Shorter Oxford English Dictionary

Shorter Oxford English Dictionary

ON HISTORICAL PRINCIPLES

Fifth edition

VOLUME 2 · N–Z

OXFORD
UNIVERSITY PRESS

OXFORD
UNIVERSITY PRESS

Great Clarendon Street, Oxford OX2 6DP

Oxford University Press is a department of the University of Oxford.
It furthers the University's objective of excellence in research, scholarship,
and education by publishing worldwide in

Oxford New York

Auckland Bangkok Buenos Aires Cape Town Chennai
Dar es Salaam Delhi Hong Kong Istanbul Karachi Kolkata
Kuala Lumpur Madrid Melbourne Mexico City Mumbai Nairobi
São Paulo Shanghai Singapore Taipei Tokyo Toronto

with an associated company in Berlin

Published in the United States
by Oxford University Press Inc., New York

First edition 1933
Second edition 1936
Third edition 1944
Reprinted with revised etymologies and enlarged addenda 1973
Fourth edition published 1993 as the *New Shorter Oxford English Dictionary*
Fifth edition 2002

British Library Cataloguing in Publication Data
Data available

Library of Congress Cataloging in Publication Data
Data available

ISBN 0-19-860575-7
ISBN 0-19-860457-2 (thumb index)

10 9 8 7 6 5 4 3 2 1

Typeset in OUP Swift, OUP Argo, and Coranto
by Interactive Sciences Ltd, Gloucester
Printed in the United States of America

Contents

VOLUME 1

VOLUME 2

Abbreviations AND SYMBOLS

In this list the abbreviations are printed in the type and with the capitalization that is normally used for them, but variation according to context will be found. Some general abbreviations, such as those for units of measurement or points of the compass, are not listed here, but can be found in the main dictionary text.

abl.	ablative
abl. absol.	ablative absolute
absol.	in absolute use, absolutely
accus.	accusative
allus.	allusion
allus.	allusively
alt.	altered, alteration
a.m.	ante meridiem, 'before noon'
Amer.	American, America
Ant. & Cl.	Antony and Cleopatra
aphet.	aphetic, aphetized
app.	apparently
approx.	approximately
Arab.	Arabic
arch.	archaic
assim.	assimilated, -ation
assoc.	associated, -ation
attrib.	attributive, -ly
Attrib. & comb.	in attributive uses and combinations
augm.	augmentative
Austral.	Australian, Australia
aux.	auxiliary (verb etc.)
AV	Authorized Version
A.Y.L.	As You Like It
back-form(s).	back-formation(s)
Brit.	British
c	*circa*, 'about'
Canad.	Canadian
cap(s).	capital(s)
cent.	century
cents.	centuries
cf.	*confer*, 'compare'
Chron.	Chronicles
cogn.	cognate
Col.	Colossians
collect.	collective, -ly
colloq.	colloquial, -ly
Com.	Comedy
Comb.	(in) combination
combs.	combinations
Com. Err.	Comedy of Errors
compar(s).	comparative(s)
compl.	complement
conf.	confused
contempt.	contemptuous, -ly
contr.	contracted, contraction
Cor.	Corinthians
Coriol.	Coriolanus
correl.	correlative
corresp.	corresponding
corrupt.	corruption
cross-refs.	cross-references
Cymb.	Cymbeline
d.	died
Dan.	Daniel
dat.	dative
def.	definite
demonstr.	demonstrative
deriv(s).	derivative(s), derivation(s)
derog.	derogatory
Deut.	Deuteronomy
devel.	development
dial.	dialect, dialectal, -ly
Dicts.	(in) Dictionaries
dim(s).	diminutive(s)
distrib.	distributive
E	early (in dates)
Eccles.	Ecclesiastes
Ecclus	Ecclesiasticus
elem(s).	element(s)
ellipt.	elliptical, -ly
Encycl. Brit.	Encyclopaedia Britannica
Eph.	Ephesians
equiv.	equivalent
erron.	erroneous, -ly
Esd.	Esdras
esp.	especially
etym.	etymology
euphem.	euphemistic, -ally
exc.	except
exclam(s).	exclamation(s)
Exod.	Exodus
exp.	exponential
expr.	expressing, expressive of
Ezek.	Ezekiel
fem.	feminine
fig.	in figurative use, figuratively
fl.	*floruit*, 'flourished'
foll.	followed
freq.	frequent, -ly
Gal.	Galatians
gen.	general, -ly
Gen.	Genesis
genit.	genitive
Hab.	Habbakuk
Haml.	Hamlet
Heb.	Hebrews
Hen.	Henry
Hist.	historical, history
hyperbol.	hyperbolically
imit.	imitative, -ly
immed.	immediately
imper.	imperative, -ly
impers.	impersonal, -ly
indef.	indefinite, -ly
indic.	indicative
inf.	infinitive
infl.	inflected, influenced
instr.	instrumental
interrog.	interrogative, -ly
intrans.	intransitive, -ly
iron.	ironical, -ly
irreg.	irregular, -ly
Isa.	Isaiah
Jer.	Jeremiah
joc.	jocular, -ly
Josh.	Joshua
Judg.	Judges
Jul. Caes.	Julius Caesar
L	late (in dates)
Lam.	Lamentations
lang(s).	language(s)
Ld	Lord
Lev.	Leviticus
lit.	literal, -ly
lit. & fig.	in literal and figurative use, literally and figuratively
L.L.L.	Love's Labour's Lost
LME	late Middle English
LOE	late Old English
Lucr.	Lucrece
M	mid (in dates)
Macb.	Macbeth
Macc.	Maccabees
masc.	masculine
Math.	Mathematics
Matt.	Matthew
ME	Middle English

Meas. for M.	Measure for Measure
Merch. V.	Merchant of Venice
Merry W.	Merry Wives of Windsor
Mids. N. D.	Midsummer Night's Dream
mod.	modern
N. Amer.	North America(n)
NEB	New English Bible
neg.	negative
neut.	neuter
N. Ir.	Northern Ireland, Northern Irish
nom.	nominative
north.	northern
north.	northern (dialect)
Num.	Numbers
NZ	New Zealand
obj.	object, -ive
obs.	obsolete
occas.	occasional, -ly
OE	Old English
OED	Oxford English Dictionary
opp.	opposed (to)
orig.	original, -ly
Oth.	Othello
pa.	past
pa. ppl	past (or passive) participial
pa. pple	past (or passive) participle
pass.	passive, -ly
pa. t.	past tense
Per.	Pericles
perf.	perfect
perh.	perhaps
pers.	personal
Pet.	Peter
Phil.	Philippians
phonet.	phonetic, -ally
phr.	phrase
phrs.	phrases
pl.	plural
pls.	plurals
poet.	poetical
possess.	possessive
ppl	participial
pple	participle
prec.	preceding (headword or main entry)
pred.	predicate
pred.	predicative, -ly
pres.	present
pres. ppl	present participial
pres. pple	present participle
pres. t.	present tense

prob.	probably
prons.	pronouns
pronunc.	pronunciation
Prov.	Proverbs
Ps.	Psalms
redupl.	reduplicated, -ation(s)
ref.	reference
refash.	refashioned, -ing
refl.	reflexive
rel.	relative
rel.	related
repl.	replaced, -ing
repr.	representative (of), represented, representing, representation(s)
Rev.	Revelation
rhet.	rhetorical, -ly
Rich.	Richard
Rom.	Romans
Rom. & Jul.	Romeo and Juliet
RV	Revised Version
S. Afr.	South Africa(n)
Sam.	Samuel
S. Amer.	South America(n)
Scot.	Scottish, Scots
Shakes.	Shakespeare
sing.	singular
S. of S.	Song of Solomon (or Songs)
Sonn.	Sonnets
sp.	spelling
spec.	specific, -ally
subj.	subject
subjunct.	subjunctive
subord.	subordinate
subsp.	subspecies
superl.	superlative
Suppl.	Supplement
Sus.	Susanna
s.v.	*sub voce*, 'under the word'
syll.	syllable
synon.	synonymous
t.	tense
Tam. Shr.	Taming of the Shrew
techn.	in technical use
Temp.	Tempest
Thess.	Thessalonians
Tim.	Timothy
Times Lit. Suppl.	Times Literary Supplement
Tit. A.	Titus Andronicus
Tr. & Cr.	Troilus and Cressida
trans.	transitive, -ly
transf.	transferred
transf. & fig.	transferred and figurative
Twel. N.	Twelfth Night

Two Gent.	Two Gentlemen of Verona
ult.	ultimate, -ly
unexpl.	unexplained
Univ.	University
Univs.	Universities
unkn.	unknown
US	United States
USA	United States of America
usu.	usually
var.	variant (of), variety
vars.	variants (of)
Ven. & Ad.	Venus and Adonis
voc.	vocative
W. Indies	West Indies
Wint. T.	Winter's Tale
Wisd.	Wisdom of Solomon
Zech.	Zechariah
Zeph.	Zephaniah

Symbols

†	obsolete
*	now chiefly in the United States (see volume 1, p. xv)
¶	introduces a note (see volume 1, p. xx)

The printing of hyphens

Hyphens introduced at line-breaks in words or formulae not otherwise hyphenated are printed ⁻. The regular form - represents a hyphen which would occur in any circumstance in the text.

Note on proprietary status

This dictionary includes words which have, or are asserted to have, proprietary status as trade marks or otherwise. Their inclusion does not imply that they have acquired for legal purposes a non-proprietary or general significance, nor any other judgement concerning their legal status. In cases where the editorial staff have some evidence that a word has proprietary status this is indicated in the entry for that word, but no judgement concerning the legal status of such words is made or implied thereby.

Pronunciation GUIDE

Vowels

a	*as in*	c**a**t, pl**ai**t
ɛ		b**e**d, d**ea**th
ɪ		s**i**t, m**y**th, beg**i**n, th**e**ology
i		cos**y**, eer**ie**, anemon**e**, *Spanish* s**i**
ɒ		h**o**t, w**a**sh, tr**ou**gh
ʌ		r**u**n, s**o**n, gl**o**ve, r**ou**gh
ʊ		p**u**t, g**oo**d, sh**ou**ld, amb**u**lance
ə		**a**go, gath**er**, flav**our**, cheet**ah**, thor**ough**, lem**o**n, s**u**ccess, mistak**e**n
ɑː		**ar**m, c**al**m, loc**a**le, br**ah**min
əː		h**er**, **ear**n, b**ir**d, sp**ur**, m**yrrh**
iː		s**ee**, p**ea**, s**ei**ze, d**e**cent, f**oe**tus, p**ae**on
ɔː		s**aw**, b**a**ll, b**oar**d, h**or**se, th**ough**t, appl**au**d
uː		t**oo**, gl**ue**, fr**ui**t, r**ou**te, thr**ough**, shr**ew**d
ɛː		h**air**, d**are**, p**ear**, th**ere**, v**a**ry

ʌɪ	*as in*	m**y**, h**igh**, **i**ce, s**ig**n, s**ei**smic, bons**ai**
aʊ		h**ow**, pl**ough**, s**ou**nd, kr**au**t
eɪ		d**ay**, g**a**te, d**ai**sy, th**ey**, r**ei**n, d**eig**n
əʊ		n**o**, c**o**c**oa**, s**ou**l, r**oe**, th**ough**, gl**ow**, b**eau**, m**au**ve, y**eo**man
ɪə		n**ear**, b**eer**, th**eo**ry, qu**e**ry, sev**ere**, em**ir**, grenad**ier**
ɔɪ		b**oy**, sp**oi**l, Fr**eu**dian
ʊə		p**oor**, r**u**ral, d**our**, liqu**eur**
ʌɪə		t**ire**, b**yre**, ch**oir**, qu**ie**t, di**a**phragm
aʊə		s**our**, fl**ower**, cow**ar**d

ɑ	*as in*	*French* p**a**s
e		*French* **été**, *Italian* v**e**rde
ɔ		*French* h**o**mme, *Italian* d**o**nna, *German* G**o**tt
o		*French* **eau**, m**o**t, *Italian* figl**io**
u		*French* t**ou**t
ø		*French* bl**eu**, *German* sp**ö**tteln
œ		*French* b**œu**f
y		*French* d**u**, *German* f**ü**nf
eː		*German* **Eh**re
oː		*German* B**oo**t
øː		*German* H**öh**le
œː		*French* doul**eu**r
yː		*German* F**üh**rer
aɪ		*German* **ei**n, fr**ei**
ɔy		*German* H**äu**ser

ː	indicates length
˜	indicates nasality

ɒ̃	*as in*	cord**on** bleu
ɒ̃ː		Ly**ons**
ɑ̃		*French* **en**
ɑ̃ː		*French* bl**an**che
ɛ̃		*French* v**in**
ɛ̃ː		*French* c**in**q
ɔ̃		*French* m**on**
ɔ̃ː		*French* m**on**de
œ̃		*French* **un**

Consonants and semivowels

b, d, f, h, k, l, m, n, p, r, s, t, v, w, and z have their usual English values.

g	*as in*	**g**et
tʃ		**ch**ip, di**tch**, **c**ello, **Cz**ech, cul**t**ure, ques**ti**on
dʒ		**j**ar, he**dg**e, ur**g**e, lo**g**ic, **g**entle, privile**g**e, sol**di**er
ŋ		ri**ng**, ba**n**k, co**n**quer, ju**n**ction
θ		**th**in, **th**rone, bir**th**, heal**th**, too**th**
ð		**th**is, clo**th**e, smoo**th**, swar**th**y
ʃ		**sh**e, a**sh**, **ch**ef, sta**ti**on, mi**ssi**on, spa**ci**ous, herba**ce**ous
ʒ		vi**si**on, era**su**re, auber**g**ine, bour**ge**ois
j		**y**es, tune, new, eulogy
x		lo**ch**, *German* a**ch**, *Spanish* Rio**j**a
ç		*German* ni**ch**t
ʎ		*Spanish* o**ll**a, **ll**amar, *Italian* **gl**i
ɲ		*French* mi**gn**on, *Spanish* pi**ñ**a, *Italian* **gn**occo
ɥ		*French* n**u**it

Stress

ˈ indicates primary stress on the following syllable

ˌ indicates secondary stress on the following syllable

For further details see volume 1, pp. xii–xiii

Nn

N, n /ɛn/.

The fourteenth letter of the modern English alphabet and the thirteenth of the ancient Roman one, repr. the Greek *nū* and the Semitic *nūn*. The sound normally represented by the letter is a (usu. voiced) nasal consonant. N in mod. English has the following values: (i) the alveolar nasal /n/; (ii) the velar nasal /ŋ/ before the consonants 'hard' *g* and *k*; (iii) silent as the final letter of a syllable after *m*, as in ***condemn***, ***hymn***. Pl. **N's**, **Ns**. See also **EN** 2.

▸ **I 1** The letter and its sound.

2 The shape of the letter.

3 *TYPOGRAPHY.* = **EN** 2.

1 n-declension declension of Germanic nouns and adjectives in which the stem ends in *n*. **2 N-shaped** *adjective* having a shape or a cross-section like the capital letter N. **3 n quadrat** = ***EN quadrat***.

▸ **II** Symbolical uses.

4 (Cap. N.) Representing the name of a person to be inserted in a written or spoken text.

5 Used to denote serial order, applied e.g. to the fourteenth (or the thirteenth, either I or J being omitted) group or section, sheet of a book, etc.

6 a *MATH.* (Italic *n*.) Used to denote an indefinite or unspecified (usu. integral) number; ***to the nth (power)***, to any required power (*fig.* to any extent, to the utmost degree). Also used in place of *bi-*, *di-*, *tri-*, etc., in words, as ***n-ary***, ***n-tuple***. ▸**b** *PHYSICS & CHEMISTRY.* (Italic *n*.) Denoting the principal quantum number of an electron in an atom, which determines its orbital energy (to the first order) and takes integral values. ▸**c** *PHYSICS.* (Cap. N.) Designating the series of X-ray emission lines of an excited atom, of longer wavelength than the *M*-series, arising from electron transitions to the atomic orbit of fourth lowest energy, of principal quantum number 4; hence ***N-shell***, this orbit; ***N-electrons***, electrons in this shell. ▸**d** *GENETICS.* (Italic *n*.) Representing the haploid or gametic chromosome number (so 2*n* = diploid or zygotic number, 3*n* = triploid, etc.). Cf. **X**, **x** 7b.

7 ***N-rays***, a form of radiation supposedly discovered in 1903 by R. Blondlot but later found to be spurious. *obsolete* exc. *Hist.* **E20.**

†**8** (Italic *n*.) A unit of neutron dosage. Only in **M20.**

▸ **III 9** Abbrevs.: (A small selection only is given here. Those all in caps. or small caps. also occur with a full stop after each letter; some of those all in caps. also occur (i) with initial cap. only, (ii) in small caps.) **N** = (*CHESS*) knight; New; (*PHYSICS*) newton; (*CHEMISTRY*) nitrogen; (*CHEMISTRY*) normal (sense A.4b); north(ern); nuclear. **n** = (as *prefix*) nano-; (*CHEMISTRY*) normal (sense A.4c) (***n-octane***: see **OCTANE** 1).

'n /(ə)n/ *conjunction*[1]. *colloq.* Also **'n'**. **M19.**
[Reduced form.]
= **AND** *conjunction*[1].

'n /(ə)n/ *conjunction*[2]. *colloq.* **M19.**
[Reduced form.]
= **THAN** *conjunction*[2].

-n *suffixes* see **-EN**[4], **-EN**[6].

Na *symbol.*
[Latin *natrium*.]
CHEMISTRY. Sodium.

†**na** *adverb*[1] & *conjunction*[1]. See also **NAE** *adverb*. **OE.**
[from **NE** + *ā* (see **AYE** *adverb*[1]). Cf. **NO** *adverb*[1] & see also **NO** *adverb*[2].]

▸ **A** *adverb*. **1** = **NOT** *adverb*. **OE–E16.**

2 = **NO** *adverb*[2]. **OE–L16.**

▸ **B** *conjunction*. **1** Nor; *rare* neither. **OE–L18.**

2 That not, but that. **LME–L18.**

na /nɑː/ *adverb*[2] & *interjection*. Chiefly *Scot.* & *north.* **ME.**
[Use of prec. Cf. **NAH** *adverb*[2], **NO** *adverb*[3] & *interjection*.]
= **NO** *adverb*[3] & *interjection*.

na /nə/ *adverb*[3]. *Scot.* & *north.* **E18.**
[Enclitic form of **NO** *adverb*[1].]
Not. Freq. joined to a preceding aux. verb, as ***canna***, ***dinna***, etc.

n/a *abbreviation.*

1 Not applicable.

2 Not available.

NAACP *abbreviation. US.*
National Association for the Advancement of Colored People.

NAAFI /ˈnafi/ *noun.* Also **Naffy**. **E20.**
[Acronym.]
The Navy, Army, and Air Force Institutes; a canteen, store, etc., run for service personnel by this organization.

naam /nɑːm/ *noun.* **OE.**
[Old Norse *nám* rel. to *niman* take, **NIM** *verb*.]
LAW (now *Hist.*). The action of taking another's goods by distraint; goods so taken.

naan *noun* var. of **NAN** *noun*[2].

naartjie /ˈnɑːtʃi, ˈnɑːki/ *noun. S. Afr.* Also **naartje**, **nartjie**, & other vars. **L18.**
[Afrikaans from Tamil *nārattai* citrus.]
A soft loose-skinned tangerine or mandarin orange.

naat /nɑːt/ *noun.* **M20.**
[Afrikaans = seam from Dutch *naad*.]
An irregularity in the structure of a diamond caused by a change in direction in the grain; a diamond containing such an irregularity.

nab /nab/ *noun*[1]. Chiefly *Scot.* & *north.* **ME.**
[Old Norse *nabbr*, *nabbi* projecting peak or knoll.]

1 A projecting part of a hill or rock; a peak, a promontory; a rocky hill, a summit. **ME.** ▸**b** A tuft, a clump. *rare.* **M19.**

2 A projection or spur on the bolt of a lock. **L17.**

nab /nab/ *noun*[2]. *slang & dial.* Now *rare* or *obsolete*. **M16.**
[Perh. a use of prec. Cf. **NOB** *noun*[1], **KNOB** *noun* 4.]

1 The head. **M16.**

2 A hat. **L17.**

nab /nab/ *noun*[3]. *slang.* **E19.**
[from **NAB** *verb*[1].]
A person who catches someone or something; *spec.* a police officer.

nab /nab/ *noun*[4]. *colloq.* Now *rare.* **M19.**
[from *nab* var. of **KNAB** *verb*[1].]
A bite.

nab *noun*[5] see **NOB** *noun*[2].

nab /nab/ *verb*[1]. *slang.* Infl. **-bb-**. **L17.**
[Origin unkn. Cf. **NAP** *verb*[3].]

1 *verb trans.* Catch (a person) and take into custody; apprehend, arrest; catch in wrongdoing. **L17.**

2 *verb trans.* Snatch or seize (a thing); steal. **E19.** ▸**b** *verb intrans.* Snatch *at* a thing. *rare.* **E19.**

📖 **1** R. CROMPTON Crumbs! . . I thought he was going to nab us. R. MACAULAY He's disqualified for driving . . for a year; he did something silly and got nabbed.

Phrases: **nab the rust** (now *dial.*) be angry, restive, or sulky.

▪ **nabber** *noun* a person who nabs someone or something; *spec.* a bailiff, a constable; a thief: **E19.**

nab *verb*[2] var. of **KNAB** *verb*[1].

nab *adverb* & *noun*[6] see **HAB**.

nabal /ˈneɪb(ə)l/ *noun.* Chiefly *Scot.* **L16.**
[Hebrew personal name *Nābāl*, with ref. to *1 Samuel* 25:3.]
A churlish or miserly person.

Nabataean /nabəˈtiːən/ *noun & adjective.* **E17.**
[from Latin *Nabat(h)aeus*, Greek *Nabat(h)aios* (cf. Arab. *Nabatī* adjective, pertaining to the Nabataeans) + **-AN**.]

▸ **A** *noun*. A member of an ancient Arabian people forming a kingdom with its capital at Petra; the language of this people. **E17.**

▸ **B** *adjective*. Of or pertaining to the Nabataeans or their language. **L19.**

nabbie /ˈnabi/ *noun*, **L19.**
[Perh. from **NOBBY** *noun*[1].]
A type of Scottish boat used esp. in herring-fishing on Loch Fyne and in the Firth of Clyde, originally having a raking mast, lugsail, and jib. Cf. **NOBBY** *noun*[1] 1.

†**nabby** *adjective & noun* see **NOBBY** *adjective & noun*[2].

nabe /neɪb/ *noun. US slang.* **M20.**
[Repr. pronunc. of 1st syll. of *neighbourhood*.]
A local cinema.

Nabeshima /nabəˈʃiːmə/ *adjective.* **L19.**
[Baronial family name in feudal Japan.]
Designating a form of Hizen ware manufactured at Okawachi on Kyushu in Japan using kilns established there by the Nabeshima family in 1722.

nabi /ˈnɑːbiː/ *noun.* Pl. (in sense 1) **nebiim** /nɛˈbiːɪm/, (in sense 2) **nabis**. Also **N-**. **L19.**
[Hebrew *nābī* prophet.]

1 *THEOLOGY.* A person inspired to speak the word of God; a prophet; *spec.* a prophetical writer of the Old Testament and Hebrew Scriptures. Also (in *pl.*) = ***the Prophets*** (b) s.v. **PROPHET. L19.**

2 A member of a group of late 19th-cent. French post-impressionists following the artistic theories of the French painter Paul Gauguin (1848–1903). **M20.**

▪ **nabism** *noun* the principles or practice of a nabi; adherence to a nabi: **E20.**

nabla /ˈnablə/ *noun.* **L19.**
[Greek = a kind of harp, prob. of Semitic origin. Cf. **NEBEL**.]
MATH. = **DEL**.

nabob /ˈneɪbɒb/ *noun.* **E17.**
[Portuguese *nababo* or Spanish *nabab* from Urdu *nawwāb*, *nawāb* deputy governor: see **NAWAB**.]

1 *Hist.* (The title of) any of certain Muslim officials acting as deputy governors of provinces or districts in the Mughal Empire; a governor of an Indian town or district. **E17.**

2 A person of great wealth or (formerly) high rank; *spec.* a person returning from India with a large fortune acquired there; a wealthy luxury-loving person. *arch.* **M18.**

▪ **nabobess** *noun* a female nabob; the wife of a nabob: **M18. nabobship** *noun* (*a*) the rank or office of nabob; the state of being a nabob; (*b*) *Hist.* the territory or district subject to a nabob: **M18.**

nabocklish /nəˈbɒklɪʃ/ *interjection. Anglo-Irish.* **M19.**
[from Irish *na* not + *bac* imper. sing. of *bacaim* I meddle + *leis* with it, lit. 'don't meddle with it'.]
Never mind! Leave it alone!

Nabokovian /nabəˈkɒfiən/ *adjective.* **M20.**
[from *Nabokov* (see below) + **-IAN**.]
Of, pertaining to, or characteristic of the Russian-born novelist and poet Vladimir Nabokov (1899–1977) or his writing.

nabs /nabz/ *noun. arch. slang* (chiefly *joc.*). Pl. same. **L18.**
[Origin unkn. Cf. **NIB** *noun*[2], **NIBS**.]
A person. Only with possess. adjective, as ***his nabs*** etc.

nacarat /ˈnakərat/ *noun.* **M18.**
[French, perh. from Spanish & Portuguese *nacarado*, from *nacar* nacre.]

1 A bright orange-red colour. **M18.**

2 A fine linen fabric dyed in this colour. **M19.**

nacelle /nəˈsɛl/ *noun.* **L15.**
[French from late Latin *navicella* dim. of Latin *navis* ship.]

▸ **I** †**1** A small boat. *rare.* Only in **L15.**

▸ **II 2** The basket or car of a balloon or airship. **M19.**

3 Orig., the cockpit of an aeroplane. Now, a streamlined bulge on an aircraft's wing or fuselage enclosing an engine etc. **E20.**

4 A similarly shaped structure on or in a motor vehicle. **M20.**

¶ In branch II reintroduced from French.

nachas *noun* var. of **NACHES**.

nache /neɪtʃ/ *noun.* Now *rare* or *obsolete* exc. *dial.* Also †**nage**, **natch** /natʃ/. **ME.**
[Old French *nache*, *nage*, pl. *naches* from late Latin *naticas* accus. pl. of *naticae*, from Latin *natis* buttock. Cf. **AITCHBONE**.]

1 In *pl.*, the buttocks; *sing.* the anus. Long *obsolete* exc. *Hist.* **ME.**

2 (The point of) the rump in an ox or cow. **ME.**

Comb.: **nache-bone** = **AITCHBONE**.

naches /ˈnʌxəs/ *noun. US.* Also **nachas**. **E20.**
[Yiddish *nakhes* from Hebrew *nakaṯ* contentment.]
A sense of pleasure or pride, esp. at the achievements of one's children; joy, gratification.

Nachlass /ˈnaːxlas/ *noun.* Pl. ***-lasse*** /-lasə/, ***-lässe*** /-lɛsə/. **M19.**
[German.]
sing. & (*rare*) in *pl.* Unpublished material left by an author after his or her death.

nacho /ˈnɑːtʃəʊ, ˈnatʃəʊ/ *noun.* Orig. *US.* Pl. **-os**. **M20.**
[Origin uncertain: perh. from Mexican Spanish *Nacho* pet-form of male forename *Ignacio* (that of a chef often credited with the dish's creation), but cf. Spanish *nacho* flat-nosed.]
A snack or appetizer consisting of fried tortilla chips covered in melted cheese, peppers, spices, etc. In *pl.* exc. when *attrib.*

Nachschlag /ˈnaːxʃlaːk/ *noun.* Pl. **-schläge** /-ʃlɛːɡə/. L19.
[German, from *nach* after + *Schlag* blow, note.]
MUSIC. A grace-note taking its value from that of the note preceding it.

Nachtlokal /ˈnaxtlokal/ *noun.* Pl. **-e** /-ə/. M20.
[German, from *Nacht* night + *Lokal* public house.]
A nightclub.

Nachtmaal *noun* see NAGMAAL.

Nacht und Nebel /naxt ʊnt ˈneːb(ə)l/ *noun phr.* M20.
[German, lit. 'night and fog'.]
A situation characterized by mystery or obscurity, esp. as associated with Nazi Germany between 1941 and 1945.

nacket /ˈnakɪt/ *noun. Scot.* L16.
[Origin unkn.]
1 A type of small loaf, *esp.* one made with fine white flour. L16.
2 A snack, a lunch; a light meal. L18.

NACODS *abbreviation.*
National Association of Colliery Overmen, Deputies, and Shotfirers.

nacre /ˈneɪkə/ *noun.* L16.
[French, prob. ult. of oriental origin.]
= MOTHER-OF-PEARL.
■ **nacred** *adjective* covered with or resembling nacre M18.

nacreous /ˈneɪkrɪəs/ *adjective.* M19.
[from prec.: see -EOUS.]
Consisting of or resembling nacre; pearly.
📖 D. J. ENRIGHT The nacreous face of a leper observed in Asia. J. BARNES A very early . . shaver, nacreous pink in its box.

nacrite /ˈneɪkrʌɪt/ *noun.* E19.
[from NACRE + -ITE[1].]
MINERALOGY. A clay mineral related to kaolinite.

nacrous /ˈneɪkrəs/ *adjective.* M19.
[from NACRE: see -OUS.]
Nacreous.

NAD *abbreviation.*
BIOCHEMISTRY. Nicotinamide adenine dinucleotide.

nada /ˈnaːda/ *noun*[1]. E20.
[Sanskrit *nāda* sound.]
HINDUISM. Inchoate or elemental sound considered as the source of all sounds and as a source of creation.

nada /ˈnaða, ˈnadə/ *noun*[2]. M20.
[Spanish = nothing, from Latin (*res*) *nata* thing born, insignificant thing.]
Nothing; nothingness, non-existence.

Na-Dene /ˈnaːdəneɪ/ *adjective & noun.* E20.
[from Athapaskan *na* cogn. with Haida *náa* dwell, Tlingit *naa* tribe + *dene* tribe.]
▶ **A** *adjective.* Designating, of, or pertaining to a N. American Indian language group including the Athapaskan and Tlingit families, and (in some classifications) Haida. E20.
▶ **B** *noun.* The Na-Dene group of languages. M20.

Naderism /ˈneɪdərɪz(ə)m/ *noun.* M20.
[from Ralph *Nader* (b. 1934), US lawyer + -ISM.]
Public agitation for greater safety and higher quality in consumer goods.
■ **Naderite** *noun & adjective* L20.

nadir /ˈneɪdɪə/ *noun.* LME.
[Old & mod. French (also Spanish, Italian) from Arab. *naẓīr* (*as-samt*) opposite (the zenith).]
†**1** ASTRONOMY. A point in the heavens diametrically opposite to some other point, esp. to the sun. Foll. by *of, to.* LME–E18.
2 ASTRONOMY. The point of the heavens diametrically opposite to the zenith; the point directly below an observer. L15.
3 The lowest point (*of* something); the place or time of greatest depression or degradation. L18.
📖 **3** C. HILL When Buckingham was assassinated . . England's international reputation was at its nadir.

NADP *abbreviation.*
BIOCHEMISTRY. Nicotinamide adenine dinucleotide phosphate.

nads /nadz/ *noun pl. coarse slang.* M20.
[Shortening of *gonads*.]
The testicles; *fig.* courage, strength.

nae *adjective* see NO *adjective.*

nae /neɪ/ *adverb. Scot. & north.* E18.
[Var. of NA *adverb*[1], NO *adverb*[1].]
Not.

naevus /ˈniːvəs/ *noun.* Also ***nevus**. Pl. **-vi** /-vʌɪ/. M19.
[Latin.]
MEDICINE. A congenital reddish or brown mark or (usu.) raised blemish on the skin, *esp.* a haemangioma; a birthmark, a mole.
■ **naevoid** *adjective* of the nature of a naevus M19.

naff /naf/ *adjective. slang.* M20.
[Origin unkn.]
Unfashionable, lacking in style. Also, worthless, faulty, rubbishy.
📖 L. CODY No electricity . . . I think it's just a naff battery connection. *Sunday Telegraph* It is naff to call your house The Gables . . or Dunroamin'.
■ **naffness** *noun* L20.

naff /naf/ *verb intrans. slang.* M20.
[Prob. euphem. substitute for FUCK *verb.* Cf. EFF *verb.*]
Foll. by *off*: go away. Freq. in *imper.*
■ **naffing** *adjective* (used as an intensifier) M20.

Naffy *noun* var. of NAAFI.

NAFTA /ˈnaftə/ *abbreviation.*
North American Free Trade Agreement.

nag /naɡ/ *noun*[1]. LME.
[Origin unkn.]
1 A small riding-horse or pony; *colloq.* a horse. LME.
†**2** A contemptible or worthless person. L16–E17.
Comb.: **nagsman** a skilled horseman employed to train or show horses.

nag /naɡ/ *noun*[2]. L19.
[from NAG *verb.*]
An act or spell of nagging; a thing that nags. Also, a persistently nagging person, esp. a woman.
📖 *New Yorker* Pam is portrayed as an airhead and a nag.

nag /naɡ/ *verb.* Infl. **-gg-**. E19.
[Origin uncertain: perh. ult. of Scandinavian origin or from Low German (cf. Swedish *nagga*, Norwegian *nagge* gnaw, nibble, irritate, Low German (*g*)*naggen* irritate, provoke).]
1 a *verb trans. & intrans.* Gnaw, nibble, (*at*). *dial.* E19.
▶**b** *verb intrans.* Of a pain etc.: ache dully but persistently. M19.
2 *verb intrans.* Find fault, complain, or urge someone, esp. persistently. (Foll. by *at.*) M19.
3 *verb trans.* Annoy or irritate (a person) with persistent fault-finding, complaining, or urging. M19.
📖 **1b** *Sunday Express* Those nagging back aches and tense neck muscles. **3a** A. GERAS I'm sorry if I made your life a misery nagging you about the piano. C. TOMALIN Fear of exposure must have nagged and tormented her.
■ **nagger** *noun* L19. **naggingly** *adverb* in a nagging manner M20. **naggingness** *noun* (*rare*) nagging quality or condition L19.

naga /ˈnɑːɡə/ *noun*[1]. L18.
[Sanskrit *nāga* serpent, snake.]
INDIAN MYTHOLOGY. A member of a race of semi-divine creatures, half-snake and half-human, that are the genii of rain, rivers, etc.

Naga /ˈnɑːɡɑː/ *noun*[2]. E19.
[Hindi *nāgā* from Sanskrit *nagnaka* cogn. with NAKED.]
HINDUISM. A naked mendicant; *spec.* such an ascetic belonging to a sect permitting its members to carry arms and serve as mercenaries.

Naga /ˈnɑːɡə/ *noun*[3] *& adjective.* M19.
[Perh. from Sanskrit *nagna* naked or *naga* mountain.]
▶ **A** *noun.* **1** A member of a group of peoples living in or near the Naga Hills of Myanmar (Burma) and in NE India; a native or inhabitant of Nagaland, a State in NE India. M19.
2 The Tibeto-Burman language of these peoples. M19.
▶ **B** *attrib.* or as *adjective.* Of or pertaining to the Nagas or their language. E20.

nagaika /nəˈɡʌɪkə/ *noun.* Pl. **-ki** /-ki/, **-kas**. M19.
[Russian *nagaĭka*, from (the same root as) NOGAY.]
A thick plaited Cossack whip.

nagana /nəˈɡɑːnə/ *noun.* L19.
[Zulu *nakane*.]
A disease of cattle, antelope, etc., in southern Africa, characterized by fever, lethargy, and oedema caused by trypanosomes transmitted by tsetse-flies.

Nagari /ˈnɑːɡəriː/ *adjective & noun.* L18.
[Sanskrit *nāgarī*, from *nagara* town.]
= DEVANAGARI.

†**nage** *noun* var. of NACHE.

nagelfluh /ˈnɑːɡ(ə)lfluː/ *noun.* Pl. **-fluhe** /-fluːə/. E19.
[German, from *Nagel* nail + Swiss German *Fluh* rock face.]
GEOLOGY. A massive Miocene conglomerate associated with the molasse of the Swiss Alps, containing pebbles supposed to look like nail-heads.

naggle /ˈnaɡ(ə)l/ *verb & noun.* M19.
[Frequentative of NAG *verb*: see -LE[3].]
▶ **A** *verb intrans.* Gnaw, bite, (chiefly *dial.*). Also, nag, quarrel, esp. in a petty manner. M19.
▶ **B** *noun.* Pettiness; nagging. *rare.* M19.
📖 K. MILLETT The regulation American mother bullying her two sons with naggle.

naggy /ˈnaɡi/ *noun.* Chiefly *Scot.* L17.
[from NAG *noun*[1] + -Y[6].]
A small nag, a pony.

naggy /ˈnaɡi/ *adjective.* L17.
[from NAG *verb* + -Y[1].]
Given to nagging; *dial.* ill-natured, bad-tempered.
📖 *Guardian* Kids . . whose mothers are tired and naggy.

Nagmaal /ˈnaxmaːl/ *noun. S. Afr.* Also (earlier) ***Nacht-*** /ˈnaxt-/. M19.
[Afrikaans *nagmaal* (Dutch *nachtmaal*), from *nag* (Dutch *nacht*) night + *maal* meal.]
The usu. quarterly celebration of the Eucharist in the Dutch Reformed Church (an occasion of family reunions and celebration).

Nago /ˈnɑːɡəʊ/ *noun & adjective.* L18.
[Ewe *anagó* a Yoruba person.]
▶ **A** *noun.* Pl. **-os**.
1 A member of a Yoruba-speaking people of W. Africa, of whom many were taken to the Americas as slaves. L18.
2 The language of this people, now *spec.* (**a**) as spoken in Benin; (**b**) the reduced form spoken in Bahia, Brazil. M20.
▶ **B** *attrib.* or as *adjective.* Of or pertaining to the Nagos or their language. L18.

nagor /ˈneɪɡɔː/ *noun.* Now *rare.* L18.
[French, arbitrarily formed by Buffon after earlier *nanguer*.]
A reedbuck, *Redunca redunca*, of savannah in equatorial Africa, with short forward-curving horns.

nag's-head /ˈnaɡzhɛd/ *noun.* M19.
[Perh. from NAG *noun*[1] + -'S[1] + HEAD *noun*.]
MUSIC HISTORY. A kind of organ swell consisting of a rising and falling shutter.

Nagualism /ˈnaɡw(ə)lɪz(ə)m, ˈnaw(ə)l-/ *noun.* L19.
[from Mexican Spanish *nagual*, *nahual* from Nahuatl *nahualli* guardian spirit.]
Belief in a personal guardian spirit thought by some Central American Indians to reside in a bird, animal, or other embodiment.

nah /nɑː/ *adverb*[1]. *non-standard.* M19.
[Repr. a pronunc. Cf. NAOW *adverb*[2].]
= NOW *adverb.*

nah /nɑː/ *adverb*[2] *& interjection. non-standard.* E20.
[Repr. a pronunc. Cf. NA *adverb*[2] *& interjection*, NAOW *adverb*[1], *interjection*, NAW.]
= NO *adverb*[3] *& interjection.*

Nah. *abbreviation.*
Nahum (in the Bible).

nahal /nəˈhɑːl/ *noun.* M20.
[Hebrew, from initials of the name of the organization, *Nō'ar Ḥălūṣī Lōḥēm* Pioneer Military Youth.]
A military youth organization in Israel; an agricultural settlement manned by members of this organization.

Nahuatl /ˈnɑːwɑːt(ə)l, nɑːˈwɑːt(ə)l/ *noun & adjective.* E19.
[Spanish from Nahuatl.]
▶ **A** *noun.* Pl. **-s**, same. A member of a group of peoples of southern Mexico and Central America, including the Aztecs. Also, the Uto-Aztecan language of these peoples. E19.
▶ **B** *attrib.* or as *adjective.* Of or pertaining to the Nahuatls or their language. L19.
■ **Nahuatlan** *adjective & noun* (of or pertaining to) the group of Nahuatl dialects E20.

naiad /ˈnʌɪad/ *noun.* Pl. **-s**, **naiades** /ˈnʌɪədiːz/. LME.
[Latin *Naiad-*, *Naias* from Greek, rel. to *naein* flow. Cf. NAÏD, NAÏS.]
1 CLASSICAL MYTHOLOGY. A nymph supposed to inhabit a river, spring, etc., as its tutelary spirit; a water-nymph. LME.
2 ENTOMOLOGY. The aquatic larva or nymph of a hemimetabolous insect. E20.
3 BOTANY. A submerged aquatic plant of the genus *Najas* (family Najadaceae). M20.

naiant /ˈneɪənt/ *adjective.* M16.
[Anglo-Norman = Old French *noiant* pres. pple of *no(i)er* swim = Italian *nuotare* from Proto-Romance alt. of Latin *natare*.]
HERALDRY. Of a fish etc.: swimming horizontally.

naib /ˈnɑːɪb, ˈneɪb/ *noun.* L17.
[Arab. *nā'ib* deputy. Cf. NAWAB.]
In Arabic-speaking countries: a deputy governor; a deputy.

naice /neɪs/ *adjective.* Chiefly *joc. & derog.* E20.
[Repr. an affected pronunc.]
= NICE *adjective.*

†**naïd** *noun. rare.* E17.
[Latin *Naïd-*, *Naïs* var. of *Naïad-*, *Naias*: see NAIAD. Cf. NAÏS.]
1 CLASSICAL MYTHOLOGY. A naiad. E17–E18.
2 ZOOLOGY. A freshwater mussel. Only in M19.

naïdes *noun* pl. of NAÏS.

naieo *noun* var. of NAIO.

naïf /nʌɪˈiːf, nɑːˈiːf/ ***adjective & noun.*** Pl. of noun pronounced same. **L16.**
[French: see NAIVE.]
▶ **A** *adjective.* **1** = NAIVE 1. **L16.** ▸**b** = NAIVE 1b. **M20.**
†**2** Of a diamond: without an imperfection, flawless. *rare.* **M–L17.**
▶ **B** *noun.* A naive person. **L19.**
¶ Formerly fully naturalized.
■ **naïfly** *adverb (rare)* **M17.**

naik /ˈnɑːɪk, ˈneɪk/ *noun.* **L16.**
[Urdu *nā'ik* from Hindi *nāyak* chief, officer from Sanskrit *nāyaka* leader.]
Chiefly *Hist.* **1** (The title of) an Indian prince or nobleman; a lord, a prince, a governor. **L16.**
2 In the Indian subcontinent: orig., a military officer; later, a corporal of infantry. **L18.**

nail /neɪl/ *noun.*
[Old English *næg(e)l* = Old Frisian *neil*, Old Saxon, Old High German *nagal* (Dutch, German *Nagel*), Old Norse *nagl*, from Germanic, from Indo-European base also repr. by Lithuanian *nāgas* nail, claw, Greek *onux*, Latin *unguis*.]
▶ **I 1** The smooth, horny, usu. oval-shaped covering of the upper surface at the end of a finger or toe in humans and other primates. Also, a claw, a talon, a hoof. **OE.**
2 A thing resembling a nail in shape or colour; *spec.* †(*a*) = HAW *noun*[3] 1; (*b*) a hard excrescence on the upper mandible of some soft-billed birds. **OE.**

1 P. H. JOHNSON An astonishingly small . . hand, with beautiful square-cut nails. M. BRADBURY Her tight-knuckled hands and bitten nails.

▶ **II 3** A small, usu. sharpened, metal spike with a broadened flat head for driving in with a hammer, to fasten things together, serve as a peg, or provide protection or decoration. Also (*rare*), a wooden peg (cf. TREENAIL). **OE.**
4 †**a** *MEDICINE.* An abscess, a carbuncle. Only in **17.** ▸**b** A defect in a stone. Long *rare* or *obsolete.* **M17.**
5 A person who overreaches another, a cunning or clever fellow. *arch. slang.* **E19.**

3 C. LAMB The countless nails that rivet the chains of habit. W. E. H. LECKY The nails of the Cross . . were converted by the emperor into a helmet. R. K. NARAYAN He took the gate key from the nail on the . . wall. ***overlap nail, rose nail, stub-nail***, etc.

▶ **III 6** *Hist.* A unit of weight of wool, beef, etc., equal to 7 or 8 lb (approx. 3.2 to 3.6 kg); = CLOVE *noun*[3]. Formerly also, a measure of land. Now *dial.* **LME.**
7 *Hist.* A unit of length for cloth, equal to 2¼ inches (approx. 57 mm). **LME.**

Phrases: ***a nail in the coffin of***: see COFFIN *noun*. **as hard as nails** (*a*) in good physical condition; (*b*) callous. ***bed of nails***: see BED *noun*. **bite one's nails** bite the ends of one's nails as a nervous habit, esp. in impatience and frustration. ***dead as a door-nail***: see DEAD *adjective*. ***hit the nail on the head***: see HIT *verb*. **off at the nail** *Scot.* crazy. **on the nail** (esp. of the payment of a debt etc.) without delay, immediately. ***tooth and nail***: see TOOTH *noun*.
Comb.: **nail-biting** *adjective* (*fig.*) causing helpless anxiety or tension; **nail bomb** a lethal weapon made from nails wrapped round a stick of gelignite; **nail-brush** a small brush for cleaning one's nails; **nail enamel** *N. Amer.* = ***nail polish*** below; **nail-file** a roughened metal or emery strip for trimming one's nails; **nail-gall** a nail-shaped gall produced on the leaves of lime and other trees by a mite of the genus *Phytoptus*; **nail-head** the head of a nail; an ornament, esp. on a garment, resembling this; ***nail-head spar***, calcite occurring as hexagonal prisms and flat rhombohedra; **nail-headed** *adjective* having a head like that of a nail; formed like a nail-head; **nail-hole** a hole made for or left by a nail; **nail-maker** a person who makes nails; **nail-making** the process of making nails; **nail-plate** a piece of iron from which nails are cut; **nail-polish** a liquid cosmetic applied to fingernails to colour them, or make them shiny; **nail-punch** a tool for sinking the head of a nail below a surface; **nail-rod** (*a*) a strip or rod of) iron for making nails; (*b*) (chiefly *Austral.*) coarse dark tobacco in the form of a thin roll or stick; **nail-scissors** small scissors for trimming one's nails; **nail-set** = ***nail-punch*** above; **nailsick** *Nautical slang* (of a ship etc.) leaky at the nail-holes; **nail-tailed** *adjective* having a nail or spur on the tip of the tail; ***nail-tailed wallaby***, any of several rare or extinct wallabies of the genus *Onychogalea*, which have a horny nail near the end of the tail; **nail varnish** = ***nail polish*** above; **nail violin** a bowed musical instrument consisting of a semicircular wooden resonator studded with nails of varying lengths.
■ **nailless** /-l-l-/ *adjective* **M19.** **naily** *adjective (rare)* provided with nails **E17.**

nail /neɪl/ *verb.*
[Old English *næglan*, from the noun. Cf. Gothic *ganagljan*.]
1 *verb trans.* Fix or fasten with a nail or nails on or on to something or in a certain place. Freq. foll. by *on, to, together, down, in, up*, etc. **OE.**
2 a *verb trans.* Pierce (a person or thing) with a nail or nails. Now *rare* or *obsolete.* **OE.** ▸**b** Stud (as) with a nail or nails; mark by driving in a nail or nails. *rare.* **OE.** ▸†**c** *MILITARY.* Spike (a cannon) by driving a nail into the vent. **L16–L18.**
3 Fix in one place or make immovable as with a nail or nails; secure. Now *rare* or *obsolete.* **ME.**
4 a Concentrate, keep fixed, (the eyes, attention, etc.) on a particular object. **L16.** ▸**b** Hold (a person) in a particular position, occupation, etc. **E17.**
5 a Secure, catch, or get hold of (a person or thing); steal; incriminate, arrest, convict. Also, catch (a person) in some fix or difficulty. *colloq.* **M18.** ▸**b** Strike or punch (a person, ball, etc.) forcefully; put out of action; kill, esp. violently or from a distance. *colloq.* **L18.** ▸**c** In *BASEBALL* (of a fielder), put (a runner) out by throwing; *gen.* in *SPORT*, defeat (an opponent), make ineffective. *colloq.* (chiefly *N. Amer.*). **L19.** ▸**d** Esp. of a man: copulate with. *coarse slang* (orig. *US*). **M20.**

1 W. COWPER Close by the threshold of a door nailed fast. I. D'ISRAELI The royal anathema was nailed on the Episcopal gate at London. S. S. BUCKMAN The draught . . prevented by a small tarpaulin nailed across the opening. *transf.*: DRYDEN The second Shaft . . pierc'd his Hand, and nail'd it to his side. **2b** R. FANSHAW Those Stars which nail Heav'ns pavement! **3** W. CONGREVE Rivet and nail me where I stand. **4a** SIR W. SCOTT I cannot nail my mind to one subject of contemplation. R. W. EMERSON The man whose eyes are nailed . . on the wages. **b** W. COWPER Those Whose headaches nail them to a noonday bed. **5a** D. C. MURRAY We shall have to wait and nail them . . when we've proved complicity. C. F. BURKE The cops . . nail Ben for havin' the cup. **b** *Boxing News* Ayala rallied . . putting punches together as he nailed Espinoza with left hooks and rights.

Phrases, & with adverbs in specialized senses: **nail a lie** expose as a falsehood. **nail down** (*a*) fasten (esp. a lid) with a nail or nails; (*b*) bind (a person) to a promise etc.; (*c*) define exactly. ***nail one's colours to the mast***: see COLOUR *noun*. **nail to the barn door, nail to the counter** expose as false or spurious. **nail up** (*a*) prevent (a door etc.) from being opened by fastening with a nail or nails; (*b*) fix (a thing) at a height with a nail or nails; †(*c*) *MILITARY* = sense 2c above.
■ **nailable** *adjective* able to be nailed; *spec.* (of construction materials etc.) able to be nailed into place: **M20.**

nailer /ˈneɪlə/ *noun.* **ME.**
[from NAIL *verb* + -ER[1].]
1 A person who makes nails; a nail-maker. **ME.**
2 A person who nails something. *rare.* **M17.**
3 A supremely efficient person or thing; a person who is exceptionally good *at* something. *slang.* **E19.**
4 A police officer, a detective. *slang.* **M19.**
5 A power tool for driving in nails. **L20.**
■ **naileress** *noun* a female nail-maker **M19.** **nailery** *noun* a place or workshop for the making of nails **L18.**

Nailsea /ˈneɪlsiː/ *noun.* **E20.**
[See below.]
In full ***Nailsea glass***. A style of glassware first manufactured at Nailsea, a town near Bristol in SW England, in the late 18th cent.

nain /neɪn/ *adjective. Scot.* **LME.**
[Var. of NOWN.]
(One's) own.
Comb.: **nainsell** *pronoun* (one's) own self.

nainsook /ˈneɪnsʊk/ *noun & adjective.* **L18.**
[Urdu (Hindi) *nainsukh*, from *nain* eye + *sukh* pleasure.]
▶ **A** *noun.* A fine soft cotton fabric, a kind of muslin or jaconet, orig. from the Indian subcontinent; a garment made of this. **L18.**
▶ **B** *attrib.* or as *adjective.* Made of nainsook. **L19.**

naio /ˈnʌɪəʊ/ *noun.* Also **naieo**. **L19.**
[Hawaiian: cf. NGAIO.]
A Hawaiian evergreen tree, *Myoporum sandwicense* (family Myoporaceae), bearing clusters of small pink or white flowers. Also called ***bastard sandalwood***.

Nair /ˈnʌɪə/ *noun.* **L16.**
[Portuguese *nayre, naire* from Malayalam *nāyar*.]
A member of the noble and military caste in Malabar, a coastal district of SW India.

naira /ˈnʌɪrə/ *noun.* Pl. same. **L20.**
[Origin uncertain: perh. ult. from *Nigeria* (see below).]
The basic monetary unit of Nigeria, equal to 100 kobo.

naïs /ˈneɪɪs/ *noun.* Pl. **naïdes** /ˈneɪdiːz/. **L17.**
[Latin *Naïs* var. of *Naias*: see NAIAD. Cf. NAÏD.]
1 *CLASSICAL MYTHOLOGY.* A naiad. **L17.**
2 *ZOOLOGY.* A small bristly freshwater oligochaete worm of the genus *Nais* or the family Naididae. Now chiefly as mod. Latin genus name. **M19.**

naissance /ˈneɪs(ə)ns/ *noun. rare.* **L15.**
[French, from *naiss-* pres. ppl stem of *naître*: see next, -ANCE.]
Origin, birth.

naissant /ˈneɪs(ə)nt/ *adjective.* **L16.**
[Old & mod. French, pres. pple of *naître* from Proto-Romance from Latin *nasci* be born: see -ANT[1].]
1 *HERALDRY.* Of a charge, esp. an animal: issuing from the middle of a fess or other ordinary. **L16.**
2 That is coming into existence or being produced. *rare.* **L19.**

nait /neɪt/ *verb trans.* Long *obsolete* exc. *dial.* **ME.**
[Old Norse *neyta* (Norwegian *nøyte*, Swedish *nöta*), ult. from Germanic ablaut stem (cf. *naut* NEAT *noun*, *nautr* gift, companion), from base also of Gothic *niutan*, Old Norse *njóta* (Swedish *njúta*), Old English *nēotan* enjoy.]
Make use of, use.

naive /nʌɪˈiːv, nɑːˈiːv/ *adjective.* Also **naïve**. **M17.**
[Old & mod. French *naïve*, fem. of *naïf* from Latin *nativus* NATIVE *adjective*. Cf. NAÏF.]
1 Unaffected, unconsciously artless. Also, foolishly credulous, simple. **M17.** ▸**b** Of art etc.: straightforward in style, eschewing subtlety or conventional technique. Cf. PRIMITIVE *adjective* 9. **M20.**
2 *MEDICINE & PSYCHOLOGY.* Not having had a particular experience before, or been the subject of a particular experiment; lacking the knowledge to guess the purpose of an experiment; *esp.* not having taken or received a particular drug. (Foll. by *to*.) **M20.**

1 R. C. HUTCHINSON Could he suppose her so naïve as to be impressed? O. MANNING He smiled in naïve pleasure. **b** ***naive painter, naive painting***, etc.

Special collocations: **naive realism** *PHILOSOPHY* the belief that an object of perception is not only real but has in reality all its perceived attributes. **naive realist** *PHILOSOPHY* an adherent of or believer in naive realism.
■ **naively** *adverb* †(*a*) naturally, true to nature; (*b*) in a naive manner, artlessly: **M17.** **naiveness** *noun (rare)* **M20.**

naïveté /naivte; nʌɪˈiːvteɪ, nɑː-/ *noun.* Pl. pronounced same. **L17.**
[French, formed as prec. + *-té* -TY[1].]
1 = NAIVETY 2. **L17.**
2 = NAIVETY 1. **E18.**

naivety /nʌɪˈiːvti, nɑːˈiːvti/ *noun.* Also **naïvety**. **E18.**
[Anglicized from prec.: see -TY[1].]
1 The state or quality of being naive. **E18.**
2 A naive action, remark, etc. **M19.**

1 J. BERGER He must have taken advantage of . . your naivety and your good heart. **2** CARLYLE Shrewd simplicities, naiveties, blundering ingenuities.

Naja /ˈneɪdʒə, ˈneɪjə/ *noun.* **M18.**
[mod. Latin (see below) from Hindi *nāg* snake.]
A cobra of the genus *Naja*. Now chiefly as mod. Latin genus name.

nake /neɪk/ *verb trans.* Long *obsolete* exc. *Scot.* **ME.**
[Back-form. from NAKED *adjective*.]
Make naked (*lit. & fig.*).

naked /ˈneɪkɪd/ *adjective & noun.*
[Old English *nacod* = Old Frisian *naked, -et*, Middle Low German, Middle Dutch *naket* (Dutch *naakt*), Old High German *nackut* (German *nackt*), Old Norse *nǫkkviðr*, Gothic *naqaþs, -ad-*, from Germanic, rel. to Latin *nudus*, Sanskrit *nagna*.]
▶ **A** *adjective.* **I 1** Of the body or a part: unclothed, stripped to the skin, not covered or protected by clothing. **OE.** ▸**b** Of a horse etc.: without a saddle or harness; barebacked. Long *obsolete* exc. *Scot.* **OE.**
2 †**a** Of a person: destitute of clothing, esp. through extreme poverty. Of an animal: deprived of its hair, wool, etc. **OE–L17.** ▸**b** Destitute of means. *arch. rare.* **E17.**
3 Without a weapon or means of defence; defenceless, unprotected; exposed *to* assault or injury. *arch.* **ME.**

1 SIR W. SCOTT His naked foot was dyed with red. G. GREENE A child naked except for a . . necklace round the waist. W. GOLDING He stripped naked and spread his clothing in the sun. **2a** SHAKES. *Lear* Poor naked wretches . . that bide the pelting of this pitiless storm. *absol.*: DRYDEN The afflicted came, The hunger-starved, the naked and the lame. **b** R. L. STEVENSON I am held naked in my prison. **3** DEFOE I scorn to take up a sword against a naked man. M. C. CLARKE Gaunt . . left him naked to the tender mercies of his priestly enemies. V. WOOLF You are all protected. I am naked.

▶ **II 4** Of a sword etc.: not in a sheath, unsheathed. **OE.**
5 Free from concealment or reserve; straightforward; outspoken. Now chiefly in ***the naked truth*** below. **ME.**
6 Exposed to view or examination; without disguise or concealment; plain, obvious, clear. **ME.**

4 G. GREENE The executioner stands by with naked blade. **5** GIBBON A fragment of the Anecdotes, somewhat too naked, was suppressed. **6** LD MACAULAY Chamberlayne laid his plan, in all its naked absurdity, before the Commons. J. GROSS With Arnold or Eliot . . the snobbishness is naked and unashamed.

▶ **III 7 a** Destitute or devoid *of* something. **OE.** ▸**b** Lacking or defective in some respect. **LME.** ▸**c** Unfilled, unoccupied. *rare.* **M17.**
8 Lacking tackle, equipment, furnishings, etc.; unfurnished; undecorated. **LME.**
9 Lacking vegetation, barren; treeless; having no foliage; (of rock etc.) without soil; exposed. **LME.**
10 *BOTANY.* **a** Of a seed: having no pericarp. Also, of varieties of oats or other cereals: having the husk easily detached (cf. PILCORN). **L16.** ▸**b** Of a stem or leaf: having no leaves or hairs. **E18.**
11 Lacking a protective case or covering; *esp.* (of a light, flame, etc.) unprotected from the wind etc., unshaded. **E17.**
12 *ZOOLOGY.* Of (part of) an animal: lacking hair, scales, or a shell, present in related forms. **E17.**

> 📖 **7a** S. PEPYS It is a remarkable thing how infinitely naked . . Covent Garden is . . of people. **8** O. MANNING A single light bulb . . hung over naked floorboards. **9** W. COWPER Sea-beaten rocks and naked shores. R. KIPLING Not only on the Naked Chalk, but also among the Trees. **11** BURKE I always felt it on the naked nerve. M. DIBDIN It was lit by a large number of naked bulbs.

▶ **IV 13** Without addition; bare, mere; not accompanied by remarks or comments; plainly expressed. Also, not otherwise supported or confirmed by proof, evidence, etc. **OE.**
14 Undiluted, neat. *rare* (chiefly *Scot.*). **E19.**
15 STOCK EXCHANGE. Of an option etc.: not secured on or backed by the underlying share. **L20.**

> 📖 **13** W. BLACKSTONE Herein they state the naked facts. JAS. MILL For the evidence of these designs, Mr. Hastings presents his own naked assertion.

Special collocations & phrases: ***naked ape***: see APE *noun*. **naked as a jay-bird** *US* completely naked. **naked as a needle** *arch.* completely naked. **naked bed** *arch.*: for a naked occupant or one who has removed his or her ordinary clothes. **naked boys** = ***naked ladies*** below. **naked eye** vision unassisted by microscope, telescope, etc. **naked flooring** timbers supporting flooring boards. **naked force** unconcealed, ruthless force. **naked ladies** meadow saffron, *Colchicum autumnale*, whose flowers appear long before the leaves. **naked singularity** ASTRONOMY a space-time singularity which is not surrounded by an event horizon and would therefore be visible to an observer. **the naked truth** the plain truth, without concealment or addition.
▶ **B** *noun*. **†1** *The* naked skin. *rare*. Only in **LME.**
2 A nude figure. Formerly also, *the* nude. **E17.**
3 *The* face or plain surface of a wall etc. **L17.**

> 📖 **2** *Zigzag* We still had to guarantee that there would be . . no more nakeds on the stage.

▪ **nakedly** *adverb* **ME. nakedness** *noun* **OE.**

naker /ˈneɪkə/ *noun*. **ME.**
[Old French *nac(a)ire* = Italian *nacchera* (cf. medieval Latin *nacara*, Greek *anakara*) from Arab. *naḳḳāra* drum.]
Chiefly *Hist.* A kettledrum.
▪ **nakerer** *noun* (long *rare* or *obsolete*) a person who plays the naker **ME.**

nakhlite /ˈnɑːklʌɪt/ *noun*. **E20.**
[from El *Nakhla* el Baharia, a village in Egypt + -ITE[1].]
GEOLOGY. An achondrite containing about 75 per cent ferroan diopside and 15 per cent olivine.
▪ **nakhlitic** /-ˈlɪtɪk/ *adjective* **M20.**

nakhoda /ˈnɑːkədɑː/ *noun*. **E17.**
[Persian & Urdu *nāḵudā*, from *nāw* boat, ship + *ḵudā* master.]
The captain or master of a local boat in Indo-Malayan waters.

nakodo /naˈkoːdo, naˈkəʊdəʊ/ *noun*. Pl. same, **-os**. **L19.**
[Japanese.]
In Japan, a person acting as go-between in the arrangement of a marriage.

nala *noun* var. of NULLAH *noun*[1].

nalbuphine /ˈnalbjʊfiːn/ *noun*. **M20.**
[from NAL(OR)PHINE with inserted BU(TYL.)]
PHARMACOLOGY. A synthetic narcotic, $C_{21}H_{27}NO_4$, which is an analgesic structurally similar to morphine.

naled /ˈneɪlɛd/ *noun*. **M20.**
[Origin unkn.]
An agricultural organophosphorus pesticide, $C_4H_7Br_2Cl_2O_4P$, of low toxicity to mammals and rapidly degradable.

NALGO /ˈnalgəʊ/ *abbreviation*.
National and Local Government Officers' Association.

nalidixic /nalɪˈdɪksɪk/ *adjective*. **M20.**
[from rearrangement of elems. (NAPHTHALENE, CARBOXYLIC, DI-[2]) of the systematic name.]
PHARMACOLOGY. ***nalidixic acid***, a heterocyclic organic acid, $C_{12}H_{12}N_2O_3$, given as a bacteriostatic antiseptic in the treatment of urinary infections.

Nalline /ˈnaliːn/ *noun*. Also **n-**. **M20.**
[from *N-allylnormorphine*: see next.]
PHARMACOLOGY. (US proprietary name for) the drug nalorphine.

nalorphine /ˈnalɔːfiːn/ *noun*. **M20.**
[Contr. of *N-allylnormorphine*, from ALLYL + NOR- + MORPHINE.]
PHARMACOLOGY. A heterocyclic base, $C_{19}H_{21}NO_3$, very similar to morphine in structure and used as an antagonist for that drug and similar narcotics.
¶ A proprietary name for this drug in the US is NALLINE.

naloxone /nəˈlɒksəʊn/ *noun*. **M20.**
[Contr. of *N-allylnoroxymorphone*: see prec., OXY-, -ONE.]
PHARMACOLOGY. A heterocyclic base resembling nalorphine in structure and action. $C_{19}H_{21}NO_4$.

naltrexone /nalˈtrɛksəʊn/ *noun*. **L20.**
[formed as prec. with arbitrary elem. *-trex-*.]
PHARMACOLOGY. A narcotic antagonist, $C_{20}H_{23}NO_4$, related to naloxone and nalorphine.

NAM *abbreviation*. *US*.
National Association of Manufacturers.

Nama /ˈnɑːmə/ *adjective & noun*. **M19.**
[Nama.]
▶ **A** *adjective*. Of, pertaining to, or designating a people living chiefly in Namaqualand (in western South Africa) and Namibia, or their language. **M19.**
▶ **B** *noun*. Pl. **-s**, same.
1 A member of the Nama people. **L19.**
2 The language of this people. **E20.**
¶ Also known by the names *Khoikhoi* and (formerly) *Hottentot*.

Namaqua /nəˈmɑːkwə/ *noun & adjective*. **L17.**
[Nama *nama gu a*.]
▶ **A** *noun*. Pl. **-s**, same. = NAMA *noun*. **L17.**
▶ **B** *adjective*. = NAMA *adjective*. **E19.**
Namaqua dove a small long-tailed dove, *Oena capensis*, found in Africa south of Sudan. **Namaqua grouse**, **Namaqua partridge**, **Namaqua sandgrouse** a game-bird, *Pterocles namaqua*, of southern Africa.

Namaqualand daisy /nəˈmakwəlan(d) ˌdeɪzi/ *noun phr.* **M20.**
[*Namaqualand*, a province of western South Africa.]
An annual daisy, *Dimorphotheca sinuata* (family Compositae), native to Namaqualand, South Africa, and now widely cultivated.

namaskar /nʌməsˈkɑː/ *noun*. **M20.**
[Hindi from Sanskrit *namaskāra*, from *namas* (see next) + *kāra* action.]
A traditional Hindu gesture of greeting made by bringing the palms together before the face or chest and bowing. Cf. WAI *noun*.

namaste /ˈnʌməsteɪ/ *noun*, *interjection*, & *verb*. **M20.**
[Hindi from Sanskrit *namas* bowing, obeisance + *te* dat. of *tvam* you (sing.).]
▶ **A** *noun*. = prec. **M20.**
▶ **B** *interjection*. Expr. respectful greeting (said when giving a namaskar). **M20.**
▶ **C** *verb intrans*. Pres. pple & verbal noun **-eing**. Give a namaskar. **M20.**

namaycush /ˈnameɪkʌʃ, -mɪk-/ *noun*. **L18.**
[Cree *name:kos* or Ojibwa *name:koss*.]
The N. American lake trout, *Salvelinus namaycush*.

namby-pamby /nambɪˈpambi/ *adjective & noun*. **M18.**
[Fanciful formation with redupl. on *Ambrose* Philips (d. 1749), author of pastorals ridiculed by Pope and by Carey (in *Namby Pamby*, 1726).]
▶ **A** *adjective*. Weakly sentimental, affectedly or childishly simple; lacking vigour. **M18.**

> 📖 B. A. STAPLES These weren't namby-pamby fights . . but brutal affairs. M. KEYES There was something very namby-pamby about a man living in the family home.

▶ **B** *noun*. **1** Namby-pamby speech, behaviour, writing, etc.; an instance of this. **M18.**
2 A namby-pamby person. **L19.**

> 📖 **2** P. SCOTT She thought him a bit of a namby-pamby.

▪ **namby-pambyism** *noun* namby-pamby quality; an instance of this: **M19.**

name /neɪm/ *noun & adjective*.
[Old English *nama*, *noma* = Old Frisian *nama*, *noma*, Old Saxon, Old High German *namo* (Dutch *naam*, German *Name*), Old Norse *nafn*, *namn*, Gothic *namo*, from Germanic from Indo-European, cogn. with Latin *nomen*, Greek *onoma*, Sanskrit *nāman*.]
▶ **A** *noun*. **I 1** A word or combination of words constituting the individual designation by which a person, animal, place, or thing is known, spoken of, etc. **OE.** ▸**b** STOCK EXCHANGE. The ticket bearing the name of the purchaser of stock, handed over to the selling broker on ticket-day. **E20.**
2 A word or combination of words designating an object of thought, *esp.* one applicable to many individuals. **OE.** ▸**†b** A title of rank or dignity. Chiefly *Scot.* **LME–L17.**

> 📖 **1** SHAKES. *Merry W.* Peter Simple you say your name is? H. E. BATES The name of the eldest . . was Dulcima. ***Christian name***, ***forename***, ***maiden name***, ***place-name***, ***street name***, etc. **2** TENNYSON Thus he bore without abuse The grand old name of gentleman. I. MCEWAN His ignorance of the names of trees and plants. ***taxonomic name***, ***trade name***, etc.

▶ **II 3** The individual designation or personality of a divine being, as God, Christ, etc., esp. as the object of formal devotion. **OE.**
4 a The individual designation of a person spoken of with admiration, commendation, etc. **ME.** ▸**b** A famous or notorious person, a celebrity; a person or organization whose individual designation is well known. **E17.** ▸**c** (Also **N-**.) An underwriting member of Lloyd's. **L19.**
5 a A person, esp. a well-known one, distinguished by an individual designation. **LME.** ▸**b** All those people collectively bearing or counted as distinguished by a particular designation; a family, a clan, a people. **LME.**

> 📖 **3** J. WESLEY Thee we adore Eternal Name. **4a** SHAKES. *Meas. for M.* My unsoil'd name, th'austereness of my life. TENNYSON If they find Some stain or blemish in a name of note. **b** J. BETJEMAN His publisher believed that a 'name' was needed to help sell the book. *Daily Express* Famous retail names are involved. Once they move out of a town centre, others . . follow. **5a** SHAKES. *Hen. V* By the hand Of that black name, Edward, Black Prince of Wales. A. ALISON Names since immortalised in the rolls of fame were . . assembled. **b** LD MACAULAY All the clans hostile to the name of Campbell were set in motion.

▶ **III 6** The reputation *of* some character or attribute; a reputation of a specified kind. **ME.**
7 A person's reputation. Freq. with specifying word, as *good*, *ill*, etc. **ME.**
8 Repute, fame, distinction. Now *rare*. **ME.**

> 📖 **6** S. AUSTIN If he were victorious, he would . . bequeath a great name to posterity. *Law Times* No profession will lightly earn for itself the name of a profession of hireling subornees of perjury. A. LURIE He's got a name in some circles, but essentially he's a fraud. **7** W. COWPER Flavia, most tender of her own good name. T. MEDWIN Hourly came Fresh followers, lured by his success and name. **8** BACON Senators that had name and opinion for general wise men. TENNYSON He lay as dead And lost to life and use and name and fame.

▶ **IV 9** A mere appellation as distinct from an actual person or thing; a thing existing only nominally. **ME.**

> 📖 **9** SHAKES. *All's Well* 'Tis but the shadow of a wife you see, The name and not the thing.

Phrases: ***a name to conjure with***: see CONJURE *verb*. **by name** called (freq. *postpositive*). **by the name of** called or known by, having, the name of. ***call out of one's name***, ***call someone names***: see CALL *verb*. ***for one's name sake***, ***for one's name's sake***: see SAKE *noun*[1]. **get the name of** *arch.* have the reputation of (being). **give it a name** *colloq.* what would you like to drink? ***have a person's name and number on it***: see NUMBER *noun*. **have a person's name on it** = ***have a person's name and number on it*** s.v. NUMBER *noun*. **have one's name in lights** (of an actor etc.) have one's name displayed in lights outside a theatre etc.; *fig.* be famous. **have — to one's name** possess. **in all but name** virtually. **in God's name**, **in Heaven's name**, etc., invoking, relying on, or calling to witness God, Heaven, etc., (freq. as *interjection* & in exclamatory phrs.). **in name (only)** as a mere formality, hardly at all. **in one's own name** independently; not on the authority of anyone else. **in the name of** (*a*) invoking, relying on, calling to witness, (freq. as *interjection* & in exclamatory phrs., as ***in the name of God***, ***in the name of goodness***, ***in the name of wonder***, etc.); (*b*) acting as a deputy for or on behalf of; (*c*) (now *rare* or *obsolete*) in the identity of, in the guise of; (*d*) indicating the stated ownership of. **keep one's name on the books** remain a member of a college, club, etc. **know by name** (*a*) know individually; (*b*) know by repute, not personally or actually. **make a name for oneself** become famous. **no names, no pack-drill** discretion will prevent punishment. **of name**, **of great name**, etc., *arch.* noted, distinguished, famous. **of no name**, **without a name**, **without name** obscure, unimportant. ***one's name is mud***: see MUD *noun*[1]. **or my name is not** —: expr. asseveration. ***over one's name***: see OVER *preposition*. **put one's name down (for)**, **put a person's name down (for)** (*a*) apply, enter, as a candidate etc. (for); (*b*) promise to subscribe (to). ***take a person's name in vain***: see VAIN *adjective*. **take one's name off the books** withdraw from membership of a college, club, etc. **the name of the game** *colloq.* the purpose or essence of an action etc. ***variable name***: see VARIABLE *noun* 1b. ***without a name***, ***without name***: see ***of no name*** above.
Comb.: **name-calling** abusive language, mere abuse; **name-check** (*a*) the public mention of a person's name, esp. in acknowledgement of his or her contribution to a particular matter; (*b*) an official check on a person's credentials, esp. for security or criminal investigation; **name-child** *arch.* a person named after another person; **name-day** (*a*) the feast-day of the particular saint after whom a person is named; (*b*) = ***ticket-day*** s.v. TICKET *noun*; **name-drop** *verb intrans.* practise name-dropping; **name-dropper** a person who name-drops; **name-dropping** familiar mention of the name of a distinguished person as implying one's own importance; **name-part** the title role of a play, book, ballet, etc.; **name-plate** a plate or panel bearing the name of the occupant of a room etc. or of the thing to which it is attached; **name-son** *arch.* a male person named after another person; **name-story** the story from which a volume of collected short stories is named; **name-tag** a tag, label, badge, etc., (to be) inscribed with a name identifying the person or object to which it is fixed; **name-tape** a piece of tape fixed to a garment etc. bearing the name of the owner.
▶ **B** *attrib.* or as *adjective*. Of or pertaining to a widely-known group of people (esp. a jazz band), commercial product, etc. **M20.**

> 📖 *Twentieth Century* A big factor in the sale of the more popular 'name' records is the personality cult.

▪ **nameworthy** *adjective* (*arch.*) noteworthy, notable **L16.**

name /neɪm/ *verb trans.*
[Old English (*ge*)*namian*, from West Germanic; partly directly from the noun.]
▶ **I 1** Give a name or names to (a person, place, etc.); call by a specified name. (Foll. by *after*, *from*, (now chiefly *N. Amer.*) *for*, and with a name as compl.) Freq. in *pass.* **OE.**
2 Call by a specified title or epithet. Formerly also, give (a person etc.) the name of being; allege, declare, (a person or thing) *to be*. *arch.* **OE.**

3 Call by the right name. **ME.**

📖 **1** T. S. ELIOT We named the child Barnabas. P. L. FERMOR He had discovered an Indian mineral which was named after him. **2** SHELLEY Silence! Oh, well are Death and Sleep and Thou Three brethren named. **3** SHAKES. *Wint. T.* There is a sickness Which puts some of us in distemper; but I cannot name the disease. R. BURNS I'm sure I've seen that bonie face, But yet I canna name ye.

▶**II 4** Nominate or appoint (a person) to an office, position, etc. Freq. foll. by *to*. **OE.**

5 Mention or specify by name. **OE.** ▶**b** Make mention of, speak about, (a fact, circumstance, etc.); cite as an instance; state, give particulars of. **M16.** ▶**c** *refl.* Announce one's own name. *arch.* **L16.** ▶**d** Of the Speaker of the House of Commons: mention (a Member of Parliament) by name as disobedient to the chair. **L18.** ▶**e** Cite as co-respondent in a divorce petition. **L20.**

6 With cognate obj.: utter, mention, (a name). Formerly also, utter (a word); say. **LME.**

7 Specify as something desired, suggested, or decided on; appoint or fix (a sum, time, etc.). **L16.**

📖 **4** SHAKES. *Macb.* He is already nam'd, and gone to Scone To be invested. T. JEFFERSON In the meantime a consul general is named to St. Domingo. **5** SHELLEY The crimes which mortal tongue dare never name. JOAN SMITH The man, who has not been named, was taken to police headquarters. **name and shame** make public details of failure, wrongdoing, or other shortcoming on the part of a specified person, institution, etc. **b** TENNYSON Hear The wish too strong for words to name. J. R. GREEN The measures we have named were only part of Henry's legislation. **c** SHAKES. *Coriol.* Necessity Commands me name myself. **6** SHAKES. *3 Hen. VI* What's worse than murderer, that I may name it? DEFOE It is a .. profane thing to name his name on slight occasions. **7** J. WAINWRIGHT I'll pay . . . Just name it.

Phrases: **name no names** refrain from naming the people involved in an incident etc. **name the day** arrange a date, esp. (of a woman) fix the date for one's wedding. **you name it** *colloq.* everything that you can think of is available, has been done, etc.

■ **namea'bility** *noun* the quality of being nameable **L19.** **nameable** *adjective* (*a*) worthy of being named; memorable; (*b*) able to be named; (earlier in **UNNAMEABLE**): **M17.** **namer** *noun* **E17.**

nameless /'neɪmlɪs/ *adjective.* **ME.**
[from **NAME** *noun* + **-LESS**.]

1 Not possessed of a distinguished or famous name; obscure, inglorious; left in obscurity. **ME.**

2 Not specified by name, left unnamed on purpose; having an undivulged name; impersonal, unknown. **LME.**

3 Orig., (of a book, letter, etc.) of undeclared source or authorship, anonymous. Later, (of a tomb etc.) not having a name or identifying inscription. **E16.**

4 a Not having any legal right to a name, illegitimate. *arch.* **L16.** ▶**b** That has not been named; unnamed. **M17.**

5 That cannot be definitely named or described; inexpressible, indefinable. **L16.**

6 That one shrinks from naming; inexpressibly loathsome and horrific. **E17.**

📖 **1** MILTON Nameless in dark oblivion let them dwell. **2** LD MACAULAY The two nameless executioners who had done their office . . on the scaffold. *Sounds* The road manager of a headlining band that shall remain nameless. M. ANGELOU A lady can't drink with a nameless man. **3** J. WESLEY One of the hearers wrote me a nameless letter upon it. A. A. PROCTER Over a nameless grave. **4a** DRYDEN And into Noble Families advance A Nameless Issue. **b** S. ROGERS A thousand nameless rills that shun the light. **5** CLIVE JAMES Nameless fears haunted the mind. **6** H. P. LIDDON Paganism allowed man to sink beneath a flood of nameless sensualities.

■ **namelessly** *adverb* **L18.** **namelessness** *noun* **E19.**

namely /'neɪmli/ *adjective.* Now only *Scot.* **LME.**
[from **NAME** *noun* + **-LY**[1].]
Distinguished, famous, notable (*for*).

namely /'neɪmli/ *adverb.* **ME.**
[from **NAME** *noun* + **-LY**[2], rendering Latin *nominatim* by name, expressly, in detail.]

1 Particularly, especially, above all. Long *obsolete* exc. *Scot.* **ME.** ▶†**b** By name, individually. *rare.* **M–L16.**

†**2** At least, at any rate. *rare.* Only in **ME.**

3 That is to say. Formerly also, (foll. by *as*) for example. **LME.**

📖 **3** J. NORRIS Namely, to consider what is meant by the Law. T. HARDY Its situation gave the house what little distinctive name it possessed, namely, 'The Knap'.

namesake /'neɪmseɪk/ *noun & verb.* **M17.**
[from **NAME** *noun* + **SAKE** *noun*[1], prob. ult. from ***for one's name's sake*** s.v. **SAKE** *noun*[1].]

▶**A** *noun.* A person or thing having the same name as another. **M17.**

▶**B** *verb trans.* Call by the same name; name *after*. *rare.* **M17.**

Namibian /nə'mɪbɪən/ *noun & adjective.* **M20.**
[from *Namibia* (see below), from *Namib* a desert on the west coast of Africa + **-IAN**.]

▶**A** *noun.* A native or inhabitant of Namibia, a country in SW Africa between Angola and Cape Province. **M20.**

▶**B** *adjective.* Of or pertaining to Namibia or the Namibians. **M20.**

Namierian /neɪ'mɪərɪən/ *noun & adjective.* **M20.**
[from *Namier* (see below) + **-IAN**.]

▶**A** *noun.* An adherent of the methods and theories of the Polish-born British historian Sir Lewis Namier (1886–1960), esp. as concerning the influence of politics on the course of history. **M20.**

▶**B** *adjective.* Of or pertaining to the historical theories or techniques of Namier. **M20.**

■ **'Namierite** *noun & adjective* = **NAMIERIAN M20.** **Namieri'zation** *noun* the application of Namier's methods and theories to a historical situation **M20.** **'Namierize** *verb intrans.* practise Namierization **M20.**

naming /'neɪmɪŋ/ *verbal noun.* **ME.**
[from **NAME** *verb* + **-ING**[1].]
The action or result of **NAME** *verb.*

naming of parts the process of becoming acquainted, or of acquainting others, with the essentials of an unfamiliar object or topic.

namma hole *noun phr.* var. of **GNAMMA HOLE.**

nan /nan/ *noun*[1]. *arch.* **L17.**
[from *Nan* familiar form of female forename *Ann(e)*.]
A serving-maid.

nan /nɑːn/ *noun*[2]. Also **naan**. **E20.**
[Persian & Urdu *nān*.]
In Indian cookery, a type of leavened bread cooked esp. in a clay oven.

nan /nan/ *noun*[3]. *nursery & colloq.* **M20.**
[from **GRAN** or abbreviation of **NANNY** *noun*.]
Grandmother. Also (occas.), a child's nursemaid.

nana /'nanə/ *noun*[1]. *nursery & colloq.* Also **nanna**. **M19.**
[formed as **NAN** *noun*[3].]
= **NAN** *noun*[3].

nana /'nɑːnə/ *noun*[2]. **M20.**
[Aphet. from **BANANA**.]

1 A banana. *nursery & joc.* **M20.**

2 A foolish person, a fool. *slang.* **M20.**

3 The head. *Austral. slang.* **M20.**

nanberry /'nanb(ə)ri/ *noun. dial.* **E18.**
[Alt. of **ANBURY**.]
= **ANBURY** 1.

nance /nans/ *noun. slang. derog.* **E20.**
[Abbreviation.]
= **NANCY** *noun*[2].

nancy /'nansi/ *noun*[1]. **E19.**
[from *Anancy, Anansi*, spider character in W. African & W. Indian folklore from Twi *ananse* spider: infl. by the female forename *Nancy*.]

nancy-story, nancy-tale, a type of folk-tale popular in W. Africa and the W. Indies.

nancy /'nansi/ *noun*[2]. *slang. derog.* **E20.**
[from ***Miss Nancy*** s.v. **MISS** *noun*[2].]
An effeminate man or boy; a homosexual man. Also ***nancy-boy***.

■ **nancified** *adjective* (of a man) effeminate; (of a thing) bland, weak, fussily overelaborated: **E20.**

Nancy Dawson /nansɪ 'dɔːs(ə)n/ *noun phr.* Now *rare* or *obsolete.* **M18.**
[Perh. from the name of a prostitute.]
A sailor's dance to the tune of the song 'Nancy Dawson'. Also (*slang*), a male homosexual.

NAND /nand/ *noun.* **M20.**
[from *not and*.]
COMPUTING. A Boolean operator which gives the value zero if and only if all the operands are unity, and is otherwise unity; = NOT AND. Usu. *attrib.*

Nandi /'nʌndiː/ *noun*[1]. **E19.**
[Sanskrit *Nandī, -din*.]
In Hindu mythology, the bull of Siva which is his vahana or vehicle and symbolizes fertility; a figure or statue of Nandi.

Nandi /'nandi/ *noun*[2] *& adjective.* **L19.**
[Nandi.]

▶**A** *noun.* Pl. same.

1 A member of an E. African people of mixed origin which inhabits an area on the Uganda–Kenya border. **L19.**

2 The Nilotic language spoken by the Nandi and some neighbouring peoples. **E20.**

▶**B** *attrib.* or as *adjective.* Of or pertaining to the Nandi or their language. **E20.**

Nandi bear a hypothetical animal resembling a bear, said to inhabit parts of E. Africa.

Nandrolone /'nandrələʊn/ *noun.* **M20.**
[from **N**(**OR-** 1 + **ANDR**(**O-** + **-OL** + **-ONE**, elems. of alternative chemical name.]
A synthetic anabolic steroid, $C_{18}H_{26}O_2$ (also called ***19-nortestosterone***), which has tissue-building properties and is used (often illegally) to enhance performance in sport.

Nanga /'naŋgə/ *adjective.* **M20.**
[Japanese, abbreviation of *Nanshuga*, from *nanshu* southern China + *ga* painting, picture.]
Designating, of, or pertaining to an intellectual style of Japanese painting.

†**nanguer** *noun.* **L18–M19.**
[French, from a local name.]
ZOOLOGY. An antelope of Senegal, probably a reedbuck.

nanism /'neɪnɪz(ə)m/ *noun.* **M19.**
[French *nanisme*, from Latin *nanus* (Greek *nanos*) dwarf: see **-ISM**.]
The condition of being abnormally small; the tendency to become stunted; an instance of this.

nankeen /naŋ'kiːn, nan-/ *noun & adjective.* Also **-kin** /-kɪn/, **N-**. **M18.**
[from *Nankin(g)* in China.]

▶**A** *noun.* **1** A kind of pale yellowish cotton cloth, orig. made from a yellow variety of cotton but now usu. dyed. Also ***nankeen cloth***. **M18.** ▶**b** A kind or variety of this cloth. **L18.** ▶**c** In *pl.* Trousers made of nankeen. **E19.**

2 The colour of nankeen; a pale yellowish buff. **L18.**

3 a (Usu. **N-**.) In full ***Nankeen porcelain***, ***Nankeen ware***, etc. A kind of usu. blue and white Chinese porcelain. **M18.** ▶**b** = ***blonde lace*** s.v. **BLOND** *adjective.* **M19.**

▶**B** *attrib.* or as *adjective.* Made of nankeen; of the pale yellowish-buff colour of nankeen. **L18.**

Comb. & special collocations: **nankeen cloth**: see sense 1 above; **nankeen cotton** the variety of cotton from which nankeen cloth was originally made; †**nankeen hawk** = ***nankeen kestrel*** below; **nankeen heron** = ***nankeen night heron*** below; **nankeen kestrel** a small Australasian falcon, *Falco cenchroides*; **nankeen night heron** a nocturnal heron, *Nycticorax caledonicus*, of Australia and the SW Pacific islands.

nanna *noun* var. of **NANA** *noun*[1].

nannie *noun & verb* var. of **NANNY.**

nannofossil /'nanəʊfɒs(ə)l, -sɪl/ *noun.* **M20.**
[formed as next + **FOSSIL**.]
GEOLOGY. A fossil of a minute planktonic organism, esp. a calcareous unicellular alga.

nannoplankton /'nanəʊplaŋkt(ə)n/ *noun.* Also **nano-**. **E20.**
[German, formed as **NANO-** + **PLANKTON**.]
BIOLOGY. Very small unicellular plankton, at the limits of resolution of light microscopy.

■ **nannoplank'tonic** *adjective* **M20.**

nanny /'nani/ *noun & verb.* Also **-ie**, (as a title) **N-**. **E18.**
[Pet-form of female forename *Ann(e)*: see **-Y**[6].]

▶**A** *noun.* **1** A person employed, esp. on a full-time basis, to look after a child; a nursemaid. Also, a grandmother. Freq. as a familiar form of address. **E18.** ▶**b** *transf.* A person, institution, etc., considered to be unduly protective or apprehensive. **M20.**

2 = **NANNY-GOAT** 1. **L19.**

📖 **1** JILLY COOPER Nanny Ellis said it was common to play with children whose friends were in trade. **b** *Listener* The top authorities . . who regulate television should [be] . . impervious to the huge army of self-appointed nannies.

Phrases: **get a person's nanny** *colloq.* = ***get a person's*** **GOAT.**

▶**B** *verb trans.* Treat in the manner of a nanny; be unduly protective towards. **M20.**

■ **nannydom** *noun* the condition of being a nanny; nannies collectively: **M20.** **nannyish** *adjective* resembling or characteristic of a nanny; overprotective, fussy: **M20.** **nannyishly** *adverb* **L20.**

nannygai /'nanɪgʌɪ/ *noun. Austral.* **L19.**
[Aboriginal.]
A reddish deep-bodied marine food fish, *Centroberyx affinis*, of S. Australia. Also called ***redfish***.

nanny-goat /'nanɪgəʊt/ *noun.* **L18.**
[from **NANNY** + **GOAT**.]

1 A female goat. **L18.**

2 a An anecdote. *rhyming slang.* **M19.** ▶**b** A totalizator ('tote'). *rhyming slang.* **M20.**

Phrases: **get a person's nanny-goat** *colloq.* = ***get a person's*** **GOAT.**

nano /'nanəʊ/ *noun.* **L20.**
[Abbreviation.]
Nanotechnology. Freq. *attrib.*

nano- /'nanəʊ, 'neɪməʊ, 'nɑːnəʊ/ *combining form.*
[from Greek *nanos*, Latin *nanus* dwarf: see **-O-**.]
Very small; *spec.* used in names of units of measurement to denote a factor of 10^{-9} (one thousand-millionth), as ***nanogram***, ***nanometre***, ***nanosecond***, etc. Abbreviation *n.*

■ **nanobac'terium** *noun*, pl. **-ria**, (MICROBIOLOGY) a kind of microorganism about a tenth the size of the smallest normal bacteria, claimed to have been discovered in living tissue and in rock **L20.**

nanomachine *noun* a machine or device of nanotechnological scale L20. **nanotechno'logical** *adjective* of or pertaining to nanotechnology L20. **nanotech'nology** *noun* the branch of technology that deals with dimensions and tolerances of 0.1 to 100 nanometres L20. **nanotube** *noun* (CHEMISTRY) a cylindrical molecule of a fullerene L20.

nanoid /'neɪnɔɪd/ *adjective. rare.* M19.
[formed as prec. + -OID.]
Resembling a dwarf, dwarfish.

nanophanerophyte /nanəʊ'fanərə(ʊ)fʌɪt/ *noun.* E20.
[French *nanophanérophyte*, formed as NANO- + PHANEROPHYTE.]
A shrub or sub-shrub between 25 cm and 2 m (approx. 10 and 80 inches) in height, bearing its resting buds above the surface of the soil.

nanoplankton *noun* var. of NANNOPLANKTON.

Nansen /'nans(ə)n/ *noun.* E20.
[from Fridtjof *Nansen* (1861–1930), Norwegian diplomat and explorer.]
1 In full ***Nansen passport***. A document of identification issued after the war of 1914–18 to a stateless person ineligible for a passport. E20.
2 OCEANOGRAPHY. ***Nansen bottle***, a device for collecting water samples at predetermined depths. M20.

nant /nant/ *noun.* M19.
[Welsh.]
In Wales: a brook, a valley.

Nantgarw /nant'garuː/ *noun.* E19.
[See below.]
In full ***Nantgarw porcelain***, ***Nantgarw ware***, etc. A kind of translucent soft-paste porcelain produced between 1813 and 1920 in Nantgarw, a village in S. Wales.

Nanticoke /'nantɪkəʊk/ *noun & adjective.* E18.
[*Nanticoke* River, on the eastern side of Chesapeake Bay.]
▶ **A** *noun.* Pl. same.
1 A member of an Algonquian people formerly inhabiting the Chesapeake Bay area of Maryland, Delaware, and Pennsylvania. E18.
2 The language of this people. L19.
▶ **B** *attrib.* or as *adjective.* Of or pertaining to the Nanticoke or their language. E20.

Nants *noun* var. of NANTZ.

Nantucketer /nan'tʌkɪtə/ *noun.* M19.
[from *Nantucket* (see below) + -ER¹.]
A native or inhabitant of Nantucket, an island off the coast of Massachusetts, USA.

Nantz /nants/ *noun. arch.* Also **Nants**. L17.
[from *Nantes* in France, a place of manufacture.]
Brandy. Also ***right Nantz***.

naology /neɪ'ɒlədʒi/ *noun.* M19.
[formed as next + -LOGY.]
The branch of knowledge that deals with sacred buildings.
■ **nao'logical** *adjective* M19.

naos /'neɪɒs/ *noun.* L18.
[Greek = temple.]
(The inner cell or sanctuary of) a temple.

naow /naʊ, 'naːʊ/ *adjective, adverb¹ & interjection. non-standard.* E20.
[Repr. a pronunc. Cf. NAH *adverb² & interjection*, NAW.]
▶ **A** *adjective.* = NO *adjective.* E20.
▶ **B** *adverb & interjection.* = NO *adverb³ & interjection.* M20.

naow /naʊ, 'naːʊ/ *adverb².* *non-standard.* E20.
[Repr. a pronunc. Cf. NAH *adverb¹*.]
= NOW *adverb.*

nap /nap/ *noun¹.* LME.
[from NAP *verb¹*.]
A short or light sleep, *esp.* one taken during the day; a doze.

> A. BROOKNER The dead hour between two and three, when sensible people . . take a nap.

nap /nap/ *noun².* Also **†knap**. LME.
[Middle Low German, Middle Dutch *noppe* (whence German, Danish *noppe*) rel. to *noppen* trim by shearing the nap.]
1 Orig. the rough layer of projecting threads or fibres on the surface of a woollen or other textile fabric. Now, a raised pile given to cloth, esp. velvet, by raising, cutting, and smoothing the short fibres. LME. ▸**b** A cloth with a nap on it. Now *rare.* M18. ▸**c** A bundle of bedding that is carried around, a swag. *Austral. slang.* L19.
2 *transf.* A soft downy surface resembling the nap of cloth. L16.
3 The smooth glossy surface of a felt, silk, etc. hat. E18.

> **1** T. DREISER His feet sinking into the soft nap of the carpet. E. WILSON Sometimes this linen twill was brushed to form a raised nap.

nap /nap/ *noun³.* E19.
[Abbreviation of *Napoleon*.]
1 = NAPOLEON 1. E19.
2 A card-game in which each player receives five cards and declares the number of tricks he or she expects to win; a call of five tricks in this game. Cf. NAPOLEON 5. M19.
3 A tipster's prediction of the horse most likely to win its race on a particular day; a horse etc. so tipped; a bet on such a horse etc. Also ***nap selection***. *colloq.* L19.

> **2 go nap** attempt to take all five tricks in nap; *fig.* risk everything in one attempt; score five goals, wins, etc. **not go nap on** *Austral. colloq.* not be keen on, not care much for.
> **3** *Times* Today's nap . . is on First Division to maintain his . . winning sequence.

Comb.: **nap hand** a hand likely to win all five tricks in nap; *fig.* a favourable position seen as inviting the taking of risks; a set of five things. ***nap selection***: see sense 3 above.

nap /nap/ *noun⁴.* *Theatrical slang.* M19.
[Perh. var. of KNAP *noun²*.]
A pretended blow. Esp. in ***give the nap***, ***take the nap***.

nap /nap/ *verb¹ intrans.* Infl. **-pp-**.
[Old English *hnappian* rel. to Old High German (*h*)*naffezan* slumber, of unkn. origin.]
Sleep lightly or for a brief time; take a short sleep.
catch napping, **take napping** find (a person) asleep; *fig.* take (a person) unawares or off guard; surprise (a person).

nap /nap/ *verb² trans.* Also **†knap**. Infl. **-pp-**. LME.
[Middle Low German, Middle Dutch *noppen*: see NAP *noun²*.]
1 Provide with a nap; raise a nap on. LME.
†2 Trim (cloth) by shearing the nap. L15–L16.

nap /nap/ *verb³ trans. slang.* Now *rare.* Infl. **-pp-**. L17.
[Origin uncertain: cf. earlier NAPPER *noun²*, also NAB *verb¹*.]
1 Seize, catch, arrest, (a person or thing); steal (a thing). L17.
2 Receive, suffer, (a blow etc.). Chiefly in ***nap it***, receive severe punishment, esp. in a boxing-match. L17.

nap /nap/ *verb⁴ trans. colloq.* Infl. **-pp-**. E20.
[from NAP *noun³*.]
Name (a horse etc.) as a nap selection; predict, forecast. Usu. in *pass.*

> *Racing Post* Sharblask . . is napped to give Nicky Vigors a perfect start to the new Flat season.

nap /nap/ *verb⁵ intrans.* Infl. **-pp-**. M20.
[Rel. to NAPPY *adjective¹* 3.]
Of a horse: refuse to go on at the rider's instruction.

Napa *noun¹* var. of NAPPA.

napa /'napə/ *noun².* L20.
[Japanese *nappa* greens.]
In full ***napa cabbage***. A form of Chinese cabbage, *Brassica rapa* var. *pekinensis*, with pale green leaves forming a tight head.

napalm /'neɪpaːm, 'na-/ *noun & verb.* Orig. *US.* M20.
[from NA(PHTHENIC + PALM(ITATE.]
▶ **A** *noun.* A thickening agent containing aluminium salts of naphthenic acids and of fatty acids of coconut oil; a thixotropic gel consisting of petrol and such a thickening agent, used in flame-throwers and incendiary bombs; jellied petrol. M20.
▶ **B** *verb trans.* Attack or destroy with napalm. M20.

> *Listener* The Greeks are told how the Turks bombed and napalmed innocent people.

nape /neɪp/ *noun.* ME.
[Origin unkn.]
1 The back of the neck. Esp. in ***nape of the neck***. ME.
2 The fleshy part left projecting from a fish's backbone after the head has been removed. Long *obsolete* exc. *Canad. dial.* L15.

napellus /nə'pɛləs/ *noun.* Now *rare* or *obsolete.* E17.
[medieval Latin, from *napus* turnip, with ref. to the turnip-shaped root.]
The plant monkshood, *Aconitum napellus*.

napery /'neɪpəri/ *noun.* ME.
[Old French *naperie*, from *nap(p)e* tablecloth: see NAPKIN, -ERY.]
1 Linen used for various household purposes; *esp.* table linen. ME.
†2 The charge or custody of the royal linen; the position or office of naperer. L15–E17.
3 A storeroom for linen. E19.
■ **naperer** *noun* (*Hist.*) a person in charge of table linen in a royal or manor house LME.

naphtha /'nafθə/ *noun.* LME.
[Latin from Greek (also *naphthos*), of oriental origin.]
Orig., liquid petroleum, esp. as occurring naturally. Now, any of various mixtures of volatile flammable liquid distillation products used esp. as solvents and in petrol, derived (***a***) from petroleum, including aliphatic and alicyclic hydrocarbons with boiling points below 200°C, (***b***) from coal tar, including toluene, xylene, and other aromatic benzene derivatives. Freq. *attrib.* and with specifying words.
¶ Rare before L16.
■ **naphthacene** *noun* [ANTHRACENE] CHEMISTRY an aromatic hydrocarbon, $C_{18}H_{12}$, whose molecule consists of four fused benzene rings and is the skeleton of the tetracyclines M20. **naphthous** *adjective* of the nature of naphtha L19.

naphthalene /'nafθəliːn/ *noun.* Also (earlier) **†-in**, **†-ine**. E19.
[from prec. + -l- + -ENE.]
CHEMISTRY. A pungent crystalline aromatic compound, $C_{10}H_8$, which is obtained as a distillation product of coal tar, and whose molecule consists of two six-membered rings fused along one side.

naphthaleneacetic /ˌnafθəliːnə'siːtɪk/ *adjective.* E20.
[from prec. + ACETIC.]
CHEMISTRY. ***naphthaleneacetic acid***: either of two crystalline compounds, $C_{10}H_7CH_2COOH$, derived from naphthalene; *spec.* (more fully ***α-naphthaleneacetic acid***) one used to stimulate the rooting of plant cuttings and prevent premature dropping of fruit.

naphthalic /naf'θalɪk/ *adjective. rare.* M19.
[formed as NAPHTHALENE + -IC.]
Naphthous; CHEMISTRY phthalic.

†naphthalin(e) *noun* see NAPHTHALENE.

naphthalize /'nafθəlʌɪz/ *verb trans.* Also **-ise**. M19.
[formed as NAPHTHALENE + -IZE.]
Mingle, saturate, or impregnate with naphtha.
■ **naphthali'zation** *noun* M19.

naphthaquinone *noun* var. of NAPHTHOQUINONE.

naphthene /'nafθiːn/ *noun.* M19.
[from NAPHTHA + -ENE.]
CHEMISTRY. **†1** A supposed constituent of naphtha (now regarded as a mixture). Only in M19.
2 Any of a class of saturated cyclic hydrocarbons (including cyclopentane and cyclohexane) present in or obtained from petroleum. L19.

naphthenic /naf'θiːnɪk/ *adjective.* L19.
[from prec. + -IC.]
CHEMISTRY. **1** ***naphthenic acid***, (a mixture of) any of the carboxylic acids obtained in the refining of petroleum, esp. one derived from a naphthene. L19.
2 Of, pertaining to, or containing naphthenes. M20.
■ **'naphthenate** *noun* a salt or ester of a naphthenic acid L19.

naphthol /'nafθɒl/ *noun.* M19.
[from NAPHTHA + -OL.]
CHEMISTRY. Either of two isomeric phenols, $C_{10}H_8O$, derived from naphthalene.

naphthoquinone /nafθə'kwɪnəʊn/ *noun.* Also **naphtha-**. L19.
[from NAPHTH(ALENE + -O- + QUINONE.]
CHEMISTRY. Each of six isomeric compounds, $C_{10}H_6O_2$, notionally obtained by replacing two of the CH groups of naphthalene by carbonyl groups; *spec.* (more fully ***1,4-naphthoquinone***, ***α-naphthoquinone***) a volatile yellow solid whose molecule forms part of the structure of vitamin K.

naphthyl /'nafθʌɪl, -θɪl/ *noun.* M19.
[from NAPHTH(ALENE + -YL.]
CHEMISTRY. Either of two isomeric radicals of naphthalene, $C_{10}H_7\cdot$. Usu. in *comb.*

Napierian /neɪ'pɪərɪən/ *adjective.* E19.
[from *Napier* (see next) + -IAN.]
Invented by or associated with John Napier.
Napierian LOGARITHM.

Napier's bones /'neɪpɪəz bəʊnz/ *noun phr. pl.* M17.
[John *Napier* (1550–1617), Scot. mathematician.]
Several narrow strips of ivory, wood, etc., divided into marked sections bearing digits, used as an aid to multiplication and division.

napiform /'neɪpɪfɔːm/ *adjective.* M19.
[from Latin *napus* turnip + -I- + -FORM.]
Formed like a turnip; BOTANY (of a root) round above and tapering below.

napkin /'napkɪn/ *noun.* LME.
[Old & mod. French *nap(p)e* tablecloth from Latin *mappa* MAP *noun¹* (for the change of *m* to *n* cf. French *natte* from Latin *matta* mat): see -KIN.]
1 A usu. square piece of linen, paper, etc., used at a meal to wipe the fingers or lips and to protect garments, or to serve food on. Also ***table napkin***. LME.
2 a A handkerchief. Now only *Scot. & north.* LME. ▸**b** A kerchief, a neckerchief. *Scot.* L18.
3 A cloth, a small towel. L16.
4 = NAPPY *noun³*. M19.
5 A sanitary towel. Also ***sanitary napkin***. Chiefly *N. Amer.* L19.

> **1** H. BELLOC Gentlefolk who say 'napkin', side by side with those . . of our modern world who say 'serviette'. JULIAN GLOAG Oliver tucked his napkin under his chin and picked up his knife and fork.

Comb.: **napkin-ring** a ring of silver, wood, etc., used to hold (and distinguish) a person's table napkin when not in use.
■ **napkined** *adjective* wrapped in or covered with a napkin; provided with or served on a napkin: M18. **napkining** *noun* (now *rare* or *obsolete*) material for napkins M17.

Naples /ˈneɪp(ə)lz/ *noun*. L17.
[A city in S. Italy.]
1 ***Naples biscuit***, a kind of rosewater-flavoured biscuit. Now *rare*. L17.
2 ***Naples yellow***, a pale yellow pigment orig. made at Naples with lead antimonate but now freq. a coloured zinc oxide; the colour produced by this. M18.
3 *Hist.* ***Naples soap***, a soft brown soap formerly used for shaving. L18.

napless /ˈnaplɪs/ *adjective*. L16.
[from NAP *noun*² + -LESS.]
Having no nap; worn, threadbare.
■ **naplessness** *noun* M19.

napoh /ˈnɑːpəʊ/ *noun*. Also (earlier) †**napu**. E19.
[Malay.]
The greater chevrotain, *Tragulus napu*, of SE Asia.

napoleon /nəˈpəʊlɪən/ *noun*. Also **N-**. E19.
[Forename of certain emperors of the French, esp. *Napoleon I* (Bonaparte) (1769–1821).]
1 A gold twenty-franc coin issued in the reign of the French emperor Napoleon I; a twenty-franc piece. E19.
2 (**N-**.) A person regarded as resembling Napoleon I, esp. in having gained supremacy through ruthless ambition. E19.
3 *Hist.* A kind of high boot. M19.
4 A kind of cannon. *US*. M19.
5 CARDS. = NAP *noun*³ 2. L19.
6 = MILLEFEUILLE. Chiefly *N. Amer.* L19.
7 A large bigarreau cherry with a red skin and white flesh. Cf. ***Royal Ann(e)*** s.v. ROYAL *adjective*. E20.
8 (Usu. **N-**.) In full ***Napoleon brandy***. Brandy of supposed great age or special merit; a glass or variety of this. M20.

> 📖 **1 double napoleon** a forty-franc piece. **2** T. S. ELIOT The Cat who all the time Just controls their operations: the Napoleon of Crime!

■ **Napoleonism** *noun* (*a*) the method of government practised by Napoleon I, *spec.* the assumption of absolute control over subject peoples or countries; (*b*) attachment to the policy or dynasty of the Napoleons; (*c*) conduct or behaviour resembling that of Napoleon I: E19. **Napoleonist** *noun & adjective* (*a*) *noun* an adherent of Napoleon I or the Napoleonic dynasty; (*b*) *adjective* pertaining or attached to Napoleon: E19. **Napoleoˈnistic** *adjective* Napoleonic; of the nature or characteristic of Napoleonism: L19. **Napoleonize** *verb trans.* govern in the style of Napoleon I E19.

Napoleonic /nəpəʊlɪˈɒnɪk/ *adjective*. M19.
[from prec. + -IC.]
Of, pertaining to, or characteristic of Napoleon I or his family or times.

> 📖 G. B. SHAW It is assumed . . that I look for the salvation of society to the despotism of a single Napoleonic Superman. A. BLOND A sense of purpose and efficiency which is almost Napoleonic. **Napoleonic Wars** a series of campaigns (1800–15) of French armies under Napoleon I against various European powers.

■ **Napoleonically** *adverb* M19.

napoo /nɑːˈpuː/ *interjection, adjective, & verb*. *slang* (orig. MILITARY). E20.
[French *il n'y en a plus* there's none left.]
▶ **A** *interjection*. Finished!, gone!, done for!; goodbye. E20.
▶ **B** *adjective*. Finished; good for nothing; dead. E20.
▶ **C** *verb trans*. Finish, kill, destroy. E20.

Nappa /ˈnapə/ *noun*. Also **Napa**, **n-**. L19.
[A county, town, and valley in California, USA.]
More fully ***Nappa leather***. A soft leather prepared from sheep- or goat-skin by a special tawing process.

nappe /nap/ *noun*. L19.
[French, lit. 'tablecloth'.]
1 A sheet of water falling over a weir or similar surface. L19.
2 GEOLOGY. A sheet of rock which has moved horizontally over neighbouring strata, as a result of overthrusting or recumbent folding. E20.

napped /napt/ *adjective*¹. LME.
[from NAP *noun*², *verb*²: see -ED², -ED¹.]
Of cloth: having a nap.

napped /napt/ *adjective*². L20.
[translating French *nappé*, pa. pple of *napper* coat (with a sauce), from *nappe* coating (see NAPPE).]
Coated (with a thick sauce); served in a sauce or other liquid.

napper /ˈnapə/ *noun*¹. LME.
[from NAP *verb*¹ + -ER¹.]
A person who naps or takes a nap.

†**napper** *noun*². *slang*. M17–E18.
[Rel. to NAP *verb*³: see -ER¹.]
A thief.
¶ The 2nd elem. of KIDNAPPER.

napper /ˈnapə/ *noun*³. *rare*. E18.
[from NAP *verb*² + -ER¹.]
A person who or machine which raises the nap on cloth.

napper /ˈnapə/ *noun*⁴. *dial. & slang*. L18.
[Origin unkn.]
The head.

napping /ˈnapɪŋ/ *noun*. LME.
[from NAP *verb*² + -ING¹.]
The action of raising a nap on cloth. Also, the nap on cloth; material used for the nap of a hat.

nappy /ˈnapi/ *noun*¹. Now *Scot. & dial.* M18.
[from NAPPY *adjective*¹.]
Strong or foaming beer; liquor.

nappy /ˈnapi/ *noun*². *N. Amer.* M19.
[Origin unkn.]
An earthenware or glass dish with sloping sides.

nappy /ˈnapi/ *noun*³. E20.
[Abbreviation of NAPKIN: see -Y⁶.]
A usu. square piece of towelling etc. wrapped and pinned on a baby to absorb or retain urine and faeces; a disposable equivalent of cotton wool etc. with a waterproof backing.

> 📖 J. DISKI Young men who are tired of life as soon as they're out of nappies.

Comb.: ***nappy-liner***: see LINER *noun*¹ 3b; **nappy pin** a kind of large curved safety pin used for fastening a nappy; **nappy rash** redness of an infant's skin where it is in persistent contact with soiled nappies.

nappy /ˈnapi/ *adjective*¹. LME.
[Prob. transf. use of next.]
1 Of beer etc.: having a head, foaming; heady, strong. LME.
2 Slightly intoxicated or exhilarated by drink. E18.
3 Of a horse: awkward, disobedient. E20.

nappy /ˈnapi/ *adjective*². L15.
[Middle Dutch *noppigh*, Middle Low German *noppich*, from *noppe* NAP *noun*²: see -Y¹.]
1 Of cloth etc.: having a nap, downy, shaggy. L15.
2 Of hair, esp. that of a black person: fuzzy, kinky. (*US slang, derog.*). E20.

†**napron** *noun & verb* see APRON.

†**napu** *noun* see NAPOH.

nar /nɑː/ *adjective, adverb, & preposition*. *obsolete* exc. *north*. Compar. & superl. **-rr-**.
[Old English *nēarra* etc. compar. of *nēah* NIGH *adverb, preposition, & adjective*: in Middle English perh. partly from Old Norse *naerri*. Cf. NEAR *adverb*¹ *& preposition*¹, NEAR *adverb*² *& preposition*².]
▶ **A** *adjective*. **1** Nearer, closer; that is the nearer of two. OE.
2 a In compar.: nearer. ME. ▸**b** In superl.: nearest. ME.
▶ **B** *adverb*. **1** Nearer, closer. Cf. NEAR *adverb*¹. ME.
2 Near, close. ME. ▸**b** Nearly, almost. *rare*. ME.
▶ **C** *preposition*. Near or close to. ME.

Nara /ˈnɑːrə/ *adjective*. E20.
[See below.]
Of, pertaining to, or designating Buddhist sculpture of the period (710–84) during which Nara in central Honshu was the capital of Japan.

naras /ˈnarəs/ *noun*. Pl. same. Also **narra** /ˈnarə/. M19.
[Nama.]
A leafless spiny shrub of the gourd family, *Acanthosicyos horrida*, occurring in the Kalahari desert and Namibia; the spiny edible fruit of this plant, which inside resembles a melon.

narc /nɑːk/ *noun*. *slang* (chiefly *N. Amer.*). M20.
[Abbreviation of NARCOTIC.]
An official narcotics agent. Cf. NARCO 2.

narceine /ˈnɑːsiːn/ *noun*. M19.
[French *narcéine*, from Greek *narkē* numbness: see -INE⁵.]
PHARMACOLOGY. A narcotic tricyclic alkaloid, $C_{23}H_{27}NO_8$, obtained from opium and formerly used therapeutically.
■ Also †**narceia** *noun* M–L19.

narcism /ˈnɑːsɪz(ə)m/ *noun*. M20.
[Contr.]
PSYCHOLOGY. Narcissism.

narciss /nɑːˈsɪs/ *noun*. Now *rare*. L16.
[Latin NARCISSUS or French *narcisse*.]
BOTANY. A narcissus.

narcissi *noun pl.* see NARCISSUS.

narcissine /nɑːˈsɪsʌɪn/ *adjective*. M17.
[Latin *narcissinus* from Greek *narkissinos* of narcissus: see NARCISSUS, -INE².]
1 Of or pertaining to a plant of the genus *Narcissus*. *rare*. Only in M17.
2 Loving or admiring oneself, narcissistic. E19.

narcissism /ˈnɑːsɪsɪz(ə)m, nɑːˈsɪs-/ *noun*. E19.
[from Latin *Narcissus* from Greek *Narkissos* a youth in Greek mythol. who fell in love with his own reflection in water and pined away: see -ISM.]
Self-love, extreme vanity; PSYCHOLOGY emotional or erotic gratification gained from contemplation of one's self or one's appearance.

> 📖 B. TRAPIDO His preening beauty, which borders upon the physically repulsive in its narcissism.

■ ˈ**narcissist** *noun* a person affected or characterized by narcissism; an excessively self-admiring person: M20.

narcissistic /nɑːsɪˈsɪstɪk/ *adjective*. E20.
[from prec.: see -ISTIC.]
Of, pertaining to, or of the nature of narcissism; marked or caused by excessive self-love.

> 📖 A. STORR Ruthlessly narcissistic people for whom the monologue is a substitute for conversation. P. D. JAMES Barbara was incapable of passing a mirror without that moment of narcissistic stillness.

■ **narcissistically** *adverb* E20.

narcissus /nɑːˈsɪsəs/ *noun*. In sense 2 also **N-**. Pl. **-ssi** /-sʌɪ/, **-ssuses**. M16.
[Latin from Greek *narkissos*, perh. from *narkē* numbness, with ref. to its narcotic effects: for sense 2 see NARCISSISM.]
1 BOTANY. Any of numerous bulbous spring-flowering plants of the genus *Narcissus* (family Amaryllidaceae), much grown for ornament; *esp.* one with a corona shorter than the perianth segments and often several flowers on the stem (cf. DAFFODIL); *spec.* (also ***pheasant's eye narcissus***) the plant *N. poeticus*, which has a fragrant white flower with a short yellow crimson-edged corona. Also, a flowering stem of such a plant. M16.
2 A (usu. physically attractive) person characterized by extreme self-regard; a narcissist. E17.

> 📖 **1** *POETAZ narcissus*. **2** *attrib.*: A. J. MUNBY His face . . seemed to me weak and self-conscious; a Narcissus face.

Comb.: **narcissus fly** a hoverfly, *Merodon equestris*, resembling a bee, whose larvae infest the bulbs of narcissus and other plants, causing them to rot.

narco /ˈnɑːkəʊ/ *noun*. *US slang*. Pl. **-os**. M20.
[Abbreviation of NARCOTIC: sense 3 perh. infl. by Spanish *narcotraficante*.]
1 = NARCOTIC *noun*. M20.
2 = NARC. M20.
3 A drug trafficker, a drug dealer. L20.

narco- /ˈnɑːkəʊ/ *combining form*.
[from Greek *narkē* numbness, deadness, or extracted from NARCOTIC: see -O-.]
Forming nouns and related adjectives with the senses 'pertaining to or involving the therapeutic use of narcotic drugs', as ***narco-hypnosis***, ***narco-therapy***; 'pertaining to the use of and trade in illegal narcotics', as ***narcodollar***.
■ **narcoˈterrorism** *noun* terrorism associated with illicit drugs, esp. directed against law enforcement L20. **narcoˈterrorist** *noun* a person who engages in narcoterrorism L20.

narcolepsy /ˈnɑːkəlɛpsi/ *noun*. L19.
[formed as prec. + *-lepsy*, after EPILEPSY.]
MEDICINE. A condition characterized by a recurrent tendency to fall asleep in circumstances conducive to relaxation.
■ **narcolept** *noun* = NARCOLEPTIC *noun* M20. **narcoˈleptic** *adjective & noun* (*a*) *adjective* characteristic of or affected by narcolepsy; (*b*) *noun* a narcoleptic person: E20.

narcomania /nɑːkəˈmeɪnɪə/ *noun*. Now *rare* or *obsolete*. L19.
[from NARCO- + -MANIA.]
MEDICINE. An uncontrollable craving for drugs.
■ **narcomaniac** *noun* L19. **narcomaˈniacal** *adjective* L19.

narcosis /nɑːˈkəʊsɪs/ *noun*. Pl. **-coses** /-ˈkəʊsiːz/. L17.
[Greek *narkōsis*, from *narkoun* make numb: see next, -OSIS.]
MEDICINE. The operation or effects of narcotics on the body; a state of insensibility or stupor, esp. as induced by a drug; the production of this state. Also, therapeutic sleep artificially prolonged by the use of drugs.

narcotic /nɑːˈkɒtɪk/ *noun & adjective*. LME.
[Old & mod. French *narcotique* or medieval Latin *narcoticus*, *-um* from Greek *narkōtikos*, *-on*, from *narkoun* make numb, from *narkē* numbness: see -OTIC.]
▶ **A** *noun*. **1** MEDICINE. A drug inducing drowsiness, sleep, or anaesthesia when ingested or injected, *esp.* an opiate. LME.
2 A drug affecting the mind and widely prohibited or controlled, but still sold and used illegally. Freq. in *pl.*, illegal drugs. Orig. *US*. E20.

> 📖 **1** K. A. PORTER Drowsy and dazed with his narcotic but unable to sleep. **2** *attrib.*: W. S. BURROUGHS The narcotics squad had a warrant for him sworn out by the State Inspector.

▶ **B** *adjective*. **1** (Of a substance etc.) having the property of a narcotic; *transf.* producing sleep through boredom, excessively dull. E16.
2 Of the nature of narcosis. M17.

> 📖 **1** C. KINGSLEY Stupid with mead made from narcotic heather honey. R. LANCIANI To lose hours upon hours in listening to silly and narcotic lecturers.

■ **narcotical** *adjective* (now *rare*) of a narcotic nature, soporific L16. **narcotically** *adverb* M17. **narcoticism** /-sɪz(ə)m/ *noun* (*rare*) narcosis E19.

narcotise *verb* var. of NARCOTIZE.

narcotism /ˈnɑːkətɪz(ə)m/ *noun*. M19.
[from NARCOTIC + -ISM. Cf. French *narcotisme*.]
1 *MEDICINE*. The condition produced by a narcotic, narcosis; the production of such a condition. M19.
2 *MEDICINE*. A pathological inclination to sleep; hypersomnia. Now *rare* or *obsolete*. M19.
3 *transf.* The narcotic influence *of* something. M19.
■ **narcotist** *noun* a person addicted to the use of narcotics M19.

narcotize /ˈnɑːkətʌɪz/ *verb trans.* Also **-ise**. E16.
[from NARCOT(IC + -IZE.]
Stupefy or make insensible with a narcotic; *transf.* dull, deaden.

🕮 *Nature* The effect of 2–5% alcohol is to narcotize the animals so that they cannot swim.

¶ Rare before M19.
■ **narcotiˈzation** *noun* the action of narcotizing a person etc.; the state induced by a narcotic: M19.

nard /nɑːd/ *noun & verb*. As noun also **nardus** /ˈnɑːdəs/. LOE.
[Latin *nardus* from Greek *nardos* ult. from Sanskrit *nalada, narada*. Cf. Old French *narde* (mod. *nard*).]
▸ **A** *noun*. **1** A fragrant ointment much prized by the ancients; the plant from whose rhizome it was prepared, prob. *Nardostachys grandiflora*, a Himalayan plant of the valerian family. Cf. SPIKENARD. Now chiefly *poet.* LOE.
2 With specifying word: (the root of) any of several other aromatic plants of the valerian family; *esp.* (in full ***Celtic nard***) *Valeriana celtica*, of the mountains of Europe. E17.
2 *nard pistic, pistic nard*: see PISTIC *adjective* 1.
▸ **B** *verb trans.* Anoint with nard. *rare*. E19.
■ **nardine** *adjective* (long *rare*) of or pertaining to nard, having the qualities of nard LME.

nardoo /nɑːˈduː, ˈnɑːduː/ *noun*. M19.
[Aboriginal.]
1 The sporocarp of the plant *Marsilea drummondii*, formerly used as food by Australian Aborigines; flour made from this. M19.
2 The plant *Marsilea drummondii* (family Marsileaceae), a four-leaved aquatic plant related to the ferns. M19.

nardus *noun* see NARD.

nare /nɛː/ *noun*. *arch.* LME.
[Latin: see next. Later partly back-form. from next.]
1 A nostril. Long *rare* exc. as in sense 2. LME.
2 *spec.* A nostril of a hawk. L15.

nares /ˈnɛːriːz/ *noun pl.* L17.
[Latin, pl. of *naris* nose, nostril.]
ANATOMY & ZOOLOGY. The nostrils (more fully ***external nares***). Also (***internal nares***), the openings of the nasal cavity into the pharynx.
■ **narial** *adjective* of the nares L19.

narghile /ˈnɑːgɪleɪ/ *noun*. Also **-eh**. M18.
[Persian *nārgīl* coconut, hookah from Sanskrit *nārikela* coconut; partly through French *narghileh*, *-guilé* from Turkish *nargile* from Persian *nārgīl*.]
A hookah.

narikin /ˈnarɪkɪn/ *noun*. E20.
[Japanese.]
In Japan, a wealthy parvenu.

naringin /nəˈrɪndʒɪn/ *noun*. L19.
[from Sanskrit *nāriṅgī* orange tree, from Tamil *nāram* orange + *kāy* fruit: see -IN¹.]
CHEMISTRY. A bitter flavonoid glucoside found in shaddock, grapefruit, and certain types of orange.

nark /nɑːk/ *noun & verb*. *slang*. M19.
[Romany *nāk* nose.]
▸ **A** *noun*. **1 a** An informer, *esp.* (also ***copper's nark***) a police informer. M19. ▸**b** A police officer. L19.
2 a An annoying, unpleasant, obstructive, or quarrelsome person. Chiefly *Austral. & NZ*. M19. ▸**b** An annoying or unpleasant thing or situation; a source of irritation; a bad mood, a fit of anger. E20.
▸ **B** *verb*. **1 a** *verb trans.* Watch, look after. M19. ▸**b** *verb intrans.* Act as an informer. M19.
2 a *verb trans.* Annoy, exasperate, infuriate. Freq. as ***narked*** *ppl adjective*. L19. ▸**b** *verb intrans.* Complain, grumble. E20.
3 *verb trans.* (usu. with *it*). Cease, stop. Freq. in *imper.* L19.

🕮 **2a** E. J. BANFIELD He'll be a bit narked at having wasted a whole bloomin' day. **3** R. HOGGART These chaps ought to pack it up. Nark it, chums.

■ **narker** *noun* an informer; a police officer; a complainer, a disparager: M20. **narky** *adjective* irascible, irritable, bad-tempered; sarcastic, disparaging: L19.

narks /nɑːks/ *noun pl. slang*. M20.
[Abbreviation of NARCOSIS (cf. BEND *noun*³) + -S¹.]
Nitrogen narcosis. Also ***the narks***.

narod /naˈrod/ *noun*. M20.
[Russian.]
In countries of the former USSR: the people; *spec.* the common people seen (in some ideologies) as the bearers of national culture.

Narodnik /nəˈrɒdnɪk, *foreign* naˈrodnjik/ *noun*. Also **n-**. Pl. **-niks**, **-niki** /-nɪki/. L19.
[Russian, formed as prec. + -NIK.]
A supporter of a type of socialism originating among the Russian intelligentsia in the 19th cent. which looked on the peasants and intelligentsia as revolutionary forces, rather than the urban working class; a person trying to give political education to a community of rural or urban poor while sharing its living conditions.
■ **Narodnikism** *noun* the doctrine of the Narodniks M20.

narp /nɑːp/ *noun*. *slang*. M19.
[Origin unkn.]
A shirt.

narr *verb* var. of GNAR *verb*.

narra /ˈnɑːrə/ *noun*¹. M19.
[Tagalog.]
A leguminous tree, *Pterocarpus indicus*, of SE Asia; the wood of this tree (also called ***amboyna wood***).

narra *noun*² see NARAS.

Narragansett /narəˈgansət/ *adjective & noun*. Also **-set** & other vars. E17.
[Narragansett.]
▸ **A** *adjective*. **1** Designating, of, or pertaining to an Algonquian people of Rhode Island or their language. E17.
2 Designating (a horse of) a now extinct breed of pacers originating in Rhode Island. L18.
▸ **B** *noun*. Pl. same, **-s**.
1 A Narragansett Indian. M17.
2 A Narragansett pacer. E19.
3 The language of the Narragansett Indians. M19.

narratage /ˈnarətɪdʒ/ *noun*. M20.
[from next + -AGE.]
A technique used in the visual media in which one of the characters has the role of storyteller.

narrate /nəˈreɪt/ *verb*. M17.
[Latin *narrat-* pa. ppl stem of *narrare* (from *gnarus* knowing), or back-form. from NARRATION: see -ATE³.]
1 *verb trans.* Give an account of, tell as a narrative; relate, recount. M17. ▸**b** Speak the commentary of (a film etc.). L20.
2 *verb intrans.* Give an account, recount a story. L18.

🕮 **1** B. JOWETT The tale of the last hours of Socrates is narrated to Echecrates. H. JAMES Some four months earlier than the occurrence lately narrated. **b** *Daily Telegraph* The Prince of Wales introduces and narrates . . a . . colour film about the . . Royal British Legion.

■ **narratable** *adjective* M19.

narratee /narəˈtiː, nəreɪˈtiː/ *noun*. L20.
[from prec. + -EE¹.]
Chiefly *LITERARY CRITICISM*. A person to whom a narrative is addressed; the recipient of a narrative.

†**narrater** *noun* var. of NARRATOR.

narration /nəˈreɪʃ(ə)n/ *noun*. LME.
[Old & mod. French *narration* or Latin *narratio(n-)*, formed as NARRATE: see -ATION.]
1 The action or an act of narrating or recounting; the fact of being recounted. LME. ▸**b** A thing narrated or recounted; a story, a narrative, an account. LME.
2 a *RHETORIC*. The part of an oration in which the facts of the matter are stated. E16. ▸**b** The narrative part or story of a poem; a narrative passage in a play etc. L16.

🕮 **1** J. BERMAN Lorenz breaks off the narration . . and begs Freud to spare him from the need to recite additional details.

■ **narrational** *adjective* M19.

narrative /ˈnarətɪv/ *adjective & noun*. LME.
[French *narratif, -ive* from late Latin *narrativus*, formed as NARRATE: see -IVE.]
▸ **A** *adjective*. **1** That tells a story; of or concerned with narration; having the character or form of narration. Formerly, biographical, historical. LME.
2 Given to narration; garrulous, talkative. L17.

🕮 **1** K. CLARK His picture of an experiment with an air pump . . is an admirable example of narrative-painting. P. GRIFFITHS Debussy's music has abandoned the narrative mode. *Observer* I see TV as a picture medium rather than a narrative medium. **narrative line** a consecutively developed story.

▸ **B** *noun*. **1 a** An account of a series of events, facts, etc., given in order and with the establishing of connections between them; a narration, a story. M16. ▸**b** The practice or art of narration; narrated material. M18.
2 *SCOTS LAW*. The part of a deed or document containing a statement of the relevant or essential facts, *spec.* the parties and the cause of granting of a deed. M16.

🕮 **1a** A. N. WILSON The story . . begins as a third-person narrative. **b** *Atlantic* The new happy ending is, as narrative, a total washout.

■ **narratively** *adverb* in a narrative manner; considered as a narrative: M17. **narrativize** *verb trans.* present or interpret in the form of a narrative L20.

narrativity /narəˈtɪvɪti/ *noun*. L20.
[French *narrativité*, formed as prec.: see -ITY.]
The quality or condition of being or presenting a narrative; (the action of) story-telling.

narratology /narəˈtɒlədʒi/ *noun*. L20.
[French *narratologie*, formed as NARRATIVE: see -OLOGY.]
The branch of knowledge that deals with the structure and function of narrative, esp. as analogous with linguistic structure; the examination and classification of the traditional themes, conventions, and symbols of the narrated story.
■ **narratoˈlogical** *adjective* L20. **narraˈtologist** *noun* L20.

narrator /nəˈreɪtə/ *noun*. Also †**-er**. E17.
[Latin, formed as NARRATE: see -OR.]
1 A person who narrates; *spec.* a character who recounts the events in a plot, esp. that of a novel or narrative poem. E17.
2 A character in a play, film, etc., who relates part of the plot to the audience; a person who speaks a commentary in a film etc. M20.

narratory /ˈnarət(ə)ri/ *adjective*. L16.
[Late Latin *narratorius*, formed as prec.: see -ORY².]
Characterized by or inclined to narration; of the nature of narrative.
■ **narraˈtorial** *adjective* of or pertaining to a narration or narrator L20.

narratress /nəˈreɪtrɪs/ *noun*. *rare*. L18.
[from NARRATE + -ESS¹.]
A female narrator.
■ Also **narratrix** *noun*, pl. **-trices** /-trɪsiːz/, **-trixes**, L18.

narrischkeit /ˈnarɪʃkʌɪt/ *noun*. *slang*. L19.
[Yiddish *naarishkeit, narrish-* from German *Närrischkeit*, from *närrisch* foolish, from *Narr* fool.]
Foolishness, nonsense.

narrow /ˈnarəʊ/ *adjective & noun*.
[Old English *nearu* (stem *nearw-*) = Old Saxon *naru* (Middle Dutch *nare, naer*, Dutch *naar*), from Germanic (repr. in Middle High German *narwe*, German *Narbe*, Middle Low German *nar(w)e* use as noun of adjective = 'scar'), with no certain cognates.]
▸ **A** *adjective*. **1** Small in breadth or width in proportion to length; lacking breadth. OE.
2 Lacking space or area, confined, constricted; confining. OE.
3 a Sparing, parsimonious, mean. Now *Scot. & dial.* ME. ▸**b** Restricted or rigid in views; intolerant, illiberal, prejudiced; unimaginative. E17. ▸**c** Reluctant to admit new members, exclusive. M19.
4 Searching, precise, careful. (Earlier in NARROWLY 1.) ME.
5 Limited in range, scope, or amount; restricted, straitened. LME. ▸**b** Of time: short, brief. *rare*. E17.
6 †**a** Approaching the truth. M16–L17. ▸**b** Barely achieved, with little margin. L16.
7 *PHONETICS*. **a** Of a vowel: pronounced with the vocal muscles relatively tense. Opp. WIDE *adjective* 6b. M19. ▸**b** Designating a phonetic transcription that distinguishes both phonemes and allophones. L19.

🕮 **1** B. MOORE A narrow window twelve feet long by two feet wide. J. GARDAM A lane so narrow that the bushes tangled their fingers together overhead. J. WILCOX Mrs. Undine hunched her narrow shoulders. ***straight and narrow***: see STRAIGHT *adjective*¹. **2** O. SITWELL An unparalleled concentration . . of human beings within the narrow borders of a small island. **3b** J. GRENFELL People are very narrow where I live. They have such little lives. **5** R. ADAMS Peasant girls . . accustomed to a narrow life of daily toil. A. THWAITE Intense concern that the boy should remain within the cage of his own narrow dogma. **6b** DAY LEWIS I attribute my narrow victory . . to a handful of aged voters. P. WARNER He had a narrow escape when an attempt was made to poison him.

Special collocations: **narrow axe** *US* an axe with a narrow head. **narrowback** *US slang* a US citizen of Irish ancestry. **narrow band** (*PHYSICS* etc.) a band of frequencies, wavelengths, etc., lying within narrowly-defined limits. **narrow boat** a long narrow canal boat, *spec.* one not exceeding 7 feet (2.1 metres) in width. **narrowcast** *verb & noun* (orig. *US*) (*a*) *verb trans. & intrans.* transmit (a television etc. programme), *esp.* by cable, to an audience limited by interests or location; (*b*) *noun* (an act of) transmitting in this way; a programme transmitted in this way. **narrowcaster** (orig. *US*) a person who or thing which narrowcasts. **narrow circumstances** poverty. **narrow-cut** *adjective* (*PHOTOGRAPHY*) (of a filter) transmitting only a narrow band of wavelengths. **narrow fabrics** braid, ribbons, bindings, etc. **narrow gauge** (*a*) a railway gauge narrower than the standard one (in Great Britain 56½ inches, approx. 1.435 metres); (*b*) *CINEMATOGRAPHY* a width of film narrower than the standard one (16 mm rather than 35 mm). **narrow goods** = *narrow fabrics* above. **narrow-minded** *adjective* rigid or restricted in one's views, intolerant. **narrow-mindedly** *adverb* in a narrow-minded manner. **narrow-mindedness** the quality or condition of being narrow-minded. **narrow money** *ECONOMICS* money in forms that can be used as a medium of exchange, generally notes, coins, and certain balances held by banks. **narrow seas** *the* seas separating Britain from Ireland on the one side and Continental Europe on the other. **narrow squeak** a narrow escape; a success barely attained. **narrow way** [*Matthew* 7:14] righteousness.

▶**B** *noun.* **1** A narrow part, place, or thing; the narrow part of something. Now *rare* exc. as below. **ME.**
2 *spec.* (*sing.* & (usu.) in *pl.*). A narrow part of a strait or river; a narrow part of a street; (chiefly *US*) a narrow part of a valley, a pass; *MINING* a narrow gallery. **M17.**
■ **narrowish** *adjective* **L18. narrowness** *noun* **ME.**

narrow /ˈnarəʊ/ *verb.* **OE.**
[from the adjective.]
1 *verb intrans.* Become narrower, decrease in width or breadth; diminish, lessen, contract. (Foll. by *down.*) **OE.**
2 *verb trans.* Make narrower; reduce the breadth of; reduce, constrict. (Foll. by *down.*) **OE.** ▸**b** Drive or press (people) closer together. **E19.**

📖 **1** T. HARDY Below the foot-bridge of the weir the stream suddenly narrowed to half its width. I. MCEWAN Stephen's concerns narrowed to practical matters: how soon he could leave. **2** M. PUZO Clemenza finally narrowed down the list of candidates to three men. M. KEANE He leaned across . . his desk as if he would narrow the distance between us.

■ **narrower** *noun* a thing that narrows something **M18.**

narrow /ˈnarəʊ/ *adverb.* Now *rare.* **OE.**
[from the adjective.]
†**1** Closely, strictly. **OE–L15.**
†**2** Carefully, keenly. **OE–L16.**
3 Narrowly, in a narrow or close manner. **ME.**

narrowly /ˈnarəʊli/ *adverb.* **OE.**
[from **NARROW** *adjective* + **-LY**[2].]
1 Carefully, closely, with close attention. **OE.**
2 In a contracted, confined, or closely circumscribed manner. **OE.**
†**3** Sparingly, parsimoniously. *rare.* **ME–M17.**
4 †**a** Barely, scarcely. *rare.* Only in **LME.** ▸**b** Only by a (very) little, only just. **E16.**
†**5** Closely, at close quarters. **M16–E18.**
6 Illiberally, rigidly; specifically, literally. **E18.**

📖 **1** S. BELLOW The old man questioned him narrowly. **2** G. GREENE Grey trousers cut a little narrowly to show off the long legs. **4b** JOAN SMITH She hastened across the road, narrowly avoiding a speeding car. **6** *Times* The lack of wisdom in such a narrowly short-sighted view of its responsibilities.

narthex /ˈnɑːθɛks/ *noun.* **L17.**
[Latin from Greek *narthēx* giant fennel, stick, casket, narthex.]
A railed-off antechamber or porch at the western end of some (esp. early and Orthodox) churches.

nartjie *noun* var. of **NAARTJIE.**

narwhal /ˈnɑːw(ə)l/ *noun.* **M17.**
[Dutch *narwal*, Danish *narhval* (whence German *Narwal*, French *narval*), from *hval* **WHALE** *noun*, rel. obscurely to Old Norse *náhvalr* (from *nár* corpse, with ref. to the colour of the skin).]
A toothed whale, *Monodon monoceros*, of Arctic seas, the male of which has one (or sometimes both) of its two teeth developed into a straight spirally-twisted tusk.

nary /ˈnɛːri/ *adjective & adverb. colloq.* **M18.**
[Alt. of *ne'er a* s.v. **NE'ER.**]
▶**A** *adjective.* Not a, not a single; no. Now *rare.* **M18.**
▶**B** *adverb.* Not a, never *a.* **M19.**

📖 *Road Racing Monthly* After the race the tyres showed nary a trace of wear!

NAS *abbreviation.*
Noise Abatement Society.

NASA /ˈnasə/ *abbreviation. US.*
National Aeronautics and Space Administration.

nasal /ˈneɪz(ə)l/ *noun.* In sense 1 also †**-el.** **ME.**
[In sense 1 from Old French (also *nasel*) from medieval Latin *nasale* use as noun of neut. of *nasalis* **NASAL** *adjective*; in sense 2 from medieval Latin; in other senses directly from **NASAL** *adjective.*]
1 A nose-piece on a helmet. **ME.**
†**2** = **ERRHINE. LME–M17.**
3 A nasal speech sound or letter. **M17.**
4 *ANATOMY & ZOOLOGY.* A nasal bone. **M19.**

nasal /ˈneɪz(ə)l/ *adjective.* **LME.**
[French, or medieval Latin *nasalis*, from *nasus* nose: see **-AL**[1].]
1 Of or pertaining to the nose. **LME.**
2 (Of a speech sound) pronounced with a flow of air through the cavity of the nose; pertaining to or characterized by such pronunciation, esp. to an unusual or disagreeable extent. **M17.**

📖 **1** *New Scientist* Obstructive growths in the nasal passages of bathers and divers. S. KITZINGER The hormone nasal spray. ***nasal artery, nasal cartilage, nasal duct,*** etc. **nasal bone** either of a pair of bones forming the bridge and base of the nose. ***nasal concha***: see **CONCHA** 1. ***nasal meatus***: see **MEATUS** 2. **nasal organ** *joc.* the nose. **2** D. WELCH His accent became more sweet and nasal.

■ **nasalism** *noun* (*rare*) nasal pronunciation **L19. naˈsality** *noun* the quality of being nasal, *esp.* in pronunciation **L18. nasally** *adverb* in a nasal manner, with a nasal pronunciation **M19.**

nasalize /ˈneɪz(ə)lʌɪz/ *verb trans.* Also **-ise.** **E19.**
[from **NASAL** *adjective* + **-IZE.**]
Make nasal in pronunciation; utter with a nasal sound.
■ **nasalizable** *adjective* **L19. nasaliˈzation** *noun* the action or result of nasalizing a speech sound etc. **M19.**

Nasara *noun pl.* see **NASRANI.**

Nasca *adjective* var. of **NAZCA.**

nascence /ˈnas(ə)ns, ˈneɪ-/ *noun. rare.* **L16.**
[formed as next: see **-ENCE.**]
Birth.

nascency /ˈnas(ə)nsi, ˈneɪ-/ *noun.* **L17.**
[Latin *nascentia*, formed as next: see **-ENCY.**]
The process or fact of being born or brought into existence; birth.

nascent /ˈnas(ə)nt, ˈneɪ-/ *adjective.* **E17.**
[Latin *nascent-* pres. ppl stem of *nasci* be born: see **-ENT.**]
1 In the act of being born. **E17.**
2 In the act or condition of coming into existence; beginning to form, grow, develop, etc.; *CHEMISTRY* (esp. of hydrogen) freshly generated in reactive form by electrolysis or chemical reaction. **E18.**

📖 **2** MOLLIE HARRIS During . . the eighteenth century, the nascent discipline of geology languished under the tutelage of scriptural authority. U. BENTLEY His look accused me of betraying his nascent respect for me. R. K. NARAYAN This girl was innocent, her mind in a nascent state.

■ **nascently** *adverb* **L19.**

NASDAQ /ˈnazdak/ *abbreviation. US.*
National Association of Securities Dealers Automated Quotations, a computerized system for trading in securities.

naseberry /ˈneɪzb(ə)ri/ *noun. W. Indies.* **L17.**
[Spanish, Portuguese *néspera* medlar, assim. to **BERRY** *noun*[1].]
The sapodilla tree, *Manilkara zapota* (also ***naseberry tree***); the edible fruit of this tree.

†**nasel** *noun* see **NASAL** *noun.*

Nash /naʃ/ *noun.* **M20.**
[John F. *Nash* (1928–), Brit. mathematician.]
GAME THEORY. Used **attrib.** to designate concepts arising out of Nash's work on non-cooperative strategies.
Nash equilibrium a stable state of a system involving the interaction of different participants, in which no participant can gain by a unilateral change of strategy if the strategies of the others remain unchanged.

nash-gab /ˈnaʃɡab/ *noun. Scot. & north.* **E19.**
[from **GNASH** + **GAB** *noun*[2].]
Impertinent talk; a pert or gossiping person.

nashi /ˈnaʃi/ *noun.* **M20.**
[Japanese, lit. 'pear'.]
More fully ***nashi pear.*** An apple-shaped variety of pear from the tree *Pyrus pyrifolia*, native to Japan and China and cultivated in Australasia and elsewhere.

Nashiji /naˈʃiːdʒi/ *noun.* **L19.**
[Japanese, lit. 'pear ground'.]
A Japanese lacquer containing gold or silver flakes; the technique of decorating with this lacquer.

Nasho /ˈnaʃəʊ/ *noun. Austral. slang.* Pl. **-os.** **M20.**
[Abbreviation of **NATIONAL** *adjective*: see **-O.**]
(A person doing) national service.

nasi /ˈnɑːsi/ *noun.* **L19.**
[Malay.]
In Malaysian and Indonesian cookery: cooked rice.

nasiform /ˈneɪzɪfɔːm/ *adjective. rare.* **M18.**
[from Latin *nasus* nose + **-I-** + **-FORM.**]
Shaped like a nose.

Nasik /ˈnɑːsɪk/ *noun.* **M19.**
[A town in India.]
MATH. Used **attrib.** to designate magic squares which are pandiagonal.

nasion /ˈneɪzɪən/ *noun.* **L19.**
[from **NASAL** *noun* + *-ion*, after *inion.*]
ANATOMY. The centre of the fronto-nasal suture.

Naskapi /ˈnaskəpi/ *adjective & noun.* **L18.**
[Montagnais (Naskapi).]
▶**A** *adjective.* Designating or pertaining to a N. American Indian people of northern Quebec and the interior of Labrador, or their Montagnais dialect. **L18.**
▶**B** *noun.* Pl. **-s**, same.
1 A member of this people. **M19.**
2 The dialect of this people. **M20.**

naskhi /ˈnaski/ *noun & adjective.* Also ***neskhi*** /ˈnɛski/. **L18.**
[Arab. *naskī* (pl.), from *nasaka* to copy.]
(Designating) the standard Arabic script.

Nasmyth /ˈneɪsmɪθ/ *noun.* **M19.**
[James *Nasmyth* (1808–90), Scot. engineer.]
Used **attrib.** and in **possess.** to designate a form of hammer or pile-driver in which the falling weight is raised by steam pressure on a piston attached to it.

Nasmyth's membrane /ˈneɪsmɪθs ˈmɛmbreɪn/ *noun phr.* **M19.**
[Alexander *Nasmyth* (d. 1848), Brit. dentist.]
ANATOMY. A transient membrane covering the crown of a newly erupted tooth.

naso- /ˈneɪzəʊ/ *combining form.*
[from Latin *nasus* nose: see **-O-.**]
Chiefly *ANATOMY.* Forming adjectives and nouns with the senses 'nasal and —', 'of the nose', as ***nasofrontal, nasopalatal.***
■ **nasoˈciliary** *adjective* designating a branch of the ophthalmic nerve that supplies the skin and mucous membrane of the nose, the eyelids, and parts of the eyeball **L19. nasoˈgastric** *adjective* (*MEDICINE*) reaching or supplying the stomach via the nose **M20. nasoˈlacrimal** *adjective* (*a*) pertaining to or connecting the lacrimal glands and the nasal cavity; (*b*) pertaining to the lacrimal and nasal bones: **M19. naˈsologist** *noun* (*rare*) a student of noses **M19. naˈsology** *noun* (*rare*) the branch of knowledge that deals with the nose or noses **M19. nasophaˈryngeal** *adjective* of or pertaining to the nasopharynx, or the nose and the pharynx **L19. nasoˈpharynx** *noun* the upper part of the pharynx, above the soft palate and connecting with the nasal cavity (cf. **OROPHARYNX**) **L19.**

Nasonov *noun* var. of **NASSANOFF.**

nasospinale /ˌneɪzəʊspɪˈnɑːli/ *noun.* **E20.**
[App. mod. Latin, from **NASO-** + late Latin *spinale*, neut. of *spinalis* spinal: cf. **SPINE.**]
ANATOMY. The point at which a line joining the lowest points of the nostrils intersects with the midsagittal plane.

Nasrani /nazˈrɑːni/ *noun.* Pl. **Nasranis**, same, **Nasara** /naˈzɑːrɑː/. **L16.**
[Arab. *Naṣrānī*, pl. *Naṣārā*, cogn. with **NAZARENE.**]
Among Muslims: a Christian.

Nass /nas/ *adjective & noun.* **E19.**
[A river in British Columbia, Canada.]
= **NISHGA.**

nassa /ˈnasə/ *noun.* **M19.**
[mod. Latin *Nassa* former genus name.]
(The shell of) a marine gastropod of the genus *Nassarius*; a dog-whelk. Also ***nassa shell.***

Nassanoff /ˈnasənɒf/ *noun.* Also **Nasonov** & other vars. **M20.**
[N. V. *Nasonov* (1855–1939), Russian entomologist.]
ENTOMOLOGY. ***Nassanoff gland***, a gland on the back of a honeybee, between the sixth and seventh abdominal segments, which secretes a pheromone (***Nassanoff pheromone***) that attracts workers.

Nassau /ˈnasɔː/ *noun.* **E20.**
[See next.]
A golfing match in which a point is scored for winning the first nine holes, another for the second nine, and a third for the complete round; a form of betting on the basis of such scoring.

Nassauvian /naˈsɔːvɪən/ *noun & adjective.* Also **Nassavian** /naˈseɪvɪən/. **E20.**
[from a Latinized form of *Nassau* (see below) + **-IAN.**]
(A native or inhabitant) of Nassau, the capital of the Bahamas.

nassella /naˈsɛlə/ *noun.* **M20.**
[mod. Latin (see below), from Latin *nassa* net + **-ELLA.**]
A coarse tussock-forming Chilean grass, *Nassella trichotoma*, that is a troublesome weed in New Zealand.

Nasserite /ˈnasərʌɪt/ *noun & adjective.* **M20.**
[from Abd al-*Nasser* (see below) + **-ITE**[1].]
▶**A** *noun.* A follower or adherent of Gamal Abdel Nasser (Abd al-Nasser) (1918–70), the first president of Egypt (1956–70), or his political principles or policies, esp. in relation to Arab nationalism. **M20.**
▶**B** *adjective.* Of or pertaining to Nasserites or Nasserism. **M20.**
■ **Nasserism** *noun* the political principles or policies of Nasser **M20. Nasserist** *noun & adjective* = **NASSERITE M20.**

nastalik /nastaˈlik/ *noun.* Also ***-liq, -ta'-.*** **L18.**
[Persian, from Arab. *naskī* **NASKHI** + *ta'līk*: see **TALIK** *noun*[1].]
A Persian cursive script, characterized by rounded forms and elongated horizontal strokes.

nastic /ˈnastɪk/ *adjective.* **E20.**
[from Greek *nastos* pressed together + **-IC.**]
BOTANY. Of a plant movement: caused by an external stimulus but unaffected in direction by it.

nastily /ˈnɑːstɪli/ *adverb.* **E17.**
[from **NASTY** *adjective* + **-LY**[2].]
In a nasty manner or state; filthily; disagreeably, unpleasantly.

nastiness /ˈnɑːstɪnɪs/ *noun.* **E17.**
[from **NASTY** *adjective* + **-NESS.**]
1 The state or quality of being nasty. **E17.**
2 That which is nasty; dirt, filth, (*lit.* & *fig.*). **E17.**
3 A filthy, disgusting, or repulsive thing. **E18.**

nasturtium /nəˈstəːʃəm/ *noun*. OE.
[Latin *nasturcium*, app. from *naris* nose + *torquere* to twist, with ref. to its pungency.]
1 Orig., any of several cruciferous plants having a pungent taste; *esp.* watercress, *Rorippa nasturtium-aquaticum* (or *Nasturtium officinale*). Now only (BOTANY), a plant of the genus *Nasturtium*. OE.
2 Any of several tropaeolums with a similarly pungent taste; esp. *Tropaeolum majus*, much grown for its showy orange, yellow, or red flowers. E18.
3 = ASPERSION 4. *joc.* E20.

nasty /ˈnɑːsti/ *noun*[1]. *colloq.* In sense 1 also **N-**. M20.
[from the adjective. In sense 1 alt. of NAZI *noun*.]
1 A Nazi. M20.
2 A nasty person, object, or event; (in full ***video nasty***) a horror video film. M20.

> **2** *Country Life* Museums . . present us with nasties as well as with fine things. *Sounds* Every chemical nasty that can be inhaled through your poor polluted nose. *TV Times* A squad . . to protect Britain from . . terrorists, saboteurs, and other organised nasties.

nasty /ˈnasti/ *noun*[2]. M20.
[German *Nastie*, from Greek *nastos*: see NASTIC, -Y[3].]
BOTANY. A nastic movement.

nasty /ˈnɑːsti/ *adjective*. LME.
[Origin unkn.]
1 Foul, filthy, dirty, esp. to a disgusting degree; offensive through filth or dirt. Now freq. a contextual use of sense 4. LME. ▸**b** Morally unclean; indecent, obscene. E17.
2 Offensive to smell or taste; unpalatable, nauseating. M16.
3 Of weather etc.: foul, dirty, wet, stormy. M17.
4 *gen.* Offensive; disagreeable, unpleasant, objectionable, annoying; in poor taste. E18.
5 Difficult to deal with or get rid of, dangerous; having unpleasant results, rather serious. E19.
6 Ill-natured, bad-tempered, spiteful. E19.

> **1** W. SPALDING Streets which are narrow, steep, and exceedingly nasty. **b** E. BLISHEN Our lavatories simply asked to have nasty things written on the walls. M. ALLINGHAM One doesn't have to have a nasty mind to wonder. **2** *Law Times* There was a nasty smell about the premises. P. LOMAS If the medicine is to be efficacious, it must have a nasty taste. **3** HENRY FIELDING It is a cursed nasty morning. **4** R. CHRISTIANSEN In 1815, most of musical Europe still identified Beethoven with nasty senseless noise. **5** E. HEMINGWAY A business enemy had been killed in a particularly nasty motor accident. I. MURDOCH Matthew got a nasty crack on the head. **6** M. ANGELOU The nasty children would have something new to tease me about. T. MALLON There is . . pleasure to be had in hearing nasty things well said about other people.

Phrases: **a nasty piece of work**, **a nasty bit of work**, **a nasty piece of goods**, **a nasty bit of goods** an unpleasant or contemptible person. ***a nasty taste in the mouth***: see TASTE *noun*[1]. ***cheap and nasty***: see CHEAP *adjective & adverb*. **something nasty in the woodshed** a traumatic experience or a concealed unpleasantness in a person's background.

nasty /ˈnɑːsti/ *verb trans. obsolete* exc. *dial.* E18.
[from the adjective.]
Make nasty or dirty.

nasus /ˈneɪzəs/ *noun*. L17.
[Latin = nose.]
BIOLOGY. A snout; *esp.* the proboscis of a nasute termite.
¶ Rare before M20.

nasute /ˈneɪsjuːt/ *adjective & noun*. M17.
[Latin *nasutus*, formed as prec.]
▶ **A** *adjective*. †**1** Having a keen critical faculty, sagacious. M17–E18.
2 ZOOLOGY. Nose-shaped; having a pronounced proboscis; *esp.* designating or describing (an insect of) a caste of soldier termites of the genus *Nasutitermes*. L19.
▶ **B** *noun*. A nasute soldier termite. M20.

nasutus /neɪˈsjuːtəs/ *noun*. Pl. **-ti** /-tʌɪ/. M19.
[formed as prec.]
= NASUTE *noun*.

NASUWT *abbreviation*.
National Association of Schoolmasters and Union of Women Teachers.

Nat /nat, *foreign* nʌt/ *noun*[1]. Also **Nut** /nʌt/. E19.
[Sanskrit *naṭa* dancer, actor, tumbler.]
In the Indian subcontinent, esp in the north: a member of an itinerant class of entertainers, fortune-tellers, etc.

nat /nɑːt/ *noun*[2]. E19.
[Burmese from Sanskrit *nātha* lord, protector.]
In the animistic native religion of the people of Myanmar (Burma): a spirit, a demon, a supernatural being.

Nat /nat/ *noun*[3]. *colloq.* M20.
[Abbreviation of NATIONAL or NATIONALIST.]
1 A member of the National Party in South Africa. M20.
2 A Scottish or Welsh Nationalist. Cf. SCOT NAT, ***Scots Nat*** s.v. SCOTS *adjective*. M20.

Nat. *abbreviation*.
1 National.
2 Natural.

Natal /nəˈtal, -ˈtɑːl/ *noun*. M19.
[See below.]
Used *attrib.* to designate things found in, obtained from, or associated with Natal, a province of South Africa (earlier a Boer republic).
Natal lily any of several southern African monocotyledonous plants with brightly coloured flowers, *esp.* = CLIVIA. **Natal mahogany** either of two evergreen timber trees, *Kiggelaria africana* (family Flacourtiaceae) and *Trichilia emetica* (family Meliaceae). **Natal plum** a spiny evergreen shrub or small tree, *Carissa grandiflora* (family Apocynaceae), which bears tubular white fragrant flowers and an edible purple fruit. **Natal sore** = ***oriental sore*** s.v. ORIENTAL *adjective*.

natal /ˈneɪt(ə)l/ *adjective*[1]. LME.
[Latin *natalis*, from *nat-* pa. ppl stem of *nasci* be born: see -AL[1].]
†**1** Presiding over birthdays or nativities. Only in LME.
2 Of or pertaining to (one's) birth; (of a place, chiefly *literary*) native; dating from one's birth; connected with one from birth. LME.

> **2** E. K. KANE The natal day of the Prince Consort. H. READ His talent suggests a natal endowment. J. M. COETZEE His mother . . was more at peace now that she was nearer her natal earth. *Horoscope* The . . interpretation of your complete natal horoscope.

natal /ˈneɪt(ə)l/ *adjective*[2]. L19.
[from NATES + -AL[1].]
Of or pertaining to the nates or buttocks.
natal cleft the furrow between the buttocks.

Natalian /nəˈtalɪən, -ˈtɑːl-/ *adjective & noun*. M19.
[from NATAL *noun* + -IAN.]
▶ **A** *adjective*. Of or pertaining to Natal (see NATAL *noun*). M19.
▶ **B** *noun*. A native or inhabitant of Natal. L19.

natalid /ˈnatəlɪd/ *adjective & noun*. M20.
[mod. Latin *Natalidae* (see below), from *Natalus* genus name: see -ID[3].]
ZOOLOGY. ▶**A** *adjective*. Of, pertaining to, or designating the family Natalidae of small long-legged insectivorous bats of Central and N. America, which have large funnel-shaped ears and lack a nose-leaf. M20.
natalid organ a glandular facial organ peculiar to natalids, of unknown function.
▶ **B** *noun*. A bat of the family Natalidae. L20.

natality /nəˈtalɪti/ *noun*. L15.
[from NATAL *adjective*[1] + -ITY. In mod. use from French *natalité*.]
1 Birth. *rare*. L15.
2 Birth-rate; the ratio of the number of births in a period to the size of the population. L19.

natant /ˈneɪt(ə)nt/ *adjective*. *rare*. LME.
[Latin *natant-* pres. ppl stem of *natare* frequentative of *nare* swim, float: see -ANT[1].]
Swimming, floating.

natation /nəˈteɪʃ(ə)n/ *noun*. Chiefly *literary*. M16.
[Latin *natatio(n-)*, from *natat-* pa. ppl stem of *natare*: see NATANT, -ATION.]
The action or art of swimming.

Natatores /neɪtəˈtɔːriːz/ *noun pl.* Now *rare* or *obsolete*. E19.
[mod. Latin, from Latin *natator* swimmer: see NATATORY *adjective*.]
ORNITHOLOGY. (A former order of) birds adapted for swimming.

natatorial /neɪtəˈtɔːrɪəl/ *adjective*. E19.
[formed as NATATORY *adjective* + -AL[1].]
= NATATORY *adjective*.

natatorium /neɪtəˈtɔːrɪəm/ *noun*. *N. Amer.* L19.
[Late Latin, use as noun of *natatorius*: see NATATORY *adjective*, -ORIUM.]
A swimming pool, *esp.* an indoor swimming pool.

natatory /ˈneɪtət(ə)ri/ *noun*. Now *rare*. ME.
[formed as prec.: see -ORY[1].]
1 A swimming pool; a bath. ME.
2 ZOOLOGY. A natatory organ. M19.

natatory /ˈneɪtət(ə)ri/ *adjective*. L18.
[Late Latin *natatorius*, from Latin *natator* swimmer, from *natat-*: see NATATION, -ORY[2].]
1 ZOOLOGY. Of an organ: adapted for or used in swimming or floating. L18.
2 Of or pertaining to swimming. M19.
3 Characterized by swimming. L19.

natch /natʃ/ *noun*[1] *& verb*. L16.
[Prob. var. of NOTCH *noun*.]
▶ **A** *noun*. **1** A notch. Now *dial.* L16.
2 A projection and corresponding notch by which sections of a mould are held together. M20.
▶ **B** *verb trans.* Cut a notch or notches in. Now *dial.* L16.

natch *noun*[2] var. of NACHE.

natch /natʃ/ *adverb*. *colloq.* M20.
[Abbreviation.]
Naturally, of course.

> M. MCLUHAN Natch I'm interested to know what Percy's latest book contains. T. PYNCHON An element of . . future blackmail, which operates, natch, in favour of professionals.

Natchez /ˈnatʃɪz/ *noun & adjective*. E18.
[French, a name in several Indian langs.]
▶ **A** *noun*. Pl. same. A member of a N. American Indian people of Mississippi; the language of this people. E18.
▶ **B** *attrib.* or as *adjective*. Of or pertaining to the Natchez or their language. L18.

nates /ˈneɪtiːz/ *noun pl.* L17.
[Latin, pl. of *natis* rump, buttock.]
ANATOMY & MEDICINE. The buttocks. Formerly also, the anterior optic lobes of the brain.

NATFHE *abbreviation*.
National Association of Teachers in Further and Higher Education.

nathe /neɪð/ *noun*. *obsolete* exc. *dial.* ME.
[Var. of NAVE *noun*[1].]
The nave of a wheel.

natheless /ˈneɪθlɪs/ *adverb & preposition*. Long *arch.* Also **nathless** /ˈnaθlɪs/. OE.
[from NA *adverb*[1] + THE *adverb* + LESS *adverb*.]
▶ **A** *adverb*. Nevertheless, notwithstanding. OE.
▶ **B** *preposition*. In spite of, notwithstanding. *rare*. M16.

†**nathemore** *adverb*. Also **-mo**. LOE–L16.
[from NA *adverb*[1] + THE *adverb* + MORE *adverb*, MO *adverb*.]
Never the more.

nathless *adverb & preposition* var. of NATHELESS.

natica /ˈnatɪkə/ *noun*. M19.
[mod. Latin *Natica* (see below), perh. from medieval Latin *natica* buttock, from Latin *natis*: see NATES.]
ZOOLOGY. A carnivorous marine gastropod of the genus *Natica*; a necklace shell. Now chiefly as mod. Latin genus name.

natiform /ˈneɪtɪfɔːm/ *adjective*. L17.
[from Latin *natis* (see NATES) + -FORM.]
Chiefly ANATOMY & MEDICINE. Resembling or having the form of buttocks.

nation /ˈneɪʃ(ə)n/ *noun*[1]. ME.
[Old & mod. French from Latin *natio(n-)* birth, race, from *nat-* pa. ppl stem of *nasci* be born: see -ION.]
1 A large aggregate of people so closely associated with each other by factors such as common descent, language, culture, history, and occupation of the same territory as to be identified as a distinct people, esp. when organized or potentially organizable as a political State. ME. ▸**b** A number of people belonging to a particular nation; a group of people representating a nation. Now *rare*. LME. ▸**c** In medieval and some Scottish universities, a body of students from a particular district, country, etc., forming a more or less distinct community. M17. ▸†**d** A country, a kingdom. *rare*. Only in M17.
†**2** Nationality. LME–M17.
3 †**a** A family, one's kindred. *rare*. LME–E16. ▸†**b** An Irish clan. LME–L16. ▸**c** A N. American Indian people. M17.
†**4** A particular class or kind of person or animal. LME–L18.

> **1** D. LESSING Africa . . has become . . a mass of nations.

Phrases: ***a nation of shopkeepers***: see SHOPKEEPER 1. ***comity of nations***: see COMITY 2a. ***grand inquest of the nation***, ***great inquest of the nation***: see INQUEST *noun*. **law of nations** international law. ***League of Nations***: see LEAGUE *noun*[2]. ***most favoured nation***: see FAVOURED *adjective*[2]. **one nation** a nation which is not divided by social inequalities. **the Five Nations** the five confederate N. American Indian peoples collectively known as the Iroquois. **the nation** the whole people of a country, esp. in contrast to some smaller or narrower body within it. **the nations** (***a***) (in and after biblical use) the heathen nations, the Gentiles; (***b***) *literary* the peoples of the earth. **two nations** two groups within a given nation divided from each other by marked social inequality. ***United Nations (Organization)***: see UNITED *adjective*.
Comb.: **nation-state** a sovereign State most of the citizens or subjects of which are also united by factors such as language, common descent, etc., which define a nation.

nation /ˈneɪʃ(ə)n/ *adjective, adverb, & noun*[2]. *dial.* & *US*. M18.
[Abbreviation of DAMNATION.]
▶ **A** *adjective*. Very large, very great. M18.
▶ **B** *adverb*. Very, extremely. L18.
▶ **C** *noun*. **1** A great deal. Used *adverbially*. L18.
2 ***how in the nation . . . ?***, ***what in the nation . . . ?***, etc., how etc. on earth . . . ?, how etc. . . . at all? L19.

national /ˈnaʃ(ə)n(ə)l/ *adjective & noun*. L16.
[French, formed as NATION *noun*[1]: see -AL[1].]
▶ **A** *adjective*. **1** Of or pertaining to a nation or country, esp. as a whole; affecting or shared by the whole nation. L16. ▸**b** Of or pertaining to the French Government during the time of the First Republic. L18. ▸**c** In the war

of 1939–45, designating foodstuffs made to official specifications for nationwide distribution. **M20.**

2 Of or pertaining to a particular nation or country, as opp. to another or others; peculiar to or identified specifically with the people of a particular country, characteristic or distinctive of a nation. **E17.**

3 Patriotic, strongly upholding one's own nation; devoted to the interests of the nation as a whole. Now *rare*. **E18.**

> 🕮 **1** BOLINGBROKE A Spirit of Liberty will be always . . concerned about national Interests. G. BORROW An officer in the national cavalry. *Listener* A large slice of the Italian national cake is now based on the motor-car industry. V. CRONIN A time of national danger, with Russia fighting a two-front war. M. BRETT The national newspapers derive a large portion of their revenue from financial advertising. **c *national flour, national loaf***, etc. **2** R. WILBUR The national habit Of allowing each sentence to trail off. M. WEST The German Academy was one of the . . most prestigious national academies in Rome.

Special collocations: ***national anthem***: see ANTHEM *noun* 3. **National Assembly** an assembly consisting of representatives of all parts of a nation; an elected house of legislature in any of various countries; *spec.* (*Hist.*) the first of the revolutionary assemblies of France, in session 1789–91. **National Assistance** a form of welfare payment provided under National Insurance in the UK between 1948 and 1965. **national bank** a bank associated with the national finances; *US* a bank whose circulating notes are secured by US bonds deposited with the Government. **national convention** (*a*) *Hist.* (**N- C-**) an assembly which governed France from 1792–5; (*b*) *US* a convention of a major political party to nominate a candidate for the presidency etc. ***National Covenant***: see COVENANT *noun*. **national curriculum** a curriculum that State schools in England and Wales have been required to follow since 1990, involving the teaching of specified subjects and assessment at specified ages. ***National Debt***: see DEBT *noun*. **national football** *Austral.* Australian Rules football. **National Front** a political group in Britain with extreme reactionary views on immigration etc. **National Government** a coalition government, *esp.* one subordinating party differences to the national interest in a time of crisis, as that in Britain under Ramsay MacDonald in 1931–5. **national grid** (*a*) a network of high voltage power lines interconnecting the major power stations and distribution centres in a country; (*b*) a metric coordinate system and reference grid used by cartographers (*spec.* in the British Isles, by the Ordnance Survey) and printed on maps. **national guard** *spec.* (*a*) (a member of) an armed force existing in France at various times between 1789 and 1871; (*b*) (with cap. initials) in the US, a militia force largely maintained by a particular State but available for federal use. **National Health (Service)** the system of national medical service in the UK, largely financed by taxation. **national holiday** a holiday observed throughout a country. **National Hunt (Committee)** the body controlling steeplechasing and hurdle-racing in Great Britain. **national income** the total money earned within a country. ***National Insurance***: see INSURANCE 2d. **national minority** a minority group, belonging historically to another nationality, feeling or felt to be distinct from the majority in a country. **national park** an area of land set aside as national property to be kept in a more or less natural state for the public benefit, preservation of wild life, etc. **National Party** any of various political parties or groups having nationalist policies or (supposedly) having national support or acting in the national interest (***Scottish National Party***: see SCOTTISH *adjective*). **national product** the monetary value of all goods and services produced in a country in one year (***gross national product***: see GROSS *adjective* 6; ***net national product***: see NET *adjective*[2] & *adverb*). **National Savings** a savings scheme run by or on behalf of a government and in which the funds deposited are available for the use of the government. **national school** a school conducted and supported to a greater or less extent by the State. **national service** service in the armed forces under conscription for a specified period. **national serviceman** a person performing national service. **National Socialism** in Germany, the doctrines of nationalism, racial purity, anti-Communism, and the all-powerful role of the State, advocated by Adolf Hitler; Nazism. **National Socialist** *noun & adjective* (*a*) *noun* in Germany, a member of the highly nationalistic and totalitarian National Socialist Workers' Party led by Adolf Hitler (from 1920), a Nazi; (*b*) *adjective* of or pertaining to this party or the doctrines of National Socialism. **national theatre** a theatre endowed by the State. **National Trust** a trust for the preservation of places of historic interest or natural beauty in England, Wales, and Northern Ireland, supported by endowment and private subscription; ***National Trust for Scotland***, a similar body in Scotland.

▶ **B** *noun*. **†1** A representative of a nation. Only in **M17.**

†2 A supporter of national as opp. to party interests. *rare*. Only in **M18.**

3 (Usu. **N-**.) A member or supporter of a nationalist political party or group; a member of a National Government or National Party. **L18.**

4 In full ***Grand National***. A steeplechase run annually at Aintree, Liverpool, in the first week of the flat-racing season. **M19.**

5 A citizen or subject of a (usu. specified) State. **L19.**

6 A national as opp. to a local newspaper, competition, etc. Usu. in *pl.* **M20.**

> 🕮 **5** *Geographical Magazine* Citizens of the EC follow one channel while non-EC nationals follow another.

■ **nationally** *adverb* in a national manner; as a nation; with regard to the nation as a whole: **M17. nationalness** *noun* (*rare*) **L17.**

nationalise *verb* var. of NATIONALIZE.

nationalism /ˈnaʃ(ə)n(ə)lɪz(ə)m/ *noun*. **M19.**
[from NATIONAL *adjective* + -ISM.]
Devotion to one's nation; national aspiration; advocacy of or support for national independence; (usu. **N-**) the political programme of a Nationalist party.

> 🕮 M. B. BROWN The nation state and . . nationalism are inextricably associated with the rise of a capitalist state. P. B. CLARKE Black nationalism, often referred to as a form of 'Black Zionism'. R. ELLMANN William Wilde's nationalism expressed itself in a love for the countryside. ***Scottish nationalism, Welsh nationalism***, etc.

nationalist /ˈnaʃ(ə)n(ə)lɪst/ *noun & adjective*. **E18.**
[formed as prec. + -IST.]
▶ **A** *noun*. A person devoted to his or her nation; an adherent or advocate of nationalism; an advocate of national independence; (usu. **N-**) a member of a Nationalist party. **E18.**

> 🕮 J. F. BRIGHT Those nationalists who regarded as righteous any act of antagonism to England. ***Scottish nationalist, Welsh nationalist***, etc.

▶ **B** *attrib.* or as *adjective*. Of or pertaining to nationalism or nationalists; characterized by nationalism; (usu. **N-**) designating or pertaining to any of various political parties or groups advocating independence for a particular nation or (supposedly) acting in the national interest. **L19.**

> 🕮 G. B. SHAW Every judge is a partisan in the nationalist conflict. A. J. P. TAYLOR Fighting a nationalist war against Germany, not an ideological one against 'fascism'. *Financial Times* The leader of the Nationalist Party . . campaigned under the slogan 'Fiji for the Fijians'.

■ **nationaˈlistic** *adjective* of the nature of or characterized by nationalism; somewhat nationalist: **M19. nationaˈlistically** *adverb* **E20.**

nationality /naʃəˈnalɪti/ *noun*. **L17.**
[formed as prec. + -ITY.]
1 National quality or character. **L17.** ▸**b** A national trait, characteristic, or peculiarity. *rare*. **L18.**

2 Nationalism; attachment to one's country or nation; national feeling. **M18.**

3 The fact of belonging to a particular nation; national origin; *spec.* the status of a citizen or subject of a particular State; the legal relationship by which this is defined, usu. involving allegiance by the individual to the State and protection by the State of the individual. Also, the legal relationship between a ship, aircraft, company, etc., and the State in which it is registered. **E19.** ▸**b** An instance of this, a particular national origin. Usu. in *pl.* **M19.**

4 Separate or complete existence as a nation; national independence or consolidation. **M19.**

5 A nation; a people potentially but not politically a nation; an ethnic group. **M19.**

> 🕮 **1** CARLYLE All true nationality vanished from its literature. **2** W. T. MILLS Nationality has made workers of different countries enemies to each other. **3** G. GREENE 'What nationality was this man?' 'He spoke English.' P. GROSSKURTH Confusion over nationality is compounded by the fact that . . Reizes was born in Galicia . . and moved to Vienna. A. BRIEN They will never hand over any legal resident, whatever his nationality. **b** M. FITZHERBERT Its members came from different . . backgrounds and nationalities. **4** H. MARTINEAU The Poles had been fighting—for nationality . . not for national freedom. **5** G. W. DASENT Welded by time and trouble into a distinct nationality.

nationalize /ˈnaʃ(ə)n(ə)lʌɪz/ *verb trans*. Also **-ise**. **E19.**
[formed as prec. + -IZE.]
1 Give a national character to, make distinctively national; make into or like a separate nation. **E19.**

2 Naturalize; admit into, or make part of, a nation. **E19.**

3 Bring (land, an industry, etc.) under State control or ownership, convert into the property of the State. **M19.**

> 🕮 **3** I. DEUTSCHER The economy remains capitalist whether or not fifteen percent . . of industry is nationalized. L. DEIGHTON Now that the Mexicans have nationalized the banks, the peso has dropped through the floor.

■ **nationaliˈzation** *noun* **E19. nationalizer** *noun* an advocate of nationalization **L19.**

nationalty /ˈnaʃ(ə)n(ə)lti/ *noun*. *rare*. **E19.**
[formed as prec. + -TY[1], after *realty* etc.]
National property.

nationhood /ˈneɪʃ(ə)nhʊd/ *noun*. **M19.**
[from NATION *noun*[1] + -HOOD.]
The state or fact of being a nation.

nationwide /*as adjective* ˈneɪʃ(ə)nwʌɪd, *as adverb* neɪʃ(ə)nˈwʌɪd/ *adjective & adverb*. **L19.**
[from NATION *noun*[1] + WIDE *adjective*.]
▶ **A** *adjective*. Extending throughout a nation, affecting or reaching the whole of a nation. **L19.**

> 🕮 *Dateline Magazine* Our very extensive nationwide membership.

▶ **B** *adverb*. Throughout a nation; so as to affect or reach the whole of a nation. **M20.**

> 🕮 *New York Times* A desire for American banks to expand nationwide.

native /ˈneɪtɪv/ *noun*. **LME.**
[Anglo-Latin *nativus*, *-va* use as noun of Latin *nativus*: see next. Later also directly from the adjective.]
▶ **I 1** A person born in bondage; a villein; a born slave. Long *obsolete* exc. *Hist.* **LME.**

▶ **II 2** ASTROLOGY. A person born under the specified planet or sign; the subject of a nativity or horoscope. **E16.**

3 A person born in a place; a person connected with a place by birth, whether subsequently resident there or not. Usu. foll. by *of*. **M16.** ▸**b** A local resident of a place. Freq. *derog.* **E19.** ▸**c** In Australia, a white person born in the country, as distinguished from an immigrant and from an Aboriginal. **E19.**

†4 In *pl.* Fellow-countrymen, compatriots. **L16–M17.**

5 One of the original or usual inhabitants of a country, as distinguished from strangers or foreigners or esp. (now) European colonists or their descendants holding power in the country; *N. Amer.* a N. American Indian; *Austral.* an Aboriginal; *S. Afr.* (*arch.*, now *derog.*) a black African. **E17.**

6 An animal, plant, or (formerly) mineral found naturally in or peculiar to a country or locality, and not introduced; = ENDEMIC *noun* 2. **L17.**

> 🕮 **2** *Tucson (Arizona) Citizen* Sagittarius natives seem constantly to turn up in your life. **3** S. MIDDLETON She spoke the language like a native, was often mistaken for a Greek. C. SIMMONS He was a native of Germany. **b** A. BRIEN The North Sea port we thought was called 'Har-wick' but natives pronounce 'Harridge'. **5** M. CHAPPELL There was nothing here when the pioneers came, Save bushveld and natives and wild animals. **astonish the natives** *colloq.* shock or otherwise profoundly impress public opinion.

▶ **III** *ellipt.* **7** One's native place or country. *obsolete* exc. *dial.* **E17.**

8 A native oyster (see NATIVE *adjective* 9b). **E19.**

9 A native cow, horse, etc. **M19.**

native /ˈneɪtɪv/ *adjective*. **LME.**
[Old & mod. French *natif*, *-ive* or Latin *nativus* produced by birth, innate, natural, from *nat-* pa. ppl stem of *nasci* be born: see -IVE.]
▶ **I 1** Belonging to or connected with a person or thing by nature or natural constitution, not acquired or superadded; *esp.* (of a quality) inherent, innate. Also (now *rare*), naturally resulting. **LME.** ▸**b** Natural *to* a person or thing. **M16.**

2 Pertaining to or connected with one by the fact of one's having been born there; that was the place or scene of one's birth; belonging to one by right or reason of the place or country of one's birth or of the nation to which one belongs. **E16.** ▸**b** Forming the source or origin of a thing or person; original, parent. *literary*. **L16.**

3 Left or remaining in a natural state; *esp.* free from or untouched by art; unadorned, simple, plain, unaffected; (of an interpretation, meaning, etc.) not forced. Now *rare*. **M16.**

> 🕮 **1** D. BREWSTER Every single star, shining by its own native light. D. DUNCAN Leave us to the native consequences of our folly. E. RHODE We find ourselves unable to exercise our native scepticism. **b** J. BARZUN This passivity is not native to the mind. **2** SHAKES. *Rich. II* The language I have learned these forty years, My native English. SIR W. SCOTT This is my own, my native land. *Observer* Dr Owen returned to his native Tunbridge Wells. **b** SHELLEY Heaps of broken stone That mingled slowly with their native earth. **3** STEELE Words . . used only . . to betray those who understand them in their native sense. S. JOHNSON Native beauty has little power to charm without the ornaments which fortune bestows.

▶ **II †4** Born in a state of bondage or villeinage. Only in **LME.**

5 Connected with one by birth, closely related. Also foll. by †*to*, *with*. Now *rare*. **L15.**

†6 Entitled to a certain position by birth; rightful. **M–L16.**

7 Of a metal or other mineral: occurring naturally in a pure or uncombined state; also, occurring in nature, as opp. to having been produced artificially. **L17.**

> 🕮 **5** SHAKES. *Haml.* The head is not more native to the heart, . . Than is the throne of Denmark to thy father. **7** G. E. HUTCHINSON The occurrence of native metallic copper as a constituent of lake mud.

▶ **III 8** Born in the particular place or country in question; belonging to a particular people, place, etc., by birth; *spec.* being one of the original inhabitants of a country where European colonists or their descendants hold power. Also foll. by †*of*, *to*. **L15.**

9 Produced in or naturally belonging to a certain country; of indigenous origin, production, or growth, not foreign or exotic. (Foll. by *to*.) **M16.** ▸**b** Of an oyster:

wholly or partially reared in British waters, esp. in artificial beds. **M18.**

10 Belonging to, connected with, used by, or characteristic of the natives of a particular place. **L18.**

11 COMPUTING. Designed for or built into a given system; *spec.* designating the language (esp. machine code) associated with a given processor, computer, or compiler, and programs written in it. **M20.**

> 📖 **8** J. CONRAD The father grumbled all day at the stupidity of native gardeners. E. HUXLEY All groups, immigrant and native alike, nourish feelings of prejudice against other groups. JOHN BROOKE The very fact that King George I was a stranger . . gave him an immense advantage over the native dynasty. **9** *Observer* Most of the species are native to . . South America. **10** C. ALLEN The native bazaar was . . out of bounds. A. BULLOCK In Yugoslavia there was at least a native Communist movement.

Phrases: **go native** (of a white person) adopt the way of life of the indigenous inhabitants of the country in which one lives, adopt a less civilized way of life.

Special collocations & comb.: **Native American** (an) American Indian. **native bear** *Austral.* = KOALA. **native-born** *adjective* †(*a*) *Scot.* having a certain position of status by birth; (*b*) belonging to a particular place or country by birth. **native bush** *NZ* woodland composed of indigenous trees and shrubs. **native cat** *Austral.* = DASYURE. **native companion** *Austral. & NZ* = BROLGA. ***native cranberry***: see CRANBERRY *noun* 2. **native dog** *Austral.* = DINGO. ***native FUCHSIA***. **native hen** either of two moorhens, *Gallinula ventralis* of mainland Australia and *G. mortierii* of Tasmania. ***native kumquat***: see KUMQUAT 2. **native oak** *Austral.* (the timber of) any of various trees of the genus *Casuarina*, which have wood similarly grained to the British oak. **native orange** *Austral.* any of several shrubs or trees bearing orange berries; *esp.* (*a*) a wild caper, *Capparis mitchellii*; (*b*) the orange-thorn, *Citriobatus pauciflorus*. **native oven** *NZ* = KOPA MAORI. ***native peach***: see PEACH *noun*[1] 2(b). ***native poplar***: see POPLAR 2. **native potato** *Austral.* a climbing plant, *Marsdenia viridiflora* (family Asclepiadaceae), with edible tubers. ***native quince***: see QUINCE 2. **native rock** rock in its original place in the ground. **native son** *US* a male native of a particular State. **native speaker** a person having the language in question as a native language (foll. by *of*). **Native State** = ***princely State*** s.v. PRINCELY *adjective* 1. ***native tamarind***: see TAMARIND 3. ***native turkey***: see TURKEY *noun*[2] 3. ***native willow***: see WILLOW *noun* 3.

■ **natively** *adverb* **M16.** **nativeness** *noun* **M16.** **nativi'zation** *noun* (LINGUISTICS) the process of nativizing a word, language, etc.; the state of being nativized: **M20.** **nativize** *verb trans.* (LINGUISTICS) make native; adapt to or adopt as a native language: **M20.**

nativism /ˈneɪtɪvɪz(ə)m/ *noun.* **M19.**
[from NATIVE *adjective* + -ISM.]
1 a Chiefly US HISTORY. The attitude, practice, or policy of protecting the interests of native-born or existing inhabitants against those of immigrants. **M19.** ▸**b** ANTHROPOLOGY. Return to or emphasis on a way of life or customs under threat from outside influences. **M20.**
2 a PHILOSOPHY. The doctrine of innate ideas. *rare.* **L19.** ▸**b** In PSYCHOLOGY, the doctrine that certain capacities or abilities, esp. those of sense perception, are innate rather than acquired. In LINGUISTICS, the theory that in the development of language an inherent connection exists in the mind between sound and sense. **L19.**
■ **nativist** *noun & adjective* (*a*) *noun* an adherent or student of nativism; (*b*) *adjective* of or pertaining to nativism or nativists: **M19.** **nati'vistic** *adjective* pertaining to or of the nature of nativism **L19.**

nativity /nəˈtɪvɪti/ *noun.* **ME.**
[Old & mod. French *nativité* from late Latin *nativitas*, from Latin *nativus*: see NATIVE *adjective*, -ITY.]
1 (One's) birth; *spec.* the birth of Jesus (the earliest use), of the Virgin Mary, or of St John the Baptist; any of the church festivals commemorating these births, esp. that of Jesus, observed on 25 December. Also, a picture representing the nativity of Jesus. **ME.** ▸**b** The time of one's birth considered astrologically; a horoscope at birth. **LME.**
2 Native status of a plant etc.; indigenousness. **M19.**

> 📖 **1** C. VERNON Those to bee paid at the Feast of the Nativity of our Lord God. RUFUS ANDERSON His Irish nativity, and consequent right to . . British protection. **b** SIR W. SCOTT I will calculate his nativity according to the rule of the Triplicities. S. PLATH The astrologer . . Selling the Welsh and English mothers Nativities.

Comb.: **nativity play** a play representing events surrounding the birth of Jesus.

NATO /ˈneɪtəʊ/ *abbreviation.*
North Atlantic Treaty Organization.

†**Natolian** *adjective & noun* var. of ANATOLIAN.

natrium /ˈneɪtrɪəm, ˈnat-/ *noun. rare.* **M19.**
[from NATRON + -IUM.]
Chiefly PHARMACOLOGY. Sodium. Cf. *Na* s.v. N, N 9.

natriuresis /ˌneɪtrɪjʊ(ə)ˈriːsɪs, ˌnat-/ *noun.* **M20.**
[from prec. + Greek *ourēsis* urination.]
MEDICINE. The excretion of abnormally large amounts of sodium in the urine.
■ **natriuretic** /-ˈretɪk/ *adjective* causing or pertaining to natriuresis **M20.**

natro- /ˈneɪtrəʊ, ˈnat-/ *combining form.*
[from NATRIUM: see -O-.]
MINERALOGY. Forming the names of minerals containing sodium as a primary constituent or as a substituent atom, as ***natroalunite***.

natrolite /ˈneɪtrəlʌɪt, ˈnat-/ *noun.* **E19.**
[from next + -LITE.]
MINERALOGY. A hydrous sodium aluminosilicate of the zeolite group, usu. occurring as transparent white acicular crystals of the orthorhombic system.

natron /ˈneɪtrən, ˈnat-/ *noun.* **L17.**
[French from Spanish *natrón* from Arab. *natrūn*, *nitrūn*, from Greek *nitron* NITRE.]
Native hydrous sodium carbonate, crystallizing in the monoclinic system and occurring chiefly in solution and in evaporative residues; a deposit containing this.
Comb.: **natron lake** a (salt) lake from which natron is obtainable.

NATSOPA /natˈsəʊpə/ *abbreviation.*
National Society of Operative Printers, Graphical and Media Personnel (orig., Printers and Assistants).

natter /ˈnatə/ *verb & noun.* Also (earlier, *dial.*) **gn-.** **E19.**
[Imit.: see -ER[5].]
▶ **A** *verb intrans.* **1** Grumble, complain; fret. *dial.* **E19.**
2 Chatter, chat idly. Also foll. by *away*, *on*. *colloq.* **M20.**
▶ **B** *noun.* Grumbling, nagging talk (*dial.*); aimless chatter, a chat, a talk, (*colloq.*). **M19.**

> 📖 E. BLISHEN We were able to have a pleasant natter over cups of coffee.

■ **natterer** *noun* **E20.** **nattery** *adjective* given to nattering **E19.**

Natterer's bat /ˈnatərəz bat/ *noun phr.* **L19.**
[Johann *Natterer* (1787–1843), Austrian naturalist.]
A greyish-brown Eurasian bat with a white underside, *Myotis nattereri*.

natterjack /ˈnatədʒak/ *noun.* **M18.**
[Origin unkn.: cf. JACK *noun*[1] IV.]
A toad, *Bufo calamita*, of western Eurasia (now rare in Britain), having a light yellow stripe down the back. Also ***natterjack toad***.

Nattier blue /natjeɪ ˈbluː/ *noun & adjectival phr.* **E20.**
[Jean Marc *Nattier* (1685–1766), French painter.]
(Of) a soft shade of blue.

natty /ˈnati/ *adjective*[1]. Orig. *slang.* **L18.**
[App. rel. to NEAT *adjective*: see -Y[1].]
Neatly smart, spruce, trim; exhibiting dainty tidiness, taste, or skill; deft.

> 📖 S. BELLOW He . . wore natty clothes. T. KENEALLY Natty plastic cloths . . covered the tables. E. SIMPSON A handsome . . man and a natty dresser.

■ **nattily** *adverb* **M19.** **nattiness** *noun* **M19.**

natty /ˈnati/ *adjective*[2] *& noun. Rastafarian slang.* **L20.**
[Repr. a (Jamaican) pronunc. of KNOTTY *adjective*.]
▶ **A** *adjective.* (Of hair) tightly ringleted as in dreadlocks; Rastafarian. **L20.**
natty dread (*a*) a dreadlock (usu. in *pl.*); (*b*) (a) Rastafarian.
▶ **B** *noun.* A Rastafarian. **L20.**

Natufian /naˈtuːfɪən/ *adjective & noun.* **M20.**
[Wādi an-*Natuf*, the type-site, north-west of Jerusalem, + -IAN.]
ARCHAEOLOGY. (Designating or pertaining to) a mesolithic culture of the Middle East and eastern Mediterranean, represented mainly in Israel.

natural /ˈnatʃ(ə)r(ə)l, *in sense 13 also foreign* natuˈral/ *noun.* In sense 13 pl. also **-es** /-es/. **E16.**
[from the adjective, partly after French *naturel*. In sense 13 from Spanish.]
▶ **I** †**1** A mental or (rarely) physical endowment of a person; a natural gift or power of mind (or body). Usu. in *pl.* **E16–L17.**
2 †**a** A natural thing or object; a matter having its basis in the natural world or in the usual course of nature. Usu. in *pl.* **E16–E18.** ▸†**b** ***in one's naturals***, ***in one's pure naturals*** [after medieval Latin *in puris naturalibus*], in a purely natural condition, not altered or improved in any way; completely naked. **L16–M18.** ▸**c** In *pl. & sing.* The genitals. *rare.* **M17.**
3 †**a** Natural disposition, inclination, or character; natural form or condition. **M16–L17.** ▸**b** ***the natural***, †(*a*) the real thing or person, the life; (*b*) that which is natural or according to the ordinary course of things. **L16.**
4 A person mentally handicapped from birth. **M16.**
5 MUSIC. **a** A note in a natural scale. **E17.** ▸**b** A sign (♮) indicating return to natural pitch after a preceding sharp or flat. **L18.** ▸**c** A white key on a piano etc. **L19.**
6 a In a gambling game, a combination or score that immediately wins the stake; *spec.* a throw of 7 or 11 at craps. **M18.** ▸**b** A hand as first dealt making 21 in pontoon. **M19.**
7 One's natural life. *colloq.* **L19.**
8 A person having a natural gift or talents (*for*); a natural expert (*at*); a thing with qualities that make it particularly suitable (*for*). **E20.**
9 ARCHAEOLOGY. Undisturbed terrain, below the levels affected by human activity; virgin rock. **M20.**
10 A hairstyle among black people in which the hair is not straightened or bleached; *spec.* an Afro haircut. *US.* **M20.**
11 An off-white or creamy beige, the colour of natural wool etc. **M20.**

> 📖 **7** C. MACKENZIE I never worked so hard in all my natural. **8** *Observer* The sort of play which should have been a natural for television. B. MALAMUD He was a natural and gradually began to pick up . . a reputation.

▶†**II 12** A native of a place or country. **E16–M18.**
▶ **III 13** BULLFIGHTING. A type of pass made facing the bull with the muleta in the left hand. **M20.**
Comb.: **natural-sign** MUSIC = sense 5b above.

natural /ˈnatʃ(ə)r(ə)l/ *adjective & adverb.* **ME.**
[Old & mod. French *naturel*, †-*al* from Latin *naturalis*, from *natura* NATURE *noun*: see -AL[1].]
▶ **A** *adjective.* **I 1** Of law or justice: based on innate moral feeling; instinctively or immediately felt to be right and fair, though not prescribed by any enactment or formal compact; having a claim to be followed or executed despite not being so prescribed. **ME.**
2 Established by nature; having a basis in the normal constitution of things; taking place in conformity with the ordinary course of nature; normal; not unusual, exceptional, irregular, or miraculous; (of death etc.) resulting from age or disease, as opp. to accident, violence, or poison. **ME.** ▸**b** MUSIC. Of a note: neither sharp nor flat. Of a key or scale: having no sharps or flats (i.e. being either C major or A minor). **E18.** ▸**c** BIOLOGY. Of (the groups in) a classification system: based on a (large) number of correlated characteristics, having a high degree of predictivity, not artificial; *spec.* in BOTANY, designating or belonging to a taxonomic system based on natural relationships, in contrast to that of Linnaeus (arbitrarily based on the number of stamens and pistils in the flower). **E19.**
3 Having a real or physical existence; not spiritual, intellectual, or fictitious; pertaining to physical things, operating or taking place in the physical (as opp. to the spiritual) world. **LME.**
4 Existing in or formed by nature; consisting of objects or material of this kind; not artificially made or constructed; not manufactured or processed; (of vegetation) growing of itself, self-sown; (of land) uncultivated. **LME.** ▸**b** (Of wool, cotton, silk, etc.) having a colour characteristic of the unbleached and undyed state; off-white, creamy beige. **M19.**
5 In a state of nature, without spiritual enlightenment; unenlightened, unregenerate; not communicated by revelation. **E16.**
6 Closely imitating nature, lifelike; free from affectation, artificiality, or constraint; having the normal form, free from disfigurement or disguise. **M16.**

> 📖 **2** SHAKES. *Temp.* These are not natural events; they strengthen From strange to stranger. F. BOWEN Natural or regular . . predication . . in which the genus is predicated of the species. P. MOYES The death certificate says 'Natural Causes'. **3** G. BERKELEY Sensible objects have an existence natural or real, distinct from their being perceived. **4** J. R. LOWELL Orchards, commonly of natural fruit. I. MURDOCH Unsymmetrical undulations suggested a natural growth. K. CLARK The delighted observation of natural objects. F. FORSYTH Enough natural daylight filtered over the horizon. P. ABRAHAMS The rock caved inward, making a natural shelter. **6** SIR W. SCOTT How natural these paintings, which seem to contend with life! N. HINTON He always sounded natural and . . never tried to make himself sound important.

▶ **II 7** Existing or present by nature or from birth; inherent in the very constitution of a person or thing; innate; not acquired or assumed. **ME.**
8 Normally or essentially connected with or pertaining to a person or thing; consonant with the nature or character of the person or thing (foll. by *for*, *to*); coming easily or spontaneously to. **ME.** ▸**b** Fully consonant with the circumstances, to be expected, not surprising; completely understandable. **LME.**
9 Being such by the nature of things or force of circumstances, inevitably such. **L15.** ▸†**b** = ***natural-born*** below. **E16–M17.**
†**10** Of a country or language: native. **L15–M17.**

> 📖 **7** A. BULLOCK Bevin had a powerful natural intelligence. **8** G. B. SHAW Home life . . is no more natural to us than a cage . . to a cockatoo. J. WILCOX It wasn't natural for me not to resent him. **b** A. S. NEILL Their reaction of fury was spontaneous and natural. W. GOLDING She lurched against him and it was natural that his arm should go round her waist. **9** *Nation* The people rejoiced that the laugh was on those whom they consider their natural enemies. A. SCHLEE I was the natural person to speak . . because of our close bond.

▶ **III 11** Having genetically the specified familial relationship (child, father, etc.) with the person(s) in question; actually begotten by one, as opp. to adopted etc., formerly esp. within a legal marriage. **LME.** ▶**b** So related genetically only, illegitimate. **LME.**

12 Having a specified character or ability by nature or from birth; being such innately, effortlessly, or without training. **LME.**

13 Feeling or exhibiting innate or spontaneous kindliness, affection, or (formerly) gratitude; having innate feeling (*to, towards*). Now *rare*. **LME.**

†**14** Native to a country; native-born. (Foll. by *of*.) **M16–E18.**

> 📖 **11** *Times* The law did not recognize the natural father at all. J. CLAVELL You don't ask if a person is adopted or natural. **b** L. SIMPSON I'm a natural son / of the Grand Duke Nicholas. **12** M. BARING He is a natural untaught musician. G. GREENE Natural prisoners, who would have found themselves prisoners . . sooner or later. A. CARTER No natural horseman he.

▶ **IV 15** Dealing with or relating to nature as an object of study or research. Now chiefly in special collocations: see below. **LME.**

Special collocations & comb.: **natural-born** *adjective* having a specified position or character by birth. **natural childbirth** childbirth with relaxation and physical cooperation by the mother; childbirth with minimal medical or technological intervention. **natural-coloured** *adjective* not given any artificial colouring; *spec.* = sense 4b above. **natural cosine**, **natural sine**, **natural tangent**, etc. *MATH.*: taken in an arc of radius 1, or a right-angled triangle with a hypotenuse of unit length. ***natural day***: see **DAY** *noun*. **natural deduction** *LOGIC*: in which formal proofs are obtained solely by the application of rules of inference without appeal to axioms. **natural food** (a) food without preservatives etc. **natural fool** a person mentally deficient or handicapped from birth (now only as a gen. term of abuse). **natural frequency** the frequency at which a mechanical or electrical system oscillates when not subjected to any external forces. **natural gas** flammable gas occurring naturally underground, consisting chiefly of methane and often found associated with petroleum. **natural historian** an expert in or student of natural history, a naturalist. **natural-historical** *adjective* of or pertaining to natural history. **natural history** *(a) arch.* a systematic account of natural phenomena; a scientific treatise; *(b)* the characteristics *of* a class of (esp. natural) things or persons; the facts relating to the flora, fauna, etc., *of* a place; *(c)* orig., the branch of science that dealt with all natural objects, animal, vegetable, and mineral; now, the science of living organisms (esp. animals), esp. as presented in a popular rather than a strictly scientific manner. **natural horn** *MUSIC* a horn without valves etc. to alter the length of the tube, producing only notes in the harmonic series. **natural killer cell** *PHYSIOLOGY* a lymphocyte able to bind to certain tumour cells and virus-infected cells without the stimulation of antigens, and kill them by the insertion of granules containing perforin. **natural language** (a) language used natively by people, as opp. to (an) artificial language or code; ***natural-language processing***, the computer processing of natural-language texts (for automatic machine translation, textual analysis, etc.). ***natural law***: see **LAW** *noun*[1]. ***natural liberty***: see **LIBERTY** *noun*. **natural life** the duration of one's life. ***natural LOGARITHM***. ***natural magic***: see **MAGIC** *noun*. ***natural marmalade***: see **MARMALADE** *noun* 2. **natural number** *MATH.* a positive whole number (1, 2, 3, etc., sometimes with the addition of 0). **natural order** *(a)* the order apparent in the constitution of matter and operation of forces in nature; *(b)* see **ORDER** *noun* 11b. †**natural parts** the genitals. ***natural person***: see **PERSON** *noun* 5. **natural philosopher** (chiefly *Hist.*) an expert in or student of natural philosophy, a scientist. ***natural philosophy***: see **PHILOSOPHY** 2a. ***natural pravity***: see **PRAVITY** 1. **natural regeneration** *FORESTRY* the growth of young trees from seed produced by those already established. **natural religion** *THEOLOGY* deism, as opp. to revealed religion. **natural right** a fundamental right of the individual which ought to be safeguarded by the State (usu. in *pl.*). **natural science** the branch of knowledge that deals with the natural or physical world; a physical science, as physics, chemistry, biology, geology, etc.; in *pl.*, these sciences collectively. **natural scientist** an expert in or student of (a) natural science. **natural selection** *BIOLOGY* the Darwinian theory of the survival and preferential propagation of organisms better adapted to their environment (cf. ***SURVIVAL of the fittest***). **natural shoulder** *US* an unpadded or only lightly padded shoulder of a jacket. ***natural sine***: see ***natural cosine*** above. **natural spirit** (*MEDICINE*, now *Hist.*) the supposed principle of growth and nutrition, originating in the liver. ***natural tangent***: see ***natural cosine*** above. **natural theologian** a student of natural theology. **natural theology** theology based on reasoning from natural facts apart from revelation. **natural trumpet** a trumpet without valves etc. to alter the length of the tube, producing only notes in the harmonic series. **natural uranium** unenriched uranium, as extracted from its ore. **natural virtue** each of the four chief moral virtues, justice, prudence, temperance, and fortitude, as distinct from the theological virtues (see **THEOLOGICAL** *adjective* 1; cf. ***cardinal virtue*** s.v. **CARDINAL** *adjective* 1). ***natural wastage***: see **WASTAGE** 2d. ***natural year***: see **YEAR** *noun*[1] 1.

▶ **B** *adverb.* Naturally. *colloq. & dial.* **L18.**

■ **natura'lesque** *adjective* having the characteristics of nature or natural objects, imitating nature **L19.**

naturales *noun pl.* see **NATURAL** *noun*.

naturalise *verb* var. of **NATURALIZE**.

naturalism /ˈnatʃ(ə)rəlɪz(ə)m/ *noun*. **M17.**
[from prec. + **-ISM**. In sense 2 after French *naturalisme*.]

1 Action arising from or based on natural instincts; a system of morality or religion having a purely natural basis. **M17.**

2 *PHILOSOPHY.* The belief that only natural (as opp. to supernatural or spiritual) laws and forces operate in the world. Also, the belief that moral concepts can be analysed in terms of concepts applicable to natural phenomena. **M18.**

3 Close adherence to and faithful representation of nature or reality in literature, art, etc. **M19.**

4 Adherence or attachment to what is natural, indifference to convention. **M19.**

naturalist /ˈnatʃ(ə)rəlɪst/ *noun & adjective*. **L16.**
[from **NATURAL** *adjective* + **-IST**, partly after French *naturaliste*.]

▶ **A** *noun*. **1** A person who studies natural, as opp. to supernatural or spiritual, things; a person who believes that only natural laws and forces operate in the world; an adherent of philosophical naturalism. **L16.** ▶**b** A person who follows the light of nature, as opp. to revelation. **E17.**

2 Orig., an expert in or student of natural science; a natural philosopher, a physicist. Now *spec.* an expert in or student of natural history; a zoologist or botanist (freq. an amateur) concerned with observation rather than experiment. **L16.**

3 A person who aims at close adherence to and faithful representation of nature or reality in art, literature, etc.; an adherent of artistic naturalism. **L18.**

▶ **B** *adjective*. Of or pertaining to naturalism or naturalists; naturalistic. **M19.**

naturalistic /natʃ(ə)rəˈlɪstɪk/ *adjective*. **M19.**
[from prec. + **-IC**.]

1 Pertaining to, of the nature of, or characterized by naturalism; in accordance with naturalism. **M19.**

2 Of or pertaining to natural history. **M19.**

> 📖 **1** K. CLARK Straight-forward naturalistic landscape-painting. D. CUPITT To study positive science and make his own thinking more stringently naturalistic.

■ **naturalistically** *adverb* **M19.**

naturality /natʃəˈralɪti/ *noun*. Now *rare*. **LME.**
[Old & mod. French *naturalité* from late Latin *naturalitas*, from Latin *naturalis*: see **NATURAL** *adjective*, **-ITY**.]

▶ **I 1** Natural character or quality; natural ability. Latterly *Scot.* **LME.**

2 Natural feeling or conduct. Latterly *Scot.* **L16.**

†**3** A state of nature, as opp. to morality. **E–M17.**

†**4** The fact of being in accordance with nature. **M–L17.**

5 An illustration drawn from nature. **M17.**

▶†**II 6** The position or rights of a natural-born subject. Chiefly *Scot.* **E16–E17.**

naturalize /ˈnatʃ(ə)rəlʌɪz/ *verb*. Also **-ise**. **M16.**
[French *naturaliser*, from †*natural*: see **NATURAL** *adjective*, **-IZE**.]

▶ **I 1** *verb trans.* Admit (an alien) to the position and rights of citizenship; invest with the privileges of a native-born subject. **M16.**

2 *verb trans.* Introduce or adopt (a word, practice, thing, etc.) into a country or into common use; introduce (an animal or plant) to a place where it is not indigenous, so that it appears native or wild. Freq. as ***naturalized*** *ppl adjective*. **L16.**

3 *verb intrans.* & (now *rare*) *refl.* Become naturalized. **M17.**

> 📖 **1** MALCOLM X How many German-born naturalized Americans were herded behind barbed wire. D. FRASER Having been born at Bagnères he had ultimately to be naturalized. *fig.*: STEELE My obligations . . are such as might . . naturalize me into the interests of it. **2** SOUTHEY To use a word which seems now to be naturalized, thus *mystified*.

▶ **II** †**4** *verb trans.* Familiarize, accustom, (*in, to*); convert *to* or *into* (something) by custom or familiarity. **L16–M18.**

5 *verb trans.* Make natural, cause to appear natural; free from conventionality; place on a naturalistic basis; remove the supernatural or miraculous from. **E17.**

6 *verb intrans.* Study natural history. **L18.**

■ **naturali'zation** *noun* **M16.** **naturalizer** *noun* **E19.**

naturally /ˈnatʃ(ə)rəli/ *adverb*. **ME.**
[from **NATURAL** *adjective* + **-LY**[2].]

1 In a natural manner; by nature. **ME.**

2 *spec.* As a natural result or consequence; as might be expected, of course. **LME.**

> 📖 **1** SHAKES. *Wint. T.* Though I am not naturally honest, I am so sometimes by chance. C. BRONTË Her face, naturally pale as marble. L. STEPHEN An antiquarian is naturally a conservative. R. HUGHES How can one speak naturally anything learnt by heart. N. SEDAKA Born with a naturally beautiful voice. P. B. CLARKE Living naturally means living on and off the land. **come naturally to** be a natural action for. **2** LD MACAULAY His situation naturally developes in him . . a peculiar class of abilities. A. CHRISTIE 'If I ask you questions I shall expect answers.' 'Naturally.' A. MILLER Naturally I was thrilled to bits and accepted with alacrity.

naturalness /ˈnatʃ(ə)r(ə)lnɪs/ *noun*. **LME.**
[formed as prec. + **-NESS**.]

The quality, state, or fact of being natural.

natura naturans /naˌtjʊərə ˈnatjʊranz/ *noun phr.* **E19.**
[from Latin *natura* (see **NATURE** *noun*) + medieval Latin *naturans* (pres. pple) creating, from *naturare*: see **NATURE** *verb*.]

PHILOSOPHY. Nature as creative; the essential creative power or act. Cf. next.

natura naturata /naˌtjʊərə natjʊˈrɑːtə/ *noun phr.* **E19.**
[formed as prec. + medieval Latin *naturata* (pa. pple) created, from *naturare*: see **NATURE** *verb*.]

PHILOSOPHY. Nature as created; the natural phenomena and forces in which creation is manifested. Cf. prec.

nature /ˈneɪtʃə/ *noun*. **ME.**
[Old & mod. French from Latin *natura*, from *nat-* pa. ppl stem of *nasci* be born: see **-URE**.]

1 The inherent or essential quality or constitution of a thing; the innate disposition or character of a person or animal or of humankind generally. Also, an individual element of character, disposition, etc.; a thing or person of a particular quality or character; a kind, a sort, a class. **ME.**

2 Vital or physical power (*of*); a person's physical strength or constitution; sexual drive. Now *dial.* **ME.** ▶**b** The strength or substance *of* a thing. **L19.**

3 Physical appetite or need; *spec.* *(a)* the excretory function, defecation (now chiefly in fixed phrases); *(b)* (now *rare*) the menstrual discharge. Formerly also, semen, sexual fluid. **ME.** ▶†**b** The external genitals of a female, esp. of a mare. **LME–M18.**

4 The inherent power or force by which physical and mental activities are sustained; the inherent dominating power or impulse (in people or animals) by which action or character is determined, directed, or controlled; (opp. ***nurture***) heredity as an influence on or determinant of personality. **ME.** ▶**b** The body as requiring nourishment. **LME.** ▶**c** Natural feeling or affection. Now *dial.* **LME.**

5 The creative and regulative physical power conceived of as operating in the material world and as the immediate cause of all its phenomena (sometimes, esp. **N-**, personified as a female being); these phenomena collectively; the material world; *spec.* plants, animals, and other features and products of the earth itself, as opp. to humans or human creations or civilization. **ME.** ▶**b** Fidelity or close adherence to nature; naturalness. **E18.**

> 📖 **1** H. MARTINEAU The fleeting nature of riches. R. W. DALE Men have a physical as well as spiritual nature. F. W. FARRAR The unquestioning truthfulness of a sunny nature. H. JAMES He is a noble little nature. R. G. COLLINGWOOD The nature of moral or political action. DAY LEWIS Children . . whose natures are so absorbed in the mere process of growing. E. CALDWELL Due to the nature of its use . . the road . . was usually referred to as Lovers' Lane. L. HELLMAN That kind of talk was a part of her Catholic convert nature. J. S. FOSTER The nature and properties of a material determine the methods used in processing. H. JACOBSON Not in the grain of my nature to be candid and confessional. **4** W. COWPER 'Twas Nature, sir, whose strong behest Impelled me to the deed. R. H. TAWNEY The contrast between nature and grace . . is not absolute, but relative. A. STORR The principal concern of psycho-analysis is with nurture rather than with nature. **b** G. BORROW The prison allowance will not support nature. **5** BURKE Nature . . frequently does most when she is left entirely to herself. W. IRVING We derive a great portion of our pleasures from the mere beauties of nature. L. STRACHEY Nature had given him beauty and brains. M. L. KING Johns loved to farm and live close to nature. J. BRONOWSKI Nature—that is, biological evolution—has not fitted man to any specific environment. F. WELDON Hello country! Nature, here we come! B. GILROY Then nature took a hand. It started to rain.

Phrases: **against nature** *(a)* unnatural, immoral; *(b)* miraculous(ly). **all nature** *US colloq.* everything, everyone, all creation. ***back to nature***: see **BACK** *adverb*. ***balance of nature***: see **BALANCE** *noun*. **by nature** in virtue of the very character or essence of the thing or person, naturally. **by the nature of things**, **by the very nature of things**, **by the nature of the case**, **by the very nature of the case** = ***in the nature of things*** below. **call of nature** a need to urinate or defecate. **contrary to nature** = ***against nature*** above. ***course of nature***: see **COURSE** *noun*[1]. ***debt of nature***, ***debt to nature***: see **DEBT** *noun*. ***ease nature***: see **EASE** *verb*. ***exonerate nature***: see **EXONERATE** *verb* 4. **from nature** using natural objects as models (for painting etc.). **from the nature of things**, **from the very nature of things**, **from the nature of the case**, **from the very nature of the case** = ***in the nature of things*** below. **GOOD NATURE**. ***human nature***: see **HUMAN** *adjective*. **ILL NATURE**. ***inanimate nature***: see **INANIMATE** *adjective* 1. **in nature** *(a)* actually existing; in actual fact, in reality; *(b)* anywhere, at all, (in superl. and neg. contexts). **in the nature of** *arch.* = ***of the nature of*** below. **in the nature of things**, **in the very nature of things**, **in the nature of the case**, **in the very nature of the case** inevitably given the circumstances or state of affairs. ***law of nature***: see **LAW** *noun*[1]. **Mother Nature** nature as a creative power personified, nature personified as benign and protective. **of a — nature** of a — kind, that is —. **of the nature of** essentially like or classifiable as. **one of nature's** — a member of the specified class of people by nature or temperament (esp. in ***one of nature's gentlemen***). **one's better nature** the good side of one's character; one's capacity for tolerance, generosity, etc. ***return to nature***: see **RETURN** *noun*, *verb* 1. ***second nature***: see **SECOND** *adjective*. ***secretary of nature***: see **SECRETARY** *noun*. ***sport of nature***: see **SPORT** *noun*. ***sporting of nature***: see **SPORTING** *noun*. **state of nature** *(a)* the unregenerate moral condition natural to humankind, as opp. to a state of grace; (**b**) the condition of humankind before or without organized society; (**c**) an uncultivated or undomesticated condition of plants or animals; (**d**) a state of bodily nakedness. **the nature of the beast** *colloq.* the (undesirable but unchangeable) inherent or essential quality or character of the thing. ***touch of nature***: see TOUCH *noun*. ***two natures***: see TWO *adjective*.

Comb.: **nature conservation** the preservation of wild fauna and flora and the habitats necessary for their continued existence in their native surroundings; **nature cure** a naturopathic treatment or cure; **nature-faker** (orig. *US*) a person who misrepresents facts about nature, a falsifier of reports of natural phenomena, esp. animal behaviour; **nature-faking** (orig. *US*) the activity of a nature-faker; **nature food** (a) natural food, (a) food without preservatives etc.; **nature-god** a power or phenomenon of nature personified as a god; **nature-notes**: recording one's observations on the natural world; **nature poem** a poem about the natural world; **nature poet** a poet who writes about the natural world; **nature poetry** poetry about the natural world; **nature print** an impression produced by nature-printing; **nature-printing** the method or process of producing a print of a natural object, esp. a leaf, by pressing it on a prepared plate to give a printing surface; **nature ramble**: to observe plants, animals, physical phenomena, etc., esp. as part of nature study in a school; **nature reserve** a tract of land managed in order to preserve its fauna, flora, physical features, etc.; **nature sanctuary** an area in which the fauna and flora are protected from disturbance; **nature-spirit** a spirit supposed to reside in some natural element or object; **nature strip** *Austral. colloq.* a strip of grass beside a pavement in a built-up area; **nature study** the practical study of plants, animals, physical phenomena, etc., esp. as a school subject; **nature trail** a signposted path through countryside for the observation of plants, animals, and other physical phenomena, usu. with the aid of descriptive literature or a guide; **nature walk** = *nature ramble* above.

■ **natureless** *adjective* (*rare*) M16.

nature /ˈneɪtʃə/ *verb*. Now *rare* or *obsolete*. LME.
[Old French *naturer* or medieval Latin *naturare*, from *natura* NATURE *noun*; later partly from the noun.]
1 *verb trans.* Give a particular, or a new, nature to. *rare*. LME.
2 *verb intrans.* Be creative, give each thing its specific nature. Chiefly in ***nature naturing***, = NATURA NATURANS. E16.

natured /ˈneɪtʃəd/ *adjective*. L16.
[from NATURE *noun* + -ED².]
Having a nature or disposition (of a specified kind). Chiefly as 2nd elem. of comb.
good-natured, ***ill-natured***, etc.

naturelle /natʃʊˈrɛl, *foreign* natyrɛl/ *adjective & noun*. L19.
[French, fem. of *naturel* NATURAL *adjective*.]
(Of) a pale pink or beige colour; skin-colour(ed).

nature morte /naty:r mɔrt/ *noun phr.* Pl. **-s -s** (pronounced same). E20.
[French.]
A still life.

naturise *verb* var. of NATURIZE.

naturism /ˈneɪtʃ(ə)rɪz(ə)m/ *noun*. M19.
[from NATURE *noun* + -ISM.]
1 Naturalism in religion or philosophy. M19.
2 Nature-worship. L19.
3 Nudism. M20.

naturist /ˈneɪtʃ(ə)rɪst/ *noun & adjective*. L17.
[from NATURE *noun* + -ISM.]
▶ **A** *noun*. **1** A follower of or believer in nature. L17.
2 A nudist. E20.
▶ **B** *attrib.* or as *adjective*. Of or pertaining to naturism or naturists. M20.

■ **natuˈristic** *adjective* (*rare*) of or pertaining to nature or naturism L19. **natuˈristically** *adverb* (*rare*) in a way suggestive of nature L19.

naturize /ˈneɪtʃ(ə)rʌɪz/ *verb trans. rare*. Also **-ise**. E17.
[from NATURE *noun* + -IZE.]
Give a particular nature to.

naturopathy /neɪtʃəˈrɒpəθi/ *noun*. E20.
[from NATURE *noun* + -O- + -PATHY.]
A theory of disease and system of therapy based on the supposition that diseases can be cured by natural agencies without the use of drugs.

■ **ˈnaturopath** *noun* an advocate or practitioner of naturopathy E20. **naturoˈpathic** *adjective* E20.

Naturphilosophie /naˈtu:rfilozo,fi:/ *noun*. E19.
[German, from *Natur* nature + *Philosophie* philosophy.]
The theory put forward, esp. by Schelling (1775–1854) and other German philosophers, that there is an eternal and unchanging law of nature, proceeding from the absolute, from which all laws governing natural phenomena and forces derive.

■ ***Naturphilosoph*** /-filo,zo:f/ *noun*, pl. **-en** /-ən/, an adherent of *Naturphilosophie* E19.

naucrary /ˈnɔ:krəri/ *noun*. Also **nauk-**. M19.
[Greek *naukraria* from *naukraros*, of unkn. origin.]
GREEK HISTORY. Any of the forty-eight political divisions of the Athenian people.

†naufrage *noun*. L15–M18.
[French from Latin *naufragium*, from *navis* ship + *frag-*, *frangere* break.]
(A) shipwreck (*lit.* & *fig.*).

Naugahyde /ˈnɔ:gəhʌɪd/ *noun*. Also **n-**. M20.
[from *Nauga(tuk* a town in Connecticut, USA, where rubber is manufactured + *-hyde* alt. of HIDE *noun*¹.]
(Proprietary name for) a material used in upholstery, consisting of a fabric base coated with a layer of rubber or vinyl resin and finished with a leather-like grain.

†nauger *noun* var. of AUGER *noun*¹.

naught /nɔ:t/ *pronoun, noun, adjective, adverb, & verb*.
[Old English *nāwiht*, *nāwuht*, *nauht*, from NA *adverb*¹ + *wiht* WIGHT *noun*. Cf. NOUGHT.]
▶ **A** *pronoun & noun*. **1** Nothing, not any thing. Now *arch.* & *literary*. OE.
†**2** Wickedness, evil, moral wrong. OE–M17. ▸**b** Something wrong or faulty in method. M16–M17.
3 †**a** A thing of no worth or value. *rare*. Only in M16. ▸†**b** In *pl.* Nothing, nought. *rare*. M–L16. ▸**c** A zero, a nought. M17. ▸**d** A bad person. M17.

🕮 **1** M. TWAIN He shall show naught of unrest to the curious. †**be naught** efface oneself, keep quiet, withdraw (usu. in *imper.*). **bring to naught** ruin; frustrate, foil. †**call all to naught** vilify, abuse. **come to naught** be ruined or frustrated. **for naught** = ***for nothing*** s.v. NOTHING *pronoun & noun*. **set at naught** disregard, despise; nullify, frustrate.

▶ **B** *adjective*. **1** Worthless, useless; bad, poor. OE. ▸**b** Of food or drink: unfit for consumption, unwholesome. Now *rare* or *obsolete*. L16. ▸†**c** Wrong in method; harmful, injurious. L16–M17.
†**2** Morally bad, wicked; immoral. M16–M18. ▸**b** In illicit sexual contact *with*. M16–L17.
†**3** Lost, ruined. Only in E17.
▶†**C** *adverb*. **1** Not. OE–LME.
2 Badly; wrongly. M16–E17.
▶ **D** *verb trans.* †**1** Refrain from, avoid. *rare*. Only in ME.
2 Ruin, frustrate, foil; annihilate. *literary*. E20.

naughty /ˈnɔ:ti/ *adjective, adverb, & noun*. LME.
[from NAUGHT *pronoun & noun* + -Y¹. Cf. NOUGHTY.]
▶ **A** *adjective*. †**1** Possessing nothing, poor, needy. Only in LME.
2 a Of a person: morally bad, wicked. *arch.* E16. ▸**b** Of a child or domestic animal: wayward, disobedient, badly behaved. Of an older person: mischievous, mildly immoral; licentious; sexually provocative. M17.
3 †**a** Bad, inferior, substandard. E16–L18. ▸**b** Of food or drink: unfit for consumption, unwholesome. Now *rare*. M16. ▸†**c** Unhealthy; connected with ill health. L16–M17.
4 Of a thing or action: involving or characterized by disobedience or mischief; improper; indecent, lewd, titillating; *arch.* morally bad. M16.
†**5** Of weather: bad, nasty. *rare*. M16–E17.
6 Unsubstantial; insignificant. *Scot. & dial.* L17.

🕮 **2b** F. M. FORD She was hitting a naughty child who had been stealing chocolates. P. H. GIBBS In her baby frock she looked absurdly young and very naughty. **4** *Liverpool Echo* Two young lads take their female pick-ups to the beach for a naughty day. **naughty bits** *colloq.* (*joc.*) the sexual organs, the breasts. **naughty nineties** the 1890s, regarded as a time of liberalism and permissiveness, *spec.* in Britain and France.

▶ **B** *adverb*. In a naughty or improper manner. M19.
▶ **C** *noun*. (An act of) sexual intercourse. Freq. in *pl. slang*. E20.

🕮 *New Musical Express* I didn't understand things like call girls and naughties. **do the naughty** behave in a sexually promiscuous way.

■ **naughtily** *adverb* E16. **naughtiness** *noun* the quality or condition of being naughty; a naughty act or trait: M16.

naukrary *noun* var. of NAUCRARY.

naumachia /nɔ:ˈmeɪkɪə/ *noun*. Pl. **-iae** /-ɪi:/, **-ias**. L16.
[Latin from Greek *naumakhia*, from *naus* ship + *makhē* fight: see -IA¹.]
ROMAN HISTORY. An imitation sea battle staged for entertainment; a place, esp. a building enclosing a stretch of water, specially constructed for such a battle.

naunt /nɑ:nt/ *noun*. Now *arch. & dial.* E17.
[from misdivision of *mine aunt* (see AUNT) as *my naunt*. Cf. NUNCLE.]
Aunt.

nauplius /ˈnɔ:plɪəs/ *noun*. Pl. **-lii** /-lɪʌɪ, -lɪi:/. M19.
[mod. Latin (orig. the name of a supposed genus), from Latin = a kind of shellfish, or *Nauplius*, Greek *Nauplios* a son of Poseidon.]
ZOOLOGY. The first larval stage in many crustaceans, characterized by an unsegmented body with a dorsal shield, a single median eye, and three pairs of legs; a larva in this stage. Freq. *attrib.*

■ **nauplial** *adjective* of or pertaining to a nauplius or nauplii L19. **naupliar** *adjective* = NAUPLIAL M20. **naupliiform** /-pli:ɪfɔ:m/ *adjective* having the form of a nauplius M19.

Nauruan /ˈnaʊrʊən/ *noun & adjective*. E20.
[from *Nauru* (see below) + -AN.]
▶ **A** *noun*. A native or inhabitant of Nauru, an island in the western Pacific. E20.
▶ **B** *adjective*. Of or pertaining to Nauru. E20.

nausea /ˈnɔ:sɪə, -z-/ *noun*. LME.
[Latin *nausea*, *-sia* from Greek *nausia*, *-tia* seasickness, nausea, from *naus* ship.]
1 A feeling of sickness, with loathing of food and inclination to vomit. LME. ▸**b** Seasickness. M18.
2 *transf.* A strong feeling of disgust, loathing, or aversion. E17.
3 Something causing sickness or loathing. M17.

🕮 **1** R. DAHL A slight nausea and a desire to vomit. D. LEAVITT Mark still feels a wave of nausea . . when he eats with them. **2** G. LORD Sally looked with nausea at the dangling animal.

Comb.: **nausea gas**: used to induce nausea in people.

nauseant /ˈnɔ:sɪənt, -z-/ *noun & adjective*. M19.
[from next + -ANT¹.]
MEDICINE. ▶**A** *noun*. A substance which produces nausea. M19.
▶ **B** *adjective*. Producing nausea. M19.

nauseate /ˈnɔ:sɪeɪt, -z-/ *verb*. M17.
[Latin *nauseat-* pa. ppl stem of *nauseare*, from *nausea*, after Greek *nausian*: see NAUSEA, -ATE³.]
1 *verb trans.* Reject (food etc.) with loathing or a feeling of nausea; *fig.* loathe, abhor, feel a strong aversion to. Now *rare*. M17.
2 *verb trans.* Affect (a person or thing) with nausea or aversion, create a loathing in. Freq. as ***nauseating*** *ppl adjective*. M17.
3 *verb intrans.* Become affected with nausea, feel sick or disgusted (*at*). M17.

🕮 **2** M. SEYMOUR Only one thing nauseated him as much as the modern bathing suit. G. NAYLOR I found treating a grown man like a five-year-old a little nauseating.

■ **nauseatingly** *adverb* in a nauseating manner, so as to nauseate someone L19. **nauseˈation** *noun* the action of nauseating, the state of being nauseated; sickness: E17.

nauseous /ˈnɔ:sɪəs, -z-/ *adjective*. E17.
[from Latin *nauseosus*, formed as NAUSEA + -OUS.]
1 Affected with nausea, sick, nauseated. Formerly also, inclined to nausea. E17.
2 Causing nausea; offensive to the taste or smell; *fig.* loathsome, disgusting, repulsive. E17.

🕮 **1** P. MONETTE The drug made him nauseous. **2** M. WESLEY Mylo took the nauseous brew.

■ **nauseously** *adverb* M17. **nauseousness** *noun* a feeling of nausea; the quality of being nauseous: E17.

Naussie /ˈnɒsi, -zi/ *noun*. *slang*. M20.
[from N(EW *adjective* + AUSSIE.]
= ***New Australian*** s.v. NEW *adjective*.

nautch /nɔ:tʃ/ *noun & verb*. E19.
[Urdu or Hindi *nāc* from Sanskrit *nṛtya* dancing, from *nṛt* to dance.]
▶ **A** *noun*. **1** In the Indian subcontinent, (a performance of) a traditional dance by one or more professional dancing-girls. E19.
2 In full ***nautch girl***. A girl who dances a nautch. M19.
▶ **B** *verb intrans.* Dance (as) at a nautch. *rare*. M19.

nautic /ˈnɔ:tɪk/ *adjective & noun*. E17.
[formed as next: see -IC.]
▶ **A** *adjective*. Nautical. Now *poet.* or *arch.* E17.
▶ **B** *noun*. **1** In *pl.* (treated as *sing.*). The art or science of sailing. Now *rare*. L18.
2 A sailor, esp. of the Royal Navy. *slang*. E20.

nautical /ˈnɔ:tɪk(ə)l/ *adjective*. M16.
[from French *nautique* or Latin *nauticus* from Greek *nautikos* from *nautēs* sailor from *naus* ship + -ICAL.]
Of, pertaining to, or characteristic of sailors, the sea, or sailing; naval, maritime.

🕮 C. JACKSON There were nautical touches such as a ship's clock. S. QUINN The journeys . . required . . nautical skills for navigating large ships through difficult waters. **nautical almanac** a yearbook containing astronomical and tidal information for navigators etc. **nautical mile** any of several similar measures of distance used in making precise measurements at sea; now *spec.* a unit equal to 1852 metres (approx. 2025 yards); cf. SEA-***mile***.

■ **nautiˈcality** *noun* the quality of being nautical L19. **nautically** *adverb* M19.

nautili *noun pl.* see NAUTILUS.

nautiloid /ˈnɔ:tɪlɔɪd/ *adjective & noun*. M19.
[from next + -OID.]
ZOOLOGY & PALAEONTOLOGY. ▶**A** *adjective*. Resembling the nautilus in form; *spec.* of, pertaining to, or designating a cephalopod of the subclass Nautiloidea. M19.
▶ **B** *noun*. A nautiloid mollusc; *spec.* a cephalopod of the subclass Nautiloidea, which includes the modern *Nautilus* and many fossil forms. M19.

nautilus /ˈnɔːtɪləs/ *noun.* Pl. **-li** /-lʌɪ, -liː/, **-luses**. E17.
[Latin from Greek *nautilos* sailor, nautilus, from *nautēs*: see NAUTICAL.]
Either of two marine cephalopod molluscs: (*a*) (more fully ***pearly nautilus***) an Indo-Pacific cephalopod, *Nautilus pompilius*, having a coiled chambered shell with nacreous septa; (*b*) (more fully ***paper nautilus***) = ARGONAUT 2. Also, any fossil resembling or related to either of these; *esp.* a nautiloid.
■ **nautilite** *noun* (*GEOLOGY*, *arch.*) a fossil nautilus M18.

NAV *abbreviation.*
COMMERCE. Net asset value.

Navaho *noun & adjective* var. of NAVAJO.

navaid /ˈnaveɪd/ *noun.* M20.
[from NAV(IGATIONAL + AID *noun.*]
A navigational device in an aircraft, ship, etc.

Navajo /ˈnavəhəʊ/ *noun & adjective.* Also **-ho**. L18.
[from Spanish *Apaches de Navajó* from Tewa *navahu:* fields adjoining arroyo.]
▶**A** *noun.* Pl. **-os**, same.
1 A member of an Athapaskan people of Arizona, Utah, and New Mexico. L18.
2 The language of this people. L19.
▶**B** *attrib.* or as *adjective.* Of, pertaining to, or characteristic of the Navajos or their language. E19.

naval /ˈneɪv(ə)l/ *adjective.* LME.
[Latin *navalis*, from *navis* ship: see -AL¹.]
1 Of, pertaining to, or characteristic of the navy or a navy; having or consisting of a navy. LME.
2 Of, pertaining to, or consisting of ships. E17.
3 Of a person: belonging to, connected with, or serving in the navy or a navy. M17.

> 📖 **1** G. RAWLINSON The naval power of Carthage. R. H. TAWNEY They were easily commanded by any naval power dominating the eastern Mediterranean. **2** A. EDEN A big naval engagement with the German fleet. **3** C. ANGIER He came from a naval family, and had been a lieutenant commander.

Special collocations: **naval academy** a college where naval officers are trained. ***naval architect***: see ARCHITECT *noun* 1b. ***naval architecture***: see ARCHITECTURE *noun* 1. **naval base** a securely held seaport from which naval operations can be carried out. **naval brass** a type of brass containing about 60 per cent copper, 39 per cent zinc, and one per cent tin, used for bolts and other small ship fittings. **naval brigade** a landing-force; a reinforcement force for land troops. **naval crown** *ROMAN ANTIQUITIES* a crown or garland given to a victor or brave fighter in a sea battle. **naval officer** an officer in a navy. ***naval station***: see STATION *noun* 3a. **naval stores** articles or materials used in shipping; *spec.* (*colloq.*) tar, turpentine, resin, etc.
■ **navalism** *noun* the importance of naval interests L19. **navalist** *noun* a person stressing the importance of having a strong navy E20. **navally** *adverb* in a naval manner; from a naval point of view: M18.

Navaratri /nʌvəˈrʌtri/ *noun.* Also **-tra** /-trə/. E20.
[Hindi from Sanskrit *navarātra*, lit. 'nine nights'.]
A Hindu autumn festival extending over the nine nights before Dussehra.

navarch /ˈnervɑːk/ *noun.* E19.
[Greek *nauarkhos*, from *naus* ship + *-arkhos* -ARCH.]
GREEK HISTORY. The commander of a fleet, an admiral; *esp.* the chief admiral of the Spartans.

navarchy /ˈneɪvɑːki/ *noun.* M17.
[Greek *nauarkhia*, formed as prec.: see -Y¹.]
†**1** Shipbuilding. *rare.* Only in M17.
2 The office or position of a navarch; the period during which such office is exercised. M19.

navarin /ˈnav(ə)rɪn, *foreign* navarɛ̃ (*pl. same*)/ *noun.* L19.
[French.]
A casserole of mutton or lamb with (esp. root) vegetables.

navarin printanier /navarɛ̃ prɛ̃tanje/ *noun phr.* Pl. **-s -s** (pronounced same). E20.
[French = spring.]
A navarin made with spring vegetables.

Navarran /nəˈvɑːrən/ *adjective & noun.* Also (earlier) †**-ean**. M17.
[formed as next + -AN, -EAN.]
▶**A** *adjective.* = NAVARRESE *adjective.* M17.
▶**B** *noun.* = NAVARRESE *noun.* M20.

Navarrese /navəˈriːz/ *noun & adjective.* M19.
[from *Navarre*, *Navarra* (see below) + -ESE.]
▶**A** *noun.* Pl. same. A native or inhabitant of Navarra, a province of northern Spain, or of Navarre, a former kingdom which also included part of SW France. M19.
▶**B** *adjective.* Of or pertaining to Navarra or Navarre. M19.
■ **Navarrois** /navəˈrwɑː/ *noun pl.* [French] the Navarrese L17.

nave /neɪv/ *noun*¹.
[Old English *nafu*, *-fa* corresp. to Middle Dutch *nave* (Dutch *naaf*), Old High German *naba* (German *Nabe*), Old Norse *nǫf*, from Germanic from Indo-European base repr. also by Sanskrit *nābhis* nave, navel. Cf. NAVEL.]
1 The central part or block of a wheel, into which the end of the axle-tree is inserted and from which the spokes radiate; a hub. OE.
†**2** The navel. *rare* (Shakes.). Only in E17.

nave /neɪv/ *noun*². L17.
[medieval Latin spec. use of Latin *navis* ship, whence Old & mod. French *nef*, Spanish, Italian *nave*. Cf. German *Schiff*, Dutch *schip* ship, nave.]
The main part or body of a church, usu. extending from the west door to the chancel and freq. separated from the aisle on each side by pillars.

navel /ˈneɪv(ə)l/ *noun.*
[Old English *nafela* = Old Frisian *navla*, *naula*, Middle & mod. Low German, Middle Dutch *navel*, Old High German *nabalo* (German *Nabel*), Old Norse *nafli*, from Germanic from Indo-European base repr. also by Latin *umbo* boss of shield, Greek *omphalos* navel, boss. Cf. NAVE *noun*¹.]
1 A rounded depression with a more or less raised or protuberant centre, situated in the middle of the abdomen where the umbilical cord was originally attached; the umbilicus. OE. ▸†**b** The junction of a leaf with a stem. *rare.* LME–L17. ▸**c** *HERALDRY.* = NOMBRIL. E19. ▸**d** *ellipt.* = ***navel orange*** below. L19.
2 The centre or central point of something, esp. a country, sea, or forest. LME.
†**3** The nave of a wheel. *rare.* LME–E17.

> 📖 **1 contemplate one's navel, gaze at one's navel, regard one's navel** engage in usu. profitless meditation or contemplation, be complacently parochial or escapist. **2** *Art & Artists* Cyprus was the navel of Byzantine culture.

Comb.: **navel-contemplation**, **navel-gazing** usu. profitless meditation, complacent introversion; **navel-ill** in calves, foals, and lambs, a general bacterial infection usu. involving inflammation around the navel; **navel orange** a usu. seedless variety of orange having a secondary row of carpels which open to form a depression like a navel at the apex of the fruit; **navel-stone** a stone marking a central point, *spec.* that at the temple of Apollo in Delphi, formerly thought to mark the centre of the earth; **navel string** the umbilical cord; **navelwort** a plant with round fleshy peltate leaves, *Umbilicus rupestris*, of the stonecrop family, growing on rocks and walls esp. in western Britain (also ***Venus's navelwort***); also called ***pennywort***.

naveta /naˈvɛtə/ *noun.* E20.
[Catalan. Cf. medieval Latin *naveta* dim. of *navis* ship.]
ARCHAEOLOGY. A type of Bronze Age megalithic chambered tomb shaped like an upturned boat and found on the Balearic Island of Minorca.

navette /naˈvɛt/ *noun.* E20.
[French = little boat, shuttle from medieval Latin *naveta* dim. of Latin *navis* ship.]
1 A cut of jewel in the shape of a pointed oval; a jewel cut in such a shape. E20.
2 A railway truck designed to shuttle cars through a tunnel under the sea, *spec.* the Channel Tunnel. L20.

navew /ˈneɪvjuː/ *noun.* Now *rare.* M16.
[Old French *navel* (mod. dial. *naveau*) from Latin *napus* NEEP. Cf. French *navet* turnip.]
Rape, *Brassica napus*, either (more fully †***navew gentle***) in the form grown for its sweet fleshy spindle-shaped root or (more fully ***wild navew***) in its supposedly wild form.

navicert /ˈnavɪsəːt/ *noun & verb.* E20.
[from Latin *navis* ship + CERT(IFICATE *noun.*]
▶**A** *noun.* A consular certificate granted to a neutral ship testifying that its cargo is correctly described in the manifest. E20.
▶**B** *verb trans.* Authorize (cargo) with a navicert. M20.

navicula /nəˈvɪkjʊlə/ *noun.* Pl. **-lae** /-liː, -lʌɪ/, **-las**. M19.
[Latin, dim. of *navis* ship: see -CULE.]
ECCLESIASTICAL. An incense-holder shaped like a boat.

navicular /nəˈvɪkjʊlə/ *adjective & noun.* LME.
[French *naviculaire* or late Latin *navicularis*, formed as prec.: see -AR¹.]
▶**A** *adjective.* **1 a** *ANATOMY* etc. ***navicular bone***, a boat-shaped bone in the ankle lying between the talus (astragalus) and cuneiform bones. Also (*rare*), the corresponding scaphoid bone of the wrist. LME. ▸**b** *VETERINARY MEDICINE.* ***navicular disease***, a disease of the region around the navicular bone in the foot of a horse. E19.
†**2** Of or pertaining to boats. M17–E18.
3 Having the form of a (small) boat. L18.
▶**B** *ellipt.* as *noun.* The navicular bone; navicular disease. E19.

naviculoid /nəˈvɪkjʊlɔɪd/ *adjective.* L19.
[formed as prec. + -OID.]
BOTANY. Having the form of a (small) boat; *spec.* designating diatoms of the genus *Navicula* or related genera.

Navier–Stokes equation /neɪvɪəˈstəʊks ɪˈkweɪʒ(ə)n/ *noun phr.* M20.
[Claude-Louis-Marie *Navier* (1785–1836), French engineer + Sir George Gabriel *Stokes* (1819–1903), Irish mathematician and physicist.]
PHYSICS. Each of the one-dimensional equations of motion for a viscous fluid. Also, the vector equation combining these.

naviform /ˈnavɪfɔːm/ *adjective. rare.* E19.
[from Latin *navis* ship + -FORM.]
Boat-shaped; navicular.

navigable /ˈnavɪgəb(ə)l/ *adjective & noun.* LME.
[French, or Latin *navigabilis*, from *navigare*: see next, -ABLE.]
▶**A** *adjective.* **1** Of a river or the sea: able to be navigated, allowing passage for a ship or boat. LME.
2 a Of a ship: able to be sailed; fit for sailing, seaworthy. M16. ▸**b** Of a balloon etc.: able to be steered, dirigible. *obsolete* exc. *Hist.* L18.

> 📖 **1** P. THEROUX The river is too shallow to be navigable by anything larger than a canoe.

▶**B** *noun.* A navigable balloon. Cf. DIRIGIBLE *noun. obsolete* exc. *Hist.* L19.
■ **navigaˈbility** *noun* M19. **navigableness** *noun* E18. **navigably** *adverb* M19.

navigate /ˈnavɪgeɪt/ *verb.* L16.
[Latin *navigat-* pa. ppl stem of *navigare*, from *navis* ship + *-ig-* comb. stem of *agere* drive: see -ATE³.]
1 *verb intrans.* Travel in a ship, sail. L16. ▸**b** Walk steadily; keep on one's course. *US slang.* M19. ▸**c** (Be competent to) sail a ship. L19.
2 *verb trans.* Sail on or across (the sea, a river, etc.). M17. ▸**b** *verb trans. & intrans. transf.* Make or find one's way across (an area of ground); *colloq.* steer (oneself, a course, etc.) through a crowd etc. M19. ▸**c** *verb trans.* Travel, fly through, (the air). E20.
3 a *verb trans.* Sail, direct, manage, (a ship). L17. ▸**b** *verb trans.* Fly, manage, direct, (an aircraft, balloon, etc.). Now *spec.* plot and supervise the course of (an aircraft or spacecraft). L18. ▸**c** *verb intrans.* Plot and supervise the course of a motor vehicle. M20.
4 *verb intrans.* Of a ship: sail, ply. M18.

> 📖 **2** J. YEATS The seas were navigated and islands visited by the aid of . . canoes. **b** P. BOWLES It was always difficult to navigate the Zoco Chico with its groups of stationary talkers. **3a** M. E. BRADDON I knew something about navigating a yacht. F. CHICHESTER Navigating Stormvogel . . to an anchorage near these rocks. **c** J. CAIRD Once they were in the car, David said: 'I'll navigate Turn left at the school gate'.

navigation /navɪˈgeɪʃ(ə)n/ *noun.* E16.
[Old & mod. French, or Latin *navigatio(n-)*, formed as prec.: see -ATION.]
1 A voyage. Now *rare.* E16.
2 The action or practice of travelling on water; sailing. M16. ▸**b** The action or practice of travelling through the air by means of an aircraft, balloon, etc.; flying. Now *rare.* E19.
3 The art or science of directing a ship, boat, or (now) aircraft, spacecraft, etc.; any of several methods of determining or planning a ship or other craft's position and course by geometry, astronomy, etc. M16. ▸**b** The action or practice of navigating a motor vehicle. M20.
4 Shipping, ships collectively. Chiefly *US.* Now *rare.* L16.
5 Trade or commerce conducted by water. Now *rare.* E17.
6 A canal, a man-made waterway. Formerly also, a natural inland channel. Now *dial.* E18.
2 inland navigation communication by means of canals and navigable rivers.
Comb.: **navigation act** a legal enactment regulating navigation or shipping; **navigation coal** steam-coal; **navigation law** = ***navigation act*** above; **navigation light** a light shown by a ship, aircraft, etc., at night; **navigation satellite** a satellite whose orbit is accurately known and made available so that observations of its position may be used for navigational purposes.
■ **navigational** *adjective* L19. **navigationally** *adverb* M20.

navigator /ˈnavɪgeɪtə/ *noun.* L16.
[Latin, formed as prec.: see -OR.]
1 A person who navigates; *spec.* (*a*) a sailor, esp. a skilled and experienced one, who navigates a ship; (*b*) a person who conducts an exploration by sea; (*c*) a person who navigates an aircraft or spacecraft; (*d*) a person who navigates a motor vehicle. L16.
2 = NAVVY *noun* 1. L18.

navvy /ˈnavi/ *noun & verb.* Also **navvie**. E19.
[Abbreviation of prec.]
▶**A** *noun.* **1** A labourer employed in excavating and constructing a road, railway, canal, etc. E19.
2 In full ***steam navvy***. A machine for excavating earth. L19.
▶**B** *verb intrans.* Work as or like a navvy. L19.

navy /ˈneɪvi/ *noun & adjective.* In sense A.3 also **N-**. ME.
[Old French *navie* ship, fleet from Proto-Romance var. of popular Latin *navia* from Latin *navis* ship: see -Y³.]
▶**A** *noun.* †**1** Ships collectively, shipping. ME–L15.
2 A number of ships collected together, esp. for war; a fleet. Now *poet. & rhet.* ME.
3 ***the navy***, (*a*) the whole body of a State's ships of war, including crews, maintenance systems, equipment, etc.;

a regularly organized and maintained naval force; (*b*) the people serving in a navy. LME.

4 a A type of revolver, esp. a Colt, used in the navy. Also ***navy revolver***. M19. ▸**b** A type of tobacco used esp. in the navy (also more fully ***navy plug***). Also, cigarette ends etc. as picked up by a tramp. L19. ▸**c** Rum as drunk in the navy; a ration of this. Also ***navy rum***. M20.

5 Navy blue. L19.

📖 **3** *Armed Forces* There are 35 shipyards producing . . warships for the navies of 16 nations. *Daily Telegraph* A 10-year-old choirboy . . was rescued by a Navy helicopter. ***merchant navy***: see MERCHANT *adjective*. ***Royal Navy***: see ROYAL *adjective*. ***Wavy Navy***: see WAVY *adjective*.

Comb.: **navy bean** = HARICOT 1; **navy blue** *noun & adjective* (of) a dark blue, the colour of the British naval uniform; **Navy Cut** (proprietary name for) a kind of finely sliced cake tobacco; **Navy Department** *US* the government department controlling the navy; **Navy League** an organization founded to arouse national interest in the Navy; **Navy List** an official publication containing a list of naval officers and other nautical information; ***navy plug***: see sense 4b above; **navy register** *US* = ***Navy List*** above; ***navy revolver***: see sense 4a above; ***navy rum***: see sense 4c above; **navy yard** (now *US*) a government shipyard with civilian labour.

▸ **B** *adjective*. Of the dark blue colour of the British naval uniform. L19.

📖 K. AMIS She wore her best suit of cream linen and a navy blouse.

naw /nɔː/ *adverb & interjection*. *Scot., north., & non-standard US*. M19.
[Repr. a pronunc. Cf. NA *adverb*[2] & *interjection*, NAOW *adverb*[1], *interjection*.]
= NO *adverb*[3] & *interjection*.

nawab /nəˈwɑːb, -ˈwɔːb/ *noun*. Also (as a title) **N-**. M18.
[Urdu *nawāb* from Urdu, Persian *nawwāb* var. of *nuwwāb* pl. (used as sing.) of (Arab.) *nā'ib* deputy. Cf. NABOB.]
1 (The title of) a governor or nobleman in the Indian subcontinent (*Hist.*); (the title of) a distinguished Muslim in the Indian subcontinent. M18.
2 = NABOB 2. *arch*. E19.

Naxalite /ˈnaksəlʌɪt/ *noun*. M20.
[from *Naxal(bari* in West Bengal, India + -ITE[1].]
In the Indian subcontinent, a supporter or adherent of Maoist Communism.
■ **Naxalism** *noun* Maoist Communism as practised in parts of the Indian subcontinent L20.

Naxian /ˈnaksɪən/ *noun & adjective*. E17.
[from Greek *Naxios*, Latin *Naxius*, from *Naxos* (see below) + -AN.]
(A native or inhabitant) of Naxos, a Greek island in the Cyclades group or a part of Sicily colonized from this island.

nay /neɪ/ *verb*. *arch*. LME.
[Old French *neier* (mod. *nier*) from Latin *negare*, or from next. Cf. DENY *verb*.]
1 †**a** *verb intrans. & trans.* Refuse (*to do*), deny (*that*). *rare*. LME–M16. ▸†**b** *verb trans.* Refuse (a thing) to a person. *rare*. LME–M16. ▸**c** *verb trans.* Give a refusal to (a person). L16.
†**2** *verb trans.* Refuse to admit the truth of (a matter). LME–L17.

nay /neɪ/ *adverb, interjection, & noun*. ME.
[Old Norse *nei*, from *né* NE + *ei* AYE *adverb*[1].]
▸ **A** *adverb & interjection*. **1** = NO *adverb*[3] & *interjection*. Now *arch. & dial.* ME.
†**2** Not. ME–E18.
3 Or rather, on the other hand; and even, moreover. L16.

📖 **1 say nay** (*a*) refuse a request, deny a statement; express dissent or contradiction; (*b*) deny or refuse (a person). **3** SHAKES. *Tam. Shr.* Nay, come again, good Kate, I am a gentleman. J. BUCHAN My worst fears—nay, what had seemed to me mere crazy imaginings—had been realised. J. CAREY It's a blameless, nay meritorious, occupation.

▸ **B** *noun*. An utterance of 'nay'; a denial, a refusal, a prohibition. Also (esp. *N. Amer.*), a negative reply or vote; a person voting in the negative. ME.

📖 J. BRYCE If one fifth of a quorum demand a call of yeas and nays, this is taken. ***yea and nay***: see YEA *adverb*[1], *interjection, & noun*.

Comb.: **nay-say** *noun & verb* (*a*) *noun* refusal, denial; (*b*) *verb trans.* refuse (a person or thing); **nay-sayer** a refuser, a person who votes against something.

naya paisa /ˈnʌɪjɑː ˈpʌɪsɑː, -zɑː/ *noun phr.* Pl. **naye paise** /ˈnʌɪjeɪ ˈpʌɪseɪ, -zeɪ/. M20.
[Hindi *nayā paisā* new pice.]
A monetary unit in India, equal to one-hundredth of a rupee.

†**nayward** *noun*. *rare* (Shakes.). Only in E17.
[from NAY *noun* + -WARD.]
to the nayward, towards denial or disbelief.

nayword /ˈneɪwəːd/ *noun*. L16.
[from *nay* of unkn. origin + WORD *noun*.]
1 A password; a catchword. *rare*. L16.
2 A byword, a proverb. E17.

nazar /ˈnazɑː/ *noun*. Also (earlier) **nuzzer** /ˈnʌzə/. L18.
[Persian, Urdu *nazr* gift, vow, dedication, from Arab. *nadr* vow, votive offering.]
In the Indian subcontinent, a present made by a social inferior to a superior.
■ Also **nuzzerana** /nʌzəˈrɑːnə/ *noun* [Persian, Urdu *nazrānah*] L18.

Nazarene /ˈnazəriːn, nazəˈriːn/ *noun & adjective*. ME.
[Christian Latin *Nazarenus* from Greek *Nazarēnos* from *Nazaret* Nazareth: see -ENE.]
▸ **A** *noun*. **1** A native or inhabitant of Nazareth in Israel; *spec.* (***the Nazarene***) Jesus Christ. ME.
2 Esp. among Jews and Muslims: a Christian. LME.
3 a A member of an early Jewish Christian sect allied to the Ebionites. L17. ▸**b** A member of a sect of Christian reformers in Hungary. L19. ▸**c** A member of a Protestant sect, known as the Church of the Nazarene. L19.
4 A member of a group of German artists who aimed to restore to art the religious quality found in medieval painting. Cf. PRE-RAPHAELITE. L19.
▸ **B** *adjective*. **1** Of or belonging to Nazareth. *rare*. ME.
2 a Belonging to the Jewish sect of the Nazarenes. L17. ▸**b** Of, pertaining to, or characteristic of the sect known as the Church of the Nazarene. E20.
3 Of, pertaining to, or characteristic of the artistic style or principles of the artists known as Nazarenes. M20.
■ **Naza'rean** *noun* = NAZARENE *noun* 3a L16. **Nazarenism** *noun* (*a*) the principles or doctrines of early Christians or the Jewish Nazarenes; (*b*) the characteristics or artistic principles of the Nazarene artists or their followers: L19.

Nazarite /ˈnazərʌɪt/ *noun*[1]. M16.
[Christian Latin *Nazaraeus* from Greek *Nazaraios*: see -ITE[1].]
1 A native or inhabitant of Nazareth. M16. ▸†**b** = NAZARENE *noun* 2. *rare*. M16–M17.
2 = NAZARENE *noun* 4. L19.

Nazarite /ˈnazərʌɪt/ *noun*[2]. Also **-irite**. M16.
[from Christian Latin *Nazaraeus* from Hebrew *nāzīr*, from *nāzar* separate or consecrate oneself + -ITE[1].]
Hist. A Hebrew who had taken certain vows of abstinence; an ascetic, (described in *Numbers* 6).
■ **Nazariteship** *noun* the state of being a Nazarite E17. **Naza'ritic** *adjective* of or pertaining to a Nazarite or Nazarites M19. **Nazaritish** *adjective* Nazaritic L17. **Nazaritism** *noun* (belief in) the practice of taking certain vows of abstinence M18.

Nazca /ˈnazkə, ˈnaskə/ *attrib. adjective*. Also **Nasca** /ˈnaskə/. E20.
[A river in Peru.]
ARCHAEOLOGY. Pertaining to or designating a culture of *c* 200 BC–AD 900 on the south coast of present-day Peru, esp. the ceramics produced by it.
Nazca lines a series of large-scale ancient line patterns found on the coastal plain of southern Peru.

naze /neɪz/ *noun*. L18.
[A var. of NESS, app. inferred from place-names, as *the Naze* in Essex.]
A promontory, a headland.

Nazi /ˈnɑːtsi, ˈnɑːzi/ *noun & adjective*. Also **n-**. M20.
[German, repr. pronunc. of *Nati-* in *Nationalsozialist*.]
▸ **A** *noun*. **1** A member of the National Socialist Party in Germany, led by Adolf Hitler from 1920 and in power 1933–45 (*Hist.*); a member of any similar organization. M20.
2 A believer in the aims or doctrines of Nazism or in any similar doctrines; a person holding extreme racist, esp. anti-Semitic, or authoritarian views or behaving in a brutal or bigoted manner. M20.

📖 **1** E. FEINSTEIN A Jew himself, he was sympathetic to me as someone displaced by fear of the Nazis.

▸ **B** *adjective*. Of, pertaining to, or characteristic of the National Socialist Party in Germany or any similar organization; intensely racist, intolerant, or right-wing. M20.

📖 *Economist* The Nazi Party stalwarts have . . been leading an anti-Semitic, anti-Catholic, anti-Protestant crusade. **Nazi salute**: in which the right arm is inclined upwards, palm down, and open (the official salute of the Nazi party).

■ **Nazidom** *noun* the concepts and institutions of the Nazis; Nazis collectively: M20. **Nazifi'cation** *noun* the action or fact of Nazifying or being Nazified M20. **Nazify** *verb trans.* cause or force (a person, country, etc.) to adopt Nazism or a similar doctrine M20. **Naziphil(e)** *noun* a person sympathetic to the ideology of Nazism M20.

Naziism, **Nazi-ism** *nouns* vars. of NAZISM.

nazir /ˈnɑːzɪə/ *noun*. L17.
[Persian, Urdu *nāzir* from Arab. *nāzir* superintendent, inspector from *nazar* sight, vision.]
(The title of) any of various officials in Muslim countries; *Hist.* an official in an Anglo-Indian court.

Nazirite *noun* var. of NAZARITE *noun*[2].

Nazism /ˈnɑːtsɪz(ə)m, ˈnɑːzɪ-/ *noun*. Also **-iism**, **-i-ism** /-ɪɪz(ə)m/. M20.
[from NAZI + -ISM.]
The political doctrines evolved and implemented by Adolf Hitler and his followers, esp. those relating to racial superiority; the German Nazi movement; *gen.* right-wing, esp. racist, authoritarianism.

NB *abbreviation*.
1 *Hist.* Nebraska.
2 New Brunswick.
3 No ball.
4 North Britain (Scotland).
5 Nota bene.

Nb *symbol*.
CHEMISTRY. Niobium.

NBA *abbreviation*.
1 National Basketball Association. *N. Amer.*
2 Net book agreement.

NBC *abbreviation*. *US*.
National Broadcasing Company.

NBG *abbreviation*. *colloq.*
No bloody good.

NC *abbreviation*.
North Carolina.

NC-17 *abbreviation*. *US*.
No children (under) 17, designating films classified as suitable for adults only.

NCB *abbreviation*. *Hist.*
National Coal Board.

NCC *abbreviation*.
1 National Consumer Council.
2 National Curriculum Council.
3 *Hist.* Nature Conservancy Council.

NCO *abbreviation*.
Non-commissioned officer.

NCR *abbreviation*.
No carbon required, denoting paper chemically treated so that the pressure of writing or typing alone produces duplicate copies.
¶ The abbreviation *NCR* is a proprietary name.

NCU *abbreviation*.
1 National Communications Union.
2 National Cyclists' Union.

ND *abbreviation*.
North Dakota.

Nd *symbol*.
CHEMISTRY. Neodymium.

n.d. *abbreviation*.
No date.

N.Dak. *abbreviation*.
North Dakota.

Ndama /(ə)nˈdɑːmə/ *noun*. Also (earlier) **N'D-**. M20.
[Wolof *ndaama*.]
(An animal of) a W. African breed of cattle, usu. fawn or light red, with long horns curved outwards in the middle.

Ndebele /(ə)ndəˈbiːli, -ˈbeɪli/ *noun & adjective*. L19.
[Bantu, from Ndebele *n-* sing. prefix + Sesotho (*lè*)*tèbèlè* Nguni, from *le-* prefix + *tēbēla* drive away.]
▸ **A** *noun*. Pl. **Indebele** /ɪndə-/, **Ndebele(s)**, (*arch.*) **Amandebele** /əmandə-/.
1 A member of a Nguni people living mainly in Zimbabwe and Transvaal. Also called, esp. in Zimbabwe, ***Matabele***. L19.
2 The language of this people, Sindebele. M20.
▸ **B** *attrib.* or as *adjective*. Of or pertaining to the Indebele or their language. M20.

Ndugu /(ə)nˈduːguː/ *noun*. L20.
[Kiswahili = relative, brother.]
In E. African countries, esp. Tanzania: a brother, a friend. Chiefly as a general form of address.

NE *abbreviation*.
1 Nebraska.
2 North-east(ern).

Ne *symbol*.
CHEMISTRY. Neon.

ne /niː/ *adverb & conjunction*. *arch.*
[Old English *ne*, *ni* = Old Frisian, Old Saxon, Old High German *ni*, *ne*, Old Norse *né*, Gothic *ni*, corresp. to Latin *ne-* (as in *nefas*, *nullus*, *numquam*), Lithuanian, Old Church Slavonic *ne*, Sanskrit *na*.]
▸ **A** *adverb*. = NOT *adverb*. OE.

📖 BYRON A youth Who ne in virtue's ways did take delight.

▸ **B** *conjunction*. **1** = NOR *conjunction*[1]. OE.
†**2** = OR *conjunction*[2]. *rare*. L15–M16.

📖 **1** COLERIDGE Ne could we laugh.

ne' /nɛ/ *adverb*. *colloq.* Also **ne**. M20.
[Abbreviation.]
= NEVER *adverb*.

né /neɪ, *foreign* ne/ *adjective*. M20.
[French = born, masc. pa. pple of *naître* be born. Cf. NÉE.]
Born with the name, originally called: placed before the name by which a man was originally known.

📖 N. MARSH Mr. St. John Ackroyd, *né* Albert Biggs.

NEA *abbreviation. US.*
National Education Association.

neal /niːl/ *verb. obsolete exc. dial.* M16.
[Aphet. from ANNEAL *verb*.]
1 *verb trans.* Subject to the action of fire; fire, bake, fuse, glaze. Cf. ANNEAL *verb* 2. Now *rare* or *obsolete.* M16. **2** *verb trans.* = ANNEAL *verb* 4. M16. †**3** *verb intrans.* Be or become annealed. Only in 17.

nealie /ˈniːli/ *noun. Austral.* Also **nelia** /ˈniːlɪə/. M19.
[Aboriginal *nhiiyi*.]
Any of several Australian wattles, esp. *Acacia rigens*, with needle-like leaves, and *A. loderi*.

Neanderthal /nɪˈandətɑːl/ *adjective & noun.* Also **-tal**, **n-**. M19.
[The valley of the River *Neander*, near Düsseldorf in western Germany (German *Tal*, older *Thal* valley).]
▶ **A** *adjective.* **1** Designating, pertaining to, or characteristic of a palaeolithic fossil hominid, *Homo sapiens neanderthalensis*, with a retreating forehead and massive brow-ridges, known from Europe, Africa, and Asia. Esp. in *Neanderthal man.* M19. **2** *fig.* Primitive, uncivilized, uncouth; reactionary, extremely conservative. *joc. & derog.* E20.

📖 **1** B. J. WILLIAMS In 1958 part of a Neandertal skull was recovered from a cave at Ma-pa. **2** *Observer* Neanderthal grunts over the cornflakes . . were the best most husbands could manage. *Times Lit. Suppl.* He tried to keep Neanderthal republicans happy.

▶ **B** *noun.* A Neanderthal hominid. Also *fig. (joc. & derog.)*, a primitive, uncivilized, or uncouth person; a reactionary or extremely conservative person. L19.
■ **Neanderthaler** *noun* a Neanderthal man E20. **Neanderthaloid** *adjective & noun* (pertaining to or designating) a Neanderthal man or similar middle palaeolithic hominid L19.

neanic /nɪˈanɪk/ *adjective.* L19.
[Greek *neanikos* youthful, from *neanias* young man + *-ikos* -IC.]
ZOOLOGY. Designating the middle or adolescent stages of the growth of an animal, esp. the pupal stage of an insect.

neanthropic /niːanˈθrɒpɪk/ *adjective.* L19.
[from NE(O- + ANTHROPIC.]
ANTHROPOLOGY. Of, pertaining to, or designating the single extant species of human as distinguished from extinct fossil forms.

neap /niːp/ *noun*[1]. L15.
[from NEAP *adjective*.]
A neap tide.

neap /niːp/ *noun*[2]. M16.
[Perh. of Scandinavian origin: cf. Norwegian dial. *neip* a forked pole etc.]
1 The pole or tongue of a cart. *north. & US dial.* M16. **2** A wooden rest for the shaft of a loaded cart. *north.* L17.

neap /niːp/ *adjective.*
[Old English *nēp* in *nēpflōd* (FLOOD *noun*) of unkn. origin.]
Of a tide: occurring just after the first and third quarters of the moon when there is least difference between high and low water. Formerly also, (of a point in time) coinciding with a neap tide.

📖 J. STRYPE The Tides were then at the Neapest. R. A. PROCTOR We have tides ranging between the highest spring tides . . and the lowest neap tides.

¶ Not recorded between LOE and L15.

neap /niːp/ *verb.* M17.
[from NEAP *adjective, noun*[1].]
1 *verb intrans.* Of a tide: become lower, tend towards or reach the highest point of a neap tide. M17. **2** *verb trans.* In *pass.* Of a ship: be kept aground, in harbour, etc., by a neap tide. E18.

Neapolitan /nɪəˈpɒlɪt(ə)n/ *noun & adjective.* LME.
[Latin *Neapolitanus*, from *Neapolites*, from Greek *Neapolis* new town, Naples: see -ITE[1], -AN.]
▶ **A** *noun.* **1** A native or inhabitant of the city or former kingdom of Naples in SW Italy. LME. **2** The Italian dialect of Naples. L16.
▶ **B** *adjective.* Of, pertaining to, or characteristic of, Naples or the Neapolitans. L16.
†**Neapolitan disease** syphilis. **Neapolitan ice** ice-cream made in layers of different colours and flavours. ***Neapolitan medlar***: see MEDLAR 1. **Neapolitan ointment** a mercurial ointment, formerly used in the treatment of syphilis. **Neapolitan violet** a double sweet-scented variety of viola. **Neapolitan yellow** = ***Naples yellow*** s.v. NAPLES 2.

near /nɪə/ *adjective.* ME.
[from NEAR *adverb*[2].]
1 Closely connected by blood or friendship; (esp. of a friend or friendship) close, intimate, familiar. ME. **2** Designating or pertaining to the left side of a horse, other animal, or vehicle (being the side from which an animal was traditionally mounted, led, or approached). Opp. OFF *adjective* 2. ME. **3** Close at hand, not distant, in space or time. M16. **4** Close, narrow. Chiefly *fig.* M16. **5** Of a road: short, direct. L16. **6** Closely affecting or touching one. E17. **7** Niggardly, stingy, mean. E17.

📖 **1** D. H. LAWRENCE The near kin of Meg were all in California. E. BOWEN She is Robert's near relative. **2** E. L. ANDERSON To mount without stirrups the rider should stand facing the near shoulder of the horse. **3** LD MACAULAY The near prospect of reward animated the zeal of the troops. R. GRAVES He marched . . to Boulogne, the nearest port to Britain. **4** J. DAVIES Having weighed one parcel, so as they may have a near guess at the rest. **5** ADDISON It is a pity . . there is not a nearer way of coming at it. **6** J. NORRIS It was of nearer consequence to Archimedes.

Special collocations, comb., & phrases: **Near East** the region comprising the countries of the eastern Mediterranean. **Near Eastern** *adjective* of or pertaining to the Near East. **nearest and dearest** (freq. *joc.*) one's closest friends and relatives collectively. **nearest neighbour** (chiefly STATISTICS) the member of a series or array nearest to that being considered. **near go** *colloq.* a narrow escape. ***near infrared***: see INFRARED *noun*. **near miss** (*a*) a shot that only just misses a target; (*b*) a situation in which a collision is narrowly avoided; (*c*) an attempt which is almost successful. **near money** a deposit, bond, etc., easily convertible into ready money. **near sight** (chiefly *US*) = ***short sight*** s.v. SHORT *adjective*. **near-sighted** *adjective* (*a*) having distinct vision only of near objects; short-sighted; (*b*) *rare* close, careful. **near-sightedly** *adverb* short-sightedly. **near-sightedness** short-sightedness. **near thing** something barely effected; a narrow escape. ***near ultraviolet***: see ULTRAVIOLET *noun*.
■ **nearish** *adjective* fairly near M19. **nearness** *noun* LME.

near /nɪə/ *verb.* E16.
[from NEAR *adverb*[2] or *adjective*.]
1 *verb intrans.* Draw or come near, approach, in space or time. E16. **2** *verb trans.* Draw near to, approach (a person, place, etc.), in space or time. E17.

near /nɪə/ *adverb*[1] *& preposition*[1]. Now *arch. & dial.*
[Old English *nēar* etc. compar. of *nēah* NIGH *adverb*, corresp. to Old Frisian *niār*, Old Saxon *nāhor*, Gothic *nehwis*, from Germanic.]
Nearer, closer, now chiefly (in neg. & interrog. contexts) to an end or purpose.

📖 SHAKES. *Macb.* The near in blood, The nearer bloody. **near and near** *arch.* nearer and nearer. †**no near!** NAUTICAL (ordering a helmsman to) come no closer to the wind.

¶ Superseded in general use by *nearer*.

near /nɪə/ *adverb*[2] *& preposition*[2]. ME.
[Old Norse *nær* orig. compar. of *ná* = Old English *nēah* NIGH *adverb*. Cf. NAR *adverb*, NEAR *adverb*[1].]
▶ **A** *adverb.* **1** To or at a short distance, to or in close proximity, in space or time. Freq. foll. by *to*. ME. ▸**b** NAUTICAL. Close to the wind. M17. **2** All but, almost, (very) nearly. Now *arch. & colloq.* ME. **3** Closely; close to or to something in relative position, condition, appearance, etc. Now *rare.* LME. **4** Closely connected (*to*) by blood or friendship. LME. **5** By a long way, anything like. Usu. in neg. contexts. LME. **6** Narrowly, only by a little. *arch. rare.* L16. **7** With the legs close together (esp. with ref. to a horse's gait). Earliest in ***near-legged*** below. *rare.* L16. **8** Thriftily; parsimoniously, meanly. E17.

📖 **1** H. B. STOWE Eva had come gradually nearer and nearer to her father. B. JOWETT Now the hour of sunset was near. G. STEIN There was uneasiness . . lest some danger might be near. **b** S. STURMY Keep her as near as she will lie. **2** S. FOOTE The knight is . . very near drunk. K. WATERHOUSE You bloody near destroyed me, Margot, do you know that? **3** CLARENDON His Majesty had another Exception against the Duke, which touched him as near. G. SHELVOCKE They are in shape and bigness the nearest like our green grasshoppers. **4** LD MACAULAY Many of them near in blood and affection to the defenders of Londonderry. **5** SOUTHEY They are not near so fine a people now as they were then. **6** C. MARLOWE See where my soldier shot him through the arm; He miss'd him near. **7** H. BRACKEN A Horse that goes wide before, and near behind. **8** DEFOE I had lived so near . . that in a whole year I had not spent the 15s.

▶ **B** *preposition.* **1** Close to, to or at a short distance from, (a place, thing, person, etc.) in space or time. ME. ▸**b** Close on, almost at, close to being in, (a state or condition); close to (*doing* something). M17. **2** Close to (a thing or person) in resemblance or achievement. ME. †**3** Closely related to, intimate with, (a person). LME–M17.

📖 **1** TENNYSON The time draws near the birth of Christ. W. GOLDING The Romans built a town near the fort. **b** *Bookman* He was perilously near showing his whole hand to the other side. J. BUCHAN The hope was near fulfilment. ***near-hysterical***, ***near-smiling***, etc. **2** A. LOVELL There are but few in the Western Parts who come near him in that. G. GREENE My desire now was nearer hatred than love. **3** SHAKES. *2 Hen. IV* I would humour his men with the imputation of being near their master.

Phrases: ***as near as a toucher***: see TOUCHER 3. **as near as dammit**, **as near as makes no difference**, etc. *colloq.* extremely near, virtually. **come near doing**, **come near to doing** be on the point of doing, almost succeed in doing. ***far and near***: see FAR *adverb*. ***go near doing***: see **go near to doing** below. **go near to do** be on the point of, almost succeed in. **go near doing**, **go near to doing** = ***come near doing*** above. **near at hand** (*a*) within easy reach; (*b*) in the immediate future. **near-death experience** an experience undergone (typically during a temporary heart stoppage) by a patient who is seriously ill or injured and who later recovers or is revived, in which he or she claims to have experienced an after-life or other supernatural phenomenon. ***nearest one's heart***, ***nearest the heart***: see HEART *noun*. ***near home***: see HOME *noun & adjective*. ***near one's heart***: see HEART *noun*. ***near the bone***: see BONE *noun*. ***near the heart***: see HEART *noun*. ***near the knuckle***: see KNUCKLE *noun*. ***near the wind***: see WIND *noun*[1]. **near upon** *arch.* not far in time from. ***not the rose but near it***: see ROSE *noun*. ***nowhere near***: see NOWHERE *adverb* 1. ***pretty near***: see PRETTY *adverb*. **so near and yet so far** apparently close but actually out of reach.

Attrib. & comb.: In the sense 'resembling, intended as a substitute for', as *near-silk*. Special combs., as **near-beer** (orig. *US*) a drink resembling beer; beer with a very low alcohol content; †**near-legged** *adjective* (*rare*, Shakes.) (of a horse) moving with the (fore)legs close together; **near-seal** *N. Amer.* fur dressed and dyed to resemble sealskin.

nearabout /ˈnɪərəbaʊt/ *adverb.* Now *dial.* LME.
[from NEAR *adverb*[2] + ABOUT *adverb*.]
Orig., in this vicinity; nearby. Later, nearly, almost; approximately.

nearby /nɪəˈbʌɪ/ *attrib. adjective.* M19.
[from next.]
Close at hand, neighbouring; not far off.

nearby /nɪəˈbʌɪ/ *adverb & preposition.* Also **near by**. LME.
[from NEAR *adverb*[2] + BY *adverb*.]
▶ **A** *adverb.* **1** Close by, close at hand. LME. **2** Nearly, almost; thereabouts. Chiefly *Scot.* LME.
▶ **B** *preposition.* Close to (a place etc.). Now *dial.* LME.

nearctic /nɪˈɑːktɪk/ *adjective & noun.* Also **N-**. M19.
[from NE(O- + ARCTIC *adjective*.]
▶ **A** *adjective.* Of, pertaining to, inhabiting, or (usu. **N-**) designating the biogeographical region which includes the cold and temperate zones of N. America and Greenland. M19.
▶ **B** *ellipt.* as *noun*. The Nearctic region. L19.

near hand /nɪə ˈhand/ *adverbial, prepositional, & adjectival phr.* Now only *Scot. & dial.* ME.
[from NEAR *preposition*[2] + HAND *noun*.]
▶ **A** *adverb.* **1** Close at hand, close by. ME. ▸**b** Close to a place or person. LME. ▸†**c** At close quarters; closely. *rare.* M16–L17. **2** Nearly, almost. ME.
▶ **B** *preposition.* Near to, close to, (a place, person, etc.). ME.
▶ **C** *adjective.* Near. M19.

nearly /ˈnɪəli/ *adverb.* M16.
[from NEAR *adjective* + -LY[2].]
1 With close inspection or scrutiny; carefully, narrowly. Formerly also, with great care. Now *rare.* M16. ▸**b** Parsimoniously; frugally. *rare.* L16. **2** With a close connection, esp. through blood or friendship; in close intimacy. M16. **3** In a special degree or manner; particularly. M16. **4** In close proximity; close in space or time. Formerly also, closely on a person, directly. M16. **5** With a close degree of agreement or similarity; with close approximation or near approach to a specified state or condition. E17. **6** Within a (very) little; almost, all but, virtually. L17. **7** In neg. contexts with *not*: (not) anything like, (not) by a long way. E19.

📖 **1** SIR W. SCOTT His liveries, his cognizance, his feats of arms . . were nearly watched. **b** J. RAY They had rather live nearly than take much pains. **2** S. JOHNSON To be nearly acquainted with the people of different countries can happen to very few. E. WAUGH There were many others . . all nearly or remotely cousins of his. *transf.*: J. HAWKES When the Barnock pits were worked out, nearly related limestones were brought from Rutland. **3** H. MARTINEAU News which nearly concerned . . our village. J. WAIN I did not expect that his death would affect me very nearly. **4** SHAKES. *Macb.* I doubt some danger does approach you nearly. **5** B. JOWETT That in which he approaches most nearly to the comic poet. M. S. POWER That wouldn't have been nearly as nice. F. WYNDHAM I was so nearly on time. **6** B. PYM It was nearly six o'clock. J. MITCHELL He had nearly drowned some of them. **7** *Model Engineer* The result was not nearly so attractive.

Comb.: **nearly man** *colloq.*: one who is relatively successful but never quite reaches the top of his profession or wins the ultimate prize.

nearmost /ˈnɪəməʊst/ *adjective.* L16.
[from NEAR *adjective* + -MOST.]
Nearest.

nearshore /ˈnɪəʃɔː/ *adjective.* L19.
[from NEAR *adverb*[2] + SHORE *noun*[1].]
Chiefly OCEANOGRAPHY. Situated or occurring (relatively) close to a shore; pertaining to or involving the study of a region located (relatively) close to a shore.

nearside /ˈnɪəsʌɪd/ *adjective & noun.* M19.
[from NEAR *adjective* + SIDE *noun.*]
(Of) the left side of a horse or other animal, a vehicle, etc. Cf. NEAR *adjective* 2.

neat /niːt/ *noun. arch.* Pl. (in sense 1) **-s**, same.
[Old English *nēat* = Old Frisian *nāt*, *naet*, Old Saxon *nōt* (Dutch *noot*), Old High German *nōz* (obsolete or dial. German *Nos(s)*), Old Norse *naut*, from Germanic base also of NAIT *verb*.]
1 A bovine animal; an ox, a bullock, a cow, a heifer. Now *rare*. OE.
2 *collect.* Cattle. OE.
Comb.: **neatherd** a cowherd; **neatherdess** a female cowherd; **neat-house** (*a*) a cowshed; (*b*) (*sing.* & in *pl.*) a locality near Chelsea Bridge in London, site of a well-known former market garden; **neat's-foot** cow-heel, esp. as used for food; ***neat's-foot oil***, oil made from boiled cow-heel, used to dress leather; **neat's-leather** leather made from oxhide; **neat's tongue** the tongue of an ox, esp. as used for food.

neat /niːt/ *adjective & adverb.* M16.
[Old & mod. French *net* from Latin *nitidus* shining, clean, from *nitere* to shine. Cf. NET *adjective*².]
▶ **A** *adjective.* **I** †**1** Clean; free from dirt or impurities. M16–M17.
†**2** Clear, bright. L16–L18.
3 Of a substance or solution, esp. alcoholic liquor: unadulterated; not mixed with water, undiluted. L16.
4 **a** Free from any reductions; clear, net. *arch.* L16. ▸**b** Exact, precise. Now *Scot. & dial.* L17.

📖 **3** A. TYLER One Pabst, one Jack Daniel's neat. H. CARPENTER They drank neat gin out of aluminium cups. **neat cement** a mortar made from cement and water only, without the addition of sand. **4a** JAS. MILL He offered to give a neat sum, to cover all expenses.

▶ **II** †**5** (Of a person) refined, elegant, smart, esp. in dress; (of dress) elegant, trim. M16–M17.
6 Characterized by an elegant simplicity of form or arrangement; nicely made or proportioned. M16.
7 **a** Of language or style: well selected or expressed; pithy, brief; epigrammatic. Cf. earlier NEATNESS 2. L16. ▸**b** Cleverly contrived or executed; involving special accuracy or precision. L16. ▸**c** Of a (freq. culinary) preparation: dainty, elegant, tasteful. *arch.* E17.
8 Tidy, methodical; well-organized; in good order. Also (*arch.*), (of a person) skilful and precise in action or expression. L16.
9 Orig. (*iron.*), rare, fine. Later, good, excellent; desirable, attractive. *slang.* E19.

📖 **5** JONSON Still to be neat, still to be drest, As you were going to a feast. **6** G. BERKELEY The gardens are neat, spacious, and kept in good order. *absol.*: J. R. LOWELL Pope had a sense of the neat rather than of the beautiful. **neat but not gaudy**, **neat not gaudy** pleasingly elegant without being showy. **7a** LD MACAULAY A clear and neat statement of the points in controversy. **b** W. GREENER The neatest part of the process . . the joining of the points of the two rods. DICKENS This was a neat and happy turn to give the subject. **c** S. PEPYS Had a mighty neat dish of custards and tarts. **8** C. M. YONGE The hair and dress . . always neat. H. JAMES He was fastidiously neat in his person. I. MURDOCH She made the beds and tidied Paul's things . . into neat piles. **9** *Washington Post* I've passed up some neat dinner invitations. J. RULE To go to some really neat place for Christmas, like Mexico.

Comb.: **neat-handed** *adjective* deft in handling things, dexterous; **neat-handedness** the quality of being neat-handed.
▶ **B** *adverb.* Neatly. *arch.* M17.
▪ **neatify** *verb trans.* (now *rare* or *obsolete*) make neat, purify L16. **neatly** *adverb* M16.

neat /niːt/ *verb.* Now *rare* or *obsolete.* L16.
[from prec.]
1 *verb trans. & intrans.* Make (something or someone) neat. Formerly also, clean. L16.
2 *verb trans.* Gain (a sum) as a net profit. L18.

neaten /ˈniːt(ə)n/ *verb trans.* L19.
[formed as prec. + -EN⁵.]
Make (something or someone) neat. Freq. foll. by *up*.

📖 R. INGALLS He'd often put out a hand to neaten her hair.

neath /niːθ/ *preposition.* Now chiefly *poet.* Also **'neath**. LME.
[Aphet. Cf. ANEATH.]
= BENEATH *preposition.*

neatness /ˈniːtnɪs/ *noun.* M16.
[from NEAT *adjective & adverb* + -NESS.]
1 *gen.* The quality or condition of being neat. M16.
2 Cleverness of expression in language or style; pithiness, brevity. M16.

neatnik /ˈniːtnɪk/ *noun. slang* (chiefly *N. Amer.*). M20.
[from NEAT *adjective* + -NIK, after *beatnik*.]
A person who is (excessively) neat in personal habits.

neato /ˈniːtəʊ/ *adjective. slang* (chiefly *US*). M20.
[from NEAT *adjective* + -O.]
Excellent, desirable, attractive.

NEB *abbreviation.*
1 National Enterprise Board.
2 New English Bible.

neb /nɛb/ *noun & verb.* Now chiefly *Scot. & north.*
[Old English *nebb* = Old Norse *nef*, *nefj-* rel. to Middle Low German, Middle Dutch *nebbe* (Dutch *neb(be)*), from Germanic. Cf. NIB *noun*¹.]
▶ **A** *noun.* **1** The beak or bill of a bird. Also (*transf.*), a person's mouth. OE.
2 The nose; the snout of an animal. OE.
†**3** The face. OE–LME.
4 **a** A projecting part or point; a tip, a spout, etc.; the extremity of something ending in a point or narrowed part. L16. ▸**b** The point or nib of a pen etc. L16.
1 *black neb*: see BLACK *adjective.*
▶ **B** *verb.* Infl. **-bb-**.
1 *verb intrans.* Kiss, bill. E17.
2 *verb trans.* Adapt the point of (a pen etc.) for writing. L19.
3 *verb intrans.* Pry; behave inquisitively and intrusively. Freq. foll. by *in*. Chiefly *north. & US dial.* E20.

Neb. *abbreviation.*
Nebraska.

nebbich *noun & adjective* var. of NEBBISH.

Nebbiolo /nɛbɪˈəʊləʊ/ *noun & adjective.* M19.
[Italian.]
▶ **A** *noun.* Pl. **-os**. A black wine grape grown in Piedmont in northern Italy; red wine made from this. M19.
▶ **B** *attrib.* or as *adjective.* Of or pertaining to this grape or this wine. M20.

nebbish /ˈnɛbɪʃ/ *noun & adjective. colloq.* Also **-ich**. L19.
[Yiddish *nebech* poor thing.]
▶ **A** *noun.* A nobody, a nonentity, a submissive timid person. Also as *interjection*, expr. commiseration, dismay, etc. L19.
▶ **B** *adjective.* Of a person: innocuous, ineffectual; timid, submissive. M20.
▪ **nebbishy** *adjective* L20.

nebbuk /ˈnɛbʊk/ *noun.* Also **nebek** /ˈnɛbɛk/, **nubk** /nʊbk/. M19.
[Arab. *nabk*, *nibk*, *nabak*, *nabik* the fruit of *Ziziphus spina-christi* or *Z. lotus*.]
Any of several thorny eastern Mediterranean shrubs of the genus *Ziziphus*, of the buckthorn family, esp. *Z. spina-christi* and *Z. lotus*. Also ***nebbuk-tree***.

nebel /ˈniːb(ə)l/ *noun.* M18.
[Hebrew *nēḇel*. Cf. NABLA.]
A kind of ancient Israelite (prob. stringed) musical instrument.

nebelwerfer /ˈneːb(ə)lvɛrfər, ˈneb(ə)lwəːfə/ *noun.* M20.
[German, from *Nebel* mist, fog + *Werfer* thrower, mortar, from *werfen* to throw.]
A six-barrelled rocket mortar used by the German forces in the war of 1939–45.

nebenkern /ˈneɪbənkəːn/ *noun. arch.* Pl. **-s**, **-e** /-ə/. L19.
[German, from *neben* near + *Kern* nucleus.]
CYTOLOGY. Any of various cytoplasmic structures associated with or resembling a cell nucleus, esp. a coiled mitochondrial structure in a sperm cell.

nebi'im *noun pl.* see NABI.

†**neble** *noun* see NIPPLE.

neb-neb /ˈnɛbnɛb/ *noun.* M19.
[Origin unkn.]
The pods and bark of an acacia tree, *Acacia nilotica*, used in N. Africa in tanning. Cf. BABUL, SUNT.

Nebr. *abbreviation.*
Nebraska.

Nebraskan /nɪˈbrask(ə)n/ *adjective & noun.* L19.
[from *Nebraska* (see below) + -AN.]
▶ **A** *adjective.* **1** Of or pertaining to the State of Nebraska in the central US. L19.
2 GEOLOGY. Designating or pertaining a Lower Pleistocene glaciation in N. America. E20.
▶ **B** *noun.* **1** A native or inhabitant of Nebraska. L19.
2 *The* Nebraskan glaciation or its deposits. M20.
¶ The use of this term in geology has been abandoned.

nebris /ˈnɛbrɪs/ *noun.* L18.
[Latin from Greek = the skin of a fawn, from *nebros* a fawn.]
GREEK ANTIQUITIES. The skin of a fawn, as worn by (a worshipper or follower of) Dionysus.

Nebuchadnezzar /ˌnɛbjʊkədˈnɛzə/ *noun.* E20.
[King of Babylon (605–562 BC), who in 586 BC captured and destroyed Jerusalem and deported its leaders.]
An extremely large wine bottle, equivalent to twenty ordinary bottles. Cf. JEROBOAM, REHOBOAM.

nebula /ˈnɛbjʊlə/ *noun.* Pl. **-lae** /-liː/, **-las**. M17.
[Latin = mist, vapour.]
1 **a** A film or clouded spot on or over the cornea of the eye. Now only MEDICINE. M17. ▸**b** MEDICINE. Cloudiness observed in the urine. *rare.* M17. ▸**c** A cloud, (a) cloudlike appearance; an indistinct, insubstantial, or nebulous thing or (*fig.*) person. M18.
2 ASTRONOMY. A hazy or indistinct luminous area in the night sky representing a distant cluster of stars; (chiefly *Hist.*) a galaxy. Now usu. *spec.*, a cloud of gas, dust, etc., in deep space, appearing lighter or darker due to the reflection, absorption, etc., of light. E18.
3 Fog, mist. *rare.* L19.
2 *crab nebula*, *emission nebula*, *planetary nebula*, *spiral nebula*, etc.

nebular /ˈnɛbjʊlə/ *adjective.* M19.
[from prec. + -AR¹.]
ASTRONOMY. Of, pertaining to, or of the nature of a nebula or nebulae.
nebular hypothesis, **nebular theory**: that the solar system originated as a diffuse nebula.

nebulate /ˈnɛbjʊleɪt/ *verb. rare.* L15.
[medieval Latin *nebulat-* pa. ppl stem of *nebulare* to cloud, from Latin NEBULA: see -ATE³.]
†**1** *verb trans.* HERALDRY. As **nebulated** *ppl adjective*: = NEBULÉ 1. Only in L15.
2 *verb intrans. & trans.* Become or make cloudy or turbid, dim. M18.

nebule /ˈnɛbjuːl/ *noun*¹. LME.
[Anglicized from NEBULA.]
A cloud; a mist, a fog; ASTRONOMY (*rare*) a nebula.

nebule /ˈnɛbjuːl/ *noun*². E19.
[App. from next.]
ARCHITECTURE. A moulding of a wavy form.

nebulé /ˈnɛbjʊleɪ/ *adjective.* Also **-ly** /-li/. M16.
[French *nébulé* from medieval Latin *nebulatus* pa. pple, formed as NEBULATE: see -ATE², -Y⁵.]
1 HERALDRY. Of a particular wavy form, used to represent clouds. M16.
2 ARCHITECTURE. Of a moulding: of a wavy form. M19.

nebulise *verb* var. of NEBULIZE.

nebulist /ˈnɛbjʊlɪst/ *noun. rare.* M19.
[from NEBULA + -IST.]
1 An artist whose work is marked by indistinctness of outline. M19.
2 ASTRONOMY. An advocate of the nebular hypothesis. M19.

nebulium /nɛˈbjuːlɪəm/ *noun.* L19.
[from NEBULA + -IUM.]
PHYSICS (now *Hist.*). A hypothetical chemical element proposed to explain certain lines in the spectra of nebulae now held to arise from forbidden transitions in nitrogen and oxygen ions.

nebulize /ˈnɛbjʊlʌɪz/ *verb.* Also **-ise**. L19.
[from NEBULA + -IZE.]
1 *verb trans.* Convert (a liquid) to fine spray, esp. for medical use. L19.
2 *verb intrans.* Become nebulous or indefinite. *rare.* L19.
▪ **nebuli'zation** *noun* (*a*) the reduction of a liquid to fine spray, esp. for medical use; (*b*) medical treatment using a nebulizer: E20. **nebulizer** *noun* a device for nebulizing a liquid L19.

nebulose /ˈnɛbjʊləʊs/ *adjective.* LME.
[Latin *nebulosus*: see next, -OSE¹.]
1 †**a** Resembling a mist; foggy, misty. *rare.* Only in LME. ▸**b** Nebulous (*lit. & fig.*). *rare.* L18.
2 ASTRONOMY. Of the nature of a nebula. *rare.* L17.

nebulosity /nɛbjʊˈlɒsɪti/ *noun.* M18.
[French *nébulosité* or late Latin *nebulositas*, from Latin *nebulosus*, formed as NEBULA: see -OSITY.]
The quality or condition of being nebulous; an instance of this; a nebula, nebular matter.

📖 B. BOVA The view from the homeworld is clear, not shrouded with nebulosity.

nebulous /ˈnɛbjʊləs/ *adjective.* LME.
[French *nébuleux* or Latin *nebulosus*, formed as NEBULA: see -ULOUS.]
1 Cloudy, foggy, misty, dank. *rare.* LME.
2 ASTRONOMY. Of the nature of or resembling a nebula or nebulae. L18.
3 Cloudlike; hazy, vague, indistinct, formless. Freq. *fig.* E19.
4 Clouded; turbid. E19.

📖 **1** P. LOWE Evill Ayre . . is that which is . . nebulous and commeth from stinking breaths. **3** LONGFELLOW The angel, expanding His pinions in nebulous bars. M. SHADBOLT Nothing nebulous now. All solid . . really solid. J. BERMAN *The Myth of Mental Illness* does away . . with nebulous psychiatric classification. **4** W. SCORESBY A little of this snow, dissolved in a wine glass, appeared perfectly nebulous.

Special collocations: **nebulous star** a small indistinct cluster of stars, a star surrounded by a luminous haze, (now *rare*) a nebula.
▪ **nebulously** *adverb* L19. **nebulousness** *noun* M17.

nebuly *adjective* var. of NEBULÉ.

NEC *abbreviation.*
1 National Executive Committee.
2 National Exhibition Centre.

nécessaire /nesɛsɛːr/ *noun*. Pl. pronounced same. E19.
[French.]
A small usu. ornamental case for pencils, scissors, tweezers, etc.

necessarian /nɛsɪˈsɛːrɪən/ *noun & adjective*. L18.
[from NECESSARY + -ARIAN.]
▸ **A** *noun*. A believer in necessity; a necessitarian. L18.
▸ **B** *attrib.* or as *adjective*. Of or pertaining to necessarians or their views. L18.
■ **necessarianism** *noun* M19.

necessarily /ˈnɛsəs(ə)rɪli, -ˈsɛrɪli/ *adverb*. LME.
[from NECESSARY + -LY².]
1 By force of necessity; unavoidably; indispensably; in accordance with a necessary law or operative principle. *obsolete* exc. as passing into sense 2. LME.
2 As a necessary result or consequence; of necessity; inevitably. E16.

📖 **1** H. COGAN He was necessarily to be assistant at this funeral pomp. **2** J. CONRAD Visits to his home were necessarily rare. R. G. MYERS More money for research . . does not necessarily improve research.

necessariness /ˈnɛsəs(ə)rɪnɪs/ *noun*. Now *rare*. M16.
[from NECESSARY + -NESS.]
The fact or quality of being necessary; indispensability, necessity.

necessarium /nɛsəˈsɛːrɪəm/ *noun*. Pl. **-ria** /-rɪə/, **-riums**. M19.
[medieval Latin, use as noun of neut. sing. of *necessarius* (prob. after accus. (*locum*) *necessarium* necessary (place)) from Latin *necessarius*: see next.]
A privy, a lavatory, esp. in a monastic building.

necessary /ˈnɛsəs(ə)ri/ *noun & adjective*. ME.
[Anglo-Norman form of Old & mod. French *nécessaire*, or Latin *necessarius*, from *necesse* (*esse*, *habere*) (be, consider) necessary: see -ARY¹.]
▸ **A** *noun*. **1** That which is indispensable; an essential, a requisite; a basic requirement of life, as food, warmth, etc. (freq. in ***the necessaries of life***). ME.
2 A privy, a lavatory. Now *arch.* & *dial.* M18.
3 That which is required for a given situation; *spec.* (*colloq.*) *the* money or action required for a particular purpose. L18.

📖 **1** TAFFRAIL Pincher . . left the ship with . . a little bundle of necessaries. **2** *Listener* When he came home he cleared a path to the necessary. **3** C. HUTTON To make the convenient give place to the necessary when their interests are opposite. O. MANNING M' dear old friend Dobbie Dobson'll advance me the necessary.

▸ **B** *adjective*. **I 1** That cannot be dispensed with or done without; requisite, essential, needful. Freq. foll. by *to*, *for*, *to do*. LME.
2 Of a person, esp. a servant: carrying out certain necessary or useful services. Now only in ***necessary woman*** below. LME.
3 Of an action: requiring to be done; that must be done. E17.

📖 **1** T. PAINE Government even in its best state is but a necessary evil. M. MOORCOCK The meeting was to be of considerable importance. My presence was absolutely necessary. **3** R. K. NARAYAN The officer will come on inspection to your village and then take necessary steps.

▸ **II 4 a** Determined by predestination or natural processes, and not by free will; happening or existing by necessity. LME. ▸**b** Of a mental concept, a truth, judgement, etc.: resulting inevitably from the nature of things or of the mind itself. M16. ▸**c** Inevitably determined or produced by a previous state of things. M19.
5 Of an agent: having no independent volition. L17.

📖 **4a** W. COWPER Of causes, how they work By necessary laws their sure effects. **b** J. F. FERRIER A necessary truth or law of reason is a truth the opposite of which is inconceivable. **c** J. L. SANFORD He was quite as incapable . . of perceiving its necessary issues. **5** J. WESLEY Man is not a free but a necessary agent.

▸†**III 6** Of a person: closely related or connected; intimate. *rare*. LME–M17.

📖 **6** T. STANLEY Such as . . neglect their necessary Friends.

Special collocations & comb.: **necessary condition** = CONDITION *noun* 2. **necessary house** = sense A.2 above. **necessary woman** a female personal attendant.

necessitarian /nɪˌsɛsɪˈtɛːrɪən/ *noun & adjective*. L18.
[from NECESSITY + -ARIAN.]
▸ **A** *noun*. A person holding the view that all action is determined by antecedent causes as opp. to by free will. L18.
▸ **B** *attrib.* or as *adjective*. Of or pertaining to necessitarians or their views. E19.
■ **necessitarianism** *noun* M19.

necessitate /nɪˈsɛsɪtət/ *pa. pple & ppl adjective*. Now *rare* exc. *Scot.* L16.
[medieval Latin *necessitatus* pa. pple, formed as next: see -ATE².]
Necessitated.

necessitate /nɪˈsɛsɪteɪt/ *verb trans*. E17.
[medieval Latin *necessitat-* pa. ppl stem of *necessitare* compel, constrain, from *necessitas*: see NECESSITY, -ATE³.]
1 Bring (a person) under some necessity; compel, oblige, force, *to do*. Usu. in *pass*. Now chiefly *US*. E17.
2 Make necessary; *esp.* require or involve as a necessary condition, accompaniment, or result. E17.
†**3** Reduce (a person) to want or necessity. Freq. in *pass*. Also foll. by *in*, *for*. M17–M19.

📖 **1** J. MOORE Each boy is necessitated to decide and act for himself. **2** W. C. WILLIAMS So many roads were blocked, necessitating detours. D. LESSING The urgency of the situation again necessitated use of space craft. **3** W. LILLY The Native shall . . be necessitated in nothing.

■ **necessiˈtation** *noun* the action or result of necessitating something or someone M17.

†**necessitied** *ppl adjective*. *rare* (Shakes.). Only in E17.
[Prob. from NECESSITY + -ED².]
Brought into a state of need or necessity.

necessitous /nɪˈsɛsɪtəs/ *adjective*. E17.
[from French *nécessiteux* or NECESSITY + -OUS.]
1 In a state of necessity or poverty; having little or nothing to support oneself by; poor, needy. E17.
2 Characterized by necessity or poverty. M17.
†**3** Necessary, requisite, (*for*). Long *rare* or *obsolete* exc. *dial.* M18.

📖 **1** A. HAMILTON He exhausts all his Revenues, and is always necessitous. **2** W. COWPER That I may turn from them that evil hour Necessitous.

■ **necessitously** *adverb* M17. **necessitousness** *noun* L17.

necessitude /nɪˈsɛsɪtjuːd/ *noun*. Long *rare*. E17.
[Latin *necessitudo*, from *necesse* necessary: see -TUDE.]
†**1** A relation, a connection. E–M17.
2 Need, necessity. M19.

necessity /nɪˈsɛsɪti/ *noun*. LME.
[Old & mod. French *nécessité* from Latin *necessitas*, from *necesse* necessary: see -ITY.]
†**1** The fact of being inevitably fixed or determined; the constraining power *of* something. LME–M16.
2 Constraint or compulsion caused by circumstances or the operation of natural processes, esp. regarded as a law prevailing throughout the material universe and governing all human action; a state of things enforcing a certain course of action. LME.
3 The state of being in difficulties, esp. through lack of means; want, poverty. LME. ▸**b** Inferior or illicitly distilled spirit. Now chiefly *arch.* & *dial.* M18.
4 A situation of hardship or difficulty; a pressing need or want (usu. in *pl.*). LME. ▸†**b** Want *of* a thing. LME–M18.
†**5** A necessary piece of business; a necessary act. LME–L17. ▸**b** Something unavoidable. *rare*. L16–E17.
†**6** That which is necessarily required. LME–M17.
7 An indispensable or necessary thing. L15.
8 The fact of being indispensable; the indispensability *of* an act, a thing, etc. M16.
9 a An unavoidable compulsion or obligation. Also foll. by *of*, *to do*. Now *rare*. M17. ▸**b** An imperative need *for*, †*of*, something. Also, imperative need. L17.

📖 **2** BURKE I know the rigour of political necessity. *Daedalus* The designation of evolution as a two-stage process of chance . . and necessity. ***logical necessity***: see LOGICAL *adjective*. ***make a virtue of necessity***, ***make virtue of necessity***: see VIRTUE. **3** C. V. WEDGWOOD An admission wrung from him by the hard necessity of his condition as a prisoner. **4** J. B. MOZLEY A habit of gratitude, which has no relation to present necessities. **b** J. SHEBBEARE You . . are in Necessity of many things. **5b** SHAKES. *Wint. T.* One of these two must be necessities. **7** M. R. MITFORD Trees and fresh air are necessities to my constitution. Q Necessity kept the machines small. **8** WELLINGTON The necessity of adopting some measures to subsist their armies. **9a** JAS. MILL A necessity of applying to the Bengal Government for aid.

Comb.: **necessity-operator** *LOGIC* a word or symbol signifying that the proposition to which it attaches is a necessary truth.

neck /nɛk/ *noun*¹.
[Old English *hnecca* corresp. to Old Frisian *hnecka*, *necke*, Middle Dutch *nac*, *necke* (Dutch *nek*), Old High German (*h*)*nac* (German *Nacken* nape), Old Norse *hnakki* nape, from Germanic from Indo-European.]
▸ **I 1 a** Orig., the back part of the portion of the body connecting the head and shoulders. Later, the whole of this portion, the narrow part below or behind the head. Also, the part of the spine in this region, the cervical vertebrae collectively (chiefly in ***break one's neck***). OE. ▸†**b** The head. *rare*. M16–M17.
2 a Orig. (*rare*), the skin from the neck of an animal. Later, the flesh of an animal's neck as food. M16. ▸**b** The part of a garment covering or lying next to the wearer's neck. M16. ▸**c** *RACING*. The length of the head and neck of a horse etc. as a measure of its lead in a race. Freq. in ***win by a neck***. E19.
3 Insolent speech or presumptuous behaviour, impudence. Chiefly in ***have the neck***. L19.

📖 **1** JONATHAN MILLER The head is mounted on a mobile neck. J. HOWKER She had glasses on with a chain that hung round her neck. *fig.*: BURKE The barbarians . . had at length submitted their necks to the Gospel. **2a** *Examiner* He . . should like to have a neck of mutton. **b** J. HIGGINS The barman . . , his collarless shirt soiled at the neck. **3** B. ASHLEY Who dared to have the neck to say what was best for other people?

▸ **II 4 a** The narrow part of a passage, cavity, or vessel, *esp.* the narrow part of a bottle just below the mouth. LME. ▸**b** *FORTIFICATION*. The narrow part *of* a bastion or embrasure. M17. ▸**c** A pass between hills or mountains; the narrow part *of* a mountain pass. E18. ▸**d** A narrow channel or inlet; the narrow part *of* a sound etc. E18.
5 a A narrow piece of land with water on each side; an isthmus, a narrow promontory. M16. ▸**b** A narrow stretch of wooded country (freq. in ***neck of the woods*** below). Also, a district, a neighbourhood. L18. ▸**c** *GEOLOGY*. A column of solidified lava etc. filling a volcanic vent, esp. when exposed by erosion. L19.
6 a A narrow part in an implement, instrument, etc.; a connecting part between two parts of a thing. L16. ▸**b** The narrow part of a cannon connecting the cascabel with the breech. Also, the part of a cannon immediately behind the muzzle. L16. ▸**c** The part of a violin or similar musical instrument connecting the head and the body. E17. ▸**d** *ARCHITECTURE*. The lower part of a capital immediately above the astragal terminating the shaft of the column. E18.
7 *ANATOMY*. A constricted part in a bone or at the base of a tooth. L16.
8 *BOTANY*. **a** A narrow, esp. supporting part in a plant; *spec.* the terminal, usu. tubular, part of the archegonium in a bryophite or fern or of a perithecium in a fungus. L17. ▸**b** Excessive elongation of the stalk of a plant. L19.

📖 **4a** M. BAILLIE The portion . . most frequently inflamed is that near the neck of the bladder. W. STYRON Upending the bottle, thrusting its neck deep into his throat. **c** R. G. CUMMING Their vast legions continued streaming through the neck in the hills. **d** H. CAINE The neck of the harbour was narrow. **5a** W. BLACK The long neck of land lying between . . the Dee and the Mersey. **b** *Back Street Heroes* A whole load o' questions relating to that neck o' Yorkshire. **6a** J. NICHOLSON The bearings on which the necks . . of the spindle are supported. **b** N. HINTON He put his hand round the neck of the guitar.

Phrases: ***a hair in one's neck***: see HAIR *noun*. ***breathe down a person's neck***. ***dead from the neck up***: see DEAD *adjective*. ***Derbyshire neck***. **get it in the neck** *colloq.* suffer a fatal or severe blow; be severely reprimanded or punished. ***little neck***: see LITTLE *adjective*. **neck and crop**, (now *dial.*) **neck and heels** headlong, bodily. **neck and neck** running level in a race etc. **neck of the woods** *colloq.* (orig. *US*) (*a*) a settlement in wooded country; (*b*) any community or locality. **neck or nothing** staking all on success; (despite) all risks. ***pain in the neck***: see PAIN *noun*¹. **risk one's neck** take the chance of being killed by falling etc. ***save one's neck***, ***save one's own neck***: see SAVE *verb*. ***screw a person's neck***: see SCREW *verb*. **stick one's neck out** *colloq.* ask for trouble, expose oneself to danger. ***stretch the neck of***: see STRETCH *verb*. **talk through the back of one's neck**, **talk through one's neck** *slang* talk foolishly or wildly. **up to one's neck (in)** *colloq.* very deeply involved (in). ***V-neck***: see V, V 2. ***with one's foot on the neck of***: see FOOT *noun*.

Comb.: **neckband** (*a*) a band for the neck; (*b*) the part of a garment around the neck; **neck-beef** *arch.* poor-quality beef from an animal's neck; the type of something inferior and cheap; **neck-bone** (*a*) the part of the spine in the neck; a cervical vertebra; †(*b*) the nape of the neck; **neck-break** *adverb* (now *dial.*) in a breakneck or headlong manner; **neck-canal** *BOTANY* a central channel in the neck of the archegonium; **neckcloth** (*a*) a cloth worn round the neck, a cravat, a neckerchief; †(*b*) a hangman's rope; **neck-collar** a collar for the neck; **neck-handkerchief** a neckerchief; **neck-hole** (*a*) (now *dial.*) the hollow in the back of the neck; the space between the back of the neck and the collar; (*b*) an opening for the neck; **neckline** (*a*) = sense 4b above; (*b*) the edge or shape of the neck-hole of a garment; (*c*) the shape of the hairline on a person's neck; (*d*) *ARCHAEOLOGY* an ornamental line around the neck of a vessel; **neck-lock** (*a*) a curl, esp. in a wig; (*b*) a form of stranglehold in judo etc.; **neck-oil** *slang* an alcoholic drink, *esp.* beer; **neck-piece** (*a*) = sense 2b above; (*b*) a piece of armour etc. covering or protecting the neck; †(*c*) = sense 1a above; (*d*) the flesh of an animal's neck as food; **neck-rein** *verb* (*a*) *verb trans.* cause (a horse) to change direction by exerting pressure on the neck with a rein; (*b*) *verb intrans.* (of a horse) change direction in response to pressure on the neck with a rein; **neck-roll** (*a*) *GYMNASTICS* a swing of the body backwards to rest on the back of the neck; (*b*) a roll of hair worn at the nape of the neck; **neck-spring** *GYMNASTICS* a vault in which the weight of the body is borne initially by the neck (and shoulders) and the hands; **necktie** a band of material (giving the appearance of) securing the shirt collar when knotted in front; ***necktie party*** (*slang*), a hanging; **neck-towel** (now *dial.*) a small towel (formerly carried round the neck by an attendant at a table) for wiping dishes; **neck-vein** a large vein in the neck, esp. of a horse; **neck-verse** *Hist.* a Latin verse printed in black letter (usu. the beginning of *Psalms* 51) by the reading of which a person's claim to benefit of clergy could be proved; **neckweed** *N. Amer.* a speedwell, *Veronica* *peregrina*, reputed to cure tuberculosis of the lymph nodes of the neck (scrofula).

■ **neckless** *adjective* E17.

neck /nɛk/ *noun*[2]. Chiefly *SW dial.* L17.
[Origin unkn.]
The last handful or sheaf of corn cut at harvest-time.

neck /nɛk/ *verb.* L15.
[from NECK *noun*[1].]
1 *verb trans.* Strike on the neck, esp. so as to stun or kill; behead; kill by pulling the neck out of (a fowl etc.). Now chiefly *dial.* L15.
2 *verb trans.* Drink, swallow. *slang.* E16.
3 a *verb intrans.* Engage in amorous fondling (*with*), (of a couple) embrace, kiss, or caress one another, clasp one another round the neck. *slang.* E19. ▸**b** *verb trans.* Hug, kiss, embrace; clasp (a lover, sweetheart, etc.) round the neck; fondle. *slang.* L19.
4 *verb trans.* Fasten (a cow etc.) by the neck to another cow etc. Freq. foll. by *to. US.* M19.
5 *verb intrans.* Be or become rapidly and irreversibly reduced in local diameter as a result of applied tension. Freq. foll. by *down.* M20.

📖 **1** J. STEVENS They would have neck'd me as they do Rabbets to kill them. **2** J. MASEFIELD I do wish . . you'd chuck necking Scotch the way you do. **3a** TOECKEY JONES I was eighteen and had necked with dozens of boyfriends. L. R. BANKS I wished we'd never started going together, necking and that. **4** J. F. DOBIE Every animal . . had been roped and led in necked to an old brindle ox.

†**neckatee** *noun. rare.* E18–E19.
[App. irreg. from NECK *noun*[1].]
A lady's neckerchief.

necked /nɛkt/ *adjective.* LME.
[from NECK *noun*[1], *verb*: see -ED[2], -ED[1].]
1 Having a neck. Freq. with qualifying adjective. LME.
2 Reduced locally in diameter as a result of applied tension. M20.

📖 **1** M. R. MITFORD A model of grace . . necked and crested like an Arabian. ***long-necked***, ***short-necked***, etc.

necker /ˈnɛkə/ *noun. slang.* E20.
[from NECK *verb* + -ER[1].]
A person who indulges in amorous fondling with another.

neckercher /ˈnɛkətʃə/ *noun.* Now *dial.* LME.
[from NECK *noun*[1] + KERCHER.]
= next.

neckerchief /ˈnɛkətʃɪf/ *noun.* LME.
[from NECK *noun*[1] + KERCHIEF.]
A square of cloth worn around the neck.

Necker cube /ˈnɛkə kjuːb/ *noun phr.* Also **Necker's cube**. E20.
[from L. A. *Necker* (1786–1861), Swiss naturalist.]
A line drawing of a transparent cube in which the lines of opposite sides are drawn parallel, so that the perspective is ambiguous and the orientation of the cube appears to alternate.

necking /ˈnɛkɪŋ/ *noun.* E19.
[from NECK *noun*[1] + -ING[1].]
1 ARCHITECTURE. The part of a column lying between the capital and the shaft. Cf. NECK *noun*[1] 6d. E19.
2 A stem or stalk resembling a neck. *rare.* M19.
3 ARCHAEOLOGY. A circlet around a projection such as the boss of a shield. M20.
Comb.: **necking-cord** any of the cords in a loom joining the pulley cords and the leashes.

neckinger /ˈnɛkɪndʒə/ *noun.* Long *dial.* L16.
[Alt. of NECKERCHER.]
A neckerchief.

necklace /ˈnɛklɪs/ *noun & verb.* L16.
[from NECK *noun*[1] + LACE *noun*.]
▶ **A** *noun.* **1** An ornamental chain or string of precious stones, precious metal, beads, links, etc., worn round the neck. L16. ▸†**b** A lace or ribbon for the neck; a necktie. M17–M18.
2 A noose, a halter. *arch. rare.* E17.
3 NAUTICAL. A chain or strop round a mast. Also, a ring of wads placed round a gun. M19.
4 A tyre soaked or filled with petrol, placed around a victim's neck and shoulders and set alight; *the* form of lynching or unofficial execution using this. *S. Afr.* L20.

📖 **1** R. K. NARAYAN She removed . . her necklace, gold bangles and rings. **4** *attrib.*: *Independent* The necklace killings, horrific brutalities in the townships.

Comb.: **necklace poplar** [from its long interrupted catkins] the cottonwood *Populus deltoides*; **necklace shell** a burrowing carnivorous gastropod mollusc of the genus *Natica*, which drills into the shells of bivalves; **necklace-tree** any of several mainly W. Indian leguminous trees of the genus *Ormosia*, with bright red seeds used as beads.

▶ **B** *verb.* **1** *verb trans. & intrans.* Form into a necklace. L16.
2 *verb trans.* Encircle or surround (as) with a necklace. M18. ▸**b** Kill (a person) by means of the necklace (sense A.4 above). Chiefly as ***necklaced** ppl adjective*, ***necklacing** verbal noun. S. Afr.* L20.

📖 **2** T. MORRISON Lines of cars necklaced the entrance.

necklet /ˈnɛklɪt/ *noun.* M19.
[from NECK *noun*[1] + -LET.]
1 An ornament for wearing round the neck; a small fur garment for the neck. M19.
2 A collar or belt for the neck. M19.

necro- /ˈnɛkrəʊ/ *combining form.* Also (occas.) **nekro-**; before a vowel also **necr-**.
[from Greek *nekros* dead person, corpse.]
Used in words adopted from Greek and in English words modelled on these, with the senses 'death', 'dead body', 'dead tissue'.

■ **necrobaciˈllosis** *noun*, pl. **-lloses** /-ˈləʊsiːz/, MEDICINE & VETERINARY MEDICINE any of several bacterial infections in (esp. domestic) animals and occas. in humans, characterized by diffuse or localized necrotic lesions E20. **neˈcrophagous** *adjective* feeding on dead bodies or carrion M19. **necroˈgenic** *adjective* arising from or produced by contact with dead bodies L19. **necrotype** *noun* an extinct form, a fossil L19.

necrobiosis /nɛkrə(ʊ)bʌɪˈəʊsɪs/ *noun.* L19.
[mod. Latin, formed as NECRO- + Greek *bios* life: see -OSIS.]
MEDICINE. The process of gradual degeneration or death in the cells of the body; necrosis.

■ **necrobiotic** /-ˈɒtɪk/ *adjective* L19.

necrolatry /nɛˈkrɒlətri/ *noun.* E19.
[ecclesiastical Greek *nekrolatreia*, formed as NECRO- + -LATRY.]
Worship of or excessive reverence for the dead.

necrology /nɛˈkrɒlədʒi/ *noun.* E18.
[medieval Latin *necrologium*, formed as NECRO- + -LOGY. In senses 2, 3 infl. by French *nécrologie*.]
1 An ecclesiastical or monastic register containing entries of the deaths of people connected with, or commemorated by, a church, monastery, etc. E18. ▸**b** A list of people who have died during a certain period; a death-roll. M19. ▸**c** An account of a number of deaths, esp. as due to a particular cause. M20.
2 An obituary notice. L18.
3 The history of the dead. M19.

■ **necroˈlogical** *adjective* of or pertaining to (a) necrology E19. **necroˈlogically** *adverb* E19. **necrologist** *noun* the author of an obituary notice E19. **necrologue** /-lɒg/ *noun* an obituary notice L19.

necromance /ˈnɛkrə(ʊ)mans/ *noun.* Long *arch. rare.* Also (earlier) †**nigro-**. ME.
[Old French *nigromance* var. of *nigromancie*: see NECROMANCY.]
Necromancy.

necromancer /ˈnɛkrə(ʊ)mansə/ *noun.* Also (earlier) †**nigro-**. LME.
[Old French *nigromansere*, from *nigromancie*: see next, -ER[2].]
1 A person who practises necromancy; a wizard, a magician, a conjuror. LME.
2 A silver or pewter dish with closely fitting lid and wide rim. M18.

necromancy /ˈnɛkrə(ʊ)mansi/ *noun.* Also (earlier) †**nigro-**. ME.
[Old French *nigromancie* from Proto-Romance (medieval Latin) *nigromantia* alt., by assoc. with Latin *nigr-*, *niger* black, of late Latin *necromantia* from Greek *nekromanteia*, formed as NECRO- + -MANCY (later refash. after Latin & Greek).]
1 The art of prediction by supposed communication with the dead; magic, enchantment, conjuration. Also, an instance of this. ME.
2 The part of the *Odyssey* describing the visit of Odysseus to Hades. E17.

📖 **1** SWIFT By his Skill in Necromancy he hath a Power of calling whom he pleaseth from the Dead. E. FEINSTEIN His voice was irresistible; it was like necromancy.

†**necromant** *noun.* Also (earlier) **nigro-**. L16–L19.
[Italian *negromante* = Spanish *nigromante*, French †*négromant* (mod. *nécro-*) from Greek *nekromantis*, formed as NECRO- + *mantis* a diviner.]
A necromancer.

necromantic /nɛkrə(ʊ)ˈmantɪk/ *noun & adjective.* Also (earlier) †**nigro-**. M16.
[Late Latin *necromanticus* or medieval Latin *nigromanticus*, from late Latin *necromantia* or medieval Latin *nigromantia*: see NECROMANCY, -MANTIC.]
▶† **A** *noun.* **1** A necromancer. M16–M17.
2 In *pl.* Conjuring tricks. *rare.* Only in M18.
▶ **B** *adjective.* **1** Practising necromancy. L16.
2 Of, belonging to, or used in necromancy; performed by necromancy; magical, enchanting. L16.

■ **necromantically** *adverb* M17.

necromantist /ˈnɛkrə(ʊ)mantɪst/ *noun. rare.* E17.
[from late Latin *necromantia* (see NECROMANCY) + -IST.]
A necromancer.

necrophilia /nɛkrə(ʊ)ˈfɪlɪə/ *noun.* L19.
[from NECRO- + -PHILIA.]
Fascination with death and dead bodies; *esp.* sexual attraction to dead bodies.

■ **ˈnecrophil(e)** *noun* a person affected by necrophilia L19. **necrophiliac** *noun & adjective* (*a*) *noun* a necrophile; (*b*) *adjective* necrophilic: M20. **necrophilic** *adjective* of, pertaining to, or (esp.) affected by necrophilia E20. **neˈcrophilism** *noun* necrophilia M19. **neˈcrophilist** *noun* a necrophile M20. **neˈcrophily** *noun* necrophilia L19.

necrophilous /nɛˈkrɒfɪləs/ *adjective.* L19.
[from NECRO- + -PHILOUS.]
1 BIOLOGY. Feeding or growing on dead organic matter; saprophytic, saprozoic, necrophagous. L19.
2 = NECROPHILIC. M20.

necrophobia /nɛkrə(ʊ)ˈfəʊbɪə/ *noun.* M19.
[from NECRO- + -PHOBIA.]
Fear or horror of death; *esp.* irrational fear of dead bodies or of anything associated with death.

■ **ˈnecrophobe** *noun* a person affected by necrophobia L20. **necrophobic** *adjective* of, pertaining to, or (esp.) affected with necrophobia M19.

necropolis /nɛˈkrɒpəlɪs, nɪ-/ *noun.* E19.
[Greek, formed as NECRO- + -POLIS.]
1 A cemetery, *esp.* a large cemetery in or near a city; an ancient burying-place. E19.
2 A dead city, a city of the dead; a city in the final stages of social and economic degeneration. *rare.* E20.

■ **necroˈpolitan** *adjective* of or belonging to a necropolis L19.

necropsy /ˈnɛkrɒpsi, nɛˈkrɒpsi/ *noun & verb.* M19.
[from NECRO- after *autopsy*.]
MEDICINE. ▶**A** *noun.* = AUTOPSY *noun* 2. M19.
▶ **B** *verb trans.* = AUTOPSY *verb.* E20.

necroscopy /nɛˈkrɒskəpi/ *noun.* Now *rare* or *obsolete.* M19.
[from NECRO- + -SCOPY.]
MEDICINE. = AUTOPSY *noun* 2.

■ **necroˈscopic**, **necroˈscopical** *adjectives* M19.

necrose /nɛˈkrəʊs, ˈnɛkrəʊs/ *verb intrans. & trans.* Now *rare.* L19.
[Back-form. from next.]
MEDICINE & BIOLOGY. = NECROTIZE. Esp. as ***necrosed***, ***necrosing** ppl adjectives.*

necrosis /nɛˈkrəʊsɪs/ *noun.* Pl. **-roses** /-ˈrəʊsiːz/. M17.
[mod. Latin, from Greek *nekrōsis* state of death, from *nekroun* kill, mortify, formed as NECRO-: see -OSIS.]
MEDICINE & BIOLOGY. The death or decay of (part of) an organ or tissue due to disease, injury, or deficiency of nutrients; mortification.

necrotic /nɛˈkrɒtɪk/ *adjective.* L19.
[from Greek *nekroun* (see prec.) + -OTIC.]
MEDICINE & BIOLOGY. Of, pertaining to, or exhibiting necrosis.

necrotize /ˈnɛkrə(ʊ)tʌɪz/ *verb intrans. & trans.* Also **-ise**. L19.
[from prec. + -IZE.]
MEDICINE & BIOLOGY. Become or make necrotic. Freq. as ***necrotized***, ***necrotizing** ppl adjectives.*
necrotizing fasciitis an acute disease (caused by the bacterium *Streptococcus pyogenes*) in which inflammation of the fasciae of muscles or other organs results in rapid destruction of overlying tissues.

■ **necrotiˈzation** *noun* the process of causing or undergoing necrosis; necrotic condition: M19.

nectar /ˈnɛktə/ *noun.* M16.
[Latin from Greek *nektar*.]
1 CLASSICAL MYTHOLOGY. The drink of the gods. M16.
2 Any delicious wine or other drink. L16.
3 A sugary fluid produced by plants to attract pollinating insects to their flowers and made into honey by bees. E17.
Comb.: **nectar-bird** a bird which feeds on nectar, *esp.* a sunbird; **nectar-guide**, **nectar-mark**, **nectar-spot** = *honeyguide* (b) s.v. HONEY *noun*.

■ **nectareal** /-ˈtɛːrɪəl/ *adjective* (*rare*) nectarean M17. **nectarean** /-ˈtɛːrɪən/ *adjective* of the nature of or resembling nectar E17. **nectared** *adjective* (*literary*) filled, flavoured, or impregnated with nectar; deliciously sweet or fragrant: L16. **nectareous** /-ˈtɛːrɪəs/ *adjective* of the nature of, consisting of, or resembling nectar E18. **nectareously** *adverb* (*rare*) M19. **nectareousness** *noun* (*rare*) M19. **nectarian** /-ˈtɛːrɪən/ *adjective* (*rare*) nectarean M17. **nectaˈriferous** *adjective* (BOTANY) producing nectar M18. **nectarious** /-ˈtɛːrɪəs/ *adjective* (*rare*) nectareous E18. **nectarous** *adjective* resembling nectar M17.

nectarine /ˈnɛktərɪn, -iːn/ *noun.* E17.
[Prob. use as noun of next.]
A fruit resembling a peach but having a thinner downless skin and a firmer pulp; the tree that bears this fruit, a variety of the peach tree.
clingstone nectarine: see CLING *verb*. ***freestone nectarine***: see FREESTONE 2.

nectarine /ˈnɛktərɪn/ *adjective*. E17.
[from NECTAR + -INE¹.]
Of the nature of nectar, sweet as nectar.

nectarium /nɛkˈtɛːrɪəm/ *noun*. Now *rare* or *obsolete*. Pl. **-ria** /-rɪə/. M18.
[mod. Latin, from Latin NECTAR: see -ARIUM.]
BOTANY. = NECTARY 2.

nectarivorous /nɛktəˈrɪv(ə)rəs/ *adjective*. L19.
[from NECTAR + -I- + -VOROUS.]
ZOOLOGY. Feeding on nectar.
■ **nectarivore** /nɛkˈtarɪvɔː/ *noun* a nectarivorous animal L20.

nectary /ˈnɛkt(ə)ri/ *noun*. L16.
[from NECTAR, or mod. Latin NECTARIUM: see -ARY¹, -Y¹.]
†**1** A nectareous fluid. *rare*. Only in L16.
2 BOTANY. A nectar-secreting gland at the base of a flower. M18.
†**3** ENTOMOLOGY. A cornicle of an aphid (formerly supposed to secrete honeydew). *rare*. Only in L19.

nectocalyx /nɛktəˈkeɪlɪks/ *noun*. Pl. **-calyces** /-ˈkeɪlɪsiːz/. M19.
[from mod. Latin *necto-*, from Greek *nēktos* swimming (from *nēkhein* swim) + CALYX.]
ZOOLOGY. A swimming-bell in some siphonophores, resembling a small jellyfish but lacking a manubrium.
■ **nectocalycine** /nɛktəˈkalɪsʌɪn/ *adjective* of or pertaining to a nectocalyx M19.

NED *abbreviation*. *arch*.
New English Dictionary (later Oxford English Dictionary).

ned /nɛd/ *noun*. *Scot. slang*. M20.
[Perh. from the forename *Ned*: see NEDDY.]
1 A hooligan, a thug, a petty criminal. M20.
2 A stupid or silly person. M20.

NEDC *abbreviation*. *Hist*.
National Economic Development Council.

neddy /ˈnɛdi/ *noun*. M16.
[Dim. of *Ned*, familiar abbreviation of male forename *Edward*: see -Y⁶. In branch II partly an acronym.]
►**I 1** A donkey, an ass. M16. ►**b** A horse, *esp*. a racehorse. *Austral. slang*. L19.
2 A stupid or silly person. E19.
3 A short stick with a heavily loaded end, a life-preserver. *slang*. M19.
►**II 4** (**N-**.) The National Economic Development Council; a sub-committee of this. *colloq*. (now *Hist*.). M20.

Nederlands /ˈneːdərlants/ *noun*. *S. Afr*. E20.
[Afrikaans from Dutch *Nederlandsch*.]
The Dutch language.

Ned Kelly /nɛd ˈkɛli/ *noun phr*. *Austral*. L19.
[The most famous Austral. bush-ranger (1857–80).]
1 A person of reckless courage or unscrupulous business dealings. *colloq*. L19.
2 The belly. *rhyming slang*. M20.
¶ See also ***game as Ned Kelly*** s.v. GAME *adjective*¹ 1.

NEDO *abbreviation*.
National Economic Development Office.

née /neɪ, *foreign* ne/ *adjective*. Also ***nee**. M18.
[French = born, fem. pa. pple of *naître* be born. Cf. NÉ.]
1 Born with the name: placed before a married woman's maiden name. M18.
2 *transf*. Formerly called. M20.

> 🕮 **1** E. BOWEN On her marriage . . Mrs Heccomb née Miss Yardes had gone to live at Seale. A. PRICE Mrs Agnes Childe was née O'Byrne. **2** W. SAFIRE The flight attendant, née stewardess, singsongs over the loudspeaker.

need /niːd/ *noun & adjective*.
[Old English *nēd*, *nēod*, (West Saxon) *nīed*, *nȳd* = Old Frisian *nēd*, *nāth*, Old Saxon *nōd* (Dutch *nood*), Old High German *nōt* (German *Not*), Old Norse *nauð*, *neyð*, Gothic *nauþs*, from Germanic.]
►**A** *noun*. †**1** Violence, force, constraint, compulsion. OE–LME.
2 Necessity for a course of action arising from facts or circumstances. Usu. with specifying word, as *what*, *little*, *no*, etc., with *there is* or *was*, & in ***if need require***, ***if need be***, ***if need were***. OE.
3 Necessity or demand for the presence, possession, etc., *of* something. OE.
4 A condition or time of difficulty, distress, or trouble; exigency, emergency, crisis. OE.
5 A condition of lacking or requiring some necessary thing, either physically or (now) psychologically; destitution, lack of the means of subsistence or of necessaries, poverty. Now also, a condition of requiring or being motivated *to do*, a necessity *to do*. OE.
6 A matter requiring action; a piece of necessary business. Long only in ***one's needs*** below. OE.
7 A particular point or respect in which some necessity or want is present or is felt; a thing wanted, a requirement. OE.

> 🕮 **2** SWIFT But what need is there of disputing. *Daily News* Clothes and household effects . . which, if need be, they can 'put away' during the winter. R. COBB There had been no *need* for him to go on working. G. W. TARGET There's no need to get nasty . . . I'm only trying to help. **3** TOLKIEN Sleep! I feel the need of it. G. VIDAL There are no real mysteries for them, no need of logic. **4** SIR W. SCOTT A short passage . . secured at time of need by two oaken doors. *Proverb*: A friend in need is a friend indeed. **5** B. THORPE They therefore lived in great poverty, and . . when need crept in, love walked out. GEO. ELIOT The great need of her heart compelled her to strangle . . suspicion. E. WAUGH His year of anarchy had filled a deep, interior need. DAY LEWIS The need for my mother . . made me warmly responsive to physical tenderness. A. HUTSCHNECKER Thinkers, writers, painters, and other people feel an inner need to create goals for themselves. J. HELLER Rembrandt had need of a woman . . to care for the infant and attend to the house. **7** E. SAINTSBURY The wealthy . . should . . provide for the needs of the poor.

Phrases: **at need** *arch*. in an emergency or crisis, in time of need. **had need** would require, ought, *to do* (or *do*). **have need** †(*a*) be in difficulties or in want; †(*b*) = ***have need of*** below; (*c*) be under a necessity or require *to do* (or †*do*). **have need of**, **have need for** require, want. **in need** requiring help. **in need of** requiring. ***make a virtue of need***: see VIRTUE. **one's needs** (*a*) (long *obsolete* exc. *Scot*.) errands, business; (*b*) (long *obsolete* exc. *dial*.) defecation or urination.
Comb.: **need-be** (chiefly *dial*.) an essential or necessary reason, a necessity; **need-blind** *adjective* (*US*) of or denoting a university admissions policy in which applicants are judged solely on their own merits, irrespective of their ability to pay tuition fees; **needfire** (now *dial*.) (*a*) fire obtained from dry wood by means of violent friction, formerly credited with various magical or medicinal properties; (*b*) a beacon, a bonfire.
►**B** *pred. adjective*. Necessary, needful. Now *rare* or *obsolete*. OE.

need /niːd/ *verb*.
[Old English *nēodian* (rare), from *nēod* NEED *noun*.]
1 a *verb intrans. impers*. (usu. with *it*) & interrog. with *what*. Be needful or necessary (*to do*, *to do*, *that*). Formerly also with indirect obj. Long *obsolete* exc. *Scot*. OE. ►**b** *verb trans. impers*. (with *it*, *there*) & †interrog. with *what*. Be a need for, require. *arch*. LME.
2 *verb intrans*. Of a thing: be needful or necessary. Formerly also with indirect obj. *arch*. ME.
†**3** *verb intrans*. Be in need *of* (or *to*). ME–L16.
4 *verb trans*. Be in need of, require (a person or thing (*to do*, *doing*, (*Scot*.) *done*)). LME.
5 *verb intrans*. Be in need or want. *arch*. LME.
6 *verb trans*. Be under a necessity or obligation *to do* (now esp. in positive & declarative contexts), *do* (now esp. in neg. & interrog. contexts). Also, be recommended or desirable *to do*. LME.

> 🕮 **1a** SPENSER Now needeth him no lenger labour spend. W. G. PALGRAVE Needs not say how lovely are the summer evenings. **b** SHELLEY There needeth not the hell that bigots frame. M. ARNOLD It needs heaven-sent moments for this skill. **2** BROWNING Lest you, even more than needs, embitter Our parting. **4** W. CATHER The moment I thought you might need me, it all looked different. SCOTT FITZGERALD The front right fender needed repair. P. BOWLES I can't see . . why Jack needs anyone . . in that little office. R. K. NARAYAN This is the natural way of taking the sugar we need. T. S. ELIOT Eliot's development, it hardly needs saying, . . calls up other questions. **5** MILTON If Nature need not, Or God support Nature without repast. **6** R. P. JHABVALA If Olivia was nervous about this meeting, she need not have been. P. LOMAS Something has gone wrong, which needs to be understood and healed. M. FLANAGAN I don't see that this need concern anyone but you and me. *Holiday Which?* The route round the mills needs to be more clearly marked. *absol*.: STEELE Some use Ten Times more Words than they need.

Phrases: ***need like a hole in the head***: see HOLE *noun*¹. ***need one's head examined***: see HEAD *noun*.
Comb.: **need-not** (now *rare*) an unnecessary thing; **need-to-know** *adjective & noun* (designating) the principle or practice of telling people only what it is necessary for them to know to carry out a task effectively.
■ **needer** *noun* M16.

†**need** *adverb*. OE–M18.
[Old English *nēde*, instr. of *nēd* NEED *noun*.]
= NEEDS *adverb*.

needcessity /niːdˈsɛsɪti/ *noun*. *dial*. M16.
[Alt. of NECESSITY after NEED *noun*.]
Necessity, need.

needful /ˈniːdfʊl, -f(ə)l/ *adjective & noun*. ME.
[from NEED *noun* + -FUL.]
►**A** *adjective*. **1** Of a person: poor, needy, without necessaries. Now chiefly *Scot*. ME.
2 Of a circumstance, occasion, etc.: characterized by need or necessity. Now chiefly *Scot*. ME.
3 Requisite, necessary, indispensable. (Foll. by *for*, *to*, (now *rare*) *to do* or *be done*; (with impers. *it*) *that*, *to do*.) ME.
4 In need *of*. *rare*. LME.

> 🕮 **3** SHAKES. *3 Hen. VI* It is more than needful Forthwith that Edward be pronounc'd a traitor. R. FRY We learn to see only so much as is needful for our purposes. J. UGLOW It is more needful to have a 'fibre of sympathy' with the tradesman . . than with heroes. **4** *Country Life* Needful of more rhubarb for forcing, I am sowing a boxful.

►**B** *noun*. **1** *The* needy people. Now *rare*. ME.
2 *The* necessary thing (esp. in ***do the needful***); *spec*. (*colloq*.) the necessary amount of money, cash. E18.
3 A necessary thing. Now *rare*. M18.

> 🕮 **2** M. EDGEWORTH I resolved to write . . only 3 or 4 lines just to say the needful. L. R. BANKS I was doing some odd jobs. Picked up a bit of the needful.

■ **needfully** *adverb* necessarily, on compulsion or constraint; urgently, pressingly: ME. **needfulness** *noun* (*a*) *rare* a condition of need; a strait; (*b*) the state or quality of being needful; necessity: ME.

needle /ˈniːd(ə)l/ *noun*.
[Old English *nǣdl* = Old Frisian *nēdle*, Old Saxon *nādla*, *nāþla*, Middle Low German *nālde*, Old High German *nādala* (Dutch *naald*, German *Nadel*), Old Norse *nál*, Gothic *nēþla*, from Germanic, from Indo-European base also of Latin *nere* to spin, Greek *nēma* thread.]
►**I 1** A thin pointed instrument for conveying one thing, esp. a thread, into or through another; *spec*. a small slender piece of polished steel etc. with a hole or eye for thread to pass through, used in sewing, surgical stitching, etc. OE. ►**b** Any of various other pointed pins or implements used in making or working fabric; *spec*. (*a*) = ***KNITTING-needle***; (*b*) = ***CROCHET hook***. L16. ►**c** *transf*. A user of a needle, a needlewoman. *rare*. M19.
2 A piece of magnetized steel (orig. a sewing-needle) used as an indicator of direction, *spec*. as a part of a compass, or in connection with magnetic or electrical apparatus in telegraphy etc. Also ***magnetic needle***. LME. ►**b** *Hist*. A small strip of gold or silver of known or standard fineness used with a touchstone in testing the purity of other pieces of those metals. LME. ►**c** A tongue or index of a scale or balance. L16. ►**d** A slender, usu. pointed, indicator on a dial or other measuring instrument, *spec*. on a speedometer. E20.
3 a A pointed instrument used in engraving or etching. M17. ►**b** In a breech-loading firearm, a slender steel pin by the impact of which a cartridge is exploded. M19. ►**c** A thin sharply pointed hollow attachment for the end of a hypodermic syringe or other injector; *slang* (orig. *US*) an injection of a drug through such a needle, a quantity of a drug for injection. L19. ►**d** A thin pointed or tapering rod used to secure fine adjustment in closing an aperture, as in a valve. L19. ►**e** A small pointed jewel or piece of metal, wood, etc., for resting in the groove of a revolving gramophone record to receive and transmit the vibrations set up; a similar device used to cut grooves in records; a stylus. E20.
4 A fit of bad temper or nervousness (freq. in ***the needle***); anger, enmity; *esp*. in SPORT, antagonism provoked by rivalry. *slang*. L19.
1 ***darning-needle***, ***larding-needle***, ***sewing-needle***, etc.
►**II 5** An obelisk, a pillar. Chiefly in proper names. LME.
6 A sharply pointed mass of rock, a peak. Chiefly in proper names. LME.
7 A beam or post of wood, *esp*. one used as a temporary support for a wall during underpinning. LME.
8 The penis. *coarse slang*. Now *rare*. M17.
9 CHEMISTRY & MINERALOGY. A long narrow pointed crystal or spicule. E18.
10 Any of the sharp stiff slender leaves characteristic of conifers. L18.
11 *sing*. & in *pl*. = ***shepherd's needle*** s.v. SHEPHERD *noun*. L18.
5 ***Cleopatra's Needle*** etc.
Phrases: **get the needle** become angry or upset, lose one's temper. **look for a needle in a haystack**, **look for a needle in a bottle of hay**, & vars., attempt an extremely difficult, impossible, or foolish task. ***naked as a needle***: see NAKED *adjective*. ***pins and needles***: see PIN *noun*¹. ***sharp as a needle***: see SHARP *adjective*. ***shepherd's needle***: see SHEPHERD *noun*. **the eye of a needle** = ***needle's eye*** below. ***variation of the needle***: see VARIATION 8. ***Whitechapel needle***: see WHITECHAPEL 2.
Comb.: **needle-and-pin** *rhyming slang* gin; **needle-and-thread** *rhyming slang* bread; **needle-beam** = sense 7 above; **needle bearing** a bearing using needle rollers; **needle beer** *US slang* (a drink of) liquor made (more) alcoholic by the addition of ethyl alcohol; **needle biopsy** MEDICINE removal of tissue with a hollow needle for analysis and diagnosis; **needle-book** a needle-case resembling a small book; **needle-bug** = ***water measurer*** s.v. WATER *noun*; **needle-bush** any of various Australian shrubs or small trees of the genus *Hakea* (family Proteaceae), with stiff needle-like leaves, esp. *H. leucoptera* and *H. tephrosperma*; **needle-case** a case for keeping needles in; **needle-cast** any of several fungal diseases of conifers, causing the leaves to go brown and drop off; *esp*. = ***larch needle-cast*** s.v. LARCH *noun*¹; **needle contest** = ***needle match*** below; **needlecord** *adjective & noun* (of) a finely ribbed corduroy; **needlecraft** the art of using a needle for sewing, embroidering, etc., skill in needlework; **needle exchange** a public health service which makes sterile hypodermic needles available to drug users; a place or building in which such a service is based; **needle fight** a closely contested fight, a fight arousing exceptional personal antagonism between the participants; **needlefish** any of various elongated fishes, esp. garfishes; **needle furze** petty whin, *Genista anglica*; **needle game** a closely contested game, a game arousing exceptional personal antagonism between the participants; **needle gap** ELECTRICITY a pair of needle-shaped electrodes placed in line, separated by a gap across which an electric discharge can take place when the potential difference between them exceeds a value

dependent on the size of the gap; **needle-grass** any of various long-awned grasses of the genera *Aristida* and *Stipa*, of dry areas in the south-western US; **needle-gun** a gun in which a cartridge is exploded by the impact of a needle; **needle ice** ice formed into thin needle-like crystals just beneath the soil surface and often pushing up through it; **needle-lace** lace made with a needle, as opp. to bobbin-lace, point lace; **needleloom** *noun & adjective* (*a*) *noun* a loom with needles rather than shuttles, *esp.* one for making carpeting by forcing fibre through a base of rubber, hessian, etc.; (*b*) *adjective* made using such a loom; **needleman** (*a*) *arch.* a man who works with a needle, *esp.* a tailor; (*b*) *US slang* (usu. ***needle-man***) a drug addict, *esp.* a person addicted to injecting drugs; **needle match** a closely contested match or contest, a contest arousing exceptional personal antagonism between the participants; **needle paper** stout black paper of a type orig. used for wrapping up needles; **needlepoint** (*a*) the point of a needle; a fine sharp point; (*b*) = ***needle-lace*** above; (*c*) embroidery worked over canvas, esp. *gros point* or *petit point*; **needle-pointed** *adjective* having a point like that of a needle, sharply pointed; **needle roller** a roller in the form of a long thin, sometimes tapered cylinder, used in roller bearings; **needle's eye** a minute opening or space (chiefly in echoes of *Matthew* 19:24 etc.); **needle shower** a shower-bath of strong fine jets of water; †**needlestone** MINERALOGY any of various minerals having needle-like crystals; **needle-threader** a device for threading a needle; **needle time** an agreed limited amount of time for broadcasting recorded music; **needle valve** a valve worked by a narrow pointed rod fitting into a conical seating; **needle-whin** = ***needle-furze*** above; **needlewoman** (*a*) a woman who works with a needle, a seamstress; (*b*) a woman who is *good*, *bad*, etc., at using a sewing-needle; **needle-wood** = ***needle-bush*** above; **needlework** (*a*) work done with a needle; sewing or embroidery; (*b*) (now *rare*) a piece or kind of this work (usu. in *pl.*); **needleworker** a worker with a needle, a sewer or embroiderer.

■ **needle-like** *adjective* resembling a needle in shape; long, slender, and pointed: L17.

needle /ˈniːd(ə)l/ *verb.* L16.
[from the noun.]
▶ **I** *verb trans.* **1** Underpin with needle-beams. L16.
2 Provide with a needle or needles. *rare.* M17.
3 Sew (*up*) or pierce with or as with a needle; apply a needle or needles to, esp. in acupuncture. E18.
4 Shape or point like a needle. Chiefly as ***needled*** *ppl adjective.* L18.
5 Pass or lead or thread (one's way) through or in and out like a needle. M19.
6 Annoy, irritate; goad; provoke into anger. *colloq.* L19.
7 Add ethyl alcohol to (liquor). Freq. as ***needled*** *ppl adjective*, designating beers. *US slang.* E20.

> 🕮 **6** G. B. SHAW Old Indian women get 'fairly needled' at the spectacle of their houses . . being burnt. R. CHRISTIANSEN She hectored and needled him to renounce his 'paganism'. **7** D. RUNYON It is sleeping so sound that I . . figure that Butch must give it . . needled beer.

▶ **II** *verb intrans.* **8** Use a needle, sew. L18.
9 Pass through or in and out like a needle; penetrate or prick like a needle. M19.

> 🕮 **9** R. B. PARKER The rain . . needled at my face as I ran.

needleful /ˈniːd(ə)lfʊl, -f(ə)l/ *noun.* L16.
[from NEEDLE *noun* + -FUL.]
The amount of thread which can be conveniently used at one time with a needle.

needler /ˈniːdlə/ *noun.* ME.
[from NEEDLE *noun, verb* + -ER¹.]
1 A person who makes needles. ME.
2 A person who annoys, goads, or provokes others to anger. *colloq.* M20.

needless /ˈniːdlɪs/ *adjective & adverb.* ME.
[from NEED *noun* + -LESS.]
▶ **A** *adjective.* **1** Not needed or wanted; unnecessary, useless, uncalled for. ME.
†**2** Not in need, not needy. LME–M17.

> 🕮 **1** J. STEINBECK He had never before spent a needless penny. K. M. E. MURRAY He did waste an enormous amount of time in writing needless . . letters. **needless to say** (parenthetically) as it is unnecessary to say, as will already have been deduced.

▶†**B** *adverb.* Without any compulsion or necessity; needlessly. ME–L15.
■ **needlessly** *adverb* in a needless or unnecessary manner, without necessity LME. **needlessness** *noun* E17.

needly /ˈniːdli/ *adjective. rare.* L17.
[from NEEDLE *noun* + -Y¹.]
Resembling a needle or needles.

needment /ˈniːdm(ə)nt/ *noun.* L16.
[from NEED *noun* or *verb* + -MENT.]
1 A thing needed, a necessary thing; *esp.* a personal requisite carried as luggage. Usu. in *pl. arch.* L16.
2 A need, a requirement. Usu. in *pl.* Now *Scot. rare.* E17.

needs /niːdz/ *adverb.* OE.
[from NEED *noun* + -S³, later identified with -S¹.]
Of necessity, necessarily. Now *rare* exc. in clauses containing *must* (*arch.* exc. as below).
must needs *spec.* (*a*) foolishly insist(s) or insisted on (foll. by *do*); (*b*) = ***needs must*** (a) below. **needs must** (*a*) cannot or could not help or avoid or get out of (foll. by *do*); (*b*) *ellipt.* it is or was necessary, one has or had to (esp. in proverb ***needs must when the Devil drives***). **will needs**, **would needs** *arch.* am, is, was, etc., determined (foll. by *do*).

needy /ˈniːdi/ *adjective & noun.* ME.
[from NEED *noun* + -Y¹.]
▶ **A** *adjective.* **1** Of a person: poor, destitute, without necessaries. ME. ▶†**b** In need *of.* M16–E17.
†**2** Needful, necessary. ME–E17.
3 Of circumstances etc.: characterized by poverty or need. L16.

> 🕮 **1** Z. TOMIN Parcels from America were still distributed . . for needy victims of war. M. M. R. KHAN I supported him financially whenever he was very needy. **3** O. W. HOLMES Some person in needy circumstances who wishes to make a living by the pen. *New Statesman* Targeting additional resources . . to the most needy council estates.

▶ **B** *absol.* as *noun. The* poor or destitute as a class. ME.

> 🕮 E. WAUGH I distribute food to the needy.

■ **neediness** *noun* LME.

Néel /ˈneɪəl/ *noun.* M20.
[L. E. F. *Néel* (1904–2000), French physicist.]
PHYSICS. Used *attrib.* to designate phenomena connected with Néel's work on magnetism.
Néel point the transition temperature for an antiferromagnetic or ferrimagnetic substance, above which it is paramagnetic (analogous to the Curie point for ferromagnetics). **Néel spike** a sharply pointed triangular domain next to a small hole or inclusion in a magnetic substance. **Néel temperature** = ***Néel point*** above. **Néel wall** a domain boundary in a thin layer of magnetic material across which the rotation of the field direction occurs in the plane of the layer.

neem /niːm/ *noun.* Also **nim**. E19.
[Hindi *nīm* from Sanskrit *nimba*.]
A tree, *Azadirachta indica* (family Meliaceae), valued in the Indian subcontinent esp. for its leaves and bitter bark which are used medicinally, and for the oil of its seeds which is used in soaps. Also called ***margosa***.

neencephalon /niːɛnˈsɛf(ə)lɒn, -ˈkɛf-/ *noun. rare.* E20.
[from NE(O- + ENCEPHALON.]
ANATOMY. The more recently evolved part of the brain, comprising the cerebral cortex and related structures.
■ **neenceˈphalic** *adjective* E20.

neep /niːp/ *noun. Scot. & north.* OE.
[Latin *napus*.]
A turnip. Now *esp.*, a swede.

ne'er /nɛː/ *adverb.* Now *poet. & dial.* ME.
[Contr.]
Never.
ne'er a never a, not a, no. **ne'er the less** nevertheless.

Ne'erday /ˈnɛːdeɪ/ *noun. Scot.* M19.
[Contr. of *NEW YEAR's Day*.]
New Year's Day.

ne'er-do-well /ˈnɛːduːˌwɛl, -dʊ-/ *noun & adjective.* Orig. *Scot.* Also **-weel** /-ˌwiːl/. M18.
[from NE'ER + DO *verb* + WELL *adverb.*]
(A person who is) good-for-nothing.

neeze /niːz/ *verb & noun. obsolete* exc. *Scot. & north.* ME.
[Old Norse *hnjósa* = Old High German *niosan*, Middle Low German *niesen* (German *niesen*, Dutch *niezen*), of imit. origin. Cf. SNEEZE.]
▶ **A** *verb intrans.* Sneeze. ME.
▶ **B** *noun.* A sneeze. M17.

nef /nɛf/ *noun.* Pl. pronounced same. L17.
[French = ship, nave, formed as NAVE *noun*².]
†**1** The nave of a church. L17–L18.
2 A usu. intricate receptacle in the shape of a ship for holding table napkins, condiments, etc. M19.

nefandous /nɪˈfandəs/ *adjective.* Now *rare.* M17.
[from Latin *nefandus*, from *ne-* not + *fandus* gerundive of *fari* speak: see -OUS.]
Not to be spoken of; unmentionable; abominable, atrocious.

nefarious /nɪˈfɛːrɪəs/ *adjective.* E17.
[from Latin *nefarius*, from *nefas* wrong, wickedness, from *ne-* not + *fas* divine permission, command, or law: see -OUS.]
Wicked, iniquitous, villainous.
■ **nefariously** *adverb* L16. **nefariousness** *noun* E18.

nefast /nɪˈfɑːst/ *adjective. rare.* M19.
[Latin *nefastus*, from *nefas*: see prec.]
Nefarious.

neg /nɛg/ *noun. colloq.* L19.
[Abbreviation.]
= NEGATIVE *noun*; *spec.* a negative photograph.

> 🕮 I. RANKIN He held the negs up to the light, but couldn't make out much.

nega- /ˈnɛgə/ *combining form. colloq.* L20.
[Abbreviation of NEGATIVE *adjective*.]
Denoting the negative counterpart of a unit of measurement, *spec.* a unit of energy saved as a result of conservation measures.
■ **negawatt** *noun* a unit of electricity which has been saved by energy conservation measures L20.

negate /nɪˈgeɪt/ *verb trans.* E17.
[Latin *negat-* pa. ppl stem of *negare* say no, deny, from *neg-*: see NEGLECT *verb*, -ATE³.]
1 Deny; deny the existence of; destroy, nullify, make ineffective. E17.
2 GRAMMAR. Turn into the negative. M20.

> 🕮 **1** B. NEIL Ben negated Eric's existence by never referring to him. L. GORDON Eliot set himself to negate the senses . . in order to become a vacuum for grace.

¶ Rare before M19.

negater /nɪˈgeɪtə/ *noun.* M20.
[from prec. + -ER¹. Cf. NEGATOR.]
COMPUTING. = INVERTER 2C.

negation /nɪˈgeɪʃ(ə)n/ *noun.* LME.
[Old & mod. French *négation* or Latin *negatio(n-)*, formed as prec.: see -ATION.]
1 The action of contradicting a statement or allegation, the making of a statement involving the use of a negative word, as 'no', 'not', 'never', etc., (foll. by *of*). Also, an instance of this; a negative statement, doctrine, etc.; a refusal, a contradiction; a denial (*of*). LME. ▶**b** In LOGIC, (an) assertion that a proposition is false; in COMPUTING, = INVERSION 15. L16.
2 The absence or opposite of a thing which is actual, positive, or affirmative. M17.
3 A negative or unreal thing, a nonentity; a thing whose essence consists in the absence of something positive. E18.
Comb.: **negation-sign** LOGIC a sign or symbol used to indicate negation.
■ **negational** *adjective* negative, using or involving negation M19. **negationist** *noun* = NEGATIVIST *noun* M19.

negatival /nɛgəˈtʌɪv(ə)l/ *adjective.* M20.
[from next + -AL¹.]
Negative; negativistic; characterized by negation.

negative /ˈnɛgətɪv/ *noun.* LME.
[Old & mod. French *négative* or late Latin *negativa* use as noun (sc. *sententia*, *propositio*) of fem. of *negativus* adjective: see next. Partly directly from the adjective.]
▶ **I** †**1** A negative command, a prohibition. LME–L16.
2 A negative statement or proposition; a negative mode of stating something. LME.
3 A negative reply or answer. Formerly also (a) denial, (a) refusal. M16.
4 A negative word or particle; a negative term. L16.
5 *The* side, position, or aspect of a question which is opposed to the affirmative or positive side etc.; *the* mode of expression in which proposals or suggestions are rejected. L16.
†**6** The right to refuse consent; a right of veto. Also, a negative or adverse vote. E17–L18.
▶ **II 7** The opposite or negation *of* something. *rare.* LME.
8 A negative quality or characteristic. M17.
9 MATH. A negative quantity. E18.
10 PHOTOGRAPHY. A developed image made on film, prepared glass, etc., showing the lights and shades (and colour values) reversed from those of the original, and from which positive prints may be made. M19.
11 The negative electrode of a voltaic cell or battery. L19.
12 A mould for, or reverse impression of, a piece of sculpture etc. E20.
13 A disc similar to a gramophone record but having ridges in place of grooves. E20.
Phrases: ***double negative***: see DOUBLE *adjective & adverb.* **in the negative** †(*a*) on the negative side of a question; (*b*) in rejection of a proposal or suggestion; with denial or negation, negatively; so as to say 'no'. ***negative pregnant***: see PREGNANT *adjective*¹.

negative /ˈnɛgətɪv/ *adjective & interjection.* LME.
[Old & mod. French *négatif*, *-ive* or late Latin *negativus*, formed as NEGATE: see -IVE.]
▶ **A** *adjective.* **I** Opp. AFFIRMATIVE *adjective.*
†**1** Of a person: making denial of something. *rare.* LME–M18.
2 Expressing, conveying, or implying negation or denial. LME. ▶**b** *spec.* in LOGIC. Expressing the disagreement of the terms of a proposition. M16.
3 Of a command, statute, etc.: prohibitory. E16. ▶**b** Expressing refusal; refusing consent. M16. ▶**c** Able to impose a veto. Long *rare.* M17.
4 THEOLOGY. = APOPHATIC. M20.
▶ **II** Opp. POSITIVE *adjective* III.
5 Consisting in, characterized by, or expressing the absence or lack of features or qualities, rather than their presence. Also, consisting in or characterized by unhelpful or destructive attitudes; pessimistic, defeatist. M16. ▶**b** Of evidence, an experimental result, etc.: providing no support for a particular hypothesis, esp. one concerning the presence or existence of something. Of a test or experiment, or the subject of one: producing such a result (freq. *postpositive* in comb.). L18. ▶**c** *attrib.* Not any, no. *colloq.* L20.

6 Of a quantity: less than zero, to be subtracted, not positive. **L17.** ▸**b** Reckoned, situated, or tending in a direction opposite to the positive and taken as the direction of decrease or reversal. **E19.**

7 Orig., designating that form of electricity produced by friction on resin, wax, rubber, etc. (= RESINOUS 5). Now, designating electric charge, potential, etc., having the same polarity as that electrode of a voltaic cell towards which the current is held to flow (and away from which the actual flow of electrons occurs); possessing such charge. **M18.** ▸**b** Designating a south-seeking pole of a magnet; having the polarity of the earth's north pole. **M19.**

8 *OPTICS.* Of, pertaining to, or displaying birefringence in which the refractive index of the extraordinary ray is less than that of the ordinary ray. **M19.**

9 Of a visual image, esp. a photograph: showing the lights and shades (and colour values) reversed from those of the original. **M19.**

10 Of, pertaining to, or designating a mould or reverse impression of an object. **E20.**

> 🕮 **5** J. BARZUN The effort to please becomes negative—the avoidance . . of pain. I. WALLACE He had been shackled by countless negative fears. D. FRANCIS The negative attitude which erects a barrier against sympathy. B. MOORE I don't want to be negative, but I don't see how we could get away. **b** *rhesus negative* etc.

Special collocations & comb.: **negative capability** (orig., the poet John Keats' term for) the ability to accept lack of knowledge and certainty, regarded as a quality of the creative artist; now also, empathy. ***negative catalysis***: see CATALYSIS 2. **negative equity** the indebtedness that occurs when the value of a property falls to below the outstanding amount of a mortgage secured on it. **negative eugenics** the practice of attempting to prevent the birth of children considered likely to be defective, degenerate, or of unfit parentage. ***negative FEEDBACK***. **negative glow** *PHYSICS* a luminous region in a low-pressure discharge tube between the Crookes dark space and the Faraday dark space. **negative-going** *adjective* increasing in magnitude in the direction of negative polarity; becoming less positive or more negative. **negative growth** *BIOLOGY* the cessation or reversal of growth in an organism in response to starvation or other unfavourable conditions. ***negative income tax***: see INCOME *noun*[1]. **negative instance** an instance of the non-occurrence of something. ***negative pedal***: see PEDAL *noun*[1] 4. **negative pole** the south-seeking pole of a magnet. **negative resistance** the phenomenon or property whereby an increase in the potential difference across the terminals of certain electrical devices (e.g. an arc lamp) causes a drop in the current flowing. **negative sign** = *MINUS sign*. **negative transfer** the transfer of effects from the learning of one skill which hinder the learning of another. **negative transference** transference of negative or hostile feelings, esp. (*PSYCHOANALYSIS*) in a patient's perception, from the patient to the analyst. **negative virtue** abstention from vice.

▸**B** *interjection.* No. Chiefly *N. Amer.* (orig. *MILITARY*). **M20.**

▪ **negatively** *adverb* **LME.** **negativeness** *noun* **L17.**

negative /ˈnɛɡətɪv/ *verb trans.* **E18.**
[from the adjective.]

1 Reject (a person) for some office; vote against; veto. *US.* **E18.**

2 Refuse to accept, act on, consider, or countenance. **L18.**

3 Disprove, show to be false; deny, contradict. **L18.**

4 Make ineffective, neutralize; negate, cancel. **M19.**

negativism /ˈnɛɡətɪvɪz(ə)m/ *noun.* **E19.**
[from NEGATIVE *adjective* + -ISM.]

1 The habit or practice of denying any accepted belief or assertion; the tendency to be negative in attitude or action; extreme scepticism, criticism, etc. **E19.**

2 *PSYCHOLOGY.* Resistance to attempts to impose a change of activity or posture, characteristic of various neuropsychiatric disorders. **L19.**

negativist /ˈnɛɡətɪvɪst/ *noun & adjective.* **L19.**
[from NEGATIVE *adjective* + -IST.]

▸**A** *noun.* A person who denies any accepted belief or assertion. **L19.**

▸**B** *attrib.* or as *adjective.* Of or pertaining to negativism or negativists. **E20.**

▪ **negatiˈvistic** *adjective* characterized by or of the nature of negativism **E20.**

negativity /nɛɡəˈtɪvɪti/ *noun.* **M19.**
[from NEGATIVE *adjective* + -ITY.]
The fact or quality of being negative.

> 🕮 J. CAIRD That universal negativity or nothingness which pertains to all finite agents. P. CAREY It's all so depressing and ugly. I can't stand all this negativity. *Times* The negativity of the finding . . was perhaps the light at the end of the tunnel.

negaton /ˈnɛɡətɒn/ *noun.* **E20.**
[from NEGAT(IVE *adjective* + -ON.]
PHYSICS. = NEGATRON 2.

negator /nɪˈɡeɪtə/ *noun.* **E19.**
[from NEGATE + -OR. Cf. NEGATER.]

1 A person who denies something. **E19.**

2 A word or particle expressing negation; = NEGATIVE *noun* 4. **M20.**

3 = NEGATER. **M20.**

negatory /ˈnɛɡət(ə)ri/ *adjective.* **L16.**
[French *négatoire* or late Latin *negatorius*, formed as NEGATE: see -ORY[2].]
Of the nature of or expressing negation.

negatron /ˈnɛɡətrɒn/ *noun.* **E20.**
[from NEGA(TIVE *adjective* + -TRON.]

1 *ELECTRONICS.* A valve with negative resistance, having an anode on one side of the cathode and a control grid and second anode on the other side. Now *rare.* **E20.**

2 *PHYSICS.* An ordinary negatively charged electron (as distinct from a positron). Also called ***negaton***. **M20.**

negentropy /nɛˈɡɛntrəpi/ *noun.* **M20.**
[from NEG(ATIVE *adjective* + ENTROPY.]
Negative entropy, as a measure of order or information.

▪ **negenˈtropic** *adjective* **M20.**

neger /ˈniːɡə/ *noun & adjective. obsolete* exc. *Scot. & north. derog. & racially offensive.* **L16.**
[French *nègre* from Spanish *negro* NEGRO.]

▸**A** *noun.* = NEGRO *noun* 1. **L16.**

▸**B** *adjective.* = NEGRO *adjective.* **M17.**

neglect /nɪˈɡlɛkt/ *noun.* **L16.**
[from (the same root as) next, partly after Latin *neglectus*.]

1 The fact of neglecting a person or thing; the fact or condition of being neglected; disregard *of*; negligence. **L16.**

2 An instance of negligence; an omission, an oversight. Now *rare.* **M17.**

> 🕮 **1** BURKE Neglect, contumely, and insult, were never the ways of keeping friends. A. C. BOULT The apathetic neglect that England maintains towards all American composers. P. GROSSKURTH Emanuel . . was constantly reminding her of her neglect in not writing to him. I. MCEWAN How rapidly a home perishes through neglect. ***benign neglect***: see BENIGN 2. **2** M. TWAIN You must try to overlook these . . little neglects on my part.

neglect /nɪˈɡlɛkt/ *verb trans.* Pa. pple & ppl adjective. **neglected**, (earlier) †**neglect**. **LME.**
[Latin *neglect-* pa. ppl stem of *neglegere* disregard, slight, from *neg-* var. of *nec* not + *legere* choose.]

1 Disregard; pay little or no respect or attention to; slight, leave unnoticed. **LME.**

2 Fail to give proper attention to, fail to take proper or necessary care of; leave unattended to or uncared for. **M16.**

3 Fail to perform, leave undone, be remiss about; fail through carelessness or negligence *to do*, omit *doing*. **M16.**

†**4** Cause (something) to be neglected. **L16–E17.**

> 🕮 **1** E. M. FORSTER If it is Mrs Grundy who is troubling you . . you can neglect the good person. M. GIROUARD They have been largely neglected by art historians as . . of no interest. **2** M. MOORCOCK I had neglected my work at the very time I should have been concentrating on it. C. ANGIER She went to see her father's grave and found it neglected, covered with weeds. **3** STEELE I did not neglect spending a considerable Time in the Crowd. D. CARNEGIE They were so busy with their own affairs that they neglected to write. **4** SHAKES. *Rich. III* I trust My absence doth neglect no great design.

▪ **neglectable** *adjective* that may be neglected, negligible **L19.** **neglectedly** *adverb* (now *rare*) (*a*) in a neglected manner; (*b*) negligently: **M17.** **neglectedness** *noun* (now *rare*) the state or condition of being neglected **M17.** **neglecter** *noun* **L16.** **neglecting** *ppl adjective* guilty of neglect **E17.** †**neglectingly** *adverb* negligently, neglectfully **L16–E17.** **neglector** *noun* **E17.**

neglectful /nɪˈɡlɛk(t)fʊl, -f(ə)l/ *adjective.* **E17.**
[from NEGLECT *noun* + -FUL.]
Characterized by neglect or inattention; negligent, heedless, careless. (Foll. by *of.*)

> 🕮 JAS. MILL A government at once insatiable and neglectful. H. ROBBINS He followed Gordon . . to his car, neglectful of the rain that was falling on him. R. COBB She was getting rather untidy and . . neglectful of her appearance.

▪ **neglectfully** *adverb* **M17.** **neglectfulness** *noun* **L17.**

neglection /nɪˈɡlɛkʃ(ə)n/ *noun.* Long *obsolete* exc. *dial.* **L16.**
[Latin *neglectio(n-)*, formed as NEGLECT *verb*: see -ION.]
Negligence, neglect.

neglective /nɪˈɡlɛktɪv/ *adjective.* Now *rare* or *obsolete.* **E17.**
[from NEGLECT *verb* + -IVE.]
Neglectful, inattentive. (Foll. by *of.*)

▪ **neglectively** *adverb* **E17.**

néglig̃é *noun* var. of NEGLIGÉE.

negligeable /ˈnɛɡlɪdʒəb(ə)l/ *adjective.* Now *rare.* **L19.**
[French *négligeable*, from *négliger* neglect: see -ABLE.]
Negligible.

negligée /ˈnɛɡlɪʒeɪ/ *noun.* Also **negligee**, **négligé** /*also foreign* neɡliʒe (*pl. same*)/. **E18.**
[French *négligé* pa. pple of *négliger* neglect.]

1 Informal, unceremonious, or incomplete attire. **E18.**

2 *Hist.* A kind of loose gown worn by women in the 18th cent. **M18.**

3 A shroud. *US.* **E20.**

4 A woman's light dressing-gown, *esp.* one of flimsy semi-transparent fabric trimmed with ruffles, lace, etc. **M20.**

negligence /ˈnɛɡlɪdʒ(ə)ns/ *noun.* **ME.**
[Old & mod. French *négligence* or Latin *negligentia*, formed as next: see -ENCE.]

1 Lack of attention to what ought to be done; failure to take proper or necessary care of a thing or person; lack of necessary or reasonable care in doing something; carelessness. (Foll. by †*of*.) **ME.** ▸**b** Disregard of a thing or person; failure to take notice. **E17.**

2 An instance of inattention or carelessness; a negligent act, a careless omission. **LME.**

3 Orig., a careless indifference, as in appearance or dress or in literary or artistic style. Later, freedom from artificiality or restraint. **LME.**

> 🕮 **1** S. JOHNSON Imputing every deficience to criminal negligence. E. TAYLOR Leaving things lying about—a habit of infuriating negligence. *Which?* The accident was clearly caused by negligence. ***contributory negligence***: see CONTRIBUTORY *adjective* 2. **3** ADDISON Nothing is so modish as an agreeable Negligence.

▪ **negligency** *noun* (*rare*) **L15.**

negligent /ˈnɛɡlɪdʒ(ə)nt/ *adjective & noun.* **ME.**
[Old & mod. French *négligent* or Latin *negligent-* pres. ppl stem of *negligere* var. of *neglegere*: see NEGLECT *verb*, -ENT.]

▸**A** *adjective.* **1** Inattentive to what ought to be done; failing to take proper, necessary, or reasonable care; guilty of negligence. (Foll. by *of.*) **ME.** ▸**b** Heedless, indifferent. *rare.* **LME.**

2 Characterized by or displaying negligence or carelessness. **E16.** ▸**b** Due to negligence. *rare.* **E17.**

> 🕮 **1** G. W. CABLE He was a great student and rather negligent of his business. B. GUEST The forsaken wife who now controlled the fate of the negligent husband. *Woman & Home* People . . will no longer have to prove . . a company was negligent—just that their drug caused the injury. **2** SIR W. SCOTT All loose her negligent attire. H. B. STOWE The person . . with a haughty, negligent air. *Daily Telegraph* Joseph Kennedy . . was fined . . for negligent driving. **b** SHAKES. *Ant. & Cl.* Till we perceiv'd both how you were wrong led And we in negligent danger.

▸**B** *noun.* **1** A negligent person. **LME.**

2 *Hist.* A type of wig worn in the 18th cent. **M18.**

▪ **negligently** *adverb* **ME.**

negligible /ˈnɛɡlɪdʒɪb(ə)l/ *adjective.* **E19.**
[French †*négligible*, from *négliger* neglect: see -IBLE. Cf. NEGLIGEABLE.]
Able to be neglected or disregarded; unworthy of notice or regard; so small or insignificant as to be ignorable.

> 🕮 J. F. W. HERSCHEL Within very negligible limits of error. A. T. ELLIS He found me too negligible to bother to disguise his ennui. Z. TOMIN We may appear ludicrously pretentious; our numbers negligible. **negligible quantity** a person who or thing which need not be considered.

▪ **negligiˈbility** *noun* **E20.** **negligibleness** *noun* **E20.** **negligibly** *adverb* **L19.**

négoce /neɡɔs/ *noun. rare.* **E17.**
[French from Latin *negotium*: see NEGOTIATE.]
sing. & †in *pl.* Business, commerce.

†**negociable** *adjective*, **negociant** *noun* vars. of NEGOTIABLE, NEGOTIANT.

négociant /neɡɔsjɑ̃/ *noun.* Pl. pronounced same. **E20.**
[French = merchant (sc. *des vins*), formed as NÉGOCE: see -ANT[1]. Cf. NEGOTIANT.]
A wine merchant.

†**negociate** *verb*, **negociation** *noun*, etc., vars. of NEGOTIATE, NEGOTIATION, etc.

negotiable /nɪˈɡəʊʃəb(ə)l, -ʃɪə-/ *adjective.* Also †**negoci-**. **M18.**
[from NEGOTIATE + -ABLE. Cf. French *négociable*.]

1 *COMMERCE.* Of a bill, draft, cheque, etc.: transferable or assignable in the course of business from one person to another simply by delivery. **M18.**

2 Of an obstacle: admitting of being crossed or being got over, round, or through. **L19.**

3 Able to be decided or arranged by negotiation or mutual agreement; subject to negotiation; subject to modification of meaning or interpretation. **M20.**

> 🕮 **1** G. LORD Honey . . sold easily; it was almost as negotiable as . . gold. *Independent* Make all cheques payable to the account only and not negotiable. **2** C. RYAN Sand and small streams made the area barely negotiable even for reconnaissance vehicles. **3** *Morning Star* Jack Lynch . . said that the constitution of a future United Ireland was negotiable. M. IGNATIEFF The more negotiable . . the past becomes, the more intense its hold. *Daily Telegraph* An excellent salary negotiable according to experience.

▪ **negotiaˈbility** *noun* **E19.**

negotiant /nɪˈɡəʊʃ(ə)nt, -ʃɪə-/ *noun.* Also †**negoci-**. **E17.**
[Latin *negotiant-* pres. ppl stem of *negotiare*: see next, -ANT[1]. Partly from French NÉGOCIANT.]
A person who conducts negotiations, a negotiator; an agent, a representative. Formerly also, a merchant, a trader.

negotiate /nɪˈɡəʊʃɪeɪt/ *verb.* Also †**negoci-**. **L16.**
[Latin *negotiat-* pa. ppl stem of *negotiari* carry on business, from *negotium* business, from *neg-* var. of *nec* not + *otium* leisure: see -ATE[3].]
1 *verb intrans.* **a** Communicate or confer (*with* another or others) for the purpose of arranging some matter by mutual agreement; have a discussion or discussions with a view to some compromise or settlement. **L16.** ▸†**b** Do business, engage in commerce. **L16–M18.**
2 *verb trans.* **a** Conduct a negotiation or negotiations about (a matter, affair, etc.). **E17.** ▸**b** Arrange for, obtain, or bring about by negotiation. **E18.**
3 *verb trans.* COMMERCE. ▸**a** Transfer or assign (a bill etc.) to another simply by delivery; convert into cash or notes; obtain or give value for (a bill, cheque, etc.) in money. **L17.** ▸**b** Deal with or carry out as a business or monetary transaction. **E19.**
4 *verb trans.* Clear (a hedge or fence) by jumping; cross, get over, round, or through (an obstacle, difficulty, etc.). **M19.**

🕮 **1a** H. T. BUCKLE Both parties were now willing to negotiate. B. MOORE You don't know a damn thing about . . negotiating with the government. P. FITZGERALD Cesare was doggedly negotiating for a low interest loan. **2a** M. DRAYTON That weightie Bus'nesse to negotiate. **b** R. THOMAS He was . . fluent and lawyer-like, negotiating an out-of-court settlement. **3b** W. M. CLARKE He was . . wrestling with the value of the remaining copyrights and finally decided to negotiate their sale himself. **4** E. L. RICE He . . negotiates the steps . . without too much difficulty. O. MANNING She had no memory of . . negotiating the traffic. J. FULLER Moving together at a variable pace to negotiate the terrain.

negotiation /nɪˌɡəʊʃɪˈeɪʃ(ə)n/ *noun.* Also †**negoci-**. **LME.**
[Latin *negotiatio(n-)*, formed as prec.: see -ATION. Cf. Old & mod. French *négociation*.]
†**1 a** An act of dealing with another person; a private or business transaction. **LME–E18.** ▸**b** Trading, commerce. **E–M17.**
2 A process or act of conferring with another or others to arrange some matter by mutual agreement, a discussion with a view to some compromise or settlement, orig. esp. in an affair of State. Freq. in *pl.* **M16.**
3 The action or process of negotiating with another or others, discussion with a view to settlement or compromise. **E17.**
4 The action of crossing or getting over, round, or through some obstacle. **L19.**

🕮 **2** *Guardian* Pay negotiations . . had broken down. E. KUZWAYO Meaningful negotiations with the government. *Business* It is not a negotiation when one person says 'this is what I want'. **3** H. KISSINGER These were subjects for negotiation; we were invited to make counterproposals. A. N. WILSON The fighting was brought to an end by negotiation.

negotiator /nɪˈɡəʊʃɪeɪtə/ *noun.* Also †**negoci-**. **L16.**
[Latin, formed as NEGOTIATE: see -OR.]
†**1** A trader, a businessman. **L16–E17.**
2 A person who conducts negotiations. **E17.**
3 A person who negotiates bills, loans, etc. **L17.**

negotiatory /nɪˈɡəʊʃət(ə)ri, -ʃɪə-/ *adjective. rare.* Also †**negoci-**. **E18.**
[from NEGOTIATE + -ORY[2].]
Of or pertaining to negotiation.

negotiatress /nɪˈɡəʊʃətrɪs, -ʃɪə-/ *noun.* **E19.**
[from NEGOTIATOR + -ESS[1].]
A female negotiator.

negotiatrix /nɪˈɡəʊʃətrɪks, -ʃɪə-/ *noun.* Also †**negoci-**. Pl. **-trices** /-trɪsiːz/, **-trixes**. **E17.**
[Late Latin, formed as NEGOTIATE: see -TRIX.]
A female negotiator.

Negress /ˈniːɡrɪs/ *noun.* Now considered *racially offensive*. Also **n-**. **L18.**
[French *négresse*, from *nègre* NEGRO: see -ESS[1].]
A female black person.

Negretti /nɪˈɡreti/ *noun.* Now chiefly *Hist.* **L18.**
[Spanish (*merino*) *negrete*, from NEGRO.]
(An animal of) a strain of merino sheep, formerly widespread, having relatively short wool and a wrinkled fleece.

Negri /ˈneɪɡriː/ *noun.* Also **n-**. **E20.**
[Adelchi *Negri* (1876–1912), Italian physician.]
MEDICINE. Used **attrib.** and (formerly) in **possess.** to designate eosinophilic cytoplasmic inclusion bodies characteristically found in the brain cells of people and animals infected with rabies.

negrification /ˌnɛɡrɪfɪˈkeɪʃ(ə)n/ *noun.* Also **N-**. **E20.**
[Irreg. from NEGRO: see -FICATION.]
The action or fact of increasing the number or influence of black people in something; placing something under the control of black people.

Negrillo /nɪˈɡrɪləʊ/ *noun.* Pl. **-os**. **M19.**
[Spanish, dim. of NEGRO.]
A member of a small-statured black people of central and southern Africa.

Negritic /niːˈɡrɪtɪk/ *adjective.* Also **n-**. **L19.**
[Irreg. from NEGRO + -ITIC. Cf. NIGRITIC.]
Of or pertaining to black people.

negritize /ˈnɛɡrɪtʌɪz/ *verb trans.* Also **N-**, **-ise**. **E20.**
[Irreg. from NEGRO or NEGRITIC + -IZE.]
Make Negroid or Negritic in character or appearance.

Negrito /nɪˈɡriːtəʊ/ *noun & adjective.* **E19.**
[Spanish, dim. of NEGRO.]
▶ **A** *noun.* Pl. **-o(e)s**. A member of a small-statured black people of the Austronesian region. **E19.**
▶ **B** *attrib.* or as *adjective.* Of or pertaining to this people. **M19.**

Negritude /ˈnɛɡrɪtjuːd/ *noun.* Also ***Négritude*** /negrityd/, **n-**. **M20.**
[French *négritude* formed as NIGRITUDE.]
The quality or characteristic of being a black person; affirmation of the value of black or African culture, identity, etc.

Negro /ˈniːɡrəʊ/ *noun & adjective.* Also **n-**. Now considered *racially offensive*. **M16.**
[Spanish & Portuguese from Latin *nigr-*, *niger* black.]
▶ **A** *noun.* Pl. **-oes**.
1 An individual (esp. a male) belonging to or descended from any of various peoples indigenous to Africa and characterized by black or dark skin, black tightly curled hair, and a broad flattish nose and full lips; a black person. **M16.**
2 Black English. Now *rare.* **E18.**
1 *New Negro*: see NEW *adjective*. *White Negro*: see WHITE *adjective*.
▶ **B** *attrib.* or as *adjective*: of, pertaining to, or characteristic of black people. **L16.**
Special collocations & comb.: **Negro cloth** *Hist.* coarse plain cloth intended to be worn by black slaves in America. **Negro dog** *Hist.* a dog used in hunting runaway black slaves in America. **Negro English** Black English. **Negroland** (now *arch. rare*) black Africa. **Negro minstrel** = ***blackface minstrel*** s.v. BLACK *adjective*. **Negro-Portuguese** *adjective & noun* (of) a pidginized form of Portuguese used as a trade language on the Atlantic coast of S. America. **Negro Renaissance** (the period of) an increase in artistic activity among American black people in the 1920s. **Negro's head** a tropical American palm, *Phytelephas macrocarpa*, the fruit of which is a source of vegetable ivory. **Negro spiritual** a religious song characteristic of the black people in the southern States of America. **Negro State** any of the Southern States of America in which slavery was legal. **Negro tamarin** a tamarin monkey *Saguinus midas*, of the lower Amazon. **Negro yam** *W. Indies* a coarse-textured yam, the tuber of *Dioscorea sativa*.
¶ Once a relatively neutral term, but now *black* is preferred when referring to people.
■ **Negrodom** *noun* (now *rare*) the region or community of black people. **M19.** **Negroish** *adjective* (now *rare*) suggestive or characteristic of black people **M18.** **Negroism** *noun* (*a*) advancement of the interests or rights of black people; (*b*) a pronunciation, expression, or idiom, characteristic of or restricted to Black English: **M19.** **Negroness** *noun* the state or quality of being black, black qualities and characteristics collectively **M20.**

negro-head /ˈniːɡrəʊhɛd/ *noun.* **L18.**
[from prec. + HEAD *noun*.]
†**1** A nest of tree-ants. *rare.* Only in **L18.**
2 In full ***negro-head tobacco***. Strong black tobacco for smoking. **E19.**
3 Indiarubber of an inferior quality. **L19.**
4 = NIGGERHEAD 2. **E20.**
Comb.: **negro-head beech** an Australian evergreen tree, *Nothofagus moorei*, related to the beech; ***negro-head tobacco***: see sense 2 above.

Negroid /ˈniːɡrɔɪd/ *adjective & noun.* Also **n-**. Now considered *racially offensive*. **M19.**
[from NEGRO + -OID.]
▶ **A** *adjective.* Resembling or having some of the characteristic physical features of black people. **M19.**
▶ **B** *noun.* A black person. **M19.**
■ **Neˈgroidal** *adjective* (now *rare*) **L19.**

negroni /nɪˈɡrəʊniː/ *noun.* Also **-ne**. **M20.**
[Italian.]
A drink made from gin, vermouth, and Campari.

Negrophile /ˈniːɡrəfʌɪl/ *noun.* Also **-phil** /-fɪl/, **n-**. **E19.**
[from NEGRO + -PHILE, -PHIL.]
A person who is friendly or well-disposed towards black people; a person who favours the advancement of the interests or rights of black people.
■ **Negrophilism** /nɪˈɡrɒfɪlɪz(ə)m/ *noun* friendliness towards black people, advocacy of the interests or rights of black people **M19.** **Negrophilist** /nɪˈɡrɒfɪlɪst/ *noun* = NEGROPHILE **M19.**

Negrophobe /ˈniːɡrəfəʊb/ *noun.* Also **n-**. **E20.**
[from NEGRO + -PHOBE.]
A person who has an intense aversion to or hatred of black people.
■ **Negroˈphobia** *noun* intense aversion to or hatred of black people **E19.**

Negus /ˈniːɡəs/ *noun*[1]. *obsolete* exc. *Hist.* **L16.**
[Amharic *nˈgus* kinged, king.]
(The title of) the supreme ruler of Ethiopia.

negus /ˈniːɡəs/ *noun*[2]. Pl. same. **M18.**
[Col. Francis *Negus* (d. 1732), its creator.]
Wine (esp. port or sherry) mixed with hot water, sweetened, and flavoured; a drink of this.

Neh. *abbreviation.*
Nehemiah (in the Bible).

Nehru /ˈnɛːruː/ *noun.* **M20.**
[Jawaharlal *Nehru* (see next), who often wore the style.]
In full ***Nehru jacket***. A long narrow jacket with a high stand-up collar.

Nehruvian /nɛːˈruːvɪən/ *adjective.* **M20.**
[from *Nehru* (see below), after *Peruvian*.]
Pertaining to or characteristic of Jawaharlal Nehru (1889–1964), first Prime Minister of independent India.

neif /niːf/ *noun. obsolete* exc. *Hist.* **M16.**
[Anglo-Norman *neif*, *nief* = Old French NAÏF.]
A person born in a state of bondage or serfdom.

neifty /ˈniːfti/ *noun. obsolete* exc. *Hist.* **L15.**
[Anglo-Norman *neifté*, formed as prec.: see -TY[1].]
The status of a neif. Chiefly in ***writ of neifty***, a writ by which a lord claimed a person as his neif.

neigh /neɪ/ *verb & noun.*
[Old English *hnǣgan* = Middle Dutch *neyen* (Dutch dial. *neijen*), Middle High German *nēgen*, of imit. origin.]
▶ **A** *verb.* **1** *verb intrans.* (Of a horse) make its characteristic prolonged cry or call; make a sound likened to this. **OE.**
2 *verb trans.* Utter in neighing, or with a sound like neighing. Now *rare.* **E17.**
▶ **B** *noun.* The prolonged natural cry or call of a horse; a sound likened to this. **E16.**
■ **neigher** *noun* (*rare*) a creature that neighs, a horse **M17.**

neighbor *noun & adjective, verb*, **neighborhood** *noun*, etc., see NEIGHBOUR *noun & adjective* etc.

neighbour /ˈneɪbə/ *noun & adjective.* Also ***-bor**.
[Old English *nēahġebūr*, *nēahhebūr*, from *nēah* NIGH *adverb* + *ġebūr* GEBUR (cf. BOOR), corresp. to Middle Dutch *nagebuer*, Old High German *nāhgibūr*. Cf. Old Saxon *nābūr*, Middle Low German, Middle Dutch *nabur*, Middle High German *nāchbūr* (German *Nachbar*, Old Norse *nábúi* (Swedish, Danish *nabo*), from *ná* NEAR *adverb*[2] + *búa* dwell. See -OUR.]
▶ **A** *noun.* **1** A person who lives near or next to another; a person who occupies a near or adjoining house, each of a number of people living close to each other, esp. in the same street or village. Freq., such a person regarded as one who should be friendly or as having a claim on the friendliness of others. Also (*obsolete* exc. *dial.*) used as a form of address. **OE.**
2 A person who lives in an adjoining or not far distant town, district, or country; the ruler of an adjacent country. Usu. in *pl.* **OE.**
3 A person or thing in close proximity to another; a person positioned near or next to another on some occasion. **LME.**
4 A thing which makes a pair with another. *Scot.* **M18.**

🕮 **1** J. K. GALBRAITH Churches have long featured the virtue of loving one's neighbour. B. GILROY Someone borrowed some smelling-salts from a neighbour, six doors away. ***beggar-my-neighbour***: see BEGGAR *verb* 1. GOOD NEIGHBOUR. **2** S. JOHNSON The Welsh . . insulted their English neighbours. **3** SHAKES. *Lucr.* His nose being shadowed by his neighbour's ear. D. FRANCIS The Updike residence was large but squashed by neighbours.

▶ **B** *attrib.* or as *adjective.* Living or situated near or close to some other person or thing, neighbouring, nearby. Formerly also, taking place between neighbours. **LME.**

🕮 R. ADAMS She . . nodded, smiling, towards the neighbour room. JAYNE PHILLIPS The neighbor woman at her elbow.

■ †**neighboured** *noun* [-RED] = NEIGHBOURHOOD **ME–L16.** **neighbouress** *noun* (*rare*) a female neighbour **LME.** **neighbourhead** *noun* (now *rare*) = NEIGHBOURHOOD **LME.**

neighbour /ˈneɪbə/ *verb.* Also ***-bor**. **M16.**
[from the noun.]
1 *verb trans.* As **neighboured** *pa. pple & ppl adjective*. Provided with neighbours or surroundings of a specified kind; (foll. by *by*, *with*) having a specified person or thing as a neighbour or close at hand. **M16.**
2 *verb trans.* Bring or place near *to* some person or thing; situate close together. Freq. in *pass.* **L16.** ▸**b** Place in conjunction *with* something. **M17.**
3 *verb trans.* Adjoin, touch, border on, be situated next or close to; live next or close to. **L16.** ▸**b** Come near to, approach. **M19.**
4 *verb intrans.* Of a person: live near to, *unto* a person, place, etc., (also foll. by *upon*). Also with *near*. Now *rare.* **L16.**
5 *verb intrans.* Of a thing or place: be situated next or close (*to*, *on*, or *upon*); be contiguous *with*. **L16.**
6 *verb trans.* with *it* & *intrans.* Be on neighbourly terms, associate in a friendly way *with*. **L16.**
■ **neighbourer** *noun* (*rare*) a neighbour **E17.**

neighbourhood /ˈneɪbəhʊd/ *noun*. Also ***-bor-**. LME.
[from NEIGHBOUR *noun* + -HOOD.]
1 Friendly relations between neighbours; neighbourly feeling or conduct. Cf. GOOD-NEIGHBOURHOOD. LME.
2 a The people living near to a certain place or within a certain range, neighbours; a community, a certain number of people who live close together. LME. ▸**b** A district or portion of a town, city, or country, esp. considered in reference to the character or circumstances of its inhabitants; a small but relatively self-contained sector of a larger urban area. L17.
3 The quality, condition, or fact of being neighbours or of being situated near to something; nearness. M16.
4 a The nearby or surrounding area, the vicinity, the near situation, (foll. by *of*). Chiefly after prepositions in ***the neighbourhood of***, somewhere close to (*lit.* & *fig.*), somewhere about. L16. ▸†**b** A nearby place. *rare* (Milton). Only in M17.
5 *MATH*. **a** The set of points whose distance from a given point is less than (or less than or equal to) some usu. small value. L19. ▸**b** Any open set containing a given point or non-empty set; any set containing such an open set. M20.

📖 **1** SWIFT The laws of charity, neighbourhood, alliance, and hospitality. E. HEWLETT Good neighbourhood does not require . . idle gossipping. **2a** GOLDSMITH The whole neighbourhood came out to meet their minister. COLERIDGE Men remain in the domestic state and form neighbourhoods, but not governments. **b** DICKENS It was a low neighbourhood; no help was near. *Country Life* One of London's greatest attractions is . . its village-like localities. In planning jargon these are called neighbourhoods. D. LEVERTOV They rose / and ran about the neighbourhood. **3** D. HUME The neighbourhood of the sun inflames the imagination of men.
4a N. HAWTHORNE Hillocks of waste . . disfigure the neighbourhood of iron-mongering towns. M. TWAIN The neighbourhood of that dental chair. K. B. MILLER Distances up to the neighbourhood of about 50 miles. *Daily Telegraph* The cost is going to be in the neighbourhood of £250m. a year.

Attrib. & comb.: In the sense 'belonging to a neighbourhood, serving a particular neighbourhood', as ***neighbourhood school***, ***neighbourhood shop***, etc. (***your friendly neighbourhood*** —: applied to a well-known and popular local person or thing (freq. *iron.*)). **neighbourhood watch** (a programme of) systematic vigilance by people to combat crime in their neighbourhood.
▪ **neighbouring** *adjective* that neighbours something or someone situated or living near, nearby, adjacent: L16. **neighbourless** *adjective* without a neighbour; solitary: M16. **neighbour-like** *adverb* & *adjective* (chiefly *Scot.*) (*a*) *adverb* in a neighbourly fashion; (*b*) *adjective* neighbourly, friendly, kindly: LME.

neighbourly /ˈneɪbəli/ *adjective*. Also ***-bor-**. M16.
[from NEIGHBOUR *noun* + -LY¹.]
Characteristic of or befitting a neighbour or neighbours; inclined to act as a neighbour; friendly, kindly.

📖 A. GHOSH They can't stand the sight of each other but their mamas have told them to be neighbourly. I. WELSH She catches me staring so I give a good neighbourly wave.

▪ **neighbourliness** *noun* M17.

neighbourship /ˈneɪbəʃɪp/ *noun*. Also ***-bor-**. ME.
[from NEIGHBOUR *noun* + -SHIP.]
1 Neighbourliness, neighbourly relations. Esp. in ***good neighbourship***, ***bad neighbourship***, etc. ME.
2 The state or fact of being a neighbour; nearness. LME.

Neil Robertson stretcher /niːəl ˌrɒbəts(ə)n ˈstretʃə/ *noun phr*. M20.
[App. from a personal name.]
A type of canvas stretcher to which a person can be strapped and lifted or lowered in an upright position.

neinei /ˈneɪneɪ/ *noun*. M19.
[Maori.]
A New Zealand shrub or small tree of the genus *Dracophyllum* (family Epacridaceae), having clusters of long, narrow leaves; esp. *D. latifolium*.

neisseria /nʌɪˈsɪərɪə/ *noun*. Pl. **-riae** /-rɪiː/. M20.
[mod. Latin (see below), from A. L. S. *Neisser* (1855–1916), German dermatologist and bacteriologist: see -IA¹.]
MICROBIOLOGY & MEDICINE. A bacterium of the genus *Neisseria* of aerobic, Gram-negative, parasitic or pathogenic diplococci, found esp. on mammalian mucous membranes and including gonococci and meningococci.

neither /ˈnʌɪðə, ˈniː-/ *adverb, conjunction, pronoun, & adjective* (in mod. usage also classed as a *determiner*).
[Old English *nawþer*, *nauþer* contr. of *nāhwæþer* (= Old Frisian *nahwedder*), formed as NA *adverb*¹ + WHETHER *adjective* etc., alt. early in Middle English after EITHER. Cf. NOTHER *pronoun* etc., NOUTHER.]
▶ **A** *adverb & conjunction*. **1** Followed by coordinate *nor*, *or*, †*neither*, introducing the first of two or more alternatives or different things: not either, not on the one hand. OE.
2 And not — either, nor yet, nor moreover, and not, also not. Now only introducing a clause or sentence with inversion of subject and verb. LME.
3 Strengthening a preceding negative (explicit or, formerly, implicit): any more than the other, likewise not. Cf. EITHER *adverb & conjunction* 5. M16. ▸**b** Introducing a reiteration (with pronouns and pro-forms of verbs) of a previous negative statement: indeed not, it is true that . . not. *colloq.* E20.

📖 **1** J. HERVEY Neither care disturbs their sleep, nor passion inflames their breast. SOUTHEY No respite neither by day nor night for this devoted city. G. W. DASENT Wasn't it true that he neither knew anything or could do anything? J. RUSKIN Neither painting nor fighting feed men. M. KEANE Jessica felt neither very well nor very kindly disposed towards Jane. A. JUDD He had neither the desire nor the time to rework old ground. ***neither here nor there***: see HERE *adverb*. ***neither more nor less than***: see MORE *adjective* etc.. **2** J. STRYPE Neither did he . . ever endeavour for it. **3** G. MEREDITH Lady Edbury would never see Roy-Richmond after that, nor the old lord neither. R. BUSBY 'Can you place either of them?' The young detective shook his head. 'Me neither'. **b** L. M. MONTGOMERY 'Davy declares he never saw her since I left.' 'Neither I did,' avowed Davy.

▶ **B** *pronoun*. Not either; not any one (of more than two). (Foll. by *of*: with sing. & (*colloq.*) pl. concord.) OE.

📖 W. R. GROVE Heat, light, electricity, magnetism . . are all correlatives . . neither, taken abstractedly, can be said to be the essential cause of the others. J. RUSKIN What at present I believe neither of us know. P. KAVANAGH They were both more than twenty-seven . . yet neither had . . kissed a girl. E. BAKER 'Would you save him or your manuscript?' 'Neither,' said Shillitoe. E. LONGFORD Two clumsy attempts to heal the breach, neither of which succeeded. M. ROBERTS Neither of the two men makes a move.

▶ **C** *adjective*. Not the one or the other, not either. LME.

📖 J. J. HENNESSY Neither side had made any effort to contact the other.

nek /nɛk/ *noun*. *S. Afr.* M19.
[Dutch = NECK *noun*¹.]
= COL 1.

nekro- *combining form* see NECRO-.

nekton /ˈnɛkt(ə)n, -tɒn/ *noun*. L19.
[Greek *nēkton* neut. of *nēktos* swimming, from *nēkhein* swim.]
BIOLOGY. Free-swimming aquatic animals collectively. Cf. BENTHOS, PLANKTON.
▪ **nekˈtonic** *adjective* E20.

nekulturny /nikʊljˈturnɪj, nɛkʊlˈtəːni/ *adjective*. M20.
[Russian *nekul'turnyĭ* uncivilized, from *ne-* not + KULTURNY.]
In countries of the former USSR: not having cultured manners, uncivilized, boorish.

nelia *noun* var. of NEALIE.

nelly /ˈnɛli/ *noun*¹. E19.
[Origin uncertain: perh. formed as next.]
A large sea bird of the petrel family; *esp.* a giant petrel.

nelly /ˈnɛli/ *noun*². M20.
[Pet-form of female forenames *Helen*, *Eleanor*.]
1 ***not on your Nelly***, (more fully) ***not on your Nelly Duff*** [rhyming slang = puff, breath of life], not on your life, not likely. *slang*. M20.
2 Cheap wine. *Austral. slang*. M20.
3 A weak-spirited or silly person. Also, a homosexual. *colloq.* M20.
4 ***sitting next to Nelly***, learning an occupation on the job by observing others. *colloq.* M20.
3 *NERVOUS Nelly*.

Nelson /ˈnɛls(ə)n/ *noun*¹. E19.
[Horatio *Nelson* (1758–1805), Brit. admiral, killed in the battle of Trafalgar, having suffered the loss of an eye and an arm in earlier conflicts.]
Used *attrib.* and in *possess.* to designate things associated with or characteristic of Nelson.
Nelson cake a cake consisting of crushed biscuits, dried fruit, etc., soaked in syrup, and sandwiched between two layers of pastry. **Nelson eye** a blind eye (chiefly in ***turn a Nelson eye (to)*** = ***turn a blind eye (to)*** s.v. BLIND *adjective*). **Nelson knife** a combined knife and fork esp. for use by a one-armed person. **Nelson's blood** Navy rum. **Nelson touch** a Nelsonian approach to a situation or problem, *esp.* a self-confident or daring approach.

nelson /ˈnɛls(ə)n/ *noun*². L19.
[App. from a personal name.]
WRESTLING. A hold in which both arms are passed under an opponent's arms from behind and the hands or wrists are clasped on the back of the opponent's neck (usu. ***double nelson***, ***full nelson***), or in which one arm is thrust under the opponent's corresponding arm and the hand placed on the back of the opponent's neck (usu. ***half nelson***).

Nelsonian /nɛlˈsəʊnɪən/ *adjective*. E20.
[from NELSON *noun*¹ + -IAN.]
Of, pertaining to, or characteristic of the British Admiral Horatio Nelson (1758–1805) or the navy at the time of his command.
▪ **Nelsoniˈana** *noun pl.* [-ANA] publications or other items concerning or associated with Nelson E20.

Nelsonic /nɛlˈsɒnɪk/ *adjective*. M19.
[formed as prec. + -IC.]
Of, pertaining to, or characteristic of the British Admiral Horatio Nelson (1758–1805).

nelumbium /nɪˈlʌmbɪəm/ *noun*. E19.
[mod. Latin (see below), from Sinhalese *nelum̆ba* or *nelum*.]
A plant of the former genus *Nelumbium* (now *Nelumbo*); = next.

nelumbo /nɪˈlʌmbəʊ/ *noun*. Pl. **-os**. L18.
[mod. Latin (see below), formed as prec.]
Either of two water lilies of the genus *Nelumbo* (family Nelumbonaceae), the sacred lotus of the East, *N. nucifera*, and the American lotus, *N. lutea*.

nema /ˈniːmə/ *noun*. E20.
[Greek *nēma* thread.]
1 *ZOOLOGY*. = NEMATODE *noun*. E20.
2 *PALAEONTOLOGY*. A threadlike extension of the sicula in some graptolites, apparently for attachment to the substrate. E20.

-nema /ˈniːmə/ *suffix*. Pl. **-nemas**, **-nemata** /-ˈniːmətə/.
[formed as prec.]
BIOLOGY. Forming nouns denoting threadlike structures, as ***diplonema***, ***pachynema***, ***treponema***, ***zygonema***.

nemacide /ˈnɛməsʌɪd/ *noun*. M20.
[from NEMA(TODE + -CIDE.]
AGRICULTURE & HORTICULTURE. = NEMATOCIDE.

-nemata *suffix* see -NEMA.

nemathecium /nɛməˈθiːʃəm, -ɪəm/ *noun*. Pl. **-cia** /-ʃə, -ʃɪə/. M19.
[from Greek *nēma* thread + *thēkē* container: see -IUM.]
BOTANY. A warty protuberance in certain red algae, usu. containing tetraspores.
▪ **nemathecial** *adjective* L19.

nemathelminth /nɛməˈtɛlmɪnθ, nɛmətˈhɛl-/ *noun*. Now *rare* or *obsolete*. L19.
[from Greek *nēmat-*, *nēma* thread + *helminth-*, *helmins* worm.]
ZOOLOGY. Any unsegmented worm of the group Nemathelminthes, which includes nematomorphs, nematodes, and (in some classifications) acanthocephalans.

nematic /nɪˈmatɪk/ *adjective & noun*. E20.
[from Greek *nēmat-*, *nēma* thread + -IC.]
PHYSICAL CHEMISTRY. ▶**A** *adjective*. Designating (the state of) a mesophase or liquid crystal in which the molecules are oriented in parallel but not arranged in well-defined planes. Opp. ***smectic***. E20.
▶ **B** *noun*. A nematic substance. L20.

nematicide /nɪˈmatɪsʌɪd, ˈnɛmət-/ *noun*. M20.
[Irreg. from NEMAT(ODE + -I- + -CIDE.]
AGRICULTURE & HORTICULTURE. = NEMATOCIDE.
▪ **nematiˈcidal** *adjective* = NEMATOCIDAL M20.

nemato- /nɪˈmatəʊ, ˈnɛmətəʊ/ *combining form*. Before a vowel also **nemat-**.
[Greek *nēmat-*, *nēma*.]
Thread; threadlike structure.
▪ **neˈmatoblast** *noun* (*BIOLOGY*) a blastema cell which develops into a sperm L19. **nemaˈtocerous** *adjective* [Greek *keras* horn] *ENTOMOLOGY* of, pertaining to, or designating the dipteran subclass Nematocera of flies having long palpi and antennae, including crane-flies, blackflies, and mosquitoes L19. **neˈmatogen** *noun* (*ZOOLOGY*) an adult form in some mesozoans which can reproduce asexually via a vermiform larval stage or give rise to the sexual adult form (rhombogen) L19. **neˈmatomorph** *noun* (*ZOOLOGY*) a worm of the phylum Nematomorpha, whose members have unsegmented threadlike bodies and develop from larvae which are parasites of arthropods (also called ***hair-worm***) M20. **neˈmatophore** *noun* (*ZOOLOGY*) a specialized organ bearing nematocysts M19. **nematoˈzooid** *noun* (*ZOOLOGY*) in colonial coelenterates, a zooid bearing nematocysts L19.

nematocide /nɪˈmatə(ʊ)sʌɪd, ˈnɛmət-/ *noun*. L19.
[from prec. + -CIDE.]
MEDICINE, AGRICULTURE, & HORTICULTURE. A substance or preparation used to kill nematode worms.
▪ **nematoˈcidal** *adjective* characteristic of or acting as a nematocide M20.

nematocyst /nɪˈmatə(ʊ)sɪst, ˈnɛmət-/ *noun*. L19.
[formed as prec. + CYST.]
ZOOLOGY. A small organ contained in cells on the body surface of jellyfishes and other coelenterates, containing a coiled thread, freq. barbed or poisoned, which is ejected as a defence or to capture prey. Also called ***lasso-cell***, ***thread-cell***.

nematode /ˈnɛmətəʊd/ *adjective & noun*. M19.
[from NEMATO- + -ODE¹.]
▶ **A** *adjective*. Designating, pertaining to, or characteristic of worms of the phylum Nematoda, comprising numerous slender, unsegmented, parasitic or free-living worms, including roundworms, hookworms, pinworms, threadworms, Guinea worms, etc. M19.
▶ **B** *noun*. A nematode worm. M19.

nematodirus /nɛmətə(ʊ)ˈdʌɪrəs/ *noun*. E20.
[mod. Latin (see below), from NEMATO(DE + Greek *deirē* neck.]
A parasitic nematode of the genus *Nematodirus* (family Trichostrongylidae) which is found in the intestines of many mammals. Also ***nematodirus worm***.

■ **nematodiriasis** /-dɪˈrʌɪəsɪs/ *noun*, pl. **-ases** /-əsiːz/, VETERINARY MEDICINE a disease of young lambs caused by larval nematodirus worms, characterized by severe dehydration M20.

nematoid /ˈnɛmətɔɪd/ *adjective & noun*. M19.
[from NEMAT(O- + -OID.]
► **A** *adjective*. = NEMATODE *adjective*. Also, resembling a nematode; related to nematodes. M19.
► **B** *noun*. = NEMATODE *noun*. M19.

nematology /nɛməˈtɒlədʒi/ *noun*. E20.
[from NEMAT(ODE + -O- + -LOGY.]
The branch of biology that deals with the nematodes.
■ **nematoˈlogical** *adjective* E20. **nematologist** *noun* M20.

nembie /ˈnɛmbi/ *noun*. *slang* (orig. *US*). M20.
[from NEMB(UTAL + -IE.]
(A capsule of) Nembutal.

Nembutal /ˈnɛmbjʊt(ə)l, -taːl/ *noun*. Also **n-**. M20.
[from *Na* symbol for sodium + E(THYL + M(ETHYL + BUT(YL, elems. of the systematic name + -AL².]
PHARMACOLOGY. (Proprietary name for) the sodium salt of pentobarbitone, or a capsule of this.
■ **nemˈbutalized** *adjective* (chiefly PHYSIOLOGY) anaesthetized with Nembutal M20.

nembutsu /nɛmˈbʊtsuː/ *noun*. M20.
[Japanese, from *nen* thought + *butsu* Buddha.]
In Japanese Buddhism, the invocation and repetition of the name of the Buddha Amida for the purpose of salvation and spiritual unity; this invocation.

nem. con. /nɛm ˈkɒn/ *adverbial phr.* L16.
[Abbreviation.]
= NEMINE CONTRADICENTE.

nem. diss. /nɛm ˈdɪs/ *adverbial phr.* L18.
[Abbreviation of Latin *nemine dissentiente*.]
With no one dissenting.

Nemean /nɪˈmiːən, ˈniːmɪən/ *adjective*. L16.
[from Latin *Nem(e)aeus*, *Nemeus* from Greek *Nemaios*, *-eos*, *-ea* Nemea (see below) + -AN.]
Of or belonging to Nemea, a wooded district near Argos in ancient Greece.
Nemean festival, **Nemean games** GREEK HISTORY one of the national festivals of ancient Greece, held at Nemea in the second and fourth years of each Olympiad. **Nemean lion** CLASSICAL MYTHOLOGY a monstrous lion which terrorized the Nemean region until killed by Hercules as the first of his twelve labours.

Nemedian /nɪˈmiːdɪən/ *noun*. M19.
[from *Nemed* (see below) + -IAN.]
IRISH MYTHOLOGY. A member of a legendary early colonizing people of Ireland, led by or descended from Nemed of Scythia, who were later driven out by the Fomorians.

nemertean /nɪˈməːtɪən, nɛməˈtiːən, ˈnɛmətiːn/ *noun & adjective*. Also **-ian** /-ɪən/. M19.
[from mod. Latin *Nemertes* genus name from Greek *Nēmertēs* a sea-nymph: see -AN.]
► **A** *noun*. A worm of the chiefly marine phylum Nemertea (or Rhynchocoela), comprising unsegmented worms which typically have an extremely elongated contractile body with an eversible proboscis, and are often brilliantly coloured. M19.
► **B** *adjective*. Of, pertaining to, or designating this phylum. L19.

nemertine /nɪˈməːtʌɪn, ˈnɛmətiːn/ *adjective & noun*. M19.
[formed as prec. + -INE¹.]
► **A** *adjective*. = NEMERTEAN *adjective*. M19.
► **B** *noun*. = NEMERTEAN *noun*. L19.

nemesia /nɪˈmiːʒə/ *noun*. E19.
[mod. Latin (see below), from Greek *nemesion* catchfly: see -IA¹.]
Any of various ornamental plants of the genus *Nemesia*, of the figwort family, with funnel-shaped flowers; *esp.* the southern African *N. strumosa* and its cultivated derivatives.

nemesis /ˈnɛmɪsɪs/ *noun*. Also **N-**. Pl. **nemeses** /ˈnɛmɪsiːz/. L16.
[Greek = righteous indignation, personified as the goddess of retribution or vengeance, from *nemein* deal out what is due, rel. to *nomos* custom, law.]
1 An agent of retribution; a person who avenges or punishes. L16. ▸**b** A persistent tormentor; a long-standing rival or enemy. *US*. M20.
2 (An instance of) retributive justice. L16.

> 🕮 **1** SHAKES. *1 Hen. VI* Is Talbot slain—the Frenchmen's only scourge, Your kingdom's terror and black Nemesis? **b** *Business Week* Juan Pablo Perez Alphonso . . long time nemesis of the oil companies. **2** R. MACAULAY The Nemesis that his crime deserved.

nemesism /ˈnɛmɪsɪz(ə)m/ *noun*. M20.
[from prec. + -ISM.]
PSYCHOLOGY. Frustration and aggression directed against oneself.
■ **nemeˈsistic** *adjective* of or connected with nemesism M20.

nemic /ˈniːmɪk/ *adjective*. E20.
[from NEMA + -IC.]
BIOLOGY. Of or pertaining to a nema or nemas; *esp.* consisting of nematodes.

nemine contradicente /ˈnɛmɪnɪ ˌkɒntrədɪˈsɛnti/ *adverbial phr.* M17.
[Latin.]
With no one contradicting.

nemmind /ˈnɛmʌɪnd, nɛˈmʌɪnd/ *verb intrans.* (*imper.*). *non-standard* (chiefly *US*). Also **-mine** /-mʌɪn/. E20.
[Repr. a pronunc.]
= ***never mind*** s.v. NEVER *adverb*.

†**nemn** *verb trans.* Pa. pple **nempt**. OE–L16.
[Old English *nemnan* = Old Frisian *namna*, *-ne*, Old Saxon *nemnian*, Middle Dutch, Middle Low German *nennen*, Old High German *nemnan*, *nennen* (German *nennen*), Old Norse *nefna*, *nemna*, Gothic *namnjan*, from Germanic base also of NAME *noun*.]
Name; call by some name; mention.

nemo /ˈniːməʊ/ *noun*. *US*. Pl. **-os**. M20.
[Origin unkn.]
A radio or television programme originating outside the studio from which it is broadcast.

nemocerous /nɪˈmɒs(ə)rəs/ *adjective*. Now *rare* or *obsolete*. M19.
[from mod. Latin *Nemocera*, irreg. from Greek *nēma* thread + *keras* horn: see -OUS.]
ENTOMOLOGY. = NEMATOCEROUS.

nemophila /nɪˈmɒfɪlə/ *noun*. M19.
[mod. Latin (see below), from Greek *nemos* wooded pasture, glade + *philos* -PHILE.]
Any of various delicate annual plants of the genus *Nemophila* (family Hydrophyllaceae), chiefly of Californian origin and freq. grown for ornament; *esp.* baby-blue-eyes, *N. menziesii*.

nemoral /ˈnɛmər(ə)l/ *adjective*. *rare*. M17.
[French *némoral* or Latin *nemoralis*, from *nemor-*, *nemus* grove + -AL¹.]
Pertaining to, living in, or frequenting groves or woods.
¶ Not recorded L17–E19.

†**nempt** *verbs pa. pple* of NEMN, NIM *verb*.

nene /ˈneɪneɪ/ *noun*. Also **néné**, **ne-ne**. E20.
[Hawaiian.]
A rare goose, *Branta sandvicensis*, native to Hawaii but now breeding chiefly in captivity. Also called ***Hawaiian goose***.

Nenets /ˈnɛnɛts/ *noun & adjective*. M20.
[Russian.]
► **A** *noun*. Pl. same; **Nentsi**, **Nentsy**, /ˈnɛn(t)si/. A member of a Samoyedic people inhabiting the far north-east of Europe and the north of Siberia; the Uralic language of this people. Also called ***Yurak Samoyed***, ***Yurak***. Cf. ENETS. M20.
► **B** *attrib.* or as *adjective*. Of or pertaining to the Nenets or their language. M20.

nenuphar /ˈnɛnjʊfaː/ *noun*. ME.
[medieval Latin (whence also French *nénuphar*) from Arab. *nīlūfar*, Persian *nīnūfar*, *nīlūpal* from Sanskrit *nīlotpala*, from *nīla* blue (see ANIL) + *utpala* water lily, lotus.]
A water lily; *esp.* (**a**) the common white water lily, *Nymphaea alba*; (**b**) the yellow water lily, *Nuphar luteum*.

neo- /ˈniːəʊ/ *combining form*.
[from Greek *neos* new: see -O-.]
New, modern, recent, a new or revived form of, as in ***neo-capitalism***, ***neo-capitalist***, ***neo-Fascism***, ***neo-Fascist***, ***neo-Freudian***, ***neo-Freudianism***, ***neo-imperialism***, ***neo-imperialist***, ***neo-Stalinism***, ***neo-Stalinist***, etc.; in scientific use freq. opp. PALAEO-. Also in CHEMISTRY, forming names of compounds in which one carbon atom is linked to four others.
■ **neoarsˈphenamine** *noun* (PHARMACOLOGY) a toxic sulphated derivative of arsphenamine formerly used to treat syphilis E20. **neoblast** *noun* (ZOOLOGY) any of the undifferentiated cells in various worms, esp. planarians, whose division provides for the regeneration of lost portions of the body L19. **neocereˈbellar** *adjective* (ANATOMY) of or pertaining to the neocerebellum E20. **neocereˈbellum** *noun* (ANATOMY) the most recently evolved part of the cerebellum, present in mammals E20. **Neo-Conˈfucianism** *noun* a later, esp. medieval, form of Confucianism M20. **neoˈcortex** *noun*, pl. **-tices** /-tɪsiːz/, ANATOMY the most recently evolved part of the cerebral cortex, which is involved in sight and hearing in advanced reptiles and in mammals E20. **neoˈcortical** *adjective* (ANATOMY) of or pertaining to the neocortex E20. **neoˈcyanine** *noun* (CHEMISTRY) a cyanine dye used in emulsions for infrared photography M20. **neoˈgenesis** *noun* (chiefly SCIENCE) the formation of a new thing, as a structure, species, etc. E20. **neo-ˈGothic** *adjective & noun* (of or in) an artistic style that originated in the 19th century, characterized by the revival of Gothic and other medieval forms including pointed arches, vaulted ceilings, and mock fortifications L19. **neoˈgraphic** *adjective* of or pertaining to a new system of writing or spelling E19. **neo-Heˈllenic** *adjective* of or pertaining to neo-Hellenism M19. **neo-ˈHellenism** *noun* the revival of the culture and ideas of ancient Greece L19. **neoˈhexane** *noun* (CHEMISTRY) 2,2-dimethylbutane, $CH_3C(CH_3)_2CH_2CH_3$, an isomer of hexane used in aviation fuels L19. **neo-ˈLatin** *adjective & noun* (**a**) *adjective* of or pertaining to a Romance language or modern Latin; (**b**) *noun* a Romance language; modern Latin: M19. **neoˈlocal** *adjective* (ANTHROPOLOGY) designating a place of residence chosen by a newly married couple which is in a location independent of their respective families M20. **neoˈlocally** *adverb* (ANTHROPOLOGY) in a neolocal manner M20. **neo-Malˈthusian** *adjective & noun* (**a**) *adjective* of or pertaining to neo-Malthusianism; (**b**) *noun* an advocate or adherent of neo-Malthusian principles or practices: E20. **neo-Malˈthusianism** *noun* the view that the rate of increase of a population should be controlled, esp. by contraception L19. **Neo-Melaˈnesian** *noun* an English-based pidgin of New Guinea, Melanesia, and NE Australia; *spec.* = BISLAMA: M20. **neoˈpallial** *adjective* (ANATOMY) of or pertaining to the neopallium E20. **neoˈpallium** *noun* (ANATOMY) = NEOCORTEX E20. **neoˈpentane** *noun* (CHEMISTRY) dimethylpropane, $C(CH_3)_4$, an isomer of pentane which is an easily condensable gas found in small amounts in petroleum L19. **neoˈpentyl** *noun* (CHEMISTRY) the radical $C(CH_3)_3CH_2\cdot$ derived from neopentane L19. **neoˈphobia** *noun* fear or dislike of what is new L19. **neoˈphobic** *adjective* fearing or disliking what is new E20. **neoˈsalvarsan** *noun* (PHARMACOLOGY) = NEOARSPHENAMINE E20. **neo-schoˈlasticism** *noun* (CHRISTIAN CHURCH) a philosophical movement of the 19th and 20th cents. based on the writings of Thomas Aquinas E20. **neoˈstigmine** *noun* (PHARMACOLOGY) the quaternary ammonium compound $(CH_3)_2N{\cdot}CO{\cdot}O{\cdot}C_6H_4N^+(CH_3)_3$ or its bromide or methylsulphate salts, which are cholinesterase inhibitors used esp. to treat ileus, glaucoma, and myasthenia gravis M20. **neostriˈatal** *adjective* (ANATOMY) of or pertaining to the neostriatum M20. **neostriˈatum** *noun*, pl. **-ta**, ANATOMY the more recently evolved part of the corpus striatum, including the caudate nucleus E20. **neoˈtechnic** *adjective* designating or belonging to the most recent stage of industrial development E20. **neoˈtechnics** *noun* neotechnic technology E20. **neotecˈtonic** *adjective* (GEOLOGY) of or pertaining to neotectonics M20. **neotecˈtonics** *noun* (GEOLOGY) the branch of geology that deals with the movements of the earth's crust since the Miocene M20. **neoˈthalamic** *adjective* (ANATOMY) of or pertaining to the neothalamus E20. **neoˈthalamus** *noun*, pl. **-mi**, ANATOMY the phylogenetically younger, lateral part of the thalamus, present in mammals E20.

neo-classic /niːəʊˈklasɪk/ *adjective*. L19.
[from NEO- + CLASSIC *adjective*.]
Neoclassical.

neoclassical /niːəʊˈklasɪk(ə)l/ *adjective*. L19.
[from NEO- + CLASSICAL.]
1 Of, pertaining to, or characteristic of a revival of classical style or treatment in the arts. L19.
2 ECONOMICS. Of, pertaining to, or characteristic of a body of theory primarily concerned with supply and demand rather than with the source and distribution of wealth. E20.

> 🕮 **1** J. N. SUMMERSON The Panthéon is the first major building which can be called neo-classical. **2** *Man* Theories of consumer choice in neoclassical economics rely upon a concept of preference devoid of social entailments in history.

■ **neoclassically** *adverb* L20.

neoclassicism /niːəʊˈklasɪsɪz(ə)m/ *noun*. L19.
[from NEO- + CLASSICISM.]
Neoclassical style or principles in the arts; *spec.* (**a**) a style in art and architecture from the mid 18th cent. inspired by a renewed interest in classical architecture and archaeology; (**b**) MUSIC a 20th-cent. trend in music characterized by a reworking in modern terms of Baroque and Classical forms, procedures, and styles. Also, adherence to neoclassical style or principles.

> 🕮 R. BARBER Neoclassicism appeals to reason and to the sense of order.

■ **neoclassicist** *noun* an expert in or student of neoclassicism; an adherent or practitioner of neoclassical style or principles: E20.

neo-colonial /ˌniːəʊkəˈləʊnɪəl/ *adjective & noun*. M20.
[from NEO- + COLONIAL.]
► **A** *adjective*. Of or pertaining to neo-colonialism. M20.
► **B** *noun*. A neo-colonialist. M20.

neo-colonialism /ˌniːəʊkəˈləʊnɪəlɪz(ə)m/ *noun*. M20.
[from NEO- + COLONIALISM.]
The practice or principles of applying economic, political, or other influential pressures on another country, esp. on a former colony.
■ **neo-colonialist** *adjective & noun* (**a**) *adjective* of or pertaining to neo-colonialists or neo-colonialism; (**b**) *noun* an adherent of neo-colonialism: M20.

neo-con /ˈniːəʊkɒn/ *adjective & noun*. Chiefly *US*. Also **neocon**. L20.
[from NEO- + CON(SERVATIVE.]
► **A** *adjective*. Of or pertaining to a form of political conservatism advocating a moderate type of democratic capitalism. L20.
► **B** *noun*. An advocate or supporter of neo-con principles or beliefs. L20.

neodamode /niːˈɒdəməʊd/ *noun*. E19.
[from Greek *neodamōdēs*, formed as NEO- + *damos*, *dēmos* people.]
GREEK HISTORY. An enfranchised Helot in ancient Sparta.

Neo-Darwinism /niːəʊˈdaːwɪnɪz(ə)m/ *noun*. Also **n-**. L19.
[from NEO- + DARWINISM 2.]
A theory of biological evolution based on Darwin's theory of natural selection but incorporating the findings of Mendelian genetics and widely accepted since the 1920s.

■ **Neo-Dar'winian** *adjective & noun* (*a*) *adjective* of, pertaining to, or characteristic of Neo-Darwinism; (*b*) *noun* = NEO-DARWINIST: L19. **Neo-Darwinist** *noun* an advocate of Neo-Darwinism L19.

neodymium /niːə(ʊ)'dɪmɪəm/ *noun*. L19.
[from NEO- + DI)DYMIUM.]
A rare metallic chemical element of the lanthanide series, atomic no. 60, which occurs in association with praseodymium. (Symbol Nd.)

Neogene /'niːə(ʊ)dʒiːn/ *adjective & noun*. L19.
[from NEO- + Greek *-genēs*: see -GEN.]
GEOLOGY. ▶**A** *adjective*. Designating or pertaining to the later part of the Tertiary period or sub-era, comprising the Miocene and Pliocene epochs. L19.
▶**B** *noun*. The Neogene period; the system of rocks dating from this time. M20.

neoglacial /niːəʊ'gleɪʃ(ə)l, -sɪəl/ *adjective & noun*. M20.
[from NEO- + GLACIAL.]
GEOLOGY. ▶**A** *adjective*. Of or pertaining to a neoglaciation. M20.
▶**B** *noun*. A neoglacial period. L20.

neoglaciation /ˌniːəʊgleɪsɪ'eɪʃ(ə)n/ *noun*. M20.
[from NEO- + GLACIATION.]
GEOLOGY. (A) minor temporary increase in the extent of glaciation after the end of the Ice Age.

neogrammarian /ˌniːəʊgrə'mɛːrɪən/ *noun & adjective*. L19.
[from NEO- + GRAMMARIAN.]
LINGUISTICS. ▶**A** *noun*. A person holding the view that phonetic changes operate without exception; *spec*. a member of the *Junggrammatiker*. Cf. NEO-LINGUIST. L19.
▶**B** *adjective*. Of or pertaining to neogrammarians. L19.

neo-impressionism /ˌniːəʊɪm'prɛʃ(ə)nɪz(ə)m/ *noun*. Also **Neo-I-**. L19.
[from NEO- + IMPRESSIONISM.]
A movement or style in art, originated by the French painter Georges Seurat (1859–91), aiming at the achievement of a subjective response in the viewer through a systematic use of divisionism.
■ **neo-impressionist** *adjective & noun* (*a*) *adjective* of or pertaining to neo-impressionism; (*b*) *noun* an adherent or practitioner of neo-impressionism: L19.

neo-linguist /niːəʊ'lɪŋgwɪst/ *noun*. M20.
[from NEO- + LINGUIST.]
LINGUISTICS. A member of a school of linguistics best known for its theories of linguistic geography, but which orig. arose in opposition to the neogrammarians and held that linguistic change arises from individual innovation. Cf. NEOGRAMMARIAN.
■ **neo-lin'guistic** *adjective* of or pertaining to the neo-linguists or their views M20.

neolithic /niːə(ʊ)'lɪθɪk/ *adjective & noun*. M19.
[from NEO- + -LITHIC.]
▶**A** *adjective*. **1** *ARCHAEOLOGY*. Designating or pertaining to the latest part of the Stone Age, following the mesolithic period, esp. as characterized by the use of ground or polished stone implements and weapons. M19.
2 Antiquated; hopelessly outdated. M20.

> 🕮 **1 Neolithic Revolution** the development in the neolithic period of agriculture and the domestication of animals in contrast to the previous practices of hunting, foraging, etc. **2** *Business Week* Politics that were so Neolithic that they created an antibusiness atmosphere as well as . . a recession.

▶**B** *noun*. *ARCHAEOLOGY*. *The* neolithic period. L19.
■ **neolithically** *adverb* M20.

neologian /niːə'ləʊdʒɪən/ *adjective & noun*. M19.
[from NEOLOGY + -IAN.]
THEOLOGY. ▶**A** *adjective*. Of, inclined to, or marked by, neologism. M19.
▶**B** *noun*. An adherent of neologism; a neologist. M19.

neologic /niːə'lɒdʒɪk/ *adjective*. *rare*. L18.
[French *néologique*, formed as NEOLOGY + -IC.]
Neological.

neological /niːə'lɒdʒɪk(ə)l/ *adjective*. M18.
[formed as prec.: see -ICAL.]
1 Dealing with or characterized by new words or expressions. *rare*. M18.
2 *THEOLOGY*. Of, pertaining to, or characterized by neologism. E19.

neologise *verb* var. of NEOLOGIZE.

neologism /nɪ'ɒlədʒɪz(ə)m/ *noun*. E19.
[French *néologisme*, formed as NEOLOGY + -ISM.]
1 The action of coining or using new words or expressions; a new word or expression. E19. ▶**b** *PSYCHOLOGY*. A nonsense word interpolated in an otherwise correct sentence by a person with a mental illness, esp. schizophrenia. E20.
2 *THEOLOGY*. The tendency to or adoption of novel or rationalistic views. E19.

neologist /nɪ'ɒlədʒɪst/ *noun*. L18.
[French *néologiste*, formed as NEOLOGY + -IST.]
1 A person who coins or uses new words or expressions. L18.
2 *THEOLOGY*. An adherent or advocate of neologism; a rationalist. E19.
■ **neolo'gistic** *adjective* of or pertaining to neologists or neologism E19.

neologize /nɪ'ɒlədʒʌɪz/ *verb intrans*. Also **-ise**. E19.
[French *néologiser*, formed as NEOLOGY + -IZE.]
1 Use or coin new words or expressions. E19.
2 *THEOLOGY*. Adopt or accept novel or rationalistic views. L19.
■ **neologiz'ation** *noun* E19.

neology /nɪ'ɒlədʒi/ *noun*. L18.
[French *néologie*, from *néo-* NEO- + *-logie* -LOGY.]
1 = NEOLOGISM 1. L18.
2 *THEOLOGY*. = NEOLOGISM 2. M19.

neomenia /niːə(ʊ)'miːnɪə/ *noun*. Pl. ***-iae*** /-ɪiː/. LME.
[ecclesiastical Latin from Greek *neomēnia*, formed as NEO- + *mēnē* moon.]
Among the ancient Hebrews and Greeks: the time of the new moon, the beginning of the lunar month; the festival held at that time.

neomorph /'niːə(ʊ)mɔːf/ *noun*. L19.
[from NEO- + Greek *morphē* form.]
1 *BIOLOGY*. An anatomical structure or feature that is of recent evolutionary origin. L19.
2 *GENETICS*. A mutant allele which affects developmental processes to produce a variant phenotype. M20.
■ **neo'morphic** *adjective* of, pertaining to, or of the nature of a neomorph E20.

neomycin /niːəʊ'mʌɪsɪn/ *noun*. M20.
[from NEO- + -MYCIN.]
PHARMACOLOGY. An antibiotic produced by a strain of *Streptomyces fradiae* and used to treat a wide variety of bacterial infections.

neon /'niːɒn/ *noun & adjective*. L19.
[Greek, neut. of *neos* new.]
▶**A** *noun*. **1** A colourless odourless gaseous chemical element, atomic no. 10, which is one of the noble gases, occurring as a trace constituent of the earth's atmosphere and used in low-pressure discharge tubes. (Symbol Ne.) L19.
2 A neon lamp or tube; neon lighting. M20.
▶**B** *attrib*. or as *adjective*. Of, pertaining to, or involving neon; resembling a neon light in colour or brilliance, harshly bright, gaudy, glowing. L19.
Special collocations & comb.: **neon fish** = *neon tetra* below. **neon lamp**, **neon light** a lamp or light in which an electric discharge is passed through neon at low pressure, giving an orange-red light, or through a mixture of neon with other gases, giving other colours. **neon lighting** neon lights collectively; illumination by neon lights. **neon sign** a sign incorporating a neon light, freq. a shaped tube serving as an advertisement. **neon tetra** a small characin, *Paracheirodon innesi*, native to the Amazon and common in aquaria, having a shining blue-green stripe along each side and a red band near the tail. **neon tube** a neon light in the form of a tube.
■ **neoned** *adjective* illuminated by a neon light or lights M20.

neonate /'niːə(ʊ)neɪt/ *noun & adjective*. M20.
[from NEO- + Latin *natus* born: see -ATE[1].]
▶**A** *noun*. *MEDICINE & BIOLOGY*. A recently born individual; *spec*. in *MEDICINE*, an infant less than four weeks old. M20.
▶**B** *attrib*. or as *adjective*. Recently born; of or pertaining to neonates, neonatal. M20.
■ **neo'natal** *adjective* of or pertaining to neonates L19. **neo'natally** *adverb* soon after birth M20. **neona'tologist** *noun* an expert in or student of neonatology M20. **neona'tology** *noun* (*MEDICINE*) the branch of medicine that deals with the disorders and problems of newly born infants M20.

neo-Nazi /niːə(ʊ)'nɑːtsi, -'nɑːzi/ *noun & adjective*. M20.
[formed as NEO- + NAZI.]
▶**A** *noun*. An adherent or supporter of a new or revived form of Nazism. M20.
▶**B** *adjective*. Of or pertaining to neo-Nazis or neo-Nazism. M20.
■ **neo-Nazism** *noun* the principles or practices of neo-Nazis M20.

Neonomian /niːə(ʊ)'nəʊmɪən/ *noun & adjective*. L17.
[formed as NEO- + Greek *nomos* law + -IAN, after *antinomian*.]
CHRISTIAN THEOLOGY. ▶**A** *noun*. A person maintaining that the gospel of Christ is a new law entirely supplanting the old or Mosaic law. L17.
▶**B** *adjective*. Of or pertaining to the Neonomians or their views. L17.
■ **Neonomianism** *noun* L17.

neontology /niːɒn'tɒlədʒi/ *noun*. L19.
[from NEO- after *palaeontology*.]
BIOLOGY. The branch of biology (esp. zoology) that deals with extant (as opp. to fossil or extinct) forms.
■ **neonto'logical** *adjective* L19. **neonto'logically** *adverb* as regards neontology, in terms of neontology L20. **neon'tologist** *noun* L19.

neopaganism /niːəʊ'peɪg(ə)nɪz(ə)m/ *noun*. L19.
[from NEO-+ PAGANISM.]
A modern religious movement which incorporates beliefs and ritual practices (such as nature worship and shamanism) from traditions outside the main world religions.
■ **neopagan** *adjective & noun* M19.

neophilia /niːə(ʊ)'fɪlɪə/ *noun*. M20.
[from NEO- + -PHILIA.]
Love for, or great interest in, what is new; a love of novelty.
■ **neophiliac** *adjective & noun* (a person) characterized by neophilia M20. **neophilic** *adjective* = NEOPHILIAC *adjective* M20.

neophron /'niːə(ʊ)frɒn/ *noun*. M19.
[mod. Latin (see below) from Latin from Greek *Neophrōn* a man who was changed into a vulture.]
The Egyptian vulture, *Neophron percnopterus*. Now chiefly as mod. Latin genus name.

neophyte /'niːə(ʊ)fʌɪt/ *noun & adjective*. LME.
[ecclesiastical Latin *neophytus* from Greek *neophutos* newly planted (with ref. to *1 Timothy* 3:6), formed as NEO- + *phuton* plant.]
▶**A** *noun*. **1** A new convert to a Church or religious body; *spec*. a recently baptized convert to the early Christian Church. Also, in the Roman Catholic Church, a newly ordained priest, a novice of a religious order. LME.
2 A person who is new to a subject; a beginner, a novice. L16.
3 *BOTANY*. A plant introduced into an area where it was previously unknown. E20.
▶**B** *attrib*. or as *adjective*. That is a neophyte, novice. L16.

> 🕮 A. MILLER Theodore had ordered Barney, as a neophyte cop, to don civilian clothes.

neoplasia /niːə(ʊ)'pleɪzɪə/ *noun*. L19.
[from NEO- + -PLASIA.]
MEDICINE & BIOLOGY. The formation of neoplasms; the state or condition of having neoplastic growth.

neoplasm /'niːə(ʊ)plaz(ə)m/ *noun*. M19.
[from NEO- + Greek PLASMA formation.]
MEDICINE & BIOLOGY. A new and abnormal growth or formation of tissue in the body; a tumour.

neoplastic /niːə(ʊ)'plastɪk/ *adjective*[1]. L19.
[from NEO- + -PLASTIC.]
MEDICINE & BIOLOGY. Of, pertaining to, or of the nature of a neoplasm.

neoplastic /niːə(ʊ)'plastɪk/ *adjective*[2]. Also **neo-plastic**. M20.
[Back-form. from next.]
Of or pertaining to neo-plasticism.

neo-plasticism /niːə(ʊ)'plastɪsɪz(ə)m/ *noun*. M20.
[French *néoplasticisme*, from *néo-* NEO- + *plasticisme* PLASTICISM.]
A movement or style in abstract art originated by the Dutch painter Piet Mondrian (1872–1944), characterized by the use of geometric shapes and primary colours.

Neoplatonic /ˌniːəʊplə'tɒnɪk/ *noun & adjective*. M19.
[from NEO- + PLATONIC.]
▶**A** *noun*. = NEOPLATONIST *noun*. M19.
▶**B** *adjective*. Of or pertaining to Neoplatonism or Neoplatonists. M19.

Neoplatonism /niːəʊ'pleɪtənɪz(ə)m/ *noun*. M19.
[from NEO- + PLATONISM.]
A philosophical and religious system based on Platonic ideas and originating with Plotinus in the 3rd cent. AD, which emphasizes the distinction between a supposed eternal world and the changing physical world, and combines this with a mystic possibility of union with the supreme being from which all reality is supposed to derive.
■ **Neoplatonist** *noun & adjective* (*a*) *noun* an originator or adherent of Neoplatonism; (*b*) *adjective* = NEOPLATONIC *adjective*: M19.

neoprene /'niːə(ʊ)priːn/ *noun*. M20.
[from NEO- + *-prene*, after *isoprene*.]
Any of various strong synthetic rubbers made by polymerizing chloroprene, which are resistant to oil, heat, and weathering.

Neorican /niːə(ʊ)'riːk(ə)n/ *noun & adjective*. Also **Neo-Rican**. M20.
[Perh. from Spanish *Neorriqueño*, but usu. regarded as from NEO- + *Rican*, 2nd elem. of PUERTO RICAN.]
▶**A** *noun*. A Puerto Rican living or formerly living in the US. M20.
▶**B** *adjective*. Of or pertaining to a Neorican or Neoricans. L20.

Neo-Synephrine /ˌniːəʊsɪ'nɛfrɪn, -iːn/ *noun*. Also **n-**. M20.
[from NEO- + SYN- + EPIN)EPHRINE.]
PHARMACOLOGY. (Proprietary name for) the drug phenylephrine.

neoteny /niː'ɒt(ə)ni/ *noun*. Also (earlier) †**-te(i)nia**. L19.
[from NEO- + Greek *teinein* keep: see -Y[3].]
ZOOLOGY. **1** The retention of juvenile characteristics in adult life; paedomorphosis. L19.
2 The possession of precocious sexual maturity by an animal still in its larval stage; paedogenesis, progenesis. L19.

📖 **1** *Scientific American* The exception to the rule of human neoteny is the chin which grows relatively larger in human beings. **2** D. NICHOLS Neoteny, .. by the acceleration of development of the gonads.

■ **neo'tenic** *adjective* L19. **neotenin** *noun* (ENTOMOLOGY) = ***juvenile hormone*** s.v. JUVENILE *adjective* M20. **neotenous** *adjective* M20. **neotenously** *adverb* M20.

neoteric /niːə(ʊ)'tɛrɪk/ *adjective & noun.* L16.
[Late Latin *neotericus* from Greek *neōterikos*, from *neōteros* compar. of *neos* new: see -IC.]
▶ **A** *adjective.* Esp. of an author, opinion, or trend: recent, new, modern. L16.
▶ **B** *noun.* A person, esp. an author, who adheres to modern views. L16.
■ **neoterical** *adjective* (*arch.*) = NEOTERIC *adjective* L16.

neoterism /niː'ɒtərɪz(ə)m/ *noun.* L18.
[Greek *neōterismos*, from *neōterizein* make innovations, from *neōteros*: see prec., -ISM.]
= NEOLOGISM 1.

neotocite /niːə'təʊkʌɪt/ *noun.* Also (earlier) †**-k-**. M19.
[from Greek *neotokos* newborn, recent (formed as NEO- + *tokos* offspring) + -ITE[1].]
MINERALOGY. A hydrated ferrous manganese silicate occurring as black amorphous masses.

neotropical /niːəʊ'trɒpɪk(ə)l/ *adjective.* Also **N-**. M19.
[from NEO- + TROPICAL.]
Of, pertaining to, or designating the biogeographical region which comprises the continent of America south of Mexico.
■ **neo'tropics** *noun pl.* E20.

neotype /'niːə(ʊ)tʌɪp/ *noun.* M19.
[from NEO- + -TYPE.]
†**1** MINERALOGY. A barytic variety of calcite. *rare*. Only in M19.
2 TAXONOMY. A specimen designated as a new type to replace original type material which has been lost or destroyed. E20.

neoza /niː'əʊzə/ *noun.* M19.
[Dzongkha *neoza*, *nioza*.]
In full ***neoza pine***. A Himalayan pine, *Pinus gerardiana*, the cones of which contain edible seeds.

Neozoic /niːə(ʊ)'zəʊɪk/ *adjective.* Now *rare*. M19.
[from NEO- after *Palaeozoic*.]
GEOLOGY. Designating or pertaining to an era following the Palaeozoic and comprising both the Mesozoic and Cenozoic eras. Also = CENOZOIC *adjective*.

nep /nɛp/ *noun*[1]. *obsolete* exc. *dial.* Also **nip** /nɪp/. LME.
[medieval Latin *nepta* from Latin NEPETA.]
Catmint, *Nepeta cataria*.

nep /nɛp/ *noun*[2] *& verb.* Chiefly *US*. L19.
[Origin unkn.]
▶ **A** *noun.* A small lump or knot on cotton-fibres, resulting from irregular growth or produced during ginning. L19.
▶ **B** *verb trans.* Infl. **-pp-**. Form knots on (cotton fibre) during ginning. L19.

Nepalese /nɛpə'liːz, -pɔː-/ *noun & adjective.* E19.
[from *Nepal* (see below) + -ESE.]
▶ **A** *noun.* Pl. same. A native or inhabitant of Nepal, a country in southern Asia, bordered by Tibet to the north and India to the south. Also, the official (Indo-Aryan) language of Nepal; Nepali. E19.
▶ **B** *adjective.* Of or pertaining to Nepal, the Nepalese, or their language. E19.
¶ Cf. NEWAR.

Nepali /nɪ'pɔːli, -'pɑːli/ *noun & adjective.* L19.
[formed as prec. + -I[2].]
▶ **A** *noun.* **1** The official (Indo-Aryan) language of Nepal. L19.
2 A Nepalese. L19.
▶ **B** *adjective.* Of or pertaining to Nepal, its official language, or its people. L19.

nepenthe /nɪ'pɛnθi/ *noun.* L16.
[Alt. of next after Italian *nepente*.]
1 = NEPENTHES 1. L16.
2 MEDICINE. A preparation containing opium. L17.

nepenthes /nɪ'pɛnθiːz/ *noun.* L16.
[Latin from Greek *nēpenthes* neut. of *nēpenthēs* banishing pain (qualifying *pharmakon* drug), from *nē-* not + *penthos* grief.]
1 A drug mentioned in Homer's *Odyssey* as liberating the mind from grief or trouble; any drug or potion bringing welcome forgetfulness. Also, a plant yielding such a drug. L16.
2 Any of various freq. climbing pitcher plants of the genus *Nepenthes* (family Nepenthaceae), chiefly of SE Asia, having brightly coloured pitchers at the end of the leaf tendrils. M18.

neper /'niːpə, 'neɪ-/ *noun.* E20.
[*Neperus*, Latinized form of *Napier*: see NAPIER'S BONES.]
A unit used in comparing voltages, currents, power levels, etc., esp. in communication circuits, the difference in nepers being equal, for voltages and currents, to the natural logarithm of their ratio or, for power differences, to half of this.

nepeta /nɪ'piːtə/ *noun.* E20.
[mod. Latin (see below) from Latin = calamint (formerly in this genus).]
Any of various labiate plants of the genus *Nepeta*; esp. *N.* × *faassenii* and *N. mussinii*, with blue or violet-blue flowers, grown to edge flower-beds.

nephalism /'nɛf(ə)lɪz(ə)m/ *noun. rare*. M19.
[Late Greek *nēphalismos*, from *nēphalios* sober: see -ISM.]
Teetotalism.

nephanalysis /nɛfə'nalɪsɪs/ *noun.* Pl. **-lyses** /-lɪsiːz/. M20.
[from Greek *nephos* cloud + ANALYSIS.]
METEOROLOGY. (A chart representing) an analysis of the amounts and kinds of cloud present over an area.

nepheline /'nɛf(ə)lɪn/ *noun.* E19.
[French *néphéline*, from Greek *nephelē* cloud (because its fragments are made cloudy by immersion in nitric acid): see -INE[5].]
A hexagonal aluminosilicate of sodium and potassium which belongs to the feldspathoid group of minerals and occurs as colourless or green to brown crystals or grains in igneous rocks.
Comb.: **nepheline-syenite** a plutonic rock resembling syenite but containing nepheline and lacking quartz.
■ **nephelinite** *noun* a rock containing nepheline M19. **nepheli'nitic** *adjective* containing or characteristic of a nephelinite E20.

nephelinization /ˌnɛf(ə)lɪnʌɪ'zeɪʃ(ə)n/ *noun.* Also **-isation**. M20.
[from NEPHELINE + -IZATION.]
GEOLOGY. The alteration of a rock to one in which nepheline is an essential constituent.
■ **'nephelinize** *verb trans.* subject to nephelinization (chiefly as ***nephelinized***, ***nephelinizing*** *ppl adjectives*) M20.

nepheloid /'nɛf(ə)lɔɪd/ *adjective.* L19.
[from Greek *nephelē* cloud + -OID.]
Cloudy; chiefly (OCEANOGRAPHY) in ***nepheloid layer***, a layer about a kilometre (3300 ft) thick in deep water, esp. in the western N. Atlantic, that is turbid owing to suspended mineral matter.
¶ Only in Dicts. before M20.

nephelometer /nɛfə'lɒmɪtə/ *noun.* L19.
[formed as prec. + -OMETER.]
1 An instrument for measuring the cloudiness of the sky. L19.
2 An instrument for measuring the turbidity of a suspension in a liquid or gas by means of the light scattered (at right angles) by it. Cf. TURBIDIMETER. L19.
■ **nephelo'metric** *adjective* of or pertaining to nephelometry E20. **nephelo'metrically** *adverb* by nephelometry E20. **nephelometry** *noun* quantitative analysis using a nephelometer L19.

nephew /'nɛfjuː, 'nɛvjuː/ *noun.* ME.
[Old & mod. French *neveu*, Old Northern French *nevu*, *nevo* from Latin *nepos*, *nepot-* grandson, nephew, descendant, corresp. to Germanic form whence Old English *nefa*, Old Frisian *neva*, Middle Dutch *neve*, *neef* (Dutch *neef*), Old High German *nevo*, *nefo* (German *Neffe*), Old Norse *nefi*.]
1 A son of a person's brother or sister; a son of a brother- or sister-in-law. ME. ▶**b** *euphem.* An illegitimate son, esp. of an ecclesiastic. Cf. NEPOTISM 2, NIECE 1b. *arch.* L16.
†**2** A grandson. ME–L17.
†**3** A descendant of a remote or unspecified degree of descent; a successor. LME–L17.
†**4** A daughter of a person's brother or sister; a niece. LME–E17.

📖 **1b** W. H. DIXON More papal 'nephews' had been stalled and mitred in the English Church.

■ **nephewship** *noun* (*a*) the state or position of a nephew; †(*b*) nepotism: M17.

nephology /nɪ'fɒlədʒi/ *noun.* L19.
[from Greek *nephos* cloud + -LOGY.]
The branch of science that deals with clouds.
■ **nephologist** *noun* L19.

nephometer /nɪ'fɒmɪtə/ *noun.* E20.
[formed as prec. + -METER.]
= NEPHELOMETER 1.

nephoscope /'nɛfəskəʊp/ *noun.* L19.
[formed as prec. + -SCOPE.]
METEOROLOGY. An instrument used to determine the direction of motion of clouds and their angular velocity relative to a given point on the ground.

nephr- *combining form* see NEPHRO-.

nephralgia /nɪ'fraldʒə/ *noun.* E19.
[formed as NEPHRO- + -ALGIA.]
MEDICINE. Pain in (the region of) the kidneys.
■ **nephralgic** *adjective* E19.

nephrectomy /nɪ'frɛktəmi/ *noun.* L19.
[from NEPHRO- + -ECTOMY.]
Surgical removal of a kidney; an instance of this.
■ **nephrectomize** *verb trans.* perform nephrectomy on E20.

nephric /'nɛfrɪk/ *adjective.* L19.
[formed as prec. + -IC.]
ANATOMY & ZOOLOGY. Of or pertaining to an excretory organ or kidney.

nephridium /nɪ'frɪdɪəm/ *noun.* Pl. **-dia** /-dɪə/. L19.
[from Greek *nephrion* dim. of *nephros* kidney: see -IDIUM.]
ZOOLOGY. An excretory or osmoregulatory tubule, typically of ectodermal origin, open to the exterior, having cells with cilia or flagella and absorptive walls, present in various invertebrate groups; a protonephridium; *esp.* a metanephridium.
■ **nephridial** *adjective* of or pertaining to a nephridium L19. **nephridiopore** *noun* the excretory opening of a nephridium L19.

nephrite /'nɛfrʌɪt/ *noun.* L18.
[from Greek *nephros* kidney (with allus. to its supposed efficacy in kidney disease) + -ITE[1].]
MINERALOGY. A hard translucent monoclinic silicate of calcium and magnesium, often pale green or white, related to actinolite and prized as jade. Cf. JADE *noun*[2] 1.

nephritic /nɪ'frɪtɪk/ *adjective*[1] *& noun.* LME.
[Late Latin *nephriticus* from Greek *nephritikos*, from NEPHRITIS: see -IC.]
▶ **A** *adjective.* **1** Orig. (of pain, a disease, etc.), affecting or originating in the kidneys, urinary, renal. Now *spec.* of the nature of or pertaining to nephritis. LME.
2 Of a person: affected with pain or disease of the kidneys, esp. (and now usu.) nephritis. LME.
†**3** Of a medicine, a treatment, etc.: acting or alleviating conditions of the kidneys. M17–L18.
3 nephritic stone jade, nephrite. **nephritic wood** a wood an infusion of which was formerly used to treat diseases of the kidneys.
▶ **B** *noun.* **1** A person with kidney disease, esp. (and now usu.) nephritis. LME.
†**2** A medicine for the kidneys. M17–E18.

nephritic /nɪ'frɪtɪk/ *adjective*[2]. E19.
[from NEPHRITE + -IC.]
MINERALOGY. Of the nature of, pertaining to, or containing nephrite.

†**nephritical** *adjective.* M17–E18.
[formed as NEPHRITIC *adjective*[1]: see -ICAL.]
= NEPHRITIC *adjective*[1].

nephritis /nɪ'frʌɪtɪs/ *noun.* L16.
[Late Latin from Greek formed as next: see -ITIS.]
MEDICINE. Inflammation of the kidney.

nephro- /'nɛfrəʊ/ *combining form.* Before a vowel also **nephr-**.
[from Greek *nephros* kidney: see -O-.]
ANATOMY, MEDICINE, & ZOOLOGY. Of or pertaining to the kidneys or a kidney or other excretory organ.
■ **nephroblast** *noun* (ZOOLOGY) a cell from which a nephridium develops L19. **nephrobla'stoma** *noun*, pl. **-mas**, **-mata** /-mətə/, MEDICINE a malignant tumour of the kidney in children, Wilms' tumour M20. **nephrocalci'nosis** *noun* (MEDICINE) the deposition of calcareous concretions in the kidneys M20. **nephrocyte** *noun* (ZOOLOGY) a cell in insects which absorbs colloidal substances from the haemocoel by pinocytosis L19. **nephro'genic** *adjective* arising in or developing into the kidneys; ***nephrogenic cord***, a ridge of tissue in an embryo which gives rise to the kidneys and gonads: L19. **nephroli'thiasis** *noun*, pl. **-ases** /-əsiːz/, MEDICINE (disease caused by) the presence of renal calculi M19. **nephroli'thotomy** *noun* (an instance of) surgical removal of a renal calculus by incision M19. **ne'phrologist** *noun* an expert in or student of nephrology L19. **ne'phrology** *noun* the branch of medicine that deals with the physiology and diseases of the kidneys M19. **nephro'mixium** *noun*, pl. **-'mixia**, ZOOLOGY a combined genital and nephridial organ in certain polychaetes E20. **nephro'pathic** *adjective* of or pertaining to nephropathy E20. **ne'phropathy** *noun* disease or dysfunction of the kidneys E20. **nephropexy** *noun* (MEDICINE) = NEPHRORRHAPHY L19. **nephroptosis** /-ɒp'təʊsɪs/ *noun*, pl. **-toses** /-'təʊsiːz/, MEDICINE abnormal descent of a movable kidney L19. **ne'phrorrhaphy** *noun* (an instance of) the surgical fixing of a movable kidney L19. **nephroscle'rosis** *noun*, pl. **-roses** /-'rəʊsiːz/, MEDICINE hardening of the walls of the blood-vessels in the kidney L19. **nephrostome** *noun* (ZOOLOGY) the funnel-shaped aperture of some nephridial organs L19. **ne'phrostomy** *noun* (an instance of) surgical creation of an opening to drain urine directly from the kidney E20. **nephrotome** *noun* (EMBRYOLOGY) a block of tissue at the edge of a somite which gives rise to the excretory organs L19. **nephro'toxic** *adjective* toxic due to the effect on the kidneys E20. **nephrotoxicity** /-tɒk'sɪsɪti/ *noun* the property or degree of being nephrotoxic M20. **nephro'toxin** *noun* a nephrotoxic substance; an antibody specific to kidney tissue: E20.

nephroid /'nɛfrɔɪd/ *adjective.* M19.
[from prec. + -OID.]
Kidney-shaped.

nephron /'nɛfrɒn/ *noun.* M20.
[from Greek *nephros* kidney.]
ANATOMY. Each of the functional units in the kidney, consisting of a glomerulus and its associated tubule, through which the glomerular filtrate passes before emerging as urine.

nephrops /'nɛfrɒps/ *noun.* Pl. same. M19.
[mod. Latin genus name, from NEPHRO- + Greek *ōps* eye, face.]
= DUBLIN BAY PRAWN. Chiefly as mod. Latin genus name.

For other words beginning with *neo-* see the entry for **neo-**

nephrosis /nɪˈfrəʊsɪs/ *noun*. Pl. **-phroses** /-ˈfrəʊsiːz/. **E20**.
[from NEPHRO- + -OSIS.]
MEDICINE. Kidney disease; now *spec.* nephrotic syndrome.

nephrotic /nɪˈfrɒtɪk/ *adjective*. **E20**.
[from prec. + -OTIC.]
MEDICINE. Of, associated with, or suffering from nephrosis.
nephrotic syndrome a syndrome characterized by oedema and the loss of protein, esp. albumin, from the plasma into the urine, usu. caused by increased glomerular permeability.

nephrotomy /nɪˈfrɒtəmi/ *noun*. **L17**.
[from NEPHRO- + -TOMY.]
Surgical incision into the kidney, esp. to remove a renal calculus.

nephsystem /ˈnɛfsɪstəm/ *noun*. **M20**.
[from Greek *nephos* cloud + SYSTEM.]
METEOROLOGY. A large-scale array of clouds associated with a weather system; a cloud system.

nepionic /niːpɪˈɒnɪk/ *adjective*. **L19**.
[from Greek *nēpios* child + *-onic* after *embryonic*: see -IC.]
ZOOLOGY. Designating or pertaining to an animal in an early stage of development; immature, larval.

ne plus ultra /niː plʌs ˈʌltrə, neɪ plʊs ˈʊltrɑː/ *noun phr.* **M17**.
[Latin = not further beyond, the supposed inscription on the Pillars of Hercules (Strait of Gibraltar) prohibiting passage by ships.]
1 A prohibition of further advance or action; an impassable obstacle or limitation. **M17**.
2 The furthest limit reached or attainable; *esp.* the point of highest attainment, the acme or highest point *of* a quality etc. **L17**.

📖 **2** *Independent* A dozen meat and fish dishes and that ne plus ultra of my childhood, kedgeree.

nepman /ˈnɛpmən/ *noun*. Also **N-**. Pl. **-men**. **E20**.
[from acronym from Russian *novaya ékonomicheskaya politika* New Economic Policy (see below) + MAN *noun*.]
Hist. A supporter of or participant in the New Economic Policy programme introduced in the Soviet Union in 1921 as a means of encouraging a limited amount of private enterprise.

nepotal /ˈnɛpət(ə)l/ *adjective*. **M19**.
[from NEPOT(ISM + -AL¹.]
Of, pertaining to, or characteristic of a nephew or nephews.

nepotic /nɪˈpɒtɪk/ *adjective*. **M19**.
[formed as prec. + -IC.]
Tending to or of the nature of nepotism; holding or pertaining to the position of a nephew.

nepotism /ˈnɛpətɪz(ə)m/ *noun*. **M17**.
[French *népotisme* from Italian *nepotismo*, from *nipote* nephew + -ISM.]
†**1** The advantages, or opportunities for advancement, conferred on a pope's nephew. Only in **M17**.
2 The showing of special favour to a nephew or other relative in conferring privileges or position, esp. (now *Hist.*) by a pope or other ecclesiastic; *gen.* the unfair preferment of relatives, friends, or protegés. **L17**.

📖 **2** A. BEVAN Entitlement to advancement on grounds of merit alone, free from any tinge of political nepotism, must be jealously guarded.

nepotist /ˈnɛpətɪst/ *noun*. **M19**.
[from prec.: see -IST.]
A person given to nepotism.
▪ **nepoˈtistic** *adjective* **M20**.

Neptune /ˈnɛptjuːn/ *noun*. **LME**.
[French, or Latin *Neptunus* Neptune (see below).]
1 In ROMAN MYTHOLOGY, the god of the sea, corresponding to the Greek Poseidon. Also (*transf.*), the sea, the ocean. **LME**.
2 The eighth planet in order of distance from the sun, whose orbit lies beyond that of Uranus. **M19**.
3 (**n-**.) A large brass or copper plate or pan, formerly used as an item of trade in Africa. **M19**.
Phrases: **Neptune's cup**, **Neptune's goblet** a sponge of the genus *Poterion*, which forms a large stalked cuplike colony; a soft coral of similar form.

Neptunian /nɛpˈtjuːnɪən/ *adjective & noun*. Also **n-**, (*rare*) **-ean**. **M17**.
[from Latin *Neptunius*, from *Neptunus* (see prec.), + -IAN.]
▶**A** *adjective*. **1** Of or pertaining to the Roman sea-god Neptune; of or pertaining to the sea. **M17**.
2 GEOLOGY. **a** = NEPTUNIC. **L18**. ▸**b** Pertaining to, of the nature of, or advocating Neptunism. **E19**.
3 Of or belonging to the planet Neptune. **M19**.
2a Neptunian dyke a deposit of sand cutting through sedimentary strata in the manner of an igneous dyke, formed by the filling of an underwater fissure.
▶**B** *noun*. **1** GEOLOGY. = NEPTUNIST 2. **L18**.
2 An (imaginary or hypothetical) inhabitant of the planet Neptune. **L19**.
▪ **Neptunianism** *noun* = NEPTUNISM **M19**.

neptunic /nɛpˈtjuːnɪk/ *adjective*. **L19**.
[from NEPTUNE + -IC.]
GEOLOGY. Of a rock or formation: formed by the action of water; sedimentary, not volcanic or plutonic.

Neptunism /ˈnɛptjuːnɪz(ə)m/ *noun*. **E20**.
[formed as prec. + -ISM.]
GEOLOGY (now *Hist.*). The theory that the rocks of the earth's crust were laid down primarily by precipitation from the sea, rather than by solidification from magma. Cf. PLUTONISM 1.

Neptunist /ˈnɛptjuːnɪst/ *noun*. **L16**.
[formed as prec. + -IST.]
†**1** A nautical person. *rare*. Only in **L16**.
2 GEOLOGY (now *Hist.*). An advocate of Neptunism. **E19**.

neptunite /ˈnɛptjuːnʌɪt/ *noun*. **L19**.
[from NEPTUNE (so called from its occurrence with AEGIRINE) + -ITE¹.]
MINERALOGY. A silicate of sodium, potassium, iron, manganese, and titanium, occurring as black monoclinic crystals.

neptunium /nɛpˈtjuːnɪəm/ *noun*. **L19**.
[from NEPTUNE + -IUM, after *uranium*.]
†**1** A supposed chemical element similar to tantalum found in a sample of tantalite. Only in **L19**.
2 A radioactive metallic chemical element of the lanthanide series, atomic no. 93, which is produced artificially. (Symbol Np.) **M20**.

neral /ˈnɪəral/ *noun*. **M20**.
[from NEROL + -AL².]
CHEMISTRY. A colourless oily aldehyde which is the *cis* form of citral and gives nerol on reduction.

neram /nɪˈrɑːm/ *noun*. **E20**.
[Malay.]
A large evergreen tree, *Dipterocarpus oblongifolius* (family Dipterocarpaceae), growing along river-banks in SE Asia.

NERC *abbreviation*.
Natural Environment Research Council.

nerd /nəːd/ *noun*. *slang* (orig. *US*). Also **nurd**. **M20**.
[Origin unkn.]
An insignificant or foolish person, a person who is boringly conventional or studious.
Comb.: **nerd pack** a plastic holder kept in the top pocket to prevent pens from soiling the fabric.
▪ **nerdiness** *noun* **L20**. **nerdish** *adjective* **L20**. **nerdishness** *noun* **L20**. **nerdy** *adjective* **L20**.

Neread /ˈnɪərɪad/ *noun*. *rare*. Also **n-**. Pl. **-ads**, **-ades** /-ədiːz/. **M16**.
[Alt. of next after *dryad*, *oread*, etc.]
= NEREID 1.

Nereid /ˈnɪərɪɪd/ *noun & adjective*. Also (in sense A.2 now usu.) **n-**. **LME**.
[Latin *Nereid-*, *Nereis* from Greek *Nērēid-*, *Nērēis*, from *Nēreus* a sea-god: see -ID³.]
▶**A** *noun*. Pl. **-s**, **-es** /-iːz/.
1 CLASSICAL MYTHOLOGY. A sea-nymph, any of the daughters of the sea-god Nereus. **LME**.
2 ZOOLOGY. A carnivorous errant polychaete worm of the marine family Nereidae, having a long body composed of many similar segments, and freq. pelagic during part of the life cycle; a ragworm. **L18**.
▶**B** *adjective*. ZOOLOGY. Of, pertaining to, or designating the family Nereidae (see sense A.2 above). **L19**.

nereis /ˈnɪərɪs/ *noun*. **M18**.
[mod. Latin (see below), formed as prec.]
ZOOLOGY. A ragworm of the genus *Nereis*. Now chiefly as mod. Latin genus name.

nerf /nəːf/ *verb intrans.* *slang* (orig. *US*). **M20**.
[Origin unkn.]
Bump another car in a drag race. Freq. as ***nerfing*** *verbal noun*.
Comb.: **nerf-bar**, **nerfing-bar** a bumper fitted to a car used in a drag race.

nerine /nɪˈrʌɪni, nəˈriːnə/ *noun*. **E19**.
[mod. Latin (see below) from Latin from Greek *Nērēis* a water-nymph: cf. NEREID.]
Any of various southern African bulbous plants of the genus *Nerine* (family Amaryllidaceae); esp. *N. bowdenii* and the Guernsey lily, *N. sarniensis*, widely cultivated for their autumn-blooming pink flowers.

Nerita /nɪˈrʌɪtə/ *noun*. Pl. **-tae** /-tiː/, **-tas**. Also **n-**. **M18**.
[mod. Latin, formed as next.]
ZOOLOGY. = next. Now chiefly as mod. Latin genus name.

nerite /ˈnɪərʌɪt/ *noun*. **E18**.
[Latin *nerita* from Greek *nēritēs* sea-mussel, from *Nēreus*: see NEREID, -ITE¹.]
ZOOLOGY. A gastropod mollusc of the prosobranch order Neritacea; *esp.* one of the genus *Nerita*, having a pyramidal or globular shell with a semilunate opening, and freq. found in brackish or intertidal habitats.

neritic /nɪˈrɪtɪk/ *adjective*. **L19**.
[Perh. formed as prec. + -IC.]
Of, pertaining to, originating in, or inhabiting the shallow part of the sea, near a coast and overlying the continental shelf.
neritic province, ***neritic zone***.

nerium /ˈnɪərɪəm/ *noun*. **L19**.
[Latin from Greek *nērion*.]
Any of several plants of the genus *Nerium* (family Apocynaceae); *esp.* the oleander, *N. oleander*.

nerk /nəːk/ *noun*. *slang*. Also **nurk**. **M20**.
[Origin uncertain: cf. NERD, JERK *noun*¹ 4.]
A foolish, objectionable, or insignificant person.
▪ **nerkish** *adjective* **L20**.

nerka /ˈnəːkə/ *noun*. **M18**.
[mod. Latin (see below), of unkn. origin.]
The sockeye salmon, *Oncorhynchus nerka*.

Nernst /nəːnst, *foreign* nɛrnst/ *noun*. **L19**.
[W. H. *Nernst* (1864–1941), German physical chemist.]
1 Used *attrib.* to designate an electric incandescent lamp in which the filament is an unenclosed ceramic rod of rare earths and other metallic oxides, and which is used esp. as a source of infrared radiation. Also, used to designate the filament of such a lamp. **L19**.
2 PHYSICS. Used *attrib.* with ref. to a thermomagnetic effect in which a temperature gradient in a metal subject to a magnetic field at right angles to the gradient gives rise to an electromotive force at right angles to both. **E20**.
3 PHYSICS. Used *attrib.* and in *possess.* with ref. to a theorem in thermodynamics which states that the change in entropy accompanying a chemical reaction between pure crystalline solids tends to zero as the temperature tends to absolute zero. **E20**.

nerol /ˈnɪərɒl/ *noun*. **E20**.
[from next + -OL.]
CHEMISTRY. A colourless oily unsaturated alcohol, $C_{10}H_{18}O$, present in neroli and some other essential oils and used in perfumery, having a similar fragrance to its stereoisomer geraniol.

neroli /ˈnɪərəli/ *noun*. **L17**.
[French *néroli*, from Italian *neroli* after an Italian princess of that name, to whom its discovery is attributed.]
An essential oil distilled from the flowers of the Seville orange and used in perfumery. Also ***neroli oil***, ***oil of neroli***.

Neronian /nɪˈrəʊnɪən/ *adjective*. **L16**.
[Latin *Neronianus*, from *Nero* Claudius Caesar, Roman Emperor 54–68: see -IAN.]
Of, pertaining to, or characteristic of the Roman Emperor Nero or his times; *esp.* cruel, tyrannical, licentious.

Neronic /nɪˈrɒnɪk/ *adjective*. **E20**.
[formed as prec. + -IC.]
Neronian.

Neronize /ˈnɪərənʌɪz/ *verb trans.* Also **-ise**. **E17**.
[formed as prec. + -IZE.]
Tyrannize over or deprave in a manner characteristic of the Roman Emperor Nero; stigmatize as resembling Nero.

nerts /nəːts/ *noun*. *slang*. **M20**.
[Repr. a colloq. pronunc. of *nuts*: see NUT *noun* 4b.]
Nonsense, rubbish.

nerval /ˈnəːv(ə)l/ *adjective*. Now *rare* or *obsolete*. **M17**.
[French, or Latin *nervalis*, formed as NERVE *noun*: see -AL¹.]
Of, pertaining to, or affecting the nerves; neural.

†**nervate** *verb trans.* **L17–L18**.
[from NERVE *noun* + -ATE³.]
Nerve, support, strengthen.

nervation /nəːˈveɪʃ(ə)n/ *noun*. **E18**.
[French, from *nerver*, formed as next: see -ATION.]
†**1** The action of strengthening as though by sinews. *rare*. Only in **E18**.
2 BOTANY. The arrangement of nerves in a leaf etc.; venation. **M19**.
▪ **ˈnervature** *noun* = NERVATION **M19**.

nerve /nəːv/ *noun*. **LME**.
[Latin *nervus* sinew, bowstring, rel. to Greek *neuron* sinew, nerve and to Latin *nere* to spin.]
▶**I** **1** **a** A sinew, a tendon, esp. as removed from an animal's body for a particular purpose. Now chiefly *poet.* and in ***strain every nerve***, make the utmost exertion. **LME**. ▸†**b** The penis. *rare*. **M–L17**. ▸**c** A bowstring. Chiefly *poet.* **E18**.
2 BOTANY. A rib or vein of a leaf, bract, etc., *esp.* a prominent unbranched vein; *spec.* the midrib of the leaf of a moss. **LME**.
†**3** A thread or narrow band of material used to ornament a garment. *Scot. rare*. Only in **M16**.
4 *fig.* A person, quality, element, etc., constituting the main strength or vigour *of* something. Freq. in *pl.* **E17**.

5 Strength, vigour, energy. Also (*rare*), the texture, body, etc., of a material. **E17.**
6 ARCHITECTURE. A rib or moulding on a vault. *rare*. **E18.**

> **4** GIBBON Prosperity had relaxed the nerves of discipline. **5** GOLDSMITH Not . . too near extreme wealth to slacken the nerve of labour.

▶**II 7 a** A fibre or bundle of fibres containing neurones and associated cells and serving to transmit electrochemical signals within a human or animal body, esp. from the sense organs to the brain and spinal cord, and from these to the muscle cells, glands, etc. **LME.** ▸**b** Nervous tissue. **L18.**
8 In *pl.* The bodily state resulting from the influence of mental or physical stimuli, esp. with regard to a person's feeling or courage. Also, disordered or heightened sensitivity; anxiety, fearfulness, tension, etc. **E17.**
9 Coolness in adversity or danger, boldness, assurance; *colloq.* audacity, impudence. **E19.**

> ***7a cranial nerve, motor nerve, optic nerve, sciatic nerve***, etc. **8** M. EDGEWORTH Not the fittest companion in the world for a person of your ladyship's nerves. C. CHAPLIN On the opening night at the Coliseum my nerves were wound tight like a clock. **9** H. CARPENTER His decision to remain in America in the face of criticism . . required no small amount of nerve. D. LODGE I didn't think you'd have the nerve to show your face in this place again.

Phrases: **bag of nerves**, **bundle of nerves**, etc., a very tense or timid person. **get on a person's nerves** (begin to) be a source of worry or irritation to a person. **have a nerve** act boldly, behave impudently. **have nerves of steel**, **have nerves of iron** (of a person etc.) be not easily frightened or unsettled. **have the nerve** be bold enough to act, behave impudently. **hit a nerve**, **touch a nerve** remark on or draw attention to a sensitive subject or point. **live on one's nerves** lead a stressful or emotionally demanding life. **lose one's nerve** experience a lack of confidence, become suddenly fearful or apprehensive. ***of all the nerve***: see OF *preposition*. ***strain every nerve***: see sense 1a above. ***touch a nerve***: see **hit a nerve** above. **war of nerves** the use of hostile or subversive propaganda to undermine morale and cause confusion.

Comb.: **nerve agent** = *nerve gas* below; **nerve block**, **nerve blocking** inactivation of a nerve serving a particular area of the body, esp. by local anaesthetic; **nerve cell** a neurone, a cell with elongated processes along which electrical impulses are propagated within a nerve; **nerve-centre** a ganglion; (chiefly *fig.*) a centre of information flow or of control; **nerve-cord** (chiefly ZOOLOGY) a major nerve, *esp.* the main axis of a nervous system; **nerve-deafness**: due to malfunction of the auditory nerve; **nerve-doctor** a neurologist; **nerve-ending** the branched or specialized end of a nerve fibre; **nerve fibre** an axon; a nerve; **nerve-force** *arch.* the force supposed to be liberated in nerve cells; **nerve gas** a poisonous gas or vapour that disrupts the functioning of the nervous system, esp. for use in warfare; **nerve impulse** a signal transmitted along a nerve fibre, consisting of a wave of electrical depolarization; **nerve-knot** a ganglion, a nerve-centre; **nerve net** ZOOLOGY a diffuse network of neurones found in coelenterates, flatworms, etc., which conducts impulses in all directions from a point of stimulus; **nerve-path** a route (inborn or developed through use) by which a specific sensory stimulus or motor response is propagated through the nervous system; **nerve-patient** a patient suffering from a nervous disorder; **nerve-racking** *adjective* stressful, frightening; **nerve-ring** ZOOLOGY a ring of nerve-cords and ganglia round the oesophagus in various invertebrates; **nerve storm** an emotional outburst; a state of nervous frenzy; **nerve war** = ***war of nerves*** above.

nerve /nəːv/ *verb trans.* **E16.**
[from the noun.]
†**1** Ornament with threads or narrow bands of some material. *Scot. rare.* **E–M16.**
2 Give strength or vigour to (the arm, the body, etc.). **M18.**
3 Imbue with courage, embolden; *refl.* brace (oneself) to face adversity etc. **L18.**

> **2** W. C. BRYANT He nerved their limbs With vigor ever new. **3** E. M. FORSTER With infinite effort we nerve ourselves for a crisis that never comes.

nerved /nəːvd/ *adjective.* **E18.**
[from NERVE *noun* + -ED².]
1 Having a nerve or nerves of a specified kind; BOTANY ribbed. Freq. with qualifying adjective, as ***strong-nerved***, ***weak-nerved***, etc. **E18.**
2 HERALDRY. Of a leaf: having the veins detailed in a different colour from their background. **E19.**

nerveless /ˈnəːvlɪs/ *adjective.* **L17.**
[from NERVE *noun* + -LESS.]
1 Lacking courage or vigour; weak, incapable of effort, lifeless. **L17.** ▸**b** Of literary or artistic style: diffuse, insipid. **M18.**
2 ANATOMY, BOTANY, & ZOOLOGY. Having no nerves or nervures. **L18.**
3 Confident; not nervous. **L20.**

> **1** *Liverpool Daily Post* A nerveless diplomatist who only has to be menaced and he will yield. D. LODGE Vic's last action is normally to detach a book from Marjorie's nerveless fingers. **b** *Blackwood's Magazine* Lord Byron retains the same nerveless and pointless kind of blank verse.

■ **nervelessly** *adverb* **M19.** **nervelessness** *noun* **M19.**

nervelet /ˈnəːvlɪt/ *noun. rare.* **M17.**
[from NERVE *noun* + -LET.]
Orig., a tendril. Later, a little nerve.

nervine /ˈnəːvʌɪn, -iːn/ *adjective & noun.* Now *rare* or *obsolete.* **M17.**
[medieval Latin *nervinus* of a sinew or sinews, or after French *nervin*: see -INE¹. Cf. NERVE *noun*.]
MEDICINE. ▶**A** *adjective.* Having a soothing effect on the nerves (or, formerly, the tendons). **M17.**
▶**B** *noun.* A nervine medicine or substance. **M18.**

nervo- /ˈnəːvəʊ/ *combining form.* Now *rare* or *obsolete.* **M19.**
[from Latin *nervus* NERVE *noun*: see -O-.]
PHYSIOLOGY. Of or pertaining to nerves.
¶ Largely replaced by NEURO-.

nervose /nəˈvəʊs/ *adjective.* **LME.**
[formed as NERVOUS: see -OSE¹.]
†**1** = NERVOUS 1. *rare.* Only in **LME.**
†**2** = NERVOUS 2. *rare.* Only in **M17.**
3 = NERVOUS 6. **L17.**
4 BOTANY. Of a leaf etc.: having (conspicuous) nerves or veins. **M18.**

nervosity /nəˈvɒsɪti/ *noun.* **LME.**
[Latin *nervositas* strength, formed as next: see -OSITY.]
†**1** The state of having or consisting of sinews or fibres. Only in **LME.**
†**2** Strength. *rare.* Only in **17.**
3 The state or quality of being nervous; nervousness; *rare* an instance of this. **L18.**

nervous /ˈnəːvəs/ *adjective.* **LME.**
[Latin *nervosus* sinewy, vigorous, formed as NERVE *noun*: see -OUS.]
▶**I** †**1** Sinewy, tendinous; resembling a sinew or a tendon in texture, fibrous. **LME–M18.**
†**2** Affecting the sinews or tendons. *rare.* Only in **LME.**
3 (Of a person, a limb, etc.) muscular, strong; (of strength, courage, etc.) vigorous, powerful. Now *rare* exc. as passing into sense 8. **LME.**
4 Of literary style etc.: vigorous, forcible; free from insipidity and diffuseness. **M17.**
†**5** BOTANY. Of a leaf etc.: nervose. **M17–L18.**

> **3** RICHARD SAUNDERS The arms strong and nervous, having the veins conspicuous. H. D. THOREAU They . . handled their paddles unskilfully, but with nervous energy and determination. **4** CARLYLE [His] own writing is . . so clear, direct and nervous.

▶**II 6** Of or pertaining to the nerves. **LME.** ▸**b** Well supplied with nerves, sensitive. **LME.**
7 Of a medicine: acting on the nerves or nervous system. Now *rare* or *obsolete.* **E18.**
8 Affecting or involving the nerves; suffering from or arising out of a disorder of the nervous system. Freq. in ***nervous exhaustion***, ***nervous headache***. **M18.**
9 Excitable, highly strung, easily agitated; characterized by a heightened sensitivity. Also, worried, anxious (*about*); reluctant; afraid (*of*). **M18.** ▸**b** STOCK EXCHANGE. Characterized or dominated by apprehension or uncertainty in the financial market. **M20.**
10 Overstimulating; exciting. *arch.* **L18.**

> **9** E. FIGES He was nervous, uneasy, . . he paced up and down the room like a caged animal. J. R. ACKERLEY She had already begun . . that nervous withdrawal from the hazardous outside world. W. TREVOR All I could do now was confess my feelings to my father, which I'd been nervous of doing. ***as nervous as a witch***: see WITCH *noun*¹. **b** *Economist* Markets were nervous ahead of the latest round of . . talks on Hong Kong's future. **10** G. CRABBE The gentle fair on nervous tea relies.

Special collocations: **nervous breakdown** failure to cope psychologically with the stresses of everyday life, manifesting in incapacitating mental and emotional disturbance and (freq.) depression; a period of this. **nervous Nelly** *colloq.* an excessively timid or anxious person. **nervous system** the network of nerves within the body; (with specifying word, as *autonomic*, *central*, *peripheral*, etc.) each of the main functional subsystems of this. **nervous tension** a state of mental stress or excitement. **nervous wreck** a person suffering from stress or emotional exhaustion.
■ **nervously** *adverb* **M17.** **nervousness** *noun* **E18.**

nervure /ˈnəːvjʊə/ *noun.* **E19.**
[Old & mod. French, from *nerf* from Latin *nervus*: see NERVE *noun*, -URE.]
1 A vein in an insect's wing. **E19.**
2 A principal vein of a leaf. **M19.**

nervy /ˈnəːvi/ *adjective.* **E17.**
[from NERVE *noun* + -Y¹.]
1 Vigorous, sinewy, full of strength. *poet.* **E17.**
2 Confident, assured, cool. Also (*N. Amer. colloq.*), audacious, impudent. **L19.**
3 Jerky, sudden. **L19.**
4 = NERVOUS 9, 9b. **L19.**

> **1** KEATS Between His nervy knees there lay a boar-spear keen. **2** E. ROBINS It is a little 'nervy' . . to walk into another man's house uninvited. **4** R. MACAULAY Barbary had been a wild baby, a nervy, excited child. *Observer* They are . . vulnerable to the nervy, post-Big Bang international financial markets.

■ **nervily** *adverb* **E19.** **nerviness** *noun* **E17.**

nescience /ˈnɛsɪəns/ *noun.* Chiefly *literary.* **E17.**
[Late Latin *nescientia*, from *nescire*: see next, -ENCE.]
Absence or lack of knowledge, ignorance, (*of*); *rare* an instance of this.

nescient /ˈnɛsɪənt/ *adjective & noun.* Chiefly *literary.* **LME.**
[Latin *nescient-* pres. ppl stem of *nescire*, from *ne* not + *scire* know: see -ENT.]
▶**A** *adjective.* **1** Ignorant. Usu. foll. by *of.* **LME.**
2 Agnostic. **L19.**
▶**B** *noun.* An agnostic. **L19.**

nese /niːz/ *noun.* Long *obsolete* exc. *Scot.* **ME.**
[Perh. from Middle Low German, Middle Dutch *nese*.]
The nose.

nesh /nɛʃ/ *adjective.* Now *dial.*
[Old English *hnesċe* = Dutch *nesch*, *nisch* soft (of eggs), damp, sodden, foolish, Gothic *hnasqus*, soft, tender: ult. origin unkn.]
1 a Soft in texture or consistency; tender, succulent, juicy. **OE.** ▸**b** Damp, moist, wet. *rare.* **LME.**
2 a Lacking in energy or diligence; slack, negligent. **OE.** ▸**b** Timid; lacking courage; faint-hearted. **LME.**
†**3 a** Inclined to pity, mercy, or other tender feelings. **OE–M16.** ▸**b** Easily yielding to temptation; inclined to lust or wantonness. **OE–LME.**
4 a Unable to endure fatigue or exposure; susceptible to cold; delicate, weak. **OE.** ▸**b** Dainty, fastidious, squeamish. **M19.**
■ **neshly** *adverb* **OE.** **neshness** *noun* **OE.**

Nesite /ˈnɛsʌɪt/ *noun & adjective.* **M20.**
[from *Nešaš* an ancient city of Asia Minor + -ITE¹.]
= KANESIAN.

neskhi *noun & adjective* var. of NASKHI.

nespola /ˈnɛspola/ *noun.* Pl. **-le** /-le/. **L19.**
[Italian.]
A medlar (the tree and its fruit).

ness /nɛs/ *noun.*
[Old English *næs(s)*, *nes(s)*, *næsse* corresp. to Low German *nesse*, Old Norse *nes* rel. to NOSE *noun*.]
A promontory, a headland, a cape.

-ness /nɪs/ *suffix.*
[Old English *-nes(s)*, *-nis(s)* = Old Frisian *-nesse*, *-nisse*, Old Saxon *-nessi*, *-nissi* (Dutch *-nis*), Old High German *-nessi*, *-nassi*, *-nissi* (German *-nis*), Gothic *-nassus*, from Germanic, from final consonant of pa. pple of strong verbs stem + suffix of weak verbs.]
Forming nouns expr. a state or condition, esp. from adjectives and (orig. pa.) pples, as ***bitterness***, ***conceitedness***, ***darkness***, ***hardness***, ***kindheartedness***, ***tongue-tiedness***, ***up-to-dateness***, etc., also occas. from adverbs, as ***everydayness***, ***nowness***, etc., and in other nonce uses. Also in extended senses 'an instance of a state or condition', as a ***kindness*** etc., 'something in a state or condition', as ***foulness*** etc., and in a few other exceptional uses, as ***witness***.

nessberry /ˈnɛsbɛri/ *noun.* **E20.**
[from Helge *Ness* (d. 1928), US horticulturist, who introduced it + BERRY *noun*¹.]
A cross between a dewberry and a raspberry.

Nesselrode /ˈnɛs(ə)lrəʊd/ *noun.* **M19.**
[Karl-Robert *Nesselrode* (1780–1862), Russian statesman.]
In full ***Nesselrode pie***, ***Nesselrode pudding***. An iced dessert made with chestnuts, cream, preserved fruits, etc., and freq. flavoured with rum.

Nessler /ˈnɛslə/ *noun.* **M19.**
[Julius *Nessler* (1827–1905), German agricultural chemist.]
CHEMISTRY. Used *attrib.* and in *possess.* with ref. to an analytical test for ammonia devised by Nessler.
Nessler's reagent, **Nessler's solution**, **Nessler reagent**, **Nessler solution** an alkaline solution of potassium mercuric iodide, which gives a yellow or brown colour or precipitate when added to an aqueous solution containing ammonia. **Nessler's tube**, **Nessler tube** a flat-bottomed glass cylinder marked with a line indicating a certain volume and depth, used in colorimetry, esp. nesslerization.
■ **nessleriˈzation** *noun* the process of testing with Nessler's reagent **L19.** **nesslerize** *verb trans.* analyse or determine with Nessler's reagent **L19.**

Nessus /ˈnɛsəs/ *noun. literary.* **E17.**
[A centaur killed by Hercules and in whose blood was soaked a tunic which consumed Hercules with fire.]
Nessus robe, ***Nessus shirt***, ***shirt of Nessus***, a destructive or expurgatory force or influence.

nest /nɛst/ *noun.*
[Old English *nest* = Middle & mod. Dutch, Old & mod. High German *nest*, from Indo-European (whence also Latin *nidus*, Old Irish *net* (mod. *nead*), Welsh *nyth*, Sanskrit *nīḍa* resting-place), from base meaning 'down' (repr. also in 1st elem. of NETHER) + base of SIT *verb*.]
1 a A structure made or a place chosen by a bird for laying and incubating its eggs and for sheltering its young. **OE.** ▸**b** A place or structure used by an animal or insect as a lair or somewhere to live, or as a spawning- or breeding-ground. **LME.**
2 a A place in which a person (or personified thing) lives or finds rest; a lodging, shelter, home, bed, etc., esp.

of a secluded or comfortable nature; a snug retreat. OE. ▸**b** A place in which a thing is lodged or deposited. L16. ▸**c** *MILITARY.* An emplaced group of machine-guns. E20.

3 A place usually inhabited or frequented by people of a certain type or class; a place or quarter in which some state of things, quality, etc. (esp. of a bad kind), is fostered or is prevalent; a haunt *of* thieves, robbers, crime, vice, etc. LME.

4 a A number of birds, insects, or other animals occupying the same nest or habitation; a brood, a swarm, a colony. LME. ▸**b** A number or collection of people, esp. of the same type or class or inhabiting or frequenting the same place. L16.

5 A set or series of similar objects, esp. designed to be contained in the same receptacle or so made that each smaller one is enclosed in or fits into the next up in size; an accumulation or collection of similar objects or immaterial things. LME. ▸**b** A connected series of cogwheels or pulleys. L18. ▸**c** A number of buildings or narrow streets lying in close proximity to one another. L18. ▸**d** *COMPUTING & LINGUISTICS.* A set of nested procedures, subroutines, or syntactic units. M20.

6 *MINERALOGY.* A small isolated deposit of a mineral or metal. E18.

> **1a** C. STEAD Along the side porch .. were five nests, two of house wrens and three .. of sparrows. **b** W. KIRBY Fishes .. sometimes .. prepare regular nests for their young. J. A. THOMSON The tree-nest of one of the Termites. **2a** ***love-nest***: see LOVE noun. **c** C. RYAN Tops of haystacks open to disclose nests of 88 and 20 mm. guns. **4b** K. WATERHOUSE There is a chattering nest of Arab women at the .. chemist's. **5** E. CAIRD The cosmological argument is a nest of dialectical assumptions. F. L. WRIGHT A nest of small tables. *New Yorker* They had a breadbox, a camp stove, a nest of aluminum pots. **c** S. SHELDON A nest of research buildings .. experimental laboratories .. and railroad spurs.

Phrases: ***empty nest***: see EMPTY *adjective & noun*. ***feather one's nest***, ***feather one's own nest***: see FEATHER *verb* 5a. ***foul one's nest***, ***foul one's own nest***: see FOUL *verb* 2. ***mare's nest***: see MARE *noun*[1].

Comb.: **nest-box** (*a*) a box containing others of graduated sizes fitted in a nest; (*b*) a box provided for a domestic fowl or other bird to make its nest in; **nest egg** (*a*) an egg, natural or artificial, left in a nest to induce a hen etc. to continue to lay there after other eggs have been removed; an inducement, a decoy; (*b*) a sum of money laid or set by as a reserve or nucleus of savings; something kept in reserve.

■ **nestful** *noun* the quantity or number (of eggs or young) that a nest can contain L16. **nestlike** *adjective* resembling (that of) a nest L18.

nest /nɛst/ *verb*.

[Old English *nist(i)an* = Middle Dutch, Old & mod. High German *nistan*, re-formed in Middle English after NEST *noun*.]

1 *verb intrans.* Of a bird etc.: make or have a nest in a particular place; engage in nest-building. OE.

2 *verb intrans.* Settle, lodge, or fit as in a nest; be contained within a similar item in a hierarchical arrangement. ME.

†**3** *verb refl.* Rest or settle in a place. ME–E18.

4 *verb trans.* As ***nested*** *ppl adjective*. ▸**a** Settled, established, or comfortably placed in or as in a nest. L16. ▸**b** Used as a nest, used for making nests *in*. M19. ▸**c** Placed or fitted one inside another, such that each item or constituent contains or is contained within another similar one in a hierarchical arrangement. L19.

5 *verb intrans.* Search for birds' nests, esp. to take the eggs, go bird's-nesting. L19.

> **1** *Country Life* As many as 100,000 .. turtles arrive to nest in the autumn. J. C. OATES Pigeons and other birds nested in the open towers. **nesting-box** = ***nest-box*** (b) s.v. NEST *noun*. **2** H. VAUGHAN These dark confusions that within me nest. C. F. HOCKETT Complex expressions built up by a series of attributive constructions, one nesting within another. **4a** J. E. HOPKINS The tender tweet! tweet! of the nested birds in the ivy. G. NAYLOR She seemed so content nested down there at the end of Tupelo Drive. **b** R. L. STEVENSON Chestnuts .. nested in by song birds. **c** D. V. HUNTSBERGER Every classification is nested within the next larger one. *Practical Computing* The result is a conglomeration of nested subroutines.

nester /ˈnɛstə/ *noun*. M19.

[from NEST *verb* + -ER[1].]

1 A bird that is building or has built a nest. M19.

2 A farmer, homesteader, etc., settled in a cattle-grazing region. *derog. N. Amer.* M19.

¶ See also ***empty nester*** s.v. EMPTY *adjective & noun*.

nestle /ˈnɛs(ə)l/ *verb*.

[Old English *nestlian* = Middle Low German, Middle & mod. Dutch *nestelen*, formed as NEST *noun* + -LE[3].]

▶ **I** *verb intrans.* **1** Of a bird etc.: make or have a nest, esp. *in* a place; = NEST *verb* 1. OE.

2 Lodge or settle more or less permanently as in a nest. Formerly, make one's home (*in*). LME.

3 Settle down as in a nest or in a snug or comfortable manner (foll. by *down, in, into, among*, etc.); draw or press (*close*) *to* or *up to* a person or thing, esp. in an affectionate manner. L17.

4 Lie half-hidden or embedded (*in*); be in a snug or sheltered situation (foll. by *among, in*, etc.). L18.

> **1** W. S. DALLAS They nestle in rocks and holes of trees, and lay five or six eggs. **3** D. H. LAWRENCE 'Yes,' she murmured, nestling very sweet and close to him. Z. TOMIN We nestled in bed with a book each. **4** R. K. NARAYAN A small village nestling at the foot of the range of mountains. A. JUDD Instead of nestling snugly under his arm, .. the bulky Browning pressed heavily against his ribs. P. CUTTING The town of Baalbek nestles in the foothills.

▶ **II** *verb trans.* **5** *refl.* Settle or establish oneself in a place. (Foll. by *in(to)*.) Now *rare*. M16.

6 Place or settle in or as in a nest; set in a secure place. Freq. as ***nestled*** *ppl adjective*. M16.

7 Provide with a nesting-place. M17.

8 Push, press, rest, or settle (one's head etc.) in a snug or affectionate manner. L17.

> **6** *Chicago* He poured me some Harvey's Bristol Cream .. from a bottle nestled in a bar. **7** E. COOK Where the citron-tree nestles the soft humming-bird. **8** CONAN DOYLE The boy cooed and nestled his head upon his father's breast.

Comb.: **nestle-chick**, **nestle-cock** (now *dial.*) the last-hatched bird or weakling of a brood; a mother's pet, a spoilt or delicate child or youth; **nestle-tripe** (now *dial.*) = NESTLING 2.

■ **nestler** *noun* (*a*) a nesting bird; (*b*) a nestling; a little child: E17.

nestling /ˈnɛs(t)lɪŋ/ *noun*. LME.

[from NEST *noun* + -LING[1], or NESTLE + -ING[3], perh. after Middle Dutch *nestelinc* (mod. *-ling*).]

1 A young bird not yet old enough to leave the nest. LME.

2 The youngest child of a family. Now *rare*. L16.

Nestor /ˈnɛstɔː, -ə/ *noun*. *literary*. L16.

[Greek *Nestōr* a Homeric hero famous for his age and wisdom.]

(A name for) an old man.

Nestorian /nɛˈstɔːrɪən/ *noun & adjective*. LME.

[Late Latin *Nestorianus*, from *Nestorius* (see below): see -AN.]

CHRISTIAN CHURCH. ▶**A** *noun*. A follower or adherent of Nestorius, patriarch of Constantinople (appointed in 428), who asserted that Christ had distinct human and divine persons. LME.

▶ **B** *adjective*. Adhering to Nestorius or his doctrine; of or pertaining to Nestorius or the Nestorians. M16.

■ **Nestorianism** *noun* the doctrine of Nestorius E17.

net /nɛt/ *noun*[1] *& adjective*[1].

[Old English *net(t)* = Old Frisian *net(te)*, Old Saxon *netti*, *net*, Middle & mod. Dutch *net*, Middle Low German, Middle Dutch *nette*, Old High German *nezzi* (German *Netz*), Old Norse *net*, Gothic *nati*.]

▶ **A** *noun*. **I 1** (A piece of) openwork fabric made of twine or strong cord, forming meshes of a suitable size, used for catching fish, birds, or other living things. OE.

2 (A piece of) open fabric of meshwork used for any of various other purposes, as covering, protecting, confining, holding, delimiting, etc.; *spec*. (a structure with) a piece of netting used as part of the equipment for a ball game, as to divide off practice wickets in cricket, to divide the court in tennis etc., to form a goal in football, hockey, netball, etc.; in *pl*. also, a practice-ground in cricket, enclosed by nets. OE. ▸**b** A let in tennis. *colloq*. E20.

3 (A piece of) fine meshwork used as a part of a person's dress, as a veil, or as a means of confining the hair; *spec*. machine-made lace composed of small meshes. LME.

> **1** GOLDSMITH When our small birds begin to migrate .. taking them with nets in their passage. A. DESAI Caught in the traffic like a fish in a net. ***butterfly net***, ***fishing net***, etc. ***bag-net***, ***drag-net***, ***drift-net***, ***lave-net***, ***purse-net***, ***stake-net***, ***trawl-net***, etc. **2** *Times* He batted in the nets before the Yorkshire game resumed. N. STREATFEILD Under the trapezes or high tight-rope act a net is stretched. *Football Monthly* Rush dribbled around the goalkeeper to place the ball in an empty net. ***life net***, ***mosquito-net***, ***safety net***, etc. ***badminton net***, ***basketball net***, ***football net***, ***table-tennis net***, etc. **3** BOBBINET, ***hair net***, etc.

▶ **II** *transf. & fig*. **4** A spider's web. OE.

5 A means of catching or securing a person; *esp*. a moral or mental snare, trap, or entanglement. OE.

6 A thing resembling a net; a number of lines, veins, fibres, etc., arranged like the threads of a net; a reticulation, a network; *spec*. (*a*) a network of spies, (*b*) a broadcasting network, (*c*) *COMPUTING* a network of interconnected computers, (*d*) (**N-**) *COMPUTING* (*colloq*.) *the* Internet. L16. ▸**b** *MATH.* A plane figure which represents the faces of a polyhedron and can be folded to make a model of it. M19. ▸**c** (Usu. **N-**.) *The* constellation Reticulum. Also ***Rhomboidal Net***. E20.

> **5** MILTON Skill'd to .. draw Hearts after them tangl'd in Amorous Nets. B. PYM Somebody who's fallen through the net of the welfare state. V. BROME Jones was working .. to help one person after another escape the .. Nazi net. **6** A. GHOSH You could have as much time on the Net as you wanted.

Phrases: **dance in a net**, **march in a net** *arch*. (*a*) act with practically no disguise or concealment, while expecting to escape notice; (*b*) do something undetected. ***old boy net***, ***old boy's net***: see OLD *adjective*. ***slip through the net***: see SLIP *verb*[1].

Comb.: **netball** a team game the object of which is to throw a large inflated ball into a net hanging from a horizontal ring attached to a high pole, and in which players may only throw or hand the ball to each other and may not run or walk with the ball in their hands; the ball used in this; **net-cord** (*a*) a cord passing along and supporting the top of a net, esp. a tennis net; (*b*) (more fully ***net-cord stroke***) in tennis, a stroke which hits the net cord but still crosses the net; **net-drifter** = ***net-layer*** below; **net-fisher** a person who fishes with a net; **net-fishing** fishing with a net; **net-layer** a naval vessel which lays anti-submarine nets; **netmaker** a maker of nets; **netsman** a person who uses a net; **net-masonry** a form of decorative masonry in which the joints resemble the meshes of a net; **netminder** a goalkeeper, *spec*. in ice hockey; **net-play** *TENNIS & BADMINTON* play from a position close to the net; **net-player** *TENNIS & BADMINTON* a player who plays from a position close to the net; **net-practice** cricket practice at the nets.

▶ **B** *attrib*. or as *adjective*. Made of net. L16.

> L. CODY Net curtains .. up the street were twitching violently.

■ **netful** *noun* as much or as many as will fill a net M19. **netlike** *adjective* resembling (that of) a net E17. **netwise** *adverb* L16.

net /nɛt/ *noun*[2]. Now *rare*.

[Old English *nette* = Old Frisian *nette*, Old Norse *netja*, formed as prec.]

A sheet or covering of connective tissue, esp. in an animal; the mesentery; the omentum.

net /nɛt/ *noun*[3]. Also **nett**. E20.

[from NET *adjective*[2].]

A net sum; a net income; *the* net result.

net /nɛt/ *adjective*[2] *& adverb*. Also **nett**. ME.

[French *net*, (fem.) *nette* NEAT *adjective*.]

▶ **I** *adjective*. †**1** Good; neat, trim, smart. ME–E19.

†**2** Clean, free from dirt etc.; bright, clear; pure, unadulterated, unmixed. ME–M19.

▶ **II** *adjective & adverb*. **3** (Of an amount, weight, etc.) free from or not subject to any deduction, remaining after all necessary deductions have been made; (of a price) to be paid in full, not reducible; (of a result etc.) final, overall, emerging after all necessary factors have been taken into consideration. LME. ▸**b** Sold at or based on a net price. L19.

> **3** S. SEWALL Weight .. 193 pounds, Net. R. R. MARETT The net result was that, despite a very fair environment .. man [in Australia] .. stagnated. B. WEBB My net impression was that the Trade Unionists .. were .. no abler than thirty years ago. M. MEYER The tickets were .. cheap, for the net takings amounted to no more than £75. M. BRETT Current liabilities .. are therefore deducted from current assets .. to give net current assets. H. EVANS If we put up the cover price by X .. but cut the trade margin by Y, we'll end up net. **net of** after a deduction has been made for.

Special collocations: **net book** a book sold at an established net price; ***Net Book Agreement***, a formal arrangement between some publishers and booksellers, binding the latter not to sell books below the net price. **net national product** the annual total value of goods produced and services provided in a country, after depreciation of capital goods has been allowed for. **net net** (of a book) not subject to any discount whatever. **net reproduction rate** a reproduction rate representing the average number of girls born to each woman of a population who can be expected to reach their mothers' age at the time of birth, calculated from the average fertility rates and death rates of each age-group during the period considered. **net system** the system of selling books only at the net price. ***net ton***: see TON *noun*[1] 2. ***net tonnage***: see TONNAGE *noun* 5.

net /nɛt/ *verb*[1]. Infl. **-tt-**. LME.

[from NET *noun*[1].]

▶ **I 1** *verb trans*. Take, catch, or capture (fish, birds, etc.) with a net or nets. LME. ▸**b** *fig*. Take, catch, or capture, as with a net; *colloq*. acquire. E19.

2 *verb trans*. Cover or confine with or as with a net or nets. L16.

3 *verb trans*. Fish (a river etc.) with a net; set or use nets in. M19.

4 *verb trans. & intrans*. In ball games in which a net is used: send (a ball) into the net, score (a goal). E20.

> **1** L. ERDRICH The fish .. swarmed to the surface and we netted them. **b** J. GALSWORTHY Dusk is falling ... Some stars are already netted in the branches of the pines. R. LINDNER His first criminal offense .. netted him a two-year sentence. **2** TENNYSON Thy fibres net the dreamless head. N. BAWDEN The strawberries were netted close to the ground. **3** R. ADAMS They made their way upstream to net some likely pool.

▶ **II 5** *verb intrans*. Make nets or network; occupy oneself with netting. L17.

6 *verb trans*. Make (a thing) by netting; cross or interlace (threads etc.) to make network; arrange as or form into a network. E18. ▸**b** Mark with a netlike pattern, reticulate. Chiefly as ***netted*** *ppl adjective*. M19.

■ **nettable** *adjective* able to be netted E19.

net /nɛt/ *verb*[2] *trans*. Also **nett**. Infl. **-tt-**. M18.

[from NET *adjective*[2].]

1 Gain as a net sum or as clear profit; succeed in clearing (a certain sum). M18.

2 Bring in or yield as a profit or net sum. L18. **3** Foll. by *off*, *out*: exclude (a non-net amount, as tax) when making a calculation, in order to reduce the amount left to a net sum. M20.

nete /ˈniːtiː/ *noun.* E17.
[Greek *nētē*, *neatē* (sc. *khordē* string) fem. of *neatos* lowest (orig. with ref. to the position of the string, not the pitch).]
In ancient Greek music, the fixed highest note of an upper tetrachord.

ne temere /neɪ ˈtɛməri/ *noun phr.* E20.
[Latin, lit. 'lest rashly', the first words of the decree.]
A papal decree of 1907 declaring any marriage between two Catholics or between a Catholic and a non-Catholic invalid unless solemnized by a Roman Catholic priest.

nether /ˈnɛðə/ *adjective.* Now *literary* or *joc.*
[Old English *neoþera*, *niþera* = Old Frisian *nithera*, *nethera*, Old Saxon *niþiri* (Dutch *neder* in compounds), Middle Low German *ned(d)er*, Old High German *nidari*, *-eri*, *-iri* (German *nieder*), Old Norse *neðri*, from Germanic base meaning 'down, downwards' (= Sanskrit *nitarām*, from *ni-* down + compar. suffix): see -ER³.]
Lower, under (in contrast to ***higher***, ***over***, or ***upper***).

> SHAKES. *Lear* You justicers, that these our nether crimes So speedily can venge! MILTON 'Twixt upper, nether, and surrounding Fires. DRYDEN The rising rivers float the nether ground. SIR W. SCOTT At the nether end of the hall, a huge . . chimney-piece projected. H. T. BUCKLE A nether jaw protruding so hideously that his teeth could never meet.

Special collocations & comb.: **nether garments** *spec.* trousers. **nether man** the lower part of a man's body, the legs etc. **nether millstone** the lower of a pair of millstones (now only in ***as hard as the nether millstone*** & vars.); *fig.* a hard heart. **nether person** the lower part of the body, the legs etc. **nether regions** (*a*) hell, the underworld (of the dead); (*b*) *euphem.* (*colloq.*) the lower part of the body, esp. the genitals and buttocks. **netherstock** (long *obsolete* exc. *Hist.*) a stocking. ***nether vert***: see VERT *noun*¹ & *adjective*. **netherworld** hell; the underworld (of the dead or of criminals etc.).
■ **nethermore** *adverb & adjective* (long *rare*) †(*a*) *adverb* lower or further down; (*b*) *adjective* lower, inferior: ME. **nethermost** *adjective* lowest, undermost, furthest down ME. **netherward** *adverb & adjective* (now *rare*) (*a*) *adverb* downwards; (*b*) *adjective* downward: OE. **netherwards** *adverb* (now *rare*) downwards OE.

Netherlander /ˈnɛðələndə/ *noun.* E17.
[from the *Netherlands*, after Dutch *Nederlander*, from *Nederland* (from *neder* NETHER + *lad* LAND *noun*¹): see -ER¹.]
A native or inhabitant of the Netherlands, a country in western Europe bordering on the North Sea with Belgium on its southern frontier, but formerly including Flanders or Belgium and Luxembourg.

Netherlandian /ˈnɛðəlandɪən/ *adjective. rare.* E17.
[formed as prec. + -IAN.]
= NETHERLANDISH *adjective*.

Netherlandic /ˈnɛðəlandɪk/ *adjective & noun.* E20.
[formed as prec. + -IC.]
= NETHERLANDISH.

Netherlandish /ˈnɛðəlandɪʃ/ *adjective & noun.* L16.
[formed as prec. + -ISH¹, after Dutch *Nederlandsch*.]
▶**A** *adjective.* Of or pertaining to the Netherlands, Dutch. L16.
▶**B** *noun.* The Germanic language of the Netherlands; Dutch. M19.

netiquette /ˈnɛtɪkɛt/ *noun.* Also **N-**. L20.
[Blend of NET *noun*¹ and ETIQUETTE.]
COMPUTING. The correct or acceptable way of using the Internet.

netizen /ˈnɛtɪzən/ *noun.* Also **N-**. L20.
[Blend of NET *noun*¹ and CITIZEN.]
A (keen or habitual) user of the Internet.

netsuke /ˈnɛtski, ˈnɛtsʊki/ *noun.* Pl. **-s**, same. L19.
[Japanese.]
A small piece of ivory, wood, or other material, carved or otherwise decorated, formerly worn, by Japanese, on a cord suspending articles from a girdle.

nett *noun, adjective & adverb, verb* vars. of NET *noun*³, *adjective*² & *adverb*, *verb*².

netter /ˈnɛtə/ *noun.* ME.
[from NET *verb*¹ + -ER¹.]
1 A netmaker. Long *rare.* ME.
2 A person who uses a net. L16.
3 A tennis player. *US colloq.* M20.

netting /ˈnɛtɪŋ/ *noun.* M16.
[from NET *noun*¹, *verb*¹ + -ING¹.]
1 NAUTICAL. A coarse network of small ropes used now or formerly for various purposes, as to prevent boarding, stow hammocks or sails in, etc. M16.
2 Meshwork or network of any of various other materials; material composed of meshes. L16.
3 The action or process of making a net or nets or network. M17.
4 The action of fishing with a net or nets. L19.
2 wire netting etc.

nettle /ˈnɛt(ə)l/ *noun.*
[Old English *net(e)le*, *netel* = Old Saxon *netila*, Middle Low German *net(t)ele*, Middle Dutch *netele* (Dutch *netel*), Old High German *nezzila* (German *Nessel*), Old Swedish *netla*, Old Danish *nætlæ*, *næd-*, Icelandic *netla*, from Germanic deriv. (see -LE¹) of base of Old High German *nazza*, Icelandic *nötu* (*gras*).]
1 Any of various plants of the genus *Urtica* (family Urticaceae), with small green flowers and usu. with stinging hairs; *esp.* the common *U. dioica*, (more fully ***stinging nettle***) which has strongly toothed ovate leaves. OE.
2 With specifying word: any of various labiate plants, esp. of the genus *Lamium*, with leaves like those of stinging nettles but without stinging hairs. LME.
1 grasp the nettle: see GRASP *verb* 2. ***in dock, out nettle***: see DOCK *noun*¹. ***Roman nettle***: see ROMAN *adjective*. ***2 blind nettle***, ***dead-nettle***, ***deaf-nettle***, ***flame nettle***, ***hemp-nettle***, ***red nettle***, etc.
Comb.: **nettle beer** a drink made with nettles; **nettle-rash** MEDICINE a rash of itching red spots on the skin caused by allergic reaction to food etc., and resembling that caused by the sting of a nettle; urticaria; **nettle-tree** (*a*) any of several trees of the genus *Celtis*, of the elm family; esp. *C. australis*, of southern Europe, and *C. occidentalis*, of N. America; (*b*) *Austral.* = ***stinging tree*** s.v. STING *verb* 2b.
■ **nettle-like** *adjective* resembling (that of) a nettle L18.

nettle /ˈnɛt(ə)l/ *verb trans.* LME.
[from the noun.]
1 Of a nettle: give a sting to (usu. in *pass.*). Of a person: beat or sting (another person or animal) with nettles. LME. ▶**b** Get (oneself, one's hands, etc.) stung by nettles. E18.
2 Irritate, vex, provoke, annoy. Freq. as ***nettled*** *ppl adjective.* LME.
3 Incite, rouse. L16.

> **1** J. RAY Ants, if they get into peoples clothes, . . will cause a . . tingling, as if they were netled. **2** S. LEACOCK Slightly nettled . . at the very casual way . . they seemed to take my announcement. S. BRETT She was nettled that her daughter hadn't told her she was going out. R. ELLMANN The prohibition on visits remained to nettle Douglas.

■ **nettling** *adjective* (*a*) irritating, provoking; (*b*) stinging: E17.

nettlesome /ˈnɛt(ə)ls(ə)m/ *adjective.* M18.
[from NETTLE *noun* or *verb* + -SOME¹.]
1 Easily nettled, irritable. M18.
2 Causing annoyance, vexatious; awkward, difficult. Chiefly *N. Amer.* M19.

> **2** *New York Times* Iran's willingness to doublecross the nettlesome Kurds. S. I. LANDAU The difficulty of distinguishing between lexical units and items in a nomenclature is especially nettlesome in specialized dictionaries.

nettly /ˈnɛtli/ *adjective.* ME.
[from NETTLE *noun* + -Y¹.]
1 Overgrown with nettles. ME.
2 Irritable. E19.

netty /ˈnɛti/ *noun. north.* E20.
[Origin unkn.: perh. alt. of *necessary*.]
An outside toilet; a lavatory.

netty /ˈnɛti/ *adjective.* Now *rare.* E17.
[from NET *noun*¹ + -Y¹.]
Netlike; netted, made of net.

network /ˈnɛtwəːk/ *noun & adjective.* M16.
[from NET *noun*¹ + WORK *noun*.]
▶**A** *noun.* **I 1** Work in which threads, wires, etc., are crossed or interlaced in the fashion of a net; *esp.* light fabric made of threads intersecting with interstices. M16.
▶**II 2** A piece of work having the form or construction of a net; a collection, arrangement, or structure with intersecting lines and interstices resembling those of a net. L16. ▶**b** A structure in a glass in which oxygen atoms form a three-dimensional array connecting other atoms (usu. of silicon). M20.
3 A chain or system of interconnected or intercommunicating immaterial things, points, or people. Also, a representation of interconnected events, processes, etc., used in the study of work efficiency. E19.
4 A complex collection or system of rivers, canals, railways, etc., or of telephone lines, power distribution cables, etc. M19.
5 a ELECTRICITY. A system of interconnected electrical conductors or components providing more than one path for a current between any two points. L19. ▶**b** MATH. A graph, esp. a digraph, in which each edge has associated with it a non-negative number. M20. ▶**c** COMPUTING. A system of interconnected computers; *spec.* (*ellipt.*) a local area network, a wide area network. Freq. *attrib.* M20.
6 A broadcasting system consisting of a series of transmitters able to be linked together to carry the same programme; *gen.* a nationwide broadcasting company, broadcasting companies collectively. E20.

> **2** K. A. PORTER His long face . . was a network of fine wrinkles. ANTHONY HUXLEY Incredibly extensive networks of very thin stems. T. O. ECHEWA Slender limbs wrapped in networks of turgid veins. G. NAYLOR A deceptively large network of smaller offices. **3** STAFFORD BEER Each of the dots in the network represents some binary situation. D. ROWE Everything that happens emerges out of a whole network of causes. B. MOORE I have a little network of friends. J. HELLER The vast network of Dutch trading posts and territorial possessions. ***old boy network***, ***old boy's network***: see OLD *adjective.* **4** *Holiday Which?* Most of the accommodation is . . on a network of lousy roads. *Jordan Times* Prince Hassan urged . . Arab countries to develop their railway systems, because these networks have beneficial results. **5c** *Datamation* The network was to consist of at least one large . . central computing system and a number of smaller 'subsidiary' systems. ***local area network***: see LOCAL *adjective*. ***wide area network***: see WIDE *adjective*. **6** *Economist* The three big American television networks, ABC, NBC and CBS.

Comb.: **network analyser** ELECTRICITY an assembly of inductors, capacitors, and resistors used to model an electrical network; **network analysis** (*a*) ELECTRICITY calculation of the currents flowing in the various meshes of a network; (*b*) (a method of) analysis of complex working procedures in terms of a network of related activities; critical path analysis; **network appliance**, **network computer** a relatively low-cost computer designed chiefly to provide network access, and featuring a graphical interface based on World Wide Web standards; **network former** (a substance containing) an atom which can become part of a network in a glass; **network modifier** (a substance containing) a metal ion which can occupy an interstice in a glass network; **network structure** METALLURGY an alloy structure in which one component forms a continuous network around grains of the other; **network theorem** any of various theorems for determining currents and voltages in an electrical network.
▶**B** *attrib.* or as *adjective.* **1** Made of network; arranged in the fashion of network. E17.
2 Heard on networked radio or television. M20.

network /ˈnɛtwəːk/ *verb.* L19.
[from the noun.]
1 *verb trans.* Cover with a network. L19.
2 *verb trans.* Broadcast simultaneously over a network of radio or television stations. M20.
3 *verb trans. & intrans.* Link (computers) together to allow the sharing of data and efficient utilization of resources; incorporate (a computer, data, etc.) into a computer network. Freq. as ***networking*** *verbal noun.* L20.
4 *verb intrans.* Communicate or foster relationships with a network of people, esp. for personal advantage. L20.

> **4** *Working Woman* Recreational activities offer time to network with colleagues. *Times* She wanted publicity for her charity and seized the opportunity to network.

■ **networkable** *adjective* that can be used in or with a network; *spec.* (COMPUTING) compatible with an existing network: M20. **networked** *adjective* M20.

networker /ˈnɛtwəːkə/ *noun.* L20.
[from NETWORK *noun*, *verb* + -ER¹.]
A person who uses a network; *spec.* (*a*) a member of an organization or computer network who operates from home or from an external office; (*b*) a person who communicates or fosters relationships with a network of people, esp. for personal advantage.

Neue Sachlichkeit /ˈnɔɪə ˈzaxlɪçkaɪt/ *noun phr.* E20.
[German, lit. 'new objectivity'.]
A movement in the fine arts, music, and literature, which developed in Germany during the 1920s and was characterized by realism and a deliberate rejection of romantic attitudes.

neum *noun* var. of NEUME.

neuma /ˈnjuːmə/ *noun.* Pl. **-mata** /-mətə/, **-mae** /-miː/. L18.
[medieval Latin: see NEUME.]
MUSIC. = NEUME.

Neumann /ˈnɔɪmən/ *noun.* L19.
[F. E. *Neumann* (1798–1895), German mineralogist and physicist.]
Used *attrib.* to designate narrow bands, lines, or lamellae parallel to crystallographic planes which are seen in α-iron (ferrite) subjected to a sudden shock, and are usu. attributed to twinning.

neumata *noun pl.* see NEUMA.

neumatic /njuːˈmatɪk/ *adjective.* L19.
[medieval Latin *neumaticus*, from NEUMA: see -ATIC.]
MUSIC. Of, pertaining to, or of the nature of neumes.

neume /njuːm/ *noun.* Also **neum**. LME.
[Old & mod. French from medieval Latin *neuma*, *neupma* from Greek *pneuma* breath.]
MUSIC. **1** In plainsong, a prolonged phrase or group of notes sung to a single syllable, esp. at the end of a melody. LME.
2 Each of a set of signs employed in the earliest plainsong notation to indicate the melody. M19.

neur- *combining form* see NEURO-.

neural /ˈnjʊər(ə)l/ *adjective & noun.* M19.
[from Greek *neuron* nerve + -AL¹.]
▶**A** *adjective.* **1** ANATOMY & ZOOLOGY. Of, pertaining to, or resembling a nerve or the nervous system. M19.

2 *ZOOLOGY.* Designating or pertaining to the side of the body in which the central nervous axis lies. **M19.**

Special collocations: **neural arch** the curved dorsal part of a vertebra enclosing the canal through which the spinal cord runs. **neural crest** *EMBRYOLOGY* a band of ectodermal tissue either side of the neural plate which gives rise to many types of cell including peripheral nerves. **neural net**, **neural network** *MATH. & COMPUTING* a system of interconnections which resembles or is based on the arrangement of neurones in the brain and nervous system; a configuration of computers designed to simulate this. **neural plate** *EMBRYOLOGY* a band of ectodermal tissue along the axis of the early embryo which develops into the neural tube. **neural spine** the dorsal process of a vertebra. **neural tube** *EMBRYOLOGY* a hollow structure from which the brain and spinal cord develop; ***neural tube defect*** any of a range of congenital abnormalities, including spina bifida, resulting from incomplete fusion of the neural tube.

▶ **B** *noun. ZOOLOGY.* Each of the plates lying along the dorsal midline of the carapace of a chelonian and attached to a neural spine. **L19.**

▪ **neurally** *adverb* by or as regards a nerve or nerves **E20.**

neuralgia /njʊəˈraldʒə/ *noun.* **E19.**
[from NEURO- + -ALGIA.]
MEDICINE. Intense burning or stabbing pain, typically along the line of a nerve, esp. in the face.
▪ **neuralgic** *adjective* **E19.** **neuralgically** *adverb* in a neuralgic manner, *fig.* painfully **L19.**

neuraminic /njʊərəˈmɪnɪk/ *adjective.* **M20.**
[from NEURO- (as orig. isolated from brain tissue) + AMINE + -IC.]
CHEMISTRY. ***neuraminic acid***, an amino sugar, $C_9H_{17}O_8$, derivatives of which occur in many animal substances, chiefly as sialic acids.
▪ **neuˈraminate** *noun* a salt or ester of neuraminic acid **L20.**

neuraminidase /njʊərəˈmɪnɪdeɪz/ *noun.* **M20.**
[from prec. + -IDE + -ASE.]
BIOCHEMISTRY. Any of several enzymes, present esp. in many pathogenic or symbiotic micro-organisms, which catalyse the breakdown of glucosides containing neuraminic acid. Also called ***sialidase***.

neurapophysis /njʊərəˈpɒfɪsɪs/ *noun.* Pl. **-physes** /-fɪsiːz/. **M19.**
[from NEURO- + APOPHYSIS.]
ANATOMY & ZOOLOGY. Either of the two processes of a vertebra which join to form the neural spine and arch (usu. in *pl.*). Also, a neural spine.
▪ **neurapoˈphyseal**, **neurapoˈphysial** *adjectives* **M19.**

neurapraxia /njʊərəˈpraksɪə/ *noun.* **M20.**
[from NEURO- + APRAXIA.]
MEDICINE. Temporary dysfunction or loss of conduction in a peripheral nerve fibre or fibres, as caused by local compression.

neurasthenia /njʊərəsˈθiːnɪə/ *noun.* **M19.**
[from NEURO- + ASTHENIA.]
An ill-defined medical condition characterized by lassitude, fatigue, headache, and irritability, associated chiefly with emotional disturbance.
¶ Not now generally considered a technical term.
▪ **neurasthenic** /-ˈθɛnɪk/ *adjective & noun* (**a**) *adjective* caused by, affected with, or characteristic of neurasthenia; (**b**) *noun* a person with neurasthenia: **L19.**

neuration /njʊəˈreɪʃ(ə)n/ *noun.* Now *rare* or *obsolete.* **E19.**
[Irreg. from Greek *neuron* nerve + -ATION.]
BOTANY & ENTOMOLOGY. = VENATION *noun*[2] 2.

neuraxis /njʊəˈraksɪs/ *noun.* Pl. **-raxes** /-ˈraksiːz/. **L19.**
[from NEURAL + AXIS *noun*[1].]
ANATOMY. The central axis of the nervous system; the brain and spinal cord.
▪ **neuraxial** *adjective* **L19.**

neurectomy /njʊəˈrɛktəmi/ *noun.* **M19.**
[from NEURO- + -ECTOMY.]
Surgical removal of all or part of a nerve; an instance of this.

neurenteric /njʊər(ə)nˈtɛrɪk/ *adjective.* **L19.**
[from NEURO- + ENTERIC.]
ANATOMY. Pertaining to the nervous system and intestines.
neurenteric cyst an abnormal structure consisting of isolated intestinal tissue.

neuric /ˈnjʊərɪk/ *adjective. rare.* **M19.**
[from Greek *neuron* nerve + -IC.]
Of or pertaining to a nerve or nerves; neural.

neuridine /ˈnjʊərɪdiːn/ *noun.* **L19.**
[from NEURO- + -IDINE.]
BIOCHEMISTRY. = SPERMINE.

neurilemma /njʊərɪˈlɛmə/ *noun.* Also **neuro-** /njʊərə-/, †**neurilema**. Pl. **-lemmata** /-ˈlɛmətə/, **-lemmas**. **E19.**
[Orig. from Greek *neuron* nerve + *eilēma* covering; later taken as from Greek *lemma* husk, skin. Cf. French *névrilème*.]
ANATOMY. **1** A sheath of connective tissue around a nerve; epineurium, perineurium. Now *rare* or *obsolete.* **E19.**
2 The thin sheath of cells which surrounds the axon of a peripheral nerve fibre (and its myelin sheath where present). Also called ***sheath of Schwann***. **M19.**
▪ **neurilemmal** *adjective* **E20.** †**neurilemmatous** *adjective* **M–L19.** **neurileˈmmoma** *noun*, pl. **-mas**, **-mata** /-mətə/, *MEDICINE* a neurofibroma **M20.**

neurine /ˈnjʊəriːn/ *noun.* **M19.**
[from NEURO- + -INE[5].]
1 *ANATOMY.* Nerve tissue; the matter contained in nerve fibres. Now *rare* or *obsolete.* **M19.**
2 *BIOCHEMISTRY.* A ptomaine, $(CH_3)_3(OH)N{\cdot}CH{:}CH_2$, present in various tissues and formed during putrefaction by dehydration of choline. **M19.**

neurinoma /njʊərɪˈnəʊmə/ *noun.* Pl. **-mas**, **-mata** /-mətə/. **E20.**
[from NEURO- + INO- + -OMA.]
MEDICINE. Neurofibroma.

neuristor /njʊəˈrɪstə/ *noun.* **M20.**
[from NEURO- + -*istor*, after *resistor*, *transistor*.]
ELECTRONICS. Any device that acts as a transmission line along which a signal will travel without attenuation (usu. with an energy supply along its length).

neurite /ˈnjʊərʌɪt/ *noun.* **L19.**
[from NEURO- + -ITE[1].]
ANATOMY. A dendrite or (formerly *spec.*) an axon of a nerve cell.

neuritic /njʊəˈrɪtɪk/ *adjective.* **E18.**
[In sense 1 from NEURO- + -ITIC. In sense 2 from NEURITIS: see -IC.]
†**1** Good for the nerves. Cf. NEUROTIC *adjective* 1. *rare.* Only in **E18.**
2 *MEDICINE.* Of, pertaining to, or of the nature of neuritis. **M19.**

neuritis /njʊəˈrʌɪtɪs/ *noun.* **M19.**
[from NEURO- + -ITIS.]
MEDICINE. Inflammation of a peripheral nerve or nerves, usu. with pain and loss of function. Also *gen.*, neuropathy.

neuro- /ˈnjʊərəʊ/ *combining form.* Before a vowel also **neur-**.
[from Greek *neuron* nerve: see -O-.]
Of nerves or the nervous system, as ***neurobiology***, ***neurochemistry***, ***neuroembryology***, ***neuroradiology***.
▪ **neuroanaˈtomical** *adjective* of or pertaining to neuroanatomy **E20.** **neuroaˈnatomist** *noun* an expert in or student of neuroanatomy **M20.** **neuroaˈnatomy** *noun* the anatomy of the nervous system **E20.** **neurobioˈtactic** *adjective* (*BIOLOGY*) of, pertaining to, or stimulating neurobiotaxis **E20.** **neurobioˈtaxis** *noun* (*BIOLOGY*) a tendency of nerve cells to migrate during development towards the source of stimuli **E20.** **neuroblast** *noun* (*BIOLOGY*) an embryonic cell from which nerve fibres originate **L19.** **neuroˈblastic** *adjective* (*BIOLOGY*) of, pertaining to, or consisting of neuroblasts **E20.** **neuroblaˈstoma** *noun*, pl. **-mas**, **-mata** /-mətə/, *MEDICINE* a tumour composed of neuroblasts, *esp.* a malignant tumour originating in the adrenal gland **E20.** **neurocircuˈlatory** *adjective* (*MEDICINE*) of or pertaining to the nervous and circulatory systems **E20.** **neurocomˈputing** *noun* the development and study of computers based on neural networks **L20.** **neuroˈcranium** *noun* (*ANATOMY*) the part of the skull enclosing the brain **E20.** **neurocrine** *adjective* (*PHYSIOLOGY*) secreting or secreted directly into nervous tissue **E20.** **neurocyte** *noun* (*ANATOMY*, now *rare*) a neurone, a nerve cell **L19.** **neurocyˈtoma** *noun*, pl. **-mas**, **-mata** /-mətə/, *MEDICINE* a malignant tumour composed of nerve cells **E20.** **neurodeˈgenerative** *adjective* (of a disease or illness) causing or characterized by degeneration of the nervous system **E20.** **neurodermaˈtitis** *noun*, pl. **-titides** /-ˈtʌɪtɪdiːz/, *MEDICINE* local thickening of the skin due to constant scratching of a persistent itch, freq. psychosomatic **L19.** **neurodermaˈtosis** *noun*, pl. **-toses** /-ˈtəʊsiːz/, *MEDICINE* = NEURODERMATITIS **E20.** **neuroeˈffector** *adjective & noun* (*PHYSIOLOGY*) (**a**) *adjective* pertaining to or composed of both a nerve and an effector; (**b**) *noun* a neuroeffector system: **M20.** **neuroeˈlectric** *adjective* (*PHYSIOLOGY*) of or pertaining to the electrical phenomena and properties of the nervous system **M19.** **neuroˈendocrine** *adjective* (*PHYSIOLOGY*) pertaining to or involving both nervous stimulation and endocrine secretion **E20.** **neuroeˈthology** *noun* (*BIOLOGY*) the branch of zoology that deals with the neuronal basis of behaviour **L20.** **neuroˈfibril** *noun* (*CYTOLOGY*) a fibril in the cytoplasm of a nerve cell, visible by light microscopy **L19.** **neurofiˈbrilla** *noun*, pl. **-llae** /-liː/, *ANATOMY* = NEUROFIBRIL (usu. in *pl.*) **E20.** **neurofiˈbrillar**, **neurofiˈbrillary** *adjectives* of or pertaining to neurofibrils **E20.** **neurofiˈbroma** *noun*, pl. **-mas**, **-mata** /-mətə/, *MEDICINE* a benign tumour of the sheath of a nerve, a neurilemmoma (also called ***Schwannoma***) **L19.** **neurofibromaˈtosis** *noun*, pl. **-toses** /-ˈtəʊsiːz/, (*MEDICINE*) any condition characterized by multiple neurofibromas; *spec.* a congenital condition in which multiple palpable neurofibromas occur on peripheral or cranial nerves (also called ***von Recklinghausen's disease***): **L19.** **neuroˈfilament** *noun* (*CYTOLOGY*) a long filament in the cytoplasm of a nerve cell, visible by electron microscopy **M20.** **neuroˈglandular** *adjective* involving or possessing both glandular and nervous tissue or functions **E20.** **neuroˈhaemal** *adjective* (*ZOOLOGY*) designating an organ, esp. in an insect, composed of a group of nerve endings closely associated with the vascular system and believed to have a neurosecretory function **M20.** **neuroˈimaging** *noun* imaging of the structure and activity of the brain by techniques such as computerized tomography, positron emission tomography, and magnetic resonance imaging **L20.** **neurolinˈguistic** *adjective* of or pertaining to neurolinguistics; ***neurolinguistic programming***, a system of alternative therapy intended to educate people in self-awareness and effective communication, and to model and change their patterns of mental and emotional behaviour: **M20.** **neurolinˈguistics** *noun* the branch of linguistics that deals with the relationship between language and the structure and function of the brain **M20.** **neuromere** *noun* (*ANATOMY*) a distinct segment of the nervous system, e.g. in an embryo **M19.** **neuroˈmuscular** *adjective* pertaining to, consisting of, or resembling both nervous and muscular tissue; *esp.* pertaining to or designating a junction between a nerve fibre and a muscle fibre: **M19.** **neuroˈpeptide** *noun* (*BIOCHEMISTRY*) a short-chain polypeptide capable of acting as a neurotransmitter **L20.** **neuropharmacoˈlogic** *adjective* (chiefly *US*) neuropharmacological **E20.** **neuropharmacoˈlogical** *adjective* of or pertaining to neuropharmacology **M20.** **neuropharmaˈcology** *noun* the branch of pharmacology that deals with the action of drugs on the nervous system **M20.** **neurophysin** /-ˈfʌɪsɪn/ *noun* (*BIOCHEMISTRY*) any of a group of proteins which are found in the neurohypophysis in complexes with oxytocin and vasopressin and are believed to act as carriers for these hormones **M20.** **neurophysioˈlogic** *adjective* (chiefly *US*) neurophysiological **M20.** **neurophysioˈlogical** *adjective* of or pertaining to neurophysiology **M19.** **neurophysioˈlogically** *adverb* with respect to neurophysiology **M20.** **neurophysiˈologist** *noun* an expert in or student of neurophysiology **M20.** **neurophysiˈology** *noun* the physiology of the nervous system **L19.** **neuroplasm** *noun* (*CYTOLOGY*) the cytoplasm of a neurone, *spec.* that of the cell body **L19.** **neuroretiˈnitis** *noun* (*MEDICINE*) inflammation of the optic nerve and retina **L19.** **neuroscience** *noun* any of the sciences (as neurochemistry, psychology) which deal with the structure or function of the nervous system and brain; such sciences collectively: **M20.** **neuroˈscientist** *noun* an expert in or student of (a) neuroscience **M20.** **neuroseˈcretion** *noun* (**a**) the process of secretion by a (specially adapted) nerve cell; (**b**) the substance secreted in this process: **M20.** **neuroseˈcretory** *adjective* performing, produced by, or pertaining to neurosecretion **M20.** **neuroˈsensory** *adjective* of, pertaining to, or consisting of sensory nerve cells; *spec.* designating a nerve cell in which the cell body (usu. situated in epithelium) is the receptor and has a single process by which impulses are transmitted: **E20.** **neuroˈsurgeon** *noun* a practitioner of neurosurgery **E20.** **neuroˈsurgery** *noun* surgery of the nervous system **E20.** **neuroˈsurgical** *adjective* of or pertaining to neurosurgery **E20.** **neuroˈtendinous** *adjective* pertaining to both nervous tissue and tendons; *esp.* pertaining to or designating a sense-organ within a tendon: **E20.** **neuroˈtoxic** *adjective* poisonous due to the effect on the nervous system **E20.** **neurotoxicity** /-tɒkˈsɪsɪti/ *noun* (**a**) the property or degree of being neurotoxic; (**b**) poisoning by a neurotoxin: **M20.** **neuroˈtoxin** *noun* a neurotoxic substance **E20.** **neuroˈtubule** *noun* a microtubule in a nerve cell **M20.**

neuroepithelial /ˌnjʊərəʊɛpɪˈθiːlɪəl/ *adjective.* **L19.**
[from next + -AL[1].]
1 *ANATOMY & ZOOLOGY.* Of, pertaining to, or consisting of sensory neuroepithelium; designating an epithelial cell that acts as a sensory receptor. **L19.**
2 *EMBRYOLOGY.* Composed of or derived from embryonic neuroepithelium. **M20.**

neuroepithelium /ˌnjʊərəʊɛpɪˈθiːlɪəm/ *noun.* **L19.**
[from NEURO- + EPITHELIUM.]
1 *ANATOMY & ZOOLOGY.* Epithelium, esp. in a sense organ, containing sensory nerve endings; sensory epithelium. **L19.**
2 *EMBRYOLOGY.* Ectoderm that develops into nervous tissue. **L19.**

neurogenesis /njʊərə(ʊ)ˈdʒɛnɪsɪs/ *noun.* **E20.**
[from NEURO- + -GENESIS.]
BIOLOGY. The growth and development of nerves.
▪ **neurogeˈnetic** *adjective* = NEUROGENIC *adjective* 2 **L19.**

neurogenic /njʊərə(ʊ)ˈdʒɛnɪk/ *adjective.* **E20.**
[from NEURO- + -GENIC.]
1 Caused, controlled by, or originating in the nervous system. **E20.**
2 Of or pertaining to neurogenesis; giving rise to nerve tissue. **E20.**

> 🕮 **1** *Nature* Synchronous, or neurogenic, muscles in which each contraction is initiated by a nerve impulse.
> **neurogenic bladder** a condition characterized by abnormal functioning of the bladder owing to disturbances of nervous control. **neurogenic theory** (*PHYSIOLOGY*, now *Hist.*) the theory that the heart depends for its action on nervous stimulation.

▪ **neurogenically** *adverb* by the nervous system, by a nerve impulse **M20.**

neuroglia /njʊəˈrɒglɪə/ *noun.* **M19.**
[from NEURO- + Greek *glia* glue.]
ANATOMY. = GLIA.
▪ **neuroglial** *adjective* **L19.**

neurogram /ˈnjʊərəgram/ *noun.* Now *rare* or *obsolete.* **E20.**
[from NEURO- + -GRAM.]
= ENGRAM.

neurohormone /njʊərəʊˈhɔːməʊn/ *noun.* **M20.**
[from NEURO- + HORMONE.]
PHYSIOLOGY. A hormone secreted by a specialized nerve cell. Also, a neurotransmitter.
▪ **neurohorˈmonal** *adjective* of or pertaining to a neurohormone; neuroendocrine: **M20.**

neurohumour /ˈnjʊərəʊhjuːmə/ *noun.* Also ***-or.** **M20.**
[from NEURO- + HUMOUR *noun* 1.]
PHYSIOLOGY. A neurohormone, *esp.* a neurotransmitter.
▪ **neuroˈhumoral** *adjective* of or involving a neurohumour or neurohumours **E20.**

neurohypophysial /ˌnjʊərəʊhʌɪpəˈfɪzɪəl, -ˈfɪsɪəl, -fɪˈsiːəl/ *adjective.* Also **-physeal**. **L19.**
[from NEURO- + HYPOPHYSIAL: cf. next.]
1 *BIOLOGY.* Pertaining to or designating the canal connecting the brain and hypophysis. Now *rare* or *obsolete.* **L19.**

2 *ANATOMY & PHYSIOLOGY.* Of or pertaining to the neurohypophysis. **M20.**

neurohypophysis /ˌnjʊərəʊhʌɪˈpɒfɪsɪs/ *noun.* Pl. **-physes** /-fɪsiːz/. **E20.**
[from NEURO- + HYPOPHYSIS.]
ANATOMY. The posterior lobe of the hypophysis (pituitary gland), which stores and releases oxytocin and vasopressin produced in the hypothalamus.

neuroid /ˈnjʊərɔɪd/ *adjective. rare.* **L19.**
[from NEURO- + -OID.]
Resembling or analogous to a nerve or nervous system.

neurolemma *noun* var. of NEURILEMMA.

neuroleptic /njʊərəˈlɛptɪk/ *adjective & noun.* **M20.**
[from NEURO- after *psycholeptic*.]
PHARMACOLOGY. ▶**A** *adjective.* Tending or able to reduce nervous tension by depressing nerve functions; having antipsychotic properties. **M20.**
▶**B** *noun.* A neuroleptic drug; a major tranquillizer. **M20.**

neurology /njʊəˈrɒlədʒi/ *noun.* **L17.**
[mod. Latin *neurologia*, formed as NEURO- + -LOGY.]
The branch of biology or esp. medicine that deals with the anatomy, functions, and organic disorders of nerves and the nervous system. Formerly also, (a treatise on) the nervous system or its operation.
■ **neuroˈlogical** *adjective* **M19.** **neuroˈlogically** *adverb* as regards neurology **M20.** **neurologist** *noun* an expert in or student of neurology, *esp.* a physician specializing in organic disorders of the nervous system **M19.**

neuroma /njʊəˈrəʊmə/ *noun.* Pl. **-mas**, **-mata** /-mətə/. **M19.**
[from NEURO- + -OMA.]
MEDICINE. A benign tumour formed from nerve fibres and fibrous tissue, esp. at the end of a severed nerve.
■ **neuromatous** *adjective* of the nature of or resembling a neuroma **M19.**

neuromast /ˈnjʊərə(ʊ)mast/ *noun.* **E20.**
[from NEURO- + Greek *mastos* breast.]
ZOOLOGY. A sensory organ forming part of the lateral line system of fishes and larval or aquatic amphibians.

neuromotor /ˈnjʊərə(ʊ)məʊtə/ *adjective.* **E20.**
[from NEURO- + MOTOR *adjective*.]
BIOLOGY. Pertaining to or involving the stimulation of movement by motor neurones; *spec.* in *ZOOLOGY*, designating a system of minute fibrils connected with the locomotory organs of some ciliates.

neurone /ˈnjʊərəʊn/ *noun.* Also **-ron** /-rɒn/. **L19.**
[Greek *neuron* sinew, cord, nerve. Cf. French *neurone*.]
ANATOMY & BIOLOGY. †**1** = NEURAXIS. *rare.* Only in **L19.**
2 A nerve cell. **L19.**
†**3** = AXON 2. **L19–M20.**
2 *motor neurone*, *sensory neurone*, etc.
Comb.: **neurone theory** (*Hist.*) the theory (now universally accepted) that the nervous system is composed of distinct cells in effective contact with one another.
■ **neuˈronal** *adjective* of or pertaining to a neurone or neurones **E20.** **neuˈronally** *adverb* by a neurone or neurones **M20.** **neuronic** /-ˈrɒnɪk/ *adjective* neuronal **L19.**

neuronophagia /ˌnjʊərɒnəˈfeɪdʒə, -dʒə/ *noun.* **E20.**
[from prec. + -O- + -PHAGIA.]
MEDICINE. The destruction of damaged neurones by phagocytes.

neuropathic /njʊərə(ʊ)ˈpaθɪk/ *adjective.* **M19.**
[from NEUROPATHY + -IC.]
MEDICINE. Of, pertaining to, or caused by neuropathy.
■ **ˈneuropath** *noun* (*a*) a person suffering from or susceptible to nervous disease or disorder; (*b*) *rare* a neuropathologist: **L19.**

neuropathology /ˌnjʊərəʊpəˈθɒlədʒi/ *noun.* **M19.**
[from NEURO- + PATHOLOGY.]
The branch of pathology that deals with diseases and disorders of the nervous system.
■ **neuropathoˈlogic** *adjective* (chiefly *US*) **M20.** **neuropathoˈlogical** *adjective* **L19.** **neuropathologist** *noun* a (medical) neurologist, an expert in diseases of the nervous system **L19.**

neuropathy /njʊəˈrɒpəθi/ *noun.* **M19.**
[from NEURO- + -PATHY.]
MEDICINE. A disease or dysfunction of one or more peripheral nerves, typically causing numbness and weakness.
■ **neuropathist** *noun* (now *rare* or *obsolete*) a neuropathologist **M19.**

neuropil /ˈnjʊərə(ʊ)pɪl/ *noun.* Also **-pile** /-pʌɪl/. **L19.**
[Prob. abbreviation of next.]
ANATOMY & ZOOLOGY. (A tissue or structure composed of) a network of interwoven unmyelinated nerve fibres and their branches and synapses, together with glial processes.

†**neuropilema** *noun.* **L19–E20.**
[from NEURO- + Greek *pilēma* felt.]
= prec.

neuropodium /njʊərə(ʊ)ˈpəʊdɪəm/ *noun.* Pl. **-ia** /-ɪə/. **L19.**
[from NEURO- + PODIUM.]
ZOOLOGY. The lower or ventral branch of a parapodium. Cf. NOTOPODIUM.
■ **neuropodial** *adjective* **L19.**

neuropsychiatry /ˌnjʊərə(ʊ)sʌɪˈkʌɪətri/ *noun.* **E20.**
[from NEURO- + PSYCHIATRY.]
Psychiatry relating mental or emotional disturbance to disordered brain function.
■ **neuropsychiˈatric** *adjective* **E20.** **neuropsychiatrist** *noun* **E20.**

neuropsychology /ˌnjʊərə(ʊ)sʌɪˈkɒlədʒi/ *noun.* **L19.**
[from NEURO- + PSYCHOLOGY.]
The branch of science that deals with the relationship between behaviour and the mind on the one hand, and the nervous system, esp. the brain, on the other; neurological psychology.
■ **neuropsychoˈlogical** *adjective* **M19.** **neuropsychologist** *noun* **M19.**

Neuroptera /njʊəˈrɒpt(ə)rə/ *noun pl.* Also **n-**. **M18.**
[mod. Latin, from NEURO- + Greek *pteron* wing: see -A[3].]
(Members of) an order of insects (including lacewings and ant-lions) having biting mouthparts and two pairs of leaf-shaped transparent wings with numerous veins, freq. held over the back like a roof when at rest.
■ †**neuropter** *noun* (*rare*) = NEUROPTERAN *noun*: only in **19.** **neuropteran** *noun* a neuropterous insect **M19.** **neuropterous** *adjective* of or pertaining to the Neuroptera **E19.**

neurosis /njʊəˈrəʊsɪs/ *noun.* Pl. **-roses** /-ˈrəʊsiːz/. **M18.**
[mod. Latin, from NEURO- + -OSIS.]
1 *PSYCHOLOGY.* (A) mild mental illness, not attributable to organic disease, characterized by symptoms of stress such as anxiety, depression, obsessive behaviour, hypochondria, etc., without loss of contact with reality. Cf. PSYCHONEUROSIS, PSYCHOSIS. **M18.**
2 Any more or less specific anxiety or malaise experienced by an individual, group, nation, etc. **E20.**
1 ***obsessional neurosis***: see OBSESSIONAL *adjective* 2.

neurosyphilis /njʊərəʊˈsɪfɪlɪs/ *noun.* **L19.**
[from NEURO- + SYPHILIS.]
MEDICINE. Syphilis involving the central nervous system.
■ **neurosyphiˈlitic** *adjective & noun* (*a*) *adjective* of, pertaining to or suffering from neurosyphilis; (*b*) *noun* a person suffering from neurosyphilis: **L19.**

neurotic /njʊəˈrɒtɪk/ *noun & adjective.* **M17.**
[Orig. from Greek *neuron* nerve + -IC, after *hypnotic* etc.: in mod. use formed as NEUROSIS + -OTIC.]
▶**A** *noun.* †**1** *MEDICINE.* A drug having an (esp. tonic) effect on the nervous system. **M17–M19.**
2 A person suffering from neurosis. **L19.**

> **2** D. M. THOMAS Everyone, not only neurotics, shows signs of an irrational compulsion to repeat. ***obsessional neurotic***: see OBSESSIONAL *adjective* 2.

▶**B** *adjective.* **1** Acting on or stimulating the nerves. Only in Dicts. **L18.**
2 Of the nature of or characterized by neurosis or nervous disorder. **L19.**
3 a Suffering from neurosis; freq. *loosely*, unnecessarily or excessively anxious, obsessive. **L19.** ▸**b** Characteristic of neurosis or of a neurotic. **E20.**

> **2** *British Medical Bulletin* Psychotic and neurotic forms of depression lie on the same continuum. **3a** A. KOESTLER The timeless case-history of the neurotic child from a problem family. A. WEST I was so afraid you might be . . neurotic about my marrying. **b** *fig.*: *Newsweek* Enslaved by its neurotic emphasis on seeking re-election . . at all costs.

■ **neurotically** *adverb* in a neurotic manner; as the result of a nervous disorder: **L19.** **neuroticism** /-sɪz(ə)m/ *noun* the condition or state of being neurotic; a tendency towards neurosis, esp. as a factor in certain types of personality assessment: **E20.**

neurotomy /njʊəˈrɒtəmi/ *noun.* **E18.**
[from NEURO- + -TOMY.]
MEDICINE. †**1** Neuroanatomy. Only in Dicts. **E–M18.**
2 The (partial or total) surgical severing of a nerve, to produce sensory loss and relief of pain, or to suppress involuntary movements; an instance of this. **M19.**

neurotransmitter /ˌnjʊərəʊtranzˈmɪtə/ *noun.* **M20.**
[from NEURO- + TRANSMITTER.]
PHYSIOLOGY. A chemical substance which is released at the end of a nerve fibre by the arrival of a nerve impulse and, by diffusing across the synapse or junction, effects the transfer of the impulse to another nerve fibre, a muscle fibre, or some other structure.
■ **neurotransmission** *noun* the transmission of nerve impulses **M20.**

neurotrophic /njʊərə(ʊ)ˈtrəʊfɪk, -ˈtrɒf-/ *adjective.* **L19.**
[from NEURO- + -TROPHIC.]
PHYSIOLOGY. Of or pertaining to the control of cells exerted by nervous tissue, esp. in relation to cellular nutrition.

neurotropic /njʊərə(ʊ)ˈtrəʊpɪk, -ˈtrɒp-/ *adjective.* **E20.**
[from NEURO- + -TROPIC.]
1 *MEDICINE.* Tending to attack or affect the nervous system preferentially. **E20.**
2 *ANATOMY.* Of or pertaining to the control or regulation of nerves, esp. in relation to their growth and regeneration. **E20.**

neurotropism /njʊərəʊˈtrəʊpɪz(ə)m, njʊəˈrɒtrəpɪz(ə)m/ *noun.* **E20.**
[formed as prec. + -ISM.]
1 *MEDICINE.* The tendency of a virus or other pathological agent to attack the nervous system preferentially. **E20.**
2 *ANATOMY.* Attraction or repulsion exerted by a substance or tissue on growing nerve fibres; the response of nerves so influenced. **E20.**

neurula /ˈnjʊərələ/ *noun.* Pl. **-lae** /-liː/. **L19.**
[from NEURO- + *-ula*, after *blastula*, *gastrula*.]
EMBRYOLOGY. An embryo at the stage succeeding the gastrula, when the neural tube develops from the neural plate.
■ **neuˈrulation** *noun* the formation of a neural tube **L19.**

neurypnology /njʊərɪpˈnɒlədʒi/ *noun.* **M19.**
[from NEUR(O- + H)YPNOLOGY.]
(The science of) hypnotism.

neuston /ˈnjuːstɒn/ *noun.* **E20.**
[German from Greek, neut. of *neustos* swimming (from *nein* to swim), after PLANKTON.]
BIOLOGY. Minute organisms inhabiting the surface layer of fresh water, considered collectively.

Neustrian /ˈnjuːstrɪən/ *noun & adjective.* **L18.**
[from *Neustria* (see below) + -AN.]
Hist. ▶**A** *noun.* A native or inhabitant of Neustria, the western part of the Frankish empire in the Merovingian period. **L18.**
▶**B** *adjective.* Of or pertaining to Neustria or its inhabitants. **L19.**

neuter /ˈnjuːtə/ *adjective, noun, & verb.* **LME.**
[Old & mod. French *neutre* or its source Latin *neuter*, from *ne* not + *uter* either (of two).]
▶**A** *adjective.* **1** *GRAMMAR.* **a** Designating the gender to which belong words classified as neither masculine nor feminine; (of a word) belonging to this gender; (of a suffix, inflection, etc.) used with or to form words of this gender. **LME.** ▸**b** Of a verb: neither active nor passive; middle or reflexive or intransitive. **LME.**
2 Neutral in a war, dispute, controversy, etc. Formerly also, not disputatious. *arch.* **L15.**
3 Belonging to neither of two specified, implied, or usual categories. *arch.* **L16.**
4 Having no sexual characteristics, neither male nor female, asexual; having no functional sexual organs, sterile. **L18.**

> **1b neuter passive** (a verb which is) semi-deponent. **2** BURKE Eleven were for it, only three against. One was neuter. J. M. JEPHSON In the wars . . the citizens flattered themselves that they could remain neuter. **stand neuter** remain neutral, declare neutrality.

▶**B** *noun.* **1** *GRAMMAR.* **a** The neuter gender; a word belonging to the neuter gender. **LME.** ▸**b** A neuter verb. **M16.**
2 A person who remains neutral in a dispute, controversy, etc. Formerly also, a neutral State in a war etc. **M16.**
3 A sexually undeveloped animal, *esp.* an insect of a sterile worker caste. **L18.**
4 A castrated or spayed animal. **E20.**
▶**C** *verb trans.* Castrate, spay; *fig.* deprive of potency, vigour, or force. **E20.**
■ **neuterdom** *noun* the state of being (sexually) neuter **L19.** **neuterly** *adverb* (now *rare*) in a neuter or neutral sense **L18.** **neuterness** *noun* the fact of being (grammatically) neuter **L19.**

neutral /ˈnjuːtr(ə)l/ *noun & adjective.* **LME.**
[French †*neutral* or Latin *neutralis* (Quintilian), from *neutr-*, NEUTER: see -AL[1].]
▶**A** *noun.* **1** A person or State remaining neutral in a war, dispute, controversy, etc.; a subject of or ship belonging to a neutral State. **LME.**
2 A chemically neutral salt. **E19.**
3 An electrically neutral point, terminal, conductor, wire, etc. **E20.**
4 In full ***Idiom Neutral***. An artificial language based on Volapük and having the roots of its vocabulary chosen on the basis of maximum internationality. **E20.**
5 A position of the driving and driven parts in a gear mechanism in which no power is transmitted; *fig.* a state of inactivity (chiefly in ***in neutral***). **E20.**

> **1** P. ZIEGLER When war broke out Philip was still a Greek citizen and therefore technically a neutral. B. CHATWIN Politically, Utz was a neutral. **5** L. CODY She had to sail along in neutral for several yards before engaging the . . second gear. *Audio Visual* Pictures of the world from space (. . a good thing to throw in when the creative imagination's in neutral).

▶**B** *adjective.* **1** Not assisting or actively taking the side of either of two belligerent States or groups of States in a war; taking neither side or view in a dispute, disagreement, or controversy. **L15.** ▸**b** Belonging to neither party or side in a war, dispute, controversy, etc.; belonging to a power which remains inactive during hostilities, exempted or excluded from the sphere of warlike operations. M16.

2 Belonging to neither of two specified, implied, or usual categories; occupying a middle position with regard to two extremes; indifferent, impartial, dispassionate. In early use also, made up of opposing elements able to neutralize each other. L15.

3 Having no sexual characteristics, having no functional sexual organs, neuter, asexual. M17.

4 *CHEMISTRY.* Having the properties of neither an acid nor a base; (of an aqueous solution) having equal concentrations of hydroxyl and hydrogen ions, having a pH of 7. M17.

5 Having no strongly marked characteristics or features; undefined, indefinite, indistinct, vague; lacking colour or intensity (*lit. & fig.*). E19.

6 *ELECTRICITY.* Neither positive nor negative. M19.

7 *PHYSICS.* Designating or situated at a point or on a line or plane where opposing forces are in equilibrium. M19.

8 Designating any of various dyes, stains, and indicators whose properties or usual conditions of use are not strongly acidic or basic. Also, designating biological stains precipitated on mixing an acid and a basic dye. L19.

9 *PHILOSOPHY.* Neither specifically mental nor physical. E20.

1 W. S. CHURCHILL The intrusion of Federal troops . . caused many citizens who had hitherto been neutral to join the ranks of Secession. M. FITZHERBERT Albania, which declared itself neutral, became a battleground. **b** J. LUBBOCK Neutral goods . . are not liable to capture under enemy's flag. *Sunday Times* Weinstock and Clark met on neutral ground . . to bury their differences. **2** P. BARKER He wasn't just indifferent to them, he wasn't neutral: he really hated them. D. ROWE Dorothy has no axe to grind. She's completely neutral. **5** GEO. ELIOT Dissatisfied with his neutral life. A. HARDY Red appears as a dull neutral colour in all but very shallow regions. A. BULLOCK Unlike Attlee, who . . could disappear into a neutral background, Bevin's personality had always provoked controversy.

Special collocations & comb.: **neutral axis** *MECHANICS* a line or plane connecting points at which no extension or compression occurs when a beam, plate, etc., is bent. **neutral corner** either of the two corners of a boxing-ring not allocated to a contestant as a base between rounds etc. **neutral-density** *adjective* designating a photographic filter that absorbs light of all wavelengths to the same extent and so causes no change in colour. ***neutral EQUILIBRIUM***. **neutral-gear** = sense A.5 above. **neutral monism** *PHILOSOPHY* the theory that there is only one stuff or substance of existence of which mind and matter are varying arrangements. **neutral monist** *PHILOSOPHY* an adherent of neutral monism. **neutral vowel** *PHONETICS* a central, usu. unstressed, vowel sound produced with the tongue slack and the lips relaxed and having indefinite quality, *esp.* schwa.

▪ **neutrally** *adverb* L16.

neutralise *verb* var. of NEUTRALIZE.

neutralism /ˈnjuːtrəlɪz(ə)m/ *noun.* L16.

[from NEUTRAL + -ISM.]

1 Maintenance of neutrality; *spec.* a policy of maintaining neutrality and attempting conciliation in conflicts between States. L16.

2 *BIOLOGY.* The neutralist theory of genetic variation. L20.

neutralist /ˈnjuːtrəlɪst/ *noun & adjective.* E17.

[from NEUTRAL + -IST.]

▸ **A** *noun.* **1** A person who maintains a neutral attitude; an adherent of political neutralism. E17.

2 *BIOLOGY.* An advocate of the theory that all or most genetic mutations have no significant phenotypic effect and are established by random drift, not by selection. Opp. ***selectionist***. L20.

▸ **B** *adjective.* Of or pertaining to neutralists or neutralism; neutral in attitude. E19.

▪ **neutraˈlistic** *adjective* characterized by a neutral attitude, of the nature of neutralism M20.

neutrality /njuːˈtralɪti/ *noun.* L15.

[Old & mod. French *neutralité* or medieval Latin *neutralitas*, from Latin *neutralis*: see NEUTRAL, -ITY.]

1 An intermediate state or condition, a neutral position, middle ground. L15.

2 *The* people or parties remaining neutral during a dispute, controversy, etc.; *the* States remaining neutral during a war. *obsolete* exc. *Hist.* L15.

3 The state or condition of remaining neutral in a war, dispute, controversy, etc.; absence of decided views, feeling, or expression, indifference; impartiality, dispassionateness; an instance of this. M16. ▸**b** The neutral character *of* a place during a war. M18.

4 *GRAMMAR.* The fact of being of the neuter gender. Now *rare.* M17.

5 The condition of having no sexual characteristics. E19.

6 The fact or state of being chemically or electrically neutral. L19.

3 J. COLVILLE Norway and Denmark are determined on neutrality. A. S. NEILL For a parent there is no sitting on the fence, no neutrality. P. LOMAS Freud . . claimed a neutrality that is beyond human reach. **b** WELLINGTON The Russian Admiral . . would claim the neutrality of the port of Lisbon.

neutralize /ˈnjuːtrəlʌɪz/ *verb.* Also **-ise**. M17.

[In branch I from medieval Latin *neutralizare*, in branch II from French *neutraliser*, formed as NEUTRAL: see -IZE.]

▸ **I** *verb intrans.* †**1** Remain neutral. Only in M17.

▸ **II** *verb trans.* **2 a** Make (an acidic or alkaline solution) chemically neutral. M18. ▸**b** Eliminate a charge difference in; make electrically neutral. M19.

3 a Counterbalance; make ineffective or void by an opposite force or effect. L18. ▸**b** *OPHTHALMOLOGY.* Annul the refractive power of (a lens) by combination with one or more other lenses (of known power). E20. ▸**c** *ELECTRONICS.* Cancel internal feedback in (an amplifier stage, valve, or transistor) by providing an additional external feedback voltage of equal magnitude but opposite phase. E20. ▸**d** *LINGUISTICS.* Remove in a particular context the contrast or distinction between (phonemes, inflections, etc.). Chiefly as ***neutralized*** *ppl adjective.* M20. ▸**e** *euphem.* Make (a person) harmless or ineffective; *spec.* kill. L20.

4 Exempt or exclude (a place) from the sphere of warlike operations. M19.

5 In motor rallying, exempt (a section of a course) from having to be covered at a set average speed, so that that section has no effect on the result of a race. E20.

3a B. HINES Smoothing out the newspaper and rolling it the other way to neutralize the first curve. R. V. JONES Eckersley's evidence had neutralised itself, because he said one thing . . before and now something quite different.

▪ **neutraliˈzation** *noun* E19. **neutralizer** *noun* †(*a*) *rare* a person who adopts a neutral attitude; (*b*) a person who or thing which neutralizes something, a neutralizing agent: E17.

neutretto /njuːˈtrɛtəʊ/ *noun.* Pl. **-os**. M20.

[from NEUTRAL *adjective* + Italian *-etto* dim. suffix (cf. -ET[1]).]

NUCLEAR PHYSICS. †**1** A neutral pion. Only in M20.

2 A muon neutrino. M20.

neutrino /njuːˈtriːnəʊ/ *noun.* Pl. **-os**. M20.

[from NEUTRAL *adjective* + Italian *-ino* dim. suffix.]

NUCLEAR PHYSICS. Each of three stable uncharged leptons (associated with the electron, muon, and tau-particle) having very low mass and an extremely low probability of interaction with matter (symbol ν). Also, an antiparticle of any of these (symbol ν̄), as produced (with an electron and a proton) in the beta decay of a neutron.

solar neutrino unit: see SOLAR *adjective*[1].

neutro- /ˈnjuːtrəʊ/ *combining form* of NEUTRAL *adjective*: see -O-.

▪ **neutroˈpenia** *noun* (*MEDICINE*) (a condition characterized by) a reduction in the number of neutrophils in the blood M20. **neutrophil(e)** *adjective & noun* (*BIOLOGY*) (*a*) *adjective* (esp. of a cell or tissue) that can be stained with neutral dyes but usu. not readily with either acidic or basic dyes; (*b*) *noun* a neutrophil cell; *spec.* a polymorphonuclear leucocyte: L19. **neutroˈphilic** *adjective* = NEUTROPHIL(E) *adjective* L19.

neutrodyne /ˈnjuːtrədʌɪn/ *noun.* E20.

[from NEUTRO- + *-dyne*, after *heterodyne*.]

RADIO. A type of high-frequency valve amplifier in which neutralization was first employed to prevent oscillation throughout a range of frequencies. Freq. *attrib.*

neutron /ˈnjuːtrɒn/ *noun.* E20.

[from NEUTRAL *adjective* + -ON.]

PHYSICS. An electrically uncharged subatomic particle of slightly greater mass than the proton, which is a constituent (with the proton) of all atomic nuclei except that of the common isotope of hydrogen.

fast neutron, ***photoneutron***, ***slow neutron***, ***thermal neutron***, etc.

Comb.: **neutron activation** the process of making a substance radioactive by irradiating it with neutrons; **neutron bomb** a kind of atomic bomb producing large numbers of neutrons but little blast, and consequently harmful to life but not destructive of property; **neutron capture** the absorption of a neutron by an atomic nucleus; **neutron diffraction**: of a beam of neutrons; **neutron excess** the excess of the number of neutrons in an atomic nucleus over the number of protons; **neutron number** the mass number of a nucleus minus its atomic number, taken as being the number of neutrons it contains; **neutron radiography**: employing a beam of neutrons; **neutron star** *ASTRONOMY* an extremely small dense star composed predominantly of closely packed neutrons and thought to form by the collapse of a star under its own gravity (cf. PULSAR); **neutron therapy** *MEDICINE* radiation therapy employing a beam of neutrons.

▪ **neuˈtronic** *adjective* of, pertaining to, or employing neutrons M20.

Nev. *abbreviation.*

Nevada.

Nevadan /nɪˈvɑːdən/ *adjective & noun.* L19.

[from *Nevada* (see below) + -AN.]

(A native or inhabitant) of the State of Nevada in the western US.

▪ Also **Nevadian** *adjective & noun* M19.

névé /neve/ *noun.* Pl. pronounced same. M19.

[Swiss French, from Latin *niv-*, *nix* snow.]

The crystalline or granular snow on the upper part of a glacier, which has not yet been compressed into ice. Also, a field or bed of this. Also called ***firn***.

nevel /ˈnɛv(ə)l/ *noun & verb. Scot. & north.* Also **kn-**. M16.

[from NIEVE + -EL[1].]

▸ **A** *noun.* A blow with the fist. M16.

▸ **B** *verb trans.* Infl. **-ll-**. Beat with the fists; pound, pummel. L16.

never /ˈnɛvə/ *adverb.* See also NE'ER.

[Old English *nǣfre*, formed as NE + EVER. Cf. NE'.]

1 At no time or moment, on no occasion, not ever. OE.

2 By an unlimited degree or amount. Only in ***never so*** in conditional clauses. OE.

3 Not at all, in no way. In later use usu. *impers.*, esp. in ***never fear***, ***never you fear*** s.v. FEAR *verb* 4, ***never mind***, ***never you mind*** below. ME.

4 In no degree, to no extent. Only in ***never the*** followed by compar. ME.

5 In emphatic denial, or expr. surprise or incredulity: definitely not, surely not. *colloq.* M19.

1 GOLDSMITH I never yet found one instance of their existence. COLERIDGE To be found . . in the realities of Heaven, but never, never, in creatures of flesh, and blood. DICKENS A frown upon its never-smiling face. J. TYNDALL I believe the fact was never before observed. E. WALLACE One never-to-be-forgotten occasion. E. BOWEN Never till now . . had Portia been the first to look away. S. BEDFORD I never knew my grandparents. F. SWINNERTON His daughters had never to his knowledge wept hysterically. M. ROBERTS I'll never get married. **2** A. C. SWINBURNE Were the critic never so much in the wrong, the author will . . put him . . in the right. **5** CONAN DOYLE It's not he—it's never the man whom we have known. B. BAINBRIDGE 'It's probably all that crouching you did under dining-room tables during the war.' 'I never.' W. TREVOR You're never selling up, Fitz? *Wire* JCN was wound up in April '85. The crux was money (never!).

Phrases & comb.: **I never did!** *colloq.*: expr. surprise or incredulity (*sc.* hear such a thing before, etc.). ***may your shadow never grow less!***: see SHADOW *noun*. **never a** — not a single —; no — at all (***never a one***, not a single one). **never again!** expr. emphatic refusal to repeat an experience etc. **never-ceasing** *adjective* unceasing, ceaseless; constant, continual. **never-dying** *adjective* (chiefly *poet.*) undying; immortal. **never-ending** *adjective* unending, endless, everlasting, perpetual. **never ever** never at all, absolutely never. **never-fading** *adjective* unfading, fadeless, ever fresh or new. **never-fail** any of several drought-resistant Australian grasses of the genus *Eragrostis*, esp. *E. setifolia* and *E. xerophila*; **never-failing** *adjective* unfailing. **never-failingly** *adverb* (now *rare*) unfailingly. ***never fear***: see FEAR *verb* 4. **Never Land** = ***Never Never Land*** (b) below. **nevermind** *N. Amer. colloq.* (an occasion of or cause for) concern, attention, (only in neg. contexts, chiefly in ***make no nevermind***, make no difference, ***pay no nevermind***, pay no attention). **never mind** *imper.* (*a*) do not be troubled or upset, take comfort; (*b*) do not think or enquire further about it (it is no business of yours); (*c*) not to mention, let alone. **never never** *adverb*: redupl. for emphasis. **never-never** *noun* (*colloq.*) *the* hire-purchase system. **never-never** *adjective* unrealistic, unrealizable, imaginary. **Never Never Country** *Austral.* = ***Never Never Land*** (a) below. **Never Never Land** (*a*) (*Austral.*) *the* unpopulated northern part of the Northern Territory and Queensland; *the* desert country of the interior of Australia; (*b*) an imaginary, illusory, or utopian place. ***never say die***: see DIE *verb*[1]. ***never you fear***: see FEAR *verb* 4. **never you mind** *imper.* = ***never mind*** (a), (b) above. **never-was**, **never-waser** *colloq.* a person who has never been great, distinguished, useful, etc. ***one never knows***: see KNOW *verb*. ***on which the sun never sets***: see SUN *noun*[1]. **well, I never!** *colloq.* expr. surprise or incredulity (*sc.* heard such a thing before, etc.). ***you never know***: see KNOW *verb*.

nevermore /nɛvəˈmɔː/ *adverb.* LOE.

[Orig. two words, from NEVER + MORE *adverb*.]

Never again, at no future time.

Nevers /nɛvɛːr/ *noun & adjective.* M19.

[A city in central France.]

(Designating) deep blue-ground faience in the style of Italian majolica, made at Nevers from the latter part of the 16th cent. to the 18th.

nevertheless /nɛvəðəˈlɛs/ *adverb.* ME.

[from NEVER + THE + LESS *adverb*.]

Despite that, but despite that, notwithstanding, all the same.

G. GREENE He was glad, nevertheless, when the Indian looked out of his room. *Daily Mirror* Nevertheless, she did speak. A. BROOKNER He disliked the more sociable aspects of his calling, but had nevertheless booked a table in a . . restaurant.

nevus *noun* see NAEVUS.

nevvy /ˈnɛvi/ *noun. dial. & colloq.* Also **nevy**. M16.

[Abbreviation.]

= NEPHEW.

new /njuː/ *adjective & noun.*

[Old English *nēowe*, *nī(o)we* = Old Frisian *nȳ*, *nī*, Old Saxon *niuwi*, *nigi*, Middle Low German *nige*, *nie*, Middle Dutch *n(ie)uwe*, *nie* (Dutch *nieuw*), Old High German *niuwi* (German *neu*), Old Norse *nýr*, Gothic *niujis*, from Germanic from Indo-European base repr. also by Greek *neos* (Ionic *neios*), Gaulish *Novio-* (in place-names), Latin *novus*, Sanskrit *nava*. Cf. NEO-.]

► **A** *adjective*. **I 1** Not existing before; now made or existing for the first time. OE. ▸**b** Of a kind now first invented or introduced; novel. LME.

2 Now known, experienced, used, etc., for the first time. OE. ▸**b** Strange or unfamiliar (*to*). ME.

3 a Starting afresh; restored or renewed after decay, disappearance, etc. OE. ▸**b** Fresh, further, additional. ME.

4 Different from a thing previously existing, known, used, etc.; in addition to others already existing or present; succeeding another person in a specified function or position. OE. ▸**b** Fundamentally, esp. spiritually or morally, changed; reformed; reinvigorated. LME.

5 (Usu. with *the*.) Of more recent origin than, superseding, or reviving a thing of the same kind; modern, advanced in method or doctrine. OE. ▸**b** In place-names: discovered or founded later than and named after. ME.

> **1** *Which?* A new law . . means a driver must give . . insurance details after an accident. **b** R. DAHL There is a new exciting music . . with subtle harmonies and grinding discords. **2** W. ABISH Why don't you come and visit . . . Meet new people. A. LURIE Her father always knew so many funny new jokes. V. BROME The disciple had nothing really new to say because the Master had . . said it all before. **b** T. HARDY The scene—so new to her, fresh from the seclusion of a seaside cottage. **3a** J. G. FARRELL The Major found himself seeing London with new and less world-weary eyes. **b** LD MACAULAY Commissions were issued for the levying of new regiments. **4** DAY LEWIS They have a new clergyman . . a very clever man. J. F. LEHMANN Virginia was at work on a new book. *Times* Mr Grimond, the new leader of the Liberals. **b** S. HILL Alida appears to be a new woman. **5** ***the new celibacy, the new economics, the new morality***, etc. **b** ***New Delhi, New Hampshire, New South Wales, New York, New Zealand***, etc.

► **II 6 a** Of recent origin; (of an event etc.) recent. OE. ▸**b** Of food or drink: freshly produced or grown, not stale; harvested early in the season. OE. ▸**c** Recently made, not yet used or worn. OE. ▸**d** Recently inhabited or settled. E19.

7 Having recently entered a certain state, position, etc.; unaccustomed *to*, inexperienced *at*. OE. ▸**b** Fresh *from* a place, state, etc. E18.

8 That is or remains fresh or vital, not declining or decaying. ME.

9 Having reached a high social standing comparatively recently; not belonging to a well-established family. E17.

> **6a** SHAKES. *Cymb.* The exile of her minion is too new; She hath not yet forgot him. **b** ***new bread, new potatoes***, etc. **c** R. BRAUTIGAN Another sign advertising new and used two and three ton hoists. W. BOYD The station—new, stone and quite impressive. **7** LD MACAULAY James's parliament contained a most unusual proportion of new members. **b** *Times* The Government was new to office. **8** MILTON Heav'ns last best gift, my ever new delight.

Special collocations & phrases: ***brave new world***: see BRAVE *adjective*. ***New Academy***: see ACADEMY 2. ***new arrival***: see ARRIVAL 2. **New Art** = ART NOUVEAU. **New Australian** a recent immigrant to Australia, *esp.* one from Europe. **new ball** a previously unused ball; *spec.* in CRICKET, a ball brought into use at the beginning of an innings or after a prescribed number of overs (***see off the new ball***: see SEE *verb*). ***new birth***: see BIRTH *noun*[1] 1. ***new blood***: see BLOOD *noun*. ***new broom***: see BROOM *noun* 2. **new boy** (*a*) a boy during his first term(s) at a school; (*b*) a (young) man newly come into a certain situation. **new bug** *School slang* = ***new boy*** (a) above. **newbuilding** [Danish *nybygning*] a newly constructed ship; the construction of ships. **New Caledonian** *noun & adjective* (a native or inhabitant) of New Caledonia, an island in the SW Pacific east of Australia. **New Canadian** an immigrant who has settled in Canada. ***new chum***: see CHUM *noun*[1]. **new-collar** *adjective & noun* (chiefly *US*) (designating) a person from a blue-collar family who is better educated and has a higher standard of living. ***New Commonwealth***: see COMMONWEALTH 5C. ***new Covenant***: see COVENANT *noun*. **New Critic** an advocate or exponent of New Criticism. **New Critical** *adjective* of or pertaining to New Criticism or New Critics. **New Criticism** an approach to the analysis of literary texts which concentrates on the organization of the text itself with particular emphasis on irony, ambiguity, paradox, etc. **new deal** a new usu. improved arrangement; *spec.* (with cap. initials) the US programme of social and economic reform launched in the 1930s by the Roosevelt administration to counteract the depression. **New Dealish** *adjective* of, pertaining to, or supporting the New Deal. **New English Bible** a modern English translation of the Bible, published in the UK in 1961–70 and revised (as the ***Revised English Bible***) in 1989 (abbreviation ***NEB***). **new entry** a recruit; *collect.* people having recently qualified, been recruited, or become eligible to do something. **new frontier** *fig.* a new approach to reform and social betterment; *spec.* (with cap. initials) a programme of social improvement advocated by US president J. F. Kennedy. **New Frontiersman** an advocate or supporter of the New Frontier programme. **new girl** (*a*) a girl during her first term(s) at a school; (*b*) a (young) woman newly come into a certain situation. **new ground** (*a*) *US* land only recently cleared and cultivated; (*b*) *Austral.* part of a goldfield only recently exploited; (*c*) ***break new ground***: see BREAK *verb*. **New Humanism** (with *the*) a school of thought emphasizing humankind's superiority to the natural order through the use of reason. **New Humanist** an advocate or adherent of the New Humanism. **New International Version** a modern English translation of the Bible published in 1973–8 (abbreviation ***NIV***). **New Journalism** (usu. with *the*) (orig. *US*) a style of journalism characterized by the use of subjective and fictional elements so as to elicit an emotional response from the reader. **New Journalist** (orig. *US*) a practitioner of New Journalism. **new kid on the block** *colloq.* a newcomer, a novice; a recent arrival to a specified position or area. **New Kingdom** *the* Eighteenth, Nineteenth, and Twentieth Dynasties, which ruled Egypt from the 16th to the 11th cents. BC; *the* period of these dynasties. **New Labour** POLITICS that section of the British Labour Party which actively supported the internal reforms initiated by Neil Kinnock (party leader 1983–92) and carried through by subsequent party leaders; the Labour Party as a whole after the implementation of those reforms; (cf. ***Old Labour***). ***new law***: see LAW *noun*[1]. **new learning** (*a*) the studies, esp. that of the Greek language, introduced into England in the 16th cent.; (*b*) the doctrines of the Reformation. ***new lease of life, new lease on life***: see LEASE *noun*[3]. **New Left** a movement originated by young left-wing radicals opposed to the philosophy of the old liberal society; *gen.* any radical left-wing movement. **New Leftist** *adjective & noun* (a supporter or member) of the New Left. **New Light** *noun & adjective* (*a*) *noun* a new, freq. more moderate, theological or ecclesiastical doctrine; a supporter or propounder of this; *Hist.* (a member of) any of various Protestant sects in Scotland and N. America; (*b*) *adjective* of or pertaining to such a doctrine or any of its supporters or propounders; *transf.* newfangled, novel. **new look** a new or revised appearance or presentation, esp. of something familiar; *spec.* (freq. with cap. initials) a style of women's clothing introduced after the war of 1939–45, featuring long wide skirts and a generous use of material in contrast to wartime austerity. **new-look** *adjective* having a new image, restyled. **new man** *spec.* (*a*) THEOLOGY a man recently converted to Christianity; (*b*) a man rejecting sexist attitudes and the traditional male role. **new mathematics**, **new maths**, (*N. Amer.*) **new math** (freq. with *the*) a system of teaching mathematics to younger children, with emphasis on investigation and discovery on their part and on set theory etc. **New Model** *Hist.* the plan for the reorganization of the Parliamentary army, passed by the House of Commons in 1644–5. **new money** (*a*) a fortune recently acquired, funds recently raised; (*b*) the new rich. **new moon** (*a*) the moon when it appears as a slender crescent shortly after its conjunction with the sun; (*b*) the time when this occurs; ASTRONOMY the time at which the moon is in conjunction with the sun; (*c*) the ancient Hebrew festival celebrated at the time of the new moon. **New Negro** *US* (*a*) *Hist.* a black slave newly brought from Africa; (*b*) a member of any of various movements striving for black rights. ***new nothing***: see NOTHING *pronoun & noun*. ***new off the irons***: see IRON *noun*. **new one** *colloq.* (orig. *US*) an anecdote, idea, situation, etc., not previously encountered (freq. in ***a new one on me***). **new order** a new system, regime, or government; *Hist.* (with cap. initials) Hitler's planned reorganization of Europe under Nazi rule. **new poor** *the* class of recently impoverished people. **new psychology** *the* new areas of psychological investigation, as experimental psychology and esp. those theories recognizing the irrational and unconscious motivations of human behaviour. **new realism** PHILOSOPHY (chiefly *US*) the doctrine of realism as revived at the beginning of the 20th cent. to refute certain tenets of idealism. **new realist** *noun & adjective* (an adherent or student) of new realism. ***New Red Sandstone***: see SANDSTONE. **New Revised Standard Version** a modern English translation of the Bible, based on the Revised Standard Version and published in 1990 (abbreviation ***NRSV***). **new rich** *the* class of people having recently acquired wealth, the ***nouveaux riches***. **New Right** (orig. *US*) a political movement reacting to the New Left, characterized by rejection of all forms of socialism and emphasis on traditional conservative values or (esp. in the US) by libertarian, esp. free-market policies; the supporters of this movement collectively. **New Rightist** *noun & adjective* (a supporter or member) of the New Right. **New Romantic** a devotee or exponent of a style of popular music and fashion popular in Britain in the early 1980s, in which both men and women wore make-up and dressed in flamboyant clothes. **new school** an advanced or liberal faction of a party or organization; *spec.* (with cap. initials) the section of the Presbyterian Church of the US separated from the rest of the Church in the 19th cent. **new star** a nova. **New Style** the method of calculating dates using the Gregorian calendar, which in England and Wales superseded the use of the Julian calendar in 1752 (cf. ***Old Style*** s.v. OLD *adjective*). **newtake** a piece of moorland newly enclosed and cultivated (esp. on Dartmoor in Devon, England). **new technology** technology that radically alters the way something is produced or performed, esp. involving labour-saving automation or computerization. **New Testament** the part of the Bible concerned with the life and teachings of Jesus and his earliest followers. **new thing** *slang* (orig. *US*) *the* latest craze, something avant-garde or innovative; *spec.* a type of experimental jazz music in the 1960s dispensing with the conventional harmonic and rhythmic framework. **New Thought** (*a*) a theory of the nature of disease and of therapeutic practice; (*b*) a religious sect believing in this theory in the guidance of an inner presence. **New Thoughter** an adherent of New Thought. **new tick** *School slang* = ***new bug*** above. **new town** a town established as a completely new settlement with government sponsorship or approval, esp. to absorb overspill population. **new towner** an inhabitant of a new town. **new wave** (*a*) = NOUVELLE VAGUE; (*b*) *spec.* (more fully ***new wave music***) a style of rock music originally associated with punk rock, popular in the late 1970s. **new waver** a performer or follower of new wave music. **new wavish** *adjective* associated with or resembling new wave music. ***new wine in old bottles***: see WINE *noun*. **new woman** *spec.* (*a*) *Hist.* a woman aspiring to freedom and independence for women, a feminist; (*b*) a woman successful in a traditionally male-dominated area. **New World** *noun & adjective* (*a*) *noun* the western hemisphere, the Americas; (*b*) *adjective* native to, characteristic of, or associated with the New World; ***New World monkey***, a monkey of the platyrrhine group, which comprises all American monkeys, typically having a prehensile tail. **New Worlder** a native or inhabitant of the New World. **New World Order** a vision of a world ordered differently from the way it is at present; a new set of conditions, principles, laws, etc., governing events in the world, *spec.* following the end of the Cold War. ***new wrinkle***: see WRINKLE *noun*[1] 7a. ***turn over a new leaf***: see LEAF *noun*[1]. **what's new?** *colloq.* what has been happening?; how are you?

► **B** *absol.* as *noun*. **1 a** That which is new. OE. ▸**b** A new thing. Cf. NEWS *noun*. *rare*. LME.

2 ***new of the moon***, the time at which the moon is new. Now *rare*. LME.

3 ***of new***, of late, recently, newly (now *Scot.*); afresh, over again (now *rare*). LME.

4 A naval cadet during his or her first term in a training ship. *slang*. E20.

> **1a** B. JOWETT In the arts . . also in politics, the new must always prevail over the old.

■ **newish** *adjective* somewhat new L16.

†new *verb*. See also NEWING.

[Old English *nīwian*, from prec. Cf. Old Saxon *niwian*, Old High German *niwōn*, Old Norse *nýja* Gothic (*ana*)*niujan*.]

1 *verb trans.* Renew, make new. OE–M16.

2 *verb intrans.* Become new again, renew itself. OE–E16.

new /njuː/ *adverb*.

[Old English *nīwe*, from the adjective.]

1 Newly, recently, lately. Exc. *Scot.* only modifying ppl adjectives. OE.

2 Anew, afresh, over again. Long chiefly modifying ppl adjectives. ME.

> **1** ***new-baked, new-coined, new-found, new-mown, new-risen***, etc. **2** J. ADAMS To correct or new-make the whole work. LYTTON The streets are new-peopled: the morning is bright.

Comb.: **new-blown** *adjective* having just come into bloom (*lit.* & *fig.*); **newborn** *adjective & noun* (*a*) *adjective* recently born; *fig.* regenerated; (*b*) *noun* a newborn human or animal; **new-come** *adjective & noun* (now *rare*) (*a*) *adjective* newly or recently arrived; (*b*) *noun* a new or recent arrival; a novice, a newcomer; **new-create** *verb trans.* (chiefly *poet.*) create anew or newly; **new-fallen** *adjective* (chiefly *poet.*) (*a*) newly or recently fallen; †(*b*) (*rare*, Shakes.) newly fallen to one; (*c*) newborn; **new-fashioned** *adjective* of a new type, of recent invention; **new-laid** *adjective* (of an egg) freshly laid; **new-model** *verb trans.* [after *New Model* s.v. NEW *adjective*] remodel or rearrange in a new way (*spec.* an army or government); **†new-modelize** *verb trans.* = ***new-model*** above.

New Age /njuː ˈeɪdʒ/ *noun & adjectival phr.* M17.

[from NEW *adjective* + AGE *noun*.]

► **A** *noun*. **1** A new era of history, *spec.* = ***Age of Aquarius*** s.v. AQUARIUS 1. M17.

2 A broad movement inspired by a belief in the approach of the Age of Aquarius and characterized by alternative approaches to (or rejection of) traditional Western culture and interest in spirituality, mysticism, holism, and environmentalism; the culture or philosophy of this movement. L20.

► **B** *attrib.* or as *adjective*. Of, pertaining to, or characteristic of the New Age; advocating or following the culture, lifestyle, etc., associated with it. M20.

Comb. & special collocations: **New Age music** a style of chiefly instrumental modern music characterized by light melodic harmonies, improvisation, and the reproduction of sounds from the natural world, intended to promote serenity; **New Age traveller** a person, esp. an adherent of New Age philosophies, who has deliberately rejected conventional ways of life and adopted a travelling existence.

■ **New Ageism** *noun* L20. **New Ager** *noun* L20. **New Agey** *adjective* L20.

Newar /niːˈwɑː/ *noun & adjective*. E19.

[Newari *newār* from Prakrit *newāla*, Sanskrit *naipāla*, from *Nepāla* the Kathmandu Valley in Nepal.]

► **A** *noun*. Pl. **-s**, same. A member of a Tibeto-Burman people of Nepal. E19.

► **B** *adjective*. Of or pertaining to the Newars. L19.

■ **Newari** /niːˈwɑːri/ *adjective & noun* (of) the Tibeto-Burman language of the Newars E19.

Newark /ˈnjuːək/ *noun*. Chiefly *US*. L18.

[A city in New Jersey, USA.]

Used *attrib.* to designate things coming from or associated with Newark.

Newark charging system a system of recording library book loans in which the date of borrowing is recorded on the book, the book card, and the borrower's ticket.

newbie /ˈnjuːbi/ *noun*. L20.

[from NEW *adjective* + -IE, perh. infl. by NEW BOY.]

A person who is new to a particular activity, profession, etc., a beginner; *spec.* a new user of the Internet.

> E. S. RAYMOND Note for the newbie: Overuse of the smiley is a mark of loserhood!

Newcastle /ˈnjuːkɑːs(ə)l/ *noun*. M18.

[A city (in full *Newcastle upon Tyne*) in northern England.]

Used *attrib.* to designate things coming from or associated with Newcastle.

Newcastle Brown (proprietary name for) a strong brown ale; a drink of this. **Newcastle disease** an acute febrile infectious disease of birds, esp. poultry, caused by a paramyxovirus; also called ***fowl pest***. **Newcastle glass** a type of colour-free glass manufactured in Newcastle. **Newcastle pottery** a type of coarse pottery manufactured around Newcastle.

¶ See also ***carry coals to Newcastle*** s.v. COAL.

newcomer /ˈnjuːkʌmə/ *noun*. LME.

[from NEW *adjective* + COMER.]

A person who has recently arrived, a new arrival; a beginner at or novice in a certain activity or situation.

📖 P. AUSTER Until they have learned the ways of the city, these newcomers are easy victims. *London Daily News* Roden . . is a newcomer to the ranks of television food pundits.

newel /'nju:əl/ *noun*. LME.
[Old French *nouel*, *noel* knob, from medieval Latin *nodellus* dim. of *nodus* knot: see -EL². Cf. NOWEL *noun*².]
1 The supporting central pillar of a spiral or winding staircase. Formerly also, any of the stones forming such a pillar. Also ***solid newel***. LME. ▸**b** ***hollow newel***, ***open newel***, a central open space or well in a spiral etc. staircase. E17.
2 A post at the head or foot of a staircase supporting a handrail. L17.
■ **newelled** *adjective* having a newel (of a specified kind) L17.

newelty /'nju:əlti/ *noun*. Now *dial*. LME.
[Old French *noueleté*, *nov-* (mod. *nouveauté*) NOVELTY, alt. after NEW *adjective*: see -TY¹.]
1 Novelty, newness. LME.
2 A novelty, a new thing. LME.

New England /nju: 'ɪŋglənd/ *noun phr*. M17.
[A part of the US comprising the six north-eastern States.]
Used *attrib*. to designate things or people native to, associated with, or characteristic of New England, USA.
New England aster a Michaelmas daisy, *Aster novae-angliae*, with deep purple flowers. **New England boiled dinner** a dish comprising root vegetables and corned or salt beef. **New England mayflower** the trailing arbutus, *Epigaea repens*. **New England theology** a movement in American Congregationalism repudiating much Calvinist doctrine.
■ **New Englander** *noun phr*. a native or inhabitant of New England M17. **New Englandish** *adjectival phr*. characteristic or typical of New England M19. **New Englandism** *noun phr*. (*a*) behaviour or temperament characteristic of New Englanders; (*b*) an idiom characteristic of New Englanders: M19. **New English** *adjectival phr*. of or pertaining to New England M17.

newfangle /nju:'faŋg(ə)l/ *adjective, noun, & verb*. Now *dial*. ME.
[from NEW *adverb* + *-fangle* repr. an Old English word rel. to FANG *verb*¹: see -LE³.]
▸**A** *adjective*. **1** = NEWFANGLED 1. ME.
2 = NEWFANGLED 2. L15.
▸**B** *noun*. A new thing or fashion; a novelty. E16.
▸**C** *verb trans*. Make newfangled. M18.

newfangled /nju:'faŋg(ə)ld/ *adjective*. LME.
[from prec. + -ED¹.]
1 (Excessively) fond of new things, fashions, or ideas; easily carried away by whatever is new. LME.
2 Newly made or existing, novel. Freq. *derog*. or *joc*., objectionably or gratuitously modern, different from what one is used to. M16.

📖 **1** F. DHONDY These new-fangled art teachers didn't know about art. **2** C. AMORY Her father-in-law pronounced the newfangled dance 'an indecorous exhibition'. D. ACHESON The summer sun . . unabated by any such newfangled contrivance as air conditioning.

■ **newfangledly** *adverb* (*rare*) E20. **newfangledness** *noun* the fact or state of being newfangled; novelty, innovation: M16.

newfanglement /nju:'faŋg(ə)lm(ə)nt/ *noun*. Now *rare*. L18.
[from NEWFANGLE *adjective* + -MENT.]
Novelty; a novel thing.

newfangleness /nju:'faŋg(ə)lnɪs/ *noun*. Now *rare*. LME.
[formed as prec. + -NESS.]
Newfangledness.

Newfie /'nju:fi/ *noun & adjective*. *colloq*. (freq. *derog*.). M20.
[Abbreviation of next: see -IE.]
▸**A** *noun*. A Newfoundlander. M20.
▸**B** *adjective*. Coming from or associated with Newfoundland. M20.

Newfoundland /'nju:f(ə)n(d)lənd, -land, nju:'faʊndlənd/ *noun*. E17.
[A large island on the east coast of Canada and a Canadian province consisting of the island and mainland Labrador.]
1 Used *attrib*. to designate things from, characteristic of, or associated with Newfoundland. E17.
2 (An animal of) a very large breed of dog with a thick coarse usu. black coat, noted for its intelligence, strength, and swimming ability. Also more fully ***Newfoundland dog***. L18.
1 Newfoundland fish codfish. **2** LANDSEER ***Newfoundland***.
■ **Newfoundlander** *noun* (*a*) a native or inhabitant of Newfoundland; (*b*) a Newfoundland dog: E17.

Newgate /'nju:geɪt/ *noun*. L16.
[See below.]
Used *attrib*. to designate things associated with Newgate, a celebrated London prison pulled down in 1902–3.
Newgate bird *arch*. a jailbird. **Newgate Calendar** *Hist*. a publication containing accounts of prisoners in Newgate. **Newgate frill**, **Newgate fringe** a fringe of beard worn under the chin. **Newgate hornpipe** *arch*. a hanging. **Newgate novel** a 19th-cent. genre of picaresque novels involving criminal characters; a novel of this genre. **Newgate novelist** a writer of Newgate novels. **Newgate school** the Newgate novelists collectively.

newie /'nju:i/ *noun*. *colloq*. Also **newy**. M20.
[from NEW *adjective* + -IE.]
1 Something new; *spec*. (*a*) a new joke or idea; (*b*) a song recently released on a record etc.; (*c*) = ***new ball*** s.v. NEW *adjective*. M20.
2 A person without previous experience in professional entertainment. M20.

📖 **1** *Melody Maker* Dave Dee's newie 'Save Me'.

newing /'nju:ɪŋ/ *noun*. LME.
[from NEW *verb* + -ING¹. Sense 3 perh. a different word.]
†**1** The action of renewing or making new. LME–L15.
2 A new thing, a novelty; in *pl*. (usu. treated as *sing*.), news, something new. Long *obsolete* exc. *dial*. LME.
3 (The working of) yeast. *dial*. M17.

new jack /'nju: dʒak/ *adjectival & noun phr*. Chiefly *US*. L20.
[from NEW *adjective* + JACK *noun*¹.]
▸**A** *adjective*. Of or relating to novice gang members or their related subculture; of or relating to new jack swing or its related subculture. *slang*. L20.
▸**B** *noun*. **1** Esp. in African-American usage: a newcomer, a recent arrival, a novice (esp. one who is a member of a street gang or involved in criminal activities). *slang*. L20.
2 = ***new jack swing***. Also: a performer or fan of this music. L20.
Comb.: **New Jack City** an urban district populated chiefly by African-Americans and characterized by violent crime and street gangs. **new jack swing** a form of music combining elements of r'n'b, soul, and rap music.

New Jersey /nju: 'dʒɜ:zi/ *noun*. M18.
[See below. Cf. JERSEY *noun*¹.]
Used *attrib*. to designate things from, characteristic of, or associated with New Jersey, a north-eastern coastal State of the US.
New Jersey tea = ***Jersey tea*** s.v. JERSEY *noun*¹.
■ **New Jerseyan**, **New Jerseyite** *nouns* a native or inhabitant of New Jersey M20.

Newlands /'nju:ləndz/ *noun*. M20.
[J. K. *Newlands* (1838–98), Brit. chemist.]
CHEMISTRY. ***Newlands' Law of Octaves*** = ***Law of Octaves*** s.v. OCTAVE *noun*.

newly /'nju:li/ *adverb*. OE.
[from NEW *adjective* + -LY².]
1 Recently, lately, a very little time before. OE.
2 Anew, afresh. OE.
†**3** Immediately; soon, quickly. ME–M16.
4 In a new or different manner. M16.
Comb.: **newly-wed** a recently married person.

Newmanism /'nju:mənɪz(ə)m/ *noun*. M19.
[from *Newman* (see below) + -ISM.]
The theological and ecclesiastical views put forward by the English churchman John Henry Newman (1801–90) before he left the Anglican for the Roman Catholic Church; the principles involved in Newman's teaching.
■ **Newmania** /nju:'meɪnɪə/ *noun* enthusiastic support for Newmanism M19. **Newmanite** *noun* a follower or adherent of Newman M19. **Newmanize** *verb intrans*. (*rare*) incline to or adopt Newmanism M19.

Newman–Keuls /nju:mən'kɔ:ls/ *noun*. M20.
[D. *Newman* (fl. 1939), English statistician and M. *Keuls* (fl. 1952), Dutch horticulturist.]
STATISTICS. Used *attrib*. to designate a test for assessing the significance of differences between all possible pairs of different sets of observations, with a fixed error rate for the whole set of comparisons.

Newmarket /'nju:mɑ:kɪt/ *noun*. L17.
[A town in Suffolk, England, famous for horse-racing.]
1 Used. *attrib*. to designate things coming from or associated with Newmarket. L17.
2 In full ***Newmarket coat***, ***Newmarket frock***. A close-fitting tailcoat of a style originally worn for riding. M18.
3 A gambling card-game in which the main object is to play off all one's cards to a matching sequence on the table. M19.

New Mexican /nju: 'mɛksɪk(ə)n/ *adjectival & noun phr*. M19.
[from *New Mexico* (see below) + -AN.]
▸**A** *adjective*. Of or pertaining to the State of New Mexico in the south-western US. M19.
▸**B** *noun*. A native or inhabitant of New Mexico. M19.

newness /'nju:nɪs/ *noun*. OE.
[from NEW *adjective* + -NESS.]
1 The state, fact, or quality of being new. OE.
2 a A new thing, a novelty. *rare*. L17. ▸**b** CHRISTIAN THEOLOGY. (**N-**.) The transcendentalism associated with New England. M19.

📖 **1** *Broadcast* You can actually taste the newness of Jersey new potatoes. P. GROSSKURTH She . . remembers the newness of the upper-income house.

New Orleans /nju:'ɔ:lɪənz, ɔ:'li:nz/ *noun phr*. E19.
[See below.]
Used *attrib*. to designate things originating in or associated with New Orleans, a city in Louisiana, USA, *spec*. a kind of traditional jazz characterized by collective improvisation.
■ **New Orleanian** /nju:ɔ:'li:ənɪən/ *noun* a native or inhabitant of New Orleans, an Orleanian M20.

news /nju:z/ *noun pl*. (now usu. treated as *sing*.). LME.
[Pl. of NEW *noun* after Old French *noveles* pl. of *novele* (mod. *nouvelle*) NOVEL *noun* or medieval Latin *nova* pl. of *novum* use as noun of Latin *novus* NEW *adjective*. Cf. ODDS *noun*.]
†**1** New things, novelties. *rare*. LME–M16.
2 (Freq. with *the*.) Information, esp. when published or broadcast, about important or interesting recent events; such events themselves as a subject of report or talk. Also, newly received or noteworthy information about matters of personal, local, etc., interest. LME. ▸**b** A person, thing, or place regarded as worthy of discussion or of reporting by the media. E20.
†**3** A piece or item of news. L16–M17.
4 a The newspapers; (*rare*) a newspaper. Freq. in titles of newspapers and periodicals. M18. ▸**b** (Usu. with *the*.) A television, radio, etc., broadcast in which news is announced and sometimes discussed. E20.

📖 **2** SHELLEY There are bad news from Palermo. E. ALBEE I have some terrible news for you. J. RATHBONE The worst news of all was the fall of gallant Saragossa. P. HOWARD The Times was . . born when there was a lot of news around. ***bad news***: see BAD *adjective*. **it is news to me**, **that is news to me**, etc. *colloq*. I did not know that. ***spot news***: see SPOT *noun* etc. ***that is news to me***: see ***it is news to me*** above. YESTERDAY'S ***news***. **b** R. MACAULAY Aunt Dot and Father Chantry-Pigg . . were . . news in three continents. **4a** SWIFT His House was burnt . . to the Ground. Yes; it was in the News. ***Daily News***, ***Garden News***, ***Illustrated London News***, etc. **b** *Sunday Times* I then listen to the 5:45 news.

Comb.: **news agency** (*a*) a business that sells newspapers and periodicals; (*b*) an organization that collects news items and distributes them to newspapers, broadcasters, etc.; **newsagent** (a proprietor of) a shop selling newspapers, periodicals, and usu. confectionery, tobacco, etc.; **newsboy**: who sells or delivers newspapers; **newsbreak** (*a*) a newsworthy item; (*b*) a newsflash; **newsbrief** a short item of news, esp. on television; a newsflash; **news bulletin** a short broadcast or published news item or collection of news items; **news butch**, **news butcher** *US colloq*. a seller of newspapers, sweets, etc., on a train; **newscast** *noun & verb* (*a*) *noun* a broadcast of the news on radio or television; (*b*) *verb intrans*. transmit or broadcast news; **newscaster** (*a*) a newsreader; (*b*) an illuminated sign which transmits news etc.; **news cinema** *Hist*. a cinema showing short films, cartoons, and newsreels; **news conference** = ***press conference*** s.v. PRESS *noun*¹; **news desk** the department of a broadcasting organization or newspaper responsible for collecting and reporting the news; **newsflash** a single item of important news broadcast separately and often interrupting other programmes; **newsgatherer** a person who researches news items esp. for broadcast or publication; **newsgirl**: who sells or delivers newspapers; **newsgroup** COMPUTING a forum on a network (esp. the Internet) for the discussion of a particular subject and the exchange of information about it; a group of Internet users who exchange email messages on a topic of mutual interest; **newshawk**, **newshound** *colloq*. (orig. *US*) a newspaper reporter; **newsletter** (*a*) a letter specially written to communicate news; (*b*) *Hist*. a printed account of the news; (*c*) an informal printed report issued periodically to members of a society, business, etc.; **newsman** (*a*) a male reporter or journalist; (*b*) a man who sells or delivers newspapers; **newsmonger** a person who collects and reports news; a gossip; **newsmongering** reporting news, gossiping; **newsprint** cheap paper made from mechanical and chemical wood pulp and used chiefly for newspapers; **newsreader** a person who reads out the news on radio or television; **newsreel** a short television or cinema programme or film dealing with news and current affairs; **news room** (*a*) a reading-room specially set apart for newspapers; (*b*) an office in a newspaper or broadcasting office where news is processed; **news-sheet** a printed sheet containing the news, a simple form of newspaper; **news-stand** a stand or stall for the sale of newspapers; **news theatre** *Hist*. = ***news cinema*** above; **news ticker** a telegraphic recording instrument which automatically prints the news on to a tape; **newsvendor** a newspaper-seller; **newswoman** (*a*) a female newspaper-seller; (*b*) a female reporter or journalist.
■ **newsful** *adjective* (*rare*) M17. **newsless** *adjective* M18. **newslessness** *noun* M19.

news /nju:z/ *verb*. Now *dial*. M17.
[from the noun.]
1 *verb trans*. Tell or spread as news. M17.
2 *verb intrans*. Tell news; gossip. E18.

newsie /'nju:zi/ *noun*. *colloq*. Also **-sy**. L19.
[from NEWS *noun* + -IE.]
1 = ***newsboy*** s.v. NEWS *noun*. Chiefly *US & Austral*. L19.
2 A journalist or news reporter; any person working in the news media. Chiefly *N. Amer*. L20.

📖 **2** T. CLANCY We'll lay down the law to the newsies on what they may and may not ask.

newspaper /'nju:zpeɪpə, 'nju:s-/ *noun*. L17.
[from NEWS *noun* + PAPER *noun*.]
1 A printed publication, now usu. daily or weekly, consisting of folded unstapled sheets and containing news, freq. with photographs, features, advertisements, etc.; (the organization responsible for or office of) any of these published under a particular title. L17. ▸**b** The low-

quality paper from which newspapers are made; the sheets of paper forming a newspaper. **E19.**
2 A prison sentence of thirty days. *slang.* **E20.**

📖 **1** *Daily Herald* To hear the news from your favourite announcer is like buying your favourite newspaper. V. BRITTAIN Events reported in the newspapers seemed too incredible to be taken seriously. C. HAMPTON Blanket censorship and the silencing of all opposition newspapers. ***newspaper article, newspaper clipping, newspaper column, newspaper cutting, newspaper office, newspaper reporter,*** etc. ***living newspaper***: see LIVING *ppl adjective.* ***quality newspaper***: see QUALITY *noun & adjective.*

Comb.: **newspaper English** the style of English used in newspapers; journalese; **newspaperland** = NEWSPAPERDOM; **newspaperman** a male journalist; **newspaperwoman** a female journalist.
■ **newspaperdom** *noun* the world or sphere of newspapers; newspapers collectively: **L19. newspapered** *adjective* provided or covered with (a) newspaper **E18. newspaperese** *noun* (*colloq.*) the characteristic language or style of newspapers, journalese **L19. newspaperish** *adjective* somewhat in the style of or like a newspaper **E19. newspaperishly** *adverb* **M19. newspaperism** *noun* the characteristic features or style of newspapers; a phrase or expression characteristic of newspapers: **M19. newspaperless** *adjective* **L19. newspapery** *adjective* in a style characteristic of newspapers; given to reading newspapers: **M19.**

newspaper /ˈnjuːzpeɪpə, ˈnjuːs-/ *verb intrans.* Now *US.* **E19.**
[from the noun.]
Orig., read a newspaper. Now, work on a newspaper, do newspaper work. Orig. & chiefly as ***newspapering*** *verbal noun.*

Newspeak /ˈnjuːspiːk/ *noun.* Also **n-**. **M20.**
[An artificial language used for official propaganda in George Orwell's novel *Nineteen Eighty-Four* (1949), from NEW *adjective* + SPEAK *verb.* Cf. -SPEAK.]
Ambiguous euphemistic language, esp. as used in official pronouncements or political propaganda.

📖 *Listener* The spokesman . . claimed, 'We had to destroy that village to save it,' . . 1984 Newspeak had come. *Times Lit. Suppl.* 'Rootless cosmopolitans'—Newspeak for Jews. *Amateur Photographer* In Newspeak it would be a very user-friendly camera.

newsworthy /ˈnjuːzwəːði/ *adjective.* **M20.**
[from NEWS *noun* + -WORTHY.]
(Regarded as) of sufficient interest to the public to warrant mention in the news; topical.
■ **newsworthily** *adverb* **M20. newsworthiness** *noun* **M20.**

newsy *noun* var. of NEWSIE.

newsy /ˈnjuːzi/ *adjective.* **E19.**
[from NEWS *noun* + -Y[1].]
1 Full of news, esp. of a personal or inconsequential nature; given to communicating news or gossiping. **E19.**
2 Likely to create news. **M20.**

📖 **1** *Atlantic Monthly* Two newsy letters every year, pictures of the children.

■ **newsily** *adverb* **M20. newsiness** *noun* **L19.**

newt /njuːt/ *noun.* **LME.**
[from misdivision of *an ewt* (see EFT *noun*) as *a newt*.]
A small aquatic or semi-aquatic urodele amphibian of the family Salamandridae, having a long tail; *esp.* any of the common Eurasian genus *Triturus.*
crested newt: see CRESTED 1. ***marbled newt***: see MARBLED *adjective* 2. PALMATE ***newt. smooth newt***: see SMOOTH *adjective & adverb.*

Newton /ˈnjuːt(ə)n/ *noun.* In sense 3 also **n-**. **E19.**
[Sir Isaac *Newton*: see next.]
1 ***Newton's law***, any of various physical laws deduced or formulated by Newton, esp.: (***a***) ***Newton's law of gravitation***, a law stating that any two bodies exert an attractive force on each other which is proportional to the product of their masses, and inversely proportional to the square of the distance between them; (***b***) ***Newton's laws of motion***, three fundamental laws of classical physics, the first stating that a body continues in a state of rest or uniform motion in a straight line unless it is acted on by an external force, the second stating that the rate of change of momentum of a moving body is proportional to the force acting to produce the change, and the third stating that if one body exerts a force on another, there is an equal and opposite force (or reaction) exerted by the second body on the first. **E19.**
2 ***Newton's rings***, a set of concentric circular fringes seen around the point of contact when a convex lens is placed on a plane surface (or on another lens), caused by interference between light reflected from the upper and lower surfaces. Also *sing.* when used *attrib.* **M19.**
3 (**n-**.) The SI unit of force, equal to the force that would give a mass of one kilogram an acceleration of one metre per second per second (equivalent to 100,000 dynes). (Symbol N.) **E20.**

Newtonian /njuːˈtəʊnɪən/ *adjective & noun.* Also **n-**. **E18.**
[formed as prec. + -IAN.]
► **A** *adjective.* **1** Pertaining to or arising from the work of the English scientist and philosopher Sir Isaac Newton (1642–1727), esp. his physical or optical theories; formulated or behaving according to the principles of classical physics. **E18.**
2 Resembling or characteristic of Newton; advocating the views of Newton. **M18.**
3 ASTRONOMY. Designating or pertaining to a kind of reflecting telescope having an oblique plane secondary mirror which produces a focus at an aperture in the side of a telescope. **M18.**

📖 **1** *Daedalus* In Newtonian theory space and time are absolute, . . unaffected by the presence and motion of matter.

► **B** *noun.* **1** A follower of Newton; a person who accepts the Newtonian or classical system of physics. **M18.**
2 ASTRONOMY. A Newtonian reflecting telescope. **L19.**
■ **Newtonianism** *noun* the Newtonian system **E19. New'tonically** *adverb* (*rare*) in the manner of Newton **M19. 'Newtonist** *noun* = NEWTONIAN *noun* 1 **M18.**

Newtown pippin /ˈnjuːtaʊn ˈpɪpɪn/ *noun phr.* **M18.**
[*Newtown*, a town on Long Island, New York.]
A yellowish-skinned variety of eating apple.

newy *noun* var. of NEWIE.

New Year /njuː ˈjɪə/ *noun phr.* **ME.**
[from NEW *adjective* + YEAR *noun*[1].]
The beginning or first few days of a year; the coming year; the year about to begin or just beginning.

📖 B. PYM She began to plan a visit, after the New Year, when the weather improved. ***Chinese New Year, Jewish New Year,*** etc. **New Year's** *ellipt.* (*N. Amer.*) New Year's Day. **New Year's Day** the first day of the year, 1 January. **New Year's Eve** the last day of the year, 31 December; *spec.* the evening of this day, often marked with a celebration. **see the New Year in** stay up until after midnight on 31 December to celebrate the start of a new year.

New York /njuː ˈjɔːk/ *noun phr.* **E18.**
[A US city and State.]
Used *attrib.* to designate things coming from, associated with, or characteristic of New York.
New York cut a cut of steak including the hip-bone. **New York dressed** *adjective* (of poultry) sold by weight without having the entrails, head, or feet removed. **New York minute** *colloq.* a very short period of time, an instant.
■ **New Yorker** *noun* a native or inhabitant of New York **M18. New Yorkese** *noun* the regional form of English used in or associated with New York City **L19. New Yorkish, New Yorky** *adjectives* suggestive or characteristic of New York **E20.**

newzak /ˈnjuːzak/ *noun. colloq.* **M20.**
[Blend of NEWS *noun* and MUZAK.]
Trivial items of news; news coverage likened to Muzak in being pervasive but unchallenging.

New Zealand /njuː ˈziːlənd/ *noun phr.* **L18.**
[A country consisting of two large islands and several smaller ones in the SW Pacific, east of Australia.]
1 *gen.* Used *attrib.* to designate plants and animals native to New Zealand or other things coming from, associated with, or characteristic of New Zealand. **L18.**
2 *spec.* Used *attrib.* to designate various American breeds of domestic rabbit used esp. for meat and fur. **E20.**
1 New Zealand ash = TITOKI. **New Zealand falcon** a reddish-brown falcon, *Falco novaezeelandiae.* ***New Zealand flax***: see FLAX *noun* 2b. **New Zealand robin** a dark grey songbird, *Petroica australis* (family Eopsaltridae). **New Zealand rug** a lined waterproof canvas etc. rug for a horse. **New Zealand spinach** an annual plant, *Tetragonia tetragonioides* (family Aizoaceae), cultivated for its thick leaves which are used as a substitute for spinach. **New Zealand thrush** = PIOPIO. **New Zealand tit** = TOMTIT 1(c). **2** ***New Zealand rabbit; New Zealand black, New Zealand red, New Zealand white,*** etc.
■ **New Zealander** *noun* a native or inhabitant of New Zealand **L18. New Zealandism** *noun* an idiom or word peculiar to or associated with the English spoken in New Zealand **M20.**

nexal /ˈnɛks(ə)l/ *adjective. rare.* **L19.**
[from Latin NEXUS + -AL[1].]
1 ROMAN LAW. Characterized by the imposition of servitude as a penalty on a defaulting debtor. **L19.**
2 LINGUISTICS. Of or pertaining to a nexus. **E20.**

next /nɛkst/ *adjective, noun, adverb, & preposition.*
[Old English *nēhsta*, (West Saxon) *nīehsta* = Old Frisian *neeste*, Old Saxon *nā(h)isto* (Dutch *naaste*), Old High German *nāhisto* (German *nächste*), Old Norse *næstr, næsti*: see -EST[1]. (Germanic superl. of NIGH *adverb, preposition, & adjective.*)]
► **A** *adjective.* **1** Lying nearest in place or position. Now, *spec.* lying nearest in a certain direction or line; by the side (of), adjoining. In *pred.* use freq. foll. by *to.* **OE.**
2 Of a person: living, dwelling, or happening to be nearest to one. Now *rare* or *obsolete.* **OE.**
3 Nearest in relationship or kinship. Now only *attrib.* (Cf. sense B. below.) **OE.**
4 a Designating the time, season, etc., occurring directly after that of writing or speaking. Also (of a day of the week etc.), the nearest but one, the second after *this* one. (With a common noun after *the* or (emphasizing imminence) *this* or *these* or without article or demonstrative; with the name of a month, of a day of the week, etc., placed before or (more formally) after the noun.) **OE.** ▸**b** Esp. of an event or an occasion: occurring directly after another in time, without anything of the same kind intervening. **LME.**
5 Immediately succeeding or preceding in order, precedence, importance, etc. Also foll. by *to, after.* **OE.** ▸**b** Other, another. Chiefly *W. Indies.* **M20.**
†**6 a** Most pressing or urgent. *rare.* Only in **ME.** ▸**b** (Of a means or remedy) most readily available; (of an end or cause) least remote, most proximate. **LME–E19.**

📖 **1** ADDISON When a Fox is very much troubled with Fleas, he goes into the next pool. E. WAUGH Music was borne in from the next room. *Esquire* Perched on a stool next to her is her friend Barbara. **4a** *Times* The trial . . has been fixed for Tuesday next. I. MURDOCH I don't know how I shall live through this next week till he comes. *Guardian* Next Saturday is the opening day of the coarse fishing season. P. AUSTER A house is there one day, and the next day it is gone. **b** P. HILL If the Christian Democrats put enough candidates up at the next election they'll walk in. **5** B. ROMANS The ground nut . . is next after this for its easy cultivation. G. BUTLER The centre spread where they put the next most important news. G. GREENE Is the next stage the stage of corrupting others? I. MCEWAN Perhaps we should get off at the next stop. J. J. HENNESSY I believe they will be the next Olympic champions.

► **B** *absol.* as *noun.* The next person or thing identified contextually; *spec.* †(***a***) a neighbour; (***b***) a relative (now only in ***next of kin*** s.v. KIN *noun*); (***c***) the next issue or episode; (***d***) the next day of the week etc. **OE.**

📖 J. MCCARTHY Some serial story which stopped . . with the words—To be continued in our next. C. SANDBURG When a member died the newspaper men . . gave the toast: 'Hurrah for the next who goes!' *Guardian* The week after next.

► **C** *adverb.* †**1** Last, on the last occasion. **OE–ME.**
2 In the nearest place or degree, immediately following in time or order. Freq. foll. by *to.* **ME.**
3 On the first future or subsequent occasion. **M16.**

📖 **2** C. R. MARKHAM The East Indian source of supply is now the most important next to Colombia. O. MANNING He never knew what she would do or say next. B. REID Next we went to the King's Palace, Preston. **3** J. M. COETZEE When he woke next there was a light on.

► **D** *preposition.* Next to. Now *colloq.* **OE.**

📖 MILTON One next himself in power, and next in crime. SWIFT The greatest punner of this town next myself. J. CONRAD He had been wearing next his bare skin . . a sort of waistcoat.

Phrases: ***knock into the middle of next week***: see KNOCK *verb.* ***next of kin***: see KIN *noun.* ***next the heart***: see HEART *noun.* **next to** (***a***) very nearly, almost (freq. in ***next to nothing***); (***b***) by the side of, beside, in comparison with; ***put next to***, put in close proximity with, *esp.* seat next to at dinner etc., *US slang* introduce to, make familiar with; ***sitting next to Nelly***: see NELLY *noun*[2] 4; (***c***) ***be next to, get next to*** (*US slang*), get to know, become familiar with; (***d***) see also senses A.1, C.2 above. **whatever next?, what next?** expr. surprise, amazement, dismay, etc.
Special collocations & comb.: **next-best** second-best, second in order of preference. **next door** (***a***) the occupant(s) of the nearest or an adjoining house, flat, etc.; (***b***) *adverb* in, at, or to the nearest or an adjoining house or an adjacent room; *fig.* very close or near *to*, almost amounting *to*; (***c***) ***Mr Next-Door, Mrs Next-Door***, the occupant of a next-door house, flat, etc.; (***d***) ***next-door-but-one***, (the occupant(s) of) a house, flat, etc., two doors away; in, to, or at a house, flat, etc., two doors away; (***e***) ***the boy next door, the girl next door***, the boy or girl living next door; the type of a familiar and reliable boy or girl, esp. when viewed as a romantic partner. **next-door** *adjective* that is next door, *esp.* living next door. **next friend** (***a***) one's nearest friend or relative; (***b***) *spec.* in LAW, a person acting for an infant or someone legally disabled. **next man, next one, next person**, etc., *the* average person, anybody. †**next way** the shortest, most convenient or direct way. **next world** *the* afterlife, a supposed life after death.
■ **nextly** *adverb* (now *rare*) in the next place, next **L16. nextness** *noun* the fact or condition of immediate succession or proximity **ME.**

nexus /ˈnɛksəs/ *noun.* Pl. same, **-es** /-ɪz/. **M17.**
[Latin, from *nex-* pa. ppl stem of *nectere* bind.]
1 A connection; a bond, a link. **M17.** ▸**b** GRAMMAR. A group of words (with or without a verb) expressing a predicative relation; a construction treated as such. **E20.**
2 A connected group or series; a network. **M19.**

📖 **1** E. GELLNER The nexus between the new growth of wealth and good government. A. STORR Embedded in a family and social nexus.

Nez Percé /nɛz ˈpɜːs, ˈpɛːseɪ/ *adjectival & noun phr.* Also **Nez Perce** /nɛz ˈpɜːs/. **E19.**
[French, lit. 'pierced nose'.]
► **A** *adjective.* Designating or pertaining to a Penutian people of north-western N. America or their language. **E19.**
► **B** *noun.* Pl. **-s**, same.
1 A member of the Nez Percé people. **M19.**
2 The language of the Nez Percé people. **M20.**
¶ Cf. ***Pierced Nose*** s.v. PIERCED.

NF *abbreviation.*
1 National Front.
2 Newfoundland.

NFL *abbreviation. US.*
National Football League.

Nfld *abbreviation.*
Newfoundland.

NFS *abbreviation.*
National Fire Service.

NFT *abbreviation.*
National Film Theatre.

NFU *abbreviation.*
National Farmers' Union.

n.g. *abbreviation.*
No good.

NGA *abbreviation. Hist.* National Graphical Association.

ngaio /ˈnʌɪəʊ/ *noun.* M19.
[Maori: cf. NAIO.]
A small New Zealand evergreen white-flowered tree, *Myoporum laetum* (family Myoporaceae), yielding a light white timber.

Ngala *noun & adjective* var. of LINGALA.

Nganasan /(ə)ŋˈganəsan/ *noun & adjective.* M20.
[Russian *nganasan* from Nganasan, lit. 'a man'.]
▶ **A** *noun.* Pl. **-s**, same.
1 A member of a Samoyedic people of the Taimyr peninsular in northern Siberia. M20.
2 The Uralic language of this people. M20.
▶ **B** *adjective.* Of or pertaining to the Nganasans or their language. L20.
¶ Also called *Tavgi.*

ngarara /ŋɑːˈrara, n-/ *noun.* L19.
[Maori.]
Any of various unidentified extinct New Zealand lizards. Also, in Maori mythology, a lizard-like monster.

Ngbaka /(ə)ŋˈbɑːkə/ *noun & adjective.* M20.
[Ngbaka.]
▶ **A** *noun.* A group of related languages spoken in the Central African Republic, Cameroon, and the north of the Democratic Republic of Congo (Zaire). M20.
▶ **B** *attrib.* or as *adjective.* Of or pertaining to any of these languages. M20.

Ngbandi /(ə)ŋˈbandi/ *noun & adjective.* M20.
[Ngbandi.]
▶ **A** *noun.* A Niger-Congo language of the north of the Democratic Republic of Congo (Zaire). Cf. SANGO. M20.
▶ **B** *attrib.* or as *adjective.* Of or pertaining to this language. M20.

NGC *abbreviation.*
ASTRONOMY. New General Catalogue (of non-stellar objects).

ngege /(ə)ŋˈgeɪgeɪ/ *noun.* E20.
[App. from an E. African lang.]
A cichlid food fish, *Tilapia esculenta*, of Lake Victoria in E. Africa. Cf. TILAPIA.

NGO *abbreviation.*
Non-governmental organization.

Ngoko /(ə)ŋˈgəʊkəʊ/ *noun.* L19.
[Javanese.]
In Indonesia, the form of Javanese used among intimates and when addressing certain people of lower status. Cf. KROMO.

ngoma /(ə)ŋˈgəʊmə/ *noun.* E20.
[Kiswahili (also *goma*) drum, dance, music.]
In E. Africa: a dance; a night of dancing.

Ngoni /(ə)ŋˈgəʊni/ *noun & adjective.* L19.
[Bantu.]
▶ **A** *noun.* Pl. same, **-s**. A member of an Nguni people now living chiefly in Malawi. L19.
▶ **B** *attrib.* or as *adjective.* Of or pertaining to the Ngoni. L19.

ngultrum /(ə)ŋˈgʊltrəm/ *noun.* Pl. same. L20.
[Dzongkha.]
The basic monetary unit of Bhutan, equal to 100 chetrum.

Nguni /(ə)ŋˈguːni/ *noun & adjective.* E20.
[Zulu.]
▶ **A** *noun.* Pl. same, **-s**.
1 A member of a Bantu-speaking people living mainly in southern Africa. E20.
2 The group of closely related Bantu languages, including Xhosa, Zulu, Swazi, and Sindebele, spoken by this people. E20.
▶ **B** *attrib.* or as *adjective.* Of or pertaining to the Nguni or their languages. E20.

ngwee /(ə)ŋˈgweɪ/ *noun.* Pl. same. M20.
[Bantu.]
A monetary unit of Zambia, equal to one-hundredth of a kwacha.

NH *abbreviation.*
New Hampshire.

NHI *abbreviation.*
National Health Insurance.

NHL *abbreviation. N. Amer.*
National Hockey League.

NHS *abbreviation.*
National Health Service.

NI *abbreviation.*
1 National Insurance.
2 Northern Ireland.

Ni *symbol.*
CHEMISTRY. Nickel.

niacin /ˈnʌɪəsɪn/ *noun.* M20.
[from *nicotinic acid* + -IN¹.]
BIOCHEMISTRY. Orig., nicotinic acid. Now also, nicotinamide.

niacinamide /nʌɪəˈsɪnəmʌɪd/ *noun.* M20.
[from prec. + AMIDE.]
BIOCHEMISTRY. = NICOTINAMIDE.

Niagara /nʌɪˈag(ə)rə/ *verb & noun.* L18.
[A N. American river, famous for its waterfalls, between Lakes Erie and Ontario.]
▶ **A** *verb intrans.* Pour in a torrent or deluge. *rare.* L18.
▶ **B** *noun.* An outpouring *of*, a torrent, a deluge. M19.

T. L. PEACOCK That Niagara of sound under which it is now the fashion to bury it.

■ **Nia'garian** *adjective* resembling Niagara M19.

niaiserie /njɛz(ə)ri (*pl. same*)/ *noun. rare.* M17.
[French, from *niais* simple, foolish + *-erie* -ERY.]
Simplicity; foolishness; an instance of this.

nialamide /nʌɪˈaləmʌɪd/ *noun.* M20.
[from NI(COTINIC + AMID(E with insertion of *-al-*.]
PHARMACOLOGY. A hydrazide, $C_{16}H_{18}N_4O_2$, which is a monoamine oxidase inhibitor used as an antidepressant.
¶ A proprietary name for this drug is NIAMID.

Niamid /ˈnʌɪəmɪd/ *noun.* M20.
[formed as prec.]
PHARMACOLOGY. (Proprietary name for) the drug nialamide.

Niam-Niam /ˈniːəmˈniːəm/ *noun & adjective.* Pl. of noun same, **-s**. M19.
[Dinka, lit. 'great eaters'.]
= ZANDE.

niaouli /nɪəˈuːli/ *noun.* E20.
[New Caledonian name.]
An evergreen tree of New Caledonia, New Guinea, and eastern Australia, *Melaleuca quinquenervia*, of the myrtle family, noted for its resistance to fire.

niata /nɪˈɑːtə/ *noun.* M19.
[Origin unkn.]
(An animal of) an extinct breed of small blunt-nosed Uruguayan cattle.

nib /nɪb/ *noun*¹. L16.
[Prob. from Middle Dutch, Middle Low German *nibbe* var. of *nebbe* beak: see NEB.]
1 = NEB *noun* 1, 2. *obsolete* exc. *dial.* L16.
2 Orig., the point of a pen (esp. a quill). Now usu., the (esp. metal) tapered part of a pen, often vertically divided at the point, which touches the writing surface and is fitted into a holder. E17. ▸**b** Either of two sections of the divided writing point of a pen. M19.
3 a Each of the two short handles projecting from the shaft of a scythe. Usu. in *pl. dial.* L17. ▸**b** The pole of an ox-cart or timber-carriage. *dial.* E19.
4 The point or tip of anything; a peak, a projecting part, a pointed extremity. E18.
5 A small lump or knot in wool or raw silk. L18.
6 In *pl.* More fully ***cocoa nibs***, ***coffee nibs***. Shelled and crushed cocoa or coffee beans. M19.
7 A speck of solid matter in a coat of paint or varnish. M20.
■ **nibful** *noun* (*rare*) as much as a nib will hold M20.

nib /nɪb/ *noun*². *slang.* E19.
[Origin unkn. Cf. NABS, NIBS.]
A person of superior social standing or wealth. Also, a person proficient in a particular activity.

W. FORTESCUE I am rather a nib at cleaning silver, and . . I was allowed to be parlourmaid.

nib /nɪb/ *verb*¹. Now *rare.* Infl. **-bb-**. M16.
[App. rel. to NIBBLE *verb*¹.]
†**1** *verb trans.* Peck, pick, prick. M16–M17.
2 *verb intrans. & trans.* Nibble. *obsolete* exc. *dial.* E17.
3 *verb trans.* Catch, arrest, nab. *arch. slang.* L18.

nib /nɪb/ *verb*² *trans.* Infl. **-bb-**. M18.
[from NIB *noun*¹.]
Provide (a pen) with a nib or point; mend the nib of (a quill pen). Cf. earlier NIBBED *adjective.*

nibbana /nɪˈbɑːnə/ *noun.* E20.
[Pali *nibbāna* = Sanskrit *nirvāṇa* NIRVANA.]
BUDDHISM. = NIRVANA.
■ ***nibbanic*** *adjective* L20.

nibbed /nɪbd/ *adjective.* L17.
[from NIB *noun*¹, *verb*²: see -ED², -ED¹.]
Provided with a nib or point. Freq. as 2nd elem. of comb., as ***gold-nibbed***, ***hard-nibbed***, ***steel-nibbed***, etc.

nibble *noun*¹ & *verb*¹ see NIPPLE.

nibble /ˈnɪb(ə)l/ *verb*² & *noun*². In sense B.3 also **nybble**. LME.
[Prob. from Low Dutch: cf. Low German *nibbeln* gnaw.]
▶ **A** *verb.* **1 a** *verb trans.* Take small bites of, bite away gradually, bite at tentatively, delicately, or playfully. LME. ▸**b** *verb intrans.* Take small repeated bites, bite something away gradually, bite at something tentatively, delicately, or playfully. Also, eat frequently in small amounts, esp. snacks etc. L16. ▸**c** *verb trans.* Shape *into*, produce, by nibbling. E19. ▸**d** *verb intrans.* CRICKET. Play indecisively at a ball bowled outside the off stump. E20.
2 *verb intrans.* Carp (*at*), make petty objections or criticisms. L16.
3 *verb intrans. & trans.* Fidget (with). Long *obsolete* exc. *dial.* L16.
4 *verb intrans.* Catch, nab; pilfer. *arch. slang.* E17.

1a T. HARDY The bases of the trees were nibbled bare by rabbits. P. READING Encircling her . . waist with a fond arm, the husband . . nibbles her throat. **b** *Living* Helen should keep . . fruit, carrot and celery sticks on hand for when she's tempted to nibble. **nibble at** show tentative interest in. **nibble off** remove with small bites.

Comb.: **nibble-nip** *verb intrans. & trans.* (*arch.*) nibble and nip (at).
▶ **B** *noun.* **1** The action or an act of nibbling; a small, delicate, tentative, or playful bite. L15.
2 A (very) small amount of food, a quantity of food sufficient for a nibble; *colloq.* (usu. in *pl.*) a small snack, *esp.* one eaten between meals. M19.
3 COMPUTING. A unit of memory equal to half a byte; four bits. L20.

1 W. IRVING [To] fish all day . . though he should not be encouraged by a single nibble. *fig.*: *New Yorker* I got two job nibbles, each interesting in its own way. **2** *Independent* The nibbles: crackers and spicy marinated olives.

■ **nibbler** *noun* (**a**) a person or thing which nibbles; (**b**) ENGINEERING a type of metal-cutting tool in which a rapidly reciprocating punch knocks out a line of overlapping small holes from sheet or plate; (**c**) *US* any of various fishes esp. of the Pacific family Kyphosidae: L16. **nibbling** *noun* the action of the verb; an instance of this; a portion nibbled: L16. **nibblingly** *adverb* in a nibbling manner M19.

Nibelung /ˈniːbəlʊŋ/ *noun & adjective.* Also **Niblung** /ˈniːblʊŋ/. E19.
[German (see below).]
GERMANIC MYTHOLOGY. ▶**A** *noun.* Pl. **-s**, **-en** /-ən/. A member of a subterranean race of dwarfs, ruled over by Nibelung, king of Nibelheim (the land of mist) guardians of a hoard of gold and treasures sought and eventually taken by the hero Siegfried. Also, any of the followers of Siegfried or any of the Burgundians who subsequently stole the hoard from him, as recounted in the 13th-cent. Germanic epic the *Nibelungenlied*. Usu. in *pl.* E19.
▶ **B** *attrib.* or as *adjective.* Of or pertaining to the Nibelungs. E19.

niblet /ˈnɪblɪt/ *noun.* L19.
[from NIB *noun*¹ or NIBBLE *verb*² & *noun*²: see -LET.]
1 A small bit, piece, or portion of something, *esp.* a small piece of food. Usu. in *pl.* L19.
2 (Also **N-**.) In *pl.* (Proprietary name for) canned kernels of sweetcorn. M20.
¶ Rare before M20.

niblick /ˈnɪblɪk/ *noun.* M19.
[Origin unkn.]
GOLF. An iron (formerly a wooden) club having a round heavy head, used esp. for playing out of a bunker. ***MASHIE-niblick***.

Niblung *noun & adjective* var. of NIBELUNG.

Nibmar /ˈnɪbmɑː/ *noun.* Also **NIBMAR**. M20.
[from *no independence before majority African rule*.]
Chiefly *Hist.* The policy of opposing recognition of the minority government which proclaimed the independence of Rhodesia (since 1979, Zimbabwe) in 1965.

nibong /ˈniːbʌŋ/ *noun.* L18.
[Malay *nibung*.]
A spiny palm of SE Asia, *Oncosperma tigillarium*, the young leaves of which are used as a vegetable.

nibs /nɪbz/ *noun. slang.* E19.
[Origin unkn.: cf. NABS, NIB *noun*[2].]
A superior; a self-important person. Chiefly in ***his nibs***, ***her nibs***, etc.

NIC *abbreviation.*
1 National Insurance contributions.
2 (Also /nɪk/.) Newly industrialized (or industrializing) country.

nicad /ˈnʌɪkad/ *noun.* Also **Nicad**, **NiCad**. M20.
[from NI(CKEL *noun* + CAD(MIUM.]
ELECTRICITY. A battery or cell with a nickel anode, a cadmium cathode, and a potassium hydroxide electrolyte, used esp. as a rechargeable power source for portable equipment. Also ***nicad battery***.
¶ Proprietary name in the US.

Nicaean /nʌɪˈsiːən/ *adjective & noun.* E18.
[from *Nicaea* (see NICENE) + -AN.]
▶ **A** *adjective.* = NICENE *adjective* 3. E18.
▶ **B** *noun.* = NICENE *noun. rare.* M19.

Nicam /ˈnʌɪkam/ *noun & adjective.* Also **NICAM**. L20.
[Acronym, from *n*ear *i*nstantaneously *c*ompanded *a*udio *m*ultiplex.]
(Designating or pertaining to) a digital system used in British television to produce high-quality stereophonic sound.

Nicaraguan /nɪkəˈragjʊən/ *noun & adjective.* M19.
[from *Nicaragua* (see below) + -AN.]
▶ **A** *noun.* A native or inhabitant of Nicaragua, a Central American republic. M19.
▶ **B** *adjective.* Of, pertaining to, or characteristic of Nicaragua or Nicaraguans. M19.

Nicaragua wood /nɪkəˈragjʊə wʊd/ *noun phr.* L17.
[from *Nicaragua* (see prec.) + WOOD *noun*[1].]
Any of several dye-woods obtained from certain tropical American leguminous trees, esp. *Haematoxylum brasiletto*.

niccolic /ˈnɪkəlɪk/ *adjective.* Now *rare* or *obsolete.* M19.
[from mod. Latin *niccolum* nickel + -IC.]
= NICKELIC.

niccolite /ˈnɪkəlʌɪt/ *noun.* M19.
[formed as prec. + -ITE[1].]
MINERALOGY. Native nickel arsenide, a pale copper-red mineral crystallizing in the hexagonal system and an important ore of nickel. Also called ***nickeline***, ***copper-nickel***.

niccolous /ˈnɪkələs/ *adjective.* Now *rare* or *obsolete.* M19.
[formed as prec. + -OUS.]
= NICKELOUS.

Nice /niːs/ *noun.* E20.
[App. from *Nice*, a city in southern France.]
More fully ***Nice biscuit***. A thin sweet coconut-flavoured biscuit with a sprinkled sugar topping.

nice /nʌɪs/ *adjective & adverb.* ME.
[Old French from Latin *nescius* ignorant, from *nescire*: see NESCIENT. Cf. NAICE.]
▶ **A** *adjective.* †**1** Foolish, stupid, senseless. ME–M16.
†**2 a** Wanton; lascivious. ME–E17. ▸**b** Of dress: ostentatious, showy. LME–M16. ▸**c** Neat, elegant, dainty; (of upbringing) refined. LME–E18.
†**3** Strange, rare, extraordinary. LME–E18.
†**4 a** Slothful, lazy. *rare.* LME–E17. ▸**b** Not capable of much endurance; delicate; *rare* effeminate, unmanly; pampered, luxurious. LME–E18.
†**5** Orig., coy, affectedly modest, reserved. Later, shy, reluctant, unwilling (foll. by *to*, *in*, *of*, *to do*). Cf. NICETY 3. LME–L17.
6 a Fastidious, hard to please; of refined or critical tastes. LME. ▸**b** Scrupulous, punctilious, particular. L16.
7 Requiring great precision or accuracy. Cf. NICETY 6. L15.
8 a Not obvious or readily understood, demanding close consideration; minute, subtle; (of differences) slight, small. E16. ▸**b** Exact, closely judged, fine. E18.
†**9** Slender, thin; *fig.*, unimportant, trivial. *rare.* L16–E17.
10 †**a** Critical, doubtful, full of risk or uncertainty. L16–E19. ▸**b** Requiring care, tact, or discrimination. E17.
11 Entering minutely into details; attentive, close. L16.
12 Delicately sensitive; finely discriminative; deft. L16.
13 Minutely or carefully accurate; (of an instrument or apparatus) showing minute differences, finely poised or graduated. L16.
14 Agreeable, pleasant, satisfactory, delightful, generally commendable; (of food) tasty, appetizing; (of a person) kind, considerate, friendly; *iron.* (very) bad, unsatisfactory. *colloq.* E18.

> 🕮 **4b** CLARENDON He . . was of so nice and tender a composition, that a little rain . . would disorder him. **5** DRYDEN Virtue is nice to take what's not her own. **6a** S. JOHNSON The mind . . becomes . . nice and fastidious, and like a vitiated palate. **b** S. BARING-GOULD I should get it back again . . and not be too nice about the means. **7** R. BOYLE The Watch I use to measure the time with in nice Experiments. **8a** S. LEACOCK The Authority, who was a man of nice distinctions . . was . . afraid that he had overstated things a little. **b** G. D. CAMPBELL The nice and perfect balance which is maintained between these two forces. **9** SHAKES. *Jul. Caes.* In such a time as this it is not meet That every nice offence should bear his comment. **10b** A. F. DOUGLAS-HOME It is a matter of so nice a judgement when these . . processes should be put in motion that few . . can mark the right moment. D. LODGE It is a nice question how far you can go . . without throwing out something vital. **11** G. WHITE Upon a nice examination . . I could find nothing resinous in them. **12** H. MARTINEAU No people on earth had so nice a sense of the morally graceful. BROWNING The nice eye can distinguish grade and grade. **13** JAS. HARRIS The nicest Hygrometer of any . . it will show . . very small Alterations. **14** E. NESBIT A very nice way to make your fortune—by deceit and trickery. L. DEIGHTON There's nothing so reviving as a nice cup of tea. B. BAINBRIDGE He dripped gravy on the nice white cloth. P. FITZGERALD Pale blue tiles with a nice design of waterlilies.

Phrases: ***have a nice day***: see HAVE *verb*. †**make it nice**, †**make nice** display reserve or reluctance. **nice and —** *colloq.* satisfactory in respect of a specified quality. ***nice as pie***: see PIE *noun*[2] 4a.
Special collocations & comb.: **nice-looking** *adjective* attractive. **nice Nelly** *N. Amer. colloq.* a respectable or prudish woman. **nice-nellyism** *N. Amer. colloq.* excessive prudishness of speech or behaviour, an instance of this; (a) genteelism. **nice one** *interjection* expr. approval or commendation. **nice work** a task well performed; ***nice work if you can get it*** (*iron.*), expr. envy of (what is perceived to be) another's more favourable situation, position, etc.
▶ **B** *adverb.* Orig., foolishly, unwisely. Later (*non-standard*), satisfactorily, agreeably, well, etc. LME.

> 🕮 N. HINTON He sings really nice and he's picked up the guitar ever so quick.

▪ **niceling** *noun* †(*a*) an effeminate or delicate person; (*b*) *arch.*, *rare* a nice thing: M16.

niceish /ˈnʌɪsɪʃ/ *adjective.* Also **nicish**. E19.
[from NICE *adjective* + -ISH[1].]
Somewhat nice, rather nice.

nicely /ˈnʌɪsli/ *adverb & adjective.* ME.
[from NICE *adjective* + -LY[2].]
▶ **A** *adverb.* In a nice manner; *colloq.* in a slightly intoxicated condition. ME.

> 🕮 M. SINCLAIR I don't mean horridly stout, dear, just nicely and comfortably stout. J. BUCHAN My ankle felt . . stiff, but . . he pronounced that it was mending nicely.

▶ **B** *adjective.* In good health or spirits; *spec.* tipsy, slightly intoxicated. *dial.* & *slang.* M19.

Nicene /ˈnʌɪsiːn, nʌɪˈsiːn/ *adjective & noun.* LME.
[Late Latin *Nicenus*, *Nicaenus*, from *Nicea*, *Nicaea*, Greek *Nikaia*, a town of ancient Bithynia. Cf. ISNIK.]
▶ **A** *adjective.* **1** ***Nicene Council***, either of two ecclesiastical Councils held at Nicaea in AD 325 and 787, convened to settle the Arian controversy and the question of images respectively. LME.
2 ***Nicene Creed***, either of two formal statements of Christian belief, (*a*) *rare* one drawn up by the first Nicene Council; (*b*) one drawn up at the first Council of Constantinople in AD 381, in regular use in Eucharistic worship. LME.
3 Connected with, originating from, or related to either of the Nicene Councils or their doctrines. L16.
▶ **B** *noun.* An adherent of the doctrine sanctioned by the first Nicene Council. *rare.* L19.

niceness /ˈnʌɪsnɪs/ *noun.* M16.
[from NICE *adjective* + -NESS.]
The quality or condition of being nice.

> 🕮 G. BERKELEY Neither need any one's niceness be offended on account of the bones. T. HARMER The niceness of Russell's observations will not allow us to doubt the truth of what he says. E. M. FORSTER 'Is it a very nice smell?' said Lucy . . 'One doesn't come to Italy for niceness' was the retort.

nicety /ˈnʌɪsɪti/ *noun.* ME.
[Old French *niceté*, formed as NICE *adjective* + -TY[1].]
▶ **I** †**1** Foolish or irresponsible conduct, stupidity; an instance of this. ME–L15.
†**2** Lasciviousness, lust. Only in LME.
†**3** Reserve, shyness, coyness; an instance of this. LME–M18.
†**4** Sloth, idleness. *rare.* Only in LME.
†**5** Overrefinement; *rare* luxuriousness. LME–M17.
6 Precision, accuracy, minuteness. LME. ▸**b** A (specified) degree of precision. Freq. in ***to a nicety***, precisely, exactly. M18.
7 a Scrupulosity, punctiliousness. L16. ▸**b** Fastidiousness. E18.
8 The quality of requiring close consideration; delicacy, intricacy, subtlety; the point at which these qualities are required. E18.

> 🕮 **6** S. JOHNSON Those who can distinguish with the utmost nicety the boundaries of vice and virtue. **8** K. AMIS Was this not excessive even for van den Haag, known as he was . . to be no strict observer of diplomatic nicety?

▶ **II 9** Orig. (now *rare*), something choice, elegant, or dainty, *esp.* something to eat. Later, a social courtesy, a point of etiquette or manners. Usu. in *pl.* LME.
10 A fine or minute distinction; a subtle point or detail; in *pl.* also, minutiae. L16.

> 🕮 **9** A. T. ELLIS She could no more be bothered with the niceties of drawing-room small talk than could a fox. **10** D. MACDONALD He was a speaker . . who paid . . more attention to the niceties of delivering a lecture than to literary technique.

nicey /ˈnʌɪsi/ *adjective & noun. nursery & colloq.* Also **nicy**. M19.
[from NICE *adjective* + -Y[1].]
▶ **A** *adjective.* Nice. M19.
▶ **B** *noun.* A nice person or thing. L19.

niche /nɪtʃ, niːʃ/ *noun & verb.* E17.
[Old & mod. French, from Old French *nichier* (mod. *nicher*) make a nest, nestle, from Proto-Romance from Latin *nidus* nest.]
▶ **A** *noun.* **1** An artificially constructed wall recess; *spec.* (*a*) a shallow ornamental recess for a statue, urn, etc.; (*b*) (now *rare*) a small vaulted recess or chamber in the thickness of a wall. E17. ▸**b** A natural hollow in a rock or hill. M19. ▸**c** More fully ***prayer niche***. A mihrab motif on an oriental prayer rug. E20.
2 *fig.* **a** A place or position suited to or intended for a person's capabilities, occupation, or status. E18. ▸**b** A place of safety or retreat. E18. ▸**c** ECOLOGY. A position or role taken by a kind of organism within its community. E20. ▸**d** COMMERCE. A position from which an opening in a market etc. can be exploited; *esp.* a specialized but profitable segment of a commercial market. M20.

> 🕮 **1** BYRON It leads through winding walls . . and obscure niches, to I know not whither. P. H. NEWBY A niche in the cloisters held a Madonna and two circles of . . candles. **2a** B. MOORE Men of his age . . have found their niche They are not greedy for further powers. **c** D. NORMAN The . . evolution of herbivorous dinosaurs to fill the niches vacated by the herbivorous cynodonts. **d** *attrib.*: *Times* Niche outlets selling lingerie, shoes and accessories are doing well.

▶ **B** *verb.* **1** *verb trans.* Place (a statue, urn, etc.) in a niche. Usu. in *pass.* M18. ▸**b** Construct as a niche. (Foll. by *into*, *in*.) E19.
2 *verb trans.* Place in a recess or nook; ensconce, settle (esp. oneself) comfortably in a corner etc. M18.
3 *verb intrans.* Nestle, settle. *rare.* E19.
▪ **niched** *ppl adjective* that has been niched; provided with a niche: L18. **nichemanship** *noun* [-MANSHIP] COMMERCE the policy of or skill in identifying and exploiting a market niche L20.

nicher /ˈnɪxə/ *verb & noun. Scot. & north.* L17.
[Imit.: cf. NICKER *verb*, *noun*[5].]
▶ **A** *verb.* **1** *verb intrans.* Neigh. L17.
2 *verb trans.* Utter with a neighing sound. M19.
▶ **B** *noun.* A neigh; a neighing sound. L18.

†**nichil** *noun & verb.* Also **-ll**. L15.
[medieval Latin from Latin *nihil* nothing: see NIHIL. Cf. NIFLE.]
▶ **A** *noun.* **1** Nothing, naught. *rare.* L15–L17.
2 LAW. The return made by a sheriff to the exchequer in cases where the party named in the writ had no goods upon which a levy could be made. Cf. NIHIL 2. L16–M18.
▶ **B** *verb trans.* Infl. **-ll-**. LAW. Of a sheriff: designate (a chargeable sum) as unable to be raised through the absence of any leviable goods. E17–E18.

Nichiren /ˈnɪ(t)ʃərən/ *adjective & noun.* L19.
[See below.]
▶ **A** *adjective.* Of or pertaining to a Japanese Buddhist sect, founded by the Japanese religious teacher Nichiren (1222–82). L19.
▶ **B** *noun.* Nichiren Buddhism. L20.

Nichrome /ˈnʌɪkrəʊm/ *noun.* E20.
[from NI(CKEL *noun* + CHROME.]
METALLURGY. (Proprietary name for) any of various alloys of nickel with chromium (10 to 20 per cent) and sometimes iron (up to 25 per cent), used esp. in high-temperature applications.

nicht wahr /nɪçt vaːr/ *interjection.* E20.
[German, lit. 'not true'.]
Is it not true? Isn't that so?

nick /nɪk/ *noun*[1]. LME.
[Rel. to or perh. from NICK *verb*[2]. Cf. NITCH *noun*[1].]
▶ **I 1** A notch, a groove, a slit; an incision, an indentation. LME. ▸**b** PRINTING. A groove on the shank of a piece of type to help ensure the correct choice and positioning of type. L17. ▸**c** SQUASH & REAL TENNIS. The junction between the side-wall and the floor of the court; a return when the ball makes contact with both surfaces simultaneously. L19. ▸**d** BIOCHEMISTRY. A short break in (one strand of) a DNA or RNA molecule. M20.
2 a A notch made to keep a score or tally. Formerly also, reckoning, account. L15. ▸**b** Any of the depressions

between the rings which form on a cow's horn giving an indication of the animal's age. Chiefly *Scot. & dial.* L18.
3 A gap in a range of hills. E17.
4 A cut in the skin, *esp.* a minor one caused in shaving etc.; an act of making such a cut. E17.

1 J. S. LE FANU Deepening a nick with his penknife in the counter. **2a** RIDER HAGGARD A number of little nicks, each . . representing a man killed in battle. **4** S. CISNEROS The nicks and cuts that never get a chance to heal.

▶ **II** †**5** A verbal correspondence or resemblance; a pun. Cf. NICK *verb*² 8. M–L16.
6 In the game of hazard, a throw which is either the same as the main, or has a fixed correspondence to it. M17.
▶ **III 7 a** The precise point of time at which something occurs; the precise moment or time *of*; the critical moment. Chiefly in ***in the nick***, ***in the very nick***. L16. ▸†**b** The exact point aimed at; the mark. E–M17.
†**8** The essential part or the exact amount *of* something. L16–L17.
9 a A critical juncture or moment. Now *rare*. E17. ▸†**b** A stage, a degree. M–L17.

7a SWIFT Ent'ring in the very nick, He saw . . Nell belabour . . his peaceful neighbour. BROWNING In the very nick Of giving up, one time more, Came a click. **9a** R. L. STEVENSON Certainly here was a man in an interesting nick of life.

▶ **IV** †**10** A false base fitted to a tankard which diminishes the vessel's actual capacity. (Cf. KICK *noun*².) Only in ***nick and froth***. E17–M18.
11 An instance of crossbreeding. E19.
12 A prison; a police station. *slang*. L19.

12 *Observer* Being a thief is a terrific life, but . . they do put you in the nick for it.

Phrases: **in good nick**, **in poor nick**, etc. *colloq.* in good, poor, etc., condition. **in the nick of time**, **in the very nick of time** just at the right or critical moment; only just in time.
Comb.: **nick-eared** *adjective* having the ears nicked.

Nick /nɪk/ *noun*². *colloq.* M17.
[Prob. abbreviation of male forename *Nicholas*.]
In full ***Old Nick***. The Devil.

nick *noun*³ var. of KNICK *noun*².

nick /nɪk/ *verb*¹. Long *arch. rare.* ME.
[Origin unkn.]
†**1** *verb intrans. & trans.* Make denial (of), deny (a person or thing). Only in ME.
2 *verb trans.* Answer (a person) in the negative. Chiefly in ***nick a person with nay***. ME–E19.

nick /nɪk/ *verb*². LME.
[Origin unkn. In sense 9 perh. partly from NICKNAME. Cf. NICK *noun*¹.]
▶ **I 1** *verb trans.* Make a nick or nicks in; indent. LME. ▸**b** Record or keep (a score) by means of a nick or nicks made on a tally or stick. E16.
2 *verb trans.* Cut into or through; cut short. E17. ▸**b** *verb trans.* Fashion or mark out by cutting. Also foll. by *out*. E17. ▸**c** *verb intrans.* MINING. Cut vertical sections in a mine; cut or shear coal after holing. M19. ▸**d** *verb trans.* Fasten (a lock etc.) with a click. *rare*. M19.
3 *verb trans.* Make an incision at the root of (a horse's tail) or at the root of the tail of (a horse) in order to make the animal carry its tail higher. M18.

1 E. LEONARD The .38 slug chipped bone, nicked the ilium. **b** SWIFT I'll get a knife and nick it down, that Mr. Neverout came. **2b** *fig.*: W. CAMDEN A Monke . . busied his braine in nicking out these nice verses. **d** V. WOOLF She nicked the catch of her paint-box to, more firmly than was necessary.

▶ **II 4 a** *verb trans.* Orig., make a winning cast against (a player), make (a winning cast), by throwing a nick in the game of hazard. Later, throw a nick against (a specified number or (esp.) the main) at hazard. M16. ▸†**b** *verb intrans.* Gamble; throw a nick at hazard. *rare*. L17–M18.
5 *verb trans.* Trick, cheat: defraud. *obsolete* exc. *dial.* L16.
†**6** *verb trans. & intrans.* Fit (a tankard) with a false base to diminish the vessel's actual capacity. Cf. NICK *noun*¹ 10. L16–M17.
7 *verb intrans.* In hunting, racing, or coursing: overtake, esp. by a short cut. Also foll. by *in*, *past*, etc. M19. ▸**b** Slip away, depart hurriedly. Also foll. by *off*, *away*, etc. *Austral. colloq.* L19.

5 SIR W. SCOTT The . . accomplished adventurer, who nicked you out of your money at White's. **7** *Daily News* That . . filly was lucky enough to nick in on the inside when the leaders ran out at the bend. **b** J. KELMAN They'll stay there as long as possible, just in case we nick away for a pint.

▶ **III** †**8** *verb trans.* Correspond to, resemble; suit exactly. L16–E18.
9 *verb trans.* Designate or call by a particular name (freq. foll. by *with*); nickname. Long *rare* or *obsolete*. L16.
10 *verb trans.* **a** Arrive at with precision, hit. Freq. in ***nick it***, hit the mark, guess correctly. E17. ▸**b** Hit *off* neatly or precisely. L17.
11 *verb trans.* Catch, take unawares. Now *spec.* (of the police) arrest, put in jail. *slang*. E17. ▸**b** Steal; rob. *slang*. M19.
12 *verb trans.* Select (exactly the right time for something). *arch. colloq.* M17. ▸†**b** Seize, take advantage of (an opportunity etc.). M17–E18. ▸**c** Catch (a boat, train, etc.) just in time. *arch. colloq.* M19. ▸**d** SQUASH & REAL TENNIS. Of a ball: strike the floor and wall simultaneously. L19.

10a CONAN DOYLE Mayhap you have nicked the truth. **11** L. GRIFFITHS He was nicked for fraud years later. **b** A. SILLITOE He'd nicked four bob from his mother's purse last week. **12** GOLDSMITH He had . . just nicked the time, for he came in as the cloth was laying. **b** MARVELL None more ready to nick a juncture of Affairs than a malapert Chaplain. **c** LYTTON I must arrive just in time to nick the vessels.

▶ **IV 13** *verb intrans.* Of (a mating between) domestic animals etc. of different breeds or pedigrees: produce offspring of high quality. M19.
14 *verb intrans.* Compare, compete. *rare*. L19.

13 *New Scientist* Where the offspring's performance is . . superior to that of its parents the mating [of poultry] is said to 'nick'.

Comb.: **nick-stick** (now *rare* or *obsolete*) a tally, a reckoning-stick; **nick-tailed** *adjective* (of a horse) having a nicked tail.

nickar *noun* var. of NICKER *noun*⁴.

nickel /ˈnɪk(ə)l/ *noun & adjective*. M18.
[Abbreviation of German *Kupfernickel* copper-nickel, niccolite, from *Kupfer* copper + *Nickel* dwarf, mischievous demon (so called because the ore yielded no copper). Cf. KUPFERNICKEL.]
▶ **A** *noun*. **1** A hard silvery-white metal which is a chemical element of the transition series, atomic no. 28, and is used esp. in special steels, magnetic alloys, and catalysts. (Symbol Ni.) M18.
2 a Orig. (*rare*), a one-cent piece. Later, a five-cent piece; in *pl.* also (*colloq.*), money. *N. Amer.* M19. ▸**b** Five dollars' worth of marijuana. *US slang*. M20.

1 white nickel (ore): see WHITE *adjective*. **2a** S. BELLOW It made him indignant that a man of such wealth should be miserly with nickels and dimes. ***accept a wooden nickel***, ***take a wooden nickel***: see WOODEN *adjective*.

▶ **B** *attrib.* or as *adjective*. Made of or with nickel. L18.
Comb. & special collocations: **nickel-and-dime** *adjective & verb* (chiefly *N. Amer.*) (*a*) *adjective* designating a store selling cheaply-priced articles, originally for five or ten cents (cf. ***FIVE-and-ten-cent store***); petty, of little importance; (*b*) *verb trans.* hinder or weaken by overattention to petty details; **nickel bag** *US slang* (a bag containing) five dollars' worth of a drug, esp. heroin or marijuana; **nickel-bloom** = ANNABERGITE; **nickel brass**, **nickel bronze**: containing a small amount of nickel; **nickel carbonyl** CHEMISTRY a toxic colourless liquid, $Ni(CO)_4$, used as a carbonylation agent; **nickel-in-the-slot** *adjective* (of a machine etc.) operated by the insertion of a nickel; **nickel-iron** *noun & adjective* (made of) any alloy of nickel and iron; **nickel note** *US slang* a five-dollar bill; **nickel nurser** *US slang* a miser; **nickel silver** an alloy of copper, zinc, and nickel, resembling silver and used in tableware etc.; **nickel-skutterudite** MINERALOGY an arsenide of nickel, usu. containing some cobalt, which crystallizes in the cubic system; **nickel steel** an alloy of iron containing nickel.
■ **nickelian** /nɪˈkiːlɪən/ *adjective* (MINERALOGY) having a constituent element partly replaced by nickel M20. **nickelic** *adjective* of, pertaining to, or containing nickel, esp. in the trivalent state E19. **nickeˈliferous** *adjective* containing or yielding nickel E19. **nickelite** *noun* = NICCOLITE L19. **nickelˈization** *noun* the action or process of plating with nickel or a nickel alloy M19. **nickelized** *adjective* plated with nickel or a nickel alloy L19. **nickelous** *adjective* of or containing nickel, esp. in the divalent state L19.

nickel /ˈnɪk(ə)l/ *verb*. Infl. **-ll-**, ***-l-**. L19.
[from NICKEL *noun*.]
1 *verb trans.* Coat with nickel. Chiefly as ***nickelled*** *ppl adjective*. L19.
2 a *verb trans.* Foul (the bore of a gun) with nickel from a bullet-casing. Chiefly as ***nickelling*** *verbal noun*. E20. ▸**b** *verb intrans.* Of the bore of a gun: become fouled with nickel from a bullet-casing. Chiefly as ***nickelling*** *verbal noun*. E20.

nickeline /ˈnɪk(ə)lʌɪn/ *adjective & noun*. L18.
[from NICKEL *noun* + -INE⁵.]
MINERALOGY. ▶ **A** *adjective*. Consisting of or containing nickel. L18.
▶ **B** *noun*. = NICCOLITE. M19.

nickelodeon /nɪkəˈləʊdɪən/ *noun*. *US*. E20.
[from NICKEL *noun* + MEL)ODEON.]
1 A theatre or cinema with an admission fee of one nickel; an amusement arcade. E20.
2 A jukebox. M20.

nicker /ˈnɪkə/ *noun*¹. Long *arch. rare.*
[Old English *nicor* = Middle Dutch, Middle Low German *nicker*, *necker* (Dutch *nikker*), Old Norse *nykr* (masc.) (Icelandic *nykur*, Norwegian *nykk*, Danish *nøkk*, Swedish *neck*), from Germanic base also of Old High German *nichus*, *nih(h)us* (masc.), *nicchessa* (fem.): see NIX *noun*², NIXIE *noun*¹.]
A supernatural being reputed to live in the sea or other waters; a water-demon, a kelpie. Formerly also, a siren, a mermaid.

nicker /ˈnɪkə/ *noun*². M17.
[from NICK *verb*² + -ER¹.]
†**1** A person who cheats at gaming. *rare*. M17–E18.
2 A member of a group of disorderly youths, active in the early 18th cent., who made a practice of breaking windows by throwing copper coins at them. E18.
3 A person who or thing which nicks or cuts something; *spec.* the part of a centre-bit which cuts the circle of a hole made by it. E19.

nicker /ˈnɪkə/ *noun*³. Also **kn-**. L17.
[Dutch *knikker* a marble, perh. from Dutch *knikken* crack, snap: see KNICK *noun*¹ & *verb*.]
A marble made of baked clay; in *pl.*, a game played with such marbles.

nicker /ˈnɪkə/ *noun*⁴. Also **nickar**. L17.
[Prob. a special use of NICKER *noun*³.]
Any of the hard round seeds of certain tropical leguminous trees, esp. *Caesalpinia bonduc*, used in the W. Indies to play marbles with (also ***nicker-nut***); any of these trees, *esp.* (also ***nicker-tree***) *Caesalpinia bonduc*.

nicker /ˈnɪkə/ *noun*⁵. *Scot. & north.* L18.
[Imit.: cf. NICKER *verb*.]
A neigh, a neighing sound; a snigger.

nicker /ˈnɪkə/ *noun*⁶. *slang*. Pl. same. L19.
[Origin unkn.]
One pound sterling.

J. SYMONS Who said there'd be trouble? Anyway, it's a hundred nicker.

nicker /ˈnɪkə/ *verb*. Chiefly *Scot. & north.* L16.
[Imit.: cf. NICHER, WHICKER.]
1 *verb intrans.* Neigh. L16.
2 *verb intrans.* Laugh loudly or shrilly. E19. ▸**b** *verb trans.* Utter (a laugh) loudly or shrilly. *rare*. E19.
3 *verb intrans.* Cry querulously for something (*lit. & fig.*). E20. ▸**b** *verb trans.* Express querulously. M20.

3 N. SHUTE He did not want to go on nickering after small commissions.

nickey /ˈnɪki/ *noun*. Also **-ie**. L19.
[Origin unkn.]
A fishing boat with lugsails, used in the waters around the Isle of Man in the Irish Sea.

nicking /ˈnɪkɪŋ/ *noun*. M16.
[from NICK *verb*² + -ING¹.]
The action of NICK *verb*²; an instance of this; a notch, an indentation; *spec.* a method of pruning in which an incision is made below the base of a bud in order to curb its growth.

nick-nack *noun* var. of KNICK-KNACK.

nickname /ˈnɪkneɪm/ *noun & verb*. LME.
[from misdivision of *an eke-name* (see EKE-NAME) as *a neke-name*: cf. NEWT.]
▶ **A** *noun*. **1** A familiar, humorous, or derogatory name added to or replacing the proper name of a person, place, etc. LME.
2 A familiar or abbreviated form of a forename. E17.

1 M. SCAMMELL When he suddenly grew much taller . . he earned the nickname of 'Ostrich'.

▶ **B** *verb trans.* **1** Call by an incorrect or improper name; misname. Also foll. by *as*, *so*. M16. ▸†**b** Mention by mistake; assert wrongly *to be* something. *rare*. L16–M17.
2 Give a nickname to (a person); call by a nickname. Also foll. by *as*, *so*. M16.

1 BYRON With no great care for what is nicknamed glory. **2** E. PIZZEY Privately she had nicknamed this particular woman 'Piranha teeth'.

■ **nicknamer** *noun* †(*a*) a rhetorical figure consisting in the use of verbal resemblances or nicknames; (*b*) a person who nicknames another person or thing: L16.

nickpoint *noun* var. of KNICKPOINT.

Nicobarese /nɪkəbəˈriːz/ *noun & adjective*. L19.
[from *Nicobar* (see below) + -ESE.]
▶ **A** *noun*. Pl. same.
1 A native or inhabitant of the Nicobar Islands in the Bay of Bengal, south of the Andaman Islands, with which the Nicobar group forms a Union Territory of India. L19.
2 The Mon-Khmer language of this people. L19.
▶ **B** *adjective*. Of or pertaining to the Nicobarese or their language. L19.
■ Also **Nicobarian** /nɪkəˈbɑːrɪən/ *noun & adjective* (now *rare*) L18.

Nicodemite /nɪkəˈdiːmʌɪt/ *noun*. *rare*. L16.
[from *Nicodemus* (see below) + -ITE¹.]
A person whose behaviour resembles that of Nicodemus, a Pharisee and member of the council of the Sanhedrin who became a secret follower of Jesus (cf. *John* 3:4); a secret or timid follower or adherent.

Niçois /niswa, niːˈswɑː/ *noun & adjective*. Fem. **-çoise** /-swaːz, -ˈswɑːz/. L19.
[French = of Nice (see below).]
▶**A** *noun*. Pl. **-çois** /-swa, -ˈswɑː/, (fem.) **-oises** /-waːz, -ˈwɑːz/. A native or inhabitant of the city of Nice in southern France. L19.
▶**B** *adjective*. Of, pertaining to, or characteristic of Nice or its inhabitants; *spec*. in COOKERY, designating food, esp. garnished with tomatoes, capers, anchovies, etc., characteristic of Nice or the surrounding region. Freq. *postpositive*. L19.
SALADE NIÇOISE.

Nicol /ˈnɪk(ə)l/ *noun*. M19.
[William *Nicol* (d. 1851), Scot. physicist and geologist.]
OPTICS. In full ***Nicol prism***, ***Nicol's prism***. A prism consisting of two pieces of Iceland spar cemented together so as to transmit only the extraordinary ray of doubly refracted light.

Nicolaitan /nɪkəˈleɪtən/ *noun & adjective*. E16.
[from Greek *Nikolaitēs*, from forename *Nikolaos* + -AN.]
ECCLESIASTICAL HISTORY. ▶**A** *noun*. A member of an early Christian sect advocating a return to pagan worship, mentioned in *Revelation* 2:6, 15. Formerly also, a married priest, an opponent of clerical celibacy. E16.
▶**B** *adjective*. Of or pertaining to the Nicolaitans or their views. L19.
■ **Nicolaitanism** *noun* L19. †**Nicolaite** *noun* LME–M17.

nicolo /ˈnɪkələʊ/ *noun*. M19.
[Italian *niccolo*, aphet. from dim. of Latin ONYX.]
A blue-black variety of onyx, used esp. in cameos and intaglios.

†**nicompoop** *noun* see NINCOMPOOP.

nicotia /nɪˈkəʊʃə/ *noun*. Now *rare*. M19.
[mod. Latin, formed as NICOTINE + -IA[1].]
Nicotine; *poet*. tobacco.

nicotian /nɪˈkəʊʃ(ə)n/ *noun & adjective*. *arch*. L16.
[formed as prec.: see -IAN.]
▶**A** *noun*. †**1** = NICOTIANA. L16–L17.
2 A tobacco-smoker. L19.
▶**B** *adjective*. Of or pertaining to tobacco; arising from the use of tobacco. E17.

nicotiana /ˌnɪkɒtɪˈɑːnə, -kəʊʃ-/ *noun*. E17.
[mod. Latin (see below), from Jaques *Nicot*, French ambassador at Lisbon, who introduced tobacco to France in 1560.]
Any of various plants of the genus *Nicotiana*, of the nightshade family, which includes *N. tabacum*, the principal source of tobacco; *spec*. any of several ornamental plants, esp. *N. alata*, grown for their night-scented trumpet-shaped flowers of various colours. Also called ***tobacco-plant***, ***tobacco***.

†**nicotin** *noun* see NICOTINE.

nicotina /nɪkəˈtʌɪnə/ *noun*. Now *rare* or *obsolete*. M19.
[Alt.]
CHEMISTRY. = NICOTINE.

nicotinamide /nɪkəˈtɪnəmʌɪd/ *noun*. L19.
[from NICOTIN(E + AMIDE.]
BIOCHEMISTRY. The amide, $(C_5H_4N)CONH_2$, of nicotinic acid which has the same role as the acid in the diet. Also called ***niacinamide***.
Comb.: **nicotinamide adenine dinucleotide** a compound of adenosine monophosphate and nicotinamide mononucleotide which is a coenzyme for the oxidation *in vivo* of a wide variety of substrates; also called ***NAD***, ***diphosphopyridine nucleotide***.

nicotinate /ˈnɪkətɪneɪt/ *noun*. L19.
[from NICOTINE + -ATE[1].]
CHEMISTRY. The anion, or a salt or ester, of nicotinic acid.

nicotine /ˈnɪkətiːn/ *noun*. Orig. †**-in**. E19.
[from NICOT(IANA + -INE[5].]
CHEMISTRY. A toxic colourless or yellowish oily liquid alkaloid which is the chief constituent of tobacco, acting as a stimulant in small doses, but in larger amounts blocking the action of autonomic nerve and skeletal muscle cells; β-pyridyl-α-N-methylpyrrolidine, $C_{10}H_{14}N_2$.
Comb.: **nicotine patch** an adhesive patch impregnated with nicotine which is worn on the skin and from which nicotine is absorbed gradually through the skin, thus reducing the wearer's craving for cigarettes.
■ **nicotined** *adjective* full of tobacco smoke; stained or impregnated with nicotine: L19. **nicoˈtinian** *adjective* = NICOTIAN *adjective* L19. **nicotinism** *noun* a pathological condition produced by excessive use of tobacco; nicotine poisoning, addiction to nicotine: L19. **nicotiniˈzation** *noun* the action of nicotinizing someone; the state of being nicotinized: M20. **nicotinize** *verb trans*. subject to the action of nicotine, drug or saturate with nicotine M19. **nicotize** *verb trans*. (now *rare*) = NICOTINIZE M19.

nicotinic /nɪkəˈtɪnɪk/ *adjective*. L19.
[from prec. + -IC.]
BIOCHEMISTRY. **1** ***nicotinic acid***, a white crystalline heterocyclic acid, $(C_5H_4N)COOH$, which is a vitamin of the B complex whose deficiency causes pellagra, is widely distributed (usu. as nicotinamide) in foods such as milk, wheat germ, and meat, and is formed by oxidation of nicotine and by synthesis in the body from tryptophan; 3-pyridinecarboxylic acid. Also called ***niacin***. L19.
2 Resembling (that of) nicotine; capable of responding to nicotine. M20.

nictate /nɪkˈteɪt, ˈnɪkteɪt/ *verb intrans*. L17.
[Latin *nictat-* pa. ppl stem of *nictare* wink: see -ATE[3]. Cf. NICTITATE.]
Wink, blink.
■ **nicˈtation** *noun* (a) wink, (a) blink E17.

nictitant /ˈnɪktɪt(ə)nt/ *adjective*. *rare*. E19.
[from medieval Latin *nictitant-* pres. ppl stem of *nictitare*: see NICTITATING, -ANT[1].]
Nictitating.

nictitate /ˈnɪktɪteɪt/ *verb intrans*. *rare*. E19.
[Back-form. from next.]
Esp. of the eyelid: wink, blink.
■ **nictiˈtation** *noun* winking, blinking; the action or habit of moving the eyelids: L18.

nictitating /ˈnɪktɪteɪtɪŋ/ *adjective*. E18.
[from medieval Latin *nictitat-* pa. ppl stem of *nictitare* frequentative of Latin *nictare* wink: -ING[1]. Cf. NICTATE.]
Winking, blinking.
nictitating membrane a third or inner eyelid which can be extended across the eye in many animals to protect it from dust etc. and keep it moist.

nid /nɪd/ *noun*. *rare*. E19.
[Alt., perh. after French *nid* nest.]
= NIDE.

nidamental /nʌɪdəˈmɛnt(ə)l/ *adjective*. M19.
[from Latin *nidamentum* (formed as NIDUS + -MENT) + -AL[1].]
Serving as a nest or nests; *esp*. in ZOOLOGY, pertaining to or serving as a receptacle for the ova of a mollusc or other marine animal.

nidation /nʌɪˈdeɪʃ(ə)n/ *noun*. L19.
[from NIDUS + -ATION.]
PHYSIOLOGY. †**1** The periodic development of the uterine lining. Only in L19.
2 = IMPLANTATION 5. L19.

niddering /ˈnɪd(ə)rɪŋ/ *noun & adjective*. Long *pseudo-arch*. Also **nidering**. L16.
[Var. of NITHING by misreading of ð. Cf. NIDING.]
▶**A** *noun*. = NITHING. L16.
▶**B** *attrib*. or as *adjective*. Cowardly, despicable. E19.
¶ Not recorded after E18 until revived by Sir Walter Scott in E19.
■ Also **nidderling** *noun* (*rare*) M17.

niddick /ˈnɪdɪk/ *noun*. Long *obsolete* exc. *dial*. M16.
[Origin unkn.]
The nape of the neck.

niddle-noddle /ˈnɪd(ə)lnɒd(ə)l/ *adjective & verb*. M18.
[Redupl. of NOD *verb*: see -LE[3]. Cf. next, NID-NOD.]
▶**A** *adjective*. Having a nodding head; nodding, unsteady. M18.
▶**B** *verb intrans. & trans*. Nod (the head), esp. continuously; nod unsteadily to and fro. M19.

niddy-noddy /ˈnɪdɪnɒdi/ *noun, verb, & adverb*. M17.
[Redupl. of NOD *verb*: see -Y[6]. Cf. prec., NID-NOD.]
▶**A** *noun*. †**1** An unsteady movement. *rare*. Only in M17.
2 A frame on which to skein and measure wool yarn. L19.
▶**B** *verb intrans. & trans*. = NIDDLE-NODDLE *verb*. M19.
▶**C** *adverb*. To and fro, unsteadily. L19.

nide /nʌɪd/ *noun*. L17.
[French *nid* or Latin *nidus* NEST *noun*. Cf. NID, NYE.]
A brood or nest of pheasants.

nidering *noun* var. of NIDDERING.

Niderviller /ˈniːdəvɪlə; *foreign* nidɛrvilɛːr/ *noun & adjective*. M19.
[A town in Lorraine, eastern France.]
(Designating) a type of porcelain and faience made at Niderviller since 1754.

nidge /nɪdʒ/ *verb*[1] *trans. & intrans*. *rare*. E19.
[Origin unkn.]
Shake (the head).

nidge /nɪdʒ/ *verb*[2] *trans*. Chiefly *Scot*. M19.
[Origin unkn.]
Trim (stone) roughly with a sharp-pointed hammer. Chiefly as ***nidged*** *ppl adjective*.

nidget /ˈnɪdʒɪt/ *noun*[1]. Long *arch*. L16.
[Repr. a pronunc. of NIDIOT.]
An idiot, a fool.

nidget /ˈnɪdʒɪt/ *noun*[2] & *verb*. L18.
[Origin unkn.]
Chiefly *Hist*. ▶**A** *noun*. A triangular horse-hoe, used in Kent and Sussex. L18.
▶**B** *verb trans*. Infl. **-tt-**.
1 Work (land) with a nidget. E19.
2 Work (lime etc.) *in* with the soil using a nidget. M19.

nidicolous /nɪˈdɪk(ə)ləs/ *adjective*. E20.
[from Latin *nidus* nest + -I- + -COLOUS.]
ORNITHOLOGY. (Having young which are) helpless at birth and confined to the nest until sufficiently developed to live without parental care; altricial. Opp. ***nidifugous***.
■ **ˈnidicole** *noun* a nidicolous bird M20.

nidification /ˌnɪdɪfɪˈkeɪʃ(ə)n/ *noun*. M17.
[from Latin *nidificat-* pa. ppl stem of *nidificare*, from *nidus* nest: see -ATION.]
The action or an act of nest-building; the manner in which this is done.
■ **ˈnidificate** *verb intrans*. make a nest E19.

nidifugous /nɪˈdɪfjʊgəs/ *adjective*. E20.
[from Latin *nidus* nest + -I- + *fugere* flee + -OUS.]
ORNITHOLOGY. (Having young which are) well developed at birth and able to leave the nest almost immediately; precocial. Opp. ***nidicolous***.
■ **ˈnidifuge** *noun* a nidifugous bird M20.

nidify /ˈnɪdɪfʌɪ/ *verb intrans*. M17.
[from Latin *nidificare*, from *nidus* nest: see -FY.]
Make a nest or nests.

niding /ˈnɪdɪŋ/ *noun*. Long *arch*. *rare*. E17.
[Alt.: cf. NIDDERING.]
= NITHING.

nidiot /ˈnɪdɪət/ *noun*. Now *joc*. Long *rare*. M16.
[from misdivision of *an idiot* (see IDIOT) as *a nidiot*. See also NIDGET *noun*[1].]
An idiot, a fool.

nid-nod /ˈnɪdnɒd/ *verb & adjective*. L18.
[Redupl. of NOD *verb*: cf. NIDDLE-NODDLE *verb*.]
▶**A** *verb intrans. & trans*. Infl. **-dd-**. Nod (the head etc.) repeatedly. L18.
▶**B** *adjective*. That nid-nods. *poet*. E20.

nidor /ˈnʌɪdə/ *noun*. Now *rare*. E17.
[Latin.]
The smell of burnt or cooked (esp. fatty) animal substances. Formerly also, a strong, esp. unpleasant, odour of any kind.

nidorous /ˈnʌɪd(ə)rəs/ *adjective*. Now *rare*. E17.
[from late Latin *nidorosus*, from (the same root as) prec.: see -OUS.]
1 Of a smell: resembling that of cooked or burnt (esp. fatty) animal substances; strong and unpleasant. E17.
2 Of a belch: having a strong, unpleasant taste or odour. M17.

nidulant /ˈnɪdjʊl(ə)nt/ *adjective*. Now *rare*. L18.
[Latin *nidulant-* pres. ppl stem of *nidulari* nestle, from *nidus* nest: see -ANT[1].]
BOTANY. Of the seeds of a berry: embedded in pulp. Also, of sporangia: lying free in a cavity.

nidulation /nɪdjʊˈleɪʃ(ə)n/ *noun*. *rare*. M17.
[from Latin *nidulat-* pa. ppl stem of *nidulari*, from *nidus* nest: see -ATION.]
Nesting, nidification.

nidus /ˈnʌɪdəs/ *noun*. Pl. **nidi** /ˈnʌɪdʌɪ/, **niduses**. E18.
[Latin = nest.]
1 a MEDICINE. A place in which bacteria or other pathogens have multiplied; a focus of infection. E18. ▶**b** ZOOLOGY. A nest or place in which a small animal, as an insect, snail, etc., lives or deposits its eggs. M18. ▶**c** BOTANY. A place or substance in which spores or seeds develop. L18.
2 A place in which something is formed, deposited, settled, or located; a site of origin. L18.
3 *fig*. A source, an origin; a place where some quality or principle is fostered. E19.
4 A collection *of* eggs, tubercles, etc. *rare*. E19.

niece /niːs/ *noun*. ME.
[Old & mod. French *nièce* from popular Latin *neptia* for Latin *neptis* corresp. to Sanskrit *naptī*, Lithuanian *neptė̃*, and Germanic base of Old English *nift*, Middle Dutch *nichte* (whence German *Nichte*), Dutch *nicht*, Old Norse *nipt*.]
1 Orig., a granddaughter; a remote female descendant. Later, a daughter of a person's brother or sister; a daughter of a brother- or sister-in-law. ME. ▶**b** *euphem*. An illegitimate daughter of an ecclesiastic. Cf. NEPHEW 1b. *arch*. M19.
†**2** *gen*. A female relative. ME–E16.
†**3** A male relative, *esp*. a nephew. *rare*. LME–E17.
Phrases: ***Welsh niece***: see WELSH *adjective*.

nief *noun* var. of NIEVE.

niello /nɪˈɛləʊ/ *noun & verb*. E19.
[Italian from Latin *nigellus* dim. of *niger* black.]
▶**A** *noun*. Pl. **-lli** /-liː/, **-llos**.
1 A black composition of sulphur with silver, lead, or copper, for filling engraved designs on silver or other metals. E19.
2 (A specimen of) such ornamental work; an article decorated with niello. M19.
3 An impression on paper of a design to be filled with niello. M19.
▶**B** *verb trans*. Inlay with niello. Chiefly as ***nielloed*** *ppl adjective*. M19.

■ **niellated** *ppl adjective* inlaid in niello L19. **niellist** *noun* a person skilled in working with niello M19.

nielsbohrium /niːlzˈbɔːrɪəm/ *noun*. L20.
[from *Niels* BOHR + -IUM.]
A name proposed for the chemical elements of atomic number 104 (now called *rutherfordium*) and (later) 107 (now called *bohrium*).

Nielsen /ˈnɪəls(ə)n/ *adjective*. *US*. M20.
[Arthur Charles *Nielsen* (1897–1980), founder of A. C. Nielsen Co. (see below).]
Designating or pertaining to a popularity rating for radio and television programmes provided by A. C. Nielsen Co. and calculated from figures obtained from a sample survey of receiving sets adapted to record automatically audience listening or viewing patterns. Freq. in ***Nielsen rating***.

📖 *Time* According to the Nielsen Index figures . . Americans will have watched 18,000 TV murders by age 18.

Niemann–Pick disease /niːmənˈpɪk dɪˌziːz/ *noun phr.* Also **Niemann–Pick's disease**. E20.
[Albert *Nieman* (1880–1921) and Ludwig *Pick* (1868–c1944), German physicians.]
MEDICINE. A rare inherited metabolic disorder, usu. fatal in childhood, characterized by the accumulation in the body cells of the lipid sphingomyelin.

nien hao /ˈnɪən haʊ/ *noun phr.* Pl. same, **-s**. L19.
[Chinese *niánhào* lit. 'reign year'.]
A title given to (part of) the reign of a Chinese emperor, used in imperial China as a system of dating. Also, a mark (signifying the reign of a particular emperor) used on Chinese pottery or porcelain to indicate an object's period of manufacture.

niente /niˈɛnte, nɪˈɛnti/ *noun, adverb, & adjective*. E19.
[Italian.]
▶ **A** *noun*. Nothing. E19.
▶ **B** *adverb & adjective*. *MUSIC*. A direction: with gradual fading away of the sound or tone to nothing. E20.
¶ Noun only recorded in (DOLCE) FAR NIENTE before E20.

Niersteiner /ˈnɪəʃtʌɪnə/ *noun*. M19.
[from *Nierstein* (see below) + *-er* German adjective suffix.]
A white Rhine wine produced in the region around Nierstein, a town in Germany.

niet /ˈnjɛt/ *adverb & noun*. Also **nyet**. E20.
[Russian *net* no.]
▶ **A** *adverb*. In Russian: = NO *adverb*³, esp. expr. a blunt refusal. E20.
▶ **B** *noun*. An utterance of 'njet'. E20.

Nietzschean /ˈniːtʃɪən/ *noun & adjective*. E20.
[from *Nietzsche* (see below): see -EAN.]
▶ **A** *noun*. A follower of the German philosopher Friedrich Nietzsche (1844–1900); a supporter of Nietzsche's principles or views, esp. his theories of the superman able to rise above the restrictive morality of ordinary men. E20.
▶ **B** *adjective*. Of, pertaining to, or characteristic of Nietzsche or his views. E20.
■ **Nietzscheanism**, **Nietzscheism** *nouns* the philosophical system of Nietzsche E20.

nieve /niːv/ *noun*. Now *arch., Scot., & north*. Also **nief** /niːf/. LME.
[Old Norse *hnefi*, *nefi*, of unkn. origin.]
A clenched hand; a fist.

nieveful /ˈniːvfʊl, -f(ə)l/ *noun*. *Scot. & north*. LME.
[from prec. + -FUL.]
A handful.

nievie /ˈniːvi/ *noun*. *Scot. & north*. L16.
[from NIEVE + -IE.]
In full ***nievie-nick-nack***, ***nievie-nievie-nick-nack***. A children's guessing game in which these words are used.

Nife /ˈnʌɪf/ *noun*. E20.
[from *Ni* symbol for nickel + *Fe* symbol for iron.]
Nickel-iron; *spec.* (the material composing) the earth's core.

nifedipine /nʌɪˈfɛdɪpiːn/ *noun*. L20.
[from NI(TRO- + *fe* (alt. of PHE(NYL *noun*) + DI-² + P(YRID)INE, elems. of the systematic name.]
PHARMACOLOGY. A calcium antagonist, $C_{17}H_{18}N_2O_6$, given as a coronary vasodilator in the treatment of cardiac and circulatory disorders.

niff /nɪf/ *noun*¹ *& verb*¹. *colloq. & dial.* L18.
[Origin unkn.]
▶ **A** *noun*. An act or instance of feeling resentment or taking offence. Freq. in ***take a niff***, take offence. L18.
▶ **B** *verb trans*. Quarrel with, offend. Chiefly as ***niffed*** *ppl adjective*. L19.

niff /nɪf/ *noun*² *& verb*². *colloq. & dial.* E20.
[Perh. from SNIFF.]
▶ **A** *noun*. A smell, *esp.* an unpleasant one. E20.

📖 *Beano* What is that revolting niff?

▶ **B** *verb intrans*. Smell, stink. E20.

📖 D. NORDEN My overcoat and woolly gloves still niff of haddock.

niffer /ˈnɪfə, ˈniː-/ *noun & verb*. *Scot. & north*. LME.
[Origin uncertain: perh. from NIEVE + FARE *noun*¹.]
▶ **A** *noun*. An exchange. LME.
▶ **B** *verb*. **1** *verb trans*. Exchange (a thing) *for* (†*with*) another. E16.
2 *verb intrans*. **a** Make an exchange, barter. L16. ▸**b** Bargain, haggle. E19.
3 *verb trans*. Make a mutual exchange of. E18.

niff-naff /ˈnɪfnaf/ *verb intrans*. *Scot. & north*. E18.
[Origin unkn.]
Trifle.
■ **niff-naffy** *adjective* = NIFFY-NAFFY E19. **niffy-naffy** *adjective* trifling, fastidious M18.

niffy /ˈnɪfi/ *adjective*. *colloq. & dial.* E20.
[from NIFF *noun*² + -Y¹.]
Having a strong smell, esp. an unpleasant one.
■ **niffiness** *noun* M20.

nifle /ˈnʌɪf(ə)l/ *noun*. Long *dial*. LME.
[Perh. from NICHIL, infl. by *trifle*.]
Orig., a trifling or fictitious tale. Later, a trifle; a thing of little or no value.

Niflheim /ˈnɪv(ə)lheɪm, -hʌɪm/ *noun*. L19.
[Old Norse *Niflheimr*, from *nifl-* (cogn. with Old English *nifol* darkness, Old High German *nebal* mist, cloud, Latin *nebula*) + *heimr* world.]
In Scandinavian mythology, the abode of those who die from old age or illness, a place of eternal cold, darkness, and mist, ruled over by the goddess Hel.

nifty /ˈnɪfti/ *adjective & noun*. *colloq*. M19.
[Origin unkn.]
▶ **A** *adjective*. Smart, stylish, splendid. Also, clever, nimble, adroit. M19.

📖 I. HAMILTON She . . cajoled her father into some nifty mortgage-juggling which eventually produced the house. *Listener* Unalloyed quality . . can still outflank nifty packaging.

▶ **B** *noun*. A joke, a witty remark or story. E20.
■ **niftily** *adverb* E20. **niftiness** *noun* E20.

†**nig** *noun*¹. ME–L17.
[Prob. of Scandinavian origin.]
= NIGGARD *noun* 1.

nig /nɪɡ/ *noun*². *slang* (*derog.* & considered *racially offensive*). E19.
[Abbreviation of NIGGER *noun*. Cf. NIG-NOG *noun*².]
A black person.

nigella /nʌɪˈdʒɛlə/ *noun*. LME.
[mod. Latin (see below), use as genus name of fem. of Latin *nigellus* dim. of *niger* black.]
Any of several plants of the genus *Nigella* of the buttercup family, with showy flowers and finely dissected leaves; *esp.* love-in-a-mist, *N. damascena*, a common garden flower, and fennel-flower, *N. sativa*, the seeds of which are used as a flavouring.

†**Niger** *noun*¹ *& adjective*. L16–M18.
[Latin: see NEGRO.]
= NEGRO *noun* 1, *adjective*.

Niger /ˈnʌɪdʒə/ *noun*². L19.
[A W. African river.]
1 In full ***Niger morocco***, ***Niger goatskin***. A type of morocco produced in regions near the River Niger and used for bookbinding. L19.
2 ***Niger seed***, the seeds of *Guizotia abyssinica*, an African plant of the composite family cultivated esp. in India for the oil obtained from its seeds. Also called ***ramtil***. L19.

Niger-Congo /nʌɪdʒəˈkɒŋɡəʊ/ *noun & adjective*. M20.
[from prec. + CONGO *noun*¹.]
(Designating or pertaining to) a group of languages which includes those of most of the indigenous peoples of western, central, and southern Africa.

Nigerian /nʌɪˈdʒɪərɪən/ *noun & adjective*. M19.
[from *Nigeria* (see below), formed as NIGER *noun*²: see -AN.]
▶ **A** *noun*. A native or inhabitant of Nigeria, a country (now a republic) in W. Africa occupying the basin of the lower Niger. M19.
▶ **B** *adjective*. Of or pertaining to Nigeria or its inhabitants. E20.
Nigerian teak: see TEAK *noun* 2.
■ **Nigeriani'zation** *noun* the process of Nigerianizing something M20. **Nigerianize** *verb trans*. make Nigerian in character; *spec.* replace foreigners by native Nigerians in (government, industry, etc.) M20.

nigga /ˈnɪɡə/ *noun & adjective*. *US*. *derog.* & considered *racially offensive* exc. *Black English*. Also **-ah**, **-uh**. E20.
[Repr. a pronunc. of NIGGER *adjective & noun*. Cf. NIGRA.]
= NEGRO *noun* 1, *adjective*.
¶ Now virtually restricted to publications in which Black English vernacular is set down.

niggard /ˈnɪɡəd/ *noun, adjective, & verb*. LME.
[Alt. of NIGON by suffix-substitution of -ARD.]
▶ **A** *noun*. **1** A mean, stingy, or parsimonious person; a miser; a person who grudgingly parts with, spends, or uses up anything. (Foll. by *of*.) LME.
2 A movable piece of iron or fire-brick placed in the side or bottom of a grate to save fuel. Also ***niggard iron***. *dial*. L17.
▶ **B** *adjective*. Now *literary*.
1 = NIGGARDLY *adjective* 1. LME.
†**2** = NIGGARDLY *adjective* 2. LME–L16.
▶†**C** *verb*. *rare*.
1 *verb intrans. & trans*. (with *it*). Act in a niggardly fashion. L16–E17.
2 *verb trans*. Be sparing or niggardly of. L16–E17.
3 *verb trans*. Put off *with* a small amount of something; treat in a niggardly fashion. Only in E17.
■ †**niggardise** *noun* [-ISE¹] niggardliness E16–M18. **niggardize** *verb* (*rare*) †(**a**) *verb intrans. & trans*. (with *it*) to be niggardly; (**b**) *verb trans*. give in a niggardly fashion: E17. **niggardness** *noun* (now *rare*) niggardliness E16.

niggardly /ˈnɪɡədli/ *adjective*. M16.
[from NIGGARD *noun* + -LY¹.]
1 Having or displaying an unwillingness to give, spend, or use anything up; mean, miserly. (Foll. by *of*, *with*.) M16.
2 Such as a niggard would give; meanly small, scanty, closely limited; given grudgingly. L16.

📖 **1** T. R. MALTHUS The earth had been so niggardly of her produce. R. K. NARAYAN Never knew people could be so niggardly with cucumber. C. G. WOLFF She was apparently not above the most niggardly retaliation. **2** *Economist* America's foreign aid has become notoriously niggardly.

■ **niggardliness** *noun* L16.

niggardly /ˈnɪɡədli/ *adverb*. M16.
[from NIGGARD *adjective* + -LY².]
In a niggardly manner, parsimoniously, grudgingly, sparingly.

nigger /ˈnɪɡə/ *adjective & noun*. Exc. *Black English* now *derog.* & considered *racially offensive* as used of people & usu. avoided in other contexts. L17.
[Var. of NEGER. Cf. NIGER *noun*¹, NIGGA, NIGRA. Cf. also NIG *noun*².]
▶ **A** *adjective*. = NEGRO *adjective*. Also (*US slang*), contemptible, despicable, inferior. L17.
▶ **B** *noun*. **1** a black person. L18. ▸**b** *loosely*. A member of any dark-skinned people. M19. ▸**c** A contemptible or inferior person; a socially or economically disadvantaged person. M19.
2 **a** A form of steam engine used on a ship; a steam-capstan employed in hauling riverboats over bars or snags. *US*. M19. ▸**b** A strong spiked timber by which logs are canted in a sawmill. *US*. M19.
3 Any of various black or mainly black animals, fishes, insect larvae, etc. (see also combs. below); *spec.* (more fully ***nigger caterpillar***) the larva of the turnip sawfly, *Athalia spinarum*. *colloq*. M19.
4 A dark shade of brown. E20.
5 *CINEMATOGRAPHY*. A screen used to absorb or direct light to cast shadows etc. *slang*. M20.
1 nigger in the woodpile, (*US*) **nigger in the fence** *slang* a concealed motive or unknown factor affecting a situation in an adverse way. ***White nigger***: see WHITE *adjective*. **work like a nigger** work exceptionally hard.
Special collocations & comb.: **nigger brown** = sense B.4 above. ***nigger caterpillar***: see sense B.3 above. **nigger cloth** *Hist.* = NEGRO *cloth*. **nigger fish** = CONY 6. **nigger goose** *N. Amer. colloq.* a cormorant. **nigger heaven** *US slang* the top gallery in a theatre. **nigger luck** *arch. US slang* exceptionally good luck. **nigger minstrel** (chiefly *Hist.*) = ***blackface minstrel*** s.v. BLACK *adjective*. **nigger-shooter** *arch. US slang* a catapult. **nigger-stick** *US slang* a stick or truncheon carried by a police officer etc. **nigger toe** *US* a Brazil nut.
¶ Of early forms, only those with *-gg-* have been regarded as belonging here. Those with single *-g-* have been attributed to NEGER or NIGER *noun*¹.
■ **niggerdom** *noun* (now *rare*) = NEGRODOM M19. **niggerish** *adjective* (now *rare*) = NEGROISH E19. **niggerism** *noun* (**a**) the state or condition of being black; (**b**) = NEGROISM (a); (**c**) = NEGROISM (b): M19. **niggery** *adjective* of, pertaining to, or characteristic of black people. M19.

nigger /ˈnɪɡə/ *verb trans*. *US*. Now *rare*. M19.
[from prec.]
1 Burn or char off a length or lengths of (a log etc.). Usu. foll. by *off*. M19.
2 With *it* as obj. Work very hard. M19.

niggerality /nɪɡəˈralɪti/ *noun*. *rare*. E17.
[from NIGGAR(D *noun* -ALITY.]
Niggardliness.

niggerhead /ˈnɪɡəhɛd/ *noun*. M19.
[from NIGGER *adjective & noun* + HEAD *noun*.]
1 **a** A tangled mass of the roots and decayed remains of sedges projecting from a swamp (*N. Amer. & NZ*). Also (*NZ*), any of several sedges forming such masses, esp. *Carex secta*. M19. ▸**b** Any of various spiny spherical cacti of the genera *Ferocactus* and *Echinocactus*. *US*. L19. ▸**c** Black-eyed Susan, *Rudbeckia hirta*. *US*. L19.

2 A rock, a black stone etc.; *esp.* a projecting stump of dead coral. **M19.**

3 = NEGRO-HEAD 2. **M19.**

4 An advocate of political rights for black people in the US. *slang (obsolete exc. Hist.). derog.* **M19.**

niggle /ˈnɪɡ(ə)l/ *verb*[1] *intrans. & trans. slang.* Now *rare.* **M16.**
[Origin unkn.: cf. next.]
Have sexual intercourse (with).

niggle /ˈnɪɡ(ə)l/ *verb*[2] *& noun.* **E17.**
[App. of Scandinavian origin: cf. Norwegian *nigla* verb. Earlier as NIGGLING *adjective.*]
▶ **A** *verb.* **I 1** *verb intrans.* Work or do something in a trifling, fiddling, or ineffective way; trifle (†*with* a thing); waste effort or time on petty details; be overelaborate in minor points. **E17.** ▸**b** Go about, keep moving *along*, in a fiddling or ineffective manner. **M18.**
†**2** *verb intrans.* Of a girl: be restless or fidgety from wantonness or sexual inclination. **E18–E19.**
3 *verb intrans.* Nag; cause slight but persistent annoyance, discomfort, or anxiety; complain, esp. in a petty or trifling way; be unnecessarily critical or overprecise. (Foll. by *at.*) **L18.**
4 *verb trans.* Execute in a petty trifling manner, or with too much petty detail or overelaboration of minor points. Chiefly as ***niggled*** *ppl adjective.* **M19.**
5 *verb trans.* Annoy, irritate; complain at, esp. in a petty or trifling way; criticize; nag at. **L19.**

> 🕮 **1** A. Y. JACKSON She niggled with small brushes while I tried . . to get her to paint with more breadth. **3** A. WEST It was like so many of our dull conversations, my mistakes being niggled over. G. PRIESTLAND I may niggle at some of their details. M. S. POWER Something niggled at the back of Pericles's mind. **5** S. BARSTOW Nothing niggles me more than cutting myself shaving.

▶ **II 6** *verb trans.* Cheat, trick. *slang & dial.* Now *rare* or *obsolete.* **E17.**
▶ **B** *noun.* **1** (An example of) small cramped handwriting. **M19.**
2 The action of nagging or finding fault. *dial.* **L19.**
3 A complaint, a criticism, *esp.* one that is petty or trifling; a worry, an annoyance. **M20.**

> 🕮 **1** *New Yorker* Her handwriting . . doesn't seem such a niggle as usual. **3** *Motorbike Monthly* Niggles . . were the difficulty of access to the port engine . . and to the adjustment nuts.

■ **niggler** *noun* **M19.**

niggling /ˈnɪɡlɪŋ/ *noun.* **E19.**
[from NIGGLE *verb*[2] + -ING[1].]
The action of NIGGLE *verb*[2]; trifling or fiddling work; overattention to details; mean or petty dealing.

niggling /ˈnɪɡlɪŋ/ *adjective.* **L16.**
[from (the same root as) NIGGLE *verb*[2] + -ING[2].]
1 Trifling, mean, petty; deficient in force or vigour; lacking in breadth of view or feeling. **L16.**
2 Showing too great elaboration of detail; deficient in boldness of execution; (of handwriting) consisting of short feeble strokes, cramped. **E19.**
3 Fiddling, troublesome, finicking; tending to niggle; causing slight but persistent annoyance, discomfort, or anxiety. **M19.**

> 🕮 **1** C. C. TRENCH The Act of Settlement had imposed many niggling . . restrictions on the power of a sovereign. *Antiquaries Journal* She had a certain impatience, especially for niggling scholars. **3** *Lancet* The niggling left iliac fossa pain of diverticular disease. R. FRAME Elegant women . . might be more demanding—niggling—about the smaller details. *Daily Star* I thought he was lying but there was a niggling doubt in my mind. *What Investment* There is a niggling fear in the markets, but some expectation of better days is returning.

niggly /ˈnɪɡli/ *adjective.* **M19.**
[from NIGGLE *verb*[2] + -Y[1].]
= NIGGLING *adjective.* Also, irritable, short-tempered.

nigguh *noun & adjective* var. of NIGGA.

nigh /nʌɪ/ *verb.* Now *rare.* **ME.**
[from the adverb.]
1 *verb trans.* Go, come, or draw near to, approach closely. Formerly also, approach so as to touch or handle. **ME.**
2 *verb intrans. &* †*trans.* with impers. *it.* Draw near or close *to*, *towards*, or (formerly) to (a certain time). **ME.**
3 *verb intrans.* Go, come, or draw near; approach. (Foll. by *to*, *toward.*) **ME.**

> 🕮 **1** SIR W. SCOTT Sooner than Walwayn my sick couch should nigh, My choice were, by leach-craft unaided to die. **3** SPENSER Now day is doen, and night is nighing fast. KEATS The laden heart Is persecuted more . . when it is nighing to a mournful house. T. HARDY The first battle nighed on the low Southern side.

nigh /nʌɪ/ *adverb, preposition, & adjective.* Now *arch., dial., & literary.* Compar. NEAR *adverb*[1] *& preposition*[1], NAR, (later) **nigher**; superl. NEXT, (later) **nighest**.
[Old English *nēah*, *nēh*, corresp. to Old Frisian *nei*, *nī*, Old Saxon, Old High German *nāh* (Dutch *na*, German *nah*), Old Norse *ná-*, Gothic *nēhw-* (*nēhw* preposition, *nēhwa* adverb), from Germanic.]
▶ **I** *adverb, preposition, & pred. adjective.* **1** Near in place, time, etc.; near to or (*un*)*to*; nearby, near at hand. **OE.**
2 Near in degree, amount, kind, etc.; nearly, almost, all but, (also ***nigh on***). **OE.**

> 🕮 **1** SHAKES. *Mids. N. D.* Never harm Nor spell nor charm Come our lovely lady nigh. J. PORY The citie of Tunis . . hath no mountaines nigh vnto it. T. GRAY Some frail memorial still erected nigh. JOHN NEAL The . . dog would not leave him; but crawled nigher. J. F. COOPER A bay nigh the northern termination of the lake. E. MYERS When man's heart is nighest heaven. *Cornish Times* Smallholders who . . have land nigh new estates. P. USTINOV Signs that the end of the world was nigh. G. SWIFT Judgement was nigh, the denouement was due. **2** LEIGH HUNT Her sarcasms . . go nigh to confirm it. TENNYSON The wood is nigh as full of thieves as leaves. D. L. SAYERS It nigh frightened my brither's wife into a fit. F. REID It took me nigh and next an hour trying to clean your clothes. *Time* All the . . highways were nigh bare of automobiles. E. JONES His father . . was now nigh on seventy. P. RYAN I nigh on missed my bus home.

▶ **II** *attrib. adjective.* **3** Near, close. **OE.**
4 Parsimonious, mean. **M16.**

> 🕮 **3** COLERIDGE The nigh thatch Smokes in the sun-thaw. SIR W. SCOTT The nigher and the safer road to Liege.

Comb.: **nigh-hand** *adverb & preposition* (*a*) near or close at hand (to); close by; (*b*) almost, nearly.
■ **nighly** *adverb* (*a*) nearly, almost; †(*b*) closely: **OE.**

night /nʌɪt/ *noun.*
[Old English *niht*, Anglian *næht*, *neaht* = Old Frisian, Middle Dutch *nacht*, Old Saxon, Old High German *naht* (Dutch, German *Nacht*), Old Norse *nátt*, *nótt*, Gothic *nahts*, from Indo-European base also of Latin *nox*, *noct-*, Greek *nux*, *nukt-*, Sanskrit *nak* (*nakt-*). Cf. NITE.]
1 a The period of darkness which intervenes between day and day; that part of the natural day (of 24 hours) during which no light is received from the sun; the time between evening and morning. **OE.** ▸**b** The darkness which prevails during this time; the dark. **ME.**
2 (A period of) figurative darkness; (a period of) depression, obscurity, ignorance, etc.; death. **OE.**
3 Each of the intervals of darkness between two days. **OE.** ▸**b** Such an interval as characterized by the kind of weather or other natural feature or by the quality of rest obtained or by the manner in which the time is spent. **LOE.** ▸**c** With *possess.* The particular night on which a person performs some duty (formerly *spec.* receives visitors), engages in a particular activity, etc. **E16.** ▸**d** With *possess.* The kind of night one has had, or usually has. **M17.** ▸**e** An evening or night devoted to a performance of a play, music, etc., or to a particular activity. Freq. with specifying word. **E18.** ▸**f** As *interjection.* (Also **'night.**) = GOOD NIGHT *interjection. colloq.* **E20.**
4 The time at which darkness comes on; the close or end of daylight. Also, bedtime. **ME.**

> 🕮 **1a** SHELLEY Evening must usher night. BYRON Her eyelashes, though dark as night, were tinged. *personified*: POPE The sable Throne behold Of Night primaeval and of Chaos old. **b** P. BOWLES Converging rows of . . lights leading off into the night. **2** DRYDEN Dido . . clos'd her Lids at last, in endless Night. M. L. KING Daybreak . . had come to end the long night of their captivity. **3** G. H. JOHNSTON 'It's early yet,' he retorted . . 'The night's young.' R. CONQUEST We got away—for just two nights. I. MCEWAN He had slept well the night before. ***wedding night*** etc. **b** T. S. ELIOT Restless nights in . . cheap hotels. J. B. PRIESTLEY To see how the people . . enjoy themselves on a damp night in autumn. **c** C. JOHNSTON The footman answered, that it was not his lady's night. **d** B. RUBENS Had his father known of his son's night, he would not have woken him. **e** W. DE LA MARE It was 'bath-night' on Saturday. H. A. JONES *Mrs Dane's Defence* ran for 200 nights. *Listener* Beethoven nights at the old Queen's Hall. **f** R. INGALLS 'Night all,' he said. **4** MILTON It was the hour of night.

Phrases: **all night (long)**, **all the night (long)** throughout the night, from nightfall to daybreak. **at night** at nightfall, in the evening; in the period from 6 p.m. to midnight. **at nights** during the night, by night. **by night** during the night, in the night-time. **by night and day** always, at any time. ***dark night (of the soul)***: see DARK *adjective.* ***day and night***: see DAY *noun.* ***early night***: see EARLY *adjective.* ***first night***: see FIRST *adjective* etc. **in the night** by night, during the night. ***ladies' night***, ***lady of the night***: see LADY *noun & adjective.* ***last night***: see LAST *adjective.* ***last thing (at night)***: see LAST *adverb* etc. ***late night***: see LATE *adjective & noun*[2]. ***make a night of it***: see MAKE *verb.* ***MORNING, noon, and night.*** ***night and day***: see DAY *noun.* **night in** a night at home, an evening on which one does not go out. **night off** a night free from work or one's usual duties. **night of the long knives** (*a*) a treacherous massacre, as (according to legend) of the Britons by Hengist in 472, or of Ernst Roehm and his associates by Hitler on 29–30 June 1934; (*b*) a ruthless or decisive action held to resemble this. †**of the night** = ***in the night*** above. **night or day**, (*arch.*) **night nor day** by night or by day, at any time. **night out** (*a*) an evening on which a domestic servant is free to go out; (*b*) an evening or night spent in enjoyment or revelling away from one's home; a spree. †**o' nights** = ***on nights*** (a) below. **on nights** †(*a*) by night (habitually); (*b*) *colloq.* working night shifts. ***queen of night***, ***queen-of-the-night***: see QUEEN *noun.* ***ships that pass in the night***: see SHIP *noun* 1. **spend the night** remain until the next day; remain with as an overnight guest; go to bed for the night *with* or *together* and have sexual intercourse. ***stag night***: see STAG *noun* etc. ***stay the night***: see STAY *verb*[1]. ***the MORNING after the night before.*** **the night** †(*a*) *adverb* during the night, by night; (*b*) the first occasion on which a play, entertainment, etc., is publicly performed (freq. in ***it will be all right on the night***, expr. optimism that an unpromising performance etc. will go well when it really matters). ***the other night***: see OTHER *adjective.* ***TOMORROW night.*** ***Twelfth Night***: see TWELFTH *adjective.* ***twilight night***: see TWILIGHT *adjective.* ***under night***: see UNDER *preposition.* ***WALPURGIS night.*** ***watch-night***: see WATCH *noun.* ***white night***: see WHITE *adjective.* ***YESTERDAY night.***

Attrib. & comb.: In the senses 'of or pertaining to night', 'existing, taking place, etc., during the night (or in the evening)', '(intended to be) worn or used during the night', 'operating, acting, or on duty during the night', as ***night-attire***, ***night-bombing***, ***night breeze***, ***night-driving***, ***night ferry***, ***night flight***, ***night porter***, ***night raid***, ***night train***. Special combs., as **night-adapted** *adjective* = *dark-adapted adjective* s.v. DARK *noun*[1]; **night adder** a nocturnal venomous African viper of the genus *Causus*, esp. *C. rhombeatus*, a grey snake with darker patches, common in southern Africa; **night bag** a travelling-bag containing necessaries for the night, an overnight bag; **night-bell** a bell to summon a person at night, *esp.* one on a street-door to summon a porter etc.; **nightbird** (*a*) a bird that is chiefly (or only) heard or seen by night; *esp.* an owl, a nightingale; (*b*) a person who habitually goes about or out at night; **night-blooming** *adjective* = ***night-flowering*** below; ***night-blooming cereus***, any of several tropical cacti of the genera *Hylocereus* and *Selenicereus*, with flowers that open only at night, esp. *H. undatus*, which has very large fragrant white flowers; **night-blind** *adjective* = NYCTALOPIC; **night-blindness** poor vision in dim light; = NYCTALOPIA; **night-blue** (of) any of various dark blues, esp. those which retain the colour under artificial light; **night boat** a passenger-boat which makes a crossing overnight; **night bolt** an inside bolt serving to secure a door by night; **night bomber** an aircraft that drops bombs at night; the pilot of such an aircraft; **night-bound** *adjective* bound, confined, or impeded by night or darkness; **night-box** a small (French) nightclub; †**night-cape** *fig.* a wife; **night-cart** a cart used in removing night-soil; **night-cellar** *Hist.* a low-class tavern or place of resort during the night, situated in a cellar; **night chain** a chain for securing a door at night; **night-chair** a close-stool or commode for use at night; **night class** = *EVENING class*; **night clock** a clock with an interior light allowing the time to be read in the dark; **nightclothes** (*a*) clothes worn in bed; †(*b*) negligée or informal dress worn in the evening; **nightclub** a club or similar establishment that opens at night, usu. providing food, drink, and entertainment; **nightclubber** a frequenter of nightclubs; **nightclubbing** the frequenting of nightclubs; **nightclubby** *adjective* characteristic or fond of nightclubs; **night coach** (*a*) a coach that travels at night; (*b*) *US* a commercial aircraft flying at night; **night crawler** *N. Amer.* a large earthworm, *esp.* one caught at night to be used as fishing bait; **night cream** (a) cosmetic cream that is applied to the face at night; **night-crow** *arch.* a bird supposed to croak or cry during the night and to be of evil omen; **nightdress** a loose garment worn in bed, now *spec.* by women and children; **night effect** irregularity of the strength and apparent direction of received radio waves of certain frequencies, especially marked at night, owing to the reception of polarized waves reflected by the ionosphere; **night error**: in direction-finding due to night effect; **night eye** (*a*) *US* = CHESTNUT 3; (*b*) an eye able to see or adapted for seeing in the dark (usu. in *pl.*); **nightfall** the coming on of night, the end of daylight, the time of dusk; **night-fighter** a fighter aircraft used or designed for use at night; the pilot of such an aircraft; **night-flower** a flower that opens or blooms during the night; **night-flowering** *adjective* having flowers that open only at night; ***night-flowering cereus*** = ***night-blooming cereus*** above; **night-fly** *verb intrans.* fly in an aircraft at night; **night flying** flying in an aircraft at night; **night-flying** *adjective* (of an insect, bird, etc.) that flies at night; **night-gear** nightclothes; **night-glass** a short refracting telescope for use at night; **nightglow** METEOROLOGY the faint light emitted by the upper atmosphere at night; **nightgown** (*a*) *Hist.* a dressing-gown; a kind of gown worn by women in the 18th cent., orig. as an evening dress; (*b*) = ***nightdress*** above; **nightgowned** *adjective* wearing a nightgown; **night-hag** (now *rare*) a hag or female demon supposed to ride in the air at night; the nightmare; **nighthawk** (*a*) a nightjar; now *spec.* one of the American genus *Chordeiles* or related genera; (*b*) *fig.* a predatory person active at night; a nocturnal prowler; a person who stays up late or who goes out or works at night; **night-herd** *noun & verb* (*N. Amer.*) (*a*) *noun* the herding or guarding of cattle at night; (*b*) *verb intrans. & trans.* herd or guard (cattle) at night; **night-herder** *N. Amer.* a person who night-herds; **night-herding** the work of a night-herder; **night heron** a heron of the genus *Nycticorax* or the genus *Gorsachius*, *esp.* the black-crowned *N. nycticorax* and (*US*) the yellow-crowned *N. violaceus* (see also ***nankeen night heron*** s.v. NANKEEN *adjective*); **night horse** a horse used for work at night; **night-house** *Hist.* a tavern, public house, etc., remaining open all night; ***night jasmine***: see JASMINE 1; **night journey** (in Muslim tradition) the miraculous journey in which, in the space of a single night, the prophet Muhammad was transported to Jerusalem, ascended to heaven, and was returned to Mecca; **night-lamp** a lamp kept burning during the night, esp. in a bedroom; **night lark** a person who habitually goes about or out at night; ***night-latch***: see LATCH *noun*[1] 1; **night letter (telegram)** *Hist.* a cheap-rate overseas telegram delivered overnight; **night-life** manifestations of life at night; *spec.* the activities of pleasure-seekers at night, urban entertainments open at night; **night-light** (*a*) faint light perceptible during the night; (*b*) a light which burns or shines during the night; *spec.* an electric bulb, small thick candle, etc., giving a dim light during the night for a child, invalid, etc.; **night-line** (*a*) a line with baited hooks set to catch fish at night; (*b*) a telephone line on which a person may call for help, advice, etc., at night; **night lizard** a small nocturnal lizard of the family Xantusiidae, having large scales or bony plates on the head, occurring from the south-western US to Central America; **night-long** *adjective & adverb* (lasting or having lasted) for the whole night; **nightman** (*a*) a man employed during the night to empty cesspools etc. and to remove night-soil; (*b*) (usu. ***night man***) a man who works during the night or on a night-shift; **night monkey** a nocturnal monkey of the genus *Aotus*, of tropical Central and S. America, with a greyish back, orange or whiteish underside, and black and white face markings, the male of which has a hooting cry; also called ***owl monkey***, ***douroucouli***; **night-night** *interjection* (*colloq.*) good-night; **night nurse** a nurse employed to attend to a patient or patients during the night; **night-office** ROMAN CATHOLIC CHURCH a part of the canonical office performed during the night hours; **night-owl** (*a*) a nocturnal owl; (*b*) *colloq.* a person who is active late at night; **night paddock** *Austral. & NZ* a field where stock, esp. dairy cows, are kept overnight; **night parrot** a nocturnal green and yellow ground parrot, *Geopsittacus occidentalis*, of the Australian interior; **night-piece** (a painting or picture representing) a scene or landscape at night; **night-primrose** = ***EVENING primrose***; **night-rail** *Hist.* a woman's loose wrap, jacket, or dressing-gown worn after undressing or before dressing; **night-raven** (now *poet.*) a (real or mythical) nocturnal bird, sometimes identified as a night-owl, night heron, or nightjar; **night rider** a person who rides by night, esp. on horseback; *spec.* (*US*) a member of a mounted gang committing acts of violence, esp. to intimidate; **night riding** the activity of a night rider; **night-robe** (now chiefly *US*) a garment worn during the night; a nightdress; (now usu.) a dressing-gown; **night safe** a safe with an opening in the outer wall of a bank etc. for the deposit of money etc. at night or otherwise outside opening hours; **nightscape** = ***night-piece*** above; **night-scene** (a picture or dramatic representation of) a scene viewed or taking place at night; **night-scented** *adjective* giving off fragrance at night; ***night-scented stock***, a small annual cruciferous plant, *Matthiola longipetala* subsp. *bicornis*, grown for its fragrant lilac flowers which open at night; **night school** a school providing evening instruction for those working during the day; the process of being educated at such a school; **night scope** a night-vision telescope, used esp. as the telescopic sight of a rifle; **night-season** *arch.* the night-time; **night shift** (*a*) a shift or garment worn in bed, esp. by women; (*b*) a shift of workers employed during the night; the time during which such a shift works; **nightshirt** a long shirt or loose garment worn in bed, esp. by boys or men; **night-side** (*a*) the dark or bad aspect of a person or thing; (*b*) the side of a planet that is facing away from the sun and is therefore in darkness; **night sight** (*a*) the faculty of seeing during the night or in the dark; (*b*) a rifle-sight designed for shooting at night; **night-singer** a bird that sings by night; *spec.* the sedge-warbler; **night snake** any of several nocturnal African snakes; **night-soil** excremental matter removed at night from cesspools etc.; **night-spell** (*a*) a spell used as a protection against harm at night; (*b*) a spell used to cause harm or trouble at night; **nightspot** *colloq.* a nightclub or similar place open at night; **nightstand** (chiefly *N. Amer.*) a small, low, bedside table, typically having drawers; **night star** = ***EVENING star***; **night starvation** hunger at night; *transf.* lack of sexual gratification; **nightstick** (orig. *US*) a stick or truncheon carried by a police officer etc., esp. at night; **night-stool** a close-stool for use at night; **night-stop** *verb intrans.* stop for the night on a journey; **night storage heater**, **night storage radiator** an electric heater in which heat can be accumulated at night and released during the day; **night-sweat** profuse perspiration occurring during the night, symptomatic of certain diseases; **night table** = ***nightstand*** above; **night telegraph letter** *Hist.* a cheap-rate inland telegram delivered overnight; **night-terrors** feelings of terror experienced during the night, esp. by children, causing wakening from sleep (cf. PAVOR 2); **night-tide** (*a*) *arch.* the time of night, night-time; (*b*) a tide of the sea occurring during the night; **night-time** *noun & adjective* (*a*) *noun* the time between evening and morning; the time of night or darkness; (*b*) *adjective* of or pertaining to this time; **night-times** *adverb* (chiefly *dial.*) at night, during the night; **night vision** (*a*) a vision or dream during the night; (*b*) the faculty of seeing during the night or in the dark; ability to see only during the night or in the dark; (*c*) *attrib.* (***night-vision***) denoting goggles or other devices enabling the user to see objects in the dark; **night-walk** *verb trans.* walk or travel across (a place) at night; **night-walker** (*a*) (now *rare*) a person who walks about at night, esp. with criminal intentions; a bully, a thief; a streetwalker, a prostitute; (*b*) an animal that moves about at night; **night-walking** *noun* (*a*) walking or going about at night; (*b*) sleepwalking; **night-walking** *ppl adjective* that walks or goes about at night; **night-wanderer** a person who or thing which wanders at night; a person travelling at night; **night-wandering** *ppl adjective* that wanders at night; **night-watch** (*a*) a watch or guard kept during the night; the time during which such a watch is kept; (*b*) a person or group of people engaged in keeping watch during the night; (*c*) each of the (three or four) watches into which the night was divided by the Jews and Romans; any similar period or division of the night; ***in the night-watches***, during the wakeful and anxious or wearisome night; **night-watcher** a person who keeps watch during the night; **night-watching** keeping watch during the night; **night-watchman** (*a*) a person employed to keep watch at night; (*b*) CRICKET an inferior batsman sent in to bat when a wicket falls just before the end of a day's play, to avoid the dismissal of a better one in adverse conditions; **night-water** water which collects or is stored during the night; **night-wind** a wind that blows during the night; **night-work** work done, or which must be done, during the night; **night-worker** a person who works during the night.

■ **nightless** *adjective* E17. **nightward** *adjective* coming, taking place, etc., towards nightfall; leading towards night: M17. **nightwards** *adverb* (*rare*) towards night, westwards M19.

night /nʌɪt/ *verb*. ME.
[from the noun.]
1 *verb intrans.* Spend or pass the night; remain or lodge for the night. Now *Scot.* ME.
†**2** *verb intrans. impers.* Turn to night; grow dark. LME–E16.
3 *verb trans.* In *pass.* & as ***nighted*** *ppl adjective*. (Be) overtaken by night, (be) benighted. Now *Scot. & literary*. LME.
4 *verb trans.* In *pass.* & as ***nighted*** *ppl adjective*. (Made) dark or black as night. *literary*. E17.

nightcap /ˈnʌɪtkap/ *noun*. LME.
[from NIGHT *noun* + CAP *noun*[1].]
1 A cap worn in bed. LME. ▸**b** *fig.* A cloud of mist covering a mountain-top. Now *rare*. E17.
2 A drink, esp. an alcoholic drink, taken before going to bed. E19.
3 The final event in one day's series of sporting contests; *spec.* the second of two baseball games played by the same two teams on a single day. *N. Amer. colloq.* M20.
■ **nightcapped** *adjective* covered with or wearing a nightcap or nightcaps M17.

nighter /ˈnʌɪtə/ *noun*. M19.
[from NIGHT *noun* + -ER[1].]
A thing operating or happening at night. See also ***ALL-nighter***, ***FIRST-nighter***.

nightie /ˈnʌɪti/ *noun*. *colloq.* Also **-y**. L19.
[from *nightdress*, *nightgown* (see NIGHT *noun*) + -IE, -Y[6].]
A nightdress, a nightgown.

nightie-night *interjection* var. of NIGHTY-NIGHT.

nightingale /ˈnʌɪtɪŋɡeɪl/ *noun*[1].
[Old English *nihtegala* = Old Saxon, Old High German *nahtagala*, *nahti-* (Dutch *nachtegaal*, German *Nachtigall*), Old Norse *nætrgali*, from Germanic base of NIGHT *noun* + base meaning 'sing' (cf. YELL *verb*): alt. by insertion of *-n-* early in Middle English.]
1 a A small reddish-brown migratory thrush, *Luscinia megarhynchos*, noted for the melodious song of the male, especially noticeable by night. OE. ▸**b** With specifying word: any of various sweet-singing birds. E18.
2 A person likened to a nightingale, a melodious singer or speaker. (Earliest as a surname.) ME.
3 In full ***Dutch nightingale***. A frog. M18.
1b ***KENTISH nightingale***. ***SWEDISH nightingale***. ***thrush nightingale***: see THRUSH *noun*[1]. ***VIRGINIAN nightingale***. **3** CAMBRIDGESHIRE NIGHTINGALE.
Comb.: **nightingale floor** in Japan, a floor that emits a high-pitched sound when trodden on.

nightingale /ˈnʌɪtɪŋɡeɪl/ *noun*[2]. L19.
[Florence *Nightingale* (1820–1910), Brit. nurse and medical reformer.]
1 *Hist.* A kind of flannel wrap used to cover the shoulders and arms of a patient while confined to bed. L19.
2 ***Nightingale ward***, a type of long hospital ward with two rows of beds and a central point for the nurse in charge. M20.

nightjar /ˈnʌɪtdʒɑː/ *noun*. M17.
[from NIGHT *noun* + JAR *noun*[1]: cf. CHIRR, CHURR.]
A nocturnal insectivorous migratory bird, *Caprimulgus europaeus*, with grey-brown cryptic plumage and a distinctive churring call. Also (freq. with specifying word), any other similar bird of the family Caprimulgidae. Also called ***fern-owl***, ***goatsucker***, etc.

nightly /ˈnʌɪtli/ *adjective*. OE.
[from NIGHT *noun* + -LY[1].]
1 Coming, happening, or occurring during the night; accomplished or done by night. OE.
2 Belonging, pertaining, appropriate, or peculiar to the night; used by night; acting by night. Now *literary*. ME. ▸**b** Dark as, or with, night; resembling night; unenlightened. Now *literary*. LME.
3 Happening or occurring every night. E18.

> 📖 **1** E. YOUNG By nightly march he purpos'd to surprize. **2** E. JENNINGS To become acquainted with nightly creatures. **3** W. ABISH She was preparing his nightly cup of cocoa.

nightly /ˈnʌɪtli/ *adverb*. LME.
[from NIGHT *noun* + -LY[2].]
Every night; at or by night, during the night.

> 📖 SHAKES. *Rom. & Jul.* Chain me with roaring bears, Or hide me nightly in a charnel house. E. WAUGH Supplies came almost nightly in great profusion. A. PRYCE-JONES Being in college by nine nightly.

nightmare /ˈnʌɪtmɛː/ *noun & adjective*. ME.
[from NIGHT *noun* + MARE *noun*[2].]
▸ **A** *noun*. **1** A female spirit or monster supposed to settle on and produce a feeling of suffocation in a sleeping person or animal. ME.
2 Orig. (usu. ***the nightmare***), a feeling of suffocation or great distress felt during sleep. Now usu., a bad dream producing these or similar sensations; an oppressive or terrifying or fantastically horrible dream, fear, or experience. M16.

> 📖 **1** TENNYSON King Arthur panted hard Like one that feels a nightmare on his bed. **2** W. GOLDING He was breathing quickly like a man in the first stages of nightmare. V. CRONIN His sleep was troubled by dreadful nightmares. E. LEONARD He needed to . . put the nightmare of prison out of his mind. *Lancaster Guardian* The tax would be . . a bureaucratic nightmare.

▸ **B** *attrib.* or as *adjective*. Of the nature of a nightmare, nightmarish. M19.

> 📖 T. S. ELIOT You've had a cream of a nightmare dream. S. NAIPAUL Nightmare visions of imminent fascist take-over and genocidal doom.

■ **nightmarey** *adjective* nightmarish M19. **nightmarish** *adjective* of the nature of a nightmare; oppressive or terrifying enough to cause nightmares: M19. **nightmarishly** *adverb* L19.

nightmare /ˈnʌɪtmɛː/ *verb trans.* Now *rare*. M17.
[from the noun.]
Trouble as by a nightmare.

nights /nʌɪts/ *adverb*. Now *colloq. & N. Amer.* OE.
[from NIGHT *noun* + -S[3], later identified with -S[1]. Cf. DAYS *adverb*.]
During the night, by night, at night.

nightshade /ˈnʌɪtʃeɪd/ *noun*.
[Old English *nihtscada* corresp. to Middle Low German, Middle Dutch *nachtschade*, Old High German *nahtscato* (German *Nachtschatten*), app. formed as NIGHT *noun* + SHADE *noun*, prob. with allus. to the poisonous or narcotic properties of the berries.]
Any of various poisonous plants of the genus *Solanum* (family Solanaceae); *esp.* (more fully ***black nightshade***) *S. nigrum*, a garden weed with white flowers and black berries, and (more fully ***woody nightshade***) *S. dulcamara*, a scrambling plant of hedges with purple flowers and bright red berries. Also (in full ***deadly nightshade***), the related and even more poisonous plant *Atropa belladonna*, with drooping lurid purple flowers and black cherry-like fruit.
Phrases: **enchanter's nightshade** [alluding to the witch *Circe*, source of the genus name] any of several woodland plants of the genus *Circaea*, of the willowherb family, having small white flowers and fruit with hooked bristles. **Malabar nightshade** a tropical plant of the goosefoot family, *Basella alba*, grown in the Indian subcontinent as a pot-herb.

nighty *noun* var. of NIGHTIE.

nighty-night /nʌɪtiˈnʌɪt/ *interjection*. *colloq.* Also **nightie-**. L19.
[Redupl. of NIGHT *noun*: see -Y[6], -IE.]
Good-night.

nigiri zushi /ˌnɪɡɪri ˈzuːʃi/ *noun phr.* Also **nigiri**. L20.
[Japanese, from *nigiri-* (combining stem of *nigiru* clasp, clench, roll in the hands) + *-zushi* SUSHI.]
A type of sushi consisting of a small ball of rice, smeared with wasabi sauce and topped with raw fish or other seafood.

nig-nog /ˈnɪɡnɒɡ/ *noun*[1]. *slang*. M20.
[Origin unkn. Cf. NING-NONG.]
A foolish person; a raw and unskilled recruit.

nig-nog /ˈnɪɡnɒɡ/ *noun*[2]. *slang*. (*derog. & racially offensive*). M20.
[Redupl. of NIG *noun*[2].]
A black person.

†**nigon** *noun & adjective*. ME–L16.
[from NIG *noun*[1] + suffix of unkn. origin.]
= NIGGARD *noun* 1, *adjective* 1.
¶ Alt. by suffix-substitution to NIGGARD.

nigra /ˈnɪɡrə/ *noun & adjective*. *US* (chiefly *Southern US*). *derog. & considered racially offensive*. M20.
[Repr. a pronunc. Cf. NIGGA.]
= NEGRO *noun* 1, *adjective*.

nigrescence /nɪˈɡrɛs(ə)ns, nʌɪ-/ *noun*. M19.
[formed as next: see -ESCENCE.]
The process of becoming black; blackness; darkness of hair, eyes, or complexion.

nigrescent /nɪˈɡrɛs(ə)nt, nʌɪ-/ *adjective*. M18.
[Latin *nigrescent-* pres. ppl stem of *nigrescere* grow black, from *nigr-*, *niger* black: see -ESCENT.]
Blackish, somewhat black.

nigricant /ˈnɪɡrɪk(ə)nt/ *adjective*. L18.
[Latin *nigricant-* pres. ppl stem of *nigricare* be blackish, from *nigr-*, *niger* black: see -ANT[1].]
Black; BOTANY blackish, nigrescent.
■ †**nigricanting** *ppl adjective* blackening: only in E18.

nigrify /ˈnɪɡrɪfʌɪ/ *verb trans.* M17.
[from Latin *nigri-*, *niger* black + -FY.]
Blacken.

Nigritian /nɪˈɡrɪʃ(ə)n/ *adjective & noun*. *arch.* M18.
[from *Nigritia* (see below), from Latin *nigr-*, *niger* black, + -AN.]
▸ **A** *adjective*. Of or pertaining to Nigritia, a region in central Africa nearly co-extensive with Sudan; Sudanese. Also, (of a person) black. M18.
▸ **B** *noun*. A native or inhabitant of Nigritia; a Sudanese. L19.

Nigritic /nɪˈɡrɪtɪk/ *adjective & noun*. L19.
[from Latin *nigr-*, *niger* black + -ITIC. Cf. NEGRITIC.]
(Of or pertaining to) the Sudanic group of languages.
■ Earlier **Nigrotic** /nɪˈɡrɒtɪk/ *adjective* (*rare*) M19.

nigritude /ˈnɪɡrɪtjuːd/ *noun*. M17.
[Latin *nigritudo*, from *nigr-*, *niger* black: see -TUDE. Cf. NEGRITUDE.]
1 Blackness. M17.
2 A black thing, a black reputation. *rare*. M19.

nigromance, **nigromancer**, **nigromancy** *nouns* etc., see NECROMANCE etc.

nigrosine /ˈnɪɡrəsɪn/ *noun*. L19.
[from Latin *nigr-*, *niger* black + -OSE[1] + -INE[5].]
CHEMISTRY. Any of several black or blackish aniline compounds used in dyes, inks, and polishes.

nigrous /ˈnɪɡrəs/ *adjective*. *rare*. M19.
[from Latin *nigr-*, *niger* black + -OUS.]
Deep black.

nigua /ˈnɪɡwə/ *noun*. M16.
[Spanish.]
= JIGGER *noun*[2] 1.

NIH *abbreviation*. *US*.
National Institutes of Health.

nihang /ˈnɪhaŋ/ *noun*. L19.
[Persian = crocodile.]
A member of a militant Sikh group in the Indian subcontinent.

nihil /ˈnɪhɪl, ˈnʌɪ-/ *noun*. Now *rare*. L16.
[Latin = nothing. Cf. NICHIL *noun*, NIL *noun*[2] & *adjective*.]
1 A thing of no worth or value. L16.
2 Nothing. Formerly *spec*. (LAW) = NICHIL *noun* 2. E17.

nihilianism /nɪˈhɪljənɪz(ə)m, nʌɪ-/ *noun*. L19.
[from Latin NIHIL + -IAN + -ISM.]
THEOLOGY. The doctrine that in the nature of Jesus there was no human, but only a divine element.

nihilism /ˈnʌɪ(h)ɪlɪz(ə)m/ *noun*. In sense 4 usu. **N-**. E19.
[from Latin NIHIL + -ISM, partly after German *Nihilismus*, (in sense 4) French *nihilisme*, Russian *nigilizm*.]
1 Total rejection of current religious beliefs or moral principles, often involving a general sense of despair and the belief that life is devoid of meaning. E19.
2 a PHILOSOPHY. An extreme form of scepticism, involving the denial of all existence. M19. ▸**b** PSYCHOLOGY. The delusional belief that something (even the outside world or the patient's self) has ceased to exist or to function. L19.
3 Nothingness, non-existence. M19.
4 *Hist*. The doctrines or principles of the Russian Nihilists. M19.

nihilist /ˈnʌɪ(h)ɪlɪst/ *noun & adjective*. In sense A.2 & corresp. uses of the adjective usu. **N-**. M19.
[formed as prec. + -IST, partly after German *Nihilist*, French *nihiliste*, Russian *nigilist*.]
▶ **A** *noun*. **1** A believer in nihilism. M19.
2 *Hist*. A member of a revolutionary party in 19th-cent. and early 20th-cent. Russia which sought the complete overthrow of the established order and was willing to use terrorism to achieve this end. L19.
▶ **B** *attrib*. or as *adjective*. Of or pertaining to nihilists or nihilism. L19.
■ **nihiˈlistic** *adjective* of, pertaining to, or characterized by nihilism; of the nature of nihilism: M19.

nihility /nɪˈhɪlɪti, nʌɪ-/ *noun*. L17.
[medieval Latin *nihilitas*, from Latin NIHIL: see -ITY.]
1 The quality or state of being nothing; non-existence, nullity. L17.
2 A mere nothing, a trifle; a non-existent thing; a nullity. M18.

nihil obstat /nʌɪhɪl ˈɒbstat, nɪhɪl/ *noun phr*. M20.
[Latin, lit. 'nothing hinders' (the censor's formula of approval).]
A certificate or statement recording that a work has been approved by the Roman Catholic Church as free of doctrinal or moral error; a statement of official approval, authorization.

-nik /nɪk/ *suffix*. M20.
[from Russian (as SPUTNIK), Hebrew, and Yiddish.]
Forming nouns from nouns and adjectives, denoting a person or thing involved in or associated with the thing or quality specified, as ***beatnik***, ***folknik***, ***kibbutznik***, etc.

nikah /ˈniːkɑː/ *noun*. L19.
[Urdu & Arab. *nikāh* marriage (contract), matrimony.]
An Islamic marriage ceremony.

nikau /ˈniːkaʊ/ *noun*. M19.
[Maori.]
A New Zealand palm, *Rhopalostylis sapida* (also ***nikau palm***); the leaves of this palm, formerly used to build huts.

nikethamide /nɪˈkɛθəmʌɪd/ *noun*. M20.
[from alt. of NICOTINIC + ETH(YL + AMIDE, elems. of the systematic name.]
PHARMACOLOGY. A derivative of nicotinic acid used as a respiratory stimulant.
¶ A proprietary name for this drug is CORAMINE.

Nikkei /ˈnɪkeɪ/ *noun*. L20.
[Japanese, abbreviation of *Nihon Keizai Shimbun* Japanese Economic Journal (Japan's principal financial daily newspaper, which calculates the rate).]
Used *attrib*. and in comb. ***Nikkei Average***, ***Nikkei Stock Average***, (formerly) ***Nikkei Dow*** [Dow *noun*[2]] to designate an index of share prices on the Tokyo Stock Exchange.

†**nil** *noun*[1]. M16.
[Persian *nīl*: see ANIL.]
1 Any of various indigo-yielding leguminous plants of the genus *Indigofera*; indigo dye. M16–M19.
2 A kind of convolvulus with blue flowers. L16–M18.

nil /nɪl/ *noun*[2] & *adjective*. E19.
[Latin, contr. of NIHIL.]
▶ **A** *noun*. †**1** LAW. = NICHIL *noun* 2. Only in E19.
2 Nothing, no number or amount, (now esp. in scoring at games etc.). M19.

> 🕮 **2** *Times* The British Isles Rugby Union tourists beat South West Africa by nine points to nil. J. WAIN Such help as the old man could give . . amounted to nil.

Comb.: **nil-grade** PHILOLOGY = ***zero grade*** s.v. ZERO *noun & adjective*.
▶ **B** *adjective*. Containing, reporting, or consisting of nothing; non-existent. M20.

> 🕮 *Punch* Dull work, with long blank intervals, offering . . a nil return. P. CUTTING The streets of West Beirut, where the authority of the state was virtually nil.

nil admirari /nɪl admɪˈrɑːri/ *noun phr*. M18.
[Latin *nil admirari* (*prope res est una . . quae possit facere et servare beatum*) to wonder at nothing (is just about the only way a man can become contented and remain so), from Horace *Epistles* I. vi. 1.]
The attitude of indifference to the distractions of the outside world advocated by the Roman poet Horace.

nilas /ˈniːlas/ *noun*. M20.
[Russian.]
Partly refrozen ice forming a thin flexible layer on the surface of water.

nil desperandum /nɪl dɛspəˈrandəm/ *interjection*. E17.
[Latin *nil desperandum* (*Teucro duce et auspice Teucro*) no need to despair (with Teucer as your leader and Teucer to protect you), from Horace *Odes*.]
Do not despair, never despair.

Nile /nʌɪl/ *noun*. L19.
[A river which flows from east central Africa northwards through Egypt to the Mediterranean Sea.]
▶ **I 1** Used *attrib*. to designate animals inhabiting the Nile river system. L19.
1 Nile crocodile the African crocodile *Crocodylus niloticus*. **Nile lechwe** a grazing antelope, *Kobus megaceros*, of flood plains of the Nile. **Nile monitor** a very large aquatic monitor lizard of sub-Saharan Africa, *Varanus niloticus*, which is brownish with bands of yellow spots. **Nile perch** a large carnivorous percoid food fish, *Lates niloticus* (family Centropomidae), of rivers and lakes in north and central Africa.
▶ **II 2** ***Nile blue*** [after French *bleu de Nil*], (**a**) (of) a pale greenish blue; (**b**) (a salt, esp. the sulphate, of) a tetracyclic quaternary ammonium ion which is an azine dye used in cytology to stain fatty acids. L19.
3 ***Nile green***, (of) a pale bluish-green. L19.

nilgai /ˈnɪlɡʌɪ/ *noun*. Also (earlier) **nylghau** /ˈnɪlɡɔː/. Pl. **-s**, same. L18.
[Hindi *nīlgāe*, *nīlgao*, from Sanskrit *nīla* blue + *-gāvī*, *-gavī* cow.]
A large Indian antelope, *Boselaphus tragocamelus*, the male of which is blue-grey with white markings and short horns, the female tawny and without horns.

nill /nɪl/ *verb*. Long *arch*. Pa. t. †**nilled**, †**nould**.
[Old English *nyle* (pres. t.) from *ne* not + WILL *verb*[1]. Cf. Old Frisian *nil*, *nel*.]
1 *verb intrans*. Be unwilling, not want. Formerly also as aux. denoting simple futurity: will not. Foll. by *do*, *to do*. Now chiefly contrasting with *will*. OE.
2 *verb trans*. Not will (a thing, †*that*); refuse, reject; negative, prevent from happening etc. OE.

> 🕮 **1** TOLKIEN I must indeed abide the Doom of Men, whether I will or I nill. ***nill he, will he*** etc., ***will he, nill he*** etc.: see WILL *verb*[1]. ***willing or nilling***, ***willing nilling***: see WILLING *adverb*. **2** E. B. PUSEY When to will the same and nill the same, maketh of twain, one spirit.

nilly-willy /nɪlɪˈwɪli/ *adverb*. L19.
[By reversal of elems.]
= WILLY-NILLY.

Nilo- /ˈnʌɪləʊ/ *combining form*.
[from NILE + -O-.]
Forming nouns and adjectives with the sense 'of or pertaining to the Nile or the region of the Nile', esp. in names of language groups common to inhabitants of the region of the Nile and of some other specified region.
■ **Nilo-ˈHamite** *noun* a member of a Nilotic people M20. **Nilo-Haˈmitic** *adjective & noun* (**a**) *adjective* = NILOTIC *adjective* 2; (**b**) *noun* = NILOTIC *noun* 2: M19. **Nilo-Saˈharan** *adjective* of or pertaining to the regions of the Nile and the Sahara; *spec*. of or designating a language family including Sudanic and other northern and E. African languages: M20.

Nilometer /nʌɪˈlɒmɪtə/ *noun*. E18.
[from NILE + -OMETER, after Greek *Neilometrion*.]
A graduated pillar or other vertical surface, serving to indicate the height to which the Nile rises during its annual floods.
■ **Niloˈmetric** *adjective* of or pertaining to a Nilometer or the measurement of the height of the Nile E20.

Nilot /ˈnʌɪlɒt/ *noun*. Also **-ote**. Pl. **-otes** /-əˈtiːz/, **-ots**. L19.
[from NILE or from Greek *Neilōtēs*, from *Neilos* NILE: see -OT[2].]
A native of the region of the Upper Nile.

Nilotic /nʌɪˈlɒtɪk/ *adjective & noun*. M17.
[Latin *Niloticus* from Greek *Neilōtikos*, from *Neilos* NILE: see -OTIC.]
▶ **A** *adjective*. **1** Of, pertaining to, restricted to, or characteristic of the Nile or the Nile region or its inhabitants. M17.
2 *spec*. Designating or pertaining to a group of Sudanic languages spoken by some E. African peoples, as the Dinka, Luo, Nuer, and Shilluk; designating or pertaining to a people or the peoples speaking a language of this group. M19.
1 Nilotic crocodile = ***Nile crocodile***. **Nilotic monitor** = ***Nile monitor***.
▶ **B** *noun*. **1** = NILOT. E20.
2 The Nilotic group of languages. M20.

nilpotent /nɪlˈpəʊt(ə)nt/ *adjective*. L19.
[from NIL *noun*[2] & *adjective* + Latin *potent-*, *potens* power.]
MATH. Becoming zero when raised to some positive integral power.

nim /nɪm/ *noun*[1]. E20.
[Origin uncertain: perh. from next or German *nimm* imper. of *nehmen* take.]
A game in which two players alternately take one or more objects from any of several heaps, each trying to take, or to compel the other to take, the last remaining object.

nim *noun*[2] var. of NEEM.

nim /nɪm/ *verb*. *arch*. Infl. **-mm-**. Pa. t. & pple †**nempt**, **nimmed**, †**nom**; pa. pple also †**num**.
[Old English *niman* = Old Frisian *nima*, Old Saxon *niman* (Dutch *nemen*), Old High German *neman* (German *nehmen*), Old Norse *nema*, Gothic *niman*, from Germanic, rel. to Greek *nemein* deal out, distribute, possess, occupy.]
†**1** *verb trans*. Take. OE–M17.
†**2** *verb intrans*. Betake oneself, go. OE–LME.
3 *verb trans*. & *intrans*. Steal, pilfer, (something). OE.
■ **nimmer** *noun* ME.

nimb /nɪmb/ *noun*. M19.
[from Latin NIMBUS. Cf. French *nimbe*.]
A nimbus, a halo.
■ **nimbed** /nɪmd/ *adjective* having a nimb M19.

nimbi *noun pl*. see NIMBUS.

nimble /ˈnɪmb(ə)l/ *adjective & adverb*.
[Old English *næmel* from *niman*: see NIM *verb*, -LE[1]. For the intrusive *b* cf. *thimble*.]
▶ **A** *adjective*. †**1** Quick to seize or grasp at something, someone, etc. (*lit*. & *fig*.); wise. OE–L15.
2 Quick and light in movement or action; agile, swift. OE. ▸**b** Of a ship: fast and easily handled. *arch*. L16. ▸**c** Of a coin or sum of money: likely to circulate briskly. *arch*. M19.
3 a Ready, prepared. Freq. foll. by *in*, *to do*. Now *rare* or *obsolete*. M16. ▸†**b** Of a physical agent: acting rapidly. L17–M18.
4 a Of the mind etc.: quick to devise or plan; clever, versatile, alert. L16. ▸**b** Cleverly contrived, ingenious. E17.

> 🕮 **2** W. COWPER Proceeding with his nimblest pace. D. FRANCIS Maisie, for all her scarlet-coated bulk, was nimble on her feet. **c** C. READE He often sold his purchase on the road, for the nimble shilling tempted him. **4a** P. G. WODEHOUSE At home with these Bohemian revels, a man has to have a nimble wit. **b** S. JOHNSON I was . . initiated in a thousand . . nimble shifts, and sly concealments.

▶ **B** *adverb*. Nimbly. Now *rare* or *obsolete*. M16.
Comb. & special collocations: **nimble-fingered** *adjective* (**a**) dexterous; (**b**) light-fingered; **nimble-footed** *adjective* quick and light of foot; **nimble Will** a fast-spreading pasture-grass, *Muhlenbergia schreberi*, of the central US; **nimble-witted** *adjective* quick-witted.
■ **nimbleness** *noun* LME. †**nimbless** *noun* (*rare*) nimbleness L16–M17. **nimbly** *adverb* LME.

nimble /ˈnɪmb(ə)l/ *verb*. Now *rare*. E16.
[from prec.]
†**1** *verb trans*. Make nimble. E16–M17.
2 *verb intrans*. Move nimbly. L16.

nimbostratus /nɪmbə(ʊ)ˈstrɑːtəs, -ˈstreɪtəs/ *noun*. L19.
[from NIMBUS + -O- + STRATUS.]
METEOROLOGY. Orig. = CUMULONIMBUS. Now, a cloud or cloud-type, usu. occurring as an extensive thick layer at low altitude, from which precipitation falls (not necessarily reaching the ground) without any lightning or thunder.

nimbu-pani /ˈnɪmbuːˌpɑːni/ *noun*. M20.
[Hindi *nimbū* lime, lemon + *pānī* water.]
A drink of the Indian subcontinent consisting of lemon juice or lime-juice with sugar and ice or water.

nimbus /ˈnɪmbəs/ *noun*. Pl. **-bi** /-bʌɪ/, **-buses**. E17.
[Latin = cloud, rain, aureole.]
1 A bright or luminous cloud or cloudlike formation investing a god etc.; *transf*. a cloud of fine particles or other matter surrounding a person or thing. E17.

2 (A representation of) a halo surrounding the head of Jesus, a saint, etc. **E18.**
3 *METEOROLOGY.* A rain-cloud. Now *rare.* **E19.**

📖 **1** H. R. REYNOLDS Manhood was lost in the nimbus of celestial glory. M. GORDON The protective nimbus cast by his father's body. **2** W. DE LA MARE The golden nimbus of the windowed saint.

■ **nimbused** *adjective* (*a*) invested with or surrounded by a nimbus; (*b*) formed into a nimbus: **M19.**

Nimby /ˈnɪmbi/ *noun. slang.* **L20.**
[Acronym, from the slogan *not in my backyard.*]
A person who objects to the siting of something unpleasant or dangerous in his or her own locality.
■ **Nimbyism** *noun* **L20.**

nimiety /nɪˈmʌɪɪti/ *noun. literary.* **M16.**
[Latin *nimietas*, from *nimis* too much: see **-ITY.**]
Excess, too much; an instance of this.

niminy /ˈnɪmɪni/ *adjective. rare.* **L19.**
[Abbreviation.]
= next.

niminy-piminy /ˌnɪmɪni ˈpɪmɪni/ *adjective.* **L18.**
[Fanciful formation based on **NAMBY-PAMBY.** Cf. **MIMINY-PIMINY.**]
Mincing, affected; without force or spirit.

📖 W. GOLDING She had an exquisite niminy-piminy lady-like air.

nimious /ˈnɪmɪəs/ *adjective.* **L15.**
[from Latin *nimius*, from *nimis* too much: see **-IOUS.**]
Orig., exceedingly great. Later (now chiefly *SCOTS LAW*), excessive and vexatious.

Nimonic /nɪˈmɒnɪk/ *noun.* Also **n-**. **M20.**
[Arbitrary formation from **NICKEL** *noun.*]
(Proprietary name for) any of various nickel-based high-temperature alloys.

Nimrod /ˈnɪmrɒd/ *noun.* **M16.**
[Hebrew *Nimrōd*, great-grandson of Noah, traditional founder of the Babylonian dynasty and noted as a mighty hunter (*Genesis* 10:8–9).]
†**1** A tyrannical ruler; a tyrant. **M16–L17.**
2 A great or skilful hunter; a person given to hunting. **L16.**
■ **Nimrodian** /nɪmˈrəʊdɪən/ *adjective* of, pertaining to, or resembling Nimrod **M17.**

Nimzo-Indian /nɪmzəʊˈɪndɪən/ *adjective.* **M20.**
[from **NIMZO(WITSCH** + **INDIAN.**]
CHESS. Designating a form of Indian defence popularized by A. Nimzowitsch (see next), in which Black develops Black's king's bishop by moving it four squares to the square b4 (Kt5) instead of fianchettoing it.

Nimzowitsch /ˈnɪmzəvɪtʃ/ *noun.* **E20.**
[See below.]
CHESS. Used *attrib.* and in *possess.* to designate various methods of opening play introduced or popularized by the Latvian-born chess-player Aaron Nimzowitsch (1886–1935).

nincom /ˈnɪŋkəm/ *noun. arch. colloq.* Also **-cum.** **E19.**
[Abbreviation.]
= **NINCOMPOOP.**

nincompoop /ˈnɪŋkəmpuːp/ *noun.* Also (earlier) †**nic-**. **L17.**
[Origin uncertain: perh. from male forename *Nicholas* or *Nicodemus* (cf. French *nicodème* simpleton) with *-n-* due to assoc. with **NINNY**, + **POOP** *verb*[2].]
A simpleton, a foolish person.

📖 P. SCOTT I felt such a nincompoop.

■ **nincompoopery** *noun* behaviour characteristic of a nincompoop **E20.** **nincompoopiˈana** *noun pl.* [**-ANA**] (orig. *derog.*) publications or other items concerning or associated with the aesthetic movement **L19.** **nincompoopish** *adjective* somewhat like a nincompoop **L19.**

nincum *noun* var. of **NINCOM.**

nine /nʌɪn/ *adjective & noun (cardinal numeral).*
[Old English *nigon* = Old Frisian *nigun*, Old Saxon *nigun*, *nigon* (Dutch *negen*) from var. of Germanic word repr. by Old High German *niun*, German *neun*, Old Norse *níu*, Gothic *niun*, from Indo-European base repr. also by Latin *novem*, Greek *ennea*, Sanskrit *nava*.]
▶ **A** *adjective.* One more than eight (a cardinal numeral represented by 9 in arabic numerals, ix, IX in roman). **OE.**

📖 SHAKES. *3 Hen. VI* When I was crown'd, I was but nine months old. *Christian Aid News* Nine countries . . form the Amazon basin. ***cat-o'-nine-tails***: see **CAT** *noun*[1] 6. **Nine Days' Queen** Lady Jane Grey (1537–54), Queen of England for nine days following the death of Edward VI. **nine days' wonder** a person who or thing which is briefly famous. ***nine men's morris***: see **MORRIS** *noun*[1]. ***nine points***: see **POINT** *noun*[1]. **nine times out of ten** nearly always. ***the nine worthies***: see **WORTHY** *adjective, adverb, & noun.*

▶ **B** *noun.* **1** Nine persons or things identified contextually, as parts or divisions, years of age, points, runs, etc., in a game, chances (in giving odds), minutes, inches, shillings (now *Hist.*), pence, etc. **OE.**
2 One more than eight as an abstract number; the symbol(s) or figure(s) representing this (9 in arabic numerals, ix, IX in roman). **LME.**
3 The time of day nine hours after midnight or midday (on a clock, watch, etc., indicated by the numeral nine displayed or pointed to). **LME.**
4 The ninth of a set or series with numbered members, the one designated nine, (usu. ***number nine***, or with specification, as ***book nine***, ***chapter nine***, etc.); a size etc. denoted by nine, a shoe, glove, garment, etc., of such a size (also ***size nine***). **E16.**
5 A set of nine; a thing having a set of nine as an essential or distinguishing feature; *spec.* (*a*) a playing-card marked with nine pips or spots; (*b*) a team of nine in baseball. **L16.**

📖 **1** SWIFT Nine of the Vessels that attended me. DAY LEWIS My mother, at the age of nine or ten. **3** B. MOORE The car . . entered Proclamation Square sometime between nine and nine fifteen. **5** C. COTTON You have in your hand a Nine and two Sixes. R. LARDNER They made him try for a place on the Yale nine.

Phrases: **dressed up to the nines** *colloq.* dressed very elaborately. ***long nine***: see **LONG** *adjective*[1]. ***on cloud nine***: see **CLOUD** *noun.* **The Nine** (*a*) the nine Muses; (*b*) (now *Hist.*) the group of countries forming the enlarged European Economic Community between 1973 and 1981, following the admission of Denmark, the UK, and the Irish Republic.

Comb.: Forming compound cardinal numerals with multiples of ten from twenty to ninety, as ***thirty-nine***, (*arch.*) ***nine-and-thirty***, etc., and (*arch.*) their corresponding ordinals, as ***nine-and-thirtieth*** etc., and with multiples of a hundred, as ***209*** (read ***two hundred and nine***, US also ***two hundred nine***), ***5009*** (read ***five thousand and nine***, US also ***five thousand nine***), etc. With nouns + **-ER**[1] forming nouns with the sense 'something (identified contextually) being or having nine —s', as ***nine-seater*** etc. Special combs., as **nine-eyed** *adjective* having nine eyes; ***nine-eyed eel*** (*Scot.*), a lamprey; **nine-holes** (*a*) a game in which the players try to roll small balls into nine holes or arches, each hole or arch having a separate scoring value; (*b*) (chiefly *dial.*) a lamprey; (*c*) ***in the nine-holes*** (US), in a difficulty; **nine-killer** a shrike; **nine-nine-nine** (also written ***999***), in the US and Canada **nine-one-one** (also written ***911***), a telephone number connecting a caller with the emergency services (ambulance service, fire brigade, police); **ninepence** nine pence, esp. of the old British currency before decimalization; *Hist.* a coin representing this; ***as neat as ninepence***, ***as right as ninepence***, etc. (*arch. colloq.*) as neat, right, etc., as possible; ***ninepence in the shilling***, ***no more than ninepence in the shilling*** (now *dial. & arch. colloq.*), of low intelligence, not very bright; **ninepenny** *adjective* worth or costing ninepence; **ninepin** (*a*) in *pl.* (usu. treated as *sing.*), a game in which nine skittles are set up and bowled at to be knocked down; (*b*) a skittle used in this game (usu. in *pl.*); (*c*) ***ninepin block*** (**NAUTICAL**), a block resembling such a pin or skittle in shape; **nine-tenths** *fig.* nearly all; **nine-to-five** *adjective* of or pertaining to (the type of) standard office hours; **nine-to-fiver** a person who works standard office hours.

■ **ninefold** *adjective, noun, & adverb* (*a*) *adjective* nine times as great or as numerous; having nine parts, divisions, elements, or units; (*b*) *noun* (*rare*) a set of nine; formerly also, a ninefold amount; (*c*) *adverb* to nine times the number or quantity: **OE.**

nineteen /nʌɪnˈtiːn, ˈnʌɪntiːn/ *adjective & noun (cardinal numeral).*
[Old English *nigontȳne* = Old Frisian *niogentena*, Old Saxon *nigentein* (Dutch *negentien*), Old High German *niunzehan* (German *neunzehn*), Old Norse *nítján*, from Germanic base of **NINE**, **-TEEN.**]
▶ **A** *adjective.* One more than eighteen (a cardinal numeral represented by 19 in arabic numerals, xix, XIX in roman). **OE.**

📖 M. S. POWER Nineteen children . . sat waiting for the lesson to start.

▶ **B** *noun.* **1** Nineteen persons or things identified contextually, as years of age, points, runs, etc., in a game, chances (in giving odds), minutes, inches, shillings (now *Hist.*), pence, etc. **ME.**
2 One more than eighteen as an abstract number; the symbols or figures representing this (19 in arabic numerals, xix, XIX in roman). **LME.**
3 The nineteenth of a set or series with numbered members, the one designated nineteen, (usu. ***number nineteen***, or with specification, as ***book nineteen***, ***chapter nineteen***, etc.); a size denoted by nineteen, a garment etc. of such a size, (also ***size nineteen***). **E16.**
4 A set of nineteen; a thing having a set of nineteen as an essential or distinguishing feature. **L18.**

📖 **1** A. WALKER She was Katherine Degos . . , nineteen and with a wasp waist. ***talk nineteen to the dozen***: see **TALK** *verb.*

Comb.: Forming compound numerals with multiples of a hundred as ***619*** (read ***six hundred and nineteen***, US also ***six hundred nineteen***), ***6019*** (read ***six thousand and nineteen***, US also ***six thousand nineteen***), etc. In dates used for one thousand nine hundred, as ***1912*** (read ***nineteen twelve***), ***nineteen-nineties***, etc. With nouns + **-ER**[1] forming nouns with the sense 'something (identified contextually) being of or having nineteen —s', as ***nineteen-pounder*** etc.

nineteenth /nʌɪnˈtiːnθ, ˈnʌɪntiːnθ/ *adjective & noun (ordinal numeral).*
[Old English *nigontēoþa* etc., repl. in Middle English by forms from **NINETEEN** + **-TH**[2].]
▶ **A** *adjective.* Next in order after the eighteenth, that is number nineteen in a series, (represented by 19th). **OE.**
the nineteenth hole *slang* (the bar-room in) a golf clubhouse.
▶ **B** *noun.* **1** The nineteenth person or thing of a category, series, etc., identified contextually, as day of the month, (following a proper name) person, esp. monarch or pope, of the specified name, etc. **LME.**
2 *MUSIC.* An interval embracing nineteen notes on the diatonic scale; a note a nineteenth above another given note; a chord of two notes a nineteenth apart. **L16.**
3 Each of nineteen equal parts into which something is or may be divided, a fraction which when multiplied by nineteen gives one. **E17.**
Comb.: Forming compound ordinal numerals with multiples of a hundred, as ***three-hundred-and-nineteenth*** (***319th***), ***five-thousand-and-nineteenth*** (***5019th***), etc.
■ **nineteenthly** *adverb* in the nineteenth place **L17.**

ninetieth /ˈnʌɪntɪɪθ/ *adjective & noun (ordinal numeral).* **OE.**
[from **NINETY** + **-TH**[2].]
▶ **A** *adjective.* Next in order after the eighty-ninth, that is number ninety in a series, (represented by 90th). **OE.**
▶ **B** *noun.* **1** The ninetieth person or thing of a category, series, etc., identified contextually. **OE.**
2 Each of ninety equal parts into which something is or may be divided, a fraction which when multiplied by ninety gives one. **L20.**
Comb.: Forming compound ordinal numerals with multiples of a hundred, as ***one-hundred-and-ninetieth*** (***190th***), ***two-thousand-and-ninetieth*** (***2090th***), etc., and (*arch.*) with numerals below ten, as ***three-and-ninetieth*** etc.

ninety /ˈnʌɪnti/ *adjective & noun (cardinal numeral).* **OE.**
[from **NINE** + **-TY**[2].]
▶ **A** *adjective.* Nine times ten (a cardinal numeral represented by 90 in arabic numerals, xc, XC in roman). **OE.**
▶ **B** *noun.* **1** Ninety persons or things identified contextually, as years of age, points, runs, etc., in a game, chances (in giving odds), etc. **OE.**
2 Nine times ten as an abstract number; the symbols or figures representing this (90 in arabic numerals, xc, XC in roman). **LME.**
3 The ninetieth of a set or series with numbered members, the one designated ninety, (usu. ***number ninety***, or with specification, as ***chapter ninety***, ***verse ninety***, etc.); a size etc. denoted by ninety (also ***size ninety***). **E16.**
4 In *pl.* The numbers from 90 to 99 inclusive, esp. denoting years of a century or units of a scale of temperature; *one's* years of life between the ages of 90 and 99. **L19.**
4 naughty nineties: see **NAUGHTY** *adjective* 4.
Comb.: Forming compound numerals (cardinal or ordinal) with numerals below ten, as ***ninety-three***, (*arch.*) ***three-and-ninety*** (***93***), ***ninety-third*** (***93rd***), etc., and (cardinals) with multiples of a hundred, as ***590*** (read ***five hundred and ninety***, US also ***five hundred ninety***), ***5090*** (read ***five thousand and ninety***, US also ***five thousand ninety***), etc.
■ **ninetyish** *adjective* (*a*) about ninety (in age, measurements, etc.); (*b*) of, pertaining to, or characteristic of the 1890s; resembling or recalling the fashions etc. of the 1890s: **E20.**

Ninevite /ˈnɪnɪvʌɪt/ *noun.* **M16.**
[ecclesiastical Latin *Ninivitae* (pl.), from *Ninive* Nineveh: see **-ITE**[1].]
A native or inhabitant of the ancient city of Nineveh, capital of Assyria from the reign of Sennacherib (704–681 BC) until its sack in 612 BC.

ning-nong /ˈnɪŋnɒŋ/ *noun.* Now chiefly *Austral. slang.* Also **†-nang.** **M19.**
[Origin unkn. Cf. **NIG-NOG** *noun*[1].]
A fool, a stupid person.

Ningre Tongo /ˈnɪŋgreɪ ˈtɒŋgəʊ/ *noun & adjectival phr.* **M20.**
[Prob. from Taki-Taki, from **NIGGER** *noun* + **TONGUE** *noun.*]
(Of) an English-based creole language of Suriname.

ninhydrin /nɪnˈhʌɪdrɪn/ *noun.* **E20.**
[from *nin-* of unkn. origin + **HYDRO-** + **-IN**[1].]
CHEMISTRY. A bicyclic compound which forms deeply coloured products with primary amines and is used in analytical tests for amino acids; 1,2,3-indantrione hydrate, $C_9H_6O_4$.

ninja /ˈnɪndʒə/ *noun.* Pl. same. **M20.**
[Japanese = spy.]
A person, esp. a Japanese samurai, expert in *ninjutsu*.

ninjutsu /nɪnˈdʒʌtsuː/ *noun.* **M20.**
[Japanese, from *nin* stealth, invisibility + *jutsu* art, science.]
The traditional Japanese technique of espionage, developed in feudal times for military purposes and subsequently used in the training of samurai.

ninny /ˈnɪni/ *noun. colloq.* **L16.**
[Origin uncertain: perh. from **INN(OCENT** with prefixed *n-*: see **-Y**[6].]
A simpleton; a fool.

> 📖 DENNIS POTTER A mealy-mouthed pasty-faced . . ninny like him.

■ **ninnyish** *adjective* characteristic of a ninny; foolish: **E19.**

ninny-hammer /ˈnɪnɪhamə/ *noun. arch.* **L16.**
[App. from prec. with unexpl. 2nd elem.]
A simpleton.

ninon /ˈniːnɒn, *foreign* ninɔ̃/ *noun & adjective.* **E20.**
[French.]
▶ **A** *noun.* A lightweight dress fabric of silk, nylon, etc. **E20.**
▶ **B** *attrib.* or as *adjective.* Made of ninon. **E20.**

ninth /ˈnʌɪnθ/ *adjective & noun (ordinal numeral).*
[Old English *nigoþa*, repl. in Middle English by forms from **NINE** + **-TH**[2].]
▶ **A** *adjective.* Next in order after the eighth, that is number nine in a series, (represented by 9th). **OE.**
ninth part *arch.* = sense B.2 below.
▶ **B** *noun.* **1** The ninth person or thing of a category, series, etc., identified contextually, as day of the month, (following a proper name) person, esp. monarch or pope, of the specified name, etc. **OE.**
2 Each of nine equal parts into which something is or may be divided, a fraction which when multiplied by nine gives one, (= ***ninth part*** above). **ME.**
3 MUSIC. An interval embracing nine consecutive notes in the diatonic scale; a note a ninth above another note; a chord of two notes a ninth apart, or based around the ninth of a note. **L16.**
Comb.: Forming compound numerals with multiples of ten, as ***forty-ninth*** (49th), ***five-thousand-and-ninth*** (5009th), etc.
■ **ninthly** *adverb* in the ninth place **LME.**

Niobe /ˈnʌɪəbi/ *noun.* **L16.**
[Greek *Niobē*, the legendary daughter of Tantalus, turned into stone while weeping for her murdered children.]
An inconsolable bereaved woman, a weeping woman.

niobium /nʌɪˈəʊbɪəm/ *noun.* **M19.**
[from **NIOBE** (from the element's association with tantalum) + **-IUM.**]
A soft greyish-white chemical element, atomic no. 41, which is one of the transition metals, occurs in tantalite, columbite, and other minerals, and is used in superconducting alloys. (Symbol Nb.)
¶ Formerly also called ***columbium***.
■ **ˈniobate** *noun* a salt containing oxyanions of niobium **M19.** **niobian** *adjective* (MINERALOGY) having a constituent element partly replaced by niobium **M20.** **niobic** *adjective* of, pertaining to, or derived from niobium; ***niobic acid***, a weakly acidic hydrated compound precipitated from niobate solutions: **M19.**

niopo /niːˈəʊpəʊ/ *noun.* Also **yopo** /ˈjəʊpəʊ/. **M19.**
[Perh. from Tupi.]
A hallucinogenic snuff used by S. American Indians, prepared from the seeds of the leguminous tree *Anadenanthera peregrina* and related species.

nip /nɪp/ *noun*[1]. **M16.**
[from **NIP** *verb*[1].]
▶ **I 1 a** An act of compressing or catching something between two edges, points, etc.; a pinch; a sharp squeeze, a bite. **M16.** ▸**b** NAUTICAL. Severe pressure exerted by ice on the sides of a vessel; the crushing effect of this. **M19.** ▸**c** NAUTICAL. The grip of a rope at a point where it is twisted round something; part of a rope held fast in this way. **M19.** ▸**d** A break or interruption in a seam of coal between strata. **M19.**
2 A sharp remark or comment; a rebuke, a reproof. Now *rare.* **M16.**
3 a A check to vegetation caused by cold; (a nipping effect of) the cold producing this. **E17.** ▸**b** The quality of being pungent; a pungent flavour. *Scot.* **E19.**
4 CRICKET. †**a** A slight touch or stroke given to the ball by a batsman. **E–M18.** ▸**b** The quality in bowling causing the ball to rise sharply. **M20.**

> 📖 **1a** R. BADEN-POWELL A judiciously applied nip of his sharp little jaws. **2** M. ARNOLD Many a shrewd nip has he . . given to the Philistines, this editor. **3a** B. PYM A fine . . autumn morning, but there was quite a nip in the air.

▶ **II 5** Orig., a cutpurse, a pickpocket. Later, a niggardly person, a person who drives hard bargains; a cheat. Now *dial. & arch. slang.* **L16.**
6 a A device which nips something; *spec.* (in apparatus for combing silk or wool) a mechanism for catching and moving the material. **L17.** ▸**b** The narrow gap or area of contact between two rollers in a mechanism. **L19.**
▶ **III 7** A small portion, *esp.* one pinched off something; a fragment, a little bit. **E17.**
8 PHYSICAL GEOGRAPHY. A low cliff cut along a gently sloping coastline by wave action. Also, a notch cut similarly along the base of a cliff. **L19.**

> 📖 **7** D. MASSON The minutest . . animalcule has its little nip of a cosmos.

Phrases: **nip and tuck** (chiefly *N. Amer.*) neck and neck. **put in the nips** *Austral. & NZ colloq.* cadge, borrow, or extort money.

nip /nɪp/ *noun*[2]. **L18.**
[Prob. abbreviation of **NIPPERKIN.**]
Orig., a half-pint of ale. Later, a small quantity of spirits.

> 📖 D. H. LAWRENCE Her father kept taking a nip of brandy.

Comb.: **nip bottle** a miniature bottle of spirits.

Nip /nɪp/ *noun*[3] *& adjective. slang (derog. & racially offensive).* **M20.**
[Abbreviation of **NIPPONESE.**]
▶ **A** *noun.* A Japanese person. **M20.**
▶ **B** *adjective.* Japanese. **M20.**

nip *noun*[4] var. of **NEP** *noun*[1].

nip /nɪp/ *verb*[1]. Infl. **-pp-**. **LME.**
[Prob. of Low Dutch origin.]
▶ **I** *verb trans.* **1** Compress or catch between two edges, points, etc.; pinch, squeeze sharply, bite. **LME.** ▸†**b** Close up (a glass vessel) by compressing the heated end of the neck or tube. Also foll. by *up.* **L16–M17.** ▸**c** NAUTICAL. Secure (a rope) by twisting it round something. **M17.** ▸**d** NAUTICAL. Of ice: squeeze or crush (the sides of a vessel). **M19.**
2 Remove by pinching etc. Freq. foll. by *off.* **LME.** ▸**b** Strip or reduce the amount of by pinching or biting. Chiefly *Scot. rare.* **L16.** ▸**c** Cadge; borrow or extort (money). Cf. ***put in the nips*** s.v. **NIP** *noun*[1]. *slang* (chiefly *Austral.*). **E20.**
3 Snatch, seize; take *away, out, up.* Chiefly *dial. & slang.* **LME.** ▸**b** Arrest. *slang.* **M16.**
4 Retard the development of; (of cold, frost, etc.) cause pain or damage to; retard the growth of (vegetation). **M16.**
†**5** Rebuke, reprove; direct sharp comments against. **M16–E17.**
6 Concern sharply and closely; affect painfully, vex. Now *rare.* **M16.**
7 Defeat narrowly in a sporting contest. *N. Amer.* **M20.**

> 📖 **1** E. M. FORSTER She caught up an old man . . and nipped him playfully upon the arm. N. ALGREN Dove . . felt his heel nipped gently. **2** J. MORTIMER The small shoots . . must be nipt off. **b** D. M. MOIR The milk-cows were nipping the clovery parks. **3** J. POYER Memling . . found the packet of cigarettes . . but the young man nipped them from his hand. **4** BROWNING Nip these foolish fronds Of hope a-sprout. G. GREENE An early fly nipped by the cold died noisily. **6** J. EARLE Not a word can bee spoke, but nips him somewhere. **7** *American Speech* Oregon nips St. Mary's.

▶ **II** *verb intrans.* **8** Give a nip; inflict a sharp pinch, squeeze, or bite. **LME.** ▸**b** Ache, smart. Chiefly *Scot.* **M18.**
†**9** Pick pockets, steal. *slang.* **L16–M17.**
10 Move rapidly or nimbly; go quickly. Foll. by adverb or preposition. *colloq.* **E19.** ▸**b** Of a cricket ball: come sharply *off* the pitch. **L19.**

> 📖 **8** R. KIPLING Machinery that . . punches and hoists and nips. **10** M. GILBERT If you nip along now . . you could catch her. C. M. OMAN The visiting English . . quietly nipped off. J. CASEY We nipped into the bird sanctuary.

Phrases: ***nip in the bud***: see **BUD** *noun*[1]. †**nip in the head** (*a*) overpower by suddenly catching by the head, make helpless in this way; (*b*) *fig.* give a decisive or final check to.
Comb.: **nipcheese** †(*a*) *slang* a ship's purser; (*b*) (now *arch. & dial.*) a miserly person; **nipfarthing** *arch.* a miserly person.
■ **nipping** *ppl adjective* (*a*) that nips; (*b*) causing sharp physical or mental pain, stinging, blighting: **M16.** **nippingly** *adverb* **M16.**

nip /nɪp/ *verb*[2] *intrans. & trans.* Infl. **-pp-**. **M19.**
[from **NIP** *noun*[2].]
Drink (spirits etc.) in nips.

nipa /ˈniːpə, ˈnʌɪpə/ *noun.* **L16.**
[Malay *nipah*.]
†**1** A toddy made from the sap of the nipa-palm. **L16–E17.**
2 A palm tree, *Nypa fruticans*, of mangrove swamps in tropical Asia and Australia, having a creeping rhizome and large feathery leaves (also ***nipa-palm***); foliage of this, used as thatch. **L18.**

Nipkow disc /ˈnɪpkɒf dɪsk/ *noun phr.* **M20.**
[from Paul *Nipkow* (1860–1940), Pomeranian electrical engineer.]
A scanning disc in some early television transmitters and receivers having a line of small apertures near the circumference arranged in a spiral of one complete turn.

Nipmuck /ˈnɪpmʌk/ *noun & adjective.* **M17.**
[Algonquian.]
▶ **A** *noun.* Pl. same, **-s.** A member of an extinct Algonquian people of southern New England. **M17.**
▶ **B** *attrib.* or as *adjective.* Of or pertaining to this people. **L18.**

nipper /ˈnɪpə/ *noun & verb.* **M16.**
[from **NIP** *verb*[1] + **-ER**[1].]
▶ **A** *noun.* **I 1 a** A person who nips. Now *rare* in *gen.* sense. **M16.** ▸**b** A miserly person. *arch.* **L16.** ▸**c** Any of several wrasses, *esp.* the American cunner. *US.* **L19.** ▸**d** Any of several burrowing prawns of the order Thalassinidea, used as bait. Also called ***yabby***. *Austral.* **L19.**
†**2** A thief, a pickpocket. *slang.* **L16–L18.**
3 a Chiefly *Hist.* A boy assisting a costermonger etc. **M19.** ▸**b** A young boy or girl; a child; the smallest or youngest of a family. *slang.* **M19.**

> 📖 **3b** G. W. TARGET Up half the night with the nipper—cutting his first tooth.

▶ **II 4** In *pl.* ▸**a** An instrument for gripping or cutting; forceps, pincers, pliers. Also ***pair of nippers***. **M16.** ▸**b** Handcuffs. *slang.* **E19.** ▸**c** Eyeglasses, pince-nez. *arch. slang.* **L19.**
5 NAUTICAL. **a** A piece of braided cordage used to prevent a cable from slipping. **E17.** ▸**b** A kind of thick woollen mitten or glove used in cod-fishing to protect the wrists and hands. *US.* **M19.**
6 a A horse's incisor. Usu. in *pl.* **L17.** ▸**b** A crustacean's claw, a chela. Usu. in *pl.* **M18.**
7 A piece of machinery for gripping and holding; *spec.* (in wool-combing machinery) a mechanism for catching and moving forward the material. **L18.**
▶ **B** *verb trans.* **1** NAUTICAL. Secure (a rope etc.) with nippers. **M16.**
2 Arrest. *slang. rare.* **M19.**

nipperkin /ˈnɪpəkɪn/ *noun.* Now *rare.* **E17.**
[Rel. to Low Dutch *nippen* sip, whence German *nippen*, Danish *nippe*: cf. **-ER**[1], **-KIN.**]
A small vessel for alcoholic liquor, containing up to half a pint; the capacity of such a vessel as a measure. Also, such a vessel and its contents; a small quantity of wine, beer, etc.

nipple /ˈnɪp(ə)l/ *noun & verb.* As noun also (earlier) †**neble**, †**nibble**. **M16.**
[Origin uncertain: perh. dim. of **NEB**: see **-LE**[1].]
▶ **A** *noun.* **1 a** The small prominence, composed of vascular erectile tissue, in which the milk ducts of the mammary glands terminate externally in all female mammals (except monotremes); *esp.* that of a woman's breast; a teat. Also, the analogous structure of a male. **M16.** ▸**b** The teat of a feeding-bottle. **L19.**
2 A device resembling a nipple in form and serving to dispense a fluid in controlled amounts. **L16.**
3 A nipple-like protuberance on the surface of the skin, *esp.* one forming the outlet of a secretory gland. **E18.**
4 a Chiefly *Hist.* A short perforated projection on a firearm for holding a percussion cap. **E19.** ▸**b** A nipple-like projection on glass, metal, etc. **M19.**
5 A small rounded elevation on the summit of a hill or mountain. **M19.**
6 A short section of pipe with a screw-thread at each end for coupling. **L19.**
Comb.: **nipplewort** a slender annual plant with small yellow heads, *Lapsana communis*, of the composite family, common by roadsides, as a garden weed, etc.
▶ **B** *verb trans.* Provide with a nipple or nipples. **L19.**
■ **nippled** *adjective* provided with or having a nipple or nipples **L19.** **nippleless** /-l-l-/ *adjective* **M19.** **nipple-like** *adjective* resembling (that of) a nipple, of the shape of a nipple **E19.**

Nipponese /nɪpəˈniːz/ *noun & adjective.* **M19.**
[from Japanese *Nippon* Japan, lit. 'land of the rising sun', from *ni(chi* the sun + *pon, hon* source: see **-ESE.**]
▶ **A** *noun.* Pl. same.
1 A Japanese person. **M19.**
2 The Japanese language. **E20.**
▶ **B** *adjective.* Japanese. **M19.**

Nippon vellum /nɪpɒn ˈvɛləm/ *noun phr.* **E20.**
[from *Nippon* (see prec.) + **VELLUM.**]
= ***Japanese vellum*** s.v. **JAPANESE** *adjective.*

Nippy /ˈnɪpi/ *noun. slang* (now *Hist.*). **E20.**
[from **NIPPY** *adjective.*]
A waitress; *spec.* a waitress in any of the restaurants of J. Lyons & Co. Ltd., London.

nippy /ˈnɪpi/ *adjective.* **L16.**
[from **NIP** *verb*[1] + **-Y**[1].]
1 Nipping; inclined to nip; (esp. of the weather) chilly, cold. **L16.**
2 Sharp, quick, active, nimble. *colloq.* **M19.**

> 📖 **1** M. ALLINGHAM It was getting kind of nippy, so I went for a walk. **2** J. D. ASTLEY I told him he would have to be pretty nippy. *Times Lit. Suppl.* To supply the new 'project managers' with nippy little cars.

■ **nippily** *adverb* **M17.** **nippiness** *noun* **E20.**

NIREX /ˈnʌɪrɛks/ *abbreviation.*
Nuclear Industry Radioactive Waste Executive.

niridazole /nʌɪˈrʌɪdəzəʊl/ *noun.* **M20.**
[from **NI(T)R(O-** + **IM)ID(E** + **AZOLE.**]
PHARMACOLOGY. An anthelmintic drug which has been used to treat schistosomiasis.

nirvana /nɪəˈvɑːnə/ *noun.* **M19.**
[Sanskrit *nirvāṇa* use as noun of pa. pple of *nirvā-* be extinguished, from *nis-* out + *vā-* to blow.]
In BUDDHISM, the experience that comes to a person in life when greed, hatred, and delusion are extinguished and enlightenment gained, and the release from the effects

of karma and the cycle of death and rebirth that comes when an enlightened person dies. In HINDUISM & JAINISM, liberation of the soul from the effects of karma and from bodily existence.

Comb.: **Nirvana principle** PSYCHOANALYSIS the attraction towards a state of oblivion, usu. (following Freud) identified as expression of an instinctive death-wish.

■ **Nirvanist** *noun* a person who experiences nirvana L19.

nis /nɪs/ *noun*. Pl. **nisses**. M19.
[Danish & Swedish *nisse*.]
In Scandinavian folklore, a kind of brownie or friendly goblin frequenting barns, stables, etc.

Nisan /ˈnɪs(ə)n, ˈniːsɑːn/ *noun*. LME.
[Hebrew *Nīsān*.]
In the Jewish calendar, the seventh month of the civil and first of the religious year, usu. coinciding with parts of March and April. Formerly called ***Abib***.

nisei /ˈniːseɪ/ *noun*. Pl. same. M20.
[Japanese, from *ni-* second + *sei* generation.]
An American whose parents were immigrants from Japan.

Nishga /ˈnɪʃgə/ *noun & adjective*. Also **Nisgha** /ˈnɪsgə/, (earlier) **Niska** /ˈnɪskə/. Pl. of noun same, **-s**. L19.
[Tsimshian *nisgueʹa*.]
A member of, of or pertaining to, a branch of the Tsimshian people of British Columbia inhabiting the Nass river basin; (of) the Tsimshian dialect of this people. Also called ***Nass***.

nisi /ˈnʌɪsʌɪ/ *postpositive adjective*. M19.
[Latin = unless.]
LAW. That takes effect only on certain conditions, not final.
decree nisi: see DECREE *noun*.

nisin /ˈnʌɪsɪn/ *noun*. M20.
[from Group *N* inhibitory substance + -IN¹.]
PHARMACOLOGY. A mixture of related polypeptides produced by the bacterium *Streptococcus lactis* which is active against Gram-positive bacteria and is used in some countries as a food preservative.

nisi prius /nʌɪsʌɪ ˈprʌɪəs/ *noun phr*. LME.
[Latin = unless previously (the opening words in a clause of the writ).]
LAW (now *Hist.*).
1 A writ directing a sheriff to provide a jury at the Court of Westminster unless the assize judges came beforehand to the county from which the jury was to be drawn; the clause in such a writ of which the opening words are '*nisi prius*'. Also, the authority to try causes conferred on judges by this clause. LME.
2 An action tried under such a writ. LME.
3 The hearing of civil causes by judges in the Crown Court or assize court; court business of this kind. M16.

Niska *noun & adjective* see NISHGA.

Nissen /ˈnɪs(ə)n/ *noun*. E20.
[Lt.-Col. Peter Norman *Nissen* (1871–1930), its Brit. inventor.]
In full ***Nissen hut***. A tunnel-shaped hut of corrugated iron with a cement floor.

nisses *noun* pl. of NIS.

Nissl /ˈnɪs(ə)l/ *noun*. L19.
[Franz *Nissl* (1860–1919), German neurologist.]
ANATOMY. Used *attrib.* and in *possess.* with ref. to a method for staining nerve cells.
Nissl body a large basophilic granule containing ribosomes and found in the cell body of neurones. **Nissl degeneration** degeneration of the body of a neurone and disintegration of its Nissl bodies after its axon is cut. **Nissl granule** = ***Nissl body*** above. **Nissl stain**, **Nissl's stain** a dye which stains the cell bodies of neurones, *esp.* methylene blue. **Nissl substance** Nissl bodies collectively.

nisus /ˈnʌɪsəs/ *noun*. L17.
[Latin, from *niti* strive, endeavour.]
Effort, endeavour, impulse.

nit /nɪt/ *noun*¹.
[Old English *hnitu* = Middle Low German, Middle Dutch *nēte* (Dutch *neet*), Old High German (*h*)*niz* (German *Niss*(*e*)), from West Germanic from Indo-European (cf. Greek *konid-*, *konis*).]
1 The egg or the young of a louse or other parasitic insect; *spec.* the egg of the head louse, esp. when attached to hair. OE. ▸†**b** A gnat, a small fly. *rare*. M16–L17.
2 A contemptible person, *esp.* a stupid or incompetent person. *slang*. L16.

> 📖 **1 as dead as a nit** *arch.* completely dead.
> **2** B. BAINBRIDGE But they're different colours, you nit.

Comb.: **nit-grass** a grass, *Gastridium ventricosum*, with shiny swollen florets resembling nits; **nitweed** a N. American St John's wort, *Hypericum gentianoides*, with scalelike leaves and small yellow flowers; also called ***orange grass***.

nit /nɪt/ *noun*². M20.
[French, from Latin *nitere* shine.]
PHYSICS. A unit of luminance equal to one candela per square metre.

nit /nɪt/ *verb intrans. Austral.* Infl. **-tt-**. L19.
[Origin unkn. Cf. NIT *interjection & noun*³.]
Escape, decamp; hurry away.

nit /nɪt/ *interjection & noun*³. *Austral.* L19.
[Origin unkn.]
▶ **A** *interjection*. Signalling or warning of a person's approach. L19.
▶ **B** *noun*. Watch, guard. Only in ***keep nit***. E20.

nital /ˈnʌɪtal/ *noun*. E20.
[from NIT(RIC + AL(COHOL.]
METALLURGY. An etchant consisting of a few per cent of concentrated nitric acid in ethanol or methanol.

nitch /nɪtʃ/ *noun*¹. Long *obsolete* exc. *Scot. & dial.* E18.
[Origin unkn. Cf. NICK *noun*¹, NOTCH *noun*.]
A slight break, notch, or incision.

nitch *noun*² var. of KNITCH *noun*.

nitch /nɪtʃ/ *verb trans. rare*. Also (*Scot.*) **knitch**. E19.
[Prob. from KNITCH *noun*.]
Unite or join together; fix together, truss.

nitchevo /niːtʃɪˈvəʊ/ *interjection & noun*. E20.
[Russian *nichego*.]
▶ **A** *interjection*. In Russian: Never mind! It does not matter! E20.
▶ **B** *noun*. The use of the word 'nitchevo'; an attitude of resignation or fatalism. M20.

nitchie /ˈnɪtʃi/ *noun*. *Canad.* L18.
[Ojibwa *niːčiː*: (voc.) friend.]
Orig. (among N. American Indians), a friend. Later (usu. considered *derog.*), a N. American Indian.

nite /nʌɪt/ *noun*. *informal* (chiefly *commercial*). M20.
[Phonetic spelling.]
Night.

†**nitency** *noun*. *rare*. M17–M18.
[from Latin *nit-* ppl stem of *niti* (see NISUS): see -ENCY.]
An impulse.

niter *noun* see NITRE.

nitery /ˈnʌɪtəri/ *noun*. *US slang*. M20.
[from NITE *noun* + -ERY.]
A nightclub.

nithing /ˈnʌɪðɪŋ/ *noun*. Now *arch.* or *Hist.* LOE.
[Old Norse *níðingr* from *níð* contumely, libel, insult = Old English *nīþ* enmity, malice, affliction, Old Frisian, Old Saxon, Old High German *nīd* (Dutch *nijd*, German *Neid* envy). Cf. NIDING, NIDDERING.]
A vile coward; an abject or contemptible person; a villain. Formerly also, a mean or miserly person; a niggard.

Nithsdale /ˈnɪθsdeɪl/ *noun*. E18.
[The Countess of *Nithsdale*, who enabled her Jacobite husband to escape from the Tower in 1716 disguised in her cloak and hood.]
Hist. A long hooded riding cloak fashionable in the 18th cent.

nitid /ˈnɪtɪd/ *adjective*. M17.
[Latin *nitidus*, from *nitere* shine: see -ID¹.]
Bright, shining, polished, glossy.

Nitinol /ˈnɪtɪnɒl/ *noun*. M20.
[from *Ni* symbol for nickel + *Ti* symbol for titanium + initial letters of Naval Ordnance Laboratory, Maryland, US.]
An alloy of nickel and titanium; *esp.* one composed of equimolar proportions of these elements, which will return to its original shape after deformation when heated to a certain transition temperature.

niton /ˈnʌɪtɒn/ *noun*. Now *rare* or *obsolete*. E20.
[from Latin *nitere* shine + -ON.]
CHEMISTRY. = RADON.

nitpick /ˈnɪtpɪk/ *verb & noun*. M20.
[Back-form. from next.]
▶ **A** *verb intrans. & trans.* Criticize pedantically; find fault (with) in a petty manner. Freq. as ***nitpicking*** *verbal noun & ppl adjective*. M20.

> 📖 *Time* The atmosphere gets very tense over the nitpicking. L. URDANG If I must nitpick, it is with the sparse treatment . . of the possessive with the gerund.

▶ **B** *noun*. A nitpicker. Also, a pedantic criticism, a petty quibble. M20.

> 📖 *Times Lit. Suppl.* Professor Laqueur's nitpicks force me to comment.

nitpicker /ˈnɪtpɪkə/ *noun*. M20.
[from NIT *noun*¹ + PICKER *noun*¹.]
A pedantic critic; a petty fault-finder.

Nitralloy /ˈnʌɪtrəlɔɪ/ *noun*. E20.
[from NITR(O + ALLOY *noun*.]
(Proprietary name for) any of a range of alloy steels specially manufactured for nitriding.

nitrate /ˈnʌɪtreɪt/ *noun & verb*. L18.
[French, formed as NITRE *noun* + -ATE¹. Cf. earlier NITRATED.]
▶ **A** *noun*. **1** CHEMISTRY. A salt or ester of nitric acid. L18.
2 a A nitrogenous fertilizer, *esp.* one containing potassium, sodium, or ammonium nitrate. M19. ▸**b** Silver nitrate, used in photographic development. M19. ▸**c** Cellulose nitrate (nitrocellulose), as formerly used as a base for cinematographic films. M20.
1 ***silver nitrate***: see SILVER *noun & adjective*.
Comb.: **nitrate reductase** an enzyme which brings about (the second step in) the reduction of nitrate to nitrite.
▶ **B** *verb trans.* CHEMISTRY. Treat, combine, or impregnate with nitric acid; introduce a nitro group into (a compound or molecule). L19.
■ **nitrating** *adjective* designating a compound, species, or mixture used to introduce a nitro group into a molecule M20.

nitrated /nʌɪˈtreɪtɪd/ *adjective*. L17.
[Orig. from NITRE + -ATE² + -ED¹. Later from prec. + -ED¹, -ED².]
Treated or combined with nitric acid or (formerly) nitre; that has been nitrated.

nitratine /ˈnʌɪtrətiːn/ *noun*. M19.
[formed as prec. + -INE⁵.]
MINERALOGY. = ***SODA nitre***.

nitration /nʌɪˈtreɪʃ(ə)n/ *noun*. L19.
[from prec. + -ATION.]
CHEMISTRY. The process of nitrating a compound; the formation of a nitro compound or nitrate.

nitrazepam /nʌɪˈtreɪzɪpam, -ˈtrazə-/ *noun*. M20.
[from NITR(O + AZ(O- + -EP(INE + AM(IDE.]
PHARMACOLOGY. A short-acting hypnotic drug of the benzodiazepine group, used to treat insomnia.
¶ A proprietary name for this drug is MOGADON.

nitre /ˈnʌɪtə/ *noun*. Also ***niter**. LME.
[Old & mod. French from Latin *nitrum* from Greek *nitron*, of Semitic origin or from Egyptian *ntrj*. In AV rendering Hebrew *neter*. Cf. NATRON.]
1 Potassium nitrate, saltpetre. Formerly also, native sodium carbonate, washing soda. LME.
†**2** A vital substance presumed to be present in the air and in rain. M17–L18.
3 A deposit of malic acid produced during the refining of maple syrup. L19.

> 📖 **1** AV *Jer.* 2:22 For though thou wash thee with nitre, . . yet thine iniquitie is marked before me. **2** R. SOUTH It is not the bare water that fructifies, but a secret spirit or nitre descending with it.

Phrases: ***cubic nitre***: see CUBIC *adjective* 2. †***fixed nitre*** potassium carbonate. ***SODA nitre***.

nitrene /ˈnʌɪtriːn/ *noun*. M20.
[from NITR(O- + -ENE.]
CHEMISTRY. Any organic compound of divalent nitrogen.

Nitrian /ˈnɪtrɪən/ *adjective*. M19.
[from *Nitria* (see below) + -AN.]
Designating, of, or pertaining to the desert region of Nitria in Egypt, west of Cairo (in the 4th cent. the site of a settlement of ascetic Christian hermits).

nitriary /ˈnʌɪtrɪəri/ *noun*. *obsolete* exc. *Hist.* M19.
[French *nitrière*, formed as NITRE.]
A place where nitre (saltpetre) is obtained from natural deposits.

nitric /ˈnʌɪtrɪk/ *adjective*. L18.
[from NITRE *noun* + -IC.]
CHEMISTRY. Orig., pertaining to, derived from, or containing nitre. Now usu., of or containing nitrogen, esp. in the pentavalent state. Cf. NITROUS.
nitric acid a highly corrosive and toxic acid, HNO_3, which in its pure state is a clear colourless or pale yellow fuming liquid with a pungent smell, and which is used in manufacturing chemicals, as a metal solvent, etc.; cf. AQUA FORTIS. **nitric oxide** a colourless gas, NO, which reacts readily with air to form nitrogen dioxide.

nitride /ˈnʌɪtrʌɪd/ *noun & verb*. M19.
[from NITR(OGEN + -IDE.]
CHEMISTRY & METALLURGY. ▶**A** *noun*. A binary compound of nitrogen with a more electropositive element or radical. M19.
▶ **B** *verb trans.* Convert into a nitride or nitrides; *spec.* heat (a ferrous alloy) in the presence of ammonia or other nitrogenous material so as to increase hardness and corrosion resistance. E20.
■ **nitriˈdation** *noun* a reaction analogous to oxidation but involving nitrogen rather than oxygen; *spec.* the action or an act of nitriding an alloy: E20.

nitrify /ˈnʌɪtrɪfʌɪ/ *verb*. E19.
[French *nitrifier*, formed as NITRE: see -FY.]
1 *verb trans.* Convert to or enrich with nitre; impregnate with nitrogen; treat with nitric acid or nitrate; *spec.* (chiefly of bacteria) convert (ammonia) to nitrite or nitrate. E19.
2 *verb intrans.* Turn into or produce nitre. E19.
■ **nitrifiable** *adjective* E19. **nitrifiˈcation** *noun* E19. **nitrifier** *noun* (BIOLOGY) a nitrifying organism or soil E20.

nitrile /ˈnʌɪtrʌɪl/ *noun*. Also (earlier) †**-yle**. M19.
[from NITRE + *-ile* alt. of -YL.]
CHEMISTRY. Any organic cyanide compound in which an alkyl group is directly attached to the carbon of a cyanide group.
Comb.: **nitrile rubber** any of several oil-resistant synthetic rubbers which are copolymers of acrylonitrile with butadiene.

nitrite /ˈnʌɪtrʌɪt/ *noun.* E19.
[from NITRE + -ITE¹.]
CHEMISTRY. A salt or ester of nitrous acid.

nitro /ˈnʌɪtrəʊ/ *noun.* E20.
[Abbreviation.]
1 = NITRO-POWDER. E20.
2 Nitroglycerine. *slang.* E20.

nitro- /ˈnʌɪtrəʊ/ *combining form.* Before a vowel also **nitr-**. Also as attrib. adjective **nitro**.
[from NITRE or Greek *nitron*: see -O-.]
Chiefly CHEMISTRY. Of or pertaining to nitre, nitric acid, or nitrogen; *spec.* in ORGANIC CHEMISTRY, designating (*a*) (compounds containing) the group $\cdot NO_2$; (*b*) compounds which are esters of nitric acid.
■ **nitro-acid** *noun* a compound of nitric acid with an organic acid M19. **nitrobacˈterium** *noun*, pl. **-ia**, a nitrifying bacterium; *spec.* one belonging to the family Nitrobacteraceae: L19. **nitroˈcellulose** *noun* a highly flammable material made by treating cellulose with concentrated nitric acid, used in explosives and celluloid L19. **Nitrochalk** *noun* (proprietary name for) a blend of chalk and ammonium nitrate, used as fertilizer E20. **nitro compound** *noun* a compound containing a nitro group M19. **nitro-cotton** *noun* gun cotton, nitrocellulose L19. **nitroˈfuran** *noun* any of a group of compounds having a nitro group attached to a furan ring, some of which have bacteriostatic properties M20. **nitrofurantoin** /-fjʊˈrantəʊɪn/ *noun* (PHARMACOLOGY) a bicyclic compound, $C_8H_6N_4O_5$, which is an antibacterial agent used to treat infections of the urinary tract M20. **nitrofurazone** /-ˈfjʊərəzəʊn/ *noun* (PHARMACOLOGY) a cyclic compound, $C_6H_6N_4O_4$, which is an antibacterial agent used locally on burns, wounds, and skin infections, and in veterinary medicine M20. **nitro group** *noun* the monovalent radical $\cdot NO_2$ L19. **Nitrolime** *noun* (US proprietary name for) a fertilizer containing calcium cyanamide E20. **nitroˈmethane** *noun* an oily liquid, CH_3NO_2, which is used as a solvent and rocket fuel and in the production of nitro compounds L19. **nitro-powder** *noun* gunpowder made using nitric acid L19. **nitro-proof** *adjective* (of a firearm) warranted as suitable for use with nitro-powder E20. **nitro-prove** *verb trans.* prove or test (a firearm to be used with nitro-powder) M20.

nitro-aerial /nʌɪtrəʊˈɛːrɪəl/ *adjective. obsolete* exc. *Hist.* L17.
[from NITRO- + AERIAL *adjective*. Cf. mod. Latin *nitro-aereus*.]
Designating (particles of) a substance presumed to be common to air and nitre and supporting combustion and life. Cf. NITRE 2.

nitrogen /ˈnʌɪtrədʒ(ə)n/ *noun.* L18.
[French *nitrogène*, formed as NITRO-: see -GEN.]
A non-metallic chemical element, atomic no. 7, which forms four-fifths of the earth's atmosphere as the colourless, tasteless, inert gas N_2, and combines to form numerous compounds, including nitrates, amino acids, and nucleic acids. (Symbol N.)
Comb.: **nitrogen cycle** BIOLOGY the cycle of changes whereby nitrogen is interconverted between its free state in the air and combined states in organisms and the soil; **nitrogen fixation** the conversion, esp. by bacteria, of gaseous nitrogen into a combined form usable by plants; **nitrogen fixer** a nitrogen-fixing organism; **nitrogen-fixing** *adjective* bringing about nitrogen fixation; **nitrogen mustard** any of a group of cytotoxic alkylating agents containing the group $\cdot N(CH_2CH_2Cl)_2$, some of which are used in chemotherapy to treat cancer; **nitrogen narcosis** a narcotic state, occurring esp. in divers, induced by breathing air under pressure.
■ **niˈtrogenize** *verb trans.* = NITROGENATE M19.

nitrogenase /nʌɪˈtrɒdʒəneɪz/ *noun.* M20.
[from prec. + -ASE.]
BIOCHEMISTRY. An enzyme which combines with molecular nitrogen as the first step in biological nitrogen fixation.

nitrogenate /nʌɪˈtrɒdʒəneɪt/ *verb trans.* E20.
[from NITROGEN + -ATE³.]
Combine with nitrogen; nitrify; nitride.
■ **nitrogeˈnation** *noun* E20.

nitrogenous /nʌɪˈtrɒdʒɪnəs/ *adjective.* E19.
[from NITROGEN + -OUS.]
Containing nitrogen in combination.

nitroglycerine /nʌɪtrə(ʊ)ˈglɪsəriːn, -ɪn/ *noun.* Also **-in** /-ɪn/. M19.
[from NITRO- + GLYCERINE.]
An explosive oily liquid made by treating glycerol with a mixture of concentrated nitric and sulphuric acids, used as an explosive and medicinally as a vasodilator. Also called ***glyceryl trinitrate***.

nitrohydrochloric /ˌnʌɪtrəʊhʌɪdrəˈklɒrɪk, -ˈklɔː-/ *adjective.* Now *rare.* M19.
[from NITRO- + HYDROCHLORIC.]
CHEMISTRY. ***nitrohydrochloric acid***, = AQUA REGIA.

nitrometer /nʌɪˈtrɒmɪtə/ *noun.* E19.
[from NITRO- + -METER.]
An instrument by which the amount of nitrogen in a substance can be determined.

nitromuriatic /ˌnʌɪtrəʊmjʊərɪˈatɪk/ *adjective. arch.* L18.
[from NITRO- + MURIATIC.]
CHEMISTRY. ***nitromuriatic acid***, = AQUA REGIA.
■ **nitroˈmuriate** *noun* a compound produced by treatment with nitromuriatic acid L18.

nitron /ˈnʌɪtrɒn/ *noun.* E20.
[German, formed as NITRO- + -ON.]
CHEMISTRY. A crystalline heterocyclic compound, $C_{20}H_{16}N_4$, which is used in analysis as a precipitant for nitrate, perchlorate, and some other ions.

nitronium /nʌɪˈtrəʊnɪəm/ *noun.* E20.
[from NITRO- + -ONIUM.]
CHEMISTRY. The cation NO_2^+, which is the nitrating agent in mixtures of concentrated nitric acid with other strong acids and is formed by dissociation of nitric acid itself. Usu. *attrib.*
¶ Orig. differently formulated.

nitrophilous /nʌɪˈtrɒfɪləs/ *adjective.* E20.
[from NITRO(GEN + -PHILOUS.]
BOTANY. Of a plant: preferring soils rich in nitrogen.
■ **ˈnitrophile** *noun* a nitrophilous plant M20.

nitroprusside /nʌɪtrə(ʊ)ˈprʌsʌɪd/ *noun.* M19.
[from NITRO- + PRUSSIC *adjective* + -IDE.]
CHEMISTRY. A complex salt containing the anion $[Fe(CN)_5NO]^{2-}$, obtained by treating a ferrocyanide with nitric acid.

nitrosamine /nʌɪˈtrəʊsəmiːn/ *noun.* L19.
[from NITROS(O- + AMINE.]
ORGANIC CHEMISTRY. Any of a class of compounds containing the group :N–N=O attached to alkyl or aryl groups, formed by the action of nitrites or nitrogen oxides on amines.

nitrosate /ˈnʌɪtrəseɪt/ *verb trans.* E20.
[from NITROS(O- + -ATE³.]
CHEMISTRY. Introduce a nitroso group into (a compound).
■ **nirosatable** *adjective* L20. **nitroˈsation** *noun* E20.

†**nitrose** *adjective. rare.* LME–M18.
[formed as next: see -OSE¹.]
Of the nature of nitre; nitrous.

nitroso- /nʌɪˈtrəʊsəʊ/ *combining form.* Also as attrib. adjective **nitroso**. M19.
[from Latin *nitrosus* nitrous: see -O-.]
CHEMISTRY. Designating or containing a nitrosyl radical.

nitrosyl /ˈnʌɪtrəsʌɪl, -sɪl/ *noun.* Also †**-yle**. M19.
[from prec. + -YL.]
CHEMISTRY. The radical ·N=O; the cation NO^+. Usu. in *comb.*

nitrous /ˈnʌɪtrəs/ *adjective.* E17.
[from NITRE *noun* + -OUS.]
Orig., pertaining to, of the nature of, or containing nitre. Now usu. *spec.*, (CHEMISTRY), of or containing nitrogen, esp. in a state of low valency. Cf. NITRIC.
nitrous acid a weak acid, HNO_2, the parent acid of nitrites, which occurs as a pale blue aqueous solution. †**nitrous air**, †**nitrous gas** a mixture of oxides of nitrogen, obtained by the action of nitric acid on most metals in air. **nitrous oxide** a colourless gas, N_2O, with a faint sweetish odour and taste, which when inhaled produces exhilaration or anaesthesia; also called ***laughing gas***.

nitroxide /nʌɪˈtrɒksʌɪd/ *noun.* E19.
[from NITR(O- + OXIDE.]
CHEMISTRY. †**1** ***nitroxide of mercury***, mercuric oxide as prepared using nitric acid. Only in E19.
2 Any compound containing the divalent group :N–O. M20.

nitroxyl /nʌɪˈtrɒksʌɪl, -sɪl/ *noun.* M19.
[from NITR(O- + OX(Y- + -YL.]
CHEMISTRY. = NITRYL. Usu. in *comb.*

nitryl /ˈnʌɪtrʌɪl, -rɪl/ *noun.* M19.
[from NITR(IC + -YL.]
CHEMISTRY. The radical $\cdot NO_2$; the nitronium ion, NO_2^+. Usu. in *comb.*

†**nitryle** *noun* see NITRILE.

nitta /ˈnɪtə/ *noun.* L18.
[App. a W. African name.]
Any of several African trees of the genus *Parkia*, whose pods contain an edible mealy pulp, esp. *P. biglobosa* and *P. filicoidea*. Also ***nitta-tree***.

nitty /ˈnɪti/ *adjective.* Now *joc.* L16.
[from NIT *noun*¹ + -Y¹.]
Having many nits; infested with nits.

nitty-gritty /nɪtɪˈgrɪti/ *noun. colloq.* M20.
[Origin unkn.]
The realities or basic facts of a situation, subject, etc.; the heart of the matter.

> M. KINGTON Let's get down to the nitty-gritty.

nitwit /ˈnɪtwɪt/ *noun. colloq.* E20.
[Perh. from NIT *noun*¹ + WIT *noun*.]
A silly or foolish person.

> J. DRUMMOND Beryl, don't be such a nitwit. *attrib.*: R. JAFFE Apparently, I have a nitwit half-brother.

■ **nitwitted** *adjective* silly, foolish M20. **nitˈwittedness** *noun* M20. **nitˈwittery** *noun* silliness, folly M20.

Niuean /nɪˈuːən, ˈnjuːɪən/ *noun & adjective.* E20.
[from *Niue* (see below) + -AN.]
▶ **A** *noun.* **1** A native or inhabitant of Niue, an island in the S. Pacific. E20.
2 The Polynesian language of the people of Niue. M20.
▶ **B** *adjective.* Of or pertaining to Niue, the Niueans, or their language. E20.

NIV *abbreviation.*
New International Version (of the Bible).

nival /ˈnʌɪv(ə)l/ *adjective.* M17.
[Latin *nivalis*, from *niv-*, *nix* snow: see -AL¹.]
†**1** Of, pertaining to, or characteristic of snow. *rare.* Only in M17.
2 Marked by perpetual snow; characteristic of or growing in a region having perpetual snow. L19.

nivation /nʌɪˈveɪʃ(ə)n/ *noun.* E20.
[from Latin *niv-*, *nix* snow + -ATION.]
PHYSICAL GEOGRAPHY. Erosion of the ground beneath and at the sides of a snowbank, mainly as a result of alternate freezing and thawing.

nivellization /nɪv(ə)lʌɪˈzeɪʃ(ə)n/ *noun. rare.* Also **-isation**. L19.
[from French *niveler* to level + -IZATION.]
Levelling, removal of distinctions; an instance of this.

niveous /ˈnɪvɪəs/ *adjective. literary.* E17.
[from Latin *niveus*, from *niv-*, *nix* snow: see -EOUS.]
Snowy, resembling snow.

Nivernois /ˈnɪvəːnwɑː, *foreign* nivɛrnwa/ *noun.* Pl. same /-wɑːz, *foreign* -wa/. M18.
[Louis Mazarini, Duc de Nivernais or *Nivernois*, from Nivernais, *Nivernois*, a former province of central France.]
Hist. A three-cornered hat with a wide rolled brim and a low crown, fashionable in the late 18th cent.

Nivose /nɪˈvəʊz/ *noun.* Also **Nivôse** /niːvoːz/. E19.
[French *Nivôse* from Latin *nivosus* snowy, from *niv-*, *nix* snow: see -OSE¹.]
Hist. The fourth month of the French Republican calendar (introduced 1793), extending from 21 December to 19 January.

nix /nɪks/ *noun*¹, *interjection, adverb, & adjective. slang.* L18.
[German, dial. & colloq. var. of *Nichts* nothing.]
▶ **A** *noun.* **1** Nothing. L18.
2 Watch, guard. Only in ***keep nix***. M19.
3 = NIXIE *noun*². *US.* L19.

> **1** CONAN DOYLE If I pull down fifty bucks a week it's not for nix. D. FRANCIS Apart from that, nix. **nix on** enough of, no more of.

▶ **B** *interjection.* Signalling or warning that a person is approaching. M19.
▶ **C** *adverb.* Not possibly, not at all, no. E20.
▶ **D** *adjective.* Not any, no. E20.

nix /nɪks/ *noun*². M19.
[German (masc.) from Middle High German *niches*, *nickes* from Old High German *nichus*, *nih(h)us*, from Germanic base also of NICKER *noun*¹. Cf. NIXIE *noun*¹.]
A water-elf.

nix /nɪks/ *verb trans. slang.* E20.
[from NIX *noun*¹.]
Cancel, forbid, refuse.

> *Maclean's Magazine* It was the inner voice that nixed the deal. **nix out** *US* get rid of, throw away.

nixie /ˈnɪksi/ *noun*¹. E19.
[from German *Nixe* (fem.) from Middle High German from Old High German *nicchessa*, from Germanic base also of NICKER *noun*¹, with ending assim. to -IE. Cf. NIX *noun*².]
A female water-elf; a water-nymph.

nixie /ˈnɪksi/ *noun*², *adverb, & interjection.* Also **-y**. L19.
[from NIX *noun*¹: see -IE, -Y⁶.]
▶ **A** *noun.* A letter, parcel, etc., unable to be forwarded through being illegibly or incorrectly addressed. *US.* L19.
▶ **B** *adverb & interjection.* Not possibly, not at all, no. E20.

Nixie tube /ˈnɪksɪ tjuːb/ *noun phr.* Also **n-**. M20.
[from numeric indicator experimental (number) 1: see -IE.]
A numerical indicator used in scientific instruments, consisting of a gas-discharge bulb containing ten cathodes bent into the shapes of numerals.
¶ Proprietary name in the US.

Nixonian /nɪkˈsəʊnɪən/ *adjective.* M20.
[from *Nixon* (see below) + -IAN.]
Of, pertaining to, or characteristic of Richard M. Nixon (1913–94), US Vice-President, 1953–61, and President, 1969–74.

■ **ˈNixonite** *noun* a supporter of Nixon or his policies **M20.** **Nixoˈnomics** *noun pl.* [from *eco*)*nomics*] the economic policies of Nixon **M20.**

Nizam /nɪˈzɑːm/ *noun.* **M18.**
[Turkish, Persian, & Urdu *nizām* (in sense 1 abbreviation of *nizām-al-mulk* administrator of the realm, in sense 2 abbreviation of *nizām askeri* regular soldier) from Arab. *nizām* good order, disposition, arrangement.]
Hist. **1** (The title of) the hereditary ruler of Hyderabad, a former State of southern India, divided in 1956 between Andhra Pradesh, Mysore (Karnataka), and Maharashtra. **M18.**
2 (The body of men composing) the Turkish regular army. **M19.**
■ **Nizamut** *noun* [Urdu *nizāmat*] *Hist.* the authority or office of the Nizam of Hyderabad **M18.**

†**nizy** *noun.* **L17–E19.**
[Origin unkn.]
A fool, a simpleton.

NJ *abbreviation.*
New Jersey.

NK *abbreviation.*
PHYSIOLOGY. Natural killer (cell).

NKVD *abbreviation.*
Russian *Narodnyĭ Komissariat Vnutrennikh Del* People's Commissariat of Internal Affairs, replacing the Ogpu.

NLP *abbreviation.*
1 Natural language processing.
2 Neurolinguistic programming.

NLRB *abbreviation. US.*
National Labor Relations Board.

NM *abbreviation*¹.
New Mexico.

nm *abbreviation*².
PHYSICS. Nanometre(s).

n.m. *abbreviation.*
Nautical mile.

N.Mex. *abbreviation.*
New Mexico.

NMOS *abbreviation.*
n-channel enhancement metal-oxide semiconductor.

NMR *abbreviation.*
Nuclear magnetic resonance.

NNE *abbreviation.*
North-north-east.

NNP *abbreviation.*
Net national product.

NNR *abbreviation.*
National Nature Reserve.

NNW *abbreviation.*
North-north-west.

no /nəʊ/ *noun*¹. Pl. **noes**. **ME.**
[from NO *adverb*³ & *interjection*.]
†**1** ***without no***, beyond denial, certainly. *rare.* Only in **ME.**
2 An utterance of the word 'no'; an instance of the use of 'no'; a denial, a refusal. **L16.**
3 A negative vote or decision. **L16.**
4 In *pl.* & †*collect. sing.* Those who vote on the negative side in a division. **E17.**

📖 **2** A. YOUNG She determined to . . give a solemn no instead of a yea. **not take no for an answer** persist in spite of refusals. **say no** refuse a request, deny a statement made. **3** GLADSTONE With you . . it rests to deliver the great Aye or No. **4** LD MACAULAY The Ayes were one hundred and eighty-two and the Noes one hundred and eighty-three. *attrib.*: J. ARCHER He followed the surge of Labour members into the Noes lobby.

Comb.: **no man** *colloq.* a man who habitually says 'no'; a person who is accustomed to disagree or resolutely refuse requests.

No *noun*² var. of NOH.

no /nəʊ/ *adjective* (in mod. usage also classed as a *determiner*). Also (*Scot. & north.*) **nae** /neɪ/. **OE.**
[Reduced form of NONE *adjective*, orig. only before consonants. Cf. NAOW *adjective*.]
1 Not any. (As the only negative of a sentence or (now *dial. & non-standard*) with other negatives.) **OE.** ▸**b** Not any possibility of (*doing*). **M16.** ▸**c** *ellipt.* In truisms, slogans, notices, etc.: (*a*) (in parallel phrases) if there is no —, then there is no —; (*b*) we will have no —, let there be no —, there will be no —, no — is allowed, etc. **M16.**
2 Not (a), quite other than (a); not in reality a, not a proper; a non-existent. **ME.** ▸**b** Hardly any. Chiefly in ***no time***. *colloq.* **M19.**

📖 **1** SCOTT FITZGERALD I've got no place to go in the evenings, so I just work. *Listener* He's not going to be put in no poorhouse. M. AMIS I looked for cabs and no cabs came. *Times of India* No violence was reported from anywhere. V. BRAMWELL No discussion on keeping . . beautiful would be complete without mention of how to sunbathe safely. *attrib.*: *Guardian* A no-hope telephonist with an invalid mother . . and a bad communication problem. *Times* Ford entered a 'no contest' plea and . . was fined . . $7m. *Business Week* A no-strike pledge to be used in 1983 bargaining in the steel industry. **b** C. HARE Once let this fellow start talking, there was no stopping him. *Proverb*: There is no accounting for tastes. ***no entry, no parking, no popery, no smoking, no surrender, no thoroughfare, no waiting***, etc. **2** SHAKES. *Merch. V.* This is no answer, thou unfeeling man. M. R. RINEHART It's no way to talk about a sister. G. S. HAIGHT Even with the new coiffure . . she is no beauty. E. BLISHEN I know people who say that *Alice* is no book for a child. D. BOGARDE So many loyal years' service, in which . . I have played no small part. ***no chicken, no fool, no joke***, etc.

Special collocations, phrases, & comb.: (A selection of cross-refs. only is included: see esp. other nouns.) ***a bit of no good***: see GOOD *noun*. ***by no means***: see MEAN *noun*¹. ***come to no good***: see GOOD *noun*. ***in no shape or form***: see SHAPE *noun*¹. **no-account** *adjective & noun* (a person who is) of no account, importance, value, or use. ***no amount of***: see AMOUNT *noun* 3. **no-ball** *noun & verb* (*a*) *noun* in cricket, a ball not delivered according to the rules of the game, counting one to the batting side if not otherwise scored from (orig. the words of the umpire declaring that a ball is of this type); *fig.* an unfair or unlawful act; (*b*) *verb trans.* declare to be or to have delivered a no-ball. **no-being** negative existence; non-existence, nonentity. **no bon** /bɔ̃/ *arch. slang* [BON *adjective*] no good. **no-brainer** *colloq.* (*a*) something that requires little mental effort or intelligence to perform, undertake, or understand (also *attrib.*); (*b*) a foolish or unintelligent person or action. **no-brand** *adjective* = ***no-name*** *adjective* below. **no-claim bonus**, **no-claims bonus** a discount allowed on a motor-vehicle insurance premium if no claim has been submitted during a preceding period. **no-'count** *adjective & noun* (*US colloq.*) = ***no-account*** above. ***no dice***: see DICE *noun*. ***no doubt***: see DOUBT *noun*. ***no end***: see END *noun*. **no-fault** *adjective* (*N. Amer.*) involving no attribution of fault or blame; *spec.* designating a form of motor-vehicle insurance in which compensation is paid for an accident regardless of whether or not it was the policyholder's fault. ***no fear***: see FEAR *noun*¹. **no-fines** *adjective & noun* (designating) concrete made from an aggregate from which lumps smaller than about 9 mm (0.35 inch) have been removed, which results in increased porosity and better thermal insulation. ***no flies on***: see FLY *noun*¹. **no-frills** *adjective* having no ornamentation or embellishment, basic. **no go** (*a*) impossible, hopeless (***it is no go, it was no go***, etc., the task is etc. impossible, the situation is etc. hopeless); (*b*) (of a contest etc.) indecisive; (see also NO-GO). **no good** *colloq.* (be) useless, worthless; (be) pointless (*doing*). **no-good** *colloq.* a useless or worthless person. **no-gooder**, **no-goodnik** *US slang* = ***no-good*** above. **no-hit** *adjective* (BASEBALL) designating a game in which a team scores no base hits. **no-hitter** BASEBALL a no-hit game. **no-hoper** *colloq.* (orig. *Austral.*) a horse with no prospect of winning, an outsider; a useless or incompetent person; a person or thing doomed to failure. **no-iron** *adjective* not requiring to be ironed. **no-jump** in a jumping competition, a jump disallowed because it does not comply with the rules. **no-knock** *adjective* (*US*) designating or pertaining to a search or raid by the police made without permission or warning. **no little** much, considerable; a good deal of. **no-load** *adjective & noun* (*a*) *adjective* corresponding to or involving an absence of any electrical load; (of shares) sold at net asset value; (*b*) *noun* (in *pl.*), no-load shares. **no man** *pronoun* no person, nobody; ***no man's land***, a piece of waste or unowned land; an intermediate place, an indeterminate state; the terrain between two opposing, esp. entrenched, armies; a stretch of disputed territory. **no-mar** *adjective* designed not to mar, spoil, etc. **no-meaning** absence of meaning or purpose; nonsense. ***no mistake***: see MISTAKE *noun*. **no-name** *adjective & noun* (chiefly *N. Amer.*) (*a*) (a product) having no brand name, (a product which is) generic or own-brand; (*b*) (a person who is) unknown, esp. in a particular profession etc. ***no names, no packdrill***: see NAME *noun*. **no-nonsense** *adjective* that does not tolerate foolish or extravagant conduct; sensible, businesslike, realistic, practical. ***no object***: see OBJECT *noun* 4. ***no offence***: see OFFENCE 5. ***no question of, no questions asked***: see QUESTION *noun*. **no-right** LAW an obligation not to prevent the exercise of a privilege. **no-show** (orig. *US*) a person who reserves a place or seat, esp. on an aircraft, and neither uses it nor cancels it; *gen.* someone who fails to appear when expected. **no side** RUGBY FOOTBALL (the announcement of) the conclusion of a game. **no-sky** *adjective* designating a line in a room from behind which no sky is visible from the height of a table. **no small** a considerable, a substantial; much, a good deal of. ***no such***: see SUCH *adjective & pronoun*. ***no sweat***: see SWEAT *noun*. ***no thanks to***: see THANK *noun*. **no thoroughfare** no public way through or right of way. **no-thoroughfare** a street, passage, etc., closed at one end; a cul-de-sac. **no through road** not a thoroughfare, not open at the far end. **no-throw** in various sports and games, a throw disallowed because it does not comply with the rules. **no-touch** *adjective* (MEDICINE) designating a surgical technique in which only sterilized instruments and swabs are allowed to touch a wound and its dressings. **no trump** CARDS = ***no trumps*** below. **no-trump** *adjective* (CARDS) with no designated trump suit. **no-trumper** CARDS a no-trump declaration or bid; a hand on which a no-trump bid can suitably be, or has been, made. **no trumps** CARDS a bid or contract with no suit designated as trumps; (usu. with preceding numeral) a bid or contract involving playing with no designated trump suit. NO WAY. ***no whit***: see WHIT *noun*¹. **no-win** *adjective* (of a contest, struggle, etc.) that cannot be won; (of a situation) that can have no favourable outcome. ***no wiser***: see WISE *adjective & noun*². ***no wonder***: see WONDER *noun*. ***to no purpose***: see PURPOSE *noun*.

no /nəʊ/ *verb intrans. & trans. rare.* **E19.**
[from NO *adverb*³ & *interjection*.]
Say no (to).

no /nəʊ/ *adverb*¹. See also NA *adverb*¹ & *conjunction*¹, NAE. **OE.**
[from NE + *ō* var. of *ā* (see AYE *adverb*¹). Partly repr. var. of NA *adverb*¹. Cf. next, NA *adverb*³.]
= NOT *adverb*. Exc. *Scot.* now only in ***whether or no*** s.v. WHETHER *pronoun, adjective, & conjunction*, ***no can do*** (*colloq.*), I cannot, it is not within my power, and ***no fair*** (orig. and chiefly children's usage) not fair, unfair.

📖 R. L. STEVENSON Oh, my dear, that'll no dae! E. SAINTSBURY A person's character . . determined whether he were a gentleman or no.

no /nəʊ/ *adverb*². **ME.**
[Var. of NA *adverb*¹.]
With comparatives: not any, not at all, to no extent, in no degree.

📖 M. KEANE This tough young man was no older than she was. *Observer* The names of no fewer than forty-one Turkish newspapermen. ***no better than one ought to be, no better than one should be***: see BETTER *adjective*. **no less** not less, as much; (emphasizing a preceding statement) and nobody or nothing less important, significant, etc. ***no longer***: see LONG *adverb*. †**no mo** no more. **no more** (*a*) nothing more or further; (*b*) not any more; no further; no longer; *spec.* no longer existent, dead, gone; (*c*) never again, nevermore; (*d*) to no greater extent, in no greater degree, (*than*); neither.

no /nəʊ/ *adverb*³ & *interjection.* **ME.**
[Use of NO *adverb*¹. Cf. NA *adverb*² & *interjection*, NAOW *adverb*¹, *interjection*, NAH *adverb*² & *interjection*, NAW, NOPE *adverb* & *interjection*.]
Equivalent to a negative sentence: esp. (*a*) giving a negative reply to a question, request, etc.; (*b*) introducing a correction or contradiction of a statement or assumption; (*c*) introducing a more emphatic or comprehensive statement, followed by *not* or *nor*; (*d*) agreeing with or affirming a negative statement. Also repeated for the sake of emphasis or earnestness.

📖 DEFOE She declares she will not marry, no, not if a peer of the realm courted her. L. M. ALCOTT Here was a genuine article—no, not the genuine article at all. OUIDA 'Do you think her attractive?' 'No, not at all.' C. M. YONGE 'One can have two friends.' 'No! no! no! not two *best* friends.' ARNOLD BENNETT 'I'm not much for these restaurants.' . . 'No?' he responded tentatively. 'I'm sorry.' J. CONRAD 'A sailor isn't a globe-trotter.' 'No,' muttered Mr. Powell. T. S. ELIOT No, ma'am, you needn't look old-fashioned at me. A. CHRISTIE 'But you didn't come here to talk to me about my books.' 'Frankly no.' **no sir** *colloq.* (chiefly *N. Amer.*) certainly not, indeed no (cf. NOSSIR). ***no siree. no you don't***: see DO *verb*. ***yes and no, yes-no, yes-or-no***: see YES *adverb & interjection*.

No. *abbreviation.*
1 Latin *numero* ablative of *numerus* number.
2 North. *US.*

n.o. *abbreviation.*
CRICKET. Not out.

noa /ˈnəʊə/ *noun & adjective.* **E20.**
[Hawaiian (Maori, Tahitian) = (a thing) free from taboo, ordinary.]
LINGUISTICS. (Designating) an expression substituted for a taboo word or phrase.

NOAA *abbreviation. US.*
National Oceanic and Atmospheric Administration.

Noachian /nəʊˈeɪkɪən/ *adjective.* **L17.**
[from *Noach* = NOAH + -IAN.]
1 Of or pertaining to the biblical patriarch Noah or his time. **L17.**
2 Very ancient or old-fashioned. **L19.**

📖 **1** *Times Lit. Suppl.* Cataclysmic events had occurred . . but he no longer saw the Noachian flood as the last. **2** T. HARDY A . . grey overcast of Noachian cut.

■ **Noachic** *adjective* = NOACHIAN **L18.** **Noachical** *adjective* (*rare*) = NOACHIAN **M17.**

Noah /ˈnəʊə/ *noun.* Earlier †**Noe**. **ME.**
[Biblical patriarch repr. as 10th in descent from Adam (*Genesis* 6 ff.).]
▸**I** ***Noah's Flood.***
1 The flood said to have been sent by God in the time of Noah (*Genesis* 6–8) to destroy humankind because of the wickedness of the human race. **ME.**
▸**II** ***Noah's ark.***
2 = ARK 3. **L16.** ▸**b** A small imitation of this, intended as a plaything for children. **E19.**
3 A small somewhat rectangular bivalve mollusc, *Arca noae*. Also ***Noah's ark shell***. **E18.**
4 A boat-shaped cloud, *esp.* a small dark cloud fragment moving below a raincloud. **L18.**
5 A thing resembling or suggestive of Noah's ark; *esp.* a large, cumbrous, or old-fashioned trunk, boat, or vehicle. **E19.**
6 Any of several N. American lady's-slipper orchids, esp. *Cypripedium acaule* and *C. pubescens*. **E19.**
7 a A police informer (cf. NARK *noun* 1a). *rhyming slang.* **L19.** ▸**b** A shark. *Austral. rhyming slang.* **M20.**
▸**III** ***Noah's Dove.***
8 = COLUMBA. Now *rare* or *obsolete*. **L16.**
■ **Noahic** /nəʊˈeɪɪk/ *adjective* = NOACHIAN **M19.**

noax *noun* var. of NOKES.

nob /nɒb/ *noun*¹. *slang*. L17.
[Perh. var. of KNOB *noun*, but cf. earlier NAB *noun*².]
1 The head. Also, an individual, a head, (chiefly in ***bob a nob*** s.v. BOB *noun*⁶). L17. ▸**b** A blow on the head. *Boxing slang*. Now *rare* or *obsolete*. E19.
2 CRIBBAGE. The jack of the same suit as the card turned up by the dealer, scoring one to its holder. Esp. in ***one for his nob***. E19.

nob /nɒb/ *noun*². *slang*. Earlier (*Scot.*, now *local*) **(k)nab** /nab/. L17.
[Origin unkn.]
A person of some wealth or social distinction.

nob *noun*³ see HOB *adverb & noun*³.

nob /nɒb/ *verb*¹. Also (*Scot.*) **knab** /nab/. Infl. **-bb-**. M16.
[Orig. perh. var. of KNOB *verb*, later from NOB *noun*¹. In Scot. use also var. of KNAP *verb*¹.]
1 *verb trans*. Beat, strike. *Scot*. M16.
2 *verb trans. & intrans*. Deliver a blow or blows to the head (of). *Boxing slang*. Now *rare* or *obsolete*. E19.
■ **nobber** *noun*¹ (*Boxing slang*, now *rare* or *obsolete*) a blow to the head E19.

nob /nɒb/ *verb*² *intrans*. Infl. **-bb-**. E17.
[Neg. corresp. to HOB *verb*¹: cf. Old English *næbbe* (see HAB).]
†**1** Take (in ***hob, nob***: see HOB *verb*¹ 1). Only in E17.
2 ***hob and nob, hob or nob***: see HOB *verb*¹ 2. M18.

nob /nɒb/ *verb*³ *trans. & intrans*. *slang*. Infl. **-bb-**. M19.
[Origin unkn.]
Collect (money), esp. after a performance.
■ **nobber** *noun*² L19.

nob *adverb* see HOB *adverb & noun*³.

nobbins /ˈnɒbɪnz/ *noun pl*. *slang*. Also **-ings** /-ɪŋz/. M19.
[from NOB *verb*³ + -ING¹.]
Coins or other money collected after a performance, the proceeds of a collection; *spec*. coins etc. thrown into a boxing ring in appreciation of a fight.

nobble /ˈnɒb(ə)l/ *verb trans*. *slang*. M19.
[Prob. var. of *knobble* KNUBBLE *verb*.]
1 a Tamper with (a horse), e.g. by drugging or laming it, in order to prevent it from winning a race. M19. ▸**b** Secure the support of (a person etc.) by bribery or other underhand methods; influence the opinion or actions of in advance of a collective decision etc.; weaken or reduce the efficiency of (a person etc.). M19.
2 a Obtain dishonestly; steal. M19. ▸**b** Swindle. (Foll. by *out of*.) Now *rare*. M19.
3 Get hold of, seize, catch. M19.

> 🕮 **1a** P. G. WODEHOUSE The bounder was liable to come sneaking in . . intent on nobbling the favourite. **b** F. M. HUEFFER You want to nobble her before she makes any business arrangements with my uncle. *Times* Unions felt . . they would be 'nobbled at the start'. *Economist* Jurors have been nobbled with bribes or threats. **2a** THACKERAY The old chap has nobbled the young fellow's money. **3** M. WOODHOUSE We've got this Shackleton we've nobbled off Coastal Command.

nobbler /ˈnɒblə/ *noun*¹. M19.
[from prec. + -ER¹.]
A person who nobbles horses etc.

nobbler /ˈnɒblə/ *noun*². *slang*. Chiefly *Austral. & NZ*. M19.
[Origin unkn.]
A small quantity of alcoholic drink. Also, a small glass or container for alcoholic drink.

nobbly *adjective* var. of KNOBBLY.

nobbut /ˈnɒbət/ *adverb, preposition, & conjunction*. Now *dial*. ME.
[from NO *adverb*¹ + BUT *preposition* etc.]
1 Only, merely, just. ME.
2 Except, unless; except that. LME.

nobby /ˈnɒbi/ *noun*¹. L19.
[Origin unkn. Cf. NABBIE.]
1 A small single-masted sailing boat of a type used esp. for fishing in the Irish Sea. L19.
2 A nodule of black opal. *Austral*. E20.

nobby /ˈnɒbi/ *adjective & noun*². *slang*. Earlier (*Scot.*) †**(k)nabby**. L18.
[from NOB *noun*² + -Y¹.]
▸**A** *adjective*. Pertaining to or characteristic of people of some wealth or social distinction; extremely smart or elegant. L18.

> 🕮 J. HAWES I was with her and her favourite beagle in some nobby restaurant.

▸**B** *noun*. *The* smart thing. M19.
■ **nobbily** *adverb* M19. **nobbiness** *noun* E20.

Nobel /nəʊˈbɛl, ˈnəʊbɛl/ *noun*. E20.
[Alfred *Nobel* (1833–96), Swedish inventor of dynamite.]
1 In full ***Nobel prize***. Each of six (orig. five) annual prizes awarded from the bequest of Alfred Nobel, for physics, chemistry, physiology or medicine, literature, the promotion of peace, and (a later addition) economic sciences. E20.
2 ***Nobel laureate***, a person who has been awarded a Nobel prize. M20.
■ **Nobelist** *noun* (chiefly *US*) a Nobel laureate M20.

nobelium /nə(ʊ)ˈbiːlɪəm, -ˈbɛl-/ *noun*. M20.
[from prec. + -IUM.]
CHEMISTRY. A radioactive metallic element of the actinide series, atomic no. 102, which is produced artificially. (Symbol No.)

nobiliary /nə(ʊ)ˈbɪljəri/ *adjective*. M18.
[French *nobiliaire*, formed as NOBLE: see -ARY¹.]
Of or pertaining to the nobility.

†**nobilitate** *verb trans*. M16–L18.
[Latin *nobilitat-* pa. ppl stem of *nobilitare*, from *nobilis*: see NOBLE, -ATE³.]
= ENNOBLE.
■ †**nobilitation** *noun* E17–L18.

nobility /nə(ʊ)ˈbɪlɪti/ *noun*. LME.
[Old & mod. French *nobilité* or Latin *nobilitas*, from *nobilis*: see NOBLE, -ITY.]
▸**I 1** The quality of being noble in respect of excellence, value, or importance. Now *rare*. LME.
2 The quality or condition of being noble in respect of rank, title, or birth. LME.
3 The quality of being noble in nature or character; nobleness or dignity of mind. L16.
4 CHEMISTRY. The property (of an element) of being noble or relatively unreactive. E20.
▸**II 5** *The* body of people forming a noble class in a country or State; the aristocracy, the hereditary peerage. LME.
6 A noble class; a body of nobles. E17.
7 A member of a noble class. M19.

noble /ˈnəʊb(ə)l/ *adjective & noun*. ME.
[Old & mod. French from Latin *nobilis*, earlier *gnobilis*, from Indo-European base repr. also by KNOW *verb*: see -BLE.]
▸**A** *adjective*. **1** Distinguished by virtue of position, character, or exploits. Usu. implying, and *obsolete* exc. as passing into, senses 2 and 4. ME.
2 Distinguished by virtue of rank, title, or birth; designating, belonging to, or pertaining to a class of people having a high social rank, esp. recognized or conferred by a (hereditary) title (in Britain now *spec*. duke, marquess, earl, viscount, baron, or their female equivalents). ME.
†**3** Distinguished by virtue of intelligence, knowledge, or skill. ME–L16.
4 Having or displaying high moral qualities or lofty ideals; of a great character; honourable, admirable; free from pettiness and meanness, magnanimous. ME.
5 Distinguished by virtue of splendour, magnificence, or stateliness of appearance; of imposing or impressive proportions or dimensions. ME.
6 Having qualities or properties of a very high or admirable kind; of very high value or importance; excellent, superior. ME. ▸**b** *spec*. (Of a metal) resisting corrosion, as by oxidation or the action of acids; relatively unreactive; (of any chemical element) low in the electrochemical series. ME. ▸**c** Of a part of the body: necessary to life. M17.
7 Splendid, admirable, surpassingly good. ME.

> 🕮 **2** *Shetland Times* Even the noble lord might see the sense in banning the landing of ungutted fish. **4** SPENSER The noblest mind the best contentment has. SHAKES. *Jul. Caes.* This was the noblest Roman of them all. J. RUSKIN The noble pride which was provoked by the insolence of the emperor. P. TILLICH The motive for withstanding pain . . courageously is . . that it is noble to do so. **5** D. FRANCIS In the background, the noble lines of a mansion. **7** W. BESANT He drank a great deal of port, of which he possessed a noble cellar.

Special collocations, phrases, & comb.: **noble gas** any of a group of very unreactive gaseous elements (helium, neon, argon, krypton, xenon, and radon) which have a filled outermost electronic orbital in the atom; also called ***inert gas***. **noble hawk** FALCONRY a long-winged high-flying hawk (e.g. a peregrine or merlin) which swoops down on its prey rather than chasing or raking after it. **noble liquid** a liquefied noble gas. **noble-minded** *adjective* having or characterized by a noble mind, magnanimous. **noble-mindedness** the quality of being noble-minded. **noble rot** = ***pourriture noble*** s.v. POURRITURE 2. **the noble art (of self-defence)**, **the noble science (of self-defence)** boxing. **the noble savage** primitive man, conceived of in the manner of Rousseau as morally superior to civilized man. ***the noble science (of self-defence)***: see ***the noble art (of self-defence)*** above.
▸**B** *noun*. **1** A man of noble birth or rank; a member of the nobility; a peer, a peeress. ME.
2 *Hist*. A former English gold coin, first minted by Edward III, with a value settled by 1550 at 6*s*. 8*d*. Also (with qualifying word), any of various forms of this or similar gold coins. LME.
2 ***angel-noble*** s.v. ANGEL *noun* 7. ***George-noble***. ***Harry noble*** s.v. HARRY *adjective & noun*². ***maille noble*** s.v. MAIL *noun*⁴. ***rose-noble*** s.v. ROSE *noun & adjective*.

nobleman /ˈnəʊb(ə)lmən/ *noun*. Pl. **-men**. ME.
[from NOBLE *adjective* + MAN *noun*.]
1 A man of noble birth or rank; a (male) peer. ME. ▸**b** *Hist*. A nobleman's son as a member of Oxford or Cambridge University. L17.
2 A superior piece in the game of chess. Usu. in *pl*. Now *rare*. L17.
■ **noblemanly** *adjective* of or befitting a nobleman E19.

nobleness /ˈnəʊb(ə)lnɪs/ *noun*. LME.
[from NOBLE *adjective* + -NESS.]
1 The state or quality of being noble, nobility. LME. ▸†**b** With possess. adjective (as ***your nobleness*** etc.): a title of respect given to a noble. LME–M18.
†**2** A noble person or thing; *collect*. members of nobility. L15–M19.
†**3** Display, splendour; an occasion of this. E16–L17.

noblesse /nəʊˈblɛs, *foreign* nɔblɛs/ *noun*. ME.
[Old & mod. French, formed as NOBLE.]
1 Noble birth or rank; nobility, nobleness. Now chiefly as below. ME.
2 *The* nobility; a class of people of noble rank, now esp. in a foreign country. L15.
1 ***noblesse oblige*** /ɔbliʒ, ɒˈbliːʒ/ privilege entails responsibility. **2** ***petite noblesse***: see PETITE *adjective* 2.

noblewoman /ˈnəʊb(ə)lwʊmən/ *noun*. Pl. **-women** /-wɪmɪn/. ME.
[from NOBLE *adjective* + WOMAN *noun*.]
A woman of noble birth or rank; a peeress.

nobly /ˈnəʊbli/ *adverb*. ME.
[from NOBLE *adjective* + -LY².]
In a noble manner.

> 🕮 J. RUSKIN Thinking it better to be nobly remembered than nobly born. M. MCLUHAN It is dark stained solid one inch oak and will age nobly. DAY LEWIS There is a photograph of me sitting beside a nobly handsome fisherman. A. LIVINGSTONE Insistence on the obligation to face life nobly and without lies. *Independent* Flu sufferers who nobly insist on struggling on rather than . . going to bed.

Nobodaddy /ˈnəʊbəʊdadi/ *noun*. L18.
[Blend of NOBODY and DADDY.]
(A disrespectful name for) God, esp. when regarded anthropomorphically; a person no longer held in esteem.
¶ Coined by the poet William Blake.

nobody /ˈnəʊbədi/ *pronoun & noun*. Orig. two words. ME.
[from NO *adjective* + BODY *noun*.]
1 No person; no one. ME.
2 a Not anybody of importance, authority, or position. Chiefly as compl. L16. ▸**b** A person of no importance, authority, or position. L16.

> 🕮 **1** L. STEPHEN Nobody ever put so much of themselves into their work. T. HARDY There was nobody in the world whose care she would more readily be under. *Vogue* Nobody dared touch his gloves. E. LEMARCHAND You can fill us in as nobody else can. C. RAYNER In their handsome house . . her presence . . would discommode nobody. H. JACOBSON 'Who are we expecting?' . . 'Nobody. We're all here.' ***nobody's BUSINESS***. ***nobody's fool***: see FOOL *noun*¹. **2a** M. SINCLAIR She was nobody in that roomful of keen, intellectual people. **b** A. PRICE You mustn't think of the Parrotts as mere nobodies; they were squires and gentlemen. T. TANNER Why her obsession with this pretty little nobody from who-knows-where?

Comb.: **nobody-crab** a pycnogonid, a sea-spider.

nocake /ˈnəʊkeɪk/ *noun*. *US*. M17.
[Narragansett *nokehick*.]
Maize parched and pounded into meal.

nocardiosis /ˌnəʊkɑːdɪˈəʊsɪs/ *noun*. Pl. **-oses** /-ˈəʊsiːz/. E20.
[from mod. Latin *Nocardia* (see below) + -OSIS.]
MEDICINE. (A disease caused by) infection with an actinomycete of the genus *Nocardia*, esp. *N. asteroides*, which sometimes affects humans and is often fatal.

nocent /ˈnəʊs(ə)nt/ *noun & adjective*. Long *rare*. LME.
[Latin *nocent-* pres. ppl stem of *nocere* hurt: see -ENT.]
▸**A** *noun*. **1** A guilty person, a criminal. LME.
2 *The* guilty as a class. M16.
▸**B** *adjective*. **1** Harmful, injurious, hurtful. L15.
2 Guilty; criminal. M16.
■ †**nocency** *noun* guilt E17–M18.

noceur /nɔsœːr/ *noun*. Pl. pronounced same. E20.
[French.]
A reveller, a rake, a libertine; a person who stays up late at night.

nocht *pronoun* etc.: see NOUGHT.

noci- /ˈnəʊsi/ *combining form*.
[from Latin *nocere* to harm: see -I-.]
Chiefly PHYSIOLOGY. Pain; harm.
■ **noci'ceptive** *adjective* (PHYSIOLOGY) (of a stimulus) painful; responding to or caused by a painful stimulus: E20. **nociceptor** *noun* (PHYSIOLOGY) a sensory receptor for painful stimuli E20. **nocifensor** *adjective* [Latin *defensor* defender] PHYSIOLOGY (of a nerve) transmitting signals arising from pain or injury M20.

nock /nɒk/ *noun*. LME.
[Middle Dutch *nocke* (Dutch *nok*), whence also German *Nock*. Branch I may be a different word.]
▶ **I 1** ARCHERY. Orig., either of the small tips of horn fixed at each end of a bow and provided with a notch for holding the string; later, such a notch cut in this or in the bow itself. Also, a small piece of horn etc. fixed in the butt-end of an arrow, provided with a notch for receiving the bowstring; such a notch. LME.
†**2** The cleft in the buttocks. M16–E18.
▶ **II** NAUTICAL. †**3** *nockline*, a part of a ship's rigging. Only in LME.
†**4** The tip or extremity of a yard-arm. *Scot.* Only in 16.
5 The foremost upper corner of some types of sail. L18.

nock /nɒk/ *verb trans*. LME.
[from the noun.]
1 Provide (a bow or arrow) with a nock or notch. Chiefly as ***nocked*** *ppl adjective*. LME.
2 Fit (an arrow) to a bowstring ready for shooting. LME.
2 nocking point the point of a bowstring to which the notch of an arrow is applied.

nockerl /ˈnɒkərl/ *noun*. Pl. **-ln** /-ln/. M19.
[Austrian German = little dumpling.]
A small light Austrian and Bavarian dumpling, made with a batter including eggs, and usu. semolina.
SALZBURGER ***nockerl***.

noctambulant /nɒkˈtambjʊl(ə)nt/ *adjective*. L17.
[from Latin *noct-*, *nox* night + *ambulant-*: see AMBULANT.]
That walks or moves about during the night; somnambulant.

noctambulation /nɒkˌtambjʊˈleɪʃ(ə)n/ *noun*. E18.
[from Latin *noct-*, *nox* night + *ambulatio(n-)*: see AMBULATION.]
The action of walking or moving about during the night; somnambulism, sleepwalking.

noctambulist /nɒkˈtambjʊlɪst/ *noun*. M18.
[from Latin *noct-*, *nox* night + *ambulare* to walk + -IST.]
A person who walks or moves about at night; a somnambulist, a sleepwalker.
■ **noctambulism** *noun* = NOCTAMBULATION M19. †**noctambulo** *noun*, pl. **-o(e)s**, **-ones**, = NOCTAMBULIST E17–M18.

noctambulous /nɒkˈtambjʊləs/ *adjective*. M18.
[formed as prec. + -OUS.]
That walks or moves about during the night; somnambulant.

nocti- /ˈnɒkti/ *combining form* of Latin *noct-*, *nox* night: see -I-.
■ **nocˈtidial** *adjective* [Latin *dies* day] comprising a night and a day L17.

noctiluca /nɒktɪˈluːkə/ *noun*. Pl. **-cae** /-kiː/. LME.
[mod. Latin from Latin = lantern, moon: cf. next.]
†**1** A glow-worm. Only in LME.
†**2** The moon. *rare*. Only in E17.
†**3** ALCHEMY. A kind of phosphorescent substance. L17–E18.
4 BIOLOGY. A roughly spherical marine dinoflagellate of the genus *Noctiluca*, which is strongly phosphorescent, esp. when disturbed. M19.

noctilucent /nɒktɪˈluːs(ə)nt/ *adjective*. L19.
[from NOCTI- + Latin *lucere* shine + -ENT.]
Shining at night; *spec.* designating a luminous cloud of a kind occasionally seen at night in summer in high latitudes, at the height of the mesopause.

noctilucous /nɒktɪˈluːkəs/ *adjective*. *rare*. L17.
[formed as prec. + -OUS.]
Shining at night, phosphorescent.

noctivagant /nɒkˈtɪvəg(ə)nt/ *adjective*. E17.
[from Latin *noctivagus*, formed as NOCTI- + *vagari* wander: see -ANT¹.]
That wanders or roams about during the night.

noctivagation /ˌnɒktɪvəˈgeɪʃ(ə)n/ *noun*. Long *obsolete* exc. *Hist*. M17.
[from NOCTI- + VAGATION.]
The action of wandering about during the night, *spec.* as an offence.
■ †**noctivagator** *noun* a person who wanders about during the night M17–E18.

noctivagous /nɒkˈtɪvəgəs/ *adjective*. E18.
[formed as NOCTIVAGANT: see -OUS.]
= NOCTIVAGANT.

noctua /ˈnɒktjʊə/ *noun*. M19.
[mod. Latin (see below) from Latin = night-owl.]
A noctuid moth, *esp.* one of the genus *Noctua*.

†**noctuary** *noun*. *rare*. E18–E20.
[from Latin *noctu* by night (from *noct-*, *nox* night) + -ARY¹, after DIARY *noun*.]
An account of what happens during a particular night or particular nights.

noctuid /ˈnɒktjʊɪd/ *adjective & noun*. L19.
[from NOCTUA + -ID³.]
ENTOMOLOGY. ▶ **A** *adjective*. Of, pertaining to, or designating the family Noctuidae of large and medium-sized moths, which are mostly night-flying and brownish in colour, with paler hindwings and an eyelike spot on the forewings. L19.
▶ **B** *noun*. A moth of this family. Also called ***miller-moth***, ***owlet-moth***. L19.

noctule /ˈnɒktjuːl/ *noun*. L18.
[French from Italian *nottola* bat.]
ZOOLOGY. A large brown vespertilionid bat, *Nyctalus noctula*, of temperate and subtropical Eurasia and N. Africa, the largest bat found in Britain. Also ***noctule bat***.
giant noctule a large bat, *Nyctalus lasiopterus*, of the Mediterranean and Middle East. **lesser noctule** = LEISLER'S BAT.

nocturia /nɒkˈtjʊərɪə/ *noun*. E20.
[from Latin *noct-*, *nox* night + -URIA.]
MEDICINE. Excessive need to urinate at night.

nocturn /ˈnɒktəːn/ *noun*. ME.
[Old & mod. French *nocturne* or ecclesiastical Latin *nocturnus*, -*um* use as noun of Latin *nocturnus* of the night, from *noct-*, *nox* night. Cf. NOCTURNE.]
ROMAN CATHOLIC CHURCH. Each of three divisions of the traditional office of matins, including a group of psalms; in *pl.* also, matins. Formerly also, each of seven groups of psalms into which the Psalter was divided.

†**nocturn** *adjective*. *rare*. E16–M18.
[Latin *nocturnus*: see prec.]
Nocturnal.

nocturnal /nɒkˈtəːn(ə)l/ *adjective & noun*. L15.
[Late Latin *nocturnalis*, from *nocturnus*: see NOCTURN *noun*, -AL¹. Cf. DIURNAL.]
▶ **A** *adjective*. **1** Of or pertaining to the night; done, held, or occurring during the night. L15.
2 Of an animal: active (only) during the night. L16.
▶**b** *transf.* Of a person: practising an activity or occupation by night; preferring to be active at night. E19.
3 Of the nature of a nocturne. *rare*. L19.

> 📖 **1** O. SACKS Attacks are nocturnal and wake the patient from deep sleep. N. LOWNDES A nocturnal blizzard had come on. ***nocturnal arc***: see ARC *noun* 1. **nocturnal emission** involuntary ejaculation of seminal fluid during sleep. **nocturnal enuresis** MEDICINE persistent involuntary urination during the night, esp. by a child.

▶ **B** *noun*. **1** Chiefly NAUTICAL (now *Hist.*). An instrument for calculating latitude from the position of the polestar. L16.
2 A person out at night, a night-walker. Now *rare*. L17.
■ **nocturnally** *adverb* †(*a*) nightly; (*b*) by night, during the night: LME.

nocturne /ˈnɒktəːn/ *noun*. M19.
[French: see NOCTURN *noun*.]
1 A musical composition of a dreamy character. M19.
2 A painting of a night scene, a night-piece. L19.

nocuous /ˈnɒkjʊəs/ *adjective*. M17.
[from Latin *nocuus*, from *nocere* to hurt: see -OUS. Cf. earlier INNOCUOUS.]
Noxious, hurtful; venomous, poisonous.

nod /nɒd/ *noun*. M16.
[from the verb.]
1 An act of nodding the head, esp. in salutation, assent, or command, or to direct attention to something. M16.
2 A forward or downward movement. *rare*. L16.
3 An involuntary forward movement of the head in a person who has fallen asleep or is drowsy; a short sleep, a nap. E17. ▶**b** A state of drowsiness brought on by narcotic drugs. *slang*. M20.

> 📖 **1** G. SANTAYANA This assumption seemed to be confirmed . . by a little nod from the Doctor. E. TEMPLETON Mr. Parker passed the table with a slight nod of his head. A. BROOKNER At a nod from the head waiter, he . . removed the half-finished bottle.

Phrases: **get the nod** (chiefly *N. Amer.*) be chosen or approved. **on the nod** (*a*) on credit; (*b*) with a merely formal assent and no discussion; without the taking of a vote; (*c*) *slang* drowsy or unconscious through taking narcotic drugs. **the land of Nod** sleep.

nod /nɒd/ *verb*. Infl. **-dd-**. LME.
[Perh. of Low German origin: cf. Middle High German *notten* move about, shake.]
▶ **I** *verb intrans*. **1** Make a brief inclination of the head, esp. in salutation, assent, or command, or to draw attention to something. LME.
2 Let the head fall forward with a quick, short, involuntary motion when drowsy or asleep; doze, esp. in an upright position. LME.
3 Swing or sway from the perpendicular, as if about to fall; bend or incline downward or forward with a swaying or jerking movement. L16.

> 📖 **1** W. CATHER She peeped through the door and nodded to the boy. W. TREVOR Two other women . . nodded wisely, agreeing with the observation. R. P. JHABVALA 'Are you alone?' she asked. He nodded. R. THOMAS The nurse nodded at a chair . . to one side of the bed. **nodding acquaintance** a slight acquaintance (*with*). **nodding terms** terms of slight acquaintance (*with*). **2** J. BUCHAN At ten I was nodding in my chair. D. BARNES She nodded and awoke again . . before she opened her eyes. **3** SHAKES. *Mids. N. D.* I know a bank . . Where oxlips and the nodding violet grows. S. BECKETT His head nods and falls forward. G. LORD Winter grass . . blew in the light wind; nodding, dying.

▶ **II** *verb trans*. **4** Incline (the head) briefly in a nod. M16.
5 Direct by a nod. E17. ▶**b** Head (a football etc.) downwards. M20.
6 Signify by or express with a nod. E18.
7 Cause to bend or sway. E19.

> 📖 **4** E. HEMINGWAY Sordo passed the wine bottle back and nodded his head in thanks. *transf.*: D. WELCH Enormous sunflowers nodding their black faces along my hedge. **5** SHAKES. *Ant. & Cl.* Cleopatra Hath nodded him to her. D. JOHNSON Mr. Cheung . . nodded his protégé into the seat beside him. **b** D. LAW I nodded the ball . . in his path. **6** STEELE Ay, ay nodded the Porter; but, Sir, whom must I say I came from? O. MANNING Mrs. Mackie nodded her acceptance of this apology. **7** KEATS By every wind that nods the mountain pine.

With *adverbs in specialized senses*: **nod off** fall asleep, esp. briefly or involuntarily. **nod through** (*a*) approve with merely formal assent and without discussion; (*b*) count (a Member of Parliament) as having voted although remaining in his or her seat through infirmity etc.
■ **nodder** *noun* E17. **nodding** *adjective* (*a*) that nods; ***nodding donkey (pump)***, a small reciprocating pump for extracting oil; (*b*) BOTANY (of an inflorescence etc.) slightly pendulous: L16. **noddingly** *adverb* with a nod or nods L19.

noda *noun* pl. of NODUM.

nodal /ˈnəʊd(ə)l/ *adjective*. M19.
[from NODE + -AL¹.]
Of or pertaining to a node or nodes, of the nature of a node.
nodal point a point constituting a node; a centre of divergence or convergence.

nodality /nəʊˈdalɪti/ *noun*. L19.
[from prec. + -ITY.]
1 The degree to which a place is a point of convergence for channels, roads, etc. L19.
2 The number of nodes of an oscillation. E20.

noddle /ˈnɒd(ə)l/ *noun*. LME.
[Origin unkn.]
1 Orig., the back of or of the head. Now, the head, as part of the body or as the seat of the mind or thought (usu. with a suggestion of dullness or emptiness). *colloq.* LME. ▶**b** A person; *spec.* a foolish person. *colloq.* E18.
†**2** The back or nape of or *of* the neck. M16–L19.

> 📖 **1** F. MUIR Wondering what goes on inside cats' noddles is what makes them seem . . beautiful. K. AMIS A bald noddle with flowing locks . . on one side only.

noddle /ˈnɒd(ə)l/ *verb trans. & (now dial.) intrans.* M18.
[Frequentative of NOD *verb*: see -LE³.]
Nod or wag (the head) quickly or slightly.

noddy /ˈnɒdi/ *noun¹ & adjective*. E16.
[Perh. from NOD *verb* + -Y¹.]
▶ **A** *noun*. **1** A fool, a simpleton. E16.
2 Any of several terns of the genera *Anous* and *Procelsterna*, mostly tropical and with dark plumage, *esp.* (more fully ***common noddy***) *A. stolidus*. L16.
▶†**B** *adjective*. Foolish, silly. E16–M17.

noddy /ˈnɒdi/ *noun²*. Now *rare*. L16.
[Origin uncertain: perh. from prec.]
1 A card-game resembling cribbage. L16.
†**2** The jack in various card-games. Also ***knave noddy***. E17–E19.

noddy /ˈnɒdi/ *noun³*. M18.
[Perh. from NOD *verb* + -Y⁶. Cf. next.]
1 A light two-wheeled hackney carriage, formerly used in Ireland and Scotland. M18.
2 An inverted pendulum fitted with a spring which tends to restore it to a vertical position. M19.

noddy /ˈnɒdi/ *noun⁴*. *slang*. L20.
[from NOD *verb* or *noun* + -Y⁶. Cf. prec.]
A brief shot in a filmed interview in which the interviewer or interviewee nods in agreement or acknowledgement. Also ***noddy-shot***.

node /nəʊd/ *noun*. LME.
[Latin *nodus* knot.]
1 MEDICINE. A hard tumour; a knotty swelling or concretion on a part of the body, esp. on a joint affected by gout or rheumatism. LME.
2 A knot, a knob, a protuberance; a knotty formation. LME. ▶**b** BOTANY. A point of a stem from which one or more leaves arise. M19. ▶**c** ANATOMY. A small mass of differentiated tissue; *spec.* = LYMPH ***gland***. Also = ***node of*** RANVIER. L19.

3 A complication; an entanglement. L16.
4 ASTRONOMY. Either of the two points at which the orbit of a planet intersects the ecliptic, or at which two great circles of the celestial sphere intersect each other. M17.
5 a A point or line of rest in a standing wave system; a point at which a spherical harmonic or similar function has the value zero. M19. ▸**b** ELECTRICITY. A point of zero current or voltage. E20.
6 a GEOMETRY. A point at which a curved line or surface crosses itself. M19. ▸**b** A vertex or end-point in a network, graph, or tree diagram. Also ***node point***. M19. ▸**c** COMPUTING & TELECOMMUNICATIONS. (A device occupying) a junction in a system of components interconnected by telecommunications lines, *esp.* one in a local or wide area network. M20.
4 *ascending node*: see ASCEND *verb* 1b. ***descending node***: see DESCEND *verb*. ***lunar node***: see LUNAR *adjective*. **6b *root node***: see ROOT *noun*[1] 13c.

nodi *noun* pl. of NODUS.

nodical /ˈnəʊdɪk(ə)l/ *adjective*. M19.
[from NODE + -ICAL.]
ASTRONOMY. Of or pertaining to the nodes.

nodosarian /nəʊdəʊˈsɛːrɪən/ *adjective & noun*. M19.
[from mod. Latin *Nodosaria* (see below), formed as next: see -ARIAN.]
PALAEONTOLOGY & ZOOLOGY. ▶**A** *adjective*. Designating, pertaining to, or resembling a foraminiferan of the genus *Nodosaria*, characterized by a linear series of chambers. M19.
▶**B** *noun*. A foraminiferan of the genus *Nodosaria*. L19.
■ Also **noˈdosarine** *adjective & noun* M19.

nodose /nəʊˈdəʊs/ *adjective*. E18.
[Latin *nodosus*, formed as NODE + -OSE[1].]
Knotty; knotted, knobbed; having or characterized by knotty swellings.

nodosity /nəʊˈdɒsɪti/ *noun*. LME.
[Late Latin *nodositas*, formed as prec.: see -ITY.]
1 A knotty swelling or protuberance. LME.
2 The state or quality of being nodose. E17.

nodous /ˈnəʊdəs/ *adjective*. M17.
[formed as NODOSE: see -OUS.]
Full of knots, knotty.

nodular /ˈnɒdjʊlə/ *adjective*. L18.
[from NODULE + -AR[1].]
1 Chiefly MINERALOGY & GEOLOGY. Having the form of a nodule, occurring as nodules. L18.
2 Chiefly MEDICINE. Of the nature of or characterized by many nodules. M19.
3 METALLURGY. Of cast iron: containing carbon in the form of small spheroids rather than flakes, as brought about by adding an inoculant to increase the strength and ductility. Also called ***spheroidal***, ***spherulitic***. M20.
■ **noduˈlarity** *noun* the state or condition of being nodular M20.

nodulate /ˈnɒdjʊleɪt/ *verb*. M20.
[from NODULE + -ATE[3], or back-form. from next.]
BOTANY. **1** *verb trans*. Produce root nodules on (a plant). M20.
2 *verb intrans*. Of a plant: undergo nodulation. M20.

nodulated /ˈnɒdjʊleɪtɪd/ *adjective*. M19.
[from NODULE + -ATE[2] + -ED[1].]
Having or characterized by nodular growths, esp. root nodules.

nodulation /nɒdjʊˈleɪʃ(ə)n/ *noun*. L19.
[from next + -ATION.]
A nodule; the process of becoming, or the state of being, nodulated.

nodule /ˈnɒdjuːl/ *noun*. LME.
[Latin *nodulus* dim. of *nodus*: see NODE, -ULE.]
1 ANATOMY. A small rounded or swollen structure in the body; a small, often hard, lump, cyst, or tumour. LME. ▸**b** The most anterior part of the inferior surface of the vermis of the cerebellum. M19.
†**2** A small bag containing spices or medicines and tied with a knot; a plug used in cauterizing. LME–M18.
3 MINERALOGY, GEOLOGY, & METALLURGY. A small discrete rounded lump of material within a matrix. L17.
4 BOTANY. A small node or knot in the stem or other part of a plant; *spec*. (more fully ***root nodule***) a lump formed on the root of a leguminous plant around a group of symbiotic (esp. nitrogen-fixing) bacteria. L18.

noduli *noun* pl. of NODULUS.

nodulize /ˈnɒdjʊlʌɪz/ *verb trans*. Also **-ise**. E20.
[from prec. + -IZE.]
METALLURGY. Convert (esp. finely-divided iron ore) into nodules.
■ **noduliˈzation** *noun* E20.

nodulose /ˈnɒdjʊləʊs/ *adjective*. E19.
[from NODULE + -OSE[1].]
BOTANY & ZOOLOGY. Having little knots or knobs.
■ Also **nodulous** *adjective* M19.

nodulus /ˈnɒdjʊləs/ *noun*. Pl. **-li** /-lʌɪ, -liː/. M17.
[Latin: see NODULE.]
†**1** = NODULE 2. M17–E19.
2 ANATOMY. = NODULE 1b. M19.

nodum /ˈnəʊdəm/ *noun*. Pl. **-da** /-də/. M20.
[mod. Latin, from Latin *nodus* knot, NODE.]
ECOLOGY. A plant community of any rank; *spec*. one below the rank of an association.

nodus /ˈnəʊdəs/ *noun*. Pl. **-di** /-dʌɪ/. LME.
[Latin: see NODE.]
†**1** MEDICINE. A hard swelling; a node. LME–E18.
†**2** MATH. = BASE *noun*[1] 7. *rare*. Only in L17.
3 A knotty point, a difficulty, a complication in the plot of a story etc. E18.

†**Noe** *noun* see NOAH.

noegenesis /nəʊɪˈdʒɛnɪsɪs/ *noun*. E20.
[formed as NOESIS + -GENESIS.]
The generating or obtaining of new knowledge from experience through observation, the inferring of relations, and the consideration of correlates.
■ **noegeˈnetic** *adjective* E20.

noel /nəʊˈɛl/ *noun*. Also **noël**. E19.
[French *noël*: see NOWEL *noun*[1].]
A Christmas carol. Also (**N-**) = NOWEL *noun*[1].

noem *noun* var. of NOEME.

noema /nəʊˈiːmə, -ˈɛmə/ *noun*. Pl. **noemata** /nəʊˈiːmətə/. E20.
[Greek *noēma* a thought.]
PHILOSOPHY. An object of perception or thought, as opp. to a process or aspect of perceiving or thinking. Cf. NOESIS 3.

noematic /nəʊɪˈmatɪk/ *adjective*. M19.
[formed as NOEMA: see -ATIC.]
PHILOSOPHY & LINGUISTICS. Of or pertaining to a noeme or a noema.

noeme /ˈnəʊiːm/ *noun*. Also **noem** /ˈnəʊɛm/. M19.
[formed as prec.: see -EME.]
PHILOSOPHY & LINGUISTICS. A meaning or concept as an aspect of a unit of speech.

noesis /nəʊˈiːsɪs/ *noun*. Pl. **noeses** /nəʊˈiːsiːz/. L19.
[Greek *noēsis*, from *noein*: see NOETIC *adjective*[1].]
1 Mental capacity or action. *rare*. L19.
2 An intellectual view of the moral and physical world. *rare*. L19.
3 PHILOSOPHY. A process or aspect of perceiving or thinking, as opp. to an object of perception or thought. Cf. NOEMA. M20.

Noetian /nəʊˈiːʃ(ə)n/ *noun & adjective*. L16.
[ecclesiastical Latin *Noetiani* (pl.), from *Noetus* presbyter of the church in Asia Minor (*c* AD 230).]
ECCLESIASTICAL HISTORY. ▶**A** *noun*. A follower of Noetus in acknowledging only one person (the Father) in the Godhead. L16.
▶**B** *adjective*. Of or pertaining to Noetus or his beliefs. E18.

noetic /nəʊˈɛtɪk/ *adjective*[1] & *noun*. M17.
[Greek *noētikos*, from *noētos* intellectual, from *noein* think, perceive, from *nous*, *noos* mind, thought: see -IC.]
▶**A** *adjective*. **1** Of or pertaining to the mind or intellect; characterized by or consisting in mental or intellectual activity. M17. ▸**b** PHILOSOPHY. Of or pertaining to the act or processes of perceiving or thinking. E20.
2 Originating or existing in the mind or intellect; purely intellectual or abstract. E19.
▶**B** *noun*. **1** *sing*. & in *pl*. (treated as *sing*.). The branch of knowledge that deals with the intellect. E19.
2 That which has a purely intellectual existence or basis. M19.
■ **noetical** *adjective* M17.

Noetic /nəʊˈɛtɪk/ *adjective*[2]. *rare*. L17.
[from *Noe* var. of NOAH: see -ETIC.]
= NOACHIAN.

nog /nɒg/ *noun*[1]. Chiefly *dial*. & *techn*. E17.
[Origin unkn.]
A peg, pin, or small block of wood serving for any of various purposes.

nog /nɒg/ *noun*[2]. Also **nogg**. L17.
[Origin unkn.]
1 A kind of strong beer, brewed in East Anglia. L17.
2 In full ***egg-nog***. A hot or cold alcoholic drink with added egg and usu. milk; egg-flip. L18.

nog /nɒg/ *verb trans*. Infl. **-gg-**. L17.
[from NOG *noun*[1].]
1 Build with brick in a timber framework. Chiefly as ***nogged*** *ppl adjective*. L17.
2 Secure by nogs or pegs. E18.

Nogai *noun & adjective* var. of NOGAY.

nogaku /ˈnoːgaku, ˈnəʊgakuː/ *noun*. E20.
[Japanese *nōgaku*, from *nō* NOH + *gaku* music.]
Noh as a dramatic form or genre.

†**nogat** *noun* see NOUGAT.

Nogay /nəˈgʌɪ/ *noun & adjective*. Also **-ai**. Pl. of noun **-s**, same. L16.
[Nogay.]
Designating or pertaining to, a member of, a Turkic-speaking people inhabiting the NW Caucasus; (of) the language of this people.

nogg *noun* var. of NOG *noun*[2].

noggin /ˈnɒgɪn/ *noun*[1]. M17.
[Origin unkn.]
1 A small drinking-vessel; a mug, a cup. M17.
2 A small quantity of alcoholic liquor, usu. a quarter of a pint; a small drink of spirits etc. L17.
3 The head. Chiefly *N. Amer*. M18.

noggin *noun*[2] see next.

nogging /ˈnɒgɪŋ/ *noun*. Also (esp. in sense 2) **-in** /-ɪn/. E19.
[from NOG *noun*[1] or *verb* + -ING[1].]
1 In full ***brick-nogging***. Brickwork in a timber frame. E19.
2 A horizontal piece of timber inserted between wall studs to prevent them from twisting (also ***nogging-piece***); a horizontal timber support or strut. E19.

no-go /nəʊˈgəʊ/ *noun & adjective*. L19.
[from NO *adjective* + GO *noun*[1], esp. ***no go*** s.v. NO *adjective*. Cf. GO *adjective*, NOT-GO.]
▶**A** *noun*. Pl. **-goes**. An impracticable situation; an impasse; an indecisive contest. L19.
▶**B** *adjective*. **1** = NOT-GO. E20.
2 Esp. of a device in a spacecraft: not functioning properly; not ready and prepared. *colloq*. M20.
3 Designating an area which is impossible to enter (because of barricades etc.) or to which entry is restricted or forbidden. L20.

> **3** *Which?* Many buildings are no-go areas for people with disabilities.

Noh /nəʊ/ *noun*. Also **No**. L19.
[Japanese *nō* (also = talent, accomplishment).]
The traditional Japanese masked drama with dance and song, evolved from Shinto rites.

> *attrib*.: I. FLEMING So thickly made up that she looked like a character out of a Noh play. S. MARCUS Billie gave me .. a Noh mask from Japan.

nohow /ˈnəʊhaʊ/ *adverb & pred. adjective*. L18.
[from NO *adjective* + HOW *adverb*.]
1 In no way, by no means; not at all. Now chiefly *non-standard* & following another negative. L18.
2 In no particular manner or condition; with no distinctive or particularly good appearance or character; out of order, out of sorts, off colour, (also ***all nohow***). *colloq*. & *dial*. L18.

> **1** W. S. LANDOR The misfortune could nohow be attributed to me. *Country Quest* You don't get nothing for nothing in this life not nowhere nor nohow. **2** DICKENS Ain't Mr. B. so well this morning? You look all nohow. E. BOWEN Her shortish, thick, stiff hair sprang about, nohow.

■ **nohowish** *adjective* (*colloq*. & *dial*.) out of order, out of sorts, off colour E19.

noia /ˈnɔɪə/ *noun*. M20.
[Italian, ult. from Latin *in odio*: see ANNOY *noun*. Cf. ENNUI.]
Boredom, weariness, ennui.

noil /nɔɪl/ *noun*. E17.
[Prob. from Old French *noel* from medieval Latin *nodellus* dim. of Latin *nodus* knot (and so earlier than the written record).]
sing. & in *pl*. Short pieces and knots of wool combed out of the long staple.

noint /nɔɪnt/ *verb trans*. Now *arch*. & *dial*. Also **ˈnoint**. ME.
[Aphet.]
= ANOINT *verb*.

noir /nwɑː/ *adjective & noun*. LME.
[French.]
1 Black (*lit*. & *fig*.). *rare* exc. in phrs. below. LME.
2 Black as one of the two colours of divisions in rouge-et-noir and roulette. Earliest in ***rouge-et-noir***. L18.
1 EN NOIR. FILM NOIR. *PINOT Noir*. ***roman noir***: see ROMAN *noun*[3].

noise /nɔɪz/ *noun*. ME.
[Old & mod. French = Provençal *nausa* from Latin NAUSEA.]
1 A sound, *esp*. a loud, harsh, disagreeable, disturbing, or intrusive sound; loud shouting; clamour; a confused sound of voices and movements; the aggregate of such sounds in a particular place or at a particular time. Formerly also, strife, contention, quarrelling. ME. ▸**b** In *pl*. Conventional remarks, sounds resembling speech without actual words. Freq. in ***make noises*** below. M20.
†**2 a** Common talk, rumour, report; slander, scandal. ME–L19. ▸**b** Repute, reputation. LME–M16.
†**3** A company or band of musicians. M16–L17.
4 A person who or organization which is much talked of or the object of general notice or comment; an important person. Chiefly in ***big noise*** s.v. BIG *adjective & adverb*. *colloq*. E20.

5 *SCIENCE.* Fluctuations or disturbances (usu. random or irregular) which are not part of a signal (whether audible or not), or which interfere with or obscure a signal. **E20.**

📖 **1** DRYDEN A buzzing noise of Bees his Ears alarms. TENNYSON Thro' the noises of the night She floated down to Camelot. A. RANSOME Down the platform milk-cans were being shifted, making a loud clanging noise. C. S. FORESTER A harsh voice could be heard . . whistles being blown, much noise and bustle. C. ISHERWOOD He makes a terrific noise in the shower . . a series of shouts. G. VIDAL There was a great noise all around her, harsh voices and much laughing. N. MONSARRAT There were aeroplane noises, and ambulance noises; the telephone rang several times. M. SPARK So great was the noise during the day that I used to lie awake at night listening to the silence.

Phrases: **make a noise**, †**keep a noise** (*a*) be much talked of; be the object of general notice and comment; (*b*) make an outcry, talk much or loudly, *about*; (*c*) ***make a noise like*** (*slang*), pretend to be. **make noises** (*a*) be vocal, make comments or enquiries, (*about*); (*b*) (with defining adjective) make remarks etc. of a specified kind. **noise and number index** a quantity used in evaluating aircraft noise in terms of its intensity and duration. **noises off** off-stage sound effects. ***pink noise***: see PINK *adjective*[2]. ***red noise***: see RED *adjective*. ***signal-to-noise ratio***: see SIGNAL *noun*. ***surface noise***: see SURFACE *noun & adjective*. ***thermal noise***: see THERMAL *adjective*. ***white noise***: see WHITE *adjective*.

Comb.: **noise contour** a line or surface (imaginary or on a diagram etc.) joining points where the noise level is the same; **noise factor**, **noise figure** *ELECTRONICS* a quantity representing the additional noise introduced by a signal-processing device such as an amplifier; **noise filter** *ELECTRONICS* a filter for selectively reducing noise; **noise limiter** *ELECTRONICS* a circuit or device for selectively reducing certain types of noise, esp. by momentarily reducing the output or the gain during peaks of greater amplitude than the desired signal; **noise-maker** a person who or thing which makes a noise; *spec.* a device for making a loud noise at a festivity etc.; **noise pollution** harmful or annoying noise; **noise storm** *ASTRONOMY* a radio emission from the sun consisting of a succession of short bursts or pips in the megahertz range that lasts for a period of hours or days and is associated with sunspots.

▪ **noiseful** *adjective* noisy **LME.** **noiseless** *adjective* (*a*) silent, quiet; making no stir or commotion; (*b*) (of signals, recording equipment, etc.) characterized by a virtual absence of noise: **E17.** **noiselessly** *adverb* **M19.** **noiselessness** *noun* **M19.**

noise /nɔɪz/ *verb.* **LME.**
[from the noun or from Old French *noisier, noiser.*]
1 *verb trans.* Report, rumour, spread (*about, abroad*). **LME.** **2** *verb trans. & intrans.* Spread rumours or a report concerning (a person etc.). Long *obsolete* exc. *dial.* **LME.** **3** *verb intrans.* Talk loudly or much *of* a thing. *arch.* **LME.** **4** *verb intrans.* Make a noise or outcry. Now *arch. & dial.* **LME.**

📖 **1** SHAKES. *L.L.L.* All-telling fame Doth noise abroad Navarre hath made a vow. LD MACAULAY It was noised abroad that he had more real power to help . . than many nobles. J. HELLER Relatives of hers noising it about that she was living extravagantly. **3** CARLYLE A plan, much noised of in those days. **4** J. CLARE Rook, crow and jackdaw—noising loud, Fly to and fro to dreary fen.

noisette /nwɑːˈzɛt/ *noun*[1]. **M19.**
[Philippe *Noisette*, French gardener, fl. 1817.]
In full ***noisette rose***. A hybrid rose, *Rosa* × *noisettiana*, that is a cross between the China rose and the musk rose.

noisette /nwɑːˈzɛt/ *noun*[2]. **L19.**
[French, dim. of NOIX nut: see -ETTE.]
A small round piece of meat.

noisome /ˈnɔɪs(ə)m/ *adjective.* Now *literary.* **LME.**
[from NOY *noun*[1] or *verb* + -SOME[1].]
1 Harmful, noxious. **LME.** **2** Disagreeable, unpleasant, offensive; evil-smelling. **LME.** †**3** Annoying, troublesome. *rare.* **M16–M17.**
▪ **noisomely** *adverb* (*rare*) **L16.** **noisomeness** *noun* **E16.**

noisy /ˈnɔɪzi/ *adjective.* **L17.**
[from NOISE *noun* + -Y[1].]
1 Making, or given to making, a loud noise; clamorous, turbulent. **L17.** **2** Full of or characterized by noise; attended with noise. **L17.** ▸**b** Producing or characterized by (visual, thermal, or electronic) noise; obscured by random fluctuations or interference. **M20.** **3** Very loud in colour, conspicuous. **E20.**

📖 **1** G. GORER Six per cent of the population complain that their neighbours are noisy. W. ABISH The bus was old . . the engine was noisy. G. LORD Sam was not a noisy dog; he rarely barked. **noisy miner** *Austral.* a grey and white honeyeater, *Manorina melanocephala*, of eastern Australia. ***noisy scrub-bird***: see SCRUB *noun*[1] *& adjective*. **2** S. JOHNSON The noisy happiness which my elder brother had the fortune to enjoy. O. MANNING They found the restaurant crowded, noisy and brilliantly lit.

▪ **noisily** *adverb* **L18.** **noisiness** *noun* **E18.**

noix /nwa/ *noun.* Pl. same. **M19.**
[French, lit. 'nut'. Cf. NOISETTE *noun*[2].]
A piece of veal cut from the rump. Also ***noix de veau*** /də vo/.

nokes /nəʊks/ *noun.* Long *obsolete* exc. *Canad. dial.* Also **noax**. **L17.**
[Origin unkn.]
A fool, a simpleton.

nolens volens /nəʊlɛnz ˈvəʊlɛnz/ *adverbial phr.* **L16.**
[Latin, pres. pples of *nolo, nolle* be unwilling, *volo, velle* be willing.]
Willing or unwilling, whether willing or not, willy-nilly.

noli me tangere /ˌnəʊlʌɪ miː ˈtan(d)ʒəri, ˌnəʊlɪ meɪ ˈtaŋg(ə)ri/ *noun phr.* **LME.**
[Latin = do not touch me (*John* 20:17 in Vulgate).]
1 *MEDICINE.* An ulcerous condition attacking bone and soft tissues esp. of the face: *spec.* = LUPUS. Now *rare* or *obsolete.* **LME.** **2** A person who or thing which must not be touched or interfered with. **LME.** †**3** *BOTANY.* = TOUCH-ME-NOT 2. **M16–M18.** **4** A warning or prohibition against meddling or interference. **M17.** **5** A painting representing the appearance of Jesus to Mary Magdalen at the sepulchre (*John* 20:17). **L17.**

†**nolition** *noun.* **M17–M19.**
[from Latin *nolo, nolle* be unwilling + -ITION, after VOLITION.]
Unwillingness.

noll /nəʊl/ *noun.* Long *obsolete* exc. *dial.*
[Old English *hnoll* = Middle Dutch *nolle*, Old High German *hnol* top, summit, crown of the head.]
1 (The top or crown of) the head. **OE.** ▸†**b** A person of a specified kind. **LME–E17.** †**2** The nape of the neck; the back of the head. **LME–E18.**

nolle /ˈnɒli/ *noun. US.* **L19.**
[Abbreviation.]
= NOLLE PROSEQUI.

nolle /ˈnɒli/ *verb trans. US.* Pres. pple & verbal noun **-eing**. **L19.**
[Abbreviation of NOLLE-PROS *verb.*]
= NOL-PROS.

nolle-pros /nɒlɪˈprɒs/ *verb trans. US.* Infl. **-ss-**. Also **-pross(e)**. **L19.**
[formed as NOL-PROS.]
= NOL-PROS.

nolle prosequi /nɒlɪ ˈprɒsɪkwʌɪ/ *noun phr.* **L17.**
[Latin = be unwilling to pursue.]
LAW. (Orig., now *US*) the relinquishment by a plaintiff or prosecutor of part or all of his or her suit or prosecution; (later) a procedure by which the Attorney-General can terminate criminal proceedings. Also, an entry of this in a court record.

nolle-pross(e) *verb* var. of NOLLE-PROS.

nolo contendere /ˌnəʊləʊ kɒnˈtɛndəri/ *noun phr.* **L19.**
[Latin = I do not wish to contend.]
US LAW. A plea by which a defendant in a criminal prosecution accepts conviction as in the case of a plea of guilty but does not admit guilt.

nol-pros /nɒlˈprɒs/ *verb trans. US.* Infl. **-ss-**. **M19.**
[Abbreviation from NOLLE PROSEQUI.]
Relinquish by a ***nolle prosequi***.

nolt *noun* see NOWT *noun*[1].

†**nom** *verb pa. t. & pple* of NIM *verb.*

nom. *abbreviation.*
Nominal.

noma /ˈnəʊmə/ *noun.* Now *rare.* **M19.**
[mod. Latin alt. of Latin *nome*, Greek *nomē*, from *nom-*, *nemein* feed.]
MEDICINE. A gangrenous ulceration of the mouth or genitals, associated with weakness or malnutrition.

nomad /ˈnəʊmad/ *noun & adjective.* **L16.**
[French *nomade* from Latin *Nomades* (pl.), *Nomas* (sing.) from Greek *nomad-*, *nomas* roaming about, esp. for pasture, from base of *nemein* to pasture: see NIM *verb*, -AD[2]. See also next.]
▸**A** *noun.* A member of a people who move from place to place to find pasture; a person who leads a roaming or wandering life. **L16.**

📖 *Petroleum Today* The pipeliner is a nomad; he goes where the job is. G. L. HARDING The Bedu are originally nomads, each tribe wandering within its own tribal boundaries.

▸**B** *attrib.* or as *adjective.* Living as a nomad; nomadic; pertaining to or characteristic of nomads. **L18.**

📖 DYLAN THOMAS I have been leading a very nomad existence. J. BRONOWSKI Before 10,000 BC nomad peoples used to follow the natural migration of wild herds.

▪ **nomadism** *noun* the practice, fact, or state of leading a nomadic life **M19.** **nomadiˈzation** *noun* the action of nomadizing a people, area, etc.; the state of being nomadized: **L19.** **nomadize** *verb* (*a*) *verb intrans.* lead a nomadic life; (*b*) *verb trans.* make nomadic in character: **L18.** **nomady** *noun* the state, condition, or life of a nomad **E20.**

nomade /ˈnəʊmeɪd/ *noun & adjective.* Now *rare.* **M17.**
[Var. of prec.; later after French See also note under next.]
▸**A** *noun.* †**1** A nomadic band. *rare.* Only in **M17.** **2** A nomad. **L18.**
▸**B** *attrib.* or as *adjective.* Nomadic. **E19.**

nomades /ˈnəʊmədiːz/ *noun pl.* Now *rare.* **M16.**
[Latin *Nomades*: see NOMAD.]
Nomadic peoples, orig. *spec.* those mentioned by ancient writers.
¶ It is sometimes uncertain whether this form or the pl. of prec. is intended.

nomadic /nə(ʊ)ˈmadɪk/ *adjective.* **E19.**
[Greek *nomadikos*, from *nomad-*: see NOMAD, -IC.]
Of, pertaining to, or characteristic of nomads; moving from place to place to find pasture; leading a roaming or wandering life.

📖 C. G. SELIGMAN To some extent nomadic owing to the necessity of fresh pasturage for their flocks. M. FITZHERBERT The nomadic life, the sounds and smells of the East, had entered his blood. M. SEYMOUR Nomadic . . in his shifts of home.

▪ **nomadical** *adjective* **L18.** **nomadically** *adverb* **M19.**

nomarch /ˈnɒmɑːk/ *noun.* **M17.**
[Greek *nomarkhēs* or *nomarkhos*, from *nomos* NOME *noun*[2]: see -ARCH.]
†**1** A local ruler or governor. *rare* (Dicts.). **M–L17.** **2** The governor of an ancient Egyptian nome. **M19.** **3** The senior administrator or (formerly) governor of a modern Greek nomarchy. **L19.**

nomarchy /ˈnɒmɑːki/ *noun.* **M17.**
[Greek *nomarkhia*, formed as prec.: see -ARCHY.]
†**1** Any of various administrative divisions of a country. *rare* (Dicts.). Only in **M17.** **2** Formerly, a province, now, a smaller administrative division, of modern Greece. **M19.**

nombril /ˈnɒmbrɪl/ *noun.* **M16.**
[French = navel.]
HERALDRY. The point on an escutcheon midway between the true centre (or fess point) and the base. Also called ***navel***.

nom de dieu /nɔ̃ də djø, nɒm də ˈdjəː/ *interjection.* **M19.**
[French = name of God.]
Expr. mild surprise or annoyance.

nom de guerre /nɔ̃ də gɛːr, nɒm də ˈgɛː/ *noun phr.* Pl. ***noms de guerre*** (pronounced same). **L17.**
[French = war-name.]
An assumed name under which a person fights or engages in some other action or enterprise.

nom de plume /nɒm də ˈpluːm, *foreign* nɔ̃ də plym/ *noun phr.* Pl. **noms de plume** (pronounced same). **E19.**
[from French *nom* name, *de* of, *plume* pen, after prec.]
An assumed name under which a person writes, a pen-name.

nom de théâtre /nɔ̃ də teaːtr, nɒm də teɪˈɑːtrə/ *noun phr.* Pl. ***noms de théâtre*** (pronounced same). **L19.**
[French = theatre-name.]
An assumed name under which a person acts or otherwise performs on stage, a stage name.

nome /nəʊm/ *noun*[1]. Now *rare* or *obsolete.* **M17.**
[French *-nôme*, 2nd elem. of *binôme* etc.: see BINOMIAL.]
MATH. Each of the terms in a binomial or polynomial.

nome /nəʊm/ *noun*[2]. **E18.**
[Greek *nomos*, from *nemein* divide.]
1 Each of the thirty-six territorial divisions of ancient Egypt. **E18.** **2** An ancient Greek musical composition of a particular genre. **M18.**

nomen /ˈnəʊmən/ *noun.* Pl. **nomina** /ˈnɒmɪnə/. **E18.**
[Latin = name.]
1 *ROMAN HISTORY.* The second personal name of a Roman citizen (as Marcus *Tullius* Cicero), distinguishing the gens. **E18.** **2** *GRAMMAR.* A noun. Chiefly in phrs. below. **M19.** **3** *TAXONOMY.* A Latin name or binomial. Chiefly in phrs. below. **E20.**

Phrases: **nomen actionis** /aktɪˈəʊnɪs/ *GRAMMAR* a noun of action. **nomen agentis** /aˈdʒɛntɪs/ *GRAMMAR* an agent-noun. **nomen dubium** /ˈdjuːbɪəm/, pl. **dubia** /ˈdjuːbɪə/, [= doubtful] *TAXONOMY* a Latin name the correct application of which is vague or uncertain. **nomen nudum** /ˈnjuːdəm/, pl. **nuda** /ˈnjuːdə/, [= naked] *TAXONOMY* a Latin name which has no standing because it was not validly published.

nomenclate /ˈnəʊmənkleɪt/ *verb trans. rare.* **E19.**
[Back-form. from NOMENCLATURE.]
Assign a name or names to.

nomenclative /ˈnəʊmənˌkleɪtɪv/ *adjective.* **M19.**
[from NOMENCLATURE + -IVE.]
Concerned with or relating to the action of naming.

nomenclator /ˈnəʊmənkleɪtə/ *noun.* **M16.**
[Latin (in senses 3, 4), from *nomen* name + *calare* call.]
†**1** A pupil appointed to supervise part of the class to which he belonged. *rare.* Only in **M16.** **2** A book containing collections or lists of names or words. Long *rare.* **L16.** ▸†**b** A compiler of lists of names or words. *rare.* Only in **E17.**

3 A person who announces, or tells to another, the names of people, esp. guests. **L16.**

4 *ROMAN HISTORY.* A servant or dependent whose duty it was to inform his master of the names of people, esp. ones canvassing for office. Also, a steward who assigned or indicated the places of guests at a banquet. **E17.**

5 A person who devises or assigns names; *spec.* a person who names or classifies natural objects. **M17.**

■ **no,mencla'torial** *adjective* of or pertaining to a nomenclator or nomenclature **L19.**

nomenclature /nə(ʊ)ˈmɛŋklətʃə, ˈnəʊmənkleɪtʃə/ *noun & verb.* **E17.**
[French from Latin *nomenclatura*, formed as prec.: see -URE.]

► **A** *noun.* **1** A name, a designation. Now *rare.* **E17.**

2 The action of assigning names (esp. systematically) to things, classes, places, etc.; the manner in which names are assigned. **E17.**

3 A list or collection of names or particulars, a catalogue. Formerly also *spec.*, a glossary, a vocabulary. Now *rare.* **M17.**

4 A set of names used, or intended to be used, to designate things, classes, places, etc.; *esp.* a system of technical terms used in a science or other discipline. **M17.** ▸**b** Names, terms, or designations collectively; terminology. **L18.**

> 📖 **2** *Edinburgh Review* The nomenclature of the frozen regions .. has exercised the ingenuity of .. explorers. E. MAYR Zoological nomenclature is the application of distinctive names to each of the groups recognized in the .. classification. **4** R. BAKEWELL The pedantic nomenclature .. recently introduced into mineralogy. *American Speech* In the nomenclature of the South-western cowboy, *sombrero* is used interchangeably for hat. **b** R. L. STEVENSON There is no part of the world where nomenclature is so rich .. and picturesque as the United States. A. J. CRONIN To explain, in tongue-twisting nomenclature, the .. selective action of the kidney tubules.

► **B** *verb trans.* Name, designate. Now *rare.* **E19.**

■ **nomencla'tural** *adjective* of or pertaining to nomenclature **E19.** **nomencla'turally** *adverb* with regard to nomenclature **M20.** **nomenclaturist** *noun* = NOMENCLATOR 5 **E19.**

nomenklatura /naˌmjɛnklaˈturə, nɒˌmɛnkləˈtjʊərə/ *noun.* **M20.**
[Russian from Latin *nomenclatura*: see NOMENCLATURE.]
In the former Soviet Union: a list of influential posts in government and industry to be filled by Party appointees; *collect.* the holders of these posts, the Soviet élite.

nomic /ˈnɒmɪk/ *adjective*[1]. **E18.**
[formed as NOME *noun*[2] + -IC.]
Pertaining to or having the character of ancient Greek musical nomes.

nomic /ˈnɒmɪk/ *adjective*[2]. **L19.**
[Greek *nomikos*, from *nomos* law: see -IC.]
PHILOSOPHY. Pertaining to or concerned with a discoverable scientific or logical law.

■ **nomically** *adverb* **E20.**

nomina *noun* pl. of NOMEN.

nominable /ˈnɒmɪnəb(ə)l/ *adjective. rare.* **M18.**
[Latin *nominabilis*, from *nomin-*, *nomen* name: see -ABLE. Cf. earlier INNOMINABLE.]
Possible to name; fit to be named.

nominal /ˈnɒmɪn(ə)l/ *adjective & noun.* **L15.**
[French, or Latin *nominalis*, from *nomin-*, *nomen* name: see -AL[1].]

► **A** *adjective.* **1** *GRAMMAR.* Of or pertaining to a noun or nouns; of the nature of a noun. **L15.**

2 Of or pertaining to nominalists; holding nominalist views. *rare.* **E16.**

3 Of or pertaining to the name or naming of things; of the nature of a name. **E17.**

4 Existing in name only, not real or actual; merely named, stated, or expressed, without reference to reality or fact; minimal in relation to the true value, token; so small or insignificant as hardly to justify the name. **E17.**

5 Containing explicit mention of a name or names; consisting of or giving a set of names. **L18.**

6 Assigned to a person by name. **M19.**

7 Functioning acceptably, normal. *slang* (orig. & chiefly *ASTRONAUTICS*). **M20.**

> 📖 **4** A. G. GARDINER The challenges were couched in the most ruthless terms. This was to be no mere nominal satisfaction of honour. A. MASSIE A ghost is employed because the nominal author has no concept of how a book should be made. N. SYMINGTON In the laboratory he was paid only a nominal sum. **5** R. A. FREEMAN The nominal roll, address book and journal of the gang.

Special collocations: **nominal account**: recording financial transactions (payments and receipts) in a particular category rather than with a person or organization. **nominal definition** (a) strict verbal definition; the definition of what a word means, as opp. to an explanation or description of what it denotes. **nominal ledger**: containing nominal accounts and real accounts. **nominal value** the face value of a coin, share, etc.

► **B** *noun.* †**1** A nominalist. **E16–L18.**

†**2** A thing existing in name only. *rare.* **E–M17.**

3 *MUSIC.* A note giving its name to a scale. **E19.**

4 *GRAMMAR.* A word or phrase functioning as a noun. **E20.**

■ **nominally** *adverb* (*a*) by name; as regards a name or names; (*b*) in name (though not really or actually); ostensibly, supposedly, theoretically: **M17.**

nominalise *verb* var. of NOMINALIZE.

nominalism /ˈnɒmɪn(ə)lɪz(ə)m/ *noun.* **M19.**
[from NOMINAL + -ISM. Cf. French *nominalisme*.]
PHILOSOPHY. The doctrine that universals or abstract concepts are mere names without any corresponding reality. Opp. REALISM 1a.

nominalist /ˈnɒmɪn(ə)lɪst/ *noun & adjective.* **M17.**
[formed as prec. + -IST.]
PHILOSOPHY. ► **A** *noun.* An adherent of nominalism. **M17.**

► **B** *attrib.* or as *adjective.* Of or pertaining to nominalists or nominalism. **M19.**

■ **nomina'listic** *adjective* of the nature of or pertaining to nominalism **M19.**

nominalize /ˈnɒmɪn(ə)lʌɪz/ *verb trans.* Also **-ise.** **M17.**
[from NOMINAL + -IZE.]
Convert into a noun.
¶ In isolated use before **M20.**

■ **nominalizable** *adjective* **M20.** **nominali'zation** *noun* the action of nominalizing; a noun formed in this way: **M20.**

nominata *noun* pl. of NOMINATUM.

nominate /ˈnɒmɪnət/ *ppl adjective & †pa. pple.* **LME.**
[Latin *nominatus*, formed as next: see -ATE[2].]

1 Named, called, entitled. Now *spec.* given or having a distinctive name. **LME.**

2 Chiefly *SCOTS LAW.* Nominated, appointed. **M16.**

3 *TAXONOMY.* Designating a subordinate taxon, esp. a subspecies, which bears the same name as the taxon of which it is a subdivision. **M20.**

■ **nominately** *adverb* (*rare*) = NOMINATIM **M17.**

nominate /ˈnɒmɪneɪt/ *verb trans.* **M16.**
[Latin *nominat-* pa. ppl stem of *nominare*, from *nomin-*, *nomen* name: see -ATE[3]. Cf. prec. (earlier).]

1 Call by the name of; call, name, entitle, designate. Now *rare.* **M16.** ▸†**b** Give a name or names to; provide with a name. **L16–L17.**

2 Specify, name, fix, establish. Exc. as passing into other senses now *spec.* in *SNOOKER*, specify as the object-ball to be next hit by the cue-ball. **M16.**

3 Appoint (a person) by name to hold some office or discharge some duty. **M16.**

4 Propose or formally enter as a candidate for election or for an honour, award, etc. **M16.** ▸**b** Enter (a horse) for or *for* a race. **L19.**

5 Mention or specify by name. Now *rare.* **L16.**

6 In horse-breeding, choose (a mare) as suitable for mating *to* a particular stallion. **M20.**

> 📖 **3** G. ORWELL A ruling group is a ruling group so long as it can nominate its successors. *Hindu* Nominated boards cannot be entirely free of Government influence. **4** *My Weekly* She was nominated for an Academy Award but did not win.

nominatim /nɒmɪˈneɪtɪm/ *adverb.* **E19.**
[Latin, from *nomin-*, *nomen* name.]
Chiefly *LAW.* By name; particularly, expressly.

nomination /nɒmɪˈneɪʃ(ə)n/ *noun.* **LME.**
[Old & mod. French, or Latin *nominatio(n-)*, formed as NOMINATE *verb*: see -ATION.]

†**1** **a** The action of mentioning someone or something by name. **LME–M17.** ▸**b** The action of specifying, naming, or fixing something. *rare.* **L16–M18.**

2 The action or right of assigning a name or names to something. **LME.**

†**3** A name, a designation. **LME–L18.**

4 The action or right, or an act or right, of nominating a person to some office (in early use *spec.* ecclesiastical) or duty; the action or an act of nominating a candidate for election or for an honour, award, etc.; the action or an act of entering a horse for a race. Also, an occasion of such nominating. **LME.**

5 The fact or position of being nominated (freq. in ***in nomination***); (a formal acknowledgement of) selection to go forward to the next stage of an election process etc. **L15.**

6 A name of a person nominated, a nominee. Also (*rare*), a set of nominees. **E19.**

7 In horse-breeding, the planned mating of a particular mare and a particular stallion. **E20.**

> 📖 **4** J. A. FROUDE He had absolute power over every nomination to an English benefice. GEO. ELIOT Using voteless miners and navvies at Nominations and Elections. A. BULLOCK His nomination to the post of Ambassador in Washington. **5** W. I. JENNINGS The influence of a great landowner .. May Secure nomination by the local Conservative association. *Village Voice* He's not going to get the nomination .. without coming to some .. arrangement with the power brokers. **6** M. PUZO The Academy Award nominations came out. *Lancaster Guardian* As there were no other nominations, the chairman and committee were re-elected en bloc.

nominative /ˈnɒmɪnətɪv, *in sense A.2* -eɪtɪv/ *adjective & noun.* **LME.**
[Old & mod. French *nominatif, -ive* or Latin *nominativus* (sc. *casus* case), formed as NOMINATE *verb*: see -ATIVE.]

► **A** *adjective.* **1** *GRAMMAR.* Designating, being in, or pertaining to a case of words in inflected languages functioning as or qualifying the subject of a verb. **LME.**

2 Nominated; appointed by nomination. **M17.**

3 Of or pertaining to the giving of a name or names. *rare.* **M19.**

4 Bearing the name of a person. **L19.**

> 📖 **3** A. BURGESS We have been taught to accept the nominative claim of Amerigo Vespucci as regards America.

► **B** *noun. GRAMMAR.* The nominative case; a word, form, etc., in the nominative case. **LME.**

nominative absolute a construction in which a nominative noun or pronoun followed by an (adjectival or non-finite verbal) adjunct forms an adverbial phrase (as in *the dictionary being completed, they celebrated*).

■ **nominatival** /-ˈtʌɪv(ə)l/ *adjective* of or pertaining to the nominative case; having the character of a nominative: **M19.**

nominativus pendens /ˌnɒmɪnəˈtʌɪvəs ˈpɛndɛnz/ *noun phr.* Pl. ***nominativi pendentes*** /ˌnɒmɪnəˈtʌɪvʌɪ pɛnˈdɛntiːz/. **M19.**
[Latin, lit. 'hanging nominative'.]
GRAMMAR. A construction in which a sentence is completed as though the subject were other than it is; the apparent subject in such a construction.

nominator /ˈnɒmɪneɪtə/ *noun.* **M17.**
[Late Latin, formed as NOMINATE *verb*: see -OR.]
A person who nominates another to some office or duty; a person who nominates a candidate for election or for an honour, award, etc.

nominatum /nɒmɪˈnɑːtəm, -ˈneɪtəm/ *noun.* Pl. **-ta** /-tə/. **M20.**
[Latin, neut. of *nominatus*: see NOMINATE *ppl adjective*.]
The thing named by a sign or expression.

nominee /nɒmɪˈniː/ *noun & adjective.* **M17.**
[from NOMINATE *verb*: see -EE[1].]

► **A** *noun.* **1** A person mentioned by name; *spec.* the person named in connection with or as the recipient of an annuity, grant, etc. **M17.**

2 A person who is nominated for some office or duty; a person nominated as a candidate for election or for an honour, award, etc. **L17.**

3 A person or group of people, not the owner(s), in whose name a stock or registered bond certificate or a company is registered. **M19.**

► **B** *attrib.* or as *adjective.* That is a nominee; that is registered in the name of a nominee. **M20.**

■ **nomineeism** *noun* the system of nominating people to offices or posts **M19.**

nominis umbra /ˌnɒmɪnɪs ˈʌmbrə/ *noun phr.* **M19.**
[Latin, lit. 'the shadow or appearance of a name' (Lucan).]
A name without substance; a thing which is not what the name implies.

nomism /ˈnəʊmɪz(ə)m/ *noun.* **E20.**
[from Greek NOMOS law + -ISM.]
Legalism in religion or ethics.

■ **no'mistic** *adjective* based on law **L19.**

nomisma /nə(ʊ)ˈmɪzmə/ *noun.* Pl. **-mata** /-mətə/. **E20.**
[Greek = money, from *nomizein* use customarily, from NOMOS usage, custom.]
Hist. = BEZANT 1.

nomo- /ˈnɒməʊ/ *combining form* of Greek NOMOS law: see -O-.

■ **nomocanon** *noun* [medieval Greek *nomokanōn, -kanon*] a collection of the canons of Church councils, together with civil laws relating to ecclesiastical matters **E18.** **no'mocracy** *noun* a system of government based on a legal code; the rule of law in a community: **M19.** **nomo'genesis** *noun* (*BIOLOGY*, chiefly *Hist.*) the theory that the evolution of living organisms results more from laws inherent in their nature than from external causes **E20.**

nomogram /ˈnɒməgram/ *noun.* **E20.**
[from NOMO- + -GRAM.]
A diagram representing the relations between three or more variables by means of a number of straight or curved scales, so arranged that the value of one variable can be found by a simple geometrical construction (e.g. drawing a straight line intersecting the other scales at the appropriate values).

nomograph /ˈnɒməgrɑːf/ *noun.* **E20.**
[from NOMO- + -GRAPH: cf. NOMOGRAPHY *noun*[2].]
= prec.

nomography /nəˈmɒgrəfi/ *noun*[1]. **M18.**
[from NOMO- + -GRAPHY.]

1 A treatise on law. *rare.* **M18.**

2 The writing or formulation of laws. Now *rare.* **M19.**

■ **nomographer** *noun*[1] (now *rare*) a writer or formulator of laws, a legislator **M17.**

nomography /nəˈmɒɡrəfi/ *noun*². E20.
[French *nomographie*, formed as NOMO- + -*graphie* -GRAPHY.]
The technique of using or devising nomograms.
■ **nomographer** *noun*² a person who employs nomography M20. **nomoˈgraphic** *adjective* involving or designating a nomogram E20. **nomoˈgraphically** *adverb* by means of a nomogram M20.

nomoli /ˈnɒmɒli/ *noun*. Also **-ri** /-ri/. Pl. same. E20.
[Mende.]
A small steatite figure of a human or animal of a type found in Sierra Leone.

nomology /nɒˈmɒlədʒi/ *noun*. E19.
[from NOMO- + -LOGY.]
1 The science of laws and legislation. E19.
2 The branch of science and philosophy that deals with the laws governing natural phenomena. M19.
■ **nomoˈlogical** *adjective* pertaining to, concerned with, or designating laws, esp. (in PHILOSOPHY) those which are not logical necessities M19. **nomoˈlogically** *adverb* M20. **nomologist** *noun* an expert in or student of nomology L19.

nomori *noun* var. of NOMOLI.

nomos /ˈnɒmɒs/ *noun*. M20.
[Greek = usage, custom, law.]
THEOLOGY. The law; the law of life.

nomothetic /nɒməˈθɛtɪk/ *adjective*. M17.
[Greek *nomothetikos*, from *nomothetēs* law-giver, legislator, from NOMOS law: see -IC.]
1 = NOMOTHETICAL. M17.
2 Of or pertaining to the study or discovery of general laws. Opp. IDIOGRAPHIC. L19.

nomothetical /nɒməˈθɛtɪk(ə)l/ *adjective*. E17.
[formed as prec.: see -ICAL.]
Law-giving; legislative.

noms de guerre *noun phr.* pl. of NOM DE GUERRE.

noms de plume *noun phr.* pl. of NOM DE PLUME.

noms de théâtre *noun phr.* pl. of NOM DE THÉÂTRE.

-nomy /nəmi/ *suffix*.
[Repr. Greek -*nomia*, rel. to *nomos* law, *nemein* distribute: see -Y³.]
Forming nouns adopted from Greek and in English formations modelled on these, with the senses 'law, body of laws, management', 'branch of knowledge, science', as ***agronomy***, ***astronomy***, ***autonomy***, ***economy***, ***gastronomy***, etc.

†**non** *noun*¹. M16.
[Latin = not.]
1 A negation, a prohibition. Only in M16.
2 = NON PLACET. L17–E18.

non /nɔ̃/ *noun*². Pl. pronounced same. L20.
[French = no.]
In France and French-speaking countries, an utterance of 'non', an absolute refusal or veto.

non- /nɒn/ *prefix*.
[Anglo-Norman *noun-* = Old French *non-*, *nom-* (mod. *non-*) or their source Latin *non-* use as prefix of *non* not.]
Used in words adopted from Anglo-Norman, Old & mod. French, and Latin, in English words modelled on these, and as a freely productive prefix to form words with the sense 'not' (usu. hyphenated but sometimes also written solid).
1 Forming nouns from nouns with the sense 'not doing, failure to do, exemption from doing', as ***non-acceptance***, ***non-attendance***, ***non-observance***, ***non-payment***, ***non-recognition***, etc.; nouns from nouns with the sense 'failure to be, not being', as ***non-belligerence***, ***non-violence***, etc.
2 Forming nouns from nouns with the sense 'a person or thing not of the kind designated', as ***non-abstainer***, ***non-Indian***, ***non-joiner***, etc.; nouns from nouns with the sense 'a person or thing not wholly, adequately, or genuinely of the kind designated', as ***non-answer***, ***non-issue***, ***non-novel***, etc.
3 Forming attrib. adjectives from nouns with the sense 'not connected with or involving the thing designated', as ***non-party***, ***non-profit***, ***non-union***, etc.
4 Forming adjectives from adjectives with the sense 'failing to be, not being', as ***non-alcoholic***, ***non-British***, ***non-commutative***, ***non-corrosive***, ***non-episcopal***, ***non-indigenous***, ***non-Indo-European***, ***non-Muslim***, ***non-perishable***, ***non-Semitic***, ***non-venomous***, ***non-visual***, etc.; adjectives from adjectives with the sense 'neither such nor its (esp. blameworthy) opposite', as ***non-moral*** etc.
5 Forming adjectives from ppl adjectives with the sense 'that does not, that has not been', as ***non-aspirated***, ***non-fattening***, ***non-naturalized***, etc.
6 Forming adjectives from verbs with the sense 'not doing, not functioning or requiring to be treated in a specified way', as ***non-crush***, ***non-iron***, ***non-shrink***, etc.
7 Forming adverbs from adverbs with the sense 'not thus, not in the manner specified', as ***non-inferentially***, ***non-spatially***, ***non-uniformly***, etc.

■ **non-aˈbelian** *adjective* M20. **non-aˈbility** *noun* (long *rare*) inability, incapacity L15. **non-abˈstainer** *noun* a person who does not abstain, esp. from alcohol L19. **non-acˈceptance** *noun* failure or refusal to accept L17. **non-ˈaccess** *noun* (LAW) impossibility of access for sexual intercourse (in questions of paternity etc.) L18. **non-act** *noun* a thing which is not an act; a failure or refusal to act: M17. **non-ˈaction** *noun* a failure or refusal to act M19. **non-aˈddictive** *adjective* (esp. of a drug) not tending to cause addiction or dependence M20. **non-adˈmission** *noun* failure or refusal to admit L17. **non-adˈvertence** *noun* lack of advertence or attention (*to*) M16. **non-aˈggression** *noun* & *adjective* (**a**) *noun* lack of or restraint from aggression; (**b**) *attrib. adjective* involving lack of or restraint from aggression (freq. in ***non-aggression pact***): E20. **non-alcoˈholic** *adjective* (of a drink etc.) not containing alcohol E20. **non-aˈligned** *adjective* that is not aligned; POLITICS (of a State etc.) not aligned with another (esp. major) power: M20. **non-aˈlignment** *noun* lack or absence of alignment; POLITICS the condition of being non-aligned: M20. **non-allerˈgenic** *adjective* not causing an allergic reaction M20. **non-aˈllergic** *adjective* not allergic; *spec.* non-allergenic: M20. **non-amˈbiguous** *adjective* unambiguous, free from ambiguity M20. **non-Aˈmerican** *adjective* & *noun* (**a**) *adjective* not American, of a nationality other than American; (**b**) *noun* a non-American person: E20. **non-aˈpparent** *adjective* not apparent, not clear or manifest M18. **non-aˈppearance** *noun* failure or refusal to appear or be present, esp. as a witness etc. in a court of law L15. **non-ˈart** *noun* (**a**) *gen.* something that is not art; (**b**) a form of art avoiding artifice or rejecting conventional modes and methods: M20. **non-ˈAryan** *adjective* & *noun* (**a**) *adjective* not Aryan or of Aryan descent; *spec.* (esp. in Nazi Germany) Jewish; (**b**) a person who is not an Aryan; *spec.* (esp. in Nazi Germany) a Jew: M19. **non-aˈssociative** *adjective* (**a**) not characterized by association (esp. of ideas); (**b**) MATH. not associative; characterized by or designating operations in which the result is dependent on the grouping of quantities or elements: M20. **non-aˈttached** *adjective* that is not attached; *fig.* unconcerned or uninvolved, esp. with material things: M19. **non-aˈttachment** *noun* the state of being non-attached M20. **non-aˈttendance** *noun* failure or refusal to attend L17. **non-aˈttributable** *adjective* that cannot or may not be attributed to a particular source etc. L20. **non-aˈttributably** *adverb* L20. **non-availaˈbility** *noun* L20. **non-bank** *adjective* not connected with or transacted by a banking house; (of an institution) not a bank: M20. **non-barˈbiturate** *noun* (PHARMACOLOGY) a drug that is not a barbiturate M20. **non-ˈbeing** *noun* (**a**) the state of not being; non-existence; (**b**) a non-existent person or thing: LME. **non-beˈliever** *noun* a person who does not believe in something, a person with no (esp. religious) faith L19. **non-beˈlligerence** *noun* the state of being non-belligerent; the position or status of a non-belligerent nation, State, etc.: M20. **non-beˈlligerency** *noun* = NON-BELLIGERENCE M20. **non-beˈlligerent** *adjective* & *noun* (**a**) *adjective* (esp. of a nation, State, etc.) not actively engaged in hostilities; not aggressive; abstaining from active involvement in a war etc. but tending to favour one side (as distinct from ***neutral***); (**b**) *noun* a non-belligerent nation, State, etc.: E20. **nonbiodeˈgradable** *adjective* M20. **non-bioˈlogical** *adjective* not belonging to biology or forming part of its subject matter; not of biological origin; not occurring in, involving, or pertaining to living organisms: M20. **non-ˈblack** *adjective* & *noun* (**a**) *adjective* not black; (**b**) *noun* (***non-black***) (a person who is) not black: E20. **non-ˈbreakable** *adjective* that is not breakable L20. **non-ˈcapital** *adjective* (of a crime etc.) not punishable by death L19. **non-ˈCatholic** *noun* & *adjective* (**a**) *noun* a person who is not a Roman Catholic; (**b**) *adjective* (of a person, institution, etc.) not Roman Catholic; not Catholic: L18. **non-ˈChristian** *noun* & *adjective* (**a**) *noun* a person who is not a Christian, *esp.* an adherent of another religion; (**b**) *adjective* of or pertaining to a non-Christian or non-Christians: L17. **non-chronoˈlogical** *adjective* = UNCHRONOLOGICAL 1 M20. **non-ˈcitizen** *noun* a person who is not a citizen, esp. of a particular State etc. (freq. *attrib.*) L19. **non-ˈclassified** *adjective* (esp. of information) that is not officially secret or classified M20. **non-ˈclerical** *adjective* not clerical, not doing or involving clerical work M19. **non-ˈclinical** *adjective* not clinical; *esp.* not accompanied by directly observable symptoms: M20. **non-coding** *adjective* (GENETICS) that does not direct the production of a peptide sequence L20. **non-coˈllegiate** *noun* & *adjective* (**a**) *noun* a person not educated in or attached to a college; a member of a non-collegiate body; (**b**) *adjective* (of a person) not educated in or attached to a college; (of a university etc.) not consisting of or having colleges: L17. **non-com** *noun* (*colloq.*) [abbreviation] a non-commissioned officer L19. **non-ˈcombatant** *noun* & *adjective* (**a**) *noun* a person who is not a combatant; *esp.* a person not participating in active fighting during a war, as a civilian, army chaplain, etc.; (**b**) *adjective* of, pertaining to, or characteristic of a non-combatant or non-combatants: E19. †**non-commission** *adjective* non-commissioned L17–M18. **non-coˈmmissioned** *adjective* (esp. of an officer) not holding a commission E18. **non-coˈmmittal** *adjective* & *noun* (orig. *US*) (**a**) *adjective* avoiding committing oneself to a definite course of action or side of a question; (**b**) *noun* a non-committal response; non-committal behaviour: E19. **non-coˈmmittalism** *noun* (orig. *US*) non-committal action, practice, state of mind, etc. M19. **non-coˈmmittally** *adverb* (orig. *US*) in a non-committal manner; without committing oneself: L19. **non-coˈmmunicant** *noun* a person who is not a communicant, *esp.* one who does not receive Holy Communion M16. **non-coˈmmunicating** *adjective* L17. **non-ˈcommunist**, **-C-** *adjective* & *noun* (**a**) *adjective* not communist; not adhering to communism; (**b**) *noun* a non-communist person: E20. **non-comˈpearance** *noun* (SCOTS LAW) failure or refusal to appear in a court of law M16. **non-comˈpetitive** *adjective* not competitive, not involving competition M20. **non-comˈpliance** *noun* failure or refusal to comply L17. **non-comˈpounder** *noun* a person who is not a compounder; (*obsolete exc. Hist.*) a supporter of the unconditional restoration of James II: M17. **non-conˈcur** *verb* (*US*) (**a**) *verb trans.* (now *rare* or *obsolete*) fail or refuse to concur in or agree to; (**b**) *verb intrans.* fail or refuse to concur, disagree, (usu. foll. by *in*, *with*): E18. **non-conˈdensing** *adjective* designating a kind of steam engine in which steam leaving the cylinder is not condensed in a condenser but discharged into the atmosphere M19. **non-conˈducting** *adjective* that does not conduct heat or electricity; that is a non-conductor: L18. **non-conˈductor** *noun* a substance or medium that does not permit the passage of some form of energy (as heat or electricity) M18. **non-confiˈdential** *adjective* L20. **non-confiˈdentially** *adverb* L20. **non-conˈjunction** *noun* (**a**) GENETICS (*rare*) the failure of homologous chromosomes to pair at meiosis; (**b**) LOGIC the relation of the terms in a proposition asserting the negative of a conjunctive proposition: E20. **non-ˈconsequence** *noun* lack of consequence in reasoning; an instance of this, a *non sequitur*: M17. **non-conˈsumption** *noun* failure or refusal to consume a specified article of food L18. **non-content** *noun* (**a**) a negative voter in the House of Lords, a person who votes 'not content' (see CONTENT *adjective* & *noun*³); (**b**) a person who is not content: L18. **non-conˈtentious** *adjective* M19. **non-conˈtingent** *adjective* L19. **non-contraˈdiction** *noun* lack or absence of contradiction M19. **non-conˈtributory** *adjective* (of a pension, a pension scheme, etc.) not involving contributions E20. **non-controˈversial** *adjective* L19. **non-coˈoperate** *verb intrans.* fail or refuse to cooperate E20. **non-coopeˈration** *noun* failure or refusal to cooperate, esp. as part of a programme of civil disobedience L18. **non-coˈoperator** *noun* a person who practises or advocates non-cooperation E20. **non-count** *adjective* (GRAMMAR) not countable L20. **non-ˈcrossover** *noun* & *adjective* (GENETICS) (designating) a gamete or individual which does not exhibit the results of crossing over between two genetic loci E20. **non-cuˈstodial** *adjective* (LAW) (**a**) (of a sentence) not involving imprisonment; (**b**) (of a divorced parent) not granted custody of a child or children: L20. **non-deˈlivery** *noun* failure or refusal to deliver M18. **non-denomiˈnational** *adjective* not restricted as regards religious denomination E20. **non-deˈstructive** *adjective* that does not involve destruction, esp. of an object or material being tested; COMPUTING that does not involve erasure of data: E20. **non-deˈstructively** *adverb* M20. **non-diˈmensional** *adjective* (of a quantity) dimensionless; (of an equation) composed of dimensionless terms: L19. **non-diˈrectional** *adjective* lacking directional properties; *esp.* equally sensitive, intense, etc., in every direction: E20. **non-disˈclosure** *noun* failure or refusal to disclose something E20. **non-disˈjunction** *noun* (**a**) GENETICS the failure of one or more pairs of homologous chromosomes or sister chromatids to separate normally during nuclear division, usu. resulting in an abnormal distribution of chromosomes in the daughter nuclei; (**b**) LOGIC the relation of the terms in a proposition asserting the negative of a disjunctive proposition: E20. **non-disˈjunctional** *adjective* pertaining to or involving non-disjunction E20. **non-diˈstinctive** *adjective* (LINGUISTICS) (esp. of speech sounds) not distinctive E20. **non-ˈdrinker** *noun* a person who does not drink (esp. alcoholic liquor) E20. **non-drip** *adjective* that does not drip M20. **non-ˈdriver** *noun* a person who does not or cannot drive (esp. a motor vehicle) M20. **non-ˈearning** *adjective* not earning (esp. a regular wage or salary) L20. **non-eˈffective** *adjective* & *noun* (**a**) *adjective* (of a soldier etc.) not available for active service; of, pertaining to, or characteristic of such a soldier etc.; *gen.* producing no effect; (**b**) *noun* a non-effective soldier etc.: M18. **non-eˈfficient** *noun* & *adjective* (now *rare* or *obsolete*) (**a**) *noun* a soldier, esp. a volunteer, who has failed to meet a training standard; (**b**) *adjective* (of a soldier, esp. a volunteer) non-efficient: M19. **non-ˈego** *noun* (PHILOSOPHY) all that is not the ego or conscious self; the object as opp. to the subject: E19. **non-ˈelastic** *adjective* not elastic, lacking in elasticity M18. **non-eˈlect** *adjective* not elect or chosen; *spec.* (THEOLOGY) not chosen for salvation: L17. **non-eˈlection** *noun* the state of not being elect or (THEOLOGY) chosen for salvation; failure to elect or to be elected: M17. **non-eˈlective** *adjective* not appointed or filled by election E20. **non-eˈlectric** *adjective* & *noun* (**a**) *adjective* not electric; not generating or powered by electricity; †(**b**) *noun* a non-electric thing or substance; *spec.* a substance which does not generate static electricity when rubbed: M18. **non-eˈlectrified** *adjective* M18. **non-ˈemptiness** *noun* (MATH. & LOGIC) the property of being non-empty M20. **non-ˈempty** *adjective* (MATH. & LOGIC) (of a class or set) not empty, having at least one member or element: M20. **non-ˈentry** *noun* (**a**) SCOTS LAW (now *Hist.*) failure of the heir of a deceased vassal to renew investiture; the feudal casualty due to the immediate superior upon such failure; (**b**) the act or fact of not entering; no entrance: L15. **non-ˈessence** *noun* (*rare*) non-existence E17. **non-eˈssential** *adjective* & *noun* (**a**) *adjective* not essential; (**b**) *noun* a non-essential thing: M18. **non-Euroˈpean** *adjective* & *noun* (**a**) *adjective* not European; (**b**) *noun* a non-European person; *esp.* (in South Africa) a non-white: L19. **non-eˈvaluative** *adjective* M20. **non-eˈvent** *noun* an unimportant or unexciting event; an anticlimatic occurrence; occas., something that did not happen: M20. **non-exeˈcution** *noun* omission or failure to execute or carry out something M17. **non-eˈxecutive** *adjective* & *noun* (**a**) *adjective* not having an executive function; (**b**) *noun* a non-executive director of a company etc.: M20. **non-exˈplosive** *adjective* (of a substance) not explosive, that does not explode M20. **non-exporˈtation** *noun* failure or refusal to export goods etc. L18. **non-fat** *noun* a substance, esp. in food, that is not a fat M20. **non-ˈfattening** *adjective* (of food etc.) not fattening, that does not fatten E20. **nonˈfeasance** *noun* (LAW) failure to perform an act required by law E17. **non-ˈferrous** *adjective* designating, of, or pertaining to metals other than iron and its alloys; not containing a significant amount of iron: L19. **non-ˈfiction** *noun* (the genre comprising) prose writings other than fiction, esp. including biography and reference books (freq. *attrib.*) M19. **non-ˈfictional** *adjective* of, pertaining to, or characteristic of non-fiction L19. **non-ˈfigurative** *adjective* not figurative; ART abstract: E20. **non-ˈfinite** *adjective* not finite; *esp.* (GRAMMAR) (of a verb part or form) not limited by person or number L19. **non-ˈflam** *adjective* = NON-FLAMMABLE E20. **non-ˈflammable** *adjective* not flammable, not likely to catch fire M20. **non-fulˈfilment** *noun* failure to fulfil something, esp. an obligation E19. **non-ˈfunctional** *adjective* not functional, not having a function E20. **non-ˈgenital** *adjective* L20. **non-governˈmental** *adjective* not belonging to or associated with a government E20. **non-ˈgreasy** *adjective* E20. **non-hero** *noun* an anti-hero, esp. in a novel; a person who is not genuinely a hero: M20. **non-Hodgkin's lymphoma** *noun phr.* (MEDICINE) a form of malignant lymphoma distinguished from Hodgkin's disease only by the absence of binucleate giant cells L20. **non-hoˈmologous**

For other words beginning with *non-* see the main alphabetic sequence of entries

adjective (esp. of a chromosome pair) not homologous E20. **non-ˈhuman** *adjective* (*a*) not of the human race, not a human being; (*b*) not characteristic of or appropriate to the human race: M19. **non-imporˈtation** *noun* failure or refusal to import goods etc. L18. **non-inˈfectious** *adjective* (esp. of a disease) not infectious E20. **non-inˈflammable** *adjective* = NON-FLAMMABLE above M19. **non-inˈflected** *adjective* not inflected; (of a language) not having inflections: M19. **non-inˈtelligence** *noun* (*rare*) †(*a*) failure to understand; (*b*) lack of intelligence: L17. **non-inˈtelligent** *noun & adjective* †(*a*) *noun* a person who is not intelligent; (*b*) *adjective* not intelligent: E17. **non-ˈintercourse** *noun* lack or prohibition of intercourse or esp. social communication; ***non-intercourse act*** (*US HISTORY*), an act of 1809 prohibiting ships from France and Great Britain from entering American ports: E19. **non-interˈference** *noun* failure or refusal to interfere, esp. in a political dispute M19. **non-interˈvene** *verb intrans.* practise non-intervention E20. **non-interˈvener** *noun* a person who does not intervene; a non-interventionist: M20. **non-interˈvention** *noun* lack of intervention; the principles or practice of not becoming involved in others' affairs, esp. as adopted by one State with regard to another: M19. **non-interˈventionism** *noun* the principle or policy of non-intervention M20. **non-interˈventionist** *noun & adjective* (*a*) *noun* a person who favours or advocates non-intervention; (*b*) *adjective* of or pertaining to non-interventionists or non-intervention: M19. **non-inˈtoxicating** *adjective* not intoxicating; (of drink) not causing intoxication: L19. **non-inˈtrusion** *noun* failure or refusal to intrude, lack of intrusion; in the Church of Scotland, the principle of resisting the intrusion of an unacceptable minister on a congregation: M19. **non-invasive** *adjective* not invasive; *spec.* in *MEDICINE* (*a*) (of a medical procedure) not requiring incision into the body or removal of tissue; (*b*) (of a pathogen, infection, etc.) not tending to spread to new sites: L20. **non-iˈonic** *adjective & noun* (*a*) *adjective* not ionic; *spec.* (esp. of a detergent) not dissociating into ions in aqueous solution; (*b*) *noun* a non-ionic substance: M20. **non-ˈiron** *adjective* (of a fabric etc.) that needs no ironing M20. **non-ˈJewish** *adjective* not Jewish; not of Jewish descent: M20. **nonˈjoinder** *noun* (*LAW*) the omission of a person who ought to be made a party to an action M19. **non-judgeˈmental** *adjective* not judgemental, avoiding moral judgements M20. **nonˈjurancy** *noun* (chiefly *Hist.*) the condition of being a nonjuror; the principles or practice of nonjurors: E18. **nonˈjurant** *adjective & noun* (chiefly *Hist.*) (*a*) *adjective* that is a nonjuror; belonging to or characteristic of nonjurors; (*b*) *noun* a nonjuror: L17. **nonˈjuring** *ppl adjective* refusing to become a juror; *spec.* (*Hist.*), refusing to take the oath of allegiance of 1689 to William and Mary or their successors: L17. **nonˈjuror** *noun* a person who is not a juror; *spec.* (*Hist.*) a beneficed clergyman refusing to take the oath of allegiance of 1689 to William and Mary or their successors: L17. **non-ˈjury** *noun & adjective* (an action, case, etc.) not having or requiring a jury L19. **non-ˈknowledge** *noun* lack of knowledge E16. **nonˈleaded** *adjective* (of petrol) unleaded M20. **non-ˈlethal** *adjective* E17. **non-life** *noun* absence or negation of life M18. **non-ˈliterary** *adjective* (esp. of writing, a text, etc.) not literary in character L19. **non-ˈliterate** *adjective & noun* (*ANTHROPOLOGY*) (*a*) *adjective* designating a person, culture, etc., having no written language; (*b*) *noun* a non-literate person: M20. **non-ˈlogical** *adjective* not involving or proceeding from logic E19. **non-magˈnetic** *adjective* (of a substance) not magnetic E19. **non-maˈlignant** *adjective* (*MEDICINE*) benign, not cancerous M20. **non-ˈmaterial** *adjective* M19. **non-ˈmember** *noun* a person who is not a member of a particular association, club, etc. M17. **non-ˈmembership** *noun* the state of being a non-member M17. **non-ˈmetal** *noun* a non-metallic element or substance M19. **non-meˈtallic** *adjective* consisting of or designating an element or substance that is not metallic E19. **non-migratory** /nɒnˈmʌɪɡrət(ə)ri, nɒnmʌɪˈɡreɪt(ə)ri/ *adjective* that does not migrate E20. **non-ˈmilitant** *adjective & noun* (*a*) *adjective* not militant; (*b*) *noun* a non-militant person: L20. **non-ˈmilitary** *adjective* not military; not involving armed forces: M19. **non-miniˈsterial** *adjective* not ministerial; *esp.* not pertaining to (the role of) a governmental minister: E20. **non-ˈmoral** *adjective* not moral; not concerned with morality: M19. **non-ˈnative** *adjective & noun* (*a*) *adjective* not native; that is not a native inhabitant, species, speaker, etc.; (*b*) *noun* a person who or thing which is a non-native: M19. **non-neˈcessity** *noun* the condition of being unnecessary; absence of necessity: L16. **non-ˈnegative** *adjective* not negative; *MATH.* either positive or equal to zero: M18. **non-neˈgotiable** *adjective* not negotiable; that cannot be negotiated, esp. commercially: L19. **non-net** /nɒnˈnɛt, ˈnɒn-/ *adjective* (of a book) not subject to a minimum or net selling price M20. **non-Newˈtonian** *adjective* not Newtonian; *esp.* pertaining to or designating fluids whose rate of shear is not proportional to the shearing stress: E20. **non-ˈnormal** *adjective* E20. **non-norˈmality** *noun* M20. **non-ˈnuclear** *adjective* (*a*) not involving or forming part of a nucleus or nuclei; (*b*) not involving nuclear energy; (*c*) (of a State etc.) not having nuclear weapons: E20. **non-oˈbedience** *noun* failure or refusal to obey L16. **non-ˈobject** *noun & adjective* (*a*) (a thing which is) not corporeal; (*b*) *GRAMMAR* (the condition of) not functioning as a grammatical object: E20. **non-obˈjective** *adjective* not objective; *ART* abstract: E20. **non-obˈservance** *noun* failure or refusal to observe, esp. an agreement, requirement, etc. M18. **non-ˈoccurrence** *noun* E19. **non-opeˈrational** *adjective* that does not operate or work; that does not involve operations: M20. **non-orˈganic** *adjective* not organic E20. **non-orientaˈbility** *noun* (*MATH.*) the property of being non-orientable M20. **non-ˈorientable** *adjective* (*MATH.*) (of a surface) such that a figure in the surface can be continuously transformed into its mirror image by taking it round a closed path in the surface; not orientable: M20. **non-paraˈmetric** *adjective* (*STATISTICS*) not involving any assumptions as to the form or parameters of a frequency distribution M20. **non-parˈticipant** *noun* a person who is not participating L19. **non-parˈticipating** *adjective* not participating, not taking part E20. **non-partiˈsan** *adjective* L19. **non-partiˈsanship** *noun* L19. **non-past** *noun & adjective* (*GRAMMAR*) (designating or pertaining to) a tense not expressing a past action or state, *esp.* the present tense or present and future tense; of or pertaining to a non-past tense: M20. **non-ˈpatrial** *noun & adjective* (designating) a person who is not a patrial L20. **non-ˈpaying** *noun* failure or refusal to pay, non-payment LME. **non-ˈpayment** *noun* failure or refusal to pay; the condition of not being paid: LME. **non-perˈception** *noun* lack of perception; failure to perceive: L17. **non-perˈformance** *noun* failure or refusal to perform or fulfil a condition, promise, etc.; the state of not being performed: E16. **non-perˈforming** *noun & adjective* (*a*) *noun* failure or refusal to perform; (*b*) *adjective* not performing or functioning; (of an investment, loan, etc.) producing no income: LME. **non-periˈodic** *adjective* not periodic; aperiodic: M19. **non-perˈsistent** *adjective* (*BIOLOGY*) that does not persist (esp. in the environment, an organism, etc.); *spec.* (of a plant virus) carried briefly in the stylets of an insect vector: M20. **non-ˈperson** *noun* a person regarded as non-existent or unimportant, or as having no rights; an ignored, humiliated, or forgotten person: M20. **non-ˈpersonal** *adjective & noun* (*a*) *adjective* not personal; (*b*) *noun* a non-personal thing; *spec.* (*GRAMMAR*) an impersonal pronoun: E20. **non-ˈphysical** *adjective* L19. **non-ˈphysically** *adverb* M20. **non-ˈplaying** *adjective* not playing or taking part, esp. in a sporting contest L19. **non-ˈplural** *noun & adjective* (*a*) *noun* the fact or condition of being only one in number; (*b*) *adjective* (*GRAMMAR*) not in the plural form: M20. **non-ˈpoisonous** *adjective* (esp. of a substance) not poisonous L19. **non-polar** *adjective* (*PHYSICS & CHEMISTRY*) not polar; *spec.* having no electric dipole moment: L19. **non-poˈlitical** *adjective & noun* (*a*) *adjective* not political; not involved in politics; (*b*) *noun* a non-political person: M19. **non-ˈporous** *adjective* (esp. of a substance) not porous M19. **non-ˈpositive** *adjective* (*MATH.*) either negative or equal to zero M20. **non-preˈscription** *adjective* (of a medicine) available for sale or purchase without a prescription; designating such sale or purchase: L20. **non-ˈpressure** *adjective* involving or designed for operation at normal (air) pressure; characterized by a lack of pressure: M20. **non-ˈprinting** *adjective* that does not print M20. **non-proˈductive** *adjective* E20. **non-proˈfessional** *adjective & noun* (*a*) *adjective* not professional; *esp.* (of a person) not belonging to or connected with a profession; (*b*) *noun* a non-professional person: E19. **non-proˈficiency** *noun* failure to make progress or improve L16. **non-ˈprofit** *adjective* not involving or making a profit; ***non-profit-making***, (of an enterprise etc.) not conducted primarily to make a profit: M20. **non-prolifeˈration** *noun* the prevention of an increase in something, esp. in the possession of nuclear weapons M20. **non-proˈprietary** *adjective* not privately owned; (of a name, term, etc.) not proprietary, generic: M20. **non-proˈvided** *adjective* (chiefly *Hist.*) (of a public elementary school) not provided by a local education authority E20. **non-ˈracial** *adjective* not involving race or racial factors E20. **non-radioˈactive** *adjective* M20. **non-ˈrandom** *adjective* not random, ordered randomly M20. **non-ˈrandomly** *adverb* L20. **non-ˈrandomness** *noun* M20. **non-ˈrational** *adjective* L19. **non-ratioˈnality** *noun* E20. **non-ˈreader** *noun* a person who does not or who cannot read M20. **non-reˈducing** *adjective* (*CHEMISTRY*) (of a sugar) that does not reduce test solutions containing copper (II) salts (cf. REDUCING *ppl adjective*) M20. **non-refeˈrential** *adjective* not referential, without reference to anything; not indicating a referent or having a referent as object: E20. **non-reˈflexive** *adjective* (*a*) *GRAMMAR* not reflexive; (*b*) *PHILOSOPHY* (of a relation) possibly but not necessarily holding between a thing and itself: M20. **†non-regardance** *noun* (*rare*, Shakes.) failure or refusal to regard something: only in E17. **non-ˈregent** *noun* (now *Hist.*) chiefly at the universities of Oxford and Cambridge, a master of arts not responsible for presiding over disputations, one who is not a regent LME. **non-reguˈlation** *adjective* not regulation; *Hist.* designating Indian provinces not having the ordinary laws in force: M19. **non-reˈsistance** *noun* failure or refusal to resist, lack of resistance (*to*); *spec.* the practice or principle of not resisting authority, even when unjustly exercised: LME. **non-reˈsistant** *adjective & noun* (*a*) *adjective* not resistant; of or pertaining to non-resistance; (*b*) *noun* a person who does not resist; *spec.* an advocate or follower of non-resistance: E18. **non-reˈsisting** *adjective* not resisting, non-resistant E18. **non-reˈstrictive** *adjective* not restrictive; *GRAMMAR* designating a word, phrase, or clause not restricting or limiting the meaning of the word or words to which it is added: E20. **nonreˈward** *noun* (*PSYCHOLOGY*) (in learning experiments) deliberate withholding of an expected reward M20. **non-ˈrhotic** *adjective* (*PHONETICS*) relating to or designating a dialect in which *r* is pronounced in pre-vocalic position only L20. **non-ˈrigid** *adjective & noun* (*a*) *adjective* (esp. of a material) not rigid; *spec.* (of an airship) having no framework to support the envelope; (*b*) *noun* a non-rigid airship: E20. **non-ˈscene** *adjective* (of a homosexual) not inclined to participate in the social environment frequented predominantly by other homosexuals L20. **non-scienˈtific** *adjective* not scientific; not involving science or scientific methods: M19. **non-ˈscientist** *noun* M20. **non-seˈcretor** *noun* a person whose saliva and other secretions do not contain blood-group antigens M20. **non-secˈtarian** *adjective* M19. **non-segˈmental** *adjective* that does not fall within certain defined segments M20. **non-seˈlective** *adjective* E20. **non-ˈsensible** *adjective* M19. **non-ˈsensitive** *noun & adjective* †(*a*) *noun* a person who or thing which is not sensitive; (*b*) *adjective* not sensitive: E17. **non-ˈsequence** *noun* (*GEOLOGY*) an interruption in the deposition of adjacent strata inferred from a gap in the fossil record E20. **non-ˈsexist** *adjective* L20. **non-ˈsexual** *adjective* not based on or involving sex M19. **non-ˈsexually** *adverb* L19. **non-sigˈnificance** *noun* the state of being non-significant M19. **non-sigˈnificant** *noun & adjective* (*a*) *noun* (long *rare* or *obsolete*) something that is not significant; (*b*) *adjective* not significant: E17. **non-ˈskid** *adjective & noun* (*a*) *adjective* that does not skid, that is designed to prevent skidding; (*b*) *noun* a non-skid object, substance, etc., *esp.* a non-skid tyre: E20. **non-ˈslip** *adjective* that does not slip, that is designed to prevent slipping E20. **non-ˈsmoker** *noun* (*a*) a person who does not smoke; (*b*) *colloq.* a train compartment etc. in which smoking is forbidden: M19. **non-ˈsmoking** *adjective* (*a*) designating a train compartment etc. in which smoking is forbidden; (*b*) designating or pertaining to a person who does not smoke: L19. **non-ˈsoluble** *adjective* (esp. of a substance) not soluble L20. **non-ˈsolvency** *noun* (long *rare* or *obsolete*) failure or inability to pay what one owes; insolvency: E18. **non-ˈspecialist** *adjective & noun* (a person who is) not a specialist, esp. in a particular subject: E20. **non-speˈcific** *adjective* not specific; not restricted in extent, effect, etc.: M20. **non-ˈstandard** *adjective* (*a*) not standard; *spec.* (of language) containing features which are widely used but generally considered incorrect; (*b*) *MATH.* involving infinitesimals and infinities, as quantities which are not defined in the real number system but can be rigorously accommodated in a model which includes that system: E20. **non-ˈstarter** *noun* (*a*) a person who or thing which does not start; *esp.* a person or animal failing to start in a race or other contest; (*b*) a person or thing unlikely to succeed or be effective; an impracticable idea: M19. **non-ˈstellar** *adjective* that is not or does not appear to be a star E20. **non-ˈstick** *adjective* that does not stick, (esp. of a cooking utensil) that is designed to prevent sticking M20. **non-stoichioˈmetric** *adjective* (*CHEMISTRY*) containing or representing atoms of different elements in numbers that do not bear a simple integral ratio to one another or are not in the ratio expected from an ideal formula M20. **non-ˈstop** *adjective, noun, & adverb* (*a*) *adjective* that does not stop; (of a train etc.) not stopping at intermediate places; (of a journey etc.) made or done without break; (of a variety show etc.) having no interval between the various acts; (*b*) *noun* a non-stop train; a non-stop journey; (*c*) *adverb* without stopping or pausing: E20. **non-subˈscriber** *noun* (*a*) a person failing or refusing to subscribe to an undertaking, a religious creed, etc.; *SCOTTISH HISTORY* a person who was not a subscriber to the National Covenant of 1638; (*b*) a person who does not pay a subscription: L16. **non-subˈscribing** *noun* the action or practice of a non-subscriber M17. **non-subˈstantial** *adjective* (chiefly *PHILOSOPHY*) not substantial, lacking substance L19. **non-sucˈcess** *noun* lack of success M17. **non-sucˈcessful** *adjective* M19. **non-ˈsummons** *noun* (*LAW*, chiefly *Hist.*) failure to serve a summons in due time M17. **non-ˈswimmer** *noun* a person who does not or who cannot swim E20. **non-syˈllabic** *adjective & noun* (*LINGUISTICS*) (*a*) *adjective* asyllabic; *spec.* designating a speech sound not constituting the peak sonority of a syllable; (*b*) *noun* a non-syllabic speech sound: M19. **non-ˈtechnical** *adjective* not technical; without technical knowledge: M19. **†non-term** *noun* the time of vacation between two terms; the end of term; *gen.* a period of inaction: E17–E19. **non-theˈmatic** *adjective* (*a*) = ATHEMATIC *adjective* 1, 2; (*b*) not conveying new information; rhematic: M20. **non-ˈtoxic** *adjective* M20. **non-transˈferable** *adjective* that may not be transferred M19. **non-ˈtreaty** *adjective & noun* (*N. Amer.*, chiefly *Hist.*) (*a*) *adjective* of or pertaining to an American Indian person or people not subject to a treaty made with the Government; (*b*) *noun* a non-treaty American Indian: L19. **non-ˈtrivial** *adjective* not trivial; significant; *spec.* in *MATH.*, such that not all variables or terms are zero: E20. **non-ˈtrivially** *adverb* M20. **non-ˈtropical** *adjective* characteristic of or occurring in regions outside the tropics; ***non-tropical sprue***, coeliac disease: L20. **non-ˈuniform** *adjective* L19. **non-uniˈformity** *noun* E20. **non-ˈunion** *noun & adjective* (*a*) *noun* failure or refusal to unite; (*b*) *adjective* not belonging to a trade union; not done or produced by members of a trade union: M19. **non-ˈunionist** *adjective & noun* (of or designating) a person not belonging to a trade union M19. **non-ˈunionize** *verb trans.* make non-union in character; not bring under trade-union organization and rules (freq. as ***non-unionized*** *ppl adjective*): E20. **non-uˈnited** *adjective* (*rare*) designating that part of the Greek Orthodox Church not in union with Rome L18. **non-ˈusage** *noun* cessation of the use of something; non-use: M16. **non-ˈuse** *noun* failure or refusal to use something M16. **non-ˈuser** *noun* [-ER[4]] *LAW* neglect to use a right, by which it may be lost M17. **non-uˈtility** *adjective* (esp. of clothing) not utility, not for utility: M20. **non-ˈvanishing** *adjective* (*MATH. & PHYSICS*) not zero, not becoming zero E20. **non-ˈvascular** *adjective* (*ANATOMY*) not consisting of, containing, or involving vessels (esp. blood-vessels) M19. **non-ˈverbal** *adjective* (*a*) not using or including words or speech; unskilful in the use of words or speech; (*b*) not using or including a verb; not constituting a verbal form: E20. **non-ˈverbalized** *adjective* M20. **non-ˈverbally** *adverb* M20. **non-ˈviable** *adjective* not viable, inviable L19. **non-ˈvintage** *adjective* (of wine etc.) not vintage M20. **non-ˈviolence** *noun* avoidance of the use of violence, esp. as a principle E20. **non-ˈviolent** *adjective* characterized by, believing in, or practising non-violence E20. **non-ˈviolently** *adverb* M20. **non-ˈvolatile** *adjective* (esp. of a substance) not volatile M19. **non-volaˈtility** *noun* the property of being non-volatile M20. **non-ˈvoter** *noun* a person who does not vote or who has no vote L19. **non-ˈvoting** *adjective* not voting or not having a vote L19. **non-ˈwhite** *adjective & noun* (a person who is) not white; E20. **non-word** *noun* an unrecorded or unused word M20. **non-ˈworker** *noun* a person who does not work or who is out of work M19. **non-ˈworking** *ppl adjective* M19. **non-ˈwoven** *adjective & noun* (*a*) *adjective* (of a fabric etc.) not woven; (*b*) *noun* a non-woven fabric etc.: M20. **non-ˈzero** *adjective* not equal to zero, having a positive or negative value E20.

nona- /ˈnɒnə, ˈnəʊnə/ *combining form.* Before a vowel **non-**.

[from Latin *nonus* ninth after *tetra-*, *penta-*, etc.]

Having nine, ninefold.

■ **nonamer** *noun* (*CHEMISTRY*) a compound whose molecule is composed of nine molecules of monomer M20. **nonaˈmeric** *adjective* (*CHEMISTRY*) of the nature of a nonamer, consisting of a nonamer or nonamers M20. **nonaˈpeptide** *noun* (*BIOCHEMISTRY*) a peptide composed of nine amino-acid residues M20.

nonage /ˈnəʊnɪdʒ, ˈnɒn-/ *noun.* LME.

[Anglo-Norman *nounage* = Old French *nonage*, formed as NON- + AGE *noun*.]

1 The state of being under full legal age; minority. LME.

2 *fig.* A period of immaturity; the early stage in the growth or development of something. L16.

nonagenarian /nɒnədʒɪˈnɛːrɪən/ *adjective & noun.* E19.

[from Latin *nonagenarius*, from *nonageni* distrib. of *nonaginta* ninety: see -ARIAN.]

▶ **A** *noun.* A person between 90 and 99 years of age. E19.

▶ **B** *adjective.* Between 90 and 99 years of age; of or pertaining to a nonagenarian or nonagenarians. L19.

nonagesimal /nɒnəˈdʒɛsɪm(ə)l/ *adjective & noun*. Now *rare* or *obsolete*. E18.
[from Latin *nonagesima* ninetieth, from *nonaginta* ninety: see -AL[1].]
Chiefly ASTRONOMY. ▶**A** *adjective*. Ninetieth. E18.
nonagesimal degree, **nonagesimal point** that point of the ecliptic which is highest above the horizon at any given time, being 90° above the point at which the ecliptic meets the horizon.
▶**B** *noun*. The nonagesimal degree. L18.

nonagon /ˈnɒnəg(ə)n/ *noun*. M17.
[from NONA- + -GON.]
A plane figure with nine straight sides and nine angles.
■ **noˈnagonal** *adjective* M20.

nonane /ˈnəʊneɪn, ˈnɒn-/ *noun*. M19.
[from NONA- + -ANE.]
CHEMISTRY. Any of a series of saturated hydrocarbons (alkanes) with the formula C_9H_{20}; *spec*. (also *n-nonane*) the unbranched isomer, $CH_3(CH_2)_7CH_3$.
■ **nonaˈnoic** *adjective*: **nonanoic acid**, a liquid fatty acid, $CH_3(CH_2)_7COOH$, used in chemical synthesis etc. (also called *pelargonic acid*) M20.

nonary /ˈnəʊnəri/ *noun & adjective*. M17.
[Irreg. from Latin *nonus* ninth + -ARY[1], after *denary* etc.]
▶**A** *noun*. **1** A group of nine. M17.
2 A fever recurring every eighth (by inclusive reckoning every ninth) day. Long *rare* or *obsolete*. M18.
▶**B** *adjective*. MATH. Designating or pertaining to a scale of numeration having a base of nine. L19.

non assumpsit /nɒn əˈsʌm(p)sɪt/ *noun phr*. M17.
[Latin, formed as NON *noun*[1] + ASSUMPSIT.]
LAW (now *Hist*.). A plea in an action of assumpsit by which the defendant denies making any promise or undertaking.

non avenu /nɔn avny/ *adjectival phr. rare*. M19.
[French.]
Not having happened.

nonce /nɒns/ *noun*[1]. ME.
[from misdivision (cf. NEWT) in Middle English of *þan anes* the one (occasion).]
1 Purpose, reason, intention. Now only in ***for the nonce***, (*a*) (*obsolete* exc. *dial*.) for the particular purpose; on purpose; expressly; (*b*) *poet. arch*. indeed, verily; also used as a virtually meaningless metrical tag. ME.
2 Occasion. Now only in ***for the nonce***, for the present occasion, for the time being; temporarily. L16.
Attrib. & comb.: Designating linguistic forms created for one occasion, as ***nonce-formation***, ***nonce use***, etc.; **nonce-word** a word coined for one occasion.

nonce /nɒns/ *noun*[2]. *slang*. L20.
[Origin unkn.]
A sexual deviant; a person convicted of a sexual offence, esp. child-molesting.

non-central /nɒnˈsɛntr(ə)l/ *adjective*. E20.
[from NON- + CENTRAL *adjective*.]
1 STATISTICS. Having or corresponding to a non-zero mean. E20.
2 PHYSICS. Of a force: not central, i.e. not in general directed along the line joining the bodies it acts between. M20.
■ **non-cenˈtrality** *noun* the property of being non-central M20.

nonchalance /ˈnɒnʃ(ə)l(ə)ns/ *noun*. L17.
[Old & mod. French, formed as next: see -ANCE.]
The state of being nonchalant; lack of enthusiasm or interest; casual indifference, unconcern.

> K. WATERHOUSE She . . re-set her face into gum-chewing nonchalance. I. BANKS Feigning nonchalance, I study a yellowed notice.

nonchalant /ˈnɒnʃ(ə)l(ə)nt/ *adjective*. M18.
[Old & mod. French, from NON- + *chalant* pres. pple of *chaloir* be concerned.]
Calm and casual; lacking in enthusiasm or interest; indifferent, unconcerned.

> A. J. CRONIN Despite his nonchalant, rather lazy manner, Hollis was plainly delighted. C. JACKSON He had settled in, completely relaxed and nonchalant.

■ **nonchalantly** *adverb* M19.

non-claim /ˈnɒnkleɪm/ *noun*. L15.
[Anglo-Norman *nounclaim*, formed as NON- + CLAIM *noun*.]
LAW (now *Hist*.). Failure or refusal to make a claim within the legal time-limit.

†**non-come** *noun*. *rare* (Shakes.). Only in L16.
[Origin uncertain: perh. a nonsensical abbreviation of NON COMPOS or a substitute for NONPLUS.]
A state of perplexity or bewilderment.

non-comedogenic /nɒnˌkɒmɪdə(ʊ)ˈdʒɛnɪk/ *adjective*. L20.
[from NON- + COMEDO + -GENIC.]
Designating a skincare product or cosmetic that is formulated so as not to block pores.

non compos /nɒn ˈkɒmpɒs/ *pred. adjectival phr*. E17.
[Latin.]
= next.

non compos mentis /nɒn ˌkɒmpɒs ˈmɛntɪs/ *pred. adjectival phr*. E17.
[Latin.]
Not compos mentis; not in one's right mind.

non-con /ˈnɒnkɒn/ *noun & adjective*. *colloq*. Also **Non-Con**. L17.
[Abbreviation from (the same root as) NONCONFORMIST.]
▶**A** *noun*. A person who is not a conformist; *esp*. a religious Nonconformist. L17.
▶**B** *attrib*. or as *adjective*. Not conformist; *esp*. Nonconformist in religion. L17.

†**nonconform** *adjective*. M17–L18.
[from NON- + CONFORM *adjective*.]
Not conforming; esp. with the usages of the Church of England.

nonconform /nɒnkənˈfɔːm/ *verb intrans*. M17.
[from NON- + CONFORM *verb*.]
Fail or refuse to conform, esp. with the usages of the Church of England. Freq. as ***nonconforming*** *verbal noun & ppl adjective*.
■ **nonconˈformance** *noun* M19.

nonconformist /nɒnkənˈfɔːmɪst/ *noun & adjective*. In sense A.1 & corresp. uses of the adjective usu. **N-**. E17.
[from NON- + CONFORMIST.]
▶**A** *noun*. **1** (Usu. **N-**.) Orig. (now *Hist*.), a person adhering to the doctrine but not the usages or discipline of the Church of England; later, a member of a Church (esp. a Protestant one) separated from the Church of England. Also (*gen*.), a person not conforming to the doctrine or discipline of any established Church. E17.
2 A person not conforming to a particular practice or course of action. L17.
▶**B** *attrib*. or as *adjective*. Nonconforming; of or pertaining to a nonconformist (or Nonconformist). M17.
■ **nonconformism** *noun* nonconformist (or Nonconformist) principles and practices M19.

nonconformity /nɒnkənˈfɔːmɪti/ *noun*. E17.
[from NON- + CONFORMITY.]
1 (Also **N-**.) Refusal to conform to the doctrine, discipline, or usages of the Church of England or (*gen*.) of any established Church; Nonconformist principles and practice; the body of Nonconformists collectively. E17.
2 Lack of conformity, failure or refusal to conform to a rule, practice, etc. Foll. by *to*, *with*. L17.
3 Lack of correspondence, agreement, or adaptability between people or things. L17.

non-contagious /nɒnkənˈteɪdʒəs/ *adjective*. E19.
[from NON- + CONTAGIOUS.]
Esp. of a disease: not propagated by contagion; non-infectious.
■ **non-contagion** *noun* the condition or property of being non-contagious E19. **non-contagionist** *noun* (now *Hist*.) a person who holds that a certain disease (esp. cholera) is not contagious E19.

noncurantist /nɒnkjʊ(ə)ˈrantɪst/ *adjective*. *literary*. L19.
[from Italian *noncurante* not caring, careless + -IST.]
Characterized by indifference, nonchalant.
■ **noncurance** *noun* indifference, nonchalance E20.

nonda /ˈnɒndə/ *noun*. M19.
[Aboriginal.]
A tree of NE Australia, *Parinari nonda* (family Chrysobalanaceae), which bears edible yellow plumlike fruit.

nondescript /ˈnɒndɪskrɪpt/ *adjective & noun*. L17.
[from NON- + DESCRIPT.]
▶**A** *adjective*. †**1** SCIENCE & MEDICINE. Of a species, condition, etc.: not previously described or identified. L17–E19.
2 Not easily described or classified; lacking distinctive characteristics; neither one thing nor another; hybrid. E19.
▶**B** *noun*. †**1** SCIENCE. An undescribed species etc. L17–M19.
2 A nondescript person or thing. E19.
■ **nondescriptly** *adverb* L20. **nondescriptness** *noun* L20.

none /nəʊn/ *noun*. M17.
[French (Spanish, Italian *nona*) from Latin *nona* (sc. *hora* hour): see NOON *noun*. Cf. NONES.]
†**1** The last part of the day, lasting from about 3 p.m. to 6 p.m. M17–E18.
2 = NONES 2. M19.
¶ Early examples of the spelling *none* represent NOON *noun*.

none /nʌn/ *pronoun, adjective, & adverb*.
[Old English *nān* = Old Frisian *nen*, Old Norse *neinn*, from NE + *ān* ONE *adjective*.]
▶**A** *pronoun*. **1** No one, not any one, *of* a number of persons or things; (now *dial*.) neither *of* two persons or things; *pl*. not any of. OE. ▸**b** *pred*. Not one *of* a particular class. LME.
2 No one, no person, nobody; *pl*. no persons. OE.
3 Not any such person, thing, etc., as that previously or subsequently mentioned. OE.
4 No part or amount *of* a thing, quality, etc. ME.

> **1** E. J. HOWARD Except for her eyes, none of her features was remarkable. G. GREENE None of our wives are invited. **b** C. LAMB He was none of your hesitating half story-tellers. RIDER HAGGARD His understanding was none of the clearest. **2** E. C. STEDMAN None but sentimentalists and dilettanti confuse their prose and verse. V. WOOLF Bare are the pillars; auspicious to none. P. ROSE People sought her . . but none was a companion. **none other** †(*a*) no other thing, nothing else; (*b*) *arch*. no other person, nobody else. **3** I. WALTON How to make a man that was none, an Angler by a book. W. S. MAUGHAM He waited for some answer . . but she gave none. **4** J. RHYS She has none of my fear of life. I. MURDOCH He said none of this to Catherine.

▶**B** *adjective*. Not any; no. *arch*. OE.

> J. SHUTE You are inimicitious to those that offer you none injury. SOUTHEY Those journalists taught . . that Europe should have none other Lord but him. M. PATTISON Poetry we have almost none.

▶**C** *adverb*. **1** †**a** = NO *adverb*[2]. *rare*. OE–L17. ▸**b** With *the* and compar.: in no way, to no extent. L18.
2 By no means, not at all. Now only modifying *too*, *so*. M17. ▸**b** At all, by any means. Usu. in neg. contexts. Chiefly *colloq*. E18.

> **1b** M. ALLINGHAM I'm none the wiser. C. HARE I hope you're none the worse, Rogers. ***none the less***: see NONETHELESS. **2** A. WESKER The farm-labourer . . is often none too clean. *Argosy* Gianpaolo himself . . seemed none too pleased. **b** E. BULLINS Don't you worry none about that, mother. We'll find a way.

Comb.: **none-so-pretty** (*a*) *Hist*. an article of haberdashery; (*b*) the plant London pride.

†**non-ens** *noun*. Pl. **nonentia**. E17–E19.
[medieval Latin, from *non* not + ENS.]
A thing which has no existence; a nonentity.

nonentity /nɒˈnɛntɪti/ *noun*. L16.
[medieval Latin *nonentitas*, from *non* not + *entitas* ENTITY.]
1 A non-existent thing; a thing which exists in the imagination only; a figment. L16. ▸**b** Non-existent matter; that which does not exist. M17.
2 The quality or condition of not existing; non-existence. M17.
3 A person or thing of no importance; a characterless person. E18.

> **1** W. HAMILTON What . . has no qualities, has no existence in thought,—it is a logical nonentity. **b** J. TAIT Total unfamiliarity with entity coming out of non-entity, by mental process. **2** H. GUNTRIP The secret isolation . . of the patient's life, giving him a feeling of unreality and nonentity. **3** J. BARNES He wasn't an authority on anything. He's a complete nonentity. C. WILSON His father . . was a nonentity, an undistinguished clergyman.

■ **nonentitious** *adjective* = NONENTITOUS M20. **nonentitous** *adjective* that is a nonentity, non-existent M19.

nones /nəʊnz/ *noun pl*. (treated as *sing*. or *pl*.). LME.
[In sense 1 from Old & mod. French from Latin *nonas* use as noun of fem. accus. pl. of *nonus* ninth, from *novem* nine. In sense 2 from (the same root as) NONE *noun* + -S[1], after *matins*, *lauds*, *vespers*, etc.]
1 The ninth day (by inclusive reckoning) before the ides in the ancient Roman calendar; the 7th of March, May, July, and October, and the 5th of the other months. LME.
2 ECCLESIASTICAL. The fifth of the daytime canonical hours of prayer, orig. appointed for the ninth hour of the day (about 3 p.m.); the office appointed for this hour. E18.

non est /nɒn ˈɛst/ *adjectival phr*. L19.
[Abbreviation formed as NON EST INVENTUS.]
Non-existent, absent.

non est factum /nɒn ɛst ˈfaktəm/ *noun phr*. Long chiefly *US*. E17.
[Latin = it was not done.]
LAW. A plea that a written agreement is invalid because the defendant was mistaken about its character when signing it.

non est inventus /ˌnɒn ɛst ɪnˈvɛntəs/ *noun phr*. L15.
[Latin = he was not found.]
LAW (now *Hist*.). A sheriff's statement in returning a writ, that the defendant is not to be found in the sheriff's jurisdiction.

nonesuch /ˈnʌnsʌtʃ/ *noun & adjective*. L16.
[from NONE *pronoun & adjective* + SUCH *adjective*. Cf. NONSUCH. In sense B.2 from *Nonsuch* Palace built by Henry VIII and demolished in 1670.]
▶**A** *noun*. **1** = NONSUCH *noun* 1. L16. ▸†**b** = NONSUCH *noun* 2. Only in 17.
2 The scarlet lychnis, *Lychnis chalcedonica*. Now *rare* or *obsolete*. L16.
3 = NONSUCH *noun* 3. M18.
▶**B** *attrib*. or as *adjective*. **1** = NONSUCH *adjective* 1. Long *rare* or *obsolete*. M17.
2 ***Nonesuch chest***, a type of wooden chest of the 16th and 17th cents., inlaid with stylized architectural designs supposedly representing Nonsuch Palace. E20.

For other words beginning with *non-* see the entry for **non-**

nonet /nəʊˈnɛt, nɒˈnɛt/ *noun*. **M19.**
[Italian *nonetto*, from *nono* ninth: see **-ET**¹.]
1 *MUSIC*. A composition for nine voices or instruments; a group of nine singers or players who perform together. **M19.**
2 *NUCLEAR PHYSICS*. A multiplet of nine subatomic particles. **M20.**

nonetheless /nʌnðəˈlɛs, ˈnʌnðəlɛs/ *adverb*. Also **none the less**. **M19.**
[from **NONE** *adverb* + **THE** + **LESS** *adverb*.]
Nevertheless.

> V. BROME His manner charming, I was nonetheless aware of the masked scrutiny of the trained analyst. D. MELTZER A newly cleared bridleway had nonetheless three . . saplings growing in the middle.

non-Euclidean /nɒnjuːˈklɪdɪən/ *adjective*. **L19.**
[from **NON-** + **EUCLIDEAN**.]
Not Euclidean; *spec.* arising from or involving the dispensation with or denial of Euclidean axioms in geometry.
non-Euclidean geometry, non-Euclidean space, etc.

non-existence /nɒnɪgˈzɪst(ə)ns/ *noun*. **M17.**
[medieval Latin *nonexistentia*, from *non-* **NON-** + late Latin *existentia* **EXISTENCE**.]
1 The condition or state of being non-existent; non-being, nonentity. **M17.**
2 A non-existent thing; that which has no existence. **M17.**

non-existent /nɒnɪgˈzɪst(ə)nt/ *noun & adjective*. **M17.**
[from **NON-** + **EXISTENT**. Cf. prec., **NON-ENS**.]
▶ **A** *noun*. A person who or thing which does not exist. **M17.**
▶ **B** *adjective*. That does not exist or have being. **L17.**
▪ **non-eˈxisting** *adjective* non-existent **L18.**

nong /nɒŋ/ *noun*. *Austral. slang*. **M20.**
[Origin unkn. Cf. **NING-NONG**.]
A fool; a stupid person.

nongenary /nɒnˈdʒiːnəri/ *noun*. **E20.**
[from Latin *nongenarius* containing nine hundred, after *centenary*.]
(The celebration of) a nine hundredth anniversary.

nonic /ˈnəʊnɪk/ *adjective & noun*. **L19.**
[from **NONA-** + **-IC**.]
MATH. ▶ **A** *adjective*. Of the ninth order or degree. **L19.**
▶ **B** *noun*. A nonic expression, equation, or curve. **L19.**

nonillion /nəʊˈnɪljən/ *noun*. **L17.**
[French, formed as **NONA-**, after *million*, *billion*, etc.]
Orig. (esp. in the UK), the ninth power of a million (10^{54}). Now usu. (orig. *US*), the tenth power of a thousand (10^{30}).

non inventus /nɒn ɪnˈvɛntəs/ *noun phr.* **M17.**
[Latin = not found.]
Hist. = **NON EST INVENTUS**.

nonius /ˈnəʊnɪəs/ *noun*. Now *Hist.* **M18.**
[Latinized form of the name of Pedro Nuñes (1502–78), Portuguese mathematician and geographer.]
A device for improving the accuracy of graduation of mathematical instruments, superseded by the vernier.

non-licet /nɒnˈlɪsɛt/ *adjective*. *arch.* **E17.**
[from Latin *non licet* it is not lawful.]
Not allowed, unlawful.

non-linear /nɒnˈlɪnɪə/ *adjective*. **M19.**
[from **NON-** + **LINEAR**.]
1 Not linear; not pertaining to, involving, or arranged in a (straight) line; *spec.* (**a**) *MATH. & PHYSICS* involving measurement in more than one dimension; involving a lack of linearity between two related qualities such as input and output; (**b**) *LINGUISTICS* representing forms other than as a linear sequence, suprasegmental.
2 *TELEVISION*. Pertaining to or designating digital editing whereby a sequence of edits is stored on computer as opposed to videotape, thus facilitating further editing. **L20.**
3 *fig.* Not straightforward; unpredictable, random. **L20.**
1 non-linear optics: involving light so intense that a non-linear relationship holds between the electromagnetic field of the light and the response of the propagating medium. **3 go non-linear** *colloq.* go crazy; rave, esp. about a particular obsession.
▪ **non-lineˈarity** *noun* **E20.** **non-linearly** *adverb* **M20.**

non liquet /nɒn ˈlɪkwɛt/ *noun phr.* **E17.**
[from Latin, lit. 'it is not clear'.]
Orig., a person uncertain as to what side to take. Later, a condition of uncertainty as to whether a thing is so or not; *LAW* (*rare*) a jury's verdict deferring a disputed matter to another day for trial.

non-natural /nɒnˈnatʃ(ə)r(ə)l/ *adjective & noun*. **E17.**
[from **NON-** + **NATURAL** *adjective*, *noun*.]
▶ **A** *adjective*. **1** *MEDICINE*. Designating, of, or pertaining to the non-naturals (see sense B.1 below). *obsolete* exc. *Hist.* **E17.**
2 Not belonging to the natural order of things; not involving natural means or process. **E19.**
3 Not in accordance with a natural interpretation or meaning. **M19.**
▶ **B** *noun*. **1** *MEDICINE*. In *pl.* The six things (air, sustenance, sleep, exercise, excretion, emotion) which are necessary to health but may through abuse, accident, etc., become a cause of disease. *obsolete* exc. *Hist.* **L17.**
2 A non-natural or unnatural thing. *rare*. **L19.**

non-naturalism /nɒnˈnatʃ(ə)rəlɪz(ə)m/ *noun*. **L19.**
[from **NON-** + **NATURALISM**.]
1 A non-natural feature or characteristic; non-natural style. **L19.**
2 *PHILOSOPHY*. A theory of ethics opposing naturalism; intuitionalism in ethics. **M20.**

non-naturalist /nɒnˈnatʃ(ə)rəlɪst/ *adjective & noun*. **M19.**
[from **NON-** + **NATURALIST**.]
▶ **A** *adjective*. **1** Of a person: not a student of natural history; not a naturalist. **M19.**
2 *PHILOSOPHY*. Of or pertaining to non-naturalism. **M20.**
▶ **B** *noun*. *PHILOSOPHY*. An adherent of non-naturalism. **M20.**
▪ **non-naturaˈlistic** *adjective* **E20.**

non nobis /nɒn ˈnəʊbɪs/ *interjection*. **E19.**
[Latin, the first words of Psalm 115 (part of Psalm 113 in the Vulgate) beginning *Non nobis, Domine, non nobis* 'Not to us, O Lord, not to us'.]
Expr. humble gratitude or thanksgiving.

†**nonny-no** *noun & interjection*. **L16.**
[Origin unkn.]
1 *noun & interjection*. Used as a meaningless refrain in songs etc. Also ***hey nonny-no***. Cf. **NONNY-NONNY**. **L16–M17.**
2 *noun*. A trifle, a bagatelle. Only in **L17.**

nonny-nonny /nɒnɪˈnɒni/ *noun & interjection*. *arch.* **M16.**
[Origin unkn.]
Used as a meaningless or (formerly) euphemistic refrain in songs etc. Also ***hey nonny-nonny***. Cf. **NONNY-NO**.

no-no /ˈnəʊnəʊ/ *noun*. *colloq.* Pl. **-os**. **M20.**
[Redupl. of **NO** *noun*¹.]
A thing that must not be done, used, etc.; a forbidden, impossible, or unacceptable thing; a failure.

non-obstante /nɒnɒbˈstanti/ *noun*. Also ***non obstante***. **LME.**
[medieval Latin *non obstante* not being in the way, from *non* not + *obstante* abl. pres. pple of *obstare* be in the way (orig. in abl. absol., as *non obstante veredicto* notwithstanding the verdict).]
1 *Hist.* In full ***clause of non-obstante***. A clause in a statute or letter patent, beginning 'non obstante', and conveying a dispensation from a monarch to perform an action despite any statute to the contrary. Also, a similar clause issued by the Pope. **LME.**
†**2** *gen.* A dispensation from or relaxation of a law or rule (foll. by *on*, *of*, *to*). Also, an exception to a rule. **E17–M18.**

nonoic /nəʊˈnəʊɪk, nɒˈnəʊɪk/ *adjective*. **L19.**
[from **NON(A-** + **-OIC**.]
CHEMISTRY. = **NONANOIC**.

nonose /ˈnəʊnəʊs, -z, ˈnɒn-/ *noun*. **L19.**
[from **NON(A-** + **-OSE**².]
CHEMISTRY. Any monosaccharide having nine carbon atoms in its molecule, esp. in an unbranched chain.

nonpareil /nɒnpəˈreɪl/ *adjective & noun*. **LME.**
[French, from *non-* **NON-** + *pareil* like, equal from popular Latin *pariculus* dim. of Latin **PAR** *noun*¹.]
▶ **A** *adjective*. **1** Having no equal; unrivalled, unique. **LME.**
2 Printed in nonpareil (see sense B.2 below); of or pertaining to this size of type. *rare*. **M17.**

> **1** SOUTHEY A truth which . . will be . . elucidated in this nonpareil history. *Times Lit. Suppl.* The canvas is vast, the picture animated, the painter nonpareil.

▶ **B** *noun*. **1** A person or thing having no equal; an unrivalled or unique person or thing. **L15.**
2 Type of a size (6 points) larger than ruby and smaller than emerald (*US*, larger than agate and smaller than minion). **L17.**
3 A kind of sweet. *arch.* **L17.**
4 An old variety of apple. **M18.**
5 a The painted bunting, *Passerina ciris*. **M18.** ▸**b** More fully ***nonpareil parrot***. The eastern rosella, *Platycercus eximius*. Chiefly *Austral.* **M18.**
6 Any of several attractively patterned moths. Orig. and now only in **CLIFDEN NONPAREIL**. **M18.**

non placet /nɒn ˈpleɪsɛt/ *noun & verb phr.* As verb also ***non-placet***. **L16.**
[Latin = it does not please, a formula used esp. in university and Church assemblies in giving a negative vote on a proposition.]
▶ **A** *noun*. Orig., an expression of dissent or disapproval. Later, a negative vote in a university or Church assembly. **L16.**
▶ **B** *verb trans.* Give a negative vote on (a proposition); reject (a measure). **E19.**

nonplus /nɒnˈplʌs/ *noun & verb*. **L16.**
[from Latin *non plus* not more, no further.]
▶ **A** *noun*. Pl. **-sses**. A state in which no more can be said or done; inability to proceed in speech or action; a state of perplexity; a standstill. Chiefly in ***at a nonplus***, ***bring to a nonplus***, ***reduce to a nonplus***. **L16.**

> A. JESSOPP Prophets are never at a nonplus, never surprised. A. MARS-JONES Abandoned members of the royal party . . in a state of paralysed nonplus.

▶ **B** *verb trans.* Infl. **-ss-**. Bring (a person etc.) to a nonplus; perplex; make (a thing) ineffective or inoperative. Freq. as **nonplussed** *ppl adjective*. **L16.**

> P. G. WODEHOUSE The spectacle . . was enough to nonplus anyone. N. MONSARRAT It was all very well to be puzzled, but one should not be completely nonplussed.

▪ **nonpluˈssation** *noun* (*rare*) the action of nonplussing someone; the condition of being nonplussed: **M19.**

non plus ultra /nɒn plʌs ˈʌltrə/ *noun phr.* **L17.**
[Latin = not more beyond.]
A ***ne plus ultra***, the highest point or culmination *of*.

non possumus /nɒn ˈpɒsjʊməs/ *noun phr.* **L19.**
[Latin = we cannot.]
A statement or answer expressing inability to act in a matter.

non-pros /nɒnˈprɒs/ *noun & verb*. Now *rare*. **L17.**
[Abbreviation of Latin *non prosequitur* he does not prosecute.]
LAW (now *Hist.*).
▶ **A** *noun*. A judgement entered against a plaintiff on the grounds that the prosecution of an action has not taken place within the time allowed. **L17.**
▶ **B** *verb trans.* Infl. **-ss-**. Enter a judgement of non-pros against. Only in *pass.* **M18.**

non-residence /nɒnˈrɛzɪd(ə)ns/ *noun*. **LME.**
[from **NON-** + **RESIDENCE** *noun*¹.]
1 Failure or refusal of a member of the clergy to reside as required by official duties; systematic absence of a member of the clergy from a benefice or charge. **LME.**
2 *gen.* The fact of sojourning in a place for a short time only or of habitually residing elsewhere. **L16.**
▪ **non-resiˈdential** *adjective* not residential; (of a college, university, etc.) not requiring to reside in college etc. accommodation: **L19.** **non-resiˈdentiary** *noun & adjective* (**a**) *adjective* not residentiary; (**b**) *noun* a non-residentiary ecclesiatic: **E17.**

non-resident /nɒnˈrɛzɪd(ə)nt/ *noun & adjective*. **LME.**
[from **NON-** + **RESIDENT**.]
▶ **A** *noun*. **1** A member of the clergy who fails or refuses to reside as required by official duties, or who is systematically absent from a benefice or charge. **LME.**
2 *gen.* A person sojourning in a place only for a short time or habitually residing elsewhere. **E17.**
3 A person using some of the facilities of a hotel etc. without residing there. **E20.**
▶ **B** *adjective*. **1** Of a member of the clergy: failing or refusing to reside as required by official duties; systematically absent from a benefice or charge. **M16.**
2 *gen.* Of a person: sojourning in a place only for a short time or habitually residing elsewhere. **M16.**
3 Of land: owned by a person not residing on it. *US*. **M19.**
4 Of a post, position, etc.: not requiring the holder to live in. **L20.**
▪ **non-residenter** *noun* (*rare*) a non-resident **M17.**

non-return /nɒnrɪˈtəːn; *as adjective also* ˈnɒnrɪtəːn/ *noun & adjective*. **M16.**
[from **NON-** + **RETURN** *noun*.]
▶ **A** *noun*. Failure or refusal to return; the condition of not being returned. **M16.**
▶ **B** *adjective*. Permitting flow of air, liquid, etc., in one direction only. **L19.**
▪ **non-returnable** *adjective & noun* (**a**) *adjective* that may or need not be returned; *spec.* (of a bottle etc.) that may not be returned empty to the suppliers; (**b**) *noun* a non-returnable bottle etc.: **E20.**

non-sane /nɒnˈseɪn/ *adjective*. Also **nonsane**. **E17.**
[Law French *non sane* (*memorie*), law Latin *non sanae* (*memoriae*): see **NON-**. Cf. **SANE** *adjective*, **MEMORY**.]
LAW. Not sane; of unsound mind.
▪ †**non-sanity** *noun* insanity **L17–M18.**

non-sched /nɒnˈʃɛd, -ˈskɛd/ *noun*. *colloq.* Also ***-sked** /-skɛd/. **M20.**
[Abbreviation of next.]
A non-scheduled airline.

non-scheduled /nɒnˈʃɛdjuːld, -ˈskɛd-/ *adjective*. **M20.**
[from **NON-** + **SCHEDULED**.]
Not scheduled; *spec.* (of an airline) operating without fixed or published flying schedules; of or pertaining to such an airline.

nonsense /ˈnɒns(ə)ns/ *noun & adjective*. In sense A.1 also **non-sense**. **E17.**
[from **NON-** + **SENSE** *noun*.]
▶ **A** *noun*. **1** That which is not sense or which differs from sense; absurd or meaningless words or ideas; foolish or

For other words beginning with *non-* see the entry for **non-**

extravagant conduct. Also as *interjection.* E17. ▸**b** An instance of this; an arrangement of which one disapproves; a muddle, a fiasco, (freq. in ***make a nonsense (of)***). M17.
†**2** Lack of feeling or physical sensation. Only in E17.
3 Absurdity, the quality of being nonsensical. M17.
4 Insubstantial or worthless matter, a trivial or worthless thing. M17.
†**5** A meaning that makes no sense. M17–E18.

1 *English Studies* A 'steep ford' is quite obvious non-sense. G. JOSIPOVICI What nonsense! . . you'll see there won't be any problems. A. BRIEN He became delirious. Started muttering nonsense. S. HILL 'She has insinuated herself.' 'Nonsense! We have known her for years.' **knock the nonsense out of** force to abandon foolish or extravagant ideas or conduct. **stand no nonsense (from)** refuse to tolerate foolish or extravagant ideas or conduct (from). ***stuff and nonsense***: see STUFF *noun.* **b** SIR W. SCOTT I shall go on scribbling one nonsense or another. *Listener* A small steel works . . is an economic nonsense. **3** LEIGH HUNT The nonsense of ill-will. **4** Z. TOMIN I'll get the boots . . you'd only buy yourself another flimsy nonsense.

▸**B** *attrib.* or as *adjective.* **1** Full of nonsense, nonsensical. E17.
2 BIOLOGY. Designating a codon which does not specify any amino acid; pertaining or giving rise to such a codon. M20.

Comb. & special collocations: **nonsense syllable** a syllable formed by putting a vowel between any two consonants, used in memory experiments and tests; **nonsense verse** comically nonsensical or whimsical verse intended to amuse by absurdity; an example of this; *spec.* a limerick; **nonsense word** a word having no accepted meaning; a nonsense syllable.
■ **non,sensifi'cation** *noun* (*rare*) the production of nonsense E19.

nonsense /ˈnɒns(ə)ns/ *verb intrans. rare.* E19.
[from prec.]
Talk nonsense.

nonsensical /nɒnˈsɛnsɪk(ə)l/ *adjective & noun.* M17.
[formed as prec. + -ICAL.]
▸**A** *adjective.* That is nonsense; of the nature of, or full of, nonsense; having no sense; absurd. M17.
▸**B** *noun.* A nonsensical, absurd, or trifling thing. M19.
■ **nonsensically** *adverb* M17. **nonsensicalness** *noun* L17. **nonsensi'cality** *noun* nonsensical quality; an instance of this: E18.

non sequitur /nɒn ˈsɛkwɪtə/ *noun phr.* LME.
[from Latin, lit. 'it does not follow'.]
†**1** A part of the collar of a shirt etc.; an unfastened collar. *rare.* Only in LME.
2 An inference or conclusion not logically following from the premisses; a response, remark, etc., not logically following from what has gone before. M16.

2 S. BELLOW Uncle couldn't have been listening . . he came up with a non sequitur.

non-sked *noun* see NON-SCHED.

nonsuch /ˈnʌnsʌtʃ/ *noun & adjective.* E17.
[Var. of NONESUCH, after *nonpareil*.]
▸**A** *noun.* **1** An unparalleled or unrivalled person or thing, a paragon. E17.
†**2** The most eminent person or thing *of* a specified class or kind. M–L17.
3 Black medick, *Medicago lupulina*, formerly grown as fodder. Also ***black nonsuch***. M17.
4 An old variety of apple. L17.
▸**B** *attrib.* or as *adjective.* **1** Unparalleled, unrivalled, incomparable. *obsolete* exc. in ***nonsuch apple*** = sense A.4 above. M17.
2 ***Nonsuch chest***, = ***Nonesuch chest*** s.v. NONESUCH *adjective* 2. E20.

nonsuit /ˈnɒnsjuːt, -suːt/ *noun.* LME.
[Anglo-Norman *no(u)nsuit*, formed as NON- + SUIT *noun*.]
LAW. The cessation of a suit as a result of the voluntary withdrawal of the plaintiff (*obsolete* exc. *US*). Now usu., the stoppage of a suit by the judge when the plaintiff fails to make out a legal case or to bring sufficient evidence.

†**nonsuit** *adjective.* LME–E19.
[from prec., app. taken as a ppl. form by analogy with *execute* etc. Cf. Anglo-Norman *nounsuy*.]
LAW. Subjected to a nonsuit; that is or has been nonsuited.

nonsuit /nɒnˈsjuːt, -ˈsuːt/ *verb trans.* M16.
[from NONSUIT *noun* or *adjective*.]
LAW (now *Hist.*). Subject (a plaintiff) to a nonsuit.

non-tenure /nɒnˈtɛnjə/ *noun.* L16.
[Anglo-Norman *nountenure*, Anglo-Latin *nontenura*, formed as NON- + TENURE *noun*.]
LAW (now *Hist.*). A plea in bar to a real action denying that a defendant held (part of) the land mentioned in the plaintiff's count or declaration.

nontronite /ˈnɒntrənʌɪt/ *noun.* M19.
[from *Nontron* a town in France + -ITE¹.]
MINERALOGY. A pale yellow or greenish crystalline clay mineral of the montmorillonite group, sometimes resembling opal. Also called ***chloropal***.

non-U /nɒnˈjuː, ˈnɒnjuː/ *adjective & noun. colloq.* M20.
[from NON- + U *adjective & noun*².]
▸**A** *adjective.* Not upper-class; (esp. of linguistic usage or social conduct) not characteristic of upper-class people. M20.
▸**B** *noun.* Non-U persons or characteristics collectively; non-U language. M20.

†**non ultra** *noun phr.* E17–E18.
[from Latin, lit. 'not beyond'.]
= NE PLUS ULTRA 2.

†**nonupla** *noun.* L16–E19.
[mod. Latin, fem. of *nonuplus*, from Latin *nonus* ninth + *-plus* after *duplus* DUPLE.]
MUSIC. A tempo or time signature having nine crotchets or quavers in a bar.

nonuplet /ˈnɒnjʊplɛt/ *noun.* L19.
[from Latin *nonus* ninth + *-plet*, after *triplet*.]
MUSIC. A group of nine notes to be performed in the time of eight or six.

non-valent /nɒnˈveɪl(ə)nt/ *adjective.* E20.
[from NON- + -VALENT.]
CHEMISTRY. **1** Not readily forming chemical bonds; inert. Now *rare.* E20.
2 Having a formal oxidation state of zero. M20.

nonyl /ˈnɒnʌɪl, -nɪl, ˈnəʊn-/ *noun.* M19.
[from NON(A- + -YL.]
CHEMISTRY. Any of the series of monovalent radicals C_9H_{19}· derived from the nonanes. Usu. in *comb.*

noodle /ˈnuːd(ə)l/ *noun*¹. *slang.* M18.
[Origin unkn.]
1 A fool, a stupid or silly person. M18.
2 The head. Cf. NODDLE *noun.* E20.
■ **noodledom** *noun* the world of fools, fools collectively; (an instance of) foolishness or stupidity: E19. **noodleism** *noun* a silly act or idea; silliness, stupidity: E19. **noodly** *adjective* (*rare*) stupid, silly L19.

noodle /ˈnuːd(ə)l/ *noun*². L18.
[German *Nudel*, of unkn. origin.]
A thin strip or ring of pasta served in soup, with a sauce, etc.

noodle /ˈnuːd(ə)l/ *verb*¹ & *noun*³. M19.
[Origin unkn.]
▸**A** *verb intrans.* & (*rare*) *trans.* Improvise or play (music) in a casual or desultory manner, esp. in jazz; do or say (something) in an unproductive or undirected way. M19.

M. PIERCY Tracy noodled around with her left hand making bluesy chords and progressions.

▸**B** *noun.* A (casual or desultory) trill or improvisation on a musical instrument, esp. in jazz. E20.

noodle /ˈnuːd(ə)l/ *verb*². *Austral. slang.* E20.
[Origin unkn.]
1 *verb intrans. & trans.* Search (an opal dump) for opals. E20.
2 *verb trans.* Obtain (an opal) in this way. M20.
■ **noodler** *noun* E20.

noogenesis /nəʊəˈdʒɛnɪsɪs/ *noun.* Also **noö-**. M20.
[French *noögenèse*, from Greek *noos* mind + GENESIS.]
The growth or development of the mind or consciousness; the coming into being of the noosphere (freq. with ref. to the writings of Teilhard de Chardin).
■ **noogenic** *adjective* pertaining to or connected with noogenesis or the noosphere M20.

Noogoora burr /nʊˈguːrə ˈbɜː/ *noun phr.* L19.
[*Noogoora*, a Queensland sheep station.]
The plant *Xanthium occidentale*, of the composite family, treated as a noxious weed in Australia because of its hooked burrs which become entangled in sheep's wool.

nook /nʊk/ *noun.* ME.
[Origin unkn.]
1 A corner of a quadrilateral or angular thing (as a piece of cloth or paper) or of a figure bounded by straight lines. Now *rare.* ME. ▸**b** A small part, a piece, a fragment. Now *rare.* ME. ▸**c** A projecting piece of land; a headland, a promontory. Now *rare.* L15. ▸**d** A corner or angular piece of land; a small triangular field. Formerly also, a measure of land. Now *rare.* E17
2 A corner of a house, street, etc. Chiefly *Scot. & north.* ME.
3 A corner in a room or other enclosed space. ME. ▸**b** A small or out-of-the-way corner or recess; a secluded or sheltered spot. LME. ▸**c** A small or sheltered creek or inlet. L16.
4 An outlying or remote part of a country, region, etc., or of the world. LME.

3 ***chimney-nook***, ***inglenook***. **b** SHERWOOD ANDERSON Little cloistered nooks, quiet places where lovers go to sit. **every nook and corner**, **every nook and cranny** *fig.* every part or aspect, the entirety. **4** BROWNING That rare nook Yet untroubled by the tourist.

Comb.: **nook-shaft** ARCHITECTURE a shaft placed in the internal angle formed by the meeting of two contiguous faces in a compound archway; **nook-shotten** *adjective* (now *arch. & dial.*) having many sharp corners or angles, jagged; out of square, crooked.
■ **nooked** *adjective* (now *dial.*) having (a specified number of) corners; having points or peaks, angular: ME. **nookery** *noun* a small or snug nook E19. **nooklet** *noun* a small nook or corner M19.

nook /nʊk/ *verb. rare.* E17.
[from the noun.]
1 *verb intrans.* Hide in a corner. E17.
2 *verb trans.* **a** Humble, check, (a person). M18. ▸**b** Chip *off* (material) so as to form corners. L18.
3 *verb trans.* Put in a corner; conceal. E19.

nooky /ˈnʊki/ *noun. slang.* Also **-ie**. E20.
[Origin uncertain: perh. from NOOK *noun* + -Y⁶.]
Sexual activity, sexual intercourse; a woman or girl considered as a sex object.

nooky /ˈnʊki/ *adjective.* E19.
[from NOOK *noun* + -Y¹.]
Having many nooks; resembling a nook.

noology /nəʊˈɒlədʒi/ *noun.* E19.
[from Greek *noos* mind + -LOGY.]
Chiefly *Hist.* The branch of learning that deals with the mind.
■ **noo'logical** *adjective* pertaining to noology E19. **noologist** *noun* a person referring the origin of certain ideas to the mind rather than to experience, a rationalist M19.

noon /nuːn/ *noun.*
[Old English *nōn* corresp. to Old Saxon *nōn(e*, Middle & mod. Dutch *noen*, Old High German *nona* (German *None*), Old Norse *nōn*, from Latin *nona* (sc. *hora* hour) fem. sing. of *nonus* ninth. Cf. NONE *noun*, NONES.]
†**1 a** The ninth hour from sunrise, about 3 p.m. OE–LME. ▸**b** ECCLESIASTICAL. The hour or office of nones. OE–M16.
2 The time when the sun reaches the meridian; twelve o'clock in the day, midday. Also ***twelve noon***. ME. ▸**b** *transf.* The most important hour of the day. Now *rare.* E18.
3 A midday meal. Long *dial.* ME.
4 The culminating or highest point, the peak. L16.
5 The time of night corresponding to midday; midnight. Chiefly in ***noon of night***. *poet.* E17.

2 *attrib.*: M. ANGELOU The noon sun called the workers to rest. ***MORNING, noon, and night***. **4** F. NORRIS Men . . were shot down in the very noon of life.

Comb.: **noonday** the middle of the day, midday; **noon-flower** (*a*) the goat's-beard, *Tragopogon pratensis*, with flowers that close at noon; (*b*) *Austral.* any of several mesembryanthemums whose flowers open about noon; **noontide**, **noontime** (*a*) the time of noon, midday; (*b*) the culminating point *of* something; **noontimes** *adverb* (*US*) at midday.
■ **nooner** *noun* (*slang*) an act of sexual intercourse in the middle of the day, esp. during the lunch hour L20.

noon /nuːn/ *verb intrans. & trans.* (with *it*). *US.* E19.
[from the noun.]
Halt or rest at noon; stop for or consume a midday meal.

no one /ˈnəʊ wʌn/ *pronoun.* Also **no-one**. E17.
[from NO *adjective* + ONE *pronoun*.]
No person; nobody.

nooning /ˈnuːnɪŋ/ *noun.* Now chiefly *US.* LME.
[from NOON *noun, verb* + -ING¹.]
1 Midday. LME.
2 a A rest or interval at noon, esp. for food. M16. ▸**b** A midday meal. M17.

noop /nuːp/ *noun. Scot. & north.* L18.
[Perh. rel. to KNOP, KNOB: cf. ***knotberry*** s.v. KNOT *noun*¹.]
(The fruit of) the cloudberry, *Rubus chamaemorus*. Also ***noop-berry***.

noose /nuːs/ *noun & verb.* LME.
[Origin uncertain: perh. from Old French *nos*, *nous* nom. sing. & accus. pl. of *no*, *nou* (later *noud*, mod. *noeud*) from Latin *nodus*, *-os* knot.]
▸**A** *noun.* **1** A loop with a running knot, which tightens as the rope etc. is pulled, as in a snare, lasso, hangman's halter, etc. (also ***running noose***); a folding or doubling of a rope etc., a loop. LME. ▸**b** *The* hangman's rope. M17.
2 *fig.* A snare, a bond; *spec.* the tie of marriage. L16.

1 DEFOE The Shark had . . got his Head through the Noose, to . . jam the running knot taut about him. G. HUNTINGTON Ropes were thrown out, and the nooses caught the posts of the landing stage. **put one's head in a noose** act in a way likely to bring about one's downfall. **b** A. RADCLIFFE Many an honest fellow has run his head into the noose that way. **2** J. TATHAM I fall Into the noose of taverns like a pigeon.

▸**B** *verb trans.* **1** Catch or enclose with or as with a noose; *fig.* ensnare. L16. ▸**b** Marry (a person), ensnare in marriage. E18.

2 Arrange (a cord etc.) in a noose or loop. E17. **3** Execute (a person) by hanging. L17.

📖 **1** F. MARRYAT G. had . . noosed the animal with his lasso. **2** ALBERT SMITH A piece of whipcord is then noosed round the victim's neck.

■ **nooser** *noun* M19.

noosphere /ˈnəʊəsfɪə/ *noun*. Also **noö-**. M20.
[French *noösphere*, from Greek *noos* mind: see -SPHERE.]
The sphere or stage of evolutionary development characterized by (the emergence or dominance of) consciousness, the mind, and interpersonal relationships (freq. with ref. to the writings of Teilhard de Chardin).
■ **noo'spheric** *adjective* M20.

Nootka /ˈnuːtkə, ˈnʊtkə/ *adjective & noun*. E19.
[*Nootka* Sound, an inlet on the coast of Vancouver Island, British Columbia, Canada.]
▶ **A** *adjective*. **1** Designating trees and plants native to the Pacific coast of N. America. E19.
2 Pertaining to or designating a N. American Indian people of Vancouver Island, or their Wakashan language. M19.
1 Nootka cypress a tall pyramidal cypress, *Chamaecyparis nootkatensis*, of western N. America; also called ***yellow cedar***. **Nootka fir** the Douglas fir, *Pseudotsuga menziesii*. **Nootka lupin** a blue-flowered lupin, *Lupinus nootkatensis*, naturalized in Scotland.
▶ **B** *noun*. Pl. same, **-s**. A member of the Nootka people; the language of this people. M19.
■ **Nootkan** *adjective & noun* (*a*) *adjective* of the Nootka or the language group Nootkan; (*b*) *noun* a Nootka; a group of Wakashan languages including Nootka: M19.

nootropic /nəʊəˈtrɒpɪk/ *adjective & noun*. L20.
[French *nootrope*, from Greek *noos* mind + *tropē* turning: see -IC.]
PHARMACOLOGY. ▶**A** *adjective*. Designating or characteristic of a drug or group of drugs considered to improve cognitive functioning, esp. memory, and used to treat some cases of dementia. L20.
▶ **B** *noun*. A nootropic drug. L20.

nopal /ˈnəʊp(ə)l/ *noun*. M18.
[French from Spanish from Nahuatl *nopalli* cactus.]
A shrubby cactus, *Nopalea cochenillifera* (related to the prickly pear), which is cultivated as a food plant of the cochineal insect.

nopalery *noun* var. of NOPALRY.

nopaline /ˈnəʊp(ə)liːn/ *noun*. L20.
[formed as NOPAL + -INE[5].]
BIOCHEMISTRY. An opine, $C_{11}H_{20}N_4O_4$, synthesized by plant cells infected with certain plasmids from the crown gall pathogen *Agrobacterium tumefaciens*. Cf. OCTOPINE *noun*.

nopalry /ˈnəʊp(ə)lri/ *noun*. Also **-ery**. L18.
[from NOPAL + -RY, after Spanish *nopalera*, French *nopalerie*, *nopalière*.]
A plantation of nopals cultivated for the production of cochineal.

nope /nəʊp/ *noun*. *obsolete* exc. *dial*. E17.
[App. var. of ALP *noun*[2], with misdivision after *an*.]
A bullfinch.

nope /nəʊp/ *adverb & interjection*. *colloq*. (orig. *US*). L19.
[Extension of NO *adverb*[3] & *interjection*. Cf. YEP *adverb & interjection*[1].]
= NO *adverb*[3] & *interjection*.

📖 C. E. MULFORD Nope, I reckon not—seven husky Apaches are too much for one man to . . fight.

noplace /ˈnəʊpleɪs/ *adverb*. *N. Amer. colloq*. Also as two words. M20.
[from NO *adjective* + PLACE *noun*[1], after NOWHERE.]
= NOWHERE *adverb*.

nor *adjective* see NOR-.

nor /nɔː, nə/ *adverb*, *conjunction*[1], & *noun*. ME.
[Contr. of NOTHER *pronoun*, *adjective*[1], *adverb*, & *conjunction*, as OR *conjunction*[2] is of OTHER *conjunction & adverb*[2].]
▶ **A** *adverb & conjunction*. **1** Following, *neither*, *nor*, *not*, or another negative, introducing the second or further of two or more alternatives or different things: and not, or not; not on the other hand. Also (now *dial*. or *slang*) followed by another negative or (chiefly *poet*.) without preceding negative. ME. ▶**b** Followed by *nor*: introducing the first of two alternatives, neither. Chiefly *poet*. L16.
2 Introducing a clause or sentence freq. following a preceding affirmative: and indeed not, neither; and no more, and not either. E16.

📖 **1** GOLDSMITH No skill could obviate nor no remedy dispel the terrible infection. TENNYSON Great brother, thou nor I have made the world. G. MEREDITH I am neither German nor French nor . . English. K. TYNAN He could not command my sympathy nor even . . my interest. S. HAZZARD Nicholas Cartledge was impassive, neither patient nor impatient. **b** POPE Now let our compact made Be nor by signal nor by word betray'd. **2** BYRON Away! nor weep! B. JOWETT Nor among the friends of Socrates must the jailer be forgotten. CONAN DOYLE I had no glimmer of what was in his mind, nor did he enlighten me. E. BOWEN I can't see that this change has done you any harm. Nor the shake-up either.

▶ **B** *noun*. (Usu. **NOR**.) COMPUTING. A Boolean operator which gives the value unity if and only if all the operands are zero, and is otherwise zero. Usu. *attrib*. M20.

nor /nɔː, nə/ *conjunction*[2]. *Scot. & dial*. LME.
[Origin unkn.]
Than.

📖 FLORA THOMPSON Can't be done, matey. Cost me more nor that.

nor' /nɔː/ *noun*, *adjective*, & *adverb*. LME.
[Contr.]
Freq. NAUTICAL. North. Usu. in *comb*., as ***nor'-nor'-east***, NOR'-WEST, NOR'-WESTER.

nor- /nɔː/ *prefix*. In sense 1 also as attrib. adjective **nor**.
[from NOR(MAL.]
Chiefly BIOCHEMISTRY. **1** Denoting the contraction of a chain or ring of carbon atoms by one methylene group, or the replacement of one or (esp. in terpenes) all the (methyl) side-chains by hydrogen atoms, as ***noradrenaline***, ***norsteroid***, ***nortestosterone***.
2 Denoting a normal (unbranched) isomer of a compound, as ***norleucine***, ***norvaline***.
■ **nor'ephedrine** *noun* = ***phenylpropanolamine*** s.v. PHENYL E20. **norethisterone** /nɔːrɛˈθɪst(ə)rəʊn/ *noun* a synthetic hormone similar to progesterone, used in contraceptives and in the treatment of amenorrhoea M20.

noradrenaline /nɔːrəˈdrɛn(ə)lɪn/ *noun*. Also **-in**. M20.
[from NOR- + ADRENALIN.]
BIOCHEMISTRY & MEDICINE. An amine that is the nor derivative of adrenalin; 1-(3,4-dihydroxyphenyl)-2-aminoethanol; $(HO)_2C_6H_3{\cdot}CHOH{\cdot}CH_2NH_2$; *spec*. the l-isomer, which is the neurotransmitter in sympathetic nerves and parts of the central nervous system, and which is given to raise the blood pressure.
■ **noradre'nergic** *adjective* releasing or involving noradrenaline as a neurotransmitter M20. **noradre'nergically** *adverb* L20.

Noraid /ˈnɔːreɪd/ *noun*. Also **NORAID**. L20.
[from Irish Northern Aid Committee.]
An organization whose principal purpose is to raise funds for Northern Irish Republican causes among sympathizers in the US.

norbergite /ˈnɔːbəgʌɪt/ *noun*. E20.
[from *Norberg*, a village in Sweden + -ITE[1].]
MINERALOGY. A basic orthorhombic silicate and fluoride of magnesium which occurs as pink or whitish crystals.

Norbertine /ˈnɔːbətɪn, -ʌɪn/ *noun & adjective*. L17.
[from St *Norbert* (*c* 1080–1134), founder of the order + -INE[1].]
ECCLESIASTICAL. ▶**A** *noun*. = PREMONSTRATENSIAN *noun*. L17.
▶ **B** *adjective*. = PREMONSTRATENSIAN *adjective*. M19.

nordcaper /ˈnɔːdkeɪpə/ *noun*. Now *rare*. M18.
[Dutch *noordkaper* or German *Nordkaper*, from Dutch *noordkaap*, German *Nordkap* North Cape.]
A N. Atlantic whale of the genus *Balaena*; a right whale.

Nordenfelt /ˈnɔːd(ə)nfɛlt/ *noun*. L19.
[Thorsten *Nordenfelt* (1842–1920), Swedish engineer.]
In full ***Nordenfelt gun***. A form of machine-gun having between one and twelve barrels mounted horizontally.

Nordhausen /ˈnɔːdhaʊz(ə)n/ *noun*. Also **n-**. M19.
[A town in Germany.]
In full ***Nordhausen acid***, ***Nordhausen sulphuric acid***. Fuming sulphuric acid (formerly made esp. in Nordhausen).

Nordic /ˈnɔːdɪk/ *adjective & noun*. L19.
[French *nordique*, from *nord* north: see -IC.]
▶ **A** *adjective*. **1** Of or pertaining to the countries of Scandinavia, Finland, and Iceland or their people or languages; *spec*. of or pertaining to a physical type of northern Germanic peoples characterized by tall stature, a bony frame, light colouring, and a dolichocephalic head. L19.
2 Of skiing: involving cross-country work and jumping. M20.

📖 **1** ALDOUS HUXLEY Hitlerian theology affirms that there is a Nordic race, inherently superior to all other. *Sunday Express* Most Icelanders are tall, blonde . . with a very strong Nordic look.

▶ **B** *noun*. **1** A person of the Nordic type or from a Nordic country. E20.
2 The northern division of the Germanic languages; North Germanic. M20.

📖 **1** H. DOOLITTLE Winters are cold, summers are hot, so we have the temperaments of Nordics and southerners both.

¶ In Nazi doctrine the 'Nordic race' was regarded as essentially superior to other races.
■ **Nordicism** /-sɪz(ə)m/ *noun* the state or condition of being Nordic, the characteristics of the Nordics; the belief in or doctrine of the cultural and racial supremacy of the Nordic peoples: E20. **Nordicist** /-sɪst/ *noun* a person believing in the supremacy of the Nordic peoples M20.

nordmarkite /ˈnɔːdmɑːkʌɪt/ *noun*. M19.
[In sense 1 from *Nordmark* a town in Sweden; in sense 2 from *Nordmarka* a region in Norway: see -ITE[1].]
1 MINERALOGY. A brown manganesian variety of staurolite. M19.
2 PETROGRAPHY. A syenite composed mainly of microperthite, with quartz and usu. oligoclase and biotite, which has a trachytoid or granitic texture. L19.
■ **nordmar'kitic** *adjective* consisting of or containing (the rock) nordmarkite M20.

norepinephrine /ˌnɔːrɛpɪˈnɛfrɪn, -riːn, nɔːrɪˈpɪnɪfriːn/ *noun*. Chiefly *US*. M20.
[from NOR- + EPINEPHRINE.]
BIOCHEMISTRY. = NORADRENALINE.

Norfolk /ˈnɔːfək/ *noun*. LME.
[A county in SE England, forming part of East Anglia.]
1 Used *attrib*. to designate things found in, originating from, or characteristic of Norfolk. LME.
2 a In full ***Norfolk jacket***. A man's loose belted jacket, usu. of tweed, having box pleats and worn chiefly for shooting, fishing, etc. M19. ▶**b** In *pl*. & more fully ***Norfolk suit***. A suit with a Norfolk jacket and knee breeches. L19.
3 The dialect of Norfolk. L19.
1 Norfolk capon a smoked herring. **Norfolk dumpling** (*a*) a plain dumpling made from bread dough; (*b*) *slang* a native or inhabitant of Norfolk. **Norfolk Howard** *slang* a bed-bug. **Norfolk plover** the stone curlew. **Norfolk reed** the common reed, *Phragmites australis*, grown in East Anglia for use as thatch. **Norfolk spaniel** *Hist*. the springer spaniel. **Norfolk terrier** the drop-eared variety of the Norwich terrier; an animal of this breed.

Norfolk Island pine /ˈnɔːfək ˈʌɪlənd ˌpʌɪn/ *noun phr*. E19.
[*Norfolk Island* an island north-west of New Zealand.]
A large pyramidal coniferous tree, *Araucaria heterophylla*, much planted in Mediterranean countries.
■ Also **Norfolk pine** *noun phr*. M20.

nori /ˈnɔːri/ *noun*. L19.
[Japanese.]
Edible seaweed of the genus *Porphyra*, eaten esp. by the Japanese either fresh or dried in sheets (used to wrap sushi). Cf. ***laver bread*** s.v. LAVER *noun*[1].

noria /ˈnɔːrɪə/ *noun*. L18.
[Spanish from Arab. *nā'ūra*.]
Esp. in Spain and the East: a device for raising water from a stream etc., consisting of a chain of pots or buckets, revolving round a wheel driven by the water current.

Noric /ˈnɔːrɪk/ *adjective*. E17.
[Latin *Noricus*, from *Noricum* a region and Roman province roughly equivalent to modern Austria, ult. from Celtic *Noreia* name of its ancient capital: see -IC.]
Designating, of, or pertaining to a part of the Alps situated in southern Austria, or (GEOLOGY, now *rare*) a division of the Upper Triassic period represented in its rocks.

norimon /ˈnɒrɪmɒn/ *noun*. E17.
[Japanese *norimono*, from *nori* to ride + *mono* thing.]
Chiefly *Hist*. A kind of litter or palanquin used in Japan.

norite /ˈnɔːrʌɪt/ *noun*. L19.
[from NOR(WAY + -ITE[1].]
PETROGRAPHY. A coarse-grained plutonic rock similar to gabbro but containing hypersthene.

nork /nɔːk/ *noun*. *slang* (chiefly *Austral*.). M20.
[Origin unkn.]
A woman's breast. Usu. in *pl*.

norland /ˈnɔːlənd/ *noun*[1]. Now *arch*. or *poet*. L16.
[Contr. of ***northland*** s.v. NORTH.]
1 A northern region, a land or country in the north. L16.
2 A person from the north, esp. of Scotland; a northerner. L18.
■ **norlander** *noun* = NORLAND *noun* 2 E18.

Norland /ˈnɔːlənd/ *noun*[2]. L19.
[See below.]
(Proprietary name) used *attrib*. to designate a nurse or children's nanny trained at or according to the methods of the Norland Nursery Training College (formerly the Norland Institute) in London.

norm /nɔːm/ *noun & verb*. E19.
[Anglicized from next. Now infl. by NORMAL.]
▶ **A** *noun*. **1** A standard, a type; what is expected or regarded as normal; customary behaviour, appearance, etc. Freq. ***the norm***. E19.
2 a MATH. The product of a complex number and its conjugate, equal to the sum of the squares of its components; the positive square root of this quantity; an analogous quantity defined on a vector space over the real or complex field which represents a generalization of the concept of length or magnitude. M19. ▶**b** A mean, an average. M20.
3 PETROGRAPHY. A hypothetical mineral composition of a rock calculated by assigning the compounds present to certain relatively simple minerals in accordance with prescribed rules. E20.
4 Esp. in a Communist country, a prescribed standard unit of work, production, etc. M20.

📖 **1** E. B. PUSEY Every expression of his . . became a norm for the party. C. S. LEWIS In her days some kind and degree of religious belief and practice were the norm. M. ARGYLE When group members deviate from the norms, various kinds of persuasion . . are exerted in order to make them conform. **4** *Survey* Real prosperity, to be experienced by the people and not measured by the overfulfilment of fictitious norms.

▶ **B** *verb trans.* MATH.
1 = NORMALIZE *verb* 4. *rare.* M20.
2 Define a norm on (a space). M20.

norma /ˈnɔːmə/ *noun.* Pl. **normae** /ˈnɔːmiː/. L17.
[Latin = carpenter's square, pattern, rule.]
1 = NORM *noun* 1. L17.
2 (Usu. **N-**.) (The name of) an inconspicuous constellation of the southern hemisphere, lying partly in the Milky Way between Lupus and Ara; the Rule. M19.

normal /ˈnɔːm(ə)l/ *adjective & noun.* L15.
[French, or Latin *normalis* made according to a square, right (-angled), (in medieval Latin) regular, (in mod. Latin) perpendicular: see -AL[1]. Cf. prec.]
▶ **A** *adjective.* †**1** Of a verb: regular. *rare.* Only in L15.
2 Right-angled, standing at right angles; perpendicular (*to*). M17.
3 Constituting or conforming to a type or standard; regular, usual, typical; ordinary, conventional. Also, physically or mentally sound, healthy. E19. ▸**b** Heterosexual. E20.
4 CHEMISTRY. **a** Of a salt: containing no acidic hydrogen. M19. ▸**b** Of (the concentration of) a solution: having one gram-equivalent of a solute or solvated ion per litre of solution. M19. ▸**c** (Composed of molecules) containing an unbranched chain of carbon atoms in an alkane molecule or alkyl radical. M19.
5 PHYSICS. **a** Of, pertaining to, or designating a mode of vibration in which every particle executes simple harmonic motion at the same frequency and in phase (or 180 degrees out of phase). M19. ▸**b** ***normal state***, = ***ground state*** s.v. GROUND *noun.* E20. ▸**c** Pertaining to or characteristic of a substance that is not in a superconducting state. E20. ▸**d** Designating a fluid that coexists at the atomic level with a superfluid, in a proportion that decreases with decreasing temperature. M20.
6 GEOLOGY. Designating a fault or faulting in which a relative downward movement occurred in the strata situated on the upper side of the fault plane. L19.
7 STATISTICS. Of a curve, function, process, etc.: = GAUSSIAN. L19.
8 MEDICINE. Of a saline solution: containing the same salt concentration as the blood. L19.

📖 **3** J. WYNDHAM A woman requires her own baby to be perfectly normal. A. BURGESS If you think I'm perverted you're completely mistaken. I'm quite normal. A. BLAISDELL Sunday morning broke bright and clear . . which was normal for Southern California after a rainstorm. I. MURDOCH She moved heavily, in a way quite unlike her normal gait. M. M. KAYE By the following week he was back to normal and feeling as fit as . . ever.

Special collocations: **normal forest** a collection of trees at various stages of development, organized to provide a regular yield of timber. **normal form** (*a*) PHILOSOPHY a standard structure or format in which all propositions in a (usu. symbolic) language can be expressed; (*b*) COMPUTING a defined standard structure for relational databases in which a relation may not be nested within another relation. **normal saline** BIOLOGY & MEDICINE = ***physiological saline*** s.v. PHYSIOLOGICAL 2. **normal school** [after French *école normale*] esp. in Continental Europe and N. America, a school or college for the training of teachers.

▶ **B** *noun.* †**1** A regular verb. *rare.* Only in M16.
2 GEOMETRY. A perpendicular; a straight line at right angles to a tangent or tangent plane to a curve or curved surface. E18.
3 An average, a mean. Now *rare.* M19.
4 The usual state or condition. L19.
5 A normal variety of anything; a sound, healthy, or unimpaired person or thing. L19. ▸**b** A heterosexual person. *slang.* M20.
■ **normalcy** *noun* (chiefly *N. Amer.*) normality M19. **normalism** *noun* (*rare*) the quality or state of being normal L19.

normalise *verb* var. of NORMALIZE.

normality /nɔːˈmalɪti/ *noun.* M19.
[from NORMAL + -ITY.]
1 The state or condition of being normal; normal things or acts collectively. M19.
2 CHEMISTRY. The concentration of a solution as a proportion of the normal concentration. E20.

📖 **1** S. KITZINGER I was offended by the unfeeling normality of the milkman delivering and the sun rising. B. GELDOF On the plane . . back I would, I suppose, have said I was returning to normality.

normalize /ˈnɔːm(ə)lʌɪz/ *verb.* Also **-ise**. M19.
[formed as prec. + -IZE.]
1 *verb trans.* Make normal or regular; cause to conform. Now *spec.* (POLITICS), make (relations) normal or stable between countries etc. M19.
2 *verb intrans.* Become or return to normal. E20.
3 *verb trans.* METALLURGY. Heat (steel) above a certain temperature (about 700°C) and allow to cool in still air at room temperature, to eliminate internal stresses and produce a finer grain structure. E20.
4 *verb trans.* MATH. & PHYSICS. Multiply (a series, function, or variable) by a factor that makes the norm or some associated quantity (as an integral) equal to a particular value, usu. unity. E20.
5 *verb trans.* COMPUTING. ▸**a** In floating-point representation: express (a number) in the standard form as regards the position of the radix point, usu. immediately preceding the first non-zero digit. M20. ▸**b** Conform (a relational database) to a normal form. Chiefly as ***normalized*** *ppl adjective.* L20.

📖 **1** *Survey* The relationship between the U.S.S.R. and the Western powers cannot be normalized . . until . . there is a change in Soviet values.

■ **normalizable** *adjective* M20. **normaliˈzation** *noun* (*a*) the action of the verb; (*b*) PSYCHOLOGY the subconscious process whereby the mental image of a shape, pattern, etc., changes after prolonged presentation to assume a more familiar form: L19. **normalizer** *noun* E20. **normalizing** *noun* = NORMALIZATION: E20.

normally /ˈnɔːm(ə)li/ *adverb.* L16.
[formed as prec. + -LY[2].]
†**1** In a regular manner; regularly. *rare.* Only in L16.
2 Under normal or ordinary conditions; as a rule, ordinarily. M19.
3 At right angles. M19.
4 In a normal manner, in the usual way. L19.
5 STATISTICS. In accordance with the normal distribution. E20.

📖 **2** H. SECOMBE A blush spread over his long, normally pale face. J. WILCOX Normally Mr. Pickens wouldn't have gone for a drive with her. **4** J. S. BLACKIE Constant action and reaction in every normally developed human mind. G. SWIFT When they are just talking normally it sounds as if they are having a fight.

normalness /ˈnɔːm(ə)lnɪs/ *noun. rare.* M19.
[formed as prec. + -NESS.]
= NORMALITY 1.

Norman /ˈnɔːmən/ *noun*[1] *& adjective.* ME.
[Old & mod. French *Normans*, *-anz*, pl. of *Normant* (mod. *-and*) from Old Norse *Norðmaðr*, pl. *-menn*, (whence Old English *Norþmann* Northman, Old High German *Nordman* (Dutch *Noorman*, German *Normanne*)), from *norðr* NORTH + *maðr* MAN *noun*.]
▶ **A** *noun.* **1** A native or inhabitant of Normandy in NW France; *Hist.* a member or descendant of the mixed Scandinavian and Frankish people inhabiting Normandy from the 10th cent., who conquered England in 1066. ME. ▸†**b** A Northman, a Norwegian. *rare.* E17–L18.
2 = ***Norman French*** below. M17.
3 The Norman style of architecture. See sense B.2 below. M19.
▶ **B** *adjective.* **1** Of, pertaining to, or characteristic of the Normans or Normandy. L16.
2 Designating or belonging to a style of Romanesque architecture developed by the Normans and prevalent in England from the Norman Conquest until the early 12th cent., characterized by round arches and heavy piers or columns. Cf. ROMANESQUE *adjective* 3. L18.
1 ***Norman Conquest***: see CONQUEST *noun.* **Norman English** *rare* English as spoken or influenced by the Normans. **Norman French** the form of French spoken by the Normans or (after 1066 and until the 14th cent.) in English lawcourts. **Norman Saxon** *rare* = ***Norman English*** above. **Norman thrush** a mistle thrush.
¶ See also ANGLO-NORMAN.
■ **Normaˈnesque** *adjective* suggestive of or resembling the Norman style of architecture M19. **Normanism** *noun* prevalence of Norman rule or characteristics; tendency to favour or imitate the Normans: M17. **Normanist** *noun* (*a*) a supporter of the Normans; (*b*) an advocate or adherent of the theory that Russia was first settled largely by Scandinavians: E17.

norman /ˈnɔːmən/ *noun*[2]. M18.
[Corresp. to Dutch *noorman*, German *Normann*. Perh. rel. to prec.]
NAUTICAL. A bar or pin inserted into a hole to guide or secure a rope etc. or a rudder.

Normandy /ˈnɔːməndi/ *noun.* E16.
[A region of NW France.]
Used *attrib.* to designate things made in or associated with Normandy.
Normandy butter butter made in Normandy. **Normandy vellum** a strong handmade paper designed to imitate the qualities of parchment.

Normanize /ˈnɔːmənʌɪz/ *verb.* Also **-ise**. E17.
[from NORMAN *noun*[1] + -IZE.]
1 *verb intrans.* Adopt the Norman language or Norman customs. E17.
2 *verb trans.* Make Norman or like the Normans. M19.
■ **Normaniˈzation** *noun* E20. **Normanizer** *noun* M19.

Normannic /nɔːˈmanɪk/ *adjective. rare.* E18.
[from NORMAN *noun*[1] + -IC.]
Of or belonging to the Normans.

Norman Rockwell /ˌnɔːmən ˈrɒkwɛl/ *adjectival phr.* L20.
[*Norman Rockwell* (1894–1978), US artist and illustrator.]
Characteristic of or resembling Norman Rockwell's depictions of small-town American life, freq. characterized (esp. with negative connotations) as being idealized, sentimental, and quaint.

normative /ˈnɔːmətɪv/ *adjective.* L19.
[French *normatif*, *-ive*, from Latin NORMA: see -ATIVE.]
1 Establishing a norm or standard; of, deriving from, or implying a standard or norm; prescriptive. L19.
2 PETROGRAPHY. Of or pertaining to the norm of a rock. E20.
■ **normatively** *adverb* M20. **normativeness** *noun* M20. **normativism** *noun* a normative approach or attitude L20. **normativist** *noun* a person having normative ideas or attitudes M20. **normaˈtivity** *noun* the quality of being normative M20.

normed /nɔːmd/ *adjective.* M20.
[from NORM + -ED[2].]
MATH. Having a norm.

normlessness /ˈnɔːmlɪsnɪs/ *noun.* M20.
[from NORM + -LESS + -NESS.]
The lack of any relevant standard or norm.

normo- /ˈnɔːməʊ/ *combining form.*
[Latin NORMA: see -O-.]
Chiefly BIOLOGY & MEDICINE. Normal; close to the average in respect of a variable character (freq. contrasted with HYPER- and HYPO-).
■ **normoblast** *noun* †(*a*) a normocyte; (*b*) a bone marrow cell which loses its nucleus to become a normocyte: L19. **normoˈblastic** *adjective* of or pertaining to a normoblast or normoblasts E20. **normoˈchromic** *adjective* characterized by or designating red blood cells with the normal content of haemoglobin M20. **normocyte** *noun* an erythrocyte which is normal (esp. in size) E20. **normoˈcytic** *adjective* of or pertaining to a normocyte; (of anaemia) characterized by the presence of erythrocytes of the normal size: E20. **normoglyˈcaemia**, ***-cemia** *noun* a normal concentration of sugar in the blood M20. **normoglyˈcaemic**, ***-cemic** *adjective* characterized by normoglycaemia M20. **normoˈtensive** *adjective & noun* (*a*) *adjective* having or designating a normal blood pressure; (*b*) *noun* a person who has a normal blood pressure: M20. **normoˈthermic** *adjective* characterized by or occurring at a normal body temperature M20. **normovoˈlaemia**, ***-lemia** *noun* the condition of having a normal volume of circulating blood in the body E20. **normovoˈlaemic**, ***-lemic** *adjective* characterized by or pertaining to normovolaemia M20.

Norn /nɔːn/ *noun*[1]. Pl. **-s**, **-ir** /-ɪə/. Also **-na** /-nə/, **-nie** /-ni/. L18.
[Old Norse, of unkn. origin.]
In Scandinavian mythology, each of the three Fates or goddesses of destiny. Usu. in *pl.*

Norn /ˈnɔːn/ *adjective & noun*[2]. ME.
[Old Norse *norrœn* adjective, *norrœnna* noun, from *norðr* north.]
▶ **A** *adjective.* Norwegian. Also, of or designating the form of Norwegian formerly spoken in Orkney and Shetland. ME.
▶ **B** *noun.* The Norn language. L15.

Norna, **Nornie** *nouns* vars. of NORN *noun*[1].

Nornir *noun pl.* see NORN *noun*[1].

Norroy /ˈnɒrɔɪ/ *noun.* LME.
[from Anglo-Norman word from Old & mod. French *nord* north + *roi* king.]
HERALDRY. (The title of) the third King of Arms, having jurisdiction in England and Wales north of the River Trent and now also (as ***Norroy and Ulster***) in Northern Ireland.

Norse /nɔːs/ *noun & adjective.* L16.
[Dutch *noor(d)sch*, from *noord* north + *-sch* -ISH[1].]
▶ **A** *noun.* Pl. same, (earlier) †**-s**.
1 *pl.* Norwegians. Also, natives or inhabitants of ancient Scandinavia. L16.
2 The Norwegian language. Also, the Scandinavian language division; North Germanic. L17.
▶ **B** *adjective.* Of or pertaining to Norway or its language, Norwegian. Also, of or pertaining to ancient Scandinavia or its inhabitants. M17.
Phrases: ***Old Norse***: see OLD *adjective.*
Comb.: **Norseland** *arch.* Norway; **Norseman** a man of Norwegian birth or nationality; a native or inhabitant of ancient Scandinavia, a Viking.
■ **Norseness** *noun* the state or quality of being Norwegian or Scandinavian M20.

Norsk /nɔːsk/ *adjective & noun.* M19.
[Swedish, Danish, & Norwegian.]
Norse.

norsteroid /nɔːˈstɪərɔɪd, -ˈstɛrɔɪd/ *noun.* M20.
[from NOR- + STEROID.]
BIOCHEMISTRY. A steroid lacking a methyl side chain or having one of its rings contracted by one methylene group.

norte /ˈnɔrte/ *noun.* M19.
[Spanish = north.]
Any of the violent gales from the north prevailing in the Gulf of Mexico from September to March. Cf. NORTHER *noun.* Usu. in *pl.*

norteamericano /ˌnɔrteameriˈkano/ *noun & adjective.* Pl. of noun **-os** /-ɔs/. Also **N-**, fem. **-cana** /-ˈkana/. **E20.**
[Spanish & Portuguese, from *norte* north + *americano* American.]
Esp. in Latin America, (a native or inhabitant) of N. America, (a) N. American.

north /nɔːθ/ *adverb, adjective, noun, & verb.*
[Old English *norþ* = Old Frisian *north, noerd*, Old Saxon *norþ* (Dutch *noord*), Old & mod. High German *nord*, Old Norse *norðr*, from Germanic.]
▶ **A** *adverb.* **1** In the direction of the part of the horizon on the left-hand side of a person facing east; towards the point or pole on the earth's surface where it is cut by the earth's axis of rotation and where the heavens appear to turn anticlockwise about a point directly overhead; towards the magnetic pole near this point, to which a compass needle points. **OE.**
2 Foll. by *of*: further in this direction than. **E17.**

📖 **1** J. SPRIGGE Lying but eighteen miles north from Oxford. F. A. STEEL If you will take my advice, come up north. J. BUCHAN I had to go north by an earlier train from Euston. I. MCEWAN Usually the canal flows north, but today it was completely still. **2** DEFOE North of the Mouth of this River is . . Cromarty Bay.

▶ **B** *adjective.* Compar. †**norther**, superl. †**northest**.
1 (Also **N-**.) Designating (a person or the people of) the northern part of a country, region, city, etc. **OE.**
2 Lying towards, at, or near the north or northern part of something; on the northerly side. **OE.** ▸**b** Facing north. **M17.**
3 Of or pertaining to the north; (esp. of a wind) coming from the north. **ME.**

📖 **1** *North Africa, North Korea, North London, North Oxford, North Yorkshire*, etc. *North African, North Korean*, etc. **2** D. H. LAWRENCE Strelley Mill lies at the north end of the long Nethermere Valley. J. F. LEHMANN I had taken a flat on the north side of Mecklenburgh Square. T. DUPUY The . . Kurds in Iraq . . . live in the highlands north and east of Mosul. **3** SHAKES. *Per.* When I was born the wind was north. OUIDA The north wind is racing in from the Polish steppes.

▶ **C** *noun.* In senses 1, 2, 3 usu. with *the*.
1 (The direction of) the part of the horizon on the left-hand side of a person facing east; *spec.* the cardinal point corresponding to this. **ME.**
2 (Freq. **N-**.) The northern part of the world relative to another part, or of a (specified) country, region, town, etc.; *spec.* (*a*) the northern part of England, regarded as extending from the boundary with Scotland approximately down to the southern boundaries of Cheshire, Yorkshire, and Humberside; (*b*) the northern countries of Europe; the Arctic; (*c*) the northern States of the US, bounded on the south by Maryland, the Ohio River, and Missouri; *Hist.* the States opposed to slavery; (*d*) the industrialized nations of the world. Also (*transf.*) the inhabitants of such a part of the world, such a country, region, etc. **ME.**
3 A north wind, *esp.* one that brings cold weather. Also, a northerly gale in the W. Indies (usu. in *pl.*). **ME.**
4 (**N-**.) In bridge, (formerly) whist, or other four-handed partnership game: the player occupying the position so designated, who sits opposite 'South'. In mah-jong, = ***north wind*** (a) below. **E20.**

📖 **1** J. H. TOOKE Directing his view to the North rather than to the East. SHELLEY The rainbow hung over the city . . from north to south. T. H. HUXLEY Draw maps in such a position that the north is towards the top. **2** *Westminster Gazette* Professionalism in Rugby football in the North of England is inevitable. *West Hawaii Today* The brushy south contrasts with Sudan's desert-like north.

▶ **D** *verb.* **1** *verb intrans.* Move northward; (of a wind) shift or veer northward. *rare.* **M19.**
2 *verb trans.* Steer to the north of (a place). *rare.* **L19.**
Special collocations, comb., & phrases: **magnetic north** (the direction of) the north magnetic pole. **northabout** *adverb* (NAUTICAL) by a northerly route, *spec.* round the north of Scotland; northwards. **North American** *noun & adjective* (a native or inhabitant) of North America, the half of the American landmass north of the Isthmus of Panama, esp. the US or Canada. **north and south** (*a*) lengthwise along a line from north to south; (*b*) *rhyming slang* the mouth. **North Atlantic Drift** a continuation of the Gulf Stream across the Atlantic Ocean and along the coast of NW Europe, where it has a significant warming effect on the climate. **northbound** *adjective & noun* (*a*) *adjective* travelling or heading northwards; (*b*) *noun* (chiefly *N. Amer.*) a northbound train. **North Britain** (now chiefly *derog.* or *joc.*) Scotland. **North Briton** (now chiefly *derog.* or *joc.*) a Scot. **north-by-east**, **north-by-west** (in the direction of) those compass points 11¼ degrees or one point east, west, of the north point. **north canoe** a type of large capacious canoe, orig. of birchbark, formerly used in N. America. **north country** the northern part of any country, *spec.* of England; the dialect of the north of England. **North countryman**, **North countrywoman** a native or inhabitant of the north country. *North Downs*: see DOWN *noun*[1] 2. **North** GERMANIC. **North Islander** a native or inhabitant of the North Island of New Zealand. **northland** (now chiefly *poet.*) the northern part of a country, region, etc., or of the world; in *pl.*, lands lying in the north. **northlander** a person from the north. **north light** (*a*) (usu. in *pl.*) the aurora borealis; (*b*) light from a northerly direction, esp. as favoured by artists and in factory design; (*c*) a window, esp. in a roof, facing north. **Northman** a native or inhabitant of Scandinavia, esp. of Norway; a Viking. **north-north-east**, **north-north-west** (in the direction) midway between north and north-east, north and north-west. **northpaw** *N. Amer. slang* a right-handed person. ***north pole***: see POLE *noun*[2]. **North Sea** the sea between Britain and the Netherlands, Germany, and Scandinavia. **North Star** the polestar; ***North Star State***, (*US*) the State of Minnesota. ***north*** TRANSEPT. **north wind** (*a*) (usu. with cap. initials) one of the four players in mah-jong, the player who takes the last four tiles, after West Wind, at the outset of the game; (*b*) each of four tiles so designated, which with east, south, and west winds make up the suit of winds in mah-jong; (see also sense B.3 above). **to the north (of)** in a northerly direction (from). **true north** (in) the direction of the earth's North Pole. **up north** (in or into) the northern part of a country.
■ **northmost** *adjective* (now *rare*) northernmost **OE.** **northness** *noun* (*rare*) **M19.**

Northants *abbreviation.*
Northamptonshire.

north-east /nɔːθˈiːst/ *adverb, noun, & adjective.* **OE.**
[from NORTH + EAST.]
▶ **A** *adverb.* In the direction midway between north and east. Foll. by *of*: further in this direction than. **OE.**

📖 *Brighouse News* Terrington Coom, north-east of York.

▶ **B** *noun.* **1** (The direction of) the point of the horizon midway between north and east; the compass point corresponding to this. Also (freq. **North-East**), *the* north-eastern part of a country, region, etc., *spec.* the area of England regarded as consisting of Northumberland, Durham, Tyne and Wear, and Cleveland. **OE.**
2 A north-east wind. **LME.**
▶ **C** *adjective.* Of or pertaining to the north-east; (esp. of a wind) coming from the north-east; situated in, directed towards, or facing the north-east. **LME.**

📖 H. H. JOHNSTON The Meru dialect . . is . . . spoken in the north-east portion of the Kikuyu area. **north-east passage** a sea passage along the north coasts of Europe and Asia, formerly thought of as a possible route to the East.

■ **north-easter** *noun* a north-east wind **L18.** **north-easterly** *adjective & adverb* (*a*) *adjective* situated towards or facing the north-east; directed towards the north-east; (esp. of a wind) coming (nearly) from the north-east; (*b*) *adverb* in a north-easterly position or direction; towards the north-east: **M18.**

north-eastern /nɔːθˈiːst(ə)n/ *adjective.* **LME.**
[from NORTH + EASTERN.]
Situated in or directed towards the north-east; of, pertaining to, or characteristic of the north-east; (esp. of a wind) coming from the north-east.
■ **north-easterner** *noun* a native or inhabitant of the north-eastern part of a country **M20.** **north-easternmost** *adjective* situated furthest to the north-east **M19.**

north-eastward /nɔːθˈiːstwəd/ *adverb, adjective, & noun.* **M16.**
[from NORTH-EAST + -WARD.]
▶ **A** *adverb.* Towards the north-east (*of*); in a north-easterly direction. **M16.**
▶ **B** *adjective.* Situated or directed towards the north-east; moving or facing towards the north-east. **M18.**
▶ **C** *noun.* The direction or area lying to the north-east or north-east *of* a place etc. **L18.**
■ **north-eastwardly** *adjective & adverb* (*a*) *adjective* moving, lying, or facing towards the north-east; (of a wind) blowing (nearly) from the north-east; (*b*) *adverb* in or from a north-easterly direction: **L18.** **north-eastwards** *adverb* = NORTH-EASTWARD *adverb* **L16.**

†**northen** *adjective.* **ME–L18.**
[from NORTH + -EN[4].]
Northern.

norther /ˈnɔːθə/ *noun.* **L18.**
[from NORTH + -ER[1].]
A (strong) northerly wind, *esp.* one blowing over Texas, Florida, and the Gulf of Mexico during the autumn and winter or on the N. American Pacific seaboard.

†**norther** *adjective* compar. of NORTH *adjective.*

norther /ˈnɔːðə/ *verb intrans.* **E17.**
[from NORTH + -ER[5].]
Of a wind: shift or veer northward.

northerly /ˈnɔːðəli/ *adjective, adverb, & noun.* **M16.**
[from †*norther* compar. of NORTH *adjective* + -LY[1], -LY[2]; partly from NORTH after *easterly*.]
▶ **A** *adjective.* **1** Situated towards or facing the north; directed towards the north. **M16.**
2 Esp. of a wind: (nearly) from the north. **M16.**

📖 **1** S. BELLOW Kolyma is one of the most northerly of the . . camps.

▶ **B** *adverb.* **1** In a northward position or direction. **M16.**
2 Esp. of a wind: (nearly) from the north. **L16.**
▶ **C** *noun.* A northerly wind. Freq. in *pl.* **M20.**
■ **northerliness** *noun* (*rare*) **M19.**

†**northermost** *adjective.* **M16–M18.**
[from †*norther* compar. of NORTH *adjective* + -MOST.]
= NORTHERNMOST.

northern /ˈnɔːð(ə)n/ *adjective & noun*[1].
[Old English *norþerne* corresp. to Old Saxon *norþrōni(wind)*, Old High German *nordrōni*, Old Norse *norðrœnn*, from Germanic base of NORTH.]
▶ **A** *adjective.* **1** Living in or originating from the north, esp. of England or Europe. **OE.** ▸**b** *spec.* Living in or originating from (any of) the States in the north of the US. **L18.**
2 Of a wind: blowing from the north. **OE.**
3 Of, pertaining to, or characteristic of the north or its inhabitants. **LME.**
4 Situated in the north; directed, facing, or lying towards the north; having a position relatively north. **L16.**

📖 **1** M. PATTISON A powerful coalition of northern princes to resist the encroachments of Rome. ***northern hartebeest***, ***northern sparrowhawk***, ***northern wren***, etc. **3** E. O'BRIEN He spoke with a clipped Northern accent. A. S. BYATT He would break a close northern habit of meanness to provide champagne. **4** SHELLEY Like the sea on a northern shore. D. H. LAWRENCE On the northern slopes lay its pasture and arable lands.

Special collocations & phrases: ***great northern diver***: see DIVER 1. **Northern blot**, **Northern blotting** [after SOUTHERN BLOT] BIOCHEMISTRY an adaptation of the Southern blot procedure used to detect specific sequences of RNA by hybridization with complementary DNA. **northern canoe** = *NORTH canoe*. ***Northern Crown***: see CROWN *noun* 8. ***Northern hemisphere***: see HEMISPHERE 1b. **northern hornworm** = ***tomato hornworm*** s.v. TOMATO *noun*. **Northern Irish** *noun pl. & adjective* (the people) of the north of Ireland or of Northern Ireland, a unit of the United Kingdom comprising the six north-eastern counties of Ireland. **northern lights** the aurora borealis. ***Northern Paiute***: see PAIUTE *noun* 1. **northern sea lion** = *STELLER's sea lion*. **Northern Spy** a red-skinned, late-ripening N. American variety of eating apple. **northern star** *spec.* = *North Star* s.v. NORTH. **Northern States** the States in the north of the US; *Hist.* the States opposed to slavery. ***northern wren***: see WREN *noun*[1] 1.
▶ **B** *noun.* †**1** *collect. sing.* Northern men. *rare.* **ME–E17.**
2 The dialect of English spoken in the north, esp. of England. **L16.**
3 a A native or inhabitant of the north. **L18.** ▸**b** A north wind. **E19.**
■ **northerner** *noun* a native or inhabitant of the north, esp. of northern England; (freq. **N-**) a person belonging to the States in the north of the US: **ME.** **northernism** *noun* (*a*) northern quality; (*b*) a northern characteristic, idiom, etc.: **L19.** **northernize** *verb trans.* make northern in character, quality, form, etc. **M19.** **northernly** *adjective & adverb* (now *rare*) = NORTHERLY *adjective*, *adverb* **L16.** **northernmost** *adjective* situated furthest to the north, most northerly **E18.** **northernness** /-n-n-/ *noun* **M19.**

†**northest** *adjective* superl. of NORTH *adjective.*

northing /ˈnɔːθɪŋ/ *noun.* **M17.**
[from NORTH + -ING[1].]
1 Chiefly NAUTICAL. (A measurement of) progress or deviation made towards the north. Freq. in ***make (so much) northing***. **M17.**
2 CARTOGRAPHY. Distance northward from a point of origin, (freq. from the south-west corner on a map); a figure representing this, expressed by convention as the second part of a grid reference (usu. in *pl.* or more fully ***northing coordinate***). Cf. EASTING 2. **M18.**
3 The apparent movement of a celestial object towards the north. **E19.**

Northumb. *abbreviation.*
Northumberland.

Northumber /nɔːˈθʌmbə/ *noun.* Now *rare.* **LME.**
[See next.]
Hist. A native or inhabitant of the Anglo-Saxon kingdom of Northumbria. Usu. in *pl.*

Northumbrian /nɔːˈθʌmbrɪən/ *noun & adjective.* **M16.**
[from *Northumbria* Latinized form of *Northumber*, from NORTH + the river *Humber* in NE England: see -AN.]
▶ **A** *noun.* **1** A native or inhabitant of the ancient Anglo-Saxon kingdom of Northumbria, stretching from the Humber to the Forth, or of modern Northumberland, a county in the extreme north-east of England. **M16.**
2 The dialect of English used in Northumbria or Northumberland. **M19.**
▶ **B** *adjective.* Of or pertaining to ancient Northumbria or modern Northumberland. **E17.**

northward /ˈnɔːθwəd/ *adverb, noun, & adjective.* **OE.**
[from NORTH + -WARD.]
▶ **A** *adverb.* Towards the north (*of*); in a northerly direction. **OE.**

📖 JEREMY COOPER The house itself faced the wrong direction, northward into the side of the hill. C. THUBRON I took a bus northward to the valley where the Ming emperors are buried.

▶ **B** *noun.* The direction or area lying to the north or north *of* a place etc. **LME.**

📖 W. F. P. NAPIER The mountains to the northward of Barcelona.

▶ **C** *adjective.* Situated or directed towards the north; moving or facing towards the north. **L16.**

THACKERAY The northward track which the expeditionary army had hewed out for itself.

■ **northwardly** *adjective & adverb* (*a*) *adjective* moving, lying, or facing towards the north; (of a wind) blowing (nearly) from the north; (*b*) *adverb* in or from a northwardly direction: L17. **northwards** *adverb* & (now *rare*) *noun* = NORTHWARD *adverb, noun* OE.

north-west /nɔːθˈwɛst/ *adverb, noun, & adjective*. OE.
[from NORTH + WEST *adverb*.]
▶ **A** *adverb*. In the direction midway between north and west. Foll. by *of*: further in this direction than. OE.
▶ **B** *noun*. (The direction of) the point of the horizon midway between north and west; the compass point corresponding to this. Also (freq. **North-West**), *the* north-western part of a country, region, etc., *spec*. (*a*) the North-West Territories of Canada; (*b*) the part of England regarded as consisting of Cheshire, Lancashire, Manchester, and Merseyside. LME.
▶ **C** *adjective*. Of or pertaining to the north-west; (esp. of a wind) coming from the north-west; situated in, directed towards, or facing the north-west. LME.

J. SCOULER The vocabularies of the languages spoken on the north-west coast. **north-west passage** a sea passage along the north coast of America, formerly thought of as a possible route between the Atlantic and the Pacific.

■ **north-wester** *noun* = NOR'-WESTER M18. **north-westerly** *adjective & adverb* (*a*) *adjective* situated towards or facing the north-west; directed towards the north-west; (esp. of a wind) coming (nearly) from the north-west; (*b*) *adverb* in a north-westerly position or direction, towards the north-west: E17.

north-western /nɔːθˈwɛst(ə)n/ *adjective*. E17.
[from NORTH + WESTERN.]
Situated in or directed towards the north-west; of, pertaining to, or characteristic of the north-west; (esp. of a wind) coming from the north-west.
■ **north-westerner** *noun* a native or inhabitant of the north-western part of a country M20. **northwesternmost** *adjective* situated furthest to the north-west L20.

north-westward /nɔːθˈwɛstwəd/ *adverb, noun, & adjective*. LME.
[from NORTH-WEST + -WARD.]
▶ **A** *adverb*. Towards the north-west (*of*); in a north-westerly direction. LME.
▶ **B** *noun*. The direction or area lying to the north-west or north-west *of* a place etc. L18.
▶ **C** *adjective*. Situated or directed towards the north-west; moving or facing towards the north-west. L20.
■ **north-westwardly** *adjective & adverb* (*a*) *adjective* moving, lying, or facing towards the north-west; (of a wind) blowing (nearly) from the north-west; (*b*) *adverb* in or from a north-westerly direction: L18. **north-westwards** *adverb* = NORTH-WESTWARD *adverb* L20.

nortriptyline /nɔːˈtrɪptɪliːn/ *noun*. M20.
[from NOR- + TRI- + HE)PTYL + -INE[5].]
PHARMACOLOGY. A tricyclic antidepressant drug, $C_{19}H_{21}N$.

norward /ˈnɔːwəd/ *adverb & noun*. E17.
[from NOR' + -WARD.]
▶ **A** *adverb*. In a northerly direction, northward. E17.
▶ **B** *noun*. A northern direction or region, the north. E17.
■ **norwards** *adverb* = NORWARD *adverb* L17.

Norway /ˈnɔːweɪ/ *noun*. L17.
[A country in Scandinavia: see next.]
Used *attrib*. to designate things coming from or associated with Norway.
Norway haddock the N. Atlantic redfish *Sebastes marinus*. ***Norway lemming***: see LEMMING 1. **Norway lobster** a long slender lobster, *Nephrops norvegicus*, found in the Atlantic, North Sea, and Mediterranean; also called ***Dublin Bay prawn***, ***scampi***. **Norway maple** a maple, *Acer platanoides*, native to the mountains of Europe and much planted elsewhere, with yellow flowers which appear before the leaves. **Norway pine** the red pine of N. America, *Pinus resinosa*. ***Norway rat***: see RAT *noun*[1] 1a. **Norway spruce** a long-coned European spruce, *Picea abies*, widely grown for its timber.

Norwegian /nɔːˈwiːdʒ(ə)n/ *adjective & noun*. E17.
[from medieval Latin *Norvegia* from Old Norse *Norvegr* Norway, from *norðr* north + *vegr* way, (in place-names) region: see -AN. The *w* is from *Norway*.]
▶ **A** *adjective*. Of or pertaining to Norway, a country occupying the northern and western part of the Scandinavian peninsula; native to or associated with Norway. E17.
Norwegian steam *slang* (chiefly NAUTICAL) hard manual work or physical effort.
▶ **B** *noun*. **1** A native or inhabitant of Norway. E17.
2 The North Germanic language of Norway. E17.

nor'-west /nɔːˈwɛst/ *noun & adjective*. LME.
[from NOR' + WEST *noun*[2], *adjective*.]
= NORTH-WEST *noun & adjective*.

nor'-wester /nɔːˈwɛstə/ *noun*. L17.
[Contr. of NORTH-WESTER: cf. prec., -ER[1].]
1 An oilskin hat worn by sailors in rough weather, a sou'wester. Also (in full ***nor'-wester coat***), a strong waterproof, esp. oilskin, coat worn in rough weather. L17.
2 A wind from the north-west. E18.
3 A glass of strong liquor. M19.

Norweyan /nɔːˈweɪən/ *adjective*. *rare*. E17.
[from NORWAY + -AN.]
Norwegian.

Norwich /ˈnɒrɪtʃ, -ɪdʒ/ *noun*. E17.
[A city in, and the county town of, Norfolk.]
Used *attrib*. to designate things coming from, made in, or associated with Norwich.
Norwich school an early 19th-cent. English school of painting which produced mostly landscapes. **Norwich terrier** (an animal of) a small thickset red or black-and-tan rough-coated breed of terrier with pricked ears; *US* a Norfolk terrier.

nose /nəʊz/ *noun*.
[Old English *nosu* = Old Frisian *nose*, Middle Dutch *nōse*, *nuese* (Dutch *neus*). Cf. Latin *nares* pl. nostrils, *nas(s)us* nose, Sanskrit *nas*. Cf. NESS.]
▶ **I 1** The organ above the mouth on the head or face of a human or animal containing the nostrils and used for smelling and breathing; this with the air passages from the nostrils to the pharynx. OE. ▸**b** An elephant's trunk. Now *joc. & colloq.* LME. ▸**c** In horse-racing etc., the nose of a competitor used as an indication of the winning margin in a close finish. E20.
2 The sense of smell; a faculty for discriminating scents, esp. in the ability to track by scent (freq. with specifying word); *fig*. a talent or knack *for* the detection of something. ME.
3 A spy, an informer, esp. for the police. *slang*. L18.
4 The odour or perfume of wine, tea, tobacco, etc.; = BOUQUET 2. L19.

1 D. JOHNSON His glasses slipped down to the end of his nose. I. MCEWAN One of the academics . . was wiping his nose with a tissue to conceal laughter. D. HALL We never see beaver, except a distant nose sticking up from the water . . as it swims. **2** A. S. NEILL The young have a sensitive nose for insincerity. **4** P. CAREY The crushed violet nose of a 1973 Cheval Blanc.

▶ **II 5** Orig., a socket on a candlestick into which the candle was inserted. Now, the open end or nozzle of a pipe, tube, gun muzzle, retort, etc. LME.
6 The prow of a ship or boat; the front end of an aircraft, motor vehicle, etc. M16.
7 A prominent or projecting part, the point or extremity of anything; *spec*. (*a*) the remains of the calyx on a gooseberry etc.; (*b*) = NOSING; (*c*) a projecting part of an electric traction motor by which it is suspended from the framework of a bogie or vehicle. L16.

Phrases: **as plain as the nose on your face** perfectly clear or obvious. **before one's nose** right in front of one. **bet on the nose** back a horse to win (as opp. to betting for a place or betting each way). †**bite a person's nose off** = *bite a person's head off* s.v. BITE *verb*. †**bite by the nose** treat with contempt. †**by one's nose** very close to one. ***cock one's nose***, ***cock the nose***: see COCK *verb*[1] 6. **count noses** = *count heads* s.v. HEAD *noun*. **cut off one's nose to spite one's face** harm oneself through acting spitefully or resentfully. **follow one's nose** go straight forward; *fig*. be guided by instinct. **get one's nose down (to)** work arduously and concentratedly (at). **get up a person's nose** *slang* annoy a person. ***Grecian nose***: see GRECIAN *adjective*. **have one's nose in a book** read intently. ***hold a person's nose to the grindstone***: see GRINDSTONE 2. **hold one's nose** compress the nostrils between the fingers to avoid a (bad) smell. ***John Crow nose***, ***John Crow's nose***: see JOHN CROW 2. ***keep a person's nose to the grindstone***: see GRINDSTONE 2. **keep one's nose clean** *slang* behave properly, keep out of trouble. ***lead by the nose***: see LEAD *verb*[1]. ***long nose***: see LONG *adjective*[1]. ***look down one's nose at***: see LOOK *verb*. **nose of wax** (now *rare*) a thing easily turned or moulded; a person easily influenced or of a weak character. **nose to nose** closely face to face, directly opposite. ***no skin off one's nose***: see SKIN *noun*. **on the nose** (*slang*) (*a*) *adverbial phr.* (*N. Amer.*) accurately, precisely, to the point; (*b*) *adjectival phr.* accurate, precise (*N. Amer.*); *Austral.* offensive, annoying, smelly. ***parson's nose***. **pay through the nose** *colloq.* have to pay an exorbitant price. **poke one's nose in** = ***stick one's nose in*** below. ***powder one's nose***: see POWDER *verb*[1] 3. **put a person's nose out of joint** make a person jealous, supplant, affront, or disconcert a person. **rub a person's nose in it** remind a person humiliatingly of an error, fault, etc. ***rub noses***: see RUB *verb*. **see no further than one's nose** be short-sighted (*lit. & fig.*) or unperceptive. ***snap a person's nose off***: see SNAP *verb* 3. ***snub nose***: see SNUB *adjective* 1. **speak through one's nose** speak in a nasal manner. **stick one's nose into** interfere or intrude in something not properly of concern to one. ***stop one's nose***: see STOP *verb*. **thumb one's nose at** put one's thumb to one's nose and extend the fingers towards (a person) as a gesture of derision; *fig*. act with blatant disregard for the feelings or status of (another). †**to one's nose** to one's face, in front of one. **turn up one's nose at** show disdain or scorn for. **under a person's nose**, **under a person's very nose** right in front of a person, regardless of his or her displeasure or without being noticed. **with one's nose in the air** haughtily.

Comb.: **nose-ape** = ***nose-monkey*** below; **nosebag** (*a*) a bag containing fodder, suspended from a horse's head and hanging below the nose; (*b*) *slang* food, a meal, (***put on the nose***, eat); a gas mask; **noseband** a strap passing round the nose of a horse, suspended by its own head-piece fitted under the bridle; **nosebleed** (*a*) the plant yarrow, *Achillea millefolium*; (*b*) an instance of bleeding from the nose; (*c*) *attrib*. (*US slang*) likely to cause a nosebleed due to excessive altitude or speed, *esp*. designating the highest (and cheapest) seats in an auditorium or stadium; **nose bot (fly)** = ***nose-fly*** below; **nose-bridge** (*a*) the part of a pair of spectacles which crosses the nose, the bridge; (*b*) ARCHAEOLOGY designating a type of handle found on pottery of the Copper Age in southern Europe; **nose-candy** *N. Amer. slang* a drug that is inhaled, *spec*. cocaine; **nose cap** the cap on the nose of an aircraft, shell, bomb, etc.; **nose-clip** a clip to prevent water from entering the nose of a swimmer or diver; **nose cone** a conical nose cap; *spec*. the cone-shaped front part of a rocket, designed to withstand the severe heating caused by atmospheric friction; **nosedive** *noun* a sudden or rapid nose-first descent by an aircraft etc. (***terminal nosedive***: see TERMINAL *adjective*); *fig*. a sudden drop or decline; **nosedive** *verb* (*a*) *verb intrans*. make a nosedive; (*b*) *verb trans*. put (an aircraft) into a nosedive; **nose door** a forward-facing door in the nose of an aircraft; **nose-down** *adjective & adverb* (chiefly AERONAUTICS) with the nose pointing downwards; **nose drops** a medicament intended to be administered as drops into the nose; **nose flute** a musical instrument blown with the nose, popular in the Pacific islands and SE Asia; **nose-fly** a fly, esp. a bot-fly, which irritates or infests the nostrils of domestic animals; spec. *Gasterophilus haemorrhoidalis*, which infests horses, and *Oestrus ovis*, which infests sheep; **nosegay** *arch*. a bunch of (esp. sweet-smelling) flowers or herbs; a bouquet, a posy; **nose-glasses** *US* = PINCE-NEZ; **nose guard** AMER. FOOTBALL = ***nose tackle*** below; **nose-heavy** *adjective* (of an aircraft etc.) having a tendency for the nose to drop relative to the tail; †**nose-herb** (*rare*, Shakes.) an aromatic plant; **nosehole** (now *slang & dial.*) a nostril; **nose job** *colloq*. an operation involving rhinoplasty or cosmetic surgery on a person's nose; **nose-leaf** the leaf-shaped structure on the nose of many bats; **nose-monkey** the proboscis monkey; **nose-nippers** = ***nose-glasses*** above; **nose-paint** *slang* intoxicating liquor; a reddening of the nose ascribed to habitual drinking; **nose paste** = ***nose putty*** below; **nose-piece** (*a*) a part of a helmet covering the nose; (*b*) = ***nose-band*** above; (*c*) OPTICS the part of a microscope to which the objective is attached; **nosepipe** a piece of piping used as a nozzle, esp. inside a blast-furnace; **nose print** a drawing of the facial characteristics of an animal, used as a means of identification; **nose putty** a putty-like substance used in the theatre for altering the shape of the nose etc.; **nose-rag** *slang* a pocket-handkerchief; **nose-ring** a ring fixed in the nose, *spec*. (*a*) of an animal (esp. a bull) for leading it; (*b*) of a person as an ornament; **nose-suspended** *adjective* supported by nose suspension; **nose suspension** the suspension of an electric traction motor by a nose (see sense 7 above) from the framework of a bogie or vehicle; **nose tackle** AMER. FOOTBALL a defensive lineman positioned opposite the offensive centre; **nose-to-tail** *adverb & adjective* (of motor vehicles) travelling or placed behind one another and very close together; **nose trick** *slang* the inadvertent inhalation or expulsion of liquid through the nose when drinking; **nose-tube** a tube used for feeding a patient through the nose; **nose-up** *adjective & adverb* (chiefly AERONAUTICS) with the nose pointing upwards; **nose wheel** a landing-wheel under the nose of an aircraft; **nose-wipe**, **nose-wiper** *slang* a handkerchief; **nose-worm** the maggot of the sheep bot-fly, *Oestrus ovis*.

■ **nosed** *adjective* having a nose, *esp*. of a specified kind (freq. as 2nd elem. of comb., as ***long-nosed***, ***snub-nosed***, etc.) LME. **noseless** *adjective* LME. **noselessly** *adverb* M19. **noselessness** *noun* M18. **noser** *noun* (*slang*) (*a*) a blow or fall on the nose; (*b*) a strong head wind: M19.

nose /nəʊz/ *verb*. L16.
[from the noun.]
▶ **I** *verb trans*. **1** Perceive the smell of, discover or notice by smell. Also foll. by *out*. L16.
2 Confront or reproach (a person), esp. *with* something. *obsolete* exc. *dial*. E17.
3 Utter or sing nasally. *rare*. M17.
4 Remove the dried calyx from (a gooseberry etc.). Chiefly *dial*. M18.
5 Push or rub the nose against or into, esp. in order to smell something; press the nose against. L18.
6 Inform on (a person) to the police etc. *slang*. E19.
7 **a** Make (one's way) cautiously forward. L19. ▸**b** Direct (a motor vehicle etc.) cautiously forward. M20.

1 M. AYRTON Picking a jar and nosing its aroma. *fig*.: J. GALSWORTHY He was always nosing out bargains. **5** TENNYSON Lambs are glad Nosing the mother's udder. W. SOYINKA A canoe . . nosed the shore-line. **7a** K. AMIS The bus nosed . . on to the crown of the road. **b** E. L. DOCTOROW He nosed the shiny car through the narrow . . streets.

▶ **II** *verb intrans*. **8** Search, esp. furtively, for something, pry; investigate by the sense of smell; sniff, smell. Also foll. by *about*, *around*. M17.
9 Inform on a person to the police etc. *slang*. E19.
10 Move cautiously forward. L19. ▸**b** Move forward and down; *spec*. (*a*) (of an aircraft) fall *over* on the nose; (*b*) (of a surfboard) plunge downward nose first. E20.

8 M. TWAIN The detectives were nosing around after Stewart's loud remains. R. LEHMANN I thought of her nosing in my room for signs. R. K. NARAYAN Pigs and piglets . . nosed about the ground. *Sunday Times* Nosing around other people's houses fascinates most of us. **10** B. BAINBRIDGE The car nosed out into the thin stream of traffic. **nose ahead** go into the lead by a small margin. **b** **nose down** AERONAUTICS produce or undergo a steepening of an aircraft's flight path, descend, esp. gently.

no-see-em /nəʊˈsiːəm/ *noun*. *N. Amer.* Also **-um**. M19.
[from NO *adverb*[1] + SEE *verb* + 'EM.]
Any of various small bloodsucking insects, esp. biting midges.

noseling /ˈnəʊzlɪŋ/ *adverb*. Long *arch*. LME.
[from NOSE *noun* + -LING[2]. Cf. NUZZLE *verb*[1].]
On the nose, face downwards.

nosema /nəʊˈsiːmə/ *noun*. E20.
[mod. Latin (see below), from Greek *nosēma* disease.]
A microsporidian protozoan parasite of the genus *Nosema*; (more fully ***nosema disease***) an infectious dysentery affecting bees and caused by *Nosema apis*. Cf. PÉBRINE.

nose-thirl *noun* see NOSTRIL.

nosey *adjective & noun* var. of NOSY.

nosh /nɒʃ/ *noun & verb*. *slang*. E20.
[Yiddish. Cf. German *naschen* to nibble.]
▶ **A** *noun*. **1** A restaurant; a snack bar. More fully ***nosh bar***, ***nosh-house***. E20.
2 Food, a meal. M20.
3 A snack eaten between meals, a titbit. Chiefly *N. Amer.* M20.
📖 **2** D. LODGE Would you . . join me for a little Italian nosh?
Comb.: ***nosh bar***, ***nosh-house***: see sense 1 above; **nosh-up** a large meal.
▶ **B** *verb trans. & intrans*. **1** Nibble or eat (a snack) (chiefly *N. Amer.*); eat (food), esp. heartily or greedily. M20.
2 Practise fellatio (with). M20.
📖 **1** S. ELKIN There's nothing to nosh but gum.
■ **noshable** *adjective* able to be eaten; *spec.* appetizing, tasty: M20. **nosher** *noun* a person who noshes; *spec.* a person who samples food before buying it: M20. **noshery** *noun* a restaurant; a snack bar: M20.

noshi /ˈnɒʃi/ *noun*. M19.
[Japanese.]
A Japanese token of esteem, forming part of the wrapping of a gift, orig. a piece of dried awabi but now usu. a specially folded piece of paper.

nosing /ˈnəʊzɪŋ/ *noun*. L18.
[from NOSE *noun* + -ING[1].]
The rounded edge of a bench or moulding or of a step projecting beyond the riser; a metal etc. shield for this.

nosism /ˈnɒsɪz(ə)m/ *noun*. Now *rare*. E19.
[from Latin *nos* we + -ISM.]
1 A selfish attitude in a group of people, corresponding to egotism in an individual. E19.
2 The use of 'we' in stating one's own opinions. E19.

noso- /ˈnɒsəʊ/ *combining form*.
[Greek, from *nosos* disease: see -O-.]
Of or pertaining to disease.
■ **nosoˈcomial** *adjective* [Greek *nosokomos* person who tends the sick] pertaining to or (esp. of disease) originating in a hospital M19. **nosoˈgraphic** *adjective* of or pertaining to nosography L19. **noˈsography** *noun* (a) systematic description of diseases, nosology M17. **nosophile** *noun* (*rare*) a person who is excessively attracted by sickness or disease L19. **nosoˈphobia** *noun* irrational or excessive fear of disease L19. **nosopoˈetic** *adjective* (*rare*) producing or causing disease, pathogenic M18.

nosode /ˈnɒsəʊd/ *noun*. L19.
[Prob. from NOSO- + -ODE[1].]
Homoeopathy. A preparation of substances produced in the course of a disease, used in the treatment of that disease.

nosology /nɒˈsɒlədʒi/ *noun*. E18.
[from NOSO- + -LOGY.]
Chiefly MEDICINE. **1** A classification, arrangement, or catalogue of diseases; a collection or combination *of* diseases. E18.
2 (The branch of medicine that deals with) the systematic naming and classification of diseases. E18.
📖 **1** CARLYLE All this fatal nosology of spiritual maladies.
■ **nosoˈlogical** *adjective* of, pertaining to, or dealing with nosology L18. **nosoˈlogically** *adverb* M19. **nosologist** *noun* an expert in nosology L18.

nossir /nəʊˈsəː/ *interjection*. *colloq*. (chiefly *N. Amer.*). M20.
[Alt. of *no sir* s.v. NO *adverb*[3] & *interjection* after YESSIR.]
Certainly not, indeed no.

nostalgia /nɒˈstaldʒə, -dʒɪə/ *noun*. L18.
[mod. Latin (translating German *Heimweh* homesickness), from Greek NOSTOS + *algos* pain: see -IA[1].]
1 Acute longing for familiar surroundings; severe homesickness. L18.
2 Regret or sentimental longing *for* the conditions of a period of the (usu. recent) past; (a) regretful or wistful memory or imagining of an earlier time. E20. ▸**b** Cause for nostalgia; objects evoking nostalgia collectively. L20.
📖 **2** A. TOFFLER This reversion to pre-scientific attitudes is accompanied . . by a tremendous wave of nostalgia. *Country Life* Nostalgia for a world . . of Norfolk jackets, muttonchop whiskers, penny-farthing bicycles. A. BROOKNER She alone remembers her father . . with nostalgia for his benevolent if abstracted presence. **b** P. DE VRIES Her potato bread was sheer mouth-watering nostalgia.
■ Also **nostalgy** *noun* (*rare*) M19.

nostalgic /nɒˈstaldʒɪk/ *adjective & noun*. E19.
[from prec. + -IC.]
▶ **A** *adjective*. Of the nature of or characterized by nostalgia; caused by or evoking nostalgia; feeling or indulging in nostalgia. E19.
📖 *Church Times* The departure of the last . . steam locomotive was . . a nostalgic occasion. R. K. NARAYAN He felt nostalgic for his brother's gruff voice. M. MEYER He retained, like so many exiles, a nostalgic longing for the simple food of his homeland.
▶ **B** *noun*. A person who is affected by or who indulges in nostalgia. M20.
■ **nostalgically** *adverb* E20.

nostalgie de la boue /nɔstalʒi də la bu/ *noun phr*. L19.
[French, lit. 'yearning for mud'.]
A desire for degradation and depravity.
📖 C. MACINNES It's the crude animal type that attracts you . . . It's simply another form of *nostalgie de la boue*.

nostalgist /nɒˈstaldʒɪst/ *noun*. M20.
[from NOSTALGIA + -IST.]
A person (habitually) feeling or indulging in nostalgia; a person attempting to recreate the (usu. recent) past.

nostoc /ˈnɒstɒk/ *noun*. M17.
[Name invented by Paracelsus.]
Any unicellular blue-green alga of the genus *Nostoc*, having the cells arranged in intertwining rows to form a gelatinous mass; a mass of such algae, formerly believed to be an emanation from the stars.

nostos /ˈnɒstɒs/ *noun*. *literary*. Pl. **nostoi** /ˈnɒstɔɪ/. L19.
[Greek.]
A homecoming, a homeward journey, *spec.* that of Odysseus and the other heroes from Troy. Also, an account of such a homecoming or homeward journey, esp. as the conclusion of a literary work.

nostra *noun pl.* see NOSTRUM.

Nostradamus /nɒstrəˈdɑːməs, -ˈdeɪ-/ *noun*. M17.
[Latinized form of the name of Michel de *Nostredame* (1503–66), French physician who published a book of prophecies in 1555.]
A person claiming the ability to foretell the future; a seer, a prophet.
■ **Nostradamic** *adjective* of or pertaining to Nostradamus; similar to that of Nostradamus: M19.

Nostratic /nɒˈstratɪk/ *adjective*. M20.
[from German *nostratisch*, from Latin *nostratis*, *nostras* of our country: see -IC.]
Of, pertaining to, or designating a hypothetical language family of which the principal members are the families Indo-European, Semitic, Altaic, and Dravidian.
■ **Nostratian** /nɒˈstreɪʃ(ə)n/ *adjective & noun* (of) this hypothetical language family M20.

nostril /ˈnɒstr(ə)l/ *noun & verb*.
[Old English *nosþyrl*, *nosterl* (= Old Frisian *nosterl*), from NOSE *noun* + THIRL *noun*[1].]
▶ **A** *noun*. Also (long *obsolete* exc. *dial.*) **nose-thirl** /ˈnəʊzθəːl/.
1 Either of the two openings in the nose in humans and most vertebrates; an analogous opening in other animals. OE.
2 A small opening, esp. in a furnace, through which gas, water, etc., may pass. M19.
📖 **1** P. BOWLES He . . inhaled a bit of snuff through each nostril. C. JACKSON A good nose, the nostrils of which flared slightly as if scenting some distant . . odour. *fig.*: BURKE Our judgements stink in the nostrils of the people.
▶ **B** *verb trans. & intrans*. Infl. **-ll-**. Inhale or exhale through the nose. E20.
■ **nostrilled** *adjective* having a nostril or nostrils, esp. of a specified kind E20. **nostrility** /nɒˈstrɪlɪti/ *noun* (*rare*) prominence of the part of the nose surrounding the nostrils L19.

nostrum /ˈnɒstrəm/ *noun*. Pl. **-trums**, **-tra** /-trə/. E17.
[Latin, neut. sing. of *noster* our.]
1 A quack remedy, a patent medicine, *esp.* one prepared by the person recommending it. E17. ▸**b** A recipe. *rare*. M18.
2 A pet scheme, a favourite remedy, esp. for bringing about social or political reform or improvement. M18.
📖 **2** C. KINGSLEY Another party's nostrum is, more churches, more schools, more clergymen.

nosy /ˈnəʊzi/ *adjective & noun*. *colloq*. Also **nosey**. E17.
[from NOSE *noun* + -Y[1].]
▶ **A** *adjective*. **1** Having a prominent nose. E17.
2 Having a distinctive smell, strong-smelling. M19.
3 Having a strong sense of smell. *rare*. L19.
4 Inquisitive, esp. objectionably or unwarrantedly so; prying. L19.
📖 **4** N. COWARD If you hadn't been so . . nosy you'd never have known a thing about it. P. LIVELY You get to looking at people, when you're on your own. It's kind of nosy.
Special collocations & comb.: **nosy parker** (also with cap. initials) an overly inquisitive or prying person. **nosy-parker** *verb intrans*. be overly inquisitive, pry (chiefly as ***nosy-parkering*** *verbal noun & ppl adjective*).
▶ **B** *noun*. **1** (A nickname for) a person having a prominent nose. L18.
2 (A nickname for) an overly inquisitive or prying person. M20.
■ **nosily** *adverb* M20. **nosiness** *noun* E20.

not /nɒt/ *noun*. In sense 3 usu. **NOT**. LME.
[Partly var. of NOUGHT *noun*, partly from the adverb.]
†**1** Nought, nothing. LME–E16.
2 The word 'not'; a negation, a negative. E17.
3 COMPUTING. (Usu. **NOT**.) A Boolean function of one variable that has the value unity if the variable is zero, and vice versa. Usu. in *comb*. M20.

not /nɒt/ *adjective*. Now *dial*. Also **nott**.
[Old English *hnot*, of unkn. origin.]
†**1** Close-cropped, short-haired. OE–M17.
2 Of sheep or cattle: hornless, polled. L16.

†**not** *verb trans. & intrans*. (*pres. sing.*). Also **note**. OE–E17.
[Contr. of *ne wot*: see NE, WIT *verb*.]
Do or does not know.

not /nɒt/ *adverb*. In senses 1, 2 also (*informal*) **n't**, freq. joined to the preceding copula or auxiliary (see also note below). ME.
[Contr. of NOUGHT *adverb*.]
The ordinary adverb of negation.
1 Negativing copular *be*: following it or, (*not* in full only) in questions (with inversion of subject and verb) its subject. ME. ▸**b** With ellipsis of the verb, esp. after *if* and in replies. LME.
2 Negativing an auxiliary verb: with constructions as sense 1. LME. ▸**b** With ellipsis of the verb, in replies. E17. ▸**c** In elliptical repetitions of questions equivalent to an answer 'yes indeed'. *colloq*. E20.
3 Negativing a finite full verb: following it (*arch*. exc. with *be*) or (*poet.*) preceding it. (Normal construction with periphrastic *do*: see DO *verb* 30c.) LME.
4 Negativing an infinitive: preceding it. Also with ellipsis of the inf. after *to* or (*colloq.*) of *to do*. LME.
5 Negativing a gerund or pres. pple (esp. of a verb of mental activity): preceding it. LME.
6 Negativing a word other than a verb or a phr., clause, or sentence to be rejected or to emphasize by contrast one already used: preceding it. Freq. foll. by *but* introducing an alternative. LME.
7 In litotes or periphrasis, negativing a word etc. of opposite meaning to that which is to be conveyed: preceding it. LME.
8 Used *ellipt*. for a negative clause, verb, or phr. expressed or implied, in a clause etc. introduced by *as*, *if*, or *or* or after a verb of thinking, saying, etc. LME.
9 Negativing a pronoun appended for emphasis after a negative statement or in a reply: preceding it. E17.
📖 **1** R. B. SHERIDAN Is he not a gay dissipated rake who has squandered his patrimony? BURKE This is not the cause of a king, but of kings. T. HARDY If the sky were not clear . . you would have to come . . in the morning. A. TATE The English translation is not good. P. CAPON An Indian, isn't he? *absol.*: G. GREENE A swimming-pool . . is common to all as a table is not. **b** BROWNING No Love! not so indeed! **2** GOLDSMITH His presence did not interrupt our conversation. T. HARDY Could you not wait a fortnight longer? B. PYM I don't suppose I shall be in very much. L. P. HARTLEY I may not be an oil-painting, but I'm all right in my way. *Listener* Did he, or did he not, want to be Prime Minister? M. SPARK We mustn't get morbid. **b** G. MEREDITH 'Ammiani will marry her, I presume,' said Lena. 'Not before he has met Captain Weisspriess.' **c** R. KIPLING 'Did *you* have a governess, then?' 'Did we not? A Greek too.' **3** S. JOHNSON They . . possessed the island, but not enjoyed it. COLERIDGE Fear not, fear not, thou Wedding Guest! W. S. MAUGHAM She would have given anything to ask him . . but dared not. *absol.*: M. WARNOCK Human thought entails the ability to think of things . . as they are not. **4** DEFOE I knew neither what to do, or what not to do. F. M. CRAWFORD I wanted to turn round and look. It was an effort not to. V. WOOLF He had eaten quickly, not to keep them waiting. K. AMIS 'Can't you just not turn up?' 'I do not turn up as much as I can.' G. CHARLES They had . . fought their feelings of shame—a Rabbi not to have children! C. AIRD Father always puts it in a book . . . I've never known him not. *Bella* He would only marry me if I vowed not to lose weight. **5** B. STARKE Dick praised me for not saying anything. **6** DRYDEN Nor cou'd his Kindred . . change his fatal Course. No, not the dying Maid. T. SHADWELL They govern for themselves and not the people. GOLDSMITH His method is still, and not without reason, adopted by many. J. BENTHAM In case of not-guiltiness. C. LAMB The remnants left at his table (not many, nor very choice fragments). J. H. NEWMAN It was a respite, not a resurrection. E. E. CUMMINGS Many voices answer . . but not mine. J. B. PRIESTLEY Not for years had she made such a noise. E. BOWEN They were riveted not to each other but to what she said. S. SPENDER One of their not-too-distant neighbours was Lytton Strachey. B. KOPS I'm not that hard up. J. WAINWRIGHT I settled myself into the not-too-comfortable seat. S. B. FLEXNER The oral history of the not-so-common common people. **7** G. C. BRODRICK A certain air of dignity, not unmingled with insolence. **8** DEFOE Shall we give battle . . or not? B. JOWETT If virtue is of such a nature, it will be taught; and if not, not. *Chambers's Journal* Is this fashionable fad a good thing? Physicians say not. *Scientific American* The specificity of the virus, i.e., whether or not it will attack a certain bacterium. E. BAKER My concern . . was . . he said it poetically. I think not. **9** B. GILROY I ain't going back . . not me.
Phrases: (A selection of cross-refs. only is included.) ***as likely as not***. DEFINITELY ***not***. ***last but not least***: see LAST *adjective*. ***not a —*** not a single —, not even a —. ***not a few***. ***not a little***: see LITTLE

adjective etc. **not all that** — not exceptionally so. **not at all** (in a polite reply to thanks) there is no need to thank me. **not a thing** nothing at all. **not at home** *spec.* not available to callers. ***not bad***: see BAD *adjective*. ***not before time***: see TIME *noun*. **not but what**, (*formal*) **not but that**, (*arch.*) **not but** although. ***not for all the tea in China***: see TEA *noun* 1. ***not half***: see HALF *adverb* 2. ***not half bad***: see BAD *adjective*. **not least** notably (*because* etc.), with considerable importance. ***not LIKELY***. ***not MUCH***. ***not much wiser***: see WISE *adjective* & *noun*². **not on** *colloq.* impossible, not allowable. ***not once or twice, not once nor twice***: see ONCE. ***not put a foot wrong***: see FOOT *noun*. ***not quite***: see QUITE *adverb*. ***not so bad***: see BAD *adjective*. **not sufficient** (as written by a banker) this cheque cannot be honoured. **not that** it is not to be inferred, however, that. **not the less** (*a*) no less; (*b*) nevertheless, nonetheless. **not to worry** never mind, don't worry.

Comb.: **not-being** non-existence; **not-I**, **not-me** that from which the personal or subjective is excluded; that which is not oneself; **not-out** *adjective* & *noun* (CRICKET) (*a*) *attrib. adjective* designating a batsman who is not out when the team's innings ends or the score or innings of such a batsman; (*b*) *noun* a not-out batsman, score, or innings; **not-quite** *adjective*, *noun*, & *adverb* (*a*) *adjective* not wholly committed or involved, not wholly acceptable or respectable; (*b*) *noun* a not-quite person; (*c*) *adverb* (modifying an attrib. adjective) not wholly, almost but not really; **not-self** that which is other than self, something different from the conscious self, the non-ego.

¶ The full form is also written joined to the preceding auxiliary in *cannot* (CAN *verb*¹). The form of the auxiliary is also modified by following *n't* in *can't* (CAN *verb*¹), *won't* (WILL *verb*¹), etc.

nota /ˈnəʊtə/ *noun*¹. *rare*. Pl. **-tae** /-tiː/. E18.
[Latin: cf. NOTE *noun*².]
A mark, a sign, a stigma.

nota *noun*² pl. of NOTUM.

†**nota** *verb trans.* (*imper.*). LME–M19.
[Latin, 2nd person sing. imper. of *notare* NOTE *verb*¹.]
Observe, take note.
¶ Cf. next.

nota bene /ˌnəʊtə ˈbɛneɪ/ *verb phr. trans.* & *intrans.* (*imper.*). E18.
[Latin, formed as prec. + *bene* well.]
Mark well, observe particularly, (usu. drawing attention to a following qualification of what has preceded). Abbreviation ***NB***.
¶ The abbreviation *NB* is recorded L17.

notabilia /nəʊtəˈbɪlɪə/ *noun pl.* M19.
[Latin, neut. pl. of *notabilis* NOTABLE *adjective*, after MEMORABILIA.]
Things worthy of note.

notability /nəʊtəˈbɪlɪti/ *noun*. LME.
[Old & mod. French *notabilité* or late Latin *notabilitas*, from *notabilis*: see next, -ITY.]
1 †**a** A notable fact or circumstance. LME–L15. ▸**b** A noteworthy object or feature. *rare*. M19. ▸**c** A notable or prominent person. M19.
2 a The quality of being notable; distinction, prominence. LME. ▸**b** Housewifely industry or management. Now *rare* or *obsolete*. L18.

notable /ˈnəʊtəb(ə)l/ *adjective* & *noun*. ME.
[Old & mod. French from Latin *notabilis*, from *notare* NOTE *verb*¹: see -ABLE.]
▸**A** *adjective*. **1** Worthy or deserving of note, esp. on account of excellence, value, or importance; remarkable, striking, eminent. ME.
2 Easily noted, attracting notice, conspicuous; able to be noted or observed, noticeable, perceptible. Now *rare*. LME.
3 †**a** Of a man: industrious, energetic, businesslike. *rare*. M17–M18. ▸**b** Of a woman: capable, managing, bustling; clever and industrious in household management or occupations. Now *rare* or *obsolete*. E18. ▸**c** Of the nature of, connected with, household management or industry. Now *rare* or *obsolete*. L18.

> 📖 **1** R. MACAULAY It was notable that the women had been greatly superior to the men. A. C. BOULT In previous years the B.B.C. had planned many notable public concerts. M. WEST You know . . for a notable scholar you're . . very naive. W. RAEPER George . . was a well-liked and notable figure in the town. **2** F. O'CONNOR Not that they could have got far, for they had a notable accent.

▸**B** *noun*. **1** A noteworthy fact or thing. *rare*. ME.
2 FRENCH HISTORY. In *pl.* During the *ancien régime*: prominent men summoned by the king as a deliberative assembly in times of national emergency. M16.
3 A person of eminence or distinction. E19.
¶ Formerly pronounced with short vowel in 1st syll., a pronunc. which survived longest in sense A.3b.
■ **notableness** *noun* LME. **notably** *adverb* (*a*) in a notable manner; remarkably, strikingly; (*b*) in particular, especially: LME.

notae *noun* pl. of NOTA *noun*¹.

notal /ˈnəʊt(ə)l/ *adjective*¹. M19.
[formed as NOTUM + -AL¹.]
Dorsal. Now only ENTOMOLOGY, of or pertaining to a notum.

notal /ˈnəʊt(ə)l/ *adjective*². *rare*. L19.
[from NOTE *noun*² + -AL¹.]
Of, pertaining to, or employing notes.

notalgia /nəʊˈtaldʒə/ *noun*. *rare*. M19.
[from Greek *nōton* back + -ALGIA.]
MEDICINE. Pain in the back without inflammatory symptoms.
■ **notalgic** *adjective* M19.

notam /ˈnəʊtəm/ *noun*. M20.
[Acronym, from *notice to airmen*.]
A (warning) notice to pilots of aircraft.

notamy /ˈnɒtəmi/ *noun*. *obsolete* exc. *dial*. L15.
[Aphet. from ANATOMY.]
A skeleton. Orig. also, a subject for dissection.

NOT AND /nɒt ˈand/ *noun phr.* M20.
[from NOT *adverb* + AND *conjunction*¹: see NOT *noun*, AND *noun*.]
COMPUTING. = NAND. Usu. *attrib.*

notandum /nəʊˈtandəm/ *noun*. Pl. **-da** /-də/. L17.
[Latin, neut. gerundive of *notare* NOTE *verb*¹.]
An entry or jotting of something to be specially noted; a memorandum, an observation, a note.

notaphily /nəʊˈtafɪli/ *noun*. L20.
[from NOTE *noun*² + -PHILY.]
The collecting of banknotes as a hobby.
■ **notaˈphilic** *adjective* of or pertaining to notaphily L20. **notaphilist** *noun* a collector of banknotes as a hobby L20.

notarial /nəʊˈtɛːrɪəl/ *adjective*. L15.
[from NOTARY + -AL¹.]
1 Of or pertaining to a notary; characteristic of notaries. L15.
2 Drawn up, framed, or executed by a notary. E17.
■ **notarially** *adverb* M19.

notarikon /nəʊˈtarɪkən/ *noun*. L19.
[Greek, formed as NOTARY.]
In cabalistic phraseology: the art of making a new word from letters taken from the beginning, middle, or end of the words in a sentence; a word so made.

notarize /ˈnəʊtərʌɪz/ *verb trans.* Chiefly *N. Amer.* Also **-ise**. M20.
[from next + -IZE.]
Have (a document) legalized by a notary. Chiefly as ***notarized*** *ppl adjective*.
■ **notariˈzation** *noun* the action or process of notarizing a document; a notarized document: M20.

notary /ˈnəʊt(ə)ri/ *noun*. ME.
[Latin *notarius* shorthand-writer, clerk, from *nota* NOTE *noun*²: see -ARY¹.]
†**1** A clerk or secretary to a person. ME–E17.
2 A person, usu. a solicitor, publicly authorized to draw up or certify contracts, deeds, etc., to protest bills of exchange etc., and discharge other legal duties of a formal character. Also ***notary public***, ***public notary***. ME.
†**3** A noter, an observer. L16–L17.

notate /nəʊˈteɪt/ *verb trans.* E20.
[Back-form. from NOTATION.]
Set down in (musical) notation.

notatin /nəʊˈteɪtɪn/ *noun*. M20.
[from mod. Latin *notatum* (see below), from Latin *notare* to mark, note: see -IN¹.]
BIOCHEMISTRY. A flavoprotein enzyme, produced by the mould *Penicillium chrysogenum* (formerly *notatum*), which catalyses the oxidation of glucose and is used in its detection and estimation. Formerly also called ***penatin***, ***penicillin A***, ***penicillin B***.

notation /nəʊˈteɪʃ(ə)n/ *noun*. L16.
[Old & mod. French, or Latin *notatio(n-)*, from *notat-* pa. ppl stem of *notare* NOTE *verb*¹: see -ATION.]
†**1** The explanation of a term on the basis of its etymology; the etymological or primary sense of a word. L16–L17.
2 A note, an annotation; a record. Now chiefly *US*. L16.
3 The action of taking or making note of something. *rare*. M17.
4 The representation of numbers, quantities, pitch, duration, etc., of musical notes, etc., by a set or system of signs or symbols; a set of such signs or symbols; a set of symbols used to represent things or relations, as chess moves, dance steps, etc., to facilitate recording or considering them. E18.
4 ***Polish notation***: see POLISH *adjective*. ***scientific notation***: see SCIENTIFIC *adjective*.
■ **notational** *adjective* L19. **notationally** *adverb* L19. **notationist** *noun* a user or advocate of a particular system of musical notation L19.

notative /ˈnəʊtətɪv/ *adjective*. M19.
[from Latin *notat-* (see prec.) + -IVE, after *connotative*.]
1 Of, pertaining to, or of the nature of notes or signs. M19.
2 Of a name etc.: descriptive of the thing denoted. M19.

notator /nəʊˈteɪtə/ *noun*. *rare*. L17.
[formed as prec. + -OR.]
†**1** An annotator. Only in L17.
2 A noter, a recorder. M19.
3 A person skilled in musical notation. L19.

notch /nɒtʃ/ *noun*. L16.
[Anglo-Norman *noche*, perh. formed as next. Cf. NATCH *noun*¹ & *verb*, NITCH *noun*¹.]
1 A V-shaped indentation or incision made, or naturally occurring, in an edge or across a surface; *spec.* (*a*) each of a series of holes for the tongue of a buckle etc.; (*b*) each of a series of indentations marking graduated points on a regulating dial etc.; (*c*) a slit in the ground made to take the roots of a seedling tree; (*d*) an incision made in a twig to stimulate the growth of a bud lower down the twig. L16.
2 A nick made on a stick etc. as a means of keeping a score or record. L16. ▸**b** A run in cricket. *slang*. M18.
3 An opening; a break, a breach; *spec.* (*a*) *N. Amer.* a narrow opening or defile through mountains, a deep narrow pass; (*b*) an opening extending above the water-level in a weir or similar structure placed across a stream or current. M17.
4 *fig.* A point in a scale; a step, a degree. Now *colloq.* L17.

> 📖 **1** J. WILKINS A little wheel, with some notches in it, equivalent to teeth. W. C. BRYANT Grasping the bowstring and the arrow's notch He drew them back. C. S. FORESTER Randall put his eye to the notch; through the sights of his rifle . . he had seen something. L. MCMURTRY Wilbarger . . automatically loosened his horse's girth a notch. ***sciatic notch***: see SCIATIC *adjective* 1. **2** J. BRADBURY To register every exploit in war, by making a notch for each on the handle of their tomahawks. A. CHRISTIE Six notches in her gun representing dead Germans. **4** *Cape Times* The notch for appointment will depend on previous experience. J. RABAN An upper working class of semi-skilled men—a clear notch or two above the Baluchis.

Comb.: **notchback** (a motor car with) a back that extends approximately horizontally from the bottom of the rear window so as to make a distinct angle with it; **notch-bar test** ENGINEERING = ***notched-bar test*** s.v. NOTCHED (a); **notch-brittle** *adjective* (ENGINEERING) susceptible to fracture at a notch when a sudden load is applied; **notch-brittleness** ENGINEERING the state or degree of being notch-brittle; **notch effect** ENGINEERING the increase caused by a notch in the susceptibility of a specimen to fracture; **notch filter** ELECTRONICS a filter that attenuates signals within a very narrow band of frequencies; **notch-house** *slang* a brothel; **notch-planting** = NOTCHING *noun* 3; **notch-sensitive** *adjective* (ENGINEERING) characterized by a high notch-sensitivity; **notch-sensitiveness**, **notch-sensitivity** ENGINEERING the ratio of apparent increase in stress in a material due to a notch etc. to that predicted by a theory of stress concentration; **notch-toughness** ENGINEERING resistance to fracture at a notch; *spec.* the result (in units of energy) of a notched-bar test on a specimen.

notch /nɒtʃ/ *verb trans.* M16.
[from Anglo-Norman verb rel. to *anoccer* add a notch to: cf. Latin *inoccare* harrow in, Old French *oche*, *osche* (mod. *hoche*), from *o(s)chier* (*hocher*) = Provençal *oscar* nick, notch.]
1 a Trim, cut (*off*). *rare*. M16. ▸†**b** *spec.* Cut (hair) unevenly; crop the hair of (a person) unevenly or closely. L16–E19.
2 a Cut or make notches in; cut or mark with notches. E17. ▸**b** Convert *into* by making notches. L18.
3 Score, mark, or record by means of notches, succeed in scoring (a run etc.); achieve (esp. an amount or quantity), register (a victory), win. Freq. foll. by *up*. E17.
4 Fit (an arrow) to a bowstring; nock. M17.
5 Fix, secure, or insert, by means of notches. M18.
6 Cut *out*. L19.

> 📖 **3** DICKENS The scorers were prepared to notch the runs. *Sporting Mirror* Their forwards . . should notch enough goals for a home win. *Sunday Express* Her earnings . . are well above the £10,000 she was notching up a few years ago. D. RUTHERFORD In about three minutes Mascot would have notched up the victory. *Cambrian News* The Prysor team notched the school's cricket championship.

¶ Earliest in UNNOTCHED.
■ **notched** *adjective* (*a*) *gen.* that has been notched; having a notch or notches cut in it; ***notched-bar test***, any of several impact tests (as the Izod test) in which the energy absorbed in breaking a notched specimen in a single blow is measured; (*b*) BOTANY (of a leaf) coarsely dentate; (*c*) ZOOLOGY having notches or incisions: M16. **notcher** *noun* (*a*) a person who notches; a scorer; (*b*) an instrument for making notches: M18.

notching /ˈnɒtʃɪŋ/ *noun*. E17.
[from NOTCH *verb* + -ING¹.]
1 The action or process of making notches, esp. in carpentry as a method of joining timbers. E17.
2 A notch, an incision resembling a notch. M19.
3 A method of planting seedling trees in which a slit is made in the earth to take the roots of the plant. M19.
4 A type of pruning in which an incision is made in a twig above a bud to stimulate growth from the bud. E20.

notchy /ˈnɒtʃi/ *adjective*. M19.
[from NOTCH *noun* + -Y¹.]
1 Having notches or indentations. M19.
2 Of a manual gear-changing mechanism: difficult to use because the lever has to be moved accurately (as if into a narrow notch). M20.
■ **notchiness** *noun* L20.

note /nəʊt/ *noun*[1]. Long *obsolete* exc. *dial.*
[Old English *notu* rel. to NEAT *noun*, NOWT *noun*[1].]
1 Use, usefulness, profit, advantage. OE.
2 Employment, occupation, work. OE.
3 A matter, an affair, a circumstance; a thing. ME.
4 The milk given by a cow; the period of giving milk; the condition of a cow when giving, or beginning to give, milk after calving. *dial.* E18.

note /nəʊt/ *noun*[2]. ME.
[Old & mod. French from Latin *nota* a mark.]
▶ **I 1** A single tone of definite pitch, such as is produced by a musical instrument or by the human voice. ME.
2 A strain of music, a melody, a tune, a song. Long only *poet.* ME.
3 (A single tone of) the musical song or call of a bird; a cry, call, or sound made by a bird. ME.
4 *transf.* **a** Any expressive or musical sound; a quality or tone in speaking; an expression of mood, attitude, etc.; an aspect, an indication, an intimation. L15. ▸**b** In perfumery, any of the basic components of the fragrance of a perfume which give it its character. E20.

📖 **1** W. IRVING She . . hummed . . and did not make a single false note. ***blue note, eighth note, fundamental note, half-note, leading note, leaning note, pedal note, recite note, sixteenth note, top note, white note***, etc. **2** MILTON Celestial voices . . responsive each to others note. **3** T. GRAY The Attic warbler pours her throat, Responsive to the cuckoo's note. GOLDSMITH The birds excel rather in . . their plumage than the sweetness of their notes. W. COWPER A bird who . . by hoarseness of his note, Might be suppos'd a crow. ***call note***: see CALL *noun*. **4a** N. MARSH 'Upon that note,' said Alleyn, 'we may . . make our plans.' H. WILLIAMSON To listen for the note of the . . engines. W. TREVOR The note of seriousness must be stressed. P. BARKER The gloves . . added an incongruous note of gentility. J. NAGENDA Only occasionally was he able to detect any . . note of envy. **b** ***top note*** etc.

▶ **II 5** A written character or sign expressing the pitch and duration of a musical sound. ME.
6 †**a** A letter of the alphabet. Only in LME. ▸**b** A sign or character (other than a letter) used in writing or printing. E16.
7 A mark, a sign, a token, an indication, (*of*); a characteristic or distinguishing feature. LME. ▸**b** *CHRISTIAN CHURCH.* Any of certain characteristics, as unity, sanctity, catholicity, and apostolicity, by which the true Church may be known; a sign or proof of genuine origin, authority, and practice. M16.
8 A stigma, a reproach. Foll. by *of*. Long *rare*. M16.
9 A key of a piano or similar instrument. M19.
6b ***note of admiration***: see ADMIRATION 1. ***Tironian notes***.

▶ **III 10** Notice, regard, or attention. ME.
11 Distinction, mark, importance; reputation, fame. Esp. in ***of note, of good note, of bad note***, etc. LME.
12 Knowledge, information. *rare*. L16.

📖 **10** E. V. NEALE We select . . what we want . . and take no note of the rest. *Nature* Another addition to the Zoo worthy of note is three young cane-rats. **11** W. H. DIXON Had he died at sixty . . he might have left behind him an obscure and blameless note. **of note** of distinction or eminence; notable.

▶ **IV 13** *LAW.* **a** An abstract of essential particulars relating to transfer of land by process of fine (see FINE *noun*[1] 6). *obsolete* exc. *Hist.* LME. ▸**b** *SCOTS LAW.* Any of various written forms of legal process and memoranda. M16.
14 A brief record or abstract of facts written down to aid the memory, or written down or (also ***mental note***) stored in the mind as a basis for a more complete statement or for future action; a brief memorandum to help in speaking on some subject. Freq. in *pl.* LME.
15 a An explanatory or critical annotation or comment appended to a passage in a book etc. M16. ▸†**b** An observation worth noticing or remembering; an interesting or noteworthy remark. L16–M17. ▸**c** A thing of note, an important matter, a surprise. *US colloq.* M19.
16 A brief statement of particulars or of some fact. Formerly also, a bill, an account. L16.
17 a A short letter or written communication of an informal kind. L16. ▸**b** A formal diplomatic or parliamentary communication. L18.
†**18** A signed receipt or voucher. E17–M18.
19 A written promise to pay a certain sum at a specified time (also ***note of hand***); *spec.* a banknote. M17. ▸**b** A banknote worth £1; the amount of a pound sterling. *Scot.* & *Austral.* L18.

📖 **14** SOUTHEY Only his memory to trust to, never having made any notes. J. A. FROUDE He spoke for more than an hour without a note. H. FAST He made mental notes to have a talk with his son. ***compare notes***: see COMPARE *verb*[1] 3. **15a** MILTON The entire Scripture translated into English with plenty of Notes. ***end-note, footnote***, etc. **16** ***covering note, credit note, demand note, head-note***, etc. ***liner note***: see LINER *noun*[1] 4. ***sick note***: see SICK *adjective*. **17a** J. DISKI We had communicated . . by notes left on the kitchen table. T. CALLENDER She wouldn't even drop a note to Courcy. **b** ***identic note***: see IDENTIC *adjective*. **19** M. DRABBLE Tales of . . call girls and twenty-pound notes. E. LEONARD I . . signed notes on everything we owned. ***banknote, currency note, judgement note***, etc. ***fractional note***: see FRACTIONAL *adjective*. ***postal note***: see POSTAL *adjective*. ***promissory note***.

Other phrases: **change one's note**, **change note** alter one's way of speaking or thinking. **hit a false note** = *strike a false note* below. **hit the right note** = *strike the right note* below. **sound a note of caution**, **sound a note of warning**, etc., say or write something cautionary etc., esp. contrasting in tone with what has preceded. **strike a false note** say or write something insincere, inappropriate, etc. **strike the right note** say or write something sincere, appropriate, etc. **take note** observe, pay attention, (foll. by *of*).

Comb.: **notebook** (*a*) a small book for or containing notes or memoranda; (*b*) a portable computer smaller than a laptop used esp. as a data store (cf. ***palmtop*** s.v. PALM *noun*[2]); **note-broker** *US* a broker who deals in promissory notes and bills of exchange; **note card** a card for a note or notes; *esp.* a decorative card with a blank space for a short message; **notecase** a wallet for holding banknotes; **note-cluster** a group of neighbouring notes played simultaneously; **note-holder** a holder of notes issued by a business company etc. promising to repay money borrowed for temporary financing; **notepad** (*a*) a pad or notebook for or containing notes or memoranda; (*b*) *COMPUTING* a small, lightweight portable computer, esp. one operated by means of a pen or stylus; **notepaper** paper of a type used for correspondence; **note-row**, **note-series** = ***tone-row*** s.v. TONE *noun*; **note-shaver** *US slang* a promoter of bogus financial companies; a usurer; **note-shaving** *US slang* the profession of a note-shaver; the making of an excessive profit on the discounting of notes.

■ **noteless** *adjective* (*a*) not of note; unmarked, undistinguished, unnoticed; (*b*) unmusical, unharmonious; voiceless: E17.

note /nəʊt/ *verb*[1] *trans.* ME.
[Old & mod. French *noter* from Latin *notare*, from *nota* NOTE *noun*[2].]
1 Observe or mark carefully; give close attention to; take notice of; observe, perceive. ME.
2 Mention separately or specially; record or write *down* as a thing to be remembered or observed. ME. ▸†**b** Set down as having a certain (good or bad) character. LME–L16.
3 a Denote, signify (something). Now chiefly in dictionary definitions. ME. ▸**b** Indicate; formerly also, point at, indicate by pointing; point *out*. Now *rare*. E16.
4 a Record in musical notation, set down the music for. Now *rare*. ME. ▸†**b** Mark; distinguish by a mark. L15–E18. ▸**c** Annotate; write notes in. E19.
†**5** Accuse *of* some fault etc.; mark or brand *with* some disgrace or defect; stigmatize. LME–L17.

📖 **1** I. MURDOCH He ran upstairs, noting Gertrude's suitcase in the . . bedroom. S. BIKO The major thing to note . . is that they never were songs for individuals. **2** A. HELPS I must just note that Bastiah's censure does not apply to England. R. K. NARAYAN She . . noted down all the names. E. NORTH A diary noting her activities.

■ **noter** *noun* OE.

†**note** *verb*[2] (*aux.*). Also **no'te**. L16–M17.
[Misuse of next.]
Could not.

†**note** *verb*[3] var. of NOT *verb*.

noted /ˈnəʊtɪd/ *adjective*. LME.
[from NOTE *verb*[1] + -ED[1].]
1 Specially noticed, observed, or marked; distinguished, celebrated, famous. (Foll. by *for*.) LME.
2 Provided with a musical score; having musical notation. LME.

📖 **1** J. HELLER The noted art dealer Joseph Duveen. G. PRIESTLAND Frank was noted for his intense interest in the opposite sex.

■ **notedly** *adverb* in a noted manner, markedly, especially, particularly E17.

notelet /ˈnəʊtlɪt/ *noun*. E19.
[from NOTE *noun*[2] + -LET.]
1 A short note or written communication. Now *rare*. E19.
2 A folded card or sheet of paper on which a note or short letter may be written, having a picture or design on the face of the first leaf. M20.

notes inégales /nɔts inegal/ *noun phr. pl.* E20.
[French, lit. 'unequal notes'.]
MUSIC. In baroque music, notes performed by convention in a rhythm different from that shown in the score.

note verbale /nɔt vɛrbal/ *noun phr.* Pl. **-s -s** (pronounced same). M19.
[French, lit. 'verbal note'.]
An unsigned diplomatic note, of the nature of a memorandum, written in the third person.

noteworthy /ˈnəʊtwəːði/ *adjective*. M16.
[from NOTE *noun*[2] + -WORTHY.]
Worthy of attention, observation, or notice; remarkable.
■ **noteworthily** *adverb* L19. **noteworthiness** *noun* L19.

not-go /ˈnɒtgəʊ/ *adjective*. E20.
[from NOT *adverb* + GO *verb*. Cf. GO *adjective*, NO-GO.]
ENGINEERING. Designating a gauge which will not pass through an aperture, or will not admit an object, of the required size.

nother /ˈnʌðə/ *pronoun, adjective*[1], *adverb, & conjunction*. *obsolete* exc. *dial.*
[Old English *noþer*, from NE + contr. of var. of *āhwæþer*, from *ā* (see AYE *adverb*[1]) + *hwæþer* WHETHER *adjective* etc. Cf. NEITHER, NOUTHER.]
1 = NEITHER. OE.
†**2** = NOR *adverb, conjunction*[1]. Usu. with preceding negative. LME–L16.

nother /ˈnʌðə/ *adjective*[2] *sing.* Long *obsolete* exc. *dial.* ME.
[from misdivision of *an other*, ANOTHER.]
Other, different: in ***a nother***, (*US*) ***a whole nother***, †***no nother***.

'nother /ˈnʌðə/ *adjective & noun*. *colloq.* M20.
[Aphet.]
Another.

nothing /ˈnʌθɪŋ/ *pronoun, noun, adverb, verb, & adjective*. Orig. two words. OE.
[from NO *adjective* + THING *noun*[1].]
▶ **A** *pronoun & noun*. **1** Not any (material or immaterial) thing; (more positively, followed by an adjective or limiting phr. or clause) not one thing. OE. ▸**b** As *interjection* (passing into *adverb*). Not at all, in no respect, (following a (partial) repetition of a previous statement and contradicting it). *colloq.* (orig. *US*). L19.
2 No part, share, etc., *of* some thing (or person). Also (now *rare*) foll. by *of* with adjective OE.
3 a (Chiefly as compl.) Not anything (or anybody) of importance, value, or concern. LME. ▸**b** A thing (or person) of no importance, value, or concern; a non-existent thing; a trifling event; a trivial remark; an insignificant person, a nobody. E17.
4 Not any quantity or number, zero, nought; the score of no points in a game etc. Also, the figure or character representing zero, a nought. LME.
5 That which does not exist. M16.
†**6** = NOTHINGNESS. *rare*. Only in 17.

📖 **1** M. KEANE She saw nothing either funny or comforting in her sister relaxing. J. C. POWYS Before, there had been nothing but the deepening of a . . golden glow. O. MANNING In Bucharest nothing can be kept secret for long. G. VIDAL There was nothing anyone could do but . . wait for the news. R. P. JHABVALA Had a bit of trouble . . today . . . Nothing we couldn't easily handle. T. O'BRIEN Don't blow no bubbles or nothing. C. P. SNOW To solve . . problems you have to . . think of nothing else. P. ACKROYD He could think of nothing to say. H. JACOBSON I knew nothing of Camilla, had never even heard of her. D. DELILLO Full professors . . who read nothing but cereal boxes. *Daily Mail* Those . . whose dream remains a separate state or nothing. *Woman & Home* Few . . possess the talent to do . . nothing. **b** M. B. HOUSTON 'He could have found it, of course.' . . 'Found it, nothing. I saw other things he'd taken.' A. E. LINDOP Poor little mite nothing . . She'd done her best to seduce him. **2** GOLDSMITH Johnson . . has nothing of the bear but his skin. A. C. SWINBURNE Nothing of common is there, nothing of theatrical. **3a** W. D. HOWELLS He would be nothing without her. V. WOOLF 'All that fuss about nothing!' a voice exclaimed. G. CHARLES The people I know think me nothing to look at. R. DAHL Don't worry about it . . . It's nothing. **b** LD HOUGHTON The little nothings of occupied life leave a man no time. J. A. FROUDE Metellus and . . Afranius, who had been chosen consuls for the year 60, were mere nothings. H. STURGIS Claude moved about . . saying little laughing nothings to everyone. S. MIDDLETON His lunch, a nothing, cheese omelette with . . peas. **5** H. SPENCER Nothing can become an object of consciousness.

Phrases: **all to nothing** *arch.* to the fullest extent; undoubtedly. **be nothing if not** be above all (the specified thing). **come to nothing** have no effect or result; break down, fail. ***dance upon nothing***: see DANCE *verb*. **for nothing**: †(*a*) by no means; on no account; (*b*) in vain, to no purpose; (*c*) for no reason, causelessly; (*d*) without payment or cost, free, gratuitously. (***free, gratis, and for nothing***: see FREE *adverb* 1). **have nothing on** (*a*) be wearing no clothes, be naked; (*b*) have no engagements; (*c*) (*on preposition*) see ***have nothing on*** — s.v. HAVE *verb*. ***have nothing to say for oneself, have nothing to say to***: see SAY *verb*[1]. ***know nothing and care less***: see KNOW *verb*. ***leave nothing to chance***: see LEAVE *verb*[1]. **like nothing on earth** *colloq.* extremely strange, ugly, wretched, etc. ***little or nothing***: see LITTLE *noun*. ***make nothing of***: see MAKE *verb*. ***neck or nothing***: see NECK *noun*[1]. **new nothing** (*obsolete* exc. *dial.*) a worthless novelty. **no nothing** *colloq.* nothing at all (concluding a list of negatives). ***nothing doing***: see DO *verb*. **nothing else for it**, **nothing for it** no alternative; (foll. by *but to do*) no possible course of action other than. ***nothing in it***: see ***there is nothing in it*** below. ***nothing less (than)***: see LESS *adjective* etc. ***nothing of the kind***: see KIND *noun*. ***nothing of the sort***: see SORT *noun*[2]. **nothing to** (as compl.) (*a*) of no consequence or concern to; (*b*) insignificant or worthless compared to. ***nothing to it***: see ***there is nothing to it*** below. ***nothing to lose***: see LOSE *verb*. ***nothing to write home about***: see HOME *adverb*. ***on a hiding to nothing***: see HIDING *noun*[2]. **stick at nothing**, **stop at nothing** not allow anything to deter one, be ruthless or unscrupulous. ***sweet nothings***: see SWEET *adjective & adverb*. ***thank you for nothing***: see THANK *verb*. **there is nothing in it**, **nothing in it** *colloq.* (*a*) it has no important feature of interest or value, there is no significant difference between the things in question, (also

nothing much in it); (***b***) = ***there is nothing to it*** below. **there is nothing to it**, **nothing to it** *colloq.* (***a***) it is very easy to do, there is no difficulty involved; (***b***) it is untrue, it is unimportant. **think nothing of** consider as unremarkable. **think nothing of it** do not apologize or feel bound to show gratitude. **to nothing** to the final point, stage, or state of the process of destruction, dissolution, etc. **to say nothing of** not to mention (see MENTION *verb*). ***want for nothing***: see WANT *verb*. **with nothing on** wearing no clothes, naked.

▶ **B** *adverb.* Not at all, in no way. (See also sense A.1b above.) Now *arch. & literary* exc. in ***nothing like*** s.v. LIKE *adjective* etc. **OE.**

🕮 T. FULLER Mustard is nothing worth unless it bite. T. HEARNE He was nothing so learned . . as he is represented to have been. W. S. LANDOR They often infect those who ailed nothing. SOUTHEY The bird was nothing the worse for what it had undergone. ***nothing loath***: see LOATH *adjective* 3.

▶ **C** *verb trans.* Reduce to nothing. Long *rare.* **M17.**

▶ **D** *attrib.* or as *adjective.* Of no account, insignificant, insipid, dull; indeterminate; (of a garment) discreet, elegantly unobtrusive. *colloq.* **M20.**

🕮 *Vogue* Little 'nothing' sweaters . . for wearing with suits. C. PHILLIPS The woman was a nothing woman to him.

■ **nothin'garian** *noun* a person who has no religious belief or political creed **L18.** **nothin'garianism** *noun* absence of any religious belief or political creed **M19.** **nothingism** *noun* (***a***) a triviality, a trifle; (***b***) nihilism: **M18.** **nothingist** *noun* a nihilist **L18.** **nothingly** *adjective* (now *rare*) of no value or effect **E19.**

nothingness /ˈnʌθɪŋnɪs/ *noun.* **M17.**
[from NOTHING + -NESS.]

1 The state or condition of being non-existent or nothing; non-existence; that which is non-existent; absence or cessation of consciousness or of life. **M17.**
2 Utter insignificance or unimportance; the condition of being worthless; that which has no value; the worthlessness or vanity *of* something. **M17.**
3 A non-existent thing; a state of non-existence or worthlessness; an absence of consciousness or of life; a thing of no value; an insignificant act or concern. **M17.**

🕮 **1** S. BECKETT All will vanish and we'll be alone again, in the midst of nothingness. *Times* Plans can slip away to nothingness. **2** BYRON Must I restrain me . . From holding up the nothingness of life? J. A. SYMONDS Many . . have found a deep peace in the sense of their own nothingness. **3** D. DURRANT Patty was busying herself with small nothingnesses. D. ROWE Where there was once a person will be a nothingness.

nothofagus /nɒθə(ʊ)ˈfeɪɡəs/ *noun.* **E20.**
[mod. Latin (see below), from Greek *nothos* (see next) + Latin *fagus* beech.]

Any of various timber trees of the genus *Nothofagus*, of the beech family, native to temperate parts of the southern hemisphere. Also called ***southern beech***.

nothomorph /ˈnɒθə(ʊ)mɔːf/ *noun.* **M20.**
[from Greek *nothos* bastard, crossbred + -MORPH.]

BOTANY. A particular form or variant of a given hybrid.

nothosaur /ˈnəʊtəsɔː, ˈnəʊθ-, ˈnɒθ-/ *noun.* **M20.**
[mod. Latin *Nothosauria* (see below), from *Nothosaurus* genus name, from Greek *nothos* false: see -SAUR.]

An extinct marine reptile of the suborder Nothosauria, known from Triassic fossil remains in Europe.

■ **notho'saurian** *adjective* **L19.** **nothosaurus** *noun*, pl. **-ruses**, **-ri** /-rʌɪ/, a nothosaur of the genus *Nothosaurus* **M19.**

notice /ˈnəʊtɪs/ *noun.* **LME.**
[Old & mod. French from Latin *notitia* being known, acquaintance, knowledge, notion, from *notus* known: see -ICE[1].]

▶ **I 1** Information, intelligence, warning; instruction *to do* something; an instance of this. Formerly also, knowledge. **LME.**
2 *spec.* **a** An announcement by one of the parties to an agreement (esp. concerning a tenancy or employment) that it is to terminate at a specified time. **M18.** ▶**b** A sign, placard, etc., conveying some information or intelligence; the text of such a sign etc. **E19.** ▶**c** An announcement read to a church congregation. Freq. in *pl.* **M19.** ▶**d** A brief mention in writing; *spec.* a paragraph or article in a newspaper or magazine on a newly published book, a performance of a play, etc.; a review. **M19.**
3 Time of a specified duration for action or preparation after receipt of information or a warning. Chiefly in preposition phrs., as ***at a few minutes' notice***, ***without any notice***. **L18.**

🕮 **1** J. CARLYLE I had the lease . . and the notice to quit. *Holiday Which?* Kemp had not given . . written notice of his condition. **2a** F. WELDON If the job doesn't suit them, they hand in their notice. **b** E. BLUNDEN I read the notice that I was under orders for France. P. CAMPBELL A notice on the door said that the plumber was closed for the month. **c** M. TWAIN The local minister had read sixteen 'notices' of . . sewing society and other meetings. **d** R. K. NARAYAN He saw his name in a notice announcing the . . debate. B. BAINBRIDGE The play . . received good notices in the local press. ROSEMARY MANNING The few notices it received were good, but there were too few to put the book on the map. **3** H. JAMES At such short notice it was impossible to find good quarters. A. GUINNESS A few hours' notice was required if one needed a bath. B. MOORE This network of people that Jan seemed able to summon up on a few minutes' notice.

▶ **II 4** Heed, cognizance, note, attention. **L16.** ▶**b** One's observation. **E17.**
†**5** A notion, an idea. **M17–L18.**

🕮 **4** BURKE A thing scarcely worthy of notice. H. ADAMS These apsidal windows have not received much notice. **b** SHAKES. *Coriol.* To my poor unworthy notice, He mock'd us when he begg'd our voices.

Phrases: **put on notice** *N. Amer.* alert or warn (a person, *that*). **take no notice** (***a***) pay no attention (foll. by *of* a person or thing, *that*, *how*); (***b***) take no action in consequence *of*. **take notice** (***a***) pay attention (foll. by *of* a person or thing, *that*, *how*); †(***b***) (foll. by *of*, *that*) point out, mention specially; (***c***) show signs of intelligence or interest; (***d***) *imper.* I warn you *that*.

Comb.: **notice-board** a board bearing a notice; a board on which notices are fixed; **notice paper** a parliamentary paper giving the current day's proceedings.

notice /ˈnəʊtɪs/ *verb.* **LME.**
[from the noun.]

†**1** *verb trans.* Notify or inform of. **LME–E17.**
2 *verb trans.* Mention; remark on; refer to, speak of (something observed); point out or mention *to*. **E17.** ▶**b** *verb trans.* Write a review or notice of (a book, play, etc.). **M19.**
3 *verb trans. & intrans.* Observe, perceive. **M18.** ▶**b** *verb intrans.* Pay attention, be observant. Freq. as ***noticing*** *ppl adjective.* **M19.**
4 *verb trans.* Treat (a person) with some degree of attention, favour, or politeness; recognize or acknowledge (a person). **M18.**
5 *verb trans.* †**a** Notify (a person) *of* a thing. *rare.* Only in **L18.** ▶**b** Serve with a notice; give notice to (a person). (Foll. by *to do*.) **M19.**

🕮 **2** E. GASKELL She looked so much better that Sir Charles noticed it to Lady Harriet. L. STRACHEY The Duke of Kent who must be noticed separately. G. HARRIS Hills began to be noticed for their beauty. **b** J. AGATE A paper for which I write . . wanted me to notice the Camargo Ballet. **3** W. GOLDING They were late home . . but nobody noticed. E. KUZWAYO I noticed that his tie matched the silk handkerchief. L. CODY She noticed a car leaving the car park. **4** G. JOSIPOVICI You barely noticed me when I was there.

Phrases: **not so as you'd notice** *colloq.* not to a noticeable degree.

¶ Rare before **M18.**
■ **noticer** *noun* (*rare*) **M18.**

noticeable /ˈnəʊtɪsəb(ə)l/ *adjective.* **M18.**
[from NOTICE *verb* + -ABLE.]

1 Able to be noticed or observed, perceptible. **M18.**
2 Worthy or deserving of notice. **L18.**

■ **noticea'bility** *noun* (***a***) *rare* a noticeable thing; (***b***) the quality, state, or fact of being noticeable: **L19.** **noticeably** *adverb* in a noticeable manner, to a noticeable degree; perceptibly, remarkably: **M19.**

notifiable /ˈnəʊtɪfʌɪəb(ə)l/ *adjective.* **L19.**
[from NOTIFY + -ABLE.]

That should be notified to some authority; (esp. of a serious transmissible disease) of a type such as to warrant notification to some authority.

🕮 *Times* Making AIDS . . a notifiable disease . . would provide powers to detain patients in hospital for treatment.

notification /ˌnəʊtɪfɪˈkeɪʃ(ə)n/ *noun.* **LME.**
[French, or medieval Latin *notificatio(n-)*, from *notificat-* pa. ppl stem of *notificare*: see next, -FICATION.]

The action or an act of notifying something; intimation, a notice.

🕮 D. DU MAURIER Have the kindness to see that notification of the death goes to the newspapers. V. BROME *Jung* . . sent the notification of the meeting to his home in Wales. *Times of India* The government . . issued a notification appointing a two-member judicial commission.

notify /ˈnəʊtɪfʌɪ/ *verb trans.* **LME.**
[Old & mod. French *notifier* from Latin *notificare*, from *notus* known: see -FY.]

†**1** Take note of, observe, notice. **LME–L17.**
2 Make known, publish; intimate, give notice of, announce. **LME.**
†**3** Indicate, denote. **LME–E18.**
4 Inform, give notice to. (Foll. by *of*, *that*.) **LME.**

🕮 **2** LD MACAULAY The king . . notified to the country his intention of holding a parliament. *Independent* More than half of all workplaces are not notified to the authorities. **4** W. C. WILLIAMS His wife was notified of the accident. W. S. CHURCHILL She notified Oxford by gesture and utterance that he must surrender the Lord Treasurer's white staff. A. TOFFLER The worker nearest the breakdown would notify his foreman.

■ **notified** *adjective* (now *dial.*) celebrated, notorious, well known **M16.** **notifier** *noun* **M18.**

notion /ˈnəʊʃ(ə)n/ *noun.* **LME.**
[Latin *notio(n-)* conception, idea, from *not-* pa. ppl stem of *(g)noscere* know: see -ION.]

1 A concept, an idea. Orig. *spec.* a general concept under which a particular thing or person is comprehended or classed; a classificatory term. **LME.** ▶†**b** The connotation or meaning *of* a term. **M17–E18.**
2 An inclination, disposition, or desire, to do something specified; a fancy for something. Usu. foll. by *of doing*, *to do*. **LME.** ▶**b** A fancy or affection for a person of the other sex. *Scot. & north.* **L18.**
3 An opinion, theory, idea, view, or belief, held by one or more people. **E17.**
†**4** Understanding, mind, intellect; imagination, fancy. Only in **17.**
5 In *pl.* Articles or wares of various kinds; *N. Amer.* small wares, cheap useful articles, now *spec.* buttons, hooks, etc., necessary for sewing a garment in addition to the fabric. **L18.**

🕮 **1** W. HAMILTON A first notion is the concept of a thing as it exists itself. W. OWEN Happy the soldier home, with not a notion How somewhere, every dawn, some men attack. H. READ Not the objective facts of nature, nor any abstract notion based on those facts. DAY LEWIS I have no notion what we talked about. J. IRVING The notion of Judgment Day was as tangible as the weather. **under the notion of** under the concept, category, designation, or name of. **2** HUGH WALPOLE I have no notion of going to anybody's house. J. R. ACKERLEY I took up . . Law with the notion of becoming a barrister. V. S. PRITCHETT She had notions of becoming an actress. **3** F. D. MAURICE It is not a new notion that . . history . . is divided into certain great periods. M. ESSLIN Without any preconceived notions and ready-made expectations. JANET MORGAN Clara's notion that premature reading was injurious. **5** ***YANKEE notions***.

■ **notionist** *noun* (now *arch. rare*) a person who holds extravagant religious opinions **M17.** **notionless** *adjective* **E19.**

notional /ˈnəʊʃ(ə)n(ə)l/ *adjective.* **LME.**
[French †*notional*, *-el* or medieval Latin *notionalis*, formed as prec.: see -AL[1].]

▶ **I 1** Of or pertaining to a notion or idea, (of a word etc.) abstract. **LME.** ▶**b** *GRAMMAR.* Of or pertaining to semantic content as opp. to grammatical structure or behaviour. **M19.**
2 Of knowledge etc.: purely speculative; not based on fact or demonstration. **L16.**
3 Existing only in thought; imaginary. **E17.**
4 Hypothetical; for the purposes of a particular interpretation or theory. **M20.**

🕮 **3** G. BERKELEY All things that exist, exist only in the mind, that is, they are purely notional. *Times Lit. Suppl.* Thackeray's narrative persona addresses a notional reader. **4** *Times* The appointment is for one notional half-day a week. *Accountant* A company . . will be able to obtain relief . . on a notional figure.

▶ **II** Of a person.
†**5** Given to abstract or fanciful speculation; holding merely speculative views. **M17–L18.**
6 Full of fancies, whims, or caprices. **L18.**
7 Inclined to think. *US.* **E19.**

¶ In isolated use before **L16.**
■ **notionalist** *noun* (now *rare*) a speculative thinker, a theorist **L17.** †**notionality** *noun* (***a***) the fact, state, or condition of being notional; (***b***) a notional or imaginary thing: **M17–E19.** **notionally** *adverb* in a notional fashion; speculatively, hypothetically, theoretically: **M17.**

notionary /ˈnəʊʃ(ə)n(ə)ri/ *adjective.* Now *rare.* **M17.**
[from NOTION *noun* + -ARY[1].]

= NOTIONAL.

notionate /ˈnəʊʃ(ə)nət/ *adjective. Scot. & US.* **M19.**
[from NOTION *noun* + -ATE[2].]

Full of notions, fanciful. Also, headstrong, obstinate.

notitia /nəʊˈtɪʃɪə, -ʃə/ *noun.* **E18.**
[Latin = knowledge, (in late Latin) list, account, etc., from *notus* known.]

†**1** Knowledge, detailed information. *rare.* Only in **E18.**
2 An account, a list; *spec.* a register or list of ecclesiastical sees or districts. **L18.**

notochord /ˈnəʊtəkɔːd/ *noun.* **M19.**
[from Greek *nōton* back + CHORD *noun*[2].]

BIOLOGY. An elastic cartilaginous band or rod which forms the primitive basis of the spine, present in all embryonic and some adult chordates.

■ **notochordal** *adjective* **M19.**

notonecta /nəʊtəˈnɛktə/ *noun.* **M17.**
[mod. Latin (see below), from Greek *nōton* back + *nēktēs* swimmer.]

An aquatic bug of the genus *Notonecta*, which swims on its back; a backswimmer. Now only as mod. Latin genus name. Cf. ***water-boatman*** s.v. WATER *noun.*

notopodium /nəʊtəˈpəʊdɪəm/ *noun.* Pl. **-ia** /-ɪə/. **L19.**
[from Greek *nōton* back + PODIUM.]

ZOOLOGY. The upper or dorsal branch of a parapodium. Cf. NEUROPODIUM.

■ **notopodial** *adjective* **L19.**

notoriety /nəʊtəˈrʌɪəti/ *noun.* **M16.**
[French *notoriété* or medieval Latin *notorietas*, formed as next: see -ITY.]

1 The state or fact of being notorious or well known. **M16.**

†**2** A notorious or well-known thing or event. *rare.* M17–M18.
3 A notorious or well-known person. M19.

📖 **1** E. M. FORSTER She would . . inveigh against those women who . . seek notoriety in print. H. CARPENTER The Inklings achieved a certain fame—or even notoriety, for they had their detractors.

notorious /nə(ʊ)ˈtɔːrɪəs/ *adjective.* M16.
[from medieval Latin *notorius* (cf. late Latin *notoria* notice, news, *notorium* information, indictment), from Latin *notus* known: see -IOUS.]
1 Well known, commonly or generally known, forming a matter of common knowledge, esp. on account of some bad practice, quality, etc., or some other thing not generally approved of or admired. (Foll. by *for*.) (Earlier in NOTORIOUSLY 1.) M16. **2** Such as is or may be generally, openly, or publicly known. Now *rare.* L16. †**3** Conspicuous; obvious, evident. (Earlier in NOTORIOUSLY 2.) E17–L18.

📖 **1** E. YOUNG My indignation at two notorious offenders. LD MACAULAY It was notorious that loyal . . men had been turned out of office . . for being Protestants. K. AMIS Beesley, notorious for his inability to get to know women. A. STORR Dons are notorious amongst analysts as being difficult patients. *Morning Star* A survivor of the notorious . . extermination camp of Natsweiler. S. BELLOW I was . . notorious for the kinkiness of my theories. A. LURIE You are a notorious gossip. **2** MARVELL Either by confession . . , or oath of witnesses, or by notorious evidence.

■ **notoriousness** *noun* notoriety E17. †**notory** *adjective* = NOTORIOUS LME–E17.

notoriously /nə(ʊ)ˈtɔːrɪəsli/ *adverb.* L15.
[from prec. + -LY².]
1 In a notorious manner; as a matter of common knowledge (and usu. disapproval); recognizedly. L15. †**2** Manifestly, evidently, obviously. L16–L17.

📖 **1** W. COBBETT Let us confine ourselves to notoriously public transactions. A. CROSS That profound indifference . . which the flu notoriously induces. J. BERMAN Hearsay is notoriously unreliable.

notornis /nə(ʊ)ˈtɔːnɪs/ *noun.* M19.
[mod. Latin former genus name, from Greek *notos* south + *ornis* bird.]
= TAKAHE.

notoungulate /nəʊtəʊˈʌŋgjʊlət/ *noun.* L20.
[from mod. Latin *Notoungulata* (see below), from Greek *notos* south: see UNGULATE.]
PALAEONTOLOGY. Any herbivorous hoofed mammal of the extinct S. American order Notoungulata.

nott *adjective* var. of NOT *adjective.*

Nottingham /ˈnɒtɪŋəm/ *noun.* E18.
[A city in the midlands of England.]
Used *attrib.* to designate things originating in or associated with Nottingham.
Nottingham catchfly a campion with drooping white flowers, *Silene nutans*, first found on the walls of Nottingham Castle. **Nottingham lace** a type of machine-made flat lace. **Nottingham reel** a type of wooden reel used in fishing. **Nottingham stoneware**, **Nottingham ware** a type of stoneware produced at Nottingham until the end of the 18th cent.

Notts. *abbreviation.*
Nottinghamshire.

notum /ˈnəʊtəm/ *noun.* Pl. **nota** /ˈnəʊtə/. L19.
[from Greek *nōton* back.]
ENTOMOLOGY. The tergum or dorsal exoskeleton of the thorax of an insect.

notwithstanding /nɒtwɪðˈstandɪŋ, -wɪθ-/ *preposition, adverb, & conjunction.* LME.
[from NOT *adverb* + *withstanding* pres. pple of WITHSTAND *verb*, after Old & mod. French *non obstant*, medieval Latin *non obstante* (see NON-OBSTANTE).]
▶ **A** *preposition.* In spite of, without regard to or prevention by. (Before or after the governed noun or pronoun.) LME.

📖 A. S. EDDINGTON We have used classical laws and quantum laws alongside one another notwithstanding the irreconcilability of their conceptions. S. WEINTRAUB The tour commenced, headaches and backaches notwithstanding.

▶ **B** *adverb.* Nevertheless, all the same. LME.

📖 GOLDSMITH Julian . . was, notwithstanding, a very good and a very valiant prince. W. S. MAUGHAM Bertha, knowing she would not read, took with her notwithstanding a book.

▶ **C** *conjunction.* Although; in spite of the fact that or *that. arch.* LME.

📖 J. LANG Notwithstanding it was enlivened by several exciting incidents, . . I was very glad when it was over. *Standard* The duty is deductible notwithstanding that payment . . may not happen to be claimed until after that date.

■ Also †**notwithstand** *preposition* (*rare*) L16–E19.

nougat /ˈnuːgɑː, ˈnʌgət/ *noun.* Also (earlier) †**nogat**. E19.
[(French from) Provençal *nogat*, from *noga* nut from Latin *nux* + *-at* from Latin *-atum* -ATE¹.]
(A sweet made from) egg-white sweetened with sugar or honey and mixed with nuts and sometimes pieces of fruit.

nougatine /nuːgəˈtiːn, nʌ-/ *noun.* L19.
[from prec. + -INE¹.]
A nougat covered with chocolate.

'nough /nʌf/ *adjective, noun, & adverb. colloq.* M19.
[Aphet. from ENOUGH. See also NUFF.]
Enough. Chiefly in **'nough said**.

nought /nɔːt/ *pronoun, noun, adverb, adjective, & verb.* Also (*Scot.*) **nocht** /nɒxt/, (*dial.*) **nowt** /naʊt/.
[Old English *nōwiht*, from NE + *ōwiht* var. of *āwiht* AUGHT *pronoun* (cf. NAUGHT). Cf. also OUGHT *noun*².]
▶ **A** *pronoun & noun.* **I 1** Nothing, not any thing; = NAUGHT *pronoun* 1. Now *dial., arch., & literary.* OE. †**2** That which does not exist. OE–E18. **3** A thing or person of no worth or value; a mere nothing. Long *obsolete* exc. *dial.* ME. **4** Not any quantity or number, zero; the score of no points in a game etc. Also, the figure or character representing zero; a cipher, a zero. LME.

📖 **1** R. TORRENCE At first, she loved nought else but flowers. †**a thing of nought** a mere nothing. **bring to nought** = *bring to naught* s.v. NAUGHT *pronoun & noun* 1. **come to nought** = *come to naught* s.v. NAUGHT *pronoun & noun* 1. **for nought** = *for nothing* s.v. NOTHING *pronoun & noun*. †**nought worth** worth nothing, of no value. **set at nought** = *set at naught* s.v. NAUGHT *pronoun & noun* 1. **4** R. C. SHERRIFF I don't like the enormous noughts you draw when a batsman . . fails to score. D. STOREY Nought point six six. A. JUDD They were aged nought to fourteen. **noughts and crosses** a game with pencil and paper, etc., in which a player using the figure nought and another a cross alternately mark one of a number (usu. nine) of spaces in a square grid with a nought or cross as appropriate, the winner being the first to fill in a row with his or her symbol.

▶†**II 5** Evil, worthless character or conduct. ME–M17.
▶ **B** *adverb.* **1** To no extent; in no way; not at all. Now *arch. & literary.* OE. **2** Not. *arch.* Long *obsolete* exc. *Scot.* OE.
▶ **C** *adjective.* **1** Good for nothing, worthless, useless; inappropriate. Formerly also, wicked, immoral, vicious. *obsolete* exc. *dial.* ME. †**2** Bad in condition or of its kind. LME–E18. †**3** Injurious (*to*), bad (*for*). M16–L17. **4** Zero. M20.
4 at nought feet AERONAUTICS very close to the ground, just above the ground.
▶ **D** *verb trans.* **1** Disregard, despise, hold in contempt. Long *obsolete* exc. *Scot. rare.* ME **2** Efface (esp. oneself). *arch. rare.* LME.

noughty /ˈnɔːti/ *adjective. obsolete* exc. *Scot.* LME.
[from NOUGHT *pronoun & noun* + -Y¹. Cf. NAUGHTY.]
†**1** Wicked, bad, immoral; abject, vile. LME–E17. **2** Good for nothing; worthless, useless; *Scot.* insignificant, puny, trifling. E16. †**3** Bad in condition or of its kind. M16–M17.

nouille /nuːj/ *noun.* Pl. pronounced same. M19.
[French.]
= NOODLE *noun*². Usu. in *pl.*

†**nould** *verb pa. t.*: see NILL *verb.*

noumena *noun pl.* of NOUMENON.

noumenal /ˈnaʊmən(ə)l, ˈnuː-/ *adjective.* E19.
[from NOUMEN(ON + -AL¹.]
Chiefly KANTIAN PHILOSOPHY. Of, pertaining to, or consisting of noumena; that can only be apprehended by intuition; not phenomenal.
■ **noumenalism** *noun* the doctrine that knowledge can only be apprehended by intuition. E20. **noumenalist** *noun & adjective* (*a*) *noun* an adherent of noumenalism; (*b*) *adjective* of or pertaining to noumenalism or noumenalists: E20. **noumeˈnality** *noun* the quality or state of being a noumenon L19. **noumenally** *adverb* in a noumenal aspect; as regards noumena: M19.

noumenon /ˈnaʊmənɒn, ˈnuː-/ *noun.* Pl. **-mena** /-mənə/. L18.
[German (Kant) from Greek, use as noun of neut. pres. pple pass. of *noein* apprehend, conceive.]
Chiefly KANTIAN PHILOSOPHY. An object of purely intellectual intuition, devoid of all phenomenal attributes.

†**noumpere** *noun* see UMPIRE *noun & verb.*

noun /naʊn/ *noun.* LME.
[Anglo-Norman = Old French *nun*, *num* (mod. *nom*) from Latin *nomen* name.]
GRAMMAR. **1** A word used as the name or designation of a person, place, or thing. (One of the parts of speech.) LME. **2** With specifying word: a word of a class comprising nouns proper (**noun substantive**) and adjectives (**noun adjective**), and formerly also occas. pronouns. *arch.* LME.
1 abstract noun, **collective noun**, **common noun**, **concrete noun**, **count noun**, **mass noun**, **proper noun**, **verbal noun**, etc.
■ **nounless** *adjective* M19. **nounness** /-n-n-/ *noun* the nature or character of a noun L20. **nouny** *adjective* having or using many nouns; of the nature or character of a noun: E20.

nounal /ˈnaʊn(ə)l/ *adjective.* L19.
[from prec. + -AL¹.]
1 GRAMMAR. Of the nature or character of a noun, nominal. L19. **2** Of style etc.: characterized by many nouns. M20.
■ **nounally** *adverb* as a noun L19.

nounou /ˈnuːnuː/ *noun.* Pl. pronounced same. L19.
[French.]
(A child's name for) a nurse; a wet-nurse.

†**nouns** *noun pl.* M16–L18.
[Alt. of *wounds* in *God's wounds*. Cf. ZOUNDS.]
Wounds. Orig. & chiefly in oaths and as *interjection.*

nourice /ˈnʌrɪs/ *noun. obsolete* exc. *Scot. arch.* Also †**nourish**. ME.
[Old French *nurice* (mod. *nourrice*) from late Latin *nutricia* fem. of Latin *nutricius*, from *nutric-*, *nutrix* (wet-)nurse, from *nutrire*: see next. Cf. NURSE *noun*¹.]
A nurse.

nourish /ˈnʌrɪʃ/ *verb.* ME.
[Old French *noriss-* lengthened stem of *norir* (mod. *nourrir*) from Latin *nutrire* feed, foster, cherish: see -ISH².]
▶ **I** *verb trans.* †**1** Bring up, rear, nurture, (a child or young person, an animal); feed with milk from the breast, suckle. ME–L17. ▸**b** Cherish (a person). LME–M16. **2** Sustain with food or proper nutriment; provide with food or sustenance; supply with something necessary for growth, formation, or good condition. ME. **3** *fig.* Promote or foster (a feeling, habit, condition, state of things, etc.); nurse (a feeling) in one's own heart or mind. ME. **4** Maintain, encourage, strengthen (one's heart, mind, etc.) in or with something. ME. †**5** Cultivate the growth of (one's hair, a plant, a tree). LME–E19.

📖 **2** AV *Gen.* 45:11 Thou shalt dwell in the land of Goshen . . and there wil I nourish thee. J. TYNDALL The mountain slopes which nourish the glacier. W. S. CHURCHILL Valleys, nourished alike by endless sunshine and abundant water. STEVIE SMITH Nourish me on an egg, Nanny. J. DISKI The wood is to be fed and nourished. *fig.*: W. H. PRESCOTT Men of umblemished purity of life, nourished with the learning of the cloister. **3** SHAKES. *Coriol.* They nourished disobedience, fed the ruin of the state. J. BUCHAN Working-class life . . nourished many major virtues. H. JACOBSON Men nourish the fantasy that women enjoy . . a thrashing.

▶ **II** *verb intrans.* **6** Provide nourishment. Chiefly as NOURISHING *adjective.* ME. †**7** Receive or take nourishment; be fed (*lit. & fig.*). LME–E17.
■ **nourishable** *adjective* (*a*) nourishing, nutritious; (*b*) able to be nourished, susceptible to nourishment: L15. **nourisher** *noun* LME. **nourishing** *noun* (*a*) the action of the verb; (*b*) nourishment, nutriment: ME. **nourishing** *adjective* that nourishes; sustaining; (esp. of food) providing much nourishment: LME. **nourishingly** *adverb* in a nourishing manner, so as to provide nourishment L19.

nourishment /ˈnʌrɪʃm(ə)nt/ *noun.* ME.
[from NOURISH *verb* + -MENT.]
1 The action, process, or fact of nourishing someone or something, nurture. ME. **2** That which nourishes or sustains someone or something; sustenance, food (*lit. & fig.*). ME.

†**nouriture** *noun.* LME.
[Old French *noureture*, *noriture* (mod. *nourriture*), from *norir*: see NOURISH *verb.* Cf. NURTURE *noun.*]
1 = NOURISHMENT 2. LME–M19. **2** = NOURISHMENT 1. LME–M17.

nous /naʊs/ *noun.* Also **nouse**. L17.
[Greek.]
1 GREEK PHILOSOPHY. Intuitive apprehension, intelligence; mind, intellect. L17. **2** Common sense, practical intelligence, gumption. *colloq.* E18.

nous autres /nuz oːtr/ *pers. pronoun, 1 pl.* L18.
[French, lit. 'we others'.]
We as opp. to somebody or anybody else.

nouse *noun* var. of NOUS.

nouther /ˈnuːðə/ *pronoun, adjective, adverb, & conjunction. obsolete* exc. *dial.* Also **nowther**.
[Old English *nowþer* contr. of *nōhwæþer*, from *nō* NO *adverb*¹ + *hwæþer* WHETHER *adjective* etc. Cf. NOTHER *pronoun* etc.]
1 = NEITHER. OE. †**2** = NOR *adverb, conjunction*¹. *rare.* ME–L16.

nouveau /ˈnuːvəʊ, nuːˈvəʊ, *foreign* nuvo/ *adjective & noun.* E20.
[French = new, extracted from ART NOUVEAU, NOUVEAU RICHE, etc.]
▶ **A** *adjective.* **1** *nouveau art*, = ART NOUVEAU. E20. **2** Of a person: possessing recently acquired wealth, *nouveau riche*; ostentatiously displaying such wealth. Of wealth etc.: recently acquired. M20. ▸**b** *nouveau poor*, = NOUVEAU PAUVRE. L20.

3 Modern, up to date. L20.
3 BEAUJOLAIS *nouveau*.
▶**B** *noun*. Pl. **-eaus**, **-eaux** /-əʊ, -əʊz, *foreign* -o/.
1 A *nouveau riche*. Usu. in *pl*. L20.
2 *ellipt*. = BEAUJOLAIS *nouveau*. *colloq*. L20.
¶ See also DE NOUVEAU (earlier).

nouveau pauvre /nuvo poːvr, nuːvəʊ ˈpɔːvrə/ *adjectival & noun phr*. Pl. ***nouveaux pauvres*** (pronounced same). M20.
[French, lit. 'new poor', after next.]
▶**A** *adjective*. Of a person: newly impoverished. M20.
▶**B** *noun*. A person who has recently become poor. L20.

nouveau riche /nuvo riʃ, nuːvəʊ ˈriːʃ/ *noun & adjectival phr*. Pl. ***nouveaux riches*** (pronounced same). E19.
[French, lit. 'new rich'.]
▶**A** *noun phr*. A person who has recently acquired wealth, *esp*. one who displays the fact ostentatiously or vulgarly. E19.
▶**B** *attrib*. or as *adjectival phr*. Of, pertaining to, or characteristic of a ***nouveau riche***; that has recently acquired wealth. L19.

nouveau roman /nuvo rɔmɑ̃/ *noun phr*. M20.
[French, lit. 'new novel'.]
A type of (esp. French) novel characterized by precise descriptions of characters' mental states and absence of interpretation of or comment on them.

nouveaux *noun pl*. see NOUVEAU.

nouveaux arrivés /nuvoz arivɛ/ *noun phr. pl*. L19.
[French, lit. 'new arrivals'.]
People who have recently acquired a higher financial and social standing.

nouveaux pauvres, ***nouveaux riches*** *noun phrs*. pls. of NOUVEAU PAUVRE, NOUVEAU RICHE.

nouvelle /nuvɛl/ *noun*. Pl. pronounced same. L17.
[French: see NOVEL *noun*. See also NOUVELLES.]
A short fictitious narrative, a short novel, *esp*. one dealing with a single situation or a single aspect of a character or characters.

nouvelle /nuːˈvɛl, *foreign* nuvɛl/ *adjective*. E18.
[French, fem. of NOUVEAU; in sense 2 extracted from NOUVELLE CUISINE.]
1 *gen*. New, novel. Now *rare*. E18.
2 Of, pertaining to, or characteristic of ***nouvelle cuisine***. L20.

nouvelle cuisine /nuvɛl kɥizin, ˌnuːvɛl kwɪˈziːn/ *noun phr*. L20.
[French, lit. 'new cooking'.]
A style of (esp. French) cooking that avoids traditional rich sauces and emphasizes the freshness of the ingredients and attractive presentation.

nouvelles /nuːˈvɛlz/ *noun pl*. L15.
[French, pl. of NOUVELLE *noun*.]
1 News. *rare*. L15.
2 Pl. of NOUVELLE *noun*. L17.

nouvellette /nuːvəˈlɛt/ *noun*. *rare*. E19.
[Alt. of NOVELETTE, after French *nouvelle*.]
A novelette.

nouvelle vague /nuvɛl vag/ *noun phr*. M20.
[French, lit. 'new wave'. Cf. VAGUE *noun*[1].]
A new movement or trend; *spec*. that in film-making originating in France in the late 1950s.

Nov. *abbreviation*.
November.

nova /ˈnəʊvə/ *noun*. Pl. **novae** /ˈnəʊviː/, **novas**. L17.
[Latin, fem. sing. of *novus* new.]
†**1** A thick ring or roll of tobacco. *rare*. Only in L17.
2 ASTRONOMY. Orig., a new star or nebula. Now *spec*. a star whose brightness suddenly increases by several magnitudes, with violent ejection of gaseous material, and then decreases more or less gradually. Formerly also, a supernova. L19.

Novachord /ˈnəʊvəkɔːd/ *noun*. Also **n-**. M20.
[from Latin NOVA + CHORD *noun*[1].]
An electronic six-octave keyboard instrument.

novaculite /nə(ʊ)ˈvakjʊlʌɪt/ *noun*. L18.
[from Latin *novacula* razor + -ITE[1].]
Orig., any of various smooth hard rocks used to make whetstones. Now *spec*. in PETROGRAPHY, a dense hard fine-grained siliceous rock resembling chert with a high content of quartz microcrystals.

novae *noun pl*. see NOVA.

Novanglian /nəʊˈvaŋglɪən/ *adjective & noun*. Chiefly *US*. Now *rare* or *obsolete*. L17.
[from *Nova Anglia* Latinized form of *New England*: see -AN.]
▶**A** *adjective*. Of or pertaining to New England. L17.
▶**B** *noun*. A New Englander. M18.

Nova Scotian /ˈnəʊvə ˈskəʊʃ(ə)n/ *noun & adjective*. M19.
[from *Nova Scotia* (see below), in Latin lit. 'New Scotland'.]
(A native or inhabitant) of the province of Nova Scotia in SE Canada.

novate /nəʊˈveɪt/ *verb trans*. *rare*. E17.
[Latin *novat-* pa. ppl stem of *novare* make new, from *novus* new: see -ATE[3].]
Replace by something new; *spec*. in LAW, replace by a new obligation, debt, etc.

Novatian /nəʊˈveɪʃ(ə)n/ *noun & adjective*. LME.
[ecclesiastical Latin *Novatiani* (pl.), from *Novatianus* (see below).]
ECCLESIASTICAL HISTORY. ▶**A** *noun*. A member of an extremely rigorous but doctrinally orthodox sect founded by Novatianus, a Roman presbyter in the middle of the 3rd cent. AD. Usu. in *pl*. LME.
▶**B** *adjective*. Of or pertaining to Novatianus or the Novatians. M17.
■ **Novatianism** *noun* the doctrine or tenets of the Novatians L16. **Novatianist** *noun & adjective* (*a*) a Novatian; (*b*) *adjective* of or pertaining to Novationism or Novations: L16.

novation /nə(ʊ)ˈveɪʃ(ə)n/ *noun*. Chiefly *Scot*. E16.
[Late Latin *novatio(n-)*, formed as NOVATE: see -ATION.]
1 The introduction of something new; a change, an innovation, *esp*. an undesirable one. Now *rare*. E16.
2 LAW. The substitution of a new contract in place of an old one, esp. one whereby debtors are substituted. E16.

novator /nə(ʊ)ˈveɪtə/ *noun*. Long *rare*. E17.
[Latin, formed as NOVATE: see -OR.]
An innovator.

novel /ˈnɒv(ə)l/ *noun*. In branch III also **-ll**. LME.
[In branch I from Old French *novelle* (mod. *nouvelle*) = Italian *novella* from Latin use as noun (treated as sing.) of neut. pl. of *novellus*, from *novus* new. In branch II directly from Italian *novella* orig. fem. (sc. *storia* story) of *novello* new. In branch III from late Latin *novella* (usu. in pl. *-ae*) use as noun (sc. *constitutio(n-)* CONSTITUTION) of fem. of Latin *novellus*: see -EL[2].]
▶**I** †**1** Something new, a novelty, (usu. in *pl*.). In *pl*. also, news, tidings. LME–E18. ▸**b** A piece of news. E17–M18.
▶**II 2** *Hist*. Any of a number of tales or fictional narratives making up a larger short work, as in the *Decameron* of Boccaccio, the *Heptameron* of Marguerite of Valois, etc.; a short narrative of this type. Usu. in *pl*. M16.
3 A fictitious prose narrative or tale of considerable length (now usu. one long enough to fill one or more volumes), esp. & orig. (freq. contrasted with a ***romance***) representing character and action with some degree of realism; a volume containing such a narrative. M17. ▸**b** (Formerly without article; now with *the*.) The literary genre constituted or exemplified by such fiction. M18.

📖 **3** STEELE I am afraid thy Brains are . . disordered with Romances and Novels. R. K. NARAYAN He was already in bed, with a novel shielding his face. E. J. HOWARD She usually re-read three Austen novels each winter. ***antinovel***, ***dime novel***, ***Gothic novel***, ***psychological novel***, etc. **graphic novel** a full-length (esp. science fiction or fantasy) story in comic-strip format, published in book form for the adult or teenage market. ***novel of terror***: see TERROR *noun*.

▶**III 4** ROMAN LAW. A new constitution, supplementary to a code, *esp*. any of those enacted by the Emperor Justinian. E17.
■ **noveldom** *noun* the world of novels; novels collectively: M19. **noveˈlese** *noun* the style of language supposedly characteristic of inferior novels E20. **novelesque** *adjective* characteristic of a novel, resembling (that of) a novel M19. **novelish** *adjective* characteristic or suggestive of a novel E19.

novel /ˈnɒv(ə)l/ *adjective*. LME.
[Old French (mod. *nouvel*, *nouveau*) from Latin *novellus*, from *novus* new: see -EL[2].]
1 †**a** Young, fresh; newly made or created. LME–M17. ▸†**b** Recent; of recent origin. *obsolete* exc. in ***novel disseisin*** s.v. DISSEISIN 1. M17.
2 Of a new kind or nature; strange; previously unknown, original. L15.

📖 **2** G. HUNTINGTON Much was novel to him, for he had little experience of the world. A. TOFFLER Technologically, novel industries will rise to process the output of the oceans. K. WATERHOUSE It was a novel and, I thought, an audacious approach.

■ **novelly** /ˈnɒv(ə)li/ *adverb* (*rare*) in a novel manner; by a novel method: E19. **novelness** *noun* (*rare*) newness, novelty L15.

novelette /nɒvəˈlɛt/ *noun*. In sense 1 also **-et**. L18.
[from NOVEL *noun* + -ETTE. Cf. NOUVELLETTE.]
1 A story of moderate length having the characteristics of a novel; *derog*. a light romantic or sentimental novel. L18.
2 MUSIC. A piano piece of free form with several themes. L19.
■ **novelettish** *adjective* characteristic or suggestive of a novelette E20. **novelettist** *noun* a writer of novelettes L19.

novelise *verb* var. of NOVELIZE.

novelism /ˈnɒv(ə)lɪz(ə)m/ *noun*. Now *rare*. E17.
[from NOVEL *noun* + -ISM.]
†**1** Innovation; novelty. E17–E18.
2 Novel-writing. E19.

novelist /ˈnɒv(ə)lɪst/ *noun*. L16.
[from NOVEL *noun* + -IST. In sense 3 from French *nouvelliste*.]
†**1** An innovator; a favourer of novelty. L16–E18.
†**2** An inexperienced person, a novice. *rare*. M17–M18.
†**3** A newsmonger, a carrier of news. E–M18.
4 A writer of novels. E18.

novelistic /nɒvəˈlɪstɪk/ *adjective*. M19.
[from NOVEL *noun* + -ISTIC.]
Of, pertaining to, or characteristic of novels; resembling a novel, esp. in style or in the treatment of character and action.
■ **novelistically** *adverb* L19.

novelize /ˈnɒv(ə)lʌɪz/ *verb*. Also **-ise**. E17.
[from NOVEL *noun* + -IZE.]
▶**I 1** *verb intrans*. Produce something new; introduce novelty. Chiefly as ***novelizing*** *ppl adjective*. E17.
†**2** *verb trans*. Bring into a new condition; make new or novel. Only in M17.
▶**II 3** *verb trans*. Convert into the form or style of a novel. E19.
4 *verb intrans*. Write novels. *rare*. E19.
■ **noveliˈzation** *noun* (*a*) conversion into a novel; (*b*) an instance of this; a novelized play, true story, etc.: L19.

novell *noun* see NOVEL *noun*.

novella /nə(ʊ)ˈvɛlə/ *noun*. L17.
[Italian: see NOVEL *noun*.]
A short fictitious prose narrative, a short novel, a long short story.

novelty /ˈnɒv(ə)lti/ *noun & adjective*. LME.
[Old French *novelté* (mod. *nouveauté*), formed as NOVEL *adjective*, -TY[1].]
▶**A** *noun*. **1** A new or unusual thing; a novel thing or occurrence; an innovation, a novel proceeding. LME. ▸†**b** A new matter or recent event, as a subject of report or talk. Usu. in *pl*. LME–L16. ▸**c** A decorative or amusing object relying for its appeal on the newness of its design. E20.
2 The quality or state of being novel; newness, strangeness, novel or unusual character (*of*). LME.

📖 **1** R. K. NARAYAN New turns and tricks and novelties to announce to the public. L. APPIGNANESI It was still something of a novelty . . for a woman to do things alone. **c** B. MASON Carnival novelties, from false noses to squeakers and rattles. **2** R. C. HUTCHINSON A young student . . delighting in the novelty of every fresh experience. E. H. GOMBRICH The pictures . . must have shocked the Egyptians . . by their novelty. B. PYM What will they talk about . . when the novelty has worn off.

▶**B** *attrib*. or as *adjective*. Having novelty, appealing through newness. L18.

📖 L. FEATHER Novelty songs . . began to edge out the jazz material in his repertoire. *Guardian* French cloth manufacturers will be showing . . novelty silks.

November /nə(ʊ)ˈvɛmbə/ *noun*. OE.
[(Old & mod. French *novembre* from) Latin *November*, also *Novembris* (sc. *mensis* month), from *novem* nine: orig. the ninth month of the Roman year. The meaning of *-ber* is unkn. (cf. *September* etc.).]
The eleventh month of the year in the Gregorian calendar. Also *fig*., with allusion to the cold, damp, or foggy days considered characteristic of the month in Britain and elsewhere in the northern hemisphere.
■ **Novemberish** *adjective* characteristic or suggestive of November; dismal, gloomy: L18. **Novembery** *adjective* = NOVEMBERISH M19.

novemdial *adjective & noun* var. of NOVENDIAL.

novena /nə(ʊ)ˈviːnə/ *noun*. Pl. **-nae** /-niː/, **-nas**. M19.
[medieval Latin, from *novem* nine, after Latin *novenarius* of nine days: see next.]
ROMAN CATHOLIC CHURCH. A devotion consisting of special prayers or services on nine successive days.

novenary /ˈnɒv(ə)n(ə)ri/ *noun & adjective*. Now *rare*. L16.
[Latin *novenarius*, from *novem* nine: see -ARY[1].]
▶**A** *noun*. **1** An aggregate or set of nine. L16.
2 = NOVENA. M17.
▶**B** *adjective*. Pertaining to, consisting of, or based on the number nine. E17.

novendial /nə(ʊ)ˈvɛndj(ə)l/ *adjective & noun*. Now *rare*. Also **novem-** /nə(ʊ)ˈvɛm-/. M16.
[Latin *novendialis*, from *novem* nine + *dies* day: see -AL[1].]
ROMAN HISTORY. ▶**A** *adjective*. Of a religious ceremony etc.: lasting for nine days. M16.
▶**B** *noun*. **1** A religious ceremony lasting for nine days. E17.
2 A funeral ceremony held on the ninth day after the burial of the deceased person. E18.

novennial /nə(ʊ)ˈvɛnɪəl/ *adjective*. *rare*. M17.
[from late Latin *novennis*, from *novem* nine + *annus* year, after BIENNIAL etc.]
Occurring every nine years.

novercal /nə(ʊ)ˈvəːk(ə)l/ *adjective*. *literary*. Now *rare*. E17.
[Latin *novercalis*, from *noverca* stepmother, from *novus* new: see -AL[1].]
Characteristic of or resembling a stepmother, stepmotherly.

Novial /ˈnəʊvɪəl/ *noun.* **E20.**
[from Latin *novus* new + initials of *international auxiliary language.*]
An artificial language created by Otto Jespersen in 1928 for use as an international auxiliary language.

novice /ˈnɒvɪs/ *noun & adjective.* **ME.**
[Old & mod. French from late Latin *novicius, -ia*, from Latin *novus* new: see **-ICE**[1].]
▶ **A** *noun.* **1** ECCLESIASTICAL. A person who has entered a religious order and is under probation or trial, before taking the required vows. **ME.**
2 An inexperienced person; a person new to the circumstances in which he or she is placed; a beginner. **ME.**
3 A newly converted person. **E16.**
4 An animal entered in a competitive event which has not previously (or before a specified date) won a major prize. **E20.**
▶ **B** *attrib.* or as *adjective.* **1** Of or pertaining to novices. **M16.**
2 That is a novice. **E17.**
■ **novicehood** *noun* the condition of a novice **M18.**

noviceship /ˈnɒvɪsʃɪp/ *noun.* **E17.**
[from prec. + **-SHIP.**]
1 a Initial stage; inexperience. *rare.* **E17.** ▸**b** = **NOVICIATE** *noun* 1. **M17.**
2 A Jesuit college where novices are trained. **E17.**

noviciate /nə(ʊ)ˈvɪʃɪət, -ɪeɪt/ *noun & adjective.* Also **novitiate. E17.**
[French *noviciat* or medieval Latin *noviciatus*, formed as **NOVICE**: see **-ATE**[1].]
▶ **A** *noun.* **1** The period of being a novice; the state or time of being a beginner; time of initiation, apprenticeship, or probation. **E17.**
2 A place housing novices during their period of probation. **E17.**
3 A novice, a beginner. **M17.**
▶ **B** *attrib.* or as *adjective.* **1** = **NOVICE** *adjective* 1. **E18.**
2 = **NOVICE** *adjective* 2. Now *rare.* **L18.**
■ **noviciateship** *noun* = **NOVICIATE** *noun* 1 **M17.**

novi homines *noun phr.* pl. of **NOVUS HOMO.**

novillada /nɒviˈʎaða, nɒvɪˈljɑːdə/ *noun.* Pl. ***-as*** /-as, -əz/. **L19.**
[Spanish, from **NOVILLO** + *-ada* **-ADE.**]
A bullfight in which three-year-old bulls are fought by novice matadors.

novillero /noviˈʎero, nɒvɪˈljɛːrəʊ/ *noun.* Pl. ***-os*** /-ɔs, -əʊz/. **E20.**
[Spanish, from **NOVILLO** + *-ero* agent-suff.]
An apprentice matador who has fought only in *novilladas.*

novillo /noˈviʎo, nəˈviːljəʊ/ *noun.* Pl. ***-os*** /-ɔs, -əʊz/. **M19.**
[Spanish, from Latin *novellus* new: see **NOVEL** *adjective.*]
A young bull; *spec.* a fighting bull not more than three years old.

novilunar /nɒvɪˈluːnə/ *adjective. rare.* **L17.**
[from medieval Latin *noviluna*, from Latin *novus* new + *luna* moon, after **LUNAR** *adjective.*]
Of or pertaining to the new moon.

novio /ˈnovjo/ *noun.* Pl. ***-os*** /-ɔs/. **E20.**
[Spanish.]
In Spain and Spanish-speaking countries: a boyfriend, a lover.

novitial /nə(ʊ)ˈvɪʃ(ə)l/ *adjective. rare.* **L18.**
[from Latin *novicius, -tius*, from *novus* new + **-AL**[1].]
Of the nature or characteristic of a novice.

novitiate *noun & adjective* var. of **NOVICIATE.**

novity /ˈnɒvɪti/ *noun.* Now *rare.* **LME.**
[Old French *novité* from Latin *novitas*, from *novus* new: see **-ITY.**]
1 An innovation; a novelty. **LME.**
2 Novelty; newness. **M16.**

novobiocin /nəʊvə(ʊ)ˈbʌɪəsɪn/ *noun.* **M20.**
[formed as next + **BIO-** + **-MY)CIN.**]
PHARMACOLOGY. A weakly acidic tetracyclic phenol produced by various bacteria of the genus *Streptomyces* and used to treat bacterial infections resistant to less toxic antibiotics.

Novocain /ˈnəʊvə(ʊ)keɪn/ *noun.* Also **-aine, n-. E20.**
[formed as next + **-CAINE.**]
PHARMACOLOGY. (Proprietary name for) the drug procaine.

Novocastrian /nəʊvəˈkastrɪən/ *noun & adjective.* **L19.**
[from Latin *novo-* combining form of *novus* new + *castrum* castle (translating *Newcastle* (see below)) + **-IAN.**]
(A native or inhabitant) of the city of Newcastle-upon-Tyne in NE England.

novodamus /nəʊvə(ʊ)ˈdeɪməs/ *noun.* **M17.**
[from Latin *de novo damus* we grant anew.]
SCOTS LAW. (A charter containing) a clause by which a feudal superior renews a former grant, now *spec.* to alter or correct it.

novolak /ˈnəʊvəlak/ *noun.* **E20.**
[from Latin *novo-* (see **NOVOCASTRIAN**) + alt. of **LAC(QUER** *noun.*]
Any of a range of soluble fusible resins formed by condensing formaldehyde with phenol using an acid catalyst, and used in varnishes.

†**novum** *noun.* **L16–E17.**
[Latin *novem* nine.]
An old game at dice played by five or six people, the two principal throws being nine and five.

novus homo /nəʊvəs ˈhɒməʊ/ *noun phr.* Pl. ***novi homines*** /nəʊvʌɪ ˈhɒmɪniːz/. **L16.**
[Latin, lit. 'new man': in ancient Rome, the first man in a family to rise to a curule office.]
A man who has recently risen to a position of importance from insignificance; an upstart.

now /naʊ/ *adverb, conjunction, noun, & adjective.*
[Old English *nu* = Old Saxon *nu* (Dutch *nu*), Old High German *nu* (German *nun* (with adverbial *-n* added)), Old Norse, Gothic *nu*, from Indo-European adverb of time repr. also by Latin *num, nunc*, Greek *nu, nun*, Sanskrit *nu, nūnam.* Cf. **NAH** *adverb*[1], **NAOW** *adverb*[2].]
▶ **A** *adverb.* **I 1** At the present time or moment; under the present circumstances. **OE.**
2 In the time directly following on the present moment; immediately, at once. **OE.**
3 In the time directly preceding the present moment. Now only in ***just now*** or (poet.) ***even now.*** **OE.**
4 At this time; at the time spoken of or referred to; (in narrative or discourse) then, next, by that time. **LOE.**

> **1** H. B. STOWE I can believe now that you could sell little Harry. A. E. HOUSMAN Then 'twas the Roman, now 'tis I. V. WOOLF It is now Thursday. J. MITCHELL Some elaborate ritual of which nothing now remains. *High Times* Right now I'm in east Tennessee. **2** P. G. WODEHOUSE He must put his fortune to the test . . . Now or never must the balloon go up. G. GREENE If only we could leave now, at once. **3** T. HARDY Mr Downe, who called just now wanting to see you. **4** SCOTT FITZGERALD Now at last she was beginning to be unhappy. G. W. KNIGHT The course of events now leagues itself with Troilus' metaphysical difficulties.

▶ **II** With temporal sense weakened or lost.
5 In or (later) as a command or request, or in a question, giving any of various tones (exclaiming, expostulating, reproving, soothing, etc.): I insist, I warn you, I ask, I pray, I beg, tell me. Also ***now then.*** **OE.**
6 As an important or noteworthy point in an argument or proof or in a series of statements: you should be told; as must be admitted; on the other hand. **OE.**
7 At the end of an ironic question repeating (with substitution of *do* for the verb phr. or ellipsis of the compl. after another auxiliary) a previous statement: indeed? really? *colloq.* **M20.**

> **5** G. BERKELEY Now, in the name of truth, I entreat you to tell me. G. CHESNEY: 'Now, Peter, behave youself.' I. MURDOCH The police barred my way . . . 'Now then!' said one of them. *Times Lit. Suppl.* These omissions cannot be . . merely . . my personal preference, now can they? **6** SHAKES. *A.Y.L.* Now, if thou wert a poet, I might have some hope thou didst feign. L. BRUCE Now, my priest uniform overshadowed General Eisenhower's in commanding respect. E. PIZZEY I just can't get into spending on myself. Now, for the children, that's different. **7** C. DEXTER 'She confirms what Martin says, sir.' 'Does she now?' 'You sound . . dubious.'

Phrases: ***be a big boy now, be a big girl now***: see **BIG** *adjective.* ***even now***: see **EVEN** *adverb.* ***every now and again, every now and then***: see **EVERY** *adjective* 1. **FROM *now on.*** ***good now*** *interjection* (*obsolete* exc. *dial.*) expr. acquiescence, entreaty, expostulation, or surprise. ***here and now***: see **HERE** *adverb.* ***how now?***: see **HOW** *adverb.* ***just now***: see **JUST** *adverb.* ***now and again***: see **AGAIN** *adverb* 4. **now and then** occasionally, fitfully, intermittently, at intervals. **now now**: reprimanding or pacifying a person. **now X, now Y**, (*arch.*) **now X and again Y**, at one moment X, at the next Y; alternately X and Y.
Comb.: **nowanights** *adverb* (*literary*) [after **NOWADAYS**] at night at the present time, nightly now; **nowcast** a description of present weather conditions and forecast of those immediately expected; **nowcasting** preparation or provision of nowcasts.

▶ **B** *conjunction.* As a consequence of or simultaneously with the fact that; since, seeing that. Also ***now that.*** **OE.**

> R. BOLDREWOOD We'd as good as got a free pardon . . now the police was away. W. STEVENS Now that the weather is growing cooler.

▶ **C** *noun.* **1** The present time or moment; (esp. after prepositions) the time spoken of or referred to. (Earliest after prepositions.) **OE.** ▸**b** *The* present; *this* moment. **M17.**
2 A present point or moment of time; one's present. *literary.* **M17.**

> **1** J. B. PRIESTLEY Think it over between now and five o'clock. *Punch* I crave a few words . . on a personal matter. 'Will now suit you?' he said simply. J. WAINWRIGHT As of now you have another job. A. BROOKNER Slightly more alert by now, she looked round the room. **b** DRYDEN With scarce a breathing space betwixt, This now becalmed, and perishing the next. B. BREYTENBACH Life is in the present, in the now. **2** J. R. LOWELL Man ever with his Now at strife. R. W. EMERSON An everlasting Now reigns in nature.

▶ **D** *attrib.* or as *adjective.* **1** Of the present time, present. Now *rare.* **LME.**
2 Modern, fashionable, up to date. *colloq.* **M20.**

> **1** BYRON His now escape may furnish A future miracle. **2** G. GREER Even a poet as *now* as Dylan has two kinds of female . . in his imagery.

nowaday /ˈnaʊədeɪ/ *adverb, adjective, & noun.* **LME.**
[from **NOW** *adverb* + **A-DAY.**]
▶ **A** *adverb.* = **NOWADAYS** *adverb. arch.* **LME.**
▶ **B** *attrib.* or as *adjective.* Of the present time or age, of these times. **M17.**
▶ **C** *noun.* = **NOWADAYS** *noun. rare.* **L19.**

nowadays /ˈnaʊədeɪz/ *adverb, noun, & adjective.* **LME.**
[from **NOW** *adverb* + **A-DAYS.**]
▶ **A** *adverb.* At the present time or age, in these days. **LME.**
▶ **B** *noun.* The present time or age. Chiefly after *of.* **LME.**
▶ **C** *attrib.* or as *adjective.* = **NOWADAY** *adjective. rare.* **E17.**

no way /nəʊ ˈweɪ/ *adverbial phr.* In sense 1 also **noway. ME.**
[from **NO** *adjective* + **WAY** *noun.*]
1 In no way or manner; not at all; by no means. **ME.**
2 *emphatic.* Equivalent to a neg. sentence, as *interjection*, or introducing a clause (usu. with inversion of subj. & obj.): under no circumstances, absolutely not, emphatically no; it is impossible (that). *colloq.* **M20.**

> **1** J. F. W. HERSCHEL Cavendish . . is therefore no way to blame for any misconception. H. B. STOWE Dem . . an't much 'count, no way! TENNYSON I have lived a virgin, and I no way doubt But that . . I can live so still. B. BEHAN The sun shone . . not white . . and no way hot, but steady, golden. **2** J. CALLAGHAN Then no way will you stop prices or unemployment going up again. J. D. MACDONALD 'All is forgiven?' 'No. No way. Never.' *Sunday Star (Toronto)* No way mail service is going to improve. K. HULME They both think I'm going to put up with him . . . No way.

■ **noways** *adverb* (now *arch.* & *dial.*) = **NO WAY** 1 **ME.**

nowed /naʊd/ *adjective.* **L16.**
[from French *noué* knotted (see **NOWY**) + **-ED**[1].]
HERALDRY. Knotted; tied in a knot; *esp.* (of a snake) displayed in the form of a horizontal figure of eight with the head and tail extending. Usu. *postpositive.*

Nowel /nəʊˈɛl/ *noun*[1]. *arch.* Also **-ll. LME.**
[Old French *nouel, noel* (mod. *noël*) obscure var. of *nael, neel*, from Latin *natalis* (sc. *dies* day) **NATAL** *adjective*[1]. Cf. **NOEL.**]
1 A word shouted or sung as an expression of joy, orig. to commemorate the birth of Jesus. Now only as retained in Christmas carols. **LME.**
†**2** The feast of Christmas; Christmas-time. **LME–L16.**

nowel /ˈnəʊəl/ *noun*[2]. **LME.**
[Var. of **NEWEL.**]
†**1** = **NEWEL** 1. **LME–L17.**
2 FOUNDING. The core of a mould for casting a large hollow cylinder. **M19.**

Nowell *noun* var. of **NOWEL** *noun*[1].

nowhat /ˈnəʊwɒt/ *pronoun & adverb. rare.* **M16.**
[from **NO** *adjective* + **WHAT** *pronoun* etc., after *somewhat.*]
▶†**A** *pronoun.* Nothing. Only in **M16.**
▶ **B** *adverb.* Not at all, not in the least. **M17.**

nowhen /ˈnəʊwɛn/ *adverb. rare.* **M18.**
[from **NO** *adjective* + **WHEN.**]
At no time, never.

nowhence /ˈnəʊwɛns/ *adverb & pronoun. rare.* **M18.**
[from **NO** *adjective* + **WHENCE.** Cf. **NOWHITHER.**]
▶ **A** *adverb.* From nowhere. **M18.**
▶ **B** *pronoun.* Nowhere. **M19.**

nowhere /ˈnəʊwɛː/ *adverb, noun, pronoun, & adjective.* **OE.**
[from **NO** *adjective* + **WHERE.**]
▶ **A** *adverb.* **1** In or to no place; not anywhere. **OE.**
2 In no part or passage of a book etc.; in no work or author. **ME.**
3 In or to no situation of achievement, success, improvement, or development. Chiefly in phrs. below. **M18.**

> **1** R. FROST I go nowhere on purpose: I happen by. W. COOPER Steve was nowhere to be seen. *Time* Nowhere in Europe have relations . . become more acrimonious. **nowhere near** (modifying an adjective or noun) not nearly, not by a long way. **2** J. CONRAD The only really honest writing is to be found in newspapers and nowhere else. J. KOSINSKI Surprised that in so many papers . . his name was nowhere mentioned. **3 be nowhere, come in nowhere** be badly beaten (in a race, contest, etc.); be hopelessly distanced, be out of the running. **get nowhere** (*a*) *verb phr. intrans.* make no progress; (*b*) *verb phr. trans.* not assist (a person) to make progress. **go nowhere** (*a*) make no progress; (*b*) (of a sum of money etc.) be quickly spent, have little buying power.

▶ **B** *noun & pronoun.* **1** No place. In early use also, the mystical state or feeling of being nowhere. **LME.**
2 Somewhere remote or inaccessible, somewhere dull or nondescript, (freq. in ***the middle of nowhere***); a place of this kind. **L19.**
3 Somewhere unidentified or unknown, obscurity. Chiefly in phrs. below. **E20.**

📖 **1** R. INGALLS There was nowhere for him to hide. J. N. ISBISTER Nowhere could quite compare . . with Paris. **2** W. MCILVANNEY Graithnock had become a kind of nowhere fixed in stone. P. LIVELY The landscape has an impersonality and uniformity that makes it a nowhere. B. HEAD We are in the middle of nowhere Most communication is by ox cart or sledge. **3 from nowhere, out of nowhere** unexpectedly or without warning from somewhere unknown or from obscurity, out of the blue.

▶**C** *adjective.* Remote, inaccessible; insignificant, unsatisfactory, dull. Chiefly *slang.* **L19.**

📖 *Melody Maker* The most nowhere record we'd made. A. BEATTIE He is so nowhere, . . I can't even believe that Lloyd likes him.

Comb.: **nowheresville** *US colloq.* (a name for) a place or situation of no significance, promise, or interest.

■ **nowhereness** *noun* **M19. nowheres** *adverb* (*US dial.*) = **NOWHERE** *adverb* **L19.**

nowhither /ˈnəʊwɪðə/ *adverb & pronoun. arch.* **OE.**
[from **NO** *adjective* + **WHITHER** *adverb* etc.]
▶**A** *adverb.* To no place; nowhere. **OE.**
▶**B** *pronoun.* Nowhere. **E19.**

nowise /ˈnəʊwʌɪz/ *adverb.* **LME.**
[from **NO** *adjective* + **-WISE.**]
In no way or manner; not at all.

nown /nəʊn/ *adjective. obsolete* exc. *Scot. dial.* **LME.**
[Var. of **OWN** *adjective*, by misdivision of *mine own, thine own.*]
(One's) own.

nowness /ˈnaʊnɪs/ *noun.* **L17.**
[from **NOW** *adverb* + **-NESS.**]
1 The quality of being always present. *rare.* **L17.**
2 The quality of taking place or existing in the present time, immediacy. **L19.**

nowt /naʊt/ *noun*[1]. *Scot. & north.* Also **nolt** /nəʊlt, nɒlt/. **ME.**
[Old Norse *naut* corresp. to Old English *nēat* **NEAT** *noun.*]
1 *pl.* Cattle, oxen. **ME.**
2 *sing.* **a** An ox, a bullock. **LME.** ▸**b** *transf.* A stupid, coarse, or clumsy person. **L18.**
Comb.: **nowtherd** a cowherd.

nowt *pronoun, noun*[2], *adjective, & adverb* see **NOUGHT.**

nowther *pronoun, adjective, adverb, & conjunction* var. of **NOUTHER.**

nowy /ˈnəʊi/ *adjective.* **M16.**
[Old French *noé* (mod. *noué*) pa. pple of *noer, nouer* knot from Latin *nodare*, from *nodus* knot: see **-Y**[5]. Cf. **NOWED.**]
HERALDRY. †**1** = **NOWED.** *rare.* Only in **M16.**
2 Esp. of a cross: having a projection or curvature in or near the middle. **M16.**

NOx /nɒks/ *abbreviation.*
Nitrogen oxides, esp. as atmospheric pollutants.

nox /nɒks/ *noun.* Chiefly *poet.* **M16.**
[Latin.]
Night (personified).

noxa /ˈnɒksə/ *noun.* Pl. **noxae** /ˈnɒksiː/. **L19.**
[Latin = hurt, damage.]
MEDICINE. A thing harmful to the body.

noxal /ˈnɒks(ə)l/ *adjective.* **E17.**
[Late Latin *noxalis*, formed as prec.: see **-AL**[1].]
ROMAN LAW. Of or pertaining to damage or injury done by a person or animal belonging to or in the power of another.

noxious /ˈnɒkʃəs/ *adjective.* **L15.**
[from Latin *noxius*, from **NOXA**: see **-OUS.**]
Injurious, hurtful, harmful; unwholesome.
noxious weed *spec.* in Australia and New Zealand, a plant considered harmful to animals or the environment.
■ **noxiously** *adverb* **M18. noxiousness** *noun* **M17.**

noy /nɔɪ/ *noun*[1]. Long *obsolete* exc. *dial.* **ME.**
[Aphet. from **ANNOY** *noun.*]
Annoyance, trouble.

noy /nɔɪ/ *noun*[2]. **M20.**
[Repr. pronunc. of the first part of *noise.*]
PHYSICS. A unit of perceived noisiness, defined so that the number of noys is proportional to the noisiness of a sound, and one noy is equal to the noisiness of a sound of specified bandwidth and intensity.

noy /nɔɪ/ *verb.* Long *obsolete* exc. *dial.* **ME.**
[Aphet. from **ANNOY** *verb.*]
1 *verb trans.* Annoy, trouble, vex, harass; harm, injure. **ME.**
2 *verb intrans.* Cause annoyance or harm. **ME.**

noyade /nwɑːˈjɑːd, *foreign* nwajad/ *noun & verb.* **E19.**
[French, from *noyer* drown from Latin *necare* kill without a weapon, (later) drown, from *nec-*, *nex* slaughter: see **-ADE.**]
▶**A** *noun.* Pl. pronounced /-ɑːdz, *foreign* -ad/. An execution carried out by drowning, esp. a mass one as in France in 1794. **E19.**
▶**B** *verb trans.* Execute by drowning, esp. *en masse.* **M19.**

†**noyance** *noun.* **ME.**
[Aphet. from (the same root as) **ANNOYANCE.**]
1 = **ANNOYANCE** 3. **ME–L17.**
2 = **ANNOYANCE** 2. **LME–M16.**
3 = **ANNOYANCE** 1. **LME–L16.**

noyau /nwɑːˈjəʊ, *foreign* nwajo/ *noun.* Pl. **-aux**, /-əʊz, *foreign* -o/. **L18.**
[French, earlier *noiel* kernel from Proto-Romance use as noun of neut. of late Latin *nucalis*, from *nuc-*, *nux* nut.]
1 A liqueur made of brandy flavoured with the kernels of certain fruits. **L18.**
2 A type of sweet similar to nougat. **E20.**

nozzle /ˈnɒz(ə)l/ *noun.* **E17.**
[from **NOSE** *noun* + **-LE**[1].]
1 A projecting part or end. **E17.**
2 A socket on a candlestick or sconce, for receiving the lower end of the candle. Now *rare.* **M17.**
3 A spout, mouthpiece, or projecting aperture, or a short terminal pipe or part of a pipe, from which something may issue or be discharged, or through which something may pass, as a spout on a watering-can or spray, the end of a pair of bellows, the muzzle of a gun barrel, the steam-port of a steam engine, a part of a turbine for directing fluid on to the rotor, a part of an internal-combustion engine for injecting fuel into the carburettor or the combustion chamber, a part of a jet engine for increasing the speed of the ejected fluid, etc. **L17.**
4 The nose. *slang.* **L18.**

NP *abbreviation.*
Notary Public.

Np *symbol.*
CHEMISTRY. Neptunium.

n.p. *abbreviation.*
1 New paragraph.
2 No place of publication.

NPA *abbreviation.*
Newspaper Publishers' Association.

NPD *abbreviation.*
German *Nationaldemokratische Partei Deutschlands* National Democratic Party of Germany.

NPL *abbreviation.*
National Physical Laboratory.

n-p-n /ɛnpiːˈɛn/ *adjective.* Also **npn**, **NPN.** **M20.**
[from *n-*, *p-* in **N-TYPE**, **P-TYPE**, repr. the structure.]
ELECTRONICS. Designating a semiconductor device in which a *p*-type region is sandwiched between two *n*-type regions.

NPV *abbreviation.*
Net Present Value.

NR *abbreviation.*
Hist. North Riding.

nr. *abbreviation.*
Near.

NRA *abbreviation.*
1 National Recovery Administration. *US.*
2 National Rifle Association. *US.*
3 National Rivers Authority.

NRDC *abbreviation.*
National Research Development Corporation.

nritta /ˈ(ə)nrɪtə/ *noun.* **E20.**
[Sanskrit *nṛtta* dancing.]
A type of Indian dance with abstract patterns of movement and neutral facial expressions.

nritya /ˈ(ə)nrɪtjə/ *noun.* **L19.**
[Sanskrit *nṛtya* dance, mime.]
A type of Indian dance through which ideas or emotions are expressed.

NRSV *abbreviation.*
New Revised Standard Version (of the Bible).

NS *abbreviation*[1].
1 New series.
2 New Style.
3 Nova Scotia.

ns *abbreviation*[2].
Nanosecond(s).

N.S. *abbreviation.*
STATISTICS. Not significant.

n/s *abbreviation.*
Non-smoker.

NSA *abbreviation. US.*
National Security Agency.

NSAID /ˈɛnsɛd/ *abbreviation.*
PHARMACOLOGY. Non-steroidal anti-inflammatory drug.

NSB *abbreviation.*
National Savings Bank.

NSC *abbreviation.*
National Security Council.

NSF *abbreviation.*
National Science Foundation.

NSPCC *abbreviation.*
National Society for the Prevention of Cruelty to Children.

NSU *abbreviation.*
MEDICINE. Non-specific urethritis.

NSW *abbreviation.*
New South Wales.

NT *abbreviation.*
1 National Trust.
2 New Testament.
3 Northern Territory (of Australia).
4 No trumps.

n't *adverb* see **NOT** *adverb.*

Nth. *abbreviation.*
North.

NTP *abbreviation.*
SCIENCE. Normal temperature and pressure.

n-type /ˈɛntʌɪp/ *adjective.* **M20.**
[from **N**(**EGATIVE** *adjective* + **TYPE** *noun.*]
PHYSICS. Designating (a region in) a semiconductor in which electrical conduction is due chiefly to the movement of electrons. Opp. **P-TYPE.**

nu /njuː/ *noun.* **LME.**
[Greek, of Semitic origin (cf. Hebrew *nūn*).]
The thirteenth letter (N, ν) of the Greek alphabet.

nu /nuː/ *interjection.* **L19.**
[Yiddish from Russian, lit. 'well, well now'.]
Expr. impatient inquiry, surprise, emphasis, doubt, etc.

nuance /ˈnjuːɑːns/ *noun & verb.* **L18.**
[French, from *nuer* show cloudlike variations in colour, from *nue* cloud from popular Latin var. of Latin *nubes*: see **-ANCE.**]
▶**A** *noun.* A slight or subtle variation in or shade of meaning, expression, colour, etc. **L18.**

📖 A. WILSON Every such relationship had a hundred overtones, a thousand nuances that made it unique. E. H. GOMBRICH The rendering of the exact nuance of facial expression is notoriously difficult. Q A phenomenally rich and expressive voice, awesome in its . . mastery of emotional nuance.

▶**B** *verb trans.* Give a nuance or nuances to. **L19.**

nuancé /nɥɑ̃se/ *adjective.* **M20.**
[French, formed as prec.]
= next.

nuanced /ˈnjuːɑːnst/ *adjective.* **E20.**
[from **NUANCE** *noun, verb*: see **-ED**[2], **-ED**[1].]
Having or characterized by nuances.

📖 *Time* The artfully nuanced language of diplomacy. *Daedalus* How complex and nuanced are the . . issues surrounding research with human subjects.

nub /nʌb/ *noun*[1]. **L16.**
[Var. of **KNUB** *noun.*]
†**1** = **KNUB** *noun* 2. *rare.* **L16–M18.**
2 A knob, a small protuberance; a lump, as of coal; a knot or irregularity in fabric, a slub. **E18.**
3 The point or gist of a story or matter. **M19.**

📖 **3** P. HOWARD A remarkable gift . . of grasping the nub of what was going on.

nub /nʌb/ *verb*[1] *& noun*[2]. *arch. slang.* **L17.**
[Origin unkn.]
▶**A** *verb trans.* Infl. **-bb-**. Hang (a person), execute by hanging. **L17.**
nubbing-cheat the gallows (***trine to the nubbing-cheat***: see **TRINE** *verb*[1] 2).
▶**B** *noun.* The gallows. *rare.* **L17.**

†**nub** *verb*[2] see **KNUB** *verb.*

Nuba /ˈnuːbə/ *noun & adjective.* **E19.**
[from Latin *Nubae*: see **NUBIAN.**]
▶**A** *noun.* Pl. same, **-s.** A member of any of several peoples inhabiting southern Kordofan in Sudan. **E19.**
▶**B** *attrib.* or as *adjective.* Of or pertaining to any of these peoples. **E20.**

nubbin /ˈnʌbɪn/ *noun. US.* **L17.**
[Dim. of **NUB** *noun*[1].]
A stunted or imperfect ear of maize etc.; *transf. & fig.* a residual part, a stub, a stump.

📖 D. BAGLEY The lipstick was worn right down . . to a nubbin.

nubble /ˈnʌb(ə)l/ *noun.* **E19.**
[from **NUB** *noun*[1] + **-LE**[1]. Cf. **KNOBBLE** *noun*, **KNUBBLE** *noun.*]
A small knob or lump.

nubble *verb* see KNUBBLE *verb*.

nubbly /ˈnʌbli/ *adjective*. E19.
[from NUBBLE *noun* + -Y¹. Cf. KNOBBLY, KNUBBLY.]
1 Having numerous small protuberances; knobby, lumpy. E19.
2 Having the form of a small lump. M19.
3 Of a garment or fabric: rough-textured, having slubs. M20.

nubby /ˈnʌbi/ *adjective*. L19.
[from NUB *noun*¹ + -Y¹.]
= NUBBLY.

NUBE *abbreviation*.
National Union of Bank Employees.

nubecula /njuːˈbɛkjʊlə/ *noun*. Now *rare* or *obsolete*. Also **N-**. Pl. **-lae** /-liː/. L17.
[Latin, dim. of *nubes* cloud: see -CULE.]
1 MEDICINE. **a** A cloudy formation in urine. L17. ▸**b** = LEUCOMA. E18.
2 ASTRONOMY. (The name of) either of the Magellanic Clouds. M19.

nubia /ˈnjuːbɪə/ *noun*. M19.
[Irreg. from Latin *nubes* cloud.]
A woman's soft fleecy scarf for the head and neck.

Nubian /ˈnjuːbɪən/ *adjective & noun*. LME.
[Partly from medieval Latin *Nubianus*, from *Nubia* Nubia, from Latin *Nubae* Nubians from Greek *Noubai*; partly from *Nubia*: see below, -AN.]
► **A** *noun*. **1** (A descendant of) a native or inhabitant of Nubia, a region and former kingdom comprising southern Egypt and northern Sudan. LME.
†**2** A member of an Eastern Christian sect. Only in LME.
3 Any of several Sudanic languages spoken by the Nubians. E17.
4 A goat of a breed distinguished by a convex profile, large pendulous ears, short hair, and long legs, probably of N. African and Indian origin. L19.
► **B** *adjective*. Of or pertaining to Nubia, its people, or their languages. E17.

nubiferous /njuːˈbɪf(ə)rəs/ *adjective*. *rare*. M17.
[from Latin *nubifer*, from *nubes* cloud: see -FEROUS.]
Cloud-bearing.

nubilate /ˈnjuːbɪleɪt/ *verb trans*. Now *rare*. L17.
[Latin *nubilat-* pa. ppl stem of *nubilare* be or make cloudy, from *nubila* (neut. pl.), from *nubes* cloud: see -ATE³.]
Cloud, obscure, (*lit.* & *fig.*).

nubile /ˈnjuːbʌɪl/ *adjective*. M17.
[Latin *nubilis*, from *nubere* be married to (a man): see -ILE.]
1 Esp. of a girl or young woman: of an age or condition suitable for marriage; sexually mature. M17.
2 Of age: suitable for marriage. M17.
3 Of a girl or woman: sexually attractive. M20.

🕮 **1** E. FEINSTEIN As I was nubile at eleven, I attracted sexual attention. **3** D. LODGE A . . not altogether disagreeable experience to have a nubile young woman throw herself at him.

■ **nuˈbility** *noun* E19.

nubilous /ˈnjuːbɪləs/ *adjective*. Now *rare*. M16.
[from Latin *nubilosus* or *nubilus*, from *nubes* cloud: see -OUS, cf. -OSE¹.]
Cloudy, foggy, misty; *fig.* obscure, indefinite.

nubk *noun* var. of NEBBUK.

nubuck /ˈnjuːbʌk/ *noun*. L20.
[Origin uncertain: perh. from respelling of NEW *adjective* + BUCK *noun*¹.]
Cowhide leather which has been rubbed on the flesh side to give it a suede-like feel, used chiefly in the manufacture of shoes.

†**nucament** *noun*. *rare*. M17–E19.
[Latin = nutlike growth, from *nuc-*, *nux* nut: see -MENT.]
BOTANY. A catkin.

nucellus /njuːˈsɛləs/ *noun*. L19.
[mod. Latin, app. irreg. dim. of *nucleus*.]
BOTANY. The central part of an ovule, containing the embryo sac.
■ **nucellar** *adjective* of, pertaining to, or derived from the nucellus E20.

nucha /ˈnjuːkə/ *noun*. LME.
[medieval Latin = medulla oblongata, from Arab. *nukāʿ* spinal marrow, medulla.]
ANATOMY. The nape of the neck. Formerly also, the hindbrain and upper spinal cord.

nuchal /ˈnjuːk(ə)l/ *adjective & noun*. M19.
[from prec. + -AL¹.]
► **A** *adjective*. ANATOMY. Of or pertaining to the nucha or nape of the neck. M19.
nuchal ligament the thick elastic ligament supporting the back of the skull, esp. in quadrupeds.
► **B** *noun*. ZOOLOGY. The bony plate next to the nape of the neck in the carapace of a chelonian. M19.

nuci- /ˈnjuːsi/ *combining form* of Latin *nuc-*, *nux*: see -I-.
■ **nuˈciferous** *adjective* bearing nuts M17. **nuciform** *adjective* nut-shaped M19. **nuˈcivorous** *adjective* (*rare*) feeding on nuts E19.

nucleal /ˈnjuːklɪəl/ *adjective*. Now *rare* or *obsolete*. M19.
[from NUCLEUS + -AL¹.]
PHYSICS & CHEMISTRY. Pertaining to or acting as a nucleus.

nucleant /ˈnjuːklɪənt/ *adjective & noun*. M20.
[from NUCLEATE *verb* + -ANT¹.]
► **A** *adjective*. Forming a nucleus. *rare*. M20.
► **B** *noun*. A particle that initiates nucleation; = NUCLEUS *noun* 4b. M20.

nuclear /ˈnjuːklɪə/ *adjective & noun*. M19.
[from NUCLEUS *noun* + -AR¹. Cf. NUKE.]
► **A** *adjective*. **1 a** Chiefly BIOLOGY & ASTRONOMY. Having the character, position, or form of a nucleus; that is a nucleus. M19. ▸**b** Central, crucial; *spec.* constituting a linguistic nucleus. E20. ▸**c** PSYCHOANALYSIS. Central to the development of the sexual components of the ego; pertaining to or being the emotional nucleus of a neurosis, esp. the Oedipus complex. E20.
2 Of, pertaining to, or affecting a nucleus or nuclei, esp. cell nuclei or atomic nuclei; with or by (atomic) nuclei. L19. ▸**b** Concerned with the science of the atomic nucleus. M20.
3 Pertaining to, connected with, or using energy from the fission or fusion of atomic nuclei as a source of power or destructive force; producing or produced by atomic energy; possessing, involving, or using atomic weapons. Freq. opp. ***conventional***. M20.

🕮 **1** R. A. PROCTOR The nuclear parts of the sun are exceedingly dense. **2** *Biological Bulletin* The time relationships between nuclear and cytoplasmic division. N. V. SIDGWICK This element has been obtained as artificial product of nuclear bombardment. G. R. CHOPPIN Nuclear scattering is a more important factor for electrons. **b** A. H. COMPTON The use of the cyclotron was of epochal importance in nuclear physics. ***nuclear chemistry***, ***nuclear physicist***, etc. **3** *Times* As a guarantee of European nuclear retaliation against a nuclear attack a N.A.T.O deterrent would be highly credible. H. KISSINGER In the nuclear age we cannot be without dialogue with Moscow. *New York Times* The Navy's projected new nuclear submarine and missile. *New Statesman* A Socialist government should actively support a new nuclear freeze in Europe. **go nuclear** acquire nuclear power stations or weapons.

Special collocations: **nuclear atom** the atom regarded as having the charges of one sign surrounding a much smaller central cluster of those of the opposite sign. **nuclear battery** an electric battery that utilizes the separation of positive and negative charges accompanying radioactivity. **nuclear bomb**: deriving its destructive power from the release of nuclear energy. **nuclear club** the nations possessing nuclear weapons. **nuclear disarmament** the renunciation of nuclear weapons. **nuclear emulsion** a fine-grained photographic emulsion designed to record the tracks of subatomic particles in it. **nuclear family** SOCIOLOGY father, mother, and children, regarded as a basic social unit (freq. opp. ***extended family***). **nuclear fission** (*a*) BIOLOGY the division of a cell nucleus; (*b*) NUCLEAR PHYSICS = FISSION *noun* 3. **nuclear force** a force that acts between nucleons; now *spec.* the strong interaction. **nuclear fuel** = FUEL *noun* 4d. **nuclear fusion** (*a*) BIOLOGY the fusion of cell nuclei; (*b*) NUCLEAR PHYSICS = FUSION *noun* 3. **nuclear holocaust** (the envisaged result of) a nuclear war or accident, *esp.* one involving widespread destruction of life and the environment. **nuclear isomer** = ISOMER *noun* 2. **nuclear magnetic resonance** PHYSICS resonance in which the transition involved is that of nuclei between different quantum states in a magnetic field (used to investigate molecular structure etc.). ***nuclear*** MAGNETON. **nuclear medicine** the branch of medicine that deals with the use of radioactive substances in research, diagnosis, and treatment. **nuclear pile** = REACTOR 4. **nuclear power** (*a*) electric or motive power generated by a nuclear reactor; (*b*) a country possessing nuclear weapons. ***nuclear reactor***: see REACTOR 4. **nuclear sap** CYTOLOGY (now *rare* or *obsolete*) = NUCLEOPLASM. **nuclear umbrella** the supposed protection gained from alliance with a country possessing nuclear weapons. **nuclear war**, **nuclear warfare**: in which nuclear weapons are used. **nuclear waste** radioactive waste material resulting from the reprocessing of spent nuclear fuel. **nuclear winter** a period of extreme cold and darkness predicted to follow a nuclear war, caused by an atmospheric layer of smoke and dust particles shutting out the sun's rays.
► **B** *ellipt.* as *noun*. **1** A nuclear weapon; a nuclear-powered submarine. M20.
2 Nuclear power, esp. as an energy source. L20.
Comb.: **nuclear-free** *adjective* (of an area) free from nuclear weapons or nuclear power.
■ **nuclearism** *noun* belief in or advocacy of the possession of nuclear weapons M20. **nuclearist** *noun* a believer in or advocate of nuclearism; a nation possessing nuclear weapons: M20. **nuclearly** *adverb* in a nuclear manner; with nuclear weapons: M20. **nucleary** *adjective* (now *rare*) of the nature of a nucleus M19.

nuclearize /ˈnjuːklɪərʌɪz/ *verb trans*. Also **-ise**. M20.
[from prec. + -IZE.]
1 Supply or equip (a nation) with nuclear weapons. M20.
2 SOCIOLOGY. Make of the character of a nuclear family. *rare*. L20.
■ **nucleariˈzation** *noun* M20.

nuclease /ˈnjuːklɪeɪz/ *noun*. E20.
[from NUCLE(IC + -ASE.]
BIOCHEMISTRY. An enzyme which catalyses the hydrolysis of polynucleotides or oligonucleotides into smaller units.

nucleate /ˈnjuːklɪeɪt/ *noun*. E20.
[from NUCLE(IC + -ATE¹.]
BIOCHEMISTRY. A salt or ester of a nucleic acid.

nucleate /ˈnjuːklɪət/ *adjective*. M19.
[from NUCLEUS *noun* + -ATE². Cf. ENUCLEATE *adjective*.]
1 Having a nucleus; nucleated. M19.
2 Designating a manner of boiling in which streams of bubbles rise from specific sites (nuclei) on a hot surface in a liquid and are recondensed in the surrounding liquid. M20.

nucleate /ˈnjuːklɪeɪt/ *verb*. M19.
[from NUCLEUS *noun* + -ATE³. Cf. ENUCLEATE *verb*.]
1 *verb trans*. **a** Form into or bring together as a nucleus. M19. ▸**b** Form nuclei in; act as or provide a nucleus for the growth of (crystals, cracks, aggregates, etc.). M20.
2 *verb intrans*. Form a nucleus or nuclei; gather or collect about a nucleus or nuclei. L19.
■ **nucleˈation** *noun* the formation of nuclei, esp. (PHYSICAL CHEMISTRY) by the aggregation of molecules into a new phase (as in boiling, condensation, crystallization, etc.); formation at or into a nucleus: M19. **nucleator** *noun* a substance which provides nuclei, esp. for crystallization etc. E20.

nucleated /ˈnjuːklɪeɪtɪd/ *adjective*. M19.
[formed as NUCLEATE *adjective* + -ED².]
1 Chiefly BIOLOGY. Having a nucleus. M19.
2 Esp. of buildings in a village: clustered together. L19.

nuclei *noun pl.* see NUCLEUS *noun*.

nucleic /njuːˈkleɪɪk, -ˈkliːɪk, ˈnjuː-/ *adjective*. L19.
[from NUCLEUS *noun* + -IC.]
BIOCHEMISTRY. ***nucleic acid***, any of the long unbranched polynucleotides which carry genetic information in living cells (esp. in chromosomes and ribosomes) or are involved in the translation of this into the structure of proteins. Cf. DNA, RNA.

nuclein /ˈnjuːklɪɪn/ *noun*. *obsolete* exc. *Hist.* L19.
[from NUCLEUS *noun* + -IN¹.]
BIOCHEMISTRY. Chromatin; nucleoprotein in a cell nucleus.

nucleo- /ˈnjuːklɪəʊ/ *combining form* of NUCLEUS, NUCLEAR, NUCLEIC: see -O-.
■ **nucleoˈcapsid** *noun* (BIOLOGY) the capsid of a virus with the enclosed nucleic acid M20. **nucleochroˈnology** *noun* (ASTRONOMY) (*a*) a technique for dating stages in stellar nucleosynthesis by examining the relative abundances of nuclear species; (*b*) a series of nuclear species arranged in supposed chronological order of formation: L20. **nucleoˌcosmochroˈnology** *noun* (ASTRONOMY) (*a*) a technique for dating the evolutionary stages of the universe by examining the present distribution of isotopes; (*b*) a chronology so devised: M20. **nucleo-cytoˈplasmic** *adjective* (BIOLOGY) existing or taking place between, or relating to, the cell nucleus and the cytoplasm E20. **nucleoˈgenesis** *noun* the formation of nuclei; *spec.* = NUCLEOSYNTHESIS: M20. **nucleoˈhistone** *noun* (BIOCHEMISTRY) a nucleoprotein in which the protein component is a histone L19. **nucleoˈprotamine** *noun* (BIOCHEMISTRY) a nucleoprotein in which the protein component is a protamine E20. **nucleoˈsomal** *adjective* (BIOLOGY) of or pertaining to a nucleosome or nucleosomes L20. **nucleosome** *noun* (BIOLOGY) a structural unit of a eukaryotic chromosome, consisting of a length of DNA coiled around a core of histones L20. **nucleoˈsynthesis** *noun* (ASTRONOMY) the cosmic formation of atoms more complicated than the hydrogen atom M20. **nucleosynˈthetic** *adjective* of, pertaining to, or designating nucleosynthesis M20.

nucleoid *noun*¹ var. of NUCLOID.

nucleoid /ˈnjuːklɪɔɪd/ *adjective & noun*². M19.
[from NUCLEUS *noun* + -OID.]
► **A** *adjective*. Like a nucleus in form or appearance. M19.
► **B** *noun*. †**1** CYTOLOGY. A fibrous or granular substance seen in red blood cells under certain conditions. Only in E20.
2 MICROBIOLOGY. The region of a bacterium or virus, or of a mitochondrion or chloroplast, containing the genetic material. M20.

nucleolar /njuːklɪˈəʊlə/ *adjective*. M19.
[from NUCLEOLUS + -AR¹.]
BIOLOGY. Of the nature of or pertaining to a nucleolus.
nucleolar organizer a region on a chromosome with which a nucleolus is typically associated.

nucleoli *noun* pl. of NUCLEOLUS.

nucleolinus /ˌnjuːklɪə(ʊ)ˈlʌɪnəs/ *noun*. Pl. **-ni** /-nʌɪ, -niː/. M19.
[mod. Latin, from NUCLEOLUS: cf. -INE⁴.]
BIOLOGY. A minute body visible within a nucleolus, *esp.* one associated with a nucleolar organizer.

nucleolus /njuːklɪˈəʊləs/ *noun*. Pl. **-li** /-lʌɪ/. M19.
[Late Latin, dim. of NUCLEUS *noun*.]
BIOLOGY. A minute rounded body within the nucleus of a cell, associated with RNA synthesis. Also occas., a paranucleus.
■ **ˈnucleolated** *adjective* having a nucleolus M19. **ˈnucleole** *noun* (now *rare* or *obsolete*) = NUCLEOLUS M19. **ˌnucleoloˈnema** *noun*,

pl. **-mas**, **-mata** /-mətə/, CYTOLOGY a threadlike aggregation of particles in a nucleolus resembling ribosomes M20.

nucleon /ˈnjuːklɪɒn/ *noun.* Also †**nuclon**. E20.
[from NUCLEUS *noun* + -ON.]
NUCLEAR PHYSICS. †**1** A proton. Only in E20.
2 A particle of which the proton and the neutron are regarded as different states. M20.
■ **nucleˈonic** *adjective* of or pertaining to nucleons or nucleonics M20.

nucleonics /njuːklɪˈɒnɪks/ *noun.* M20.
[from prec. after *electronics*.]
The branch of science and technology that deals with nucleons and the atomic nucleus, esp. with the applications of nuclear energy.

nucleophile /ˈnjuːklɪə(ʊ)fʌɪl/ *noun.* M20.
[Back-form. from next: see -PHILE.]
CHEMISTRY. A nucleophilic substance or molecule.

nucleophilic /ˌnjuːklɪə(ʊ)ˈfɪlɪk/ *adjective.* M20.
[from NUCLEO- + -PHILIC: cf. ELECTROPHILIC.]
CHEMISTRY. **1** Having an affinity for atomic nuclei; tending to donate electrons or react at relatively electron-poor sites. M20.
2 Of a reaction: brought about by a nucleophilic reagent. M20.
■ **nucleophilically** *adverb* L20. **nucleophilicity** /-fɪˈlɪsɪti/ *noun* nucleophilic character M20.

nucleoplasm /ˈnjuːklɪə(ʊ)plaz(ə)m/ *noun.* L19.
[from NUCLEO- + PROTO)PLASM.]
BIOLOGY. The substance of a cell nucleus or nucleoid, *esp.* that not forming part of a nucleolus; karyoplasm.
■ **nucleoˈplasmic** *adjective* L19.

nucleoprotein /ˌnjuːklɪə(ʊ)ˈprəʊtiːn/ *noun.* E20.
[from NUCLEO- + PROTEIN.]
BIOCHEMISTRY. A substance consisting of a protein combined with a nucleic acid.

nucleoside /ˈnjuːklɪəsʌɪd/ *noun.* E20.
[from NUCLEO- + GLYCO)SIDE.]
BIOCHEMISTRY. A compound in which a sugar (usu. ribose or deoxyribose) is linked to a purine or pyrimidine base to form a glycoside; *spec.* such a compound derived from a nucleic acid by hydrolysis.
■ **nucleoˈsidase** *noun* an enzyme which catalyses the hydrolysis of a nucleoside into its constituent base and sugar, or catalyses the reaction between a nucleoside and phosphate to yield a base and a sugar phosphate E20.

nucleotide /ˈnjuːklɪətʌɪd/ *noun.* E20.
[from NUCLEO- + euphonic *-t-* + -IDE.]
BIOCHEMISTRY. A compound in which a phosphate group is linked to the sugar of a nucleoside; *spec.* such a compound obtained by partial hydrolysis of a nucleic acid (polynucleotide).
■ **nucleoˈtidase** *noun* an enzyme which catalyses the hydrolysis of a nucleotide to a nucleoside and phosphate E20.

nucleus /ˈnjuːklɪəs/ *noun & verb.* E18.
[Latin = nut, kernel, inner part, var. of *nuculeus*, formed as NUCULE.]
▶ **A** *noun.* Pl. **-clei** /-klɪʌɪ/, **-cleuses**.
1 ASTRONOMY. **a** The dense core of the head of a comet. E18. ▸**b** A dense, usu. bright, central part in a galaxy or nebula. L18.
†**2** Each of a supposed series of concentric layers within the earth. Only in E18.
3 BOTANY. The kernel of a nut or seed; the nucellus of an ovule. Also, the hilum of a starch granule. Now *rare.* E18.
4 The central part or thing around which others are grouped or collected; the centre or kernel of an aggregate or mass; an initial part or collection of things to which others may be added. M18. ▸**b** A small particle in a fluid on which crystals, droplets, or bubbles can form; a particle that initiates nucleation. M19. ▸**c** A small colony of bees, including a queen, esp. as used to found a new colony. L19.
5 ANATOMY. A discrete collection of neurones of similar type in the central nervous system. Chiefly with specifying word. E19.
6 ARCHAEOLOGY. A stone from which flakes have been removed to make implements; a core. M19.
7 BIOLOGY. A cell organelle present in most living cells (though not those of bacteria), usu. as a single rounded structure bounded (except when undergoing division) by a double membrane within which lie the chromosomes, and functioning as a store of genetic information and as the director of metabolic and synthetic activity in the cell. Also occas., a nucleoid. Cf. EUKARYOTE, PROKARYOTE. M19.
8 CHEMISTRY. A ring structure or other arrangement of atoms which is characteristic of a group of compounds. M19.
9 PHYSICS. The positively charged central core of an atom, comprising most of its mass but occupying only a very small part of its volume and composed of protons and (usu.) neutrons. E20.
10 LINGUISTICS. **a** The most prominent syllable or syllables in a word or utterance. E20. ▸**b** The main or central word or words in a derivative, phrase, or sentence. M20.

> 🕮 **4** J. H. BENNET A very fair collection of modern books . . as the nucleus of a library. *Christian Aid News* Those units were eventually to form the nucleus of the new Sudan People's Liberation Army. JAN MORRIS The tight, tough island quarter . . the original nucleus of the city. *attrib.*: *Westminster Gazette* They will have nucleus crew of two-fifths of their war complement. **5** *caudate nucleus*, *lenticular nucleus*, *olivary nucleus*, etc.

▶ **B** *verb trans.* Make into or provide with a nucleus, concentrate (something). *rare.* E19.

nuclide /ˈnjuːklʌɪd/ *noun.* M20.
[from NUCLEUS *noun* + *-ide* (from Greek *eidos* form, kind).]
NUCLEAR PHYSICS. A distinct kind of atom or nucleus, as defined by the numbers of protons and neutrons in the nucleus. Cf. ISOTOPE 1.
mirror nuclide: see MIRROR *noun*.
■ **nuclidic** /-ˈklɪdɪk/ *adjective* M20.

nucloid /ˈnjuːklɔɪd/ *noun.* *Nautical slang.* Also **-cleoid** /-klɪɔɪd/. E20.
[from NUCL(EUS + -OID.]
A ship of the reserve fleet with a skeleton crew.

†**nuclon** *noun* var. of NUCLEON.

nuculanium /njuːkjʊˈleɪnɪəm/ *noun.* Now *rare* or *obsolete.* E19.
[mod. Latin, irreg. formed as NUCULE: see -IUM.]
BOTANY. Orig., a fleshy fruit formed of several distinct nutlets. Later, a fleshy stony-seeded fruit (e.g. a grape) formed from a superior ovary.

nucule /ˈnjuːkjuːl/ *noun.* E19.
[Latin *nucula* dim. of *nuc-*, *nux* nut: see -ULE.]
BOTANY. **1** Each of the nutlets or hard seeds of a fleshy fruit formed of several distinct nutlets. Now *rare.* E19.
2 The female reproductive structure of a charophyte (stonewort). Cf. GLOBULE 1b. M19.

nud /nʌd/ *verb trans. & intrans. rare* (long *dial.*). Infl. **-dd-**. L17.
[Origin unkn. Cf. next.]
Press or butt (a person or thing) with the head.

nuddle /ˈnʌd(ə)l/ *verb.* Now *dial.* M17.
[Origin unkn.: see -LE[3]. Cf. prec., NUZZLE *verb*[1].]
1 *verb intrans.* **a** Push with the nose; press close, nestle. M17. ▸**b** Move with the head stooped or close to the ground. M17.
2 *verb trans.* †**a** Beat, pummel. *rare.* Only in M17. ▸**b** Squeeze, press; nuzzle. L19.

nuddy /ˈnʌdi/ *noun. slang.* M20.
[Prob. from NUDE *noun* + -Y[6].]
= NUDE *noun* 2b. Chiefly in ***in the nuddy***.

nude /njuːd/ *adjective & noun.* LME.
[Latin *nudus* bare, naked.]
▶ **A** *adjective.* †**1** Mere, plain; open, explicit. LME–M17.
2 LAW. Of a statement, promise, etc.: not formally attested or recorded. Of an executor etc.: receiving no profit from supervising a transaction. Now usu. in ***nude contract***, ***nude pact*** below. L15.
3 a Of a person or (part of) the body: naked, unclothed, bare. M19. ▸**b** Involving or portraying a naked or scantily clad person or persons; performed without clothing. L19. ▸**c** Of hosiery etc.: flesh-coloured. E20.
4 Of a thing: lacking natural covering, foliage, etc.; lacking furniture or decoration, unadorned. M19.
5 MEDICINE. Of a mouse: homozygous for a mutant gene which causes apparent hairlessness and (usu.) immunosuppression due to gross underdevelopment of the thymus gland. M20.

> 🕮 **2** ***nude contract***, ***nude pact***: lacking a consideration and therefore void unless made by deed. **3a** J. HELLER A nude ridiculous man with a blushing scar. **b** *Daily Telegraph* An Italian magazine published . . nude photographs of her. *Holiday Which?* Nude bathing is best kept to . . designated beaches.

▶ **B** *noun.* **1** A painting, sculpture, photograph, or other representation of a nude human figure; such a figure. Also, a nude person. E18.
2 a *The* undraped human figure; *the* representation of this as a genre in art. M18. ▸**b** The condition of being unclothed. Chiefly in ***in the nude***. M19.
3 MEDICINE. A nude mouse. M20.

> 🕮 **1** *Observer* Our notorious nude . . was towed across the . . gallery. *New Statesman* Red paint marks . . to indicate a vague . . intention to paint a female nude. **2a** P. ROSE Innocence of the female nude and . . shock when confronted with one. **b** A. HIGGINS I . . stripped and ran round in the nude.

■ **nudely** *adverb* (*rare*) †(*a*) simply, plainly; (*b*) without clothing: E17. **nudeness** *noun* L19.

nude /njuːd/ *verb trans. rare.* M16.
[Latin *nudare*, or from the adjective.]
†**1** Denude or deprive (a person) *of* something. Only in M16.
2 Strip, unclothe, (a person). M19.

nudge /nʌdʒ/ *verb & noun.* L17.
[Perh. rel. to Norwegian dial. *nugga*, *nyggja* push, rub, and in much earlier use.]
▶ **A** *verb.* **1** *verb trans.* Touch or prod (a person) gently, esp. with the elbow, to attract attention etc.; push gently or gradually. L17. ▸**b** *fig.* Coax or pressurize gently *into* something; give a gentle reminder to. Also, approach, come near to, (freq. as ***nudging*** *ppl adjective*). M19.
2 *verb intrans.* Give a gentle push or prod; *fig.* move *up*, *ahead*, etc., slightly or by gradual pushing. E19.

> 🕮 **1** L. R. BANKS I opened my mouth to say yes but Connie nudged me. F. RAPHAEL Pamela and Miriam were nudging the trolley over . . the carpet. **b** A. MACVICAR I was big, nudging six feet two. W. RAEPER He talked . . to his father who tried to nudge him into the ministry. **2** A. T. ELLIS Younger . . they would have nudged, giggled and snorted. *Daily Telegraph* Interest rates in the London money market nudged up about 1/16 per cent.

▶ **B** *noun.* An act of nudging; a gentle push or prod, esp. with the elbow; *fig.* a gentle reminder. M19.

> 🕮 L. HUDSON The poet . . relies on nudges and hints to control . . his reader. **nudge, nudge, wink, wink** (*a*) *interjection & adverb* used to imply a sexual innuendo in the preceding phr. or clause; (*b*) (with hyphens) sexually suggestive.

■ **nudger** *noun* (*a*) a person who nudges; (*b*) *dial.* a bowler hat: E20.

nudibranch /ˈnjuːdɪbraŋk/ *noun & adjective.* M19.
[from next.]
ZOOLOGY. ▶**A** *noun.* A marine gastropod mollusc of the order Nudibranchia, freq. brightly coloured and having exposed gills and a vestigial shell which is usu. discarded during development; a sea-slug. M19.
▶ **B** *adjective.* = NUDIBRANCHIATE *adjective.* M19.

nudibranchiate /njuːdɪˈbraŋkɪət/ *adjective & noun.* M19.
[from mod. Latin *Nudibranchia* (see below), formed as NUDE *adjective & noun* + BRANCHIATE: see -ATE[2].]
ZOOLOGY. ▶**A** *adjective.* Having naked gills; *spec.* of or pertaining to the gastropod order Nudibranchia. M19.
▶ **B** *noun.* = NUDIBRANCH *noun.* L19.

nudie /ˈnjuːdi/ *noun. colloq.* M20.
[from NUDE *adjective & noun* + -IE.]
▶ **A** *noun.* A nude person; a film, photograph, magazine, etc., featuring nudity. M20.
▶ **B** *adjective.* = NUDE *adjective* 3b. M20.

nudism /ˈnjuːdɪz(ə)m/ *noun.* E20.
[from NUDE *adjective & noun* + -ISM.]
The practice of going unclothed; this as a cult; naturism.

nudist /ˈnjuːdɪst/ *noun & adjective.* E20.
[formed as prec. + -IST.]
▶ **A** *noun.* A person who advocates or practises nudism; a naturist. E20.
▶ **B** *attrib.* or as *adjective.* Of or pertaining to nudists or nudism. E20.

> 🕮 *attrib.*: G. MITCHELL There is a nudist colony on the island.

nudity /ˈnjuːdɪti/ *noun.* E17.
[French *nudité* or late Latin *nuditas*, from NUDE *adjective & noun*: see -ITY.]
1 The state or condition of being nude; appearance in the nude; nakedness. E17.
2 A nude figure, esp. in art. Now *rare.* M17.
†**3** In *pl.* The genitals when exposed. L17–M18.

> 🕮 **1** H. JAMES The room had a certain vulgar nudity, the bed and the window were curtainless. M. CICCONE I loved the script . . but I couldn't deal with all the nudity in it.

nudnik /ˈnʊdnɪk/ *noun. US slang.* Also **-ick**. M20.
[Yiddish, from Russian *nudnyĭ* tedious, boring: see -NIK.]
A pestering, nagging, or irritating person; a bore.

nuée ardente /nɥe ardɑ̃t/ *noun phr.* Pl. **-s -s** (pronounced same). E20.
[French, lit. 'burning cloud'.]
GEOLOGY. A hot dense cloud of ash and fragmented lava suspended in a mass of gas, typically ejected from the side of the dome of certain volcanoes and flowing downhill like an avalanche.

Nuer /ˈnuːə/ *noun & adjective.* M19.
[Dinka.]
▶ **A** *noun.* Pl. same, **-s**. A member of an African people of SE Sudan and Ethiopia; the Nilotic language of this people. M19.
▶ **B** *attrib.* or as *adjective.* Of or pertaining to the Nuer or their language. L19.

nuff /nʌf/ *adjective, noun, & adverb. non-standard.* Also **'nuff**. M19.
[Repr. pronunc. of 'NOUGH.]
Enough. Chiefly in ***nuff said***, ***sure nuff*** or (esp. *US Black English*) ***sho' nuff***.

nuffin /ˈnʌfɪn/ *pronoun, noun, & adverb. non-standard.* Also **-ffin'**; **-ffink** /-fɪŋk/. L19.
[Repr. a pronunc.]
Nothing.

nug /nʌɡ/ *noun. dial.* M19.
[Origin unkn.]
A lump, a piece, a rough mass.

nugacious /njuːˈɡeɪʃəs, nuː-/ *adjective.* Now *rare.* M17.
[from Latin *nugac-, -ax* + -OUS: see -ACIOUS.]
Trivial, trifling, unimportant.

nugacity /njuːˈɡasɪti, nuː-/ *noun.* L16.
[Late Latin *nugacitas*, formed as prec.: see -ACITY.]
1 Triviality, frivolity. L16.
2 A trivial or frivolous thing or idea. M17.

nugae /ˈnjuːdʒiː, ˈnuːɡʌɪ/ *noun pl.* E18.
[Latin.]
Trifles. Chiefly in ***nugae difficiles*** /ˈdɪfɪkɪleɪz/, PHILOSOPHY matters of trifling importance occupying a disproportionate amount of time owing to their difficulty.

nugation /njuːˈɡeɪʃ(ə)n, nuː-/ *noun.* Long *rare.* LME.
[Latin *nugatio(n-)*, from *nugat-*: see next, -ATION.]
Triviality, trifling; a trivial act, a trifle.

nugatory /ˈnjuːɡət(ə)ri, ˈnuː-/ *adjective.* E17.
[Latin *nugatorius*, from *nugat-* pa. ppl stem of *nugari* trifle, from NUGAE jests, trifles: see -ORY².]
1 Trifling, of no value or importance, worthless. E17.
2 Not valid, inoperative; useless, futile. E17.

🕮 **1** A. BROOKNER She could feel her contentment ebbing away, felt it . . to be nugatory, laughable. **2** W. E. H. LECKY The law . . was evaded and made almost nugatory.

■ **nuga'toriness** *noun* M19.

nuggar /ˈnʌɡə/ *noun.* L19.
[Prob. from Arab. *nukur* pl. of *nakīra* nuggar.]
A type of large broad cargo boat used on the upper Nile.

nugget /ˈnʌɡɪt/ *noun & verb.* M19.
[App. dim. of NUG: see -ET¹.]
▶ **A** *noun.* **1** A lump of gold or other metal as found in the earth; *gen.* a lump of anything; *transf.* a small and valuable (esp. abstract) thing concealed in a larger mass. M19.
2 A small compact stocky animal or person; a runt; an unbranded calf. *Austral. slang.* M19.

🕮 **1** *Sunday Times* Hyde's book . . has nuggets of information.

▶ **B** *verb. Austral.*
1 *verb trans. & intrans.* Search for or obtain (nuggets of gold) close to the earth's surface. M19.
2 *verb trans.* Steal (an unbranded calf). L19.
■ **nuggety, -tty** *adjectives* having the form of nuggets; rich in nuggets; *Austral. & NZ* stocky, thickset, compact: M19.

NUGMW *abbreviation.*
National Union of General and Municipal Workers.

nuisance /ˈnjuːs(ə)ns/ *noun.* LME.
[Old & mod. French (now arch.) = hurt, from *nuis-* stem of *nuire* injure from Latin *nocere*: see -ANCE.]
1 Injury, hurt, harm. *arch.* LME.
2 Something harmful or offensive to the public or a member of it and for which there is a legal remedy. LME.
3 Any person or thing causing annoyance, inconvenience, or trouble; an irksome situation or circumstance, a source of irritation. M17.

🕮 **2** *Law Times* Repair the drain so as to abate the nuisance complained of. **3** V. WOOLF The pigeons were a nuisance . . making a mess on the steps. R. K. NARAYAN It'll be a nuisance to maintain the garden. *Lancaster Guardian* Potential nuisances, such as dust, noise and increased traffic.

Comb. & phrases: **nuisance ground** *Canad.* a rubbish dump; **nuisance raid** a bombing attack intended only to inconvenience or disrupt the enemy; **nuisance value** the value or importance of a person or thing arising from the capacity to be a nuisance; PUBLIC ***nuisance***.
■ **nuisancey, -cy** *adjectives* annoying, irritating L20.

nuit blanche /nɥi blɑ̃ʃ/ *noun phr.* Pl. ***-s -s*** (pronounced same). M19.
[French, lit. 'white night'.]
A sleepless night.

Nuits St Georges /ˌnwiː sã ˈʒɔːʒ/ *noun phr.* M20.
[The name of the capital town of the Côte de Nuits, in the department of Côte d'Or, France.]
A red wine of Burgundy, from the district of Nuits St Georges.
¶ Until 1892 the town was called *Nuits*. In 1892 the town's most famous vineyard was commemorated in the name of the town, which became *Nuits St Georges*.

NUJ *abbreviation.*
National Union of Journalists.

Nujol /ˈnjuːdʒɒl/ *noun.* E20.
[Origin uncertain: perh. from *New J(ersey* location of original manufacturing company + Latin *oleum* oil.]
(Proprietary name for) a paraffin oil used as an emulsifying agent in pharmacy and for making mulls in infrared spectroscopy.

nuke /njuːk/ *noun & verb. colloq.* M20.
[Abbreviation of NUCLEAR *noun*.]
▶ **A** *noun.* A nuclear bomb, weapon, etc.; a nuclear power station. M20.

🕮 T. O'BRIEN I suddenly didn't give a damn about fallout or nukes.

▶ **B** *verb trans.* **1** Attack or destroy with a nuclear weapon or weapons. M20.
2 = MICROWAVE *verb* 1. *US slang.* L20.

🕮 **1** M. AMIS Don't wait for the war to escalate. Nuke them, right off.

null /nʌl/ *adjective & noun.* LME.
[Old & mod. French *nul(le)* or Latin *nullus*, from *ne* not + *ullus* any, from *unus* one.]
▶ **A** *adjective.* **1** Non-existent, amounting to nothing. Orig. SCOTS LAW. LME.
2 Of no legal or binding force; void, invalid. Freq. in ***null and void***. M16.
3 a Of no value or importance; insignificant, ineffective. L18. ▸**b** Devoid of character, expression, or distinctive personality. M19.
4 Chiefly MATH. Associated with, producing, or having the value zero; designating or pertaining to a point or region in which no effect or force occurs or in which effects or forces cancel each other out. E19. ▸**b** MATH. & LOGIC. (Of a class or set) having no members; (of a propositional function or relation) not applying in any case, having the null class as its range. E20. ▸**c** PHYSICS. Existing between or joining points in space–time between which the interval is zero. E20. ▸**d** ELECTRICITY & RADIO. Having no signal present or detectable. E20.

🕮 **1** J. PINKERTON Its influence on that element was absolutely null. **2** A. THWAITE His appointment had been pronounced null and void. **3a** T. R. MALTHUS We take . . pains to weaken and render null the ties of nature.

Special collocations: **null cone** = ***light cone*** s.v. LIGHT *noun*. **null hypothesis** in a statistical test, the hypothesis that there is no significant difference between specified populations (any apparent difference being due to sampling or experimental error). **null space** MATH. a space composed of all quantities that are transformed into zero by some given transformation.
▶ **B** *noun.* **1** A nought, a zero. E17.
2 CRYPTOGRAPHY. A meaningless letter or symbol used to impede decipherment. L17.
3 ELECTRICITY & RADIO. A condition of no signal; a direction in which no radiation is detected or emitted. Freq. *attrib.* E20.
■ **nullness** *noun* M20.

null /nʌl/ *verb trans.* M16.
[from the adjective after ANNUL, perh. after medieval Latin *nullare*, French †*nuller*.]
1 Annul, cancel, make void. Also foll. by *out*. M16.
†**2** Reduce to nothing; destroy or efface completely. M17–E18.
■ **nullable** *adjective* (*rare*) E18.

nulla /ˈnʌlə/ *noun. Austral.* Also **-ah**. L19.
[Abbreviation.]
= NULLA-NULLA.

nulla bona /nʌlə ˈbəʊnə/ *noun phr.* E19.
[Latin = no goods.]
The return made by a sheriff upon an execution when the party has no goods to be distrained.

nullah /ˈnʌlə/ *noun*¹. Also **nala** /ˈnɑːlə/. L18.
[Hindi *nālā*.]
In the Indian subcontinent, a deep ditch or (esp. dry) river-bed.

nullah *noun*² var. of NULLA.

nulla-nulla /ˈnʌlənʌlə/ *noun. Austral.* Also **nullah-nullah** & other vars. L18.
[Aboriginal.]
A hardwood club used as a weapon by Aborigines.

nulli- /ˈnʌli/ *combining form.*
[Latin, from *nullus* no, none: see -I-.]
Forming chiefly scientific words with the sense 'having no —'.
■ **nullipore** *noun* (BOTANY) any of various red algae which secrete a crust of calcium carbonate M19. **nulliverse** *noun* (*rare*) a world without any unifying principle or plan M19.

nullibiety /nʌlɪˈbʌɪəti/ *noun. rare.* M17.
[from Latin *nullibi* nowhere + euphonic *e* + -TY¹.]
The condition of existing nowhere.
■ Also **nullibicity** *noun* E19.

nullibist /ˈnʌlɪbɪst/ *noun.* Now *rare* or *obsolete.* M17.
[formed as prec. + -IST.]
A person who affirms that a spirit or incorporeal being exists nowhere in the physical world.

nullification /ˌnʌlɪfɪˈkeɪʃ(ə)n/ *noun.* M17.
[from NULLIFY: see -FICATION.]
†**1** Reduction to nothing. *rare.* Only in M17.
2 The action of making null or of no effect; *spec.* (US HISTORY) the refusal of a State legislature to allow a federal law to be enforced within the State; an instance of this. L18.
■ **nullificationist**, ˈ**nullificator** *nouns* (US HISTORY) an advocate or supporter of nullification M19.

nullifidian /nʌlɪˈfɪdɪən/ *noun & adjective.* M16.
[from medieval Latin *nullifidius*, formed as NULLI- + *fides* faith: see -AN, -IAN.]
▶ **A** *noun.* **1** A person having no faith or religion, an atheist. M16.
2 *gen.* A disbeliever (*in* something), a sceptic. M17.
▶ **B** *adjective.* Having no faith or belief. M17.

nullify /ˈnʌlɪfʌɪ/ *verb trans.* L16.
[from NULL *adjective* + -I- + -FY.]
1 Make legally null and void; annul, invalidate. L16.
2 Make of no value or use; cancel out. E17.

🕮 **1** *Sanity* A long line of referenda had nullified . . the island's constitution. **2** *Royal Air Force Journal* Wet clay and exposed conditions tend to nullify the advantages of . . greater sun heat.

■ **nullifier** *noun* a person who nullifies something; *spec.* (US HISTORY) an advocate of the right of a State to annul within its own boundaries a federal law: M19.

nulling /ˈnʌlɪŋ/ *noun.* M19.
[Alt.]
= KNURLING; *esp.* knurled work in wood-carving.

nullipara /nʌˈlɪp(ə)rə/ *noun.* L19.
[mod. Latin, formed as NULLI- + *-para* fem. of *-parus*: see -PAROUS.]
An adult female who has never given birth to a child, or *spec.* to a child capable of survival beyond birth.
■ **nulliˈparity** *noun* L19. **nulliparous** *adjective* that has not borne a child M19.

nulliplex /ˈnʌlɪplɛks/ *adjective.* E20.
[from NULLI- + *-plex* as in *duplex, simplex*, etc.]
GENETICS. Of a polyploid individual: having the dominant allele of a particular gene not represented (i.e., usu., homozygous for the recessive allele).

nulli secundus /ˌnʌlɪ sɪˈkʌndəs/ *adjectival phr.* Also ***nulli secundum*** /ˌnʌlɪ sɪˈkʌndəm/. M19.
[Latin.]
Second to none.

nullisomic /nʌlɪˈsəʊmɪk/ *adjective & noun.* M20.
[from NULLI- + *-somic* as in *trisomic, monosomic*, etc.]
GENETICS. ▶ **A** *adjective.* Of the nature of or having a diploid chromosome complement in which a pair, or more than one pair, of homologous chromosomes is lacking. M20.
▶ **B** *noun.* A nullisomic individual or variety. M20.
■ ˈ**nullisome** *noun* an absent chromosome pair; a nullisomic individual: M20. ˈ**nullisomy** *noun* nullisomic character or condition M20.

nullity /ˈnʌlɪti/ *noun.* M16.
[French *nullité* or medieval Latin *nullitas*, from Latin *nullus* no, none: see -ITY.]
1 The fact of being null and void; invalidity, esp. of marriage; an instance of this; a fact or circumstance causing invalidity. M16. ▸**b** An act or thing which is null or invalid. E17.
2 The condition of being non-existent; nothingness. L16.
3 A mere nothing; a nonentity. L16.
4 MATH. The number of columns of a matrix minus its rank; the dimension of the null space of a matrix or linear transformation (equal to the dimension of its domain minus that of its range). L19.

nullo /ˈnʌləʊ/ *noun.* Pl. **-os**. L16.
[Italian from Latin *nullus*: see NULL *adjective & noun*.]
1 A nought, a zero. *obsolete* exc. TYPOGRAPHY. L16.
2 *sing.* & in *pl.* (treated as *sing.*). CARDS. A type of bridge or a contract in which the object is to lose rather than gain tricks or in which tricks gained count against a player. L19.

nully /ˈnʌli/ *noun. slang.* L20.
[App. from NULL *adjective* + -Y⁶.]
A fool, a stupid or insignificant person.

NUM *abbreviation.*
National Union of Mineworkers.

num /nʌm/ *noun & interjection.* Also redupl. **num-num**. L19.
[Var. of YUM. Cf. NUMMY.]
(A cry or noise) expr. pleasure from eating or at the prospect of eating.

†**num** *verb pa. pple* of NIM *verb*.

Num. *abbreviation.*
Numbers (in the Bible).

numb /nʌm/ *adjective.* LME.
[from *num* pa. pple of NIM *verb*. For parasitic *b* cf. *thumb*. Cf. BENUMB.]
1 Deprived of feeling or the power of movement, esp. through extreme cold; incapable of sensation (*lit. & fig.*); (of a quality etc.) resulting from or characteristic of such deprivation. LME.

†**2** Causing numbness. *rare* (Shakes.). Only in **L16**.

> 1 A. PATON His feet were cold and numb. P. G. WODEHOUSE Steve's faculties were rapidly becoming numb. S. KITZINGER She may be numb with shock. **2** SHAKES. *Rich. III* He . . did give himself, All thin and naked, to the numb cold night.

Special collocations & comb.: **numb fish** the electric ray or torpedo. **numb hand** *arch. slang* an inexpert and clumsy person. **numbhead** *US colloq.* [after *numskull*] a numskull, a blockhead. **numbheaded** *adjective* resembling a numskull, blockheaded. †**numb palsy** paralysis.

■ **numbly** *adverb* **L16**. **numbness** *noun* **L16**. **numby** *adjective* (*rare*) numbed; somewhat numb: **E17**.

numb /nʌm/ *verb trans.* **L16**.
[from prec., or back-form. from NUMBED *adjective*.]
Make numb.

> R. GRAVES Has the chill night numbed you? M. BINCHY A whiskey-flavoured piece of cotton wool on the gum to numb the pain. *Listener* Violence has . . numbed viewers into anaesthetised . . voyeurs.

■ **numbingly** *adverb* in a numbing manner **M18**.

numbat /ˈnʌmbat/ *noun.* **E20**.
[Aboriginal.]
A small rare termite-eating marsupial, *Myrmecobius fasciatus*, of SW Australia, having red-brown fur with white bars on the face and rump. Also called ***banded anteater***.

numbed /nʌmd/ *adjective.* **M16**.
[from NUMB *adjective* + -ED[1]. Cf. NUMB *verb*.]
That has been numbed.

> W. JONES To warm the traveller, numb'd with winter's cold. H. E. MANNING Anxiously chafing . . numbed limbs to life. DENNIS POTTER Shocked, numbed, Eileen closed her eyes.

■ **numbedness** *noun* (long *rare* or *obsolete*) **E17**.

number /ˈnʌmbə/ *noun.* **ME**.
[Anglo-Norman *numbre*, Old & mod. French *nombre* from Latin *numerus*.]
► **I 1** The precise sum or aggregate *of*; a sum or aggregate of individuals of a specified kind. **ME**. ▸**b** In *pl.* (treated as *sing.*) & (*rare*) †*sing.* (**N-**.) A book of the Old Testament and Hebrew Scriptures, containing a census of the Israelites. **ME**.

2 An abstract entity representing a quantity, used to express how many things are being referred to, or how much there is of some thing or property; an arithmetical value corresponding to a particular quantity of something. Also, an analogous entity or value used in mathematical operations without reference to actual things. **ME**. ▸**b** A word, symbol, figure, or group of these, representing graphically an arithmetical unit; a numeral. Also, a total, value, etc., expressed in figures, a statistic (usu. in *pl.*). **ME**. ▸**c** In *pl.* An illegal form of gambling in which bets are taken on the occurrence of numbers in a lottery or in the financial columns of a newspaper. Freq. in ***play the numbers***. Also ***numbers game***, ***numbers racket***. *N. Amer. slang.* **L19**.

3 In *pl.* Arithmetic. Also *sing.* (*Austral. & NZ*), elementary arithmetic at primary school level. **ME**.

4 An arithmetical value showing position in a series, esp. for identification, reference, etc., (freq. preceding a numeral, as ***number five***, ***number thirty-nine***, etc.); *spec.* (*a*) that assigned to a particular telephone or group of telephones and used in making connections to it (also ***phone number***, ***telephone number***); (*b*) the series of letters and figures assigned to a motor vehicle on registration (also ***registration number***). **ME**.

5 A person or thing having a place in a series; *spec.* (*a*) a single part or issue of a magazine etc.; (*b*) any of a collection of songs or poems; (*c*) an item in a programme of musical entertainment; a song, a tune; (*d*) *colloq.* a person, esp. a girl or young woman, or thing regarded appreciatively or tolerantly (freq. with specifying word); (*e*) *colloq.* a job, an assignment (freq. with specifying word); (*f*) = DENIER *noun*[2] 4. **M18**.

> **1** M. L. KING The number of cars swelled to about three hundred. B. LOPEZ Changed both the type and the numbers of animals living in the Arctic. *Bird Watching* Greylag numbers were very low during March. **2** MILTON Distance inexpressible, By Numbers that have name. BARNARD SMITH A Mixed Number is composed of a whole number and a fraction. D. R. HOFSTADTER The hard-edged rules that govern 'ideal' numbers constitute arithmetic. ***atomic number***, ***Avogadro's number***, ***complex number***, ***irrational number***, ***natural number***, ***prime number***, ***quantum number***, ***real number***, ***whole number***, etc. **b** U. LE GUIN There was a number; a 5 he thought at first, then took it for 1. G. JOSIPOVICI I . . examined the numbers on each of the doors. **3** STEELE None of . . these Things could be done . . without the Exercise of his Skill in Numbers. **4** F. MARRYAT A strange sail, who had not . . shown her number. G. B. SHAW 'What is Dr Paramore's number in Savile Row?' 'Seventy-nine.' L. GARFIELD He tramped into Newport Court . . where . . he resided on the top floor of Number Fourteen. *Omni* The palm-size cellular phone . . can remember 120 numbers for easy speed dialing. ***box number***, ***plate number***, ***private number***, ***serial number***, etc. **5** H. JAMES *The Ambassadors*, which first appeared in twelve numbers of *The North American Review*. J. GRENFELL I sang the Ave Maria. I do all Deanna Durbin's numbers. J. J. HENNESSY The bouncy little number is the English girl. *New Yorker* One of his specially made shirts—an Italian-silk number.

► **II 6** The full count of a collection of persons, things, etc., of a specified category; an example of this, a company, a collection, a group. **ME**. ▸†**b** The body or aggregate of persons or things specified. **E16–E17**. ▸†**c** The class or category *of* something. **L16–M18**. ▸†**d** Those forming a specified class; the multitude, the public. *rare.* **L16–M18**.

7 A (*large*, *small*, etc.) collection or aggregate *of* or of persons or things. **ME**.

8 A certain, esp. large or considerable, collection or aggregate *of* or of persons or things, not precisely reckoned or counted. **ME**.

9 In *pl.* ▸**a** A multitude of people or things; many people or things. **LME**. ▸**b** Numerical preponderance. **M17**.

†**10** A quantity, an amount. *rare.* **LME–E18**.

> **6** MILTON Hell, her numbers full, Thence-forth shall be forever shut. TENNYSON To . . miss the wonted number of my knights. K. TYNAN One of their number is about to be ritually strangled. **b** SHAKES. *A.Y.L.* Every of this happy number, That have endur'd shrewd days and nights with us. **c** R. BAKER I count not Amazons in the Number of women, but of Monsters. **d** POPE The Number may be hang'd, but not be crown'd. **7** *Pall Mall Magazine* A considerable number are employed in . . workshops. JULIETTE HUXLEY A very small number of centimes . . allotted to us each week as pocket money. **8** SOUTHEY A number of little forts are erected about the adjoining coast. **9** GOLDSMITH There are numbers in this city who live by writing new books. WELLINGTON The French have lost immense numbers of men. **b** J. MARSHALL European policy, numbers and skill prevailed. F. METCALFE They overpowered the foreigners by force of numbers. **10** R. WHITINTON An honest man hath . . brought a great nombre of wheate in the derth tyme.

► **III 11** That aspect of things involved in considering them as separate units of which one or more may be distinguished. **ME**. ▸**b** PHRENOLOGY. The faculty of numbering or calculating. **M19**.

12 GRAMMAR. The classification of word forms according to the number of entities to which they refer (usu. one or more than one); a particular form so classified. **LME**.

†**13** Harmony; conformity, in verse or music, to a certain regular beat or measure; rhythm. **LME–M17**.

14 In *pl.* Musical periods or groups of notes. Also, metrical periods or feet; lines, verses. **LME**.

> **11** MILTON Speed, to describe whose swiftness Number failes. G. D. CAMPBELL Laws of number and proportion pervade all Nature. **12** L. MURRAY The singular number expresses but one object. **13** MILTON With Heav'nly touch of instrumental sounds In full harmonic number joined. **14** N. ROWE When some skilful Artist strikes the Strings The magick Numbers rouze our sleeping Passions. POPE But most by Numbers judge a Poet's song.

Phrases & comb.: **a number of** some, several. ***back number***: see BACK-. **by numbers** following simple instructions (as if) identified by numbers. ***cardinal number***: see CARDINAL *adjective* 1. **do a number on** *N. Amer. slang* disparage, speak or write of with contempt; deceive. ***golden number***: see GOLDEN *adjective*. **have a person's name and number on it**, **have a person's number on it** (of a bullet etc.) be destined to kill a particular person. **have a person's number** understand a person's real motives, character, etc. ***index number***: see INDEX *noun*. ***law of large numbers***: see LARGE *adjective* 8. ***lose the number of one's mess***: see MESS *noun*. **number-average** CHEMISTRY an average of some parameter of the molecules of a mixture calculated as an arithmetic mean with each individual molecule contributing equally, regardless of size. **number board** a board on which numbers are displayed. **number-cloth** the cloth bearing a horse's number in a race. **number-crunch** *verb intrans.* (*slang*) make complex calculations (chiefly as ***number-crunching*** *verbal noun*). **number-cruncher** *slang* a machine capable of complex calculations etc. **number-form** the shapes into which series of numbers are formed in a person's mental imagery. **number line** a graduated line used to illustrate simple numerical concepts and operations. **number one** (*a*) oneself, one's own person and interests (freq. in ***look after number one***, ***take care of number one***); (*b*) *nursery & euphem.* an act of urination; (*c*) *colloq.* the finest quality, the best obtainable (freq. *attrib.*); ***number ones***, a best dress uniform worn esp. in the Navy. **number opera**: in which arias and other sections are clearly separable. **number-plate** a plate bearing a number, or series of numbers; *spec.* the registration plate of a motor vehicle. **numbers game** (*a*) = sense 2c above; (*b*) *transf.* the practice of adducing statistics, esp. in support of an argument (freq. in ***play the numbers game***). **number six** (*a*) *US colloq.* a household medicinal remedy (orig. placed sixth on the pharmaceutical list of its inventor); (*b*) a curl dressed on to the forehead in the shape of a figure six. **Number Ten** 10 Downing Street, the official London home of the Prime Minister; *transf.* the British Government, the Prime Minister. **number theory** the branch of mathematics that deals with the properties and relationships of numbers, esp. the positive integers. **number two** (*a*) *colloq.* something second-rate (freq. *attrib.*); (*b*) *colloq.* a second in command; (*c*) *nursery & euphem.* an act of defecation. **one's number is up** *colloq.* one is finished or doomed to die. ***opposite number***: see OPPOSITE *adjective* 1. ***ordinal number***: see ORDINAL *adjective* 2. ***quiet number***: see QUIET *adjective*. ***sacred number***: see SACRED *adjective*. **without number** innumerable.

■ **numberless** *adjective* (*a*) innumerable, countless, beyond computation; (*b*) *rare* without a number or numbers: **L16**. †**numberous** *adjective* numerous **M16–E18**.

number /ˈnʌmbə/ *verb trans.* **ME**.
[Old & mod. French *nombrer* from Latin *numerare*, from *numerus*: see prec.]
1 Count, ascertain the number of, (individual things or people). **ME**. ▸†**b** Ascertain the amount or quantity of. *rare.* **LME–E17**. ▸†**c** Compute, calculate, measure. **LME–L18**.

2 a Enumerate, count *up*. *arch.* **LME**. ▸**b** Fix the number of; reduce to a definite number; make few in number; bring near to a close. Usu. in *pass.* **LME**. ▸†**c** Collect (a body of soldiers etc.) up to a certain number. **LME–E17**.

3 Count or class among people or things of a specified category. Freq. foll. by *among*, *in*, *with*. **LME**.

4 Assign a number to (a thing); *spec.* mark or distinguish by a numerical symbol. **LME**.

5 †**a** Expend (money or time); pay *down* (money). **L15–M19**. ▸**b** Check, control, or verify the number of; count *over*. *arch.* **M16**. ▸†**c** Appoint or allot *to* a specified fate. Only in **E17**.

6 Have lived, have to live, (a specified number of years). **L16**.

7 Include or comprise in a number; have or comprise (a specified number of things or people). **M17**. ▸**b** Equal, amount to, (a specified total). **M19**.

> **1** W. GOLDING Glumly I numbered the things I . . had not done. **c** T. TAYLOR Accurately numbering the interval of time from one . . festival to another. **2a** R. H. HUTTON If . . you numbered up the acts of trust. **b** T. SHARPE The days of the Dean's influence are numbered. M. SPARK My days with Mackintosh & Tooley were numbered. **c** AV 1 *Kings* 10:25 And number thee an armie, like the armie that thou hast lost. **3** J. N. ISBISTER Freud numbered in his relations two rabbis. SAKI A colleague whose House had the embarrassing distinction of numbering Comus among its inmates. **4** J. CONRAD One . . was numbered 37. V. S. NAIPAUL I never numbered my pages. **numbered account** a bank account (esp. in a Swiss bank) identified only by a number and not bearing the owner's name. **5a** MILTON His ransom . . shall willingly be paid And numbered down. J. W. WARTER Days of this life's pilgrimage spared to me . . to number wisely. **b** SHELLEY Thou delight'st In numbering o'er the myriads of thy slain. **c** AV *Isa.* 65:12 Therefore will I number you to the sword. **6** W. COWPER My birth (Since which I number three-score winters past). **7** G. F. KENNAN A pro-Allied force, numbering forty to fifty thousand men. **b** G. GREENE A full complement of passengers would have numbered only fourteen.

■ **numberable** *adjective* (*rare*) (*a*) able to be numbered; numerable; †(*b*) *Scot.* numerous: **ME**. **numberer** *noun* **LME**.

numbles /ˈnʌmb(ə)lz/ *noun pl. arch.* **ME**.
[Old French (also *nombles*) ult. from Latin *lumbulus* dim. of *lumbus* loin. Cf. UMBLES.]
Orig., part of the back and loins of a hart. Later, the edible entrails of an animal, esp. a deer.

numbskull *noun* var. of NUMSKULL.

numdah /ˈnʌmdə/ *noun.* Also (earlier) †**nummud**. See also NUMNAH. **E19**.
[Urdu *namdā* from Persian *namad* felt, carpet, rug.]
1 In the Indian subcontinent and the Middle East: a kind of felt or coarse woollen cloth, freq. embroidered; a rug or carpet made from this (also ***numdah rug***). **E19**.
2 = NUMNAH. **L19**.

numen /ˈnjuːmən/ *noun.* Pl. **numina** /ˈnjuːmɪnə/. **E17**.
[Latin, rel. to *nuere* nod, Greek *neuein* incline the head.]
Divinity; a local or presiding god.

numerable /ˈnjuːm(ə)rəb(ə)l/ *adjective.* **M16**.
[Latin *numerabilis*, from *numerare*: see NUMBER *verb*, -ABLE.]
Able to be numbered.
■ **numeraˈbility** *noun* (*rare*) **E20**.

numeracy /ˈnjuːm(ə)rəsi/ *noun.* **M20**.
[from NUMERATE *adjective* + -ACY, after *literacy*.]
The quality or state of being numerate; ability with or knowledge of numbers.

numeraire /ˈnjuːmərɛː/ *noun.* **M20**.
[French *numéraire* from late Latin *numerarius*, from Latin *numerus* NUMERAL.]
ECONOMICS. The function of money as a measure of value or unit of account; a standard for currency exchange rates.

numeral /ˈnjuːm(ə)r(ə)l/ *adjective & noun.* **LME**.
[Late Latin *numeralis*, from Latin *numerus* NUMBER *noun*: see -AL[1].]
► **A** *adjective.* **1** Expressing or denoting a number or numbers. **LME**.
2 Belonging or pertaining to a number or numbers; numerical. **E17**.

> **1** L. MURRAY *One* is a numeral adjective. **2** HENRY MORE Those letters, in their numeral value, make just 666.

► **B** *noun.* **1** A word expressing a number. **M16**.
2 A figure or symbol, or a group of these, denoting a number. **L17**.

📖 **1** ***cardinal numeral***: see CARDINAL *adjective* 1. ***ordinal numeral***: see ORDINAL *adjective* 2. **2** J. O'HARA The little clock had no numerals. ***arabic numeral***: see ARABIC *adjective* 2. ***Roman numeral***: see ROMAN *adjective*.

numerary /'nju:m(ə)rəri/ *adjective & noun*. E18.
[medieval Latin *numerarius* (in late Latin used as noun = arithmetician, accountant), from Latin *numerus*: see NUMBER *noun*, -ARY[1].]
▶ **A** *adjective*. †**1** ECCLESIASTICAL. Of a canon: being a member of a body of regular canons. Only in E18.
2 Of or pertaining to a number or numbers. M18.
▶ **B** *noun*. A member of the highest of the three ranks of the Roman Catholic organization Opus Dei. L20.

numerate /'nju:m(ə)rət/ *adjective*. LME.
[In sense 1 from Latin *numeratus* pa. pple of *numerare* (see NUMBER *verb*); in sense 2 from Latin *numerus* NUMBER *noun* after *literate*: see -ATE[2].]
†**1** Numbered; counted. LME–L17.
2 Acquainted with the basic principles of mathematics, esp. arithmetic. M20.

📖 **2** *Country Life* Children are much less literate and numerate than ever before.

numerate /'nju:məreɪt/ *verb trans. rare*. E18.
[Latin *numerat-* pa. ppl stem of *numerare*: see NUMBER *verb*, -ATE[3].]
Compute, calculate.

numeration /nju:mə'reɪʃ(ə)n/ *noun*. LME.
[Latin *numeratio(n-)* (in late Latin sense numbering, in classical Latin = payment), formed as prec.: see -ATION.]
1 (A method or process of) counting, computing, or calculation. LME.
2 The action, process, or result of ascertaining the number *of* people etc. of a specified category, enumeration. LME.
3 The expression in words of a number written in figures. M16.

numerative /'nju:m(ə)rətɪv/ *adjective & noun*. L18.
[from NUMERATE *verb* + -IVE.]
▶ **A** *adjective*. Of or pertaining to numeration. L18.
▶ **B** *noun*. GRAMMAR. A numeral classifier. M19.

numerator /'nju:məreɪtə/ *noun*. M16.
[French *numérateur* or late Latin *numerator*, formed as NUMERATE *verb*: see -OR.]
1 The number written above the line in a vulgar fraction, which shows the number of parts of an integer which are represented; the dividend in an algebraic fraction; (correl. to ***denominator***). Formerly also, the word, symbol, figure, or group of these expressing the number of people or things specified. M16.
2 A person who or thing which numbers something. L17.

numeric /nju:'mɛrɪk/ *adjective & noun*. M17.
[from Latin *numerus* NUMBER *noun* + -IC: origin & use of sense A.1 unexpl.]
▶ **A** *adjective*. †**1** Identical. M17–E18.
2 Numerical. M20.
▶ **B** *noun*. A number. *rare*. L19.

numerical /nju:'mɛrɪk(ə)l/ *adjective & noun*. E17.
[from medieval Latin *numericus*, from Latin *numerus* NUMBER *noun*: see -ICAL.]
▶ **A** *adjective*. **1** Of, pertaining to, or characteristic of a number or numbers; (of a figure, symbol, etc.) expressing a number. E17.
†**2** Identical; particular, individual. E17–E18.
1 numerical analysis the branch of mathematics that deals with the development and use of numerical methods for solving problems.
▶ **B** *noun*. A number. M18.
■ **numerically** *adverb* E17.

numerist /'nju:mərɪst/ *noun*. *rare*. M17.
[from Latin *numerus* NUMBER *noun* + -IST.]
A person who attaches importance to or is concerned with numbers.

†**numero** *noun*. Pl. **-oes**. E17.
[Latin, abl. sing. of *numerus* NUMBER *noun*.]
1 A copy of a book. Only in E17.
2 A numbered thing. M17–E18.

numéro /nymero/ *noun*. Pl. **-os** /-o/. E20.
[French.]
= NUMBER *noun* 5. Also, a remarkable or strange person.

numerology /nju:mə'rɒlədʒi/ *noun*. E20.
[from Latin *numerus* NUMBER *noun* + -OLOGY.]
Divination by numbers; the branch of knowledge that deals with the occult or esoteric significance of numbers.
■ **numero'logical** *adjective* of or pertaining to numerology E20. **numero'logically** *adverb* E20. **numerologist** *noun* a student of or expert in numerology E20.

numerosity /nju:mə'rɒsɪti/ *noun*. M16.
[Late Latin *numerositas*, from Latin *numerosus*: see NUMEROUS, -ITY.]
1 Rhythmic quality. M16.
2 The state or condition of being numerous; condition in respect of number; numerousness. E17.

numero uno /nju:mərəʊ 'u:nəʊ/ *noun phr*. Pl. **numero unos**. L20.
[Italian = number one.]
The best or most important person. Cf. ***number one*** s.v. NUMBER *noun*.

numerous /'nju:m(ə)rəs/ *adjective*. LME.
[from Latin *numerosus*, from *numerus* NUMBER *noun*: see -OUS.]
1 a Plentiful, abundant, copious; comprising many separate things. Now *rare* exc. *Canad. dial.* LME. ▸**b** Consisting of many individuals. E17.
2 Rhythmic, harmonious. *arch*. L16.
3 Many; great in number. E17.
4 Containing or including many individuals; crowded. Also foll. by *of*. Now *rare*. E17.

📖 **1** T. RANDOLPH A cloud of numerous sand. GIBBON The free use of a numerous and learned library. **b** LD MACAULAY The commoners . . formed a numerous assembly. **2** H. HALLAM Blank verse . . falling . . almost into numerous prose. **3** H. JAMES The numerous ribbons . . with which she was bedecked. W. S. CHURCHILL Troops . . twice as numerous as their opponents. **4** SOUTHEY Both Universities are already sufficiently numerous.

■ **numerously** *adverb* E17. **numerousness** *noun* (*a*) the state or condition of being numerous; (*b*) *arch*. the quality of being numerous or rhythmic: M17.

numerus clausus /nju:mərəs 'klaʊsəs/ *noun phr*. E20.
[Latin, lit. 'closed number'.]
A fixed maximum number of entrants admissible to an academic institution.

Numic /'nju:mɪk/ *adjective & noun*. M20.
[Shoshonean = person.]
(Of or pertaining to) a branch of the Shoshonean language family.

Numidian /nju:'mɪdɪən/ *noun & adjective*. M16.
[from Latin *Numidia* (see below) + -AN.]
Chiefly *Hist*. ▶**A** *noun*. A native or inhabitant of Numidia, an ancient kingdom (later a Roman province) in N. Africa, east of Mauritania and west of Carthage, now part of Algeria. M16.
▶ **B** *adjective*. Of or pertaining to Numidia or the Numidians. E17.
Numidian crane = DEMOISELLE 2.

numina *noun* pl. of NUMEN.

numinal /'nju:mɪn(ə)l/ *adjective*. *rare*. M17.
[formed as NUMINOUS + -AL[1].]
Divine.

numinosum /nju:mɪ'nəʊzəm/ *noun*. M20.
[mod. Latin from German *Numinose* the numinous, formed as next.]
That which is numinous.

numinous /'nju:mɪnəs/ *adjective*. M17.
[from Latin *numin-* stem of NUMEN + -OUS.]
Divine, spiritual; revealing or indicating the presence of a divinity; awe-inspiring. Also, aesthetically appealing, uplifting.

📖 H. CARPENTER To children, the earth appears . . beautiful and numinous. R. SILVERBERG He felt shrouded in a numinous aura.

■ **numi'nosity** *noun* numinousness M20. **numinously** *adverb* M17. **numinousness** *noun* the condition or state of being numinous M20.

numismatic /nju:mɪz'matɪk/ *adjective*. L18.
[French *numismatique*, from Latin *numismat-*, *-sma* var. (infl. by *nummus* coin) of *nomisma* from Greek = current coin, from *nomisein* have in use: see -ISM, -ATIC.]
1 Of, pertaining to, or concerned with coins or medals. L18.
2 Consisting of coins or medals. M19.
■ **numismatical** *adjective* (*rare*) numismatic E18. **numismatically** *adverb* L19.

numismatics /nju:mɪz'matɪks/ *noun*. E19.
[formed as prec.: see -ICS.]
The branch of knowledge that deals with coins and medals, esp. from an archaeological or historical standpoint.

numismatist /nju:'mɪzmətɪst/ *noun*. L18.
[French *numismatiste*, from Latin *numismat-*: see NUMISMATIC, -IST.]
An expert in or student of numismatics.

numismatology /ˌnju:mɪzmə'tɒlədʒi/ *noun*. E19.
[from Latin *numismat-* (see NUMISMATIC) + -OLOGY.]
Numismatics.
■ **numismatologist** *noun* a numismatist M19.

nummary /'nʌm(ə)ri/ *adjective*. Now *rare*. E17.
[Latin *nummarius*, from *nummus* coin: see -ARY[1].]
1 Of or pertaining to money or coinage. E17.
2 Of a person: concerned or occupied with money or coinage. L17.

nummion /'nu:mɪɒn/ *noun*. Pl. **-ia** /-ɪə/. E20.
[Greek *noum(m)ion* dim. of *noummos* coin.]
Hist. A Byzantine copper coin, equal to one fortieth of a follis.

†**nummud** *noun* see NUMDAH.

nummular /'nʌmjʊlə/ *adjective*. M18.
[from Latin *nummulus* dim. of *nummus* coin + -AR[1].]
1 = next. *rare*. M18.
2 MEDICINE. Resembling a coin or coins; characterized by discoid structures or inclusions. M19.

nummulary /'nʌmjʊləri/ *adjective*. M18.
[formed as prec. + -ARY[1].]
Of or pertaining to money.

nummulated /'nʌmjʊleɪtɪd/ *adjective*. L19.
[formed as NUMMULAR: see -ATE[2], -ED[1].]
MEDICINE. = NUMMULAR 2.

nummulite /'nʌmjʊlʌɪt/ *noun*. E19.
[from mod. Latin *Nummulites* (see below), formed as NUMMULAR: see -ITE[1].]
ZOOLOGY & PALAEONTOLOGY. A fossil or extant foraminiferan of the genus *Camerina* (formerly *Nummulites*) or a related genus, having a calcareous and typically disc-shaped skeleton, and numerous in certain Tertiary strata.
■ **nummuline** *adjective & noun* (now *rare*) (*a*) *adjective* = NUMMULITIC; (*b*) *noun* = NUMMULITE: M19. **nummulitic** /-'lɪtɪk/ *adjective* (GEOLOGY) (esp. of limestone) containing or consisting of nummulites M19. **nummulitid** *noun* any foraminiferan of the family Nummulitidae L19.

nummy /'nʌmi/ *noun & interjection*. Also redupl. **nummy-nummy**. E20.
[Var. of YUMMY. Cf. NUM *noun & interjection*.]
(A cry) expr. pleasure from eating or at the prospect of eating.

numnah /'nʌmnə/ *noun*. M19.
[Var. of NUMDAH.]
A saddle-cloth; a pad placed under a saddle to prevent soreness.

num-num /nʊm'nʊm/ *noun*[1]. *S. Afr.* E19.
[Afrikaans *noem-noem*, perh. from Nama.]
Any of various white-flowered southern African spiny evergreen shrubs or small trees of the genus *Carissa* (family Apocynaceae), which includes the Natal plum, *C. grandiflora*; the edible red or purple fruit of such a plant.

num-num *noun*[2] *& interjection* see NUM *noun & interjection*.

numps /nʌmps/ *noun*. Long *arch. joc.* Also **nump** /nʌmp/. L16.
[Origin unkn.]
A silly or stupid person.

numpty /'nʌmpti/ *noun*. *Scot.* L20.
[from prec. + -TY[1].]
A stupid or ineffectual person.

📖 J. BYRNE A right pair of numpties we're gonnae look turnin' up on wur tod.

numskull /'nʌmskʌl/ *noun*. Also **numbskull**. E18.
[from NUMB *adjective* + SKULL *noun*[1].]
1 A stupid or foolish person; a dolt. E18.
2 The head, *esp*. that of a stupid or foolish person. E18.
■ **numskulled** *adjective* stupid, foolish E18.

nun /nʌn/ *noun*[1] *& verb*.
[Old English *nunne* = Old High German *nunna* (Middle High German, German dial. *nunne*), Old Norse *nunna*; partly from Old French *nonne*= Middle Dutch *nonne* (Dutch *non*), German *Nonne*, from ecclesiastical Latin *nonna* fem. of *nonnus* monk, orig. a title given to an elderly person.]
▶**A** *noun*. **1** A member of a Christian community of women living under vows of poverty, chastity, and obedience, according to the rule of a particular order, and devoted chiefly to religious duties, prayer, and often social, educational, or medical work. OE. ▸**b** A priestess or votaress of a god. Long *rare* or *obsolete*. OE. ▸**c** *transf*. A courtesan. *arch. slang*. L16.
2 Any of various birds whose plumage resembles a nun's habit, *esp*. (*a*) the blue tit; (*b*) the smew; (*c*) a black and white variety of the domestic pigeon; (*d*) *Austral*. the white-faced chat, *Ephthianura albifrons*. L16.
3 A tussock moth, *Lymantria monacha*, which is a pest of Eurasian forests. Also called ***black arches***. M19.
Comb.: **nunbird** any of several puffbirds of the genera *Monasa* and *Hapaloptila*; **nun's cloth** a thin light woollen fabric; †**nun's flesh** a cold or ascetic temperament; **nun's veiling** a thin light dress fabric.
▶**B** *verb trans*. Infl. **-nn-**. Confine or shut *up* as in a nunnery; cause to take vows as a nun. *rare*. M18.
■ **nunhood** *noun* the state or profession of being a nun; life as a nun: E19. **nunlike** *adverb & adjective* (*a*) *adverb* in the manner of a nun; (*b*) *adjective* resembling (that of) a nun: L16. **nunnish** *adjective* of, pertaining to, or characteristic of a nun; nunlike: L16. **nunship** *noun* the state or condition of being a nun E17.

nun /nʌn/ *noun*[2]. Long *obsolete* exc. in NUN-BUOY. L16.
[Origin uncertain: perh. rel. to prec.]
A child's top.

nunatak /'nʌnətak/ *noun*. L19.
[Inupiaq (Greenlandic) *nunataq*.]
An isolated peak of rock projecting above a surface of the inland ice or snow in Greenland, Norway, etc.

nunation /nʌˈneɪʃ(ə)n/ *noun.* Also **nunn-**. L18.
[mod. Latin *nunnatio(n-)*, from *nun* Arab. name of letter *n*: see -ATION.]
1 The addition of a final *n* in the indefinite declension of Arabic nouns. L18.
2 A similar addition of *n* in Middle English nouns etc. M19.

nun-buoy /ˈnʌnbɔɪ/ *noun.* E18.
[from NUN *noun*² + BUOY *noun*.]
A buoy circular in the middle and tapering towards each end.

nunc dimittis /nʌŋk dɪˈmɪtɪs/ *noun phr.* M16.
[Latin = now you let (your servant) depart (see below).]
1 A canticle forming part of the Christian liturgy at evensong and compline, comprising the song of Simeon in *Luke* 2:29–32 (in the Vulgate beginning *Nunc dimittis, Domine*). M16.
2 Permission to depart; dismissal. L16.
1 *sing one's nunc dimittis* *arch.* declare oneself willing or pleased to depart from life, an occupation, etc.

nunchaku /nʌnˈtʃakuː/ *noun.* L20.
[Japanese from Okinawa dial.]
More fully ***nunchaku stick***. A Japanese martial arts weapon consisting of two hardwood sticks joined together by a strap, chain, etc. Usu. in *pl.*

nuncheon /ˈnʌnʃ(ə)n/ *noun.* Now *arch. & dial.* ME.
[from NOON *noun* + SHENCH *noun*.]
A drink taken in the afternoon; a light refreshment between meals, a snack.

nunciate /ˈnʌnʃɪeɪt/ *noun. arch.* L16.
[Irreg. from Latin NUNCIUS or *nunciare* announce, perh. after *legate*.]
A person who or thing which announces something; a messenger, a nuncio.

nunciative /ˈnʌnʃɪətɪv/ *adjective. rare.* M17.
[medieval Latin *nunciativus*, from Latin *nunciat-* pa. ppl stem of *nunciare* announce: see -ATIVE.]
Conveying a message or messages; making an announcement.

nunciature /ˈnʌnʃətjʊə/ *noun.* E17.
[Italian *nunziatura*, from *nunzio* NUNCIO.]
ROMAN CATHOLIC CHURCH. **1** The representation of the Pope by a nuncio; the office or position of a nuncio. E17.
2 The tenure of office of a papal nuncio. E17.

nuncio /ˈnʌnsɪəʊ, ˈnʌnʃɪəʊ/ *noun.* Pl. **-os**. E16.
[Italian †*nuncio*, †*nuntio* (now *nunzio*) from Latin NUNCIUS, NUNTIUS.]
1 ROMAN CATHOLIC CHURCH. A papal ambassador to a foreign court or government. E16.
2 A person bearing a message; a messenger. E17.
3 *Hist.* A member of the Polish diet. L17.

nuncius /ˈnʌnʃɪəs, ˈnʌnʃəs/ *noun. rare.* E17.
[Latin, from *nunciare* announce.]
A messenger.

nuncle /ˈnʌŋk(ə)l/ *noun.* Now *arch. & dial.* L16.
[from misdivision of *mine uncle* (see UNCLE *noun*) as *my nuncle*. Cf. NAUNT, NUNK, NUNKY.]
Uncle.

nunc stans /nʌŋk ˈstanz/ *noun phr.* M17.
[from Latin *nunc* now + *stans* pres. pple of *stare* stand.]
PHILOSOPHY. Eternity regarded as a state outside time in which there is no past or future.

nuncupate /ˈnʌŋkjʊpeɪt/ *verb trans.* Pa. t. & pple **-ated**, **†-ate**. M16.
[Latin *nuncupat-* pa. ppl stem of *nuncupare* name, designate, declare: see -ATE³.]
†**1** Dedicate (a work) *to* a person. M16–M17.
†**2** Call, name, designate. M16–M17.
†**3** Express (a solemn promise) in words. E17–L18.
4 Declare (a will or testament) orally as opposed to in writing. L17.

nuncupation /nʌŋkjʊˈpeɪʃ(ə)n/ *noun.* LME.
[Latin *nuncupatio(n-)*, formed as prec.: see -ATION.]
†**1** The action of calling, naming, or designating; an instance of this. LME–M17.
†**2** The expression in words *of* a solemn promise. Only in 17.
3 The oral declaration of a will or testament. E18.

nuncupative /ˈnʌŋkjʊpətɪv/ *adjective.* M16.
[Late Latin *nuncupativus*, formed as NUNCUPATE: see -ATIVE.]
1 Of a will or testament: declared orally. M16.
†**2** Nominal; so-called. *rare.* M16–M17.
3 Designative. *rare.* E17.
■ **nuncupatively** *adverb* (now *rare* or *obsolete*) M17.

nuncupatory /nʌŋkjʊˈpeɪt(ə)ri/ *adjective. rare.* E17.
[medieval Latin *nuncupatorius*, formed as NUNCUPATE: see -ORY².]
†**1** = NUNCUPATIVE 1. E17–E18.
2 = NUNCUPATIVE 3. M20.

nundinal /ˈnʌndɪn(ə)l/ *adjective.* M17.
[French, in *lettres nundinales*, from *nundine* NUNDINE: see -AL¹.]
Of or pertaining to a fair or market; ROMAN HISTORY of or pertaining to a nundine.
nundinal letter each of the eight letters A to H used to indicate the days of the ancient Roman nundinal period.

nundination /nʌndɪˈneɪʃ(ə)n/ *noun.* Now *rare.* L16.
[Latin *nundinatio(n-)*, from *nundinat-* pa. ppl stem of *nundinari* attend or hold market, from *nundinae*: see next, -ATION.]
Traffic, trade, buying and selling; sale; an instance of this.

nundine /ˈnʌndʌɪn/ *noun.* M16.
[Latin *nundinae* fem. pl., from *novem* nine + *dies* day.]
1 ROMAN HISTORY. *sing.* & in *pl.* A market-day held every eighth (by inclusive reckoning, ninth) day. M16.
2 A recurring period of eight days. M19.
■ †**nundinary** *adjective* (*rare*) nundinal M17–M18.

nunk /nʌŋk/ *noun. arch. colloq.* Also **nunks** /nʌŋks/. M19.
[Abbreviation.]
= NUNKY 1.

nunky /ˈnʌŋki/ *noun. arch. colloq.* L18.
[Var. of NUNCLE: see -Y⁶.]
1 = NUNCLE. L18.
2 A pawnbroker. Cf. UNCLE *noun* 2. *slang.* E20.

nunlet /ˈnʌnlət/ *noun.* L19.
[from NUN *noun*¹ + -LET.]
Any of several mainly brown-backed puffbirds of the genus *Nonnula*.

nunnation *noun* var. of NUNATION.

nunnery /ˈnʌn(ə)ri/ *noun.* ME.
[Anglo-Norman, from *nonne* NUN *noun*¹: see -ERY.]
1 A place of residence for a community of nuns; a building or group of buildings in which nuns live as a religious community; a convent. ME. ▸**b** *transf.* A brothel. *arch.* L16.
†**2** The institution of conventual life for women; nunship. M–L17.
3 A group of nuns. Chiefly *fig. rare.* M17.

nuntius /ˈnʌnʃɪəs, ˈnʌnʃəs/ *noun.* Pl. **-tii** /-ʃɪʌɪ/. E17.
[Latin, var. of NUNCIUS.]
A nuncio.

nuoc mam /nwɒk ˈmɑːm/ *noun phr.* E20.
[Vietnamese.]
A spicy Vietnamese fish sauce.

NUPE /ˈnjuːpi/ *abbreviation.*
National Union of Public Employees.

Nupe /ˈnuːpeɪ/ *adjective & noun.* E19.
[A former kingdom at the junction of the Niger and Benue rivers in W. Africa.]
▸ **A** *adjective.* Of, pertaining to, or designating a people of central Nigeria, or the Sudanic language of this people. E19.
▸ **B** *noun.* Pl. same, **-s**.
1 A member of this people. L19.
2 The language of this people. L19.

Nupercaine /ˈnjuːpəkeɪn/ *noun.* E20.
[from *nu-* repr. NEW *adjective* + PERCAINE.]
PHARMACOLOGY. (Proprietary name for) a preparation of cinchocaine.

nuphar /ˈnjuːfə/ *noun.* Chiefly *poet.* M19.
[Arab. from Persian *nūfar*, reduced form of *nīnūphar* NENUPHAR.]
The yellow water lily, *Nuphar lutea* (family Nymphaeaceae).

nuplex /ˈnjuːplɛks/ *noun.* M20.
[from NU(CLEAR *adjective* + COM)PLEX *noun*.]
A combined agricultural and industrial complex built around a nuclear reactor which generates all the necessary power.

nuppence /ˈnʌp(ə)ns/ *noun. slang.* L19.
[from NO *adjective* + PENCE, after *tuppence*.]
No money.

nuptial /ˈnʌpʃ(ə)l/ *adjective & noun.* L15.
[Old & mod. French, or Latin *nuptialis*, from *nuptiae* wedding, from *nupt-* pa. ppl stem of *nubere*: see NUBILE, -IAL.]
▸ **A** *adjective.* **1** Of or pertaining to marriage or a wedding. L15.
2 ZOOLOGY. Of, pertaining to, or characteristic of mating or the breeding season; *esp.* designating characteristic breeding coloration or behaviour. M19.

> **1** A. N. WILSON The extended nuptial celebrations . . of the bride and groom. †**nuptial father** a man representing the bride's father at a wedding. **nuptial mass**: celebrated as part of a wedding ceremony. **2 nuptial pad** a swelling on the inner side of the hand in some male frogs and toads, assisting grip during amplexus.

▸ **B** *noun.* A marriage, a wedding. Usu. in *pl.* M16.

> **1** C. THIRLWALL The nuptials were solemnized according to Persian usage.

nuptiality /nʌpʃɪˈalɪti/ *noun.* M18.
[from prec. + -ITY.]
†**1** In *pl.* A couple about to be married. *rare.* Only in M18.
2 Conjugal virtues or character. L18.
3 In *pl.* Nuptial ceremonies. M19.
4 The frequency or incidence of marriage within a population. E20.

nuque /njuːk/ *noun. rare.* L16.
[French. Cf. NUCHA.]
The nape of the neck.

NUR *abbreviation.*
Hist. National Union of Railwaymen.

nuragh /ˈnʊərag/ *noun.* Pl. **-i** /-i/. E19.
[Sardinian.]
ARCHAEOLOGY. A type of massive stone tower found in Sardinia, dating from the Bronze and Iron Ages. Cf. TALAYOT.
■ **nuˈraghic** *adjective* of, pertaining to, or designating the principal Bronze Age culture of Sardinia, characterized by the building of nuraghi E20.

nurd *noun* var. of NERD.

Nuremberg /ˈnjʊərəmbəːg/ *noun.* E17.
[English name of *Nürnberg*, a city in Bavaria, S. Germany.]
1 Used *attrib.* to designate a type of porcelain manufactured in Nuremberg. E17.
2 *Hist.* Used *attrib.* to designate things associated with the German Nazi party which occurred in or were connected with Nuremberg. M20.
2 Nuremberg Laws laws promulgated in 1935 barring Jews from German citizenship and forbidding intermarriage between Aryans and Jews. **Nuremberg rally** any of the mass meetings of the German Nazi party held annually in Nuremberg from 1933 to 1938. **Nuremberg trials** a series of trials of former Nazi leaders for alleged war crimes, crimes against peace, and crimes against humanity, presided over by an International Military Tribunal representing the victorious Allied Powers and held in Nuremberg in 1945–6.

Nuremberger /ˈnjʊərəmbəːgə/ *noun.* L17.
[from prec. + -ER¹.]
A native or inhabitant of Nuremberg in Bavaria, S. Germany.

nurk *noun* var. of NERK.

nurl *noun & verb* var. of KNURL.

Nurofen /ˈnjʊərəfɛn/ *noun.* L20.
[Invented name after IBUPROFEN.]
PHARMACOLOGY. (Proprietary name for) ibuprofen.

nurse /nəːs/ *noun*¹. LME.
[Contr. of NOURICE.]
1 a Orig., a wet-nurse. Later, a woman employed or trained to take charge of a young child or children. *arch.* LME. ▸**b** *transf. & fig.* A source of nourishment and care; a person who takes care of or looks after another. LME.
2 A person, esp. a woman, caring for the sick or infirm, *spec.* one professionally qualified for this purpose; a person professionally qualified to provide advice on health and to treat minor medical problems. Freq. with specifying word. L16.
3 FORESTRY. A tree planted to shelter others. Also ***nurse-tree***. L18.
4 ENTOMOLOGY. A worker ant, bee, etc., which cares for the larvae. E19.
5 ZOOLOGY. In some invertebrates, esp. tunicates, an asexual individual. M19.

> **1b** SHAKES. *Two Gent.* Time is the nurse and breeder of all good. **2 *charge-nurse***, ***district nurse***, ***geriatric nurse***, etc. ***DENTAL nurse***.

Phrases: **at nurse** in the care or charge of a nurse. **put out to nurse**, **put to nurse** commit to the care or charge of a nurse.
Comb.: **nurse cell** any cell whose function appears to be to support or nourish another, esp. an ovum; **nurse-child** *arch.* a child in relation to his or her nurse; a foster-child; **nurse-crop**: planted to protect another; †**nurse-father** a foster-father; **nurse-frog** the midwife toad; **nurse-mother** (now *rare* or *obsolete*) a foster-mother; **nurse-plant**: which is host to a parasite; **nurses' home** a hostel providing residential accommodation for the nurses employed by a hospital; **nurse-tend** *verb trans. & intrans.* care for (a sick or infirm person); **nurse-tender** (chiefly *Anglo-Irish*) a nurse who cares for a sick or infirm person; ***nurse-tree***: see sense 3 above.

nurse /nəːs/ *noun*². Also †**nuss(e)**. L15.
[Perh. var. of HUSS, with added *n* from misdivision of *an* (cf. *newt*); later assim. to prec.]
Any of various dogfishes and sharks. Also ***nurse-fish***.
grey nurse: see GREY *adjective*.
Comb.: ***nurse-fish***: see above; **nurse hound** any of several dogfishes, *esp.* the large-spotted dogfish, *Scyliorhinus stellaris*; **nurse shark** a broad-headed brownish shark, *Ginglymostoma cirratum*, of warm, mainly Atlantic, waters.

nurse /nəːs/ *verb.* LME.
[Alt. of NOURISH *verb*, assim. to NURSE *noun*¹.]
1 a *verb trans.* Of a woman: breast-feed and look after (a baby); take maternal charge of (a young child or children). LME. ▸**b** *verb intrans.* Breast-feed; act as wet-nurse. L18. ▸**c** *verb intrans.* Be fed at the breast or teat. L19.

2 *verb trans.* In *pass.* Be reared or brought up in a certain place or under certain conditions etc. Chiefly *poet.* **E16.**
3 *verb trans.* **a** Foster; promote the development of; harbour, nurture, (a feeling etc.). **M16.** ▸**b** Supply (a plant) with warmth or moisture; tend or cultivate carefully. **L16.** ▸**c** Manage (land) carefully or economically. *arch.* **M18.** ▸**d** Help or cause (a person or thing) to develop *into* or *to* a certain form, size, state, etc. **L18.** ▸**e** Guide or manoeuvre (a mount, vehicle, etc.) in a specified direction, esp. in circumstances requiring exceptional care or skill. Freq. foll. by *along.* **M19.**
4 *verb trans.* Bring or rear *up* with care. **L16.**
5 *verb trans.* Cheat *out of*; obtain by cheating. *slang. rare.* **M17.**
6 a *verb trans.* Care for during sickness or infirmity. **M18.** ▸**b** *verb trans.* Try to cure (an illness) or heal (an injury) by taking care of oneself. **L18.** ▸**c** *verb intrans.* Work as a nurse providing health care. **M19.**
7 *verb trans.* Hold closely and carefully, esp. in the arms or on the lap; clasp in one's hands. **M19.** ▸**b** Consume (a drink) slowly, holding the glass etc. in the hand between sips. **M20.**
8 *verb trans.* Keep in touch with or influence, pay special attention to, (a constituency). **M19.**
9 BILLIARDS. Keep (the balls) close together to enable a series of cannons to be made. **M19.**

🕮 **1a** S. HASTINGS Sydney was determined to nurse the baby herself. **b** S. KITZINGER Women are naturally thirsty when nursing. **c** M. K. RAWLINGS The fawn nuzzled her full udders and began to nurse. B. SPOCK As the baby nurses, the suction engorges his painful gums. **2** SHELLEY The fierce savage, nursed in hate. TENNYSON Thou wert not nursed by the waterfall. **3a** W. COWPER To nurse with tender care the thriving arts. R. K. NARAYAN Gandhi trained us not to nurse any resentment. **b** C. MARSHALL The pots are to be nursed and preserved moderately warm. **d** S. JOHNSON Kindness was employed to nurse them into mischief. E. EDWARDS To nurse the embers of the old enmity into a flame. **e** C. A. LINDBERGH Once in the air, I can nurse my engine all the way. **4** SHAKES. *Meas. for M.* A Bohemian born; but here nurs'd up and bred. **6a** D. H. LAWRENCE Mrs Bolton had once nursed him through scarlet fever. **b** LD HOUGHTON I am nursing an influenza which came on the evening I got here. J. NAGENDA He was nursing a torrid hangover. **c** F. NIGHTINGALE Bad arrangements often make it impossible to nurse. DAY LEWIS She was known as 'The Angel' in the . . hospital where she had nursed. **7a** W. BLACK A gentleman . . was sitting on the grass, nursing his knees. E. LYALL They . . drove home again, Francesca nursing a Dying Gladiator in terra-cotta. J. HIGGINS Nursing a mug of strong black coffee. **8** W. S. MAUGHAM Enough money to nurse the constituency.

■ **nurser** *noun* (now *rare*) **LME.**

nurseling *noun* var. of NURSLING.

nursemaid /ˈnəːsmeɪd/ *noun & verb.* **M17.**
[from NURSE *noun*¹ + MAID *noun*.]
▸**A** *noun.* **1** A woman employed to look after a young child or children. **M17.**
2 A person who watches over or carefully guides another. *colloq.* **M20.**

🕮 **1** P. GAY The nursemaid who took care of him until he was about two.

▸**B** *verb trans.* Look after (a person) in the manner of a nursemaid; watch over with care, tend, (a thing). *colloq.* **E20.**

🕮 C. S. FORESTER The engine . . was greased and cleaned and nurse-maided. A. YORK Nursemaiding princesses . . is not really my line.

nursery /ˈnəːs(ə)ri/ *noun.* **LME.**
[Prob. from Anglo-Norman, from *norice* NOURICE with assim. to NURSE *noun*¹, *verb*: see -ERY.]
†**1** Fosterage, upbringing. **LME–L17.**
2 a A room or place set aside and equipped for babies and young children, esp. in the care of a nurse. **L15** ▸**b** = ***nursery class***, ***nursery school*** below. Also = ***day-nursery*** (b) s.v. DAY *noun.* **E20.**
3 A practice, institution, etc., in or by which a quality etc. is fostered or bred; a place in which people are trained or educated, a school *of* or *for* a specified profession, job, or activity. **E16.**
4 A place, esp. a commercial garden, where plants and trees are grown and raised for sale or for transplantation (now also ***nursery garden***). **M16.**
5 a A place which breeds or supports animals; a pond etc. in which young fry are reared. **M17.** ▸**b** The brood cells or chambers in which the larvae and pupae of ants, bees, etc., develop. Also *gen.*, a place or structure in which organisms grow and develop. **L18.**
6 BILLIARDS. A close group of balls which enables a series of cannons to be made (cf. NURSE *verb* 9). Also (in full ***nursery cannon***), each of a series of cannons which keep the balls close together. **M19.**
7 More fully ***nursery stakes***. A race for two-year-old horses. **L19.**

🕮 **1** M. CASAUBON Two brothers preserved by the milk and nursery of a she-wolf. **2a** M. FITZHERBERT Three years later Aubrey was joined in the nursery by his brother Mervyn. S. WEINTRAUB Wooden Dutch dolls . . lived in a large box in the nursery. **b** *attrib.*: H. JOLLY Learning to read and write . . is not what nursery education is about. **3** BURKE All . . treasuries, as nurseries of mismanagement . . ought to be dissolved. J. GROSS Older universities . . proving . . as much a training-ground for journalists as a nursery for philosophers. S. T. FELSTEAD They constituted the nursery for most of the famous artistes. **4** *Forestry* Shoots growing on logs in the nursery are less likely to become infected.

Comb.: ***nursery cannon***: see sense 6 above; **nursery class** a class for the education of children usu. between the ages of three and five; ***nursery garden***: see sense 4 above; **nursery language** a contrived form of language used by or to a young child; **nurseryman** a person who owns or works in a nursery for plants; **nursery-nurse** a person trained to take charge of babies and young children; **nursery rhyme** a simple traditional song or story in rhyme for children; **nursery school** a school for children below the age for compulsory education, usu. between the ages of three and five; **nursery slope** SKIING a gentle slope suitable for beginners; ***nursery stakes***: see sense 7 above; **nursery word** a non-standard word used by or to a young child.
■ **nurseryful** *noun* a quantity that fills a nursery, as much or as many as a nursery will hold **L19.**

nursey /ˈnəːsi/ *noun. nursery & colloq.* Also **nursie**. **E19.**
[Dim. of NURSE *noun*¹: see -IE, -Y⁶.]
A nurse.

nursing /ˈnəːsɪŋ/ *noun.* **E16.**
[from NURSE *verb* + -ING¹.]
1 The action of NURSE *verb.* **E16.**
2 The practice or profession of providing health care as a nurse; the duties of a nurse. **M19.**
Comb.: **nursing bra**: designed to facilitate breast-feeding; **nursing home** an institution, esp. a small private one, providing health care esp. for the elderly; **nursing officer** a senior nurse; ***senior nursing officer***, a person in charge of nursing services in a hospital.

nursing /ˈnəːsɪŋ/ *ppl adjective.* **M16.**
[from NURSE *verb* + -ING².]
That nurses.
nursing-father *arch.* a foster-father. **nursing-mother** (*a*) *arch.* a foster-mother; (*b*) a mother who is breast-feeding her baby.
■ **nursingly** *adverb* (*rare*) **M19.**

nursle /ˈnəːs(ə)l/ *verb trans.* **L16.**
[Var. of NUZZLE *verb*², assim. to NURSE *verb*.]
1 = NUZZLE *verb*² 1. *arch.* **L16.**
2 Nurse, foster, cherish. *poet.* **M17.**

nursling /ˈnəːslɪŋ/ *noun.* Also **nurseling**. **L15.**
[from NURSE *noun*¹ + -LING¹, after *suckling*.]
A baby or young child, esp. in relation to his or her nurse; *spec.* an infant that is being breast-fed; *fig.* a person or thing bred in or fostered by a particular place, conditions, etc.

🕮 S. JOHNSON Peevishness . . is much oftener . . the child of vanity and nursling of ignorance. CARLYLE She saw . . her little nurseling grown to be a brilliant man.

nurturance /ˈnəːtʃər(ə)ns/ *noun.* **M20.**
[from NURTURE *verb* + -ANCE.]
PSYCHOLOGY. (Ability to provide) emotional and physical nourishment and care.

nurturant /ˈnəːtʃər(ə)nt/ *adjective.* **M20.**
[formed as prec. + -ANT¹.]
PSYCHOLOGY. Caring or nourishing (emotionally or physically); pertaining to or exhibiting nurturance.

nurture /ˈnəːtʃə/ *noun.* **ME.**
[Old French *nourture* contr. of *noureture*: see NOURITURE.]
1 Breeding, upbringing, education, as received or possessed by a person. Now *rare.* **ME.** ▸†**b** Moral training or discipline. **E16–M17.**
2 That which nourishes; nourishment, food. **ME.**
3 The process of bringing up or training a person, esp. a child; tutelage; fostering care (freq. foll. by *of*). Also, social environment as an influence on or determinant of personality (opp. ***nature***). **L17.**

🕮 **1** R. HUGHES This crime . . done by one of her years and nurture . . was unspeakable. **2** BYRON Where . . from the heart we took Our first and sweetest nurture. **3** W. COWPER Things so sacred as a nation's trust, The nurture of her youth. J. M. SYNGE All should rear up lengthy families for the nurture of the earth.

■ **nurtural** *adjective* of, pertaining to, or due to nurture; esp. (PSYCHOLOGY) designating a characteristic etc. attributable to training, environment, etc., as distinct from being natural or inherited: **L19.** **nurtureless** *adjective* (*rare*) **M19.**

nurture /ˈnəːtʃə/ *verb trans.* **LME.**
[from the noun.]
1 Feed, nourish; support and bring up to maturity; rear. **LME.** ▸**b** Foster, cherish. **E19.**
2 Train, educate. Freq. as ***nurtured*** *ppl adjective.* **LME.** ▸†**b** Discipline, punish. **E16–M17.**

🕮 **1** SHELLEY By solemn vision, and bright silver dream, His infancy was nurtured. H. BELLOC Most of our trees were planted and carefully nurtured. W. C. WILLIAMS Bred of the . . country itself, nurtured from its plains and streams. **b** W. BLACK The Lieutenant began to nurture a secret affection for Scotland. **2** BURKE Persons . . nurtured in office do admirably well as long as things go on in . . order.

■ **nurturer** *noun* **L18.**

NUS *abbreviation.*
1 *Hist.* National Union of Seamen.
2 National Union of Students.

†**nuss(e)** *nouns* vars. of NURSE *noun*².

Nusselt number /ˈnʊs(ə)lt nʌmbə/ *noun phr.* **M20.**
[E. K. W. *Nusselt* (1882–1957), German engineer.]
PHYSICS etc. A dimensionless parameter used in calculations of heat transfer between a moving fluid and a solid body, equal to hD/k, where h is the rate of heat loss per unit area per degree difference in temperature between the body and its surroundings, D is a characteristic length of the body, and k is the thermal conductivity of the fluid.

NUT *abbreviation.*
National Union of Teachers.

nut /nʌt/ *noun & adjective.*
[Old English *hnutu* = Middle Low German *note*, Middle Dutch *note*, *neute* (Dutch *noot*, *neut*), Old High German *(h)nuz* (German *Nuss*), from Germanic. Cf. KNUT.]
▸**A** *noun.* **I 1** (The kernel of) any edible or oil-yielding usu. woody or hard-shelled fruit or seed; *spec.* (BOTANY) a hard indehiscent one-seeded fruit (e.g. an acorn, a hazelnut), freq. surrounded by a cupule. **OE.** ▸**b** Any of the seeds in a pine cone. *obsolete* exc. in ***pine nut*** s.v. PINE *noun*². **OE.** ▸**c** In *pl.* The testicles. *coarse slang.* **E20.**
2 A cup made from a coconut shell mounted in metal; one made of other materials to resemble this. Long *arch.* **ME.**
3 A difficult question, problem or undertaking; a difficult person to deal with etc. Now chiefly in ***a hard nut to crack***, ***a tough nut to crack*** below. **M16.**
4 a The head. *slang.* **M19.** ▸**b** In *pl.* Nonsense, rubbish (cf. NUTS *adjective*). Usu. as *interjection.* **M20.**
5 a A person. *arch. colloq.* exc. in ***tough nut*** below. **L19.** ▸**b** A mad or eccentric person. *slang.* **E20.** ▸**c** An enthusiast, a devotee. Freq. with specifying word. *colloq.* **M20.**
6 A fashionable or showy young man, = KNUT. *arch. slang.* **E20.**

🕮 **1** SIR W. SCOTT My Lord of Rothsay who . . was cracking nuts with a strolling musician. P. BENSON People couldn't gather nuts and berries without baskets. ***Brazil-nut***, ***cashew-nut***, ***hazelnut***, ***peanut***, ***pistachio nut***, etc. **c** L. MICHAELS If I stopped talking . . I might kick you in the nuts. A. SILLITOE I'd be sweating my nuts off for nine quid a week. **4a** H. ROBBINS You're beating your nut against a stone wall. **b** D. FRANCIS 'I'll give you a hundred.' 'Nuts.' 'A hundred and fifty.' **5b** D. RUNYON This Count Saro is some kind of a nut. J. GARDNER When a plain ordinary human being thinks he's God, the fact is he's a nut. **c** L. GOULD If you're such a health nut, how come you take all those pills? **6** R. MACAULAY He always looked . . calm, unruffled, tidy, the exquisite nut.

▸**II 7** A small toothed metal projection on a spindle of a clock etc., engaging in a cog-wheel; a small spur-wheel. **LME.**
8 A revolving claw that holds back the bowstring of a crossbow until released by the trigger. **E16.**
9 a A small usu. square or hexagonal flat piece of metal, wood, etc., with a hole through it for screwing on to a bolt to secure or adjust it. **E17.** ▸**b** A part of a wooden printing-press in which the screw plays. **M17.** ▸**c** A screw at the lower end of the bow of a stringed instrument for adjusting the tension of the horsehair etc. **M17.**
10 NAUTICAL. A projection on the end of the stock of an anchor designed to make it lie flat. **E17.**
11 The fixed ridge on the neck of a stringed instrument over which the strings pass. **L17.**

🕮 **9a** N. TINBERGEN Nuts, bolts and various small pieces of scrap iron. *Scientific American* The bolts . . were held in place by wrought-iron or wood nuts. **11** C. FORD A nut that is too high makes playing very difficult.

▸**III** †**12** The glans penis. **M16–M18.**
13 †**a** = POPE'S EYE. Only in **17.** ▸**b** A small usu. oval piece of food, formerly of meat, now esp. of butter, for cooking. Usu. foll. by *of.* **M18.** ▸**c** The pancreas. Also, part of the omentum. *obsolete* exc. *dial.* **E19.**
14 A small rounded biscuit or cake. Only as 2nd elem. of comb., as ***doughnut***, ***ginger-nut***, etc. **L18.**
15 In *pl.* Small lumps of coal. **L19.**
16 The amount of money required for a venture; overhead costs; *transf.* any sum of money. *US slang.* **E20.**

🕮 **13b** *Times* With a nut of butter and some fresh rosemary . . inside.

▸**IV 17** TYPOGRAPHY. More fully **nut quad**, **nut quadrat**. = EN ***quadrat***. **E20.**
Phrases: **a hard nut to crack** *colloq.* a difficult problem; a person not easily understood or influenced. ***deaf nut***: see DEAF *adjective* &

noun. ***do one's nut***: see DO *verb.* **for nuts** *colloq.* even tolerably well (only in neg. contexts). ***from soup to nuts***: see SOUP *noun.* **nuts and bolts** *colloq.* the practical details. **nuts in May**: a children's singing game (more fully ***here we come gathering nuts in May***). **nuts to** *arch. slang* a source of pleasure and delight to. **off one's nut** *slang* out of one's mind, insane, crazy. **sound as a nut**, **sweet as a nut** very sound or sweet, in good order. ***take a sledgehammer to crack a nut***: see SLEDGEHAMMER *noun.* **the nuts** *US slang* an excellent or first-rate person or thing. **tough nut** *colloq.* (*a*) = ***tough guy*** s.v. TOUGH *adjective*; (*b*) ***tough nut to crack***, = ***hard nut to crack*** above. ***use a sledgehammer to crack a nut***: see SLEDGEHAMMER *noun.* ***where the monkey keeps his nuts***, ***where the monkey puts his nuts***: see MONKEY *noun.*

Comb.: **nut-brown** *adjective & noun* (*a*) (of) the colour of a ripe hazelnut, (of) a warm reddish-brown colour; (*b*) *arch.* (designating) ale of such a colour; **nutburger** (a bread bun containing) a savoury round flat cake or patty made from chopped nuts and other vegetarian ingredients; **nut-butter** a substitute for butter obtained from the oil of nuts; **nut-cake** (*a*) *US* a doughnut or other fried cake; (*b*) a cake containing (usu. chopped or ground) nuts; **nutcase** *colloq.* a mad or eccentric person; **nut chocolate** chocolate containing nuts; **nut-crack** (*a*) (now *rare* or *obsolete*) = NUTCRACKER *noun* 1; (*b*) ***Nut-crack Night*** (*arch.*), Hallowe'en; **nut cutlet**; **nut factory** *US slang* = ***nut-house*** below; **nutgall** a gall from an oak of Asia Minor, *Quercus infectoria*, used chiefly to give astringency to ointments; **nut-grass** a small plant of the sedge family, *Cyperus rotundus*, with roots which form nutlike tubers, a weed in some tropical countries; **nut-hook** (*a*) a hooked stick used when nutting to pull down the branches of the trees; †(*b*) a beadle, a constable; **nut-house** *slang* a mental home or hospital; **nut loaf** a nut roast (see below) in the shape of a loaf; **nut-meat** the kernel of a nut; **nut milk chocolate** milk chocolate containing nuts; **nut-oil** oil obtained from the kernels of nuts, esp. hazelnuts and walnuts, used in the manufacture of paints and varnishes, in cookery, etc.; **nut-pine** any of several pines of south-western N. America and the Rocky Mountains which produce edible seeds, esp. *Pinus monophylla*; **nut roast** a baked vegetarian dish made from a mixture of ground or chopped nuts, vegetables, and herbs; **nut runner** a power tool for tightening nuts; **nut-steak** a steak-shaped savoury cake made from chopped nuts and other vegetarian ingredients; **nut tree** a tree that bears nuts, *esp.* the hazel, *Corylus avellana*; **nut-weevil** a small yellow-scaled beetle, *Curculio nucum*, which lays its eggs in green hazel- and filbert-nuts; **nut-wood** wood from a nut-bearing tree, esp. the walnut.

▶ **B** *attrib.* or as *adjective.* Mad, eccentric. Cf. earlier NUTS *adjective. slang.* E20.

> 🕮 S. LEWIS Woofums—kind of a nut name . . that's what she calls me sometimes. S. BRILL He took the nut calls that still came in.

■ **nutlike** *adjective* resembling a nut M19. **nuttish** *adjective* (*rare*) nutlike L19.

nut /nʌt/ *verb.* Infl. **-tt-**. E17.
[from the noun.]
1 *verb intrans.* Look for or gather nuts. E17.
2 *verb trans.* Curry favour with, court, (a person). *arch. slang.* E19.
3 *verb trans.* Think (a thing) out. Freq. foll. by *out*, *up.* Cf. NUT *noun* 4a. *slang.* E20.
4 *verb trans.* Butt with the head. *slang.* M20.
5 *verb trans.* Kill. Also foll. by *off.* Usu. in *pass. slang.* L20.

> 🕮 **1** LD MACAULAY A schoolboy who goes nutting in the wood. **3** M. SHADBOLT I haven't nutted out what I'm going to say. **4** *Sounds* Like the school bully about to nut someone with his forehead.

nutant /ˈnjuːt(ə)nt/ *adjective.* M18.
[Latin *nutant-* pres. ppl stem of *nutare*: see next, -ANT¹.]
Chiefly BOTANY. Nodding, pendulous.

nutate /njuːˈteɪt/ *verb intrans.* L19.
[Latin *nutat-* pa. ppl stem of *nutare* nod, from base of *-nuere* nod: see -ATE³.]
Undergo or exhibit nutation.

nutation /njuːˈteɪʃ(ə)n/ *noun.* E17.
[Latin *nutatio(n-)*, formed as prec.: see -ATION.]
1 The action or an act of nodding the head. E17.
2 a Chiefly ASTRONOMY. An oscillation of the axis of a spinning body. Now usu. *spec.*, a variation in the inclination of an axis from the vertical, *esp.* that which makes the precession of the earth's poles follow a wavy rather than a circular path. E18. ▸**b** Rotation of an axis (of a beam, aerial, etc.) so as to describe a cone. M20.
3 BOTANY. The bending of a growing plant, esp. alternately in opposite directions, due to variation in growth-rate on different sides. Cf. CIRCUMNUTATION. L18.
■ **nutational** *adjective* L19.

nutcracker /ˈnʌtkrakə/ *noun & adjective.* M16.
[from NUT *noun* + CRACKER.]
▶ **A** *noun.* **1** A device for cracking the shell of a nut to reach the (edible) kernel; *esp.* (now usu. ***nutcrackers***, ***pair of nutcrackers***) such a device consisting of two curved pivoted limbs. M16.
2 †**a** The cardinal grosbeak. *rare.* Only in L17. ▸**b** Either of two crows, the brown *Nucifraga caryocatactes* of Eurasia and the black, white, and grey *Nucifraga columbiana* of western N. America. M18.
▶ **B** *attrib.* or as *adjective.* **1** Designating a nose and chin with the points naturally, or through loss of teeth, near each other. L17.
2 ***Nutcracker Man***, (a nickname for) an E. African fossil hominid, *Australopithecus boisei*, with massive jaws and powerful premolar teeth. M20.

nut-cut /ˈnʌtkʌt/ *adjective & noun. rare.* M19.
[Hindi *natkhat.*]
In the Indian subcontinent: (a person who is) roguish or rascally.

nuthatch /ˈnʌthatʃ/ *noun.* ME.
[from NUT *noun* + 2nd elem. connected with HACK *verb*¹ or HAG *verb*¹ (from the bird's habit of hacking with the beak at nuts wedged in a crevice).]
Any of various small passerine birds of the genus *Sitta* or the family Sittidae, which creep up and down trees or rocks, esp. the common Eurasian species *S. europaea.* ***white-breasted nuthatch***: see WHITE *adjective.*

nuthin /ˈnʌθɪn/ *pronoun & noun. non-standard.* E20.
[Repr. a pronunc.]
Nothing.

nutjobber /ˈnʌtdʒɒbə/ *noun. obsolete* exc. *dial.* M16.
[from NUT *noun* + JOB *verb*¹ + -ER¹.]
= NUTHATCH.

nutlet /ˈnʌtlɪt/ *noun.* M19.
[from NUT *noun* + -LET.]
BOTANY. A small achene, esp. of a labiate plant.

nutmeg /ˈnʌtmɛg/ *noun & verb.* ME.
[Partial translation of Anglo-Norman alt. of Old French *nois mug(u)ede* (also *musguete*, mod. *noix muscade*) from medieval Latin *nux muscata* lit. 'musk-scented nut'.]
▶ **A** *noun.* **1** The hard spherical aromatic seed of the kernel of the fruit of *Myristica fragrans* (family Myristicaceae), an evergreen tree of the Moluccas; this kernel grated or ground and used as a spice in cooking (cf. MACE *noun*²); (in full ***nutmeg tree***) the tree itself. Also (with specifying word), (a similar spice obtained from) any of several other, mostly unrelated, trees. ME. ▸†**b** In *pl.* The testicles. *slang.* L17–M19. ▸**c** FOOTBALL. An act of kicking a ball between the legs of an opponent. *slang.* M20.
2 Any of several old varieties of peach, plum, etc. M17.
3 A small noctuid moth, *Discestra trifolii*, with grey-brown forewings. E20.

> 🕮 **1** R. K. NARAYAN What *halva* would be worth its name if you did not crush a little nutmeg into it? **Brazilian nutmeg** (the spicy fruit of) a S. American tree, *Cryptocarya moschata*, of the laurel family. **calabash nutmeg**, **West African nutmeg** (the spicy seed of) a W. African tree, *Monodora myristica* (family Annonaceae). **wooden nutmeg** *US* [cf. ***Nutmeg State*** below] a false or fraudulent thing. **2 *white nutmeg***: see WHITE *adjective.*

Comb.: **nutmeg-apple** the fruit of the nutmeg tree; **nutmeg-bird** a brown speckled finch, *Lonchura punctulata*, of southern and eastern Asia; **nutmeg-coloured** *adjective* dark grey-brown with a reddish tinge; **nutmeg hickory** a hickory of the southern US, *Carya myristicaeformis*, bearing a fruit resembling a nutmeg; **nutmeg liver** MEDICINE a congested state of the liver, which presents a mosaic of light and dark brown patches in cross-section; **nutmeg melon** a musk melon with a netted rind like a nutmeg; **Nutmeg State** *US* the State of Connecticut, whose inhabitants reputedly passed off as the spice nutmeg-shaped pieces of wood; ***nutmeg tree***: see sense 1 above.

▶ **B** *verb trans.* Infl. **-gg-**. FOOTBALL. Deceive (an opponent) by kicking the ball through his or her legs. *slang.* L20.
■ **nutmegged** *adjective* = NUTMEGGY M18. **nutmeggy** *adjective* (*a*) flavoured with or scented like nutmeg; †(*b*) MEDICINE affected with nutmeg liver: M19.

nutraceutical /njuːtrəˈsjuːtɪk(ə)l/ *noun.* L20.
[Blend of NUTRITIONAL and PHARMACEUTICAL.]
A foodstuff, food additive, or dietary supplement that has (or is claimed to have) medicinal properties; a functional food. Usu. in *pl.*

nutria /ˈnjuːtrɪə/ *noun & adjective.* E19.
[Spanish = otter.]
▶ **A** *noun.* The skin or fur of the coypu; *N. Amer.* the animal itself. Also, the mid-brown colour of this fur. E19.
▶ **B** *adjective.* Made of nutria. E20.

nutrice /ˈnjuːtrɪs/ *noun. rare.* M16.
[Latin *nutric-*, *nutrix*: see NOURICE.]
A wet-nurse.

nutrient /ˈnjuːtrɪənt/ *adjective & noun.* M17.
[Latin *nutrient-* pres. ppl stem of *nutrire* nourish: see -ENT.]
▶ **A** *adjective.* **1** Serving as nourishment; possessing nourishing qualities. M17.
2 ANATOMY & ZOOLOGY. Conveying nourishment. M17.
▶ **B** *noun.* A nutritious substance. E19.

> 🕮 N. CALDER Rain and rivers bring abundant fresh water, rich in nutrients.

nutrify /ˈnjuːtrɪfʌɪ/ *verb.* Now *rare.* L15.
[from Latin *nutrire* nourish: see -FY.]
1 *verb trans.* Nourish. L15.
2 *verb intrans.* Provide nourishment. M17.

nutriment /ˈnjuːtrɪm(ə)nt/ *noun.* LME.
[Latin *nutrimentum*, from *nutrire* nourish: see -MENT.]
1 That which nourishes; food, nourishment; a nourishing food. LME.
2 *fig.* Spiritual, intellectual, artistic, etc., nourishment or stimulus. E17.

> 🕮 **1** ST G. J. MIVART It . . helps to keep the body warm and serves as a store of nutriment. **2** W. H. DIXON Homer and Thucydides might yield them richer nutriment.

■ **nutriˈmental** *adjective* (*a*) nutritious, nourishing; (*b*) conveying nourishment: LME.

nutrition /njʊˈtrɪʃ(ə)n/ *noun.* LME.
[Old & mod. French, or late Latin *nutritio(n-)*, from *nutrit-* pa. ppl stem of *nutrire* nourish: see -ITION.]
1 The action or process of supplying or receiving nourishment. LME. ▸†**b** The practice of adding oil etc. to a preparation to make an ointment or unguent. Cf. NUTRITUM. *rare.* E17–E18.
2 That which nourishes; food, nourishment; diet. L15.
3 The branch of science that deals with (esp. human) nutrients and nutrition. E20.

> 🕮 **1** T. R. MALTHUS The kind of food . . best suited to the purposes of nutrition. **2** S. KITZINGER Nutrition can play a part in preventing bones becoming fragile. S. BELLOW Lichens could take nutrition from the atmosphere. **3** J. YUDKIN Twenty-five or so scientists who have made notable contributions to . . nutrition.

■ **nutritional** *adjective* M19. **nutritionalist** *noun* = NUTRITIONIST M20. **nutritionally** *adverb* with respect to nutrition L19. **nutritionist** *noun* an expert in or student of (esp. human) nutrients and nutrition E20.

nutritious /njʊˈtrɪʃəs/ *adjective.* M17.
[Latin *nutritius*, *-icius*, from *nutric-*, *nutrix*: see NOURICE, -ITIOUS².]
1 Serving as nourishment; capable of nourishing; efficient as food. M17.
2 ANATOMY & ZOOLOGY. Conveying nourishment. *rare.* M18.

> 🕮 **1** *Stock & Land (Melbourne)* A sheep's diet shifts from grass to pellets . . a more nutritious food. **2** A. MONRO The Holes for the Passage of the nutritious Vessels.

■ **nutritiously** *adverb* M18. **nutritiousness** *noun* E18.

nutritive /ˈnjuːtrɪtɪv/ *adjective & noun.* LME.
[French *nutritif*, *-ive* from medieval Latin *nutritivus*, from Latin *nutrit-*: see NUTRITION, -IVE.]
▶ **A** *adjective.* **1** Capable of nourishing; nutritious. LME.
2 Of, pertaining to, or concerned in nutrition. LME.
3 Giving or providing nourishment. LME.
▶ **B** *noun.* A nourishing item of food. *rare.* LME.
■ **nutritively** *adverb* L19. **nutritiveness** *noun* E18.

†**nutritum** *noun. rare.* LME–M18.
[Latin, use as noun of neut. pa. pple of *nutrire* nourish.]
An ointment, an unguent. Cf. NUTRITION 1b.

nutriture /ˈnjuːtrɪtʃə/ *noun.* M16.
[Late Latin *nutritura*, from Latin *nutrit-*: see NUTRITION, -URE.]
1 †**a** Nourishment, nutrition. M16–M18. ▸**b** Condition with respect to nourishment. E17.
†**2** Fostering; careful rearing or bringing up. M16–L17.
¶ In sense 1b obsolete by E17; revived in M20.

nuts /nʌts/ *adjective. slang.* L18.
[Pl. of NUT *noun*: see -S¹.]
Mad; eccentric.

> 🕮 C. SANDBURG He was nuts and belonged in a booby hatch. B. SCHULBERG 'Mr Manheim, you're nuts,' he said sympathetically. 'It's driving me nuts,' I said. **nuts about**, **nuts on** enthusiastic about, very fond of, devoted to.

nutshell /ˈnʌtʃɛl/ *noun & verb.* Also (earlier) †**-shale**. ME.
[from NUT *noun* + SHALE *noun*¹, SHELL *noun.*]
▶ **A** *noun.* **1** The hard or woody pericarp enclosing the kernel of a nut. ME.
2 An object regarded as the type of something without value or of extremely small capacity or extent. ME.

> 🕮 **2** J. COLLIER Dont stake your life against a nutshell. DICKENS A little cracked nutshell of a wooden house.

Phrases: **in a nutshell** in a few words, concisely stated.
▶ **B** *verb trans.* Sum up in a few words; state concisely. L19.

nutso /ˈnʌtsəʊ/ *noun & adjective. US colloq.* L20.
[from NUTS + -O. Cf. FATSO.]
▶ **A** *noun.* Pl. **-os**. A mad or eccentric person. Freq. as a term of abuse. L20.

> 🕮 R. SILVERBERG Hey, crazy man! Hey, nutso!

▶ **B** *adjective.* Mad, eccentric. L20.

nutsy /ˈnʌtsi/ *adjective. colloq.* M20.
[from NUTS + -Y¹.]
Mad, eccentric.

nutted /ˈnʌtɪd/ *adjective.* L17.
[from NUT *noun* + -ED².]
1 Provided with or fastened by a nut (NUT *noun* 9). L17.
2 Having many nuts (NUT *noun* 1). *rare.* M19.

nutter /ˈnʌtə/ *noun*¹. LME.
[from NUT *noun, verb*: see -ER¹.]
†**1** A nut tree. LME–L15.
2 A person who gathers nuts. E19.
3 A mad or eccentric person. *slang.* M20.

Nutter /ˈnʌtə/ *noun*². E20.
[from NUT *noun* + BUT)TER *noun*¹.]
(Proprietary name for) a butter-substitute made from the oil of nuts.

nuttery /ˈnʌt(ə)ri/ *noun*. E19.
[from NUT *noun* + -ERY.]
1 A place in which nut trees grow or are raised. E19.
2 A place in which nuts are stored. L19.
3 A mental hospital. *slang*. M20.

nutty /ˈnʌti/ *adjective & noun*. LME.
[from NUT *noun* + -Y¹.]
► **A** *adjective*. **1** Nutlike; tasting like nuts; having a rich mellow flavour. LME.
2 Having many nuts; producing nuts. M17.
3 a Amorous, fond; enthusiastic. Freq. foll. by *on*. *arch. colloq*. E19. ►**b** Mad; eccentric. Freq. in ***nutty as a fruit cake*** s.v. FRUIT *noun*. L19.
4 Smart, spruce. *arch. slang*. E19.

1 H. WILLIAMSON The bird has a nutty flavour, equal with a full-bodied burgundy. **nutty slack** coal slack in small lumps or nuts. **2** R. BROUGHTON The nutty, briary hedgerows. **3a** *Fraser's Magazine* Being so nutty upon one another. **b** D. HAMMETT You mean he's really insane . . not just nutty? DENNIS POTTER It was . . a pretty nutty thing to say. **4** BYRON So prime, so swell, so nutty, and so knowing.

► **B** *noun*. Chocolate, sweets. *Nautical slang*. M20.
■ **nuttiness** *noun* M19.

nux vomica /nʌks ˈvɒmɪkə/ *noun phr*. LME.
[medieval Latin, lit. 'emetic nut', from Latin *nux* nut + adjective from *vomere* to vomit.]
The highly poisonous seeds of the tree *Strychnos nux-vomica* (family Loganiaceae), used as a major source of strychnine and in homoeopathic remedies; this tree, a native of southern Asia.

Nuzi /ˈnjuːzi/ *noun & adjective*. M20.
[See below.]
► **A** *noun*. A dialect of Akkadian, known from cuneiform inscriptions discovered at Nuzi, the site of an ancient city in northern Iraq. M20.
► **B** *adjective*. Of or pertaining to this city or dialect. M20.
■ **Nuzian** *noun & adjective* (*a*) *noun* a member of a Hurrian people whose culture flourished at Nuzi in the second millennium BC; (*b*) *adjective* of or pertaining to this people: M20.

nuzzer *noun* see NAZAR.

nuzzle /ˈnʌz(ə)l/ *verb*¹. See also SNUZZLE. LME.
[from NOSE *noun* + -LE³, perh. partly back-form. from NOSELING, also infl. later by Dutch *neuzelen* poke with the nose, from *neus* nose. Cf. NUDDLE, SNOOZLE.]
► **I** *verb intrans*. †**1** Bring the nose towards the ground; grovel. *rare*. Only in LME.
2 Burrow or dig with the nose; thrust the nose into the ground or something lying on the ground. M16.
3 Poke or push with the nose *at*, *in*, or *into* something; rub the nose *against* something. L16. ►**b** Of a dog: sniff at something. E19. ►**c** Poke or press with the fingers. *rare*. E19.
4 Nestle, esp. close to a person; lie close or snug; *fig*. associate closely *with*. L16.

2 T. HARDY Like sows nuzzling for acorns. **3** R. KIPLING The red mare . . nuzzled against his breast. G. LORD Robin tried to nuzzle into my neck. **b** J. BERESFORD A large bulldog . . with his muzzle nuzzling about your calf. **4** H. CAINE Pete nuzzled up to Philip's side. D. DELILLO Elvis and Gladys liked to nuzzle and pet. *American Poetry Review* It would nuzzle next to my arm.

► **II** *verb trans*. **5** Nestle (oneself, the body); lay close. Long *rare* or *obsolete*. M16.
6 Thrust in (the nose or head). L16.
7 a Root *up* with the nose; push *aside* with the nose. *rare*. E17. ►**b** Touch or rub (a person or thing) with the nose. E19.

6 J. A. SYMONDS Six stalwart horses . . nuzzling their noses to the brimful stalls. J. BUCHAN He nuzzled his face into the neck of a most astonished cow! **7b** W. ABISH She leaned forward, nuzzling his neck. B. MOORE A . . Dalmatian dog came up to him, nuzzling his hand.

nuzzle /ˈnʌz(ə)l/ *verb*² *trans*. Now *rare*. E16.
[Origin uncertain: perh. from prec.]
†**1** Train, educate, nurture, (a person), esp. *in* a particular opinion, habit, or custom. Freq. foll. by *up*. E16–L17. ►**b** Impose upon, deceive. *rare*. L17–E18.
†**2** Accustom (a dog or hawk) to attacking other animals or birds. M16–L17.
3 Nurse, cherish; provide with a snug place of rest. L16.

NV *abbreviation*.
Nevada.

nvCJD *abbreviation*.
New variant Creutzfeldt–Jakob disease.

NVQ *abbreviation*.
National Vocational Qualification.

NW *abbreviation*.
North-west(ern).

NY *abbreviation*.
New York.

nyala /ˈnjɑːlə/ *noun*. Pl. **-s**, same. Also (earlier) **inyala** /ɪˈnjɑːlə/. M19.
[Zulu *i-nyala*.]
A large gregarious antelope, *Tragelaphus angasii*, of southern Africa, the male of which is grey-brown with white stripes and spiral black horns, the female red-brown and hornless. Also (more fully ***mountain nyala***), *T. buxtoni* of Ethiopia.

Nyamwezi /njamˈweɪzi/ *adjective & noun*. L19.
[Bantu.]
► **A** *noun*. Pl. same, **-s**. A member of a Bantu-speaking people of western Tanzania; the Bantu language of this people. L19.
► **B** *adjective*. Of or pertaining to the Nyamwezi or their language. E20.

Nyanja /ˈnjandʒə/ *noun & adjective*. M19.
[Bantu.]
► **A** *noun*. Pl. same, **-s**. A member of a Bantu-speaking people inhabiting Malawi; the Bantu language of this people. M19.
► **B** *attrib*. or as *adjective*. Of or pertaining to the Nyanja or their language. M19.

†**nyas** *noun & adjective* see EYAS.

Nyasa /nʌɪˈasə, nɪ-/ *noun & adjective*. M19.
[Bantu.]
► **A** *noun*. Pl. same, **-s**. A member of a Bantu-speaking people inhabiting Malawi; the Bantu language of this people. M19.
► **B** *attrib*. or as *adjective*. Of or pertaining to the Nyasa or their language. L19.

nybble *noun* see NIBBLE *verb*² & *noun*².

NYC *abbreviation*.
New York City.

nychthemera *noun pl*. see NYCHTHEMERON.

nychthemeral /nɪkˈθiːm(ə)r(ə)l/ *adjective*. E20.
[from next + -AL¹.]
SCIENCE. Occurring with a variation matching that of night and day.

nychthemeron /nɪkˈθiːmərɒn/ *noun*. *arch*. Pl. **-rons**, **-ra** /-rə/. L17.
[Greek *nukhthēmeron* neut. of *nukhthēmeros* lasting for a day and a night, from *nukt-*, *nux* night + *hēmera* day.]
A period of twenty-four hours, of a day and a night.

nyctalope /ˈnɪktələʊp/ *noun*. Now *rare* or *obsolete*. E17.
[formed as NYCTALOPS.]
A person or animal exhibiting nyctalopia; = NYCTALOPS 2. Usu. in *pl*.

nyctalopia /nɪktəˈləʊpɪə/ *noun*. Also Anglicized as †**nyctalopy**. L17.
[Late Latin, formed as next + -IA¹.]
1 Chiefly MEDICINE. Reduction or loss of vision in dim light, due to disorder of the retinal rods, as caused by vitamin A deficiency; night-blindness. L17.
2 [By confusion.] = HEMERALOPIA 1. Now *rare*. L17.
■ **nyctalopic** *adjective* of the nature of or exhibiting nyctalopia M19.

nyctalops /ˈnɪktəlɒps/ *noun*. *rare*. M17.
[Greek *nuktalōps*, *-ōp-*, from *nukt-*, *nux* night + *alaos* blind + *-ōps* eye.]
†**1** Nyctalopia. M17–E18.
2 A person exhibiting nyctalopia. Cf. earlier NYCTALOPE. E19.

†**nyctalopy** *noun* see NYCTALOPIA.

nycti- /ˈnɪkti/ *combining form*.
[Greek *nukti-* combining form (properly locative) of *nukt-*, *nux* night: see -I-.]
Of or pertaining to night. Cf. NYCTO-.
■ **nyctiˈnastic** *adjective* (BOTANY) (of periodic movements of flowers or leaves) caused by regular (esp. nightly) changes in light intensity or temperature E20. **nyctinasty** *noun* [Greek *nastos* pressed] BOTANY a nyctinastic movement M20. **nyctitropic** /-ˈtrəʊpɪk, -ˈtrɒpɪk/ *adjective* exhibiting nyctitropism L19. **nyctitropism** /-ˈtrəʊp-/ *noun* (BOTANY) the tendency of leaves or other parts of a plant to take up a different position at night from that occupied in the day L19.

nycticorax /nɪkˈtɪkəraks/ *noun*. Pl. ***nycticoraces*** /nɪktɪˈkɒrəsiːz/. L17.
[Latin from Greek *nuktikorax*, formed as prec. + *corax* raven.]
A night heron. Now only as mod. Latin genus name.

nycto- /ˈnɪktəʊ/ *combining form*.
[Greek *nukto-* combining form of *nukt-*, *nux* night: see -O-.]
Of or pertaining to night. Cf. NYCTI-.
■ **nyctoˈhemeral** *adjective* = NYCHTHEMERAL M20. **nyctoˈphobia** *noun* extreme fear of the night or of darkness E20. **nyctoˈphonia** *noun* (PSYCHOLOGY) inability or refusal to speak except at night L19.

nye /nʌɪ/ *noun*. Long *dial*. LME.
[Old French *ni* (mod. *nid*) from Latin *nidus* nest. Cf. NIDE.]
A brood of pheasants.

nyet *adverb & noun* var. of NIET.

nylghau *noun* see NILGAI.

nylon /ˈnʌɪlɒn/ *noun & adjective*. M20.
[Invented word, after *rayon*, *cotton*.]
► **A** *noun*. **1** Any of various synthetic thermoplastic polymers whose molecules are linear polyamides, many of which are tough, lightweight, and resistant to heat and chemicals, and may be produced as filaments (widely used in textiles) or sheets, or as moulded objects; *esp*. (more fully ***nylon 66***), that made from adipic acid and hexamethylenediamine. M20.
2 Fabric made from nylon yarn. M20.
3 In *pl*. Stockings or tights made of nylon. M20.
Comb.: **nylon salt** a salt formed by the reaction of diamine (esp. hexamethylenediamine) with a dibasic acid (esp. adipic acid) and polymerizable to give nylon.
► **B** *attrib*. or as *adjective*. Made or consisting of nylon. M20.
¶ Proprietary names for this substance include PERLON, RILSAN.
■ **nyloned** *adjective* clad in nylon or nylons M20.

-nym /nɪm/ *suffix*.
[Repr. Greek *onuma* (Aeolic), *onoma* name; in later use extracted from HOMONYM, SYNONYM.]
Forming nouns with the sense 'name', as ***acronym***, ***hyponym***, etc.

nymph /nɪmf/ *noun*. LME.
[Old French *nimphe* (mod. *nymphe*) from Latin *nympha* from Greek *numphē* bride, nymph, rel. to Latin *nubere* be married to (a man). Cf. earlier NYMPHET.]
1 a CLASSICAL MYTHOLOGY. Any of a class of semi-divine spirits regarded as maidens inhabiting the sea, rivers, hills, woods, and trees. LME. ►**b** A stream, a river. *literary*. L16.
2 A beautiful young woman. Chiefly *poet. & joc*. L16.
3 a A larva of a hemimetabolous insect, resembling the adult but immature. Also occas., a pupa. L16. ►**b** A fishing-fly made to resemble the aquatic larva of a mayfly. E20.

1 W. S. MAUGHAM The nymph flying through the woods of Greece with the satyr in hot pursuit. ***sea-nymph***, ***wood nymph***, etc. **b** W. DRUMMOND Having to these Seas of Joy . . added this small Brook or Nymph of mine. **2** W. HAGGARD Counsellor of Embassy living with fellow-travelling nymph.

■ **nymphean** *adjective* of or pertaining to a nymph or nymphs; nymphlike: M18. **nymphic** *adjective* (*rare*) of or pertaining to a nymph or nymphs L19. **nymphical** *adjective* (*arch. rare*) pertaining to or characteristic of a nymph or nymphs L18. **nymphish** *adjective* (*arch*.) (*a*) of, pertaining to, or consisting of nymphs; (*b*) *rare* nymphlike, bewitching: L16. **nymphlike** *adjective & adverb* (*a*) *adjective* resembling (that of) a nymph; graceful, beautiful; (*b*) *adverb* (long *rare* or *obsolete*) in the manner of a nymph: E17.

nymph /nɪmf/ *verb intrans*. M20.
[from the noun.]
Of fish, esp. trout: feed on insect larvae near the surface of the water.

nympha /ˈnɪmfə/ *noun*. Pl. **-phae** /-fiː/. E17.
[Latin: see prec.]
1 ENTOMOLOGY. = NYMPH *noun* 3a. E17.
2 ANATOMY. In *pl*. The labia minora of the vulva. Now *rare*. L17.

nymphaea /nɪmˈfiːə/ *noun*¹. M16.
[Latin from Greek *numphaia* fem. of *numphaios* sacred to the nymphs.]
Any water lily of or formerly included in the genus *Nymphaea* (family Nymphaeaceae); *esp*. the common white water lily, ***Nymphaea alba***.

nymphaea *noun*² pl. of NYMPHAEUM.

nymphaeum /nɪmˈfiːəm/ *noun*. Pl. **-phaea** /-ˈfiːə/. Also †**-pheum**, pl. **-phea**. L18.
[Latin from Greek *numphaion*, *-eion* temple or shrine of the nymphs, neut. of *numphaios*, *-eios* sacred to the nymphs, from *numphē* NYMPH *noun*.]
CLASSICAL ANTIQUITIES. A grotto or shrine dedicated to a nymph or nymphs; (a part of) a building built to represent this.

nymphal /ˈnɪmf(ə)l/ *noun & adjective*. E17.
[Late Latin *nymphalis*, from Latin *nympha* NYMPH *noun*; in sense A.2 from French *nymphale*, formed as NYMPH *noun*: see -AL¹.]
►† **A** *noun*. **1** A meeting or gathering of nymphs. Only in E17.
2 = NYMPHALID *noun*. Only in L18.
► **B** *adjective*. **1** Pertaining to a mythological nymph or nymphs; consisting of mythological nymphs. M17.
2 Pertaining to or of the nature of an insect nymph. M19.

nymphalid /nɪmˈfalɪd/ *adjective & noun*. L19.
[mod. Latin *Nymphalidae* (see below), from *Nymphalis* genus name, from *nympha* nymph: see -ID³.]
► **A** *adjective*. Of, pertaining to, designating, or belonging to the large family Nymphalidae of butterflies with

degenerate forelegs (sometimes held to include danaids and satyrids). L19.
▶ **B** *noun*. A butterfly of this family. L19.

†**nymphea** *noun*² pl. of NYMPHAEUM.

Nymphenburg /ˈnɪmf(ə)nbəːg/ *adjective*. M19.
[A former village in Bavaria, Germany, now a suburb of Munich.]
Designating porcelain manufactured at Nymphenburg from 1761.

nymphet /ˈnɪmfɛt, nɪmˈfɛt/ *noun*. OE.
[In sense 1 from Latin *nympha* (see NYMPH *noun*); in senses 2 and 3 directly from NYMPH *noun*: see -ET¹.]
†**1** The white water lily, *Nymphaea alba*. Only in OE.
2 A young or small nymph. Chiefly *poet*. E17.
3 An attractive and sexually mature young girl. M20.

📖 **2** M. DRAYTON Of the Nymphets sporting there In Wyrall and in Delamere. **3** SNOO WILSON I'm in love with a thirteen-year-old nymphet. F. RAPHAEL Eleven-year-old Lady Charlotte, a nymphet much to Byron's prepubescent taste.

nymphette /nɪmˈfɛt/ *noun*. M20.
[French, formed as NYMPH *noun* + -ETTE.]
= NYMPHET 3.

†**nympheum** *noun* var. of NYMPHAEUM.

nympho /ˈnɪmfəʊ/ *noun & adjective*. *colloq*. Pl. of noun **-os**. M20.
[Abbreviation.]
= NYMPHOMANIAC *noun*, *adjective*.

nympholepsy /ˈnɪmfəlɛpsi/ *noun*. L18.
[from next after *epilepsy*.]
A state of rapture supposedly inspired in men by nymphs; an ecstasy or frenzy caused by desire for the unattainable.

nympholept /ˈnɪmfəlɛpt/ *noun*. E19.
[from Greek *numpholēptos* caught by nymphs, from *numphē* NYMPH *noun* + *lambanein* take hold of.]
A person inspired by a violent enthusiasm, esp. for an unattainable ideal. (Foll. by *of*.)

nympholeptic /nɪmfəˈlɛptɪk/ *adjective*. E19.
[from prec. + -IC.]
1 Of or pertaining to nympholepsy. E19.
2 Affected with nympholepsy; enraptured. M19.

nymphomania /nɪmfəˈmeɪnɪə/ *noun*. L18.
[mod. Latin, from Latin *nympha* NYMPH *noun* + -O- + -MANIA.]
Excessive or uncontrollable sexual desire in a female. Freq. *hyperbol*. Cf. SATYRIASIS, SATYROMANIA.
■ **nymphomaniac** *adjective & noun* (*a*) *adjective* of, pertaining to, or exhibiting nymphomania; (*b*) *noun* a woman exhibiting nymphomania: L19. **nymphomaˈniacal** *adjective* = NYMPHOMANIAC *adjective* E20. **nymphomanic** /-ˈman-/ *adjective* (*rare*) = NYMPHOMANIAC *adjective* M19.

nymphon /ˈnɪmfɒn/ *noun*. M19.
[mod. Latin *Nymphon* (see below) from Greek *numphōn* bride-chamber, from *numphē* bride.]
ZOOLOGY. A pycnogonid (sea-spider) of the genus *Nymphon*. Chiefly as mod. Latin genus name.

Nynorsk /ˈnjyːnɔːsk, ˈnjuː-/ *noun*. M20.
[Norwegian, from *ny* new + *Norsk* Norwegian.]
A literary form of Norwegian based on elements common to the (esp. western) Norwegian dialects and intended to be a purer form of Norwegian than ***Bokmål***. Formerly called LANDSMÅL.

Nyon /ˈniːən/ *noun & adjective*. M19.
[A commune in Switzerland.]
(Designating) porcelain manufactured at Nyon from *c* 1780.

NYPD *abbreviation*.
New York Police Department.

Nyquist /ˈnʌɪkwɪst/ *noun*. M20.
[Harry *Nyquist* (1889–1976), Swedish-born US engineer.]
ELECTRONICS. Used *attrib*. to designate various methods, rules, etc., devised by Nyquist.
Nyquist criterion a method of determining the stability or instability of a feedback system according to whether the plot of a Nyquist diagram encircles the point (−1, 0). **Nyquist diagram** a representation of the vector response of a feedback system (esp. an amplifier) as a complex graphical plot showing the relationship between feedback and gain. **Nyquist frequency** the minimum frequency at which it is necessary to sample a signal in order that it can be uniquely reconstructed, equal to twice the frequency of the highest-frequency component present.

NYSE *abbreviation*.
New York Stock Exchange.

nyssa /ˈnɪsə/ *noun*. L19.
[mod. Latin (see below), from *Nysa* the name of a water-nymph, with ref. to the swamp habitat of some species.]
BOTANY & HORTICULTURE. Any of several chiefly N. American trees constituting the genus *Nyssa* (family Nyssaceae), allied to the cornels, having small greenish flowers, berry-like fruits, and often bright foliage in autumn. Cf. PEPPERIDGE, TUPELO.

nystagmus /nɪˈstagməs/ *noun*. E19.
[mod. Latin from Greek *nustagmos* nodding, drowsiness, from *nustazein* nod, be sleepy.]
MEDICINE. A rapid involuntary, usu. lateral, oscillation of the eyeball.
■ **nystagmic** *adjective* L19. **nystagmoid** *adjective* designating jerking movements of the eyes when tired L19. **nystagmoˈgraphic** *adjective* of or pertaining to nystagmography M20. **nystagˈmography** *noun* recording of nystagmic movements of the eyeball E20.

nystatin /ˈnʌɪstətɪn/ *noun*. M20.
[from *New York State* (where developed) + -IN¹.]
PHARMACOLOGY. A yellow antibiotic produced by the bacterium *Streptomyces noursei* and applied locally to treat various fungal infections.

nytril /ˈnʌɪtrɪl/ *noun*. Orig. *US*. M20.
[from elems. of the semi-systematic name of the chief component, *vinylidene dinitrile*.]
A synthetic fibre, usu. soft and elastic, used in textiles.

Nyungar /ˈnjʊŋə/ *noun*. L19.
[Nyungar, = an Aboriginal, a man.]
1 An Australian aboriginal language formerly spoken in the area around Perth and Albany in Western Australia and now extinct.
2 (Pl. same.) A member of an aboriginal people speaking a dialect of Nyungar.

NZ *abbreviation*.
New Zealand.

Nzima /(ə)nˈziːmə/ *noun & adjective*. Also **Nzema**. E20.
[Nzima.]
(Of, pertaining to, or designating) a Niger-Congo language spoken in Ghana and Ivory Coast.

Oo

O, o /əʊ/.
The fifteenth letter of the modern English alphabet and the fourteenth of the ancient Roman one, corresp. to Greek *o*, repr. the sixteenth letter of the Phoenician and ancient Semitic alphabet. The sound orig. represented by the letter was probably a mid-back rounded or labial vowel. For its principal mod. sounds see the Key to the Pronunciation. Pl. **oes**, **O's**, **Os**.
▶ **I 1** The letter and its sound.
2 The shape of the letter.
2 O-ring a gasket or seal (usu. of rubber) in the form of a ring with a circular cross-section.
▶ **II** Symbolical uses.
3 Used to denote serial order; applied e.g. to the fifteenth (or fourteenth, I or J being omitted) group or section, sheet of a book, etc.
4 LOGIC. (Cap. O.) A particular negative proposition.
5 (Cap. O.) The blood group characterized by the absence of both the A and B agglutinogens.
▶ **III 6** Abbrevs.: **O** = Ohio; old; ordinary (in *O level* (*Hist.*), of the General Certificate of Education examination); oxygen.

O /əʊ/ *noun*[1]. LME.
[from O *interjection*.]
1 An utterance of 'O!' LME.
2 ECCLESIASTICAL. An anthem, meditation, etc., containing an invocation to Christ beginning with *O*, as ***O Sapientia***, ***O Adonai***, etc.; *spec.* (also ***O-antiphon***) each of a group of such antiphons sung in the days preceding Christmas Eve. M16.

O /əʊ/ *noun*[2] & *adjective*. Pl. **O's**, **oes**. L16.
[from resemblance in shape to the letter O.]
▶ **A** *noun*. **1** A round thing, as a circle, round spot, etc. L16. ▸†**b** In *pl.* Small circular spangles used to ornament clothing. Only in 17.
2 The arabic zero, o; a cipher, a mere nothing. E17.
▶ **B** *attrib.* or as *adjective*. Designating a gauge of track in model railways (now 32 mm). E20.
Comb.: **OO** *adjective* designating a model railway gauge of 16.5 mm. **OOO** *adjective* designating a model railway gauge of 10 mm.

O /əʊ/ *interjection*. ME.
[Natural exclam.]
1 Expr. appeal, surprise, lament, etc. Freq. before a name in the vocative. *arch.* ME.
2 Appended to lines in ballads and other popular verse for metrical reasons. Cf. -A[4]. Chiefly *Scot.* E18.

📖 **1** AV *Ps.* 147:12 Praise the Lord, O Jerusalem. I. WATTS But O! how exceedingly difficult it is. TENNYSON O for the touch of a vanished hand. ***O be joyful***: see JOYFUL 1.

O' /əʊ/ *noun*. M18.
[Irish *ó*, *ua* grandson, Old Irish *aue*: see OE.]
A person whose surname begins with the Irish patronymic prefix *O'*, indicating descent from an ancient Irish family. Also, this prefix.

o' /əʊ, ə/ *preposition*[1]. Long *arch.* & *dial.* ME.
[Reduced form.]
= ON *preposition*.

📖 SHAKES. *Hen. VIII* Mercy o' me. W. A. WALLACE He went to church twice o' Sundays.

o' /əʊ, ə/ *preposition*[2]. ME.
[Reduced form.]
= OF *preposition*. Now chiefly *arch.* & *dial.* exc. in ***o' clock*** and certain phrs.

📖 BROWNING Just a spirt O' the proper fiery acid. ***Jack o' lantern***, ***John o' Groats***, ***Tom o' Bedlam***, ***will o' the wisp***, etc.

-o /əʊ/ *suffix*.
[Perh. repr. O *interjection*, reinforced by the final syll. of abbreviated forms as *compo*, *hippo*, *photo*, etc.]
Forming words constituting slang or colloq. variants or derivatives, as ***beano***, ***boyo***, ***pinko***, ***preggo***, ***starko***, ***wino***, etc.

-o- /əʊ/ *combining form* (*connective*).
Repr. Greek *-o-* as a stem-vowel or connective, forming the terminal vowel of combining forms of words adopted from Greek through Latin or directly from Greek, or of English words modelled on these, as ***Anglo-***, ***chemico-***, ***dynamo-***, ***Franco-***, ***hydro-***, ***medico-***, etc.

oaf /əʊf/ *noun*. Also (earlier) †**auf(e)**. E17.
[Old Norse *álfr* cogn. with Old English *ælf*: see ELF *noun*[1]. Cf. OUPH.]
Orig., a child of an elf or a goblin, a supposed fairy changeling; a deformed or idiot child. Now, a halfwit, a fool; an awkward lout, a rude and boorish (esp. male) person.

📖 T. ROETHKE I was like a country boy at his first party—such an oaf . . such a blockhead. W. S. MAUGHAM You are an ill-mannered oaf.

oafish /ˈəʊfɪʃ/ *adjective*. E17.
[from OAF + -ISH[1].]
Characteristic of or resembling an oaf; dull-witted, foolish; loutish, rude.

📖 DYLAN THOMAS The poems . . are a poor lot . . with . . many oafish sentiments.

■ **oafishly** *adverb* L19. **oafishness** *noun* E18.

oafo /ˈəʊfəʊ/ *noun*. *colloq.* Pl. **-os**. M20.
[from OAF + -O.]
A lout, a hooligan.

oak /əʊk/ *noun* & *adjective*.
[Old English *āc* (pl. *ǣc*) = Old Frisian, Middle Low German *ēk* (Dutch *eik*), Old High German *eih* (German *Eiche*), Old Norse *eik*, from Germanic.]
▶ **A** *noun*. **1** Any of numerous trees (rarely shrubs) of the genus *Quercus*, of the beech family, with acorns borne in cupules and freq. with sinuately lobed leaves; *spec.* (more fully ***common oak***, ***English oak***, ***pedunculate oak***) *Q. robur* and (more fully ***durmast oak***, ***sessile oak***) *Q. petraea*. Also ***oak tree***. OE.
2 The timber of the oak, an important building material, esp. for ships. Freq. in allusive phrases with ref. to its hardness and durability. LME. ▸**b** A wooden outer door, usu. of university rooms. Chiefly in ***sport one's oak***, shut this door as a sign that one does not wish to be disturbed. *colloq.* L18. ▸**c** Furniture or domestic fittings made of oak. E19.
3 In certain biblical translations: the terebinth tree, *Pistacia terebinthus*. LME.
4 The leaves of the oak, esp. as worn in wreaths. LME. ▸**b** A shade of brown like that of a young oak-leaf. L19.
5 Any of various trees resembling the English oak or having wood similarly grained; *esp.* = CASUARINA. Cf. SHE-OAK. *Austral.* L18.
6 The taste, flavour, or aroma imparted to wine by the use of oak casks, usu. characterized as coconut-like or vanillic. L20.

📖 **1** ***kermes oak***, ***live oak***, ***quercitron oak***, ***robur-oak***, etc. **5** ***native oak***: see NATIVE *adjective*. ***silky oak***: see SILKY *adjective* 4. **6** C. CLARK A monster wine with . . lots of spicy oak.

Other phrases: ***heart of oak***: see HEART *noun*. ***lungs of oak***, ***lungs of the oak***: see LUNG. **oak of Jerusalem** an aromatic goosefoot, *Chenopodium botrys*, with oaklike leaves. ***poison oak***: see POISON *noun*, *adjective*, & *adverb*. ***royal oak***: see ROYAL *adjective*. **the Oaks** [from the name of an estate near Epsom] an annual horse-race for three-year-old fillies run at Epsom on the Friday after the Derby.
▶ **B** *adjective*. Made of, decorated with, or resembling the wood of the oak. M17.
Comb. & special collocations: **oak-apple** a globular spongy gall formed on the leaves and stems of the oak by the gall-wasp *Biorhiza pallida*; ***oak-apple day***, the anniversary of Charles II's restoration (29 May), when oak-apples or oak-leaves used to be worn in memory of his hiding in an oak after the battle of Worcester; **Oak-boy** a member of an Irish rebel society of the 1760s, whose badge was an oak-sprig worn in the hat; **oak cist**, **oak coffin** ARCHAEOLOGY a coffin made from a split and hollowed oak log, used in Bronze-Age Europe; ***oak* EGGAR**; **oak fern** †(*a*) the polypody *Polypodium vulgare*, regarded as specially efficacious against disease when epiphytic on the oak; (*b*) a fern of rocky or mountainous woods, *Gymnocarpium dryopteris*; **oak-fly** ANGLING (an artificial fly imitating) a long-legged yellowish dipteran fly, *Rhagio scolopacea*; **oak-gall** a gall on an oak, *esp.* one of a rounded form; **oak land** (chiefly *US*) land bearing a growth of oak trees; **oak leaf** (*a*) a leaf of an oak tree; (*b*) a red or green variety of lettuce which has leaves with serrated edges and a slightly bitter taste; **oak moss** a tree-lichen, *Evernia prunastri*, found on oaks and used as a basis for perfumes; **oak-opening** a clearing or thinly wooded space in an oak forest; **oak-pruner** = ***twig-pruner*** s.v. TWIG *noun*[1]; **oak-spangle** a kind of flat gall caused by some gall-flies on the underside of oak-leaves; **oaktag** = ***tagboard*** (a) s.v. TAG *noun*[1]; ***oak tree***: see sense 1 above; **oak-web** *dial.* a cockchafer; **oak wilt** *US* a disease of oaks etc. caused by the fungus *Ceratocystis fagacearum*, which makes the foliage wilt and eventually kills the tree; **oak-wood** (*a*) the wood or timber of the oak; (*b*) a wood or forest consisting of oaks; **oak-worm** any of various moth caterpillars that live on oaks.

■ **oaklet** *noun* L19. **oaklike** *adjective* resembling (that of) an oak M19. **oaky** *adjective* M17.

oaken /ˈəʊk(ə)n/ *adjective*. ME.
[from prec. + -EN[4].]
1 Made of the wood of the oak. ME.
2 Of, pertaining to, or forming part of the oak. *arch.* LME.
3 Fashioned from oak leaves or twigs. *arch.* E17.
4 Consisting of oak trees. Now *arch.* & *poet.* M17.

📖 **1** M. CHABON His father's laughter coming through the oaken door. ***oaken towel***: see TOWEL *noun* 3. **2** DRYDEN Jove . . shook from Oaken Leaves the liquid Gold. **3** W. FALCONER Around her head an oaken wreath was seen.

oakling /ˈəʊklɪŋ/ *noun*. M17.
[from OAK *noun* + -LING[1].]
A young or small oak.

oakum /ˈəʊkəm/ *noun*.
[Old English *ācumbe*, *ācum(b)a* lit. 'off-combings', formed as A-[3] + *camb-* stem of *cemban* KEMB.]
†**1** = TOW *noun*[1] 1b. Also, trimmings, shreds. Only in OE.
2 Loose fibre obtained by untwisting and picking old rope and used esp. in caulking ships' seams (the picking of which was formerly a task assigned to convicts and inmates of workhouses). L15.

📖 **2** P. ACKROYD My eyesight began to fail, from the strain of picking oakum in my cell.

oaky /ˈəʊki/ *adjective*. M17.
[from OAK + -Y[1].]
1 Resembling oak; strong, firm, hard. M17.
2 Having many oaks. L18.
■ **oakiness** *noun* M19.

O. and M. *abbreviation*.
Organization and methods.

OAP *abbreviation*.
Old age pensioner.

OAPEC /əʊˈeɪpɛk/ *abbreviation*.
Organization of Arab Petroleum Exporting Countries.

oar /ɔː/ *noun* & *verb*.
[Old English *ār*, Old Norse *ár*, from Germanic, perh. rel. to Greek *eretmos* oar, *eretēs* rower, *eressein* row.]
▶ **A** *noun*. **1** A long pole widened and flattened at one end into a blade, used to propel or steer a boat by pressure against the water. OE.
2 *fig.* An object resembling an oar in function or shape. L16.
3 *transf.* **a** A rowing boat. Freq. in ***pair of oars*** below. L16. ▸**b** *sing.* & in *pl.* An oarsman. Freq. in ***first oars*** below. M18.
4 A pole or other implement with which something is stirred; BREWING a pole for stirring the mash in the tun. M18.

📖 **1** G. HUNTINGTON To the quiet dipping of oars the boat went evenly forward. **3b** *Daily Telegraph* He . . trained on into a first-rate College oar.

Phrases: **first oars** a person who rows stroke; *fig.* a person taking the first place. **lay on one's oars** *US* = **rest on one's oars** below. **pair of oars** a boat rowed by two people. ***ply the* LABOURING *oar***. ***pull the* LABOURING *oar***. **put one's oar in** *colloq.* interfere, be (or become) meddlesomely involved with. **rest on one's oars** lean on the handles of one's oars and thereby raise them horizontally out of the water; *fig.* relax one's efforts. **shove one's oar in** *colloq.* = ***put one's oar in*** above. ***stretch to the oar***: see STRETCH *verb*. ***toss oar(s)***, ***toss one's oar(s)***: see TOSS *verb*. ***tug at the oar***: see TUG *verb*. ***tug the* LABOURING *oar***.
Comb.: **oarfish** a large, very long deep-water marine fish, *Regalecus glesne* (family Regalecidae) with a ribbon-like dorsal fin; **oar-hole** (chiefly *Hist.*) a hole in the side of a galley through which an oar passes; **oar-lop** (*obsolete* exc. *Hist.*) a lop-eared rabbit with its ears sticking out at right angles to its head; **oar-port** (chiefly *Hist.*) = ***oar-hole*** above.
▶ **B** *verb*. Chiefly *poet.*
1 *verb intrans.* Row; advance, as if propelled by oars. LME.
2 *verb trans.* Row; propel with or as with oars. E17.
3 *verb trans.* Move (the hands etc.) like oars. L19.

📖 **1** A. TYLER He was moving toward the target . . oaring through the weeds. **2** SOUTHEY Now oaring with slow wing her upward way. **3** R. PRICE He raised his arms above his chest, oared them as if taking delicate signals.

■ **oarless** *adjective* having no oars; undisturbed by oars: L16.

oarage /ˈɔːrɪdʒ/ *noun.* **M18.**
[from **OAR** *noun, verb* + **-AGE.**]
1 The action or practice of oaring; rowing. **M18.**
2 Apparatus or fittings pertaining to or resembling oars; rowing equipment. **E19.**

> **2** *Times Lit. Suppl.* Hazards will persist as the ship tries out its complicated oarage in real waves.

oared /ɔːd/ *adjective.* **M18.**
[from **OAR** *noun* + **-ED**².]
Having an oar or oars, esp. of a specified number.

> J. M. NEALE Where shall go no oared galley. ***four-oared, six-oared***, etc.

oarlock /ˈɔːlɒk/ *noun.* Now chiefly *N. Amer.* **OE.**
[from **OAR** *noun* + **LOCK** *noun*². Cf. **ROWLOCK.**]
A rowlock.

oarman /ˈɔːmən/ *noun. rare.* Pl. **-men.** **E17.**
[formed as next + **MAN** *noun.*]
= next.

oarsman /ˈɔːzmən/ *noun.* Pl. **-men.** **LME.**
[from **OAR** *noun* + **-'S**¹ + **MAN** *noun.*]
A person who uses oars; a rower.
■ **oarsmanship** *noun* the art of rowing; skill in rowing: **L19.**

oarswoman /ˈɔːzwʊmən/ *noun.* Pl. **-women** /-wɪmɪn/. **L19.**
[formed as prec. + **WOMAN** *noun.*]
A female rower.

oarweed /ˈɔːwiːd/ *noun.* Also (earlier) **oreweed.** **L16.**
[from dial. var. of **WARE** *noun*¹ + **WEED** *noun*¹, by assoc. with **OAR** *noun.*]
Any large marine alga with long strap-shaped fronds; *esp.* one of the genus *Laminaria*, often found along shores.

oary /ˈɔːri/ *adjective. arch.* or *poet.* **L16.**
[from **OAR** *noun* + **-Y**¹.]
1 Provided with oars; having (things resembling) oars. **L16.**
2 Resembling or having the function of an oar or oars. **M17.**

OAS *abbreviation.*
1 On active service.
2 Organization of American States.

oasis /əʊˈeɪsɪs/ *noun.* Pl. **oases** /əʊˈeɪsiːz/. **E17.**
[Late Latin from Greek, app. of Egyptian origin.]
1 A fertile spot in a desert where water can be found, esp. in N. Africa. **E17.** ▸**b** *fig.* A place or period of calm in the midst of trouble or bustle. **E19.**
2 (Usu. **O-**.) (Proprietary name for) a rigid foam used as a matrix for flower arrangements. **M20.**

> **1b** S. BRETT One oasis of calm in the turmoil of rehearsals.

oast /əʊst/ *noun.*
[Old English *āst* = West Frisian *iest*, Middle Low German *eist* (Dutch *eest*), from Germanic, from Indo-European base meaning 'burn'.]
Orig., a kiln. Later *spec.*, a kiln for drying hops or (formerly) malt; a building containing this.
Comb.: **oast-house** a building containing a kiln for drying hops.

oat /əʊt/ *noun.* Also (*Scot. & north.*) **ait** /eɪt/.
[Old English *āte*, pl. *ātan*, peculiar to English and of unkn. origin. App. *oat* (unlike other cereal names) denoted primarily an individual grain: cf. *groats*.]
1 a In *pl.*, the grains of a hardy cereal plant of the genus *Avena*, usu. *A. sativa*, used as food for people (in porridge etc.) and animals, esp. horses; *sing.* (*rare*), one such grain. **OE.** ▸**b** (A particular kind or strain of) the plant yielding this grain. Usu. in *pl.*, this plant as a crop. **ME.**
2 Any of various wild grasses related to or resembling the cultivated oat. **OE.**
3 A shepherd's pipe made of a straw from an oat-plant. *poet.* **M17.**
4 In *pl.* Sexual gratification. Chiefly in ***get one's oats, have one's oats.*** *slang.* **E20.**
1a *rolled oats*: see **ROLL** *verb.* **2 *false oat*** a common grass of hedgerows, *Arrhenatherum elatius.* **wild oat** a cornfield weed, *Avena fatua*, resembling the cultivated oat but with the florets hairy at the base. **yellow oat** a grass of pasture-land, *Trisetum flavescens*, with small golden spikelets.
Phrases: **be off one's oats** *colloq.* have no appetite for food. **feel one's oats** *colloq.* be lively or (*US*) self-important. **wild oats** youthful follies or excesses committed before settling down (chiefly in ***sow one's wild oats***).
Comb.: **oat burner** *N. Amer. colloq.* a horse; **oatcake** a thin unleavened cake similar to a biscuit, made with oatmeal; **oat cell** *MEDICINE* a small oval cell with little cytoplasm and a densely staining nucleus, characteristic of carcinoma of the bronchus; **oat-celled** *adjective* (*MEDICINE*) containing oat cells; **oat-grass** any of several grasses resembling the cultivated oat; *esp.* (**a**) (in full ***tall oat-grass***) = ***false oat*** above; (**b**) either of two grasses of calcareous soils, *Helictotrichon pubescens* (in full ***downy oat-grass***), and *H. pratense* (in full ***meadow oat-grass***); **oat-plant** the plant that yields oats.
■ **oater** *noun* (chiefly *US*) = ***horse opera*** s.v. **HORSE** *noun* **M20.**

oat /əʊt/ *verb trans. & intrans. US.* **M18.**
[from prec.]
Feed (a horse etc.) with oats.

oaten /ˈəʊt(ə)n/ *adjective.* **LME.**
[from **OAT** *noun* + **-EN**⁴.]
1 Made of the grain of oats; made of oatmeal. **LME.**
2 Of or belonging to the oat-plant; *esp.* (of a musical pipe) made of a straw or stem from one. **LME.**

oath /əʊθ/ *noun.* Also (*Scot. & north.*) **aith** /eɪθ/. Pl. **-ths** /-ðz/.
[Old English *āþ* = Old Frisian *ēth*, *ēd*, Old Saxon *ēþ* (Dutch *eed*), Old & mod. High German *eid*, Old Norse *eiðr*, Gothic *aiþs*, from Germanic.]
1 A solemn declaration (often invoking God, a deity, etc.), as to the truth of something, or as an absolute commitment to future action, behaviour, etc.; an act making such a declaration. Also, (the words of) a statement or promise made by such a declaration. **OE.** ▸**b** *gen.* A firm asseveration. *arch. rare.* **E17.**
2 A casual or careless declaration (often naming God, a deity, etc., without intent of reverence) made in corroboration of a statement etc.; (the words of) a careless use of the name of God, a deity, etc., in asseveration or imprecation; a profane or blasphemous utterance, an expletive, a curse. **ME.**

> **1** G. MEREDITH Rose . . made an oath to her soul she would rescue him. *TV Times* Masons pride themselves on loyalty to their oath. ***assertory oath, Bible oath, coronation oath, gospel oath, Hippocratic oath, promissory oath*** etc. **2** J. LONDON Oaths and obscene allusions were frequent on their lips. HENRY MILLER Instead of wild oaths there were now nothing but blessings.

Phrases: ***ABJURATION oath.*** ***Commissioner for Oaths***: see **COMMISSIONER** 1. **my oath!** *Austral. & NZ slang* yes! of course! upon my word! ***oath of abjuration***: see **ABJURATION** 2. **oath of allegiance** an oath affirming allegiance to the monarch, as taken before accepting certain official positions or a seat in Parliament, or on becoming a naturalized subject. **on oath** accompanied by a binding oath, having sworn an oath. ***PROMISSORY oath.*** **swear an oath, take an oath** bind oneself by an oath. ***tender an oath***: see **TENDER** *verb*² 2. **under oath** having sworn an oath.
Comb.: **oath-helper** *Hist.* = **COMPURGATOR** 1.

oath /əʊθ, əʊð/ *verb. rare.* **ME.**
[from prec.]
†**1** *verb trans.* Impose an oath on, put under oath. Only in **ME.**
2 *verb intrans. & trans.* (with *it*). Utter an oath or oaths; swear; take an oath. **L15.**
3 *verb trans.* Address or call with oaths. **M19.**

oathable /ˈəʊðəb(ə)l/ *adjective. rare.* **E17.**
[from **OATH** *noun* or *verb* + **-ABLE.**]
Capable of taking an oath; able to be sworn.

oatmeal /ˈəʊtmiːl/ *noun & adjective.* **LME.**
[from **OAT** *noun* + **MEAL** *noun*¹.]
▶**A** *noun.* **1** Meal made from ground oats, used esp. in porridge and oatcakes. **LME.** ▸**b** Porridge made from this. Also (US) ***oatmeal mush.*** **L19.**
2 A greyish-fawn colour with flecks of brown. **E20.**
Comb.: ***oatmeal mush***: see sense 1b above; **oatmeal soap**: containing oatmeal as a mild abrasive.
▶**B** *attrib.* or as *adjective.* Of the colour oatmeal. **M20.**

OAU *abbreviation.*
Organization of African Unity.

Oaxacan /wəˈhɑːk(ə)n/ *adjective.* **M20.**
[from *Oaxaca* (see below) + **-AN.**]
Of, pertaining, or belonging to the southern Mexican State of Oaxaca.

OB *abbreviation.*
1 Obstetric(s), obstetrician. *US.*
2 Off-Broadway.
3 Old Boy.
4 Order of battle.
5 Outside broadcast.

†**ob** *noun.* **LME–M17.**
[Abbreviation of **OBOLUS.**]
A halfpenny (the sum or the coin).

ob /ɒb/ *preposition. non-standard.* **M19.**
[Repr. a pronunc.]
= **OF** *preposition.*

ob- /ɒb/ *prefix.* Before *c* **oc-** /ɒk/; before *f* **of-** /ɒf/; before *p* **op-** /ɒp/.
[Repr. Latin *ob* towards, against, in the way of, *ob-* prefix usu. denoting opposition or confrontation. In sense 2 app. taken from **OB(VERSE).**]
1 Used in words adopted from Latin.
2 Forming words (chiefly technical and scientific) with the sense 'inversely, in a direction or manner contrary to the usual', as ***obconical, obovate.***
■ **obˈconic** *adjective* (*BOTANY*) = **OBCONICAL** **E19.** **obˈconical** *adjective* (chiefly *BOTANY & ZOOLOGY*) inversely conical, with the apex downward or inward **E19.** **obˈcordate** *adjective* (*BOTANY*) inversely cordate, with the pointed end serving as the base or point of attachment **L18.** **obˌdiploˈstemonous** *adjective* (*BOTANY*) inversely diplostemonous, having the stamens of the outer whorl opposite the petals and those of the inner whorl opposite the sepals **L19.** **obˌdiploˈstemony** *noun* (*BOTANY*) obdiplostemonous condition **L19.** **obˈlanceolate** *adjective* (*BOTANY*) inversely lanceolate, with the pointed end serving as the base or point of attachment **M19.** **obˈovate** *adjective* (*BOTANY & ZOOLOGY*) inversely ovate, with the broader end uppermost or forward **L18.** **obˈovoid** *adjective* (*BOTANY & ZOOLOGY*) somewhat obovate **E19.**

ob. *abbreviation.*
Latin *Obiit* died.

oba /ˈɒbə/ *noun.* **E20.**
[Yoruba.]
Orig., (the title of) the absolute ruler of the ancient W. African kingdom of Benin, now part of Nigeria. Now, (the title of) a local chief in Nigeria.

Obad. *abbreviation.*
Obadiah (in the Bible).

Obaku /ˈəʊbakuː/ *noun.* **L19.**
[Japanese *Ōbaku* from Chinese *Huángbò* the mountain where the founder studied (used in the name of a temple established near Kyoto).]
One of the three branches of Zen Buddhism, the others being Rinzai and Soto.

obambulation /əbambjʊˈleɪʃ(ə)n/ *noun.* Long *rare* or *obsolete.* **E17.**
[from Latin *obambulat-* pa. ppl stem of *obambulare*, from **OB-** + *ambulare* walk: see **-ATION.**]
The action or an act of walking about or wandering here and there.

obang /ˈəʊbaŋ/ *noun.* **M17.**
[Japanese *ō-ban*, from *ō* great, major + *ban* part, share, division: cf. **KOBANG.**]
Hist. An oblong gold coin with rounded corners, formerly current in Japan; the sum of money represented by this, equal to ten kobangs.

Obanian /əʊˈbeɪnɪən/ *adjective & noun.* **M20.**
[from *Oban* (see below) + **-IAN.**]
ARCHAEOLOGY. ▶**A** *adjective.* Designating or pertaining to a local mesolithic culture first recognized in the neighbourhood of Oban on the west coast of Scotland. **M20.**
▶**B** *noun.* The Obanian culture; a person of this culture. **M20.**

obbligato /ɒblɪˈgɑːtəʊ/ *adjective & noun.* Also **obli-.** **L18.**
[Italian = obliged, obligatory.]
MUSIC. ▶**A** *adjective.* Indispensable; that cannot be omitted: designating a part or accompaniment forming an integral part of a composition, and the instrument on which it is played. **L18.**
▶**B** *noun.* Pl. **-os.** An obbligato part or accompaniment, *esp.* one of particular prominence in a piece. **M19.**

obbo /ˈɒbəʊ/ *noun. slang.* **E20.**
[Abbreviation of **OBSERVATION**: see **-O.**]
Observation, esp. in police work.

> B. GRAEME We're keeping a man, suspected of robbery . . under obbo.

†**obduce** *verb trans.* **M–L17.**
[Latin *obducere*: see next.]
Cover, envelop; draw over as a covering.

obduct /ɒbˈdʌkt/ *verb trans.* **E17.**
[Latin *obduct-* pa. ppl stem of *obducere*, from *ob-* **OB-** + *ducere* lead, draw.]
†**1** = **OBDUCE.** **E–M17.**
2 *GEOLOGY.* Cause to undergo obduction. Chiefly as ***obducted*** *ppl adjective.* **L20.**

obduction /ɒbˈdʌkʃ(ə)n/ *noun.* **L16.**
[Latin *obductio(n-)*, formed as prec.: see **-ION.**]
†**1** The action of covering or enveloping. **L16–M17.**
2 *GEOLOGY.* The movement of a lithospheric plate sideways and upwards over the margin of an adjacent plate. **L20.**

obduracy /ˈɒbdjʊrəsi/ *noun.* **L16.**
[from (the same root as) next: see **-ACY.**]
1 The state or quality of being obdurate. **L16.**
2 The state of being physically hard or hardened. *rare.* **E19.**

obdurate /ˈɒbdjʊrət/ *adjective.* **LME.**
[Latin *obduratus* pa. pple of *obdurare*, from *ob-* **OB-** + *durare* harden, from *durus* hard: see **-ATE**².]
1 Hardened, esp. in wrongdoing, against moral influence or persuasion; stubbornly impenitent; obstinate, unyielding, hard-hearted. **LME.**
†**2** Physically hardened or hard. **L16–L18.**

> **1** SIR W. SCOTT The obdurate conscience of the old sinner. N. ANNAN The dons remained obdurate until . . forced . . to change their tune.

■ **obdurately** *adverb* **E18.** **obdurateness** *noun* (now *rare*) **L16.**

obdurate /ˈɒbdjʊreɪt, ɒbˈdjʊəreɪt/ *verb.* **M16.**
[from prec. or Latin *obdurat-* pa. ppl stem of *obdurare*: see prec., **-ATE**³.]
1 *verb trans.* Make obdurate. **M16.**
†**2** *verb trans. & intrans.* Harden physically. **L16–M17.**

For other words beginning with *ob-* see the main alphabetic sequence of entries

obduration /ɒbdjʊˈreɪʃ(ə)n/ *noun.* LME.
[Latin *obduratio(n-)*, from *obdurat-*: see prec., -ATION.]
1 The action or fact of making or becoming obdurate. LME.
2 Physical hardening. *rare.* M17.

obdure /ɒbˈdjʊə/ *adjective.* Long *arch. rare.* L16.
[from OB- + Latin *durus* hard, after Latin *obdurare*: see OBDURATE *adjective*.]
1 = OBDURATE *adjective* 1. L16.
†**2** = OBDURATE *adjective* 2. E–M17.

obdure /ɒbˈdjʊə/ *verb.* Now *rare* or *obsolete.* LME.
[Latin *obdurare*: see OBDURATE *adjective*.]
1 *verb trans.* = OBDURATE *verb* 1. Freq. as ***obdured** ppl adjective.* LME.
†**2** *verb trans.* Harden physically. E–M17.
†**3** *verb intrans.* Become hard; become or remain obdurate. E17–M18.

OBE *abbreviation.*
Officer of (the Order of) the British Empire.

obe /əʊb/ *noun.* M19.
[Greek *ōba*.]
GREEK HISTORY. A village or district in ancient Laconia; a subdivision of a phyle or clan.

obeah /ˈəʊbɪə/ *noun & verb.* Also **obi** /ˈəʊbi/. M18.
[Twi *ɔ-bayifo* sorcerer, from *bayi* sorcery.]
▶ **A** *noun.* A kind of sorcery or witchcraft practised esp. in the W. Indies. M18.
Comb.: **obeahman**, **obeahwoman**, a male, female, practitioner of obeah.
▶ **B** *verb trans.* Bewitch by obeah, practise obeah on. E19.
■ **obeahism** *noun* the practice of or belief in obeah M19.

obeche /əʊˈbiːtʃi/ *noun.* E20.
[Local name in Nigeria.]
A large W. African tree, *Triplochiton scleroxylon* (family Sterculiaceae); the light-coloured timber of this tree.

obedience /əˈbiːdɪəns/ *noun.* ME.
[Old & mod. French *obédience* from Latin *oboedientia*, from *oboedient-*: see next, -ENCE.]
1 The action or practice of obeying; the fact of being obedient; submission to another's rule or authority; compliance with a law, command, etc. ME.
2 The fact or position of being obeyed or in authority over others, now esp. in an ecclesiastical context; authority, command, rule. ME. ▸**b** A sphere of authority; a district or body of people subject to a rule, esp. an ecclesiastical one. M17.
3 = OBEISANCE 3. Freq. in ***make obedience***, ***make one's obedience***. Now *arch. & dial.* LME.
4 ECCLESIASTICAL. A duty or a position of responsibility in a monastery or convent, esp. as assigned to a particular member under a superior; the room or place relating to such a duty or position. E18.

> 🕮 **1** A. F. DOUGLAS-HOME Obedience to the thoughts of Chairman Mao appeared to be absolute. **in obedience to** actuated by or in accordance with. ***passive obedience***: see PASSIVE *adjective*. **2** T. FULLER To abjure the authority and obedience of the Bishop of Rome. H. HALLAM Reducing Spain to the archduke's obedience. **b** E. A. FREEMAN All the English land-owners within William's obedience.

Comb.: **obedience class** a class for teaching dogs to obey orders; **obedience test** = ***obedience trial*** below; **obedience-train** *verb trans.* train (a dog) to obey orders; **obedience trial** a competition designed to test a dog's obedience.
■ †**obediencer** *noun* = OBEDIENTIARY *noun* LME–E18. **obediency** *noun* (*rare*) = OBEDIENCE 1 E17.

obedient /əˈbiːdɪənt/ *adjective & noun.* ME.
[Old & mod. French *obédient* from Latin *oboedient-* pres. ppl stem of *oboedire* OBEY: see -ENT.]
▶ **A** *adjective.* **1** That obeys or is willing to obey; submissive to another's rule or authority; complying with a law, command, etc. (Foll. by *to*.) ME. ▸†**b** Owing allegiance, subject. ME–E16.
†**2** Yielding to desires or wishes. LME–L15.
3 Moving or yielding as actuated or affected by something else. *arch.* LME.

> 🕮 **1** D. H. LAWRENCE The continual influx of more servile Europeans . . provided America with an obedient labouring class. H. T. LANE They were unusually obedient to a direct command. D. MADDEN She was a docile and obedient child. **obedient plant** the ornamental labiate plant *Physostegia virginiana*, whose flowers, if moved sideways, remain in their new position. **your obedient** *arch.* a conventional expression of respect and courtesy at leave-taking etc. (now chiefly in ***your obedient servant***, a formula for closing a business or formal letter). **3** J. LEONI The Ash is accounted very obedient in all manner of Works.

▶†**B** *noun.* A person subject to authority; a subordinate. LME–M17.
■ **obediently** *adverb* LME. **obedientness** *noun* (long *rare* or *obsolete*) L16.

obediential /ə(ʊ)ˌbiːdɪˈɛnʃ(ə)l/ *adjective.* L15.
[medieval Latin *oboedientialis*, from Latin *oboedientia* OBEDIENCE: see -IAL.]
1 Of, pertaining to, or characterized by obedience, esp. to God or the Church. L15.
2 SCOTS LAW. Designating an obligation imposed by law, esp. one arising from a family relationship. L17.
■ **obedientially** *adverb* (long *rare*) M17. **obedientialness** *noun* (long *rare*) M17.

obedientiary /ə(ʊ)ˌbiːdɪˈɛnʃ(ə)ri/ *noun & adjective.* M16.
[medieval Latin *oboedientiarius*, from *oboedientia* OBEDIENCE: see -ARY[1].]
▶ **A** *noun.* **1** A person practising or owing obedience; a subject; a liegeman. Long *arch.* M16.
2 A member of a monastery or convent to whom a particular duty is assigned; the holder of a position of responsibility in a monastery or convent under a superior. L18.
▶ **B** *adjective.* Practising or professing obedience; obedient. *rare.* E18.
■ **obedientiar** *noun* (*rare*) = OBEDIENTIARY *noun* 2 L19.

obeisance /ə(ʊ)ˈbeɪs(ə)ns/ *noun.* LME.
[Old & mod. French *obéissance*, from *obéissant* pres. pple of *obéir* OBEY: see -ANCE.]
†**1** = OBEDIENCE 1. LME–M17.
†**2** = OBEDIENCE 2. LME–M17. ▸**b** = OBEDIENCE 2b. LME–E17.
3 An act or gesture expressing submission, respect, or salutation, *esp.* a bending or prostration of the body; a bow, a curtsy. Freq. in ***make an obeisance***. Now chiefly *literary.* LME.
4 Respectfulness of manner or bearing, deference; homage, submission. Freq. in ***do obeisance***, ***make obeisance***, ***pay obeisance***. Now usu. taken as *fig.* from sense 3. LME.

> 🕮 **3** A. HIGGINS Making a profound obeisance before the altar. **4** F. RAPHAEL The cult . . to which . . he would make effortful obeisance.

obeisant /ə(ʊ)ˈbeɪs(ə)nt/ *adjective & noun.* ME.
[Old & mod. French *obéissant*: see prec., -ANT[1].]
▶ **A** *adjective.* **1** = OBEDIENT *adjective* 1, 1b. *obsolete* exc. as passing into sense 3. ME.
†**2** = OBEDIENT *adjective* 3. LME–E19.
3 Showing respect or deference, deferential; obsequious. M17.
▶†**B** *noun.* A person subject to authority; a subordinate. ME–E17.
■ **obeisantly** *adverb* (long *rare*) LME.

obeli *noun* pl. of OBELUS.

obelion /ə(ʊ)ˈbiːlɪən/ *noun.* L19.
[from Greek *obeliaios* sagittal + *-ion*, after *inion*.]
ANATOMY. The point on the skull where an imaginary line joining the parietal foramina crosses the sagittal suture.

obeliscal /ɒbəˈlɪsk(ə)l/ *adjective.* M18.
[formed as OBELISK + -AL[1].]
Of or pertaining to an obelisk; resembling an obelisk.

obeliscoid /ɒbəˈlɪskɔɪd/ *adjective.* Also **-koid**. L19.
[formed as prec. + -OID.]
Resembling an obelisk.

obelise *verb* var. of OBELIZE.

obelisk /ˈɒb(ə)lɪsk/ *noun & adjective.* M16.
[Latin *obeliscus* from Greek *obeliskos* dim. of *obelos* spit, pointed pillar.]
▶ **A** *noun.* **1** A tapering, four-sided stone pillar with a pyramidal apex, set up as a monument or landmark. M16. ▸†**b** A column or pillar of any form. L16–L17. ▸**c** A natural formation, esp. a mountain, resembling an obelisk. M17.
2 = OBELUS. L16.
2 double obelisk = ***double dagger*** s.v. DAGGER *noun*[1].
▶ **B** *attrib.* or as *adjective.* Having the shape of an obelisk. *rare.* M17.

obeliskoid *adjective* var. of OBELISCOID.

obelize /ˈɒb(ə)lʌɪz/ *verb trans.* Also **-ise**. M17.
[Greek *obelizein*, from *obelos*: see OBELISK, -IZE.]
Mark (a word, passage, etc.) with an obelus.

obelus /ˈɒb(ə)ləs/ *noun.* Pl. **-li** /-lʌɪ, -liː/. LME.
[Latin = spit, critical obelus from Greek *obelos*: see OBELISK.]
A straight horizontal stroke (–), sometimes with a dot above and below (÷), used in ancient manuscripts to mark a word, passage, etc., esp. as spurious. Also, a dagger-shaped reference mark (†) used in printed matter as a reference to a footnote etc., and in some dictionaries to denote obsoleteness. Also called ***obelisk***.

oberek /ə(ʊ)ˈbɛrɪk/ *noun.* M20.
[Polish.]
A lively Polish dance in triple time, related to the mazurka but usually faster.

Oberleutnant /əʊbəˈlɔɪtnənt/ *noun.* M19.
[German, from *ober* senior + *Leutnant* lieutenant.]
In the German, Austrian, and Swiss armies: a lieutenant.

Oberstleutnant /əʊbəːstˈlɔɪtnənt/ *noun.* M20.
[German, from *Oberst* colonel (from superl. of *ober* senior) + *Leutnant* lieutenant.]
In the German, Austrian, and Swiss armies: a lieutenant colonel.

obertas /ə(ʊ)ˈbɛːtəs/ *noun.* L19.
[Polish.]
= OBEREK.

obese /ə(ʊ)ˈbiːs/ *adjective.* M17.
[Latin *obesus* having eaten oneself fat, from *ob-* OB- + *esus* pa. pple of *edere* eat.]
Very fat; extremely corpulent.

> 🕮 C. BRONTË A woman of robust frame . . and though stout, not obese.

¶ Rare before 19.
■ **obesely** *adverb* E19. **obeseness** *noun* M17.

obesity /ə(ʊ)ˈbiːsɪti/ *noun.* E17.
[French *obésité* or Latin *obesitas*, formed as prec.: see -ITY.]
The condition of being obese; extreme corpulence.

obex /ˈəʊbɛks/ *noun.* Now *rare* or *obsolete.* E17.
[Latin = barrier, bolt, from *obicere* cast in front of, from *ob-* OB- + *jacere* to throw.]
An impediment, an obstacle.

obey /ə(ʊ)ˈbeɪ/ *verb.* ME.
[Old & mod. French *obéir* from Latin *oboedire*, *obedire*, from *ob-* OB- + *audire* hear.]
1 *verb trans.* (orig. with *dat.*). ▸**a** Comply with the bidding of; do what one is told to do by (a person); be obedient to. ME. ▸**b** Comply with, execute (a command etc.). LME. ▸**c** Submit to; follow (a principle, authority, etc.). Now *rare* or *obsolete.* LME. ▸**d** Of a thing: be actuated by, respond to, (a force, impulse, etc.); act in accordance with (a law of nature, a constraint, etc.). L16.
†**2** *verb intrans.* Be obedient *to*. ME–M17.
3 *verb intrans.* Do what one is told to do; comply with a command etc.; be obedient. LME.
†**4** *verb refl.* Submit oneself *to*. LME–L15.
5 *verb intrans.* ASTROLOGY. Of a zodiacal sign or planet: be subject to the influence of another zodiacal sign or planet. LME.
†**6** *verb intrans. & trans.* Make an obeisance *to* or to; salute respectfully. LME–M17.

> 🕮 **1** R. THOMAS Provided that he was obeyed her father was his . . kindly self. **b** G. GISSING Reuben had no choice but to obey the artist's directions. H. BELLOC He went on obeying orders. **c** MILTON What obeyes Reason, is free. **d** N. COWARD She obeyed her instincts. *Model Engineer* Coil springs . . obey Hooke's Law. **2** AV *Rom.* 6:16 His servants ye are to whom ye obey. **3** TENNYSON Man to command and woman to obey. TOLKIEN 'Take the rope off, Sam!' said Frodo. Reluctantly Sam obeyed.

■ **obeyable** *adjective* (*rare*) that can or should be obeyed LME. **obeyance** *noun* obedience; obeisance, homage: LME. **obeyer** *noun* M16.

obfuscate /ˈɒbfʌskeɪt/ *adjective.* Now *rare* or *obsolete.* M16.
[Late Latin *obfuscatus* pa. pple, formed as next: see -ATE[2].]
Darkened, obscured, obfuscated.

obfuscate /ˈɒbfʌskeɪt/ *verb trans.* Pa. pple & ppl adjective **-ated**, (earlier) †**-ate**. LME.
[Late Latin *obfuscat-* pa. ppl stem of *obfuscare*, from *ob-* OB- + *fuscare* darken, from *fuscus* dark: see -ATE[3].]
1 Dim (the sight); obscure, confuse, (the understanding, judgement, etc.); stupefy, bewilder. LME.
2 Make (a topic etc.) obscure or confused; deprive of clarity or impact. M16.
3 Darken; deprive of light or brightness. (Earlier in OBFUSCATION 1.) Now *rare.* L16.

> 🕮 **1** H. VIZETELLY He was obfuscated with brandy and water. **2** L. A. ECHARD To obfuscate the brightness of the Gospel. ROSEMARY MANNING Details were altered or obfuscated.

■ **obfuscatory** *adjective* that obfuscates (esp. a topic, the understanding, etc.); bewildering; intended to confuse or deceive: M20.

obfuscation /ɒbfʌˈskeɪʃ(ə)n/ *noun.* LME.
[Late Latin *obfuscatio(n-)*, formed as prec.: see -ATION.]
1 The action of making darker; darkness, dimness; an instance of this. LME.
2 The action of making obscure or confused; stupefaction, bewilderment. E17.
3 *transf.* A thing that darkens or obscures. M17.

> 🕮 **1** E. DARWIN In cataracts and obfuscations of the cornea. **2** M. DODS His conscience was in a state of obfuscation. J. M. BREWER One looks for . . meaning instead of obfuscation. **3** JOHN OWEN Too often theologians . . escape pursuit by enveloping themselves in their self-raised obfuscations.

†**obfusk** *verb.* L15–M18.
[Old French *obfusquer* from late Latin *obfuscare*: see OBFUSCATE *verb*.]
= OBFUSCATE *verb*.

obi /ˈəʊbi/ *noun*[1]. E19.
[Japanese = belt.]
A sash worn round the waist with Japanese clothing.

obi /ˈəʊbi/ *noun*². M20.
[Igbo.]
In Nigeria: a hut, a house, *esp.* one for ceremonial purposes.

obi *noun*³ var. of OBEAH.

Obie /ˈəʊbi/ *noun. US colloq.* M20.
[Repr. pronunc. of *ob* abbreviation of *off-Broadway*.]
Any of a number of annual awards for off-Broadway experimental theatre productions.

obit /ˈɒbɪt, ˈəʊ-/ *noun.* LME.
[Old & mod. French from Latin *obitus* going down, setting, death, from *obit-* pa. ppl stem of *obire* perish, die (from *mortem obire* meet death), from *ob-* OB- + *ire* go. In sense 3 partly abbreviation of OBITUARY.]
†**1** Departure from life, death, decease. LME–L17.
2 †**a** A ceremony performed at the burial of a deceased person; a funeral service. LME–E18. ▸**b** *Hist.* A ceremony (usu. a mass) commemorating, or commending to God, a deceased person, esp. a founder or benefactor of an institution on the anniversary of his or her death; an annual or other regular memorial service. LME.
3 Orig., a record or notice of (the date of) a person's death. Later (*colloq.*), an obituary. LME.

📖 **2b** J. HACKET Obits, Dirges, Masses are not said for nothing. **3** B. MEGGS Doc had been given a very nice obit . . on page 42.

Comb.: **obit-day** *Hist.*: on which an obit (sense 2b above) was celebrated.

†**obital** *adjective & noun.* L17.
[from OBIT *noun* + -AL¹. Cf. OBITUAL.]
▸ **A** *adjective.* = OBITUAL *adjective.* L17–E18.
▸ **B** *noun.* = OBITUAL *noun*, OBITUARY *noun* 1. Only in L17.

obiter /ˈɒbɪtə/ *adverb, noun, & adjective.* L16.
[Latin, orig. two words, *ob itur* by the way.]
▸ **A** *adverb.* By the way, in passing, incidentally. L16.
▸ **B** *noun.* A thing said, done, or occurring by the way; an incidental matter. Also, an *obiter dictum.* E17.
▸ **C** *adjective.* Made or said by the way; incidental. M18.

obiter dictum /ˌɒbɪtə ˈdɪktəm/ *noun phr.* Pl. ***obiter dicta*** /ˈdɪktə/. E19.
[Latin, formed as prec. + DICTUM.]
A judge's expression of opinion uttered in discussing a point of law or in giving judgement, but not essential to the decision and so without binding authority; *gen.* an incidental remark.

obitual /ə(ʊ)ˈbɪtjʊəl/ *adjective & noun. rare.* E18.
[from Latin *obitus* OBIT + -AL¹. Cf. earlier OBITAL.]
▸ **A** *adjective.* Of, pertaining to, or recording an obit. E18.
▸ **B** *noun.* = OBITUARY *noun* 1. E18.

obituary /ə(ʊ)ˈbɪtʃʊəri/ *noun & adjective.* E18.
[medieval Latin *obituarius*, from *obitus*: see OBIT, -ARY¹.]
▸ **A** *noun.* **1** A register of deaths or (*Hist.*) of obit-days. E18.
2 A record or announcement of a death, esp. in a newspaper, usu. comprising a brief biographical sketch of the deceased. M18.
▸ **B** *attrib.* or as *adjective.* Relating to or recording a death; of the nature of an obituary (sense A.2 above). E19.

📖 J. COLVILLE Father . . and I composed an obituary notice at the request of the *Sunday Times.*

■ **obituˈarial** *adjective* of, pertaining to, or characteristic of an obituary L20. **obituˈarian** *noun* (*US*) an obituarist E20. **obituarily** *adverb* in the manner of an obituary M19. **obituarist** *noun* the writer of an obituary notice L18. **obituarize** *verb intrans. & trans.* write (as) an obituary notice L19.

object /ˈɒbdʒɪkt/ *noun.* LME.
[In branch I partly use as noun of *object* pa. pple of OBJECT *verb*, partly from medieval Latin *objectum* thing presented to the mind, use as noun of neut. pa. pple of Latin *obicere*. In branch II directly from Latin *objectus* pa. pple of *obicere*: see OBJECT *verb*.]
▸ **I** †**1** A statement introduced in opposition; an objection. Latterly *Scot.* LME–E19.
†**2** An obstacle, a hindrance. LME–M16.
3 a A thing placed before the eyes or presented to one of the senses; a material thing (that can be) seen or perceived; *spec.* the thing of which an observation is made or an image produced. LME. ▸**b** A person or thing of affecting appearance; *colloq.* (freq. *derog.*) a pitiable- or ridiculous-looking person, a sight, a fright. L16.
4 The end to which effort is directed; a thing sought or aimed at; a purpose, an end, an aim. LME.
5 A thing or person to which action, thought, or feeling is directed; a thing or person to which something is done, or on or about which something acts or operates. (Foll. by *of.*) L16.
6 PHILOSOPHY. A thing or being of which a person thinks or has cognition; a thing external to the thinking mind or subject; the non-ego as distinguished from or related to the ego. M17.
7 GRAMMAR. A noun or noun equivalent dependent on or governed by a verb, esp. an active transitive one, or a preposition. E18.
8 COMPUTING. A package of information and a description of its manipulation. L20.

📖 **3a** T. MEDWIN The torch's glare gave horrible indistinctness to objects. A. LURIE In the spare bedroom . . surrounded by more and more objects. ***material object***: see MATERIAL *adjective.* **object of art** = OBJET D'ART. ***object of virtu. physical object***: see PHYSICAL *adjective.* **b** MILTON To sit idle on the household hearth . . to visitants a gaze Or pitied object. **4** R. MACAULAY To tear him out of her heart—that was her constant object. E. WAUGH Walking without any particular object except to take the air. **no object** not an important or restricting factor. ***the object of the exercise***: see EXERCISE *noun.* **5** J. H. NEWMAN To substitute objects of sense for objects of imagination. J. THURBER Men were the frequent object of her colourful scorn. A. NIN They had once been an object of veneration and superstition. ***intentional object***: see INTENTIONAL *adjective* 2. ***internal object***: see INTERNAL *adjective.* **6** H. L. MANSEL A conscious subject, and an object of which he is conscious. ***transcendental object***: see TRANSCENDENTAL *adjective.* **7** N. CHOMSKY In 'I believed your testimony,' the noun phrase is the grammatical object of 'believe'. ***cognate object***: see COGNATE *adjective.* ***direct object***: see DIRECT *adjective.* INDIRECT ***object. retained object***: see RETAIN 3C.

▸†**II 9** The fact of becoming a hindrance or obstruction; interposition, obstruction. *rare.* E–M16.
10 The presentation of something to the eye or perception. Only in E17.

Comb.: **object-ball** (BILLIARDS & SNOOKER etc.), the ball at which a player aims the cue-ball; **object choice** PSYCHOANALYSIS a thing or (usu.) a person external to the ego chosen as an object of desire; **object code** COMPUTING code produced by a compiler or assembler; **object complement** LINGUISTICS a word complementing the object of a verb, expressing the state or condition of the object at the time of the action or resulting from it; a complement clause in the position of an object; **object-finder** a contrivance for registering the position of an object on a mounted microscopic slide, so as to make it possible to find it again; **object-glass** = OBJECTIVE *noun* 1; **object language** (*a*) a language described by means of another language (a metalanguage); (*b*) PHILOSOPHY a language consisting only of words having meaning in isolation; (*c*) COMPUTING a language into which a program is translated by means of a compiler; **object-lesson** a lesson in which a pupil's examination of a material object forms the basis for instruction; now chiefly *fig.* a striking practical illustration of some principle; **object libido** PSYCHOANALYSIS the part of psychic energy which is directed to objects other than the ego; **object love** PSYCHOANALYSIS love for something external to the ego or self; **object-oriented** *adjective* (COMPUTING) (of a programming language) based on a methodology which enables a system to be modelled as a set of objects which can be controlled and manipulated in a modular manner; **object program** COMPUTING a program into which some other program is translated by an assembler or compiler; **object-relationship** PSYCHOANALYSIS a relationship felt, or the emotional energy directed, by the self or ego towards a chosen object; **objects clause** LAW in a memorandum of association, a clause specifying the objects for which the company was established; **object word** a word designating an object or material thing; *spec.* one the meaning of which can be learned independently of the rest of the linguistic system; **object-world** the world external to the self, apprehended through the objects in it.

object /əbˈdʒɛkt/ *verb.* Pa. pple & ppl adjective **objected**, (earlier) †**object**. LME.
[Latin *object-* pa. ppl stem of *objectare* frequentative of *obicere*, from *ob-* OB- + *jacere* to throw.]
†**1** *verb trans.* Place so as to interrupt, hinder, or intercept something; put in the way, interpose; expose *to.* LME–M19.
2 *verb trans.* State as an objection; adduce as contrary or damaging to a case, contention, etc. Now usu. foll. by quoted words or obj. clause; also (now *rare*) foll. by *to, against.* LME.
3 *verb intrans.* State or have an objection; express or feel opposition, disapproval, or reluctance. Usu. foll. by *to, against.* LME. ▸†**b** Bring a charge or accusation. *rare* (AV). Only in E17.
4 *verb trans.* Bring as a charge against a person; attribute to a person as a fault or crime; accuse a person of, reproach a person with. (Foll. by *to, against*, obj. clause.) *arch.* LME. ▸†**b** Impute or attribute *to.* E17–L18.
†**5** *verb trans.* Place before the eyes; present to one of the other senses. L15–M19.
†**6** *verb trans.* Present in argument; bring forward as a reason or instance; adduce. L15–M19.

📖 **1** R. CODRINGTON He commanded him to be objected to a hungry . . Lyon. N. GREW A very white . . piece of Ashwood . . objected to a proper Light. SOUTHEY The Goth objects His shield, and on its rim received the edge. **2** H. N. COLERIDGE Bryant objects this very circumstance to the authenticity of the Iliad. *Listener* Mr Johnston objected: 'But we already have . . a shop stewards' movement.' *New Yorker* Estonian officials . . objected that the steel treads of the vehicles were chewing up the streets. **3** C. PETERS Isabella objected to Thackeray's ardour. *New Yorker* Bress . . objected to this line of questioning. C. FREEMAN His mother would object to his going to a prize fight. **4** STEELE I have heard it objected against that Piece, that its Instructions are not of general use. D. HUME This subtlety, which has been frequently objected to Charles.

■ **objectable** *adjective* †(*a*) able to be urged as an objection; (*b*) able to be objected to, objectionable: M17. **objectant** *noun* †(*a*) *rare* a person who or thing which objectifies something; (*b*) a person who puts forward an objection: E17. **objecˈtee** *noun* a person against whom an objection is made: M19.

objectification /ɒbˌdʒɛktɪfɪˈkeɪʃ(ə)n/ *noun.* M19.
[from next: see -FICATION.]
The action or an act of objectifying something; the condition of being objectified; a thing that has been objectified.

objectify /ɒbˈdʒɛktɪfʌɪ/ *verb trans.* M19.
[from OBJECT *noun* + -I- + -FY.]
Make into or present as an object of perception; make objective; express in an external or concrete form.
■ **objectifiable** *adjective* E20. **objectifier** *noun* M20.

objection /əbˈdʒɛkʃ(ə)n/ *noun.* LME.
[Old & mod. French, or late Latin *objectio(n-)*, formed as OBJECT *verb*: see -ION.]
1 The action or an act of stating something in opposition or protest; counter-argument; an adverse reason or statement, a feeling of disapproval or reluctance. Formerly also, a charge or accusation against a person. LME.
†**2** An attack, an assault. LME–L16.
†**3** The action of interposing something. M16–E17.
†**4** Presentation to the mind or one of the senses; representation. M16–M17.

📖 **1** P. G. WODEHOUSE She tried to analyse her objection to these men. J. LE CARRÉ Objection! . . Where's the Stewards . . ? That horse was pulled! N. SHERRY There were family objections to the engagement. R. S. WOOLHOUSE Hobbes's view . . is open to objection.

■ **objectional** *adjective* (*a*) of the nature of or involving objection; (*b*) open to objection, objectionable: M17. **objectionist** *noun* (*rare*) an objector E17.

objectionable /əbˈdʒɛkʃ(ə)nəb(ə)l/ *adjective & noun.* L18.
[from prec. + -ABLE.]
▸ **A** *adjective.* Open to objection; undesirable, unpleasant, offensive, disapproved of. M18.

📖 P. H. GIBBS It would be pleasanter for both of us . . if you would avoid objectionable expressions.

▸ **B** *noun.* An objectionable person or thing. *rare.* L19.
■ **objectionableness** *noun* (*rare*) M19. **objectionably** *adverb* M19.

objectise *verb* var. of OBJECTIZE.

objectivate /ɒbˈdʒɛktɪveɪt/ *verb trans.* L19.
[from OBJECTIVE *adjective* + -ATE³.]
= OBJECTIFY.
■ **objectiˈvation** *noun* L19.

objective /əbˈdʒɛktɪv/ *adjective & noun.* E17.
[medieval Latin *objectivus*, from *objectum*: see OBJECT *noun*, -IVE.]
▸ **A** *adjective.* †**1** PHILOSOPHY. **a** Pertaining to or considered in relation to its object; constituting or belonging to an object of action, thought, or feeling; material as opp. to formal. Only in 17. ▸†**b** Of or pertaining to an object or end as a cause of action. Only in 17.
2 PHILOSOPHY. †**a** Existing as an object of consciousness as opp. to having a real existence; considered as presented to the mind rather than in terms of inherent qualities. M17–M18. ▸**b** Existing as an object of consciousness, as opp. to being part of the conscious subject; external to or independent of the mind. M17.
3 Of a line or point: of or belonging to an object to be delineated in perspective. *rare.* E18.
4 That is an object of sensation or thought *to* a person, faculty, etc. M18.
5 OPTICS. Of a lens: that is an objective (sense B.1 below). M18.
6 GRAMMAR. Expressing, designating, or referring to the object of an action; *spec.* (of a case or word) constructed as or appropriate to the object of a verb, esp. a transitive active one, or preposition. M18.
7 Characterized by objecting; that states objections. (Earlier in OBJECTIVELY 1.) *rare.* E19.
8 a Dealing with or laying stress on what is external to the mind; concerned with outward things or events; presenting facts uncoloured by feelings, opinions, or personal bias; disinterested. M19. ▸**b** Of a symptom: observable by another and not felt only by the patient. L19.
9 Sought or aimed at. Orig. & chiefly in ***objective point*** below. M19.

📖 **1b** R. CUDWORTH Aristotle's first mover is . . only the final and objective cause, of the heavenly motions. **2b** E. WAUGH Because the validity of a sacrament is objective . . the personal virtue of the priest does not affect it. P. GROSSKURTH The world is not an objective reality, but a phantasmagoria. **4** GIBBON Operations . . made objective to sense by the means of speech, gesture and action. **8a** A. BRINK I'm a journalist, I'm supposed to be objective and not to get drawn into things. **b** A. CLARE Others pay as little attention to objective symptoms and . . immerse themselves in . . their patients' inner world.

▸ **B** *noun.* **1** OPTICS. The lens or combination of lenses in a telescope, microscope, etc., that is nearest the object observed. M19.
2 GRAMMAR. (A word or form in) the objective case. M19.

For other words beginning with *ob-* see the entry for **ob-**

3 A thing aimed at or sought; a target, a goal, an aim. **L19.**
4 A thing external to or independent of the mind. **L19.**

> 📖 **3** R. V. JONES It would be possible to attack selected objectives, such as oil plants. S. BELLOW His main objective was to pile up a huge personal fortune. **4** *Christian Commonwealth* The value and attraction of the externals and objectives.

Special collocations & comb.: **objective complement** *LINGUISTICS* = *object complement* s.v. **OBJECT** *noun*. **objective correlative** the artistic technique of representing or evoking a particular emotion by means of symbols which become indicative of that emotion and are associated with it. **objective function** in linear programming, the function that it is desired to maximize or minimize. **objective point** (orig. *MILITARY*) the point to which an advance of troops is directed; the point aimed at.
¶ Cf. **SUBJECTIVE.**

objectively /əbˈdʒɛktɪvli/ *adverb.* **L16.**
[from **OBJECTIVE** *adjective* + **-LY**[2].]
†**1** By way of objection or counter-argument. **L16–M17.**
2 In an objective manner or relation. **E17.**

> 📖 **2** R. HOLMES How far Nerval was justified in thinking like this was difficult to establish objectively.

objectiveness /əbˈdʒɛktɪvnɪs/ *noun.* **L17.**
[formed as prec. + **-NESS.**]
The quality or character of being objective; objectivity.

objectivise *verb* var. of **OBJECTIVIZE.**

objectivism /əbˈdʒɛktɪvɪz(ə)m/ *noun.* **M19.**
[formed as prec. + **-ISM.**]
1 The tendency to lay stress on what is external to or independent of the mind; *PHILOSOPHY* the belief that certain things (esp. moral truths) exist apart from human knowledge or perception of them; the quality or character of being objective. **M19.**
2 In Communist theory: an objective attitude towards existing conditions as opp. to a concern for change according to revolutionary principles. Chiefly *derog.* **M20.**
■ **objectivist** *noun & adjective* (***a***) *noun* an adherent of objectivism; (***b***) *adjective* of or pertaining to objectivists or objectivism: **L19.** **objectiˈvistic** *adjective* characterized by objectivism **L19.**

objectivity /ɒbdʒɛkˈtɪvɪti/ *noun.* **E19.**
[formed as prec. + **-ITY.**]
The quality or character of being objective; *esp.* the ability to present or view facts uncoloured by feelings, opinions, or personal bias.

> 📖 A. FRANCE I have moved from . . distanced objectivity to a more personal account of my own therapies.

objectivize /əbˈdʒɛktɪvʌɪz/ *verb trans.* Also **-ise.** **M19.**
[formed as prec. + **-IZE.**]
Make objective; objectify.
■ **objectiviˈzation** *noun* the action or an act of objectivizing something; a thing that externalizes an idea, principle, etc.: **E20.**

objectize /ˈɒbdʒɪktʌɪz/ *verb trans. rare.* Also **-ise.** **M17.**
[from **OBJECT** *noun* + **-IZE.**]
Make into an object; objectify.

objectless /ˈɒbdʒɪktlɪs/ *adjective.* **L18.**
[formed as prec. + **-LESS.**]
Having no object or objects; aimless, purposeless.

> 📖 COLERIDGE The whole Country is a flat objectless hungry heath. S. NAIPAUL Another wave of objectless fear rolled over her.

■ **objectlessly** *adverb* **M19.** **objectlessness** *noun* **M19.**

object-matter /ˈɒbdʒɪk(t)matə/ *noun.* **M17.**
[In sense 1 from *object* pa. pple of **OBJECT** *verb* + **MATTER** *noun*. In sense 2 from **OBJECT** *noun* + **MATTER** *noun*.]
†**1** Matter presented to view, or to be employed as an instrument or means to an end. Only in **M17.**
2 The matter that is the object of an action or study; the matter dealt with or treated. **M19.**

objectness /ˈɒbdʒɪk(t)nɪs/ *noun.* **M20.**
[from **OBJECT** *noun* + **-NESS.**]
The state or quality of being objective or an object. ***material objectness***: see **MATERIAL** *adjective*.

objector /əbˈdʒɛktə/ *noun.* **E17.**
[from **OBJECT** *verb* + **-OR.**]
A person who objects or makes an objection; one bringing forward a reason or argument against or expressing disapproval of or disagreement with.

> 📖 *Guardian* Objectors . . said that to continue with the plan was a waste of public money. ***CONSCIENTIOUS objector.***

objet /ɔbʒɛ, ˈɒbʒeɪ/ *noun.* Pl. pronounced same. **M19.**
[French.]
1 An object displayed as an ornament. **M19.**
2 A person forming the object of another's attentions or affection. Cf. **OBJECT** *noun* 5. *rare.* **M19.**

> 📖 **1** V. C. CLINTON-BADDELEY All those lamentable *objets* on the window-sills.

Phrases: ***objet de luxe*** /də lyks, ˈluːks/, pl. ***objets de luxe***, [lit. 'of luxury'] an especially fine or sumptuous article of value, a luxury item. ***objet de virtu*** /də vɛrty, vəːˈtuː/, pl. ***objets de virtu***, [pseudo-French translation of *object of virtu* after *objet d'art*] = ***object of VIRTU.*** ***objet trouvé*** /truve, ˈtruːveɪ/, pl. ***objets trouvés*** (pronounced same), [lit. 'found'] an object found or picked up at random and presented as a rarity or a work of art.

objet d'art /ɔbʒɛ ˈdaːr, ɒbʒeɪ ˈdɑː/ *noun phr.* Pl. ***objets d'art*** (pronounced same). **M19.**
[French, lit. 'object of art'. Cf. prec.]
A small decorative object.

objicient /əbˈdʒɪʃ(ə)nt/ *noun.* **M19.**
[Latin *objicient-* pres. ppl stem of *obicere*: see **OBJECT** *verb*, **-ENT.**]
A person who objects; an opponent of a motion or proposition.

objuration /ɒbdʒʊˈreɪʃ(ə)n/ *noun. rare.* **M16.**
[Latin *objuratio(n-)*, from *objurat-* pa. ppl stem of *objurare*: see next, **-ATION.**]
The action of binding by oath. Also, a solemn command or entreaty.

objure /əbˈdʒʊə/ *verb. rare.* **E17.**
[Latin *objurare*, from *ob-* **OB-** + *jurare* swear.]
†**1** *verb trans.* Bind by oath. Only in **E17.**
2 *verb intrans.* Utter an oath, swear. **M19.**

objurgate /ˈɒbdʒəgeɪt/ *verb trans. & intrans. literary.* **E17.**
[Latin *objurgat-* pa. ppl stem of *objurgare*, from *ob-* **OB-** + *jurgare* quarrel, scold, from *jurgium* quarrel: see **-ATE**[3].]
Give a severe rebuke (to); scold, chide.
■ **objurˈgation** *noun* the action or an act of objurgating; a severe rebuke: **L15.** **obˈjurgative** *adjective* (*rare*) = **OBJURGATORY** **M19.** **obˈjurgatorily** *adverb* in an objurgatory manner **M17.** **obˈjurgatory** *adjective* having the character of scolding or chiding; conveying or uttering a severe rebuke: **L16.**

oblast /ˈɒblast/ *noun.* **L19.**
[Russian *oblast'*.]
In countries of the former USSR and earlier in Russia: a second-order administrative division, a province, a region. Cf. **OKRUG.**

†**oblat** *noun* see **OBLATE** *noun*.

oblata /ɒˈbleɪtə/ *noun pl.* Now *rare.* **M17.**
[mod. Latin, use as noun of neut. pl. of Latin *oblatus*: see next.]
LAW (now *Hist.*). Old debts to the Exchequer remaining unpaid and put in the sheriff's charge. Also, gifts or offerings made by a subject or subjects to the monarch.

oblate /ˈɒbleɪt/ *noun.* Also (earlier) †**oblat.** **L17.**
[French *oblat* from medieval Latin *oblatus* use as noun of pa. pple of Latin *offerre* **OFFER** *verb*. Cf. **OBLEY.**]
A person dedicated to monastic or religious life or work; *spec.* (***a***) *Hist.* a child offered by his or her parents to a monastery and placed there to be brought up; (***b***) a lay person attached to a religious community without having taken vows; (***c***) a member of any of various congregations of secular priests or communities of women devoted to some special work.
Oblate of Mary Immaculate, Oblate of St Charles Borromeo, etc.

oblate /ˈɒbleɪt, ɒˈbleɪt/ *adjective.* **E18.**
[mod. Latin *oblatus*, from *ob-* **OB-** + *-latus*, after Latin *prolatus* **PROLATE** *adjective*.]
Flattened at the poles; designating a spheroid produced by the revolution of an ellipse about its shorter axis. Opp. ***prolate.***
■ **oblately** *adverb* **M18.** **oblateness** *noun* **L18.**

†**oblate** *verb trans. rare.* **M16–L19.**
[from Latin *oblat-*: see next, **-ATE**[3].]
Offer, esp. as an oblation.

oblation /əˈbleɪʃ(ə)n/ *noun.* **LME.**
[Old & mod. French, or late (eccl.) Latin *oblatio(n-)*, from Latin *oblat-* pa. ppl stem of *offerre* **OFFER** *verb*: see **-ATION.**]
▶ **I 1** The action of offering or presenting something to God or a god; *spec.* (*CHRISTIAN CHURCH*) the offering or presentation of the bread and wine in the Eucharist. **LME.**
2 A thing presented or offered to God or a god; a sacrifice; *spec.* an offering made to God for the service of the Church, the clergy, the needy, etc.; a pious donation or bequest. **LME.**

> 📖 **1** JER. TAYLOR These men . . enumerate many glories of the Holy Sacrament . . calling it . . the paschal oblation. DAY LEWIS The ponds, on whose dark glass the water-lilies rested like hands cupped in oblation. **2** R. HEBER Vainly we offer each ample oblation; Vainly with gifts would his favour secure. A. G. GARDINER I shall want some oblation to lay on the altar.

▶†**II** *gen.* **3** A gratuity; a gift; the action of offering or giving something. **LME–L17.**
4 A subsidy, a tax; a gift to the monarch. Cf. **OBLATA.** **E–M17.**
■ **oblational** *adjective* of or pertaining to an oblation; of the nature of an oblation: **M19.** **oblationary** *adjective* (*ECCLESIASTICAL*) that receives the oblations in the Eucharist **L19.**

oblatory /ˈɒblət(ə)ri/ *adjective.* **E17.**
[French †*oblatoire* or medieval Latin *oblatorius*, from Latin *oblat-*: see prec., **-ORY**[2].]
Of or pertaining to an oblation.

†**oblectation** *noun.* **E16–M19.**
[Latin *oblectatio(n-)*, from *oblectat-* pa. ppl stem of *oblectare* to delight, from *ob-* **OB-** + *lectare* frequentative of *lacere* entice: see **-ATION.**]
(A) delight, (a) pleasure, (an) enjoyment.

obley /ˈɒbli/ *noun.* **ME.**
[Old French *ublee, oubleie, oblie* (mod. *oublie*) from ecclesiastical Latin *oblata* use as noun of fem. of pa. pple of Latin *offerre* **OFFER** *verb*. Cf. **OBLATE** *noun*, **OBLATION.**]
†**1** An offering, an oblation. Only in **ME.**
2 *ECCLESIASTICAL HISTORY.* A Eucharistic wafer. **ME.**
†**3** A thin cake of pastry. **LME–E17.**

oblietjie /ɒˈbliːki/ *noun. S. Afr.* **L19.**
[Afrikaans, from French *oublie* (see prec.) + *-tjie* dim. suffix.]
A rolled wafer-thin teacake.

obligable /ˈɒblɪgəb(ə)l/ *adjective. rare.* **M17.**
[from **OBLIGE** + **-ABLE.**]
Able to be brought, or capable of bringing, under an obligation.

obligant /ˈɒblɪg(ə)nt/ *noun.* **L16.**
[Latin *obligant-* pres. ppl stem of *obligare*: see **OBLIGE** *verb*, **-ANT**[1].]
SCOTS LAW. A person who binds himself or herself, or is legally bound, to pay or perform something.

obligate /ˈɒblɪgət/ *adjective* (orig. *pa. pple*). **LME.**
[Latin *obligatus* pa. pple, formed as next: see **-ATE**[2].]
†**1** Bound by oath, law, or duty; obliged. **LME–M16.**
2 *attrib. BIOLOGY.* That has to be such; *esp.* (of an organism) restricted to a particular (specified) function; (of a mode of life) obligatory, necessary. Opp. **FACULTATIVE** 1b. **M18.**
■ **obligately** *adverb* (*BIOLOGY*) of necessity **M20.**

obligate /ˈɒblɪgeɪt/ *verb trans.* **M16.**
[Latin *obligat-* pa. ppl stem of *obligare*: see **OBLIGE** *verb*, **-ATE**[3].]
†**1** Bind, connect, attach; fasten up. **M–L16.**
†**2** Make (a thing) a security; pledge, pawn, mortgage. **M16–L19.**
3 Bind (a person) morally or legally. Usu. in *pass.*, be bound or compelled (*to do*). **M17.**
4 Confer a favour on, place under an obligation; oblige. Usu. in *pass.* Now chiefly *dial. & N. Amer.* **L17.**

> 📖 **3** W. ANDERSON You are not only warranted but obligated to vindicate yourself. T. DREISER He feared to obligate himself to do something. **4** SHELLEY I am much obligated by the trouble you have taken. A. LURIE Gerry feels obligated to expand his consciousness in every available direction.

obligation /ɒblɪˈgeɪʃ(ə)n/ *noun.* **ME.**
[Old & mod. French from Latin *obligatio(n-)*, formed as **OBLIGATE** *verb*: see **-ATION.**]
1 The action of constraining oneself by promise or contract to a particular course of action; a mutually binding agreement. Also, the course of action etc. to which one commits oneself, a formal promise. *arch.* **ME.**
2 *LAW.* A binding agreement committing a person to a payment or other action; the document containing such an agreement, a written contract or bond. Also, the right created or liability incurred by such an agreement. **LME.**
3 Moral or legal constraint; the condition of being morally or legally bound; the constraining power of a law, duty, contract, etc.; *rare* an instance of this. **LME.**
4 An act or course of action to which a person is morally or legally obliged; what one is bound to do; (a) duty; an enforced or burdensome task or responsibility. **E17.**
5 a A benefit, a service; a kindness done or received. **E17.** ▶**b** A debt of gratitude. **M17.**
†**6** Legal liability. **L17–M18.**

> 📖 **1** G. B. SMITH A valid obligation could not be made with the Court of Rome without communication with the Pope. **2** JAS. MILL Security for the discharge of the obligations which the Company held upon the government of Oude. **3** LD MACAULAY He had a strong sense of moral and religious obligation. *Choice* For a free colour brochure . . , sent to you without obligation, please complete your name and address. **day of obligation** *ROMAN CATHOLIC CHURCH* a day on which all are required to attend mass. **of obligation** obligatory. **4** J. RABAN The host tribe were under an obligation to provide the traveller with food and drink. A. E. STEVENSON We are doing more to meet our obligations to our older citizens today. B. PYM An aunt was not a very high priority on most people's list of obligations. **5b** F. MARRYAT You have no right to put her under an obligation.

obligative /ˈɒblɪgətɪv/ *adjective & noun.* **L16.**
[formed as **OBLIGATE** *verb* + **-IVE.**]
▶ **A** *adjective.* **1** Imposing obligation; obligatory. **L16.**
2 *GRAMMAR.* Of a verb form, mood, etc.: implying obligation. **L19.**
▶ **B** *noun. GRAMMAR.* An obligative verb form, mood, etc. **M20.**
■ **obligativeness** *noun* **L17.**

obligato *adjective & noun* var. of **OBBLIGATO.**

obligator /ˈɒblɪgeɪtə/ *noun. rare.* **L16.**
[medieval Latin, formed as **OBLIGATE** *verb* + **-OR.**]
†**1** *LAW.* = **OBLIGOR.** Only in **L16.**
2 = **OBLIGER** 2. **L18.**

obligatory /əˈblɪɡət(ə)ri/ *adjective*. LME.
[Late Latin *obligatorius*, formed as OBLIGATE *verb*: see -ORY[2].]
1 Imposing obligation, legally or morally binding; compulsory and not merely permissive. LME.
2 Creating or constituting an obligation. LME.
3 *BIOLOGY*. = OBLIGATE *adjective* 2. L19.

1 H. CARPENTER Betjeman was sent down . . for failing the obligatory University examination in Divinity. F. POHL They did not relish standing in the blowing snow . . for the obligatory identity check.

■ **obligatorily** *adverb* M16. **obligatoriness** *noun* M17.

oblige /əˈblʌɪdʒ/ *verb*. ME.
[Old & mod. French *obliger* from Latin *obligare*, from *ob-* OB- + *ligare* bind.]
▸ **I 1 a** *verb trans.* Bind (a person) by oath, promise, or contract; put under an obligation, commit. Of an oath etc.: make legally or morally bound; be binding on. (Foll. by *to do*, *to* a person or course of action.) *arch.* exc. *LAW*. ME. ▸**b** *verb trans.* Constrain, esp. morally or legally; compel, force. Foll. by *to do*, (now *rare*) *to* a course of action. LME. ▸**c** *verb intrans.* Pledge, promise. *Scot.* E16. ▸†**d** *verb intrans.* & *trans.* Restrain (a person) *from* action etc. M17–E18.
†**2** *verb trans.* Make (property etc.) a guarantee for the discharge of a promise or debt; pledge, pawn, mortgage. ME–M18.
3 *verb trans.* †**a** Make (a person) subject or liable *to* a bond, penalty, etc. ME–M17. ▸**b** *refl.* Render oneself liable to punishment, involve oneself in guilt. Now *rare* or *obsolete*. LME.

1a W. G. PALGRAVE The names of those whom vicinity obliges to attendance are read over morning and evening. **b** DEFOE Self-preservation obliged the people to these severities. R. GRAVES The Parthian king was obliged to sign a humiliating peace. J. RHYS I've been obliged to stop working.

▸†**II 4** *verb trans.* Fetter, ensnare. Only in ME.
5 *verb trans.* Fasten or attach closely; bind, tie up. M17–E18.
▸ **III 6** *verb trans.* Make indebted by conferring a favour; gratify *with*, *by doing*; perform a service or kindness for, confer a favour on. M16. ▸**b** *verb intrans.* Do something desired or pleasing, *esp.* entertain a gathering (*with*). *colloq.* M18. ▸**c** *verb intrans.* & *trans.* Act as a charwoman (for); assist (a person) with housework. *colloq.* M20.
7 *verb trans.* In *pass.* Be bound *to* a person by gratitude; be indebted *to* a person or thing *for* something. Now *literary* & *joc.* M16.
†**8** *verb trans.* Gratify, please. M17–E18.
9 *verb trans.* Make imperative; necessitate. M17.

6 J. SINCLAIR Your early attention to this application, will much oblige, Sir, your . . obedient servant. DICKENS Oblige me with the milk. R. DAVIES None of them seemed anxious to oblige the escape-artist by tying him up. **b** ARNOLD BENNETT Miss Florence Simcox . . , the champion female clog-dancer of the Midlands, will now oblige. **c** J. CANNAN I'm not in service. I oblige by the hour. **7** R. BENTLEY To those Hills we are obliged for all our Metals. CONAN DOYLE I am exceedingly obliged to you for your co-operation. **much obliged**: expr. thanks. **your obliged servant** *arch.*: a formula for closing a business or formal letter. **9** *Cornhill Magazine* The custom of the Elizabethan theatre obliged this double authorship.

■ **obligedly** *adverb* in an obliged manner M17. **obligedness** *noun* the condition or fact of being obliged L17.

†**obligeant** *adjective*. M17–M18.
[French, pres. pple of *obliger* OBLIGE *verb*: see -ANT[1].]
Obliging.

obligee /ɒblɪˈdʒiː/ *noun*. L16.
[from OBLIGE + -EE[1].]
1 *LAW*. A person to whom another is bound by contract or to whom a bond is given. Correl. to *obligor*. L16. ▸†**b** A person who undertakes an obligation. L16–L17.
2 A person under obligation to another on account of a service or kindness received. E17.

obligement /əˈblʌɪdʒm(ə)nt/ *noun*. L16.
[from OBLIGE + -MENT.]
1 The fact of binding oneself by formal promise or contract; a contract, a covenant; = OBLIGATION 2. *obsolete* exc. *SCOTS LAW*. L16.
2 Moral or legal obligation; obligation for a service or kindness received; a kindness, a favour. *arch.* exc. *Scot.* E17.

obliger /əˈblʌɪdʒə/ *noun*. M17.
[from OBLIGE + -ER[1].]
1 A person who binds another to the performance of a contract, duty, etc.; a person who imposes obligation. Formerly also = OBLIGEE 1. M17.
2 A person who does a service or kindness. M17.
3 A person who obliges another domestically; a charwoman. *colloq.* M20.

obliging /əˈblʌɪdʒɪŋ/ *adjective*. M17.
[from OBLIGE + -ING[2].]
1 Legally or morally binding; obligatory. Now *rare*. M17.
2 Of a person, disposition, etc.: ready to do a service or kindness; courteous, civil, accommodating. M17. ▸**b** Of an action, word, etc.: courteous, polite. Formerly also, gratifying, pleasing. M17.

2 LD MACAULAY Keppel had a sweet and obliging temper. S. T. WARNER She was most obliging to us, lowered the rent by two pound ten.

■ **obligingly** *adverb* M17. **obligingness** *noun* M17.

obligor /ˈɒblɪɡɔː/ *noun*. M16.
[from OBLIGE + -OR.]
LAW. A person who is bound to another by contract or who gives a bond to another. Correl. to *obligee*.

obliquangular /ɒblɪˈkwaŋɡjʊlə/ *adjective*. M17.
[from mod. Latin *obliquangulus*, from Latin *obliquus* OBLIQUE *adjective* + *angulus* ANGLE *noun*[3]: see -AR[1].]
Of a figure: having all its angles oblique.

†**obliquation** *noun*. LME–E19.
[Latin *obliquatio(n-)*, from *obliquat-* pa. ppl stem of *obliquare*, from *obliquus* OBLIQUE *adjective*: see -ATION.]
Orig., strabismus. Later *gen.*, a bending aside; a twisting obliquely.
■ †**obliquate** *verb trans.* (*rare*) bend, twist M17–E18.

oblique /əˈbliːk/ *adjective*, *noun*, & *adverb*. LME.
[Old & mod. French from Latin *obliquus*, from *ob-* OB- + unexpl. 2nd elem.]
▸ **A** *adjective*. **1** Having a slanting direction or position; not vertical or horizontal; diverging from a straight line or course. LME.
2 *fig.* **a** Not taking the direct course; not going straight to the point; indirectly stated or expressed; indirect. LME. ▸**b** Of an end, result, etc.: indirectly aimed at; resulting or arising indirectly. E16. ▸**c** Diverging from right conduct or thought; perverse, aberrant. *arch.* L16.
3 a *GEOMETRY*. (Of a line or surface) inclined at an angle other than a right angle; (of an angle) less than 180 degrees but not equal to a right angle; (of a solid) having its axis not perpendicular to the plane of its base. E16. ▸**b** *ANATOMY*. Having a direction neither parallel nor at right angles to the long axis of the body, a limb, etc.; *spec.* designating various muscles of the head, abdomen, eyeball, etc. L16. ▸**c** *BOTANY*. Of a leaf: having unequal sides. M19.
4 *GRAMMAR*. Designating any case not as basic, *esp.* one other than the nominative or vocative. Also = INDIRECT 1b. M16.

1 GIBBON Advancing their whole wing of cavalry in an oblique line. A. NIN He edged sideways, with an oblique glance. **2a** P. ABRAHAMS You will evade me with oblique responses. **b** M. DRAYTON The love we bear our friends . . Hath in it certain oblique ends. **c** J. JORTIN There are persons . . who grow rich and great . . by various oblique and scandalous ways. **4** GLADSTONE He is mentioned six times in oblique cases . . and five times in the nominative. F. W. FARRAR There is scarcely a single oblique sentence throughout St. John's Gospel.

Special collocations: **oblique ascension**: see ASCENSION 2. **oblique circular cone**, **oblique cone**: see CONE *noun* 3. **oblique motion** *MUSIC*: in which one part remains stationary while another ascends or descends. **oblique oration** indirect speech. **oblique pedal**: see PEDAL *noun*[1] 4. **oblique perspective**: in which neither side of the principal object is parallel to the plane of delineation, so that their horizontal lines converge to a vanishing point. **oblique photograph** = sense B.3 below. **oblique speech** indirect speech. **oblique sphere** the celestial or terrestrial sphere when its axis is oblique to the horizon (as it is at any point except the poles and the equator). **oblique stroke** = sense B.4 below.

▸ **B** *ellipt.* as *noun*. **1** *GRAMMAR*. An oblique case. Usu. in *pl.* LME.
2 An oblique muscle. Usu. with specifying word. M19.
3 A photograph, esp. an aerial one, taken at an oblique angle. E20.
4 An oblique line; *spec.* a solidus. M20.
▸ **C** *adverb*. Obliquely, diagonally, slantwise. *arch.* M17.

MILTON They with labour push'd Oblique the Centric Globe.

■ **obliquely** *adverb* E16. **obliqueness** *noun* E17. †**obliquous** *adjective* (*rare*) oblique E17–M18.

oblique /əˈbliːk/ *verb*. LME.
[French *obliquer* march in an oblique direction, formed as prec.]
†**1** *verb trans.* Turn askew or in an oblique direction. Chiefly as **obliqued** *ppl adjective*. LME–L18.
2 *verb intrans.* Advance in an oblique direction, esp. (*MILITARY*) by making a half-face to the right or left and then marching forward. L18.
¶ Rare before L18.

obliquity /əˈblɪkwɪti/ *noun*. LME.
[Old & mod. French *obliquité* from Latin *obliquitas*, from *obliquus* OBLIQUE *adjective*: see -ITY.]
1 The quality of being oblique in direction, position, or form; (degree or extent of) inclination at an oblique angle to a line or plane. LME.
2 *fig.* **a** Divergence from right conduct or thought; perversity, aberration; an instance of this. *arch.* LME. ▸**b** Indirectness in action, speech, etc.; a way or method that is not direct or straightforward. E17. ▸†**c** Deviation from a rule or order. *rare*. M17–M18.

1 C. DARWIN The obliquity of the eye, which is proper to the Chinese and Japanese. **2a** DONNE The perversenesse and obliquity of my will. GLADSTONE Mr. Ward evinces the same thorough one-sidedness and obliquity of judgment. **b** JAS. MILL The obliquities of Eastern negotiation wore out the temper of Lally. A. BROOKNER A mild and subtle influence compounded of glancing opinions, smiling obliquities, tender and persuasive flatteries.

■ **obliquitous** *adjective* characterized by obliquity M19.

obliterate /əˈblɪt(ə)rət/ *adjective* (orig. *pa. pple*). Now *poet.* L16.
[Latin *oblit(t)eratus* pa. pple, formed as next: see -ATE[2].]
Blotted out; obliterated.

obliterate /əˈblɪtəreɪt/ *verb trans.* L16.
[Latin *oblit(t)erat-* pa. ppl stem of *oblit(t)erare* strike out, erase, from *ob-* OB- + *lit(t)era* LETTER *noun*[1]: see -ATE[3].]
1 Blot out, leaving no clear traces; cause to disappear from view; completely conceal; erase, efface. L16. ▸**b** Cancel (a postage stamp etc.) to prevent further use. M19.
2 *fig.* Completely get rid of from the mind; do away with, destroy, (qualities, characteristics, etc.). L16.
3 *MEDICINE* & *BIOLOGY*. Close up or destroy (a passage or cavity). E19.

1 LYTTON The colours were half obliterated by time and damp. H. E. BATES Snow . . had obliterated everything . . and I could not find the way. C. FRANCIS Driving rain obliterated the Lizard, a couple of miles to starboard. **2** R. L. STEVENSON One brief impression follows and obliterates another. M. SPARK Freddy had obliterated these days from his memory.

■ **obliteratingly** *adverb* in an obliterating manner; so as to obliterate: M19. **obliterator** *noun* a person who or thing which obliterates something; *spec.* an engraved block or stamping-tool used to cancel a postage stamp: M19.

obliteration /əblɪtəˈreɪʃ(ə)n/ *noun*. M17.
[Late Latin *oblit(t)eratio(n-)*, formed as prec.: see -ATION.]
1 The action of obliterating something; the fact of being obliterated. M17. ▸**b** A postmark used to cancel a postage stamp to prevent further use. L19.
2 *MEDICINE* & *BIOLOGY*. The disappearance or effective destruction of a structure; *esp.* the blocking or collapsing of a vessel or cavity. M19.
Comb.: **obliteration bombing** heavy bombing intended to destroy a target completely.

obliterative /əˈblɪt(ə)rətɪv/ *adjective*. E19.
[from OBLITERATE *verb*: see -ATIVE.]
1 Characterized by obliteration; tending to obliterate something. E19.
2 *ZOOLOGY*. Of coloration or shading: cryptic. E20.

oblivescence /ɒblɪˈvɛs(ə)ns/ *noun*. L19.
[Alt. of OBLIVISCENCE: see -ESCENCE.]
= OBLIVISCENCE.

I. MURDOCH Would that our sins had built-in qualities of oblivescence such as our dreams have.

oblivial /əˈblɪvɪəl/ *adjective* & *noun*. *rare*. E18.
[from Latin *oblivium* from *oblivio(n-)* OBLIVION: see -AL[1].]
(A thing) that causes forgetfulness.

obliviate /əˈblɪvɪeɪt/ *verb trans.* Now *rare* or *obsolete*. M17.
[formed as prec.: see -ATE[3].]
Forget.

oblivion /əˈblɪvɪən/ *noun*. LME.
[Old & mod. French from Latin *oblivio(n-)*, from *obliv-* stem of *oblivisci* forget: see -ION.]
1 The state or fact of forgetting or having forgotten; forgetfulness, esp. as resulting from inattention or carelessness; disregard. LME. ▸**b** Intentional overlooking of an offence, esp. a political one; amnesty, pardon. E17.
2 The state or condition of being forgotten. LME.

1 GOLDSMITH Thither no more the peasant shall repair To sweet oblivion of his daily care. P. SAYER He would drink himself into some kind of oblivion. **b** WELLINGTON There shall be a mutual oblivion and pardon of all injuries on both sides. **act of oblivion** a parliamentary etc. act granting a general pardon for political offences; *spec.* (*Hist.*) each of two acts, of 1660 and 1690, granting exemption from the penalties attached to those who had acted against Charles II and William III respectively. **2** *Times Lit. Suppl.* The work returns to oblivion for the next five years. **fall into oblivion** become forgotten or disused.

■ **oblivionize** *verb trans.* consign to oblivion L16.

oblivious /əˈblɪvɪəs/ *adjective*. LME.
[Latin *obliviosus*, from *oblivio(n-)*: see prec., -IOUS.]
1 That forgets, given to forgetting; forgetful. (Foll. by *of*.) LME. ▸**b** Unaware or unconscious of, indifferent to. (Foll. by *of*, *to*.) M19.
2 Of or pertaining to forgetfulness; attended by or associated with oblivion. *arch.* M16.
†**3** Forgotten. *rare*. M16–E19.

1 BURKE The slow formality of an oblivious and drowsy exchequer. J. WAIN Oblivious even of his wish to get home, Robinson watched. **b** D. R. KOONTZ She strolled back and forth, . . oblivious of the stingingly cold air. *Times* Seemingly oblivious to Israel's incursion into west Beirut.

For other words beginning with *ob-* see the entry for **ob-**

■ **obliviously** *adverb* L15. **obliviousness** *noun* M16.

obliviscence /ɒblɪˈvɪs(ə)ns/ *noun*. L18.
[from Latin *obliviscent-* pres. ppl stem of *oblivisci* forget: see -ENCE.]
The fact of forgetting; the state of having forgotten; forgetfulness.

†**oblocution** *noun*. LME–M18.
[Late Latin *oblocutio(n-)*, from Latin *oblocut-* pa. ppl stem of *obloqui* contradict, from *ob-* OB- + *loqui* talk, speak: see -ION.]
Evil-speaking, obloquy, slander.

Oblomov /ˈɒblə(ʊ)mɒf/ *noun*. Also **-off**. E20.
[The hero of Ivan Goncharov's novel *Oblomov* (1855).]
An inactive, weak-willed, and procrastinating person.
■ **Oblomovism** *noun* conduct characteristic of an Oblomov; sluggishness, inertia: E20.

oblong /ˈɒblɒŋ/ *adjective & noun*. LME.
[Latin *oblongus* somewhat long, oblong, elliptical, from *ob-* OB- + *longus* long.]
▶ **A** *adjective*. Elongated in one direction; *esp.* rectangular with adjacent sides unequal; (of a sheet of paper, a picture, etc.) rectangular with the breadth greater than the height. LME.
oblong WOODSIA.
▶ **B** *noun*. An oblong figure or object; *esp.* an oblong rectangle. E17.
■ **oblongish** *adjective* (*rare*) somewhat oblong L17. **oblongly** *adverb* (*rare*) M17. **oblongness** *noun* (*rare*) E18.

oblongo- /ɒbˈlɒŋgəʊ/ *combining form*. Now *rare*. L18.
[from prec. + -O-.]
BOTANY. Forming adjectives with the sense 'with oblong modification of another shape', as ***oblongo-elliptic***, ***oblongo-lanceolate***.

obloquy /ˈɒbləkwi/ *noun*. LME.
[Late Latin *obloquium* contradiction, from *ob-* OB- + *loqui* talk, speak.]
1 Abuse, calumny, slander. Formerly also, an abusive or calumnious speech or utterance. LME. ▸**b** The state of being generally ill spoken of; bad repute; disgrace. LME.
†**2** A cause, occasion, or object of detraction or reproach; a reproach, a disgrace. L16–E17.

📖 **1** A. STORR It required considerable courage to advance his theories . . against a current of almost universal obloquy. **2** SHAKES. *All's Well* An honour . . Which were the greatest obloquy i' th' world In me to lose.

obmutescence /ɒbmjuːˈtɛs(ə)ns/ *noun*. Now *rare*. M17.
[from Latin *obmutescere*, from *ob-* OB- + *mutescere* grow mute: see -ESCENCE.]
The state or condition of becoming wilfully mute, speechless, or dumb; the action of obstinately remaining mute.

obnebulate /ɒbˈnɛbjʊleɪt/ *verb trans. rare*. M16.
[from OB- + NEBULA + -ATE³.]
Obscure (as) with a mist; cloud.

obnounce /ɒbˈnaʊns/ *verb intrans. rare*. M18.
[Latin *obnuntiare*, from *ob-* OB- + *nuntiare* to tell, alt. after *announce*, *pronounce*, etc.]
ROMAN HISTORY. Of a magistrate: announce an inauspicious omen (and thus prevent or make void some public transaction).

obnoxious /əbˈnɒkʃəs/ *adjective*. L16.
[from Latin *obnoxiosus* or *obnoxius* exposed to harm, subject, liable, from *ob-* OB- + *noxa* hurt, injury: see -IOUS. Later infl. by assoc. with NOXIOUS.]
1 Subject or liable *to* harm or injury. Now *rare*. L16. ▸†**b** Liable *to be*; apt to do. E17–M18.
†**2** Subject to the rule or authority of another; answerable, amenable, (*to* some authority); submissive, obsequious. (Foll. by *to*.) L16–M18.
†**3** Open to punishment or censure; blameworthy, reprehensible. E17–L18.
4 That is an object of aversion or dislike; offensive, objectionable, odious; acting objectionably. Formerly also, hurtful, injurious. L17.

📖 **1** BUNYAN The town of Mansoul . . now lies obnoxious to its foes. **b** M. HALE The time of Youth is most obnoxious to forget God. **2** W. WOLLASTON An existence that is not dependent upon or obnoxious to any other. **3** GOLDSMITH A late work has appeared to us highly obnoxious in this respect. **4** E. FITZGERALD Carlyle . . is becoming very obnoxious now that he has become popular. R. SUTCLIFF An obnoxious little boy . . silly and a bully to boot.

■ **obnoxiety** /-nɒkˈsʌɪti/ *noun* (*rare*) liability (*to* something) M17. **obnoxiously** *adverb* E17. **obnoxiousness** *noun* E17. **obnoxity** *noun* an objectionable person or thing E20.

obnubilate /ɒbˈnjuːbɪleɪt/ *verb trans.* Chiefly *literary*. L16.
[Latin *obnubilat-* pa. ppl stem of *obnubilare* cover with clouds or fog, from *ob-* OB- + *nubilare*: see NUBILATE, -ATE³.]
Darken, dim, or conceal (as) with a cloud; obscure.
■ **obnubiˈlation** *noun* obscuration; *spec.* clouding of the mind or faculties: E17.

obo /ˈəʊbəʊ/ *noun*. Pl. same, **-os**. E20.
[Mongolian *obu* stone shrine, cairn.]
In Mongolia and northern Tibet: a sacred cairn of stones; an inscribed slab of stone.

oboe /ˈəʊbəʊ/ *noun*. E18.
[Italian formed as HAUTBOY.]
1 A double-reed woodwind instrument, forming the treble to the bassoon; a player of this instrument. E18.
2 An organ reed-stop imitating the oboe's penetrating tone. M19.
3 (**O-**.) A radar system used esp. in the 1940s to guide military aircraft, involving signals between two ground stations and a transponder in the aircraft. M20.
■ **oboist** *noun* a player of the oboe M19.

oboe da caccia /ˌəʊbəʊ da ˈkatʃə/ *noun phr*. Pl. **oboi da caccia** /ˈəʊbɔɪ/. L19.
[Italian, lit. 'hunting oboe'.]
Chiefly *Hist.* An obsolete type of tenor oboe with a pitch a fifth lower than the ordinary oboe.

oboe d'amore /ˌəʊbəʊ daˈmɔːreɪ/ *noun phr*. Pl. **oboes d'amore**, **oboi d'amore** /ˈəʊbɔɪ/. L19.
[Italian, lit. 'oboe of love'.]
A type of alto oboe with a pear-shaped bell and a pitch a minor third below that of the ordinary oboe, now used esp. in baroque music.

oboi da caccia *noun phr*. pl. of OBOE DA CACCIA.

oboi d'amore *noun phr*. pl. of OBOE D'AMORE.

obol /ˈɒb(ə)l/ *noun*. L16.
[Latin *obolus* from Greek *obolos* var. of *obelos* OBELISK.]
ANTIQUITIES. A silver (later bronze) coin of ancient Greece representing one-sixth of a drachma.

obole /ˈɒbəʊl/ *noun*. E17.
[French formed as prec.]
†**1** = OBOLUS 1. E–M17.
2 *Hist.* A small French silver (later billon) coin of the value of half a denier, in use from the 10th to the 15th cents. M17.

obolus /ˈɒb(ə)ləs/ *noun*. Pl. **-li** /-lʌɪ, -liː/. LME.
[Latin: see OBOL.]
†**1** An apothecaries' weight of 10 grains (approx. 0.648 gram). LME–M17.
2 *Hist.* Any of various low-value coins formerly current in Europe, *esp.* the French obole; any small coin. LME.
3 ANTIQUITIES. = OBOL. L16.

obosom /əʊˈbəʊsəm/ *noun*. Pl. ***abo-*** /əˈbəʊ-/. M19.
[Twi *ɔ-bósôm*.]
Any of various minor deities or spirits in the religious system of the Ashanti peoples of Ghana.

obreption /əˈbrɛpʃ(ə)n/ *noun*. LME.
[French, or Latin *obreptio(n-)*, from *obrept-* pa. ppl stem of *obrepere* creep up to, steal up on, from *ob-* OB- + *repere* creep: see -ION.]
The action of obtaining something by fraud; an attempt to do this; *spec.* in ECCLESIASTICAL & SCOTS LAW, the obtaining of a dispensation, gift, etc., by false statement. Cf. SUBREPTION 1.

obreptitious /ɒbrɛpˈtɪʃəs/ *adjective*. E17.
[from late Latin *obrepticius*, from Latin *obrept-*: see prec., -ITIOUS¹.]
Characterized by obreption; containing a false statement made for the purpose of obtaining something.
■ **obreptitiously** *adverb* L19.

obrogate /ˈɒbrəgeɪt/ *verb trans. rare*. M17.
[Latin *obrogat-* pa. ppl stem of *obrogare*, from *ob-* OB- + *rogare* ask, propose a law: see -ATE³.]
Repeal (a law) by passing a new law. Formerly also, interrupt (a person).
■ **obroˈgation** *noun* M17.

obs /ɒbz/ *noun*. *slang*. Pl. same. M20.
[Abbreviation.]
(An) observation.

obscene /əbˈsiːn/ *adjective*. L16.
[French *obscène* or Latin *obsc(a)enus* ill-omened, abominable, indecent.]
1 Highly offensive, morally repugnant; *arch.* repulsive, foul, loathsome. L16.
2 Offensively or grossly indecent, lewd; LAW (of a publication) tending to deprave and corrupt those who are likely to read, see, or hear the contents. L16.
†**3** Ill-omened, inauspicious. M17–M19.

📖 **1** *Times* The obscene proposals of the Monday Club to initiate repatriation. **2** B. VINE An anonymous phone-caller who had said obscene things to Felicity.

■ **obscenely** *adverb* L16. **obsceneness** *noun* (*rare*) M17.

obscenity /əbˈsɛnɪti/ *noun*. L16.
[Latin *obscaenitas*, from *obscaenus*: see prec., -ITY.]
The character or quality of being obscene; an instance of this, *esp.* an obscene expression.

📖 *Times* The hideous obscenity of gang violence. R. CHRISTIANSEN The carousing obscenities of the prostitutes offended her sensibilities.

obscurant /ɒbˈskjʊər(ə)nt/ *noun & adjective*. L18.
[German, from Latin *obscurant-* pres. ppl stem of *obscurare*: see OBSCURE *verb*, -ANT¹.]
▶ **A** *noun*. A person who obscures something; an obscurantist. L18.
▶ **B** *adjective*. That makes obscure; obscurantist. L19.
■ **obscurancy** *noun* (*rare*) E19.

obscurantism /ɒbskjʊˈrantɪz(ə)m/ *noun*. M19.
[from prec. + -ISM.]
Opposition to reform and enlightenment.
■ **obscurantist** *noun & adjective* (**a**) *noun* a person characterized by obscurantism; = OBSCURANT *noun*; (**b**) *adjective* of the nature of an obscurantist; pertaining to or characterized by obscurantism: M19.

obscuration /ɒbskjʊˈreɪʃ(ə)n/ *noun*. L15.
[Latin *obscuratio(n-)*, from *obscurat-* pa. ppl stem of *obscurare*: see OBSCURE *verb*, -ATION.]
The action of making something obscure, dim, or dark; the process of becoming obscure; a dimmed state or condition; ASTRONOMY occultation.

📖 A. C. GIMSON Weak accent in OE led to the obscuration of short vowels.

obscure /əbˈskjʊə/ *adjective & noun*. LME.
[Old & mod. French *obscur* Latinized form of earlier *oscur*, *escur* from Latin *obscurus* dark.]
▶ **A** *adjective*. **1** Dark, dim; gloomy, dismal. LME.
2 *fig.* Not clear or plain to the mind; vague, uncertain; not easily understood; not clearly expressed. LME.
3 a Indistinctly perceived, felt, or heard; *spec.* (of a vowel) weak and centralized (cf. *INDETERMINATE vowel*). LME. ▸**b** Lacking clarity of form or outline; indistinct, faint. L16.
4 Of colour: almost black, sombre; dingy, dull. L15.
5 Of a place: remote from observation; hidden, secret. L15.
6 Inconspicuous, undistinguished; (of a person) not illustrious or famous; humble. (Earlier in OBSCURELY 1.) M16.
7 Of, pertaining to, or frequenting the darkness; concealed from sight by darkness. E17.
8 Of a ray or radiation: invisible. *arch.* L18.

📖 **1** E. K. KANE The day misty and obscure. **2** T. H. HUXLEY The origin of hail is obscure. H. E. BATES Out of her obscure reflections she suddenly emerged clear-headed. L. GORDON Eliot was at his most obscure in these poems. **3b** S. JOHNSON What is distant is in itself obscure, and . . easily escapes our notice. **5** ALDOUS HUXLEY Gumbril Senior occupied a . . house in a little obscure square not far from Paddington. **6** V. WOOLF Quite obscure people, people of no importance whatsoever.

▶ **B** *noun*. **1** Obscurity, darkness. Chiefly *poet.* M17.
2 Indistinctness of outline or colour. L18.
■ **obscureness** *noun* (now *rare*) E16. †**obscurify** *verb trans.* (*rare*) make obscure; hide: E17–E19.

obscure /əbˈskjʊə/ *verb trans.* LME.
[Old French *obscurer* from Latin *obscurare*, from *obscurus* dark.]
1 a Make obscure or dark; dim. LME. ▸**b** Make less distinct in quality of sound; *spec.* articulate (a vowel) in a weaker, more centralized position. M17.
2 Conceal from knowledge or observation; disguise. Now *rare*. E16.
3 Lessen the lustre or glory of; overshadow. M16.
4 Make vague, indistinct, or unintelligible; blur the significance of. L16.
5 Cover or hide from view; conceal. E17.

📖 **1a** POPE See gloomy clouds obscure the cheerful day! **2** *Omni* Humans often obscure their feelings with words. **3** J. R. GREEN The fortunes of the University were obscured by the glories of Paris. **4** CONAN DOYLE The interesting personality of the accused does not obscure the clearness of the evidence. **5** G. ADAIR The enclosed terrace was at present obscured by a fleet of CRS vans.

■ **obscuredly** /-rɪdli/ *adverb* in an obscured manner E17. **obscurement** *noun* (*rare*) M17. **obscurer** *noun* (*rare*) M17.

obscurely /əbˈskjʊəli/ *adverb*. LME.
[from OBSCURE *adjective* + -LY².]
1 In obscurity; inconspicuously. LME.
2 *fig.* With obscurity of meaning; not plainly or clearly. E16.
3 Darkly; dimly, dully; indistinctly; with a dark or sombre colour. L16.

📖 **1** V. WOOLF He was an unknown man exhibiting obscurely. **2** M. MOORCOCK People had begun to weep and she felt obscurely guilty for not joining in. **3** W. M. PRAED There my Whole, obscurely bright, still shows his little lamp by night.

obscurity /əbˈskjʊərɪti/ *noun*. LME.
[Old & mod. French *obscurité* from Latin *obscuritas*, from *obscurus*: see OBSCURE *adjective*, -ITY.]
1 a An obscure point; a wholly or partially unintelligible speech or passage. LME. ▸**b** Lack of clarity of

expression; uncertainty of meaning; unintelligibility. M16.

2 Absence of light; darkness, dimness; indistinctness. Also, a dark place. L15.

3 The quality or condition of not being clearly known or understood. L15.

4 The quality or condition of being unknown, inconspicuous, or insignificant. Also, an obscure or unknown person. E17.

> 🕮 **1a** B. JOWETT The obscurities of early Greek poets. **b** M. SEYMOUR Confronted with the veiled obscurity of Henry's later work . . he was puzzled. **2** J. MCPHEE Mount McKinley, veiled in snow haze, was fast removing itself to obscurity. **3** H. N. HUMPHREYS The precise date of the origin of coined money is lost in obscurity. **4** H. KISSINGER His advisers are suddenly catapulted from obscurity into the limelight.

obscurum per obscurius /əbˌskjʊərəm pər əbˈskjʊərɪəs/ *noun phr.* L19.
[Late Latin, lit. 'the obscure by the still more obscure'.]
= IGNOTUM PER IGNOTIUS.

obsecration /ɒbsɪˈkreɪʃ(ə)n/ *noun.* LME.
[Latin *obsecratio(n-)*, from *obsecrat-* pa. ppl stem of *obsecrare* entreat, beseech (orig. by the name of the gods), from *ob-* OB- + *sacrare* hold sacred: see -ATION.]
1 Entreaty, supplication. LME. ▸**b** *RHETORIC.* A figure of speech in which assistance is implored. E17.
2 *ECCLESIASTICAL.* Any of the intercessory petitions of the Litany introduced by the word 'by' (Latin *per*). L19.
■ **ˈobsecrate** *verb trans.* (*rare*) entreat, implore; beg (a thing): L16.

obsequence /ˈɒbsɪkw(ə)ns/ *noun.* Now *rare.* E17.
[Latin *obsequentia*, from *obsequent-* pres. ppl stem of *obsequi* from *ob-* OB- + *sequi* follow: see -ENCE.]
Compliance, obsequiousness.

obsequent /ˈɒbsɪkw(ə)nt, əbˈsiːkw(ə)nt/ *adjective & noun.* L19.
[from OB- + *-sequent*, after *consequent* etc.]
PHYSICAL GEOGRAPHY. ▶**A** *adjective.* **1** Of a stream, valley, etc.: having a course or character opposite to the direction of dip of the strata. Cf. CONSEQUENT *adjective* 5, SUBSEQUENT *adjective* 2b. L19.
2 Of a fault-line scarp, etc.: having (as a result of erosion) a relief the reverse of that originally produced by the faulting. E20.
▶**B** *noun.* An obsequent stream. L19.

obsequies /ˈɒbsɪkwɪz/ *noun pl.* Also sing. †**obsequy**. LME.
[Anglo-Norman *obsequie(s* = Old French *obsèque(s* (mod. *obsèques*) from medieval Latin *obsequiae* prob. alt. of Latin *exequiae* (see EXEQUY) by assoc. with *obsequium* dutiful service (see OBSEQUY *noun*¹).]
Funeral rites or ceremonies; a funeral. Formerly also, a commemorative rite or service.
■ **obsequial** /-ˈsiː-/ *adjective* L17.

obsequious /əbˈsiːkwɪəs/ *adjective.* L15.
[from Latin *obsequiosus*, from *obsequium* compliance, from *ob-* OB- + *sequi* follow: see -IOUS.]
1 Compliant with the will or wishes of another; prompt to serve, please, or follow directions; obedient; dutiful. Now *rare.* L15. ▸†**b** [Infl. by OBSEQUIES.] Dutiful in showing respect for the dead; appropriate to obsequies. L15–L17.
2 Unduly or servilely compliant; manifesting or characterized by servility; fawning, sycophantic. E17.

> 🕮 **1** LD MACAULAY An army may be so constituted as to be . . efficient against an enemy, and yet obsequious to the . . magistrate. **2** O. MANNING He adopted an obsequious whine quite different from his usual sardonic tone.

■ **obsequiously** *adverb* L16. **obsequiousness** *noun* LME.

obsequy /ˈɒbsɪkwi/ *noun*¹. Now *rare* or *obsolete.* LME.
[French †*obsèque* or Latin *obsequium* compliance, from *ob-* OB- + *sequi* follow.]
Ready compliance with the will of another; deferential service; obsequiousness.

†**obsequy** *noun*² see OBSEQUIES.

observable /əbˈzəːvəb(ə)l/ *adjective & noun.* E17.
[Latin *observabilis*, from *observare* OBSERVE *verb*: see -ABLE.]
▶**A** *adjective.* **1** That must or may be adhered to, followed, or kept. E17.
2 Worthy of observation, attention, or mention; noteworthy. Formerly also, remarkable, notable. Now *rare.* E17.
3 Able to be observed; perceptible. E17.

> 🕮 **1** H. SPENCER Forms observable in social intercourse. **2** I. D'ISRAELI A very observable incident in the history of Charles. **3** E. NORTH Being courted by the Viking had wrought no observable change in her.

▶**B** *noun.* †**1** A noteworthy thing. Usu. in *pl.* M17–E19.
2 a A thing that may be observed or noticed; a thing that can be perceived; a thing that is knowable through the senses. (*rare* before M20.) M17. ▸**b** *PHYSICS.* A quantity that can (in principle) be measured. M20.

> 🕮 **1** SOUTHEY Among other observables, it ought to be noticed that she has peculiar names for her domestic implements. **2a** *Listener* The observables of a science must be potentially observable 'by all normal people'.

■ **observaˈbility** *noun* the quality of being observable; ability to be observed: M20. **observably** *adverb* noticeably, perceptibly M17.

observance /əbˈzəːv(ə)ns/ *noun.* ME.
[Old & mod. French from Latin *observantia*, from *observant-* pres. ppl stem of *observare*: see OBSERVE *verb*, -ANCE.]
1 An act performed in accordance with prescribed usage, *esp.* one of religious or ceremonial character; a customary rite or ceremony. ME. ▸**b** An ordinance; *esp.* the rule, or a regulation, of a religious order. LME.
2 The action or practice of following or heeding a law, custom, etc.; adherence to a practice, principle, etc.; the keeping of a prescribed or traditional ritual. LME.
3 The giving of due respect or deference to a person; respectful or courteous attention. *arch.* LME.
†**4** Attentive care, heed. LME–M17.
5 The action of observing or noticing what is said or done; observation. *arch.* L16.

> 🕮 **1** D. M. THOMAS From that day she had ceased her religious observances. DRYDEN To do the observance due to sprightly May. **2** A. MASON He may be defied by breaking every law whose observance he has commanded. *Sunday observance.* **4** R. SHARROCK This observance is absolutely necessary to Damask roses. **5** J. RUSKIN Consider how much intellect was needed in the architect, and how much observance of nature.

observancy /əbˈzəːv(ə)nsi/ *noun.* M16.
[from Latin *observantia*: see prec., -ANCY.]
1 Orig., the action of observing, observation. Later, the quality of being observant or observing. M16.
2 Respectful or obsequious attention. *arch.* E17.

observant /əbˈzəːv(ə)nt/ *noun & adjective.* LME.
[French, pres. pple of *observer*: see OBSERVE *verb*, -ANT¹.]
▶**A** *noun.* †**1** A person who observes a law, custom, etc. LME–E17.
2 (Usu. **O-**.) A member of a branch of the Franciscans in which the friars follow a strict rule. Cf. ***Conventual***. LME.
†**3** A dutiful or attentive servant or follower; an obsequious attendant. Only in E17.

> 🕮 **3** SHAKES. *Lear* Twenty silly ducking observants That stretch their duties nicely.

▶**B** *adjective.* **1** (Usu. **O-**.) Designating or pertaining to the Franciscan Observants. L15.
†**2** Showing respect or deference; considerately attentive; assiduous in service; obsequious. (Foll. by *of, to.*) L16–M18.
3 Attentive in adhering to a law, custom, principle, etc., or a set of these. E17.
4 Carefully particular; heedful. E17.
5 Diligent in taking notice; perceptive. E17.

> 🕮 **2** POPE Observant of the Gods, and sternly just. **3** C. POTOK The stores that were run by observant Jews were all closed on Shabbos. **4** G. HAKEWILL Of their weight they were so . . observant, that they had them weighed many times. **5** J. LONDON Sharply observant, every detail of the . . interior registering itself on his brain.

■ **observantly** *adverb* M17.

Observantine /əbˈzəːv(ə)ntɪn/ *noun & adjective.* E17.
[French *Observantin*, formed as prec.: see -INE¹.]
▶**A** *noun.* = OBSERVANT *noun* 2. E17.
▶**B** *adjective.* = OBSERVANT *adjective* 1. L18.

observation /ɒbzəˈveɪʃ(ə)n/ *noun.* LME.
[Latin *observatio(n-)*, from *observat-* pa. ppl stem of *observare*: see OBSERVE *verb*, -ATION.]
1 = OBSERVANCE 1. LME.
2 = OBSERVANCE 2. Now *rare.* LME.
3 a The action or an act of observing or noting; *MILITARY* the watching of an enemy's position, movements, etc.; the fact or condition of being noticed. M16. ▸**b** The faculty or habit of perceiving or taking notice. E17. ▸†**c** An act of augury or divination. E17–E18.
4 The careful watching and noting of an object or phenomenon for the purpose of scientific investigation; an instance of this; a measurement or other piece of information so obtained, an experimental result. M16. ▸**b** *spec.* The measurement of the altitude of the sun (or other celestial object) used to find latitude or longitude; an instance of this. M16.
5 An utterance as to something observed; a remark, a comment. M16.
6 An observed truth or fact; a thing learned by observing; a maxim gathered from experience. Now *rare.* M16.
†**7** = OBSERVANCE 4. Only in 17.
†**8** Respectful or courteous attention; = OBSERVANCE 3. M17–E18.

> 🕮 **1** W. J. LOCKE The daily calls to inquire after her health and happiness had grown to be sacred observation. **2** G. GORER Post-war rationing had weakened the general observation of the law. **3a** J. REED We were suddenly aware of observation, and looked up to encounter the . . gaze of half a dozen . . soldiers. *Guardian* He briefly escaped from a psychiatric hospital where he had been transferred for observation. **b** R. RENDELL His powers of observation in general so sharp, were less acute than usual. **4** W. SCORESBY This observation was . . made at a different hour almost every day. J. H. MASSERMAN A . . theory that cannot be verified by observation. *Daily Colonist* The physicists hope to make the first observation of 'quarks'. **5** R. CARVER I'm just saying we drink too much . . It's just an observation. **6** C. MARSHALL It may prove an observation of some use, that trees . . raised from seed grow the largest.

Phrases: **lunar observation**: see LUNAR *adjective.* **mass observation**: see MASS *noun*² & *adjective.* **place of observation** a place favourable for watching from or in. **under observation** being watched methodically; *spec.* (of a hospital patient) being monitored as to the symptoms, progress, etc., of a medical condition, esp. without specific treatment; (of a suspect) being kept under surveillance by the police etc.

Comb.: **observation car** (chiefly *N. Amer.*) a railway carriage designed to provide good views of passing scenery; **observation officer** *MILITARY* = OBSERVER 4b; **observation post** *MILITARY* a post for watching the effect of artillery fire etc.; **observation-sentence** *PHILOSOPHY* in a scientific theory, a sentence that reports, or directly relates to, observed phenomena; **observation-statement** an (utterance of) an observation-sentence; **observation ward** a hospital ward for patients under observation.

observational /ɒbzəˈveɪʃ(ə)n(ə)l/ *adjective.* M19.
[from prec. + -AL¹.]
Of or pertaining to observation.
■ **observationally** *adverb* by means of observation, with regard to observation L19.

observationalism /ɒbzəˈveɪʃ(ə)n(ə)lɪz(ə)m/ *noun.* L19.
[from prec. + -ISM.]
The theory that all knowledge is based on observation. Also, the doctrine that observation, rather than theory, is the basis of science.
■ **observationalist** *adjective & noun* (**a**) *adjective* adhering to observationalism; practising observational as opp. to theoretical work; (**b**) *noun* an adherent of observationalism: M20.

observative /əbˈzəːvətɪv/ *adjective.* Now chiefly *US.* E17.
[from OBSERVATION + -ATIVE, after *conservation*, *conservative* etc.]
Of or pertaining to observation; given to observation, attentive, heedful.

†**observator** *noun.* E16.
[French *observateur* or Latin *observator*, from *observat-*: see OBSERVATION, -OR.]
1 = OBSERVER 1. E16–M17.
2 a A person who keeps watch over or looks after something; a school monitor. E17–E18. ▸**b** = OBSERVER 2a. Formerly also, the editor or writer of a newspaper etc. M17–L18.
3 = OBSERVER 4a. M17–L18.
4 A person who makes a remark. M–L17.

observatory /əbˈzəːvət(ə)ri/ *noun.* L17.
[from (the same root as) OBSERVATION + -ORY¹.]
1 A building or place equipped with instruments for making observations of natural phenomena, esp. in astronomy or meteorology. L17.
2 A position or building affording an extensive view. L17.

observatory /əbˈzəːvət(ə)ri/ *adjective.* M19.
[from OBSERVATION + -ORY², after *conservation*, *conservatory*, etc.]
Of or pertaining to scientific observation.

observe /əbˈzəːv/ *verb & noun.* LME.
[Old & mod. French *observer* from Latin *observare* watch, attend to, guard, from *ob-* OB- + *servare* watch, keep.]
▶**A** *verb.* **I 1** *verb trans.* Pay practical regard to (a law, custom, principle, etc.); adhere to, keep, follow. LME.
2 *verb trans.* Hold or keep to (a manner of life or behaviour, a habit); maintain (a quality, state, etc.). LME. ▸†**b** Foll. by *to do*: be in the habit of doing. M17–M18.
3 *verb trans.* Mark or acknowledge (a festival, anniversary, etc.) by due rites; perform (a ceremony, rite, etc.); = KEEP *verb* 9. LME.
†**4** *verb trans.* Show regard for; show respectful or courteous attention to (a person); humour; gratify. LME–M18.

> 🕮 **1** P. NORMAN There was a 5 m.p.h. speed limit for cars . . which Dad observed with . . care. A. MASON When procedures were correctly observed, results followed. **2** J. H. NEWMAN Othman observed the life of a Turcoman, till he became a conqueror. J. NEEL The meeting observed a thirty-second silence. **3** S. BUTLER The rigour with which the young people were taught to observe the Sabbath. **4** SHAKES. *Jul. Caes.* Must I observe you? Must I stand and crouch under your testy humour?

▶**II 5 a** *verb trans.* Inspect for purposes of divination; watch or take note of (omens). *arch.* LME. ▸**b** *verb trans.* Watch attentively or carefully. M16. ▸†**c** *verb intrans.* Make observations; keep watch. E17–L18.
†**6** *verb trans.* Give heed to (a point); take care *that*, *to do*. E16–L18.

For other words beginning with *ob-* see the entry for **ob-**

†**7** *verb trans.* Watch for in order to take advantage of (a suitable time, an opportunity). M16–M17.
8 *verb trans.* Take notice of; be aware of seeing; remark, perceive, see. (Foll. by *that, to be, to do.*) M16.
9 a *verb trans.* Take note of or detect scientifically; watch or examine methodically, esp. without experimental or therapeutic intervention. M16. ▸**b** *verb intrans.* Make scientific observations; *spec.* (now *rare* or *obsolete*) make an astronomical measurement to determine latitude or longitude. M18.

📖 **5b** D. MURPHY Gloom enveloped me at the thought of Old Brigid . . vigilantly observing our table-manners. **7** W. MONSON They must observe the Spring-Tides to come over the Barr. **8** T. HARDY At last he observed the white waistcoat of the man he sought. *Scientific American* In such circumstances crocodiles have been observed to move the carcass toward another crocodile.

▸**III 10** *verb trans.* Say by way of comment; remark, mention. (Foll. by *that.*) E17. ▸**b** *verb intrans.* Foll. by *on*: make a remark about, comment on. Now *rare.* E17.

📖 **10** T. HARDY 'Well, 'tis a curious place . . ,' observed Moon. J. CONRAD Captain Vincent . . observed abstractedly that he was not a man to put a noose round a dog's neck.

▸**B** *noun.* **1** = OBSERVATION 5, 6. Now *Scot. dial.* M17. †**2** = OBSERVATION 3, 4. Chiefly *Scot.* L17–M19.
■ **observingly** *adverb* in an observant manner L16.

observer /əbˈzəːvə/ *noun.* M16.
[from prec. + -ER¹.]
1 An adherent or follower of a law, custom, principle, etc. M16.
2 a A person who watches, or takes notice (freq. in titles of newspapers); an interested spectator; a person who observes without participating; *spec.* (**a**) one who attends a conference, inquiry, etc., to note the proceedings; (**b**) one posted in an official capacity to an area of conflict to monitor events, supervise a cease-fire, etc. L16. ▸**b** An interpreter of omens. *arch.* L16.
†**3** A person showing respect or dutiful attention; an obsequious follower. E–M17.
4 a A person who makes scientific observations; such a person (real or hypothetical) regarded as having a particular viewpoint or effect. Also, a person in charge of an observatory. L18. ▸**b** MILITARY. A person responsible for observation; *esp.* (**a**) a member of an artillery group trained to identify the target; (**b**) a person trained to spot and identify aircraft, or to reconnoitre the enemy positions from the air; *spec.* a rank in an air force. L19.

📖 **1** L. WALLACE They were rigorous observers of the Law as found in the books of Moses. **2a** A. N. WILSON It was becoming clear to most observers that . . the war would soon be over in Europe. **c** E. PAWEL He remained the detached and critical observer. *attrib.*: *Guardian* The French and the Pope have . . called for a new observer force. **4a** *attrib.*: *Nature* This study was not double blind and hence subject to observer bias.

obsess /əbˈsɛs/ *verb.* LME.
[Latin *obsess-* pa. ppl stem of *obsidere* sit down before, besiege, occupy, from *ob-* OB- + *sedere* sit.]
1 *verb trans.* Of an evil spirit: haunt, torment, possess. Now *rare* or *obsolete.* LME.
†**2** *verb trans.* = BESIEGE 1. E16–M17.
3 *verb trans.* Orig., beset, harass (cf. BESIEGE 2). Now, fill the mind of (a person) continually (and often intrusively); preoccupy; haunt (the mind) as an obsession. Usu. in *pass.* (foll. by *with, by*). M16.
4 *verb intrans.* Worry persistently. Also, express oneself anxiously and at length. Orig. *N. Amer.* L20.

📖 **3** L. W. MEYNELL The one idea that obsessed him with overpowering force was to . . finish his man. *Independent* French tale of a middle-aged voyeur . . obsessed with a young girl. **4** M. PIERCY The conversation was studded with silences . . when she would begin to obsess about Nina. HELEN FIELDING He indulged me while I obsessed to him about my unattractiveness crisis.

¶ Obsolete after E18 until revived in L19.

obsession /əbˈsɛʃ(ə)n/ *noun.* E16.
[Latin *obsessio(n-)*, formed as prec.: see -ION.]
†**1** The action of besieging a place; a siege. E16–M17.
2 The supposed action of an evil spirit in besetting a person; the supposed state or fact of being affected by an evil spirit from outside. Now *rare.* E17.
3 (The action of) an idea or image which continually or persistently fills the mind; PSYCHOLOGY an idea or image that repeatedly intrudes on the mind of a person against his or her will and is usually distressing; the state of being affected in this way. L17.

📖 **2** E. B. TYLOR These cases belong rather to obsession than possession. **3** R. CLAY I never had her obsession about cleanliness. *Lifestyle* Supermarket aisles are devoted to a modern obsession for chemically-induced cleanliness. *Guardian* An egalitarian obsession with redistribution had eroded incentives.

¶ Not recorded between L17 and M19.

■ **obsessionist** *noun* a person who is obsessed, or is subject to obsession E20.

obsessional /əbˈsɛʃ(ə)n(ə)l/ *adjective & noun.* M19.
[from prec. + -AL¹.]
▸**A** *adjective.* **1** Of or pertaining to a siege. *rare.* M19.
2 Characterized by or caused by an obsession. E20.
2 obsessional neurosis PSYCHOLOGY a neurosis in which the main symptom is the occurrence of obsessional thoughts. **obsessional neurotic** a person with an obsessional neurosis.
▸**B** *noun.* A person whose personality is dominated by an obsession. E20.
■ **obsessionalism** *noun* obsessional behaviour M20. **obsessionally** *adverb* M20.

obsessive /əbˈsɛsɪv/ *adjective & noun.* E20.
[from OBSESS + -IVE.]
▸**A** *adjective.* (Of an idea or image) affecting the mind as an obsession; characteristic of or characterized by (an) obsession. E20.

📖 *Independent* He was meticulous about his appearance and obsessive about cleanliness. *Times Educ. Suppl.* He developed obsessive behaviours. B. BETTELHEIM An anxiously obsessive desire to maintain sameness.

▸**B** *noun.* A person characterized by obsessive behaviour. M20.
Comb.: **obsessive-compulsive** *adjective & noun* (PSYCHOLOGY) (**a**) *adjective* designating or pertaining to a disorder in which a person has an obsessive compulsion to perform meaningless acts repeatedly; (**b**) *noun* a person whose compulsive behaviour is due to obsessive thoughts.
■ **obsessively** *adverb* in an obsessive manner; insistently, beyond reason: M20. **obsessiveness** *noun* M20.

obsidian /əbˈsɪdɪən/ *noun.* M17.
[Latin (*lapis*) *obsidianus* erron. form of *obsianus*, from Greek *opsianos* (*lithos*) a black stone, named after its supposed discoverer Obsius: see -IAN.]
MINERALOGY. A dark-coloured vitreous lava or volcanic rock, of varying composition and conchoidal fracture, resembling common glass; volcanic glass. Also †*obsidian stone*.

obsidianite /əbˈsɪdɪənʌɪt/ *noun.* Now *rare.* L19.
[from prec. + -ITE¹.]
GEOLOGY. = TEKTITE.

obsidional /əbˈsɪdɪən(ə)l/ *adjective.* LME.
[Latin *obsidionalis*, from *obsidio(n-)* siege, from *obsidere*: see OBSESS, -AL¹.]
Of or pertaining to a siege.
obsidional coin a coin struck in a besieged city when current coins are unobtainable. **obsidional crown**, **obsidional coronet**, etc., a wreath of grass or weeds conferred as a mark of honour upon a Roman general who raised a siege.

obsidious /əbˈsɪdɪəs/ *adjective. rare.* E17.
[from Latin *obsidium* siege, from *obsidere*: see OBSESS, -IOUS.]
Besieging; besetting.

obsignation /ɒbsɪgˈneɪʃ(ə)n/ *noun.* Now *rare.* M16.
[Latin *obsignatio(n-)*, from *obsignat-* pa. ppl stem of *obsignare* seal, seal up, from *ob-* OB- + *signare* mark, seal, SIGN *verb*: see -ATION.]
1 Formal ratification or confirmation of something. M16.
†**2** The action of sealing up. M–L17.

obsignatory /əbˈsɪgnət(ə)ri/ *adjective.* Now *rare.* M17.
[from prec. + -ORY².]
Ratifying, confirming; pertaining to ratification.

obsolesce /ɒbsəˈlɛs/ *verb intrans.* L19.
[Latin *obsolescere*, from *ob-* OB- + *solere* be accustomed: see -ESCE.]
Be obsolescent; fall into disuse.

📖 E. V. LUCAS The Mayor . . still clung to the steadily obsolescing topper.

¶ Rare before M20.

obsolescence /ɒbsəˈlɛs(ə)ns/ *noun.* E19.
[formed as next: see -ESCENCE.]
1 The process or state of becoming obsolete or falling into disuse. E19. ▸**b** A diminution in the value or usefulness of consumer goods, machinery, etc., owing to technological advances, changes in demand, etc. L19.
2 BIOLOGY. The penultimate stage in the evolutionary loss of a character or part, or in the extinction of a species. M19.

📖 **1** A. N. WILSON Old heresies, like old jokes, acquire their own . . kind of pathetic obsolescence. **b** *New Scientist* Household equipment with built-in obsolescence. PLANNED *obsolescence*.

obsolescent /ɒbsəˈlɛs(ə)nt/ *adjective.* M18.
[Latin *obsolescent-* pres. ppl stem of *obsolescere*: see OBSOLESCE, -ESCENT.]
1 Becoming obsolete; going out of use, out of production, or out of date. M18.
2 BIOLOGY. Of an organ or structure: in the process of (apparent) disappearance or atrophy. M19.

📖 **1** *Time* Jazz lingo becomes obsolescent almost as fast as it reaches the public ear.

For other words beginning with *ob-* see the entry for **ob-**

obsolete /ˈɒbsəliːt/ *adjective & noun.* L16.
[Latin *obsoletus* grown old, worn out, pa. pple of *obsolescere*: see OBSOLESCE.]
▸**A** *adjective.* **1** No longer practised or used; outmoded, out of date. L16.
2 Chiefly BIOLOGY. Indistinct; rudimentary, vestigial, almost or entirely absent. M18.
3 Effaced through erosion, atrophy, or deterioration. M19.

📖 **1** T. BENN The House of Lords should be abolished as an obsolete and unnecessary part of our constitution. B. BRYSON Even when you strip out its obsolete senses, *round* still has twelve uses as an adjective. **3** G. DOWNES The . . Tomb of Nero . . is embellished with carving, and bears a nearly obsolete inscription.

▸**B** *noun.* A thing which is out of date or has fallen into disuse; a person who is out of date or behind the times. M17.
■ **obsoletely** *adverb* E19. **obsoleteness** *noun* E17. **obsoˈletion** *noun* (*rare*) obsoleteness; obsolescence: E19. **obsoletism** *noun* (**a**) an obsolete term, phrase, custom, etc.; (**b**) obsoleteness: L18.

obsolete /ˈɒbsəliːt/ *verb trans.* Now chiefly *N. Amer.* M17.
[from prec. or Latin *obsolet-* pa. ppl stem of *obsolescere*: see OBSOLESCE.]
Make or consider as obsolete; discard as being out of date; cease to produce or use.

📖 *Daily Telegraph* We're trying to stimulate the business by obsoleting last year's designs.

obstacle /ˈɒbstək(ə)l/ *noun & adjective.* ME.
[Old & mod. French from Latin *obstaculum*, from *obstare* stand in the way, from *ob-* OB- + *stare* stand.]
▸**A** *noun.* **1** A thing that stands in the way and obstructs progress; a hindrance, an obstruction. ME.
†**2** Opposition, objection: only in ***make obstacle***, offer opposition. LME–M17.

📖 **1** M. GIROUARD Drunkenness was as much of an obstacle to enlightenment as lack of education. *Independent* Her racial background need pose no obstacle to advancement.

Comb.: **obstacle course** an area (used for military training etc.) containing an assortment of obstacles to be negotiated; **obstacle-race**: in which the competitors have to negotiate a series of obstructions.
▸†**B** *adjective.* Obstinate, stubborn. M–L16.

📖 SHAKES. *1 Hen. VI* Fie, Joan, that thou wilt be so obstacle!

■ **obstacular** /ɒbˈstakjʊlə/ *adjective* of the nature of an obstacle; presenting many or a series of obstacles: M20.

obstacle /ˈɒbstək(ə)l/ *verb trans. rare.* M16.
[French †*obstacler*, formed as prec.]
Place obstacles or difficulties in the way of.

obstetric /əbˈstɛtrɪk/ *adjective.* M18.
[mod. Latin *obstetricus* from Latin *obstetricius*, from *obstetrix* midwife, lit. 'woman who is present', i.e. to receive the child, from *obstare*: see OBSTACLE *noun*, -IC.]
Orig., of or pertaining to a midwife or accoucheur. Now, of or pertaining to childbirth and the practice of obstetrics.

obstetrical /əbˈstɛtrɪk(ə)l/ *adjective.* L18.
[formed as prec. + -AL¹.]
= prec.
obstetrical toad = ***midwife toad*** s.v. MIDWIFE *noun*.

obstetrically /əbˈstɛtrɪk(ə)li/ *adverb.* M18.
[from OBSTETRIC + -ALLY.]
As regards obstetrics; from an obstetric point of view.

†**obstetricate** *verb intrans. rare.* E17–E19.
[Latin *obstetricat-* pa. ppl stem of ecclesiastical Latin *obstetricare*, from Latin *obstetrix*: see OBSTETRIC, -ATE³.]
Act as midwife; aid a woman in childbirth.

obstetrician /ɒbstəˈtrɪʃ(ə)n/ *noun.* E19.
[from OBSTETRICS + -ICIAN.]
A physician qualified to practise obstetrics. Formerly also, a person skilled in midwifery.

obstetrics /əbˈstɛtrɪks/ *noun.* E19.
[from OBSTETRIC: see -ICS.]
The branch of medicine that deals with childbirth and the care and treatment of the mother before and after birth; the practice of midwifery.

obstetrix /əbˈstɛtrɪks/ *noun. rare.* L18.
[Latin: see OBSTETRIC, -TRIX.]
A midwife.

obstinacy /ˈɒbstɪnəsi/ *noun.* LME.
[medieval Latin *obstinacia*, from *obstinatus* pa. pple of *obstinare*: see OBSTINATE *adjective & noun*, -ACY.]
1 The quality or condition of being obstinate; stubbornness; inflexibility; persistency. LME.
2 An act or instance of this. Usu. in *pl.* E17.

📖 **1** E. F. BENSON She . . had a quiet obstinacy that wore down opposition.

obstinance /ˈɒbstɪnəns/ *noun. rare.* LME.
[medieval Latin *obstinantia*, from *obstinant-* pres. ppl stem of *obstinare*: see OBSTINATE *adjective & noun*, -ANCE.]
Stubborn or self-willed persistence; obstinacy.

obstinancy /ˈɒbstɪnənsi/ *noun. rare.* E17.
[formed as prec.: see -ANCY.]
Obstinacy.

obstinate /ˈɒbstɪnət/ *adjective & noun.* ME.
[Latin *obstinatus* pa. pple of *obstinare* persist, from *ob-* OB- + causative deriv. of *stare* STAND verb: see -ATE[2].]
▶ **A** *adjective.* **1** Firmly adhering to one's chosen course of action or opinion despite persuasion or argument; stubborn, self-willed. ME.
2 Stiff, rigid; refractory; *spec.* (of a disease etc.) not responding readily to treatment. L16.

📖 **1** J. GALSWORTHY He had no hope of shaking her resolution; She was as obstinate as a mule. G. GREENE He could see Ali's face in the .. mirror, set, obstinate, closed and rocky like a cave mouth.

▶ **B** *noun.* An obstinate person. Now *rare* or *obsolete.* LME.
■ **obstinately** *adverb* LME.

obstinate /ˈɒbstɪneɪt/ *verb trans.* Now *rare.* LME.
[Latin *obstinat-* pa. ppl stem of *obstinare*: see prec., -ATE[3].]
Make obstinate; cause to persist stubbornly.

📖 *refl.*: T. CARTWRIGHT One that hath obstinated himselfe against the Church.

obstination /ɒbstɪˈneɪʃ(ə)n/ *noun. rare.* ME.
[French from Latin *obstinatio(n-)* determination, resolution, formed as prec.: see -ATION.]
Obstinacy.

obstipation /ɒbstɪˈpeɪʃ(ə)n/ *noun.* L16.
[Alt. of CONSTIPATION: see OB-.]
The action of blocking; the state of being blocked; MEDICINE severe or complete constipation.
■ †**obstipate** *verb trans.* (*rare*) block up M17–E18.

obstreperous /əbˈstrɛp(ə)rəs/ *adjective.* E16.
[from Latin *obstreperus*, from *obstrepere* make a noise against: see -OUS.]
1 Noisy; vociferous; characterized by clamorous opposition. E16.
2 Turbulent, unruly; noisily resisting control, advice, etc. M16.

📖 **1** *National Observer (US)* He can appeal not only to the party main stream but to its obstreperous minority. **2** A. MAY Much of her own childhood had been lost to .. amusing obstreperous toddlers.

■ **obstreperously** *adverb* E17. **obstreperousness** *noun* M17.

obstriction /əbˈstrɪkʃ(ə)n/ *noun.* L17.
[medieval Latin *obstrictio(n-)*, from *obstrict-* pa. ppl stem of *obstringere*, from *ob-* OB- + *stringere* tie, bind: see -ION.]
The state of being subject to a moral or legal obligation.

obstruct /əbˈstrʌkt/ *verb trans.* L16.
[Latin *obstruct-* pa. ppl stem of *obstruere* build against, block up, from *ob-* OB- + *struere* pile, build.]
1 Place or be an obstacle in (a passageway, opening, etc.); make difficult or impossible to pass through. L16.
2 Retard the passage or progress of; impede, hinder the motion of; SPORT impede (a player) in a manner which constitutes an offence. M17.
3 *fig.* Stand in the way of, oppose, retard the course of, (proceedings, a proposed action, etc.); frustrate (a person, intention, etc.). M17.
4 Get in the way of, shut out, (a sight or view). E18.

📖 **1** MILTON Both Sin, and Death, .. obstruct the mouth of Hell .. and seal up his ravenous Jawes. W. LEWIS The sidewalks are obstructed by hobbling women. **2** P. CAREY He edged around the boy ... He imagined the boy was deliberately obstructing him. **obstructing the field**, †**obstructing the ball** CRICKET (of a batsman) deliberately hindering a fieldsman or interfering with the ball in order to avoid being caught, stumped, etc., in contravention of the laws of the game. **3** GOLDSMITH I don't know if it be just thus to obstruct the union of man and wife. *Daily Chronicle* The conviction of two men for obstructing the police. **4** J. RABAN One could not .. see through their windows, since the view was obstructed by .. shutters.

■ **obstructedly** *adverb* in an obstructed manner M17. **obstructingly** *adverb* in an obstructing manner L19.

obstruction /əbˈstrʌkʃ(ə)n/ *noun.* M16.
[Latin *obstructio(n-)*, formed as prec.: see -ION.]
1 The action or an act of obstructing something or someone; the condition of being obstructed; MEDICINE blockage of a bodily passage, esp. the gut; LAW the action of impeding the movement of traffic on a highway. M16.
2 A thing impeding or preventing passage or progress; an obstacle, a blockage. L16.

📖 **1** SHAKES. *Twel. N.* This does make some obstruction in the blood, this cross-gartering. A. E. STEVENSON In every field Democratic proposals .. are met by Republican indifference, obstruction and opposition. *Independent* All they can be arrested for is causing an obstruction. **cold obstruction** *poet.* death, rigor mortis. **2** W. MARCH She had to get out .. and move the obstruction before she could put her car away.

Comb.: **obstruction light** a light placed on a tall structure as a warning to aircraft.
■ **obstructionary** *adjective* (*rare*) tending to obstruct something M20. **obstructionism** *noun* the practice of systematic obstruction, as in a legislative assembly L19. **obstructionist** *noun & adjective* (*a*) *noun* an advocate or systematic practitioner of obstruction, *esp.* one who delays the proceedings of a legislative assembly; (*b*) *adjective* of or pertaining to obstructionists or obstructionism: M19.

obstructive /əbˈstrʌktɪv/ *adjective & noun.* E17.
[from OBSTRUCT + -IVE.]
▶ **A** *adjective.* **1** Causing (an) obstruction; tending to obstruct something. (Foll. by *of*, *to*.) E17.
2 Of, pertaining to, or of the nature of obstruction of a passage in the body, esp. the gut or the bronchi. E17.

📖 **1** M. ARNOLD Academies may be said to be obstructive to .. inventive genius. **2 obstructive jaundice**: resulting from blockage of the bile ducts or abnormal retention of bile in the liver.

▶ **B** *noun.* **1** An obstructive agent, instrument, or force; a hindrance. M17.
2 A person who obstructs or delays progress. M19.

📖 **1** J. TYNDALL The leading mule .. proved a mere obstructive. **2** G. A. SALA A meddlesome .. body of political obstructives who called themselves the Constitutional Association.

■ **obstructively** *adverb* M19. **obstructiveness** *noun* E18.

obstructor /əbˈstrʌktə/ *noun.* M17.
[from OBSTRUCT + -OR.]
A person who or thing which obstructs something; an opponent of progress.

obstruent /ˈɒbstrʊənt/ *adjective & noun.* M17.
[Latin *obstruent-* pres. ppl stem of *obstruere*: see OBSTRUCT, -ENT.]
▶ **A** *noun.* **1** An obstruction. M17.
†**2** MEDICINE. A medicine or substance which closes the natural passages or pores of the body. M17–L19.
3 PHONETICS. A fricative or plosive speech sound. M20.

📖 **1** SLOAN WILSON Some obstruent to clear away. **3** N. CHOMSKY If the second consonant is a liquid, the first must be an obstruent.

▶ **B** *adjective.* = OBSTRUCTIVE *adjective* 1. M18.

📖 J. WAINWRIGHT The object .. was to demolish any obstruent bushel likely to get in the way of *his* .. light.

†**obstruse** *adjective.* E17–M18.
[Alt.]
Abstruse.

obstupefy /əbˈstjuːpɪfʌɪ/ *verb trans.* E17.
[from Latin *obstupefacere* make stupid, after STUPEFY.]
Stupefy, make insensible.

†**obstupescence** *noun. rare.* L16–L19.
[from Latin *obstupescent-* pres. ppl stem of *obstupescere* (*obstipescere*) become stupefied: see -ESCENCE.]
The condition of being in a stupor.

obtain /əbˈteɪn/ *verb.* LME.
[Old & mod. French *obtenir* from Latin *obtinere*, from *ob-* OB- + *tenere* hold.]
1 *verb trans.* Come into the possession or enjoyment of; secure or gain as the result of request or effort; acquire, get. Formerly also foll. by obj. clause expr. what was gained. LME. ▶†**b** Foll. by *of*, *from*: prevail on (a person) *to do*. L17–M18.
†**2** *verb trans.* Win (a victory, battle, etc.). LME–M17.
3 *verb intrans.* Prevail; succeed, prosper. *arch.* LME.
4 a *verb trans.* & †*intrans.* (with *to*). Attain, reach, get as far as. *arch.* L15. ▶†**b** *verb intrans.* Come *to be*, *to do*; manage *to do*. E16–E18.
†**5** *verb trans.* Hold; possess; occupy. L15–E18.
6 *verb intrans.* Be prevalent, customary, or established; subsist, hold good; be in force or in vogue. E17.

📖 **1** W. WHISTON Macheras .. earnestly begged and obtained that he would be reconciled. H. BELLOC Life is very hard for some of our town dwellers in spite of the high wages they obtain. DAY LEWIS I could recognise the distinctive pleasure I obtained from being driven in a car. P. CUTTING Those few who had managed to obtain a .. work permit .. had lost their jobs. *absol.*: J. G. WHITTIER The simple heart, that freely asks in love, obtains. **b** S. RICHARDSON The Gentlemen .. obtained of Miss to play several Tunes on the Spinnet. **4a** P. SIDNEY The Poets have obtained to the .. top of their profession. SIR W. SCOTT The vivacity of fancy .. dies within us when we obtain the age of manhood. **b** H. MAUNDRELL It was not without much importunity that we obtain'd to have the use of .. the House. **6** P. ACKROYD The exasperated affection which obtained between them. ROSEMARY MANNING Secrecy was made necessary by the hostile climate of opinion that obtained throughout .. this century.

■ **obtainal** *noun* (*rare*) = OBTAINMENT E19. **obtainer** *noun* a person who obtains something, a winner; a getter: M16. **obtainment** *noun* the action of obtaining or getting something L16.

obtainable /əbˈteɪnəb(ə)l/ *adjective.* E17.
[from OBTAIN + -ABLE.]
Able to be obtained or got.

📖 A. STORR Writers came predominantly from the middle class in which privacy is more easily obtainable.

■ **obtainaˈbility** *noun* M20.

For other words beginning with *ob-* see the entry for **ob-**

obtect /əbˈtɛkt/ *adjective.* L19.
[formed as next.]
ENTOMOLOGY. Designating or characterized by a pupa in which the limbs are glued by a secretion to the body and usu. covered by a hard case.

obtected /əbˈtɛktɪd/ *adjective.* E19.
[from Latin *obtectus* pa. pple of *obtegere* cover over, from *ob-* OB- + *tegere* cover: see -ED[1].]
ENTOMOLOGY. **1** Covered by a neighbouring part, like the hemelytra of some bugs by the enlarged scutellum. E19.
2 = OBTECT. L19.

obtemper /əbˈtɛmpə/ *verb.* LME.
[Old & mod. French *obtempérer* from Latin *obtemperare* obey, from *ob-* OB- + *temperare* qualify, temper, restrain oneself: see TEMPER *verb*[1].]
†**1** *verb trans.* Temper, restrain. *rare.* LME–M16.
2 *verb trans.* & †*intrans.* (with *to*). Comply with, submit to, obey. Now only in SCOTS LAW, obey (a judgement or court order). L15.

obtemperate /əbˈtɛmpəreɪt/ *verb.* Now *rare.* LME.
[Latin *obtemperat-* pa. ppl stem of *obtemperare*: see prec., -ATE[3].]
1 *verb trans.* Comply with, submit to, obey. LME.
2 *verb intrans.* Be obedient *to*. M16.

†**obtend** *verb trans.* L16.
[Latin *obtendere* spread in front of, from *ob-* OB- + *tendere* stretch.]
1 Put forward as a statement, reason, etc.; pretend, allege. L16–E18.
2 Proffer (in opposition); oppose. L17–E18.

obtenebrate /əbˈtɛnɪbreɪt/ *verb trans.* L16.
[ecclesiastical Latin *obtenebrat-* pa. ppl stem of *obtenebrare*, from *ob-* OB- + *tenebrare* darken: see -ATE[3].]
Cast a shadow over; overshadow, darken.
■ **obteneˈbration** *noun* the action of overshadowing something; the condition of being overshadowed: E17.

obtention /əbˈtɛnʃ(ə)n/ *noun.* E17.
[French, or late Latin *obtentio(n-)*, from *obtent-* pa. ppl stem of *obtinere* OBTAIN: see -ION.]
The action of obtaining something; obtainment.

📖 *Sun (Baltimore)* The charges involved the alleged obtention by Siegel of $200 from Russell Long.

obtest /əbˈtɛst/ *verb.* M16.
[Latin *obtestari* call to witness, protest by, from *ob-* OB- + *testari* bear witness, call upon as witness.]
1 *verb trans.* Call on in the name of something sacred, adjure; implore, entreat, (a person *that*, *to do*). M16. ▶†**b** Beg earnestly for (a thing). *rare.* L16–L17.
2 *verb intrans.* Make earnest entreaty; call heaven to witness. (Foll. by *that*, *against*.) E17.
3 *verb trans.* Call (God, heaven, etc.) to witness; appeal to in confirmation of something. *rare.* E17.

📖 **1** SIR W. SCOTT Other Chiefs .. obtested their Chieftain to leave them .. to the leading of Ardenvohr. **2** R. BAXTER He .. obtested with them that they .. take in good part what was delivered with a good intention. POPE Eumaeus heav'd His hands obtesting.

■ **obteˈstation** *noun* the action or an act of obtesting; entreaty, supplication; a solemn appeal: M16.

†**obtrectation** *noun.* L15–E18.
[Latin *obtrectatio(n-)*, from *obtrectat-* pa. ppl stem of *obtrectare* disparage, detract from, from *ob-* OB- + *tractare* drag, haul: see -ATION.]
Detraction, disparagement, slander; an instance of this.

obtrude /əbˈtruːd/ *verb.* M16.
[Latin *obtrudere*, from *ob-* OB- + *trudere* thrust.]
1 *verb trans.* Thrust (a thing) forward forcibly or without invitation; press or impose (a matter, a person, one's presence, etc.) *on*. Formerly also foll. by *to*. M16. ▶**b** *verb intrans.* Be or become obtrusive; intrude. (Foll. by *on*.) L16.
2 *verb trans.* Eject, force out. L16.

📖 **1** T. FULLER A man of low birth .. obtruded on them .. by the king for their general. *refl.*: E. BOWEN His masculinity did not obtrude itself upon the conversation. **b** K. CLARK The world of his imagination is so clear .. that nothing obtrudes, nothing is commonplace. **2** *refl.*: *Examiner* He .. ripped him open, and the bowels obtruded themselves.

■ **obtruder** *noun* a person who imposes himself or herself on someone in an unwelcome manner M17.

obtruncate /əbˈtrʌŋkeɪt/ *verb trans. rare.* L16.
[Latin *obtruncat-* pa. ppl stem of *obtruncare* cut off, lop away, from *ob-* OB- + *truncare* cut off, maim: see -ATE[3].]
Cut off the head or top of. Now chiefly as ***obtruncated*** *ppl adjective.*

obtrusion /əbˈtruːʒ(ə)n/ *noun.* L16.
[Alt. of INTRUSION by substitution of OB-.]
1 The action or an act of forcing oneself or one's presence on a person; the action or an act of imposing one person or thing on another. Also, a thing so imposed, an unwelcome intrusion. L16.
2 The forcible pushing or thrusting of something into or against something else. M19.

1 *Cornhill Magazine* The obtrusion of these topics upon persons not conversant with . . technicalities.

obtrusive /əbˈtruːsɪv/ *adjective*. M17.
[from Latin *obtrus-* pa. ppl stem of *obtrudere* OBTRUDE + -IVE.]
Unduly or unpleasantly noticeable or prominent.

ROSEMARY MANNING My father regarded Dr. Montague's intervention as obtrusive if not impertinent. *Highways & Transportation* Blacktop roads harmonise with the country-side, and are less obtrusive.

■ **obtrusively** *adverb* L18. **obtrusiveness** *noun* E19.

obtund /əbˈtʌnd/ *verb trans*. LME.
[Latin *obtundere* from *ob-* OB- + *tundere* to beat.]
Chiefly MEDICINE. Dull the sensitivity of; deprive of sharpness or vigour.

S. JOHNSON No man can at pleasure obtund or invigorate his senses.

obtundent /əbˈtʌnd(ə)nt/ *adjective & noun*. M19.
[Latin *obtundent-* pres. ppl stem of *obtundere*, or from prec.: see -ENT.]
MEDICINE. (A substance) having the property of dulling sensitivity; (acting as) a demulcent or local anaesthetic.

obturate /əbˈtjʊəreɪt, ˈɒbtjʊr-/ *verb trans*. M17.
[Latin *obturat-* pa. ppl stem of *obturare* stop up, from *ob-* OB- + *turare* close up: see -ATE³.]
Block up, close, obstruct.

obturation /ɒbtjʊˈreɪʃ(ə)n/ *noun*. E17.
[Late Latin *obturatio(n-)*, formed as prec.: see -ATION.]
The action of stopping something up; the obstruction of an opening or channel; *spec.* the sealing of the breech of a gun.

obturator /ˈɒbtjʊreɪtə/ *noun*. E18.
[medieval Latin = obstructor, formed as prec.: see -OR.]
1 ANATOMY. More fully ***obturator muscle***. Either of two paired muscles which partly cover the obturator foramen and serve to move the thigh and hip. E18. ▸**b** *attrib.* Designating structures associated with these muscles or with the obturator foramen. M18.
2 An artificial device for blocking an opening; *spec.* (***a***) MEDICINE a plate which is fitted to cover a perforated or cleft palate and may also carry false teeth; (***b***) MEDICINE a wire or rod running inside a cannula or hollow needle; (***c***) GUNNERY a cap, pad, etc., for preventing the escape of gas through a joint or hole, esp. through the breech of a gun. L19.

Comb.: **obturator foramen** a large opening in the hip-bone between the pubis and the ischium. ***obturator muscle***: see sense 1 above.

obtuse /əbˈtjuːs/ *adjective*. LME.
[Latin *obtusus* pa. pple of *obtundere* OBTUND.]
1 Chiefly BOTANY & ZOOLOGY. Not sharp or pointed, blunt. LME.
2 Not acutely sensitive or perceptive; dull; stupid. E16. ▸**b** Of pain: indistinctly felt or perceived, dull. E17.
3 GEOMETRY. Of a plane angle: greater than 90 degrees and less than 180 degrees. L16.

2 U. BENTLEY How obtuse I had been not to suspect some trouble at home behind Grass's aggressive behaviour.

■ **obtusely** *adverb* E16. **obtuseness** *noun* the quality of being obtuse, bluntness; *esp.* dullness of feeling, insensitivity, stupidity: M17. **obtusity** *noun* obtuseness E19.

Ob-Ugrian /ɒbˈuːgrɪən/ *noun & adjective*. M20.
[from *Ob*, a Siberian river + UGRIAN.]
(Designating) a group of Finno-Ugric languages spoken in Siberia, comprising Khanty and Vogul.
■ Also **Ob-Ugric** *noun & adjective* M20.

†**obumbrate** *adjective*. LME.
[Latin *obumbratus* pa. pple, formed as next: see -ATE².]
1 Overshadowed, darkened. LME–M17.
2 ZOOLOGY. Concealed under an overhanging part. *rare*. Only in E19.

obumbrate /ɒˈbʌmbreɪt/ *verb trans*. Now *rare*. M16.
[Latin *obumbrat-* pa. ppl stem of *obumbrare*, from *ob-* OB- + *umbrare* to shade, from *umbra* shadow: see -ATE³.]
1 Overshadow, darken; obscure (*lit. & fig.*). M16.
2 Adumbrate, prefigure, foreshadow. M17.
■ **obumˈbration** *noun* (now *rare*) (***a***) the action or an act of overshadowing; the condition of being overshadowed; (***b***) adumbration: LME.

obus /ˈɒbʊs/ *noun*. L19.
[French from German *Haubitze* HOWITZ.]
A howitzer shell.

obvelation /ɒbvɪˈleɪʃ(ə)n/ *noun*. *rare*. M17.
[Latin *obvelatio(n-)*, from *obvelat-* pa. ppl stem of *obvelare* cover over, conceal, from *ob-* OB- + *velare* cover, veil: see -ATION.]
The action or an act of concealing something.

obvention /əbˈvɛnʃ(ə)n/ *noun*. LME.
[Old & mod. French, or late Latin *obventio(n-)* revenue, from *obvent-* pa. ppl stem of *obvenire* come in the way of, happen to, from *ob-* OB- + *venire* come: see -ION.]
ECCLESIASTICAL LAW. An incoming fee or revenue, *esp.* one of an occasional or incidental character.

†**obversant** *adjective*. L16–M18.
[Latin *obversant-* pres. ppl stem of *obversari* take position over against, formed as next: see -ANT¹.]
Opposite, contrary; placed in front of; well known.

obverse /ˈɒbvəːs/ *adjective & noun*. M17.
[Latin *obversus* pa. pple of *obvertere* turn towards, from *ob-* OB- + *vertere* turn.]
▸ **A** *adjective*. **1** Turned towards or facing the observer. M17.
2 Narrower at the base or point of attachment than at the apex or top. E19.
3 Corresponding to something else as its counterpart. L19.
4 LOGIC. Of a proposition: obtained from another proposition by the process of obversion. L19.

3 E. POSTE To every mode of obligation there is an obverse mode of liberation.

▸ **B** *noun*. **1** The side of a coin, medal, seal, etc., bearing the head or the main design; the design or inscription on this side. Opp. REVERSE *noun* 2. M17.
2a The facing side, front, or top of something; the side etc. intended to be seen. M19. ▸**b** *fig.* The counterpart of a fact or truth. M19.
3 LOGIC. A proposition obtained by obversion. L19.

1 M. WARNER A single coin . . with Demeter's . . head on the obverse. **2b** P. MONETTE The obverse of this optimism was the hair ball of fear at the pit of my stomach. **3** A. BAIN No men are gods. The obverse is . . all men are no-gods.

■ **obversely** *adverb* M18.

obversion /əbˈvəːʃ(ə)n/ *noun*. M19.
[Irreg. from OBVERSE + -ION, after *version*.]
1 The action of turning towards a person or thing. *rare* (only in Dicts.). M19.
2 LOGIC. A form of immediate inference in which the predicate of the contrary of a proposition is negated, so as to obtain another proposition logically equivalent to the original. Also called ***permutation***. L19.

obvert /əbˈvəːt/ *verb trans*. E17.
[Latin *obvertere*, from *ob-* OB- + *vertere* to turn.]
†**1** Turn (something) towards; place (something) facing. E17–L18.
2 LOGIC. Change (a proposition) by obversion. L19.
■ **obvertend** *noun* (LOGIC) a proposition to be obverted L19.

obviate /ˈɒbvɪeɪt/ *verb trans*. L16.
[Late Latin *obviat-* pa. ppl stem of *obviare* meet in the way, prevent, from *ob-* OB- + *via* way: see -ATE³. Cf. OBVIOUS.]
1 Encounter and dispose of; get round, do away with, (esp. a difficulty, need, etc.). L16.
†**2** Meet; withstand, oppose. E17–E18.

1 M. N. COX *Analogies* can . . convey meaning in such a vivid . . form that many pages of . . arid description are obviated. *Independent* The new emphasis does not obviate the need for financial assistance to developing countries.

■ **obviˈation** *noun* (***a***) the action of obviating something; prevention; (***b***) LINGUISTICS the use, in some N. American Indian languages, of the obviative: LME.

obviative /ˈɒbvɪətɪv, -eɪtɪv/ *noun & adjective*. L19.
[from prec. + -IVE, after French *obviatif*.]
LINGUISTICS. ▸**A** *noun*. A case in the Algonquian family of N. American Indian languages that marks a third person other than the principal one in a given context. L19.
▸ **B** *adjective*. Designating, in, or pertaining to this case. L19.

obvious /ˈɒbvɪəs/ *adjective & noun*. L16.
[from Latin *obvius*, from *obviam* in the way, from *ob-* against + *via* way: see -IOUS. Cf. OBVIATE.]
▸ **A** *adjective*. †**1** Frequently encountered; commonly occurring. L16–M18.
2 Situated in the way; positioned in front of or opposite to; facing. Now *rare* or *obsolete*. E17.
†**3** Exposed or open *to* (an action or influence). E17–M18.
4 Plain and evident to the mind, perfectly clear or manifest; such as common sense might suggest; (esp. ZOOLOGY) clearly visible. M17.

1 J. WOODWARD The next Quarry, or Chalk-pit . . these are so ready and obvious in almost all places. **2** H. L'ESTRANGE Paris being obvious to him, and in his way to Spain, he delaid there one day. **3** H. BROOKE She was artless, and obvious to seduction. **4** CONAN DOYLE I should have thought . . that your obvious way was to advertise in the agony columns. A. LURIE It is obvious as they turn on to campus that something unusual is happening.

▸ **B** *absol.* as *noun*. ***the obvious***, the obvious thing; what is obvious. E20.

P. LOMAS It often takes a genius to bring the obvious to our attention.

■ **obviously** *adverb* M17. **obviousness** *noun* M17.

obvolute /ˈɒbvəluːt/ *adjective*. M18.
[Latin *obvolutus* pa. pple of *obvolvere*: see OBVOLVE.]
BOTANY. (Of a leaf etc.) having a margin that alternately overlaps and is overlapped by that of an opposing leaf; characterized by such an arrangement.

For other words beginning with *ob-* see the entry for **ob-**

obvolution /ɒbvəˈluːʃ(ə)n/ *noun*. *rare*. L16.
[Latin *obvolutio(n-)*, from *obvolut-* pa. ppl stem of *obvolvere*: see next.]
Formerly, a fold, twist, or turn of something coiled. Now, the wrapping or folding of a bandage round a limb.

obvolve /əbˈvɒlv/ *verb trans*. Now *rare* or *obsolete*. E17.
[Latin *obvolvere* wrap round, from *ob-* OB- + *volvere* to roll.]
Wrap round; *fig.* disguise.

OC *abbreviation*.
1 MILITARY. Officer commanding.
2 Officer of the Order of Canada.

oc- *prefix* see OB-.

oca /ˈəʊkə/ *noun*. Also **oka**. E17.
[Amer. Spanish from Quechua *ócca*.]
A S. American oxalis, *Oxalis tuberosa*, cultivated for its edible tubers.

ocarina /ɒkəˈriːnə/ *noun*. L19.
[Italian, from *oca* goose (with ref. to its shape): see -INA¹.]
A simple wind instrument in the form of a hollow egg-shaped body with finger-holes and a hole to blow at.

Occam /ˈɒkəm/ *noun*. In sense 1 also **Ockham**. M19.
[William of *Occam* (d. c 1350), English scholastic philosopher.]
1 ***Occam's razor***, the principle that in explaining a thing no more assumptions should be made than are necessary. Also called ***law of parsimony***. M19.
2 COMPUTING. A programming language devised for use in parallel processing. L20.
■ **Occamism** *noun* the theological or philosophical doctrine of William of Occam, characterized by rejection of realism and a revival of nominalism M19. **Occamist** *noun* a follower or adherent of William of Occam L16.

occamy /ˈɒkəmi/ *noun*. Now *rare* or *obsolete*. L16.
[Alt. of ALCHEMY.]
A metallic composition imitating silver.

occasion /əˈkeɪʒ(ə)n/ *noun*. LME.
[Old & mod. French, or Latin *occasio(n-)* juncture, opportunity, motive, cause, from *occas-* pa. ppl stem of *occidere* go down, set, from *ob-* OB- + *cadere* fall: see -ION.]
▸ **I 1** A set of circumstances allowing something to be done or favourable to a purpose; an opportunity, a chance. Formerly *spec.*, an opportunity for finding fault or of giving or taking offence. LME.
2 An occurrence, fact, or consideration giving grounds for an action or state; a (good) reason, a motive. (Foll. by *for*, *of*, *to do*.) LME. ▸†**b** A pretext, an excuse. LME–M17.
3 A thing or person that causes something; now *esp.* a subordinate or incidental cause. (Foll. by *of*.) LME. ▸†**b** The action of causing or occasioning something; a thing caused or occasioned. M16–E17.
†**4** A matter considered or discussed. LME–M17.

1 T. S. ELIOT First of all I must take the occasion To wish Miss Angel every happiness. **2** A. EDEN A few years ago . . I had occasion to pass along the Great North Road. T. C. BOYLE Only human activity was occasion for a wager.
3 B. T. WASHINGTON The occasion of the trouble was that a dark-skinned man had stopped at the local hotel.

▸ **II** †**5** An occurrence, an event, an incident. LME–M17. ▸**b** The course of events or circumstances; chance. *rare* (Shakes.). Only in L16.
6 (The time of occurrence of) a particular event or happening. Formerly also, a case, an instance. M16.
7 A religious function or ceremony; *spec.* (*Scot.*), a Eucharist. *arch.* M18.
8 A special ceremony or celebration; a significant or noteworthy happening. M19.

6 *Athenaeum* An article of his appearing on the occasion of the death of Gogol. P. G. WODEHOUSE He could not recall a single occasion on which they had fallen out. R. INGALLS He saw her in town on three different occasions.
8 T. CALLENDER It was a big occasion, held at the Hilton.

▸ **III 9** A set of circumstances requiring action; necessity, need. M16. ▸**b** A particular need, want, or requirement. Usu. in *pl.* *arch.* L16.
10 Necessary business; a matter, a piece of business. Usu. in *pl.*, affairs, business. *arch.* L16.

9 W. S. MAUGHAM When the occasion for firmness no longer existed she gave way. **10** R. MACAULAY Guests arrived to find their hostess gone out on her own occasions.

Phrases: †**do one's occasions** defecate; urinate. **for one's occasion** on one's account, for one's sake. **give occasion to** give rise to, cause. **on occasion** as need or opportunity arises; now and then, occasionally. **on occasion of** in connection with, on account of, with reference to. **on one's occasion** = ***for one's occasion*** above. ***rise to the occasion***: see RISE *verb* 13b. **take occasion** make use of an opportunity (*to do*). ***take occasion by the forelock***: see FORELOCK *noun*¹. **upon occasion** = ***on occasion*** above.

occasion /əˈkeɪʒ(ə)n/ *verb trans*. LME.
[from the noun. Cf. French *occasionner*.]
†**1** Induce, urge; impel by circumstances; accustom. (Foll. by *to*, *to do*.) LME–L17.

2 Be the occasion or cause of; give rise to, bring about, esp. incidentally. Also with pers. indirect obj., cause to experience or have. LME. ▸**b** Cause (a person or thing) *to do*. E17.

📖 **2** H. J. LASKI A book which, even in those days, occasioned some controversy. F. TUOHY This curiosity from a bystander occasioned them some surprise.

▪ **occasioner** *noun* (now *rare*) LME.

occasional /əˈkeɪʒ(ə)n(ə)l/ *adjective & noun*. LME.
[medieval Latin *occasionalis*, from Latin *occasion-*: see OCCASION *noun*, -AL¹.]
▸ **A** *adjective*. **1** Happening on, made for, or associated with a particular occasion. LME.
†**2** Happening casually or incidentally, incidental. M16–M17.
3 Occurring or met with now and then; irregular and infrequent; sporadic. M17.
4 Constituting or serving as the occasion or incidental cause of something. M17.
5 Of furniture etc.: made or adapted for use on a particular occasion or for irregular use. Of a person: acting or employed for a particular occasion or on an irregular basis. M18.

📖 **1** N. FRYE *Lycidas* is an occasional poem, called forth by a specific event. **occasional conformist** *Hist.* a practitioner of occasional conformity. **occasional conformity** *Hist.* the receiving of Holy Communion in the Church of England by a practising Nonconformist in order to qualify for an official position. **3** E. WAUGH The streets were empty save for an occasional muffled figure. D. WALCOTT She took an occasional whisky. A. BRINK She . . only came home for the occasional weekend. **4 occasional cause** *PHILOSOPHY* a secondary cause, an occasion. **5 occasional table** a small side-table for irregular and varied use.

▸ **B** *noun*. †**1** An occasional speech or writing. Usu. in *pl.* M–L17.
2 An occasional worker, visitor, etc. M19.
▪ **occasionalism** *noun* (*PHILOSOPHY*) the Cartesian doctrine ascribing the connection between mental and bodily events to the continuing intervention of God, either being produced by him on the occasion of the other M19. **occasionalist** *noun* †(*a*) an occasional conformist; (*b*) *PHILOSOPHY* an adherent or student of occasionalism: E18. **occasionaˈlistic** *adjective* of or pertaining to occasionalists or occasionalism L19. **occasioˈnality** *noun* the quality or fact of being occasional, esp. of being specially prepared for an occasion M18.

occasionally /əˈkeɪʒ(ə)n(ə)li/ *adverb*. LME.
[from prec. + -LY².]
1 On or for a particular occasion or occasions; when occasion arises. *obsolete* exc. *dial.* LME. ▸†**b** Incidentally. M–L17.
2 Now and then, at times, sometimes; irregularly and infrequently. LME.
†**3** By chance, casually, accidentally. E17–E18.

📖 **2** T. HARDY Next day Mr. Torkingham, who occasionally dropped in to see St. Cleeve, called again. E. F. BENSON Sometimes Maud rode with her, sometimes Charlie, occasionally both.

Occident /ˈɒksɪd(ə)nt/ *noun & adjective*. Chiefly *poet. & rhet.* Also (esp. in sense 1) **o-**. LME.
[Old & mod. French from Latin *occident-*, *occidens* setting, sunset, west, use as noun of pres. pple of *occidere* go down, set: see OCCASION *noun*, -ENT.]
▸ **A** *noun*. **1** *The* region of the sky in which the sun sets; *the* west. Now *rare*. LME.
2 *The* part of the world to the west of some recognized part, i.e. western Europe, Europe and America, or the western hemisphere; *the* civilization or culture of the West. LME.
▸†**B** *adjective*. Situated in the west, western. E–M16.
¶ Opp. ***orient***.

occidental /ɒksɪˈdɛnt(ə)l/ *adjective & noun*. Also (esp. as noun) **O-**. LME.
[Old & mod. French, or Latin *occidentalis*, formed as prec.: see -AL¹.]
▸ **A** *adjective*. **1** Of, in, or directed towards the west; western, westerly; *spec.* in *ASTROLOGY* (of a planet), seen after sunset or in the western part of the sky. LME.
2 Of, situated in, or characteristic of western countries or regions; of the West, Western. Also, of, in, or characteristic of the western US. M16.
3 Of a precious stone: inferior in value and brilliance. M18.
2 ***occidental topaz***: see TOPAZ *noun* 1. ***occidental turquoise***: see TURQUOISE *noun* 2.
▸ **B** *noun*. **1 a** A native or inhabitant of the West. M16. ▸†**b** A western country or region. L16–L19.
2 An artificial language based chiefly on the Romance languages. E20.
¶ Opp. ***oriental***.
▪ **occidentalism** *noun* occidental quality, style, or character; Western customs, institutions, characteristics, etc.: M19. **occidentalist** *noun* (*a*) a person who favours or advocates Western customs, ideas, etc.; (*b*) a student of Western languages and institutions; (*c*) an advocate or user of the language Occidental: L19. **occidenˈtality** *noun* the quality or state of being occidental or Western M17. **occidentaliˈzation** *noun* the process of occidentalizing a people, culture, etc. L19. **occidentalize** *verb trans.* make occidental; imbue with Western ideas or characteristics: L19. **occidentally** *adverb* in the West; in a Western manner: M19.

occipital /ɒkˈsɪpɪt(ə)l/ *adjective & noun*. M16.
[French, from medieval Latin *occipitalis*, formed as OCCIPUT: see -AL¹.]
▸ **A** *adjective*. Chiefly *ANATOMY & ZOOLOGY*. Belonging to, or situated in or on, the occiput. M16.
occipital bone the bone which forms the back and base of the skull and encircles the spinal cord. **occipital condyle** either of two rounded knobs at the base of the skull which articulate the first vertebra. **occipital lobe** the rearmost lobe in each cerebral hemisphere of the brain.
▸ **B** *noun*. The occipital bone. M18.

occipito- /ɒkˌsɪpɪtəʊ/ *combining form*.
[from OCCIPITAL: see -O-.]
ANATOMY & MEDICINE. Of, pertaining to, or involving the occiput.
▪ **occipito-anˈterior** *adjective* designating a position of the foetus in which the occiput is directed away from the mother's sacrum M19. **occipitoˈfrontal** *adjective* pertaining to, or extending between, the back of the head and the forehead E19. **occipitopoˈsterior** *adjective* designating a position of the foetus in which the occiput is directed towards the mother's sacrum M19. **occipitoˈtemporal** *adjective* pertaining to the occipital and temporal bones L19.

occiput /ˈɒksɪpʌt/ *noun*. LME.
[Latin, from *ob-* OB- + *caput* head.]
Chiefly *ANATOMY*. **1** The back of the head. LME.
2 The occipital bone. L16.

Occitan /ˈɒksɪt(ə)n, *foreign* ɔksitɑ̃/ *noun & adjective*. M20.
[French.]
(Of or pertaining to) the Provençal language or the French dialect of Provence.
▪ Also **Occitanian** /ɒksɪˈteɪnɪən/ *noun & adjective* M20.

occlude /əˈkluːd/ *verb*. L16.
[Latin *occludere*, from *ob-* OB- + *claudere* to close.]
1 *verb trans.* Block or stop up (an opening, esp. an orifice or pore); obstruct (a passage). L16.
2 *verb trans.* Shut in, enclose; cover, hide; *spec.* cover (an eye) to prevent its use. E17.
3 *verb trans. CHEMISTRY*. ▸**a** Of a metal or other solid: absorb and retain (a gas). M19. ▸**b** Remove (a substance) from solution by occlusion in the crystals of a precipitate. E20.
4 *verb intrans.* Of a tooth: come into contact with a tooth or teeth of the other jaw. (Foll. by *with*.) L19.
5 *verb intrans. METEOROLOGY*. Of a front or frontal system: undergo occlusion. M20.

📖 **1** J. G. FARRELL The new and astonishing growth of bamboo . . threatened to occlude the entrance entirely. **2** *fig.*: I. COLEGATE When she faltered, when her brightness was occluded by doubt. **5 occluded front** a front at which occlusion has occurred.

▪ **occludent** *noun & adjective* (*rare*) (a thing) that occludes M18. **occluder** *noun* (*OPHTHALMOLOGY*) a device for occluding an eye M20.

occlusal /əˈkluːs(ə)l/ *adjective*. L19.
[from OCCLUSION + -AL¹.]
DENTISTRY. Of, pertaining to, or involved in the occlusion of teeth; *spec.* designating a surface of a tooth that comes into contact with a tooth in the other jaw.
▪ **occlusally** *adverb* from or on an occlusal surface E20.

occluse /əˈkluːs/ *adjective*. *rare*. E17.
[formed as next.]
Occluded; stopped up, closed; shut up, enclosed.

occlusion /əˈkluːʒ(ə)n/ *noun*. M17.
[from Latin *occlus-* pa. ppl stem of *occludere*: see OCCLUDE, -ION.]
1 Chiefly *SCIENCE*. The action of occluding something; the fact of being occluded; *MEDICINE* the partial or total closure of a blood-vessel due to an obstacle or to the swelling of an adjacent organ. M17. ▸**b** *fig.* The blocking out of an idea or thought from one's mind; the exclusion of a subject from a discourse; a mental block. M20.
2 *DENTISTRY*. The position assumed by the two sets of teeth relative to each other when the mouth is closed; the state of having the jaws closed and the teeth in contact. L19.
3 *PHONETICS*. The momentary closure of the breath passage during the articulation of an orally released consonant, or of the mouth passage during the articulation of a nasal consonant. E20.
4 *METEOROLOGY*. The overtaking of the warm front of a depression by the cold front, so that the warm air between them is forced upwards off the earth's surface by two wedges of cold air; the occluded front so formed. E20.

occlusive /əˈkluːsɪv/ *adjective & noun*. L19.
[formed as prec. + -IVE.]
▸ **A** *adjective*. Having the property or function of occluding something; characterized by occlusion. L19.
▸ **B** *noun*. *PHONETICS*. A consonantal sound produced with stoppage of breath; a stop with suppression of the explosive sound. E20.

occluso- /əˈkluːsəʊ/ *combining form* of OCCLUSAL, OCCLUSION: see -O-. Forming chiefly adjectives in *DENTISTRY*, as ***occlusogingival***.

occlusor /əˈkluːsə/ *noun*. L19.
[from OCCLUSION + -OR.]
ZOOLOGY. A structure which serves to close an opening or passage. Usu. *attrib.*
occlusor apparatus, ***occlusor muscle***, etc.

occult /ɒˈkʌlt, ˈɒkʌlt/ *adjective & noun*. L15.
[Latin *occultus* pa. pple of *occulere*, prob. from *ob-* OB- + *celare* conceal.]
▸ **A** *adjective*. **1** Hidden from sight, concealed (now *rare* or *obsolete*); not disclosed; secret, clandestine. L15. ▸†**b** Of a line etc.: drawn as an aid in constructing a figure but intended to be erased or covered. M17–E19. ▸**c** *MEDICINE*. Difficult to detect; (of a disease or process) unaccompanied by readily discernible signs or symptoms. Formerly also, inexplicable. E19.
2 Beyond ordinary understanding or knowledge; abstruse, recondite, mysterious. M16. ▸**b** *HISTORY OF SCIENCE*. (Of a property of matter) not manifest, discoverable only by experiment, latent; dealing with such qualities, experimental. M17.
3 Of or pertaining to practical arts held to involve agencies of a secret or mysterious nature; of the nature of such an art; dealing with or knowledgeable in such matters; magical, mystical. M17.

📖 **1** I. D'ISRAELI Printing remained . . a secret and occult art. **c occult blood**: abnormally present (esp. in faeces) but detectable only chemically or microscopically. ***occult spavin***: see SPAVIN *noun*¹. **3** R. W. EMERSON He is versed in occult science, In magic, and in clairvoyance. *Punch* One could fill a library with . . ghost stories, studies of occult phenomena. T. LEARY The ancient wisdom of gnostics, hermetics . . yogis, occult healers.

▸ **B** *noun*. †**1** A hidden or secret thing. *rare*. Only in M17.
2 ***the occult***, occult phenomena, influences, etc., generally; the art or science that deals with such things. L19.
▪ **occultism** *noun* the doctrine, principles, or practice of occult science L19. **occultist** *noun* an expert in or adherent of occultism L19. **occultly** *adverb* M17. **occultness** *noun* E18.

occult /ɒˈkʌlt/ *verb*. L15.
[Latin *occultare* frequentative of *occulere*: see prec.]
1 *verb trans.* Cut off from view by interposing something; hide, conceal. L15. ▸**b** *spec.* in *ASTRONOMY*. Of a celestial body: conceal from view by passing or being in front of (an apparently smaller body). M18.
2 *verb intrans.* Of a lighthouse light: be cut off from view as part of its cycle of light and dark. L19.
▪ **occulter** *noun* an apparatus for occulting a light E20.

occultation /ɒk(ə)lˈteɪʃ(ə)n/ *noun*. LME.
[French, or Latin *occultatio(n-)*, from *occultare*: see prec., -ATION.]
1 Orig., hiding, concealment. Now (*SCIENCE*), the fact of being cut off from view, esp. by something interposed; *ASTRONOMY* the concealment of a celestial body by an apparently larger body passing between it and the observer. LME.
2 *fig.* Disappearance from view or notice. E19.

occupancy /ˈɒkjʊp(ə)nsi/ *noun*. L16.
[from next.: see -ANCY.]
1 The act, condition, or fact of occupying something or of being occupied; actual possession or residence, esp. of a dwelling or land; *spec.* in *LAW*, the action of taking possession of something having no owner, as constituting a title to it. (Foll. by *of*.) L16.
2 a The state of being occupied or busy. E19. ▸**b** The proportion of accommodation occupied or used; the extent to which accommodation is occupied. E19. ▸**c** *TELEPHONY*. The proportion of the time during which a circuit or device is handling calls. M20.

📖 **1** D. WORDSWORTH The first signs of occupancy and labour we had noticed . . were felled trees. C. C. HARRISON Country cottage fitted up for summer occupancy. ***open occupancy***: see OPEN *adjective*. **2b** *Debonair (India)* Hoteliers . . grumble about low occupancy rates.

▪ **occupance** *noun* = OCCUPANCY 1; *GEOGRAPHY* the inhabiting and modification of an area by humans: E19.

occupant /ˈɒkjʊp(ə)nt/ *noun*. L16.
[French, or Latin *occupant-* pres. ppl stem of *occupare*: see OCCUPY, -ANT¹.]
1 *LAW*. A person who establishes a title to something without an owner by taking possession of it. L16.
2 *gen.* A person who occupies, resides in, or is in a place; a person occupying or holding in actual possession property or a position; an occupier. L16.

📖 **2** J. BUCHAN I recognised him as the occupant of the flat on the top floor. P. FARMER In the train the lights were dim. The occupants of the carriage still sat up.

†**occupate** *adjective*. E17–M19.
[Latin *occupat-*: see OCCUPATION, -ATE².]
Occupied; taken into and held in possession.

occupatio /ɒkjʊˈpeɪʃɪəʊ, -ˈpɑːtɪəʊ/ *noun.* L16.
[Latin: see next.]
RHETORIC. = PRETERITION 1.

occupation /ɒkjʊˈpeɪʃ(ə)n/ *noun.* ME.
[Anglo-Norman *ocupacioun* (in sense 4) = Old & mod. French *occupation* from Latin *occupatio(n-)*, from *occupat-* pa. ppl stem of *occupare*: see OCCUPY, -ATION.]
1 a The state of having one's time or attention occupied; employment. ME. **▸b** What a person is (habitually) engaged in, esp. to earn a living; a job, a business, a profession; a pursuit, an activity. ME. **▸†c** *spec.* Mechanical or mercantile employment; (a) trade. M16–E17.
2 The action or condition of residing in or holding a place or position; the state of being so occupied; tenure, occupancy. ME. **▸b** A piece of land occupied by a tenant; a holding. *dial.* L18.
†3 Use, employment, (*of* a thing). LME–E18.
4 The action of taking or maintaining possession of a country, building, etc., by force; the state of being so occupied; the duration or an instance of this. M16.

📖 **1a** E. A. FREEMAN Harold and Swend . . by their invasion . . gave him full occupation throughout the year. **b** A. G. GARDINER I find that there is no occupation that stimulates thought more than digging. C. MCCULLOUGH By profession he was a shearer of sheep, a seasonal occupation. J. CALDER Thomas . . took his occupation and his religion very seriously. **2** J. DISKI There are small signs of occupation: the breakfast things are . . stacked in the sink. **4** T. PYNCHON Civilian prisoners brought in from countries under German occupation. B. CHATWIN The occupation of Czechoslovakia had been completed in a day. **army of occupation** an army left to occupy a newly conquered region until the conclusion of hostilities or establishment of a settled government.

Attrib. & comb.: In the senses 'pertaining to military occupation', as ***occupation army***, ***occupation forces***, etc.; 'pertaining to the occupation of an archaeological site', as ***occupation layer***, ***occupation site***, etc. Special combs., as **occupation bridge** a bridge for the use of the occupiers of land, as one connecting parts of a farm etc. separated by a canal or railway; **occupation centre** an establishment where occupational therapy is practised or where mentally handicapped people are trained or employed; **occupation disease** = *OCCUPATIONAL disease*; **occupation neurosis** MEDICINE a painful and disabling spasm affecting muscles subject to heavier use than normal because of the person's occupation; **occupation number** PHYSICS the number of particles in a system that are in any given state; **occupation road** a private road for the use of the occupiers of land.
■ **occupationist** *noun* an advocate of military occupation L19. **occupationless** *adjective* E19.

occupational /ɒkjʊˈpeɪʃ(ə)n(ə)l/ *adjective.* M19.
[from prec. + -AL¹.]
Of, pertaining to, derived from, or characteristic of an occupation or occupations.

📖 J. HELLER Nervous breakdowns do occur regularly in all age and occupational groups. **occupational disease** (a) disease to which a particular occupation makes a person especially liable; *joc.* a trait or failing supposedly common in a particular group of people. **occupational hazard** a risk accepted as a consequence of a particular occupation; *joc.* a frequent consequence or accompaniment of a particular activity. **occupational psychology** the study of human behaviour at work, including methods of selecting personnel, improving productivity, and coping with stress. **occupational psychologist** a person who studies occupational psychology. **occupational risk** = ***occupational hazard*** above. **occupational therapy** mental or physical activity prescribed to assist recovery from disease, injury, or impairment. **occupational therapist** a person skilled in supervising occupational therapy.

■ **occupationally** *adverb* M20.

occupative /ˈɒkjʊpətɪv/ *adjective. rare.* M17.
[from Latin *occupat-*: see OCCUPATION, -IVE.]
Characterized by occupying or being occupied; LAW held by a tenure based on occupation.

occupiable /ˈɒkjʊpʌɪəb(ə)l/ *adjective. rare.* M19.
[from OCCUPY + -ABLE.]
Able or fit to be occupied.

occupier /ˈɒkjʊpʌɪə/ *noun.* LME.
[Anglo-Norman *occupiour*, or from next + -ER¹.]
1 A person holding possession *of* property, esp. a dwelling or land, or a position or office; *spec.* a person living in a dwelling as its owner or tenant; a holder, an occupant. LME.
†2 A person practising or employed in a specified occupation; a person dealing in something, a trader, a merchant. (Foll. by *of*.) LME–E17.

📖 **1** R. RENDELL The letter had been sent to 'the occupier' and perhaps had not been meant for her.

occupy /ˈɒkjʊpʌɪ/ *verb.* ME.
[Anglo-Norman var. of Old & mod. French *occuper* from Latin *occupare*, from *ob-* OB- + *capere* take, seize.]
1 *verb trans.* Orig., take possession of, seize. Now *spec.* take possession of (a country, town, strategic position, etc.) by military conquest or by settlement. ME. **▸b** Enter and remain in (a building etc.) forcibly or without authority, esp. as a form of protest. M20.
2 *verb trans.* Take up, use, fill, (space or time); be situated in or at (a place or position). ME.
3 *verb trans.* Keep busy, engage, employ, (a person, or the mind, attention, etc.). (Foll. by *by*, *in*, *with*.) Freq. in *pass.* or *refl.* ME.
4 *verb trans.* Hold (a position or office); live in, tenant, (a place). LME.
†5 *verb trans.* Make use of, use; *spec.* invest, trade with, (money). LME–L18.
†6 a *verb trans.* Follow or ply as one's business or occupation. LME–E19. **▸b** *verb intrans.* Do business, work; trade, deal. LME–M19.
†7 *verb trans. & intrans.* Have sexual intercourse or relations (with); cohabit (with). E16–L17.

📖 **1** R. MACAULAY I asked Xenophon what he thought about the Turks going into Greece and occupying Athens. G. SWIFT He used to be dropped into occupied France and . . keep watch on German installations. **b** *Globe & Mail (Toronto)* Mount Pleasant residents occupied Mayor Michael Harcourt's office overnight to press for action. **2** R. G. COLLINGWOOD Lessons occupied only two or three hours each morning. I. MURDOCH Hugo's flat occupied a corner position. G. VIDAL Paul's offices occupied an entire floor of a small skyscraper. M. SPARK Two or three other tables on the terrace were occupied. **3** H. T. LANE The citizens are occupied chiefly with earning a living. A. BRINK There must be many bigger and more serious problems to occupy you? **4** *Westminster Gazette* The managing-director still . . occupies the position he has held from the start. D. H. LAWRENCE The Bishop no longer occupied the great episcopal palace. M. SPARK The other room on the attic floor . . was occupied by a medical student.

¶ Rare in 17 and much of 18, perh. because of connotations of sense 7.

occur /əˈkəː/ *verb.* Infl. **-rr-**. L15.
[Latin *occurrere* run to meet, present itself, befall, from *ob-* OB- + *currere* run.]
1 *verb intrans.* **a** Of an event or process: happen, take place, come about, esp. without being arranged or expected. L15. **▸b** Be met with or found, appear, exist, (*in* some place, conditions, context, etc.). M16.
†2 *verb intrans. & trans.* Meet, encounter; resist, oppose; reply, argue. (Foll. by *against*, *to*, *upon*, *with*.) E16–M18.
3 *verb intrans.* Foll. by *to*: come into the mind of, be realized or considered by, (*that*, *to do*). Freq. *impers.* in ***it occurs***, ***it occurred***, etc. E17.

📖 **1a** T. HARDY That she consented to the novel proposition . . was apparent by what occurred a little later. D. JUDD The death of a child is one of the most disturbing . . events that can occur. P. FUSSELL The bombing attack was to occur on July 25. **b** W. BERRY This sometimes occurs as a bearing in coat-armour. *Melody Maker* Fox-trots . . occur in feature pictures to accompany dancing. **3** R. L. STEVENSON It occurred to us at last to go forth together and seek help. J. STEINBECK Two things only occur to Cornelia, love and fighting. J. MARK It had never occurred to him that she would leave the baby behind.

occurrence /əˈkʌr(ə)ns/ *noun.* M16.
[Orig. prob. from *occurrents* pl. of OCCURRENT *noun*: later from next + -ENCE. Cf. French *occurrence*, medieval Latin *occurrentia*.]
1 A thing that occurs, happens, or is met with; an event, an incident. Formerly also, that which occurs. Cf. OCCURRENT *noun.* M16.
2 The action or an instance of occurring, being met with, or happening. Also, the rate or measure of occurring; incidence. E18.

📖 **1** A. MERRITT Observing a series of ordinary occurrences through the glamour of an active imagination. J. E. T. ROGERS Evidence of the occurrence of that fish on the Kentish coast. M. GOWING Occurrences of ore were known to be much more widespread than those of uranium minerals. **2** *Parent* The high occurrence of so-called 'baby blues' . . shows us that the birth of a child is a very stressful event. **of frequent occurrence** occurring frequently, common.

Comb.: **occurrence book**, **occurrences book** a record of events kept at a police station, drawn from the diaries of police officers.
■ Also **occurrency** *noun* (*rare*) M17.

occurrent /əˈkʌr(ə)nt/ *adjective & noun.* Now *rare.* L15.
[French, or Latin *occurrent-* pres. ppl stem of *occurrere*: see OCCUR, -ENT.]
▸A *adjective.* That occurs, occurring, esp. incidentally; current. L15.
▸B *noun.* = OCCURRENCE 1. Long *arch.* M16.

occursion /əˈkəːʃ(ə)n/ *noun.* Long *rare.* M16.
[Latin *occursio(n-)*, from *occurs-* pa. ppl stem of *occurrere*: see OCCUR, -ION.]
An attack; an encounter; a collision.

OCD *abbreviation.*
Obsessive-compulsive disorder.

ocean /ˈəʊʃ(ə)n/ *noun.* ME.
[Old French *occean(e)* (mod. *océan*) from Latin *oceanus* from Greek *ōkeanos* (*potamos*) the great river encompassing the earth, the great sea, the Atlantic.]
1 The continuous body of salt water covering the greater part of the earth's surface and surrounding its land masses; *the* sea (orig. *spec.* regarded as encompassing the earth's single land mass, as opp. to the Mediterranean and other inland seas). Formerly also, ***ocean sea***, ***ocean stream***. Now chiefly *US* in *gen.* use. ME.
2 Each of the main areas or regions into which this body of water is divided geographically; any large expanse of sea. LME.
3 *transf. & fig.* An immense quantity or expanse (*of*), in *pl.*, lots *of*. L16.

📖 **1** E. YOUNG See how earth smiles, and hear old ocean roar. R. MACDONALD I turned on to Maritime Drive, which took us along the ocean. A. TYLER On the beach—where the ocean curled and flattened. ***a drop in the ocean***: see DROP *noun* 3. **2** ***Antarctic Ocean***, ***Arctic Ocean***, ***Atlantic Ocean***, ***Indian Ocean***, ***Pacific Ocean***. ***German ocean***: see GERMAN *adjective*¹. ***TETHYS Ocean***. **3** LD MACAULAY Ale flowed in oceans for the populace. M. LASKI Children . . had oceans of pocket money. R. WHELAN Two days of heavy rains . . transformed the terrain into an ocean of mud.

Comb.: **ocean-basin** a depression of the earth's surface in which an ocean lies; **ocean-going** *adjective* (of a ship) capable of crossing oceans; **ocean pipefish** a long slender pipefish, *Entelurus aequoreus*, of the Atlantic Ocean; also called ***snake pipefish***; ***ocean pout***: see POUT *noun*¹; ***ocean sea***: see sense 1 above; **ocean spray** *N. Amer.* an ornamental shrub of western N. America, *Holodiscus discolor*, of the rose family, allied to the spiraeas and bearing arching panicles of small white flowers; ***ocean stream***: see sense 1 above; ***ocean tramp***: see TRAMP *noun* 6a; **ocean wave** *rhyming slang* a shave; ***ocean whitetip (shark)***: see ***whitetip*** s.v. WHITE *adjective*.
■ **oceanful** *noun* as much as an ocean contains; *hyperbol.* a large quantity: L19. **oceˈanity** *noun* = OCEANICITY E20. **oceanwise** *adverb* (*rare*) by way of an ocean L19.

oceanarium /əʊʃəˈnɛːrɪəm/ *noun.* Orig. *US.* Pl. **-ia** /-ɪə/, **-iums**. M20.
[from prec. + -ARIUM. Cf. *dolphinarium*.]
(An establishment having) a seawater aquarium in which large sea-creatures are kept and observed, esp. for public entertainment.

Oceanian /əʊʃɪˈɑːnɪən, -eɪnɪən, əʊsɪ-/ *adjective & noun.* M19.
[from *Oceania* (see below) from French *Océanie* from Latin *oceanus* (see OCEAN) + -IAN.]
▸A *adjective.* Of or pertaining to Oceania, comprising the islands and island-groups of the Pacific Ocean and its adjacent seas, including Melanesia, Micronesia, and Polynesia, and sometimes also Australasia and the Malay archipelago. M19.
▸B *noun.* A native or inhabitant of Oceania; *spec.* a Polynesian. M19.

oceanic /əʊʃɪˈanɪk, əʊsɪ-/ *adjective.* M17.
[from OCEAN + -IC.]
▸I 1 Of or pertaining to the ocean or sea. M17. **▸b** BIOLOGY & GEOLOGY. Of or pertaining to the open sea beyond the edge of a continental shelf. M19.
2 Resembling an ocean; immense, vast. M19.
3 Of a climate: influenced by proximity to an ocean or sea and thus having a relatively small diurnal and annual range of temperature and relatively great precipitation. L19.
▸II 4 (**O-**.) = OCEANIAN *adjective.* M19.
Special collocations: **oceanic crust** GEOLOGY the relatively thin type of crust, lacking a sialic layer, which underlies the ocean-basins. **oceanic feeling**, **oceanic longing** a longing for something vast and eternal, interpreted by Freud as nostalgia of the psyche for the completeness of infancy. **oceanic province**, **oceanic zone** BIOLOGY & GEOLOGY the region of the sea deeper than the littoral and neritic zones, beyond the continental shelf.
■ **oceanicity** /-ˈnɪsɪti/ *noun* the extent to which a particular climate is oceanic; the state of being or having an oceanic climate: M20.

Oceanid /əʊˈsiːənɪd, ˈəʊʃ(ə)nɪd/ *noun.* Pl. **Oceanids**, **Oceanides** /əʊsɪˈanɪdiːz/. M19.
[French *Océanide* from Greek *ōkeanid-*, from *ōkeanos*: see OCEAN, -ID³.]
GREEK MYTHOLOGY. A sea-nymph, any of the daughters of the sea-god Oceanus, personification of the ocean, and his sister and wife Tethys.

oceanisation *noun* var. of OCEANIZATION.

oceanite /ˈəʊʃ(ə)nʌɪt/ *noun.* E20.
[from OCEAN(IC + -ITE¹.]
GEOLOGY. Any of various basalts which are very rich in olivine.

oceanization /əʊʃ(ə)nʌɪˈzeɪʃ(ə)n/ *noun.* Also **-isation**. M20.
[from OCEAN(IC + -IZATION.]
GEOLOGY. The conversion of continental crust into oceanic crust.

oceanography /əʊʃəˈnɒgrəfi/ *noun.* M19.
[from OCEAN + -OGRAPHY.]
The branch of science that deals with the physical and biological properties and phenomena of the sea. Cf. next.
■ **oceanographer** *noun* L19. **oceanoˈgraphic**, **oceanoˈgraphical** *adjectives* L19. **oceanoˈgraphically** *adverb* L19.

oceanology /əʊʃəˈnɒlədʒi/ *noun.* M19.
[from OCEAN + -OLOGY.]
Oceanography. Also *spec.*, the branch of technology and economics dealing with human use of the sea.
■ **oceanoˈlogical** *adjective* M20. **oceanologist** *noun* M20.

oceanward /ˈəʊʃ(ə)nwəd/ *adverb & adjective.* M19.
[from OCEAN + -WARD.]
▸ **A** *adverb.* Towards or in the direction of the ocean. M19.
▸ **B** *adjective.* Moving or directed towards the ocean. E20.
■ Also **oceanwards** *adverb* M19.

ocellar /əˈsɛlə/ *adjective.* L19.
[from OCELLUS + -AR¹.]
1 ZOOLOGY. Of or pertaining to an ocellus or simple eye. L19.
2 PETROGRAPHY. Having or designating a structure of igneous rocks in which minute crystals of one mineral are arranged in radiating aggregations round crystals of another. L19.

ocellated /ˈɒsɪleɪtɪd/ *adjective.* E18.
[from Latin *ocellatus*, from OCELLUS: see -ATE², -ED¹.]
ZOOLOGY & BOTANY. **1** Marked with an ocellus or ocelli; having spots resembling eyes. E18.
2 Forming an ocellus; (of a small round marking) surrounded by a ring of a different colour. E19.
1 *ocellated turkey*: see TURKEY *noun*².
■ Also **ocellate** *adjective* M19.

ocellus /əˈsɛləs/ *noun.* Pl. **-lli** /-lʌɪ, -liː/. E19.
[Latin, dim. of *oculus* eye.]
1 ZOOLOGY. Each of the small simple, as distinct from the compound, eyes of insects, other arthropods, etc.; a simple or rudimentary eye or visual spot which is sensitive to light but does not form a focused image. Also occas., a facet of a compound eye, an ommatidium. E19.
2 A coloured spot surrounded by a ring or rings of different colour, as on some feathers, butterflies' wings, etc.; an eyelike spot. E19.

ocelot /ˈɒsɪlɒt, ˈəʊs-/ *noun.* L18.
[French from Nahuatl *tlatlocelotl* lit. 'field tiger'.]
1 A nocturnal carnivorous mammal of the cat family, *Felis pardalis*, of Central and S. American forests and scrub, whose coat is tan with light black-edged patches. L18.
2 The skin or fur of an ocelot; a garment made of this. L19.

och /ɒk, ɒx/ *interjection. Scot. & Anglo-Irish.* E16.
[Gaelic & Irish.]
Expr. regret, irritation, etc.: ah! oh!
📖 W. CORLETT Och, leave it, Andy.

oche /ˈɒki/ *noun.* Also **hockey** /ˈhɒki, ˈɒki/. M20.
[Origin uncertain: perh. ult. connected with Old French *ocher* cut a deep notch in.]
Chiefly DARTS. The line behind which a player must stand when throwing.

ocher *noun, adjective, & verb*, **ocherous**, **ochery** *adjectives* see OCHRE etc.

ochlocracy /ɒkˈlɒkrəsi/ *noun.* L16.
[French *ochlocratie* or mod. Latin *ochlocratia* from Greek *okhlokratia*, from *okhlos* crowd: see -CRACY.]
Government by the populace; mob rule; a State etc. ruled or dominated by the populace.
■ ˈ**ochlocrat** *noun* an advocate or adherent of ochlocracy L19. **ochloˈcratic** *adjective* of, pertaining to, or of the nature of ochlocracy; upholding ochlocracy: M19. **ochloˈcratical** *adjective* = OCHLOCRATIC M17. **ochloˈcratically** *adverb* M19.

ochlophobia /ɒkləˈfəʊbɪə/ *noun.* L19.
[from Greek *okhlos* crowd + -PHOBIA.]
Irrational fear of or aversion to crowds.
■ **ochlophobic** *adjective* L20. **ochlophobist** *noun* (*rare*) a person afflicted with ochlophobia M19.

ochlospecies /ˈɒkləʊˌspiːʃiːz, -ʃɪz/ *noun. rare.* Pl. same. M20.
[from Greek *okhlos* crowd + SPECIES.]
TAXONOMY. A species which exhibits a complex pattern of variation amongst its members, not separable into distinct groups.

ochone /əʊˈhəʊn, əʊˈxəʊn/ *interjection & noun. Scot. & Anglo-Irish.* Also **ohone**. LME.
[Irish *ochón*, Gaelic *ochòin*.]
▸ **A** *interjection.* Expr. lamentation: oh! alas! LME.
▸ **B** *noun.* An utterance of 'ochone!'. L17.

ochraceous /əʊˈkreɪʃəs/ *adjective.* L18.
[from Latin *ochra* OCHRE *noun* + -ACEOUS.]
= OCHREOUS.

ochratoxin /əʊkrəˈtɒksɪn/ *noun.* L20.
[from mod. Latin *ochraceus* (see below), formed as prec. + TOXIN.]
BIOCHEMISTRY. Any of several nephrotoxins present in the grain mould *Aspergillus ochraceus* and other moulds of the genera *Aspergillus* and *Penicillium*.

ochre /ˈəʊkə/ *noun, adjective, & verb.* Also ***ocher**. ME.
[Old & mod. French *ocre* from Latin *ochra* from Greek *ōkhra* from *ōkhros* pale yellow, paleness.]
▸ **A** *noun.* **1** Any of various earthy pigments containing a mixture of hydrated iron oxides, freq. with some proportion of clay, and varying in colour from yellow to deep orange-red or brown; the colour of any of these, *esp.* a light brownish yellow; any pigment of this colour. ME.
2 With specifying word: any of various earthy oxides of metals other than iron. M19.
3 Money (with ref. to the colour of gold coin). *slang.* M19.
4 GENETICS. The nonsense codon UAA; a mutant fragment of genetic material containing this. M20.
📖 **1** *Time* Sunflower colors change . . burnished gold, burnt lemon, dusty ocher and pumpkin orange. ***brown ochre***, ***burnt ochre***, ***Oxford ochre***, ***red ochre***, ***white ochre***, ***yellow ochre***, etc. **2** ***antimony ochre***, ***chrome ochre***, ***tungsten ochre***, etc.
▸ **B** *adjective.* Of the colour of ochre, *esp.* light brownish yellow. L16.
📖 L. GRANT-ADAMSON The South of France was a sepia print: ochre valleys gouged from brown mountains.
▸ **C** *verb trans.* Pres. pple & verbal noun **ochreing**. Colour, mark, or rub with ochre. Chiefly as ***ochred*** *ppl adjective.* E17.
■ **ochreish** *adjective* = OCHREOUS M19.

ochrea /ˈɒkrɪə/ *noun.* Also (now *rare*) **ocrea**. M19.
[Latin = greave, protective legging.]
BOTANY. A scarious sheath round a stem formed by the cohesion of two or more stipules, characteristic of the knotgrass family Polygonaceae.

ochreate *adjective* see OCREATE.

ochreous /ˈəʊkrɪəs/ *adjective.* E18.
[from mod. Latin *ochreus*, from *ochra* OCHRE *noun*: see -EOUS.]
Of the nature of or containing ochre; of the colour of ochre, *spec.* light brownish yellow.

ochroid /ˈəʊkrɔɪd/ *adjective. rare.* L19.
[Greek *ōkhroeidēs*, from *ōkhra* OCHRE *noun*: see -OID.]
Pale yellowish.

ochronosis /əʊkrəˈnəʊsɪs/ *noun.* Pl. **-noses** /-ˈnəʊsiːz/. M19.
[from OCHRE + -O- + *-n-* + -OSIS.]
MEDICINE. An abnormal brown pigmentation of tissue, esp. cartilage, that is typically a symptom of alkaptonuria resulting from accumulation of homogentisic acid.
■ **ochronotic** /-ˈnɒt-/ *adjective* E20.

ochrous /ˈəʊkrəs/ *adjective.* Also ***ocherous** /ˈəʊk(ə)rəs/. M18.
[from OCHRE *noun* or directly from Latin *ochra*: see -OUS.]
= OCHREOUS.

ochry /ˈəʊkri/ *adjective.* Also ***ochery** /ˈəʊk(ə)ri/. M16.
[from OCHRE *noun* + -Y¹.]
= OCHREOUS.

†**ociosity** *noun* see OTIOSITY.

-ock /ɒk/ *suffix* (not productive).
[Old English *-oc*, *-uc*.]
Forming nouns with (orig.) diminutive sense, as ***hillock***, ***dunnock***, ***haddock***, ***pollock***, etc. In other words, as ***bannock***, ***hassock***, ***mattock***, app. of different origin.

ocker /ˈɒkə/ *noun*¹ *& verb.* Chiefly *derog.* Long *obsolete* exc. *Scot.* ME.
[Old Norse *okr* (Swedish *ocker*, Danish *okker*) corresp. to Old English *wōcor*, Old Frisian, Middle Low German *wōker*, Middle & mod. Dutch *woeker*, Old High German *wuchhar*, Middle High German *wuocher* (German *Wucher*), Gothic *woks*, increase, usury from Germanic: perh. ult. from base also of Latin *augere* to increase, Gothic *aukan* to add.]
▸†**A** *noun.* The lending of money at (excessive) interest, usury; interest gained from this. ME–E18.
▸ **B** *verb.* †**1** *verb intrans.* Of money: grow (as) with the addition of interest. Of a person: lend at interest, take usury. Only in ME.
2 *verb trans.* Orig., increase (money) by usury. Later, increase (a thing) in value or price. ME.
■ **ockerer** *noun* ME.

ocker /ˈɒkə/ *noun*². *Austral. slang.* L20.
[A nickname, esp. as an alt. of the personal name *Oscar*, used for a character in a series of Austral. television sketches.]
A rough, uncultivated, or aggressively boorish Australian man (esp. as a stereotype).
📖 *Sunday Express* He is Crocodile Dundee, the ocker whose outspokenness trounces cityslickers.
■ **ockerdom** *noun* ockers collectively L20. **ockerism** *noun* behaviour characteristic of an ocker L20.

Ockham *noun* see OCCAM.

o'clock /əˈklɒk/ *adverb.* Also (earlier) †**a clock**. L15.
[Contr. of ***of the clock*** s.v. OF *preposition*.]
1 Of or according to the clock: used to express time, after a numeral indicating the hour and (passing into *noun*) after an interrog. L15.
2 *transf.* Used following a numeral to indicate direction or bearing with reference to an imaginary clock-face, twelve o'clock being thought of as directly above or in front of the observer or at the top of a circular target etc. E20.
📖 **1** DICKENS I . . asked him what o'clock it was. CONAN DOYLE I'll meet the seven o'clock train and take no steps till you arrive. *Listener* The worst time of the week for me is between three o'clock and twenty to five every Saturday afternoon. ***like one o'clock***: see ONE *adjective* etc.. **2** H. WILLIAMSON There's another tip I learned in racing—to hold the wheel at four o'clock and eight o'clock. *New Yorker* The sun lay at about two o'clock to our course.

ocnophil /ˈɒknəfɪl/ *noun. rare.* Also **ok-**. M20.
[from Greek *oknein* hesitate + -O- + -PHIL.]
PSYCHOLOGY. A person who relies on external objects or other people for emotional security. Opp. PHILOBAT.
■ **ocnoˈphilic** *adjective* pertaining to or characteristic of an ocnophil M20.

ocote /əˈkəʊteɪ/ *noun.* E20.
[Amer. Spanish from Nahuatl *ocotl* torch.]
(The wood of) a resinous Mexican pine, *Pinus montezumae*.

ocotillo /əʊkəˈtiːjəʊ/ *noun. US.* Pl. **-os**. M19.
[Amer. Spanish, dim. of OCOTE.]
A desert shrub, *Fouquieria splendens* (family Fouquieriaceae), of Mexico and the south-western US, bearing panicles of scarlet flowers on stiff spiny stems.

OCR *abbreviation.*
Optical character recognition.

ocracy /ˈɒkrəsi/ *noun.* Chiefly *derog.* or *joc.* M19.
[Use as noun of *-ocracy*: see -CRACY.]
Any form of government, organization, or domination of a specified or distinctive character or type.
📖 *Sunday Telegraph* He has a profound contempt for all 'ocracies' and 'isms,' above all American liberalism.

-ocracy *suffix* see -CRACY.

ocrea *noun* see OCHREA.

ocreate /ˈɒkrɪət/ *adjective.* In sense 1 now usu. **och-**. M19.
[formed as OCHREA + -ATE².]
1 BOTANY. Having the stipules united by cohesion into a sheath surrounding the stem. M19.
2 ORNITHOLOGY. Having the tarsal envelope undivided; = BOOTED 2. L19.

oct- *combining form* see OCTA-, OCTO-.

Oct. *abbreviation*¹.
October.

oct. *abbreviation*².
Octavo.

octa- /ˈɒktə/ *combining form.* Before a vowel **oct-**.
[Greek *okta-* combining form of *oktō* eight. Cf. OCTO-.]
Having eight, eightfold.
■ **octaˈdecanol** *noun* (CHEMISTRY) any alcohol of the formula $C_{18}H_{37}OH$, of which many isomers exist; *spec.* (in full ***n-octadecanol***) the unbranched primary alcohol, found in whale oils (also called ***stearyl alcohol***): E20. **octamethylˌcycloˌtetrasiˈloxane** *noun* (CHEMISTRY) a colourless oily liquid formed during silicone manufacture, with a cyclic tetrameric molecule of formula $[(CH_3)_2SiO]_4$ M20. **ocˈtandrous** *adjective* (BOTANY) having eight stamens E19. **octaˈpeptide** *noun* (BIOCHEMISTRY) a peptide with eight amino acids in its molecule M20. **octapody** *noun* (PROSODY) a line of verse consisting of eight metrical feet E20. **octarch** *adjective* (BOTANY) (of a vascular bundle) having eight strands of xylem, formed from eight points of origin L19. **octastich** /ˈɒktəstɪk/ *noun* (PROSODY) a group of eight lines of verse L16.

octachord /ˈɒktəkɔːd/ *adjective & noun.* M18.
[In senses A.1, B.2 from Latin *octachordos* adjective, late Latin *octachordon* noun, from Greek *oktakhordos* adjective, *oktakhordon* noun, formed as OCTA- + *khordē* string (see CORD *noun*¹). In senses A.2, B.1 from OCTA- + CHORD *noun*¹.]
MUSIC. ▸**A** *adjective.* **1** Having eight strings. M18.
2 Of or pertaining to an eight-note scale. M18.
▸ **B** *noun.* **1** A series of eight notes, as the ordinary diatonic scale. L18.
2 A musical instrument having eight strings. E19.

octad /ˈɒktad/ *noun.* M19.
[Greek *oktad-*, *oktas* a group of eight, from *oktō* eight: see -AD¹.]
1 MATH. †**a** Each of a system of eight numbers analogous to quaternions. Only in M19. ▸**b** GEOMETRY. The set of eight intersections of three quadric surfaces. L19.
2 *gen.* A group of eight; *spec.* a unit in the Archimedean system of arithmetical notation representing a power of 10^8. L19.
3 CHEMISTRY. An octavalent element or group. Now *rare* or *obsolete*. L19.
■ **ocˈtadic** *adjective* L19.

octadrachm /ˈɒktədram/ *noun.* Also **octo-**. L19.
[from Greek *oktadrakhmos* adjective, formed as OCTA-, OCTO- + *drakhmē* DRACHMA.]
An ancient Greek silver coin worth eight drachmas.

octaeteris /ɒktʌɪˈtɪərɪs/ *noun.* Pl. **-terides** /-ˈtɪərɪdiːz/. E18.
[Greek *oktaetēris*, formed as OCTA- + *etos* year.]
In the ancient Greek calendar, a period of eight years, during which three months of 30 days each were intercalated so as to make the year of 12 lunar months correspond with the solar year.
■ **octaeteric** *adjective* of or pertaining to this period M19.

octagon /ˈɒktəg(ə)n/ *noun & adjective.* Also †**octo-**. L16.
[Latin *octagonum*, *octo-* noun, *octagonos*, *octo-* adjective, from Greek *octagōnon* use as noun of *oktagōnos* eight-cornered, formed as OCTA-, OCTO-: see -GON.]
▶ **A** *noun.* A plane figure with eight straight sides and eight angles; a building or object of octagonal shape or cross-section. L16.
▶ **B** *adjective.* = next. L17.

octagonal /ɒkˈtag(ə)n(ə)l/ *adjective.* Also †**octo-**. L16.
[from (the same root as) prec.: see -AL[1].]
Having the form of an octagon; having eight sides.
■ **octagonally** *adverb* M18.

octagynous *adjective* var. of OCTOGYNOUS.

octahedra *noun pl.* see OCTAHEDRON.

octahedral /ɒktəˈhiːdr(ə)l, -ˈhɛd-/ *adjective.* Also **octo-**. M18.
[from late Latin *octa(h)edros* from Greek *oktaedros*: see OCTAHEDRON, -AL[1].]
Having the form of an octahedron; having eight plane (esp. triangular) faces.
■ **octahedrally** *adverb* L19. **octahedrical** *adjective* (*rare*) = OCTAHEDRAL M17.

octahedrite /ɒktəˈhiːdrʌɪt, -ˈhɛd-/ *noun.* E19.
[from next + -ITE[1].]
1 MINERALOGY. = ANATASE. E19.
2 GEOLOGY. An iron meteorite which shows a Widmanstätten structure on etching due to octahedrally oriented plates of kamacite and taenite. E20.

octahedron /ɒktəˈhiːdrən, -ˈhɛd-/ *noun.* Also **octo-**. Pl. **-dra** /-drə/, **-drons**. L16.
[Greek *oktaedron* use as noun of *oktaedros* eight-sided, formed as OCTA-, OCTO-: see -HEDRON.]
A solid figure or object with eight plane faces; *esp.* (more fully ***regular octahedron***) one with eight equilateral triangular faces (representable as two equal pyramids on one square base).
truncated octahedron a fourteen-sided solid formed from a regular octahedron by truncating its six corners to form six square faces and eight (usu. regular) hexagonal faces.

octal /ˈɒkt(ə)l/ *adjective & noun.* M20.
[from OCTA- + -AL[1].]
▶ **A** *adjective.* **1** ELECTRONICS. Designating (plugs, sockets, etc. having) a standard circular arrangement of eight pins with a central moulded key for determining the orientation. M20.
2 MATH. & COMPUTING. Pertaining to or designating a system of numerical notation in which the base is 8 rather than 10. M20.
▶ **B** *noun.* The octal system; an octal number. M20.

octamer /ˈɒktəmə/ *noun.* E20.
[from OCTA- + -MER.]
CHEMISTRY. A compound whose molecule is composed of eight molecules of monomer.
■ **octaˈmeric** *adjective* of the nature of an octamer, consisting of an octamer or octamers M20.

octamerous /ɒkˈtam(ə)rəs/ *adjective.* Also **octom-** /ɒkˈtɒm-/. M19.
[from OCTA-, OCTO- + -MEROUS.]
BIOLOGY. Having parts arranged in groups of eight.
■ **octamerism** *noun* the condition of being octamerous L19.

octameter /ɒkˈtamɪtə/ *noun.* M19.
[from OCTA- + -METER, after *hexameter*, *pentameter*.]
PROSODY. A line of eight metrical feet.

octane /ˈɒkteɪn/ *noun.* L19.
[from OCTA- + -ANE.]
1 CHEMISTRY. Any of a series of saturated hydrocarbons (alkanes) with the formula C_8H_{18}; *esp.* (also n-***octane***) the unbranched isomer, $CH_3(CH_2)_6CH_3$. Cf. ISOOCTANE. L19.
2 *ellipt.* An octane number. Usu. with preceding numeral or adjective, as ***105 octane***, ***high octane***. M20.
Comb.: **octane number**, **octane rating** a number indicating the antiknock properties of a motor or aviation fuel, equal to the percentage by volume of isooctane in an isooctane/heptane mixture of equivalent performance, or (for numbers above 100) to the number of millilitres of tetraethyl lead per gallon of isooctane required to give an equivalent performance.
■ **octaˈnoate** *noun* a salt or ester of octanoic acid M20. **octaˈnoic** *adjective*: ***octanoic acid***, any unsaturated fatty acid of the formula $C_7H_{15}COOH$, of which several isomers exist; *spec.* = CAPRYLIC ***acid***: E20. **octanoyl** /ˈɒktənəʊʌɪl, -əʊɪl/ *noun* a radical of the formula $C_7H_{15}CO$-; *spec.* = CAPRYLYL: M20.

†**octangle** *adjective & noun.* E17.
[Latin *octangulus* eight-angled, from OCTO- + *angulus* ANGLE *noun*[3].]
▶ **A** *adjective.* Octagonal. Only in E17.
▶ **B** *noun.* An octagon. M17–E18.

octangular /ɒkˈtaŋgjʊlə/ *adjective.* M17.
[from (the same root as) prec. + -AR[1].]
Having eight angles, octagonal.

Octans /ˈɒktanz/ *noun.* E19.
[Latin *octans*, OCTANT.]
(The name of) an inconspicuous constellation containing the south celestial pole; the Octant.

octant /ˈɒkt(ə)nt/ *noun.* L17.
[Latin *octant-*, *-ans* half-quadrant, from OCTO-. Cf. QUADRANT *noun*[1], SEXTANT.]
1 ASTROLOGY & ASTRONOMY. The aspect of two planets which are one-eighth of a circle (45 degrees) apart in the sky; *spec.* each of the four points at which the moon is 45 degrees from conjunction with or opposition to the sun. Cf. OCTILE. Now *rare* or *obsolete*. L17.
2 An arc of a circle or of the horizon forming one-eighth of the whole; one-eighth of the area of a circle, contained within two radii at an angle of 45 degrees. M18. ▸**b** Each of the eight parts into which a space or solid figure is divided by three planes (usually mutually at right angles) intersecting at the central point. L18.
3 An instrument in the form of a graduated eighth of a circle, used for making angular measurements, esp. in astronomy and navigation. M18.
4 (Usu. **O-**.) *The* constellation Octans. M19.
■ **ocˈtantal** *adjective* L18.

octapla /ˈɒktəplə/ *noun.* Also **octaple** /ˈɒktəp(ə)l/. L17.
[Greek *oktapla* neut. pl. of *oktaplous* eightfold, after HEXAPLA.]
A text consisting of eight versions in parallel columns, esp. of the Old or New Testament.

octaploid *adjective & noun* var. of OCTOPLOID.

octapole *noun* var. of OCTUPOLE.

octarchy /ˈɒktɑːki/ *noun.* L18.
[from OCTA- + -ARCHY, after HEPTARCHY.]
Government by eight rulers; an aggregate of eight districts or kingdoms, each under its own ruler; *spec.* the supposed eight kingdoms of the Angles and Saxons in Britain in the 7th and 8th cents. Cf. HEPTARCHY.

octaroon *noun* var. of OCTOROON.

octastyle /ˈɒktəstʌɪl/ *adjective & noun.* Also **octo-**. E18.
[Latin *octastylus* adjective from Greek *oktastulos*, formed as OCTA-, OCTO- + *stulos* column.]
ARCHITECTURE. (A building or portico) having eight columns at the end or in front.

Octateuch /ˈɒktətjuːk/ *noun.* Also **Octo-**. L17.
[Late Latin *octateuchus*, from Greek *oktateukhos* containing eight books, formed as OCTA-, OCTO- + *teukhos* book.]
The first eight books of the Old Testament and Hebrew Scriptures collectively; the Pentateuch together with the books of Joshua, Judges, and Ruth. Also, a manuscript or edition of the Octateuch.

octavalent /ɒktəˈveɪl(ə)nt/ *adjective.* Also **octo-**. E20.
[from OCTA-, OCTO- + -VALENT.]
CHEMISTRY. Having a valency of eight.

octave /ˈɒktɪv/ *noun & verb.* In sense A.1 also †**utave**. ME.
[Old & mod. French from Latin *octava* (sc. *dies* day) fem. of *octavus* eighth, from *octo* eight. See also UTAS *noun*.]
▶ **A** *noun.* **1** ECCLESIASTICAL. The seventh day after a festival (the eighth day when counted inclusively). Also, a period of eight days beginning with the day of a festival. Orig. in *pl.* ME.
2 MUSIC. An interval embracing eight notes on the diatonic scale, the highest note having twice the frequency of and the same alphabetical name as the lowest; a series of notes or instrument keys etc. extending through this interval. Also, the note an octave below or (usu.) above a given note; two notes an octave apart sounding together. Cf. EIGHTH *noun* 2. L16. ▸**b** An organ-stop sounding an octave higher than the ordinary pitch; a principal. E18. ▸**c** PHYSICS. An interval, analogous to the musical octave, between two electromagnetic waves one of which has twice the frequency of the other. L19.
3 A group or stanza of eight lines of verse, an octet; *spec.* = OTTAVA RIMA. L16.
4 FENCING. Orig. (now *rare*) ***octave parade***. The last of eight recognized parrying positions, used to protect the lower outside of the body, with the sword-hand to the right in supination and the tip of the blade pointing at the opponent's head; a parry in this position. L18.
5 = OCTET 3. E19.
6 A small wine-cask containing an eighth of a pipe, 13½ gallons (approx. 61.4 litres). L19.

> **2** V. BRITTAIN My hands were too small to stretch an octave easily. K. AMIS His voice was . . an octave higher than she . . expected. **5** *Tit-Bits* The . . tallest brother of this remarkable octave.

Phrases: **Law of Octaves** CHEMISTRY (now *Hist.*) the principle according to which, when the lighter elements are arranged in order of their atomic weights, similar properties recur at every eighth term of the series; also called ***Newlands' Law of Octaves***. ***short octave***: see SHORT *adjective*.
Comb.: **octave coupler** a device in an organ etc. enabling a note an octave higher or lower to be sounded with the note being played; **octave flute** (*a*) a piccolo; (*b*) a flute stop in an organ sounding an octave higher than the ordinary pitch; **octave key** a key on a wind instrument used to produce a note an octave higher than the note that is being fingered; **octave stanza** = sense 3 above; **octave stop** = sense 2b above.
▶ **B** *verb intrans.* Play music in octaves. *rare.* L19.
■ **octaval** /ɒkˈteɪv(ə)l/ *adjective* of or pertaining to an octave; proceeding by octaves or eights: L19.

octavian /ɒkˈteɪvɪən/ *noun.* L16.
[Latin *octavus* eighth + -IAN.]
SCOTTISH HISTORY. Each of the eight members of a finance committee appointed by James VI to control the royal exchequer.

octavic /ɒkˈteɪvɪk/ *adjective.* Now *rare*. M19.
[from Latin *octavus* eighth + -IC.]
MATH. = OCTIC.

octavo /ɒkˈtɑːvəʊ, -ˈteɪ-/ *noun.* Pl. **-os**. L16.
[Latin (*in*) *octavo* in an eighth (sc. of a sheet), from *octavus* eighth.]
1 A size of book or paper in which each leaf is one-eighth of a standard printing-sheet. L16.
2 A book or page of this size. E18.
1 ***royal octavo***: see ROYAL *adjective*.

octennial /ɒkˈtɛnɪəl/ *adjective.* M17.
[from late Latin *octennium* period of eight years, formed as OCTO- + *annus* year: see -AL[1]. Cf. *biennial* etc.]
Of or pertaining to a period of eight years; lasting for eight years; occurring every eight years.
■ **octennially** *adverb* every eight years M19.

octet /ɒkˈtɛt/ *noun.* Also **-ette**. M19.
[Italian *ottetto* or German *Oktett*, assim. to OCTA-, OCTO-, -ET[1], after *duet*, *quartet*.]
1 MUSIC. A composition for eight voices or instruments. M19.
2 A group of eight lines of verse; *spec.* the first eight lines of a sonnet. L19.
3 A group of eight persons or things; *esp.* (MUSIC) a group of eight singers or instrumentalists. L19. ▸**b** PHYSICS & CHEMISTRY. A stable group of eight electrons in an electron shell of an atom. E20. ▸**c** NUCLEAR PHYSICS. A multiplet of eight subatomic particles. M20.

octic /ˈɒktɪk/ *adjective & noun.* L19.
[from OCTA- + -IC.]
MATH. (A curve or polynomial) of the eighth order or degree.

†**octile** *adjective & noun.* L17–E18.
[mod. Latin *octilis*, from Latin OCTO- + *-ilis* -ILE after *sextile*, *decile*, etc.]
ASTROLOGY. (Designating) the aspect of two planets which are one-eighth of a circle (45 degrees) apart in the sky. Cf. OCTANT 1.

octillion /ɒkˈtɪljən/ *noun.* L17.
[from OCTA- after *million*, *billion*, etc.]
Orig. (esp. in the UK), the eighth power of a million (10^{48}). Now usu. (orig. *US*), the ninth power of a thousand (10^{27}).
■ **octillionth** *adjective & noun* M19.

octli /ˈəʊktli/ *noun.* M19.
[Mexican Spanish.]
= PULQUE.

octo- /ˈɒktəʊ/ *combining form.* Before a vowel **oct-**.
[from Latin *octo* eight, or (occas.) as OCTA-: see -O-.]
Having eight, eightfold.
■ **octocoral** *noun* (ZOOLOGY) a coral of a group characterized by polyps with eight tentacles, an alcyonarian M20. **octocoˈrallian** *adjective* (ZOOLOGY) designating or pertaining to a coral with eightfold symmetry M20. **octode** *noun* (RADIO) a thermionic valve with eight electrodes M20. **octofid** *adjective* (BOTANY) (of a calyx or corolla) divided into eight segments M18. **octofoil** *adjective & noun* (*a*) *adjective* having or consisting of eight leaves or lobes; (*b*) *noun* an octofoil ornamental or heraldic figure: M19. **octofoiled** *adjective* = OCTOFOIL *adjective* M19. **ocˈtoic** *adjective* (CHEMISTRY) = OCTANOIC L19. **octoˈpetalous** *adjective* having eight petals M18. **octose** *noun* (CHEMISTRY) any monosaccharide sugar with eight carbon atoms in its molecule L19. **octoˈsepalous** *adjective* (BOTANY) having eight sepals L19.

octobass /ˈɒktə(ʊ)beɪs/ *noun.* L19.
[French *octobasse*, formed as prec. + *basse* BASS *noun*[2].]
A very large instrument of the viol family, having three strings stopped by keys worked by the fingers and feet.

October /ɒkˈtəʊbə/ *noun.* LOE.
[Latin *october*, also *Octobris* (sc. *mensis* month), from *octo* eight: orig. the eighth month of the Roman year. The meaning of *-ber* is unkn. (cf. *September* etc.).]
1 The tenth month of the year in the Gregorian calendar. LOE.
2 Chiefly *Hist.* A kind of strong ale traditionally brewed in October. E18.
Comb.: **October Revolution** *Hist.* the Russian Bolshevik revolution in November (October Old Style) 1917, in which the provisional government was overthrown, leading to the establishment of the USSR. **October surprise** US POLITICS an unexpected but popular political act or speech made just prior to a November election in an attempt to win votes; *spec.* an alleged Republican conspiracy to make an arms deal with Iran to delay the release of American hostages until after the 1980 election.

Octobrist /ɒkˈtəʊbrɪst/ *noun.* Also **-berist** /-b(ə)rɪst/. **E20.**
[In sense 1 from Russian *oktyabrist*, in sense 2 from *oktyabryonok*, from *oktyabr'* OCTOBER + -IST.]
1 *Hist.* A member of the moderate party in the Russian Duma, supporting the Imperial Constitutional Manifesto of October 1905. **E20.**
2 A member of a Soviet Communist organization for young people below the normal age of the Pioneers. (Cf. PIONEER *noun* 3c.) **E20.**

octocentenary /ˌɒktəʊsɛnˈtiːnəri, -ˈtɛn-, ɒktəʊˈsɛntɪn-/ *noun.* **L19.**
[from OCTO- + CENTENARY.]
(A celebration of) an eight-hundredth anniversary.
■ **octocentennial** /ˌɒktəʊsɛnˈtɛnɪəl/ *adjective* of or pertaining to an octocentenary **L19.**

octodecimo /ɒktəʊˈdɛsɪməʊ/ *noun.* Pl. **-os.** **M19.**
[Latin (*in*) *octodecimo* in an eighteenth (sc. of a sheet), from *octodecimus* eighteenth.]
A size of book or paper in which each leaf is one-eighteenth of a standard printing-sheet. Also, a book or page of this size.

octodrachm *noun* var. of OCTADRACHM.

octogenarian /ˌɒktə(ʊ)dʒɪˈnɛːrɪən/ *noun & adjective.* **E19.**
[from Latin *octogenarius*, from *octogeni* distrib. of *octoginta* eighty: see -ARIAN.]
► **A** *noun.* A person between 80 and 89 years of age. **E19.**
► **B** *adjective.* Between 80 and 89 years of age; of or pertaining to an octogenarian or octogenarians. **E19.**
■ **ocˈtogenary** *adjective & noun* (now *rare*) = OCTOGENARIAN **L17.** **octogenarianism** *noun* the state or fact of being an octogenarian **L19.**

†**octogon** *noun & adjective*, **octogonal** *adjective* vars. of OCTAGON, OCTAGONAL.

octogynous /ɒkˈtɒdʒɪnəs/ *adjective.* Also **octagynous** /ɒkˈtadʒ-/. **M19.**
[from OCTO-, OCTA- + -GYNOUS.]
BOTANY. Having eight styles.

octohedron *noun* var. of OCTAHEDRON.

octomerous *adjective* var. of OCTAMEROUS.

octonal /ˈɒktən(ə)l/ *adjective.* **L19.**
[from Latin *octoni* (see OCTONARY) + -AL[1].]
= OCTONARY *adjective.*

octonarius /ɒktə(ʊ)ˈnɛːrɪəs/ *noun.* Pl. **-narii** /-ˈnɛːrɪʌɪ/. **E19.**
[from Latin *octonarius* (*versus*), formed as next.]
PROSODY. A verse of eight feet, an octapody.
■ **octonarian** *adjective & noun* (a verse) of eight feet **L19.**

octonary /ˈɒktə(ʊ)n(ə)ri/ *noun & adjective.* **M16.**
[from Latin *octonarius* containing eight, from *octoni* distrib. of *octo* eight: see -ARY[1].]
► **A** *noun.* A group of eight; *spec.* a stanza of eight lines of verse, esp. of Psalm 119 (118 in the Vulgate). **M16.**
► **B** *adjective.* Pertaining to the number eight: consisting of eight; proceeding by eights; *spec.* = OCTAL *adjective* 1. **E17.**

octopamine /ɒkˈtəʊpəmiːn/ *noun.* **M20.**
[from OCTOPUS (from which it was first extracted) + AMINE.]
BIOCHEMISTRY. A weakly sympathomimetic amine which under the influence of monoamine oxidase inhibitors may accumulate in nerves in place of the closely related noradrenaline and cause a rise in blood pressure; 1-(3-hydroxyphenyl)-2-aminoethanol, $HO{\cdot}C_6H_4{\cdot}CHOH{\cdot}CH_2NH_2$.

octopartite /ɒktə(ʊ)ˈpɑːtʌɪt/ *adjective.* **M18.**
[from OCTO- after *bipartite*, *tripartite*.]
Divided into or consisting of eight parts. Formerly *spec.* in *LAW*, (of a contract etc.) drawn up in eight corresponding parts, one for each party.

octopean /ˈɒktəpiːən, ɒkˈtəʊpɪən/ *adjective.* **L19.**
[from OCTOPUS + -EAN.]
Pertaining to or like (that of) an octopus; octopoid.

octoped /ˈɒktəpɛd/ *noun.* Also **-pede** /-piːd/. **E19.**
[from Latin *octo* eight + *ped-*, *pes* foot.]
An eight-footed animal or thing.

octopi *noun pl.* see OCTOPUS.

octopian /ˈɒktəpiːən, ɒkˈtəʊpɪən/ *adjective.* **E20.**
[from OCTOPUS + -IAN.]
= OCTOPEAN.
■ Also **octopic** /-ˈtɒp-, -ˈtəʊp-/ *adjective* **M20.**

octopine /ˈɒktəpiːn/ *noun.* **E20.**
[from OCTOPUS + -INE[5].]
BIOCHEMISTRY. An opine, $C_9H_{18}N_4O_4$, present in octopus muscle and also synthesized by plant cells infected with certain plasmids from the crown gall pathogen *Agrobacterium tumefaciens*. Cf. NOPALINE.

octopine /ˈɒktəpʌɪn/ *adjective.* **E20.**
[from OCTOPUS + -INE[1].]
= OCTOPEAN.

octoploid /ˈɒktəplɔɪd/ *adjective & noun.* Also **octa-.** **E20.**
[from OCTO-, OCTA- + -PLOID.]
BIOLOGY. ► **A** *adjective.* (Of a cell) containing eight sets of chromosomes; (of an individual) composed of octoploid cells. **E20.**
► **B** *noun.* An octoploid individual. **E20.**
■ **octoploidy** *noun* octoploid condition **M20.**

octopod /ˈɒktəpɒd/ *adjective & noun.* **E19.**
[from Greek *oktōpod-* stem of *oktōpous*: see OCTOPUS, -POD.]
► **A** *adjective.* Eight-footed. **E19.**
► **B** *noun.* An eight-footed animal; *spec.* an octopus or other cephalopod of the order Octopoda. **M19.**
■ **octopodan** /-ˈpəʊd-/ *adjective & noun* **L19.** **octopodous** /-ˈpəʊd-/ *adjective* **M19.**

octopodes *noun pl.* see OCTOPUS.

octopoid /ˈɒktəpɔɪd/ *adjective.* **M20.**
[from OCTOPUS + -OID.]
Like an octopus (*lit.* & *fig.*).

octopole *noun* var. of OCTUPOLE.

octopus /ˈɒktəpəs/ *noun.* Pl. **octopuses**, **octopi** /ˈɒktəpʌɪ/, **octopodes** /ɒkˈtəʊpədiːz/. **M18.**
[mod. Latin from Greek *oktōpous*, from *oktō* eight + *pous* foot.]
1 A cephalopod mollusc of the genus *Octopus* or the order Octopoda, having a beaklike mouth surrounded by eight arms or tentacles bearing suckers, and with the shell vestigial or absent. **M18.**
2 *fig.* An organized, esp. harmful or destructive, power or influence having extended ramifications. **L19.**
3 A fairground ride in the form of a set of eccentrically rotating spokes with passenger cars suspended from their ends. **M20.**

📖 **2** N. FREELING The great bureaucratic octopus got in the way.

octopush /ˈɒktəpʊʃ/ *noun.* **M20.**
[Alt. of prec. by assoc. with PUSH *noun*[1].]
A game similar to ice hockey in which a weight is pushed along on the bottom of a swimming pool by two teams of divers.
■ **octopusher** *noun* **M20.**

octoroon /ɒktəˈruːn/ *noun.* Also **octa-.** **M19.**
[from OCTO-, OCTA- after QUADROON.]
A person having one-eighth black blood; the offspring of a quadroon and a white person.

octostyle *adjective & noun* var. of OCTASTYLE.

octosyllabic /ˌɒktəʊsɪˈlabɪk/ *adjective & noun.* **L18.**
[from OCTO- + SYLLABIC. Cf. late Latin *octosyllabus*, late Greek *octasullabos* adjectives.]
► **A** *adjective.* Consisting of eight syllables; composed of lines of eight syllables each. **L18.**
► **B** *noun.* A line of eight syllables. **M19.**

octosyllable /ˈɒktə(ʊ)ˌsɪləb(ə)l/ *adjective & noun.* **L18.**
[from OCTO- + SYLLABLE *noun.* Cf. prec.]
► **A** *adjective.* = OCTOSYLLABIC *adjective.* **L18.**
► **B** *noun.* A line or word of eight syllables. **L18.**

Octoteuch *noun* var. of OCTATEUCH.

octovalent *adjective* var. of OCTAVALENT.

octroi /ˈɒktrwɑː, *foreign* ɔktrwa (*pl. same*)/ *noun.* Also †**octroy.** **L16.**
[French, formed as next.]
†**1** A concession, a grant; a privilege granted by a government, *esp.* an exclusive right of trade etc. **L16–E18.**
2 A duty levied on certain goods entering a town, esp. in some European countries. **E18.** ▸**b** The point at which goods are examined for liability to this duty; the body of officials responsible for this. **M19.**

📖 **2b** *attrib.*: B. STOKER There are . . customs and octroi officers to pass.

octroy /ˈɒktrɔɪ/ *verb trans.* **L15.**
[French *octroyer*, *ott-* grant from Proto-Gallo-Romance from medieval Latin *auctorizare* AUTHORIZE.]
Of a government etc.: concede or grant (a privilege etc.).

OCTU /ˈɒktuː/ *abbreviation.*
Officer Cadets Training Unit.

octuor /ˈɒktjuːɔː/ *noun.* **M19.**
[French, irreg. from Latin *octo* eight after *quatuor* four.]
MUSIC. = OCTET 1.

octuple /ˈɒktjʊp(ə)l, ɒkˈtjuːp(ə)l/ *adjective, noun, & verb.* **E17.**
[French, or Latin *octuplus*, from OCTO- + *-plus* as in *duplus* double.]
► **A** *adjective.* Consisting of eight parts or things; eight times as many or as much, eightfold; *MUSIC* (of a rhythm or time) having eight beats in a bar. **E17.**
► **B** *noun.* An eightfold number or amount. **L17.**
► **C** *verb trans. & intrans.* Multiply by eight; make or become eight times as large, numerous, etc. **M19.**
■ **octuplet** *noun* a set or combination of eight; *spec.* in *MUSIC*, a group of eight notes to be played in the time of six: **M19.**

octuplicate /ɒkˈtjuːplɪkət/ *noun.* **M20.**
[from OCTA-, OCTUPLE after *duplicate* etc.]
in octuplicate, in eight identical copies.

octupole /ˈɒktjʊpəʊl/ *noun & adjective.* Also **octa-**, **octo-** /ˈɒktə(ʊ)-/. **E20.**
[from OCTA-, OCTO- after *quadrupole*.]
PHYSICS. (Of or pertaining to) a multipole of order 3.

octyl /ˈɒktʌɪl, -tɪl/ *noun.* **M19.**
[from OCTA- + -YL.]
CHEMISTRY. A radical, $C_8H_{17}{\cdot}$, derived from an octane. Usu. in *comb.*

ocular /ˈɒkjʊlə/ *adjective & noun.* **L16.**
[French *oculaire* from late Latin *ocularis*, from Latin *oculus* eye: see -AR[1].]
► **A** *adjective.* **1** Of, pertaining to, or in the region of the eye; of the nature, form, or function of an eye; expressed by the eye; *spec.* in *ENTOMOLOGY*, pertaining to a compound eye (opp. ***ocellar***). **L16.**
2 Of, pertaining to, performed by, or obtained by the sense of sight; visual. Formerly also, visible. **L16.**

📖 **1** R. W. EMERSON The eyes of men converse as much as their tongues . . the ocular dialect needs no dictionary. **ocular dominance** the priority of one eye over the other as regards preference of use etc. **2** G. SANTAYANA This . . might . . have been confirmed by ocular proof, if you had watched.

► **B** *noun.* †**1** A visible or manifest thing. Only in **M17.**
2 The eye. *joc.* **E19.**
3 The eyepiece of an optical instrument. **M19.**
■ **ocularly** *adverb* **E17.**

ocularist /ˈɒkjʊlərɪst/ *noun.* **M19.**
[French *oculariste*, formed as prec.: see -IST.]
A maker of artificial eyes.

oculate /ˈɒkjʊlət/ *adjective.* **M16.**
[Latin *oculatus*, from *oculus* eye: see -ATE[2].]
†**1** Possessing (good) sight; sharp-eyed; observant. **M16–M17.**
2 *BOTANY* & *ZOOLOGY.* Having eyelike spots or holes resembling eyes, ocellate. **M17.**
■ **oculated** *adjective* = OCULATE *adjective* 2 **E18.**

oculi *noun* pl. of OCULUS.

oculiform /ˈɒkjʊlɪfɔːm/ *adjective.* **E19.**
[from Latin *oculus* eye+ -I- + -FORM.]
Eye-shaped; eyelike.

oculist /ˈɒkjʊlɪst/ *noun.* **L16.**
[French *oculiste*, formed as prec.: see -IST.]
1 A specialist or expert in the treatment of eye disorders and defects; an ophthalmologist; an optician. **L16.**
†**2** A sharp-eyed or observant person. *rare.* **M17–M19.**
Comb.: **oculist's stamp**, **oculist-stamp** = ***medicine seal*** s.v. MEDICINE *noun*[1].
■ **oculism** *noun* (*rare*) (*a*) the business of an oculist; (*b*) knowledge of defects and disorders of the eye: **E20.** **ocuˈlistic** *adjective* of or pertaining to an oculist; practising as an oculist: **M19.**

oculo- /ˈɒkjʊləʊ/ *combining form.*
[from Latin *oculus* eye: see -O-.]
Of or pertaining to the eye or visual sense.
■ **oculo-aˈgravic** *adjective* designating an illusion of upward movement of objects in the visual field, experienced when the net force acting on a person is reduced **M20.** **oculoˈgravic** *adjective* designating an illusion of apparent tilting experienced when a person undergoes acceleration that changes the direction of the net force acting on him or her **M20.** **oculoˈgyral** *adjective* designating an illusion of apparent rotation experienced during or just after rotational acceleration of the body **M20.** **oculoˈgyric** *adjective* relating to or involving the turning of the eyeball in its socket; ***oculogyric crisis***, an attack during which the eyeball becomes fixed in an extreme position: **E20.** **oculoˈmotor** *adjective & noun* (*a*) *adjective* of or pertaining to motion of the eye; *spec.* designating or pertaining to the third pair of cranial nerves, which supply most of the muscles around and within the eyeballs; (*b*) *noun* either of the oculomotor nerves: **L19.** **oculoˈnasal** *adjective* relating to the eye and the nose **L19.**

oculus /ˈɒkjʊləs/ *noun.* Pl. **-li** /-lʌɪ, -liː/. **LME.**
[Latin = eye.]
†**1** ***oculus Christi*** [lit. 'of Christ'], wild clary, *Salvia verbenaca*, a plant reputed to be good for the eyes. **LME–M17.**
†**2** ***oculus mundi*** [lit. 'of the world'], = HYDROPHANE. **L17–L18.**
3 *ZOOLOGY* & *BOTANY.* An eye, *esp.* a compound eye; a structure or marking resembling an eye. *rare.* **E18.**
4 *ARCHITECTURE.* A round or eyelike opening or design; *spec.* a circular window (esp. in a church); the central boss of a volute; an opening at the apex of a dome. **M19.**

OD *abbreviation.*
1 Ordnance datum.
2 Overdose; (as a verb) take an overdose (esp. in ***OD'd***, overdosed, dead of an overdose). Chiefly *N. Amer. slang.*

od /ɒd/ *noun*[1]. Now *arch.* & *dial.* Also **'od.** **L16.**
[Alt. of GOD *noun*: cf. AGAD, GAD *noun*[2], GAWD.]
God: chiefly as interjection & in exclamatory phrs. corresp. to those s.v. GOD *noun* 5.
ods bodikins, ***odso***, ***odzooks***, etc.

od /ɒd, əʊd/ *noun*[2]. *obsolete* exc. *Hist.* **M19.**
[Arbitrary formation, intended also as a word-forming elem.]
A hypothetical force proposed by Baron von Reichenbach (1788–1869) as pervading all nature, being manifest in certain people of sensitive temperament and accounting for the phenomena of mesmerism and animal magnetism. Also ***od force***. Also called ***odyl***.

o.d. *abbreviation.*
Outer diameter.

oda /ˈəʊdə/ *noun.* **E17.**
[Turkish *oda* chamber, hall.]
A chamber, a room, *spec.* in a harem.

odal *noun* var. of **UDAL.**

odalisque /ˈəʊd(ə)lɪsk/ *noun.* **L17.**
[French from Turkish *ödalık*, formed as **ODA** + *lık* suffix expr. function.]
A female slave or concubine in an Eastern harem, esp. in the seraglio of the Sultan of Turkey (now *Hist.*); *transf.* an exotic sexually attractive woman.

ODC *abbreviation.*
Order of Discalced Carmelites.

odd /ɒd/ *adjective, noun, & adverb.* **ME.**
[from Old Norse *odda-* in *odda-maðr* third or odd man who gives a casting vote, from *oddi* point, angle. Cf. **ODDS** *noun.*]
▶ **A** *adjective.* **I 1** Remaining over after division into pairs or equal parts; that is one in addition to a pair. **ME.**
2 Of a whole number: having one left over as remainder when divided by two. Of a thing in a series: numbered with or known by such a number. Opp. ***even***. **LME.** ▸**b** *MATH.* Of a function of one variable: having the property that changing the sign of the argument changes the sign, but not the magnitude, of the function (i.e. $f(-x) = -f(x)$). **L19.** ▸**c** *PHYSICS.* Having odd parity. **M20.**
3 Forming indefinite compound cardinal numerals or quantifiers with multiples of ten or similar units (as ***dozen***): somewhat more than (the preceding number). Also ***and odd***. **LME.**
4 Of a surplus over a definite sum: by which a given sum of money, weight, etc., is slightly exceeded. **LME.**

> 🕮 **1** D. BAGLEY I was invited as a makeweight for the odd girl. **2** SHAKES. *Merry W.* This is the third time; I hope good luck lies in odd numbers. **3** M. ARNOLD The eighty and odd pigeons. W. SHEED Forty-odd years before. **4** ADDISON Two hundred Pounds Five Shillings, and a few odd Pence.

▶ **II 5** That exists or stands alone; single, solitary. Now *dial.* **ME.**
†**6** Distinguished; unique, remarkable; renowned. **LME–L17.**
†**7** Not level or aligned, uneven; diverse, different. **LME–L16.** ▸**b** *fig.* At variance or strife (*with*). **M16–E17.**
8 Not regulated, connected, or planned; occasional, irregular, casual; occurring randomly or haphazardly. **LME.** ▸**b** Of a place: out of the way; secluded. Now chiefly in ***odd corner***. **L16.** ▸†**c** Extra; given over and above. Only in **E17.** ▸**d** Forming part of an incomplete pair or set; that does not match with other garments etc. **M18.**
9 Different from what is expected or usual; strange, extraordinary, unusual; eccentric, bizarre, peculiar; unexpected, surprising. **L16.**

> 🕮 **8** S. RADLEY He didn't . . drink . . more than the odd pint. M. COREN He still wrote in . . the odd moments . . left free. **b** TENNYSON From some odd corner of the brain. **d** H. MAYHEW Odd numbers of periodicals and broadsheets. P. CAREY He . . sat down . . to reveal footballer's legs and odd socks. **9** R. L. STEVENSON A marshy tract . . of . . odd, outlandish, swampy trees. T. HARDY Modern attire looking . . odd where everything else was old-fashioned. I. ORIGO It is odd how used one can become to uncertainty.

▶ **B** *noun.* **1** An odd number; an odd or extra person or thing. Long *rare* or *obsolete*. **LME.**
2 A surplus over a definite sum; the amount by which a given sum of money, weight, etc., is slightly exceeded. Also in indefinite numerals and quantifiers: see sense A.3 above. **LME.**
3 *GOLF.* A handicap of one stroke at each hole (now *rare*). Also, a stroke which makes a player's total for the hole one more than the opponent's (cf. **LIKE** *noun*[2] 5). **M19.**

> 🕮 **1 odd and even, odd or even** a children's game in which a player has to guess at the number of objects held in another player's closed hand. **2** T. HOOD His death . . At forty-odd befell.

Special collocations & comb.: **oddball** *noun & adjective* (*colloq.* orig. *US*) (*a*) *noun* an eccentric or odd person; (*b*) *adjective* eccentric, peculiar. **odd bod** *slang* a strange or eccentric person. **odd-come-short** *arch.* (*a*) a remnant, a remainder (orig. of cloth); (*b*) in *pl.*, odds and ends. **odd-come-shortly** *arch.* some day or other in the near future. **odd-even** *adjective* (*NUCLEAR PHYSICS*) (*a*) pertaining to nuclei of odd and those of even mass number; (*b*) designating nuclei containing an odd number of protons and an even number of neutrons. **Oddfellow** a member of a social and charitable society or fraternity, resembling the Freemasons, founded in the 18th cent. **Oddfellowship** the status of an Oddfellow; the principles and organization of the Oddfellows. **odd job** a casual isolated piece of (esp. domestic or routine) work; ***odd job man***, a person who does odd jobs. **odd jobber** = ***odd job man*** above. **odd lot** an incomplete set or random mixture (of goods). **odd-lot** *adjective* (*STOCK EXCHANGE*) involving a number of shares smaller than is normally dealt in. **odd man** the person in an odd-numbered group able to give the casting vote; ***odd man out***, a method of selecting one person from a group of three or more, e.g. by tossing a coin; a person or thing differing from all others of a group in some respect. **odd-odd** *adjective* (*NUCLEAR PHYSICS*) (*a*) pertaining to nuclei of odd mass number only; (*b*) designating nuclei containing odd numbers of protons and neutrons. ***odd parity***: see **PARITY** *noun*[1] 3d. **odd-pinnate** *adjective* (*BOTANY*) (of a leaf) pinnate with an odd terminal leaflet. **oddside** *FOUNDING* a temporary cope in which part of a pattern is bedded while the final mould is made of the upper, exposed portion. **odd-toed** *adjective* having an odd number of toes. **odd trick** *CARDS* in whist, the thirteenth trick, won by one side after each side has won six; in bridge, each trick after six won by the declarer.
▶ **C** *adverb.* In an odd manner, oddly. Now *non-standard.* **LME.**
■ **oddish** *adjective* **E18.** **oddly** *adverb* in an odd manner; strangely, unusually; surprisingly: **LME.** **oddness** *noun* the quality or fact of being odd; something odd, a discrepancy, a peculiarity: **LME.**

Oddi /ˈɒdi/ *noun.* **E20.**
[Ruggero *Oddi* (1864–1913), Italian physician.]
ANATOMY. ***Oddi's sphincter***, ***sphincter of Oddi***, the sphincter which controls the flow of fluids into the duodenum through the united biliary and pancreatic duct.

odditorium /ɒdɪˈtɔːrɪəm/ *noun.* **E20.**
[from next + **-ORIUM.**]
A shop or venue for the display or sale of oddities or oddments.

oddity /ˈɒdɪti/ *noun.* **L16.**
[from **ODD** *adjective* + **-ITY.**]
1 a An odd or peculiar thing; a strange event. **L16.** ▸**b** An odd or peculiar person. **M18.**
2 An odd characteristic or trait, a peculiarity. **E18.**
3 The quality or character of being odd or peculiar; peculiarity, strangeness. **M18.**

> 🕮 **2** W. MARCH Always . . something strange about the child, but they . . ignored her oddities. **3** SIR W. SCOTT Such oddity of gestures . . befitted their bizarre . . appearance.

oddling /ˈɒdlɪŋ/ *noun.* Chiefly *dial.* **M19.**
[from **ODD** *adjective* + **-LING**[1].]
An oddment, a remnant. Usu. in *pl.*

oddment /ˈɒdm(ə)nt/ *noun.* **L18.**
[from **ODD** *adjective* + **-MENT**, after *fragment*.]
1 An odd or extra article, a fragment, a remnant. In *pl.* also, odds and ends, miscellaneous articles, *esp.* those offered for sale from broken or incomplete sets. **L18.**
2 *PRINTING.* In *pl.* The parts of a book other than the main text, as the title page, preface, etc. **L19.**

> 🕮 **1** G. LORD Inside . . were penknives . . and other oddments that might come in handy. I. MURDOCH A clean neat room with oddments of furniture. K. MOORE Separate heaps of oddments: one for . . jumble, one for Oxfam.

odds /ɒdz/ *noun pl.* (occas. treated as *sing.*). **E16.**
[App. pl. of **ODD** *noun.* Cf. **NEWS** *noun.*]
1 Unequal matters or conditions, inequalities. Freq. in ***make odds even***. **E16.**
2 a Items additional to and slightly in excess of a given number or amount; something over, a surplus. Chiefly in ***some odds***. *Scot.* **E16.** ▸**b** ***odds and ends***, also (*colloq.*) ***odds and bobs***, ***odds and sods***, miscellaneous articles or remnants, oddments. **M18.**
3 a Disparity in number, amount, or quality; inequality; amount of disparity or difference. Now *rare.* **M16.** ▸**b** Difference in advantage, effect, or significance. Now chiefly in ***what's the odds?***, ***it makes no odds*** below. **M17.**
4 Conflict, variance, strife. Now chiefly in ***at odds*** below. **L16.**
5 a Difference in favour of one of two contending parties; balance of advantage. **L16.** ▸†**b** Superior position, advantage. **L16–M18.** ▸**c** Equalizing advantage given to a weaker side or competitor. **L16.**
6 The ratio between the amounts staked by the parties in a bet, based on the expected probability either way; *transf.* the chances or balance of probability in favour of something happening or being the case. **L16.**

> 🕮 **2b** DICKENS Odds and ends of spoiled goods. **4** R. PARK Mrs. Pond's tirade, so much at odds with her demure . . gestures. **5a** T. MEDWIN The odds were now greatly in their favour. L. APPIGNANESI Against all the odds . . she managed to get a permit. **6** C. J. LEVER The odds are he'd pull me up . . for doing so. J. BUCHAN The odds were a thousand to one that I might have missed it. *Times* The Commons' bookie . . offers odds of 7–4 against her still being prime minister by . . next year.

Phrases: **ask no odds** *US* desire no advantage, seek no favour. **at odds** in conflict or at variance (*with*). **by all odds** *US* by far. ***fixed odds***: see **FIXED** *adjective*. **give odds, lay odds** offer a bet with odds favourable to the other better. **it makes no odds** *colloq.* it does not matter. ***lay odds***: see ***give odds*** above. ***long odds***: see **LONG** *adjective*[1]. ***odds and bobs***, ***odds and ends***, ***odds and sods***: see sense 2b above. **over the odds** past the limit, above a generally agreed or usual rate. **shout the odds** talk loudly and opinionatedly; boast; complain. ***stack the odds against***: see **STACK** *verb*. **take odds** accept a bet; offer a bet with odds unfavourable to the other better. **what's the odds?** *colloq.* what does it matter?
Comb.: **oddsmaker** *N. Amer.* a person who calculates or predicts the outcome of a contest, race, etc., and sets betting odds; **odds-on** *adjective* rated at odds of better than 1:1 to win; very likely to succeed or happen.
¶ Before **19** usu. treated as *sing.*

odds /ɒdz/ *verb trans.* **M19.**
[from the noun.]
1 Make different, alter; balance. *dial.* **M19.**
2 Elude, evade. *slang.* **M20.**

ode /əʊd/ *noun.* **L16.**
[French from Latin *oda*, *ode* from Greek *ōidē* Attic form of *aoidē* song, singing, from *aeidein* sing.]
1 Orig., a poem intended or adapted to be sung. Now, a lyric poem, usu. rhymed and in the form of an address, in varied or irregular metre and of moderate length. **L16.**
2 *GREEK ORTHODOX CHURCH.* Each of the nine Scripture canticles; each song or hymn of the canon. **L19.**
1 Choral Ode a song of the chorus in a Greek play etc.
■ **odelet** *noun* a short or little ode **L16.** **odeling** *noun* (*rare*) = **ODELET L18.** **odist** *noun* (*rare*) a writer of an ode **L18.**

-ode /əʊd/ *suffix*[1].
[Repr. mod. Latin *-odium* or its source Greek *-ōdēs*, *-ōdes* adjective ending, contr. of *-oeidēs*: see **-OID.**]
In nouns adopted from Greek or mod. Latin and in English words modelled on these, with the sense 'something of the nature of', as ***cestode***, ***geode***, ***phyllode***, etc.

-ode /əʊd/ *suffix*[2].
[Greek *hodos* way, path; partly extracted from **ANODE.**]
Forming nouns and corresp. adjectives with the sense 'way, pathway', as ***centrode***; *esp.* forming names of thermionic valves with a specified number of electrodes, as ***diode***, ***triode***, ***tetrode***, etc.

odea *noun pl.* see **ODEUM.**

odeon /ˈəʊdɪən/ *noun.* In sense 1 also now **odeion** /əʊˈdʌɪən/. **M19.**
[Greek *ōideion*: see **ODEUM.**]
1 = **ODEUM. M19.**
2 (**O-**.) Any of numerous large lavish cinemas in a chain built in the 1930s; *gen.* a cinema, *esp.* one resembling these. **M20.**

odeum /ˈəʊdɪəm/ *noun.* Pl. **odeums**, **odea** /ˈəʊdɪə/. **E17.**
[French *odéum* or Latin *odeum* from Greek *ōideion* from *ōidē*: see **ODE.**]
A building for the performance of vocal and instrumental music, esp. among the ancient Greeks and Romans.

odic /ˈəʊdɪk/ *adjective*[1]. *rare.* **M19.**
[from **ODE** + **-IC.**]
Of the nature of or pertaining to an ode.

odic /ˈɒdɪk, ˈəʊdɪk/ *adjective*[2]. Now *rare* or *obsolete.* **M19.**
[from **OD** *noun*[2] + **-IC.**]
Of or pertaining to the hypothetical force called od.

odiferous /əʊˈdɪf(ə)rəs/ *adjective.* **L15.**
[Contr.]
= **ODORIFEROUS.**

Odinism /ˈəʊdɪnɪz(ə)m/ *noun.* **E19.**
[from *Odin* (see below) + **-ISM.**]
The worship of Odin, in Scandinavian mythology the supreme god and creator, god of victory and of the dead; the mythology and religious doctrine of the ancient Scandinavians.
■ **Oˈdinic** *adjective* of or pertaining to Odin or Odinism **M19.** **Odinist** *adjective & noun* (*a*) *adjective* = **ODINIC**; (*b*) *noun* a worshipper of Odin; a student or follower of Odinism: **M19.** **Odiˈnitic** *adjective* (*rare*) = **ODINIC L19.**

odious /ˈəʊdɪəs/ *adjective.* **LME.**
[Old French *odious*, *odieus* (mod. *odieux*) from Latin *odiosus*, formed as **ODIUM**: see **-OUS.**]
Deserving of or causing hatred or repugnance; hateful, offensive, repugnant.

> 🕮 E. BOWEN To disoblige any friend of the family was odious to her. A. G. GARDINER The slum-owner, . . the profiteer, and all the odious people . . exploiting others. A. PRYCE-JONES I was an odious child.

■ **odiously** *adverb* **LME.** **odiousness** *noun* **L15.**

Odissi *noun* var. of **ORISSI.**

odium /ˈəʊdɪəm/ *noun.* **E17.**
[Latin = hatred, from *odi* I hate.]
The fact or state of being hated; general or widespread unpopularity or opprobrium.

> 🕮 J. A. FROUDE On him had fallen the odium of the proscription. A. FRASER He incurred a great deal of odium. **odium theologicum** /θɪəˈlɒdʒɪkəm/ [mod. Latin] the hatred which proverbially characterizes theological disputes.

odometer /əʊˈdɒmɪtə/ *noun.* Also **ho-** /hɒʊ-/. **L18.**
[French *odomètre*, or from Greek *hodos* way + **-METER.**]
An instrument for measuring the distance travelled by a wheeled vehicle; a milometer. Also, an instrument for measuring distances in surveying.

-odon /ədɒn/ *suffix.*
[from Greek *odōn* Ionic var. of *odous, odont-* tooth.]
ZOOLOGY & PALAEONTOLOGY. Forming names of animals, chiefly after mod. Latin genus names, indicating some characteristic of the teeth, as ***iguanodon***, ***mastodon***, ***solenodon***, etc. Cf. -ODONT.

odonate /ˈəʊdəneɪt/ *adjective & noun.* E20.
[mod. Latin *Odonata* (see below), irreg. from Greek *odōn* var. of *odous, odont-* tooth (with ref. to the insect's mandibles): see -ATE².]
ENTOMOLOGY. ▶**A** *adjective.* Of, pertaining to, or characteristic of (an insect of) the order Odonata, which includes dragonflies and damselflies. E20.
▶**B** *noun.* An odonate insect; a dragonfly, a damselfly. E20.

odont- *combining form* see ODONTO-.

-odont /ədɒnt/ *suffix.*
[from Greek *odont-, odous* tooth.]
ZOOLOGY & PALAEONTOLOGY. Forming adjectives and corresp. nouns indicating some characteristic of the teeth or toothlike formations, as ***conodont***, ***diprotodont***, ***labyrinthodont***, etc. Cf. -ODON, ODONTO-.

odontalgia /ɒdɒnˈtaldʒə, -dʒɪə/ *noun.* Also Anglicized as **-gy** /-dʒi/. M17.
[Greek, formed as ODONTO- + -ALGIA.]
Toothache.
■ **odontalgic** *adjective & noun* (**a**) *adjective* of or pertaining to toothache; (**b**) *noun* a medicine for toothache: E18.

odonto- /ɒˈdɒntəʊ/ *combining form.* Before a vowel also **odont-**. L19.
[from Greek *odont-, odous* tooth: see -O-.]
Of or pertaining to a tooth or teeth.
■ **odontoblast** *noun* a cell in the pulp of a tooth that produces dentine, a tooth-forming cell L19. **odontoˈblastic** *adjective* of or pertaining to odontoblasts L19. **odontocete** /-siːt/ *adjective & noun* (**a**) *adjective* of or designating a cetacean having teeth rather than whalebone; (**b**) *noun* a toothed whale: L19. **odontoˈgenic** *adjective* of or pertaining to the origin and development of teeth L19. **odonˈtogeny** *noun* the generation and development of teeth M19.

odontoglossum /ədɒntəˈglɒsəm/ *noun.* M19.
[mod. Latin (see below), formed as ODONTO- + Greek *glōssa* tongue.]
BOTANY. Any of various American tropical epiphytic orchids constituting the genus *Odontoglossum*, much grown for their flowers.

odontoid /əˈdɒntɔɪd/ *adjective & noun.* E19.
[Greek *odontoeidēs*, formed as ODONTO- + -OID.]
▶**A** *adjective.* Resembling or having the form of a tooth; toothlike. Also, of or associated with the odontoid process. E19.
odontoid process a toothlike projection on the axis or second cervical vertebra of mammals and some other vertebrates, formed by fusion with the centrum of the atlas vertebra.
▶**B** *noun.* A toothlike structure; *spec.* the odontoid process. M19.

odontology /ɒdɒnˈtɒlədʒi/ *noun.* E19.
[from ODONTO- + -LOGY.]
The branch of anatomy that deals with the structure and development of teeth.
■ **odontoˈlogical** *adjective* pertaining to teeth or to odontology M19. **odontologist** *noun* L18.

odontome /əˈdɒntəʊm/ *noun.* Also **odontoma** /əʊdɒnˈtəʊmə/, pl. **-mas**, **-mata** /-mətə/. L19.
[French, formed as ODONTO- + -OME, -OMA.]
MEDICINE. A small growth of abnormal calcified dental tissue.

odontophore /əˈdɒntəfɔː/ *noun.* L19.
[from Greek *odontophoros* bearing teeth, formed as ODONTO- + -PHORE.]
ZOOLOGY. An organ bearing teeth; *spec.* a cartilaginous projection in the mouth of a mollusc on which the radula is supported; occas., the radula itself.
■ **odonˈtophoral** *adjective* of or pertaining to an odontophore L19. **odonˈtophorous** *adjective* tooth-bearing; having an odontophore: L19.

odoom *noun* var. of ODUM.

odor *noun* see ODOUR.

odorant /ˈəʊd(ə)r(ə)nt/ *adjective & noun.* LME.
[Old & mod. French, pres. pple of *odorer* from Latin *odorare* give a smell or fragrance to, from *odor*: see ODOUR, -ANT¹.]
▶**A** *adjective.* Odorous, odoriferous. Now *rare.* LME.
▶**B** *noun.* An odoriferous substance, *spec.* one used to give a particular scent or odour to a product. M20.

odorate /ˈəʊd(ə)rət/ *adjective.* Now *rare.* LME.
[Latin *odoratus* pa. pple of *odorare*: see prec., -ATE².]
Scented, fragrant.

odoriferant /əʊdəˈrɪf(ə)r(ə)nt/ *adjective.* Now *rare.* M16.
[French *odoriférant* pres. pple of *odoriférer*, formed as next: see -ANT¹.]
Odoriferous, odorous.

odoriferous /əʊdəˈrɪf(ə)rəs/ *adjective.* LME.
[from Latin *odorifer* (from *odor* ODOUR) + -OUS: see -FEROUS.]
Having or emitting a (pleasant or unpleasant) scent or odour; odorous; fragrant.
■ **odoriferously** *adverb* E17. **odoriferousness** *noun* L16.

odorimeter /əʊdəˈrɪmɪtə/ *noun.* L19.
[from Latin *odori-*, *odor* ODOUR + -METER.]
An instrument for measuring the intensity of odours.
■ **odoriˈmetric** *adjective* E20. **odorimetry** *noun* the measurement of the intensity of odours L19.

odoriphore /ˈəʊd(ə)rɪˌfɔː/ *noun.* E20.
[formed as prec. + -PHORE.]
= OSMOPHORE 1.
■ **odoriˈphoric** *adjective* M20.

odorise *verb* var. of ODORIZE.

odorivector /ˈəʊd(ə)rɪvɛktə/ *noun.* E20.
[from Latin *odori-*, *odor* ODOUR + VECTOR *noun*.]
Any substance the molecules of which stimulate the olfactory system.

odorize /ˈəʊdərʌɪz/ *verb trans. rare.* Also **-ise**. L19.
[from Latin *odor* ODOUR + -IZE.]
Give a scent or odour to; make fragrant.

odorous /ˈəʊd(ə)rəs/ *adjective.* LME.
[from Latin *odorus* fragrant (from *odor* ODOUR) + -OUS.]
Having or emitting a smell or scent; odoriferous, scented, fragrant; malodorous.

> 📖 SHAKES. *Mids. N. D.* An odorous chaplet of sweet summer buds. P. H. JOHNSON A street of boarding-houses odorous with meals to come.

■ **odoˈrosity** *noun* (*rare*) odorousness M19. **odorously** *adverb* M19. **odorousness** *noun* E18.

odour /ˈəʊdə/ *noun.* Also ***odor**. ME.
[Anglo-Norman, Old French *odor*, *odur* (mod. *odeur*) from Latin *odor* smell, scent.]
1 The property of a substance that is perceptible by the sense of smell; a scent, a smell. ME.
2 a A pervasive quality or trace attaching to something. ME. ▸**b** Good or bad repute, regard, or estimation. E19.
3 A thing or substance emitting a sweet smell or scent; a perfume. Now *rare* or *obsolete.* LME.

> 📖 **1** E. F. BENSON The odour of the flower-beds and the smell of the dewy grass. A. GIBBS A strong odour of paper and printers' ink. **odour of sanctity** [French *odeur de sainteté*] a sweet or balsamic odour reputedly emitted by the bodies of saints at or after death; *fig.* a state of holiness or saintliness; *joc. & derog.* sanctimoniousness. **2a** J. H. BURTON No odour of religious intolerance attaches to it. **b** N. MITFORD St. Germain fell into bad odour with the police.

Comb.: **odour-blindness** an inability to perceive a particular smell or range of smells.
■ **odoured** *adjective* having an odour or scent (of a specified kind) LME. **odourful** *adjective* = ODOROUS L19. **odourless** *adjective* M19. **odourlessness** *noun* L19.

†**odso** *interjection.* L17–M19.
[from OD *noun*¹ + GAD)SO.]
Expr. surprise or asseveration.

odum /əʊˈduːm/ *noun.* Also ***odoom***. L19.
[Twi *o-dom.*]
In Ghana, (the wood of) the iroko *Chlorophora excelsa.*

odyl /ˈəʊdɪl, ˈɒdɪl/ *noun. obsolete* exc. *Hist.* Also **-yle**. M19.
[from OD *noun*² + Greek *hulē* material: see -YL.]
= OD *noun*².
■ **oˈdylic** *adjective* M19.

odynometer /ɒdɪˈnɒmɪtə/ *noun. rare.* L19.
[from Greek *odunē* pain + -OMETER.]
An instrument for measuring pain.
■ **odynoˈmetrical** *adjective* of or pertaining to the measurement of pain L19.

odynophagia /ˌɒdɪnəˈfeɪdʒɪə, -dʒə/ *noun.* Also (earlier) **odynphagia** /ɒdɪnˈfeɪdʒɪə, -dʒə/. L19.
[from Greek *odunē* pain + -PHAGIA.]
MEDICINE. Pain behind the sternum during swallowing, esp. as a symptom of oesophagitis.

odyssey /ˈɒdɪsi/ *noun.* L19.
[Title of a Greek epic poem attributed to Homer, describing the adventures of Odysseus (Ulysses) on his way home to Ithaca after the fall of Troy, from Latin *Odyssea* from Greek *Odusseia* from *Odusseus* Odysseus.]
A long series of wanderings, a long adventurous journey; *fig.* an extended process of development or change.

> 📖 *Observer* A day-long odyssey . . began when the aircraft . . stopped for re-fuelling at Dubrovnik . . Palermo . . and Cagliari. A. C. CLARKE The four-billion-year odyssey from amoeba to Man.

■ **Odyssean** /ɒdɪˈsiːən/ *adjective* of or pertaining to the Odyssey; of the nature of an odyssey: E18.

Œ, œ
A ligature. (Orig. and now usu. (and in this dictionary) written as a digraph *oe*.)
1 In Old English, the symbol of a simple vowel (short and long) intermediate between *o* and *e*, in early Middle English replaced by *e*.
2 In mod. English reproduces usual Latin spelling of Greek *oi*, which was often treated in medieval Latin and Proto-Romance like simple long *e*. When thoroughly Anglicized and popularized this becomes *e*, *oe* being retained only in some Greek and Latin proper names, terms of Greek and Roman antiquity, and some scientific and techn. terms (where, however, *e* is usual in the US).

OE *abbreviation.*
Old English.

oe /ɔɪ, ˈəʊi/ *noun. Scot.* (now *dial.*). Also **oy**. LME.
[Gaelic *ogha*, *odha* = Old Irish *aue*, *úa* descendant, grandson. Cf. O' *noun.*]
1 A grandchild. LME.
2 A nephew. Formerly also, a niece. Now *rare* or *obsolete.* L16.

OECD *abbreviation.*
Organization for Economic Cooperation and Development.

oecist /ˈiːsɪst, ˈiːkɪst/ *noun.* Also **oek-** /ˈiːk-/, **oik-** /ˈiːk-, ˈɔɪk-/. M19.
[Greek *oikistēs*, from *oikizein*: see EKISTICS, -IST.]
In ancient Greece, the founder of a colony.

†**oecological** *adjective*, **oecology** *noun* vars. of ECOLOGICAL, ECOLOGY.

oeconomi *noun pl.* see OECONOMUS.

†**oeconomic**, **oeconomical** *adjectives*, **oeconomics** *noun* see ECONOMIC etc.

oeconomus /ɪˈkɒnəməs/ *noun.* Pl. **-muses**, **-mi** /-mʌɪ, -miː/. M16.
[Latin from Greek *oikonomos*: see ECONOMY.]
Hist. The steward or manager of the temporalities of a religious foundation or society; the steward of a college.

oecumene /ɪˈkjuːməni/ *noun.* Also **oik(o)u-** /*also* ɔɪˈkjuː-/. E20.
[Greek *oikoumenē*: see ECUMENICAL.]
The inhabited world as known to a particular civilization, *spec.* the ancient Greeks; the Greeks and their neighbours regarded in the context of development in human society.

oecumenical *adjective* see ECUMENICAL.

OED *abbreviation.*
Oxford English Dictionary.

oedema /ɪˈdiːmə/ *noun.* Also ***edema**. Pl. **-mata** /-mətə/, **-mas**. LME.
[Late Latin from Greek *oidēma*, from *oidein* swell.]
MEDICINE. (A) local or general swelling produced by the accumulation of fluid in the body tissues or cavities; dropsy.
■ **oedeˈmatic** *adjective* (now *rare* or *obsolete*) oedematous M17. **oedematose** /ɪˈdiːmətəʊs, ɪˈdɛm-/ *adjective* oedematous E18. **oedematous** /ɪˈdiːmətəs, ɪˈdɛm-/ *adjective* pertaining to or of the nature of oedema; affected with oedema, dropsical: M17. **oedematously** /ɪˈdiːm-, ɪˈdɛm-/ *adverb* L18.

Oedipal /ˈiːdɪp(ə)l/ *adjective.* Also **oe-**, ***Ed-** /ˈɛd-/. M20.
[from next + -AL¹.]
PSYCHOANALYSIS. Characterized by an Oedipus complex; of or pertaining to subconscious sexual desire felt by a child for a parent of the opposite sex, and conflict with the parent of the same sex.

> 📖 *New Left Review* They interpreted the assassination in Oedipal terms, Trotsky being . . the hated father-substitute.

Oedipus /ˈiːdɪpəs/ *noun.* M16.
[Greek *Oidipous*, *-pod-* a legendary Theban king who solved the riddle of the Sphinx and unknowingly killed his father and married his mother.]
1 A person clever at guessing riddles. M16.
2 PSYCHOANALYSIS. Used ***attrib.*** with ref. to the use by Freud of the Oedipus legend to exemplify desires felt for the parent of the opposite sex by a child at an early stage of sexual development. Chiefly in ***Oedipus complex***, a complex of emotions aroused in a young (esp. male) child by a subconscious sexual desire for the parent of the opposite sex and a fear of the jealousy of the parent of the same sex. Cf. ELECTRA. E20.
3 ***Oedipus effect***, the influence of a prediction on the predicted event. M20.
■ **Oediˈpean** *adjective* pertaining to or reminiscent of the legend of Oedipus; Oedipal; clever at guessing a riddle: E17. **Oedipoˈdean** *adjective* = OEDIPEAN M20.

oedometer /ɪˈdɒmɪtə/ *noun.* E20.
[from Greek *oidein* swell + -OMETER.]
A device for measuring the swelling of a gel when water is absorbed, or the compressibility of soil.

OEEC *abbreviation.*
Hist. Organization for European Economic Cooperation.

oeil-de-boeuf /œjdəbœf/ *noun.* Pl. **oeils-de-boeuf** (pronounced same). M18.
[French, lit. 'ox-eye'.]
1 A small round window. Cf. BULL'S-EYE 3. M18.
2 A small vestibule or antechamber in a palace (*spec.* one in Versailles lighted by a small round window); *transf.* (a part of) a monarch's court. L18.

oeil-de-perdrix /œjdəpɛrdri/ *noun.* M19.
[French, lit. 'partridge-eye'.]
1 In French pottery and porcelain, a design of dotted circles, usu. on a coloured background, freq. used on Sèvres porcelain. Also **oeil-de-perdrix pattern** etc. M19. ▸**b** A similar design used as a ground in lace-making. L19.
2 In full **oeil-de-perdrix wine**, **oeil-de-perdrix champagne**. Pink or pale red wine or champagne. L19.

oeillade /œjad/ *noun. arch.* Pl. pronounced same. L16.
[French, from *oeil* eye after Italian *occhiata*, from *occhio* eye: see -ADE.]
A glance of the eye, *esp.* an amorous one; an ogle.
¶ Formerly naturalized.

oeils-de-boeuf *noun* pl. of OEIL-DE-BOEUF.

oekist *noun* var. of OECIST.

OEM *abbreviation.*
Original equipment manufacturer.

oenanthic /iːˈnanθɪk/ *adjective.* Also **en-**. M19.
[from Latin *oenanthe* from Greek *oinanthē* vine-shoot, vine-blossom (from *oinē* vine + *anthē* blossom): see -IC.]
CHEMISTRY. Containing the unbranched heptyl radical, C_7H_{15}·; heptanoic.
oenanthic ether a heptyl ether which gives to wine its characteristic odour.
■ **oenanthol** *noun* a simple aldehyde, $C_6H_{13}CHO$, used in perfumery M19.

oeno- /ˈiːnəʊ/ *combining form* of Greek *oinos* wine: see -O-. Also **oino-** /ˈiːnəʊ, ˈɔɪnəʊ/, ***eno-**.
■ **oenocyte** *noun* (*ZOOLOGY*) a large apparently secretory cell in insects, usu. occurring in groups associated with the epidermis or the fat-body L19. **oeˈnology** *noun* the knowledge or study of wines E19. **oenoˈlogical** *adjective* of or pertaining to oeonology E19. **oeˈnologist** *noun* an expert in or connoisseur of wines M19. **oenomancy** *noun* divination by means of wine M17. **oenoˈmania** *noun* (*a*) a mania or craving for wine or other alcoholic drink; (*b*) mania resulting from intoxication, delirium tremens: L19. **oenoˈmaniac** *noun* a person affected with oenomania M19. **oenophile** *noun* a lover of wine, an oenologist M20. **oenoˈphilic** *adjective* loving wine, of or pertaining to an oenophile or oenophiles M20. **oeˈnophilist** *noun* = OENOPHILE M19.

oenochoe /iːˈnɒkəʊi/ *noun.* Also **oi-** /iː-, ɔɪ-/. L19.
[Greek *oinokhoē*, formed as OENO- + *khoas*, *khoē* pouring.]
GREEK ANTIQUITIES. A vessel used for ladling wine from a bowl into a cup.

oenomel /ˈiːnəmɛl/ *noun.* Also **oi-** /ˈiː-, ˈɔɪ-/. L16.
[Late Latin *oenomeli*, *-um* from Greek *oinomeli*, formed as OENO- + *meli* honey.]
1 In ancient Greece, a drink made from wine mixed with honey. L16.
2 *fig.* Language, thought, etc., in which strength and sweetness are combined. M19.

oenothera /iːnə(ʊ)ˈθɪərə, ɪˈnɒθ(ə)rə/ *noun.* E17.
[mod. Latin (see below), from Greek *oinothēras* an unknown narcotic plant, lit. 'wine-trap', from *oinos* wine (but prob. a false reading for *onothēras*, from *onos* ass).]
Any plant of the genus *Oenothera*, of the willowherb family, comprising chiefly N. American plants with large, often yellow, flowers.
¶ Those which open in the day are alternatively called **sundrops**, those which open in the evening, **evening primrose**.

OEO *abbreviation. US.*
Office of Economic Opportunity.

OEP *abbreviation. US.*
Office of Economic Preparedness.

o'er *adverb, preposition* see OVER *adverb, preposition.*

Oerlikon /ˈɔːlɪk(ə)n/ *noun.* Also **o-**. M20.
[A suburb of Zurich, the place of manufacture.]
(Proprietary name for) any of various guns and fittings, *spec.* a light anti-aircraft cannon.

oersted /ˈɔːstɛd/ *noun.* L19.
[H. C. *Oersted* (1777–1851), Danish physicist.]
PHYSICS. †**1** A unit of reluctance in the cgs system, defined as one gilbert per maxwell. L19–M20.
2 A unit of magnetic field strength in the cgs system, equal to that produced at a distance of one centimetre by a unit magnetic pole or by a thin straight wire carrying half an electromagnetic unit (five amperes) of current; one maxwell per square centimetre. Cf. GAUSS. M20.

oesophagi *noun pl.* see OESOPHAGUS.

oesophago- /ɪˈsɒfəgəʊ/ *combining form* of OESOPHAGUS: see -O-. Before a vowel also **oesophag-**. Also ***esophag(o)-**.
■ **oesophaˈgectomy** *noun* (an instance of) surgical removal of a part of the oesophagus L19. **oesophagitis** /-ˈdʒʌɪtɪs/ *noun* inflammation of the oesophagus M19. **oesophagocele** *noun* protrusion of the mucous membrane of the oesophagus through an opening in its muscular wall M19. **oesophagoscope** *noun* an instrument for the inspection or treatment of the oesophagus L19. **oesophaˈgostomy** *noun* (an instance of) surgical creation of an opening from the oesophagus to the outside of the neck L19. **oesophaˈgotomy** *noun* (an instance of) surgical incision into the oesophagus M19.

oesophagus /ɪˈsɒfəgəs/ *noun.* Pl. **-guses**, **-gi** /-gʌɪ/. Also ***eso-**. LME.
[medieval Latin *ysophagus*, *iso-* from Greek *oisophagos*, from unkn. 1st elem. + (app.) *-phagos* eating, eater. Current spelling after mod. Latin.]
ANATOMY & ZOOLOGY. The canal (in humans and other vertebrates, a muscular tube) leading from the back of the mouth, through which food and drink pass to the stomach; the gullet.
■ **oesophagal** *adjective* = OESOPHAGEAL L18. **oesophageal** /iːˌsɒfəˈdʒiːəl/ *adjective* of or pertaining to the oesophagus E19.

oestradiol /iːstrəˈdʌɪɒl, ɛstrə-/ *noun.* Also ***estra-**. M20.
[from OESTRANE + DI-[2] + -OL.]
BIOCHEMISTRY. A major oestrogen produced in the ovarian follicles of female mammals.

oestral /ˈiːstr(ə)l, ˈɛstr(ə)l/ *adjective.* Also ***estral**. L19.
[from OESTRUS + -AL[1].]
= OESTROUS.

oestrane /ˈiːstreɪn, ˈɛstreɪn/ *noun.* Also ***estrane**. M20.
[from next + -ANE.]
BIOCHEMISTRY. The parent molecule of most oestrogens, a saturated methylsteroid, $C_{18}H_{30}$.

oestrin /ˈiːstrɪn, ˈɛstrɪn/ *noun.* Also ***estrin**. E20.
[from OESTRUS + -IN[1].]
BIOCHEMISTRY. An oestrogenic substance or material; oestrogen (esp. as formerly considered a single substance).

oestriol /ˈiːstrɪɒl, ˈɛstrɪɒl/ *noun.* Also ***estriol**. M20.
[from OESTRANE + TRI- + -OL.]
BIOCHEMISTRY. An oestrogen which is one of the metabolic products of oestradiol.

oestrogen /ˈiːstrədʒ(ə)n, ˈɛstrə-/ *noun.* Also ***estro-**. E20.
[from OESTRUS + -O- + -GEN.]
PHYSIOLOGY & BIOCHEMISTRY. Any of a number of natural or synthetic substances, mainly steroids, which control sexual development in female mammals, including development of sexual characteristics and maintenance of the menstrual or oestrous cycle, and which may be used to treat menopausal and menstrual disorders and in contraceptives.
■ **oestroˈgenic** *adjective* of the nature of, pertaining to, or acting as an oestrogen M20. **oestroˈgenically** *adverb* as regards oestrogenic properties M20. **oestrogenicity** /-ˈnɪsɪti/ *noun* oestrogenic property M20. **oestrogeniˈzation** *noun* the action or result of treating with oestrogen M20. **oestrogenized** *adjective* treated with oestrogen M20.

oestrone /ˈiːstrəʊn, ˈɛstrəʊn/ *noun.* Also ***estrone**. M20.
[from OESTRANE + -ONE.]
BIOCHEMISTRY. An oestrogen similar to but less potent than oestradiol.

oestrous /ˈiːstrəs, ˈɛstrəs/ *adjective.* Also ***estrous**. E20.
[from OESTRUS + -OUS.]
ZOOLOGY & PHYSIOLOGY. Pertaining to or involving (an) oestrus; menstrual; (of a female animal) on or in heat.
oestrous cycle the cyclic series of physiological changes preceding, including, and following oestrus that takes place in most female mammals and involves esp. the reproductive and endocrine systems.
■ **oestrual** *adjective* [irreg., app. after *menstrual*] pertaining to or affected by (an) oestrus; menstrual; oestrous: M19. **oestruˈation** *noun* the state of being in oestrus M19.

oestrum /ˈiːstrəm, ˈɛstrəm/ *noun.* Also ***estrum**. M17.
[medieval Latin, var. of next.]
1 = OESTRUS 1. M17.
2 = OESTRUS 2. M17.
3 = OESTRUS 3. L18.

oestrus /ˈiːstrəs, ˈɛstrəs/ *noun.* Also ***estrus**. L17.
[Latin from Greek *oistros* gadfly, breeze, sting, frenzy.]
1 A parasitic insect; now *spec.* a biting fly of the genus *Oestrus* or the family Oestridae whose larvae are parasitic on various animals; a botfly. Now chiefly as mod. Latin genus name. L17.
2 *fig.* A sharp stimulus; (a) passion, (a) frenzy. Now *rare.* E19.
3 *ZOOLOGY & PHYSIOLOGY.* (The period of) a female animal's readiness to mate, accompanied by certain physiological changes; the rut, heat. L19.

> 📖 **2** E. FITZGERALD The Impetus, the Lyrical oestrus, is gone.

oeufs en cocotte /øf ɑ̃ kɔkɔt/ *noun phr. pl.* E20.
[French = eggs in a cocotte.]
A French dish of eggs in butter baked and served in individual cocottes or ramekins.

oeuvre /œvr, ˈəːvrə/ *noun.* Pl. pronounced same. L19.
[French = work.]
A work of art, music, literature, etc.; the whole body of work produced by an artist, composer, etc. Cf. CHEF-D'ŒUVRE.

> 📖 R. FRY A general study of Cézanne's oeuvre. **oeuvre de vulgarisation** /də vylgarizasjɔ̃/ [= of popularization] a work attempting to make an academic or esoteric subject accessible to the general public.

of /əv/ *aux. verb. non-standard.* M19.
[Repr. an unstressed pronunc.: cf. A *verb.*]
Have: esp. in compound tenses after another aux. verb, as *could, might, must, would.*

†**of** *adverb* see OFF *adverb* etc.

of /ɒv, *unstressed* (ə)v/ *preposition.*
[Old English *of* (also adverb: treated s.v. OFF *adverb*), orig. unstressed var. of *æf* corresp. to Old Frisian *af, of*, Old Saxon *af*, Middle Low German, Middle Dutch *ave, af*, Old High German *aba* (adverb & preposition), Middle High German *abe, ab* (Dutch *af*, German dial. *ab*), Old Norse *af*, Gothic *af*, from Germanic adverb & preposition from Indo-European, repr. also by Latin *ab*, Greek *apo*, Sanskrit *apa* away from. See also A *preposition*[2], O' *preposition*[2], OB *preposition.*]
▶**I** Of motion, direction, distance.
1 Indicating the thing, place, or direction from which something goes, comes, or is driven or moved, or from which action is directed: from, away from, out of; so as no longer to lie, rest, or lean on. *obsolete* exc. as OFF *preposition* 1 & following and closely connected to an adverb, as **out of**, (now only *poet.*) **forth of**, (now *colloq.* & *dial.*) **off of**. OE.
2 Orig., indicating a point of time (or stage of life, etc.) from which something begins or proceeds: from (now only in **as of**: see AS *adverb* etc.). Now (in **of late**, **of recent years**, **of old**, **of yore**, etc.), indicating a period during which something takes place or obtains: during, in the course of. OE.
†**3** Indicating a situation, condition, or state into or out of which something moves: from, out of. OE–L16.
4 Indicating a point of departure in terms of which some position is defined. Now only following a point of the compass & in **within a mile of**, **within an hour of**, **within an ace of**, etc., **wide of**, (chiefly *N. Amer.*) **back of**, **upwards of** (a number or amount), etc. OE. ▸**b** In expressing the time: from or before (a specified hour), to. *N. Amer.* & *dial.* E19.

> 📖 **1** N. WATTS She took the material off of the wall. **2** SHAKES. *Two Gent.* One that I brought up of a puppy. I. MURDOCH Hugh's relations with his son . . had unaccountably improved of late. **4** *Country Life* About 100 miles south of the western Pyrenees. **b** L. STEWART 'What time is it now?' 'Quarter of six.' A. BEATTIE He told her it was ten of three in the morning.

▶**II 5** Indicating separation or removal of something from an owner or affected person or thing. After (chiefly trans.) verbs, adjectives, & (now *rare*) some verbal nouns and nouns of action. OE.
5 cure of, **cleanse of**, **clear of**, etc.; **bring to bed of**, **deliver of** (a child), **empty of**, **lighten of**, **rid of**, etc.; **deprive of**, **divest of**, **drain of**, **rob of**, **strip of**, etc.; **recover of**, etc.; **whole of** (a wound); **free of**, **pure of**, etc.; **bare of**, **barren of**, **destitute of**, **devoid of**, **void of**, etc.
▶**III** Of origin or source.
6 Indicating a thing, place, or person from which or whom something originates, comes, or is acquired or sought. After certain verbs & verbal derivs., & after a noun (with a pple of such a verb implied or understood). OE.

> 📖 **6** R. BURNS Three noble chieftains, and all of his blood. THACKERAY Of English parents, and of a good English family of clergymen, Swift was born in Dublin. **borrow of**, **buy of**, **receive of**, **win of**, etc.; **take advantage of**, **take leave of**, etc.; **ask of**, **beg of**, **demand of**, **desire of**, **expect of**, **inquire of**, **request of**, **require of**, etc.; **learn of**, **hear of**.

▶**IV** Of the source or starting-point of action, emotion, etc.
7 Indicating the mental or non-material source or spring of action, emotion, etc., or the cause, reason, or ground of an action, occurrence, fact, feeling, etc.: out of, from, as an outcome, expression, or consequence of; because of, on account of. OE.
7 of one's own accord, **of choice**, **of course**, **of necessity**, **of right**, **of one's own free will**, etc.; **die of**, **perish of**, etc.; **savour of**, **smell of**, **taste of**, etc.; **sick of**, **weary of**, etc.; **ashamed of**, **afraid of**, **fearful of**, etc.; **glad of**, **proud of**, **vain of**, etc.
▶**V** Indicating the agent or doer.
8 Introducing the agent after a passive verb (most frequently after pa. pples expressing a continued non-physical action): by. Now *arch.* & *literary.* OE.
9 After a noun, indicating its doer, maker, or author. ME.
10 Indicating the doer of something characterized by an adjective (alone or qualifying a noun) or a pa. pple qualified by an adverb. (Foll. by *to do*, (less frequently) *that he, she*, etc., *did*.) M16.

🕮 **8** AV *Acts* 12:23 Hee was eaten of wormes, and gaue vp the ghost. E. A. FREEMAN Otho was not loved of his kinsfolk. **9** G. GROVE A composition of Haydn's dating about 1785. N. FRYE The tremendous finales of Beethoven. I. MURDOCH Which are the most important plays of Shakespeare? **10** F. W. NEWMAN It was not a proud thing of Paul to say. L. CARROLL It was most absurd of you to offer it! *Listener* It seems . . niggling of Graham Hough to complain. ***bad of, clever of, foolish of, good of, kind of, right of, rude of, silly of, stupid of, wrong of,*** etc.

▸ **VI** Indicating means or instrument.
11 Indicating a thing by means of or with which something is done: with. *obsolete* exc. *dial.* OE.
12 Indicating a substance on which a person, animal, etc., lives or feeds, or a means of sustenance or livelihood: on. *arch.* LME.

▸ **VII 13** Indicating the material or substance of which something is made or consists. After verbs, after a noun (connecting the material immediately with the thing). OE. ▸**b** Indicating former condition from which a transformation has taken place into a specified condition. *arch.* OE.
14 Connecting two nouns of which the former denotes the class of which the latter is a particular example or of which the former is a connotative and the latter a denotative term. OE.
15 Connecting two nouns of which the former is a collective term, a classificatory word, a quantitative or numeral word, or the name of something having component parts, and the latter is the substance or elements of which this consists. ME.
16 Connecting two nouns in sense-apposition: in the form of; *arch.* in the person of, in respect of being, to be, for. ME.

🕮 **13** J. D. CLARK The knife or scraper . . was also made of wood. L. BRUCE Yea, brothers, I was of mortal flesh. V. S. PRITCHETT The headboard was of monumental walnut. ***make a fool of, make much of, make the best of,*** etc. **b** SPENSER Streight of beasts they comely men became. **14 *the city of Rome, the Isle of Wight,*** etc. **15** LD MACAULAY A reward of five hundred pistoles. A. WHITE Any sort of coercion . . makes me feel like an animal in a trap. **16** CHESTERFIELD Allowed to be the best scholar of a gentleman in England. BYRON Juan was quite 'a broth of a boy'.

▸ **VIII 17** Indicating the subject-matter of thought, feeling, or action: concerning, about, with regard to, in reference to. After intrans. verbs & some trans. verbs and their objects, esp. of learning, knowing, thinking, and expressing thought, after adjectives, & *arch.* after nouns OE.

🕮 **17** D. ABSE This Dr Aristotle—everybody has heard of him. W. GOLDING A junior saint of whom next to nothing is known. ***read of, think of, dream of, tell of, write of,*** etc.

▸ **IX 18** Indicating things or a thing of which a part is expressed by the preceding words. Preceded by a word of number or quantity (which may be equal to the whole), by a noun denoting a class (also followed by the same noun in the pl., in intensive phrs., by a superl. or compar. or equivalent, & after the verb *partake* (formerly also *part, participate*). Also (*literary*) followed by an adjective used absol. OE. ▸**b** Without preceding partitive word: a portion of, one of, a member of, some of, some. *arch.* OE.
19 Followed by a possess.: orig. distinguishing the preceding word(s) from others of the same class possessed by the referent of the noun or pronoun, later indicating simple possession. ME.

🕮 **18** W. COWPER The sagacious of mankind. BYRON All that it had of holy he has hallowed. G. GREENE There's a good many of us, ma'am. DAY LEWIS Thirty men of us here Came out to guard the star-lit village. A. SAMPSON The fellows . . are supposed to be the cream of Oxford intellectuals. I. MURDOCH They had read most of Scott, Jane Austen, Trollope, Dickens. H. CARPENTER Edward Lear . . was the youngest of twenty children. *New Yorker* Sixty-six thousand people, all of them intelligent-looking. *Lancet* A Scot of Scots, he was born in 1912. J. A. DUDGEON One of the earliest and most significant discoveries. **b** KEATS As though of hemlock I had drunk. BROWNING Shakespeare was of us, Milton was for us. J. D. CHAMBERS The bread should be of the whitest and finest. **19** DEFOE This was . . a false step of the . . general's. A. WHITE I wish I had something . . to send you of my own. D. E. WESTLAKE James Stewart put on that sheepskin-lined jacket of his.

▸ **X** Expr. possession and being possessed.
20 Belonging to (a place) as a native or resident, as situated, existing, or taking place there, as forming part of it, as deriving a title from it, etc. OE.
21 Related to (a thing or person) as ruler, superior, possessor, holder of that office, etc.; with responsibility for, in charge of. OE.
22 Belonging to (a person or thing) as something that he, she, or it has or possesses, or as a quality or attribute; having a specified relationship to (a person). ME.
23 Related to (a thing) in a way defined, specified, or implied by the preceding words; belonging to (an action etc.) as that to which it relates. ME.
24 Belonging to (a time) as existing or taking place in it; typical or characteristic of (a particular period). E16.

🕮 **20** T. HARDY They were all young fellows of . . the neighbourhood. W. S. MAUGHAM The sight of the . . houses of Calais filled him with elation. ***the Archbishop of Canterbury, the King of Spain, the President of the United States, the Queen of England,*** etc. **21** J. G. FRAZER The king of the Matabeles. ***Chancellor of the Exchequer, Minister of Health, Secretary of State,*** etc. **22** M. MCLUHAN The value of the movie medium. E. TAYLOR Boy-friend of my mother's just came in. D. ABSE He buckled the bumper of the car. G. HOUSEHOLD The force and speed of the tide. **23 *cause of, effect of, origin of, reason of, result of,*** etc.; ***correlative of, counterpart of, opposite of, original of,*** etc.; ***copy of, derivative of, image of, likeness of,*** etc.; ***square of, cube of, logarithm of, tangent of, differential of,*** etc. **24** *Listener* It is absolutely of its time. F. WILKINSON Both men and women of the period used muffs. A. F. LOEWENSTEIN She wished for her rage of earlier in the day.

▸ **XI 25** Expressing an objective relation. After a noun of action, after a verbal noun in *-ing* (also (now *dial.*) what was formerly a verbal noun governed by *in* or *a*, now identified with a pres. pple), & after an agent-noun. OE.

🕮 **25** ADDISON Notions and Observations . . made in his reading of the Poets. T. HARDY Want of breath prevented a continuance of the story. J. RUSKIN We must cease throwing of stones. C. DAWSON A food-gatherer and an eater of shellfish. *Observer* The singing of devotional songs called *bhajans*. *Atlantic* A rival to the border collie in the management of sheep.

▸ **XII 26** Repr. an original genitive dependent on a verb or adjective. After intrans. verbs (now *rare*, formerly esp. with verbs of sense and asking); with trans. verbs with a personal obj., introducing a secondary or non-personal obj.; & with adjectives. (In meaning often passing into other branches but sometimes distinct and sometimes with hardly more than a constructional force.) ME.

26 *balk of, defraud of, disappoint of, frustrate of,* etc.; ***accuse of, convict of, suspect of,*** etc.; ***avail oneself of, bethink oneself of,*** etc.; ***fruitful of, redolent of,*** etc.; ***prodigal of, scant of, short of, sparing of,*** etc.; ***capable of, incapable of, susceptible of,*** etc.; ***worthy of, guilty of, guiltless of, innocent of,*** etc.; ***certain of, uncertain of, confident of, doubtful of, sure of,*** etc.; ***aware of, conscious of, ignorant of,*** etc.; ***careful of, careless of, forgetful of, hopeful of, hopeless of, mindful of, regardless of, neglectful of, observant of, watchful of,*** etc.; ***desirous of, enamoured of, envious of, fond of, jealous of, suspicious of,*** etc.; ***apprehensive of, descriptive of, destructive of, expressive of, indicative of, productive of,*** etc.; ***characteristic of, symbolic of,*** etc.

▸ **XIII 27** Indicating that in respect of which a quality is attributed, or a fact is predicated: in respect of, in the matter of, in point of, in. After an adjective (now *arch.* & *literary* exc. in certain phrs., as ***hard of hearing***), a noun (*arch.* exc. in ***of age***), & (formerly) a verb. ME.

🕮 **27** *Cornhill Magazine* Hard he was of hand and harder of heart. *Punch* A lethal chamber for all over fifty years of age.

▸ **XIV 28** Indicating a quality or other distinguishing mark by which a person or thing is characterized, identified, or described. ME.
29 Indicating quantity, age, extent, price, or other measurable thing. ME.
30 Indicating an action, fact, or thing that distinguishes, characterizes, identifies, or specifies a time, place, etc. (Passing into branch X.) ME.
31 Followed by a noun of action with possess., equivalent to a pass. ppl phr., indicating the agent and action of which something is the object or product. E16.

🕮 **28** H. MACKENZIE The man of feeling. JOYCE Birds of prey . . swooping from eyries. V. S. PRITCHETT It is felt unnatural for a man of his size to be living alone. F. TUOHY This had been a country of coffee plantations. **29** *Guardian* Most . . were probably Leftist rebels at the age of twenty. C. A. W. GUGGISBERG With a length of twenty-eight feet and standing seventeen to eighteen feet at the shoulder. **30 *country of one's birth, land of one's birth,*** etc. ***in time of drought, in time of need, in time of war,*** etc. **31** KEATS Its feet were tied, With a silken thread of my own hand's weaving.

▸ **XV 32** Indicating a point or space of time: at some time during, in the course of, on, (now only implying repetition or regularity, in ***of an evening, of a Sunday afternoon, of nights,*** etc.); *arch.* during, for (a space of time), (latterly only in neg. contexts). LME.

Phrases: (A selection of cross-refs. only is included.) **all of a —** *colloq.* completely in or into a specified state. ***all of a sudden***: see SUDDEN *noun* 1. **have a bad — of it, have a good — of it,** etc., have a thoroughly bad etc. —. **of all people** etc. (in apposition to a noun or pronoun) as the least expected, likely or desirable person etc. (to do the thing in question). **of all the cheek, of all the nerve,** etc.: expr. indignation at a person's impudence. ***of a sudden***: see SUDDEN *noun* 1. ***of a truth***: see TRUTH *noun*. ***of kin***: see KIN *noun*. **of late** lately, recently. ***of no** CONSEQUENCE.* **of old** formerly, long ago. **of oneself** by one's own impetus or motion, spontaneously, without the instigation or aid of another. **of sorts**: see SORT *noun*². **of the clock** *arch.* = O'CLOCK. **of yore** *arch.* = ***of old*** above. **send of an errand** *arch. colloq.* send on an errand.

¶ The primary sense 'away, away from' is retained only as OFF *preposition*. From its original sense, *of* was naturally used in the expression of the notions of removal, separation, privation, derivation, origin or source, starting-point, spring of action, cause, agent, instrument, material, etc. Its scope was enlarged even in Old English, by its use to render Latin *ab, de,* or *ex*, in constructions where the native idiom would not have used it, and from early Middle English by its use as the equivalent of French *de*, which represented not only Latin *de* in its various prepositional uses, but which had also come to substitute for the Latin genitive case. A selection only of words foll. by *of* is mentioned here: see the main noun, verb, adjective, etc., of the phrase.

of- *prefix*¹ see OFF-.

of- *prefix*² see OB-.

ofay /ˈəʊfeɪ/ *noun & adjective. US Black slang. derog.* E20.
[Origin unkn. Cf. FAY *noun*⁴.]
▸ **A** *noun.* A white person. E20.
▸ **B** *attrib.* or as *adjective.* Of a person: white. E20.

†**ofdrad** *adjective* see ADRAD.

off /ɒf/ *verb.* ME.
[from the adverb, with ellipsis of a verb: inflected forms rare before 19.]
▸ **I** *verb intrans. non-standard & joc.* exc. in *imper.* **1** Foll. by *with*: take off, chop off, remove. ME.
2 Come off, be taken off. LME.
3 Go off, make off, leave. E17.

🕮 **1** K. GRAHAME When the Queen said 'Off with his head!' she'd have offed with your head. **3** *Listener* He ups and offs from wife, job, kids.

▸ **II** *verb trans.* †**4** Put off; defer. Only in M17.
5 Take off, remove; eat off, swallow. *rare.* L19.
6 Kill. *slang* (orig. *US Black English*). M20.

🕮 **6** S. PARETSKY She might off a cop, but she wouldn't shoot her boyfriend.

off /ɒf/ *adverb, preposition, noun, & adjective.* As adverb earlier †**of**. See also OF *preposition*. OE.
[Var. of OF *preposition* (also adverb: treated here), gradually appropriated to the emphatic form.]
▸ **A** *adverb.* **1** To or at a distance, away, quite away, (in space and time). After trans. verbs also, so as to send the obj. of the verb to a distance away. OE. ▸**b** *fig.* Distant or remote in fact, nature, character, feeling, thought, etc. M16. ▸**c** NAUTICAL. Away from land, to seaward; away from the ship. Also, away from the wind. E17. ▸**d** *ellipt.* Gone off, just going off, about to go, leaving, on one's way; off to sleep, fallen or falling asleep. L18. ▸**e** *ellipt.* = ***off one's head*** s.v. HEAD *noun. colloq. & dial.* M19. ▸**f** In bad condition; wrong, abnormal, odd; *spec.* (**a**) off form; slightly unwell; (**b**) (of food) stale, sour, beginning to decay, contaminated; (**c**) (of behaviour etc.) unacceptable, ill-mannered, esp. in ***a bit off***. M19.
2 Out of position; not on or touching or attached; (so as to be) loose or separate. OE. ▸**b** *ellipt.* Come, cut, fallen, or taken off; (of clothes) removed, no longer on. LME. ▸**c** Off-stage. Also, opening out of or leading off another room etc. L18.
3 So as to interrupt continuity or cause discontinuance; so as to cause temporary disconnection, inactivity, or cessation of operation (as of an electrical or mechanical device). ME. ▸**b** Discontinued, stopped, given up; no longer in operation or going on; cancelled; (of a person) disengaged. E18. ▸**c** Away or free from one's work, school, service, or other regular commitment. M19. ▸**d** (Of an item of food) deleted from the menu; not available as a choice. *colloq.* E20.
4 So as to exhaust or finish; so as to leave none; to the end; entirely, completely, to a finish. LME. ▸**b** Finished, worked off; done with work. Now *rare*. L17.
5 So as to (cause to) lessen, abate, diminish, or decay. E17. ▸**b** Down or lower in value or price (by a specified amount or numbered points); down or reduced in price by a specified amount. E20.
6 Situated in a specified way (*well, badly, comfortably*, etc.) as regards money or supplies or other personal circumstances. M18.
7 With a preceding numeral: produced or made at one time. Chiefly in ***one-off***. M20.

🕮 **1** T. HARDY Casterbridge, the county-town, was a dozen or fifteen miles off. J. B. PRIESTLEY And off he went. G. HOUSEHOLD Marrin considered the Severn his private property from which trespassers must be warned off. M. ROBERTS Bean poles strung with black cotton to keep the birds off. D. AYERST The 'glorious twelfth' only three days off. ***afar off, far off.*** **d** K. AMIS Now I must be off, or I shall miss my bus. M. INGATE He's been crying all night. I've just got him off. **2** W. S. MAUGHAM She was arranging flowers . . and broke off the stalks savagely. G. GREENE She took off thick winter gloves. A. CARTER Victoria tore the fringes off the hassocks. **b** J. LOGAN We walked in the small cool creek Our shoes off. **c** T. S. ELIOT *Lady Elizabeth Mulhammer's voice off*: Just open the case. D. HALLIDAY My room had a balcony, and a bathroom off. **3** SCOTT FITZGERALD Claude, who was checking stock, broke off his work. K. H. COOPER The point where anaerobics leave off and aerobics begin. **b** E. BOWEN The only wireless . . had been turned off. **c** T. DREISER How about tomorrow night? I'm off then. G. CHARLES She had been paid while she was off two mornings. **d** N. FREELING Sorry sir, said the waitress . . the pudding's off. **4** G. A. SMITH We do not . . kill them off by gladiatorial combats. F. M. FORD She poured out a wineglassful and drank it off. P. G. WODEHOUSE I polished off the steak. **5** D. H. LAWRENCE Although he was very steady at work, his wages fell off. I. MURDOCH The first shock seemed . . to have worn off. **b** J. T. FARRELL His stocks were off eight points. J. ASHFORD Soup was . . sold at three-pence a tin off.

Phrases: (A selection of cross-refs. only is included.) ***badly off***: see BADLY *adverb*. ***be off***: see BE *verb*. FIRST ***off***. **get off to sleep** (cause to) fall asleep, esp. after wakefulness. ***hands off!***: see HAND *noun*. ***noises off***: see NOISE *noun*. **off and on** (*a*) intermittently, at intervals, now and again; (*b*) NAUTICAL on alternate tacks, away from and then towards the shore. **off and running** making good progress. **off from**, (now *colloq. & dial.*) **off of**, (*US & dial.*) **off on** = sense B.I below. ***right off***: see RIGHT *adverb*. ***straight off***: see STRAIGHT *adverb*[1]. **they're off!** *colloq.* the race has begun. ***well off***: see WELL *adverb*.

▶**B** *preposition*. **I** Of motion or direction.

1 Away from, down from, up from; so as no longer to lie, rest, or lean on; so as to be no longer attached to or in contact with. Also ***from off***. LME.

2 From the hands, charge, or possession of. M16. ▸**b** Derived from, taken from (also ***from off***); CRICKET from the delivery of (a ball), from the bowling of (a bowler), from all the balls in (an over). M18.

3 Using as a source, stock, or supply. E19.

4 As a deduction from or lessening of. M19.

🕮 **1** E. BOWEN A step or two off the hearthrug. I. MURDOCH I simply dived into deep water off the rocks. W. GOLDING To clean the dirt . . off the old masters. **2** R. BARNARD Alison . . hadn't had any money off me recently. A. BURGESS I bought it off a Spaniard. **b** J. TEY A frayed . . tartan ribbon off a box of Edinburgh rock. **3** R. R. MARETT The Mousterians who dined off woolly rhinoceros. **4** A. ALISON The sums . . she saved off her allowance.

▶**II** Of position.

5 Distant from (in space, time, likeness, etc.). E17. ▸**b** To seaward of; at a short distance to sea from. M17.

6 Away from being on; not on; *esp.* no longer on; not occupied with, relieved from, disengaged or free from, esp. temporarily; abstaining from; having lost interest in, averse to. L17.

7 Opening or turning out of, leading from; not far from. M19.

🕮 **5** F. CHICHESTER The difference . . would tell me how far I was off the right track. **b** P. AUSTER On an island off the coast of Chile. **6** L. URIS I hope . . to have you completely off drugs. A. CARTER To see me off my feed was the first cause of . . concern I'd given her. A. LURIE She's probably off him for good. **7** P. O'DONNELL I'll show you your room. There's a shower off it. P. ACKROYD The offices . . were in a small street off Piccadilly.

▶**C** *noun*. **1** *NAUTICAL*. = OFFING 1. *rare*. L16.

2 The condition or fact of being off; an instance or period of being off; the position in which an electrical device etc. is off. M17.

3 *CRICKET*. The off side. M19.

4 The start of a race; the start, the beginning; departure; a signal to start or depart. *colloq.* M20.

▶**D** *adjective*. (Freq. with hyphen: cf. OFF-.)

1 Situated further off, more distant, further, far. In earliest use *NAUTICAL*, further from the shore; seaward. M17.

2 Designating or pertaining to the right side of a horse, other animal, or vehicle, as being opposite to the near side. Opp. NEAR *adjective* 2. L17.

3 *CRICKET*. Designating or pertaining to the side of the field (as divided lengthways through the pitch) to which the batsman's feet are pointed. L18.

4 Designating or pertaining to a day, evening, time, etc., when a person is away or free from work, business, school, or other regular commitment. Also, designating a time when a person is off form or slightly unwell, or when any performance is not up to the usual standard. E19.

5 Corresponding to or producing the state (of an electrical device) of being disconnected (cf. sense A.3 above). L19.

6 *PHYSIOLOGY*. Of, pertaining to, or exhibiting the brief electrical activity that occurs in some optic nerve fibres when illumination of the retina ceases. E20.

Phrases, special collocations, & comb. (of preposition & adjective: cf. OFF-): (A selection of cross-refs. only is included.) **off-air** *adjective & adverb* (*a*) involving or by the transmission of programmes by broadcasting; (*b*) involving or from broadcast transmissions. **off-axis** *adjective & adverb* (situated) away from an axis. ***off balance***: see BALANCE *noun*. ***off base***: see BASE *noun*[1] 5. ***off beam***: see BEAM *noun*. **off-board** *adjective* (*US*) designating or pertaining to stocks, bonds, etc., dealt in or sold elsewhere than at a stock exchange. **off-Broadway** *adjective & noun* (designating or pertaining to) New York theatres, theatrical productions, or theatre life outside the area of Broadway, characteristically being more experimental and less commercial. ***off camera***: see CAMERA 4. **off-campus** *adjective & adverb* away from a university or college campus. **off-centre** *adverb, adjective, & verb* (*a*) *adverb & adjective* (slightly) away from the centre, not quite coinciding with a central position; awry, wrong; (*b*) *verb trans.* place or position off-centre. **off chance** a remote chance or possibility. **off colour** (*a*) (usu. **off-colour**) of the wrong or an inferior colour; *spec.* (of a diamond) neither white nor any definite colour; (*b*) slightly unwell, not in the best of health; (*c*) (chiefly *N. Amer.*) slightly indecent or obscene. ***off course***: see COURSE *noun*[1]. **off-course** *adjective* situated or taking place away from a racecourse. **off cutter** CRICKET a cutter that turns from the off side. **off-design** *adjective* not allowed for or expected. **off-diagonal** *adjective & noun* (MATH.) (designating) an element of a square matrix that is not on the diagonal running from the upper left to the lower right. **off-dry** *adjective* (of wine) almost dry, with just a trace of sweetness. ***off duty***: see DUTY *noun*. ***off form***: see FORM *noun*. **off-gauge** *adjective & noun* (designating steel strip having) thickness outside the permitted tolerance. **off-grain** *adverb* against the direction of the threads of a fabric. ***off guard***: see GUARD *noun*. **off-key** *adverb & adjective* out of tune; inappropriate(ly), wrong(ly). ***off limits***: see LIMIT *noun*. ***off message***: see MESSAGE *noun*. **off microphone**, (*colloq.*) **off mike** away from a microphone, distant from or not facing a microphone. **off-off-Broadway** *adjective & noun* (designating or pertaining to) New York theatrical productions or theatre life outside off-Broadway, characteristically being avant-garde, small scale, and informal. ***off one's base***: see BASE *noun*[1] 5. ***off one's block***: see BLOCK *noun* 6b. ***off one's chump***: see CHUMP *noun* 3. **off one's feet** *colloq.* (*a*) to a condition of no longer being able to stand, to a point of collapse; (*b*) into a state of exhilaration or excitement. ***off one's game***: see GAME *noun*. ***off one's guard***: see GUARD *noun*. ***off one's hands***: see HAND *noun*. ***off one's rocker***. **off-peak** *adjective* designating or pertaining to a time when demand is not at the maximum; used or for use at times other than those of greatest demand. **off-piste** *adjective* (of skiing) away from prepared ski runs. **off-pitch** *adjective* (*MUSIC*) not of the correct pitch. **off-plan** *adverb & adjective* (of the selling or purchasing of property) before the property is built and with only the plans available for inspection. **off-road** *adjective* used, for use, or taking place away from roads; on or for rough terrain. **off-roader** an off-road vehicle. **off-roading** driving over rough terrain, driving off-road vehicles, esp. as a sport. **off-screen** *adverb & adjective* (while) not appearing or occurring on a cinema or television screen or on a VDU etc. **off-set** *adverb* out of range of the cameras in a film or television set or studio. **off-shears** *adjective* (*Austral. & NZ*) (of a sheep) recently shorn. ***off site***: see SITE *noun*. **off spin** CRICKET a type of spin which causes the ball to turn from the off side towards the leg side after bouncing. **off-spinner** CRICKET a bowler who bowls with off spin. **off-stage** *adverb & adjective* (while) not appearing or occurring on a stage, (so as to be) invisible or inaudible to a theatre audience. **off-street** *adjective* (esp. of parking facilities) other than on a street; not taking place on a street. **off-target** *adverb & adjective* so as to miss, that misses, a target; inaccurate(ly); on the wrong track, not as forecast. ***off the air***: see AIR *noun*[1] 1b. **off the ball** (FOOTBALL etc.) (with the player(s) in question) not in contact with or playing the ball. ***off the beam***: see BEAM *noun* 6. **off-the-course** *adjective* = *off-course adjective* above. ***off the cuff***: see CUFF *noun*[1]. **off-the-face** *adjective* (of a hat) not covering or shading any part of the face. **off theory** CRICKET a theory that favours concentrating the fielders on the off side and bowling the ball at or outside the off stump. ***off the peg***: see PEG *noun*[1]. ***off the point***: see POINT *noun*[1]. ***off the record***: see RECORD *noun*. **off-the-road** *adjective* = *off-road adjective* above. ***off the shelf***: see SHELF *noun*[1]. **off-the-shoulder** *adjective* (of a dress, blouse, etc.) not covering the shoulders. **off-the-wall** *adjective* (*slang*) crazy, absurd, outlandish. **off-time** a time when business etc. is slack. **off-track** *adjective* situated or taking place away from a racetrack. **off-verse** [translating German *Abvers*] the second half-line of a line of Old English verse. **off year** *spec.* in the US, a year in which there is a Congressional election but no Presidential election.

¶ Also used idiomatically with many verbs.

off- /ɒf/ *prefix*. Earlier †**of-**.
[from OFF *adverb*. Corresp. to Old Saxon *af-*, Old Norse *af-*, Gothic *af-*, Old High German *ab*, also Latin *ab-*, Greek *apo-*, Sanskrit *apa-*. Cf. combs. of OFF *preposition*, OFF *adjective*.]

1 In various senses of 'off', forming verbs (chiefly *obsolete*), adjectives from pples, verbal nouns & nouns of action (sometimes concrete), as ***offload***, ***off-putting***, ***offset***; also forming other types of noun, as ***off-drive***, ***off-rhyme***, etc.

2 Prefixed to the names of colours in the sense 'closely resembling but not truly', as ***off-blue***, ***off-white***, etc.

¶ With absence of hyphen passing into OFF *adjective*.

Off. *abbreviation*.

1 Office.

2 Officer.

offa /ˈɒfə/ *preposition*. *non-standard US*. M20.
[Repr. an informal pronunc. of *off of* s.v. OFF *adverb*.]
Off from, from off.

offal /ˈɒf(ə)l/ *noun & adjective*. LME.
[from OFF *adverb* + FALL *verb*, prob. after Middle & mod. Dutch *afval*.]

▶**A** *noun*. **1** *sing.* & (now *rare*) in *pl.* Refuse or waste from some process, as milling grain, dressing wood, etc.; less valuable by-products. LME. ▸†**b** In *pl.* Fragments, crumbs; remnants. L16–L18.

2 *sing.* & †in *pl.* The edible parts cut off as less valuable in dressing the carcass of an animal meant for food, esp. the entrails and internal organs. LME.

3 *sing.* & †in *pl.* The parts of a slaughtered or dead animal unfit for human consumption; decomposing flesh; carrion. L16.

4 *sing.* & †in *pl.* Refuse in general; rubbish, garbage, dregs, scum (*lit.* & *fig.*). L16.

🕮 **1** G. E. EVANS The miller . . used to charge us . . but we got the offal as well as the flour. **2** V. BRAMWELL Liver and other offal. **3** J. BUCHAN The kites that batten on the offal of war. I. FLEMING The circling buzzard had found its offal. J. CLAVELL They emptied the . . rotting fish offal . . onto the heads of the prisoners. **4** LD MACAULAY Wretches . . whom every body now believes to have been . . the offal of gaols and brothels.

▶**B** *attrib.* or as *adjective*. Rejected, waste; worthless. *obsolete* exc. *dial.* L16.

off-bear /ˈɒfbɛː/ *verb trans. techn.* Pa. t. **-bore** /-bɔː/; pa. pple **-borne** /-bɔːn/. L19.
[from OFF- + BEAR *verb*[1].]
Carry off, remove, *spec.* in a brickyard or sawmill.
▪ **off-bearer** *noun* M19.

offbeat /ˈɒfbiːt, *as adjective also* ɒfˈbiːt/ *noun & adjective*. E20.
[from OFF- or (as adjective) OFF *preposition* + BEAT *noun*[2].]

▶**A** *noun*. *MUSIC*. An unaccented beat; any of the normally unaccented beats in a bar, as the second or fourth beat in common time. E20.

🕮 *Early Music* The deliberate . . accentuation of the offbeats in the Sanctus.

▶**B** *adjective*. **1** Of, pertaining to, or comprising offbeats; having a marked rhythm on the offbeats; not coinciding with the beat. E20.

2 Unusual, unconventional; strange, eccentric. *colloq.* M20.

🕮 **1** W. GADDIS Their steps matched in a precise, off-beat, ordained syncopation. A. HOPKINS A new theme marked by strong off-beat accents. **2** *Observer* It is the off-beat things, the eccentricities, that help give . . surprise. E. BLISHEN He liked visiting specialists . . to be offbeat, to contradict the . . tidy British image.

▪ **offbeatness** *noun* (*colloq.*) unusualness, unconventionality, eccentricity M20.

off-bore, **off-borne** *verbs* see OFF-BEAR.

off-brand /ˈɒfbrand/ *noun & adjective*. M20.
[from OFF- + BRAND *noun*.]
(Designating an item of goods of) an unknown, unpopular, or inferior brand.

off-break /ˈɒfbreɪk/ *noun*. M19.
[from OFF- + BREAK *noun*[1].]

1 The act or result of breaking off; a schism. M19.

2 *CRICKET*. A ball bowled in such a way that, on pitching, it changes direction towards the leg side; a change of a ball's direction towards the leg side. L19.

off-cap /ɒfˈkap/ *verb intrans. rare*. Infl. **-pp-**. E17.
[from OFF- (cf. OFF *verb*) + CAP *noun*[1].]
Take off or doff one's cap *to* (a person).

offcast /ˈɒfkɑːst/ *verb & noun*. LME.
[from OFF- + CAST *verb*.]

▶**A** *verb trans.* Pa. t. & pple **-cast**. Cast off, discard, reject. Chiefly as ***offcast*** *ppl adjective*. LME.

▶**B** *noun*. A thing or person cast off, discarded, or rejected. LME.

▪ **offcasting** *noun* (*a*) discarded material, waste; a thing cast off; (*b*) the action of the verb: LME.

offcome /ˈɒfkʌm/ *noun*. M16.
[from OFF- + COME *verb*.]

†**1** *MATH*. The product of multiplication. M16–L17.

†**2** A conclusion of an argument. Only in M17.

3 The way in which a person emerges from or succeeds in an affair; (good or ill) success. *Scot.* L17.

4 A way of avoiding something; an excuse. *Scot.* L17.

5 An outsider, a stranger; a relative newcomer to a district. *north.* M19.

▪ **offcomed** *ppl adjective* (*north.*) coming or having come from outside L19. **offcomer** *noun* (*north.*) = OFFCOME *noun* 5 L19.

off-corn /ˈɒfkɔːn/ *noun*. Now *dial.* ME.
[from OFF- + CORN *noun*[1].]
Corn thrown out or separated in winnowing, either as being light, or not separated from the chaff.

offcut /ˈɒfkʌt/ *noun*. M17.
[from OFF- + CUT *verb*.]
A piece cut off, *spec.* in making or shaping something else, as an odd or waste piece of timber left after sawing, a piece of paper cut off in reducing a sheet to the required size.

off-drive /ˈɒfdrʌɪv/ *noun & verb*. M19.
[from OFF- + DRIVE *noun*.]
CRICKET. ▶**A** *noun*. A drive to the off side. M19.

▶**B** *verb trans.* Pa. t. **-drove** /-drəʊv/, pa. pple **-driven** /-drɪv(ə)n/. Drive (a ball) to the off side; drive a ball delivered by (a bowler) to the off side. L19.

offen /ˈɒf(ə)n/ *preposition*. *US & dial.* Also **off'n**. E19.
[Repr. a pronunc. of *off of* or *off on* s.v. OFF *adverb*.]
Off from, from off.

Offenbachian /ɒf(ə)nˈbɑːkɪən/ *adjective*. M19.
[from *Offenbach* (see below) + -IAN.]
Of, pertaining to, or characteristic of the French composer Jacques Offenbach (1819–80) or his music; *esp.* (of an opera) witty, satirical.

offence /əˈfɛns/ *noun*. Also ***offense**. LME.
[Old & mod. French *offens* from Latin *offensus* annoyance, and Old & mod. French *offense* from Latin *offensa* striking against something, hurt, wrong, displeasure, both Latin forms from *offens-* pa. ppl stem of *offendere* OFFEND *verb*.]
†**1** In biblical use: striking the foot against something; stumbling. *rare*. LME–E17.
2 A stumbling-block; a cause of spiritual or moral stumbling; an occasion of unbelief, doubt, or apostasy. *arch*. LME.
3 The action of attacking or taking the offensive; attack, assault, aggressive action. LME. ▸**b** SPORTS & GAMES. The attacking team or players, the attack. *N. Amer*. E20.
†**4** Hurt, harm, injury, damage, pain, (inflicted or felt). LME–E18.
5 The act or fact of offending, wounding the feelings of, or displeasing another; offended or wounded feeling; displeasure, annoyance, resentment; umbrage. LME. ▸†**b** Disfavour, disgrace. *rare*. LME–E17.
6 †**a** The fact of being annoying, unpleasant, or repulsive; offensiveness. LME–M17. ▸**b** A cause of annoyance or disgust; an offensive person or thing; a nuisance. Long *rare*. LME.
7 A breach of law, rules, duty, propriety, or etiquette; an illegal act, a transgression, a sin, a wrong, a misdemeanour, a misdeed; a fault. LME.

📖 **5 give offence (to)** offend, displease. **no offence** *colloq*. no offence is meant, or taken. **take offence** be offended, feel resentment, take umbrage, (*at*). **without offence** without giving, or taking, offence. **6b** A. G. GARDINER The over-dressed man . . is an offence. **7** G. GORER Those . . imprisoned for civil offences . . are full of resentment. A. HALEY She committed the unthinkable offense of raising her voice to her husband. A. CLARE Offences ranging from . . petty theft . . to breaking and entering. ***summary offence***: see SUMMARY *adjective* 1c.

■ **offenceful** *adjective* (*rare*) full of offence, sinful E17. **offenceless** *adjective* without offence; unoffending, inoffensive; incapable of offence or attack: E17. **offencelessly** *adverb* without offence M17.

offend /əˈfɛnd/ *verb*. LME.
[Old French *offendre* or its source Latin *offendere*, formed as OB- + *-fendere* strike.]
†**1** *verb intrans*. Strike with the feet against something, stumble. *rare*. Only in LME.
2 *verb intrans*. Make a false step or stumble morally; commit a sin or crime, break a rule; fail in duty; do wrong, transgress. (Foll. by *against*.) LME.
†**3** *verb trans*. Sin against; wrong (a person); violate or transgress (a law etc.). LME–M17.
†**4** *verb intrans*. & *trans*. Be caused or cause to stumble or make a false step; be shocked or shock spiritually or morally. LME–M17.
†**5** **a** *verb trans*. Attack, assault, assail. LME–M18. ▸**b** *verb intrans*. Act on the offensive. LME–L19.
†**6** *verb trans*. Wound or hurt physically; harm, injure. LME–M18.
7 *verb trans*. Hurt or wound the feelings or susceptibilities of; be displeasing or disagreeable to; excite a feeling of personal annoyance, resentment, or disgust in. LME. ▸**b** *verb intrans*. Excite feelings of annoyance, resentment, or disgust; give offence. M19.

📖 **2** A. S. NEILL If I offend . . the community will punish me with ostracism. **7** J. BETJEMAN Nor constant here offend the ear Low-flying aeroplanes. G. BODDY The way he ate his boiled eggs offended her. M. LANE He never minded whom he offended.

■ **offendable** *adjective* (*rare*) able or liable to be offended M19. **offendant** *adjective* & *noun* (long *rare*) †(**a**) *adjective* causing injury or mischief; (**b**) *noun* an offender: M16. **offended** *adjective* that has been offended; *esp*. displeased, annoyed, resentful, hurt in the feelings, (*at*, *with*, *that*): LME. **offendedly** *adverb* E19. **offendedness** *noun* M20. **offending** *adjective* that offends; *esp*. that has caused the hurt or offence in question: M16.

offender /əˈfɛndə/ *noun*. LME.
[from prec. + -ER¹.]
A person who or (occas.) thing which offends; a person who breaks a law, rule, or regulation; a person who commits an offence; a person who gives offence, displeases, or excites resentment. Formerly also, an assailant.

📖 L. R. BANKS Giving young offenders a short sharp shock. A. STORR Prisons . . herding offenders together. P. QUILLIN Beans are . . nourishing food. They are also prime offenders in producing flatus. ***FIRST offender***. ***old offender***: see OLD *adjective*.

offense *noun* see OFFENCE.

offensive /əˈfɛnsɪv/ *adjective* & *noun*. M16.
[French *offensif*, *-ive* or medieval Latin *offensivus*, from Latin *offens-*: see OFFENCE, -IVE. As noun after French *l'offensive* after Italian *l'offensiva*.]
▶**A** *adjective*. **1** Of or pertaining to attack; attacking; aggressive; serving or intended for attack; having the function of or aimed at attacking an opponent. M16.
†**2** Hurtful, harmful, injurious. M16–E19.
3 Causing offence; giving or liable to give offence; displeasing; annoying; insulting; disgusting, nauseous. L16.
†**4** Having the quality of committing an offence; of the nature of an offence or crime. E–M17.

📖 **1** J. F. KENNEDY It . . depends . . which end of a revolver one is facing whether it is an offensive or a defensive weapon. J. LEHANE To force a smaller defensive player to . . cover a taller offensive player. R. C. A. WHITE Prohibited articles include offensive weapons (articles made . . for causing injury). **3** *Law Times* Permitting offensive smells . . to emanate from drains. J. P. HENNESSY He described in what seemed offensive detail the exact sum of money. W. STYRON I knew my curiosity would be offensive. E. LEONARD He was assuming she was a whore and it was offensive to her.

▶**B** *noun*. The position or attitude of attack; aggressive action; an aggressive act; forceful action or movement directed towards a particular end; a sustained campaign or effort. E18.

📖 C. THIRLWALL The council now . . felt itself strong enough to act on the offensive. J. COLVILLE Every effort is being made by the Germans for their great peace offensive. F. FITZGERALD Westmoreland took the offensive . . against enemy units. *Marxism Today* A supporter of the equality offensive . . by the trade union movement.

■ **offensively** *adverb* M16. **offensiveness** *noun* E17.

OFFER /ˈɒfə/ *abbreviation*.
Office of Electricity Regulation, a regulatory body supervising the operation of the UK electricity industry.

offer /ˈɒfə/ *noun*. LME.
[from the verb. Cf. French *offre*.]
▶**I 1** An act of offering something for acceptance or refusal; an expression of intention or willingness to give or do something if desired; a proposal; an invitation. LME. ▸**b** *spec*. A proposal of marriage. M16.
2 An act of offering a price or equivalent for something; a bid. M16.
3 The condition of being offered; the fact of being offered for sale, esp. at a reduced price. L18.

📖 **1** L. HELLMAN I had an offer to write movies for Samuel Goldwyn. *Woman* You'll be made an offer you can't refuse and may have to change your plans accordingly. **3 on offer** available for taking or choosing; on sale, esp. at a reduced price. **under offer** having had a price offered or bid made for its purchase.

▶**II 4** A thing or amount offered. Formerly *spec*., an offering. M16.
5 An attempt. *obsolete* exc. *Scot*. L16.
6 A knob or bud showing on a stag's antler. L19.

📖 **4** *Financial Times* The Government was not prepared to improve on its latest offer of 7.5 per cent for nurses. *Which?* To snip out the coupons . . to send off for the offer.

Comb.: **offer document** a document containing details of a takeover bid which is sent to the shareholders of the target company; **offer price** the price at which shares or units are offered for sale by a market-maker or institution, esp. a unit trust (cf. ***bid price*** s.v. BID *noun*).

offer /ˈɒfə/ *verb*.
[Old English *offrian* = Old Frisian *off(a)ria*, Old Saxon *offron* (Dutch *offeren*), Old Norse *offra*, from Germanic from Latin *offerre*, formed as OB- + *ferre* bring. Reinforced from Old & mod. French *offrir*.]
1 *verb trans*. Present or sacrifice (something) to God, a deity, a saint, etc., as an act of worship or devotion; formerly also *gen*., give, present, *spec*. to a superior as an act of homage etc. Also foll. by *up*. OE.
2 *verb intrans*. Present a sacrifice or offering; make a donation as an act of worship. OE.
3 *verb trans*. Present or tender for acceptance or refusal; hold out (a thing) to a person to take if he or she so desires. Foll. by indirect and direct obj.; direct obj. and *to*, †*unto*; (now *rare*) indirect obj. and *to do*; †*that*. LME. ▸**b** *verb intrans*. Make an offer or proposal; *spec*. make an offer of marriage, propose. L16. ▸**c** *verb trans*. Make available or put up for sale. M17. ▸**d** *verb refl*. Put (oneself) forward, *spec*. as a suitor. M18. ▸†**e** *verb intrans*. Stand as a candidate for office. M18–M19. ▸**f** *verb trans*. With direct speech as obj.: say tentatively or helpfully. L19. ▸**g** *verb trans*. TELEPHONY. Direct (a call) *to*. M20.
4 *verb trans*. Propose or express readiness *to do* something if desired. LME.
5 *verb trans*. Attempt to inflict, deal, or bring to bear (violence or injury); make an effort in (an attack), (attempt to) show (resistance). M16. ▸**b** Attempt, try, or intend *to do*. M16. ▸**c** *verb intrans*. Make an attempt *at*; aim *at*. *obsolete* exc. *Scot*. E17.
6 *verb intrans*. Give an opportunity for (battle etc.) to an enemy. M16.
7 *verb trans*. **a** Bring or put forward for consideration, propound. L16. ▸**b** Put in place, hold up, or display to test or assess appearance or correctness. Usu. foll. by *up*. *dial*. & *techn*. M19.
8 *verb trans*. Of a thing: present to sight, notice, etc.; afford, give an opportunity for. L16.
9 *verb intrans*. Present itself; occur. E17.

📖 **1** B. MOORE Offering up the daily sacrifice of the Mass to God. T. O'BRIEN Reverend Stenberg offered a prayer. **2** G. L. KITTREDGE Those who offered to his relics and receive his absolution. **3** C. MORLEY I offered him to go in the bathroom to wash. E. HEMINGWAY Robert . . offered the cigarettes to the gipsy. R. L. FOX Alexander had received envoys . . offering him friendship. A. C. BOULT I was offered a job. J. HARVEY The price . . offered was . . too low. J. RATHBONE Isabella kissing me . . her sister offering me her hand. **c** C. RAYNER Flower-sellers . . were offering bunches of violets and primroses. **d** O. WILDE I beg to offer myself as a candidate. **f** A. BROOKNER 'I've seen you on television,' offered Tissy. **4** M. SPARK Milly offered to make a cup of tea. **5a** R. GRAVES They would be afraid to offer violence to Castor's . . son. **b** W. VAN T. CLARK Kincaid . . never offered to say anything. **7a** OED On this I wish to offer a few remarks. **b** J. S. FOSTER The infill panels are offered up and bolted in position. **8** A. S. DALE Publishing . . offered fewer risks. **9** J. BUCHAN I seized a chance that offered and went into business.

■ **offerable** *adjective* (*rare*) L16. **offeˈree** *noun* a person to whom something is or has been offered L19. **offerer** *noun* LME. **offeror** *noun* a person who offers something, esp. shares, for sale E20.

offering /ˈɒf(ə)rɪŋ/ *noun*. OE.
[from prec. + -ING¹.]
▶**I 1** The action of OFFER *verb*. OE.
▶**II 2** A thing presented or sacrificed to God, a deity, a saint, etc., in worship or devotion; a contribution, esp. of money, to a Church. OE.
3 A thing offered for acceptance, esp. in tribute or as a token of esteem; a present, a gift; a thing offered as entertainment, *spec*. a theatrical production; a thing offered for sale. OE.

📖 **2** ***drink-offering***, ***meat-offering***, etc. BURNT ***offering***. **3** B. TRAPIDO The headmaster . . turned down his . . offering as unsuitable. S. WEINTRAUB The Jubilee offerings included bejewelled bowls. *Marketing* Chocolates . . of a better quality . . than the standard British offerings.

offertory /ˈɒfət(ə)ri/ *noun*. LME.
[ecclesiastical Latin *offertorium* place of offering, oblation, from late Latin *offert-* for Latin *oblat-*: see OBLATION, -ORY².]
1 CHRISTIAN CHURCH. The part of the Eucharist, usu. following the readings and the Creed, during which the bread and wine are placed on the altar and any collection is taken; an anthem sung or said during this; the making of offerings or the gifts offered during the Eucharist. LME.
†**2** An act of offering something, esp. to God. (Foll. by *of*.) Only in 17.
3 An offering or collection of money made at a religious service. M19.

off-flavour /ˈɒfˌfleɪvə/ *noun*. Also ***-or**. M20.
[from OFF- + FLAVOUR *noun*.]
A stale, rancid, or unnatural flavour in food.

off-gas /ˈɒfgas/ *noun* & *verb*. M20.
[from OFF- or OFF *preposition* + GAS *noun*¹.]
▶**A** *noun*. A gas which is given off, esp. one emitted as the by-product of a chemical process. M20.
▶**B** *verb intrans*. Infl. **-ss-**. Give off gas or vapour; be emitted in the form of gas or vapour. Freq. as ***off-gassing*** *verbal noun*. L20.

off-glide /ˈɒfglʌɪd/ *noun*. L19.
[from OFF- + GLIDE *noun*.]
PHONETICS. A glide terminating the articulation of a speech sound, when the vocal organs either return to a neutral position or adopt a position anticipating the formation of the next sound. Cf. ON-GLIDE.

offhand /*as adverb & pred. adjective* ɒfˈhand, *as attrib. & pred. adjective* ˈɒfhand/ *adverb* & *adjective*. Also **off-hand**. L17.
[from OFF *preposition* + HAND *noun*.]
▶**A** *adverb*. **1** At once, straightaway; without preliminary deliberation or preparation, extempore. Also, in a curt or casual manner. L17.
2 SHOOTING. From the hand without other support. *US*. M19.

📖 **1** R. CAMPBELL It was done off-hand without consulting . . the book. E. FERBER A big clip with a lot of sapphire scatter pins is smart worn just somewhere offhand. T. ROETHKE Offhand I don't know anyone who's tried this.

▶**B** *adjective*. **1** Done, made, or acting offhand; unpremeditated, extemporaneous, impromptu; free and easy, unstudied, unceremonious; curt or casual in manner. E18.
2 Of a shot: fired from a gun held in the hand without other support. *US*. M19.
3 ENGINEERING. Carried out with the workpiece held in the hand. M20.
4 GLASS-MAKING. Made or done by hand, without a mould. M20.

📖 **1** M. RENAULT Greeted by a couple of men . . he gave an off-hand nod. E. LEONARD He tried to think of a . . quick offhand comment. J. ARCHER It would be offhand not to be . . polite.

■ **offhanded** *adjective* = OFFHAND *adjective* M19. **offhandedly** *adverb* L19. **offhandedness** *noun* E19. **offhandish** *adjective* somewhat offhand L19.

office /ˈɒfɪs/ *noun*. ME.
[Old & mod. French from Latin *officium* (orig.) performance of a task, (in medieval Latin) office, rite, divine service, from comb. from *opus* work + *fic-*, *facere* do.]

1 A duty attaching to a person's position or employment; a service or task to be performed; a person's business, function, or part. Formerly also, duty towards others; a moral obligation. ME. ▸†**b** An act of performing a duty or task or of doing a service. ME–E17.

2 A thing done or intended to be done by a particular thing; a thing's function. *arch.* ME. ▸**b** A bodily or mental function; *spec.* the discharging of faeces or urine excretion. Long *obsolete* exc. in ***house of office*** s.v. HOUSE *noun*[1]. LME.

3 a A position or place to which certain duties are attached, *esp.* one of a more or less public character; a position of trust, authority, or service. ME. ▸**b** Tenure of an official position, official employment, *spec.* that of a minister of State or of the party forming a government (freq. in ***hold office***, ***out of office***). ME.

4 ECCLESIASTICAL. An authorized form of divine service or worship; *spec.* (***a***) (more fully ***divine office***) a non-Eucharistic service prescribed for daily use; (***b***) the introit sung while the priest approaches the altar to celebrate the Eucharist; the whole Eucharistic service; (***c***) an occasional service; a special form of service appointed for some particular occasion. ME.

5 A ceremonial duty or service; a religious or social observance; *esp.* the rite or rites due to the dead, obsequies. Now chiefly in ***last office(s)***. LME.

6 A service done, a kindness, a piece of attention, esp. of a specified kind, as ***good office***, ***kind office***. LME.

7 = ***inquest of office*** s.v. INQUEST 1. LME.

8 A room or building or other place for business; a room or department for clerical or administrative work; a counting-house; a room or department for a particular business (freq. of a specified kind); a local centre of a large business or organization; *N. Amer.* a professional person's consulting-room. Also, the staff of a particular office; the collective power or responsibility of the staff of a particular office. LME. ▸**b** The company or corporation established in a particular place of business; *esp.* an insurance company. M17. ▸**c** (**O-**.) The building or set of rooms or other place in which the business of a specified department of government administration is carried on; the staff of such a department, esp. the responsible head and senior officials; the collective power or responsibility of the staff of such a department. E18. ▸**d** The cockpit of an aircraft. *Aeronautics slang.* E20.

9 a In *pl.* The parts of a house, or buildings attached to a house, specially devoted to household work or service, or to storage etc. Also, the barns and outhouses of a farm. M16. ▸**b** *sing.* & in *pl.* A privy, a lavatory. Freq. ***usual office(s)***. L17.

10 A hint, a signal, a private intimation. Esp. in ***give the office***. *slang.* E19.

📖 **1** C. V. WEDGWOOD He would himself perform the executioner's office. **3a** M. HUGHES I have held this office for just six years. **b** A. BEVAN When in office the Conservatives reduce parliamentary intervention in economic processes. P. F. BOLLER When he left office, the United States was half again as large. *fig.*: SHAKES. *Haml.* The insolence of office. **4** H. ALLEN The voice of Brother François saying the office for the dead. T. KENEALLY The nuns were . . singing their office. **6** J. COLVILLE The kind offices of Lord Kemsley . . might be solicited. **8** W. VAN T. CLARK It's not the place of a judge. It lies in the sheriff's office. DAY LEWIS No.1 was a house-agent's office. ***box office***, ***Heralds' Office***, ***inquiry office***, ***land office***, ***law office***, ***patent office***, ***post office***, etc. **b** C. MARSHALL Some offices allow the policyholder to increase his sum assured. **c** ***Colonial Office***, ***Foreign Office***, ***Home Office***, ***India Office***, ***Public Record Office***, etc. **9a** E. E. EVANS The house and offices enclose a square . . yard.

Phrases: **find an office** return a verdict in favour of the Crown at an inquest of office. ***front office***: see FRONT *noun, adjective, & adverb*. ***head office***: see HEAD *noun & adjective*. ***Holy Office***: see HOLY *adjective*. ***inquest of office***: see INQUEST 1. ***Jack-in-office***, ***Jack out of office***: see JACK *noun*[1]. **office found** a verdict in favour of the Crown at an inquest of office. **office of arms** the College of Arms; a similar body in a country other than England or Wales. ***Oval Office***: see OVAL *adjective* 1. PUBLIC ***office***. ***the seals of office***: see SEAL *noun*[2].

Comb.: **office-bearer** a person who holds office; an officer, an official; **office block** a large building or block designed to contain offices; **office boy**, **office girl** a young man or woman employed to do minor jobs in an office; **office hours** the hours of work at an office; the hours during which business is conducted; **office-house** (now *rare*) †(***a***) = sense 9b above; (***b***) in *pl.* = sense 9a above; **office hymn** a hymn sung during the divine office; **office junior** the youngest or newest member of the staff of an office, employed esp. in minor jobs; **office-man** †(***a***) *Scot.* an officer, an official; (***b***) a man who works in an office; *spec.* (*slang*) a detective who remains at headquarters; **office party** a party held for members of the staff of an office; **office wife** *colloq.* a businessman's female secretary; **office-worker** an employee in an office, esp. engaged in clerical or administrative work.

■ **officeful** *noun* as many or as much as an office will hold M20. **officeless** *adjective* (*rare*) having no office, out of office L15.

office /ˈɒfɪs/ *verb*. LME.
[from the noun.]

†**1** *verb intrans.* Officiate at a religious service. LME–E16.

†**2** *verb trans.* Perform in the way of duty or service. *rare* (Shakes.). Only in E17.

†**3** *verb trans.* Appoint to or place in office. *rare*. E17–M18.

†**4** *verb trans.* Drive away *from* by virtue of one's office. *rare* (Shakes.). Only in E17.

5 *verb trans.* Give a hint or signal to; give private notice of. *slang*. E19.

6 *verb intrans.* Have or work in an office; share an office *with*. *US*. L19.

officer /ˈɒfɪsə/ *noun*. ME.
[Anglo-Norman (Old & mod. French *officier*) from medieval Latin *officiarius*, from *officium*: see OFFICE *noun*, -ER[2].]

1 A person who holds a public, civil, or ecclesiastical office (in early use, esp. in the administration of law or justice); an appointed or elected functionary (usu. with specification of the nature of the office). ME.

2 A person holding a military or naval command, or occupying a position of authority in an army, navy, air force, or mercantile marine, or on a passenger ship; *spec.* one holding a commission in the armed services. LME.

3 A servant or functionary in a royal household; a manager of the domestic affairs of a large household or estate, or of a college etc. Formerly also, a subordinate of such an officer, a menial, a domestic. LME.

†**4** *gen.* A person who performs a duty, service, or function; a minister, an agent. LME–M17.

5 A person holding an office in law enforcement; a sheriff's serjeant, a bailiff; a member of a police force (now also used as a mode of address to such an officer). Formerly also, a jailer; an executioner. E16.

6 A person holding office and taking part in the management or direction of a society or institution, *esp.* one holding the office of president, treasurer, or secretary. M17.

7 A chess-piece, *spec.* one ranking above a pawn. E19.

8 A member of a certain grade in some honorary orders, as the grade next below commander in the Order of the British Empire. M19.

📖 **1** ***attendance officer***, ***health officer***, ***house officer***, ***information officer***, ***law-officer***, ***medical officer***, ***probation officer***, ***relieving officer***, ***returning officer***, ***senior nursing officer***, etc. **officer of arms**, **officer at arms** a herald, a pursuivant. ***sabbatical officer***: see SABBATICAL *adjective*. **2** E. O'NEILL I give you my word of honour as an officer and a gentleman. ***air officer***, ***branch officer***, ***commissioned officer***, ***company officer***, ***field officer***, ***first officer***, ***flag officer***, ***Flight Officer***, ***Flying Officer***, ***line officer***, ***non-commissioned officer***, ***petty officer***, ***warrant officer***, etc. **Officers Training Corps** an organization set up in schools and universities for the preliminary training of boys and young men who may later become officers in the armed services. **5** J. GALSWORTHY Pardon me officer . . but where is Wren Street? ***police officer***, ***sheriff's officer***, etc.

■ **officerless** *adjective* L19. **officerlike** *adjective* resembling (that of) an officer L18. **officerly** *adjective* characteristic or suggestive of an officer in the armed services, appropriate to an officer M20. **officership** *noun* (***a***) the position or rank of an officer; the function or conduct of an officer; (***b***) a staff of officers: L16.

officer /ˈɒfɪsə/ *verb trans*. L17.
[from the noun.]

1 Provide (esp. military or naval) officers for; lead, command, or direct as an officer. Usu. in *pass.* L17.

2 *gen.* Command, direct; lead, conduct, manage; escort. M19.

officese /ɒfɪˈsiːz/ *noun*. M20.
[from OFFICE *noun* + -ESE.]
= COMMERCIALESE.

official /əˈfɪʃ(ə)l/ *noun*. ME.
[Partly from Old & mod. French, partly from the adjective.]

†**1** A person who holds office in a household. Only in ME.

2 ECCLESIASTICAL. (Usu. **O-**.) The presiding officer or judge of an archbishop's, bishop's, or archdeacon's court. Now usu. ***Official Principal***. ME.

3 A person holding public office; a person having official duties. M16.

📖 **3** E. MANNIN Officials . . sat at a table examining tickets. *Times* Some district matches are being played without an official in charge.

official /əˈfɪʃ(ə)l/ *adjective*. LME.
[Latin *officialis*, from *officium* OFFICE *noun*: see -AL[1].]

†**1** Performing some office or service; *spec.* (of a bodily organ) serving the needs or purposes of a vital organ. LME–M17.

†**2** Of, pertaining to, or required by duty. L16.

3 Of or pertaining to an office or position of trust, authority, or service; of or pertaining to the duties or tenure of an office; formal, ceremonious. E17.

4 Emanating from or having the sanction of a person or persons in office; authorized or supported by a government etc.; properly authorized, formally accepted or agreed. L18. ▸**b** MEDICINE. Of a drug etc.: authorized as standard by a pharmacopoeia or recognized formulary. L19.

5 Holding office; employed in a public capacity; authorized to exercise a specific function. M19.

📖 **3** D. H. LAWRENCE She had spoken with him . . in his official capacity as inspector. **4** N. PEVSNER Only in . . the fourteenth century did English become the . . official language of England. G. VIDAL I never accept the official reason for anything. S. WEINTRAUB Before the official month of mourning . . was over.

Special collocations: **official birthday** the day chosen for the annual observance of the birthday of the British monarch. ***official receiver***: see RECEIVER 2b. **official secrets**: the disclosure of which outside official circles would constitute a breach of national security. ***Official Solicitor***: see SOLICITOR 4.

officialdom /əˈfɪʃ(ə)ldəm/ *noun*. M19.
[from OFFICIAL *noun* or *adjective* + -DOM.]
The position of an official; official routine; the domain, sphere, or ways of officials, officials collectively, esp. as regarded as inefficient or obstructive.

officialese /əfɪʃəˈliːz/ *noun*. L19.
[formed as prec. + -ESE.]
Language supposedly characteristic of officials or official documents; turgid or pedantic official prose.

officialise *verb* var. of OFFICIALIZE.

officialism /əˈfɪʃ(ə)lɪz(ə)m/ *noun*. M19.
[formed as OFFICIALESE + -ISM.]
The mode of action supposedly characteristic of officials; perfunctory and literal discharge of the duties of office; official system or routine; officials collectively or in the abstract.

officiality /əfɪʃɪˈalɪti/ *noun*. L16.
[Old & mod. French *officialité* or medieval Latin *officialitas*, from Latin *officialis*: see OFFICIAL *adjective*, -ITY.]
ECCLESIASTICAL HISTORY. The office or jurisdiction of an Official Principal; (the building housing) the court of an Official Principal.

officialize /əˈfɪʃ(ə)lʌɪz/ *verb*. Also **-ise**. M19.
[from OFFICIAL *adjective* + -IZE.]

1 *verb intrans.* Do official work. *rare*. M19.

2 *verb trans.* Make official, give an official character to; bring under official control. L19.

officially /əˈfɪʃ(ə)li/ *adverb*. L18.
[from OFFICIAL *adjective* + -LY[2].]
In an official manner or capacity; by virtue or in consequence of one's office; with or according to official authority, sanction, or formality; by or in the presence of an official; for official purposes; in official or public statements, reports, etc. (but not in actuality).

📖 DICKENS Some gentle-hearted functionary who . . was officially present at the Inquest. L. DEIGHTON 'Does anyone have phones going . . across Berlin?' 'Officially one.' *Navy News* Dolphin . . was officially opened by Cdr. Graham Laslett. M. FORSTER She was twenty-one and officially an adult.

†**officialship** *noun*. L15–M18.
[from OFFICIAL *noun* + -SHIP.]
ECCLESIASTICAL. The office or dignity of an Official Principal; a body of Officials Principal.

officiant /əˈfɪʃɪənt, -ʃ(ə)nt/ *noun*. M19.
[medieval Latin *officiant-*, *-ans* use as noun of pres. pple of *officiare*: see OFFICIATE *verb*, -ANT[1].]
A person who officiates at a religious ceremony; an officiating priest or minister.

officiary /əˈfɪʃɪəri, -ʃ(ə)ri/ *noun*. E16.
[medieval Latin *officiarius*: see OFFICER *noun*, -ARY[1].]
▶ **I 1** An officer, an official. *rare*. E16.

2 A body of officers; an official body. *US*. L19.
▶ **II 3** SCOTTISH HISTORY. A division of a Highland estate, orig. in the charge of one officer. Formerly also, the position or function of an officer in charge of such a division. L16.

officiary /əˈfɪʃɪəri, -ʃ(ə)ri/ *adjective*. Now *rare*. E17.
[medieval Latin *officiarius*, from *officium*: see OFFICE *noun*, -ARY[1].]

1 Of a title etc.: attached to or derived from an office held. Of a dignitary: having a title or rank derived from office. E17.

2 Of, pertaining to, or holding office; official. M18.

officiate /əˈfɪʃɪət/ *noun*. *rare*. E16.
[medieval Latin *officiatus*, formed as next: see -ATE[1].]

1 An official, an officer. E16.

2 A body of officials or officers. M19.

officiate /əˈfɪʃɪeɪt/ *verb*. M17.
[medieval Latin *officiat-* pa. ppl stem of *officiare* perform divine service, from Latin *officium*: see OFFICE *noun*, -ATE[3].]
▶ **I** *verb intrans.* **1** Discharge the office of a priest or minister; perform divine service, or any religious rite or ceremony. M17.

†**2** Of a bodily organ etc.: perform its function, operate. M17–M18.

3 Perform the duties attaching to an office or position, perform any particular duty or service; act as an official. L17.

1 *Discovery* The officiating priest was a Franciscan friar. S. WEINTRAUB The Archbishop of Canterbury officiated. **3** M. R. MITFORD His unmarried daughter who officiated as his private secretary. *Times* I am always an admirer of strong officiating in sport.

▶ **II** *verb trans.* †**4** Perform or celebrate as a priest or minister. **M17–E18.**
†**5** Perform the duties of (an office or position); execute, fulfil. **M17–E18.**
†**6** Minister, supply. *rare.* Only in **M17.**
7 Serve (a church). *rare.* **L19.**
■ **offici'ation** *noun* the action of officiating; performance of a religious, ceremonial, or public duty: **L18.** **officiator** *noun* a person who officiates **M19.**

officina /ɒfɪˈsʌɪnə, -ˈsiːnə/ *noun.* Pl. ***-nae*** /-niː, -nʌɪ/. **E19.**
[Latin = workshop etc., contr. of *opificina*, from *opifex* workman.]
A workshop; a place of production (freq. *fig.*).
officina gentium /ɒfɪˌsʌɪnə ˈdʒɛntɪəm, ɒfɪˌsiːnə ˈɡɛntɪəm/ a country or area from the inhabitants of which several nations develop.

officinal /əˈfɪsɪn(ə)l/ *adjective & noun.* **L17.**
[medieval Latin *officinalis*, from *officina* (in medieval Latin a storeroom for medicines etc. in a monastery): see prec., -AL¹.]
▶ **A** *noun.* An officinal drug or medicine. Now *rare* or *obsolete.* **L17.**
▶ **B** *adjective.* Of a herb, drug, etc.: regularly sold or used as a medicine. Of a medicinal substance: kept as a standard preparation by apothecaries and pharmacists. Formerly also *spec.* = OFFICIAL *adjective* 4b. Cf. MAGISTRAL *adjective* 2a. **E18.**
■ **officinally** *adverb* in officinal use; according to the pharmacopoeia: **E19.**

officious /əˈfɪʃəs/ *adjective.* **L15.**
[from Latin *officiosus*, from *officium* OFFICE *noun*: see -OUS.]
†**1 a** Performing its office or function, serving its purpose, efficacious. *rare.* **L15–L19.** ▸**b** Active or zealous in doing one's duty. **L16–M18.**
†**2** Doing or ready to do kind offices; intended to help or please; attentive, obliging, kind. **M16–E19.**
3 Unduly forward in offering one's services, too inclined to do things personally; aggressive in asserting one's interest or authority; interfering with what is not one's concern; intrusive, meddlesome; domineering. **L16.**
†**4** Pertaining to an office or business, official; formal. **E17–M19.**
5 In diplomats' use: unofficial, informal. **M19.**

2 officious lie a lie told as an act of kindness to further another's interests. **3** L. W. MEYNELL An officious inspector warned him, trying to bar his way. M. HUGHES Some officious person would . . come up and ask if they could help.

■ **officiously** *adverb* **E17.** **officiousness** *noun* **L16.**

offie *noun* var. of OFFY.

offing /ˈɒfɪŋ/ *noun.* **E17.**
[Perh. from OFF *adverb* + -ING¹.]
1 NAUTICAL. The part of the visible sea that is distant from the shore or beyond an anchoring-ground. **E17.**
2 NAUTICAL. A position at a distance off a shore. **L17.**
3 ***in the offing***, †(*a*) *rare* in the distant future; (*b*) nearby, at hand, in prospect, likely to appear or happen in the near future. **L18.**

offish /ˈɒfɪʃ/ *adjective. colloq.* **M19.**
[from OFF *adverb* + -ISH¹.]
Inclined to keep aloof; distant in manner.
■ **offishly** *adverb* **M20.** **offishness** *noun* **L19.**

off-island /*adverb & corresp. adjective uses* ɒfˈʌɪlənd, *noun & corresp. adjective uses* ˈɒfʌɪlənd/ *adverb, noun, & adjective.* **E20.**
[from OFF *preposition* (as adverb), OFF- (as noun) + ISLAND *noun*¹.]
▶ **A** *adverb.* Away from an island; *spec.* (US) away from the island of Nantucket. **E20.**
▶ **B** *noun.* An island off the shore of a larger or central island. **M20.**
▶ **C** *adjective.* Visiting or temporarily residing on an island. Also, of or pertaining to an off-island. **M20.**
■ **off-islander** *noun* (*a*) a visitor or temporary resident on an island, *spec.* (US) in Nantucket; (*b*) a native or inhabitant of an offshore island: **L19.**

offlap /ˈɒflap/ *noun.* **E20.**
[from OFF- + LAP *verb*², after *overlap*.]
GEOLOGY. A progressive decrease in the lateral extent of conformable strata in passing upwards from older to younger strata, so that each stratum leaves a portion of the underlying one exposed; a set of strata exhibiting this. Cf. ONLAP.

offlet /ˈɒflɪt/ *noun.* Orig. *Scot.* **M18.**
[from OFF- + LET *verb*¹.]
A channel or pipe for letting water run away.

off-licence /ˈɒflʌɪs(ə)ns/ *noun.* Also ***-license**. **L19.**
[from OFF- + LICENCE *noun.*]
A shop or other establishment, or a counter in a public house or hotel, where alcoholic drink is sold for consumption elsewhere; a licence permitting such sales.
■ **off-licensed** *adjective* having a licence permitting such sales **L19.** **off-licen'see** *noun* a person having a licence permitting such sales, the proprietor or manager of an off-licence **L19.**

offline /ɒfˈlʌɪn, *as attrib. adjective* ˈɒflʌɪn/ *adjective & adverb.* **E20.**
[from OFF *preposition* + LINE *noun*².]
▶ **A** *adjective.* **1** Not situated or performed on a railway or by rail. **E20.**
2 COMPUTING. Not online. Also, not connected, not in operation. **M20.**
▶ **B** *adverb.* COMPUTING. With a delay between the production of data and its processing; not under direct computer control. **M20.**

offload /ˈɒfləʊd, ɒfˈləʊd/ *verb.* Orig. *S. Afr.* **M19.**
[from OFF- + LOAD *verb*, after Dutch *afladen*.]
1 *verb trans. & intrans.* Unload. **M19.**
2 *transf. & fig.* Discard, get rid of, relieve oneself of (esp. an unpleasant or unwanted person or thing), *spec.* on to someone else. **M20.**
■ **offloader** *noun* **L20.**

off-lying /ˈɒflʌɪɪŋ/ *adjective.* **M19.**
[from OFF- + LYING *adjective*¹.]
Lying off, at a distance, or out of the way; remote; situated away from the central or main part.

off'n *preposition* var. of OFFEN.

off-price /ˈɒfprʌɪs/ *adjective. N. Amer.* **L20.**
[from OFF- + PRICE *noun.*]
Designating or pertaining to merchandise sold at a retail price lower than that recommended by the manufacturer.
■ **off-pricer** *noun* a seller of off-price merchandise **L20.**

offprint /ˈɒfprɪnt/ *noun.* **L19.**
[from OFF- + PRINT *noun.* Cf. Dutch *afdruk*.]
A separately printed copy of an article etc. which originally appeared as a part of a larger publication.

offprint /ɒfˈprɪnt, ˈɒfprɪnt/ *verb trans.* **L19.**
[from OFF- + PRINT *verb.*]
Print off or reprint as an excerpt or offprint.

off-put /ˈɒfpʊt/ *verb & noun.* **LME.**
[from OFF- + PUT *verb*¹.]
▶ **A** *verb trans.* Infl. as PUT *verb*¹; pres. pple & verbal noun **-putting**, pa. t. & pple usu. **-put**. Put off; disconcert; repel. Chiefly as ***off-putting** verbal noun*, OFF-PUTTING *adjective.* Chiefly *north.* **LME.**
▶ **B** *noun.* An act of putting something or someone off. Also, a person who puts a thing off, a procrastinator, a timewaster. **M18.**
■ **off-putter** *noun* **L18.**

off-putting /ˈɒfpʊtɪŋ, ɒfˈpʊtɪŋ/ *adjective.* **E19.**
[from prec. + -ING².]
That puts something or someone off; *spec.* creating an unfavourable impression, causing displeasure, disconcerting, repellent.
■ **off-puttingly** *adverb* **M20.**

off-ramp /ˈɒframp/ *noun. N. Amer.* **M20.**
[from OFF- + RAMP *noun*¹.]
A sloping one-way road leading off a main highway.

off-reckoning /ˈɒfrɛk(ə)nɪŋ/ *noun.* **L17.**
[from OFF- + RECKONING *noun.* Cf. Dutch *afreckening*, German *Abrechnung* deduction, settlement of accounts.]
A deduction; *spec.* (*Hist.*) a deduction from the pay of a British soldier or marine towards clothing or other expenses, according to a special account between the Government and the commanding officers of regiments. Usu. in *pl.*

off-rhyme /ˈɒfrʌɪm/ *noun.* **M20.**
[from OFF- + RHYME *noun.*]
A partial or near rhyme.

offsaddle /ˈɒfsad(ə)l/ *verb trans. & intrans.* Chiefly *S. Afr.* **M19.**
[from OFF- + SADDLE *verb*, after Dutch *afzadelen*.]
Take the saddle off (a horse) for a rest, feeding, etc.; unsaddle.

off-sale /ˈɒfseɪl/ *noun.* **L19.**
[from OFF- + SALE *noun.*]
The sale of alcoholic drink for consumption elsewhere than at the place of sale; an instance of this, an alcoholic drink sold for consumption elsewhere, (usu. in *pl.*).

offscape /ˈɒfskeɪp/ *noun.* Now *rare.* Also (*arch.*) **-skip** /-skɪp/. **E18.**
[from OFF- after LANDSCAPE *noun.*]
A distant view or prospect; the distant part of a view or prospect, the distance, background.

offscouring /ˈɒfskaʊərɪŋ/ *noun.* **E16.**
[from OFF- + SCOURING.]
sing. & (usu.) in *pl.* Refuse, rubbish, dregs, (*lit.* & *fig.*). (Foll. by *of*.)

J. M. JEPHSON Having carefully picked my way through the off-scourings of the lofty houses. F. W. LINDSAY Thugs, gamblers and the off-scourings of the world.

offscum /ˈɒfskʌm/ *noun.* Now *rare.* **L16.**
[from OFF- + SCUM *noun.*]
Scum, dross, refuse. Chiefly *fig.*

off-season /ˈɒfsiːz(ə)n/ *noun & adjective.* **M19.**
[from OFF- + SEASON *noun.* Adj. partly from OFF *preposition.*]
▶ **A** *noun.* A period when ordinary business is slack or does not occur; a time of year other than the busiest or most popular time for a particular activity. **M19.**
▶ **B** *attrib.* or as *adjective.* Of or pertaining to an off-season. **E20.**

offset /ˈɒfsɛt/ *noun.* **M16.**
[from OFF- + SET *noun*¹. Cf. SET-OFF.]
1 The act of setting off (on a journey or course of action); the outset, a start, a beginning. **M16.**
2 A short lateral shoot, esp. from the lower stem, bulb, or corm, of a plant, serving for propagation; *transf. & fig.* a lateral branch, an offshoot, a collateral descendant; a spur of a mountain range. **E17.**
3 A thing that acts as a foil to embellish, or throws something else into prominence. **L17.**
4 SURVEYING. A short distance measured perpendicularly from a main line of measurement. **E18.**
5 ARCHITECTURE. A horizontal or sloping break or ledge on the face of a wall, pier, etc., formed where the portion above is reduced in thickness. **E18.**
6 A counterbalance to or compensation for something else; a consideration or amount diminishing or neutralizing the effect of a contrary one; a set-off. **M18.**
7 PRINTING. The transfer of ink from a freshly printed surface; a printing process in which ink is transferred from a plate (orig. a stone) to a rubber-covered cylinder and then transferred to paper. **L19.**
8 A bend in a pipe, made to carry it past an obstruction. **E20.**
9 ELECTRICITY. A small deviation from a correct or normal voltage, current, etc.; a small bias introduced to ensure correct operation of a circuit. **M20.**
7 ***lithographic offset***, ***photolitho offset***. ***offset litho***, ***offset lithography***, ***offset printing***, ***offset process***.
Comb.: **offset purchase** ECONOMICS a purchase made abroad by agreement to counterbalance revenues spent in the buying country by the selling country; **offset well** an oil or gas well drilled in a particular area to counteract drainage of oil or gas from there caused by drilling in an adjacent area.

offset /ɒfˈsɛt, ˈɒfsɛt/ *verb.* Infl. **-tt-**. Pa. t. & pple **-set**. **L17.**
[from OFF- + SET *verb*¹.]
1 *verb trans.* Set off as an equivalent *against*; cancel out by, balance by something on the other side or of contrary nature; counterbalance, compensate. **L17.**
2 *verb intrans.* Spring, branch off, or project as an offset *from*. Now *rare.* **M19.**
3 *verb trans.* Set at an angle; place off-centre or out of line. Chiefly as ***offset** ppl adjective.* **M19.**
4 *verb intrans.* PRINTING. Of ink, a freshly printed page: transfer an impression to the next leaf or sheet. **L19.**

1 R. W. EMERSON In human action, against the spasm of energy we offset the continuity of drill. L. NAMIER The debit balances . . would be offset by the credit balances. G. HUNTINGTON The negative beginning . . had been somewhat offset by the positive end.

offshoot /ˈɒfʃuːt/ *noun.* **L17.**
[from OFF- + SHOOT *noun*¹.]
†**1** An emanation. *rare.* Only in **L17.**
2 A collateral branch or descendant of a (specified) family etc. **E18.**
3 A shoot springing from the stem or other part of a plant; a lateral branch projecting from the main part of anything material, as a mountain-range, street, etc. **E19.**
4 A thing which originated as a branch of something else; a derivative. **E19.**

offshore /*as adverb* ɒfˈʃɔː, *as adjective* ˈɒfʃɔː/ *adverb & adjective.* Also **off-shore**. **E18.**
[from OFF *preposition* + SHORE *noun*¹.]
▶ **A** *adverb.* In a direction away from a shore; at some distance from a shore. **E18.**
▶ **B** *adjective.* **1** Moving or directed away from a shore. **M19.**
2 Situated, existing, or operating at a distance from a shore. Also, away from the mainland. **L19.**
3 Chiefly with ref. to commercial or financial activity: pertaining to, derived from, or involving another country; foreign, international; not domestic or native. **M20.**
2 offshore island an island close to the mainland. **offshore islander** a native or inhabitant of an offshore island. **3 offshore purchase**: with American dollars by and from countries other than the US.

offside /ˈɒfsʌɪd/ *verb intrans. Austral. colloq.* **L19.**
[Back-form. from next.]
Act as an offsider or assistant.

offside /*as adverb & noun* ɒfˈsʌɪd, *as adjective* ˈɒfsʌɪd/ *adverb, adjective, & noun.* Also **off-side**, (*N. Amer.*) **offsides** /-ˈsʌɪdz/. **M19.**
[from OFF *preposition* + SIDE *noun*.]
▶ **A** *adverb.* In FOOTBALL, HOCKEY, etc., away from one's own side, between the ball and the opponent's goal, esp. in a situation where a player may not play the ball or is penalized; *transf. & fig.* on the wrong side, out of favour *with*. **M19.**
▶ **B** *attrib.* or as *adjective.* Involving being offside. **L19.**
▶ **C** *noun.* The fact or an occasion of being offside; a minor penalty for being offside. **L19.**

offsider /ˈɒfsʌɪdə/ *noun. Austral. & NZ colloq.* **L19.**
[from OFF *adjective* + SIDE *noun* + -ER[1].]
An animal on the off side of a team; an assistant, formerly *spec.*, a bullock-driver's assistant; a companion, a deputy, a partner.

offskip *noun* see OFFSCAPE.

offspring /ˈɒfsprɪŋ/ *noun.* **OE.**
[from OFF- + SPRING *verb*[1].]
▶ **I 1** *collect.* & (later, less usu.) in *pl.* A person's children or descendants; an animal's young; progeny. **OE.**
2 *sing.* A person's child; a person or animal in relation to a parent or ancestor. **L15.**
3 *fig. collect.* & †in *pl.* The products or results of something. **L16.**
4 A family of young, a line of descendants. Usu. with an adjective of size or number. **M17.**

> 1 *South Wales Guardian* They do all they can to encourage their off-springs to learn Welsh. D. LODGE All had moments of great . . pride in their offspring. *fig.*: W. M. PRAED Beautiful Athens, we will weep for thee; For thee and for thine off-spring! **2** W. PLOMER She wanted her offspring to work, to be happy, to find his proper level.

▶†**II 5** A generation. **ME–L16.**
6 A person's family or stock; ancestry. **ME–E17.**
7 The fact of descending from some ancestor or source; derivation, origin. **LME–E18.**
8 A source, a spring, a fountain, an original. **E16–E17.**

offtake /ˈɒfteɪk/ *noun.* **L19.**
[from OFF- + TAKE *noun*.]
The action of taking something off; *spec.* (**a**) the taking of commodities off the market; purchase of goods; (**b**) the removal of oil from a reservoir or supply.

off-trade /ˈɒftreɪd/ *noun.* **L20.**
[from OFF- + TRADE *noun*.]
That part of the market in alcoholic liquors which is made up of off-sales.

offuscate /ˈɒfʌskeɪt/ *verb trans.* Now *rare.* Pa. pple & ppl adjective **-ate**, **-ated**. **E17.**
[Latin *offuscat-* pa. ppl stem of *offuscare* var. of *obfuscare*: see OBFUSCATE *verb*.]
= OBFUSCATE *verb*.
■ **offuˈscation** *noun* = OBFUSCATION **E16.**

offward /ˈɒfwəd/ *adjective & adverb.* **M16.**
[from OFF *adverb* + -WARD.]
▶ **A** *adjective.* †**1** Turned or directed off or away; averse. **M16–E17.**
†**2** = OFF *adjective* 2. *rare.* Only in **E18.**
▶ **B** *adverb.* In a direction or position off or away from something; to the off side; NAUTICAL away from a shore. **E17.**

off-white /ɒfˈwʌɪt, *attrib. adjective* ˈɒfwʌɪt/ *noun & adjective.* **E20.**
[from OFF- + WHITE *noun, adjective*.]
▶ **A** *noun.* A colour closely resembling but not truly white, usu. with a grey or yellow tinge. **E20.**
▶ **B** *adjective.* Closely resembling but not truly white; *fig.* not standard, not socially acceptable. **M20.**

offy /ˈɒfi/ *noun. colloq.* Also **offie**.
[from OFF(-LICENCE + -Y[6].]
An off-licence.

Ofgas /ˈɒfgas/ *abbreviation.*
Office of Gas Supply, a regulatory body supervising the operation of the UK gas industry.

†**ofhungered** *adjective.* Also **afingered**. **OE–M16.**
[from Old English *of-* OFF- + pa. pple of *hyngrian* HUNGER *verb*: see -ED[1].]
Famished, very hungry.
¶ May survive as AHUNGERED.

oficina /ɒfɪˈsiːnə/ *noun.* **L19.**
[Spanish from Latin OFFICINA.]
A factory in Spanish-speaking S. America or Mexico.

Oflag /ˈɒflag/ *noun.* **M20.**
[German, contr. of *Offizier(s)lager* officers' camp. Cf. STALAG.]
Hist. In Nazi Germany: a prison-camp for captured enemy officers.

Oflot /ˈɒflɒt/ *abbreviation.*
Office of the National Lottery, a regulatory body set up in 1993 to supervise the operation of the British National Lottery.

OFM *abbreviation.*
Order of Friars Minor.

OFr. *abbreviation.*
Old French.

Ofrail /ˈɒfreɪl/ *abbreviation.*
(An unofficial name for) the Office of the Railway Regulator, a regulatory body created in 1993 to supervise the privatization of British Rail. (Officially called *ORR*.)

OFS *abbreviation.*
Orange Free State.

Ofsted /ˈɒfstɛd/ *abbreviation.*
Office for Standards in Education, a UK organization monitoring standards in schools by means of regular inspections.

OFT *abbreviation.*
Office of Fair Trading.

oft /ɒft/ *adverb & adjective.* Now *arch., poet., & dial.*
[Old English *oft* = Old Frisian *ofta*, Old Saxon *oft(o)*, Old High German *ofto* (German *oft*), Old Norse *opt*, *oft*, Gothic *ufta*, from Germanic.]
= OFTEN.
many a time and oft: see TIME *noun*.
■ **oftly** *adverb* (*rare*) = OFTEN *adverb* **L16.**

OFtel /ˈɒftɛl/ *abbreviation.*
Office of Telecommunications, a regulatory body supervising the operation of the UK telecommunications industry.

often /ˈɒf(ə)n, ˈɒft(ə)n/ *adverb & adjective.* **ME.**
[Extended from OFT, prob. after *selden* SELDOM.]
▶ **A** *adverb.* Many times; on numerous occasions; frequently; at short intervals; in many instances; in cases frequently occurring. **ME.**

> H. JAMES Oftenest . . he wished he were a vigorous young man of genius. DAY LEWIS I am often assumed to be Welsh. F. CHICHESTER Through this voyage I had been . . changing the sails more often. E. BOWEN Francis . . often either lay down or took a short walk. E. FIGES I heard about it often enough. **as often as not** in (about) half the instances. ***every so often***: see EVERY *adjective* 1. ***many a time and often***: see TIME *noun*. **more often than not** in more than (about) half the instances. ***once too often***: see ONCE *adverb* etc..

▶ **B** *adjective.* Done, made, happening, or occurring many times; frequent. *arch.* **LME.**

> CARLYLE The greatest and oftenest laughter. W. D. HOWELLS I knew those lemons . . from often study of them.

■ †**oftenly** *adverb* (*rare*) = OFTEN *adverb* **L16–M18.** **oftenness** /-n-n-/ *noun* (now *rare*) the fact or condition of occurring often; frequence: **M16.** **oftens** *adverb* (long *obsolete* exc. *dial.*) [-s[3], later identified with -s[1]] = OFTEN *adverb* **M16.**

oftentime /ˈɒf(ə)ntʌɪm, ˈɒft(ə)n-/ *adverb.* Now *arch. rare.* **LME.**
[Extended from OFT-TIME, after OFTEN.]
= OFTEN *adverb*.

oftentimes /ˈɒf(ə)ntʌɪmz, ˈɒft(ə)n-/ *adverb.* Now *arch. & literary* exc. *US*. **LME.**
[Extended from OFT-TIMES, after OFTEN.]
= OFTEN *adverb*.

oft-time /ˈɒf(t)tʌɪm/ *adverb.* Now *arch. rare.* **LME.**
[from OFT + TIME *noun*.]
= OFTEN *adverb*.

oft-times /ˈɒf(t)tʌɪmz/ *adverb.* Now *arch. & literary.* **LME.**
[from OFT + TIME *noun* + -S[1].]
= OFTEN *adverb*.

ofuro /əʊˈfʊərəʊ, *foreign* oˈfuro/ *noun.* Pl. **-os**. **M20.**
[Japanese, from *o* honorific prefix + *furo* bath.]
A communal hot bath, as taken by Japanese.

OFwat /ˈɒfwɒt/ *abbreviation.*
Office of Water Services, a regulatory body supervising the operation of the UK water industry.

oga /ˈəʊgə/ *noun. W. Afr.* **L20.**
[W. African.]
Boss, master. Also, as a form of address, sir.

ogam *noun* var. of OGHAM.

ogbanje /əʊgˈbanʒiː/ *noun.* **M20.**
[Igbo.]
In Nigeria, a child believed to be a reincarnation of another dead child.

ogdoad /ˈɒgdəʊad/ *noun.* **E17.**
[Late Latin *ogdoad-*, *ogdoas* from Greek, from *ogdoos* eighth, *oktō* eight: see -AD[1].]
The number eight; a group, set, or series of eight; *spec.* in Gnosticism, a group of eight divine beings or aeons.

ogee /ˈəʊdʒiː, əʊˈdʒiː/ *noun & adjective.* **ME.**
[Prob. reduced form of OGIVE, perh. through the pl. form *ogi(v)es*.]
ARCHITECTURE. ▶**A** *noun.* †**1** = OGIVE 1. **ME–E17.**
2 (A moulding having) a curved surface S-shaped in cross-section, concave above and convex below; a cyma recta. Also occas., such a moulding convex above and concave below; a cyma reversa. **L17.**
▶ **B** *attrib.* or as *adjective.* Consisting of an ogee or a series of ogees; having the outline of an ogee or an ogee arch. **L17.**
ogee curve, ***ogee moulding***, ***ogee shape***, ***ogee window***, etc. **ogee arch** an arch formed by two contrasted ogees which meet at its apex.
■ **ogeed**, **ogee'd** *adjective* having (the form of) an ogee or ogees **M19.**

Ogen /ˈəʊgɛn/ *noun.* **M20.**
[A particular kibbutz in Israel.]
In full ***Ogen melon***. A small melon with pale orange flesh and an orange skin ribbed with green.

-ogen /əˈdʒɛn/ *suffix.*
Form of **-GEN** with *-o-* provided by first element (***androgen***, ***hydrogen***) or merely connective (***fibrinogen***, ***pepsinogen***).

oggin /ˈɒgɪn/ *noun. Nautical slang.* **M20.**
[Alt. of ***hogwash*** s.v. HOG *noun*.]
The sea.

ogham /ˈɒgəm/ *noun.* Also **ogam**, **O-**. **E18.**
[Old Irish *ogam*, *ogum* (genit. *oguim*), mod. Irish *ogham*, pl. *-aim*, Gaelic *oghum*, connected with its mythical inventor *Ogma*.]
An ancient British and Irish system of writing using an alphabet of twenty or twenty-five characters; any of these characters, consisting of a line or stroke, or a group of two to five parallel strokes, arranged alongside or across a continuous line or the edge of a stone (usu. in *pl.*). Also, an inscription in this alphabet.
■ **oghamic** /ˈɒgəmɪk, ɒˈgamɪk/ *adjective* of or pertaining to ogham; consisting of oghams: **L19.**

Oghuz /əʊˈguːz/ *noun & adjective.* **M19.**
[Turkic *Oğuz* (also a legendary Turkish hero). Cf. GHUZZ.]
▶ **A** *noun.* Pl. same, **-es** /-ɪz/. A member of a group of Turkic peoples who invaded Persia, Syria, and Asia Minor from central Asia in the 11th cent. **M19.**
▶ **B** *attrib.* or as *adjective.* Of or pertaining to these peoples. Also, designating or pertaining to the SW division of the Turkic languages, including Turkish and Azerbaijani. **M20.**
■ Also **Oghuzian** *adjective & noun* (now *rare*) **E17.**

ogi /ˈəʊgi/ *noun. W. Afr.* **M20.**
[W. African.]
(Porridge made from) a kind of maize meal.

ogival /əʊˈdʒʌɪv(ə)l, ˈəʊdʒɪv(ə)l/ *adjective & noun.* **M19.**
[from next + -AL[1], or from French *ogival*.]
▶ **A** *adjective.* ARCHITECTURE.
1 a Having the form or outline of an ogive or pointed arch. **M19.** ▸**b** Characterized by ogives or pointed arches. **M19.**
2 Having the shape of an ogee. **M20.**
▶ **B** *noun.* A head of a projectile shaped like an ogive. **L19.**

ogive /ˈəʊdʒʌɪv, əʊˈdʒʌɪv/ *noun.* **LME.**
[French from Hispano-Arab. *al-jibb*, Arab. *al-jubb* cistern.]
1 ARCHITECTURE. The diagonal groin or rib of a vault, two of which cross each other at the vault's centre. **LME.**
†**2** ARCHITECTURE. An ogee moulding. Only in **E18.**
3 a ARCHITECTURE. A pointed or Gothic arch. **M19.** ▸**b** A thing, esp. the head of a projectile, having the profile of an ogive; such a profile. **E20.**
4 STATISTICS. A graph in which each ordinate represents the frequency with which a variate has a value less than or equal to that indicated by the corresponding abscissa, which for many unimodal frequency distributions has the form of an ogee. Formerly, the inverse of this. **L19.**
5 GEOLOGY. A stripe or band of dark material stretching across the surface of a glacier, usu. arched in the direction of flow and arranged with others in a parallel series. **M20.**
■ **ogived** *adjective* consisting of an ogive or ogives; having the form of an ogive or ogee: **E17.**

Oglala /ɒˈglɑːlə/ *adjective & noun.* Pl. of noun **-s**, same. **M19.**
[Sioux.]
Designating or pertaining to, a member of, the chief division of the Lakota (Sioux).

ogle /ˈəʊg(ə)l/ *noun.* **L17.**
[from or cogn. with the verb.]
1 An eye. Usu. in *pl. arch. slang.* **L17.**
2 An amorous, coquettish, or lecherous look; an act of ogling. **E18.**

ogle /ˈəʊg(ə)l/ *verb.* **L17.**
[Prob. from Low Dutch (cf. Low German *oegeln* frequentative of *oegen* look at, also early mod. Dutch *oogheler*, *oegeler* flatterer, *oogen* make eyes at): see -LE[3]. Orig. a cant word.]
1 *verb intrans.* Cast amorous, coquettish, or lecherous glances. **L17.**
2 *verb trans.* Eye amorously, admiringly, or lecherously. **L17.**
3 *verb trans.* Keep one's eyes on; eye, look at. **E19.**

📖 **1** M. W. MONTAGU He sighs and ogles so, that it would do your heart good to see him. **2** M. SCAMMELL The rest . . continued to promenade and ogle the girls. L. GARFIELD He was ogling her! How disgusting! He was winking at her and grinning. **3** W. C. RUSSELL He stood ogling the wreck through his binocular.

■ **ogler** *noun* L17.

ogmic /ˈɒɡmɪk/ *adjective*. L19.
[formed as OGHAM + -IC.]
= OGHAMIC.

o'goblin *noun* see GOBLIN *noun*².

Ogopogo /əʊɡəʊˈpəʊɡəʊ/ *noun*. *Canad.* E20.
[Invented word, said to be from a Brit. music hall song.]
(The name of) a water monster alleged to live in Okanagan Lake, British Columbia.

o-goshi /əʊˈɡɒʃi/ *noun*. Also **ogoshi**. M20.
[Japanese, from *ō* great, major + *koshi* waist, hips.]
A major hip throw in judo.

Ogpu /ˈɒɡpuː/ *noun*. Also **ogpu**, **OGPU**. E20.
[Russian acronym, from *Ob"edinënnoe Gosudarstvennoe Politicheskoe Upravlenie* United State Political Directorate.]
Hist. An organization for investigating and combating counter-revolutionary activities in the USSR, which existed from 1922 to 1934, replacing the Cheka.

O'Grady /ə(ʊ)ˈɡreɪdi/ *noun*. M20.
[Irish surname.]
A children's game resembling Simon Says but with the instructions prefaced by 'O'Grady says'. Also ***O'Grady Says***.

-ography /ˈɒɡrəfi/ *suffix*.
Form of -GRAPHY with -O- provided by first element or merely connective (***discography***, ***hydrography***).

ogre /ˈəʊɡə/ *noun*. E18.
[French, of unkn. origin.]
A man-eating monster, usu. represented as a hideous giant. Also, a cruel, irascible, or ugly person.
the CORSICAN *ogre*.

ogreish /ˈəʊɡ(ə)rɪʃ/ *adjective*. Also **ogrish** /ˈəʊɡrɪʃ/. M19.
[from prec. + -ISH¹.]
Resembling or characteristic of an ogre.
■ **ogreishly** *adverb* L19.

ogress /ˈəʊɡrɪs/ *noun*¹. E18.
[from OGRE + -ESS¹.]
A female ogre.

ogress /ˈəʊɡrɪs/ *noun*². L16.
[Origin unkn.]
HERALDRY. A solid black circle forming a charge, supposed to represent a cannon-ball: a roundel sable, a pellet, a gunstone.

ogrish *adjective* var. of OGREISH.

Ogygian /əˈdʒɪdʒɪən/ *adjective*. Now *rare*. E17.
[from *Ogyges* (see below) + -IAN.]
Of or pertaining to (the time of) the mythical Attic or Boeotian king Ogyges. Also, of obscure antiquity, of great age.

OH *abbreviation*.
Ohio.

oh /əʊ/ *noun*¹. E20.
[Repr. pronunc. of *O*, *o* as the letter's name.]
The letter **O**, **o**; the figure zero.

oh /əʊ/ *interjection*, *noun*², & *verb*. M16.
[Var. of O *interjection*, infl. by French, Latin *oh*. Cf. AH *interjection*, OH-OH.]
▶ **A** *interjection*. Expr. surprise, pain, frustration, entreaty, disappointment, sorrow, relief, hesitation, disdain, doubt, etc. (freq. with other interjections, as ***oh damn!***, ***oh my!***, ***oh no!***, ***oh well!***, etc). Also (*poet. & rhet.*), (***a***) preceding a vocative in address and apostrophe, (***b***) introducing an emphatic statement or declaration, (***c***) expr. a wish *for* a thing or *that* a thing might be the case. M16.

📖 COVERDALE *Ps.* 6:4 Oh saue me, for thy mercies sake. W. COWPER Oh! for a closer walk with God. J. BUCHAN Oh, God be thanked, it's our friends. B. PYM Oh, rubbish! I never heard such far-fetched excuses. C. EKWENSI 'Oh! —' she exclaimed suddenly. 'I nearly sat on this!' ALIVE ***oh***. ***oh be joyful***: see JOYFUL *adjective* 1. ***oh boy!***: see BOY *noun* 5. ***oh dear!***: see DEAR *interjection*. **oh well** expr. resignation. **oh yeah** (*colloq.*, orig. *US*) expr. incredulity, disbelief, or scepticism, freq. prefacing a contradiction.

▶ **B** *noun*. An utterance of 'oh'. M16.

📖 SOUTHEY With throbs and throes, and ahs and ohs.

▶ **C** *verb intrans.* Say 'oh'. M19.

📖 R. BRADBURY The audience ohed and ahed as the captain talked.

o.h.c. *abbreviation*.
overhead camshaft.

OHG *abbreviation*.
Old High German.

†**oh ho** *interjection* var. of OHO.

ohia /əʊˈhiːə/ *noun*. E19.
[Hawaiian.]
In the Hawaiian Islands, (the fruit of) either of two trees of the myrtle family: (***a***) (more fully ***ohia lehua***) the lehua, *Metrosideros collina*; (***b***) the Malay apple, *Syzygium malaccense*.

Ohian /əʊˈhʌɪən/ *noun & adjective*. E19.
[from *Ohi(o* (see next) + -AN.]
▶ **A** *noun*. = OHIOAN *noun*. E19.
▶ **B** *adjective*. = OHIOAN *adjective*. M19.

Ohioan /əʊˈhʌɪəʊən/ *noun & adjective*. E19.
[from *Ohio*, a State (see below) and the river which forms its southern boundary + -AN.]
▶ **A** *noun*. A native or inhabitant of Ohio, a State of the north-eastern US. E19.
▶ **B** *adjective*. Of or pertaining to Ohio. E20.

ohm /əʊm/ *noun*. M19.
[Georg Simon *Ohm* (1787–1854), German physicist.]
PHYSICS etc.
1 The SI unit of electrical resistance, defined as the resistance that exists between two points when a potential difference between them of one volt produces a current of one ampere. (Symbol Ω.) M19.
2 ***Ohm's law***, either of two laws propounded by Ohm: (***a***) that the strength of a constant electric current in a circuit is proportional to the electromotive force divided by the resistance of the circuit, and that the potential difference between any two points of it is proportional to the resistance between them; (***b***) that a complex musical sound is heard as the sum of a number of distinct pure tones which can be resolved by Fourier analysis. M19.
■ **ohmage** *noun* electrical resistance measured in ohms E20. **ohmic** *adjective* of or pertaining to electrical resistance; *esp.* behaving in accordance with Ohm's law: L19. **ohmically** *adverb* by or as a result of ohmic resistance E20. **ohmmeter** *noun* an instrument for measuring electrical resistance in ohms L19.

OHMS *abbreviation*.
On Her or His Majesty's Service.

ohnosecond /ˈəʊnəʊsɛk(ə)nd/ *noun*. *colloq.* L20.
[from OH *interjection* + NO *interjection* + SECOND *noun*¹.]
COMPUTING. A moment in which one realises that one has made an error, typically by pressing the wrong key.

oho /əʊˈhəʊ/ *interjection*. Also †**oh ho**, †**o ho**. ME.
[from O *interjection* + HO *interjection*¹. Cf. AHA.]
Expr. surprise, mockery, exultation, etc., or (occas.) attracting attention.

oh-oh /ˈə-əʊ, əˈəʊ/ *interjection*. Also **oh, oh**. E18.
[Redupl. of OH *interjection*.]
Expr. alarm, dismay, derisive astonishment, or realization of a difficulty.

-oholic *suffix* var. of -AHOLIC.

ohone *interjection*, *noun*, & *verb* var. of OCHONE.

OHP *abbreviation*.
Overhead projector.

oh-so /ˈəʊsəʊ/ *adverb*. Freq. *iron.* Also as two words. L19.
[from OH *interjection* + SO *adverb*.]
Ever so, extremely: used as an intensive before an adjective or adverb

📖 J. GORES The mailboxes were set against the oh-so-rustic redwood slat fence.

o.h.v. *abbreviation*.
Overhead valve.

Oi /ɔɪ/ *pers. pronoun*. *dial.* E20.
[Repr. a pronunc.]
= I *pers. pronoun*.

oi /ɔɪ/ *interjection*¹. *slang*. M18.
[Repr. a pronunc. of HOY *interjection*.]
Attracting attention; = HOY *interjection*.

oi *interjection*² var. of OY *interjection*².

-oic /ˈəʊɪk/ *suffix*.
[from -O- + -IC, app. first in *caproic*, perh. after *benzoic*.]
ORGANIC CHEMISTRY. Forming adjectives designating carboxylic acids and their anhydrides, as ***hexanoic***, ***isatoic***, ***methanoic***, etc.

oick *noun* see OIK.

-oid /ɔɪd/ *suffix*.
[Repr. mod. Latin *-oides*, Greek *-oeidēs*, from *-o-* of the preceding elem. or connective + *-eidēs* having the form of, like, from *eidos* form (cf. Latin *-formis*: see -FORM). Cf. -ODE¹.]
Forming nouns and adjectives adopted from Greek or Latin, or English words modelled on these, with the sense '(a thing) having the form of, like, similar to' as ***android***, ***colloid***, ***metalloid***, ***ovoid***, ***spheroid***, ***steroid***, etc.; in *ZOOLOGY* also, '(a member) of a specified superfamily, suborder, or similarly ranked taxon (with a name ending in *-oidea*, *-oidei*)', as ***hominoid***, ***lemuroid***.

oidium /əʊˈɪdɪəm/ *noun*. Pl. **-ia** /-ɪə/. M19.
[mod. Latin (see below), from Greek *ōion* egg + -IDIUM.]
MYCOLOGY. Any of several kinds of fungal spore; *esp.* any member of the form-genus *Oidium*, which includes linked conidia of powdery mildews of the order Erysiphales; (a) disease caused by such a mildew, *spec.* vine mildew, caused by *Uncinula necator* (= *Oidium tuckeri*).
■ **oidiomy'cosis** *noun*, pl. **-coses** /-ˈkəʊsiːz/, *MEDICINE & VETERINARY MEDICINE* infection (now esp. infection of poultry) with a fungus formerly classified in the form-genus *Oidium*; *esp.* candidiasis (sour crop): E20.

oik /ɔɪk/ *noun*. *colloq.* (orig. *School slang*). Also (earlier) **oick**. E20.
[Origin unkn.]
An uncouth or obnoxious person; a fool, an idiot.

oikist *noun* var. of OECIST.

oikoumene, **oikumene** *nouns* vars. of OECUMENE.

oil /ɔɪl/ *noun*. ME.
[Anglo-Norman, Old Northern French *olie*, Old French *oile* (mod. *huile*) from Latin *oleum* (olive) oil (cf. Latin *olea* olive).]
1 Any of numerous liquids with a smooth sticky feel that are immiscible with water (but miscible with organic solvents), flammable, and chemically neutral; *spec.* crude oil (or a refined product of this), lubricating oil, or (formerly) olive oil. Also, a particular kind of this. Freq. with specifying word. ME. ▸**b** *CHEMISTRY*. Orig. (*ALCHEMY*), one of the five supposed principles of matter; a substance, esp. a viscous liquid, thought to represent this. Now only in *arch.* phrs. LME. ▸**c** Nitroglycerine. *US slang*. E20.
2 *fig. & allus.* **a** A thing which heals, comforts, or soothes; soothing or flattering words; nonsense, falsehood. ME. ▸**b** Laborious study (with allus. to the use of an oil-lamp for nightly study). Chiefly in phrs. below. M16. ▸**c** Money, esp. given as a bribe. Cf. GREASE *noun* 4. *US slang*. E20. ▸**d** Information, news, the true facts. Esp. in ***dinkum oil*** s.v. DINKUM *adjective & adverb*. *Austral. & NZ slang*. E20.
3 **a** *sing.* & (usu.) in *pl.* Paints made by grinding pigments in oil; oil-colours, oil-paints. M16. ▸**b** An oil-painting, a picture painted in oils. M19.
4 *ellipt.* In *pl.* Oilskin garments, an oilskin suit. *colloq.* L19.
5 In *pl.* Shares in an oil company. E20.

📖 **1** E. DAVID Add a little more oil so that the mushrooms do not dry up. R. P. JHABVALA His hair was thickly plastered with sweetly-smelling oil. *Daily Telegraph* Converting more power stations from oil to coal would push up electricity charges. M. WESLEY Petrol tank's full. I checked the oil, water, and tyres. ***almond oil***, ***black oil***, ***boiled oil***, ***castor oil***, ***cod liver oil***, ***diesel oil***, ***drying oil***, ***essential oil***, ***fixed oil***, ***gas oil***, ***hair oil***, ***heavy oil***, ***light oil***, ***linseed oil***, ***mineral oil***, ***olive oil***, ***sperm oil***, ***suntan oil***, ***vegetable oil***, ***volatile oil***, ***whale oil***, etc. ***oil of cloves***, ***oil of lavender***, ***oil of turpentine***, ***oil of wintergreen***, etc. **2a** AV *Isa.* 61:3 To giue vnto them . . the oyle of ioy for mourning. P. G. WODEHOUSE Coo to him, and give him the old oil. **3b** N. FREELING A large oil of three splendid horses.

Phrases: **animal oil** any oil obtained as an animal product. **burn midnight oil**, **burn the midnight oil** study late into the night. ***crude oil***: see CRUDE *adjective*. **good oil** = ***dinkum oil*** s.v. DINKUM *adjective & adverb*. **holy oil** oil used in religious or sacred rites. **oil and vinegar**, **oil and water** *fig.* two elements or factors which do not agree or blend together. **oil of vitriol** oleum, concentrated sulphuric acid. **oil on the fire**, **oil on the flames** further aggravation of existing anger, conflict, etc. **oil on water**, **oil on the water(s)** a means of appeasing conflict or disturbance (cf. ***pour oil on the waters***, ***pour oil on troubled waters*** s.v. POUR *verb* 1). **oil to the fire**, **oil to the flames** = ***oil on the fire*** above. ***smell of oil***: see SMELL *verb* 8a. **strike oil** (orig. *US*) *lit.* succeed in reaching oil (petroleum) by sinking a shaft through the overlying rock; *fig.* (*colloq.*) hit upon a source of rapid profit and affluence.

Attrib. & comb.: Esp. in the senses 'using oil as fuel', as ***oil heater***, ***oil lamp***, ***oil stove***, etc., 'pertaining to the international trade in petroleum and petroleum products', as ***oil company***, ***oil derrick***, ***oil industry***, ***oil minister***, ***oil refinery***, ***oil sheikh***, ***oil terminal***, etc. Special combs., as **oil baron** a magnate in the oil trade; **oil bath** (***a***) a receptacle containing oil, esp. for cooling, heating, lubricating, or insulating apparatus immersed in it; (***b***) the process of covering the body with oil (and then bathing to remove the oil); **oil-beetle** a beetle of the family Meloidae, which exudes an oily liquid when alarmed; **oil-berg** [after *iceberg*] a large body of oil floating freely in the sea; a ship carrying a large quantity of oil; **oil-bird** a gregarious nocturnal fruit-eating bird, *Steatornis caripensis*, of mountain caves in S. America and Trinidad, resembling a nightjar and having very fat nestlings which yield oil; **oil-box** (***a***) a box in which oil is stored; (***b***) a reservoir in a machine from which lubricating oil is dispensed; **oil-break** *adjective* designating a circuit-breaker in which the contacts are immersed in oil; **oil burner** (***a***) a device in which oil is vaporized and burned to produce heat; (***b***) a vehicle or ship which burns oil as fuel; (***c***) *slang* a vehicle which uses an excessive amount of lubricating oil; **oilcake** the substance that results when seeds such as rapeseed, linseed, etc., are compressed so as to drive out the oil, used as fodder or fertilizer; **oilcan** a can for holding oil, *esp.* one with a long nozzle for oiling machinery; †**oil-case** oilskin cloth; **oil circuit-breaker** a circuit-breaker in which the contacts are immersed in oil; **oil-colour** (a) paint made by grinding a pigment in oil (usu. in *pl.*); **oil-cooled** *adjective* (of machinery) using circulating oil to remove heat; **oil-cup** a cup-shaped reservoir which provides a supply of lubricating oil; **oil-drop** a drop of oil or lipid (freq. *attrib.* with ref. to an experiment to measure the charge of the electron); **oil drum** a metal cylindrical container used to transport oil; **oil engine** an internal-combustion engine in which the fuel enters the cylinder as a liquid; **oilfield** an area of land or seabed underlain by strata which bear oil, usu. in amounts that justify commercial exploitation; **oil-fired** *adjective* fuelled by the combustion of oil; **oilfish** a large violet or purple-brown escolar, *Ruvettus pretiosus*, the flesh of which is oily and unpalatable; **oil-gas** a gaseous mixture derived from mineral oils by destructive distillation; **oil-gauge** a meter for measuring the level or condition of oil, esp. in an engine; **oil-gilding** gilding in which gold leaf is laid on a surface formed of linseed oil mixed with a yellow pigment; **oil-gland** a gland which secretes oil; *spec.* the uropygial or coccygeal gland of a bird, which secretes the oil used for preening; **oilman** (*a*) *arch.* a maker or seller of animal and vegetable oils and eatables preserved in these; (*b*) an owner or employee of an oil company; **oil-meal** ground oilcake; **oil-mill** a machine or a factory in which seeds, fruits, etc., are crushed or pressed to extract oil; **oil-nut** the oil-rich nut or large seed of any of various plants, esp. the castor oil plant, *Ricinus communis*, the N. American white walnut, *Juglans cinerea*, or the buffalo nut, *Pyrularia pubera*; any of the plants producing these nuts or seeds; **oil-paint** = *oil-colour* above; **oil-painter** a painter in oils; **oil-painting** (*a*) the action or art of painting in oils; (*b*) a picture painted in oils; ***be no oil-painting***, (of a person) be physically unattractive; **oil-palm** a W. African palm tree, *Elaeis guineensis*, bearing fruit whose pericarp and seed-kernels are a valuable source of oil; **oil-pan** the sump of an engine; **oil-paper**: made transparent or waterproof by soaking in oil; **oil-plant** any of various plants yielding an oil; *spec.* sesame, *Sesamum indicum*; **oil pollution** contamination with an escape or discharge of oil, esp. from a ship; ***oil pool***: see POOL *noun*[1] 5; **oil-press** an apparatus for pressing oil from fruit, seeds, etc.; **oil province** an extensive area containing a number of oil-fields that are geologically related; **oil-rich** *adjective* containing or yielding much oil; **oil rig** a structure with equipment for drilling an oil well; **oil-ring** a ring which dips into an oil reservoir and continuously lubricates a bearing around which it revolves; **oil-sand** a rock stratum, esp. of sandstone, which yields oil; **oil-seed** any of various seeds (as sesame, cottonseed, castor bean, etc.) cultivated as a source of oil (***oil-seed rape***: see RAPE *noun*[3] 2 (b)); **oil shale** (a) shale containing an organic deposit (kerogen), which yields oil on distillation (freq. in *pl.*); **oil-shark** a shark from which oil may be obtained, *esp.* the soupfin, *Galeorhinus zyopterus*; **oil-silk** oiled silk; **oil slick** a film or layer of oil floating on an expanse of water, *esp.* one which has escaped or been discharged from a ship; **oil spill** an escape of oil into the sea, an estuary, etc.; **oil-spot** an oily patch or mark; *spec.* a silvery marking on brown Chinese porcelain (esp. of the Song period) caused by precipitation of iron in firing (usu. *attrib.*); **oil-strike** a discovery of an oilfield by drilling; **oil string** the innermost length of casing (tubing) in an oil well, extending down to the oil-producing rock; **oil switch** = *oil circuit-breaker* above; **oil tanker** a vehicle or vessel designed to transport oil; **oil-tight** *adjective* [after *watertight*] sealed so as to prevent oil from passing through; **oil trade** the international trade in petroleum and petroleum products; ***oil trap***: see TRAP *noun*[1] 6C; **oil-way** a channel for the passage of lubricating oil; **oil well** an artificially made well or shaft in rock from which mineral oil is drawn.

■ **oildom** *noun* the world of petroleum production and marketing M19. **oilless** /-l-l-/ *adjective* devoid of oil; containing no oil; not lubricated, or not requiring to be lubricated, with oil: M17. **oillessness** *noun* M19.

oil /ɔɪl/ *verb.* LME.
[from the noun.]
1 *verb trans.* †**a** Anoint; pour oil on ceremonially, esp. when consecrating as monarch. LME–M19. ▸**b** Put oil on; apply oil to; moisten, smear, cover, or lubricate with oil; *spec.* rub (a person) with suntan oil to protect against sunburn. LME. ▸**c** Treat with oil; *esp.* cover (water) with a surface film of oil to kill mosquito larvae. E20.
2 *verb trans.* Bribe; flatter. E17.
3 a *verb trans.* Supply with oil as fuel. E17. ▸**b** *verb intrans.* Take on oil as fuel. E20.
4 a *verb intrans.* Of butter or other food: become oily, esp. when heated or melted. E18. ▸**b** *verb trans.* Make (butter etc.) oily, esp. by heating or melting. M18.
5 *verb intrans.* Move or go in a smooth or stealthy manner. *colloq.* E20.
1b oil the wheels *fig.* help things to go smoothly. **2 oil a person's hand**, **oil a person's palm** bribe (a person). **oil one's tongue** *arch.* adopt or use flattering speech. **oil the knocker** *slang* bribe or tip a doorman.
With adverbs in specialized senses: **oil in** *colloq.* enter stealthily; *fig.* interfere. **oil out** (*a*) PAINTING moisten (parts of a picture) with oil before retouching; (*b*) *colloq.* leave stealthily; *fig.* extricate oneself. **oil up** (*a*) clog up with oil; (*b*) rub or polish with oil; cover (the body) with suntan oil.

oilcloth /ˈɔɪlklɒθ/ *noun.* L17.
[from OIL *noun* + CLOTH *noun*.]
1 A fabric, usu. of cotton, waterproofed with an oil or resin and used for clothing etc; oilskin; in *pl.*, oilskin garments. L17.
2 A canvas painted or coated with linseed or other oil, used to cover floors, tables, etc; linoleum. L18.
■ **oil-clothed** *adjective* covered with oilcloth L19.

oiled /ɔɪld/ *adjective.* M16.
[from OIL *verb* + -ED[1].]
1 a Smeared, moistened, or lubricated with oil; covered with oil. Formerly, (of a person) anointed. M16. ▸**b** Prepared with or preserved in oil. M16. ▸**c** Of a fabric etc.: impregnated with oil, esp. so as to be waterproof. E17.
2 Converted or melted into oil. M18.
3 (Mildly) drunk, tipsy. Freq. preceded by qualifying adverb, as *nicely*, *well*. M18.

> 🕮 **1c** J. R. L. ANDERSON A heavyweight oiled-wool pullover. A. S. BYATT Two parcels, wrapped in oiled silk, and tied with black ribbon.

Comb.: **oiled-down** *adjective* smoothed or plastered down with (hair) oil; **oiled-up** *adjective* fouled or choked with oil.

oiler /ˈɔɪlə/ *noun.* ME.
[from OIL *noun*, *verb* + -ER[1].]
†**1** A maker or seller of oil. Long *rare*. ME–E19.
2 A person who oils or lubricates with oil. M19.
3 A device for oiling machinery; *spec.* an oilcan. M19.
4 In *pl.* Oilskin garments, an oilskin suit. *colloq.* (orig. *US*). L19.
5 An oil well. *US colloq.* L19.
6 A vessel or vehicle transporting oil. L19.
7 A vessel or vehicle using oil as its fuel; an oil engine. E20.

oilskin /ˈɔɪlskɪn/ *noun & adjective.* L18.
[from OIL *noun* + SKIN *noun*.]
▶ **A** *noun.* Cloth waterproofed with oil, oilcloth; a piece of this; a garment or (in *pl.*) a suit made of this. L18.

> 🕮 *Highlife* A hairy old fisherman in a stiff black oilskin.

▶ **B** *adjective.* Made of oilskin. L18.
■ **oilskinned** *adjective* dressed in oilskin(s) M19.

oilstone /ˈɔɪlstəʊn/ *noun & verb.* L16.
[from OIL *noun* + STONE *noun*.]
▶ **A** *noun.* A smooth, fine-grained stone lubricated with oil for sharpening tools; a whetstone. L16.
▶ **B** *verb trans.* Sharpen on an oilstone. *rare.* L19.

oily /ˈɔɪli/ *adjective & noun.* E16.
[from OIL *noun* + -Y[1].]
▶ **A** *adjective.* **1** Of, pertaining to, or resembling oil; full of or impregnated with oil. E16.
2 Smeared or covered with oil; greasy. L16.
3 *fig.* Smooth in behaviour or (esp.) speech; insinuating, fawning, unctuous, obsequious, servile. L16.
Special collocations: **oily wad** *Nautical slang* †(*a*) a torpedo boat burning oil as fuel; (*b*) a seaman without a special skill.
▶ **B** *noun.* An oilskin garment. Usu. in *pl.* L19.
■ **oilily** *adverb* M19. **oiliness** *noun* oily quality or condition (*lit.* & *fig.*); *spec.* in ENGINEERING, lubricating power: L16.

oime /oiˈmɛ/ *interjection. rare.* M17.
[Italian *oimè*, *ohimè*, from *ohi!* alas! + *me* me.]
Alas! Ah me!

oink /ɔɪŋk/ *verb, noun, & interjection.* M20.
[Imit.]
▶ **A** *verb intrans.* Of a pig: utter its characteristic deep grunting sound. Of a person: make a similar sound; grunt like a pig. M20.
▶ **B** *noun & interjection.* (Repr.) the grunt of a pig; an act of grunting like a pig; a sound resembling this. M20.

oino- *combining form* see OENO-.

oinochoe *noun* var. of OENOCHOE.

oint /ɔɪnt/ *verb trans.* Long *arch.* or *poet.* ME.
[Old French, pa. pple of *oindre*, from Latin *unguere* anoint.]
= ANOINT.

ointment /ˈɔɪntm(ə)nt/ *noun.* ME.
[Alt., after prec., of Old French *oignement*, from popular Latin form of Latin *unguentum* UNGUENT: see -MENT.]
1 A cosmetic or (now usu.) medicinal preparation in the form of a soft smooth paste. ME.
†**2** Anointing, unction. E16–E17.
1 ***fly in the ointment***: see FLY *noun*[1]. ***Neapolitan ointment***: see NEAPOLITAN *adjective.*

oiran /ˈɔɪrən/ *noun.* Pl. same. L19.
[Japanese.]
A Japanese courtesan of high standing.

Oireachtas /ˈɛrəktəs, *foreign* ˈɛrəxtəs/ *noun.* E20.
[Irish = assembly, convocation.]
1 A cultural festival held annually by the Gaelic League of Ireland. E20.
2 The legislature or parliament of the Republic of Ireland, consisting of the president, a lower house of elected representatives (Dáil Éireann), and a partially nominated senate or upper house (Seanad Éireann). E20.

oiticica /ɔɪtɪˈsiːkə/ *noun.* E20.
[Portuguese from Tupi *oitisica*, from *uita* plant-name + *isika* resin.]
Any of several tropical S. American trees, esp. *Licania rigida* (family Chrysobalanaceae), whose crushed seeds yield an oil used in paints and varnishes.

Ojibwa /ə(ʊ)ˈdʒɪbweɪ/ *noun & adjective.* Also **-way** & other vars. E18.
[Ojibwa *ojibwe*, said to mean 'puckered', with ref. to a type of puckered moccasin worn by this people. Cf. CHIPPEWA.]
▶ **A** *noun.* Pl. same, **-s**.
1 A member of an Algonquian people of central Canada, esp. the area around Lake Superior. E18.
2 The language of this people. M19.
▶ **B** *attrib.* or as *adjective.* Of or pertaining to the Ojibwa or their language. M19.

¶ *Chippewa* is the more usual name in the US, and *Ojibwa(y)* in Canada.

ojime /ˈəʊdʒɪmeɪ, *foreign* ˈoːdʒime/ *noun.* Pl. same, **-s**. L19.
[Japanese, from *o* string + *shime* fastening, fastener.]
A bead or beadlike object, often very elaborate, used in Japan as a sliding fastener on the strings of a bag, pouch, or inro.

OK *abbreviation.*
Oklahoma.

OK /əʊˈkeɪ/ *adjective, interjection, noun, adverb, & verb. colloq.* (orig. *US*). Also **O.K.**, **ok**, **o.k.** See also OKAY. M19.
[App. from the initials of *orl korrect* joc. alt. of *all correct*, but also popularized as a slogan in the US election campaign of 1840, repr. the initials of *Old Kinderhook*, a nickname (derived from his birthplace) of President Martin Van Buren (1782–1862), who was seeking re-election.]
▶ **A** *adjective.* **1** All correct, all right; satisfactory, good; well, in good health; (in weakened sense) adequate, not bad, so-so. M19.
2 Socially or culturally acceptable; correct; fashionable, modish. M19.

> 🕮 **1** D. H. LAWRENCE At first Joe thought the job O.K. *Zigzag* We could have had a great album, rather than an OK album. **OK by**, **OK with** acceptable to (a person). **2** *Times Lit. Suppl.* Handy quotations from such OK literary luminaries as Macaulay, Nietzsche, Strindberg.

▶ **B** *interjection.* Expr. (or, interrog., seeking) assent, acquiescence, or approval (esp. in response to a question or statement); expr. readiness; introducing an utterance. Also (orig. in slogans) appended to a statement or declaration as a challenge demanding agreement (freq. in — ***rules OK!***). M19.

> 🕮 D. LODGE If it happens, it doesn't matter, OK? *She* OK—but be quick. C. BRAYFIELD OK, let's go.

▶ **C** *noun.* The letters 'OK', esp. as written on a document etc. to express approval; *gen.* an endorsement, an approval, an authorization. Freq. in ***give the OK (to)***. M19.
▶ **D** *adverb.* In a satisfactory or acceptable manner. L19.

> 🕮 J. REITH He said . . that if things went OK I should get a rise soon.

▶ **E** *verb trans.* Pa. t. & pple **OK'd**, **OKed**. Endorse, esp. by marking with the letters 'OK'; approve, agree to, sanction, pass. L19.

> 🕮 P. DICKINSON But you know quite well head office wouldn't OK it.

■ **OK-ness** *noun* the fact or quality of being OK; acceptability: M20.

oka /ˈɒkə/ *noun*[1]. Also **oke** /əʊk/. E17.
[Italian *oca*, French *oque* from Turkish *okka* from Arab. *ūkiya*, prob. through Syriac from Greek *ougkia* from Latin *uncia* OUNCE *noun*[1].]
An Egyptian and former Turkish unit of weight, variable but now usu. equal to approx. 1.3 kg (2¾ lb). Also, a unit of capacity equal to approx. 0.2 litre (⅓ pint).

oka *noun*[2] var. of OCA.

Oka /ˈəʊkə/ *noun*[3]. M20.
[The name of a town in southern Quebec, where the cheese is made.]
In full ***Oka cheese***. A variety of cured Canadian cheese, made by Trappist monks.

okapi /ə(ʊ)ˈkɑːpi/ *noun.* Pl. same, **-s**. E20.
[African name.]
A rare ungulate mammal of the giraffe family, *Okapia johnstoni*, which is reddish-brown with horizontal white stripes on the legs, and is native to the Congolese rainforest.

okay /əʊˈkeɪ/ *adjective, interjection, noun, adverb, & verb. colloq.* (orig. *US*). E20.
[Repr. pronunc. of OK.]
= OK.

Okazaki /əʊkəˈzɑːki/ *noun.* M20.
[Reiji *Okazaki* (1930–75), Japanese molecular biologist.]
BIOLOGY. Used *attrib.* to designate fragments formed during the replication of chromosomal DNA.

oke *noun* var. of OKA *noun*[1].

oke /əʊk/ *adjective & interjection. colloq.* (orig. *US*). E20.
[Abbreviation of OKAY, OK.]
= OK *adjective, interjection.*

okey-doke /əʊkɪˈdəʊk/ *adjective & interjection. colloq.* (orig. *US*). Also **-dokey** /-ˈdəʊki/ & other vars. M20.
[Redupl. of OKAY, OK.]
= OK *adjective, interjection.*

Okhrana /ɒkˈrɑːnə/ *noun.* L19.
[Russian *okhrana* lit. 'guarding, protection'.]
Hist. An organization set up in 1881 in Russia after the assassination of Alexander II to maintain State security and suppress revolutionary activities, replaced after the Revolution of 1917 by the Cheka.

Okie /ˈəʊki/ *noun. colloq. Chiefly US.* **M20.**
[formed as OK(LAHOMA + -IE.]
A migrant agricultural worker; *spec.* one from Oklahoma who had been forced to leave a farm during the depression of the 1930s. Also, a native or inhabitant of Oklahoma.

okimono /əʊkɪˈməʊnəʊ, *foreign* oːkiˈmoːno/ *noun.* Pl. same, **-s**. **L19.**
[Japanese, from *oki* putting + *mono* thing.]
A Japanese standing ornament or figure, *esp.* one put in a guest room of a house.

Okinawan /əʊkɪˈnɑːwən, ɒk-/ *noun & adjective.* **M20.**
[from *Okinawa* (see below) + -AN.]
▶ **A** *noun.* A native or inhabitant of Okinawa, a region of Japan in the southern Ryukyu islands, esp. of the largest of the islands, from which the region takes its name. Also, the dialect of Japanese spoken in Okinawa. **M20.**
▶ **B** *adjective.* Of or pertaining to the region or island of Okinawa or the dialect spoken there. **M20.**

Okla. *abbreviation.*
Oklahoma.

Oklahoma /əʊkləˈhəʊmə/ *noun.* **M20.**
[A State of the south-western US.]
A kind of rummy, prob. orig. played in Oklahoma. Also more fully ***Oklahoma gin***, ***Oklahoma rummy***.

Oklahoman /əʊkləˈhəʊmən/ *noun & adjective.* **L19.**
[formed as prec. + -AN.]
(A native or inhabitant) of the State of Oklahoma.

oknophil *noun* var. of OCNOPHIL.

okoume /əʊˈkuːmeɪ/ *noun.* **E20.**
[African name.]
Gaboon mahogany; the tree which yields this, *Aucoumea klaineana*.

okra /ˈɒkrə, ˈəʊkrə/ *noun.* **E18.**
[App. W. African: cf. Igbo *okuro* okra, Twi *nkrakra* broth.]
1 A tall African plant of the mallow family, *Abelmoschus esculentus*, widely cultivated in tropical and subtropical regions; the mucilaginous fruit of this plant, gathered when young and used as a vegetable and for thickening soup and stews. Also called ***gumbo***, ***lady's fingers***. **E18.**
2 With specifying word: any of various other mallows of the genera *Abelmoschus* and *Hibiscus*. **M19.**

okrug /ˈɒkrʊɡ/ *noun.* **L19.**
[Russian *okrug*, Bulgarian *okrǎg*.]
In Russia and Bulgaria, a territorial division for administrative and other purposes. Cf. OBLAST.

okta /ˈɒktə/ *noun.* Pl. **-s**, same. **M20.**
[Alt. of OCTA-.]
METEOROLOGY. A unit of cloud cover, equal to one-eighth of the sky.

Okun /ˈəʊk(ə)n/ *noun.* **L20.**
[Arthur M. *Okun* (1928–80), US economist.]
ECONOMICS. Used *attrib.* and in *possess.* to designate a law propounded by Okun that increased national unemployment is directly related to a decreased gross national product.

ol /ɒl/ *noun.* **E20.**
[from -OL.]
CHEMISTRY. Used *attrib.* and in *comb.* to designate a hydroxyl group of which the oxygen atom is bonded to two metal atoms, and a polynuclear complex containing such a group.

ol' *adjective* var. of OLE *adjective*.

-ol /ɒl/ *suffix.*
[In sense 1 from ALCOH)OL. In sense 2 from Latin *oleum* oil: cf. -OLE[2].]
CHEMISTRY. **1** Forming the names of substances which are alcohols in the wider sense (including aromatic alcohols or phenols), as ***cholesterol***, ***diol***, ***geraniol***, ***methanol***, ***naphthol***, ***thymol***, or compounds analogous to alcohol, as ***thiol***. ▶**b** Forming trivial names of substances related to or derived from phenols, as ***creosol***.
2 Forming the names of oils and oil-derived substances, as **benzol** etc. (in *CHEMISTRY* use now formally replaced by -OLE[2]). Also, forming proprietary names of various kinds of substance, as ***Lysol*** etc.

-ola /ˈəʊlə/ *suffix.* Chiefly *US.*
[Prob. from PIANOLA.]
Forming nouns, as ***granola***, ***payola***, etc.

olam /əʊˈlɑːm/ *noun. rare.* **L19.**
[Hebrew *ʿōlām*.]
A vast period of time, an age of the universe. Cf. AEON.
■ **olamic** *adjective* of or belonging to an olam **L19.**

-olater /ˈɒlətə/ *suffix.*
Form of -LATER with *-o-* provided by first element or merely connective (***idolater***, ***Mariolater***).

olation /ɒˈleɪʃ(ə)n/ *noun.* **M20.**
[from OL + -ATION.]
CHEMISTRY. Conversion of a complex into an ol form; linking of metal atoms by hydroxyl ligands (esp. with ref. to chromium compounds used in tanning).
■ **olate** *verb intrans.* form an ol group or compound (chiefly as ***olated*** *ppl adjective*) **M20.**

-olatry /ˈɒlətri/ *suffix.*
Form of -LATRY with *-o-* provided by first element or merely connective (***demonolatry***, ***idolatry***).

Olbers' paradox /ˈɒlbəz ˌparədɒks/ *noun phr.* **M20.**
[H. W. M. *Olbers* (1758–1840), German astronomer.]
ASTRONOMY. The apparent paradox that if stars are distributed evenly throughout an infinite universe, the sky should be as bright by night as by day, since more distant stars would be fainter but more numerous (resolved by the observation that distant stars are of finite age, and recede from the observer as the universe expands).

†**old** *noun*[1]. Also **ald**. **ME.**
[Old Norse *ǫld* (genit. sing. *aldar*) age, an age from Germanic base of OLD *adjective*; later perh. from OLD *adjective* or alt. of ELD *noun*.]
1 Age, duration of life; an age of the world. Only in **ME.**
2 Old age. Also, the waning of the moon. **ME–E17.**

old /əʊld/ *adjective, noun*[2], *& adverb.*
[Old English *ald*, (West Saxon) *eald* = Old Frisian, Old Saxon *ald* (Dutch *oud*), Old & mod. High German *alt*, from West Germanic; pa. ppl formation from Germanic base of Old English *alan*, Old Norse *ala* nourish, Gothic *alan* grow up, app. with the sense 'grown up, adult', rel. to Latin *alere* nourish. Cf. ELD *noun, adjective*, ELDER *adjective & noun*[2], ELDEST, also AULD.]
▶ **A** *adjective.* **I** Having lived or existed for a relatively long time.
1 That has lived long; advanced in age; far on in the natural span of life; not young. **OE.**
2 That has been relatively long in existence or use. Also, worn with age or use; decayed, shabby, stale; disused, outdated. **OE.** ▶†**b** Wearing old clothes. *rare* (Shakes.). Only in **L16.**
3 *pred.* & *in comb.* Of a specified age. **OE.** ▶**b** *transf.* Of an activity, as a game, run, etc.: having covered a specified number of laps, overs, yards, etc. **M20.**
4 Practised, experienced, skilled, (*in* a specified matter or respect). **OE.**
5 Of, pertaining to, or characteristic of old people or advanced years. Freq. in ***old age***. **ME.**
6 Great, plentiful, abundant, excessive. Now *rare* exc. as intensifier after *good*, *grand*, etc. **LME.**

📖 **1** TENNYSON All my children have gone before me, I am so old. *Sunday Express* Delroy . . bought his car last year before he was old enough to drive. *Bella* I've been seeing a much older man who . . only wants to be friends. **2** THACKERAY Cracked old houses where the painters . . are always at work. G. VIDAL He was dressed in old clothes and looked like a beggar. **b** SHAKES. *Tam. Shr.* The rest were ragged, old, and beggarly. **3** J. RUSKIN A wall which was just eighteen hundred years old. *Daily News* A five-year-old girl. B. BAINBRIDGE 'How old?' demanded Mary O'Leary. 'Twenty-three,' Bridget said. **b** *Observer* The innings was . . three overs old when Bedi came on. **4** B. ASHLEY He was a younger man, but old in the ways of beer. **5** AV *Gen.* 25:8 Abraham . . died in a good old age. F. MARRYAT An old head upon very young shoulders. **6** C. COTTON There was old drinking and . . singing. E. O'NEILL We'll go on a grand old souse together.

▶ **II** Existing since an earlier period; long established.
7 a Dating from ancient times; made or formed long ago, primeval. **OE.** ▶**b** Long-standing; not new or recent; familiar from of old. **OE.**
8 Used in casual, familiar, or affectionate forms of address or reference. Now freq. *joc.* & *colloq.* **L16.**

📖 **7a** MILTON An old, and haughty Nation. *South African Panorama* Hinduism, one of the oldest religions still practised today. **b** SHELLEY Another piece of fun, One of his old tricks. F. WELDON She was in no position either to make new friends, or renew old acquaintances. **8** G. BERKELEY Hath not old England subsisted for many ages? D. FRANCIS 'They didn't take my advice,' 'Silly old them.' ***old bean***, ***old fruit***, ***old son***, ***old sport***, etc.

▶ **III** Belonging to a bygone period; former.
9 Of or pertaining to antiquity or the distant past; ancient, bygone. **OE.** ▶**b** Of ancient character, form, or appearance; antique. **LME.** ▶**c** Associated with ancient, esp. classical, times; renowned in history. Chiefly *poet.* **M17.**
10 Belonging to an earlier period (of time, one's life, etc.) or to the earliest of two or more periods, times, or stages; designating the earlier of two specified things of the same kind; former, previous. **OE.** ▶**b** Designating a country, region, etc., known or inhabited by a person or his or her ancestors at an earlier period; *spec.* designating the oldest district or historic centre of a town etc. **L16.** ▶**c** Designating a former member of a particular institution or society, esp. a school. **E19.** ▶**d** Designating a monetary unit that has been replaced by another of the same name. **M20.**

📖 **9** SHAKES. *1 Hen. VI* The nine sybils of old Rome. MILTON City of old or modern Fame. **b** POPE Some by old words to fame have made pretence, Ancients in phrase. **c** M. PATTISON The old historical lands of Europe. **10** WORDSWORTH My old remembrances went from me wholly. TENNYSON The old order changeth, yielding place to new. N. SEDAKA My old girlfriend . . came back into my life. P. AUSTER Back in the old days, eighteen, twenty years ago. **b** N. MAGENS The Ship called St. George, belonging to London in old England. *Weekly New Mexican* Albuquerque . . has an old town like nearly all of the New Mexico cities. **c** C. MACKENZIE Cyril Bailey . . was an Old Pauline who had left before I went to St Paul's. **d** *Listener* In those pre-decimal days, you could buy a loaf . . for 15 old pennies.

Special collocations, phrases, & comb.: **an old one** a familiar joke. **any old** — any — whatever. **any old how** *colloq.* in any way whatever. ***come the old soldier over***: see COME *verb*. ***for old sake's sake***, ***for old times' sake***: see SAKE *noun*[1]. **good old** worthy, worthwhile; much valued or appreciated, freq. in a sentimental way. ***Grand Old Party***: see GRAND *adjective*[1]. ***high old time***: see HIGH *adjective*. **little old**: an affectionate or mildly depreciatory form of reference. ***new wine in old bottles***: see WINE *noun*. ***of old***: see OF *preposition*. ***Old Academy***: see ACADEMY 2. **old age pension** a pension paid in the UK by the State to retired people above a certain age. **old age pensioner** an old person, *esp.* one receiving an old age pension. ***old as the hills***: see HILL *noun*. ***Old Bailey***: see BAILEY 2. **Old Believer** *ECCLESIASTICAL HISTORY* a member of a Russian Orthodox group which refused to accept the liturgical reforms of the patriarch Nikon (1605–81); a Raskolnik. ***old BETSY***. **Old Bill** (***a***) [with allus. to a cartoon character created during the war of 1914–18 by Bruce Bairnsfather (1888–1959), Brit. cartoonist] a grumbling veteran soldier, usu. having a large moustache; (***b***) = BILL *noun*[4]. **old bird** *slang* a wary astute person. **old boot** *slang* (freq. *derog.*) a woman *esp.* an unattractive one, a wife. **old boy** (***a***) *colloq.* an elderly man; (***b***) *colloq.* an affectionate or familiar form of address or reference to a man or boy; (***c***) a former male pupil of a school or college, esp. of an English public school; ***old boy net***, ***old boy network***, ***old boys' net***, ***old boys' network***, mutual assistance, esp. preferment in employment, shown among old boys or others with a shared social background. ***Old British***: see BRITISH *noun* 1. ***Old* CATHOLIC**. ***Old* CELTIC**. ***Old Church Slavonic***: see SLAVONIC *noun*. **old clothes man** a dealer in second-hand clothes. ***Old Commonwealth***: see COMMONWEALTH 5c. ***Old Contemptibles***: see CONTEMPTIBLE *noun*. ***Old Covenant***: see COVENANT *noun*. ***old crumpet***: see CRUMPET 4. **old days**, **old times** past times. ***old dog***: see DOG *noun* 8. ***Old English***: see ENGLISH *adjective & noun*. **Old English sheepdog** (an animal of) a breed of large sheepdog with a shaggy blue-grey and white coat. **old-face** *noun & adjective* (*TYPOGRAPHY*) (designating or pertaining to) a typeface with oblique stress, bracketed serifs, and little contrast between thick and thin strokes, orig. modelled on characters derived from classical inscriptions and early humanist hands. ***old firm***: see FIRM *noun*. ***old fogy***: see FOGY *noun* 1. **Old French** the French language of the period before *c* 1600, esp. before *c* 1400. **old gang** *colloq.* a clique, esp. of politicians, accustomed to supporting each other. ***Old Gentleman***: see GENTLEMAN. **old girl** (***a***) a former female pupil of a school or college; (***b***) *colloq.* a familiar form of address or reference to a woman. **Old Glory** *US* the national flag of the US. ***old gold***: see GOLD *noun*[1]. ***old gooseberry***: see GOOSEBERRY *noun* 3. **old-growth** *adjective* (of a tree, forest, etc.) mature, never felled. **old guard** the original, established, or conservative members of a group, party, etc. **old hand** (***a***) a person with long experience, an expert; (***b***) an ex-convict. ***Old Harry***: see HARRY *noun*[2]. ***old hat***: see HAT *noun*. **Old High German** High German of the period before *c* 1200. **old ice** in polar regions, ice formed before the most recent winter. **Old Icelandic** the western branch of Old Norse spoken and written in Norway, Iceland, the Orkneys, etc. up to the 16th cent.; the Icelandic language before the 17th cent. ***old identity***: see IDENTITY 4. ***old Indian***: see INDIAN *noun* 1b. **Old Irish** the Celtic language of Ireland in the period before *c* 1000. **Old Italian** the Italian language between the 4th and the 10th cents. **Old Kingdom** (***a***) (*collect.*) *the* Third, Fourth, Fifth, and Sixth Dynasties, which ruled Egypt from the 27th to the 22nd cent. BC; (***b***) *the* period of Hittite history from the 18th to the 16th cent. BC. **Old Labour** *POLITICS* the UK Labour Party before the introduction of the internal reforms initiated by Neil Kinnock (see ***NEW Labour***); that section of the Labour Party which actively opposed those reforms. **old lady** (***a***) *colloq.* one's mother, wife, or female partner; (***b***) a brown noctuid moth, *Mormo maura*; (***c***) ***the Old Lady in Threadneedle Street***, ***the Old Lady of Threadneedle Street***, the Bank of England. ***old lag***: see LAG *noun*[5] 2b. ***Old Latin***: see LATIN *adjective & noun*. ***old law***: see LAW *noun*[1]. **old leaven** [with allus. to *1 Corinthians* 5:6, 7] *CHRISTIAN THEOLOGY* traces of the unregenerate condition, former prejudices inconsistently retained by a convert. **Old Left** (of or relating to) the older liberal elements in the socialist movement. **Old Light** (esp. *SCOTTISH ECCLESIASTICAL HISTORY*) a traditional, freq. more conservative, theological or ecclesiastical doctrine; a supporter or propounder of this. **old master** (a painting by) a great artist of former times, esp. of the 13th to 17th cents. in Europe. **old money** old-established wealth. **old moon** the moon in its last quarter, before the new moon. ***old moustache***: see MOUSTACHE 4. ***Old Nick***: see NICK *noun*[2]. **Old Norse** the old N. Germanic language from which the Scandinavian languages derive; *spec.* = ***Old Icelandic*** above. **old offender** a habitual criminal. **old pal** an old friend, *esp.* a business associate; ***Old Pals Act***, (the practice of giving) favour or mutual help based on prior acquaintance. ***Old Peg***: see PEG *noun*[2] 2. ***Old Pharaoh***: see PHARAOH 2. ***old poker***: see POKER *noun*[2]. **Old Prussian** *noun & adjectival phr.* (*Hist.*) (***a***) *noun phr.* a member of a medieval people, related to the Lithuanians, who inhabited the shores of the Baltic Sea east of the Vistula; the language of this people (see PRUSSIAN *noun* 2); (***b***) *adjectival phr.* pertaining to this people or their language. ***old* QUANTUM *theory***. ***Old Red Sandstone***: see SANDSTONE. **old religion** a religion replaced or ousted by another; *spec.* (***a***) paganism, (***b***) witchcraft, (***c***) Roman Catholicism. ***old retainer***: see RETAINER *noun*[2] 1. **Old Ritualist** *ECCLESIASTICAL HISTORY* = ***Old Believer*** above. **old rope** rank tobacco (*slang*); ***money for old rope***: see MONEY *noun*. ***Old* SAXON**. ***Old***

Scratch: see SCRATCH *noun*². **old ship** *Nautical slang* an old shipmate. **old sledge** = ALL FOURS 2. **old snow** snow formed before the most recent winter. *old* SOAKER. *old soldier*: see SOLDIER *noun*. **Old South** the Southern States of the US, before the civil war of 1861–5. *old Spanish custom*, *old Spanish practice*: see SPANISH *adjective*. **old-spelling** the unstandardized early spelling of English. **old squaw** the long-tailed duck, *Clangula hyemalis*. *old stager*: see STAGER 1. **old-standing** *adjective* long-standing. **old story** a familiar tale, *esp.* an excuse. *Old Stripes*: see STRIPE *noun*² 1b. **old style** (*a*) (**O- S-**) the method of calculating dates using the Julian calendar, used in England and Wales until superseded by the Gregorian calendar in 1752 (cf. *New Style* s.v. NEW *adjective*); (*b*) TYPOGRAPHY a typeface modelled on old-face, but more regular in design; *US* old-face. **old sweat** *slang* a veteran soldier. **Old Testament** the part of the Bible concerned with the Mosaic dispensation. **old thing** (*a*) a familiar form of address; (*b*) *Austral.* a meal of beef and damper. **old Thirteen** *US HISTORY* the original thirteen American colonies, which declared their independence in 1776. *old times*: see *old days* above. **Old Tom** (proprietary name for) a kind of strong gin. **Old Welsh** the Welsh language of the period before *c* 1150. **old witch-grass** a N. American panic-grass, *Panicum capillare*. **Old World** Europe, Asia, and Africa; the eastern hemisphere. **old-world** *adjective* belonging to or associated with old times or the Old World; *Old World monkey*, a monkey of the catarrhine family Cercopithecidae, comprising Eurasian and African monkeys and including guenons, macaques, langurs, and baboons. **old-worldish** *adjective* characteristic of a past era. **old year** the year just ended or about to end. *pay off old scores*: see SCORE *noun*. *play old gooseberry*: see GOOSEBERRY *noun* 3. **the old country** one's mother country. **the Old Dart** *Austral. & NZ colloq.* Great Britain, *esp.* England. *the oldest profession*: see PROFESSION 3. *the Old Pretender*: see PRETENDER 2. *the Old Reaper*: see REAPER 1. *the old regime*: see REGIME 2. *the old sod*: see SOD *noun*¹. *tough as old boots*: see TOUGH *adjective*.

► **B** *noun*. †**1** An old man, an old woman. ME–M16.

2 An earlier time or period. Only in *of old*. LME.

3 a In *pl. The* old members, esp. *the* old people (of a set or category). *colloq.* (now *rare*). L19. ▸**b** *collect. pl. The* class of old people. L19.

4 a In *pl.* Hops between two and four years old. L19. ▸**b** A type of beer noted for its strength. E20.

> 📖 **2** R. ELLIS You of old did hold them Something worthy.

► **C** *adverb*. In ancient times, long ago. *rare* (Shakes.) exc. in *comb.* M16.

> 📖 NEB *Matt.* 15:2 Why do your disciples break the old-established tradition?

■ **oldish** *adjective* M17. **oldly** *adverb* (*rare*) (*a*) in the manner of an old person; (*b*) in a bygone manner; (*c*) long ago: ME. **oldness** *noun* LOE. **oldster** *noun* (*a*) NAUTICAL a midshipman of four years' standing; (*b*) *colloq.* a person who is no longer young, an elderly person: E19.

†**old** *verb intrans.* OE–M18.
[from OLD *adjective*.]
Grow old.

olde /əʊld, ˈəʊldi/ *adjective*. *pseudo-arch.* E20.
[Alt. of OLD *adjective*. Cf. *ye* pseudo-arch. var. of THE *demonstr. adjective*.]
Old; quaint. Freq. implying (usu. spurious) antiquity. Chiefly in *olde English(e)*, *olde worlde*.

olden /ˈəʊld(ə)n/ *adjective*. *arch. & literary*. LME.
[from OLD *noun*¹ + -EN⁴.]
Belonging to a bygone age; ancient.

olden /ˈəʊld(ə)n/ *verb trans. & intrans. rare*. E19.
[from OLD *adjective* + -EN⁵.]
(Cause to) grow old, age.

old-fangled /əʊl(d)ˈfaŋg(ə)ld/ *adjective*. M19.
[from OLD *adjective* after NEWFANGLED: cf. FANGLE.]
Characterized by adherence to what is old, old-fashioned.

old-fashioned /əʊl(d)ˈfaʃ(ə)nd/ *adjective, noun, & adverb*. L16.
[from OLD *adjective* + FASHIONED.]
► **A** *adjective*. **1** In, reflecting, or according to the style, fashion, or tastes of an earlier period; antiquated, outdated. L16. ▸**b** Of a plant: belonging to a species or variety no longer in common cultivation. E20.

2 Attached to old fashions or ways; having out-of-date tastes. L17.

3 Unusually mature; precocious, intelligent, knowing. Chiefly *dial.* M19.

4 Disapproving, reproachful. E20.

> 📖 **1** M. KINGSLEY Good, old-fashioned, long skirts. **2** A. POWELL He was old-fashioned enough to retain the starched shirt and cuffs of an earlier generation. **4** D. BARLOW Men . . are receiving old-fashioned looks as they ask for a half-pint of lime juice.

Special collocations: **old-fashioned cocktail** = sense B. below. **old-fashioned rose** = OLD ROSE *noun* 1. **old-fashioned waltz** a waltz played in quick time. **old-fashioned winter** a winter marked by snow and hard frost.

► **B** *noun*. A cocktail consisting chiefly of whisky, bitters, water, and sugar; a low tumbler in which such a cocktail is served. *N. Amer.* E20.

► **C** *adverb*. In a disapproving, reproachful, or quizzical manner. E20.

■ †**old-fashion** *adjective* = OLD-FASHIONED L16–L18. **old-fashionedly** *adverb* E19. **old-fashionedness** *noun* E19.

old field /əʊld fiːld/ *noun phr. US*. M17.
[from OLD *adjective* + FIELD *noun*.]
(A piece of) formerly cultivated land.

Comb.: **old-field birch** any of several N. American birches; *esp.* the grey birch, *Betula populifolia*; **old-field lark** a meadowlark; **old-field mouse** a white-footed pale brown deer-mouse, *Peromyscus polionotus*, of sandy regions in the south-eastern US; **old-field pine** any of several N. American pines; *esp.* the loblolly pine, *Pinus taeda*.

oldie /ˈəʊldi/ *noun*. *colloq.* L19.
[from OLD *adjective* + -IE.]
1 An old or elderly person; an adult. Freq. *joc.* or *iron.* L19.

2 A thing that is old or familiar; *esp.* an old song, tune, or film. M20.

old land /əʊld land/ *noun phr.* In sense 1 usu. **olland** /ˈɒlənd/; in sense 3 usu. **oldland**. L17.
[from OLD *adjective* + LAND *noun*¹.]
1 (A piece of) land newly ploughed after lying uncultivated for some time; (a piece of) arable land sown with grass for more than two years. *dial.* L17.

2 Land that has been cultivated for a long time; land exhausted by long cultivation. *US*. E18.

3 GEOLOGY. Land which lies behind a coastal plain of more recent origin, esp. where this plain has been built up from sedimentary material derived from that land. Also, an area of very ancient crystalline rocks, esp. when reduced to low relief. L19.

old maid /əʊld ˈmeɪd/ *noun phr.* M16.
[from OLD *adjective* + MAID *noun*.]
1 An elderly spinster. Freq. *derog.* M16. ▸**b** A prim, fussy, or nervous person. M19.

2 The common soft-shelled clam, *Mya arenaria*. M19.

3 a A garden zinnia, *Zinnia elegans*. *US*. M19. ▸**b** The Madagascar periwinkle, *Catharanthus roseus*. Chiefly *W. Indies*. L19.

4 A card-game with one card (usu. a queen) removed from the pack, in which the players draw cards from one another, discarding pairs, until only the unpaired card is left. Also, the holder of the unpaired card at the end of this game. M19.

> 📖 **1b** *Chicago Tribune* He . . seems more prissy old maid than confirmed old bachelor.

■ **old-ˈmaidenhood** *noun* the state or condition of being an old maid M19. **old-ˈmaidenism** *noun* = OLD-MAIDENHOOD L18. **old-ˈmaidenly** *adjective* = OLD-MAIDISH L18. **old-ˈmaidish** *adjective* resembling or characteristic of an old maid M18. **old-ˈmaidishly** *adverb* L20. **old-ˈmaidishness** *noun* E19. **old-ˈmaidism** *noun* the state of being or characteristics of an old maid L18. **old-ˈmaidy** *adjective* = OLD-MAIDISH L19.

old man /əʊld ˈman/ *noun & adjectival phr.* ME.
[from OLD *adjective* + MAN *noun*.]
► **A** *noun phr.* Pl. **old men** /ˈmɛn/.

1 a *lit.* An elderly or aged man; *spec.* one's father. Now also, a woman's husband or partner. ME. ▸**b** THEATRICAL. An actor playing an old man, *esp.* one who specializes in such roles. Also, such a role. M18. ▸**c** A person in authority over others, as (*a*) a ship's captain; (*b*) a commanding officer; (*c*) a boss. *colloq.* M19. ▸**d** Used as a familiar form of address between men. L19.

2 THEOLOGY. Unregenerate human nature. LME.

3 MINING. An exhausted or long-abandoned vein or working. Also, waste devoid of ore left from the working of a mine. M17.

4 = *chestnut-bellied* CUCKOO. *Jamaican*. L17.

5 A full-grown male kangaroo. *Austral.* E19.

6 The herb southernwood, *Artemisia abrotanum*, so called from its hoary foliage. E19.

7 The penis. *slang*. E20.

> 📖 **1a** F. O'CONNOR She gave the old man a pair of glasses this Christmas. R. J. CONLEY An old man sitting beside the road carving a pipe. **c** P. B. YUILL The old man wants to hear a progress report. **d** R. BOLDREWOOD Take another tumbler, old man.

Phrases: *dirty old man*: see DIRTY *adjective*. *grand old man*: see GRAND *adjective*¹. **old man of the mountains** [with allus. to the nickname of an early leader of the assassins] a political assassin; a ruthlessly ambitious person. **old man of the sea** [with allus. to the sea-god in the *Arabian Nights' Entertainments* who forced Sinbad the Sailor to carry him on his shoulders for many days and nights] a person from whose company one cannot easily escape; a tiresome heavy burden.

► **B** *attrib.* or as *adjectival phr.* That is or resembles an old man; *Austral. & NZ colloq.* of great size or significance. M19.

Special collocations & comb.: **old-man bird** = sense A.4 above. **old-man cactus** a Mexican cactus, *Cephalocereus senilis*, covered with long grey hairs. **old-man kangaroo** = A.5 above. **Old Man River** the Mississippi. **old man saltbush** a shrubby Australian orache, *Atriplex nummularia*, with grey-green leaves, used as food for sheep in dry areas. **old man's beard** (*a*) *N. Amer.* Spanish moss, *Tillandsia usneoides*; (*b*) traveller's joy, *Clematis vitalba*, or (*Austral.*) its close ally *C. aristata*, which both have grey-bearded fruits.

■ **old-mannish** *adjective* characteristic or suggestive of an old man M19.

Oldowan /ˈɒldəʊwən/ *adjective*. M20.
[from *Oldoway* alt. of Olduvai Gorge, Tanzania + -AN.]
Belonging to an African culture of the early Pleistocene period, characterized by primitive stone tools.

old rose /əʊld ˈrəʊz/ *noun & adjectival phr.* L19.
[from OLD *adjective* + ROSE *noun & adjective*.]
► **A** *noun phr.* **1** Any of various double-flowered rose varieties or hybrids evolved before the development of the hybrid tea rose. L19.

2 A shade of deep pink. L19.

► **B** *adjectival phr.* Of the deep pink shade old rose. E20.

old school /əʊld skuːl/ *noun & adjectival phr.* M18.
[from OLD *adjective* + SCHOOL *noun*¹.]
► **A** *noun phr.* A group of people or a section of society noted for its conservative views or principles. Also, a school which one used to attend. M18.

► **B** *attrib.* or as *adjectival phr.* Designating (a holder of) conservative or traditional (esp. religious) views. E19.

Phrases: **in the old school** according to traditional or old-fashioned methods. **of the old school** traditional, old-fashioned. **old school tie** (*a*) a necktie with a characteristic pattern worn by former members of a particular (usu. public) school; (*b*) the attitudes of group loyalty and traditionalism associated with the wearing of such a tie.

Oldspeak /ˈəʊldspiːk/ *noun*. M20.
[from OLD *adjective* + SPEAK *verb*, as opp. to NEWSPEAK, in George Orwell's novel *Nineteen Eighty-Four* (1949).]
Standard English; normal English usage as opp. to technical or propagandist language.

old-time /ˈəʊldtʌɪm/ *adjective*. L18.
[from OLD *adjective* + TIME *noun*.]
1 Of, belonging to, or characteristic of an ancient or earlier time. L18.

2 Designating a usu. slow or romantic style of ballroom dancing and music particularly fashionable in the 19th and early 20th cents. L19.

3 Applied to traditional or folk styles of American popular music, as gospel, Cajun, bluegrass, etc. *US*. E20.

■ **old-ˈtimer** *noun* (orig. *US*) (*a*) a person of long experience (in a place or position); (*b*) an old-fashioned person or thing: L19. **old-timey** *adjective* old-fashioned, (nostalgically or sentimentally) recalling the past M19.

old wife /əʊld ˈwʌɪf/ *noun phr.* Pl. **old wives** /ˈwʌɪvz/. ME.
[from OLD *adjective* + WIFE *noun*.]
1 An old woman. Now usu. *derog.* ME.

2 Any of various marine fishes, as (*a*) a wrasse; (*b*) the black sea bream, *Spondyliosoma cantharus*; (*c*) the queen trigger fish, *Balistes vetula*; (*d*) *Enoplosus armatus*, a brown and white striped fish with pink fins, of Australasian coasts. L16.

3 The long-tailed duck, *Clangula hyemalis*. Cf. *old squaw* s.v. OLD *adjective*. M17.

4 A cap or cowl to prevent a chimney from smoking. *Scot.* M19.

1 old wives' tale an old but foolish story or belief.

■ **old-wifish** *adjective* M16.

old woman /əʊld ˈwʊmən/ *noun phr.* Pl. **old women** /ˈwɪmɪn/. LME.
[from OLD *adjective* + WOMAN *noun*.]
1 An elderly or aged woman; *spec.* one's wife or mother. Also (*derog.*), a person (esp. a man) of timid and fussy character. LME.

2 THEATRICAL. An actress playing an old woman, *esp.* one who specializes in such roles. M19.

Phrases: **old woman's tooth** a simple kind of wooden router plane used by cabinet-makers.

■ **old-womanish** *adjective* resembling or characteristic of an old woman; fussy, timid: L18. **old-womanishness** *noun* M20. **old-womanism** *noun* the characteristics of an old woman E19. **old-womanly** *adjective* = OLD-WOMANISH E19. **old-womanry** *noun* (*rare*) an old-womanish trait or practice E19.

ole /ˈole/ *noun*. M19.
[Spanish.]
A Spanish folk-dance which is accompanied by castanets and singing.

ole /əʊl/ *adjective*. *colloq., dial., & Black English*. Also **ol'**. M19.
[Repr. a pronunc.]
= OLD *adjective*
Grand Ole Opry: see OPRY.

-ole /əʊl/ *suffix*¹.
[Repr. Latin dim. ending *-olus*, *-ola*, *-olum*.]
Chiefly BIOLOGY. Forming dim. nouns, as ***ovariole***, ***tracheole***.

-ole /əʊl/ *suffix*².
[from Latin *oleum* oil, in gen. use after *pyrrole* etc.]
CHEMISTRY. Forming names of organic compounds, now esp. those containing a five-membered unsaturated ring with at least one hetero-atom, as ***carbazole***, ***indazole***, ***indole***, ***pyrrole***, ***thiazole***, ***triazole***.

olé /oˈle, əʊˈleɪ/ *interjection & noun*. E20.
[Spanish.]
► **A** *interjection*. Bravo! E20.
► **B** *noun*. A cry of '*olé!*'. M20.

¶ Usu. associated with Spanish music and dance and with bullfighting.

olea *noun* pl. of OLEUM.

oleaceous /əʊlɪˈeɪʃəs/ *adjective. rare.* M19.
[from mod. Latin *Oleaceae*, from Latin *olea* olive tree: see -ACEOUS.]
BOTANY. Of or pertaining to the family Oleaceae, which includes olive, jasmine, lilac, privet, ash, and other trees and shrubs.

oleaginous /əʊlɪˈadʒɪnəs/ *adjective.* LME.
[from Old & mod. French *oléagineux* from Latin *oleaginus* oily, from *oleum* oil: see -OUS.]
1 a Having the character or properties of oil; containing oil or an oily substance; oily, greasy. LME. ▸**b** Producing oil. L17. **2** *fig.* Smooth; unctuous; obsequious; = OILY *adjective* 3. M19.

📖 **2** B. MASON His voice, smooth and oleaginous, would have charmed a tartar.

■ **oleagiˈnosity**, **oleaginousness** *nouns* L17. **oleaginously** *adverb* E20.

oleander /əʊlɪˈandə/ *noun.* M16.
[medieval Latin *oleander*, *oliandrum*. Cf. French *oléandre*.]
A poisonous evergreen shrub, *Nerium oleander* (family Apocynaceae), of the Mediterranean region, with leathery lanceolate leaves and fragrant pink or white flowers, freq. grown for ornament (also called ***rosebay***). Also, any of several related shrubs.
yellow oleander a tropical American shrub, *Thevetia peruviana*, with fragrant yellow flowers.
Comb.: **oleander hawk**, **oleander hawkmoth** a large hawkmoth, *Daphnis nerii*, whose caterpillars feed on oleander or periwinkle leaves.

oleandomycin /ˌəʊlɪandəˈmʌɪsɪn/ *noun.* M20.
[from OLEAND(RINE + -O- + -MYCIN.]
PHARMACOLOGY. (The phosphate of) a macrolide antibiotic, $C_{35}H_{61}NO_{12}$, produced by a streptomycete and active against a wide range of Gram-positive bacteria, which has been used to treat staphylococcal enteritis and skin infections.

oleandrine /əʊlɪˈandriːn/ *noun.* Also **-in** /-ɪn/. L19.
[from OLEANDER + -INE[5], -IN[1].]
CHEMISTRY. A bitter poisonous yellow alkaloid found in the leaves of the oleander.

olearia /əʊlɪˈɛːrɪə/ *noun.* M19.
[mod. Latin (see below), from Johann Gottfried *Olearius* (1635–1711), German horticulturist: see -IA[1].]
Any of numerous Australasian evergreen shrubs and trees of the genus *Olearia*, of the composite family, which bear daisy-like white, mauve, etc., flowers and are freq. grown in coastal districts. Also called ***daisy-bush***.

oleaster /əʊlɪˈastə/ *noun.* LME.
[Latin, from *olea* olive tree: see -ASTER.]
A wild variant of the cultivated olive, *Olea europaea* var. *sylvestris*, with thorny branches and small unproductive fruit. Also, any of several small southern European trees of the genus *Elaeagnus* (family Elaeagnaceae), resembling the oleaster in their narrow silvery leaves.

oleate /ˈəʊlɪeɪt, -lɪət/ *noun.* M19.
[from OLEIC + -ATE[1].]
CHEMISTRY & PHARMACOLOGY. A salt or ester of oleic acid; a medicine in which such a compound is the solvent.

olecranon /əʊˈlɛkrənɒn, əʊlɪˈkreɪnən/ *noun.* E18.
[Greek *ōlekranon* abbreviation of *ōlenokranon* head or point of the elbow, from *ōlenē* elbow + *kranion* head.]
ANATOMY. The process at the upper end of the ulna which forms the bony prominence of the elbow. Also ***olecranon process***.
■ **olecranal**, **oleˈcranial** *adjectives* M19.

olefiant /ˈəʊlɪfʌɪənt/ *adjective. obsolete* exc. *Hist.* E19.
[French *(gaz) oléfiant*, formed as pres. pple of verb in *-fier* -FY from Latin *oleum* oil: see -ANT[1].]
CHEMISTRY. ***olefiant gas***, ethylene.

olefin /ˈəʊlɪfɪn/ *noun.* Also (now *rare*) **-ine** /-iːn/. M19.
[from prec. + -IN[1], -INE[5].]
CHEMISTRY. = ALKENE.
■ **oleˈfinic** *adjective* of the nature of or characteristic of an olefin; of an olefin; *spec.* = ETHYLENIC: L19.

oleic /əʊˈliːɪk, ˈəʊlɪɪk/ *adjective.* E19.
[from Latin *oleum* oil + -IC.]
CHEMISTRY. ***oleic acid***, a straight-chain unsaturated fatty acid, $CH_3(CH_2)_7CH{=}CH(CH_2)_7COOH$, which occurs in most fats and soaps and is a colourless tasteless oily liquid; *cis*-9-octadecenoic acid. Cf. ELAIDIC.

oleiferous /əʊlɪˈɪf(ə)rəs/ *adjective.* E19.
[from Latin *oleum* oil + -I- + -FEROUS.]
Producing or yielding oil.

olein /ˈəʊlɪɪn/ *noun.* M19.
[French *oléine*, from Latin *oleum* oil + *-ine* -IN[1], after *glycerine*.]
CHEMISTRY. Glyceryl trioleate, $C_3H_5(C_{18}H_{33}O_2)_3$, a colourless oily liquid which is a very common natural fat. Also, a glyceride of oleic acid (usu. in *pl.*).

olenellid /ɒləˈnɛlɪd/ *noun & adjective.* L19.
[mod. Latin *Olenellidae* (see below), from *Olenellus* genus name: see -ID[3].]
PALAEONTOLOGY. ▸**A** *adjective.* Of or pertaining to the trilobite family Olenellidae. L19.
▸**B** *noun.* A trilobite of this family. L19.

olent /ˈəʊl(ə)nt/ *adjective. rare.* E17.
[Latin *olent-* pres. ppl stem of *olere* smell: see -ENT.]
Giving out a smell or scent.

oleo /ˈəʊlɪəʊ, ˈɒlɪəʊ/ *noun*[1]. *US.* Pl. **-os**. L19.
[Abbreviation.]
= OLEOMARGARINE; *esp.* artificial butter, margarine.

oleo /ˈəʊlɪəʊ/ *adjective & noun*[2]. E20.
[from next.]
AERONAUTICS. ▸**A** *adjective.* Designating (a system containing) a telescopic strut, used esp. in aircraft undercarriages, which absorbs shocks by causing oil to be forced through a small valve into a hollow piston when the strut is compressed. E20.
▸**B** *absol.* as *noun.* Pl. **-os**. An oleo strut or leg. E20.

oleo- /ˈəʊlɪəʊ, ˈɒlɪəʊ/ *combining form* of Latin *oleum* oil: see -O-.
■ **oleoˈchemical** *noun* a compound derived industrially from animal or vegetable oils or fats M20. **oleograph** *noun* (*obsolete* exc. *Hist.*) a form of chromolithograph, usu. varnished and often embossed, that imitates an oil-painting L19. **oleoˈgraphic** *adjective* (*obsolete* exc. *Hist.*) of, pertaining to, or resembling an oleograph L19. **oleˈography** *noun* (*obsolete* exc. *Hist.*) the art or process of printing oleographs L19. **oleˈometer** *noun* an instrument for determining the density and purity of oils M19. **oleoˈphilic** *adjective* having an affinity for oils or oily materials; readily absorbing oil: M20. **oleoˈphobic** *adjective* tending to repel, or not to absorb, oils or oily materials M20. **oleo-pneuˈmatic** *adjective* (of a device or mechanism) absorbing shocks by a combination of forcing oil through an orifice and compressing gas E20. **oleoˈresin** *noun* a natural or artificial mixture of a (volatile) oil and a resin, a balsam M19. **oleoˈresinous** *adjective* of the nature of an oleoresin M19. **oleoˈthorax** *MEDICINE* (now *Hist.*) the introduction of light oil into the pleural cavity, formerly used to treat tuberculosis E20.

oleomargarine /ˌəʊlɪəʊmɑːdʒəriːn, -ˈmɑːgəriːn/ *noun.* L19.
[from OLEO- + MARGARINE.]
The liquid portion of clarified beef fat, extracted by pressure and allowed to solidify, freq. used in the manufacture of artificial butter or margarine; *US* (a) margarine.

oleose /ˈəʊlɪəʊs, əʊlɪˈəʊs/ *adjective.* Now *rare.* L17.
[formed as next: see -OSE[1].]
= next.

oleous /ˈəʊlɪəs/ *adjective.* Now *rare.* E17.
[from Latin *oleosus*, from *oleum* oil: see -OUS.]
Of the character or consistency of oil; containing oil; oily.

oleraceous /ɒləˈreɪʃəs/ *adjective.* L17.
[Latin *(h)oleraceus*, from *(h)oler-*, *(h)olus* pot-herb: see -OUS, -ACEOUS.]
Of the character of a pot-herb or culinary vegetable; obtained from a pot-herb.

Olestra /ɒˈlɛstrə/ *noun.* L20.
[Invented word, based on letters of POLYESTER.]
(Proprietary name for) a synthetic sucrose polyester used as a calorie-free substitute for fat in various foods because of its ability to pass through the body without being absorbed.

oleum /ˈəʊlɪəm/ *noun.* Pl. **oleums**, **olea** /ˈəʊlɪə/. E20.
[Latin = oil.]
Fuming sulphuric acid, an oily corrosive liquid produced by dissolving sulphur trioxide in concentrated sulphuric acid and used in sulphonation and nitration.

oleyl /ˈəʊlɪʌɪl, -lɪl/ *noun.* E20.
[from OLEIC + -YL.]
CHEMISTRY. The radical $C_{18}H_{35}\cdot$, derived from oleic acid. Usu. in *comb.*
Comb.: **oleyl alcohol** an oily liquid, $C_{18}H_{35}OH$ (*cis*-9-octadecen-1-ol), which occurs in fish oils and is used in the manufacture of surfactants.

olfact /ɒlˈfakt/ *verb trans. rare.* M17.
[Latin *olfact-* pa. ppl stem of *olfacere*: see OLFACTORY.]
Detect with the sense of smell.
■ **olfactible** *adjective* able to be smelled E18.

olfaction /ɒlˈfakʃ(ə)n/ *noun.* M19.
[from OLFACT(IVE + -ION.]
The action of smelling; the sense of smell.

olfactive /ɒlˈfaktɪv/ *adjective.* M17.
[from Latin *olfactus* smell, from *olfacere*: see OLFACTORY, -IVE.]
Of or pertaining to the sense of smell; olfactory.

olfactometer /ɒlfakˈtɒmɪtə/ *noun.* L19.
[formed as OLFACT + -OMETER.]
1 An instrument for measuring the intensity of an odour or the sensitivity of a subject to an odour. L19. **2** A device for investigating the responses of an animal to odours. E20.

olfactometry /ɒlfakˈtɒmɪtri/ *noun.* L19.
[formed as OLFACT + -OMETRY.]
Measurement of the intensity of odours or the sensitivity of the sense of smell.
■ **olfactoˈmetric** *adjective* L19.

olfactorium /ɒlfakˈtɔːrɪəm/ *noun.* Pl. **-ia** /-ɪə/. M20.
[formed as OLFACT + -ORIUM.]
A large odour-proof enclosure in which olfactory experiments are conducted.

olfactory /ɒlˈfakt(ə)ri/ *adjective & noun.* M17.
[from Latin *olfactor-* (in *olfactoria* nosegay), from *olfactare* frequentative of *olfacere* to smell, from *olere* to smell + *facere* make: see -ORY[2]. Cf. OLFACT.]
▸**A** *adjective.* Of or pertaining to the sense of smell or the action of smelling. M17.
olfactory nerve either of the first pair of cranial nerves, which supply the smell receptors in the mucous membrane of the nose.
▸**B** *noun.* An organ of smell. E19.
■ **olfactorily** *adverb* in the sense of smell L19.

olfactronics /ɒlfakˈtrɒnɪks/ *noun.* M20.
[formed as OLFACT + ELEC)TRONICS.]
The detection, analysis, and measurement of vapours by means of instruments.
■ **olfactronic** *adjective* M20.

†**oliaginose** *adjective* see OLEAGINOUS.

olibanum /ɒˈlɪbənəm/ *noun.* Also Anglicized as **oliban** /ˈɒlɪb(ə)n/. LME.
[medieval Latin, ult. repr. Greek *libanos* frankincense tree, incense (of Semitic origin: cf. Hebrew *lĕbōnāh* incense) prob. through Arab. *al-lubān* storax (see AL-[2]).]
An aromatic gum from the N. African tree *Boswellia sacra* (family Burseraceae), formerly used in medicine but now chiefly as incense. Now usu. ***gum olibanum***.

olid /ˈɒlɪd/ *adjective.* L17.
[Latin *olidus* smelling, from *olere* to smell: see -ID[1].]
Having a strong disagreeable smell; fetid, rank.

olig- *combining form* see OLIGO-.

oligaemia /ɒlɪˈgiːmɪə/ *noun.* Also ***-gemia**. M19.
[French *oligaimie* from Greek *oligaimia*, formed as OLIGO- + -AEMIA.]
MEDICINE. = HYPOVOLAEMIA.
■ **oligaemic** *adjective* M19.

oligarch /ˈɒlɪgɑːk/ *noun.* E17.
[Greek *oligarkhēs*, from *oligos* few: see -ARCH.]
A member of an oligarchy; any of a small group holding power in a State. Also, an advocate or supporter of oligarchy.

📖 *Survey* The ageing oligarchs of the Politbureau.

■ **oligarchist** *noun* an advocate or supporter of oligarchy M17. **oligarchiˈzation** *noun* movement towards oligarchy M20. **oligarchize** *verb trans.* convert into or subject to an oligarchy M19.

oligarch /ˈɒlɪgɑːk/ *adjective.* L19.
[from OLIGO- + Greek *arkhē* beginning, origin.]
BOTANY. Of primary xylem or woody tissue: proceeding from few points of origin.

†**oligarchia** *noun* see OLIGARCHY.

oligarchic /ɒlɪˈgɑːkɪk/ *adjective.* M17.
[Greek *oligarkhikos*, formed as OLIGARCH *noun*: see -ARCH, -IC.]
Of, pertaining to, or of the character of an oligarchy; practised, administered, or governed by an oligarchy; supporting or advocating oligarchy.
■ **oligarchical** *adjective* = OLIGARCHIC L16. **oligarchically** *adverb* M19.

oligarchy /ˈɒlɪgɑːki/ *noun.* Also (earlier) in Latin form †**-ia**. L15.
[Old & mod. French *oligarchie* or medieval Latin *oligarchia* from Greek *oligarkhia*, formed as OLIGARCH *noun*: see -ARCHY.]
(A form of) government by a small group of people; the members of such a government; a State governed in this way.

📖 *transf.*: *Observer* The Civil Service is a self-perpetuating oligarchy, and what better system is there?

oligemia *noun* see OLIGAEMIA.

oligist /ˈɒlɪdʒɪst/ *noun.* E19.
[from Greek *oligistos* least, superl. of *oligos* small, little, (pl.) few (so called as containing less iron than magnetite).]
MINERALOGY. More fully ***oligist iron***. = HAEMATITE.
■ **oliˈgistic** *adjective* containing or resembling oligist E19.

oligo /ˈɒlɪgəʊ/ *noun.* Pl. **-os**. L20.
[Abbreviation.]
BIOCHEMISTRY. = OLIGONUCLEOTIDE.

oligo- /ˈɒlɪgəʊ/ *combining form.* Before a vowel **olig-**.
[from Greek *oligos* small, little, (pl.) few: see -O-.]
Forming nouns and adjectives adopted from Greek and English formations modelled on these, with the sense 'having few, having little' (freq. contrasted with words in ***poly-***).

■ **oli'gandrous** *adjective* (BOTANY) having fewer than twenty stamens L19. **oligar'ticular** *adjective* (MEDICINE) = PAUCIARTICULAR L19. **oligo'carpous** *adjective* (BOTANY) having few fruits or spore-cases M19. **oligody'namic** *adjective* acting or being active at very low concentrations L19. **oligo'ester** *noun* (CHEMISTRY) an oligomer in which adjacent monomeric units are linked by an ester grouping, ·CO·O· M20. **oligo'haline** *adjective* characterized by salinity in the range immediately above that of fresh water M20. **oligohy'dramnios** *noun* (MEDICINE) a deficiency in the amount of amniotic fluid L19. **oligo'lectic** *adjective* (ZOOLOGY) (of a bee) gathering pollen from only a few closely related plants E20. **oligomeno'rrhoea** *noun* abnormally infrequent, sporadic, or scanty menstruation L19. **oligomeno'rrhoeic** *adjective* of, pertaining to, or affected with oligomenorrhoea M20. **oli'gomerous** *adjective* (ZOOLOGY) having a small number of segments or compartments; BOTANY having fewer divisions than normal: M19. **oli'gomery** *noun* (BOTANY) oligomerous state L19. **oligo'mycin** *noun* (PHARMACOLOGY) (any of) a group of antifungal antibiotics produced by the bacterium *Streptomyces diastatochromogenes*, which inhibit certain mitochondrial phosphorylation reactions M20. **oligo'nucleotide** *noun* (BIOCHEMISTRY) a polynucleotide whose molecules contain a relatively small number of nucleotides M20. **oligo'peptide** *noun* (BIOCHEMISTRY) a peptide whose molecules contain a relatively small number of amino-acid residues M20. **oli'gophagous** *adjective* (ZOOLOGY) (of an insect) feeding on a limited number of plants E20. **oli'gophagy** *noun* oligophagous feeding M20. **oligo'phrenia** *noun* (MEDICINE, now *rare* or *obsolete*) feeble-mindedness, mental subnormality L19. **oligopod** *adjective* (ENTOMOLOGY) (of an insect larva) having well-developed thoracic limbs E20. **oligo'saccharide** *noun* (BIOCHEMISTRY) a carbohydrate whose molecules contain a relatively small number of monosaccharide residues M20. **oligo'saprobe** *noun* (ECOLOGY) an oligosaprobic organism M20. **oligosa'probic** *adjective* (ECOLOGY) of, designating, or inhabiting an aquatic environment that is rich in dissolved oxygen and relatively free of decayed organic matter E20. **oligo'spermia** *noun* (MEDICINE) deficiency of sperm cells in the semen M19. **oligosy'llabic** *adjective* having fewer than four syllables E19. **oligotropic** /-'trəʊpɪk, -'trɒpɪk/ *adjective* (ZOOLOGY) (of a bee) collecting nectar from only a few kinds of flower L19. **oli'guria** *noun* (MEDICINE) (a condition characterized by) the production of abnormally small amounts of urine L19. **oli'guric** *adjective & noun* (*a*) *adjective* of, pertaining to, or involving oliguria; (*b*) *noun* a person affected with oliguria: L19.

Oligocene /'ɒlɪgəsiːn/ *adjective & noun*. M19.
[from OLIGO- + Greek *kainos* new, recent.]
GEOLOGY. ▶**A** *adjective*. Designating or pertaining to the third epoch of the Tertiary period or sub-era, following the Eocene and preceding the Miocene. M19.
▶ **B** *noun*. The Oligocene epoch; the series of rocks dating from this time. M19.

oligochaete /'ɒlɪgəkiːt/ *adjective & noun*. L19.
[mod. Latin *Oligochaeta* (see below), formed as OLIGO- + Greek *khaitē* mane, taken as meaning 'bristle'.]
▶ **A** *adjective*. Of, pertaining to, or characteristic of the division Oligochaeta of annelid worms, which includes earthworms. L19.
▶ **B** *noun*. An oligochaete worm. L19.
■ **oligo'chaetous** *adjective* (now *rare* or *obsolete*) L19.

oligoclase /'ɒlɪgəkleɪz/ *noun*. M19.
[from OLIGO- + Greek *klasis* breaking, cleavage (as thought to have a less perfect cleavage than albite).]
MINERALOGY. A sodium-rich plagioclase feldspar containing more calcium than albite, common in siliceous igneous rocks.

oligodendrocyte /ˌɒlɪgə'dɛndrəsʌɪt/ *noun*. M20.
[from next + -CYTE.]
ANATOMY. A glial cell similar to an astrocyte but with fewer processes, concerned with the production of myelin in the central nervous system.

oligodendroglia /ˌɒlɪgədɛndrə'glʌɪə/ *noun*. E20.
[from OLIGO- + DENDRO- + NEURO)GLIA.]
ANATOMY. The part of the glia which consists of oligodendrocytes; now usu. (treated as *pl.*), oligodendrocytes collectively.
■ **oligodendroglial** *adjective* E20. ˌ**oligodendrogli'oma** *noun*, pl. **-mas**, **-mata** /-mətə/, a tumour derived from oligodendroglia E20.

oligomer /ə'lɪgəmə, 'ɒlɪg-/ *noun*. M20.
[from OLIGO- + -MER.]
CHEMISTRY. A polymer whose molecules consist of relatively few repeating units.
■ **oligo'meric** *adjective* of the nature of a oligomer, consisting of an oligomer or oligomers M20. **oligomeri'zation** *noun* M20. **oligomerize** *verb trans.* form an oligomer of (a monomer) M20.

oligomictic /ˌɒlɪgə'mɪktɪk/ *adjective*. M20.
[from OLIGO- + Greek *miktos* mixed + -IC.]
1 GEOLOGY. Of a rock: consisting of a small number of dominant minerals. M20.
2 PHYSICAL GEOGRAPHY. Of a lake: that exhibits a stable thermal stratification and only rarely undergoes an overturn. M20.

oligopoly /ɒlɪ'gɒp(ə)li/ *noun*. L19.
[from OLIGO- + Greek *pōlein* sell, after MONOPOLY.]
ECONOMICS. A state of limited competition, in a market having a small number of producers or sellers.
■ **oligopolist** *noun* each of the few producers or sellers in a particular market M20. **oligopo'listic** *adjective* of or pertaining to oligopoly M20.

oligopsony /ɒlɪ'gɒps(ə)ni/ *noun*. M20.
[from OLIGO- + Greek *opsōnein* buy provisions, after MONOPSONY.]
ECONOMICS. A state of the market in which only a small number of buyers exists for a product.
■ **oligopso'nistic** *adjective* of or pertaining to oligopsony M20. **oligopsonist** *noun* each of the few buyers for a particular product M20.

oligotrophic /ˌɒlɪgə'trəʊfɪk, -'trɒf-/ *adjective*. M20.
[formed as OLIGO- + Greek *trofē* nourishment.]
ECOLOGY. Relatively poor in plant nutrients and (*spec.* of a lake) containing abundant oxygen in the deeper parts.
■ **oligotrophy** *noun* oligotrophic condition E20.

olim /əʊ'liːm/ *noun pl.* M20.
[Hebrew *'ōlīm* pl. of *'ōleh* person who ascends.]
Jewish immigrants who settle in the State of Israel.

olim /'əʊlɪm/ *adverb*. M17.
[Latin.]
At one time; formerly.

olingo /ɒ'lɪŋgəʊ/ *noun*. Pl. **-os**. E20.
[Amer. Spanish from Maya name.]
A small nocturnal mammal of the genus *Bassaricyon* (family Procyonidae), native to Central and S. American forests and distinguished from the kinkajou by a straight, non-prehensile tail.

olio /'əʊlɪəʊ/ *noun*. Pl. **-os**. M17.
[Alt. of Spanish *olla* (Portuguese *olha*) from Proto-Romance var. of Latin *olla* pot, jar. Cf. OLLA *noun*¹.]
1 A highly spiced stew of various meats and vegetables, of Spanish and Portuguese origin; *gen.* any dish containing a great variety of ingredients. M17.
2 *fig.* **a** Any mixture of heterogeneous things or elements; a hotchpotch, a medley. M17. ▶**b** A collection of various artistic or literary pieces; a miscellany; a musical medley; *spec.* a variety act or show. M17.

oliphant *noun* see ELEPHANT.

oliprance /'ɒlɪprɑːns/ *noun*. *obsolete* exc. *dial.* ME.
[Origin unkn.]
†**1** Pride, vanity, ostentation. ME–M16.
2 Merrymaking, jollity; a romp. L15.

olisbos /'ɒlɪzbəs/ *noun*. L19.
[Greek.]
= DILDO *noun* 1.

olistostrome /ɒ'lɪstəstrəʊm/ *noun*. M20.
[from Greek *olisth-* stem of *olisthēma* slip, slide + -O- + *strōma* bed.]
GEOLOGY. A heterogeneous sedimentary deposit formed by the sliding or slumping of semifluid sediment.
■ **olistolith** *noun* each of the discrete bodies in the matrix of an olistostrome M20.

olitory /'ɒlɪt(ə)ri/ *adjective & noun*. Now *rare*. M17.
[Latin *(h)olitorius*, from *(h)olitor* kitchen gardener, from *(h)olus* pot-herb: see -ORY¹, -ORY².]
▶ **A** *adjective*. Of or pertaining to a pot-herb or culinary vegetable, or a kitchen garden. M17.
▶†**B** *noun*. **1** A pot-herb, a culinary vegetable. Only in L17.
2 A kitchen garden. E18–E20.

oliva /ə'lʌɪvə/ *noun*. M19.
[Latin: see OLIVE *noun*¹.]
In full ***oliva shell***. = OLIVE *noun*¹ 8.

olivaceous /ɒlɪ'veɪʃəs/ *adjective*. L18.
[from OLIVE *noun*¹ + -ACEOUS.]
Chiefly BIOLOGY & PALAEONTOLOGY. Of a dull yellowish-green colour; olive-green; olive.

olivary /'ɒlɪv(ə)ri/ *noun & adjective*. LME.
[Latin *olivarius* pertaining to olives, from *oliva* OLIVE *noun*¹: see -ARY¹.]
▶ **A** *noun*. MEDICINE. A cautery with an oval head. Long *rare* or *obsolete*. LME.
▶ **B** *adjective*. ANATOMY. Shaped like an olive, oval. Only in collocations below. M19.
olivary body either of two oval swellings on each side of the upper medulla oblongata; also called ***olive***. **olivary nucleus** the mass of grey matter within an olivary body.

olive /'ɒlɪv/ *noun*¹ *& adjective*. ME.
[Old & mod. French from Latin *oliva* from Greek word meaning 'oil'.]
▶ **A** *noun*. **1** An evergreen tree, *Olea europaea* (family Oleaceae), with narrow leaves hoary on the underside and small whitish flowers, long cultivated in the Mediterranean region for its fruit and the oil obtained from this. Also ***olive tree***. ME. ▶**b** Any of various wild trees or shrubs of the genus *Olea*; (with specifying word) any of various trees and shrubs allied to the common olive, or resembling it in appearance or in providing oil. L16.
2 The small oval fruit of *Olea europaea*, usu. green when unripe and black when ripe, with a hard stone and a bitter pulp, which yields abundant oil and is also eaten pickled either ripe or unripe. LME.
3 A leaf, branch, or wreath of an olive tree, as an emblem of peace. Also (*fig.*), any emblem of peace. See OLIVE BRANCH 1b. LME. ▶**b** A child; = OLIVE BRANCH 2. E19.
4 The wood of the olive tree. Also ***olive-wood***. LME.
5 COOKERY. A slice of beef or veal rolled and stuffed with onions and herbs, usu. stewed in brown sauce. Usu. ***beef olive***, ***olive of veal***. L16.
6 An oval or olive-shaped thing; *spec.* †(*a*) a kind of oval bit for a horse; (*b*) = ***olive button*** below; (*c*) a metal ring or fitting which is tightened under a threaded nut to form a seal, as on a compression joint. E17.
7 Olive-green. Also, a yellowish-brown colour, esp. of the skin. E17.
8 Any of various gastropod molluscs of the genus *Oliva* or the family Olividae; the elongated, usu. highly polished oval shell of one of these. Also ***olive-shell***. M19.
9 A greenish-brown noctuid moth, *Ipimorpha subtusa*, of Europe and northern Asia. M19.
10 ANATOMY. An olivary body. L19.
11 **a** A mayfly with an olive-coloured body, of the genus *Baetis* (usu. with transparent wings), or the genus *Ephemerella*, esp. *E. ignita* (which has blue wings). L19. ▶**b** ANGLING. An artificial fly made in imitation of such an insect. L19.

📖 **1b American olive** the devil-wood, *Osmanthus americanus*. **black olive** = ***olive-bark*** (b) below. **Chinese olive** any of several East Asian trees of the genus *Canarium* (family Burseraceae) whose fruits have oily seeds, esp. *C. album*. ***mock olive***: see MOCK *attrib. adjective*. ***Russian olive***. ***sweet olive***: see SWEET *adjective*. **2** *Independent* A little dish of juicy olives with warm bread. ***stuffed olive***. **7** W. C. SMITH The sun has dyed Her cheek with olive.

▶ **B** *attrib.* or as *adjective*. **1** Of, pertaining to, or containing olives (the fruit or usu. the tree). E16.
2 Of olive-green. Also (of the skin or complexion), yellowish-brown. E17.

📖 **1** *Times* Vineyards and olive groves. **2** J. G. STRUTT The Oak, whose early leaf has generally more of the olive cast. M. FORSTER Black hair and long legs and a beautiful olive skin.

Special collocations & comb.: **olive-back**, **olive-backed thrush** Swainson's thrush, *Catharus ustulatus*. **olive-bark** (*a*) the bark of the olive; (*b*) *W. Indies* a tree, *Bucida buceras* (family Combretaceae), with an olive-like fruit and a bark used in tanning. **olive button** an oval button or fastener fitting into a corresponding loop. **olive-coloured** *adjective* = sense B.2 above. **olive crescent** a pale greenish-brown Eurasian noctuid moth, *Trisateles emortualis*. **olive-crown** a garland of olive leaves as a token of victory. **olive drab** (of) a brownish-green colour; *spec.* (of) the colour of the US Army uniform. **olive dun** = sense 11a above. **olive-fly**, **olive fruit fly** a fruit fly, *Dacus oleae*, which is a pest of olive trees. **olive-green** *adjective & noun* (*a*) (of) the colour of an unripe olive, a dull yellowish green; (*b*) (of) the colour of the foliage of the olive tree, a greyish or silvery green. **olive oil** (*a*) a pale, light, faintly scented oil extracted from olive pulp, used esp. in cookery; (*b*) [repr. a joc. pronunc. of AU REVOIR] goodbye. **olive pie**: made with olives of veal (see sense A.5 above). **olive-plant** (*a*) = sense A.1 above; (*b*) a child (see OLIVE BRANCH 2). **olive-plum** (the olive-like fruit of) any of various tropical trees of the genus *Cassine* (family Celastraceae). **olive-shaped** *adjective* shaped like an olive, oval. **olive thrush** (*a*) = ***olive-back*** above; (*b*) a brownish thrush, *Turdus olivaceus*, of eastern, central, and southern Africa. ***olive tree***: see sense 1 above. **olive whistler** a flycatcher, *Pachycephala olivacea*, of SE Australia. **olive-yard** an enclosure or piece of ground in which olive trees are cultivated.
■ **olived** *adjective* (*rare*) (*a*) cut up into olives (see OLIVE *noun*¹ 5); (*b*) provided or decorated with olive trees or olive branches: M17. **olive-like** *adjective* resembling the olive, *esp.* resembling the fruit of the olive L19.

olive /'ɒlɪv/ *noun*². *local*. M16.
[Origin uncertain: perh. rel. to female forename *Olive*.]
An oystercatcher.

olive branch /'ɒlɪv brɑːn(t)ʃ/ *noun phr.* ME.
[from OLIVE *noun*¹ + BRANCH *noun*.]
1 A branch of an olive tree. ME. ▶**b** This as an emblem of peace (with allus. to *Genesis* 8:11); *fig.* any token of peace or goodwill. ME.
2 A child (with allus. to *Psalms* 128:3). Usu. in *pl.* Now *joc.* L17.

📖 **1b** *Pall Mall Gazette* Here comes Mr. Balfour with his olive branch, ingeminating peace.

olivenite /ə'lɪv(ə)nʌɪt, 'ɒlɪv-/ *noun*. E19.
[from German *Oliven-erz* olive ore + -ITE¹.]
MINERALOGY. Native basic copper arsenate occurring as orthorhombic crystals or masses, freq. of olive-green colour.

Oliver /'ɒlɪvə/ *noun*¹. *slang*. L18.
[from male forename *Oliver*.]
The moon (perh. with allus. to Oliver Cromwell).
¶ See also ***a Roland for an Oliver***.

oliver /'ɒlɪvə/ *noun*². M19.
[Perh. formed as prec.]
A tilt-hammer worked with the foot by a treadle, used esp. to shape nails, bolts, links of chains, etc.

Oliverian /ɒlɪ'vɪərɪən/ *noun & adjective*. M17.
[from *Oliver* (see below) + -IAN.]
▶ **A** *noun*. A follower or adherent of Oliver Cromwell, a Cromwellian. M17.
▶ **B** *adjective*. Cromwellian. L17.

olivet /ˈɒlɪvɛt/ *noun*[1]. Now *rare* or *obsolete*. Also **-ette**. **LME**.
[Latin *olivetum* olive grove. In sense 2 with allus. to the Mount of Olives (proper name *Olivet*) on the east side of Jerusalem, the scene of the Ascension.]
1 A place in which olive trees are grown; an olive grove. **LME**.
2 (A sign or symbol of) redemption or reward. **M19**.

olivet /ˈɒlɪvɛt/ *noun*[2]. Also **-ette**. **E19**.
[French *olivette* dim. of *olive* **OLIVE** *noun*[1]: see **-ET**[1].]
= ***olive button*** s.v. **OLIVE** *noun*[1] *& adjective*.

Olivetan /ɒlɪˈviːt(ə)n/ *noun*. **L17**.
[from Monte *Oliveto* near Siena (see below) + **-AN**.]
A member of an order of monks founded at Monte Oliveto in 1313 by John Tolomei of Siena, and later subjected to the Benedictine rule.

olivette *noun* var. of **OLIVET** *noun*[1], *noun*[2].

olivine /ˈɒlɪviːn, -ʌɪn/ *noun*. **L18**.
[from Latin *oliva* **OLIVE** *noun*[1] + **-INE**[5].]
MINERALOGY & GEOLOGY. An olive-green, grey-green, or brown orthorhombic silicate of magnesium and iron which is a common mineral in basic igneous rocks. Also, (a member of) a group of isomorphous silicate minerals also including fayalite and forsterite, which contain varying proportions of magnesium, iron, manganese, and calcium.
olivine basalt, ***olivine group***, ***olivine rock***, etc.

olla /ˈɒlə/ *noun*[1]. Pl. **ollas**, (in sense 3) **ollae** /ˈɒliː, ˈɒlʌɪ/. **E17**.
[Spanish from L; in sense 3 directly from Latin.]
1 In Spain and Spanish-speaking countries: an earthen jar or pot used for cooking etc.; a dish of (esp. stewed) meat and vegetables cooked in this. Cf. **OLIO** *noun* 1, **OLLA PODRIDA** 1. **E17**.
2 In Spanish America: a large porous earthen jar for keeping drinking-water cool by evaporation from its outer surface. **M19**.
3 An ancient cinerary urn. **M19**.

olla /ˈɒlə/ *noun*[2]. **E17**.
[Portuguese from Malayalam *ōla*.]
In (esp. the southern part of) the Indian subcontinent: (a letter or document written on) a strip of palm leaf, esp. of the palmyra, prepared for writing.

ollamh /ˈɒləv/ *noun*. Also **-am**, **-av(e)**. **E18**.
[Irish *ollamh*, Old Irish *ollam* learned man, doctor.]
IRISH HISTORY. An expert in an art or branch of learning; a learned man of a rank corresponding to that of a university professor.

olland *noun* see **OLD LAND**.

olla podrida /ˌɒlə pə(ʊ)ˈdriːdə/ *noun phr*. **L16**.
[Spanish, lit. 'rotten pot', formed as **OLLA** *noun*[1] + *podrida* putrid.]
1 = **OLIO** *noun* 1. **L16**.
2 = **OLIO** *noun* 2. **M17**.

ollav(e) *noun* var. of **OLLAMH**.

Ollendorffian /ɒlɪnˈdɔːfɪən/ *adjective*. **L19**.
[from Heinrich Gottfried *Ollendorff* (1803–65), German educator and grammarian + **-IAN**.]
Exhibiting or characterized by the stilted language of some foreign phrase-books.

> 🕮 *Sketch* She persisted in firing off Ollendorffian French at the waiters.

ollie /ˈɒli/ *noun & verb*. *slang*. **L20**.
[Origin unkn.]
▶ **A** *noun*. In skateboarding, snowboarding, etc.: a jump performed without the aid of a take-off ramp, executed by pressing the foot down on the tail of the board to make the deck rebound off the ground. **L20**.
▶ **B** *verb intrans*. Pres. pple & verbal noun **ollieing**. Perform an ollie. **L20**.

olm /əʊlm/ *noun*. **E20**.
[German.]
An aquatic salamander of the genus *Proteus*, having persistent gills and eyes covered with skin, found in deep caves in Austria.

Olmec /ˈɒlmɛk/ *noun & adjective*. **L18**.
[Nahuatl *Olmecatl*, pl. *Olmeca* lit. 'inhabitants of the rubber country'.]
▶ **A** *noun*. Pl. **-s**, same, (in sense 1 also) **-a(s)** /-ə(z)/.
1 In *pl*. A native American people or peoples, probably orig. of the Mexican altiplano, inhabiting the coast of southern Veracruz and western Tabasco during the 15th and 16th cents. **L18**.
2 A member of a prehistoric people inhabiting this same area *c* 1200–100 BC. **M20**.
▶ **B** *attrib*. or as *adjective*. Designating the culture or characteristic artistic style of the prehistoric Olmecs. **M20**.
■ **Olˈmecan** *adjective* of or pertaining to the prehistoric Olmecs **E20**. **Olmecoid** *adjective* resembling the art or culture of the prehistoric Olmecs **M20**.

-ologic /əˈlɒdʒɪk/ *suffix*.
[from **-OLOG(Y** + **-IC**.]
Forming adjectives corresp. to nouns in ***-ology***; = **-LOGIC**.
¶ See note s.v. **-LOGICAL**.

-ological /əˈlɒdʒɪk(ə)l/ *suffix*.
[from **-OLOG(Y** + **-ICAL**.]
Forming adjectives corresp. to nouns in ***-ology***; = **-LOGICAL**.

ologist /ˈɒlədʒɪst/ *noun*. *colloq*. (*joc*.). **M19**.
[from next.]
An expert in or student of some subject of study or branch of knowledge.

> 🕮 *Nature* 'Ologists' of the Select Committee on Science and Technology often feel that key questions are not asked.

-ologist /ˈɒlədʒɪst/ *suffix*.
[from **-OLOG(Y** + **-IST**.]
Forming nouns corresp. to nouns in ***-ology***, with the sense 'an expert in or student of a specified subject of study or branch of knowledge'.

ology /ˈɒlədʒi/ *noun*. *colloq*. (*joc*.). Also **'ology** **E19**.
[from next.]
A subject of study, a branch of knowledge.

> 🕮 E. NARES To understand . . Geology, Philology and a hundred other ologies.

-ology /ˈɒlədʒi/ *suffix*.
[formed as **-O-** + **-LOGY**.]
Forming nouns from or after Greek, with the sense 'a subject of study or interest, a branch of knowledge', as ***phenology***, ***psychology***, ***sexology***, etc.

ololiuqui /əʊləʊˈl(j)uːki/ *noun*. **E20**.
[Amer. Spanish *ololiuque* from Nahuatl, from *ololoa* to cover + *qui* agent-suff.]
A Mexican climbing plant, *Turbina corymbosa*, related to morning glory; the hallucinogenic drug prepared from the seeds of this plant.

Olonetsian /ɒləˈnɛtsɪən/ *noun & adjective*. **M20**.
[from *Olonets*, a region of NW Russia + **-IAN**.]
(Of) a Finno-Ugric language spoken in NW Russia.
■ Also **Olonets** *noun & adjective* **M20**.

oloroso /ɒləˈrəʊsəʊ/ *noun*. Pl. **-os**. **L19**.
[Spanish = fragrant.]
A heavy, dark, medium-sweet sherry; a glass of this.

olpe /ˈɒlpeɪ/ *noun*. **L19**.
[Greek *olpē*.]
GREEK ANTIQUITIES. A leather flask for oil, wine, etc. Also, a pear-shaped jug with a handle.

Olympiad /əˈlɪmpɪad/ *noun*. **LME**.
[French *Olympiade* or Latin *Olympiad-*, *-as*, from Greek *Olumpiad-*, *-as*, from *Olumpios* adjective of *Olumpos* **OLYMPUS**: see **-AD**[1].]
1 A period of four years between Olympic games, by which the ancient Greeks calculated time. **LME**. ▸**b** A four-yearly celebration of the ancient Olympic games. **L15**.
2 A (four-yearly) celebration of the modern Olympic Games. Also, a regular international competition in a particular game or sport, as chess or bridge. **E20**.

> 🕮 **1b** *Journal of Hellenic Studies* The well-known string of Spartan victories in running events at the early Olympiads. **2** *Radio Times* In the following six Olympiads the Soviet Union . . won over 500 medals.

¶ In the US *Olympiad* may only be used with the agreement of the United States Olympic Committee (or the International Olympic Committee).

Olympian /əˈlɪmpɪən/ *adjective & noun*. **L15**.
[from Latin *Olympus* or **OLYMP(IC** + **-IAN**.]
▶ **A** *adjective*. **1** Of, pertaining to, or characteristic of Olympus or its inhabitants, the gods of Greek mythology; heavenly, celestial; godlike, majestic; aloof, superior in manner. **L15**.
2 Of or pertaining to Olympia; = **OLYMPIC** *adjective* 1a. **E16**.

> 🕮 **1** G. B. SHAW The Olympian majesty with which a mane . . of . . hair is thrown back from an imposing brow. J. S. HUXLEY In Olympian detachment from popular feeling.

▶ **B** *noun*. **1** A native or inhabitant of Olympia. Also, a competitor in the ancient Olympic games. **E17**. ▸**b** A competitor in the modern Olympic games. **L20**.
2 Each of the twelve greater gods of Greek mythology, traditionally believed to inhabit Olympus; spec. *the* god Zeus or Jupiter. **M19**.
3 *transf*. A person resembling the gods of Olympus in power, majesty, or detachment; a person of apparently superhuman ability or achievement. Cf. **TITAN** *noun* 3a. **L19**.

> 🕮 **1** *Bookcase* The memory of the giant Olympians of the past, who have shaped today's Games. **3** A. C. SWINBURNE The ranks of great men are . . divisible, not into thinkers and workers, but into Titans and Olympians.

■ **Olympianism** *noun* (*a*) the polytheism of the ancient Greeks, centred on the gods of Olympus; (*b*) an Olympian sense of power, superiority, etc.: **L19**.

Olympia oyster /əˌlɪmpɪə ˈɔɪstə/ *noun phr*. **E20**.
[*Olympia*, a town at the southern end of Puget Sound and the capital of the State of Washington, in the US.]
A small northern variety of the Californian oyster, *Ostrea lurida*.

Olympic /əˈlɪmpɪk/ *adjective & noun*. **L16**.
[Latin *Olympicus* from Greek *Olumpikos* of Olympus or Olympia: see **-IC**.]
▶ **A** *adjective*. **1 a** Of or pertaining to Olympia, a district of Elis in southen Greece, or the ancient games which were held there. **L16**. ▸**b** Of or pertaining to the modern Olympic games. **L19**.
2 Of or pertaining to Olympus; = **OLYMPIAN** *adjective* 1. *rare*. **L16**.

> 🕮 **1b** *Japan Times* Gao, the Olympic gold medallist. *Independent* Tennis . . is recognized again as an Olympic sport.

Special collocations & comb.: **Olympic games** (*a*) an ancient Greek festival held at Olympia every four years in honour of Zeus, with athletic, literary, and musical competitions; (*b*) (**O- G-**) a modern international sports festival inspired by this and now under the auspices of an International Olympic Committee, held every four years (except during world wars) since 1896 in different venues. **Olympic-size**, **Olympic-sized** *adjectives* of the dimensions prescribed for modern Olympic competitions.
▶ **B** *noun*. In *pl*., the Olympic games, *esp*. the modern Olympic Games; *transf*. (*sing*. & in *pl*.) a regular international competition in chess etc. **E17**.

> 🕮 R. HOLT Britain only won one gold medal in the 1952 Olympics.

¶ In the US *Olympic(s)* may only be used with the agreement of the United States Olympic Committee (or the International Olympic Committee).

Olympism /əˈlɪmpɪz(ə)m/ *noun*. Chiefly *US*. **M20**.
[French *olympisme*: cf. **OLYMPIC**, **-ISM**.]
The spirit, principles, and ideals of the modern Olympic Games; commitment to or promotion of these.

Olympus /əˈlɪmpəs/ *noun*. **L16**.
[Latin from Greek *Olumpos*, the name of several tall mountains, esp. that mentioned below.]
1 The traditional home of the twelve greater gods of Greek mythology, a mountain in N. Thessaly; *transf*. heaven; the abode of a divinity or divinities. **L16**.
2 *fig*. An acme, an ideal, a pinnacle of achievement, etc.; an impressive or majestic thing. **E17**.

OM *abbreviation*.
(Member of) the Order of Merit.

om /əʊm/ *interjection & noun*. **L18**.
[Sanskrit *om*, *oṃ*, sometimes regarded as composed of three sounds, *a-u-m*, symbolizing the three major Hindu deities: see also **OM MANI PADME HUM**.]
HINDUISM & TIBETAN BUDDHISM. ▶ **A** *interjection*. Used as a mantra or auspicious formula at the beginning of prayers etc. **L18**.
▶ **B** *noun*. An utterance of 'om'. **L19**.

om- *combining form* see **OMO-**.

-oma /ˈəʊmə/ *suffix*.
[Repr. Greek *-ōma* suffix, chiefly from verbs in *-ousthai*. See also **-OME**.]
Forming nouns adopted from Greek, and English nouns modelled on these, with the sense 'tumour, abnormal growth', as ***carcinoma***, ***glaucoma***, ***tuberculoma***, with pls. in *-omata* (after Greek) or (increasingly) in *-omas*.

omadhaun /ˈɒmədɔːn/ *noun*. Orig. & chiefly *Anglo-Irish* (*derog*.). Also **omad(h)awn** & other vars. **E19**.
[Irish *amadán*.]
A foolish person.

Omaha /ˈəʊməhɑː/ *noun & adjective*. Also (earlier) †**Maha**. **E19**.
[Omaha *umonhon* upstream people.]
▶ **A** *noun*. Pl. same, **-s**. A member of a Siouan people of NE Nebraska; the language of this people. **E19**.
▶ **B** *adjective*. Of or pertaining to the Omaha or their language. **E19**.

omalgia /əʊˈmaldʒə/ *noun*. Now *rare*. **L19**.
[from **OM(O-** + **-ALGIA**.]
MEDICINE. Pain, esp. rheumatism, in the shoulder.

Oman /əʊˈmɑːn/ *attrib. adjective*. **E19**.
[See **OMANI**.]
= **OMANI** *adjective*.

omander /əʊˈmandə/ *noun*. **M19**.
[Origin unkn.]
An Indian ebony resembling calamander, from the tree *Diospyros digyna*.

omanhene /ˈəʊmanheneɪ/ *noun*. **E20**.
[Twi ɔ-*mâŋ-hene* chief, king.]
Among the Ashanti people: a paramount chief of a state or district.

Omani /əʊˈmɑːni/ *noun & adjective.* As adjective also **Oman**. **E19.**
[Arab., from *ʿUmān* (see below) + *-ī* adjectival suffix.]
▶ **A** *noun.* A native or inhabitant of Oman, a coastal region in the south-east of the Arabian peninsula. **E19.**
▶ **B** *adjective.* Of or pertaining to Oman or its inhabitants. **E19.**

Omarian /əʊˈmɑːrɪən/ *adjective & noun.* **L19.**
[from *Omar* (see below) + **-IAN**.]
▶ **A** *adjective.* Of or pertaining to the Persian astronomer and poet Omar Khayyam (*c* 1048–*c* 1123) or his writing; resembling the poetry of Omar Khayyam, esp. his quatrains as translated and adapted by Edward Fitzgerald, esp. in the celebration of earthly pleasures. **L19.**
▶ **B** *noun.* An admirer or student of Omar Khayyam or his writing. **L19.**
■ **Omarianism**, **ˈOmarism** *nouns* the doctrines or cult of Omar Khayyam **L19.** **Omarite** *adjective & noun* = **OMARIAN** **E20.**

omasum /əʊˈmeɪsəm/ *noun.* Pl. **omasa** /-sə/. **E18.**
[Latin = bullock's tripe.]
The muscular third stomach of a ruminant.

omble chevalier *noun phr.* var. of **OMBRE CHEVALIER**.

ombre /ˈɒmbə, ˈɒmbreɪ/ *noun.* **M17.**
[Spanish **HOMBRE**. Cf. French *(h)ombre* (chief player at) ombre.]
1 A card-game played by three people, with forty cards, popular in the 17th and 18th cents. **M17.**
2 The player at this and other card-games who undertakes to win the pool. **E18.**

ombré /ɔ̃bre/ *noun & adjective.* **L19.**
[French, pa. pple of *ombrer* to shade.]
(A fabric or design) having gradual shading of colour from light to dark.

ombre chevalier /ɔ̃ːbr ʃəvalje/ *noun phr.* Also ***omble chevalier*** /ɔ̃ːbl/. **L19.**
[French.]
A variety of the char, *Salvelinus alpinus*, found in Alpine lakes, esp. Lake Geneva.

ombrellino /ombrelˈliːno, ɒmbrɛˈliːnəʊ/ *noun.* Pl. ***-ni*** /-ni/, ***-nos*** /-nəʊz/. **M19.**
[Italian.]
ROMAN CATHOLIC CHURCH. A small umbrella-like canopy held over the sacraments when they are moved from one place to another.

ombres chinoises /ɔ̃br ʃinwaz/ *noun phr. pl.* **L18.**
[French = Chinese shadows.]
Hist. A European version of Chinese shadow-puppets, used in a galanty show.

ombro- /ˈɒmbrəʊ/ *combining form* of Greek *ombros* shower of rain: see **-O-**.
■ **omˈbrogenous** *adjective* (ECOLOGY) (of a bog, peat, etc.) dependent on rain or other precipitation for its formation (cf. **SOLIGENOUS**, **TOPOGENOUS**) **M20.** **ombroˈlogical** *adjective* of or pertaining to ombrology **M19.** **omˈbrology** *noun* the branch of meteorology that deals with rain **M19.** **omˈbrometer** *noun* (now *rare*) a rain-gauge **M18.** **ombrophile** *noun* an ombrophilous plant **L19.** **omˈbrophilous** *adjective* (of a plant) able to withstand prolonged rainfall **L19.** **ombrophobe** *noun* an ombrophobous plant **L19.** **omˈbrophobous** *adjective* (of a plant) intolerant of prolonged rainfall **L19.** **ombrotrophic** /-ˈtrəʊfɪk, -ˈtrɒfɪk/ *adjective* (of a bog etc. or its vegetation) dependent on atmospheric moisture for its nutrients **M20.**

ombú /ɒmˈbuː/ *noun.* **E17.**
[Amer. Spanish from Guarani *umbú*.]
A large S. American evergreen tree, *Phytolacca dioica* (family Phytolaccaceae).

ombudsman /ˈɒmbʊdzmən/ *noun.* Pl. **-men**. **M20.**
[Swedish, from *ombud* commissioner, agent, repr. Old Norse *umboð* charge, commission, *umboðsmaðr* commissary, manager. Cf. **UMBOTH**.]
An official appointed to investigate complaints by individuals against maladministration by public authorities; *esp.* a British official of this kind (officially called the Parliamentary Commissioner for Administration), first appointed in 1967.

> 🕮 *fig.*: A. TOFFLER A technology ombudsman could serve as an official sounding board for complaints.

■ **ombudsmanship** *noun* the office or function of an ombudsman **M20.** **ombudsperson** *noun* an ombudsman or ombudswoman **L20.** **ombudswoman** *noun* a female ombudsman **M20.**

omdah /ˈɒmdə/ *noun.* Also ***omdeh***. **E20.**
[Arab. *ʿumda* lit. 'column, support', from *ʿamada* to support.]
In Arab countries: the headman of a village.

-ome /əʊm/ *suffix.*
[Anglicized from **-OMA** (partly through influence of German *-om*, French *-ome*).]
Chiefly BOTANY. Forming nouns denoting a structure or group of cells normally present, as ***caulome***, ***rhizome***, ***trichome***. Formerly also in words now written with *-oma*, as ***tuberculome***.

omee /ˈəʊmi/ *noun. slang* (chiefly THEATRICAL). Also **omie** & other vars. **M19.**
[Alt. of Italian *uomo* man.]
A man, *esp.* (***a***) a landlord, (***b***) an itinerant actor.

omega /ˈəʊmɪɡə/ *noun.* **E16.**
[Greek *ō mega* lit. 'great O', opp. *o mikron* **OMICRON**.]
1 The last letter (Ω, ω) of the Greek alphabet, having originally the value of a long open *o*; *fig.* the last of a series; the last word, the final development. **E16.**
2 PARTICLE PHYSICS. Either of two subatomic particles: (***a***) (in full ***omega meson***) a neutral meson with a mass of 784 MeV and zero spin that usually decays into three pions (freq. written ω); (***b***) (in full ***omega minus***) a negatively charged baryon with a mass of 1672 MeV and a spin of $\frac{3}{2}$, the discovery of which led to the concept of quarks (freq. written Ω^-). **M20.**

> 🕮 **1** *Athenaeum* These two volumes may be considered as the omega of Hebrew bibliography. ***Alpha and Omega***: see **ALPHA**.

Comb.: **Omega point** (in the work of P. Teilhard de Chardin) a hypothesized point of convergence, absorption, or transformation which is the divine end, or God, towards which the forces of evolution are moving; **omega-3** BIOCHEMISTRY (usu. *attrib.*) any of a class of polyunsaturated fatty acids, found chiefly in fish oils, which contain a double bond at the third to last carbon atom in the hydrocarbon chain; **omega-6** BIOCHEMISTRY (usu. *attrib.*) any of a class of polyunsaturated fatty acids, found especially in nuts, seeds, and vegetable oils, which contain a double bond at the sixth to last carbon atom in the hydrocarbon chain.

omegatron /ˈəʊmɪɡətrɒn/ *noun.* **M20.**
[from prec. (used as symbol for angular momentum) + **-TRON**.]
PHYSICS. A mass spectrometer used to identify and measure gases at very low pressures by applying a radio-frequency electric field at right angles to a magnetic field.

omelette /ˈɒmlɪt/ *noun.* Also **omelet**; earlier †**amulet**, †**aumelet**, & other vars. **E17.**
[French *omelette*, †*aume-*, †*ame-* metath. alt. of †*alumette* by-form of †*alumelle*, †*alemel(l)e*, from *lemele* knife-blade (by misdivision of *la lemelle* as *l'alemelle*) from Latin **LAMELLA**, presumably with ref. to the thin flat shape of an omelette.]
A dish of beaten eggs cooked in a frying-pan and served, usu. folded over, either plain or with a savoury or sweet filling.

> 🕮 *Proverb*: One can't make an omelette without breaking eggs. ***Spanish omelette***: see **SPANISH** *adjective*.

Comb.: **omelette soufflé** an omelette made with separated eggs, the beaten whites being folded into the yolks.

omen /ˈəʊmən/ *noun & verb.* **L16.**
[Latin *omen*, *omin-*.]
▶ **A** *noun.* A phenomenon or circumstance thought to portend good or evil; a prophetic sign, an augury. Also, prophetic significance. **L16.**

> 🕮 T. KENEALLY A bad place full of miserable omen. A. DAVIS Like an omen from hell . . a woman's screams shattered the silence. *Which?* The omens for the future may not be so bleak.

▶ **B** *verb trans.* Presage, prognosticate. **L18.**

> 🕮 SIR W. SCOTT The yet unknown verdict, of which, however, all omened the tragical contents.

■ **omened** *adjective* having omens (of a specified kind) **E18.**

omentum /əʊˈmɛntəm/ *noun.* Pl. **-ta** /-tə/. **LME.**
[Latin.]
ANATOMY. A fold of the peritoneum which connects the stomach with the liver, spleen, colon, etc; the epiploon. **greater omentum**, **great omentum** a fatty, highly folded part of the omentum covering the intestines. **lesser omentum** a part of the omentum linking the liver to the stomach.
■ **omental** *adjective* of, pertaining to, or situated in the omentum **M18.** **omentopexy** *noun* (an instance of) the surgical attachment of the omentum to another structure, usu. the heart or the abdominal wall **E20.**

omer /ˈəʊmə/ *noun.* **E17.**
[Hebrew *ʿōmer*.]
1 An ancient Hebrew dry measure, the tenth part of an ephah. **E17.**
2 JUDAISM. (Usu. **O-**.) A sheaf of corn or omer of grain presented as an offering on the second day of Passover; the period of 49 days between this day and Pentecost. **M19.**
2 counting of the omer the formal enumeration of the 49 days from the offering at Passover to Pentecost.

omertà /omerˈtaː/ *noun.* **L19.**
[Italian dial. var. of *umiltà* humility, orig. with ref. to the Mafia code which enjoins submission of the group to its leader.]
A code of silence observed by members or associates of the Mafia or (*transf.*) others engaged in clandestine activities.

ometer /ˈɒmɪtə/ *noun. joc. rare.* **M19.**
[from next.]
A meter, a measuring instrument.

> 🕮 *Farmer's Magazine* The barometers, thermometers, saccharometers, and other ometers.

-ometer /ˈɒmɪtə/ *suffix.*
Form of **-METER** with *-o-* provided by first element (***barometer***, ***hydrometer***) or merely connective (***accelerometer***, ***Fade-Ometer***). Cf. **-IMETER**.
■ **-ometry** *suffix*: forming corresp. nouns (cf. **-METRY**).

omicron /əʊˈmʌɪkrɒn/ *noun.* **M17.**
[Greek *o mikron* lit. 'little O', opp. *ō mega* **OMEGA**.]
The fifteenth letter (Ο, ο) of the Greek alphabet, having the value of a short *o*.

omie *noun* var. of **OMEE**.

†**ominate** *verb.* **L16.**
[Latin *ominat-* pa. ppl stem of *ominari*, *-are*, formed as **OMEN**: see **-ATE**[3].]
1 *verb trans. & intrans.* Prognosticate (the future) from omens, augur. **L16–M18.**
2 *verb trans. & intrans.* Be a prognostic (of), presage. **L16–E19.**

ominous /ˈɒmɪnəs/ *adjective.* **L16.**
[from Latin *ominosus*, formed as **OMEN**: see **-OUS**.]
1 Serving as an omen; portentous. **L16.**
†**2** Of good omen, auspicious; fortunate. **L16–M17.**
3 Indicative or suggestive of future misfortune; boding ill, menacing. **L16.** ▸**b** Marked by evil omens, disastrous. Now *rare* or *obsolete*. **M17.**

> 🕮 **1** GOLDSMITH An ominous circumstance that happened the last time we played together. **3** B. MOORE The ominous air of frailty of a bomb-damaged building. M. MAHY They agreed about many of them—an ominous sign. B. VINE His look had become ominous, like that of a messenger come to break bad news.

■ **ominously** *adverb* **L16.** **ominousness** *noun* **E17.**

omissible /ə(ʊ)ˈmɪsɪb(ə)l/ *adjective.* **E19.**
[from Latin *omiss-* pa. ppl stem of *omittere* **OMIT** + **-IBLE**.]
Able to be omitted.
■ **omissiˈbility** *noun* **M20.**

omission /ə(ʊ)ˈmɪʃ(ə)n/ *noun.* **ME.**
[Old & mod. French, or late Latin *omissio(n-)*, formed as prec.: see **-ION**.]
1 The action or an act of neglecting or failing to perform something, esp. a duty. **ME.**
2 The action of omitting or failing to include something or someone, the fact of being omitted; an instance of this. **ME.**

> 🕮 **1** H. E. BATES It was an omission that would have to be remedied. **sin of omission** a failure to perform something that should have been done (opp. ***sin of commission***). **2** ***great omission***: see **GREAT** *adjective*.

omissive /ə(ʊ)ˈmɪsɪv/ *adjective.* **L15.**
[from Latin *omiss-* (see **OMISSIBLE**) + **-IVE**.]
Characterized by neglecting to perform something or leaving something or someone out.

omit /ə(ʊ)ˈmɪt/ *verb trans.* Infl. **-tt-**. **LME.**
[Latin *omittere*, formed as **OB-** + *mittere* send, let go.]
1 Leave out; fail to include. **LME.**
2 Fail to perform, leave undone; neglect *to do*. **M16.**
▸†**b** Take no notice of. *rare* (Shakes.). **L16–E17.**
†**3** Cease to retain; let go. **E–M17.**

> 🕮 **1** A. WILSON She told him nearly all, only omitting the dreadful remarks. **2** R. FORD No traveller . . should omit visiting the two latter. W. S. CHURCHILL Its English Governor . . omitted to accompany his request with a suitable bribe. **b** SHAKES. *2 Hen. IV* Therefore omit him not; blunt not his love . . by seeming cold.

■ †**omittance** *noun* (*rare*) omission: only in **E17.** **omitter** *noun* **E17.**

omlah /ˈɒmlɑː/ *noun.* **L18.**
[Arab. *ʿumalāʾ*.]
In the Indian subcontinent: the body of officials who staff a court-house.

om mani padme hum /əʊm ˌmʌni pʌdmeɪ ˈhuːm/ *noun phr. & interjection.* **L18.**
[Sanskrit *Om mani-padme hūm* lit. 'oh (goddess) Manipadma', reinterpreted as 'oh jewel in the lotus', from *maṇi* jewel, *padma* lotus. Cf. **OM**.]
(Used as) a mantra or auspicious formula in prayer and meditation in Tibetan Buddhism.

ommateum /ɒməˈtiːəm/ *noun.* Pl. **-tea** /-ˈtiːə/. **L19.**
[mod. Latin, from Greek *omma(t-)* eye.]
ZOOLOGY. Orig., the soft tissue (excluding the lens) of a simple eye in an invertebrate. Now usu., a compound eye.
■ **ommateal** *adjective* **L19.**

ommatidium /ɒməˈtɪdɪəm/ *noun.* Pl. **-dia** /-ˈdɪə/. **L19.**
[formed as prec. + **-IDIUM**.]
ZOOLOGY. Each of the conical structural elements of a compound eye.
■ **ommatidial** *adjective* **L19.**

ommatin /ˈɒmətɪn/ *noun.* Also (earlier) **-ine** /-iːn/. **M20.**
[from Greek *omma(t-)* eye + **-IN**[1], **-INE**[5].]
BIOCHEMISTRY. Any of the group of ommochromes characterized by weaker colours, lower stability to alkalis, and lower molecular weights than ommins.

ommatophore /ˈɒmətəfɔː/ *noun.* L19.
[formed as prec. + -O- + -PHORE.]
ZOOLOGY. A part of an invertebrate animal, esp. a tentacle, which bears an eye.

Ommayyad *adjective & noun* var. of UMAYYAD.

ommin /ˈɒmɪn/ *noun.* Also (earlier) **-ine** /-iːn/. M20.
[from Greek *omma* eye + -IN[1], -INE[5].]
BIOCHEMISTRY. Any of the group of sulphur-containing ommochromes characterized by stronger colours, greater stability to alkalis, and higher molecular weights than ommatins.

ommochrome /ˈɒməkrəʊm/ *noun.* M20.
[formed as prec. + -O- + Greek *khrōma* colour.]
BIOCHEMISTRY. Any of a group of insect pigments derived by condensation reactions from kynurenine, giving yellow, red, and brownish body colours and commonly also found in the accessory cells of insect eyes. Cf. OMMATIN, OMMIN.

omneity /ɒmˈniːɪti/ *noun. rare.* M17.
[from Latin *omnis*, *omne* all + -ITY, prob. immed. from a medieval Latin word corresp. to *haeccitas* (HAECCEITY), *seitas* (SEITY), etc.]
The condition of being all; allness.

omni- /ˈɒmni/ *combining form.*
[Latin *omnis* all, every: see -I-.]
Used in words adopted from Latin or in English words modelled on these, with the sense 'all, of everything, in every way'.
■ **omni-anˈtenna** *noun* an omnidirectional aerial L20. **omniˈfocal** *adjective & noun* (designating) a lens whose power changes continuously from top to bottom M20. **omniˈlateral** *adjective* facing all directions; representing all points of view: M20. **omniˈlingual** *adjective* speaking all languages L19. **omniˈlucent** *adjective* (*rare*) shining everywhere or on all M17. **omniˈpatient** *adjective* having unlimited endurance M19. **omniperˈcipient** *adjective* perceiving all things M17. **omniˈprevalent** *adjective* (*a*) all-prevailing; (*b*) universally prevalent: M17. **omnirange** *noun* (part of) a navigation system in which short-range omnidirectional VHF transmitters serve as radio beacons M20. **omniˈsexual** *adjective* of or involving sexual activities of all kinds; widely diverse in sexual orientation: L20. **omnisexuˈality** *noun* the quality or condition of being omnisexual L20. **omniˈsubjugant** *adjective* subjugating everything or everyone E20. **omniˈtemporal** *adjective* relating to all times or tenses L19. **omniˈtolerant** *adjective* tolerant of everything M19. †**omnivalent** *adjective* all-prevailing E17–L18.

omniana /ɒmnɪˈɑːnə/ *noun pl.* E19.
[from Latin *omnis* all, *omnia* all things + -ANA.]
Notes or scraps of information about all kinds of things.

omnibus /ˈɒmnɪbəs/ *noun, adjective, & verb.* E19.
[French, also *voiture omnibus* carriage for all (Latin *omnibus* dat. pl. of *omnis* all): cf. BUS *noun.*]
▶ **A** *noun.* Pl. **-buses**, ***-busses**, (chiefly *joc.*) **-bi** /-bʌɪ/.
1 A large public road vehicle for carrying numerous passengers, running on a fixed route; a bus. Now chiefly *formal* or *Hist.* (esp. with ref. to a horse-drawn vehicle of this kind). E19.
2 A publication containing a variety of items; *esp.* = ***omnibus volume*** below. E19.
3 A waiter's assistant who clears tables etc. Cf. ***busboy*** s.v. BUS *noun.* L19.
1 ***the man on the Clapham omnibus***: see CLAPHAM 2.
▶ **B** *adjective.* Esp. of a legislative bill: relating to, covering, or containing numerous disparate or unrelated items. M19.
Special collocations & comb.: †**omnibus-bar** = ***busbar*** s.v. BUS *noun.* **omnibus book** = ***omnibus volume*** below. **omnibus box** *Hist.* a large theatre box allocated to a considerable number of subscribers. **omnibus edition**, **omnibus programme** an edition of a radio or television serial containing all the week's episodes. **omnibus train**: stopping at all the stations on a route. **omnibus volume** an economically priced volume containing several reprinted works by a single author or stories etc. of a similar kind.
▶ **C** *verb.* Infl. **-s-**, ***-ss-**.
1 *verb intrans. & trans.* Travel or convey by omnibus. M19.
2 *verb trans.* Publish an omnibus edition of (an author). M20.

omnicompetent /ɒmnɪˈkɒmpɪt(ə)nt/ *adjective.* E19.
[from OMNI- + COMPETENT *adjective.*]
Competent to deal with everything; *spec.* possessing jurisdiction to act in all matters.
■ **omnicompetence** *noun* E20.

omnidirectional /ˌɒmnɪdɪˈrɛkʃ(ə)n(ə)l, -dʌɪ-/ *adjective.* E20.
[from OMNI- + DIRECTIONAL.]
Of equal sensitivity or power in all (esp. horizontal) directions.
■ **ˌomnidirectioˈnality** *noun* M20. **omnidirectionally** *adverb* M20.

omnifarious /ɒmnɪˈfɛːrɪəs/ *adjective.* M17.
[from Latin *omnifarius* (formed as OMNI-: cf. *multifarious*) + -OUS.]
Comprising or dealing with all kinds of things.
■ **omnifariousness** *noun* E19.

omnific /ɒmˈnɪfɪk/ *adjective.* M17.
[from OMNI- + -FIC, after *omnipotent* etc.]
All-creating.
> MILTON Silence, ye troubl'd waves, and thou Deep, peace, Said then th' Omnific Word.

omnificent /ɒmˈnɪfɪs(ə)nt/ *adjective.* L17.
[formed as OMNI- + *-ficent*, after *magnificent* etc.]
= prec.
■ **omnificence** *noun* L19.

omniform /ˈɒmnɪfɔːm/ *adjective.* M17.
[Late Latin *omniformis*, formed as OMNI-: see -FORM.]
Of all shapes; taking every form.
■ **omniˈformity** *noun* M17.

omnify /ˈɒmnɪfʌɪ/ *verb trans.* E17.
[from OMNI- + -FY, after *magnify*.]
†**1** Make everything of, regard as all in all. E–M17.
2 Make universal. E19.

†**omnigatherum** *noun.* LME–E19.
[from OMNI- + GATHER *verb* + *-um* after Latin nouns in *-um*.]
= OMNIUM GATHERUM; *spec.* (*Scot.*) the unincorporated craftsmen of a burgh.

omnigenous /ɒmˈnɪdʒɪnəs/ *adjective.* M17.
[from Latin *omnigenus* (formed as OMNI- + GENUS) + -OUS.]
Of all kinds.

Omnimax /ˈɒmnɪmaks/ *noun.* L20.
[from OMNI- + MAX(IMUM, after IMAX.]
(Proprietary name for) a technique of wide-screen cinematography in which 70mm film is projected through a fish-eye lens on to a hemispherical screen. Freq. *attrib.*

omnipotence /ɒmˈnɪpət(ə)ns/ *noun.* LME.
[Late Latin *omnipotentia*, from Latin *omnipotent-*: see next, -ENCE.]
The quality of having infinite or unlimited power (esp. as an attribute of God). Also, (God as) an omnipotent force.
■ Also †**omnipotency** *noun* L15–E18.

omnipotent /ɒmˈnɪpət(ə)nt/ *adjective & noun.* ME.
[Old & mod. French from Latin *omnipotent-*, formed as OMNI- + POTENT *adjective*[2].]
▶ **A** *adjective.* **1** Of God, a deity, etc.: almighty, infinite in power. ME.
2 *gen.* All-powerful; having unlimited or very great power, force, or influence. L16. ▶†**b** Unparalleled, arrant; huge, mighty. *joc.* Only in L16.
> **2** I. MURDOCH He was omnipotent, the . . despot of his little world. **b** SHAKES. *1 Hen. IV* This is the most omnipotent villain that ever cried 'Stand' to a true man.

▶ **B** *noun.* An omnipotent being; spec. *the* Almighty, God. E17.
> G. MEREDITH The open mind, The Omnipotent's prime gift.

■ **omnipotently** *adverb* M17.

omnipresent /ɒmnɪˈprɛz(ə)nt/ *adjective.* E17.
[medieval Latin *omnipraesent-*, formed as OMNI- + PRESENT *adjective.*]
1 Of God etc.: present in all places at the same time. E17.
2 *hyperbol.* Widely or constantly met with; widespread. E18.
> **1** A. WILLET It is proper to the diuine nature to be infinite, omnipotent, omnipresent. **2** *Wine & Spirits* The . . rarely glimpsed but omnipresent and ever-hungry wild boar.

■ **omnipresence** *noun* E17. **omnipresently** *adverb* E18.

omniscient /ɒmˈnɪsɪənt/ *adjective & noun.* E17.
[medieval Latin *omniscient-*, formed as OMNI- + SCIENT *adjective.*]
▶ **A** *adjective.* **1** Esp. of God: having infinite knowledge. E17.
2 *hyperbol.* Having very extensive knowledge. L18.
▶ **B** *noun.* An omniscient being; spec. *the* Almighty, God. L18.
■ **omniscience** *noun* E17. **omnisciency** *noun* (long *arch.*) M17. **omnisciently** *adverb* M19.

†**omniscious** *adjective.* L16–E18.
[from medieval Latin *omniscius* (formed as OMNI- + *scire* know) + -OUS.]
Omniscient.

omnitude /ˈɒmnɪtjuːd/ *noun. rare.* M19.
[from OMNI- + -TUDE.]
The fact of being all, universality; the total sum.

omnium /ˈɒmnɪəm/ *noun.* M18.
[Latin, lit. 'of all (things, sorts),' genit. pl. of *omnis* all: cf. next.]
1 STOCK EXCHANGE. **a** *Hist.* The total value of the stock and other interests offered by the Government to each subscriber when raising a loan. M18. ▶**b** Any combined stock the constituents of which can be dealt with separately. *colloq.* L19.
2 The sum of what one values; one's all. M18.
3 A piece of furniture with open shelves for ornaments; a whatnot. M19.

omnium gatherum /ˌɒmnɪəm ˈɡaðərəm/ *noun phr. colloq.* Pl. **-rums**, (*rare*) **-ra** /-rə/. M16.
[Pseudo-Latin, from Latin OMNIUM + GATHER *verb* + *-um*: see OMNIGATHERUM.]
1 A gathering or collection of all sorts of persons or things; a confused medley. M16.
†**2** STOCK EXCHANGE. = OMNIUM 1a. M–L18.

omnivore /ˈɒmnɪvɔː/ *noun.* L19.
[French formed as next, or back-form. from next.]
An omnivorous person or animal.

omnivorous /ɒmˈnɪv(ə)rəs/ *adjective.* M17.
[from Latin *omnivorus*: see OMNI-, -VOROUS.]
1 Feeding on every kind of food available; *spec.* eating both plant and animal food. M17.
2 *fig.* Reading, observing, etc., whatever comes one's way. L18.
> **1** *Natural World* The brown rat . . is an omnivorous scavenger. **2** LD BRAIN His intellectual appetite was omnivorous.

■ **omnivorously** *adverb* M19. **omnivorousness** *noun* E18. **omnivory** *noun* omnivorousness M20.

Omnopon /ˈɒmnəpɒn/ *noun.* E20.
[from OMNI- + OP(IUM + *-on*.]
PHARMACOLOGY. (Proprietary name for) a mixture of the hydrochlorides of the opium alkaloids. Cf. PANTOPON.

omo- /ˈəʊməʊ/ *combining form.* Before a vowel also **om-**.
[from Greek *ōmos* shoulder: see -O-.]
ANATOMY. Of, pertaining to, or connected with the shoulder, as ***omalgia***. Cf. OMOPLATE.
■ **omo-ˈhyoid** *adjective & noun* (*a*) *adjective* pertaining to or connecting the shoulder and the hyoid bone; (*b*) *noun* the omohyoid muscle: M19.

omomyid /əʊməˈmʌɪɪd/ *noun & adjective.* M20.
[mod. Latin *Omomyidae* (see below), from *Omomys* genus name: see -ID[3].]
ZOOLOGY & PALAEONTOLOGY. ▶**A** *noun.* A tarsioid primate of the extinct family Omomyidae, known from Palaeogene fossils in N. America and Europe. M20.
▶ **B** *adjective.* Of or pertaining to the family Omomyidae. M20.

omophagia /əʊməˈfeɪdʒɪə, -dʒə/ *noun. rare.* Also Anglicized as **omophagy** /ə(ʊ)ˈmɒfədʒi/. E18.
[Greek *ōmophagia*, from *ōmos* raw: see -PHAGIA.]
The eating of raw food, esp. raw flesh.
■ **omophagic** /-ˈfadʒɪk/, **omophagous** /ə(ʊ)ˈmɒfəɡəs/ *adjectives* M19. **omophagist** /ə(ʊ)ˈmɒfədʒɪst/ *noun* L19.

omophorion /əʊməˈfɔːrɪən/ *noun.* M19.
[Greek *ōmophorion* lit. 'garment worn over the shoulders'.]
GREEK ORTHODOX CHURCH. A vestment resembling the pallium of the Latin Church, worn by patriarchs and bishops.

omoplate /ˈəʊməpleɪt/ *noun. arch.* L16.
[Greek *ōmoplatē*, formed as OMO- + *platē* broad surface, blade.]
The shoulder-blade, the scapula.

omphalo- /ˈɒmfələʊ/ *combining form.* Before a vowel **omphal-**.
[Greek, combining form of *omphalos* navel: see -O-.]
Of, pertaining to, or involving the navel or umbilicus.
■ **omphaˈlitis** *noun* inflammation of the umbilicus M19. **omphalocele** /-siːl/ *noun* umbilical hernia E18. **omphalo-mesenˈteric** *adjective* of, pertaining to, or connecting the navel and the mesentery E18. **omphaˈloscopy** *noun* contemplation of the navel M20. **omphaloˈskepsis** *noun* = OMPHALOSCOPY E20. **omphaˈlotomy** *noun* (an instance of) the surgical division of the umbilical cord E19.

omphaloi *noun* pl. of OMPHALOS.

omphaloid /ˈɒmfəlɔɪd/ *adjective. rare.* M19.
[Greek *omphaloeidēs*, from *omphalos* navel: see -OID.]
Resembling the navel.

omphalos /ˈɒmfəlɒs/ *noun.* Pl. ***-loi*** /-lɔɪ/. M19.
[Greek, lit. 'navel'.]
1 GREEK ANTIQUITIES. **a** A boss on a shield etc. M19. ▶**b** A stone, in the temple of Apollo at Delphi, reputed to mark the central point of the earth. M19.
2 *fig.* A central point, a centre. M19.

omrah /ˈɒmrɑː/ *noun.* E17.
[Urdu *umarā*, orig. Arab. pl. of *ʼamīr* AMIR, used already in Urdu in sing. sense.]
A grandee of a Muslim court, esp. that of the Great Mogul.

omul /ˈəʊmʊl/ *noun.* Pl. same. L19.
[Russian *omulʼ*.]
A whitefish, *Coregonus autumnalis*, found in Lake Baikal and regions bordering the Arctic Ocean. Also called ***Arctic cisco***.

ON *abbreviation.*
Old Norse.

on /ɒn/ *adverb, adjective, noun, & verb.*
[Old English *on*, *an*, from (the same root as) the preposition.]
▶ **A** *adverb.* **1** In or into the position of being in contact with, supported by, or attached to something, or of

covering something; *esp.* (of clothing etc.) on the body. OE.

2 In a particular direction; towards something specified or understood; onward, forward, (in space, time, or condition); further forward, in advance. OE. ▸**b** The worse for drink. *slang.* E19. ▸**c** Chiefly CRICKET. In advance of the opposing side. L19. ▸**d** (Of betting odds) in favour of a particular horse etc. winning. Opp. ***against***. E20.

3 With continued movement or action. OE.

4 In or into action or operation; functioning; so as to be activated; in progress; *spec.* (of a person) on the stage, on the field, on duty, etc.; (of an event) arranged, going to happen, (of a film, show, etc.) to be shown or performed; (of food etc.) on the stove etc., cooking; (of an electrical etc. appliance) switched on. M16. ▸**b** Having agreed to a wager, bargain, etc. Chiefly in ***you are on***, ***you're on***: the bet or bargain is agreed. *colloq.* E19. ▸**c** In favour of or willing to take part in something. *colloq.* L19. ▸**d** In a state of knowledge or awareness regarding something. Cf. ON TO *preposition* 2. *US slang.* L19. ▸**e** Acceptable, allowable, possible, likely. Usu. in neg. contexts. *colloq.* M20. ▸**f** Of an item of food: on the menu, available. *colloq.* M20. ▸**g** Addicted to or regularly taking a drug or drugs; under the influence of drugs. *US slang.* M20.

5 Directed towards or in a line *with* something. E19.

> 🕮 **1** DISRAELI I will doff my travelling cap and on with the monk's cowl. T. HARDY A coat was laid on and polished. E. BOWEN Marda . . began screwing on the lids of her little pots. R. LEHMANN My red silk dressing-gown on, tied tightly. J. WILSON Change the sheets . . although they were clean on yesterday. **2** C. KINGSLEY But no; he must on for honour's sake. T. HARDY Sunset passed and dusk drew on. D. H. LAWRENCE The boy was small and frail at first, but he came on quickly. M. SINCLAIR I saw you stampeding on in front of me. D. H. LAWRENCE The year drew on, in the hedges the berries shone red. E. BOWEN Roses were on . . into their second blooming. **3** J. CONRAD 'They see,' he went on, 'that . . this . . island won't turn turtle.' G. GREENE I'll be walking on . . or it will be breakfast time. I. MURDOCH We just went on arguing, neither of us would stop. **4** R. H. FROUDE At last it came on to rain. E. COXHEAD 'I left the potatoes on,' she muttered. J. GILL I've nearly done, just putting the rice on. E. BOWEN Emmeline strolled . . into the bathroom and turned her bath on. D. ABSE My father switched on the wireless. C. POTOK My father worked . . with the desk lamp on. *Scottish Daily Express* With Miller on for Parlane, Rangers continued to push forward. R. FRAME The hunt is on for the missing envoy. K. MOORE They're enemy outposts—there's a war on. **b** J. SEYMOUR 'Let you have the . . cottages . . for ten pounds a year.' 'You're on,' I said. **c** P. G. WODEHOUSE This jamboree is . . Monday week. The question is, Are we on? **e** E. NORTH Marriage is not really on these days. **5** J. A. FROUDE The ship lay rolling in the sea broadside on to the waves.

Phrases: **on and on** on continually or at tedious length. **on and off** intermittently, at intervals, now and then.

▸ **B** *adjective*. (Freq. with hyphen: cf. ON-.)

1 CRICKET. Designating or pertaining to that side of the field (as divided lengthways through the pitch) away from which the batsman's feet are pointed, esp. that part in front of the batsman's wicket. M19.

2 Corresponding to or designating the state (of an electrical etc. device) of being operative. L19.

3 PHYSIOLOGY. Of, pertaining to, or exhibiting the electrical activity occurring briefly in some optic nerve fibres on commencement of illumination of the retina. E20.

Comb.: **on-ramp** *N. Amer.* (*a*) a sloping one-way road leading on to a highway; (*b*) COMPUTING a means of gaining access to a network, esp. the Internet; **on-verse** [translating German *Anvers*] the first half-line of a line of Old English verse.

▸ **C** *noun*. CRICKET. The on side. M19.

▸ **D** *verb intrans*. Pa. t. & pple **on'd**, **onned**, pres. pple **onning**. Foll. by *with*: place or put on. *dial.* M19.

¶ The adverb is also used idiomatically with many verbs.

on /ɒn/ *preposition*.

[Old English *on*, orig. unstressed var. of *an* = Old Frisian *an*, Old Saxon, Old High German *ana*, *an* (Dutch *aan*, German *an*), Old Norse *á*, Gothic *ana* rel to Greek *ana* on, upon, Sanskrit, Avestan *anu* along, Old Church Slavonic *na*. See also O' *preposition*¹.]

I Of position.

1 Above and in contact with, above and supported by. OE. ▸**b** Supported by (one's feet, legs, etc.). OE. ▸**c** So as to be transported by; using as a means of conveyance. OE. ▸**d** With respect to or around (an axis, pivot, etc.). OE. ▸**e** With or as with the hands touching (a bible etc.) in making an oath; using or invoking as the basis of an affirmation etc. OE. ▸**f** Named in (a list etc.); having membership of (a body), employed as one of (a staff). E18.

2 In contact with (a surface, object, etc.); covering, enclosing, clothing. Also, attached as to a support, restraint, or lead. OE. ▸**b** Above or against (a background, a colour providing this). M18. ▸**c** Carried with, about the person of. Also, indicating possession of physical features. M19.

3 Close to, beside, near, just by, at; on the bank or coast of. OE.

4 Expr. position with reference to a place or thing, with reference to. As obj. esp. *side*, *hand*, *front*, *back*, etc., and compass points. OE.

5 Within the limits or bounds of, in (long *colloq.* & *dial.* exc. *N. Amer.*); at (chiefly *Austral.*). OE.

> 🕮 **1** V. WOOLF Boating on the lake by moonlight. D. LESSING Beans on toast, with chips. R. HARDY He felt Maclaren's hands on his shoulders. P. O'DONNELL The sail-wing rested on the grass. W. KENNEDY He walked north on Broadway. W. GOLDING Trees that stand . . here and there on the downs. **b** SOUTHEY One of these unipeds is represented in a print, lying on his back, under the shade of his . . foot. E. BOWEN She rose on her tiptoes. **c** T. HARDY On her arm she carried a basket. LADY BIRD JOHNSON The press arrived . . on the bus. G. SAYER They set out on borrowed bicycles. **d** J. N. LOCKYER All the planets rotate, or turn on their axes. **e** J. BOUVIER In courts of equity peers . . answer on their honor only. G. GREENE I won't go . . . I swear on the Bible I won't. **f** M. LASKI I don't want to stay on a magazine like that. F. FORSYTH Passport . . mailed . . to the address on the application form. E. TAYLOR They have steak-and-kidney pie on the set menu. *Daily Telegraph* A Turin court . . recessed . . for lack of citizens willing to serve on the jury. **2** SHAKES. *Temp.* Come, hang them on this line. W. WILLIAMS A brewer's yard dog, always on the chain. DYLAN THOMAS Tomatoes ripening on the wall. *New York Times* As . . pitted as the vaccination mark on her arm. **b** G. B. SHAW A design of . . purple wreaths on a . . yellow background. **c** M. TWAIN One brute had a neck on him like a bowsprit. D. L. SAYERS Do you happen to have a railway time-table on you? *South Wales Echo* She only had about £1 on her. **3** H. ANGELO His residence . . on the Uxbridge Road. **4** R. MACAULAY Gideon was a Russian Jew on his father's side. G. GREENE My . . village was bounded on the south by New Oxford Street. D. WELCH A bit further down, on the left. I. MURDOCH Clumps of . . nettles on the other side of the road. V. S. PRITCHETT She was on the stout side herself. **5** *Time* What is now called the Barsky Unit on the grounds of the Cho Ray Hospital.

▸ **II** Of time, or action implying time.

6 During, or at some time during (a specified day or part of a day); contemporaneously with (an occasion). Also (now chiefly *US* & *Austral.*) in or at (any period of time); *dial.* & *US* used redundantly with *tomorrow*, *yesterday*. OE. ▸†**b** Within the space of; in (a length of time). OE–L17. ▸**c** Exactly at or just coming up to (a specified time), just before or after in time. M19.

7 On the occasion of (an action); immediately after (and because of or in reaction to), as a result of. L16.

> 🕮 **6** GOLDSMITH The day . . on which we were to disperse. DICKENS Mrs. Tibbs . . looked like a wax doll on a sunny day. W. S. MAUGHAM Entertaining their friends to supper on Sunday evenings. J. STEINBECK That check has zeroed in on the first of every month. *Scholarly Publishing* My work as an assistant editor is only a sideline . . . I do it largely on my own time. **7** C. S. FORESTER The captain came instantly on hearing your summons. F. TUOHY Roland's first decision on leaving . . was entirely conventional.

▸ **III** Of order, arrangement, manner, state.

8 Indicating physical arrangement or grouping: in (a row, a heap, pieces, etc.). Long *arch.* OE.

9 Indicating manner: in (a certain way). Long *arch.* exc. in colloq. phrs. with *the*, as ***on the cheap***, ***on the sly***, etc. OE.

10 In (a particular state or condition), engaged in or occupied with (an activity). Foll. by noun or (*obsolete*) verbal noun. Now chiefly in established phrs., as ***on fire***, ***on sale***, ***on the move***, ***on watch***, etc. OE. ▸**b** Using as a musical instrument, playing; by means of or employing (a device). LME. ▸**c** Using as a medium of communication, by means of (the telephone etc.); broadcast by or as part of (a channel, programme, etc.). E20. ▸**d** Drinking, esp. excessively; addicted to, regularly using or receiving (a drug or drugs). *colloq.* M20.

11 Indicating the basis or reason of action, opinion, etc.; having as a motive. OE. ▸**b** In the style of, using as a model, according to, after. E19.

12 Indicating risk or penalty; at the risk of; BETTING in expectation of the success of, (with specified odds) with that likelihood of success of. LME.

13 Indicating the basis of income, taxation, borrowing, or lending, profit or loss, etc; having as standard, confirmation, or guarantee. L17.

> 🕮 **9** TINDALE *Matt.* 1:18 The byrthe off Christe was on thys wyse. *Chicago Sun* The glee of a schoolkid reading Playboy on the sneak. **10** LD MACAULAY But fortune was already on the turn. D. FRANCIS He was in France on business. **b** *Radio Times* Neither . . Anderson on trumpet nor . . Brown on trombone were able to make this tour. *Scientific American* Our entire simulation . . could be rerun . . on any fast modern computer. **c** *Listener* Millions more saw the coronation . . on television. P. O'DONNELL Get on the phone and book three seats. *Custom Car* Anyone with that kind of money contact Richard on . . 71619. **d** M. NA GOPALEEN Seen you were on the beer last night. *Lancet* She was . . on tranylcypromine 30 mg. daily. P. HILL Are you on the pill? **11** V. WOOLF She had got them there on false pretences. *Economist* Brought to trial . . on evidence provided by an electronic device. **b** E. BOWEN The inner frame . . and the mantelpiece are on the Roman pattern. A. CARTER She performed . . variations on the basic bread-pudding recipe. **12** JER. TAYLOR Let no man, on his own head, reprove the religion . . established by law. A. WHITE The Church . . asks you to believe her . . on pain of loss of salvation. **13** J. HANWAY The king borrowed considerable sums on his jewels. *Oxford Times* Armed with a credit card, . . an American can have meals, buy clothes, stay at hotels—all on credit.

▸ **IV** Of motion, direction, or relation.

14 To or towards (and into a position expressed by sense 1 or 2); on to. Also denoting cumulative addition or repetition. (Cf. UPON *preposition* 4.) OE.

15 Into proximity, contact, or collision with; (of a blow) striking; so as to threaten (physically or otherwise); with hostility towards, against. (Cf. UPON *preposition* 4.) OE.

16 In the direction of, so as to face; towards; so as to affect or have as its object; (expr. advantage) over. OE. ▸**b** Of a cheque etc.: payable by or at. L17. ▸**c** Of a joke, laugh, etc.: against or at the expense of. M19. ▸**d** Indicating who is to pay, esp. for a treat: at the expense of. *colloq.* L19. ▸**e** While in the presence or charge of (and usu. to the inconvenience or detriment of). *colloq.* L19. ▸**f** MATH. (Defined or expressed) in terms of (a set, an element of a set). M20.

17 Indicating that which forms the means of subsistence; having as food (whether usually or at a particular occasion); supported financially by. OE.

†**18** To a position within, into. OE–LME.

19 Into, or to (some action or condition). Formerly esp. with verbal noun. OE.

20 In reference to, with respect to, as to; concerning, about. OE. ▸**b** Compared with (a previous situation, figure, etc.). L19.

†**21** (Won, taken, etc.) from. OE–L17.

22 Of. *arch.* & *dial.* ME.

23 To (a person) by descent or marriage. *obsolete* exc. *Scot.* ME.

> 🕮 **14** R. HARDY Asians . . load it on dhows and ship it to the Far East. V. S. PRITCHETT She flopped down on the chair. **15** DRYDEN He bears his Rider headlong on the Foe. F. MARRYAT I received a blow on the head. S. BARING-GOULD If he drew his knife on her and attacked. **16** C. THIRLWALL The title of Admiral was conferred on Aracus. TENNYSON Philip's dwelling fronted on the street. G. PALEY He was a big guy with a few years on me. G. HOUSEHOLD Look on me as a wandering friar. **b** THACKERAY Here . . is a cheque on Child's. **c** L. M. MONTGOMERY A nice laugh he will have on me. **d** J. A. LEE 'I must have a drink.' Here, have one on the house. **e** M. BUTTERWORTH He's passed out on me . . . Had some kind of seizure. *Photography* Occasionally one claps out on me but so would any camera. **17** S. PEPYS Dined at home on a poor Lenten dinner. J. BRAINE We used to live on onions and cheese. **19** BACON That might . . set the Plough on going. LD MACAULAY The fanaticism of Cromwell never urged him on impracticable undertakings. **20** JOYCE Father Conmee reflected on the providence of the Creator. W. S. MAUGHAM He wanted to be . . an expert on a subject of which most Labour members were . . ignorant. B. SCHULBERG What's the real story on you and Sammy? D. ABSE I'm not keen on curly hair. L. BRUCE His articles on narcotic addiction. **b** *Daily Telegraph* Average earnings . . were . . up on the previous year. **21** SHAKES. *Lear* But what art thou That hast this fortune on me? **22** STEELE Nay, you are in the Right on't. TAFFRAIL Ere's another on 'em.

Phrases & comb.: (A selection of cross-refs. only is included: see esp. other nouns.) ***have a down on***: see DOWN *noun*³ 4. ***have nothing on***: see HAVE *verb*. ***on account***: see ACCOUNT *noun*. ***on average***: see AVERAGE *noun*² 4. ***on behalf of***: see BEHALF *noun* 1. ***on board***: see BOARD *noun*. **on-board** *adjective* (COMPUTING) designating or controlled from a facility or feature incorporated into the main circuit board of a computer or computerized device. ***on camera***: see CAMERA 4. ***on course***: see COURSE *noun*¹. ***on duty***: see DUTY *noun*. ***on form***: see FORM *noun*. ***on guard***: see GUARD *noun*. ***on hand***: see HAND *noun*. **on it** (*a*) *dial.* (with preceding adverb or adjective) in a particular (usu. distressing) condition or situation; (*b*) *Austral. colloq.* drinking heavily. ***on message***: see MESSAGE *noun*. ***on one's game***: see GAME *noun*. ***on one's guard***: see GUARD *noun*. ***on purpose***: see PURPOSE *noun*. **onscreen** *adverb* & *adjective* (while) appearing or occurring on a cinema, television, VDU, etc., screen; (while) appearing within the view presented by a cinema screen. ***on site***: see SITE *noun*. **on-stage** *adverb* & *adjective* (while) appearing or occurring on a stage; (so as to be) visible or audible to a theatre audience. **on-target** *adverb* & *adjective* so as to hit, that hits, a target; accurate(ly); on the right track, as forecast. ***on the air***: see AIR *noun*¹ 1b. ***on the ball***: see BALL *noun*¹ 2. ***on the beam***: see BEAM *noun*. ***on the hour***: see HOUR *noun*. ***on the shelf***: see SHELF *noun*¹.

¶ See also ON TO, ONTO, UPON *preposition*.

on- /ɒn/ *prefix*.

[Unstressed form of Old English *an*, ON *preposition* A *preposition*¹. Cf. combs. of ON *preposition*, ON *adjective*.]

In various senses of 'on' forming verbs (chiefly obs.), adjectives from pples, verbal nouns & nouns of action (sometimes concrete), as ***oncoming***, ***onlay***, ***onset***; also forming other types of noun, as ***on-drive***.

-on /ɒn/ *suffix*.

[In sense 1 first in *electron*, from the ending of ION, but in this and other senses infl. by Greek *on* being (cf. -ONT), *-on* ending of neut. nouns, or (in names of substances) the ending of *cotton*, *nylon*, or German *-on* -ONE.]

1 *PHYSICS.* Forming names of subatomic particles, as ***electron***, ***hyperon***, ***fermion***, ***proton***, and quanta, as ***graviton***, ***phonon***.
2 Forming names of other entities conceived of as units, esp. in molecular biology, as ***codon***, ***mnemon***, ***operon***, and anatomy, as ***osteon***, ***pleon***.
3 Forming names of substances, as ***interferon***, ***parathion***.

onager /ˈɒnəɡə/ *noun*. ME.
[Latin from Greek *onagros*, from *onos* ass + *agrios* wild.]
1 A wild ass; *esp.* an animal of the central Asian race of *Equus hemionus*. ME.
2 *Hist.* A kind of military engine for throwing rocks. LME.

onagraceous /ɒnəˈɡreɪʃəs/ *adjective*. M19.
[from mod. Latin *Onagraceae*, from *onagra* former name of genus *Oenothera* + -OUS.]
BOTANY. Of or pertaining to the family Onagraceae, which includes the willowherbs and evening primroses.

onanism /ˈəʊnənɪz(ə)m/ *noun*. E18.
[French *onanisme* or mod. Latin *onasismus*, from *Onan*, son of Judah, who practised coitus interruptus (*Genesis* 38:9): see -ISM.]
Masturbation. Also, coitus interruptus.
■ **onanist** *noun* a person who practises onanism M19. **onaˈnistic** *adjective* L19.

Onazote /ˈɒnəzəʊt/ *noun*. E20.
[Prob. from AZOTE.]
(Proprietary name for) a type of expanded cellular rubber made by forcing a neutral gas into the rubber during vulcanization, used for making lifebelts, floats, etc.

onbethink *verb* see UNBETHINK.

ONC *abbreviation*.
Ordinary National Certificate.

once /wʌns/ *adverb, conjunction, noun, & adjective*. ME.
[from ONE *adjective* + -S³.]
▶**A** *adverb*. **1** On one occasion, for one time only. Also, multiplied by one, by one degree. ME. ▸†**b** In the first place, firstly. Only in 16.
2 Chiefly in conditional and negative statements: on any occasion, under any circumstances; ever, at all, only, merely. ME.
3 *emphatic*. = ***once and for all*** below. Also, to sum up; in short. Now only *US dial.* ME.
4 At some point or period in the past; on some past occasion; formerly. ME.
5 At some future time; one day. Now *rare*. LME.

📖 **1** J. B. PRIESTLEY Miss Trant read it through once. S. BEDFORD The curé was asked to dinner once a year. **2** W. BLACK Once past the turnpike, the highway runs along an elevated ridge. OED If we once lose sight of him we shall never set eyes on him again. R. LEHMANN I haven't seen her fussed once. **4** E. WAUGH Years of war had left their marks on the once gay interior. I. MCEWAN The whole house had once belonged to his grandfather. **5** DRYDEN Britons and Saxons shall be once one people.

▶**B** *conjunction*. When once, if once; as soon as. ME.

📖 O. MANNING Once the treasure is secure, I mean to ease Lomay into publishing.

▶**C** *noun*. One occasion, a single time (chiefly after a preposition or demonstrative); *ellipt.* the action or fact of doing something once. ME.

📖 OED Once a week is enough for me. L. P. HARTLEY On most occasions . . Isabel was pleased . . but for this once she wasn't.

▶**D** *adjective*. **1** Done or performed once. Now *rare*. M16.
2 That once was; former. L17.

📖 **1** W. ABNEY Once coating is generally sufficient. **2** R. BROUGHTON Nothing remains but for the once enemies to say farewell. T. H. WHITE The once and future king.

Phrases: **all at once** (*a*) without warning, suddenly; (*b*) all together. **at once** (*a*) immediately, without delay; (*b*) simultaneously. **cousin once removed**: see COUSIN *noun*. **every once in a while** = ***once in a while*** below. **for once and all** *arch.* = ***once and for all*** below. **for once (in one's life)** on this occasion, if on no other. **not once** on no occasion, never. **not once nor twice**, **not once or twice** many times. **once again** on a further occasion, not for the first time. **once and again** *arch.* more than once. **once and for all**, (*arch.*) **once and away** once as a final act; conclusively, so as to end uncertainty. ***once in a blue moon***: see BLUE *adjective*. **once in a way** rarely, exceptionally. **once in a while** from time to time; very occasionally. **once more** on one more occasion, once again. **once or twice** a few times. **once too often** once more than necessary or tolerable (and so as to incur unpleasant repercussions). **once upon a time** at some vague time in the past (usu. as a conventional opening of a story). ***THAT once***. **this once**: see THIS *pronoun & adjective*.

Comb.: **once-born** *adjective* not born-again, unregenerate; **once-off** *adjective* happening only once; **once-over** *colloq.* a quick (and usu. cursory) inspection or search; a rapid superficial assessment; an appraising glance.
■ **onceness** *noun* the fact or quality of happening only once, or all at once M19.

oncer /ˈwʌnsə/ *noun*. *colloq.* L19.
[from ONCE + -ER¹.]
1 A person who or thing which does a particular thing only once; a thing that occurs only once. L19.
2 A one-pound note. Now *Hist.* M20.
3 (An election of) an MP thought likely only to serve one term. *Austral.* L20.

onchocerciasis /ˌɒŋkəʊsəːˈsʌɪəsɪs, -ˈkʌɪəsɪs/ *noun*. Pl. **-ases** /-əsiːz/. E20.
[from mod. Latin *Onchocerca* (see below), from Greek *ogkos* barb + *kerkos* tail: see -IASIS.]
MEDICINE. Infestation with filarioid worms of the genus *Onchocerca*; *spec.* disease caused by *O. volvulus* and transmitted by biting flies of the genus *Simulium*, which occurs in tropical Africa and America and is marked by characteristic lesions of subcutaneous tissue and the eyes, often causing blindness (also called ***river blindness***).
■ **onchoˈcercal** *adjective* of the genus *Onchocerca*; caused by worms of this genus: M20. **onchocerˈcosis** *noun*, pl. **-coses** /-ˈkəʊsiːz/, = ONCHOCERCIASIS E20.

oncidium /ɒnˈsɪdɪəm/ *noun*. L19.
[mod. Latin (see below), from Greek *ogkos* swelling, with ref. to the basal swelling of the labellum: see -IDIUM.]
Any of numerous American epiphytic orchids (often with bright yellow flowers) consituting the genus *Oncidium*, many species of which are grown for ornament.

onco- /ˈɒŋkəʊ/ *combining form* of Greek *ogkos* mass, bulk, swelling: see -O-. Freq. in *MEDICINE & BIOLOGY* with the sense 'of or pertaining to swelling, esp. tumours'.
■ **oncolite** *noun* (*GEOLOGY*) a spheroidal stromatolite M20. **oncoˈlitic** *adjective* (*GEOLOGY*) of, pertaining to, or consisting of oncolites M20. **oncolysis** /ɒŋˈkɒlɪsɪs/ *noun* (*BIOLOGY*) the absorption or destruction of a tumour E20. **oncoˈlytic** *adjective* (*BIOLOGY*) of, pertaining to, or causing oncolysis. E20. **oncometer** /ɒŋˈkɒmɪtə/ *noun* (*MEDICINE*) an instrument for measuring variations in the size of an organ L19. **oncosphere** *noun* (*ZOOLOGY*) a tapeworm embryo in a hexacanth and spheroidal form E20.

oncogene /ˈɒŋkədʒiːn/ *noun*. M20.
[from ONCO- + GENE.]
BIOLOGY. A viral gene held to be responsible for transforming a host cell into a tumour cell.

oncogenesis /ɒŋkə(ʊ)ˈdʒɛnɪsɪs/ *noun*. M20.
[from ONCO- + -GENESIS.]
BIOLOGY. The formation or production of a tumour or tumours.

oncogenic /ɒŋkəˈdʒɛnɪk/ *adjective*. M20.
[from ONCO- + -GENIC.]
BIOLOGY. Causing the development of a tumour or tumours; of or pertaining to oncogenesis.
■ **oncogenicity** /-ˈnɪsɪti/ *noun* M20.

oncology /ɒŋˈkɒlədʒi/ *noun*. M19.
[from ONCO- + -LOGY.]
The branch of medicine that deals with tumours.
■ **oncoˈlogic** *adjective* (chiefly *US*) E20. **oncoˈlogical** *adjective* L19. **oncologist** *noun* E20.

oncome /ˈɒnkʌm/ *noun*. ME.
[from ON- + COME *verb*. See also ANCOME, UNCOME, & cf. INCOME *noun*².]
1 Something (harmful) that comes suddenly, a calamity. Long only *Scot.*, an attack of disease. ME.
2 A coming on, the onset. Chiefly *Scot.* L19.

oncoming /ˈɒnkʌmɪŋ/ *noun & adjective*. LME.
[from ON- + COMING *noun*, *adjective*.]
▶**A** *noun*. The action or fact of coming on; an advance, an approach, the onset. LME.
▶**B** *adjective*. **1** Coming on; advancing, approaching from the front. M19.
2 Ready to be sociable; friendly, welcoming. E20.

oncornavirus /ɒŋˈkɔːnəvʌɪrəs/ *noun*. L20.
[from ONCO- + RNA + VIRUS.]
MICROBIOLOGY. = LEUKOVIRUS.

oncosine /ˈɒŋkəsiːn/ *noun*. Also (earlier) †**-in**. M19.
[German *Onkosin*, from Greek *onkōsis* swelling (from its behaviour when heated with a blowpipe): see -INE⁵.]
MINERALOGY. A variety of muscovite forming rounded masses.

oncost /ˈɒnkɒst/ *noun*. LME.
[from ON- + COST *noun*².]
An overhead expense, overhead expenses collectively; *Scot.* extra expense, contingent costs.
¶ Before 20 only in Scot. use.

oncotic /ɒŋˈkɒtɪk/ *adjective*. M20.
[from ONCO- + -OTIC.]
MEDICINE & PHYSIOLOGY. Of or pertaining to a swelling, as an oedema, a tumour, etc. Orig. & chiefly in ***oncotic pressure***, osmotic pressure exerted by a colloid, esp. plasma protein.

OND *abbreviation*.
Ordinary National Diploma.

Ondes Martenot /ɔ̃d martəno, ɔ̃ːd ˈmɑːt(ə)nəʊ/ *noun phr.* Pl. same. M20.
[from French *ondes* (*musicales* musical) waves (original name of the instrument) + Maurice *Martenot* (1898–1980), French inventor.]
A kind of electronic keyboard musical instrument producing one note of variable pitch.

ondine *noun* var. of UNDINE.

on-ding /ˈɒndɪŋ/ *noun*. *Scot.* L18.
[from ON- + DING *verb*¹.]
A heavy fall of rain or snow.

on dit /ɔ̃ di/ *noun*. Pl. ***on dits*** (pronounced same). E19.
[French = they say.]
An item of gossip; something reported on hearsay.

📖 D. FRANCIS The *on dit* . . is that he is even thicker than anyone thought.

on-drive /ˈɒndrʌɪv/ *noun & verb*. M19.
[from ON- + DRIVE *noun*, *verb*.]
CRICKET. ▶**A** *noun*. A drive to the on side. M19.
▶**B** *verb trans.* Pa. t. **-drove** /-drəʊv/, pa. pple **-driven** /-drɪv(ə)n/. Drive to the on side; drive a ball delivered by (a bowler) to the on side. L19.

one /wʌn/ *adjective, noun, & pronoun*. See also ANE.
[Old English *ān* = Frisian *ān*, *ēn*, Old Saxon *ēn* (Dutch) *een*, Old & mod. High German *ein*, Old Norse *einu*, Gothic *ains*, from Germanic from Indo-European, whence also Old Latin *oinos*, Latin *unus*. The pronunc. with /w-/ developed in 15.]
▶**A** *adjective* (in some senses *cardinal numeral*, in others in mod. usage also classed as a *determiner*).
▶**I** Simple or emphatic numeral.
1 Of the lowest of the cardinal numerals (represented by 1 in arabic numerals, i, I in roman); single and integral in number, without any more. OE.
2 a A single as opp. to two or more; only such, sole. OE. ▸**b** A single as opp. to none at all; at least one. L15. ▸**c** A very, an extremely, a noteworthy example of. *colloq.* E19.
†**3** A, an. OE–M16.
4 *pred.* †**a** Alone. OE–M16. ▸**b** Single, individual. ME.

📖 **1** *Westminster Gazette* One officer, two non-coms., and twenty men. **2a** E. BLOUNT Tell me if . . I have omitted any one point of importance. D. HUME One person alone of the garrison escaped. E. LEONARD My one concern was to get Amelita out of there. **b** S. FOOTE That's one comfort, however. **c** *Q* This is one strange novel and this John Buck . . is one strange character. *New Yorker* As the . . sun began to penetrate the trees, we were looking out on one lovely scene. **4b** W. WOLLASTON We know no such thing as a part of matter purely one (or indivisible).

▶**II** United, uniform, the same.
5 Forming a unity; made up of separate components united. OE.
6 The same in substance, quality, or bearing; the same in mind, intention, etc.; identical. OE. ▸**b** *spec. pred.* The same; the same thing. Often in ***all one***. LME.
7 Uniformly the same; the same in all parts, at all times, or in all circumstances. ME.

📖 **5** LD MACAULAY One cry of grief and rage rose from . . Protestant Europe. **6** SHELLEY He is made one with Nature. J. N. LOCKYER All the planets revolve round the sun in one direction. **b** F. L. WRIGHT Form and function . . become one in design and execution.

▶**III** In particular or partitive sense.
8 A particular of several or from amongst others; an individual. OE.
9 Another. Contrasted with **one**. Now *rare*. OE.
10 A particular (but undefined). Contrasted with ***another***, ***other***, ***others***. ME.
11 A person now being identified as, a certain. *colloq.* ME.

📖 **8** I. MURDOCH But Rosa's only one shareholder among others. G. GORDON Some . . friends . . had at one period of their overlapping lives had boats. **10** M. KEANE His life was spent in uprooting one species and planting the other. W. GASS Corn is grown one year, soybeans another. **11** *Law Times* He died . . leaving the property . . to one Anne Duncan.

▶**B** *noun* (*cardinal numeral*) & *pronoun*. **I** *noun & pronoun*. **1** One person or thing identified contextually, as a part or division, a year of age, a point, run, etc., in a game, a chance (in giving odds), a minute, an inch, *Hist.* a shilling, etc. OE.
2 A single or particular person or thing; *esp.* one of several or from amongst others. Also contrasted with ***another***, ***other***, ***others***. OE.
3 A person or thing of a particular or specified kind, or of a kind already mentioned. Freq. preceded by a demonstr. or other determiner or an interrog. adjective, as *this*, *that*, *each*, *which*, etc. OE. ▸**b** *spec.* A joke, a story. *colloq.* E19. ▸**c** A blow. *colloq.* E20. ▸**d** An alcoholic drink. *colloq.* E20.
4 A single unit as an abstract number; the symbol or figure representing this (1 in arabic numerals, i, I in roman). ME.
5 A unit, a unity; a single thing or person; a thing having oneness as an essential or distinguishing feature;

spec. (**a**) a domino or die marked with one pip or spot; (**b**) a one-pound note (chiefly *Hist.*) or coin, a one-dollar bill. ME.

6 ***the one***, a single person or thing of which two are referred to; the first, the former. Contrasted with ***the other***. ME.

7 The first of a set or series with numbered members, designated one (usu. ***number one***, or with specification as ***book one***, ***chapter one***, etc.); a size etc. denoted by one, a shoe, glove, garment, etc., of such a size, (also ***size one***). LME.

8 The time of day one hour after midnight or midday (on a clock, watch, etc., indicated by the numeral one displayed or pointed to). Also ***one o'clock***. M16.

9 A remarkable or extraordinary person; a person who is distinctive in some way. *colloq.* L19.

📖 **1** *Hamilton (Ontario) Spectator* Twelve per cent of Haitian babies die before the age of one. ***a hundred to one***, ***a million to one***, ***ten to one***, etc. **c** P. Reading I'm sorry, Sarge, but I caught him one with my ring. **2** M. Keane They . . crossed the hall one behind another. J. Rhys One of the things I hate most about being hard up. R. P. Jhabvala One played a drum, others sang. J. Simms There is only one that seems at all appropriate. **3** T. Hardy There are bad women about, and they think me one. *Daily Chronicle* Since Bacon . . broke all other records, why not this one as well? G. Greene You want a cup of coffee. And you shall have one. I. Murdoch Catherine pleaded, speaking as one that fears a refusal. **b** *Listener* Have you heard the one about the Queen Mother? **4** J. Vanbrugh One, two, three, and away! **5** T. Callender People going down the road in ones and twos. **6** A. M. Fairbairn The exchange and the cathedral stand together, the one for administration, the other for business. **7** S. Foote A coach of his grandfather's built in the year 1. *Maclean's Magazine* Her last six singles all shot to number one on the national country music charts. **8** M. Prior St Dunstan's, as they pass'd, struck one. Z. M. Pike At one o'clock we bid adieu to our friendly hostess. **9** J. B. Priestley You're a bit of a one, aren't you. J. Winterson Such a one for figures as you never saw.

▶ **II** *pers. pronoun 3 sing.* & in sense 12 *1 sing. & pl. subjective (nom.) & objective (dat. & accus.).*

†**10** A person or being whose identity is undefined; someone; a certain one; an individual. ME–M18.

11 A person or being identified by a following noun, clause, or phrase. ME.

12 Any person of undefined identity, as representing people in general; I, him, her, as an example; a person, anyone. Also (*colloq.* or *affected*) I or me as an individual. ME.

13 Oneself. Now *rare*. M16.

📖 **12** O. Wilde I don't mind waiting in the carriage . . provided there is somebody to look at one. N. Mitford One is not exactly encouraged to use one's brain. J. Rhys I do know how one longs for company. M. Renault Ralph would never let one do anything for him. *Real Estate* Rehabilitation allows one to upgrade his housing.

Comb., special collocations, & phrases: (A selection of cross-refs. only is included.) Forming compound cardinal numerals with multiples of ten from twenty to ninety, as ***thirty-one***, (*arch.*) ***one-and-thirty***, etc., and (*arch.*) their corresponding ordinals, as ***one-and-thirtieth*** etc., and with multiples of a hundred as ***201*** (read ***two hundred and one***, US also ***two hundred one***) etc. With nouns + -ER[1] forming nouns with the sense 'something (identified contextually) being of or having one —', as ***one-seater*** etc. ***a good one***: see GOOD *adjective*; ***a great one for***: see GREAT *adjective*; ***all one***: see ALL *adverb* 1; **at one** in agreement; ***at one swoop***, ***at one fell swoop***: see SWOOP *noun*; ***back to square one***: see SQUARE *noun*; ***Evil One***: see EVIL *adjective*; ***fast one***: see FAST *adjective*; **for one** as one person, even if the only one; ***for one thing***: see THING *noun*[1]; **get it in one** succeed at the first attempt (cf. ***in one*** (e) below); ***hang one on***: see HANG *verb*; ***hole in one***: see HOLE *noun*[1]; ***I for one***: see FOR *preposition*; **in one** (**a**) in or into one place, company, or mass; together; (**b**) in unison, agreement, or harmony; †(**c**) in one course; straight on, without ceasing; (**d**) combined in one; in combination; (**e**) at one stroke or attempt; ***in one fell swoop***: see SWOOP *noun*; ***in one piece***: see PIECE *noun*; ***in one swoop***: see SWOOP *noun*; ***in one word***: see WORD *noun*; ***Jimmy the One***: see JIMMY *noun*[2] 3; ***kill two birds with one stone***: see BIRD *noun*; **like one o'clock** vigorously, quickly; excellently; enthusiastically; ***new one***: see NEW *adjective*; ***number one***: see NUMBER *noun*; **one-act** *adjective* (of a short play or other production) consisting of a single act; **one-acter** a one-act play; ***one and all***: see ALL *pronoun* & *noun* 4; **one and another** more than one, two or more in succession; **one and only** one's sweetheart; one's only child or love; something unique or of great personal value; **one and the same**, (*arch.*) **one and the selfsame** the same, the identical; **one-and-thirty** (now *rare*) a card-game resembling vingt-et-un; **one another** each other reciprocally; **one argument** LOGIC the variable of a function or operator of only one variable; **one-arm** *adjective* having one arm; ***one-arm bandit***: see BANDIT 1; ***one-arm joint*** (*US*), a cheap eating-house where the seats have one arm wide enough to hold a plate of food etc.; **one-armed** *adjective* having one arm; ***one-armed bandit***: see BANDIT 1; **one-bar** *adjective* (of an electric fire) having only one heating element; **one-base** *adjective* (BASEBALL) designating a hit that enables the batter to reach the first base; **one-baser** BASEBALL a one-base hit; **one-berry** (**a**) herb Paris, *Paris quadrifolia*, which bears a single black berry; (**b**) *US* the partridge berry, *Mitchella repens*; **one by one** singly, successively; **one-coloured** *adjective* of one colour, of uniform colour throughout; **one day** *adverbial* (**a**) on an unspecified day; (**b**) at some unspecified future date; **one-design** *adjective* & *noun* (NAUTICAL) (designating) a yacht built from a standard design, or a class of such ships which are almost identical; **one-dimensional** *adjective* having or pertaining to a single dimension; **one-dimensionality** one-dimensional quality; **one-directional** *adjective* having or pertaining to a single direction; **one down** one point behind in a game; inferior in one respect; disadvantaged; **one-downmanship** the art or practice of being one down on another person; **one-downness** the fact or state of being one down; **one-eyed** *adjective* (**a**) having only one eye; blind in one eye; (**b**) narrow in outlook; prejudiced, narrow-minded; (**c**) *colloq.* small, inferior, unimportant; **one-for-one** *adjective* designating a situation, arrangement, etc., in which one thing corresponds to or is exchanged for another; **one for the book**, **one for the end book** *N. Amer. colloq.* a notable or extraordinary event, action, saying, etc.; **one for the road** a final drink before departure; **one-girl** *adjective* = ***one-woman*** below; **one-handed** *adjective & adverb* (**a**) *adjective* having only one hand, or only one hand capable of use; used, worked, or performed with one hand; (**b**) *adverb* using only one hand; **one-handedly** *adverb* with one hand; **one-handedness** the state of being one-handed; **one-horse** *adjective* (**a**) using a single horse; (**b**) *colloq.* on a small scale; petty; inferior; ***one-horse town***, a small or rural town, *esp.* one where nothing important or exciting happens; (**c**) ***one-horse race***, a competition etc. in which there is a clear winner from or before the outset; **one-idea'd** *adjective* having or possessed by a single idea; **one-inch** *adjective* (of a map) having a scale of one inch to the mile; **one in five**, **one in six**, etc. (designating or pertaining to) a slope or gradient in which the vertical height changes by one foot (or other measure) in the specified number of feet etc. horizontally; ***one in the eye***: see EYE *noun*; **one-legged** *adjective* (**a**) having only one leg; (**b**) *fig.* that is or does only one half of what is required; one-sided; **one-liner** (**a**) a headline consisting of only one line of print; (**b**) a short witty remark, a joke consisting of only one sentence; **one-lunger** (**a**) a person with only one lung; (**b**) *slang* (a vehicle or boat driven by) a single-cylinder engine; **one-man** *adjective* (**a**) consisting of, done, or operated by one man only; (**b**) committed or attached to one man only; (**c**) ***one-man band***, a solo musician playing several instruments simultaneously; *fig.* a person who does everything personally, one who operates alone without assistance; (**d**) ***one-man show***, a show, entertainment, etc., presented or performed by one man only, *esp.* an exhibition of the work of one artist; **one man, one vote** a policy that each individual should have a single vote; **one–many** *adjective* (of a correspondence or relation) in which each member of one set can be associated with or related to more than one member of a second set; ***one nation***: see NATION *noun*[1]; **one-night** *adjective* (**a**) lasting, residing, or used for a single night; (**b**) ***one-night stand***, a single performance of a play etc. in one place; *colloq.* a sexual liaison lasting only one night: **one-nighter** (**a**) a person who stays at a place for a single night; (**b**) *colloq.* a one-night stand; **one-of-a-kind** (**a**) of only one kind; (**b**) unique; **one-off** *noun & adjective* (**a**) *noun* the only example of a manufactured product; something not repeated; (**b**) *adjective* made or done as the only one, not repeated; †**one of the fairest**, †**one of the truest**, †**one of the wisest**, etc. the most fair, true, wise, etc.; ***one of these days***, ***one of those days***: see DAY *noun*; **one of those things** *colloq.* something inevitable or inexplicable; **one of us** a member of our group; *spec.* a homosexual; **one-old-cat** *US* a form of baseball in which a batter runs to one base and home again, remaining as batter until put out (to be succeeded by the player who put him or her out); **one–one** *adjective* = ***one-to-one*** below; **one-on-one** *adjective* (**a**) *N. Amer.* designating or pertaining to a situation in which two opponents etc. come into conflict; (**b**) = ***one-to-one*** (b) below; **one or other** whichever way it is viewed; **one or two** a very few, a small number of; **one-over-one** *adjective & noun* (BRIDGE) (designating) a bid of one in a suit, made in response to a preceding bid of one in a suit; **one-parent** *adjective* of, pertaining to, or designating a family in which one person brings up a child or children without a partner; **one-piece** *adjective & noun* made or consisting of a single piece; (an article of clothing) comprising a single garment; **one-pip**, **one-pipper** *Military slang* a second lieutenant (entitled to wear one pip on the shoulder of his or her uniform); **one-pipe** *adjective* (of a hot-water central heating system) in which all radiators and the boiler use the same pipe, which runs in a complete circuit, to take and return water; (of a plumbing system) that uses the same pipe to convey waste from all sinks, water-closets, etc., to the sewer; **one-place** *adjective* (LOGIC) designating an assertion etc. in which only one thing is postulated or involved; **one-plus-one** *adjective* (COMPUTING) designating an instruction which has the address of an operand and that of the next instruction; **one-reeler** a film lasting for one reel, usu. for ten minutes or less; **one-ring** *adjective* (of a circus) having only one ring, small; **one-shot** *adjective & noun* (**a**) *adjective* achieved or done with a single shot, stroke, or attempt; consisting of a single shot; occurring, produced, used, etc., only once; (**b**) *noun* an event or process that occurs only once; something used or intended for use only once; **one-sided** *adjective* (**a**) occurring or having the constituent parts on one side; (**b**) leaning to one side; larger or more developed on one side; (**c**) relating to, considering, or dealing with only one side of a question, subject, etc.; partial, unfair; **one-sidedly** *adverb* in a one-sided manner; **one-sidedness** the quality of being one-sided; **one-star** *adjective* (**a**) (of a hotel, restaurant, etc.) given one star in a grading system in which this denotes the lowest standard; (**b**) (of a general) of the fifth-highest military rank, distinguished in the US armed forces by one star on the uniform; **one-step** *noun & verb* (**a**) *noun* an early kind of foxtrot in quadruple time; a piece of music for this; (**b**) *verb intrans.* dance the one-step; **one-stop** *adjective* (of a shop etc.) capable of supplying all a customer's needs within a particular range of goods or services; ***one-striper***: see STRIPER 1; **one-suiter** *N. Amer.* a suitcase designed to hold one suit; **one-tail**, **one-tailed** *adjectives* (STATISTICS) designating a test for deviation from the null hypothesis in one direction only; **one thing** something acceptable or satisfactory, contrasted with ***another (thing)***; **one-time pad** a pad of keys for a cipher each page of which is destroyed after being used once, so that each message is sent using a different key; **one-to-many** *adjective* = ***one–many*** *adjective* above; **one-to-one** *adjective* (**a**) in which each member of one set is associated with one member of another; ***one-to-one correspondence***; (**b**) involving direct individual communication; **one-touch** (**a**) (of an electrical device) that can be operated simply at the touch of a button; (**b**) FOOTBALL designating fast-moving play in which each player manages to control or pass the ball with the first touch of the foot; **one-track** *adjective* (of a person's mind) preoccupied with one subject or line of thought; **one-trick pony** *colloq.* someone or something specializing in only one area or having only one talent; someone or something of limited ability; **one-two** (**a**) BOXING a delivery of two punches in quick succession with alternate hands; (**b**) (FOOTBALL & HOCKEY etc.) an (often quick) interchange of the ball between two players; **one up** scoring one point more than an opponent; ahead of another person; *fig.* having a psychological advantage; **one-up** *verb trans.* do better than (someone); **one-upmanship** the art or practice of gaining or maintaining a psychological advantage; **one-upness** the fact or state of being one up; **one-up, one-down** *adjective* designating a house consisting of one main room upstairs and one downstairs; **one-valued** *adjective* (MATH.) single-valued; **one with another** †(**a**) together; (**b**) one taken with another so as to deduce an average; on average; **one-woman** *adjective* of, pertaining to, or done by one woman only; *spec.* committed or attached to one woman only; **one-world** *adjective* designating, pertaining to, or holding the view that there is only one world, or that the world's inhabitants are interdependent and should behave accordingly; **one-worlder** a person who holds a one-world view; ***public enemy number one***: see PUBLIC *adjective & noun*; ***quick one***: see QUICK *adjective*; ***Radio One***: see RADIO *noun* 3; ***stiff one***: see STIFF *adjective*; ***the year one***: see YEAR *noun*[1]; ***Three in One***: see THREE *noun* 1.

■ **onefold** *adjective* (**a**) having only one part, division, element, or unit; single; simple; (**b**) simple in character; simple-minded; free from duplicity: OE. **onefoldness** *noun* singleness, unity; simplicity: L17.

one /wʌn/ *verb*. Now *rare*. Pres. pple **oneing**. ME.
[from prec.]
1 *verb trans.* Make into one; unite. ME.
†**2** *verb refl.* & *intrans.* Agree, unite; come to terms. Only in ME.

-one /əʊn/ *suffix*.
[Greek *-ōnē* feminine patronymic, in gen. use after *acetone* etc.]
CHEMISTRY. Forming names of organic compounds, *spec.* ketones, as ***acetone***, ***hydrazone***, ***quinone***, etc.

Oneida /ə(ʊ)ˈnʌɪdə/ *noun & adjective*. M17.
[Oneida *onẽˀyóteˀ* erected stone (the name of the main Oneida settlement at successive locations, near which, traditionally, was a large syenite boulder).]
▶ **A** *noun*. Pl. **-s**, same. A member of an Iroquois people, one of the five of the original Iroquois confederation, formerly inhabiting upper New York State; the language of this people. M17.
▶ **B** *attrib.* or as *adjective*. Of or pertaining to the Oneida or their language. M18.

oneing /ˈwʌnɪŋ/ *noun*. ME.
[from ONE *adjective, noun, & pronoun* + -ING[1].]
A making one, uniting, union, fusion.
¶ App. obsolete in 15 and revived in 20.

oneiric /ə(ʊ)ˈnʌɪrɪk/ *adjective*. M19.
[from Greek *oneiros* a dream + -IC.]
Of or pertaining to dreams or dreaming.

oneiro- /ə(ʊ)ˈnʌɪrəʊ/ *combining form*. Before a vowel also **oneir-**. Also **oniro-**.
[from Greek *oneiros* a dream + -O-.]
Forming words with the sense 'of, by, or relating to dreams or dreaming'.
■ **oneiˈrocracy** *noun* = ONEIROCRITICISM M17. **oneiroˈcritic** *noun* (**a**) *sing.* & (usu.) in *pl.*, the art of interpreting dreams, oneirocriticism; (**b**) an interpreter of dreams: E17. **oneiroˈcritical** *adjective* pertaining to, practising, or expert in the interpretation of dreams L16. **oneiroˈcriticism** *noun* the art or practice of interpreting dreams E17. **oneiromancy** *noun* divination by dreams M17. **oneiromancer** *noun* a person who divines by dreams M17. **oneiˈroscopist** *noun* an expert in interpreting dreams E18.

†**oneliness** *noun*, †**onely** *adjective*, etc., vars. of ONLINESS, ONLY *adjective*, etc.

†**onement** *noun*. LME–L16.
[from ONE *verb* + -MENT. Cf. later ATONEMENT.]
The fact of being made into one; physical union; mental or emotional union, agreement.

oneness /ˈwʌnnɪs/ *noun*. OE.
[from ONE *adjective, noun, & pronoun* + -NESS.]
1 The quality of being one in number; singleness; *esp.* the singleness of the divine unity. OE. ▸**b** The fact or quality of being the only one of its kind; uniqueness. E18.
2 The fact or quality of being alone; solitariness, loneliness. *rare*. OE.
3 The quality of being one body or whole, though formed of two or more parts; undividedness, unity. Also, the fact of forming one whole; combination, union. OE.
4 Unity of mind, feeling, or purpose; agreement, harmony, concord. ME.
5 The fact or quality of being or remaining the same; sameness, identity; unchangingness. E17.

🕮 **1** J. PORDAGE The Holy Trinity are one, and yet three in that oneness. D. BLOODWORTH The . . Cosmos is One, and since you are of that oneness, you have no separate ego. **3** D. PITTS A tremendous, overwhelming feeling of oneness and equality. J. BERMAN The mother, the most primitive object of the child's search for oneness.

¶ Not recorded between **ME** and **16**.

oner /ˈwʌnə/ ***noun.*** **M19.**
[from **ONE** *adjective, noun, & pronoun* + **-ER**[1].]
1 A person or thing of a unique or remarkable kind; *esp.* a person keen on or expert at something. *slang.* **M19.**
2 A single thing; *spec.* one pound (of money). *colloq.* **L19.**

🕮 **2** G. F. NEWMAN Worth a oner to you. **in a oner** in one go.

†**onerate** ***verb trans.*** **LME–E19.**
[Latin *onerat-* pa. ppl stem of *onerare*, from *oner-*: see **ONEROUS**, **-ATE**[3].]
Load, burden, charge, oppress.

onerosity /əʊnəˈrɒsɪti, ɒn-/ ***noun.*** *rare.* **L17.**
[formed as next + **-ITY**.]
The quality of being onerous; *SCOTS LAW* the fact of something being done or given in return for payment.

onerous /ˈəʊn(ə)rəs, ˈɒn-/ ***adjective.*** **LME.**
[from Old & mod. French *onéreux*, †*-ous* from Latin *onerosus*, from *oner-*, *onus* load burden: see **-OUS**.]
1 Of the nature of a burden; oppressive, difficult, troublesome. **LME.** ▸**b** Of the nature of a legal burden or obligation. **M16.**
2 *SCOTS LAW.* Done or given in return for money, goods, or services of equivalent value; not gratuitous. **E17.**

🕮 **1** S. UNWIN The final terms . . were onerous, and involved my taking great risks. *Antiquity* Greece and its people have a role of great honour fraught with onerous responsibility.

■ **onerously** *adverb* **M19.** **onerousness** *noun* **M19.**

one's /wʌnz/ ***possess. adjective*** (in mod. usage also classed as a ***determiner***) *3 sing.* & *1 sing.* & *pl.* Orig. †**ones**. **LME.**
[from **ONE** *pers. pronoun* + **-'S**[1].]
Of one; of oneself; which belongs or pertains to oneself.

🕮 W. IRVING That soft vernal temperature, that seems to thaw all the frost out of one's blood. H. C. KING The many-sidedness of truth and the necessary partialness of one's own view.

oneself /wʌnˈsɛlf/ ***pronoun.*** Also **one's self**. **M16.**
[Orig. from prec. + **SELF** *noun*. Later assim. to *himself*, *itself*, etc.]
1 Refl. form of **ONE** *pers. pronoun*: (to, for, etc.) the person in question. **M16.**
2 Emphatic use in apposition to a personal noun (subjective or objective) or to a subjective pronoun: that particular person; the person in question personally; himself, herself. **E17.**

🕮 **1** W. S. MAUGHAM One couldn't only think of oneself, could one? C. D. SIMAK It was one way . . to tell one's self that only . . part of life had changed. **2** J. CONRAD His friend was not a person to give oneself away to. I. MURDOCH Must one, really, to help the sufferer, suffer oneself?

Phrases: **be oneself** (*a*) act in one's normal unconstrained manner; (*b*) feel as well as one usually does (usu. in neg. contexts). **by oneself** on one's own, alone.

one-time /ˈwʌntʌɪm/ ***adjective & adverb.*** Also **onetime**. **M19.**
[from **ONE** *adjective* + **TIME** *noun*.]
▶ **A** *adjective.* **1** Former. **M19.**
2 Of or pertaining to a single occasion. **M19.**

🕮 **1** J. UPDIKE His onetime patroness and confidante. **2** M. ANGELOU What we were seeing was a one-time phenomenon, so we were determined to enjoy it. **one-time-cipher**: in which the cipher representation of the alphabet is changed at random for each letter of a message, generating a key as long as the message. **one-time pad** a pad of keys for a one-time cipher, each page being destroyed after one use, so that each message is sent using a different key.

▶ **B** *adverb.* **1** Simultaneously. **L19.**
2 On one occasion, at one time, formerly, once. Also, at once, immediately. **L19.**

one-way /ˈwʌnweɪ, wʌnˈweɪ/ ***adjective.*** **E17.**
[from **ONE** *adjective* + **WAY** *noun*.]
†**1** Designating a kind of bread. Only in **E17.**
2 *gen.* Leading, pointing, developing, or going in one direction only. **E19.**
3 Of a plough: able to turn furrows in one direction only. **L19.**
4 *ELECTRICITY.* Of a switch etc.: providing only one possible path for current. **L19.**
5 Of a ticket: valid for a journey in one direction only; single. **E20.**
6 (Of a road or system of roads) along which traffic may travel in only one direction; (of traffic) travelling only in one direction. Also, of or pertaining to such traffic. **E20.**
7 Of a window, mirror, etc.: permitting vision from one side; transparent from one side only. **M20.**

🕮 **6** P. LAURIE They put up temporary one-way signs, controlling junctions. **7** F. POHL The cameras . . activated . . behind every one-way mirror in the room.

onewhere /ˈwʌnwɛː/ ***adverb.*** *rare.* **E17.**
[from **ONE** *adjective, noun, & pronoun* + **WHERE**, after *somewhere*, *nowhere*.]
In one place as opposed to another; in one place only.

onfall /ˈɒnfɔːl/ ***noun.*** **LOE.**
[from **ON-** + **FALL** *noun*[2].]
1 An attack or onset of disease, plague, or disaster. Now *Scot.* **LOE.** ▸**b** *gen.* An attack, an assault. **E19.**
2 a A fall of rain or snow. *Scot.* **E19.** ▸**b** Nightfall. *Scot.* **E19.**

onflow /ˈɒnfləʊ/ ***verb & noun.*** **M19.**
[from **ON-** + **FLOW** *verb*, *noun*[1].]
▶ **A** *verb intrans.* Flow on. **M19.**
▶ **B** *noun.* The action or fact of flowing on; onward flow. **M19.**

on-glaze /ˈɒnɡleɪz/ ***noun & adjective.*** **L19.**
[from **ON** *preposition* + **GLAZE** *noun*.]
(Of, pertaining to, or designating) overglaze decoration on porcelain etc.

on-glide /ˈɒnɡlʌɪd/ ***noun.*** **L19.**
[from **ON-** + **GLIDE** *noun*.]
PHONETICS. A glide produced at the beginning of articulating a speech sound. Cf. **OFF-GLIDE**.

ongoing /ˈɒnɡəʊɪŋ/ ***noun & adjective.*** **M17.**
[from **ON-** + **GOING** *noun, adjective*.]
▶ **A** *noun.* **1** The action of going on; process, continued movement or action. **M17.**
2 In *pl.* Goings-on; proceedings, doings. **L17.**
▶ **B** *adjective.* Going on, in progress; continuous; current. **L19.**

🕮 *Spaceflight* Michael Wilhite . . identifies the main ongoing developments in . . manned space operations. *Private Investor* The need for on-going support and consultancy is readily accepted.

■ **ongoingly** *adverb* continuously, progressively **L20.** **ongoingness** *noun* **M20.**

ongon /ˈɒnɡəʊn/ ***noun.*** **E20.**
[Mongolian.]
In the shamanist religion of the Buriats of Mongolia: an image of a god or spirit supposed to be endowed with a certain power; a fetish.

onhanger /ˈɒnhaŋə/ ***noun.*** **E19.**
[from **ON-** + **HANGER** *noun*[2].]
A hanger-on, a dependant.

Oni /ˈəʊni/ ***noun.*** **E20.**
[Yoruba.]
The ruler of the town of Ife in western Nigeria.

-onic /ɒnɪk/ ***suffix.***
[from **-ONE** + **-IC** or extracted from **GLYCUR)ONIC**.]
CHEMISTRY. Forming adjectives designating acids, *esp.* carboxylic acids obtained by oxidation of aldoses, as ***gluconic***, ***sulphonic***, etc.

oniomania /əʊnɪəˈmeɪnɪə/ ***noun.*** **L19.**
[from Greek *ōnios* for sale, from *ōnos* price, purchase: see **-MANIA**.]
The compulsive urge to buy things.

onion /ˈʌnjən/ ***noun.*** **ME.**
[Anglo-Norman *union*, Old & mod. French *oignon*, from Proto-Gallo-Romance alt. of Latin *unio(n)-* kind of onion.]
1 A plant, *Allium cepa*, of the lily family, cultivated for its edible bulb; this bulb which has a strong pungent flavour and smell and consists of fleshy concentric leaf-bases, eaten raw, cooked, or pickled. **ME.** ▸**b** With specifying word: any of various mainly bulbous plants of other genera. **LME.**
†**2** A pearl. Cf. **UNION** *noun*[1]. **ME–M18.**
†**3** A bunion. **L18–M19.**
4 A seal worn on a watch-chain. *slang.* **E19.**
5 *NAUTICAL.* A fraction of the speed of one knot. **E20.**

1 ***Egyptian onion***, ***pearl onion***, ***potato onion***, ***spanish onion***, ***spring onion***, ***top onion***, ***tree onion***, ***Welsh onion***, etc. **b bog onion** any of several plants with onion-like roots, esp. the royal fern, *Osmunda regalis*. **dog's onion** the star of Bethlehem, *Ornithogalum umbellatum*. **sea onion** (*a*) the squill, *Drimia maritima*; (*b*) *dial.* spring squill, *Scilla verna*.

Phrases: **know one's onions** be experienced in or knowledgeable about something. **off one's onion** *colloq.* crazy.

Comb.: **onion-couch** a tuberous form of false oat, *Arrhenatherum elatius*, occurring as a cornfield weed etc.; **onion dome** a bulbous dome on a church, palace, etc.; †**onion-eyed** *adjective* (*rare*) having eyes full of tears, as if from the effect of raw onions; **onion-fly** a dipteran fly, *Delia antiqua*, the larva of which is very destructive to onions; **onion-grass** = ***onion-couch*** above; **onion-maggot** the larva of the onion-fly; **onion set** a small onion bulb planted instead of seed to yield a mature bulb; **onion-skin** (*a*) the outermost or any outer coat of an onion; (*b*) very fine smooth translucent paper; **onion-twitch** = ***onion-couch*** above.

■ **onion-like** *adjective* resembling (that of) an onion **M20.** **oniony** *adjective* flavoured with onions; tasting or smelling of onions: **M19.**

onion /ˈʌnjən/ ***verb trans.*** *rare.* **M18.**
[from the noun.]
1 Season or flavour with onions. **M18.**
2 Apply an onion to; produce (tears) by using an onion. **M18.**

oniro- *combining form* var. of **ONEIRO-**.

onisciform /əˈnɪsɪfɔːm, -ˈnɪsk-/ ***adjective.*** **E19.**
[from Latin *oniscus* woodlouse + **-I-** + **-FORM**.]
ZOOLOGY. Of certain myriapods and lepidopteran larvae: resembling a woodlouse.

onium /ˈəʊnɪəm/ ***noun.*** **E20.**
[from next.]
CHEMISTRY. Used ***attrib.*** and in ***comb.*** to designate (compounds containing) ions of the kind with names ending in *-onium*.

-onium /əʊnɪəm/ ***suffix.***
[Extracted from **AMMONIUM**.]
1 *CHEMISTRY.* Forming names of complex cations of a more or less electronegative element, often bonded to protons, as ***carbonium***, ***diazonium***, etc.
2 *PHYSICS.* Forming names of bound states of a particle and its antiparticle, as ***charmonium***.

onlaid *verb pa. t. & pple* of **ONLAY** *verb*.

onlap /ˈɒnlap/ ***noun.*** **M20.**
[from **ON** *adverb* + **LAP** *verb*[2], after *offlap*.]
GEOLOGY. A progressive increase in the lateral extent of conformable strata in passing upwards from older to younger strata, so that each stratum is hidden by the one above; a set of strata exhibiting this. Cf. **OFFLAP**.

onlay /*as verb* ɒnˈleɪ; *as noun* ˈɒnleɪ/ ***verb & noun.*** **ME.**
[from **ON-** + **LAY** *verb*[1].]
▶ **A** *verb trans.* Pa. t. & pple **-laid** /-ˈleɪd/. Lay on. Now *rare*. **ME.**
▶ **B** *noun.* **1** Something fixed on the surface of something else, esp. as decoration, as on the cover of a book. **L19.**
2 *DENTISTRY.* An occlusal rest covering the whole occlusal surface of a tooth. **E20.**

Comb.: **onlay graft** *SURGERY* a bone graft in which a piece of bone is fixed over a fracture.

on-lend /ˈɒnlɛnd/ ***verb trans. & intrans.*** Pa. t. & pple **-lent** /-lɛnt/. **L20.**
[from **ON-** + **LEND** *verb*.]
COMMERCE. Lend (borrowed money) to a third party.

🕮 *Times* Capital intermediaries borrowing funds from one part of the world and on-lending to another part.

onlie, **onliest** *adjectives* see **ONLY** *adjective*.

online /*as adjective* ˈɒnlʌɪn; *as adverb* ɒnˈlʌɪn/ ***adjective & adverb.*** Also **on-line**, (in sense B.2) **on line**. **M20.**
[from **ON** *preposition* + **LINE** *noun*[2].]
▶ **A** *adjective.* **1** *COMPUTING.* Directly connected, so that a computer immediately receives an input from or sends an output to a peripheral process etc.; carried out while so connected or under direct computer control. **M20.**
2 Occurring on the current authorized routes of an airline. **M20.**
3 Chiefly *ENGINEERING.* = **IN-LINE** *adjective* 2. **L20.**
▶ **B** *adverb.* **1** *COMPUTING.* With processing of data carried out simultaneously with its production; while connected to a computer or under direct computer control. **M20.**
2 = **ON-STREAM** *adverb.* **M20.**

onliness /ˈəʊnlɪnɪs/ ***noun.*** Now *rare*. Also †**oneliness**. **ME.**
[from **ONLY** *adjective* + **-NESS**.]
†**1** The fact or condition of being alone; solitariness, solitude. **ME–E17.**
2 The fact or quality of being the only one of a kind; singularity, uniqueness. **M17.**

onlooker /ˈɒnlʊkə/ ***noun.*** **E17.**
[from **ON-** + **LOOKER**.]
A person who looks on, a looker-on; a (mere) spectator.

🕮 D. H. LAWRENCE She was outside of life, an onlooker, whilst Ursula was a partaker. *Observer* Onlookers threw stones at the procession.

onlooking /ˈɒnlʊkɪŋ/ ***noun.*** *rare.* **M17.**
[from **ON-** + **LOOKING**.]
The action of looking on, (mere) spectating.

onlooking /ˈɒnlʊkɪŋ/ ***adjective.*** **M17.**
[from **ON-** + **LOOK** *verb* + **-ING**[2].]
That looks on, (merely) spectating; looking at something.

only /ˈəʊnli/ ***noun.*** **OE.**
[from the adjective.]
†**1** The only one. **OE–L17.**
2 The only chance. Now *rare* or *obsolete*. **L19.**
3 An only child. **M20.**

🕮 **3** J. BETJEMAN I was a delicate boy—my parents' only.

only /ˈəʊnli/ *adjective.* Also †**onely**, (in sense 2, *pseudo-arch.*) **onlie**. Superl. (in sense 2, now *colloq.*) **onliest**.
[Old English *ānlīc* late var. of *ǣnlīc* corresp. to Middle Low German *einlīk*, Middle Dutch *een(e)lijc*, from Germanic bases of ONE *adjective, noun, & pronoun*, -LY[1].]
▶ **I 1** Without companions; solitary, lonely. Long *obsolete* exc. *dial.* OE.
▶ **II** *attrib.* **2** Unique in quality, character, rank, etc.; pre-eminent, unparalleled, best, alone worth knowing. Passing into hyperbol. use of sense 3. OE.
3 Of a kind of which there exist no more or no others. OE. ▶**b** *spec.* Of a child: having no brothers or sisters. L15.
4 Single, sole, one, lone. *arch.* LME. ▶†**b** Acting or existing alone; mere, sole. LME–E17.

📖 **2** T. CALLENDER The onliest thing to do is to get up and see. **onlie begetter** *pseudo-arch.* the sole originator. **3** J. CONRAD Reason is my only guide. I. MURDOCH You're the only person I can tell. *Holiday Which?* The only way through the western Lake District is by mountain passes. ***one and only***: see ONE *adjective, noun, & pronoun*. ***the only pebble on the beach***: see PEBBLE *noun*. **b** DAY LEWIS It is said that an only child develops a particularly vivid fantasy-life. **4** GOLDSMITH One only master grasps the whole domain.

only /ˈəʊnli/ *adverb, conjunction, & preposition.* Also †**onely**.
[Late Old English *ǣnlīce*, formed as ONE *adjective* etc. + -LY[2], after ONLY *adjective*, later alt. partly directly from ONLY *adjective*.]
▶ **A** *adverb.* †**1** Singularly, uniquely, pre-eminently. LOE–E17.
2 As a single or solitary thing or fact; no more than; nothing other than; no one or nothing more besides; solely, merely, exclusively; as much as, just. Also, with no better result than. ME.
†**3** By itself, alone, without anything else. LME–E19.
4 With adverbs and adverbial phrs. expr. time: not until, not earlier than, no longer ago than. L17.

📖 **2** G. K. CHESTERTON The police novel . . permits privacy only to explode and smash privacy. SCOTT FITZGERALD If Violet had only kept her mouth shut I could have fixed it. G. VIDAL Since he had only two suitcases, he carried them himself. J. OSBORNE He's not only got guts, but sensitivity as well. J. JOHNSTON It seems like only yesterday you were down here. H. SECOMBE She had only married him for the hyphen in his name. J. SIMMS Only a child would ask so many questions. A. BROOKNER A cool room which got the morning sun only. **4** E. BOWEN They . . have come from Paris only today. *Times* He reached the first drop shot only at its second bounce.

Phrases: ***if and only if***: see IF *conjunction*. ***if only***: see IF *conjunction*. ***only just***: see JUST *adverb*. **only not** *arch.* all but, little else than. **only too** extremely, very, regrettably.
▶ **B** *conjunction & preposition.* **1** Used to introduce a statement that forms an exception to a statement just made; but, on the other hand. LME.
2 Except (*for, that*); were it not (*for, that*). M16.

📖 **1** W. BOYD I'd come with you . . only I'm tied up with work. **2** E. DE ACTON Something like a castle in miniature, only that its windows were modern. E. O'NEILL And only for me, . . we'd be being scoffed by fishes this minute! T. COLLINS I didn't see anybody—nothing only Morgan's big white pig.

only-begotten /ˌəʊnlɪbɪˈɡɒt(ə)n/ *adjective. arch.* LME.
[translating Latin *unigentus*, Greek *monogenēs*.]
Begotten as the only child.

onmun /ˈɒnmʊn/ *noun.* Now *rare.* M20.
[Korean *ŏnmun* popular script.]
= HANGUL *noun*[2].

onnagata /ɒnəˈɡɑːtə/ *noun.* Pl. same. E20.
[Japanese, from *onna* woman + *kata* figure.]
In Japanese kabuki theatre: a man who plays female roles.

o.n.o. *abbreviation.*
Or near offer.

onocentaur /ɒnə(ʊ)ˈsɛntɔː/ *noun.* E16.
[Late Latin *onocentaurus* from Greek *onokentauros*, from *onos* ass + *kentauros* CENTAUR.]
GREEK MYTHOLOGY. A centaur with the body of an ass (rather than of a horse).

on-off /ɒnˈɒf, ˈɒnɒf/ *adjective.* M20.
[from ON *adverb* + OFF *adverb*.]
1 Of a switch etc.: that turns something on or off. M20.
2 Intermittent, off and on. M20.

📖 **1** E. GUNDREY An on-off lever on the head of the spray controls the flow. **2** A. DAVIES She started an on-off affair with a lecturer.

onolatry /əʊˈnɒlətri/ *noun. rare.* E20.
[from Greek *onos* ass + -LATRY.]
Worship of the donkey.

onomancy /ˈɒnəmansi/ *noun.* Also (earlier) †**onomantia**. E17.
[medieval Latin *onomantia* (whence also French *onomancie*, Italian *onomantia*), irreg. from Greek *onoma* name: see -MANCY.]
Divination from names, as from the number of letters in a name.

onomasiology /ˌɒnə(ʊ)meɪsɪˈɒlədʒi/ *noun.* E20.
[from Greek *onomasia* name + -OLOGY.]
The branch of knowledge that deals with the principles of nomenclature, esp. with regard to regional, social, or occupational variation.
■ **onomasioˈlogical** *adjective* E20. **onomasiologist** *noun* L20.

onomastic /ɒnəˈmastɪk/ *noun & adjective.* L16.
[Greek *onomastikos* pertaining to naming, from *onoma* name: see -IC.]
▶ **A** *noun.* †**1** = ONOMASTICON. Only in L16.
†**2** A writer of an onomasticon; a lexicographer. L16–E18.
3 In *pl.* (treated as *sing.*). The branch of knowledge that deals with the origin and formation of (esp. personal) proper names. M20.
▶ **B** *adjective.* **1** Of or relating to names, naming, or nomenclature. E18.
2 Of a signature on a legal document: (orig.) made by signing one's name as opp. to leaving a seal or mark; (later) applied by a person to a document in the handwriting of another. E19.

📖 **1** *American Speech* An interesting . . onomastic question is whether names can be said to be translatable.

■ **onomastician** /-ˈstɪʃ(ə)n/ *noun* an expert in or student of onomastics L20.

onomasticon /ɒnə(ʊ)ˈmastɪkɒn/ *noun.* E18.
[Greek, use as noun (sc. *biblion* book) of neut. of *onomastikos*: see prec.]
A vocabulary or alphabetic list of (esp. personal) proper names. Also, a vocabulary of nouns; a general lexicon.

onomato- /ɒnəˈmatəʊ/ *combining form.*
[Greek, from *onoma* name: see -O-.]
Of or pertaining to names, naming, or nomenclature, as ***onomatophobia***.

onomatology /ɒnə(ʊ)məˈtɒlədʒi/ *noun. rare.* M19.
[from ONOMATO- + -LOGY.]
The science of the formation of names or terms; terminology.
■ **onomatoˈlogical** *adjective* M20. **onomatologist** *noun* L17.

onomatomania /ˌɒnə(ʊ)matəˈmeɪnɪə/ *noun. rare.* L19.
[from ONOMATO- + -MANIA.]
Irrational fear of a particular word. Also, a preoccupation with words in general or with word-making.

onomatop /ɒˈnɒmətɒp/ *noun.* Also **-ope** /-əʊp/. E19.
[Abbreviation of next.]
= ONOMATOPOEIA 2.

onomatopoeia /ˌɒnə(ʊ)matəˈpiːə/ *noun.* L16.
[Late Latin from Greek *onomatopoiia* making of words, from *onomatopoios*, formed as ONOMATO- + *-poios* making, from *poiein* make, create: see -IA[1].]
1 The formation of a word by an imitation of the sound associated with the thing or action designated; the principle or practice of forming words by this process. L16.
2 A word formed by this process. M19.
3 RHETORIC. The use of naturally suggestive language for rhetorical effect. M19.
■ **onomatopoeian** *adjective* = ONOMATOPOEIC M19. **onomatopoeic** *adjective* of, pertaining to, or characterized by onomatopoeia; imitative in sound: M19. **onomatopoeically** *adverb* E20. **onomatopoeics** *noun pl.* (treated as *sing.* or *pl.*) = ONOMATOPOEIA M20.

onomatopoesis /ˌɒnəmatəpəʊˈiːsɪs/ *noun.* M19.
[Greek *onomatopoiēsis* the making of a name, formed as ONOMATO- + *poiēsis* making, from *po(i)ein* make, create.]
= ONOMATOPOEIA 1.
■ **onomatopoetic** *adjective* = ONOMATOPOEIC M19. **onomatopoetically** *adverb* M19.

onomatopy /ɒnəˈmatəpi/ *noun.* M17.
[formed as ONOMATOPOEIA, or French *onomatopée*.]
= ONOMATOPOEIA.

Onondaga /ɒnənˈdɑːɡə/ *noun & adjective.* L17.
[Onondaga *onǫ̃tàʔke* on the hill (the name of the main Onondaga settlement).]
▶ **A** *noun.* Pl. **-s**, same. A member of an Iroquois people, one of the five of the original Iroquois confederation, formerly inhabiting an area near Syracuse, New York; the language of this people. L17.
▶ **B** *attrib.* or as *adjective.* Of or pertaining to the Onondaga or their language. M18.

onrush /ˈɒnrʌʃ/ *noun.* M19.
[from ON- + RUSH *noun*[2].]
The act of rushing on; an onward rush, an impetuous onward movement.

📖 M. LEITCH He felt a sudden onrush of sentiment.

onrush /ˈɒnrʌʃ/ *verb intrans.* M19.
[from ON- + RUSH *verb*[2].]
Rush on. Chiefly as ***onrushing*** *ppl adjective.*

📖 E. SIMPSON Delmore grabbed my arm . . for protection against the onrushing traffic.

onsell /ˈɒnsɛl/ *verb trans.* Also **on-sell**. Pa. t. & pple **onsold** /ɒnˈsəʊld/. L20.
[from ON- + SELL *verb*.]
COMMERCE. Sell (an asset) to a third party, usu. for a profit, esp. shortly after acquisition.

onsen /ˈɒnsɛn/ *noun.* Pl. same. M20.
[Japanese, from *on* hot + *sen* spring.]
In Japan: a hot spring, *esp.* one thought to have medicinal properties; a hot spring resort.

onset /ˈɒnsɛt/ *noun.* E16.
[from ON- + SET *noun*[1].]
1 (An) attack, (an) assault. E16.
2 a The beginning of some (esp. unpleasant) operation, situation, condition, etc.; the commencement, the start. M16. ▶**b** PHONETICS. The movement of the speech organs preparatory to, or at the start of, the articulation of a speech sound. Also, the consonant or consonants at the beginning of a syllable. M20.

📖 **1** B. JOWETT His argument could not sustain the first onset of yours. **2a** W. GERHARDIE It grew markedly colder, and one felt the onset of winter. R. THOMAS Walking . . like a man at the onset of paralysis.

onsetter /ˈɒnsɛtə/ *noun.* M16.
[from ON- + SETTER *noun*[1].]
†**1** A person who urges another on; an inciter. M16–M17.
2 A person who makes an attack; an assailant. *arch.* L16.
3 MINING. A worker who loads tubs into the cage at the bottom of a shaft. L18.

onshore /*as adverb* ɒnˈʃɔː, *as adjective* ˈɒnʃɔː/ *adverb & adjective.* Also **on-shore**. M19.
[from ON *preposition* + SHORE *noun*[1].]
▶ **A** *adverb.* In a direction towards a shore; on or on to a shore. M19.
▶ **B** *adjective.* **1** Esp. of a wind: directed or moving from the sea towards the land. L19.
2 Existing or occurring on the shore or on land. L19.

onside /*as adverb* ɒnˈsʌɪd, *as adjective* ˈɒnsʌɪd/ *adverb & adjective.* Also **on-side**. M19.
[from ON *preposition* + SIDE *noun*.]
FOOTBALL & HOCKEY etc. In a position where a player may lawfully play the ball; not offside.

onsight /ˈɒnsʌɪt/ *noun. rare.* M19.
[from ON- + SIGHT *noun*, after *insight*.]
The action or faculty of looking forward into the future.

onslaught /ˈɒnslɔːt/ *noun.* E17.
[Early Middle Dutch *aenslag* (mod. *aan-*), from *aan* on + *slag* blow, stroke, rel. to Dutch *slagen* strike (see SLAY *verb*[1]), assim. to SLAUGHTER *noun*.]
An onset, an attack; *esp.* a vigorous or destructive assault or attack.

📖 A. KENNY The second great air onslaught on Liverpool was in the spring of 1941. *fig.*: *Time* They were besieged . . by onslaughts launched by critics in the Carter Administration.

¶ Not recorded in 18. App. revived by Sir Walter Scott.

onsold *verb pa. t. & pple* of ONSELL.

onstead /ˈɒnstɛd/ *noun. Scot. & north.* LME.
[from ON- + STEAD *noun*.]
A farmhouse with its attached stables and other buildings; a farmstead. Now also *spec.*, the offices of a farm as distinct from the farmer's house.

on-stream /*as adverb* ɒnˈstriːm; *as adjective* ˈɒnstriːm/ *adverb & adjective.* Also **onstream**, (as adverb) **on stream**. M20.
[from ON *preposition* + STREAM *noun*.]
▶ **A** *adverb.* In or into (industrial) production or useful operation. M20.
▶ **B** *adjective.* Of or pertaining to normal (industrial) production, productive. M20.

Ont. *abbreviation.*
Ontario.

-ont /ɒnt/ *suffix.*
[from Greek *ont-*, *on* being, pres. pple of *einai* be, exist.]
BIOLOGY. Forming nouns denoting individuals of particular type, as ***diplont***, ***symbiont***.

ontal /ˈɒnt(ə)l/ *adjective.* Now *rare.* E20.
[from Greek *ont-*, *ōn* being (see ONTO-) + -AL[1].]
PHILOSOPHY. Relating to or comprising reality as opp. to mere phenomena.

Ontarian /ɒnˈtɛːrɪən/ *adjective & noun.* L19.
[from *Ontari(o* (see below) + -AN.]
▶ **A** *adjective.* Of or pertaining to the Canadian province of Ontario or the Great Lake after which it is named. L19.
▶ **B** *noun.* A native or inhabitant of the province of Ontario. M20.

ontic /ˈɒntɪk/ *adjective.* M20.
[from Greek *ont-*, *ōn* being (see ONTO-) + -IC.]
PHILOSOPHY. Of or pertaining to entities and the facts about them; relating to real as opp. to phenomenal existence.

■ **ontical** *adjective* = ONTIC M20. **ontically** *adverb* M20.

onto /ˈɒntuː/ *preposition & adjective.* E18.
[Var. of ON TO.]
▶ **A** *preposition.* **1** = ON TO. E18.
2 *MATH.* Expr. the relationship of a set to its image under a mapping when every element of the image set has an inverse image in the first set. Cf. INTO. M20.

📖 **1** D. BOGARDE Blackett screwed the top onto his hip flask. *Private Eye* Short stories recorded onto cassettes. R. SUTCLIFF The window opened directly onto the pavement.

▶ **B** *adjective. MATH.* Designating a mapping of one set onto another. M20.
¶ Although in wide use, and despite the similarity to *into*, the form *onto* is still not fully accepted. It is however useful in distinguishing sense as between *we drove on to the beach* (i.e. in that direction) and *we drove onto the beach* (i.e. into contact with it).

onto- /ˈɒntəʊ/ *combining form.*
[Greek *ont-*, *ōn* being, neut. pres. pple of *einai* to be: see -O-.]
Forming words with the sense 'of or pertaining to being', as ***ontogenetic***, ***ontology*** etc.
■ **ontotheˈology** *noun* (*a*) the cognition of a supreme being through mere conceptions as opp. to experience; (*b*) theology in which God is regarded as a (supreme) being: L18.

on to /ˈɒn tuː/ *preposition.* See also ONTO. L16.
[from ON *adverb* + TO *preposition*, with the same relation to *on* as *into* has to *in*.]
1 To a position or state on or upon; into contact with. L16.
2 Aware of, knowledgeable about. *colloq.* (orig. *US*). L19.

📖 **1** DICKENS Assisting Mr. Pickwick on to the roof. H. MAUDSLEY If laid on its back, it struggles on to its legs again. *Independent* There's no news—I've been on to the cops every hour. **2** M. GEE Maybe she knew he was on to her.

ontogenesis /ɒntə(ʊ)ˈdʒɛnɪsɪs/ *noun.* L19.
[from ONTO- + -GENESIS.]
BIOLOGY. The development of the individual organism from the earliest embryonic stage to maturity. Also, the development of a particular (anatomical, behavioural, etc.) feature of an organism. Cf. PHYLOGENESIS.

ontogenetic /ɒntə(ʊ)dʒɪˈnɛtɪk/ *adjective.* L19.
[from ONTO- + -GENETIC.]
BIOLOGY. Of, pertaining to, or characteristic of ontogenesis; relating to the development of the individual organism.
■ **ontogenetical** *adjective* (*rare*) E20. **ontogenetically** *adverb* L19.

ontogeny /ɒnˈtɒdʒəni/ *noun.* L19.
[from ONTO- + -GENY.]
1 *BIOLOGY.* The origin and development of the individual organism; ontogenesis. L19.
2 The branch of science that deals with ontogenesis. L19.

📖 **1** J. B. WATSON The recapitulation theory . . holds . . that ontogeny repeats phylogeny.

■ **ontoˈgenic** *adjective* = ONTOGENETIC L19. **ontoˈgenically** *adverb* L19. **ontogenist** *noun* L19.

ontologic /ɒntəˈlɒdʒɪk/ *adjective.* M18.
[formed as next + -IC.]
= next.

ontological /ɒntəˈlɒdʒɪk(ə)l/ *adjective.* L18.
[formed as next + -ICAL.]
PHILOSOPHY. Of or pertaining to ontology; metaphysical.

📖 D. CUPITT The ordinary person does not make a clear distinction between mythical and ontological realities. **ontological argument**: for the objective existence of God from the idea or essence of God.

■ **ontologically** *adverb* M19.

ontology /ɒnˈtɒlədʒi/ *noun.* E18.
[mod. Latin *ontologia*, from Greek ONTO-: see -LOGY.]
PHILOSOPHY. The science or study of being; that part of metaphysics which relates to the nature or essence of being or existence.
■ **ontologism** *noun* (*THEOLOGY*) a form of mysticism based on a belief in an immediate cognition of God M19. **ontologist** *noun* a person who studies ontology; a metaphysician: E18. **ontologize** *verb* (*a*) *verb intrans.* apply or deal with ontology; (*b*) *verb trans.* treat ontologically: M19.

onus /ˈəʊnəs/ *noun.* M17.
[Latin = load, burden.]
A burden, a responsibility, a duty.

📖 R. FRAME My father fell seriously ill . . so the onus of responsibility became mine. *Which?* The onus should be on the card issuer to prove that the customer was at fault. **onus probandi** /prə(ʊ)ˈbandʌɪ/ [Latin = the burden of proving] *LAW* the obligation to prove an assertion or allegation one makes, the burden of proof.

onward /ˈɒnwəd/ *preposition, adverb, & adjective.* ME.
[from ON *adverb* + -WARD, after *inward*, *forward*, etc.]
▶†**A** *preposition.* On; over. Long *rare.* ME–M17.
▶ **B** *adverb.* †**1** In advance; towards the final settlement, provisionally. LME–M16.
2 a Situated further on; ahead. Now *rare.* LME. ▸**b** Further on in time. Now *rare* or *obsolete.* LME.
3 a In the direction of what is ahead; towards the front; with advancing motion; forward. LME. ▸**b** Forward in time; in succession. M17.

📖 **3a** T. HARDY Johns and my man have gone onward to the little inn. **b** P. GAY From his earliest days onward Freud had been surrounded by women.

▶ **C** *adjective.* **1** In advance in time or space; advanced. Long *rare* or *obsolete.* L16.
2 Directed or moving onward or forward; advancing. L17.

📖 **2** TENNYSON Vast eddies in the flood Of onward time.

■ **onwardness** *noun* the state or condition of moving onward; advance, progression, progress: M16. **onwards** *adverb* †(*a*) = ONWARD *adverb* 1; (*b*) onward, esp. in time: LME.

onycha /ˈɒnɪkə/ *noun.* LME.
[Latin = Greek *onukha* accus. of *onux* nail, from the resemblance of the molluscan operculum to a fingernail.]
An ingredient of incense used in Mosaic ritual, consisting of the opercula of marine molluscs.

onychia /əʊˈnɪkɪə/ *noun.* M19.
[from Greek *onukh-*, *onux* nail + -IA[1].]
MEDICINE. Inflammation of the matrix of the nail. Cf. PARONYCHIA.

onycho- /ˈɒnɪkəʊ/ *combining form* of Greek *onukh-*, *onux* nail, claw: see -O-.
■ **onychogryˈphosis** *noun* [Greek *grupōsis* hooking of the nails] *MEDICINE* gross thickening and curvature of one or more nails M19. **onychomancy** *noun* (*rare*) divination from the fingernails M17. **onychomyˈcosis** *noun*, pl. **-coses** /-ˈkəʊsiːz/, *MEDICINE* fungal infection of a finger or toenail, causing brittleness and discoloration M19. **onychophagia** /ˌɒnɪkə(ʊ)ˈfeɪdʒɪə/ *noun* [see -PHAGY] the habit of biting one's nails E20. **onychophagist** /ɒnɪˈkɒfədʒɪst/ *noun* [from Greek *-phagos* eating + -IST] a person who bites his or her nails M19.

onychophoran /ɒnɪˈkɒf(ə)rən/ *noun & adjective.* L19.
[from mod. Latin *Onychophora* (see below), from ONYCHO- + *-phoros* bearing: see -AN.]
ZOOLOGY. ▶**A** *noun.* An animal of the arthropod class Onychophora, sometimes regarded as a distinct phylum intermediate between annelids and arthropods. Also called ***velvet-worm***. L19.
▶ **B** *adjective.* Of, pertaining to, or designating this group of animals. L19.

onymatic /ɒnɪˈmatɪk/ *adjective.* M19.
[from Greek (Aeolic) *onumat-*, *onuma* var. of *onoma* name + -IC.]
Of or pertaining to names, onomastic.

onymous /ˈɒnɪməs/ *adjective. rare.* L18.
[Extracted from ANONYMOUS.]
Having a name; (of a writing) bearing the name of the author; (of an author) giving his or her name. Usu. in collocation with ***anonymous***.
■ **oˈnymity** *noun* the condition of being onymous L19. **onymously** *adverb* with the writer's name given L19.

o'nyong-nyong /əʊˈnjɒŋnjɒŋ/ *noun.* M20.
[Acholi *ɔ̀nyɔ̀ŋ-nyɔ̀ŋ*.]
MEDICINE. A mosquito-borne viral disease similar to dengue, occurring in E. Africa.

onyx /ˈɒnɪks, ˈəʊnɪks/ *noun & adjective.* ME.
[Old French *oniche*, *onix*, from Latin *onych-*, *onyx*, from Greek *onukh-*, *onux* nail, claw, onyx.]
▶ **A** *noun.* **1** A form of chalcedony consisting of plane layers of different colours, much used for cameos. Also ***onyx stone***. ME.
†**2** = ONYCHA. *rare.* Only in E17.
3 *MEDICINE.* An opacity of the lower part of the cornea of the eye, caused by an infiltration of pus and resembling a fingernail. Now *rare* or *obsolete.* E18.
▶ **B** *adjective.* Of, pertaining to, or resembling onyx. L19.

📖 R. KIPLING His big onyx eyes.

oo *noun*[1], *noun*[2] vars. of O-O, OOH *noun.*

oo /uː/ *pronoun*[1]. *nursery & colloq.* Also **'oo**. E18.
[Repr. a pronunc.]
= YOU *pers. pronoun.*

oo /uː/ *pronoun*[2]. *non-standard.* Also **'oo**. M19.
[Repr. a pronunc.]
= WHO *pronoun.*

oo *interjection, verb* var. of OOH *interjection, verb.*

oo- /ˈəʊə/ *combining form* of Greek *ōion* egg, ovum, used esp. in *BIOLOGY*: see -O-. Cf. OVI-[1], OVO-.
¶ Also, though now less commonly, written with a diaeresis, oö-.
■ **oocyst** *noun* (*a*) a cyst containing a zygote formed by a parasitic protozoan; (*b*) = ***ovicell*** (a) s.v. OVI-[1]: L19. **ooˈgenesis** *noun* the production or development of an ovum L19. **oogeˈnetic** *adjective* of or pertaining to oogenesis L19. **oophyte** *noun* (*BOTANY*) = PROTHALLUS L19. **oosphere** *noun* (*BOTANY*) the female reproductive cell of certain algae, fungi, etc., which is formed in the oogonium and when fertilized becomes the oospore L19. **oospore** *noun* (*BOTANY*) the thick-walled zygote of certain algae, fungi, etc., formed by fertilization of an oosphere M19.

o-o /ˈəʊəʊ/ *noun.* Also **oo**. L19.
[Hawaiian.]
Any of various extinct or very rare Hawaiian honeyeaters of the genus *Moho*, esp. *M. braccatus* of the island of Kauai.

oocyte /ˈəʊəsʌɪt/ *noun.* L19.
[from OO- + -CYTE.]
BIOLOGY. An egg mother cell, which gives rise to a mature ovum by meiosis. Also, a polar body so produced. Cf. OVOCYTE.
primary oocyte: see PRIMARY *adjective.* ***secondary oocyte***: see SECONDARY *adjective.*

oodles /ˈuːd(ə)lz/ *noun pl. colloq.* M19.
[Origin unkn.]
A very great amount; large or unlimited quantities; lots, heaps.

📖 *Family Circle* The Rayburn Nouvelle . . gives you oodles of hot water (up to 100 gallons every 24 hours). *Natural History* We have oodles to learn about how evolution happened.

oo-er /uːˈɜː/ *interjection.* Also **ooer**. E20.
[from OOH *interjection* + ER *interjection.*]
Expr. surprise, wonder, etc.

oof /uːf/ *noun. slang.* L19.
[Abbreviation of OOFTISH.]
Money, cash.
Comb.: **oof-bird** a source of money, a wealthy person.
■ **oofless** *adjective* without cash L19.

oof *interjection* var. of OUF.

ooftish /ˈuːftɪʃ/ *noun. slang.* Now *rare.* L19.
[Yiddish *ooftisch* for German *auf* (*dem*) *Tische* on (the) table, i.e. (money) laid on the table, (money) down.]
Money, = OOF *noun.*

oofy /ˈuːfi/ *adjective. slang.* L19.
[from OOF *noun* + -Y[1].]
Wealthy, rich.
■ **oofiness** *noun* M20.

oogamy /əʊˈɒgəmi/ *noun.* L19.
[from OO- + -GAMY.]
BIOLOGY. The union of dissimilar gametes, usu. of a small motile male gamete and a larger non-motile female gamete.
■ **oogamete** /əʊəˈgamiːt/ *noun* either gamete in oogamous reproduction L19. **oˈogamous** *adjective* designating, pertaining to, or involving the union of dissimilar gametes L19.

oogonium /əʊəˈgəʊnɪəm/ *noun.* Pl. **-nia** /-nɪə/. M19.
[from OO- + Greek *gonos* generation: see -IUM.]
1 *BOTANY.* The female gametangium of certain algae, fungi, etc., usu. a rounded cell or sac containing one or more oospheres. M19.
2 *BIOLOGY.* A primordial female reproductive cell that gives rise to primary oocytes by mitosis. L19.
■ **oogonial** *adjective* E20.

ooh /uː/ *interjection, noun, & verb.* Also **oo**. E20.
[Natural exclam. Cf. OH *interjection, noun*[2], *& verb.*]
▶ **A** *interjection.* Expr. pain, surprise, wonder, disapprobation, etc. E20.
▶ **B** *noun.* An utterance of 'ooh!'. Freq. in ***oohs and ahs***. M20.
▶ **C** *verb intrans. & trans.* Say or express with 'ooh!'. Freq. in ***ooh and ah***. M20.

ooh-la-la /ˈuːlɑːlɑː, uːlɑːˈlɑː/ *interjection, noun, & adjective.* E20.
[French *ô là! là!*]
▶ **A** *interjection.* Expr. surprise, appreciaton, etc. E20.
▶ **B** *noun.* **1** An utterance of 'ooh-la-la!'. M20.
2 Impropriety or naughtiness as popularly associated with the French. Also, an attractive or provocative girl or woman. *slang.* M20.

📖 **2** I. CROSS If this red-haired ooh-la-la gets out of hand, I'll fix her for you.

▶ **C** *adjective.* Sexually attractive or provocative. *slang.* M20.

📖 *Spectator* The ooh-la-la French maid.

ooid /ˈəʊɔɪd/ *noun.* M20.
[German, from Greek *ōoeidēs* egg-shaped, from *ōion* egg: see -OID.]
GEOLOGY. = OOLITH.

oojah /ˈuːdʒɑː/ *noun. slang.* Also **ooja-ka-piv** /ˌuːdʒɑːkəˈpɪv/, (*Army slang*) **oojiboo** /ˈuːdʒɪbuː/, & other vars. E20.
[Origin unkn.]
A thing whose name one forgets, or does not know, or does not wish to mention; a gadget, a thingummy.

ook /ʊk/ *noun. slang.* M20.
[Symbolic.]
Something slimy, sticky, or otherwise unpleasant.
■ **ooky** *adjective* M20.

ookinete /əʊəkɪˈniːt, -ˈkʌɪniːt/ *noun.* E20.
[German *Ookinet*, formed as OO- + KINET(IC.]
BIOLOGY. A zygote capable of autonomous movement, esp. as a stage in the life cycle of some parasitic protozoans.

oolichan *noun* var. of EULACHON.

oolite /ˈəʊəlʌɪt/ *noun.* E19.
[French *oölithe*, mod. Latin *oolites*: see OO-, -LITE.]
GEOLOGY. **1** Orig., any limestone composed of small rounded granules like the roe of a fish. Now *spec.* any of a series of such limestones and other sedimentary rocks of the Jurassic system, lying above the lias. E19.
2 = OOLITH. M19.
■ **ooˈlitic** *adjective* of or pertaining to oolite; of the nature of oolite: L18.

oolith /ˈəʊəlɪθ/ *noun.* L18.
[from OO- + -LITH.]
GEOLOGY. Any of the small rounded granules of which oolite is composed.

oology /əʊˈɒlədʒi/ *noun.* M19.
[French *oölogie*, mod. Latin *oologia*: see OO-, -LOGY.]
The branch of knowledge that deals with birds' eggs; a description of birds' eggs; the collecting of birds' eggs.
■ **ooˈlogical** *adjective* M19. **oologist** *noun* a person who studies oology; an egg-collector: M19.

oolong /ˈuːlɒŋ/ *noun.* M19.
[Chinese *wūlóng*, from *wū* black + *lóng* dragon.]
A dark variety of cured China tea.

ooloo *noun* var. of ULU *noun*[1].

oom /ʊəm/ *noun. S. Afr.* E19.
[Afrikaans from Dutch *oom*: see EME *noun*[1].]
Uncle. Freq. used by children or young people as a respectful form of address to any older or elderly man.

oomiak *noun* var. of UMIAK.

oompah /ˈuːmpɑː/ *noun.* Also **oom-pah**. L19.
[Imit.]
A repetitive rhythmical sound of or as of a bass brass musical instrument; an instrument that makes such a sound.
📖 *attrib.*: *Daily Telegraph* The oompah world of moustachioed military bandmasters.

oomph /ʊmf, uːmf/ *noun. slang.* Also **umph**. M20.
[Origin uncertain: perh. imit.]
Sex appeal, glamour, attractiveness. Also, energy, enthusiasm.
📖 *Daily Telegraph* This strictly-tailored suit has more oomph than any see-through ever had. *New Scientist* The substance that puts the oomph into most fireworks is gunpowder.

oomycete /əʊəˈmʌɪsiːt/ *noun & adjective.* Orig. only in pl. **-mycetes** /-ˈmʌɪsiːts, -mʌɪˈsiːtiːz/. E20.
[Anglicized sing. of mod. Latin *Oomycetes* (see below), formed as OO- + Greek *mukētes* pl. of *mukēs* fungus.]
BOTANY. ▶**A** *noun.* A fungus of the class Oomycetes, characterized by having a zoospore with two flagella. E20.
▶**B** *attrib.* or as *adjective.* Of or designating a fungus of this class. E20.

-oon /uːn/ *suffix.*
[Repr. French *-on* = Italian *-one*, Spanish *-on*, from Latin *-o(n-)*.]
In nouns from Romance languages, esp. French, adopted between the 16th and 18th cents., usu. equivalent to French words stressed on final *-on*, as ***balloon***, ***dragoon***, ***festoon***, ***platoon***, ***saloon***, etc., less commonly from Spanish, as ***barracoon***, ***quadroon***, etc., and Italian, as ***cartoon***. Occas. in English formations as ***spittoon***, ***tenoroon***, etc.
¶ Older and modern borrowings, and those from unstressed *-on*, take *-on*, as *baron*, *felon*, etc.

oons /uːnz/ *interjection. arch.* L16.
[Contr. of *wounds* in ***God's wounds*** s.v. GOD *noun* 5.]
= ZOUNDS.

oont /uːnt/ *noun. slang* (orig. *Anglo-Indian*). M19.
[Hindi, Urdu *ūṭ* from Sanskrit *uṣṭra*.]
A camel.

oophorectomy /ˌəʊəfəˈrɛktəmi/ *noun.* L19.
[formed as next + -ECTOMY.]
MEDICINE. Surgical removal of one or both ovaries; an instance of this.
■ **oophorectomize** *verb trans.* perform oophorectomy on M20.

oophoritis /ˌəʊəfəˈrʌɪtɪs/ *noun.* L19.
[from next + -ITIS.]
MEDICINE. Inflammation of an ovary.

oophoron /əʊˈɒfərɒn/ *noun. rare* exc. in Dicts. M19.
[Use as noun of neut. of Greek *ōophoros* egg-bearing, formed as OO- + *phoros* -PHORE.]
An ovary.
¶ Cf. EPOOPHORON, PAROOPHORON.

ooplasm /ˈəʊəplaz(ə)m/ *noun.* L19.
[from OO- + -PLASM.]
1 *ZOOLOGY.* The cytoplasm of an egg. L19.
2 *BOTANY.* In an oomycete: the central portion of the cytoplasm of the oogonium, which becomes the oosphere. L19.
■ **ooˈplasmic** *adjective* E20.

oops /uːps, ʊps/ *interjection.* M20.
[Natural exclam.]
Expr. apology, dismay, or surprise, esp. after an obvious mistake, a near miss, etc.

oops-a-daisy *interjection* var. of UPSY-DAISY.

oorali *noun* var. of URARI.

†**oorial** *noun* see URIAL.

Oort /ʊət/ *noun.* M20.
[Jan Hendick *Oort* (1900–92), Dutch astronomer.]
ASTRONOMY. **1** ***Oort constant***, ***Oort's constant***, either of two constants in an equation relating the radial velocity of a star in the Galaxy to its distance from the sun. M20.
2 ***Oort cloud***, ***Oort comet cloud***, ***Oort's cloud***, ***Oort's comet cloud***, a cloud of small bodies postulated to orbit the sun well beyond the orbit of Pluto and act as a reservoir of comets. M20.

ootheca /əʊəˈθiːkə/ *noun.* Pl. **-cae** /-siː, -kiː/. M19.
[from OO- + Greek *thēkē* case, receptacle.]
ZOOLOGY. The egg-case of certain invertebrates, esp. the orthopteroid insects.
■ **oothecal** *adjective* E20.

ootid /ˈəʊətɪd/ *noun.* E20.
[from OO- after *spermatid*.]
BIOLOGY. A haploid cell formed by the meiotic division of a secondary oocyte; *esp.* the ovum, as distinct from the polar bodies.

ooze /uːz/ *noun*[1].
[Old English *wōs* corresp. to Middle Low German *wōs(e* scum, Old Norse *vás* (Middle Swedish *oss*, *os*, *oos*, Middle Danish *oss*, *oess*, *voos*). Now assoc. with OOZE *noun*[2], *noun*[4].]
†**1** Juice, sap; the liquid from a plant, fruit, etc. OE–LME.
2 *TANNING.* The liquor of a tan-vat; an infusion of oak-bark, sumac, etc., in which hides are steeped. L16.
Comb.: **ooze-calf**, **ooze leather** calf-skin through which the dye has been mechanically forced, used for the uppers of boots and shoes, and by bookbinders.

ooze /uːz/ *noun*[2].
[Old English *wāse* = Old Frisian *wāse*, Old Norse *veisa* stagnant pool, puddle.]
1 a Wet mud or slime; *esp.* that in the bed of a river or estuary. OE. ▸**b** A stretch or extent of mud; a mudbank; a marsh, a fen. L15.
2 *OCEANOGRAPHY.* (A deposit or layer of) white or grey calcareous matter largely composed of foraminiferan remains, covering large areas of the ocean floor. M19.
📖 **1b** CARLYLE There are thickets, intricacies, runlets, boggy oozes. **2** ***globigerina ooze***, ***pteropod ooze***, ***radiolarian ooze***, etc.

ooze /uːz/ *noun*[3]. Now *rare* or *obsolete.* M16.
[Origin unkn.]
Sea-weed.

ooze /uːz/ *noun*[4]. E18.
[from OOZE *verb.*]
The action or fact of oozing or flowing gently; exudation. Also, that which oozes, a sluggish flow.
📖 *New Yorker* The paramedics rescue a man trapped in the ooze of a gushing oil well.

ooze /uːz/ *verb.* LME.
[from OOZE *noun*[1].]
1 *verb intrans.* Of moisture: pass slowly or in small quantities through the pores of a body or through small openings or interstices; exude, seep. Also foll. by *out*, *up*, etc. LME. ▸**b** *transf.* & *fig.* Pass slowly, gradually, or imperceptibly. Also foll. by *out*, *up*, etc. L18.
2 *verb intrans.* Of a substance: exude moisture. LME.
3 *verb trans.* Emit or give out (moisture etc.) slowly, gradually, or liberally; exhibit (a feeling etc.) to a high degree. Also foll. by *out*. LME.
📖 **1** J. F. W. HERSCHEL When a crack takes place in ice, the water oozes up. **b** A. HIGGINS Grease oozed out from the wheel socket at the whim of the rising and falling plunger. B. NEIL The sound of laughter and music oozed down the stairwell. **3** R. ADAMS Several of the wounds were putrescent, oozing a glistening green matter. V. GLENDINNING He . . bought them great hot doughnuts oozing jam. B. EMECHETA The space of the . . house seemed to be oozing out heat.

oozi /ˈuːzi/ *noun.* E20.
[Burmese *ù-zì* a person seated at the head of an elephant or at the prow of a boat, from *ù* head + *sì* ride on, mount.]
An elephant-driver; a mahout.

oozlum bird /ˈuːzlʌm bəːd/ *noun phr.* L19.
[Fanciful: see BIRD *noun.*]
A mythical or unrecognized bird.

oozy /ˈuːzi/ *adjective.* OE.
[from OOZE *noun*[1], *noun*[2], *verb*: see -Y[1].]
▶†**I 1** Full of moisture, juicy. Only in OE.
▶**II 2** Of water: filled with ooze or mud; muddy. LME.
3 Composed of or resembling ooze; muddy, slimy. Also (of a sea bottom) consisting of ooze or fine mud. LME.
▶**III 4** Exuding moisture; damp with exuded or deposited moisture. E18. ▸**b** Of seaweed: slimy, damp. M18.
■ **oozily** *adverb* L19. **ooziness** *noun* L17.

OP *abbreviation.*
1 Observation post.
2 *THEATRICAL.* Opposite prompt.
3 Latin *Ordo Praedicatorum* Order of Preachers, the Dominican Order.

op /ɒp/ *noun*[1]. As a written abbreviation also **op.** (point), pl. **opp.** (point). L18.
[Abbreviation of OPUS *noun.*]
A numbered opus of a composer's output, an opus number.

op /ɒp/ *noun*[2]. *colloq.* E20.
[Abbreviation of OPERATION.]
1 A surgical operation. E20.
2 A military operation. E20.

op /ɒp/ *noun*[3]. *colloq.* E20.
[Abbreviation of OPERATIVE *noun.*]
A detective; *esp.* a private investigator.

op /ɒp/ *noun*[4]. *colloq.* M20.
[Abbreviation of OPERATOR.]
A radio or telephone operator.

op /ɒp/ *noun*[5]. *colloq.* Also **opp**. L20.
[Abbreviation.]
= OPPORTUNITY. Chiefly in ***photo op*** s.v. PHOTO *noun & adjective.*
Comb.: **op shop** (*Austral. & NZ*) a charity shop.

op /ɒp/ *adjective. colloq.* M20.
[Abbreviation of OPTICAL *adjective.*]
Of a form of art: optical, generating illusions of movement in its patterns.

op- *prefix* see OB-.

op. *abbreviation.*
= OP *noun*[1].

o.p. *abbreviation.*
1 Out of print.
2 Overproof.

opacate /ə(ʊ)ˈpeɪkeɪt/ *verb trans. rare.* M17.
[Latin *opacat-* pa. ppl stem of *opacare*, from *opacus* OPAQUE: see -ATE[3].]
Make dim or opaque.

opacify /ə(ʊ)ˈpasɪfʌɪ/ *verb trans. & intrans.* E20.
[from OPACI(TY + -FY.]
Make or become opaque.
■ **opacifiˈcation** *noun* E20. **opacifier** *noun* a substance which makes something opaque E20.

opacimeter /ə(ʊ)ˈpasɪmiːtə/ *noun.* E20.
[from OPACI(TY + -METER.]
An instrument for measuring opacity, esp. by reflection.

opacious /ə(ʊ)ˈpeɪʃəs/ *adjective.* Now *rare.* M17.
[from Latin *opacus* OPAQUE + -IOUS. Cf. OPACOUS.]
= OPAQUE *adjective* 1, 2.

opacity /ə(ʊ)ˈpasɪti/ *noun.* M16.
[French *opacité* from Latin *opacitas*, from *opacus* OPAQUE: see -ACITY.]
1 Obscurity of meaning; resistance to interpretation. Also, denseness or obtuseness of intellect or understanding. M16. ▸**b** *LINGUISTICS.* Inability (of a rule) to be extrapolated from every occurrence of the phenomenon. M16.
2 a The state of being in shadow; dimness, obscurity; an instance of this. E17. ▸**b** The fact or condition of not reflecting light. L18.
3 The quality or condition of being impervious to light; lack of transparency or translucence; *spec.* the ratio of the intensity of the light incident on a sample or object to that of the light transmitted through it. M17. ▸**b** *transf.* Imperviousness to other forms of radiation, heat, sound, etc. L19.

opacous /ə(ʊ)ˈpeɪkəs/ *adjective.* Now *rare.* E17.
[from Latin *opacus* OPAQUE + -OUS. Cf. OPACIOUS.]
†**1** = OPAQUE *adjective* 1. E17–E18.
2 = OPAQUE *adjective* 2. E17.

opacular /ə(ʊ)ˈpakjʊlə/ *adjective. rare.* M18.
[from Latin *opacus* OPAQUE + -ULAR.]
Somewhat opaque.

opah /ˈəʊpə/ *noun.* M18.
[W. African.]
A large rare fish of deep ocean waters, *Lampris guttatus*, having a compressed oval body, silver-blue above, with white spots and crimson dorsal and anal fins. Also called ***kingfish***, ***moonfish***, ***sunfish***.

For other words beginning with *oo-* see the entry for **oo-**

†**opake** *adjective, noun, & verb* see OPAQUE.

opal /ˈəʊp(ə)l/ *noun & adjective*. L16.
[French *opale* or Latin *opalus*, prob. ult. (like late Greek *opallios*) from Sanskrit *upala* stone, precious stone.]
▶ **A** *noun*. **1** An amorphous form of hydrated silica resembling chalcedony, often white or colourless, but varying through blue-green and orange almost to black and valued in those forms showing colourful iridescence. Also, a stone of (an iridescent form of) this, usu. cut *en cabochon*. L16. ▸**b** *fig.* Something variegated or changing like the colours of an opal. L16. ▸**c** The colour or colours of an opal. L19.
2 Semi-translucent white glass; = OPALINE *noun* 2. L19.
3 *BIOLOGY*. The nonsense codon UGA; a mutant fragment of genetic material containing this. Freq. *attrib.* M20.
1 *fire-opal*, *moss-opal*, etc. **common opal** semi-translucent white opal without iridescence.
Comb.: **opal-agate** a form of opal with a banded structure of different colours; **opal dirt** *Austral.* the type of earth in which opal is found; **opal glass** (*a*) = OPALINE *noun* 2; (*b*) glass iridescent like precious opal; **opal ware** (*a*) ware made of opal glass; (*b*) *Opalware*, (proprietary name for) a type of heat-resistant opalescent ware.
▶ **B** *adjective*. **1** Of or resembling an opal; of the colour or colours of opal; opalescent. M17.
2 Of a light bulb: made of translucent glass. E20.
■ **opaˈlesque** *adjective* opalescent M19.

opalescent /əʊpəˈlɛs(ə)nt/ *adjective*. E19.
[from OPAL + -ESCENT.]
Showing varying colours like an opal; having a milky iridescence.
■ **opalescence** *noun* the quality of being opalescent E19.

opaline /ˈəʊp(ə)lʌɪn, -lɪn/ *adjective & noun*. L18.
[from OPAL + -INE[1].]
▶ **A** *adjective*. Resembling opal, esp. in colour or iridescence. L18.
▶ **B** *noun*. **1** A variety of yellow chalcedony which presents an opaline semi-opacity. Now *rare*. M19.
2 A semi-translucent glass, whitened by the addition of various ingredients (also called ***milk-glass***). Also, translucent glass of a colour other than white. L19.
3 An opaline colour, surface, or expanse. L19.

opalise *verb* var. of OPALIZE.

opalite /ˈəʊp(ə)lʌɪt/ *noun*. E20.
[from OPAL + -ITE[1].]
Opal glass made into tiles or bricks.
¶ Formerly a proprietary name.

opalize /ˈəʊp(ə)lʌɪz/ *verb*. Also **-ise**. E19.
[from OPAL + -IZE.]
1 *verb intrans*. Show varying colours like an opal. *rare*. E19.
2 *verb trans*. Make iridescent like an opal; make opaline or opalescent; *MINERALOGY* convert into (a form resembling) opal. Chiefly as ***opalized*** *ppl adjective*. E19.

op-amp /ˈɒpamp/ *noun*. L20.
[Abbreviation.]
ELECTRONICS. = OPERATIONAL ***amplifier***.

opanka /ɒˈpankə/ *noun*. Pl. **-s**, **opanci** /ɒˈpantsi/. E19.
[Croatian *opanak*.]
In the Balkans: a kind of footwear made of soft leather and fastened with straps, similar in style to a moccasin.

opaque /ə(ʊ)ˈpeɪk/ *adjective, noun, & verb*. Also (earlier) †**opake**. LME.
[Latin *opacus* shaded dark; partly through French *opaque*.]
▶ **A** *adjective*. **1** †**a** Lying in shadow; not illuminated, darkened, obscure. LME–L18. ▸**b** Of a body or surface: not reflecting light; not shining or lustrous; dull, dark. Now *rare*. L18.
2 Not transmitting light, not transparent or translucent; impenetrable to sight. M17. ▸**b** *transf.* Not transmitting other forms of radiation, heat, sound, etc. L19.
3 Hard to understand or make out; not clear, obscure. M18. ▸**b** *LINGUISTICS*. Of a rule: that cannot be extrapolated from every occurrence of the phenomenon; to which there are exceptions. Opp. TRANSPARENT 2b. L20.
4 Impervious to reason; dense, obtuse. M19.

> 🕮 **2** J. CONRAD A great body of motionless and opaque clouds. WILFRED BUCKLEY An opaque red glass resembling jasper. M. FRAYN Her spectacles were so dirty as to be almost opaque. **3** J. BARZUN Words and phrases now opaque to a generation neither scholastic nor Latinate. *Times* Hongkong & Shanghai's motives . . are more opaque.

▶ **B** *noun*. **1** An opaque thing; a medium or space through which light cannot pass. M18. ▸**b** A shade for the eyes. E20.
2 *PHOTOGRAPHY*. **a** A substance for producing opaque areas on negatives. E20. ▸**b** A print made on opaque paper. M20.
▶ **C** *verb trans*. Make opaque. L19.
■ **opaquely** *adverb* M18. **opaqueness** *noun* M17.

op. cit. /ɒp ˈsɪt/ *noun & adverbial phr*. L19.
[Abbreviation of Latin *opus citatum* the work quoted, or *opere citato* in the work quoted.]
(In) the work already quoted.

opcode /ˈɒpkəʊd/ *noun*. M20.
[Abbreviation.]
COMPUTING. = OPERATION ***code***.

ope /əʊp/ *pred. adjective & noun*. ME.
[Reduced form of OPEN *adjective, noun*.]
▶ **A** *adjective*. Open. Now *arch. & poet.* ME.
▶ **B** *noun*. †**1** = OPEN *noun* 2, OPENING *noun* 6. Only in E17.
2 = OPEN *noun* 1, OPENING *noun* 2a. M19.

ope /əʊp/ *verb trans. & intrans*. Chiefly *poet*. LME.
[Reduced form of OPEN *verb*.]
= OPEN *verb*.

OPEC /ˈəʊpɛk/ *abbreviation*.
Organization of Petroleum Exporting Countries.

Op-Ed /ɒpˈɛd/ *noun*. *N. Amer.* L20.
[Abbreviation of opposite editorial.]
In full ***Op-Ed page***. A newspaper page opposite the editorial page, devoted to personal comment, feature articles, etc.

opelet /ˈəʊplɪt/ *noun*. M19.
[Irreg. from OPE *adjective* + -LET.]
A sea anemone, *Anemonia sulcata*, so called because the tentacles cannot be retracted.

open /ˈəʊp(ə)n/ *noun*. ME.
[Partly from OPEN *verb*, partly from OPEN *adjective*.]
▶ **I 1** An aperture; = OPENING *noun* 2a. Now *rare*. ME.
2 An opportunity; = OPENING *noun* 6. Now *rare*. E18.
▶ **II** †**3** Open or unconcealed circumstances or condition. LME–M17.
4 ***the open***: ▸**a** Countryside or air without enclosures; ground without buildings, trees, cover, etc.; that part of the sea or river which is well away from land. E17. ▸**b** Public knowledge or notice; general attention. M20.
5 An open or clear space or expanse of ground. L18.
6 *ELECTRICITY*. An accidental break in the conducting path for a current. E20.
7 A competition, tournament, etc., which anyone can enter. E20.

> 🕮 **4a** D. H. LAWRENCE A miner could be seen washing himself in the open on this hot evening. L. MCMURTRY They would have a fine chance of catching them out in the open. **b** V. BROME Jung now came right out into the open and told Freud.

open /ˈəʊp(ə)n/ *adjective & adverb*.
[Old English *open* = Old Frisian *open*, Old Saxon *opan* (Dutch *open*), Old High German *offan* (German *offen*), Old Norse *opin*, from Germanic base having the form of a strong pa. pple from UP *adverb*[1].]
▶ **A** *adjective*. **I** Physical senses.
1 Of a door, gate, etc.: not closed, shut, or locked; set so as to allow access or free passage through. OE.
2 a Of an enclosed space, a house, room, box, etc.: having its gate, door, lid, or some part of its enclosing boundary drawn aside or removed so that there is free access to its interior; not shut up. Also *spec.*, (of the mouth) with lips apart, esp. in surprise or incomprehension, or to receive food. OE. ▸**b** Of a shop, public house, etc.: accessible to customers, esp. at a particular time; available for business. E19. ▸**c** Of a prison etc.: in which the inmates are seldom or never locked up. M20.
3 a Of a space: not enclosed or confined; not walled, fenced, or otherwise shut in; to which there is free access or passage on all or nearly all sides. OE. ▸**b** Of a battle: fought in the open as opp. to in a fortress or stronghold, and so with full forces. M16.
4 Not covered over or covered in; having no roof, lid, or other covering. OE.
5 Not covered so as to be concealed or protected; bare, exposed. OE. ▸**b** *MEDICINE*. (Of a wound) exposed to the air; (of a surgical operation) involving the exposure of an interior part of the body. L18. ▸**c** Of a telephone line or other transmission line: above ground. L19. ▸**d** *MEDICINE*. Of (a case of) tuberculosis: accompanied by the discharge of infectious material. M20.
6 a (Of a passage or space) not occupied by something that prevents access or view; free from objects or obstructions; unobstructed, clear; (of an expanse of ground) free from a covering of trees, buildings, etc.; (of a river, port, etc.) not frozen over, free from ice. LME. ▸**b** Not constipated. M16. ▸**c** *SPORT*. Of a player: unmarked by a member of the opposite team. M20.
7 Not having the marginal parts drawn, folded, or rolled together; expanded, spread out. LME.
8 *NAUTICAL*. Seen with an opening between; clear, detached. Formerly also, in full view. L15.
9 (Of a vocal sound) made or uttered with the mouth open; *PHONETICS* (of a vowel) articulated with the tongue in a relatively low position. L15.
10 a Of a line, fabric, etc.: having apertures or spaces; containing interstices or gaps; perforated; porous. E17. ▸**b** *SPORT*. Of a game or style of play: characterized by action which is spread out over the field. M20.
11 a (Of weather or a season) free from frost or (*NAUTICAL*) fog or mist. E17. ▸**b** Of soil: unbound by frost or heat; loose, permeable. M17.
12 *MUSIC*. Of a (part of) a musical instrument: not stopped or muted in the production of a sound or note. Also, (of a note) sounded without restriction of the instrument, string, etc., producing it. L17.
13 *ELECTRICITY*. Having a break in the conducting path for an electric current. E19.
14 *MEDICINE*. Designating a method of administering anaesthetics in which the patient's respiratory tract is in communication with the air so that exhaled air is not rebreathed. L19.
15 a *MATH*. Of a set of points: not containing any of its boundary points. Of an interval in the real line: not containing either of its end points. E20. ▸**b** *MATH. & LOGIC*. Of a statement or equation: containing at least one free variable or undetermined quantity. M20. ▸**c** *ASTRONOMY*. Of the universe: having a negative or zero radius of curvature; spatially infinite and always expanding. M20.

> 🕮 **1** TENNYSON The voice of Enid . . rang Clear thro' the open casement of the Hall, Singing. M. ROBERTS Helen has left the hall door propped open. J. IRVING He lay with his head by the open tent flap. **2a** OUIDA The earth had yawned open in many places. C. ISHERWOOD Closes the empty drawer in his desk, which has been pulled open a little. A. SILLITOE Smoke drifted from his open mouth. **b** P. FITZGERALD The market was open every week-day. **3a** O. MANNING The army men slept under an open sky. R. DAHL We were out in the open water beyond the chain of islands. **4** R. C. HUTCHINSON Except that his eyes were open he might have been in the deepest sleep. G. V. HIGGINS A small four-passenger open car with a canvas roof. R. WHELAN A soldier standing in the open turret of his tank. **5** A. THWAITE I took the open razor to my throat. **6a** E. A. FREEMAN The besieged must have had the river and the sea open to them during . . the siege. *Punch* His decision to move to the wide open spaces of Montana. **7** A. TROLLOPE Having an open letter in his hand. **11a** D. C. MURRAY The weather being fine and open and dry. **12** *Guitar Player* Notice how the left-hand fingering combines open and stopped notes.

▶ **II** Non-physical senses.
16 Exposed to the mental view, brought to light; evident, clear. OE.
17 a Exposed to general view or knowledge; existing or performed without concealment; public; (of a person) acting publicly or without concealment; (of a style of administration or government) in which the public is kept well-informed and may participate. OE. ▸**b** Of a workplace: in which both union and non-union workers are employed. L19.
18 Not confined or limited to a few; generally accessible or available; that may be used, shared, entered, or competed for without restriction. Also, accessible *to* someone or something specified. OE. ▸**b** Of a person: having won an open championship, scholarship, tournament, etc. L19.
19 Of a person: not given to concealing thoughts or feelings; frank, candid. Also (of a quality, manner, etc.) showing or marked by candour. ME.
20 Free in giving or communicating; generous, bounteous. LME.
21 Without (esp. mental or spiritual) defence or protection; exposed, liable, or subject *to*. L15.
22 Of a thing, course of action, etc.: not closed or shut against access; not denied; accessible or available without hindrance *to*. E16.
23 Of a matter, discussion, etc.: not finally settled or determined; that may be decided according to circumstances or at will; uncertain. Formerly also, (of a period of time) not completed. M16.
24 Of a person: accessible to appeals, emotions, or ideas; ready to receive impressions, respond to sympathy, etc.; amenable or receptive *to*. L17.

> 🕮 **16** W. IRVING They . . laid open to him the whole scheme. **17a** W. GERHARDIE This open display of hostility. G. SANTAYANA Mother and son avoided an open rupture by never referring to their differences. M. FOOT In the interests of open government . . it may now be revealed. *USA Today* There is a need for an open press. **18** J. WILSON Even the house of God Was open to the Plague. V. WOOLF All professions are open to women of your generation. *Times* The match was a curtain-raiser to the Wills Open Tournament. P. ERDMANN Get yourself an open airplane ticket. **19** A. KOESTLER The barber, whose broad open face he liked. M. GORDON She had been too trusting, too open with her stories. **21** W. N. HARBEN I'm open to criticism. R. V. JONES I could hardly believe the extent to which he had left himself open. E. NEWMAN Should I tell my boy . . not to hit his boy when he's open? **22** *Manchester Examiner* There are three, or perhaps four, courses open to us. **23** *Law Times* Lord Justice Cotton . . left the matter open for future consideration. **24** A. FRANCE He . . was open to new suggestions.

Special collocations, phrases, & comb.: **be open with** speak frankly to. ***cut open***: see CUT *verb* 9. **in open court** in a public court of justice, before the judge and the public. ***keep an eye open***, ***keep one's eye(s) open***: see EYE *noun*. ***keep one's options open***: see OPTION *noun* 1. ***keep open house***: see *open house* s.v. HOUSE *noun*[1]. **lay open to** make liable to expose to. **open access** ease of availability; availability to all; *spec.* a system whereby users of a library have direct access to bookshelves. **open-access** *adjective* easily available; available to all. **open admission** *US* = *open enrolment* below. **open air** (*the*) free or unenclosed space outdoors; the unconfined atmosphere. **open-air** *adjective* existing, taking place in, or characteristic of the open air. **open-and-shut** *adjective* & *noun* (*a*) *adjective* simple, straightforward; in which there is no doubt; also, (of weather) alternately sunny and cloudy; (*b*) *noun* a simple or straightforward operation, case, etc.; also, alternately sunny and cloudy conditions. **open-armed** *adjective* cordial, warm, receptive. **open-arse** (now *dial.*) [in ref. to the wide gap between the persistent calyx lobes] (the fruit of) the medlar, *Mespilus germanica*. **open bar** a bar at a special function at which the drinks have been paid for by the host or are prepaid through the admission fee. **open-bill (stork)** either of two storks of the genus *Anastomus* found in Africa and Asia, having bills which when shut are in contact only at the ends. **open bite** DENTISTRY lack of occlusion of the front teeth when the jaw is closed normally. **open book** *fig.* a person who or thing which can be readily understood; a person who conceals nothing. **open-breasted** *adjective* (*a*) with the breast exposed; (*b*) not secretive, frank. ***Open Brethren***: see BROTHER *noun*. **opencast** *noun* & *adjective* (MINING) (*a*) *noun* an open working; also, a method of mining coal, ore, etc., by removing surface layers and working from above, rather than from shafts; (*b*) *adjective* designating or pertaining to this method of mining. **open chain** CHEMISTRY an open-ended chain of atoms with no closed rings. **open cheque** (*a*) an uncrossed cheque; (*b*) a cheque for an unstated amount. **open circuit** a circuit, esp. an electric circuit, that is incomplete. **open-circuited** *adjective* consisting of or containing an open circuit. **open city** an undefended city; *spec.* one declared as such and exempt from enemy bombardment. **open class** a class of which the numbers cannot be specified. **open classroom**: in which instruction is informal, individual, and free-ranging. **open cluster** ASTRONOMY an open or loose grouping of stars. **open college** an adult-education college having few if any restrictions on admission, and usu. teaching mainly by correspondence and broadcasting. ***open Communion***: see COMMUNION. **open community** ECOLOGY an area in which plants do not completely cover the ground. **open compound** a compound word printed or written with a space between the component elements. **open cover** marine insurance that covers all shipments made by a person or firm without advance specification of the details of each shipment. **open cycle** a cycle of operations in which a working fluid, coolant, etc., is used only once. **open date** (*a*) *US* SPORT a future available date for which no fixture has yet been arranged; (*b*) a future unspecified date, *esp.* one left undetermined when a travel ticket is bought; (*c*) a date on which perishable goods were prepacked, or by which they should be sold. **open dating** the marking of packaged goods with an open date for consumption, sale, etc. **open day** a day when a school, university, or other institution normally closed to the public is made accessible to visitors. **open door** a free or available way in; free admission or access; *spec.* free admission to a country of foreign imports and immigrants. **open-door** *adjective* done publicly or with doors open; (of a policy, system, etc.) unrestricted, advocating or providing freedom of access etc.; (of a prison etc.) allowing freedom of access or movement where locking in is more usual. **open-end**, **open-ended** *adjectives* having an open end; *fig.* having no predetermined limit, boundary, or outcome; *spec.* (of a question or test) not limiting the respondent in the range of his or her answer. **open-endedness** the quality of being open-ended. **open enrolment** *US* the unrestricted enrolment of students at schools, colleges, etc., of their choice. **open-eyed** *adjective* having or done with the eyes open; aware, perceptive. **open-faced** *adjective* (*a*) having the face uncovered; (*b*) having a frank or ingenuous face; (*c*) (of a sandwich, pie, etc.) without an upper layer of bread or pastry. **open field** an unenclosed field; arable land without physical division by hedges, ditches, etc. **open fire**, **open fireplace**: that is not enclosed in a stove etc. **open fracture** MEDICINE: in which the broken bone protrudes through the skin. **open go** *Austral. colloq.* an unimpeded opportunity; a fair chance. **open goal** (FOOTBALL & HOCKEY etc.) an undefended goal(-mouth); a goal scored into this. **open-handed** *adjective* generous. **open-handedly** *adverb* generously. **open-handedness** generosity. **open harmony** MUSIC: in which the chords are separated by wide intervals. **open-heart** *adjective* pertaining to or designating surgery in which the heart has been temporarily by-passed and opened. **open-hearted** *adjective* unreserved, frank; kindly, generous. **open-heartedness** open-hearted quality. **open-hearth furnace** a shallow reverberatory furnace for making steel. **open-hearth process** the making of steel in an open-hearth furnace. ***open house***: see HOUSE *noun*[1]. **open housing** *US* property that can be rented or bought without restriction on racial or ethnic grounds. **open interest** COMMERCE the number of contracts or commitments outstanding in financial trading at any one time. ***open interval***: see INTERVAL *noun*. **open juncture** LINGUISTICS the type of juncture found at word boundaries or marked syllable division in the word. **open learning**: based on independent study or initiative rather than formal classroom instruction. **open letter** a letter, esp. of protest, addressed to a particular person or persons but made public, esp. in a newspaper etc. **open line** a telephone line on which conversations can be overheard or intercepted by others. **open-line** *adjective* designating a radio or television programme in which the public can participate by telephone. **open loop** a control loop without feedback, each operation or activity being affected only by those earlier in the sequence. **open market** an unrestricted market with free competition both of buyers and sellers. **open marriage** a marriage in which partners agree that each may have sexual relations with other people. **open-mic**, **open-mike** *adjective* denoting a session in a club where anyone who chooses is welcome to sing, perform stand-up comedy, etc. **open mind** a mind accessible to new arguments or ideas; a mind open to influence or persuasion. **open-minded** *adjective* having an open mind. **open-mindedly** *adverb* in an open-minded manner. **open-mindedness** the quality of being open-minded. **open-mouthed** *adjective* with the mouth open, esp. in surprise or incomprehension. **open-neck** a collar of a kind that leaves the neck unrestricted; an unbuttoned collar. **open-necked** *adjective* (of a shirt) worn with the collar unbuttoned, without a tie. ***open newel***: see NEWEL *noun* 1b. **open occupancy** *US* occupancy of housing available to people of any racial or ethnic group. **open outcry** COMMERCE a system of financial trading in which dealers shout their bids and contracts aloud. **open-pit** *adjective* (chiefly *N. Amer.*) = *opencast* (b) above. **open-plan** *adjective* (of a house, office, etc.) having few or no internal walls or partitions. **open question** a matter on which differences of opinion are legitimate, a matter not yet decided. **open range** *N. Amer.* a tract of land without fences etc. **open-range** *adjective* = ***free-range*** *adjective* s.v. FREE *adjective*, *noun*, & *adverb*. **open-reel** *adjective* using tape reels which are accessible and require individual threading, as opp. to being contained in cassettes etc. **open road** (*a*) *US* a road that is not private; (*b*) a country road; a main road outside an urban area; a road along which one can travel without care or hindrance. **open sandal** an open-toed sandal. **open sandwich** a sandwich without a top slice of bread. **open score** MUSIC: in which each voice is written on a separate staff. **open season** the season when hunting or fishing is allowed; *transf.* a time when something is unrestricted. ***open secret***: see SECRET *noun*. **open shelf** a shelf that is not shut in by doors etc.; a bookshelf in a library from which readers can take books themselves. **open shop** a system whereby employees in a company etc. do not have to join a union; a company etc. which follows this system. **open-skies**, **open-sky** *adjectives* designating or pertaining to a system whereby aircraft of any nation may fly over a particular territory or whereby two or more nations permit air surveillance of one another. ***open slather***: see SLATHER *noun*. **open society**: characterized by a flexible structure, freedom of belief, wide dissemination of information, and much contact with other peoples. **open space** (*a*) an area without buildings in a city or town; a small public park etc.; (*b*) in *pl.*, tracts of open country (freq. in ***wide open spaces***). **open stage** a stage in the same area as the audience; *esp.* one surrounded on three sides by the audience. **open-stock** *N. Amer.* goods, esp. sets of crockery, that are always kept in stock by a shop etc. **open subroutine** COMPUTING a routine that is written, in full, directly into a program wherever it occurs. **open syllable**: ending in a vowel. **open system** (*a*) a material system in which mass or energy can be lost or gained from the environment; an incomplete or alterable system of ideas, things, etc.; (*b*) COMPUTING a system in which the components and protocols conform to standards independent of a particular supplier. **open texture** PHILOSOPHY the inability of certain concepts etc. to be fully or precisely defined. **open-toe**, **open-toed** *adjectives* designating a shoe or sandal in which the upper does not cover the toes. **open-top** *adjective* & *noun* (designating) a vehicle, trailer, etc. without a (fixed) top. **open-topped** *adjective* not having a (fixed) top. **open town** (*a*) *US* a town characterized by a lack of restrictions on places for drinking, gambling, etc.; (*b*) = ***open city*** above. **open-tread** *adjective* (of a staircase) having no risers. **open university** a university having few if any restrictions on admission, *spec.* (with cap. initials) a university in the UK which accepts people without qualifications and teaches mainly by correspondence and broadcasting. ***open verdict***: see VERDICT *noun*. **open ward** a hospital ward allowing relative freedom of movement to patients. **open water** *spec.* (chiefly *Canad.*) the melting of ice on rivers and lakes in spring; the time when this happens; a stretch of water with little or no ice. **open window unit** ACOUSTICS = SABIN. **open woods** *N. Amer.* a patch of woodland in which there is no undergrowth. **openwork** metalwork, needlework (as lace or embroidery), etc., having ornamental gaps or openings. **openworked** *adjective* made in openwork. ***pound open***: see POUND *noun*[2] 1a. ***seize the open file***: see FILE *noun*[2]. ***under the open sky***: see SKY *noun*. ***wide open***: see WIDE *adverb*. ***with one's eyes open***: see EYE *noun*. ***with open arms***: see ARM *noun*[1]. †**with open face** with uncovered face; confidently, brazenly. **with open mouth**: esp. in surprise or incomprehension.

▶ **B** *adverb*. = OPENLY. ME.

open /ˈəʊp(ə)n/ *verb*.

[Old English *openian* = Old Saxon *oparion* (Dutch *openen*), Old High German *offanōn* (German *öffnen*), from Germanic base of OPEN *adjective*.]

▶ **I** *verb trans.* **1** Move or turn (a door, gate, etc.) away from a closed or obstructing position, esp. so as to allow passage; part or separate (the lips, eyelids, etc.). OE.

2 Spread apart or out; expand, unfold, unroll, extend. OE.

3 Uncover, disclose to sight, display; *spec.* uncover (an eye) by separating the eyelids. OE.

4 Make known to the mental or spiritual view; reveal, disclose, or divulge (now only one's mind, feelings, feeling, etc.). OE.

5 Make (a building, box, other enclosing object, or enclosed space) open by moving or turning a door, gate, lid, or some other part of the enclosing boundaries, or by clearing away something that obstructs passage; break open, undo; provide free access to or egress from; *fig.* make mentally or emotionally receptive (*to*). ME. ▸**b** *spec.* Give access to for a particular purpose; make (esp. a shop, public house, etc.) accessible to a person, the public (*for* some purpose). M16. ▸**c** Ceremonially declare (a building, park, fête, shop, etc.) to be completed and available for use or open for business for the first time. M19.

6 a Make an opening in; cut or break into; make a hole or incision in. Also, break up (ground) by ploughing, digging, etc. ME. ▸**b** Make or cause (an opening or open space of some kind) by cutting, breaking in, or breaking up. ME. ▸**c** Cut open (the leaves of a book); = CUT *verb* 9. E19. ▸**d** Polish part of (a rough gem) so as to view the interior. Also foll. by *up*. E20.

7 Make less or no longer tight, dense, stiff, etc. Formerly also, untie, unfasten, break apart (a seal). ME. ▸†**b** Dissolve, decompose. L17–M19.

8 Explain the sense of; expound, interpret. Now *rare* or *obsolete*. ME.

9 Make more intelligent, enlightened, or sympathetic; expand, enlighten (the mind or heart). ME.

10 a Clear of obstruction or hindrance; make (a road etc.) free for passage. LME. ▸**b** Clear a bodily passage of (esp. digestive) obstructions; cause evacuation of (the bowels); clear (obstructions) from a bodily passage. L16. ▸**c** ELECTRICITY. Break or interrupt (an electric circuit); put (a switch or circuit-breaker) into a condition in which it interrupts an electric circuit. M19.

11 Make accessible or available for settlement, use, trade, communication, etc. Cf. ***open up*** (a) below. LME.

12 a Begin, start, commence; set in action, initiate, (proceedings, operations, or business); take the action required, as making an initial deposit, to establish (a bank account etc.). LME. ▸**b** BRIDGE. Make the first statement in (the bidding); offer as a particular bid. M20.

13 LAW. State (a case, the substance of the pleadings, etc.) to a court, before calling witnesses or (esp.) before any statement from the other side. Also, state (an argument, assertion, etc.) in opening a case. E17.

14 NAUTICAL. Come in sight of by rounding or passing some intervening object. M18.

15 Undo or set aside (a judgement, settlement, sale, etc.) so as to allow for further action, discussion, or negotiation. L18.

> 🕮 **1** J. BRAINE He seemed to be able to speak and scarcely open his lips. I. MURDOCH Danby opened a door .. and marched in. R. P. JHABVALA She had not allowed the servants to .. open the shutters. **2** T. DAY He .. had a library, although he never opened a book. H. ROTH She opened her palms in a gesture of emphasis. E. WELTY Every spring .. it opened its first translucent flowers. **3** M. AMIS I opened an eye to see the .. self-righteous figure. **5** LYTTON She saw Evelyn opening the monthly parcel from London. M. E. BRADDON Daphne .. opened her colour-box. T. O'BRIEN He gazed at the girl .. opening himself to whatever she might answer. J. FOWLES My father opened champagne. **6b** SHELLEY Alpheus bold .. With his trident .. opened a chasm In the rocks. **9** G. BERKELEY His Understanding wants to be opened and enlarged. **12a** J. REED Cossack artillery opened fire on the barracks. D. CAUTE Opening the debate, Harry said that the demand went too far. *Which?* Open the new account and transfer all standing orders.

▶ **II** *verb intrans.* **16** Become physically open; become no longer shut or closed; be open for business etc.; come apart so as to reveal a space, display the interior, or allow access or free passage through. OE. ▸**b** ELECTRICITY. Of a circuit or device: suffer a break in its conducting path. M19.

17 a Expand, extend, spread out or apart. Also, (of a collective body) move apart so as to present gaps. Also foll. by *out*. LME. ▸**b** *fig.* Increase in intellect or sympathy. E18.

18 Of a hound: begin to bay or cry out in pursuit of a scent. LME.

19 Declare one's knowledge, thoughts, or feelings; speak out; speak freely; explain. Also foll. by *out*. M16.

20 Of a door, room, etc.: give access, have or provide an opening, *into*, *on to*, *to*, etc. E17.

21 a Begin to appear; become increasingly visible, esp. on nearer approach or change of position. E18. ▸**b** NAUTICAL. Become distinct or separate to the view. M18.

22 Begin; start or commence operations; *spec.* (*a*) begin speaking, writing, etc.; (*b*) open fire; (*c*) THEATRICAL make a début, be performed for the first time, begin a season or tour; (*d*) CARDS make the first bid or bet, lead on a hand. E18.

> 🕮 **16** W. CATHER The door of the front office opened. J. STEINBECK Kino's eyes opened, and he looked .. at the lightening square. G. GREENE The wound opened again. *Hamilton (Ontario) Spectator* Do you think all stores should .. open on Sunday? *fig.*: P. ABRAHAMS The skies opened and the rain fell. **17a** E. K. KANE The little flag .. opened once more to the breeze. T. O'BRIEN Flares opened high over blue-tile domes. **20** *Law Times* An outer door opening on to a .. stairway. **22** L. DURRELL The first chapter of guns opens from the south. *Times Lit. Suppl.* The story opens with lobstering in the Orkneys. M. HAMBURGER The year opens with frozen pipes. JOHN BROOKE In the spring of 1761 peace negotiations opened between Great Britain and France. S. HASTINGS The play .. opened at the Lyric in London.

Phrases: **not open one's mouth** say nothing, remain silent. ***open a gate for***, ***open a gate to***: see GATE *noun*[1]. ***open a person's eyes***: see EYE *noun*. ***open a door for***, ***open a door to***: see DOOR *noun*. ***open one's budget***: see BUDGET *noun* 1. ***open one's ears***: see EAR *noun*[1]. ***open one's heart (to)***: see HEART *noun*. ***open one's mind (to)***: see MIND *noun*[1]. ***open one's shop window***: see SHOP *noun*. ***open the ball***: see BALL *noun*[2] 1. ***open the shoulders***: see SHOULDER *noun*. ***the SCENE opens***.

With adverbs in specialized senses: **open out** *verb phr. trans.* (*a*) make visible or accessible by removing something which covers or conceals; (*b*) develop, bring out; (*c*) disclose, reveal, tell; (*d*) = **open up** (e) below; (see also senses 17a, 20 above). **open up** (*a*) *verb phr. trans.* make accessible or available to view or for use, passage, etc., esp. by the removal of obstructions; unlock (premises); lay open or initiate (a new line of enquiry); bring to notice, reveal; (*b*) *verb phr. intrans.* become accessible or available for passage, view, enterprise, etc., esp. by the removal of obstructions; (*c*) *verb phr. trans. & intrans.* (*Austral. & NZ*) shear wool from (some part, esp. the neck, of a sheep); (*d*) *verb phr. intrans.* talk or speak openly; (*e*) *verb phr. trans. & intrans.* increase the speed of (an engine) by widening the throttle (cf. **open out** (d) above); (*f*) *verb phr. intrans.* start shooting (*at, on*).

■ **openable** *adjective* able to be opened L18.

opener /ˈəʊp(ə)nə/ *noun.* LME.
[from OPEN *verb* + -ER¹.]
1 A person who opens something; *spec.* (*a*) CARDS a player who opens betting or bidding; (*b*) CRICKET either of the two batsmen who open an innings. LME.
2 A laxative. Now *US slang.* E17.
3 A machine or device which opens something; *spec.* (*a*) a device for opening tins, bottles, etc.; (*b*) a machine for loosening matted cotton fibres and removing impurities. M19.
4 CARDS. In *pl.* Cards which entitle the holder to open the betting. E20.
5 The first of a series of items, events, etc.; the first item on a programme; an opening remark etc. *colloq.* M20.

📖 **1** A. DESAI 'Shall I let him in?' called the opener of the door. **5** A. C. H. SMITH I'll tell you what's going to win the opener. G. PALEY That was the opener After that Eddie said other things. **for openers** to start with.

opening /ˈəʊp(ə)nɪŋ/ *noun.* ME.
[from OPEN *verb* + -ING¹.]
▸ **I 1** The action of OPEN *verb.* Also foll. by *out, up.* ME. ▸**b** The process of loosening matted fibres with an opener. L19.
▸ **II 2 a** A vacant space between portions of solid matter; a gap, a passage; an aperture. ME. ▸**b** A bay, a gulf. Now *rare.* E18. ▸**c** A part of a book etc. consisting of two facing pages. E20.
3 A beginning; the commencement; the part, act, words, etc., with which something opens; *spec.* (LAW) a preliminary statement of a case made to a court before witnesses are called. M17. ▸**b** CHESS. A recognized sequence of moves at the beginning of a game. M18. ▸**c** An introductory or burlesque part of a traditional pantomime preceding the harlequinade. E19. ▸**d** THEATRICAL. The first performance of a play etc.; a première. Chiefly *N. Amer.* M19. ▸**e** The start of an art exhibition, fashion show, etc. E20.
4 In the Society of Friends: a divine revelation; an intuitive insight. L17.
5 A tract of ground over which trees are sparsely scattered in comparison with adjoining areas. *US.* E18.
6 An opportunity; a favourable situation; a chance of advantage, success, or gratification. L18.

📖 **2a** J. K. JEROME Where there occurred an opening among the trees you could . . see the sky. S. COOPER Cally hauled herself out through the opening. **3** I. HAY I attempted one or two conversational openings. V. BROME The opening of the Congress. **e** D. AMES Paris for the autumn dress openings. **6** U. LE GUIN There never was an opening in his line of work.

Comb.: **opening-time** the time at which a public house may legally open for custom.

opening /ˈəʊp(ə)nɪŋ/ *adjective.* LME.
[from OPEN *verb* + -ING².]
1 a That opens something; *spec.* that opens the bowels; laxative. LME. ▸**b** Initial; introductory; first; *spec.* in CRICKET, of or designating the batsmen who open the innings, or the bowlers who open the attack. M19.
2 That opens; expanding, beginning. M17.

📖 **1b** J. WAIN Any rehearsal greeting or opening speech, he forgot. **opening night** the first night of a theatrical play, entertainment, etc. **2** SCOTT FITZGERALD A wedge of light came out of the opening door.

openly /ˈəʊp(ə)nli/ *adverb.* OE.
[from OPEN *adjective* + -LY².]
1 In an open manner; publicly. OE.
†**2** Manifestly; clearly, plainly. OE–L17.
3 Without concealment of thought or feeling; frankly, unreservedly. ME.

📖 **1** J. UGLOW The woman . . defied convention by living openly with a married man. **3** N. CHOMSKY They began speaking more openly to people whom they . . could trust.

openness /ˈəʊp(ə)nnɪs/ *noun.* M16.
[from OPEN *adjective* + -NESS.]
1 The quality or condition of being open. M16.
2 *spec.* Absence of dissimulation, secrecy, or reserve; frankness, candour, sincerity. E17.

Open Sesame /ˌəʊp(ə)n ˈsɛsəmi/ *noun phr.* E19.
[The magic words by which, in the tale of Ali Baba and the Forty Thieves in the *Arabian Nights' Entertainments*, the door of the robbers' cave was made to open. Cf. SESAME.]
A (marvellous or irresistible) means of securing access to what would usu. be inaccessible.

opepe /əʊˈpiːpi/ *noun.* L19.
[Yoruba.]
A W. African tree, *Nauclea diderichii*, of the madder family; the hard yellowish-brown wood of this tree.

opera /ˈɒp(ə)rə/ *noun*¹. M17.
[Italian (whence also French *opéra*) from Latin = labour, work produced, fem. noun from *oper-, opus* work. See also OPRY.]
1 A dramatic musical work in one or more acts, in which singing forms an essential part, chiefly consisting of recitatives, arias, and choruses, with orchestral accompaniment; a performance of such a work; a libretto or musical score for such a work. M17.
2 The place where an opera is performed; an opera-house. M17.
3 Such works as a genre. Also ***the opera.*** M18.
Phrases: ***comic opera***: see COMIC *adjective.* ***grand opera***: see GRAND *adjective*¹. ***horse opera***: see HORSE *noun.* PEKING ***opera.*** ***Savoy opera***: see SAVOY 3. ***soap opera***: see SOAP *noun*¹ 3. ***space opera***: see SPACE *noun.*
Comb.: **opera cloak** a cloak of rich material worn over evening clothes, esp. by women; **opera glass(es)** small binoculars for use at the opera, theatre, etc.; **opera hat** a man's tall collapsible hat; **opera-house** a theatre for the performance of operas; ***opera recital***: see RECITAL 3b; **opera window** *N. Amer.* a small, typically triangular window at the side of a motor car, usually behind a rear side window.

opera *noun*² *pl.* see OPUS *noun.*

operable /ˈɒp(ə)rəb(ə)l/ *adjective.* M17.
[Late Latin *operabilis*, from *operari*: see OPERATE *verb*, -ABLE. In sense 2 from OPERATE *verb.*]
1 Able to be operated. M17.
2 MEDICINE. Able to be operated on; suitable for treatment by a surgical operation. E20.

📖 **1** H. S. HARRISON How could this principle be . . reduced to an operable law?

■ **operaˈbility** *noun* E20.

opéra bouffe /ɔpera buf, ˌɒp(ə)rə ˈbuːf/ *noun phr.* Pl. ***opéras bouffe(s)*** (pronounced same). L19.
[French formed as next.]
= OPERA BUFFA; (an example of) French comic opera.

opera buffa /ˌɒp(ə)rə ˈbuːfə, *foreign* ˈɔːpera ˈbuffa/ *noun phr.* Pl. **operas buffa**, ***opere buffe*** /ˈɔːpere ˈbuffe/. E19.
[Italian = comic opera.]
(Italian) comic opera, with dialogue in recitative and characters drawn from everyday life; an example of this.

opéra comique /ɔpera kɔmik, ˌɒp(ə)rə kɒˈmiːk/ *noun phr.* Pl. ***opéras comiques*** (pronounced same). M18.
[French = comic opera.]
A type of opera (orig. humorous, later romantic) characterized by spoken dialogue; an example of this.

operance /ˈɒp(ə)r(ə)ns/ *noun. rare.* E17.
[from OPERANT: see -ANCE.]
The quality or fact of being operant; operation.
■ Also **operancy** *noun* E19.

operand /ˈɒpərand/ *noun.* L19.
[Latin *operandum* neut. gerundive of *operari*: see OPERATE, -AND.]
MATH. & LOGIC. A quantity on which a mathematical or logical operation is (to be) performed.

operant /ˈɒp(ə)r(ə)nt/ *adjective & noun.* LME.
[Latin *operant-* pres. ppl stem of *operari*: see OPERATE, -ANT¹.]
▸ **A** *adjective.* **1** That operates or produces effects, operative. Formerly also, powerful in effect. LME.
2 PSYCHOLOGY. Involving the modification of behaviour by the reinforcing or inhibiting effect of its own consequences. M20.

📖 **1** SHAKES. *Timon* Sauce his palate With thy most operant poison. *English World-Wide* The respondents . . had difficulty with those items in which code-shifting was operant.

▸ **B** *noun.* **1** A person who or thing which operates or exerts force or influence. E18.
2 PSYCHOLOGY. An item of behaviour held not to be a response to a prior stimulus but something initially spontaneous, operating on or affecting the environment so as to produce consequences which may reinforce or inhibit recurrence of that behaviour. M20.

opéras bouffe(s) *noun phrs.* pls. of OPÉRA BOUFFE.

operas buffa *noun phr. pl.* see OPERA BUFFA.

opéras comiques *noun phr.* pl. of OPÉRA COMIQUE.

opera seria /ɒp(ə)rə ˈsɪərɪə, *foreign* ˌɔːpera ˈsɛːrja/ *noun phr.* Pl. **operas seria**, ***opere serie*** /ˌɔːpere ˈsɛːrje/. L19.
[Italian = serious opera.]
A type of opera prevalent in the 18th cent., with elaborate arias and usu. based on mythological themes; an example of this. Cf. TRAGÉDIE LYRIQUE.

operate /ˈɒpəreɪt/ *verb.* E17.
[Latin *operat-* pa. ppl stem of *operari* to work, expend labour on, from *oper-, opus* work: see -ATE³.]
▸ **I** *verb intrans.* **1** Exercise force or influence; produce an effect. Usu. foll. by (*up*)*on.* E17. ▸**b** Esp. of a drug, medicine, etc.: produce the intended effect; act. E18.
2 a Conduct a military or naval action; carry on commercial, professional, etc., activities; *spec.* deal in stocks or shares. E17. ▸**b** Be in action; be functioning. M20.
3 Perform an operation or series of operations; *spec.* perform a surgical operation. (Foll. by (*up*)*on.*) L17.

📖 **1** T. HARDY Rivalry usually operates as a stimulant to esteem. **2a** P. KAVANAGH He was . . on terms of good will . . in the districts through which he operated. G. GREENE Before the last war MI6 had never operated on British territory. **b** J. W. KRUTCH Not enough manufactured goods were being consumed . . to keep the factories operating at full capacity. ANTHONY SMITH The cat (whose brain . . operates in a similar fashion in this regard to that of humans). L. MCMURTRY His instincts needed privacy in which to operate. **3** *Language* A successful asymmetrical derivation rule must operate on a P-marker. A. CARTER He was successfully operated upon at St Bartholomew's Hospital. V. BRAMWELL Surgeons believe in telling a patient when the lump is cancerous before operating further.

▸ **II** *verb trans.* **4** Effect by action or the exertion of force or influence; bring about. M17.
5 Cause or direct the functioning of; control the working of (a machine etc.). M19.
6 Manage, direct the operation of (a business, enterprise, etc.). L19.
7 Operate on surgically. E20.

📖 **4** *Nature* Energy in the form of light operates changes in the surface of bodies. **5** K. AMIS He operated the till without looking at where his fingers were going. *Which Micro?* Allowing . . both a disk drive and an RS 232 serial module . . to be operated at the same time. *Money & Family Wealth* The child can operate the account from age seven. **6** F. A. WALKER State railways and private companies' lines were operated side by side.

■ **operatable** *adjective* (*rare*) able to be operated on surgically, = OPERABLE 2 L19.

operatic /ɒpəˈratɪk/ *adjective & noun.* M18.
[Irreg. from OPERA *noun*¹ after *dramatic* etc.]
▸ **A** *adjective.* Pertaining to or of the nature of opera; characteristic of opera; extravagantly theatrical, histrionic. M18.

📖 W. MCILVANNEY They were both laughing. She tapered her's off into an operatic groan.

▸ **B** *noun.* In *pl.* (treated as *sing.*). The production or performance of operas. E20.
■ †**operatical** *adjective* = OPERATIC M18–E19. **operatically** *adverb* E19.

operating /ˈɒpəreɪtɪŋ/ *verbal noun.* M17.
[from OPERATE *verb* + -ING¹.]
The action of OPERATE *verb*; an instance of this.
Comb.: **operating profit** ACCOUNTANCY gross profit before deduction of expenses; **operating room** (chiefly *N. Amer.*) a room in a hospital where operations are performed, an operating theatre; **operating system** COMPUTING a set of programs for organizing the resources and activities of a computer; **operating-table**: on which the patient is placed during an operation; ***operating theatre***: see THEATRE *noun* 5b.

operation /ɒpəˈreɪʃ(ə)n/ *noun.* LME.
[Old & mod. French *opération* from Latin *operatio(n-)*, formed as OPERATE: see -ATION.]
†**1** An action, (a) deed. LME–M16.
2 Exertion of force or influence; working, activity; an instance of this. Also, the way in which a thing works. LME. ▸**b** The condition of functioning or being active. Chiefly in ***in operation, come into operation, put into operation.*** E19.
3 a Power to operate or produce effects; efficacy, force. Now *rare.* LME. ▸**b** Effect produced, influence. Now *rare* or *obsolete.* E17.
4 a An act of a practical or technical nature, *esp.* one forming a step in a process. LME. ▸**b** A business transaction, esp. of a speculative kind. Also, a business concern or enterprise. Orig. *US.* M19.
†**5** Something made; a product. LME–L18.
6 An active process; a discharge of a function. L16. ▸**b** PSYCHOLOGY. Esp. in Piaget's theory of children's development, a mental activity whereby the effect of actions or ideas is understood or predicted. M20.
7 A surgical procedure performed on a patient, esp. with the object of removing or repairing a diseased or damaged part. L16.
8 MATH. & LOGIC etc. A process in which a number, quantity, expression, etc. is altered or manipulated according to set formal rules, as those of addition, multiplication, differentiation, negation, etc. E18.
9 A strategic movement of troops, ships, etc., for military action; *gen.* a piece of planned and coordinated activity involving a number of people. (Freq. preceding a code-name.) M18.

10 The action of operating a machine, business, etc. L19.

🕮 **2** C. TOURNEUR The Starres whose operations make The fortunes and destinies of men. R. STUART The operation of the condenser pump is very simple. B. SPOCK Psychological concepts . . can seriously interfere with the operation of the parents' good sense. **b** G. LORD He'd put his plan into operation. **3b** MONMOUTH Many remedies had been applyed . . yet none . . procured the desired operation. **4a** J. S. FOSTER An orderly sequence of operations ensures the necessary continuity of work. A. FRANCE The establishment of a trusting relationship is a delicate operation. **b** *Marketing Week* The . . new Sharedrug operation and Northern-based . . Tip Top have both gone public. **6** T. REID By the operations of the mind we understand every mode of thinking. **b concrete operations** *PSYCHOLOGY* in Piaget's theory, those mental processes characteristic of the third stage of cognitive development, in which a child develops the ability to think logically but only about concrete problems. **formal operations** *PSYCHOLOGY* in Piaget's theory, those mental processes characteristic of the fourth and final stage of cognitive development, in which an individual is capable of abstract thought. **7** P. CUTTING She . . was having a series of operations on her legs. ***Caesarean operation***, ***Taliacotian operation***, etc. ***illegal operation***: see ILLEGAL *adjective*. **8** *LOGICAL* ***operation***. **9** *Listener* General Westmoreland launched 'Operation Final Solution' to sweep the enemy from the surroundings of Saigon. F. FITZGERALD The U. S. forces launched over six search-and-destroy operations. *Hamilton (Ontario) Spectator* Money seized in drug operations is turned over to the Federal government. ***combined operation***: see COMBINED 2. ***psychological operations***: see PSYCHOLOGICAL *adjective*.

Comb.: **operation code** *COMPUTING* the part of a machine code instruction that defines the operation to be performed; **operations research** *US* = *OPERATIONAL* ***research***; **operations room**: from which military or police etc. operations are directed.

operational /ɒpəˈreɪʃ(ə)n(ə)l/ *adjective.* E20.
[from OPERATION + -AL[1].]
1 Of or pertaining to operations; used in the operation of something; *spec.* engaged in or connected with active (military) operations (as opp. to being under training, in reserve, etc.). E20. ▸**b** In a condition of readiness to perform some intended (esp. military) function; able and ready to function. M20.
2 *MATH.* Of, pertaining to, or employing operators. E20.
3 Of, pertaining to, or in accordance with operationalism. E20.

🕮 **1** L. DEIGHTON Stinnes was my operational name and I have retained it. **b** I. MURDOCH A huge primitive . . machine, obsolete yet still operational.

Special collocations: **operational amplifier** an amplifier with high gain and high input impedance (usu. with external feedback), used esp. in circuits for performing mathematical operations on an input voltage. **operational research** a method of mathematically-based analysis for providing a quantitative basis for management decisions (orig. for military planning).
▪ **operatioˈnality** *noun* L20. **operationally** *adverb* in terms of, or as regards, operation(s), esp. those required to define a concept or term (cf. OPERATIONALISM) E20.

operationalise *verb* var. of OPERATIONALIZE.

operationalism /ɒpəˈreɪʃ(ə)n(ə)lɪz(ə)m/ *noun.* M20.
[from OPERATIONAL + -ISM.]
PHILOSOPHY. A form of positivism which defines scientific concepts in terms of the operations used to determine or prove them.
▪ **operationalist** *noun & adjective* (**a**) *noun* an adherent of operationalism; (**b**) *adjective* of or pertaining to operationalists or operationalism: M20.

operationalize /ɒpəˈreɪʃ(ə)n(ə)lʌɪz/ *verb trans.* Also **-ise**. M20.
[from OPERATIONAL + -IZE.]
1 Express in operational terms. M20.
2 Put into effect, realize. L20.
▪ **operationaˈlizable** *adjective* L20. **operationaliˈzation** *noun* M20.

operationism /ɒpəˈreɪʃ(ə)nɪz(ə)m/ *noun.* M20.
[from OPERATION + -ISM.]
PHILOSOPHY. = OPERATIONALISM.
▪ **operationist** *adjective & noun* = OPERATIONALIST M20.

operatise *verb* var. of OPERATIZE.

operative /ˈɒp(ə)rətɪv/ *adjective & noun.* LME.
[Late Latin *operativus*, formed as OPERATE: see -IVE.]
▶ **A** *adjective.* **1** Being in operation or force; exerting force or influence. Also, designating the part of a legal document which expresses the intention to effect the transaction concerned. LME.
2 Effective, efficacious. L16. ▸**b** Significant, important; (of a word) essential to the meaning of the whole, having the principal relevance. E20.
3 Concerned with manual or mechanical work; practical. E17.
4 Pertaining to or based on surgical operations. L18.
5 Of a person: actively engaged in work or production, esp. as a skilled worker or artisan. E19.

🕮 **1** P. GROSSKURTH How infantile phantasies . . remained operative in the adult. **2** JAS. MILL Fraud was an operative instrument in the hands of this aspiring general. **b** N. MARSH 'It was nice getting your occasional letters,' Patrick said . . . 'Operative word "occasional".'

▶ **B** *noun.* †**1** An operative mood or condition. Only in E17.
†**2** A thing, esp. a drug, which operates. L17–E18.
3 A worker, *esp.* a skilled one; *spec.* a factory worker, an artisan. E19.
4 An agent employed by a detective agency or secret-service; a private investigator. Cf. OP *noun*[3]. Orig. & chiefly *US*. E20.

🕮 **3** J. E. C. BODLEY Lawyers and other unproductive operatives. J. S. FOSTER Assembly on site by operatives with specialized skill. **4** *New York* Arafat . . rejected the notion that Sebai's killers were PLO operatives.

▪ **operatively** *adverb* E17. **operativeness** *noun* E17.

operatize /ˈɒp(ə)rətʌɪz/ *verb trans.* Also **-ise**. M19.
[Irreg. from OPERA *noun*[1] + -IZE, after *dramatize*: cf. *operatic*.]
Put into operatic form.

operator /ˈɒpəreɪtə/ *noun.* L16.
[Late Latin, formed as OPERATE: see -OR.]
1 A person (professionally) engaged in performing the practical or mechanical operations of a process, business, etc. L16. ▸†**b** A person dealing in quack medicines etc. L17–E18. ▸**c** A secret-service agent. M20.
2 An operating surgeon. L16.
3 A person by whose agency something is done. Formerly also, a creator. E17.
4 A person who carries on (speculative) financial operations; a person who operates or acts in a specified way (esp. in ***fast operator***, ***sharp operator***, ***smooth operator***); a plausible or manipulative person. E19.
5 A person operating a machine; *spec.* a person who works at the switchboard of a telephone exchange. M19. ▸**b** A person licensed to drive a motor vehicle. *N. Amer.* M20.
6 A person who or company which runs a business, enterprise, etc. M19.
7 *MATH. & LOGIC.* A symbol or group of symbols indicating an operation or series of operations to be carried out (on a following expression). M19.
8 *LINGUISTICS.* A form word. Also, in Basic English: an article, particle, preposition, etc., or any of certain words used as substitutes for verbs. E20.
9 *BIOLOGY.* A segment of chromosomal DNA believed to control the activity of the structural gene(s) of an operon. M20.

🕮 **1** SIR T. BROWNE Culinary operators observe that flesh boyles best, when the bones are boyled with it. **4** *Daily News* The market . . eventually improved, due to local operators covering. R. CARVER Harry was an operator That is to say he always had something going. **5** *Pall Mall Gazette* A machine operator, making nine shirts a day. B. F. CONNERS Operator, I'd like to call person to person to Officer Dolan. **6** *Outing (US)* A . . distillery . . where owner and operator divide the result of the year's working.

▪ **operatorship** *noun* (**a**) the position of an operator; (**b**) (in the oil and gas industries) the right to operate a well, field, etc.: L20.

opercle /əˈpəːk(ə)l/ *noun.* L16.
[Latin OPERCULUM.]
†**1** A cover, a covering. Only in L16.
2 *ZOOLOGY & BOTANY.* = OPERCULUM. Now *rare* or *obsolete*. M19.

opercula *noun* pl. of OPERCULUM.

opercular /ə(ʊ)ˈpəːkjʊlə/ *adjective.* M19.
[from OPERCULUM + -AR[1].]
ZOOLOGY & BOTANY. Of, pertaining to, or of the nature of an operculum; characterized by the presence of an operculum.

operculate /ə(ʊ)ˈpəːkjʊlət/ *adjective & noun.* L18.
[from OPERCULUM + -ATE[2].]
ZOOLOGY & BOTANY. ▶**A** *adjective.* Provided with or having an operculum; effected by means of an operculum. L18.
▶ **B** *noun.* Pl. **operculates**, in Latin form **operculata** /əpəːkjʊˈleɪtə/. A mollusc which bears an operculum. M19.
▪ **operculated** *adjective* (now *rare*) = OPERCULATE *adjective* L17.

operculum /ə(ʊ)ˈpəːkjʊləm/ *noun.* Pl. **-la** /-lə/. E18.
[Latin = lid, covering, from *operire* to cover: see -CULE.]
1 *ZOOLOGY.* Any of various structures covering or closing an aperture; *esp.* (**a**) the bony flap covering the gills of a fish; (**b**) the calcareous, horny, or fibrous plate secreted by some gastropod molluscs, serving to close the aperture of the shell when the animal is retracted. E18.
2 *BOTANY.* **a** The lid of the capsule in mosses, covering the peristome. L18. ▸**b** The cap of the ascus in certain ascomycetous fungi. L19.
3 *gen.* A cover. M19.

🕮 **3** *Time* The . . 'grandfather clock' pediment with its round operculum.

opere buffe, ***opere serie*** *noun phrs. pl.* see OPERA BUFFA, OPERA SERIA.

operetta /ɒpəˈrɛtə/ *noun.* L18.
[Italian, dim. of OPERA *noun*[1].]
A short, orig. one-act, opera, usu. on a light or humorous theme.
Savoy operetta: see SAVOY 3.
▪ **operettist** *noun* a writer or composer of operettas E20.

operette /ɒpəˈrɛt/ *noun.* Also in French form ***opérette*** /ɔperɛt (*pl. same*)/. L19.
[French *opérette* from Italian OPERETTA.]
= OPERETTA.

operon /ˈɒpərɒn/ *noun.* M20.
[French *opéron*, from *opérer* to effect, work: see -ON.]
BIOLOGY. A unit of linked genes which is believed to regulate other genes responsible for protein synthesis, and is usu. conceived as comprising an operator, a promoter, and one or more structural genes.

operose /ˈɒpərəʊs/ *adjective.* L17.
[Latin *operosus*, from *oper-*, *opus* work: see -OSE[1].]
1 Made with or displaying much industry or effort; laborious. L17.
2 Of a person: industrious, busy. L17.

🕮 **1** *New Scientist* Operose and scholarly collected editions. **2** R. NORTH We cannot think such an operose Compiler of History . . should be ignorant of so remarkable a Passage.

▪ **operosely** *adverb* M17. **operoseness** *noun* M17. **opeˈrosity** *noun* E17. †**operous** *adjective* = OPEROSE M17–L18.

Ophelian /əˈfiːlɪən/ *adjective.* E20.
[from *Ophelia* (see below) + -AN.]
Resembling or characteristic of Ophelia, the tragic heroine of Shakespeare's *Hamlet*.

ophicalcite /ɒfɪˈkalsʌɪt/ *noun.* M19.
[from Greek *ophis* snake + CALCITE.]
GEOLOGY. A form of marble consisting of a mixture of serpentine and calcite.

ophicleide /ˈɒfɪklʌɪd/ *noun.* M19.
[French *ophicléide*, from Greek *ophis* snake + *kleid-*, *kleis* key.]
MUSIC. **1** A deep wind instrument consisting of a U-shaped brass tube with eleven keys, forming a bass version of the key-bugle; a performer on this. M19.
2 A powerful reed-stop on the organ, a variety of the tuba. M19.

ophidian /əˈfɪdɪən/ *adjective & noun.* E19.
[from mod. Latin *Ophidia* (see below), from Greek *ophid-*, *ophis* snake: see -IA[2], -AN.]
▶ **A** *adjective.* Of or pertaining to the reptile suborder Serpentes (formerly Ophidia), which includes the snakes; of or pertaining to snakes, snakelike. E19.
▶ **B** *noun.* A snake. M19.

ophio- /ˈɒfɪəʊ/ *combining form* of Greek *ophis* snake: see -O-.
▪ **ophiˈolater** *noun* a snake-worshipper L19. **ophiˈolatry** *noun* snake-worship E19. **ophiˈologist** *noun* an expert on or student of snakes E19. **ophiˈology** *noun* the branch of zoology that deals with snakes E19. **ophiomancy** *noun* (*rare*) divination by means of snakes M18. **ophioˈmorphic** *adjective* (*rare*) having the form of a snake, snakelike E20.

ophiolite /ˈɒfɪəlʌɪt/ *noun.* M19.
[from OPHIO- + -LITE.]
1 Serpentine; an ornamental marble containing this; verd-antique. Now *rare*. M19.
2 *GEOLOGY.* Any of a group of basic and ultrabasic igneous rocks consisting largely of serpentine and thought to have been formed from the submarine eruption of oceanic crustal and upper mantle material. M19.
Comb.: **ophiolite association suite** *GEOLOGY* an assemblage of ophiolites, pillow lava, and radiolarian chert occurring in a characteristic pattern of layers in the Alps and elsewhere.
▪ **ophioˈlitic** *adjective* E20.

ophiophagous /ɒfɪˈɒfəgəs/ *adjective.* M17.
[from OPHIO- + -PHAGOUS.]
Feeding on snakes.

ophite /ˈɒfʌɪt/ *noun*[1]. M17.
[Latin *ophites* from Greek *ophitēs* serpentine stone, from *ophis* snake: see -ITE[1].]
GEOLOGY. Any of various eruptive or metamorphic rocks which are usually green and have spots or markings like a snake; serpentine.
▪ **oˈphitic** *adjective*[1] characterized by or designating a rock texture in which crystals of feldspar are interposed between plates of augite L19. **oˈphitically** *adverb* with an ophitic texture E20.

Ophite /ˈɒfʌɪt/ *noun*[2]. L17.
[Late Latin *Ophitae* from Greek *Ophitai* pl. of *Ophitēs*, from *ophis* snake: see -ITE[1].]
A member of an early Gnostic sect which exalted the serpent (*Genesis* 3) as the liberator of humankind.
▪ **Oˈphitic** *adjective*[2] M19. **Ophitism** *noun* the doctrine of the Ophites L19.

Ophiuchus /ɒˈfjuːkəs/ *noun*. **M16.**
[Latin from Greek *Ophioukhos*, formed as OPHIO- + *ekhein* to hold.]
A large constellation on the celestial equator immediately south of Hercules; the serpent-bearer. Cf. SERPENS.

ophiuran /ɒfɪˈ(j)ʊərən/ *noun & adjective*. **M19.**
[from mod. Latin *ophiura* (see below), from Greek *ophis* snake + *oura* tail, from the long, snakelike arms: see -AN.]
ZOOLOGY. ▶**A** *noun*. A star-shaped echinoderm of the subclass Ophiuroidea or the genus *Ophiura*, comprising species with small bodies and well-defined slender arms; a brittle-star, a sand-star. **M19.**
▶**B** *adjective*. Of or pertaining to this genus or subclass. **E20.**
■ **ophiurid** *adjective & noun* (*a*) *noun* any member of the subclass Ophiuroidea, *esp.* one of the family Ophiuridae; (*b*) *adjective* of or pertaining to this subclass or family: **L19.** ˈ**ophiuroid** *noun & adjective* (*a*) *noun* any member of the subclass Ophiuroidea; a brittle-star; (*b*) *adjective* of or pertaining to this subclass: **L19.**

ophrys /ˈɒfrɪs/ *noun*. **L18.**
[mod. Latin (see below), use as genus name of Latin name of an unidentified plant, from Greek *ophrus* eyebrow.]
Any of various orchids of, or formerly included in, the genus *Ophrys*, noted for the resemblance of the flowers to insects and including the bee orchid, *O. apifera*, and the fly orchid, *O. insectifera*.

ophthalm- *combining form* see OPHTHALMO-.

ophthalmia /ɒfˈθalmɪə/ *noun*. **LME.**
[Late Latin from Greek, from *ophthalmos* eye: see -IA[1].]
MEDICINE. Inflammation of the eye; *esp.* conjunctivitis.
ophthalmia neonatorum /ˌniːəʊnəˈtɔːrəm/ [mod. Latin = of the newborn: cf. NEONATE] a form of conjunctivitis occurring in newborn infants. ***sympathetic ophthalmia***: see SYMPATHETIC *adjective*.

ophthalmic /ɒfˈθalmɪk/ *adjective & noun*. **E17.**
[Latin *ophthalmicus* from Greek *ophthalmikos*, from *ophthalmos* eye: see -IC.]
▶**A** *adjective*. **1** Good for diseases of the eye; that performs or is used for operations on the eye. **E17.**
2 Pertaining to or connected with the eye; (of a disease) affecting the eye. **M18.**
3 Suffering from eye disease. **M19.**
2 ophthalmic artery, ophthalmic nerve, etc. **ophthalmic acid** BIOCHEMISTRY a tripeptide found in the lenses of various mammals. **ophthalmic optician** an optometrist.
▶**B** *noun*. †**1** A remedy for diseases of the eye. **M17–L19.**
2 The ophthalmic or orbital nerve. **E18.**

ophthalmitis /ɒfθalˈmʌɪtɪs/ *noun*. **E19.**
[from Greek *ophthalmos* eye + -ITIS.]
MEDICINE. Inflammation of the eye.

ophthalmo- /ɒfˈθalməʊ/ *combining form* of Greek *ophthalmos* eye: see -O-. Before a vowel **ophthalm-**.
■ **ophthalˈmometer** *noun* = KERATOMETER **M19.** **ophthalmoˈmetric** *adjective* of or pertaining to measurement of the eye **L19.** **ophthalˈmometry** *noun* measurement of the eye **L19.** **ophthalmoˈplegia** *noun* (MEDICINE) paralysis of one or more of the muscles of the eye **L19.** **ophthalmoˈplegic** *adjective* (MEDICINE) suffering from ophthalmoplegia **L19.** **ophthalˈmotomy** *noun* (an instance of) surgical incision into the eyeball **M19.** **ophthalmotoˈnometer** *noun* (MEDICINE) an instrument for measuring the tension of the eyeball **E20.**

ophthalmology /ɒfθalˈmɒlədʒi/ *noun*. **M19.**
[from OPHTHALMO- + -LOGY.]
The branch of medicine that deals with the structure, functions, and diseases of the eye.
■ **ophthalmoˈlogic** *adjective* (chiefly *US*) **M19.** **ophthalmoˈlogical** *adjective* **M19.** **ophthalmoˈlogically** *adverb* **L19.** **ophthalmologist** *noun* **E19.**

ophthalmoscope /ɒfˈθalməskəʊp/ *noun*. **M19.**
[from OPHTHALMO- + -SCOPE.]
An instrument for inspecting the interior of the eye, esp. the retina.
■ **ophthalmoˈscopic** *adjective* of or pertaining to the ophthalmoscope or its use **M19.** **ophthalmoˈscopical** *adjective* = OPHTHALMOSCOPIC **L19.** **ophthalmoˈscopically** *adverb* **M19.**

ophthalmoscopy /ɒfθalˈmɒskəpi/ *noun*. **M18.**
[formed as prec. + -SCOPY.]
1 A branch of physiognomy by which character is inferred from the appearance of the eyes. Now *rare* or *obsolete*. **M18.**
2 Inspection of the interior of the eye by means of an ophthalmoscope. **M19.**
■ **ophthalmoscopist** *noun* **M19.**

ophthalmy /ˈɒfθalmi/ *noun*. Now *rare* or *obsolete*. **M16.**
[French *ophthalmie* from Latin OPHTHALMIA: see -Y[3].]
= OPHTHALMIA.

-opia /ˈəʊpɪə/ *suffix*. Also (now *rare*) Anglicized as **-opy** /ˈɒpi/.
[Greek *-ōpia*, from *ōps*, *ōp-* eye, face: see -IA[1], -Y[3].]
Forming nouns denoting visual disorders and abnormalities, as ***amblyopia***, ***myopia***.

opiate /ˈəʊpɪət/ *noun & adjective*. **LME.**
[medieval Latin *opiatus* adjective, *opiatum* noun, from *opiat-* pa. ppl stem of *opiare*, from Latin *opium*: see OPIUM, -ATE[2].]
▶**A** *noun*. **1** Any of various drugs derived from opium and used as narcotics, hypnotics, sedatives, and analgesics. **LME.** ▶**b** *fig.* Something that soothes or dulls the senses or causes drowsiness or inaction. **M17.**
2 Any drug having similar addictive effects to those of the opium-derived drugs morphine and cocaine. **M20.**

> 🕮 **1** J. B. MORTON She popped a subtle Oriental opiate in his milk, and he fell asleep. **b** ALDOUS HUXLEY Mass opiates in the form of television . . and cigarettes. **2** *attrib.*: *Nature* Most people consider opiate addiction to comprise three major elements: tolerance, physical dependence, and compulsive craving.

▶**B** *adjective*. Containing opium; (of a drug etc.) narcotic, soporific; *fig.* that soothes or dulls the senses, causing drowsiness or inaction. **M16.**
■ **opiˈatic** *adjective* of or pertaining to opiates **L17.**

opiate /ˈəʊpɪeɪt/ *verb trans*. **L16.**
[medieval Latin *opiat-* pa. ppl stem of *opiare* (see prec.); in mod. use from OPIUM: see -ATE[3].]
1 Put to sleep by means of opium; *fig.* dull the senses or sensibility of. **L16.**
2 Mix with opium. Chiefly as ***opiated*** *ppl adjective*. **E17.**

> 🕮 **1** SOUTHEY One who can let his feelings remain awake, and opiate his reason.

†**opificer** *noun*. **M16–M18.**
[from Latin *opifex*, *opificem*: see -ER[1].]
A person who makes or constructs something; a maker; a worker.

opihi /əʊˈpiːhi/ *noun*. **E20.**
[Hawaiian.]
A black limpet, *Cellana exarata*, commonly eaten in Hawaii; the shallow shell of this. Also ***opihi shell***.

opiism /ˈəʊpɪɪz(ə)m/ *noun*. *rare*. **L19.**
[from OPI(UM + -ISM.]
Intoxication induced by taking opium; the habit of taking opium.

opilionid /ɒˌpɪlɪˈəʊnɪd/ *noun & adjective*. **M20.**
[from mod. Latin *Opiliones* (see below), from Latin *opilio(n-)* shepherd (a former name for these animals): see -ID[3].]
ZOOLOGY. ▶**A** *noun*. An arachnid belonging to the order Opiliones; a harvestman. **M20.**
▶**B** *adjective*. Of or pertaining to this order. **L20.**

Opimian /əʊˈpɪmɪən/ *adjective & noun*. **E17.**
[Latin *Opimianus* of or pertaining to Opimius (fl. 121 BC), a Roman consul.]
ROMAN ANTIQUITIES. (Designating) a celebrated ancient Roman wine.

†**opinative** *adjective*. **LME.**
[Late Latin *opinativus*, from Latin *opinat-* pa. ppl stem of *opinari*: see OPINION *noun*, -ATIVE.]
1 Of the nature of, or expressing, an opinion; conjectural, uncertain. **LME–E19.**
2 Sticking obstinately to one's own opinion; opinionated. **M16–M17.**

opine /ˈəʊpiːn/ *noun*. **L20.**
[Back-form. from OCTOPINE *noun*.]
BIOCHEMISTRY. Any of various amino acids containing a guanidino group.

opine /ə(ʊ)ˈpʌɪn/ *verb*. **LME.**
[Latin *opinari* think, believe.]
1 *verb trans.* Hold or express as one's opinion; be of the opinion *that*; think, suppose. **LME.**
2 *verb intrans.* Express an opinion, *spec.* (now *rare*) an authoritative opinion in a council etc. **L16.**

> 🕮 **1** L. M. MONTGOMERY No boys were allowed in—although Ruby Gillis opined that their admission would make it more exciting. **2** *Independent* Men who spend their days opining on the share price of their past employer.

■ **opiner** *noun* **E17.**

opiniated /əˈpɪnɪeɪtɪd/ *adjective*. Now *rare*. **L16.**
[App. from shortened stem of Latin *opinio(n-)* OPINION *noun* + -ATE[2] + -ED[1]. Cf. next.]
†**1** Having a conceited opinion *of*; thinking much *of*. **L16–E18.**
2 Sticking to one's own opinion; = OPINIONATED 2. **L16.**

opiniative /əˈpɪnɪətɪv/ *adjective*. Now *rare*. **L16.**
[formed as prec. + -IVE. Cf. medieval Latin *opiniativus*.]
= OPINIONATED 2.
■ **opiniativeness** *noun* **E17.**

†**opiniatre** *adjective & noun*. Also **-astre**. **L16.**
[French †*opiniastre*, now *opiniâtre*: cf. OPINION *noun*, -ASTER.]
▶**A** *adjective*. = OPINIONATED 2. **L16–E18.**
▶**B** *noun*. An opinionated person. **E17–E18.**
■ †**opiniatrety** *noun* obstinate adherence to one's own opinion **E17–M18.** †**opiniatry** *noun* = OPINIATRETY **M17–M18.**

†**opiniatre** *verb trans. & intrans.* **M17–L18.**
[French *opiniâtrer*, from *opiniâtre*: see prec.]
Persist obstinately in (an opinion, a course of action).

opinicus /əˈpɪnɪkəs/ *noun*. Pl. **-ci** /-kʌɪ, -kiː/. **M16.**
[Origin unkn.]
HERALDRY. An imaginary creature resembling a griffin, having a lion's body and legs, an eagle's head, and wings and a short tail.

opinion /əˈpɪnjən/ *noun*. **ME.**
[Old & mod. French from Latin *opinio(n-)*, from stem of *opinari* think, believe: see -ION.]
1 A view held about a particular subject or point; a judgement formed; a belief. **ME.**
2 a What or how one thinks about something; judgement or belief of something as probable, though not certain or established. **LME.** ▶**b** Such judgement or belief on the part of a particular group, or the majority, of people; what is generally thought about something. Usu. with specifying adjective **LME.**
3 A formal statement by a member of an advisory body, an expert, etc., of what he or she judges or advises on a matter; professional advice. **LME.**
4 a What one thinks *of* a person or thing; an estimate of character, quality, or value. Formerly also (*spec.*), a good or favourable estimate; esteem. **LME.** ▶†**b** Favourable estimate of oneself; conceit, arrogance; self-confidence. *rare* (Shakes.). **L16–E17.**
†**5** What is thought of one by others; the (esp. good) estimation in which one stands; reputation, standing. **LME–E18.**
†**6** The thought of what is likely to happen; expectation; apprehension. **LME–M17.**

> 🕮 **1** E. M. FORSTER He has no tact . . and will not keep his opinions to himself. J. B. PRIESTLEY His considered opinion was that prices were far too high. *Observer* Give your honest opinion of the film. *Which?* Opinions on the usefulness of home banking varied widely. **2a** B. JOWETT Opinion is based on perception, which may be correct or mistaken. **b** A. FRASER His prolonged march had given him no opportunity to feel the pulse of English opinion. J. BARZUN Professional opinion was divided about what he really meant. ***common opinion***, ***general opinion***, ***popular opinion***, etc. **3** ***legal opinion***, ***medical opinion***, etc. **4a** E. J. HOWARD She didn't clear up . . and his opinion of her dropped further still. G. BOYCOTT He has an inflated opinion of his ability.

Phrases: **a matter of opinion** a matter about which each may have his or her own opinion; a disputable point. **a second opinion** the opinion of a second (esp. medical) expert or adviser. **be of the opinion (that)**, **be of opinion (that)** hold the belief or view, think, (that). ***golden opinions***: see GOLDEN *adjective*. ***high opinion***: see HIGH *adjective*. ***horseback opinion***: see HORSEBACK *noun*. **in one's opinion** according to one's thinking; as one thinks. ***low opinion***: see LOW *adjective*. ***public opinion***: see PUBLIC *adjective & noun*.
Comb.: **opinion poll**, (*rare*) **opinion survey** an assessment of public opinion taken by questioning a random or representative sample, esp. as the basis for forecasting the results of voting (cf. POLL *noun*[1] 7).
■ **opinional** *adjective* (*rare*) of the nature of or based on opinion **LME.** **opinionless** *adjective* having no opinion of one's own **M19.**

†**opinion** *verb trans.* **M16–M19.**
[from the noun, perh. after Old French *opinionner*.]
= OPINIONATE 1a.

opinionate /əˈpɪnjəneɪt/ *verb*. **L16.**
[from OPINION *noun* + -ATE[3], perh. after Old French *opinionner*.]
1 a *verb trans.* Believe, suppose; hold the opinion *that*. **L16.** ▶**b** *verb intrans.* Form, hold, or state an opinion. **M17.**
†**2** *verb refl.* Be or become opinionated or dogmatic. Only in **E17.**

> 🕮 **1a** O. HENRY I set apart with my eye the one I opinionated to be the boss. **b** W. MCILVANNEY They came here simply to . . opinionate on matters of national importance.

■ **opinionator** *noun* a person who holds an opinion, a theorist **L17.**

opinionated /əˈpɪnjəneɪtɪd/ *adjective*. **L16.**
[from prec. + -ED[1].]
†**1** Having a particular opinion or estimate of a person or thing; *spec.* having a favourable opinion *of*. **L16–M18.**
2 Thinking too highly of or sticking obstinately to one's own opinion; conceited; dogmatic. **E17.** ▶**b** Obstinate, self-willed. **M17.**
3 Having firm esp. articulately expressed opinions; authoritative. *US*. **L20.**

> 🕮 **2** P. MAILLOUX A brusque, contentious, opinionated man, Ernst was not at all to Kafka's liking. **3** A. S. DALE Belloc . . was an intense, brooding, brilliant and opinionated talker.

■ **opinionatedly** *adverb* **L20.** **opinionatedness** *noun* **M19.** **opinioˈnation** *noun* the state or condition of sticking obstinately to one's own opinion **E20.**

opinionative /əˈpɪnjənətɪv/ *adjective*. **M16.**
[from OPINION *noun* + -ATIVE.]
†**1** Based on opinion or belief; imagined; conjectural, speculative; doctrinal as opp. to practical. **M16–L19.**
2 Sticking obstinately to one's own opinion; opinionated. **M16.**

> 🕮 **2** C. M. YONGE Since her engagement she had become much quieter and less opinionative.

■ **opinionatively** *adverb* (*rare*) (**a**) as an expression of opinion; (**b**) in an opinionated manner; conceitedly, obstinately: M16. **opinionativeness** *noun* L16.

opinioned /əˈpɪnjənd/ *adjective*. Now *rare*. L16.
[from OPINION *noun* + -ED².]
1 Having an opinion, esp. of a specified kind. L16.
2 Holding a particular (esp. favourable) opinion *of* oneself or another. E17.
📖 **2** J. NORRIS A man well opinioned of himself.

opinionist /əˈpɪnjənɪst/ *noun*. E17.
[formed as prec. + -IST.]
†**1** A holder of an opinion or doctrine against the generally accepted view; a dissenter. E17–M18. ▸**b** *ECCLESIASTICAL HISTORY*. A member of a sect in the 15th cent. who held that the only true Popes were those who practised voluntary poverty. L17–E18.
2 The holder of any specified opinion. M17.
3 A person whose business is to give a professional opinion. E19.

opinionnaire /əpɪnjəˈnɛː/ *noun*. M20.
[from OPINION *noun* + *-aire*, after QUESTIONNAIRE.]
A series of questions designed to gauge the opinion of a group on an issue; a questionnaire.

opioid /ˈəʊpɪɔɪd/ *noun & adjective*. M20.
[from OPI(UM + -OID.]
PHARMACOLOGY & BIOCHEMISTRY. ▸**A** *noun*. Any compound resembling cocaine and morphine in its addictive properties or in its neurochemical (and esp. analgesic) effects. Cf. OPIATE *noun* 2. M20.
▸**B** *adjective*. Of, pertaining to, or of the nature of an opioid. M20.

opisometer /ɒpɪˈsɒmɪtə/ *noun*. L19.
[from Greek *opisō* backwards + -METER.]
An instrument for measuring curved lines on a map etc., consisting of a wheel running on a screw and then returning to its original position by rolling along a straight scale. Cf. ROTOMETER.

opistho- /əˈpɪsθəʊ/ *combining form*. Before a vowel **opisth-**.
[from Greek *opisthen* behind: see -O-.]
Forming nouns and adjectives with the sense 'posterior, rear'.
■ **opisˈthognathous** *adjective* having retreating jaws or teeth M19. **opisthoˈpulmonate** *adjective* (*ZOOLOGY*) designating those pulmonate or air-breathing gastropod molluscs which have the pulmonary sac behind the heart (cf. OPISTHOBRANCHIATE) L19. **opisthoˈsoma** *noun* (*ZOOLOGY*) the posterior section of the body in certain types of invertebrate; *spec.* (**a**) the abdomen or metasoma of an arachnid or merostome; (**b**) the segmented posterior end of the body of a pogonophoran worm: M20.

opisthobranch /əˈpɪsθəbraŋk/ *noun & adjective*. M19.
[from next.]
ZOOLOGY. = next.

opisthobranchiate /ɒpɪsθəˈbraŋkɪət/ *adjective & noun*. M19.
[from mod. Latin *Opisthobranchiata* (see below), formed as OPISTHO- + Greek *bragkhia* gills: see -ATE².]
ZOOLOGY. ▸**A** *adjective*. Belonging to or characteristic of the subclass Opisthobranchiata of gastropod molluscs, comprising marine forms (mostly sea-slugs) having the gills behind the heart. Cf. PROSOBRANCHIATE, PULMONATE. M19.
▸**B** *noun*. An opisthobranchiate gastropod. E20.

opisthocoelous /ɒpɪsθəˈsiːləs/ *adjective*. Also ***-celous**. L19.
[from OPISTHO- + Greek *koilos* hollow + -OUS.]
ANATOMY & ZOOLOGY. Hollow behind; *spec.* (of vertebral centra) concave posteriorly. Cf. AMPHICOELOUS, PROCOELOUS.
■ Also **opisthocoelian** *adjective* M19.

opisthodomos /ɒpɪsˈθɒdəməs/ *noun*. E18.
[Greek, formed as OPISTHO- + *domos* house, room.]
ARCHITECTURE. An apartment or vestibule (usu. open) at the rear of an ancient Greek temple, equivalent to the Roman posticum.

opisthoglyph /əˈpɪsθəglɪf/ *noun & adjective*. L19.
[mod. Latin *Opisthoglypha*, from Greek OPISTHO- + *gluphē* carving.]
ZOOLOGY. ▸**A** *noun*. A venomous colubrid snake with grooved fangs in the rear of the upper jaw. L19.
▸**B** *adjective*. Of a snake: having such fangs. L19.
■ **opisthoˈglyphous** *adjective* = OPISTHOGLYPH *adjective* L19.

opisthograph /əˈpɪsθəgrɑːf/ *noun*. E17.
[Greek *opisthographos*, formed as OPISTHO- + *-graphos* -GRAPH.]
CLASSICAL ANTIQUITIES. A manuscript written on both the back and front of the papyrus or parchment; a slab inscribed on both sides.
■ **opisthoˈgraphic** *adjective* written or inscribed on both the back and front E19. **opisthoˈgraphical** *adjective* = OPISTHOGRAPHIC M17.

opisthotic /ɒpɪsˈθɒtɪk, -ˈθəʊtɪk/ *adjective & noun*. L19.
[from OPISTHO- + Greek *otikos* of the ear.]
ANATOMY & ZOOLOGY. (Designating or pertaining to) one of the periotic bones, situated in the back of the ear and in humans represented by an embryonic ossification centre of the temporal bone.

opisthotonos /ɒpɪsˈθɒt(ə)nəs/ *noun*. Also **-us**. M17.
[Late Latin *opisthotonus* from Greek *opisthotonos* drawn backwards, formed as OPISTHO- + *-tonos* stretched.]
MEDICINE. Spasm of the muscles causing the head, neck, and spine to be arched backwards, as in severe tetanus, some kinds of meningitis, strychnine poisoning, etc.
■ **opisthoˈtonic** *adjective* E17.

†**opitulation** *noun*. L16–E18.
[Late Latin *opitulatio(n-)* aid.]
Help, aid, assistance.

opium /ˈəʊpɪəm/ *noun*. ME.
[Latin from Greek *opion* poppy juice, opium, dim. of *opos* vegetable juice, from Indo-European base meaning 'water'.]
1 A reddish-brown strong-scented addictive drug prepared from the thickened dried juice of the unripe capsules of the opium poppy (see below), used (formerly esp. in the East) as a stimulant and intoxicant, and in medicine as a sedative and analgesic. ME.
2 *fig.* Something that soothes or dulls the senses. E17.
📖 **2** N. ANNAN Kingsley might protest that religion was being used as opium for the people. *Scientific American* Formalism is the opium of the thinking classes.

Comb.: **opium den** a haunt of opium-smokers; **opium dream** a dream during an opium-induced sleep; **opium joint** *US* = *opium den* above; **opium poppy** the plant which yields opium, *Papaver somniferum*, a glaucous poppy with chiefly white or lilac flowers; **Opium War**: waged by Britain against China (1839–42) following China's attempt to prohibit the importation of opium.

opobalsamum /ɒpəʊˈbalsəməm/ *noun*. Also **-balsam** /-ˈbɔːls(ə)m/. LME.
[Latin from Greek *opobalsamon*, from *opos* juice + *balsamon* BALSAM *noun*.]
= ***balm of Gilead*** (a) s.v. BALM *noun*¹. Also, the tree producing this, *Commiphora opobalsamum*.

opodeldoc /ɒpə(ʊ)ˈdɛldɒk/ *noun*. M17.
[Prob. invented by Paracelsus.]
†**1** A medical plaster. M17–M18.
2 Soap liniment; a preparation resembling this. M18.

opopanax /əˈpɒpənaks/ *noun*. LME.
[Latin from Greek, from *opos* juice + *panax*: see PANACEA.]
1 A fetid gum resin from the root of *Opopanax chironium*, a yellow-flowered umbelliferous plant of southern Europe. LME.
2 A gum resin obtained from a kind of myrrh tree, *Commiphora kataf*; a perfume made from this. M19.
3 More fully ***opopanax-tree***. A spiny acacia, of tropical and subtropical America, with fragrant yellow flowers *Acacia farnesiana*, which yield an essential oil. Also called ***cassie***, ***sponge tree***. L19.

opossum /əˈpɒs(ə)m/ *noun*. E17.
[Virginia Algonquian *opassom*, from *op* white + *assom* dog, doglike animal. Cf. POSSUM.]
1 Any of various small or medium-sized marsupial mammals, mostly arboreal, of the mainly neotropical family Didelphidae, which have an opposable thumb on the hind foot and a usu. prehensile and hairless tail; *esp.* (more fully ***Virginian opossum***) the common N. American species, *Didelphis virginiana*, which is the size of a cat. E17.
2 = POSSUM *noun* 2. L18.
1 ***mouse opossum***, ***vulpine opossum***, etc.
Comb.: **opossum-shrimp** a shrimp of the genus *Mysis* or the family Mysidae, so called from the brood-pouch in which the female carries her eggs; **opossum wood** (the wood of) an Australian timber tree, *Quintinia sieberi*.
■ **opossuming** *noun* (*rare*) the hunting of opossums M19.

opp *noun* var. of OP *noun*⁵.

opp. *abbreviation*.
Opposite (see also OP *noun*¹).

opp. *noun pl.* see OP *noun*¹.

oppida *noun* pl. of OPPIDUM.

oppidan /ˈɒpɪd(ə)n/ *noun & adjective*. M16.
[Latin *oppidanus* belonging to a town (other than Rome), from *oppidum* (fortified) town: see -AN.]
▸**A** *noun*. **1** An inhabitant of a town. M16.
2 At Eton College: a student who is not on the foundation and who boards with a housemaster (orig. with a private family in the town). Opp. ***colleger***. M16.
▸**B** *adjective*. Of or pertaining to a town; civic; urban. Formerly also (*spec.*), pertaining to a university town as opp. to the university itself. M17.

oppidum /ˈɒpɪdəm/ *noun*. Pl. **-da** /-də/ M19.
[Latin: see prec.]
Hist. An ancient Celtic fortified town, esp. one under Roman rule.

†**oppignorate** *verb trans.* Also **-erate**. E17–M19.
[Latin *oppignorat-*, *-erat-* pa. ppl stem of *oppignorare*, *-erare* pledge.]
Pawn, pledge.

oppilate /ˈɒpɪleɪt/ *verb trans.* Now *rare* or *obsolete*. LME.
[Latin *oppilat-* pa. ppl stem of *oppilare* stop up, formed as OB- + *pilare* ram down, stop up: see -ATE³.]
MEDICINE. Stop or block up, obstruct.
■ **oppiˈlation** *noun* the action of obstructing, the condition of being obstructed; an obstruction: LME. †**oppilative** *adjective* tending to stop up or obstruct, constipating LME–E18.

†**oppletion** *noun*. E17–M18.
[from Latin *opplet-* pa. ppl stem of *opplere* fill up, formed as OB- + *plere* fill: see -ION.]
MEDICINE. The action of filling up, the condition of being filled up; an instance of this.

oppo /ˈɒpəʊ/ *noun*. *slang* (orig. *MILITARY*). Pl **-os**. M20.
[Abbreviation of *opposite number*.]
A friend; a colleague.

†**oppone** *verb trans. & intrans.* ME–M18.
[Latin *opponere*: see OPPONENT.]
Oppose; speak in opposition (against).

opponency /əˈpəʊnənsi/ *noun*. E18.
[from OPPONENT + -ENCY.]
1 The action of opposing; antagonism, opposition. E18.
2 The action or position of the opponent in an academic disputation. Cf. OPPONENT *noun* 1. *obsolete* exc. *Hist.* M18.

opponens /əˈpəʊnənz/ *noun*. L18.
[Latin, pres. pple of *opponere*: see next.]
ANATOMY. Either of two muscles in the hand that bring the thumb and the fingers into opposition. Also, an analogous muscle in the foot. Also ***opponens muscle***. Chiefly in mod. Latin combs.

opponent /əˈpəʊnənt/ *noun & adjective*. L16.
[Latin *opponent-* pres. ppl stem of *opponere* set against, formed as OB- + *ponere* place: see -ENT, cf. OPPONE.]
▸**A** *noun*. **1** A person who maintains a contrary argument in a disputation; *esp.* the person who opens an academic disputation by proposing objections to a philosophical or theological thesis. Cf. OPPOSE *verb* 2. *obsolete* exc. *Hist.* L16.
2 A person who takes the opposite side in a struggle or contest; an antagonist, an adversary. E17.
3 *ANATOMY*. An opponens muscle. *rare*. M18.
📖 **2** *New Society* Better accepted as a friend . . than as a formidable opponent. A. N. WILSON He was an entrenched opponent of modern biblical scholarship. P. GROSSKURTH Opponents have accused her of never being willing to learn from anyone.

▸**B** *adjective*. **1** Antagonistic, contrary, opposed, (*to*). M17.
2 Situated opposite; opposing. E18.
3 *ANATOMY*. Designating an opponens muscle; (of a digit) opposable. M19.

opportune /ˈɒpətjuːn, ɒpəˈtjuːn/ *adjective & adverb*. LME.
[Old & mod. French *opportun(e)* from Latin *opportunus* (orig. of wind) driving towards the harbour, (hence) seasonable (cf. *Portunus* the protecting god of harbours), formed as OB- + *portus* harbour. Cf. IMPORTUNE *adjective*.]
▸**A** *adjective*. †**1** Advantageous, useful. LME–M17.
†**2** Conveniently exposed; liable or open (*to* attack or injury). *rare*. LME–M17.
3 Of a time or (formerly) a place: appropriate for a particular action; suitable, fit. LME.
4 Of an event, action, or thing: fitting with regard to time or circumstances. Now chiefly *spec.*, occurring at a favourable time; timely, well timed. LME.
5 Adopted with a view to present expediency. Cf. OPPORTUNISM. *rare*. M19.
📖 **2** MILTON Behold alone The Woman opportune to all attempts. **3** ALEXANDER RICHARDSON The time is . . opportune for trade unions to recognise their responsibility. D. BAGLEY At an opportune moment, when their masters were otherwise occupied, the slaves had risen. **4** MAX-MÜLLER The opportune death of Philip alone prevented the breaking out of a rebellion. S. WEINTRAUB Seeing Victoria's enfeeblement as opportune, Sir John confronted her with a paper.

▸†**B** *adverb*. Opportunely. *rare*. M17–M18.
■ **opportunely** *adverb* †(**a**) in an opportune manner; (**b**) at an opportune time: LME. **opportuneness** *noun* E18.

opportunism /ɒpəˈtjuːnɪz(ə)m, ˈɒpətjuːn-/ *noun*. L19.
[from prec. + -ISM after Italian *opportunismo*, French *opportunisme*, etc., terms first of Italian, later of French, politics.]
1 The adaptation of (political) policy, actions, or judgement to circumstance or opportunity, esp. regardless of principle; *gen.* the seizing of opportunities when they occur. L19. ▸**b** In Communism, the policy of making concessions to bourgeois elements of society in the development towards socialism. E20.
2 *MEDICINE & ECOLOGY*. Opportunistic state or activity. M20.

opportunist /ɒpəˈtjuːnɪst/ *noun & adjective*. L19.
[formed as prec. + -IST.]
▸**A** *noun*. **1** A person who advocates or practises opportunism, esp. in politics; *Hist.* a person who in 1870 held that the time was opportune for the promulgation of the doctrine of papal infallibility (cf. INOPPORTUNIST). Now

esp., a person who practises opportunism in an aggressive or exploitative manner. L19.

2 *MEDICINE.* An opportunistic fungus or micro-organism. M20.

3 *ECOLOGY.* An opportunistic species. L20.

> **1** C. FRANCIS Drake was an opportunist who traded, robbed or raided to achieve his aims. S. ROSENBERG The Party was becoming corrupt with more opportunists . . than honest communists.

▶**B** *adjective.* Of or pertaining to opportunism or an opportunist; opportunistic. L19.

opportunistic /ɒpətjuːˈnɪstɪk/ *adjective.* L19.
[from prec. + -IC.]

1 Of, pertaining to, or characteristic of an opportunist. L19.

2 *ECOLOGY.* Of a species: especially suited to rapid propagation and dispersal through unexploited or newly formed habitats. M20.

3 *MEDICINE.* Of a fungus or micro-organism: not normally pathogenic except in certain circumstances, as when the body is made vulnerable by other agencies. Of an infection: caused by such an organism. M20.

> **1** J. CAREY His method of composition was essentially opportunistic, relying on ideas coming as he wrote.

■ **opportunistically** *adverb* M20.

opportunity /ɒpəˈtjuːnɪti/ *noun.* LME.
[Old & mod. French *opportunité* from Latin *opportunitas*, from *opportunus*: see OPPORTUNE, -ITY.]

1 A time or condition favourable for a particular action or aim; occasion, chance. LME. ▸**†b** A time when there is occasion or need for something. *rare.* E16–L17.

2 The quality or fact of being opportune; timeliness, opportuneness. Now *rare.* LME.

†3 Fitness, aptitude, competency. M16–E17.

†4 Convenience or advantageousness of site or position. M16–L18.

†5 Importunity. L16–M17.

> **1** W. K. HANCOCK Equality of opportunity implies free scope for natural talent. E. ROOSEVELT I had plenty of opportunity to meet . . interesting men and women. G. BORROW The chance of visiting Bethlehem . . was too great an opportunity to be missed. L. MCMURTRY Texas was the land of opportunity. *Proverb:* Opportunity never knocks twice at any man's door. **5** SHAKES. *Merry W.* If opportunity and humblest suit Cannot attain it, why then—hark you hither.

Phrases: ***equal opportunity***: see EQUAL *adjective.* ***photo opportunity***: see PHOTO *noun & adjective.* ***the opportunity of a lifetime***.

Comb.: **opportunity cost** ECONOMICS the loss of other alternatives when one alternative is chosen; an alternative lost in this way; **opportunity shop** *Austral. & NZ* = CHARITY *shop* (cf. ***op shop*** s.v. OP *noun*[5]); **opportunity State** a country which offers many opportunities for advancement.

opposable /əˈpəʊzəb(ə)l/ *adjective.* E19.
[from OPPOSE + -ABLE.]

1 Able to be opposed, withstood, or placed in opposition (*to*). *rare.* E19.

2 Of a digit, esp. the thumb: able to be opposed to another digit. M19.

¶ Earlier in UNOPPOSABLE.

■ **opposaˈbility** *noun* M19.

†opposal *noun.* LME.
[from next + -AL[1].]

▶**I 1** The putting of hard or searching questions; examination, interrogation; a searching question. Cf. APPOSAL. LME–E17.

▶**II 2** = OPPOSITION 4, 4b. Only in M17.

3 = OPPOSITION 1, 2. L17–M19.

oppose /əˈpəʊz/ *verb.* LME.
[Old & mod. French *opposer* based on Latin *opponere* (see OPPONE, OPPONENT), but re-formed on Latin *oppositus* (pa. pple of *opponere*) and Old & mod. French *poser*: see POSE *verb*[1].]

▶**I †1** *verb trans.* Confront with objections or hard questions; examine, interrogate; = APPOSE *verb*[1] 1. LME–E17.

2 *verb intrans.* Put objections or hard questions; *spec.* put forward objections to be answered by a person maintaining a philosophical or theological thesis, esp. as a means of qualifying for a degree etc. *obsolete* exc. *Hist.* LME.

†3 *verb trans.* Examine as to accounts; audit; = APPOSE *verb*[1] 2. *rare.* Only in L15.

▶**II 4** *verb trans.* Set oneself against (a person or thing); fight or argue against; resist, combat; stand in the way of, obstruct. LME. ▸**b** *verb refl.* & *†intrans.* Fight or contend *against*; be hostile, act in resistance, *to*. Long *arch.* L16.

5 *verb trans.* Set (a thing) against another thing by way of resistance; place as an obstacle. Also, set (a person) up as an antagonist. Usu. foll. by *to*. L16.

6 *verb trans.* Place or position directly before or in front. Usu. foll. by *to*. L16. ▸**b** Expose, subject, (*to*). Long *rare* or *obsolete.* L16.

7 *verb trans.* Set (a thing) against or on the other side of another thing, as a balance or contrast; contrast; put in opposition. Usu. foll. by *to*. L16.

8 *verb trans.* Look towards, face. Now *rare.* E17.

9 *verb trans.* Bring (a digit, esp. the thumb) into a position opposite another digit on the same hand (or foot), so that the pads may be pressed together, or so that an object may be gripped. (Foll. by *to*.) M19.

> **4** L. NAMIER Osbaldston, previously a follower of Fox, now openly opposed him. *Observer* Opposing false reporting is a huge duty still facing us. **7** E. NEWMAN Opposing the probity and sobriety of his black costume to the gangster black of Barbetta.

■ **opposeless** *adjective* (*poet. & rhet.*) not to be opposed; irresistible: E17.

opposed /əˈpəʊzd/ *adjective.* LME.
[from prec. + -ED[1].]

1 a Placed against; facing, opposite. LME. ▸**b** *MECHANICS.* (Having pistons) arranged in pairs moving in opposite directions along the same straight line. E20.

2 Standing in opposition or contrast; conflicting; opposite or contrary *to*. LME.

3 Of a person: hostile to or *to* another person; adverse *to* a measure, system, etc. L16.

4 Of a digit: opposable, that is or has been opposed (OPPOSE *verb* 9) to another. M19.

> **1a** *leaf-opposed*: see LEAF *noun*[1]. **2** C. CAUDWELL Their interests—reconciled during the period of wage-labour shortage—are now opposed. **as opposed to** in contrast with. **3** T. CAPOTE Most of the ministers are opposed to capital punishment. A. TUTUOLA We are opposed to all your proposals.

■ **opposedness** /-zɪdnɪs/ *noun* (*rare*) L19.

opposer /əˈpəʊzə/ *noun.* L15.
[from OPPOSE + -ER[1].]

†1 A person who checks accounts. Cf. OPPOSE 3. Only in L15.

2 a A person who opposes the defender of a thesis in an academic disputation. Cf. OPPOSE 2, OPPONENT *noun* 1. *obsolete* exc. *Hist.* L15. ▸**b** Either of two examiners formerly appointed to carry out at Winchester College the elections to New College, Oxford. *rare.* L19.

3 A person who opposes or contends against a person, measure, system, etc. E17.

opposing /əˈpəʊzɪŋ/ *adjective.* E17.
[from OPPOSE + -ING[2].]

That opposes, opposite; contrasting; adverse.

> H. MOORE This conflict . . represents two opposing sides in me, the 'tough' and the 'tender'.

■ **opposingly** *adverb* M19.

opposit /əˈpɒzɪt/ *verb trans. rare.* M17.
[Latin *opposit-* pa. ppl stem of *opponere*: see OPPONENT.]

†1 Oppose, resist. Only in M17.

2 *METAPHYSICS.* Posit as a contradictory. L19.

opposite /ˈɒpəzɪt, -sɪt/ *adjective, noun, adverb, & preposition.* LME.
[Old & mod. French from Latin *oppositus* pa. pple of *opponere*: see OPPONENT.]

▶**A** *adjective.* **1** Situated on the other or further side; on either side of an intervening space or thing; contrary in position; facing. (Foll. by *to*, *from*.) LME. ▸**b** Of angles: on opposite sides of the intersection of two lines. E17. ▸**c** *BOTANY.* Of leaves etc.: arising in pairs at the same level on opposite sides of a stem (opp. ***alternate***); placed straight in front of another organ. E18.

2 Turned or moving the other way; contrary, reverse. L16.

3 a Contrary in nature, character, or tendency; diametrically different. (Foll. by *to*, *from*.) L16. ▸**b** Being the other of a contrasted pair; *the* contrary —, *the* other —. M17.

†4 a Opposed in will or action; hostile, antagonistic. (Foll. by *to*, *against*.) L16–M18. ▸**b** Of a thing: adverse, repugnant. (Foll. by *to*.) L16–E18.

> **1** W. H. SMYTH An iron ladle with a . . spout opposite to the handle. H. JAMES The opposite bank of the Seine. J. DISKI We undressed on opposite sides of the bed. **opposite number** a person holding an equivalent position in another organization, country, etc.; a counterpart, a partner. **opposite prompt** the off-stage area of a theatre stage to the right of an actor facing the audience. **2** J. GASKELL We started . . racing around in opposite directions to each other. **3a** J. GALSWORTHY His mind . . was the junction of two curiously opposite emotions. H. E. BATES We were . . an oddly opposite pair . . with almost nothing in common. **b** G. P. R. JAMES After the king's death, you continued in office under the opposite faction. **the opposite sex** females in relation to males or vice versa.

▶**B** *noun.* **†1** The opposite point, esp. of the heavens. Cf. OPPOSITION 2. LME–E17. ▸**b** = OPPOSITION 2. *rare* (Milton). Only in M17.

2 A person who stands in opposition to another; an antagonist, an opponent. Now *rare* or *obsolete.* LME.

3 That which is opposite or contrary; an object, fact, or quality that is the reverse of something else; in *pl.*, two things or people the most different of their kind. LME. ▸**b** *LOGIC.* Orig., a contrary argument. Now, a contrary term or proposition. M16.

> **3** J. R. SEELEY The opposite of conventionalism is freshness of feeling, enthusiasm. N. MOSLEY She had the sensuality of opposites—the youth and experience, the leanness and voluptuousness. V. BROME Temperamentally opposites, the two men followed different paths. ***direct opposite***: see DIRECT *adjective.*

▶**C** *adverb.* **†1** In opposition, by way of balance. *rare.* Only in E16.

2 In an opposite position or direction. M17.

> **2** J. CONRAD Flashes of red sunlight on the roofs and windows opposite. S. BEDFORD Caroline sat on the seat opposite.

▶**D** *preposition.* In a position opposite to; fronting on the other side of; facing; *THEATRICAL* in a complementary leading role to (another performer, esp. of the opposite sex). M18.

> E. WAUGH Opposite him at the table . . sat a middle-aged man. T. CALLENDER Maysie moved into the house opposite his.

■ **oppositely** *adverb* in an opposite or contrary manner; on the contrary; in an opposite position or direction: M16. **oppositeness** *noun* E17.

opposition /ɒpəˈzɪʃ(ə)n/ *noun.* LME.
[Old & mod. French from Latin *oppositio(n-)*, from *opposit-* pa. ppl stem of *opponere*: see OPPONENT, -ION.]

1 Position opposite something; opposite situation or direction. Now *rare.* LME.

2 *ASTROLOGY & ASTRONOMY.* The apparent position of two celestial objects directly opposite to each other in the sky as viewed from the earth; *esp.* the position of a superior planet when opposite to the sun. Also, the time when this occurs. LME.

3 †a *RHETORIC.* A contrast of arguments; a contrary argument; a counter-thesis. Cf. ANTITHESIS 2, 3. LME–L17. ▸**b** The action of placing one thing in contrast with another; the condition of being opposed or contrasted; distinction, antithesis. L16. ▸**†c** That which is contrary; that which contrasts or counterbalances. L16–E18. ▸**d** *LOGIC.* The relation between two propositions which have the same subject and predicate but differ in quantity or quality or both. L16. ▸**e** The state or condition of being opposite in meaning; antonymy. L19. ▸**f** *LINGUISTICS.* A functional contrast between esp. phonological elements. M20.

4 The fact or condition of being opposed or hostile; hostile action, antagonism, resistance. L16. ▸**†b** Encounter, combat. L16–M17.

5 †a The action of setting one person or thing against another. *rare* (Shakes.). Only in E17. ▸**b** *spec.* The action of touching the fingertips with the tip of the thumb. L19.

6 A political party opposed to that in office; *esp.* (usu. ***the Opposition***) the principal party opposed to the governing party in the British Parliament. Also (*gen.*), any body of opponents. E18.

> **3b** E. A. FREEMAN In the English Chronicles . . the opposition is made between 'French' and 'English'. **4** G. STEIN Jane had met Anna with sharp resistance, in opposition to her ways. A. N. WILSON Her mother's opposition to her marrying Belloc was absolute. M. MAHY He had gone from one . . victory to another without any opposition. **6** J. F. KENNEDY The National Government . . gained the tremendous Parliamentary majority of 554 seats to 56 for the opposition. *attrib.*: *Hansard* The Government . . cannot accept views expressed from the Opposition Benches. H. WILSON The relationship between the leader (be he prime minister or Opposition leader) and his party.

Phrases: **in opposition** (of a political party) opposed to the party in office. ***Leader of the Opposition***: see LEADER 3.

■ **oppositional** *adjective* of the nature of or pertaining to opposition; connected with the parliamentary opposition: L17. **oppositionary** *adjective* (*rare*) = OPPOSITIONAL E20. **oppositionist** *noun & adjective* (**a**) *noun* a person who professes or practises opposition; *esp.* a member of the parliamentary opposition; (**b**) *adjective* of or pertaining to opposition or an oppositionist: L18. **oppositionless** *adjective* (*rare*) M18.

oppositive /əˈpɒzɪtɪv/ *adjective.* L15.
[medieval Latin *oppositivus*, from Latin *opposit-*: see prec., -IVE.]

1 Characterized by opposing or contrasting; expressive of opposition or antithesis; adversative. L15.

†2 = OPPOSITE *adjective* 1. L16–M19.

3 Inclined to opposition; contentious. *rare.* M19.

■ **†oppositively** *adverb* E–M17. **oppositiveness** *noun* (*rare*) E19.

oppositive /əˈpəʊzɪv/ *adjective. rare.* L17.
[Irreg. from OPPOSE + -IVE.]

Inclined to oppose, contradictory.

oppress /əˈprɛs/ *verb trans.* ME.
[Old & mod. French *oppresser* from medieval Latin *oppressare*, from Latin *oppress-* pa. ppl stem of *opprimere*, formed as OB- + *premere* PRESS *verb*[1].]

†1 Put down, suppress; subdue, overwhelm; check, put an end to. ME–E19.

2 †a Press down on forcefully and harmfully; trample; smother. LME–L18. ▸**b** Crush in battle; overwhelm with numbers. Now *rare.* LME. ▸**c** *fig.* Of sleep etc.: overpower, weigh down. Chiefly *poet.* L16.

3 Affect with a feeling of pressure, constraint, or distress; weigh down mentally, disturb. LME.
4 Subdue or keep in subservience by cruel or unjust exercise of authority or power; govern or treat harshly; tyrannize. LME.
†**5** Of an enemy, disaster, etc.: reduce to straits; trouble, distress. LME–E17.
†**6** Come upon unexpectedly, take by surprise. LME–E17.
†**7** Violate, rape. LME–E17.
8 *HERALDRY.* = DEBRUISE *verb* 2. L16.

> **2c** KEATS Until the poppied warmth of sleep oppress'd Her soothed limbs. **3** S. MIDDLETON The heat of the place . . oppressed him. P. MAILLOUX He is oppressed by his work, which leaves him too tired to do anything else. **4** N. CHOMSKY The Khmer minority, oppressed by Saigon's policies of racial discrimination. *Peace News* Events in the Philippines . . have given hope to oppressed peoples around the world.

■ **oppressed** *ppl adjective & noun* (*a*) *ppl adjective* that is oppressed; (*b*) *noun the* class of oppressed people: LME. **oppressingly** *adverb* (*rare*) oppressively E20. **oppressor** *noun* a person who or thing which oppresses someone LME.

oppression /ə'prɛʃ(ə)n/ *noun.* ME.
[Old & mod. French from Latin *oppressio(n-)*, from *oppress-*: see prec., -ION.]
1 Cruel or unjust exercise of authority or power; harsh government or treatment; tyranny. ME.
2 †**a** The action of weighing down mentally someone or something; pressure of circumstances, grief, pain, etc.; straitened condition, distress. LME–M19. ▸**b** The feeling of being weighed down mentally; uneasiness, mental distress. Also, a thing causing this. LME.
†**3** Violation, rape. Only in LME.
†**4** The action of forcibly putting down or crushing someone or something; repression. LME–M16.
5 The action of pressing or weighing down physically someone or something; pressure. Chiefly *poet.* LME.

> **1** V. CRONIN Reforming the code of laws . . to end oppression . . of serf by master. **2b** B. PYM The stultifying oppression of the suburbs seemed particularly heavy on this early winter evening. A. DESAI Baumgartner found any relationship at all a relief from the oppression of solitude.

oppressive /ə'prɛsɪv/ *adjective.* L16.
[French *oppressif, -ive* from medieval Latin *oppressivus*, from Latin *oppress*: see prec., -IVE.]
1 Of the nature of or characterized by cruel or unjust exercise of authority or power; unreasonably harsh; tyrannical. L16.
2 Weighing heavily on the mind, spirits, or senses; depressing; *spec.* (of weather conditions etc.) unpleasantly hot and close. E18.

> **1** W. MCILVANNEY He's still sanctioning an oppressive regime. **2** V. WOOLF The hostility, the indifference of other people dining here is oppressive. G. LORD It was a heavy oppressive day with an afternoon storm building up. R. THOMAS Everything went quiet, but the silence was oppressive where it had once been tranquil.

■ **oppressively** *adverb* M18. **oppressiveness** *noun* E18.

opprobriate /ə'prəʊbrɪeɪt/ *verb trans.* Now *rare.* M17.
[medieval Latin *opprobriat-* pa. ppl stem of *opprobriare*, from Latin OPPROBRIUM.]
Speak abusively or contemptuously of or to; reproach.

opprobrious /ə'prəʊbrɪəs/ *adjective.* LME.
[Late Latin *opprobriosus*, formed as next: see -OUS.]
1 Involving shame or disgrace; held in dishonour; infamous, shameful. Now *rare.* LME.
2 (Of language etc.) reproachful, abusive, attaching disgrace; (of a person) using such language. L15. ▸†**b** Of an action, feeling, etc.: insulting, insolent. L16–E18.

> **2** M. M. KAYE The term . . became an opprobrious word, signifying members of an inferior—and coloured—race.

■ **opprobriously** *adverb* L15. **opprobriousness** *noun* M16.

opprobrium /ə'prəʊbrɪəm/ *noun.* Pl. **-ia** /-ɪə/. M17.
[Latin = infamy, reproach, formed as OB- + *probrum* shameful deed, disgrace, use as noun of neut. of *probus* disgraceful. Cf. next.]
1 An occasion or cause of reproach; shameful conduct; something that brings disgrace. M17.
2 Disgrace attached to conduct considered shameful; the expression of this disgrace; shame, reproach. L17.

> **2** A. MASSIE His vanity was bruised by the scandals and opprobrium she attracted.

†**opprobry** *noun.* LME.
[formed as prec.: see -Y[4].]
1 = OPPROBRIUM 2. LME–M18.
2 Accusation of shameful conduct; an utterance of reproach. LME–M18.
3 = OPPROBRIUM 1; an indignity, an insult. LME–L18.

oppugn /ə'pjuːn/ *verb.* LME.
[Latin *oppugnare*, formed as OB- + *pugnare* fight.]
†**1** *verb trans.* Fight against, attack, assault. LME–M19.
2 *verb trans.* Assail or oppose with words, action, etc.; *esp.* call into question, dispute the truth or validity of (a statement, belief, etc.). E16. ▸**b** *verb trans.* Of a thing: conflict with, run counter to. Now *rare.* L16. ▸**c** *verb intrans.* Fight, contend. L16.
†**3** *verb trans.* Oppose (a statement, argument, etc.) to another; maintain in opposition. L18–M19.

> **2** W. PRYNNE Such of those Tenets which haue beene constantly oppugned, repelled, disclaimed.

■ **oppugnable** *adjective* (*rare*) L19. †**oppugnate** *verb trans. & intrans.* (*rare*) = OPPUGN M18–E19. **oppug'nation** *noun* (now *rare*) [Latin *oppugnatio(n-)*] the action of oppugning M16. **oppugner** *noun* M16.

oppugnant /ə'pʌgnənt/ *adjective & noun.* E16.
[Latin *oppugnant-* pres. pple of *oppugnare* OPPUGN: see -ANT[1].]
▶ **A** *adjective.* Opposing, antagonistic, contrary. E16.
▶ **B** *noun.* A person who opposes something or someone, an opponent. *rare.* M19.
■ **oppugnance** *noun* = OPPUGNANCY M19. **oppugnancy** *noun* the quality of being oppugnant; the fact or action of oppugning: E17.

opry /'ɒpri/ *noun. US.* E20.
[Repr. a pronunc.]
1 = OPERA *noun*[1]. *dial.* E20.
2 *Grand Ole Opry*, (proprietary name for) a concert of country music broadcast from Nashville, Tennessee; the type of music forming part of this. M20.

opsimathy /ɒp'sɪməθi/ *noun. rare.* M17.
[Greek *opsimathia*, from *opsimathēs* late in learning, from *opsi-* late + *math-* learn: see -Y[3].]
Learning or study late in life.
■ **'opsimath** *noun* a person who begins to learn or study late in life L19.

opsin /'ɒpsɪn/ *noun.* M20.
[Back-form. from RHODOPSIN.]
BIOCHEMISTRY. A protein combined with retinal in the visual pigment rhodopsin and released by the action of light.

opsit /'ɔpsɪt/ *verb intrans.* Infl. **-tt-**. L19.
[Afrikaans from Dutch *opzitten* sit up.]
S. AFR. HISTORY. Of a young couple: sit up together into the night by candlelight, for a period determined by the length of the candle provided by the girl's family, in a Boer custom of courtship.

opsonin /'ɒpsənɪn/ *noun.* E20.
[from Latin *opsonare* buy provisions, cater, from Greek *opsōnein*: see -IN[1].]
MEDICINE & BACTERIOLOGY. A substance (often an antibody) in blood plasma which combines with foreign cells and makes them more susceptible to phagocytosis.
■ **op'sonic** *adjective* of or pertaining to opsonins; produced by or involving opsonins: E20. **opsoni'zation** *noun* the process of opsonizing cells etc. E20. **opsonize** *verb trans.* make more susceptible to phagocytosis E20. **opsonocyto'phagic** *adjective* (now *rare*) opsonic; *spec.* designating or pertaining to a test of immunity involving opsonic phagocytosis: E20.

opt /ɒpt/ *verb intrans.* L19.
[French *opter* from Latin *optare* choose, desire. Cf. ADOPT.]
Choose, make a choice; decide. (Foll. by *for, to do.*)

> J. C. OATES They wished her to opt for an early retirement. A. N. WILSON He opted . . to read Modern History. **opt in** choose to participate. **opt out** choose not to participate in something (foll. by *of*); *spec.* (of a school or hospital) decide to withdraw from the control of a local authority.

■ **optable** *adjective* (now *rare*) desirable M16.

optant /'ɒpt(ə)nt/ *noun.* E20.
[German, Danish, from Latin *optant-* pres. ppl stem of *optare* choose: see -ANT[1].]
A person who, when the region which he or she inhabits changes sovereignty, may choose either to retain the same nationality or to change it.

optate /'ɒpteɪt/ *verb intrans. rare.* E17.
[Latin *optat-*: see next, -ATE[3].]
Opt, choose.

optation /ɒp'teɪʃ(ə)n/ *noun.* L16.
[Latin *optatio(n-)*, from *optat-* pa. ppl stem of *optare* choose: see -ATION.]
The action of wishing; a wish, a desire; *spec.* (*RHETORIC*) the expression of a wish in the form of an exclamation.

optative /'ɒptətɪv, ɒp'teɪtɪv/ *adjective & noun.* M16.
[French *optatif, -ive* from late Latin *optativus*, from Latin *optat-*: see prec., -IVE.]
▶ **A** *adjective.* **1** *GRAMMAR.* Designating or pertaining to a mood expressing wish or desire. M16.
2 Characterized by desire or choice; expressing desire. E17.
▶ **B** *noun. GRAMMAR.* (A verb in) the optative mood. M16.
■ **optatively** *adverb* in an optative manner; in the optative mood: E17.

optic /'ɒptɪk/ *adjective & noun.* LME.
[Old & mod. French *optique* or medieval Latin *opticus* from Greek *optikos*, from *optos* seen, visible: see -IC.]
▶ **A** *adjective.* **1** Now chiefly *ANATOMY & MEDICINE.* Of, pertaining to, or connected with the eyes, the faculty of sight, or the process of vision; of or pertaining to light, esp. as the medium of vision. LME.
†**2** Of, pertaining to, or skilled in optics (see sense B.1 below). M16–E18.
3 = OPTICAL *adjective* 3. *arch.* E17.
Special collocations: **optic angle** (*a*) = *visual angle* s.v. VISUAL *adjective*; (*b*) the angle between the optic axes of the eyes when directed to the same object; (*c*) the angle between the optic axes of a biaxial doubly-refracting crystal. **optic axis** (*a*) the straight line through the centres of the pupil and the crystalline lens, the axis of the eye; the axis of a lens; (*b*) a line in a doubly-refracting crystal such that a ray of light passing in the direction of it suffers no double refraction. ***optic chiasma***: see CHIASMA 1. **optic commissure** the optic chiasma. **optic cup** *EMBRYOLOGY* a cuplike depression in the front of the optic vesicle of the embryo which eventually forms the retina. **optic disc** the raised disc on the retina at the point of entry of the optic nerve, lacking visual receptors and so forming a blind spot. **optic lobe** *ANATOMY* each of two or (in mammals) four lobes of the dorsal part of the midbrain from which in part the optic nerves arise. **optic measure** a device fastened to the neck of an inverted bottle for measuring out spirits etc. (cf. sense B.4 below). **optic nerve** either of the second pair of cranial nerves, which supply the retinas, *esp.* that part of either between the optic chiasma and the eye. **optic neuritis** *MEDICINE* inflammation of an optic nerve. **optic papilla** = *optic disc* above. ***optic pencil***: see PENCIL *noun*. ***optic tectum***: see TECTUM 2. **optic thalamus** *ANATOMY* either of two lateral geniculate bodies which relay visual information from the optic tract. **optic tract** the pathway between the optic chiasma and the brain. **optic vesicle** a vesicle connected with the forebrain of the embryo, from which the optic nerve and retina are developed.
▶ **B** *noun.* **1** In *pl.* (now treated as *sing.*) & †*sing.* The branch of physics that deals with the properties and phenomena of light. M16.
2 The eye. Usu. in *pl.* Now *joc.* E17. ▸†**b** In *pl.* Visual power. M17–E18.
3 a An eyeglass, a magnifying glass; a microscope, a telescope, a photographic lens. Now *rare.* E17. ▸**b** In *pl.* The optical components of an instrument or apparatus. M20.
4 (Usu. **O-**). (Proprietary name for) an optic measure. E20.
1 ***physical optics***: see PHYSICAL *adjective*.
■ **opticity** /ɒp'tɪsɪti/ *noun* (in the brewing and food industries) the degree of optical activity of carbohydrates in a solution, as a measure of concentration E20.

optical /'ɒptɪk(ə)l/ *adjective & noun.* L16.
[from prec. + -AL[1].]
▶ **A** *adjective.* **1** Of or pertaining to sight, esp. in relation to the physical action of light; pertaining to light as the medium of sight, or in relation to its physical properties; of or pertaining to optics; *spec.* operating in or employing the visible part of the spectrum. L16. ▸**b** Relating to the transmission of electromagnetic radiation of any wavelength, or of beams of particles analogous to light. M20. ▸**c** Designating a form of abstract art in which the precise use of pattern and colour generates illusions of movement. Cf. OP *adjective.* M20.
2 Of a person: concerned with or skilled in optics. L16.
3 Constructed to assist vision; acting by means of sight or light; devised on the principles of optics. E17.
4 Designating a detergent additive which produces a whitening effect on textiles by fluorescing in ultraviolet light. M20.
5 *COMPUTING.* Designating (a part of) a computer requiring electromagnetic radiation for its operation, esp. as a means of storing, retrieving, or transmitting data. M20.
Special collocations: **optical activity** *CHEMISTRY* (the property of causing) optical rotation. **optical axis** = *optic axis* s.v. OPTIC *adjective.* **optical bench** a straight rigid bar, usu. graduated, to which supports for lenses, light sources, etc., can be attached. **optical centre** that point in the axis of a lens where all rays passing through it remain unrefracted. **optical character reader** a device which performs optical character recognition and produces coded signals corresponding to the characters identified. **optical character recognition** identification of printed or written characters using photoelectric devices. **optical comparator** an instrument for facilitating comparisons of two objects by projecting shadows or transparencies of them on to a screen. **optical density** (*a*) the degree to which a refractive medium retards transmitted rays of light; (*b*) the logarithm to the base 10 of opacity. **optical disk** *COMPUTING* a smooth non-magnetic disk with a special coating that allows data to be recorded on it by means of a laser beam and read by a laser scanner. **optical double** *ASTRONOMY* two stars which appear to constitute a double star due to their being in the same line of sight as seen from the earth, but are actually at different distances. **optical fibre** a transparent fibre used to transmit light signals by total internal reflection (cf. *FIBRE optics*). ***optical flat***: see FLAT *noun*[1] 7c. **optical glass**: of specially high homogeneity manufactured for use in optical components. **optical illusion** (an instance of) something having an appearance so resembling something else as to deceive the eye; mental misapprehension caused by this. **optical isomer** *CHEMISTRY* a compound exhibiting optical isomerism. ***optical isomerism***: see ISOMERISM 1. ***optical microscope***: see MICROSCOPE *noun* 1. **optical path** *PHYSICS* the distance which in a vacuum would contain the same number of wavelengths as the actual path taken by a ray of light. **optical printer** = *PROJECTION printer.* **optical pyrometer** a device for measuring the temperature of an incandescent body by comparing its brightness with that of a heated filament in the instrument. **optical rotation** *CHEMISTRY* the rotation of the plane of

polarization of plane-polarized light by a substance through which it passes; *spec.* = ***specific rotation*** s.v. SPECIFIC *adjective*. **optical scanner** = ***optical character reader*** above. **optical sound** CINEMATOGRAPHY sound recorded by optical (photographic) means on a film. **optical square** SURVEYING a reflecting instrument used to establish lines of sight at right angles to each other.
▶**B** *noun*. **1** CINEMATOGRAPHY & TELEVISION. An optical effect created in a processing laboratory. M20.
2 An example of optical art. *rare*. M20.
■ **optically** *adverb* by means of or in relation to sight, light, or optics; ***optically active*** (CHEMISTRY), causing optical rotation: L16.

optician /ɒpˈtɪʃ(ə)n/ *noun*. L17.
[French *opticien*, from medieval Latin *optica* optics: see -ICIAN.]
1 An expert in or student of optics. Now *rare* or *obsolete*. L17.
2 A maker of or dealer in optical instruments; *spec.* a person who tests eyes and makes up and dispenses spectacles and corrective lenses. M18.
2 ***ophthalmic optician***: see OPHTHALMIC *adjective* 2.
■ **opticist** *noun* (*rare*) an expert in or student of optics L19.

optico- /ˈɒptɪkəʊ/ *combining form* of Greek *optikos* OPTIC: see -O-.
■ **opticokiˈnetic** *adjective* = OPTOKINETIC M20.

optima *noun pl.* see OPTIMUM *noun*.

optimacy /ˈɒptɪməsi/ *noun*. Now *rare*. L16.
[mod. Latin *optimatia*, from Latin *optimas*: see OPTIMATE, -ACY.]
1 = ARISTOCRACY 2. L16.
2 = ARISTOCRACY 4. L16.

optimal /ˈɒptɪm(ə)l/ *adjective*. L19.
[from Latin *optimus* best + -AL[1].]
Orig. BIOLOGY. Best, most favourable, esp. under a particular set of circumstances; = OPTIMUM *adjective*. Cf. PESSIMAL.

> D. C. HAGUE An optimal decision . . comes as close as possible to achieving a given objective. N. F. DIXON There are optimal levels of information flow for proper functioning of the human brain. **optimal foraging** ECOLOGY utilizing prey resources in a manner that optimizes net energy gain per unit feeding time.

■ **optimally** *adverb* M20. **optiˈmality** *noun* M20. **optimaliˈzation** *noun* = OPTIMIZATION M20.

optimate /ˈɒptɪmət/ *noun*. Pl. **optimates** /ɒptɪˈmeɪtiːz, ˈɒptɪməts/. E17.
[Latin *optimates* (pl.) aristocrats use as noun of *optimas* aristocratic, from *optimus* best.]
A member of the patrician order in Rome; *gen.* a noble, an aristocrat. Usu. in *pl.*

optime /ˈɒptɪmeɪ/ *noun*. M18.
[Latin = best, very well, from *optime disputasti* you have disputed very well.]
In the mathematical tripos at Cambridge University, a student placed in the second or third division. Also (respectively) ***senior optime***, ***junior optime***.

optimific /ɒptɪˈmɪfɪk/ *adjective*. M20.
[from Latin *optimus* best + -I- + -FIC.]
PHILOSOPHY. Producing the maximum good consequences.

optimise *verb* var. of OPTIMIZE.

optimism /ˈɒptɪmɪz(ə)m/ *noun*. M18.
[French *optimisme*, from Latin OPTIMUM. Cf. PESSIMISM.]
1 The doctrine, esp. as propounded by the German philosopher Leibniz, that the actual world is the best of all the possible worlds that could have been created. M18. ▸**b** *gen.* Any view which supposes the ultimate predominance of good over evil in the universe. M19.
2 The character or quality of being the best or for the best. Now *rare*. L18.
3 The tendency to hope for the best or to take a favourable view of circumstances or prospects; hopefulness, confidence in the future. E19.

> **3** J. F. KENNEDY I am astounded at the wave of optimism . . There is a veritable tide of feeling that all is well. *Times of India* Mr. Shevardnadze expressed optimism that an agreement . . would emerge.

optimist /ˈɒptɪmɪst/ *noun & adjective*. M18.
[formed as prec.: see -IST.]
▶**A** *noun*. **1** A person inclined to optimism or hopefulness; a person who takes a favourable view of circumstances or prospects. M18.
2 A person who believes in the doctrine of optimism. L18.

> **1** P. CUTTING Optimists would announce that peace was at hand.

▶**B** *adjective*. Characterized by optimism; optimistic. M19.
■ **optiˈmistic** *adjective* of or pertaining to optimism; characterized by optimism: M19. **optiˈmistically** *adverb* L19.

optimity /ɒpˈtɪmɪti/ *noun*. *rare*. M17.
[from late Latin *optimitas*, from Latin *optimus* best: see -ITY.]
The quality or fact of being very good or for the best; excellence.

optimize /ˈɒptɪmʌɪz/ *verb*. Also **-ise**. E19.
[from Latin *optimus* best + -IZE.]
1 *verb trans.* Make the best or most of, develop to the utmost; make optimal; *transf.* develop in size, enlarge, swell. E19.
2 *verb intrans.* Act as an optimist; take a favourable view of circumstances. M19.
3 *verb intrans.* Become optimal. L20.

> **1** *Verbatim* The transportation system must be optimized for people . . to move at the lowest achievable total cost.

■ **optimiˈzation** *noun* the action of making the best of something; the state or condition of being optimal: M19. **optimizer** *noun* a person who optimizes or seeks to optimize something; (esp. in MATH. & COMPUTING) a thing which optimizes something: L20.

optimum /ˈɒptɪməm/ *noun & adjective*. L19.
[Latin, use as noun of neut. of *optimus* best.]
Orig. BIOLOGY. ▶**A** *noun*. Pl. **-mums**, **-ma** /-mə/. The conditions most favourable for growth, reproduction, or other vital process; *gen.* the best, a level, condition, etc., regarded as the best or most favourable. Cf. PESSIMUM. L19.

> B. MAGEE The maximum possible tolerance or freedom is an optimum, not an absolute.

▶**B** *adjective*. Best, most favourable, esp. under a particular set of circumstances; = OPTIMAL. L19.

> S. UNWIN The optimum size of a publisher's business, beyond which it is inexpedient to go. N. F. DIXON In one respect . . information is much like good. We need an optimum amount.

option /ˈɒpʃ(ə)n/ *noun*. M16.
[French, or Latin *optio(n-)*, from *opt-* stem of *optare*: see OPT, -ION.]
1 The action of choosing; choice; *esp.* a thing that is or may be chosen, an alternative, a possibility, a choice. M16. ▸**b** An item available in addition to the standard features of a product, esp. of a motor vehicle; an optional extra. M20. ▸**c** N. AMER. FOOTBALL. A play in which a quarter- or half-back chooses whether to pass or to run with the ball. M20.
†**2** A wish, a desire. E17–M18.
3 The right to choose; power or freedom of choice. M17.
4 *Hist.* The right which an archbishop formerly had on consecration of a bishop, of choosing one benefice within the see of the latter, to be in his own patronage for the next presentation. E18.
5 COMMERCE. The or a right, obtained by payment, to buy or sell shares etc. at a fixed price within a specified time. M18.

> **1** *USA Today* As long as there are other options, war is a fool's course. JOAN SMITH She didn't like any of the options open to her. F. WELDON We really have no option but to put up with anything she chooses to do. **keep one's options open** not commit oneself. **soft option** a choice which entails no difficult actions or decisions. **b** *Which?* Cortina option packs . . Carpets, reclining seats, . . adjustable back quarter lights. **3** P. G. WODEHOUSE A sentence of thirty days . . without the option of a fine. ***local option***: see LOCAL *adjective*. ***zero option***: see ZERO *noun & adjective*. **5** *European Investor* It would be pointless to exercise your option until the shares rose far enough. ***TRADED option***.

Comb.: **option card** (*a*) COMPUTING an expansion card; (*b*) a credit card issued for use in a particular store or chain of stores.
■ **optionless** *adjective* (*poet.*) E20.

option /ˈɒpʃ(ə)n/ *verb trans.* Chiefly *US*. M20.
[from the noun.]
Buy or sell under option; have an option on.

> *Times Lit. Suppl.* Film rights have already been optioned.

optional /ˈɒpʃ(ə)n(ə)l/ *adjective & noun*. M18.
[from OPTION *noun* + -AL[1].]
▶**A** *adjective*. **1** That leaves something to choice. M18.
2 That may be chosen; dependent on choice or preference; not obligatory. L17.

> **1** W. BLACKSTONE Original writs are either optional or peremptory. **2** *Which?* A permanent venting kit is usually an optional extra when you buy a tumble drier.

▶**B** *noun*. An optional subject or course; a class studying an optional subject. Orig. *US*. M19.
■ **optioˈnality** *noun* the quality of being optional; opportunity or freedom of choice: L19. **optionally** *adverb* in an optional way, by choice M19. **optionalize** *verb trans.* make optional E20.

opto /ˈɒptəʊ/ *adjective*. L20.
[Abbreviation.]
Optoelectronic; of or pertaining to optoelectronics.

opto- /ˈɒptəʊ/ *combining form*.
[Greek *optos* seen, visible: see -O-.]
Forming (chiefly scientific) words with the sense 'of sight or vision, optic'.
■ **optoaˈcoustic** *adjective* designating, pertaining to, or involving the effect whereby a light beam periodically interrupted at an audio frequency produces sound when made to irradiate an enclosed body of gas L20. **opto-ˈcoupler** *noun* (ELECTRONICS) a device containing light-emitting and light-sensitive components, used to couple isolated circuits L20. **optoelecˈtronic** *adjective* involving or pertaining to the interconversion or interaction of light and electronic signals M20. **optoelecˈtronics** *noun* the study and application of optoelectronic effects M20. **optotype** *noun* (OPHTHALMOLOGY) a letter or figure of definite size used for testing acuteness of vision; a test-type: L19.

optokinetic /ˌɒptəʊkɪˈnɛtɪk, -kʌɪ-/ *adjective*. E20.
[from OPTO- + KINETIC.]
MEDICINE. Pertaining to or designating a form of nystagmus produced by attempting to fixate objects which are rapidly traversing the visual field. Also = OPTOMOTOR.
■ **optokinetically** *adverb* M20.

optometer /ɒpˈtɒmɪtə/ *noun*. M18.
[from OPTO- + -METER.]
OPHTHALMOLOGY. Any of various instruments for measuring or testing vision, *esp.* one for measuring the refractive power of the eye.

optometry /ɒpˈtɒmɪtri/ *noun*. L19.
[from OPTO- + -METRY.]
OPHTHALMOLOGY. (The occupation concerned with) the measurement of vision, esp. the measurement of the refractive power of the eyes and the prescription of corrective lenses; the use of an optometer.
■ **optoˈmetric** *adjective* of or pertaining to optometry L19. **optoˈmetrical** *adjective* = OPTOMETRIC M19. **optoˈmetrically** *adverb* M19. **optometrist** *noun* a person who practises optometry; an ophthalmic optician: E20.

optomotor /ˈɒptəməʊtə/ *adjective*. E20.
[from OPTO- + MOTOR *adjective*.]
PHYSIOLOGY. Of, pertaining to, or characterized by turning of the eyes or body in response to the visual perception of a moving object.

opt-out /ˈɒptaʊt/ *noun*. M20.
[from *opt out* s.v. OPT.]
1 (An instance of) the action of opting out of something; *spec.* an act (by a school or hospital) of opting out of local authority control. M20.
2 A television or radio programme broadcast locally by a regional station in place of the national network programme. M20.

optronics /ɒpˈtrɒnɪks/ *noun pl.* M20.
[Abbreviation.]
= OPTOELECTRONICS.

opulence /ˈɒpjʊləns/ *noun*. E16.
[Latin *opulentia*, from *opulent-*: see next, -ENCE.]
1 Riches, wealth, affluence. E16.
2 *transf.* & *fig.* Abundance of resources or power; abundance *of* hair etc.; plumpness. L18.
■ Also †**opulency** *noun* E17–M18.

opulent /ˈɒpjʊl(ə)nt/ *adjective*. M16.
[Latin *opulent-*, from *opes* resources, wealth: see -ULENT.]
1 Rich, wealthy, affluent. M16. ▸**b** Yielding great wealth, lucrative. M17.
2 Rich or profuse in some property or quality; luxurious, plentiful; *transf.* plump. E19.
3 Of a flower or plant: having a wealth of blossom, colour, or fragrance; splendid. M19.

> **1** J. K. GALBRAITH The prices of mink pelts reflect the demand of an opulent minority. **2** J. UPDIKE The novel is opulent in its display of accents, imagery, and emotions. L. WHISTLER Opulent suede-coloured dressing-cases, with gilded initials on the lids.

■ **opulently** *adverb* in an opulent manner; richly, splendidly: M16.

opuntia /əˈpʌnʃɪə/ *noun*. E17.
[Latin, from *Opus* (accus. *Opuntem*) (see below), later used as a genus name: see -IA[1].]
Orig., a plant said to grow about the Locrian city of Opus, in Greece. Now, any cactus of the genus *Opuntia*, which includes the prickly pears.

opus /ˈəʊpəs, ˈɒp-/ *noun*. Pl. **opuses** /ˈəʊpəsɪz, ˈɒp-/, **opera** /ˈɒp(ə)rə/. E18.
[Latin = work.]
An artistic work, a composition; *esp.* a musical composition or set of compositions as numbered among the works of a composer in order of publication. (Abbreviation ***op.***)

> L. APPIGNANESI His vast philosophical opus *Being & Nothingness* was published. **opus magnum** = MAGNUM OPUS.

opus /ˈəʊpəs, ˈɒp-/ *verb trans.* *rare*. E20.
[from the noun.]
Include and number among the works of a composer of music.

opus Alexandrinum /ˌɒpəs ˌalɛksɑːnˈdriːnəm/ *noun phr.* M19.
[medieval Latin, lit. 'Alexandrian work'.]
A pavement mosaic work widely used in Byzantium in the 9th cent. and later in Italy, consisting of coloured stone, glass, and semiprecious stones arranged in intricate geometric patterns.

opus anglicanum /ˌɒpəs aŋglɪˈkɑːnəm/ *noun phr.* Also **A-**. M19.
[medieval Latin, lit. 'English work': see ANGLICAN.]
Fine pictorial embroidery produced in England in the Middle Ages and used esp. on ecclesiastical vestments.

opus Anglicum /ɒpəs ˈaŋglɪkəm/ *noun phr.* Now *rare*. M19.
[medieval Latin, lit. 'English work': cf. prec.]
A style of manuscript illumination regarded as characteristically English.

opus araneum /ˌɒpəs aˈrɑːnɪəm/ *noun phr.* M19.
[medieval Latin, lit. 'spider's work'.]
Darned netting; delicate embroidery done on a net and resembling a spider's web. Also called ***spider-work***.

opus consutum /ˌɒpəs kɒnˈsuːtəm/ *noun phr.* L19.
[medieval Latin, lit. 'work sewn together'.]
= APPLIQUÉ *noun*.

opuscule /əˈpʌskjuːl/ *noun*. Also in Latin form **-culum** /-kjʊləm/, pl. **-la** /-lə/. M17.
[Old & mod. French from Latin *opusculum* dim. of *opus*: see OPUS *noun*, -CULE.]
A minor (esp. literary or musical) work.
■ **opuscular** *adjective* (*rare*) pertaining to or of the nature of a minor work E19.

opus Dei /ɒpəs ˈdeɪiː/ *noun phr.* L19.
[medieval Latin.]
1 ECCLESIASTICAL. The work of God; *spec.* liturgical worship regarded as man's primary duty to God. L19.
2 (With cap. initials.) A Roman Catholic organization of priests and lay people founded in Spain in 1928 with the aim of re-establishing Christian ideals in society. E20.

opus sectile /ɒpəs ˈsɛktɪleɪ/ *noun phr.* M19.
[Latin, lit. 'cut work'.]
An orig. Roman floor decoration made up of pieces shaped individually to fit the pattern or design, as distinct from mosaic which uses regularly shaped pieces.

opus signinum /ˌɒpəs sɪgˈniːnəm/ *noun phr.* M18.
[Latin, lit. 'work of Signia', a town (now Segni) in Central Italy famous for its tiles.]
An orig. Roman flooring material consisting of broken tiles etc. mixed with lime mortar.

OR *abbreviation*.
1 Operational research.
2 Oregon.
3 MILITARY. Other ranks.

or /ɔː/ *noun*[1]. LME.
[Old & mod. French, ult. from Latin *aurum* gold.]
Orig., gold. Later (HERALDRY), the tincture gold or yellow in armorial bearings.

or /ɔː, ə/ *adverb, preposition, & conjunction*[1]. Now *arch. & dial.* or *Scot.*
[Old English *ār*, or later from Old Norse *ár* = Old English *ǣr* ERE. Cf. AIR *adverb*.]
▸†**A** *adverb*. **1** Early, soon; = AIR *adverb* 2, ERE *adverb* 1. OE–LME.
2 Sooner, earlier; = ERE *adverb* 2. Only in ME.
3 On a former occasion; formerly, before; = AIR *adverb* 1, ERE *adverb* 3. ME–L15. ▸**b** Before something else, in the first place. Only in ME.
▸**B** *preposition*. Before (in time); = ERE *preposition*. Freq. in adverbial phrs. ***or long***, ***or now***, etc. OE.

📖 G. CAVENDISH It was midnight or they departed.

▸**C** *conjunction*. **1** Of time: before. Also ***or e'er***, ***or ever***, †***or than***, †***or that***. ME.
2 Of preference: rather than; = ERE *conjunction* 2. ME.
3 After a comparative or *other*: than. ME.

📖 **1** T. WILSON Wil you drink or you go?

or /ɔː, ə/ *conjunction*[2], *noun*[2], *& verb*. ME.
[Reduced form of OTHER *conjunction & adverb*[2].]
▸**A** *conjunction*. **1** Introducing the second of two, or all but the first or only the last of several, alternatives. ME. ▸**b** Introducing an emphatic repetition of a rhetorical question. *colloq.* M20.
2 Introducing the only remaining possibility or choice of two or more quite different or mutually exclusive alternatives. Freq. following *either*, †*other*, (in neg. contexts, *colloq.*) *neither*. ME.
3 Followed by *or*: as an alternative; either. Formerly also, introducing alternative questions. Now *arch. & poet.* ME.
4 Introducing, after a primary statement, a secondary alternative, or consequence of setting aside the primary statement; otherwise, else; if not. ME.
5 Connecting two words denoting the same thing, or introducing an explanation of a preceding word etc.; otherwise called, that is. ME.
6 Introducing a significant afterthought, usu. in the form of a question, which casts doubt on a preceding assertion or assumption. E20.

📖 **1** R. MACAULAY A periodical . . with which you may or may not be familiar. F. REID Cockroaches or no cockroaches he must get his shoes. R. ADAMS Four or five mounds of newly-turned earth. J. WILSON He was often called a nut-case or a twit or a weirdo. **b** P. CHEYNEY Has that dame gotta swell voice or has she? **2** SOUTHEY Morality can neither be produced or preserved in a people . . without true religion. F. IRWIN You can either double the two hearts or go 'two no-trumps'. **3** COLERIDGE Without or wave or wind. **4** S. O'FAOLÁIN He'll marry the girl or he'll have no house . . by morning. V. S. PRITCHETT Rain was pouring down . . or I would have gone after her. **5** OED An inhabitant . . of the Netherlands or Holland. *New Scientist* The common or garden inter-city train of the future. **6** I. MURDOCH She must surely . . be fourteen now. Or was she?

Phrases: ***or else***: see ELSE *adverb* 3.

▸**B** *noun*. (Usu. **OR**.) COMPUTING. A Boolean operator which gives the value unity if at least one of the operands is unity, and is otherwise zero. Usu. *attrib.* M20.
inclusive OR = sense B. above. **exclusive OR** a function that has the value unity if at least one, but not all, of the variables are unity.

▸**C** *verb trans.* (Usu. **OR**.) COMPUTING. Combine using a Boolean OR operator. Chiefly as ***ORed*** *ppl adjective*. L20.

-or /ə, LAW ɔː/ *suffix*.
1 Forming nouns of condition from or after Anglo-Norman -(*o*)*ur*, Old French -*or*, -*ur* (mod. -*eur*) or Latin -*or*, as ***error***, ***horror***, ***pallor***, ***stupor***, ***tremor***. Now chiefly *US* exc. in those words conformed to Latin spelling in the Renaissance: cf. -OUR 1.
2 a Forming agent-nouns from or after Anglo-Norman -*eour*, Old French -*or*, -*ur* (mod -*eur*) or Latin -*or*, as ***actor***, ***creator***, ***doctor***, ***elevator***, ***monitor***, ***sculptor***, ***successor***. Freq. in legal terms (opp. -EE[1]), as ***guarantor***, ***lessor***, ***mortgagor***. ▸**b** Forming agent-nouns from or after Anglo-Norman -*eour*, Old French -*ëor*, -*ëur* (mod. -*eur*) or Latin -*ator*, -*etor*, -*itor*, as ***conqueror***, ***donor***, ***governor***, ***solicitor***, ***tailor***, ***visitor***. ▸**c** Var. of -ER[2], as ***bachelor***, ***chancellor***. ▸**d** Var. of -ER[1], as ***sailor***. Freq. forming inanimate agent-nouns, as ***conveyor***, ***resistor***, ***sensor***.
3 Forming nouns from Old & mod. French -*oir*, as ***manor***, ***mirror***.
4 Forming adjectives of comparison from Anglo-Norman -*our* or Latin -*or*, as ***major***, ***minor***. Cf. -IOR.
5 Var. of -OUR 2. *US*.

ora /ˈɔːrə/ *noun*[1]. OE.
[App. from Old Norse *aurar* pl.; commonly regarded as from Latin *aureus* golden. Cf. URE *noun*[2].]
Hist. **1** A Danish monetary unit introduced into England with the Danish invasion. OE.
2 A unit of weight equal to an ounce. E17.

ora /ˈɔːrə/ *noun*[2]. E19.
[Latin = border, brim, coast, etc.]
An edge, a border. Chiefly (ANATOMY) in ***ora serrata*** /sɛˈrɑːtə/, the serrated edge of the retina, just behind the ciliary body.

ora *noun*[3] pl. of OS *noun*[2].

orache /ˈɒrətʃ/ *noun*. Also (earlier) †**-age**, **-ach**. ME.
[Anglo-Norman *arasche*, Old French *arache*, *arrace* (mod. *arroche*), from Latin *atriplex*, -*plic*- (or some intermediate form between this and its source) from Greek *atraphaxus*, -*is*.]
Any of various inconspicuous-flowered plants constituting the genus *Atriplex*, of the goosefoot family, which includes the garden orache, *A. hortensis*, grown as a substitute for spinach, and several common weeds (*A. patula*, *A. prostrata*).
Comb.: **orache moth** a noctuid moth, *Trachea atriplicis*, whose caterpillars feed on the orache.

oracle /ˈɒrək(ə)l/ *noun*. In sense 9 usu. **O-**. LME.
[Old & mod. French from Latin *oraculum*, from *orare* speak, plead, pray: see -CLE.]
▸**I 1** CLASSICAL MYTHOLOGY. The agency or medium by which the gods were supposed to speak or prophesy; the mouthpiece of the gods; the place or seat of this, at which advice or prophecy was sought from the gods. LME.
2 A freq. ambiguous or obscure response or message given at an oracle, supposedly from a god and usu. delivered by a priest or priestess. M16.

📖 **1** F. FERGUSSON Laius and Jocasta . . are told by the oracle that their son will . . kill his father. **2** C. THIRLWALL An oracle was procured exactly suited to the purpose of the leaders of the expedition. *transf.*: A. WILSON We're not going to get very far if we talk in Delphic oracles.

▸**II** In religious use.
3 a The most sacred sanctuary of the Jewish Temple, regarded as a place of divine communication; the holy of holies. LME. ▸**b** A person who or thing which expounds or interprets the will of God; a divine teacher. LME.
4 Divine inspiration or revelation; an instance of this. LME.
†**5** An injunction or command of the Pope. L16–E17.

📖 **3b** MILTON God hath now sent his living Oracle Into the World. **4** ***Sibylline oracles***: see SIBYLLINE *adjective*.

▸**III** *fig.* **6** An utterance of deep import or wisdom; a saying etc. regarded as offering infallible guidance; undeniable truth. LME.
7 A person of great wisdom or knowledge, regarded as an infallible authority. L16.
8 a Something reputed to give oracular replies or advice. E17. ▸**b** Something regarded as an infallible guide or indicator, esp. when its action could be thought of as mysterious. E18.
9 (Usu. **O-**.) (Proprietary name for) a teletext system developed for British commercial television. L20.

📖 **6** W. WOTTON His Words were received as Oracles. **7** K. M. E. MURRAY He longed for an oracle . . who would give him a clear Yes or No. A. KENNY Heard was . . impressive . . and some of us treated him as an oracle.

Phrases: **work the oracle** gain something to one's advantage by influence or manipulation.
Comb.: **oracle bones** bones used in ancient China for divination.

oracle /ˈɒrək(ə)l/ *verb*. *rare*. L16.
[from the noun.]
1 *verb trans.* Utter or pronounce as an oracle. L16.
2 *verb intrans.* Speak as an oracle. M17.

oracular /ɒˈrakjʊlə/ *adjective*. M17.
[from Latin *oraculum* (see ORACLE *noun*) + -AR[1].]
1 Of, pertaining to, or of the nature of an oracle. M17. ▸**b** *spec.* Ambiguous or mysterious, like an ancient oracle. M18.
2 Of a person: that delivers oracular responses; *transf.* that speaks or writes like an oracle. E19.
3 Delivered, uttered, or decreed by an oracle. E19.

📖 **1** C. C. FELTON Delphi—one of the richest oracular sites in the world. LD MACAULAY Whatever he said . . was considered oracular by his disciples. **3** J. A. SYMONDS When Oedipus slays his father, he does so in contempt of oracular warnings.

■ **oracuˈlarity** *noun* the quality or character of being oracular E19. **oracularly** *adverb* in an oracular manner; solemnly, authoritatively; obscurely, ambiguously: L18. **oracularness** *noun* oracularity E18.

oraculate /ɒˈrakjʊleɪt/ *verb trans. & intrans.* *rare*. E19.
[formed as prec. + -ATE[3].]
Say or speak oracularly.

oraculous /ɒˈrakjʊləs/ *adjective*. Now *rare* or *obsolete*. E17.
[formed as ORACULAR + -OUS, perh. after *miraculous*.]
= ORACULAR.
■ **oraculously** *adverb* (long *rare*) M17.

oraculum /ɒˈrakjʊləm/ *noun*. *rare*. Pl. **-la** /-lə/. E18.
[Latin: see ORACLE *noun*.]
1 = ORACLE *noun*. E18.
2 = ORATORY *noun*[1] 1. M19.

oracy /ˈɔːrəsi/ *noun*. M20.
[from Latin *or*-, *os* mouth + -ACY, after *literacy*.]
The ability to express oneself fluently in speech.

orage /ɔːˈrɑːʒ/ *noun*[1]. Long *rare*. Pl. pronounced same. L15.
[French from popular Latin *auraticum*, from Latin *aura* breeze.]
A violent or tempestuous wind; a storm.

†**orage** *noun*[2] var. of ORACHE.

oragious /ɒˈreɪdʒəs/ *adjective*. *rare*. L16.
[from French *orageux*, -*euse*, formed as ORAGE *noun*[1]: see -IOUS.]
Stormy, tempestuous.

oraison funèbre /ɔrɛzɔ̃ fynɛbr/ *noun phr.* Pl. **-s -s** (pronounced same). L19.
[French.]
A funeral oration.

oral /ˈɔːr(ə)l/ *adjective & noun*. E17.
[Late Latin *oralis*, from Latin *or*-, *os* mouth: see -AL[1].]
▸**A** *adjective*. **1** Uttered or communicated in spoken words; conducted by word of mouth; spoken, verbal; *spec.* (of verse etc.) delivered or transmitted verbally, of or pertaining to such verse etc. E17.
2 a Done or performed with or by the mouth as the organ of eating and drinking, *spec.* with ref. to the Eucharist. *rare*. E17. ▸**b** (Of medication etc.) administered or taken through the mouth; involving such administration. M20.
3 Of or pertaining to the mouth, as a part of the body. M17.
4 Designating or involving sexual activity in which the genitals of one partner are stimulated by the mouth of the other. Cf. CUNNILINGUS, FELLATIO. L19.
5 PSYCHOANALYSIS. Of or concerning a supposed stage of infantile psychosexual development in which the mouth is the main focus of energy and feeling. E20.
6 PHONETICS. Of a sound: articulated with the velum raised, so that there is no nasal resonance. E20.

1 H. BELLOC Fragments preserved by oral tradition. H. A. L. FISHER Information . . derived from oral sources only was . . fragmentary. **2b** J. H. BURN Ring worm . . responds well to oral treatment with antibiotic Griseofulvin. W. J. BURLEY A sachet of oral contraceptives. **4** S. FISHER Most of the women . . received manual and often oral stimulation of the clitoral region.

Special collocations & comb.: **oral-formulaic** *adjective* of or pertaining to (usu. early) poetry belonging to a spoken tradition characterized by the use of poetic formulae. **oral history** (a collection of) tape-recorded historical information drawn from the speaker's personal knowledge; the use or interpretation of this as an academic subject. **Oral Law** the part of Jewish religious law believed to have been passed down by oral tradition before being collected in the Mishnah.

▶ **B** *absol.* as *noun*. **1** PHONETICS. An oral sound. L19.

2 An oral examination or test. L19.

2 L. APPIGNANESI Following the written part there would be an oral.

▪ **oralism** *noun* a method of instructing deaf mutes by ordinary speech and lip-reading, instead of by sign language L19. **oralist** *noun* (*a*) *rare* an expert in oral delivery; (*b*) a person who teaches deaf mutes by oralism: M19. **orally** *adverb* by, through, or with the mouth E17.

orality /ɒˈralɪti/ *noun*. M17.

[from prec. + -ITY.]

1 The quality of being spoken or verbally communicated; preference for or tendency to use spoken forms of language. M17.

2 PSYCHOANALYSIS. The focusing of sexual energy and feeling on the mouth. M20.

3 PHONETICS. The quality or state of being oral. M20.

1 R. C. A. WHITE The trial proceeds on the basis of orality; almost every document . . is read out. **2** H. SEGAL Orality may express itself in greed.

orang /ɒˈraŋ/ *noun*. L18.

[Abbreviation.]

= ORANG-UTAN.

orange /ˈɒrɪn(d)ʒ/ *noun & adjective*[1]. LME.

[Old French *orenge* in *pomme d'orenge*, ult. from Arab. *nāranj* from Persian *nārang* (whence also Spanish *naranja* etc.) from Sanskrit *nāraṅga*.]

▶ **A** *noun*. **1** Any of several large round citrus fruits with segmented juicy pulp enclosed in a tough reddish-yellow rind; *spec.* (also ***sweet orange***, ***China orange***) a common dessert fruit, borne by *Citrus sinensis*. LME.

2 More fully ***orange tree***. Any of the trees, widely cultivated in warm-temperate or subtropical regions, which bear such fruit and are noted for their fragrant white flowers. LME.

3 HERALDRY. A roundel tenné. M16.

4 The colour of an orange, between red and yellow in the spectrum. Also, a pigment of this colour (freq. with specifying word). L16.

5 Any of several reddish-yellow varieties of apple or pear. M18.

6 With specifying word: any of various plants thought to resemble the orange tree in flower or fruit; the fruit of such a plant. M18.

7 An orange-flavoured soft drink; orange squash, orange juice; a drink of this. M20.

1 ***blood orange***, ***Jaffa orange***, ***navel orange***, ***Seville orange***, ***Valencia orange***, etc. **4** TENNYSON Till all the crimson changed and past Into deep orange o'er the sea. **7** C. HOPE Gabriel and Looksmart Dladla were given bottles of fizzy orange to drink.

Phrases: **Agent Orange** a highly poisonous herbicide used as a defoliant for crops and forest cover, esp. by US forces during the Vietnam war. ***bitter orange***: see BITTER *adjective*. ***China orange***: see CHINA *noun*[1] 1. ***Cox's orange pippin***: see COX *noun*[2]. INTERNATIONAL ***orange***. ***Kaffir orange***: see KAFFIR *adjective*. ***Lombard Street to a China orange***: see LOMBARD *noun*[1] *& adjective*. ***Mexican orange***. ***mock orange***: see MOCK *adjective*. ***native orange***: see NATIVE *adjective*. **oranges and lemons** a nursery game, in which a song beginning with these words is sung, and the players take sides. ***Osage orange***. ***poor man's orange***: see POOR MAN 2. ***sea-orange***. ***Seville orange***: see SEVILLE 2. ***sour orange***: see SOUR *adjective*. **squeeze an orange**, **suck an orange** *fig.* take all that is profitable out of something. ***wild orange***: see WILD *adjective*.

▶ **B** *adjective*. Of the colour of an orange, reddish-yellow; of the flavour of an orange. M16.

P. ABRAHAMS The setting sun . . threw pale orange fingers of light into the darkening sky. F. WELDON Red and orange flowers grew in tidy patterns.

Comb. & special collocations: **orange bat** a leaf-nosed bat of northern Australia, *Rhinonycteris aurantius*, the male of which has bright orange fur; **orange blossom** (*a*) the white fragrant blossom of the orange tree, traditionally worn by the bride at a wedding ceremony; (*b*) a cocktail flavoured with orange juice; **orange-brandy** brandy flavoured with orange peel; **orange-chip** a slice of orange peel prepared for eating; **orange-colour** *noun & adjective* (of) the colour of an orange; reddish-yellow; **orange-coloured** *adjective* of the colour of an orange, reddish-yellow; **orange dove** a Fijian dove, *Ptilinopus victor*, the male of which has bright orange plumage; **orange flower** a flower of an orange tree; orange blossom; **orange grass** = **nitweed** S.V. NIT *noun*[1]; **orange juice** the juice of an orange, esp. when extracted from the orange; a drink of this; **orange lily** a cultivated lily, *Lilium bulbiferum* var. *croceum*, with orange flowers; **orange moth** a geometrid moth, *Angerona prunaria*, the males of which have speckled orange wings; **orange-oil** an essential oil obtained from the rind of the orange; **orange peel** (*a*) the rind or skin of an orange, esp. when separated from the pulp; (*b*) a rough surface resembling this; (*c*) ***orange-peel bucket***, ***orange-peel grab***, a suspended bucket or grab made up of several curved, pointed segments that are hinged at the top and come together to form a container; (*d*) ***orange-peel fungus***, a cup-shaped fungus, *Aleuria aurantia*, which resembles orange peel; (*e*) ***orange-peel skin*** [cf. French PEAU D'ORANGE], skin dimpled like that of an orange, esp. when resulting from subcutaneous fat deposits; cellulite; **orange pekoe** a type of black tea made from very small leaves; **orange-quarter** (*a*) any of the segments of an orange; (*b*) a fourth part of an orange; **orangequit** [QUIT *noun*[1]] a Jamaican tanager, *Euneornis campestris*; **orange-red** *adjective & noun* (of) a shade of red approaching orange; **orange-root** the golden seal, *Hydrastis canadensis*; **orange squash** a soft drink made from oranges, sugar, and water, often sold in concentrated form, orange-flavoured squash; **orange stick** a short stick, usu. of orange-wood, used for manicuring the nails; **orange-strainer** a utensil for straining the juice of an orange; **orange-tawny** *adjective & noun* (of) a dull yellowish-brown colour; brownish-yellow with a tinge of orange; **orange thorn** an Australian thorny shrub bearing orange berries, *Citriobatus pauciflorus* (family Pittosporaceae); **orange-tip (butterfly)** any of various pierid butterflies of the genus *Anthocharis*, the males having wings tipped with orange, esp. (in Britain) *A. cardamines* and (in *US*) *A. genutia*; ***orange tree***: see sense 2 above; **orange upperwing** a European noctuid moth, *Jodia croceago*, which has orange-brown forewings; **orange-wood** the wood of the orange tree; **orange-yellow** *adjective & noun* (of) a shade of yellow approaching orange.

▪ **oranged** *adjective* (*rare*) coloured orange, tinted with orange M16. **orangey** *adjective* (*a*) resembling an orange in colour, taste, etc.; (*b*) covered in or sticky with orange: L18. **orangish** *adjective* having an orange tinge; somewhat orange: L19.

Orange /ˈɒrɪn(d)ʒ/ *adjective*[2]. M17.

[A town and principality on the River Rhône in France.]

1 Of or pertaining to the Dutch family or dynasty, later the Dutch royal house, descended from the House of Nassau and who in 1530 took possession of the town of Orange. M17.

2 Of, pertaining to, or designating an extreme Protestant political society or order formed in 1795 to defend and uphold Protestant supremacy in Ireland, whose supporters wear orange badges etc. as a symbol of their attachment to William III (William of Orange) and his principles. L18.

2 B. BEHAN It was an Orange district, but . . some of them were Liverpool-Irish trying to prove their solidarity. L. MACNEICE A framed Certificate of admission Into the Orange Order. *Scotland on Sunday* One of the less-attractive sides of the city's cultural life—an advancing Orange walk.

Special collocations & comb.: **Orange Lodge** the Orange Order (believed to have started as a Freemasons' lodge in Belfast). **Orangeman** a member of the Orange Order.

▪ **Orangeism**, **Orangism** *noun* the principles of the Orange Order; the principle of Protestant political supremacy in Ireland: E19. **Orangist** *noun* (*a*) *Hist.* a supporter of the Dutch family or dynasty descended from the House of Nassau; (*b*) an Orangeman: L18.

orangeade /ɒrɪn(d)ʒˈeɪd/ *noun*. E18.

[from ORANGE *noun* + -ADE, after *lemonade*.]

A usu. fizzy soft drink flavoured with orange; a drink of this.

†orangeado *noun*. L16–L18.

[Cf. Spanish *naranjada* conserve of oranges, French *orangeat*: see -ADO.]

Candied orange peel.

orangery /ˈɒrɪndʒ(ə)ri/ *noun*. Also **-erie**. M17.

[In sense 1 from French *orangerie*, from *oranger* orange tree: see -ERY. In sense 2 unexpl. deriv. of ORANGE *noun & adjective*[1].]

1 A place, esp. a special protective structure, where orange trees are cultivated. M17.

2 A scent or perfume extracted from orange-flowers; snuff scented with this. Now *rare* or *obsolete*. L17.

orang-utan /ɔːˌraŋuːˈtan, əˈraŋuːtan/ *noun*. Also (earlier) **-outang** /-uːˈtaŋ/. L17.

[Malay *orang hutan* forest person.]

An arboreal anthropoid ape, *Pongo pygmaeus*, native to Borneo and Sumatra, having long reddish hair and characteristic long arms with hooked hands and feet.

orans /ˈɔːranz/ *noun*. Pl. **orantes** /ɒˈrantiːz/. E20.

[Latin *orans*, *orantem* pres. pple of *orare* pray.]

ART. A representation of a person in a kneeling or praying position.

Oraon /əʊˈrɑːɒn/ *noun & adjective*. Pl. of noun same, **-s**. M19.

[Kurukh.]

= KURUKH.

orarion /ɒˈrɑːrɪɒn/ *noun*. L18.

[Graecized from next.]

In the Orthodox Church, a deacon's stole.

orarium /ɒˈrɛːrɪəm/ *noun*. Pl. ***-ia*** /-ɪə/, **-iums**. E18.

[Latin = napkin, from *or-*, *os* mouth, face: see -ARIUM.]

ECCLESIASTICAL. A stole; *spec.* = ORARION.

orate /ɔːˈreɪt, ɒˈreɪt/ *verb intrans*. E17.

[Latin *orat-* pa. ppl stem of *orare* speak, plead: see -ATE[3]. Sense 2 re-formed in US in M19, as back-form. from ORATION *noun*.]

†1 Pray; plead. Only in E17.

2 Deliver an oration; hold forth pompously or at length. Now chiefly *joc.* or *derog.* M17.

oration /ɒˈreɪʃ(ə)n/ *noun*. LME.

[Latin *oratio(n-)* discourse, speech, (ecclesiastical) prayer, formed as ORATE: see -ATION.]

1 CHRISTIAN CHURCH. A prayer or supplication to God. *obsolete* exc. *Hist.* LME.

2 A formal speech or discourse delivered in elevated and dignified language, esp. on a particular occasion. E16.

3 Speech, language; a way of speaking. M17.

2 L. M. MONTGOMERY Mark Antony's oration over the dead body of Caesar. **3** ***direct oration***: see DIRECT *adjective*. ***oblique oration***: see OBLIQUE *adjective*.

▪ **orational** *adjective* (*rare*) of or pertaining to prayer in religious worship L19.

oration /ɒˈreɪʃ(ə)n/ *verb intrans. colloq.* M17.

[from the noun.]

Make a speech or oration.

▪ **orationer** *noun* (*rare*) M18.

oratio obliqua /ɒˌrɑːtɪəʊ ɒˈbliːkwə, ɒˌreɪʃ(ɪ)əʊ əˈblʌɪkwə/ *noun phr*. M19.

[Latin, formed as ORATION *noun* + *obliqua* fem. of *obliquus* OBLIQUE *adjective*.]

Indirect speech.

oratio recta /ɒˌrɑːtɪəʊ ˈrɛktə, ɒˌreɪʃ(ɪ)əʊ ˈrɛktə/ *noun phr*. M19.

[Latin, formed as ORATION *noun* + *recta* fem. of *rectus* straight, direct.]

Direct speech.

orator /ˈɒrətə/ *noun*. LME.

[Anglo-Norman *oratour* = Old & mod. French *orateur* from Latin *orator* speaker, pleader, formed as ORATE: see -OR.]

†1 A person who pleads or argues in favour of a person or cause; an advocate, *spec.* a professional one. LME–M17.

2 †a A person who offers a prayer or petition; a petitioner, a suppliant. LME–E18. ▶**b** LAW. A plaintiff or petitioner in a case in a court of chancery. *obsolete* exc. *US*. L16.

3 A person who delivers a public speech or oration; an eloquent public speaker. LME.

†4 A person sent to plead or speak for another; an ambassador, an envoy, a messenger. L15–L17.

5 More fully ***public orator***. An official at a university, esp. Oxford and Cambridge, who speaks for the university on ceremonial occasions, and who performs other written and spoken duties of a formal and representational nature. E17.

3 H. J. LASKI An able speaker, without being a great orator.

▪ **oratorize** *verb intrans.* play the orator; deliver an oration; orate: E17. **oratorship** *noun* the position or office of orator, esp. in a university L16.

oratorial /ɒrəˈtɔːrɪəl/ *adjective*. M16.

[In sense 1 from Latin *oratorius* of or pertaining to an orator, from *orator* ORATOR + *-ius*: see -ORY[2]; in sense 2 from ORATORIO: see -AL[1].]

1 Of, pertaining to, or proper to an orator. M16.

2 Of or pertaining to an oratorio. E19.

1 *Times* The conference's new oratorial hero, Scargill.

▪ **oratorially** *adverb* M16.

oratorian /ɒrəˈtɔːrɪən/ *adjective & noun*. E17.

[from Latin *oratorius* of or pertaining to an orator, *oratorium* place of prayer, ORATORY *noun*[1] + -AN.]

▶ **A** *adjective*. **†1** Of or pertaining to an orator; oratorial. E17–M18.

2 Of or pertaining to an Oratory. M19.

▶ **B** *noun*. A father or priest of an oratory; *spec.* (**O-**) a member of an Oratory, esp. that at Rome. E17.

▪ **Oratorianism** *noun* the system, principles, or practice of the Oratorians M19. **Oratorianize** *verb intrans.* follow the methods of the Oratorians M19.

oratoric /ɒrəˈtɒrɪk/ *adjective*. M17.

[from Latin ORATOR + -IC, after *historic*, *rhetoric*.]

= next.

oratorical /ɒrəˈtɒrɪk(ə)l/ *adjective*. L16.

[formed as prec. + -AL[1].]

1 Of, pertaining to, or characteristic of an orator or oratory; rhetorical. Also, according to the rules of oratory. L16.

†2 = ORATORIAN *adjective* 2. Only in E17.

3 Given to the use of oratory. E19.

1 V. BROME One of his rolling oratorical utterances.

▪ **oratorically** *adverb* L17.

oratorio /ɒrəˈtɔːrɪəʊ/ *noun*. Pl. **-os**. M17.

[Italian from ecclesiastical Latin *oratorium* ORATORY *noun*[1]. Sense 2 named from the musical services in the church of the Oratory of St Philip Neri in Rome.]

†**1** A pulpit. *rare*. Only in **M17.**
2 A semi-dramatic extended musical composition, usually based on a Scriptural theme, performed by a choir with soloists and a full orchestra, without costume, action, or scenery. **E18.** ▸**b** The genre of musical composition or drama characterized by such a theme and such performance. **L19.**

> 🕮 **2** *Early Music* No Venetian oratorio from the 17th century survives.

oratory /ˈɒrət(ə)ri/ *noun*[1]. **ME.**
[Anglo-Norman *oratorie* = Old & mod. French *oratoire* from ecclesiastical Latin *oratorium* use as noun (sc. *templum* temple) of neut. of *oratorius*: see **ORATORIAL, -ORY**[1].]
1 A place of prayer; a small chapel or shrine; a room or building for private worship. **ME.**
†**2** A place for public speaking. **E17–E18.**
3 *ROMAN CATHOLIC CHURCH*. (**O-**.) A religious society of priests without vows founded in Rome in 1564 and providing plain preaching and popular services; any of the branches of this in other countries. **M17.**
†**4** A faldstool used by a worshipper at prayer. **L17–L18.**

oratory /ˈɒrət(ə)ri/ *noun*[2]. **E16.**
[Latin *oratoria* use as noun (sc. *ars* art) of fem. of *oratorius*: see **ORATORIAL, -ORY**[1].]
1 The art of public speaking; the art of speaking formally and eloquently; rhetoric. **E16.**
2 The delivery of orations or speeches; the language of these; rhetorical or exaggerated language. **L16.**

> 🕮 **1** R. WARNER What he said seemed to need no tricks of oratory to make it emphatic.

oratress /ˈɒrətrɪs/ *noun*. **L16.**
[from **ORATOR** + **-ESS**[1].]
†**1** A female petitioner or plaintiff. **L16–M19.**
2 A female public speaker. **L16.**

oratrix /ɒˈreɪtrɪks, ˈɒrətrɪks/ *noun*. Pl. **-trices** /-trɪsiːz/. **LME.**
[Latin, fem. of *orator* **ORATOR**: see **-TRIX**.]
†**1** = **ORATRESS** 1. **LME–M19.**
2 = **ORATRESS** 2. **L16.**

orb /ɔːb/ *noun*[1]. **LME.**
[Latin *orbis*.]
▸ **I** A circle, & derived senses.
1 A circle; anything of circular form, as a disc, wheel, or ring. Now *rare*. **LME.**
†**2** *ASTRONOMY*. (The plane of) the orbit of a planet etc. **LME–M18.**
†**3** A recurring period; a cycle. **M17–M18.**
4 *ASTROLOGY*. The space on either side of a planet across which its influence is held to extend, so that aspects need not be exact. **E18.**

> 🕮 **1** J. CLEVELAND The Wheels, or Orbs, upon which Providence turns. **2** *fig.*: A. TUCKER Whenever we venture to move in an eccentric orb. **3** DRYDEN Mighty Years, begun From their first Orb, in radiant Circles run.

▸ **II** A sphere, & derived senses.
5 Each of the concentric hollow spheres formerly believed to surround the earth and carry the planets and stars with them in their revolutions. Cf. **SPHERE** *noun* 2. *obsolete* exc. *Hist.* **E16.**
6 A spherical body; *spec.* a planetary or celestial body. Chiefly *poet. & rhet.* **L16.** ▸†**b** The world. *rare* (Shakes.). Only in **E17.**
7 The eye-ball; the eye. *poet. & rhet.* **E17.**
8 *fig.* †**a** A sphere of action; rank, station. **E17–M18.** ▸**b** An organized or collective whole. **E17.**
9 A golden globe surmounted by a cross, forming part of the regalia of a monarch etc. **E18.**

> 🕮 **6** C. THIRLWALL They worshipped the elements, the heavens, and the orbs of day and night. **b** SHAKES. *Twel. N.* Foolery, sir, does walk about the orb like the sun—it shines everywhere. **7** E. HARDWICK Nice, empty, withdrawn and staring eyes—orbs in a porcelain head. **8a** T. ELLWOOD My Station, not being so Eminent . . as others who have moved in higher Orbs. **b** E. H. SEARS The race in its totality, as an organic whole . . making one orb of being.

Comb.: **orb-weaver** a spider which builds an orb-web; **orb-web** a circular web formed of threads radiating from a central point, crossed by others spiralling out, typical of spiders of the family Araneidae.
■ **orbless** *adjective* **E19.** **orblet** *noun* **M19.**

orb /ɔːb/ *noun*[2]. *obsolete* exc. *Hist.* **E16.**
[Anglo-Norman *orbe*, Anglo-Latin *orba*, perh. use as noun of fem. of Latin *orbus* deprived, devoid (of), rel. to **ORPHAN** *noun*. Cf. French *mur orbe* blind wall.]
ARCHITECTURE. A blank or blind window. Also, a plain stone panel, a blank panel.

orb /ɔːb/ *verb*. Chiefly *poet.* **E17.**
[from **ORB** *noun*[1].]
1 *verb trans.* Form into a circular or spherical body. **E17.**
2 *verb trans.* Enclose (as) in a circle; surround with a rim. **M17.**
3 **a** *verb trans.* Cause to move in an orbit. *rare*. **M17.** ▸**b** *verb intrans.* Move in an orbit or as a celestial orb. *rare*. **E19.**

> 🕮 **1** O. W. HOLMES Two large tears orbed themselves beneath the Professor's lids. **2** ADDISON The wheels were orb'd with gold. **3b** KEATS Golden Crown, Orbing along the serene firmament Of a wide empire, like a glowing moon.

orbat /ˈɔːbat/ *noun*. **L20.**
[Abbreviation.]
MILITARY. = *order of* **BATTLE**.

†**orbation** *noun*. **E17–L18.**
[Latin *orbatio(n-)*, from *orbat-* pa. ppl stem of *orbare* bereave: see **-ATION**.]
Bereavement.

orbed /ɔːbd/ *adjective*. **L16.**
[from **ORB** *noun*[1], *verb*: see **-ED**[2], **-ED**[1].]
Formed into or having the form of an orb; circular; spherical.

orbic /ˈɔːbɪk/ *adjective*. *rare*. **E17.**
[Irreg. from Latin *orbis* **ORB** *noun*[1] + **-IC**.]
Round, orbicular.

orbicle /ˈɔːbɪk(ə)l/ *noun*. Now *rare* or *obsolete*. **E17.**
[Latin *orbiculus* dim. of *orbis* **ORB** *noun*[1]: see **-CLE**.]
A small spherical body; a globule.

orbicular /ɔːˈbɪkjʊlə/ *adjective*. **LME.**
[Late Latin *orbicularis*, formed as prec.: see **-AR**[1].]
1 Round, circular; *spec.* (*ANATOMY*) designating an orbicularis muscle. **LME.**
2 Spherical, globular; *loosely* having a rounded or convex (rather than a flat) form or surface. **LME.**
3 *fig.* Rounded, complete. **L17.**
4 *PETROGRAPHY*. Containing orbicules. **E19.**
■ **orbicuˈlarity** *noun* orbicular form or character **M17.** **orbicularly** *adverb* **E16.**

orbicularis /ɔːˌbɪkjʊˈlɑːrɪs/ *noun*. Pl. **-lares**. /-ˈlɑːriːz/. **L17.**
[formed as prec.]
ANATOMY. Any of various circular, discoidal, or ring-shaped muscles, esp. those around the eyes and mouth. Also *orbicularis muscle*.

orbiculate /ɔːˈbɪkjʊlət/ *adjective*. **M18.**
[Latin *orbiculatus*, from *orbiculus*: see **ORBICLE, -ATE**[2].]
Chiefly *BOTANY & ZOOLOGY*. Rounded, orbicular.
■ **orbiculated** *adjective* (now *rare*) = **ORBICULATE** **M17.** **orbiculately** *adverb* **M19.** †**orbiculation** *noun* (*a*) the formation of a circle or sphere; (*b*) an orbicular structure: **M17–L18.**

orbicule /ˈɔːbɪkjuːl/ *noun*. **M20.**
[Back-form. from **ORBICULAR** *adjective*: cf. Latin *orbiculus* (see **ORBICLE**), **-CULE**.]
PETROGRAPHY. An igneous spheroidal inclusion, *esp.* one composed of a number of concentric layers.

orbit /ˈɔːbɪt/ *noun*. **M16.**
[Latin *orbita* wheel-track, orbit, from *orbis* wheel, circle.]
1 *ANATOMY*. The bony cavity of the skull containing the eye and associated structures; the eye socket. **M16.** ▸**b** The eye-ball; the eye. *poet.* **E18.** ▸**c** *ZOOLOGY*. The border or region surrounding the eye in a bird, insect, etc. **L18.**
2 *ASTRONOMY*. The regularly repeated elliptical course of a celestial object or spacecraft about a star or planet. Also, one complete circuit round an orbited body. **L17.** ▸**b** = **ORB** *noun*[1] 5. *obsolete* exc. *Hist.* **E18.** ▸**c** *gen.* A circular or elliptical path traced by a moving body, (e.g. by an electron round a nucleus or an aircraft around an airfield). **E19.** ▸**d** The state of being on or moving in such an elliptical course. Chiefly in ***in orbit, into orbit***. **M20.**
3 *fig.* Sphere of activity or influence. **E20.**
4 *MATH.* A subset whose elements are related by a permutation belonging to a given group, or, more generally, are generated by the iteration of a function and its inverse. **M20.**

> 🕮 **1** J. MAY His eyes . . were very pale blue . . and sunken deep into bony orbits. **2** A. S. EDDINGTON A planet with a sharp elliptical orbit. A. KOESTLER The gravitational force which holds the earth in its orbit. U. LE GUIN One cycle, one orbit around the sun, is a year, isn't it? ***lunar orbit***: see **LUNAR** *adjective*. ***polar orbit***: see **POLAR** *adjective*. ***transfer orbit***: see **TRANSFER** *noun*. **d go into orbit** *fig.* (*colloq.*) achieve a high level of success, value, indignation, etc.; become very high. **3** F. FITZGERALD Vietnam has always lived in the orbit of China. V. GLENDINNING One's near and dear like to keep one from moving too far out of their orbit.

orbit /ˈɔːbɪt/ *verb*. **M20.**
[from the noun.]
1 *verb trans.* Travel round (esp. a celestial object) in an orbit. **M20.**
2 *verb intrans.* Move in or go into orbit. **M20.** ▸**b** Fly in a circle. **M20.**
3 *verb trans.* Put into orbit. **M20.**

> 🕮 **1** A. C. CLARKE Orbiting Saturn was Titan, the largest satellite in the Solar System. **2** *fig.*: *Daily Telegraph* The shares should orbit in next to no time.

■ **orbiter** *noun* (*ASTRONAUTICS*) a spacecraft in orbit or intended to go into orbit, *esp.* one that does not subsequently land: **M20.**

orbital /ˈɔːbɪt(ə)l/ *adjective & noun*. **M16.**
[Prob. from medieval Latin *orbitalis*, formed as **ORBIT** *noun*: see **-AL**[1].]
▸ **A** *adjective*. **1** *ANATOMY & ZOOLOGY*. Of or pertaining to the orbit or eye socket. **M16.**
2 Of, pertaining to, or of the nature of an orbit, esp. that of a celestial object; moving or taking place in an orbit or circular path. **M19.**
3 Of a road etc.: encircling a large town. Cf. ***ring-road*** s.v. **RING** *noun*[1]. **M20.**
1 orbital index *ANATOMY* one hundred times the ratio of the height of an orbit to its width. **2 orbital sander**: having a circular rather than an oscillating motion.
▸ **B** *noun*. **1** *PHYSICS & CHEMISTRY*. An actual or potential pattern of electron density around an atomic nucleus or nuclei which may be formed by either one or two electrons in a bound state in an atom or molecule; the wave function of a single electron corresponding to any such pattern. **M20.**
2 An orbital road. **L20.**

orbitale /ɔːbɪˈteɪli, -ˈtɑːli/ *noun*. **E20.**
[medieval Latin, neut. of *orbitalis*: see prec.]
ANATOMY. The lowest point on the lower edge of the orbit.

orbitar /ˈɔːbɪtə/ *adjective*. Now *rare*. **M18.**
[French *orbitaire*, from *orbite* **ORBIT** *noun*: see **-AR**[1].]
ANATOMY. = **ORBITAL** *adjective* 1.

orbito- /ˈɔːbɪtəʊ/ *combining form* of Latin *orbita* **ORBIT** *noun*: see **-O-**.
■ **orbitoˈsphenoid** *adjective & noun* (*ANATOMY & ZOOLOGY*) (forming or pertaining to) a bone of the floor of the cranium in the region of the optic nerve (in the human skull, either of the lesser wings of the sphenoid bone). **M19.**

†**orbity** *noun*. **L16–E19.**
[Latin *orbitas*, from *orbus* orphaned, bereaved: see **-ITY**.]
The condition of being bereaved of one's children. Also, childlessness.

orbivirus /ˈɔːbɪvʌɪrəs/ *noun*. **L20.**
[from Latin *orbis* ring, circle (from the shape of the capsomeres) + **VIRUS**.]
BIOLOGY. Any of a group of arthropod-borne RNA viruses which cause disease chiefly in mammals and are similar to reoviruses.

orby /ˈɔːbi/ *adjective*. *rare*. **E17.**
[from **ORB** *noun*[1] + **-Y**[1].]
Of the form of, or moving as in, a circle; pertaining to an orb or celestial object.

orc /ɔːk/ *noun*. Also **ork**. **L16.**
[In sense 1 from French *orque* or Latin **ORCA**. In sense 2 perh. repr. or infl. by Latin *orcus* hell, Italian *orco* demon, monster, (in Tolkien) Old English *orcneas* (pl.).]
†**1** Any of various ferocious sea-creatures; *spec.* the killer whale. **L16–M19.**
2 A devouring monster, an ogre. In the stories of J. R. R. Tolkien (1892–1973): a member of an imaginary warlike race of short stature and ogreish characteristics. **L16.**

orca /ˈɔːkə/ *noun*. **M19.**
[mod. Latin *Orca* former genus name from Latin *orca* large sea-creature (prob. = killer whale). Cf. prec.]
The killer whale.

Orcadian /ɔːˈkeɪdɪən/ *noun & adjective*. **M17.**
[Latin *Orcades* Orkney Islands (see **ORKNEY**) + **-IAN**.]
▸ **A** *noun*. A native or inhabitant of Orkney. **M17.**
▸ **B** *adjective*. Of or pertaining to Orkney. **E19.**

Orcagnesque /ɔːkəˈnjɛsk/ *adjective*. **E20.**
[from Italian dial. *Orcagna* archangel, nickname of Andrea di Cione (see below) + **-ESQUE**.]
Resembling the style, subject-matter, etc., of Andrea di Cione, Florentine painter, sculptor, and architect, fl. *c* 1308–*c* 1368.

orcanet /ˈɔːkənɪt/ *noun*. **M16.**
[Old French *orcanette* alt. of *arcanette* dim. of *arcanne* alt. of *alcanne* from medieval Latin *alkanna* formed as **ALKANET**.]
(The red dye obtained from) the alkanet *Alkanna lehmannii*.

orcein /ˈɔːsiːɪn/ *noun*. **M19.**
[Alt. of **ORCIN**.]
CHEMISTRY. A red dye which is a constituent of orchil, and may be obtained from orcinol by reaction with ammonia and oxygen.

orch- *combining form* see **ORCHO-**.

orch. *abbreviation*.
1 Orchestra.
2 Orchestrated by.

orchard /ˈɔːtʃəd/ *noun*.
[Old English *ortgeard*, *orċġeard*, *orċe(a)rd* = Gothic *aurtigards* garden (cf. *aurtja* farmer, Old High German *kaorzōn* cultivate); 1st elem. repr. Latin *hortus* garden, 2nd **YARD** *noun*[1].]
Orig., a garden for herbs and fruit trees. Now *spec.* an enclosure for the cultivation of fruit trees.
marble orchard: see **MARBLE** *noun & adjective*.
Comb.: **orchard grass** any grass grown in an orchard; *spec.* (*US*) cock's-foot, *Dactylis glomerata*; **orchard-house** a greenhouse for

the protection of fruit too delicate to be grown in the open air or required to ripen earlier; **orchardman** an orchardist; **orchard oriole** a N. American oriole, *Icterus spurius*, which suspends its nest from the boughs of fruit and other trees.

■ **orcharded** *adjective* having orchards; planted with fruit trees: M18. **orcharding** *noun* (*a*) the cultivation of fruit trees in orchards; (*b*) (chiefly *US*) land planted with fruit trees: M17. **orchardist** *noun* a person who cultivates an orchard or orchards, a fruit-grower L18.

orchata *noun* var. of HORCHATA.

orchella *noun* var. of ORCHILLA.

orchesography /ɔːkɪˈsɒɡrəfi/ *noun*. *rare*. E18.
[French *orchésographie*, irreg. from Greek *orkhēsis* dancing + -O- + -GRAPHY.]
The description or notation of dancing by means of diagrams etc.

orchester *noun* var. of ORCHESTRE.

orchestic /ɔːˈkɛstɪk/ *adjective & noun*. *rare*. M19.
[Greek *orkhēstikos*, from *orkhēstēs* dancer: see -IC.]
► **A** *adjective*. Of or pertaining to dancing. M19.
► **B** *noun sing.* & in *pl.* The art of dancing. M19.

orchestra /ˈɔːkɪstrə/ *noun*. L16.
[Latin from Greek *orkhēstra*, from *orkheisthai* to dance.]
†**1** Dancing. *rare*. Only in L16.
2 a CLASSICAL ANTIQUITIES. In a Greek theatre, the semicircular area in front of the stage where the chorus danced and sang; in a Roman theatre, the area in front of the stage containing the seats of senators and other important people. E17. ▸**b** The (front) stalls of an auditorium. Chiefly *N. Amer.* M18.
3 The part of a theatre, opera-house, etc., in which the musicians play, now usu. (more fully ***orchestra pit***) in front of the stage and on a lower level. E18.
4 A usu. large group of assorted instrumentalists, *esp.* one combining string, woodwind, brass, and percussion sections. E18. ▸**b** The set of instruments played by such a group. M19.
4 ***Schrammel orchestra***: see SCHRAMMEL 2. ***symphony orchestra***: see SYMPHONY 5C.
Comb.: ***orchestra pit***: see sense 3 above; **orchestra seat**, **orchestra stall** *N. Amer.* a seat in the (front) stalls.

orchestral /ɔːˈkɛstr(ə)l/ *adjective*. E19.
[from prec. + -AL[1].]
Of, pertaining to, composed for, or performed by an orchestra.
■ **orchestralist** *noun* a writer of orchestral music L19. **orchestrally** *adverb* L19.

orchestrate /ˈɔːkɪstreɪt/ *verb trans.* L19.
[from ORCHESTRA + -ATE[3], perh. after French *orchestrer*.]
1 Compose or arrange for an orchestra; score for orchestral performance. L19.
2 *fig.* Combine harmoniously, like instruments in an orchestra; carefully direct or coordinate the elements of (a plan, situation, etc.). L19.

📖 **2** *Times* Mrs. Gandhi's Home Minister, had for days been orchestrating a campaign about . . law and order. W. RAEPER MacDonald orchestrated his fairy story to achieve certain conscious ends.

■ **orcheˈstration** *noun* the action of orchestrating; the manner of this; an orchestrated piece: M19. **orchestrator** *noun* E20.

orchestre /ˈɔːkɪstə/ *noun*. Also **-ter**. E17.
[French from Latin ORCHESTRA.]
= ORCHESTRA.
¶ Formerly with stress on 2nd syll.

orchestrelle /ˈɔːkɪstrɛl/ *noun*. E20.
[from ORCHESTRA + French *-elle* -EL[2].]
A kind of organ which can also be made to function like a player-piano.

orchestric /ɔːˈkɛstrɪk/ *adjective*. L18.
[from ORCHESTRA + -IC.]
1 Of or pertaining to dancing. Cf. ORCHESTIC *adjective*. L18.
2 Orchestral. M19.

orchestrion /ɔːˈkɛstrɪən/ *noun*. M19.
[from ORCHESTRA after *accordion*.]
Any of several chiefly mechanical instruments designed to imitate the sound of an entire orchestra.
■ Also **orchestrina** /ɔːkɪˈstriːnə/ *noun* [after *concertina* etc.] M19.

orchi- *combining form* see ORCHIO-.

orchid /ˈɔːkɪd/ *noun & adjective*. M19.
[from mod. Latin *Orchidaceae* (or earlier *Orchideae*): see next, -ID[2].]
► **A** *noun*. **1** Any of numerous (freq. epiphytic) monocotyledonous plants of the family Orchidaceae, characterized by having one perianth segment (the labellum) differentiated from the rest and by commonly having only one anther, united with the style in a central body (the column), and often having brilliantly coloured or bizarrely shaped flowers. Also, a flowering stem of such a plant. M19.
2 A purplish colour. E20.

1 ***bee orchid***, ***butterfly orchid***, ***early purple orchid***, ***frog orchid***, ***lizard orchid***, ***military orchid***, ***musk orchid***, ***pyramidal orchid***, ***spotted orchid***, etc. POOR MAN'S ***orchid***.
Comb.: **orchid cactus** = EPIPHYLLUM; **orchid house** a hothouse for growing tropical orchids.
► **B** *adjective*. Of a purplish colour. M20.

orchid- /ˈɔːkɪd/ *combining form*. Before a consonant **orchido-** /ˈɔːkɪdəʊ/.
[mod. Latin, erron. taken as stem of Latin ORCHIS or Latinized stem of Greek *orkhis* testicle (after nouns in *-is*, *-id-*), in sense 1 now freq. taken as from ORCHID *noun*: see -O-. Cf. ORCHIO-, ORCHO-.]
1 Of or pertaining to orchids.
2 ANATOMY & MEDICINE. Of or pertaining to a testicle or the testicles.
■ **orchidectomize** *verb trans.* perform orchidectomy on M20. **orchiˈdectomy** *noun* (an instance of) surgical removal of one or both testicles; castration: L19. **orchidopexy** *noun* (an instance of) the surgical fixing in position of an undescended testicle L19. **orchiˈdotomy** *noun* (an instance of) surgical incision into a testicle, usu. to obtain biopsy material L19.

orchidaceous /ɔːkɪˈdeɪʃəs/ *adjective*. M19.
[from mod. Latin *Orchidaceae* (see below): see ORCHID-, -ACEOUS.]
1 Of or pertaining to the Orchidaceae or orchid family. M19.
2 *fig.* Resembling an orchid, esp. in flamboyancy or exoticness. M19.

📖 **2** R. LE GALLIENNE The simple old type of manhood is lost long since in endless orchidaceous variation.

■ **orchidacity** *noun* flamboyancy, exoticness L19.

orchideous /ɔːˈkɪdɪəs/ *adjective*. Now *rare* or *obsolete*. E19.
[from mod. Latin *Orchideae* (now Orchidaceae): see ORCHID-, -OUS.]
BOTANY. = ORCHIDACEOUS.
■ Also **orchideal**, **orchidean** *adjectives* (*rare*) M19.

orchidist /ˈɔːkɪdɪst/ *noun*. L19.
[from ORCHID *noun* + -IST.]
A cultivator of orchids.

orchido- *combining form* see ORCHID-.

orchidology /ɔːkɪˈdɒlədʒi/ *noun*. L19.
[formed as ORCHID *noun* + -OLOGY.]
The branch of botany or horticulture which deals with orchids.
■ **orchidologist** *noun* L19.

orchil /ˈɔːtʃɪl/ *noun*. L15.
[Spanish ORCHILLA, *urchilla*: cf. Italian *orcello*, *oricello*, French *orseille*.]
A red or violet dye prepared from certain lichens, esp. *Roccella tinctoria*; any of these lichens.

orchilla /ɔːˈtʃɪlə/ *noun*. Also **-chella** /-ˈtʃɛlə/. E18.
[Spanish, of unkn. origin.]
The dye or (in full ***orchilla-weed***) the lichen orchil.

orchio- /ˈɔːkɪəʊ/ *combining form*. Before a vowel **orchi-**.
[from Latin ORCHIS, Greek *orkhis*, as a correction of *orchido-*, ORCHID-: see -O-. Cf. ORCHO-.]
MEDICINE. = ORCHID- 2.
■ **orchiˈectomy** *noun* = ORCHIDECTOMY L19. **orchiopexy** *noun* = ORCHIDOPEXY E20.

orchis /ˈɔːkɪs/ *noun*. M16.
[Latin from Greek *orkhis* testicle, with ref. to the shape of the tuber.]
Any of various orchids belonging to or formerly included in the genus *Orchis*, with spikes of often purple flowers and the outer perianth segments freq. united in a helmet. Also (now *rare*), any of various wild orchids of other genera.

orcho- /ˈɔːkəʊ/ *combining form*. Before a vowel **orch-**.
[Greek *orkho-* combining form of *orkhis* testicle: see -O-. Cf. ORCHID-, ORCHIO-.]
MEDICINE. = ORCHID- 2.
■ **orchitis** /ɔːˈkʌɪtɪs/ *noun* inflammation of a testicle L18. **orˈchotomy** *noun* [cf. Greek *orkhotomia* castration] = ORCHIDOTOMY M18.

orcin /ˈɔːsɪn/ *noun*. M19.
[from mod. Latin *orcina*, Italian *orcello* ORCHIL: see -IN[1].]
= next. Cf. ORCEIN.

orcinol /ˈɔːsɪnɒl/ *noun*. L19.
[from prec. + -OL.]
A colourless crystalline substance, $C_7H_8O_2{\cdot}H_2O$, obtained from various species of orchil, which turns red, brown, or yellow in contact with air or when treated with various compounds; 2-hydroxyphenylmethanol. Cf. ORCEIN.

orciprenaline /ɔːsɪˈprɛn(ə)liːn/ *noun*. M20.
[from ORCI(NOL + ISO)PRENALINE.]
PHARMACOLOGY. A sympathomimetic amine that is closely related to isoprenaline in structure, taken for the relief of bronchitis and asthma.

ord. *abbreviation*.
Ordinary.

ordain /ɔːˈdeɪn/ *verb*. ME.
[Anglo-Norman *ordeiner* = Old French *ordener* (tonic stem *ordein-*), later *ordoner* (mod. *-onner*) from Latin *ordinare*, from *ordo*, *ordin-* ORDER *noun*.]
► **I** Put in order, arrange, prepare.
†**1** *verb trans.* Arrange in rows, ranks, or other regular order; *esp.* draw up in order of battle. ME–L16.
†**2** *verb trans.* Set in proper order or position; regulate, manage, conduct. ME–L15.
3 *verb trans.* Establish or found by ordinance; set up, institute. *arch.* ME.
†**4** *verb trans.* Plan, devise; organize, arrange. ME–L17.
†**5** *verb trans.* Put into a particular mental condition, esp. into a right or fitting frame of mind. ME–E16.
†**6** *verb trans.* Put in order, esp. for a purpose; prepare, provide. ME–M16. ▸**b** Fit out, equip, provide, (a person etc.) *with*, *in*, *of*. LME–M16.
†**7 a** *verb refl.* Prepare oneself, make ready; set or apply oneself (*to do* something). ME–L15. ▸**b** *verb intrans.* Make preparation, prepare (*for*). ME–M16.
► **II** Appoint, decree, order.
†**8** *verb trans.* Appoint (a person etc.) to an official duty or position. (Foll. by *to do*, *to* some office, etc.) ME–E19.
9 *verb trans.* ECCLESIASTICAL. Appoint or admit to the ministry of the Christian Church; confer holy orders on. ME.
10 *verb trans.* **a** Assign or appoint, esp. *to* or *for* a special purpose etc. *obsolete* exc. *dial.* & *Canad.* ME. ▸**b** Assign (*to* a person) as a share or allowance; allot. LME–L16.
11 *verb trans.* & *intrans.* Of God, fate, a supernatural power, etc.: prescribe as part of the order of the universe or of nature; decree. (Foll. by *that*, *to do*, †*to*.) ME.
12 *verb trans.* Decree as a thing to be observed; appoint, enact; determine, decide or *that*. ME.
13 *verb trans.* Order, command (a person *to do* something, *that* a thing be done or made). Now *rare* or *obsolete*. ME.

📖 **9** D. CUPITT He was . . ordained deacon and priest by the Bishop of Oxford. **10a** W. RALEIGH That day was ordayned by him to be their Sabbaoth. **11** E. YOUNG But fate ordains that dearest friends must part. C. KINGSLEY So the gods have ordained, and it will surely come to pass. K. CROSSLEY-HOLLAND No Viking believed he could change his destiny, ordained . . by the Norns. **12** W. H. PRESCOTT By this edict . . it was ordained that all who were convicted of heresy should suffer death. E. BOWEN The following morning, at the hour ordained, round came the chauffeur-driven Daimler.

■ **ordainment** *noun* the action or fact of ordaining; appointment; authoritative order; (divine) ordinance: LME.

ordainer /ɔːˈdeɪnə/ *noun*. ME.
[from prec. + -ER[1].]
1 A person who ordains something or someone; *spec.* an ordaining bishop, priest, or minister. ME.
2 ENGLISH HISTORY. (**O-**.) Any of a commission of twenty-one barons and bishops appointed in 1310 to draw up ordinances for improved administration of the kingdom. M18.

ordeal /ɔːˈdiːl, ɔːˈdiːəl/ *noun*.
[Old English *ordāl*, *ordēl* (whence Anglo-Latin *ordalium*, *ordela*, *-elum*) = Old Frisian *ordēl*, Old Saxon *urdēli* (Dutch *oordeel*), Old High German *urteili* (German *Urteil*) judgement, judicial decision, from Germanic, corresp. to Old English *ādǣlan*, Old Saxon *ādēljan*, Old High German *arteilen*, *ir-* (German *urteilen*) adjudge as one's share, decide, give judgement, from Germanic base meaning 'share out'. Cf. DEAL *verb*.]
1 *Hist.* A test of guilt or innocence used by Germanic peoples in which an accused person was subjected to severe pain or torture, the result being regarded as the immediate judgement of God. Later also, any similar method of determining innocence or guilt. OE.
2 Anything which severely tests character or endurance; a painful or trying experience, a severe trial. M17.

📖 **2** N. SEDAKA I kept dreading the ordeal of standing on the stage of Festival Hall. M. MOORCOCK The freezing journey home at night . . had been one of his worst ordeals.

Comb.: **ordeal bean** = CALABAR BEAN.

order /ˈɔːdə/ *noun*. ME.
[Old & mod. French *ordre*, earlier *ordene* from Latin *ordin-*, *ordo* row, series, course, array, rank (of soldiers), class, degree, captaincy, command, (ecclesiastical) rank in the Church; rel. to *ordiri* begin, *ornare* ADORN *verb*.]
► **I** Rank, class.
1 In Christian theology, each of the nine ranks of angelic beings, as seraphim, cherubim, etc., forming the ninefold celestial hierarchy (see note below). Also, any similar class of spiritual or demonic beings. ME.
2 ECCLESIASTICAL. **a** A grade or rank in the Christian ministry, as bishop, priest, etc., or in any ecclesiastical hierarchy; (now only in *pl.*, more fully ***holy orders***) the rank or position of a member of the clergy or an ordained minister of the Church. ME. ▸**b** The conferment of holy orders, the rite of ordination. ME.
3 a A society of monks, nuns, or friars living under the same religious, moral, and social regulations and discipline; a monastic society. Also, monasticism as an institution. ME. ▸**b** *Hist.* A society of knights bound by a

common rule of life and having a combined military and monastic character. LME.

4 An institution founded (usu. by a monarch and in imitation of certain orders of monks) for the purpose of rewarding meritorious service by conferring an honour or honours. Also, the badge or insignia of such an honour. ME.

5 A rank in a community, consisting of people of the same status; a social division or grade. Esp. in ***higher orders, lower orders***. ME. **▸b** A definite rank in a State. LME. **▸c** *gen.* Rank, position. *poet.* M17.

6 A body of people of the same profession or occupation, or united by the same special interest or activity. LME.

7 A rank, a row; any of several parallel series behind or above one another. Now *rare* or *obsolete*. LME. **▸b** *PHYSICS*. Each of a successive series of spectra or fringes formed by interference or diffraction; a number characterizing a particular spectrum or fringe, equal to the number of wavelengths by which the optical paths of successive contributing rays differ. E18. **▸c** *ARCHITECTURE*. A series of mouldings. M19.

8 *ARCHITECTURE*. A system or style of building subject to certain uniform established proportions; *esp.* each of the five classical styles of architecture (Tuscan, Doric, Ionic, Corinthian, and Composite) based on the proportions of columns, the amount of decoration, etc. M16.

9 A kind, group, or class of person or thing, distinguished from others by character, quality, or importance. E17.

10 a *MATH*. The degree of complexity of an analytical or geometrical form, equation, expression, operator, etc., as denoted by an ordinal numeral (e.g. the power of the largest derivative in an equation). E18. **▸b** *MATH*. The dimension of a determinant or square matrix; the number of elements in a group; the smallest positive integer *m* for which g^m is equal to the identity element of a group, *g* being any given element. M19. **▸c** Chiefly *LOGIC & PSYCHOLOGY*. Each of the ranks or levels in a hierarchy in which every member above the lowest rank is a function of members of the next lower rank. Freq. with preceding ordinal numeral. E20. **▸d** *CHEMISTRY*. The sum of the exponents of the concentrations of reactants, or the exponent of that of any particular reactant, in the expression for the rate of a chemical reaction. E20.

11 a *BIOLOGY* (orig. only *ZOOLOGY*). A basic taxonomic grouping ranking above family and below class. M18. **▸b** *BOTANY* (now *Hist.*). Orig., a grouping of genera in the artificial system of Linnaeus, based on the number of stamens and carpels. Later (more fully ***natural order***), a natural grouping of related genera based on other criteria; a family. M18.

> 📖 **1** T. HEYWOOD In the third order Principates . . Next them Arch-Angels. **3a** ***Benedictine order, Cistercian order, Franciscan order***, etc. **4** R. DAVIES A very stout, shortish man in uniform and a blaze of orders. ***Order of Merit, Victorian Order***, etc. **5c** MILTON These were the prime in order and in might. **6** GIBBON A generous . . enthusiasm seemed to animate the military order. **9** GOLDSMITH Every order . . of animals seems fitted for its situation in life. H. KELLER Miss Sullivan's talents are of the highest order. D. H. LAWRENCE A large meal of the high-tea order.

▸ II Sequence, arrangement.

12 Arrangement of things in which one thing follows another; sequence in space or time; succession of acts or events. Also, the way in which this occurs. ME.

13 A method by which things act or events take place in the world, society, etc.; a natural, moral, spiritual, or social system in which things proceed according to definite laws. ME.

14 Orig. *gen.*, regular procedure; customary practice; an established usage. Later *spec.*, the prescribed or customary mode of proceeding in the conduct of a legislative body, public meeting, debate, etc. See also ***order of the day*** below. ME.

15 Formal, regular, or methodical arrangement in the position of the things in any area or group. Also more widely, the condition in which everything has its proper place and function. LME.

16 *ECCLESIASTICAL*. A stated form of liturgical service, or of administration of a rite or ceremony, prescribed by ecclesiastical authority; the service so prescribed. LME.

17 A condition in which the laws regulating the public conduct of members of a community are maintained and observed; the rule of law or constituted authority; absence of riot or violent crimes. L15.

18 Measures or steps taken for the accomplishment of a purpose; suitable action in view of some end. Chiefly in ***take order***. Now *rare* or *obsolete*. M16.

19 General state or condition; *spec.* normal, healthy, or efficient condition. M16.

20 Orig. & chiefly *MILITARY*. Equipment, uniform, etc., for a specified purpose or of a specified type. M19.

21 *MILITARY*. The position in which a rifle is held after ordering arms (see ***order arms*** s.v. ORDER *verb* 1). M19.

> 📖 **12** C. STEAD He . . marshaled them in order of age. R. DAHL Arrange words in their right order according to the rules of grammar. **13** R. W. DALE Christ's death is the foundation of a new spiritual order. J. MORLEY Two generations of men had almost ceased to care whether there be any moral order or not. **14** A. TODD The leader of the House of Commons is at liberty to arrange the order of business. A. S. DALE As chairman, Gilbert tried to keep order. **15** J. C. POWYS Oases of order in the midst of chaos. D. HALBERSTAM He loved order, his own desk clean every night. **17** H. MAYHEW Policemen, with their . . truncheons speedily restored order. J. R. GREEN The old social discontent . . remained a perpetual menace to public order. **18** J. STRYPE They had taken order to meet these again . . in the morning. **19** W. R. GROVE The machinery of the truck is apparently in good order. **20** ***drill order, review order, shirtsleeve order***, etc.

▸ III Regulation, direction.

†**22** The action of putting or keeping in order; regulation, control. E16–L17.

23 An authoritative direction, an injunction, a mandate; a command, an instruction. Freq. in ***under orders***. M16.

24 *spec.* **a** *FINANCE*. A written direction to pay money or deliver property; *esp.* a postal order. L17. **▸b** *LAW*. A written decision of a court or judge; a direction of a court or judge (esp. in the Supreme Court or county courts) other than a final judgement. E18. **▸c** A pass for free or reduced admission to a theatre, museum, private house, etc. M18. **▸d** *COMMERCE*. A direction or commission to make or provide something at the responsibility of the person ordering. M19. **▸e** A request for food or drink in a restaurant, public house, etc.; the food or drink served in response to such a request. M19. **▸f** *COMPUTING*. An instruction or command, *esp.* one in machine language. M20.

> 📖 **23** A. DJOLETO Each class teacher stood in front of his class and barked orders. **24a** W. OWEN I have cashed the Order long ago. **b** *Times Educ. Suppl.* Juvenile supervision orders under the 1969 children and Young Persons Act. ***court order, demolition order, exclusion order, preservation order, probation order***, etc. **d** *Which?* As soon as the . . company accepts your order. **e** *Listener* Should you require your vegetables well done, please advise on placing your order.

Phrases: **a large order** *slang* a large requirement, demand, etc. ***apple-pie order***: see APPLE-PIE *noun*. ***a tall order***: see TALL *adjective*. ***Attic order***: see ATTIC *adjective*[1]. **banker's order** = ***standing order*** below. **by order** by authoritative direction or command. ***compound order***: see COMPOUND *adjective*. **doctor's orders** instructions from one's doctor; *fig.* any instructions which cannot be evaded. **five orders** *ARCHITECTURE* the five classical styles of architecture (see sense 8 above). ***FRATERNAL order***. ***GIANT order***. ***holy orders***: see sense 2a above. **in holy orders, in orders** belonging to the clergy, in the position of an ordained minister of the Church. **in order** (*a*) in proper sequence, according to rank, size, position, date, etc.; (*b*) in proper condition; in accordance with some rule or custom; (*c*) (orig. *US*) appropriate to the occasion, suitable; in fashion, current, correct; (*d*) ***in order that*** so that; (*e*) ***in order to*** with the purpose of doing, with a view to. ***in orders***: see ***in holy orders*** above. **in short order** (orig. *US*) without delay, immediately. **in the order of** = ***of the order of*** (b) below. ***law and order***: see LAW *noun*[1] 3a. **Letters of Orders** a certificate of ordination given by a bishop to a priest or deacon. ***loose order***: see LOOSE *adjective*. ***lower orders***: see LOWER *adjective*. ***mail order***: see MAIL *noun*[3]. ***MARCHING order***. ***matched orders***: see MATCH *verb*[1]. ***minor orders***: see MINOR *adjective & noun*. ***new order***: see NEW *adjective*. ***of the FIRST order***. **of the order of** (*a*) *MATH*. (also ***of order —***) having a ratio to (the quantity specified) that is neither a large number nor a small fraction, or that tends in the limit to a finite number; (*b*) *gen.* in the region of; approximately. **on the order of** = ***of the order of*** (b) above. **Order in Council** (*a*) an order issued by the British monarch on the advice of the Privy Council; (*b*) an order issued by a government department under powers bestowed by Act of Parliament. ***order of battle***: see BATTLE *noun*. **order of magnitude** approximate number or magnitude in a scale in which steps correspond to a fixed factor (usu. of 10); a range between one power of 10 and the next. **order of the day** (*a*) in a legislative body, the business set down for debate on a particular day; (*b*) instructions issued by a commanding officer to the troops under his command; (*c*) the prevailing custom or state of things. **orders are orders** commands must be obeyed. **order to view** a request from an estate agent to an occupier to allow inspection of his or her premises by a client. **out of order** (*a*) not in proper sequence; in disorder, unsettled; (now usu. of a mechanical or electrical device) not working properly, broken; (*b*) in breach of the rules of an organization, meeting, etc. ***point of order***: see POINT *noun*[1]. ***postal order***: see POSTAL *adjective*. **public order** = sense 17 above. ***put one's house in order***: see HOUSE *noun*[1]. ***sacred order***: see SACRED *adjective*. ***SEALED orders***. ***set one's house in order***: see HOUSE *noun*[1]. ***short order***: see SHORT *adjective*. ***social order***: see SOCIAL *adjective*. **standing order** (*a*) an instruction to a bank to make regular fixed payments from an account usu. to another party; (*b*) an instruction for the regular provision of a commodity, newspaper, etc.; (*c*) in *pl.* the rules governing the manner in which all business shall be conducted in a parliament, council, society, etc. **take orders** enter the ministry of the Church, be ordained. ***under STARTER's orders***. ***walking-orders***: see WALKING *noun*. ***working order***: see WORKING *noun*.

Comb.: **order-form** a form to be filled in by a customer giving a business order; **order man** a man who takes or makes out orders; **order mark** *arch.* a punishment in a school for bad behaviour; **order pad** a pad of order-forms; **order-paper** (*a*) a paper on which questions etc. for debate in a legislative assembly are entered; (*b*) esp. in the House of Lords, a publication of future business for the remainder of a session, an agenda; **order wire** *TELECOMMUNICATIONS* a channel or path in a communication system used for signals controlling or directing system operations.

¶ The ranks of the celestial hierarchy as originally proposed were seraphim, cherubim, thrones; dominations, virtues, powers; principalities, archangels, angels. Later speculation exchanged the ranking of virtues and principalities.

■ **orderless** *adjective* devoid of order, regularity, or method; disorderly: M16.

order /ˈɔːdə/ *verb*. ME.

[from the noun.]

▸ I 1 *verb trans.* Put in order; arrange methodically or suitably; *spec.* marshal, draw up in order of battle. *arch.* ME.

2 a *verb refl.* Conduct oneself, behave. *arch.* L15. **▸b** *verb trans.* Set or keep in order or proper condition; adjust or carry on according to rule; regulate, govern, manage; settle. E16. **▸c** *verb trans.* Of God, fate, etc.: determine (events etc.); ordain. M17.

†**3** *verb trans.* Make ready, prepare. E16–E18.

†**4** *verb trans.* Take a certain course with (a person or thing); treat, deal with, manage, esp. in a specified way. E16–L18.

†**5** *verb trans.* Cause to submit to lawful authority; chastise, punish. M16–M17.

> 📖 **1** W. D. HOWELLS Ordering her hair, some coils of which had been loosened. **order arms** *MILITARY* position a rifle so it is held vertically against the right side with the butt on the ground. **2b** K. AMIS Dixon . . was bad at ordering his thoughts. C. SAGAN Direction to human beings on how to order their affairs.

▸ II 6 *verb trans. ECCLESIASTICAL*. Admit to holy orders; ordain. Formerly also, admit ceremonially into a monastic order or to a benefice. Now *rare* or *obsolete*. ME.

▸ III 7 *verb trans.* Give orders for (something to be done etc.); bid, command, direct. Also, prescribe medically. M16.

8 *verb trans.* Give orders to, command, authoritatively direct (a person *to do* something, *to go* somewhere, etc.). E17.

9 *verb trans.* Give an order or commission for; direct (a thing) to be provided or supplied. Also foll. by *up*. M18.

> 📖 **7** G. VIDAL He ordered Domitian arrested on a charge of lese-majesty. *Oxford Art Journal* Somoza ordered the complete destruction of the parish. **8** R. MACAULAY His battalion was ordered east, to fight the Japanese. *Daily Telegraph* He was . . ordered to pay £150 towards legal aid. **9** L. DURRELL I went to Pastrouli and ordered a double whisky. M. ATWOOD The Smeaths get their clothes that way . . order them out of the Eaton's Catalogue. ***what the doctor ordered, just what the doctor ordered***: see DOCTOR *noun*.

With adverbs in specialized senses: **order about, order around** continually give peremptory orders to, treat as a subordinate. **order up** in the game of euchre, order (the suit of a card turned up by an opponent who is dealing) to be adopted as trumps.

■ **orderable** *adjective* (*rare*) able to be ordered M17. **orderer** *noun* L15.

order book /ˈɔːdə bʊk/ *noun phr.* L18.

[from ORDER *noun* + BOOK *noun*.]

A book in which orders are entered; *spec.* (*a*) *MILITARY* a book in which general and regimental orders or regulations are entered; (*b*) *NAUTICAL* a book kept on a man-of-war for recording occasional orders of the commander; (*c*) *POLITICS* in the House of Commons, a book in which motions to be submitted to the House must be entered; (*d*) *COMMERCE* a book in which the orders of customers are entered; *transf.* the number of orders to be fulfilled.

ordered /ˈɔːdəd/ *ppl adjective*. ME.

[from ORDER *verb* + -ED[1].]

†**1** In holy orders, ordained. Also, belonging to a religious order. ME–E17.

2 Set in order, arranged; disciplined, regulated, controlled. Formerly also, made ready, prepared. L16. **▸b** *MATH*. Of a set: having the property that there is a transitive binary relation '>' such that for any elements *a* and *b* of the set, $a > b$, $b > a$, or $b = a$. E20.

3 Commanded, bidden, prescribed. L18.

> 📖 **2** A. BRINK An ordered and patterned life, with a place and time for everything. **b** **ordered pair, ordered triple**, etc. a pair, triple, or higher multiple of elements *a, b,* (*c*, . .) having the property that $(a, b, \ldots) = (u, v, \ldots)$ if and only if $a = u$, $b = v$, etc.

■ **orderedness** *noun* E18.

orderly /ˈɔːd(ə)li/ *adjective & noun*. M16.

[from ORDER *noun* + -LY[1].]

▸ A *adjective*. **1 a** Arranged in order; characterized by regular sequence or arrangement; regular, methodical. M16. **▸b** Of a person, a person's disposition, etc.: observant of order or method; systematic, methodical. L16.

2 Observant of order or discipline; well-conducted, well-behaved. L16.

3 *MILITARY*. Pertaining to orders; charged with the conveyance or execution of orders. E18.

4 Pertaining to a system of keeping the streets clean by sweeping and the removal of dirt, litter, etc. Now *rare*. M19.

1a V. Woolf In what orderly procession they advance. C. S. Forester His world dissolved into chaos compared with which what had gone before was orderly. **2** *Manchester Examiner* Elections are now conducted in an orderly manner.

Special collocations: **orderly book** = ORDER BOOK (a). **orderly corporal**, **orderly officer**, **orderly sergeant** (*a*) a corporal, officer, or sergeant who carries orders or messages for a superior officer; (*b*) a corporal, officer, or sergeant whose turn it is to attend to the domestic affairs of the corps or regiment. **orderly room** a room in a barracks used for company business. ***orderly sergeant***: see ***orderly corporal*** above.

► **B** *noun*. **1** A non-commissioned officer or private soldier who carries orders or messages for a superior officer. L18.

2 An attendant in a hospital responsible for the non-medical care of patients and the maintenance of order and cleanliness. E19.

3 A person whose job is to keep the streets clean. Now *rare*. M19.

1 P. Fitzgerald He had to be wakened by his orderly before every battle. **2** E. Welty A pair of orderlies came . . to take Mr. Dalzell to the operating room.

¶ Earlier in UNORDERLY *adjective*.

■ **orderliness** *noun* L16.

orderly /ˈɔːd(ə)li/ *adverb*. Now *rare*. LME.
[from ORDER *noun* + -LY².]

1 According to established order or procedure; in a disciplined or well-behaved manner. LME.

2 In order; with proper arrangement or distribution; methodically. L15.

ordinaire /ɔːdɪˈnɛː/ *noun*. M19.
[French = ordinary.]
= VIN ***ordinaire***.

ordinal /ˈɔːdɪn(ə)l/ *noun*¹. ME.
[medieval Latin *ordinale* use as noun of neut. sing. of *ordinalis* (sc. *liber* book): see next, -AL¹.]

A book setting out the order or form of Church services; a service-book. Also, a book prescribing ecclesiastical rules, esp. those for the ordination of deacons and priests and the consecration of bishops.

ordinal /ˈɔːdɪn(ə)l/ *adjective & noun*². LME.
[Late Latin *ordinalis* denoting order in a series, from *ordo*, *ordin-* ORDER *noun*: see -AL¹.]

► **A** *adjective*. †**1** Conforming to order, rule, or custom; regular, orderly. LME–L15.

2 Marking position in an order or series. L16.

3 BIOLOGY. Of or pertaining to an order of animals or plants, or (now *Hist.*) a natural order. E19.

4 Relating to, or consisting of, a row or rows. *rare*. L19.

2 ordinal number, **ordinal numeral** any of the positive whole numbers defining a thing's position in a series (first, second, third, etc.); cf. ***cardinal number***, ***cardinal numeral*** s.v. CARDINAL *adjective* 1.

► **B** *noun*. An ordinal numeral. L16.

ordinance /ˈɔːdɪnəns/ *noun*. ME.
[Old French *ordenance* (mod. *ordonnance*) from medieval Latin *ordinantia*, from Latin *ordinare* ORDAIN: see -ANCE. Cf. ORDNANCE, ORDONNANCE.]

†**1** Arrangement in ranks or rows; *esp*. battle array. ME–E17.

2 The action of ordering or regulating; direction, management, control. *arch*. ME. ▸**b** That which is ordained by God or fate; a dispensation or decree of providence, destiny, etc. ME. ▸†**c** Ordained or appointed place, condition, etc. *rare*. LME–E17.

3 Authoritative direction on how to act; an established set of principles; a system of government or discipline. *arch*. ME.

4 An authoritative decree or command; *spec*. a public injunction or rule of less constitutional character than a statute, e.g. a decree of a monarch, a local authority, etc. ME.

5 An authoritatively prescribed practice or usage; *esp*. a religious or ceremonial observance, e.g. the sacraments. ME. ▸**b** *spec*. The sacrament of the Lord's Supper. M19.

6 †**a** Arrangement in regular sequence or proper position; regulated condition; order. LME–L17. ▸**b** *spec*. Arrangement of literary material or architectural parts in accordance with some plan or rule of composition. Also, a characteristic series of architectural parts. Cf. ORDONNANCE 1. LME.

†**7** The action or process of preparing or providing; a preparatory step or measure. Also, the thing prepared or provided. LME–E17. ▸**b** Equipment, apparatus, furniture. L15–E17.

†**8** Rank or order in a State. *rare* (Shakes.). Only in E17.

2c Shakes. *Jul. Caes.* If you would consider the true cause . . Why all these things change from their ordinance. **4** F. Fitzgerald He issued an ordinance calling for the arrest . . of persons deemed dangerous to the state. SELF-DENYING ***ordinance***. **6b** J. Fergusson To ascertain how far the ordinance of the present building was influenced by his designs.

ordinand /ˈɔːdɪnand, ɔːdɪˈnand/ *noun*. M19.
[Latin *ordinandus* gerundive of *ordinare* ORDAIN: see -AND.]

A person about to be ordained, a candidate for ordination.

ordinant /ˈɔːdɪnənt/ *adjective & noun*. *rare*. LME.
[Orig. from Old French, pres. pple of *ordiner*; in mod. use from Latin *ordinant-* pres. ppl stem of *ordinare*: see ORDAIN, -ANT¹.]

► **A** *adjective*. That orders, regulates, or directs. LME.

► **B** *noun*. **1** MILITARY. An officer who assigns soldiers to their places in the ranks. *obsolete* exc. *Hist*. LME.

2 A person who ordains or confers holy orders. M19.

ordinar /ˈɔːdnə, -dɪnə/ *adjective & noun*. Chiefly & now only *Scot*. LME.
[Old French *ordinaire*, *orden-* adjective & noun, from Latin *ordinarius*: see ORDINARY *adjective*, *noun*.]
= ORDINARY *adjective*, *noun*.

ordinarily /ˈɔːd(ə)n(ə)rɪli, -d(ə)nˈɛrɪli/ *adverb*. LME.
[from ORDINARY *adjective* + -LY².]

†**1** In accordance with a rule or established custom; according to regular practice or occurrence. LME–L17.

2 In the ordinary course of events; in most cases; usually, commonly. M16.

3 To an ordinary degree; to the usual extent. L17.

4 In an ordinary or unexceptional way; as is normal or usual. M19.

2 P. Roth He could hardly manage the small talk at which he was ordinarily so proficient. **3** H. Sturgis Lady Charmington, never a great talker, was more than ordinarily silent. **4** J. H. Newman Materials . . to be found in any ordinarily furnished library.

ordinary /ˈɔːdɪn(ə)ri, -d(ə)n-/ *noun*. ME.
[Anglo-Norman, Old French *ordinarie* (later and mod. *ordinaire*) from medieval Latin *ordinarius* (sc. *judex* judge etc.) and in neut. sing. *ordinarium*: see next.]

► **I** Rule, ordinance.

†**1 a** A formula or rule prescribing a certain order or course of action; an ordinance, a regulation. Only in ME. ▸**b** A prescribed or customary procedure. Only in 16.

2 ECCLESIASTICAL. A rule prescribing, or book containing, the order or form of a religious service, esp. the Mass; the service of the Mass; *spec*. (usu. **O-**) the unvarying parts of a Roman Catholic service, *esp*. those which form a sung Mass. L15.

2 *Gramophone* Two well-known items of the Ordinary, Sanctus I and Sanctus XI.

► **II** A person, a group of people.

3 LAW. A person who has immediate jurisdiction in ecclesiastical cases, as the archbishop in a province, or the bishop in a diocese. LME.

†**4** A courier conveying letters etc. at regular intervals. Also, post, mail. L16–M18.

5 LAW. A judge having authority to attend to cases by right of office and not by delegation; *spec*. (*a*) SCOTS LAW (now *rare*) = ***Lord Ordinary*** s.v. ORDINARY *adjective*; (*b*) US LAW a judge of a probate court. E17.

†**6** NAUTICAL. A group of officers, labourers, etc., in charge of warships laid up in harbour. Treated as *pl*. M17–M18.

7 *Hist*. A diocesan officer, *spec*. the chaplain of Newgate prison, who gave condemned prisoners their neck-verses and prepared them for death. L17.

7 W. Besant The prisoner was conveyed . . in a cart . . while the ordinary sat beside him and exhorted him.

► **III** Something ordinary, regular, or usual.

†**8** A lecture read at regular or stated times. LME–E16.

†**9** A regular allowance or portion, *esp*. a regular daily meal or allowance of food. L15–M17.

10 HERALDRY. **a** A dictionary of heraldic bearings, arranged by design. Also ***ordinary of arms***, ***ordinary of crests***, etc. E16. ▸**b** A charge of the earliest, simplest, and commonest kind, bounded in its simple form by straight lines. E17.

11 a A meal regularly available at a fixed price in a restaurant, public house, etc. Formerly also, *the* body of people eating such a meal. L16. ▸**b** (A dining-room in) a restaurant, public house, etc., where such meals are provided. L16. ▸**c** In parts of the US, a public house, an inn. M17.

12 a *The* ordinary or usual condition, course, or degree; customary or usual thing. Now *colloq*. L16. ▸**b** An ordinary or commonplace thing or person. *rare*. E17.

13 *Hist*. An early ungeared bicycle with one large and one very small wheel; a penny-farthing. L19.

14 COMMERCE. An ordinary share (as opp. to a preference share etc.). L19.

11b K. Boyle Carrie sat in the Ordinary . . shaking with fear of what they might serve her. **12a** N. Sedaka The roller coaster . . is an escape from the ordinary.

Phrases: **in ordinary** (*a*) = ORDINARY *adjective* 1b; used postpositively in titles, as ***painter-in-ordinary***, ***physician-in-ordinary***, etc.; ***Lord of Appeal in Ordinary***: see LORD *noun*; (*b*) NAUTICAL HISTORY (of a ship) laid up, out of commission. ***ordinary of arms***, ***ordinary of crests***: see sense 10a above. **out of the ordinary** unusual.

Comb.: **ordinary table** *Hist*. (*a*) a table at which an ordinary was served, cleared afterwards for gambling; (*b*) a gambling table, a gambling house.

ordinary /ˈɔːdɪn(ə)ri, -d(ə)n-/ *adjective & adverb*. LME.
[Latin *ordinarius* orderly, usual, from *ordo*, *ordin-* ORDER *noun*: see -ARY¹.]

► **A** *adjective*. **1 a** Belonging to or occurring in regular custom or practice; normal, customary, usual. LME. ▸**b** Of an official etc.: belonging to a regular or permanent staff. Cf. EXTRAORDINARY *adjective* 2, ***in ordinary*** s.v. ORDINARY *noun*. M16. ▸**c** Of language, usage, etc.: widely found or attested; not specialized; *spec*. not having the precision of the language of symbolic logic. L17.

2 (Of a judge) exercising authority by virtue of office and not by special deputation; (of jurisdiction etc.) exercised by virtue of office. LME.

†**3** Conforming to order or rule; regular, methodical. L15–M17.

†**4** Of common or everyday occurrence; frequent, abundant. L16–E18.

5 a Of the usual kind, not singular or exceptional; commonplace, mundane. Also, plain in appearance. L16. ▸**b** COMMERCE. Of shares, stock, etc.: forming part of the common stock entitling holders to a dividend from net profits. Cf. ***preference share***, ***preference stock*** s.v. PREFERENCE. M19. ▸**c** Of a person: typical of a particular group; average; without exceptional experience or expert knowledge. M19.

†**6** Not distinguished by rank or position; characteristic of the common people; vulgar, unrefined, coarse. M17–E19.

1a J. Buchan His ordinary manner was a composed geniality. *Hamilton (Ontario) Spectator* The artists mainly produced typical, ordinary Dutch scenes. A. Storr Holidays are escapes from the routine of ordinary day-to-day existence. **4** Shakes. *2 Hen. IV* These fits Are with his Highness very ordinary. **5a** B. Pym The most ordinary things done with someone one loves are full of new significance. C. Ekwensi Why could she be so unglamorous, ordinary and unsophisticated? *Beano* Hm! Pretty ordinary lumps of stone. **c** *Times* A government claiming that it wants to involve ordinary people in decision-making.

Phrases: **Judge Ordinary** (*a*) *Hist*. the judge of the Court for Divorce, a branch of ecclesiastical judicature; (*b*) SCOTS LAW the sheriff of a county. **Lord Ordinary** SCOTS LAW a judge in the Court of Session sitting in the Outer House. **more than ordinary** *arch*. & *dial*. (*a*) *adjectival phr*. more than usual; of a greater amount or to a greater degree than usual; (*b*) *adverbial phr*. unusually, exceptionally.

Special collocations: ***ordinary*** AMBASSADOR. **ordinary grade** *Hist*. the lower of the two main levels of examination of the Scottish Certificate of Education. **ordinary level** *Hist*. the lower of the two main levels of examination of the General Certificate of Education in England and Wales. **ordinary ray** OPTICS in double refraction, the ray that obeys the ordinary laws of refraction (cf. ***extraordinary ray*** s.v. EXTRAORDINARY *adjective* 1). **ordinary seaman** a seaman of the lowest rank in the Royal Navy. **ordinary wine** *rare* = VIN ***ordinaire***.

► **B** *adverb*. In an ordinary manner; as a matter of regular practice; commonly, ordinarily. Now *colloq*. L16.

■ **ordinariness** *noun* the quality or condition of being ordinary; an instance of this quality: E17.

ordinate /ˈɔːdɪnət/ *adjective & noun*. LME.
[Latin *ordinatus* pa. pple, formed as next: see -ATE¹, -ATE².]

►† **A** *adjective*. **1** Ordered, arranged; ordained, destined. LME–M17.

2 Ordered, regulated; orderly, regular, moderate. LME–L17.

3 GEOMETRY. Of a figure: = REGULAR *adjective* 2b. E17–E18.

► **B** *noun*. MATH.

1 Orig., any of a series of parallel chords of a conic section, in relation to the diameter which bisects each of them. Now usu., half of such a chord. L17.

2 In Cartesian coordinates: orig., a straight line parallel to one of the coordinate axes and meeting the other; now, the distance of a point from the *x*-axis measured parallel to the *y*-axis. L17.

■ †**ordinately** *adverb* (*a*) in an ordinate, ordered, or regulated manner; (*b*) MATH. so as to form an ordinate or a regular figure: LME–M18.

ordinate /ˈɔːdɪneɪt/ *verb trans*. E16.
[Latin *ordinat-* pa. ppl stem of *ordinare*: see ORDAIN, -ATE³.]

1 Appoint authoritatively to a position or office; *spec*. admit to holy orders, ordain. Now *rare* or *obsolete*. L16.

2 Regulate, control, govern. Now *rare* or *obsolete*. L16.

3 Establish, ordain, predestine. Now *rare* or *obsolete*. E17.

4 Place side by side in a series, coordinate. *rare*. L19.

5 STATISTICS. Subject to ordination (see ORDINATION 4c). M20.

■ **ordinator** *noun* †(*a*) a person who ordains or admits someone to holy orders; (*b*) a person who regulates, controls, or governs: L15.

ordination /ɔːdɪˈneɪʃ(ə)n/ *noun*. LME.
[Old & mod. French, or Latin *ordinatio(n-)*, formed as prec.: see -ATION.]

1 a The fact or (esp. divine) action of ordaining or decreeing. LME. ▸†**b** The fact of being destined or appointed (*to* an end or purpose); destined or ordained function. E17–E19.

2 The action of ordaining or conferring holy orders; admission to the ministry of the Church; the fact of being ordained. LME.

†**3** That which is ordained; an ordinance, a decree, a law. L15–M17.

4 a The action of arranging in ranks or order; the condition of being ordered or arranged; an arrangement. M16. ▸**b** Arrangement in classes; classification. M17. ▸**c** *STATISTICS.* Numerical analysis in which communities etc. are represented as points in a multidimensional space. M20.

> 📖 **1a** A. LIVELY The notes slid . . into place as though under the force of God or Fate's ordination. **2** *Derby Diocesan News* The conference voted on the contentious subject of the ordination of women.

ordinative /ˈɔːdɪnətɪv/ *adjective & noun.* E17.
[Late Latin *ordinativus*, formed as ORDINATE *verb*: see -IVE.]
▶ **A** *adjective.* Having the character or function of ordaining, ordering, or regulating. E17.
▶ **B** *noun. GRAMMAR.* A particle which ordinates or coordinates clauses. M19.

ordinee /ɔːdɪˈniː/ *adjective & noun.* ME.
[Old French *ordiné* pa. pple of *ordiner* ORDAIN: see -EE[1].]
▶†**A** *adjective.* Admitted to holy orders, or into a religious order; ordained. Only in ME.
▶ **B** *noun.* An ordained member of the clergy. Now usu. (*spec.*), a newly ordained deacon. ME.

ordnance /ˈɔːdnəns/ *noun.* LME.
[Contr. of Old French *ordenance*, ORDINANCE.]
1 Military stores or supplies; missiles discharged in war; artillery. LME.
2 a Engines for discharging missiles; = ARTILLERY 2. LME. ▸†**b** The artillery as a branch of the army. M17–L18.
3 A branch of the government service concerned esp. with the supply of military stores and materials. L15.

> 📖 **2a** *Antique* As pieces of ordnance they were formidable weapons. **3 Board of Ordnance** *Hist.* a board (dissolved in 1855) which managed all affairs relating to the artillery and engineers of the army.

Comb.: **ordnance datum** the datum-line or mean sea level to which all heights are referred in the Ordnance Survey; **ordnance map**: produced by the Ordnance Survey; **Ordnance Survey** (a formal body set up to conduct) an official survey of Great Britain and Ireland, producing detailed maps of the whole country.

ordo /ˈɔːdəʊ/ *noun.* Also **O-**. Pl. **-os**. M19.
[Latin = row, series, order.]
ECCLESIASTICAL. An ordinal, directory, or book of rubrics; an office or service with its rubrics.

ordonnance /ˈɔːdənəns, *foreign* ɔrdɔnɑ̃s (*pl. same*)/ *noun.* M17.
[French, alt. of Old French *ordenance* after Old & mod. French *ordonner*: see ORDINANCE.]
1 Systematic arrangement, esp. of literary material or architectural parts; a plan or method of literary or artistic composition; an architectural order. Cf. ORDINANCE 6b. M17.
2 In various European countries, esp. France, an ordinance, a decree, a law. M18.
3 *FRENCH HISTORY.* In full ***company of ordonnance***. Any of those organized companies of men-at-arms who formed the beginnings of a standing army in France. M18.

> 📖 **1** *Daedalus* No symmetrical ordonnance in Michelangelo's composition is likely to be rigid.

Ordovician /ɔːdəˈvɪʃɪən/ *adjective & noun.* L19.
[from Latin *Ordovices*, an ancient Brit. tribe in N. Wales + -IAN.]
GEOLOGY. ▶**A** *adjective.* Designating or pertaining to the second period of the Palaeozoic era, following the Cambrian and preceding the Silurian. L19.
▶ **B** *noun.* The Ordovician period; the system of rocks dating from this time. L19.

ordure /ˈɔːdjʊə/ *noun.* ME.
[Old & mod. French, from *ord* filthy from Latin *horridus* HORRID: see -URE.]
1 Filth, dirt. *arch.* ME.
2 Excrement, dung. LME.
3 *fig.* Moral defilement, corruption; obscene language, (an) obscene action. LME.

> 📖 **2** DENNIS POTTER The glistening sewers with their floating lumps of ordure. **3** T. JEFFERSON These ordures are rapidly depraving the public taste.

ore /ɔː/ *noun*[1].
[Old English *ōra*, (for sense) corresp. to Dutch *oer*, Low German *ūr*, of unkn. origin; in form prob. repr. *ār* = Old Saxon, Old High German *ēr*, Old Norse *eir*, Gothic *aiz*, from Germanic, corresp. to Latin *aes* crude metal, bronze, money.]
1 A native mineral containing a precious or useful substance, esp. metal, in such quantity and form as to make its extraction profitable. OE.
2 Metal; *esp.* precious metal. Chiefly *poet.* M17.

> 📖 **1** J. BRONOWSKI The extraction of metals from their ores . . was begun rather over seven thousand years ago. ***copper ore***, ***iron ore***, ***lead ore***, ***silver ore***, etc. ***bog ore***, ***feather ore***, ***kidney ore***, ***pitch-ore***, ***potter's ore***, ***tile-ore***, etc. *fig.*: W. GODWIN To work upon the ore of their native language.

Comb.: **orebody** a connected mass of ore in a mine or suitable for mining; **ore-shoot** a usu. elongated mass of ore in a vein.

ore /ɔː/ *noun*[2]. In sense 2 also **öre**, **øre** /ˈɔːrə/, pl. same. E17.
[In sense 1 from ORA *noun*[1]; in sense 2 from Danish, Norwegian *øre*, Swedish *öre*.]
1 = ORA *noun*[1]. Now *Hist.* E17.
2 (A coin representing) a monetary unit of Denmark and Norway (now usu. *øre*), and Sweden (now usu. *öre*), equal to one-hundredth of a krone or krona. E18.

Ore. *abbreviation.*
Oregon.

oread /ˈɔːrɪad/ *noun.* LME.
[Latin *Oread-*, *Oreas* from Greek *Oreiad-*, *Oreias*, from *oros* mountain: see -AD[1].]
CLASSICAL MYTHOLOGY. A nymph supposed to inhabit mountains, a mountain nymph.

†**orebi** *noun* var. of ORIBI.

orecchiette /ɒrəˈkjɛti/ *noun pl.* L20.
[Italian, = little ears.]
Small pieces of pasta shaped like ears.

orectic /ɒˈrɛktɪk/ *noun & adjective.* L17.
[Greek *orektikos* appetitive, from *orektos*, from *oregein* stretch out, grasp after, desire: see -IC.]
▶†**A** *noun.* A stimulant for the appetite. *rare.* Only in L17.
▶ **B** *adjective.* Chiefly *PHILOSOPHY.* Pertaining to or characterized by appetite or desire; appetitive. L18.

Oreg. *abbreviation.*
Oregon.

oregano /ɒrɪˈgɑːnəʊ, əˈrɛgənəʊ/ *noun.* L18.
[Spanish & Amer. Spanish var. of ORIGANUM.]
A seasoning prepared from the (usu. dried) leaves of wild marjoram, *Origanum vulgare*, or, esp. in Central and S. America, from shrubs of the genus *Lippia*, of the verbena family, esp. *L. graveolens*.

Oregon /ˈɒrɪg(ə)n/ *noun.* M19.
[A State on the Pacific coast of the US.]
Used ***attrib.*** to designate plants, animals, etc., found in or associated with Oregon.
Oregon cedar = LAWSON'S CYPRESS. **Oregon grape** a N. American evergreen shrub, *Mahonia aquifolium*, of the barberry family, with spiny-toothed leaves and racemes of yellow flowers, much planted in Europe as cover for game-birds; the dark blue-black berry of this plant. **Oregon pine** (the wood of) the Douglas fir, *Pseudotsuga menziesii*.
■ **Ore'gonian** *noun & adjective* (a native or inhabitant) of Oregon M19.

oreillet /ˈɒrɪlɛt/ *noun.* Now *rare.* Also ***oreillette*** /ɔrɛjɛt (*pl. same*)/. M16.
[French *oreillette* little ear, covering or ornament for the ear, dim. of *oreille* ear: see -ET[1].]
Orig., a defensive or decorative covering for the ears. Later *spec.*, the earpiece of a helmet.

oremus /ɒˈreɪmʊs/ *noun.* L18.
[Latin, lit. 'let us pray'.]
ROMAN CATHOLIC CHURCH. A liturgical prayer introduced by the word *oremus*.

orenda /ɒˈrɛndə/ *noun.* E20.
[Coined in English as expected Huron form of Mohawk *orė́:naˀ*.]
Invisible magic power believed by the Iroquois to pervade all natural objects as a spiritual energy.

Oreo /ˈɔːrɪəʊ/ *noun. US slang. derog.* Pl. **-os**. M20.
[US proprietary name for a chocolate biscuit with a white cream filling.]
A black American who is seen, esp. by other black people, as part of the white establishment.

†**oreography** *noun* var. of OROGRAPHY.

†**oreology** *noun* var. of OROLOGY.

ore rotundo /ˌɔːrɪ rəˈtʌndəʊ/ *adverbial phr.* E18.
[Latin, lit. 'with round mouth', from abl. of *os* mouth + abl. of *rotundus* round.]
With round, well-turned speech. Cf. OROTUND.

oreweed *noun* see OARWEED.

orey *adjective* var. of ORY.

orf /ɔːf/ *noun.* M19.
[Prob. from Old Norse *hrufa*: see ROVE *noun*[2].]
VETERINARY MEDICINE. An infectious disease of sheep and goats caused by a poxvirus, characterized by skin lesions, esp. on the lips, and secondary bacterial infection.

orf /ɔːf/ *preposition & adverb. non-standard.* L19.
[Repr. a pronunc.]
= OFF *adverb, preposition*.

orfe /ɔːf/ *noun.* L19.
[German: cf. French *orphe*, †*orfe*, Latin *orphus* from Greek *orphos* sea-perch.]
A freshwater cyprinid fish of northern Eurasia, *Leuciscus idus*; *esp.* (also ***silver orfe***) the normal silvery form, fished commercially.
golden orfe a yellow variety of the orfe, domesticated as an ornamental fish. ***silver orfe***: see above.

orfèvrerie /ɔrfɛvrəri/ *noun.* ME.
[French, from *orfèvre* from popular Latin *aurifabrum* worker in gold, goldsmith.]
Goldsmiths' work. Formerly also, the goldsmiths' quarter in London.

orfray *noun* var. of ORPHREY.

orfrayed *adjective* var. of ORPHREYED.

orful /ˈɔːfʊl, -f(ə)l/ *adjective. non-standard.* L19.
[Repr. a pronunc.]
= AWFUL.

org /ɔːg/ *noun. colloq.* M20.
[Abbreviation.]
= ORGANIZATION.

organ /ˈɔːg(ə)n/ *noun*[1]. LOE.
[Old French *organe*, *orgene* (mod. ORGUE), from Latin *organum* instrument, engine, musical instrument, (ecclesiastical) church organ, from Greek *organon*, from Indo-European base also of WORK *noun, verb.* Cf. ORGY.]
▶ **I 1** *gen.* Any of various musical (esp. wind) instruments. Long *obsolete* exc. in ***mouth-organ*** s.v. MOUTH *noun.* LOE.
2 *spec.* A usu. large musical instrument consisting of a number of pipes, supplied with compressed air from bellows, sounded by keys, which on being pressed down let air into the pipes by opening valves. Orig. in *pl.* ME. ▸**b** Any of a number of separate groups of sets or stops, each with its own keyboard, which make up an organ. E17.
3 a = ***barrel-organ*** s.v. BARREL *noun.* M19. ▸**b** A keyboard instrument with metal reeds, bellows mostly worked by treadles, and (usu.) a number of stops; a harmonium; a reed-organ. Now also = ***electric organ*** s.v. ELECTRIC *adjective.* L19.
2b ***choir organ***, ***great organ***, ***pedal organ***, ***swell organ***, etc. **3b** ***American organ***, ***cabinet organ***, ***pipe-organ***, ***reed-organ***, etc.
▶ **II 4** A part of an animal or plant adapted for a particular function, such as digestion, respiration, excretion, reproduction, locomotion, perception, etc. LME. ▸**b** The human organs of speech or voice collectively; the larynx and its accessories as used in speaking or singing. *rare.* E17. ▸**c** *PHRENOLOGY.* Each of the regions of the brain held to be the site of particular mental faculties. E19. ▸**d** The penis. Also more fully ***male organ***. *colloq.* E20.
5 *Hist.* A mechanical device, *esp.* a firearm, a machine-gun. LME.
6 a A means of action or operation; an instrument. Now *esp.*, a person, body of people, or thing by which some purpose is carried out or some function is performed. LME. ▸**b** A mental or spiritual faculty regarded as an instrument of the mind or soul. M17. ▸**c** A means or medium of communication; *spec.* a newspaper or journal which serves as the mouthpiece of a particular party, movement, etc. L18.

> 📖 **4** ***internal organ***, ***Jacobson's organ***, ***nasal organ***, ***pit organ***, ***sense-organ***, ***sexual organ***, etc. ***electric organ***: see ELECTRIC *adjective*. ***organ of Corti***, ***organ of Rosenmüller***. **6a** G. M. TREVELYAN County Councils . . the administrative organs of country life. *Accountancy* Enforcement has to be by an organ of government, preferably the Secretary of State. **b** W. HAMILTON Faith,— Belief,—is the organ by which we apprehend what is beyond our knowledge. **c** B. GUEST The . . magazine was originally begun as an organ for the philosophy of Dora Marsden.

Comb.: **organ-bird** either of two Australian birds of the family Cracticidae having a melodious song, the pied butcher-bird *Cracticus nigrogularis*, and the black-backed magpie *Gymnorhina tibicen*; **organ-blower** a person who or mechanical device which works the bellows of an organ; **organ-cactus** = ***organ-pipe cactus*** s.v. ORGAN-PIPE 2; **organ clock** a clock which plays a small pipe-organ at regular intervals; **organ-coral** = ***ORGAN-PIPE coral***; **organ-grinder** (*a*) a street musician who works a barrel-organ (cf. GRINDER 1c); (*b*) *fig.* [with ref. to the tradition of an organ-grinder's keeping a monkey trained to collect money] a person in control, a boss (as opposed to an underling); **organ-gun** a firearm with several charged chambers set side by side like organ-pipes (cf. sense 5 above); **organ-loft** a loft or gallery for an organ; **organ-man** (*a*) a man who builds or repairs organs; (*b*) an organ-grinder; **organ-metal** = ***pipe-metal*** s.v. PIPE *noun*[1]; **organ-point** = ***pedal point*** s.v. PEDAL *noun*[1]; **organ-screen** an ornamental screen on which an organ is placed in a church, cathedral, etc.; ***organ-stop***: see STOP *noun*[2] 14.
■ **orga'nific** *adjective* having the property or power of forming organs or organized structures; formative, organizing: E19. **organless** *adjective* (*a*) having no (bodily) organs; (*b*) having no musical organ: M19.

organ /ˈɔːg(ə)n/ *noun*[2]. *obsolete* exc. *dial.* LOE.
[Alt. of Latin ORIGANUM, Greek *origanon*.]
= ORIGANUM. Also, pennyroyal, *Mentha pulegium*.

organ /ˈɔːg(ə)n/ *verb. rare.* L16.
[from ORGAN *noun*[1].]
1 *verb trans.* Provide with an organ or organs. *obsolete* or *arch.* L16.
2 *verb intrans. & trans.* Play (something) on an organ. E19.

organa *noun* pl. of ORGANUM.

organal /ˈɔːg(ə)n(ə)l/ *adjective. rare.* E16.
[Old French, from Latin *organum*: see ORGAN *noun*[1], -AL[1].]
†**1** ***organal vein***, the jugular vein. Only in E16.
†**2** Of or pertaining to a musical organ. Only in M17.
3 MEDIEVAL MUSIC. Of or pertaining to (the) organum. E20.

organdie /ˈɔːg(ə)ndi, ɔːˈgandi/ *noun & adjective.* Also **-y**. E19.
[French *organdi*, of unkn. origin.]
(Made of) very fine translucent muslin, usu. stiffened.

organelle /ɔːgəˈnɛl/ *noun.* E20.
[mod. Latin *organella*, from *organum*: see ORGAN *noun*[1], -EL[2].]
BIOLOGY. Any of various specialized structures in the cytoplasm of an individual cell or unicellular organism, analogous to the organs of multicellular organisms.
■ **organellar** *adjective* L20.

organette /ɔːgəˈnɛt/ *noun.* L19.
[from ORGAN *noun*[1] + -ETTE.]
A small musical organ.

organetto /ɔːgəˈnɛtəʊ/ *noun.* Pl. **-os**. L19.
[Italian.]
Hist. A small portable organ used in the Middle Ages.

organic /ɔːˈganɪk/ *adjective & noun.* LME.
[French *organique* from Latin *organicus* from Greek *organikos* pertaining to an organ, instrumental, from *organon* ORGAN *noun*[1]: see -IC.]
▶ **A** *adjective.* **1** BIOLOGY & MEDICINE. Of, pertaining to, or of the nature of a bodily organ or organs; (of a disease) resulting from physical or metabolic disorder, accompanied by actual physical change in body tissue. LME.
2 Serving as an instrument or means; instrumental. *rare.* E16.
3 a MUSIC. Resembling an organ or the musical tones of an organ. E17. ▸†**b** MEDIEVAL MUSIC. Of or pertaining to (the) organum. Only in L18.
4 a Of, pertaining to, or derived from a living organism; having the characteristics of a living organism. L17. ▸**b** CHEMISTRY. Of, pertaining to, or designating carbon compounds, (orig. those naturally existing as the constituents of living organisms or derived from such compounds); containing carbon in combination. Also, (of an element) contained in an organic compound. Cf. INORGANIC *adjective* 1b. E19. ▸**c** (Of a fertilizer) produced from (only) natural substances; (of farming, gardening, etc.) involving the growing of plants without the use of artificial fertilizers, pesticides, etc.; (of food) produced without the use of such chemicals. M19.
5 a Inherent in the organization or constitution of a living being; constitutional; fundamental. L18. ▸**b** Belonging to the constitution of an organized whole; structural. L19.
†**6 a** MUSIC. Of or pertaining to musical instruments; instrumental. Only in E19. ▸**b** Done by means of technical instruments; mechanical. Only in L19.
7 a Of, pertaining to, or characterized by connection or coordination of parts in one whole; organized; systematic. E19. ▸**b** Organizing, constitutive. Chiefly in ***organic law***. *rare.* M19. ▸**c** Characterized by continuous or natural development suggestive of the growth of a living being. L19. ▸**d** ARCHITECTURE. Of a building, architectural style, etc.: reminiscent of or resembling a natural organism; *spec.* designating architecture that attempts to unify a building with its surroundings. E20.

🕮 **1** T. HARDY This fear . . rather than any organic disease . . was eating away the health of John South. **4a** G. LORD The soil was . . easily worked with a reasonable amount of organic stuff in it. **b** N. G. CLARK Cellulose and starch, are probably the most abundant organic substances known. **c** *Here's Health* Chemical-free food is now becoming . . appreciated and organic fruit and vegetables easier to buy. *Environment Now* If an organic farmer needs to apply more phosphate . . he uses rock minerals. **5a** F. FERGUSSON Euripedes' choruses are . . incidental music rather than organic parts of the action. A. BROOKNER Her inability to speak was not organic but deliberate. **7a** A. BEVAN Their teaching had an organic relationship with . . political and social realities. F. L. WRIGHT The work shall grow more truly simple . . more fluent . . more organic. **c** J. UGLOW Change . . must be gradual, organic, natural. *Times* Organic growth accounted for sales 8 per cent higher. **d** N. GORDIMER After heavy rains the concrete buildings have a . . bloom . . that makes them look organic.

Special collocations: **organic chemistry** the branch of chemistry that deals with the properties and reactions of organic compounds, i.e. those containing carbon (see note s.v. INORGANIC). **organic composition (of capital)** ECONOMICS in Marxist use, the ratio of constant capital or means of production to variable capital or labour-power. **organic soil**: composed mainly of organic material.
▶ **B** *noun.* An organic compound. Usu. in *pl.* M20.

■ **organicity** /-ˈnɪsɪti/ *noun* the quality or state of being organic M20.

organical /ɔːˈganɪk(ə)l/ *adjective.* LME.
[formed as prec. + -AL[1].]
†**1 a** BIOLOGY & MEDICINE. = ORGANIC *adjective* 1. LME–E19. ▸**b** Serving as an instrument, instrumental. Only in 17.
†**2** Of music: performed on an instrument, instrumental. E16–M18.
3 = ORGANIC *adjective* 4a. Now *rare* or *obsolete*. M16.
†**4** Of the nature of or pertaining to an instrument or machine; mechanical. L16–E18.
5 Of the nature of or pertaining to an organized structure; organized; structural. Now *rare* or *obsolete*. M17.
■ **organicalness** *noun* (long *rare*) L17.

organically /ɔːˈganɪk(ə)li/ *adverb.* L17.
[from ORGANIC *adjective* or prec.: see -ICALLY.]
In an organic manner.

organicism /ɔːˈganɪsɪz(ə)m/ *noun.* M19.
[French *organicisme*: cf. ORGANIC, -ISM.]
†**1** MEDICINE. The doctrine or theory which refers all disease to a localized organic cause. M–L19.
2 The doctrine that everything in nature has an organic basis or is part of an organic whole. E20.
3 The use or advocacy of literary or artistic forms in which the parts are connected or coordinated in the whole. M20.
■ **organicist** *noun & adjective* (*a*) *noun* an advocate or supporter of organicism; (*b*) *adjective* of or pertaining to organicism: L19. **organiˈcistic** *adjective* E20.

organification /ɔːˌganɪfɪˈkeɪʃ(ə)n/ *noun.* M20.
[from ORGANIC + -FICATION.]
Incorporation into an organic compound.

organigram /ɔːˈganɪgram/ *noun.* Also **-nogram**. M20.
[from ORGANI(ZATION + -GRAM.]
= ORGANIZATION ***chart***.

organisable *adjective*, **organisation** *noun*, **organise** *verb*, etc., vars. of ORGANIZABLE etc.

organism /ˈɔːg(ə)nɪz(ə)m/ *noun.* E18.
[In sense 1 from ORGANIZE + -ISM; in senses 2, 3 from French *organisme*.]
1 Organic structure; organization. Now *rare.* E18.
2 a An organized or organic system; a whole consisting of dependent and interdependent parts, resembling a living being. M18. ▸**b** PHILOSOPHY. The theory that in science everything is ultimately an organic part of an integrated whole. E20.
3 An organized living body; *esp.* (the material structure of) an individual animal, plant, bacterium, etc. Also ***living organism***. M19.
■ **orgaˈnismal** *adjective* of, pertaining to, or relating to an organism or organisms M19. **orgaˈnismic** *adjective* of or pertaining to an organism, expressed in terms of an organism L19. **orgaˈnismically** *adverb* (*rare*) M20.

organist /ˈɔːg(ə)nɪst/ *noun.* E16.
[French *organiste* or medieval Latin *organista*, formed as ORGAN *noun*[1]: see -IST.]
†**1** A maker of organs; an organ-builder. E16–M17.
2 A person who plays an organ; *spec.* a person appointed to play the organ at church services. M16. ▸**b** A player on a barrel-organ. L18.
†**3** MEDIEVAL MUSIC. = ORGANIZER 1b. L18–E19.
■ **orgaˈnistic** *adjective* (*rare*) (*a*) MUSIC of or pertaining to an organist or organ; (*b*) of or pertaining to an organism; based on organisms: M19. **organistship** *noun* the position or office of an organist M19.

organistrum /ɔːgəˈnɪstrəm/ *noun.* L19.
[medieval Latin, from Latin *organum*: see ORGAN *noun*[1].]
An old form of hurdy-gurdy.

organity /ɔːˈganɪti/ *noun. rare.* M17.
[Irreg. from ORGAN *noun*[1] + -ITY.]
†**1** The condition of being organic; organization. Only in M17.
2 An organized whole; an organism. E20.

organizable /ˈɔːg(ə)nʌɪzəb(ə)l/ *adjective.* Also **-isable**. L17.
[from ORGANIZE + -ABLE.]
Able to be organized; *spec.* in BIOLOGY, able to be converted into organized or living tissue.
■ **organizaˈbility** *noun* M19.

organization /ɔːg(ə)nʌɪˈzeɪʃ(ə)n/ *noun.* Also **-isation**. LME.
[from ORGANIZE + -ATION; in early use and sense 3 from medieval Latin *organizatio(n-)*.]
1 a The action of organizing or the condition of being organized as a living being; connection and coordination of parts for vital functions or processes. Also, the way in which a living being is organized; the structure of (any part of) a living organism; constitution. LME. ▸**b** An organized structure, body, or being; an organism. E18. ▸**c** The fact or process of becoming organized or organic; MEDICINE the conversion of a fibrin clot into fibrous tissue during the healing of a wound. E19.
2 a The condition of being organized; the way in which something is organized; coordination of parts in an organic whole; systematic arrangement. L18. ▸**b** The action of organizing or putting into systematic form; the arranging and coordinating of parts into a systematic whole. E19. ▸**c** An organized body, system, or society. E19.
3 MEDIEVAL MUSIC. The singing of the organum. L18.

🕮 **1a** H. JAMES The princess is a massive lady with the organisation of an athlete. **2a** A. S. DALE In organization, the *Nation* was . . run like a family affair. A. LIVELY He explained . . in detail the organization of the railroad company. **c** M. MEAD Different forms of marriage . . and age-grading . . resulted in a rich and complex form of social organization. *South African Panorama* An organisation run by the students themselves . . renders a very important community service.

Phrases: **organization and methods** management techniques and work study applied in office administration with a view to increasing efficiency.
Comb.: **organization centre** EMBRYOLOGY = ORGANIZER 2; **organization chart** a graphic representation of the structure of an organization showing the relationships of the positions or jobs within it; **organization man** (orig. *US*) a man who subordinates his individuality and personal life to the organization he serves.
■ **organizational** *adjective* of or pertaining to organization. M20. **organizationally** *adverb* M20. **organizationist** *noun* a person who advocates or practises organization L19. **organizatory** *adjective* of or pertaining to organization E20.

organize /ˈɔːg(ə)nʌɪz/ *verb.* Also **-ise**. LME.
[Old & mod. French *organiser* from medieval Latin *organizare*, from *organum*: see ORGAN *noun*[1], -IZE.]
1 *verb trans.* Give organic structure to; provide with the structure and interdependence of parts which subserves vital processes; form into a living being or living tissue; MEDICINE convert into fibrous tissue during healing. Usu. in *pass.* and as ORGANIZED 1. LME.
2 a *verb trans. gen.* Form into a whole with mutually connected and dependent parts; give a definite and orderly structure to; systematize; frame and put into working order (an institution, enterprise, etc.); arrange (something involving united action). M17. ▸**b** *verb intrans.* Become a systematic whole; become coordinated; attain orderly structure or working order. L19. ▸**c** *verb trans.* Provide for (a person); make arrangements for. L19. ▸**d** *verb trans.* Arrange personally; take responsibility for providing (something); fix up. M20.
3 *verb trans. & intrans.* MEDIEVAL MUSIC. Sing (a melody, line, etc.) as the organum. M17.
4 *verb trans.* Acquire deviously or illicitly; obtain cleverly. *slang* (orig. MILITARY). M20.

🕮 **2a** A. CARNEGIE I had organized among the railroad men a club of a hundred. W. S. CHURCHILL A formidable conspiracy was organised against him. **b** *Times Lit. Suppl.* By the 1890s they began to organize politically. **c** S. HILL You never organised yourself in those days, you always . . forgot things. *ASTMS Industry News* ASTMS has organised engineers and scientists . . since the first world war. **d** G. DURRELL We spent the rest of the day organizing a car to take us to Mexico City. WILLY RUSSELL Julia's organized a few people to come round for dinner. **4** H. ROOSENBURG Frenchwomen . . were busy organizing some sausages from a reluctant butcher.

organized /ˈɔːg(ə)nʌɪzd/ *adjective.* Also **-ised**. L16.
[from prec. + -ED[1].]
1 Provided with organs; composed of parts connected and coordinated for vital functions or processes; endowed with physical life, living; organic. L16.
2 MUSIC. Made or sounding like an organ. E17.
3 a *gen.* Formed into a whole with interdependent parts; coordinated so as to form an orderly structure; systematically arranged. E19. ▸**b** Of a person: having one's affairs in order; ready, prepared; efficient. M20.
4 Of or pertaining to a coordinated organization directing (esp. illegal) operations on a large or widespread scale. Esp. in ***organized crime***. E20.
5 Acquired deviously, illicitly, or cleverly. *slang* (orig. MILITARY). M20.

🕮 **3a organized games** athletics or sports as organized in a school, college, etc. **organized labour** workers affiliated by membership in trade unions. **b** S. BRETT Charles was very organized He got up at five o'clock. **4** *Times Lit. Suppl.* Organized religion has been the greatest psychotherapeutic ever invented.

organizer /ˈɔːg(ə)nʌɪzə/ *noun.* Also **-iser**. E19.
[from ORGANIZE + -ER[1].]
1 a A person who organizes or arranges something systematically; a person skilled in organization. Also (*spec.*), a person who organizes criminal activity. E19. ▸**b** MEDIEVAL MUSIC. A person who sings the organum. L19.
2 EMBRYOLOGY. A region of an embryo capable of causing induction (see INDUCTION 8c); an inductor. E20.
3 A thing which helps organize belongings or which is used in organizing systematically; *spec.* an object, as a purse, folder, etc., with compartments for filing or storing items separately. Also = ***personal organizer*** s.v. PERSONAL *adjective*. Orig. *US*. M20.

📖 **1a** V. BROME Brill, who was a good organiser, founded the New York Psycho Analytic Society. **2** *NUCLEOLAR organizer.* **3** *Office* Desk Organizer with three extra wide horizontal shelves.

organo- /'ɔːg(ə)nəʊ, ɔː'ganəʊ/ *combining form.*
[from Greek *organon* ORGAN *noun*[1], or from ORGANIC *adjective*: see -O-.]
1 Forming chiefly adjectives & nouns with the senses 'of bodily organs', 'of organic matter', 'of organic compounds'.
2 *spec.* in CHEMISTRY, forming (*a*) adjectives designating compounds containing a particular element bonded to an organic radical, as ***organochlorine***, ***organolead***, ***organomercury***, ***organosilicon***, etc.; (*b*) nouns denoting compounds of a particular type in which an organic radical is present, as ***organoborane***, ***organophosphate***.
■ **organo'leptic** *adjective* [French *organoleptique*, from Greek *lēptikos*, from *lambanein* apprehend by the senses] acting on the senses and bodily organs; involving the use of the senses: M19. **organo'leptically** *adverb* by means of or as regards the bodily senses M20. **or,ganome'tallic** *adjective & noun* (CHEMISTRY) (*a*) *adjective* (of a compound) in which an organic radical is bonded directly to a metal atom; of or pertaining to such compounds; (*b*) *noun* an organometallic compound: M19. **organo'phosphorus** *adjective* designating an organic compound that contains phosphorus M20. **or,gano'plastic** *adjective* (BIOLOGY) having the property of forming or producing the bodily organs M19. **orga'noscopy** *noun* (MEDICINE) examination of the organs, esp. visualization of abdominal contents by an endoscope inserted through the abdominal wall M19. **organosedi'mentary** *adjective* (GEOLOGY) produced by or involving sedimentation as affected by living organisms M20.

organogenesis /ɔːg(ə)nəʊ'dʒɛnɪsɪs/ *noun.* M19.
[from ORGANO- + -GENESIS.]
BIOLOGY. = ORGANOGENY.
■ ,**organoge'netic** *adjective* = ORGANOGENIC M19.

organogenic /ɔːg(ə)nə'dʒɛnɪk/ *adjective.* M19.
[from ORGANO- + -GENIC.]
1 BIOLOGY. Of or pertaining to organogeny. M19.
2 GEOLOGY. = ORGANOGENOUS. M20.
■ **organogenically** *adverb* M20.

organogenous /ɔːgə'nɒdʒɪnəs/ *adjective.* L19.
[from ORGANO- + -GENOUS.]
PETROGRAPHY. Of a rock: formed from organic materials.

organogeny /ɔːgə'nɒdʒəni/ *noun.* M19.
[from ORGANO- + -GENY.]
BIOLOGY. The production or development of the organs of an animal or plant; the branch of biology that deals with this.
■ **organogenist** *noun* L19.

organogram *noun* var. of ORGANIGRAM.

organography /ɔːgə'nɒgrəfi/ *noun.* M16.
[from ORGANO- + -GRAPHY.]
†**1** A description of instruments. M16–L17.
2 The description of the organs of animals or (esp.) plants. E19.
■ **organo'graphic**, **organo'graphical** *adjectives* E19.

organoid /'ɔːg(ə)nɔɪd/ *adjective & noun.* M19.
[mod. Latin *organoides*: see ORGANO-, -OID.]
▶**A** *adjective.* Resembling an organ or organism in structure; having an organic appearance. M19.
▶**B** *noun.* BIOLOGY. = ORGANELLE. Now *rare.* M20.

organology /ɔːgə'nɒlədʒi/ *noun.* E19.
[from ORGANO- + -LOGY.]
1 The branch of knowledge that deals with the supposed organs of the mental faculties etc. indicated by regions of the cranium; phrenology. E19.
2 The branch of anatomy and physiology that deals with the organs of animals and plants. M19.
3 The study of anything as an organ or means of doing something. M19.
4 The branch of knowledge that deals with the history of musical instruments. M20.
■ **organo'logical** *adjective* M19. **organologist** *noun* M19.

organon /'ɔːg(ə)nɒn/ *noun.* L16.
[Greek = instrument, organ, etc. See ORGAN *noun*[1].]
†**1** A bodily organ, esp. as an instrument of the soul or mind. L16–E17.
2 An instrument of thought or knowledge; a means of reasoning, discovery, etc.; *spec.* a system of logical rules of demonstration or investigation, *esp.* the logical treatises of Aristotle. E17.

organonomy /ɔːgə'nɒnəmi/ *noun. rare.* E19.
[from Greek ORGANON + -NOMY.]
The branch of knowledge that deals with the laws of organic life.
■ ,**organo'nomic** *adjective* M19.

organosol /ɔː'ganəsɒl/ *noun.* L19.
[from ORGANO- + SOL *noun*[5].]
A dispersion of a substance in an organic liquid; *spec.* one of a synthetic resin in a liquid containing a plasticizer, which can be converted into a solid plastic simply by heating (cf. PLASTISOL).

organotherapy /ɔːg(ə)nəʊ'θɛrəpi/ *noun.* L19.
[from ORGANO- + THERAPY.]
MEDICINE. Treatment by the administration of preparations made from animal organs, esp. glands.
■ ,**organothera'peutic** *adjective* E20.

organ-pipe /'ɔːg(ə)npʌɪp/ *noun.* LME.
[from ORGAN *noun*[1] + PIPE *noun*[1].]
1 Any of the tubes by which sounds are produced in an organ. LME.
2 More fully ***organ-pipe cactus***. Any of several large cacti of the south-western US with columnar stems or branches, esp. *Lemaireocereus marginatus* and the saguaro, *Carnegiea gigantea*. M19.

📖 **1** *fig.*: SHAKES. *Temp.* The thunder, That deep and dreadful organ-pipe.

Comb.: ***organ-pipe cactus***: see sense 2 above; **organ-pipe coral** a coral of the genus *Tubipora*, which forms tall pipelike structures.

organum /'ɔːg(ə)nəm/ *noun.* Pl. **-na** /-nə/. E17.
[Latin from Greek ORGANON.]
1 = ORGANON 1. Long *rare* or *obsolete.* E17.
2 MEDIEVAL MUSIC. A part sung as an accompaniment below or above the melody or plainsong, usu. at an interval of a fourth or fifth; this method of singing in parts. L18.

organy /'ɔːg(ə)ni/ *noun.* Now *rare* or *obsolete.* M16.
[Alt.]
= ORIGANUM.

organza /ɔː'ganzə/ *noun.* E19.
[formed as next.]
A thin stiff transparent dress fabric of silk or synthetic fibre.

organzine /'ɔːg(ə)nziːn/ *noun & verb.* L17.
[French *organsin* from Italian *organzino*, of unkn. origin.]
▶**A** *noun.* A strong thread, made of strands of silk twisted together in a direction contrary to that of each individual strand. Also (in full ***organzine silk***), a fabric made from this thread. L17.
▶**B** *verb trans. & intrans.* Make (silk or silk threads) into organzine. L18.

orgasm /'ɔːgaz(ə)m/ *noun & verb.* L17.
[French *orgasme* or mod. Latin *orgasmus* from Greek *orgasmos*, from *organ* swell as with moisture, be excited.]
▶**A** *noun.* **1** Excitement or violent action in a bodily organ or part, accompanied by turgescence. Now only *spec.* (also ***sexual orgasm***), this centred in the genitals as the climax of sexual excitement; an experience of orgasm, a sexual climax. L17.
2 Violent excitement, rage, fury; a paroxysm. Now only as fig. use of sense 1. M18.

📖 **1** *British Medical Journal* Patients used a vibrator to achieve orgasm. **2** J. R. LOWELL He saw man . . vibrated by the orgasm of a national emotion.

▶**B** *verb intrans.* Experience a sexual orgasm. L20.
■ **or'gasmal** *adjective* = ORGASMIC M20. **or'gasmic** *adjective* of or pertaining to (sexual) orgasm; in a state of (sexual) orgasm; able or likely to experience orgasm: M20. **or'gasmically** *adverb* L20.

orgasmatron /ɔː'gazmətrɒn/ *noun.* L20.
[from prec. + *-atron* after *betatron*, *thetatron*, etc.]
A (fictional or hypothetical) automated booth or machine designed to provide sexual pleasure.
¶ Introduced in the Woody Allen film *Sleeper* (1973).

orgastic /ɔː'gastɪk/ *adjective.* E19.
[Greek *orgastikos*, from *organ*: see ORGASM.]
Pertaining to or characterized by (sexual) orgasm.
■ **orgastically** *adverb* M20.

orgeat /'ɔːdʒɪət; *foreign* ɔrʒa (*pl. same*)/ *noun.* LME.
[French from Provençal *orjat*, from *ordi* barley from Latin *hordeum*.]
A syrup or cooling drink made from barley (later from almonds) and orange-flower water.

orgia /'ɔːdʒɪə/ *noun pl.* L15.
[Latin & Greek: see ORGY.]
Orgies, esp. in honour of Dionysus or Bacchus.

orgiac /'ɔːdʒɪak/ *noun & adjective. rare.* M19.
[from Greek ORGIA + -AC.]
▶**A** *noun.* An orgy. M19.
▶**B** *adjective.* Of or pertaining to an orgy. L19.

orgiast /'ɔːdʒɪast/ *noun.* L18.
[Greek *orgiastēs*, from *orgiazein* celebrate orgies, from ORGIA.]
A person who celebrates orgies.

orgiastic /ɔːdʒɪ'astɪk/ *adjective.* L17.
[Greek *orgiastikos*, formed as prec.: see -IC.]
Characterized by or of the nature of orgies; marked by extravagance, licentiousness, or dissolute revelry.
■ **orgiastical** *adjective* (*rare*) of orgiastic character or tendency L19. **orgiastically** *adverb* M20. **orgiasticism** /-sɪz(ə)m/ *noun* (*rare*) (advocacy of) orgiastic behaviour M20.

orgic /'ɔːdʒɪk/ *adjective. rare.* L18.
[Irreg. from ORGY + -IC.]
= ORGIAC *adjective.*

orgie *noun* see ORGY.

orgillous *adjective* var. of ORGULOUS.

orgone /'ɔːgəʊn/ *noun.* M20.
[from ORG(ANISM, ORG(ASTIC + *-one*, after HORMONE.]
In the psychoanalytical theory of Wilhelm Reich (1897–1957), a supposed excess sexual energy or life-force distributed throughout the universe which can be collected and stored for subsequent therapeutic use. Freq. *attrib.*

📖 E. JONG They seemed to give off blue light as they fucked . . . If there was such a thing as orgone energy . . they had discovered it.

■ **or'gonomy** *noun* the study or investigation of orgone M20.

orgue /ɔːg/ *noun. obsolete* exc. *Hist.* M17.
[French = organ, instrument, warlike machine, etc.: see ORGAN *noun*[1].]
1 A musical organ; something resembling an organ or organ-pipes. M17.
2 FORTIFICATION. Any of several thick pieces of wood hung over a gate to act as a portcullis. E18.
¶ See also ***point d'orgue*** s.v. POINT *noun*[2] 3.

†**orgueil** *noun & adjective.* Also **orguil**, **orgul**. ME.
[Anglo-Norman *orguil*, Old French *orgoill*, *orguill* (mod. *orgueil*) from Frankish noun meaning 'pride'.]
▶**A** *noun.* Pride, haughtiness. ME–L18.
▶**B** *adjective.* Proud, haughty, presumptuous. ME–M16.

orguinette /ɔːgɪ'nɛt/ *noun. rare.* L19.
[French ORGUE or Old French *orguine* var. of *organe* ORGAN *noun*[1]: see -ETTE.]
A mechanical musical instrument in which the wind from a bellows is admitted to a set of reeds through holes in a strip of paper which is moved along by turning a crank.

†**orgul** *noun & adjective* var. of ORGUEIL.

orgulous /'ɔːgjʊləs/ *adjective. arch.* Also **orgillous** /'ɔːgɪləs/. ME.
[from Old French *orguillus*, Anglo-Norman *orguillous* (mod. *orgueilleux*): see -ULOUS. Cf. ORGUEIL.]
1 Proud, haughty. ME.
2 Swelling, violent. L15.

orgy /'ɔːdʒi/ *noun.* Also (now *rare*) **orgie**. M16.
[Orig. in pl. from French *orgies*, from Latin ORGIA (neut. pl.) secret rites; secret frantic revels, from Indo-European base also of WORK *noun*, *verb* (cf. ORGAN *noun*[1]): see -Y[3].]
1 CLASSICAL HISTORY. In *pl.*, secret rites or ceremonies practised in the worship of various deities of Greek and Roman mythology; *esp.* festivals in honour of Dionysus or Bacchus, celebrated with extravagant dancing, singing, drinking, etc. Occas. *sing.*, an occasion of such rites etc. M16.
2 *gen.* In *pl.*, any rites, ceremonies, or secret observances. Occas. *sing.*, an occasion of such rites etc. L16.
3 An occasion of feasting or revelry, esp. marked by excessive indulgence, drunkenness, sexual activity, etc.; a debauch. Also (*transf.*), an occasion of excessive indulgence in any activity. E18.

📖 **2** *Nineteenth Century* Edward Colston . . in whose honour pious orgies are still annually celebrated. **3** M. HUNTER A three-day orgy of drinking, dancing in the streets. *Oxford Star* Burglars ransacked a family's home in a sickening orgy of destruction.

oribatid /ɒ'rɪbətɪd/ *noun & adjective.* E20.
[from mod. Latin *Oribata* genus name, perh. from Greek *oreibatēs* mountain-ranging: see -ID[3].]
▶**A** *noun.* Any of various small dark oval-bodied acariform mites of the suborder Oribatida, which includes non-parasitic mites with a thickened leathery integument. E20.
▶**B** *adjective.* Of, pertaining to, or designating this suborder. E20.

oribi /'ɒrɪbi/ *noun.* Also †**ourebi**, †**orebi**, & other vars. L18.
[Afrikaans, app. from Nama.]
A small antelope, *Ourebia ourebi*, of open grassy plains in southern and eastern Africa.

orichalc /'ɒrɪkalk/ *noun.* Also **aur-**, & in Latin form **-chalcum** /-kalkəm/. LME.
[Latin *orichalcum*, *auri-*, from Greek *oreikhalkon* lit. 'mountain copper': the var. *aurichalcum* by assoc. with *aurum* gold.]
A yellow metal prized by the ancients and often known of only by repute, prob. a form of brass or similar alloy.

oriel /'ɔːrɪəl/ *noun.* LME.
[Old French *oriol*, *eurieul* passage, gallery, of unkn. origin: cf. medieval Latin *oriolum* porch, anteroom, upper chamber.]
1 A portico, a gallery, a balcony, etc. Now only (*dial.*), a porch or balcony at the head of an outdoor staircase. LME.
2 A large polygonal recess with a window, projecting usu. from the upper storey of a building, and supported from the ground or on corbels. LME. ▸**b** In full ***oriel***

window. A window in such a recess; a projecting upper-floor window. **M18.**
■ **orielled** *adjective* (*rare*) provided with oriels **E20.**

oriency /ˈɔːrɪənsi/ *noun*. Now *poet. rare*. **M17.**
[from **ORIENT** *adjective*: see **-ENCY**.]
Orient quality, brilliancy, lustre.
■ Also **orience** *noun* **M19.**

orient /ˈɔːrɪənt, ˈɒr-/ *noun & adjective*. Also (esp. in senses A.1, 2) **O-**. **LME.**
[Old & mod. French from Latin *orient-* pres. ppl stem of *oriri* to rise: see **-ENT**.]
▶ **A** *noun*. **1** *The* part of the heavens in which the sun and other celestial objects rise; *the* corresponding region of the world or quarter of the compass, *the* east. Now *poet. & rhet.* **LME.**
2 The part of the earth east of a given point; *spec.* the countries east of the Mediterranean, *esp.* those of eastern Asia. Usu. ***the Orient***. Now *poet. & literary*. **LME.**
3 The rising of the sun etc.; dawn. Now *rare* or *obsolete*. **E16.**
4 The special lustre of a pearl of the best quality; a pearl having this lustre. **M18.**

1 POPE All the ruddy Orient flames with day. **2** A. BEVAN The awakening of the Orient under the impact of Western ideas. **3** *fig.*: W. DRUMMOND His life having set in the orient of his age. **4 pearl of orient** a pearl from the Indian seas, as opp. to those of less beauty found in European mussels; *gen.* a brilliant pearl.

Comb.: **Orient Express** a train which ran (from 1883 to 1961) between Paris and Istanbul and other Balkan cities, via Vienna, popularly associated with espionage and intrigue; a successor to this train following a similar route.
▶ **B** *adjective*. **1** Situated in or belonging to the east; oriental. Now *poet.* **LME.**
2 Of a pearl or other precious stone, orig. one coming from the East: of superior value and brilliancy, lustrous, precious. **LME.** ▸**b** *gen.* Shining, radiant, resplendent. Also, shining like the dawn, bright red. *arch.* **LME.**
3 Of the sun, daylight, etc.: rising. **M16.**

1 COLERIDGE A richer dowry Than orient kings can give! **2** E. YOUNG Orient gems around her temples blazed. **b** T. FULLER A shrub, whose red berries . . gave an orient tincture to cloth. D. G. ROSSETTI Its flowering crest impearled and orient.

¶ Opp. ***Occident***.

orient /ˈɔːrɪɛnt, ˈɒr-/ *verb*. **E18.**
[French *orienter*, formed as **ORIENT** *noun*.]
1 *verb trans.* Place or arrange to face the east; *spec.* build (a church) with the longer axis running due east and west. **E18.**
2 *verb trans.* Position or align (a structure etc.) in a particular way relative to the points of the compass or other defined data (foll. by *to*, *with*). Also, ascertain the bearings of. **M19.** ▸**b** *fig.* Bring into a defined relationship to known facts or principles; *refl.* put oneself in the right position or relation. Also, give a specific direction or tendency to. **M19.**
3 *verb intrans.* Turn to the east, or (by extension) in any specified direction. **L19.**
4 CHEMISTRY. **a** *verb intrans.* Of a substituent in a ring: direct further substituents to a specified (meta, ortho, or para) position in the ring. **E20.** ▸**b** *verb trans.* Ascertain the relative positions of the substituents in (a cyclic molecule). **M20.**
5 *verb trans.* Cause the molecules of (a plastic etc.) to align with their axes parallel. **M20.**

2 W. FAULKNER Trying to orient himself by looking back . . to establish whether he was above or below the tree. E. LYNAM All early maps were oriented with the East at the top. **b** R. MAY Man needs relations with other people in order to orient himself. *Scientific American* The program is oriented toward the long-range goal of providing . . power sources. **3** *fig.*: *Times* Orienting to a Labour victory through pushing back the Alliance.

■ **orientaˈbility** *noun* the property of being orientable **M20.** **orientable** *adjective* able to be oriented **M20.** **oriented** *adjective* (*a*) having (a particular) orientation; (*b*) (with preceding noun or adverb) having a specified emphasis, bias, or interest: **E20.**

oriental /ɔːrɪˈɛnt(ə)l, ɒr-/ *adjective & noun*. Also (esp. in senses A.2, B.2) **O-**. **LME.**
[Old & mod. French, or Latin *orientalis*, from *orient-*: see **ORIENT** *noun*, **-AL**[1].]
▶ **A** *adjective*. **1** Belonging to or situated in the eastern part of the sky or (formerly) of a specified country or region. Also (ASTROLOGY), (of a planet) seen in the east or eastern part of the sky, seen before sunrise. **LME.**
2 *spec.* Belonging to, occurring in, or characteristic of, the countries east of the Mediterranean, esp. those of eastern Asia; of or pertaining to the Orient, its affairs, or civilization. **LME.**
3 Of a precious stone, esp. a pearl: superior in brilliancy or lustre; = **ORIENT** *adjective* 2. **LME.**

2 *Independent* A dance which for decades has stood for female voluptuousness and oriental mystique. *Country Homes* An extensive range of beautiful oriental silks for curtains & soft furnishings. *Here's Health* Health remedies unique to Oriental traditional medicine.

Special collocations: **oriental carpet**, **oriental rug**: hand-knotted (as) made in the Orient. **Oriental Jew** a Jewish person from the Middle or Far East, esp. from Yemen, Ethiopia, Iraq, or India. **Oriental languages** those languages native to Oriental countries. **Oriental Lowestoft** Chinese porcelain made for export to Europe (erron. thought to have been made at Lowestoft, England). ***oriental medlar***: see **MEDLAR** 1. ***Oriental Orthodox***: see **ORTHODOX** *adjective* 5. ***oriental plane***: see **PLANE** *noun*[2] 1. **oriental poppy** a perennial garden poppy, *Papaver orientale*, with showy usu. scarlet flowers, native to SW Asia. ***oriental rug***: see ***oriental carpet*** above. **oriental sore** a form of leishmaniasis occurring in Asia and Africa, causing open ulcers. **oriental stitch** EMBROIDERY a long straight stitch across an area to be filled, secured with a short diagonal stitch in the centre. ***oriental topaz***: see **TOPAZ** *noun* 1. ***oriental verd-antique***: see **VERD-ANTIQUE** 3.
▶ **B** *noun*. †**1** A precious stone, *esp.* an oriental pearl. **LME–M18.**
2 A native or inhabitant of the East; *spec.* an Asian. Now sometimes *offensive*. **L15.**
†**3** In *pl.* Oriental languages. **L17–M18.**
4 = ***Oriental Lowestoft*** above. **M19.**
5 An oriental rug. **M20.**

2 J. H. BURTON A solemn, bearded, . . robed Oriental.

¶ Opp. *occidental*.
■ **orientally** *adverb* **L18.**

orientalia /ɔːrɪɛnˈteɪlɪə, ɒr-/ *noun pl*. **E20.**
[Latin, neut. pl. of *orientalis* **ORIENTAL** *adjective*: see **-IA**[2].]
Things, esp. books, relating to or characteristic of the Orient.

orientalise *verb* var. of **ORIENTALIZE**.

orientalism /ɔːrɪˈɛnt(ə)lɪz(ə)m, ɒr-/ *noun*. **M18.**
[from **ORIENTAL** *adjective* + **-ISM**.]
1 Oriental character or style; an oriental trait or idiom. **M18.**
2 Oriental scholarship; knowledge of Oriental languages. **E19.**
■ **orientalist** *noun* †(*a*) a member of the Greek Orthodox Church; †(*b*) = **ORIENTAL** *noun* 2; (*c*) an expert in or student of Oriental languages and literature: **L17.**

orientality /ɔːrɪənˈtalɪti, ɒr-/ *noun*. **M17.**
[from **ORIENTAL** *adjective* +**-ITY**.]
1 Chiefly ASTROLOGY. Visibility of a planet in the eastern part of the sky or before sunrise. **M17.**
2 Eastern style or character. **M18.**

orientalize /ɔːrɪˈɛnt(ə)lʌɪz, ɒr-/ *verb*. Also **-ise**. **E19.**
[from **ORIENTAL** *adjective* + **-IZE**.]
1 *verb trans.* Make oriental; give an oriental character to. **E19.**
2 *verb intrans.* Become oriental in character; act or speak like an Oriental. **E19.**
■ **orientaliˈzation** *noun* **L19.** **orientalizing** *ppl adjective* that orientalizes; *esp.* (of artistic or literary style, etc.) displaying oriental influence: **M19.**

orientate /ˈɔːrɪənteɪt, ˈɒr-/ *verb trans. & intrans.* **M19.**
[Prob. back-form. from **ORIENTATION**.]
= **ORIENT** *verb*.
■ **orientated** *adjective* = **ORIENTED** **L19.**

orientation /ˌɔːrɪənˈteɪʃ(ə)n, ˌɒr-/ *noun*. **M19.**
[App. from **ORIENT** *verb* + **-ATION**.]
1 The placing or arranging of something to face the east; *spec.* the construction of a church with the longer axis running due east and west. **M19.** ▸**b** The action of turning to the east, *esp.* in an act of worship. **L19.**
2 Position or arrangement of a building, natural object, etc., relative to the points of the compass or other defined data. **M19.**
3 The action or process of ascertaining one's bearings or relative position, or of taking up a known bearing or position; the faculty of doing this, sense of relative position. **M19.** ▸**b** CHEMISTRY. The orienting effect of a substituent in a ring; the process of ascertaining the relative positions of the substituents in a ring. **L19.**
4 *fig.* A person's attitude or adjustment in relation to circumstances, ideas, etc; determination of one's mental or emotional position. **L19.** ▸**b** An introductory talk, course, etc., given esp. to newcomers to a university, organization, etc. Also ***orientation course***, ***orientation programme***, etc. Chiefly *N. Amer.* **M20.**

2 *Independent* The southerly orientation of its slopes is an asset. **4** E. FROMM A culture in which the marketing orientation prevails. J. GATHORNE-HARDY An adult's sexual orientation is determined between the ages of one and five.

Comb.: ***orientation course***, ***orientation programme***: see sense 4b above; **orientation triad** the three elements of the body's orientation system, i.e. sight, mechanoreceptors, and inner ear.
■ **orientational** *adjective* **M20.** **orientationally** *adverb* **L20.**

orienteer /ˌɔːrɪənˈtɪə, ˌɒr-/ *noun & verb*. **M20.**
[Back-form. from next.]
▶ **A** *noun*. A person who engages in orienteering. **M20.**
▶ **B** *verb intrans.* Practise orienteering. **M20.**

orienteering /ˌɔːrɪɛnˈtɪərɪŋ, ˌɒr-/ *noun*. **M20.**
[Swedish *orientering* orienteering, orig. 'orientating': cf. **ORIENT** *verb*, **-ING**[1].]
A competitive sport in which participants have to find their way on foot, skis, etc., across rough country with the aid of map and compass.

orientite /ɔːrɪˈɛntʌɪt, ɒr-/ *noun*. **E20.**
[from *Oriente* a Cuban province + **-ITE**[1].]
MINERALOGY. An orthorhombic hydrated silicate of calcium and manganese, usu. occurring as light brown or pink crystals.

orifacial *adjective* see **OROFACIAL**.

orifice /ˈɒrɪfɪs/ *noun*. Also †**orifex**. **LME.**
[Old & mod. French from late Latin *orificium*, from *or-*, *os* mouth + *-fic-* var. of *fac-* stem of *facere* make.]
A (small) opening or aperture; *esp.* the mouth of a bodily organ or other cavity.

A. N. WILSON Tristram Shandy's obscene fascination with his mother's body and its various orifices.

■ **oriˈficial** *adjective* of or pertaining to an orifice or orifices, esp. (MEDICINE) those of the rectum and urogenital system **LME.**

oriflamme /ˈɒrɪflam/ *noun*. **LME.**
[Old & mod. French *oriflambe*, *-amme*, in medieval Latin *auriflamma*, from *aurum* gold + *flamma* **FLAME** *noun*.]
1 *Hist.* The sacred red or orange-red silk banner of St Denis, given to early kings of France by the abbot of St Denis on setting out for war. **LME.**
2 *transf.* & *fig.* **a** A banner, principle, ideal, etc., that serves as a rallying point in a struggle. **E17.** ▸**b** A bright conspicuous object, colour, etc. **M19.**

2a D. MACDONALD A copy of *Ulysses*, whose light-blue-and-white cover was then an oriflamme for such as me. **b** GEO. ELIOT The new-bathed Day With oriflamme uplifted o'er the peaks.

origami /ɒrɪˈɡɑːmi/ *noun*. **M20.**
[Japanese, from *oru*, *-ori* fold + *kami* paper.]
The Japanese art of folding paper into decorative shapes and objects.

origanum /ɒˈrɪɡ(ə)nəm/ *noun*. Also (now *rare*) **origan** /ˈɒrɪɡ(ə)n/. **ME.**
[Latin from Greek *origanon*, perh. from *oros* mountain + *ganos* brightness, joy: cf. **OREGANO**.]
Any of various aromatic labiate plants of the genus *Origanum*, much grown as herbs; *esp.* wild marjoram, *O. vulgare*.

Origenist /ˈɒrɪdʒɪnɪst/ *noun*. **M16.**
[from *Origen* (see below) + **-IST**.]
A person holding any of the doctrines attributed to the Alexandrian biblical scholar and theologian Origen (*c* 185–254), esp. the belief that all moral beings, including the fallen angels, will ultimately be saved.
■ **Origenism** *noun* **E18.** **Origeˈnistic** *adjective* **M19.**

origin /ˈɒrɪdʒɪn/ *noun*. **M16.**
[French *origine* or Latin *origin-*, *origo*, from *oriri* to rise.]
1 The beginning, cause, or ultimate source of something; that from which a thing is derived, a source, a starting-point. Freq. in *pl.* **M16.** ▸**b** A person's parentage or ancestry. **E17.**
2 ANATOMY. The place or point at which a muscle, nerve, etc., arises; the proximal attachment of a muscle; the root of a nerve in the brain or spinal cord. **L17.**
3 MATH. A fixed point from which measurement or motion begins; *spec.* (*a*) the point of intersection of the axes in Cartesian coordinates; (*b*) the pole in polar coordinates. **E18.**

1 R. DAWKINS Begin at the beginning, with the very origin of life itself. T. BENN The origins of socialism can be traced back as far as the time of Christ. **certificate of origin** a custom-house document certifying the place of origin of a commodity imported. **b** A. HARDING So little did I know of my origins that even the existence of my mother seemed . . a fancy. E. FEINSTEIN Both my parents were Jewish in origin. **3 *pedal origin***: see **PEDAL** *adjective* 2.

original /əˈrɪdʒɪn(ə)l, ɒ-/ *adjective & noun*. **ME.**
[Old & mod. French, or Latin *originalis*, from *origin-*: see prec., **-AL**[1].]
▶ **A** *adjective*. **1** Existing at or from the beginning or earliest stage; primary, initial, innate. Earliest in ***original sin*** below. **ME.** ▸**b** That is such by birth, born. *rare*. **E18.**
2 That is the origin or source of something; *spec.* (of a picture, text, etc.) from which another is copied, translated, etc. **ME.**
3 Proceeding directly from its source; not derivative or imitative; *spec.* made, composed, etc., by a person himself or herself. **E18.**
4 Given to or displaying independent exercise of the mind or imagination; inventive, fresh, creative. **M18.**

📖 **1** S. BELLOW His original vexation with Max revived. *Daily Telegraph* Quiet and peaceful inside with original panelling and tapestries. **2** T. GRAY Shake her own creation To its original atoms. M. WOODHOUSE Copies of Lorca in the original Spanish. **3** J. RUSKIN A certain quality about an original drawing which you cannot get in a woodcut. **4** H. C. MERIVALE Even on the .. mysteries of Aristotle's Ethics he could throw an original light. A. LURIE Some of the stories .. are conventionally sentimental .. others are startlingly original.

Special collocations: **original equipment manufacturer** an organization that makes devices to its own design and under its own brand name from component parts bought from other manufacturers (*abbreviation OEM*). **original gravity** BREWING the relative density of the wort before it is fermented to produce beer (this value depending chiefly on the quantity of fermentable sugars in solution and hence being a guide to the alcoholic strength of the finished beer). **original instrument** (a copy of) a musical instrument dating from the time when the music played on it was composed. ***original pravity***: see PRAVITY 1. **original print**: made directly from an artist's own woodcut, etching, etc., and printed by the artist or under his or her supervision. **original sin** THEOLOGY the tendency to evil supposedly innate in all humans, held to be inherited from Adam in consequence of the Fall of Man (opp. ***actual sin***). **original writ** LAW (now *Hist.*) a writ issuing from the Court of Chancery, which formed the foundation of a real action at common law.

▶ **B** *noun*. **1** Origin, derivation; parentage, descent. *arch.* & *Scot.* LME. ▸†**b** Beginning, earliest stage. E16–M18. ▸†**c** ANATOMY. The fact of springing or arising (as a nerve, vein, etc.) from some part. Also, = ORIGIN 2. L16–M17.

2 A person or thing from which something proceeds; a source, a cause. *arch.* LME. ▸**b** LAW (now *Hist.*). = ***original writ*** above. LME.

3 A picture, document, photograph, etc., from which another is copied; the text or literary work from which a translation is made. LME. ▸**b** A person represented in a picture; a person on whom a literary character is based. L18.

4 In *pl.* ▸†**a** Original or fundamental elements. LME–M17. ▸**b** Original inhabitants, members (of a society), etc. *rare*. E18.

5 A work of literature or art that is not a copy or imitation. L17. ▸**b** A garment specially designed for exhibition in a fashion collection; a copy of such a garment made to order. M20. ▸**c** MUSIC (chiefly JAZZ). A piece written by its performer(s). M20.

6 a A person who acts in an original way; a singular or eccentric person. L17. ▸**b** A thing of unique character. *rare*. E18.

📖 **1** H. HALLAM Some word of barbarous original. **2** R. L. STEVENSON The unmistakeable original of the deed in question. **3** B. BOVA He knew which were the originals and which the copies. P. GROSSKURTH Learning German in order to read Freud in the original. **5** *House & Garden* The intricately gilded furniture .. the Sevres porcelain—all are .. copies of well-known originals. **6a** C. LAMBERT An 'original' like Gesualdo, Berlioz or Busoni. **b** *Antiquity* This self bow is an original of unknown origin.

■ **originally** *adverb* (*a*) in respect of origin or derivation; (*b*) in the first place, primarily; (*c*) at or from the beginning: LME.

originality /əˌrɪdʒɪˈnalɪti/ *noun*. M18.
[French *originalité*, from ORIGINAL: see -ITY.]
1 The quality or fact of being original; *spec.* (*a*) authenticity, genuineness; primariness; (*b*) inventiveness, creativity; (*c*) novelty, freshness, esp. of literary or artistic style. L18.
2 An original trait, act, remark, etc. M19.

originant /əˈrɪdʒɪnənt, ɒ-/ *adjective*. *rare*. M17.
[from ORIGIN(ATE + -ANT¹.]
That gives origin to a thing.

originary /əˈrɪdʒɪn(ə)ri, ɒ-/ *adjective* & *noun*. Now *rare*. L16.
[Late Latin *originarius*, from Latin *origin-*: see ORIGIN, -ARY¹.]
▶ **A** *adjective*. †**1** Native to or *of* a given place. L16–E18.
2 That is the origin or source of a person or thing. M17.
†**3** Arising directly; primary, underived. L17–E18.

📖 **2** C. FREILICH Even prohibition has its place, but its place is not originary or fundamental.

▶†**B** *noun*. An aboriginal inhabitant. L16–E18.

originate /əˈrɪdʒɪneɪt, ɒ-/ *verb* pa. pple **-ated**, †**-ate**. M17.
[medieval Latin *originat-* pa. ppl stem of *originare*, formed as prec.: see -ATE³. Cf. Latin *originatio(n-)* etymology.]
1 *verb trans.* Cause to begin; initiate. M17.
2 *verb intrans.* Take its origin; arise, commence, be derived. Usu. foll. by *from*, *in*, *with*. L18.

📖 **1** H. L. MENCKEN The Legislature .. seldom originates a really sound piece of legislation. *Economist* The cost of originating a loan .. is about 150 basis points. **2** W. B. CARPENTER The points whence the legs and wings originate. E. WAUGH The scandal originated with the Connollys. P. GROSSKURTH She .. sees anxiety as originating from .. the death instinct within the self.

■ **origiˈnation** *noun* (*a*) rise, origin; commencement; formerly (*spec.*), derivation of a word; (*b*) the action of causing to begin; initiation; (*c*) ***origination fee***, a fee charged by a lender on entering into a loan agreement to cover the cost of processing the loan: E17. **originative** *adjective* having the quality or power of originating; creative: M19. **originator** *noun* an initiator E19.

orignal /ɒrɪˈnjal/ *noun*. *Canad.* (now *rare*). Also (earlier) †**oriniack**. M17.
[Canad. French, alt. of Basque *oregna*, pl. *oregnac*.]
The moose, *Alces alces*.

orihon /ˈɒrɪhɒn/ *noun*. E20.
[Japanese, from *ori* fold + *hon* book.]
A book formed by folding a printed roll alternately backwards and forwards between the columns, and usu. fastening it with cord down one side.

orillion /əˈrɪljən/ *noun*. M17.
[Old & mod. French *orillon*, *oreillon*, ear-shaped appendage, from *oreille* ear.]
FORTIFICATION (now *Hist.*). A projecting tower or shoulder of a bastion.

Orimulsion /ɒrɪˈmʌlʃ(ə)n/ *noun*. L20.
[Blend of *Orinoco* (the bitumen being originally extracted from the Orinoco oil belt in Venezuela) and EMULSION.]
(Proprietary name for) a fuel consisting of an emulsion of bitumen in water.

orinasal /ɔːrɪˈneɪz(ə)l/ *adjective* & *noun*. Also **oro-** /ɔːrə-/. M19.
[from Latin *ori-* combining form of *or-*, *os* mouth + NASAL *noun*, *adjective*.]
▶ **A** *adjective*. Pertaining to the mouth and nose; *spec.* in PHONETICS, (of a vowel) sounded with the oral and nasal passages both open, as the nasal vowels in French, nasalized. M19.
▶ **B** *noun*. PHONETICS. An orinasal vowel. L19.
■ **orinasally** *adverb* by means of the mouth and nose L20.

oriole /ˈɔːrɪəʊl, ˈɔːrɪəl/ *noun*. L18.
[medieval Latin *oriolus* from Old French *oriol* from Latin *aureolus* dim. of *aureus* golden, from *aurum* gold: see -OLE¹.]
1 Any of various mainly tropical Old World passerine birds of the genus *Oriolus* or the family Oriolidae, noted for the melodious song and brilliant plumage of the males; *esp.* (in full ***golden oriole***) *Oriolus oriolus*, the male of which is yellow and black. L18.
2 Any of various mainly tropical birds, esp. New World passerines of the genus *Icterus* (family Icteridae), which resemble the true orioles in the bright plumage of the males. L18.
2 ***Baltimore oriole***, ***orchard oriole***, ***regent oriole***, etc.

Orion /əˈrʌɪən/ *noun*. LME.
[Latin from Greek *Ōriōn* mighty hunter in Greek mythol., (also the constellation).]
(The name of) a conspicuous constellation lying on the celestial equator, at the edge of the Milky Way, and interpreted as a hunter with belt and sword.
Orion's belt a short line of three bright stars across the middle of Orion. **Orion's hound** Sirius, the dog-star.
■ **Orionid** *noun* & *adjective* (designating) any of a shower of meteors seeming to radiate from the constellation Orion, in October L19.

Orisha /əˈrɪʃə/ *noun*. Pl. same, **-s**. E20.
[Yoruba.]
In southern Nigeria, any of several minor gods. Usu. in *pl.*

orismology /ɒrɪzˈmɒlədʒi/ *noun*. *rare*. E19.
[from Greek *horismos* definition + -OLOGY.]
(An explanation of) technical terms collectively; terminology.
■ **orismoˈlogical** *adjective* E19.

orison /ˈɒrɪz(ə)n, -s(ə)n/ *noun*. *arch.* ME.
[Old French *oreison*, *orison* (mod. *oraison*), Anglo-Norman *ureison*, from Latin *oratio(n-)* speech, oration: see ORATION *noun*.]
1 A prayer. In later use usu. in *pl.* ME. ▸**b** The action of praying. Now *rare*. ME.
†**2** A speech, an oration. Chiefly *Scot.* LME–E17.

📖 **1** SHAKES. *Haml.* Nymph, in thy orisons Be all my sins rememb'red.

Orissi /ɒˈrɪsi/ *noun*. Also **Odissi** /ɒˈdɪsi/. M20.
[Oriya, adjective from *Orisā*, from Sanskrit *odradeśa*, from *Odra* (see ORIYA) + *deśa* country, province.]
An Indian classical dance which originated in Orissa in eastern India. Freq. *attrib.*

-orium /ˈɔːrɪəm/ *suffix*. Pl. **-iums**, **-ia** /-ɪə/.
[Latin, neut. sing. ending of adjectives in *-orius* -ORY².]
Forming nouns with the sense 'a place for or belonging to, a thing or part used for' as ***auditorium***, ***exploratorium***, ***haustorium***, ***sanatorium***, etc.

Oriya /ɒˈriːjə/ *noun* & *adjective*. Also **Uriya** /ˈʊrɪə/. E19.
[Oriya *Oriyā*, Bengali, Hindi *Uriyā*, ult. from Sanskrit *Oḍra* Odra (see sense A.2).]
▶ **A** *noun*. Pl. same, **-s**.
1 The Indo-Aryan language of the State of Orissa in eastern India. E19.
2 A native or inhabitant of Orissa or Odra, an ancient region of India corresponding to present-day Orissa. M19.
▶ **B** *adjective*. Of or pertaining to Orissa or Odra. E19.

ork /ɔːk/ *noun*¹. *slang* (orig. & chiefly *US*). M20.
[Abbreviation.]
An orchestra; *spec.* a jazz or dance band.

ork *noun*² var. of ORC.

Orkney /ˈɔːkni/ *noun*. M19.
[A group of islands off the north coast of Scotland.]
Used ***attrib.*** to designate things found or produced in Orkney.
Orkney cheese a type of cheese, resembling Cheddar, made in Orkney. **Orkney sheep** a small feral sheep distinguished by backward-curving horns, a brown, white, or speckled fleece, and the habit of feeding on seaweed on the shore. **Orkney vole** a large vole, of a subspecies of the common European vole, *Microtus arvalis*, found only in Orkney.

Orkneyman /ˈɔːknɪmən/ *noun*. Pl. **-men**. L18.
[from *Orkney* (see prec.) + MAN *noun*.]
A native or inhabitant of Orkney.

orl /ɔːl/ *noun*. *dial.* exc. in ***orl-fly*** below. LME.
[Alt.]
= ALDER.
Comb.: **orl-fly** an alder fly, *esp.* the common *Sialis lutaria*, used for trout-fishing.

orle /ɔːl/ *noun*. L16.
[Old & mod. French, also †*ourle* (cf. mod. *ourlet* hem), from *ourler* to hem, from Proto-Romance dim. of Latin *ora* edge, border, prob. from *or-*, *os* mouth.]
1 HERALDRY. A narrow bordure following the outline of a shield but not extending to its edge; a number of charges forming such a bordure. L16.
2 *Hist.* The chaplet or wreath round the helmet of a knight, bearing the crest. M19.

Orleanian /ɔːˈliːnɪən/ *noun*. M20.
[from NEW) ORLEAN(S + -IAN.]
A native or inhabitant of New Orleans, Louisiana.

Orleanist /ˈɔːlɪənɪst, ɔːˈliːənɪst/ *noun* & *adjective*. M19.
[French *Orléaniste*, from *Orléans*: see next, -IST.]
Hist. A person supporting the claim to the French throne of the descendants of the Duke of Orleans (1640–1701), younger brother of Louis XIV, esp. Louis-Philippe, who reigned as King of France, 1830–48.
■ **Orleanism** *noun* L19. **Orleaˈnistic** *adjective* M19.

Orleans /ˈɔːlɪənz, ɔːˈliːənz/ *noun*. L17.
[*Orléans*, a city in France.]
1 In full ***Orleans plum***. An old variety of plum. L17.
2 In full ***Orleans cloth***. A fabric of cotton warp and worsted weft, brought alternately to the surface in weaving. M19.
¶ See also ***the maid of Orleans*** s.v. MAID *noun*.

orlo /ˈɔːləʊ/ *noun*. Pl. **-os**. M17.
[Italian = border, hem, etc., from Latin *ora*: see ORLE.]
ARCHITECTURE. **1** The fillet under the ovolo of a capital. M17.
2 The plinth under the base of a column. E18.

Orlon /ˈɔːlɒn/ *noun*. Also **o-**. M20.
[Invented name: cf. NYLON.]
(Proprietary name for) a polyacrylonitrile fibre and fabric for textiles and knitwear.

orlop /ˈɔːlɒp/ *noun*. LME.
[Middle & mod. Dutch *overloop*, from *overloopen* run over: see OVER-, LEAP *verb*.]
NAUTICAL. A platform over the hold of a ship forming the lowest deck, esp. in a ship of more than three decks. Also ***orlop deck***.

ormer /ˈɔːmə; *foreign* ɔrmɛr (*pl. same*)/ *noun*. M17.
[Channel Islands French = French *ormier*, from Latin *auris maris* ear of the sea, so called from its resemblance to the ear.]
A sea-ear or abalone of northern and Mediterranean waters, of the genus *Haliotis*; esp. *H. tuberculata*, used as food in the Channel Islands.
■ **ormering** *noun* the collecting of ormers (in the Channel Islands) E20.

orming /ˈɔːmɪŋ/ *adjective*. *dial.* E20.
[Origin unkn.]
Tall and ungainly. Also, gawping.

ormolu /ˈɔːməluː/ *noun* & *adjective*. M18.
[from French *or moulu* lit. 'powdered gold'.]
▶ **A** *noun*. Orig., gold or gold leaf prepared for gilding brass, bronze, etc. Later, gilded bronze or a gold-coloured alloy of copper, zinc, and tin used to decorate furniture, make ornaments, etc.; articles made of or decorated with this. M18.
▶ **B** *adjective*. Made of ormolu. E19.

ornament /ˈɔːnəm(ə)nt/ *noun*. ME.
[Anglo-Norman *urnement*, Old French *o(u)rnement* (mod. *orne-*) from Latin *ornamentum* equipment, ornament, from *ornare* adorn: see -MENT. Refash. after Latin from 15.]
1 †**a** An adjunct, an accessory; equipment, furniture, attire. ME–M18. ▸**b** ECCLESIASTICAL. In *pl.* The accessories or furnishings of the Church and its worship, as the altar, sacred vessels, vestments, etc. LME.
2 a Something used or serving to adorn, beautify, or embellish; a decoration, an embellishment, *esp.* a small trinket, vase, figure, etc. ME. ▸**b** *fig.* A quality or circumstance that confers beauty, grace, or honour. M16. ▸**c** A person who adds honour or distinction to his or her

sphere, time, etc. L16. ▸**d** MUSIC. A grace note; a decorative figure used to embellish a melody. M17.
3 a The action of adorning; the fact of being adorned; adornment, embellishment, decoration. L15. ▸†**b** Mere adornment; outward show or display. *rare* (Shakes.). Only in L16.

📖 **2a** E. WELTY The new green shoes placed like ornaments on top of the mantel shelf. *Sunday Express* Expensive ornaments and knicknacks anoint every available surface. **c** LD MACAULAY He was very severe on Erasmus, though the most distinguished ornament of his own College. **d** *Opera Now* When it comes to arias they sing absolutely straight . . adding no ornaments. **3a** F. O'BRIEN Certain porcelain articles related more to utility than ornament. K. CLARK The pages of pure ornament are almost the richest . . pieces of abstract decoration ever produced. *Independent* Another Norman church . . distinguished by its rich carving and ornament.

Comb.: **ornaments rubric** the rubric immediately preceding the Order for Morning and Evening Prayer in the *Book of Common Prayer*, referring to the ornaments to be used in the Church of England.

ornament /ˈɔːnəm(ə)nt, -mɛnt/ *verb trans.* E18.
[from prec.]
Provide with ornaments, make ornamental; adorn, embellish, beautify.
▪ **ornamenter** *noun* a person who or thing which ornaments; *spec.* an artist skilled in decoration: E19. **ornamentist** *noun* a professional decorator; a designer of ornaments: M19.

ornamental /ɔːnəˈmɛnt(ə)l/ *adjective & noun.* M17.
[from ORNAMENT *noun* + -AL[1].]
▸**A** *adjective.* Of the nature of an ornament, serving as an ornament; decorative. M17.

📖 E. WAUGH A long, ornamental sword hung at his side.

▸**B** *noun.* **1** In *pl.* Things that are ornamental; adornments, embellishments, esp. as opp. to essentials. M17.
2 A tree, shrub, or plant grown for its attractive appearance. E20.
▪ **ornamentalism** *noun* the principle or practice of being ornamental M19. **ornamentalist** *noun* a person skilled (esp. artistic) in ornamentation M19. **ornamenˈtality** *noun* the condition of being ornamental; a thing which is ornamental: M19. **ornamentalize** *verb trans.* make ornamental L19. **ornamentally** *adverb* E18.

ornamentation /ɔːnəm(ə)nˈteɪʃ(ə)n, -mɛn-/ *noun.* M19.
[from ORNAMENT *verb* + -ATION.]
1 The action or process of ornamenting; the state of being adorned; *spec.* detailed artistic decoration or embellishment. M19.
2 Ornament; a thing which is ornamented; the ornaments which adorn something. M19.
3 MUSIC. The use of grace notes to embellish a melody. L19.

ornate /ɔːˈneɪt/ *adjective.* LME.
[Latin *ornatus* pa. pple of *ornare* adorn: see -ATE[2].]
1 Adorned, ornamented (*with*) (long *rare*); highly decorated, elaborately embellished. LME.
2 Of literary or oratorical style: embellished with flowery language or rhetoric. LME.

📖 **1** S. QUINN A luxurious hotel, with chandeliers even more ornate than any she had seen in Europe. **2** H. ROGERS The imagery is too profuse, the diction too ornate . . There is too much . . rhetoric.

▪ **ornately** *adverb* L15. **ornateness** *noun* L16.

ornation /ɔːˈneɪʃ(ə)n/ *noun. rare.* L15.
[Latin *ornatio(n-)*, from *ornat-*: see next, -ATION.]
The action of adorning; the condition of being adorned; (an) adornment, (an) ornamentation.

ornature /ˈɔːnətjʊə/ *noun. rare.* L15.
[French from late Latin *ornatura*, from Latin *ornat-* pa. ppl stem of *ornare* adorn: see -URE.]
Ornamentation, adornment, decoration; embellishment; an instance of this.

ornery /ˈɔːnəri/ *adjective. dial. & colloq.* (chiefly *N. Amer.*). E19.
[Dial. var. of ORDINARY *adjective*.]
Commonplace, inferior, unpleasant; mean, cantankerous.

📖 A. HAILEY His partner . . might just be ornery enough to make trouble later.

▪ **orneriness** *noun* meanness, cussedness L19.

ornithic /ɔːˈnɪθɪk/ *adjective.* Now *rare* or *obsolete.* M19.
[Greek *ornithikos* birdlike, from *ornis* bird: see -IC.]
Of, pertaining to, or characteristic of birds; avian. Also, dealing with or skilled in birds.

ornithine /ˈɔːnɪθiːn/ *noun.* L19.
[from ORNITHO- + -INE[5].]
BIOCHEMISTRY. An amino acid, $NH_2(CH_2)_3CH(NH_2)COOH$, produced by the body and important in protein metabolism.

ornithischian /ɔːnɪˈθɪskɪən, -ˈθɪʃɪən/ *adjective & noun.* E20.
[from mod. Latin *Ornithischia* (see below), from ORNITHO- + ISCHIUM: see -IA[2], -IAN.]
PALAEONTOLOGY. ▸**A** *adjective.* Of, pertaining to, or designating the order Ornithischia of herbivorous dinosaurs, which includes forms having a birdlike pelvic structure as hadrosaurs, stegosaurs, iguanodons, etc. E20.
▸**B** *noun.* A dinosaur of this order. M20.

ornitho- /ˈɔːnɪθəʊ/ *combining form* of Greek *ornith-*, *ornis* bird: see -O-.
▪ **ornithocoˈprophilous** *adjective* (esp. of lichen) growing on bird droppings E20. †**ornitholite** *noun* a fossil of (part of) a bird: only in 19. **ornithomancy** *noun* divination by means of the flight and cries of birds M17. **ornithoˈmorphic** *adjective* having the form and appearance of a bird, birdlike L19. **orniˈthoscopy** *noun* observation of birds for the purpose of divination M19.

ornithogalum /ɔːnɪˈθɒg(ə)ləm/ *noun.* Formerly Anglicized as †**ornithogal**. L16.
[mod. Latin (see below), from Latin *ornithogale*, Greek *ornithogalon*, formed as ORNITHO- + *gala* milk.]
Any plant of the genus *Ornithogalum*, of the lily family; = ***star of Bethlehem*** s.v. STAR *noun*[1] *& adjective*.

ornithoid /ˈɔːnɪθɔɪd/ *adjective.* M19.
[from ORNITHO- + -OID.]
ZOOLOGY. Esp. of certain reptiles: resembling a bird (in structure).

ornithology /ɔːnɪˈθɒlədʒi/ *noun.* L17.
[mod. Latin *ornithologia*, from Greek *ornithologos* treating of birds: see ORNITHO-, -LOGY.]
The branch of zoology that deals with birds.
▪ **ornithologer** *noun* (*rare*) = ORNITHOLOGIST M17. ˌ**ornithoˈlogic** *adjective* (chiefly *US*) M19. ˌ**ornithoˈlogical** *adjective* E19. ˌ**ornithoˈlogically** *adverb* M19. **ornithologist** *noun* L17. **ornithologize** *verb intrans.* look for or study birds in the wild L19.

ornithophily /ɔːnɪˈθɒfɪli/ *noun.* L19.
[from ORNITHO- + -PHILY.]
1 Love of birds. Now *rare*. L19.
2 BOTANY. Pollination by birds. E20.
▪ ˈ**ornithophile** *noun* (*a*) a lover of birds; (*b*) BOTANY an ornithophilous plant: M20. **ornithophilist** *noun* (now *rare*) = ORNITHOPHILE (a) L19. **ornithophilous** *adjective* (BOTANY) pollinated by birds L19.

ornithopod /ˈɔːnɪθəpɒd/ *adjective & noun.* L19.
[mod. Latin *Ornithopoda* (see below), formed as ORNITHO- + -POD.]
PALAEONTOLOGY. ▸**A** *adjective.* Of, pertaining to, or designating the suborder Ornithopoda of herbivorous ornithischian dinosaurs, whose hind feet somewhat resembled those of birds. L19.
▸**B** *noun.* A dinosaur of this suborder. L19.
▪ **orniˈthopodous** *adjective* L19.

ornithopter /ˈɔːnɪθɒptə/ *noun. obsolete* exc. *Hist.* E20.
[French *ornithoptère* coined to repl. *orthoptère* ORTHOPTER 1.]
AERONAUTICS. A machine designed to achieve flight by means of flapping wings.

ornithorhynchus /ˌɔːnɪθəˈrɪŋkəs/ *noun.* E19.
[mod. Latin genus name, formed as ORNITHO- + Greek *rhugkhos* bill.]
= PLATYPUS. Chiefly as mod. Latin genus name.

ornithosaur /ˈɔːnɪθəsɔː/ *noun.* L19.
[mod. Latin *Ornithosauria* former order name (now Pterosauria), formed as ORNITHO-: see -SAUR.]
= PTEROSAUR.
▪ **ornithoˈsaurian** *adjective & noun* L19.

ornithosis /ɔːnɪˈθəʊsɪs/ *noun.* Pl. **-thoses** /-ˈθəʊsiːz/. M20.
[from ORNITHO- + -OSIS.]
MEDICINE. Psittacosis, esp. as communicated to humans.
▪ **ornithotic** /-ˈθɒtɪk/ *adjective* M20.

orobanche /ɒrəˈbaŋki/ *noun.* M16.
[Latin from Greek *orobagkhē*, from *orobos* OROBUS + *agkhein* to throttle.]
A broomrape of the genus *Orobanche*.

orobus /ˈɒrəbəs/ *noun.* LME.
[Latin from Greek *orobos* a Mediterranean fodder plant, *Vicia ervilia*.]
Any of various leguminous plants of the genera *Vicia* and *Lathyrus*; *spec.* any of those (e.g. the spring-flowering *Lathyrus montanus*) constituting the former genus *Orobus* (also called ***bitter-vetch***).

orocratic /ɒrəˈkratɪk/ *adjective.* E20.
[from Greek *oros* mountain + *kratos* strength: see -IC.]
GEOLOGY. Designating a period when crustal upheaval predominates over erosion, leading to an overall increase in relief.

orofacial /ɔːrəˈfeɪʃ(ə)l/ *adjective.* Also (now *rare*) **ori-** /ɔːrɪ-/. E19.
[from Latin *or-*, *os* mouth + -O-, -I- + FACIAL *adjective*.]
ANATOMY. Pertaining to the mouth and face; located on or directed at the mouth and adjacent part of the face.
▪ **oroˈfacially** *adverb* L20.

orogen /ˈɒrədʒ(ə)n/ *noun.* E20.
[from Greek *oros* mountain + -GEN.]
GEOLOGY. An orogenic belt.

orogenesis /ɒrəˈdʒɛnɪsɪs/ *noun.* L19.
[from Greek *oros* mountain + -GENESIS.]
GEOLOGY. The formation of mountains.
▪ **orogeˈnetic** *adjective* = OROGENIC *adjective* L19. **orogeˈnetically** *adverb* E20.

orogenic /ɒrəˈdʒɛnɪk/ *adjective.* L19.
[formed as prec. + -GENIC.]
GEOLOGY. Mountain-forming; connected with or characterized by the formation of mountains.
▪ **oroˈgenically** *adverb* M20.

orogenital /ɔːrəʊˈdʒɛnɪt(ə)l/ *adjective.* M20.
[Irreg. from Latin *or-*, *os* mouth + -O- + GENITAL *adjective*.]
Of sexual activity: involving contact between the mouth of one person and genitals of another.

orogeny /ɒˈrɒdʒəni/ *noun.* L19.
[from Greek *oros* mountain + -GENY.]
GEOLOGY. **1** = OROGENESIS. L19.
2 A geological period of mountain-building. E20.

orographic /ɒrəˈgrafɪk/ *adjective.* M19.
[from Greek *oros* mountain + -GRAPHIC.]
Of or pertaining to orography; relating to the physical features and relative position of mountains; (of precipitation) resulting from moist air being forced upwards by mountains.
▪ **orographical** *adjective* E19. **orographically** *adverb* L19.

orography /ɒˈrɒgrəfi/ *noun.* Also †**oreog-**. M19.
[from Greek *oros*, *ore-* mountain + -GRAPHY.]
The branch of physical geography which deals with the formation and features of mountains. Also, the orographical features of a region.

orohydrography /ˌɒrəʊhʌɪˈdrɒgrəfi/ *noun.* L19.
[from Greek *oros* mountain + HYDROGRAPHY.]
The branch of hydrography that deals with the role of mountains in determining drainage patterns, esp. with regard to watersheds.
▪ **orohydroˈgraphic**, **orohydroˈgraphical** *adjectives* E20.

orology /ɒˈrɒlədʒi/ *noun.* Also †**oreol-**. L18.
[from Greek *oros*, *ore-* mountain + -LOGY.]
The branch of science that deals with mountains; orography.
▪ **oroˈlogical** *adjective* E19. **orologist** *noun* E19.

orometric /ɒrəˈmɛtrɪk/ *adjective.* L18.
[from Greek *oros* mountain + -METRIC.]
Of or pertaining to the measurement of mountains.
▪ **oˈrometry** *noun* the measurement of forms of relief L19.

oronasal *adjective & noun* var. of ORINASAL.

oronoco /ɔːrəˈnəʊkəʊ/ *noun.* Also **-nooko** /-ˈnuːkəʊ/. M17.
[Origin unkn.: app. unconnected with the River Orinoco.]
A variety of tobacco.

oropendola /ɒrəˈpɛndələ/ *noun.* L19.
[Spanish = golden oriole.]
Any fruit-eating bird of the neotropical genus *Psarocolius* (family Icteridae), the members of which are noted for their long hanging nests.

Oropesa /ɒrəˈpiːzə/ *noun.* M20.
[The name of the trawler first used to test this float.]
More fully ***Oropesa float***, ***Oropesa sweep***. A kind of minesweeping float introduced during the war of 1914–18.

oropharynx /ɔːrə(ʊ)ˈfarɪŋks/ *noun.* Pl. **-pharynges** /-fəˈrɪndʒiːz/, **-pharynxes**. L19.
[Irreg. from Latin *or-*, *os* mouth + -O- + PHARYNX.]
ANATOMY. The part of the pharynx that lies between the soft palate and the hyoid bone. Cf. NASOPHARYNX.
▪ **orophaˈryngeal** *adjective* of or pertaining to the oropharynx L19.

oro-rotundity /ˌɒrəʊrə(ʊ)ˈtʌndɪti/ *noun.* Now *rare*. M19.
[from ORO(TUND + ROTUNDITY.]
= OROTUNDITY.

orotic /ɒˈrɒtɪk/ *adjective.* E20.
[Italian *orotico*, formed as Greek *oros* serum, whey + -OTIC.]
BIOCHEMISTRY & MEDICINE. **1** ***orotic acid***, a colourless crystalline heterocyclic acid, $C_4HN_2(OH)_2COOH$, which is found in milk and is a growth factor for some micro-organisms. E20.
2 ***orotic aciduria***, a rare genetic disorder in which the metabolism of orotic acid is impaired, resulting in anaemia and excessive amounts of the acid in the blood and urine. M20.
▪ ˈ**orotate** *noun* a salt or ester of orotic acid E20. **orotidine** *noun* a nucleoside containing an orotic acid residue, involved in the biosynthesis of pyrimidine nucleotides M20.

orotund /ˈɒrə(ʊ)tʌnd, ˈɔːr-/ *adjective.* L18.
[Contr. of Latin ORE ROTUNDO.]
1 Of a voice, utterance, etc.: full, round, imposing; clear, resonant. L18.
2 Of writing, style of expression, etc.: inflated, pretentious. L19.

🕮 **1** N. LOWNDES In an unexpectedly orotund voice he began to pray aloud. **2** R. ALTER A monosyllabic muscularity in Johnson's spoken diction . . marks it off from the more orotund rhetoric of his prose.

■ **oro'tundity** *noun* the quality of being orotund E20.

Oroya fever /ɒˈrɔɪə ˌfiːvə/ *noun phr.* L19.
[from La *Oroya*, a town in central Peru.]
MEDICINE. An acute (frequently fatal) febrile haemolytic disease which is a form of bartonellosis. Cf. CARRION'S DISEASE, VERRUGA.

orphan /ˈɔːf(ə)n/ *noun & adjective.* LME.
[Late Latin *orphanus* from Greek *orphanos* without parents, bereft, rel. to Latin *orbus* bereft.]
▶ **A** *noun.* **1** A child whose parents are dead; a fatherless or motherless child. Now also, a child abandoned by his or her parents. LME.
2 A person bereft of former protection, advantages, etc. L15.
3 *transf.* A discontinued model of a motor vehicle. *slang.* M20.
4 TYPOGRAPHY. Esp. in word processing and desktop publishing: a word or line undesirably separated by a page break from the paragraph to which it belongs. Cf. WIDOW *noun*¹ 4. L20.

🕮 **1** K. GIBBONS That lady would take in anything from orphans to stray cats.

Comb.: **orphan asylum** (now *rare*) an orphanage; **Orphan's Court** in some States of the US (formerly also in England), a probate court having jurisdiction over the estates and persons of orphans.
▶ **B** *adjective.* That is an orphan, having no parents; *fig.* lacking protection or identity such as a parent would provide. L15.
orphan drug a synthetic drug which remains commercially undeveloped. **orphan virus** any virus that is not known to be the cause of a disease.
■ **orphancy** *noun* orphanhood L16. **orphandom** *noun* (*rare*) orphanhood L19. **orphanhood** *noun* the state or condition of being an orphan E19. †**orphanism** *noun* orphanhood L16–M19. **orphanize** *verb trans.* make an orphan of L18.

orphan /ˈɔːf(ə)n/ *verb trans.* E19.
[from the noun.]
Make an orphan of; bereave of a parent or parents; abandon. Chiefly as ***orphaned*** *ppl adjective.*

🕮 E. GRIFFITH He is orphan'd both of father and mother. DICKENS She saw she had no father upon earth, and ran out, orphaned, from his house. *Daily Progress* Two cars have been orphaned on Market Street . . and have sat there—abandoned.

orphanage /ˈɔːf(ə)nɪdʒ/ *noun.* M16.
[from ORPHAN *noun* + -AGE.]
†**1** The guardianship formerly exercised by the Lord Mayor and Aldermen of London over the persons and property of orphans within the City not yet of age. M16–M18.
2 The state or condition of being an orphan, orphanhood. L16.
3 Orphans collectively. *rare.* M19.
4 An institution or home for orphans. M19.

orpharion /ɔːˈfarɪən/ *noun.* L16.
[from *Orph(eus* + *Arion*, musicians in Greek mythol.]
A large instrument resembling a lute, with six to nine pairs of metal strings usu. played with a plectrum, popular in the 16th and 17th cents.

Orphean /ɔːˈfiːən/ *adjective & noun.* L16.
[from Latin *Orpheus* from Greek *Orpheios*, from *Orpheus* (see below): see -AN, -EAN.]
▶ **A** *adjective.* **1** Of or pertaining to (the musical abilities of) Orpheus, a mythical Greek musician and poet the strains of whose lyre were said to be able to move rocks and trees. Also, melodious, entrancing. L16.
2 = ORPHIC *adjective* 1. L17.

🕮 **1** W. COWPER As if conven'd By magic summons of th' Orphean lyre. **Orphean warbler** a grey and white migratory warbler, *Sylvia hortensis*, with a whitish eye, of Southern Europe, SW Asia, and Africa north of the equator.

▶ **B** *noun.* An adherent of Orphic philosophy. E19.

orphenadrine /ɔːˈfɛnədriːn/ *noun.* M20.
[from OR(THO- + contr. of DIPHENHYDRAMINE.]
PHARMACOLOGY. A derivative of diphenhydramine used as an antispasmodic, esp. in the treatment of Parkinsonism.

orpheonist /ˈɔːfɪənɪst/ *noun.* M19.
[French *orphéoniste* from *Orphéon* a school of vocal music established in Paris in 1833, from *Orpheus*: see ORPHEAN, -IST.]
A member of any of a number of French schools of vocal music founded in the 19th cent.; a choral singer.

Orphic /ˈɔːfɪk/ *adjective & noun.* L17.
[Latin *Orphicus* from Greek *Orphikos*, from *Orpheus*: see -IC.]
▶ **A** *adjective.* **1** Of or pertaining to Orpheus (see ORPHEAN), esp. with respect to the philosophical mysteries associated with his name, or the writings or doctrines subsequently attributed to him. Also, oracular. L17.
2 Of the nature of the music of or poems attributed to Orpheus; melodious, entrancing, ravishing. E19.
3 Of, pertaining to, or characteristic of Orphism in cubist art. M20.

🕮 **1** *Daily Telegraph* The mosaic . . contains symbols . . similar to those mentioned in the Orphic writings. **Orphic egg** the earth, the world (formerly held to be egg-shaped).

▶ **B** *noun.* **1** An Orphic song or hymn. Usu. in *pl.* M19.
2 An adherent of the Orphic school of philosophy. L19.
■ **Orphically** *adverb* after the manner of the Orphic writings, doctrines, or mysteries. L17.

Orphism /ˈɔːfɪz(ə)m/ *noun.* L19.
[from prec. + -ISM.]
1 The system of mystic philosophy embodied in Orphic poems, and taught to those initiated in Orphic mysteries. L19.
2 A movement within cubist art which emphasized the lyrical use of colour in pure abstract designs. E20.
■ **Orphist** *noun* a follower of Orphism in cubist art E20.

orphrey /ˈɔːfri/ *noun.* Also **orfray**. ME.
[Old French *orfreis* (mod. *orfroi*) from medieval Latin *aurifrisium* alt. of *auriphrygium* gold embroidery, i.e. *aurum Phrygium* Phrygian gold.]
1 (A piece of) rich, esp. gold, embroidery. Now *arch.* or *Hist.* ME.
2 An ornamental sometimes richly embroidered border or band, esp. on an ecclesiastical vestment. LME.

orphreyed /ˈɔːfrɪd/ *adjective.* Also **orfrayed**. LME.
[from prec. + -ED².]
Embroidered with gold; bordered with an orphrey.

orpiment /ˈɔːpɪm(ə)nt/ *noun.* LME.
[Old & mod. French from Latin *auripigmentum*, from *aurum* gold + *pigmentum* PIGMENT.]
Arsenic trisulphide, a bright yellow monoclinic mineral occurring naturally as prismatic crystals or (more usu.) massive deposits, or made artificially, and formerly used as a dye and artist's pigment (also more fully ***yellow orpiment***). Also (in full ***red orpiment***) = REALGAR.

orpine /ˈɔːpɪn/ *noun.* Also **orpin**. ME.
[In sense 1 from Old & mod. French *orpin* (cf. Anglo-Latin *orpina*); in sense 2 from Old French *orpine* yellow arsenic, presumably shortening of *orpiment* (see prec.).]
1 A stonecrop, *Sedum telephium*, with smooth flat fleshy leaves and corymbs of reddish-purple flowers, which grows on woodland banks etc. and is an old-fashioned garden plant. Also called ***livelong***. ME.
†**2** = ORPIMENT. M16–E18.

Orpington /ˈɔːpɪŋtən/ *noun.* L19.
[A town in Kent, England.]
(A bird of) a breed of poultry occurring in several colour varieties.

orra /ˈɒrə/ *adjective. Scot.* L16.
[Origin unkn.]
Odd, unmatched; occasional, miscellaneous; unattached, unemployed.
orra man an odd-job man.

Orrefors /ˈɒrɪfɔːz/ *noun & adjective.* E20.
[A town in Sweden.]
(Designating) glassware produced in Orrefors or the characteristic style of its decoration.

orrery /ˈɒrəri/ *noun.* E18.
[Charles Boyle, 4th Earl of *Orrery* (1676–1731), for whom such a device was made.]
A mechanical, usu. clockwork, model of the solar system.

†**orrice** *noun* var. of ORRIS *noun*².

orright /ɔːˈrʌɪt/ *adjective & adverb. non-standard.* M20.
[Repr. a pronunc.]
= ALL RIGHT *adverb & adjective.*

orris /ˈɒrɪs/ *noun*¹. M16.
[App. unexpl. alt. of IRIS.]
1 In full ***orris root***. The dried fragrant root of an orris (see sense 2), used in perfumery. M16.
2 Any of several bearded irises, *esp.* one cultivated for its fragrant rhizomes, such as the Florentine iris and *Iris pallida*. E17.
Comb.: **orris-powder** powdered orris root.

orris /ˈɒrɪs/ *noun*². Also †**orrice** & other vars. E18.
[Perh. alt. of obsolete var. of ORPHREY.]
Lace with patterns in gold and silver; gold lace embroidery.

orsedue *noun* var. of ARSEDINE.

ort /ɔːt/ *noun.* LME.
[Middle Low German *orte* refuse of food = early mod. Dutch †*oorœte* (cf. Swedish dial. *oräte* refuse, fodder, Low German *orten*, *verorten* to leave remains of food or fodder), perh. from Dutch *oor-* out (as in ORDEAL) + *eten* EAT *verb*.]
Usu. in *pl.* Fragments of food left over from a meal; fodder left by cattle; refuse scraps. Also more widely, anything left over; remains.

🕮 A. S. BYATT The orts and fragments of the owl's compressed package of bone, tooth and fur.

ortanique /ɔːtəˈniːk/ *noun.* M20.
[from OR(ANGE *noun* + TAN(GERINE + UN)IQUE.]
A citrus fruit cultivated in the W. Indies, resembling a slightly flattened orange and produced by crossing an orange and a tangerine.

orteguina /ɔrteˈgina, ɔːtəˈgiːnə/ *noun.* Pl. **-as** /-as, -əz/. M20.
[Spanish, from Domingo *Ortega* (1906–88), Spanish bullfighter who practised this pass, + *-uina*.]
BULLFIGHTING. = MANOLETINA.

orterde /ˈɔːtɛːdə/ *noun.* M20.
[German, from *Ort* place + *Erde* earth.]
SOIL SCIENCE. A dark sandy layer in soil containing redeposited materials from the upper layers, but not cemented into a hardpan. Cf. ORTSTEIN.

ortet /ˈɔːtət/ *noun.* E20.
[from Latin *ortus* origin + -ET¹.]
BIOLOGY. The original organism (usu. a plant) from which a clone has been produced. Cf. RAMET.

orth- *combining form* see ORTHO-.

orthesis /ɔːˈθiːsɪs/ *noun.* Pl. **ortheses** /ɔːˈθiːsiːz/. M20.
[from ORTHO- + *-esis* after PROSTHESIS.]
MEDICINE. = ORTHOSIS.

orthian /ˈɔːθɪən/ *adjective.* E17.
[from Greek *orthios* upright, high-pitched + -AN.]
Of singing etc.: very high-pitched.

orthicon /ˈɔːθɪkɒn/ *noun.* M20.
[Contr. of ORTHO- + ICONOSCOPE.]
An early form of television camera tube similar to the iconoscope but with a low-velocity scanning beam which strikes the (transparent) target plate on the opposite side to that on which the image is projected.
image orthicon an orthicon incorporating a separate image stage which is used to collect the image and focus it on to the target electrode.

orthite /ˈɔːθʌɪt/ *noun.* E19.
[from Greek *orthos* straight + -ITE¹.]
MINERALOGY. Allanite, esp. of a variety occurring as elongated crystals.

ortho /ˈɔːθəʊ/ *adjective & adverb.* Freq. italicized. L19
[from ORTHO-.]
▶ **A** *adjective.* **1** CHEMISTRY. Characterized by or relating to (substitution at) two adjacent carbon atoms in a benzene ring; at a position adjacent *to* some (specified) substituent in a benzene ring. L19.
2 PHOTOGRAPHY. Orthochromatic. E20.
▶ **B** *adverb.* CHEMISTRY. So as to form ortho-substituted compounds. M20.

ortho- /ˈɔːθəʊ/ *combining form.* Before a vowel also **orth-**.
[from Greek *orthos* straight, right + -O-.]
1 Used in words with the senses 'straight, rectangular, upright', 'normal, proper, correct'.
2 CHEMISTRY. (Freq. italicized.) ▸**a** Forming names of salts and acids containing one molecule of water more than a corresponding *meta*-compound. ▸**b** Denoting substitution in a benzene ring at adjacent carbon atoms.
3 PHYSICS & CHEMISTRY. Denoting the fact of having parallel spins (opp. PARA-¹ 4).
■ **orthocentre** *noun* (GEOMETRY) the point of intersection of the three altitudes of a triangle M19. **ortho'clastic** *adjective* (MINERALOGY) having cleavages at right angles to each other (cf. ORTHOCLASE, PLAGIOCLASTIC) L19. **orthocone** *noun & adjective* (PALAEONTOLOGY) (***a***) *noun* the straight shell typical of early nautiloid cephalopods; a fossil characterized by such a shell; (***b***) *adjective* having such a shell: E20. **ortho'conic** *adjective* (PALAEONTOLOGY) of or pertaining to a fossil or shell of the orthocone type E20. **ortho-cousin** *noun* either of two cousins who are children of siblings of the same sex E20. **ortho'ferrite** *noun* (CHEMISTRY) any compound of formula $AFeO_3$ (where A is yttrium or a rare earth), having an orthorhombic crystal structure and exhibiting weak ferromagnetism M20. **orthoform** *noun* (PHARMACOLOGY) [after CHLOROFORM] methyl *m*-amino-*p*-hydroxybenzoate, $C_8H_9NO_3$, a crystalline compound used as a local anaesthetic L19. **orthogeosyn'clinal** *adjective* (GEOLOGY) of, pertaining to, or of the nature of an orthogeosyncline M20. **orthogeo'syncline** *noun* (GEOLOGY) a linear geosyncline between a continental and an oceanic craton, typically comprising a miogeosyncline and an adjacent eugeosyncline M20. **orthogneiss** *noun* (GEOLOGY) gneiss derived from igneous rocks E20. **orthoki'nesis** *noun*, pl. **-neses** /-ˈniːsiːz/, ZOOLOGY a kinesis in which the movement is linear M20. **orthoki'netic** *adjective* (ZOOLOGY) of, pertaining to, or of the nature of an orthokinesis M20. **orthomo'lecular** *adjective* (MEDICINE) the treatment of mental illness by the provision of optimal bodily concentrations of vitamins and other substances M20. **orthoper'cussion** *noun* (MEDICINE) light diagnostic percussion of the chest using one finger to strike the knuckles of another bent at right angles E20. **ortho'phonic** *adjective* (***a***) pertaining to orthophony; (***b***) reproducing sounds accurately: L19. **orthophony** /ɔːˈθɒf(ə)ni/ *noun* the art of correct speaking or enunciation M19. **ortho'phoria** *noun* (OPHTHALMOLOGY) the state of perfect oculomotor balance in which the visual axes are parallel L19. **ortho'phoric** *adjective* (OPHTHALMOLOGY) pertaining to or exhibiting orthophoria L19. **orthophoto**, **ortho'photograph** *nouns* an

image produced optically or electronically from aerial photographs by eliminating distortions of angles and scales so as to give a result corresponding to a planimetric map M20. **ortho'photomap** *noun* a relief map made up from orthophotographs M20. **ortho'pinacoid** *noun* (CRYSTALLOGRAPHY) the plane parallel to the vertical axis and the axis of symmetry in the monoclinic system L19. **orthopy'roxene** *noun* (MINERALOGY) any orthorhombic pyroxene E20. **ortho'rrhaphous** *adjective* [Greek *rhaphē* seam] ENTOMOLOGY of or pertaining to the more primitive groups of dipteran insects (formerly constituting the suborder Orthorrhapha), characterized by the emergence of the adult from the pupa through a straight or longitudinal split L19. **orthose'lection** *noun* (BIOLOGY) natural selection acting in the same direction over a long period and giving rise to orthogenesis E20. **ortho'silicate** *noun* (CHEMISTRY) any compound containing the anion SiO_4^{4-} M19. **orthostichy** /ɔːˈθɒstɪki/ *noun* [cf. PARASTICHY] BOTANY a vertical row of leaves etc. inserted on an axis or stem one directly above another L19. **orthotec'tonic** *adjective* (GEOLOGY) designating or formed by a deformation believed to be characteristic of orthogeosynclines, producing complicated systems of fold belts (such as those of the Alps), and characterized by much magmatism and lateral thrusting M20. **ortho'topic** *adjective* (MEDICINE & ZOOLOGY) designating or involving transplantation of a structure to the same site in the recipient as it occupied in the donor E20. **ortho'topically** *adverb* (MEDICINE & ZOOLOGY) in an orthotopic manner E20. **or'thotropal** *adjective* (BOTANY) = ORTHOTROPOUS M19. **orthotropic** /-ˈtrəʊpɪk, -ˈtrɒpɪk/ *adjective* (*a*) BOTANY growing vertically upwards or downwards, as a root or stem; (*b*) ENGINEERING having three mutually perpendicular planes of elastic symmetry at each point: L19. **or'thotropous** *adjective* (BOTANY) (of an ovule) having the nucleus straight, i.e. not inverted, so that the micropyle is at the end opposite the base; (of an embryo) having the radicle directed towards the hilum: M19. **or'thotropy** *noun* (BOTANY & ENGINEERING) the condition of being orthotropous or orthotropic M19. **ortho'voltage** *noun* (MEDICINE) a voltage of the magnitude used in deep X-ray therapy (200–400 kV) (usu. *attrib.*) M20.

orthocephalic /ˌɔːθəʊsɪˈfalɪk, -kɛˈfalɪk/ *adjective*. M19.
[from ORTHO- + -CEPHALIC.]
Having a head of an average or relatively low shape; *spec.* having a cranial length–height index below 75 (in living people below 63). Also = MESOCEPHALIC.
■ **ortho'cephalous** *adjective* orthocephalic L19. **ortho'cephaly** *noun* orthocephalic condition L19.

orthochromatic /ˌɔːθəʊkrəˈmatɪk/ *adjective*. L19.
[from ORTHO- + CHROMATIC.]
1 PHOTOGRAPHY. Having a sensitivity which is more nearly uniform throughout the visible range than that of silver halide used alone but which is relatively low in the red and high in the blue part of the spectrum. Cf. PANCHROMATIC *adjective* 1. L19.
2 BIOLOGY. Exhibiting or characterized by staining of the same colour as that of a stain solution applied. Cf. METACHROMATIC. L19.
■ **ortho'chromatize** *verb trans.* make orthochromatic L19.

orthoclase /ˈɔːθəkleɪz/ *noun*. M19.
[from ORTHO- + Greek *klasis* breaking, cleavage.]
MINERALOGY. The common potassium feldspar, a monoclinic silicate of aluminium and potassium characterized by two cleavages at right angles, which occurs widely in rocks and as free crystals.

orthodiagraphy /ˌɔːθəʊdʌɪˈagrəfi/ *noun*. Now *rare*. E20.
[from ORTHO- + DIA-¹ + -GRAPHY.]
MEDICINE. A technique for determining the size of an organ etc. by measuring the area of its shadow projected on to a fluorescent screen using a beam of X-rays.
■ **ortho'diagram** *noun* a shadow projection used in orthodiagraphy E20. **orthodia'graphic** *adjective* E20.

orthodigita /ɔːθə(ʊ)ˈdɪdʒɪtə/ *noun*. M20.
[pseudo-Latin, formed as ORTHO- + DIGIT + -A³.]
MEDICINE. The non-surgical correction of toe deformities and malalignments.
■ **orthodigital** *adjective* M20.

orthodontia /ɔːθəˈdɒntɪə/ *noun*. Now *rare*. M19.
[formed as next + -IA¹.]
DENTISTRY. Orthodontics.

orthodontic /ɔːθəˈdɒntɪk/ *adjective*. E20.
[from ORTHO- + Greek *odont-*, *odous* tooth + -IC.]
Serving to correct irregularities of the teeth and jaws; of or pertaining to orthodontics.
■ **orthodontically** *adverb* M20.

orthodontics /ɔːθəˈdɒntɪks/ *noun*. E20.
[formed as prec. + -S¹.]
The branch of dentistry that deals with the treatment and prevention of irregularities of the teeth and jaws.
■ **orthodontist** *noun* a person who practises orthodontics E20.

orthodox /ˈɔːθədɒks/ *adjective & noun*. LME.
[ecclesiastical Latin *orthodoxus* from Greek *orthodoxos*, formed as ORTHO- + *doxa* opinion.]
▸**A** *adjective*. **I 1** Holding correct, or currently accepted opinions, esp. on matters of religious belief; not independent-minded, conventional. LME.
2 Of opinion, doctrine, etc.: right, correct, in accordance with what is accepted or authoritatively established. LME.
3 In accordance with what is regarded as proper or usual; conventional, approved. M19.
4 Of sleep: characterized by the absence of rapid eye movements and (probably) dreams, and by a lower level of physiological activity than paradoxical sleep. M20.

> **1** G. ORWELL If one thinks fearlessly one cannot be politically orthodox. S. QUINN He was not a rigidly orthodox Freudian . . he was in fact a believer in heterodoxy. **2** H. CARPENTER His own orthodox . . Christian faith had . . inclined him to accept the theology of *Paradise Lost*. **3** H. T. LANE The effects of the orthodox method of feeding to a time-table are definitely bad. H. E. BATES Lydia and Blackie were not really dancing the orthodox steps of the waltz.

▸**II** Usu. **O-**.
5 Designating or pertaining to (any of) the family of Christian Churches originating in the East (including the national Churches of Greece, Russia, Romania, etc.) which recognize the headship of the Patriarch of Constantinople and separated from the Western Church in or around the 11th cent. Also (more fully ***Oriental Orthodox***) or with specifying word), designating or pertaining to any of various Eastern Churches which earlier separated from both the Western Church and Constantinople. (See note below.) L17.
6 Of Judaism or Jews: adhering strictly to the rabbinical interpretation of Jewish law and its traditional observances. M19.

> **5** *Tablet* The fourth plenary session . . was hampered by two Orthodox delegations walking out. D. M. THOMAS The long and, compared with an Orthodox mass, rather colourless service. ***Coptic Orthodox***, ***Syrian Orthodox***, etc. **6** *Independent* The long coats and earlocks adopted by . . strictly orthodox Jews.

▸**B** *noun*. Pl. same.
1 An orthodox person; a member of the Orthodox Church; an Orthodox Jew. L16.
†**2** An orthodox opinion. E–M17.
¶ The designation 'Orthodox' was orig. adopted by the Eastern Churches to distinguish themselves from the Monophysite Churches.
■ **orthodoxal** *adjective* (long *rare* or *obsolete*) = ORTHODOX *adjective* 1, 2 L16. **ortho'doxian** *noun* (*rare*) a person who holds orthodox beliefs E17. **ortho'doxical** *adjective* (now *rare*) = ORTHODOX *adjective* 1, 2 L16. **orthodoxly** *adverb* E17. **orthodoxness** *noun* (long *rare*) M17.

orthodoxism /ˈɔːθədɒksɪz(ə)m/ *noun*. M17.
[from prec. + -ISM.]
†**1** The quality of being orthodox; orthodoxy. Only in M17.
2 The deliberate or stubborn adherence to orthodox beliefs or opinions. E19.
■ **orthodoxist** *noun* M19.

orthodoxy /ˈɔːθədɒksi/ *noun*. M17.
[Late Latin *orthodoxia* from late (eccl.) Greek = right opinion, sound doctrine, from *orthodoxos*: see ORTHODOX, -Y³.]
1 The quality or character of being orthodox; belief in or agreement with what is, or is currently held to be, right, esp. in religious matters; the body of orthodox doctrine. M17.
2 An orthodox belief or opinion. L19.
3 The orthodox practice of Judaism; the body of Orthodox Jews or Orthodox Christians. L19.
Phrases: **Feast of Orthodoxy** a festival celebrated in the Orthodox Church on the first Sunday in Lent.

orthodromic /ɔːθəˈdrəʊmɪk/ *adjective*. L18.
[from ORTHO- + Greek *dromos* course + -IC.]
1 Travelling along the arc of a great circle; (of a projection) representing great circles as straight lines. L18.
2 PHYSIOLOGY. Of an impulse: travelling in the normal direction in a nerve fibre. Opp. ANTIDROMIC. M20.
■ **'orthodrome** *noun* (a route forming part of) a great circle M19. **orthodromically** *adverb* M20. †**orthodromics** *noun* navigation by means of great circles E18–E19.

orthoepic /ɔːθəʊˈɛpɪk/ *adjective*. M19.
[formed as next + -IC.]
Of or pertaining to orthoepy; relating to correct or accepted pronunciation.
■ **orthoepical** *adjective* (now *rare*) E19. **orthoepically** *adverb* M19.

orthoepist /ˈɔːθəʊɛpɪst, -iːpɪst, ɔːˈθəʊɪpɪst/ *noun & adjective*. L18.
[from next + -IST.]
▸**A** *noun*. An expert in orthoepy; a person who studies the pronunciation of words; *esp.* (*Hist.*) any of a group of 16th- and 17th-cent. writers who sought to establish a standard pronunciation of English and to reform the spelling system in accordance with it. L18.
▸**B** *attrib.* or as *adjective*. Of orthoepists; orthoepistic. L20.
■ **orthoe'pistic** *adjective* pertaining to or characteristic of orthoepists M19. **orthoe'pistical** *adjective* E20.

orthoepy /ˈɔːθəʊɛpi, -iːpi, ɔːˈθəʊɪpi/ *noun*. M17.
[Greek *orthoepeia* correctness of diction, ult. formed as ORTHO- + *epe-*, *epos* word: see -IA¹, -Y³.]
1 The branch of grammar that deals with (correct) pronunciation, esp. the relationship between pronunciation and spelling. M17.
2 Correct, accepted, or customary pronunciation. E19.

orthogenesis /ɔːθə(ʊ)ˈdʒɛnɪsɪs/ *noun*. L19.
[from ORTHO- + -GENESIS.]
BIOLOGY. Evolutionary change in one direction, esp. as supposedly caused by internal tendency rather than external influence.

orthogenetic /ˌɔːθəʊdʒɪˈnɛtɪk/ *adjective*. L19.
[from ORTHO- + -GENETIC.]
BIOLOGY. Of, pertaining to, or characterized by orthogenesis.
■ **orthogenetically** *adverb* E20. **orthogenetics** *noun* the branch of biology that deals with orthogenesis M20.

orthognathous /ɔːθəgˈneɪθəs, ɔːˈθɒgnəθəs/ *adjective*. M19.
[from ORTHO- + Greek *gnathos* jaw + -OUS.]
Having straight jaws; having the jaws not projecting beyond a vertical line drawn from the forehead, and a facial angle of about 90 degrees. Cf. PROGNATHOUS.
■ **orthognathic** /ɔːθəgˈnaθɪk/ *adjective* = ORTHOGNATHOUS M19. **orthognathism** *noun* orthognathous condition L19.

orthogonal /ɔːˈθɒg(ə)n(ə)l/ *adjective*. L16.
[medieval Latin *orthogonalis*, from late Latin *orthogonus* right-angled: see -AL¹.]
1 GEOMETRY. Pertaining to or involving right angles, at right angles; right-angled; rectangular. L16.
2 MATH. (Of a linear transformation) preserving lengths and angles; (of two vectors or functions) having a scalar product equal to zero; (of a square matrix) representing an orthogonal transformation, and hence equal to the inverse of its transpose. M19.
3 STATISTICS. (Of variates) statistically independent; (of an experiment) having variates which can be treated as statistically independent. M20.
1 orthogonal projection: in which the rays are at right angles to the plane of projection.
■ **orthogo'nality** *noun* L19. **orthogonali'zation** *noun* (MATH.) the action or process of orthogonalizing E20. **orthogonalize** *verb trans.* (MATH.) make orthogonal; freq. *spec.* = ORTHONORMALIZE: M20. **orthogonally** *adverb* in an orthogonal manner; at right angles: L16.

orthograde /ˈɔːθəgreɪd/ *adjective*. E20.
[from ORTHO- + Latin *-gradus* walking.]
Of a primate: carrying its body upright.

orthographic /ɔːθəˈgrafɪk/ *adjective*. M17.
[Sense 1 from ORTHO- + -GRAPHIC; sense 2 from ORTHOGRAPHY + -IC.]
1 Of a projection used in maps and elevations: depicted as if seen from an infinite distance, so that horizontal lines are parallel. M17.
2 = ORTHOGRAPHICAL 1. M19.

orthographical /ɔːθəˈgrafɪk(ə)l/ *adjective*. L16.
[Sense 1 from ORTHOGRAPHY; sense 2 from sense 1 of prec.: see -ICAL.]
1 Of or pertaining to orthography; relating to (correct) spelling; correct in spelling. L16.
2 = ORTHOGRAPHIC 1. E18.
■ **orthographically** *adverb* E17.

orthography /ɔːˈθɒgrəfi/ *noun*. LME.
[Old French *ortografie*, later *-graphie* (mod. *orthographie*) from Latin *orthographia* from Greek, formed as ORTHO- + -GRAPHY.]
1 Correct or proper spelling; spelling according to accepted usage or convention. Also, a particular mode or system of spelling. LME. ▸**b** The branch of grammar which deals with letters and their combination to represent sounds and words; the subject of spelling. L16. ▸†**c** An orthographer. *rare* (Shakes.). Only in L16.
2 (A representation in) orthographic projection, a vertical elevation. M17.
■ **orthographer** *noun* a person skilled in orthography; a person who spells in accordance with accepted usage: L16. **orthographist** *noun* = ORTHOGRAPHER E17. **orthographize** *verb* (*rare*) †(*a*) *verb trans.* school in orthography; spell (a word) correctly; (*b*) *verb intrans.* follow the rules of orthography, spell correctly: L16.

orthohelium /ɔːθə(ʊ)ˈhiːlɪəm/ *noun*. E20.
[from ORTHO- + HELIUM.]
PHYSICS. The form of helium whose spectrum exhibits a fine structure of triplets owing to the spins of the two orbital electrons being parallel. Cf. PARAHELIUM.

orthohydrogen /ɔːθə(ʊ)ˈhʌɪdrədʒ(ə)n/ *noun*. E20.
[from ORTHO- + HYDROGEN.]
PHYSICS. The form of molecular hydrogen in which the two nuclei in the molecule have parallel spins (so that the spectrum exhibits a hyperfine structure of triplets) and which forms about 75 per cent of hydrogen under normal conditions. Cf. PARAHYDROGEN.

orthologous /ɔːˈθɒləgəs/ *adjective*. L20.
[from ORTHO- + HOMO)LOGOUS.]
BIOLOGY. Of, pertaining to, or designating homologous genes in different species which are descended from the same gene in the nearest common ancestor; (of a single gene) descended from the same gene as another specified gene (foll. by *with*).
■ **orthologously** *adverb* L20.

orthology /ɔːˈθɒlədʒi/ *noun. rare.* E17.
[Greek *orthologia* correctness of language, formed as ORTHO- + -LOGY.]
The branch of grammar that deals with the correct use of words.

orthometric /ɔːθəˈmɛtrɪk/ *adjective.* M19.
[from ORTHO- + -METRIC.]
1 *CRYSTALLOGRAPHY.* Designating those crystal systems (cubic, tetragonal, and orthorhombic) in which the axes are mutually at right angles. Now *rare.* M19.
2 *SURVEYING.* Designating or pertaining to a height above the geoid. E20.
■ **orthometrically** *adverb* M20.

orthometry /ɔːˈθɒmɪtri/ *noun. rare.* L18.
[from ORTHO- + -METRY.]
PROSODY. The art of correct versification.

orthomorphic /ɔːθəˈmɔːfɪk/ *adjective.* M19.
[from ORTHO- + -MORPH + -IC.]
†**1** *ZOOLOGY.* Attaining full size before sexual maturity. *rare.* M–L19.
2 Of a map projection: preserving the correct shape of small areas. L19.
■ **orthomorphism** *noun* the property of being orthomorphic E20.

orthonormal /ɔːθəˈnɔːm(ə)l/ *adjective.* M20.
[from ORTHO(GONAL + NORMAL *adjective.*]
MATH. Both orthogonal and normalized.
■ **orthonorˈmality** *noun* M20. **orthonormalize** *verb trans.* make (a set of vectors or functions) orthonormal by orthogonalizing them and then multiplying each by an appropriate factor M20. **orthonormaliˈzation** *noun* the action or process of orthonormalizing vectors or functions M20.

orthopaedic /ɔːθəˈpiːdɪk/ *adjective.* Also ***-pedic.** M19.
[French *orthopédique*, from *orthopédie* orthopaedics, formed as ORTHO- + Greek *paideia* rearing of children: see -IC.]
MEDICINE. Pertaining to or concerned with the treatment of disorders of the bones and joints, and the correction of deformities in general (orig. in children); *spec.* (of a bed etc.) designed to relieve back problems and usu. having a very firm mattress or board; (of footwear) designed to ease or correct deformities of the feet.
■ **orthopaedist** *noun* a person who practises orthopaedics; an orthopaedic surgeon: M19. **orthopaedically** *adverb* L20.

orthopaedics /ɔːθəˈpiːdɪks/ *noun.* Also ***-ped-.** M19.
[from prec. + -S¹.]
MEDICINE. Orthopaedic medicine; orthopaedic surgery.

orthopantomography /ˌɔːθə(ʊ)pantəˈmɒgrəfi/ *noun.* M20.
[from ORTHO- + PANTOMOGRAPHY.]
DENTISTRY. A modification of pantomography in which the X-rays are made to be perpendicular to the line of the jaws, so that a radiograph can be obtained showing the teeth of both sides on one film.
■ **orthopanˈtomogram** *noun* a radiograph obtained by orthopantomography M20. **orthopanˈtomograph** *noun* an instrument for performing orthopantomography M20.

orthopedic *adjective*, **orthopedics** *noun* see ORTHOPAEDIC, ORTHOPAEDICS.

orthophosphoric /ˌɔːθəʊfɒsˈfɒrɪk/ *adjective.* M19.
[from ORTHO- + PHOSPHORIC.]
CHEMISTRY. ***orthophosphoric acid***, the tribasic parent acid, H_3PO_4, of most phosphates, which is a colourless crystalline solid when pure and forms syrupy solutions with water. Cf. ***phosphoric acid*** s.v. PHOSPHORIC 2.
■ **orthoˈphosphate** *noun* a salt or ester of orthophosphoric acid M19.

orthophyre /ˈɔːθəfʌɪə/ *noun.* L19.
[French, formed as ORTHO- + por)phyre PORPHYRY.]
PETROGRAPHY. Porphyry in which the phenocrysts are chiefly of orthoclase.
■ **orthoˈphyric** *adjective* having a groundmass containing short stout feldspar crystals of rectangular or quadratic cross-section L19.

orthopnoea /ɔːθɒpˈniːə/ *noun.* E17.
[Latin from Greek *orthopnoia*, from *orthos* upright + *pnoē* breathing: see -A¹.]
MEDICINE. A severe form of dyspnoea in which breathing is possible only in an upright position.
■ **orthopnoeic**, †**-pnoic** *adjective* of, pertaining to, or affected with orthopnoea E17.

orthopod /ˈɔːθəpɒd/ *noun. slang.* M20.
[Alt. of ORTHOPAED(IC.]
An orthopaedic surgeon.

orthopoxvirus /ɔːθə(ʊ)ˈpɒksvʌɪrəs/ *noun.* L20.
[from ORTHO- + ***poxvirus*** s.v. POX *noun.*]
Any poxvirus of the genus *Orthopoxvirus*, which includes those causing cowpox, monkey pox, and smallpox.

orthopraxy /ˈɔːθəpraksi/ *noun.* M19.
[from ORTHO- + Greek *praxis* action: see -Y³.]
Rightness of action, esp. in the expression of religious faith; practical righteousness; correct practice.
■ Also **orthopraxis** *noun* M20.

orthopsychiatry /ˌɔːθəʊsʌɪˈkʌɪətri/ *noun.* M20.
[from ORTHO- + PSYCHIATRY.]
MEDICINE. The branch of psychiatry concerned especially with the prevention of mental or behavioural disorders.
■ **orthopsychiˈatric** *adjective* M20. **orthopsychiatrist** *noun* E20.

orthopter /ɔːˈθɒptə/ *noun.* In sense 1 also **-ere.** M19.
[French *orthoptère*, formed as ORTHO- + Greek *pteron* wing.]
1 *AERONAUTICS.* = ORNITHOPTER. *obsolete* exc. *Hist.* M19.
2 = ORTHOPTERAN *noun. rare.* L19.

Orthoptera /ɔːˈθɒpt(ə)rə/ *noun pl.* Rarely in sing. **-ron** /-rən/. E19.
[mod. Latin, neut. pl. of *orthopterus*, from Greek ORTHO- + *pteron* wing: see -A³.]
(Members of) a large order of insects (the crickets, grasshoppers, etc.) having the hind legs usually enlarged and modified for jumping, and characterized by biting mouthparts and incomplete metamorphosis.
¶ Formerly also including the cockroaches and stick insects, now included in the separate orders Dictyoptera and Phasmida.
■ **orthopteran** *noun & adjective* (***a***) *noun* a member of the order Orthoptera; (***b***) *adjective* = ORTHOPTEROUS: M19. **orthopterist** *noun* a person who studies Orthoptera L19. **orthopteroid** *adjective & noun* (***a***) *adjective* of, pertaining to, or designating a group of insect orders closely related to the Orthoptera; (***b***) *noun* an orthopteroid insect: L19. **orthopterous** *adjective* belonging or pertaining to the order Orthoptera E19.

orthoptere *noun* see ORTHOPTER.

Orthopteron *noun* see ORTHOPTERA.

orthoptics /ɔːˈθɒptɪks/ *noun.* M20.
[from ORTHO- + *optics* (see OPTIC *noun* 1).]
MEDICINE. The branch of medicine that deals with the treatment of defective binocular vision by means of eye exercises.
■ **orthoptic** *adjective* employing the principles of orthoptics; of or pertaining to orthoptics: L19. **orthoptically** *adverb* M20. **orthoptist** *noun* a person who practises orthoptics M20.

orthorexia /ɔːθəˈrɛksɪə/ *noun.* L20.
[from ORTHO- + Greek *orexis* appetite, after ANOREXIA.]
MEDICINE. An obsession with eating the 'right' foods; *esp.* (in full ***orthorexia nervosa*** /nəːˈvəʊsə/) a condition whereby the sufferer systematically eliminates specific foods or food groups that he or she believes are harmful to health.
■ **orthorexic** *noun & adjective* L20.

orthorhombic /ɔːθəˈrɒmbɪk/ *adjective.* M19.
[from ORTHO- + RHOMBIC.]
CRYSTALLOGRAPHY. Designating or pertaining to a crystal system in which the three axes are mutually at right angles and of unequal length.

orthoroentgenography /ˌɔːθə(ʊ)rʌntjəˈnɒgrəfi/ *noun.* M20.
[from ORTHO- + ROENTGENOGRAPHY.]
MEDICINE. A technique for producing radiographs showing the exact sizes of organs or bones by using a narrow beam of X-rays perpendicular to the plate or film.
■ **orthoˈroentgenogram** *noun* a radiograph produced by orthoroentgenography M20. **ˌorthoroentgenoˈgraphic** *adjective* M20.

orthoscopic /ɔːθəˈskɒpɪk/ *adjective.* M19.
[from ORTHO- + Greek *-skopos* viewing: see -IC.]
Having normal vision; yielding an image free from distortion.

orthosis /ɔːˈθəʊsɪs/ *noun.* Pl. **orthoses** /ɔːˈθəʊsiːz/. M20.
[Greek *orthōsis* making straight, from *orthoun* set straight: see -OSIS.]
MEDICINE. An artificial external device, as a brace or splint, serving to prevent or assist relative movement in the limbs or the spine; = ORTHOTIC *noun* 2.

orthostat /ˈɔːθəstat/ *noun.* Also **-state** /-steɪt/. E20.
[Greek *orthostatēs*, formed as ORTHO- + *statos* standing.]
ARCHAEOLOGY. An upright stone or slab forming part of a structure or set in the ground.

orthostatic /ɔːθəˈstatɪk/ *adjective.* E20.
[from ORTHO- + STATIC *adjective.*]
1 *MEDICINE.* Relating to or caused by an upright posture; manifested or occurring while a person is standing up. E20.
2 *ARCHAEOLOGY.* Set on end; constructed of stones or slabs set on end. Cf. prec. E20.
■ **orthostatically** *adverb* M20.

orthostereoscopic /ˌɔːθə(ʊ)stɛrɪəˈskɒpɪk/ *adjective.* L19.
[from ORTHO- + STEREOSCOPIC.]
Showing a correct three-dimensional image.
■ **orthostereoscopically** *adverb* M20. **orthostereˈoscopy** *noun* the production of orthostereoscopic images E20.

orthotic /ɔːˈθɒtɪk/ *adjective & noun.* M20.
[from ORTHOSIS: see -OTIC.]
MEDICINE. ▶**A** *adjective.* Serving as an orthosis; of or employing an orthosis or orthoses. M20.
▶**B** *noun.* **1** In *pl.* (treated as *sing.*). The use of orthoses. M20.
2 An orthosis. L20.
■ ˈ**orthotist** *noun* a person who practises orthotics M20.

orthotomic /ɔːθəˈtɒmɪk/ *adjective. rare.* M19.
[from ORTHO- + Greek *-tomos* cutting + -IC.]
MATH. Intersecting at right angles.

orthotone /ˈɔːθətəʊn/ *adjective & noun.* L19.
[Greek *orthotonos*, formed as ORTHO- + *tonos* tone, accent.]
▶**A** *adjective.* Of a word: having an independent stress pattern, not enclitic or proclitic. L19.
▶**B** *noun.* An orthotone word. L19.

orticant /ˈɔːtɪk(ə)nt/ *adjective & noun.* M20.
[Italian *orticante* stinging, URTICANT.]
MEDICINE. ▶**A** *adjective.* Irritating to the skin. M20.
▶**B** *noun.* An orticant agent. M20.

ortolan /ˈɔːt(ə)lən/ *noun.* E16.
[French from Provençal = gardener, from Latin *hortulanus*, from *hortulus* dim. of *hortus* garden: see -AN.]
†**1** A gardener. *rare.* Only in E16.
2 A bunting, *Emberiza hortulana*, found throughout much of the western Palaearctic, distinguished by the greenish head and yellow throat of the male, and formerly esteemed as a delicacy (also ***ortolan bunting***). Also (*US & W. Indies, rare*) any of certain other birds of similar gastronomic reputation; *esp.* (***a***) the bobolink; (***b***) the sora rail. M17.

Ortonesque /ɔːtəˈnɛsk/ *adjective.* L20.
[from the name of John Kingsley (Joe) *Orton* (1933–67), Brit. playwright + -ESQUE.]
Characteristic of Orton's work; *esp.* displaying an anarchic, black humour.

ortstein /ˈɔːtʃtʌɪn/ *noun.* E20.
[German, from *Ort* place + *Stein* stone.]
SOIL SCIENCE. A hardpan; *esp.* an iron pan in a podzol. Cf. ORTERDE.

Ortygian /ɔːˈtɪdʒɪən/ *adjective.* M17.
[from Latin *Ortygius*, from Greek *Ortugia* Ortygia (see below), from *ortux* a quail: see -AN.]
1 Of or pertaining to Ortygia (now Delos), a Greek island in the Cyclades, reputed birthplace of Apollo and Artemis. M17.
2 Of or pertaining to Ortygia, an island forming part of the city of Syracuse in Sicily. *rare.* E19.

Orvietan /ɔːvɪˈeɪt(ə)n/ *noun.* Long *obsolete* exc. *Hist.* L17.
[French *orviétan* or Italian *orvietano*, from *Orvieto* (see next), the inventor's birthplace: see -AN.]
A composition held to be a universal antidote against poisons.

Orvieto /ɔːvɪˈeɪtəʊ/ *noun & adjective.* M19.
[A city in Italy.]
▶**A** *noun.* Pl. **-os.** A white wine made near Orvieto; an example of this. M19.
▶**B** *adjective.* Designating a type of majolica ware manufactured at Orvieto. E20.

Orwellian /ɔːˈwɛlɪən/ *adjective.* M20.
[from *Orwell* (see below) + -IAN.]
Characteristic or suggestive of the works of the English writer George Orwell (Eric Blair, 1903–50); *esp.* pertaining to or characteristic of the kind of totalitarian society portrayed in his futuristic novel *Nineteen Eighty-Four* (1949).

> M. McCARTHY A leap into the Orwellian future. J. M. McPHERSON This Orwellian definition of liberty as slavery provoked ridicule north of the Potomac.

ory /ˈɔːri/ *adjective.* Now *rare.* Also **orey.** M16.
[from ORE *noun*¹ + -Y¹.]
Of the nature of, bearing, or resembling ore.

-ory /əri/ *suffix*¹.
[Latin *-oria*, *-orium*, freq. Old Northern French, Anglo-Norman *-orie*, Old French *-oire*.]
Forming nouns denoting a place, object, etc., having a particular purpose, as ***dormitory***, ***refectory***, ***repository***, etc., or (less usu.) a particular character, as ***promontory***, ***territory***.

-ory /əri/ *suffix*².
[Latin *-orius*, freq. Anglo-Norman *-ori(e)*, Old French *-oir(e)*.]
Forming adjectives and occas. nouns relating to a verbal action, as ***accessory***, ***compulsory***, ***predatory***, etc.

orycto- /ɒˈrɪktəʊ/ *combining form* of Greek *oruktos* dug up: see -O-. Used (now rarely) in the senses 'fossil', 'mineral'.
■ †**oryctognosy** *noun* the knowledge of minerals; mineralogy: E–M19. †**oryctography** *noun* the description of fossils or minerals; descriptive mineralogy: M18–M19.

oryctology /ɒrɪkˈtɒlədʒi/ *noun. obsolete* exc. *Hist.* M18.
[from prec. + -LOGY.]
The branch of geology that deals with rocks, minerals, and fossils dug out of the earth.
■ **oryctoˈlogical** *adjective* E19. **orycˈtologist** *noun* L18.

oryx /ˈɒrɪks/ *noun.* Pl. same. LME.
[Latin from Greek *orux* lit. 'stonemason's pickaxe' from its pointed horns.]
Orig., a N. African antelope of uncertain identity. Now, any large antelope of the genus *Oryx*, occurring in arid regions of Africa and Arabia, having long straight (or slightly curved) pointed horns in both sexes, and including the gemsbok, *O. gazella*, *O. leucoryx* (more fully ***Arabian oryx***), and *O. dammah* (more fully ***scimitar oryx***).
BEISA oryx.

oryzenin /ɒˈrʌɪzɪnɪn/ *noun.* E20.
[from Latin *oryza* rice (from Greek *oruza*) + *-enin*, prob. after GLUTENIN.]
BIOCHEMISTRY. The chief protein present in rice.

orzo /ˈɔːtsəʊ/ *noun.* E20.
[Italian, lit. 'barley'.]
Pasta in small pieces shaped like grains of barley or rice.

OS *abbreviation.*
1 Old Style.
2 COMPUTING. Operating system.
3 Ordinary seaman.
4 Ordnance Survey.
5 Out of stock.
6 Outsize.

Os *symbol.*
CHEMISTRY. Osmium.

os /ɒs/ *noun*[1]. Pl. **ossa** /ˈɒsə/. LME.
[Latin.]
ANATOMY. A bone. Only in mod. Latin names of particular bones.
os intermedium, ***os pubis***, ***os sacrum***, etc. **os frontis** *joc.* [pseudo-Latin, after mod. Latin *os frontale* frontal bone] the forehead. **os penis** the bone of the penis, found in many mammals (not man); also called ***penis-bone***, ***baculum***.

os /ɒs/ *noun*[2]. Pl. **ora** /ˈɔːrə/. M18.
[Latin (stem *or-*) = mouth.]
ANATOMY. An opening or entrance to a passage; *spec.* one at either end of the cervix of the womb. Orig. only in mod. Latin names of particular structures.

OSA *abbreviation.*
Order of St Augustine.

osaekomi waza /ˈoːsaekoːmi ˈwaza, ˈəʊsəeɪˌkəʊmi ˈwɑːzə/ *noun phr.* M20.
[Japanese, lit. 'art of holding', from *osae* press on or against + *komi* be packed up + *waza* technique.]
JUDO. The technique or practice of holding down one's opponent.

Osage /əʊˈseɪdʒ, ˈəʊseɪdʒ/ *noun & adjective.* L17.
[Alt. of Osage *Wazhazhe*, one of three bands composing the people.]
▶**A** *noun.* Pl. **-s**, same.
1 A member of a N. American Indian people formerly inhabiting the Osage river valley, Missouri. L17.
2 The Siouan language of this people. M19.
▶**B** *adjective.* Of or pertaining to the Osages or their language. E19.
Osage orange (the fruit or wood of) the maclura, *Maclura pomifera*.

osar /ˈəʊsɑː/ *noun.* Pl. same, **-s**. M19.
[Swedish *åsar* pl. of *ås* ridge (of a roof or hill).]
GEOLOGY. = ESKER.

osazone /ˈəʊsəzəʊn/ *noun.* L19.
[from -OSE[2] + AZO- + -ONE. Orig. as suffix.]
CHEMISTRY. Any of the compounds (mostly yellow crystalline solids) whose molecules contain two adjacent hydrazone groups, used for characterizing sugars.

OSB *abbreviation.*
Order of St Benedict.

Osborne /ˈɒzbɔːn/ *noun.* L19.
[A former Brit. royal residence on the Isle of Wight.]
In full ***Osborne biscuit***. A type of sweetish plain biscuit.

Oscan /ˈɒsk(ə)n/ *adjective & noun.* L16.
[from Latin *Oscus* + -AN.]
▶**A** *adjective.* Of or pertaining to a people inhabiting Campania in southern Italy before the Sabellians, or their language. L16.
▶**B** *noun.* **1** A member of this people. M18.
2 The Italic language of this people, surviving only in inscriptions. E19.

Oscar /ˈɒskə/ *noun*[1]. *Austral. & NZ slang.* Also **o-**. E20.
[Rhyming slang for *Oscar Asche* (1871–1936), Austral. actor.]
Cash; money.

Oscar /ˈɒskə/ *noun*[2]. M20.
[App. after the supposed resemblance of the statuette to an Academy employee's uncle called *Oscar*.]
1 Any of the statuettes awarded annually in Hollywood, USA, by the Academy of Motion Picture Arts and Sciences for excellence in film acting, directing, etc. Also, the award represented by this. M20.
2 *transf.* Any award for an outstanding performance or achievement. M20.
Comb.: **Oscar-winning** *adjective* (of a performance etc.) that has been awarded or is worthy of an Oscar; *fig.* outstanding; histrionic, overdone.

oscar /ˈɒskə/ *noun*[3]. M20.
[Origin unkn.]
A S. American cichlid fish, *Astronotus ocellatus*, with velvety brown young and multicoloured adults, popular in aquaria.

oscheo- /ˈɒskɪəʊ/ *combining form.*
[from Greek *oskheon* scrotum: see -O-.]
ANATOMY & MEDICINE. Of or pertaining to the scrotum.
■ **oscheocele** *noun* scrotal hernia E18.

oscillate /ˈɒsɪleɪt/ *verb.* E18.
[Latin *oscillat-* pa. ppl stem of *oscillare* swing: see -ATE[3].]
1 *verb intrans.* Swing or move to and fro, esp. between two points; vibrate. E18. ▸**b** ELECTRONICS. Of a circuit or device: cause oscillations in a current flowing in it. Of a radio receiver or (*transf.*) a user of one: transmit radio waves owing to faulty operation. E20.
2 *verb trans.* Cause to swing or move to and fro. M18.
3 *verb intrans. fig.* Fluctuate between or *between* two opinions, principles, purposes, etc.; vacillate; waver. L18.
4 *verb intrans.* MATH. Of a series or function: increase and decrease alternately as successive terms are taken or as the variable tends to infinity. L19.

> 📖 **1** CARLYLE Look at the waves oscillating hither, thither on the beach. **3** H. MACMILLAN Political life oscillates between tragedy and comedy.

■ **oscillator** *noun* (**a**) a person who or thing which oscillates; (**b**) an apparatus for generating oscillatory electric currents by non-mechanical means (***local oscillator***: see LOCAL *adjective*; ***master oscillator***: see MASTER *adjective*): M19. **oscillatory** /əˈsɪlət(ə)ri, ˈɒsɪlət(ə)ri/ *adjective* characterized by oscillation; oscillating, tending to oscillate: M18.

oscillating /ˈɒsɪleɪtɪŋ/ *ppl adjective.* M18.
[from prec. + -ING[2].]
1 Swinging or moving to and fro; vibrating; (of a machine etc.) characterized by the oscillatory motion of a part. M18.
2 MATH. Of a series or function: alternately increasing and decreasing in value. L19.
3 ELECTRONICS. (Of an electric current) undergoing very rapid periodic reversal of direction; characterized by or produced by such a current. E20.

oscillation /ɒsɪˈleɪʃ(ə)n/ *noun.* M17.
[Latin *oscillatio(n)-*, formed as OSCILLATE: see -ATION.]
1 The action of oscillating; (esp. SCIENCE) a single movement to and fro. M17.
2 *fig.* (A) fluctuation between two opinions, principles, purposes, etc.; vacillation. L18.
3 MATH. The difference between the greatest and the least values of a function in any given interval. L19.

> 📖 **1** E. REVELEY He stayed . . motionless save for the slow ruminative oscillation of his jaw. **2** R. MACAULAY These oscillations of fortune would . . always occur. L. HUDSON A violent oscillation between states of drunken orgy and . . spirituality.

oscillatoria /ˌɒsɪləˈtɔːrɪə/ *noun.* M19.
[mod. Latin (see below), formed as OSCILLATE: see -ORY[1], -IA[1].]
Any of various blue-green algae constituting the genus *Oscillatoria* (family Oscillatoriaceae), which form dark slimy unbranched filaments capable of gliding or undulating motion.

oscillogram /əˈsɪləgram/ *noun.* E20.
[formed as next + -GRAM.]
A record produced by an oscillograph.

oscillograph /əˈsɪləgrɑːf/ *noun & verb.* L19.
[from OSCILL(ATION + -O- + -GRAPH.]
▶**A** *noun.* **1** An instrument for detecting and measuring the motion of a ship or the sea. L19.
2 An instrument for displaying or for recording as a continuous curve the form of a varying voltage. L19.
3 = OSCILLOGRAM. M20.
▶**B** *verb trans.* Record or display by means of an oscillograph. E20.
■ **osciloˈgraphic** *adjective* of, pertaining to, or using an oscillograph E20. **oscilloˈgraphically** *adverb* by means of or as an oscillograph E20. **osciˈllography** *noun* the use of oscillographs M20.

oscillometer /ɒsɪˈlɒmɪtə/ *noun.* L19.
[formed as prec. + -OMETER.]
†**1** A gyroscopic form of nautical oscillograph. Only in L19.
2 MEDICINE. An instrument for indicating or recording the amplitude and rhythm of the pulse and fluctuations in blood pressure. E20.
■ **oscilloˈmetric** *adjective* M20. **osciˈllometry** *noun* the use of an oscillometer M20.

oscilloscope /əˈsɪləskəʊp/ *noun.* E20.
[formed as OSCILLOGRAPH + -O- + -SCOPE.]
†**1** A stroboscopic apparatus used to make visible any irregularities in the motion of rapidly rotating or oscillating machinery. Only in E20.
2 An oscillograph. Now *spec.* (more fully ***cathode-ray oscilloscope***), an electronic instrument in which the position of a moving spot on the screen of a cathode-ray tube represents the relationship between two variables, usu. a signal voltage (vertically) and time (horizontally), and which is capable of displaying a periodic variation in voltage as a stationary curve. E20.
■ **oscilloscopic** /-ˈskɒpɪk/ *adjective* M20. **oscilloscopically** /-ˈskɒpɪk-/ *adverb* by means of an oscilloscope M20.

oscine /ˈɒsiːn/ *noun.* L19.
[from HY)OSCINE.]
CHEMISTRY. A tropane alkaloid which is an isomer of scopine and a degradation product of hyoscine. Also called ***scopoline***.

oscine /ˈɒsʌɪn/ *adjective.* L19.
[from next: see -INE[1].]
Of, pertaining to, or belonging to the Oscines.

oscines /ˈɒsɪniːz/ *noun pl.* In sense 2 **O-**. E17.
[Latin, pl. of *oscin-*, *oscen* singing or divining bird, formed as OB- + *canere* sing.]
1 *Hist.* The birds (esp. ravens or owls) from whose voices auguries were taken by the Romans. E17.
2 ORNITHOLOGY. An extensive group of birds (the songbirds) containing those families of advanced passerine birds which have the muscles of the syrinx attached to the extremities of the bronchial semi-rings. L19.

oscitancy /ˈɒsɪt(ə)nsi/ *noun.* E17.
[formed as next: see -ANCY.]
1 The condition or fact of being drowsy or listless; an instance of inattention or negligence. E17.
2 = OSCITATION 1. E18.

> 📖 **1** W. COWPER Her, whose winking eye, And slumb'ring oscitancy mars the brood.

oscitant /ˈɒsɪt(ə)nt/ *adjective.* Now *rare* or *obsolete.* E17.
[Latin *oscitant-* pres. ppl stem of *oscitare* gape: see -ANT[1].]
Yawning from drowsiness; drowsy, dull; negligent.

oscitation /ɒsɪˈteɪʃ(ə)n/ *noun.* M16.
[Latin *oscitatio(n-)*, from *oscitat-* pa. ppl stem of *oscitare* gape: see -ATION.]
1 The action or an act of yawning from drowsiness. M16.
2 = OSCITANCY 1. M17.

Oscotian /ɒˈskəʊʃ(ə)n/ *noun & adjective.* E19.
[from *Oscott* (see below) + -IAN.]
▶**A** *noun.* A past or present member of the Roman Catholic college and seminary of St Mary's at Oscott, now part of Birmingham. E19.
▶**B** *adjective.* Of or pertaining to this college or its members. E19.

Osco-Umbrian /ɒskəʊˈʌmbrɪən/ *noun & adjective.* L19.
[from OSC(AN + -O- + UMBRIAN.]
▶**A** *noun.* **1** A group of ancient Italic languages including Oscan, Umbrian, and related dialects. L19.
2 A member of any of the peoples who spoke a language in this group. L19.
▶**B** *adjective.* Of or pertaining to these peoples or their languages. L19.

oscula *noun* pl. of OSCULUM.

osculant /ˈɒskjʊl(ə)nt/ *adjective.* E19.
[from OSCULATE *verb* + -ANT[1].]
BIOLOGY (now *Hist.*). Situated between and connecting two groups of organisms (represented by osculating circles in the quinary system of classification); intermediate.

oscular /ˈɒskjʊlə/ *adjective.* E19.
[from Latin OSCULUM + -AR[1].]
1 Of or pertaining to kissing. E19.
2 ZOOLOGY. Of or pertaining to an osculum. L19.

osculate /ˈɒskjʊleɪt/ *verb.* M17.
[Latin *osculat-* pa. ppl stem of *osculari* to kiss, formed as OSCULUM: see -ATE[3].]
1 *verb trans. & intrans.* Kiss. Now *joc.* M17.
2 GEOMETRY. **a** *verb trans.* Of a curve or surface: touch (another curve or surface) without crossing, so as to have a common tangent. E18. ▸**b** *verb intrans.* Of two curves or surfaces: have a common tangent. M19.
3 *verb intrans.* Come into close contact or union; come together. M18.

osculation /ɒskjʊˈleɪʃ(ə)n/ *noun.* M17.
[Latin *osculatio(n-)*, formed as prec.: see -ATION.]
1 The action or an act of kissing. Now *joc.* M17.
2 Close contact; *spec.* (**a**) the mutual contact of blood-vessels; (**b**) GEOMETRY contact of curves or surfaces at a common tangent. L18.

osculatory /ˈɒskjʊlət(ə)ri/ *noun.* Also in Latin form **osculatorium** /ˌɒskjʊləˈtɔːrɪəm/, pl. **-ia** /-ɪə/. M18.
[medieval Latin *osculatorium*, formed as OSCULATE *verb*: see -ORY[1], -ORIUM.]
ECCLESIASTICAL HISTORY. = PAX *noun* 2.

osculatory /ˈɒskjʊlət(ə)ri/ *adjective.* M18.
[formed as prec.: see -ORY².]
1 MATH. Osculating; of or pertaining to osculation. M18.
2 Involving a kiss or kissing. *rare.* M19.

osculum /ˈɒskjʊləm/ *noun.* Pl. **-la** /-lə/. In sense 2 also Anglicized as **oscule** /ˈɒskjuːl/. E17.
[Latin = little mouth, a kiss, hypocoristic dim. of *os* noun²: see -CULE.]
1 ECCLESIASTICAL HISTORY. ***osculum pacis*** /ˈpɑːtʃɪs/, = ***kiss of peace*** s.v. KISS noun. E17.
2 ZOOLOGY. A pore, an orifice; *esp.* a large opening in a sponge through which water is expelled. E17.

-ose /əʊs, əʊz/ *suffix*¹.
[Repr. Latin *-osus*. Cf. -OUS.]
Forming adjectives from Latin words in *-osus* with the sense 'full of, having much or many of', as ***bellicose***, ***grandiose***, ***morose***, ***verbose***.

-ose /əʊz, əʊs/ *suffix*².
[from GLUC)OSE.]
CHEMISTRY. Forming the names of sugars and other carbohydrates, as ***dextrose***, ***hexose***, ***lactose***, ***ribose***, ***sucrose***, etc.

Osetian *noun & adjective* var. of OSSETIAN.

OSF *abbreviation.*
Order of St Francis.

Osgood–Schlatter /ɒzgʊdˈʃlatə/ *noun.* E20.
[R. B. *Osgood* (1873–1956), US surgeon, and Carl *Schlatter* (1864–1934), Swiss surgeon.]
MEDICINE. Used *attrib.* and in *possess.* to designate inflammatory necrosis of the tibial tuberosity, freq. associated with chronic stress on the knee.

OSHA *abbreviation. US.*
Occupational Safety and Health Administration.

oshibori /ˈoːʃibori, ˈəʊʃɪbɒri/ *noun.* M20.
[Japanese, from *o-* deferential prefix + *shibori* that which has been wrung out.]
In Japan, a small dampened towel offered to guests or customers to refresh themselves. Also ***oshibori towel***.

Osiandrian /əʊzɪˈandrɪən/ *noun & adjective.* L16.
[from *Osiander* Latinized form of the name of Andreas *Hosemann* (1498–1552), German theologian: see -IAN.]
ECCLESIASTICAL HISTORY. ▶**A** *noun.* A member of a 16th-cent. group of German Protestants who opposed the Lutheran doctrine of atonement and justification by faith. L16.
▶**B** *adjective.* Of or pertaining to the Osiandrians. L19.

-oside /əsʌɪd/ *suffix.*
[from -OSE² + -IDE, after *glucoside*, *glycoside*.]
CHEMISTRY. Forming the names of glycosides, as ***furanoside***, ***ganglioside***, ***pyranoside***, etc.

osier /ˈəʊzɪə/ *noun & adjective.* ME.
[Old & mod. French, masc. form corresp. to fem. (dial.) *osière* from medieval Latin *auseria*, which has been referred to a Gaulish word for 'river-bed'.]
▶**A** *noun.* (A shoot of) any of several willows with tough pliant branches used in basketwork, esp. *Salix viminalis*, which has long narrow leaves silky on the underside. ME.
purple osier: see PURPLE *adjective.* ***red osier***: see RED *adjective.*
Comb.: **osier-bed** an area of land where osiers are grown, esp. for basket-making.
▶**B** *attrib.* or as *adjective.* Of, pertaining to, or made of osiers. L16.
■ **osiered** *adjective* covered or planted with osiers; twisted like osiers: E16. **osiery** *noun* (*a*) a place where osiers are grown; a thicket or plantation of osiers; (*b*) (articles made of) osier branches: M18.

Osirian /əʊˈsʌɪrɪən/ *adjective.* M19.
[from *Osiris* (see below) + -IAN.]
Of, pertaining to, or representing Osiris, the ancient Egyptian god of fertility and ruler of the underworld.

Osiride /əʊˈsʌɪrɪd/ *adjective.* M19.
[formed as prec.: see -ID².]
= prec.
Osiride column, **Osiride pillar** ARCHITECTURE a square pier with a standing figure of Osiris in front of it.

-osis /ˈəʊsɪs/ *suffix.*
[Latin, or Greek *-ōsis*.]
Forming (esp. MEDICINE) nouns of action or condition from or after Latin or Greek, as ***anadiplosis***, ***apotheosis***, ***metamorphosis***, ***sclerosis***, ***thrombosis***, ***tuberculosis***.

-osity /ˈɒsɪti/ *suffix.*
[from -OSE¹ or -OUS + -ITY, from or after (French *-osité* from) Latin *-ositas*.]
Forming nouns of state corresp. to adjectives in -OSE¹ or -OUS, as ***luminosity***, ***pomposity***, ***verbosity***, etc.

Oslo breakfast /ˈɒzləʊ ˈbrɛkfəst/ *noun phr.* M20.
[*Oslo*, capital of Norway.]
A type of meal orig. introduced into Norwegian schools, designed to correct nutritional deficiencies in children's diets.

OSM *abbreviation.*
Order of Servants of Mary, the Servite Order.

Osmanli /ɒzˈmanli/ *noun & adjective.* L18.
[Turkish *Osmānlı*, from *Osman* (from Arab. *ʿUṯmān*: see OTTOMAN noun¹ & adjective) + adjectival suffix *-lı*.]
▶**A** *noun.* Pl. same, **-s**.
1 = OTTOMAN noun¹. L18.
2 The language of the Ottoman Turks; Turkish. M19.
▶**B** *adjective.* = OTTOMAN *adjective.* L19.

osmanthus /ɒzˈmanθəs/ *noun.* L19.
[mod. Latin (see below), from Greek *osmē* scent + *anthos* flower.]
Any of various mainly Chinese evergreen shrubs and trees constituting the genus *Osmanthus*, of the olive family, with white or cream, usu. fragrant, flowers.

osmate /ˈɒzmeɪt/ *noun.* M19.
[from OSMIUM + -ATE¹.]
CHEMISTRY. A salt or ester of osmic acid in which osmium has an oxidation state of 6. Cf. PEROSMATE.

osmeterium /ɒzmɪˈtɪərɪəm/ *noun.* Also (earlier) †**osma-**. Pl. **-ria** /-rɪə/. E19.
[mod. Latin from Greek *osmasthai* to smell + *-tērion* instr. suffix: see -IUM.]
ENTOMOLOGY. An organ which emits a (usu. noxious) smell; *spec.* a forked eversible gland on the first thoracic segment of papilionid caterpillars.

osmiate /ˈɒzmɪət/ *noun.* Now *rare.* M19.
[from OSMIUM + -ATE¹.]
CHEMISTRY. †**1** = PEROSMATE. M–L19.
2 = OSMATE. E20.

osmic /ˈɒzmɪk/ *adjective*¹. M19.
[from OSMIUM + -IC.]
CHEMISTRY. Containing osmium, esp. in one of its higher oxidation states.
osmic acid (*a*) = ***osmium tetroxide***; (*b*) the acid H_2OsO_4, known chiefly as salts (osmates).

osmic /ˈɒzmɪk/ *adjective*². M20.
[from Greek *osmē* smell + -IC.]
Of or pertaining to odours or the sense of smell.
■ **osmically** *adverb* as regards smell M20.

osmicate /ˈɒzmɪkeɪt/ *verb trans.* E20.
[from OSMIC *adjective*¹ + -ATE³.]
BIOLOGY. Stain or treat with osmium tetroxide.
■ **osmiˈcation** *noun* L19.

osmics /ˈɒzmɪks/ *noun.* E20.
[formed as OSMIC *adjective*²: see -ICS.]
The branch of science that deals with odours and the sense of smell.

osmiophilic /ˌɒzmɪə(ʊ)ˈfɪlɪk/ *adjective.* E20.
[from OSMIUM + -O- + -PHILIC.]
BIOLOGY. Having an affinity for, or staining readily with, osmium tetroxide.

osmious /ˈɒzmɪəs/ *adjective.* Now *rare.* M19.
[from OSMIUM + -OUS.]
CHEMISTRY. Containing osmium, esp. in the divalent state.

osmiridium /ɒzmɪˈrɪdɪəm/ *noun.* L19.
[from OSMIUM + IRIDIUM.]
Orig. = IRIDOSMINE. Now usu., a native alloy of iridium and osmium containing less than one-third osmium.

osmium /ˈɒzmɪəm/ *noun.* E19.
[from Greek *osmē* odour + -IUM (with ref. to the peculiar pungent smell of the tetroxide).]
A hard heavy white metal which is a chemical element, atomic no. 76, belonging to the platinum group and used esp. in catalysts. (Symbol Os.)
Comb.: **osmium tetroxide** a poisonous pale yellow solid, OsO_4, with a distinctive pungent smell, used in solution as a biological stain, esp. for lipids, and as a fixative; also called ***osmic acid***.

osmo- /ˈɒzməʊ/ *combining form*¹.
[Greek *osmo-* combining form of *osmē* smell, odour: see -O-.]
Of or pertaining to smells or the sense of smell.
■ **osmoceptor** *noun* (PHYSIOLOGY) a sensory receptor for the sense of smell M20.

osmo- /ˈɒzməʊ/ *combining form*².
[from OSMO(SIS.]
Of or pertaining to osmosis.
■ **osˈmometer** *noun* an instrument for demonstrating or measuring osmotic pressure M19. **osmoˈmetric** *adjective* of, pertaining to, or involving an osmometer E20. **osmoˈmetrically** *adverb* by means of an osmometer M20. **osˈmometry** *noun* the use of an osmometer E20.

osmol *noun* var. of OSMOLE.

osmolal /ɒzˈməʊləl/ *adjective.* M20.
[Blend of OSMOTIC and MOLAL.]
CHEMISTRY. Of the concentration of a solution: expressed as an osmolality.
■ **osmoˈlality** *noun* the number of osmotically effective dissolved particles per unit quantity of a solution, esp. when expressed as (milli)osmoles per kilogram of solvent M20.

osmolar /ɒzˈməʊlə/ *adjective.* M20.
[Blend of OSMOTIC and MOLAR *adjective*³.]
Of the concentration of a solution: expressed as an osmolarity.
■ **osmoˈlarity** *noun* the number of osmotically effective dissolved particles per unit quantity of a solution, esp. when expressed as (milli)osmoles per litre of solution M20.

osmole /ˈɒzməʊl/ *noun.* Also **-ol** /-ɒl/. M20.
[Blend of OSMOTIC and MOLE *noun*⁵.]
A thousand milliosmoles.

osmophilic /ɒzməˈfɪlɪk/ *adjective*¹. E20.
[from OSMO-² + -PHILIC.]
BIOLOGY. Of a micro-organism, esp. a yeast: tolerating or thriving in an environment of high osmotic pressure (e.g. due to high sugar or salt concentration).
■ **osmophile** *noun* an osmophilic micro-organism M20.

osmophilic /ɒzməˈfɪlɪk/ *adjective*². M20.
[from OSMIUM + -O- + -PHILIC.]
BIOLOGY. = OSMIOPHILIC.

osmophore /ˈɒzmə(ʊ)fɔː/ *noun.* E20.
[from OSMO-¹ + -PHORE.]
1 A chemical group whose presence in the molecules of a substance causes it to have a smell. Also called ***odoriphore***. E20.
2 A scent gland found in the flowers of certain plant families, esp. the Orchidaceae. M20.
■ **osmoˈphoric** *adjective* of, pertaining to, or of the nature of an osmophore E20.

osmoregulation /ˌɒzməʊrɛgjʊˈleɪʃ(ə)n/ *noun.* M20.
[from OSMO-² + REGULATION.]
PHYSIOLOGY. The maintenance of a more or less constant osmotic pressure in the body fluids of an organism.
■ **osmoˈregulate** *verb intrans.* maintain the osmotic pressure of the body fluids at a constant level M20. **osmoˈregulator** *noun* an organ concerned with osmoregulation; an organism capable of or considered with respect to osmoregulation: M20. **osmoˈregulatory** *adjective* of, pertaining to, or effecting osmoregulation E20.

osmose /ˈɒzməʊs/ *noun & verb.* M19.
[Common elem. of *endosmose* and *exosmose*: cf. Greek *ōsmos* a push.]
▶**A** *noun.* Osmosis. Now *rare* or *obsolete.* M19.
▶**B** *verb intrans.* Pass by osmosis (*lit.* & *fig.*). *rare.* L19.
📖 *Daily Telegraph* Publishing companies osmose like amoebae into ever larger . . conglomerates.

osmosis /ɒzˈməʊsɪs/ *noun.* M19.
[Latinized form of prec.: see -OSIS.]
1 The process by which a solvent passes through a semipermeable membrane into a region of greater solute concentration, so as to make the concentrations on the two sides more nearly equal. M19.
2 *fig.* Gradual, usu. unconscious assimilation or absorption of ideas, knowledge, etc. E20.
📖 **1** ***reverse osmosis***: see REVERSE *adjective.* **2** P. AUSTER Whatever I . . learned from her . . I absorbed it by a kind of osmosis.

osmotic /ɒzˈmɒtɪk/ *adjective.* M19.
[from OSMOSE or OSMOSIS: see -OTIC.]
Of, pertaining to, or caused by osmosis (*lit.* & *fig.*).
📖 *Economist* In the osmotic way these things happen, virtually all . . were absorbed by other local industries. **osmotic pressure** a measure of the tendency of a solution to draw solvent through a semipermeable membrane by osmosis, equal to the pressure that must be applied to the solution to keep it in equilibrium with pure solvent. **osmotic shock** a sudden lowering of the osmotic pressure of the liquid surrounding a cell or virus, causing inflow of liquid and consequent rupture.
■ **osmotically** *adverb* by the process of osmosis; as regards osmosis: L19.

osmund /ˈɒzmənd/ *noun*¹. ME.
[Anglo-Norman *osmunde*, Old & mod. French *osmonde*, of unkn. origin.]
Hist. **1** A type of high-quality iron formerly produced in the Baltic, and used for the manufacture of arrow-heads, fish-hooks, etc. Also ***osmund iron***. ME.
2 A small bar or rod of osmund. LME.

osmund /ˈɒsmənd, ˈɒz-/ *noun*². Now *rare.* LME.
[Anglo-Norman *osmunde* (Anglo-Latin *osmunda*), Old & mod. French *osmonde*: ult. origin unkn.]
More fully ***osmund royal***. The royal fern, *Osmunda regalis*; formerly, any of various other ferns.

osmunda /ɒzˈmʌndə/ *noun.* L18.
[Anglo-Latin (see prec.), adopted as genus name.]
1 Any fern of the genus *Osmunda*; *esp.* the royal fern, *O. regalis*. L18.
2 In full ***osmunda fibre***. A fibre made from the roots of *Osmunda cinnamomea* or *O. claytoniana*, used as a potting medium for orchids. E20.

osmundine /ˈɒzməndiːn/ *noun. N. Amer.* M20.
[from prec. + -INE⁴.]
= OSMUNDA 2.

osnaburg /ˈɒznəbəːg/ *noun & adjective.* Also **O-**. M16.
[Alt. of *Osnabrück*, a town in northern Germany.]
(Made of) a kind of coarse linen (later cotton) used for pillowcases, sacks, etc., orig. from Osnabrück.

oso-berry /ˈəʊsəʊbɛri/ *noun.* **L19.**
[from Spanish *oso* bear + **BERRY** *noun*[1].]
A shrub or small tree, *Oemleria cerasiformis*, of western N. America which bears racemes of greenish-white flowers; the blue-black fruit of this plant.

osone /ˈəʊsəʊn/ *noun.* **L19.**
[from -**OSE**[2] + -**ONE**.]
CHEMISTRY. Any compound containing two adjacent carbonyl groups, obtained by hydrolysing an osazone.

O-soto-gari /ɔːˌsoːtoˈgaːri, əʊˌsəʊtəʊˈgɑːri/ *noun.* **M20.**
[Japanese, from *ō* great, major + *soto* outside + *gari* from *kari* mow, reap.]
JUDO. A major throw executed with a sweeping movement of the leg.

osphradium /ɒsˈfreɪdɪəm/ *noun.* **L19.**
[from Greek *osphradion* strong scent, dim. of *osphra* smell: see -**IUM**.]
ZOOLOGY. An olfactory organ in some molluscs, consisting of a group of elongated sense-cells over each gill.
■ **osphradial** *adjective* **L19.**

osprey /ˈɒspri, -preɪ/ *noun.* **LME.**
[Old French *ospres*, app. ult. from Latin *ossifraga* **OSSIFRAGE**.]
1 A large brown and white bird of prey, *Pandion haliaetus*, which preys on marine and freshwater fish and is of almost cosmopolitan distribution, though now extinct in much of Europe. Also called ***fish-hawk***. **LME.**
2 = **AIGRETTE**. **L19.**

oss /ɒs/ *verb.* Now *dial.* Also **osse**. **LME.**
[Prob. rel. to **HALSE** *verb*[1].]
†**1** *verb trans. & intrans.* Prophesy, forecast; divine; wish (esp. good luck). **LME–E17.**
2 *verb trans. & intrans.* Give promise of (a good or bad outcome); show readiness, offer, intend, (*to do*); attempt, dare, (*to do*). **L17.**
3 *verb trans.* Direct (a person) *to* an advantageous place or thing. **L19.**

ossa *noun*[1] pl. of **OS** *noun*[1].

Ossa *noun*[2] see **PELION**.

ossature /ˈɒsətjʊə/ *noun. rare.* **L19.**
[French, from Latin *os(s-)* **OS** *noun*[1] after *musculature*: see -**URE**.]
The arrangement of the bones of a skeleton.

osse *verb* var. of **OSS**.

ossein /ˈɒsɪɪn/ *noun.* **M19.**
[from Latin *osseus* bony + -**IN**[1].]
BIOCHEMISTRY. The collagenous organic component of bone.

osselet /ˈɒsəlɪt, ˈɒslɛt/ *noun. rare.* **L17.**
[French, from Latin *os(s-)* **OS** *noun*[1]: see -**LET**.]
1 A small bone, an ossicle; *esp.* each of the small bones of the carpus or tarsus. **L17.**
2 *PALAEONTOLOGY.* A (fossil) cuttle-bone. **M19.**

osseous /ˈɒsɪəs/ *adjective.* **LME.**
[from Latin *osseus*, from *os(s-)* **OS** *noun*[1]: see -**EOUS**.]
1 Of, pertaining to, consisting of, or resembling bone; *fig.* hard or firm as bone. **LME.**
2 *GEOLOGY.* Of a deposit: containing many fossil bones, ossiferous. **E19.**
3 Of a fish: having a bony skeleton, osteichthyan. **M19.**
■ **osseously** *adverb* as regards bone; in a bony manner: **L19.**

Ossete /ˈɒsiːt/ *noun & adjective.* **E19.**
[Russian *osetin* from Georgian *ovs*ʻ*i* Ossetia.]
▶ **A** *noun.* A native or inhabitant of Ossetia, a region of the central Caucasus partly in Russia and partly in Georgia. **E19.**
▶ **B** *adjective.* Of or pertaining to Ossetia or the Ossetes. **M20.**
■ **Ossetic** /ɒˈsɛtɪk/ *noun & adjective* (**a**) *noun* = **OSSETIAN** *noun* 1; (**b**) *adjective* = **OSSETE** *adjective*: **M19.**

Ossetian /ɒˈsiːʃ(ə)n/ *noun & adjective.* Also **Osetian**. **M19.**
[from *Ossetia* (see **OSSETE** *noun*) + -**AN**.]
▶ **A** *noun.* **1** The Iranian language of the Ossetes. **M19.**
2 = **OSSETE** *noun.* **E20.**
▶ **B** *adjective.* Of or pertaining to the Ossetes or their language. **M19.**

Ossi /ˈɒsi/ *noun. colloq.* (freq. *derog.*). Pl. -**is**, -**ies**. **L20.**
[German, prob. abbreviation of *Ostdeutsche* East German.]
A term used in Germany (esp. since reunification) to denote a citizen of the former German Democratic Republic; an East German. Cf. **WESSI**.

ossia /ɒˈsiːə, ˈɒsjə/ *conjunction.* **L19.**
[Italian.]
MUSIC. In directions: or, alternatively (indicating an alternative and usu. easier way of playing a passage).

Ossianic /ɒsɪˈanɪk, ɒʃ-/ *adjective.* **E19.**
[from *Ossian* Anglicized form of *Oisin* + -**IC**.]
Of or pertaining to Ossian (Oisín), a legendary Irish warrior and bard of the 3rd cent. AD whose poems James Macpherson (1736–96) claimed to have collected and translated, or the poems ascribed to him. Also, resembling the style or character of the poems by Macpherson ascribed to Ossian; inflated, bombastic.
■ ˈ**Ossianism** *noun* **M19.**

ossicle /ˈɒsɪk(ə)l/ *noun.* **L16.**
[formed as **OSSICULUM**.]
1 *ANATOMY & ZOOLOGY.* A small bone; *esp.* each of the small bones (malleus, incus, and stapes) which transmit sound through the middle ear. **L16.**
2 *ZOOLOGY.* A small skeletal plate, joint, etc.; *esp.* each of the calcareous plates forming the skeleton of an echinoderm. **M19.**
1 *Weberian ossicles*: see **WEBERIAN** *adjective*[1].

ossicula *noun* pl. of **OSSICULUM**.

ossicular /ɒˈsɪkjʊlə/ *adjective.* **M19.**
[from next + -**AR**[1].]
ANATOMY & ZOOLOGY. Pertaining to or consisting of an ossicle or ossicles.

ossiculum /ɒˈsɪkjʊləm/ *noun.* Pl. -**la** /-lə/. **E18.**
[Latin, dim. of *os(s-)* **OS** *noun*[1]: see -**CULE**.]
ANATOMY & ZOOLOGY. An ossicle.
■ **ossicuˈlectomy** *noun* (an instance of) surgical removal of the auditory ossicles **E20.**

ossiferous /ɒˈsɪf(ə)rəs/ *adjective.* **E19.**
[from Latin *os(s-)* **OS** *noun*[1] + -**I**- + -**FEROUS**.]
Of a cave etc.: containing or yielding deposits of bone.

ossific /ɒˈsɪfɪk/ *adjective.* **L17.**
[from Latin *os(s-)* **OS** *noun*[1] + -**I**- + -**FIC**.]
Forming bone; pertaining to or capable of ossification.

ossification /ˌɒsɪfɪˈkeɪʃ(ə)n/ *noun.* **L17.**
[French, formed as **OSSIFY**: see -**FICATION**.]
1 The formation of bone; the process of becoming or changing into bone or bony tissue; the condition of being ossified. **L17.**
2 A bony formation or concretion. **E18.**
3 *fig.* The process of becoming hardened, callous, or fixed in attitude etc. **L19.**

> 🕮 **1 centre of ossification** the place where cartilage or connective tissue begins to ossify. **3** M. FLANAGAN Ossification had set in and . . spiritual death was only a matter of time.

ossifrage /ˈɒsɪfrɪdʒ/ *noun.* **E17.**
[Latin *ossifragus*, *-fraga* use as noun of adjective = bone-breaking, from *os(s-)* **OS** *noun*[1] + base of *frangere* break. Cf. **OSPREY**.]
1 A bird of prey mentioned by Pliny, usu. identified with the lammergeyer. **E17.**
2 An osprey. **M17.**

ossify /ˈɒsɪfʌɪ/ *verb trans. & intrans.* **E18.**
[French *ossifier*, from Latin *os(s-)* **OS** *noun*[1]: see -**FY**.]
1 Turn into bone or bony tissue. **E18.**
2 *fig.* (Cause to) become emotionally hardened or callous; (cause to) become rigid or fixed in attitude etc. Now chiefly as ***ossified ppl adjective***. **M19.**

> 🕮 **2** R. H. HUTTON Doubt . . must in the end ossify the higher parts of the mind. *Independent* The omnipotent but ossified Soviet Academy of Sciences.

osso bucco /ɒsəʊ ˈbuːkəʊ/ *noun phr.* **M20.**
[Italian = marrowbone.]
(An Italian dish of) shin of veal containing marrowbone stewed in wine with vegetables.

ossuary /ˈɒsjʊəri/ *noun & adjective.* As noun also in Latin form **ossuarium** /ɒsjʊˈɛːrɪəm/, pl. -**ria** /-rɪə/. **M17.**
[Late Latin *ossuarium*, from *ossu* var. of Latin **OS** *noun*[1]: see -**ARY**[1], -**ARIUM**.]
▶ **A** *noun.* **1** A receptacle or vault for the bones of the dead; a charnel-house. **M17.**
2 *transf.* A cave containing deposits of ancient bones; a pile of bones or carcasses resulting from carnage. **M19.**
▶ **B** *adjective.* Used for the deposit of bones. **M19.**

OST *abbreviation. US.*
Office of Science and Technology.

ostectomy /ɒˈstɛktəmi/ *noun.* **L19.**
[from **OST**(**EO**- + -**ECTOMY**.]
Surgical removal of all or part of a bone; an instance of this.

osteichthyan /ɒstɪˈɪkθɪən/ *noun & adjective.* **M20.**
[from mod. Latin *Osteichthyes* (see below), from Greek *osteon* bone + *ikhthus* fish: see -**AN**.]
ZOOLOGY. ▶**A** *noun.* Any fish of the class Osteichthyes, comprising fishes with a bony endoskeleton. **M20.**
▶ **B** *adjective.* Of, belonging to, or characteristic of the class Osteichthyes. **M20.**

osteitis /ɒstɪˈʌɪtɪs/ *noun.* **M19.**
[from **OSTE**(**O**- + -**ITIS**.]
MEDICINE. (A disease involving) inflammation of bone.
osteitis deformans /dɪˈfɔːmanz/ [Latin = deforming] Paget's disease (of the bones). **osteitis fibrosa cystica** /fʌɪˌbrəʊsə ˈsɪstɪkə/ [mod. Latin = fibrous cystic] von Recklinghausen's disease (of the bones).

ostend /ɒˈstɛnd/ *verb trans.* Now *rare.* **LME.**
[Latin *ostendere*: see next.]
Show, reveal; exhibit.

ostensible /ɒˈstɛnsɪb(ə)l/ *adjective & noun.* **M18.**
[French from medieval Latin *ostensibilis*, from Latin *ostens-* pa. ppl stem of *ostendere* stretch out to view, from Latin *ob-* **OB**- + *tendere* stretch: see -**IBLE**.]
▶ **A** *adjective.* †**1** Able to be shown or exhibited; presentable. Also, made or intended to be shown. **M18–E19.**
2 Declared, professed, esp. while concealing the actual or genuine; pretended; apparent but not necessarily real. **M18.**
†**3** That presents itself to or is open to view; conspicuous, ostentatious. **L18–M19.**

> 🕮 **2** C. BRONTË My ostensible errand . . was to get measured for . . shoes.

▶ **B** *noun.* A thing that is able or intended to be shown. *rare.* **M18.**
■ **ostensiˈbility** *noun* **L18.** **ostensibly** *adverb* **M18.**

ostension /ɒˈstɛnʃ(ə)n/ *noun.* **LME.**
[Old & mod. French from Latin *ostensio(n)-*, from *ostens-*: see prec., -**ION**.]
1 The action of showing or exhibiting; (a) display. *obsolete* exc. as in sense 2. **LME.**
2 *ECCLESIASTICAL HISTORY.* The showing of the consecrated elements to the congregation at the Eucharist. **E17.**
3 *LOGIC.* An ostensive definition. **M20.**

ostensive /ɒˈstɛnsɪv/ *adjective.* **M16.**
[Late Latin *ostensivus*, from Latin *ostens-*: see **OSTENSIBLE**, -**IVE**.]
1 Manifestly or directly demonstrative; declarative, denotative; *spec.* in *LOGIC*, (of a proof, method, etc.) direct, proceeding by the processes of conversion, permutation, and transposition, (opp. ***indirect***). **M16.** ▸**b** *PHILOSOPHY.* Of a definition: indicating by direct demonstration that which is signified by a term. **E20.**
2 = **OSTENSIBLE** *adjective* 2. **L18.**
■ **ostensively** *adverb* **L18.** **ostensiveness** *noun* **M20.**

ostensory /ɒˈstɛns(ə)ri/ *noun.* Also in French form **ostensoir** /ɒstɛnˈswɑː/, & in Latin form **ostensorium** /ɒstɛnˈsɔːrɪəm/, pl. -**ia** /-ɪə/. **E18.**
[medieval Latin *ostensorium*, formed as *ostens-*: see **OSTENSIBLE**, -**ORY**[1].]
ROMAN CATHOLIC CHURCH. An open or transparent vessel used to display the Host to the congregation at mass; a monstrance.

ostent /ɒˈstɛnt/ *noun.* Now *rare.* **L16.**
[In branch I from Latin *ostentum* something shown, prodigy, use as noun of neut. pa. pple of *ostendere*; in branch II from Latin *ostent-* pa. ppl stem of *ostendere*: see **OSTENSIBLE**.]
▶ **I 1** A sign, a portent; a prodigy. **L16.**
▶ **II 2** = **OSTENTATION** 2. **L16.**
3 = **OSTENTATION** 3. **L16.**

ostentate /ˈɒstənteɪt/ *verb trans.* Now *rare.* **M16.**
[Latin *ostentat-*: see next, -**ATE**[3].]
Display ostentatiously; make a show of.

ostentation /ɒstɛnˈteɪʃ(ə)n/ *noun.* **LME.**
[Old & mod. French from Latin *ostentatio(n-)*, from *ostentat-* pa. ppl stem of *ostentare* exhibit, display, frequentative of *ostendere*: see **OSTENSIBLE**, -**ATION**.]
†**1** The presaging of future events; a portent. *rare.* **LME–E17.**
2 The action or an act of showing or exhibiting; (a) display or demonstration of a feeling, quality, etc. *arch.* **L15.** ▸†**b** Mere or false show; pretence. **E–M17.**
3 Display intended to attract notice or admiration; pretentious and vulgar display, esp. of wealth or luxury. **L15.**

> 🕮 **2** SHAKES. *Ant. & Cl.* You are come . . and have prevented the ostentation of our love. **3** J. K. GALBRAITH A time . . of incredible ostentation. Great limestone mansions were rising. P. CAREY The Reverend Mr Nelson . . found himself criticised for the ostentation of his vestments.

ostentatious /ɒstɛnˈteɪʃəs/ *adjective.* **L16.**
[from prec. + -**IOUS**.]
1 Characterized by ostentation; intended or intending to attract attention or admiration, esp. of wealth or luxury; pretentious, showy. **L16.**
†**2** Likely to attract attention; conspicuous. **E18–L19.**

> 🕮 **1** J. G. BALLARD A group of long-term unemployed . . provoked by the ostentatious display of privilege and prosperity.

■ **ostentatiously** *adverb* **E18.** **ostentatiousness** *noun* **M17.**

†**ostentive** *adjective.* Chiefly *Scot.* **L16–M18.**
[from Latin *ostent-*: see **OSTENT** *noun*, -**IVE**.]
Ostentatious.

osteo- /ˈɒstɪəʊ/ *combining form* of Greek *osteon* bone, forming terms chiefly in *ANATOMY & MEDICINE*: see -**O**-.
■ **osteoarˈthritic** *adjective* of, pertaining to, or affected by osteoarthritis **E20.** **osteoarˈthritis** *noun* degeneration of the cartilage in the joints of the body, which occurs esp. in middle age and later and causes pain and stiffness **L19.** **osteoarˈthropathy** *noun* a disease which affects bone and cartilage around the joints; *esp.* a syndrome marked by deposition of bony tissue at joints, associated with some chronic chest diseases **L19.** **osteoarˈthrosis** *noun* osteoarthritis **M20.** **osteoarˈthrotic**

adjective osteoarthritic **M20.** **osteoblast** *noun* a mesodermal cell which secretes the substance of bone **L19.** **osteoˈblastic** *adjective* of, pertaining to, or of the nature of an osteoblast **L19.** **osteochonˈdritis** *noun* painful inflammation of bone with deposition of bony tissue or release of fragments into a joint **L19.** **osteochonˈdroma** *noun*, pl. **-mas**, **-mata** /-mətə/, a bone tumour containing cartilage-forming cells **L19.** **osteoclasia** /-ˈkleɪzjə/ *noun*, **osteoclasis** /ɒstɪˈɒkləsɪs, ɒstɪə(ʊ)ˈkleɪsɪs/ *noun*, (pl. **-clases** /-kləsiːz, -ˈkleɪsiːz/). [Greek *klasis* breaking] (**a**) *SURGERY* deliberate fracture of a bone to correct a deformity; (**b**) the absorption of bone by osteoclasts, as during healing of a fracture: **M19.** **osteocyte** *noun* an osteoblast that has ceased bone-forming activity and is enclosed in a lacuna in the bone matrix **M20.** **osteoderm** *noun* (*ZOOLOGY*) a bony plate in the skin, esp. in reptiles **L19.** **osteoˌdontokeˈratic** *adjective* (*ANTHROPOLOGY*) of, pertaining to, or utilizing implements of bone, tooth, and horn **M20.** **osteodyˈstrophia** *noun* = **OSTEODYSTROPHY M20.** **osteodyˈstrophic** *adjective* of, pertaining to, or affected by osteodystrophy **E20.** **osteoˈdystrophy** *noun* any bone disease caused by faulty metabolism **M20.** **osteˈolysis** *noun* the pathological destruction or disappearance of bone tissue **L19.** **osteoˈlytic** *adjective* causing or characterized by osteolysis **L19.** **osteomalacia** /-ˈleɪʃ(ɪ)ə/ *noun* softening of the bones in adults due to vitamin D deficiency and consequent decalcification (cf. **RICKETS**) **E19.** **osteomalacic** /-ˈlasɪk/ *adjective* pertaining to or affected with osteomalacia **E20.** **osteˈometry** *noun* the measurement of bones, esp. with regard to their relative proportions in different populations **L19.** **osteomyeˈlitis** *noun* inflammation of the bone and bone marrow due to infection **M19.** **osteoneˈcrosis** *noun* necrosis of bone tissue **M19.** **osteophyte** *noun* [Greek *phyton* growth] a bony projection esp. associated with degeneration of articular cartilage **M19.** **osteophytic** /-ˈfɪtɪk/ *adjective* of, pertaining to, or of the nature of an osteophyte **L19.** **osteoscleˈrosis** *noun* hardening or abnormal increase in density of a bone **M19.** **osteotome** *noun* an instrument for cutting bone **M19.** **osteˈotomy** *noun* (an instance of) the anatomical or surgical cutting of a bone, esp. to allow realignment **M19.**

osteoclast /ˈɒstɪəklast/ *noun*. **L19.**
[from **OSTEO-** + Greek *klastēs* breaker.]
ANATOMY & MEDICINE. A large multinucleate bone cell which absorbs bone tissue during growth and healing.
■ **osteoˈclastic** *adjective* acting to destroy bone tissue; pertaining to or of the nature of an osteoclast or osteoclasts: **M20.** **osteoclaˈstoma** *noun*, pl. **-mas**, **-mata** /-mətə/, a rare bone tumour involving proliferation of osteoclasts **E20.**

osteocolla /ɒstɪəˈkɒlə/ *noun*. **M17.**
[from **OSTEO-** + Greek *kolla* glue, from its supposed property of knitting broken bones.]
A deposit of calcium carbonate round the roots and stems of plants, found in sandy ground, esp. in parts of Germany.

osteogenesis /ɒstɪəˈdʒɛnɪsɪs/ *noun*. **M19.**
[from **OSTEO-** + **-GENESIS**.]
The formation of bone; ossification.
osteogenesis imperfecta /ɪmpəˈfɛktə/ [Latin = imperfect] an inherited disorder characterized by extreme fragility of the bones.
■ **osteogeˈnetic**, **osteogenic** *adjectives* of or pertaining to osteogenesis **M19.** †**osteogeny** *noun* = **OSTEOGENESIS M18–M19.**

osteoid /ˈɒstɪɔɪd/ *adjective & noun*. **M19.**
[from **OSTEO-** + **-OID**.]
ANATOMY & MEDICINE. ▶**A** *adjective*. Resembling bone in appearance or structure; bony, osseous; *spec.* consisting of or designating the uncalcified protein matrix on which bone is formed. **M19.**
▶**B** *noun*. †**1** A kind of malignant tumour composed of osteoid tissue. Only in **M19.**
2 Osteoid tissue, uncalcified bone. **M20.**

osteology /ɒstɪˈɒlədʒi/ *noun*. **L17.**
[from **OSTEO-** + **-LOGY**.]
1 The science, esp. the branch of human anatomy, which deals with bones and related structures. **L17.**
2 The structure and arrangement of the bones of an animal. **M19.**
■ **osteoˈlogic** *adjective* (*rare*) = **OSTEOLOGICAL E19.** **osteoˈlogical** *adjective* of or pertaining to osteology; forming part of the subject-matter of osteology: **L18.** **osteoˈlogically** *adverb* as regards osteology **E19.** **osteologist** *noun* **M18.**

osteoma /ɒstɪˈəʊmə/ *noun*. Pl. **-mata** /-mətə/, **-mas**. **M19.**
[from **OSTEO-** + **-OMA**.]
MEDICINE. A benign tumour of bone.

osteomancy /ˈɒstɪəmansi/ *noun*. **E17.**
[from **OSTEO-** + **-MANCY**.]
Divination by means of bones.

osteon /ˈɒstɪɒn/ *noun*. Also **-one** /-əʊn/. **E20.**
[Greek = bone: see **-ON**.]
ANATOMY. Each of the minute cylindrical passages which make up the Haversian system of a bone.

osteopathy /ɒstɪˈɒpəθi/ *noun*. **M19.**
[from **OSTEO-** + **-PATHY**.]
1 Disease of the bones. Now *rare* or *obsolete*. **M19.**
2 A system of healing based on the theory that some disorders can be alleviated by treatment of the skeleton and musculature using manipulation and massage. **L19.**
■ **ˈosteopath** *noun* a practitioner of osteopathy **L19.** **osteoˈpathic** *adjective* **L19.** **osteoˈpathically** *adverb* **L19.** **osteopathist** *noun* a believer in osteopathy; an osteopath: **L19.**

osteopetrosis /ˌɒstɪəʊpɛˈtrəʊsɪs/ *noun*. Pl. **-troses** /-ˈtrəʊsiːz/. **E20.**
[from **OSTEO-** + Latin, Greek *petra* rock + **-OSIS**.]
MEDICINE & VETERINARY MEDICINE. A rare hereditary disease characterized by excessive formation of dense, brittle trabecular bone. Also called ***Albers-Schönberg disease***, ***marble bone(s)***.
■ **osteopetrotic** /-ˈtrɒtɪk/ *adjective* pertaining to or affected by osteopetrosis **M20.**

osteoporosis /ˌɒstɪəʊpəˈrəʊsɪs/ *noun*. Pl. **-roses** /-ˈrəʊsiːz/. **M19.**
[from **OSTEO-** + **PORE** *noun* + **-OSIS**.]
MEDICINE. A reduction in the protein and mineral content of bone tissue, resulting in fragile porous bones and occurring esp. in post-menopausal women and elderly men.
■ **osteoporotic** /-ˈrɒtɪk/ *adjective* **L19.**

osteosarcoma /ˌɒstɪəʊsɑːˈkəʊmə/ *noun*. Pl. **-mas**, **-mata** /-mətə/. **E19.**
[from **OSTEO-** + **SARCOMA**.]
MEDICINE. A malignant tumour of bone, *spec.* one involving proliferation of osteoblasts.
■ **osteosarcomatous** *adjective* **M19.**

osteospermum /ɒstɪəʊˈspəːməm/ *noun*. **M19.**
[mod. Latin (see below), formed as **OSTEO-** + Greek *sperma* seed.]
Any of various plants and shrubs of the genus *Osteospermum* (family Compositae), native to Africa and the Middle East, some species of which are cultivated for their yellow or violet flowers.

osteria /əʊstəˈriːə/ *noun*. **E17.**
[Italian, from *oste* **HOST** *noun*[2].]
In Italy: an inn, a hostelry.

ostia *noun* pl. of **OSTIUM**.

ostial /ˈɒstɪəl/ *adjective*. **E20.**
[from **OSTIUM** + **-AL**[1].]
ANATOMY & ZOOLOGY. Of, pertaining to, or having an ostium or ostia; of the nature of an ostium.

ostiary /ˈɒstɪəri/ *noun*. **LME.**
[Latin *ostiarius*, formed as **OSTIUM**: see **-ARY**[1].]
1 *Hist.* A doorkeeper, esp. of a church; *spec.* a member of the lowest of the four lesser orders in the pre-Reformation Western Church, and later in the Roman Catholic Church. **LME.**
†**2** = **OSTIUM 1. M–L17.**

ostinato /ɒstɪˈnɑːtəʊ/ *adjective & noun*. **L19.**
[Italian = obstinate, persistent.]
MUSIC. ▶**A** *adjective*. Of a melodic or rhythmical figure: continuously repeated. **L19.**
BASSO *ostinato*.
▶**B** *noun*. Pl. **-ti** /-ti/, **-tos**. A melodic phrase repeated through all or part of a piece. **E20.**

ostiole /ˈɒstɪəʊl/ *noun*. **M19.**
[Latin *ostiolum* dim. of **OSTIUM**: see **-OLE**[1].]
BOTANY. A small orifice or opening; *spec.* a small pore in the conceptacles of certain algae and the perithecia of certain fungi, through which the spores are discharged.

ostium /ˈɒstɪəm/ *noun*. Pl. **-ia** /-ɪə/. **E17.**
[Latin = door, opening, river mouth.]
†**1** The mouth of a river. Only in **17.**
2 *ANATOMY & ZOOLOGY.* An opening into a vessel or cavity of the body (also in mod. Latin names of particular openings); in arthropods, each of the slits or valves by which the heart opens to the body cavity; in sponges, an inhalant opening. **E19.**

> 🕮 **2** *Journal of Pediatrics* At open-heart surgery . . ostium primum and secundum defects were corrected.

ostler /ˈɒslə/ *noun*. **LME.**
[Var. of **HOSTLER**.]
Hist. A stableman or groom at an inn.
■ **ostleress** *noun* a female ostler **M17.**

Ostman /ˈəʊs(t)mən/ *noun*. Pl. **-men**. **ME.**
[Old Norse *Austmaðr*, pl. *Austmenn* (Latinized *Ostmanni*). Cf. **EAST**, **MAN** *noun*.]
Hist. A Norse invader of Ireland in the 9th cent.; a descendant of the Norse invaders in towns on the Irish east coast.

Ostmark /ˈɒstmɑːk/ *noun*. **M20.**
[German, from *Ost* east + *Mark* **MARK** *noun*[2].]
Hist. The basic monetary unit of the German Democratic Republic (superseded in 1990 by the Deutschmark).

Ostmen *noun* pl. of **OSTMAN**.

ostomy /ˈɒstəmi/ *noun*. Orig. *US*. **M20.**
[Extracted from *colostomy*, *ileostomy*, etc.: see **-STOMY**.]
MEDICINE. An operation that involves making a permanent artificial opening in the body; an opening so made.
■ **ostomate** *noun* a person who has had an ostomy **M20.**

Ostpolitik /ˈɒstpɒlɪˌtiːk/ *noun*. **M20.**
[German, from *Ost* east + *Politik* policy.]
Hist. The foreign policy (esp. of détente) of a western country with reference to the Communist bloc; *spec.* that of the Federal Republic of Germany.

ostraca *noun pl.* see **OSTRACON**.

ostraceous *adjective* var. of **OSTREACEOUS**.

ostracion /ɒˈstreɪsɪɒn/ *noun*. **M17.**
[mod. Latin (see below) from Greek *ostrakion* dim. of *ostrakon* hard shell.]
ZOOLOGY. A trunkfish, *esp.* one of the genus *Ostracion*. Now only as mod. Latin genus name.

ostracise *verb* var. of **OSTRACIZE**.

ostracism /ˈɒstrəsɪz(ə)m/ *noun*. **L16.**
[French *ostracisme* or mod. Latin *ostracismus* from Greek *ostrakismos*, from *ostrakizein*, from *ostrakon* shell, potsherd (because the Greek vote was effected with potsherds): see **-ISM**.]
1 *GREEK HISTORY.* The custom in ancient Greek cities of voting to banish for five or ten years a citizen regarded as unpopular or too powerful; a vote to effect such a banishment. **L16.**
2 Banishment by general consent; exclusion from favour, common privileges, or a particular social group. **M17.**

> 🕮 **2** N. Annan Nor was he likely to suffer social ostracism in London where a great thinker was by no means unique.

ostracite /ˈɒstrəsʌɪt/ *noun*. **M17.**
[Latin *ostracites* from Greek *ostrakitēs* earthen, testaceous, from *ostrakon* shell: see **-ITE**[1].]
PALAEONTOLOGY. A fossil shell of an oyster-like mollusc.

ostracize /ˈɒstrəsʌɪz/ *verb trans.* Also **-ise**. **M17.**
[Greek *ostrakizein*: see **OSTRACISM**, **-IZE**.]
1 Exclude (a person) from favour, common privileges, or a particular social group; refuse to associate with. **M17.**
2 *GREEK HISTORY.* Banish temporarily from a city. **M19.**

> 🕮 **1** K. Chernin Someone had gone about urging the boys and girls from the social clubs to ostracize me. J. Uglow Ostracised from polite society because she was living with a married man.

■ **ostraciˈzation** *noun* ostracism **L19.**

ostracod /ˈɒstrəkɒd/ *noun & adjective*. Also **-code** /-kəʊd/. **M19.**
[mod. Latin *Ostracoda* (see below), from Greek *ostrakōdēs* testaceous, from *ostrakon* shell.]
▶**A** *noun*. A crustacean of the class Ostracoda, which comprises very small organisms enclosed within a hinged shell. **M19.**
▶**B** *adjective*. Of or pertaining to an ostracod or ostracods. **L19.**

ostracoderm /ɒˈstrakədəːm/ *noun & adjective*. **L19.**
[mod. Latin *Ostracodermi* (former taxonomic name), formed as next + Greek *derma* skin.]
PALAEONTOLOGY. ▶**A** *noun*. An early fossil fish belonging to any of four extinct agnathan orders, characterized by heavy armour and known from the Cambrian to the Devonian. **L19.**
▶**B** *adjective*. Of or pertaining to this group of fossils. **L19.**

ostracon /ˈɒstrəkɒn/ *noun*. Pl. **-ca** /-kə/. Also **-kon**, pl. **-ka** /-kə/. **L19.**
[Greek *ostrakon* hard shell, potsherd.]
ARCHAEOLOGY. A potsherd used as a writing surface. Usu. in *pl.*

ostreaceous /ɒstrɪˈeɪʃəs/ *adjective*. Also **ostraceous** /ɒˈstreɪʃəs/. **L17.**
[from Latin *ostrea* oyster (mod. Latin *Ostrea* genus name, *Ostracea* former family name): see **-ACEOUS**.]
Of the nature of an oyster; resembling an oyster or an oyster's shell.

ostreger /ˈɒstrɪdʒə/ *noun*. **ME.**
[Old French *ostruchier*, *aus-*, from *ostour* (mod. *autour*) hawk, from Proto-Gallo-Romance *auceptore* alt. (by assoc. with Latin *avis* bird) of *acceptore*, from Latin *accipter*.]
A keeper of goshawks; = **AUSTRINGER**.

ostreiculture *noun*, **ostreicultural** *adjective*, etc., vars. of **OSTREOCULTURE** etc.

ostreiform /ˈɒstreɪfɔːm/ *adjective*. **M19.**
[from Latin *ostrea*, Greek *ostreon* oyster + **-I-** + **-FORM**.]
Having the form of an oyster.

ostreoculture /ˈɒstrɪəkʌltʃə/ *noun*. Also **ostrei-** /ˈɒstrɪ-/. **M19.**
[formed as prec. + **-O-** + **CULTURE** *noun*.]
The breeding of oysters for food or pearls.
■ **ostreoˈcultural** *adjective* **L19.** **ostreoˈculturist** *noun* a person engaged in ostreoculture **M19.**

ostreophagous /ɒstrɪˈɒfəgəs/ *adjective*. **M19.**
[formed as prec. + **-PHAGOUS**.]
Feeding on or eating oysters.

ostrich /ˈɒstrɪtʃ/ *noun & adjective*. Also †**-idge**, †**est-**. **ME.**
[Old French *ostrice*, *-iche*, *-usce* (mod. *autruche*) from Proto-Romance, from Latin *avis* bird + late Latin *struthio* from Greek *strouthiōn* ostrich, from *strouthos* sparrow, ostrich.]
▶**A** *noun*. **1** A very large swift flightless bird, *Struthio camelus*, with long legs and two toes on each foot, and inhabiting desert plains in Africa and the Middle East. **ME.**

2 = RHEA *noun*[1]. *rare*. E19.

Comb.: **ostrich farm**: on which ostriches are reared for their feathers; **ostrich-feather** a feather of an ostrich; *esp.* a long curly quill-feather from the wings or tail used as an ornament; **ostrich-fern** an ornamental fern, *Matteuccia struthiopteris*, with the sterile fronds arranged like a shuttlecock round the smaller fertile fronds; **ostrich-plume** an ostrich-feather; a bunch of these.

▶ **B** *attrib.* or as *adjective*. **1** Of or pertaining to an ostrich; *fig.* (*a*) that refuses to face facts, that deludes himself or herself (from the popular belief that ostriches bury their heads in the sand when pursued); †(*b*) capable of digesting anything (from the belief that ostriches could digest iron objects). LME.

2 Made of ostrich skin. M20.

1 *Pall Mall Gazette* The facts . . are too damning to leave much room for an ostrich policy.

■ **ostrichism** *noun* the policy of refusing to face facts M19. **ostrich-like** *adjective & adverb* like (that of) an ostrich; characterized by or with a refusal to face facts: L16.

ostringer *noun* var. of AUSTRINGER.

ostrobogulous /ɒstrəˈbɒgjʊləs/ *adjective*. *slang*. M20.
[Prob. invented word.]
Risqué, indecent.

ostrog /ɒˈstrɒg/ *noun*. M18.
[Russian.]
In Russia, a fortified house or village surrounded by a palisade.

Ostrogoth /ˈɒstrəgɒθ/ *noun & adjective*. LME.
[Late Latin *Ostrogothi* (pl.), from Germanic base of EAST + Latin *Gothus* Gothic.]
▶ **A** *noun*. A member of the eastern branch of the Goths which towards the end of the 5th cent. AD conquered Italy. Cf. VISIGOTH. LME.
▶ **B** *adjective*. = OSTROGOTHIC *adjective*. E20.
■ **Ostroˈgothic** *adjective* of or pertaining to the Ostrogoths E19.

Ostwald /ˈɒstwəld/ *noun*. E20.
[W. F. *Ostwald* (1853–1932), Russian chemist.]
Used *attrib.* and in *possess.* to designate apparatus invented and principles enunciated by Ostwald.
Ostwald dilution law, **Ostwald's dilution law**: that for dilute solutions of a binary electrolyte the square of the degree of dissociation of the solute, multiplied by its concentration, and divided by one minus the degree of dissociation, is a constant for the solute.

Ostyak /ˈɒstɪak/ *noun & adjective*. E18.
[Russian from Tartar *uştyak* one of another tribe.]
= KHANTY.
Ostyak Samoyed = SELKUP. *YENISEI-Ostyak*.

osu /ˈɒsuː/ *noun*. *W. Afr.* M20.
[Igbo.]
An outcast, a person regarded as belonging to the lowest class of society.

Oswego /ɒˈzwiːgəʊ, ɒˈswiː-/ *noun*. Pl. **-os**. M18.
[A river and town in the northern part of New York State.]
1 In full ***Oswego bass***. The large-mouth bass, *Micropterus salmoides*. *US local*. M18.
2 (Proprietary name for) a type of cornflour. L19.
Comb.: ***Oswego bass***: see sense 1 above; ***Oswego biscuit***, ***Oswego cake***: made with Oswego; ***Oswego tea*** a N. American bergamot, *Monarda didyma*, grown for its showy heads of scarlet flowers.

OT *abbreviation*.
Old Testament.

-ot /ət/ *suffix*[1] (not productive).
[Repr. Old & mod. French, orig. dim.]
Forming nouns, as in ***ballot***, ***mascot***, ***parrot***.

-ot /ət/ *suffix*[2]. In sense 2 also **-ote** /əʊt/.
[Repr. French *-ote*, Latin *-ota*, Greek *-ōtes* suffix meaning 'nativity'.]
1 Forming nouns with the sense 'a person of a particular type or character', as ***idiot***, ***patriot***, ***zealot***.
2 Forming nouns with the sense 'a native or inhabitant of', as ***Cypriot***, ***Epirot***, ***Italiot***.

†**otacoustic** *noun & adjective*. *rare*. E17.
[from Greek *ōt-*, *ous* ear + *akoustikos* ACOUSTIC.]
▶ **A** *noun*. An instrument to assist hearing. E17–E18.
▶ **B** *adjective*. Used to assist hearing. Only in Dicts. L18–E19.
■ †**otacoustical** *adjective*: only in E19. †**otacousticon** *noun* = OTACOUSTIC *noun* E17–E18.

Otaheite /əʊtəˈhiːti/ *adjective & noun*. L18.
[Tahitian *Otaheite* Tahiti.]
= TAHITIAN *adjective & noun*. Now only in the names of fruits or plants introduced from or associated with Tahiti.
Otaheite apple the edible yellow plumlike fruit of *Spondias cytherea* (family Anacardiaceae); also (*W. Indies*) (the fruit of) the Malay apple, *Syzygium malaccense*. **Otaheite gooseberry** (the astringent fruit of) a tree of the spurge family, *Phyllanthus acidus*. **Otaheite orange** a variety of an acid mandarin orange grown as a pot plant.

†**Otaheitean** *adjective & noun*. L18–M19.
[formed as prec. + -AN. Cf. TAHITIAN.]
= TAHITIAN *adjective & noun*.

otaku /əʊˈtɑːkuː/ *noun*. L20.
[Japanese = your house, home (in formal speech), from *o-* honorific prefix + *taku* house, home: with allus. to the poor social skills of such people (such as excessive formality or a reluctance to leave the house).]
In Japan: young people who are highly skilled in or obsessed with computer technology (or any other subject) to the detriment of their social skills.

otalgia /əʊˈtaldʒə/ *noun*. M17.
[Greek *ōtalgia* earache, from *ōt-*, *ous* ear: see -ALGIA.]
MEDICINE. Pain in the ear, earache.

otariid /əʊˈtɛːrɪɪd/ *noun & adjective*. L19.
[mod. Latin *Otariidae* (see below), from *Otaria* genus name, from Greek *ōt-*, *ous* ear: see -ID[3].]
▶ **A** *noun*. Any of various carnivorous marine mammals of the family Otariidae, comprising eared seals (fur seals and sea lions) and formerly walruses. L19.
▶ **B** *adjective*. Of or pertaining to the otariids. L20.
■ **otarioid** *noun & adjective* (*a*) *noun* a member of the superfamily Otarioidea, which comprises the otariids together with walruses; (*b*) *adjective* of or pertaining to this superfamily: L19.

otary /ˈəʊtəri/ *noun*. Now *rare*. M19.
[mod. Latin *Otaria*: see prec., -Y[3].]
An eared seal; an otariid.

OTC *abbreviation*.
1 Officers' Training Corps.
2 Over the counter.

OTE *abbreviation*.
COMMERCE. On-target (or on-track) earnings.

-ote *suffix* see -OT[2].

other /ˈʌðə/ *adjective* (in mod. usage also classed as a *determiner*), *pronoun*, *noun*, & *adverb*[1].
[Old English *ōþer* = Old Frisian *ōther*, Old Saxon *ōþar*, *andar*, Old High German *andar* (Dutch, German *ander*), Old Norse *annarr*, Gothic *anþar*, from Indo-European (cf. Latin *alter* (see ALTER *verb*), Avestan, Sanskrit *ántara*).]
▶ **A** *adjective*. †**1** One — of two. *rare*. OE–L16.
2 That remain(s) from a specified or implied group of two or (later) more. Usu. preceded by *the*, *my*, etc. OE.
†**3** That follows the first; second. OE–L16.
4 Existing besides or distinct from that or those already specified or implied; further, additional. (Also following or (now only in ***other such*** below) preceding a numeral or determiner.) See also ANOTHER 1. OE.
5 Different in kind or quality. Formerly also used pleonastically before adjectives. (Foll. by *than*, †*but*, (arch.) *from*.) See also ANOTHER 2. ME.

2 D. H. LAWRENCE The boy tried to creep over . . the roof and escape down the other side. SCOTT FITZGERALD The first song he had chosen . . followed, after a slight interval, by his other choice. P. NEWTON The other four . . were playing pitch and toss. I. MURDOCH That's what the Mafia do, they frighten all the other villains. A. N. WILSON He told them to turn the other cheek if they were struck. **4** JAS. ROBERTSON St Bridget and other nine virgins. H. JAMES His face told clearly of youth and kindness . . but it had little other beauty. G. GREENE It was by no means certain that there would not be other deaths. E. MCBAIN The minister and two other people were killed. G. GORDON Easily absorbed . . into the fabric of their lives, like any other experience. U. BENTLEY She had a distressing appetite for romantic slush, and, indeed, other kinds of slush. **5** R. BENTLEY Immortal Vellum . . that could last . . in spite of all damp and moisture, that moulders other mortal skins. SIR W. SCOTT Far other scene her thoughts recall. D. ADAMS We get in his tri-jet which he had souped up into something totally other. A. BROOKNER At home with Christine, who did not urge her to be other than she was.

Phrases & comb.: **do the other thing** *colloq.* (*a*) do the opposite of what has been suggested or specified previously; (*b*) have sexual intercourse. **every other** — every second —, every alternate —. ***go to the other extreme***: see EXTREME *noun*. ***in other words***: see WORD *noun*. ***laugh on the other side of one's face***, ***laugh on the other side of one's mouth***: see LAUGH *verb*. ***on the other hand***: see HAND *noun*. †**otherguise** *adjective* = OTHERGUESS. ***other half***: see HALF *noun*. **otherkins** *adjective* (long obsolete exc. *dial.*) [KIN *noun*, -S[3]] of another kind. **other life** *the* life after death. **other ranks** MILITARY non-commissioned officers and ordinary soldiers, seamen, etc. **other some** (now *arch.* & *dial.*) (*a*) some other —; (*b*) some others. **other such** *adjectival & noun phr.* (*a*) *adjectival phr.* other similar; also pleonastically with *like*; (*b*) *noun phr.* others of a similar kind. **other than** besides; (see also sense 5 above). †**othertimes** *adverb* at other times. **otherways** *adverb* (obsolete exc. *dial.*) otherwise. **otherwhere** *adverb & noun* (*arch.*) (in or to) another place. **otherwheres** *adverb* (*arch.*) in or to another place. **otherwhile(s)** *adverb* (obsolete exc. *dial.*) (*a*) at times; now and then; (*b*) at another time, or at other times. **other world** (*a*) a world supposedly inhabited after death, as heaven, hell, etc. (***the other world***, heaven, hell); (*b*) an imaginary ideal or fantastic world. ***pull the other one***: see PULL *verb*. ***quite other***: see QUITE *adverb*. **the other day**, **the other night**, **the other week**, etc. †(*a*) the following or next day, night, week, etc.; †(*b*) the preceding day, night, week, etc.; (*c*) a few days, nights, weeks, etc., ago. **the other man**, **the other woman** the lover of a married or similarly attached woman or man. ***the other night***: see ***the other day*** above. **the other place** (*a*) hell (as opp. to heaven); (*b*) *joc.* Oxford University as regarded from Cambridge University and vice versa; (*c*) the House of Lords as regarded from the House of Commons and vice versa. **the other side** (*a*) heaven, hell; the abode of the dead; (*b*) *Austral. & NZ slang* a place (as a State) separated by a border etc. or otherwise distant from the speaker; *spec.* a place in the northern hemisphere; (*c*) an opponent, an opposing side; (*d*) ***the other side of the coin***: see COIN *noun*; ***the other side of the hill***: see SIDE *noun*. ***the other way about***, ***the other way around***, ***the other way round***: see WAY *noun*. ***the other week***: see ***the other day*** above. ***the other woman***: see ***the other man*** above. ***the other world***: see ***other world*** above. ***the shoe is on the other foot***: see SHOE *noun*.

▶ **B** *pronoun & noun*. **I** †**1** One of (the) two. OE–ME.
†**2** That which follows the first; the second. OE–ME.
3 The remaining one of two or (later) more, after enumeration or allusion. OE. ▶**b** Each preceding one (in turn). Long *obsolete* exc. *Scot. dial.* ME.
4 In *pl.* & (orig.) †*sing.* treated as *pl.* The remaining ones, the rest. OE.
5 a *sing.* Another person or thing of a kind specified or understood contextually; another person. Now only preceded by *any*, *no*, *none*, *one*, *some* (see also ANOTHER) and in ***one — or other***; ***some — or other***, an unspecified —. OE. ▶**b** In *pl.* & (arch.) *sing.* treated as *pl.* Other persons or things of a kind specified or understood contextually; other people. OE. ▶**c** Another thing; something else. Usu. in neg. contexts. *arch.* OE.
6 *sing.* & †in *pl.* Each other, one another. Long only *Scot.* ME.

3 C. ISHERWOOD Neither one of us would want to keep on the animals if the other wasn't there. I. MURDOCH The spires . . heavily shadowed on one side and defined on the other. J. SIMMS We waited in silence for the other to speak. **b** SHAKES. *Meas. for M.* Every letter he hath writ hath disvouch'd other. **4** SHAKES. *Mids. N. D.* Awaking when the other do. C. S. LEWIS They decided to play hide-and-seek. Susan was 'It' and . . the others scattered to hide. **5a** J. CONRAD For some reason or other this last statement of hers brought me immense comfort. C. JACKSON He was the man for her, and she felt there would be no other. **b** J. BUCHAN A diary of a pilgrimage . . might interest others who travel a like road. E. WAUGH One can write, think and pray exclusively of others. C. BRAYFIELD His office and several others were ransacked. *Encounter* Not . . the kind of person who undertook, as other of our friends . . to argue.

▶ **II 7** ***the other***, sexual activity; sexual intercourse. *slang*. E20.

7 D. H. LAWRENCE She loved me . . to kiss her . . . But the other, she just didn't want.

Phrases & comb.: EACH **other**. ***go in at one ear and out at the other***, ***go in one ear and out the other***: see EAR *noun*[1]. **of all others** out of the many possible or likely. **other-directed** *adjective* governed by external circumstances and trends. ***significant other***: see SIGNIFICANT *adjective*. ***something or other***: see SOMETHING *pronoun & noun*. ***this, that, and the other***, ***this, that, or the other***: see THIS *pronoun* etc.

▶ **C** *adverb*. Otherwise *than*. ME.

Law Times It is impossible to refer to them . . other than very cursorily. L. GRANT-ADAMSON It was too late to do other than let him race about the back garden.

■ **otherness** *noun* the quality or fact of being other or different; a different or separate thing (to something previously specified): L16.

†**other** *conjunction & adverb*[2].
[Old English *oþþe*, earlier *oþþa*, superseded in late Old English by *oþer*, of unkn. origin.]
▶ **A** *conjunction*. Or. OE–L16.
▶ **B** *adverb*. Followed by *or* or *other*: = EITHER *adverb & conjunction* 2. ME–L16.

othergates /ˈʌðəgeɪts/ *adverb & adjective*. *obsolete* exc. *dial.* ME.
[from OTHER *adjective* + GATE *noun*[2] + -S[3].]
▶ **A** *adverb*. In another way, differently. ME.
▶ †**B** *adjective*. Of another kind, different. L16–M17.

otherguess /ˈʌðəgɛs/ *attrib. adjective*. *arch.* M17.
[Alt. of prec., spelt after *guess*: cf. GUESS *adjective*.]
Of another kind, different.

otherwise /ˈʌðəwʌɪz/ *adverb & adjective*. ME.
[from OTHER *adjective* + -WISE, ellipt. from Old English *on ōþre wīsan* in other wise or manner.]
▶ **A** *adverb*. **1** In another way, or in other ways; by other means; differently. Also foll. by *than*. ME.
2 In another case; in other circumstances; if not; else. ME.
3 In other respects. LME.
†**4** On the other hand. LME–L17.

1 H. JAMES She made no attempt to contradict him; she simply said she had supposed otherwise. I. MURDOCH If she had played her cards otherwise she could have made a much better bargain. E. FIGES She felt . . this was her home and . . pretending otherwise was becoming too much. L. KOPPETT Slipping on a rain-soaked or otherwise tricky surface. **2** G. GREENE Nobody . . knows how long a parting is for, otherwise we would pay more attention to . . the formal words. I. MURDOCH Often one identifies with what would otherwise prove a menace. R. DINNAGE I'm very glad someone gave me the push . . I might not have done it otherwise. **3** D. HAMMETT His lips were dry and rough in a face otherwise pale and damp. O. SACKS Somewhat deaf, but otherwise in good health.

▶ **B** *adjective.* **1** *pred.* Different; other. ME.
2 That would otherwise be —. *rare.* E17.

📖 **1** T. S. ELIOT I had very much rather that the facts were otherwise. W. BRONK Would it be otherwise in a real world? S. BRETT 'Frances, I'm sorry I'm late.' 'When were you ever otherwise?'

Phrases: **or otherwise**, **and otherwise**: used to indicate the opposite or negation of a preceding noun, adjective, adverb, or verb.

otherworldly /ˈʌðəwəːldli/ *adjective.* L19.
[from *other world* s.v. OTHER *adjective*: see -LY[1].]
1 Of or pertaining to an imaginary ideal or fantastic world. L19.
2 Of, pertaining to, or concerned with a world inhabited after death. L19.

📖 **1** *Antiquity* It is less eerily otherworldly than . . others of the stone heads. **2** C. LASCH Even the most . . otherworldly religions expressed a hope of social justice. D. CUPITT Celibate clerics with a very other-worldly outlook.

¶ Opp. THIS-WORLDLY.
■ **otherworldliness** *noun* M19.

Othman *noun & adjective* see OTTOMAN *noun*[1] *& adjective.*

otic /ˈəʊtɪk, ˈɒtɪk/ *adjective.* M17.
[Greek *ōtikos*, from *ōt-*, *ous* ear: see -IC.]
ANATOMY & MEDICINE. Of or pertaining to the ear; auricular.

-otic /ˈɒtɪk/ *suffix.*
[Repr. (through French *-otique*, Latin *-oticus*) Greek *-ōtikos*, from nouns in *-ōtēs* or adjectives in *-ōtos* + *-ikos* -IC.]
Forming adjectives: (*a*) corresp. to nouns in -OSIS, as ***hypnotic***, ***narcotic***, ***osmotic***; (*b*) from or after Greek, as ***chaotic***, ***demotic***, ***erotic***, ***exotic***.

otiose /ˈəʊtɪəʊs, ˈəʊʃɪ-/ *adjective.* L18.
[Latin *otiosus*, from *otium* leisure: see -OSE[1].]
1 Having no practical result; futile. L18. ▸**b** Having no practical function; superfluous. M19.
2 At leisure, at rest; idle; indolent. M19.

📖 **1** C. RYCROFT Both explanations can be seen to be erroneous and indeed otiose. **b** M. FRAYN Sections of the English language were . . rendered otiose by replacing long words with small words hyphenated together. **2** J. HELLER No chance ever of staring this otiose, imperturbable . . friend out of countenance.

■ **otiosely** *adverb* L19. **otioseness** *noun* M19.

otiosity /əʊtɪˈɒsɪti, əʊʃɪ-/ *noun.* Orig. †**oci-**. L15.
[French †*ociosité*, from *ociose* from Latin *otiosus*: see prec., -ITY.]
The condition or state of being unoccupied or idle; ease, leisure; idleness, indolence.

otitis /əʊˈtʌɪtɪs/ *noun.* L18.
[mod. Latin, from Greek *ōt-*, *ous* ear: see -ITIS.]
MEDICINE. Inflammation of (part of) the ear. Usu. with mod. Latin qualifying adjective
otitis externa /ɛkˈstəːnə/ inflammation of the external ear. **otitis interna** /ɪnˈtəːnə/ inflammation of the inner ear. **otitis media** /ˈmiːdɪə/ inflammation of the middle ear.
■ **otitic** /əʊˈtɪtɪk/ *adjective* E19.

otium /ˈəʊʃɪəm/ *noun.* E18.
[Latin.]
Leisure, ease, idleness. Chiefly in ***otium cum dignitate*** /kʌm dɪgnɪˈtɑːteɪ/, dignified leisure or ease.

oto- /ˈəʊtəʊ/ *combining form* of Greek *ōtos*, *ous* ear, used chiefly in *ANATOMY & MEDICINE*: see -O-.
■ **otoˈconium** *noun*, pl. **-onia**, = OTOLITH M19. **otocyst** *noun* the auditory vesicle or organ of hearing in some invertebrates; an embryonic precursor of the inner ear in mammals: L19. **otomyˈcosis** *noun*, pl. **-coses** /-ˈkəʊsiːz/, a fungal infection of the ear, causing irritation and inflammation of the external auditory meatus L19. **otophone** *noun* an ear-trumpet M19. **otoplasty** *noun* plastic surgery of the ear L19. **otoˈrrhoea** *noun* purulent discharge from the ear E19. **oˈtotomy** *noun* orig., dissection of the ear; now, (an instance of) surgical incision into the ear: M19. **otoˈtoxic** *adjective* having a toxic effect on the ear or its nerve supply M20. **ototoˈxicity** *noun* the property of being ototoxic M20.

otolaryngology /ˌəʊtə(ʊ)larɪŋˈgɒlədʒi/ *noun.* L19.
[from OTO- + LARYNGOLOGY.]
The branch of medicine that deals with the ear and larynx. Also = OTORHINOLARYNGOLOGY.
■ **otolaryngoˈlogic** (chiefly *US*), **otolaryngoˈlogical** *adjectives* L19. **otolaryngologist** *noun* E20.

otolith /ˈəʊtəlɪθ/ *noun.* M19.
[from OTO- + -LITH.]
ANATOMY. Any of the calcareous bodies found in the inner ear of vertebrates, important as sensors of gravity and acceleration.
■ **otolite** *noun* = OTOLITH M19. **otoˈlithic** *adjective* of the nature of or pertaining to an otolith; containing otoliths: L19. **otoˈlitic** *adjective* = OTOLITHIC M19.

otology /əʊˈtɒlədʒi/ *noun.* M19.
[from OTO- + -LOGY.]
The branch of medicine that deals with the anatomy, functions, and diseases of the ear.
■ **otoˈlogical** *adjective* L19. **otologist** *noun* L19.

Otomi /əʊtəˈmiː/ *noun & adjective.* L18.
[Amer. Spanish *Otomí* from Nahuatl *otomih* lit. 'unknown'.]
▶ **A** *noun.* Pl. same, **-s**. A member of an American Indian people inhabiting parts of central Mexico; the language of this people. L18.
▶ **B** *attrib.* or as *adjective.* Of or pertaining to the Otomi or their language. L19.

otorhinolaryngology /ˌəʊtərʌɪnəʊˌlarɪŋˈgɒlədʒi/ *noun.* E20.
[from OTO- + RHINO- + LARYNGOLOGY.]
The branch of medicine that deals with the ear, nose, and throat. Cf. OTOLARYNGOLOGY.
■ **otorhinolaryngoˈlogical** *adjective* M20. **otorhinolaryngologist** *noun* M20.

otosclerosis /ˌəʊtəʊskləˈrəʊsɪs, -sklɪə-/ *noun.* Pl. **-roses** /-ˈrəʊsiːz/. E20.
[from OTO- + SCLEROSIS.]
MEDICINE. A hereditary disorder causing deafness, resulting from overgrowth of bone in the inner ear.
■ **otosclerotic** /-ˈrɒtɪk/ *adjective & noun* (*a*) *adjective* of, pertaining to, or affected with otosclerosis; (*b*) *noun* a person affected with otosclerosis: M20.

otoscope /ˈəʊtəskəʊp/ *noun.* M19.
[from OTO- + -SCOPE.]
MEDICINE. **1** A stethoscope for listening to sounds in the ear. Now *rare.* M19.
2 = AURISCOPE. M19.
■ **otoscopic** /-ˈskɒpɪk/ *adjective* L19.

Otshi-herero /əʊtʃɪˈhɪərərəʊ, -hɛˈrɛːrəʊ/ *noun.* M19.
[Bantu, from *otyi-* noun class prefix + HERERO.]
= HERERO *noun* 1. Also, the Herero people.

OTT *abbreviation. slang.*
= ***over the top*** (c) s.v. TOP *noun*[1].

ottava rima /otˌtaːva ˈriːma, ɒˌtɑːvə ˈriːmə/ *noun.* L18.
[Italian = eighth rhyme.]
A stanza of eight lines, 11-syllabled in Italian, 10-syllabled in English, rhyming as *abababcc*.

Ottawa /ˈɒtəwə/ *adjective & noun.* L17.
[Canad. French *Outaouais* from Ojibwa *otāwā*.]
▶ **A** *adjective.* Of, pertaining to, or designating an Algonquian people inhabiting the area near Lake Huron in Canada. L17.
▶ **B** *noun.* Pl. same, **-s**. A member of this people. M18.

otter /ˈɒtə/ *noun & verb.*
[Old English *otr*, *ot(t)or* = Middle Low German, Dutch *otter*, Old High German *ottar* (German *Otter*), Old Norse *otr*, from Germanic, from Indo-European word repr. by Avestan, Sanskrit *udra*, Greek *hudros* water snake, *hudra* HYDRA.]
▶ **A** *noun.* **1** Pl. **-s**, same. Any of various semi-aquatic fish-eating mustelid mammals of the subfamily Lutrinae, with short legs, webbed feet, and dense fur, and swimming with great agility; esp. *Lutra lutra* of European rivers. OE.
2 The fur or skin of the otter. ME.
3 A piece of freshwater tackle consisting of a float with line and a number of hooks. Also = ***otter-board*** (b) below. M19. ▸**b** A paravane. E20.
1 *SEA otter.*
Comb.: **otter-board** (*a*) a piece of fishing tackle consisting of a board with several hooks attached; (*b*) = DOOR 4; **otter civet** an Indo-Chinese semi-aquatic viverrid, *Cynogale bennettii*, which resembles an otter; **otter-dog**, **otter-hound** (an animal of) a breed of dog used for hunting otters; **otter-shell** any of various marine bivalve molluscs of the genus *Lutraria*; **otter shrew** any of various central African semi-aquatic insect-eating mammals of the family Tenrecidae; *esp.* (more fully ***giant otter shrew***) *Potamogale velox*, which resembles a small otter; **otter tail** an otter's tail; a dog's tail resembling this; **otter-trawl** a trawl fitted with an otter-board; **otter-trawling** fishing with an otter-trawl.
▶ **B** *verb intrans.* Fish with an otter. M19.

Otto /ˈɒtəʊ/ *noun*[1]. L19.
[N. A. *Otto* (1832–91), German engineer.]
Used *attrib.* to designate (an engine using) the four-stroke cycle employed in most petrol and gas engines.

otto *noun*[2] see ATTAR.

ottocento /ɒtəʊˈtʃɛntəʊ/ *noun.* Also **O-**. E20.
[Italian = eight hundred.]
The nineteenth century in Italy; the style of Italian art, architecture, music, etc., of this period.

📖 *attrib.*: *Financial Times* No other living conductor I would rather hear in early Ottocento Italian opera.

Ottoman /ˈɒtəmən/ *noun*[1] *& adjective.* Also (*arch.*) **Othman** /ˈɒθmən/. L16.
[French, or Italian *Ottomano*, medieval Latin *Ottomanus*, medieval Greek *Othōmanoi*, from Arab. *ʿUṯmānī* adjective of personal name *ʿUṯmān*: cf. OSMANLI.]
▶ **A** *noun.* A member of the former Turkish dynasty founded by Othman or Osman I in *c* 1300; a Turkish subject under this dynasty. L16.
▶ **B** *adjective.* Of or belonging to the dynasty of the Ottomans, the branch of the Turks to which they belonged, or the empire ruled by them until 1922. E17.
Ottoman Porte: see PORTE.
■ **Ottomanism** *noun* the culture of the Ottomans E20. **Ottomaniˈzation** *noun* the process of Ottomanizing people, an institution, etc. E20. **Ottomanize** *verb trans.* make Ottoman or Turkish M19.

ottoman /ˈɒtəmən/ *noun*[2]. E19.
[French *ottomane* fem. of *ottoman* (adjective) Ottoman.]
1 A low cushioned seat without a back or arms, often serving as a footstool or a chest. E19.
2 A heavy ribbed fabric of a mixture of silk and wool or cotton. Also more fully ***ottoman silk***. L19.

†**Ottomite** *noun.* E17–E19.
[from OTTO(MAN + -ITE[1].]
= OTTOMAN *noun*[1].

📖 SHAKES. *Oth.* This present wars against the Ottomites.

Ottonian /ɒˈtəʊnɪən/ *adjective.* L19.
[Late Latin *Ottonianus*, from *Otto*: see below, -IAN.]
Of or pertaining to the East Frankish dynasty of the Holy Roman Empire founded by Otto I (912–73), which ruled from 962 to 1002; *spec.* pertaining to or characteristic of the art of this period.

OU *abbreviation.*
1 Open University.
2 Oxford University.

ou /ˈəʊuː/ *noun*[1]. L19.
[Hawaiian *ʻōʻū*.]
A green and yellow Hawaiian honeycreeper, *Psittirostra psittacea*, of the family Drepanididae.

ou /əʊ/ *noun*[2]. *S. Afr. colloq.* Pl. **ouens** /ˈəʊənz/, **ous**. M20.
[Afrikaans, perh. from Dutch *ouwe* old man. Cf. next.]
A man, a fellow. Cf. OUTJIE.

📖 J. DRUMMOND The ou that shot Loder—he is dangerous.

ou /əʊ/ *adjective. S. Afr. colloq.* M19.
[Afrikaans from Dutch *oud* old. Cf. prec.]
Old, elder. Freq. in terms of affection or casual reference.

ouabain /ˈwɑːbeɪɪn, -bʌɪn, wɑːˈbeɪɪn/ *noun.* L19.
[French, from Somali *wabayo* tree yielding arrow poison containing ouabain: see -IN[1].]
CHEMISTRY & PHARMACOLOGY. A potentially poisonous polycyclic glycoside that is obtained from certain trees of the African genera *Strophanthus* and *Acokanthera* (family Apocynaceae) and is used as a very rapid cardiac stimulant. Also called ***G-strophanthin***.

ouananiche /wanəˈniːʃ/ *noun.* L19.
[Canad. French from Montagnais.]
A lake variety of the Atlantic salmon, *Salmo salar*, occurring in Labrador and Newfoundland.

oubaas /ˈəʊbɑːs/ *noun. S. Afr.* M19.
[Afrikaans, from OU *adjective* + BAAS.]
A head of a family; an elderly man. Freq. as a form of address to an older man.

oubit *noun* var. of WOUBIT.

oubliette /uːblɪˈɛt/ *noun.* L18.
[French, from *oublier* forget: see -ETTE.]
A secret dungeon accessible only through a trapdoor.

ouch /aʊtʃ/ *noun*[1] *& verb*[1]. *arch.* ME.
[Old French *nosche*, *nouche* from Old Frankish (= Old High German) *nuskja* buckle, clasp, perh. of Celtic origin. The initial *n* was lost by misdivision, as in *adder*, *apron*, etc.]
▶ **A** *noun.* A clasp, buckle, or brooch, esp. one set with precious stones, for holding together the two sides of a garment; a buckle or brooch worn as an ornament. Also, the setting of a precious stone. ME.
▶ **B** *verb trans.* Adorn (as) with ouches. *rare.* LME.

ouch /aʊtʃ/ *verb*[2], *interjection, & noun*[2]. M17.
[Natural exclam.]
▶ **A** *verb intrans.* Cry out with pain. M17.
▶ **B** *interjection.* Expr. pain. M19.
▶ **C** *noun.* A cry of 'ouch!' M19.

oud /uːd/ *noun.* M18.
[Arab. *al-ʿūd*: see LUTE *noun*[1]. Cf. LAUD *noun*[2].]
A form of lute or mandolin played principally in Arab countries.

OUDS *abbreviation.*
Oxford University Dramatic Society.

oudstryder /ˈəʊtstreɪdə/ *noun. S. Afr.* M20.
[Afrikaans = ex-soldier.]
A veteran of the South African War (1899–1902) who fought on the side of the Boer republics; *gen.* any war veteran.

oued /wɛd/ *noun.* M19.
[French from Arab. *wādī*.]
= WADI.

ouens *noun pl.* see OU *noun*[2].

ouf /uːf, ʊf/ *interjection.* Also **oof**. M19.
[Natural exclam.]
1 Expr. alarm or annoyance. M19.
2 Expr. relief. E20.

ough /uːx, ɔːx/ *interjection.* Now *dial.* M16.
[Natural exclam.]
Expr. disgust; = UGH 2.

ought /ɔːt/ *noun*[1]. L16.
[from the verb.]
The action or an act of what is expressed by the verb *ought*; (a) duty, (an) obligation; a thing which one ought to have.

> 🕮 GEO. ELIOT The will supreme, the individual claim, The social Ought, the lyrist's liberty.

ought /ɔːt/ *noun*[2]. M19.
[from NOUGHT by misdivision as in *adder, apron*.]
A nought, a cipher.

ought *pronoun, adjective, & adverb* var. of AUGHT *pronoun, adjective, & adverb.*

ought /ɔːt/ *verb.* As aux. pres. & pa. (all persons) **ought**; neg. **ought not**, (*informal*) **oughtn't** /ˈɔːt(ə)nt/; no other parts used exc. pa. pple (*non-standard*) **ought**. In senses 5, 6 also (*Scot.*) **aucht** /ɔːxt/, **aught**.
[Old English *āhte* pa. t. of OWE.]
▶ **I 1** Pa. t. & pple of OWE. OE.
▶ **II** *aux.* Foll. by *to be, to do*; (arch.) *be, do*; also without inf., or foll. by *to* only.
2 As pres. t. (indic. & subjunct.): ▸**a** Am (is, are) bound or under moral obligation; it is my (your, his, their, etc.) duty; it is right or proper for me (you, him, them, etc.). Cf. earlier OWE 2. ME. ▸**b** Am (is, are) advised or recommended; am (is, are) expected or assumed, it is probable that I (you, he, they, etc.) will. ME. ▸†**c** *impers.* Is due or proper to, behoves, befits, (a person) *to do, do.* ME–E16.
3 As pa. t. (indic. & subjunct.); now only with perf. inf. (*ought to have done*) or (*non-standard*) with *did* (*did ought*), exc. in reported speech, action, etc., and in conditional clauses: ▸**a** Was (were) bound or under moral obligation; it was my (your, his, their, etc.) duty; it was right or proper for me (you, him, them, etc.). ME. ▸**b** Was (were) advised or recommended; was (were) expected or assumed, it was probable that I (you, he, they, etc.) would. ME. ▸†**c** *impers.* Was due or proper to, behoved, befitted, (a person) *to do, do.* ME–L15.

> 🕮 **2a** BROWNING How ought I address thee, how ought I revere thee? E. WAUGH You ought to think yourself lucky . . to get a good position like that. G. VIDAL If it benefits . . people to confiscate your father's money then it ought to be confiscated. F. KING The kind of person who tells you, not what you want to do, but what you ought to do. **b** E. NESBIT Father says so, and he ought to know. T. S. ELIOT You ought to see your face! **c** CHAUCER Hym oughte now to have the lesse peyne. **3a** J. CONRAD He never offered to take Winnie to theatres, as such a nice gentleman ought to have done. D. L. SAYERS I did ought to have spoke up at the time. I. MURDOCH Ought I to have told her about Daisy, Tim wondered. *Guardian* He suggested that they ought to be revealing how much they earn. **b** V. WOOLF They ought to have been asleep hours ago. J. FOWLES He ought to have looked sallow. **c** MALORY I have no thynge done but that me ought for to doo.

▶ **III** As full verb, with inflections.
†**4** *verb intrans.* Be under moral obligation; have as a duty; be advised. Foll. by *to do, to be.* LME–M17.
5 *verb trans.* Have to pay; = OWE 4. *Scot.* M16.
6 *verb trans.* Possess; = OWE 1, OWN *verb* 2. *Scot.* L18.

> 🕮 **4** A. COKAINE The cause is common to all, Kings oughting not to suffer usurpation. **5** SIR W. SCOTT We aught him the siller, and will pay him wi' our convenience. **6** R. L. STEVENSON There's naebody but you and me that ought the name.

Phrases: **no better than one ought to be**: see BETTER *adjective.* **ought not** am (is, are) bound not to, am (is, are) obliged not to, etc.
■ **oughtness** *noun* (a) moral obligation or duty L19.

oughta /ˈɔːtə/ *aux. verb. colloq.* Also **oughter**. M19.
[Repr. an informal pronunc.]
I (you, he, they, etc.) ought to.

†**ougly** *adjective* see UGLY *adjective.*

ouguiya /uːˈgiːjə/ *noun.* Also **ougiya**. L20.
[French from Mauritanian Arab. *ūgiyya* from Arab. *ʼūkiyya* from Greek *ougkia* from Latin *uncia* OUNCE *noun*[1].]
The basic monetary unit of Mauritania, equal to five khoums.

Ouidaesque /wiːdəˈɛsk/ *adjective.* E20.
[from *Ouida*, nom-de-plume: see below, -ESQUE.]
Characteristic of the novels of the English novelist Ouida (Marie Louise de la Ramée, 1839–1908); characterized by extravagance.

Ouija /ˈwiːdʒə/ *noun.* Also **o-**. L19.
[French *oui* yes + German *ja* yes.]
More fully ***Ouija board***. (Proprietary name for) a board having letters or signs at its rim at which a planchette, movable pointer, or upturned glass points in answer to questions from attenders at a seance etc.

ouistiti /ˈwɪstɪti/ *noun.* Now *rare.* Also **wistiti**. L18.
[French, imit. of the animal's cry. Cf. OUSTITI.]
A marmoset; *esp.* the common marmoset, *Callithrix jacchus.*

oukha *noun* var. of UKHA.

ouklip /ˈəʊklɪp/ *noun. S. Afr.* L19.
[Afrikaans, from *oud* old + KLIP.]
GEOLOGY. A lateritic conglomerate found in southern Africa.

ould /aʊld/ *adjective. Anglo-Irish.* L17.
[Repr. Irish pronunc.]
= OLD *adjective.*

Ouled Nail /uːlɪd ˈnɑːiːl, ˈnʌɪl/ *noun.* L19.
[French from Arab. *Awlād Nāʼil* lit. 'sons of Nail'.]
A member of an Arab people of Algeria; a professional dancing girl in some N. African cities.

ouma /ˈəʊmə/ *noun. S. Afr.* E20.
[Afrikaans = grandmother, formed as OU *adjective* + *ma* mother.]
A grandmother; an elderly woman. Chiefly as a respectful or affectionate form of address or reference.

oumer *noun, verb* see UMBER *noun*[1], *verb*[1].

ounce /aʊns/ *noun*[1]. ME.
[Old French *unce* (mod. *once*) from Latin *uncia* twelfth part (cf. INCH *noun*[1]), from *unus* ONE *adjective*, prob. intended orig. to express a unit.]
1 A unit of weight of (*a*) (orig.) 1/12 of a pound in troy and apothecaries' measure, equal to 480 grains (approx. 31.1 grams), (*b*) 1/16 of a pound in avoirdupois measure (approx. 28.3 grams). ME.
2 *fig.* A small quantity. LME.
3 [Spanish *onza*.] A Spanish or Sicilian coin of varying value. *obsolete* exc. *Hist.* L18.

> 🕮 **1** ***fluid ounce***: see FLUID *adjective.* **2** J. P. DONLEAVY Can't get an ounce of work out of them these days.

■ **ouncer** *noun* (as 2nd elem. of comb.) a thing that weighs a specified number of ounces L19.

ounce /aʊns/ *noun*[2]. ME.
[Anglo-Norman = Old French *once, lonce* (the *l* of which was taken for the def. article) = Italian *lonza* from Latin *lync-*, LYNX.]
†**1** The Eurasian lynx; any of various other felids of moderate size, such as the Canadian lynx and the cheetah. ME–E19.
2 = ***snow leopard*** s.v. SNOW *noun*[1]. L18.

†**'ounds** *interjection.* L16–E18.
[Contr. of *wounds* in ***God's wounds*** s.v. GOD *noun* 5(h). Cf. ZOUNDS *interjection.*]
Expr. anger, surprise, etc.

oung /aʊŋ/ *verb trans. & intrans.* Also **aung**. E20.
[Burmese.]
In Myanmar (Burma) (of an elephant): move or transport (logs).

OUP *abbreviation.*
Oxford University Press.

oupa /ˈəʊpə/ *noun. S. Afr.* E20.
[Afrikaans = grandfather, formed as OU *adjective* + *pa* father.]
A grandfather; an elderly man. Chiefly as a respectful or affectionate form of address or reference.

ouph /aʊf/ *noun. literary.* E17.
[Alt. of OAF *noun*, perh. by scribal error.]
= OAF *noun.*
¶ First recorded in Shakes. First Folio.

our /aʊə/ *possess. pronoun & adjective* (in mod. usage also classed as a *determiner*), *1 pl.*
[Old English *ūre* genit. of WE *pronoun* = Old Frisian, Old Saxon *ūser*, Old High German *unsēr*, Old Norse *vár*, Gothic *unsara*. Cf. OURN, OURS.]
▶†**A** *pronoun.* **1** Genit. of WE *pronoun*; of us. OE–LME.
2 = OURS. OE–M17.
▶ **B** *attrib. adjective.* **1** Of us; which belongs or pertains to us or ourselves. OE. ▸**b** Of or pertaining to humanity or (orig., CHRISTIAN THEOLOGY) the body of Christians. OE.
2 Used by a monarch or ruler: = MY *possess. adjective.* Cf. WE *pronoun* 2a. ME.
3 Whom or which we have in mind; of whom or which we are speaking; of the writer, or the writer and his or her readers. Cf. WE *pronoun* 2b. E17.
4 (Before a personal name) that has a familial relationship with me, *esp.* that is my son, daughter, or sibling; (before a surname etc.) that belongs to the same company, organization, etc., as me. *colloq.* M19. ▸**b** In the speech of a doctor, nurse, etc.: the part of a patient's person that concerns him or her. *joc.* M19.

> 🕮 **1** I. MURDOCH It is our duty, yours and mine, to assist and protect her. **b** *Wilson Quarterly* We can only know reality through our minds. ***Our Father*** (*a*) the Lord's Prayer; (*b*) God. ***Our Lady***: see LADY *noun* 3. ***Our Lord***: see LORD *noun* 6. ***Our Saviour***: see SAVIOUR 2. **3** T. SHERIDAN The whole body of the works, not only of our author, but of . . other . . writers. *Early Music* Our knowledge of the early history of the orchestra is seriously muddled. **4** N. ROYDE-SMITH I sent up our Mr Wilkinson, who has lived in Russia. ***our kid***: see KID *noun*[1] 4d. **b** DICKENS Now, lets see . . how our ribs are?

-our /ə/ *suffix.*
1 Earlier form of -OR. Now chiefly in (the British spelling of) nouns whose spelling was not conformed to Latin in the Renaissance, as ***colour***, ***honour***, ***splendour***.
2 Forming nouns repr. various other endings of Old French or Germanic origin, as ***arbour***, ***behaviour***, ***endeavour***, ***harbour***, ***neighbour***, ***parlour***.

†**ouranography** *noun* var. of URANOGRAPHY.

†**ourebi** *noun* var. of ORIBI.

ouricury *noun* var. of URUCURI.

ourie /ˈaʊri, ˈuːri/ *adjective. Scot.* (formerly also *north.*). ME.
[Origin unkn.]
Shabby; dull; dreary, melancholy.

ourn /aʊən/ *possess. pronoun.* Long *obsolete* exc. *dial.* LME.
[from OUR *pronoun* after *my* and *mine, thy* and *thine*, etc.]
= OURS.
¶ See note s.v. OURS.

ouroboros *noun* var. of UROBOROS.

ours /ˈaʊəz/ *possess. pronoun.* ME.
[from OUR *pronoun* + -'S[1]. Cf. OURN.]
1 Our one(s); that or those belonging or pertaining to us; *spec.* our group, organization, regiment, or side. ME.
2 ***of ours***, belonging or pertaining to us. LME.

> 🕮 **1** E. WAUGH We cherish our friends not for their ability to amuse us but for ours to amuse them. W. OWEN They were not ours: We never heard to which front these were sent. **2** T. HARDY He is a great friend of ours—our best friend.

¶ Orig. northern.

ourself /aʊəˈsɛlf/ *pronoun.* See also OURSELVES. ME.
[from OUR *pronoun* + SELF *adjective* (but long interpreted as from OUR *adjective* + SELF *noun*).]
▶ **I** *refl.* **1** Refl. form (indirect, direct, & after prepositions) corresp. to the subjective pronoun *we*: (to, for, etc.) our particular group of people personally, us as individuals; (to, for, etc.) me, oneself personally. ME.

> 🕮 **1** *Times* The answer . . becomes evident the moment we immerse ourself in Eckhart's writings.

▶ **II** Orig. *emphatic.*
2 In apposition to the subjective pronoun *we* or (rarely) *us*: our particular group of people personally; myself, oneself personally. LME.
3 (Not appositional.) ▸**a** Subjective: we ourselves, I myself (now *arch.* & *rhet.*); (pred. after *be* & after *than, as*) us as individuals. LME. ▸**b** Objective: our particular group of people; myself, oneself. *arch.* E16.

> 🕮 **3a** TENNYSON Were you sick, ourself Would tend upon you. M. WARNOCK When we are telling our own story the central figure is, of course, ourself.

¶ Orig. treated as *pl.* (= OURSELVES), now chiefly *sing.*, corresp. to OUR *adjective* 3, 4. Used in place of *ourselves* esp. when *we* refers to an individual or is not definitely plural, as in royal pronouncements or newspaper editorials.

ourselves /aʊəˈsɛlvz/ *pronoun pl.* L15.
[from OURSELF + -S[1], or from OURSELVEN by suffix substitution.]
▶ **I** *refl.* **1** Refl. form (indirect, direct, & after prepositions) corresp. to the subjective pronoun *we*: (to, for, etc.) our particular group of people personally, us. L15.

> 🕮 **1** G. GREENE I wonder if we ought to involve ourselves any further. D. M. THOMAS There are things we are afraid to reveal even to ourselves.

▶ **II** Orig. *emphatic.*
2 In apposition to the subjective pronoun *we* or (rarely) *us*: our particular group of people personally. E16.
3 (Not appositional.) ▸**a** Subjective: we ourselves (now *arch.* & *rhet.*); (pred. after *be* & after *than, as*) us. L16. ▸**b** Objective: our particular group of people (*arch.* in emphatic use). L16.

> 🕮 **2** M. O. W. OLIPHANT When we are ourselves poor. *Times Educ. Suppl.* Targets and outcomes that we ourselves set. **3a** E. WAUGH 'There's only ourselves, Jo,' she said. **b** *Independent* Beliefs about ourselves are self-fulfilling.

Phrases: **be ourselves** (*a*) act in our normal unconstrained manner; (*b*) feel as well as we usually do (usu. in neg. contexts). **by ourselves** on our own.
■ Earlier †**ourselven** *pronoun pl.* [from OURSELF + -EN[3]]: only in ME.

oursin /ˈɔːsan, *foreign* ursɛ̃/ *noun.* E20.
[French.]
A sea urchin, *esp.* an edible one.

-ous /əs/ *suffix.*
[Old French *-os, -us, -ous* from Latin *-osus*. Cf. -OSE[1].]
1 Forming adjectives from or after French or Latin, with the sense 'having many or much, characterized by, of the nature of', as ***dangerous***, ***glorious***, ***murderous***, ***viscous***, etc. Also forming adjectives in same sense from other Latin adjectives, esp. in *-ax, -er, -ris, -us*, as ***capacious***, ***adulterous***, ***ferocious***, ***hilarious***, ***arduous***.
2 CHEMISTRY. Forming adjectives denoting a lower valence or degree of oxidation than those ending in ***-ic***, as ***cuprous***, ***manganous***.

ousel *noun* var. of OUZEL.

oust /aʊst/ *verb trans.* L16.
[Anglo-Norman *ouster* = Old French *oster* (mod. *ôter*) take away, remove from Latin *obstare* oppose, hinder, from *ob-* OB- + *stare* stand.]
1 LAW. Eject from a possession, deprive of an inheritance; = DISSEISE 1. (Foll. by *of*.) L16. ▸**b** Exclude or take away (a right, privilege, etc.). M17.
2 Eject or expel from a place or position; drive or turn out; displace, supersede. (Foll. by *from*.) M17.

> 🕮 **2** G. ORWELL English flower names . . are being ousted by Greek ones. *Scotland on Sunday* Mr Maclean may . . attempt to oust ministers who have already signed the deed of separation. P. MAILLOUX His sanguine indifference to . . efforts to oust him from his job.

ouster /ˈaʊstə/ *noun.* M16.
[Legal Anglo-Norman, use as noun of inf.: see prec., -ER[4].]
1 LAW. Ejection from a possession; deprivation of an inheritance. M16.
2 Dismissal, expulsion; the action of manoeuvring someone out of a place or position. Chiefly *N. Amer.* M20.

> 🕮 **2** *Illustrated Weekly of India* Expelled Marxist leader . . talks about his ouster from the party.

ouster-le-main /aʊstələˈmeɪn/ *noun.* L15.
[Anglo-Norman *ouster la main*, in medieval Latin *amovere manum* remove the hand: see prec.]
FEUDAL LAW. **1** (A judgement or writ granting) a legal delivery of land out of the monarch's hands on grounds that the monarch has no title to hold it. L15.
2 The delivery of lands out of a guardian's hands on a ward's coming of age. L15.

oustiti /ˈuːstɪti/ *noun.* M20.
[French OUISTITI.]
= OUTSIDER 4.

out /aʊt/ *noun.* L15.
[from OUT *adverb*.]
1 †**a** An exit. Only in L15. ▸**b** A means of escape; an excuse, a defence, an alibi. *slang.* E20.
†**2** Something one has or may run out of. Only in ***drink the three outs***, drink until one is out of wit, money, and alcohol, get very drunk. E–M17.
3 The outside; something external. E18.
4 a POLITICS. A member of a party which is out of office; a member of an official opposition party. Usu. in *pl.*, contrasted with *ins*. M18. ▸**b** In some games: a member of a side which is not actively playing but fielding. E19. ▸**c** A person who lacks money, popularity, status, etc. Usu. in *pl. colloq.* M20.
5 An excursion, an outing. *dial.* M18.
6 a PRINTING. An accidental omission; something omitted. L18. ▸**b** A defect, a disadvantage, a flaw. *colloq. & dial.* (chiefly *US*). L19.
7 An attempt, an undertaking; an achievement; progress, success. *colloq. & dial.* M19. ▸**b** BASEBALL. The action or an act of putting a player out. Chiefly *N. Amer.* M19.

> 🕮 **1b** C. BROWN It gave them an out, a reason for not doing it. **7b** R. ANGELL Tom Seaver . . came within two outs of a perfect game.

Phrases: **at outs** *colloq. & dial.* at variance or enmity (*with*). ***drink the three outs***: see sense 2 above. **from out to out** from one end to the other; in total external length or breadth. ***ins and outs***: see IN *noun* 1. **on the outs** = *at outs* above. ***outs and ins***: see IN *noun* 1.

out /aʊt/ *attrib. adjective.* ME.
[from OUT *adverb*.]
1 That is on the outside or external surface of anything; external, exterior. Now *rare.* ME.
2 Outlying; at a distance; situated on the outer edge. ME.
3 SPORT. Of a match: played away from one's home ground. L19.
4 Unfashionable. Opp. IN *adjective* 2. M20.
2 out island, **out isle**: situated away from the mainland.

out /aʊt/ *verb.*
[Old English *ūtian* = Old Frisian *utia*, Old High German *uzōn*. Perh. re-formed in Middle English.]
1 *verb trans.* **a** Expel, reject, or dismiss from or *from* a place, office, rank, etc.; deprive (*of* a possession). OE. ▸**b** Extinguish; blot out. E16. ▸**c** In a ball game, esp. tennis: send (the ball) outside the court or playing area. M19. ▸**d** Make unconscious; BOXING knock out, defeat, (an opponent); kill, esp. by a blow. *slang.* L19.
2 *verb intrans.* Be expelled or extinguished; go out. Usu. in *imper.* ME.
3 *verb trans.* Bring out; exhibit; disclose; utter. LME. ▸**b** Publicly reveal or expose the homosexuality of (a well-known person), esp. in order to promote a homosexual cause; *gen.* expose, publicly reveal. L20.
4 *verb intrans.* Of information, news, etc.: become known. LME.
5 *verb intrans.* Go out, esp. on a pleasure-trip. Cf. OUTING 3a. *colloq.* M19.

> 🕮 **1a** E. FITZGERALD My pictures . . are now got back to the Room they were outed from. E. WAUGH They had outed Asquith quite easily. **b** I. GURNEY Stars are routed And street lamps outed. **2** TENNYSON: O drunken ribaldry! Out, beast! . . begone! **3** S. MIDDLETON As soon as she'd outed the words, she began to cry. **4** W. WESTALL 'Murder will out.' They say so, because they have no idea how often murders don't out.

Phrases: **out with** (*a*) have out, bring out; disclose; ***out with it***, say what you are thinking or hesitating over; (*b*) expel, extinguish.

out /aʊt/ *adverb.*
[Old English *ūt* = Old Frisian, Old Saxon *ūt* (Dutch *uit*), Old High German *ūz* (German *aus*), Old Norse *út*, Gothic *ūt*, from Germanic adverb rel. to Sanskrit prefix *ud-* out.]
▸**I** Of motion or direction.
1 Expr. motion or direction from within (a space, as a room, building, dam, etc.) esp. to a point outside. OE. ▸**b** From among others; from those available; from one's company or surroundings. ME.
2 Expr. motion or direction away from oneself, a centre, a familiar place, the shore, etc., esp. to a remote point, to sea, to war, etc. Now also *spec.*, (of a boat, train, post, etc.) going out, departing. OE. ▸**b** From one's control or possession into that of others. LME.
3 Expr. movement, removal, exclusion, etc., from its or one's proper place or from one's or its position when in. OE. ▸**b** From an appropriate, normal, or equable state; into disharmony, disturbance, confusion, etc. M16.
4 From containment or quiet into action, accessibility, etc. OE.
5 a So as to extend or prolong (in space or time). ME. ▸**b** So as to project or protrude. M16.
6 To an end; completely, fully, thoroughly; to the utmost degree. ME. ▸**b** To an intelligible or explicit result or solution. M16.
7 So as to be heard or seen; aloud; visibly; openly; publicly. ME. ▸**b** Into public attention, circulation, knowledge, employment, etc. M16.
8 So as to be no longer alight or burning; into darkness. LME. ▸**b** From being in existence; from being fashionable or in season; into obsolescence. E16.

> 🕮 **1** T. HARDY Dorothy . . had gone out one day for an airing. I. MURDOCH The big hand-mirror which they had brought out . . onto the terrace. E. WELTY She saw him out . . then shut the door on him. **b** F. KITCHEN You could pick out the Lincolnshire 'fenners' by their . . bright blue cords. J. M. COETZEE The real war had come to Sea Point and found them out. **2** J. CONRAD We had very fine weather on our passage out. W. S. MAUGHAM His vitality was intense, shining out upon others. I. MURDOCH Powerful arms reached out towards me. R. INGALLS I just jumped on the first train out. **b** GOLDSMITH The officers appointed to dole out public charity. H. RASHDALL The Stationer's primary business was to let out books on hire to scholars. **3** THACKERAY Volunteering . . to have a tooth out. **b** HAZLITT Friends not unfrequently fall out and never meet again. A. BIRRELL Neither he nor any other sensible man puts himself out about new books. **4** H. T. BUCKLE The war that now broke out lasted seven years. **5a** S. BOWLES Looking out on the starry heavens. **b** W. MOTLEY Behind Ma's back Ang . . stuck out her tongue. **6** J. A. SYMONDS A procession of . . little girls dressed out in white. I. MURDOCH I felt that I must . . have it out with him. **b** *Independent* The book has 15 walks, each carefully thought out and delightfully described. **7** M. ARNOLD The stars came out. TENNYSON The old echoes . . Rang out like hollow woods at huntingtide. *Face* You came right out and said you were a virgin. **b** LD HOUGHTON My sister in town bringing out a young sister-in-law. *Bookman* Mr Hare's Autobiography . . is apparently not to come out this season. **8** T. HARDY These everlasting stars . . burn out like candles. **b** S. SMILES Nations that are idle and luxurious . . must inevitably die out.

▸**II** Of position.
9 Expr. position or situation beyond the bounds of or not inside (a space, as a room, building, dam, etc.). OE. ▸**b** Not included or inserted; omitted. Freq. in ***leave out***. LME. ▸**c** Impossible; unwanted, unacceptable, prohibited; out of place, irrelevant. M20.
10 Away or at a distance from oneself, a centre, a familiar place, the shore, etc.; *esp.* at sea, gone to war, etc.; *spec.* (of the tide) with the water lower and further away, (of a river etc.) flooding adjacent ground. OE. ▸**b** Not in one's possession or control; let, leased. L16.
11 On the outside; externally. OE.
12 Removed from one's or its place or from one's or its position when in; displaced, dislocated, extracted. ME. ▸**b** No longer in prison. ME. ▸**c** Abroad, away from home. E17. ▸**d** Not in office; removed from a post. Also, out of work, unemployed; on strike. E17. ▸**e** In some games: no longer in play, dismissed or excluded from play; *esp.* (CRICKET & BASEBALL etc.) dismissed from batting, not batting but fielding. Also as *interjection*, notifying the dismissal of a player. E17.
13 No longer burning or alight; extinguished. ME. ▸**b** Finished, at an end, exhausted; expired, elapsed. Also, out of stock of a particular thing. ME. ▸**c** No longer in fashion; not in season; obsolete. M17. ▸**d** Unconscious; *spec.* (BOXING) defeated through failing to rise within ten seconds of being knocked down. Also as *interjection*, notifying the defeat of a boxer in this situation. L19. ▸**e** No longer functioning, inoperative; unusable. M20.
14 In existence. LME. ▸**b** Manifest, apparent; displayed; disclosed; in the open; *spec.* (of (a part of) a plant) unfolded, in leaf or flower. L16. ▸**c** Introduced to the public or into society; in the public realm. E17. ▸**d** Openly acknowledging one's homosexuality or bisexuality. Cf. ***come out of the closet*** s.v. CLOSET *noun & adjective. colloq.* L20.
15 a Projecting, protruding. M16. ▸**b** Extended, displayed, unfurled. E18.
16 Astray from what is appropriate, correct, or right; in disharmony, disturbance, confusion, etc.; in error, mistaken; at variance. Formerly also, at a loss, puzzled, nonplussed. M16. ▸**b** Out of pocket; minus (a sum). M17.

> 🕮 **9** M. SINCLAIR She dared not light her candle out there in the passage. G. GREENE The dustbins were all out. *Word Study* Many English teachers . . issue pronouncements, both in the classroom and out. **c** *Woman's Own* Crying, she decided, was not going to help . . . From then on, tears were out. **10** *Columbus (Montana) News* Annin remained publisher . . with two years out during active service. V. WOOLF There was a hurricane out at sea. P. MONETTE There were people out there who knew more than anyone told us. **12** SHAKES. *Macb.* When the brains were out the man would die. **d** G. MEREDITH His party was out and he hoped for higher station on its return to power. *National Observer (US)* Help . . to keep him in funds when he is out on strike. **13b** G. ALLEN Before the week was out, he had been duly installed. J. McCLURE Got a smoke? I'm out. **c** CLIVE JAMES Some cafés are in and others are out. **d** R. SILVERBERG Alleluia was out cold: they had had to hit her with an anaesthetic dart. **e** H. ROOSENBURG There is only one place where the rivers can be crossed . . the other bridges are out. **14** *Times* A Triumph is still the best bike out. **b** TOLKIEN The stars were out in a dark sky. R. WEST The second lilac in that row . . is almost out. **c** LD HOUGHTON Wordsworth's new poem will be out next week. W. H. AUDEN At last the secret is out. **16** *Daily Colonist* 'My watch must be out', and so you are late. B. MAGEE A clearcut statement which is slightly out is more serviceable than one which is . . vague. *Rolling Stone* Westinghouse and General Electric are out more than $500 million apiece.

▸**III 17** As *interjection.* Expr. lamentation, reproach, abhorrence, etc. Freq. in ***out upon it***, ***out upon you***, ***out upon him***, etc. *arch.* or *dial.* LME.
Phrases: (A selection of cross-refs. only is included.) ALL OUT. ***day in, day out***: see IN *adverb*. ***keep an eye out***, ***keep one's eye(s) out***: see EYE *noun*. **from here on out**, **from there on out**, **from this out** *colloq.* henceforth, from now on. **not out** CRICKET (of a side or a batsman) not having been caught, bowled, etc., out. ***out and about***: see ABOUT *adverb* 2b. ***out and away***: see AWAY *adverb* 2. OUT AND OUT. ***out at elbows***: see ELBOW *noun*. ***out at heels***: see HEEL *noun*[1]. **out for** having one's interest or effort directed to; intent on. ***out for the count***: see COUNT *noun*[1] 1b. OUT OF. **out there** *colloq.* (*a*) *Hist.* in the war of 1914–18, at the Western Front or in France; (*b*) in the world outside. **out to** keenly striving to *do*; intent on. ***out to lunch***: see LUNCH *noun* 2. ***over and out***: see OVER *adverb*. ***take it out on a person***: see TAKE *verb*. ***week in, week out***, ***year in, year out***: see IN *adverb*.

out /aʊt/ *preposition.* ME.
[Ellipt. for OUT OF.]
1 From within, out of, away from. ME.
2 Outside, beyond (the limits of); out of. Now *arch.* or *dial.* ME.
†**3** Without, lacking. *rare.* LME–L16.

> 🕮 **1** P. KAVANAGH He stared out the window at the hills beyond. *New Yorker* Out the back of the machine . . ran a huge block cable. **2** W. D. HOWELLS Its history . . could not be known out the family.

out- /aʊt/ *combining form.*
[Repr. OUT *adverb, preposition, adjective*.]
Forming combs. with verbs, nouns, adjectives, & adverbs in various relations and with various senses, esp. indicating (*a*) position outside, external to, away from, or beyond, as **outboard**, **outdoor**, **outline**, **out-patient**, etc.; (*b*) motion or direction out of or outward, as **outburst**, **outgoing**, **outlet**, etc.; (*c*) completion, completeness, thoroughness, as **outcome**, **outfit**, etc.; (*d*) surpassing, exceeding, overcoming, or outdoing, as **outlast**, **outlive**, **outnumber**, **outrun**, etc.

■ **out'act** *verb trans.* surpass in acting or performing; excel, outdo: M17. **out'argue** *verb trans.* defeat in argument M18. **out'arm** *verb trans.* exceed in possession or acquisition of weapons; provide (oneself) with more arms than a competitor: M20. **out-'ask** *verb trans.* †(*a*) ask in excess of; (*b*) *dial.* proclaim the marriage banns of (a couple) for the final time: M17. **out'balance** *verb trans.* outweigh; exceed in effect, importance, etc.: M17. **out-basket** *noun* (a basket used as) an out-tray M20. **out'bawl** *verb trans.* outdo in bawling or shouting M17. **out'bear** *verb trans.* (*a*) *poet.* carry out or away; †(*b*) endure; (*c*) NAUTICAL = OUTCARRY (b): ME. **out'bellow** *verb trans.* (*a*) bellow louder than; (*b*) overcome by bellowing: E17. **outbent** *adjective* bent out or outwards E17. **outbirth** *noun* a product, a progeny M17. **out'blaze** *verb* (*a*) *verb intrans.* blaze or burst out; (*b*) *verb trans.* obscure by a brighter blaze; outshine: E18. **out'bloom** *verb trans.* surpass in bloom M18. **out'blossom** *verb trans.* = OUTBLOOM L17. **out'blossoming** *noun* the act of blossoming out; a flowering: E20. **out'blot** *verb trans.*

(*poet.*) blot out M16. **out'blush** *verb trans.* outdo in blushing; surpass in rosy colour: M17. **outbound** *adjective* outward-bound L16. †**out-bounds** *noun pl.* the extreme boundaries or limits M16–L17. **out'brag** *verb trans.* (*a*) outdo in bragging; (*b*) (*rare*, Shakes.) surpass in beauty: M16. **out'branch** *verb intrans.* (*rare*) branch out, ramify M19. **out'brave** *verb trans.* (*a*) face with defiance; (*b*) outdo, surpass, esp. in bravery or splendour: L16. **out'brazen** *verb trans.* (*a*) brazen out; face defiantly; (*b*) surpass in brazenness: L17. **out'breathe** *verb trans.* & (*rare*) *intrans.* (now *poet.*) exhale or be exhaled M16. **outbreathed** /-ˈbriːðd/ *adjective*[1] breathed out L16. **outbreathed** /-ˈbrɛθt/ *adjective*[2] put out of breath L16. **out'build** *verb trans.* (*a*) surpass in (durability of) building; (*b*) *poet.* build out: M18. **out'burn** *verb* (*a*) *verb intrans.* (*rare*, Shakes.) burn out or away, be consumed; (*b*) *verb trans.* burn longer than: L16. **out'buy** *verb trans.* †(*a*) ransom, buy out or off; (*b*) outdo in buying, buy more than: ME. **out-'by** *adverb & adjective* (*Scot. & north.*) (*a*) *adverb* (to the) outside; (*b*) *adjective* a short distance away or out; outside, in the open: LME. **outcall** *noun* a visit made to a client in his (or her) own home by a prostitute L20. **outcamp** *noun* (chiefly *N. Amer.*) a camp at some distance from a main camp: M19. **out'cant** *verb trans.* surpass or excel in using cant M17. **out'carry** *verb trans.* †(*a*) carry out, accomplish; (*b*) NAUTICAL carry more sail than; outsail: M16. **outcaste** *noun & adjective* (a person who is) outside or put out of his or her caste, (a person) without a caste: L19. **out'caste** *verb trans.* deprive (a person) of his or her caste: M19. **out'charm** *verb trans.* charm better than E18. **out'climb** *verb trans.* outdo in climbing; climb or ascend beyond: E17. **out-college** *adjective* (of a college member) not living in college M19. **outcom'pete** *verb trans.* surpass, excel, or outdo in competition; overpower or defeat: L19. **out'countenance** *verb trans.* (long *arch.*) put out of countenance, outface L16. **out-county** *adjective* coming from or situated outside a particular county M20. †**outcrafty** *verb trans.* (*rare*, Shakes.) outwit: only in E17. **out-cricket** *noun* (CRICKET) bowling and fielding as opp. to batting L19. **out-cue** *noun* (BROADCASTING) a cue indicating or announcing the end of a particular recording or transmission M20. †**outcut** *verb trans.* cut out or away, excise M17–M19. **out'dance** *verb trans.* surpass in dancing M17. **out'dare** *verb trans.* (now *rare*) (*a*) overcome by daring, defy; (*b*) surpass in daring: L16. **out'date** *verb trans.* make out of date or obsolete M17. **out'dated** *adjective* out of date; obsolete; antiquated: E17. **out'datedness** *noun* the state of being outdated M20. **out'dazzle** *verb trans.* outshine E18. **out'distance** *verb trans.* leave (a competitor) far behind; outstrip: M19. **outdraught** *noun* an outward draught or current, esp. of air M19. **out'dream** *verb trans.* (*rare*) †(*a*) expel by dreams; (*b*) dream to an end: E17. **out'dress** *verb trans.* dress more finely than L18. **out'drink** *verb trans.* outdo in drinking, drink more than LME. †**outdwell** *verb trans.* (*rare*, Shakes.) stay beyond (a time): only in L16. **outdweller** *noun* a person who lives outside or away from a certain place LME. **out'eat** *verb trans.* (*a*) outdo in eating, eat more than; †(*b*) erode, eat away: M16. **outfall** *noun* (*a*) an outlet, esp. the mouth of a river; (*b*) (long *rare* or *obsolete*) a sally, a sortie; (*c*) *Scot. & north.* a quarrel: E17. **out'fast** *verb trans.* outdo in fasting, fast longer than M17. **out'fight** *verb trans.* †(*a*) take by assault, conquer; (*b*) fight better than, beat in a fight: LME. **outfighting** *noun* fighting that is not at close quarters M19. **outflame** *noun* a fiery outburst L19. **out'flame** *verb* (*poet.*) (*a*) *verb trans.* surpass in fieriness; (*b*) *verb intrans.* burst into flame or brilliancy: M19. **outflash** *noun* (chiefly *fig.*) an act of flashing out M19. **out'flash** *verb* (*a*) *verb trans.* outshine; (*b*) *verb intrans.* flash out: M19. **out'fling** *verb trans. & intrans.* (*poet.*) fling (oneself) out LME. **out'flourish** *verb trans.* (*a*) unsheath and flourish (a weapon); (*b*) flourish longer than: L16. **outflush** *noun* an outward movement like that of blood flushing the face M19. **out'fly** *verb* (*a*) *verb intrans.* (*poet.*) fly out; (*b*) *verb trans.* outstrip or surpass in flying: ME. **out'fool** *verb trans.* outdo in folly or fooling M17. **out'foot** *verb trans.* outpace, outstrip M18. **outfort** *noun* an outlying fort E17. **out'fox** *verb trans.* outdo in cunning, outwit M20. **out'front** *verb trans.* confront, face M17. **out'frown** *verb trans.* outdo in frowning; prevail over by frowning: E17. **out'gallop** *verb trans.* outstrip in galloping E17. **out'general** *verb trans.* outdo in generalship; get the better of by superior strategy or tactics: M18. **out'give** *verb* (*a*) *verb intrans.* & †*trans.* give out; (*b*) *verb trans.* give more than: L15. **outgiving** *noun & adjective* (*a*) *noun* the action or fact of giving something out; a thing which is given out; in *pl.*, payments; (*b*) *adjective* generous, open-hearted: M16. **out'glare** *verb trans.* outdo in dazzling effect; be more glaring or flagrant than: M17. **out'glitter** *verb trans.* surpass in glitter or splendour M17. **out'glow** *verb trans.* glow more brightly than L19. **out'gross** *verb trans.* surpass (another film, project, etc.) in gross takings or profit M20. **out-guard** *noun* a guard placed at a distance from the main body of an army; an advanced guard: E17. **out'guess** *verb trans.* outwit by guessing more shrewdly; anticipate the actions etc. of (a person): E20. **out'gun** *verb trans.* (*a*) be more heavily armed than, surpass in power or strength; (*b*) shoot better than: L17. **outgush** *noun* the act of gushing out; a sudden strong outflow: M19. **out'gush** *verb intrans.* gush out M16. **out-half** *noun* (RUGBY FOOTBALL) a fly-half M20. **out'hector** *verb trans.* outdo in hectoring; bully, intimidate: L17. **out'hold** *verb trans.* (*rare*) †(*a*) hold out, extend; †(*b*) hold back; withstand; (*c*) continue to hold: LME. **out'howl** *verb trans.* outdo in howling; howl louder than: M17. **out'humour** *verb trans.* (*rare*) †(*a*) disrupt the humour or mood of; (*b*) outdo in humour: E17. **outjet** *noun* a part that juts out, a projection M18. **out'jockey** *verb trans.* outwit by cunning E18. **out'juggle** *verb trans.* outdo in juggling E17. **out'jump** *verb trans.* surpass in jumping M17. **out'jut** *verb intrans.* jut out, project E17. **out'kick** *verb trans.* (*rare*) (*a*) outdo in kicking; (*b*) dismiss: L18. **out'labour** *verb trans.* surpass in labour or endurance M17. **out'last** *verb trans.* last longer than or beyond; survive: L16. **out'laugh** *verb trans.* †(*a*) deride, ridicule; (*b*) outdo in laughing: L15. **outleap** *noun* an act of leaping out; an escape, a sally; *fig.* an outburst: ME. **out'leap** *verb* (*a*) *verb trans.* leap over or beyond; surpass or excel in leaping; (*b*) *verb intrans.* (*poet.*) leap out or forth: E17. **out'lie** *verb*[1] (*rare*) (*a*) *verb intrans.* lie out in the open air, camp out; (*b*) *verb trans.* lie beyond or on the outside of: E19. **out'lie** *verb*[2] *trans.* outdo in telling lies L16. **out-lot** *noun* (*US*, *obsolete* exc. *Hist.*) a plot of ground outside a town or other area M17. **out'love** *verb trans.* outdo in loving E17. **out'lung** *verb trans.* (*rare*) surpass in lung-power, outshout M18. **out'lustre** *verb trans.* surpass in lustre, outshine E17. †**outmaking** *noun* the discernment of meaning L17–E18. †**outman** *noun* a person who lives or works outside an area; an outsider: L15–L19. **out'man** *verb trans.* (*a*) outnumber; (*b*) surpass in manly qualities: L17. **outmarch** *noun* an outward march on an expedition, an advance M19. **out'march** *verb trans.* outdo or outstrip in marching M17. **out'master** *verb trans.* overcome in a struggle for mastery L18. **out'match** *verb trans.* be more than a match for (an adversary etc.); surpass: E17. **out'measure** *verb trans.* exceed in quantity or extent M17. **outmigrant** *noun* a person who has migrated from one place to another, esp. in the same country M20. **outmigration** *noun* the action of migrating from one place to another, esp. in the same country M20. †**out-mouth** *noun* a projecting mouth M17–M18. **out'mouth** *verb trans.* speak more loudly than; outdo in boasting: E17. †**outmove** *verb trans.* surpass in moving; defeat by a move, as in chess: M17–L19. **out'muscle** *verb trans.* dominate or defeat by virtue of superior strength or force L20. **out'noise** *verb trans.* make more noise than M17. **out'number** *verb trans.* exceed in number L16. **out'paint** *verb trans.* outdo in painting L17. **out'peep** *verb intrans.* (*poet.*) peep out E17. **out-pension** *noun* a pension paid by a residential institution to a person not required to live in it E18. **out-pensioner** *noun* a person receiving an out-pension E18. **out'plan** *verb trans.* outdo in planning L18. **out'plot** *verb trans.* outmanoeuvre L17. **out'pocketing** *noun* (BIOLOGY) an outward movement of part of a surface to form a protruding pocket-like cavity; the cavity so formed: E20. **out'poise** *verb trans.* outweigh M17. **out'poll** *verb trans.* receive more votes than (an opponent) E18. **outpo'sition** *verb trans.* gain a positional advantage over (an opponent), esp. on a sports field E20. **out'power** *verb trans.* exceed in power or strength, now esp. in a sport or game M17. **out'pray** *verb* †(*a*) *verb intrans.* pray vehemently; (*b*) *verb trans.* outdo in praying: LME. **out'preach** *verb trans.* (*a*) outdo in preaching, preach more or better than; (*b*) put out of existence by preaching: M17. †**outprize** *verb trans.* exceed in value or estimation E17–M19. **out'promise** *verb trans.* outdo in promising L17. **out'punch** *verb trans.* (BOXING) surpass (an opponent) in punching ability M20. **outquarter** *noun* a military station away from a regiment's headquarters (usu. in *pl.*) M17. †**outquench** *verb trans.* extinguish: only in 16. **outquencher** *noun* (*Hist.*) = SNUFFER *noun*[1] M16. **out'race** *verb trans.* outrun, outstrip M17. **out'rail** *verb* †(*a*) *verb intrans.* rail at a person; (*b*) *verb trans.* outdo in railing: M17. **out'range** *verb trans.* (of a firearm) exceed in range M19. **out'rank** *verb trans.* be superior in rank to; take priority over: M19. **out'rant** *verb trans.* exceed in ranting M17. **out'rate** *verb trans.* (orig. *Scot.*) surpass, outdo, esp. in ratings, points scored, etc. L19. **out'read** *verb trans.* †(*a*) read to the end of; (*b*) outdo in reading, read more than: E17. **out'reason** *verb trans.* overcome by reasoning or argument M17. **out'reckon** *verb trans.* †(*a*) exceed in reckoning; (*b*) *rare* overestimate: E17. **out'reign** *verb* †(*a*) *verb intrans.* reign longer than all others; (*b*) *verb trans.* reign longer than or beyond: LME. †**out-rent** *noun* rent paid out L15–L18. **out'roll** *verb trans.* roll out, unroll, unfurl L16. **outroom** *noun* an outlying room; an outbuilding: E17. **out'row** *verb trans.* outdo or outstrip in rowing M16. **out'sail** *verb trans.* sail faster or better than; *fig.* outstrip, surpass: E17. **out'scold** *verb trans.* get the better of in scolding L16. **out'score** *verb trans.* score more than in a game M20. **out'search** *verb trans.* (*rare*) search out; explore: E16. **out'see** *verb trans.* (*a*) surpass in sight or insight; (*b*) see beyond: E17. **outsettlement** *noun* an outlying or remote settlement M18. **outsettler** *noun* (*a*) a settler outside a district or in its outlying parts; (*b*) an emigrant: M18. **out'shame** *verb trans.* outdo in shamefulness; put to shame: M17. **out'shop** *verb trans.* send (a vehicle) out from a workshop or factory as a newly finished product M20. **out'shout** *verb trans.* shout louder than M17. **out'shove** *verb trans.* shove harder or more effectively than M20. **out'shrill** *verb trans.* (*poet.*) make a shriller noise than, exceed in shrillness E17. **out'sin** *verb trans.* (now *rare* or *obsolete*) (*a*) sin more than; (*b*) forfeit or exhaust (the grace of God etc.) by sinning: E17. **out'sing** *verb trans.* outdo or excel in singing E17. **out'sit** *verb trans.* sit beyond the time or duration of (something); sit longer than (another person): M17. **out'sleep** *verb trans.* sleep through or beyond; sleep longer than: L16. **out'soar** *verb trans.* (*poet.*, chiefly *fig.*) soar higher than; rise above or beyond: L17. **outsole** *noun* the outer sole of a boot or shoe, esp. a sports shoe L19. **outsource** *verb trans.* (COMMERCE, chiefly *N. Amer.*) obtain (goods etc.) by contract from an outside source; contract (work) out: L20. **outsourcing** *noun* (COMMERCE, chiefly *N. Amer.*) the obtaining of goods or contracting of work from sources outside a company or area L20. **out'sparkle** *verb trans.* outdo in sparkling; sparkle more than: M17. **out'speed** *verb trans.* surpass in speed; move, run, etc., faster than: M17. **out'spend** *verb trans.* (*a*) exhaust or use up (a resource etc.); (*b*) spend more than: LME. **out'spin** *verb* †(*a*) *verb intrans.* (*rare*, Spenser) gush out; (*b*) *verb trans.* spin out (a thread etc.): L16. **out'stare** *verb trans.* stare longer or harder than; abash by staring: L16. **out'stay** *verb trans.* (*a*) stay beyond the limit of; overstay (*outstay one's welcome*: see WELCOME *noun*[2] 1); (*b*) stay or endure longer than: E17. **out'steal** *verb trans.* & †*intrans.* (*poet.*) steal or slip away (from) furtively ME. **out'stink** *verb trans.* smell or stink more than E17. **out'strain** *verb trans.* (*poet.*) strain or stretch out tightly L16. **out'stream** *verb intrans.* (*poet.*) stream or flow out ME. **out'stride** *verb trans.* (*literary*) overtake by striding; exceed in length of stride: E17. **out'strike** *verb trans.* (*poet.*) †(*a*) strike out (writing etc.); (*b*) strike more or heavier blows than: LME. **out'strip** *verb*[1] *trans.* (*a*) pass in running etc.; outrun; (*b*) *fig.* surpass in competition; exceed in comparison with: L16. **out'strip** *verb*[2] *trans.* (*joc.*) outdo in stripping; wear or be reduced to less clothing than: L19. **out'swagger** *verb trans.* outdo in swaggering E17. **out'swear** *verb trans.* outdo in swearing; overcome or defeat by swearing: L16. **out'sweeten** *verb trans.* (*poet.*) surpass in sweetness E17. **out'swell** *verb trans.* (*a*) swell out more than; (*b*) swell beyond (a limit etc.): E17. **out'swim** *verb trans.* swim faster or further than E17. **out-'talk** *verb trans.* outdo in talking; overwhelm by talking: L16. **out-'tell** *verb trans.* (*rare*) tell about; express, declare: LME. **out-'think** *verb trans.* (*a*) *rare* devise by thinking; (*b*) outwit; think one's way out of: LME. **out-'thunder** *verb trans.* thunder louder than E17. **out-'toil** *verb trans.* †(*a*) exhaust with toil; (*b*) toil harder or longer than: E17. **out-'tongue** *verb trans.* (*poet.*) †(*a*) silence (a person, speech, etc.); (*b*) surpass in power of speech or eloquence: E17. **out-'top** *verb trans.* rise above; surmount: E17. **out-'trade** *verb trans.* surpass or outdo in trading L17. **out-'travel** *verb trans.* travel beyond or further than; travel faster than: E17. **out-tray** *noun* a tray for outgoing documents in an office M20. **out-'trick** *verb trans.* surpass in or defeat by trickery L17. **out-'trot** *verb trans.* excel in or overtake by trotting M16. **out-'trump** *verb trans.* (chiefly *fig.*) outdo in or defeat by trumping at cards E19. **out'value** *verb trans.* surpass in value E17. **out'vie** *verb trans.* (now *rare*) outdo in competition or rivalry L16. **out'villain** *verb trans.* (*rare*) surpass in villainy E17. **out'voice** *verb trans.* (now *rare*) speak louder than; make a louder noise than: L16. **out'vote** *verb trans.* obtain more votes than; defeat (as) by a majority of votes: M17. **out-vote** *noun* (*Hist.*) the vote of an out-voter; such votes collectively: L18. **out-voter** *noun* (*Hist.*) in the UK, a non-resident qualified to vote in a parliamentary constituency by holding property there M19. **out'wait** *verb trans.* wait longer than E17. **outwale** *noun* (now *Scot. & dial.*) (*a*) the rejected part of something; refuse, dregs; (*b*) an outcast: LME. **out'walk** *verb trans.* (*a*) walk faster or further than (another person); (*b*) walk beyond (a point etc.): E17. †**outwander** *verb intrans.* (chiefly *poet.*) wander out or away ME–E20. †**out-ward** *verb trans.* (*rare*, Spenser) ward off: only in L16. **out'watch** *verb trans.* watch beyond or longer than; watch (an object) until it disappears: E17. **out'weary** *verb trans.* (*poet.*) exhaust in endurance E17. **out'weep** *verb trans.* (*a*) *poet.* expel by weeping; (*b*) surpass in weeping: L16. **out'weigh** *verb trans.* (*a*) exceed in weight; (*b*) exceed in value, importance, or influence: M16. **out'well** *verb intrans.* pour out, flow ME. †**out-win** *verb trans. & intrans.* (*rare*) get out (of) ME–L16. †**outwind** *verb*[1] (*rare*, *poet.*) (*a*) *verb intrans.* become unwound; (*b*) *verb trans.* disentangle, extricate: M16–M17. **outwind** /-ˈwɪnd/ *verb*[2] *trans.* put out of wind or breath E18. †**outwind** *noun* a wind blowing inshore L17–M18. **out'wing** *verb trans.* (*a*) MILITARY outflank; (*b*) *poet.* fly beyond or faster than: M17. **out'winter** *verb trans.* keep (an animal) outside in winter M20. **outwood** *noun* (*Hist.*) (*a*) a wood outside a castle, park, etc.; (*b*) the outer border of a wood or forest: LME. **outworld** *noun* (*literary*) the external or outside world M17. †**outwrest** *verb trans.* (*poet.*) draw out by force L16–M17. **out'wrestle** *verb* †(*a*) *verb intrans.* (*rare*) escape by wrestling; (*b*) *verb trans.* defeat in wrestling; wrestle better than: M16. **out'write** *verb trans.* †(*a*) write out (a story etc.); (*b*) surpass in writing; (*c*) get over (a feeling) by writing: LME. **out'yell** *verb* †(*a*) *verb intrans.* yell out; (*b*) *verb trans.* yell louder than: L16. **out'yield** *verb trans.* yield or produce more than E20.

outa /ˈaʊtə/ *preposition. colloq.* (orig. *US*). L19.
[Repr. a pronunc.]
= OUT OF.

outage /ˈaʊtɪdʒ/ *noun.* Orig. & chiefly *N. Amer.* E20.
[from OUT *adverb* + -AGE.]
A period during which an (esp. electrical) apparatus is not operating; a power cut or failure.

out and out /aʊt (ə)nd ˈaʊt/ *adverbial & adjectival phr.* Also (the usual form as adjective) **out-and-out**. ME.
[from OUT *adverb* + AND *conjunction*[1] + OUT *adverb*.]
▶ **A** *adverb.* Thoroughly, completely, entirely. ME.
▶ **B** *adjective.* Complete; thorough; unqualified. E19.
■ **out-and-'outer** *noun* (*slang*) a person who possesses some quality thoroughly or absolutely; an enthusiast, an extremist: E19.

outasight /aʊtəˈsʌɪt/ *adjective. colloq.* L19.
[Contr. Cf. OUTA, SIGHT *noun*.]
= OUT OF SIGHT *adjectival phr.*

outback /ˈaʊtbak/ *adverb, adjective, & noun.* Chiefly *Austral. & NZ.* M19.
[from OUT- + BACK *adverb*.]
▶ **A** *adverb.* **1** In or to the (Australian) outback. M19.
2 (**out back.**) Outside at the back of a house etc.; in or into a back garden or back yard. Chiefly *N. Amer.* L19.
▶ **B** *adjective.* Of, pertaining to, or characteristic of the (Australian) outback. L19.
▶ **C** *noun.* **1** The remote, uncultivated, and usu. uninhabited inland districts of Australia. L19.
2 *transf.* Any remote or sparsely populated region. M20.
■ **outbacker** *noun* a native or inhabitant of the outback E20. **outbackery** *noun* (the cultivation of) attitudes and values characteristic of the outback M20.

outbid /aʊtˈbɪd/ *verb trans.* Infl. **-dd-**. Pa. t. & pple **-bid**. L16.
[from OUT- + BID *verb*.]
1 Outdo in bidding; offer a higher price than. L16.
2 *fig.* Offer or provide more than; outdo or surpass in any quality, action, etc. L16.
†**3** Overestimate, overrate. L17–E18.

> 🕮 **2** *Sounds* Blackfoot are packing the Marquee but Charles F easily outbids them in the . . rock stakes.

outboard /ˈaʊtbɔːd/ *adjective, adverb, & noun.* E19.
[from OUT- + BOARD *noun*.]
Orig. & chiefly NAUTICAL. ▶ **A** *adjective.* **1** Esp. of a motor: portable and situated on the outside or away from the centre of a boat, aircraft, etc. Also, (of a boat etc.) having such a motor. E19.
2 Of a piece of electronic equipment: separate from the device with which it is used, peripheral to a main device. L20.
▶ **B** *adverb.* Outward from, outside, or away from the centre or side of a boat, aircraft, etc. M19.

> 🕮 *Which Motorcaravan* The door mirrors were . . not positioned far enough outboard. *transf.*: *Pilots International* A position about 1 ft outboard of the left fuel selector.

▶ **C** *noun.* (A boat equipped with) an outboard motor. M20.

outbreak /ˈaʊtbreɪk/ *noun*. E17.
[from OUT- + BREAK *noun*¹.]
1 A sudden occurrence; an eruption; an outburst (of emotion, action, energy, disease, etc.). E17.
2 GEOLOGY. An outcrop of a stratum; an intrusive mass of igneous rock. M18.

> 📖 **1** R. BERTHOUD Thanks to the outbreak of war, the . . visit did not take place till 1946. *Holiday Which?* Problems that could lead to an outbreak of infection.

outbreak /aʊtˈbreɪk/ *verb intrans*. Now chiefly *poet*. Pa. t. **-broke** /-ˈbrəʊk/; pa. pple **-broken** /-ˈbrəʊk(ə)n/. OE.
[from OUT- + BREAK *verb*.]
Break or burst out.

outbreed /ˈaʊtbriːd, *in sense* 2 aʊtˈbriːd/ *verb*. Pa. t. & pple **-bred** /-brɛd/. E20.
[from OUT- + BREED *verb*.]
1 *verb trans. & intrans.* Breed from parents not closely related. E20.
2 *verb trans.* Be quicker or more prolific in breeding than. E20.
■ **ˈoutbreeder** *noun* a plant which is not self-fertile; an animal in which breeding pairs are not closely related: M20.

outbroke, **outbroken** *verbs pa. t. & pple* of OUTBREAK *verb*.

outbuilding /ˈaʊtbɪldɪŋ/ *noun*. E17.
[from OUT- + BUILDING *noun*.]
A detached building, esp. a shed, barn, garage, etc., within the grounds of a main building.

outburst /ˈaʊtbəːst/ *noun*. M17.
[from OUT- + BURST *noun*.]
1 An act of bursting out; a (violent) eruption; an outbreak or explosion of emotion, speech, action, etc. M17. ▸**b** ASTRONOMY. An intense solar radio emission of several minutes' duration which occurs in conjunction with a solar flare. M20.
2 GEOLOGY. An outcrop of a stratum, esp. a coal seam. Now *rare* or *obsolete*. E18.

> 📖 **1** *Nature* A new outburst of activity which culminated . . with Gödel's incompleteness theorem. S. HASTINGS Victor Cunard . . retaliating with a furious outburst. J. UGLOW Marian responded to this warm feminist outburst.

outburst /aʊtˈbəːst/ *verb intrans. rare*. Pa. t. & pple **-burst**. LME.
[from OUT- + BURST *verb*.]
Burst out.

outcast /ˈaʊtkɑːst/ *noun*¹. ME.
[Use as noun of OUTCAST *adjective*.]
An outcast person or thing. Now *esp.* an exile, a vagabond.

outcast /ˈaʊtkɑːst/ *noun*². E17.
[from OUT- + CAST *noun*¹.]
1 The act of casting or throwing out. *rare*. E17.
2 A falling out, a quarrel. *Scot.* E17.

outcast /ˈaʊtkɑːst/ *adjective*. ME.
[from OUT- + CAST *ppl adjective*.]
Rejected, despised, discarded; homeless; banished, forsaken.

outcast /aʊtˈkɑːst/ *verb trans*. Now *rare* or *poet*. Pa. t. & pple **-cast**. ME.
[from OUT- + CAST *verb*.]
Cast out.
■ **ˈoutcasting** *noun* †(*a*) something which is thrown away or rejected; (*b*) the action of casting out; ejection, expulsion: ME.

outclass /aʊtˈklɑːs/ *verb trans*. L19.
[from OUT- + CLASS *noun*.]
Be or become of a higher quality or class than; defeat easily.

> 📖 W. S. CHURCHILL Outclassed and left behind at the very beginning of the race. D. ARKELL This second garden-party . . was a truly grand affair, quite out-classing Clarrie's.

outcome /ˈaʊtkʌm/ *noun*. ME.
[from OUT- + COME *verb*.]
1 The action or fact of coming out. *obsolete* exc. *dial*. ME. ▸**b** Lengthening or prolongation, esp. of the days of spring and summer. *Scot.* E18.
2 A (visible or practical) result, effect, or product; *spec.* (MEDICINE) the result or effect of treatment. L18.

> 📖 **2** P. VAN SOMMERS There have been some disputes about the outcome of Schachter's original experiment. S. QUINN With . . birth control unreliable, pregnancy was a likely outcome.

outcoming /ˈaʊtkʌmɪŋ/ *noun*. ME.
[from OUT- + COMING *noun*.]
†**1** A coming out or forth; a place of issue or emergence. ME–M16.
2 An event; a result, a product. ME. ▸**b** Emanation. M19.

outcrier /ˈaʊtkrʌɪə/ *noun*. Now *rare*. M16.
[from OUT- + CRIER.]
A person who cries out, a person who raises an outcry.

outcrop /ˈaʊtkrɒp/ *noun & verb*. E19.
[from OUT- + CROP *noun*.]
▶ **A** *noun*. **1** GEOLOGY & MINING. A part of a rock stratum, vein, or soil layer which emerges at the surface. Also more widely, an area or mass of bare rock. E19.
2 *fig.* (An) outward manifestation. M19.
▶ **B** *verb intrans*. Infl. **-pp-**.
1 GEOLOGY & MINING. Crop out; (of a stratum or vein) emerge at the surface. M19.
2 *fig.* Emerge or come out. M19.
■ **outcropping** *noun* (*a*) appearance, emergence; (*b*) MINING & GEOLOGY the action or fact of cropping out; an outcrop: M19.

outcross /ˈaʊtkrɒs/ *noun & verb*. L19.
[from OUT- + CROSS *noun*.]
▶ **A** *noun*. A cross with an unrelated breed or race. L19.
▶ **B** *verb trans. & intrans.* Cross (an animal or plant, a breed or stock) with one not closely related. E20.

outcry /ˈaʊtkrʌɪ/ *noun*. ME.
[from OUT- + CRY *noun*.]
1 The action or an act of crying out; an exclamation, a shout; noise, uproar. Also, (a) strong public protest. ME.
2 A public sale to the highest bidder; an auction. Now chiefly *US*. L16.

> 📖 **1** E. A. FREEMAN The wild outcries of William's enemies at a drunken revel. R. BERTHOUD His carvings had already been the subject of outcry and scandal. **2** W. MUIR The remainder was sold by outcry. ***open outcry***: see OPEN *adjective*.

outcry /aʊtˈkrʌɪ/ *verb*. LME.
[from OUT- + CRY *verb*.]
1 *verb intrans.* Cry out. Now *rare*. LME. ▸**b** *verb trans.* Cry (something) aloud, exclaim; proclaim. Now *rare*. M16.
2 *verb trans.* Cry or shout louder than; shout down. M16.
■ **ˈoutcrying** *noun* a crying out; clamour, shouting: M16.

outcurve /ˈaʊtkəːv/ *noun*. M19.
[from OUT- + CURVE *noun*.]
1 BASEBALL. The curving of a pitched ball away from the batter; (the course of) a ball pitched so as to curve in this way. M19.
2 *gen.* An outward curve or prominence. E20.

outcurved /ˈaʊtkəːvd/ *adjective*. M20.
[from OUT- + *curved* pa. pple of CURVE *verb*.]
Of the bow of a violin etc.: curved away from the hair.

outdo /aʊtˈduː/ *verb trans*. Infl. as DO *verb*; pa. t. usu. **-did** /-ˈdɪd/, pa. pple usu. **-done** /-ˈdʌn/. ME.
[from OUT- + DO *verb*.]
†**1** Force out. ME–E17.
2 Surpass, excel; be superior to. L16. ▸**b** Defeat, overcome. L17.

> 📖 **2** N. SEDAKA Howie outdid himself. The collection was brilliant. A. KENNY The Christmas office was far outdone by the ceremonies of Holy Week.

outdoor /ˈaʊtdɔː/ *adjective*. M18.
[from OUT- + DOOR.]
1 Situated, performed, or used out of doors; open-air; (of a person) fond of open-air pursuits. M18.
2 *Hist.* Relieved or administered outside or apart from residence in a workhouse, almshouse, etc. M19.

> 📖 **1** P. CAMPBELL He loved fishing and any kind of outdoor life.

Special collocations: **outdoor department** a part of a public house selling liquor etc. for consumption off the premises. **outdoor relief** *Hist.* financial help given, esp. by the State, to people not living in a workhouse etc. **outdoor things** clothing worn out of doors.
■ **out-ˈdooring** *noun* in W. Africa, a traditional ceremony in which a baby is brought outside for the first time to be named M20. **outdoorish** *adjective* having an outdoor appearance or effect L19. **outdoorness** *noun* the quality of being outdoor L18.

†**out-door** *noun*. M17–E19.
[from OUT- + DOOR.]
An exterior or outer door.

outdoors /aʊtˈdɔːz/ *adverb & noun*. E19.
[from OUT *preposition* + DOOR + -S¹.]
▶ **A** *adverb*. Out of doors; in or into the open air. E19.
▶ **B** *noun*. = OUT-OF-DOORS *noun*. M19.
Phrases & comb. (of adverb & noun): **all outdoors** *US colloq.* the whole world, everybody. **outdoorsman** a person who likes outdoor activities. ***the great outdoors***: see GREAT *adjective*.
■ **outdoorsy** *adjective* associated with or characteristic of the outdoors; fond of an outdoor life: E20.

outdrive *verb & noun*. OE.
[from OUT- + DRIVE *verb & noun*.]
▶ **A** *verb trans.* /aʊtˈdrʌɪv/
†**1** Drive out, expel. OE–M17.
2 Drive faster than. M17.
3 GOLF. Drive further than. E20.
▶ **B** *noun* /ˈaʊtdrʌɪv/ SAILING. A mechanism for driving a motor boat, consisting of an inboard engine mounted towards the stern and connected to an outboard unit containing the gears, shaft, and propeller. M20.

outen /ˈaʊt(ə)n/ *adverb, preposition, & adjective*.
[Old English *ūtan(e)* (= Old Saxon *ūtan*, Old High German *ūzan*, *uzana*, Old Norse *útan*, Gothic *ūtana*), deriv. of *ūt*: see OUT *adverb*.]
▶ **A** *adverb*. †**1** From outside. Only in OE.
2 Outside, on the outside. *obsolete* exc. *dial*. OE.
▶ **B** *preposition*. †**1** Outside, away from. Only in ME.
2 Out of; out from. *colloq.* Chiefly *Scot.* & *US*. M19.
▶†**C** *adjective*. Coming from outside, foreign. Only in ME.

outer /ˈaʊtə/ *adjective, noun, & verb*. LME.
[from OUT *adjective* + -ER³, replacing earlier UTTER *adjective*.]
▶ **A** *adjective*. **1** Situated further out than another; removed from the centre or inside; situated relatively far out. Also, situated on the outside, external; of or pertaining to the outside. LME.
2 Designating things or conditions external to the mind or soul; objective; physical. LME.

> 📖 **1** J. CONRAD Disclosing to the outer world a long table. G. GORDON Removing her outer clothes to reveal a bathing costume. U. HOLDEN A stiff outer wrapping and transparent paper inside. **2** A. HUTSCHNECKER Ready to blame outer conditions for . . inner turmoil. A. STORR Complete harmony between inner and outer worlds.

Special collocations & phrases: **outer forme** PRINTING the printing surface (orig. type) containing the pages from which the outer side of a sheet is printed and including matter for the first page of the printed sheet. **outer garments** clothes worn over other garments or outdoors. **Outer House** SCOTS LAW a court of first instance at which judges of the Court of Session sit singly. **outer man**, **outer woman** the body; personal appearance, dress. **outer planet**: with an orbit beyond the asteroids. **outer space** the regions of space beyond the earth's atmosphere. **outer suburb** any of the more remote suburbs of a city or town. **outerwear** clothing designed to be worn outside other garments. ***outer woman***: see ***outer man*** above. ***the outer bar***: see BAR *noun*¹ 17a. **the outer world** people outside one's own circle.
▶ **B** *noun*. **1** That part of a target outside the circles surrounding the bull's-eye. M19. ▸**b** A shot that strikes this. L19.
2 *Austral.* The part of a racecourse outside the enclosure; the unsheltered part of a sports ground. E20.
3 An outer container in which objects already in their own containers are packed for transport or display. E20.
4 ELECTRICITY. In a three-phase distribution system, either of the two conductors with potentials above or below that of the earth. E20.
2 on the outer *transf.* (*Austral.* & *NZ slang*) penniless; out of favour, neglected.
▶ **C** *verb trans.* Make outer; externalize. *rare*. E19.

outer /ˈaʊtə/ *preposition*. *informal*. M19.
[Repr. a pronunc. Cf. OUTA.]
= OUT OF.

outercourse /ˈaʊtəkɔːs/ *noun*. L20.
[Blend of OUTER *adjective* and INTERCOURSE.]
Any form of non-penetrative sexual stimulation.

outerly /ˈaʊtəli/ *adverb & adjective*. *obsolete* exc. *dial*. ME.
[Alt. of UTTERLY.]
▶ **A** *adverb*. **1** Utterly. ME.
2 In an outward direction. L17.
▶ **B** *adjective*. Of a wind: blowing offshore or from an offshore direction. M17.

outermost /ˈaʊtəməʊst/ *adjective*. L16.
[from OUTER *adjective* + -MOST, after *innermost*, *uppermost*.]
Most outward; furthest from the inside or centre.

†**outface** *noun*. L16–E18.
[from OUT- + FACE *noun*.]
The outer face; the surface.

outface /aʊtˈfeɪs/ *verb trans*. E16.
[from OUT- + FACE *verb*.]
1 Disconcert, silence, or defeat (a person) by face-to-face confrontation or a display of confidence, arrogance, etc.; stare down. E16. ▸†**b** Force to turn *from* by confrontation. *rare* (Shakes.). Only in L16.
2 Face boldly, defiantly, or shamelessly; defy. L16.
†**3** Contradict defiantly or impudently. L16–L17.
†**4** Maintain (something false or shameful) with boldness or effrontery; brazen out. L16–L17.

> 📖 **1** E. FEINSTEIN He outfaced bullies with his nimble wits. **2** *Times* To outface the unconcealed disapproval of learned men.

†**outfang** *noun*. *Scot. rare*. M16–E19.
[Abbreviation.]
= OUTFANGTHIEF.

outfangthief /ˈaʊtfaŋθiːf/ *noun*. LOE.
[from OUT *adverb* + pa. pple of FANG *verb*¹ + THIEF, after *infangthief*.]
LAW (now *Hist.*). The right of a lord of a private jurisdiction to pursue a thief (esp. one who is the lord's tenant) outside that jurisdiction and bring him or her back for trial and punishment.

outfence /aʊtˈfɛns/ *verb trans*. L18.
[from OUT- + FENCE *verb*.]
1 Divide (land) by fences. Now *rare* or *obsolete*. L18.
2 Outdo in fencing or swordplay. L19.

For other words beginning with *out-* see the entry for **out-**

outfield /ˈaʊtfiːld/ *noun.* M17.
[from OUT- + FIELD *noun*.]
1 The outlying land of a farm; *spec.* (*a*) unenclosed and untilled moorland or pasture; (*b*) land that has been occasionally cropped but not manured. M17. ▸**b** An outlying field. Long *rare* or *obsolete.* L17.
2 CRICKET. (The fielders or a fielder occupying) the part of the field furthest from the wicket. M19.
3 BASEBALL. (The fielders or a fielder occupying) the part of the field beyond the diamond. M19.
1 *infield and outfield*: see INFIELD *noun* 1.

outfield /*in sense 1* ˈaʊtfiːld, *in sense 2* aʊtˈfiːld/ *verb.* M19.
[sense 1 from the noun; sense 2 from OUT- + FIELD *verb*.]
CRICKET & BASEBALL. **1** *verb intrans.* Field in the outfield. Chiefly as ***outfielding*** *verbal noun.* M19.
2 *verb trans.* Surpass in fielding. Usu. in *pass.* L19.

outfielder /ˈaʊtfiːldə/ *noun.* M19.
[from OUT- + FIELDER.]
CRICKET & BASEBALL. A player positioned in the outfield.

outfit /ˈaʊtfɪt/ *noun & verb.* M18.
[from OUT- + FIT *verb*¹.]
▸ **A** *noun.* **1** The action of fitting out or equipping a ship etc. for a journey, expedition, etc. Also, the expense of this. M18.
2 Equipment for a particular purpose, esp. for a journey, expedition, etc. L18. ▸**b** A set of clothes selected or designed to be worn together. M19. ▸**c** The apparatus used by a drug addict for the injection of drugs. M20.
3 A year. Orig. *spec.*, a financial year of the Hudson's Bay Company. *Canad.* L18.
4 A group of people, a team; *spec.* (*a*) a party travelling together; (*b*) a business firm or concern; (*c*) MILITARY a regiment, a squadron, etc.; (*d*) a group of musicians. M19.
5 A person. *derog. slang* (chiefly *US*). M19.

🕮 **2** *Muscle Power* Perform muscle building exercises with this outfit. *Traveller* A few filters are a useful addition to a camera outfit. *fig.*: H. P. LIDDON An indispensable part of man's moral and mental outfit. **b** *Élan* His favourite outfit of crumpled jeans and an open-necked shirt. **4** O. HENRY The worst outfit of desperadoes . . in Texas. *National Times* Outfits like Boeing, McDonalds, Procter and Gamble. A. BLOND The secret code-breaking outfit at Bletchley. A. J. AUGARDE Tenorist Michael Brecker joined his trumpeting brother Randy to form one of the best jazz-rock outfits ever.

▸ **B** *verb.* Infl. **-tt-**.
1 *verb trans.* Provide with an outfit, fit out. Also, provide or supply *with.* M19.
2 *verb intrans.* Equip oneself. L19.

🕮 **1** K. TENNANT She was smartly outfitted: white shoes, white hat. *Scientific American* Each . . destroyer is outfitted with . . missiles.

■ **outfitter** *noun* a person who or shop which supplies outfits; *esp.* one selling menswear or (*Canad.*) equipment for outdoor expeditions: M19.

outflank /aʊtˈflaŋk/ *verb trans.* M18.
[from OUT- + FLANK *verb*¹.]
MILITARY. Extend one's flank beyond that of (an opposing army); outmanoeuvre (an adversary) by a flanking movement. Also *gen.*, get the better of, confound.

🕮 BOSW. SMITH Outflanking the enemy, and riding round towards their rear. *Japan Times* To outflank the party, some opposition groups may . . move further to the right.

outflow /ˈaʊtfləʊ/ *noun.* L18.
[from OUT- + FLOW *noun*¹.]
The act or fact of flowing out; an efflux (*lit. & fig.*).

🕮 E. M. GOULBURN The outflow of His Divine compassion. *Irish Press* A net outflow of 6,760 people from Ireland.

outflow /aʊtˈfləʊ/ *verb intrans. poet.* L16.
[from OUT- + FLOW *verb*.]
Flow out.

outflowing /ˈaʊtfləʊɪŋ/ *noun.* L17.
[from OUT- + FLOWING *noun*.]
The action or an act of flowing out, (an) efflux.

outflux /ˈaʊtflʌks/ *noun.* M18.
[from OUT- + FLUX *noun*.]
Outflow; an outlet. Now *spec.* (BIOLOGY), the outward movement of ions through a cell membrane.

out-front /aʊtˈfrʌnt/ *adjective.* Chiefly *US.* M20.
[from OUT *adverb* + FRONT *noun* or *adverb*.]
Frank, open. Also, progressive, in the forefront of a movement etc.

out front /aʊt ˈfrʌnt/ *adverbial phr.* Chiefly *N. Amer.* E20.
[from OUT *adverb* + FRONT *noun*.]
At or to the front, in front; *spec.* (THEATRICAL) in the auditorium.

outgang /ˈaʊtgaŋ/ *noun. obsolete* exc. *Scot.* & *north.*
[Old English *ūtgang*: cf. Dutch *uitgang*, German *Ausgang*.]
1 A going out, a departure; *spec.* the giving up of the occupancy or tenure of property. OE.
2 A way out; an outlet, an exit. OE.

outgas /aʊtˈgas/ *verb.* Infl. **-ss-**. E20.
[from OUT- + GAS *verb*¹.]
1 *verb trans.* Drive off adsorbed or dissolved gas or vapour from. E20.
2 *verb trans. & intrans.* Give off or release as gas or vapour (an adsorbed or dissolved substance). M20.

outgate /ˈaʊtgeɪt/ *noun & adverb. obsolete* exc. *Scot. & north.* ME.
[from OUT- + GATE *noun*².]
▸ **A** *noun.* **1** The action of going out; exit, egress. ME.
2 A way out, an outlet; *fig.* a way of escape or deliverance. LME. ▸**b** An outcome. *Scot.* M16.
3 Usu. in *pl.* Goods going out of a town or port; duty on these. Cf. INGATE 3. *obsolete* exc. *Hist.* E17.
▸ **B** *adverb.* Outwards; outside. L16.

outgo /ˈaʊtgəʊ/ *noun.* Pl. **-goes**. M17.
[from OUT- + GO *noun*¹.]
1 The fact of going out; that which goes out; *spec.* outlay, expenditure. M17.
2 The action or means of going out; efflux, outflow. M19.

outgo /aʊtˈgəʊ/ *verb.* Infl. as GO *verb*; pa. t. usu. **-went** /-ˈwɛnt/, pa. pple usu. **-gone** /-ˈgɒn/. OE.
[from OUT- + GO *verb*.]
1 *verb intrans.* Go out, go forth. Now only *poet.* or as OUTGOING *adjective.* OE.
2 *verb trans.* Go faster than, outstrip; surpass, excel. *arch.* M16.

outgoer /ˈaʊtgəʊə/ *noun.* LME.
[from OUT- + GOER.]
A person who goes out; *esp.* one who departs or is dismissed from a place, position, etc.

outgoing /ˈaʊtgəʊɪŋ/ *noun.* ME.
[from OUT- + GOING *noun*.]
1 The action or an act of going out or forth; (a) departure. ME.
2 a A way out, an exit. Now *poet.* LME. ▸†**b** The extremity, the outer limit. LME–E19.
3 *sing.* & (usu.) in *pl.* Expenditure, outlay. E17.

🕮 **3** *Best* List all your outgoings and expenses over a few weeks.

outgoing /ˈaʊtgəʊɪŋ/ *adjective.* M17.
[from OUT- + GOING *ppl adjective*.]
1 That goes out. M17.
2 Going out of or retiring from office, position, etc. E19.
3 Of clothes: suitable for wearing when going out. M19.
4 Extrovert, sociable, open-hearted, friendly. M20.

🕮 **1** L. DEIGHTON Outgoing flights were hours behind their scheduled times. **2** *Independent* Brazil's outgoing president . . has offered to step down early. **4** P. ROTH Her mixture of outgoing vitality and good-natured gentility.

■ **outgoingness** *noun* M19.

outgone *verb pa. pple* of OUTGO *verb.*

outgrew *verb pa. t.* of OUTGROW.

out-group /ˈaʊtgruːp/ *noun.* E20.
[from OUT- + GROUP *noun*.]
Those people who do not belong to a specific in-group.

outgrow /aʊtˈgrəʊ/ *verb trans.* Pa. t. **-grew** /-ˈgruː/; pa. pple **-grown** /-ˈgrəʊn/. L16.
[from OUT- + GROW *verb*.]
1 Surpass in growth, grow more or faster than. L16.
2 Grow too large for (clothes etc.); *fig.* grow out of, mature beyond, (a habit, ailment, stage of development, etc.). M17.

🕮 **1** H. BROOKE His avarice outgrew even . . his wealth. **2** *Independent* Clothes and shoes were outgrown by toddlers who seemed . . to be growing like the infant Hercules. *Lancet* Most children outgrow the habit. P. ACKROYD One never outgrows one's early enthusiasms.

Phrases: **outgrow one's strength** become lanky and weak through excessively rapid growth.

outgrowing /ˈaʊtgrəʊɪŋ/ *noun.* L16.
[from OUT- + GROWING.]
The action of OUTGROW *verb.* Also, a sprout, an outgrowth.

outgrown *verb pa. pple* of OUTGROW.

outgrowth /ˈaʊtgrəʊθ/ *noun.* M19.
[from OUT- + GROWTH.]
1 The process of growing out. M19.
2 That which grows or develops out of something, a growth, an offshoot. M19.

outhaul /ˈaʊthɔːl/ *noun.* M19.
[from OUT- + HAUL *noun*.]
NAUTICAL. An appliance for hauling out; *spec.* a rope used to haul out the clew of a sail.
■ Also **outhauler** *noun* L18.

For other words beginning with *out-* see the entry for **out-**

out-Herod /aʊtˈhɛrəd/ *verb trans.* E17.
[from OUT- + *Herod* a blustering tyrant in miracle plays, representing Herod the ruler of Judaea at the time of Jesus' birth (see HERODIAN).]
Outdo in cruelty, evil, or extravagance. Chiefly in ***out-Herod Herod.***

🕮 SHAKES. *Haml.* I would have such a fellow whipp'd for o'erdoing Termagant; it out-herods Herod.

outhouse /ˈaʊthaʊs/ *noun.* Pl. **-houses** /-haʊzɪz/. ME.
[from OUT- + HOUSE *noun*¹.]
1 A subsidiary building in the grounds of or adjoining a house, as a stable, barn, shed, etc. ME.
2 An outside lavatory. Chiefly *N. Amer.* E19.
3 A schoolhouse separate from the main or central school building. E20.
■ **outhousing** /-haʊzɪŋ/ *noun*¹ a collection of outhouses E17.

outhouse /ˈaʊthaʊz/ *verb trans.* M20.
[from OUT- + HOUSE *verb*¹.]
Store (books etc.) in a building or area away from the main collection.
■ **outhousing** *noun*² the action of the verb; (provision for) accommodation or storage away from the main site: M20.

outing /ˈaʊtɪŋ/ *noun.* LME.
[from OUT *verb* + -ING¹.]
†**1** The action of going out or forth. Only in LME.
†**2** The action of putting or driving out; expulsion. LME–L17.
3 a An excursion, *esp.* one lasting (part of) a day; a brief pleasure-trip. E19. ▸**b** An appearance in an outdoor match, race, or other sporting event. M20.
4 CRICKET. The situation or position of the team which is fielding. M19.
5 The remote distance out at sea. L19.
6 The revelation or exposure of the homosexuality of a well-known person, esp. in order to promote a homosexual cause. L20.

🕮 **3a** *Delaware Today* A trip to the . . zoo is also a good idea for an outing. **b** *Sports Illustrated* Kile hadn't thrown more than 34 pitches in an outing this season.

Comb.: **outing flannel** *US* a type of flannelette.

outjie /ˈəʊki, -tʃi/ *noun. S. Afr.* M20.
[Afrikaans, formed as OU *noun*² + *-tjie* dim. suffix.]
A child, a little fellow. Also (chiefly *joc.* or *derog.*), an adult.

outlaid *verb pa. t. & pple* of OUTLAY *verb.*

outland /ˈaʊtland, -lənd/ *noun & adjective.* OE.
[from OUT- + LAND *noun*¹.]
▸ **A** *noun.* **1** Outlying land; *spec.* (*Hist.*) the outer part of an estate, feudal manor, etc., assigned to tenants (opp. INLAND *noun* 1). OE. ▸**b** Chiefly US HISTORY. In *pl.* The outlying lands of a province, district, or town. M17.
2 A foreign land. *arch.* OE.
3 A foreigner, a stranger. *obsolete* exc. *Scot.* ME.
▸ **B** *adjective.* **1** Foreign, alien. Now *arch. & Scot.* ME.
2 Outlying; lying outside the precincts of a town etc. L18.

outlander /ˈaʊtlandə/ *noun.* L16.
[from prec. + -ER¹, after Dutch *uitlander*, German *Ausländer*.]
A foreigner, an alien, a stranger.

outlandish /aʊtˈlandɪʃ/ *adjective & noun.* OE.
[from OUTLAND + -ISH¹.]
▸ **A** *adjective.* **1** Foreign, alien; not native or indigenous. *arch.* OE.
2 Looking or sounding foreign; unfamiliar, strange; odd, unlikely, bizarre. L16.
3 Out-of-the-way, remote; far removed from civilization. Now usu. *derog.* L18.

🕮 **2** W. S. MAUGHAM He was an outlandish figure, with his wide-brimmed hat and pointed beard. A. FRANCE Willing to explore almost any idea . . however outlandish.

▸ **B** *ellipt.* as *noun.* (A) foreign language. Now *rare* or *obsolete.* E17.
■ **outlandishly** *adverb* L19. **outlandishness** *noun* E17.

outlaw /ˈaʊtlɔː/ *noun & adjective.* LOE.
[Old Norse *útlagi*, from *útlagr* outlawed, banished, from *út* out (of) + pl. of *lag* law: see OUT *adverb*, LAW *noun*¹.]
▸ **A** *noun.* **1** Orig., a person deprived of the benefits and protection of the law, a person under sentence of outlawry. Later also, a fugitive from the law; an exile. LOE. ▸**b** *fig.* A wild, unmanageable, or untamed animal. L16. ▸**c** A lawless person; a professional criminal. L19.
†**2** (A sentence or proclamation of) outlawry. *rare.* LME–M17.
▸ **B** *attrib.* or as *adjective.* Designating or of the nature of an outlaw. E20.
outlaw strike an unofficial strike.

outlaw /ˈaʊtlɔː/ *verb trans.* LOE.
[from the noun.]
1 Deprive of the benefit and protection of the law, declare an outlaw (*obsolete* exc. *Hist.*); make illegal, proscribe. Formerly also, banish. LOE.
2 Deprive of legal force. *obsolete* exc. *US.* M17.

outlawry /ˈaʊtlɔːri/ *noun.* LME.
[Repr. Anglo-Norman *utlagerie*, Anglo-Latin *utlagaria*, from OUTLAW *noun* (whence Anglo-Latin *utlaga*) + Proto-Romance *-erie* -ERY, -RY.]
1 The action of putting a person outside the protection of the law, the legal process by which a person was made an outlaw (*obsolete* exc. *Hist.*); the condition of being outlawed. Formerly also, exile, banishment. LME.
†**2** Outlaws collectively. M16–L19.
3 Disregard or defiance of the law. M19.

outlay /ˈaʊtleɪ/ *noun.* Orig. *Scot.* M16.
[from OUT- + LAY *verb*¹.]
†**1** A thing that lies outside or away from something else; *spec.* an out-of-the-way lair. *rare.* M16–E17.
2 An act or the fact of spending; (an) expenditure. L18.

outlay /aʊtˈleɪ/ *verb trans.* Pa. t. & pple **-laid** /-ˈleɪd/. M16.
[formed as prec.]
1 Lay out; expose, display. Long *rare.* M16.
2 Expend, spend, (money). E19.

outlearn /aʊtˈləːn/ *verb trans.* Pa. t. & pple **-learned** /-ˈləːnd/, **-learnt** /-ˈləːnt/. M16.
[from OUT- + LEARN.]
1 Progress beyond the learning or study of. M16.
†**2** Find out, learn from others. *rare* (Spenser). Only in L16.
3 Outstrip in learning. M17.

outlet /ˈaʊtlɪt/ *noun.* ME.
[from OUT- + LET *verb*¹.]
1 a An opening by which something escapes or is released; a means of issue or exit. ME. ▸**b** *fig.* An escape; a means of expressing emotion, energy, talent, etc. E17. ▸**c** ANATOMY. The opening of a cavity of the body; *esp.* the lower aperture of the pelvic, thoracic, etc., cavities (cf. INLET *noun* 5). L18. ▸**d** A power point; an output socket in an electrical device. L19. ▸**e** A shop, a retail store; an agency, distributor, or market for goods. E20.
†**2** In *pl.* The outlying parts of something, esp. a town; the suburbs. L16–M19.
3 The action of letting out or discharging (*lit.* & *fig.*). M17.
4 A place into which something is released; *spec.* a pasture for cattle. M18.

📖 **1a** J. S. FOSTER The outlet of a flue should be well above the roof. *South African Panorama* South of the Bay's original outlet to the sea. **b** R. MACAULAY Maurice found an outlet from domestic irritation in political excitement. S. ROSENBERG I found an outlet in writing long letters.

Comb.: **outlet box** a box giving access to connections to electrical wiring where it is led out of conduits.

outlet /aʊtˈlɛt/ *verb trans.* Now *rare* or *obsolete.* Infl. **-tt-**. Pa. t. & pple **-let**. ME.
[formed as prec.]
Let out, pour forth.

†**outlicker** *noun* var. of OUTLIGGER.

outlier /ˈaʊtlʌɪə/ *noun.* E17.
[from OUT- + LIE *verb*¹ + -ER¹.]
1 a An outsider; a person who avoids acceptable or expected behaviour. E17. ▸**b** An animal, esp. a deer, that has its lair outside an enclosure or away from a main herd. M17. ▸**c** A person who sleeps or lives in the open air or away from his or her place of business, duty, etc. L17.
2 a GEOLOGY. A large detached stone or boulder; ARCHAEOLOGY a single standing stone or other feature set away from a group or formation of such features. E17. ▸**b** GEOLOGY. A portion of a geological formation separated from the main body by erosion, faulting, or folding. M19. ▸**c** *gen.* An outlying portion or member of something, detached from a main mass, body, or system. M19.
3 STATISTICS. An observation or result of a value well outside the set of values considered likely. M20.

📖 **1c** R. BENTLEY The party . . sent messengers to all their outliers within twenty miles of Cambridge. **2c** R. F. BURTON They took leave of him . . departing to the outliers of the city.

†**outligger** *noun.* Also **-licker**. L15.
[from OUT- + LIGGER. Cf. Dutch *uitligger*, OUTRIGGER.]
NAUTICAL. **1** A projecting spar for extending a sail, making a greater angle for a rope etc.; *esp.* a long stout spar extended from the poop to haul down the mizzen-sail. L15–M18.
2 = OUTRIGGER 2. L17–M18.

outline /ˈaʊtlʌɪn/ *noun & verb.* M17.
[from OUT- + LINE *noun*².]
▶ **A** *noun.* **I 1 a** *sing.* & in *pl.* The (real or apparent) line or lines defining the contour or bounds of a figure or object viewed from a particular point. M17. ▸**b** A contour, an outer boundary. E19.
2 a A sketch or drawing in which an object is represented by contour lines only. M18. ▸**b** A representation of a word in shorthand. M19. ▸**c** TYPOGRAPHY. A typeface in which the letters are drawn in outline, occas. with added shading. L19.

📖 **1a** R. RENDELL Mountainous cumulus against which the outlines of buildings took on a curious clarity. *Essentials* Melanie . . snipped layers into the hair around her face to soften the outline. **b** J. TYNDALL A mountain wall projected its jagged outline against the sky.

▶ **II 3 a** In *pl.* The main features or general principles of a subject. E18. ▸**b** A usu. brief verbal description giving a general idea of a whole; a summary; a rough draft. Now also, a précis of a proposed article, novel, etc. M18.

📖 **3b** R. W. DALE A bare outline of the contents. *Plays International* Two playscripts and an outline for a short play.

Phrases: **in outline** with only the outline drawn, represented, or visible. ***working outline***: see WORKING *noun.*
Comb.: **outline plan** a draft or sketch lacking many details; **outline planning permission**: sought by or from a public authority, to go ahead in principle with building, demolition, or industrial development; **outline stitch** EMBROIDERY: used to indicate an outline; *spec.* stem stitch.

▶ **B** *verb trans.* **1** Draw, trace, indicate, or define the outline of; draw in outline. L18.
2 Describe the main features of; sketch in general terms, summarize. M19.

📖 **1** E. WILSON Outline the shapes first and then fill them in. G. NAYLOR Tiny electrical stars . . outlined the driveways.

■ **outlinear** /-ˈlɪnɪə/ *adjective* of the nature of an outline M19. **outliner** *noun* a computer program or routine which allows its user to create and edit a hierarchically-arranged outline of the logical structure of a document L20.

outlive /aʊtˈlɪv/ *verb.* L15.
[from OUT- + LIVE *verb.*]
1 *verb trans.* **a** Live or last longer than; survive, outlast. L15. ▸**b** Live through or beyond (a specified time, an experience, etc.); pass through; outgrow. E17.
†**2** *verb intrans.* Survive. *rare* (Shakes.). Only in L16.

outlook /ˈaʊtlʊk/ *noun.* M17.
[from OUT- + LOOK *noun.*]
1 A place from which a person may look out or keep watch. M17.
2 a A mental attitude or point of view. M18. ▸**b** A view or prospect from a place or point. E19. ▸**c** The prospect for the future. M19.
3 The act or practice of looking out. E19.

📖 **2a** *Guardian* Happy integrated children with a positive outlook on life. **b** C. KINGSLEY The dreary outlook of chimney-tops and smoke. **c** *Field* It is not only in residential housing that the outlook is bleak. **3 on the outlook** on the lookout.

outlook /aʊtˈlʊk/ *verb.* L16.
[from OUT- + LOOK *verb.*]
1 *verb trans.* Disconcert by looking; stare down; outstare. L16.
2 *verb intrans.* Look out or forth. *rare.* E17.
†**3** *verb trans.* Outdo in looks or appearance. *rare.* Only in M18.

outly /ˈaʊtli/ *adverb. obsolete* exc. *dial.* ME.
[from OUT *adverb* + -LY².]
1 Utterly, completely. ME.
2 Outwardly, externally. L16.

outlying /ˈaʊtlʌɪɪŋ/ *adjective.* M17.
[from OUT- + LYING *adjective*¹.]
1 Lying or situated outside certain limits; *spec.* (of an animal) having its lair outside an enclosure. M17.
2 Situated far from a centre; remote, out-of-the-way. L17.

outmanoeuvre /aʊtməˈnuːvə/ *verb trans.* Also ***-maneuver**. L18.
[from OUT- + MANOEUVRE *verb.*]
Outdo in manoeuvring; get the better of by superior skill or strategy.

outmode /aʊtˈməʊd/ *verb trans.* E20.
[from OUT- + MODE, after French *démoder.*]
Put out of fashion, make outdated. Chiefly as **outmoded** *ppl adjective.*

📖 G. ADAIR Her grandmother's outmoded garments.

outmost /ˈaʊtməʊst/ *adjective & noun.* ME.
[Var. of UTMOST: see -MOST.]
▶ **A** *adjective.* **1** Furthest from the inside or centre; outermost. Later also, most remote, furthest away. ME.
†**2** Final; most complete; most extreme, utmost. ME–L16.
▶ **B** *noun.* The utmost point, degree, or limit; the outermost part. Now *rare.* M17.
¶ Rare before 16.

outnal /ˈaʊtn(ə)l/ *noun. obsolete* exc. *Hist.* Also †**-ll**. E17.
[Origin unkn.]
A kind of linen thread.

outness /ˈaʊtnɪs/ *noun.* E18.
[from OUT- + -NESS.]
The quality, fact, or condition of being external, esp. to the mind; externality.

For other words beginning with out- see the entry for **out-**

out of /ˈaʊt əv/ *prepositional phr.* OE.
[from OUT *adverb* + OF *preposition.*]
▶ **I** Of motion or direction. Opp. ***into***.
1 From inside a containing space (as a room, building, dam, etc.). Also as *imper.*, get, go, etc., from inside (a room etc.). OE. ▸**b** From within; so as to point, project, or lead away from. LME. ▸**c** From among (a number), from the members of (a group). L16.
2 So as to be deprived of (property, a possession, etc.). ME. ▸**b** So as to be removed from (a position or office). L16.
3 From within the range or limit of (an influence, action, faculty, etc.). ME.
4 a From (something) as a source or origin; *spec.* (of a horse) given birth to by (a particular dam). ME. ▸**b** From (something) as a cause or motive; as a result or effect of. M16. ▸**c** By the use of (a material). E17. ▸**d** From a base in; using (a place) as a centre of operations. M20.
5 From (a condition or state); so as to be no longer in or experiencing. Also, from one language (*into* another). LME.

📖 **1** M. KEANE The coffee was boiling over out of its glass container. **b** A. CARTER They came out of the wood into a bare field. **c** *Life* One out of every five U.S. homes has one. **2** B. JOWETT You are . . mean to cheat us out of a whole chapter. **3** J. BUCHAN The man I once knew had dropped out of the world's ken. *Daily Progress* The boat sailed out of reach. **4a** *Field* Many men who were not shooters made money out of dogs. **b** A. CARTER Doing cartwheels and handstands out of sheer exhilaration. **c** E. WIGGINTON Wooden wedges . . were hewn out of . . thick sections of hardwood. **d** E. JONG Hummel ran a printing business out of a tiny office in the old town. **5** LD MACAULAY His majesty . . was thought by the physicians to be out of danger.

▶ **II** Of position. Opp. ***in***.
6 Not within (a space, as a room, building, pen, dam, etc.); beyond the confines of; outside. ME. ▸**b** Away or at a (specified) distance from (a centre, familiar place, particular point, etc.). LME. ▸**c** Taken from among, occurring among or in, (a number or group). M16.
7 Beyond the range or limits of. ME. ▸**b** In error concerning (a fact or action); having deviated from the proper course of. L17.
8 Not or no longer in (a condition or state); deprived of, having lost, or without (a faculty, quality, possession, etc.). ME.
9 Obtained, made, or derived from; *spec.* (of a horse) borne by (a particular dam). LME.

📖 **6** E. WAUGH She was out of bed and out of the room. *fig.*: *New Yorker* Bert . . out of makeup looked as a clown should look—funny. **b** J. CARLYLE Ealing, some seven miles out of London. **c** *Newsweek* Nine out of 10 owners buy another Mercedes. **7** A. MCCOWEN Going into the Hall during lunch-hour, when it was out of bounds. V. S. PRITCHETT A bank on the seaward side out of the wind. *Which?* Some of the wine kits we tested were quaffable, though nothing out of the ordinary. **b** W. NICHOLLS He is a little out of his chronology again. **8** OED It was foolish to try it, when he was out of training. T. MORRISON She photographed everything . . until she was out of film. S. BELLOW His excuse for being . . out of work was that his true talent was for campaigning strategies. **9** D. LESSING To get everything he could out of a world . . organised for the profit of others. *Sunday Express* He was out of a Dartmoor mare . . by a stallion called Golden Surprise.

Phrases: (A selection of cross-refs. only is included.) FROM **out of**. ***out of bounds***: see BOUND *noun*¹ 1. ***out of*** BREATH. ***out of date***: see DATE *noun*². ***out of drawing***: see DRAWING *noun* 2. ***out of hand***: see HAND *noun.* **out of it** (*a*) not used or included in (an action or event); (*b*) astray or distant from the centre or heart of anything; (*c*) *slang* thoroughly inebriated. ***out of one's hair***: see HAIR *noun.* ***out of order***: see ORDER *noun.* ***out of pocket***: see POCKET *noun.* ***out of sorts***: see SORT *noun*². ***out of the loop***: see LOOP *noun*². ***out of the question***: see QUESTION *noun.* ***out of the running***: see RUNNING *noun.* ***ten out of ten***: see TEN *noun* 3.

out of all sight *adverbial phr.* see OUT OF SIGHT.

out-of-area /aʊt əv ˈɛːrɪə/ *adjectival & adverbial phr.* L20.
[from OUT OF + AREA.]
▶ **A** *adjective.* Of military operations: conducted away from the place of origin or normal place of action of the force concerned.
▶ **B** *adverb.* Outside the region in which a country is situated.

out-of-body /aʊt əv ˈbɒdi/ *adjectival phr.* L20.
[from OUT OF + BODY.]
Characterized by the sensation that one's consciousness is located outside one's body. Chiefly in ***out-of-body experience***.

out-of-court /aʊt əv ˈkɔːt/ *adjectival phr.* L20.
[from OUT OF + COURT *noun*¹.]
Of agreements, deals, etc.: arrived at without the intervention of a court. Chiefly in ***out-of-court settlement***.

out-of-doors /aʊtəvˈdɔːz/ *attrib. adjective & noun.* Also (as adjective) **-door** /-ˈdɔː/. L18.
[from **out of doors** S.V. DOOR *noun.*]
▶ **A** *adjective.* Situated, used, or occurring outside a building; *spec.* outside the Houses of Parliament. L18.

▶**B** *noun.* The world outside a building, esp. one's house; the open air; the countryside. **E19.**

outoffice /ˈaʊtɒfɪs/ *noun.* **E17.**
[from OUT- + OFFICE *noun.*]
A separate building forming an office or serving some other purpose for a mansion, farmhouse, etc.; an out-house.

📖 *Irish Press* Outoffices include implement shed . . fuel house . . cow byre.

out of print /aʊt əv ˈprɪnt/ *adjectival & adverbial phr.* **L17.**
[from OUT OF + PRINT *noun.*]
▶**A** *adjective.* Of a book, record, tape, etc.: no longer available from the publisher or maker. **L17.**
▶**B** *adverb.* So as to be no longer available from the publisher or maker. **M19.**

out of sight /aʊt əv ˈsʌɪt/ *adverbial & adjectival phr.* Also (as adverb) **out of all sight.** **E19.**
[from OUT OF + SIGHT *noun.*]
▶**A** *adverb.* Beyond all comparison. **E19.**
▶**B** *adjective.* Excellent, delightful, incomparable. **L19.**

out-of-state /ˈaʊtəvsteɪt/ *adjective. US.* Also **-State.** **M20.**
[from OUT OF + STATE *noun.*]
Originating from outside a particular State of the United States.
■ **out-of-Stater** *noun* a person from outside a particular State **M20.**

out-of-the-way /aʊtəvðəˈweɪ/ *adjective & adverb.* **E18.**
[from *out of the way* s.v. WAY *noun.*]
▶**A** *adjective.* **1** Seldom met with, unusual; extraordinary, odd, peculiar, remarkable. **E18.**
2 Departing from the proper path; devious. **M18.**
3 Remote; far from a main road or centre of population; unfrequented, secluded. **L18.**

📖 **1** CONAN DOYLE He has amassed a lot of out-of-the-way knowledge. R. GITTINGS He had the most out-of-the-way sense of humour. **3** W. BOYD For such an out of the way place it was . . incredible what goods were on sale.

▶**B** *adverb.* Oddly; exceptionally, extraordinarily. **E18.**
■ **out-of-the-wayness** *noun* **E19.**

out-of-town /aʊtəvˈtaʊn/ *adjective.* **E19.**
[from OUT *adverb* + OF *preposition* + TOWN *noun.*]
Situated, originating from, or occurring outside a town. Also, unsophisticated.
■ **out-of-towner** *noun* a person originating from outside a particular town **E20.**

out-over /aʊtˈəʊvə/ *preposition & adverb.* Now *Scot.* Also **outour**, **out-ower** /aʊtˈaʊə/. **ME.**
[from OUT *adverb* + OVER *preposition.*]
▶**A** *preposition.* Outwards and over, over the top of; over, across; above (*lit. & fig.*); in excess of. **ME.**
▶**B** *adverb.* Over, across; at a distance; throughout, completely; besides. **ME.**

outpace /aʊtˈpeɪs/ *verb.* **L16.**
[from OUT- + PACE *verb.*]
†**1** *verb intrans.* Pass or go out. *rare.* Only in **L16.**
2 *verb trans.* Exceed in speed; outdo in a race or rivalry, do better than. **E17.**

📖 **2** L. DEIGHTON Why choose a car that can be outpaced by . . a local bus. *Hamilton (Ontario) Spectator* Bonds outpaced short-term securities.

out-parish /ˈaʊtparɪʃ/ *noun.* **L16.**
[from OUT- + PARISH *noun.*]
A parish lying outside the walls or boundary of a city or town, but for some purpose regarded as belonging to it. Also, an outlying parish.

outpart /ˈaʊtpɑːt/ *noun.* **LME.**
[from OUT- + PART *noun.*]
An outer, outlying, or exterior part; *esp.* (in *pl.*), the parts of a town lying outside its walls or boundary.

outpass /aʊtˈpɑːs/ *verb.* **ME.**
[from OUT- + PASS *verb.*]
†**1** *verb intrans.* Go or come out. **ME–E17.**
2 *verb trans.* Pass out of or beyond. **LME.**
3 *verb trans. fig.* Surpass. **L16.**

out-patient /ˈaʊtpeɪʃ(ə)nt/ *noun.* **E18.**
[from OUT- + PATIENT *noun.*]
1 A patient who attends a hospital without staying there overnight. Opp. ***in-patient.*** **E18.**
2 In *pl.* The department of a hospital where out-patients attend. **E20.**

outpeer /aʊtˈpɪə/ *verb trans.* **E17.**
[from OUT- + PEER *verb*¹.]
Outrival, excel.

outperform /aʊtpəˈfɔːm/ *verb trans.* **M20.**
[from OUT- + PERFORM.]
Perform better than; surpass in a particular activity or function.

📖 J. MALCOLM Georgian silver has outperformed the stock market.

■ **outperformance** *noun* the action or fact of outperforming something, esp. on the stock market **L20.**

outplace /aʊtˈpleɪs/; *in sense 2 also* ˈaʊtpleɪs/ *verb trans.* Orig. *US.* **E20.**
[from OUT- + PLACE *verb.*]
1 Displace, oust (*rare*). Now *spec.* make redundant, dismiss. **E20.**
2 Assist (a redundant employee, esp. an executive) in finding new employment. **L20.**
■ **ˈoutplacement** *noun* the action or task of outplacing people; the state of being outplaced: **L20.** **ˈoutplacer** *noun* a person or agency that outplaces people **L20.**

out-place /ˈaʊtpleɪs/ *noun.* **M16.**
[from OUT- + PLACE *noun*¹.]
An out-of-the-way place.

outplay /aʊtˈpleɪ/ *verb trans.* **M17.**
[from OUT- + PLAY *verb.*]
Surpass in playing, play better than.

outpoint /aʊtˈpɔɪnt/ *verb trans.* **L16.**
[from OUT- + POINT *verb*¹.]
†**1** Point out, indicate. *poet.* Only in **L16.**
2 YACHTING. Outdo in pointing; sail closer to the wind than. **L19.**
3 In various sports and games, esp. boxing: score more points than; defeat on points. **E20.**

outport /ˈaʊtpɔːt/ *noun.* **M17.**
[from OUT- + PORT *noun*¹.]
1 a A port outside some defined place; *spec.* a British port other than that of London. **M17.** ▸**b** In Labrador and Newfoundland: a small remote fishing village. **E19.** ▸**c** A small port located to support the commerce of a main port. **M20.**
2 A port of embarkation or exportation. **L18.**
■ **outporter** *noun* a native or inhabitant of an outport **E20.**

outpost /ˈaʊtpəʊst/ *noun & adjective.* **M18.**
[from OUT- + POST *noun*².]
▶**A** *noun.* **1** A detachment placed at a distance from the main body of a force, esp. as a guard against surprise. **M18.**
2 A trading settlement situated near a frontier or at a remote place in order to facilitate the commercial contacts of a larger and more centrally situated town or settlement; any remote or isolated branch or settlement. **E19.**
3 The furthest territory of an empire, esp. (more fully ***outpost of Empire***) of the British Empire. **E20.**

📖 **2** W. J. ENTWISTLE The Dravidian languages . . have left behind them a solitary outpost in the Brahui. L. VAN DER POST A small African outpost on the edge of . . Northern Bechuanaland. **3** *Holiday Which?* This powerful last outpost of the Byzantine empire.

▶**B** *attrib.* or as *adjective.* Constituting or stationed at an outpost. **L18.**

📖 *Royal Air Force Journal* On airfields and outpost stations, the R.A.F. has taken root. *Discovery* The scheme for building a metal outpost satellite.

outpour /ˈaʊtpɔː/ *noun.* **M19.**
[from OUT- + POUR *noun.*]
An act of pouring out; an outpouring, an overflow.

📖 V. NABOKOV He would . . use binoculars to decipher from where he stood that outpour of illicit affection.

outpour /aʊtˈpɔː/ *verb.* Chiefly *poet.* **L17.**
[from OUT- + POUR *verb.*]
1 *verb trans.* Pour or send out in or as in a stream. Cf. earlier OUTPOURING *noun* 1. **L17.**
2 *verb intrans.* Flow out in or as in a stream. **M19.**

outpouring /ˈaʊtpɔːrɪŋ/ *noun.* **LME.**
[from OUT- + *pouring* verbal noun of POUR *verb.*]
1 The action or an act of pouring out. **LME.**
2 A thing which is poured out; an effusion; *esp.* (freq. in *pl.*) a lengthy spoken or written expression of emotion. **E19.**

📖 **1** B. THORPE An incessant outpouring of Northlanders in quest of booty. G. BLACK The American style of newscasting, a breathless outpouring of words. **2** THACKERAY These artless outpourings of paternal feeling. *Daily Telegraph* The . . outpourings of smoke . . sink earthward. *Independent* An outpouring of remorse, bitterness and heady triumphalism.

outpsych /aʊtˈsʌɪk/ *verb trans. colloq.* (chiefly *US*). **L20.**
[from OUT- + PSYCH *verb.*]
Gain a psychological advantage over (another person); defeat by psychological influence.

output /ˈaʊtpʊt/ *noun.* **M19.**
[from OUT- + PUT *noun*¹. Cf. earlier INPUT *noun.*]
1 (The amount of) what is produced by an industry or process, or by mental or artistic effort. **M19.** ▸**b** Energy produced by a machine; *spec.* an electrical signal delivered by or available from an electronic device. **L19.** ▸**c** Data or results produced by a computer; the physical medium on which these are represented. **M20.**
2 The action or process of supplying an output; production. **M20.**
3 A place where, or device through which, an output (esp. an electrical signal) is delivered by a system. **M20.**

📖 **1** J. AGATE I have written . . very nearly double Balzac's output. V. PACKARD Goods producers were achieving a fabulous output. **2** A. BURGER The output of epinephrine by the adrenal gland. **3** *Opera Now* The Systemline link . . will operate from the tape outputs.

output /ˈaʊtpʊt/ *verb trans.* Infl. **-tt-**. Pa. t. & pple **-put**, (sense 4 also) **-putted.** **ME.**
[In branch I from OUT- + PUT *verb*¹. In branch II from the noun.]
▶**I 1** Expel, eject, dismiss. Long *obsolete* exc. *Scot.* **ME.**
†**2** Fraudulently circulate (false coin) as legal tender. *Scot.* **M16–E18.**
†**3** Provide (men) for military service. Only in **M17.**
▶**II 4** Produce, deliver, or supply as output. **M19.**

📖 **4** *Your Computer* The two parts can be used to output data to a serial . . printer.

outputter /ˈaʊtpʊtə/ *noun.* **LME.**
[from OUT- + PUTTER *noun*¹.]
1 An accomplice of thieves and rustlers; a person who handles stolen property. Long *obsolete* exc. *Hist.* **LME.**
†**2** A person who fraudulently circulated false coin as legal tender. *Scot.* **L16–M17.**
†**3** A person under an obligation to provide men for military service. Only in **M17.**

outrage /ˈaʊtreɪdʒ/ *noun.* **ME.**
[Old & mod. French, from Old French *outrer* exceed, exaggerate, from *outre* beyond from late Latin ULTRA-: see -AGE.]
†**1 a** Lack of moderation, intemperance; extravagance, exaggeration. **ME–L16.** ▸**b** Foolhardiness; presumption. **LME–M16.**
2 Violent or disorderly action or behaviour; tumult of passion, disorder; violence of language, insolence; (an) uproar, a loud cry. *arch.* **ME.**
3 A violent injury or deed, *esp.* one committed against a person or against society. **LME.** ▸**b** A gross or wanton injury done to feelings, principles, etc. **M18.** ▸**c** Fierce anger or indignation. **E20.**
†**4** A violent exertion of force. *rare.* **L15–E16.**
5 A person of strange or wild appearance; a person who is extravagant in behaviour. **M19.**

📖 **2** S. JOHNSON I bore the diminution of my riches without any outrages of sorrow. W. COWPER Wherever there is war there is misery and outrage. **3** J. COLVILLE Bomb outrages occurred in London. **b** *Times* The very idea of having to pay a parking charge seems . . an outrage. **c** *New York Times* The President expressed his outrage over this latest . . military action.

outrage /ˈaʊtreɪdʒ/ *verb.* **ME.**
[from the noun. In sense 3 infl. by RAGE *verb.*]
†**1** *verb intrans.* Behave immoderately or extravagantly; run riot. **ME–E18.**
2 *verb trans.* Treat with gross violence or indignity; injure; mistreat. **LME.** ▸**b** Violate or infringe flagrantly (a law, authority, principle, etc.). **E18.** ▸**c** Arouse fierce anger or indignation in; deeply offend. Freq. as ***outraged*** *ppl adjective.* **E20.**
†**3** *verb intrans.* Burst into a rage, be furious. **L15–E17.**

📖 **2** *Weekend World (Johannesburg)* 'Now let us lie down, my wife'. Langton then outraged her for the whole night. **b** H. G. WELLS You are living . . under a definitely Christian moral code and my son . . has persuaded you to outrage it. **c** E. BOWEN Throughout tea the outraged Harriet had not suffered in silence. *Music & Letters* Elgar had been outraged by the royalty (4d.) offered him.

■ **outrager** *noun* a person who causes outrage, a violater **L19.** **outraging** *adjective* = OUTRAGEOUS *adjective* 2, 3 **M16.**

outrageous /aʊtˈreɪdʒəs/ *adjective & adverb.* **ME.**
[Old French *outrageus* (mod. *-eux*), formed as OUTRAGE *noun*: see -OUS.]
▶**A** *adjective.* **1** Immoderate, intemperate, extravagant; enormous, extraordinary. **ME.**
2 Unrestrained in action; violent, furious. Formerly also, excessively bold or fierce. **LME.**
3 Excessively injurious or cruel; of the nature of a violent wrong or offence; grossly immoral or offensive. **LME.**

📖 **1** *Holiday Which?* British tourists . . continue to make unacceptable and . . outrageous demands on consular staff. S. J. LEONARDI She smoked cigars, said outrageous things. **3** A. COHEN What . . arouses me to fury is the outrageous suffering of the young.

▶†**B** *adverb.* Outrageously. **LME–E16.**
■ **outrageously** *adverb* **ME.** **outrageousness** *noun* **LME.**

outrake /ˈaʊtreɪk/ *noun.* Long *obsolete* exc. *Scot. & north.* **ME.**
[from OUT- + RAKE *noun*².]
1 An extensive open pasture; a way to such a pasture from enclosed fields. **ME.**
2 An expedition, a raid, a journey. **M18.**

For other words beginning with *out-* see the entry for **out-**

outran *verb pa. t.* of OUTRUN.

†**outrance** *noun.* LME–E19.
[Old French *oultrance*, (also mod.) *outrance* going beyond bounds, from Old & mod. French *ou(l)trer* pass beyond, from *oltre*, *outre*: see OUTRAGE *noun*, -ANCE.]
A degree which goes beyond bounds or beyond measure. Only in phrs. below.
at outrance at the last extremity. **to outrance**, **to the outrance** = À OUTRANCE.
¶ See also À OUTRANCE.

outrang *verb pa. t.* of OUTRING *verb*.

outray /aʊtˈreɪ/ *verb*[1]. Long *obsolete* exc. *dial.* ME.
[Anglo-Norman *ultreier*, *outreier*, Old French *ultreer*, *outreer*, *outrer*, from late Latin ULTRA-; practically identical with Old French *ou(l)trer*: see OUTRANCE.]
†**1** *verb intrans.* Go beyond or exceed bounds; break or run away (*from*); be or get out of array. ME–M17.
2 *verb intrans.* Go beyond the bounds of moderation or propriety; be extravagant. LME.
3 *verb trans.* Overcome; vanquish; surpass, excel. LME.
†**4** *verb intrans.* Be outrageous, commit outrages. Only in LME.
†**5** *verb trans.* Treat outrageously; injure, insult. LME–M16.
†**6** *verb trans.* Put out (of bounds), turn out, expel. LME–L15.

outray /aʊtˈreɪ/ *verb*[2]. *rare.* M17.
[from OUT- + RAY *noun*[1], *verb*[2].]
1 *verb intrans.* Radiate, emanate. M17.
2 *verb trans.* Surpass in radiance. M17.

outré /utre, ˈuːtreɪ/ *adjective.* E18.
[French, pa. pple of *outrer*: see OUTRANCE.]
Beyond the bounds of what is usual or proper; eccentric, unusual, out-of-the-way.
■ **outréness** *noun* M19.

outreach /ˈaʊtriːtʃ/ *noun.* L19.
[from OUT- + REACH *noun*.]
1 The action of reaching out; the extent or length of reaching out. L19.
2 The activity of an organization, esp. a Church, in making contact and fostering relations with people who are not connected with it; the fact or extent of this activity. M20.

> 🕮 **2** *Gleaner* Methods of furthering the outreach of the Jamaican church.

outreach /aʊtˈriːtʃ/ *verb.* LME.
[from OUT- + REACH *verb*[1].]
1 *verb trans. & intrans.* Reach out, stretch out, extend. *poet.* LME.
2 *verb intrans.* Go beyond bounds, stray. LME.
3 *verb trans.* Exceed in reach, reach or extend beyond; surpass. M16.
†**4** *verb trans.* Deceive, cheat; outwit. L16–M17.

outrecuidance /uːtəˈkwiːd(ə)ns, *foreign* utrəkɥidɑ̃s/ *noun. arch.* LME.
[Old & mod. French, from *outrecuider*, from *outre* (see OUTRANCE) + *cuider* think from Latin *cogitare*: see -ANCE.]
Excessive self-esteem; overweening self-confidence or self-conceit; arrogance; presumption.

out-relief /ˈaʊtrɪliːf/ *noun.* L19.
[from OUT- + RELIEF *noun*[1].]
Hist. Financial assistance given by the State to very poor people not living in a workhouse, almshouse, etc.; outdoor relief.

outridden *verb pa. pple* of OUTRIDE *verb*.

outride /ˈaʊtrʌɪd/ *noun.* M18.
[from the verb.]
†**1** The action or an act of riding out; an excursion. *rare.* Only in M18.
2 The territory of a commercial traveller. *local.* L19.
3 PROSODY. An additional unstressed syllable in a metrical foot that is not counted in the nominal scanning. L19.

outride /aʊtˈrʌɪd/ *verb.* Pa. t. **-rode** /-ˈrəʊd/; pa. pple **-ridden** /-ˈrɪd(ə)n/. LOE.
[from OUT- + RIDE *verb*.]
1 *verb intrans.* Ride out; *spec.* go marauding. Long *obsolete* exc. *poet.* LOE.
2 *verb trans.* †**a** Drive by riding, ride to exhaustion. Only in LME. ▸**b** Ride better, faster, or further than; leave behind by riding. M16.
3 *verb trans.* Of a ship: survive the violence of (a storm). M17.
4 *verb trans. & intrans.* Ride along the boundaries of (a tract of land) to check for straying cattle, note the condition of the grass, etc. *US.* L19.
■ ˈ**outriding** *ppl adjective* (*a*) that outrides; (*b*) PROSODY designating a syllable that is an outride: E19.

outrider /ˈaʊtrʌɪdə/ *noun.* ME.
[from OUT- + RIDER *noun*.]
†**1** An officer of the sheriff's court whose duties included collecting dues, delivering summonses, etc. ME–E17.
2 †**a** An officer of an abbey or convent who saw to the external domestic requirements of the community and looked after its manors. LME–M16. ▸**b** A fellow of New College, Oxford, who accompanies the Warden on an official visitation of the estates of the college. E20.
3 A person on horseback or in a motor vehicle who goes in front of or beside a vehicle as an escort. M16.
†**4** A forager of an army; a highwayman. L16–E17.
5 A commercial traveller; a tradesman's travelling agent. *dial.* M18.
6 A mounted herdsman who prevents cattle from straying beyond a certain limit. *US.* L19.
7 A mounted official who escorts racehorses to the starting post. *US.* M20.

> 🕮 **3** *Belfast Telegraph* A convoy, with Gardai motorcycle outriders halting traffic.

outrig /ˈaʊtrɪɡ/ *verb trans.* Infl. **-gg-**. M19.
[Back-form. from next, OUTRIGGING.]
Provide (esp. a boat) with outriggers. Chiefly as ***outrigged*** *ppl adjective.*

outrigger /ˈaʊtrɪɡə/ *noun.* M18.
[Perh. an alt. (by assoc. with RIG *noun*[5], *verb*[2]) of OUTLIGGER.]
1 NAUTICAL. A strong beam passed through the portholes of a sailing ship to secure the masts and counteract the strain in the act of careening; any spar or framework rigged up and projecting from a ship. M18.
2 A float or pontoon, together with its securing struts, fixed to a small boat parallel to and at some distance from it, to increase stability. M18.
3 Each of a set of supports extending out from a trailer or farm wagon to increase its carrying capacity. L18. ▸**b** A supporting structure that projects outwards from the main part of an aircraft or spacecraft. E20. ▸**c** A framework extending from the main chassis of a motor vehicle and supporting the body. M20.
4 An extension of the splinter-bar of a carriage to enable a second horse to be harnessed outside the shafts; an extra horse running outside the shafts. E19.
5 An iron bracket with a rowlock at the end that is fixed to the side of a rowing boat to increase the leverage of the oar; (also ***outrigger boat***) a light boat fitted with such brackets. M19.
6 Any of various structures that project from the face of a wall, a frame, etc. M19.
■ **outriggered** *adjective* fitted with an outrigger L19. **outriggerless** *adjective* lacking an outrigger M18.

outrigging /ˈaʊtrɪɡɪŋ/ *noun.* M19.
[from OUT- + RIGGING *noun*[2].]
A thing with which something is rigged out; outside rigging.

outright /*as adverb* aʊtˈrʌɪt, *as adjective* ˈaʊtrʌɪt/ *adverb & adjective.* ME.
[from OUT *adverb* + -RIGHT.]
▶ **A** *adverb.* †**1** (With ref. to direction in space) straight out or ahead, directly onward; (with ref. to time) straight away, immediately, without delay. ME–M19. ▸**b** Without a break, consecutively, continuously. L16–E17.
2 Fully, completely; without reservation or limitation; without reserve of manner or expression; not gradually or tentatively. ME.
3 So that the act is finished at once; altogether, entirely. E17.

> 🕮 **2** B. JOWETT Some bold man who . . will say outright what is best. **3** P. CHAPLIN He was killed outright in an air crash. *Japan Times* To win outright, Menem needs at least 301 of the 600 electors. *Business Franchise* Equipment can be leased rather than purchased outright.

▶ **B** *adjective.* **1** Direct; downright, thorough; undisputed; complete, total. M16.
2 Directed or going straight on. *rare.* E17.

> 🕮 **1** A. LURIE Adding an outright lie to an earlier lie of omission. *Guardian* He did it on the first ballot, achieving an outright majority over all his rivals.

■ ˈ**outrightly** *adverb* (*rare*) = OUTRIGHT *adverb* 3 M17. ˈ**outrightness** *noun* the quality of being outright in speech or thought; directness, straightforwardness: M19.

outring /ˈaʊtrɪŋ/ *adjective.* M18.
[from OUT- + RING *noun*[1].]
Designating the outer drain and bank of a drainage area.

outring /aʊtˈrɪŋ/ *verb.* Pa. t. **-rang** /-ˈraŋ/; pa. pple **-rung** /-ˈrʌŋ/. LME.
[from OUT- + RING *verb*[1].]
1 *verb intrans. & (poet.) trans.* Ring out, sound with a clear loud note. LME.
2 *verb trans.* Outdo in ringing, ring louder than. M17.

outrival /aʊtˈrʌɪv(ə)l/ *verb trans.* Infl. **-ll-**, ***-l-**. E17.
[from OUT- + RIVAL *verb*.]
Outdo as a rival; surpass in a competition.

For other words beginning with *out-* see the entry for **out-**

†**outrive** *verb.* Infl. as RIVE *verb.* M16.
[from OUT- + RIVE *verb*.]
1 *verb intrans.* Tear or burst apart. *Scot.* Only in M16.
2 *verb trans.* Pull out or tear apart forcibly; break up (rough land). L16–M18.

outro /ˈaʊtrəʊ/ *noun. colloq.* Pl. **-os**. L20.
[from OUT *adverb* after INTRO.]
A concluding section, esp. of a broadcast programme or musical work.

†**outroad** *noun.* M16–M19.
[from OUT- + ROAD *noun*.]
An act of riding out; *esp.* a raid, a sally.

outroar /ˈaʊtrɔː/ *noun.* M19.
[from OUT- + ROAR *noun*[1].]
A loud noise or cry, an uproar.

outroar /aʊtˈrɔː/ *verb trans.* E17.
[from OUT- + ROAR *verb*.]
Roar louder or more than; drown the roaring of.

outrode *verb pa. t.* of OUTRIDE *verb*.

outroot /aʊtˈruːt/ *verb trans.* LME.
[from OUT- + ROOT *verb*[1], prob. after Latin *eradicare*.]
Pluck out or up by the root, root out; eradicate, exterminate.

outrun /aʊtˈrʌn/ *verb.* Infl. **-nn-**. Pa. t. **-ran** /-ˈran/; pa. pple **-run**. ME.
[from OUT- + RUN *verb*.]
1 *verb intrans.* Run out (now only *lit.*, formerly also *fig.*). ME.
2 *verb trans.* Run faster or further than; leave behind by greater speed; escape, elude; *fig.* get ahead of, go beyond. E16.
†**3** *verb trans.* Run through; pass, spend, (time); wear out (clothes etc.). Only in 17.

> 🕮 **2** J. A. SYMONDS The poet's imagination had probably outrun the fact. **outrun the constable**: see CONSTABLE *noun* 4.

out-run /ˈaʊtrʌn/ *noun.* LOE.
[from OUT- + RUN *verb*.]
1 The act or fact of running out; *spec.* the outward run of a sheepdog. LOE.
2 An outlying or distant run for livestock; outlying or surrounding pasture land. L19.
3 A level stretch at the foot of a ski slope. E20.
¶ Rare before L19.

outrung *verb pa. pple* of OUTRING *verb*.

outrunner /ˈaʊtrʌnə/ *noun.* L16.
[from OUT- + RUNNER.]
A person who or thing which runs out; *spec.* an attendant who runs in front of or beside a carriage; the leading dog of a team of sledge dogs; *fig.* a forerunner, a herald.
¶ Rare before L19.

outrush /ˈaʊtrʌʃ/ *noun.* L19.
[from OUT- + RUSH *noun*[2].]
A rushing out; a violent outflow.

outrush /aʊtˈrʌʃ/ *verb.* E17.
[from OUT- + RUSH *verb*[2].]
1 *verb intrans.* Rush out. E17.
2 *verb trans.* AMER. FOOTBALL. Excel or outdo in rushing. M20.

outscourer /ˈaʊtskaʊrə/ *noun. arch.* M16.
[from OUT- + SCOURER *noun*[1].]
A scout, a lookout.

outscourings /ˈaʊtskaʊərɪŋz/ *noun pl.* E19.
[from OUT- + SCOURING *noun* + -S[1].]
Material washed out or removed by scouring; dregs.

†**outscout** *noun.* E18–M19.
[from OUT- + SCOUT *noun*[3].]
= OUTSCOURER.

outseg /aʊtˈsɛɡ/ *verb trans. US colloq.* Infl. **-gg-**. M20.
[from OUT- + SEG *noun*[4].]
Support or advocate a more segregationist policy than.

outsell /aʊtˈsɛl/ *verb trans.* Pa. t. & pple **-sold** /-ˈsəʊld/. E17.
[from OUT- + SELL *verb*.]
1 Exceed in price when sold; *fig.* exceed in value. Long *rare.* E17.
2 Sell more than; have a larger sale than. L17.

> 🕮 **2** *National Observer (US)* Washington outsold the Soviet Union, its nearest rival. G. SAYER The book . . outsells all the other volumes.

†**outsend** *verb trans.* Pa. t. & pple **-sent**. LME–M19.
[from OUT- + SEND *verb*[1].]
Send out or forth; emit.

out-sentry /ˈaʊtsɛntri/ *noun*. **L17**.
[from OUT- + SENTRY *noun*^{1}.]
A sentry placed at a distance ahead.

outsert /ˈaʊtsəːt/ *noun*. **M20**.
[from OUT- + IN)SERT *noun*.]
1 BOOKBINDING. A signature which is placed outside another signature during binding. **M20**.
2 Promotional material which is placed on the outside of a package, publication, etc. **M20**.

outset /ˈaʊtsɛt/ *noun*. **L15**.
[from OUT- + SET *noun*^{1}.]
†**1** The advancing of a sum of money; the payment of a promised sum; in *pl.*, outgoings, expenditure. **L15–M18**.
2 An enclosure from outlying moorland, pasture, or common; an enclosure detached from the estate to which it belongs. *Scot.* **E16**.
3 The action or fact of setting off or embellishing; a thing which sets something off. *Scot.* **L16**.
†**4** That with which a venture starts; an initial outlay. **E–M18**.
5 The action or fact of setting out on a journey, course of action, business, etc.; a start, a beginning. Now chiefly in ***at the outset***, ***from the outset***. **M18**.

> **5** W. IRVING A good outset is half the voyage. H. JAMES I made up my mind at the outset. P. GROSSKURTH From the outset Freud had been suspicious of him.

outsetter /ˈaʊtsɛtə/ *noun*. **L16**.
[from OUT- + SETTER *noun*^{1}.]
†**1** A person who sets out. *Scot.* Only in **L16**.
2 An outdweller. **L17**.

outsetting /ˈaʊtsɛtɪŋ/ *noun & adjective*. **M16**.
[from OUT- + SETTING *noun*, *adjective*.]
▶ **A** *noun*. †**1** Proclamation; publishing, promotion. *Scot.* **M16–E17**.
2 The action of setting out on a journey, course of action, undertaking, etc. **L17**.
▶ **B** *adjective*. †**1** That lives in the open or outside an enclosure etc. Only in **M17**.
2 That flows steadily outward. **M18**.

outshew *verb* see OUTSHOW.

outshifts /ˈaʊtʃɪfts/ *noun pl.* Long *obsolete* exc. *dial.* **L16**.
[from OUT- + *shift* (use unidentified) + -S^1.]
The outskirts of a town.

outshine /aʊtˈʃʌɪn/ *verb*. Pa. t. & pple **-shone** /-ˈʃɒn/. **L16**.
[from OUT- + SHINE *verb*.]
1 *verb trans.* Surpass in shining or brightness, shine brighter than; *fig.* surpass in ability, excellence, etc. **L16**.
2 *verb intrans.* Shine forth or out. **L19**.

> **1** R. PLAYER Doctor Clayton was . . determined not to be outshone.

outshining /ˈaʊtʃʌɪnɪŋ/ *adjective & noun*. **LME**.
[from OUT- + SHINING *adjective*, *verbal noun* of SHINE *verb*.]
▶ **A** *adjective*. Shining out, effulgent, resplendent. **LME**.
▶ **B** *noun*. The action of shining out, the emission of light or brightness. **L17**.

outshone *verb pa. t. & pple* of OUTSHINE.

outshoot /ˈaʊtʃuːt/ *noun*. **M16**.
[from OUT- + SHOOT *noun*^{1}.]
1 A thing that shoots out or projects; a projection, an extension; *fig.* an offshoot. **M16**.
2 BASEBALL. = OUTCURVE 1. **L19**.

outshoot /aʊtˈʃuːt/ *verb*. Pa. t. & pple **-shot** /-ˈʃɒt/. **LME**.
[from OUT- + SHOOT *verb*.]
1 *verb trans.* & †*intrans.* Shoot out, project. **LME**.
2 *verb trans.* Shoot further or better than; defeat in shooting; (of a shoot, twig, etc.) grow beyond. **M16**.
3 *verb trans.* Of an archer etc.: shoot beyond (a mark or limit). Long *rare*. **M16**.

> **1** D. M. MOIR The woods outshoot their shadows dim. **2** T. MAYNARD He could outshoot any of the royal guard at the butts. J. VAN DE WETERING He is armed . . . With the carbine we could probably outshoot him.

outshot /ˈaʊtʃɒt/ *noun*. In sense 1 also **-shut** /-ʃʌt/. **LME**.
[from OUT- + SHOT *noun*^{1}.]
1 A part of a building projecting beyond the general line; a part built on as an extension. *north.* **LME**.
2 [Cf. OUTSHOT *adjective* 2.] In *pl.* Second-quality hemp or white rags. **L19**.

outshot /ˈaʊtʃɒt/ *adjective*. **ME**.
[from OUT- + SHOT *ppl adjective*.]
1 Shot or thrust out, projected. **ME**.
2 Designating second-quality Russian hemp. **L18**.
3 Projecting, made to extend beyond the general line of a building. **E19**.

outshot *verb pa. t. & pple* of OUTSHOOT *verb*.

outshow /aʊtˈʃəʊ/ *verb trans. poet.* Pa. pple **-shown** /-ˈʃəʊn/, **-showed**. Also **-shew**, pa. pple **-shewn**, **-shewed**. **LME**.
[from OUT- + SHOW *verb*.]
Show, exhibit, manifest.

outshut *noun* see OUTSHOT *noun*.

outside /aʊtˈsʌɪd, *as adjective also* ˈaʊtsʌɪd/ *noun, adjective, adverb, & preposition*. **E16**.
[from OUT- + SIDE *noun*.]
▶ **A** *noun*. **1** The outermost side or surface of something; the exterior. **E16**. ▸**b** The outer part or parts of something. **L16**. ▸**c** FENCING. The left-hand side of a sword. Now *rare*. **M19**.
2 *gen.* The area adjacent to and beyond the outer side of something. **E16**. ▸**b** In northern Canada and Alaska, the rest of the world, *esp.* a settled or urbanized area. **E19**. ▸**c** *Austral.* The unsettled parts of the outback. **M19**. ▸**d** The world out of prison. Also, the world out of the army, civilian life. *slang*. **E20**.
3 The outward or visible form of something, as distinct from its substance; *esp.* a person's outward aspect, as distinct from his or her inner nature. **L16**.
4 a (A part of) a thing which forms an outer edge or border; *spec.* (in *pl.*), the outer sheets of a ream of paper. **E17**. ▸**b** *Hist.* A passenger travelling on the outer side of a coach etc. **L18**. ▸**c** FOOTBALL & HOCKEY etc. A player in an outside position. **L19**.
5 The upper limit of an estimate; the utmost. Chiefly in ***at the outside***. *colloq.* **E18**.

> **1** *Times* Coats . . are all reversible with soft knitted mohair on the outside and . . dishcloth of knitting inside. R. DAHL It looked like a suitcase because the outside was sheathed in leather. **outside in** = *inside out* s.v. INSIDE *noun* 2. **b** DOUGLAS STUART The outside of the camp was a blaze of vincas. F. O'CONNOR Parker began at the outside of the field and made circles inward. **2** DICKENS Can I open the door from the outside, I wonder? **be on the outside looking in** be excluded from some group, activity, etc. **d** *Sound Choice* He only lasted 10 months on the outside before having his ass hauled back to prison. **3** J. M. BROWNJOHN On the outside . . I'm just a business man . . but at heart I'm a person of wide interests. E. S. PERSON Some marriages . . judged from the outside to be successful are . . dead. **4c** *Times* Although their forwards were playing . . a solid game the Westminster outsides were too slow. **5** A. PRICE You've got him for a week . . or ten days at the outside.

▶ **B** *adjective*. **1** Situated on or belonging to the outer side, surface, or edge; exterior. **M17**. ▸**b** FOOTBALL & HOCKEY etc. Designating (a player in) a position on or towards the side boundary of the field. **L19**.
†**2** Having only an outward form; insubstantial, superficial. **M17–E18**.
3 Existing, occurring, or originating away from a place or area, esp. a place of work; external. **M19**. ▸**b** In northern Canada and Alaska, of or pertaining to the rest of the world, esp. to any settled or urbanized area. **L19**. ▸**c** *spec.* Of a lavatory: situated outside a house or other main building. **M20**.
4 (Of an estimate etc.) the greatest or highest possible; (of a chance) remote, unlikely. **M19**.
5 Not of or belonging to some community, organization, institution, etc.; *spec.* (of a broker) not a member of a stock exchange. **L19**.

> **1** E. LEONARD There were three cars . . Jack watched them in his outside mirror. *Which?* The machine has to be sited near a window or outside wall. **b outside forward**, ***outside left***, ***outside right***, etc. **3** N. HAWTHORNE An outside perception of his degree and kind of merit. B. SPOCK To learn at first-hand about the outside world, about the jobs of the . . workers. A. THWAITE The Museum had . . been protesting about the . . outside work he was taking on. **c** D. LODGE At Gran's house . . with an outside toilet, you didn't go unless you really had to. **4** A. TROLLOPE The outside period during which breath could be supported. *Guardian* There was still an outside chance that Shelford might change his mind. **5** S. BELLOW Two outside parties had come between them. *Highlife* The distinction . . is sometimes obscure to an outside observer.

Special collocations: **outside broadcast** a radio or television broadcast not transmitted from or recorded inside a studio. **outside broadcasting** the action of making an outside broadcast. **outside cabin** a ship's cabin with an outside window or porthole. **outside edge** each of the edges of an ice skate which face outwards when both feet are together. **outside interest** an interest or hobby not connected with one's work or day-to-day life. **outside job** *colloq.* a crime committed in a building etc. by a person not connected with the building etc. concerned. **outside lane** the outermost lane of a sports track etc., which is longest because of the curve. **outside line** a telephone connection with an external exchange. **outside loop** a looping movement made by an aeroplane etc. in which the back of the aeroplane etc. is on the outside of the curve. **outside man** *US slang* a person playing a special role in a confidence trick or robbery. **outside seat** a seat at the end of a row in a cinema etc. **outside track** = *outside lane* above.

▶ **C** *adverb*. **1** On or to the outside or exterior; *esp.* out in the open air; beyond a limit or boundary; not within some community, organization, etc. **E19**.
2 *spec.* **a** In northern Canada and Alaska, in or to the rest of the world, esp. a settled or urbanized area. **L19**. ▸**b** Out of prison; in civilian life. *slang*. **E20**.

> **1** H. JAMES I was hanging about outside, on the steps. M. SINCLAIR Outside in the passage, she stood . . listening. V. WOOLF The wind rushed outside, but the small flame . . burnt quietly. G. CHARLES That was all right at home. But outside, . . he didn't mix much.

Phrases: **outside of** (*a*) = OUTSIDE *preposition*; **get outside of**, (*slang*) eat, drink; (*b*) (*colloq.*, chiefly *N. Amer.*) apart from, except for.

▶ **D** *preposition*. **1** Of position: on the outer side of; external to; *spec.* beyond the limits of (an action, sphere, etc.). **E19**.
2 Of motion etc.: to the outer side or exterior of; beyond (the limits of). **M19**.

> **1** M. SINCLAIR He wouldn't accept any statement outside the Bible. J. MITCHELL A precise . . meaning closed to anyone outside the inner circle. A. CARTER Sitting outside the house and not being able to get in. **2** *Daily News* Be so kind as to go outside the door and shut it.

■ **out'sidedness** *noun* (*a*) the quality of having an outside or surface; (*b*) = OUTSIDENESS: **M19**. **out'sideness** *noun* the quality or state of being outside; externality, externalism: **M17**.

outsider /aʊtˈsʌɪdə/ *noun*. **E19**.
[from prec. + -ER^1.]
1 A person who or thing which is situated outside an enclosure, boundary, etc., or on the outside of a group or series. **E19**.
2 *fig.* **a** A person who does not belong to a particular circle, community, or profession; *spec.* an uninitiated person, a layman. **M19**. ▸**b** A person isolated from conventional society, either by choice or by some social or intellectual constraint; a misfit. **E20**.
3 A horse not included among the favourites in a particular race, and not generally expected to win; *transf.* a competitor, applicant, etc., considered unlikely to succeed. **M19**.
4 In *pl.* A pair of long nippers which can be inserted into a keyhole from the side opposite the key so as to grasp and turn the key. *Criminals' slang*. **M19**.

> **1** THOMAS HUGHES Bursting through the outsiders . . straight to the heart of the scrummage. **2a** DICKENS He is only an outsider, and not in the mysteries. J. CHEEVER The sense of being an outsider would change . . when he knew the language. E. S. PERSON An outsider can't break up a healthy marriage. **3** JOHN BROOKE Very much an outsider in the matrimonial stakes.

Comb. & phrases: **outsider art** art produced by untrained artists, esp. children or the mentally ill; **outsider artist** a creator of outsider art; **rank outsider** (*a*) in a race etc., an outsider at very long odds; (*b*) a person considered a social inferior.

■ **outsiderdom** *noun* the condition or state of being a social outsider **M20**. **outsiderish** *adjective* of the nature or character of a social outsider **M20**. **outsiderishness** *noun* **M20**. **outsiderism** *noun* the state or practice of being a social outsider **M20**. **outsiderly** *adjective* characteristic of a social outsider **M20**.

†**outsight** *noun*^{1}. *Scot. & north.* **M16–E19**.
[Origin uncertain: cf. INSIGHT *noun*^{2}.]
More fully ***outsight plenishing***. Goods (esp. implements) used or kept out of doors. Opp. INSIGHT *noun*^{2}.

outsight /ˈaʊtsʌɪt/ *noun*^{2}. **L16**.
[from OUT- + SIGHT *noun*.]
†**1** Prospect, outlook. **L16**.
2 Vision or perception of external things. **E17**.

outsize /ˈaʊtsʌɪz/ *noun & adjective*. **M19**.
[from OUT- + SIZE *noun*^{1}.]
▶ **A** *noun*. An exceptionally large person or thing; *esp.* (an item of clothing of) a size above the standard or stock sizes. **M19**.
▶ **B** *adjective*. Exceptionally large; *esp.* (of an item of clothing) above the standard or stock sizes. **M19**.

> D. LODGE Youths in outsize hats. B. CHATWIN Outside the Presidential Palace hung an outsize poster of the head of State.

■ **outsized** *adjective* = OUTSIZE *adjective* **L19**.

outskirt /*as noun* ˈaʊtskəːt, *as verb* aʊtˈskəːt/ *noun & verb*. **L16**.
[from OUT- + SKIRT *noun*.]
▶ **A** *noun*. (An area within) an outer border or fringe. Now *esp.* in *pl.*, the outer border of a town, city, district, etc. **L16**.

> T. HARDY The outskirt of the garden . . had been left uncultivated. HUGH WALPOLE She . . lived in a little green house . . in the Polchester outskirts. E. TEMPLETON The new villa on the outskirts of the town. *fig.*: C. LAMB The remote edges and outskirts of history. E. WHARTON A social outskirt which Lily had always . . avoided.

▶ **B** *verb trans.* Skirt, border; pass along the outskirts of. **E19**.

■ **outskirter** *noun* (*rare*) a person on the outskirts of an area, subject, etc. **M19**.

For other words beginning with *out-* see the entry for **out-**

outsmart /aʊtˈsmɑːt/ *verb trans. colloq.* E20.
[from OUT- + SMART *adjective*.]
Defeat or get the better of by superior craft or ingenuity; outwit.

outsold *verb pa. t. & pple* of OUTSELL.

outspan /ˈaʊtspan/ *verb*[1] & *noun*. *S. Afr. arch.* E19.
[Dutch *uitspannen*, from *uit* out + *spannen* to span.]
▶ **A** *verb*. Infl. **-nn-**.
1 *verb intrans.* Unharness oxen etc. from a wagon; break a wagon journey in this way. Also, encamp. E19.
2 *verb trans.* Unharness (oxen etc.) from a wagon; unhitch (a wagon). M19.
▶ **B** *noun*. A place for grazing or encampment when travelling by wagon. E19.

outspan /aʊtˈspan/ *verb*[2] *trans. rare.* Infl. **-nn-**. L19.
[from OUT- + SPAN *verb*[1].]
Extend beyond the span of.

outspeak /aʊtˈspiːk/ *verb*. Infl. as SPEAK *verb*; pa. t. usu. **-spoke** /-ˈspəʊk/, pa. pple usu. **-spoken** /-ˈspəʊk(ə)n/. LME.
[from OUT- + SPEAK *verb*.]
1 *verb intrans. & trans.* Speak (something) out, esp. frankly or unreservedly. *rare.* LME.
†**2** *verb trans.* Express or signify more than. Only in E17.
3 *verb trans.* Outdo in speaking; speak more forcibly than. E17.

outspoken /aʊtˈspəʊk(ə)n/ *adjective*. Orig. *Scot.* E19.
[from OUT- + SPOKEN *adjective*.]
1 Given to speaking out; unreserved or frank in one's opinions or speech. E19.
2 Of an opinion, statement, etc.: candid, frank. M19.

> 📖 **1** D. PAE He is very outspoken; but he does not mean to be rude. G. PRIESTLAND Sylvia . . gets rather outspoken after her second cocktail. **2** *Independent* He has acquired . . notoriety . . for his outspoken views.

■ **outspokenly** *adverb* M19. **outspokenness** /-n-n-/ *noun* M19.

outsprang *verb pa. t.* of OUTSPRING *verb*.

outspread /*as verb* aʊtˈsprɛd, *as noun* ˈaʊtsprɛd/ *verb & noun*. ME.
[from OUT- + SPREAD *verb, noun*.]
▶ **A** *verb trans. & intrans.* Pa. t. & pple **-spread**. Spread or stretch out; expand, extend. ME.
▶ **B** *noun*. The action or an act of spreading out; (an) expansion. M19.

outspring /*as verb* aʊtˈsprɪŋ, *as noun* ˈaʊtsprɪŋ/ *verb & noun*. *poet.* ME.
[from OUT- + SPRING *verb*[1], *noun*[1].]
▶ **A** *verb*. Pa. t. **-sprang** /-ˈspraŋ/; pa. pple **-sprung** /-ˈsprʌŋ/.
1 *verb intrans.* Spring out; issue forth. ME. ▸†**b** Be born. M–L16.
2 *verb trans.* Spring beyond. *rare.* L16.
▶ **B** *noun*. The action or an act of springing out. M16.

outstand /aʊtˈstand/ *verb*. Pa. t. & pple **-stood** /-ˈstʊd/. L16.
[from OUT- + STAND *verb*.]
1 *verb trans.* Stand out against; resist or endure successfully. Now *dial.* L16. ▸**b** Maintain (a view etc.) in opposition; contradict (a person). *dial.* M17.
2 *verb trans.* Stay beyond the time of or duration of; overrun. *poet.* E17.
3 *verb intrans.* Stand out conspicuously. Cf. earlier OUTSTANDING *noun. poet.* M18.
■ **ˈoutstander** *noun* (*Scot.*) a dissenter; *spec.* (*Hist.*) an opponent of the National Covenant or its adherents: M17.

outstanding /aʊtˈstandɪŋ/ *noun*. LME.
[from OUT- + STANDING *noun*. In sense 3 absol. use of next.]
†**1** The action or an act of standing or jutting out; (a) projection. LME–E17.
2 Dissent. *Scot.* M17.
3 In *pl.* Unsettled debts. M19.

> 📖 **3** *Banker* Dealers . . should take their fair share of placing total outstandings.

outstanding /aʊtˈstandɪŋ/ *adjective*. E17.
[from OUTSTAND *verb* + -ING[2].]
1 That stands or juts out conspicuously; projecting. *arch.* E17.
2 Unresolved, pending; *esp.* (of a debt etc.) unsettled. M17.
3 Noteworthy, remarkable; exceptional. M19.

> 📖 **2** R. GITTINGS A bill of £30 was left outstanding. *Japan Times* Cossiga asked De Mita to stay on to handle outstanding business. **3** D. HALBERSTAM He had just won a coveted George Peabody Award for outstanding reporting. *Early Music* He must . . have been an outstanding musician.

■ **outstandingly** *adverb* E20.

outstart /*as verb* aʊtˈstɑːt, *as noun* ˈaʊtstɑːt/ *verb & noun*. LME.
[from OUT- + START *verb, noun*[2].]
▶ **A** *verb*. **1** *verb intrans.* Rush out suddenly, spring out. Long *obsolete* exc. *poet.* LME.
2 *verb trans.* Orig., go beyond, exceed. Later, go ahead of, precede. Now *rare* or *obsolete*. L16.
▶ **B** *noun*. The action or an act of starting out; the outset. *rare.* M19.

outstate /ˈaʊtsteɪt/ *adjective*. *US.* M20.
[from OUT- + STATE *noun*.]
1 Of or pertaining to a part of a State away from the main population centre. M20.
2 = OUT-OF-STATE. M20.

outstation /ˈaʊtsteɪʃ(ə)n/ *noun*. E19.
[from OUT- + STATION *noun*.]
1 A station, settlement, etc., in a remote area or far from a centre of population or business; *Austral.* & *NZ* a part of a farming estate separate from the main estate. E19.
2 A subordinate branch of an organization, business, etc., usu. at a considerable distance from the headquarters. L19.

outstep /*as verb* aʊtˈstɛp, *as noun* ˈaʊtstɛp/ *verb & noun*. M17.
[from OUT- + STEP *verb, noun*[1].]
▶ **A** *verb trans.* Infl. **-pp-**. Step outside of or beyond; overstep, deviate from. M17.
▶ **B** *noun*. **1** A marching pace. *rare.* M19.
2 An explorative or additional oil well sited beyond an area already drilled. Also ***outstep well***. M20.

outstood *verb pa. t. & pple* of OUTSTAND.

outstretch /*as verb* aʊtˈstrɛtʃ, *as noun* ˈaʊtstrɛtʃ/ *verb & noun*. LME.
[from OUT- + STRETCH *verb, noun*.]
▶ **A** *verb trans.* **1** Stretch or reach out (esp. one's hands or arms). LME.
2 Spread out or extend (land etc.) over an area. Freq. in *pass.*, be extended. L15.
3 Stretch beyond (a limit etc.); overreach. L16.
4 Stretch to the limit; strain. Now *rare* or *obsolete*. E17.
†**5** Surpass in competition. M17–E18.
▶ **B** *noun*. **1** The action or an act of stretching out. M19.
2 An outstretched tract of land; an extent. M19.

outsucken /ˈaʊtsʌk(ə)n/ *noun*. L16.
[from OUT- + SUCKEN *noun*.]
SCOTS LAW (now *Hist.*). More fully ***outsucken multure***. Multure payable to a particular mill for the grinding of corn grown outside its sucken.

outswinger /ˈaʊtswɪŋə/ *noun*. E20.
[from OUT- + SWINGER *noun*[1].]
1 CRICKET. (The bowler of) a ball bowled with a swerve or swing from the leg to the off. E20.
2 FOOTBALL. A pass, usu. across the goal-mouth, which curves away from the centre of the goal. M20.
■ **outswing** *noun* [back-form.] CRICKET the swerve or swing imparted to an outswinger M20.

outta /ˈaʊtə/ *preposition*. *informal* (orig. & chiefly *N. Amer.*). M20.
[Repr. a pronunc. Cf. OUTA.]
= OUT OF.

out-take /ˈaʊtteɪk/ *noun*. M19.
[from OUT- + TAKE *noun*.]
1 **a** Durability; capacity to last. *Scot.* M19. ▸**b** Yield; profit. *Scot.* M19.
2 CINEMATOGRAPHY & TELEVISION. A length of film or tape rejected in editing. M20.

out-take /aʊtˈteɪk/ *verb trans.* Long *obsolete* exc. *Scot.* Pa. t. **-took** /-ˈtʊk/; pa. pple **-taken** /-ˈteɪk(ə)n/. ME.
[from OUT- + TAKE *verb*.]
1 Take or lift out; extract; deliver, set free. Long only as ***out-taking*** *verbal noun*. ME.
†**2** Exclude from a class or category; except. ME–M19.

†**out-take** *preposition & conjunction* see OUT-TAKEN *preposition & conjunction*.

out-taken *verb pa. pple* of OUT-TAKE *verb*.

†**out-taken** *preposition & conjunction*. Also **out-take**. ME.
[pa. pple of OUT-TAKE *verb*.]
▶ **A** *preposition*. **1** = EXCEPT *preposition* 1. ME–E19.
2 = EXCEPT *preposition* 2. Only in ME.
▶ **B** *conjunction*. **1** = EXCEPT *conjunction* 3. Only in ME.
2 = EXCEPT *conjunction* 1. LME–L15.
¶ Revived by Sir Walter Scott in 19.

out-throw /*as verb* aʊtˈθrəʊ, *as noun* ˈaʊtθrəʊ/ *verb & noun*. ME.
[from OUT- + THROW *verb, noun*[2].]
▶ **A** *verb trans.* Pa. t. **-threw** /-ˈθruː/; pa. pple **-thrown** /-ˈθrəʊn/.
1 Throw or cast out; throw or thrust outward. Now *rare* exc. as OUT-THROWN. ME.
2 Throw beyond (a point); throw further than (another person). E17.
▶ **B** *noun*. The action or an act of throwing out; (an) ejection. Also, matter ejected, output. M19.
■ **ˈout-thrown** *adjective* thrown or cast out L19.

For other words beginning with *out-* see the entry for **out-**

out-thrust /*as verb* aʊtˈθrʌst, *as noun* ˈaʊtθrʌst/ *verb & noun*. LME.
[from OUT- + THRUST *verb, noun*.]
▶ **A** *verb trans.* Pa. t. & pple **-thrust**. Thrust outwards; project, extend. LME.

> 📖 C. D. SIMAK He lay back in the chair, with . . his long legs out-thrust . . underneath the radio console.

▶ **B** *noun*. The action or an act of thrusting outwards; an outward projection or pressure. M19.

> 📖 TOLKIEN An out-thrust of the eastward hill.

out-took *verb pa. t.* of OUT-TAKE *verb*.

out-turn /ˈaʊttəːn/ *noun*. E19.
[from OUT- + TURN *noun*.]
1 The quantity produced or yielded; output, product; ECONOMICS an amount or result attained, as opp. to an estimate. E19. ▸**b** The result of a process or sequence of events. *rare.* L19.
2 CURLING. An outward turn of the elbow and an inward turn of the hand made in delivering a stone. L19.

> 📖 **1** A. ALEXANDER There were two . . orders based upon the actual out-turn of expenditure.

outwall /ˈaʊtwɔːl/ *noun*. M16.
[from OUT- + WALL *noun*[1].]
1 The outer wall of a building or enclosure. Now *rare* or *obsolete*. M16.
2 *fig.* Orig., the clothing, the body. Later, a person's outer self or persona. Long *rare*. E17.

outward /ˈaʊtwəd/ *adjective & noun*. OE.
[from OUT- + -WARD.]
▶ **A** *adjective*. **1** Situated on or nearer the outside; outer, outermost. OE.
2 Of or pertaining to the outer or visible form of something, as opp. to its inner substance; external; *esp.* of or pertaining to the body as opp. to the mind, soul, or spirit. ME.
3 Of or pertaining to the external or material world. Formerly also *spec.*, temporal, secular. ME. ▸**b** Of a circumstance, relationship, etc.: external to oneself; extrinsic; (of a feeling etc.) directed outside oneself. E17.
†**4** Outside a country etc.; foreign; *fig.* lying outside some sphere of work, interest, etc. LME–L17.
5 Directed or proceeding towards the outside; (of a journey etc.) away from home. E18.

> 📖 **1** I. MURDOCH Tim sat . . looking out of the window . . . Gertrude turned on the lamp and the outward scene disappeared. **2** E. SAINTSBURY He loved the outward symbols of the Celtic way of life. D. LODGE The economy and outward appearance of the area have changed. **outward man** THEOLOGY the body; *joc.* clothing. ***outward visible sign***: see SIGN *noun*. **to outward seeming** apparently. **3** WORDSWORTH Those obstinate questionings Of sense and outward things. **b** J. MARTINEAU The law must define men's outward rights and relations. J. LE CARRÉ Whatever his outward longings, he was still living . . inside his head. **5** W. H. SMYTH A journey by sea . . usually includes the outward and homeward trips. *Physics Bulletin* The outward motion of the plasma.

▶ **B** *noun*. †**1** The outer part of something. LME–M16.
2 Outward form or appearance. E17.
3 In *pl.* Outside circumstances or things; externals. E17.
4 The external or material world. M19.
■ **outwardly** *adverb* LME. †**outwardmost** *adjective* outermost L16–E18. **outwardness** *noun* (*a*) the quality or condition of being outward; externality; objectivity; (*b*) preoccupation with or belief in outward things or externalities: L16.

outward /ˈaʊtwəd/ *adverb*. OE.
[formed as prec.]
1 **a** On the outside; externally. Now *rare* or *obsolete*. OE. ▸†**b** Outside one's house, country, etc.; abroad. ME–L17.
2 Towards the outside or exterior; away from some point or place. ME.
†**3** In outward form or appearance as opp. to inner substance; externally; publicly. LME–L17. ▸**b** On the outside of the body. E–M16.

> 📖 **2** SHAKES. *Twel. N.* How quickly the wrong side may be turn'd outward! H. CRANE Freight rafts and occasional liners starting outward. E. BOWEN Everyone started moving outward from the encampment.

outward-bound /aʊtwədˈbaʊnd/ *adjective*. In sense 2 **Outward Bound**. E17.
[from OUTWARD *adverb* + BOUND *adjective*[1].]
1 Proceeding outward; *esp.* (of a ship, person, voyage, etc.) going away from home. E17. ▸**b** *fig.* Dying. E19.
2 Designating or pertaining to a British organization providing naval and adventure training and other outdoor activities for young people. M20.

> 📖 **2** M. MORSE He had been sent on the Outward Bound course by his firm.

■ **outward-bounder** *noun* (*a*) *colloq.* an outward-bound ship etc.; (*b*) (with cap. initials) a person attending an Outward Bound school, course, etc., or advocating Outward Bound methods: M19.

outwards /ˈaʊtwədz/ *adverb.* OE.
[from OUTWARD *adverb*, with adverbial genit. *-es*, *-s*, as in *besides* etc.: see -s[3].]
1 = OUTWARD *adverb* 2. OE.
†**2** = OUTWARD *adverb* 1a. *rare*. OE–M16.

outwash /ˈaʊtwɒʃ/ *noun.* L19.
[from OUT- + WASH *noun*.]
GEOLOGY. Material such as sand, gravel, silt, etc., carried out from a glacier by melt water and deposited beyond the end moraine.
attrib.: ***outwash deposit***, ***outwash gravel***, ***outwash plain***, etc.

outwear /ˈaʊtwɛː/ *noun.* M20
[from OUT- + WEAR *noun*.]
Outerwear.

outwear /aʊtˈwɛː/ *verb trans.* Pa. t. **-wore** /-ˈwɔː/; pa. pple **-worn** /-ˈwɔːn/. M16.
[from OUT- + WEAR *verb*[1].]
1 Wear away; waste or destroy (as) by wearing. M16. ▸**b** Exhaust in strength or endurance. Earlier as OUTWORN *adjective*. E17.
2 *poet.* **a** Waste or spend (a period of time). L16. ▸**b** Overcome in the process of time. L16.
3 Outlast in wear. L16.

outwent *verb pa. t.* of OUTGO *verb*.

out West /aʊt ˈwɛst/ *adverbial phr.* M19.
[from OUT *adverb* + WEST *adverb*.]
Orig., in or towards the territory west of the early American settlements. Now, in or towards the West of the United States as regarded by inhabitants of the East.

> 🕮 *Guardian* He worked . . out west on the Union Pacific railroad.

outwick /*as noun* ˈaʊtwɪk, *as verb* aʊtˈwɪk/ *noun & verb.* *Scot.* E19.
[from OUT *adverb* + WICK *verb*[1].]
CURLING. ▸**A** *noun.* A shot intended to strike the outside of another stone and move it elsewhere. E19.
▸**B** *verb intrans.* Take or make an outwick. M19.

outwit /aʊtˈwɪt/ *verb trans.* Infl. **-tt-**. M17.
[from OUT- + WIT *noun*.]
1 Surpass in wisdom or knowledge. *arch.* M17.
2 Get the better of by superior skill or ingenuity. M17.

outwith /ˈaʊtwɪθ/ *preposition & adverb.* Chiefly *Scot. & north.* ME.
[from OUT *adverb* + WITH *preposition*.]
▸**A** *preposition.* **1** Of position: outside of, beyond. ME.
2 Of motion: out of, away from. LME.

> 🕮 **1** *Stornoway Gazette* The . . use of the games hall outwith school hours. M. HUNTER My country's history is largely unfamiliar to those outwith her borders. *Independent* Any such decision was . . outwith the protection of section 41.

▸**B** *adverb.* **1** Of position: on the outside, out of doors. ME.
2 Of direction: outward. LME.

outwore *verb pa. t.* of OUTWEAR *verb*.

outwork /ˈaʊtwəːk/ *noun.* E17.
[from OUT- + WORK *noun*.]
1 A detached outer part of a fortification or defence. E17.
†**2** = HORS D'OEUVRE. L17–E18.
3 Work done on an outside or exterior. Now *rare* or *obsolete*. L17.
4 Orig., work done out of doors. Now *esp.* work done away from an employer's premises. L18.

> 🕮 **1** *fig.*: DONNE All our moralities are but our outworks, our Christianity is our citadel.

■ **outworker** *noun* a person who works out of doors or away from an employer's premises E19.

outwork /aʊtˈwəːk/ *verb trans.* Pa. t. & pple **-worked**, (*arch.*) **-wrought** /-ˈrɔːt/. ME.
[from OUT- + WORK *verb*.]
1 †**a** Produce by work. *rare*. Only in ME. ▸**b** Work out to a conclusion. *poet.* L16.
2 †**a** Surpass in workmanship. L16–L18. ▸**b** Work harder or faster than. E17.

> 🕮 **1b** T. HARDY I saw, in web unbroken, Its history outwrought.

■ **ˈoutworking** *noun* the action or process of working out; practical operation: M19.

outworn /aʊtˈwɔːn, ˈaʊtwɔːn/ *adjective.* E16.
[pa. pple of OUTWEAR *verb*.]
1 Worn away; wasted or destroyed (as) by wear or by the action of time. Now chiefly *fig.*, (of a belief, institution, etc.) obsolete, out of date. E16.
2 Of a person, faculty, etc.: worn out, exhausted; spent. *literary*. L16.

> 🕮 **1** SHELLEY The earth doth like a snake renew Her winter weeds outworn. ROSEMARY MANNING Old intolerances based on outworn moral and social codes. **2** MILTON Inglorious, unemployed, with age outworn.

outworn *verb pa. pple* of OUTWEAR *verb*.

outwrought *verb pa. t. & pple* of OUTWORK *verb*.

outy /ˈaʊti/ *noun. colloq.* M20.
[from OUT *adverb* + -Y[6].]
sing. & in *pl.* An act of walking or letting out a pet, esp. a dog.

ouvert /uvɛːr/ *noun.* Pl. pronounced same. E20.
[French = open.]
BALLET. An open position of the feet.

ouvreuse /uvrøːz/ *noun.* Pl. pronounced same. L19.
[French.]
In France: an usherette.

ouvrier /uvrije/ *noun.* Fem. **-ière** /-ijɛːr/. Pl. pronounced same. M19.
[French.]
In France: a manual or industrial worker; a labourer.

ouvrierism /ˈuːvrɪərɪz(ə)m, *foreign* ˈuvrjerɪsm/ *noun.* M20.
[French, or from prec. + -ISM.]
Support for or advocacy of the rights of manual or industrial workers.

ouzel /ˈuːz(ə)l/ *noun.* Also **ousel**.
[Old English *ōsle* rel. to Old High German *amusla*, *amsala* (German *Amsel* blackbird).]
1 The blackbird, *Turdus merula*. Long *arch.*, *poet.*, & *dial.* OE. ▸**b** = ***ring ouzel*** s.v. RING *noun*[1]. LME.
2 Any of several other birds thought to resemble the blackbird (usu. with specifying word). Now *esp.* (in full ***water ouzel***), the dipper, *Cinclus cinclus*. E17.
1b ***rock ouzel***, ***tor ouzel***, etc.

ouzo /ˈuːzəʊ/ *noun.* Pl. **-os**. L19.
[mod. Greek.]
(A glass of) an aniseed-flavoured spirit from Greece.

ova *noun* pl. of OVUM.

Ovaherero /əʊvəhəˈrɪərəʊ/ *noun pl.* M19.
[Bantu, from *ova-* pl. prefix + HERERO.]
The Herero; *esp.* the majority group among the Herero-speaking peoples.

oval /ˈəʊv(ə)l/ *adjective, noun, & verb.* M16.
[medieval Latin *ovalis*, formed as OVUM: see -AL[1].]
▸**A** *adjective.* **1** Having the outline of an egg as projected on a surface; *loosely* elliptical. M16.
2 Of a solid or three-dimensional surface: egg-shaped; ellipsoidal. L16.
3 Of or pertaining to an egg. *rare*. M17.

> 🕮 **1** A. KOESTLER Planets move in oval, and not circular orbits. G. SAYER A heavily built man . . with a fleshy oval face. **Oval Office** the private office of the President of the United States in the White House.

▸**B** *noun.* **1** A plane figure resembling the longitudinal section of an egg; (a curve enclosing) a rounded shape without concave portions, elongated along one axis; *loosely* an ellipse. L16.
2 A body resembling an egg in shape or appearance; *spec.* †(***a***) = OVUM 1; (***b***) ARCHITECTURE an egg-shaped moulding. E17.
3 An object, area, etc., with an oval or elliptical outline; *spec.* (*Austral.*) a ground for Australian Rules football. M17.

> 🕮 **3** P. GALLICO The sensitive oval of her face.

▸**C** *verb.* Infl. **-ll-**, ***-l-**. *rare*.
1 *verb trans.* Make oval in shape. M17.
2 *verb intrans.* Move in oval-shaped curves. E20.
■ **oˈvaliform** *adjective* (*rare*) = OVAL *adjective* 2 E19. **oˈvality** *noun* = OVALNESS M20. **ovally** *adverb* M17. **ovalness** *noun* the quality of being oval E18.

ovalbumin /əʊv(ə)lˈbjuːmɪn, əʊˈvalbjʊ-/ *noun.* Also (earlier) **-en** /-ən/. M19.
[from Latin *ovi albumen* albumen of egg, alt. after ALBUMIN.]
BIOCHEMISTRY. Orig., the albumen or white of egg. Now usu. *spec.*, the albumin that is the principal protein of egg-white.

Ovaltine /ˈəʊv(ə)ltiːn/ *noun.* Also **o-**. E20.
[Prob. extension of OVAL *adjective*.]
(Proprietary name for) a powder made from malt extract, milk, and eggs; the drink made from this.

Ovambo /ɒˈvambəʊ/ *noun & adjective.* M19.
[Bantu, from *ova-* pl. prefix + *ambo* man of leisure.]
▸**A** *noun.* Pl. same, **-os**.
1 A member of a Bantu-speaking people living in northern SW Africa. M19.
2 The Bantu language of this people. M20.
▸**B** *attrib.* or as *adjective.* Of or pertaining to the Ovambo or their language. E20.

ovar-, **ovari-** *combining forms* see OVARIO-.

ovaria *noun* pl. of OVARIUM.

ovarial /əʊˈvɛːrɪəl/ *adjective. rare.* M19.
[formed as next + -AL[1].]
= next.

ovarian /əʊˈvɛːrɪən/ *adjective.* M19.
[from OVARY + -AN.]
ANATOMY, MEDICINE, & ZOOLOGY. Of, pertaining to, or of the nature of an ovary or ovaries.
ovarian follicle an egg and its surrounding cells at any stage of its development in the ovary.

ovario- /əʊˈvɛːrɪəʊ/ *combining form.* Before a vowel **ovar-**, **ovari-**.
[from OVARIUM: see -O-.]
Of, pertaining to, or involving an ovary.
■ **ovariˈectomize** *verb trans.* perform ovariectomy on E20. **ovariˈectomy** *noun* (an instance of) surgical removal of an ovary, oophorectomy L19. **ovariˈotomized** *adjective* that has undergone (an) ovariotomy E20. **ovariˈotomy** *noun* (***a***) oophorectomy; (***b***) (an instance of) surgical incision into an ovary (e.g. to remove a tumour): M19. **ovaˈritis** *noun* (MEDICINE) inflammation of the ovary, oophoritis M19.

ovariole /əʊˈvɛːrɪəʊl/ *noun.* L19.
[from OVARIUM + -OLE[1].]
ZOOLOGY. A small ovary; *spec.* each of the (freq. tubular) structures in the ovary of an insect in which oocytes are formed.

ovarium /əʊˈvɛːrɪəm/ *noun.* Pl. **-ria** /-rɪə/. L17.
[mod. Latin, from Latin OVUM: see -ARIUM.]
1 = OVARY 1. L17.
2 = OVARY 2. M18.

ovary /ˈəʊv(ə)ri/ *noun.* M17.
[from (the same root as) prec.: see -ARY[1].]
1 ANATOMY & ZOOLOGY. The female organ of reproduction (paired in humans and other vertebrates) in which the ova or eggs are produced. M17.
2 BOTANY. The swollen basal part of a carpel or gynoecium in an angiosperm, which contains the ovules. M18.
2 ***inferior ovary***: see INFERIOR *adjective*. ***superior ovary***: see SUPERIOR *adjective*.

ovate /ˈɒvət/ *noun*[1]. E18.
[from Greek *ouateis* pl. (rel. to Latin VATES) repr. a Gaulish word.]
Orig., an ancient Celtic priest or natural philosopher. Later also, a member of an order of Welsh bards recognized at an eisteddfod.

ovate /ˈəʊveɪt/ *adjective & noun*[2]. M18.
[Latin *ovatus* egg-shaped, formed as OVUM: see -ATE[2].]
▸**A** *adjective.* Chiefly BOTANY. Shaped like the longitudinal section of an egg, i.e. with the broadest part near the base. Of a solid body: ovoid. M18.
▸**B** *noun.* ARCHAEOLOGY. An oval-shaped implement; *esp.* a type of oval hand-axe with a continuous cutting edge, of the lower palaeolithic period. M20.

ovate /əʊˈveɪt/ *verb trans. joc.* M19.
[Prob. from next after *orate*.]
Give an ovation to.

ovation /ə(ʊ)ˈveɪʃ(ə)n/ *noun.* M16.
[Latin *ovatio(n-)*, from *ovat-* pa. ppl stem of *ovare* celebrate a lesser triumph: see -ATION.]
1 ROMAN HISTORY. A processional but not triumphal entrance into Rome by a victorious commander. M16.
†**2** Exultation. M17–E19.
3 *transf.* An enthusiastic reception; *esp.* a sustained burst of applause. M19.

> 🕮 **3** B. CASTLE Wedgie . . got an ovation for a rousing speech. **standing ovation** a prolonged burst of applause during which the crowd or audience rise to their feet.

■ **ovational** *adjective* of, pertaining to, or resembling an ovation M19. **ovationed** *adjective* (*colloq.*) given an ovation, enthusiastically received L19.

ovator /əʊˈveɪtə/ *noun.* M17.
[Latin, from *ovat-*: see prec., -OR.]
1 ROMAN HISTORY. A recipient of an ovation. *rare*. M17.
2 A participant in an ovation or enthusiastic reception. *colloq.* L19.

oven /ˈʌv(ə)n/ *noun & verb.*
[Old English *ofen* = Old Frisian, Middle & mod. Low German, Middle & mod. Dutch *oven*, Old High German *ovan* (German *Ofen*), Old Norse *ofn*, *ogn*, from Germanic.]
▸**A** *noun.* **1** A furnace. Now only *spec.*, a small furnace or kiln used in chemistry, metallurgy, etc. OE.
2 An enclosed compartment of brick, stone, or metal, for cooking food by continuous radiation of heat from the walls, roof, or floor. OE. ▸**b** *transf.* A small tomb built above ground. M19. ▸**c** A cremation chamber; *spec.* a cremation chamber in a Nazi concentration camp. M20. ▸**d** *fig.* The womb. Only in phrs. below. *slang.* M20.

> 🕮 **2** *transf.*: A. HALL The Toyota had become an oven—I couldn't always park in the shade. ***convection oven***, ***electric oven***, ***fan oven***, ***gas oven***, ***microwave oven***, ***toaster oven***, etc. **Dutch oven** (now chiefly *Hist.*) (***a***) a covered cooking-pot for braising etc.; (***b***) a small metal cooking utensil with an open side for placing in front of a fire. ***sirocco oven***: see SIROCCO *noun* 3. **c** C. POTOK Where else could the remnant of Jewry that had escaped Hitler's ovens go? **d bun in the oven** *slang* a child in the womb. **have something in the oven** *slang* be pregnant. **pudding in the oven** *slang* = **bun in the oven** above.

For other words beginning with *out-* see the entry for **out-**

Comb.: **ovenbird** any of various birds which build a domed or globular nest of mud; *spec.* (*a*) a bird of the S. American family Furnariidae, which includes the horneros; (*b*) a N. American warbler, *Seiurus auricapillus*; **oven-bottom** *adjective* (of bread etc.) baked at the bottom of an oven; **oven-bread**, **oven cake**: baked in an oven; **oven chip** a frozen fried potato chip intended to be reheated in an oven; **oven-cloth** a protective cloth for handling dishes in an oven; **oven-cook** *verb trans.* (*rare*) cook in an oven; **oven-glass** ovenproof glassware; **oven glove**, **oven mitt** a padded glove or mitten for handling dishes in an oven; **ovenproof** *adjective* (of a dish, bowl, etc.) suitable for use in an oven, heatproof; **oven-ready** *adjective* (of food) prepared before sale for immediate cooking in an oven; **oven timer** a device for switching an oven on or off at a pre-set time; **oven-to-table** *adjective* (of a dish, bowl, etc.) designed both for use in an oven and for serving at table; **ovenware** ovenproof dishes, bowls, etc.

▶ **B** *verb trans.* **1** Enclose or confine as in an oven. *poet.* L16.

2 Bake in an oven. Long *obsolete* exc. *Scot.* & *dial.* L17.

▪ **ove'nette** *noun* a small oven for cooking E20.

over /ˈəʊvə/ *noun*. L16.

[Absol. use of OVER *adverb*.]

1 a An excess, an extreme. *rare*. L16. ▸**b** An amount in excess or remaining over; an extra; in *pl.*, copies printed in excess of the number ordered, to allow for wastage. L19.

2 CRICKET. The number of balls (orig. four, five, or six, now six, or sometimes eight) bowled from either end of the wicket before a change is made to the other end; the portion of the game comprising a single turn of bowling from one end. M19.

3 MILITARY. A missile that passes beyond its target. Usu. in *pl. colloq.* E20.

over /ˈəʊvə/ *adjective*.

[Old English *ufer(r)a*, *yf-* from Germanic compar. of OVER *adverb*, in Middle English assim. to OVER *adverb*.]

1 *The* upper, *the* higher in position. Long *obsolete* exc. *dial.* & in place-names. OE. ▸**b** Covering something else; upper, outer. OE.

2 a That is in excess or in addition; surplus, extra. OE. ▸**b** That is in excess of what is right or proper; excessive. M16.

†**3** Later, after. OE–ME.

4 Higher in power, authority, or rank. ME.

¶ In all current senses exc. 2b, now usu. joined to the following noun (cf. OVER-).

over /ˈəʊvə/ *verb*. LME.

[from OVER *adverb*.]

†**1** *verb trans.* Get the better of, master. *Scot.* Only in LME.

†**2** *verb trans.* & *intrans.* Make (an amount) larger. M16–E17.

3 *verb trans.* Get over, recover from. *dial.* E19.

4 *verb trans.* Jump over; clear. M19.

over /ˈəʊvə/ *adverb*. Also (*arch.* & *poet.*) **o'er** /ɔː/.

[Old English *ofer* = Old Frisian, Old Saxon *oƀar* (Dutch *over*), Old High German *ubar* preposition, *ubiri* adverb (German *über*, also, from MG, *ober*), Old Norse *yfir*, Gothic *ufar*, from Germanic from Indo-European compar. formation rel. to Sanskrit *upari*, Greek *huper* (see HYPER-), Latin *super* (see SUPER-), the Indo-European positive being repr. by Latin *sub*: see SUB-.]

▶ **I** With ref. to motion and position.

1 With ref. to motion or a course: so as to pass across or above something, usu. rising before it and descending after it; so as to pass above and beyond (instead of reaching or hitting). OE. ▸**b** Above, on high. *rare*. OE. ▸**c** Forward and downward from an edge or an upright position. ME. ▸**d** So as to make what was an upper surface a lower one. LME.

2 From one side to the other of an intervening space; to a particular place, *spec.* one's home. OE. ▸**b** (Of measurement) across from one side to the other; in outside measurement. L16. ▸**c** CRICKET. As an umpire's call: change ends (at the end of an over). L18.

3 On the far side of an intervening space; at some distance. Now usu. with following preposition or adverb ME.

4 So as to cover or touch the whole of a surface. Cf. ALL OVER *adverbial phr.* 2. LME.

5 From one person, hand, etc., to another; with transference of position, allegiance, ownership, etc. L16. ▸**b** In two-way radio communication: indicating that the speaker has finished and awaits a reply. E20.

📖 **1** OED Climb over into the garden. P. GALLICO They placed one short and one over. ***boil over***, ***spill over***, etc. **c** *Observer* Detergent-packets . . almost always fall over and spill. *Globe & Mail (Toronto)* You could have knocked me over with a feather. *Motoring Which?* The steering . . means that you have to lean over . . to make the craft go round corners. **d** J. CONRAD Mr. Powell . . began to turn the leaves of the agreement over. **2** V. WOOLF The moors . . brightened as the clouds went over. W. ABISH We must have her over for dinner. J. M. COETZEE He walked over to the gate. **3** *Irish Press* Papa was postmaster over in Richmond. *Arena* Look at those men over there. **4** J. CONRAD A black dress sewn over with gold half moons. A. LURIE Windows had been painted over in irregular rectangles. **5** GOLDSMITH The profits . . I made over to the orphans and widows. *Listener* A Soviet general . . would go over to the mujahideen.

▶ **II** With ref. to quantity and time.

6 Remaining beyond what is taken; present beyond the quantity in question; in addition. OE.

7 Beyond what is normal or proper; too much; too. Chiefly modifying a following adjective or adverb, and now as OVER-. ME.

†**8** Beyond or in addition to what has been said; moreover, besides. LME–E16.

9 a Remaining unpaid, unsettled, or uncompleted after the time of settlement; until a later occasion. LME. ▸**b** Until the next season or the next day. M19.

10 Through its whole extent, from beginning to end, esp. (with *talk*, *think*) with detailed consideration. LME.

11 Used redundantly before *again* or after a numeral adverb to express repetition. M16. ▸**b** Again, once more. Now chiefly *N. Amer.* L16.

12 Past, finished, done with, at an end. E17.

📖 **6** E. NESBIT We bought . . bullseyes with the fourpence I had over. **7** J. S. BLACKIE Be not over anxious about mere style. **9a** A. TROLLOPE The matter was allowed to stand over till after Christmas. **b** ***sleep over***, ***stay over***, etc. **10** W. S. MAUGHAM She read over the great names of the past. M. BRAGG She tried to store up every detail so as to be able to tell it over to John. **11** GOLDSMITH He read it twice over. D. L. SAYERS She would rather be tried for life over again. **b** C. BROWN He had already seen the movie, but it was good, so he was seeing it over. E. SEGAL Whether you could take going back to a classroom and starting over. **12** S. BARING-GOULD Now the day is over, Night is drawing nigh. E. H. YOUNG The geraniums are over.

Phrases: ALL OVER *adverbial phr.* ***come it over***, ***come over***: see COME *verb*. **get it over with** do an unpleasant task so as to be rid of it. ***give over***: see GIVE *verb*. ***go over***: see GO *verb*. ***over again***: see AGAIN *adverb*. **over against** in an opposite situation to; adjacent to; in contrast to. **over and done with** thoroughly or definitely finished or at an end. **over and out** (in two-way radio communication): indicative that the speaker has finished and transmission ends. **over and over** (*a*) repeatedly, many times (***over and over again***: see AGAIN *adverb*); (*b*) (*roll*, *turn*, etc.) so that the same point comes up repeatedly. **over to** (*a*) *dial.* over at, at; (*b*) ***over to you***, = sense 5b above. ***remainder over***: see REMAINDER *noun* 1.

Comb. (see also OVER-): **over-and-under** *adjective* & *noun* (designating) a shotgun with one barrel mounted above the other (cf. OVER-UNDER).

over /ˈəʊvə/ *preposition*. Also (*arch.* & *poet.*) **o'er** /ɔː/. OE.

[from (the same root as) the adverb.]

▶ **I 1** In or to a position vertically up from, above; MATH. (of a number) divided by (another). OE.

2 On the upper or outer surface of; so as to cover; so as to rest on. OE. ▸**b** With ref. to a person or animal: in or into a position in which water (or *fig.* trouble, delight) rises above (a specified part of the body). E16.

3 (With ref. to position) on all parts of the surface of, here and there on; (with ref. to motion) from place to place on the surface of, throughout. Also placed after its obj., esp. in ***the world over***, ***all the world over***. Cf. ALL OVER *prepositional phr.* OE. ▸**b** Through every part of. Chiefly with verbs expr. perusal or scrutiny. M17.

4 While considering or observing; while concerned or occupied with. OE. ▸**b** In relation to, concerning. OE.

5 MATH. In terms of the elements of; *esp.* having (elements with) coefficients or coordinates in. M20.

📖 **1** T. HARDY They had at least a roof over their heads. V. WOOLF She lies with the brambles curving over her. A. WHITE The blast . . tore a large hole in the wall over the bed. **2** A. TROLLOPE Sitting with his hat low down over his eyes. I. MCEWAN He leaned back, one arm slung over the back of his chair. R. MACAULAY Sentimentalism spread a rosy veil over the ugliness. **b** J. WESLEY My horse got into a ditch over his back in water. D. MACMILLAN I am always over head and ears with one trouble or another. **3** D. LIVINGSTONE Cattle-stations . . are dotted over the landscape. E. BOWEN She had . . scattered letters over her table. **b** S. JOHNSON A wild notion, which extends over marriage. ***go over***, ***look over***, ***see over***. **4** S. CHITTY Over coffee my host asked me if I had heard of . . Gwen John. **b** T. HARDY Dr Grove . . whose taste for lonely meditation over metaphysical questions had diminished his practice. E. BOWEN He hesitated over two pairs of evening shoes. D. ABSE The arguments over money. **5** A. G. HOWSON The polynomials form a subring . . called the ring of polynomials over K.

▶ **II 6** Above and across; across and down; down from the edge of. OE.

7 To the other side of; from end to end of. OE. ▸**b** By the agency of (a telephone or other means of telecommunication). L19.

8 On the other side of, beyond. OE. ▸**b** Having recovered from, no longer suffering from. E20.

†**9** *fig.* In transgression of; in contravention of. OE–E16.

📖 **6** F. M. CRAWFORD A dainty lace-covered parasol fell over the edge. D. ABSE I stood looking over the railings. I. MURDOCH The northern view over a big hop field. *New Yorker* I . . fell over a rock-maple chair. **7** I. MURDOCH He became interested in Tibet . . and was constantly disappearing over the border. **b** F. L. ALLEN Thousands . . hear the play-by-play story over the radio. **8** KEATS O'er the southern moors I have a home for thee. **b** A. T. ELLIS I'm over Finn . . I don't seem to care any more.

▶ **III 10** Above in power, authority, or rank; (so as to be) in charge of. OE.

11 Above in degree, quality, or action; in preference to; more than. OE. ▸**b** In excess of or more than (a specified number or amount). Also placed after a statement of size, price, etc., in ***and over***, ***or over***. ME.

12 In addition to. Long *obsolete* exc. in OVER AND ABOVE *prepositional phr.* 2. OE.

📖 **10** J. ERSKINE A magistrate appointed by the King over special lands. W. BLACKSTONE The black intrigues of the Jesuits, so lately triumphant over Christendom. J. AUSTEN Oh that my dear Mother had more command over herself. **11** *Ecologist* We prefer *cassini* over the . . more cumbersome *cassinii*. *Village Voice* Mr Bate has a few years and a few winters over me. **b** M. ROBERTS Haven't seen you for over a year. *Times* Children aged 8 and over.

▶ **IV 13** After (in time). Long *obsolete* exc. *dial.* OE.

14 During, in the course of. OE.

15 Until the end of, for the duration of. (Now usu. interpreted as the adverb in ***stay over***, ***stop over***: cf. OVER *adverb* 9b.) OE.

📖 **14** L. BRUCE They told me to read the script over the weekend. **15** E. NOËL If we only live over to-day. J. CARLYLE In case you should stay over Wednesday.

Phrases: ***over one's head***: see HEAD *noun*. **over one's signature**, **over one's name** with one's name at the foot of what is written, as indicating authorship or assent. ***over the air***: see AIR *noun*¹. ***over the counter***: see COUNTER *noun*¹ 5. ***over the fence***: see FENCE *noun*. ***over the hill***: see HILL *noun*. ***over the top***: see TOP *noun*¹. **over the way** across the road, in a nearby street.

over- /ˈəʊvə/ *combining form*. Also (*arch.* & *poet.*) **o'er-** /ɔː/.

[Repr. OVER *adverb*, *preposition*, *adjective*.]

Prefixed freely to verbs, nouns, adjectives, & adverbs in various relations and with various senses, esp. indicating (*a*) position or motion over or beyond; (*b*) excess (cf. OVERLY *adverb*), repetition; (*c*) superiority; (*d*) completeness, thoroughness.

▪ **overa'ffectionate** *adjective* excessively or unduly affectionate L19. **overar'ticulate** *verb trans.* articulate with excessive precision or extra care E20. **overarticu'lation** *noun* the action or practice of overarticulating words M20. **overa'ttention** *noun* excessive or undue attention (*to*) L18. **overaward** *adjective* (*Austral.*) paid in addition to an agreed or basic wage or salary M20. **over'ballast** *verb trans.* overload, esp. with ballast E17. **overbank** *noun* (AERONAUTICS) the action or an act of overbanking E20. **over'bank** *verb trans.* & *intrans.* (AERONAUTICS & WATCHMAKING) bank excessively L19. **over'bark** *adjective* (of measurements) taken before the bark has been removed from a log M20. **over'beat** *verb trans.* (*rare*) beat down, overpower E17. **overbelief** *noun* (*a*) a belief which determines other beliefs, an overriding belief; (*b*) belief in more than the evidence warrants or more than can be verified; belief that goes beyond what is usual among members of a faith or sect: L19. †**overbias** *verb trans.* bias to one side M17–E18. **overbite** *noun* (DENTISTRY) the overlapping of the lower by the upper teeth; *esp.* vertical overlapping of the incisors: L19. **over'bitter** *adjective* too bitter E17. **over'bitterly** *adverb* in an overbitter manner LME. **over'bitterness** *noun* excessive bitterness OE. **overblanket** *noun* an electric blanket that should not be lain on but used over a person in bed L20. **over'bleach** *verb trans.* bleach excessively, so that the material is damaged E20. †**overblind** *adjective* (*rare*) excessively blind LME–M18. **overblouse** *noun* a long blouse to be worn not tucked in to a waistband E20. **over'boil** *verb* (*a*) *verb trans.* boil too much; (*b*) *verb intrans.* boil over; freq. *fig.* (of emotion etc.): L16. **overboot** *noun* a boot worn over another boot or shoe M20. **over'bright** *adjective* excessively bright L16. **over'brim** *verb* (*a*) *verb intrans.* (of a liquid or its container) overflow at the brim; (*b*) *verb trans.* flow over the brim of: E17. **over'brood** *verb trans.* (*poet.*) brood or hover over L18. **over'brow** *verb trans.* (*poet.*) overhang like a brow M18. **over'budget** *adjective*, *adverb*, & *verb* (*a*) *adjective* costing more than budgeted; (*b*) *adverb* beyond what has been budgeted; (*c*) *verb trans.* & *intrans.* budget too generously (for): L20. **over'bull** *verb trans.* (STOCK EXCHANGE) bid up the price of (shares etc.) excessively E20. **overbump** *noun* & *verb* (*a*) *noun* in bumping races, a bump in which the bumping boat goes up more than one place because the boat it bumps has just bumped also; (*b*) *verb trans.* bump in an overbump: E20. **over'canopy** *verb trans.* extend over like a canopy L16. **over'catch** *verb trans.* (long *obsolete* exc. *dial.*) (*a*) overtake, catch up; †(*b*) *fig.* outwit, deceive: L16. **overcentrali'zation** *noun* excessive centralization of administrative functions, leading to reduced efficiency L19. **over'centralized** *adjective* characterized by overcentralization M20. **overchosen** *adjective* designating members of a sociometric group that are chosen more than the average number of times M20. **over'civil** *adjective* showing excessive civility (usu. with neg. in litotes) L17. **over'civilized** *adjective* too highly civilized E19. **over'clamour** *verb trans.* overcome or subdue by clamour E18. **overclass** *noun* a privileged, wealthy, or powerful section of society L20. **overcloak** *noun* (BUILDING) the part of the upper sheet of lead in a flat joint which extends beyond the joint itself L19. **over'cloy** *verb trans.* cloy excessively, satiate L16. **overcoil** *noun* the last coil of a Breguet hairspring, with the end raised and bent towards the centre to improve time-keeping L19. **overcon'cern** *noun* undue concern or anxiety M19. **overcon'cerned** *adjective* unduly concerned or anxious M20. **overcon'solidated** *adjective* (of soil or clay) consolidated to a greater degree than could have been produced by the present-day pressure of overburden M20. **overconsoli'dation** *noun* the production or presence of an overconsolidated state M20. **over'cook** *verb* (*a*) *verb trans.* cook too much or for too long; (*b*) *verb trans.* & *intrans.* (of a motorist or motorcyclist) fail to take (a bend or a hill) or to accomplish (a stunt) (also foll. by it): E20. **over'cool** *verb trans.* cool to below the proper temperature, chill L16. **over'count** *verb trans.* (*a*) overestimate; (*b*) outnumber: L16. **over'cover** *verb trans.* cover over, cover completely, bury LME. **over'creep** *verb trans.* creep over M17. **over'critical** *adjective* excessively critical M19. **over'cross** *verb trans.* (*rare*) pass, lie, or fall across LME. **over'crow** *verb trans.* crow over; overpower: M16. **over'crust** *verb trans.* cover over with a crust or layer E17. **over'cunning** *noun & adjective* (possessing) excess of cunning E17. **overcup** *adjective* designating either of two N. American oaks, *Quercus macrocarpa* and *Q. lyrata*, in which the acorn is almost covered by its cup L18. **overcurrent** *noun* an electric current in excess of what is normal, safe, or allowed for M20. **over'damp** *verb trans.* damp to a greater extent than the minimum needed to prevent oscillations E20. **over'daring** *adjective* unduly daring, foolhardy L16. **overdate** *noun* a date on a coin which has been superimposed upon another, of which traces are still visible; a coin bearing such a date (freq. *attrib.*): M20. **over'dated** *adjective* (now *rare*) antiquated, out of date M17. **overday** *adjective & noun* (designating) a herring that is not freshly caught L19. **over'dear** *adjective* excessively dear, exceedingly dear ME. **over'decorated** *adjective* excessively decorated, overelaborately decorated E20. **overde'sign** *verb & noun* (*a*) *verb trans.* design to a standard of safety or reliability higher than the usual or minimum standard; (*b*) *noun* the action of overdesigning something; an instance of this: M20. **overde'sire** *noun* excessive desire M17. **overdifferenti'ation** *noun* (LINGUISTICS) unnecessary differentiation M20. **overdi'lute** *verb trans.* dilute too much, make too dilute E20. **overdis'charge** *verb trans.* discharge (an accumulator or storage battery) beyond a certain limit, an operation harmful to it L19. **overdi'spersed** *adjective* (ECOLOGY) exhibiting overdispersion M20. **overdi'spersion** *noun* (ECOLOGY) a greater unevenness in the distribution of individuals than would be the case if the existence and position of each were independent of the rest, so that an increased proportion of the area has either a large or a small concentration of individuals M20. **overdoor** *noun* a piece of decorative woodwork above a door L19. **over'dot** *verb trans.* (MUSIC) play (a note) so that it is longer than indicated by one following dot, and the succeeding note is correspondingly shortened; play so as to exaggerate a dotted rhythm: L20. †**overdrip** *verb trans.* drip over; overhang; overshadow: L16–L19. **over'dye** *verb trans.* dye (a thing already dyed) with a second or subsequent dye E17. **over'early** *adverb & adjective* too early, premature(ly) LME. **over'educate** *verb trans.* educate to excess or for too long M19. **overe'ffusive** *adjective* excessively or unduly effusive E20. **over'egg** *verb trans.* use too much egg or too many eggs in; only in ***overegg the pudding***, argue a point with disproportionate force or elaboration L19. **overe'motional** *adjective* excessively or unduly emotional E20. **overengi'neer** *verb trans.* engineer to a standard higher than is technically necessary, or to an extent greater than is technically desirable M20. **overe'rupt** *verb intrans.* (of teeth) undergo or exhibit overeruption M20. **overe'ruption** *noun* excessive extension of a tooth in the direction of the opposing teeth M20. **overexert** /-ɪɡ'zəːt, -ɛɡ-/ *verb refl.* exert oneself too much M19. **overexertion** /-ɪɡ'zəːʃ(ə)n, -ɛɡ-/ *noun* excessive exertion E19. **overexpand** /-ɛk'spand/ *verb trans. & intrans.* expand too much or too quickly M20. **overexploit** /-ɛk'splɔɪt/ *verb trans.* exploit excessively, *esp.* use (a natural resource) too much or too fast E20. **overexploi'tation** *noun* the action of overexploiting something M20. †**overeye** *verb trans.* watch, observe; watch over: L16–L17. **over'far** *adverb* (now *rare*) too far; to too great an extent: ME. **over'fat** *adjective* excessively fat LOE. **overfa'tigue** *noun & verb* (*a*) *noun* excessive fatigue; (*b*) *verb trans.* overtire: E18. **over'favour** *verb trans.* favour or like excessively E17. **over'favourable** *adjective* excessively favourable M16. **over'film** *verb trans.* cover with a film L16. **over'fine** *adjective* excessively fine or refined L16. **over'fire** *verb trans.* fire (pottery) or heat (metal) too much E17. **overflight** *noun* a flight of an aircraft or (formerly) birds over a country without making a landing L16. **over'flood** *verb trans.* pour over in a flood E19. **overflush** *noun* (*obsolete* exc. *dial.*) a surplus, a superfluity L16. **over'flush** *adjective* having an abundance (*of*); also foll. by *with*: M19. **over'flush** *verb trans.* (*a*) flush excessively; (*b*) cover with a flush: M17. **over'fraught** *adjective* (*arch. & poet.*) too heavily laden L16. **over'free** *adjective* excessively free M17. **over'freight** *verb & noun* (*a*) *verb trans.* overload; (*b*) *noun* an overload: M16. **overfur** *noun* the outer layer of an animal's fur E20. **over'furnished** *adjective* having too much furniture E18. **overgarment** *noun* a garment worn over others, an outer garment LME. **over'gaze** *verb trans.* (*rare*) (*a*) in *pass.*, (of the eyes) be dazzled with gazing; (*b*) gaze over, overlook: E17. **over'generous** *adjective* excessively generous (freq. with neg. in litotes) M19. **over'generously** *adverb* in an overgenerous manner L20. **over'glad** *adjective* excessively glad, very glad LME. †**overglance** *verb trans.* glance over L16–L19. **over'glide** *verb trans.* (*poet.*) pass over gently or smoothly ME. **over'gloom** *verb trans.* overshadow (*lit. & fig.*) L18. **over'glut** *verb trans.* glut to excess L16. **over'gorge** *verb trans.* cram with food L15. **over'grainer** *noun* a brush used in interior decorating to give a marbled or woodgrain effect L19. **over'graze** *verb trans.* allow (grassland) to be so heavily grazed that the vegetation is damaged and the ground becomes liable to erosion (chiefly as ***overgrazed*** *ppl adjective*, ***overgrazing*** *verbal noun*) E20. **over'great** *adjective* too great, excessive LME. **over'greedy** *adjective* excessively greedy LOE. †**overgreen** *verb trans.* (*rare*, Shakes.) cover so as to conceal a defect: only in L16. **overhair** *noun* the long straight hair that grows over or beyond the fur in fur-bearing quadrupeds L19. **over'happy** *adjective* very happy, excessively happy L16. **over'hard** *adjective & adverb* excessively hard ME. **over'hardy** *adjective* (long *rare*) excessively bold ME. **over'harsh** *adjective* excessively harsh M17. **over'heap** *verb trans.* (*a*) heap up excessively; (*b*) overlay with a large quantity, fill to excess: LME. **over'high** *adjective & adverb* very high, too high OE. **overhill** *adjective* situated or living beyond a hill or hills M18. **over'hit** *verb trans.* (*a*) affect unduly in an adverse way; (*b*) go beyond in one's aim: E19. †**overhold** *verb trans.* (*rare*) (*a*) delay to do, neglect; (*b*) overestimate; (*c*) hold back, withhold: OE–M19. **over'horse** *verb trans.* (*a*) *rare* provide with too many horses; (*b*) provide with a horse requiring a higher standard of riding than that possessed (chiefly as ***overhorsed*** *ppl adjective*): E19. **over'housed** *adjective* having housing in excess of one's needs or one's means M19. **over'hunt** *verb trans.* deplete the stock of (a species of animal) by excessive hunting; hunt in (an area) too much: M19. **overhy'drated** *adjective* affected with overhydration M20. **overhy'dration** *noun* the condition of having an excessive amount of water in the body or part of it M20. **overin'clusion** *noun* (PSYCHOLOGY) the indiscriminate inclusion of irrelevant responses to a stimulus, as a feature of some mental illnesses M20. **overin'form** *verb trans.* (*rare*) animate to excess; impart too much knowledge to: L17. **overin'surance** *noun* insurance of goods, property, etc., in excess of the real value M18. **overin'sure** *verb trans. & intrans.* insure (goods, property, etc.) for more than the real value E20. **overinte'llectual** *adjective* excessively intellectual M19. **overinte'llectualize** *verb trans.* make excessively intellectual E20. **overjacket** *noun* a large jacket for outdoor wear L19. **overjet** *noun* (DENTISTRY) = OVERBITE M20. **over'jump** *verb trans.* (*a*) (now *rare*) jump over; *fig.* transcend; (*b*) jump too far over: E17. **over'keep** *verb trans.* †(*a*) keep or observe too strictly; (*b*) keep too long: E17. **over'kind** *adjective* excessively kind E17. **over'kindly** *adverb* in an excessively kindly manner E17. **over'kindness** *noun* excessive kindness L15. **overking** *noun* (*obsolete* exc. *Hist.*) a king superior to other rulers having the title of king ME. **over'knee** *adjective* (esp. of socks) reaching above the knee M19. **over'knowing** *adjective* (*rare*) too knowing M17. **over'labour** *verb trans.* (*a*) overwork; fatigue with excessive labour; (*b*) take excessive pains with, elaborate to excess: M16. **over'lard** *verb trans.* intersperse or provide (speech, writing, etc.) with an excessive number of words, ideas, etc. E17. **over'large** *adjective* excessively large LME. **over'largely** *adverb* to too great an extent L15. **over'late** *adjective & adverb* excessively late ME. **over'lavish** *adjective* excessively lavish L16. **over'lavishly** *adverb* in an overlavish manner L16. †**overlead** *verb trans.* (*a*) oppress, tyrannize; (*b*) rule, govern; (*c*) lead astray, mislead: OE–E18. **over'lean** *verb trans.* lean over M18. **over'learn** *verb trans.* learn excessively; *spec.* (PSYCHOLOGY) learn beyond the stage of initially successful performance: L19. †**overleather** *noun* the upper leather of a shoe LME–M17. †**over'leaven** *verb trans.* cause to rise or swell excessively (chiefly *fig.*) E–M17. **over'length** *adjective & noun* (that is of) excessively great length E19. **over'lenient** *adjective* excessively lenient E20. **over'liberal** *adjective* excessively liberal E17. †**overliberality** *noun* L17–E19. **overlight** *noun* (*rare*) an excess of light E17. **over'light** *adjective* excessively light; too insubstantial, frivolous, or easy: M16. **over'lightly** *adverb* †(*a*) too easily; (*b*) too frivolously: LME. **overline** *noun* a line above something, *spec.* (*a*) the caption above an illustration in a book or newspaper; (*b*) a line of type printed above a newspaper's main headline: E20. **over'line** *verb trans.* (*a*) draw a line over or above (a piece of writing); (*b*) insert (a translation, correction, etc.) above a line of text: M19. **overlip** *noun* (now *dial.*) the upper lip ME. **over'listen** *verb trans.* (*rare*) overhear; eavesdrop: E17. **over'live** *verb* (now *rare*) (*a*) *verb trans.* outlive; (*b*) *verb intrans.* survive, continue in life: OE. **over'lock** *verb* (*a*) *verb trans.* interlock or intertwine with; (*b*) turn (the bolt of a lock) beyond the normal or first locking point; (*c*) *verb trans. & intrans.* strengthen and prevent fraying of (an edge of cloth) by oversewing: M17. **overlocker** *noun* a sewing-machinist specializing in overlocking E20. **over'long** *adverb & adjective* (*a*) *adverb* for too long a time; (*b*) *adjective* too long: ME. **over'loud** *adjective & adverb* too loud OE. **overloup** *noun* (*Scot. & north.*) (*a*) the change of the moon, a new or full moon; (*b*) a leap over a barrier; *transf.* an encroachment, a transgression: E18. **over'love** *noun & verb* (*a*) *noun* excessive love; (*b*) *verb trans. & intrans.* love (a person) too much: LOE. **over'low** *adjective* too low ME. †**overlusty** *adjective* too lusty L15–E17. **overmantel** *noun* a piece of ornamental cabinet-work, often with a mirror, placed over a mantelpiece L19. **over'mantle** *verb trans.* (*rare*) cover over as with a mantle M17. **over'many** *adjective* too many ME. **over'mark** *verb trans.* †(*a*) *rare* provide with too distant a target; (*b*) award too many marks to (a candidate in an examination, competition, etc.): M16. **over'mast** *verb trans.* provide (a ship) with too high or too heavy a mast or masts E17. **overmatter** *noun* surplus matter L19. **over'measure** *adverb, noun, & verb* (*a*) *adverb* in excess; (*b*) *noun* excess, surplus; (*c*) *verb trans.* measure or calculate above the correct amount: ME. **over'mickle** *adjective & adverb* (now *Scot. & north.*) too much OE. **overmitt** *noun* a mitten worn over another mitten or glove, by a climber etc. L20. **over'modest** *adjective* too modest M17. **over'modestly** *adverb* too modestly E17. **over'modulate** *verb trans. & intrans.* (ELECTRONICS) subject to, cause, or suffer overmodulation E20. **overmodu'lation** *noun* (ELECTRONICS) amplitude modulation which is so great that unacceptable distortion results E20. **overmost** *adjective* (long *dial.*) uppermost ME. **over'mount** *verb* (now *rare*) (*a*) *verb trans.* rise above, transcend; †(*b*) *verb intrans.* mount or rise too high: LME. **over'name** *verb trans.* (*rare*) name over or in succession L16. **over'net** *verb trans.* (*a*) cover (as) with a net; (*b*) use nets to excess in fishing: M19. †**overoffice** *verb trans.* (*rare*, Shakes.) exercise one's office over: only in E17. **overo'fficious** *adjective* excessively officious M17. **overo'fficiousness** *noun* excessive officiousness E17. **over'old** *adjective* excessively old LME. **over'optimism** *noun* excessive or unjustified optimism M20. **overopti'mistic** *adjective* excessively or unjustifiably optimistic M20. **overopti'mistically** *adverb* in an overoptimistic manner, too optimistically M20. **over'park** *verb intrans.* (*US*) park a motor vehicle for longer than the permitted period M20. **over'parted** *adjective* having too difficult a part, or too many parts, to play L16. **over'partial** *adjective* too partial L16. **overpar'ticular** *adjective* excessively particular, fussy M19. **over'pedal** *verb intrans. & trans.* use a piano's sustaining pedal excessively in playing (a piece) M20. **over'peer** *verb trans.* (*a*) tower over; *fig.* excel; (*b*) peer over, look down on: M16. **over'peopled** *adjective* having an excess of people, overpopulated L17. †**overperch** *verb trans.* (*rare*, Shakes.) fly over: only in L16. **overper'suade** *verb trans.* persuade (a person) against his or her own judgement or inclination E17. **overper'suasion** *noun* the action of overpersuading M18. **over'picture** *verb trans.* represent or depict in an exaggerated form E17. **over'pitch** *verb trans.* (*a*) CRICKET pitch (a ball) too far in bowling; (*b*) *fig.* exaggerate: M19. **over'please** *verb trans.* please excessively E17. **over'ply** *verb trans.* ply or exercise too much M17. **over'pole** *verb trans.* (*a*) (now *rare*) provide (hops or a hop-ground) with too long a pole or poles; (*b*) METALLURGY pole (copper) too much in refining, so as to remove too much oxide and render it brittle (see POLE *verb*[1] 5): E18. †**overpost** *verb trans.* (*rare*, Shakes.) cover (ground) quickly and easily (*lit. & fig.*): only in L16. **overpo'tential** *noun* = OVERVOLTAGE 1, 2 E20. **over'preach** *verb trans.* †(*a*) preach beyond (a person's understanding); (*b*) exhaust (oneself) with preaching: M17. **overpre'cise** *adjective* excessively precise E17. **overpre'cision** *noun* excessive or inappropriate precision E20. **overpre'scribe** *verb trans. & intrans.* prescribe an excessive amount of (a drug) or too many (drugs) M20. **over'privileged** *adjective & noun* (those people) possessing or enjoying too many privileges M20. **over'prize** *verb trans.* (*a*) prize or esteem too highly, overrate; †(*b*) exceed in value: L16. **overpro'duce** *verb trans.* (*a*) produce (a commodity) in excess of the demand or of a specified amount; (*b*) pay excessive attention to the quality of production of (a record, film, etc.) to the detriment of the immediacy of the performance: L19. **overpro'duction** *noun* (*a*) production in excess of the demand; (*b*) excessive attention to the quality of production of a record, film, etc.: E19. **overproof** *adjective & noun* (a spirit) containing more alcohol than proof spirit E19. **over'proud** *adjective* excessively proud LOE. **over'publicize** *verb trans.* give excessive importance to by publicizing M20. **overpunch** *noun & verb trans.* (COMPUTING) (represent by) a hole (position) in the upper portion of a punched card M20. **over'punish** *verb trans.* punish excessively or more than is deserved M17. **over'qualified** *adjective* too highly qualified, esp. for a particular job etc. M20. **overquantity** *noun* (now *rare*) an excessive or surplus amount E17. **over'quick** *adjective* too quick M16. †**overrake** *verb trans.* (of waves) break or sweep over (a ship) L16–M19. **over'rank** *adjective* (long *rare* or *obsolete*) excessively rank or vigorous in growth LOE. **over'rapid** *adjective* excessively rapid, too fast M19. **over'rash** *adjective* (*rare*) excessively rash M16. **over'rashly** *adverb* (*rare*) in an overrash manner M17. **over'read** *verb* †(*a*) *verb trans.* read over (again); (*b*) *verb intrans.* read too much: LOE. **over'readiness** *noun* excessive or undue readiness L19. **over'ready** *adjective* too ready E17. **over'reckon** *verb trans.* (*a*) overcharge (a person); (*b*) overestimate: E17. **overre'cord** *verb trans.* (*a*) record (sound) using too large a signal, so that playback is distorted; (*b*) record (a work or performer) too frequently: M20. †**overred** *verb trans.* cover over with red, redden E17–E19. **overrent** *noun* (long *rare* or *obsolete*) a higher or extra rent M16. **over'rent** *verb trans.* charge too high a rent (for) L16. **over'rich** *adjective* excessively rich L16. **over'rider** *noun* either of two projecting pieces fitted to the bumper of a motor vehicle for extra protection to the bodywork M20. **over'right** *adverb & preposition* (*obsolete* exc. *dial.*) (*a*) right across; (*b*) right opposite: LME. **over'rigid** *adjective* excessively rigid E17. **over'rigorous** *adjective* excessively rigorous L16. **over'ripe** *adjective* (*a*) (of fruit etc.) excessively ripe, spoilt; (*b*) *fig.* past the prime of life, ageing, declining: L17. **over'ripen** *verb trans.* (*rare*) ripen too much L16. **over'ripeness** *noun* the fact or condition of being overripe E19. **over'rise** *verb trans.* rise over or above (a certain point) LME. **over'risen** *adjective* that has risen or is raised too high M17. **over'roast** *verb trans.* roast too much E16. **over'roll** *verb trans.* (*a*) roll or push over; (*b*) cover up with a roll: E16. **over'roof** *verb trans.* roof over E19. **oversales** *noun pl.* speculative sales of more than can be supplied by the delivery date L19. **over'salt** *adjective* too salty LME. **over'salt** *verb trans.* make too salty L16. **over'saturated** *adjective* supersaturated; GEOLOGY (of a rock or magma) in which there is free silica or other (specified) oxide: E20. **oversatu'ration** *noun* the property of being oversaturated M20. **over'say** *verb* (*rare*) (*a*) *verb intrans.* say too much; (*b*) *verb trans.* exaggerate, overstate: L15. **overscan** *noun* (COMPUTING & ELECTRONICS) (the formation of) a display which extends beyond the edge of a computer or television screen; the portion of such a display which cannot be seen: L20. **over'score** *verb trans.* (*a*) cross out with scores, obliterate; (*b*) score (music) elaborately: M19. **over'scrupulous** *adjective* excessively scrupulous M16. **over'scrupulously** *adverb* in an overscrupulous manner L19. **over'scrupulousness** *noun* the state of being overscrupulous M18. †**overscutched** *adjective* worn out by repeated whipping or other ill treatment L16–E19. **overself** *noun* the finer, higher, or stronger part of one's being L19. †**oversensible** *adjective* excessively sensible or sensitive L16–E19. **over'sensitive** *adjective* excessively sensitive M19. **oversensi'tivity** *noun* the state or condition of being oversensitive M20. **over'sexed** *adjective* having excessive sexual propensities or desires L19. **over'shade** *verb trans.* (now *rare*) overshadow (something) OE. **over'sharp** *adjective* excessively sharp L15. **over'sharpness** *noun* the quality or condition of being oversharp M19. **over'shine** *verb trans.* (*a*) shine over, illumine; (*b*) outshine: OE. **overshoe** *noun* a shoe of rubber, felt, etc., worn over the ordinary shoe as a protection from wet, dirt, cold, etc. E19. **over-'shoe** *adverb* up to the tops of the shoes L16. **over'short** *adjective* too short ME. **over'shroud** *verb trans.* cover over as with a shroud E16. †**overskip** *verb trans.* skip over, pass without notice, omit LME–L17. **overskirt** *noun* an outer skirt, worn over the skirt of a dress L19. **oversleeve** *noun* an outer sleeve covering an ordinary sleeve M19. **over'slow** *adjective* excessively or unduly slow LME. **overslung** *adjective* (of a part) supported above the main structure or some other part M20. **over'smoke** *verb* (*a*) *verb trans.* (*rare*) cover as if with smoke; (*b*) *verb intrans.* smoke too much: M19. **over'snow** *verb trans.* (*poet.*, long *rare* or *obsolete*) whiten over with or as with snow L16. **over'soar** *verb trans.* soar above, fly over the summit of L16. **overso'licitous** *adjective* excessively solicitous M17. **overso'licitude** *noun* the state of being oversolicitous; oversolicitous behaviour, an instance of this: M18. **over'soon** *adverb* †(*a*) too quickly or readily; (*b*) too soon: ME. **overso'phisticated** *adjective* excessively sophisticated E20. **oversoul** *noun* (in Emersonian thought) the absolute spirit which includes and animates the universe M19. **over'sparred** *adjective* (of a ship) top-heavy through having too many or too heavy spars L19. **overspeciali'zation** *noun* too much specialization, esp. in education or in evolution M20. **over'specialize** *verb intrans.* specialize too much (*in* a particular endeavour) E20. **overspe'cific** *adjective* excessively specific M20. **overspecifi'cation** *noun* the fact or an instance of overspecifying something M20. **over'specify** *verb trans.* specify too narrowly or in excessive detail M20. **overspeech** *noun* loquacity, verbal indiscretion M19. **overspray** *noun* sprayed liquid that does not adhere to the object or area being sprayed M20. **over'spring** *verb trans.* spring or leap over LME. **over'sprinkle** *verb trans.* besprinkle M16. **over'sprung** *ppl adjective* fitted with too many or too flexible springs E20. **over'square** *adjective* (of a cylinder or engine) having a bore greater than the stroke M20. **over'staff** *verb trans.* provide (an organization etc.) with too large a staff M20. **over'state** *verb trans.* state (a case, argument, etc.) too strongly, exaggerate E19. **overstatement** *noun* the action or an instance of overstating a case, argument, etc.; exaggeration: E19. **over'stay** *verb trans.* stay longer than or beyond (a certain time, limit, etc.) (*overstay one's welcome*: see WELCOME *noun*[2] 1) M17. **overstayer** *noun* a person who stays beyond the expiry of a work permit etc. L20. **over'stimulate** *verb trans.* stimulate or excite excessively, esp. by a drug L18. **overstimu'lation** *noun* the fact or action of overstimulating M19. †**overstink** *verb trans.* (*rare*, Shakes.) stink more than; drown the stench of: only in E17. **overstorey** *noun* the uppermost canopy level of a forest ecosystem, formed by the taller trees M20. †**overstrait** *adjective* excessively strict, severe, or narrow ME–M18. **over'stream** *verb trans.* stream over or across E17. **over'strew** *verb trans.* (*a*) strew or sprinkle (something) over something else; (*b*) strew or sprinkle something over (something else): L16. **overstroke** *noun* (SWIMMING) an overarm stroke E20. **over'strong** *adjective* excessively strong ME. **over'study** *verb & noun* (*a*) *verb trans. & intrans.* study too much; (*b*) *noun* excessive study: M17. **over'stuff** *verb trans.* stuff more than is necessary M20. **over'stuffed** *adjective* (*a*) (of furniture) completely upholstered with a thick layer of stuffing; (*b*) *gen.* that has been overstuffed: E20. **oversub'scribe** *verb trans.* subscribe for more than the available quantity of (shares, places, a commodity, etc.) L19. **oversub'scription** *noun* the fact or an instance of oversubscribing L19. **over'subtle** *adjective* excessively subtle, not plain or clear L15. **over'subtlety** *noun* the quality of being oversubtle M19. **over'sum** *verb trans.* (long *rare*) overestimate, overrate E17. **oversu'sceptible** *adjective* too susceptible M20. **over'swarm** *verb* (*a*) *verb intrans.* swarm to excess; (*b*) *verb trans.* swarm over (a place or region): L16. **over'sweep** *verb trans.* sweep over or across, pass over with a sweeping motion E17. **over'sweet** *adjective* excessively sweet L16. **over'swim** *verb trans.* swim or float on, over, or across OE. **overswing** *noun* (*a*) an excessive swing; (*b*) GYMNASTICS a movement in which the body swings or turns over: E20. **over'talk** *verb* (*a*) *verb intrans. & refl.* talk too much; (*b*) *verb trans.* win over or overcome by talking: M17. **over'task** *verb trans.* be too heavy a task for; impose too heavy a task on: E17. **over'tedious** *adjective* too tedious L16. **over'teem** *verb* (*a*) *verb intrans.* breed excessively; be excessively productive; (*b*) *verb trans.* exhaust by excessive breeding or production: E17. **over'tell** *verb trans.* exaggerate in reckoning or narration E16. **over'tender** *adjective* excessively or unduly tender LME. **over'terve** *verb* (long *obsolete* exc. *Scot.*) overturn, overthrow, upset ME. **over'tilt** *verb trans.* tilt over, upset, overthrow LME. **over'tip** *verb trans. & intrans.* give an excessive gratuity (to) E20. **over'toil** *verb trans.* exhaust by excessive toil L16. **over'topple** *verb trans. & intrans.* (cause to) topple over; overthrow (esp. an unstable thing): M16. **over'torture** *verb trans.* overcome with torture; torture beyond endurance: L16. **over'tower** *verb trans.* tower over or above, overtop M17. **over'trace** *verb trans.* (*a*) trace over; cover or mark with tracery or tracings; (*b*) trace one's way over, pursue the track over: LME. **over'trade** *verb intrans. & trans.* (COMMERCE) trade in excess of or beyond (the requirements of the market, one's capital, stock, or means of payment, etc.) E17. **over'train** *verb trans. & intrans.* train too much; debilitate or injure (a person or thing) by excessive training: L19. **over'trample** *verb trans.* trample over or upon; tread down: L16. **over'trap** *verb trans.* trap excessively in (a region); deplete the stock of (an animal) by excessive trapping: M20. **over'trawl** *verb trans.* trawl excessively in (a fishing-ground); deplete the stock of (a fish) by excessive trawling: E20. **overtrick** *noun* (BRIDGE etc.) a trick taken in excess of the number contracted for E20. **over'trim** *verb trans.* (*a*) SAILING overadjust (a boat, a sail, etc.); (*b*) adorn (a dress etc.) with too much trimming: L16. †**overtrip** *verb trans.* (*rare*) trip or skip over; pass lightly over: only in L16. **overtrousers** *noun pl.* waterproof trousers worn (usu. over trousers or shorts) to keep the legs dry, esp. when cycling, hiking, etc. L20. **over'trow** *noun* (*rare*) (*a*) overconfidence; (*b*) excessive belief, faith, etc.: OE. **over'trump** *verb* (*a*) *verb trans. & intrans.* (BRIDGE) play a higher trump than (another player); (*b*) *verb trans. fig.* exceed or surpass (another person): M18. **over'trust** *noun & verb* (*a*) *noun* excessive trust; overconfidence; (*b*) *verb intrans. & trans.* trust or confide too much (in); be overconfident (about): ME. **over'tumble** *verb* †(*a*) *verb intrans.* tumble or fall over; capsize; (*b*) *verb trans.* (now *poet.*) cause to fall over; upset, overthrow: LME. **overvalu'ation** *noun* the action or an act of overvaluing something E17. **overvalue** *noun* †(*a*) excess or surplus of value; (*b*) a value or estimate greater than the worth of a thing: L16. **over'value** *verb trans.* (*a*) overestimate the value of; (*b*) surpass (a thing) in value: L16. **over'vault** *verb trans.* vault or arch over E17. **over'veil** *verb trans.* (chiefly *poet.*) cover or obscure (as) with a veil L16. **over'ventilate** *verb trans. & intrans.* = HYPERVENTILATE *verb* E20. **overventi'lation** *noun* = HYPERVENTILATION E20. **over'violent** *adjective* too violent L16. **over'vulcanize** *verb trans.* subject (rubber) to excessive vulcanization E20. **over'walk** *verb* (*a*) *verb trans.* walk over, traverse by walking; (*b*) *refl.* fatigue oneself with too much walking: M16. **over'wander** *verb trans.* (*rare*, *poet.*) wander over M16. **overward** *noun* the upper or superior guard L15. **over'warm** *adjective* too warm E18. **over'watch** *verb trans.* (*a*) fatigue or exhaust with excessive watching or keeping awake; †(*b*) (*rare*) watch all through (a night); (*c*) (keep) watch over: E16. **over'watching** *noun* too much watching; an excessively long vigil: M16. **overwater** *adjective* (*a*) performed or occurring on, above, or across water; (*b*) located on or over water: E20. **over'water** *verb trans.* (*a*) water thoroughly; (*b*) water too much; (*c*) *rare* cover with water: M17. **over'weak** *adjective* too weak M16. **over'wear** *verb trans.* wear out; wear away: L16. **over'weary** *verb & adjective* (*a*) *verb trans.* overtire; (*b*) *adjective* too weary: L15. †**overweathered** *ppl adjective* (*rare*, Shakes.) worn or damaged by the weather: only in L16. **over'weep** *verb trans.* (*poet.*) (*a*) *rare* weep again for; (*b*) weep over (something): L16. **over'weigh** *verb trans.* (*a*) exceed in weight or significance, outweigh; (*b*) weigh down, overburden, oppress: ME. **over'well** *adverb* too well ME. **over'wet** *adjective & verb* (*a*) *adjective* too wet; (*b*) *verb trans.* wet excessively: E17. **over'willing** *adjective* too willing L16. **over'win** *verb trans.* overcome, conquer, vanquish utterly OE. **overwind** *noun* an instance of overwinding L19. **over'wind** *verb trans.* wind (a mechanism, esp. a watch) beyond the proper stopping point LME. **over'winder** *noun* a device which guards against overwinding L19. **over'wing** *verb trans.* †(*a*) MILITARY outflank; (*b*) *poet.* fly over: E17. **over'winter** *verb* (*a*) *verb intrans.* survive through the winter (now only of a plant or animal); (*b*) *verb intrans.* spend the winter, esp. in a specified place; (*c*) *verb trans.* keep (a plant or animal) alive through the winter: OE. **over'wise** *adjective* too wise; exceedingly or affectedly wise: LME. **over'wisely** *adverb* in an overwise manner M19. **overwood** *noun* = OVERSTOREY L19. **overword** *noun* (chiefly *Scot.*) a repeated word or phrase; *esp.* the refrain of a song: E16. **overworld** *noun* (*a*) the celestial or immaterial world; (*b*) the terrestrial world as viewed from under water; (*c*) the community of conventional law-abiding citizens (opp. *underworld*): M19. **over'worn** *adjective* (*a*) worn by excessive use; shabby, faded; *fig.* (*rare*) hackneyed, stale; (*b*) exhausted by age, work, etc.; (*c*) spent in time; passed away: M16. **over'wrap** *verb trans.* wrap over or round; envelop: E19. **over'year** *adverb & adjective* (*dial.*) kept through the year or until next year LME. **over'zeal** *noun* excessive zeal M18. **over'zealous** *adjective* excessively zealous M17.

overabound /əʊv(ə)rə'baʊnd/ *verb intrans.* LME.
[from OVER- + ABOUND.]
†**1** Be more plentiful. Only in biblical allusions. LME–E17.
2 Abound too much (*in*, *with*); be too abundant. LME.

overabundance /əʊv(ə)rə'bʌnd(ə)ns/ *noun.* LME.
[from OVER- + ABUNDANCE.]
Too great a quantity, (an) excess.
■ **overabundant** *adjective* too abundant, excessive LME. **overabundantly** *adverb* E17.

overachiever /əʊv(ə)rə'tʃiːvə/ *noun.* M20.
[from OVER- + ACHIEVER.]
A person who achieves more than is expected or predicted (e.g. on the basis of intelligence tests).
■ **overachieve** *verb* (*a*) *verb intrans.* achieve more than is expected or predicted; (*b*) *verb trans.* achieve more than (an expected or predicted goal, objective, etc.): M20. **overachievement** *noun* M20.

overact /əʊvər'akt/ *verb.* E17.
[from OVER- + ACT *verb.*]
1 *verb trans. & intrans.* Act or render (a part) with exaggerated or unnecessary action or emphasis. E17.
†**2** *verb intrans.* Act in excess of what is proper, necessary, or right. Only in 17.
■ **overaction** *noun* excessive or exaggerated action M18.

overactive /əʊvər'aktɪv/ *adjective.* M19.
[from OVER- + ACTIVE.]
Excessively active.
■ †**overactiveness** *noun*: only in M17. **overac'tivity** *noun* M19.

overage /'əʊv(ə)rɪdʒ/ *noun.* M20.
[from OVER *adjective* + -AGE.]
An excess; an additional amount; *spec.* an actual amount, esp. of money, greater than that estimated.

overage /*attrib.* 'əʊv(ə)reɪdʒ, *pred.* əʊvər'eɪdʒ/ *adjective.* L19.
[from OVER- + AGE *noun.*]
That is over a certain age or limit of age; too old.

📖 A. MILLER No one in his store was to be fired for being overage. S. BELLOW He was an overage volunteer.

overaged /əʊvər'eɪdʒɪd, -'eɪdʒd/ *adjective.* L15.
[from OVER- + AGED.]
1 Overage; out of date, antiquated. L15.
2 METALLURGY. Subjected to overageing. M20.

overageing /əʊvər'eɪdʒɪŋ/ *noun.* Also **-aging.** M20.
[from OVER- + AGEING *noun.*]
METALLURGY. Prolonged artificial ageing of metal so that its hardness begins to decrease.

overall /'əʊvərɔːl/ *noun.* L18.
[from OVER- + ALL.]
1 In *pl.* Protective trousers or leggings; *spec.* (*a*) trousers or leggings of strong material worn over ordinary clothing for protection against bad weather; (*b*) close-fitting trousers worn as part of an army uniform; (*c*) loose-fitting trousers combined with a bib and strap top worn esp. by workmen for protection against dirt, wet, etc. L18.
2 A protective outer garment; now *esp.*, a loose coat or smock worn to keep the clothes beneath clean. E19.
■ **overalled** *adjective* wearing an overall or overalls M19.

overall /'əʊvərɔːl/ *adjective.* L19.
[from (the same root as) next.]
Including everything between the extreme points, measured from end to end; considered over the whole range of components, features, or aspects; total, inclusive of all.

📖 *Country Life* The overall balance of trade . . is important. *Ships Monthly* The *Klaasje* has an overall length of 24 metres.

overall /əʊvər'ɔːl/ *adverb.* Also **over all.** OE.
[Orig. two words, from OVER *preposition* + ALL.]
†**1 a** Everywhere; in every place or direction. OE–L16. ▸**b** In every part; all over, all through. ME–L16.
†**2** Beyond everything; pre-eminently; especially. ME–L17.
3 Taking all aspects into consideration; as a whole; generally. M20.

📖 **3** *Physics Bulletin* Overall, an excellent . . book. *Oxford Mail* These figures are up. So is crime overall.

overambition /əʊvəram'bɪʃ(ə)n/ *verb & noun.* M17.
[from OVER- + AMBITION *verb, noun.*]
▸†**A** *verb trans.* Desire too strongly. Only in M17.
▸**B** *noun.* Excessive ambition. E20.

overambitious /əʊvəram'bɪʃəs/ *adjective.* M20.
[from OVER- + AMBITIOUS.]
Excessively ambitious.

over and above /ˌəʊvər (ə)nd ə'bʌv/ *prepositional & adverbial phr.* LME.
[from OVER *preposition* + AND *conjunction*[1] + ABOVE *preposition.*]
▸**A** *prepositional phr.* †**1** = OVER *preposition* 10. *rare.* LME–M18.
2 In addition to, besides. Cf. OVER *preposition* 12. E16.

📖 **2** *Howard Journal* Over and above this there is the fact of who those governors were.

▸**B** *adverbial phr.* **1** In addition, besides. Cf. OVER *adverb* 6, 8. L16.
2 Modifying an adjective: overmuch, too. Cf. OVER *adverb* 7. *obsolete* exc. *dial.* M18.

overanxious /əʊvər'aŋ(k)ʃəs/ *adjective.* M18.
[from OVER- + ANXIOUS.]
Excessively or unduly anxious.
■ **overanxiety** /-aŋ'zʌɪəti/ *noun* E19. **overanxiously** *adverb* L18.

overarch /əʊvər'ɑːtʃ/ *verb & noun.* M17.
[from OVER- + ARCH *verb*[1], *noun*[1].]
▸**A** *verb trans.* Form an arch over, bend over in or like an arch. M17.
▸**B** *noun.* An arching over, an arch overhead. L19.
■ **overarching** *adjective* that forms an arch overhead; all-embracing, comprehensive: E18.

overarm /'əʊvərɑːm/ *adjective, adverb, & noun.* M19.
[from OVER- + ARM *noun*[1].]
▸**A** *adjective.* **1** (Of a throw, a delivery in cricket, a serve in tennis, etc.) performed with the hand raised above the level of the shoulders; (of a person) using such an action in throwing, bowling, or serving. M19.
2 Designating a swimming stroke in which one or both arms are lifted out of the water and brought forward and down to recover their original position; (of a swimmer) using such a stroke. L19.
▸**B** *adverb.* With an overarm action. L19.
▸**C** *noun.* An overhanging arm, *esp.* that which extends over the work table of a milling machine. E20.

overate *verb pa. t.* of OVEREAT.

overawe /əʊvər'ɔː/ *verb trans.* L16.
[from OVER- + AWE.]
Restrain by awe, keep in awe by superior influence; fill with awe.

📖 D. LODGE He was the youngest of the senior management team and rather overawed by Vic.

overbalance /əʊvə'bal(ə)ns/ *verb & noun.* E17.
[from OVER- + BALANCE *verb.*]
▸**A** *verb.* **1 a** *verb trans.* Do more than balance; outweigh. E17. ▸**b** *verb intrans.* Preponderate, have greater power or influence. M17.
2 a *verb trans.* Destroy the balance or equilibrium of; cause to capsize. M19. ▸**b** *verb intrans.* Lose one's balance; fall over or capsize through loss of balance. M19.

📖 **1a** *Review of English Studies* The distresses . . are not allowed to overbalance the aesthetic elegance of the play.

▸**B** *noun.* **1** Excess of weight, value, or amount; imbalance; preponderance. E17.
†**2** *spec.* Excess of exports over imports. E17–E18.

overbear /əʊvə'bɛː/ *verb.* Pa. t. **-bore** /-'bɔː/; pa. pple **-borne** /-'bɔːn/. LME.
[from OVER- + BEAR *verb*[1].]
†**1** *verb trans.* Carry over, transfer; remove. Only in LME.
2 *verb trans.* Bear down by weight or physical force; thrust, push, or drive over; overthrow; overwhelm. M16.
3 *verb trans. & intrans.* Exercise an oppressive influence (on); overcome or repress by power, authority, emotional pressure, etc. M16.
4 *verb trans.* Surpass in importance, cogency, etc.; outweigh. E18.
5 *verb intrans.* Of a plant: produce too much fruit. M19.
■ **overbearance** *noun* †(*a*) the fact of weighing down or weighing more; (*b*) overbearing behaviour: M17. **overbearing** *noun* the action of overbearing something; an instance of this; (an) imperious or dictatorial action: L16. **overbearing** *adjective* †(*a*) weighing down; overpowering, oppressing; (*b*) inclined not to heed other people's wishes or feelings; imperious, domineering: L17. **overbearingly** *adverb* E19. **overbearingness** *noun* L18.

overbend /'əʊvəbɛnd/ *noun.* M20.
[from OVER- + BEND *noun*[3].]
The curved stretch of pipe above the point of inflection in the S-shaped length of pipeline being lowered on to the seabed from a barge. Cf. SAGBEND.

overbend /əʊvəˈbɛnd/ *verb*. Pa. t. & pple **-bent** /-ˈbɛnt/. E17.
[from OVER- + BEND *verb*.]
1 a *verb trans.* Bend (something) over or to one side. E17.
▸b *verb trans. & intrans.* Bend over (something). M19.
▸c *verb intrans.* Bend over. M19.
2 *verb trans. & intrans.* Bend (something) excessively. E17.

overbid /*as verb* əʊvəˈbɪd, *as noun* ˈəʊvəbɪd/ *verb & noun*. ME.
[from OVER- + BID *verb*.]
▸ A *verb*. Infl. **-dd-**; pa. t. & pple **-bid**.
▸ I †1 *verb trans.* Overburden. Only in ME.
▸ II 2 *verb trans.* Make a higher bid than (a person); outbid. LME.
3 *verb trans.* Offer more than the value of (a thing). M17.
4 *verb trans. & intrans.* CARDS. Bid more on (a hand) than is warranted; overcall (an opponent). L19.
▸ B *noun*. CARDS. An act or instance of overbidding; a bid that is higher than is justified by one's cards, or higher than a previous bid. E20.
■ **overˈbidder** *noun* (CARDS) a person who overbids M20.

overblow /*as verb* əʊvəˈbləʊ, *as noun* ˈəʊvəbləʊ/ *verb & noun*. LME.
[from OVER- + BLOW *verb*[1].]
▸ A *verb*. Pa. t. **-blew** /-ˈbluː/; pa. pple **-blown** /-ˈbləʊn/.
1 *verb trans.* Blow (a thing) over the top of something; blow away. LME.
2 *verb intrans.* (Of a storm) blow over, abate in violence; *fig.* (of danger, anger, passion, etc.) pass away, be past. LME.
3 *verb trans.* Blow over the surface of; cover by blowing over (as sand or snow does). LME.
4 *verb trans.* Blow (a thing) over or down, overthrow or upset by blowing. Long *rare*. M16.
†5 *verb intrans.* NAUTICAL. Of the wind: blow very strongly; blow too hard for topsails to be carried. L16–E19.
6 *verb trans.* MUSIC. Blow (a wind instrument) so hard as to produce a harmonic instead of the fundamental; *refl.* (of a wind instrument) sound a harmonic instead of the fundamental. M19.
7 *verb trans.* METALLURGY. Subject (a charge) to an excessive length of blast. M19.
▸ B *noun*. METALLURGY. A period or instance of overblowing a charge. L19.

overblown /əʊvəˈbləʊn/ *ppl adjective*[1]. L16.
[pa. pple of prec.]
1 That has blown over or passed away. L16.
2 Inflated with conceit or vanity; overdone, exaggerated. M19.
3 METALLURGY. Of metal in the Bessemer process: injured or burnt by continuance of the blast after all the carbon has been removed from the metal. L19.

> 🕮 **2** *Far Eastern Economic Review* Although some voices are .. warning of a glut, these fears appear overblown.

overblown /əʊvəˈbləʊn/ *ppl adjective*[2]. E17.
[from OVER- + *blown* pa. pple of BLOW *verb*[2].]
Of a flower: more than full blown, past its best.

> 🕮 *fig.*: S. RUSHDIE Drawn to the painted lady by her overblown charms.

overboard /əʊvəˈbɔːd, ˈəʊvəbɔːd/ *adverb*. OE.
[from OVER- + BOARD *noun*.]
Over the side of a ship or boat, out of or from a ship into the water.

> 🕮 E. A. FREEMAN He fell overboard and was drowned. **go overboard** *fig.* behave immoderately, go too far, display excessive enthusiasm. **throw overboard** *fig.* cast aside, discard, reject, renounce.

overbody /*as noun* ˈəʊvəbɒdi, *as verb* əʊvəˈbɒdi/ *noun & verb*. LME.
[from OVER- + BODY *noun*.]
▸ A *noun*. **†1** *overbody of heaven*, a celestial object. Only in LME.
2 *Hist.* An upper or outer bodice. L16.
▸ B *verb trans.* **†1** Make too material. *rare*. Only in M17.
2 Give too large a body to (a car or engine). M20.

overbold /əʊvəˈbəʊld/ *adjective*. ME.
[from OVER- + BOLD *adjective*.]
Excessively or unduly bold; presumptuous.
■ **overboldly** *adverb* M16. **overboldness** *noun* LME.

overbook /əʊvəˈbʊk/ *verb trans. & intrans.* E20.
[from OVER- + BOOK *verb*.]
Make more bookings for (a theatre, hotel, aircraft, etc.) than there are places or seats available; book in (a number of people) for a greater number of places or seats than are available.

overbore, **overborne** *verbs pa. t. & pple* of OVERBEAR.

overbought *verb pa. t. & pple* of OVERBUY.

overbound /əʊvəˈbaʊnd/ *verb intrans. rare*. L16.
[Alt.]
= OVERABOUND *verb* 2.

overbow /əʊvəˈbaʊ/ *verb*[1] *trans.* M17.
[from OVER- + BOW *verb*[1].]
1 Bend (something) to excess. *rare*. M17.
2 Arch over (something). M19.

overbow /əʊvəˈbəʊ/ *verb*[2] *trans.* L19.
[from OVER- + BOW *noun*[1].]
Provide with a bow that is too strong. Usu. *refl.* or in *pass.*

overbreathe /əʊvəˈbriːð/ *verb*. L16.
[from OVER- + BREATHE.]
†1 *verb trans.* Put out of breath. L16–L18.
2 *verb intrans.* Breathe over something. Chiefly as *overbreathing verbal noun*. E19.
3 *verb intrans.* = HYPERVENTILATE 1. E20.

overbridge /ˈəʊvəbrɪdʒ/ *noun*. L19.
[from OVER- + BRIDGE *noun*[1].]
A bridge over a railway or a road.

overbridge /əʊvəˈbrɪdʒ/ *verb trans.* OE.
[from OVER- + BRIDGE *verb*.]
Make a bridge over.
¶ Rare before E19.

overbuild /əʊvəˈbɪld, ˈəʊvəbɪld/ *verb*. Pa. t. & pple **-built** /-ˈbɪlt/. E17.
[from OVER- + BUILD *verb*.]
1 *verb trans.* Erect too many buildings on (an area). E17.
2 *verb trans.* Build over or on; cover or surmount with a building. Chiefly *fig.* M17.
3 *verb trans. & intrans.* Build too elaborately or to excess. M17.

overburden /ˈəʊvəbəːd(ə)n/ *noun*. L16.
[from OVER- + BURDEN *noun*.]
1 (An) excessive burden. L16.
2 a The overlying rock etc. which has to be removed in quarrying or mining in order to get at the deposit worked. M19. **▸b** The material lying over a point underground, esp. over a tunnel or pipeline; the pressure due to the weight of this material. M20. **▸c** Loose unconsolidated material lying above bedrock. M20.

overburden /əʊvəˈbəːd(ə)n/ *verb trans.* Also (*arch.*) **-then** /-ð(ə)n/. M16.
[from OVER- + BURDEN *verb*.]
Put too great a burden on; burden too much; overload, esp. (*fig.*) with work or responsibility.

> 🕮 *Archives of Pediatrics* The anorectic child should not be overburdened with .. school work. *Punch* If some hulking great brute .. were to straddle an already overburdened warhorse, the whole caboodle would collapse.

overburdensome /əʊvəˈbəːd(ə)ns(ə)m/ *adjective*. E17.
[from OVER- + BURDENSOME.]
Excessively burdensome.

overburn /əʊvəˈbəːn/ *verb*. Infl. as BURN *verb*; pa. t. & pple usu. **-burned**, **-burnt** /-ˈbəːnt/. LME.
[from OVER- + BURN *verb*.]
†1 *verb trans.* Destroy or corrupt with heat. LME–E17.
2 *verb trans. & intrans.* Burn too much or to excess. E18.

overburthen *verb* see OVERBURDEN *verb*.

overbusy /əʊvəˈbɪzi/ *adjective*. LME.
[from OVER- + BUSY *adjective*.]
Excessively busy; obtrusively officious.

overbusy /əʊvəˈbɪzi/ *verb trans.* L16.
[from OVER- + BUSY *verb*.]
Busy (esp. oneself) to excess; engage or occupy too assiduously.

overbuy /əʊvəˈbʌɪ/ *verb*. Pa. t. & pple **-bought** /-ˈbɔːt/. LME.
[from OVER- + BUY *verb*.]
†1 *verb trans.* Pay too much for. LME–E18.
2 *verb trans. & intrans.* Buy in excess of what is immediately needed or what is allowed; accumulate surplus stock; *refl.* buy beyond one's means or to too great an extent. M18.

over-by /əʊvəˈbʌɪ, ˈəʊvəbʌɪ/ *adverb*. *Scot. & north.* M18.
[from OVER *adverb* + BY *adverb*.]
Over or across the way.

overcall /*as verb* əʊvəˈkɔːl, *as noun* ˈəʊvəkɔːl/ *verb & noun*. E20.
[from OVER- + CALL *verb*.]
CARDS. **▸A** *verb trans. & intrans.* Make a bid higher than (a previous bid or an opponent); overbid (a hand). E20.
▸ B *noun*. An act or instance of overcalling; a bid which is higher than an opponent's bid. E20.

overcame *verb pa. t.* of OVERCOME *verb*.

overcapacity /əʊvəkəˈpasɪti/ *noun*. M20.
[from OVER- + CAPACITY.]
Excess capacity; *spec.* a situation in which an industry or factory cannot sell as much as its plant is designed to produce.

overcapitalize /əʊvəˈkapɪt(ə)lʌɪz/ *verb trans.* Also **-ise**. L19.
[from OVER- + CAPITALIZE.]
Provide (a business) with more capital than is appropriate or useful; estimate the capital of (a business) at too high an amount. Chiefly as ***overcapitalized*** *ppl adjective*.
■ **ˌovercapitaliˈzation** *noun* L19.

overcare /əʊvəˈkɛː, ˈəʊvəkɛː/ *noun*. Now *rare*. L16.
[from OVER- + CARE *noun*.]
Undue or excessive care.

overcareful /əʊvəˈkɛːfʊl, -f(ə)l/ *adjective*. L16.
[from OVER- + CAREFUL.]
Excessively or unduly careful.
■ **overcarefully** *adverb* M19. **overcarefulness** *noun* L19.

overcarry /əʊvəˈkari/ *verb trans.* Now *rare*. LME.
[from OVER- + CARRY *verb*.]
†1 Carry over, across, or to the other side of something. LME–E16.
†2 *fig.* Carry (a person) beyond the bounds of moderation, carry away. L16–M17.
3 Carry (action or proceedings) too far, overdo. E17.
4 Carry or convey physically beyond the proper point. L19.

overcast /ˈəʊvəkɑːst/ *noun*. L15.
[from OVER- + CAST *verb*.]
†1 The action or an act of casting something over or down. Only in L15.
2 An outcast. Long *obsolete* exc. *dial.* M16.
3 A covering, a coating; *spec.* (a) cloud covering all or part of the sky, as in dull or threatening weather; AERONAUTICS cloud which restricts visibility and necessitates reliance on instruments for navigation. L17.
4 A crossing of one underground passage or airway over another without intercommunication. M19.
5 Overcast sewing. M19.

> 🕮 **3** B. F. CONNERS He felt the sun starting to burn through the overcast.

overcast /ˈəʊvəkɑːst, əʊvəˈkɑːst/ *adjective*. E17.
[pa. pple of next.]
1 Covered with cloud; overshadowed, darkened, made dull or gloomy (*lit.* & *fig.*). E17.
2 That has been overthrown or upset. Long *rare*. L17.
3 Sewn by overcasting; designating or pertaining to the stitch by which overcasting is done. M19.

> 🕮 **1** W. C. WILLIAMS It was a cold, slightly overcast December day. R. BANKS Week after week of zinc-gray overcast skies.

overcast /əʊvəˈkɑːst/ *verb*. Pa. t. & pple **-cast**. ME.
[from OVER- + CAST *verb*.]
1 *verb trans.* **a** Overthrow, overturn, upset, (*lit.* & *fig.*). *obsolete* exc. *dial.* ME. **▸†b** Turn over. LME–L16.
2 *verb trans.* Throw (a thing) over or above something else. Now *rare*. ME.
3 a *verb trans.* Cover with cloud; overshadow, darken, make dull or gloomy (*lit.* & *fig.*). ME. **▸b** *gen.* Cover or overlay (*with* something). Now *rare*. LME. **▸c** *verb intrans.* Become covered with cloud; be or become overcast. Long *obsolete* exc. *dial.* LME.
†4 *verb trans.* Transform. Only in ME.
5 *verb trans.* Orig., cast away (sorrow), repudiate (a promise). Now (*Scot.*), throw off or get over (illness or misfortune). LME.
†6 *verb trans.* Overestimate. E17–M18.
7 *verb trans.* Stitch over (a raw edge of cloth) to prevent fraying, esp. with long slanting stitches; strengthen or decorate (an edge) by buttonhole or blanket stitch; sew together (the leaves or signatures of a book) with an overcast stitch. E18.

> 🕮 **3a** D. C. PEATTIE Bronze was overcasting the salt bush foliage. E. WAUGH The threat of just such a surrender .. overcast Guy. D. CECIL Sunshine started to pierce the clouds that had long overcast his days.

■ **overˈcasting** *noun* (*a*) the action of the verb; (*b*) a covering of cloud; *fig.* a darkening, an overshadowing; (*c*) overcast stitching: LME.

overcaution /əʊvəˈkɔːʃ(ə)n/ *noun*. L18.
[from OVER- + CAUTION *noun*.]
Excessive caution.

overcautious /əʊvəˈkɔːʃəs/ *adjective*. E18.
[from OVER- + CAUTIOUS.]
Excessively cautious.
■ **overcautiously** *adverb* M19. **overcautiousness** *noun* L19.

overcharge /ˈəʊvətʃɑːdʒ/ *noun*. E17.
[from OVER- + CHARGE *noun*.]
A charge (of money, explosive, etc.) that is too great; an instance of overcharging.

overcharge /əʊvəˈtʃɑːdʒ/ *verb*. ME.
[from OVER- + CHARGE *verb*.]
1 *verb trans.* Load, fill, or supply to excess (*with* something); overload, fill too full. ME. **▸b** Put too great a charge into (a battery, gun, etc.). L17. **▸c** Make or

represent as greater than the reality; put too much detail into (a description, picture, etc.); exaggerate. **E18.**
2 *verb trans. & intrans.* Orig., overburden (a person) with expense. Later, charge (a person) a price that is too high; charge too high a price for (a thing). **ME.** ▸**b** *verb trans.* Charge (an amount) in excess of the right price. **M17.**
3 *verb trans.* Overpower by superior force; oppress, overtax. Long *rare*. **ME.** ▸**b** Accuse too severely or extravagantly. Long *rare*. **E17.**

📖 **1** J. AUSTEN Her parting words . . seemed to burst from an overcharged heart. **2** BYRON He was . . overcharged by his washerwoman. **3** G. GREENE The . . warrant officer mooning around . . with a mournful overcharged air.

overcheck /ˈəʊvətʃɛk/ *noun*¹ *& adjective*¹. **L19.**
[from OVER- + CHECK *noun*¹.]
(Designating) a strap passing over a horse's head between the ears and down the neck, so as to pull upward on the bit and raise the head to facilitate breathing.

overcheck /ˈəʊvətʃɛk/ *noun*² *& adjective*². **E20.**
[from OVER- + CHECK *noun*².]
▶**A** *noun.* (A fabric with) a combination of two check patterns of different sizes. **E20.**
▶**B** *adjective.* Marked or woven with such a pattern; made of such a fabric. **E20.**
■ **overˈchecked** *adjective* **E20.**

overclad *verb pa. t. & pple*: see OVERCLOTHE.

overclimb /əʊvəˈklʌɪm/ *verb trans.* Infl. as CLIMB *verb*. Pa. t. & pple usu. **-climbed**. **OE.**
[from OVER- + CLIMB *verb*.]
Climb over; get over by climbing.

overclose /əʊvəˈkləʊs/ *adjective & adverb*. **LME.**
[from OVER- + CLOSE *adjective & adverb*.]
Too close.
■ **overclosely** *adverb* **E20.** **overcloseness** *noun* **E19.**

overclosure /əʊvəˈkləʊʒə/ *noun*. **M20.**
[from OVER- + CLOSURE.]
DENTISTRY. A condition in which the lower jaw is raised more than normal in relation to the upper jaw when in the rest position.

overclothe /əʊvəˈkləʊð/ *verb trans.* Pa. t. & pple **-clothed**, (*arch., techn., & formal*) **-clad** /-ˈklad/. **LME.**
[from OVER- + CLOTHE.]
Cover (as) with clothing.

overcloud /əʊvəˈklaʊd/ *verb*. **L15.**
[from OVER- + CLOUD *verb*.]
1 *verb trans.* Make dim or obscure; deprive of clearness of perception; mar, detract from. **L15.**
2 *verb trans.* Cover with a cloud or clouds, or with something that dims or conceals like a cloud. **L16.**
3 *verb intrans.* Become overclouded; cloud over. **M19.**

📖 **1** H. E. MANNING The passing thoughts of evil which overcloud his soul. *Financial Times* A daughter whose life is overclouded by . . a domineering mother.

overcoat /ˈəʊvəkəʊt/ *noun*. **E19.**
[from OVER- + COAT *noun*.]
1 A thick coat for wearing over ordinary clothing, esp. in cold weather. **E19.**
2 *transf. & fig.* An outer covering or layer, *esp.* one that gives protection; *slang* a means of concealing and disposing of a body, (also ***pine overcoat*** (US), ***wooden overcoat***) a coffin. **M19.**

📖 **1** ***Inverness overcoat***: see INVERNESS 2. **2** DYLAN THOMAS Onions boiled in their overcoats.

■ **overcoated** *adjective* wearing an overcoat **L19.** **overcoating** *noun* (*a*) material for overcoats; (*b*) an added coating: **L19.** **overcoatless** *adjective* not having or not wearing an overcoat **E20.**

overcold /əʊvəˈkəʊld/ *adjective*. **OE.**
[from OVER- + COLD *adjective*.]
Too cold, excessively cold (*lit. & fig.*).

overcolour /əʊvəˈkʌlə/ *verb trans.* Also ***-or**. **E19.**
[from OVER- + COLOUR *verb*.]
Represent too strongly or in an exaggerated way.

overcome /ˈəʊvəkʌm/ *noun*. *Scot.* **LME.**
[from OVER- + COME *noun*¹, *verb*.]
†**1** A surplus, an excess. **LME–L19.**
2 A recurring or hackneyed phrase, a refrain, a chorus. **L18.**
3 A thing that overwhelms or prostrates a person; a sudden attack or shock. **E19.**
4 A voyage, a crossing. **M19.**

overcome /əʊvəˈkʌm/ *verb*. Pa. t. **-came** /-ˈkeɪm/; pa. pple **-come**. **OE.**
[from OVER- + COME *verb*.]
†**1** *verb trans.* Come upon, get at, reach, overtake. Only in **OE.**
2 a *verb trans.* Get the better of, defeat, prevail over; surmount (a difficulty or obstacle); recover from (a blow, disaster, etc.). In later use chiefly with non-material obj. **OE.** ▸**b** *verb intrans. & †trans.* Be victorious, win (a battle). **ME.**
3 *verb trans.* **a** Of emotion, feeling, etc.: make (a person) helpless, affect or influence excessively. Freq. in *pass.* (foll. by *with*, *by*). **LOE.** ▸†**b** Dominate (a person's mind or conduct). *rare*. **LME–E17.**
†**4** *verb trans.* Get through or to the end of; master, accomplish. **ME–L17.**
5 *verb trans.* Come or pass over, traverse (a road, space, etc.). Now *rare*. **ME.**
6 *verb trans.* Exceed, surpass, outstrip. *arch.* **ME.**
7 *verb trans.* **a** Overrun; spread over, cover. Now *rare*. **ME.** ▸†**b** Take by surprise. *rare* (Shakes.). Only in **E17.**
8 *verb intrans.* Revive, recover from a faint. Now *dial.* **LME.**

📖 **2a** W. GREENER We have studied long and hard to overcome those objections. L. GARFIELD She could not overcome her own distress sufficiently to say more. **b** *Black World* The Christian strains of 'We shall Overcome' gave way to . . 'We Shall be heard!' **3a** H. ROTH His aunt was so overcome that her tongue hung out in awe. I. MURDOCH A wild glee overcame them, and they began to dance. Q. BELL Seeing his . . distressed face, she was overcome with guilt and misery.

■ **overcomable** *adjective* able to be overcome, surmountable **LME.** **overcomer** *noun* a victor, a conqueror **LME.** **overcomingly** *adverb* in an overcoming manner; presumptuously; oppressively: **M17.**

overcompensate /əʊvəˈkɒmpɛnseɪt/ *verb*. **M18.**
[from OVER- + COMPENSATE.]
1 *verb trans.* Compensate excessively for. **M18.**
2 *verb intrans.* Attempt to make up for what is felt as a weakness or defect in one's character by exaggerating; exhibit overcompensation. **E20.**
■ **ˌovercompenˈsation** *noun* compensation that is excessive or more than appropriate; *esp.* an exaggerated reaction by a person to what is felt as a weakness or defect in his or her character: **E20.** **ˌovercompenˈsatory** *adjective* pertaining to or of the nature of overcompensation **E20.**

overcompound /əʊvəˈkɒmpaʊnd/ *adjective*. **M20.**
[from OVER- + COMPOUND *adjective*.]
ELECTRICAL ENGINEERING. Of a dynamo: overcompounded.

overcompound /əʊvəkəmˈpaʊnd/ *verb trans.* **L19.**
[from OVER- + COMPOUND *verb*.]
ELECTRICAL ENGINEERING. Provide (a dynamo) with so many series turns compared with the shunt turns that the voltage increases with load.

overconfidence /əʊvəˈkɒnfɪd(ə)ns/ *noun*. **E18.**
[from OVER- + CONFIDENCE.]
Confidence greater than is justified by the facts, excess of confidence.

overconfident /əʊvəˈkɒnfɪd(ə)nt/ *adjective*. **E17.**
[from OVER- + CONFIDENT.]
More confident than is justified by the facts; excessively confident.
■ **overconfidently** *adverb* **M19.**

overcorrect /əʊvəkəˈrɛkt/ *verb*. **E19.**
[from OVER- + CORRECT *verb*.]
1 *verb trans.* Correct (a lens) so that there is an aberration opposite to that of the uncorrected lens; *spec.* correct for chromatic aberration to such an extent that violet light is focused beyond red light. **E19.**
2 *verb trans. & intrans.* Make an excessive correction to or in (a thing); correct (a person) too frequently. **M20.**
■ **overcoˈrrection** *noun* (an) excessive correction; (a) correction which results in error in the opposite direction; LINGUISTICS (a) hypercorrection: **L19.**

overcredulous /əʊvəˈkrɛdjʊləs/ *adjective*. **E17.**
[from OVER- + CREDULOUS.]
Excessively credulous, unusually easy to deceive.
■ **overcreˈdulity** *noun* **L17.**

overcroft /ˈəʊvəkrɒft/ *noun*. **E20.**
[from OVER- + CROFT *noun*².]
A series of small rooms below the roof of a medieval or earlier church.

overcrop /əʊvəˈkrɒp/ *verb*. Infl. **-pp-**. **M16.**
[from OVER- + CROP *verb*.]
†**1** *verb trans.* Rise above, overtop. Only in **M16.**
2 *verb trans. & intrans.* Crop (land) to excess, exhaust by continuous cropping. **L18.**

overcrowd /əʊvəˈkraʊd/ *verb trans.* **M18.**
[from OVER- + CROWD *verb*¹.]
Fill (a room, container, etc.) with more than is usual or comfortable. Chiefly as ***overcrowded*** *ppl adjective*, ***overcrowding*** *verbal noun*.

📖 *Listener* The shortage of shopping times for working people . . causes overcrowding.

■ **overcrowdedness** *noun* the state or fact of being overcrowded **E20.**

overcure /*as verb* əʊvəˈkjʊə, *as noun* ˈəʊvəkjʊə/ *verb & noun*. **E20.**
[from OVER- + CURE *verb*, *noun*¹.]
▶**A** *verb*. **1** *verb trans. & intrans.* Cure (plastic or rubber) for longer than the optimal period; overvulcanize. **E20.**
2 *verb intrans.* Undergo overcuring. **M20.**
▶**B** *noun*. The process or result of overcuring; overvulcanization. **E20.**

overcurious /əʊvəˈkjʊərɪəs/ *adjective*. **L16.**
[from OVER- + CURIOUS.]
Excessively curious. Formerly also, excessively fastidious.
■ **overcuriˈosity** *noun* **M19.** **overcuriously** *adverb* **M16.** **overcuriousness** *noun* **L16.**

overcut /ˈəʊvəkʌt/ *noun*. **M17.**
[from OVER- + CUT *noun*².]
†**1** A cut or direct way over a hill etc. Only in **M17.**
2 MINING. A cut at or near roof level in a seam. **M20.**
3 In electrochemical machining, the distance between the outside surface of the cathode and the side of the cut in the part being machined. **M20.**

overcut /əʊvəˈkʌt/ *verb*. Infl. **-tt-**; pa. t. & pple **-cut**. **E20.**
[from OVER- + CUT *verb*.]
1 *verb trans.* Fell too many trees in (a forest) at once, upsetting the regular supply of trees suitable for cutting. **E20.**
2 *verb trans. & intrans.* MINING. Cut by machine at or near roof level. **E20.**
3 *verb intrans.* Produce a groove in a gramophone record with such amplitude that it runs into an adjacent groove. **M20.**
■ **overcutter** *noun* a machine for overcutting **M20.**

overdeck /əʊvəˈdɛk/ *verb trans.* **E16.**
[from OVER- + DECK *verb*.]
†**1** Cover over. Only in **16.**
2 Adorn to excess. **E18.**

overdeepen /əʊvəˈdiːp(ə)n/ *verb trans.* **E20.**
[from OVER- + DEEPEN.]
PHYSICAL GEOGRAPHY. Erode (a valley) more deeply by glacial action than would occur by water erosion alone. Chiefly as ***overdeepened*** *ppl adjective*, ***overdeepening*** *verbal noun*.

overdelicate /əʊvəˈdɛlɪkət/ *adjective*. **LME.**
[from OVER- + DELICATE.]
Excessively delicate.
■ **overdelicacy** *noun* (a) delicacy that is excessive **M18.**

overdetermine /əʊvədɪˈtəːmɪn/ *verb trans.* **L19.**
[from OVER- + DETERMINE.]
Determine, account for, or cause in more than one way, or with more conditions than are necessary; in *pass.*, have more determining factors than the minimum necessary, have more than one cause, PSYCHOANALYSIS give expression to more than one need or desire.
■ **ˌoverdetermiˈnation** *noun* **E20.**

overdevelop /əʊvədɪˈvɛləp/ *verb trans.* **M19.**
[from OVER- + DEVELOP.]
Develop too much or to excess; PHOTOGRAPHY treat with developer for too long or with developer that is too strong.

📖 G. FISHER Majorca's over-developed coastline.

■ **overdevelopment** *noun* **M19.**

overdid *verb pa. t.* of OVERDO.

†**overdight** *verb*. Pa. pple **-dight**. **L16–E17.**
[from OVER- + DIGHT.]
Cover overhead; clothe or deck all over. Chiefly as pa. pple.

overdo /əʊvəˈduː/ *verb*. Pa. t. **-did** /-ˈdɪd/; pa. pple **-done** /-ˈdʌn/. **OE.**
[from OVER- + DO *verb*.]
1 *verb trans. & intrans.* Do to excess or too much; carry to excess; exaggerate, carry too far. Freq. in ***overdo it***, ***overdo things***, do too much for one's health, overtax one's strength. **OE.**
2 *verb trans.* Surpass or exceed in performance; outdo. *arch.* **E17.**
3 *verb trans.* Overcook. Chiefly as ***overdone*** *ppl adjective*. **L17.**
4 *verb trans.* Overtax the strength of; fatigue, exhaust. Usu. in *pass.* **E19.**

📖 **1** D. CECIL From an anxiety to make his readers smile, he can overdo his jokes. J. UPDIKE Her ease of invention sometimes leads her to overdo.

■ **overdoer** *noun* **L17.**

overdog /ˈəʊvədɒg/ *noun*. **E20.**
[from OVER- + DOG *noun*, after *underdog*.]
A superior dog. Chiefly *fig.*, a dominant or victorious person.

overdone *verb pa. pple* of OVERDO.

overdose /*as noun* ˈəʊvədəʊs, *as verb* əʊvəˈdəʊs/ *noun & verb*. **E18.**
[from OVER- + DOSE *noun*, *verb*.]
▶**A** *noun*. A dose that is too large. **E18.**
▶**B** *verb*. **1** *verb trans.* Give (medicine etc.) in too large a dose. Now *rare*. **E18.**
2 *verb trans.* Give too large a dose to. **E18.**
3 *verb intrans.* Take an overdose of a drug. **L20.**

📖 **2** *Which?* Taking vitamin pills isn't likely to do you any real harm (unless you overdose yourself). **3** *Times* She is believed to have overdosed on heroin.

■ **over'dosage** *noun* the giving or taking of too large a dose **E20.**

overdraft /ˈəʊvədrɑːft/ *noun.* **M19.**
[from OVER- + DRAFT *noun*.]
1 A debt with a bank arising from drawing more from an account than the account holds; a bank's authorization for an account-holder to incur such a debt. **M19.**
2 See OVERDRAUGHT.

overdrank *verb pa. t.* of OVERDRINK.

overdraught /ˈəʊvədrɑːft/ *noun.* Also ***-draft.** **L19.**
[from OVER- + DRAUGHT *noun*.]
A draught passing over or above a fire, e.g. in a kiln.

overdraw /*as verb* əʊvəˈdrɔː, *as noun* ˈəʊvədrɔː/ *verb & noun.* **LME.**
[from OVER- + DRAW *verb*.]
▶ **A** *verb.* Pa. t. **-drew** /-ˈdruː/; pa. pple **-drawn** /-ˈdrɔːn/.
†**1** *verb trans. & intrans.* Draw or move over or across; pass over or away. Only in **LME.**
2 a *verb trans.* Draw money from (one's bank account) in excess of what the account holds. Formerly also, incur an overdraft with (one's banker). **E18.** ▸**b** *verb intrans.* Incur an overdraft. **M18.**
3 *verb intrans. & refl.* In card-games, exceed the maximum permissible score by drawing too many cards. **E19.**
4 *verb trans.* Exaggerate in describing or depicting. **E19.**

📖 **2a** R. BARNARD I was twenty-five quid overdrawn. **b** *Which?* More than half overdrew without arranging it beforehand. **4** D. WELCH This person seemed a caricature, an over-drawing of some novel character.

▶ **B** *noun.* **1** An overdraft. **L19.**
2 An overcheck for a horse. Also ***overdraw check.*** *US.* **E20.**
■ **overdrawn** *adjective* (**a**) that has been overdrawn; (**b**) (of tea) that has infused for too long; (**c**) having an overdraft, esp. of a specified amount: **M18.**

overdress /ˈəʊvədrɛs/ *noun.* **E19.**
[from OVER- + DRESS *noun*.]
An outer dress or garment; a dress that can be worn over another dress, a blouse, etc.

overdress /əʊvəˈdrɛs/ *verb.* **E18.**
[from OVER- + DRESS *verb*.]
1 *verb intrans. & refl.* Dress with too much display or formality. **E18.**
2 *verb trans.* Dress or cook (food) too much. **L18.**
3 *verb trans. fig.* Embellish too elaborately. **M19.**

overdrew *verb pa. t.* of OVERDRAW.

overdried *verb pa. t. & pple* of OVERDRY *verb*.

overdrink /əʊvəˈdrɪŋk/ *verb intrans. & refl.* Infl. as DRINK *verb*; pa. t. usu. **-drank** /-ˈdraŋk/, pa. pple **-drunk** /-ˈdrʌŋk/. **OE.**
[from OVER- + DRINK *verb*.]
Drink too much alcohol.
¶ Not recorded between **OE** and **L16.**

overdrive /ˈəʊvədrʌɪv/ *noun.* **E20.**
[from OVER- + DRIVE *noun*.]
1 A speed-increasing gear which may be brought into operation in addition to the ordinary (reducing) gears of a motor vehicle, so providing a gear higher than direct drive (the usual top gear) and enabling engine speed to be reduced for a given road speed. **E20.**
2 *fig.* A state of enhanced or excessive activity, esp. of the mental faculties. **M20.**
3 A device which permits the exceeding of normal levels in an electronic device, esp. the amplifier of an electric guitar; the use of such a device. **M20.**

📖 **1** MEXICAN *overdrive.* **2** *Guardian* He went into overdrive and tied up a deal . . in a few weeks.

overdrive /əʊvəˈdrʌɪv/ *verb.* Infl. as DRIVE *verb*; pa. t. usu. **-drove** /-ˈdrəʊv/, pa. pple **-driven** /-ˈdrɪv(ə)n/. **OE.**
[from OVER- + DRIVE *verb*.]
†**1** *verb trans.* Drive away, dispel; overthrow. **OE–L16.**
†**2 a** *verb trans.* Cause (time) to pass, bring to an end; pass, spend, (a night etc.). *Scot.* **LME–L16.** ▸**b** *verb intrans.* Of time: pass away, elapse. Of a person: let the time pass; delay. *Scot.* **LME–M16.**
3 *verb trans.* Drive too hard; drive or work to exhaustion; place too great a demand on (machinery or equipment). **LME.**

📖 **3** *fig.*: *Gramophone* His brilliant tempi never seem over-driven.

overdrove *verb pa. t.* of OVERDRIVE *verb*.

overdrunk *verb pa. pple* of OVERDRINK.

overdry /əʊvəˈdrʌɪ/ *adjective.* **LME.**
[from OVER- + DRY *adjective*.]
Too dry.
■ **overdryness** *noun* **L16.**

overdry /əʊvəˈdrʌɪ/ *verb intrans. & trans.* Pa. t. & pple **-dried** /-ˈdrʌɪd/. **LME.**
[from OVER- + DRY *verb*.]
Become or make too dry.

overdub /*as verb* əʊvəˈdʌb, *as noun* ˈəʊvədʌb/ *verb & noun.* **M20.**
[from OVER- + DUB *verb*[5].]
▶ **A** *verb intrans. & trans.* Infl. **-bb-**. Impose (additional sounds) on to an existing recording; record on top of (a recording previously made) so as to produce a combined recording. **M20.**
▶ **B** *noun.* An act or instance of overdubbing. **L20.**

overdue /əʊvəˈdjuː/ *adjective & noun.* **M19.**
[from OVER- + DUE *adjective*.]
▶ **A** *adjective.* More than due; past the time when due; *spec.* (of a debt etc.) remaining unpaid after the assigned date; (of a bus, train, etc.) that has not arrived at the scheduled time; (of a library book) that has been kept by the borrower longer than the period allowed; *colloq.* (of a woman) not having had a menstrual period at the expected time. **M19.**
▶ **B** *noun.* An overdue library book. **L19.**

overeager /əʊvərˈiːgə/ *adjective.* **L16.**
[from OVER- + EAGER.]
Excessively eager.
■ **overeagerly** *adverb* **L15.** **overeagerness** *noun* **E18.**

overearnest /əʊvərˈəːnɪst/ *adjective.* **E17.**
[from OVER- + EARNEST *adjective*.]
Excessively earnest.
■ **overearnestly** *adverb* **L16.** **overearnestness** *noun* **M19.**

overeasy /əʊvərˈiːzi/ *adjective.* **E17.**
[from OVER- + EASY *adjective, adverb*.]
1 Excessively easy. **E17.**
2 Usu. ***over-easy.*** Of fried eggs: turned over when almost cooked and fried briefly on the reverse side; cf. SUNNY ***side up.*** *N. Amer.* **L20.**
■ **overeasily** *adverb* **L16.** **overeasiness** *noun* **M19.**

overeat /əʊvərˈiːt/ *verb.* Pa. t. **-ate** /-ˈeɪt/; pa. pple **-eaten** /-ˈiːt(ə)n/. **E16.**
[from OVER- + EAT *verb*.]
†**1** *verb trans.* Eat more than (another). Only in **E16.**
2 *verb intrans. & refl.* Eat too much. **L16.**
†**3** Eat or nibble all over or on all sides. Only in **E17.**

overelaborate /əʊv(ə)rɪˈlab(ə)rət/ *adjective.* **L19.**
[from OVER- + ELABORATE *adjective*.]
Excessively elaborate.
■ **overelaborately** *adverb* **M20.** **overelaborateness** *noun* **E20.**

overelaborate /əʊv(ə)rɪˈlabəreɪt/ *verb trans.* **E20.**
[from OVER- + ELABORATE *verb*.]
Elaborate in excessive detail.
■ ˌ**overelaboˈration** *noun* **E20.**

overemphasis /əʊvərˈɛmfəsɪs/ *noun.* Pl. **-phases** /-fəsiːz/. **E20.**
[from OVER- + EMPHASIS.]
Excessive emphasis; an instance of this.

overemphasize /əʊvərˈɛmfəsʌɪz/ *verb trans. & intrans.* Also **-ise.** **E20.**
[from OVER- + EMPHASIZE.]
Emphasize (a thing) excessively, lay too much emphasis on.

overemployment /əʊv(ə)rɪmˈplɔɪm(ə)nt/ *noun.* **M20.**
[from OVER- + EMPLOYMENT.]
A situation in which the number of vacancies for jobs exceeds the number of people unemployed, producing a labour shortage.

†**over-end** *noun.* **ME–E18.**
[from OVER *adjective* + END *noun*.]
The top.

overenthusiasm /əʊv(ə)rɪnˈθjuːzɪaz(ə)m, -rɛn-/ *noun.* **M20.**
[from OVER- + ENTHUSIASM.]
Excessive enthusiasm.
■ ˌ**overenthusiˈastic** *adjective* **E20.** ˌ**overenthusiˈastically** *adverb* **L20.**

overesteem /əʊv(ə)rɪˈstiːm, -rɛ-/ *verb trans.* **M17.**
[from OVER- + ESTEEM *verb*.]
Esteem too highly, think too highly of.

overestimate /*as noun* əʊvərˈɛstɪmət, *as verb* əʊvərˈɛstɪmeɪt/ *noun & verb.* **E19.**
[from OVER- + ESTIMATE *noun, verb*.]
▶ **A** *noun.* An estimate that is too high. **E19.**
▶ **B** *verb trans.* Attribute too high an estimated value to; value too highly, have too high an opinion of. **E19.**

📖 J. D. MACDONALD You are a miserable, sycophantic weakling . . and your uncle overestimated you. J. HELLER Plato overestimated greatly the power of education to reform.

■ **overestiˈmation** *noun* the action of overestimating someone or something; an overestimate: **E19.**

For other words beginning with *over-* see the entry for **over-**

overexcite /əʊv(ə)rɪkˈsʌɪt, -rɛk-/ *verb trans.* **E19.**
[from OVER- + EXCITE.]
Excite excessively
■ ˌ**overexcitaˈbility** *noun* the condition of being overexcitable **M19.** **overexcitable** *adjective* excessively excitable **M19.** **overexcitement** *noun* the state of being overexcited **E19.**

overexercise /əʊvərˈɛksəsʌɪz/ *noun & verb.* **L19.**
[from OVER- + EXERCISE *noun, verb*.]
▶ **A** *noun.* Excessive exercise. **L19.**
▶ **B** *verb.* **1** *verb trans.* Exercise (the body, muscles, etc.) too much; overexert (one's authority). **L20.**
2 *verb intrans.* Take too much exercise; overexert oneself. **L20.**

overexpose /əʊv(ə)rɪkˈspəʊz, -rɛk-/ *verb trans. & intrans.* **M19.**
[from OVER- + EXPOSE.]
Expose too much; *spec.* (**a**) PHOTOGRAPHY use too long an exposure or too wide an aperture with (a film or plate) or when taking (a photograph), resulting in a pale or washed-out picture; (**b**) expose too much to the public eye.
■ **overexposure** *noun* **L19.**

overextend /əʊv(ə)rɪkˈstɛnd, -rɛk-/ *verb trans.* **M20.**
[from OVER- + EXTEND.]
1 Take on (oneself) or impose on (another) an excessive burden of work, commitments, etc.; freq. in *pass.*, have too many commitments. **M20.**
2 Extend or reach further than; extend (a thing) too far. *rare.* **M20.**
■ **overextension** *noun* **M20.**

overface /əʊvəˈfeɪs/ *verb trans.* **L15.**
[from OVER- + FACE *verb*.]
Abash or overcome, esp. by boldness or effrontery; alarm or intimidate (a person, animal, etc.) by presenting too great a task or obstacle.

overfall /ˈəʊvəfɔːl/ *noun.* **M16.**
[from OVER- + FALL *noun*[2].]
1 A turbulent stretch of sea etc. with short breaking waves, caused by a strong current over a submarine ridge or shoal, or by the meeting of contrary currents. **M16.**
2 A waterfall, a rapid. **L16.**
3 A sudden drop in the sea bottom, as at the edge of a ledge. **L18.**
4 A structure in a canal, dam, etc., to allow the water to overflow when it exceeds a certain level. **L18.**

overfall /əʊvəˈfɔːl/ *verb.* Pa. t. **-fell** /-ˈfɛl/; pa. pple **-fallen** /-ˈfɔːl(ə)n/. **OE.**
[from OVER- + FALL *verb*.]
1 *verb trans.* Attack, assail. Long *rare.* **OE.**
2 *verb trans.* Fall on, come down on. Long *rare.* **ME.**
3 *verb intrans.* Fall over; *Scot.* be very dilapidated. **M16.**

overfamiliar /əʊvəfəˈmɪlɪə/ *adjective.* **E16.**
[from OVER- + FAMILIAR.]
Excessively familiar.
■ ˌ**overfamiliˈarity** *noun* **L17.** **overfamiliarly** *adverb* (*rare*) **L15.**

overfeed /əʊvəˈfiːd/ *verb.* Pa. t. & pple **-fed** /-ˈfɛd/. **E17.**
[from OVER- + FEED *verb*.]
1 *verb trans. & intrans.* Give too much food (to). **E17.**
2 *verb intrans.* Take too much food. **L18.**

overfell *verb pa. t.* of OVERFALL *verb*.

overfill /*as verb* əʊvəˈfɪl, *as noun* ˈəʊvəfɪl/ *verb & noun.* **OE.**
[from OVER- + FILL *verb*.]
▶ **A** *verb.* **1** *verb trans.* Fill to overflowing or to excess. **OE.**
2 *verb intrans.* Become full to overflowing. **E17.**
▶ **B** *noun.* METALLURGY. A projection on rolled metal due to the metal being too large for the aperture through which it was forced, so that the excess spread between the junction of the rolls; a bar etc. that is too large for the rolling it is to undergo. **E20.**

overfish /əʊvəˈfɪʃ/ *verb trans.* **M19.**
[from OVER- + FISH *verb*[1].]
Fish (a stream etc.) too much; deplete the stock of (a fish) by excessive fishing.

overfit /ˈəʊvəfɪt/ *adjective.* **E20.**
[from OVER- after MISFIT *noun & adjective*.]
PHYSICAL GEOGRAPHY. Designating or pertaining to a stream which, on the basis of its present-day flow, would have eroded a larger valley than it has done. Cf. MISFIT *adjective* 2, UNDERFIT.

overfleet /əʊvəˈfliːt/ *verb trans. & intrans.* Long only *Scot.* Pa. pple †**-floten.** **ME.**
[from OVER- + FLEET *verb*[1].]
Flow over, overflow.

overflew *verb pa. t.* of OVERFLY.

overfloat /əʊvəˈfləʊt/ *verb trans.* **E17.**
[from OVER- + FLOAT *verb*. In sense 1 perh. orig. confused with *overfloten*: see OVERFLEET.]
†**1** Overflow. Only in **17.**
2 Float over. **M17.**

†**overfloten** *verb pa. pple* of OVERFLEET.

overflourish /əʊvəˈflʌrɪʃ/ *verb.* L16.
[from OVER- + FLOURISH *verb*.]
†**1** *verb intrans.* Flourish or thrive exceedingly. Also, be excessively embellished *with*. Only in L16.
2 *verb trans.* Cover with blossom or verdure. E17.
†**3** *verb trans.* Embellish excessively. Only in E18.

overflow /ˈəʊvəfləʊ/ *noun.* L16.
[from OVER- + FLOW *noun*¹.]
1 The action or fact of overflowing; an inundation, a flood; COMPUTING the generation of a number having more digits than the assigned location. L16.
2 An excess, a superabundance. L16.
3 A quantity that overflows; an amount or number in excess of what can be accommodated. M17.
4 An outlet or drain for carrying off excess water. Also *overflow pipe* etc. L19.

📖 **1** E. GUNDREY If overflow continues, draw off water supply. **3** M. LASKI The overflow from London's got to go somewhere.

Comb.: **overflow meeting**: attended by those who cannot be accommodated at the main gathering; ***overflow pipe***: see sense 4 above.

overflow /əʊvəˈfləʊ/ *verb.* Pa. t. **-flowed**; pa. pple **-flowed**, (*arch.*) **-flown** /-ˈfləʊn/. OE.
[from OVER- + FLOW *verb*.]
▶ **I** *verb trans.* **1** Flow over; overspread or cover with water or other liquid, flood; pass or spread over so as to pervade, fill, submerge, overwhelm, etc. OE.
2 a Flow over (the brim, banks, or sides). M16. ▸**b** Cause to overflow; fill (a vessel) so full that the contents spill over. M17.
†**3** Overflow with, pour out. *rare*. Only in L16.

📖 **1** AV *Jer.* 47:2 Waters rise vp . . and shall ouerflow the land. H. CAINE The river had overflowed the meadows. P. KAVANAGH He overflowed the shoemaker with enthusiastic greetings. **2a** J. UGLOW The river overflows its banks. **b** R. BRIDGES Again shall pleasure overflow Thy cup with sweetness.

▶ **II** *verb intrans.* **4** Flow over the sides or brim by reason of fullness; exceed the limits of something. OE. ▸†**b** *fig.* Get beyond bounds, become excessive. ME–E17. ▸**c** Leave one part for another owing to lack of room or other pressure. M19.
5 (Of a receptacle etc.) be so full that the contents spill over the brim; *fig.* be very full or abundant. (Foll. by *with*.) LME.

📖 **4c** DAY LEWIS The horde of relations . . which littered Dublin and overflowed into England. **5** G. BANCROFT Benevolence gushed prodigally from his ever overflowing heart. N. SEDAKA As the party progressed the house began to overflow. A. LURIE It was great to have Jeanne in good spirits again, overflowing with affection.

■ **overflowingly** *adverb* in an overflowing or superabundant manner M17. **overflowingness** *noun* †(*a*) luxury, extravagance; (*b*) the condition of being superabundant: ME.

overflowing /əʊvəˈfləʊɪŋ/ *noun.* LME.
[from OVERFLOW *verb* + -ING¹.]
1 The action of OVERFLOW *verb*; a flood, an inundation. Now chiefly in ***full to overflowing***, more than full, so as to overflow. LME.
2 A quantity that overflows; an excess, a superabundance. L16.

overflown *verb*¹ *pa. pple*: see OVERFLOW *verb*.

overflown *verb*² *pa. pple* of OVERFLY.

overfly /əʊvəˈflʌɪ/ *verb.* Pa. t. **-flew** /-ˈfluː/; pa. pple **-flown** /-ˈfləʊn/. M16.
[from OVER- + FLY *verb*.]
1 *verb trans. & intrans.* Fly over (place or object), pass over by flying; fly beyond. M16.
2 *verb trans.* Surpass in flight; fly higher, faster, or further than. L16.

📖 **1** *Scientific American* A laser-based system . . to detect submarines . . from overflying aircraft. *Japan Times* Soviet aircraft have overflown North Korea since December 1984.

overfold /*as verb* əʊvəˈfəʊld, *as noun* ˈəʊvəfəʊld/ *verb & noun.* LME.
[from OVER- + FOLD *verb*¹, *noun*².]
▶ **A** *verb trans.* **1** Cover over; enfold. Now *rare* exc. *Scot.* LME.
2 GEOLOGY. In *pass.* Of folded strata: be pushed beyond the vertical, so as to form an overfold. L19.
▶ **B** *noun.* GEOLOGY. A fold in which both the limbs dip in the same direction so that the strata in the middle of the fold are upside down. L19.

overfond /əʊvəˈfɒnd/ *adjective.* L16.
[from OVER- + FOND *adjective*.]
1 Too foolish. Long *obsolete* exc. *dial.* L16.
2 Having too great an affection or liking for a person or thing. (Foll. by *of*.) Usu. in neg. contexts. E17.

📖 **2** B. BAINBRIDGE He was not overfond of being called Ted.

■ **overfondly** *adverb* E17. **overfondness** *noun* L17.

overforward /əʊvəˈfɔːwəd/ *adjective.* Now *rare*. M17.
[from OVER- + FORWARD *adjective*.]
Excessively forward.
■ **overforwardly** *adverb* M17. **overforwardness** *noun* L16.

overfulfil /əʊvəfʊlˈfɪl/ *verb trans.* Infl. **-ll-**. Also ***-fill**. LME.
[from OVER- + FULFIL.]
†**1** Fill more than full, fill too full. LME–M16.
2 Fulfil (a plan, goal, etc.) beyond expectation or before the expected time. M20.
■ **overfulfilment** *noun* M20.

overfull /əʊvəˈfʊl/ *adjective.* OE.
[from OVER- + FULL *adjective*.]
Excessively full, full to overflowing.
■ **overfullness** *noun* E17.

overgang /əʊvəˈgaŋ/ *verb trans.* Now only *Scot. & north.* OE.
[from OVER- + GANG *verb*¹.]
1 = OVERGO 5a. OE.
†**2** = OVERGO 2. OE–ME.
3 = OVERGO 4. ME.
4 = OVERGO 5b. M18.

overgave *verb pa. t.* of OVERGIVE.

overgeneralize /əʊvəˈdʒɛn(ə)rəlʌɪz/ *verb.* Also **-ise**. E20.
[from OVER- + GENERALIZE.]
1 *verb intrans.* Draw general conclusions from inadequate data; argue more widely than is justified by available evidence or by circumstances. E20.
2 *verb trans.* Make more general than is justified; draw too general a conclusion from (data, circumstances, etc.). M20.

📖 **1** *Scientific American* Sherrington was careful not to overgeneralize from his findings. **2** R. V. REDINGER Slanted and overgeneralized as are many of its discussions.

■ **overgenerali'zation** *noun* M19.

overget /əʊvəˈgɛt/ *verb trans.* Infl. as GET *verb*; pa. t. usu. **-got** /-ˈgɒt/, pa. pple usu. **-got**, ***-gotten** /-ˈgɒt(ə)n/. ME.
[from OVER- + GET *verb*.]
1 Overtake. *obsolete* exc. *dial.* ME.
2 Get the better of. Long *rare* or *obsolete*. LME.
3 Get over (a difficulty), recover from the effects of (an illness, shock, etc.). E19.
4 Prevail on; take possession of (a person). E20.

overgild /əʊvəˈgɪld/ *verb trans.* Pa. t. & pple **-gilded**, (now chiefly in lit. sense) **-gilt** /-ˈgɪlt/. ME.
[from OVER- + GILD *verb*¹.]
Cover with gilding; *fig.* tinge with a golden colour. Chiefly as ***overgilded***, ***overgilt*** *ppl adjectives*.

overgive /əʊvəˈgɪv/ *verb trans.* Long *obsolete* exc. *Scot.* Pa. t. **-gave** /-ˈgeɪv/; pa. pple **-given** /-ˈgɪv(ə)n/. LME.
[from OVER- + GIVE *verb*.]
Give up, hand over.

overglaze /ˈəʊvəgleɪz/ *noun & adjective.* L19.
[from OVER- + GLAZE *noun*.]
▶ **A** *noun.* A glaze applied over another, *spec.* in CERAMICS, over printed or painted decoration done on the glazed surface of porcelain etc. Cf. UNDERGLAZE *noun*. L19.
▶ **B** *adjective.* Of, pertaining to, or suitable for an overglaze. L19.

overglaze /əʊvəˈgleɪz/ *verb trans.* L16.
[from OVER- + GLAZE *verb*¹.]
Cover with a glaze or polish; apply an overglaze to. Formerly also, coat or plate with a thin covering of something better, veneer.
■ **overglazing** *noun* (*a*) the action of the verb; (*b*) = OVERGLAZE *noun*: M20.

overgo /əʊvəˈgəʊ/ *verb.* Pa. t. **-went** /-ˈwɛnt/; pa. pple **-gone** /-ˈgɒn/. OE.
[from OVER- + GO *verb*.]
▶ **I** *verb trans.* †**1** Come upon suddenly; catch, apprehend, detect. OE–L16.
2 Cross (a river, boundary, or line). *obsolete* exc. *dial.* OE. ▸†**b** *fig.* Pass (a moral limit), transgress. OE–M16.
†**3** Pass in front of so as to hide. OE–M17.
4 Pass or spread over in a hostile or injurious way; overrun, infest. Now *Scot. & dial.* OE.
5 a Overcome, overpower, get the better of; oppress. Now *Scot. & dial.* ME. ▸**b** Surpass, exceed. ME. ▸†**c** Deceive, cheat. ME–L16.
6 Go over the surface or extent of; traverse. ME.
†**7** Live through (a specified length of time); (of time) pass over (a person). ME–L16.
†**8** Rise higher than, surmount. LME–E17.
†**9** Go faster than, leave behind in going, overtake. M16–M17.
†**10** Pass over, let alone, omit. E17–L19.
▶ **II** *verb intrans.* **11** Go or pass by; (of time) pass. Now *Scot. & dial.* OE.

¶ Cf. OVERGANG.

overgot, **overgotten** *verbs* see OVERGET.

overgovern /əʊvəˈgʌv(ə)n/ *verb trans.* L15.
[from OVER- + GOVERN.]
†**1** Rule over. Only in L15.
2 Govern too much; subject to too much government interference. M19.
■ **overgovernment** *noun* (*a*) excessive government, too much government interference; (*b*) higher government or control: M19.

overgrew *verb pa. t.* of OVERGROW.

overground /*as noun* ˈəʊvəgraʊnd, *as adjective & adverb also* əʊvəˈgraʊnd/ *noun, adjective, & adverb.* E17.
[from OVER- + GROUND *noun*.]
▶ **A** *noun.* †**1** Higher ground. Only in E17.
2 A thing regarded as the antithesis of an underground. M20.
▶ **B** *adjective.* **1** Situated above ground; raised above the ground. L19.
2 *fig.* Overt; unconcealed; publicly acknowledged. M20.
▶ **C** *adverb.* Above the ground; into the open. M20.

overgrow /əʊvəˈgrəʊ/ *verb.* Pa. t. **-grew** /-ˈgruː/; pa. pple **-grown** /-ˈgrəʊn/. ME.
[from OVER- + GROW *verb*.]
1 *verb trans.* Grow over, cover with growth; grow over so as to choke; *fig.* overcome, overwhelm. ME.
2 *verb intrans.* Grow too large; grow beyond the natural size; increase unduly. LME.
†**3** *verb trans.* Surpass, exceed. LME–M17.
4 *verb trans.* Grow too big or tall for; outgrow (a garment); *refl.* grow beyond one's strength, proper size, etc. M16.

📖 **1** *Journal of Bacteriology* Occasionally colonies fuse or overgrow each other. E. JOLLEY Some of them . . had neglected overgrown gardens. **2** S. RAVEN Lionel's nothing but an overgrown schoolboy.

overgrowth /ˈəʊvəgrəʊθ/ *noun.* E17.
[from OVER- + GROWTH.]
1 Growth that is excessive or too rapid; an instance of this. E17.
2 A growth over or on something; an accretion. L19.

†**overhale** *verb trans.* LME.
[from OVER- + HALE *verb*¹.]
1 Cover, overspread; draw over as a covering. LME–M17.
2 Harass, molest, oppress; abuse; compel *to do*. M16–L17.
3 Overpower, overmaster. M16–E17.
4 Pass over, disregard, overlook. L16–E17.
5 Examine thoroughly. M18–E19.

overhand /ˈəʊvəhand/ *noun. obsolete* exc. *Scot. dial.* ME.
[Sense 1 from OVER *adjective* + HAND *noun*, sense 2 from OVERHAND *adjective*.]
1 The upper hand; mastery, superiority. Chiefly in ***get the overhand***, ***have the overhand***, etc. ME.
2 An overarm swimming stroke. L19.

overhand /ˈəʊvəhand/ *adverb, adjective, & verb.* L16.
[formed as prec.]
▶ **A** *adverb.* †**1** Upside down. Only in L16.
†**2** Aside. Only in E19.
3 With the hand over or above the object which it grasps; (in cricket, baseball, etc.) with an overarm action. M19.
▶ **B** *adjective.* **1** Performed with the hand brought from above downwards; (in cricket, baseball, etc.) bowled, pitched, etc., with an overarm action. M17. ▸**b** Of a swimming stroke: overarm. L19.
2 Designating a simple knot made by passing the end of a rope, string, etc., over the standing part and through the loop or bight so formed. M19.
▶ **C** *verb trans.* = OVERSEW. L19.

overhanded /əʊvəˈhandɪd/ *adjective.* M18.
[Partly from OVER- + (as) HANDED, partly from OVERHAND *adverb* + -ED¹.]
1 Supplied with too many workers; overstaffed. M18.
2 = OVERHAND *adjective* 1. M19.
3 = OVERHAND *adjective* 2. L19.

overhang /ˈəʊvəhaŋ/ *noun.* M19.
[from the verb.]
1 The fact of overhanging or projecting; the extent to which something overhangs; an overhanging or projecting part; *spec.* (*a*) the projection of the upper parts of a ship, fore and aft, beyond the water-line; (*b*) (the length of) the part of a wing beyond its outermost point of support; in a biplane or multiplane, (the length of) the part of a wing that extends beyond the tip of an adjacent wing; (*c*) in a turntable unit, the distance of the stylus point beyond the centre of the turntable when the pickup arm is aligned with a radius. M19.

For other words beginning with *over-* see the entry for **over-**

2 *ECONOMICS.* An excess of (estimated) expenditure over available or budgeted funds; a quantity of securities or commodities large enough to exert downward pressure on prices if offered for sale. **M20.**

3 *AUDIO.* The (usu. undesired) continued oscillation of a system, esp. a loudspeaker, after the cessation of the signal causing the oscillation. **L20.**

overhang /əʊvəˈhaŋ/ *verb.* Pa. t. & pple **-hung** /-ˈhʌŋ/. **LME.**
[from OVER- + HANG *verb.*]
1 *verb trans. & intrans.* Hang over, be suspended (above); project or jut out above; (of a hill, building, etc.) rise steeply up (from). **LME.**
2 *verb trans.* Be as if about to fall on; loom over; threaten. **M17.**

> 1 J. TYNDALL I . . found my friend beneath an overhanging rock. E. LANGLEY An ancient family hotel, which overhung the street.

■ **overhanging** *noun* (*a*) the action of the verb; (*b*) a thing that overhangs: **M16.**

overhaste /əʊvəˈheɪst/ *noun.* **LME.**
[from OVER- + HASTE *noun.*]
Excessive haste.

overhasten /əʊvəˈheɪs(ə)n/ *verb trans.* **E17.**
[from OVER- + HASTEN.]
Hasten excessively.

overhasty /əʊvəˈheɪsti/ *adjective.* **LME.**
[from OVER- + HASTY.]
Excessively hasty; rash, precipitate.
■ **overhastily** *adverb* **LME.** **overhastiness** *noun* **L16.**

overhaul /ˈəʊvəhɔːl/ *noun.* **E19.**
[from the verb.]
The action or an act of overhauling something; a thorough examination with a view to repairs, and any necessary action taken for this purpose.

overhaul /əʊvəˈhɔːl/ *verb trans.* **E17.**
[from OVER- + HAUL *verb.* Prob. of Low German origin: all three senses are repr. in German *überholen*.]
1 *NAUTICAL.* Slacken (a rope) by pulling in the opposite direction to that in which it is drawn in hoisting; release and separate the blocks of (a tackle) in this way. **E17.**
2 Take apart to examine in detail; examine thoroughly with a view to repairs and take any necessary action for this purpose. **E18.** ▸**b** Change (something) significantly; revise, rework, improve, or update. **M20.**
3 Overtake, catch up with; gain on. **L18.**

> 2 G. A. BIRMINGHAM I'll . . look at the *Spindrift* . . . I'm having her overhauled and fitted out for a cruise. 3 *Times* Time has run out for her to overhaul Miss Dare, who now has a lead of four.

overhead /*as adverb* əʊvəˈhɛd; *as noun & adjective* ˈəʊvəhɛd; *in sense B.2 also* əʊvəˈhɛd/ *adverb, noun, & adjective.* **OE.**
[from OVER- + HEAD *noun.*]
▶ **A** *adverb.* **1** Taken together, overall; on average. Formerly also, in each case, one with another. Long *obsolete* exc. *Scot.* **OE.**
2 a Above one's head; on high, in the sky, *esp.* in or near the zenith; on the floor above. **LME.** ▸**b** So as to be completely submerged or immersed. Freq. also *fig.* (foll. by *in*). **M17.**
†**3** Headlong, precipitately. **LME–L16.**

> 2a M. MITCHELL The dark cedars on either side . . met in an arch overhead. G. GREENE In Herr Braun's cellar the husbands heard the knocker hammering overhead. G. LORD Overhead, the . . cloud had covered nearly half the sky.

▶ **B** *noun.* †**1** A blow over the head in fencing. Only in **ME.**
2 The sky, the firmament. **M19.**
3 In *pl.* & (chiefly *N. Amer.*) *sing.* Overhead expenses (see sense C.4 below). **E20.**
4 An overhead stroke in tennis, badminton, etc. **M20.**
5 An overhead projector; an overhead transparency. **L20.**
▶ **C** *adjective.* **1** Placed or situated overhead or at a distance above the ground; (of a mechanism) situated above the object driven. **L19.**
2 Overall, average. Chiefly *Scot.* **L19.**
3 Of a stroke in tennis, badminton, etc.: made with the racket above one's head. **E20.**
4 Of expenses: incurred in the upkeep of plant and premises, not attributable to individual products or items. **E20.**

> 1 T. HEGGEN The wardroom, where one overhead light burned dimly.

Special collocations: **overhead camshaft**: mounted above the cylinder block of an internal-combustion engine. **overhead projector** a projector which projects an image from a horizontally-positioned transparency on to a vertical screen by means of light passed upwards through the transparency and then through lenses mounted above it. **overhead transparency** a sheet of acetate film containing an image for projection by an overhead projector. **overhead valve**: seated in the top of the combustion chamber of an internal-combustion engine, facing the piston.

overhear /əʊvəˈhɪə/ *verb.* Pa. t. & pple **-heard** /-ˈhəːd/. **OE.**
[from OVER- + HEAR *verb.*]
†**1** *verb trans.* Disregard, disobey. Only in **OE.**
†**2** *verb trans.* Hear; hear out. **OE–LME.**
3 *verb trans. & intrans.* Hear (words etc.) spoken or hear the words of (a person) contrary to the intention or without the knowledge of the speaker(s). **M16.**
†**4** *verb trans.* Hear again. *rare* (Shakes.). Only in **L16.**
■ **overhearer** *noun* **M17.**

overheat /ˈəʊvəhiːt/ *noun.* **L16.**
[from OVER- + HEAT *noun.*]
Excessive heat; overheated condition; *fig.* excessive ardour, vehemence, etc.

overheat /əʊvəˈhiːt/ *verb.* **LME.**
[from OVER- + HEAT *verb.*]
1 *verb trans.* Heat too much, make too hot; *fig.* excite to excessive warmth of feeling; make too passionate about something. **LME.** ▸**b** Produce in (a country's economy) a condition of marked inflation by placing excessive pressure on resources during a period of expansion in demand. Chiefly as ***overheated*** *ppl adjective*, ***overheating*** *verbal noun.* **M20.**
2 *verb intrans.* Become too hot; become overheated. **E20.**

> 1 A. CROSS I'm . . inclined to attribute other feelings to my overheated imagination.

†**overhent** *verb trans.* Pa. t. & pple **-hent.** **ME–E18**
[from OVER- + HENT *verb.*]
Lay hold on; overtake.

overhie /əʊvəˈhʌɪ/ *verb trans. obsolete* exc. *Scot.* **LME.**
[from OVER- + HIE.]
Overtake by hastening after.

overhung /əʊvəˈhʌŋ/ *ppl adjective.* **E18.**
[pa. pple of OVERHANG *verb.*]
1 That projects or juts out above. **E18.**
2 Having something hanging over it. **M19.**
3 Supported from above. **L19.**
4 = ***hung-over*** s.v. HUNG 4. **M20.**

> 2 J. FENTON There was a river overhung with trees.

overhung *verb pa. t. & pple* of OVERHANG *verb.*

overindulge /əʊv(ə)rɪnˈdʌldʒ/ *verb trans. & intrans.* **M18.**
[from OVER- + INDULGE.]
Indulge too much or to excess.
■ **overindulgence** *noun* (an) excessive indulgence **M18.** †**overindulgency** *noun* (*rare*) overindulgence: only in **M17.** **overindulgent** *adjective* excessively indulgent **M17.**

overissue /əʊvərˈɪʃuː, -ˈɪsjuː/ *noun & verb.* **E19.**
[from OVER- + ISSUE *noun, verb.*]
▶ **A** *noun.* The action or an act of issuing notes, shares, etc., in excess; excess issued notes, shares, etc. **E19.**
▶ **B** *verb trans.* Issue in excess; issue (notes, shares, etc.) beyond the authorized amount or the issuer's ability to pay. **M19.**

overjoy /əʊvəˈdʒɔɪ/ *noun.* **L16.**
[from OVER- + JOY *noun.*]
Excess of joy.

overjoy /əʊvəˈdʒɔɪ/ *verb.* **LME.**
[from OVER- + JOY *verb.*]
†**1** *verb intrans.* Rejoice. Only in **LME.**
2 *verb trans.* Fill with extreme joy. Now chiefly as ***overjoyed*** *ppl adjective.* **L16.**

> 2 E. LONGFORD Antonia was overjoyed to have him back. She had missed him sorely.

overkill /ˈəʊvəkɪl, *as verb also* əʊvəˈkɪl/ *noun & verb.* **M20.**
[from OVER- + KILL *noun*[1], *verb*[2].]
▶ **A** *noun.* **1** Excessive killing; *spec.* the amount by which destruction or the capacity for destruction by a nuclear weapon exceeds that required for victory or annihilation. **M20.**
2 *transf. & fig.* Excess action leading to too much of something. **M20.**

> 1 A. TOFFLER Present-day commercial fishing . . results in ruthless overkill and threatens . . many forms of marine life. 2 *City Limits* Their sonic overkill of noise and fuzziness demands you prick up your ears. J. BAYLEY His art has a tendency to go for overkill.

▶ **B** *verb trans. & intrans.* Practice overkill (against), subject (a thing) to overkill. **M20.**

overlade /əʊvəˈleɪd/ *verb trans.* Pa. pple †**-laded**, **-laden** /-ˈleɪd(ə)n/. **ME.**
[from OVER- + LADE *verb.*]
†**1** Lade or draw water out of. Only in **ME.**
2 Load with too heavy a burden, overload. Chiefly as ***overladen*** *ppl adjective.* **LME.**

overlaid *verb pa. t. & pple* of OVERLAY *verb*[1].

overlain *verb pa. pple* of OVERLIE.

overland /ˈəʊvəland, *as adverb & adjective also* əʊvəˈland/ *adverb, adjective, & verb.* **ME.**
[from OVER- + LAND *noun*[1].]
▶ **A** *adverb.* Over or across land; by land as opp. to by sea. **ME.**

> P. HILL In Australia . . he joined a party going overland in a converted London Transport bus.

▶ **B** *adjective.* Proceeding over or across land; performed by land; for or connected with a journey over land. **E19.**

> *Daily Colonist* The northbound Southern Pacific overland express. J. COLVILLE An overland line of communication with Bergen.

▶ **C** *verb. Austral.*
1 *verb trans.* Drive (livestock) overland for long distances. Cf. earlier OVERLANDER 1. **L19.**
2 *verb intrans.* Go overland from one part of Australia to another. **L19.**

overlander /ˈəʊvəlandə/ *noun.* **M19.**
[from (the same root as) OVERLAND *verb* + -ER[1].]
1 A person who journeyed from one part of Australia to another (*obsolete* exc. *Hist.*); a person who drives livestock overland; *slang* a tramp. *Austral.* **M19.** ▸**b** A migrant. *obsolete* exc. *N. AMER. HISTORY.* **M19.**
2 *gen.* A traveller taking a long overland route to a country. **M20.**

overlap /ˈəʊvəlap/ *noun.* **M17.**
[from the verb.]
†**1** In full ***overlap nail***. A nail to secure overlapping planks. *Scot.* Only in **M17.**
2 An instance of overlapping; the point at or degree by which one thing overlaps another. Also, an overlapping thing, *esp.* a piece of material etc. which partially overlies or covers and extends beyond another. **E19.** ▸**b** *GEOLOGY.* Onlap, esp. of a transgressive sequence of strata unconformably over the underlying strata. Cf. OFFLAP, ONLAP. **M19.** ▸**c** *SAILING.* A position in racing in which the sternmost part of one yacht is, or is deemed to be, ahead of the foremost part of another, and in which the yacht which is overtaking and not yet clear ahead must give room. **L19.** ▸**d** The distance beyond a railway signal that must be clear before a train is allowed to approach it past the previous signal. **E20.** ▸**e** *COMPUTING.* The simultaneous performance of two or more operations during the execution of a program. **M20.** ▸**f** *RUGBY FOOTBALL.* A situation in which the team in possession has more players in its attack than can be marked by the defenders. **M20.** ▸**g** *SOCCER.* A situation in which a player moves up on the outside of, and overtakes, the player in possession, esp. so as to receive a pass. **M20.**

overlap /əʊvəˈlap/ *verb.* Infl. **-pp-.** **E17.**
[from OVER- + LAP *verb*[2].]
†**1** *verb trans.* Construct (esp. a boat) of planks each of which extends downwards to cover part of the plank below. *Scot.* Only in **E17.**
2 *verb trans. & intrans.* Lie or be situated so as to cover part of (a thing), overlie (something) partially; *fig.* coincide partly with (a person or thing). **E18.** ▸**b** *verb trans.* Cause to overlap. **M19.**
3 *verb trans.* Cover and extend beyond (a thing); *fig.* exceed in number or degree. **E19.** ▸**b** *verb trans. GEOLOGY.* Of a formation: extend beyond the edge of (an older underlying formation). **M19.** ▸**c** *verb intrans. & trans. SOCCER.* Move up on the outside of and overtake (the player in possession), esp. so as to receive a pass. **L20.**

> 2 *Nature* The Dans produced five children, whose upbringing overlapped World War II. M. ESSLIN This is an even more difficult dividing line to draw, for the two approaches overlap. W. MCILVANNEY There is a great gallery of photographs, so numerous . . that they overlap. E. LONGFORD Edward Longford, though two years younger than Christine, had overlapped with her at Oxford. 3 H. CRANE Its present length will slightly overlap two pages.

■ **overlapping** *noun* the action or an act of the verb; *spec.* (*PHONETICS*) coincidence in the form of a phone of one phoneme with that of another phone of a different phoneme: **L17.**

overlay /ˈəʊvəleɪ/ *noun.* **LME.**
[from the verb.]
1 A thing laid (esp. as a covering) over something else. **LME.** ▸**b** *PRINTING.* A piece of paper pasted over the impression-surface of a printing-press in order to make parts of the impression darker. **E19.** ▸**c** A transparent sheet with instructions or additional material, to be placed over artwork, esp. a map or diagram. **M20.** ▸**d** A layer of coloured glass added on top of clear glass in decorative glassware. Usu. *attrib.* **M20.** ▸**e** *BIOLOGY.* A layer of gel spread over a cell culture and containing an indicator of the presence of some cell product. **M20.**
2 A necktie, a collar. *Scot.* **L16.**
3 *DENTISTRY.* = ONLAY *noun* 2. **M20.**
4 Unjustifiably high betting odds. *US.* **M20.**
5 *COMPUTING.* The process of transferring a block of data to internal storage in place of what is already there; a section of program so transferred. **M20.**

🕮 **1** M. Tripp When Eve pulled back the quilted overlay the sheets seemed startlingly white. *Nature* Prospecting techniques will be hampered by the enormous overlay of ice. *fig.*: *English World-Wide* Such varieties represent an overlay of the English lexicon upon the several native language grammars.

overlay /əʊvəˈleɪ/ *verb*¹ *trans.* Pa. t. & pple **-laid** /-ˈleɪd/. ME.
[from OVER- + LAY *verb*¹.]
▶ **I** Lay over.
1 Cover the surface of (a thing) *with* a coating, covering, etc. ME. ▸**b** *PRINTING.* Put an overlay on. L19.
†**2** Cover excessively; overrun. ME–M18.
3 Lay or place over, above, or on top of something else. *rare.* L16. ▸**b** Surmount or span *with*. *rare.* E17.
▶ **II** Lie over.
4 Lie over. ME. ▸**b** = OVERLIE 2. LME. ▸**c** *NAUTICAL.* Cross the cable or anchor of another vessel so as to cause chafing or obstruction. L18.
5 †**a** Overwhelm; oppress. ME–M18. ▸**b** Overburden, encumber, weigh down. *arch.* E17.
6 Conceal or obscure as if by covering up. E17.

🕮 **4** T. Hardy The track had . . been a well-kept winding drive, but . . moss and leaves overlaid it now. *Which Computer?* A third screen which will overlay the others. **b** Arnold Bennett A certain baby was dead . . . Its parents had been censured . . for criminal carelessness in overlaying it. **6** M. Keane A habit of obedience overlaid the tumultuous desires and suppressions of her young daughters. Y. Menuhin California laid ideal landscapes in my mind which nothing later was to overlay.

■ **overlayer** *noun* E16. **overlaying** *noun* (*a*) the action or an act of the verb; (*b*) a covering: LME.

overlay *verb*² *pa. t.* of OVERLIE.

overleaf /əʊvəˈliːf/ *adverb.* E19.
[from OVER- + LEAF *noun*¹.]
On the other side of the leaf (esp. of a book).

overleap /əʊvəˈliːp/ *verb trans.* Pa. t. & pple **-leaped**, **-leapt** /-ˈlɛpt/. OE.
[from OVER- + LEAP *verb*.]
1 Leap over or across; *fig.* pass over, omit, leave out. OE.
2 *fig.* Surpass, excel. *rare.* ME. ▸†**b** *refl.* Leap too far. *rare* (Shakes.). Only in E17.

🕮 **1** R. C. Trench All the intervening steps of these tardier processes were overleaped. **2** J. C. Oates She was confronted with her own viciousness, which threatened at times to overleap *his*.

overlie /əʊvəˈlʌɪ/ *verb trans.* Pa. t. **-lay** /-ˈleɪ/, pres. pple **-lying** /-ˈlʌɪɪŋ/, pa. pple **-lain** /-ˈleɪn/. Also †**overlig**, infl. **-gg-**. ME.
[from OVER- + LIE *verb*¹.]
1 Lie over or on top of. ME.
2 *spec.* Smother (a child etc.) by lying on him or her. Cf. OVERLAY *verb*¹ 4b. ME.
†**3** *fig.* Oppress. ME–M16.

🕮 **1** *Discovery* Dunshauglin crannóg during excavation, showing the brushwood layer, the overlying timbers.

■ ˈ**overlier** *noun* †(*a*) a person who is a burden or encumbrance; (*b*) a thing, *spec.* a timber, which lies over or on top of something else: LME.

overling /ˈəʊvəlɪŋ/ *noun.* ME.
[from OVER- + -LING¹. Cf. UNDERLING.]
A superior.
¶ Not recorded between LME and E20.

overload /*as verb* əʊvəˈləʊd, *as noun* ˈəʊvələʊd/ *verb & noun.* M16.
[from OVER- + LOAD *verb*, *noun*.]
▶ **A** *verb.* Pa. pple **-loaded**, (*arch.*) **-loaden**.
1 *verb trans.* Load with too great a burden or cargo, put an excessive load on. M16.
2 *verb intrans.* Become overloaded. M20.

🕮 **1** J. Raban The electricity supply in Dona gets frequently overloaded. G. Naylor The teachers will be overloaded with a lot of remedial cases. **2** *New Scientist* The system overloaded as soon as it was switched on.

▶ **B** *noun.* An excessive load or burden; *spec.* a current or voltage in excess of that which is normal or allowed for. M17.

🕮 V. Seth A quite sufficient overload of nitrogen oxides to gobble up half our ozone.

overlook /ˈəʊvəlʊk/ *noun.* L16.
[from OVER- + LOOK *noun*.]
1 A considering glance or look; an inspection. L16.
2 A (high) place affording a view of the scene below. Chiefly *US.* M19.
3 A failure to see or notice something; an oversight. L19.
Comb.: **overlook bean** *W. Indies* the jack bean, *Canavalia ensiformis*, traditionally believed to guard the crops it is planted round.

overlook /əʊvəˈlʊk/ *verb trans.* LME.
[from OVER- + LOOK *verb*.]
1 Look (a thing) over or through; examine, scrutinize, inspect. *arch.* LME.
2 Look down at; survey from above or from a higher position; (of a place etc.) afford a view of. LME.
†**3** *fig.* Despise, treat with contempt. LME–L18.
4 Watch over officially, superintend, oversee. LME.
5 Fail to see or observe; pass over without noticing; disregard, ignore. E16.
6 Look over the top of; be higher than. M16.
7 Look on with the evil eye; bewitch. L16.

🕮 **2** B. Bainbridge Edward made me draw the shutters . . . He doesn't like being overlooked. H. Kissinger A . . living room overlooking a lawn. A. Maupin They ate lunch overlooking the water. A. Miller A sixth-story window that overlooks Central Park. **5** J. Steinbeck Turning . . bits of wood to see whether anything . . had been overlooked. S. Quinn Psychoanalysis . . tended to overlook the female experience.

■ **overlooker** *noun* a person who overlooks someone or something; *spec.* a superintendent, an overseer; an observer; a spy: LME.

overlord /*as noun* ˈəʊvəlɔːd, *as verb* əʊvəˈlɔːd/ *noun & verb.* ME.
[from OVER- + LORD *noun*.]
▶ **A** *noun.* **1** A lord superior to other lords or rulers; a supreme lord. ME.
2 *transf.* Any person in a position of superiority or supreme power. M20.
▶ **B** *verb trans.* Domineer over; rule as an overlord. E17.

🕮 *Daily Telegraph* A single executive to overlord . . the business.

■ **overlordship** *noun* the position or authority of an overlord M19.

overly /ˈəʊvəli/ *adjective. obsolete* exc. *dial.* ME.
[from OVER *adverb* + -LY¹.]
†**1** Supreme. Only in ME.
2 Superficial; careless, cursory. LME.
3 Supercilious, imperious, haughty. E17.
■ **overliness** *noun* E17.

overly /ˈəʊvəli/ *adverb.* OE.
[from OVER *adverb* + -LY².]
1 Above or beyond the proper amount or degree; excessively, over-. OE.
2 **a** Superficially, carelessly. *obsolete* exc. *Scot.* LME. ▸**b** Incidentally, casually. *Scot.* E19.
†**3** Superciliously, haughtily. E–M17.

🕮 **1** P. Kavanagh Peter was not overly worried about this laziness. B. Guest He became protective of her, probably overly so. M. Moorcock Relieving the tedium of overly secure habits.

overlying *verb pres. pple* of OVERLIE.

overman /ˈəʊvəmən, *in sense 4* -man/ *noun.* Pl. **-men** /-mən, *in sense 4* -mɛn/. ME.
[from OVER- + MAN *noun*.]
1 A man having authority or rule over others. Long *obsolete* in *gen.* sense. ME.
2 An arbitrator, an umpire. *rare.* LME.
3 A man in charge of a body of workers; a foreman, an overseer. E17.
4 [translating German *Übermensch*.] = SUPERMAN. L19.

overman /əʊvəˈman/ *verb trans.* Infl. **-nn-**. E17.
[from OVER- + MAN *verb*.]
1 Overcome, overpower. *rare.* E17.
2 Provide with too many men or (now esp.) too many workers. Chiefly as ***overmanning*** *verbal noun.* M17.

overmaster /əʊvəˈmɑːstə/ *verb trans.* ME.
[from OVER- + MASTER *verb*.]
1 Master completely; overcome, conquer, overpower, (esp. a feeling, force, etc.). Chiefly as ***overmastering*** *ppl adjective.* ME.
†**2** Be master over; hold in one's power or possession. M16–M17.

🕮 **1** Saki He was possessed by an overmastering desire to keep the dish. J. Buchan The place had an overmastering silence.

■ **overmasteringly** *adverb* to an overmastering degree M19.

overmasterful /əʊvəˈmɑːstəfʊl, -f(ə)l/ *adjective. rare.* LME.
[from OVER- + MASTERFUL.]
Excessively masterful.
¶ Not recorded between LME and L19.

overmastery /əʊvəˈmɑːst(ə)ri/ *noun. rare.* LME.
[from OVER- + MASTERY.]
†**1** Superiority in a contest. Only in LME.
2 Supreme authority, sovereignty. E20.

overmatch /*as verb* əʊvəˈmatʃ, *as noun* ˈəʊvəmatʃ/ *verb & noun.* LME.
[from OVER- + MATCH *verb*¹, *noun*¹.]
▶ **A** *verb trans.* Be more than a match for; defeat by superior strength or skill. LME.

🕮 A. Duggan A feeling of sympathy for an overmatched swordsman.

▶ **B** *noun.* †**1** The condition of being overmatched; a contest in which one side is superior to the other. M–L16.
2 A person who or thing which is more than a match for another. L16.

🕮 **2** A. B. Paterson A third-class pro is an overmatch for the best of the amateurs.

overmen *noun* pl. of OVERMAN *noun*.

overmuch /əʊvəˈmʌtʃ/ *adjective, noun, & adverb.* ME.
[from OVER- + MUCH.]
▶ **A** *adjective.* Too great in amount; excessive. ME.

🕮 M. Meyer Ibsen may not have devoted overmuch time to books.

▶ **B** *noun.* Too great an amount; excess. ME.

🕮 E. Waugh I have inherited overmuch of my father's homely sentiments.

▶ **C** *adverb.* Excessively. ME.

🕮 E. Templeton Never had concerned himself overmuch with his daughter's well-being.

■ **overmuchness** *noun* excess M17.

overnice /əʊvəˈnʌɪs/ *adjective.* ME.
[from OVER- + NICE *adjective*.]
Excessively punctilious, fastidious, or particular; over-scrupulous.
■ **overnicely** *adverb* E18. **overniceness** *noun* L17. **overnicety** *noun* M18.

overnight /əʊvəˈnʌɪt/ *adverb, noun, adjective, & verb.* ME.
[from OVER- + NIGHT *noun*.]
▶ **A** *adverb.* **1** On the preceding evening; the night before (with implication of continuation until the following morning). ME.
2 During the night; for the duration of a night. LME.
3 During the course of a single night; *transf.* suddenly, instantaneously, rapidly. M20.

🕮 **2** G. S. Haight Mary Ann went . . to visit . . staying overnight with the Samuel Evanses. **3** A. Brookner Suddenly, it seemed overnight, the false spring was eclipsed.

▶ **B** *noun.* **1** The preceding evening. Now chiefly *US.* L16.
2 A stop or stay lasting for one night. Also, something that arrived or happened during the night. M20.

🕮 **2** M. Binchy He did get back . . for an overnight now and then.

▶ **C** *adjective.* **1** Of or pertaining to the previous evening; done, happening, operating, etc., overnight. E19.
2 For the duration of one night; (of a person) staying overnight; for use on a stay of one night. E20. ▸**b** Designating the price of a share etc. at the close of business on the previous day. E20.
3 *transf.* Sudden, instant, rapid. M20.

🕮 **1** J. Galt The broken weapons of the overnight assault. S. Rosenberg An overnight train was taking us to Leningrad. **2** A. Lurie He retrieves his briefcase . . and overnight bag. **3** N. Sedaka The show went over, and . . I was an overnight sensation.

▶ **D** *verb.* **1** *verb intrans.* Stay for the night (*at* or *in*). L19.
2 *verb trans.* Convey (goods) overnight. *N. Amer.* L20.

🕮 **1** *Drive* You could trek deep into the forest, overnighting in a bivouac.

■ **overnighter** *noun* (*a*) a bag for use overnight; (*b*) a person who stops at a place overnight; (*c*) *N. Amer.* an overnight trip or stop: M20.

overpaid *verb pa. t. & pple* of OVERPAY *verb*.

overpaint /*as verb* əʊvəˈpeɪnt, *as noun* ˈəʊvəpeɪnt/ *verb & noun.* E17.
[from OVER- + PAINT *verb*, *noun*.]
▶ **A** *verb trans.* **1** Cover with another colour or layer of paint. E17.
2 *fig.* Depict too highly. M18.
▶ **B** *noun.* A layer of paint applied over another. M20.
■ **overpainting** *noun* (*a*) the action of the verb; (*b*) = OVERPAINT *noun*; (a part of) a painting overlying earlier work: E20.

overpass /ˈəʊvəpɑːs/ *noun.* Chiefly *N. Amer.* E20.
[from OVER- + PASS *noun*¹.]
A road or railway bridge which passes over a road or railway line; a flyover.

overpass /əʊvəˈpɑːs/ *verb.* Pa. pple **-passed**, †**-past**. ME.
[from OVER- + PASS *verb*.]
1 *verb trans.* Travel over (esp. a specified distance), move across or along. ME.
2 *verb intrans.* Pass across or overhead. ME.
3 *verb trans.* Get beyond or to the other side of; cross. ME. ▸**b** Rise above. LME.
4 *verb trans.* Get to the end of (a period of time, an action, etc.), esp. successfully or safely; endure. ME.
5 *verb intrans.* Of time, an action, etc.: come to an end, be over. ME.
6 *verb trans.* Exceed in amount, value, excellence, etc.; excel, surpass. Formerly also, (of a feeling etc.) affect, overcome. ME. ▸**b** *verb trans.* Go beyond the restrictions of, transgress. LME. ▸†**c** Be in excess, be over. LME–M16.

7 †**a** *verb intrans.* Pass or remain unnoticed. Chiefly in ***let it overpass***. ME–L16. ▸**b** *verb trans.* Pass over, leave unnoticed, ignore. Now *rare*. LME.
†**8** *verb trans.* Pass by; come up to or alongside of and go beyond. LME–M16.

📖 **4** T. HARDY To consider how best to overpass a more general catastrophe. **5** S. LESLIE The Celebrant . . hid the Host at an altar . . until the storms were overpast.

overpay /*as verb* əʊvəˈpeɪ, *as noun* ˈəʊvəpeɪ/ *verb & noun*. L16.
[from OVER- + PAY *verb*¹, *noun*.]
▸ **A** *verb trans.* Pa. t. & pple **-paid** /-ˈpeɪd/.
1 Pay or recompense (a person, service, etc.) beyond what is due or deserved; *fig.* do more than compensate for. L16.
2 Pay more than (an amount or price); pay (money) in excess of what is due. L17.

📖 **1** *Spectator* Too many overpaid, under-employed non-publishing executive personnel.

▸ **B** *noun*. A sum of money paid in excess of what is due. E19.
■ **overpayment** *noun* L16.

overplant /əʊvəˈplɑːnt/ *verb trans.* OE.
[from OVER- + PLANT *verb*.]
†**1** Transplant. OE–LME.
2 Plant to excess. L18.

overplay /əʊvəˈpleɪ/ *verb trans.* LME.
[from OVER- + PLAY *verb*.]
1 Play better than and so defeat. *rare*. LME.
2 Play (a part etc.) to excess; overact. L17.
3 a In CARDS, play on the basis of an overestimate of one's strength. Chiefly *fig.* in ***overplay one's hand***, spoil a situation by excessive confidence in its outcome or in one's own abilities. M20. ▸**b** Attach undue importance to; overemphasize. M20.

overplus /ˈəʊvəplʌs/ *noun, adverb, & adjective*. LME.
[from OVER- + SURPLUS, as partial translation of Old & mod. French *surplus* or medieval Latin *su(pe)rplus*.]
▸ **A** *noun*. **1** An amount left over from the main amount, or from what is required; a surplus. LME.
2 Excess, superabundance; an instance of this. E18.

📖 **1** H. J. S. MAINE The overplus is returned to the tenant. **2** M. ANDERSON An overplus of beans in the diet.

▸ **B** *adverb*. In addition, in excess, besides, over. Now *rare* or *obsolete*. LME.
▸ **C** *adjective*. Additional, surplus; excessive. LME.

overpoise /*as verb* əʊvəˈpɔɪz, *as noun* ˈəʊvəpɔɪz/ *verb & noun*. *arch.* M16.
[from OVER- + POISE *verb*, *noun*¹.]
▸ **A** *verb trans.* **1** Weigh more than, outweigh. Chiefly *fig.* M16.
†**2** Weigh down, overload. L16–M17.
▸ **B** *noun*. The action or fact of outweighing something; an instance of this; a thing which outweighs another. L17.

overpopulate /əʊvəˈpɒpjʊleɪt/ *verb trans.* M19.
[from OVER- + POPULATE *verb*.]
1 Exceed in population. *rare*. M19.
2 Overstock with people. Chiefly as ***overpopulated*** *ppl adjective*. L19.
■ **overpopuˈlation** *noun* E19.

overpower /əʊvəˈpaʊə/ *verb trans.* L16.
[from OVER- + POWER *verb*.]
1 Overcome with superior power or force; reduce to submission. L16.
2 Make (a quality etc.) ineffective or imperceptible by excess of force or intensity. M17.
3 Be too intense for; overwhelm. M17.

📖 **1** A. CROSS A man could have overpowered her. **2** J. BUCHAN The searching odour was apt to overpower the wafts of lilac. **3** P. GAY Charcot's scientific style and personal charm overpowered Freud.

■ **overpoweringly** *adverb* in an overpowering manner, to an overpowering degree E19.

overpraise /*as verb* əʊvəˈpreɪz, *as noun* ˈəʊvəpreɪz/ *verb & noun*. ME.
[from OVER- + PRAISE *verb*, *noun*.]
▸ **A** *verb trans.* Praise excessively. ME.
▸ **B** *noun*. Excessive praise. L17.

overpress /əʊvəˈprɛs/ *verb trans.* LME.
[from OVER- + PRESS *verb*¹.]
1 Afflict with severity or cruelty; oppress beyond endurance. Now *rare*. LME.
†**2** Overthrow or overwhelm with physical force. L15–M17.
3 Overburden, overload. Now only *fig.* L16.
4 Press or insist on unduly. M19.
5 Subject to excessive pressure (esp. of work etc.). L19.

overpressure /əʊvəˈprɛʃə, ˈəʊvəprɛʃə/ *noun*. M17.
[from OVER- + PRESSURE *noun*.]
1 Excessive pressure; *esp.* subjection to excessive pressure of work. M17.
2 Pressure (of a fluid) in excess of that normal or allowed for; *spec.* the difference between the (highest) instantaneous pressure at a point subjected to a shock wave and the ambient atmospheric pressure. M20.

overprice /əʊvəˈprʌɪs/ *verb & noun*. L16.
[from OVER- + PRICE *verb*, *noun*.]
▸ **A** *verb trans.* Assign an excessive price to (a commodity); price a commodity beyond the means of. L16.

📖 D. LODGE He . . sits gloomily . . drinking overpriced beer.

▸†**B** *noun*. An excessive price. E17–E18.

overprint /ˈəʊvəprɪnt/ *noun*. L19.
[from OVER- + PRINT *noun*.]
1 = OFFPRINT *noun*. *rare*. L19.
2 The action or result of overprinting; overprinted matter, esp. on a postage stamp; a postage stamp with overprinted matter. L19.

overprint /əʊvəˈprɪnt/ *verb*. M19.
[from OVER- + PRINT *verb*.]
1 *verb trans.* PHOTOGRAPHY. Print (a positive) darker than was intended. M19.
2 *verb trans.* **a** Print additional matter on (a surface already printed). (Foll. by *with*.) M19. ▸**b** Print (additional matter) on a surface already printed; print in one colour on top of another. E20.
3 *verb trans. & intrans.* Print too many copies of (a book etc.). E20.

📖 **2a** D. MADDEN A white cotton dress . . which is overprinted with a black lattice.

overprotect /əʊvəprəˈtɛkt/ *verb trans.* M20.
[from OVER- + PROTECT *verb*.]
Be excessively protective of (esp. a child).
■ **overprotection** *noun* M20. **overprotective** *adjective* M20.

overran *verb pa. t.* of OVERRUN *verb*.

overrate /ˈəʊvəreɪt/ *noun*. Long *rare* or *obsolete*. E17.
[from OVER- + RATE *noun*¹.]
An excessive or extra rate.

overrate /əʊvəˈreɪt/ *verb trans.* E17.
[from OVER- + RATE *verb*¹.]
1 Rate or assess too highly; overestimate. Freq. as ***overrated*** *ppl adjective*. E17.
2 ROWING. Row at a faster rate than (an opponent). M20.

†**overraught** *verb pa. t. & pple*: see OVERREACH *verb*.

overreach /ˈəʊvəriːtʃ/ *noun*. M16.
[from next.]
1 *gen.* The action of overreaching; an instance of this. M16.
2 The action, by a horse etc., of striking a forefoot with the corresponding hind foot; an injury resulting from this. E17.
3 A circumvention of someone by cunning or artifice; a trick. E17.

overreach /əʊvəˈriːtʃ/ *verb*. Pa. t. & pple **-reached**, †**-raught**. ME.
[from OVER- + REACH *verb*¹.]
1 *verb trans.* Rise above, extend beyond. Now *rare*. ME.
2 *verb trans.* Reach or get at (a person etc.) across an intervening space; overtake. Formerly also, overcome, overpower. *obsolete* exc. *dial.* ME.
3 *verb trans. &* †*intrans.* Spread over (something) so as to form a covering. LME.
4 *verb intrans.* Of a horse etc.: bring a hind foot against the corresponding forefoot in walking or running, esp. so as to strike and injure the heel of the forefoot; *gen.* bring a hind foot in front of or alongside a forefoot. E16.
5 *verb trans.* Overshoot (a target); reach past (an object). M16.
6 *verb refl.* Strain oneself by trying to reach something beyond one's strength, capacity, etc.; *fig.* defeat one's object by excessive effort or ambition. M16. ▸**b** *verb intrans. & trans.* Stretch out (an arm etc.) too far in an effort to touch or grasp something. L19.
†**7** *verb intrans. & trans.* Exaggerate, overestimate (something). M16–E19.
8 *verb trans. & (rare) intrans.* Circumvent, outwit; *esp.* get the better of (a person) by cunning or artifice. L16.
■ **overreacher** *noun* L16.

overreact /əʊvərɪˈakt/ *verb intrans.* M20.
[from OVER- + REACT.]
Respond more forcibly than is justified, react too strongly.
■ **overreaction** *noun* the action or an act of overreacting M20.

For other words beginning with *over-* see the entry for **over-**

overrefine /əʊvərɪˈfʌɪn/ *verb trans. & intrans.* E18.
[from OVER- + REFINE.]
Refine too much; *spec.* make excessively subtle distinctions in (an argument etc.).

overrefinement /əʊvərɪˈfʌɪnm(ə)nt/ *noun*. E18.
[from OVER- + REFINEMENT.]
The action or process of overrefining something; excessive refinement, an instance of this.

override /ˈəʊvərʌɪd/ *noun*. M20.
[from the verb.]
The action or process of suspending an automatic function; a device for this.

override /əʊvəˈrʌɪd/ *verb trans.* Infl. as RIDE *verb*; pa. t. usu. **-rode** /-ˈrəʊd/, pa. pple **-ridden** /-ˈrɪd(ə)n/. OE.
[from OVER- + RIDE *verb*.]
1 *gen.* Ride over, cross by riding. OE. ▸**b** Ride over (the fallen); trample down or underfoot by riding. ME. ▸**c** Ride across (hostile or enemy country), esp. with an armed force, harry. LME.
2 Reach or overtake by riding; outride. Long *rare* or *obsolete*. OE.
3 a Supersede, esp. arrogantly; have or claim precedence or superiority over; intervene and make ineffective, dominate. M16. ▸**b** Cause the operation of (an automatic device) to be suspended, esp. in favour of manual control. M20.
4 Exhaust (a horse etc.) by hard or excessive riding. E17.
5 Extend over; *esp.* (of a part of a fractured bone) overlap (another part). M19.

📖 **1** W. S. BLUNT A large portion of your hunting field overrode their smallholding. **3a** P. G. WODEHOUSE Sternly overriding the preferences of the man who paid . . his wages. K. LINES No decrees issued by . . a mere man can override the law of the gods. **override one's commission** act beyond one's powers or authority, discharge one's office high-handedly and arbitrarily.

■ **overriding** *adjective* (*a*) that overrides, *esp.* that has precedence or superiority over; (*b*) ***overriding commission*** (COMMERCE), an extra or additional commission: M19. **overridingly** *adverb* M20.

overruff /*as verb* əʊvəˈrʌf, *as noun* ˈəʊvərʌf/ *verb & noun*. E19.
[from OVER- + RUFF *verb*².]
▸ **A** *verb trans. & intrans.* Overtrump. E19.
▸ **B** *noun*. An act or instance of overruffing. E20.

overrule /əʊvəˈruːl/ *verb trans.* L16.
[from OVER- + RULE *verb*.]
1 Rule over, have authority over; control or modify the action of by superior power or authority. L16.
2 Prevail over, overcome; *spec.* (*a*) overcome the objections of or reject the wishes or requests of (a person); (*b*) overcome (the objections) or reject (the wishes or requests) of a person. L16.
3 LAW. Rule against or set aside by superior authority; *spec.* (*a*) set aside the authority of (a previous action or decision) as a precedent, annul; (*b*) reject (an argument, plea, objection, etc.), disallow (an action); (*c*) disallow or set aside the argument, plea, or objection of (a person). L16.

📖 **2** N. SYMINGTON He allowed the evidence to overrule his previous hypothesis. S. WOODS Graham protested a little, but was overruled. **3** *transf.*: *Sports Illustrated* The decision by veteran ref. Jack Madden to allow himself to be overruled on a key . . decision.

■ **overruler** *noun* L16.

overrun /ˈəʊvərʌn/ *noun*. ME.
[Prob. from next.]
†**1** Excess or superiority in running. *rare*. Only in ME.
2 An instance of overrunning; the amount or degree by which a thing overruns something. L19. ▸**b** The proportional increase in bulk occurring when butterfat is made into butter or an ice-cream mix into ice-cream. E20. ▸**c** Motion of a vehicle at a speed greater than that being imparted by the engine; the tendency of a towed vehicle to run into the back of a decelerating towing vehicle. E20. ▸**d** An overspend. Also, an excess of production. M20.
3 A length of extra track, runway, road, etc., provided to accommodate vehicles which go past their intended stopping point. Also, an instance of a vehicle etc. running too far. E20.

overrun /əʊvəˈrʌn/ *verb*. Infl. as RUN *verb*; pa. t. usu. **-ran** /-ˈran/, pa. pple usu. **-run**. OE.
[from OVER- + RUN *verb*.]
1 *verb trans.* †**a** Run over, cross or traverse by running. OE–M17. ▸**b** Of water etc.: flow over or across; *esp.* flood (land etc.). LME
†**2** *verb trans.* Go or look rapidly through or over (a book, subject, etc.), esp. cursorily. OE–M17.
†**3** *verb trans.* Overwhelm forcibly (*lit.* & *fig.*); run down, trample underfoot. OE–M17.
4 *verb intrans.* Of a container, liquid, etc.: overflow. ME.

5 *verb trans.* Ride over or traverse (hostile or enemy country) with an armed force, conquer or ravage (territory). ME.

6 *verb trans.* Spread or grow widely over (land etc.), esp. harmfully; (of vermin, weeds, etc.) swarm or spread profusely over. Freq. in *pass.* (foll. by *with*). LME.

7 *verb trans.* **a** Run faster than, outrun; *fig.* surpass. Now chiefly MECHANICS, rotate faster than. LME. ▸**b** Run away from, escape by running; *fig.* leave unfinished. *obsolete* exc. *dial.* and in **overrun the constable**: see CONSTABLE *noun* 4. L16.

†**8** *verb intrans.* Of time: run to an end, run out. LME–E16.

9 *verb trans. & intrans.* Of time, expenditure, production, etc.: exceed (a certain point, limit, quantity, etc.). L16.

10 *verb trans. & intrans.* TYPOGRAPHY. Carry over (text) on to another line or page to allow for insertions or excisions; (cause to) run over. L17.

11 *verb trans.* Operate (a mechanism etc.) excessively; cause (something) to work too frequently or at too high a rate. L19.

> 🕮 **1** W. DRUMMOND Mountains, dales, and plains I overrun. **5** C. C. TRENCH Saxe proceeded to overrun most of Flanders. **6** W. IRVING The mouldering ruin of an abbey overrun with ivy. **7a overrunning clutch** a clutch in which the driven part can rotate faster than the driving part. **overrun oneself** run too far or beyond one's strength, overreach oneself. **9** *Sunday Express* Borge overran by 15 minutes—and was kept on the air. M. SCAMMELL I overran deadline after deadline.

■ **overrunner** *noun* LME. **overrunningly** *adverb* (*rare*) in an overrunning manner M16.

oversail /əʊvəˈseɪl/ *verb*¹. Long *rare*. LOE.
[from OVER- + SAIL *verb*¹.]
1 *verb trans.* & †*intrans.* Sail over or across. LOE.
†**2** *verb trans.* Run down or sink (a vessel) by sailing over it. ME–E17.

oversail /*as verb* əʊvəˈseɪl, *as noun* ˈəʊvəseɪl/ *verb*² *& noun*. Orig. *Scot.* L17.
[App. from OVER- + French *saillir* project.]
▶ **A** *verb*. **1** *verb intrans.* Of a stone, brick, etc.: project beyond a supporting base, overhang. L17.
2 *verb trans.* Project beyond or overhang (a base). E20.
▶†**B** *noun*. The projection of a thing beyond its base; overhang. L17–E19.
■ **oversailing** *adjective* (of a part of a building) projecting beyond what is below M19.

oversampling /əʊvəˈsamplɪŋ/ *noun*. L20.
[from OVER- + SAMPLING.]
ELECTRONICS & AUDIO. A process used in CD players by which each component of the digital signal is repeated electronically so as to increase the apparent sampling frequency by a simple factor (e.g. 4 or 8), making it easier to remove spurious signals introduced by the original sampling process.

oversaw *verb pa. t.* of OVERSEE.

oversea /*as adverb* əʊvəˈsiː, *as adjective* ˈəʊvəsiː/ *adverb & adjective*. LOE.
[from OVER- + SEA.]
▶ **A** *adverb*. = OVERSEAS *adverb*. LOE.
▶ **B** *adjective*. = OVERSEAS *adjective*. LME.

overseas /*as adverb* əʊvəˈsiːz, *as adjective & noun* ˈəʊvəsiːz/ *adverb, adjective, & noun*. L16.
[formed as prec. + -S³.]
▶ **A** *adverb*. Across or beyond the sea; abroad. L16.
▶ **B** *adjective*. That is overseas; of or pertaining to transport over or countries beyond the sea; foreign. L19.

> 🕮 R. DAHL One of the London banks has an overseas branch in Khartoum. *Independent* An overseas posting is often toughest for the . . family. **overseas Chinese** a native of China residing in another country.

▶ **C** *noun*. **from overseas**, from a country overseas, from foreign countries. E20.

oversee /əʊvəˈsiː/ *verb*. Pa. t. **-saw** /-ˈsɔː/; pa. pple **-seen** /-ˈsiːn/. OE.
[from OVER- + SEE *verb*.]
▶ **I** Look.
1 *verb trans.* Look at (as) from a higher position; survey; keep watch over. OE. ▸**b** *spec.* Observe or catch sight of (a person) without being detected. M18.
2 a *verb trans.* Officially supervise (workers, work, etc.); superintend. ME. ▸†**b** *verb trans.* Ensure *that*. LME–L17. ▸**c** *verb intrans.* Act as overseer. M16.
3 *verb trans.* Look through, peruse; inspect, examine. *arch.* ME.
▶ **II** Overlook, miss.
4 a *verb trans.* Fail or omit to see, overlook; disregard. *obsolete* exc. *dial.* OE. ▸**b** *verb refl. & intrans.* Overlook what is right or fitting for one, forget oneself; act imprudently or unbecomingly; fall into error, err. *obsolete* exc. *dial.* LME.
■ **overseen** *adjective* (*a*) (now *arch.* & *dial.*) deluded, mistaken, imprudent; (*b*) (*obsolete* exc. *dial.*) drunk, intoxicated; †(*c*) skilled or expert in a subject: LME.

overseer /ˈəʊvəsɪə/ *noun & verb*. LME.
[from prec. + -ER¹.]
▶ **A** *noun*. †**1** A person appointed by a testator to supervise or assist the executor of a will. Cf. SUPERVISOR 1b. LME–M17.
†**2** A person who watches or looks down at something. LME–M17.
3 A person who supervises a job, workforce, etc.; *spec.* (the title of) any of various people with supervisory duties, as (*a*) *US* a member of a board of officials which manages the affairs of a college or university; (*b*) a member of the Society of Friends responsible for the pastoral supervision of his or her congregation. E16. ▸**b** *Hist.* In full **overseer of the poor**. A parish officer appointed annually for administrative duties mainly concerned with poor relief. E17.
†**4** A critic, censor, or reviser of a book. L16–L17.
▶ **B** *verb trans.* Act as overseer to. E18.
■ **overseership** *noun* the office or position of an overseer M17.

oversell /*as verb* əʊvəˈsɛl, *as noun* ˈəʊvəsɛl/ *verb & noun*. L16.
[from OVER- + SELL *verb*.]
▶ **A** *verb trans.* Pa. t. & pple **-sold** /-ˈsəʊld/.
1 †**a** Sell at more than the real value. L16–M18. ▸**b** Make excessive or unrealistic claims for; give (a person) an exaggerated idea of the value of something. E20.
2 Sell more of (a stock etc.) than exists or can be delivered. L19.
▶ **B** *noun*. Excessively ambitious promotion of commercial goods etc. M20.

overset /*as verb* əʊvəˈsɛt, *as noun* ˈəʊvəsɛt/ *verb & noun*. ME.
[from OVER- + SET *verb*¹.]
▶ **A** *verb*. Infl. **-tt-**; pa. t. & pple **-set**.
†**1** *verb trans.* Oppress; overcome, overpower; overthrow, overwhelm. ME–L17.
†**2** *verb trans.* Cover (a surface, garment, etc.) *with* jewels, ornaments, etc. LME–M18.
†**3** *verb trans.* **a** Put off, postpone. LME–E16. ▸**b** Pass over, omit. LME–M17.
4 *verb trans.* Get over or recover from (an illness etc.). *dial.* M16.
5 a *verb trans. & intrans.* (Cause to) turn or fall over; (be) upset, overturn, capsize. L16. ▸**b** *verb trans.* Disturb the normal condition of (a person); discompose, disorder. L16. ▸**c** *verb trans.* Subvert the order of (an institution, country, etc.); cause to fall into confusion. Now *rare*. L17. ▸**d** *verb intrans.* Lose one's balanced condition; fall into disorder. M18.
6 *verb trans.* TYPOGRAPHY. Set up (type) in excess of the available space. L19.
▶ **B** *noun*. The action or fact of oversetting; an instance of this. LME.

oversew /ˈəʊvəsəʊ/ *verb trans.* Pa. t. **-sewed** /-səʊd/; pa. pple **-sewed**, **-sewn** /-səʊn/. M19.
[from OVER- + SEW *verb*¹.]
Sew (two edges) together, passing the needle through always from the same side so that the thread returns over the edges; *spec.* join the sections of (a book) in this way.

overshadow /əʊvəˈʃadəʊ/ *verb trans.*
[Old English *ofersceadwian* = Gothic *ufarskadwjan*, formed as OVER- + SHADOW *verb*, translating Latin *obumbrare*.]
1 Cast a shadow over; cover or obscure with gloom or darkness, overcloud (*lit.* & *fig.*). OE.
2 Shelter or protect with some superior power or influence. *arch.* OE.
3 Tower above so as to cast a shadow over (*lit.* & *fig.*); make (an event, problem, etc.) appear less important; appear much more significant or important than. L16.

> 🕮 **1** E. WAUGH A stuffed ferret, whose death . . had overshadowed . . one Easter holiday. **2** AV *Luke* 1:35 The holy Ghost shall come vpon thee, and the power of the Highest shall ouershadow thee. **3** DICKENS No neighbouring architecture of lofty proportions had arisen to overshadow Staple Inn. S. QUINN Political and economic events overshadowed . . psychological questions.

overshoot /ˈəʊvəʃuːt/ *noun*. M20.
[from the verb.]
The action or result of overshooting; an instance of this; *spec.* (*a*) ECONOMICS an overspend; (*b*) ELECTRONICS transient exaggeration of the magnitude of the edge of a steep signal or waveform; (*c*) the degree to which a thermostatically-controlled device heats or cools beyond the set temperature.

overshoot /əʊvəˈʃuːt/ *verb*. Pa. t. & pple **-shot** /-ˈʃɒt/. LME.
[from OVER- + SHOOT *verb*.]
1 *verb trans. & intrans.* **a** Go past or pass beyond (a point, limit, stage, etc.), esp. unintentionally or accidentally. LME. ▸**b** *spec.* Fly beyond (a designated landing-point) while attempting to land; taxi too far along (a runway) when landing or taking off. E20.
2 *verb trans. & intrans.* Shoot a missile etc. over or beyond (a target); (of a missile etc.) pass over or beyond (a target). L15.
3 *verb refl.* Shoot over or beyond one's mark; *fig.* overreach oneself; exaggerate. E16.
†**4** *verb trans.* Utter (a word) too violently. M16–E17.
5 *verb trans.* Force beyond the proper limit. M17.
6 *verb trans.* Shoot or dart over or above. L18.

> 🕮 **1a** P. DRISCOLL Filipe missed a turning . . . 'I always overshoot in the dark,' he muttered. He drove back. *Observer* British Rail overshot its 1981–82 external financing limit. **b** C. A. LINDBERGH Bank around for final glide . . . I'll overshoot if I keep on at this rate. *Observer* A Philippine Airlines Airbus crashed on to the service road . . after overshooting the runway. **2** C. BERMANT An ink pellet . . overshot its target and landed . . on the teacher's desk. **overshoot the mark**: see MARK *noun*¹.

overshot /əʊvəˈʃɒt, *in sense 2* ˈəʊvəʃɒt/ *adjective*. M16.
[pa. pple of OVERSHOOT *verb*.]
†**1** **be overshot**, be wide of the mark, be mistaken or deceived. M16–M17.
2 Of a water-wheel: driven by the weight of a flow of water passing over the wheel and falling into buckets attached to its periphery. M16.
3 Intoxicated, drunk. *slang*. E17.
4 VETERINARY MEDICINE. Of a fetlock joint: partially dislocated through having the upper bone driven over or in front of the lower bones. L19.
5 Having the upper jaw projecting beyond the lower. L19.
6 Of a pattern or weave: characterized by lines of weft where the yarn passes over two or more warp threads before re-entering the fabric. M20.

overshot *verb pa. t. & pple* of OVERSHOOT *verb*.

overside /*as adjective* ˈəʊvəsʌɪd, *as adverb* əʊvəˈsʌɪd/ *adjective & adverb*. L19.
[from OVER- + SIDE *noun*.]
(Effected) over the side of a ship, into a smaller boat or into the sea.

oversight /ˈəʊvəsʌɪt/ *noun*. ME.
[from OVER- + SIGHT *noun*.]
1 The action or an act of overseeing something; supervision, inspection; charge, care, control. ME.
2 The action or fact of omitting or failing to see or notice something; an instance of this; an inadvertent mistake. L15.

> 🕮 **2** A. N. WILSON He had simply missed Parsons out by an oversight.

oversimplify /əʊvəˈsɪmplɪfʌɪ/ *verb trans. & intrans.* M20.
[from OVER- + SIMPLIFY.]
Treat, state, or explain (a problem, argument, etc.) in an unduly simple way.
■ **,oversimplifiˈcation** *noun* the action of oversimplifying; an instance or result of this: M20. **oversimplifier** *noun* M20.

oversize /ˈəʊvəsʌɪz/ *noun & adjective*. M19.
[from OVER- + SIZE *noun*¹.]
▶ **A** *noun*. **1** A size exceeding the usual size(s). M19.
2 Material whose particles are above a certain size. E20.
▶ **B** *adjective*. Of more than the usual size; outsize. E20.
■ **oversized** *adjective* abnormally large M19.

oversize /əʊvəˈsʌɪz/ *verb*¹ *trans.* E17.
[from OVER- + SIZE *verb*¹.]
Orig., exceed in size. Now usu., make too large, increase beyond the usual size.

oversize /əʊvəˈsʌɪz/ *verb*² *trans.* E17.
[from OVER- + SIZE *verb*².]
†**1** Cover over with size. *rare* (Shakes.). Only in E17.
2 Size too much or too heavily. L19.

overslaugh /ˈəʊvəslɔː/ *noun*. M18.
[Dutch *overslag*, from *overslaan*: see next. In sense 2 from next.]
1 A bar or sandbank impeding the navigation of a river. *US*. M18.
2 MILITARY. The passing over of one's ordinary turn of duty in consideration of a duty which takes precedence. L18.

overslaugh /ˈəʊvəslɔː/ *verb trans.* M18.
[Dutch *overslaan* pass over, from *over-* OVER- + *slaan* strike.]
1 a MILITARY. Pass over or remit (the ordinary turn of duty of an officer etc.) in consideration of another duty which takes precedence. M18. ▸**b** Pass over (a person) in favour of another; omit consideration of, ignore. *US*. M19.
2 Stop the course or progress of; obstruct, hinder. M19.

oversleep /əʊvəˈsliːp/ *verb*. Pa. t. & pple **-slept** /-ˈslɛpt/. LME.
[from OVER- + SLEEP *verb*.]
1 *verb intrans. & refl.* Sleep too long; continue sleeping beyond the usual time of waking. LME.
2 *verb trans.* Sleep beyond (a particular time). *rare*. E16.

For other words beginning with *over-* see the entry for **over-**

overslide /əʊvəˈslʌɪd/ *verb.* Infl. as **SLIDE** *verb*; pa. t. & pple usu. **-slid** /-ˈslɪd/. **LME.**
[from **OVER-** + **SLIDE** *verb*.]
†**1** *verb intrans. & trans.* (Let) slip away; (let) pass unnoticed. **LME–E17.**
2 *verb trans.* & †*intrans.* Slide, slip, or glide over (a place or thing). **E16.**

overslip /əʊvəˈslɪp/ *verb.* Now *rare* or *obsolete.* Infl. **-pp-**. **L15.**
[from **OVER-** + **SLIP** *verb*[1].]
1 a *verb trans.* Pass over without notice; let slip, let pass; omit to notice, mention, use, etc. **L15.** ▸†**b** *verb intrans.* Act inadvertently, make a slip. **L16–M17.**
†**2** *verb intrans.* Slip or pass by; pass unnoticed or unused. **L15–E17.**
3 *verb trans.* Slip away from or escape (a person); slip past, esp. secretly or covertly; *fig.* escape the notice of. **L16.**

†**overslop** *noun.* **OE–LME.**
[from **OVER-** + unexpl. 2nd elem., corresp. to Middle Dutch *overslop*, Old Norse *yfirsloppr*, ult. from Germanic.]
A loose upper garment; a cassock, a gown; a stole, a surplice.
¶ 2nd elem. survives as **SLOP** *noun*[1].

oversold *verb pa. t. & pple* of **OVERSELL** *verb.*

oversow /əʊvəˈsəʊ/ *verb trans.* Pa. t. **-sowed** /-ˈsəʊd/; pa. pple **-sowed**, **-sown** /-ˈsəʊn/. **OE.**
[from **OVER-** + **SOW** *verb*[1], repr. late Latin *superseminare*.]
1 Sow (seed) over other seed or a previously sown crop; sow (ground) *with* additional seed. **OE.**
2 Scatter seed over, sow *with* seed. **E17.**

overspan /əʊvəˈspan/ *verb*[1] *trans.* Infl. **-nn-**. **E16.**
[from **OVER-** + **SPAN** *verb*[1].]
1 Go above and across, span. **E16.**
†**2** Construct (a bridge etc.) to span a space. **E18–E19.**

overspan *verb*[2] *pa. t.*: see **OVERSPIN**.

overspeak /əʊvəˈspiːk/ *verb trans.* Now *rare* or *obsolete.* Infl. as **SPEAK** *verb*; pa. t. usu. **-spoke** /-ˈspəʊk/, pa. pple usu. **-spoken** /-ˈspəʊk(ə)n/. **E17.**
[from **OVER-** + **SPEAK** *verb*.]
†**1** Speak of too much or too strongly; exaggerate. Only in **17.**
2 Surpass or outdo in speaking. **E19.**
■ **overspeaking** *noun* the action of the verb; loquacity; exaggeration: **E17.**

overspeed /*as verb* əʊvəˈspiːd, *as noun* ˈəʊvəspiːd/ *verb & noun.* **E20.**
[from **OVER-** + **SPEED** *verb*.]
▶ **A** *verb intrans.* Pa. t. & pple **-sped** /-ˈspɛd/, **-speeded**. Drive or operate faster than allowed (for). **E20.**
▶ **B** *noun.* (An instance of) overspeeding. **E20.**

overspend /*as verb* əʊvəˈspɛnd, *as noun* ˈəʊvəspɛnd/ *verb & noun.* **E17.**
[from **OVER-** + **SPEND** *verb*.]
▶ **A** *verb.* Pa. t. & pple **-spent** /-ˈspɛnt/.
1 *verb trans.* Use until no longer fit for service; exhaust, wear out. Chiefly as ***overspent*** *ppl adjective.* **E17.**
2 a *verb trans.* Spend in excess of (a specified sum, limit, etc.). **M17.** ▸**b** *verb intrans. & refl.* Spend too much or beyond one's means. **L19.**

> 🕮 **2a** *Guardian* They are overspending their budget and will have to cut back.

▶ **B** *noun.* The action of overspending a specified sum, limit, etc.; an instance of this. Also, the amount by which a specified sum, limit, etc. is overspent. **L20.**

overspill /*as verb* əʊvəˈspɪl, *as noun* ˈəʊvəspɪl/ *verb & noun.* **M19.**
[from **OVER-** + **SPILL** *verb*.]
▶ **A** *verb.* Pa. t. & pple **-spilled**, **-spilt** /-ˈspɪlt/.
1 *verb trans. & intrans. gen.* Spill out over (something); spill over, overflow. *rare.* **M19.**
2 *verb trans.* Cause (a surplus population) to move from an overcrowded to a less heavily populated area. **M20.**
3 *verb intrans.* Of a surplus population: move from an overcrowded to a less heavily populated area. **M20.**
▶ **B** *noun.* That which is overspilt or overspills; *spec.* a surplus population moving from an overcrowded to a less heavily populated area; the movement of such a population; a place designed to accommodate such a population. **L19.**

> 🕮 *Nature* Proposals for dealing with Manchester's overspill in a new town at Mobberley.

overspin /*as verb* əʊvəˈspɪn, *as noun* ˈəʊvəspɪn/ *verb & noun.* **M17.**
[from **OVER-** + **SPIN** *verb*.]
▶ **A** *verb trans.* Infl. **-nn-**; pa. t. **-spun** /-ˈspʌn/, **-span** /-ˈspan/, pa. pple **-spun**.
†**1** Spin out, protract too much. *rare.* Only in **M17.**
2 *MUSIC.* Coil thin ductile wire around (a bass string) to increase mass and lower pitch without reducing flexibility. Chiefly as ***overspun*** *ppl adjective.* **E20.**
▶ **B** *noun.* Topspin. **E20.**

overspoke, **overspoken** *verbs* see **OVERSPEAK**.

overspread /əʊvəˈsprɛd/ *verb trans.* Pa. t. & pple **-spread**, (*arch. & poet.*) **-spreaded**. **OE.**
[from **OVER-** + **SPREAD** *verb*.]
1 Spread or diffuse (a thing) over. **OE.**
2 Spread or become diffused over (something); cover (*with*). *lit. & fig.* **ME.**

> 🕮 **2** G. ANSON High mountains overspread with trees. B. VINE A slow, mysterious smile . . overspread her face.

overspun *verb pa. t. & pple*: see **OVERSPIN**.

overstain /əʊvəˈsteɪn/ *verb.* **L16.**
[from **OVER-** + **STAIN** *verb*.]
†**1** *verb trans.* Cover with a stain or stains. *rare* (Shakes.). Only in **L16.**
2 *verb trans. & intrans. BIOLOGY.* Stain (tissue) excessively, usu. in order that certain parts may be differentiated by selective removal of some of the stain. **L19.**

overstand /əʊvəˈstand/ *verb.* Pa. t. & pple **-stood** /-ˈstʊd/. **E17.**
[from **OVER-** + **STAND** *verb*.]
1 *verb trans.* Stand over. **E17.**
†**2** *verb trans.* Endure or stay to the end of; get through; outstay. **E17–L18.**
3 *verb trans.* Of a boat: pass over, cross, (a mark or line). **M20.**
4 *verb intrans.* ***be overstanding for honours***, (at Oxford University) unable to obtain honours in an examination because of the lapse of more than the permitted number of terms (normally twelve) since matriculation. **M20.**

oversteepen /əʊvəˈstiːp(ə)n/ *verb trans.* **E20.**
[**OVER-** + **STEEPEN**.]
PHYSICAL GEOGRAPHY. Steepen (a valley or slope) by glacial action to a greater degree than would occur by water erosion alone. Chiefly as ***oversteepened*** *ppl adjective*, ***oversteepening*** *verbal noun.*

oversteer /*as verb* əʊvəˈstɪə, *as noun* ˈəʊvəstɪə/ *verb & noun.* **M20.**
[from **OVER-** + **STEER** *verb*[1].]
▶ **A** *verb intrans.* Of a motor vehicle: (have a tendency to) turn more sharply than intended by the driver. **M20.**
▶ **B** *noun.* A tendency to oversteer. **M20.**

overstep /əʊvəˈstɛp/ *verb & noun.*
[Old English *ofersteppan* (= Old High German *ubarstephen*, Dutch *overstappen*), formed as **OVER-** + **STEP** *verb*.]
▶ **A** *verb.* Infl. **-pp-**.
1 *verb trans.* Step over or across; pass beyond (a boundary or thing); violate (a standard). **OE.**
2 *verb trans. & intrans.* (foll. by *on to*). *GEOLOGY.* Of the upper strata of an unconformity: extend over (underlying strata) so as to form an overstep. **L19.**

> 🕮 **1** P. AUSTER The author feels it is his duty not to overstep the bounds of the verifiable. *absol.*: A. TYLER If I come too close, they'll say I'm overstepping. ***overstep the mark***: see **MARK** *noun*[1].

▶ **B** *noun.* **1** An act of overstepping something. **E19.**
2 *GEOLOGY.* The truncation of strata by an overlying stratum with a different dip. **L19.**
■ **overstepping** *verbal noun* the action of the verb; *spec.* in *CRICKET*, the action of bowling with a foot illegally positioned in relation to the creases: **M19.**

overstitch /ˈəʊvəstɪtʃ/ *noun & verb.* **E20.**
[from **OVER-** + **STITCH** *noun*[1], *verb*[1].]
NEEDLEWORK. ▶**A** *noun.* A stitch worked over an edge (or another stitch) in oversewing, usu. for binding or strengthening or to provide a decorative finish. **E20.**
▶ **B** *verb trans.* Sew with an overstitch. **E20.**
■ **overstitching** *noun* the action of the verb; overstitches collectively: **L20.**

overstock /*as noun* ˈəʊvəstɒk, *as verb* əʊvəˈstɒk/ *noun & verb.* **M16.**
[from **OVER-** + **STOCK** *noun*[1], *verb*[1].]
▶ **A** *noun.* †**1** In *pl.* Knee-breeches. **M–L16.**
2 A supply in excess of demand or requirement. **E18.**
▶ **B** *verb trans.* Stock to excess; supply with more than is required. **M17.**

overstood *verb pa. t. & pple* of **OVERSTAND**.

overstrain /*as verb* əʊvəˈstreɪn, *as noun* ˈəʊvəstreɪn/ *verb & noun.* **L16.**
[from **OVER-** + **STRAIN** *verb*[1], *noun*[2].]
▶ **A** *verb.* †**1** *verb trans.* Stretch or extend (a thing) over or across something. *rare.* Only in **L16.**
2 a *verb trans.* Strain too much, subject to excessive strain; *spec.* strain (a metal) beyond the yield point. **L16.** ▸**b** *verb intrans.* Exert too much effort, try too hard. **E17.**
2b overstraining disease = *capture myopathy* s.v. **CAPTURE** *noun.*
▶ **B** *noun.* Excessive strain; the action of overstraining, the fact of being overstrained. **M18.**

overstress /*as verb* əʊvəˈstrɛs, *as noun* ˈəʊvəstrɛs/ *verb & noun.* **E20.**
[from **OVER-** + **STRESS** *verb*[1], *noun*.]
▶ **A** *verb trans.* Stress too much, lay too much stress on (something). **E20.**
▶ **B** *noun.* Excessive stress. **E20.**

overstretch /*as verb* əʊvəˈstrɛtʃ, *as noun* ˈəʊvəstrɛtʃ/ *verb & noun.* **LME.**
[from **OVER-** + **STRETCH** *verb*.]
▶ **A** *verb trans.* **1** Stretch too much; *fig.* make excessive demands on (resources etc.). Freq. as ***overstretched*** *ppl adjective.* **LME.**
2 Stretch (a thing) over or across something; stretch or extend across (a thing). **LME.**
▶ **B** *noun.* The fact or an instance of overstretching. **M18.**

overstrict /əʊvəˈstrɪkt/ *adjective.* **L16.**
[from **OVER-** + **STRICT**.]
Excessively strict.
■ **overstrictly** *adverb* **M17.** **overstrictness** *noun* **M17.**

overstride /əʊvəˈstrʌɪd/ *verb.* Pa. t. **-strode** /-ˈstrəʊd/; pa. pple **-stridden** /-ˈstrɪd(ə)n/, (*colloq.*) **-strode**. **ME.**
[from **OVER-** + **STRIDE** *verb*.]
1 *verb trans.* Stride over or across; stand or sit astride, straddle. **ME.**
2 *verb trans.* Stride or extend beyond; *fig.* go beyond, surpass. **M17.**
3 *verb intrans.* Take excessively long strides. **L19.**

overstrike /*as verb* əʊvəˈstrʌɪk, *as noun* ˈəʊvəstrʌɪk/ *verb & noun.* **LME.**
[from **OVER-** + **STRIKE** *verb*.]
▶ **A** *verb.* Infl. as **STRIKE** *verb*; pa. t. & (usu.) pple **-struck** /-ˈstrʌk/.
†**1** *verb trans.* Bring down a stroke on. **LME–L16.**
2 a *verb trans.* Strike (a coin) with a new die, imposing a second design on the original; strike (a new design) on a coin. **E20.** ▸**b** *verb trans. & intrans. COMPUTING.* Print (a diacritic etc.) on top of an existing character; type (two or more characters) in the same position. **L20.**
▶ **B** *noun.* **1** An overstruck coin. **E20.**
2 *COMPUTING.* The action or result of overstriking. **L20.**

overstring /əʊvəˈstrɪŋ/ *verb trans.* Pa. t. & pple **-strung** /-ˈstrʌŋ/. **L19.**
[from **OVER-** + **STRING** *verb*.]
Arrange the strings of (a piano) in sets crossing over one another obliquely.

overstrode *verb pa. t. & pple*: see **OVERSTRIDE**.

overstruck *verb pa. t. & pple*: see **OVERSTRIKE**.

overstrung /*in sense 1* əʊvəˈstrʌŋ, *in sense 2* ˈəʊvəstrʌŋ/ *adjective.* **E19.**
[Sense 1 from **OVER-** + **STRUNG** *ppl adjective*; sense 2 pa. pple of **OVERSTRING**.]
1 Of a person, temperament, etc.: highly strung, intensely strained. **E19.**
2 Of a piano: having the strings arranged in sets crossing obliquely over one another. **L19.**

overstrung *verb pa. t. & pple* of **OVERSTRING**.

oversupply /əʊvəsəˈplʌɪ/ *noun & verb.* **M19.**
[from **OVER-** + **SUPPLY** *noun*, *verb*[1].]
▶ **A** *noun.* An excessive supply. **M19.**
▶ **B** *verb trans.* Supply in excess. **M19.**

oversway /*as verb* əʊvəˈsweɪ, *as noun* ˈəʊvəsweɪ/ *verb & noun.* Now *rare.* **L16.**
[from **OVER-** + **SWAY** *verb*, *noun*.]
▶ **A** *verb.* †**1** *verb trans.* **a** Rule over, govern; exercise power over; overpower. **L16–L17.** ▸**b** Surpass in authority; prevail over by superior authority. **L16–L19.**
†**2** *verb trans.* Lead or persuade into some action; prevail on. **L16–E18.**
3 *verb trans. & intrans.* (Cause to) sway, swing, or lean over. **E17.**
▶ **B** *noun.* (Superior) command over a person, ascendancy; overlordship. **E18.**

overswell /əʊvəˈswɛl/ *verb.* Infl. as **SWELL** *verb*; pa. pple **-swollen** /-ˈswəʊlən/. **L16.**
[from **OVER-** + **SWELL** *verb*.]
1 *verb trans. & (rare) intrans.* Swell unduly or excessively. Chiefly as ***overswollen*** *ppl adjective.* **L16.**
2 *verb trans. &* †*intrans.* Of a body of water etc.: overflow. **L16.**

overt /əʊˈvəːt, ˈəʊvət/ *adjective.* **ME.**
[Old French (mod. *ouvert*), pa. pple of *ovrir* (mod. *ouvrir*) open from Latin *aperire*.]
1 Open, not closed; (esp. of a building) uncovered. Long *rare.* **ME.**

For other words beginning with *over-* see the entry for **over-**

2 Exposed to view or knowledge; done openly or publicly; unconcealed, not secret. ME.

📖 **2** A. LURIE Some . . have already gone much further in terms of overt hostility. L. GORDON His life had become an inner waste, despite its overt success.

Phrases & special collocations: ***market overt***: see MARKET *noun*. **overt act** LAW an act which can be proved to have been done, implying criminal intent. ***pound overt***: see POUND *noun*² 1a.

▪ **overtly** *adverb* ME. **overtness** *noun* L19.

overtake /əʊvəˈteɪk/ *verb*. Pa. t. **-took** /-ˈtʊk/; pa. pple **-taken** /-ˈteɪk(ə)n/. ME.
[from OVER- + TAKE *verb*.]
1 *verb trans. & intrans.* Catch up with and pass (a person, vehicle, etc., going in the same direction). ME. ▸**b** *verb trans.* Orig. (*rare*), undertake to do. Later (chiefly *Scot.*), accomplish (a task), esp. when pressed for time. ME.
†**2** *verb trans.* Get at, reach with a blow. ME–L17.
†**3** *verb trans.* Catch, surprise, or detect in a fault or offence; convict. ME–M16.
4 *verb trans.* Learn; comprehend, understand. Long *obsolete* exc. *Scot.* ME.
5 *verb trans.* (Of an illness, misfortune, etc.) come suddenly or unexpectedly on; (of a condition etc.) affect gradually. LME.
6 *verb trans.* Overcome the will, senses, or feelings of; win over, captivate. *obsolete* exc. *dial.* LME. ▸†**b** Overcome the judgement of; deceive. L16–E18. ▸**c** Overcome with drink; intoxicate. Usu. in *pass.* Now *dial.* L16.
7 *verb intrans. & trans.* BRIDGE. Play a higher card than (the card played by one's partner). E20.

📖 **1** E. BOWEN Meeting or overtaking other couples. R. HILL He swung out sharply to overtake. J. RABAN Old ladies on bicycles were prone to overtake me on hills. *fig.*: *Japan Times* Western Europe overtook North America as the world's largest car market. **5** P. TOYNBEE As if my own death were about to overtake me at any moment. M. FRAYN Rowe awoke from the drowsiness that was overtaking him. **6** S. PEPYS We were all so overtaken with this good news.

▪ **overtakable** *adjective* able to be overtaken M19. **overtaker** *noun* L15. **overtaking** *verbal noun* the action or fact of overtaking something, esp. a vehicle going in the same direction L16.

overtax /əʊvəˈtaks/ *verb trans.* M17.
[from OVER- + TAX *verb*.]
Tax too heavily; *fig.* make excessive demands on (a person's strength etc.).

over-the-board /əʊvəðəˈbɔːd/ *adjective*. M20.
[from OVER *preposition* + THE + BOARD *noun*.]
Of chess: played with the participants present and facing each other across the chessboard.

overthink /əʊvəˈθɪŋk/ *verb*. Long *rare*. Pa. t. & pple **-thought** /-ˈθɔːt/. ME.
[from OVER- + THINK *verb*².]
▶ **I** †**1** *verb trans. impers.* (with dat. obj.). Displease, vex, grieve. Only in ME.
▶ **II** †**2** *verb trans.* Think over, consider. L15–L17.
3 †**a** *verb refl.* Exhaust (oneself) with too much thinking. Only in M17. ▸**b** *verb intrans.* Think too much or too seriously. Chiefly as ***overthinking*** *verbal noun*. E18.

overthought /ˈəʊvəθɔːt/ *noun*. Chiefly *literary*. M19.
[from OVER- + THOUGHT *noun*¹.]
1 Excessive thought, too much thinking. M19.
2 Conscious thought; an explicit idea. L19.

overthought *verb pa. t. & pple* of OVERTHINK.

overthoughtful /əʊvəˈθɔːtfʊl, -f(ə)l/ *adjective*. LME.
[from OVER- + THOUGHTFUL.]
Too thoughtful or anxious.

overthrew *verb pa. t.* of OVERTHROW *verb*.

overthrow /ˈəʊvəθrəʊ/ *noun*. E16.
[Partly from next, partly from OVER- + THROW *noun*².]
1 The action or an act of overthrowing something; the fact, state, or condition of being overthrown; an instance of this; (a) defeat, (a) deposition. E16. ▸**b** An act of overthrowing a ball; *spec.* (**a**) CRICKET a fielder's return of the ball which passes over or beyond the wicket; a run permitted by this; (**b**) BASEBALL a fielder's throw which passes over or beyond a baseman. M18.
2 ARCHITECTURE. A panel of decorated wrought-iron work forming the architrave of a gateway or arch. E20.

📖 **1** S. HASTINGS In favour of war and of the overthrow of the established order. *World Monitor* The violent . . overthrow of the Ceausescus in Romania.

overthrow /əʊvəˈθrəʊ/ *verb*. Infl. as THROW *verb*; pa. t. usu. **-threw** /-ˈθruː/, pa. pple **-thrown** /-ˈθrəʊn/. ME.
[from OVER- + THROW *verb*.]
1 *verb trans.* Upset; overturn; knock down. ME.
2 *verb trans.* Cast down from a position of prosperity, power, influence, etc.; defeat, overcome; ruin, destroy; *esp.* overturn (an established order, practice, custom, etc.); depose (a ruler, government, etc.). ME.
†**3** *verb intrans.* Fall over or down, tumble; prostrate oneself or be prostrated. ME–M16.
4 *verb trans.* Throw (a ball etc.) too far; *spec.* (**a**) CRICKET (of a fielder) return (the ball) so that it passes over or beyond the wicket; (**b**) BASEBALL (of a fielder) throw (the ball) over or beyond a baseman. M19.

📖 **1** B. JOWETT One who is already prostrate cannot be overthrown. **2** C. LAMBERT Debussy overthrew the old romantic rhetoric. A. J. TOYNBEE The Spaniards overthrew the Inca Empire. K. LINES One of his children would overthrow him and seize the throne. M. FORSTER Revolutionaries, out to overthrow absolutism.

▪ **overthrowal** *noun* the action or an act of overthrowing something; (a) defeat, (a) deposition: E20. **overthrower** *noun* M16. **overthrowing** *noun* the action or an act of overthrowing; (an) overthrowal: ME.

overthrust /*as noun* ˈəʊvəθrʌst, *as verb* əʊvəˈθrʌst/ *noun & verb*. L19.
[from OVER- + THRUST *noun, verb*.]
GEOLOGY. ▶**A** *noun*. The (extent of) thrusting forward of one series of rocks or strata over another, esp. along a fault plane at a relatively small angle to the horizontal; a large-scale reverse thrust fault in which this occurs (also ***overthrust fault***). L19.
▶ **B** *verb trans.* Pa. t. & pple **-thrust**. Thrust (a mass of rock) over or *on to* another, esp. at a low angle; obduct. Chiefly as ***overthrust*** *ppl adjective*, ***overthrusting*** *verbal noun*. L19.

overthwart /ˈəʊvəθwɔːt/ *adjective & noun*. *obsolete* exc. *dial.* ME.
[formed as OVERTHWART *adverb*.]
▶ **A** *adjective*. **1** Lying crosswise or across something else; transverse. ME.
2 *fig.* Inclined to cross or oppose; perverse, contentious, contrary, hostile. ME.
†**3** (Situated) opposite. M16–L17.
▶†**B** *absol.* as *noun*. **1** (A thing lying in) a transverse or cross direction. LME–M17.
2 (An) opposite point. *rare*. Only in L17.

overthwart /əʊvəˈθwɔːt/ *verb trans. obsolete* exc. *dial.* LME.
[from next.]
1 Pass or lie across; traverse, cross. LME.
2 *fig.* †**a** Make contrary; pervert. *rare*. Only in LME. ▸**b** Act in opposition to; cross, oppose; hinder, thwart. E16.

overthwart /əʊvəˈθwɔːt/ *adverb & preposition*. *obsolete* exc. *dial.* ME.
[from OVER *adverb* + THWART *adverb*.]
▶ **A** *adverb*. **1** From side to side, or so as to cross something; crosswise, transversely. ME.
†**2** *fig.* Amiss, perversely; contrarily; angrily. ME–M16.
†**3** Opposite. *rare* (Spenser). Only in L16.
▶ **B** *preposition*. **1** From side to side of; so as to cross; across. ME.
2 On the opposite side of; across, beyond, over (a path, stream, etc.). L18.

overtime /ˈəʊvətʌɪm/ *noun & adverb*. M16.
[from OVER- + TIME *noun*.]
▶ **A** *noun*. **1** Extra time, esp. added to one's regular working day or to a set minimum number of working hours; (payment for) work performed in such extra time. M16.
2 In sport, extra time added to a contest in the event of a draw. *N. Amer.* E20.
Comb.: **overtime ban** a prohibition on the working of overtime, esp. as a form of industrial action.
▶ **B** *adverb*. During overtime; in addition to regular or minimum hours. Freq. in ***work overtime***. M19.

overtire /əʊvəˈtʌɪə/ *verb trans.* M16.
[from OVER- + TIRE *verb*¹.]
Tire excessively, exhaust, wear out the strength of.
▪ **overtired** *adjective* excessively tired, exhausted, worn out E17.

overtone /ˈəʊvətəʊn/ *noun*. M19.
[from OVER- + TONE *noun*, after German *Oberton* contr. of *Oberpartialton* upper partial tone.]
1 ACOUSTICS & MUSIC. An upper partial tone; a harmonic. M19. ▸**b** PHYSICS. An analogous component of any kind of oscillation, having a frequency that is an integral multiple of the fundamental frequency. E20.
2 *fig.* A subtle or elusive implication or association, a connotation. Freq. in *pl.* L19.

📖 **2** F. KAPLAN *Bleak House* . . is visibly dark with overtones of . . personal dissatisfaction.

overtone /əʊvəˈtəʊn/ *verb trans.* M19.
[from OVER- + TONE *verb*.]
Tone too much or too strongly; give too deep or powerful a tone to.

overtook *verb pa. t.* of OVERTAKE.

overtop /əʊvəˈtɒp/ *verb trans.* Infl. **-pp-**. M16.
[from OVER- + TOP *verb*¹.]
1 Rise above in power or authority; be superior to, esp. in degree or quality; excel, surpass. M16.
2 Rise higher than; surpass in height; surmount. L16.
3 Overburden. Orig. *spec.*, make (a ship) top-heavy. Long *obsolete* exc. *Canad. dial. rare*. M17.

📖 **1** DAY LEWIS A victor over-topping all other men. **2** O. WELLES He seemed . . even larger than before, overtopping me by a good head and a half.

overtop /əʊvəˈtɒp/ *adverb & preposition*. Now chiefly *N. Amer.* L18.
[from OVER- + TOP *noun*¹.]
▶ **A** *adverb*. Over the top; overhead. L18.
▶ **B** *preposition*. Over the top of, over. L20.

📖 D. MCBAIN A fresh surge of river water came flushing around the horseshoe bend, spilling overtop the dyke.

¶ Adverb rare before 20.

overtravel /ˈəʊvətrav(ə)l/ *noun*. M19.
[from OVER- + TRAVEL *noun*.]
1 Excessive travel, too much travelling. M19.
2 Movement of part of a machine beyond the desired point; an allowance made for this. Freq. *attrib.* E20.

overtravel /əʊvəˈtrav(ə)l/ *verb*. Infl. **-ll-**, ***-l-**. M17.
[from OVER- + TRAVEL *verb*.]
1 *verb refl.* Travel too much or beyond one's power of endurance. M17.
2 *verb intrans.* MECHANICS. Travel further than necessary to perform a particular act or function. E20.

overtread /əʊvəˈtrɛd/ *verb trans.* Now *rare*. Pa. t. **-trod** /-ˈtrɒd/; pa. pple **-trodden** /-ˈtrɒd(ə)n/. OE.
[from OVER- + TREAD *verb*.]
Tread over, trample under foot; *fig.* oppress, subdue.

overture /ˈəʊvətj(ʊ)ə/ *noun & verb*. LME.
[Old French (mod. *ouverture*) from Latin *apertura* APERTURE, infl. by French *ouvrir* open.]
▶ **A** *noun*. †**1** An aperture, an orifice, a hole. LME–M18.
2 An opening of negotiations towards some proceeding or settlement; a formal proposal or offer. Usu. in *pl.* LME.
†**3** The disclosure of information about something; a revelation; a declaration. M16–M17.
4 a SCOTTISH HISTORY. A proposal for consideration by a legislative body; *spec.* a bill placed before the Scottish Parliament for enactment. M16. ▸**b** ECCLESIASTICAL. A formal motion proposing or calling for legislation, presented to the supreme court of a Presbyterian Church. L16.
†**5** (An) overturning of something, (an) overthrow. M16–M17.
†**6** A beginning, a commencement; *fig.* a first indication or hint *of* something. L16–E18.
†**7** A favourable situation or opportunity. E17–M18.
8 MUSIC. An orchestral piece opening or introducing (and freq. based on themes from) an opera or other extended composition; a one-movement composition in this style. M17.
9 The opening or introductory part of a poem. L19.

📖 **2** W. S. MAUGHAM She repelled the overtures of friendship. F. ASTAIRE I . . made overtures to them about releasing me from my coming options. **8** C. IVES Let him . . try to put that glory into an overture . . chuck-full of Scotch tunes.

▶ **B** *verb trans.* **1** *gen.* Offer as a suggestion or proposal; propose (*that*). *rare*. M17.
2 ECCLESIASTICAL. **a** Present as an overture to the supreme court of a Presbyterian Church. L17. ▸**b** Present as an overture to (the supreme court of a Presbyterian Church). M19.
3 MUSIC. Introduce as with an overture or prelude. L19.

overturn /*as verb* əʊvəˈtəːn, *as noun* ˈəʊvətəːn/ *verb & noun*. ME.
[from OVER- + TURN *verb, noun*.]
▶ **A** *verb*. †**1** *verb intrans.* Of a wheel: turn round, revolve. ME–M17.
2 *verb trans.* Cause to fall over or down, upset. ME. ▸**b** *verb intrans.* Fall over, capsize; fall down. LME.
3 *verb trans.* Overthrow (a person, institution, principle, etc.); subvert; abolish; invalidate. ME. ▸**b** *spec.* Reverse (a judicial etc. decision). M20.
†**4** *verb trans.* Turn away; change from one thing, state, condition, etc., to another; pervert. LME–L16.

📖 **2** M. LEITCH Our sole aim must be to overturn the social iceberg, stand it on its head. P. AUSTER I ransacked the closet . . , overturning boxes. **b** J. T. STORY Trying to haul down the sail. **3** F. SPALDING The Greco-Roman tradition was being overturned in favour of a new, geometric art. **b** *Guardian* The ruling was overturned in the Lords.

▶ **B** *noun*. **1** The action of overturning, the fact of being overturned; an instance of this; (a) subversion; (a) revolution. L16.
2 = TURNOVER 5. *rare*. L19.
3 GEOLOGY. = OVERFOLD *noun*. L19.
4 The mixing or circulation of the water in a thermally stratified lake, usu. occurring once or twice a year on cooling or warming of the epilimnion. E20.
▪ **overturner** *noun* L16.

For other words beginning with *over-* see the entry for **over-**

over-under /əʊvər'ʌndə/ *adjective & noun.* M20.
[from OVER *adverb* + UNDER *adverb*.]
(Designating) a type of shotgun having one barrel fixed over the other. Cf. ***over-and-under*** s.v. OVER *adverb*.

overuse /əʊvə'ju:s/ *noun.* Also **over-use**. M19.
[from OVER- + USE *noun*.]
Too much or too frequent use.

overuse /əʊvə'ju:z/ *verb trans.* Also **over-use**. L17.
[from OVER- + USE *verb*.]
Use too much or too frequently; injure by excessive use.

overview /*as verb* əʊvə'vju:, *as noun* 'əʊvəvju:/ *verb & noun.* M16.
[from OVER- + VIEW *verb, noun*.]
▶ **A** *verb trans.* **1** View from above, look down on; survey. Also, of a place: afford a view from above, overlook. M16.
2 Look over or all through; examine, inspect; take an overview of. M16.
▶ **B** *noun.* †**1** Inspection; supervision. L16–M17.
2 A general survey; a comprehensive review of facts or ideas; a concise statement or outline of a subject, a summary. Also (*lit.*), a view from above. M20.

🕮 **2** K. WARREN Men with expert knowledge . . maintained an overview of the whole system. *City Limits* An introductory overview outlines Spanish power politics.

■ **overviewer** *noun* M20.

overvoltage /'əʊvəvəʊltɪdʒ, -vɒlt-/ *noun.* E20.
[from OVER- + VOLTAGE.]
1 A voltage in excess of some threshold value, or of that which is normal, safe, or allowed for. E20.
2 CHEMISTRY. The extra potential above the theoretical value which must be applied to an electrolytic cell to liberate a substance at an electrode. E20.

overwash /*as verb* əʊvə'wɒʃ, *as noun* 'əʊvəwɒʃ/ *verb & noun.* LME.
[from OVER- + WASH *verb*.]
▶ **A** *verb trans.* Wash or flow over (something). LME.
▶ **B** *noun.* The action or process of washing over something; *esp.* in PHYSICAL GEOGRAPHY (*a*) the deposition over or beyond a moraine of material carried by running water from a glacier; (*b*) the flow of water from a lake, the sea, etc., over a low spit, berm, etc.; water carried or left behind by such a flow. Freq. *attrib.* L19.

overween /əʊvə'wi:n/ *verb.* Now *rare.* ME.
[from OVER- + WEEN *verb*.]
1 *verb intrans.* Have unreasonably high expectations or too good an opinion of oneself; be conceited, arrogant, or presumptuous; be excessively self-confident. Cf. next. ME.
2 *verb intrans.* Think too highly *of*, overrate something. Chiefly as ***overweening*** *verbal noun.* M16.
†**3** *verb trans.* Think too highly of, overrate. L16–L17.

overweening /əʊvə'wi:nɪŋ/ *adjective.* ME.
[from prec. + -ING[2].]
1 Having unreasonably high expectations or too good an opinion of oneself; conceited, arrogant, presumptuous; excessively self-confident. ME.
2 Of an opinion, emotion, etc.: excessive, exaggerated; immoderate. L15.

🕮 **1** *Times Lit. Suppl.* The overweening cleverboots whom the critics have insufficiently chastised. **2** M. ARNOLD Her airs of superiority and her overweening pretensions. E. PAWEL All the classic symptoms of an overweening aggression turned inward.

■ **overweeningly** *adverb* E17. **overweeningness** *noun* E17.

overweight /*as noun* 'əʊvə,weɪt, *as adjective* əʊvə'weɪt/ *noun & adjective.* M16.
[from OVER- + WEIGHT *noun*.]
▶ **A** *noun.* **1** Something beyond an allowed or suitable weight; extra weight, excess of weight. M16.
2 Too great weight, excessive weight. L16. ▸**b** An overweight or obese person. L19. ▸**c** The condition of being overweight; obesity. E20.
3 Greater weight; preponderance. E17.

🕮 **2** H. HALIBURTON With overweight of care on my mind.

▶ **B** *adjective.* **1** Above or in excess of an allowed or suitable weight; too heavy. M17.
2 Of a person: weighing more than is normal or desirable for his or her height or build; obese. L19.

🕮 **1** *Pall Mall Gazette* I was charged for a few pounds of overweight luggage. **2** M. SPARK I was immensely too fat. I was overweight.

overweight /əʊvə'weɪt/ *verb trans.* E17.
[from OVER- + WEIGHT *verb*.]
†**1** Give too much weight or importance to. Only in E17.
2 Impose an excessive weight on; overload (*with*). M18.

overwent *verb pa. t.* of OVERGO.

overwhelm /əʊvə'wɛlm/ *verb & noun.* ME.
[from OVER- + WHELM *verb*.]
▶ **A** *verb trans.* **1** Overturn, overthrow, upset; turn upside down. *obsolete* exc. *dial.* ME.
2 Bury or drown beneath a great mass of earth, water, etc.; submerge completely. ME. ▸†**b** Overhang, esp. so as to cover. *rare* (Shakes.). Only in L16.
3 *fig.* Overpower with an excess of work, responsibility, etc. Also, bring to sudden ruin or destruction; crush. E16. ▸**b** Overpower with emotion. M16. ▸**c** Deluge or inundate (*with*). E19.

🕮 **2** *Climber* They were overwhelmed by an avalanche. *Journal of Navigation* She was suddenly overwhelmed by an immense breaking sea. **3** A. C. CLARKE If we dumped it all on you . . you'd be overwhelmed. *Japan Times* Japan also overwhelmed the Soviets 4–1. **b** R. KIPLING 'Never have I seen such a man as thou art', Kim whispered, overwhelmed. **c** W. GERHARDIE He overwhelmed us with surprise.

▶ **B** *noun.* The action of overwhelming; the fact of being overwhelmed. *rare.* M18.
■ **overwhelmer** *noun* E16. **overwhelming** *adjective* †(*a*) (*rare*, Shakes.) overhanging; (*b*) that overwhelms; irresistible, esp. by strength of numbers, influence, etc.: L16. **overwhelmingly** *adverb* M17. **overwhelmingness** *noun* the state of being overwhelming M19. **overwhelmment** *noun* = OVERWHELMINGNESS M19.

overwork /əʊvə'wə:k/ *noun.* OE.
[from OVER- + WORK *noun*.]
†**1** A structure, monument, building, etc., placed or raised over something. OE–ME.
2 Extra work, overtime. L18.
3 Excessive work; work beyond one's capacity or strength. E19.

🕮 **3** A. BISHOP His health was beginning to weaken under the strain of overwork.

overwork /əʊvə'wə:k/ *verb.* Pa. t. & pple (in branch I, *arch.* in branch II) **-wrought** /-'rɔ:t/, (in branch II) **-worked**. OE.
[from OVER- + WORK *verb*.]
▶ **I 1** *verb trans.* Cover with decorative work, decorate the surface of. Usu. in *pass.* OE.
2 *verb trans.* Work too much on; make overelaborate. Usu. in *pass.* or as OVERWROUGHT *adjective.* M17.
3 *verb trans.* Make overexcited, distraught, or nervous; agitate excessively. Usu. in *pass.* or as OVERWROUGHT *adjective.* M17.
▶ **II 4** *verb trans.* Cause to work too hard; weary or exhaust with excessive work; make excessive use of. Freq. in *pass.* M16.
5 *verb intrans.* Work too hard or too much. L19.

🕮 **4** L. A. G. STRONG As . . general dog's body, she was grossly overworked. T. STERLING That phrase is overworked. **5** J. WAINWRIGHT He deliberately overworked; driving himself to the point of exhaustion.

overwrite /əʊvə'raɪt/ *verb.* Pa. t. **-wrote** /-'rəʊt/; pa. pple **-written** /-'rɪt(ə)n/. L17.
[OVER- + WRITE *verb*.]
▶ **I 1** *verb trans.* Write (something) over other writing; write on (a surface, other writing, etc.); cover with writing. L17. ▸**b** COMPUTING. Destroy (data) by putting new data in its place; place new data in (a location, file, etc.) and destroy the existing contents. M20.
2 *verb trans.* Rewrite. L19.

🕮 **1b** *Which Computer?* Information so recorded can be overwritten or erased.

▶ **II 3 a** *verb refl.* Exhaust oneself by or injure one's abilities by excessive writing. E19. ▸**b** *verb trans.* Write too much about (a subject). E19.
4 *verb intrans.* Write too much or too elaborately. M19.
5 *verb trans.* Write in too elaborate or ornate a style. Usu. in *pass.* E20.

🕮 **4** M. SEYMOUR Ford overwrote—of his eighty-one books, only a dozen deserve to be kept in print. **5** F. M. FORD A story of his . . is extremely over-written.

▶ **III 6** *verb intrans.* In (marine) insurance: accept more risk than limits allow; underwrite excessively. Usu. as ***overwriting*** *verbal noun.* L20.

overwrought /əʊvə'rɔ:t/ *adjective.* LME.
[pa. pple of OVERWORK *verb*.]
That has been overwrought; *spec.* (*a*) overexcited, nervous, distraught; (*b*) too elaborate, overdone.

🕮 *Q* Linda's overwrought, crystalline perfection. *Guardian* If . . you are overwrought, stressed or worried.

overwrought *verb pa. t. & pple*: see OVERWORK *verb*.

ovest /'əʊvɪst/ *noun. obsolete* exc. *dial.* Also (earlier) †**ovet**.
[Old English *obet* = Old High German *obaz* (Middle High German *obez*, German *Obst*), Old Low German, Middle Low German *ovet* (Middle Dutch, Dutch *ooft*).]
Orig., fruit. Later *spec.*, beechmast and acorns, esp. as fodder for pigs.

For other words beginning with *over-* see the entry for **over-**

ovi- /'əʊvi/ *combining form*[1].
[from Latin *ovum* egg: see -I-.]
Of or pertaining to eggs or ova. Cf. OVO-.
■ **ovi'capsule** *noun* (ZOOLOGY) a capsule or sac containing an ovum or a number of ova, an egg-case M19. **ovicell** *noun* (BIOLOGY) (*a*) a chamber in which the early embryos of some bryozoans develop; (*b*) an egg cell, an ovum: M19. **oviducal** /-'dju:k(ə)l/ *adjective* [irreg. from Latin *ducere* lead] = OVIDUCTAL M19. **o'viferous** *adjective* = OVIGEROUS E19. **ovisac** *noun* = OVICAPSULE M19. **ovi-vi'viparous** *adjective* (*rare*) = OVOVIVIPAROUS E19.

ovi- /'əʊvi/ *combining form*[2].
[from Latin *ovis* sheep: see -I-.]
Of or pertaining to sheep, as ***ovicide***.

ovibos /'əʊvɪbɒs/ *noun.* Pl. same. E20.
[from OVI-[2] + Latin *bos* ox.]
The musk ox. Now chiefly as mod. Latin genus name.

ovicide /'əʊvɪsʌɪd/ *noun*[1]. *joc.* M19.
[from OVI-[2] + -CIDE.]
The killing of a sheep.
■ **ovi'cidal** *adjective*[1] (*a*) of or pertaining to the killing of sheep; (*b*) that kills sheep: M19.

ovicide /'əʊvɪsʌɪd/ *noun*[2]. M20.
[from OVI-[1] + -CIDE.]
An agent that kills eggs, esp. those of insects.
■ **ovi'cidal** *adjective*[2] (*a*) of or pertaining to the killing of eggs; (*b*) that kills eggs: M20.

ovicular /ə(ʊ)'vɪkjʊlə/ *adjective. rare.* L18.
[from medieval or mod. Latin *oviculum*, dim. of *ovum* egg: see -CULE, -AR[1].]
Of the shape or nature of an egg.

Ovidian /ɒ'vɪdɪən, ə(ʊ)-/ *adjective.* E17.
[from *Ovidius* (see below): see -IAN.]
Pertaining to or characteristic of the Roman poet Ovid (Publius Ovidius Naso, 43 BC–AD 17) or his poetry.

oviduct /'əʊvɪdʌkt/ *noun.* M18.
[from OVI-[1] + DUCT *noun*.]
ANATOMY & ZOOLOGY. A duct or canal by which ova or eggs pass from an ovary; in mammals, a Fallopian or uterine tube.
■ **ovi'ductal** *adjective* of or pertaining to an oviduct, oviducal M19.

oviform /'əʊvɪfɔ:m/ *adjective.* L17.
[from OVI-[1] + -FORM.]
1 Egg-shaped. L17.
†**2** Consisting of small particles like the eggs or roe of fishes. *rare.* L18–E19.
2 oviform limestone oolitic limestone.

ovigerous /əʊ'vɪdʒ(ə)rəs/ *adjective.* M19.
[from OVI-[1] + -GEROUS.]
ANATOMY & ZOOLOGY. Bearing or carrying eggs.
ovigerous FRAENUM.

ovine /'əʊvʌɪn/ *adjective & noun.* E19.
[Late Latin *ovinus*, formed as OVI-[2]: see -INE[1].]
▶ **A** *adjective.* Of, pertaining to, or characteristic of, a sheep or sheep; resembling a sheep or sheep. E19.

🕮 G. B. SHAW The ovine members who do not know how to vote until a Party Whip tells them.

▶ **B** *noun.* A member of the genus *Ovis*; a sheep. *rare.* L19.

oviparous /əʊ'vɪp(ə)rəs/ *adjective.* M17.
[from OVI-[1] + -PAROUS.]
ZOOLOGY. Producing eggs; reproducing by means of eggs which are hatched outside the body of the parent (as in birds). Cf. VIVIPAROUS, OVOVIVIPAROUS.
■ **ovi'parity** *noun* the condition or character of being oviparous M19. **oviparously** *adverb* E19.

oviposit /əʊvɪ'pɒzɪt/ *verb.* E19.
[from OVI-[1] + Latin *posit-* ppl stem of *ponere* to place (cf. DEPOSIT *verb*).]
ZOOLOGY. **1** *verb intrans.* Deposit or lay an egg or eggs, esp. (as in insects) by means of a special organ (an ovipositor). E19.
2 *verb trans.* Deposit or lay (an egg). M19.

oviposition /,əʊvɪpə'zɪʃ(ə)n/ *noun.* E19.
[formed as prec.: see -ITION.]
ZOOLOGY. The action of depositing or laying an egg or eggs, esp. with an ovipositor.
■ **ovipositional** *adjective* L20.

ovipositor /əʊvɪ'pɒzɪtə/ *noun.* E19.
[formed as prec.: see -OR.]
ZOOLOGY. A pointed tubular organ at the end of the abdomen of the female of some animals, esp. insects, by which eggs are deposited and (in many cases) with which a hole is bored to receive them.

ovist /'əʊvɪst/ *noun.* M19.
[from OVI-[1] + -IST.]
BIOLOGY (now *Hist.*). An advocate of the theory that the ovum holds all the material necessary for development of the embryo, the sperm merely initiating the process. Cf. SPERMATIST.
■ **ovism** *noun* the theory of the ovists L19. **o'vistic** *adjective* L19.

ovivorous /əʊˈvɪv(ə)rəs/ *adjective*. E19.
[from OVI-¹ + -VOROUS.]
Egg-eating, feeding on eggs.

ovo- /ˈəʊvəʊ/ *combining form*.
[from Latin *ovum* egg: see -O-.]
Forming chiefly nouns with the sense 'of or pertaining to ova or eggs', and (occas.) compound adjectives with the sense 'partly oval and partly — in shape'. Cf. OO-, OVI-¹.
■ **ovocyte** *noun* (BIOLOGY) = OOCYTE E20. **ovoˈgenesis** *noun* (BIOLOGY) = OOGENESIS L19. **ovogeˈnetic** *adjective* (BIOLOGY) = OOGENETIC L19. **ovoˈmucin** *noun* (BIOCHEMISTRY) a water-insoluble proteoglycan in egg-white L19. **ovoˈmucoid** *noun* (BIOCHEMISTRY) a water-soluble proteoglycan in egg-white (also *ovomucoid* α); *ovomucoid* β = OVOMUCIN: L19.

ovoid /ˈəʊvɔɪd/ *adjective & noun*. E19.
[French *ovoïde* from medieval Latin *ovoides*, from Latin *ovum* egg: see -OID.]
Chiefly ZOOLOGY & BOTANY. ▶**A** *adjective*. Resembling an egg; (of a solid) egg-shaped; (of a plane figure) oval with one end more pointed than the other. E19.
▶**B** *noun*. An ovoid body or figure. M19.
■ **oˈvoidal** *adjective* = OVOID *adjective* L18.

ovolo /ˈəʊvələʊ/ *noun*. Pl. **-li** /-li/. M17.
[Italian, dim. of *uovo*, †*ovo* from Latin *ovum* egg.]
ARCHITECTURE. A rounded convex moulding.

ovonic /əʊˈvɒnɪk/ *adjective*. M20.
[from S. R. Ovshinsky (b. 1922), US physicist + ELECTR)ONIC.]
ELECTRONICS. Pertaining to, involving, or utilizing the property of certain amorphous semiconductors of making a rapid reversible transition from a non-conducting to a conducting state on the application of an electric field above a threshold value.
■ **ovonics** *noun* the study and application of ovonic effects and devices M20.

ovotestis /əʊvəʊˈtɛstɪs/ *noun*. Pl. **-testes** /-ˈtɛstiːz/. L19.
[from OVO- + TESTIS.]
In ZOOLOGY, a reproductive organ of some invertebrates which produces both ova and spermatozoa. In MEDICINE, an abnormal organ combining features of an ovary and a testis.

ovoviviparous /ˌəʊvəʊvɪˈvɪp(ə)rəs/ *adjective*. E19.
[from OVO- + VIVIPAROUS.]
ZOOLOGY. Reproducing by means of eggs which hatch in the body of the parent, so that the young do not develop in direct physiological contact with the parent, but are born alive (as in some reptiles and fishes, and many invertebrates). Cf. OVIPAROUS, VIVIPAROUS.
■ **ovoviviˈparity** *noun* the condition or character of being ovoviviparous L19.

†**ovula** *noun pl.* see OVULE.

ovular /ˈɒvjʊlə, ˈəʊv-/ *adjective*. M19.
[from OVULE + -AR¹.]
BIOLOGY. Of, pertaining to, or of the nature of an ovule.
■ Also **ovulary** *adjective* (rare) M19.

ovulate /ˈɒvjʊlət, ˈəʊ-/ *adjective*. M19.
[from (the same root as) OVULE + -ATE².]
BIOLOGY. Having or containing an ovule or ovules. Usu. as 2nd elem. of comb., as in ***biovulate***, ***multi-ovulate***, etc.

ovulate /ˈɒvjʊleɪt/ *verb*. L19.
[formed as prec. + -ATE³, or back-form. from next.]
1 *verb intrans.* Produce or discharge ova or an ovum (from the ovary). Also, (of an ovum) be discharged. L19.
2 *verb trans.* Discharge (an ovum). E20.
■ **ovuˈlatory** *adjective* of or pertaining to ovulation M20.

ovulation /ɒvjʊˈleɪʃ(ə)n/ *noun*. M19.
[from (the same root as) prec. + -ATION.]
ZOOLOGY & PHYSIOLOGY. The formation, development, or (esp.) discharge from the ovary of ova or an ovum. Also (*rare*), the development and laying of eggs by oviparous animals.

ovulator /ˈɒvjʊleɪtə/ *noun*. M20.
[from OVULATE *verb* + -OR.]
ZOOLOGY. An animal that ovulates (in a specified way).

ovule /ˈɒvjuːl, ˈəʊv-/ *noun*. Also in Latin form **†-lum**, pl. **†-la**. E19.
[French *ovule*, medieval and mod. Latin *ovulum* dim. of *ovum* egg: see -ULE.]
1 BOTANY. The structure in a flowering plant which contains the female gamete and after fertilization becomes the seed, consisting of a mass of tissue (the nucellus), usu. surrounded by protective layers, and attached to the ovary by the funicle. E19.
2 ZOOLOGY & PHYSIOLOGY. The ovum of an animal. Now *rare*. E19.
■ **ovuˈliferous** *adjective* bearing or producing ovules M19.

ovulite /ˈəʊvjʊlʌɪt/ *noun*. M19.
[from Latin *ovulum* (see OVULE) + -ITE¹.]
GEOLOGY. Orig., a fossil egg. Now = OOLITH.

†**ovulum** *noun* see OVULE.

ovum /ˈəʊvəm/ *noun*. Pl. **ova** /ˈəʊvə/. E17.
[Latin = egg.]
1 ROMAN HISTORY. Any of a number of egg-shaped objects used in the circus to indicate the number of laps in a race. Usu. in *pl.* E17.
2 BIOLOGY. The female gamete or reproductive cell in animals, usu. produced by an ovary and capable of developing into a new individual (after, or in some cases without, fertilization by the male sperm); an egg, an egg cell. Also *loosely*, a secondary oocyte (immature egg cell); a mass of cells formed by the first few divisions of a fertilized ovum. E18. ▶**b** BOTANY. Orig. (*rare*), the ovule or seed of a plant. Now, the egg cell in the nucellus of an ovule. M18.
3 ARCHITECTURE. An egg-shaped ornament or carving. E18.

ow /aʊ/ *interjection*. E20.
[Natural exclam.]
Expr. sudden pain.

> 🕮 M. WESLEY 'Ow! God! Ow!' She is seized with cramp.

owdacious /aʊˈdeɪʃəs/ *adjective*. *colloq.* (orig. *US*). M19.
[Perh. blend of AUDACIOUS and OUTRAGEOUS.]
Impertinent, mischievous, bold.

owe /əʊ/ *verb*. Pa. t. **owed**, †**ought**; pa. pple **owed**, †**owen**, †**ought**. See also OUGHT *verb*.
[Old English *āgan* = Old Frisian *āga*, Old Saxon *ēgan*, Old High German *eigan*, Old Norse *eiga*, Gothic *aigan*, ult. from Indo-European bases repr. also in Sanskrit *īś* possess, own: Germanic preterite-present verb. Cf. OWN *adjective*, OUGHT *verb*.]
▶**I** Have; possess; own.
1 *verb trans.* = OWN *verb* 2. Long *obsolete* exc. *dial.* OE. ▶†**b** = OWN *verb* 1. Only in ME. ▶†**c** = OWN *verb* 5. LME–E17.

> 🕮 **1** S. PEPYS Fine storehouses . . but of no great profit to him that oweth them.

▶**II** Have it as a duty or obligation.
†**2** *verb trans.* Be under a moral obligation, have as a duty, (*to do*, *do*). LOE–M16.
†**3** *verb intrans.* with indirect obj. & *trans. impers.* Be due or proper to, behove, befit, (a person) *to do*, *do*. ME–E16.

> 🕮 **2** T. CRANMER As obedient . . as a true Christian oweth to be.

▶**III** Have to or be required to pay.
4 *verb trans.* Be required or obliged to pay or repay (money, or in kind) in return for something received; be indebted to the amount of; be under an obligation to give (obedience, honour, allegiance, etc.). (Foll. by double obj., *to*.) ME. ▶**b** *verb intrans.* Be in debt, be required to pay, (*for*). LME. ▶**c** *verb trans.* Be in debt to (a person). L15.
5 *verb trans. transf.* Have or bear towards another (a feeling yet to be expressed in action). *obsolete* exc. in ***owe a grudge against***. ME.
6 *verb trans. fig.* Ascribe or attribute (a thing) to a person or thing; have, as received from or caused by; be indebted or beholden for. Foll. by *to*, (now *rare*) double obj. L16. ▶†**b** *verb intrans.* & (*rare*) *trans.* Be indebted or beholden to or *to* a person or thing for or *for* a thing. Only in 17.

> 🕮 **4** E. A. FREEMAN The land to which they owed a temporary allegiance. A. S. BYATT Lucas had fed and lectured and admired him: something was owed in return. L. R. BANKS What do I owe you for the first night in the camping site? M. SPARK They owe me seven pounds. P. VAN SOMMERS She had no justification for . . indignation. Her lover owed her nothing. M. WEST I could leave now, . . except that I owe you dinner. **owe it to oneself** need to do something in order to avoid unfairness to oneself. **b** J. CARLYLE I owed for my summer bonnet and cloak. **c** D. ANTHONY 'Another job.' . . 'I couldn't turn this one down,' I said. 'I owe the lady.' **6** J. BUCHAN A fine practical wisdom which owed nothing to books. DAY LEWIS To them I owe a capacity for relishing the everyday. W. MAXWELL Small towns in central Illinois nearly all owe their existence to the railroads.

owelty /ˈəʊəlti/ *noun*. L16.
[Anglo-Norman *owelté*, from Old French *owel* from Latin *aequalis* EQUAL *adjective*: see -TY¹.]
LAW (now *Hist.*). Equality as established by a compensatory sum of money etc. given after an exchange of pieces of land of differing values.

Owen /ˈəʊɪn/ *noun*. M20.
[E. E. Owen (1915–49), Austral. inventor.]
In full ***Owen gun***. A type of sub-machine-gun first used in the war of 1939–45.

†**owen** *verb pa. pple*: see OWE.

Owenism /ˈəʊɪnɪz(ə)m/ *noun*. E19.
[from *Owen* (see below) + -ISM.]
The theory or system of social reform proposed and practised by Robert Owen (1771–1858), based on communistic cooperation.
■ **Owenist** *noun & adjective* E19. **Owenite** *noun & adjective* E19.

owing /ˈəʊɪŋ/ *noun*. LME.
[from OWE + -ING¹.]
1 The action of OWE. LME.
2 That which is owed, a debt. L15.

owing /ˈəʊɪŋ/ *pred. adjective*. LME.
[from OWE + -ING².]
1 That owes something; indebted or beholden *to* a person *for* a thing. Long *rare* or *obsolete*. LME.
2 Of a thing: that is yet to be paid or rendered; owed, due. (Foll. by *to*.) LME.
3 ***owing to***: ▶**a** *adjectival phr.* Attributable to; arising from, caused by, consequent on. M17. ▶**b** *prepositional phr.* On account of, because of. E19.

> 🕮 **2** F. BURNEY She discharged all that was owing for the children. **3a** H. DAVY The effect is owing to the presence of light. F. SPALDING It was possibly owing to Hulme's influence. **b** V. WOOLF She had had to dismiss Lily . . owing to her misbehaviour. R. MACAULAY Owing to the helpful influence of Mr Potter . . Jane obtained a quite good post.

owl /aʊl/ *noun*.
[Old English *ūle* = Old Norse *ugla*, Old Low German word (whence Middle Low German, Middle Dutch *ūle*, Dutch *uil*), from Germanic base repr. by Old High German *ūwila* (Middle High German *iule*, German *Eule*).]
1 Any bird of prey of the order Strigiformes, typically nocturnal, feeding on mice, small birds, etc., and characterized by a large rounded head, raptorial beak, soft plumage, and large eyes directed forwards and surrounded by radiating feathers. OE.
2 *transf.* A person likened to an owl, esp. in looking solemn or wise or in being active at night. LME.
3 (A bird of) a fancy variety of the domestic pigeon characterized by an owl-like head and prominent ruff. Also ***owl-pigeon***. E18.
4 More fully ***owl ray***. = ***sandy ray*** s.v. SANDY *adjective*. M19.

> 🕮 **1** ***barn owl***, ***brown owl***, ***church owl***, ***eagle owl***, ***hoot owl***, ***horned owl***, ***little owl***, ***screech owl***, ***snowy owl***, ***tawny owl***, etc. **2** L. MACDONALD A frightfully learned owl of a female. *Times* Some of us are owls who spend the mornings half asleep.

Phrases etc.: **sea-owl** (now *rare* or *obsolete*) lumpfish. STUFFED **owl**.
Comb.: **owl bus** *N. Amer.*: running during the night; **owl-butterfly** any very large dusk-flying American butterfly of the family Brassolidae, *esp.* any of the genus *Caligo* having large ocelli on the hindwings; **owl-faced monkey** = ***owl-monkey*** below; **owl-fly** (*a*) = ***orl-fly*** s.v. ORL; (*b*) = ***owl midge*** below; (*c*) any predatory neuropteran insect of the chiefly tropical family Ascalaphidae, related to ant-lions; **owlglass** [translating German Till *Eulenspiegel*, a German peasant of the 14th cent. whose practical jokes were the subject of a 16th-cent. collection of satirical tales (cf. ESPIEGLE)] a jester, a buffoon (cf. ***owlspiegle*** below); **owl jug** a porcelain jug shaped like an owl; **owl-light** twilight, dusk; dim or poor light; **owl midge** = ***moth fly*** s.v. MOTH *noun*¹; **owl-monkey** = ***night monkey*** s.v. NIGHT *noun*; **owl-moth** a very large Brazilian noctuid moth, *Erebus strix*; **owl-parrot** (now *rare*) = KAKAPO; **owl-pigeon**: = sense 3 above; **owl-ray** = sense 4 above; †**owlspiegle** *noun & verb* (*rare*) (*a*) *noun* = ***owlglass*** above; (*b*) *verb trans.* cause to resemble an owlglass; **owl-swallow** a frogmouth; **owl train** *US*: running during the night.
■ **owl-like** *adjective* resembling (that of) an owl E17. **owly** *adjective* = OWLISH L16.

owl /aʊl/ *verb*. LME.
[from the noun, in sense 3 perh. with allus. to the bird's nocturnal habits, but it may repr. a separate word.]
†**1** *verb trans.* Collect (money). Only in LME.
2 *verb intrans.* Behave like an owl; *esp.* go or wander about at night. Now chiefly *dial.* M16.
3 *verb trans.* Smuggle (wool or sheep) out of England. Chiefly as ***owling*** *verbal noun*. *obsolete* exc. *Hist.* L17.
■ **owler** *noun* a person or ship engaged in owling L17.

owlery /ˈaʊləri/ *noun*. E19.
[from OWL *noun* + -ERY.]
1 A place where owls live or are kept. E19.
2 Owlishness. *rare*. M19.

owlet /ˈaʊlɪt/ *noun*. M16.
[from OWL *noun* + -ET¹. Cf. HOWLET.]
An owl; a young or small owl. Also *spec.*, any of several small owls of the genera *Glaucidium*, *Xenoglaux*, and *Athene*.
Comb.: **owlet-frogmouth**: see FROG *noun*¹; **owlet-moth** (chiefly *N. Amer.*) a noctuid moth; **owlet-nightjar** = ***owlet-frogmouth*** s.v. FROG *noun*¹.

owlish /ˈaʊlɪʃ/ *adjective*. E17.
[from OWL *noun* + -ISH¹.]
Resembling (that of) an owl; suggestive of an owl; *esp.* solemn.

> 🕮 *Times* Without being too owlish, we have to define . . romantic love. *Observer* A medium-sized man with owlish glasses.

■ **owlishly** *adverb* E20. **owlishness** *noun* L19.

own /əʊn/ *adjective & pronoun*. Also (*Scot.*) **ain** /eɪn/.
[Old English *āgen* pa. pple of OWE = Old Frisian *ēgen*, *ēin*, Old Saxon *ēgan*, Old High German *eigan* (Dutch, German *eigen*), Old Norse *eiginn*, from Germanic. Cf. NAIN, NOWN.]
▶**A** *adjective*. **1 a** Following a possess. or (now *arch. rare*) an article (latterly only indef.) or (in early use) without qualification: of or belonging to oneself or itself; individual, particular. Also (*rare*) in *superl.* with intensive force. Used to emphasize possession or ownership. OE.

▸**b** Following a possess. adjective: for or to oneself. Used to emphasize the identity of the subject. **LME.**
2 *spec.* Of a relative: related by blood and not marriage, adoption, etc. Now *arch. rare.* **ME.**

📖 **1a** W. D. WHITNEY Each should . . have an own name. T. HARDY The cottage . . had been built . . by the occupier's own hands. E. TEMPLETON Each social class has its own sort of suffering. J. D. SALINGER She wants her own Christmas tree ornaments . . not her mother's. **b** W. WINDHAM Gentlemen, who in the game-season . . became their own butchers and poulterers. SCOTT FITZGERALD He . . did his own reasoning without benefit of books. O. MANNING They had been told to bring their own food. R. INGALLS Once you've been your own boss, every other . . job seems servile. **2** C. MERIVALE Octavia was own sister to Octavius.

▸**B** *pronoun.* Following a possess.: that which belongs to a person; one's own possessions, kinsfolk, etc. **OE.**

📖 GEO. ELIOT Well, my own I will spare you all further ground for solicitude. THACKERAY Her teeth [were] as regular and bright as Lady Kew's own. F. L. WRIGHT I had an idea (it still seems to be my own). G. GREENE 'Got any testimonials?' 'I could hardly write my own, could I?' V. GLENDINNING The British army, like all the professions, looks after its own.

Phrases etc.: (A selection of cross-refs. only is included: see esp. other nouns.) **be one's own man, be one's own woman** (*a*) have command or control of oneself; be in full possession of one's senses, faculties, or powers; (*b*) be free to act, be independent. ***call one's own***: see CALL *verb*. **come into one's own** (*a*) get possession of one's rightful property; (*b*) achieve due recognition. **hold one's own** maintain one's position; not be defeated or lose strength. ***get one's own back (on), get some of one's own back (on)***: see GET *verb*. **of one's own** that is one's own; belonging to oneself (alone). **on one's own** (*a*) alone; (*b*) independently, without help. ***pick-your-own***: see PICK *verb*[1]. ***the Devil's own job***: see JOB *noun*[1].
Comb. & special collocations: **own brand** *noun & adjective* (designating) an article manufactured for a retailer and sold under the retailer's name; **own-categories** *adjective* designating a psychological test or technique in which the subject selects suitable categories for grading controversial statements so that his or her own emotional involvement may be assessed; **own goal** (*a*) a goal scored (usu. by mistake) against the scorer's own side; (*b*) an act or initiative having the unintended effect of harming one's own interests; **own-label** *adjective* own brand.

own /əʊn/ *verb.*
[Old English *āgnian*, formed as prec. Cf. OUGHT *verb*.]
†**1** *verb trans.* Make (a thing) one's own, appropriate, take or get possession of. **OE–ME.**
2 *verb trans.* Have or hold as one's own, be the proprietor of, possess. **OE.** ▸**b** HUNTING. Of a hound: show recognition of (the scent of a quarry). **L18.**
3 *verb trans.* Acknowledge as approved or accepted; accept, countenance. *arch.* **LME.**
†**4** *verb trans.* Acknowledge (a thing) as due to a person. Foll. by double obj. *rare.* **M16–L17.**
5 *verb trans.* **a** Acknowledge as or call one's own; *spec.* acknowledge paternity or authorship of. **E17.** ▸**b** Acknowledge or recognize as an acquaintance. *obsolete* exc. *dial.* **M17.** ▸†**c** Claim as being one's own. **M17–E19.**
6 *verb trans.* Acknowledge to be as claimed; admit or confess to be valid, true, or actual; *spec.* (*arch.*) acknowledge the supremacy or power of. **M17.** ▸**b** *verb intrans.* Admit, confess, *to*. **L18.** ▸**c** *verb intrans.* Foll. by *up*: confess frankly, make a full confession, (*to*). *colloq.* **M19.**

📖 **2** N. SEDAKA We picked her up . . in a borrowed car, as we didn't own one. A. SILLITOE He owned no property and lived by his labour. **3** MILTON Piracy become a project own'd and authoriz'd against the Subject. **5a** SHAKES. *Temp.* Two of these fellows you Must know and own. ANTHONY WOOD He hath also published little trivial things . . which he will not own. **b** S. PEPYS I . . met my Lord Chaimberlaine . . who owned and spoke to me. **6** SHELLEY Light, sound, and motion own the potent sway. R. L. STEVENSON I own myself an ass. E. M. FORSTER The ladies' voices grew animated, and—if the truth be owned—a little peevish. A. STORR He was extremely reluctant to own that he was indebted to other men's work. **b** P. LEVI I must own to having put off this poet. **c** H. CARPENTER If a boy broke any of his promises he was expected to own up. D. W. WINNICOTT Greed . . the thing we are all frightened to own up to.

owner /ˈəʊnə/ *noun.* **ME.**
[from prec. + -ER[1].]
1 A person who owns something; a proprietor; *spec.* a person who owns a racehorse. **ME.**
2 The captain of a ship or aircraft. *slang.* **E20.**

📖 **1** C. THUBRON They drove their family cars with the cautious pride of the owners. JULIETTE HUXLEY Emile was a vineyard owner.

Comb.: **owner-occupier** a person who owns the house or flat that he or she lives in.
■ **ownerless** *adjective* **E19.**

ownership /ˈəʊnəʃɪp/ *noun.* **L16.**
[from prec. + -SHIP.]
The fact or state of being an owner; legal right of possession; proprietorship.
public ownership: see PUBLIC *adjective*. ***social ownership***: see SOCIAL *adjective*.

owney-oh /ˈəʊnɪəʊ/ *pronoun. joc.* Also **ownio.** **E20.**
[Extension of OWN *pronoun* after the words of a popular song *Antonio & his Ice-cream Cart* (1907).]
on one's owney-oh, on one's own, alone.

ownhood /ˈəʊnhʊd/ *noun.* Now *rare.* **M17.**
[from OWN *adjective & pronoun* + -HOOD, translating German *Eigenheit*.]
PHILOSOPHY. The condition of considering oneself, one's will, etc., as one's own or at one's own disposal.

ownio *pronoun* var. of OWNEY-OH.

ownness /ˈəʊnnɪs/ *noun.* **M17.**
[from OWN *adjective* + -NESS.]
The fact or quality of being one's own or peculiar to oneself.

ownself /əʊnˈsɛlf/ *pronoun.* Long *arch. & dial.* **M17.**
[from OWN *adjective* + SELF *noun*, after *herself, oneself*, etc.]
One's own self.

📖 Z. N. HURSTON You know your ownself how looking backwards slows people up.

ownsome /ˈəʊns(ə)m/ *pronoun. colloq.* **M20.**
[from OWN *pronoun* after LONESOME *adjective*.]
on one's ownsome, on one's own, alone.

owt *pronoun* see AUGHT *pronoun*.

owzat /aʊˈzat/ *interjection.* Also **howzat** /haʊˈzat/. **L20.**
[Repr. a pronunc. Cf. ZAT.]
CRICKET. = ***how's that*** (b) s.v. HOW *adverb*.

ox /ɒks/ *noun.* Pl. **oxen** /ˈɒks(ə)n/.
[Old English *oxa* = Old Frisian *oxa*, Old Saxon, Old High German *ohso* (Dutch *os*, German *Ochse*), Old Norse *uxi, oxi*, Gothic *auhsa*, from Germanic, from Indo-European base repr. also by Sanskrit *ukṣán* bull.]
1 A large cloven-hoofed, freq. horned ruminant mammal, *Bos taurus*, derived from the extinct Eurasian aurochs and long domesticated for its milk, meat, and hide, and as a draught animal; a cow, a bull; freq. *spec.*, a castrated adult male of this animal, a steer; in *pl.*, cattle. **OE.**
2 Any bovine animal, *esp.* any of the genus *Bos*, as a zebu, a yak, or a gaur; a buffalo, a bison. **OE.**
3 *fig.* A fool, a stupid person; *esp.* a large clumsy person. **M16.**
4 An ancient Greek coin bearing a representation of an ox. *obsolete* exc. *Hist.* **E17.**
2 musk ox: see MUSK *noun*.
Phrases: **play the giddy ox** = *play the giddy* GOAT. **the black ox** misfortune, adversity; old age.
Comb.: **ox-beef** the flesh of an ox as food; **ox-berry** black bryony, *Tamus communis*; **oxbird** any of various shore-birds, *esp.* the dunlin; **ox-biter** (*a*) = ***ox-pecker*** below; (*b*) *US* = **cowbird** s.v. COW *noun*[1]; **ox-blood** *adjective & noun* (*a*) (of or resembling) the blood of an ox; (*b*) (of) a dark reddish brown; **ox-bot** = ***ox-warble*** (b) below; **ox-botfly** = ***ox-warble*** (a) below; **ox cart**: drawn by an ox; †**oxen-and-kine** any of several shore birds, *esp.* the ruff; **ox-fence** a strong fence for confining cattle; *spec.* one consisting of a hedge with a strong guard-rail on one side and (usu.) a ditch on the other; **ox-fenced** *adjective* provided with or surrounded by an ox-fence; **ox-foot** the foot of an ox, esp. as food; **ox-frame** a frame for holding oxen while they are being shod; **ox-gall** the gall of an ox, formerly used esp. in cleaning, painting, etc.; **ox-harrow** a large powerful harrow used on clay lands, (originally drawn by oxen); **ox-head** (*a*) the head of an ox; a representation of this, *spec.* as a symbol of cuckoldry; (*b*) *fig.* a stupid person; **ox-heart (cherry)** a large heart-shaped variety of cherry; **oxherd** a cowherd; **oxhide** *noun & adjective* (*a*) *noun* (leather made from) the hide of an ox; (*b*) *adjective* made of oxhide; **oxhouse** (now *dial.*) a shed for sheltering oxen; †**oxland** = OXGANG; **ox-pecker** either of two African birds of the starling family, *Buphagus africanus* and *B. erythrorhynchus*, which feed on skin parasites of cattle and other large mammals; **ox-ray** a large Indo-Pacific ray, *Mobula diabolus*; **oxtail** the tail of an ox, esp. as an ingredient in soups, stews, etc.; **oxtongue** (*a*) the tongue of an ox, esp. as food; (*b*) any of several plants with rough tongue-shaped leaves; *esp.* (more fully ***bristly oxtongue***) *Picris echioides*, a yellow-flowered plant of the composite family (cf. LANGUE DE BOEUF); **ox-warble** (*a*) (more fully ***ox-warble fly***) either of two flies of the family Oestridae, *Hypoderma bovis* and *H. lineatum*, whose larvae live under the skin of cattle; (*b*) a swelling on the back of an ox caused by the larva of the ox-warble fly; the larva itself.
■ **oxlike** *adjective* resembling (that of) an ox **E17.**

ox- *combining form* see OXA-, OXY-.

oxa- /ˈɒksə/ *combining form.* Before a vowel **ox-**. **E20.**
[from OX(Y- + *-a-*.]
ORGANIC CHEMISTRY. Denoting the presence of an oxygen atom regarded as replacing a methylene (·CH_2·) group.

oxacillin /ɒksəˈsɪlɪn/ *noun.* **M20.**
[from IS)OXA(ZOLE + PENI)CILLIN.]
PHARMACOLOGY. A semisynthetic penicillin, used as an alternative to methicillin, which can be taken orally. Also ***oxacillin sodium, sodium oxacillin***.

oxal- *combining form* see OXALO-.

oxalic /ɒkˈsalɪk/ *adjective.* **L18.**
[French *oxalique* from Latin OXALIS: see -IC.]
CHEMISTRY. ***oxalic acid***, a poisonous and intensely sour dicarboxylic acid, $(COOH)_2$, which occurs in wood sorrel and rhubarb and whose uses include bleaching and cleansing; ethanedioic acid.
■ **ˈoxalate** *noun & verb* (*a*) *noun* a salt or ester of oxalic acid; (*b*) *verb trans.* (MEDICINE) add an oxalate to (blood) to prevent coagulation: **L18.**

oxalis /ˈɒksəlɪs, ɒkˈsɑːlɪs/ *noun.* **E17.**
[Latin from Greek = sorrel, from *oxus* sour, acid (with ref. to the sharp-tasting leaves).]
Formerly, sorrel, *Rumex acetosa*. Now, any of various plants of the genus *Oxalis* (family Oxalidaceae), with delicate pentamerous flowers and usu. trifoliate leaves.

oxalo- /ˈɒksələʊ/ *combining form* of OXALIC: see -O-. Before a vowel also **oxal-**.
■ **oxaˈlacetate** *noun* the anion, or an ester or salt, of oxalacetic acid **L19.** **oxalaˈcetic** *adjective*: ***oxalacetic acid***, a dicarboxylic acid, HOOCC(OH)= CHCOOH, important in metabolism, esp. as the starting-point of the Krebs cycle **L19.** **oxaloˈacetate** *noun* = OXALACETATE **M20.** **oxaloaˈcetic** *adjective* = OXALACETIC **M20.** **oxaˈlosis** *noun* (MEDICINE) a rare metabolic disorder in which crystals of calcium oxalate are deposited in the kidneys and elsewhere, often causing death during childhood as a result of renal failure **M20.** **oxaloˈsuccinate** *noun* the anion, or an ester or salt, of oxalosuccinic acid **E20.** **oxalosucˈcinic** *adjective*: ***oxalosuccinic acid***, a tricarboxylic acid, $HOOC{\cdot}CO{\cdot}CH(COOH){\cdot}CH_2{\cdot}COOH$, which is an intermediate in the Krebs cycle **E20.** **oxaˈluria** *noun* (MEDICINE) the presence of excessive calcium oxalate in the urine **M19.** **oxalyl** /-laɪl, -lɪl/ *noun* the divalent radical $\cdot(CO)_2\cdot$ of oxalic acid **M19.**

oxamniquine /ɒkˈsamnɪkwiːn/ *noun.* **L20.**
[from OXY- + *-amni-* (perh. from AMINO-) + QUIN(OLIN)E.]
An anthelmintic drug given in the treatment of schistosomiasis.

oxathiin /ɒksəˈθʌɪɪn/ *noun.* **M20.**
[from OXA- + THIO- + -IN[1].]
CHEMISTRY. Any of a group of compounds (many of them fungicidal) whose molecule is a ring of one oxygen, one sulphur, and four carbon atoms.

oxazepam /ɒkˈseɪzɪpam, -ˈsazə-/ *noun.* **M20.**
[from OXY- + AZO- + -EPINE + AM(IDE).]
PHARMACOLOGY. A tricyclic tranquillizer given to relieve anxiety states and to control the withdrawal symptoms of alcoholism.
¶ A proprietary name for this drug is SERAX.

oxazine /ˈɒksəziːn/ *noun.* **L19.**
[from OXY- + AZO- + -INE[5].]
CHEMISTRY. Any compound whose molecule contains a ring of one nitrogen, one oxygen, and four carbon atoms; *spec.* (*a*) (more fully ***oxazine dye***) a dye of this kind derived from phenoxazine; (*b*) any of the group of monocyclic compounds of the formula C_4H_5NO.

oxazole /ˈɒksəzəʊl/ *noun.* **L19.**
[from OXY- + AZO- + -OLE[2].]
CHEMISTRY. A weakly basic heterocyclic compound, C_3H_3NO, which is a volatile liquid; a substituted derivative of this.
■ **oxazolidine** /-ˈzɒl-/ *noun* [-IDINE] any substituted derivative of the hypothetical heterocyclic compound C_3H_7NO, some of which are anticonvulsants **E20.** **oxazolone** /ɒkˈsaz-/ *noun* any compound containing the nucleus obtained by hydrogenating one of the double bonds of oxazole and replacing a methylene group by a carbonyl group **L19.**

oxbow /ˈɒksbəʊ/ *noun.* **ME.**
[from OX + BOW *noun*[1].]
1 A bow-shaped piece of wood forming a collar for a yoked ox, with the ends fastened to the yoke. **ME.**
2 A pronounced meander or horseshoe-shaped loop in a river. Also, the land within this. **L18.** ▸**b** In full ***oxbow lake***. A curved lake formed when a river cuts across the neck of an oxbow and the ends become silted up. **L19.**
Comb.: **oxbow key**: for fastening the end of an oxbow; ***oxbow lake***: see sense 2b above; **oxbow stirrup**: a bow-shaped stirrup.

Oxbridge /ˈɒksbrɪdʒ/ *noun & adjective.* **M19.**
[from Oxford + Cambridge (see below). Cf. CAMFORD.]
▸**A** *noun.* The universities of Oxford and Cambridge regarded together, esp. in contrast to other universities. **M19.**
▸**B** *attrib.* or as *adjective*. Of, pertaining to, or characteristic of Oxbridge. **M19.**
■ **Oxˈbridgean** *adjective & noun* (*a*) *adjective* = OXBRIDGE *adjective*; (*b*) *noun* a member or graduate of the universities of Oxford or Cambridge: **M20.**

oxen *noun* pl. of OX.

oxer /ˈɒksə/ *noun.* **M19.**
[from OX + -ER[1].]
An ox-fence; a fence resembling this; *spec.* in SHOWJUMPING, a jump consisting of a brush fence with a guard-rail on one side (more fully ***single oxer***) or both sides (more fully ***double oxer***).

ox-eye /ˈɒksʌɪ/ *noun.* **LME.**
[from OX + EYE *noun*.]
1 Any of various plants of the composite family with conspicuously rayed flowers; *esp.* (*a*) a central European plant, *Buphthalmum salicifolium*, grown for its bright yellow flowers; (*b*) (more fully ***yellow ox-eye***) the corn

marigold, *Chrysanthemum segetum*; (**c**) (more fully ***ox-eye daisy***) a plant of grassland, *Leucanthemum vulgare*, with large white-rayed flowers; (**d**) a N. American plant, *Heliopsis helianthoides*, resembling a sunflower. **LME.**

2 Any of various small hedge-birds, *esp.* the great tit. Also = ***oxbird*** s.v. **OX. L16.**

3 A small cloud presaging a violent storm, usu. appearing off the African coast. *Nautical slang*. **L16.**

4 An eye like that of an ox, a large protuberant eye. **L17**

Comb.: **ox-eye arch** an acutely pointed or Gothic arch; ***ox-eye daisy***: see sense 1 above; **ox-eye tarpon** an Indo-Pacific game-fish, *Megalops cyprinoides*.

■ **ox-eyed** *adjective* (**a**) having large protuberant eyes like those of an ox; (**b**) of the form of an acutely pointed or Gothic arch: **E17.**

Oxf. *abbreviation.*
Oxford.

Oxfam /ˈɒksfam/ *abbreviation.*
Oxford Committee for Famine Relief.

Oxford /ˈɒksfəd/ *adjective & noun.* **L16.**
[An English city in the SE Midlands.]
▶ **A** *adjective.* **1** Of or pertaining to Oxford University; characteristic of a member of the University; *spec.* (of manner, speech, etc.) overrefined, affected. **L16.**
2 Of, pertaining to, or associated with the city of Oxford. **M18.**

🕮 **1** D. H. LAWRENCE In a voice more expostulatingly Oxford than ever.

Special collocations: **Oxford bags** trousers cut very wide in the legs. **Oxford blue** (of) a dark occas. purple-tinged blue (adopted as the colour of Oxford University). **Oxford chrome** yellow ochre, formerly dug near Oxford. **Oxford clay** *GEOLOGY* a stiff blue fossiliferous Jurassic clay of central England. **Oxford cloth** (of) a heavy cotton cloth used chiefly for shirting. **Oxford corners** *TYPOGRAPHY* (now *Hist.*) ruled border lines crossing and extending slightly beyond each other at the corners. **Oxford Down** (an animal of) a breed of sheep produced by crossing Cotswold and Hampshire Down sheep. **Oxford frame** a picture-frame having sides which cross each other and project slightly at the corners. **Oxford grey** = ***Oxford mixture*** below. **Oxford Group (Movement)** a religious movement founded at Oxford University in 1921 by Frank Buchman (see **BUCHMANISM**), characterized by the discussion of personal problems by groups (cf. ***Moral Re-Armament*** s.v. **MORAL** *adjective*). **Oxford hollow** a flattened paper tube inserted between the spine of a book and its cover so as to strengthen the spine and allow the book to be opened flat more easily. **Oxford marmalade** a kind of coarse-cut marmalade. **Oxford mixture** (of) a kind of very dark grey woollen cloth. **Oxford Movement** *Hist.* a movement for the revival of Catholic doctrine and observance in the Church of England, begun at Oxford University in 1833. **Oxford ochre** = ***Oxford chrome*** above. **Oxford ragwort** a yellow-flowered plant of the composite family, *Senecio squalidus*, native to central and southern Europe and now widely naturalized in Britain after escaping from Oxford Botanic Garden. **Oxford sausage** a kind of skinless sausage. **Oxford scholar** *rhyming slang* a dollar. **Oxford School** *Hist.* the school of thought represented by the Oxford Movement. **Oxford shirt**: made of Oxford cloth. **Oxford shirting** = ***Oxford cloth*** above. **Oxford shoe** a low shoe laced over the instep. **Oxford Tracts** a series of pamphlets properly called 'Tracts for the Times', issued 1833–41 in advocacy of the principles of the Oxford Movement. **Oxford trousers** = ***Oxford bags*** above. **Oxford weed** ivy-leaved toadflax, *Cymbalaria muralis*.

▶ **B** *noun.* **1** (The members of) Oxford University. **L17.**
2 *ellipt.* Oxford mixture; an Oxford shoe; in *pl.*, Oxford bags. **M19.**

■ **Oxfordish** *adjective & noun* (**a**) *adjective* of, pertaining to, or characteristic of (a member of) Oxford University; (**b**) *noun* (*rare*) Oxford University slang: **M19. Oxfordism** *noun* (now *rare*) (**a**) a characteristic of or habit peculiar to a member of Oxford University; (**b**) *Hist.* the principles and practices of the Oxford Movement: **M19. Oxfordy** *adjective* = **OXFORDISH E20.**

Oxfordian /ɒksˈfɔːdɪən/ *adjective & noun.* **M19.**
[from prec. + **-IAN.**]
▶ **A** *adjective.* **1** *GEOLOGY.* Of, pertaining to, or designating (part of) a division of the Upper Jurassic. **M19.**
2 Of or pertaining to Oxford. **M20.**
3 Designating or pertaining to the theory that Edward de Vere (1550–1604), Earl of Oxford wrote the plays attributed to Shakespeare. **M20.**
▶ **B** *noun.* **1** *GEOLOGY.* The Oxfordian period. **M19.**
2 A supporter of the Oxfordian theory. **M20.**

oxgang /ˈɒksgaŋ/ *noun.* **OE.**
[from **OX** + **GANG** *noun.*]
Hist. A measure of land equivalent to an eighth of a carucate.

oxic /ˈɒksɪk/ *adjective.* **M20.**
[from **OX(IDE, OX(YGEN** + **-IC.**]
1 *SOIL SCIENCE.* Designating a subsurface mineral soil horizon more than 30 cm (approx. 12 inches) thick which lacks any weatherable materials and contains hydrated oxides of iron and aluminium, highly insoluble minerals such as quartz, and clays of the kaolinite type. **M20.**
2 [Back-form. from **ANOXIC.**] Involving, characterized by, or related to the presence of oxygen. **L20.**

†oxid *noun* see **OXIDE.**

oxidable /ˈɒksɪdəb(ə)l/ *adjective.* Now *rare.* **L18.**
[French (now *oxydable*), from *oxider*: see **OXIDATE, -ABLE.**]
CHEMISTRY. Oxidizable.
■ **oxidaˈbility** *noun* **E19.**

oxidant /ˈɒksɪd(ə)nt/ *noun.* **L19.**
[French (now *oxydant*), from *oxider*: see **OXIDATE, -ANT**[1].]
= **OXIDIZER.**

oxidase /ˈɒksɪdeɪz/ *noun.* **L19.**
[French *oxydase*, from *oxyde* **OXIDE**: see **-ASE.**]
BIOCHEMISTRY. Orig., any oxidoreductase. Now, one which reacts with molecular oxygen, *esp.* one catalysing the transfer of hydrogen from a substrate to oxygen to form water or hydrogen peroxide.
MONOAMINE *oxidase*.

oxidate /ˈɒksɪdeɪt/ *verb.* Now *rare.* **L18.**
[from French *oxider* + **-ATE**[3].]
CHEMISTRY. **1** *verb trans.* = **OXIDIZE** 1. **L18.**
2 *verb intrans.* = **OXIDIZE** 2. **E19.**

oxidation /ɒksɪˈdeɪʃ(ə)n/ *noun.* **L18.**
[French (now *oxydation*), formed as prec.: see **-ATION.**]
CHEMISTRY. The action or process of oxidizing; the loss or removal of hydrogen from a compound, or of an electron from an atom or molecule; an increase in the proportion of electronegative constituents in a molecule or compound. Opp. **REDUCTION** 8a.

🕮 H. DAVY A deep grey metallic powder, which became brown by oxidation. B. D. PORRITT The oxidation of rubber . . is technically known as 'perishing'.

Comb.: **oxidation number** the charge (expressed in units of the negative of the electron charge) which is assigned to an atom on the assumption that the bonding in the substance or radical containing it is completely ionic; the average formal charge so assigned to atoms of a particular element in a compound or radical; **oxidation potential** the electrode potential required to bring about a particular oxidation reaction at the electrode; **oxidation-reduction** = **REDOX** (freq. *attrib.*); **oxidation state** oxidation number; the state of having a particular oxidation number.

■ **ˈoxidative** *adjective* involving, pertaining to, or characterized by oxidation; ***oxidative phosphorylation*** (*BIOCHEMISTRY*), the synthesis of ATP from ADP and phosphate ions in mitochondria, utilizing energy produced in oxidative reactions: **L19. ˈoxidatively** *adverb* by an oxidative process **M20.**

oxide /ˈɒksʌɪd/ *noun.* Also **†-id**, **†-yde**. **L18.**
[French (now *oxyde*), formed as **OXYGEN** + *-ide* after *acide* **ACID** *adjective, noun.*]
CHEMISTRY. A compound of oxygen with another element or with an organic radical.
aluminium oxide, ***ethylene oxide***, ***nitric oxide***, ***nitrous oxide***, etc.

oxidize /ˈɒksɪdʌɪz/ *verb.* Also **-ise**. **E19.**
[from prec. + **-IZE.**]
CHEMISTRY. **1** *verb trans.* Cause to combine with oxygen or to undergo oxidation; remove an electron from; convert into an oxide; *spec.* cover (metal) with a coating of oxide, make (metal) rusty. Opp. **REDUCE** 10c. **E19.**
2 *verb intrans.* Become combined with oxygen; undergo oxidation; *spec.* (of metal) become coated with rust. **E19.**

🕮 **1** N. G. CLARK The organic carbon is oxidized to carbon dioxide. **2** W. HENRY A piece of zinc, immersed under water which is freely exposed to the atmosphere, oxidizes very slowly.

■ **oxidizaˈbility** *noun* the property of being oxidizable **L19. oxidizable** *adjective* able to be oxidized **E19. oxidiˈzation** *noun* = **OXIDATION E19. †oxidizement** *noun* = **OXIDATION E–M19. oxidizer** *noun* a substance that oxidizes another, an oxidizing agent; *spec.* one used to support the combustion of fuel in a rocket engine or fuel cell: **L19.**

oxidoreduction /ˌɒksɪdəʊrɪˈdʌkʃ(ə)n/ *noun.* **M20.**
[from **OXID(ATION** + **-O-** + **REDUCTION.**]
BIOCHEMISTRY. A process in which one substance is oxidized and electrons from it reduce another substance.
■ **oxidoreductase** *noun* an enzyme which catalyses oxidoreduction **E20. oxidoreductive** *adjective* involving oxidoreduction **M20.**

†oxidulated *adjective.* Also (earlier) **oxy-**. **E–M19.**
[French †*oxidulé*, from *oxidule* protoxide, dim. of *oxyde* **OXIDE** after Latin *acidus*, *acidulus*: see **-ULE, -ATE**[2], **-ED**[1].]
CHEMISTRY. Combined with a smaller proportion of oxygen than in another compound.
oxidulated iron magnetite.
■ Also **†oxidulous** *adjective* **E–M19.**

oxime /ˈɒksiːm/ *noun.* **L19.**
[from **OX(Y-** + **IM(ID)E.**]
CHEMISTRY. Any compound containing the group :C=N(OH). Cf. **ALDOXIME, KETOXIME.**

oximeter /ɒkˈsɪmɪtə/ *noun.* Also **oxy-**. **M19.**
[from **OX(Y-** + **-IMETER.**]
MEDICINE. An instrument for measuring the proportion of oxygenated haemoglobin in the blood.
■ **oxiˈmetric** *adjective* employing an oximeter **M20. oximetry** *noun* the use of an oximeter **M20.**

oxine /ˈɒksiːn/ *noun.* **E20.**
[German *Oxin*, from *Oxychinolin* hydroxyquinoline.]
CHEMISTRY. A crystalline phenol, C_9H_7NO, which forms water-insoluble complexes with many metal ions and is used in analysis and as a deodorant and antibacterial agent; 8-hydroxyquinoline.

Oxisol /ˈɒksɪsɒl/ *noun.* **M20.**
[from **OXIC** + **-SOL.**]
SOIL SCIENCE. A soil of an order comprising stable, highly weathered, tropical mineral soils with oxic horizons.

oxlip /ˈɒkslɪp/ *noun.* **OE.**
[from **OX** + **SLIP** *noun*[1]: cf. **COWSLIP.**]
Any of several kinds of *Primula* having flowers in a stalked umbel like the cowslip, *P. veris*, but larger and paler; orig. (more fully ***false oxlip***), the hybrid between the cowslip and the primrose, *P. vulgaris*; later (more fully ***true Bardfield oxlip***, ***Bardfield oxlip***), *P. elatior*, a woodland species restricted in Britain to Essex and parts of East Anglia.

oxo- /ˈɒksəʊ/ *combining form.* Before a vowel occas. **ox-**. Also as attrib. adjective **oxo**. **E20.**
[from **OX(YGEN**: see **-O-.**]
CHEMISTRY. **1** Designating or containing an oxygen atom linking two other atoms. Now *rare*.
2 Containing one or more oxygen atoms bonded to another atom; *spec.* in *ORGANIC CHEMISTRY*, denoting the presence of a carbonyl group.
3 (Freq. **OXO, Oxo.**) Designating or pertaining to the hydroformylation process or reaction.

Oxon /ˈɒks(ə)n, -sɒn/ *noun & adjective.* Also **Oxon.** (point). **L15.**
[from *Oxoniensis* or (as noun) its source *Oxonia*: see next.]
▶ **A** *noun.* Orig., the city, diocese, or university of Oxford. Now usu., the county of Oxfordshire. **L15.**
▶ **B** *adjective.* Of Oxford University. **L17.**

Oxonian /ɒkˈsəʊnɪən/ *noun & adjective.* **M16.**
[from *Oxonia* Latinized form of Old English *Ox(e)naford* **OXFORD**: see **-AN, -IAN.**]
▶ **A** *noun.* **1** A native or inhabitant of Oxford; *spec.* a member of Oxford University. **M16.**
2 A kind of shoe with a buttoned instep. **M19.**
▶ **B** *adjective.* Of or pertaining to Oxford or (*spec.*) Oxford University. **M17.**

oxonium /ɒkˈsəʊnɪəm/ *noun.* **L19.**
[from **OXY-** after *ammonium*.]
CHEMISTRY. The hydroxonium ion, H_3O^+; any analogue of this in which one or more of the hydrogen atoms are replaced by organic radicals. Usu. in *comb.*

oxosteroid /ɒksəʊˈstɪərɔɪd, -ˈstɛrɔɪd/ *noun.* **M20.**
[from **OXO-** + **STEROID.**]
BIOCHEMISTRY. = **KETOSTEROID.**

oxotremorine /ɒksəʊˈtrɛməriːn/ *noun.* **M20.**
[from **OXO-** + **TREMORINE.**]
BIOCHEMISTRY. An oxidized metabolite of tremorine, which can induce the symptoms of Parkinsonism and is used in research into this disease.

oxprenolol /ɒksˈprɛnəlɒl/ *noun.* **M20.**
[from **OX(Y-** + *-pren-* (cf. **ISOPRENALINE**) + **-OL**, redupl. after **PROPRANOLOL.**]
PHARMACOLOGY. An adrenergic blocking agent, $C_{15}H_{23}NO_3$, used mainly to treat cardiac arrhythmia, angina, and hypertension.

oxter /ˈɒkstə/ *noun & verb.* Chiefly *Scot., Anglo-Irish, & north.*
[Old English *ōxta*, *ōhsta*, from base also of Old English *ōxn* = Old High German *ōchasa* (Dutch *oksel*), *ahsala* (German *Achsel*), cogn. with Latin **AXILLA**: extended in late Middle English by *-er* suffix.]
▶ **A** *noun.* The armpit; the underside of the upper arm. Also, the corresponding part of an animal's forelimb. **OE.**
▶ **B** *verb trans.* Support by the arm, walk arm in arm with; put one's arm around. **L18.**

oxy- /ˈɒksi/ *combining form.* Before a vowel also **ox-**. In sense 2 also as attrib. adjective **oxy**.
[Greek *oxu-* combining form of *oxus* sharp, acute, acid, etc.; in sense 2 extracted from **OXYGEN.**]
1 Sharp, keen, acute; pungent, acid.
2 Oxygen. Formerly also = **HYDROXY-.**
■ **oxyaˈcetylene** *noun* a flammable mixture of oxygen and acetylene, used esp. in blowlamps (usu. *attrib.*) **E20. oxy-arc** *noun* (*ENGINEERING*) an arc struck between a workpiece and a hollow electrode through which the oxygen is piped, used in cutting metals (usu. *attrib.*) **M20. oxyˈbromide** *noun* = **BROMATE M19. oxyˈcellulose** *noun* any of various substances obtained by oxidation of cellulose, some of which are used in medical gauze and lint **L19. oxycephalic** /-sɪˈfal-, -kɛˈfal-/ *adjective* (*MEDICINE*) having or designating a skull of (abnormally) pointed or conical shape **L19. oxyˈcephaly** *noun* (*MEDICINE*) oxycephalic condition **L19. oxyˈchloride** *noun* a salt containing oxygen and chlorine; *spec.* = **CHLORATE: M19. oxy-gas** *noun* a flammable mixture of oxygen and another gas (esp. natural gas or coal gas) (usu. *attrib.*) **M20. oxygon** *noun* (now *rare* or *obsolete*) an acute-angled triangle **L16. oxyhaemoˈglobin**, ***-hem-*** *noun* the oxygenated form of haemoglobin **L19. oxy-ˈhelium** *noun* a mixture of oxygen and helium, used as a breathing mixture in deep-sea diving **M20.**

oxy-ˈhydrogen *noun* a flammable mixture of oxygen and hydrogen, used in brazing metals etc. (usu. *attrib.*) M19. **oxyluˈciferin** *noun* (BIOCHEMISTRY) the oxidized form of a luciferin produced by the action of luciferase E20. †**oxymuriate** *noun* (CHEMISTRY) a chloride; a chlorate: L18–M19. †**oxymuriatic** *adjective* (CHEMISTRY): ***oxymuriatic acid***, ***oxymuriatic gas***, chlorine (as a supposed compound of oxygen and hydrochloric ('muriatic') acid) L18–M19. **oxymyoˈglobin** *noun* the oxidized form of myoglobin M20. **oxyphil(e)** *adjective* = ACIDOPHIL(E) L19. **oxyˈphilic** *adjective* = ACIDOPHIL(E) E20. **oxyphilous** /ɒkˈsɪfɪləs/ *adjective* = ACIDOPHIL(E) L19. **oxyˈphosphate** *noun* (CHEMISTRY) a salt containing hydroxide and phosphate anions; *esp.* hydrated zinc phosphate, used in dental cements: E19. **oxyˈproline** *noun* = HYDROXYPROLINE E20. **oxy-ˈpropane** *noun* a flammable mixture of oxygen and propane (usu. *attrib.*) M20. **oxy-salt** *noun* (CHEMISTRY) a salt containing oxygen and another anion; a salt of an oxyacid: M19. **oxyˈsulphide** *noun* (CHEMISTRY) a compound containing oxygen and sulphur; now usu. *spec.* a compound oxide and sulphide of a metal: M19.

oxyacid /ˈɒksɪˌasɪd/ *noun.* M19.
[from OXY- + ACID *noun*.]
1 CHEMISTRY. An acid whose molecules contain oxygen, e.g. sulphuric acid, H_2SO_4. Cf. HYDRACID. M19.
2 ORGANIC CHEMISTRY. A carboxylic acid with at least one hydroxyl group in its molecule. Usu. in *pl.* Now *rare* or *obsolete*. L19.

oxyanion /ɒksɪˈanʌɪən/ *noun.* M20.
[from OXY- + ANION.]
CHEMISTRY. An anion containing one or more atoms each linked to one or more oxygen atoms.

oxybaphon /ɒkˈsɪbəf(ə)n/ *noun.* Pl. **-pha** /-fə/. L17.
[Greek *oxubaphon* vinegar-saucer, formed as OXY- + *baph-* stem of *baptein* dip.]
†**1** A sour or acidic liquid. Only in L17.
2 GREEK ANTIQUITIES. A bell-shaped cup or vase. M19.

†**oxycrate** *noun.* L16–M18.
[Greek *oxukrat-*, formed as OXY- + *-kratos* (in comb.) mixed.]
A mixture of vinegar and water.

†**oxyde** *noun*, †**oxydulated** *adjective* see OXIDE, OXIDULATED.

oxygen /ˈɒksɪdʒ(ə)n/ *noun.* L18.
[French (sc. *principe*) *oxygène* acidifying principle (oxygen being orig. supposed an essential component of acids): see OXY-, -GEN.]
A non-metallic chemical element, atomic no. 8, which as a colourless odourless gas (O_2) makes up about 20 per cent of the air, is essential for aerobic respiration, and is the chief agent of combustion, rusting of metals, etc., and which is combined with hydrogen to form water, with carbon in organic compounds, and with most elements to form the majority of the earth's minerals. (Symbol O.)
Comb.: **oxygen acid** = OXYACID; **oxygen bar** a place where customers pay to inhale oxygen for therapeutic effects; **oxygen debt**, **oxygen deficit** PHYSIOLOGY the condition or degree of temporary oxygen shortage in the tissues arising from exercise; **oxygen lance** (*a*) a thermic lance that uses oxygen; (*b*) see LANCE *noun* 7b; **oxygen mask** an apparatus fitting over the nose and mouth through which oxygen or oxygen-enriched air is supplied to relieve breathing difficulties or hypoxia; **oxygen tent** MEDICINE a tentlike enclosure placed over a patient and containing an oxygen-enriched atmosphere.
■ **oxygenless** *adjective* containing no oxygen M20.

oxygenase /ˈɒksɪdʒəneɪz/ *noun.* E20.
[from OXYGEN + -ASE.]
BIOCHEMISTRY. Orig., an oxidase producing hydrogen peroxide. Now, an enzyme which catalyses the incorporation of molecular oxygen into a substrate.

oxygenate /ˈɒksɪdʒəneɪt, ɒkˈsɪdʒ-/ *verb.* L18.
[from OXYGEN + -ATE[3], after French *oxygéner*.]
1 *verb trans.* Supply, treat, mix, or combine with oxygen; charge or impregnate (esp. the blood) with oxygen. Formerly also, oxidize. Freq. as ***oxygenated*** *ppl adjective*. L18.
2 *verb intrans.* Become oxygenated; absorb or combine with oxygen. L20.

> 🕮 **1** *fig.*: *Pall Mall Gazette* A much needed oxygenating of the life-blood of the nation.

■ †**oxygenant** *noun* (CHEMISTRY) an oxidizing agent E–M19. **oxygeˈnation** *noun* the action of oxygenating; the condition of being oxygenated: L18. **oxygenator** *noun* an apparatus for oxygenating something, esp. water or blood; an aquatic plant providing oxygen for an aquarium, pond, etc.: M19.

oxygenic /ɒksɪˈdʒɛnɪk/ *adjective.* M19.
[from OXYGEN + -IC, or (in sense 2) -GENIC.]
1 CHEMISTRY. Consisting of or containing oxygen. *rare.* M19.
2 BIOLOGY. Esp. of photosynthesis and photosynthetic organisms: generating oxygen. L20.

oxygenize /ˈɒksɪdʒənʌɪz/ *verb trans.* Now *rare* or *obsolete*. Also **-ise**. E19.
[from OXYGEN + -IZE.]
= OXYGENATE *verb* 1. Chiefly as ***oxygenized*** *ppl adjective*.

oxygenous /ɒkˈsɪdʒɪnəs/ *adjective.* L18.
[formed as OXYGEN + -OUS.]
Orig., producing acids, acidifying. Now, consisting of or containing oxygen.
†**oxygenous gas** oxygen.

oxylith /ˈɒksɪlɪθ/ *noun.* Now *rare* or *obsolete*. Also **-lithe**. E20.
[French *oxylithe*, formed as OXY- + -LITH.]
Calcium peroxide, as used in breathing apparatus to provide oxygen by reaction with carbon dioxide.

oxymel /ˈɒksɪmɛl/ *noun.* Now *Hist.* LME.
[Latin (also *oxymeli*) from Greek *oxumeli*, formed as OXY- + *meli* honey.]
A medicinal drink or syrup of vinegar and honey.

oxymeter *noun* var. of OXIMETER.

oxymoron /ɒksɪˈmɔːrɒn/ *noun.* M17.
[Greek *oxumōron* use as noun of neut. sing. of *oxumōros* pointedly foolish, from *oxus* (see OXY-) + *mōros* foolish (see MORON).]
A rhetorical figure of speech in which markedly contradictory terms appear in conjunction so as to emphasize the statement; *gen.* a contradiction in terms.

> 🕮 *New Yorker* That familiar oxymoron a weak tyrant.

■ **oxymoˈronic** *adjective* of or pertaining to an oxymoron; incongruous, self-contradictory: L20. **oxymoˈronically** *adverb* E20.

oxyntic /ɒkˈsɪntɪk/ *adjective.* L19.
[from Greek *oxunteos*, verbal adjective of *oxunein* sharpen, make acid, formed as OXY-: see -IC.]
ANATOMY. Designating (a secretory cell of) any of the gastric glands in the main part of the stomach which produce hydrochloric acid.

oxyrhynchus /ɒksɪˈrɪŋkəs/ *noun.* E17.
[Greek *oxurrugkhos* sharp-snouted, formed as OXY- + *rhugkhos* snout.]
A fish with a pointed snout; *spec.* a mormyrid fish, *Mormyrus kannume*, of the River Nile, venerated by the ancient Egyptians.

†**oxyrrhodin** *noun.* Also **-rhod**. M16–M18.
[mod. Latin *oxyrrhodinum* from Greek *oxurrodinon*, formed as OXY- + *rhodinos*: see RHODINOL.]
A medicinal preparation of vinegar and oil of roses.

oxytetracycline /ˌɒksɪtɛtrəˈsʌɪkliːn/ *noun.* M20.
[from OXY- + TETRACYCLINE.]
PHARMACOLOGY. The 5-hydroxy derivative of tetracycline, produced by the bacterium *Streptomyces rimosus* and used as a broad-spectrum antibiotic.
¶ A proprietary name for this drug is TERRAMYCIN.

oxytocic /ɒksɪˈtəʊsɪk/ *noun & adjective.* M19.
[from Greek *oxutokia* sudden delivery, formed as OXY- + *tokos* childbirth: see -IC.]
MEDICINE. ▶**A** *noun.* A drug which causes uterine contraction and hence induces or accelerates labour. M19.
▶**B** *adjective.* Of the nature of or pertaining to an oxytocic. L19.

oxytocin /ɒksɪˈtəʊsɪn/ *noun.* E20.
[from prec. + -IN[1].]
MEDICINE. A mammalian pituitary hormone which stimulates contraction of the uterus and the milk ducts, and is synthesized for use in inducing and accelerating labour and controlling postnatal bleeding.
■ **oxytocinase** *noun* an enzyme which inactivates oxytocin M20.

oxytone /ˈɒksɪtəʊn/ *noun & adjective.* M18.
[Greek *oxutonos*, formed as OXY- + *tonos* pitch, accent, TONE *noun*.]
Chiefly GREEK GRAMMAR. (A word) having an acute accent on the last syllable.

oxytonic /ɒksɪˈtɒnɪk/ *adjective.* M20.
[from prec. + -IC.]
Characterized by an oxytone; *esp.* designating a language in which the majority of words are oxytones.
■ **oxytonical** *adjective* L19.

oxytropis /ɒkˈsɪtrəpɪs/ *noun.* Also Anglicized as **oxytrope** /ˈɒksɪtrəʊp/ M19.
[mod. Latin (see below), formed as OXY- + *tropis* keel.]
Any of various freq. alpine leguminous plants of the genus *Oxytropis* (allied to *Astragalus*), with pinnate leaves and racemes of flowers, often purple or yellow.

oxyuris /ɒksɪˈjʊərɪs/ *noun.* Pl. **-rides** /-rɪdiːz/. M19.
[mod. Latin genus (or subgenus) name.]
ZOOLOGY. A pinworm. Chiefly as mod. Latin genus (or subgenus) name.

oy *noun*[1] var. of OE.

oy /ɔɪ/ *interjection*[1], *noun*[2], & *verb.* M18.
[Natural exclam. Cf. HOY *interjection, verb, & noun*[2].]
▶**A** *interjection & noun.* (A cry) attracting attention. M18.
▶**B** *verb intrans.* Cry 'oy!' E19.

oy /ɔɪ/ *interjection*[2]. Also **oi**. L19.
[Yiddish.]
Used by Yiddish-speakers as an exclamation of dismay, grief, etc. Also ***oy vay***, ***oy vey*** /veɪ/ [Yiddish *vey* woe].

oyama /əʊˈjɑːmə/ *noun.* Pl. same. M20.
[Japanese.]
= ONNAGATA.

oyer /ˈɔɪə/ *noun.* LME.
[Anglo-Norman = Old French *oïr*: see next, -ER[4].]
LAW. **1** The hearing of a case. Only in ***oyer and determiner***, ***oyer determiner***, ***oyer and terminer*** below. LME.
2 A criminal trial held under the commission of oyer and terminer (see below). LME.
3 *Hist.* The hearing of a document read in court, esp. an instrument in writing pleaded by one party in a suit. E17.
Phrases: **oyer and determiner**, **oyer determiner** (*obsolete* exc. *Hist.*) = ***oyer and terminer*** (a), (b) below. **oyer and terminer** (*a*) (in full ***commission of oyer and terminer***, ***writ of oyer and terminer***) a commission authorizing a judge on circuit to hold courts (formerly only for the hearing of certain specified offences); †(*b*) = sense 2 above; (*c*) a court of higher criminal jurisdiction in some States of the US.

oyez /əʊˈjɛs, -ˈjɛz, -ˈjeɪ/ *verb & noun.* Also **oyes** /əʊˈjɛs/. LME.
[Anglo-Norman, Old French (also *oiez*) imper. pl. of *oïr* (mod. *ouïr*) from Latin *audire* hear.]
▶**A** *verb intrans.* (*imper.*). Listen! 'Hear ye!' Uttered (usu. three times) by a public crier or a court officer to command silence and attention. LME.
▶**B** *noun.* Pl. same, †**oyesses**. A call or cry of 'oyez!' LME.

-oyl /əʊʌɪl, ɔɪl/ *suffix.*
[from -O(IC + -YL.]
ORGANIC CHEMISTRY. Forming names of acid radicals from names of the corresponding carboxylic acids ending in *-ic* or *-oic*, as ***benzoyl***, ***fumaroyl***.

oyster /ˈɔɪstə/ *noun, verb, & adjective.* ME.
[Old French *oistre*, *uistre* (mod. *huître*) from Latin *ostrea*, *ostreum* from Greek *ostreon* rel. to *osteon* bone, *ostrakon* shell, tile. Cf. OSTRACIZE.]
▶**A** *noun.* **1** Any of various bivalve molluscs of the family Ostreidae, several of which are eaten (esp. raw) as a delicacy and may be farmed for food or pearls; *esp.* the common European *Ostrea edulis*, and members of the widespread genus *Crassostrea*. Also (usu. with specifying word), any of various similar bivalves. ME. ▸**b** *fig.* A thing regarded as containing all one desires. Esp. in ***the world is one's oyster***. L16. ▸**c** *fig.* A reserved or uncommunicative person. E20. ▸**d** A type of unmoored submarine mine detonated magnetically or acoustically as a vessel passes over it. Freq. *attrib.* M20.
2 An oyster-shaped piece of meat in the front hollow of the side bone of a fowl, esp. a chicken. M19.
3 A greyish-white colour resembling that of an oyster. E20.
4 Any of the cross-sections of wood in an oyster-veneer. E20.
1 ***mangrove oyster***, ***Olympia oyster***, ***pearl oyster***, ***saddle-oyster***, ***thorny oyster***, etc.
Phrases: **green oyster** a cultivated oyster fed on diatoms. MOUNTAIN **oyster**. PRAIRIE **oyster**. **vegetable oyster** salsify (see ***oyster-plant*** (b) below).
Comb.: **oyster-bank** (*a*) a part of the seabed where oysters breed or are bred; (*b*) GEOLOGY a layer or stratum containing fossil oysters; **oyster bar** (*a*) = ***oyster-bank*** (a) above; (*b*) a bar at which oysters are served as food; **oyster-bed** = ***oyster-bank*** above; **oyster blenny** a blenny of the western Pacific, *Petroscirtes anolius*, which lives in empty oyster-shells; **oyster-boat**: used in oyster-fishing or oyster-farming; **oyster-brood** the spat of oysters in its second year; **oyster-cellar** *Hist.* a shop (orig. in a basement) selling oysters; ***oyster drill***: see DRILL *noun*[2] 1b; **oyster-farm** an area of the seabed where oysters are bred for food or pearls; **oyster-farmer** a person engaged in oyster-farming; **oyster-farming** the breeding and rearing of oysters for food or pearls; **oyster-fish** any of various fishes which frequent oyster-beds, *esp.* (*a*) = ***oyster toadfish*** s.v. TOADFISH 3; (*b*) the tautog; **oyster-grass** any of various seaweeds, *esp.* sea lettuce, *Ulva lactuca*; **oyster-knife** a strong knife adapted for opening oysters; ***oyster loaf***: see LOAF *noun*[1]; **oyster-man** a man who gathers or sells oysters; **oyster mushroom** an edible fungus, *Pleurotus ostreatus*, which grows on trees; **oyster-piece** a piece of oyster-veneer; **oyster-plant** (*a*) a glaucous plant of northern beaches, *Mertensia maritima*, of the borage family, with cymes of tubular blue flowers; (*b*) salsify, *Tragopogon porrifolius*, whose roots are said to taste like oysters; **oyster-plover** = OYSTERCATCHER; **oyster roast** *US* a social gathering at which oysters are roasted and eaten; **oyster-shaped** *adjective* of the shape of an oyster; of irregular rounded shape, tapered slightly at one end; ***oyster toadfish***: see TOADFISH 3; **oyster-tongs**: used for gathering oysters in shallow water and having inward-bending teeth and long handles; **oyster-veneer** a whorled veneer obtained esp. from small boughs of trees (freq. *attrib.*); **oyster-veneered** *adjective* made in oyster-veneer; **oyster-white** *noun & adjective* (of) a greyish-white colour; **oyster-woman** a woman who gathers or sells oysters.
▶**B** *verb intrans.* Fish for or gather oysters. M17.
▶**C** *adjective.* Of a greyish-white colour. L19.

> 🕮 J. CANNAN A handsome dress of oyster satin.

■ **oysterage** *noun* an oyster-bed M19. **oysterer** *noun* (*a*) a person who gathers or sells oysters; (*b*) an oyster-boat: E17. **oystering** *noun* (*a*) the action of the verb; (*b*) (work done with) oyster-veneer: M17. **oysterish** *adjective* resembling (that of) an oyster M19. **oyster-like** *adjective* (*a*) resembling (that of) an oyster; (*b*) *fig.* reserved, uncommunicative: L18. **oysterous** *adjective* resembling an oyster, esp. in colour M19. **oystery** *adjective* (*a*) having many oysters; (*b*) having the quality of an oyster: M19.

oystercatcher /ˈɔɪstəkatʃə/ *noun*. M18.
[from OYSTER + CATCHER.]
A wading shore-bird of the genus *Haematopus* (family Haematopodidae), with black or black and white plumage and brilliant red bill and feet; *esp.* the common European *Haematopus ostralegus* and the N. American *H. palliatus*.

oyster-shell /ˈɔɪstəʃɛl/ *noun*. LME.
[from OYSTER *noun* + SHELL *noun*.]
1 A shell of an oyster. LME.
2 More fully ***oyster-shell veneer***. = ***oyster-veneer*** s.v. OYSTER *noun*. E20.
Comb.: **oyster-shell scale** *N. Amer.* (the disease caused by) a scale insect, *Lepidosaphes ulmi*, which attacks many trees and shrubs, including commercial fruit and hardwood trees; ***oyster-shell veneer***: see sense 2 above.

Oz /ɒz/ *noun & adjective*. *slang* (chiefly *Austral.*). E20.
[Repr. pronunc. of abbreviation of *Australia*, *Australian*: cf. OZZIE.]
▶ **A** *noun*. Australia; an Australian. E20.
▶ **B** *adjective*. Australian. L20.

oz. *abbreviation*.
[Italian *onza*.]
Ounce(s).

ozaena /əʊˈziːnə/ *noun*. Also ***ozena**. LME.
[Latin from Greek *ozaina*, from *ozein* to smell.]
MEDICINE. A fetid discharge from the nose due to ulceration and atrophy of the mucous membrane and bone.

Ozalid /ˈɒzəlɪd, ˈɒz-/ *noun*. E20.
[from reversal of DIAZO with insertion of *l*.]
(Proprietary name for) a diazo copying process in which the paper coating contains both the coupler and the diazonium salt, so that the image develops on exposure to ammonia; a photocopy produced by this process.

Ozark /ˈəʊzɑːk/ *noun & adjective*. Also **Os-**. E19.
[French *Aux Arcs*, early French trading post among the Quapaw, *Arcs* abbreviation formed as ARKANSAS.]
▶ **A** *noun*. Pl. same, **-s**.
1 A member of a division of Quapaw Indians. E19.
2 ***the Ozarks***, the Ozark Mountains. E20.
▶ **B** *adjective*. **1** Of or pertaining to the Ozark. E19.
2 *spec.* Designating or pertaining to the mountains or the region in which the Ozark lived. M19.
■ **Ozarker** *noun* a native or inhabitant of the Ozark region E20. **Oˈzarkian** *noun & adjective* (*a*) *noun* = OZARKER; the American English dialect of the Ozarkers; (*b*) *adjective* = OZARK *adjective* 2: E20.

ozena *noun* see OZAENA.

ozocerite /əʊˈzɒsərʌɪt, əʊzəˈsɪərʌɪt/ *noun*. Also (earlier) **ozokerite** /-ˈzɒk-, -zəˈkɪər-/. M19.
[German *Ozokerit*, from Greek *ozein* to smell + *kēros* beeswax: see -ITE[1].]
MINERALOGY. A brown or black natural paraffin wax occurring in some bituminous shales and sandstones and formerly used to make candles, polishes, electrical insulators, etc.

ozonation /əʊzəˈneɪʃ(ə)n/ *noun*. M19.
[from OZONE + -ATION.]
CHEMISTRY. Ozonization.

ozone /ˈəʊzəʊn/ *noun*. M19.
[from Greek *ozein* to smell + -ONE.]
CHEMISTRY. An allotropic form of oxygen, a bluish toxic gas, O_3, with a characteristic sharp odour, produced from molecular oxygen by electrical discharge and in the upper atmosphere by ultraviolet light, and formerly supposed to have a tonic effect. Also (*colloq.*), fresh invigorating air.
Comb.: **ozone-friendly** *adjective* not containing or producing substances (such as chlorofluorocarbons) thought to deplete the ozone layer; **ozone hole** a region of marked abnormal attenuation of the ozone layer, esp. seasonally above the poles; **ozone layer** (the ozone present in) the ozonosphere.
■ **ozoned** *adjective* supplied with ozone E20. **ozoneless** *adjective* having no ozone L19. **ozonic** /əʊˈzɒnɪk/ *adjective* of the nature of, pertaining to, or containing ozone M19. **ozoˈniferous** *adjective* containing or producing ozone M19.

ozoner /ˈəʊzəʊnə/ *noun*. *US slang*. M20.
[from OZONE + -ER[1].]
A drive-in cinema.

ozonide /ˈəʊzənʌɪd/ *noun*. M19.
[from OZONE + -IDE.]
CHEMISTRY. †**1** An oxy-salt which is a strong oxidizing agent. M–L19.
2 a Any of a class of unstable cyclic compounds formed by the addition of ozone to a carbon–carbon double bond. E20. **▸b** (A salt of) the ion O_3^-. M20.

ozonify /əʊˈzəʊnɪfʌɪ/ *verb trans*. M19.
[from OZONE + -I- + -FY.]
= OZONIZE.
■ **ozonifiˈcation** *noun* M19.

ozonise *verb*, **ozoniser** *noun* vars. of OZONIZE, OZONIZER.

ozonize /ˈəʊzənʌɪz/ *verb trans*. Also **-ise**. M19.
[from OZONE + -IZE.]
1 Convert (oxygen) into ozone. M19.
2 Impregnate, enrich, or treat with ozone; cause to react with ozone, esp. in ozonolysis. M19.
■ **ozoniˈzation** *noun* M19.

ozonizer /ˈəʊzənʌɪzə/ *noun*. Also **-iser**. L19.
[from prec. + -ER[1].]
An apparatus for producing ozone.

ozonolysis /əʊzəˈnɒlɪsɪs/ *noun*. M20.
[from OZONE + -O- + -LYSIS.]
CHEMISTRY. The cleavage of double or triple carbon–carbon bonds by reaction with ozone.
■ **ozonoˈlytic** *adjective* involving ozonolysis M20.

ozonometer /əʊzəˈnɒmɪtə/ *noun*. M19.
[from OZONE + -OMETER.]
An instrument or device for measuring the amount of ozone in the air.
■ **ozonoˈmetric** *adjective* pertaining to the measurement of ozone M19. **ozonometry** *noun* the measurement of the amount or proportion of ozone in the air M19.

ozonoscope /əʊˈzəʊnəskəʊp/ *noun*. L19.
[from OZONE + -O- + -SCOPE.]
An instrument or device for indicating the presence or amount of ozone in the air.
■ **ozonoˈscopic** *adjective* serving to indicate the presence or amount of ozone L19.

ozonosphere /əʊˈzəʊnəsfɪə/ *noun*. M20.
[from OZONE + -O- + -SPHERE.]
The region of the upper atmosphere, at an altitude of 10 to 50 km (6 to 30 miles), containing significant amounts of ozone, which absorbs short ultraviolet light; *esp.* the region of maximum ozone concentration between 20 and 25 km (12 and 15 miles) up.

Ozzie /ˈɒzi/ *noun & adjective*. *slang*. E20.
[from (the same root as) OZ + -IE. Cf. AUSSIE.]
▶ **A** *noun*. An Australian; Australia. E20.
▶ **B** *adjective*. Australian. E20.

Pp

P, p /piː/.

The sixteenth letter of the modern English alphabet and the fifteenth of the ancient Roman one, corresp. to Greek *pi*, Phoenician and Semitic *pe*. The simple letter has always represented a voiceless bilabial stop, but it is usually silent in the combinations *pn-*, *ps-*, *pt-* (repr. Greek), and sometimes also medially between *m* and another consonant, esp. in words where it is not etymological (***Hampstead***, ***Simpson***). The digraph *ph-* is used (after Latin usage) to transliterate the Greek letter *phi*, the phonet. value of which is now identical with that of *F*; *ph* is thus in effect a separate consonant: see **PH**. Pl. **P's**, **Ps**.

▸**I 1** The letter and its sound.

2 The shape of the letter.

1 mind one's P's and Q's be careful or particular as to one's words or behaviour. ***P-Celtic***. **2 P trap** a trap consisting of a U-bend the upper part of whose outlet arm is bent horizontal or nearly so.

▸**II** Symbolical uses.

3 Used to indicate serial order; applied e.g. to the sixteenth (or often the fifteenth, either I or J being omitted) group or section, sheet of a book, etc.

4 [Initial letter of *primary*.] ***P wave***, an earthquake wave of alternate compression and rarefaction (the faster of the two main kinds of wave transmitted through the earth: cf. ***S wave*** s.v. **S, S** 4).

5 *CHEMISTRY*. [After *pH*.] (Lower-case p.) Used to denote the negative of the common logarithm of a concentration or activity expressed in moles per litre (e.g. pOH, that of hydroxyl ion concentration). Also ***pK***, the negative of the common logarithm of a dissociation constant.

6 *ASTRONOMY*. [Initial letter of *proton*.] ***p-process***, a process believed to occur in stars by which heavy proton-rich nuclei are formed from other nuclei, esp. in circumstances of high proton flux (e.g. in supernovae).

▸**III 7** Abbrevs.: **P** = parking (on road signs); (*CHESS*) pawn; (*PHYSICS*) (as *prefix*) peta-; (*CHEMISTRY*) phosphorus; (*LINGUISTICS*) phrase (as in ***P-marker***); (*CHEMISTRY*) poly- (in ***PCB*** etc. below); (*PHYSICS*) poise; pressure; (*TELEPHONY*) private (in ***PABX*** etc. below); proprietary. **p** = page; (*CHEMISTRY*) (as *prefix*) para-; (*BIOLOGY*) parental generation; penny, pence (in decimal currency); (*MUSIC*) piano, softly; (as *prefix*) pico-; pressure; (*PHYSICS & CHEMISTRY*) principal: orig. designating one of the four main series (S, P, D, F) of lines in atomic spectra, now more frequently applied to electronic orbitals, states, etc., possessing one unit of angular momentum (as ***p-electron***, ***p-orbital***, etc.).

PA *abbreviation*[1].

1 Pennsylvania.

2 Personal assistant.

3 [*Pierre Allain*, French mountaineer, designer.] A canvas climbing boot with a rubber sole strengthened with a steel plate.

4 Power amplifier.

5 Press Association.

6 Also **pa**. Public address (system).

Pa *abbreviation*[2].

PHYSICS. Pascal(s).

Pa *symbol*.

CHEMISTRY. Protactinium.

pa /pɑː/ *noun*[1]. Also **pah**. **M18.**

[Maori *pà*, from *pā* block up.]

A Maori fortification (*Hist.*); a Maori village or settlement.

pa /pɑː/ *noun*[2]. *colloq.* **E19.**

[from **PAPA** *noun*[2]. Cf. **PAW** *noun*[2].]

Father.

pa-in-law, pl. **pas-in-law**, *colloq.* a father-in-law.

Pa. *abbreviation*.

Pennsylvania.

p.a. *abbreviation*.

Per annum.

pa'anga /pɑːˈɑːŋɡə/ *noun*. **M20.**

[Tongan.]

The basic monetary unit of Tonga, equal to 100 seniti.

PABA /ˌpiːeɪbiːˈeɪ, ˈpɑːbɑː/ *abbreviation*.

PHARMACOLOGY. Para-aminobenzoic acid.

Pablum /ˈpabləm/ *noun*. Also **p-**. **M20.**

[Alt. of **PABULUM**.]

1 (Proprietary name for) a children's breakfast cereal. **M20.**

2 (**p-**.) = **PABULUM** 4. **L20.**

pabouch /pəˈbuːʃ/ *noun*. **L17.**

[Persian *pāpoš*: see **BABOUCHE**.]

= **BABOUCHE**.

pabulum /ˈpabjʊləm/ *noun*. **M17.**

[Latin, from stem of *pascere* feed. Cf. **PABLUM**.]

1 Food, nutriment, esp. for plants or animals or their tissues. **M17.**

2 That which feeds a fire. **L17.**

3 That which nourishes and sustains the mind or soul. **M18.**

4 Bland intellectual fare; an insipid or undemanding diet of words, entertainment, etc. **L20**

> 🕮 **3** H. ACTON A theatre whose comedies and tragedies could afford . . perennial entertainment as well as literary pabulum. **4** A. CARTER The radio . . fed me an aural pabulum of cheapjack heartbreak.

▪ **pabulary** *adjective* of or pertaining to pabulum **M19.**

PABX *abbreviation*.

Private automatic branch exchange.

PAC *abbreviation*.

Pan-Africanist Congress.

pac /pak/ *noun*[1]. *N. Amer.* Also **'pac**. **L19.**

[Abbreviation.]

= **SHOEPACK**.

PAC /pak/ *noun*[2]. *US*. Also **pac**. **M20.**

[Acronym, from *political action committee*.]

1 *Hist.* The Political Action Committee of the US Congress of Industrial Organizations, established to support labour interests. **M20.**

2 A committee formed within an organization to collect voluntary contributions to electoral funds when the organization is barred from contributing to them directly. **L20.**

paca /ˈpakə/ *noun*. **M17.**

[Spanish & Portuguese from Tupi *páca*.]

Either of two rodents of Mexico and northern S. America related to the agoutis and cavies and constituting the genus *Agouti*; esp. *A. paca*, hunted locally for food.

pacable /ˈpeɪkəb(ə)l/ *adjective*. **M19.**

[from Latin *pacare* pacify, subdue, from *pac-*, *pax* peace: see **-ABLE**.]

= **PLACABLE** 2.

Pacamac /ˈpakəmak/ *noun*. Also **Pakamac** & other vars. **M20.**

[Respelling of *pack a mac*.]

(Proprietary name for) a kind of lightweight plastic mackintosh that can be folded up into a small pack when not required.

pacarana /pakəˈrɑːnə/ *noun*. **M20.**

[Tupi, lit. 'false paca'.]

A slow-moving S. American cavy-like rodent, *Dinomys branickii*, which has coarse dark hair with white stripes along the back and a short furry tail.

pacation /pəˈkeɪʃ(ə)n/ *noun*. *rare*. **M17.**

[Latin *pacatio(n-)*, from *pacat-* pa. ppl stem of *pacare*: see prec., **-ATION**.]

Pacifying, placation.

pacay /pəˈkʌɪ, pəˈkeɪ/ *noun*. Also **paccay**, **pacaya** /pəˈkʌɪə/. **M18.**

[(Spanish *pacaya* from) Quechua *pa'qay*.]

A Peruvian leguminous tree, *Inga feuillei*, resembling a mimosa and cultivated for its large white edible pods.

paccay *noun* var. of **PACAY**.

Pacchionian /pakɪˈəʊnɪən/ *adjective*. **E19.**

[from *Pacchioni* (1665–1726), Italian anatomist + **-IAN**.]

ANATOMY. Designating the villous enlargements of the arachnoid membrane into the veins and sinuses of the dura mater, through which cerebrospinal fluid is reabsorbed into the bloodstream.

PACE *abbreviation*.

Police and Criminal Evidence Act (1984).

pace /peɪs/ *noun*[1]. **ME.**

[Old & mod. French *pas* from Latin *passus* step, pace, lit. 'stretch (of the leg)', from *pass-* pa. ppl stem of *pandere* stretch, extend, spread. Cf. **PASS** *noun*[1].]

▸**I** A step.

1 A single separate movement made by the leg in walking, running, or dancing; a step. **ME.** ▸†**b** A step or stage in any process. Only in **17.**

2 The distance covered in a step by an individual; this as a unit of length, either the distance from where one foot is set down to where the other is set down (about 75 cm or 30 inches), or the distance between successive stationary positions of the same foot (about 1½ metres or 5 feet). **ME.**

> 🕮 **1** R. DAHL She took a couple of paces backwards. **2** H. MAUNDRELL Five hundred and seventy of my paces in length. J. CLAVELL His blow was so savage . . that the oil seller had walked on a pace before falling.

▸**II** The action or rate of stepping.

3 a The manner or action of stepping when walking or running, esp. as regards speed; gait, step. **ME.** ▸†**b** One's course or way when walking or running. **ME–E18.** ▸†**c** Movement, motion; manner of going on. **LME–E17.**

†**4** A walking pace, walking as distinguished from running etc. Only in **ME.**

5 A gait of a horse, mule, etc.; *spec.* (*a*) any of the recognized trained gaits of a horse etc., as walk, trot, canter, gallop; (*b*) the lateral gait of a horse etc. in which both legs on the same side are lifted together. **LME.**

6 Rate of movement in general, or of action represented as movement; the speed with which a story unfolds or a fictional plot develops; *SPORT* (esp. *CRICKET*) the speed of a ball or of its delivery; the state of a wicket as affecting the speed of a ball. **LME.**

> 🕮 **3a** LONGFELLOW I steal with quiet pace, My pitcher at the well to fill. J. B. PRIESTLEY Mr. Oakroyd walked on . . quickening his pace. **5** E. HARTLEY EDWARDS The American gaited horses . . used paces which are now lost to Europe. **6** *Athletic Journal* A pitcher cannot always deceive the batter but a change of pace will . . assist him. *Times* Imagine how dangerous he might be on wickets with any pace in them. S. BRETT The dialogue which ran up to it showed good pace. J. UGLOW The pace of life had accelerated. *Wall Street Journal* The U.S. Mint sold 86,500 ounces of the coins, more than double . . January's pace.

▸**III** Other senses.

7 A step of a stair or the like; a part of a floor raised by a step; a stage, a platform. Long *rare*. **ME.**

†**8** A passage, a narrow way; *esp.* a pass between mountains, bogs, woods, etc.; a strait. **ME–M17.**

†**9** A passage in or section of a narrative; a chapter, a canto. **ME–E17.**

†**10** An aisle of a church. **L15–E19.**

11 A company or herd of asses. *rare*. **L15.**

Phrases: ***force the pace***: see **FORCE** *verb*[1]. **go the pace** to go along at great speed; *fig.* proceed with reckless vigour; indulge in dissipation. **hold pace**, **keep pace** advance at an equal rate, keep up, (*with*). **last the pace** = ***stand the pace*** below. ***mend one's pace***: see **MEND** *verb*. **off the pace** slower than the leading horse in the early part of a race; *gen.* behind the leader in any race or contest, not performing satisfactorily. **put through his or her paces**, **put through its paces** test or prove the abilities in action of (esp.) a person or a horse. **set the pace** set the speed of something, esp. by leading. ***snail's pace***: see **SNAIL** *noun*. **stand the pace**, **stay the pace** be able to keep up with others.

Comb.: **pace bowler** *CRICKET*: who delivers the ball at high speed without spin; **pace car**: that sets the pace for the first lap of a race but does not take part in it, or that controls the pace in temporarily hazardous conditions; **pace lap**: made before a race by all the participating cars, to warm up the engines; **paceman** *CRICKET* = ***pace bowler*** above; **pace-note**: in rally driving, providing information about the characteristics of a particular course, esp. with regard to advisable speeds for each section (usu. in *pl.*); **pace-setter** a person who sets the pace, trend, or fashion; a leader in a particular field; **pace-setting** *adjective* that sets the pace, trend, or fashion; **pace-stick** *MILITARY*: used to measure paces.

pace /peɪs/ *noun*[2]. *Scot. & north.* Also **P-**. **LME.**

[Alt. of **PASCH**.]

Easter. Now usu. in *comb.*, as ***pace egg***.

pace /peɪs/ *verb*. **E16.**

[from the noun.]

1 *verb intrans. & trans.* (with cognate obj. or †*it*). Move with paces or steps; walk with a slow or regular pace, esp. repeatedly or methodically. Usu. foll. by adverb, preposition, or cognate obj. **E16.** ▸†**b** *transf. & fig.* Proceed or advance in speech or action. **E–M17.**

2 *verb trans.* Traverse with paces or steps; walk with a slow or regular pace along, about, etc., esp. repeatedly or methodically. Also, measure by pacing. **L16.**

3 *verb intrans.* Of a horse etc.: move with a recognized pace; move with a lateral gait in which both legs on the same side are lifted together. **E17.**

4 *verb trans.* Train (a horse) to pace; exercise in pacing. **E17.**

5 *verb trans.* **a** Set the pace for, esp. in a race or in training for a race. **L19.** ▸**b** Make (the heart) beat at an appropriate rate by stimulating it with pulses of electricity. **M20.**

> 📖 **1** LD MACAULAY Sentinels paced the rounds day and night. R. MACAULAY The camel paced briskly after the jeep. J. I. M. STEWART He . . was pacing up and down his minute room. **2** R. W. EMERSON He could pace sixteen rods more accurately than another man could measure them with rod and chain. J. WAINWRIGHT And, as he talked, he paced the room. **3** *Your Horse* A . . part-bred Arab . . . He will suddenly pace for a few steps, then go back into normal walk. **5** *Scientific American* The remarkable military reconnaissance programs . . indirectly paced civilian technology. D. ROWE I have to keep my life paced to meet . . Emily's demands. *Stage* Neville has learned to pace himself.

pace /ˈpɑːtʃeɪ, ˈpeɪsi/ *preposition.* **L18.**
[Latin, abl. sing. of *pax* peace, as in *pace tua* by your leave.]
With due deference to (a person named): used esp. as a courteous or ironical apology for a contradiction or difference of opinion.

> 📖 D. PIPER Illustrations will be confined to . . British poets, *pace* an immigrant . . like Yeats. **pace tanti viri** /tanti: ˈviri:/ by the leave or favour of so great a man.

pacemaker /ˈpeɪsmeɪkə/ *noun.* **L19.**
[from PACE *noun*[1] + MAKER.]
1 A competitor who sets the pace for another in racing or training for a race; a leading competitor. **L19.**
2 A person who sets the rate of working for, or the standards to be achieved by, others; a thing that sets a trend. **E20.**
3 The part of the heart which determines the rate at which it contracts and where the contractions begin (in humans and other mammals normally the sino-atrial node); a structure which controls the rhythm of any other organ. **E20.**
4 A device which supplies electrical signals to the heart, stimulating it to beat at an appropriate rate. **M20.**

pacer /ˈpeɪsə/ *noun.* **E17.**
[from PACE *verb* + -ER[1].]
†**1** A person who trains a horse to pace. **E–M17.**
2 A horse that paces or whose natural gait is a pace; *spec.* one bred to take part in harness-racing. **M17.**
3 A person who paces or sets the pace. **M19.**
4 A thing that goes at a great pace. *colloq.* **L19.**
5 = PACEMAKER 4. **M20.**

pacey /ˈpeɪsi/ *adjective.* **E20.**
[from PACE *noun*[1] + -Y[1].]
Having a fast pace.

pacha *noun* var. of PASHA.

pachalic *noun* var. of PASHALIC.

pachinko /pəˈtʃɪŋkəʊ/ *noun.* **M20.**
[Japanese.]
A variety of pinball popular in Japan.

pachisi /pəˈtʃiːziː/ *noun.* Also **parcheesi** /pɑːˈtʃiːzi/, **P-**. **E19.**
[Hindi *pac(c)īsī* (throw of) twenty-five (the highest in the game), ult. from Sanskrit *pañcaviṃśati* twenty-five.]
A four-handed board game of the Indian subcontinent, played with six cowries for dice.

pachuco /pəˈtʃuːkəʊ, *foreign* paˈtʃuko/ *noun.* Pl. **-os** /-əʊz, *foreign* -ɔs/. **M20.**
[Mexican Spanish, lit. 'flashily dressed'.]
A juvenile delinquent of Mexican-American descent, esp. in the Los Angeles area; *derog.* any Mexican-American.

pachy- /ˈpaki/ *combining form* of Greek *pakhus* thick, large, massive.
■ **pachyˈmeninx** *noun* (ANATOMY) the dura mater **L19.** **pachyˈnema** *noun* [-NEMA] CYTOLOGY = PACHYTENE **E20.** **pachytene** *noun* [-TENE] CYTOLOGY the stage of the prophase of meiosis following zygotene, during which the paired chromosomes shorten and thicken, the two chromatids of each separate, and exchange of segments between chromatids may occur **E20.**

pachycaul /ˈpakɪkɔːl/ *noun & adjective.* **M20.**
[from PACHY- + Greek *kaulos* stalk.]
BOTANY. (A tree) having or characterized by a thick primary stem and few or no branches. Cf. LEPTOCAUL.
■ **pachyˈcaulous** *adjective* = PACHYCAUL *adjective* **M20.** **pachycauly** *noun* pachycaul development **M20.**

pachycephalosaur /pakɪˈsɛfələsɔː, -ˈkɛf-/ *noun.* **L20.**
[from mod Latin *Pachycephalosaurus* (see below), formed as PACHY- + CEPHALO- + *saurus* (see SAUR).]
PALAEONTOLOGY. A bipedal herbivorous dinosaur of the late Cretacean infraorder Pachycephalosauria (and *spec.* of the genus *Pachycephalosaurus*), members of which were characterized by thick dome-like skulls.

pachyderm /ˈpakɪdəːm/ *noun.* **M19.**
[French *pachyderme* from Greek *pakhudermos* thick-skinned, formed as PACHY- + *derma* skin.]
1 A thick-skinned quadruped, *esp.* an elephant, a hippopotamus, or a rhinoceros. Formerly, any of the obsolete group Pachydermata, comprising hoofed quadrupeds that do not chew the cud. **M19.**
2 *fig.* A thick-skinned person. **M19.**
■ **pachyˈdermatous** *adjective* designating or pertaining to a pachyderm; *fig.* thick-skinned, not sensitive to criticism or rebuff: **E19.** **pachyˈdermatously** *adverb* **E20.** **pachyˈdermatousness** *noun* pachydermatous condition **M19.** **pachyˈdermoid** *adjective* (now *rare*) pachydermatous **M19.**

pachysandra /pakɪˈsandrə/ *noun.* **E19.**
[Irreg. from Greek *pakhus* thick + *andr-*, *anēr* man, male (with ref. to the thick stamens): see -A[1].]
Any of various N. American and eastern Asian evergreen shrubs of the genus *Pachysandra*, of the box family; *esp.* the Japanese *P. terminalis*, grown as ground cover.

pacifarin /pəˈsɪf(ə)rɪn/ *noun.* **M20.**
[from Latin *pacif(ic)are* PACIFY + -IN[1].]
MEDICINE. A biologically produced substance which, when introduced into an organism, protects it from the harmful effects of an infection without killing the pathogen.

pacific /pəˈsɪfɪk/ *adjective & noun.* **M16.**
[(Old & mod. French *pacifique* from) Latin *pacificus*, from *pac-*, *pax* peace: see -I-, -FIC.]
▸**A** *adjective.* **I 1** Making, or tending to the making of, peace, leading to reconciliation; conciliatory, appeasing; calming. **M16.**
2 Of peaceful disposition or character, peaceable; characterized by peace or calm, tranquil. **M17.**

> 📖 **1** C. ANGIER He was . . too pacific; he would not fight back. **2** E. BOWEN It had been pacific, their relationship; neither . . would have admitted a crescendo . . a decrescendo. *New Yorker* Mrs. Evert, trim, pacific, and invisibly helpful.

▸**II 3** ***Pacific Ocean***, †***Pacific Sea***, the largest of the world's oceans, situated between America to the east and Asia to the west (orig. supposed to be calmer than the Atlantic). **M17.** ▸**b** (**P-**.) Of or pertaining to the Pacific Ocean; (of or involving countries) bordering the Pacific Ocean. **E19.**

> 📖 **3b** F. RIESENBERG Craft . . could go into the 'holes in the wall' along the ragged Pacific coast. D. MORRIS The largest bats of this group are the Flying Foxes of the Pacific region. ***Pacific halibut***, ***Pacific pompano***, ***Pacific salmon***, etc.

Special collocations: **pacific blockade** a blockade of ports of one country by another country not at war with it. **Pacific Islander** a native or inhabitant of any of the islands in the South Pacific, esp. an aboriginal native of Polynesia. **Pacific rim** the group of countries etc. that border the western Pacific, *esp.* those regarded as having potential for economic development. **Pacific slope** (*a*) the part of N. America west of the Rocky Mountains; (*b*) *Austral.* & *NZ slang* an escape across the Pacific Ocean to avoid arrest. **Pacific Standard Time**, **Pacific Time** the standard time used on the Pacific coast of N. America, being that of 120° W., 8 hours behind GMT.

▸**B** *noun.* †**1** An offer or overture of peace; in *pl.*, peace offerings. Only in **17.**
2 (**P-**.) *The* Pacific Ocean. **E19.**
3 (**P-**.) A steam locomotive of 4-6-2 wheel arrangement. **E20.**

pacifical /pəˈsɪfɪk(ə)l/ *adjective.* **LME.**
[medieval Latin *pacificalis*, or from Latin *pacificus*: see prec., -AL[1].]
Of peaceful disposition or character.

pacifically /pəˈsɪfɪk(ə)li/ *adverb.* **L18.**
[from PACIFIC *adjective* or prec.: see -ICALLY.]
In a pacific manner; peacefully, peaceably.

pacificate /pəˈsɪfɪkeɪt/ *verb.* **M17.**
[Latin *pacificat-* pa. ppl stem of *pacificare* PACIFY: see -ATE[3].]
1 *verb intrans.* Make peace (*with*). *rare.* **M17.**
2 *verb trans.* Give peace to, pacify. **E19.**

pacification /ˌpasɪfɪˈkeɪʃ(ə)n/ *noun.* **LME.**
[Old & mod. French from Latin *pacificatio(n-)*, formed as prec.: see -ATION.]
1 The action or fact of pacifying or appeasing a person, country, etc.; the condition of being pacified; appeasement, conciliation; *spec.* (*US*) an operation (usu. a military one) designed to secure the peaceful cooperation of a population or area in which enemies are thought to be active. **LME.**
2 A peace treaty. **M16.**

pacificator /pəˈsɪfɪkeɪtə/ *noun.* **M16.**
[Latin, formed as PACIFICATE: see -OR.]
A pacifying person or agent; a peacemaker.

pacificatory /pəsɪfɪˈkeɪt(ə)ri/ *adjective.* **L16.**
[from prec. + -ORY[2], or Latin *pacificatorius*, formed as prec.]
Tending to make peace.

pacificism /pəˈsɪfɪsɪz(ə)m/ *noun.* **E20.**
[from PACIFIC + -ISM.]
= PACIFISM. Also, advocacy of a peaceful policy in a particular instance.
■ **pacificist** *noun & adjective* (*a*) *noun* a pacifist; an advocate of a peaceful policy; (*b*) *adjective* of, pertaining to, or characterized by pacificism: **E20.**

pacifico /pəˈsɪfɪkəʊ/ *noun.* Pl. **-os.** **L19.**
[Spanish.]
A person of peaceful character; *spec.* (*Hist.*) a native or inhabitant of Cuba or the Philippines who submitted without active opposition to Spanish occupation.

pacifism /ˈpasɪfɪz(ə)m/ *noun.* **E20.**
[French *pacifisme*, from *pacifique*, formed as PACIFIC: see -ISM.]
The policy or doctrine of rejecting war and every form of violent action as means of solving disputes, esp. in international affairs; the belief in and advocacy of peaceful methods as feasible and desirable alternatives to war.
■ **pacifist** *noun & adjective* (*a*) *noun* a person who believes in or advocates pacifism; (*b*) *adjective* of, pertaining to, or characterized by pacifism: **E20.** **paciˈfistic** *adjective* suggestive of or inclined to pacifism **M20.** **paciˈfistically** *adverb* **E20.**

pacify /ˈpasɪfʌɪ/ *verb.* **L15.**
[(Old & mod. French *pacifier* from) Latin *pacificare*, from *pac-*, *pax* peace: see -I-, -FY.]
1 *verb trans.* Allay the anger, excitement, or agitation of (a person); soothe (a person, strong feelings); appease. **L15.**
2 *verb trans.* Bring (a country) to a state of peace; calm (strife, a rebellion, etc.). **L15.** ▸†**b** Reconcile (parties at strife, one party *with* or *to* another). **L15–E19.**
3 *verb intrans.* Become peaceful, calm down. **E16.**

> 📖 **1** V. BROME To pacify the infuriated Ferenczi, Freud wrote a sadly conciliatory letter to him. **2** F. FITZGERALD The French succeeded in pacifying all but the northern mountains with a very few men.

■ **pacifier** *noun* (*a*) a pacificator; (*b*) *N. Amer.* a baby's dummy: **M16.** **pacifyingly** *adverb* in a pacifying manner **M19.**

pacing /ˈpeɪsɪŋ/ *noun.* **LME.**
[from PACE *verb* + -ING[1].]
1 The action of PACE *verb.* **LME.**
2 CYCLING & ATHLETICS. The action of tactical pacemaking, esp. of artificially increasing a competitor's speed by allowing him or her to proceed in the slipstream of a vehicle. Also, the action of distributing effort carefully over a race to ensure optimum performance, esp. by utilizing the wind resistance offered by other competitors. **L19.**
3 Harness-racing for pacers. **M20.**

pacing /ˈpeɪsɪŋ/ *ppl adjective.* **L16.**
[from PACE *verb* + -ING[2].]
That paces; *spec.* (of a horse) that is a pacer, that takes part in pacing.

Pacinian /pəˈsɪnɪən/ *adjective.* **M19.**
[from F. *Pacini* (1812–83), Italian anatomist + -IAN.]
ANATOMY. Designating an encapsulated ending of a sensory nerve that acts as a receptor for pressure and vibration. Chiefly in ***Pacinian corpuscle***.

pack /pak/ *noun.* **ME.**
[Corresp. to Middle & mod. Flemish, Middle & mod. Dutch, Middle & mod. Low German *pak*, of unkn. origin.]
1 A collection of things wrapped up or tied together compactly, esp. to be carried, transported, used, or sold together; a package, a parcel, *esp.* one of considerable size or weight; a bale; *spec.* (*a*) a bundle of goods carried by a pedlar; (*b*) the container into which a parachute is packed; a parachute in its container. **ME.** ▸†**b** A stock of cash. **LME–L16.** ▸**c** PHOTOGRAPHY. A set of two or three superimposed plates or films sensitive to different colours which are exposed simultaneously. **E20.** ▸**d** A knapsack, a rucksack, *esp.* one with a frame. Chiefly *Austral.* & *NZ.* **E20.** ▸**e** A packet, esp. of cigarettes. **E20.**
2 A company or set of people. Now chiefly *derog.* or *contempt.* **LME.**
3 A number of animals kept or naturally congregating together; *spec.* (*a*) a company of hounds kept for hunting; (*b*) a group of certain animals, esp. wolves, which naturally associate for purposes of attack or defence. **LME.** ▸**b** A shepherd's own sheep grazing along with the tended flock; one of these sheep (also ***pack sheep***). Now *Scot. dial.* **E19.**
4 A measure of certain commodities, as fur or yarn. **L15.**
5 A person of low or worthless character. Chiefly in ***naughty pack***. *obsolete* exc. *dial.* **E16.**
6 a A large group *of* similar, usu. abstract, things, *spec.* lies. Chiefly *contempt.* **L16.** ▸**b** RUGBY FOOTBALL. The forwards of a team, who form one half of the scrum; the scrum. **L19.** ▸**c** The main body of competitors behind the leader(s) of a race, esp. when bunched together; any chasing group. **E20.** ▸**d** An organized group of Cub Scouts or Brownies. **E20.** ▸**e** In the war of 1939–45, a number of German submarines operating together. **M20.**
7 A complete set of playing-cards. **L16.**
8 An act or the action of packing. **E17.** ▸**b** The wrapping of a person's body in a wet (or dry) sheet or blanket, as a hydropathic treatment; the state of being so packed; the sheet etc. used. **M19.**
9 An expanse of large pieces of floating ice driven together into a nearly continuous mass, as occurs in polar seas. **L18.**
10 A mass of rough stones etc. built up to support the roof of a mine. **M19.**
11 *ellipt.* A packhorse; a pack-animal. **M19.**

12 The quantity of a particular foodstuff that is packed or canned in a particular season or year. **L19.**

13 a *SURGERY.* A soft pad usu. composed of several layers of gauze sewn together, used esp. for wedging organs of the body during an operation. **E20.** ▸**b** *DENTISTRY.* A substance applied in a plastic state to the gums around and between the teeth, subsequently hardening, to serve as a dressing after disease or surgery of periodontal tissue. **E20.** ▸**c** A hot or cold pad of absorbent material for treating a wound etc.; a face-pack, a mud-pack. **M20.**

📖 **1e** R. WHELAN Cigarettes cost about five dollars a pack. **2** R. BROOKE I go . . to our filthy academy in the Fens . . with a pack of women. **3** R. ADAMS A tussling pack of . . sparrows flew down. J. A. MICHENER An individual sloth . . was a match for one wolf, but if caught by a pack, he could be torn down. *transf.: New Yorker* The buses on Eighth tend to travel in packs. **7** I. MCEWAN A conversation Maisie and I had had about the Tarot pack. G. BRANDRETH The pack is cut to decide first deal. **12** *Sun (Baltimore)* Morgan county's . . tomato pack, normally one of the largest . . will be less than half.

Phrases: ***break the pack***: see BREAK *verb*. ***go to the pack*** *Austral. & NZ slang* suffer a collapse, deteriorate shockingly. ***joker in the pack***: see JOKER 3.

Attrib. & comb.: In the sense 'used for carrying a pack', as ***pack-animal***, ***pack-dog***, ***pack-mule***, etc. Special combs., as **pack-cloth** (a piece of) a stout coarse cloth used for packing; **pack-drill** a military punishment of walking up and down carrying full equipment; ***no names no pack-drill***: see NAME *noun*. **pack-frame** a frame into which a knapsack or other pack is fitted to make it easier to carry; **packhorse** a horse for carrying packs of goods or belongings; *fig.* a drudge; **pack-house** a warehouse, now *esp.* one for perishable goods; **pack ice** ice forming a pack (sense 9 above); **pack-leader** the leader of a pack of animals; **pack-needle** a large needle for sewing up packages in stout fabric; **pack-pedlar**: who travels about with a pack of small items for sale; **pack-rat** a N. American wood rat, *esp.* the bushy-tailed wood rat, *Neotoma cinerea*; *fig.* a person who hoards things; **pack-road**: along which pack animals are driven; **pack-sack** the container into which goods forming a pack are put, a rucksack; **pack-saddle**: adapted for supporting packs; ***sawbuck pack-saddle***: see SAWBUCK 1b; **packshot** in television advertising, a close-up picture of the advertised product in its wrappings; **packstaff** a staff on which a pedlar can support his or her pack when stood at rest; chiefly in †***plain as a packstaff*** (where repl. by ***pikestaff***); **pack-strap(s)** the strap(s) securing a load round the forehead or shoulders of a person or to the back of a pack-animal; **packthread** stout thread for sewing or tying up packs; **pack-track**, **pack-trail**: suitable for pack-animals; **pack-train** a train of pack-animals with their packs; **pack-way** a pack-road.

pack /pak/ *adjective. Scot.* **E18.**
[Origin uncertain: perh. from *packed* pa. pple of PACK *verb*².]
Of people: intimate, close.

pack /pak/ *verb*¹. **ME.**
[Middle & mod. Dutch, Middle & mod. Low German *pakken* (cf. Anglo-Norman *(en)paker*, Anglo-Latin *(im)paccare*): ult. origin unkn.]

▸**I 1** *verb trans.* Put together into a pack or package, or compactly into a receptacle, esp. for transport, storage, or subsequent sale. **ME.**

2 *verb trans.* Fill (a receptacle or space) with something packed in; fill (any space) as full as possible (also foll. by *out*); cram, crowd, (*with*). Freq. in *pass.* **LME.**

3 a *verb trans.* Carry or convey in a pack or packs; carry in any manner; carry (esp. a gun) habitually; possess. **L15.** ▸**b** *verb intrans.* Travel with one's goods or merchandise in packs. **M19.** ▸**c** *verb trans.* Be capable of delivering (a blow) with force. Esp. in ***pack a punch***. *colloq.* **E20.**

4 a *verb trans.* Put together closely or compactly; crowd together. **M16.** ▸**b** *verb trans.* Press (anything loose) into a compact or solid mass. **M19.** ▸**c** *verb trans. & intrans. COMPUTING.* Compress (stored data) in a way that permits subsequent recovery; *spec.* represent (two or more items of data) in a single word. **M20.**

5 *verb trans.* Load (an animal) with a pack. **L16.**

6 *verb trans.* Form (hounds) into a pack; place (cards) together in a pack; drive (ice) into a pack. **M17.**

7 *verb intrans.* Pack clothes and other necessaries for a journey. Also foll. by *up*. **L17.**

8 *verb trans.* Cover, surround, or protect with something pressed tightly around; *MEDICINE* envelop (the body or a part of it) in a pack; *SURGERY* fill or wedge with a pack. **L18.**

9 *verb intrans.* **a** Collect or crowd together; form a pack. **E19.** ▸**b** Admit of being packed, be suitable for packing. **M19.** ▸**c** *RUGBY FOOTBALL.* Of forwards: form or take their places in the scrum. Also foll. by *in*, *down*. **L19.**

📖 **1** GEO. ELIOT The contents of the library were all packed and carried away. B. W. ALDISS Pack your night things . . while I lay on transport. **2** A. CRAWLEY Having seen that capture was inevitable . . he had . . packed three large suitcases. *Nature* Two thousand five hundred people packed Westminster Central Hall to hear him speak. R. RENDELL A huge market square, usually packed tight with parked cars. *Woman's Own* Our biggest issue . . packed with everything you (and we) could think of. **3a** J. C. FREMONT A work of great . . labor to pack our baggage across the ridge. R. CHANDLER Don't you pack no rod? *Washington Post* Actress Ali McGraw 'packs all the glamor of a worn-out sneaker'. **c** *transf.: Daily Telegraph* Ford's refined diesel engine packs bags of punch. **4a** R. G. CUMMING Tents and waggons . . drawn up on every side of the farmhouse . . packed together in 'lagers' or encampments. **7** J. JOHNSTON I have to catch the Dublin train. I should go and pack. **b** J. CANNAN I'm packed, but I must . . tell them I'm leaving. **8** *Your Horse* Stockholm Tar . . can be used successfully to pack foot injuries.

▸**II 10** *verb intrans. & †refl.* Take oneself off with one's belongings, be off; go away, depart, esp. when summarily dismissed. Esp. in ***send packing***, dismiss summarily. **LME.**

11 *verb trans.* Send or drive away, dismiss summarily, get rid of. Now usu. foll. by *off*. **L16.**

📖 **11** A. N. WILSON He packed his wife off to stay with his mother.

Phrases, & with adverbs & prepositions in specialized senses: ***pack and peel***: see PEEL *verb*¹. **pack in** = ***pack up*** (b) below; (see also sense 9c above). **pack it in**, **pack it up** *slang* stop working, abandon an attempt; in *imper.*, be quiet, behave yourself. **pack off** (*a*) die; (*b*) *SURGERY* wedge (an internal organ) to keep it out of the way; (see also sense 11 above). **pack on all sail** *NAUTICAL* put on or hoist all possible sail for the sake of speed. **pack one's bags** *colloq.* (prepare to) leave. ***pack or peel***: see PEEL *verb*¹. **pack them** *Austral. slang* hold back defecation caused by nervousness; be terrified. **pack them in** attract a capacity audience. **pack up** (*a*) put together in a pack, make a pack or package of; (*b*) *colloq.* give up an enterprise, stop what one is doing; surrender; die; (of a machine etc.) cease working, break down; (see also sense 7a above). ***send packing***: see sense 10 above.

Comb.: **pack-flat** *adjective* able to be made into a flat package.

pack /pak/ *verb*². **E16.**
[Prob. from PACT *verb*, by apprehending the final *t* as the inflection *-ed*.]

▸**I †1** *verb intrans.* Enter into a private arrangement, agree to a secret design; conspire, intrigue. **E16–E17.**

†2 *verb trans.* Bring or let (a person) into a plot, engage as a conspirator; in *pass.*, be an accomplice. **L16–E17.**

†3 *verb trans.* Contrive or plan in an underhand way; plot. Only in **17.**

▸**II 4** *verb trans.* Select or make up (a jury, deliberative body, etc.) in such a way as to secure a biased decision or further a particular end. **L16.**

5 *verb trans.* Arrange or shuffle (playing-cards) so as to cheat or obtain a fraudulent advantage; *fig.* make a cheating arrangement *with*. *arch.* **L16.**

📖 **4** *Australian Financial Review* Roosevelt got into serious political difficulties when he tried to pack the Supreme Court.

packable /ˈpakəb(ə)l/ *adjective.* **L19.**
[from PACK *verb*¹ + -ABLE.]
Able to be packed.
■ **packaˈbility** *noun* ability to be packed, esp. (with ref. to clothing) in a suitcase without harm **M20.**

package /ˈpakɪdʒ/ *noun.* **M16.**
[from PACK *verb*¹ + -AGE. Cf. Anglo-Latin *paccagium*.]

1 The action of packing goods etc.; the mode in which goods are packed. **M16.**

2 A bundle of things packed up or tied up together; *esp.* one of small or moderate size, as an item of luggage; a packet, a parcel. **E18.** ▸**b** A set of interdependent or related abstract entities; *spec.* (*a*) = ***package deal*** below; (*b*) = ***package holiday*** below; (*c*) a series of television programmes sold or bought as a whole; a single television programme completed and available for sale or transmission. **M20.** ▸**c** A group of related objects viewed or organized as a unit; *COMPUTING* a general-purpose program or group of programs for use by a wide range of users. **M20.**

3 A box, parcel, etc., in which goods are packed. **E19.**

4 a A person who is kidnapped. *slang.* **M20.** ▸**b** A girl, *esp.* an attractive one. *slang.* **M20.**

📖 **2** *New Yorker* An enormous, fenced-in storage area piled high with crates and packages. **b** *Observer* The package would link the future of Berlin with a settlement of the German problem. *Broadcast* Three plays . . among 50 hours taken in a mainly drama package by . . ITN. *Times* The total employment package, including a performance related element, will exceed £30,000 per annum. *Which?* If you are booking a package with transport . . book with an ABTA company. **c** *Australian Personal Computer* Other facilities need to be available to make a complete . . software package. **3** J. BALDWIN His mother had unwrapped the package and was opening a bottle.

Comb.: **package deal** a set of proposals or terms offered or agreed as a whole; **package holiday**: for which all the arrangements are made by an agent at an inclusive price; **package show**: offered, presented, or toured in its entirety; **package tour**: for which all the arrangements are made by an agent at an inclusive price.

package /ˈpakɪdʒ/ *verb trans.* **E20.**
[from the noun.]
Make into or enclose in a package; present or occur as (part of) a package (esp. as ***packaged*** *ppl adjective*).

📖 *Daily Telegraph* Ghost-hunters have been offered a package tour of the haunted houses. *Scientific American* Each piece of genetic material is packaged into a small . . particle.

■ **packageable** *adjective* **M20.** **packager** *noun* **M20.**

packaging /ˈpakɪdʒɪŋ/ *noun.* **L19.**
[from PACKAGE *noun*, *verb* + -ING¹.]

1 The action, process, or manner of making something up into a package; the material in which something is packaged, esp. for sale.

2 The presentation of a person, product, or action in a particular way, esp. for promotional purposes. **M20.**

📖 **1** L. F. R. WILLIAMS Much attention is being paid to grading, packaging and marketing. **2** S. ORBACH The packaging of youth . . has become a dominant motif in American life.

packaway /ˈpakəweɪ/ *adjective.* **M20.**
[from PACK *verb*¹ + AWAY.]
Able to be folded into a small space when not in use.

packed /pakt/ *ppl adjective*¹. **L15.**
[from PACK *verb*¹ + -ED¹.]

1 That has been packed; put into a pack or package; (of a meal) made up into a small pack that can be taken away, e.g. on a picnic; put or placed closely together. **L15.** ▸**b** *COMPUTING.* Designating or pertaining to a decimal number stored with successive digits represented by successive half-bytes and the sign by the rightmost half-byte. **M20.**

2 Filled with something packed in; as full as possible; crammed, crowded. **L19.**

📖 **1** LEIGH HUNT All the chaos of packed trunks. H. MARTINEAU A closely packed assembly of business-like men. *Which?* Testers measured braking performance . . on packed snow. **be packed** (of a person) have finished one's packing. **packed cells** *MEDICINE* blood cells that have been separated from plasma; ***packed-cell volume***, the proportion of a sample of blood, by volume, occupied by cells after they have been allowed to settle. **2** G. BORDMAN Playing to packed houses. ***jam-packed***, ***packed like sardines***, etc.

packed /pakt/ *ppl adjective*². **M17.**
[from PACK *verb*² + -ED¹.]
Of a jury, deliberative body, etc.: selected or made up in such a way as to secure a biased decision or further a particular end.

packer /ˈpakə/ *noun*¹. **LME.**
[from PACK *verb*¹ + -ER¹.]

1 A person who packs things; *esp.* one who packs goods for transportation and sale. **LME.**

2 a A person who transports goods by means of pack-animals. Now *N. Amer., Austral., & NZ.* **L17.** ▸**b** A pack-animal. *Canad. & Austral.* **L19.** ▸**c** A person who carries goods in a backpack; a person who carries a rucksack containing all the necessities for travel. Chiefly *Canad.* **L19.**

3 A machine or appliance used for packing. **L19.**

4 A device inserted into an annular space in an oil well (e.g. between the casing and the tubing) in order to block the flow of oil and gas. **L19.**

📖 **1** M. E. BRADDON Some valets are bad packers. *Grimsby Evening Telegraph* His mother works as a packer at the pet food manufacturers.

packer /ˈpakə/ *noun*². **L16.**
[from PACK *verb*² + -ER¹.]
A person who packs a jury, deliberative body, etc. Formerly also, a conspirator, a plotter.

packet /ˈpakɪt/ *noun & verb.* Also †**pa(c)quet**. **M16.**
[from PACK *noun* + -ET¹, perh. of Anglo-Norman formation: cf. Anglo-Latin *paccettum*.]

▸**A** *noun.* **1** A small pack, package, or parcel. Orig., a parcel of letters or dispatches, *esp.* the State parcel or mail to and from foreign countries. Also in titles of newspapers. **M16.** ▸**b** *fig.* A small group of similar things (or persons), *spec.* lies. Chiefly *contempt.* **L16.**

2 In full ***packet-boat***. A boat travelling at regular intervals between two ports (orig. for the conveyance of mail). **M17.**

3 Esp. *MILITARY.* A bullet, a shell; *fig.* trouble, misfortune. Chiefly in ***stop a packet***, ***catch a packet***, ***cop a packet*** below. *slang.* **E20.**

4 A large sum of money. Freq. in ***cost a packet***, ***lose a packet***, ***make a packet***. *slang.* **E20.**

5 *PHYSICS.* A localized disturbance of a field or medium that retains its identity as it travels; *spec.* = ***wave packet*** s.v. WAVE *noun*. **E20.**

📖 **1** J. BRAINE There was a packet of cigarettes on the locker. A. HARDING A small packet neatly tied with a brown ribbon. B. CHATWIN I had brought . . some packets of his favourite Earl Grey tea. **b sell a person a packet** *colloq.* deceive or swindle a person. **2** F. RAPHAEL Byron . . set off for Falmouth to board the Lisbon packet. **3 stop a packet**, **catch a packet**, **cop a packet** be killed or wounded; *fig.* get into trouble; be reprimanded. **4 *pretty packet***: see PRETTY *adjective*.

Attrib. & comb.: In the senses 'made up into or sold in packets', as ***packet soup***, ***packet tobacco***, etc.; 'operating as a packet-boat', as ***packet ship***, ***packet steamer***, etc. Special combs., as ***packet-boat***: see sense 2 above; **packet network** a data transmission network using packet-switching; **packet radio** a method of broadcasting that makes use of radio signals carrying packets of data; **packet rat** *derog.* a seaman, *spec.* one who specialized in the

Atlantic crossing; **packet-switched** *adjective* employing packet-switching; **packet-switching** a mode of data transmission in which a message is broken into a number of parts which are sent independently, over whatever route is optimum for each packet, and re-assembled at the destination.
▶ **B** *verb trans.* Make up into or wrap up in a packet. E17.

packetarian /pakɪˈtɛːrɪən/ *noun. US.* L19.
[from PACKET *noun* + -ARIAN.]
A member of the crew of a packet-boat.

packetize /ˈpakɪtʌɪz/ *verb trans.* Also **-ise**. L20.
[from PACKET *noun* + -IZE.]
COMPUTING. Partition or separate (data) into units for transmission in a packet-switching network.

packie /ˈpaki/ *noun. NZ colloq.* M20.
[from PACK *noun* + -IE.]
= PACKMAN 3.

packing /ˈpakɪŋ/ *noun*^{1}. LME.
[from PACK *verb*^{1} + -ING^1.]
1 The action of PACK *verb*^{1}. LME.
2 Material used to fill up a space round or in something, e.g. to protect a breakable article in transit or to make a joint watertight or airtight. E19. ▸**b** Food, *esp.* poor food. *slang.* L19.
3 An extra charge added to the cost of delivered goods to cover the cost of packing them. E20.
4 SCIENCE. The spatial arrangement of a number of objects, esp the constituent atoms of a crystalline structure, relative to one another. E20.

🕮 **1** J. SCOTT From its rough state . . to the packing of the pure salt in casks.

Comb.: **packing box** a box for packing goods in; a packing-case; **packing-case** a usu. wooden case or framework for packing goods in, esp. for transportation; **packing density** COMPUTING the density of stored information in terms of bits per unit of storage medium; **packing fraction** PHYSICS a parameter of an atomic nucleus equal to 10,000 times the difference between its atomic weight and its mass number, divided by the former (or the latter); **packing needle** = *pack-needle* s.v. PACK *noun*; **packing-sheet** (*a*) a sheet for packing goods in; (*b*) MEDICINE a wet sheet in which a patient is wrapped in hydropathic treatment; **packing station** *spec.* an official depot where eggs are graded and packed.

packing /ˈpakɪŋ/ *noun*^{2}. E16.
[from PACK *verb*^{2} + -ING^1.]
†**1** Private or underhand arrangement; fraudulent contriving, plotting. E16–M17.
2 The action of PACK *verb*^{2}; the selection or making up of a jury, deliberative body, etc., in such a way as to secure a biased decision or further a particular end. E16.

packman /ˈpakmən/ *noun.* Pl. **-men**. L16.
[from PACK *noun* + MAN *noun*.]
1 A pedlar. L16.
2 A person who transports goods by means of pack-animals or in a backpack. *N. Amer.* L16.
3 A sheep-station handyman who transports goods by pack-animal from camp to camp and sees to the cooking. *NZ.* M20.

packmen *noun* pl. of PACKMAN.

Pac-Man /ˈpakman/ *adjective.* L20.
[Proprietary name for a computer game.]
COMMERCE. Designating or pertaining to a takeover bid in which the company facing the takeover threatens to take over the company attempting the bid.

paco /ˈpɑːkəʊ, *foreign* ˈpako/ *noun.* Pl. **-os** /-əʊz, *foreign* -ɔs/. E17.
[Spanish (in sense 2 with ref. to the brown and white colour) from Quechua *pako* red, reddish yellow.]
1 An alpaca. E17.
2 MINERALOGY. An earthy brown oxide of iron, containing particles of silver. M19.

†**Pacolet** *noun.* L16–E18.
[A dwarf in the medieval French romance of Valentine and Orson, who had a magical horse of wood by which he could instantly convey himself to any desired place.]
In full *Pacolet's horse*. A swift steed.

†**pacquet** *noun* & *verb* var. of PACKET.

pact /pakt/ *noun* & *verb.* LME.
[Old & mod. French *pacte*, †*pact* from Latin *pactum*, *-us* uses as noun of pa. pple of *pacisci* make a covenant, from base also of *pax* PEACE *noun*. Cf. PACK *verb*^{2}.]
▶ **A** *noun.* An agreement between individuals or parties; a treaty. LME.

🕮 H. WOUK The Nazi-Soviet pact broke on the world . . as one of the most stunning surprises. C. THUBRON We had an unspoken pact not to use the word 'love'. ***nude pact***: see NUDE *adjective* 2.

▶ **B** *verb trans.* & *intrans.* Stipulate; agree to; enter into a pact with or *with*. *rare.* M16.

paction /ˈpakʃ(ə)n/ *noun.* Now chiefly *Scot.* LME.
[Old French from Latin *pactio(n-)*, from *pact-* pa. ppl stem of *pacisci*: see prec., -ION.]
The action of making a pact; a bargain, an agreement, a covenant.

▪ **pactional** *adjective* of, pertaining to, or of the nature of a pact or covenant E17.

paction /ˈpakʃ(ə)n/ *verb. Scot.* M17.
[French *paction(n)er*, formed as prec.]
1 *verb trans.* Agree to. M17.
2 *verb intrans.* Make a pact. E18.

pactolian /pakˈtəʊlɪən/ *adjective. literary.* E17.
[from *Pactolus* (see below) + -IAN.]
Of, pertaining to, or typical of the River Pactolus in Lydia, famous in ancient times for its golden sands.

pacu /paˈkuː, ˈpakuː/ *noun.* L18.
[Tupi *pacú*.]
ZOOLOGY. A large herbivorous freshwater fish of the characin family, *Colossoma nigripinnis*, of northern S. America.

pad /pad/ *noun*^{1}. *obsolete* exc. *dial.* ME.
[Prob. from Old Norse *padda* = Old Frisian, Middle Dutch *paddle* (Dutch *pad*), Middle Low German *padde*, *pedde*. Cf. PADDOCK *noun*^{1}.]
1 A toad, a frog. Cf. PADDOCK *noun*^{1}. ME.
2 A starfish. E17.
1 pad in the straw (long *arch. rare*) a lurking or hidden danger.

pad /pad/ *noun*^{2}. M16.
[Low German, Dutch *pad* PATH *noun*^{1}.]
1 a A path, a track; *the* road, *the* way. *slang* & *dial. arch.* M16. ▸**b** *spec.* A track made by animals, esp. cattle. Usu. with specifying word. *Austral.* & *NZ.* L19.
2 A horse with a naturally easy pace, a horse for use on the road. *arch.* E17.
3 Highway robbery. *slang* (now *Hist.*). M17. ▸†**b** A highwayman, a footpad. *slang.* L17–M19.

🕮 **1a on the pad** on the road, on the tramp. ***rum pad***: see RUM *adjective*^{1}. **stand pad** beg by the roadside. **2** T. H. WHITE Could I waylay some knight . . mounted on an ambling pad?

Comb.: **pad-nag** *noun* & *verb* (*arch.*) (*a*) *noun* = sense 2 above; (*b*) *verb intrans.* ride at an easy pace, amble.

pad /pad/ *noun*^{3}. M16.
[Prob. of Low Dutch origin: cf. Flemish †*pad*, *patte*, Low German *pad* sole of the foot. Cf. POD *noun*^{1}, PUD *noun*^{1}.]
▶ **I 1** †**a** A bundle of straw etc. to lie on. M16–E18. ▸**b** A bed. Also, a lodging, a person's residence, *esp.* a bedsitting-room, a flat. *colloq.* (orig. *slang*). E18.
2 a A stuffed treeless riding-saddle used esp. by learners. L16. ▸**b** The part of a double harness to which the girths are attached. E19.
3 *gen.* A soft cushion-like object for reducing or giving protection from jarring, friction, or pressure between two surfaces, filling out or expanding an area or mass, holding or absorbing liquid, etc. E17. ▸**b** Orig., (a print made by) the foot or paw of a fox, hare, etc. Now chiefly, any cushion-like part of the human or animal body (freq. with specifying word); *spec.* a fleshy elastic cushion forming (part of) the sole of the foot in many mammals and birds; ENTOMOLOGY a pulvillus. L18. ▸**c** An article of clothing worn in various sports for protection; *spec.* a guard for the leg or ankle. M19. ▸**d** A padded cell. *slang.* M20. ▸**e** A pressure-sensitive strip or patch of usu. rubber material, esp. fitted in a road for operating traffic signals. M20.
4 A package of yarn of a definite amount or weight. *dial.* M18.
5 A number of sheets of blank paper fastened together at one edge. M19.
6 Any of the broad floating leaves of a water lily, a lily-pad. M19.
7 A piece of animal dung; *esp.* a cow-pat. Orig. *dial.* L19.
8 A flat-topped structure or area used as a take-off or landing point for a helicopter or spacecraft. Cf. LAUNCHING ***pad***. M20.

🕮 **1b** A. BLOND The inaugural meeting was held . . in a bachelor pad. **3** J. F. SOUTH A . . tourniquet with a bandage and a pad. *Guardian* Cotton wool pads laid on my eyelids. ***brake pad***, ***ink pad***, ***sanitary pad***, ***shoulder pad***, etc. **b** J. A. MICHENER Plishippus . . evolved . . with the pads on which his ancestors had run eliminated. A. CAMPBELL The tips, rather than the pads, of the fingers are used. ***c elbow-pad***, ***leg-pad***, etc. **5** L. DUNCAN The detective drew out a pad of letter-sized forms. ***drawing-pad***, ***notepad***, ***writing-pad***, etc. **8** J. MCPHEE The 'airstrip' there is so short it looks like a helicopter pad. M. MCCONNELL She had seen Challenger launched from the neighbouring pad.

▶ **II 9** MECHANICS. The socket of a brace, in which the end of the bit is inserted; a tool-handle into which tools of different gauges, etc., can be fitted, as in a padsaw. Cf. earlier POD *noun*^{1}. L17.
10 A projection engaging with the escapement of a watch or clock; a pallet. E18.
11 DYEING. = PADDER *noun*^{2} 2. M20.
12 ELECTRICITY. A resistance network inserted into a transmission line to attenuate all frequencies equally by a known amount. M20.
13 Money paid to a police officer etc. by an establishment for ignoring its illegal activities. Freq. in ***on the pad***, (of a police officer etc.) receiving regular payments of such money. *US slang.* M20.

Comb.: **pad-cloth** a saddle-cloth; **pad eye** ENGINEERING a flat metal plate with a projecting loop or ring, made all in one piece; **pad mangle** = PADDER *noun*^{2} 2; **pad money** *US slang* money paid for lodgings; **pad-play** CRICKET the use of leg-pads by a batsman to protect the wicket; **pad room** *US colloq.* a waiting-room for performers in a theatre; **pad-saddle** = sense 2a above; **padsaw** a saw consisting of a narrow blade in a wooden handle, used for cutting holes; **pad-steam** *adjective* & *noun* (DYEING) (designating) a process in which fabric is first padded and then steamed; **pad stitch** = PADDING ***stitch***; **padstone** a stone or concrete block built into a wall to distribute pressure.

pad /pad/ *noun*^{4}. *obsolete* exc. *Hist.* L16.
[Var. of PED *noun*^{1}.]
An open basket, usu. made of osier, used esp. as a variable measure for fish, fruit, etc.

pad /pad/ *verb*^{1}, *adverb*, & *noun*^{5}. M16.
[from PAD *noun*^{2} or Low German *padden* tread, tramp; in sense A.2b prob. partly imit.]
▶ **A** *verb.* Infl. **-dd-**.
▶ **I 1 a** *verb trans.* Tread, trudge, or tramp along (a road etc.). M16. ▸**b** *verb intrans.* Travel on foot; tread, tramp, or trudge *along* (a road etc.). E17.
2 *verb intrans.* †**a** Of a horse: pace. E–M18. ▸**b** Of a person or animal: walk or run with soft steady footsteps. Cf. PAT *verb* 3b. L19.
3 *verb trans.* Tread or beat down by frequent walking; form (a path) by treading. *dial.* M18.

🕮 **2b** V. WOOLF They heard the dog's paws padding on the carpet behind him. K. TYNAN Mr. Wanamaker pads ferally through the debris. E. NORTH Mo got out of bed . . and padded barefoot . . towards the window.

▶ **II 4** *verb intrans.* Rob on the highway; be a footpad. Cf. PAD *noun*^{3} 3. *slang* (*obsolete* exc. *Hist.*). M17.
Phrases: **pad the hoof** *slang* go on foot, tramp.
▶ **B** *adverb.* With the sound of soft steady footsteps. L16
▶ **C** *noun.* The sound of soft steady footsteps. L19.

🕮 B. HINES The pad of the rubber studs on the concrete hardly differed from that in the changing room.

pad /pad/ *verb*^{2} *trans.* Infl. **-dd-**. E19.
[from PAD *noun*^{3}.]
1 Fill out or stuff with a pad or padding, esp. so as to give shape, protect, or make comfortable. E19.
2 *fig.* Fill out or expand (spoken or written material) with superfluous words or matter. Usu. foll. by *out*. E19. ▸**b** Increase (an official list, claim for payment, etc.) with unauthorized or fraudulent items. E20.
3 DYEING. Impregnate *with* a liquid or paste by pressing between rollers. M19.

🕮 **1** LYTTON But, sir, we must be padded; we are much too thin. S. MIDDLETON He would turn to his fire, lifting it, or padding it round with fuel. **padded cell** a room for violent patients in a mental hospital, having walls padded to prevent self-injury. **2a** W. C. WILLIAMS Stretching the story, padding it up a bit . . wouldn't help to clarify it. B. PYM I did make it a bit longer . . . Difficult to pad things out, though.

pada /ˈpʌdə/ *noun*^{1}. L19.
[Sanskrit = step.]
An Indian lyric poem, set to music.

pada /ˈpʌdə/ *noun*^{2}. L19.
[Sanskrit = word.]
A mode of presenting and reciting the Vedic texts.

pada /ˈpɑːdə/ *noun*^{3}. E20.
[mod. Sanskrit *pāda* foot, quarter.]
A line of Sanskrit verse, usu. a quarter of a four-line stanza.

padang /ˈpadaŋ/ *noun.* E20.
[Malay.]
In Malaysia and Indonesia: an open grassy space; a playing field.

padauk *noun* var. of PADOUK.

padayatra /pɑːdəˈjɑːtrɑː, -trə/ *noun.* M20.
[mod. Sanskrit, from *pāda* foot + *yātrā* journey.]
In the Indian subcontinent: a pilgrimage, a political and religious tour or march.

padder /ˈpadə/ *noun*^{1}. *slang* (now *Hist.*). E17.
[from PAD *noun*^{2}, *verb*^{1} + -ER^1.]
A footpad, a highwayman, a robber.

padder /ˈpadə/ *noun*^{2}. E19.
[from PAD *verb*^{2} + -ER^1.]
1 A person who wears pads or padding. *rare.* E19.
2 DYEING. A machine for impregnating material with a liquid or paste by pressing between rollers. E20.
3 ELECTRONICS. A usu. adjustable capacitor connected in series in a tuned circuit in order to improve low frequency tracking with another tuned circuit. Also ***padder capacitor***, ***padder condenser***. Cf. TRIMMER 9. M20.

padding /ˈpadɪŋ/ *noun.* E19.
[from PAD *verb*^{2} + -ING^1.]
1 a Soft material (esp. cotton, felt, foam, etc.) used to pad or stuff something. E19. ▸**b** Superfluous matter introduced simply to lengthen or expand a book, speech, etc. M19.

2 The action of PAD *verb*[2]; an instance of this. M19.
3 *ELECTRONICS.* The use of a padder. M20.
Comb.: **padding capacitor**, **padding condenser** = PADDER *noun*[2] 3; **padding stitch** an embroidery stitch used as a foundation for another stitch, esp. satin stitch.

paddle /ˈpad(ə)l/ *noun*[1]. LME.
[Origin uncertain: cf. PATTLE *noun*. Cf. also SPADDLE.]
▸ **I 1** A small spadelike implement with a long handle, used for cleaning earth from a plough, digging, etc. LME.
▸ **II 2** A short broad-bladed oar used without a rowlock, being dipped more or less vertically into water and pulled backwards to propel a canoe, boat, etc. E17.
3 Each of the (orig.) arms or spokes or (later) boards or floats fitted round the circumference of a revolving drum or axle to propel a ship etc.; *esp.* each of the boards or floats of a paddle-wheel or mill-wheel. Also = ***paddle-wheel*** below. L17.
4 *ZOOLOGY.* A flattened limb used for locomotion in an aquatic animal, as a turtle, whale, or plesiosaur; a flipper. Also *esp.* (*a*) the foot of a duck; (*b*) the wing of a penguin; (*c*) each of the ciliated plates of a ctenophore; (*d*) each of the swimming limbs of a crustacean. M19.

> 🕮 **2** C. RYAN Eight paddles, four feet long, were supposed to accompany each boat. J. AUEL Antlers, with some trimming, make good paddles . . for pushing . . through water. ***double paddle***: see DOUBLE *adjective & adverb*. **3** W. GOLDING Projecting from her were the biggest wheels in the world and each . . bore a dozen paddles.

▸ **III** *transf.* **5** A flat-bladed instrument or tool; *spec.* (*a*) such an instrument used for stirring or mixing in any of various technical or industrial processes; (*b*) (chiefly *N. Amer.*) an instrument for administering corporal punishment; (*c*) a short-handled bat used in various ball games, esp. table tennis; (*d*) *COMPUTING* a device with a handle used to control the movement of an image on a VDU or television screen; (*e*) *MEDICINE* a plastic-covered electrode used in cardiac stimulation. M17.
6 A sliding panel which is raised or lowered to regulate the flow of something; *spec.* (*a*) a sluice in a weir or lock-gate; (*b*) a panel controlling the flow of grain from a hopper. L18.
7 The long flat snout of a paddlefish. L19.
8 *ASTRONAUTICS.* A flat array of solar cells projecting from a spacecraft. M20.
Comb.: **paddle ball** a game played with a light ball and wooden bat in a four-walled handball court; **paddle board** (*a*) each of the floats or boards of a paddle-wheel; (*b*) a surfboard; **paddle-boat** a boat propelled by a paddle-wheel; **paddle-box** the casing which encloses the upper part of a steamer's paddle-wheel; **paddle-crab** a swimming crab, *esp.* the edible N. American crab *Callinectes sapidus*; **paddlefish** either of two large fishes resembling sturgeons and constituting the family Polyodontidae, *Polyodon spathula* of the Mississippi river and *Psephurus gladius* of the Yangtze river, both having a very long flat snout; **paddle foot** *US slang* (*a*) an infantryman; (*b*) a member of an airforce ground crew; **paddle-steamer** a steamer propelled by paddle-wheels; **paddle tennis** a type of tennis played in a small court with a sponge-rubber ball and wooden or plastic bat; **paddle-wheel** (*a*) a wheel for propelling a ship etc., having paddle-boards fitted radially which press backwards against the water; (*b*) a device of a similar shape used in a game of chance; **paddle-wheeler** *N. Amer.* = *paddle-steamer* above; **paddle-wood** the light elastic wood of a S. American tree, *Aspidosperma excelsum* (family Apocynaceae), used esp. for canoe-paddles.
▪ **paddle-like** *adjective* resembling a paddle in shape or function M19.

paddle /ˈpad(ə)l/ *noun*[2]. *Scot. & north.* L16.
[Origin unkn.]
More fully ***paddle-cock***. The lumpfish; = ***cock-paddle*** s.v. COCK *noun*[1].

paddle /ˈpad(ə)l/ *verb*[1] & *noun*[3]. In sense 4 also (*dial.*) **poddle** /ˈpɒd(ə)l/. M16.
[Prob. of Low Dutch origin: cf. Low German *paddeln* tramp about, frequentative of *padden* PAD *verb*[1] & see -LE[3].]
▸ **A** *verb*. **1** *verb intrans.* Walk or wade about in mud or shallow water; dabble the feet or hands in shallow water etc. M16.
2 *verb intrans.* Finger or play idly or fondly *with* (a thing). Also foll. by *in*. Now *rare* or *obsolete*. E17. ▸†**b** *verb trans.* Finger or play with idly or fondly. Only in E17.
†**3** *verb trans. & intrans.* Waste or squander (money etc.). E17–M19.
4 *verb intrans.* Walk with short unsteady or uncertain steps; toddle. M18. ▸**b** *verb trans.* Trample down or over, esp. with wet or muddy feet. *dial.* L18.

> 🕮 **1** C. ISHERWOOD Peter paddled idly in the water with his fingers. C. P. SNOW They had been paddling in the fringe of one pond. *fig.*: S. ROSENBERG To talk about Stalin was to paddle in dangerous waters. **paddling pool** a shallow artificial pool or portable water-tub for children to play in. **2** SHAKES. *Oth.* Didst thou not see her paddle with the palm of his hand? **4a** THACKERAY A hundred little children are paddling up and down the steps to St. James's Park.

▸ **B** *noun*. †**1** Fuss, ado. *rare*. Only in M17.
2 The action or an act of paddling in mud or shallow water. M19.
▪ **paddler** *noun*[1] a person who paddles or wades about L17.

paddle /ˈpad(ə)l/ *verb*[2] & *noun*[4]. L17.
[from PADDLE *noun*[1].]
▸ **A** *verb*. **1** *verb intrans.* Move through water propelled by a paddle or paddles. Freq. foll. by *along*, *away*, *off*, etc. L17. ▸**b** Row lightly or gently; *spec.* (of a racing crew) row without exerting full power. L17.
2 *verb trans.* Propel (a canoe, boat, etc.) by means of a paddle or paddles; make (one's way etc.) by paddling. Also, transport (a person) by this method. M18.
3 *verb trans.* Beat (a person) with a paddle or strap; spank. *colloq.* (chiefly *N. Amer.*). M19.
4 *verb trans.* Stir or mix using a paddle. L19.

> 🕮 **1** P. F. BOLLER He planned to paddle across the river in a canoe and swim back. M. WESLEY Duck cruised, coots paddled in desperate haste to reach the reeds. **2** P. THEROUX The brown Magdalena River on which men paddled dugout canoes. N. SHAVE Paddling her way to a Bronze Medal. ***paddle one's own canoe***: see CANOE *noun*.

▸ **B** *noun*. The action or an act of paddling. M19.
▪ **paddler** *noun*[2] †(*a*) = PADDLE *noun*[1] 2; (*b*) a person who paddles a canoe etc.; (*c*) *colloq.* a paddle-steamer: L17

paddock /ˈpadək/ *noun*[1]. *arch.* exc. *Scot. & north.* Also (*Scot. & north.*) **puddock** /ˈpʌdək/. ME.
[from PAD *noun*[1] + -OCK.]
1 A frog, a toad; *fig.* a contemptible person. ME.
2 A wooden (usu. triangular) sledge for transporting heavy goods. *Scot.* M18.
Comb.: **paddock-hair** the soft hair or down on a newborn baby or bird; **paddock-pipe** any of several marsh or aquatic horsetails, esp. *Equisetum fluviatile*; **paddock-stone** a toadstone; **paddock-stool** a toadstool; a mushroom.

paddock /ˈpadək/ *noun*[2] & *verb*. E17.
[Alt. of PARROCK.]
▸ **A** *noun*. **1** A small field or enclosure; *esp.* one for horses adjoining a house or stable. E17. ▸**b** An enclosure adjoining a racecourse where horses or motor cars are assembled before a race. M19.
2 Any field or plot of land enclosed by fencing. *Austral. & NZ.* E19.
3 *MINING.* An open excavation in a superficial deposit. Also, a store-place for ore etc. Chiefly *Austral. & NZ.* M19.
1b ***saddling paddock***: see SADDLE *verb* 1.
Comb.: **paddock-grazing** in dairy farming, a method of pasture management involving field rotation.
▸ **B** *verb*. **1** *verb intrans.* *MINING.* Excavate washdirt in shallow ground. Also, store (ore etc.) in a paddock. M19.
2 *verb trans.* Enclose in or as in a paddock; *Austral. & NZ* enclose or fence in (a sheep-run etc.). M19.

paddy /ˈpadi/ *noun*[1]. In sense 1 usu. **padi**. E17.
[Malay *padi* corresp. to Javanese *pari*, Kannada *bhatta*.]
1 Rice before threshing; *COMMERCE* rice in the husk. Also, the rice plant. E17.
2 A paddy-field. M20.
Comb.: **paddy-bird** any of various birds which frequent paddy-fields, esp. a java sparrow, an egret; **paddy-field** a field where rice is grown.

Paddy /ˈpadi/ *noun*[2]. Also **p-**. L18.
[Pet-form of Irish male forename *Pádraig* Patrick: see -Y[6]. Cf. PAT *noun*[2].]
1 (A nickname for) an Irishman. *slang. derog.* L18.
2 A bricklayer's or builder's labourer. Now *dial.* M19.
3 A fit of temper, a rage. *colloq.* L19.
4 A white person. *Black slang.* M20.
5 A train for conveying coal from a pit-head. *slang.* M20.
Comb.: **Paddy Doyle** *Military slang* confinement in the cells; **Paddyland** *derog.* Ireland; **Paddy's hurricane** *Nautical slang* a flat calm; **Paddy's lantern** *Nautical slang* the moon; **Paddy's lucerne** *Austral.* a tropical evergreen shrub of the mallow family, *Sida rhombifolia*, formerly grown for the fibre of its stem and now a serious weed; also called ***Queensland hemp***; **Paddy mail** = sense 5 above; **Paddy wagon** (chiefly *N. Amer.*) a van for conveying prisoners; occas., a police car; **Paddy Wester** *Nautical slang* an inefficient or inexperienced seaman; **paddywhack** (*a*) = sense 1 above; (*b*) = sense 3 above; (*c*) *dial.* a severe beating, a thrashing.
▪ **Paddyism** *noun* (*slang, derog.*) (*a*) Irish quality or character; (*b*) an Irishism: E19.

paddy /ˈpadi/ *adjective*. *rare*. M19.
[from PAD *noun*[3] + -Y[1].]
Cushion-like; soft, mild; *fig.* placidly self-satisfied.

paddymelon /ˈpadɪˌmɛlən/ *noun*[1]. Orig. *Austral.* Also (esp. *SCIENCE*) **pademelon**. E19.
[Alt. of Aboriginal name.]
Any of several small brush wallabies, esp. one of the genus *Thylogale*.

paddymelon /ˈpadɪˌmɛlən/ *noun*[2]. *Austral.* L19.
[Perh. from PADDY *noun*[2] + MELON *noun*[1].]
Any of various plants of the gourd family; *esp.* a trailing or climbing annual, *Cucumis myriocarpus*, native to Africa, which has bristly melon-like fruits and has become naturalized in inland Australia.

padge /padʒ/ *noun*. Chiefly *dial.* M19.
[Perh. var. of PUDGE *noun*[2].]
A barn owl, = PUDGE *noun*[2] 2. Also ***padge-owl***.

padi *noun* see PADDY *noun*[1].

Padishah /ˈpɑːdɪʃɑː/ *noun*. Also **Padshah** /ˈpɑːdʃɑː/. E17.
[Persian *pād(i)šāh*, Pahlavi *pātakšā(h*, from *pati* lord + *šāh* SHAH.]
Hist. (A title of) the ruler of a Muslim country or empire, esp. (formerly) the Shah of Iran, the Sultan of Turkey, the Mughal emperor.

padkos /ˈpatkɔs/ *noun*. *S. Afr.* M19.
[Afrikaans, from *pad* road + *kos* (Dutch *kost*) food.]
Food for a journey; provisions.

padlock /ˈpadlɒk/ *noun & verb*. L15.
[from unkn. 1st elem. + LOCK *noun*[2].]
▸ **A** *noun*. A detachable lock designed to hang on the object fastened, having a pivoted or sliding shackle for passing through a staple, ring, etc., before being locked into a device resembling a socket. L15.
▸ **B** *verb trans.* Secure by means of a padlock. M17.

> 🕮 L. GRANT-ADAMSON The gates of the villa were still padlocked but light came from a ground floor window. *fig.*: SIR W. SCOTT My mouth shall never be padlocked by any noble of them all.

padma /ˈpʌdmə/ *noun*. M19.
[Sanskrit = lotus.]
(The flower of) the lotus-plant; an emblematic representation of this; *spec.* (**P-**) one given as a civil decoration in India, the title of this award.

padmasana /pʌdˈmɑːsənə/ *noun*. L19.
[Sanskrit *padmāsana*, from prec. + *āsana* seat, posture.]
YOGA. = LOTUS 4b.

padouk /paˈdaʊk/ *noun*. Also **padauk**. M19.
[Burmese.]
Any of various large leguminous trees of the genus *Pterocarpus*, esp. *P. soyauxii* of W. Africa, *P. dalbergioides* of the Andaman Islands, and *P. macrocarpus* of Myanmar (Burma) and Thailand; the reddish hardwood obtained from any of these trees, which resembles rosewood.

Padovan /ˈpadəv(ə)n/ *noun & adjective*. *rare*. L20.
[from Italian *Padova* Padua + -AN.]
▸ **A** *noun*. = PADUAN *noun* 1. L20.
▸ **B** *adjective*. = PADUAN *adjective*. L20.

padre /ˈpɑːdri, -dreɪ/ *noun*. L16.
[Italian, Spanish, Portuguese from Latin *patre-*, *pater* FATHER *noun*.]
In Italy, Spain, Portugal, Latin America, and other areas of Spanish influence: (a title of) a Christian clergyman, esp. a Roman Catholic priest. Now chiefly (*colloq.*), a chaplain in the armed services.

padrino /paˈdriːnəʊ, *foreign* paˈðrino/ *noun*. Pl. **-os**. M19.
[Spanish, dim. of *padre* father.]
In Spanish-speaking parts of America: a godfather or best man; a sponsor or patron.

padrone /paˈdrəʊni, *foreign* paˈdroːne/ *noun*. Pl. **-nes** /-nɪz/, **-ni** /-ni/. Fem. (esp. in sense (c)) **-na** /-nə/, *foreign* -na/, pl. **-nas** /-nəz/, **-ne** /-ne/. L17.
[Italian.]
A patron, a master; *spec.* (*a*) (*obsolete* exc. *Hist.*) the master of a trading-vessel in the Mediterranean; (*b*) (now chiefly *US colloq.*) an employer, a manager; *esp.* an exploitative employer of unskilled immigrant workers; (*c*) the proprietor of an inn or hotel in Italy.

Padshah *noun* var. of PADISHAH.

pad thai /pad ˈtʌɪ/ *noun phr.* L20.
[Thai.]
A Thai dish based on rice noodles.

Paduan /ˈpadjʊən, ˈpadʊən/ *noun & adjective*. E17.
[from *Padua* (*Padova*) (see below) + -AN. Cf. PAVANE.]
▸ **A** *noun*. **1** A native or inhabitant of Padua, a city in NE Italy. E17.
2 *Hist.* A bronze or silver counterfeit coin forged in 16th-cent. Padua in imitation of an ancient coin. M18.
3 = PAVANE. L19.
▸ **B** *adjective*. Of or pertaining to Padua. L17.

paduasoy /ˈpadjʊəsɔɪ/ *noun & adjective*. L16.
[from French *pou-de-soie* (earlier *pout de soie*) of unkn. origin, by assoc. with earlier *Padua say* (SAY *noun*[1]) from Padua, Italy.]
(Made of) a heavy rich corded or embossed silk fabric, popular in the 18th cent.

paean /ˈpiːən/ *noun*. L16.
[Latin from Greek *paian*, (Altic) *paiōn* hymn to Apollo invoked by the name *Paian*, *Paiōn*, orig. the Homeric name of the physician of the gods. Cf. PAEON.]
1 *GREEK HISTORY.* An invocation or hymn of thanksgiving addressed to a god or goddess; *esp.* a song to invoke or celebrate victory in battle; *gen.* any solemn song or chant. Also more fully ***Io paean***. L16.
2 Orig., a song of praise or thanksgiving; a shout of triumph or exultation. Now usu., a written or spoken attribution of praise. L16.

> 🕮 **2** CLIVE JAMES Dunne's excellent long article about California . . is an unbroken paean. A. BURGESS The novel is a paean to marriage.

paedagogy *noun* see PEDAGOGY.

paedeia *noun* var. of PAIDEIA.

paederasty *noun* var. of PEDERASTY.

paedeutics /piːˈdjuːtɪks/ *noun. rare.* Also **pai-** /pai-/. M19.
[from Greek *paideutikos* of or for teaching, from *paideutikē* education: see -ICS.]
The science, art, or practice of education.

paediatric /piːdɪˈatrɪk/ *adjective.* Also ***ped-**. L19.
[from PAED(O- + Greek *iatrikos* (see IATRIC).]
Of or pertaining to paediatrics or the diseases of children.
▪ **paediatrician** /-ˈtrɪʃ(ə)n/ *noun* a doctor who specializes in paediatrics E20. **paediatrist** /piːˈdʌɪətrɪst, piːdɪˈatrɪst/ *noun* = PAEDIATRICIAN L19.

paediatrics /piːdɪˈatrɪks/ *noun.* Also ***ped-**. L19.
[formed as prec.: see -ICS.]
The branch of medical science that deals with childhood and the diseases of children.

paedication, **paedicator** *nouns* vars. of PEDICATION, PEDICATOR.

paedicator *noun* see PEDICATOR.

paedo- /ˈpiːdəʊ/ *combining form.* Also ***pedo-** /ˈpiːdəʊ, ˈpɛdəʊ/. Before a vowel **paed-**, ***ped-**.
[from Greek *paid-*, *pais* child, boy + -O-.]
Forming nouns with the senses 'of a child or children' or (occas.) *spec.* 'of a boy or boys'.
▪ **paedarchy** *noun* rule or government by children M19. **paedoˈbaptism** *noun* infant baptism M17. **paedoˈbaptist** *noun* an adherent of paedobaptism M17. **paeˈdocracy** *noun* government by children M17. **paedoˈdontic** *adjective* of or pertaining to paedodontics M20. **paedoˈdontics** *noun* the branch of dentistry that deals with children's teeth E20. **paedoˈdontist** *noun* a dentist specializing in the treatment of children E20.

paedogamy /piːˈdɒɡəmi/ *noun.* Also ***ped-**. E20.
[from PAEDO- + -GAMY.]
BIOLOGY. In certain protists, reproduction by the fusion of gametes derived from the same parent cell.
▪ **paedogamous** *adjective* E20.

paedogenesis /piːdə(ʊ)ˈdʒɛnɪsɪs/ *noun.* Also ***ped-**. L19.
[from PAEDO- + -GENESIS.]
ZOOLOGY. Reproduction (usu. parthenogenetic) by a larval or immature form.
▪ **paedogeˈnetic** *adjective* pertaining to or characterized by paedogenesis L19.

paedomorphic /piːdə(ʊ)ˈmɔːfɪk/ *adjective.* Also ***ped-**. L19.
[from PAEDO- + MORPHIC.]
BIOLOGY. Exhibiting paedomorphism or paedomorphosis; occas. *gen.*, childlike.

paedomorphism /piːdə(ʊ)ˈmɔːfɪz(ə)m/ *noun.* Also ***ped-**. L19.
[from PAEDO- + -MORPHISM.]
BIOLOGY. The retention of juvenile characteristics in adult forms; = NEOTENY 1.

paedomorphosis /piːdə(ʊ)ˈmɔːfəsɪs, -mɔːˈfəʊsɪs/ *noun.* Also ***ped-**. E20.
[from PAEDO- + MORPHOSIS.]
BIOLOGY. The retention of juvenile characteristics of an ancestral form in the more mature forms of its descendants.

paedophile /ˈpiːdə(ʊ)fʌɪl/ *noun & adjective.* Also ***ped-** /ˈpɛd-, ˈpiːd-/. M20.
[from Greek *paidofilos* loving children, formed as PAEDO-: see -PHILE.]
▶ **A** *noun.* A person who exhibits paedophilia. M20.
▶ **B** *adjective.* = PAEDOPHILIAC *adjective.* M20.

paedophilia /piːdə(ʊ)ˈfɪlɪə/ *noun.* Also ***ped-** /ˈpɛd-, ˈpiːd-/. E20.
[from PAEDO- + -PHILIA.]
Sexual desire directed towards children.
▪ **paedophiliac** *noun & adjective* (**a**) *noun* = PAEDOPHILE *noun*; (**b**) *adjective* of, pertaining to, or characterized by paedophilia: M20. **paedophilic** *noun & adjective* (a) paedophiliac E20.

paedotribe /ˈpiːdə(ʊ)trʌɪb/ *noun.* Also **ped-** /ˈpɛd-, ˈpiːd-/. L16.
[Greek *paidotribēs*, formed as PAEDO- + *-tribēs*, from *tribein* rub.]
GREEK HISTORY. A teacher of gymnastic exercises, esp. wrestling.

paedotrophy /piːˈdɒtrəfi/ *noun. rare.* Also ***ped-** /ˈpɛd-, ˈpiːd-/. M19.
[Greek *paidotrophia*, formed as PAEDO-: see -TROPHY.]
The rearing of children.

Paelignian /pɛˈlɪɡnɪən, pʌɪ-/ *noun & adjective.* Also **Pel-**. E17.
[from Latin *Paeligni*, *Pel-* Paelignians + -AN.]
Hist. ▶ **A** *noun.* **1** A member of an Oscan-Umbrian people centred on Corfinium in ancient southern Italy. E17.
2 The language of this people. M20.
▶ **B** *adjective.* Of or pertaining to the Paelignians or their language. M19.

paella /pʌɪˈɛlə, pɑː-/ *noun.* L19.
[Catalan from Old French *paele* (mod. *paêle*), from Latin *patella* pan, dish.]
A Spanish dish of rice, saffron, chicken, seafood, vegetables, etc., cooked and served in a large shallow pan.

paenula /ˈpiːnjʊlə/ *noun.* Pl. **-lae** /-liː/. LME.
[Latin.]
ROMAN ANTIQUITIES. A type of sleeveless cloak or tabard covering the whole body, worn esp. as part of senatorial dress.

paeon /ˈpiːən/ *noun.* E17.
[Latin from Greek *paiōn*: see PAEAN.]
A metrical foot of one long and three short syllables in varying order.
first paeon, **second paeon**, etc.: whose first, second, etc., syllable is long.
▪ **paeˈonic** *adjective & noun* (**a**) *adjective* of, pertaining to, or having the characteristics of, a paeon or paeons; composed of paeons; (**b**) *noun* a paeonic verse or foot: E17.

paepae /ˈpʌɪpʌɪ/ *noun.* Pl. same. M19.
[Polynesian.]
In parts of Polynesia: a raised stone platform around the foundation of a house or other building; a paved area or courtyard in front of a building.

paff /paf/ *interjection. rare.* Also **paf**. L19.
[Imit.]
Repr. the sound of a sharp blow or impact. Also, expr. contempt.

pagan /ˈpeɪɡ(ə)n/ *noun & adjective.* LME.
[Latin *paganus* villager, rustic, civilian, non-militant, opp to *miles* soldier, one of the army, in Christian Latin heathen as opp. to Christian or Jewish, from *pagus* (rural) district, the country: see -AN. Cf. HEATHEN.]
▶ **A** *noun.* **1** A person holding religious beliefs other than those of any of the main religions of the world, *spec.* a non-Christian; (*derog.*) a follower of a polytheistic or pantheistic religion. Also *transf.*, a person holding views not consonant with a prevailing system of belief etc. (now *rare*); a person considered as being of irreligious or unrestrained character or behaviour. LME.
†**2** An illicit or clandestine lover; a prostitute. L16–M17.

> 🕮 **1** W. BLACK 'But what are his politics?' said the Lady Sylvia to their political pagan. C. S. LEWIS Christians and Pagans had much more in common with each other than either has with a post-Christian. *Daughters of Sarah* I am a practicing Pagan I follow the old religion of Wicca.

▶ **B** *adjective.* Of, pertaining to, or characteristic of a pagan or pagans. LME.

> 🕮 M. PYKE In pagan antiquity every tree . . had its own *genius-loci*—its own guardian spirit. E. F. BENSON It was a sort of pagan harvest festival, full of folk-lore, and was tremendously picturesque.

▪ **pagandom** *noun* paganism; pagans collectively: M19. **paganish** *adjective* (now *rare*) pagan; paganistic: L16. **paˈganity** *noun* (now *rare* or *obsolete*) = PAGANISM LME. **paganiˈzation** *noun* the action of making or fact of becoming pagan in character, beliefs, etc. M19. **paganize** *verb trans. & intrans.* make or become pagan in character, beliefs, etc. E17. **paganry** *noun* (now *rare* or *obsolete*) = PAGANISM LME.

paganism /ˈpeɪɡ(ə)nɪz(ə)m/ *noun.* LME.
[Late (eccl.) Latin *paganismus*: see prec., -ISM.]
The belief and practices of pagans; pagan character or quality. Formerly also (*rare*), pagans collectively.
▪ **pagaˈnistic** *adjective* of or pertaining to pagans or paganism M20.

page /peɪdʒ/ *noun*[1] *& verb*[1]. ME.
[Old & mod. French, perh. from Italian *paggio* from Greek *paidion* dim. of *paid-*, *pais* boy.]
▶ **A** *noun.* †**1** A boy, a youth. ME–L16.
†**2** A male person of low status or uncouth manners. *derog.* ME–E16.
3 A male servant (esp. a boy) employed as a helper or apprentice to a more experienced servant or officer. Now only (*dial.*), a shepherd's assistant. ME.
4 *Hist.* A boy in training for knighthood, ranking next below a squire in the personal service of a knight and following the latter on foot. ME. ▸†**b** A foot-soldier. ME–M16.
5 **a** *Hist.* A man or boy (orig. esp. of gentle birth) employed as the personal attendant of a person of rank; *spec.* an officer in a royal or princely household, an equerry. ME. ▸**b** A young person (esp. in uniform) employed in a hotel, club, or other large establishment, to attend to the door, run errands, etc. L18. ▸**c** A messenger or errand boy employed by a legislative body. *N. Amer.* M19. ▸**d** A young boy attending a bride at a wedding. L19.
6 ENTOMOLOGY. A black and green S. American moth of the family Uraniidae. L19.

> 🕮 **3** T. H. WHITE As a page, Wart had learned to lay the tables . . and to bring meat from the kitchen. **5** SHAKES. *Rom. & Jul.* Where is my page? Go, villain, fetch a surgeon.

Comb.: **page-boy** (**a**) a boy serving as a page; *esp.* = sense 5b above; (**b**) a woman's hairstyle consisting of a long shoulder-length bob with the ends rolled under.
▶ **B** *verb trans.* **1** Attend (to) or follow as or like a page. Now *rare* or *obsolete.* M16.
2 Search for (a person) as a page or messenger, esp. by calling out the name of the person sought for; call for (an individual) by name over a public address system; have (a person) searched for in this way. Now also, contact by means of a radio pager. E20.

> 🕮 **2** M. BINCHY David was paged urgently, and rushed to the phone.

▪ **pagehood** *noun* the state or condition of being a page E19. **pager** *noun*[1] a radio device with a bleeper, activated from a central point to alert the wearer M20. **pageship** *noun* the office or position of a page; *joc.* (with possess. adjective, as ***your pageship*** etc.) a mock title of respect given to a page: M19.

page /peɪdʒ/ *noun*[2] *& verb*[2]. L16.
[Old & mod. French, reduced form of *pagene* from Latin *pagina* vine-trellis, column of writing, page or leaf, from *pangere* fasten, fix in or together.]
▶ **A** *noun.* **1** Either side of a leaf of a book, manuscript, letter, etc. Also, a complete leaf of a book etc. L16. ▸**b** That which is (actually or notionally) written, printed, etc., on a page, or which fills a VDU screen. E19. ▸**c** COMPUTING. A division of the main store of a computer, or of the data stored. M20.
2 *fig.* Written or printed material; *spec.* (*arch. & poet.*) an author's collected work; a memorable event or episode such as would fill a page in a written history etc. E17.
3 PRINTING. **a** The type set or made up for printing a page. E18. ▸**b** A parcel of new type made up by a type-founder. L19.

> 🕮 **1** C. ISHERWOOD Turning over the pages of a book I have been reading. J. FRAME They saw the morning paper, the headlines on the front page. ***full-page***: see FULL *adjective*. ***Yellow Pages***: see YELLOW *adjective*. **b** E. B. BROWNING I offer these pages as a small testimony of . . gratitude. A. N. WILSON The narrator creates, for perhaps a page and a half, the illusion that we are really there. **2** SHELLEY His page Which charms the chosen spirits of the time. *Daily Telegraph* A bright page in her military history.

Comb.: **page charge** a fee per page of a published article levied by a periodical etc. upon the academic body or institution to which the author belongs; **page-galley** (**a**) a galley containing enough type to print a page; (**b**) a galley proof with type divided into pages and numbered; **page-one** *adjective* (*N. Amer.*) worthy of being featured on the front page of a newspaper etc.; **page-paper** PRINTING stiff paper or board used to support a page of type before imposition; **page printer** a machine that prints or types text in paged form; **page-proof** a pull or print taken from type in paged form; **page reference**: to a specific page or group of pages in a book, periodical, etc.; **page three girl** [after the standard page position in the *Sun*, a Brit. newspaper] a nude or semi-nude model whose photograph appears usu. as part of a regular series in some tabloid newspapers; **page-turn** each point in a musical score where the page must be turned; **page-turner** (**a**) a person who turns the pages of a musician's score, esp. during a performance; (**b**) *fig.* an exciting book; **page-turning** *adjective* (of a book) very exciting.
▶ **B** *verb.* **1** *verb trans.* = PAGINATE. E17.
2 *verb trans.* PRINTING. ▸**a** Make up (composed type) into pages. L19. ▸**b** Pack up (new type) into pages for sending out. E20.
3 *verb intrans.* Look *through* the pages of a book etc.; peruse text on a VDU one screenful at a time (foll. by *down, through, up*). M20.

> 🕮 **1** G. B. SHAW Kindly send me the proofs. They ought not to be paged. **3** S. BIKO The police only need to page at random through their statute book to be able . . to charge a victim. A. LURIE Polly was . . idly paging through the *New York Times* travel section.

▪ **paged** *adjective* (**a**) (of a book etc.) having the pages numbered; (**b**) (with prefixed adjective or numeral) having pages of a specified kind or number; (**c**) COMPUTING divided into pages: M19. **pageful** *noun* as much text etc. as fills a page or VDU screen L19. **pager** *noun*[2] (**a**) (with prefixed numeral) a book, letter, etc., having a specified number of pages; (**b**) ***front-pager***: see FRONT *noun & adjective*: M20. **paging** *noun* (**a**) = PAGINATION; (**b**) COMPUTING division (of storage) into pages; the transfer of pages between a central and an auxiliary store: L18.

pageant /ˈpadʒ(ə)nt/ *noun & adjective.* LME.
[Origin unkn.]
▶ **A** *noun.* **1** A scene acted on a stage; *spec.* a scene or act of a medieval mystery play. *obsolete* exc. *Hist.* LME. ▸**b** *fig.* A person's role or part in a series of events. Formerly also, a performance intended to deceive, a trick. *arch.* LME.
2 A stage or platform for presenting theatrical scenes or tableaux; *esp.* a movable structure used in the open air performance of a mystery play. *obsolete* exc. *Hist.* LME. ▸†**b** A piece of stage machinery. Also *gen.*, any mechanical device. E16–M19.
3 A tableau, allegorical representation, etc., erected on a fixed stage or movable float for public exhibition; *gen.* any show or temporary exhibit forming part of a public celebration. *obsolete* exc. *Hist.* LME.
4 *fig.* A specious display of an emotion etc., a thing without substance or reality. E17.

5 A sumptuous spectacle arranged for effect; *esp.* an elaborate or stately procession. E19. ▸**b** *spec.* A play or parade illustrating historical events, esp. ones of local occurrence or significance. L19.

▶ **B** *attrib.* or as *adjective.* Of or pertaining to a pageant or pageants; *fig.* specious, insubstantial, vain. M17.

Comb. & special collocations: ***beauty pageant***: see BEAUTY *noun*; **pageant master** a person supervising the production of a pageant or spectacle; **pageant-play** = sense 5b above.

■ **pagean'teer** *noun* (*rare*) a person taking part in a pageant E17.

pageant /ˈpadʒ(ə)nt/ *verb. rare.* E17.
[from prec.]
†**1** *verb trans.* Imitate as in a pageant or play; mimic. (Shakes.) Only in E17.
†**2** *verb trans.* Carry about or exhibit (as) in a pageant. Only in M17.
3 *verb intrans.* Present a pageant or spectacle. Only as ***pageanting*** *verbal noun.* L19.

pageantry /ˈpadʒ(ə)ntri/ *noun.* E17.
[from PAGEANT *noun* + -RY.]
1 Pageants or tableaux collectively; the public performance of these. Now *rare* or *obsolete.* E17.
2 (An) elaborate or sumptuous display or spectacle. M17.
3 *fig.* (An) empty or specious display. M17.

Paget /ˈpadʒɪt/ *noun.* L19.
[Sir James Paget (1814–99), English surgeon.]
MEDICINE. **1** ***Paget's disease***, (*a*) a chronic disease of the elderly characterized by alteration of bone tissue, esp. in the spine, skull or pelvis; also called ***osteitis deformans***; (*b*) inflammation, esp. of the nipple, resembling eczema and associated with underlying cancer. L19.
2 ***Paget cell***, an enlarged epidermal cell associated with Paget's disease of the nipple. E20.
■ **Pagetic** /pəˈdʒɛtɪk/ *adjective* pertaining to or characteristic of Paget's disease of bone L20.

paginal /ˈpadʒɪn(ə)l/ *adjective.* M17.
[Late Latin *paginalis*, from *pagina* PAGE *noun*[2]: see -AL[1].]
Of, pertaining to, or consisting of a page or pages; corresponding page for page.

paginary /ˈpadʒɪn(ə)ri/ *adjective.* E19.
[from Latin *pagina* PAGE *noun*[2] + -ARY[1].]
= prec.

paginate /ˈpadʒɪneɪt/ *verb trans.* L19.
[French *paginer*, from Latin *pagina* PAGE *noun*[2]: see -ATE[3].]
Assign consecutive numbers to the pages of (a book, manuscript, etc.). Cf. FOLIATE *verb* 5.
■ **pagi'nation** *noun* (*a*) the action or an act of paginating; (*b*) the sequence of numbers assigned to any set of pages: M19.

pagle *noun* var. of PAIGLE.

pagne /pan, *foreign* paɲ (*pl. same*)/ *noun.* L17.
[French from Spanish *paño* from Latin *pannus* cloth.]
In W. Africa: a length of cloth; *esp.* one worn draped around the waist or forming a tunic, as a traditional dress for both men and women.

pagoda /pəˈɡəʊdə/ *noun.* Orig. (esp. in sense 2, now *rare* or *obsolete*) **pagod** /ˈpaɡəd/. L16.
[Portuguese *pagode*, prob. ult. from Persian *butkada* idol temple, from *but* idol + *kada* habitation, alt. by assoc. with Prakrit *bhagodī* divine, holy.]
1 A Hindu or Buddhist temple or sacred building, usu. in the form of a many-tiered tower with storeys of diminishing size, each with an ornamented projecting roof, in China, India, Japan, and elsewhere in the Far East. L16. ▸**b** An ornamental structure built in imitation of such a temple. L18.
2 An image of a god, an idol; *fig.* a person superstitiously or extravagantly reverenced. Now *rare* or *obsolete.* L16.
3 *Hist.* A (usu.) gold or silver coin formerly current in southern India. L16.

Comb.: **pagoda sleeve** (chiefly *Hist.*) a funnel-shaped outer sleeve turned back to expose the inner sleeve and lining; **pagoda stone** a fossil shell resembling a pagoda; **pagoda-tree** (*a*) (*joc.*, now *rare*) an imaginary tree said to produce pagodas (coins); (*b*) an ornamental Chinese leguminous tree, *Sophora japonica*, with pendulous racemes of cream-coloured flowers.

pagurid /pəˈɡjʊərɪd/ *adjective & noun.* L19.
[mod. Latin *Paguridae* (see below), from Latin *pagurus*, Greek *pagouros* a kind of crab: see -ID[3].]
ZOOLOGY. (Of, pertaining to, or designating) a decapod crustacean of the family Paguridae or the genus *Pagurus*, which includes hermit crabs.

pah *noun* var. of PA *noun*[1].

pah /pɑː/ *interjection.* L16.
[Natural exclam.]
Expr. disgust or disdain.

paha /ˈpɑːhə/ *noun.* Pl. same. M19.
[Malay.]
A unit of weight in Malaysia and Indonesia formerly used esp. for gold, equal to ¼ tahil (approx. 9.4 grams).

Pahari /pəˈhɑːriː/ *noun & adjective.* Also **Pahariya** /pəˈhɑːriːjə/. E19.
[Hindi *pahārī*, *pahāriyā* (language) of the mountains, from *pahār*: see -I[2].]
▶ **A** *noun.* **1** A member of any of several peoples inhabiting the Himalayan regions of Nepal and northern India. E19.
2 (Any of) a group of Indo-Aryan languages or their dialects spoken in this area, *esp.* Nepali. M19.
▶ **B** *adjective.* Of or pertaining to (any of) these peoples or languages. L19.

pahit /ˈpɑːhɪt/ *noun.* E20.
[Malay = bitter.]
More fully ***gin pahit***. In SE Asia: gin and bitters.

Pahlavi /ˈpɑːləvi/ *adjective & noun.* Also **Pehlevi** /ˈpeɪləvi/. L18.
[Persian *pahlawī*, from *pahlav* from *parthava* Parthia: see -I[2].]
▶ **A** *noun.* The main form of the Middle Persian language, existing from the 3rd to the 10th cents., evidenced esp. in Zoroastrian texts and commentaries. Also, the writing system, of Aramaic origin, in which these texts were written. L18.
▶ **B** *adjective.* Designating, of, or pertaining to this language or writing system. E19.

paho /ˈpɑːhəʊ/ *noun.* Pl. **-os**. L19.
[Hopi *pá:ho.*]
Among the Hopi Indians: a ceremonial prayer-stick, usu. painted and decorated with feathers, serving as an invocation or offering to the spirits.

pahoehoe /pəˈhəʊɪhəʊi/ *noun.* M19.
[Hawaiian.]
GEOLOGY. Smooth, undulating or corded lava. Cf. AA.

Pah-utah *noun* see PAIUTE.

paiche /pɑːˈɪʃeɪ/ *noun.* M20.
[Amer. Spanish.]
= ARAPAIMA.

paid *verb pa. t. & pple* of PAY *verb*[1].

paideia /pʌɪˈdʌɪə/ *noun.* Also **paed-**. M20.
[Greek.]
GREEK HISTORY. Education, upbringing; the ideal result of this; a society's culture.

paideutics *noun* var. of PAEDEUTICS.

paigle /ˈpeɪɡ(ə)l/ *noun.* Chiefly *dial.* Also **pagle**; **peagle** /ˈpiːɡ(ə)l/. LME.
[Origin unkn.]
The cowslip, *Primula veris*. Also, the oxlip, *P. elatior*.

pai-hua /ˈpʌɪhwɑː/ *noun.* E20.
[Chinese *báihuà* (Wade–Giles *pai-hua*), from *bái* white, clear, plain + *huà* language, speech.]
The standard written form of modern Chinese, based on the northern dialects, esp. that of Beijing. Cf. PUTONGHUA.

paik /peɪk/ *noun & verb. Scot. & north.* E16.
[Origin unkn.]
▶ **A** *noun.* A hard blow, esp. to the body. Chiefly in ***get one's paiks***, get one's deserts. E16.
▶ **B** *verb trans.* Beat with a stick, stone, fist, etc.; punch, pummel. E16.

pai kau /pʌɪ ˈkaʊ/ *noun.* E20.
[Chinese (Cantonese) *p'aai kaú*, from *p'aai* tile + *kaú* nine.]
A Chinese gambling game played with dominoes.

pail /peɪl/ *noun.*
[Old English *pæġel* = Middle & mod. Dutch *pegel* gauge, scale, mark, Low German *pegel* half a pint, of unkn. origin. Later forms assoc. with Old French *paielle*, *paelle* (mod. *poêle*) pan, bath, liquid measure, from Latin *patella* pan.]
†**1** A gill, a small measure. *rare.* Only in OE.
2 A usu. round vessel, made of wood, metal, or (now) plastic and having a hooped handle and sometimes a detachable lid, used for holding or carrying liquids etc., a bucket, (in early use also (*rare*) a wine-vessel. Also, a pailful. OE.
2 ***milk-pail***, ***slop-pail***, etc. ***dinner-pail***: see DINNER *noun*.
■ **pailful** *noun* the amount of liquid etc. contained in a pail, as much as a pail will hold; in *pl.*, large quantities of rain etc.: L16.

pailleted *adjective* see PAILLETTED.

paillette /palˈjɛt, pʌɪˈjɛt/ *noun.* M19.
[French, dim. of *paille* straw, chaff: see -ETTE.]
1 A small piece of glittering foil, shell, etc., used to decorate a garment; a spangle. M19.
2 A decorative piece of coloured foil or bright metal used in enamel painting. L19.

pailletted /palˈjɛtɪd, pʌɪˈjɛtɪd/ *adjective.* Also ***-eted**. E20.
[from prec. + -ED[2].]
Decorated with paillettes, spangled.

pailou /pʌɪˈləʊ/ *noun.* Pl. same, **-s**. M19.
[Chinese, from *pái* tablet + *lóu* tower.]
A (usu. elaborate) Chinese commemorative or ornamental archway, freq. of temporary construction.

pain /peɪn/ *noun*[1]. ME.
[Old & mod. French *peine* from Latin *poena* penalty, punishment, (later) pain, grief. Cf. earlier PINE *noun*[1].]
1 Suffering or loss inflicted as punishment for a crime or offence; *spec.* a fine. *obsolete* exc. in ***on pain of***, ***under pain of***, ***pains and penalties*** below. ME.
2 The state or condition of consciousness arising from mental or physical suffering; (now *rare*) an unpleasurable feeling or effect. Formerly *spec.*, the sufferings of hell or purgatory. Opp. ***pleasure***. ME.
3 Bodily suffering; strongly unpleasant feeling in the body (usu. in a particular part), such as arises from illness, injury, or harmful physical contact; a single sensation of this nature. ME. ▸**b** In *pl.* & †*sing.* Such sensations experienced during childbirth. Also ***labour pains***. ME. ▸**c** = ***pain in the neck*** below. *colloq.* E20.
4 In *pl.* (also treated as *sing.*) or †*sing.* Trouble taken in accomplishing or attempting something; careful and attentive effort. Esp. in ***be at pains (to do)***, ***take pains (to do)***. ME.
5 Mental distress or trouble; *esp.* grief, sorrow. Formerly also, anxiety, apprehension. LME.

> 🕮 **2** A. BARRATT The simple reaction . . is expressed . . psychically as the Principle of following Pleasure and avoiding Pain. **3** P. CAREY He moved jerkily . . out of breath with a pain in his side. *Independent* Signs of a heart attack are pain in the centre of the chest. ***back pain***, ***period pains***, ***stomach pain***, etc. **b** D. H. LAWRENCE The pains began, Mrs. Brangwen was put to bed, the midwife came. **c** *Fast Forward* Our teacher always seems to pick on us. She is a pain. **4** G. DURRELL The beasts seemed positively afraid of the worms . . we had taken such pains to collect. L. APPIGNANESI He was always at pains to assert his independence from any individual woman. **5** DAY LEWIS I can remember no pain, no perturbation, no sense of parting. T. IRELAND Catherine thought of her own most secret pain. V. BROME Jones at once apologized for any unintentional pain he had caused.

Phrases: ***aches and pains***: see ACHE *noun*[1]. **for one's pains** in return for one's (esp. futile) labour or trouble. ***grinding pains***: see GRINDING 3. **in pain** suffering pain. ***labour pains***: see sense 3b above. **on pain of death**, **under pain of death** with death as the penalty. **pain in the arse**, **pain in the butt** *slang* = ***pain in the neck*** below. **pain in the neck** *colloq.* an annoying or tiresome person or thing. **pains and penalties**: inflicted as punishment for a crime or offence. ***PHANTOM pain***. **put out of its pain** destroy, put down a wounded animal etc. ***under pain of death***: see ***on pain of death*** above.

Comb.: **pain barrier** a state of greatest pain, esp. during physical exertion, beyond which the pain diminishes; **pain-free** *adjective* free from pain; **painkiller** a drug etc. that alleviates pain; **painkilling** *adjective* that acts as a painkiller; **pain point** PHYSIOLOGY = ***pain spot*** below; **pain-proof** *adjective* having immunity from pain; **pain spot** PHYSIOLOGY a small region on the surface of the skin that is sensitive to pain; **pain threshold** (*a*) the point beyond which a stimulus causes pain; (*b*) the upper limit of tolerance to pain.

pain /pɛ̃/ *noun*[2]. LME.
[Old & mod. French from Latin *panem*.]
Bread, *spec.* in French bakery.
pain perdu /pɛrdy/ [French PERDU] toasted stale bread, usu. sweetened and flavoured with cinnamon.
¶ Formerly naturalized.

pain /peɪn/ *verb.* ME.
[from PAIN *noun*[1].]
▶ **I** †**1** *verb trans.* Inflict a penalty on; punish. ME–E17.
2 *verb trans.* Cause mental or bodily suffering to; hurt or afflict in mind or body. LME.

> 🕮 **2** SIR W. SCOTT But your arm, my lord . . . Does it not pain you? A. MASSIE Only her mother could cause her to lie . . and the act pained her.

▶ **II 3** *verb intrans.* †**a** Of a person: suffer mental or bodily pain. ME–L19. ▸**b** Of part of the body: be affected with pain; hurt. Chiefly *US.* M20.
4 *verb refl.* & †*intrans.* Take pains or trouble; exert oneself with care and attention. *arch.* ME.

> 🕮 **3b** W. STYRON My shoulders pain something fierce.

pained /peɪnd/ *adjective.* ME.
[from PAIN *noun*[1], *verb*: see -ED[2], -ED[1].]
Affected with mental or bodily pain; hurt, distressed; expressing or indicating pain. Now chiefly *fig.*

> 🕮 *Guardian* His rigid posture and slightly pained expression.

painful /ˈpeɪnfʊl, -f(ə)l/ *adjective.* ME.
[from PAIN *noun*[1] + -FUL.]
1 Accompanied by or causing mental distress or suffering; hurtful, grievous. Also, annoying, vexatious. ME. ▸**b** Inflicting punishment; tormenting. Now *rare* or *obsolete.* LME.
2 Accompanied by or causing bodily pain or suffering; (esp. of a part of the body) affected with pain, hurting. LME.
3 Causing or involving trouble or difficulty, irksome, laborious. Now *rare* exc. as passing into sense 1. LME.
4 a = PAINSTAKING *adjective* 2. *arch.* LME. ▸**b** = PAINSTAKING *adjective* 1. *arch.* M16.

📖 **1** A. HARDING Isabella coloured suddenly, and looked away, as though some painful thought disturbed her. **2** G. HARRIS Forollkin made a painful effort to turn his head. **3** DRYDEN By quick and painful Marches hither came.

■ **painfully** *adverb* in a painful manner; to a painful extent or degree; *colloq.* excessively, exceedingly: **LME**. **painfulness** *noun* **LME**.

painless /ˈpeɪnlɪs/ *adjective*. **LME**.
[from PAIN *noun*[1] + -LESS.]
1 Orig., not suffering pain. Later, causing no pain; not accompanied by pain.
2 Involving little effort or stress. *colloq.* **L20**.

📖 **1** T. WATADA My mother claims that his was a painless birth. **2** N. HORNBY There are any number of quick and painless methods of turning yourself into a Good Bloke.

■ **painlessly** *adverb* **M19**. **painlessness** *noun* **M17**.

†**painstaker** *noun*. *rare*. **E17–E18**.
[formed as next + TAKER.]
A painstaking person.

painstaking /ˈpeɪnzteɪkɪŋ/ *noun*. Now *rare*. **M16**.
[formed as next + TAKING *noun*.]
The taking of pains; the application of careful and attentive effort towards the accomplishment of something.

painstaking /ˈpeɪnzteɪkɪŋ/ *adjective*. **L17**.
[from PAIN *noun*[1] + -S[1] + TAKING *adjective*.]
1 Of a person: that takes pains or applies careful and attentive effort towards the accomplishment of something; assiduous. **L17**.
2 Of an action etc.: performed with or characterized by attentive care. **M19**.

📖 **2** *Country Homes* Painstaking attention to detail had become her hallmark.

■ **painstakingly** *adverb* **M19**. **painstakingness** *noun* **E20**.

paint /peɪnt/ *noun*. **ME**.
[from the verb.]
1 A substance consisting of a solid colouring matter dissolved in a liquid vehicle as water, oil, etc., which when spread over a surface, dries to leave a thin decorative or protective coating. Also, the solid colouring matter used in this substance; a type of this, a pigment. **ME**. ▸**b** Cosmetic make-up; *spec.* (*a*) rouge; (*b*) nail varnish. **M17**. ▸**c** PHARMACOLOGY. A liquid medicine applied to the skin or mucous membranes, freq. with a brush. **L19**.
2 The action or an act of painting something; the fact of being painted. **E17**.
3 *fig.* Colour, colouring; adornment; outward show. **E17**.
4 A piebald horse. Freq. *attrib.* Chiefly *US*. **M19**.
5 BASKETBALL. The rectangular area marked near the basket at each end of the court. **L20**.
6 COMPUTING. The function or capability of producing graphics, esp. those that mimic the effect of real paint. **L20**.

📖 **1** M. DICKENS Now the paint and plaster had fallen in lumps and not been replaced. J. DISKI A rich, deep white that comes from many coats of good-quality paint. *Science News* The organic carbon in ancient paints derives from blood. ***latex paint***, ***oil-paint***, ***plastic paint***, ***powder paint***, etc. **b** BYRON One has false curls, another too much paint. **2** OED Give it a paint, and it will look all right. **3** E. YOUNG Virtue's paint that can make wrinkles shine. **4** *New Yorker* Emily was running her paint, Diamond Lil, in fast, narrowing circles around a fat heifer.

Phrases: **as smart as paint**, **as pretty as paint**, etc., extremely smart, pretty, etc. ***fresh as paint***: see FRESH *adjective*. ***Red Paint***: see RED *adjective*.
Comb.: **paint bomb** a balloon etc. containing paint, which bursts or otherwise opens on impact, thrown in demonstrations etc.; **paint box** (*a*) a box of solid paints or pigments, usu. watercolours; (*b*) (**Paintbox**) COMPUTING (proprietary name for) an electronic system used to create video graphics by storing filmed material on disk and manipulating it using a graphics tablet; **paint-bridge** THEATRICAL a platform on which a scene-painter stands; **paintbrush** (*a*) a brush for applying paint; (*b*) *N. Amer.* (more fully ***Indian paintbrush***) any of various plants of the genus *Castilleja*, of the figwort family, with showy coloured bracts; (*c*) ***devil's paintbrush***: see DEVIL *noun*; **paint chip** (*a*) a small area on a painted surface where the paint has been chipped away; (*b*) *N. Amer.* a card showing a colour or range of colours available in a type of paint; **paint-frame** THEATRICAL a movable iron framework for moving scenes from the stage to the paint-bridge; **paint kettle** a container with a handle for holding paint during use; **paint-pot** a container for usu. liquid paint; **paint roller** a roller covered in an absorbent material for applying paint to a surface; **paint-root** = ***red-root*** (b) s.v. RED *adjective*; **paint shop** the part of a factory where goods are painted, esp. by spraying; **paint spray**, **paint sprayer** a device for spraying paint on to a surface; **paint stick** a stick of water-soluble paint used like a crayon; **paint stripper** a substance for dissolving and removing old paint from doors, furniture, etc.; **paintwork** (*a*) painted surfaces collectively; (*b*) the work of painting.
■ **paintiness** *noun* the quality of being painty **L19**. **paintless** *adjective* devoid of paint **M19**. **painty** *adjective* (*a*) of or covered in paint; (*b*) (of a picture) overcharged with paint, having paint that is too obtrusive: **E19**.

paint /peɪnt/ *verb*. **ME**.
[Old & mod. French *peint(e* pa. pple of *peindre* from Latin *pingere* embroider, tattoo, paint, embellish.]
1 *verb trans.* Cover the surface of (a wall, door, etc.) with paint; apply paint to (an object); colour (a surface or object), *spec.* with a wash or coating of paint. **ME**. ▸**b** *fig.* Adorn with or as with colours; beautify, decorate, ornament. **LME**.
2 a *verb trans.* Produce (a picture, pattern, or representation) on a surface in colours; represent (an object, scene, etc.) or portray (a person or thing) on a surface wih paint. **ME**. ▸**b** *verb trans.* Adorn (a wall etc.) *with* a painting or paintings. Usu. in *pass.* **LME**. ▸**c** *verb intrans.* Practise the art of painting; make pictures. **LME**.
3 *verb trans. & intrans.* Apply cosmetics to (the face, skin, etc.). **ME**.
4 *verb trans.* Misrepresent, give a false colouring to; embellish, esp. deceitfully. Now *rare* or *obsolete*. **LME**.
5 *verb trans.* Depict or describe in words; present or display vividly. **LME**.
†**6** *verb trans. & intrans.* Fawn on (a person); deceive with specious words. **LME–M17**.
7 *verb trans.* Apply (a liquid) with a brush. Usu. foll. by *on*, *over*. **M19**.
8 *verb intrans.* Drink. *slang*. **M19**.
9 a *verb trans.* Cause to be displayed or represented on the screen of a cathode-ray tube. Usu. in *pass.* **M20**. ▸**b** *verb intrans.* Show (*up*) on the screen of a cathode-ray tube (esp. in a radar system). **M20**.
10 COMPUTING. Create (a graphic or screen display) using a paint program. **L20**.

📖 **1** OED Are you going to paint or varnish the wood-work? **b** B. TAYLOR Spring, that paints These savage shores. **2a** M. GEE She had been painted, by a professional artist, in oils. *South African Panorama* Sue paints delicate scenes on silk. A. ROBERTSON Still-life compositions which Grimshaw would then paint. **c** W. M. CRAIG To paint also implies to draw. **3** K. AMIS Used to paint her nails and put too much rouge on her cheeks. J. RATHBONE She painted much, especially round her eyes. **5** J. FORDYCE What words can paint the guilt of such a conduct? ISAIAH BERLIN [They] paint individuals or classes or societies as heroes and villains, wholly white or unimaginably black.

Phrases: ***not so black as one is painted***: see BLACK *adjective*. **paint by number(s)** paint a picture divided in advance into sections containing numbers indicating the colour to be used. ***paint in bright colours***: see COLOUR *noun*. ***paint oneself into a corner***: see CORNER *noun*. **paint out** (*a*) efface by covering with paint; (*b*) NAUTICAL apply a coat of paint to (part of) a craft. ***paint the lily***: see LILY *noun*. **paint the town red** *colloq.* (orig. *US*) enjoy oneself flamboyantly, go on a boisterous or riotous spree.
Comb.: **paint-in** *colloq.* a gathering for the purpose of painting something, esp. a previously shabby or neglected building.
■ **paintaˈbility** *noun* the quality of being paintable **M20**. **paintable** *adjective* (*a*) able to be painted; (*b*) suitable for painting: **M19**.

paintball /ˈpeɪntbɔːl/ *noun*. **L20**.
[from PAINT *noun* + BALL *noun*[1].]
1 A war game in which participants use weapons that fire capsules of paint that break on impact. **L20**.
2 A capsule of paint for such a weapon. **L20**.
■ **paintballer** *noun* a person who participates in paintball **L20**. **paintballing** *noun* **L20**.

painted /ˈpeɪntɪd/ *adjective*. **ME**.
[from PAINT *verb* + -ED[1].]
1 That has been painted. **ME**.
2 *fig.* Deceptively coloured, unreal, artificial; feigned. **LME**.
3 Brightly coloured; variegated. **LME**.
Special collocations: **painted bat** a SE Asian bat, *Kerivoula picta*, with scarlet or orange fur and fingers and black wing membranes. **painted beauty** a large N. American butterfly, *Cynthia virginiensis*, that is brownish yellow with black and white markings; also called ***American painted lady***. **painted bunting** a brightly coloured N. American bunting, *Passerina ciris*. ***painted cloth***: see CLOTH *noun* 1. **painted cup** = ***paintbrush*** (b) s.v. PAINT *noun*. **painted finch** any of various brightly coloured finches, *esp.* (*a*) *Emblema pictum* of central Australia; (*b*) = ***painted bunting*** above. **painted grass** = ***ribbon-grass*** s.v. RIBBON *noun*. **painted lady** (*a*) any of several migratory butterflies that are brownish yellow or orange with black and white markings; spec. *Vanessa cardui*; ***American painted lady*** = ***painted beauty*** above; (*b*) any of several plants with particoloured flowers; *esp.* (*S. Afr.*) any of various kinds of gladiolus. **painted quail** any of various quails and birds resembling them with mottled plumage, *esp.* (*a*) any of the genus *Excalfactoria*; (*b*) an Australasian button quail, *Turnix varia*. **painted snipe** a small long-billed wading bird, *Rostratula benghalensis*, having brown plumage with bold and colourful markings and native to warmer regions of the Old World. **painted terrapin** a small American freshwater turtle, *Chrysemys picta*, that is black or olive with red and yellow markings on the head and shell. **painted top-shell** a littoral gastropod mollusc, *Calliostoma zizyphinum*, with a vividly coloured conical shell. **painted tortoise**, **painted turtle** = ***painted terrapin*** above.

painter /ˈpeɪntə/ *noun*[1]. **ME**.
[Old French *peintour*, (also mod.) *peintre* from Proto-Romance alt. of Latin *pictor*, from *pict-* pa. ppl stem of *pingere* PAINT *verb*: see -ER[1].]
1 A person who paints something; *spec.* (*a*) a person who paints pictures, an artist; (*b*) a person who applies paint for decoration and protection to doors, walls, etc.; a decorator. **ME**.
2 A person who describes something in a pictorial or graphic style. **L16**.
3 (Usu. **P-**.) *The* constellation Pictor. **M20**.
Comb. & phrases: ***painter and decorator***; **painter's brush** a plant, = ***paintbrush*** (b) s.v. PAINT *noun*; **painter's colic** lead or mercury poisoning caused by handling toxic pigments; **Painter's Easel** (now *rare*) = sense 3 above; **painter's mussel**, **painters' mussel** a freshwater mussel, *Unio pictorum*, the shell of which was formerly used as a palette; ***Sunday painter***.
■ **painterliness** *noun* the quality of being painterly **M20**. **painterly** *adjective* (*a*) like, characteristic of, or pertaining to a painter, artistic; (*b*) *spec.* (of a painting or style of painting) characterized by qualities of colour, stroke, and texture rather than of contour or line: **L16**.

painter /ˈpeɪntə/ *noun*[2]. **ME**.
[App. from Old French *penteur* rope running from masthead.]
NAUTICAL. **1** Now only more fully ***shank-painter***. A short rope or chain by which the shank of an anchor is held fast to a ship's side when not in use. **ME**.
2 A rope attached to the bow of a boat for tying it to a ship, quay, etc. **E18**.
2 cut the painter, **slip the painter** *fig.* effect a separation.

painter /ˈpeɪntə/ *noun*[3]. *US*. **E19**.
[Alt. of PANTHER.]
= PUMA.

painting /ˈpeɪntɪŋ/ *noun*. **ME**.
[from PAINT *verb* + -ING[1].]
1 The action of PAINT *verb*. **ME**.
2 The result or product of applying paint; colouring, pictorial decoration or representation. Also, an instance of this, a picture. **ME**.
†**3** Pigment, paint. **L16–M17**.
1 ***Poona painting***.

paintress /ˈpeɪntrɪs/ *noun*. **LME**.
[Old French *peintresse* fem. of *peintre* PAINTER *noun*[1]: see -ESS[1].]
A female painter.

†**paintrix** *noun*. *rare*. **M16–M18**.
[from PAINT *verb* + -TRIX.]
A female painter.

†**painture** *noun*. **ME**.
[Old & mod. French *peinture*, from Proto-Gallo-Romance alt. of Latin *pictura*, from *pict-*: see PAINTER *noun*[1], -URE.]
1 That which is painted; (a) painting; a picture. **ME–M17**.
2 The action or art of painting; style of painting. **LME–E18**.
3 A paint, a pigment. **LME–E17**.

†**paiock** *noun*. *rare* (Shakes.). Only in **E17**.
[Origin uncertain: perh. alt. of PEACOCK.]
A peacock.

pair /pɛː/ *noun*[1]. Pl. **-s**, after numeral sometimes (now chiefly *non-standard*) same. **ME**.
[Old & mod. French *paire*, from Latin *paria* neut. pl. of *par* equal.]
▸ **I** A couple; a set of two.
1 A set of two individual persons or things, esp. of the same kind, that are associated or complementary in use, purpose, position, etc. Also, the second member of such a set as related to the first. **ME**. ▸**b** *ellipt.* A pair of breasts, cards, horses, oars, spectacles, etc. **E18**. ▸**c** Either or both of two members of a legislative assembly on opposite sides who absent themselves from a vote by mutual arrangement so as not to affect the outcome. Also, an agreement to do this. **E19**. ▸**d** MECHANICS. Two mechanical elements that together constitute a kinematic set. **L19**. ▸**e** In basket-making, two rods of willow or cane worked alternately over and under one another. **L19**.
2 A single article of clothing, tool, etc., consisting of two joined or corresponding parts not used separately. **ME**.
3 *gen.* Foll. by *of*: a couple, a few. Now *rare*. **ME**.
4 Two individuals of opposite sexes; *spec.* (*a*) two animals mated together; (*b*) two persons engaged or married to each other; (*c*) two partners in a dance. **LME**.

📖 **1** T. CALLENDER It had four pairs of buttons down the double-breast. V. BROME Jones had to face the formidable pair in person. ***pair of gloves***, ***pair of lips***, ***pair of shoes***, ***pair of stirrups***, ***pair of wings***, etc. **b** M. AMIS Who was that tart? . . She's got a right pair on her. **c** *New Statesman* One minister . . was flatly refused a pair by his Tory opposite number. J. ARCHER I'm the Labour member . . and I was hoping you hadn't yet found yourself a pair. **2** ***pair of compasses***, ***pair of scissors***, ***pair of tights***, ***pair of trousers***, etc. **3** J. SPEED Fewer by a paire of thousands.

▸ **II** A collection.
5 A set of separate things or parts collectively forming a whole, as (*a*) a string *of* beads; (*b*) a pack *of* cards. Now *dial.* *rare*. **ME**.
6 A company of miners working together. *dial.* **M19**.
Phrases: (A selection of cross-refs. only is included: see esp. other nouns) ***another pair of shoes***: see SHOE *noun*. **be a pair** *colloq.* (of two people) (*a*) be of the same kind; (*b*) be as bad as one another.

happy pair: see HAPPY *adjective*. *lone pair*: see LONE *adjective* etc. *LONG-TAIL pair*. *MINIMAL pair*. *ordered pair*: see ORDERED 2b. **pair of arrows** a set of three arrows. *pair of bagpipes*: see BAGPIPE 1. *pair of breeches*: see BREECH *noun* 1b. **pair of cards** †(*a*) a pack of cards; (*b*) two cards of the same denomination or value. *pair of colours*: see COLOUR *noun* 7b. **pair of hands** *fig.* a person *esp.* one available for a menial task. **pair of horses** two horses harnessed abreast and running together. *pair of knickers*: see KNICKERS 2. *pair of knives*: see KNIFE *noun*. *pair of oars*: see OAR *noun*. *pair of spectacles*: see SPECTACLE *noun*[1]. **pair of stairs** a flight of stairs. *pair of stays*: see STAY *noun*[2] 3. **pair of steps** (*a*) (now *rare* or *obsolete*) a flight of steps; (*b*) a portable self-supporting set of steps for use in a library etc., a stepladder. **pair of wheels** *colloq.* a two-wheeled vehicle. **pair royal** a set of three persons or things of the same kind, *esp.* three cards of the same denomination (cf. PRIAL). *post and pair*: see POST *noun*[3]. *show a clean pair of heels*: see CLEAN *adjective*. *stereo pair*: see STEREO *noun*[2] & *adjective*[1]. *TWISTED pair*. **two pair (of stairs)**, **three pair (of stairs)**, etc., a second, third, etc., floor or storey. *would not touch with a pair of TONGS*.

Comb.: **pair-bond** *noun & verb* (*a*) *noun* the relationship formed during courtship and mating of a pair of animals or two people; (*b*) *verb intrans.* form a pair-bond; **pair-bonding** (the patterns of behaviour that establish) the formation of a pair-bond; **pair-feed** *verb trans.* feed two groups of (experimental animals) with a diet identical except for an item whose effects are being tested; **pair-formation** the pairing of animals, esp. birds, in preparation for breeding; **pair-horse** *attrib. adjective* having or intended for a pair of horses; **pair-mate** *verb trans.* test the sexual compatibility of (experimental animals) by allowing mating within and between either of two groups; control the mating of (experimental animals) so that each male mates with only one female, or vice versa; **pair-oar** a boat rowed by a pair of oars; **pair-oared** *adjective* (of a boat) rowed by a pair of oars; **pair production** *NUCLEAR PHYSICS* the conversion of a gamma-ray photon into an electron and a positron; **pair-skating** skating performed by pairs; **pair-toed** *adjective* (of a bird) having the toes in pairs, two in front and two behind.

pair /pɛːr/ *noun*[2] *& adjective*. Pl. of noun same. M19.
[French = equal.]
ROULETTE. (Of) an even number; (of) the even numbers collectively.

pair /pɛː/ *verb*[1]. E17.
[from PAIR *noun*[1].]
1 *verb trans.* Make a pair or couple by matching (two persons or things, one person or thing *with* another); bring into association as adapted or suited to each other or another; *spec.* (*a*) join (two persons, one person *with* another) in love or marriage, mate (two animals, one animal *with* another); (*b*) associate (two members, one member *with* another) as a pair for a vote in a legislative assembly (freq. in *pass.*). E17.
2 *verb intrans.* (Of two persons or things) come together as a pair or couple; (of one person or thing) unite *with* another to form a pair or couple; *spec.* (*a*) unite in love or marriage, mate; (*b*) form a pair for a vote in a legislative assembly, come to an arrangement not to vote as (one of) a pair, (also foll. by *off*). E17.

> 📖 **1** SIR W. SCOTT The . . stag is paired with the doe. LD MACAULAY The French ambassador and the French general were well paired. G. GREENE The great characters of fiction are often paired: Quixote and Sancho, . . Pickwick and Weller. H. WILSON All who are not paired . . troop off into the division lobby. **2** T. KEN Tho' no Marriages are there, We yet may, like the Cherubs, pair. *New Statesman* It is further alleged that one Conservative . . saw fit to pair with two Labour members.

With adverbs in specialized senses: **pair off** (*a*) put or arrange in a pair or pairs; (*b*) go off or apart in pairs; **pair off with** (*colloq.*) form a couple with, marry; (*c*) see sense 2(b) above. **pair up** form a couple or couples, esp. in preparation for mating.

pair /pɛː/ *verb*[2]. Long *obsolete* exc. *dial.* ME.
[Aphet.]
1 *verb trans.* = IMPAIR *verb* 1. ME.
2 *verb intrans.* = IMPAIR *verb* 2. ME.
▪ **pairment** *noun* impairment, injury, deterioraton ME.

paired /pɛːd/ *ppl adjective*. E17.
[from PAIR *verb*[1] + -ED[1].]
Associated together in pairs or twos; coupled.
paired-associate *attrib. adjective* (*PSYCHOLOGY*) involving paired associates. **paired associates** *PSYCHOLOGY* stimulus material presented in pairs to test the strength of associations set up between them at a subsequent presentation of either of the pair; **paired association** *PSYCHOLOGY* (the association of stimuli in) paired-associate learning; **paired comparison** a method of testing the discrimination between similar stimuli by presenting them for comparison in pairs.

pairing /ˈpɛːrɪŋ/ *noun*. E17.
[from PAIR *verb*[1].]
The action of PAIR *verb*[1]; an arrangement or match resulting from this.
Comb.: **pairing-call** a call used by birds during the mating season; **pairing-season**, **pairing-time** the season at which birds pair.

pairwise /ˈpɛːwʌɪz/ *adverb & adjective*. M19.
[from PAIR *noun*[1] + -WISE.]
▶ **A** *adverb*. In or by pairs; with regard to pairing. M19.
▶ **B** *adjective*. Of, pertaining to, or forming a pair or pairs. M20.

pais /peɪs/ *noun*. *arch.* M17.
[Old French (mod. *pays*), lit. 'country'.]
LAW. The country; a jury (cf. COUNTRY *noun* 7). Now only in phrs. below.
estoppel in pais estoppel in respect of things said outside the court. **trial per pais** trial by jury.

paisa /ˈpʌɪsɑː/ *noun*. Pl. **-se** /-seɪ/, same. L19.
[Hindi *paisā*: cf. POISHA. Cf. also PICE.]
1 = PICE. L19.
2 A monetary unit equal to one-hundredth of a rupee (in India, Pakistan, and Nepal) or (formerly) to one-hundredth of a taka (in Bangladesh). M20.
¶ See also NAYA PAISA.

paisan /pʌɪˈzɑːn/ *noun*. *US colloq.* M20.
[Italian *paesano* countryman, compatriot, infl. by next.]
A fellow-countryman, a friend, of Italian or (occas.) Spanish descent. Freq. as a form of address.

paisano /pʌɪˈsɑːnəʊ, *foreign* paiˈsano/ *noun*. Pl. **-os** /-əʊz, *foreign* -os/. M19.
[Spanish = peasant, rustic.]
1 In Spain and Spanish-speaking areas, esp. in the south-western US: a fellow-countryman; a peasant. M19.
2 In Mexico and the south-western US: a road-runner. L19.

paise *noun* pl. of PAISA.

Paisley /ˈpeɪzli/ *adjective & noun*. E19.
[A town in central Scotland, the original place of manufacture.]
(Designating, pertaining to, or made of) a soft woollen material with a distinctive pattern of curved feather-shaped figures; (designating) a garment made of this material or having this pattern; (designating or having) this pattern.

Paisleyite /ˈpeɪzlɪʌɪt/ *noun & adjective*. M20.
[from Ian R. K. *Paisley* (b. 1926), Northern Irish politician and Presbyterian minister + -ITE[1].]
▶ **A** *noun*. A supporter of Ian Paisley and his beliefs, *spec.* his advocacy of Protestant interests in Northern Ireland through the continued maintenance of Northern Ireland's union with Great Britain and independence from the Republic of Ireland. M20.
▶ **B** *adjective*. Of or pertaining to Ian Paisley or his followers. M20.
▪ **Paisleyism** *noun* the religious and political principles of Paisleyites M20.

Paiute /ˈpʌɪuːt/ *noun & adjective*. Also (now *rare*) **Pah-Utah** /pɑːˈjuːtɔː, -tɑː/. E19.
[Spanish *Payuchi*, *Payuta* from a widespread term of unkn. origin (cf. Ute *payó:ċı*) infl. by UTE.]
▶ **A** *noun*. Pl. same, **-s**.
1 A member of a Shoshonean people inhabiting parts of Utah, N. Arizona, and SE Nevada (also ***Southern Paiute***); a member of a culturally similar but geographically separate and linguistically distinct Shoshonean people of W. Nevada and adjacent parts of California, Oregon, and Idaho (also ***Northern Paiute***). E19.
2 The language of either of these peoples. E20.
▶ **B** *attrib.* or as *adjective*. Of or pertaining to the Paiute or their languages. M19.

paiwari /pʌɪˈwɒri/ *noun*. M18.
[Portuguese *paiauaru* from Tupi *paiaúru*.]
In Guyana, an alcoholic drink prepared from cassava.

pajala /ˈpɑːdʒələ/ *noun*. M20.
[Malay.]
An open boat with a distinctive tripod mast used in the waters of Indonesia and Malaysia.

pajamas *noun & adjective* see PYJAMAS.

Pajarete *noun* var. of PAXARETE.

Pak /pak/ *noun*. *slang* (considered *racially offensive*). M20.
[Abbreviation.]
Pakistan; a Pakistani.

Pakamac *noun* var. of PACAMAC.

pakapoo /ˈpakəpuː, pakəˈpuː/ *noun*. Chiefly *Austral.* Also **-pu**. L19.
[Chinese *bái gē piào* (Wade–Giles *pai ko p'iao*) lit. 'white pigeon ticket', perh. referring to a Cantonese competition which involved releasing pigeons and predicting the distance they would fly and the numbers expected to return.]
A Chinese form of lottery played with slips of paper marked with columns of characters.
like a pakapoo ticket *slang* (of writing) illegible, indecipherable.

pak-choi /pakˈtʃɔɪ/ *noun*. M19.
[Chinese (Cantonese) *paāk ts'oi* white vegetable: cf. PE-TSAI.]
A kind of Chinese cabbage with smooth-edged tapering leaves, *Brassica chinensis*.

pakeha /ˈpɑːkɪhɑː/ *noun & adjective*. *NZ*. E19.
[Maori.]
▶ **A** *noun*. A white person (as opp. to a Maori). E19.
▶ **B** *adjective*. Of, pertaining to, or designating a pakeha. M19.

pakhal /pəˈkɑːl/ *noun*. M19.
[Hindi *pakhāl* large water-skin. Cf. PUCKAULY.]
A container, esp. a leather skin, for carrying or keeping water.

pakhawaj /pəˈkɑːwədʒ/ *noun*. M19.
[Hindi *pakhāwaj*.]
A double-headed drum used in Indian music.

Pakhtun /pəkˈtuːn/ *noun & adjective*. Also **Pash-** /pəʃ-/. E19.
[Pashto *paštūn*. Cf. PATHAN.]
= PATHAN.

Paki /ˈpaki/ *noun*. *slang* (considered *racially offensive*). M20.
[Abbreviation.]
An immigrant, or descendant of immigrants, from the Indian subcontinent, orig. *spec.* Pakistan.

pakihi /ˈpɑːkɪhi/ *noun*. M19.
[Maori.]
In New Zealand, an area of stony open land, freq. waterlogged, esp. in NW parts of the South Island; the type of soil associated with such land.

Pakistani /pɑːkɪˈstɑːni, pak-/ *noun & adjective*. M20.
[from *Pakistan* (see below) + -I[2].]
▶ **A** *noun*. A native or inhabitant of Pakistan, a country in the northern part of the Indian subcontinent, originally comprising both West and East Pakistan (now Bangladesh). M20.
▶ **B** *adjective*. Of or pertaining to Pakistan. M20.

Pakkawood /ˈpakəwʊd/ *noun*. Also **p-**. M20.
[Perh. rel. to PUKKA: cf. WOOD *noun*[1].]
(Proprietary name for) a hard wooden heat-resistant laminate used to make handles for cutlery, cooking utensils, etc.

pakora /pəˈkɔːrə/ *noun*. M20.
[Hindi *pakorā* a dish of vegetables in gram-flour.]
A savoury Indian dish consisting of diced or chopped vegetables coated in batter and deep fried.

pak pai /pak ˈpʌɪ/ *noun*. Pl. **pak pais**. L20.
[Chinese (Cantonese) *paāk p'aaī* white licence.]
In Hong Kong, a car used illegally as a taxi.

paktong /ˈpaktɒŋ/ *noun*. L18.
[Chinese (Cantonese) *paāk t'ūng* white copper.]
An alloy of copper, zinc, and nickel, resembling silver, used esp. in 18th-cent. fireplace furniture.

pa-kua /pɑːˈkwɑː/ *noun*. L19.
[Chinese *bāguà* (Wade–Giles *pà-kua*), from *bā* eight + *guà* divinatory symbols.]
1 *ART*. Any of various decorative and religious motifs incorporating the eight trigrams of *I Ching*; *spec.* an arrangement of these trigrams in a circle round the yin-yang symbol. L19.
2 A Chinese martial art in which fighters are arranged around a circle according to the trigram sequence in positions which they must defend. M20.

PAL /pal/ *abbreviation*.
Phase alternation line (name of the colour television system used in the UK and most of Europe).

pal /pal/ *noun & verb*. *colloq.* L17.
[English Romany = pal, brother (= Turkish *pral*, Romany *plal*), ult. from Sanskrit *bhrātṛ* brother.]
▶ **A** *noun*. A friend, a comrade, a mate, an associate. Formerly also, an accomplice. L17.

> 📖 J. PORTER Be a pal and shove the marge across. E. LEONARD That's what I get for helping out a pal. ***old pal***: see OLD *adjective*.

▶ **B** *verb intrans.* Infl. **-ll-**. Be on friendly terms (*with* a person); associate *with* or go *around with* a person; start *up* a friendship *with* a person. L19.

> 📖 J. R. ACKERLEY He met and quickly palled up with a local youth. *Time* He occasionally palled around with gangsters on golf courses.

▪ **palship** *noun* the relation of being pals, comradeship M19.

pala /ˈpɑːlə/ *noun*. Pl. **palae** /ˈpɑːliː/ L19.
[Latin = spade.]
ENTOMOLOGY. A shovel-shaped structure; *spec.* an extension of the fore tarsus in many aquatic heteropteran bugs.

palabra /pəˈlɑːbrə/ *noun*. Now *rare*. L16.
[Spanish = word, rel. to Portuguese *palura*: cf. PALAVER.]
A word; talk, palaver.
¶ Recorded esp. L16–E17 in (corruptions of) Spanish phr. *pocas palabras* few words.

palace /ˈpalɪs/ *noun*. ME.
[Old French *paleis* (mod. *palais*) from Latin *palatium* orig. called the Palatine Hill, later the house of Augustus built there, then the palace of the Caesars which covered the hill.]
1 An official residence of a monarch, president, or other ruler. ME. ▸**b** *The* monarch, *the* monarchy. M20.
2 An (esp. official) residence of an archbishop or bishop. ME.
3 A dwelling-place of palatial splendour; a stately, luxurious, or imposing building, a splendid mansion. ME.

4 A building, usu. spacious and colourful, intended as a place of amusement, entertainment, or refreshment. M19.

📖 **1** *Independent* Her weekly audience with the Queen at Buckingham Palace. **b** *Times* Primacy of the palace in the decision-making process was the principal feature of the constitution. MAYOR ***of the palace***. **3** *fig.*: R. CAMPBELL Now each small seed . . Builds up its leafy palace out of dust. **4** B. BETTELHEIM Watching funny scenes in these pleasure palaces. **palace of varieties** a variety theatre.

Comb.: **palace car** a luxurious railway carriage; **palace coup** = ***palace revolution*** below; **palace guard** a person who guards a palace or protects a monarch, president, etc.; **palace hotel** a hotel of (supposedly) palatial splendour; **palace revolution** the (usu. non-violent) overthrow of a monarch, president, etc., esp. by members of the ruling group; **palace style** ARCHAEOLOGY (an imitation of) a type of pottery associated with the Minoan palaces.

■ **palaced** *adjective* having or living in a palace E19. **palaceward(s)** *adverb* (*rare*) towards a palace LME.

palacio /paˈlaθjo, pəˈlasɪəʊ/ *noun*. Pl. **-os** /-ɒs, -əʊz/. M19.
[Spanish from Latin *palatium*: see PALACE.]
In Spain and Spanish-speaking countries: a palace, a country seat, an imposing official building.

palacsinta /paləts'sɪntə/ *noun*. Pl. same, **-s**. M20.
[Hungarian: see PALATSCHINKEN.]
In Hungarian cuisine: a thin pancake eaten as a dessert, filled esp. with jam, cheese, nuts, or chocolate.

paladin /ˈpalədɪn/ *noun*. L16.
[French, from Italian *paladino*, from Latin *palatinus*: see PALATINE *adjective*[1] & *noun*[1].]
Each of the Twelve bravest and most famous warriors of Charlemagne's court. Also, a knight errant, a champion.

palae *noun* pl. of PALA.

palae- *combining form* see PALAEO-.

palaeanthropic /ˌpalɪanˈθrɒpɪk, ˌpeɪ-/ *adjective*. Also **palaeo-** /ˌpalɪəʊ-, ˌpeɪ-/, ***pale(o)-**. L19.
[from PALAEO- + ANTHROPIC.]
Of, pertaining to, or designating extinct prehistoric forms of man.

palaearctic /palɪˈɑːktɪk, peɪ-/ *adjective* & *noun*. Also ***pale-**, **P-**. M19.
[from PALAE(O- + ARCTIC.]
▶ **A** *adjective*. Of, pertaining to, or (usu. **P-**) designating the biogeographical region which includes the cold and temperate zones of the Old World (i.e. Europe, N. Africa, and Asia north of the Himalayas). M19.
▶ **B** *ellipt*. as *noun*. The Palaearctic region. L19.

palaeencephalon /ˌpalɪɛnˈsɛf(ə)lɒn, -ˈkɛf-, ˌpeɪ-/ *noun*. *rare*. Also ***paleen-**. E20.
[from PALAEO- + ENCEPHALON.]
ANATOMY. The phylogenetically older portion of the brain, as contrasted with the neencephalon.

palaeo- /ˌpalɪəʊ, ˌpeɪlɪəʊ/ *combining form*. Also ***paleo-**. Before a vowel also **palae-**, ***pale-**.
[Greek *palaios*: see -O-.]
Ancient, old; of or belonging to ancient (esp. prehistoric) times; ANATOMY of relatively ancient development phylogenetically. Freq. opp. NEO-.

■ **palaeobathyˈmetric** *adjective* (GEOLOGY) of, pertaining to, or depicting the palaeobathymetry of an area M20. **palaeobaˈthymetry** *noun* (GEOLOGY) the bathymetric features of an area as they were at some period in the past M20. **palaeobioˈchemical** *adjective* of or pertaining to palaeobiochemistry M20. **palaeobioˈchemistry** *noun* the biochemistry of fossils and of organisms of the geological past, esp. as a means of investigating phylogeny; the investigation of the evolutionary development of biochemical processes: M20. **palaeobiogeˈographer** *noun* an expert in or student of palaeobiogeography M20. **palaeobiogeoˈgraphic**, **palaeobiogeoˈgraphical** *adjectives* of or pertaining to palaeobiogeography M20. **palaeobiogeˈography** *noun* the branch of science that deals with the distribution of extinct plants and animals M20. **palaeobioˈlogic**, **palaeobioˈlogical** *adjectives* of or pertaining to palaeobiology M20. **palaeobiˈologist** *noun* an expert in or student of palaeobiology E20. **palaeobiˈology** *noun* the biology of extinct plants and animals L19. **palaeocereˈbellar** *adjective* (ANATOMY) of or pertaining to the palaeocerebellum M20. **palaeocereˈbellum** *noun* (ANATOMY) a phylogenetically older portion of the cerebellum, comprising mainly the anterior lobe, pyramid, and uvula E20. **palaeoˈchemical** *adjective* of or pertaining to palaeochemistry E20. **palaeoˈchemistry** *noun* the chemical features of something as they were in the geological past; the branch of science that deals with such features: M19. **palaeoclimate** *noun* the climate at a period in the geological past E20. **palaeocliˈmatic** *adjective* of or pertaining to a palaeoclimate L19. **palaeoclimatoˈlogic** *adjective* palaeoclimatological M20. **palaeoclimatoˈlogical** *adjective* of or pertaining to palaeoclimatology E20. **palaeoclimatoˈlogically** *adverb* as regards palaeoclimatology M20. **palaeoclimaˈtologist** *noun* an expert in or student of palaeoclimatology E20. **palaeoclimaˈtology** *noun* the branch of science that deals with palaeoclimates E20. **palaeoconˈservative**, (*colloq.*) **palaeocon** *nouns* (*N. Amer.*) a person who advocates old or traditional forms of conservatism; an extremely right-wing conservative: L20. **palaeoˈcortex** *noun*, pl. **-tices** /-tɪsiːz/, ANATOMY a phylogenetically older portion of the cerebral cortex, coextensive with the palaeopallium E20. **palaeoˈcortical** *adjective* (ANATOMY) of or pertaining to the palaeocortex E20. **palaeocurrent** *noun* (GEOLOGY) a current, usu. of water, which existed at some period in the past, as inferred from the features of sedimentary rocks M20. **palaeodeˈmography** *noun* the branch of knowledge that deals with the demographic features of past populations and cultures M20. **palaeo-environment** *noun* an environment at a period in the geological past M20. **palaeoenvironˈmental** *adjective* of, pertaining to, or occurring in a palaeoenvironment M20. **palaeo-equator** *noun* the equator as it was at a period in the geological past M20. **palaeo-equaˈtorial** *adjective* of, pertaining to, or occurring at a palaeoequator M20. **palaeoethnoboˈtanical** *adjective* of or pertaining to palaeoethnobotany M20. **palaeoethnoˈbotanist** *noun* an expert in or student of palaeoethnobotany M20. **palaeoethnoˈbotany** *noun* the branch of ethnobotany that deals with the remains of cultivated or utilized plants in archaeological contexts M20. **palaeofield** *noun* (the strength of) the earth's magnetic field at a period in the geological past M20. **palaeogeˈographer** *noun* an expert in or student of palaeogeography E20. **palaeogeoˈgraphic** *adjective* of or pertaining to palaeogeography E20. **palaeogeoˈgraphical** *adjective* palaeogeographic L19. **palaeogeoˈgraphically** *adverb* as regards palaeogeography M20. **palaeogeˈography** *noun* the geographical features of an area in the geological past; the branch of science that deals with the investigation of such features: L19. **palaeogeoˈlogic** *adjective* palaeogeological M20. **palaeogeoˈlogical** *adjective* of or pertaining to palaeogeology L19. **palaeogeˈologist** *noun* an expert in or student of palaeogeology M20. **palaeogeˈology** *noun* the geological features of an area in the geological past; the branch of science that deals with the investigation of such features: M20. **palaeogeomagˈnetic** *adjective* of or pertaining to the magnetic field of the earth in the geological past M20. **palaeogeoˈmorphic** *adjective* (GEOLOGY) of, pertaining to, or formed by buried relief features; palaeogeomorphological: M20. **palaeogeomorphoˈlogic**, **palaeogeomorphoˈlogical** *adjectives* (GEOLOGY) of or pertaining to palaeogeomorphology M20. **palaeogeomorˈphologist** *noun* (GEOLOGY) an expert in or student of palaeogeomorphology M20. **palaeogeomorˈphology** *noun* (GEOLOGY) the geomorphology of ancient landscapes, esp. as represented today by features that are buried or newly exhumed M20. **palaeogeoˈphysical** *adjective* of or pertaining to palaeogeophysics M20. **palaeogeoˈphysics** *noun* the branch of science that deals with the physical characteristics of the earth at periods in the geological past M20. **palaeoˈgravity** *noun* the strength of the earth's gravity at some time in the past L20. **palaeohyˈdrography** *noun* the hydrographic features of an area in the geological past; the branch of science that deals with the investigation of such features: M19. **palaeohyˈdrology** *noun* (*a*) the branch of science that deals with hydrologic features of past times; (*b*) the branch of science that deals with the use and management of water in the past: M19. **palaeoinˈtensity** *noun* the intensity of a palaeomagnetic field M20. **palaeolatitude** *noun* the latitude of a place at some period in the past M20. **palaeolatiˈtudinal** *adjective* expressed in terms of palaeolatitude; involving changes in palaeolatitude: M20. **palaeolimnoˈlogical** *adjective* of or pertaining to palaeolimnology M20. **palaeolimˈnologist** *noun* an expert in or student of palaeolimnology M20. **palaeolimˈnology** *noun* the conditions and processes occurring in lakes in the geological past; the branch of science that deals with the investigation of these: M20. **palaeolithoˈlogic** *adjective* designating a map showing the lithological features of an area at some period in the past M20. **palaeometeoroˈlogical** *adjective* of or pertaining to palaeometeorology E20. **palaeometeoˈrologist** *noun* an expert in or student of palaeometeorology E20. **palaeometeoˈrology** *noun* the branch of science that deals with atmospheric conditions in the geological past M19. **palaeoneuroˈlogical** *adjective* of or pertaining to palaeoneurology M20. **palaeoneuˈrologist** *noun* an expert in or student of palaeoneurology M20. **palaeoneuˈrology** *noun* the branch of science that deals with the neurology of fossil animals and esp. the evolutionary development of the human nervous system E20. **palaeoˈpallial** *adjective* (ANATOMY) of or pertaining to the palaeopallium M20. **palaeoˈpallium** *noun*, pl. **-lia**, ANATOMY a phylogenetically older portion of the pallium of the brain, which comprises mainly the pyriform lobe E20. **palaeopedoˈlogical** *adjective* of or pertaining to palaeopedology E20. **palaeopeˈdologist** *noun* an expert in or student of palaeopedology M20. **palaeopeˈdology** *noun* the features of soils in the geological past; the branch of science that deals with the investigation of these: E20. **palaeophysiˈographer** *noun* an expert in or student of palaeophysiography L19. **palaeophysioˈgraphic** *adjective* palaeophysiographical M20. **palaeophysioˈgraphical** *adjective* of or pertaining to palaeophysiography L19. **palaeophysiˈography** *noun* the physical and topographical features of the earth's surface in the geological past; the branch of science that deals with these: L19. **palaeophytoˈlogical** *adjective* palaeobotanical L19. **palaeophyˈtologist** *noun* a palaeobotanist L19. **palaeophyˈtology** *noun* palaeobotany M19. **palaeoplain** *noun* (PHYSICAL GEOGRAPHY) a peneplain which existed at some period in the past and became overlain by other strata, being now buried or re-exposed E20. **palaeopole** *noun* a magnetic pole of the earth as it was situated at a period in the geological past M20. **palaeoradius** *noun* the radius of the earth or another planet at a time in the geological past M20. **palaeosaˈlinity** *noun* (GEOLOGY) the salinity of the environment in which a sedimentary deposit was laid down M20. **palaeoslope** *noun* (GEOLOGY) the former or original slope of a region; the direction of such a slope: M20. **palaeosol** *noun* a soil horizon which was formed as a soil in the geological past M20. **palaeoˈsolic** *adjective* of or pertaining to a palaeosol M20. **palaeospecies** *noun* (PALAEONTOLOGY) a species including a group of fossils from different geological formations that make up a chronological series M20. **palaeostriˈatal** *adjective* (ANATOMY) of or pertaining to the palaeostriatum E20. **palaeostriˈatum** *noun*, pl. **-ta**, ANATOMY the phylogenetically older portion of the corpus striatum, consisting essentially of the globus pallidus E20. **palaeostructure** *noun* (GEOLOGY) the structure of an area at some period in the past M20. **palaeotechnic** /-ˈtɛknɪk/ *adjective* designating or pertaining to the stage of industrial development before the present one E20. **palaeotecˈtonic** *adjective* (GEOLOGY) of or pertaining to tectonic features or events of previous stages in the earth's history M20. **palaeotemperature** *noun* (GEOLOGY) (a measure of) the (average) temperature of a region etc. at some time in the past M19. **palaeoˈthalamus** *noun*, pl. **-mi** /-mʌɪ, -miː/, ANATOMY the phylogenetically older portion of the thalamus, usu. taken to include its anterior and medial parts E20. **palaeotherˈmometry** *noun* the investigation of the temperature of climates and oceans in the geological past M20. **palaeotopoˈgraphic**, **palaeotopoˈgraphical** *adjectives* of or pertaining to palaeotopography M20. **palaeotopoˈgraphically** *adverb* from the point of view of palaeotopography M20. **palaeotoˈpography** *noun* the topography of ancient landscapes, esp. as represented today by features that are buried or newly exhumed M20. **palaeoˈtropical** *adjective* belonging to the tropical parts of the Old World or eastern hemisphere, considered as a zoogeographical region M19. **palaeowind** *noun* a prevailing wind that existed at some period in the geological past M20. **palaeozoogeoˈgraphic** *adjective* of or pertaining to palaeozoogeography M20. **palaeozoogeˈography** *noun* the branch of science that deals with the distribution of fossil animal remains M20.

palaeoanthropic *adjective* var. of PALAEANTHROPIC.

palaeoanthropology /ˌpalɪəʊanθrəˈpɒlədʒi, ˌpeɪ-/ *noun*. Also ***paleo-**. E20.
[from PALAEO- + ANTHROPOLOGY.]
The branch of anthropology that deals with fossil hominids.
■ **ˌpalaeoanthropoˈlogical** *adjective* M20. **palaeoanthropologist** *noun* M20.

Palaeo-Asiatic /ˌpalɪəʊeɪʃɪˈatɪk, -ɛɪʒ-, ˌpeɪ-/ *noun* & *adjective*. Also ***Paleo-**. E20.
[from PALAEO- + ASIATIC.]
= PALAEO-SIBERIAN.

palaeobotany /ˌpalɪəʊˈbɒtəni, ˌpeɪ-/ *noun*. Also ***paleo-**. L19.
[from PALAEO- + BOTANY.]
The branch of botany that deals with extinct and fossil plants.
■ **ˌpalaeoboˈtanic**, **ˌpalaeoboˈtanical** *adjectives* L19. **ˌpalaeoboˈtanically** *adverb* in terms of or as regards palaeobotany M20. **palaeobotanist** *noun* L19.

Palaeocene /ˈpalɪəsiːn, ˈpeɪ-/ *adjective* & *noun*. Also ***Paleo-**.
[from PALAEO- + Greek *kainos* new, recent, after *Eocene*, *Miocene*, etc.]
GEOLOGY. ▶**A** *adjective*. Designating or pertaining to the earliest epoch of the Tertiary period or sub-era, preceding the Eocene. L19.
▶ **B** *noun*. The Palaeocene epoch; the series of rocks dating from this time, bearing evidence of the emergence and development of mammals. L19.
¶ Formerly often not recognized as a distinct epoch but incorporated in the Eocene.

palaeocrystic /ˌpalɪə(ʊ)ˈkrɪstɪk, ˌpeɪ-/ *adjective*. Also ***paleo-**. L19.
[from PALAEO- + Greek *krustallos* ice + -IC.]
Designating or consisting of polar ice that is old (orig., ice believed to have remained frozen from remote ages, now, ice more than about ten years old).

palaeoecology /ˌpalɪəʊɪˈkɒlədʒi, ˌpeɪ-/ *noun*. Also ***paleo-**. L19.
[from PALAEO- + ECOLOGY.]
The branch of science that deals with the ecology of extinct and fossil plants and animals.
■ **ˌpalaeoecoˈlogic**, **ˌpalaeoecoˈlogical** *adjectives* M20. **ˌpalaeoecoˈlogically** *adverb* from the point of view of palaeoecology M20. **palaeoecologist** *noun* M20.

palaeoethnology /ˌpalɪəʊɛθˈnɒlədʒi, ˌpeɪ-/ *noun*. Also ***paleo-**. M19.
[from PALAEO- + ETHNOLOGY.]
The branch of ethnology that deals with peoples of past times.
■ **ˌpalaeoethnoˈlogical** *adjective* L19. **palaeoethnologist** *noun* L19.

Palaeogene /ˈpalɪə(ʊ)dʒiːn, ˈpeɪ-/ *adjective* & *noun*. Also ***Paleo-**. L19.
[from PALAEO- + Greek *genēs*: see -GEN.]
GEOLOGY. ▶**A** *adjective*. Designating or pertaining to the first part of the Tertiary period or sub-era, comprising the Palaeocene, Eocene, and Oligocene epochs. L19.
▶ **B** *noun*. The Palaeogene period; the system of rocks dating from this time. L19.

palaeography /palɪˈɒgrəfi, peɪ-/ *noun*. Also ***paleo-**. E19.
[French *paléographie* from mod. Latin *palaeographia*, formed as PALAEO- + -GRAPHY.]
Ancient writing; an ancient style or method of writing; the science or art of deciphering and determining the date of ancient documents or systems of writing.
■ **palaeographer** *noun* an expert in or student of palaeography M19. **ˌpalaeoˈgraphic**, **ˌpalaeoˈgraphical** *adjectives* M19. **ˌpalaeoˈgraphically** *adverb* as regards palaeography M19. **palaeographist** *noun* a palaeographer M19.

palaeoichthyology /ˌpalɪəʊɪkθɪˈɒlədʒi, ˌpeɪ-/ *noun.* Also ***paleo-**. L19.
[from PALAEO- + ICHTHYOLOGY.]
The branch of science that deals with extinct and fossil fishes.
■ **ˌpalaeoichthyoˈlogical** *adjective* L19. **palaeoichthyologist** *noun* L19.

Palaeo-Indian /ˌpalɪəʊˈɪndɪən, ˌpeɪ-/ *adjective & noun.* Also ***Paleo-**. M20.
[from PALAEO- + INDIAN.]
▶ **A** *adjective.* Designating, of, or pertaining to the earliest Indian inhabitants of the Americas. M20.
▶ **B** *noun.* The Palaeo-Indian culture; a Palaeo-Indian inhabitant. M20.

palaeolithic /ˌpalɪə(ʊ)ˈlɪθɪk, ˌpeɪ-/ *adjective & noun.* Also ***paleo-**. M19.
[from PALAEO- + -LITHIC.]
ARCHAEOLOGY. ▶ **A** *adjective.* Designating or pertaining to the earliest of the three major divisions of the Stone Age, now regarded as ending at about the same time as the Pleistocene (about 8000 BC), and followed by the mesolithic. M19.
▶ **B** *noun.* **1** A palaeolith. Now *rare* or *obsolete.* L19.
2 *The* palaeolithic period. L19.
■ **ˈpalaeolith** *noun* (now *rare*) a palaeolithic stone implement L19.

palaeomagnetism /ˌpalɪə(ʊ)ˈmagnɪtɪz(ə)m, ˌpeɪ-/ *noun.* Also ***paleo-**. M19.
[from PALAEO- + MAGNETISM.]
GEOLOGY. The natural magnetism of rocks, which they are believed to have acquired at the time of their formation and which is used as evidence for the past relationship of the rocks to each other and to the earth's magnetic field; the branch of science that deals with this.
■ **ˌpalaeomagˈnetic** *adjective* of or pertaining to palaeomagnetism M20. **ˌpalaeomagˈnetically** *adverb* by means of or as regards palaeomagnetism M20. **palaeomagnetist** *noun* an expert in or student of palaeomagnetism M20.

palaeoniscoid /ˌpalɪə(ʊ)ˈnɪskɔɪd, ˌpeɪ-/ *noun & adjective.* L19.
[mod. Latin *Palaeoniscoidei*, from *Palaeoniscus* genus name, from PALAEO- + Greek *oniskos* a marine fish resembling the cod: see -OID.]
▶ **A** *noun.* Any of a group of extinct chondrostean fishes of Palaeozoic times characterized by heterocercal tails and diamond-shaped scales, and from which the sturgeon and paddlefish are descended; *spec.* any of the suborder Palaeoniscoidei. L19.
▶ **B** *adjective.* Pertaining to or characteristic of a palaeoniscoid, esp. in respect of its ganoid scales. L19.
■ **palaeoniscid** /-sɪd/ *noun & adjective* (*a*) *noun* a palaeoniscoid fish (in the broader sense); (*b*) *adjective* pertaining to or characteristic of a palaeoniscid: L19.

palaeontography /ˌpalɪɒnˈtɒgrəfi, ˌpeɪ-/ *noun.* Also ***paleo-**. M19.
[formed as next + -GRAPHY.]
The description of fossil remains of animals and plants; descriptive palaeontology.
■ **palaeontographer** *noun* L20. **ˌpalaeontoˈgraphical** *adjective* M19.

palaeontology /ˌpalɪɒnˈtɒlədʒi, ˌpeɪ-/ *noun.* Also ***paleo-**. M19.
[from PALAEO- + Greek *onta* neut. pl. of *ōn* being, pres. pple of *einai* be: see -OLOGY.]
The branch of science that deals with extinct and fossil animals and plants.
■ **ˌpalaeontoˈlogic**, **ˌpalaeontoˈlogical** *adjectives* M19. **ˌpalaeontoˈlogically** *adverb* as regards palaeontology, from the palaeontological point of view M19. **palaeontologist** *noun* M19.

palaeo-oceanography /ˌpalɪəʊəʊʃəˈnɒgrəfi, ˌpeɪ-/ *noun.* Also **palaeoceanog-** /ˌpalɪəʊʃəˈnɒg-/, ***paleo-**. M20.
[from PALAEO- + OCEANOGRAPHY.]
The conditions and processes occurring in oceans in the geological past; the branch of science that deals with these.
■ **palaeo-oceanographer** *noun* M20. **ˌpalaeo-oceanoˈgraphic** *adjective* M20. **ˌpalaeo-oceanoˈgraphical** *adjective* L20.

palaeopathology /ˌpalɪəʊpəˈθɒlədʒi, ˌpeɪ-/ *noun.* Also ***paleo-**. L19.
[from PALAEO- + PATHOLOGY.]
The branch of science that deals with the pathological conditions found in ancient human and animal remains.
■ **ˌpalaeopathoˈlogic**, **ˌpalaeopathoˈlogical** *adjectives* E20. **palaeopathologist** *noun* M20.

Palaeo-Siberian /ˌpalɪəʊsʌɪˈbɪərɪən, ˌpeɪ-/ *noun & adjective.* Also ***Paleo-**. E20.
[from PALAEO- + SIBERIAN.]
▶ **A** *noun.* **1** A member of any of several peoples of northern and eastern Siberia who are held to represent the earliest inhabitants of Siberia and whose languages do not belong to any of the major families. E20.
2 Any of the languages spoken by these peoples; these languages collectively. M20.
▶ **B** *adjective.* Of or pertaining to the Palaeo-Siberians or their languages. E20.

palaeothere /ˈpalɪə(ʊ)ˌθɪə, ˈpeɪ-/ *noun.* Also in mod. Latin form **palaeotherium** /ˌpalɪə(ʊ)ˈθɪərɪəm/, ***paleo-**. E19.
[mod. Latin *palaeotherium*, from PALAEO- + Greek *thērion* wild animal.]
A fossil perissodactyl of a group that included the ancestor of the tapir.
■ **palaeoˈtherian** *adjective* of or pertaining to a palaeothere; characterized by palaeotheres: M19.

Palaeozoic /ˌpalɪə(ʊ)ˈzəʊɪk, ˌpeɪ-/ *adjective & noun.* Also ***Paleo-**. M19.
[from PALAEO- + -ZOIC.]
▶ **A** *adjective.* **1** GEOLOGY. Designating or pertaining to the earliest era of the Phanerozoic eon, extending from the Cambrian to the Permian (orig., to the Silurian), following the Proterozoic, and marked by the development of marine and terrestrial plants and animals, esp. invertebrates. M19.
2 *fig.* Belonging to the most ancient or the lowest stage. M19.
▶ **B** *noun.* GEOLOGY.
1 A Palaeozoic rock or stratum. Usu. in *pl.* M19.
2 The Palaeozoic era; the rocks collectively dating from this time. M19.

palaeozoology /ˌpalɪəʊzəʊˈɒlədʒi, -zuː-, ˌpeɪ-/ *noun.* Also ***paleo-**. M19.
[from PALAEO- + ZOOLOGY.]
The branch of zoology that deals with extinct and fossil animals.
■ **palaeozooˈlogical** *adjective* M19. **palaeozoologist** *noun* E20.

palaestra /pəˈliːstrə, pəˈlʌɪstrə/ *noun.* Also **-lestra** /-ˈliːstrə, -ˈlɛstrə/. Pl. **-strae** /-striː/. LME.
[Latin from Greek *palaistra*, from *palaiein* wrestle.]
CLASSICAL HISTORY. **1** A place devoted to the public teaching and practice of wrestling and athletics. LME.
2 Wrestling, athletics. LME.
■ **palaestral** *adjective* LME. **palaestric** *adjective* L18. †**palaestrical** *adjective* L16–M17.

palafitte /palafit (*pl. same*), ˈpaləfɪt/ *noun.* Now *rare.* L19.
[French from Italian *palafitta* a fence of stakes, from *palo* stake + *fitto* fixed.]
ARCHAEOLOGY. A prehistoric hut or settlement built on stakes driven into the bed of a lake, esp. in Switzerland or northern Italy; a lake village.

palagi *noun & adjective* var. of PAPALAGI.

palagonite /pəˈlag(ə)nʌɪt/ *noun.* M19.
[from *Palagonia* in Sicily + -ITE[1].]
MINERALOGY. A brown to yellow amorphous or fibrous constituent of pyroclastic rocks, formed by the hydration of basaltic glass (sideromelane or tachylite).
■ **palagonitic** /-ˈnɪtɪk/ *adjective* of, pertaining to, or of the nature of palagonite L19. **paˌlagonitiˈzation** *noun* the hydration of basaltic glass to form palagonite E20. **palagonitized** *adjective* (partly or wholly) converted into palagonite M20.

Palaic /pəˈleɪɪk/ *noun & adjective.* E20.
[from *Pala*, app. a district of Asia Minor + -IC.]
(Of or pertaining to) an Anatolian language, known from the Hittite archives.

palais /ˈpaleɪ/ *noun.* Pl. same /-z/. E20.
[Abbreviation.]
= PALAIS DE DANSE. Freq. *attrib.*
Comb.: **palais glide** a ballroom dance with high kicks and gliding steps performed by large groups linking arms in a row.

palais de danse /ˌpaleɪ də ˈdɒ̃s/ *noun phr.* Pl. same. E20.
[French.]
A public hall for dancing.

Palais de Justice /palɛ də ʒystis/ *noun phr.* Pl. same. L18.
[French, lit. 'palace of justice'.]
In France and French-speaking countries, a court of law.

Palais Royal /paleɪ ˈrɔɪ(ə)l, *foreign* palɛ rwajal/ *adjectival phr.* L19.
[See below.]
Designating a type of indelicate farce said to be typical of the Palais Royal theatre in Paris.

Palamite /ˈpaləmʌɪt/ *noun & adjective.* M19.
[from St Gregory *Palamas*, an intellectual leader of the Hesychasts + -ITE[1].]
ECCLESIASTICAL HISTORY. ▶ **A** *noun.* A Hesychast. M19.
▶ **B** *adjective.* Of or pertaining to the Hesychasts or their doctrines. L19.

palampore /ˈpalampɔː/ *noun.* L17.
[Prob. from Portuguese *palangapuz(es)* pl., from Urdu, Persian *palangpoš* bed-cover (cf. Hindi *palang* bed, Persian *poš* cover) or perh. from *Pālanpur*, a town and former merchanting centre in Gujarat, India.]
A kind of chintz bed-cover, originally made in the Indian subcontinent.

palander /ˈpaləndə/ *noun. obsolete* exc. *Hist.* M16.
[App. from Italian *palandra*, *palandaria*, Spanish *palandre*, French †*palandre*, medieval Latin *palandaria*, all of unkn. origin.]
†**1** A fire-ship. M16–L17.
2 A flat-bottomed vessel used esp. (by the Turks) for transporting horses. L16.

palang /pəˈlaŋ/ *noun.* M20.
[Austronesian name.]
In Borneo and (formerly) the Philippines: a metal crosspiece driven horizontally through the penis near its head. Also, the practice of piercing the penis in this way.

palank /pəˈlaŋk/ *noun.* Long *rare.* Also **-ka** /-kə/. L17.
[French *palanque* or its source Italian *palanca* a defence made of large poles or stakes.]
A kind of fortified camp in Turkey.

palanquin /palənˈkiːn/ *noun.* Also **-keen**. L16.
[Portuguese *palanquim* from Oriya *pālaṅki*, Hindi *pālkī* (whence PALKEE), prob. through Malay *palangki*, ult. from Sanskrit *palyaṅka*, *paryaṅka* bed, litter.]
A covered conveyance for one person, consisting of a large box carried on two horizontal poles by four or six bearers, used in the Indian subcontinent and other Eastern countries.

Palantype /ˈpaləntʌɪp/ *noun.* Also **p-**. M20.
[from Clementine Camille Marie *Palanque*, English manufacturer + TYPE *noun*.]
(Proprietary name for) a machine for typing in shorthand. Also, the system of shorthand used with this machine.
■ **palantypist** *noun* M20.

palapa /pəˈlapə/ *noun. US.* L20.
[Mexican Spanish = (the leaves and branches of) the palm *Orbignya cohune*.]
A traditional Mexican shelter roofed with palm leaves or branches. Also, any structure imitating this, esp. on a beach.

palar /ˈpeɪlə/ *adjective*[1]. *rare.* M18.
[Latin *palaris*, from *palus* stake: see PALE *noun*[1], -AR[1].]
Of the nature of or resembling a pale or stake.

palar /ˈpɑːlə, ˈpeɪlə/ *adjective*[2]. M20.
[from PALA *noun* + -AR[1].]
ENTOMOLOGY. Of, pertaining to, or of the nature of a pala.

palari /pəˈlɑːri/ *noun.* M20.
[Malay.]
A two-masted Malaysian sailing vessel, used as a pleasure-boat or for trade.

palarie /pəˈlɑːri/ *verb & noun. slang.* Also **-ri**, **polari**. M19.
[Italian *parlare*.]
▶ **A** *verb trans.* Talk or speak (slang). *arch.* M19.
▶ **B** *noun.* = PARLYAREE. M19.

palas /pəˈlɑːs/ *noun.* Also **-sh** /-ʃ/. L18.
[Hindi *palās*, Sanskrit *palāśa*.]
= DHAK.

palatable /ˈpalətəb(ə)l/ *adjective.* M17.
[from PALATE + -ABLE.]
1 Agreeable to the palate; pleasant to taste. M17.
2 *fig.* Pleasing or agreeable to the mind or feelings; acceptable; enjoyable. L17.

> **1** R. L. STEVENSON A diet which was palatable to myself. **2** A. S. NEILL Learning should not be deliberately seasoned with play to make it palatable. S. HASTINGS The unendurable can be borne, the unpleasant made palatable or dismissed.

■ **palataˈbility** *noun* L19. **palatableness** *noun* (now *rare* or *obsolete*) E18. **palatably** *adverb* L17.

palatal /ˈpalət(ə)l/ *adjective & noun.* E18.
[French, from Latin *palatum* PALATE *noun*: see -AL[1].]
▶ **A** *adjective.* **1** PHONETICS. **a** Of a speech sound: articulated with the tongue against the palate, esp. the hard palate. E18. ▸**b** Of a sound change: occurring in the articulatory environment of a palatal sound. L19.
2 ANATOMY & ZOOLOGY etc. Of, pertaining to, or situated in or on the palate; palatine. E19.
▶ **B** *noun.* **1** PHONETICS. A palatal sound; *esp.* a palatal consonant. E19.
2 ANATOMY & ZOOLOGY. A palatine bone. *rare.* L19.
■ **palatality** /-ˈtalɪti/ *noun* (PHONETICS) the quality of being palatal M19. **palatally** *adverb* towards or by means of the palate M20.

palatalize /ˈpalət(ə)lʌɪz/ *verb.* Also **-ise**. M19.
[from prec. + -IZE.]
PHONETICS. **1** *verb trans.* Make palatal; *esp.* change (a velar) to a palatal by moving the point of contact between tongue and palate further forward in the mouth. M19.
2 *verb intrans.* Become palatal. M20.
■ **palataliˈzation** *noun* M19.

palate /ˈpalət/ *noun & verb.* LME.
[Latin *palatum*.]
▶ **A** *noun.* **1** The roof of the mouth of a vertebrate, esp. a human; the structures of bone and flesh separating the oral from the nasal cavity. LME. ▸**b** This as the seat of taste. Also *transf.*, the sense of taste. E16.
2 *fig.* Mental taste or liking. LME.
3 BOTANY. A convex projection of the lower lip of certain two-lipped flowers, e.g. the snapdragon, which closes the throat. M18.

For other words beginning with *palaeo-* see the entry for **palaeo-**

4 ENTOMOLOGY. The hypopharynx of an insect. M19.
5 The taste or flavour of wine or beer. L20.

1 A. BURGESS The dog . . yawned, showing a clean tongue and a pink ribbed palate. ***cleft palate***: see CLEFT *ppl adjective*. **hard palate** the front part of the palate, consisting of bone covered with thick mucous membrane. **soft palate** the back part of the palate, consisting of a fold of mucous membrane terminating in the uvula, which closes the nasal passages during swallowing. **b** M. RICHLER A man with your educated palate could . . tell not only the vineyard, but the vintage! W. M. CLARKE He insisted that nothing the palate relished could be hurtful to the system. **2** GEO. ELIOT I heard a little too much preaching . . and lost my palate for it. **5** *Wine* A lively floral Vinho Verde with a fresh, crisp palate.

▶**B** *verb trans.* **1** Taste; gratify the palate with; relish. Chiefly *fig. rare.* E17.
†**2** Make palatable. *rare.* E17–M19.
■ **palateless** *adjective* without a palate; *fig.* lacking discerning taste: M19.

palatial /pəˈleɪʃ(ə)l/ *adjective.* M18.
[from Latin *palatium* (see PALACE) + -AL¹.]
Of the nature of a palace; magnificent, splendid; pertaining to or befitting a palace.

S. WEINTRAUB He maintained a palatial estate. W. DALRYMPLE Mozaffar . . lived with his canvasses and library in a palatial house in Shah Jamal.

■ **palatially** *adverb* L19.

palatian /pəˈleɪʃ(ə)n/ *adjective. rare.* M19.
[formed as prec. + -AN.]
Palatial.

palatic /pəˈlatɪk/ *noun & adjective.* M17.
[from PALATE *noun* + -IC.]
▶**A** *noun.* PHONETICS. A palatal sound. Long *rare* or *obsolete.* M17.
▶**B** *adjective.* Of or belonging to the palate. *rare.* E19.

palatinate /pəˈlatɪnət/ *noun.* L16.
[from PALATINE *noun*¹ + -ATE¹.]
Chiefly *Hist.* **1** ***the Palatinate***, the territory of the German Empire ruled by the Count Palatine of the Rhine; the area of modern Germany corresponding to this. L16.
2 A county palatine in England or Ireland. Also, an American colony whose proprietors had palatine rights. E17.
3 The territory under the jurisdiction of a palatine. M17.
4 A native or inhabitant of the German Palatinate. E18.

palatine /ˈpalətʌɪn, -tɪn/ *adjective*¹ *& noun*¹. LME.
[Old & mod. French *palatin(e)* from Latin *palatinus* (adjective) of the palace, (noun) officer of the palace, chamberlain, from *palatium*: see PALACE, -INE¹.]
Chiefly *Hist.* ▶**A** *adjective.* **1** Of an official or feudal lord: having privilege and authority within a territory which elsewhere belongs only to a monarch. Usu. *postpositive.* Earliest in ***county palatine*** below. LME. ▸**b** Of or pertaining to a palatine official or lord, or a palatinate. M17.
2 Of or belonging to a palace, esp. a palace of the Caesars or the German emperors; palatial. L16.
3 Of or belonging to the German Palatinate. M17.
Phrases & special collocations: **Countess Palatine** the wife of a Count Palatine. **Count Palatine** (*a*) a count of the imperial palace in the later Roman Empire, having supreme judicial authority in the imperial court; (*b*) any of several counts in the German Empire, each having supreme jurisdiction within his own territory; (*c*) (with lower-case initials) the earl or lord of a county palatine in England or Ireland. **county palatine** (*a*) the dominion of a count palatine; (*b*) a county in which royal privileges and exclusive rights of jurisdiction were held by its earl or lord. **earl palatine** = ***Count Palatine*** (c) above. **palatine earldom** = ***county palatine*** above. **Palatine Hill** [translating Latin *Mons Palatinus*] one of the seven hills of Rome.
▶**B** *noun.* **I 1** An officer (orig. the chamberlain, mayor, or major) of an imperial palace; a chief minister of an empire. L16. ▸**b** An official or a feudal lord having sovereignty over a territory of an empire; a vassal exercising royal privileges in his province. L16. ▸**c** A count or earl palatine in England or Ireland; the lord of a county palatine. E17. ▸**d** A title of the senior proprietor of any of various American colonies, esp. Carolina. M17.
2 In *pl.* The troops of the imperial palace in the later Roman Empire; the praetorians. E17.
3 A native or inhabitant of a palatinate. E17.
▶**II 4** [from the Princess *Palatine*, wife of a 17th cent. Duke of Orleans.] A fur tippet worn by women. L17.

palatine /ˈpalətʌɪn, -tɪn/ *adjective*² *& noun*². M17.
[French *palatin(e)*, from Latin *palatum* PALATE *noun*: see -INE¹.]
▶**A** *adjective.* **1** Of or pertaining to the palate; situated in or on the palate, palatal; *spec.* (ANATOMY & ZOOLOGY) designating or pertaining to either of two bones in the skull (see sense B.2 below). M17.
†**2** PHONETICS. = PALATAL *adjective* 1. M17–L18.
1 ***palatine uvula***: see UVULA 1.
▶**B** *noun.* †**1** PHONETICS. = PALATAL *noun* 1. L17–E19.
2 ANATOMY & ZOOLOGY. Either of two bones in the vertebrate skull which in mammals form much of the hard palate, nasal cavity, and orbit on either side of the midline. M19.

palative /ˈpalətɪv/ *adjective. rare.* L17.
[from PALATE *noun* + -IVE.]
Appealing to the palate or taste.

palato- /ˈpalətəʊ, pəˈleɪtəʊ/ *combining form* of Latin *palatum* PALATE *noun* or of PALATINE *adjective*² *& noun*²: see -O-.
■ **palato-alˈveolar** *adjective* (PHONETICS) (of a consonant) articulated with the tongue raised towards the palate and the tip of the tongue against the alveolar ridge M20. **palato-ˈdental** *adjective & noun* (PHONETICS) (*a*) *adjective* pertaining to the palate and the teeth; (of a consonant) articulated with the tongue against the palate immediately behind the teeth; (*b*) *noun* a consonant articulated in this way: M19. **ˈpalatogram** *noun* (PHONETICS) a diagram produced by palatography E20. **palatoˈgraphic** *adjective* (PHONETICS) of or pertaining to palatography E20. **palaˈtography** *noun* (PHONETICS) a technique of recording the position of the tongue during articulation from its contact with the hard palate E20. **palato-maˈxillary** *adjective* (ANATOMY & ZOOLOGY) of or pertaining to the palate and the jaw (*spec.* the maxilla) L18. **palato-phaˈryngeal** *adjective* (ANATOMY) of or pertaining to the palate and the pharynx L19. **ˈpalatoplasty** *noun* plastic surgery of the palate, esp. to repair cleft palate L19. **palato-ˈquadrate** *adjective & noun* (ZOOLOGY) (*a*) *adjective* of, pertaining to, or consisting of the palatine and quadrate bones; (*b*) *noun* a bone or cartilage of the upper jaw of some vertebrates, consisting of a fused palatine and quadrate: L19. **palatorrhaphy** /paləˈtɒrəfi/ *noun* (SURGERY) suturing of a cleft palate M19. **palato-ˈvelar** *adjective* (PHONETICS) (*a*) articulated with the tongue simultaneously or successively touching the palate and velum; (*b*) either palatal or velar: L19.

palatschinken /palatˈʃɪŋkən/ *noun pl.* E20.
[Austrian German from Hungarian *palacsinta* from Proto-Romance *placinta* from Latin *placenta* cake.]
Austrian (stuffed) pancakes.

Palauan /pəˈlaʊən/ *noun & adjective.* Also **Belauan** /bɪˈlaʊən/. E20.
[from *Palau*, now *Belau* (see below) + -AN.]
▶**A** *noun.* A native or inhabitant of the Palau Islands, a group of islands in the Caroline Islands of Micronesia, now the Republic of Belau. Also, the Austronesian language of the people of these islands. E20.
▶**B** *adjective.* Of or pertaining to the Palauans or their language. M20.

Palaung /pəˈlaʊŋ/ *noun & adjective.* M19.
[Palaung.]
▶**A** *noun.* Pl. same, **-s**.
1 A member of a people of the northern Shan States of Myanmar (Burma). M19.
2 The Mon-Khmer language of this people. E20.
▶**B** *attrib.* or as *adjective.* Of or pertaining to the Palaung or their language. M20.

palaver /pəˈlɑːvə/ *noun & verb.* M18.
[Portuguese *palavra* from Latin *parabola* PARABLE *noun*.]
▶**A** *noun.* **1** *Hist.* A talk, a conference, a parley, esp. between (African) tribespeople and traders or travellers. M18.
2 a Unnecessary, profuse, or idle talk. M18. ▸**b** Cajolery, flattery. M18. ▸†**c** In W. Africa: a dispute, a contest. M–L18.
3 Business, concern. *W. Afr. colloq.* L19.
4 A tiresome or lengthy business; (a) fuss, (a) bother; trouble. *colloq.* L19.

4 P. BAILEY What a palaver . . before the coach left! Chattering away, rushing around. JO GRIMOND All the palaver of the court . . the 'Yes m'lud' and 'No, m'lud'.

▶**B** *verb.* **1** *verb intrans.* Talk unnecessarily, profusely, or idly; jabber. M18.
2 *verb trans.* Cajole, flatter, wheedle, (a person). Also foll. by *into*, *out of*. M18.
■ **palaverer** *noun* L18.

palazzo /pəˈlatsəʊ/ *noun & adjective.* M17.
[Italian from Latin *palatium*: see PALACE *noun*.]
▶**A** *noun.* Pl. **-zzos**, (in sense 1) **-zzi** /-tsi/.
1 A palatial mansion; a large imposing building. M17.
2 *sing.* & (usu.) in *pl.* Loose wide-legged trousers worn by women. L20.
▶**B** *attrib.* or as *adjective.* Designating a loose wide-legged garment, outfit, etc. M20.

pale /peɪl/ *noun*¹. ME.
[Old & mod. French *pal* from Latin *palus* stake. Cf. PALLET *noun*³, PEEL *noun*¹.]
1 A stake; a pointed piece of wood intended to be driven into the ground, esp. along with others to form a fence. Now usu., any of the bars or strips of wood nailed vertically to a horizontal rail or rails to form a fence. ME.
2 A fence of pales. Also, an enclosing barrier. Now *arch.* & *poet.* ME. ▸**b** *fig.* A limit, a boundary; a restriction. Formerly also, a defence. Freq. in ***within the pale of***, ***outside the pale of***. LME.
3 An area or place enclosed by a fence; any enclosed area. LME.
4 A district within determined bounds, or subject to a particular jurisdiction. LME.
5 †**a** A vertical stripe on cloth or a garment. Only in LME. ▸**b** HERALDRY. An ordinary consisting of a central vertical stripe usu. occupying one third of a shield. Formerly also (in *pl.*), a number of vertical stripes on a shield. Cf. PALLET *noun*⁴, PALY *adjective*¹. L15.

1 STEVIE SMITH The churchyard pales are black against the night. **2** M. BERESFORD The Park pale runs to the north of the old village site. **b** JOYCE He had not been in the pale of the Church for twenty years. H. H. ASQUITH 'Enthusiasm' seemed to him to be outside the pale of rational Christianity. *Times* As if a pale had been built round the British Isles.

Phrases: **beyond the pale** outside the boundaries of acceptable behaviour. **in pale** HERALDRY (of a charge or row of charges) in the position of a pale, arranged vertically. **per pale** HERALDRY (of a shield) divided by a central vertical line. **the English pale** *Hist.* = ***the Pale*** (a), (b) below. **the Pale** *Hist.* (*a*) Calais when under English jurisdiction; (*b*) an area of Ireland (varying in extent at different times) under English jurisdiction; (*c*) the area(s) of Russia to which Jewish residence was restricted.
Comb.: **palesman** *rare* a native or inhabitant of the English pale in Ireland.

pale /peɪl/ *noun*². Now *rare* or *obsolete.* M16.
[from PALE *adjective*.]
Paleness, pallor.

pale /peɪl/ *noun*³. M19.
[Latin PALEA.]
BOTANY. Either of the two bracts enclosing the floret of a grass; *spec.* the inner bract; = PALEA 2(a).

pale /peɪl/ *adjective.* ME.
[Old French *pal(l)e* (mod. *pâle*) from Latin *pallidus* PALLID.]
1 Of a person, a complexion, etc.: whitish or ashen in appearance; pallid; wan. ME. ▸**b** *gen.* Of a shade of colour approaching white; lacking intensity or depth of colour. LME.
2 Lacking in brightness; faint, dim. LME.
3 *fig.* Feeble, faint; lacking intensity, vigour, or strength; fearful, timorous. E16.

1 D. H. LAWRENCE She was pale now with emotion and anxiety. **b** I. MURDOCH Her large eyes were of a blue so pale as to be almost white. R. P. JHABVALA Her tongue which looked very pale in contrast with her lipstick. RACHEL ANDERSON He had pale sandy hair. **2** DENNIS POTTER A pale September sunshine, unsure of itself.

Comb. & special collocations: ***pale brindled beauty***: see BRINDLED *adjective*; **pale crêpe (rubber)** a pale yellowish high-quality rubber made by chemical treatment of the latex to prevent its turning brown; **paleface** (orig. *US*) (*a*) a person with a pale face; supposedly among N. American Indians, a white person; (*b*) (chiefly *US Black slang*) a white person; **pale-faced** *adjective* having a pale face or complexion.
■ **palely** *adverb* with a pale look or appearance; dimly, wanly: M16. **paleness** *noun* ME.

pale /peɪl/ *verb*¹ *trans.* Now *rare.* ME.
[Old French *paler*, formed as PALE *noun*¹.]
1 Enclose with pales or a fence; fence in. ME. ▸**b** *transf.* & *fig.* Encircle, encompass, enclose. Also foll. by *in*, *up*. L16.
†**2** Mark or adorn with vertical stripes. Chiefly as ***paled*** *ppl adjective.* LME.
■ †**paler** *noun* a person who puts up a paling or fence, esp. one responsible for keeping the fences of a park in repair ME–E19.

pale /peɪl/ *verb*². LME.
[Old French *palir* (mod. *pâlir*), formed as PALE *adjective*.]
1 *verb intrans.* Become pale or dim; lose colour or brightness; *fig.* weaken, diminish in importance. LME.
2 *verb trans.* Make pale; lose colour or brightness. LME.

1 L. STRACHEY All these influences paled before a new star . . which . . immediately dominated her life. B. CHATWIN He had paled with excitement. **pale into insignificance** lose importance (esp. in comparison with a greater achievement). **2** H. WOUK A bright moon was paling the stars.

pale- *combining form* see PALAEO-.

palea /ˈpeɪlɪə/ *noun.* Pl. **-eae** /-ɪiː/, **-eas**. LME.
[Latin = chaff.]
†**1** A straw. Only in LME.
2 BOTANY. A thin dry bract or scale; *esp.* (*a*) (in the floret of a grass) orig., either of the bracts enclosing the stamens and pistil; now, the delicate inner bract (cf. LEMMA *noun*² 2); (*b*) a receptacular scale in certain plants of the composite family. M18.
3 ORNITHOLOGY. A wattle, a dewlap. L19.
■ **paleaceous** /peɪlɪˈeɪʃəs/ *adjective* (BOTANY) covered with paleae or thin dry scales; of the consistency of chaff: M18.

paleanthropic *adjective*, **palearctic** *adjective & noun*, **paleencephalon** *noun* see PALAEANTHROPIC etc.

palefrenier *noun* var. of PALFRENIER.

Palekh /ˈpɑːlɛk/ *adjective.* M20.
[See below.]
Designating a type of iconography for which the town of Palekh, NE of Moscow, was renowned in the 18th cent., and a type of miniature painting on boxes, trays, etc., developed in Palekh in the 19th cent.

paleo- *combining form* see PALAEO-.

paleoanthropic *adjective* var. of PALAEANTHROPIC.

paleoanthropology *noun*, **Paleo-Asiatic** *noun & adjective* see PALAEOANTHROPOLOGY, PALAEO-ASIATIC, etc.

Palermitan /pəˈləːmɪt(ə)n/ *noun & adjective.* L17.
[Italian *palermitano* alt. of Latin *panormitanus* from Greek *panormitēs*, from *Panormos* Palermo: see below, -ITE[1], -AN.]
▸ **A** *noun.* A native or inhabitant of the Sicilian town or province of Palermo. L17.
▸ **B** *adjective.* Of, pertaining to, or characteristic of Palermo. M19.

Palestine /ˈpaləstʌɪn/ *adjective.* M19.
[formed as next.]
Designating a cream soup made from Jerusalem artichokes.

Palestinian /ˌpaləˈstɪnɪən/ *adjective & noun.* L19.
[from *Palestine* (see below) + -IAN.]
▸ **A** *adjective.* Of or pertaining to Palestine, a territory in SW Asia on the eastern Mediterranean coast (historically of variable extent, freq. *spec.* as (*a*) in biblical times comprising the kingdom of Israel and Judah; (*b*) comprising territory west of the Jordan mandated to Britain between 1920 and 1948). L19.
▸ **B** *noun.* A native or inhabitant of Palestine in ancient or modern times; *spec.* an Arab, or descendant of Arabs, born or living in the area of the former mandated territory of Palestine. E20.

palestra *noun* var. of PALAESTRA.

Palestrinian /paləˈstrɪnɪən/ *adjective.* M20.
[from *Palestrina* (see below) + -IAN.]
Of, pertaining to, or in the style of the Italian composer Giovanni Pierluigi da Palestrina (*c* 1525–94).

paletot /ˈpalətəʊ/ *noun.* M19.
[French, of unkn. origin.]
A short loose outer garment, coat, or cloak. Also, a fitted jacket worn by women in the 19th cent.
■ **paletoted** /ˈpalətəʊd/ *adjective* provided with or wearing a paletot M19.

palette /ˈpalɪt/ *noun.* L18.
[French: see PALLET *noun*[3].]
1 A thin (oval) board or slab, usu. with a hole for the thumb, on which an artist lays and mixes colours. L18. ▸**b** *transf.* The range of colours used by a particular artist or in a particular picture, or in which a particular product is available. L19. ▸**c** The range or variety of tonal or instrumental colour in a musical piece, composer's work, etc.; the verbal range of a writer etc. M20. ▸**d** COMPUTING. In computer graphics, the range of colours or shapes available to the user. L20.
2 ZOOLOGY. A disclike structure; *spec.* (ENTOMOLOGY) a flat expanded part on the legs of some insects (esp. aquatic beetles). Cf. PALLET *noun*[3] 6. M19.
3 A device used by the banker in certain card-games to move cards and money. M20.

> 🕮 **1** D. FRANCIS He scooped up the paint-laden palette with his right hand. **c** *Music Paper* A whirlwind palette of sound, riddled in enigma.

Comb.: **palette-knife** (*a*) a thin flexible steel blade with a handle, used for mixing colours on a palette, spreading paint or ink for printing, etc.; (*b*) a kitchen knife with a long blunt rounded-ended flexible blade, used for scraping and spreading.

paleways /ˈpeɪlweɪz/ *adjective & adverb.* Now *rare* or *obsolete.* E17.
[from PALE *noun*[1] + -WAYS.]
HERALDRY. ▸**A** *adjective.* = PALY *adjective*[1]. E17.
▸ **B** *adverb.* = PALEWISE. L17.

palewise /ˈpeɪlwʌɪz/ *adverb.* E18.
[from PALE *noun*[1] + -WISE.]
HERALDRY. Vertically.

Paleyan /ˈpeɪlɪən/ *noun & adjective.* Also (earlier) †**-ian**. E19.
[from *Paley* (see below) + -AN, -IAN.]
▸ **A** *noun.* A follower or adherent of the English theologian William Paley (1743–1805) or of his rationalist and utilitarian moral philosophy, and his theology which styled God as the supreme craftsman in a mechanistic universe. E19.
▸ **B** *adjective.* Of, pertaining to, or characteristic of Paley or his views. E19.

palfrenier /palfrəˈnɪə/ *noun. arch.* Also **pale-**. L15.
[Old & mod. French *palefrenier* from Provençal *palafrenier*, from *palafren* var. of *palafre* PALFREY: see -IER.]
A man in charge of horses; a groom.

palfrey /ˈpɔːlfri, ˈpal-/ *noun.* Now *Hist.* or *poet.* ME.
[Old French *palefrei* (mod. *palefroi*) from medieval Latin *palefredus* alt. of late Latin *paraveredus*, from Greek *para* beside, extra (see PARA-[1]) + Latin *veredus* light horse, of Gaulish origin.]
A horse for ordinary riding as opp. to a warhorse; *esp.* a small saddle horse for a woman.

†**Palgrave** *noun* var. of PALSGRAVE.

Pali /ˈpɑːli/ *noun*[1] *& adjective.* L18.
[Pali *pāli* (the) canonical text(s) (as opp. to commentary).]
▸ **A** *noun.* The literary Indo-Aryan language of Buddhist canonical books; the language of the later Theravada Buddhist chronicles, commentaries, and other literature; the related language of early Indian inscriptions. L18.
▸ **B** *attrib.* or as *adjective.* Of or pertaining to Pali. L18.

pali /ˈpɑːliː/ *noun*[2]. Pl. same, **-s**. E19.
[Hawaiian.]
In Hawaii: a steep cliff or precipice; *spec.* (*the Pali*) a particular precipice and pass on the island of Oahu.

palii *noun* pl. of PALIO.

palikar /ˈpalɪkɑː/ *noun.* E19.
[mod.Greek *palikari*, *pallēkari*, dim. of Greek *pallax*, *pallēx* youth.]
A follower of a Greek or Albanian military chief, esp. during the war of independence (1821–30).

palilalia /palɪˈleɪlɪə/ *noun.* E20.
[French *palilalie*, from Greek *palin* again: see -LALIA.]
MEDICINE. A speech disorder characterized by involuntary repetition of words, phrases, or sentences.

palilogy /pəˈlɪlədʒi/ *noun.* Also **palillogy**. M17.
[Late Latin *palilogia* from Greek, from *palin* again + *-logia* -LOGY.]
RHETORIC. The (esp. immediate) repetition of a word or phrase, for emphasis.

palimbacchius /ˌpalɪmbəˈkʌɪəs/ *noun.* Long *rare.* Pl. **-cchii** /-ˈkʌɪʌɪ/. L16.
[Latin from Greek *palimbakkheios*, from *palin* back + *bakkheios* BACCHIUS.]
PROSODY. A metrical foot of three syllables, two long and one short; a reversed bacchius.
■ Also **palimbacchic** *noun* M18.

palimony /ˈpalɪməni/ *noun. colloq.* (chiefly *US*). L20.
[Blend of PAL *noun* and ALIMONY.]
Compensation made by one member of an unmarried couple to the other after separation.

> 🕮 *attrib.*: *Sunday Express* The Michele Marvin palimony case, which established rights for unmarried couples in California.

palimpsest /ˈpalɪm(p)sɛst/ *noun, adjective, & verb.* Orig. in Latin & Greek forms †**-sestus**, †**-seston**. M17.
[Latin *palimpsestus* from Greek *palimpsestos*, *-on*, from *palin* again + *psestos* pa. ppl formation on *psēn* rub smooth.]
▸ **A** *noun.* †**1** Paper, parchment, etc., prepared for writing on and wiping out, like a slate. M17–E18.
2 A paper, parchment, etc., on which the original writing has been effaced to make way for other writing; a manuscript in which a later writing is written over an effaced earlier writing. E19.
3 A monumental brass slab turned and re-engraved on the reverse side. L19.

> 🕮 **2** G. ORWELL All history was a palimpsest, scraped clean and re-inscribed exactly as often as was necessary.

▸ **B** *adjective.* **1** Of a manuscript: having the original writing effaced and superseded by later writing. M19.
2 Of a monumental brass: turned and re-engraved on the reverse. M19.
3 GEOLOGY. Exhibiting features produced at two or more distinct periods; *spec.* in PETROGRAPHY, (of a rock) partially preserving the texture it had prior to metamorphism. E20.
▸ **C** *verb trans.* Make into a palimpsest; write again on (paper, parchment, etc.) after effacing the original writing. E20.
■ **palimpˈsestic** *adjective* that is or that makes a palimpsest E18.

palinal /ˈpalɪn(ə)l/ *adjective.* L19.
[Irreg. from Greek *palin* back + -AL[1].]
PHYSIOLOGY. Characterized by or involving backward motion of the lower jaw in chewing.

palindrome /ˈpalɪndrəʊm/ *noun & adjective.* E17.
[Greek *palindromos* running back again, from *palin* back, again + *drom-*, *dramein* run.]
▸ **A** *noun.* **1** A word, phrase, etc., that reads the same backwards as forwards. E17.
2 *transf.* **a** MUSIC. A piece in which the second half is a retrograde repetition of the first half. M20. ▸**b** BIOLOGY. A palindromic sequence of nucleotides in a DNA or RNA molecule. L20.
▸ **B** *adjective.* That reads or runs the same backwards as forwards. M17.
■ **palinˈdromic** *adjective* (*a*) of the nature of a palindrome, having a structure that is the same in both directions; (*b*) MEDICINE characterized by frequent or worsening recurrences or relapses: M19. **palindromist** *noun* a writer or inventor of palindromes L19.

paling /ˈpeɪlɪŋ/ *noun.* LME.
[from PALE *verb*[1] + -ING[1].]
†**1** Decoration with pales or vertical stripes. Only in LME.
2 The action of making a fence, or of enclosing a place, with pales. LME.
3 a *sing.* & in *pl.* A fence of pales. Also in *sing.*, each of the pales forming a fence. M16. ▸**b** Wood prepared for or made into pales; pales collectively; fencing. L18.

> 🕮 **3a** R. L. STEVENSON They had cleared a wide space . . completed by a paling six feet high. *Independent* The 10-feet high palings, with their broad central gates and twin gas lamps.

palingenesia *noun* var. of PALINGENESY.

palingenesis /palɪnˈdʒɛnɪsɪs/ *noun.* E19.
[from Greek *palin* again + *genesis* birth.]
1 = PALINGENESY. E19.
2 BIOLOGY. **a** Development of organisms in accordance with the ancestral type; *spec.* the exact reproduction of ancestral characteristics in ontogenesis. Cf. RECAPITULATION *noun* 1b. L19. ▸**b** Metamorphosis. Now *rare* or *obsolete.* L19.
3 GEOLOGY. The formation of a new magma by the remelting of existing rocks. E20.
■ **palingeˈnetic** *adjective* of, belonging to, or resembling palingenesis M19. **palingeˈnetically** *adverb* L19.

palingenesy /palɪnˈdʒɛnɪsi/ *noun.* Also (earlier) in Latin form **palingenesia** /ˌpalɪndʒɪˈniːsɪə/. E17.
[(French *palingénésie* from) medieval Latin *palingenesia* from Greek *paliggenesia* rebirth, formed as prec.: see -Y[3].]
Regeneration, rebirth; revival, re-animation, resuscitation.
■ ˌ**palingeˈnesian** *adjective* E19.

palinode /ˈpalɪnəʊd/ *noun.* L16.
[(French †*palinode*, *palinodie* from) Latin *palinodia* from Greek *palinōdia*, from *palin* again + *ōdē* song, ode.]
An ode in which the writer retracts a view or sentiment expressed in an earlier poem. Also *gen.*, a recantation; *spec.* in SCOTS LAW, a recantation in court of a defamatory statement.

palinody /ˈpalɪnəʊdi/ *noun.* Now *rare* or *obsolete.* Also in Latin form **-dia** /-dɪə/. L16.
[(French *palinodie* from) Latin *palinodia* PALINODE: see -Y[3].]
= PALINODE.

palinspastic /palɪnˈspastɪk/ *adjective.* M20.
[from Greek *palin* again + *spastikos* drawing in: see SPASTIC.]
GEOLOGY. Of a map, diagram, etc.: representing layers of rock as returned to their supposed former positions.
■ **palinspastically** *adverb* by means of a palinspastic map M20. **palinspastics** *noun* the production of palinspastic maps M20.

palio /ˈpɑːlio, ˈpalɪəʊ/ *noun.* Pl. ***-ii*** /-ii, -ɪiː/. L17.
[Italian from Latin *pallium* covering, cover.]
A traditional horse-race held in Italy, esp. in Siena, every July and August. Also, the cloth or banner of velvet, silk, etc., given as the prize for winning this race.

paliotto /paliˈɔtto, palɪˈɒtəʊ/ *noun.* Pl. ***-tti*** /-t(t)i/, ***-ttos*** /-təʊz/. M20.
[Italian.]
The frontal painting on an altarpiece.

palisade /palɪˈseɪd/ *noun & verb.* E17.
[French *palissade* from Provençal *palissada*, from *palissa* fence of pales from Proto-Gallo-Romance, from Latin *palus* PALE *noun*[1]: see -ADE.]
▸ **A** *noun.* **1 a** A fence of pales or iron railings fixed in the ground, forming an enclosure or defence. E17. ▸†**b** A light fence or trellis on which trees or shrubs are trained; *transf.* a row of trees or shrubs trained on this, or forming a close hedge. M17–E18. ▸**c** MILITARY. A strong pointed wooden stake fixed deeply in the ground with others in a close row, as a defence. L17.
2 *fig.* **a** A thing resembling or likened to (one stake of) a fence of stakes. E17. ▸**b** *spec.* In *pl.* A line of high cliffs, *esp.* (*the Palisade*) such a line extending about 24 km or 15 miles along the western bank of the Hudson River above New York. *US.* M19. ▸**c** BIOLOGY. A region of parallel elongated cells, often at right angles to the surface of the structure of which they form part; *esp.* in BOTANY, the parenchyma immediately below the upper epidermis of most leaves. E20.

> 🕮 **1a** *Independent* A backyard bounded by a palisade of rusty corrugated iron. **2c** ***palisade cell***, ***palisade parenchyma***, ***palisade tissue***, etc.

Comb.: **palisade-worm** any of various strongyles (parasitic nematodes) which infest horses.
▸ **B** *verb trans.* Provide, surround, or fortify with a palisade or palisades; fence in. M17.
■ **palisading** *noun* (*a*) the action of the verb; (*b*) a palisade, a paling; (*c*) ANATOMY & MEDICINE arrangement of cells in a palisade: E18.

palisado /palɪˈsɑːdəʊ/ *noun & verb. arch.* L16.
[Spanish *palizada* from Proto-Gallo-Romance base also of prec.: see -ADO.]
▸ **A** *noun.* Pl. **-o(e)s**. = PALISADE *noun* 1, 2a, b. L16.
▸ **B** *verb trans.* = PALISADE *verb.* L16.

palisander /palɪˈsandə/ *noun.* M19.
[French *palissandre*, *palisandre*, prob. of S. Amer. Indian origin.]
Any of several ornamental woods used in cabinet-work, *esp.* that of Brazilian rosewood, *Dalbergia nigra*, and (*US*) that of purpleheart.

palish /ˈpeɪlɪʃ/ *adjective.* LME.
[from PALE *adjective* + -ISH[1].]
Somewhat pale, rather pale.

Palissy /ˈpalɪsi/ *adjective.* M19.
[Bernard *Palissy* (c 1510–c 1590), French master potter.]
Designating pottery made by Palissy or his successors or imitators.

palkee /ˈpɑːkiː/ *noun.* Also **-ki**. L17.
[Hindi *pālkī*: cf. PALANQUIN.]
= PALANQUIN.

pall /pɔːl/ *noun*[1]. OE.
[Latin PALLIUM covering, Greek mantle, philosopher's cloak.]
1 Fine or rich (esp. purple) cloth for robes. Long *arch.* OE.
2 a *ECCLESIASTICAL.* A cloth used at or on an altar; *spec.* (*a*) *arch.* a corporal; (*b*) *arch.* a frontal; (*c*) a small piece of cloth, usu. stiffened with cardboard, for covering a chalice. OE. ▸**b** A rich cloth spread on or over something. Now *esp.*, a (usu. velvet) cloth spread over a coffin, hearse, or tomb. ME. ▸**c** *fig.* Something that covers or conceals; *spec.* a dark or gloomy covering that extends over a thing or region. LME.
3 A (usu. rich) robe, cloak, or mantle. *arch.* in *gen.* sense. OE. ▸**b** *ECCLESIASTICAL.* = PALLIUM 1. LME. ▸**c** A robe or mantle put on a monarch at his or her coronation. M17.
4 *HERALDRY.* A charge representing the front half of an archbishop's pallium, consisting of three bands in the form of a capital Y, charged with crosses. Also ***cross pall***. M16.

> 🕮 **2b** CLARENDON When the Coffin was put in, the black Velvet Pall . . was thrown over it. A. S. BYATT An accordion placed under a velvet pall out of reach of all. **c** *Guardian* The eternal pall of grey pollution that . . starves the place of any sunlight. *Independent* Torture and murder have cast a pall of terror over most villages.

Comb.: **pallbearer** a person accompanying or helping to carry a coffin at a funeral.

pall *noun*[2] var. of PAWL *noun*.

pall /pɔːl/ *verb*[1]. LME.
[Aphet. from APPAL.]
▶ **I** *verb intrans.* †**1** Become pale or dim. Long *rare.* LME–M19.
†**2** Become faint; lose strength, virtue, etc. LME–E17.
3 Of fermented liquor etc.: become flat, stale, or insipid, esp. by exposure to air. Now only as ***palled*** *ppl adjective. arch.* LME.
4 a Of a thing: become unappetizing, unattractive, or uninteresting. Also foll. by *on* or *upon* the mind, the senses, etc. E18. ▸**b** Of a person or sense: become satiated (*with*). M18.

> 🕮 **4a** W. H. DIXON The pastimes . . began to pall on him. C. BRAYFIELD Sometimes she would . . go out to dinner . . but the novelty of being considered desirable had palled.

▶ **II** *verb trans.* †**5** Make faint; weaken. LME–L17.
†**6** Make pale or dim. M–L16.
†**7** Make flat, stale, or insipid. E17–E19.
8 Deprive (a person) of relish for something; satiate, cloy, (the appetite or senses). E17.

pall /pɔːl/ *verb*[2] *trans.* LME.
[from PALL *noun*[1].]
Cover with or as with a cloth; drape with a pall.

pall *verb*[3] var. of PAWL *verb*.

palla /ˈpalə/ *noun.* Pl. **-llae** /-liː/. E18.
[Latin, perh. rel. to PALLIUM.]
1 *ROMAN ANTIQUITIES.* A loose outer garment or outdoor wrap, usu. worn by women; an outer robe, a mantle. E18.
2 *ECCLESIASTICAL.* An altar-cloth; a cloth for covering a chalice. Cf. PALL *noun*[1] 2. *arch. rare.* E18.

palladia *noun* pl. of PALLADIUM *noun*[1].

Palladian /pəˈleɪdɪən/ *adjective*[1]. Now *rare* or *obsolete.* M16.
[from Latin *palladius*, *-um* (see PALLADIUM *noun*[1]) + -AN.]
Of or pertaining to Pallas (Athene), the goddess of wisdom in classical mythology; *transf.* pertaining to wisdom, knowledge, or study.

Palladian /pəˈleɪdɪən/ *adjective*[2]. E18.
[from *Palladio* (see below) + -IAN.]
ARCHITECTURE. Of, pertaining to, or according to the neo-classical style or school of the Italian architect Andrea Palladio (1518–80).
Palladian window (chiefly *US*) a large window consisting of a central arched section flanked by two narrow rectangular sections.
■ **Palladianism** *noun* M19. **Palladianize** *verb trans.* make Palladian in style L19.

palladic /pəˈladɪk, -ˈleɪdɪk/ *adjective.* M19.
[from PALLADIUM *noun*[2] + -IC.]
CHEMISTRY. Of or containing palladium in the tetravalent state.

palladious *adjective* see PALLADOUS.

palladium /pəˈleɪdɪəm/ *noun*[1]. Pl. **-dia** /-dɪə/. LME.
[Latin from Greek *palladion*, from *Pallad-*, *Pallas* epithet of the goddess Athene: see -IUM.]
1 *CLASSICAL MYTHOLOGY.* An image of the goddess Pallas (Athene), in the citadel of Troy, on which the safety of the city was supposed to depend, later reputed to have been taken to Rome. LME.
2 *transf. & fig.* A thing on which the safety of a nation, institution, privilege, etc., is believed to depend; a safeguard. E17.

palladium /pəˈleɪdɪəm/ *noun*[2]. E19.
[from *Pallas* (see prec.), after an asteroid discovered shortly before this element + -IUM: cf. CERIUM.]
CHEMISTRY. A hard white ductile metallic element, atomic no. 46, belonging to the platinum group, which resembles silver and is used in precious alloys and as a catalyst, esp. in reactions involving hydrogen. (Symbol Pd.)
■ **palladiumize** *verb trans.* coat with palladium M19.

palladous /pəˈleɪdəs, ˈpaládəs/ *adjective.* Also (earlier) **palladious** /pəˈleɪdɪəs/. M19.
[from PALLADIUM *noun*[2] + -OUS.]
CHEMISTRY. Of or containing palladium in the divalent state.

pallah /ˈpalə, ˈpɑːlə/ *noun.* Now *rare.* E19.
[Setswana *phala*: cf. IMPALA.]
= IMPALA.

Pallas /ˈpaləs/ *noun.* M19.
[P. S. *Pallas* (1741–1811), German naturalist and traveller.]
ZOOLOGY. Used in *possess.* and *attrib.* to designate birds and animals described by Pallas.
Pallas cat, **Pallas's cat** = MANUL.

pallasite /ˈpaləsʌɪt/ *noun.* M19.
[formed as prec. + -ITE[1].]
GEOLOGY. A stony-iron meteorite consisting largely of iron (usu. with some nickel) and olivine.
■ **pallasitic** /paləˈsɪtɪk/ *adjective* M20.

pallavi /ˈpaləvi/ *noun.* L19.
[Tamil, Telugu, ult. from Sanskrit *pallava* shoot, extension.]
MUSIC. In the music of southern India, the first section of a song.

pallescent /pəˈlɛs(ə)nt/ *adjective. rare.* M17.
[Latin *pallescent-* pres. ppl stem of *pallescere* become pale, from *pallere* be or look pale: see -ESCENT.]
Growing or becoming pale.

pallet /ˈpalɪt/ *noun*[1]. ME.
[Anglo-Norman *paillete*, from *paille* straw from Latin *palea* chaff, straw; in sense 2 perh. a different word: see -ET[1].]
1 A straw bed or mattress; a mean or makeshift bed or couch. ME.
†**2** *NAUTICAL.* A small room for ballast in the hold of a ship. E18–M19.

†**pallet** *noun*[2]. ME.
[Old French *palet* dim. of *pal* PALE *noun*[1]: see -ET[1].]
1 A helmet; a (usu. leather) headpiece. ME–L15.
2 *transf.* The head. ME–L19.

pallet /ˈpalɪt/ *noun*[3]. LME.
[Old & mod. French *palette* dim. of *pale* spade, blade from Latin *pala* spade, shovel, rel. to *palus* stake: see -ET[1]. Cf. PALE *noun*[1], PEEL *noun*[1].]
1 A flat wooden blade attached to a handle; *spec.* one used in pottery for shaping clay. LME.
2 a An artist's palette. E17. ▸†**b** The flat blade of an oar or float of a paddle-wheel. E18–E19. ▸**c** A board for carrying away a newly moulded brick. M19. ▸**d** A small platform on which goods can be moved, stacked, and stored, esp. with the aid of a fork-lift truck. E20.
3 Any of the valves in the upper part of the wind-chest of an organ which, when a key is pressed, open to admit compressed air to a groove below a set of pipes corresponding to that key. E18.
4 A projection on a machine part which engages with the teeth of a wheel to interconvert reciprocating and rotary motions; *spec.* (in a clock or watch) a projection transmitting motion from an escapement to a pendulum or balance-wheel. E18.
5 A tool for impressing letters or figures on the back of a book. L19.
6 *ZOOLOGY.* Either of a pair of calcareous plugs or lids at the entrance of the siphon tube of a shipworm or related mollusc. Cf. PALETTE 2. L19.
■ **palletiˈzation** *noun* the action or process of palletizing goods etc. M20. **palletize** *verb trans.* place, stack, or transport (goods etc.) on a pallet M20.

pallet /ˈpalɪt/ *noun*[4]. L16.
[from PALE *noun*[1] + -ET[1].]
HERALDRY. An ordinary resembling a pale but of half its breadth. Cf. PALE *noun*[1] 5b.

pallia *noun* pl. of PALLIUM.

pallial /ˈpalɪəl/ *adjective.* M19.
[from PALLIUM + -AL[1].]
1 *ZOOLOGY.* Of or pertaining to the pallium or mantle of a mollusc. M19.
2 *ANATOMY & ZOOLOGY.* Of or pertaining to the pallium of the brain. E20.

†**palliament** *noun* Only in L16.
[Old French *palliement*, from *pallier* from Latin *palliare*: see PALLIATE *verb*, -MENT.]
A white gown worn by a candidate for the Roman consulship.

> 🕮 SHAKES. *Tit. A.* The people of Rome . . Send thee . . This palliament of white and spotless hue; And name thee in election.

palliard /ˈpalɪəd/ *noun & adjective. arch.* L15.
[Old & mod. French *paillard*, from *paille* straw: see -ARD.]
▶ **A** *noun.* A professional beggar or vagabond; *transf.* a dissolute or knavish fellow; a lecher, a debauchee. L15.
▶†**B** *adjective.* Knavish; dissolute. L15–M17.

palliasse /ˈpalɪas/ *noun.* Also (earlier, now esp. *US*) **paillasse**. E16.
[Old & mod. French *paillasse* from Italian *pagliacchio* from Proto-Romance, from Latin *palea* straw, chaff.]
A straw mattress made with sacking or other strong material.

palliate /ˈpalɪət/ *adjective.* M16.
[Latin *palliatus* cloaked, formed as PALLIUM: see -ATE[2]. Cf. next.]
†**1** Cloaked, covered, concealed (*lit. & fig.*). M16–M17.
†**2** Of a cure: superficial, temporary. Only in 17.
3 *ZOOLOGY.* Having a pallium. *rare.* L19.

palliate /ˈpalɪeɪt/ *verb trans.* LME.
[Late Latin *palliat-* pa. ppl stem of *palliare* cover, hide, conceal, from Latin PALLIUM: see -ATE[3].]
1 Alleviate the symptoms of (a disease) without effecting a cure; relieve or ease (suffering) superficially or temporarily. LME.
2 Disguise the gravity of (an offence or evil), esp. by excuses; extenuate, excuse. LME. ▸†**b** Cover with or as with a cloak; hide, conceal. M16–E19.
†**3** Make less emphatic or pronounced; moderate or tone down (a statement, action etc.). M17–L18.

> 🕮 **1** J. E. T. ROGERS That which cannot be cured must be palliated. **2** W. ROBERTSON They endeavoured to palliate what they could not justify.

■ **palliator** *noun* a person who offers extenuating considerations L18. **palliatory** /ˈpalɪət(ə)ri/ *adjective* (*rare*) = PALLIATIVE *adjective* M17.

palliation /palɪˈeɪʃ(ə)n/ *noun.* LME.
[Old & mod. French from medieval Latin *palliatio(n-)*, formed as prec.: see -ION.]
1 Alleviation of the symptoms of (a) disease or suffering without effecting a cure; temporary relief. LME.
2 †**a** The action or a means of cloaking, hiding, or concealing something. L16–L18. ▸**b** The action or an act of disguising the gravity of an offence etc. by excuses and apologies; (an) extenuation, (an) excuse. E17.

> 🕮 **1** *Science News Letter* With advanced ovarian cancer and extensive spread, only palliation can be achieved. E. S. PERSON The palliation afforded by love on the rebound. **2b** E. A. FREEMAN The tyrant's plea of necessity in palliation of his evil deeds. ALDOUS HUXLEY There were excuses, of course, palliations.

palliative /ˈpalɪətɪv/ *adjective & noun.* LME.
[Old & mod. French, or medieval Latin *palliativus*, formed as PALLIATE *adjective*, *verb*: see -IVE.]
▶ **A** *adjective.* **1** Serving to palliate a disease, suffering, etc. LME.
2 Serving to extenuate or excuse an offence etc. L18.
1 palliative care care for the terminally ill and their families, esp. that provided by an organized health service.
▶ **B** *noun.* **1** A thing which gives superficial or temporary relief; a thing which palliates a disease, suffering, etc. E18.
2 An extenuation. M18.

> 🕮 **1** M. WILLIAMSON Anything else is just a temporary palliative, . . a treatment of the symptom but not a cure.

■ **palliatively** *adverb* E18.

pallid /ˈpalɪd/ *adjective.* L16.
[Latin *pallidus* rel. to *pallere* be pale: see -ID[1].]
Lacking depth or intensity of colour; *spec.* (of a human face) pale, esp. from illness, shock, etc.

> 🕮 P. CUTTING We were pallid creatures, after so long indoors. E. SEGAL His inner torment made him pallid, and dark circles accentuated his eyes.

■ **pallidity** /pəˈlɪdɪti/ *noun* E19. **pallidly** *adverb* M17. **pallidness** *noun* M17.

pallio- /ˈpalɪəʊ/ *combining form.* M19.
[from PALLIUM: see -O-.]
ZOOLOGY. Of or pertaining to the pallium or mantle of a mollusc or brachiopod, of the pallium and —, as ***palliocardiac***, ***palliopedal***, ***pallioviscera***l, etc.

pallion /ˈpaljən/ *noun*. L18.
[Origin uncertain: cf. Spanish *pallon* a quantity of gold or silver from an assay, Italian *pallone*, augm. of *palla* ball.]
A small piece or pellet of solder.

pallium /ˈpalɪəm/ *noun*. Pl. **-lia** /-lɪə/, **-liums**. ME.
[Latin: cf. PALL *noun*[1].]
1 ECCLESIASTICAL. A woollen vestment conferred by the Pope on an archbishop in the Latin Church, consisting of a narrow circular band placed round the shoulders with a short lappet hanging from front and back. Also (*transf.*), the office or dignity of an archbishop. ME.
2 ANTIQUITIES. A man's large rectangular cloak, worn esp. by Greek philosophical and religious teachers. M16.
3 a ZOOLOGY. The mantle of a mollusc or brachiopod. L19. ▸**b** ANATOMY & ZOOLOGY. The outer wall of the cerebrum, the cerebral cortex. Cf. NEOPALLIUM. L19.
4 METEOROLOGY. A sheet of cloud, esp. nimbostratus, covering the whole sky. Now *rare* or *obsolete*. L19.

pall-mall /pəlˈmal, pɛlˈmɛl/ *noun*. Also †**pell mell**. M16.
[French †*pal(le mail(le* from Italian *pallamaglio*, from *palla* var. of *balla* BALL *noun*[1] + *maglio* mallet: cf. MALL *noun*, MALLET *noun*[1].]
Hist. A game, played in a long alley, in which players tried to drive a boxwood ball through a suspended iron ring in as few strokes as possible.

pallone /palˈloːne/ *noun*. M19.
[Italian, augm. of *palla* ball.]
An Italian game, partially resembling tennis, in which a large ball is struck with a cylindrical wooden guard, worn over the hand and wrist.

pallor /ˈpalə/ *noun*. LME.
[Latin, rel. to *pallere* be pale: see -OR.]
Paleness, pallidness.

pally /ˈpali/ *noun*. *colloq*. E20.
[Abbreviation.]
= PALAIS DE DANSE.

pally /ˈpali/ *adjective*. *colloq*. L19.
[from PAL + -Y[1].]
Friendly.

> M. AMIS From the outset the whole team here at the hospital was instinctively pally and collegial.

palm /pɑːm/ *noun*[1].
[Old English *palm(a)* = Old Saxon, Old High German *palma* (Dutch *palm*, German *Palme*), Old Norse *pálmr*, from Germanic from Latin *palma* PALM *noun*[2] (the palm leaf being likened to a spread hand).]
1 Any tree or shrub of the large, chiefly tropical, monocotyledonous family Palmae, typically having an unbranched stem with a crown of very large leaves either palmate or pinnate in shape. Also (with specifying word), any of various palmlike plants of other families, such as cycads. OE.
2 A palm leaf, *esp*. one used as a symbol of victory or triumph. ME. ▸**b** *fig*. Victory, triumph; supreme honour; excellence. Also, a prize for this. LME. ▸**c** A representation of a palm leaf, *esp*. one awarded as a French military decoration in addition to the *Croix de Guerre*. E20.
3 A branch or sprig of any of various trees or shrubs used instead of a palm leaf in non-tropical countries, esp. in celebrating Palm Sunday. Also, a tree or shrub providing this; *spec*. (the catkins of) several willows, esp. the goat willow, *Salix caprea*. LME.
1 ***cabbage palm***, ***coconut palm***, ***date-palm***, ***fan palm***, ***feather palm***, ***rattan palm***, ***sago palm***, etc. **2b** ***award the palm***, ***bear the palm***, ***yield the palm***.
Comb.: **palm-bird** a weaver-bird which nests in palm trees; **palm-borer** a weevil or beetle whose larvae bore into palm trees; **palm branch** a palm leaf with its stalk, *esp*. one used as a symbol of victory; **palm-cabbage** = *palm-heart* below; **palm cat** (*a*) = *palm civet* below; (*b*) an ocelot; **palm civet** any of various spotted or striped arboreal civets of Africa, SE Asia, and the Indian subcontinent, as the toddy cat, *Paradoxurus hermaphroditus*, and the African civet *Nandinia binotata*; **palm crab** = COCONUT *crab*; **palm-grub** the larva of a palm-borer; **palm-heart** the terminal bud of any of various palms, eaten in salads (usu. in *pl.*); **palm honey** the refined sap of the coquito palm; **palm-kernel** the endosperm of the fruit of the oil palm, *Elaeis guineensis*; ***palm-kernel oil***, the oil from this, used in the manufacture of margarine, soap, etc.; **palm-lily** the cabbage tree of New Zealand, *Cordyline australis*; **palm-room** a room, usu. in a hotel, adorned by potted palms, a Palm Court; **palm squirrel** any of several small grey-brown tree squirrels of the Indian subcontinent with three white stripes along the back, of the genus *Funambulus*; **palm sugar**: from the sap of certain palms, esp. *Caryota urens*; **Palm Sunday** CHRISTIAN CHURCH the Sunday before Easter, on which Jesus' entry into Jerusalem is commemorated; **palm swift** either of two small swifts, *Tachornis phoenicobia* of the Caribbean and *T. squamata* of S. America, which nest in palm leaves; **palm tree** = sense 1 above; ***palm-tree justice***, justice summarily administered, in the manner once ascribed to an Islamic cadi; **palm viper** any of various venomous S. American snakes of the genus *Bothrops*; **palm warbler** a warbler, *Dendroica palmarum*, of eastern N. America; **palm-wasp** a social wasp, *Polybius palmarum*, which nests in palm trees; **palm wax** a waxy substance produced by various palms, esp. *Ceroxylon alpinum*; **palm weevil** a large tropical weevil, *Rhynchophorus ferrugineus*, whose larvae bore into the wood of coconut and toddy palms; **palm wine**: made from the fermented sap of the palm tree; **palm-worm** = *palm-grub* above.
■ **palmlike** *adjective* resembling (that of) a palm E19.

palm /pɑːm/ *noun*[2]. ME.
[Old & mod. French *paume* from Latin *palma*.]
1 The part of the hand between the wrist and the fingers, esp. & now usu. its inner surface on which the fingers close. Later also, the part of a glove that covers this surface. ME.
2 A flat expanded part of a palmate antler. LME.
3 a The flat, padded part of the foot (esp. the forefoot) of a quadruped. Also occas., a broad grasping surface on a bird's foot, on a spider-monkey's tail, etc. LME. ▸**b** The sole of the foot. E19.
4 A linear measure approx. equal either to the breadth or to the length of the hand. Cf. HAND *noun* 10. Now *rare*. LME.
5 = ***palm-play*** below. Long *obsolete* exc. *Hist*. LME.
6 A flat widened part at the end of an arm or armlike projection; *spec*. (*a*) the blade of an oar; (*b*) the inner surface of the fluke of an anchor. E16.
7 [from PALM *verb* 2.] The act of palming a card etc. M17.
8 A hard shield worn on the hand by sailmakers to protect the palm. M18.

> **1** CONAN DOYLE A return ticket in the palm of your left glove. R. THOMAS His fists clenched . . so that his fingernails dug into the palms of his hands.

Phrases: ***grease a person's palm***: see GREASE *verb* 3. **in the palm of a person's hand** under a person's control or influence. ***itching palm***: see ITCH *verb*. ***tickle in the palm***: see TICKLE *verb*.
Comb.: **palm-ball** BASEBALL a pitch with the ball gripped by the thumb and palm rather than the fingers; **palm-greasing** bribery; **palm-play** *Hist.* an old game resembling tennis, in which the ball was struck with the palm of the hand instead of a racket; **palm-print** an impression made on a surface by the palm of the hand; **palmtop** [after *desktop*, *lap-top*] a computer small and light enough to be held in one hand.
■ **palmful** *noun* a quantity that fills the palm of the hand, as much or as many as a palm can hold E19.

palm /pɑːm/ *verb trans*. L15.
[from PALM *noun*[2].]
1 Touch, slap, or stroke with the palm; handle; grasp the hand of (a person). Also, convey with the palm. L15.
2 Conceal (a card, die, or other small object) in the palm of the hand, usu. dishonestly or deceptively. L17.
3 a Usu. foll. by *off*: impose or thrust (a thing) fraudulently (*on* or *upon* a person); pass off by trickery or fraud; dispose of by misrepresentation or deceit. L17. ▸**b** Fob (a person) *off with* something. M19.
4 Offer an inducement to, bribe (a person). M18.

> **1** T. HARDY Nervously palming his hip with his left hand. *New Yorker* The water Maria palmed to her face gave a shine to her eyes. *Guardian* Neither player could do much with the ball, but Rogan unaccountably palmed it away. **2** F. HERBERT It had been easy to palm Dr. Yueh's sleeping tablet, to pretend to swallow it. **3a** C. LAMB Have you not tried to palm off a yesterday's pun. L. M. MONTGOMERY The clerks . . know they can palm anything off on him. **b** *Idler Magazine* The public . . is frequently palmed off with books which it does not . . care about. B. KOPS We were palmed off with promises.

palmaceous /palˈmeɪʃəs/ *adjective*. M18.
[from mod. Latin *Palmaceae* fem. pl., from Latin *palma* PALM *noun*[1]: see -ACEOUS.]
BOTANY. Of or pertaining to the Palmae (formerly Palmaceae) or palm family.

Palmach /ˈpalmax/ *noun*. M20.
[Hebrew, abbreviation of *pĕluggōt mahaṣ* shock troops.]
Hist. A commando force of the Jewish Haganah, incorporated in the Israeli national army in 1948.

palma Christi /ˌpalmə ˈkrɪsti/ *noun phr*. Also (*arch.*) Anglicized as **palmchrist** /ˈpɑːmkrʌɪst/. LME.
[medieval Latin = palm or hand of Christ.]
The castor oil plant, *Ricinus communis*, which has palmately divided leaves. Formerly, a medicinal herb with similar leaves, perhaps motherwort, *Leonurus cardiaca*.

palmar /ˈpalmə/ *adjective* & *noun*. M17.
[Latin *palmaris*, from *palma* PALM *noun*[2]: see -AR[1].]
▸ **A** *adjective*. ANATOMY & ZOOLOGY. Of or relating to the palm of the hand, or the corresponding part of an animal's forefoot. M17.
▸ **B** *noun*. **1** ANATOMY. A palmar muscle, nerve, etc. L19.
2 ZOOLOGY. A subterminal joint in the arms of some branched crinoids. Now *rare* or *obsolete*. L19.
¶ Only in Dicts. before M19.

palmarian /palˈmɛːrɪən/ *adjective*. *rare*. E19.
[from PALM *noun*[1] + -ARIAN.]
= PALMARY *adjective*[1].

palmarosa /palməˈrəʊsə/ *noun*. L19.
[Italian, lit. 'rose palm'.]
1 ***palmarosa oil***, an essential oil distilled from the grass *Cymbopogon martinii* (see sense 2 below) and used in perfumery etc. L19.
2 In full ***palmarosa grass***. A tropical grass, *Cymbopogon martinii*, cultivated, esp. in India, for the essential oil it produces. M20.

palmary /ˈpalməri/ *adjective*[1]. M17.
[Latin *palmarius* that carries off the palm of victory, from *palma* PALM *noun*[1]: see -ARY[1].]
(Worthy of) holding the first place or the palm which symbolizes this; pre-eminent, principal.

palmary /ˈpalməri/ *adjective*[2]. *rare*. L17.
[Latin *palmaris*, from *palma* PALM *noun*[2]: see -ARY[2].]
= PALMAR *adjective*.

palmate /ˈpalmeɪt/ *adjective*. M18.
[Latin *palmatus*, from *palma* PALM *noun*[2]: see -ATE[2].]
BOTANY & ZOOLOGY. **1** Shaped like the outspread palm of the hand; *spec*. (*a*) BOTANY (of a leaf) having (usu. five or more) lobes whose midribs all radiate from one point; (of a tuber) having divisions like fingers, as in the spotted orchid, *Dactylorhiza fuchsii*; (*b*) ZOOLOGY (of an antler) in which the angles between the tines are partly filled in to form a broad flat surface, as in reindeer and moose. M18.
2 Of the foot of a bird or animal: webbed. E19.
Special collocations: **palmate newt** a small smooth-skinned newt, *Triturus helveticus*, of western Europe, the male of which has webbed hind feet.
■ **palmated** *adjective* = PALMATE *adjective*; esp. in ***palmated newt***, = PALMATE *newt*: M18. **palmately** *adverb* (chiefly BOTANY) in a palmate manner M19.

palmati- /palˈmeɪti, -ˈmati/ *combining form* of Latin *palmatus* PALMATE *adjective*, in botanical terms relating to leaves: see -I-.
■ **palmatifid** *adjective* palmately divided up to halfway to the base M19. **palmatiform** *adjective* approaching a palmate form; having the ribs palmately arranged: M19. **palmatiˈpartite** *adjective* [Latin *partitus* divided] = PALMATISECT M19. **palmatisect** *adjective* [Latin *sectus* cut] palmately divided nearly to the base E20.

palmation /palˈmeɪʃ(ə)n/ *noun*. L17.
[formed as PALMATE *adjective*: see -ATION.]
Chiefly ZOOLOGY. Palmate formation; a broad surface in a palmate structure.

Palm Beach /pɑːm ˈbiːtʃ/ *noun phr*. E20.
[A coastal resort in Florida, USA.]
A kind of lightweight fabric used for clothing. Usu. *attrib.*
¶ Proprietary name in the US.

palmchrist *noun* see PALMA CHRISTI.

palmcorder /ˈpɑːmkɔːdə/ *noun*. L20.
[from PALM *noun*[2] + RE)CORDER *noun*[1].]
A small hand-held camcorder.

Palm Court /pɑːm ˈkɔːt/ *noun phr*. E20.
[from PALM *noun*[1] + COURT *noun*[1].]
1 A large room or patio, esp. in a hotel, decorated with palm trees. E20.
2 The kind of light music associated with a Palm Court. Freq. ***attrib.*** M20.

palmed /pɑːmd/ *adjective*. LME.
[from PALM *noun*[2] + -ED[2].]
†**1** (Esp. of an antler) palmate; (of a deer) having palmate antlers (freq. with specifying word). LME–M18.
2 *gen*. Having a palm or palms (of a specified kind). M19.

> **1** M. DRAYTON The proud palmed deer Forsake the closer woods. **2** R. S. SURTEES The smart dogskin wash-leather palmed glove.

†**palmeira** *noun* see PALMYRA.

palmelloid /palˈmɛlɔɪd/ *adjective*. L19.
[from mod. Latin *Palmella* (see below) + -OID.]
BOTANY. Pertaining to or characteristic of photosynthetic freshwater protists of the genus *Palmella* or the order or family Palmellaceae, which multiply by fission within a thick gelatinous integument; *spec*. designating a stage in the life cycle of various protists in which several generations are formed by fission within a gelatinous envelope.
■ **palmella** *attrib. adjective* designating a palmelloid stage in a life cycle L19. **palmellin** *noun* a red pigment found in the alga *Palmella cruenta* L19.

palmer /ˈpɑːmə/ *noun*[1]. ME.
[Anglo-Norman = Old French *palmier*, from medieval Latin *palmarius*, from Latin *palma* PALM *noun*[1]: see -ER[2].]
1 *Hist.* A pilgrim, *esp*. one returned from the Holy Land with a palm branch or palm leaf. Also, an itinerant monk travelling from shrine to shrine under a perpetual vow of poverty. ME.
2 More fully ***palmer-worm***. A many-legged insect, a myriapod, a woodlouse. Now *esp*. any of various caterpillars covered in stinging hairs, as the fruit pests *Euproctis chrysorrhoea* and *Dichomeris ligulella*. M16. ▸**b** ANGLING. An artificial fly covered with bristling hairs. M17.
2b ***soldier palmer***: see SOLDIER *noun*.

palmer /ˈpɑːmə/ *noun*². L17.
[from PALM *verb* 2 + -ER¹.]
A person who palms cards, dice, etc.

Palmerin /ˈpalmərɪn/ *noun*. Long *rare* or *obsolete*. E17.
[from *Palmerin de Oliva* the legendary eponymous hero of a 16th-cent. collection of Spanish romances.]
Any of the knightly heroes of the romances concerning Palmerin de Oliva; *transf.* a redoubtable knightly champion.

Palmerstonian /pɑːməˈstəʊnɪən/ *adjective*. M19.
[from *Palmerston* (see below) + -IAN.]
Of, pertaining to, or characteristic of Henry John Temple (1784–1865), the third Viscount Palmerston and a prominent British statesman, or the forceful diplomacy associated with him.
■ **ˈPalmerstonism** *noun* M19.

†palmestry *noun* see PALMISTRY.

palmette /palˈmɛt/ *noun*. M19.
[French, dim. of *palme* PALM *noun*¹: see -ETTE.]
ARCHAEOLOGY. An ornament (in sculpture or painting) with radiating petals like a palm leaf.

palmetto /palˈmɛtəʊ/ *noun*. Also (earlier) **-mito** /-ˈmiːtəʊ/. Pl. **-o(e)s**. M16.
[Spanish *palmito* dwarf fan palm, dim. of *palma* PALM *noun*¹, later assim. to Italian dims. in *-etto*.]
Any of various usu. small and sometimes stemless fan palms; *esp.* (*a*) the dwarf fan palm, *Chamaerops humilis*, of the Mediterranean; (*b*) (in full ***cabbage palmetto***) *Sabal palmetto*; (*c*) (in full ***saw palmetto***) *Serenoa repens* of the south-eastern US. Also ***palmetto tree***.
Comb.: **palmetto flag** *US* the flag of the State of South Carolina, which bears a figure of a cabbage palmetto tree; **Palmetto State** *US* the State of South Carolina; ***palmetto thatch***: see THATCH *noun* 2b.

palmier /palmje/ *noun*. Pl. pronounced same. E20.
[French, lit. 'palm tree'.]
A small crisp cake shaped like a palm leaf, made from puff pastry and sugar.

palmiet /ˈpalmiːt/ *noun*. L18.
[Afrikaans from Dutch, formed as PALMITE.]
A southern African plant of the rush family, *Prionium serratum*, which grows thickly in swamps and streams, and has long sharp leaves formerly used to make woven hats.

palmiferous /palˈmɪf(ə)rəs/ *adjective*. *rare*. M17.
[from Latin *palmifer* palm-bearing, from *palma* PALM *noun*¹: see -FEROUS.]
Carrying palm branches in token of victory.

palmiped /ˈpalmɪpɛd/ *noun* & *adjective*. Now *rare*. Also **-pede** /-piːd/, pl. **-des** /-dz, -diːz/. E17.
[Latin *palmiped-*, *-pes*, from *palma* PALM *noun*² + *ped-*, *pes* foot.]
▶ **A** *noun*. A web-footed bird. E17.
▶ **B** *adjective*. Of a bird: web-footed. M17.

palmistry /ˈpɑːmɪstri/ *noun*. Orig. **†-estry**. LME.
[from PALM *noun*² + *-estry* of unkn. origin, later alt. to *-istry* perh. after *sophistry*.]
Divination by examination of the lines and configurations of the palm of the hand; chiromancy.
■ **palmist** *noun* a person who practises palmistry L19. **palmister** *noun* (now *rare* or *obsolete*) a palmist L15.

palmite /ˈpalmʌɪt/ *noun*. Now *rare* or *obsolete*. M16.
[Spanish & Portuguese *palmito*: see PALMETTO.]
†**1** A kind of palm or palmetto. M–L16.
2 = PALMIET. M19.

palmitic /palˈmɪtɪk/ *adjective*. M19.
[French *palmitique*, from *palme* PALM *noun*¹: see -IC.]
CHEMISTRY. ***palmitic acid***, a solid saturated fatty acid, $CH_3(CH_2)_{14}COOH$, found in palm oil and in many vegetable and animal fats.
■ **palmitate** /ˈpalmɪteɪt/ *noun* a salt or ester of palmitic acid L19.

palmitin /ˈpalmɪtɪn/ *noun*. M19.
[French *palmitine*, formed as prec.: see -IN¹.]
CHEMISTRY. A glyceride of palmitic acid; *spec.* = TRIPALMITIN.

palmito *noun* see PALMETTO.

palm leaf /ˈpɑːm liːf/ *noun phr.* & *adjective*. M17.
[from PALM *noun*¹ + LEAF *noun*¹.]
▶ **A** *noun*. Pl. **palm leaves** /liːvz/.
1 A leaf of the palm tree; *spec.* one used for thatching, or for making hats, baskets, etc., and, esp. in the southern US, as a fan. M17.
2 *ellipt.* A palm-leaf fan or hat. M19.
▶ **B** *attrib.* or as *adjective*. Made from a palm leaf or palm leaves. M19.

palm oil /ˈpɑːm ɔɪl/ *noun phr.* E17.
[Sense 1 from PALM *noun*² (now interpreted as having joc. allus. to sense 2), sense 2 from PALM *noun*¹ + OIL *noun*.]
1 Money given as a bribe. *joc.* E17.
2 Oil produced by any of various palms; *esp.* that obtained from the mesocarp of the fruit of the W. African oil palm, *Elaeis guineensis*, which is used as food in W. Africa and for making soap, lubricants, pharmaceuticals, etc. E18.

palmula /ˈpalmjʊlə/ *noun*. *rare*. E19.
[mod. Latin, dim. of Latin *palma* PALM *noun*²: see -ULE.]
ENTOMOLOGY. = PULVILLUS 2.

palmy /ˈpɑːmi/ *adjective*. L16.
[from PALM *noun*¹ + -Y¹.]
1 (Worthy of) bearing the palm, triumphant; flourishing. Chiefly in ***palmy state***, ***palmy days***. L16.
2 Containing (many) palms; of or pertaining to a palm or palms. Chiefly *poet.* M17.
■ **palmily** *adverb* (*rare*) L19. **palminess** *noun* (*rare*) L19.

palmyra /palˈmʌɪrə/ *noun*. Orig. **†palmeira**. L17.
[Portuguese *palmeira* palm tree, erron. respelt like *Palmyra* (see next).]
A tall fan palm of tropical Asia, *Borassus flabellifer*, commonly cultivated in the Indian subcontinent for its leaves which are used for thatch, matting, paper, etc., for its sap which yields palm wine and palm sugar, and for its edible fruit.

Palmyrene /ˈpalmɪriːn, palˈmʌɪriːn/ *noun* & *adjective*. E17.
[Latin *Palmyrenus*, from Greek *Palmura* Palmyra (see below).]
▶ **A** *noun*. **1** A native or inhabitant of the ancient city of Palmyra in Syria. E17.
2 The Aramaic dialect of Palmyra. Also, the script in which this is written. M20.
▶ **B** *adjective*. Of or pertaining to the Palmyrenes or their language. L17.

palo blanco /ˌpaləʊ ˈblaŋkəʊ/ *noun*. *US*. Pl. same. E19.
[Amer. Spanish = white tree.]
A small tree or shrub of the genus *Celtis*, of the elm family; *esp.* a hackberry, *C. reticulata*, native to south-western N. America, distinguished by its light-coloured bark.

palo de hierro /ˌpaləʊ deɪ hɪˈɛːrəʊ/ *noun*. *US*. Also **palo fierro** /fɪˈɛːrəʊ/. Pl. same. L19.
[Amer. Spanish = tree of iron.]
Any of several trees of south-western N. America with very tough wood; *esp.* the desert ironwood, *Olneya tesota*. Also, the wood of such a tree.

palolo /pəˈləʊləʊ/ *noun*. Pl. **-os**. L19.
[Samoan or Tongan.]
In full ***palolo worm***. Any of various marine polychaete worms of the families Eunicidae and Nereidae which reproduce by breaking in half at the same time each year, the tail portion rising to the surface to release eggs and sperm; *spec.* the worm *Palola siciliensis* (*P. viridis*, *Eunice viridis*), of reefs of the S. Pacific.

palomino /paləˈmiːnəʊ/ *noun*. Pl. **-os**. L19.
[Spanish from Latin *palumbinus* of or resembling a dove.]
1 A variety of white grape, orig. grown around Jerez in southern Spain, used esp. to make sherry and fortified wines; a wine made from this grape. L19.
2 A horse with light golden-brown coat and white or pale mane and tail. Also ***palomino horse*** etc. Orig. *US*. E20.
3 A pale golden-brown colour. M20.

palone /pəˈləʊn/ *noun*. *slang*. *derog.* Also **polone**. M20.
[Origin unkn.]
A young woman; an effeminate man.

palooka /pəˈluːkə/ *noun*. *slang* (chiefly *US*). E20.
[Origin unkn.]
An inferior or average prizefighter; a stupid or mediocre person; an oaf, a lout.
Comb.: **Palookaville** *noun* (the name of) a town inhabited by palookas; mediocrity, obscurity (esp. in phr. ***a one-way ticket to Palookaville***): M20.

palourde /palurd/ *noun*. Pl. pronounced same. M20.
[French from late Latin *pelorida* from Latin *pelorid-*, *peloris* from Greek = giant mussel.]
A marine bivalve mollusc of the genus *Venerupis*, used in France as an article of food; a Venus clam.

paloverde /paləʊˈvəːdi/ *noun*. *US*. Pl. **-s**, same. Also **palo verde**, pl. same. E19.
[Amer. Spanish = green tree.]
Any of various leguminous shrubs and small trees of the genera *Cercidium* and *Parkinsonia*, which are native to the arid regions of south-western N. America and have green bark and racemes of yellow flowers.

palp /palp/ *noun*. M19.
[French *palpe* from Latin PALPUS.]
1 ZOOLOGY. An elongated segmented appendage near the mouth in many invertebrates, usu. paired and concerned with sensation or locomotion. M19.
2 The fleshy part of a fingertip. E20.

palp /palp/ *verb trans.* *rare*. M16.
[Latin *palpare*: see PALPATE.]
Touch, feel; handle gently, pat; *fig.* flatter, cajole.

palpable /ˈpalpəb(ə)l/ *adjective*. LME.
[Late Latin *palpabilis*, from Latin *palpare*: see PALPATE, -ABLE.]
1 Able to be touched, felt, or handled; *fig.* (of heat, darkness, etc.) intense, so extreme as to be almost felt. LME.
▸**b** MEDICINE. Perceptible by palpation. L19.
2 Readily perceived by one of the other senses or (esp.) by the mind; plain, evident, obvious. LME.

> **1** E. MANNIN Eleven o'clock . . even at that hour the heat was almost palpable. **2** R. F. BURTON The words Tanganenka and Tanganenko used by Dr. Livingstone . . are palpable mispronunciations. M. E. BRADDON 'Head's very hot,' said the surgeon, a fact also palpable to the patient.

■ **palpaˈbility** *noun* E17. **palpableness** *noun* E17. **palpably** *adverb* LME.

palpal /ˈpalp(ə)l/ *adjective*. M19.
[from PALP *noun*, PALPUS + -AL¹.]
ZOOLOGY. Of the nature of, pertaining to, or serving as a palp.

palpate /palˈpeɪt/ *verb trans.* & *intrans.* M19.
[Latin *palpat-* pa. ppl stem of *palpare* touch gently: see -ATE³.]
Make an examination (of) by the sense of touch, esp. for medical purposes.

palpation /palˈpeɪʃ(ə)n/ *noun*. L15.
[Latin *palpatio(n-)* stroking, flattering, flattery, formed as prec.: see -ATION.]
Touching, handling; gentle handling; *spec.* medical examination by feeling.

palpebra /ˈpalpɪbrə/ *noun*. Pl. **-brae** /-briː/. LME.
[Latin.]
ANATOMY. An eyelid.
■ **palpebral** *adjective* M19.

palpi *noun* pl. of PALPUS.

palpi- /ˈpalpi/ *combining form* of PALP *noun*, Latin PALPUS: see -I-.
■ **palpifer** *noun* a part of an insect bearing a palp, *spec.* the sclerite bearing the maxillary palp M19. **palˈpiferous** *adjective* having a palpifer or palp M19. **palpiform** *adjective* having the form of or resembling a palp E19. **palpiger** *noun* [Latin *-ger*: see -GEROUS] a part of an insect bearing a palp, *spec.* the sclerite bearing the labial palp M19. **palˈpigerous** *adjective* having a palpiger or palp E19.

palpitant /ˈpalpɪt(ə)nt/ *adjective*. M19.
[French, pres. pple of *palpiter* from Latin *palpitare*: see next, -ANT¹.]
Palpitating.

palpitate /ˈpalpɪteɪt/ *verb*. E17.
[Latin *palpitat-* pa. ppl stem of *palpitare* frequentative of *palpare*: see PALPATE.]
1 *verb intrans.* Esp. of the heart: beat rapidly and strongly as the result of exercise, strong emotion, or disease; *gen.* tremble, quiver; throb. E17.
2 *verb trans.* Cause to palpitate. L18.

> **1** W. COWPER She rushed with palpitating heart and frantic air. R. L. STEVENSON The engine was in full blast, the mill palpitating to its strokes.

■ **palpitatingly** *adverb* in a way that causes palpitations M19.

palpitation /palpɪˈteɪʃ(ə)n/ *noun*. LME.
[Latin *palpitatio(n-)*, formed as prec.: see -ATION.]
The action, esp. of the heart, of palpitating; an instance or feeling of this (usu. in *pl.*); *gen.* a trembling, quivering, or throbbing motion.

> M. FORSTER Her blood pressure soared and the . . palpitations began.

palpus /ˈpalpəs/ *noun*. Pl. **-pi** /-pʌɪ/. E19.
[Latin = feeler, from *palpare*: see PALPATE.]
ZOOLOGY. = PALP *noun* 1.

palsa /ˈpalsə/ *noun*. M20.
[Swedish *palse*, *pals* (pl. *palsar*) from Finnish and Lappish *palsa*.]
A landform of subarctic regions, consisting of a mound or ridge of peat covered with vegetation and containing a core of frozen peat or mineral soil in which are numerous ice lenses.

Palsgrave /ˈpɔːlzgreɪv/ *noun*. Also **†Palgrave**. M16.
[Early Dutch *paltsgrave* (mod. *paltsgraaf*), from *palts* palatinate + *†grave*, *graaf* count, GRAVE *noun*².]
Hist. A Count Palatine; *spec.* the Count Palatine of the Rhine.
■ **Palsgravine** *noun* a Countess Palatine M19.

palsied /ˈpɔːlzɪd/ *adjective*. M16.
[from PALSY *noun*¹, *verb*: see -ED², -ED¹.]
Affected with palsy, paralysed; *fig.* deprived of power of action; tottering, trembling.

palsie(-walsie) *nouns* & *adjectives* see PALSY *noun*² & *adjective*².

palsify /ˈpɔːlzɪfʌɪ/ *verb trans.* *rare*. L18.
[from PALSY *noun*¹ + -FY.]
= PALSY *verb* 2.

palstave /ˈpɔːlsteɪv/ *noun*. **M19.**
[Danish *paalstav* from Old Norse *pálstavr*, from *páll* hoe, spade (from Latin *palus* stake, **PALE** *noun*[1]) + *stafr* **STAFF** *noun*[1].]
ARCHAEOLOGY. A metal celt shaped to fit into a split handle, instead of having a socket into which the handle fits.

palsy /ˈpɔːlzi/ *noun*[1] & *adjective*[1]. **ME.**
[Old French *paralisie* (Anglo-Norman *parlesie*) from Proto-Romance alt. of Latin **PARALYSIS**.]
▶ **A** *noun*. **1** = **PARALYSIS** 1; *esp.* paralysis with involuntary tremors. Now chiefly with specifying word. **ME.**
†**2** A palsied person, a paralytic. **ME–E16.**
3 *fig.* An influence which destroys or seriously impairs activity or sensibility; a condition of utter powerlessness; an irresistible tremor. **LME.**
1 ***Bell's palsy, cerebral palsy, creeping palsy, Saturday night palsy, scrivener's palsy, shaking palsy***, etc.
▶†**B** *attrib. adjective*. Affected with palsy, palsied. **E16–E18.**

palsy /ˈpalzi/ *noun*[2] & *adjective*[2]. *slang*. Also **-sie**; redupl. **palsy-walsy, palsie-walsie**. **M20.**
[from **PAL** *noun* + **-SY**.]
▶ **A** *noun*. A friend. Chiefly as a form of (ostensibly) friendly address. **M20.**
▶ **B** *adjective*. Friendly. **M20.**

palsy /ˈpɔːlzi/ *verb*. **L16.**
[from **PALSY** *noun*[1].]
1 *verb intrans.* Become palsied; shake or tremble as if palsied. *rare*. **L16.**
2 *verb trans.* Affect with palsy, paralyse. Chiefly *fig.*, make powerless or inert. Cf. earlier **PALSIED**. **E17.**

> 📖 **1** C. BRONTË The heaviness . . of pining and palsying faculties.

palsy-walsy *noun* & *adjective* see **PALSY** *noun*[2] & *adjective*[2].

†**palt** *verb*. **M16.**
[By-form of **PELT** *noun*[2].]
1 *verb intrans.* Go with effort; trudge. Only in **M16.**
2 *verb trans.* Pelt (*with* missiles); *fig.* assail with obloquy or reproaches. **L16–M18.**

palter /ˈpɔːltə/ *verb*. **M16.**
[Origin unkn.]
†**1** *verb intrans.* & *trans.* Speak or say indistinctly or idly; mumble, babble. **M16–L19.**
†**2** *verb trans.* Squander. **E17–E18.**
3 *verb intrans.* **a** Equivocate or prevaricate in speech or action; deal crookedly or evasively; use trickery. Usu. foll. by *with*. **E17.** ▸**b** Haggle, bargain, esp. in a matter of duty or honour. **E17.** ▸**c** Deal flippantly, trifle, *with*. **E19.**

> 📖 **3a** SIR W. SCOTT If you palter or double in your answers, I will have thee hung alive. **b** DICKENS Hatred of the girl who had dared to palter with strangers. **c** *Nature* It would . . be paltering with the truth to pretend that our activities do as much.

■ **palterer** *noun* **L16.**

palterly /ˈpɔːltəli/ *adjective*. *obsolete* exc. *dial.* **M17.**
[App. alt. of **PALTRY** *adjective* as if from prec. + **-LY**[1].]
Paltry, shabby.

palting /ˈpɔːltɪŋ/ *adjective*. *obsolete* exc. *dial.* **L16.**
[By-form of **PELTING** *adjective*[1]: cf. **PALT**.]
Petty, paltry; trifling.

paltry /ˈpɔːltri/ *noun* & *adjective*. **M16.**
[App. from a var. of **PELT** *noun*[3] + **-RY**. For the adjective cf. **TRUMPERY**, also Middle Low German *palter-* in *palterlappen* rags, Low German *paltrig* ragged, torn. Cf. also **PELTING** *adjective*[1], **PELTRY** *noun*[2].]
▶ **A** *noun*. Rubbish, trash; something worthless. Now *dial.* **M16.**
▶ **B** *adjective*. Trashy, worthless; petty, trifling; contemptible. **L16.**

> 📖 D. H. LAWRENCE And now he looked paltry and insignificant. H. WOUK The French premier did not know what a paltry air force America had.

■ **paltriness** *noun* **E18.**

paludal /pəˈljuːd(ə)l, -ˈluː-, ˈpaljʊd(ə)l, -lʊ-/ *adjective*. **E19.**
[from Latin *palud-*, *palus* marsh + **-AL**[1].]
(Of a plant) growing in marshy ground, requiring a marshy habitat; *MEDICINE* malarial; *gen.* marshy.
■ **paludine** /ˈpaljʊdɪn, -dʌɪn; -ˈlʊ-/ *adjective* of or pertaining to a marsh, marshy **M19.**

paludament /pəˈljuːdəm(ə)nt, -ˈluː-/ *noun*. **E17.**
[Latin *paludamentum*.]
A military cloak worn by Roman generals and chief officers; a royal cloak; a herald's coat.

paludina /paljʊˈdʌɪnə/ *noun*. Pl. **-nae** /-niː/, **-nas**. **M19.**
[mod. Latin *Paludina* (see below), formed as **PALUDAL**: see **-INA**[2].]
ZOOLOGY. Any pond snail of the genus *Paludina*.

Paludrine /ˈpaljʊdrɪn, -lʊ-, -iːn/ *noun*. **M20.**
[formed as **PALUDAL** + *-rine*, after **ATABRINE**, **MEPACRINE**.]
PHARMACOLOGY. (Proprietary name for) the drug proguanil hydrochloride.

palustral /pəˈlʌstr(ə)l/ *adjective*. *rare*. **L19.**
[from Latin *palustris*, from *palus* marsh: see **-AL**[1].]
Pertaining to or inhabiting marshes.
■ Also **palustrine** *adjective* (*rare*) **L19.**

paly /ˈpeɪli/ *adjective*[1]. **LME.**
[Old & mod. French *palé*, from *pal* **PALE** *noun*[1]: see **-Y**[5].]
HERALDRY. Divided vertically into an even number of equal stripes of alternate tinctures. (Foll. by *of* the number of stripes.)

paly /ˈpeɪli/ *adjective*[2]. Chiefly *poet.* & *literary*. **M16.**
[from **PALE** *adjective* + **-Y**[1].]
Pale; somewhat pale.

palynology /palɪˈnɒlədʒi/ *noun*. **M20.**
[from Greek *palunein* sprinkle (cf. *palē* fine meal = Latin **POLLEN**) + **-OLOGY**.]
The branch of science that deals with the structure and dispersal of pollen grains and other spores, as indicators of plant geography or taxonomy, means of dating geological formations or archaeological remains, or causative agents of allergic reactions.
■ **palynoˈlogical** *adjective* **M20.** **palynoˈlogically** *adverb* **M20.** **palynologist** *noun* **M20.**

palynomorph /ˈpalɪnəmɔːf/ *noun*. **L20.**
[from **PALYNO(LOGY** + **-MORPH**.]
A pollen grain or other spore as an object for palynological analysis.
■ **palynoˈmorphic** *adjective* **L20.**

Pam /pam/ *noun*. **L17.**
[App. from French *pamphile* from Greek *Pamphilos* beloved of all.]
CARDS. **1** The jack of clubs, esp. in the game of five-card loo, in which this card is the highest trump. **L17.**
2 A card-game in which this card is the highest trump. **L17.**

pamaquin /ˈpaməkwɪn/ *noun*. **M20.**
[from **P(ENTYL** + **A(MINO-** + **M(ETHOXY-** + *-a-* + **QUIN(OLINE**.]
PHARMACOLOGY. A toxic quinoline derivative formerly used as an antimalarial drug.
¶ Proprietary names for this drug are **PLASMOCHIN** and **PLASMOQUINE**.

pamby /ˈpambi/ *adjective*. *rare*. **E19.**
[Abbreviation.]
= **NAMBY-PAMBY** *adjective*.

pamé /ˈpɑːmeɪ/ *adjective*. *rare*. **M19.**
[French *pâmé* pa. pple of *pâmer* swoon from popular Latin *pasmare* from *spasmare* lit. 'have a spasm'.]
HERALDRY. Of a fish: having a gaping mouth. Usu. *postpositive*.

pamment *noun* var. of **PAVEMENT**.

Pampangan /pɒmˈpɒŋg(ə)n/ *noun* & *adjective*. Also **-ga** /-gə/, **-go** /-gəʊ/. **E18.**
[Pampangan *kapampangan* from *pampang* river-bank.]
▶ **A** *noun*. Pl. same, **-s**.
1 The Austronesian language spoken by a people inhabiting areas of Luzon Island in the Republic of the Philippines, esp. its central plain. **E18.**
2 A member of this people. **M19.**
▶ **B** *adjective*. Of or pertaining to Pampangan or the Pampangan. **E19.**

pampano *noun* see **POMPANO**.

pampas /ˈpampəs, -z/ *noun pl.*, also used as *sing*. Also in sing. form **pampa**. **E18.**
[Spanish, pl. of *pampa* from Quechua = a plain: see **-S**[1].]
1 *pl.* (treated as *sing.* or *pl.*). The extensive treeless plains of S. America south of the Amazon. Also in *sing.*, these plains considered collectively; any one of these plains. **E18.**
2 *pl.* (treated as *sing.*). A yellowy-green colour, esp. used for bathroom suites. Usu. ***attrib.*** **L20.**

> 📖 **1** G. DURRELL You could approach fairly close to most of the bird-life on the pampa. P. THEROUX We began speeding across the pampas, a cool immense pasture.

Comb.: **pampas cat** a large wild cat of the pampas, *Felis colocolo*, with long yellow-grey fur marked with oblique brownish stripes; **pampas deer** a small deer of S. American grassland, *Odocoileus bezoarticus*; **pampas flicker** a black, white, and yellow woodpecker, *Colaptes campestris*, of eastern S. America; **pampas fox** any of several small mammals resembling a fox or a dog, *esp.* the fox *Dusicyon gymnocercus* of eastern and southern parts of S. America; **pampas-grass** a very tall grass, *Cortaderia selloana*, with silky panicles of a silvery hue, native to S. America and grown elsewhere as an ornamental plant.

pampean /pamˈpiːən, ˈpampɪən/ *adjective*. **M19.**
[from *pampa* sing. form of **PAMPAS** + **-EAN**.]
Of, pertaining to, or characteristic of (the) pampas.

pampelmoes, pampelmouse *nouns* see **POMPELMOUS**.

pamper /ˈpampə/ *verb*. **LME.**
[Prob. of Low German or Low Dutch origin: cf. German dial. *pampen*, *pampfen* cram, gorge, Western Flemish *pamperen*, perh. nasalized vars. of base of **PAP** *noun*[2].]
1 *verb trans.* Overindulge with rich food; feed luxuriously. *obsolete* exc. as passing into sense 2. **LME.**
2 *verb trans.* Overindulge the tastes and likings of (a person); accede to every wish of (esp. a child); spoil with luxury; *gen.* overindulge (any mental appetite, feeling, etc.). **M16.**
†**3** *verb intrans.* Indulge oneself with food, feed luxuriously. **L16–M17.**

> 📖 **2** E. F. BENSON Pamper your passion for all the things that are lovely. J. G. BALLARD A box-kite for one of the pampered children of the estate.

■ **pamperedness** *noun* the state of being pampered **E17.** **pamperer** *noun* **L18.**

pampero /pamˈpɛːrəʊ/ *noun*. Pl. **-os**. **L18.**
[Spanish, formed as **PAMPAS** + *-ero*.]
A piercing cold wind which blows from the Andes across the S. American pampas to the Atlantic.

pamphlet /ˈpamflɪt/ *noun* & *verb*. **LME.**
[Use of *Pamphilet*, familiar name of a 12th-cent. Latin love poem *Pamphilus, seu de Amore*.]
▶ **A** *noun*. A group of several printed or (formerly) written pages, fewer than would make a book, fastened together without a hard cover and issued as a single or (formerly) periodical work; *esp.* one of which the text is of a minor, ephemeral, or controversial nature; a booklet; a leaflet. **LME.**
▶ **B** *verb*. **1** *verb intrans.* Write a pamphlet or pamphlets. Long *rare* or *obsolete*. **L16.**
2 *verb trans.* Report or describe in a pamphlet. Now *rare* or *obsolete*. **E18.**
3 *verb trans.* Distribute pamphlets to. **L20.**
■ **pamphletary** *adjective* pertaining to or of the nature of a pamphlet **E17.** **pamˈphletic** *adjective* (*rare*) = **PAMPHLETARY** **E18.** **pamphletize** *verb intrans.* & *trans.* write a pamphlet or pamphlets (on) **M17.**

pamphleteer /pamfləˈtɪə/ *noun* & *verb*. **L16.**
[from prec. + **-EER**.]
▶ **A** *noun*. A writer of pamphlets; the author of a pamphlet. **L16.**
▶ **B** *verb intrans.* Write and issue pamphlets; engage in propaganda by means of pamphlets. Freq. as ***pamphleteering*** *verbal noun* & *ppl adjective*. **L17.**

†**pampination** *noun*. *rare*. **LME–M18.**
[Latin *pampinatio(n-)*, from *pampinat-* pa. ppl stem of *pampinare*, from *pampinus*: see next, **-ATION**.]
The pruning or trimming of vines.

pampiniform /pamˈpɪnɪfɔːm/ *adjective*. **M17.**
[from Latin *pampinus* vine-shoot + **-I-** + **-FORM**.]
ANATOMY. Designating a convoluted plexus of veins from the testis or ovary.

pampootie /pamˈpuːti/ *noun*. **L19.**
[Origin unkn.]
A kind of slipper or sandal of undressed cow-skin worn in the Isles of Aran off the west coast of Ireland.

pan /pan/ *noun*[1].
[Old English *panne* = Old Frisian, Old Saxon *panna* Middle & mod. Low German, Middle Dutch *panne* (Dutch *pan*), Old High German *phanna* (German *Pfanne*), from West Germanic, perh. from popular var. of Latin *patina* (see **PATEN**).]
1 A broad usu. metal vessel, with a flat base and often a handle, used for domestic purposes; *esp.* one for heating food in. **OE.**
2 a The skull, *esp.* its upper part. *obsolete* exc. *Scot. dial.* & in ***brain-pan*** s.v. **BRAIN** *noun*. **ME.** ▸†**b** The patella. **M17–M18.**
3 A hollow in the ground, *esp.* one in which water stands; *spec.* a basin in which salt is obtained by evaporation of seawater. **ME.** ▸**b** A shallow depression that contains water or mud in the rainy season. *S. Afr.* **M19.**
4 a A usu. large vessel used in a technical or manufacturing process for subjecting a material to heat or a mechanical or chemical process, e.g. evaporation or grinding; a circular metal dish in which gold is separated from gravel etc. by agitation and washing. **L15.** ▸**b** The part of the lock that held the priming in an old type of gun. **L16.** ▸**c** A broad open container or concavity forming part of something; *spec.* (***a***) each of those of a balance for holding the weight(s) or the object to be weighed; (***b***) the bowl of a lavatory. **E17.**
5 Orig., the socket of the thigh bone. Now *gen.*, the socket for a hinge. **L16.**
6 The contents of a pan. **M18.**
7 A hard substratum of soil, usually more or less impervious to moisture. **M18.**
8 A small ice floe. **L18.**
9 The face. *US slang*. **E20.**
10 A metal drum in a West Indian steel band. Also, steel-band music; the way of life associated with this. **M20.**
11 Severe or dismissive criticism. *colloq.* **M20.**

> 📖 **1** J. FOWLES Great copper pans on wooden trestles. P. V. WHITE The strength to . . drag him up on the pillows . . and stick the pan under him. ***bedpan, frying-pan, fry-pan, milk pan, saucepan, warming-pan***, etc. **6** RACHEL ANDERSON Humphrey stirred a pan of gruel.

Phrases: ***down the pan***: see **DOWN** *preposition*. ***flash in the pan*** [orig. with ref. to an ineffective ignition of powder in a gun] a promising start followed by failure, a one-off success. ***hard pan***: see **HARD** *adjective, adverb, & noun*. ***iron pan***: see **IRON** *noun & adjective*.

on the pan *US* under reprimand or adverse criticism. **out of the frying-pan into the fire**, **out of the pan into the fire** from one evil into an even worse one. **shut one's pan** *slang* keep silent. ***turn cat in pan***, ***turn the cat in the pan***: see CAT *noun*[1].

Comb.: **pan-broil** *verb trans.* heat (meat) in a pan with little or no fat; **pandrop** *Scot.* a hard peppermint-flavoured sweet shaped like a flattened sphere; **panfish** *US* a fish suitable for frying whole in a pan, *esp.* one caught by an angler rather than bought; **panfry** *verb trans. & intrans.* fry (something) in a pan with a shallow depth of fat; **pan-ice** loose ice in blocks which form on the shores of Labrador and break away; **pan juice**: from the roasting of meat; **pan-loaf** *noun & adjective* (chiefly *Scot.*) **(a)** *noun* a loaf baked in a pan or tin; **(b)** *adjective* (of an accent) affected, cultured; (of a person) pretentious; **pan-man** **(a)** a man in charge of a pan in a manufacturing process; **(b)** a man who plays the pan in a steel band; **pan-mug** *local* a large earthenware vessel; **pan-pie** *US* = PANDOWDY; **pan-pudding** (now *rare*) a pudding cooked or baked in a pan; ***stand one's pan-pudding***, stand firm; **pan-scourer**, **pan-scrubber** a scourer, often in the form of a wire pad, for cleaning pans; **panstick** a kind of matt cosmetic in the form of a stick; **pan-washing** the separating of gold from gravel etc. by stirring it in water in a pan.

pan /pan/ *noun*[2]. ME.

[French *panne*, medieval Latin *panna*, of unkn. origin.]

A horizontal beam supporting the rafters in a timber-framed house.

pan /pɑːn/ *noun*[3]. E17.

[Hindi *pān* betel leaf from Sanskrit *parṇa* feather, leaf.]

In the Indian subcontinent: the leaf of the betel, esp. as used to enclose slices of areca nut mixed with lime for chewing; the mixture for chewing so formed.

pan /pan/ *noun*[4]. M18.

[French = part (of a wall) etc.: see PANE *noun*[1].]

†**1** FORTIFICATION. A face of a bastion. M18–E19.

2 In a timber-framed or half-timbered house, a compartment of timber framework filled in with bricks or plaster. M19.

2 ***post-and-pan***: see POST *noun*[1].

pan /pan/ *noun*[5]. L19.

[Chinese *bǎn* (Wade–Giles *pan*) slab.]

A Chinese wooden percussion instrument used for beating time, in which one piece of wood is struck against two others tied together.

pan /pan/ *noun*[6]. E20.

[from (the same root as) PAN *verb*[2].]

An act of panning a camera; a panning movement; a film sequence obtained by this.

🕮 *Listener* The opening shot of *Exodus* is a huge 200-degree pan across the landscape.

Comb.: **pan-and-tilt** *adjective* designating a tripod etc. that allows a camera to move in both horizontal and vertical planes.

Pan /pan/ *noun*[7]. Also **pan**. E20.

[French *panne* breakdown.]

An international radio distress signal of less urgency than a mayday signal.

pan /pan/ *noun*[8]. M20.

[Abbreviation.]

= PANGUINGUE.

pan /pan/ *noun*[9] & *adjective*. M20.

[Abbreviation.]

Panchromatic (film).

pan /pan/ *verb*[1]. Infl. **-nn-**. E19.

[from PAN *noun*[1].]

1 *verb intrans.* Of soil: cake on the surface; form a hard surface layer. *Scot. & dial.* E19.

2 a *verb trans.* Wash (gold-bearing gravel, sand, etc.) in a pan, in order to separate the gold; separate by washing in a pan. Also foll. by *off*, *out*. M19. ▸**b** *verb intrans.* Search for gold with a pan. M19.

3 *verb intrans.* Turn out in a specified way (orig. of gravel etc., when panned for gold); *spec.* turn out well, have a successful outcome. Usu. foll. by *out*. M19. ▸**b** Speak freely or at length; expatiate. L19.

4 *verb trans.* Foll. by *out*: produce, yield. *US & Austral.* L19.

5 *verb trans.* Cook or prepare in a pan. L19.

6 *verb trans.* Criticize severely; judge (a performance) to be unsuccessful or inadequate. *colloq.* E20.

7 *verb trans.* Hit (a person); punch. *slang.* M20.

🕮 **3** P. G. WODEHOUSE He was hoping all along that this fight would pan out big. ALDOUS HUXLEY I shall see how things pan out. **4** V. PALMER Work them with pick and shovel and they pan out three or four ounces to the ton. **6** *Times* The play was roundly panned.

pan /pan/ *verb*[2]. Infl. **-nn-**. E20.

[from PAN(ORAMA, PAN(ORAMIC.]

CINEMATOGRAPHY. **1** *verb trans.* Turn (a cine, television, etc., camera) in a horizontal plane, esp. to give a panoramic effect or to keep a moving object in view; keep in view or pass along by panning the camera. E20.

2 *verb intrans.* Of a camera or (*transf.*) a camera operator: swing (usu. horizontally) to take in a scene too large for a fixed shot or to follow a moving object. M20.

🕮 **1** F. POHL The cameras were panning the crowd. **2** N. KNEALE The camera pans, to take in . . a little working-class street.

pan- /pan/ *combining form*.

[Greek *pan* neut. of *pas* all.]

Of, pertaining to, or including all of or the whole of, or (*spec.*) all the parts of a continent or a racial, ethnic, or religious group.

▪ **pan-Afriˈcander** *adjective* (*rare*) of or pertaining to all Afrikaners, or a government or State which would include all South Africans of Dutch descent or sympathies L19. **pan-ˈAnglican** *adjective* of, pertaining to, or involving (representatives of) all the Churches of the Anglican Communion M19. **pan-Briˈtannic** *adjective* †**(a)** of or comprising (representatives of) all the Britons or all parts of Britain; **(b)** of, pertaining to, or involving (representatives of) all countries of the British Commonwealth or (formerly) the British Empire: E18. **pan-ˈCelt** *noun* a person who believes in the unity of all Celtic peoples E20. **pan-ˈCeltic** *adjective* of or involving (representatives of) all Celts, or all the Celtic peoples L19. **pan-ˈChristian** *adjective* involving (representatives of) all or many of the different Christian denominations; ecumenical, interdenominational: L19. **panˈcosmic** *adjective* pertaining to or involving the whole universe; of or pertaining to pancosmism M19. **panˈcosmism** *noun* the doctrine that the material universe is all that exists M19. **panˈcultural** *adjective* common to all cultures; containing elements from all cultures: M20. **pancytoˈpenia** *noun* (MEDICINE) a condition in which the blood shows a relative deficiency of all three cellular components (erythrocytes, leucocytes, and platelets) M20. **pandiˈagonal** *adjective* (MATH.) designating a magic square with the property that, if any number of columns be removed from one side of the diagram and added *en bloc* to the other, another magic square results L19. **pandiaˈlectal** *adjective* (LINGUISTICS) covering all the dialects of a language M20. **pandiaˈtonic** *adjective* (MUSIC) employing any notes of the diatonic scale in a single chord M20. **pandiaˈtonicism** *noun* (MUSIC) pandiatonic technique or composition M20. **panencephaˈlitis** *noun* encephalitis in which both the grey matter and the white matter are affected and there is a gradual but progressive loss of mental and motor functions M20. **panˈentheism** *noun* the belief or doctrine that God includes and interpenetrates the universe while being more than it L19. **panˈentheist** *adjective & noun* **(a)** *adjective* of or constituting panentheism; **(b)** *noun* a person with panentheist beliefs or views: M20. **panentheˈistic** *adjective* panentheist E20. **pan-Euroˈpean** *adjective* pertaining to, affecting, or extending over the whole of Europe E20. **pan-Euroˈpeanism** *noun* (advocacy of) close cooperation between the countries of Europe; possession of a pan-European disposition or outlook: M20. **pangeˈometry** *noun* (*obsolete* exc. *Hist.*) non-Euclidean geometry L19. **pangram** *noun* a sentence etc. containing every letter of the alphabet M20. **pangraˈmmatic** *adjective* containing every letter of the alphabet M20. **panˈgrammatist** *noun* a writer who tries to use every letter of the alphabet in a line of poetry etc. M18. **panharˈmonicon** *noun* (*obsolete* exc. *Hist.*) a mechanical musical instrument resembling a barrel-organ, capable of imitating many orchestral instruments E19. **pan-ˈhuman** *adjective* of or pertaining to all human beings E20. **pan,hypopiˈtuitarism** *noun* (MEDICINE) diminished activity of the pituitary gland in respect of all its functions M20. **panidioˈmorphic** *adjective* (PETROGRAPHY) composed of crystals that are mostly idiomorphic L19. **pan-ˈIndian** *adjective* **(a)** denoting or relating to a cultural movement or religious practice participated in by many or all American Indian peoples; **(b)** of or relating to the whole of India, or to all its ethnic, religious, or linguistic groups: M20. **pan-Iˈonian** *adjective* (GREEK HISTORY) of or comprising (representatives of) all Ionians M19. **panˈlectal** *adjective* [-LECT] LINGUISTICS covering all the regional and social varieties of a language L20. **panlogism** *noun* (PHILOSOPHY) the view (held by Hegel) that only the rational is truly real L19. **panoˈistic** *adjective* [Greek *ōion* egg] BIOLOGY (of an ovariole) producing ova only, without nurse cells L19. **panophthalˈmitis** *noun* inflammation of the whole eyeball M19. **panˈoral** *adjective* (DENTISTRY) of or pertaining to radiography of the whole mouth in one exposure M20. **pan-ˈOrthodox** *adjective* of, pertaining to, or involving (representatives of) all the Orthodox Churches L19. **panˈpharmacon** *noun* (*rare*) a remedy for all diseases, a panacea M17. **pan-Presbyˈterian** *adjective* of, pertaining to, or involving (representatives of) all Presbyterian Churches L19. **pan,proctocoˈlectomy** *noun* (an instance of) surgical removal of the entire rectum and colon (with the creation of a stoma for removal of faeces) M20. **pan-ˈProtestant** *adjective* of, pertaining to, or involving (representatives of) all Protestants L19. **pan-ˈRoman** *noun* an artificial language invented for universal use and based on Latin E20. **panseˈlectionism** *noun* (BIOLOGY) the theory or belief that natural selection is the predominant cause of variation at all levels of evolution L20. **panseˈlectionist** *noun & adjective* (BIOLOGY) **(a)** *noun* a person who believes in or advocates panselectionism; **(b)** *adjective* of or characteristic of panselectionism or panselectionists: L20. **panˈsporoblast** *noun* (ZOOLOGY) a structure formed by protozoans of the class Myxosporea, comprising several sporoblasts and two other cells L19. **pantropic** /-ˈtrəʊpɪk, -ˈtrɒpɪk/ *adjective* (MEDICINE) attacking or affecting many kinds of tissue indiscriminately M20. **pan-ˈtropical** *adjective* (of a plant or animal) found in all regions of the tropics; including all tropical areas: M20. **pan-Tuˈranian** *adjective* (now *rare*) embracing all the speakers of languages regarded as Turanian E20. **pan-Tuˈranianism** *noun* (now *rare*) the principle of a political union of all speakers of languages regarded as Turanian E20.

p'an /pan/ *noun*. Pl. same. M20.

[Chinese *pán*.]

ARCHAEOLOGY. A kind of shallow dish-shaped ritual vessel of ancient China.

panace /ˈpanəsi/ *noun*. Chiefly *poet.* E16.

[Latin *panax*, *panaces* vars. of *panacea*: see next.]

A mythical herb to which was ascribed the power of healing all diseases.

panacea /panəˈsiːə/ *noun*. M16.

[Latin from Greek *panakeia*, from *panakēs* all-healing, formed as PAN- + base of *akos* remedy: see -A[1].]

1 A remedy for all diseases; a thing for solving all difficulties or adopted in every case of difficulty. M16.

†**2** = PANACE. L16–E18.

🕮 **1** B. PYM 'Buy yourself a new hat, my dear'—his panacea for most feminine ills.

▪ **panacean** *adjective* of the nature of a panacea M17. **panaceist** *noun* a person who believes in or applies a panacea E19.

panache /pəˈnaʃ/ *noun*. M16.

[French from Italian *pennacchio* from late Latin *pinnaculum* dim. of *pinna* feather.]

1 A tuft or plume of feathers, esp. as a head-dress or a decoration for a helmet. Formerly also, a decoration like a plume of feathers, e.g. a tassel. M16.

2 Flamboyantly or stylishly confident behaviour; a manner marked by this. L19.

🕮 **2** *Listener* He plays the piano with panache, but cannot read music. V. BROME A panache which marked him out in any company.

▪ **panached** *adjective* having coloured stripes M17.

panada /pəˈnɑːdə/ *noun*. Also **-nade** /-ˈneɪd/. L16.

[Spanish, Portuguese = Italian *panata*, repr. Proto-Romance deriv. of Latin *panis* bread: see -ADE.]

Bread boiled in water to a pulp and flavoured. Also, a paste of flour, water, etc., used for thickening.

Panadol /ˈpanədɒl/ *noun*. M20.

[Origin unkn.]

PHARMACOLOGY. (Proprietary name for) the drug paracetamol.

pan-African /panˈafrɪk(ə)n/ *adjective*. E20.

[from PAN- + AFRICAN.]

Of or pertaining to all people of African birth or descent; of, pertaining to, or comprising (representatives of) all the peoples of Africa.

▪ **pan-Africanism** *noun* the idea of, or advocacy of, the political union of all the indigenous inhabitants of Africa M20. **pan-Africanist** *noun & adjective* **(a)** *noun* an advocate of pan-Africanism; **(b)** *adjective* of or pertaining to pan-Africanism: M20.

Panagia /panaˈjiːə/ *noun*. Also **-ghia**. L18.

[Greek, fem. of *panagios* all-holy, formed as PAN-, HAGIO-.]

CHRISTIAN CHURCH. (A title of) the Virgin Mary in the Eastern Orthodox Church. Also, an image of the Virgin Mary.

panagraphic *adjective* var. of PANOGRAPHIC.

Panama /ˈpanəmɑː, panəˈmɑː/ *noun*. M19.

[See below.]

1 Used *attrib.* to designate things found in or associated with Panama, a country in Central America. M19.

2 (Also **p-**.) A hat of plaited material resembling straw (orig. the young leaves of the jipijapa). M19.

1 **Panama disease** a fungal disease of bananas producing yellowing and wilting of the leaves; also called ***vascular wilt disease***, ***vascular wilt***. **Panama hat** = sense 2 above; ***Panama hat palm***, ***Panama hat plant*** = JIPIJAPA 1.

▪ **ˈPanaman** *adjective & noun* = PANAMANIAN E20.

Panamanian /panəˈmeɪnɪən/ *adjective & noun*. M19.

[formed as prec. + euphonic *-n-* + -IAN.]

▸**A** *adjective*. Of or pertaining to the Central American State of Panama. M19.

▸**B** *noun*. A native or inhabitant of Panama. M19.

Panamax /ˈpanəmaks/ *adjective*. L20.

[from *Panama* (see below) + MAX(IMUM.]

Denoting a ship of not more than 69,000 tons deadweight, the maximum size for a ship able to navigate the Panama canal connecting the Atlantic and Pacific Oceans.

pan-American /panəˈmɛrɪk(ə)n/ *adjective*. L19.

[from PAN- + AMERICAN.]

Of, pertaining to, or involving (representatives of) all the countries of North and South America.

▪ **pan-Americanism** *noun* the idea of a political alliance of all the countries of North and South America; advocacy of better commercial and cultural relations among these countries: E20.

pan-Arabism /panˈarəbɪz(ə)m/ *noun*. M20.

[from PAN- + ARAB + -ISM.]

The idea of, or advocacy of, political alliance or union of all the Arab States.

▪ **pan-Arab** *adjective & noun* **(a)** *adjective* of, pertaining to, or advocating pan-Arabism; **(b)** *noun* an advocate of pan-Arabism: M20. **pan-Arabic** *adjective* pan-Arab M20.

panarchy /ˈpanɑːki/ *noun*. *rare*. M19.

[from PAN- + Greek *arkhē*, *-arkhia* rule: cf. ARCH-. See -Y[3].]

The universal realm.

panary /ˈpanəri/ *adjective*. E19.

[from Latin *panis* bread + -ARY[1].]

Of or pertaining to bread. Chiefly in ***panary fermentation***.

panatela /panəˈtɛlə/ *noun*. M19.

[Amer. Spanish = long thin biscuit, sponge cake from Spanish from Italian *panatello* small loaf, dim. of *panata*: see PANADA, -EL[2].]

1 A long slender cigar, *esp.* one tapering at the sealed end. Also more fully ***panatela cigar***. M19.

2 *transf.* A cigarette made of Central or S. American marijuana. *slang.* M20.

Panathenaea /paˌnaθɪˈniːə/ *noun.* E17.
[Greek *panathēnaia* neut. pl. adjective (sc. *hiera* solemnities), formed as PAN- + *Athēnaios* Athenian, from *Athēnai* Athens or *Athēnē* Athene.]
GREEK HISTORY. A national festival held annually (also ***lesser Panathenaea***) or every fifth or, by modern reckoning, fourth year (also ***greater Panathenaea***) in Athens, with a procession to the shrine of the goddess Athene, gymnastic games, and musical competitions.
■ **Panathenaean** *adjective* of, pertaining to, or characteristic of the Panathenaea L18. **Panathenaic** *adjective* Panathenaean E17.

Panatrope /ˈpanətrəʊp/ *noun.* Also **p-**. E20.
[from *pana-* of unkn. origin + Greek *tropē* turn, turning.]
(Proprietary name for) a device for playing records, *esp.* one that plays them loudly enough for fairground or similar use.

pancake /ˈpankeɪk/ *noun & verb.* ME.
[from PAN *noun*[1] + CAKE *noun.*]
▶ **A** *noun.* **1** A thin flat cake made of batter, usu. lightly fried and turned in a pan and often rolled up with a filling. ME.
2 NAUTICAL. A piece of pancake-ice. M19.
3 A flat hat. Also ***pancake beret***, ***pancake hat***, etc. *US.* L19.
4 More fully ***pancake landing***. A landing in which an aircraft drops vertically after having levelled out close to the ground, e.g. when its landing gear is damaged or as a result of an unintended stall. E20.
5 (Also **Pan-Cake**.) (Proprietary name for) make-up, *esp.* foundation in the form of a flat cake. M20.
1 (as) flat as a pancake completely flat. ***Scotch pancake***: see SCOTCH *adjective.*
Comb.: **pancake batter** the mixture from which pancakes are made; **pancake-bell** *Hist.*: rung on the morning of Shrove Tuesday; **pancake coil** ELECTRICITY a flat or very short inductance coil; **Pancake Day** Shrove Tuesday (from the custom of eating pancakes on that day); **pancake-ice** floating ice in thin flat pieces, forming in polar seas at the approach of winter; ***pancake landing***: see sense 4 above; **pancake race** a race held in some places on Shrove Tuesday, in which the participants toss pancakes as they run; **pancake roll** a rolled pancake with a savoury meat or vegetable filling; **Pancake Tuesday** = ***Pancake Day*** above.
▶ **B** *verb.* **1** *verb trans.* Flatten, esp. destructively; knock down. L19.
2 *verb intrans.* AERONAUTICS. (Of an aircraft) descend rapidly in a level position in stalled flight, make a pancake landing; (of a pilot) cause an aircraft to pancake. E20.

†**pancart** *noun.* L16–M18.
[French *pancarte* formed as PANCHART.]
= PANCHART. Also, a placard bearing a public notice.

pancetta /panˈ(t)ʃɛtə, *foreign* panˈtʃetta/ *noun.* M20.
[Italian, dim. of *pancio* belly from Proto-Romance word whence also PAUNCH *noun*[1]: see -ET[1].]
Italian cured belly of pork.

panch *noun* var. of PAUNCH *noun*[2].

panchakarma /pʌntʃəˈkɑːmə/ *noun.* L20.
[from Sanskrit *panca* five + *karman* action.]
In Ayurvedic medicine: a fivefold detoxification treatment involving massage, herbal therapy, and other procedures.

panchama /ˈpʌntʃəmə/ *noun.* E19.
[Sanskrit *pañcama* fifth.]
A member of the fifth and lowest division of early Indian society, outside the four brahminic divisions; a pariah, an outcaste.

†**panchart** *noun.* L16–M18.
[medieval Latin *panc(h)arta*, formed as PAN- + Latin *charta* papyrus-leaf, paper, (in medieval Latin) charter.]
A charter, orig. one of a general or inclusive character, but later almost any written record.

panchayat /pʌnˈtʃʌɪjət/ *noun.* Also **pun-**. E19.
[Hindi *pañcāyat* prob. from Sanskrit *pañcāyatta*, from *pañca* five + *āyatta* depending on.]
In the Indian subcontinent: a council (orig. of five people) assembled as a jury, a court of arbitrators, or a village or community council.

Panchen /ˈpantʃ(ə)n/ *noun.* Also **p-**. M18.
[Tibetan, abbreviation of *pandi-tachen-po* great learned one (cf. PUNDIT).]
A Tibetan Buddhist title of respect, applied esp. (***a***) to the lama (***Panchen Lama***) of the monastery of Tashilhunpo, formerly next in spiritual authority to the Dalai Lama, (***b***) to a religious teacher held in high regard (***Panchen Rinpoche***) among Tibetan Buddhists.

pancheon /ˈpan(t)ʃ(ə)n/ *noun.* E17.
[App. from PAN *noun*[1]. Cf. LUNCHEON.]
A large shallow earthenware bowl or vessel, wider at the top than at the bottom, used to stand milk in to let the cream separate.

†**panchreston** *noun.* M17–E18.
[Greek *pagkhrēston* neut. adjective = good for everything, formed as PAN- + *khrēstos* useful.]
A universal remedy, a panacea.

panchromatic /pankrə(ʊ)ˈmatɪk/ *adjective & noun.* E20.
[from PAN- + CHROMATIC.]
▶ **A** *adjective.* **1** PHOTOGRAPHY. Sensitive (though not equally so) to light of all colours in the visible range. E20.
2 Multicoloured. L20.
▶ **B** *noun.* PHOTOGRAPHY. A panchromatic film, plate, or emulsion. E20.
■ **panˈchromatize** *verb trans.* make panchromatic E20.

panchronic /panˈkrɒnɪk/ *adjective.* M20.
[French *panchronique*, formed as PAN-, CHRONIC.]
LINGUISTICS. Of (a theory of) grammar, phonetics, etc.: applied or applicable to all languages at all stages of their development.
■ **panchronically** *adverb* M20. **panchroˈnistic** *adjective* = PANCHRONIC M20. **ˈpanchrony** *noun* treatment of language from a panchronic point of view M20.

panchshila /pɑːnˈʃiːlə, pan-/ *noun.* M20.
[Sanskrit *pañcaśīla*, from *pañca* five + *śīla* moral principle.]
The five principles of peaceful relations formulated between India and China (and, by extension, other Communist countries).

panchway /ˈpantʃweɪ/ *noun.* M18.
[Hindi *pansoī*, *pansuiyā*, Bengali *pānsi*.]
A light rowing boat with a mast and a roof used on the rivers of West Bengal and Bangladesh.

†**panchymagogue** *noun.* M17–L19.
[from PAN- + Greek *khuma* fluid, humour + *agōgos* leading, eliciting.]
MEDICINE. A purgative effective against all kinds of bodily humours.

Pancoast /ˈpaŋkəʊst/ *noun.* M20.
[Henry K. *Pancoast* (1875–1939), US radiologist.]
MEDICINE. **1** ***Pancoast tumour***, ***Pancoast's tumour***, a carcinoma of the apex of the lung. M20.
2 ***Pancoast syndrome***, ***Pancoast's syndrome***, a syndrome caused by a Pancoast tumour, with pain and numbness on the inner surface of the arm and atrophy of the smaller hand muscles. M20.

pancratiast /panˈkreɪʃɪast/ *noun.* E17.
[Latin *pancratiastes* from Greek *pagkratiastēs*, from *pagkratiazein* practise the pancratium: see PANCRATIUM.]
GREEK HISTORY. A combatant or victor in the pancratium.
■ **pancratiˈastic** *adjective* of, pertaining to, or characteristic of a pancratiast M18.

pancratic /panˈkratɪk/ *adjective.* M17.
[In sense 1 from next + -IC. In sense 2 from PAN- + Greek *kratos* strength.]
1 GREEK HISTORY. Of or pertaining to the pancratium; fully disciplined or exercised in mind; having every kind of skill or accomplishment. M17.
2 Of an eyepiece: having a power that can be varied. M19.
■ †**pancratical** *adjective* = PANCRATIC 1 L16–E18. **ˈpancratist** *noun* = PANCRATIAST L18.

pancratium /panˈkreɪʃɪəm/ *noun.* Also in Greek form **-tion** /-ʃɪən, -tɪən/. E17.
[(Latin from) Greek *pagkration*, formed as PAN- + *kratos* strength: see -IUM.]
1 GREEK HISTORY. An athletic contest combining both wrestling and boxing. E17.
2 BOTANY. Any of various bulbous African and Mediterranean plants of the genus *Pancratium* (family Amaryllidaceae), bearing an umbel of fragrant white flowers; *esp.* the sea daffodil, *P. maritimum*. M17.

pancreas /ˈpaŋkrɪəs/ *noun.* L16.
[mod. Latin from Greek *pagkreas*, *-kreat-*, formed as PAN- + *kreas* flesh.]
A large lobular gland near the stomach which secretes a clear alkaline digestive fluid into the duodenum and insulin and other hormones into the blood.
■ **pancreaˈtectomize** *verb trans.* perform pancreatectomy on E20. **pancreaˈtectomy** *noun* (an instance of) surgical removal of the pancreas E20. **pancreˈatic** *adjective* of or pertaining to the pancreas; ***pancreatic juice***, the clear alkaline digestive fluid secreted by the pancreas: M17. **pancreˈatico-** *combining form* [-O-] connecting or pertaining to the pancreas and —, as ***pancreaticoduodenal*** *adjective*: M19. **pancreatin** *noun* (BIOCHEMISTRY & PHARMACOLOGY) a mixture of enzymes present in pancreatic juice; such a mixture prepared from animal pancreases for therapeutic use, e.g. as a digestive: L19. **pancreaˈtitis** *noun* inflammation of the pancreas M19. **pancreatiˈzation** *noun* the process of pancreatizing something L19. **pancreatize** *verb trans.* treat with pancreatin to make more digestible L19. **pancreˈato-** *combining form* [-O-] = PANCREATICO- E20. **pancreaˈtography** *noun* radiological examination of the pancreas L20. **pancreoˈzymin** *noun* (BIOCHEMISTRY) a hormone which stimulates the production of enzymes by the pancreas M20.

pancuronium /pankjʊˈrəʊnɪəm/ *noun.* M20.
[from *pan-* of unkn. origin + CU(RARE + -ONIUM.]
PHARMACOLOGY. A steroid used as a neuromuscular blocking agent.
¶ A proprietary name for this drug is PAVULON.

pand /pand/ *noun. Scot.* M16.
[Middle Dutch, Middle Flemish = Old & mod. French *pan*, †*pand* PANE *noun*[1], or perh. directly from Old French *pandre* hang from Latin *pendere*.]
The valance of a bed.

panda /ˈpandə/ *noun*[1]. M19.
[Local word in Nepal.]
1 More fully ***red panda***, ***lesser panda***. An animal of the racoon family, *Ailurus fulgens*, of the Himalayas and parts of eastern Asia, about the size of a large cat, with reddish-brown fur and a long bushy ring-marked tail. M19.
2 A large bearlike herbivorous mammal with characteristic black and white markings, *Ailuropoda melanoleuca*, native to a few mountainous areas of forest in China and Tibet. Also ***giant panda***. E20.
3 More fully ***panda car***. A British police car, orig. one with a broad white stripe on it. *colloq.* M20.

panda /ˈpʌndə/ *noun*[2]. E20.
[Hindi, from Sanskrit *pandita* learned, wise.]
A Brahmin holding as a hereditary position the superintendence of a place of pilgrimage, temple, or ghat.

pandal /ˈpand(ə)l, panˈdɑːl/ *noun.* E18.
[Tamil *pantal*.]
In the Indian subcontinent: a shed or shelter, esp. for temporary use.

pandan /ˈpandən/ *noun.* Also **pandang** /-daŋ/. L18.
[Malay.]
= PANDANUS.

pandanny /panˈdani/ *noun. Austral.* Also **-n(n)i**. M20.
[from prec. + -Y[6].]
A large Tasmanian tree or shrub, *Richea pandanifolia* (family Epacridaceae), resembling a pandanus.

pandanus /panˈdeɪnəs, -ˈdan-/ *noun.* M19.
[mod. Latin (see below) from Malay PANDAN.]
1 BOTANY. Any of various trees and shrubs of the genus *Pandanus* (family Pandanaceae), of Malaysia, tropical Africa, and Australia, that have twisted stems and aerial roots, long narrow usu. spiny leaves in tufts at the top, and large, sometimes edible, conelike fruits. Also called ***screw pine***. M19.
2 The fibre produced from pandanus leaves; the material woven from this fibre. L19.

pandar *noun & verb* var. of PANDER.

pandaram /pənˈdɑːrəm/ *noun.* E18.
[Tamil *pantāram*.]
A low-caste Hindu priest or ascetic mendicant of the Indian subcontinent.

pandean /panˈdiːən/ *adjective & noun.* E19.
[Irreg. from *Pan* (see below).]
▶ **A** *adjective.* Of or pertaining to Pan, a rural god of Greek mythology. E19.
pandean pipe a pan-pipe.
▶ **B** *noun.* A member of a group of itinerant musicians. E19.

pandect /ˈpandɛkt/ *noun.* M16.
[(French *pandecte* from) Latin *pandecta*, *-tes* from Greek *pandektēs* all-receiver, formed as PAN- + *dekhesthai* receive.]
1 *sing.* & in *pl.* A complete body or system of laws; *spec.* (usu. **P-** & in *pl.*) a compendium in fifty books of Roman civil law made by order of the Emperor Justinian in the 6th cent., systematizing opinions of eminent jurists and given the force of law. M16.
2 A treatise covering the whole of a subject. L16.
3 A manuscript volume containing all the books of the Bible. L19.
■ **panˈdectist** *noun* a person skilled in the Pandects E20.

Pandee *noun* var. of PANDY *noun*[2].

pandemic /panˈdɛmɪk/ *adjective & noun.* M17.
[from Greek *pandēmos* public, formed as PAN- + *dēmos* people: see -IC. In sense 2 repr. Greek *pandēmos (erōs)* common, vulgar (love), as opp. to *ouranios* heavenly, spiritual.]
▶ **A** *adjective.* **1** (Of a disease) prevalent throughout a country, a continent, or the world; of or pertaining to such a disease. M17. ▸**b** *gen.* Chiefly of something deprecated: universal, general. L19.
2 Of or pertaining to sensual love. E19.
1 *National Observer (US)* If . . enough people aren't protected . . it could spread to pandemic proportions.
▶ **B** *noun.* A pandemic disease. M19.

pandemonium /pandɪˈməʊnɪəm/ *noun.* M17.
[mod. Latin *Pandaemonium*, from PAN- + Greek *daimōn* DEMON *noun*[1]: see -IUM.]
1 (**P-**.) The abode of all demons, hell. Orig. & *spec.* the capital of hell in Milton's *Paradise Lost*. M17.
2 A centre of vice or wickedness; a place or state of utter confusion and uproar. L18. ▸**b** Utter confusion, uproar. M19.

For other words beginning with *pan-* see the entry for **pan-**

2 J. I. M. STEWART Naples roared and screeched around us. It was a pandemonium of a place. **b** G. DURRELL I set up my camera . . Immediately, pandemonium broke loose.

■ **pandemoniac** *adjective* of or pertaining to Pandaemonium or (a) pandemonium; of all divinities: M19. **pandemoniacal** /-ˈnʌɪək(ə)l/ *adjective* characteristic of Pandaemonium; *esp.* rowdy, noisy: M19. **pandemonic** /-ˈmɒn-/ *adjective* pandemoniac L19.

pander /ˈpandə/ *noun & verb.* Also **-dar**. LME.
[*Pandare*, a character in Chaucer's *Troilus & Criseyde* who procured for Troilus the love of Criseyde, from Italian *Pandaro*, similar character in Boccaccio, from Latin *Pandarus* from Greek *Pandaros*.]
▶ **A** *noun.* **1** A go-between in illicit love-affairs; a person who provides another with a means of gratifying lust; a pimp, a procurer, *esp.* a male one. LME.
2 A person who assists the baser passions or evil designs of others. E17.
▶ **B** *verb.* **1** *verb intrans.* Act as a pander. Now usu. foll. by *to*: assist in the gratification of (a desire, weakness, etc.), indulge (a person); be subservient to. E17.
2 *verb trans.* Pander to; assist in the gratification of. E17.

1 *Times* In his quest for popular support, he panders to the least responsible elements in the community. M. MEYER A young poet who did not seek to pander to fashion. N. ANNAN She pandered to Leslie's fetish for economy. M. FLANAGAN He accused you of pandering in my affair with Felix.

■ **panderer** *noun* = PANDER *noun* 1 M19. **panderess** *noun* (now *rare*) a female pander, a procuress E17. **panderism** *noun* the practice or occupation of a pander E17. †**panderly** *adjective* of the nature of or befitting a pander L16–E19.

pandiculation /pan,dɪkjʊˈleɪʃ(ə)n/ *noun.* E17.
[from Latin *pandiculat-* pa. ppl stem of *pandiculari* stretch oneself, from *pandus* bent (with dim. elem.), from *pandere* stretch, spread: see -ATION.]
An instinctive action in which a person stretches the legs, raises and stretches the arms, throws back the head and trunk, and yawns. Also, yawning.

pandit *noun* see PUNDIT *noun.*

P & L *abbreviation.*
Profit and loss (account).

P. & O. *abbreviation.*
Peninsular and Oriental Shipping Company (or line).

pandoor *noun* var. of PANDORE *noun*[1], PANDOUR.

pandora /panˈdɔːrə/ *noun.* In sense 1 also **pandore** /panˈdɔː/. L16.
[Italian (also *pandura*) from Latin *pandura* from Greek *pandoura*.]
1 = BANDORE *noun*[1]. L16.
2 Any bivalve mollusc of the genus *Pandora*, freq. having one convex and one flat valve (and so resembling the soundbox of a stringed instrument). Also ***pandora-shell***. M19.

Pandora's box /pan,dɔːrəz ˈbɒks/ *noun phr.* M16.
[from Greek *Pandōra*, lit. 'all-gifted', name in Greek mythol. of the first mortal woman, on whom, when made by Hephaestus, all the gods and goddesses bestowed gifts, formed as PAN- + *dōron* gift.]
In Greek mythology, the gift of Zeus to Pandora, a box enclosing all human ills, which flew out when the box was foolishly opened (or in a later version, containing all the blessings of the gods, which with the exception of hope escaped and were lost when the box was opened); *gen.* a thing which once activated will give rise to many unmanageable problems.

Times They would open a Pandora's box of complaints if they decided to have an inquiry.

pandore /panˈdɔː/ *noun*[1]. *Scot.* Now *rare* or *obsolete*. Also **-door**. E18.
[Origin unkn.]
A kind of large oyster.

pandore *noun*[2] see PANDORA.

pandour /ˈpandʊə/ *noun.* Also **-door**. M18.
[French *pandour*, German *Pandur* from Serbo-Croat *pandur* constable, bailiff, etc., prob. from medieval Latin *banderius* guard of cornfields and vineyards.]
1 *Hist.* A member of an 18th-cent. military force that was orig. the private army of a Croatian nobleman and later served under him as a regiment of the Austrian Army, where its members became feared for their rapacity and brutality; any brutal Croatian soldier. M18.
2 In parts of eastern Europe: a guard; an armed servant; a member of the local mounted constabulary. L19.

pandowdy /panˈdaʊdi/ *noun. US.* M19.
[Origin unkn.]
A kind of spiced apple pudding baked in a deep dish.

p. & p. *abbreviation.*
postage and packing.

pandurate /ˈpandjʊrət/ *adjective.* L18.
[from Latin *pandura* PANDORA + -ATE[2].]
= next.

panduriform /panˈdjʊərɪfɔːm/ *adjective.* M18.
[formed as prec. + -I- + -FORM.]
Chiefly BOTANY & ENTOMOLOGY. Rounded at both ends and narrowed in the middle; fiddle-shaped.

pandurina /pandjʊˈriːnə/ *noun.* L19.
[Italian, from *pandura* PANDORA + *-ina* dim. suffix.]
A small musical instrument of the mandolin type.

pandy /ˈpandi/ *noun*[1] & *verb.* Chiefly *Scot.* M18.
[Latin *pande (manum)* stretch out (the hand) imper. of *pandere* stretch, spread.]
▶ **A** *noun.* A stroke on the extended palm with a tawse, rod, etc., given as a punishment. M18.
▶ **B** *verb trans.* Strike in this way. M18.

Pandy /ˈpandi/ *noun*[2]. *colloq.* (now *Hist.*). Also **-dee**. M19.
[Perh. from the Indian surname *Pande*, common among high-caste sepoys in the Bengal army.]
Any sepoy who revolted in the Indian Mutiny of 1857–9.

Pandy /ˈpandi/ *noun*[3]. E20.
[Kálmán *Pándy* (1868–1944), Hungarian neurologist.]
MEDICINE. Used *attrib.* and in *possess.* to designate a test for globulins in spinal fluid, in which a sample is treated with a dilute aqueous solution of phenol.

pane /peɪn/ *noun*[1]. ME.
[Old & mod. French *pan* from Latin *pannus* (piece of) cloth.]
▶ **I** A piece of cloth.
†**1 a** A cloth; a piece of cloth; a distinct portion of a garment. ME–L16. ▶**b** = COUNTERPANE *noun*[2]. LME–L16.
2 a A piece or strip of cloth of which several (often of different colours or materials) were joined side by side, so as to make one cloth, curtain, or garment. *obsolete* exc. *Hist.* L15. ▶†**b** In *pl.* Strips made by cutting a garment lengthwise for ornamental purposes. E–M17.
▶ **II** A portion of something.
3 A side of a quadrangle, cloister, court, or town. Long *rare*. LME.
†**4** A section of a wall or fence, e.g. between successive posts or angles. LME–L17.
5 A flat side of an object with several sides. Long *rare* exc. *techn.* LME.
▶ **III** A division of a window, & derived senses.
6 A part of a window formed by a single piece of glass etc. held in place by a frame; such a piece of glass. Formerly also, any of the lights of a mullioned window. Also ***window-pane***. LME.
7 A rectangular division of a surface; any of the compartments of a chequered pattern; a panel. M16.
8 A plot of ground more or less rectangular in shape. E19.
9 A sheet or page of stamps. E20.
10 COMPUTING. A separate defined area within a window for displaying or interacting with a specified part of that window's application or output. L20.

6 R. FRAME The wind rattled the loose panes in the windows.

pane /peɪn/ *noun*[2]. L19.
[App. from French *panne* from Dutch *pen*, Middle Flemish *penne* peg from Latin *pinna* point, pinnacle. Cf. PEEN *noun*.]
= PEEN *noun*.

Pane *noun*[3] & *adjective* var. of PAWNEE *noun*[2] & *adjective*.

pane /peɪn/ *verb trans.* E16.
[from PANE *noun*[1].]
1 Make up (a piece of cloth, a garment) of pieces or strips joined side by side. Chiefly as ***paned*** *ppl adjective.* E16.
2 Fit or provide (a window, door, etc.) with panes (esp. of a specified kind or number). Chiefly as ***paned*** *ppl adjective.* E18.

1 SIR W. SCOTT His paned hose were of black velvet. **2** MORTIMER COLLINS Casements diamond-paned.

paneer /paˈnɪə/ *noun.* Also **-nir**. M20.
[Urdu or Persian *panīr* cheese.]
A type of milk curd cheese used in Indian, Iranian, and Afghan cooking.

†**panegyre** *noun.* E17.
[formed as PANEGYRIS.]
1 = PANEGYRIC *noun* 1. Only in E17.
2 A general assembly, a panegyris. Only in M18.

panegyric /panɪˈdʒɪrɪk/ *noun & adjective.* E17.
[French *panégyrique* from Latin *panegyricus* public eulogy, use as noun of adjective from Greek *panēgurikos*, formed as PANEGYRIS: see -IC.]
▶ **A** *noun.* **1** A public speech or published text in praise of someone or something; a laudatory discourse; a eulogy. (Foll. by *on*, †*of*.) E17.
2 High praise; = EULOGY 1. E17.
▶ **B** *adjective.* †**1** = PANEGYRICAL 2. Only in E17.
2 = PANEGYRICAL 1. M17.

panegyrical /panɪˈdʒɪrɪk(ə)l/ *adjective.* L16.
[formed as prec. + -AL[1].]
1 Of the nature of a panegyric; publicly or elaborately expressing praise or commendation; laudatory. L16.
†**2** Of the nature of a general assembly. Only in 17.
■ **panegyrically** *adverb* in or by means of a panegyric L17.

panegyris /pəˈniːdʒɪrɪs, -ˈnɛdʒ-/ *noun.* M17.
[Greek *panēguris*, formed as PAN- + *aguris* AGORA *noun*[1].]
GREEK HISTORY. A general assembly; *esp.* a festal assembly in honour of a god.

panegyrise *verb* var. of PANEGYRIZE.

panegyrist /panɪˈdʒɪrɪst/ *noun.* E17.
[from (the same root as) next + -IST.]
A person who delivers or writes a panegyric.

panegyrize /ˈpanɪdʒɪrʌɪz/ *verb trans.* Also **-ise**. E17.
[Greek *panēgurizein* celebrate a panegyris, formed as PANEGYRIS: see -IZE.]
Speak or write in praise of; eulogize.
■ ˈ**panegy,rizer** *noun* = PANEGYRIST E19.

panegyry /pəˈniːdʒɪri, -ˈnɛdʒ-/ *noun.* E17.
[formed as PANEGYRIS with change of ending.]
†**1** A panegyric. E–M17.
2 = PANEGYRIS; any religious festival. M17.

paneity /pəˈniːɪti, pəˈneɪɪti/ *noun.* Long *rare*. L17.
[from Latin *panem*, *panis* bread after *corporeity* etc.]
The quality or condition of being bread.

panel /ˈpan(ə)l/ *noun*[1]. Also †**-nn-**. ME.
[Old French = piece of cloth, saddle-cushion, piece (mod. *panneau* panel) from Proto-Romance dim. of Latin *pannus*: see PANE *noun*[1], -EL[2].]
▶ **I** A piece of cloth, & derived senses.
1 Orig., (a piece of) cloth, *esp.* a piece placed under a saddle. Now, the padded underpart of a saddle. ME.
2 A kind of saddle, *esp.* a rough treeless pad. M16.
▶ **II** A distinct part of a surface, and related uses.
3 A distinct portion of a surface, usually rectangular and contained in a frame or border; *spec.* (*a*) a usu. solid section of a fence or railing; (*b*) a usu. rectangular portion of a door, shutter, etc., generally thinner than the surround; (*c*) a distinct portion of the body of a motor vehicle; (*d*) a part of a wall or piece of furniture that is sunk below or raised above the general level. LME.
4 A compartment in a stained-glass window, containing a separate subject. Formerly also = PANE *noun*[1] 6. M16.
5 A thin board such as might form a panel of a door etc.; *esp.* one used as a working surface. E17. ▶**b** A rigid support for a painting (as opp. to a canvas); a painting on such a support. E18. ▶**c** A leaf or section of a folding screen or triptych. L19.
6 a A usu. rectangular division of a coalmine delimited by pillars of coal. Formerly, a piece of coal left uncut. M18. ▶**b** A pile of dressed ore. M19. ▶**c** A stratum, esp. of limestone, within stratified rock. L19.
7 A section of a tapestry or other ornamental work, usu. one surrounded by a decorative border; a tapestry regarded as a whole. M19. ▶**b** A piece of material often of different kind or colour inserted lengthwise in a woman's skirt; any of several usu. wedge-shaped pieces of material joined lengthwise to form a skirt; a rectangular piece of embroidery etc. for insertion in drapery. L19. ▶**c** Each of the shaped sections of a parachute. M20.
8 = ***control panel*** s.v. CONTROL *noun*, ***instrument panel*** s.v. INSTRUMENT *noun*. L19.

3 W. COBBETT A stage-coach . . with 'Bath and London' upon its panels. *Stamps* A Scottish 10½p air letter, the panel . . showing a burning Viking ship. R. THOMAS Annie . . looked out of the glass panel in the back door. ***solar panel***: see SOLAR *adjective*[1]. **4** *Stained Glass* The team . . climbed scaffolds to find panels generally decipherable only . . with binoculars. **5** T. L. PEACOCK Such things as sliding panels and secret closets. *Antique Collector* 'The Milkmaid'. James Digman Wingfield Signed. Oil on panel. **8** *Gramophone* The bottom section of the panel is completed by four variable control knobs.

▶ **III** A small piece of parchment, and related uses.
9 *Hist.* A slip or roll of parchment, *esp.* the slip on which a sheriff entered the names of jurors and which was affixed to the writ. LME.
10 A list of jurors or available jurors; a jury. LME. ▶**b** Any list of persons (or animals); *spec.* a usu. small group of people called on to be participants in a (freq. broadcast) game or quiz, advisers to an inquiry, etc. L16. ▶**c** A list of medical practitioners or patients registered for a particular practice under the British National Health Service or (formerly) under the National Health Insurance Act. E20.
11 SCOTS LAW. A person or persons indicted; an accused. M16.

10b *Which?* Our technical tests have been backed up by ratings from a panel of real people.

Comb.: **panel analysis** SOCIOLOGY analysis of attitude changes by means of panel studies; **panel-back** *adjective & noun* (designating) a wooden chair with a high back and heavy legs and stretchers, made esp. in Tudor and Jacobean times; **panel-beater** a person who beats out the metal panels of motor vehicles; **panel board** (a) heavy or dense fibreboard; **panel doctor** *Hist.* a doctor registered as accepting patients under the British National Insurance

For other words beginning with *pan-* see the entry for **pan-**

Act of 1913; **panel fence** *US*: constructed in panels or sections; **panel game** (*a*) a (freq. broadcast) quiz or similar game played before an audience by a small group of people; (*b*) the action of stealing in a panel-house; **panel gauge**: wide enough to gauge the width of a board or panel; **panel heater** a panel mounted in a wall or other surface with a concealed source of heat; **panel heating** the heating of a room, building, etc., by means of panel heaters; **panel-house** a brothel in which the walls have sliding panels for the purpose of robbery; **panel painter** an artist who specializes in panel painting; **panel painting** a painting on a panel rather than a canvas; the art of creating such paintings, esp. as practised in medieval times; **panel patient** *Hist.*: who received treatment from a doctor under the British National Insurance Act of 1913; **panel pin** a light thin nail with a small head, for securing panels; **panel plane** (*a*) a plane for shaping the edge of a raised panel; (*b*) a plane for fine smoothing and trueing; **panel saw** a light saw with a narrow blade of fine teeth, for cutting wood thinly; **panel show** = *panel game* (a) above; **panel stamp** a stamp for decorating the panels in the binding of a book; **panel study** SOCIOLOGY an investigation of attitude changes using a constant set of people and comparing each individual's opinions at different points in time; **panel technique** SOCIOLOGY the technique used in panel studies; **panel-thief** a thief in a panel-house; **panel truck** *US* a small van; **panel van** (now *Austral.*) a small van, *esp.* one with windows and passenger seats; **panel wall** (*a*) a wall of unmined coal separating two panels in a mine; (*b*) a wall in a building that does not bear weight; **panel-work** (*a*) work consisting of or containing panels, *esp.* panelled woodwork; (*b*) the working of a mine by division into panels.

panel /ˈpɑːn(ə)l/ *noun*². *obsolete* exc. *dial.* Also (earlier) †**parnel**. LME.
[Old French female name *Peronele*, *Pernele* from Latin *Petronilla*.]
A priest's concubine or mistress; a promiscuous or wanton woman.

panel /ˈpan(ə)l/ *verb trans.* Infl. **-ll-**, ***-l-**. LME.
[from PANEL *noun*¹.]
1 = EMPANEL *verb*. LME.
2 Provide or fit with a panel or panels; cover or decorate with panels. Freq. as *panelled ppl adjective*. E16.
3 Put a panel on (an animal, esp. a mule or ass); saddle with a panel. M16.
4 SCOTS LAW. Bring to trial; indict. M16.

📖 **2** W. BOTTRELL The cosy, old, panelled settle. *Daily Chronicle* The skirt panelled with lace. H. KEMELMAN A white panelled door. B. OKRI Oak-panelled, soundproofed walls with . . rare art pieces hanging on them.

†**panele** *noun*. M16–L18.
[Spanish *panela*: cf. German *Panelle*.]
(A) brown unpurified sugar from the Antilles.

paneless /ˈpeɪnlɪs/ *adjective*. M18.
[from PANE *noun*¹ + -LESS.]
Of a window: having no panes.

paneling *noun* see PANELLING.

panelist *noun* see PANELLIST.

panelling /ˈpan(ə)lɪŋ/ *noun*. Also ***-eling**. E17.
[from PANEL *noun*¹ + -ING¹.]
Wood or other material made or for making into a panel or panels; panels collectively, panelled work.

panellist /ˈpan(ə)lɪst/ *noun*. Also ***-elist**. M20.
[from PANEL *noun*¹ + -IST.]
A member of a panel, esp. in a radio or television programme.

panem et circenses /ˌpanɛm ɛt sɜːˈkɛnziːz, kəːˈkɛnseɪz/ *noun phr*. L18.
[Latin = bread and games (in the Circus in Rome).]
= ***bread and circuses*** s.v. CIRCUS 7.

Paneth /ˈpaneθ/ *noun*. L19.
[Joseph *Paneth* (1857–90), Austrian physiologist.]
ANATOMY. Used *attrib.*, in *possess.*, and with *of* to designate (*a*) a secretory cell present at the base of the crypts of Lieberkühn in the small intestine, (*b*) the eosinophilic granules characteristic of their cytoplasm.

panettone /panɪˈtəʊni, *foreign* panetˈtoːne/ *noun*. Also **panetone** /panɪˈtəʊni, *foreign* paneˈtoːne/. Pl. **-ni** /-ni/. E20.
[Italian, from *panetto* cake, bar, dim. of *pane* bread from Latin *panis*: see -ET¹.]
A rich Italian bread made with eggs, fruit, and butter.

panfan /ˈpanfan/ *noun*. E20.
[from PAN- + FAN *noun*¹.]
PHYSICAL GEOGRAPHY. = PEDIPLAIN.

panforte /panˈfɔːti, *foreign* panˈforte/ *noun*. L19.
[Italian, from *pane* bread + *forte* strong.]
A hard spicy Sienese cake containing nuts, candied peel, and honey.

panful /ˈpanfʊl, -f(ə)l/ *noun*. ME.
[from PAN *noun*¹ + -FUL.]
The quantity that fills a pan, the contents of a pan.
¶ Rare before L19.

pang /paŋ/ *noun*¹. L15.
[Unexpl. alt. of PRONG *noun*.]
1 A sudden sharp feeling of pain or painful emotion. Freq. in *pl.* (orig. in *pangs of death*). L15.
†**2** A sudden sharp feeling or emotion of any kind; a sudden brief sensation. M16–L17.

📖 **1** E. J. HOWARD Felix felt a pang of irritation. L. DEIGHTON The first sharp pang . . had by now become a dull wet ache. C. TOMALIN Kennedy . . was suffering the pangs of rejected love. **2** J. TILLOTSON He . . fell into a pang of devotion.

■ **pangful** *adjective* (*rare*) sorrowful M18. **pangless** *adjective* without a pang E19.

pang /paŋ/ *noun*². E20.
[Imit.]
A short resonant sound such as that produced by a drum, a horse's hoof, etc.

pang /paŋ/ *adjective*. *Scot.* M16.
[Origin unkn. Cf. PANG *verb*².]
Packed tight, crammed; completely full.

pang /paŋ/ *verb*¹ *trans. & intrans.* Now *rare*. E16.
[from PANG *noun*¹.]
Afflict with pangs; cause a pang.

pang /paŋ/ *verb*² *trans. Scot. & north.* M17.
[Rel. to PANG *adjective*.]
Pack tight; press close together.

panga /ˈpɑːŋɡə/ *noun*¹. Also **ponga** /ˈpɒŋɡə/. E20.
[Amer. Spanish.]
A flat-bottomed boat with rising stem and stern, used esp. in Latin America.

panga /ˈpaŋɡə/ *noun*². M20.
[E. African name.]
In Africa, a large knife used either as a tool or a weapon.

Pangaea /panˈdʒiːə/ *noun*. E20.
[from PAN- + Greek *gaia* earth.]
A supercontinent thought to have comprised all the continental crust of the earth in Palaeozoic times before breaking up into Gondwanaland and Laurasia.

Pangan /ˈpaŋɡ(ə)n/ *noun*. M19.
[Malay = forest country.]
= NEGRITO *noun*.

Pangasinan /ˌpɑːŋɡɑːsɪˈnɑːn/ *noun & adjective*. Pl. of noun **-s**, same. M19.
[Pangasinan = area of salt ponds.]
A member of, of or pertaining to, a people inhabiting the central area of the island of Luzon in the Philippines; (of) the Austronesian language of this people.

pangene /panˈdʒiːn/ *noun*. *obsolete* exc. *Hist.* Also †**-gen**. L19.
[from PAN- + stem of Greek *genos* kind, race, offspring.]
BIOLOGY. A supposed ultimate unit of living matter or of heredity.

pangenesis /panˈdʒɛnɪsɪs/ *noun*. M19.
[from PAN- + GENESIS.]
BIOLOGY. A former theory of heredity according to which each constituent unit of an organism reproduced itself individually, the resulting particles going to make up the reproductive cells.
■ **pangeˈnetic** *adjective* L19.

pangeran /paŋɡəˈran/ *noun*. E19.
[Javanese & Malay.]
Hist. (A title of) a male of high nobility or importance in Indonesia and Malaysia.

pan-German /panˈdʒəːmən/ *adjective & noun*. L19.
[from PAN- + GERMAN *noun*¹ & *adjective*¹.]
▶ **A** *adjective*. Of, pertaining to, or advocating pan-Germanism. L19.
▶ **B** *noun*. An advocate of pan-Germanism. L19.
■ **pan-Gerˈmanic** *adjective* pan-German E20.

pan-Germanism /panˈdʒəːmənɪz(ə)m/ *noun*. L19.
[formed as prec. + -ISM.]
The idea or principle of a political unification of all Europeans speaking German, or all speaking a Germanic language.
■ **pan-Germanist** *noun* = PAN-GERMAN *noun* E20.

panglima /pənˈɡliːmə/ *noun*. M19.
[Malay *pĕnglima*.]
Hist. A Malay chief or leader.

Pangloss /ˈpanɡlɒs/ *noun*. M19.
[The philosopher and tutor in Voltaire's *Candide* (1759).]
A person who is optimistic regardless of the circumstances.
■ **Panˈglossian** *adjective & noun* (of, pertaining to, or characteristic of) a Pangloss M19. **Panglossism** *noun* an unrealistically optimistic attitude or saying M20.

pangolin /paŋˈɡəʊlɪn/ *noun*. L18.
[Malay *peng-guling* lit. 'roller', from its habit of rolling itself up.]
A mammal of the order Pholidota and family Manidae, comprising anteating animals of southern Asia and Africa that have a body covered with large horny scales, a small head with an elongated snout and tongue, and a tapering tail. Also called ***scaly anteater***.

panguingue /paŋˈɡiːŋɡi/ *noun*. E20.
[Tagalog *pangginggi*.]
A card-game resembling rummy played with several packs.

For other words beginning with *pan-* see the entry for **pan-**

panhandle /ˈpanhand(ə)l/ *noun & verb*. *N. Amer.* M19.
[from PAN *noun*¹ + HANDLE *noun*¹.]
▶ **A** *noun*. **1** A narrow strip of territory projecting into the territory of another State or surrounded on three sides by the territory of other States; *spec.* (**P-**) that of West Virginia, USA. M19.
2 Begging. *slang*. M19.
▶ **B** *verb trans. & intrans.* [Back-form. from PANHANDLER.] Beg (from); steal. *slang*. E20.
■ **panhandler** *noun* (*a*) a beggar; (*b*) (**P-**) a native or inhabitant of a panhandle: L19.

Panhard rod /panhɑːd ˈrɒd, panɑːd/ *noun phr*. M20.
[*Panhard*–Levassor, French motor company.]
A torsion bar attached to the rear axle on some motor vehicles.

Panhellenic /panhɛˈlɛnɪk, -hɛˈliː-/ *adjective*. M19.
[from PAN- + HELLENIC.]
Of, concerning, or representing all people of Greek origin or ancestry; of or pertaining to Panhellenism.
■ **Panˈhellenism** *noun* the idea of, or advocacy of, a political union of all Greeks M19. **Panˈhellenist** *noun* a believer in or advocate of Panhellenism L19.

panic /ˈpanɪk/ *noun*¹. LME.
[Latin PANICUM, rel. to *panus* thread wound on a bobbin, swelling, ear of millet, from Greek *pēnos* web (*pēnion* bobbin): cf. PANICLE.]
More fully ***panic-grass***. Any of various cereals and other grasses of the genus *Panicum* or of allied genera (esp. *Setaria* and *Echinochloa*) formerly included in it; orig. *spec.*, foxtail millet, *Setaria italica*.

panic /ˈpanɪk/ *adjective & noun*². E17.
[French *panique* from mod. Latin *panicus* (in *panicus terror*) from Greek *panikos* (also neut. *panikon* used as noun), from *Pan*, Greek god of nature to whom woodland noises were attributed and whose appearance or unseen presence was held to induce terror.]
▶ **A** *adjective*. (Of fear, a fright, etc.) such as may be attributed to the action of the god Pan, sudden, unreasoning; of the nature of or caused by (a) panic. Now often regarded as *attrib.* use of the noun E17.

📖 R. L. STEVENSON A panic selfishness, like that produced by fear.

▶ **B** *noun*. †**1** (An) infectious emotion such as was ascribed to the influence of the god Pan. M17–E18.
2 An excessive or unreasoning feeling of alarm or fear leading to extravagant or foolish behaviour, such as that which may suddenly spread through a crowd of people; emotion of this kind. M17. ▸**b** A condition of widespread apprehension in relation to financial and commercial matters leading to hasty measures to guard against possible loss. M18. ▸**c** An agitated busyness as when making hurried preparations for something. E20.
3 A noteworthy or amusing person, thing, or situation. *slang*. M20.

📖 **2** J. A. FROUDE Caesar's soldiers were seized with panic. J. HERSEY In panic . . he dashed out into the street. I. MURDOCH When she could not find a hotel she had felt total panic. **b** LYNDON B. JOHNSON The London gold market was in a panic. Each day brought new losses. **c** M. TRIPP What's the panic? . . There's another hour and a half till breakfast.

Comb. & special collocations: **panic attack** a sudden overwhelming feeling of intense and disabling anxiety; **panic bar** a panic bolt in the form of a horizontal bar that is operated by pressing it; **panic bolt** a special bolt enabling a door to unfasten quickly in an emergency; *esp.* a panic bar; **panic button** a switch or button for operating a device in an emergency; (***hit the panic button***, ***press the panic button***, become overexcited, take emergency measures); **panic buying** the buying in of large quantities of goods of which a shortage is threatened or suspected; **panic-monger** a person who seeks to bring about or foster a panic, esp. on a political, social, or financial question; an alarmist; **panic party** a group of crew members assigned to feign a panic departure from a ship in order to lure or mislead an enemy; **panic stations** *colloq.* a state of alarm or panic in which immediate action is felt necessary; freq. in ***at panic stations***; **panic-stricken** *adjective* affected with panic; very apprehensive; **panic-striking** *adjective* causing or likely to cause (a) panic; **panic-struck** *adjective* = *panic-stricken* above.
■ **panical** *adjective* (*rare*) = PANIC *adjective* E17.

panic /ˈpanɪk/ *verb*. Infl. **-ck-**. E19.
[from PANIC *noun*².]
1 *verb trans.* Affect with panic. E19. ▸**b** Make (an audience) enthusiastic, excite or impress greatly. *US slang*. E20.
2 *verb intrans.* Get into a panic, lose one's head. E20.

📖 **1** *Daily Telegraph* A radio dramatisation of H. G. Wells's 'War of the Worlds' panicked thousands throughout America. **2** *Radio Times* Their headmaster . . rather panicked at the word 'drug'.

panicky /ˈpanɪki/ *adjective*. *colloq.* M19.
[from PANIC *noun*² + -Y¹.]
Affected with panic, panic-stricken; symptomatic or expressive of panic. Also, apt to panic.

📖 *Sun (Baltimore)* The panicky condition of the market. R. K. NARAYAN Jagan threw a panicky look at his cousin. D. W. GOODWIN I grew panicky even thinking I might not have alcohol.

panicle /ˈpanɪk(ə)l/ *noun*. L16.
[Latin *panicula* dim. of *panus*: see PANIC *noun*[1], -CLE.]
BOTANY. A racemose or cymose inflorescence in which the pedicels are themselves branched, so forming a loosely branching cluster of flowers.
▪ **panicled** *adjective* arranged in or bearing a panicle L17.

paniculate /pəˈnɪkjʊleɪt, -ət/ *adjective*. E18.
[mod. Latin *paniculatus*, formed as prec. + -ATE[2].]
BOTANY. Arranged in or bearing a panicle; panicled.
▪ **paniculated** *adjective* (*rare*) = PANICULATE E18. **paniculately** *adverb* L19.

panicum /ˈpanɪkəm/ *noun*. M19.
[Latin = foxtail millet, adopted by Linnaeus as a genus name: see PANIC *noun*[1].]
Any grass of the genus *Panicum*, which includes the European millet, *P. miliaceum*, and several other important cereals and fodder grasses. Cf. PANIC *noun*[1].

panier de crabes /panje də krab/ *noun phr*. Pl. ***paniers de crabes*** (pronounced same). M20.
[French, lit. 'basket of crabs'.]
A competitive struggle.

panification /ˌpanɪfɪˈkeɪʃ(ə)n/ *noun*. L18.
[French, from *panifier* make into bread, from Latin *panis* bread: see -FICATION.]
Conversion into bread, esp. considered as a chemical process.

Paninean /paˈnɪnɪən/ *adjective*. Also **-ian**. E19.
[from Sanskrit *Pāṇinīya* in same sense, from *Pāṇini* Panini (see below): see -EAN.]
Of or pertaining to the Sanskrit grammar of Panini (6th or 5th cent. BC); adhering to the rules formulated by Panini.

panino /paˈniːno/ *noun*. Pl. **-ni** /-niː/. M20.
[Italian.]
An Italian bread roll or sandwich.

pani puri /ˈpɑːnɪ ˌpuːri/ *noun phr*. L20.
[from Hindi *pānī* water + PURI *noun*[2].]
In Indian cookery: a puff-pastry ball filled with spiced mashed potato and tamarind juice and fried.

panir *noun* var. of PANEER.

panisc /ˈpanɪsk/ *noun*. E17.
[Greek *paniskos*, Latin *Paniscus*, dims. of *Pan*: see PANIC *adjective* & *noun*[2], -ISH[1].]
MYTHOLOGY. A little Pan; an inferior god representing or attending on Pan.

Panislamic /panɪzˈlamɪk, -ɪs-/ *adjective*. Also **Pan-Islamic**. L19.
[from PAN- + ISLAMIC.]
Of, pertaining to, or advocating an alliance or union of all Islamic States; of or pertaining to the whole Muslim world.
▪ **Panˈislamism** *noun* (advocacy of) the Panislamic idea L19.

pani-wallah /ˈpɑːnɪwɒlə/ *noun*. M20.
[from Hindi *pānī* water + WALLAH.]
In the Indian subcontinent: a water-carrier; a person who applies lubricating grease.

Panjabi *noun* & *adjective* see PUNJABI.

panjandrum /panˈdʒandrəm/ *noun*. L19.
[Invented word occurring, as *Grand Panjandrum*, in an 18th-cent. nonsense composition.]
(A mock title for) an imaginary or mysterious personage of much power, or a person of great pretensions; a pompous or pretentious official; an important or authoritative person. Freq. in ***Grand Panjandrum***, ***Great Panjandrum***.

> 🕮 *Washington Post* The panjandrums may next advise local citizens to stop drinking water. *Nature* R. V. Jones, the great panjandrum of the arcana of scientific intelligence.

panji *noun* see PUNJI.

pankin /ˈpankɪn/ *noun*. Now *dial*. LME.
[from PAN *noun*[1] + -KIN: cf. PANNIKIN.]
An earthenware pan or jar, *esp*. a small one.

panmixia /panˈmɪksɪə/ *noun*. Also **-mixis** /-ˈmɪksɪs/. L19.
[mod. Latin from German *Panmixie*, formed as PAN- + Greek *mixia*, from *mixis* mixing, mixing.]
BIOLOGY. **1** The transmission of a wide variety of heritable characteristics outside the influence of natural selection (as in an organ which has ceased to be useful). *obsolete* exc. *Hist*. L19.
2 Random mating within a breeding population. M20.
▪ **panmictic** *adjective* characterized by panmixia M20.

pannag /ˈpanag/ *noun*. *rare*. E17.
[Hebrew.]
A foodstuff mentioned in the Old Testament.

pannage /ˈpanɪdʒ/ *noun*. LME.
[Old French (mod. *panage*) from medieval Latin *pastionaticum*, from *pastio(n-)* feeding, pasturing, from *past-*: see PASTURE *noun*, -AGE.]
1 LAW. The feeding of pigs (or other animals) in a wood; the right or privilege of doing this; pasturage for pigs; payment made to, or income received by, the owner of a wood for this right. LME.
2 Acorns, beech-mast, etc., on which pigs feed. LME.

pannam /ˈpanəm/ *noun*. *Criminals' slang*. Also **-um**. M16.
[Prob. alt. of Latin *panem* accus. of *panis* bread.]
Bread.

panne /pan/ *noun*. L18.
[French, of unkn. origin.]
A soft silk or rayon fabric with a flattened pile, resembling velvet. Also ***panne velvet***.

†**pannel** *noun* var. of PANEL *noun*[1].

†**pannicle** *noun*. LME.
[Old French *pan(n)icle* from Latin *panniculus* rag, dim. of *pannus* cloth: see -CLE.]
1 a A membrane or membranous structure in a human or animal body; *esp*. (more fully ***fleshy pannicle***) a layer of muscular fibres lying just beneath the skin that is specially developed in some quadrupeds. LME–E18. ▸**b** BOTANY. A membranous covering in a plant, e.g. the scales covering a leaf-bud. L17–M18.
2 [By assoc. with PAN *noun*[1].] The cranium, the skull. *rare* (Spenser). Only in L16.

pannier /ˈpanɪə/ *noun*[1] & *verb*. ME.
[Old & mod. French *panier*, †*pannier* from Latin *panarium* bread basket, from *panis* bread: see -IER.]
▸ **A** *noun*. **1 a** A basket; *esp*. a large one for carrying provisions, fish, or other commodities. Now chiefly, a basket carried by a beast of burden (usu. either of a pair, one on each side, slung across the back), or on a person's shoulders. ME. ▸**b** The amount contained in a pannier. E18.
2 *Hist*. A covered basket for holding surgical instruments and medicines for a military ambulance. M19.
3 A frame formerly used to distend the skirt of a woman's dress at the hips. Also, a part of a dress looped up at the hips, or attached so as to drape over them. M19.
4 In full ***pannier bag***. A bag or box attached beside the rear wheel of a bicycle or motorcycle (usu. either of a pair, attached one on each side). M20.
Comb.: **pannier bag**: see sense 4 above; **pannierman** (*obsolete* exc. *Hist*.) (*a*) a paid officer at the Inns of Court who brought provisions from market and had duties relating to the serving of meals; (*b*) a man in charge of a pannier or panniers, or who took goods to market in panniers; **pannier pocket** a large pocket attached to the side of a skirt or dress; **pannier tank** a small steam locomotive with a protruding water tank on each side of the boiler.
▸ **B** *verb trans*. Provide with a pannier or panniers; place (as) in a pannier. *rare*. L16.
▪ **panniered** *adjective* laden with a pannier or panniers M18.

pannier /ˈpanɪə/ *noun*[2]. E19.
[Origin unkn.]
Hist. A robed waiter at table in the Inner Temple.

panniform /ˈpanɪfɔːm/ *adjective*. L19.
[from Latin *pannus* cloth + -I- + -FORM.]
BOTANY. Having the appearance or texture of woollen cloth; felted.

pannikin /ˈpanɪkɪn/ *noun*. E19.
[from PAN *noun*[1] after CANNIKIN.]
1 A small metal drinking-vessel, a cannikin; the contents of such a vessel. E19.
2 The head. Only in ***off one's pannikin***, = ***off one's head*** s.v. HEAD *noun*. *Austral. slang*. L19.
Comb.: **pannikin-boss** *Austral. slang* a minor overseer on a sheep station; a foreman.

panning /ˈpanɪŋ/ *noun*. M19.
[from PAN *verb*[1] + -ING[1].]
1 The action of PAN *verb*[1]. M19.
2 In *pl*. The gold obtained by panning gravel etc. L19.

Pannonian /paˈnəʊnɪən/ *adjective*. E17.
[from *Pannonia* (see below) + -AN.]
Of or pertaining to Pannonia, a province of the Roman Empire comprising parts of present-day Hungary, Austria, Slovenia, and Croatia.
▪ Also **Pannonic** /-ˈnɒn-/ *adjective* (long *rare*) L16.

pannum *noun* var. of PANNAM.

pannus /ˈpanəs/ *noun*. LME.
[Perh. from Latin = cloth.]
ANATOMY & MEDICINE. A layer of vascular fibrous tissue extending over the surface of a specialized structure, esp. the cornea; the condition of having such a layer.

Pano /ˈpanəʊ/ *noun* & *adjective*. M19.
[Amer. Spanish.]
▸ **A** *noun*. Pl. same, **-os**.
1 A member of a S. American Indian people of the upper Amazon basin. M19.
2 The Panoan language of this people. M19.
▸ **B** *attrib*. or as *adjective*. Designating or pertaining to the Pano or their language. L19.

Panoan /paˈnəʊən/ *adjective* & *noun*. E20.
[from prec. + -AN.]
▸ **A** *adjective*. **1** Designating or pertaining to a group of S. American Indian peoples (including the Pano) inhabiting Peru and neighbouring parts of Bolivia and Brazil. E20.
2 Of or pertaining to the group of related languages spoken by these peoples. M20.
▸ **B** *noun*. A member of any of these peoples; the Panoan language group. E20.

panocha, **panoche** *nouns* vars. of PENUCHE.

panographic /panəˈgrafɪk/ *adjective*. Also **pana-**. M20.
[from PANO(RAMIC + RADIO)GRAPHIC.]
Pertaining to or designating radiography of several teeth and the adjacent bones in a single exposure by means of a small X-ray source placed inside the mouth and a film outside it.
▪ **ˈpanograph** *noun* (*a*) a panographic radiograph; (*b*) an X-ray machine for use in panography: M20. **paˈnography** *noun* panographic radiography M20.

Panomphaean /panɒmˈfiːən/ *adjective*. *literary*. Also **-phean**. E17.
[from Greek *panomphaios*, formed as PAN- + *omphē* voice of a god, oracular response: see -AN.]
Of or pertaining to the god Zeus, as sender of all oracular voices. Also, universally understood.

panophobia /panəˈfəʊbɪə/ *noun*. L18.
[from Greek *Pan*, genit. *Panos* (see PANIC *adjective* & *noun*[2]) + -PHOBIA.]
Irrational or excessive terror; sudden panic.

panoply /ˈpanəpli/ *noun* & *verb*. L16.
[French *panoplie* or mod. Latin *panoplia* from Greek *panoplia* full armour of a hoplite, formed as PAN- + *hopla* arms: see -Y[3].]
▸ **A** *noun*. **1 a** Complete protection for spiritual or mental warfare; any complete defence or protection. Freq. with allus. to *Ephesians* 6:11, 13. L16. ▸**b** A complete covering, *esp*. one that is magnificent or impressive. E19. ▸**c** An impressive collection *of*; the trappings or accessory features (*of*). M20.
2 A complete suit of armour. Freq. in ref. to its brightness and splendour. M17.

> 🕮 **1a** R. LANDER Another charm . . a panoply, for preserving all persons while bathing from the fangs of the crocodiles. **b** L. STRACHEY That night the Faery . . appeared in a glittering panoply of enormous uncut jewels. **c** Y. MENUHIN The panoply of statehood—the army, the militarism, the flag-waving. *Illustrated London News* It would be wrong to try to introduce a complete new panoply of union law. *Economist* The panoply of police cars, blue lights and motorised outriders.

▸ **B** *verb trans*. Arm completely, provide with a panoply; *fig*. array with something magnificent or impressive. M19.

panoptic /paˈnɒptɪk/ *adjective*. E19.
[from Greek *panoptos* seen by all, *panoptēs* all-seeing, formed as PAN- + *optos* visible: see -IC.]
1 From which all can be seen; giving a panoramic view. E19.
2 All-embracing, comprehensive; universal in scope. E20.

panopticon /panˈɒptɪk(ə)n/ *noun*. M18.
[from PAN- + Greek *optikon* neut. of *optikos* OPTIC.]
1 A kind of telescope; a combined telescope and microscope. *obsolete* exc. *Hist*. M18.
2 *Hist*. A circular prison with cells built round and fully exposed towards a central well, from which prisoners could at all times be observed. L18. ▸**b** *transf*. & *fig*. A place where everything is visible; a showroom for novelties. M19.

panoram /panəˈram/ *noun*, *adjective*, & *verb*. L19.
[Abbreviation of PANORAMIC.]
▸ **A** *noun*. A panoramic camera. L19.
▸ **B** *adjective*. Panoramic. E20.
▸ **C** *verb intrans*. Infl. **-mm-**, **-m-**. = PAN *verb*[2] 2. E20.

panorama /panəˈrɑːmə/ *noun*. L18.
[from PAN- + Greek *orama* view.]
1 A picture of a landscape or other scene, either arranged on the inside of a cylindrical surface with the spectator in the centre (a cyclorama), or unrolled or unfolded and made to pass before the spectator so as to show the various parts in succession. L18.
2 A continuous passing scene; a mental vision in which a series of images passes before the mind's eye. E19.
3 An unbroken view of the whole region surrounding an observer. E19.
4 A complete and comprehensive survey or presentation of a subject. E19.

> 🕮 **1** *Independent* An enormous 360-degree panorama painted in 1881. **2** J. HILTON A panorama of one's past . . is more accurate in perspective. **3** A. C. CLARKE He was not looking at the panorama of reefs and islands spread out below. **4** G. GREENE Like a panorama of the Boer War in an old *Illustrated London News*.

For other words beginning with *pan-* see the entry for **pan-**

■ **panoramal** *adjective* (*rare*) passing everything under review; panoramic: E19. **panoramic** /-ˈram-/ *adjective* of, pertaining to, or of the nature of a panorama; ***panoramic camera***, a camera that rotates in synchronism with the gradual exposure of the film or plate, so as to get more than its field of view in a single photograph: E19. **panoramically** /-ˈram-/ *adverb* after the manner of a panorama M19. **panoramist** *noun* a painter of panoramas L19.

panorpa /paˈnɔːpə/ *noun*. L19.
[mod. Latin *Panorpa* genus name, of unkn. origin.]
A scorpion fly.
■ **panorpoid** *adjective* of, pertaining to, or designating a group of insect orders closely related to the scorpion-flies (order Mecoptera) L19.

pan-pipe /ˈpanpʌɪp/ *noun*. E19.
[from *Pan*, Greek god to whom its invention was attributed (see PANIC *adjective & noun*[2]) + PIPE *noun*[1].]
sing. & (now usu.) in *pl*. A simple wind instrument made of a series of short pipes (orig. reeds) graduated in length so as to form a scale and fixed together with their mouth ends in line; a syrinx.

panplain /ˈpanpleɪn/ *noun*. M20.
[from PAN- + PLAIN *noun*[1].]
PHYSICAL GEOGRAPHY. A plain formed by the coalescence of previously separate flood plains.
■ **panplaˈnation** *noun* the formation of a panplain M20.

panpot /ˈpanpɒt/ *noun & verb*. M20.
[from PAN(ORAMIC) + POT(ENTIOMETER.]
▶ **A** *noun*. A potentiometer used to vary the apparent position of a sound source by varying the strengths of the signals to individual speakers without changing the total signal strength. M20.
▶ **B** *verb trans*. Infl. **-tt-**. Process (sound) by means of a panpot. L20.

panpsychism /panˈsʌɪkɪz(ə)m/ *noun*. L19.
[from PAN- + PSYCHISM.]
PHILOSOPHY. The doctrine or belief that all matter, however small, has a psychical aspect or component.
■ **panpsychic** *adjective* pertaining to or based on panpsychism L19. **panpsychist** *noun & adjective* (*a*) *noun* a believer in panpsychism; (*b*) *adjective* panpsychic: E20. **panpsyˈchistic** *adjective* panpsychic E20.

pansala /ˈpʌnsələ/ *noun*. M19.
[Sinhalese (from *pan* leaf + *sala* dwelling) from Sanskrit *parṇaśālā*, Pali *pannasālā*.]
A Buddhist temple or monastery; the home of a Buddhist religious teacher.

pan-sexual /panˈsɛksjʊəl, -ʃʊəl/ *adjective*. E20.
[from PAN- + SEXUAL.]
Of or pertaining to pan-sexualism. Also, not limited or inhibited in sexual choice.
■ **pan-sexualism** *noun* the view that the sex instinct plays a part in all human thought and activity and is the chief or only source of energy E20. **pan-sexuˈality** *noun* the state or condition of being pan-sexual E20.

pansied /ˈpanzɪd/ *adjective*. L18.
[from PANSY + -ED[2].]
Adorned with pansies, having many pansies.

pansified /ˈpanzɪfʌɪd/ *adjective*. *colloq*. M20.
[from PANSY + -FY + -ED[1].]
Excessively stylized or adorned; affected, effeminate.

Panslavism /panˈslɑːvɪz(ə)m/ *noun*. M19.
[from PAN- + SLAV + -ISM, after German *Panslavismus*.]
The idea of, or advocacy of, the union of all Slavs or all Slavonic peoples in one political organization.
■ **Panslav** *adjective* Panslavonic E20. **Panslavic** *adjective* (*a*) of or pertaining to all Slavonic peoples; (*b*) = PANSLAVISTIC (a): M19. **Panslavist** *noun & adjective* (*a*) *noun* a person who believes in or promotes Panslavism; (*b*) *adjective* Panslavistic: L19. **Panslaˈvistic** *adjective* (*a*) of, pertaining to, or favouring Panslavism; (*b*) = PANSLAVIC (a): M19. **Panslaˈvonic** *adjective* Panslavistic M19.

pansophy /ˈpansəʊfi/ *noun*. M17.
[from PAN- + Greek *sophia* wisdom: see -Y[3].]
1 Universal or encyclopedic knowledge; a scheme or work claiming to embrace the whole of human knowledge. M17.
2 The claim or pretension to universal knowledge. L18.
■ **pansophic** /-ˈsɒf-/ *adjective* L19. **pansophical** /-ˈsɒf-/ *adjective* M17. **pansophism** *noun* = PANSOPHY 2 M19.

panspermia /panˈspəːmɪə/ *noun*. M19.
[Greek = doctrine that the elements were a mixture of all the seeds of things, from *panspermos* containing all kinds of seed, formed as PAN- + *sperma* SPERM.]
Orig., the theory that the atmosphere is full of minute germs which develop on finding a favourable environment. Now, the idea that micro-organisms or chemical precursors of life are present in outer space and able to initiate life on reaching a suitable environment.
■ Also **panspermism** *noun* (now *rare*) L19.

pansy /ˈpanzi/ *noun, adjective, & verb*. Also (earlier) **†pensee**, **†pensy**. LME.
[Old & mod. French *pensée* thought, pansy, from *penser* think from Latin *pensare* weigh, consider, (in Proto-Romance) think.]
▶ **A** *noun*. **1** Any of various plants of the genus *Viola* (which differ from violets in their leafy stipules and upwardly directed lateral petals); *esp*. a garden flower, *V. wittrockiana*, bearing large velvety flowers in various colours and freq. with a dark central blotch; (with specifying word) any of several related wild plants with smaller yellow, purple, or particoloured flowers. Also, a flower of such a plant. LME.
2 The colour of a pansy; *spec*. a shade of blue or purple. L19.
3 An effeminate man; a male homosexual. *colloq*. (*derog*.) E20.
1 mountain pansy a plant of upland pastures, *Viola lutea*. **wild pansy** either of two cornfield weeds, *Viola tricolor* and *V. arvensis*; heartsease.
▶ **B** *adjective*. Effeminate; homosexual; affected. *colloq*. (*derog*.). E20.
▶ **C** *verb trans*. Dress or adorn in an affected or effeminate manner. Freq. *refl*. or foll. by *up*. *colloq*. (*derog*.). M20.
■ **pansyish** *adjective* (*colloq. derog*.) somewhat effeminate, suggestive of a homosexual M20.

pant /pant/ *noun*[1]. E16.
[from PANT *verb*.]
1 Each of a series of short quick laboured breaths, caused by exertion or agitation; a gasp, a catching of the breath. E16.
2 A throb or heave of the chest in laboured breathing; a palpitation of the heart. L16.
3 *transf*. The regular throb and gasping sound of a steam engine. M19.

> 🕮 **1** S. O'FAOLÁIN Rory gabbled between every pant after his climb.

pant /pant/ *noun*[2]. *north*. L16.
[Origin unkn.]
1 A public fountain, cistern, or well, *esp*. one with a spout. L16.
2 A pool into which water or moisture drains; a puddle. E19.

pant /pant/ *noun*[3]. *US* exc. in attrib. use & comb. L19.
[Back-form. from PANTS.]
= PANTS.
Comb.: **pantcoat** a women's coat designed for wearing with trousers; **pantdress** a dress with a divided skirt; **pantskirt** a divided skirt; **pant suit** a trouser suit.

pant /pant/ *verb*. ME.
[Rel. to Old French *pantaisier* be agitated, gasp, pant from Proto-Romance from Greek *phantasioun* cause to imagine, make game of, from *phantasia*: see FANTASY *noun*.]
1 *verb intrans*. Breathe hard or with quick short breaths, as from exertion or agitation; gasp for breath. ME. ▸**b** Go or run (as if) panting. E18. ▸**c** Of an engine etc.: emit hot air, vapour, etc., in loud puffs. M18.
2 *verb intrans*. Of the heart or chest: throb or heave violently or rapidly, esp. from strong emotion; palpitate, pulsate. LME.
3 *verb intrans*. Gasp for air, water, etc.; *fig*. long with breathless eagerness; yearn *for*, *after*, or *to do*. M16.
4 *verb trans*. **a** Say gaspingly; gasp *out*. E17. ▸**†b** Drive *forth* or *out* by agitated gasping. *poet*. E17–E19.
5 *verb intrans*. Of a ship: have its hull move in and out as a result of the stress produced by the movement of the water. Chiefly as ***panting verbal noun***. M19.

> 🕮 **1** R. THOMAS Amy was panting slightly from her climb. *fig*.: POPE The dying gales that pant upon the trees. **2** M. PRIOR For breath his panting bosom heaves. SHELLEY Her very name, But spoken by a stranger, makes my heart Sicken and pant. **3** E. YOUNG All the bliss I pant for, is . . a refuge from severer pain. **4a** A. RANSOME 'It's just the wind we want,' panted Daisy.

■ **pantingly** *adverb* with quick short breaths E17.

pant- *combining form* see PANTO-.

†pantable *noun* var. of PANTOFLE.

pantagamy /panˈtagəmi/ *noun*. M19.
[from alt. of PANTO- + -GAMY.]
A communal system of marriage, in which all the men and women of a household or community are regarded as married to each other, formerly practised by the Perfectionists.

Pantagruelian /pantəgruːˈɛlɪən/ *adjective*. L17.
[from *Pantagruel* (see below) + -IAN.]
Of, pertaining to, characteristic of, or appropriate to Pantagruel, the last of the giants in Rabelais's work *Gargantua and Pantagruel*, represented as an extravagant and coarse humorist who deals satirically with serious subjects; enormous, gargantuan.
■ **Pantagruelically** *adverb* in the manner of Pantagruel E19. **Pantaˈgruelism** *noun* extravagant and coarse humour with a satirical or serious purpose M19. **Pantaˈgruelist** *noun* an imitator, admirer, or student of Pantagruel or Rabelais E17.

pantaleon /panˈtalɪən/ *noun*. M18.
[*Pantaleon* Hebenstreit (1667–1750), German inventor of the instrument.]
Hist. A kind of large dulcimer with one or two hundred strings of metal and gut.

pantalette /pantəˈlɛt/ *noun*. Chiefly *N. Amer*. Also **-let**. M19.
[Dim. of next: see -ETTE.]
In *pl*. & (*rare*) *sing*. Long loose pants with a frill at the bottom of each leg, worn as underwear by women and girls in the 19th cent. Also, women's cycling trousers.
■ **pantaletted** *adjective* wearing pantalettes M19.

pantaloon /pantəˈluːn/ *noun*. L16.
[French *pantalon* from Italian *pantalone*: see -OON.]
▶ **I** Also **P-**.
1 The Venetian character in Italian *commedia dell'arte*, represented as a lean and foolish old man, wearing spectacles, pantaloons (see sense 4), and slippers; in modern harlequinade or pantomime, a character represented as a foolish and vicious old man who is the clown's stooge. L16.
2 A feeble tottering old man; a dotard. *derog*. *obsolete* exc. with allus. to Shakes. L16.
†3 A Scottish courtier in the period after the Restoration. M–L17.

> 🕮 **2** SHAKES. *A.Y.L.* The lean and slipper'd pantaloon . . His youthful hose . . too wide for his shrunk shank.

▶ **II** Usu. (now always) in *pl*.
†4 [from the dress of the stage Pantaloon of the period.] Any of various close-fitting garments for the legs, usu. resembling breeches or hose, worn in the 17th and 18th cents. M17–M18.
5 Tight-fitting trousers fastened with ribbons or buttons below the calf or by straps passing under the instep, which were introduced late in the 18th cent. and began to supersede knee-breeches (*Hist*.); trousers of any kind (*colloq*.); *spec*. women's loose baggy trousers. L18.
■ **pantalooned** *adjective* wearing pantaloons L18. **pantaloonery** *noun* the performance of a pantaloon in pantomimes E19.

†pantarbe *noun*. L16–M18.
[Old French from Greek *pantarbē*.]
A precious stone fabled to act as a magnet to gold.

†pantas *noun*. L16–M19.
[French *pantais*, *-ois*, from Old French *pantoiser*, *pantaisier*: see PANT *verb*.]
A lung disease of hawks. Also, jaundice in cattle.

pantec /panˈtɛk/ *noun*. *Austral*. Also **-tech**. L20.
[Abbreviation of next.]
A large van forming the rear part of an articulated lorry.

pantechnicon /panˈtɛknɪk(ə)n/ *noun*. M19.
[from PAN- + Greek *tekhnikon* neut. of *tekhnikos*: see TECHNIC.]
1 A large warehouse for storing furniture. Orig. (the name of) a large building in London constructed to house a bazaar of all kinds of artistic work but converted into a furniture repository. M19.
2 A furniture van. Also ***pantechnicon van***. L19.

pantellerite /panˈtɛlərʌɪt/ *noun*. L19.
[from *Pantelleria*, an island between Sicily and Tunis + -ITE[1].]
GEOLOGY. A kind of rhyolite containing feldspar, quartz, and aegirine.

panter /ˈpantə/ *noun*[1]. *obsolete* exc. *Hist*. ME.
[Anglo-Norman *paneter* = Old & mod. French *panetier* from Proto-Romance (cf. medieval Latin *panetarius*) from late Latin *panarius* bread-seller, from *panis* bread: see -ER[2].]
The officer of a household who supplied the bread and was in charge of the pantry.

panter /ˈpantə/ *noun*[2]. *obsolete* exc. *dial*. ME.
[Old French (mod. *pantière*), in medieval Latin *panthera* from Latin = hunting-net, Greek *panthēra* large net, formed as PAN- + *thēran* to hunt.]
A fowling net, a fowler's snare; a trap, a noose.

panter /ˈpantə/ *noun*[3]. L17.
[from PANT *verb* + -ER[1].]
1 The heart. *slang*. L17.
2 A person who or thing which pants. E18.

panterer /ˈpant(ə)rə/ *noun*. LME.
[Expanded form of PANTER *noun*[1] (see -ER[1]): cf. *adulterer*, *upholsterer*, etc.]
Hist. = PANTER *noun*[1].

Panthalassa /panθəˈlasə/ *noun*. L19.
[from PAN- + Greek *thalassa* sea.]
GEOLOGY. A universal sea or single ocean, such as would have surrounded Pangaea.

panthea *noun* pl. of PANTHEUM.

pantheism /ˈpanθiːɪz(ə)m/ *noun*. M18.
[formed as next + -ISM.]
1 The belief or philosophical theory that God and the universe are identical (implying a denial of the personality and transcendence of God); the identification of God with the forces of nature and natural substances. M18.
2 Worship that admits or tolerates all gods. M19.

pantheist /ˈpanθiːɪst/ *noun*. E18.
[from PAN- + Greek *theos* god + -IST.]
A person who holds the doctrine of pantheism.
■ **pantheˈistic** *adjective* M18. **pantheˈistical** *adjective* M19. **pantheˈistically** *adverb* M19.

pantheology /panθɪˈɒlədʒi/ *noun*. M17.
[from PAN- + THEOLOGY.]
†**1** The whole sum of theology or divinity. Only in M17.
2 A synthetic theology comprehending all gods and all religions. L17.

pantheon /ˈpanθɪən/ *noun*. ME.
[Latin from Greek *pantheion*, formed as PAN- + *theios* divine, *theos* god.]
1 A temple dedicated to all the gods, or where images or other memorials of all the gods of a nation are collected; *spec.* (**the Pantheon**) the circular building in Rome orig. built for this purpose. ME. ▸**b** A building resembling or compared to the Pantheon at Rome; *esp.* a building in which the illustrious dead of a nation are buried or have memorials. E18.
2 A dwelling-place of all the gods. Also, an assemblage of gods; all the gods acknowledged or worshipped by a people; *transf.* a group of individuals who are admired, respected, or distinguished. M16.
3 A treatise on all the gods. L17.
†**4** A place of public entertainment. Only in L18.

📖 **2** G. F. MACLEAR Highest in the Celtic Pantheon was the golden-handed sun. Y. MENUHIN Furtwängler in my personal pantheon ranks with Walter as an exponent of the German tradition. *Washington Post* With Ella Fitzgerald and Sara Vaughan, she is in the pantheon of great . . jazz vocalists.

panther /ˈpanθə/ *noun*. ME.
[Old French *pantere* (mod. *panthère*) from Latin *panthera* from Greek *panthēr*.]
1 Orig., an exotic animal of the cat family that was supposedly distinct from and larger than the leopard. Now, a leopard, *esp.* a black one. ME.
2 The puma; the jaguar. *US*. L17.
3 Strong liquor, usu. spirits, esp. of a local or home manufacture. *US slang*. M20.
4 *ellipt.* A member of the Black Panthers. M20.
Comb.: **panther juice** = sense 3 above; **panther-lily** *US* a lily, *Lilium pardalinum*, of the south-western US; also called ***leopard lily***; **panther piss** = sense 3 above.
■ **pantheress** *noun* a female panther; *fig.* a woman who is fierce or cruel but beautiful: M19. **pantherine** /-rʌɪn, -rɪn/ *adjective* [Latin *pantherinus*] resembling a panther in appearance or fierceness; of, pertaining to, or characteristic of a panther: M17. **pantherish** *adjective* somewhat resembling or characteristic of a panther L19.

pantheum /panˈθiːəm/ *noun*. Pl. ***-thea*** /-ˈθiːə/. E18.
[Late Latin, use as noun of neut. of Latin *pantheus* in SIGNUM PANTHEUM.]
= SIGNUM PANTHEUM.

pantie /ˈpanti/ *noun*. *colloq.* Also **-ty**, (in comb.) **panti-**. M19.
[Dim. of PANTS: see -Y⁶, -IE.]
1 In *pl.* Men's trousers or shorts. Chiefly *derog.* M19.
2 In *pl.* & (*rare* exc. *attrib.* or in *comb.* & *US*) *sing.* Short-legged or legless pants worn as underwear by women and girls. E20.
Comb.: **pantie-girdle** a woman's girdle with a crotch shaped like pants; **pantie hose**, **pantihose** women's tights; **pantie leg** the leg part of a pair of panties; **pantie raid** *N. Amer.* a prank involving the raiding of women's rooms for trophies of underwear; **pantie-waist** *noun* & *adjective* (*N. Amer.*) (**a**) *noun* a sissy, a coward; also (*rare*), a garment, usu. for children, consisting of panties attached to a bodice; (**b**) *adjective* effeminate, weak.

pantile /ˈpantʌɪl/ *noun*. M17.
[from PAN *noun*¹ + TILE *noun*, prob. after Dutch *dakpan* roof pan (cf. German *Dachpfanne*, *Pfannenziegel* pantile).]
1 a A roofing-tile curved to an ogee shape, one curve being much larger than the other so that the greater part forms a concave channel for the descent of water while the other forms a narrow ridge overlapping the edge of the adjoining tile. Also, a simply curved tile laid so that a convex one overlaps the join of two adjacent concave ones. M17. ▸**b** Pantiles collectively or as a material. L17. ▸†**c** A flat Dutch or Flemish paving tile. L18–E19.
2 A hard flat biscuit (chiefly NAUTICAL); a flat cake with jam on it. *slang*. L19.
Comb.: **pantile-lath** an extra stout lath used for supporting pantiles on a roof.
■ **pantiled** *adjective* covered with pantiles L18. **pantiler** *noun* [from the pantile roofs of rural Nonconformist chapels] *Hist.* a Nonconformist M19. **pantiling** *noun* the covering of a roof with pantiles; pantiles collectively: E19.

pantine /panˈtiːn/ *noun*. *obsolete* exc. *Hist.* M18.
[French *pantin*, †-*ine*.]
A pasteboard human figure with a jointed neck, body, and limbs, which move when pulled by a thread or wire, fashionable as a toy in the mid 18th cent.

pantisocracy /pantɪˈsɒkrəsi/ *noun*. Now chiefly *Hist.* L18.
[from PANTO- + ISOCRACY.]
A Utopian form of social organization in which all are equal in social position and responsibility.
■ **panˈtisocrat** *noun* a person who advocates or promotes pantisocracy L18. **pantisoˈcratic** *adjective* L18. **pantisoˈcratical** *adjective* E19. **pantisocratist** *noun* E19.

pantle /ˈpant(ə)l/ *verb intrans.* *obsolete* exc. *dial.* M17.
[from PANT *verb* + -LE³.]
Pant.

pantler /ˈpantlə/ *noun*. *obsolete* exc. *Hist.* ME.
[App. alt. of PANTER *noun*¹, PANTERER, perh. after BUTLER.]
= PANTER *noun*¹.

pantless /ˈpantlɪs/ *adjective*. L19.
[from PANT *noun*³ + -LESS.]
Wearing no pants.

panto /ˈpantəʊ/ *noun* & *adjective*. *colloq.* Pl. of noun **-os**. M19.
[Abbreviation.]
= PANTOMIME *noun* 3, *adjective*.

panto- /ˈpantəʊ/ *combining form*. Before a vowel **pant-**.
[Greek, combining form of *pan*: see PAN-, -O-.]
Used in words adopted from Greek and in English words modelled on these, with the sense 'all'.
■ **Panˈtocrator** *noun* (CHRISTIAN CHURCH) (**a**) the Almighty; God, Christ; (**b**) an artistic representation of Christ, esp. as a characteristic form in Byzantine art: L19. **pantoˈlogic** *adjective* pantological M19. **pantoˈlogical** *adjective* of or pertaining to pantology E19. **panˈtologist** *noun* a person studying or versed in universal knowledge M19. **panˈtology** *noun* (**a**) a survey of all branches of knowledge; universal knowledge; (**b**) a compendium of universal information: E19. **panˈtometer** *noun* an instrument for measuring angles, distances, and heights L17. **pantoˈmetric** *adjective* of or pertaining to pantometry E19. **panˈtometry** *noun* (*obsolete* exc. *Hist.*) universal measurement M17. **panˈtophagist** *noun* (*rare*) a person or animal which eats things of all kinds, an omnivore E19. **panˈtophagy** *noun* (*rare*) omnivorousness M19. **pantopragˈmatic** *adjective* & *noun* (*joc.*) (**a**) *adjective* meddling in or occupied with everything; (**b**) *noun* a pantopragmatic person; in *pl.*, the practice of meddling in or with everything: M19. **pantoscope** *noun* (*Hist.*) (**a**) a type of photographic lens with a very wide angle; (**b**) a pantoscopic camera: L19. **pantoˈscopic** *adjective* having a wide range of vision; ***pantoscopic camera***, a panoramic camera: L19. **pantothere** *noun* (PALAEONTOLOGY) a small early therian mammal of the extinct order Pantotheria of the American Jurassic M20.

Pantocain /ˈpantə(ʊ)keɪn/ *noun*. Also **p-**, **-caine**. M20.
[German, formed as PANTO- + -CAINE.]
PHARMACOLOGY. (Proprietary name for) the anaesthetic amethocaine.

pantofle /ˈpantəf(ə)l, panˈtɒf(ə)l/ *noun*. *arch.* Also **-toufle** /-ˈtuːf(ə)l/, †**-table**, & other vars. L15.
[French *pantoufle* from Italian *pantofola*, †*pantufola*, of unkn. origin.]
A (high-heeled or oriental) slipper or loose shoe. Also, an outdoor overshoe.
†**on one's pantofles** on one's dignity.
¶ Cf. EN PANTOUFLES.

pantograph /ˈpantə(ʊ)grɑːf/ *noun*. Also **pent-** /ˈpɛnt-/. E18.
[from PANTO- + -GRAPH.]
1 An instrument for mechanically copying a diagram etc., esp. on a different scale, consisting of a jointed adjustable parallelogram with tracing points at opposite corners. E18.
2 A jointed self-adjusting framework on the top of an electric vehicle for conveying the current from overhead wires. E20.
■ **panˈtographer** *noun* †(**a**) = PANTOGRAPH 1; (**b**) a person who produces diagrams etc. with a pantograph: M18. **pantoˈgraphic** *adjective* M18. **pantoˈgraphical** *adjective* E19. **pantoˈgraphically** *adverb* L19. **panˈtography** *noun* (*rare*) (**a**) complete description; (**b**) use of a pantograph: E19.

pantoic /panˈtəʊɪk/ *adjective*. M20.
[formed as PANTOYL + -IC.]
CHEMISTRY. ***pantoic acid***, an unstable carboxylic acid of which pantothenic acid is a derivative; 1,3-dihydroxy-2-dimethylbutanoic acid, $CH_2OH{\cdot}C(CH_3)_2{\cdot}CHOH{\cdot}COOH$.
■ **ˈpantoate** *noun* a salt or ester of pantoic acid M20.

pantomime /ˈpantəmʌɪm/ *noun*, *adjective*, & *verb*. Also (earlier) in Latin form †**-mimus**, pl. **-mimi**. L16.
[French, or Latin *pantomimus* from Greek *pantomimos* adjective & noun: see PANTO-, MIME.]
▸ **A** *noun*. **1** *Hist.* A mimic actor, esp. in ancient Rome; a person who expressed meaning through gesture and action without words. L16.
2 A dramatic entertainment in which performers express meaning through gestures accompanied by music. M17.
3 A traditional theatrical performance, orig. in mime, now consisting of a dramatized fairy tale or nursery story, with music, dancing, topical jokes, and conventional characters, freq. played by actors of the opposite sex from the characters, chiefly performed in Britain around Christmas. M18. ▸**b** *fig.* An absurd or outrageous piece of behaviour. *colloq.* M20.
4 (A) significant gesture without speech; (a) mime. L18.

📖 **3** *Times Lit. Suppl.* The annual pantomime . . opens on boxing day. *Guardian* Last Christmas he was back on stage in pantomime in Manchester. **b** I. MURDOCH He waved his camera case rhythmically and clapped his hands . . . Dora stared at this pantomime. **4** H. KELLER She drops the signs and pantomime she used before, as soon as she has words.

▸ **B** *adjective*. Of, pertaining to, or characteristic of (a) pantomime. M18.

📖 *Mail on Sunday* One of the greatest pantomime artists I ever saw. *Independent* The pantomime horse would distract the players by galloping across the stage.

▸ **C** *verb*. **1** *verb intrans.* Express oneself in mime. Also, behave as though in a pantomime. M18.
2 *verb trans.* Express or represent by pantomime. M19.

📖 **1** J. UPDIKE Van Horne . . pantomimed with his uncanny hands.

■ **pantomimist** *noun* a person who writes or acts in a pantomime. M19.

pantomimic /pantəˈmɪmɪk/ *noun* & *adjective*. E17.
[Latin *pantomimicus*, from *pantomimus* PANTOMIME: see -IC.]
▸†**A** *noun*. = PANTOMIME *noun* 1. Only in 17.
▸ **B** *adjective*. **1** Of the nature of pantomime; expressed by mime. L17.
2 Of, belonging to, or characteristic of (a) pantomime. E19.

📖 **1** M. ALLINGHAM Ritchie wrinkled his nose and achieved . . pantomimic disapproval.

■ **pantomimical** *adjective* (now *rare*) = PANTOMIMIC *adjective* M17. **pantomimically** *adverb* M19.

†**pantomimus** *noun*, *adjective*, & *verb* see PANTOMIME.

pantomography /pantəˈmɒgrəfi/ *noun*. M20.
[from PAN(ORAMIC + TOMOGRAPHY.]
MEDICINE. A form of tomography for obtaining radiographs of curved layers of an object, esp. the teeth and jaws, by rotation of the body and film during exposure.
■ **panˈtomogram** *noun* a radiograph obtained by pantomography M20. **panˈtomograph** *noun* an instrument used in pantomography M20. **pantomoˈgraphic**, **pantomoˈgraphical** *adjectives* M20.

pantonal /panˈtəʊn(ə)l/ *adjective*. M20.
[from PAN- + TONAL *adjective*.]
Including all tonalities; in twelve-tone music, atonal.

Pantone /ˈpantəʊn/ *noun*. M20.
[from PAN- + TONE *noun*.]
(Proprietary name for) a system for matching colours, used in specifying printing inks.

pantopod /ˈpantə(ʊ)pɒd/ *noun*. L19.
[mod. Latin *Pantopoda*, formed as PANTO- + Greek *pod-*, *pous* foot.]
ZOOLOGY. = PYCNOGONID.

Pantopon /ˈpantə(ʊ)pɒn/ *noun*. Also **p-**. E20.
[from PANT(O- + OP(IUM + -*on*.]
PHARMACOLOGY. A mixture of the hydrochlorides of opium alkaloids. Cf. OMNOPON.
¶ Proprietary name in the US.

pantothenic /pantə(ʊ)ˈθɛnɪk/ *adjective*. M20.
[from Greek *pantothen* from every side + -IC.]
BIOCHEMISTRY. ***pantothenic acid***, a vitamin of the B complex, consisting of β-alanine linked to a pantoyl residue, which is widely distributed in animal and plant tissues and is essential (mainly as part of coenzyme A) for the oxidation of fats and carbohydrates.
■ **pantothenate** *noun* a salt or ester of pantothenic acid M20.

pantoufle *noun* var. of PANTOFLE.

pantoum *noun* var. of PANTUN.

pantoyl /ˈpantəʊʌɪl, -əʊɪl, -ɔɪl/ *noun*. M20.
[from PANTO(THENIC + -YL.]
BIOCHEMISTRY. The optically active radical $HOCH_2C(CH_3)_2CH(OH)CO{\cdot}$, present in pantothenic acid.
Comb.: **pantoyltaurine** a sulphonic acid, $C_8H_{17}O_6NS$, which inhibits the action of pantothenic acid in micro-organisms.

pantry /ˈpantri/ *noun*. ME.
[Anglo-Norman *panetrie*, Old French *paneterie*, from *panetier* PANTER *noun*¹: see -RY.]
1 A small room or a cupboard in which provisions, crockery, cutlery, table linen, etc., are kept. ME.
2 A tearoom, a café, a food bar. Only in proper names, with cap. initial. M20.
Comb.: **pantryman** a man in charge of or employed in a pantry; a butler, a butler's helper.

pants /pan(t)s/ *noun pl.* & *adjective*. Orig. *N. Amer.* M19.
[Abbreviation of *pantaloons*: see PANTALOON, -S¹. Cf. PANT *noun*³.]
1 Trousers. Chiefly *N. Amer.* M19.
2 A pair of underpants. Cf. KNICKERS 2. E20.
3 Rubbish; drivel. Also as *adjective*: useless, substandard. *slang*. L20.

📖 **1** ***loon pants***, ***toreador pants***, etc. **3** *Total Film* He's pleasantly surprised by our acting . . . He thought we were going to be absolute pants. *Pi Mag* You . . don't realise how pants it all is until it's all done and dusted.

For other words beginning with *pan-* see the entry for **pan-**

Phrases: **beat the pants off**, **bore the pants off**, **charm the pants off**, **scare the pants off** beat, bore, charm, scare, completely or utterly. **by the seat of one's pants** (of handling an aeroplane, a car, etc.) by instinct or experience as opp. to technology or science; barely; with difficulty. ***charm the pants off***: see ***beat the pants off*** above. **keep one's pants on** keep calm, not panic or get angry. ***scare the pants off***: see ***beat the pants off*** above. ***take the lead out one's pants***: see LEAD *noun*[1]. ***wear the pants***: see WEAR *verb*[1]. ***wet one's pants***: see WET *verb*. **with one's pants down** *colloq.* in a compromising situation, in a state of embarrassing unpreparedness.

Comb.: **pants rabbit** *US slang* (chiefly MILITARY) a body louse; **pants suit** a trouser suit.

pantun /pan'tu:n/ *noun*. Also **-toum** /-'tu:m/. L18.
[Malay.]
A Malay verse-form, also imitated in French and English, with an *abab* rhyme scheme.

panty *noun* var. of PANTIE.

panung /'pɑ:nʊŋ/ *noun*. M19.
[Thai.]
A Thai garment consisting of a long piece of cloth draped round the lower body (orig. worn by both sexes but now chiefly by females in rural areas).

panurgic /pa'nə:dʒɪk/ *adjective*. *rare*. L19.
[Late Greek *panourgikos* knavish, from *panourgos* ready to do anything, formed as PAN- + *ergon* work.]
Able or ready to do anything.

panyar /pə'njɑ:/ *verb trans. arch.* Infl. **-rr-**. E18.
[Portuguese *penhorar* seize as a pledge or security from Latin *pignorare*, *-erare* pledge, (in medieval Latin) take in pledge, plunder, invade.]
In W. Africa: seize as a guarantee or security; *euphem.* seize as plunder, steal, *esp.* kidnap as a slave.

panzanella /panzə'nɛlə, pantsə-, *foreign* ˌpantsa'nɛlla/ *noun*. M20.
[Italian, from *pane* bread + *zanella* small basket.]
A type of Tuscan salad made with anchovies, chopped salad vegetables, and bread soaked in dressing.

panzer /'panzə, *foreign* 'pantsər/ *noun & adjective*. Also **P-**. M20.
[German = mail, coat of mail.]
▶ **A** *noun*. (A member of) a German armoured unit. Also, a German tank. M20.
▶ **B** *attrib*. or as *adjective*. Of, pertaining to, or designating a panzer; *transf.* heavily armoured. M20.

📖 N. BARBER He's leading a crack new panzer division.

paolo /'paʊləʊ/ *noun*. Pl. **-li** /-li/. E17.
[Italian, from Latin *Paulus* Paul.]
Hist. An obsolete Italian silver coin, named after Pope Paul V, worth about five old pence.

pap /pap/ *noun*[1]. Now *arch.* & *dial.* ME.
[Prob. from Scandinavian base imit. of the sound of sucking. Cf. Latin *papilla* nipple.]
1 a A woman's nipple or breast. ME. ▶**b** A man's nipple or pectoral swelling. LME. ▶**c** An animal's teat. M17.
2 *transf.* **a** A small round tumour or swelling; a pimple. Now only in ***pap of the hause*** *Scot.*, the uvula. LME. ▶**b** A conical hill summit or small peak. Now *rare* exc. in place-names. M17.

pap /pap/ *noun*[2] & *verb*. LME.
[Prob. from Middle & mod. Low German *pappe* corresp. to Middle German *pap* (German *Pappe*), Middle Dutch *pappe* (Dutch *pap*) prob. from medieval Latin, from Latin *pappare* eat.]
▶ **A** *noun*. **1** Soft or semi-liquid food for infants or invalids, made of bread, meal, etc., with water or milk. LME. ▶**b** *fig.* Something easy or pleasant to get, have, understand, etc.; *spec.* light or trivial reading matter, entertainment, etc. M16. ▶**c** *transf.* A political appointment or grant; patronage. *US colloq.* E19.
2 A mash, a paste, a pulp of powder and liquid. LME. ▶†**b** The pulp of an apple, esp. when roasted. L16–M18. ▶**c** In Africa and the Caribbean: porridge, usu. made with maize meal. M19.

📖 **1** P. TOYNBEE Lost my false teeth again .. the bloody inconvenience of eating pap. **b** *Scotland on Sunday* Is this .. the best reason .. for dishing out pap like *Wheel of Fortune*?

Comb.: **pap-boat** *arch.* a boat-shaped vessel for holding pap for feeding infants.
▶ **B** *verb trans.* Infl. **-pp-**.
1 Feed with pap; feed *up*. LME.
2 Treat with pap; apply a pap or pulp to. *rare*. M17.

pap /pap/ *noun*[3]. Chiefly *US*. M19.
[Abbreviation.]
= PAPA *noun*[2]. Also, any older man.

Pap /pap/ *attrib. adjective*. Also **p-**. M20.
[Abbreviation of PAPANICOLAOU.]
Designating a test used to detect (vaginal, uterine, or esp. cervical) cancer by the Papanicolaou technique.

papa /pə'pɑ:/ *noun*[1]. In sense 1 also †**pape**, (esp. as a title) **P-**. In sense 2 also in Greek form **papas** /'pɑ:pəs/. OE.
[ecclesiastical Latin = bishop, later spec. the Bishop of Rome: see POPE *noun*[1]. In sense 2 translating Greek *papas*.]
1 The Pope. Now chiefly as a form of address or a title. OE.
2 A parish priest; any member of the lower ranks of the clergy in the Eastern Orthodox Church. L16.

papa /pə'pɑ:, 'pɑ:pə/ *noun*[2]. L17.
[French from late Latin *papa* from Greek *pappas*, *papas* father. Cf. POPPA.]
1 Father. Chiefly as a child's form of address. *arch.* L17.
2 *transf.* A male lover. *US slang*. E20.
2 ***sweet papa***: see SWEET *adjective & adverb*.
■ **pa'paship** *noun* (*joc.*) the position of being a papa, fatherhood E19.

papa /'pɑ:pɑ:/ *noun*[3]. L19.
[Maori.]
A soft bluish clay or mudstone found in the North Island of New Zealand.

papabile /papa'bi:le, pə'pɑ:bɪli/ *adjective & noun*. Also (as adjective) **-li** /-li/. M20.
[Italian: see PAPA *noun*[1].]
▶ **A** *adjective*. (Of a prelate) worthy of or eligible to be elected Pope; *gen.* suitable for high office. M20.
▶ **B** *absol.* as *noun*. Pl. **-li** /-li/. A prelate regarded as eligible to be elected Pope; *gen.* one regarded as suitable for high office. Usu. in *pl.* M20.

papable /'peɪpəb(ə)l/ *adjective*. *rare*. L16.
[French from Italian PAPABILE: see -BLE.]
Eligible to be elected Pope; qualified for the papacy.

papacy /'peɪpəsi/ *noun*. LME.
[medieval Latin *papatia*, formed as PAPA *noun*[1]: see -ACY.]
1 The position or office of Pope (of Rome); the tenure of office of a pope. LME.
2 The (system of) government headed by the Pope; *Hist.* the papal government regarded as a European State. M16.

Papago /'papəgəʊ, 'pɑ:-/ *noun & adjective*. M19.
[Spanish from Amer. Indian name.]
▶ **A** *noun*. Pl. same, **-os**.
1 A member of an American Indian people of the south-western US and northern Mexico. M19.
2 The Uto-Aztecan language of this people or (occas.) of the closely related Pima Indians; Pima. E20.
▶ **B** *attrib.* or as *adjective*. Of or pertaining to the Papago or their language. M19.

papain /pə'peɪn, pə'pʌɪn/ *noun*. L19.
[from *papaya* var. of PAWPAW *noun*[1] + -IN[1].]
BIOCHEMISTRY. A mixture of proteolytic enzymes obtained from the unripe fruit and latex of the pawpaw, *Carica papaya*, which is used esp. as a meat tenderizer and in clarifying liquids for drinking. Also, a pure protease extractable from this.

papal /'peɪp(ə)l/ *adjective*. LME.
[Old & mod. French from medieval Latin *papalis*, formed as PAPA *noun*[1]: see -AL[1].]
1 Of or pertaining to a pope, the Pope, or the papacy. LME.
2 Supporting or following the Pope; belonging to the Roman Catholic Church. Now *rare*. L16.

📖 **1** J. GARDNER Hildebrand accepted of the papal tiara under the title of Gregory VII.

Special collocations: **papal court** (chiefly *Hist.*) (***a***) the entourage of the Pope; (***b***) = CURIA 3. **papal cross**: with three transoms. **Papal See** = SEE *noun*[1] 2b. **Papal States** *Hist.* the Pope's temporal dominions, *esp.* those in central Italy. **papal system** the system of organization within the Roman Catholic Church, in which the Pope is both religious and political leader. ***papal vicar***: see VICAR 3. ***Papal Zouave***: see ZOUAVE 1b.
■ **papalism** *noun* L19. **papalist** *noun & adjective* (***a***) *noun* a supporter of the Pope or the papacy; (***b***) *adjective* of or pertaining to papalism or papalists: M18. **papally** *adverb* in a papal manner; from a papal point of view; as a pope: E17. †**papalty** *noun* = PAPALITY 1 L16–M19.

papalagi /pɑ:'pɑ:lɑŋi/ *noun & adjective*. *NZ & Samoa*. Also ***papalangi*** /pɑ:'pɑ:lɑŋi/, ***palagi*** /'pɑ:lɑŋi/. L19.
[Samoan *papālagi*.]
▶ **A** *noun*. Pl. same. A white person, esp. a European (as opp. to a Samoan). L19.
▶ **B** *adjective*. Of, pertaining to, or designating a *papalagi*. E20.

†**Papalin** *noun*. Also **-ine**. E17–L18.
[French *papalin* from Italian *papalino* from *papale*, from medieval Latin *papalis*: see PAPAL, -INE[1].]
A supporter of the Pope or papal system.

papalise *verb* var. of PAPALIZE.

†**papality** *noun*. LME.
[Old & mod. French *papalité* (mod. *papauté*) from medieval Latin *papalitas*, from *papalis*: see PAPAL, -ITY.]
1 Papal authority or office. LME–M17.
2 A papal doctrine. *rare*. Only in E19.

papalize /'peɪp(ə)lʌɪz/ *verb*. Also **-ise**. E17.
[from PAPAL + -IZE.]
1 *verb intrans.* Become papal in practice or sympathies; romanize. Chiefly as ***papalizing*** *ppl adjective*. E17.
2 *verb trans.* Make papal; imbue with papal principles or doctrines. M19.

papaloi /'pap(ə)lwɑ:/ *noun*. Pl. **-s**, same. L19.
[Haitian creole *papalwa*, from *papa* father + *lwa* LOA *noun*[2].]
A voodoo priest. Cf. MAMALOI.

Papanicolaou /ˌpapənɪkə'lɑ:u:, papə'nɪkəlaʊ/ *noun*. M20.
[German. N. *Papanicolaou* (1883–1962), Greek-born US anatomist.]
MEDICINE. Used *attrib.* with ref. to a technique devised by Papanicolaou for examining exfoliated or secreted cells, chiefly as a means of detecting (vaginal, cervical, or uterine) cancer. Chiefly in ***Papanicolaou technique***, ***Papanicolaou test***. Cf. PAP *adjective*.

paparazzo /papə'ratsəʊ/ *noun*. Pl. **-zzi** /-tsi/. M20.
[Italian.]
A (freelance) photographer who pursues celebrities to take their pictures.

paparchy /'peɪpɑ:ki/ *noun*. *rare*. M19.
[from PAPA *noun*[1] + -ARCHY.]
Papal rule or sovereignty; government by a pope.

papas *noun* see PAPA *noun*[1].

papauma /papa'ʊmə/ *noun*. *NZ*. Also **-mu** /-mʊ/. L19.
[Maori.]
A small evergreen tree or shrub, *Griselinia littoralis*, of the dogwood family, having large thick shiny leaves. Also called ***broad-leaf***.

papaveraceous /pəpeɪvə'reɪʃəs/ *adjective*. M19.
[from mod. Latin *Papaveraceae*, from Latin *papaver* poppy: see -ACEOUS.]
BOTANY. Of or pertaining to the Papaveraceae or poppy family.

papaverine /pə'peɪvərʌɪn, -'pav-, -i:n/ *noun*. M19.
[from Latin *papaver* POPPY *noun* + -INE[5].]
BIOCHEMISTRY. A colourless insoluble alkaloid, $C_{20}H_{21}NO_4$, found in opium and used to alleviate muscle spasm and asthma.

papaverous /pə'peɪv(ə)rəs, -'pav-/ *adjective*. *rare*. M17.
[formed as prec. + -OUS.]
Pertaining to, resembling, or allied to the poppy; *fig.* soporific.

papaw *noun*[1] var. of PAWPAW *noun*[1].

Papaw *noun*[2] var. of PAWPAW *noun*[2].

papaya *noun* see PAWPAW *noun*[1].

†**pape** *noun* see PAPA *noun*[1].

paper /'peɪpə/ *noun & adjective*. ME.
[Anglo-Norman *papir*, Old & mod. French *papier* from Latin *papyrus* PAPYRUS.]
▶ **A** *noun*. **1** Material in the form of thin flexible (freq. white) sheets made from the pulp of wood or other fibrous matter which is dried, pressed, bleached, etc., and used for writing, printing, or drawing on, or for wrapping, covering, etc.; a particular kind of this; a sheet or piece of this. ME. ▶**b** Material similar to paper in function, consistency, or texture, but differently made; a particular kind of this; a sheet or piece of this. LME. ▶**c** Material used in building etc. in the form of thick boards made from paper pulp. L17.
2 Paper bearing writing; written documents collectively. LME.
3 A sheet or piece of paper bearing writing; a document written or printed on paper. In *pl.*, written notes, letters, official documents, etc.; formerly *spec.*, State papers. LME. ▶†**b** A notice fastened on the back of a criminal undergoing punishment, specifying his or her offence. E16–L17. ▶**c** In *pl.* Documents attesting the identity, credentials, etc., of a person, esp. as required for travel to or in a certain country; documents carried by a ship indicating ownership, nationality, destination, etc. L17. ▶**d** A printed set of questions to be answered at one session in an examination; the written answers given to these. M19.
4 a A piece of paper serving as a wrapper or receptacle, esp. when containing an amount *of* a commodity; *spec.* a cigarette-paper. E16. ▶**b** A curl-paper. Usu. in *pl.* M18. ▶**c** A measure or dose of a drug contained in a folded piece of paper. M20.
5 A newspaper. M17.
6 An essay, a dissertation, an article, *esp.* one read at a conference etc. or sent for publication in a journal. M17.
7 COMMERCE. Negotiable documents, bills of exchange, etc., collectively; banknotes as opp. to coin. L17.
8 Wallpaper. M18.
9 *slang*. **a** THEATRICAL. Free tickets or passes to a theatrical performance. Also, the people admitted by free tickets or passes. L18. ▶**b** A forged cheque or document. *US*. M19. ▶**c** A playing-card; *esp.* (*collect. sing.*) marked playing-cards.

For other words beginning with *pan-* see the entry for **pan-**

US. M19. ▸**d** A poster, a placard; posters or publicity material collectively. *US.* L19.

> 📖 **1** ***airmail paper, bond paper, brown paper, carbon paper, corrugated paper, crêpe paper, drawing paper, graph paper, India paper, lavatory paper, parcel paper, scrap paper, tissue-paper, toilet paper, tracing-paper, writing-paper***, etc. **b** ***hieratic paper, rice paper, straw paper***, etc. **3** A. J. CRONIN He consulted a paper on the desk. A. BULLOCK Attlee had circulated to the Cabinet a paper dealing with policy towards Germany. JANET MORGAN Bills preserved among Frederick's papers. ***Government paper, Green Paper, order-paper, voting-paper***, etc. **c** O. MANNING Recalled to his regiment. His papers came yesterday. R. MACAULAY I crossed . . into Israel . . among great difficulties and a great fuss about my papers. **d** A. WILSON Gerald sat . . marking the History Finals papers. ***examination paper, test paper***, etc. **4** M. K. RAWLINGS I need me some thread and a paper o' needles. R. L. SIMON I . . took out some papers and started to roll a joint. **5** ***comic paper, evening paper, local paper, quality paper, trade paper***, etc. **6** C. P. SNOW He had written two good papers on molecular structure. B. BOVA The subject of a paper he'll deliver at an international conference of psychiatrists. **7** *Wall Street Journal* The ever-narrowing spread between five-year and 10-year paper. **8** C. RAYNER A ferociously plushed and crimsoned paper which was patterned with festoons of feathers.

▸**B** *adjective.* **1** Made or consisting of paper. L16. ▸**b** Resembling paper, *esp.* thin, flimsy; *fig.* feeble, insubstantial. E17.

2 *fig.* **a** Consisting of or carried on by means of letters written to journals etc. L16. ▸**b** Existing only in written form and not in reality; theoretical; unrealized. M17.

> 📖 **1** ALDOUS HUXLEY He . . decreed . . that we should be given paper hats. *Parents* Stick paper shapes on for eyes and nose. **b** R. SOUTH What Paper Walls such persons are apt to inclose themselves with. **2a** J. BENTHAM A paper war between the Dutchess of Kingston and Foote. **b** *Country Life* This enormous capital appreciation may have made some landowners paper millionaires. *ASTMS Industry News* A real and not a paper equal opportunity employer.

Phrases etc.: **commit to paper** write down. ***end-paper***: see END *noun*. ***filter-paper***: see FILTER *noun*. ***height to paper***: see HEIGHT *noun*. ***iron paper***: see IRON *noun & adjective*. ***LIQUID paper***. ***low to paper***: see LOW *adjective*. **make the papers** gain publicity, become famous or notorious. **on paper** (*a*) in writing; (*b*) in theory; according to written or printed evidence. ***put pen to paper***: see PEN *noun*². ***scrap of paper***: see SCRAP *noun*¹. **send in one's papers** (of a military officer) resign one's commission. ***vessel of paper***: see VESSEL *noun*². ***walking-papers***: see WALKING *noun*. ***waste paper***: see WASTE *adjective*. ***White Paper***: see WHITE *adjective*.

Special collocations & comb.: **paper bag** a small bag made of paper. **paper-bank** †(*a*) a bank issuing banknotes; (*b*) a receptacle for the collection of waste paper for recycling. **paper-bark** (*a*) *Austral.* any of several trees with papery bark which peels off in layers, *esp.* the cajuput, *Melaleuca leucadendron*, and other trees of this genus; the durable bark of the cajuput; (*b*) ***paper-bark maple***, a Chinese maple, *Acer griseum*, with flaky, light brown bark. **paper birch**: see BIRCH *noun* 1. **paperboard** (*a*) pasteboard; (*b*) in *pl.*, boards with a paper cover, used in bookbinding. **paperbound** (chiefly *US*) = PAPERBACK *noun*. **paper-boy**: who delivers or sells newspapers. **paper cable** an electric cable insulated with paper. **paper carriage** the part of a typewriter or printer which holds the paper in place. **paper chain** a chain made of usu. coloured paper, used as a decoration esp. at Christmas. **paper-chase** a game in which runners follow a trail marked by torn-up paper. **paper chromatogram** CHEMISTRY a chromatogram made by paper chromatography. **paper chromatography** CHEMISTRY separation of substances by chromatography on an absorbent paper support. **paper-clip**: of bent wire or of plastic for holding several sheets of paper together. **paper-coal** a thinly foliated variety of coal. **paper cover** (*a*) a stiff paper cover, used to bind a book; (*b*) = PAPERBACK *noun*. **paper cup** a drinking cup made of thin cardboard. **paper-cutter** (*a*) a machine for cutting the edges of paper; (*b*) = ***paper-knife*** below. **paper doll** a doll-shaped figure cut or folded from a sheet of paper. **paper-faced** *adjective* (*a*) having a thin or pale face; (*b*) faced with paper. **paper-fastener** = ***paper-clip*** above. **paper-feed** a device for inserting sheets of paper into a typewriter, printer, etc. **paper flower** (*a*) an imitation flower made from paper; (*b*) any of several plants with flowers of a papery texture; *esp.* (*sing.* & in *pl.*) *Psilostrophe cooperi*, a small shrub of the composite family, native to desert areas of the south-western US and bearing panicles of yellow flowers. **paper-folding** origami. **paper game** a game involving writing or drawing on paper. **paper-girl**: who delivers or sells newspapers. **paper guide** an adjustable device on a typewriter, printer, etc., for ensuring that the left edge of each sheet of paper is inserted at the same place. **paper handkerchief** a disposable handkerchief made from soft tissue-paper. **paper-hanger** (*a*) a person who as a profession decorates the walls of rooms with wallpaper; (*b*) *US slang* a person who passes forged cheques. **paper-hanging** (*a*) in *pl.*, wallpaper; (*b*) the decorating of a room with wallpaper; (*c*) *US slang* the passing of forged cheques. **paper hanky** *colloq.* = ***paper handkerchief*** above. **paper-knife** a usu. thin knife for opening letters etc. **paper-machine** a machine for making paper. **paper-making wasp** = ***paper-wasp*** below. **paper man** (*a*) a man who sells newspapers; (*b*) *US slang* a musician, esp. a drummer, who cannot improvise and plays from written music only. **paper-mill**: in which paper is made. **paper money**: in the form of banknotes. **paper-mulberry** a small tree of the mulberry family, *Broussonetia papyrifera*, from the inner bark of which paper is made in China and Japan. **paper napkin** a disposable table-napkin made of paper. ***paper* NAUTILUS**. **paper pattern** a pattern cut out of paper; *spec.* a dressmaking pattern printed on tissue-paper with instructions. **paper plate** a disposable plate made of cardboard. ***paper pulp***: see PULP *noun* 4. **paper-pusher** *slang* a menial clerical or office worker. **paper-pushing** *slang* menial or routine clerical or office work. **paper-reed** the papyrus plant. **paper ribbon** (*a*) = ***paper tape*** below; (*b*) = ***paper streamer*** below. **paper-round**, (*N. Amer.*) **paper route**, (*NZ*) **paper run** a job of regularly delivering newspapers; a route taken doing this. **paper sack** (*a*) *US* a paper bag; (*b*) a large sacklike bag made of strong paper. †**paper sailor** = ARGONAUT 2. **paper shale** GEOLOGY shale which readily splits into very thin laminae. **paper-shell** *adjective & noun* (*a*) (designating) a type of nut with a very thin shell; (*b*) (designating) a crab whose shell has not fully hardened after moulting. **paper-shelled** *adjective* having a very thin shell. **paper shredder** a machine for cutting (esp. secret) documents etc. into small unreadable pieces. **paper-spar** calcite occurring as very thin plates. **paper-stainer** *arch.* (*a*) *slang* an inferior writer; a clerk; (*b*) a wallpaper-maker. **paper streamer** a long narrow strip of coloured paper used as a decoration. **paper-taffeta** *adjective & noun* (of) a lightweight taffeta with a crisp papery finish. **paper tape** tape made of paper, esp. having holes representing data punched in it. **paper tiger** an apparently threatening but actually ineffectual person or thing. **paper towel** a small disposable towel made of absorbent paper. **paper town** *N. Amer.* (*a*) a town that is planned but not actually founded; (*b*) a town or city whose main industry is paper manufacture. **paper trail** a series of documents giving evidence on, information about, or verification of a particular issue, person, or thing. **paper ware** articles made of papier mâché. **paper-wasp** a wasp that constructs its nest of a papery substance made from wood shavings moistened into a paste; *spec.* a social wasp of the genus *Polistes*. **paperweight** a small heavy (usu. ornamental) object for keeping loose papers in place. **paper window** *Hist.*: in which paper is used instead of glass. **paperwork** (*a*) routine clerical or administrative work; written documents used in or created by such work; (*b*) *arch.* the written work of a student in a class or examination. **paper-works** a set of buildings in which paper is made, a paper-mill.

■ **paperless** *adjective* lacking paper; *spec.* (of an office, automated business system, etc.) in which paper is not used as a medium for the storage or transmission of information, computerized: L20.

paper /ˈpeɪpə/ *verb.* L16.
[from the noun.]

1 *verb trans.* Write or set down on paper; write about, describe in writing. Now chiefly (*Scot.*), issue a written notice for or about. L16.

2 *verb trans.* Enclose in, cover, or parcel *up* with paper. Now *rare.* L16.

3 *verb trans.* Stick paper to; *esp.* decorate (the walls of a room) with wallpaper. L18. ▸**b** *verb intrans.* Foll. by *over*: cover or conceal (a hole or blemish) with paper; *fig.* disguise or try to hide (a fault etc.). M20.

4 *verb trans.* Fill (a theatre etc.) by means of free passes or tickets. *Theatrical slang.* M19.

5 *verb trans.* **a** Supply with paper. L19. ▸**b** Display posters on or at, distribute leaflets at (a meeting etc.). *colloq.* M20.

6 *verb trans. & intrans.* Pass forged cheques (to); defraud (a person) by issuing forged cheques. *US slang.* E20.

7 *verb trans.* Preserve (an insect) by storing in a folded paper packet. *rare.* M20.

> 📖 **3** *Practical Wireless* The members have turned their hands to papering and painting the clubroom. **b** J. DEAKIN Not even the impressive legislative accomplishments under Lyndon Johnson can paper over Congress's serious . . frailties.

■ **paperer** *noun* (*a*) a person who as a profession decorates the walls of rooms with wallpaper, a paper-hanger; (*b*) *Theatrical slang* a person who issues or receives free passes or tickets to a theatrical performance: M19. **papering** *noun* (*a*) the action of the verb; *spec.* decoration with wallpaper; (*b*) wallpaper; (*c*) the use of curlpapers for curling the hair: L18.

paperasserie /paprasri/ *noun.* E20.
[French.]

Excessive official paperwork or routine; bureaucracy.

paperback /ˈpeɪpəbak/ *noun, adjective, & verb.* L19.
[from PAPER *adjective* + BACK *noun*¹.]

▸**A** *noun.* A book bound in flexible card or stiff paper covers. L19.

in paperback in a paperback edition.

▸**B** *attrib.* or as *adjective.* (Of a book) bound in flexible card or stiff paper covers; of or pertaining to a paperback or the publication of paperbacks. M20.

▸**C** *verb trans.* Publish in a paperback edition. M20.

■ **paperbacked** *adjective* (of a book) paperback; *fig.* feeble, weak: L19.

papery /ˈpeɪp(ə)ri/ *adjective.* E17.
[from PAPER *noun* + -Y¹.]

Resembling paper in thinness or texture.

> 📖 P. BARKER The heads of the daffodils were brown and papery.

■ **paperiness** *noun* L19.

papess /ˈpeɪpɪs/ *noun.* E17.
[French *papesse*, Italian *papessa* from medieval Latin *papissa*, from ecclesiastical Latin *papa* POPE *noun*¹: see PAPA *noun*¹, -ESS¹.]

A female pope, a popess.

papeterie /pap(ə)tri (*pl. same*), ˈpapətri/ *noun.* M19.
[French = paper manufacture, stationer's shop, writing-case, from *papetier* paper-maker.]

A (usu. ornamental) case or box for paper and other writing materials.

Paphian /ˈpeɪfɪən/ *noun & adjective.* L16.
[from Latin *Paphius* adjective, from *Paphos* (see below): see -AN.]

▸**A** *noun.* **1** A prostitute. *literary.* L16.

2 A native or inhabitant of Paphos, a Cypriot city formerly sacred to Aphrodite or Venus. E20.

▸**B** *adjective.* Of or pertaining to Paphos; *transf.* (*literary*) of or pertaining to (esp. illicit) sexual love. E17.

Paphlagonian /paflәˈɡəʊnɪən/ *adjective & noun.* L16.
[from Greek *Paphlagōnia*, Latin *Paphlagonia* (see below) + -AN.]

Hist. ▸**A** *adjective.* Of or pertaining to Paphlagonia, an ancient region in northern Asia Minor, or its inhabitants. L16.

▸**B** *noun.* A native or inhabitant of Paphlagonia. E17.

Papiamento /papɪəˈmɛntəʊ/ *noun & adjective.* Also **-tu** /-tuː/. M20.
[Spanish.]

(Of) a Spanish-based creole language of the islands of Curaçao, Aruba, and Bonaire, in the Caribbean.

papier /papje/ *noun.* M18.
[French: see PAPER *noun & adjective.*]

The French for 'paper', occurring in various phrases used in English

■ ***papier collé*** /kɔle/, pl. **-s -s** (pronounced same), [= stuck, glued] a collage made from paper; the use of paper for collage: M20. ***papier déchiré*** /deʃire/, pl. **-s -s** (pronounced same), [= torn] paper torn haphazardly for use in collage; a collage made of such paper: M20. PAPIER MÂCHÉ. ***papier poudré*** /pudre/, pl. **-s -s** (pronounced same), [= powdered] a paper impregnated with face-powder E20.

papier mâché /ˌpapɪeɪ ˈmaʃeɪ, *foreign* papje mɑʃe/ *noun & adjectival phr.* M18.
[formed as prec. + French *mâché* pa. pple of *mâcher* chew, from Latin *masticare.*]

▸**A** *noun.* Material made from pulped paper; paper reduced to a pulp mixed with glue etc. or (for fine work) sheets of paper pasted together, used for making moulded boxes, jars, trays, etc. M18.

▸**B** *adjective.* Made of papier mâché. M18.

papilio /pəˈpɪlɪəʊ/ *noun.* Pl. **-os.** L18.
[Latin = butterfly (adopted as mod. Latin genus name).]

Orig., any butterfly. Now *spec.* any of various swallowtail butterflies belonging to the large genus *Papilio.*

papilionaceous /pəpɪlɪəˈneɪʃəs/ *adjective.* M17.
[from mod. Latin *papilionaceus*, from Latin *papilio(n-)* butterfly: see -ACEOUS.]

1 Of or pertaining to a butterfly or butterflies; of the nature of a butterfly. Now *rare* or *obsolete.* M17. ▸**b** *fig.* Showy, frivolous. M19.

2 BOTANY. Of a flower corolla: arranged in the form of a butterfly, i.e. with a large erect upper petal or standard, two lateral petals or wings, and two narrow lower petals between these fused to form a keel, (as typical of many leguminous plants, esp. those of the subfamily Papilionoideae). Also, (of a plant) having this type of corolla. M17.

papilionid /pəˌpɪlɪˈəʊnɪd/ *adjective & noun.* L19.
[mod. Latin *Papilionidae* (see below): see PAPILIO, -ID³.]

ENTOMOLOGY. ▸**A** *adjective.* Of, pertaining to, or designating the widespread family Papilionidae of mainly brightly coloured tropical butterflies, including swallowtails and parnassians. L19.

▸**B** *noun.* A butterfly of this family. L20.

papilla /pəˈpɪlə/ *noun.* Pl. **-llae** /-liː/. L17.
[Latin = nipple, dim. of *papula* PAPULE.]

1 ANATOMY & ZOOLOGY. **a** A nipple, a mamilla. *rare.* L17. ▸**b** A minute, usu. soft and fleshy, nipple-like protuberance on a part or organ of the body, as at the base of a hair or feather, on the tongue bearing the taste buds, in the embryo giving rise to the teeth, etc. E18. ▸**c** MEDICINE. A small swelling or lump. L18.

2 BOTANY. A small conical projection, *esp.* one formed by an epidermal cell. M19.

1b ***optic papilla, renal papilla, vallate papilla, Vater's papilla***, etc.

■ **papiˈllectomy** *noun* (an instance of) surgical removal of a papilla or papillae E20. **papiˈlliferous** *adjective* bearing papillae E19. **papilliform** *adjective* of the form of a papilla; shaped like a nipple: E19.

papillary /pəˈpɪləri, ˈpapɪləri/ *adjective.* M17.
[from prec. + -ARY².]

Chiefly ANATOMY & BIOLOGY. Of the form or nature of a papilla; containing, possessing, or consisting of papillae; of, pertaining to, or affecting papillae.

papillary muscle each of the conical bundles of muscle fibre arising from the walls of the ventricles of the heart and attached by the chordae tendineae to the valves.

■ Also **papillar** *adjective* M19.

papillate /ˈpapɪleɪt, pəˈpɪlət/ *adjective.* **M19.**
[formed as prec. + -ATE².]
Chiefly *ANATOMY & BIOLOGY.* Having or covered with papillae.
■ Also **papillated** *adjective* **E19.**

papilledema *noun* see PAPILLOEDEMA.

papillitis /papɪˈlʌɪtɪs/ *noun.* **L19.**
[from PAPILLA + -ITIS.]
MEDICINE. Inflammation of a papilla, esp. (*OPHTHALMOLOGY*) of the optic disc.

papilloedema /ˌpapɪliːˈdiːmə/ *noun.* Also ***papilledema**. **E20.**
[from PAPILLA + OEDEMA.]
MEDICINE. Non-inflammatory swelling of the optic papilla due to increased intracranial pressure, usu. as a result of a brain tumour or abscess.

papilloma /papɪˈləʊmə/ *noun.* Pl. **-mas**, **-mata** /-mətə/. **M19.**
[from PAPILLA + -OMA.]
MEDICINE. A benign tumour of the skin or of a mucous membrane (e.g. in the nasal cavity or the uterus) consisting of overgrown and thickened epidermis or epithelium, as a wart, corn, polyp, or condyloma.
■ **papillomaˈtosis** *noun* the formation or presence of numerous papillomas **L19.** **papillomatous** *adjective* of, pertaining to, or of the nature of a papilloma **L19.**

papillon /ˈpapɪlɒn, ˈpapɪjɒ̃/ *noun.* **E20.**
[French = butterfly.]
(An animal of) a breed of toy spaniel, having erect ears resembling the shape of a butterfly's wings and a white coat with a few darker patches.

papillose /ˈpapɪləʊs/ *adjective.* **M18.**
[from PAPILLA + -OSE¹.]
ANATOMY & BIOLOGY. Full of or covered with papillae; papillate.
■ **papiˈllosity** *noun* papillose condition **L19.**

papillote /ˈpapɪləʊt, -ɒt; *in sense 2 usu.* ˈpapɪjɒt/ *noun.* **M18.**
[French.]
1 A curl-paper. *obsolete exc. Hist.* **M18.**
2 A usu. greased paper wrapper in which a fillet etc. of meat or fish is cooked. Freq. in ***en papillote*** /ɒ̃/, in a paper wrapper. **E19.**

papillous /pəˈpɪləs/ *adjective.* Now *rare* or *obsolete.* **E18.**
[from PAPILLA + -OUS.]
= PAPILLOSE.

papirosa /papɪˈrɒsə/ *noun.* Also **papy-**. Pl. **-si** /-si/. **L19.**
[Russian Cf. Greek *papūros* PAPYRUS.]
A type of Russian cigarette consisting of a hollow tube filled with tobacco at one end.

papish /ˈpeɪpɪʃ/ *adjective & noun.* Now *colloq.* or *dial.* (*derog.*). **M16.**
[from PAPIST: see -ISH¹.]
► **A** *adjective.* = PAPIST *adjective.* **M16.**
► **B** *noun.* = PAPIST *noun* 1. **E17.**
■ **papisher** *noun* = PAPISH *noun* **E19.**

papism /ˈpeɪpɪz(ə)m/ *noun.* Chiefly *derog.* **M16.**
[French *papisme* or mod. Latin *papismus*, from ecclesiastical Latin *papa* POPE *noun*¹: see PAPA *noun*¹, -ISM.]
The papal system; Roman Catholicism.

papist /ˈpeɪpɪst/ *noun & adjective.* Chiefly *derog.* **M16.**
[French *papiste* or mod. Latin *papista*, from ecclesiastical Latin *papa* POPE *noun*¹: see PAPA *noun*¹, -IST.]
► **A** *noun.* **1** An advocate of papal supremacy; *gen.* a Roman Catholic. **M16.**
2 (**P-**.) An imitator or follower of the English poet Alexander Pope (1688–1744). **M19.**
► **B** *adjective.* Of, pertaining to, or characteristic of Roman Catholics or Roman Catholicism. **E19.**
■ **papistly** *adverb* (now *rare* or *obsolete*) **M17.** **papistry** *noun* Roman Catholicism **M16.**

papistic /pəˈpɪstɪk, peɪ-/ *adjective.* Chiefly *derog.* **M16.**
[from (the same root as) prec. + -IC.]
= PAPIST *adjective.*
■ **papistical** *adjective* = PAPIST *adjective* **M16.** **papistically** *adverb* **L16.**

†**papize** *verb intrans. derog.* Also **-ise**. **E17–M19.**
[from ecclesiastical Latin *papa* POPE *noun*¹ + -IZE.]
Support the Pope or papal system.

papoose /pəˈpuːs/ *noun.* **M17.**
[Algonquian *papoos.*]
A young N. American Indian child.
Comb.: **papoose-root** a N. American plant, *Caulophyllum thalictroides*, of the barberry family, whose root has medicinal properties.

papoosh /pəˈpuːʃ/ *noun.* Also **papouche**. **L17.**
[Persian *pāpūš* BABOUCHE.]
A Turkish or oriental slipper.

papovavirus /pəˈpəʊvəvʌɪrəs/ *noun.* **M20.**
[from PA(PILLOMA + PO(LYOMA + VA(CUOLATING + VIRUS.]
MICROBIOLOGY. Any of a group of small animal viruses including those causing polyoma, papilloma, sarcoma, and warts, and consisting of double-stranded DNA in an icosahedral capsid with no envelope.

pappardelle /papɑːˈdeleɪ/ *noun pl.* **L19.**
[Italian, from *pappare* eat hungrily.]
Pasta in the form of broad flat ribbons, traditionally served with a game sauce.

Pappenheimer body /ˈpap(ə)nhʌɪmə ˌbɒdi/ *noun phr.* Also **Pappenheimer's body** /-hʌɪməz/. **M20.**
[Alwin M. *Pappenheimer* (b. 1908), US biochemist.]
MEDICINE. A siderosome, *esp.* one that stains with Romanowsky's or Wright's stain. Usu. in *pl.*

pappi *noun* pl. of PAPPUS.

pappose /paˈpəʊs/ *adjective.* **L17.**
[from next + -OSE¹.]
BOTANY. Having or of the nature of a pappus.
■ Also †**pappous** *adjective* **M17–E19.**

pappus /ˈpapəs/ *noun.* Pl. **pappi** /ˈpapʌɪ, -iː/. **E18.**
[Latin from Greek *pappos* lit. 'grandfather'.]
BOTANY. An arrangement of hairs on certain fruits, esp. achenes in plants of the composite family, which assists their aerial dispersal (as in dandelions and thistles); *gen.* the reduced calyx, consisting of hairs, scales, bristles, or teeth, etc., present in most plants of the composite family.

pappy /ˈpapi/ *noun. colloq.* (*nursery*). **M18.**
[from PAPA *noun*² + -Y⁶.]
Father.

pappy /ˈpapi/ *adjective.* **L17.**
[from PAP *noun*² + -Y¹.]
1 Of the nature or consistency of pap; soft and wet. **L17.**
2 *fig.* Feeble. **E19.**

paprika /ˈpaprɪkə, pəˈpriːkə/ *noun & adjective.* **L19.**
[Hungarian.]
► **A** *noun.* **1** A condiment made from the dried ground fruits of certain (esp. red) varieties of the sweet pepper, *Capsicum annuum.* **L19.** ►**b** The bright orange-red colour of this. **M20.**
2 Any of several European varieties of the sweet pepper, *Capsicum annuum*, bearing mildly flavoured fruits. **E20.**
► **B** *adjective.* **1** Of a dish: flavoured with (esp. the condiment) paprika. **M20.**
2 Of the colour of paprika. **M20.**

†**Papua** *noun.* **E17–L19.**
[Malay *papuah, pĕpuah* frizzed, tightly curled.]
= PAPUAN *noun* 1.

Papuan /ˈpapjʊən, ˈpɑː-, -ˈpʊən/ *noun & adjective.* **E19.**
[from *Papua* (see below), formed as prec. + -AN.]
► **A** *noun.* **1** A native or inhabitant of Papua, a territory consisting of the SE part of the island of New Guinea (formerly, of the whole island) and now incorporated into the State of Papua New Guinea. **E19.**
2 The Papuan language group. **E20.**
► **B** *adjective.* **1** Of, pertaining to, or characteristic of Papua or its inhabitants. **M19.**
2 *spec.* Designating or pertaining to languages native to Papua New Guinea and not in the Austronesian family. **L19.**

papule /ˈpapjuːl/ *noun.* Also (earlier) in mod. Latin form **papula** /ˈpapjʊlə/, pl. **-lae** /-liː/. **E18.**
[Latin *papula*: see -ULE.]
1 *MEDICINE.* A small, solid, somewhat pointed swelling, often forming part of a rash on the skin, and usu. inflammatory but without suppuration; a pimple. **E18.**
2 *ZOOLOGY & BOTANY.* A small rounded protuberance; a papilla. **L19.**
■ **papular** *adjective* pertaining to, characterized by, or of the nature of papules or pimples **E19.** **papulated** *adjective* covered with or marked by papules or pimples **E19.** **papuˈlation** *noun* the formation of papules or pimples **L19.** **papulose** *adjective* covered with papules or papillae; papillose: **L18.** **papuˈlosity** *noun* papulose condition **M17.** **papulous** *adjective* (now *rare* or *obsolete*) = PAPULAR **E19.**

papulo- /ˈpapjʊləʊ/ *combining form* of PAPULE: see -O-.
■ **papulo-eryˈthema** *noun* erythema accompanied by papules **L19.** **papulo-eryˈthematous** *adjective* characterized by or of the nature of papulo-erythema **L19.** **papulo-ˈpustular** *adjective* characterized by swellings resembling papules but containing pus **L19.** **papulo-ˈsquamous** *adjective* characterized by (a rash consisting of) papules covered by scales **L19.** **papulo-ˈvesicle** *noun* a swelling resembling a papule, but containing fluid **L19.** **papulo-veˈsicular** *adjective* characterized by papulo-vesicles **L19.**

papyraceous /papɪˈreɪʃəs/ *adjective.* **M18.**
[from Latin PAPYRUS + -ACEOUS.]
ANATOMY & BIOLOGY. Of the texture or thinness of paper; papery.

papyri *noun* pl. of PAPYRUS.

papyriferous /papɪˈrɪf(ə)rəs/ *adjective. rare.* **M17.**
[from Latin *papyrifer* papyrus-bearing: see -FEROUS.]
Producing or yielding papyrus or paper.

papyrin /ˈpapɪrɪn/ *noun.* **M19.**
[from Latin PAPYRUS + -IN¹.]
Parchment paper.

papyro- /ˈpapɪrəʊ, pəˈpʌɪrəʊ/ *combining form* of Greek *papuros* PAPYRUS, PAPER *noun*: see -O-.
■ **paˈpyrograph** *noun* (*Hist.*) an apparatus for copying documents by chemical agents acting through a porous paper-stencil **L19.** **paˌpyrographic** *adjective* (*Hist.*) pertaining to or produced by papyrography **M19.** **papyˈrography** *noun* (*Hist.*) a process for copying writing or drawings by transferring the design to a zinc plate for printing **M19.** **papyroˈlogical** *adjective* pertaining to or dealing with papyrology **E20.** **papyˈrologist** *noun* an expert in or student of papyrology **E20.** **papyˈrology** *noun* the branch of archaeology that deals with papyri **L19.**

papyrosa *noun* var. of PAPIROSA.

papyrus /pəˈpʌɪrəs/ *noun & adjective.* **LME.**
[Latin from Greek *papuros* paper-reed, of unkn. origin. Cf. PAPER *noun & adjective.*]
► **A** *noun.* Pl. **-ri** /-rʌɪ, -riː/.
1 An aquatic plant of the sedge family, *Cyperus papyrus*, with stems up to 10 feet high bearing spikelets in a very large terminal umbel, formerly abundant in Egypt and the source of the writing material papyrus. Also called ***paper-reed***. **LME.**
2 Material in the form of thin sheets made from fine slices or strips of the stem of the papyrus plant soaked in water, pressed together, and dried, used as writing-material by the ancient Egyptians, Greeks, Romans, etc. **E18.**
3 An ancient manuscript or document written on this. **E19.**
► **B** *adjective.* Made or consisting of papyrus. **L19.**

†**paquet** *noun & verb* var. of PACKET.

par /pɑː/ *noun*¹. **L16.**
[Latin = equal, equality.]
1 Equality of value or standing; an equal status or level (now chiefly in ***on a par***). Formerly also *spec.*, something that is equal to another thing. **L16.**
2 a *ECONOMICS.* In full ***par of exchange***. The recognized value of the currency of one country in terms of that of another. **E17.** ►**b** *STOCK EXCHANGE.* Equality between the market value of stocks, shares, bonds, etc., and the face value. Chiefly in phrs. below. **E18.**
3 An average or normal amount, quality, degree, or condition. **L18.**
4 *GOLF.* The number of strokes a scratch player should need for a hole or for a course, calculated from the length of the holes and sometimes taking account of any difficulties or obstacles. **L19.**

> 📖 **1** N. MAILER Gilmore had struck him as being on an intellectual par with the Court. R. HAYMAN Her . . sensitivity was more nearly on a par with his own. **3** P. G. WODEHOUSE Mrs Chavender's Pekinese . . had woken up that morning a little below par. S. RAVEN He'd certainly see that the food and drink were up to par.

Phrases: **above par** at a premium. **at par** at the face value. **below par** at a discount; *fig.* less good than usual in health or other quality. **par for the course** *colloq.* what is normal or expected in any given circumstances. ***par of exchange***: see sense 2a above.

par /pɑː/ *noun*². *dial.* **E19.**
[Rel. to PAR *verb*¹. Cf. PARROCK.]
An enclosure for farm animals.

par /pɑː/ *noun*³. *colloq.* (chiefly *PRINTING & JOURNALISM*). Also **par.** (point). **M19.**
[Abbreviation.]
= PARAGRAPH *noun* 3.

par *noun*⁴ var. of PARR.

par /pɑː/ *verb*¹ *trans. obsolete* exc. *dial.* Infl. **-rr-**. **ME.**
[Rel. to PAR *noun*². Cf. PARROCK.]
Confine or shut up in an enclosure.

par /pɑː/ *verb*² *trans.* Infl. **-rr-**. **L19.**
[from PAR *noun*¹.]
1 Equate in value. *rare.* **L19.**
2 *GOLF.* Complete (a hole or course) with a score equal to par. **M20.**

par /par, pɑː/ *preposition.* **ME.**
[Old & mod. French from Proto-Romance comb. of Latin *per* through + *ad* to.]
The French for 'through, by', occurring in various phrases used in English
par amour: see PARAMOUR. ***par avion*** /avjɔ̃, ˈavjɔ̃/ by air; by airmail. †***par charité*** out of charity. †***par cœur*** by heart. ***par éminence*** /eminɑ̃s, ˈɛmɪnəns/ pre-eminently. PAR EXCELLENCE. ***par exemple*** /ɛgzɑ̃ːpl, ɛgˈzɒmp(ə)l/ for example. ***par parenthèse*** /parɑ̃tɛːz/ by way of parenthesis.

par- /pɑː/ *prefix*¹ (not productive).
Repr. French *par-* from Latin *per-* through, thoroughly, occurring in words from French, as *parboil*, *pardon*, etc.

par- *prefix*² see PARA-¹.

para /ˈpɑːrə/ *noun*[1]. L17.
[Turkish from Persian *pāra* piece, portion, para.]
A monetary unit of Serbia and neighbouring States, equal to one-hundredth of a dinar; *Hist.* a monetary unit of Turkey, equal to one-fortieth of a piastre.

para /ˈpɑːrə/ *noun*[2]. *NZ.* M19.
[Maori.]
A large tropical evergreen fern, *Marattia fraxinea*; its swollen rhizome, formerly used by Maoris as food.

para /ˈparə/ *noun*[3]. M19.
[Abbreviation.]
A paragraph.

para /ˈparə/ *noun*[4]. L19.
[The ending of *nullipara*, *primipara*, *multipara*.]
A woman who has had a specified number of confinements, as indicated by a preceding or following numeral.

para /ˈparə/ *noun*[5]. M20.
[Abbreviation of PARATROOP (orig., of French *parachutiste*).]
A soldier belonging to a parachute regiment.

para /ˈparə/ *adjective & adverb.* Freq. italicized. L19.
[from PARA-[1].]
CHEMISTRY. ▶**A** *adjective.* Characterized by or relating to (substitution at) two opposite carbon atoms in a benzene ring; at a position opposite *to* some (specified) substituent in a benzene ring. L19.

R. O. C. NORMAN The inductive effect is relayed through one more carbon atom than is the case for . . *para* substitution. **para red, Para red** any of various dyes that consist chiefly of the coupling product of diazotized paranitraniline and β-naphthol and are used in printing inks and paints.

▶**B** *adverb.* So as to form para-substituted compounds. M20.

para- /ˈparə/ *prefix*[1]. Before a vowel or *h* also **par-**.
[Greek *para*, *par-* beside, beyond, past, (in comb. also) to one side, amiss, irregular, and expr. subsidiary relation, alteration, etc.]
1 Esp. ANATOMY & MEDICINE. Denoting (*a*) adjacency or proximity, esp. of a part of the body; (*b*) a disordered function or faculty.
2 In words with the sense 'beyond or distinct from, but analogous or parallel to'; CHEMISTRY denoting alteration or modification.
3 CHEMISTRY. (Freq. italicized.) Denoting substitution in a benzene ring at diametrically opposite carbon atoms.
4 PHYSICS & CHEMISTRY. Denoting the fact of having antiparallel spins (opp. ORTHO- 3).
■ **para-aminobenˈzoic** *adjective*: ***para-aminobenzoic acid***, the *para* isomer of aminobenzoic acid, which is sometimes considered a member of the vitamin B group, is widely distributed in plant and animal tissue, and has been used to treat rickettsial infections E20. **para-aˈortic** *adjective* (ANATOMY) situated beside the aorta; *spec.* designating certain paraganglia E20. **paraˈbronchus** *noun*, pl. **-chi**, ZOOLOGY any of the minutest ramifications of the bronchi in a bird's lung L19. **paraˈcasein** *noun* (CHEMISTRY) a phosphoprotein produced in the form of a curd by the action of rennet on milk E20. **paraˈcaseinate** *noun* (CHEMISTRY) a compound of paracasein with a metal E20. **paraˈcellular** *adjective* passing or situated alongside and between cells E20. **paracervical** /-ˈsəː-, -ˈvʌɪ-/ *adjective* (ANATOMY) pertaining to or designating the region surrounding the cervix E20. **parachor** /-kɔː/ *noun* [Greek *khoros* dance, in mistake for *khōra* space] CHEMISTRY a numerical quantity (found empirically to be constant over a wide range of temperature) equal to the molecular weight of a liquid multiplied by the fourth root of its surface tension and divided by the difference between its density and that of its vapour E20. **paraˈchordal** *adjective & noun* (ANATOMY) (designating) either of a pair of cartilaginous plates situated beside the notochord, forming the foundation of the skull in mammalian embryos L19. **para-church** *noun* a non-institutional church such as a house church L20. **paraˈclinical** *adjective* of or pertaining to the branches of medicine, esp. the laboratory sciences, that provide a service for patients without direct involvement in care M20. **paracone** *noun* (ZOOLOGY) a cusp on the anterior buccal corner of the tribosphenic upper molar tooth L19. **paraconˈformity** *noun* (GEOLOGY) = NON-SEQUENCE M20. **paraˈconid** *noun* (ZOOLOGY) a cusp on the anterior lingual corner of the tribosphenic lower molar tooth L19. **paracrine** /-krʌɪn, -krɪn/ *adjective* (PHYSIOLOGY) of, pertaining to, or designating a hormone whose effects are confined to the vicinity of the gland secreting it L20. **paracrystal** *noun* (SCIENCE) an object that is not a true crystal but has some degree of order in its structure M20. **paraˈcrystalline** *adjective* (SCIENCE) of the nature of a paracrystal M20. **paracrystaˈllinity** *noun* (SCIENCE) the property of being paracrystalline M20. **para-dichloroˈbenzene** *noun* (CHEMISTRY) a crystalline compound, $C_6H_4Cl_2$, used as a mothproofing agent L19. **paradiploˈmatic** *adjective* that is based on other than strictly diplomatic or textual evidence M19. **paraˈfiscal** *adjective* ancillary to what is fiscal; containing elements not usually regarded as fiscal: M20. **parafoˈllicular** *adjective* (ANATOMY) designating cells situated between the follicles of the mammalian thyroid gland which secrete calcitonin M20. **paraform** *noun* (CHEMISTRY) paraformaldehyde E20. **paraforˈmaldehyde** *noun* (CHEMISTRY) a white solid polymer, $(H{\cdot}CHO)_n$, of formaldehyde L19. **paraˈfovea** *noun* (ANATOMY) an annular area of the retina surrounding the fovea M20. **paraˈfoveal** *adjective* (ANATOMY) of or pertaining to the parafovea; adjacent to the fovea: E20. **paraˈfoveally** *adverb* (ANATOMY) in a parafoveal manner; by means of the parafovea: M20. **paraˈgaster** *noun* [Greek *gastēr* stomach] ZOOLOGY the central cavity of a simple sponge L19. **paraˈgastric** *adjective* (ZOOLOGY) situated next to the stomach or gastric cavity of an organism; pertaining to the paragaster of a sponge: M19. **parageosynˈclinal** *adjective* (GEOLOGY) of, pertaining to, or of the nature of a parageosyncline M20. **parageoˈsyncline** *noun* (GEOLOGY) a geosyncline situated within an older craton or (formerly) at the edge of a continental craton E20. **parageusia** /-ˈgjuːzɪə, -sɪə/ *noun* [Greek *geusis* sense of taste] disordered perception of taste L19. **paraˈglossa** *noun*, pl. **-ssae**, ENTOMOLOGY each of the pair of outer lobes of the ligula in some insects E19. **paragnath** /ˈparəgnaθ/ (also **paragnathus** /pəˈragnəθəs/, pl. **-tha** /-θə/) *noun* [Greek *gnathos* jaw] ZOOLOGY (*a*) either of two lobes forming the lower lip in most crustaceans; (*b*) either of the pair of lobes forming the hypopharynx in certain insects; (*c*) any of several paired tooth-like scales inside the mouth of certain annelid worms: L19. **paragneiss** *noun* (GEOLOGY) gneiss derived from sedimentary rocks E20. **paraˈgnosis** *noun* knowledge which is beyond that which can be obtained by normal means M20. **paragnost** *noun* a person allegedly possessing powers of clairvoyance or foreknowledge M20. **paragraˈmmatic, paragraˈmmatical** *adjectives* of or pertaining to paragrammatism M20. **paraˈgrammatism** *noun* the confused or incomplete use of grammatical structures found in certain forms of speech disturbance E20. **paraˈgutta** *noun* a material derived from rubber and gutta-percha used for insulating telephone cables M20. **parahippoˈcampal** *adjective* (ANATOMY) designating a gyrus on the inferior surface of each cerebral hemisphere that posteriorly is continuous with the cingulum and anteriorly ends in the uncus M20. **paraˈhormone** *noun* (PHYSIOLOGY) a product of metabolism which has a secondary hormonal role E20. **parakeraˈtosis** *noun* (MEDICINE & VETERINARY MEDICINE) a disease characterized by abnormal development of the horny layer of the skin, occurring in domestic animals, and occasionally in humans, as a result of zinc deficiency L19. **parakeraˈtotic** *adjective* (MEDICINE & VETERINARY MEDICINE) affected by or symptomatic of parakeratosis M20. **paraˈlalia** *noun* disordered articulation of speech L19. **paraˈlexia** *noun* [Greek *lexis* word] a form of sensory aphasia in which one word is read for or transposed with another L19. **paraˈlexic** *adjective* marked by or symptomatic of paralexia E20. **paraliˈturgical** *adjective* parallel or ancillary to the liturgy L20. **paraˈmedian** *adjective* (ANATOMY) situated or occurring alongside the median line L19. **paraˈmenstruum** *noun* the eight-day period consisting of the first four days of each menstrual cycle and the preceding four days M20. **paramesoˈnephric** *adjective* (ANATOMY): ***paramesonephric duct***, = ***Müllerian duct*** s.v. MÜLLERIAN *adjective*[1] M20. **paramˈnesia** *noun* (*a*) disordered memory, esp. of the meaning of words; (*b*) = DÉJÀ VU 1: L19. **paramˈnesic** *adjective* of, pertaining to, or characterized by paramnesia L19. **paramorph** *noun* (MINERALOGY) a pseudomorph formed by a change of physical characteristics without a change in chemical composition L19. **paraˈmorphic** *adjective* (MINERALOGY) of or pertaining to a paramorph; characterized by paramorphism: M19. **paraˈmorphism** *noun* (MINERALOGY) the change of one mineral to another with the same chemical composition but a different molecular structure M19. **paraˈmylum** *noun* [Latin *amylum* starch] BIOCHEMISTRY a carbohydrate related to starch that occurs as a storage product in some infusorians E20. **paramyoˈclonus** *noun* (MEDICINE) a condition in which there is myoclonic contraction of various muscles; ***paramyoclonus multiplex***, a chronic disorder in which there are sudden contractions, esp. of some limb muscles, at intervals of a few seconds: L19. **paraˈmyosin** *noun* (CHEMISTRY) a protein which forms the thick filaments of the contractile units of molluscan muscle M20. **paraˈnasal** *adjective* (ANATOMY) designating certain sinuses situated beside the nose E20. **paraˈnatal** *adjective* (MEDICINE) of or pertaining to the time shortly before and after birth M20. **paraniˈtraniline** *noun* (CHEMISTRY) a crystalline compound, $H_2NC_6H_4NO_2$, used in making azo dyes L19. **paraˈnotal** *adjective* of or pertaining to the paranotum of an insect E20. **paraˈnotum** *noun*, pl. **-nota**, [Greek *nōton* back] a lateral expansion of the dorsal part of a thoracic segment in certain insects E20. **paraˈnucleus** *noun* (CYTOLOGY) = NEBENKERN L19. **paraoxon** /parəˈɒksɒn/ *noun* [after PARATHION] an insecticide that is the oxygen analogue of parathion M20. **parapaˈresis** *noun* (MEDICINE) paresis of the lower limbs L19. **paraˈpatric** *adjective* [Greek *patra* fatherland] BIOLOGY (of species, speciation, etc.) occurring in distinct but contiguous areas M20. **paraˈpatrically** *adverb* (BIOLOGY) by means of parapatric speciation; without physical isolation: L20. **parapatry** *noun* (BIOLOGY) parapatric speciation; the occurrence of parapatric forms: M20. **paraˈphasia** *noun* disordered speech characterized by the incorrect use of words L19. **paraˈphasic** *adjective* marked by or symptomatic of paraphasia L19. **para-ˌphenyleneˈdiamine** *noun* (CHEMISTRY) a crystalline compound, $C_6H_4(NH_2)_2$, used as a photographic developer, for dyeing hair and fur, and for making safranine and sulphur dyes L19. **paraˈphilia** *noun* a condition characterized by abnormal sexual desires E20. **paraˈphiliac** *noun & adjective* (*a*) *noun* a person with paraphilia; (*b*) *adjective* paraphilic: M20. **paraˈphilic** *adjective* characteristic of or having paraphilia M20. **paraphiˈmosis** *noun* irreducible retraction of the prepuce L17. **paraphyˈletic** *adjective* (TAXONOMY) (of a group of taxa) descended from a common ancestral taxon but not including all its descendant taxa; *esp.* designating such a group formerly regarded as a taxon in its own right: M20. **paraˈphysical** *adjective* subsidiary or collateral to what is physical; of, pertaining to, or designating physical phenomena for which no adequate scientific explanation exists: E19. **paraˈpodial** *adjective* (ZOOLOGY) of or pertaining to a parapodium L19. **paraˈpodium** *noun*, pl. **-ia**, ZOOLOGY a jointless muscular lateral appendage occurring in pairs in polychaete worms, bearing setae, and variously used for locomotion, respiration, or sensation; a similar structure in some molluscs: L19. **parapoˈlitical** *adjective* political in a smaller context than that of the State or society M20. **paraˈprotein** *noun* (CHEMISTRY & MEDICINE) any of various proteins found in the blood only in certain diseases such as myelomatosis M20. **paraˌproteiˈnaemia** *noun* (MEDICINE) the presence of paraproteins in the blood M20. **parapsoˈriasis** *noun*, pl. **-ases**, MEDICINE any of various rare chronic skin diseases which resemble psoriasis, characterized by red scaly patches and lack of subjective symptoms E20. **paraˈpsychic, paraˈpsychical** *adjectives* of, pertaining to, or designating mental phenomena for which no adequate scientific explanation exists E20. **parareˈligious** *adjective* existing parallel to, or outside, the sphere of orthodox religion M20. **pararoˈsaniline** *noun* a colourless crystalline alcohol, $(H_2NC_6H_4)_3COH$, which is used in making certain dyes and whose red hydrochloride is used as a biological stain L19. **paraˈsagittal** *adjective* (ANATOMY) situated adjacent or parallel to the sagittal plane E20. **paraˈsphenoid** *adjective & noun* (ZOOLOGY) (designating) a bone extending medially along the base of the skull in birds, reptiles, amphibians, and fishes L19. **paraˈsternal** *adjective* (ANATOMY) situated beside the sternum L19. **paraˈsymbiont** *noun* [-BIONT] BIOLOGY an organism involved in parasymbiosis E20. **parasymbiˈosis** *noun* (BIOLOGY) the relationship between a free-living lichen and an organism (either a fungus or another lichen) which infests that lichen and establishes a symbiotic relationship with the algae L19. **parasymbiˈotic** *adjective* (BIOLOGY) of or pertaining to parasymbiosis E20. **paratecˈtonic** *adjective* (GEOLOGY) (*a*) (now *rare*) accompanying deformation; (*b*) formed by, or of the nature of, a deformation believed to be characteristic of parageosynclines, which is chiefly epeirogenic and produces relatively simple, broad folds: M20. **paraˈterminal** *adjective* (ANATOMY) designating a strip of cortex in the rhinencephalon at the anterior end of the third ventricle E20. **parathecium** *noun*, pl. **-ia**, BOTANY in cup-fungi and lichens, the outer, dark-coloured layer of an apothecium E20. **paˈratomy** *noun* (ZOOLOGY) in certain annelid worms, asexual reproduction in which new organs are developed before the division of the animal into two or more parts M20. **para-transit** *noun* transport for individuals other than private transport and conventional bus and train services (e.g. taxis and car pools) L20. **paratrophic** /-ˈtrəʊfɪk, -ˈtrɒfɪk/ *adjective* (BIOLOGY) needing live organic matter for nutrition E20. **paravenˈtricular** *adjective* (ANATOMY) situated next to a ventricle of the brain M20. **paraˈvertebral** *adjective* (ANATOMY) situated or occurring beside the vertebral column or a vertebra L19. **paraˈvisual** *adjective* conveying information visually but not needing to be looked at directly M20. **paraˈxylene** *noun* (CHEMISTRY) a low-melting solid isomer of xylene obtained from petroleum naphtha and used esp. as a source of terephthalic acid L19.

para- /ˈparə/ *prefix*[2]. M19.
[French from Italian, imper. of *parare* defend, shield, cover from, (orig.) prepare, from Latin *parare*.]
Forming nouns from nouns with the senses 'protector of', 'protection against', in words adopted from French, as ***parachute***, and in a few English words.

para- /ˈparə/ *prefix*[3].
[from PARA(CHUTE *noun*.]
Forming nouns with the senses 'dropped by parachute', 'trained or equipped for descending by parachute', etc.
■ **parabrake** *noun* a parachute which can be opened behind an aircraft to act as a brake M20. **paradoctor** *noun* a doctor who is dropped by parachute to patients in remote areas M20. **paradrop** *noun & verb* (*a*) *noun* a dropping of personnel or supplies by parachute; (*b*) *verb trans.* drop (such items) by parachute: M20. **parafoil** *noun* a fabric structure designed to function as both a parachute and an aerofoil, providing lift that enables the wearer to glide M20. **paraglider** *noun* (*a*) a large structure like a kite, composed of two flexible triangular sections joined side by side, and designed to glide with a passive load or with a pilot to control its flight; (*b*) a wide parachute-like canopy which allows a person to soar to a height or glide to the ground on thermal air-currents: M20. **paragliding** *noun* the action or sport of gliding in a paraglider L20. **parajump** *noun* a descent by parachute L20. **parakite** *noun* (*a*) *Hist.* a large kite designed to be inflated by the wind like a parachute; (*b*) a kite in the form of a parachute that is towed by a car, motor boat, etc.: L19. **parakiting** *noun* the sport of soaring while harnessed to a parakite L20. **paraˈmotor** *noun* (US proprietary name for) a motorized steerable parachute, powered by a motor and propeller strapped to the pilot's back L20. **parapack** *noun* a pack dropped by parachute M20. **paraplane** *noun* a pair of fabric wings attached to a rigid framework which a parachutist can wear to allow gliding M20. **para-rescue** *noun* a rescue carried out by a parachutist; usu. *attrib.*: M20. **paraski** *adjective* (*a*) (of a parachutist) trained to ski from the landing-place; (*b*) designating a sport in which skiers ski from a place to which they have dropped by parachute: M20. **paraskier** *noun* a paraski trooper M20. **parawing** *noun* a form of parachute with a flat inflatable wing in place of the usual umbrella, to give greater manoeuvrability M20.

Pará /pəˈrɑː/ *noun.* M19.
[See below.]
1 Used *attrib.* to designate plants found in and products obtained from Belém (formerly Pará), a Brazilian seaport on the Amazon, or the State of Pará in which Belém is situated. M19.
2 In full ***Pará rubber***. Rubber from the latex of *Hevea brasiliensis*. L19.
1 Pará cress a plant of the composite family, *Spilanthes oleracea*, cultivated in tropical countries as a salad. **Pará grass** a creeping forage grass, *Brachiaria mutica*, native to Brazil and W. Africa and widely cultivated in the tropics. **Pará-nut** a Brazil nut.

parabasal /parəˈbeɪs(ə)l/ *adjective.* L19.
[from PARA-[1] + BASAL *adjective*.]
1 ZOOLOGY. **a** Situated next to and articulated with a basal plate of a crinoid. *rare.* L19. ▸**b** Designating the kinetoplast of a protozoan. Chiefly in ***parabasal body***. E20.
2 MEDICINE. Designating cells from the layers of stratified epithelium just above the deepest (basal) layer of cells. M20.

parabasis /pəˈrabəsɪs/ *noun.* Pl. **-ases** /-əsiːz/. E19.
[Greek, from *parabainein* go aside, step forward, formed as PARA-[1] + *bainein* to step, walk.]
In ancient Greek comedy, a part unconnected with the action of the drama that was sung by the chorus to the audience in the poet's name; *transf.* a digression in which

For other words beginning with *para-* see the main alphabetic sequence of entries an author addresses the audience on personal or topical matters.

Parabellum /parəˈbɛləm/ *noun.* Also **p-**. **E20.**
[from Latin *para bellum* prepare for war, from *para* imper. of *parare* prepare + *bellum* war.]
A make of automatic pistol or machine-gun.

parabema /parəˈbiːmə/ *noun.* Pl. **-mata** /-mətə/. **M19.**
[mod. Greek *parabēma*, formed as PARA-¹, BEMA.]
CHRISTIAN CHURCH. The part of an Orthodox church on each side of the bema, when separated from the latter by a wall.

parabiosis /parəbʌɪˈəʊsɪs/ *noun.* **E20.**
[from PARA-¹ + Greek *biōsis* way of life, from *bios* life.]
BIOLOGY. The anatomical union of a pair of organisms, either naturally (as in Siamese twins) or surgically; the state of being so joined.
■ **paraˈbiont** *noun* an animal that is in a parabiotic union **M20.** **parabiˈotic** *adjective* of, pertaining to, or existing in parabiosis **E20.** **parabiˈotically** *adverb* so as to produce parabiosis **E20.**

parable /ˈparəb(ə)l/ *noun.* **ME.**
[Old & mod. French *parabole* from Latin *parabola* comparison, (in ecclesiastical Latin) allegory, proverb, discourse, speech, from Greek *parabolē* comparison, analogy, proverb, from *paraballein* put alongside, compare, formed as PARA-¹ + *ballein* to cast, throw.]
1 A saying in which something is expressed in terms of something else; an allegory; a proverb, a maxim; an enigmatical, mystical, or dark saying. *arch.* exc. as in sense 2. **ME.**
2 A narrative of imagined events used to illustrate or convey a moral or spiritual lesson; *spec.* one of those used by Jesus in the Gospels. **LME.**
3 Something that may be pointed to as an example (to follow or to avoid). *dial.* **L19.**

> **2** P. CAREY A conscientious Christian with a great fondness for the parable of the talents.

†parable *adjective.* **M16–M18.**
[Latin *parabilis*, from *parare* prepare, procure: see -ABLE.]
Able to be readily prepared, procured, or got; procurable.

parable /ˈparəb(ə)l/ *verb. rare.* **L16.**
[from PARABLE *noun.*]
1 *verb intrans.* Compose or utter a parable; speak in parables. **L16.**
2 *verb trans.* Represent or express by means of a parable. **M17.**

parablepsy /ˈparəblɛpsi/ *noun.* Also in Latin form **parablepsia** /parəˈblɛpsɪə/. **M19.**
[Greek *parablepsis*, from *parablepein* look aside at, overlook, formed as PARA-¹ + *blepein* see: see -Y³, -IA¹.]
False vision; oversight.

parabola /pəˈrab(ə)lə/ *noun.* Pl. **-las**, **-lae** /-liː/. **L16.**
[mod. Latin from Greek *parabolē* application: cf. PARABLE *noun.*]
1 One of the conic sections, a curve formed where a plane intersects a cone and is parallel to a side of the cone; the curve traced by a point whose distance from a given point (the focus) is equal to its distance from a given straight line (the directrix); a curve that is the graph of an equation of the type $y = ax^2$. **L16.**
2 A curve of higher degree resembling a parabola. **M17.**

> **1** *New Yorker* Graebner muscles one down the line so fast that Ashe's volley makes a high, awkward parabola.

■ **paraboliform** *adjective* (*rare*) of the form of a parabola **E18.**

parabolanus /parəbəˈleməs/ *noun.* Pl. **-ni** /-nʌɪ/. **L17.**
[Late Latin, from *parabolus* reckless man from Greek *parabolos* reckless, formed as PARA-¹ + *ballein* to throw: see -AN.]
In the Church in Alexandria and Constantinople in the 5th and 6th cents., a lay helper who attended the sick during the plague etc.

parabolic /parəˈbɒlɪk/ *adjective & noun.* **LME.**
[Late Latin *parabolicus* from late Greek *parabolikos* figurative, from *parabolē*: see PARABLE *noun*, -IC.]
▶ **A** *adjective.* **1** Of, pertaining to, or of the nature of a parable; expressed by parable; metaphorical, figurative. **LME.**
2 Of the form of or resembling a parabola; having a shape whose cross-section is a parabola; pertaining to the parabola. **E18.**

> **1** J. P. STERN The prophetic or parabolic nature of Christ's sayings. **2** *Practical Wireless* A parabolic mirror of 83 ft diameter . . scans the sky. **parabolic spiral** a two-armed spiral in which the length of the radius vector is proportional to the square root of the angle it makes with a fixed line.

▶**†B** *noun.* A parabolic curve or surface. *rare.* **M17–E19.**

parabolical /parəˈbɒlɪk(ə)l/ *adjective.* **M16.**
[from prec. + -AL¹.]
1 = PARABOLIC *adjective* 1. **M16.** ▶**†b** Fond of using parables or allegories. **L17–E19.**
2 = PARABOLIC *adjective* 2. Now *rare.* **L16.**

parabolically /parəˈbɒlɪk(ə)li/ *adverb.* **E17.**
[from PARABOLIC *adjective* or prec.: see -ICALLY.]
1 With parable or allegory; metaphorically, figuratively. **E17.**
2 In (the manner of) a parabola. *rare.* **M18.**

parabolise *verb* var. of PARABOLIZE.

parabolist /pəˈrab(ə)lɪst/ *noun. rare.* **M17.**
[from Greek *parabolē*: see PARABLE *noun*, -IST.]
A person who narrates, uses, or deals with parables or allegories.

parabolize /pəˈrab(ə)lʌɪz/ *verb trans.* Also **-ise**. **E17.**
[Orig. from medieval Latin *parabolizare* speak in parables; in mod. use formed as prec. + -IZE.]
1 Express or represent by means of or in a parable. **E17.**
2 Make parabolic or paraboloidal in shape. **M19.**

paraboloid /pəˈrab(ə)lɔɪd/ *noun & adjective.* **M17.**
[from PARABOLA + -OID.]
GEOMETRY. ▶**A** *noun.* **†1** = PARABOLA 2. **M17–E18.**
2 A solid or surface of which the cross-sections in two mutually perpendicular directions are parabolas and those in the third are ellipses or hyperbolas; *spec.* one with circular cross-sections, generated by the rotation of a parabola about its axis of symmetry (also more fully ***paraboloid of revolution***). **E18.**
▶ **B** *adjective.* Paraboloidal. *rare.* **M19.**
■ **paraboˈloidal** *adjective* of the form of a paraboloid **E19.**

Paracelsian /parəˈsɛlsɪən/ *noun & adjective.* **L16.**
[from *Paracelsus* (see below) + -IAN.]
HISTORY OF SCIENCE. ▶**A** *noun.* A follower or adherent of the Swiss physician, chemist, and natural philosopher Paracelsus (*c* 1493–1541), or of his medical or philosophical principles; an iatrochemist. **L16.**
▶ **B** *adjective.* Of, pertaining to, or characteristic of Paracelsus; iatrochemical. **L16.**
■ **Paracelsianism** *noun* the medical principles of Paracelsus **M17.** **Paracelsist** *noun* = PARACELSIAN *noun* **E17.**

paracentesis /parəsɛnˈtiːsɪs/ *noun.* Pl. **-teses** /-ˈtiːsiːz/. **L16.**
[Latin = couching of a cataract from Greek *parakentēsis*, from *parakentein* pierce at the side, formed as PARA-¹ + *kentein* prick, stab.]
SURGERY. The operation of making a perforation into a cavity of the body, usu. with a hollow needle to remove fluid or gas. Also, the couching of a cataract.

paracentral /parəˈsɛntr(ə)l/ *adjective.* **L19.**
[from PARA-¹ + Latin *centrum* CENTRE *noun* + -AL¹.]
ANATOMY. Situated beside or alongside the centre.

paracentric /parəˈsɛntrɪk/ *adjective.* **E18.**
[from PARA-¹ + -CENTRIC.]
†1 Designating motion to or from an attracting centre, such as was supposed to form part of the motion of the planets. Also, designating simple motion about a centre. Only in **18.**
2 CYTOLOGY. Involving only the part of a chromosome at one side of the centromere. Opp. PERICENTRIC 2. **M20.**

paracetamol /parəˈsiːtəmɒl, -ˈsɛt-/ *noun.* **M20.**
[from *para-acetylaminophenol*, chemical name: see PARA-¹, ACETYL, AMINO-, PHENOL.]
PHARMACOLOGY. A drug, $C_8H_9NO_2$, with mild analgesic and antipyretic properties; a tablet of this.
¶ A proprietary name for this drug is PANADOL.

parachronism /pəˈrakrənɪz(ə)m/ *noun.* **M17.**
[from PARA-¹ + Greek *khronos* time + -ISM, or alt. of ANACHRONISM.]
An error in chronology; *esp.* the placing of an event later than its real date. Cf. PROCHRONISM.

parachute /ˈparəʃuːt/ *noun & adjective.* **L18.**
[French, formed as PARA-² + *chute* fall.]
▶ **A** *noun.* **1** A device to prevent an unsafe increase in the rate of fall of a person or object from a great height (esp. from an aircraft), consisting when open of a large umbrella-like sheet of fabric with wires or ropes attached round the edge and converging on a harness, basket, etc., attached to their lower end; a similar umbrella-like device released from an aircraft on landing to act as a brake; *transf.* a thing acting like or resembling a parachute, *spec.* = ***golden parachute*** s.v. GOLDEN *adjective.* **L18.**
†2 A broad-brimmed hat with a bulging crown, worn by women in the late 18th cent. **L18–L19.**
▶ **B** *attrib.* or as *adjective.* Dropped or meant for dropping by parachute; involving the use of a parachute. **M19.**
parachute flare, ***parachute jump***, ***parachute troops***, etc.
■ **parachutage** *noun* a drop of supplies etc. by parachute **M20.** **parachutist** *noun* a person who makes a descent by parachute, esp. habitually; a soldier trained in making parachute descents: **L19.**

parachute /ˈparəʃuːt/ *verb.* **E19.**
[from prec.]
1 *verb trans.* Convey or drop by means of a parachute. **E19.**
2 *verb intrans.* Descend by or as by a parachute; use a parachute. **M19.**
3 *verb trans.* (freq. in *pass.*). *fig.* Appoint or elect (an outsider) to a position in an organization without regard to the existing hierarchy. More widely, send (a person) to rectify a bad situation or act as an emergency reinforcement. Foll. by *in*, *into*. **M20.**
■ **parachuter** *noun* a parachutist **L19.**

Paraclete /ˈparəkliːt/ *noun.* **ME.**
[Old & mod. French *paraclet* from ecclesiastical Latin *paracletus* from Greek *paraklētos* advocate, intercessor, from *parakalein* call to one's aid, formed as PARA-¹ + *kalein* to call.]
1 CHRISTIAN THEOLOGY. A title of the Holy Spirit, esp. as an advocate or intercessor. **ME.**
†2 (**p-**.) *gen.* An advocate, an intercessor. **M16–E18.**

†parada *noun.* Also **-do**, pl. **-oes**. **E17.**
[Alt. of French *parade* after Spanish: see next, -ADO.]
1 = PARADE *noun* 1. Only in **17.**
2 = PARADE *noun* 2. **E–M17.**
3 A relay of horses; a halt made when riding or driving. **M17–M19.**
4 = PARADE *noun* 4, 5; *spec.* (**P-**) *the* Prado in Madrid. **M–L17.**
5 = PARADE *noun* 7. Only in **M19.**

parade /pəˈreɪd/ *noun & verb.* **M17.**
[French from Spanish *parada*, Italian *parata* display, parry, pulling-up of a horse, from Proto-Romance use as noun of fem. pa. pple of Latin *parare* prepare: see -ADE.]
▶ **A** *noun.* **I 1** Ostentatious display, (a) show. Freq. in ***make a parade of***. **M17.**
2 An assembling or mustering of troops for inspection or display, *esp.* a formal or ceremonial one; the troops appearing on parade. **M17.**
3 a A public march or procession that is conducted in a formal or ceremonial manner. **L17.** ▶**b** An assembly of people; *esp.* a crowd of people promenading. **E18.**
4 A public square or promenade; a short row of or *of* shops; a street formed by such a square or row. **L17.**
5 More fully ***parade ground***. A place where troops assemble for parade. **E18.**
6 A broadcast sequence describing forthcoming programmes. **M20.**

> **1** F. RAPHAEL A parade of their innocence was taken for a show of shamelessness. **2** *New Statesman* The weekly parade by the band of the Royal Anglian Regiment. **3a** *Boston Journal* A parade two miles long . . composed of gay floats. **4** *Daily Telegraph* I would have saved if I had shopped . . in the local parade.

▶ **II 7** A parry in fencing. **L17.**
Phrases: ***Easter Parade***: see EASTER *noun*. **on parade** (***a***) taking part in a display; (***b***) on display. ***sick parade***: see SICK *adjective*.
Comb.: **parade drum** a large drum played in parades; ***parade ground***: see sense 5 above; **parade ring** a circuit at a racecourse round which horses can be walked to warm up before a race.
▶ **B** *verb.* **1** *verb trans.* Assemble (troops etc.) for inspection or review; cause to go on parade. **L17.**
2 *verb intrans.* **a** Assemble for parade; go or march on parade. **M18.** ▶**b** Walk up and down in a public place, esp. in order to be seen; walk proudly or ostentatiously. **E19.** ▶**c** Appear falsely *as*; masquerade. **M20.**
†3 *verb intrans. & trans.* (with *it*). Behave, talk, or write ostentatiously; show off. **M18–E19.**
4 *verb trans.* Walk ostentatiously through (a town) or along (a street). **L18.**
5 *verb trans.* Make (a person) go up and down or through the streets, esp. so as to be admired or treated with contempt; display in a parade. **E19.**
6 *verb trans.* Make an ostentatious display of; reveal, expose. **E19.**

> **1** K. AMIS Sergeant Ulmanis paraded the troop and reported all present and correct to Alexander. **2a** *New Statesman* The Royal Anglian paraded the following morning. **b** W. S. GILBERT Whose middle-class lives are embarrassed by wives Who long to parade as 'My Lady'. A. N. WILSON A sandwich man was hired to parade up and down outside Isaac's office. U. HOLDEN Long ago there had been peacocks on the lawns to parade amongst the flowerbeds. **5** A. J. CRONIN Earnestly, indefatigably, she paraded me round the royal and ancient borough. H. MACMILLAN Russian weapons were paraded through the streets, and Russian aeroplanes gave a display. **6** M. E. BRADDON The very last . . to parade his feelings . . before the eyes of his fellow men. JOHN BROOKE He had no wish to parade openly the ill feeling between them.

■ **paradeful** *adjective* (*rare*) ostentatious **M18.** **parader** *noun* a person who parades **M18.** **paradingly** *adverb* with much display, ostentatiously **L18.**

paradiddle /ˈparədɪd(ə)l/ *noun.* **E20.**
[Imit.]
MUSIC. A basic drum roll, consisting of four even strokes played in the order 'left right left left' or 'right left right right'.

paradidymis /parəˈdɪdɪmɪs/ *noun.* Pl. **-didymides** /-dɪˈdɪmɪdiːz/. **L19.**
[from PARA-¹ + EPI)DIDYMIS.]
ANATOMY. A group of vestigial tubules in the male just above the epididymis, derived from the mesonephros. Cf. PAROOPHORON.

■ **paradidymal** *adjective* L19.

paradigm /ˈparədʌɪm/ *noun.* L15.
[Late Latin *paradigma* from Greek *paradeigma* example, from *paradeiknunai* show side by side, formed as PARA-[1] + *deiknunai* to show.]
1 An example; a pattern followed; a typical instance; an epitome; *PHILOSOPHY* a mode of viewing the world which underlies the theories and methodology of science in a particular period of history. L15.
2 *GRAMMAR.* A list serving as an example or pattern of the inflections of an inflected part of speech. L16.

1 T. EAGLETON In the drive for order . . history . . selects criticism as both paradigm and instrument of such a project. *Scientific American* The momentous discovery of universal gravitation . . became the paradigm of successful science.

Comb.: **paradigm case** a case or instance to be regarded as representative or typical; **paradigm shift** a major conceptual or methodological change in the theory or practice of a particular science or discipline.
■ **paradigmatic** /-dɪɡˈmatɪk/ *adjective* [Greek *paradeigmatikos*] of the nature of a paradigm; exemplary; *LINGUISTICS* belonging to a set of linguistically associated or interchangeable forms: M17. †**paradigmatical** *adjective* paradigmatic L16–L18. **paradigmatically** /-dɪɡˈmatɪk(ə)li/ *adverb* (chiefly *LINGUISTICS*) as a paradigm, by means of a paradigm, in terms of a paradigm M19. †**paradigmatize** *verb trans.* present as a model, make an example of M17–E18.

paradisaic /parədɪˈseɪɪk/ *adjective.* M18.
[from PARADISE after *Judaic, Mosaic*, etc.]
= PARADISIACAL.
■ **paradisaical** *adjective* E17. **paradisaically** *adverb* M19.

paradise /ˈparədʌɪs/ *noun & verb.* ME.
[Old & mod. French *paradis* from ecclesiastical Latin *paradisus* from Greek *paradeisos* royal park, garden, enclosure, paradise from Avestan *pairidaēza* enclosure, from *pairi* around (= PERI-) + *diz* to mould, form. Cf. PARVIS.]
▶**A** *noun.* **1** The garden of Eden described in *Genesis* 2, 3. Also ***earthly paradise***. ME.
2 Heaven, in Christian and Muslim theology. Now chiefly *poet.* ME. ▶**b** *CHRISTIAN THEOLOGY.* An intermediate place or state where the departed souls of the righteous await resurrection and the last judgement. L17.
3 A region of surpassing beauty or delight; a place or state of supreme bliss. LME.
4 a *Hist.* A garden, an orchard; *spec.* the garden of a convent. LME. ▶**b** An oriental park or pleasure-ground, *esp.* one enclosing wild animals for hunting. E17.
5 *ellipt.* The plumage of a bird of paradise. E20.

3 I. MCEWAN She tasted paradise on earth. H. R. LANDON The Vienna of 1791 appeared to a later generation to have been a musical paradise.

Phrases: ***bird of paradise***: see BIRD *noun*. ***fool's paradise***: see FOOL *noun*[1]. ***grains of Paradise***: see GRAIN *noun*[1] 3a.
Comb.: **paradise apple** a variety of apple (cf. ***paradise stock*** below); **paradise-bird** = ***bird of paradise*** (a) s.v. BIRD *noun*; **paradise crane** = *STANLEY crane*; **paradise duck** a brightly coloured New Zealand sheldrake, *Tadorna variegata*; **paradise-fish** a small hardy and aggressive labyrinth fish, *Macropodus opercularis* (family Belontiidae), of SE Asia that is kept as an aquarium fish; ***comb-tailed paradise-fish***, a Sri Lankan fish, *Belontia signata*, of the same family, also kept as an aquarium fish; **paradise flycatcher** a monarch flycatcher of the genus *Terpsiphone*, with very long middle tail feathers; **paradise stock** any of several types of hardy slow-growing apple trees used as stocks for dwarfing the trees grown on them; **paradise-tree** a small W. Indian tree, *Quassia simarouba* (family Simaroubaceae).
▶**B** *verb trans.* Make into paradise; place in paradise; make supremely blessed or beautiful. Now *poet.* L16.
■ **paraˈdisal** *adjective* = PARADISIACAL M16. **paradisean** /-ˈdɪs-/ *adjective* (*rare*) = PARADISIACAL M17. **paradisial** /-ˈdɪs-, ˈdɪz-/ *adjective* = PARADISIACAL L18. **paradisian** /-ˈdɪs-, ˈdɪz-/ *adjective* = PARADISIACAL M17. **paradisic** /-ˈdɪs-, ˈdɪz-/ *adjective* = PARADISIACAL M18. **paradisical** /-ˈdɪs-, ˈdɪz-/ *adjective* = PARADISIACAL M17. **paraˈdisically** *adverb* L19.

paradisiacal /parədɪˈsʌɪək(ə)l/ *adjective.* M17.
[from ecclesiastical Latin *paradisiacus* from Greek *paradeisiakos*, from *paradeisos* PARADISE *noun*: see -ACAL.]
Of, pertaining to, or belonging to paradise; like that of paradise, supremely blessed; peacefully beautiful; celestial.
■ **paraˈdisiac** *adjective* = PARADISIACAL M17. **paradisiacally** *adverb* L19.

†**parado** *noun* var. of PARADA.

parador /ˈparədɔː/ *noun.* Pl. **-dores** /-dɔːrez/, **-dors**. M19.
[Spanish.]
A hotel owned and administered by the Spanish government. Formerly, any Spanish hotel or inn.

parados /ˈparədɒs, *foreign* parado/ *noun.* Pl. **-oses** /-ɒsɪz/, same. M19.
[French, formed as PARA-[2] + *dos* back.]
An elevation of earth behind a defended place as a protection against attack from the rear; the mound along the back of a trench.

paradoses *nouns pl.* see PARADOS, PARADOSIS.

paradosis /pəˈradəsɪs/ *noun.* Pl. **-oses** /-əsiːz/. M20.
[Greek, formed as PARA-[1]: see DOSE *noun*.]
THEOLOGY. A historical tradition, *esp.* one relating to the teachings of Jesus and his disciples; teaching based on this tradition.

paradox /ˈparədɒks/ *noun & adjective.* M16.
[Late Latin *paradoxum*, *-doxon* use as noun of neut. of *paradoxus* from Greek *paradoxos*, formed as PARA-[1] + *doxa* opinion.]
▶**A** *noun.* **1** A statement or tenet contrary to received opinion or belief, *esp.* one that is incredible, absurd, or fantastic. Long *rare.* M16.
2 a A seemingly absurd or self-contradictory statement or proposition which when investigated or explained may prove to be well-founded or true. M16. ▶**b** A proposition or statement that is actually self-contradictory, absurd, or false. L16. ▶**c** *LOGIC.* In full ***logical paradox***. A statement or argument which, despite sound reasoning from an acceptable premiss, leads to a conclusion that is against sense, logically unacceptable, or self-contradictory. E20.
3 Paradoxical character, condition, or quality. L16.
4 *transf.* A phenomenon that exhibits some contradiction or conflict with preconceived notions of what is reasonable or possible; a person of perplexingly inconsistent life or behaviour. E17.

2a E. FROMM In love the paradox occurs that two beings become one and yet remain two. P. AUSTER The paradox of the word 'cleave', which means both 'to join together' and 'to break apart'. ***twin paradox***: see TWIN *adjective & noun*. **b** D. STEWART It was perfectly impossible . . to detect the flaw to which Berkeley's paradox owed its plausibility. ***SEMANTIC paradox***. **c** ***paradox of the liar, the liar paradox***: see LIAR 1. RUSSELL'S PARADOX. **4** C. ODETS A paradox in human behaviour: . . he shoots you for a nickel . . for fifty bucks he sends you flowers!

▶†**B** *adjective.* Paradoxical. E–M17.
■ †**paradoxal** *adjective* paradoxical L16–L19.

paradox /ˈparədɒks/ *verb. rare.* M17.
[from the noun.]
1 *verb intrans. & trans.* (with *it*). Utter paradoxes. M17.
2 *verb trans.* Affect with a paradox, cause to show a paradox or contradiction. M17.

paradoxer /ˈparədɒksə/ *noun.* M19.
[from PARADOX *noun*, *verb* + -ER[1].]
A propounder of paradoxes.

paradoxical /parəˈdɒksɪk(ə)l/ *adjective.* L16.
[from PARADOX *noun* + -ICAL.]
1 Of the nature of a paradox, exhibiting or involving paradox; *esp.* apparently inconsistent with itself or with reason, though in fact true. L16.
2 Fond of or given to paradox; characterized by paradox. E17.
3 Of a phenomenon, circumstance, etc.: exhibiting some contradiction with itself or with known laws, esp. laws of nature; deviating from the normal. M17. ▶**b** Of sleep: characterized by increased physiological and mental activity (e.g. rapid eye movements and dreaming in humans) and normally alternating with longer periods of orthodox sleep. M20.

1 E. A. FREEMAN True, though it might sound paradoxical, to say that the Norman Conquest made England Saxon. **2** P. GOODMAN In this paradoxical atmosphere . . young persons grow up. It looks busy and expansive, but it is rationally at a stalemate.

■ **paradoxic** *adjective* (*rare*) = PARADOXICAL M17. **ˌparadoxiˈcality** *noun* paradoxical character or quality E19. **paradoxically** *adverb* in a paradoxical manner; in such a way or sense as to involve a paradox: L16. **paradoxicalness** *noun* paradoxicality M17.

paradoxism /ˈparədɒksɪz(ə)m/ *noun.* L16.
[from PARADOX *noun* + -ISM.]
The utterance or practice of paradox.
■ **paradoxist** *noun* a paradoxer L17.

paradoxographical /ˌparədɒksəˈɡrafɪk(ə)l/ *adjective.* E19.
[from Greek *paradoxographos* writer of paradoxes from *paradoxos* (see PARADOX *noun*, -GRAPH) + -ICAL.]
Belonging or devoted to the writing of paradoxes.

paradoxology /parədɒkˈsɒlədʒi/ *noun.* M17.
[Greek *paradoxologia*, from *paradoxologos* telling of paradoxes, from *paradoxos*: see PARADOX *noun*, -OLOGY.]
The maintaining or expression of paradoxical opinions; speaking by paradox.

paradoxure /parəˈdɒksjʊə/ *noun.* M19.
[mod. Latin *Paradoxurus* (see below), from Greek *paradoxos* (see PARADOX *noun & adjective*) + *oura* tail.]
A palm civet, *esp.* one of the genus *Paradoxurus*.

paradoxy /ˈparədɒksi/ *noun.* M17.
[Greek *paradoxia*, from *paradoxos*: see PARADOX *noun & adjective*, -Y[3].]
†**1** A paradox. *rare.* Only in M17.
2 Paradoxicality. L18.

paraenesis /pəˈriːnɪsɪs/ *noun.* Also **-ren-** /-ˈrɛn-/. Pl. **-eses** /-ɪsiːz/. L16.
[Late Latin from Greek *parainesis*, from *parainein* exhort, formed as PARA-[1] + *ainein* speak of, praise.]
An exhortatory composition; exhortation.
■ **paraenetic** /-ˈnɛt-/ *adjective* hortatory, advisory M17. **paraenetical** /-ˈnɛt-/ *adjective* (now *rare*) paraenetic L16.

paraesthesia /parɪsˈθiːzɪə/ *noun.* Also ***-res-**. Pl. **-iae** /-ɪiː/. L19.
[from PARA-[1] + Greek *aisthēsis* sensation: see -IA[1].]
MEDICINE. Orig., a sensory hallucination. Now (*sing.* & in *pl.*) apparently spontaneous sensations of tingling, numbness, etc., in the skin.
■ **paraesthetic** /-ˈθɛtɪk/ *adjective* of, pertaining to, or affected with paraesthesia M19.

parafango /parəˈfaŋɡəʊ/ *noun.* M20.
[from PARA(FFIN + FANGO.]
A mixture of mud and paraffin wax used for medicinal purposes.

paraffin /ˈparəfɪn/ *noun & verb.* M19.
[German, from Latin *parum* too little, barely + *affinis* related, with ref. to the low affinity of paraffin for other substances.]
▶**A** *noun.* **1** A whitish translucent waxy combustible solid consisting of a mixture of hydrocarbons, obtained as residue from the distillation of petroleum and shale and used esp. in candles, cosmetics, and polishes, and for coating and sealing. M19.
2 In full ***paraffin oil***. = KEROSENE. Also, paraffin (sense 1) in liquid form. M19.
3 *CHEMISTRY.* = ALKANE. L19.
2 ***liquid paraffin***: see LIQUID *adjective & noun*.
Comb.: ***paraffin oil***: see sense 2 above; **paraffin test** a test to ascertain whether a person fired a gun, in which the hand is coated with hot paraffin which is then peeled off and tested for the presence of powder; **paraffin wax** paraffin (sense 1) in solid form.
▶**B** *verb trans.* Cover, impregnate, or treat with paraffin. Usu. in *pass.* L19.
■ **paraˈffinic** *adjective* consisting or of the nature of (a) paraffin L19. **paraffinized** *adjective* treated with paraffin L19. **paraffiny** *adjective* of or suggestive of paraffin; covered or smeared with paraffin; smelling of paraffin: E20.

paraffle /pəˈraf(ə)l/ *noun. Scot.* Also **parafle**. E19.
[Perh. alt. of French *parafe*: see PARAPH, -LE[1].]
Ostentatious display; a flourish.

paraganglion /parəˈɡaŋɡlɪən/ *noun.* Pl. **-ia** /-ɪə/. E20.
[from PARA-[1] + GANGLION.]
ANATOMY. Any of several highly vascular groups of cells that are similar to those of the adrenal medulla and are closely associated with the sympathetic nerve trunks.
■ **ˌparaganglіˈoma** *noun*, pl. **-mas**, **-mata** /-mətə/, a tumour thought to arise from a paraganglion or the adrenal medulla, *esp.* one of non-chromaffin tissue E20. **paragangliˈonic** *adjective* M20.

†**parage** *noun.* ME.
[Old & mod. French, from *per* (mod. *pair*): see PEER *noun*[1], -AGE.]
1 Lineage, descent, rank; *esp.* noble or high lineage. ME–M19.
2 Equality of birth, as in members of the same family. LME–M17.
3 *FEUDAL LAW.* Tenure of inherited land by virtue of descent or rank, with no liability for homage or service. LME–M18.
4 Worth, value. *rare.* L15–E16.

paragenesis /parəˈdʒɛnɪsɪs/ *noun.* Pl. **-geneses** /-ˈdʒɛnɪsiːz/. M19.
[from PARA-[1] + -GENESIS.]
The occurrence together of different minerals, esp. as reflecting the conditions of their formation; a set of minerals occurring together or with a given mineral. Also, the sequence and periods of formation of the constituent minerals.
■ **parageˈnetic** *adjective* (*a*) involving or pertaining to paragenesis; (*b*) (of twin crystals) originating side by side; (of crystallization) giving rise to such twins: M19. **parageˈnetically** *adverb* M20.

paragoge /parəˈɡəʊdʒi/ *noun.* M16.
[Late Latin from Greek *paragōgē* derivation, addition to the end of a syllable, formed as PARA-[1] + *agōgē* carrying, leading.]
PHILOLOGY. The addition of a letter or syllable to a word, either in the course of a language's development (e.g. English *peasan-t*), or, as in Hebrew, to give emphasis or modify the meaning.
■ **paragogic** /-ˈɡɒdʒ-/ *adjective & noun* (*a*) *adjective* of, pertaining to, or of the nature of paragoge; (of a sound or letter) added to a word by paragoge; (*b*) *noun* a paragogic sound or letter: L16. **paragogical** /-ˈɡɒdʒ-/ *adjective* paragogic E17.

paragon /ˈparəɡ(ə)n/ *noun & adjective.* Also (*obsolete* exc. in sense 6) **paragone** /parəˈɡəʊni/. M16.
[Obsolete French (now *parangon*) from Italian *para(n)gone* touchstone, comparison, from medieval Greek *parakonē* whetstone.]
▶**A** *noun.* **I 1** A pattern or model of excellence; *esp.* a person supreme in merit or excellence; a person who is an exemplar *of* a virtue or a model *of* a character. M16.
†**2** A match; a companion; a partner in marriage; a rival, a competitor. M16–E19.

†**3** Comparison; competition, emulation, rivalry. L16–M17.

> 1 A. J. CRONIN Her unsparing devotion to her brother, her unstinted loyalty . . made her almost a paragon. S. MIDDLETON Even the children applauded this paragon of a father. F. KAPLAN He seemed to many a paragon of cheerfulness.

▶ **II 4** A perfect diamond. Now *spec.* one weighing more than 100 carats. E17.
†**5** A kind of double camlet used for clothing and upholstery in the 17th and early 18th cents. E17–M18.
6 (Usu. **paragone**.) A kind of Italian black marble. M17.
7 A former size of type equal to about 20 points. E18.
▶ **B** *attrib.* or as *adjective.* Of surpassing excellence. Now *rare.* M16.
†**paragon stone** = sense A.4 above.

paragon /ˈparəg(ə)n/ *verb trans.* Now *poet.* L16.
[from the noun.]
1 Place side by side; compare *to.* Also foll. by *with.* L16.
†**2** Excel, surpass. *rare* (Shakes.). Only in E17.
†**3** Present as a paragon or perfect model. *rare* (Shakes.). Only in E17.
4 Match, mate. E17.

paragone *noun & adjective* see PARAGON *noun & adjective.*

paragonimiasis /ˌparəgəʊnɪˈmʌɪəsɪs/ *noun.* Pl. **-ases** /-əsiːz/. E20.
[from mod. Latin *Paragonimus* (see below), from PARA-¹ + Greek *gonimos* productive, from *gen-*, *gon-* produce: see -IASIS.]
MEDICINE. Infestation with lung flukes (worms of the genus *Paragonimus*), which results from eating infected crustaceans and is usu. marked by abdominal pains, a persistent cough, and expectoration of blood.

†**paragram** *noun.* L17–M18.
[from Greek *ta para gramma skōmmata* jokes by the letter.]
A play on words consisting in the alteration of one letter or group of letters of a word, esp. an initial letter.

paragraph /ˈparəgrɑːf/ *noun & verb.* L15.
[Old & mod. French *paragraphe* or medieval Latin *paragraphus*, *-um* from Greek *paragraphos* short horizontal stroke written below the beginning of a line in which a break of sense occurs, passage so marked, formed as PARA-¹ + *-graphos* -GRAPH.]
▶ **A** *noun.* **1 a** A distinct passage of a text, dealing with a particular point of the subject, the words of one speaker, etc., and now marked by beginning on a new line, often indented and ending on a separate line from the text that follows; a passage of text beginning and ending in this way; any passage which, from its nature, might or ought to be so presented in writing or print. L15. ▶**b** A distinct, usually numbered, article or section of a legal document. M16. ▶**c** A distinct passage or section in a musical composition. M20.
2 More fully ***paragraph mark***, ***paragraph sign***. A symbol (now usually ¶ or ⁋) formerly used to mark the beginning of a new section of a text, now to introduce an editorial comment or as a reference to a footnote. M16.
3 A short article in a newspaper or periodical, with no headline; a printed item of news. M18.
4 A figure in which an ice skater traces complete circles with turns or loops incorporated. Also ***paragraph figure***. M20.

> **1** ***hanging paragraph***: see HANGING *adjective.* **3** J. K. JEROME Some paragraphs . . had been appearing in the papers concerning the sea-serpent.

▶ **B** *verb trans.* †**1** = PARAPH *verb* 2. Only in 17.
2 Mention in a paragraph; write a newspaper paragraph about. Also with adverbial adjunct expr. the result achieved. M18.
3 Divide into or arrange in paragraphs. Usu. in *pass.* L18.

> **2** *Examiner* The Politician must be . . paragraphed . . into notoriety. G. B. SHAW The much paragraphed 'brilliancy' of *Arms and the Man.* **3** *American Journal of Theology* I have reproduced the punctuation and paragraphing of the MS.

■ **paragrapher** *noun* a paragraphist E19. **paragraphism** *noun* the system or practice of composing or printing newspaper paragraphs M19. **paragraphist** *noun* (orig. *US*) a professional writer of newspaper paragraphs L18.

paragraphia /parəˈgrafɪə/ *noun.* L19.
[from PARA-¹ + Greek *-graphia* writing.]
The aphasic symptom of writing one letter, syllable, or word for another.

paragraphic /parəˈgrafɪk/ *adjective.* L18.
[from PARAGRAPH *noun*, PARAGRAPHIA + -IC.]
1 Of, pertaining to, or of the nature of a paragraph or paragraphs. L18.
2 Of or pertaining to paragraphia. L19.
■ **paragraphical** *adjective* = PARAGRAPHIC 1 M18. **paragraphically** *adverb* (*a*) in or by means of paragraphs; paragraph by paragraph; (*b*) in the style of, or by means of, newspaper paragraphs: E18.

Paraguay /ˈparəgwʌɪ/ *noun.* E18.
[A river and country of S. America.]
In full ***Paraguay tea***. = MATÉ 2.

Paraguayan /parəˈgwʌɪən/ *adjective & noun.* L17.
[from *Paraguay* (see below) + -AN.]
▶ **A** *noun.* A native or inhabitant of Paraguay, an inland country of S. America. L17.
▶ **B** *adjective.* Of or belonging to Paraguay or its inhabitants; produced in or characteristic of Paraguay. L17.

paraheliotropic /ˌparəhiːlɪəˈtrəʊpɪk, -ˈtrɒpɪk/ *adjective.* L19.
[from PARA-¹ + HELIOTROPIC.]
BOTANY. Designating or exhibiting a type of tropism in which a plant's leaves move to avoid intense sunlight, usu. by keeping their blades parallel to the sun's rays.
■ **paraheliˈotropism** *noun* L19.

parahelium /parəˈhiːlɪəm/ *noun.* L19.
[from PARA-¹ + HELIUM.]
PHYSICS. The form of helium whose spectrum does not exhibit the fine structure of orthohelium, the spins of the two orbital electrons being antiparallel.

parahydrogen /parəˈhʌɪdrədʒ(ə)n/ *noun.* E20.
[from PARA-¹ + HYDROGEN.]
PHYSICS. The form of molecular hydrogen in which the two nuclei in the molecule have antiparallel spins (so that the spectrum exhibits no hyperfine structure) and which forms about 25 per cent of hydrogen under normal conditions. Cf. ORTHOHYDROGEN.

para-influenza /ˌparəɪnfluˈɛnzə/ *noun.* M20.
[from PARA-¹ + INFLUENZA.]
BIOLOGY. In full ***para-influenza virus***. Any of a group of paramyxoviruses which resemble the influenza viruses and include the one causing croup.

parajournalism /parəˈdʒəːn(ə)lɪz(ə)m/ *noun.* Orig. *US.* M20.
[from PARA-¹ + JOURNALISM.]
A type of unconventional journalism not primarily concerned with the reporting of facts.
■ **parajournalist** *noun* M20. ˌ**parajournaˈlistic** *adjective* L20.

parakeelya /parəˈkiːljə/ *noun.* L19.
[Aboriginal.]
Any of several succulent Australian plants of the purslane family, esp. *Calandrinia balonensis* and *C. polyandra.*

parakeet /ˈparəkiːt/ *noun.* Also **paroquet** /ˈparəkɪt/, ***parra-**; †**-keeto**, †**-quito**, pl. **-os**. M16.
[Old French *paroquet* (mod. *perroquet* parrot), Italian *parrocchetto*, *perro-*, Spanish *periquito*, perh. ult. based on a dim. (French *Pierrot*, Spanish *Perico*) of the name 'Peter' (French *Pierre*, Spanish *Pedro*: see PETER *noun*¹).]
Orig., a parrot. Now, any of various small, usu. long-tailed parrots.

paralanguage /ˈparəlaŋgwɪdʒ/ *noun.* M20.
[from PARA-¹ + LANGUAGE *noun*¹.]
LINGUISTICS. The system of non-phonemic but vocal factors in speech, such as tone of voice, tempo of speech, and sighing, by which communication is assisted.

paraldehyde /pəˈraldɪhʌɪd/ *noun.* M19.
[from PARA-¹ + ALDEHYDE.]
CHEMISTRY & PHARMACOLOGY. A colourless liquid cyclic polymer of acetaldehyde, $(CH_3{\cdot}CHO)_3$, used medicinally in the treatment of status epilepticus, and formerly as a narcotic and sedative, and industrially as a solvent, intermediate, etc.

paralegal /parəˈliːg(ə)l/ *noun & adjective.* Chiefly *N. Amer.* L20.
[from PARA-¹ + LEGAL.]
▶ **A** *noun.* A person trained in subsidiary legal matters but not fully qualified as a lawyer; a legal aide. L20.
▶ **B** *adjective.* Of or pertaining to auxiliary aspects of the law. L20.

paraleipomenon, **paraleipsis** *nouns* vars. of PARALIPOMENON, PARALIPSIS.

paralic /pəˈralɪk/ *adjective.* E20.
[from Greek *paralios* by the sea, formed as PARA-¹ + *hal-*, *hals* sea: see -IC.]
GEOLOGY. Formed or having occurred in shallow water near the sea.

paralinguistic /parəlɪŋˈgwɪstɪk/ *adjective.* M20.
[from PARA-¹ + LINGUISTIC.]
LINGUISTICS. Of or pertaining to paralanguage or paralinguistics.
■ **paralinguistically** *adverb* M20.

paralinguistics /parəlɪŋˈgwɪstɪks/ *noun.* M20.
[from PARA-¹ + LINGUISTICS.]
The branch of linguistics that deals with paralanguage; non-phonemic factors of vocal communication.

paralipomenon /parəlɪˈpɒmɪnən/ *noun.* Also **-leipo-** /-lʌɪˈpɒ-/. Pl. **-ena** /-ɪnə/. ME.
[ecclesiastical Latin *paralipomena* pl. from Greek *paraleipomena* (things) left out, from *paraleipein* leave on one side, omit, formed as PARA-¹ + *leipein* leave. In sense 1 repr. Greek *Paraleipomenōn* genit. (sc. *biblia* books), title of Chronicles in Septuagint and Vulgate.]
†**1** (**P-**.) The Books of Chronicles in the Old Testament (so called as containing particulars omitted in the Books of Kings). ME–E18.
2 A thing omitted in the body of a work and appended as a supplement. Usu. in *pl.* L17.

paralipsis /parəˈlɪpsɪs/ *noun.* Also **-leip-** /-ˈlʌɪp-/. Pl. **-pses** /-psiːz/. M16.
[Late Latin from Greek *paraleipsis* passing by, omission, from *paraleipein*: see prec.]
RHETORIC. The emphasizing of something by affecting to pass it by without notice, usually with such phrases as 'not to mention', 'to say nothing of'.

†**paralize** *verb* var. of PARALYSE.

parallax /ˈparəlaks/ *noun.* L16.
[French *parallaxe* from mod. Latin *parallaxis* from Greek = change, alternation, angle between two lines, from *parallassein* alter, alternate, formed as PARA-¹ + *allassein* to exchange, from *allos* other.]
1 The fact of seeing wrongly or in a distorted way. Long *rare* exc. as *fig.* use of sense 2. L16.
2 Difference or change in the apparent position or the direction of an object as seen from two different points; *spec.* (*ASTRONOMY*) such a difference or change in the position of a celestial object as seen from different points on the earth's surface or opposite points in its orbit. Also, (half of) the angular amount of such a difference or change; *spec.* (*ASTRONOMY*) the angle subtended at a celestial object by the radius of the earth's orbit, as a measure of its distance. L16.
Comb.: **parallax error** error in reading an instrument caused by parallax when the scale and the indicator are not precisely coincident.
■ **paraˈllactic** *adjective* [Greek *parallaktikos*] pertaining to or resulting from parallax M17. †**parallactical** *adjective* parallactic L17–E18.

parallel /ˈparəlɛl/ *adjective, noun, & adverb.* M16.
[French *parallèle* from Latin *parallelus*, from Greek *parallēlos*, formed as PARA-¹ + *allēlos* one another.]
▶ **A** *adjective.* **1** Of lines (esp. straight ones), surfaces, or concrete things, or of one in relation to another: lying or extending alongside each other or the other and always at the same distance apart; continuously equidistant. (Foll. by *to*, *with*.) M16.
2 *transf.* Of an object, esp. an instrument, appliance, etc.: involving geometrical parallelism in some way; having essential parts that are parallel or are used to produce parallel movement; *ELECTRICITY* involving connection in parallel. L16.
3 *fig.* **a** Having the same or a like course, tendency, or purport; running on the same or similar lines; resembling something else, or each other, throughout the whole extent; precisely similar, analogous, or corresponding. E17. ▶†**b** Equal in amount or worth. Only in 17.
4 Running through the same period of time; contemporary in duration; *COMPUTING* involving the concurrent or simultaneous performance of certain operations; functioning in this way. M18.
5 *MUSIC.* Designating (the movement of) parts which move so that the interval between them remains the same (major and minor intervals of the same name, e.g. thirds or sixths, being in this case reckoned the same); (of intervals) = CONSECUTIVE 4. M19.

> **1** R. KIRWAN Cut in two, in a direction parallel to the axis. J. TYNDALL The planes of cleavage were everywhere parallel. *Physics Bulletin* A plane parallel to the earth's surface. **3a** C. PRIEST For a time our lives were running parallel. **4** *Australian Personal Computer* A parallel processor is constructed by adding more arithmetic operation modules into the system.

Special collocations & comb.: **parallel bars** two parallel horizontal rails supported on posts for use in gymnastic exercise or display. **parallel cousin** an ortho-cousin. **parallel development** *S. Afr.* separate development. **parallel distributed processing** = CONNECTIONISM. **parallel evolution** = PARALLELISM 4a. **parallel importing** the importation of goods by unlicensed distributors with a view to selling at less than the price approved by the manufacturer. **parallel market** (*a*) an unofficial market in goods or currency, esp. in a country with a controlled economy; (*b*) a stock market operating alongside one that is more regulated. **parallel-medium** *adjective* (*S. Afr.*) designating schooling or a school in which instruction is given through the medium of more than one language. **parallel-park** *verb trans.* (*N. Amer.*) park (a vehicle) parallel to the roadside. **parallel port** *COMPUTING* a connector for a device that sends or receives several bits of data simultaneously by using more than one wire. **parallel ruler(s)** an instrument for drawing parallel lines, consisting of two or more rulers connected by jointed crosspieces so as to be always parallel, at whatever distance they are set. **parallel text** either of two or more versions of a literary work etc. printed in a format which allows direct textual comparison, freq. on facing or consecutive pages of the same volume; a text of different versions of a work set out in such a way. **parallel tracking**: in which a gramophone pick-up is kept tangential to the record groove by a rectilinear motion of the arm. **parallel turn** a swing in skiing with the skis kept parallel to each other. **parallel universe**, **parallel world** a universe or world conceived of as existing alongside or in addition to that which is known, having many similarities to it but usu. differing in some significant way.
▶ **B** *noun.* **I 1** A thing running parallel or having a parallel direction; *esp.* a parallel line. Usu. in *pl.* M16.
2 Each of the imaginary parallel circles of constant latitude on the earth's surface (also more fully ***parallel of***

latitude); ASTRONOMY each of the analogous circles on the celestial sphere. Also, a representation of such a circle on a map. M16.

3 MILITARY. A trench (usually one of three) parallel to the general face of a building etc. under siege, serving as a means of communication between the different parts of the siege-works. L16.

4 *fig.* A thing or person agreeing with another in essential particulars; something precisely analogous, comparable, or of equal worth or force; an analogue, a counterpart. L16.

5 A pair of parallel vertical lines (||) used in printing as a reference mark. L18.

> **2** H. KISSINGER We bombed supply complexes south of the twentieth parallel. **4** JONSON Why, this is without parallel. A. MASSIE The relations between Sido and Colette may find a parallel in the . . love of Mme de Sévigné for her daughter.

▶ **II 6** The placing of things mentally or descriptively side by side so as to show their correspondence; (a) comparison; *esp.* a comparison of things as being alike, a statement of analogy. L16.

7 Agreement in essential particulars; a close correspondence, an analogy. E17.

8 The state of being parallel; parallel position. Long *rare* exc. in ***in parallel*** below. M17.

> **6** *Times* The Archbishop . . drew a parallel yesterday between . . political . . and ecclesiastical *apartheid*. **7** *New York Times* When you think of . . pregnant women and children, with no place to stay, the parallel to Christmas is . . obvious. J. KLEIN Parallels can be perceived between what good parents do and what good psychotherapists do.

Phrases: **in parallel** (*a*) (of two or more wires, pipes, etc.) separately joining the same two points; (*b*) so as to be in parallel; while in parallel; concurrently, simultaneously; contemporaneously; (foll. by *with*).

▶ **C** *adverb*. In a parallel direction or manner. M17.

> JOSEPH HALL Their thoughts running parallel are not like to clash. I. MURDOCH She began to swim to and fro parallel to the shore.

■ **para'llelity** *noun* the state of being parallel (*lit.* & *fig.*) M20. **parallelly** /-l-li/ *adverb* = PARALLEL *adverb* E17. †**parallelwise** *adverb* = PARALLEL *adverb* E17–M18.

parallel /'parəlɛl/ *verb*. M16.

[from prec.]

1 *verb trans.* Mentally place (one thing) beside another or (two or more things) side by side, so as to exhibit a likeness; compare; liken, compare as being like. (Foll. by *with*.) M16.

2 *verb trans.* Adduce a parallel to; serve as or be a parallel to; correspond to; match. L16. ▶†**b** Adduce as a parallel. *rare* (Shakes.). Only in E17.

†**3** *verb trans.* Bring into conformity *with*. E–M17.

4 *verb intrans.* Correspond, match, be comparable, (*with*). E17.

5 *verb trans.* Run parallel with or alongside of; go or tend in the same direction as. Chiefly *US*. L19.

6 *verb trans.* Connect (electrical components etc.) in parallel. (Foll. by *with*.) E20.

> **2** W. SPALDING An era of such grandeur as even their ancient history had not paralleled. JOHN BRIGHT A state of things which could not be paralleled in any other country. G. GREENE These tortuous . . women are paralleled through . . Miss Potter's art. **6** *Popular Hi-Fi* Amplifiers which use parallelled output transistors.

parallelepiped /ˌparəlɛlə'pʌɪpɛd, parəlɛ'lɛpɪpɛd/ *noun*. Also †**paralleli-**, **parallelopiped** /ˌparəlɛlə'pʌɪpɛd/, & (earlier) in Greek form †**parellelepipedon**, pl. **-da**, **-dons**. L16.

[Greek *parallēlepipedon*, from *parallēlos* PARALLEL *adjective* + *epipedon* plane, surface, use as noun of neut. of *epipedos* plane, flat, formed as EPI- + *pedon* ground.]

GEOMETRY. A solid figure bounded by six parallelograms, of which opposite pairs are parallel.

■ ˌ**parallele'pipedal** *adjective* having the form of a parallelepiped M18. **parallele'pipedous** *adjective* parallelepipedal E19.

parallelise *verb* var. of PARALLELIZE.

parallelism /'parəlɛlɪz(ə)m/ *noun*. E17.

[Greek *parallēlismos* comparison of parallels, from *parallēlizein*: see PARALLELIZE, -ISM.]

1 The state, position, or character of being parallel (*lit.* & *fig.*); an instance of this; a parallel case, passage, etc. E17. ▶**b** *spec.* Correspondence, in sense or construction, of successive clauses or passages, esp. in Hebrew and Old English poetry; a sentence or passage exemplifying this. L18.

2 The state or fact of maintaining the same direction. M17.

3 PSYCHOLOGY. (Belief in) a correspondence or correlation between mental phenomena and physical events in the brain or nervous system. M19.

4 a BIOLOGY. The development of similar characteristics by two related groups of animals or plants, in response to similar environmental pressures. L19. ▶**b** ANTHROPOLOGY. A similarity between the evolution and achievements of different cultures. M20.

5 COMPUTING. The execution of operations concurrently by separate parts of a computer, esp. separate microprocessors; the ability to operate in this way. L20.

> **1** HOBBES The parallelism of two concentric circles. C. CAUDWELL Marlowe, Shelley, Lawrence, and Dali have a certain parallelism.

parallelist /'parəlɛlɪst/ *noun & adjective*. E19.

[from PARALLEL *adjective & noun* + -IST.]

▶ **A** *noun*. **1** A person who draws a parallel or comparison. E19.

2 An advocate of parallelism in biology or anthropology. L19.

▶ **B** *adjective*. Of or pertaining to parallelists or parallelism. E20.

■ **paralle'listic** *adjective* pertaining to or characterized by parallelism M19.

parallelize /'parəlɛlʌɪz/ *verb trans.* Also **-ise**. E17.

[Greek *parallēlizein*, from *parallēlos* PARALLEL *adjective*: see -IZE.]

1 = PARALLEL *verb* 1. Usu. foll. by *with*. E17.

2 †**a** Cause to correspond; equalize. Only in E17. ▶**b** Place so as to be parallel; align. E20.

3 = PARALLEL *verb* 2. Usu. in *pass.* *rare*. M17.

■ **paralleli'zation** *noun* the action or an act of parallelizing; the state of being parallelized: E17.

parallelogram /parə'lɛləgram/ *noun*. L16.

[French *parallélogramme* from late Latin *parallelogrammum* from Greek *parallēlogrammon*, from *parallēlos* PARALLEL *adjective*: see -GRAM.]

1 GEOMETRY. A plane rectilinear figure with four sides, of which opposite ones are parallel. L16.

2 †**a** A pantograph. M17–E18. ▶**b** An area or a division of a surface with the shape of a parallelogram. E19.

Phrases: **parallelogram of forces** (a parallelogram illustrating) the theorem that if two forces acting at a point are represented in magnitude and direction by two sides of a parallelogram, their resultant is represented by the diagonal drawn from that point.

■ **parallelogra'mmatic** *adjective* parallelogrammic E18. ˌ**parallelo'grammic** *adjective* pertaining to or of the form of a parallelogram M18. ˌ**parallelo'grammical** *adjective* (now *rare* or *obsolete*) parallelogrammic M17.

parallelopiped *noun* var. of PARALLELEPIPED.

paralogia /parə'ləʊdʒɪə/ *noun*. E19.

[from PARA-[1] + Greek *-logia* -LOGY.]

MEDICINE. **1** Illogical or incoherent speech, as in delirium or schizophrenia. E19.

2 Impaired power of reasoning or logical thinking. E20.

paralogise *verb* var. of PARALOGIZE.

paralogism /pə'ralədʒɪz(ə)m/ *noun*. M16.

[French *paralogisme* or late Latin *paralogismus* from Greek *paralogismos*, from *paralogizesthai* reason falsely, from *paralogos* contrary to reason, formed as PARA-[1] + *logos* reasoning, discourse: see LOGOS, -ISM.]

1 A piece of false reasoning; an illogical argument; a fallacy, *esp.* one of which the reasoner is unaware. M16.

2 False reasoning; illogical argument. *rare*. L17.

■ **para'logical** *adjective* involving or characterized by false reasoning; illogical, unreasonable: M17. **paralogist** *noun* a person who reasons falsely E17. **paralo'gistic** *adjective* of the nature of a paralogism, fallacious L17.

paralogize /pə'ralədʒʌɪz/ *verb intrans.* Long *rare*. Also **-ise**. L16.

[French *paralogiser* or medieval Latin *paralogizare* from Greek *paralogizesthai*: see prec., -IZE.]

Reason falsely or illogically.

paralogous /pə'raləgəs/ *adjective*. L20.

[from PARA-[1] + HOMO)LOGOUS.]

BIOLOGY. Of two or more genes, esp. in organisms of different species: descended from the same gene by gene duplication in the course of evolution.

■ **paralogously** *adverb* L20.

paralogy /pə'ralədʒi/ *noun*. M17.

[Sense 1 from Greek *paralogia* fallacy, from *paralogos* (see PARALOGISM); sense 2 from PARA-[1] + -LOGY.]

1 Paralogical reasoning; fallacy. M17.

2 GENETICS. The state of being paralogous. L20.

Paralympics /parə'lɪmpɪks/ *noun pl.* M20.

[from PARA(PLEGIC + O)*lympics* pl. of OLYMPIC *noun*.]

The Paraplegic Games.

■ **Paralympic** *adjective* M20.

paralyse /'parəlʌɪz/ *verb trans.* Also **-yze*, †**-ize**. LME.

[French *paralyser*, from *paralysie*: see PALSY *noun*[1], and cf. ANALYSE *verb*.]

†**1** Wound. *rare*. Only in LME.

2 Deprive of the power to act; make powerless, helpless, inactive, or ineffective; halt the normal activity of (a factory, community, etc.). L18.

3 Affect with paralysis. E19.

> **2** *Sun (Baltimore)* A railway strike will paralyse the nation on the eve of the holiday week. A. HIGGINS His presence paralysed her; she could not open her mouth. **3** P. CUTTING Wounded by a sniper's bullet, paralysing him from the waist down.

■ **paraly'sation** *noun* the action of paralysing something; the state of being paralysed: M19. **paralysed** *adjective* (*a*) affected with paralysis; (*b*) *slang* (chiefly *US*) temporarily incapacitated through drink: M19. **paralyser** *noun* a paralysing agent M19. **paralysingly** *adverb* in a paralysing manner E20.

paralysis /pə'ralɪsɪs/ *noun*. Pl. **-lyses** /-lɪsiːz/. LOE.

[Latin from Greek *paralusis*, from *paraluesthai* be disabled at the side, pass. of *paraluein*, formed as PARA-[1] + *luein* loosen. Cf. PALSY *noun*[1].]

1 Loss of the ability to move a part of the body, as a result of disease of or injury to a part of the nervous system. LOE.

2 *fig.* A condition of utter powerlessness, inability to act, or suspension of activity; the state of being powerless, helpless, inactive, or ineffective. E19.

> **1** *Science* In botulism the immediate cause of death is . . a paralysis of the skeletal musculature. J. H. BURN As the poison is absorbed, the deer then suffers from a rapidly increasing paralysis. ***creeping paralysis***. **general paralysis (of the insane)** = PARESIS 2; abbreviation *GPI*. ***infantile paralysis***: see INFANTILE 1. **paralysis agitans** /'adʒɪtanz/ [Latin = shaking] Parkinson's disease. ***spastic paralysis***: see SPASTIC *adjective*. **2** N. YOUNG The paralysis of . . CND in Cuba week.

paralytic /parə'lɪtɪk/ *adjective & noun*. LME.

[Old & mod. French *paralytique* from Latin *paralyticus* from Greek *paralutikos*, from *paraluein*: see prec., -IC.]

▶ **A** *adjective*. **1** Affected with, suffering from, or subject to paralysis. LME.

2 *fig.* Deprived or destitute of power to act; powerless, ineffective. M17. ▶**b** Intoxicated; incapably drunk. *slang*. E20.

3 Of the nature of or pertaining to paralysis; characterized by paralysis. E19.

> **1** DICKENS He glanced . . at his shabby clothes and paralytic limb. **2b** A. T. ELLIS It's a miracle . . how Hywel got home . . . I have seldom seen a person so paralytic. **3** JAS. MILL The General, who had sustained a second paralytic attack. ***paralytic stroke***: see STROKE *noun*[1] 2b.

▶ **B** *noun*. A person affected with paralysis. LME.

■ †**paralytical** *adjective* = PARALYTIC *adjective* L16–L18. **paralytically** *adverb* in a paralytic manner; (as) by paralysis: E18.

paralyze *verb* see PARALYSE.

paramagnetic /parəmag'nɛtɪk/ *adjective & noun*. M19.

[from PARA-[1] + MAGNETIC.]

▶ **A** *adjective*. **1** Of a body or substance: attracted by the poles of a magnet; having a positive magnetic susceptibility. Now only as in sense 2 below. M19.

2 Of a body or substance: very weakly attracted by the poles of a magnet but not retaining any permanent magnetism and not exhibiting hysteresis; having a permeability only slightly greater than unity. L19.

▶ **B** *noun*. A paramagnetic body or substance. M19.

■ **para'magnet** *noun* = PARAMAGNETIC *noun* E20. **para'magnetically** *adverb* L19.

paramagnetism /parə'magnɪtɪz(ə)m/ *noun*. M19.

[from PARA-[1] + MAGNETISM.]

The quality of being paramagnetic; the phenomena exhibited by paramagnetic bodies.

paramatta *noun* var. of PARRAMATTA.

paramecium /parə'miːsɪəm/ *noun*. Pl. **-ia** /-ɪə/. M18.

[mod. Latin (see below), from Greek *paramēkēs* oval, formed as PARA-[1] + *mēkos* length: see -IUM.]

A protozoan of the genus *Paramecium*, comprising freshwater ciliates with a characteristic oval shape.

paramedic /parə'mɛdɪk/ *noun*[1]. M20.

[from PARA-[3] + MEDIC *noun*[1] & *adjective*[1].]

A person trained to be dropped by parachute to give medical aid. Cf. PARAMEDICAL *adjective*[2].

paramedic /parə'mɛdɪk/ *noun*[2] *& adjective*. L20.

[from next. Cf. MEDIC *noun*[1] & *adjective*[1].]

A paramedical worker, *esp.* one who works in ambulances and is trained in first aid, emergency care, etc.

paramedical /parə'mɛdɪk(ə)l/ *adjective*[1] *& noun*. E20.

[from PARA-[1] + MEDICAL.]

▶ **A** *adjective*. Supplementary to or supporting the work of medically qualified personnel. E20.

▶ **B** *noun*. = prec. L20.

paramedical /parə'mɛdɪk(ə)l/ *adjective*[2]. M20.

[from PARA-[3] + MEDICAL.]

Trained in parachuting and competent to give medical aid. Cf. PARAMEDIC *noun*[1].

parament /'parəm(ə)nt/ *noun*. LME.

[Old French (also *parement*) from late Latin *paramentum*, from Latin *parare* prepare, adorn: see -MENT.]

1 An ornament, a decoration; *esp.* an ecclesiastical ornament. Long *obsolete* exc. *Hist.* LME.

†**2** A decorated robe, a robe of state. LME–M17.

paramese /parəˈmɛsiː/ *noun.* E17.
[Greek *paramesē* string next to the middle one, from *paramesos* next to the middle, formed as PARA-¹ + *mesos* middle. Cf. MESE *noun*².]
In ancient Greek music, a fixed note which is the lowest note in the upper of two adjacent tetrachords which do not share a note in common.

parameter /pəˈramɪtə/ *noun.* M17.
[mod. Latin (also *-metrum*), from PARA-¹ + Greek *metron* measure: see -METER.]
1 GEOMETRY. (The length of) a chord passing through the focus of a conic section which is bisected by a given diameter; *spec.* the latus rectum. M17.
2 ASTRONOMY. Each of six numerical quantities that jointly specify the path of a planet, comet, etc. Usu. in *pl.* M17.
3 CRYSTALLOGRAPHY. The length of the intercept made on any of the axes of a crystal by a face, expressed in convenient arbitrary units. M19.
4 MATH. & COMPUTING. A quantity which is constant in a particular case considered, but which varies in different cases; *spec.* (*a*) a constant occurring in the equation of a curve or surface, by the variation of which the equation is made to represent a family of such curves or surfaces; (*b*) an independent variable in terms of which each coordinate of a point is expressed. M19.
5 ELECTRICITY. Any of several numerical quantities that can be used jointly to characterize a circuit or network. E20.
6 STATISTICS. A numerical characteristic of a population, as opp. to a statistic obtained by sampling. E20.
7 A distinguishing or defining characteristic or feature, *esp.* one that may be measured or quantified; an element or aspect *of* something; a boundary, a limit. E20.

📖 **4** *Computers & the Humanities* Thus input parameters were included to specify page width and length. **7** *Journal of General Psychology* Three phenomena corresponding to the three major parameters of colour—brightness, hue and saturation. *New York Times* The liberal presumption that . . man can . . comprehend the major parameters of the world. H. EVANS By the end of the series we had broken every single parameter.

■ **parametral** *adjective* (chiefly CRYSTALLOGRAPHY) parametric L19.

parameterize /pəˈramɪt(ə)rʌɪz/ *verb trans.* Also **-tr-** /-tr-/, **-ise.** M20.
[from prec. + -IZE.]
Describe or represent in terms of a parameter or parameters.
■ **parameteriˈzation** *noun* (esp. MATH.) the action of parameterizing something; a parametric representation: M20.

parametric /parəˈmɛtrɪk/ *adjective.* M19.
[from PARAMETER after *meter*, *metric*.]
1 Chiefly MATH. Of or pertaining to a parameter or parameters. M19.
2 ELECTRONICS. Designating devices and processes in which amplification or frequency conversion is obtained by applying a signal to a non-linear device modulated by a pumping frequency, so that there is a transfer of power from the latter. M20.
1 parametric curve: obtained by keeping constant one of the parameters in the parametric equations of a surface. **parametric equalizer** an electronic device or computer program which allows a part of the frequency range of a signal to be selected and altered in strength. **parametric equation** any of a set of equations each of which expresses one of the coordinates of a curve or surface as a function of one or more parameters.
■ **parametrically** *adverb* in terms of a parameter or parameters L19.

parametritis /parəmɪˈtrʌɪtɪs/ *noun.* L19.
[from PARA-¹ + Greek *mētra* uterus + -ITIS.]
MEDICINE. Inflammation of the parametrium.
■ **parametritic** /-ˈtrɪt-/ *adjective* L19.

parametrium /parəˈmiːtrɪəm/ *noun.* L19.
[formed as prec. + -IUM.]
ANATOMY. The connective tissue surrounding the uterus.
■ **parametrial** *adjective* E20.

parametrize *verb* var. of PARAMETERIZE.

parametron /pəˈramɪtrɒn/ *noun.* M20.
[from PARAMETR(IC + -ON.]
ELECTRONICS. A digital storage element consisting of a parametric oscillator in which the digit is represented by the phase of the output signal relative to that of an applied reference signal of the same frequency.

paramilitary /parəˈmɪlɪt(ə)ri/ *adjective & noun.* M20.
[from PARA-¹ + MILITARY.]
▶ **A** *adjective.* Designating, of, or pertaining to an organization or unit which is not a professional military force but which has an ancillary or analogous function or status. M20.

📖 N. MANDELA He then proceeded to set up a paramilitary underground organisation.

▶ **B** *noun.* A paramilitary force. L20.

paramo /ˈparəməʊ/ *noun.* Pl. **-os.** M18.
[Spanish, Portuguese *páramo* from Iberian Latin *paramus* bare plain.]
A high plateau in the tropical parts of S. America, bare of trees and exposed to wind and thick cold fogs.

paramoudra /parəˈmuːdrə/ *noun.* E19.
[Local name in Ireland.]
GEOLOGY. A large flint, pear-shaped, barrel-shaped, or cylindrical and with a hole running lengthwise through it, found standing erect in the chalk of Norfolk and NE Ireland.

paramouncy *noun* var. of PARAMOUNTCY.

paramount /ˈparəmaʊnt/ *adjective, preposition, & noun.* M16.
[Anglo-Norman *paramont* use as adjective of *paramont* above, from Old & mod. French *par* by + *amont*: see AMOUNT *verb*.]
▶ **A** *adjective.* **1** Of a person, people, nation, etc.: above others in rank or order; highest in power or jurisdiction. Chiefly in ***lord paramount***, ***paramount chief*** below. M16.
2 *gen.* Pre-eminent; superior to others in importance, influence, etc. (Foll. by *to*.) E17.

📖 **1 lord paramount** an overlord; *Hist.* the supreme lord of a fee, from whom other feudatories held, but who himself held from none. **paramount chief** esp. in African countries: a tribal chief of the highest order, whose authority extends over an entire district. **2** J. D. CHAMBERS Matters of paramount importance. I. FLEMING The safety factor is paramount in all underwater operations.

▶ **B** *preposition.* Of higher rank or importance than; greater than, above. L16.
▶ **C** *noun.* An overlord; a supreme ruler or proprietor. E17.
■ **paramountly** *adverb* E19. **paramountship** *noun* paramountcy M18.

paramountcy /ˈparəmaʊn(t)si/ *noun.* Also **-ncy** /-nsi/. M17.
[from prec. + -CY.]
The condition or status of being paramount; *spec.* (*Hist.*) the supremacy of the British Crown as acknowledged by Indian princes during the Raj.

paramour /ˈparəmʊə/ *adverb & noun.* ME.
[Old French *par amour(s)* by or through love, formed as PAR *preposition*, AMOUR.]
▶ **A** *adverb.* Orig. two words.
†**1** Through or by way of love; out of (your) love, for love's sake. Also, as a favour, if you please. ME–E17.
2 For or by way of sexual love. Formerly chiefly in ***love paramour***, love amorously, be in love with, have a love affair with. *arch.* ME.
▶ **B** *noun.* †**1** Love; *esp.* sexual love; an amour. LME–L16.
2 A person beloved by one of the opposite sex; a lover, a sweetheart. Also, an animal's mate. *arch. & poet.* LME. ▸†**b** (As used by a man) the Virgin Mary; (as used by a woman) Jesus Christ. Also, God. LME–L16. ▸**c** The lady for whom a knight did battle; an object of chivalrous admiration and attachment. *poet.* E16.
3 An illicit or clandestine lover taking the place of a husband or wife; an illicit partner of a married person. LME.

paramyxovirus /parəˈmɪksəvʌɪrəs/ *noun.* M20.
[from PARA-¹ + MYXOVIRUS.]
BIOLOGY. Any of a group of viruses similar to the myxoviruses but larger and haemolytic, including the parainfluenza viruses and those causing mumps, measles, distemper, and rinderpest.

Paraná pine /parəˈnɑː pʌɪn/ *noun phr.* E20.
[*Paraná*, a river and province of Brazil.]
A large evergreen coniferous tree, *Araucaria angustifolia*, of SW Brazil and neighbouring regions; its soft light-coloured timber.

paranatellon /pəranəˈtɛlɒn/ *noun.* E19.
[from PARA-¹ + Greek *anatellōn* rising.]
ASTROLOGY. A star that rises at the same time as another star or stars. Foll. by *of*.

paranemic /parəˈniːmɪk/ *adjective.* M20.
[from PARA-¹ + Greek *nēma* thread + -IC.]
Chiefly BIOCHEMISTRY. Pertaining to or designating two or more similar helices coiled together side by side in such a way that they may be fully separated without being unwound. Opp. PLECTONEMIC.

paranete /parəˈniːti/ *noun.* E17.
[Latin from Greek *paranētē*, formed as PARA-¹, NETE.]
In ancient Greek music, the second note down in an upper tetrachord, immediately below the nete.

parang /ˈpɑːraŋ/ *noun*¹. M19.
[Malay *parang*.]
A large heavy knife used in Malaysia for clearing vegetation etc.

parang /paˈraŋ/ *noun*². M20.
[Spanish creole, based on Spanish *parranda* spree, binge.]
A variety of Trinidadian folk music, traditionally played at Christmas by groups which travel from house to house.

parangi /pəˈraŋgi/ *noun.* E19.
[Sinhalese *parangi(ledē)* lit. '(disease of) foreigners' (i.e. the Portuguese) from Persian *farangī* name given to Europeans, rel. to FERINGHEE, FRANK *noun*¹.]
In Sri Lanka: yaws.

paranjah /parənˈdʒɑː/ *noun.* E20.
[Russian *parandzha* yashmak.]
A long wide robe with a veil worn by Muslim women.

paranoia /parəˈnɔɪə/ *noun.* E19.
[mod. Latin from Greek, from *paranoos* distracted, formed as PARA-¹ + *noos*, *nous* mind: see -IC.]
1 Orig., dementia. Now, a mental illness characterized by delusions of persecutions, unwarranted jealousy, or exaggerated self-importance. E19.
2 A tendency to suspect and distrust others or to believe oneself unfairly used. *colloq.* M20.

📖 **2** I. MURDOCH You always had a suspicious mind, but this is paranoia.

■ **paranoiac** *adjective & noun* (a person) affected with paranoia L19. **paranoiacally** *adverb* M20. **paranoic** /-ˈnəʊɪk, -ˈnɔɪk/ *adjective* paranoiac M19. **paranoically** /-ˈnəʊɪk-, -ˈnɔɪk-/ *adverb* L20. ˈ**paranoid** *adjective & noun* (*a*) *adjective* resembling or characterized by paranoia; *colloq.* very suspicious and distrustful of others; (*b*) *noun* a person affected with or showing symptoms of paranoia: E20.

paranormal /parəˈnɔːm(ə)l/ *adjective.* E20.
[from PARA-¹ + NORMAL *adjective*.]
▶ **A** *adjective.* Designating, pertaining to, or involving phenomena or powers, such as telekinesis or clairvoyance, whose operation is outside the scope of the known laws of nature or normal objective investigation. E20.
▶ **B** *noun.* ***the paranormal***, paranormal phenomena collectively. M20.
■ **paranorˈmality** *noun* the state or character of being paranormal M20. **paranormally** *adverb* by paranormal means, in a paranormal manner M20.

Paranthropus /pəˈranθrəpəs, paranˈθrəʊpəs/ *noun.* M20.
[mod. Latin (orig. assigned as the genus name of the fossil), from PARA-¹ + Greek *anthrōpos* man.]
A fossil hominid known from remains found in southern Africa, now usually included in the species *Australopithecus robustus*.

paranumismatica /ˌparənjuːmɪzˈmatɪkə/ *noun pl.* L20.
[from PARA-¹ + NUMISMATIC + -A³.]
Collectable items that are similar to coins and medals, such as tokens and medallions.

paranymph /ˈparənɪmf/ *noun.* M16.
[Late Latin *paranymphus* from Greek *paranumphos*, formed as PARA-¹, NYMPH *noun*.]
1 In ancient Greece: the friend who accompanied a bridegroom when he went to fetch home the bride; the bridesmaid who escorted a bride to the bridegroom. Also, a present-day best man or bridesmaid. M16.
†**2** A person who or thing which woos or solicits for another; an advocate. M16–L17.

parapegma /parəˈpɛgmə/ *noun.* Pl. **-mata** /-mətə/. Also Anglicized as **parapegm** /ˈparəpɛm/. M17.
[Latin from Greek *parapēgma* lit. 'thing fixed beside or near', formed as PARA-¹ + *pēgma* a thing fastened.]
GREEK ANTIQUITIES. A tablet set up and inscribed with some public information or announcement, e.g. a law, proclamation, or calendar; a canon, a rule; a fixed date or epoch.

parapente /ˈparəpɒnt/ *noun & verb.* L20.
[French, from *para-* initial elem. of PARACHUTE + *pente* slope.]
▶ **A** *noun.* **1** The activity or sport of gliding by means of an aerofoil parachute launched from high ground. L20.
2 The parachute used for this purpose. L20.
▶ **B** *verb intrans.* Descend from high ground by parapente. Freq. as ***parapenting*** *verbal noun.* L20.

parapet /ˈparəpɪt/ *noun & verb.* L16.
[(French from) Italian *parapetto* lit. 'a wall breast-high', formed as PARA-² + *petto* breast from Latin *pectus*.]
▶ **A** *noun.* **1** MILITARY. A bank built to provide protection from the enemy's observation and fire; *esp.* one on top of a wall or rampart, or in front of a trench. L16.
2 A low wall or barrier at the edge of a balcony, roof, etc., or along the sides of a bridge, pier, etc. L16.
3 The pavement of a street or road. *local.* L18.

📖 **2** *fig.*: SOUTHEY The brows of the Surrey hills bear a parapet of modern villas.

Comb.: **parapet line** the line of the bottom of the parapet, esp. on a roof; **parapet wall** a low wall serving as a parapet.
▶ **B** *verb trans.* Provide or defend with a parapet. Chiefly as ***parapeted*** *ppl adjective.* M17.

paraph /ˈparaf/ *noun & verb.* LME.
[French *paraphe*, *-afe* from medieval Latin *paraphus* syncopated form of *paragraphus* PARAGRAPH *noun*.]
▶ **A** *noun.* †**1** A paragraph. LME–L16.
2 A flourish made after a signature. L16.
▶ **B** *verb trans.* †**1** Divide into paragraphs. Only in LME.
2 Add a paraph to; sign, esp. with one's initials. M17.

parapherna /parəˈfəːnə/ *noun pl.* E18.
[Late Latin: see PARAPHERNALIA.]
1 ROMAN LAW. Those articles of property held by a wife over and above the dowry she brought to her husband, and which remained under her own control. Long *rare*. E18.
2 = PARAPHERNALIA 2. L19.

paraphernal /parəˈfəːn(ə)l/ *adjective & noun.* E16.
[French from late Latin *paraphernalis*: see next, -AL[1].]
LAW (now *Hist.*).
▶ **A** *noun.* An item of paraphernalia. E16.
▶ **B** *adjective.* Of the nature of paraphernalia. L18.

paraphernalia /parəfəˈneɪlɪə/ *noun pl.* M17.
[medieval Latin, use as noun of neut. pl. of *paraphernalis*, from Latin *parapherna* from Greek, formed as PARA-[1] + *phernē* dowry: see -IA[2].]
1 *Hist.* Those articles of personal property which the law allowed a married woman to keep and deal with as her own, when most of her personal or movable property vested in her husband. M17.
2 Personal belongings, esp. of dress or adornment; the miscellaneous objects that go to make up a thing or are associated with it; trappings, bits and pieces. Also treated as *sing.* M18.

📖 **2** R. LEHMANN The nursery bathroom, with its . . well-worn paraphernalia of sponges, face-cloths . . and pumice-stone. H. MACMILLAN Our way was barred by all the usual paraphernalia of Press and television.

paraphonia /parəˈfəʊnɪə/ *noun.* L18.
[Greek = harmony, formed as PARA-[1]: see -PHONIA.]
1 In ancient Greek music, the harmony or concord of fourths and fifths. L18.
2 Alteration of the voice from physiological or pathological causes. Now *rare*. L18.
■ **paraphonic** *adjective* M19.

paraphrase /ˈparəfreɪz/ *noun & verb.* M16.
[(French from) Latin *paraphrasis* from Greek, from *paraphrazein* tell in other words, formed as PARA-[1] + *phrazein* tell.]
▶ **A** *noun.* **1** An expression in other words, usually fuller and clearer, of the sense of a written or spoken passage or text; a free rendering. Also, the use of these as a mode of literary treatment. M16.
†**2** A comment, a gloss. E17–M18.
3 In the Church of Scotland and other Presbyterian Churches: a hymn that is a paraphrase of a passage from the Bible. E18.
4 ART. The representation of a subject in a realistic or other manner so as to convey its essential qualities. M20.

📖 **1** W. APEL Liszt's paraphrases on Wagnerian operas. A. BISHOP I have avoided paraphrase in favour of quotation. **3** *Presbyterian Herald* The singing of . . Psalms, Paraphrases, or Hymns at almost every service

▶ **B** *verb.* **1** *verb intrans.* Make a paraphrase; comment or enlarge *on* a passage so as to clarify its meaning. L16.
2 *verb trans.* Express the meaning of (a word, phrase, passage, or work) in other words, usually with the object of clarification; render or translate freely; ART capture the essence of (a subject). E17.
†**3** *verb intrans.* Comment or enlarge *on* a subject. M–L17.
■ **paraphrasaˈbility** *noun* ability to be paraphrased M20. **paraphrasable** *adjective* able to be paraphrased E20. **paraphraser** *noun* M16. **paraphrasis** /pəˈrafrəsɪs/ *noun*, pl. **-ases** /-əsiːz/, [Latin] = PARAPHRASE *noun* 1 M16.

paraphrast /ˈparəfrast/ *noun.* M16.
[medieval Latin *paraphrastes* from Greek *paraphrastēs*, from *paraphrazein*: see PARAPHRASE.]
A person who paraphrases; a paraphraser.
■ **paraˈphrastic** *adjective* [medieval Latin *paraphrasticus*] of, pertaining to, or of the nature of paraphrase; fond of using paraphrase: E17. **paraˈphrastical** *adjective* paraphrastic M16. **paraˈphrastically** *adverb* M16.

paraphrenia /parəˈfriːnɪə/ *noun.* L19.
[French *paraphrénie*, formed as PARA-[1] + Greek *phrēn* mind: see -IA[1].]
A form of mental illness of a paranoid or schizophrenic type.
■ **paraphrenic** *adjective* M20.

paraphysis /pəˈrafɪsɪs/ *noun.* Pl. **-physes** /-fɪsiːz/. M19.
[mod. Latin, formed as PARA-[1] + Greek *phusis* growth.]
BOTANY. A sterile hairlike filament present among the reproductive organs in many cryptogams, esp. bryophytes, algae, and fungi. Usu. in *pl.*

paraplegia /parəˈpliːdʒə/ *noun.* M17.
[mod. Latin from Greek *paraplēgia* stroke on one side, from *paraplēssein* strike at the side, formed as PARA-[1] + *plēssein* strike: see -IA[1].]
Symmetrical paralysis of both legs (and often some or all of the trunk), usu. caused by disease or injury of the spinal cord.
■ **paraplegic** *adjective & noun* (**a**) *adjective* accompanied by or characteristic of paraplegia; affected with paraplegia; ***Paraplegic Games***, an international athletic competition for disabled people; (**b**) *noun* a person with paraplegia: E19.

parapluie /paraplɥi/ *noun.* Pl. pronounced same. L18.
[French.]
An umbrella.
¶ Most common in 19.

parapophysis /parəˈpɒfɪsɪs/ *noun.* Pl. **-physes** /-fɪsiːz/. M19.
[from PARA-[1] + APOPHYSIS.]
ANATOMY & ZOOLOGY. Either of a pair of transverse processes on the anterior or ventral side of a vertebra.
■ **parapoˈphysial** *adjective* M19.

parapraxis /parəˈpraksɪs/ *noun.* Pl. **-praxes** /-ˈpraksiːz/. Also **-praxia** /-ˈpraksɪə/. E20.
[from PARA-[1] + Greek *praxis* action.]
The faulty performance of an intended action, esp. (PSYCHOLOGY) as indicative of a subconscious motive or attitude.

paraprofessional /parəprəˈfɛʃ(ə)n(ə)l/ *noun & adjective.* M20.
[from PARA-[1] + PROFESSIONAL.]
▶ **A** *noun.* A person without professional training to whom a particular aspect of a professional task is delegated. M20.
▶ **B** *adjective.* Designating, of, or pertaining to such a person. M20.

parapsychology /parəsʌɪˈkɒlədʒi/ *noun.* E20.
[from PARA-[1] + PSYCHOLOGY.]
The field of study that deals with paranormal phenomena in psychology.
■ ˌ**parapsychoˈlogical** *adjective* E20. ˌ**parapsychoˈlogically** *adverb* M20. **parapsychologist** *noun* M20.

paraquat /ˈparəkwɒt, -kwat/ *noun.* M20.
[from PARA-[1] + QUAT(ERNARY: so called because the bond between the two rings of the molecule is in the *para* position relative to their quaternary nitrogen atoms.]
A quick-acting contact herbicide that is rendered inactive by the soil and is highly toxic.

†**paraquito** *noun* var. of PARAKEET.

para-rhyme /ˈparərʌɪm/ *noun.* M20.
[from PARA-[1] + RHYME *noun*.]
A half-rhyme.

parasail /ˈparəseɪl/ *verb & noun.* M20.
[from PARA-[3] + SAIL *verb*[1].]
▶ **A** *verb intrans.* Glide through the air while sustained by a parachute and towed by a speedboat. Chiefly as ***parasailing*** *verbal noun.* M20.
▶ **B** *noun.* A parachute for use in parasailing. L20.

parasang /ˈparəsaŋ/ *noun.* L16.
[Latin *parasanga* from Greek *parasaggēs*, from Persian (rel. to FARSANG).]
An Iranian unit of length, usually reckoned as equal to between 3 and 3½ miles (5 to 5½ km).

📖 *fig.*: P. G. WODEHOUSE 'You don't get the subtle strategy?' 'Not by several parasangs.'

parascending /ˈparəsɛndɪŋ/ *noun.* L20.
[from PARA-[3] + *ascending* (from ASCEND *verb* + -ING[1]).]
A sport in which a parachutist is towed behind a vehicle to gain height before release for a conventional descent, usu. towards a target area.
■ **parascend** *verb intrans.* L20. **parascender** *noun* a person who takes part in this sport L20.

parascene /ˈparəsiːn/ *noun.* Also in Latin form **parascenium** /parəˈsiːnɪəm/, pl. **-ia** /-ɪə/. E18.
[French *parascène* from Greek *paraskēnion*, formed as PARA-[1] + *skēnē* stage.]
The part of an ancient Greek or Roman theatre on either side of the stage, comprising rooms to which the actors retired.

parascience /ˈparəsʌɪəns/ *noun.* M20.
[from PARA-[1] + SCIENCE.]
The field of study that deals with phenomena assumed to be beyond the scope of scientific inquiry or for which no scientific explanation exists.
■ **parascienˈtific** *adjective* M20. **paraˈscientist** *noun* L20.

paraselene /parəsɪˈliːni/ *noun.* Pl. **-nes**, **-nae** /-niː/. M17.
[mod. Latin, formed as PARA-[1] + Greek *selēnē* moon.]
A bright spot on a lunar halo, resembling the moon itself. Also called ***mock moon***.

parasexual /parəˈsɛksjʊəl, -ʃʊəl/ *adjective.* M20.
[from PARA-[1] + SEXUAL.]
GENETICS. Designating a process by which recombination of genes from different individuals occurs without meiosis, as in some fungi; involving or exhibiting such a process.
■ ˌ**parasexuˈality** *noun* the parasexual process M20.

parashah /ˈparəʃɑː/ *noun.* Pl. **-shiot(h)** /-ʃɪəʊt/, **-shahs**. E17.
[Hebrew *pārāšāh* division, from *pāraš* divide.]
In Jewish liturgy, any of several portions of the Torah read at a Sabbath morning synagogue service; these portions collectively, a sidra.

parasite /ˈparəsʌɪt/ *noun.* M16.
[Latin *parasitus* from Greek *parasitos* lit. (as adjective) 'feeding beside', (as noun) 'person who eats at the table of another', formed as PARA-[1] + *sitos* food.]
1 A person who lives at the expense of another person or of society in general; a person who obtains the hospitality, patronage, or favour of the wealthy or powerful by obsequiousness and flattery. M16.
2 GREEK HISTORY. A person allowed to share in the food provided for a public official, or in the feast after a sacrifice. L17.
3 An animal or plant which lives in or on another and draws its nutriment directly from it, harming it in the process. Also, a commensal, a symbiont; an epiphyte, a saprophyte; *poet.* a climbing or creeping plant. E18.
4 PHILOLOGY. A parasitic vowel or consonant. L19.

📖 **1** D. ATHILL He was going to continue living as a parasite on his friends.

Comb.: **parasite drag** AERONAUTICS drag other than that induced by the lift or due to the lifting surface; **parasite fighter** AERONAUTICS a fighter aircraft carried by and operating from another aircraft.
■ **parasitaemia** /parəsɪˈtiːmɪə/ *noun* the demonstrable presence of parasites in the blood M20. **parasital** *adjective* parasitic M19.

parasite /ˈparəsʌɪt/ *verb.* E17.
[from the noun.]
1 *verb intrans.* Behave as a parasite; live *off* as a parasite (also foll. by *on*). E17.
2 *verb trans.* Infest as a parasite. M19.

parasitic /parəˈsɪtɪk/ *adjective & noun.* E17.
[Latin *parasiticus* from Greek *parasitikos*, from *parasitos*: see PARASITE *noun*, -IC.]
▶ **A** *adjective.* **1** Of, pertaining to, or characteristic of parasites; of the nature of a parasite; living *in* or *on* an organism as a parasite. E17. ▸**b** Of a condition, disease, etc.: caused by parasites. M19.
2 Attached or adjacent to something and subsidiary to it. E19.
3 PHILOLOGY. Of a sound or letter: developed out of or added to an adjacent sound, not original, (e.g. *d* in ***thunder***). L19.
4 Occurring as an unwanted accompaniment or by-product, esp. in electronic devices and electrical machinery. L19.
5 Of an aerial: not electrically connected to a transmitter or receiver. M20.

📖 **1b parasitic bronchitis** hoose. **parasitic stomatitis** = THRUSH *noun*[2] 1. **2** T. H. HUXLEY Mount Etna . . having its flanks studded with parasitic cones.

▶ **B** *noun.* ELECTRONICS, in *pl.* Parasitic oscillations. M20.
■ **parasitical** *adjective* parasitic L16. **parasitically** *adverb* M17. **parasiticalness** *noun* E18.

parasiticide /parəˈsɪtɪsʌɪd/ *noun.* M19.
[from Latin *parasitus* PARASITE *noun* + -I- + -CIDE.]
An agent that destroys parasites.
■ ˌ**parasitiˈcidal** *adjective* L19.

parasitise *verb* var. of PARASITIZE.

parasitism /ˈparəsʌɪtɪz(ə)m/ *noun.* E17.
[from PARASITE *noun* + -ISM.]
1 The practice of living as a parasite; the condition of being a parasite; parasitic quality or habits; (in some countries) the state of being without a job or of indulging in an activity proscribed as antisocial. E17.
2 MEDICINE. Parasitic infestation; disease caused by parasites. L19.

parasitize /ˈparəsʌɪtʌɪz, -sɪ-/ *verb trans.* Also **-ise**. L19.
[from PARASITE *noun* + -IZE.]
Infest as a parasite.
■ **parasitiˈzation** *noun* M20.

parasitoid /ˈparəsɪtɔɪd/ *noun & adjective.* E20.
[mod. Latin *Parasitoidea*, formed as PARASITE *noun*: see -OID.]
(Designating, of, or pertaining to) an insect, esp. one belonging to the orders Hymenoptera and Diptera, whose larvae live as internal parasites which eventually kill their hosts.

parasitology /parəsʌɪˈtɒlədʒi, -sɪ-/ *noun.* L19.
[from PARASITE *noun* + -OLOGY.]
The branch of biology and medicine that deals with parasites and parasitism.
■ ˌ**parasitoˈlogical** *adjective* L19. ˌ**parasitoˈlogically** *adverb* L20. **parasitologist** *noun* M19.

parasitopolis /parəsʌɪˈtɒp(ə)lɪs/ *noun.* E20.
[from PARASITE *noun* + -O- + -POLIS.]
A city that is overdeveloped and economically nonproductive.

parasol /ˈparəsɒl/ *noun & verb.* E17.
[French from Italian *parasole*, formed as PARA-[2] + *sole* sun.]
▶ **A** *noun.* **1** A light portable screen or canopy carried to give shade from the sun, *esp.* a small light umbrella, often ornamental or gaily coloured. Also *gen.* (now *rare* or *obsolete*), a thing providing shade from the sun. E17.
2 In full ***parasol mushroom***. An edible fungus, *Lepiota procera*, with a shaggy convex cap raised in the centre. L19.
3 An aircraft with wings raised above the fuselage. E20.
2 SHAGGY *parasol*.
Comb.: **parasol ant** a leaf-cutting ant; ***parasol mushroom***: see sense 2 above; **parasol pine** (*a*) the stone pine, *Pinus pinea*; (*b*) = ***umbrella pine*** (b) s.v. UMBRELLA.
▶ **B** *verb trans.* Serve as a parasol for, shade from the sun. L18.
■ **parasoled** *adjective* having a parasol M19.

parastades /pəˈrastədiːz/ *noun pl.* E18.
[Greek, pl. of *parastas*, formed as PARA-[1] + base *sta-* standing.]
ARCHITECTURE. = ANTAE.

parastatal /parəˈsteɪt(ə)l/ *adjective & noun.* M20.
[from PARA-[1] + STATE *noun*, or from next, + -AL[1].]
▶ **A** *adjective.* Of an organization or industry: taking on some of the roles of the government, through which a government operates indirectly. M20.
▶ **B** *noun.* A parastatal organization etc. M20.

para-state /ˈparəsteɪt/ *noun & adjective.* M20.
[from PARA-[1] + STATE *noun.*]
= PARASTATAL *adjective & noun.*

parastichy /pəˈrastɪki/ *noun.* L19.
[from PARA-[1] + Greek *-stikhia*, from *stikhos* row, rank: cf. ORTHOSTICHY.]
BOTANY. Any of several secondary spirals or oblique rows of leaves, scales, etc., round a stem or axis, in a spiral phyllotaxis in which the leaves, scales, etc., are close together.

parasuicide /parəˈsuːɪsʌɪd, ˈsjuː-/ *noun.* M20.
[from PARA-[1] + SUICIDE *noun.*]
The action of making an apparent attempt at suicide by deliberately harming oneself without intending death; a person who does this.

parasympathetic /ˌparəsɪmpəˈθɛtɪk/ *adjective & noun.* E20.
[from PARA-[1] + SYMPATHETIC (some of the nerves concerned running alongside sympathetic nerves).]
ANATOMY. ▶**A** *adjective.* Of, pertaining to, or designating one of the major divisions of the autonomic nervous system, whose nerves leave the spinal cord in the cranial or sacral region and have acetylcholine as a transmitter, and which is associated more with calmness and rest than with alertness. E20.
▶ **B** *noun.* The parasympathetic system; a parasympathetic nerve. E20.
■ **parasympathetically** *adverb* M20. **parasympathoˈlytic** *adjective & noun* (PHARMACOLOGY) (a substance) that annuls or opposes the physiological action of the parasympathetic nervous system M20. **paraˌsympathomiˈmetic** *adjective & noun* (PHARMACOLOGY) (a substance) that produces physiological effects characteristic of the action of the parasympathetic nervous system by promoting stimulation of parasympathetic nerves M20.

parasynthesis /parəˈsɪnθɪsɪs/ *noun.* Pl. **-theses** /-θɪsiːz/. M19.
[from PARA-[1] + SYNTHESIS.]
PHILOLOGY. Derivation from a compound; word-formation involving both combination and derivation, as in English ***top-hatted***.
■ **parasynˈthetic** *adjective* M19. **parasyntheton** *noun*, pl. **-theta**, a parasynthetic formation L19.

parataxis /parəˈtaksɪs/ *noun.* Pl. **-taxes** /-ˈtaksiːz/. M19.
[Greek = placing side by side, from *paratassein* place side by side, formed as PARA-[1] + *tassein* arrange: see TAXIS.]
GRAMMAR. The placing of clauses or phrases one after another, without the use of connecting words to indicate the relation (of coordination or subordination) between them. Opp. HYPOTAXIS.
■ **paratactic**, **paratactical** *adjectives* L19. **paratactically** *adverb* L19.

paratha /pəˈrɑːtə/ *noun.* M20.
[Hindi *parāṭhā*.]
INDIAN COOKERY. A flat piece of unleavened bread fried in butter, ghee, etc., on a griddle.

parathesis /pəˈraθɪsɪs/ *noun.* Pl. **-theses** /-θɪsiːz/. M17.
[mod. Latin from Greek = a putting beside, from *paratithenai* put beside, formed as PARA-[1] + *tithenai* put: see THESIS.]
†**1** GRAMMAR. = APPOSITION *noun*[1] 2. M–L17.
†**2** The interpolation of something in the middle of a sentence or discourse by way of explanation or exposition; a bracket used in pairs to enclose such an interpolation. M17–L18.
3 In Greek and Latin, the simple juxtaposition of two words without modification. M19.

parathion /parəˈθʌɪən/ *noun.* M20.
[from PARA-[1] + THIO- + -ON.]
A sulphur-containing organophosphorus insecticide which is also highly toxic to mammals.

parathormone /parəˈθɔːməʊn/ *noun.* E20.
[from PARATH(YROID + H)ORMONE.]
PHYSIOLOGY. The parathyroid hormone.

parathyroid /parəˈθʌɪrɔɪd/ *adjective & noun.* L19.
[from PARA-[1] + THYROID.]
▶ **A** *adjective.* Designating any of several glands adjoining or within the thyroid gland; designating the hormone produced by these glands in higher vertebrates, which increases the amount of calcium in the blood and the excretion of phosphate by the kidneys. L19.
▶ **B** *noun.* Any of the parathyroid glands. L19.
■ **ˌparathyroiˈdectomize** *verb trans.* perform parathyroidectomy on E20. **ˌparathyroiˈdectomy** *noun* (an instance of) surgical removal of some or all of the parathyroids E20.

paratonnerre /paratɔnɛːr/ *noun.* Pl. pronounced same. E19.
[French, formed as PARA-[2] + *tonnerre* thunder.]
A lightning-conductor.

paratragoedia /parətrəˈdʒiːdɪə/ *noun.* Also Anglicized as **-tragedy** /-ˈtradʒɪdi/. L19.
[mod. Latin, from Greek *paratragōidos* pseudo-tragic (formed as PARA-[1], *tragōidia* TRAGEDY) + -IA[1].]
Mock tragedy.

paratroop /ˈparətruːp/ *noun.* M20.
[Orig. in pl., from PARA-[3] + *troops* pl. of TROOP *noun.*]
A soldier trained to be dropped from aircraft by parachute. Usu. in *pl.* exc. ***attrib.***
■ **paratrooper** *noun* (*a*) = PARATROOP; (*b*) an aircraft designed to transport paratroops: M20.

paratype /ˈparətʌɪp/ *noun.* L19.
[from PARA-[1] + -TYPE.]
TAXONOMY. A specimen other than the holotype from a group that includes the holotype.

paratyphoid /parəˈtʌɪfɔɪd/ *noun & adjective.* E20.
[from PARA-[1] + TYPHOID.]
MEDICINE. (Designating, in ***paratyphoid fever***) a fever similar to typhoid but less severe and caused by a different though related bacterium.

parautochthonous /parɔːˈtɒkθ(ə)nəs/ *adjective.* E20.
[from PARA-[2] + AUTOCHTHONOUS.]
GEOLOGY. Intermediate in character between autochthonous and allochthonous; formed from material that has travelled a short distance.

paravail /ˈparəveɪl/ *postpositive adjective.* *obsolete* exc. *Hist.* L16.
[Old French *par aval* down, from Old & mod. French *par* through, by + *aval*, *à val* down (adverb & preposition) from Latin *ad vallem* to the valley (cf. PARAMOUNT).]
Below others in rank.
tenant paravail a tenant who held from another who was himself a tenant, *spec.* the lowest tenant, who actually worked or occupied the land etc.

paravane /ˈparəveɪn/ *noun.* E20.
[from PARA-[2] in sense 'protector', + VANE.]
A device attached by wire to a ship and having vanes or planes to keep it at the desired depth, *esp.* one used to cut the moorings of mines.

†**paravant** *adverb. rare* (Spenser). Also **-vaunt**. Only in L16.
[Old French, from Old & mod. French *par* through, by + *avant* before.]
Before the rest; pre-eminently.

paraxial /pəˈraksɪəl/ *adjective.* M19.
[from PARA-[1] + AXIS *noun*[1] + -AL[1], after *axial*.]
1 ANATOMY & ZOOLOGY. Lying alongside, or on each side of, the axis of the body. M19.
2 Situated close to the axis of an optical system and (if linear, as a ray) virtually parallel to it; of or pertaining to such a region. E20.
■ **paraxially** *adverb* adjacent to or virtually parallel to an axis E20.

parazoan /parəˈzəʊən/ *adjective & noun.* E20.
[from mod. Latin *Parazoa* (see below), formed as PARA-[1] after *Metazoa*, *Protozoa*: see -AN.]
ZOOLOGY. (A member) of the subkingdom Parazoa, coextensive with the phylum Porifera (the sponges).

parazonium /parəˈzəʊnɪəm/ *noun.* Pl. **-ia** /-ɪə/. E17.
[Latin from Greek *parazōnion*, from *parazōnidios* at the girdle, formed as PARA-[1] + *zōnē* girdle, belt.]
Hist. A small sword or dagger worn at the girdle by the ancient Greeks; a similar medieval weapon.

parbleu /parblø/ *interjection.* E18.
[French, alt. of *pardieu* lit. 'by God': see PARDI.]
Expr. asseveration.

parboil /ˈpɑːbɔɪl/ *verb trans.* LME.
[Old French *parbo(u)illir* from late Latin *perbullire* boil thoroughly, from Latin *per* PAR-[1] (later confused with PART *adverb*) + *bullire* BOIL *verb*.]
†**1** Boil thoroughly. LME–M17.
2 Boil partially; partly cook by boiling. LME.

> **2** *Weight Watchers* Parboil parsnips for one minute until just tender. *fig.*: W. IRVING Being squeezed, and smothered, and parboiled at nightly balls.

†**parbrake** *verb* see PARBREAK *verb.*

parbreak /ˈpɑːbreɪk/ *noun.* Long *arch. rare.* L16.
[from next.]
Vomit.

†**parbreak** *verb trans. & intrans.* Orig. **-brake.** LME–L18.
[from PAR-[1] + BRAKE *verb*[2] (later referred to BREAK *verb*).]
Spew, vomit; belch. Freq. *fig.*

parbuckle /ˈpɑːbʌk(ə)l/ *noun & verb.* As noun orig. †**-bunkle.** E17.
[Origin unkn. Later form by assoc. with *buckle*.]
▶ **A** *noun.* A rope arranged like a sling, for raising or lowering heavy objects, esp. casks or cylindrical objects. E17.
▶ **B** *verb trans.* Raise or lower (a cask, gun, etc.) with a parbuckle. M19.

parcel /ˈpɑːs(ə)l/ *noun, adverb, & adjective.* ME.
[Old & mod. French *parcelle* from Proto-Romance, from Latin *particula* PARTICLE.]
▶ **A** *noun.* †**1** An item, *esp.* an item of an account; a detail, a particular, a point. Orig. & usu. in *pl.* ME–M17.
2 A part, portion, or division of a thing. *arch.* exc. as below. LME.
3 *spec.* **a** A portion or piece of land, esp. as part of an estate. LME. ▶†**b** A small sum (*of* money); an instalment. L15–M18. ▶†**c** A short passage from a sacred book, esp. the Bible. L16–M17.
4 A separate portion *of* a material; a (small) piece, particle, or fragment; a (usu. small or moderate) quantity or amount. *obsolete* in *gen.* sense. LME. ▶**b** *spec.* A small quantity of new-mown hay spread out to dry. *dial.* M19. ▶**c** MINING. A heap or arbitrary quantity of ore etc. L19. ▶**d** A packet of mixed diamonds offered together for sale. E20. ▶**e** SCIENCE. A small volume of fluid forming part of a larger body of the same fluid, but considered (in calculations) as a discrete element, or physically extracted as a sample. L20.
5 A group, a collection; *spec.* †(*a*) a small community or gathering (of people); (*b*) (now *rare*) a herd or flock of animals; (*c*) (now chiefly *US* (*colloq.*, freq. *derog.*)) an indeterminate number or quantity, a lot, a bunch, (of persons, animals, or things). Cf. PASSEL. LME.
6 a An item or quantity of goods etc. wrapped up in a single (usu. fairly small) package or bundle; a package, usu. wrapped in paper, containing (an item of) goods. L17. ▶**b** A (definite) quantity of shares or a commodity dealt with in one commercial transaction; a consignment. L18. ▶**c** A large amount of money gained or lost. *slang.* E20.
7 LAW. In *pl.* The words in a conveyance, lease, etc., containing the description of the property dealt with. M18.

> **1** SHAKES. *1 Hen. IV* I will die a hundred thousand deaths Ere break the smallest parcel of this vow. **2** W. CRUISE Franchises . . which were originally parcel of the royal prerogative. M. ARNOLD Truth more complete than the parcel of truth any momentary individual can seize. **by parcels** a part at a time, piecemeal. **of a parcel with** of a piece with, consonant with. ***part and parcel***: see PART *noun.* **3a** *American Ethnologist* That land ownership is communal does not imply that the distribution of parcels is . . egalitarian. **5** SHAKES. *L.L.L.* A holy parcel of the fairest dames. ADDISON Let posterity see their forefathers were a parcel of blockheads. A. YOUNG Sheep are kept in small parcels. **6a** DEFOE He sees the bills of parcels of goods bought. C. CAUSLEY A parcel at Christmastime Of socks and nutty and wine. L. LAWRENCE She carried a parcel under her arm. **b** *Australian Business* The failure of an agreement . . to purchase a parcel of Haoma shares. **c** P. G. WODEHOUSE Put you in the way of winning a parcel on the Mothers' Sack Race.

Comb.: **parcel bomb**: wrapped up so as to look deceptively like a parcel; **parcel delivery** = ***parcels delivery*** below; **parcel paper** stout paper, usually brown and unsized, for wrapping parcels; **parcel post** the branch of a postal service that deals with parcels; **parcels delivery** the action of, or an agency for, delivering parcels; **parcel shelf**, **parcels shelf**: on which parcels may be placed, esp. in a motor vehicle; **parcel tanker** a vessel designed to carry a cargo of different liquids with separate piping and tanks;
▶ **B** *adverb.* Partly, partially, to some degree or extent. Long used only to qualify adjectives LME.

> SIR W. SCOTT The worthy dame was parcel blind, and more than parcel deaf. PARCEL-GILT.

▶ **C** *adjective.* That is partly (what is denoted by the noun); part-time, amateur. Usu. *derog.* E17.

> L. BARRY Parcel lawyer, parcel devil, all knave. J. R. LOWELL Gilbert, Hawkins, Frobisher and Drake, parcel-soldiers all of them. †**parcel bawd** a part-time pimp.

■ **parceliˈzation**, **-ll-** *noun* the division of land into small parcels M20. **parcelize**, **-ll-** *verb trans.* (*rare*) = PARCEL *verb* 1 E17. **parcellate** *verb trans.* divide (land etc.) into separate parcels M20.

parce'llation *noun* L19. **parcel-wise** *adverb* bit by bit, piecemeal M17.

parcel /ˈpɑːs(ə)l/ *verb trans.* Infl. **-ll-**, ***-l-**. LME.
[from prec.]
1 Divide into or distribute in (small) portions. Usu. foll. by *out*. LME.
2 NAUTICAL. Make (a caulked seam etc.) watertight with a covering of canvas strips daubed with pitch; wrap (a rope) round with parcelling. E17.
3 Make (*up*) into a parcel or parcels; wrap (*up*) as a parcel. L18.

📖 **1** HARPER LEE Jem parcelled out our roles. W. S. CHURCHILL They .. parcelled out the country into the eighty-six departments that still exist. **3** J. CROLL The mechanical art of weighing and parcelling up the tea.

parcel-gilt /ˈpɑːs(ə)lgɪlt/ *adjective & noun.* LME.
[from PARCEL *adverb* + *gilt* pa. pple of GILD *verb*[1].]
► **A** *adjective.* Of silverware etc.: partly gilded; having the inner surface gilt. LME.
► **B** *noun.* Parcel-gilt ware. LME.
■ **parcel-gilding** *noun* the partial gilding of silverware etc. M19.

parcelling /ˈpɑːs(ə)lɪŋ/ *noun.* Also ***-eling**. LME.
[from PARCEL *verb* + -ING[1].]
1 The action of PARCEL *verb.* LME.
2 NAUTICAL. A strip of canvas (usu. tarred) for binding round a rope, which is then served with spun yarn, to give a smooth surface and keep the interstices water-tight. M18.

parcener /ˈpɑːs(ə)nə/ *noun.* ME.
[Anglo-Norman = Old French *parçonier*, from Proto-Romance, from Latin *partitio(n-)* PARTITION *noun*: see -ER[2]. Cf. PARTNER.]
†**1** A person who shares or partakes in something with another or others; a partner. ME–E17.
2 LAW. = COPARCENER. ME.
■ **parcenary** *noun* (LAW) = COPARCENARY *noun* 1 LME.

parc fermé /pɑːk ˈfɛːmeɪ/ *noun phr.* Also **parc ferme**. M20.
[French, lit. 'enclosed area'.]
In motor sports, an enclosure or paddock used by vehicles before or after a race.

parch /pɑːtʃ/ *noun. rare* exc. in comb. LME.
[from next.]
The action of parching; the condition of being parched.
Comb.: **parch mark** ARCHAEOLOGY a localized discoloration of the ground in dry weather over buried remains.

parch /pɑːtʃ/ *verb.* ME.
[Origin unkn.]
1 *verb trans.* **a** Dry by exposure to heat; *spec.* (**a**) roast (corn, peas, etc.) lightly; (**b**) (of the sun's heat, of fever or thirst) deprive of water, cause to be in need of water. Also in *pass.*, have an extreme thirst (*for*); long *for* on account of thirst. ME. ►**b** *transf.* Dry, shrivel, or wither with cold. Chiefly *poet.* L16.
2 *verb intrans.* Become (very) dry and hot; shrivel up with heat. M16.

📖 **1a** H. BELLOC For very many days the intense heat had parched the Weald. S. E. MORISON Once ashore, they managed to light a fire and parch corn. **b** SOUTHEY Who .. felt the storm Of the bleak winter parch his shivering form. **2** W. COBBETT The grass never parches upon these downs. W. BLACK He would sooner parch with thirst.

■ **parched** *adjective* dried up; extremely thirsty: LME. **parchedness** /ˈpɑːtʃɪdnɪs/ *noun* M17.

parcheesi *noun* var. of PACHISI.

parchment /ˈpɑːtʃm(ə)nt/ *noun, adjective, & verb.* ME.
[Old & mod. French *parchemin* from Proto-Romance, ult. from blend of Latin *pergamina* writing material from Pergamum (see PERGAMENIAN) and *Parthica pellis* Parthian skin (a kind of scarlet leather).]
► **A** *noun.* **1 a** The skin of an animal, esp. a sheep or goat, dressed and prepared for writing, painting, bookbinding, etc. ME. ►**b** A high-grade paper manufactured to resemble parchment. M19.
2 a A skin, piece, scroll, or roll of parchment; a manuscript or document on parchment. ME. ►**b** *spec.* A certificate. L19.
3 A skin or membrane resembling parchment; *spec.* the husk of the coffee bean. L17.
4 A pale yellow colour resembling that of parchment. M20.
1b vegetable parchment = *parchment paper* below.
► **B** *attrib.* or as *adjective.* Made of, pertaining to, or existing only on parchment; of the nature or colour of parchment. L16.
Comb. & special collocations: **parchment-beaver** beaver skin taken in summer after the hair has been shed; **parchment-coffee** the coffee bean while still enclosed in its husk; **parchment glue** a glue made from parchment cuttings; **parchment-lace** (*obsolete* exc. *Hist.*) a kind of lace, braid, or cord, the core of which was parchment; **parchment paper** a tough, translucent, glossy kind of paper resembling parchment, made by soaking ordinary unsized paper in dilute sulphuric acid; **parchment-skin** a piece of parchment; dry rough skin resembling parchment, as formed in xeroderma.
► **C** *verb trans.* = PARCHMENTIZE. Chiefly as ***parchmented*** *ppl adjective.* L19.
■ **parchmenter** *noun* (long *obsolete* exc. *Hist.*) a maker or seller of parchment LME. **parchmenty** *adjective* of the nature of parchment M19.

parchmentize /ˈpɑːtʃm(ə)ntʌɪz/ *verb trans.* Also **-ise**. L19.
[from prec. + -IZE.]
Convert into parchment; make like parchment in texture.

parclose /ˈpɑːkləʊz/ *noun.* ME.
[Old French, use as noun of fem. pa. pple of *parclore*: see next.]
†**1** The close or conclusion of a sentence, letter, discourse, etc. ME–L17.
2 A screen or railing serving to partition off a space in a building. Now only *spec.*, one in a church enclosing an altar, tomb, etc., or partitioning off a side-chapel. LME.
†**3** An enclosed space; *esp.* one in a building, separated from the main area by a screen or railing. Only in 16.

parclose /pɑːˈkləʊz/ *verb trans.* L16.
[Old French *parclos*, *-se* pa. pple of *parclore*, formed as PAR-[1] + *clore* from Latin *claudere* to close.]
1 Enclose (with a parclose). *rare.* L16.
†**2** (Bring to a) close, conclude. E–M17.

parcy *noun* see PERSUE.

pard /pɑːd/ *noun*[1]. *arch. & poet.* ME.
[Old French from Latin *pardus* from Greek *pardos*, earlier fem. *pardalis*, of Indo-Iranian origin.]
A panther; a leopard.
■ **parded** *adjective* spotted like a leopard E19.

pard /pɑːd/ *noun*[2]. *slang* (chiefly *US*). M19.
[Abbreviation of PARDNER.]
A partner, a mate.

†**pardal** *noun.* M16–L17.
[Latin *pardalis* from Greek: see PARD *noun*[1].]
= PARD *noun*[1].

pardalote /ˈpɑːdələʊt/ *noun.* M19.
[mod. Latin *Pardalotus* (see below), from Greek *pardalōtos* spotted like a leopard, from *pardalis*: see PARD *noun*[1].]
ORNITHOLOGY. Any small insectivorous bird of the Australian genus *Pardalotus*, having spotted or striped plumage and related to the flower-peckers. Also called ***diamond-bird***.

pardessus /pardəsy/ *noun.* Pl. same. M19.
[French = a thing that is over another, spec. a man's overcoat, from *par-dessus* (adverb) over, above.]
†**1** A kind of lady's cloak. M–L19.
2 MUSIC. In full ***pardessus de viole*** /də vjɔl/. A small treble viol, played esp. in France during the 18th cent. L19.

pardi /pɑːˈdiː/ *interjection & adverb. arch.* Also **-die**; **perdie** /pəˈdiː/. ME.
[Old French *par dé* (French *pardieu*, colloq. *pardi*) lit. 'by God', from Latin *per deum*: see PAR-[1].]
► **A** *interjection.* Expr. asseveration. ME.
► **B** *adverb.* Certainly, assuredly, indeed. ME.

pardner /ˈpɑːdnə/ *noun. colloq.* (orig. *US*). L18.
[Repr. a pronunc. of PARTNER *noun*.]
A partner, a comrade. Freq. as a form of address.

pardon /ˈpɑːd(ə)n/ *noun.* ME.
[Old French *pardun*, *perdun* (mod. *pardon*), from *pardoner*: see next.]
► **I** Forgiveness.
1 The passing over of an offence without punishment; the overlooking or forgiveness of an offence, error, sin, etc. ME.
2 Courteous forbearance or indulgence; the excusing of a (presumed) fault. Freq. in phrs. expr. polite apology, dissent, etc. M16. ►†**b** Permission. M16–E17. ►**c** As *interjection ellipt.* I beg your pardon. *colloq.* L19.

📖 **1** D. HUME Craved pardon for his offences, and offered to purchase forgiveness by any atonement. J. GILBERT Pardon supposes law and sin. **2** V. WOOLF Tore her chicken bones, asking Jacob's pardon, with her own hands. **beg a person's pardon**: express polite apology, or disagreement, request a remark etc. to be repeated. **b** SHAKES. *Haml.* I shall, first asking your pardon thereunto, recount the occasion of my .. return. **c** J. CANNAN Julian said, 'That's all nonsense. You're drunk.' .. 'Pardon?' said Eric. A. P. HERBERT She said 'Pardon?' and Mr. Baxter had to repeat his question. E. TAYLOR And Dad not particular about saying 'pardon' when he belches.

► **II** Remission.
3 Remission of a payment or penalty that is due. Long *obsolete* exc. as below. ME.
4 *spec.* **a** ROMAN CATHOLIC CHURCH. An indulgence. Later also, a (usu. local) church festival at which an indulgence is granted. ME. ►**b** LAW. A duly authorized remission of the legal consequences of a crime or conviction. ME.
5 A document conveying an indulgence or a legal pardon. LME.

📖 **4a** J. DAUS The ignoraunt people .. put the whole trust of their salvation in pardons. **b** D. HUME The farmers and officers of the customs .. were .. glad to compound for a pardon by paying a fine. **free pardon** an unconditional pardon. **general pardon** a pardon for all the offences of an individual or for offences by a number of unnamed individuals. **5** SHAKES. *Meas. for M.* Sign me a present pardon for my brother.

Comb.: **pardon-bell** = ANGELUS *bell*.
■ **pardonless** *adjective* unpardonable; without pardon: M16.

pardon /ˈpɑːd(ə)n/ *verb trans.* LME.
[Old French *pardoner*, *perduner* (mod. *pardonner*), from medieval Latin *perdonare*, from Latin *per-* (see PAR-[1] + *donare* give.]
1 Refrain from exacting the due penalty for (an offence etc.); pass over (an offence or offender) without punishment or blame; duly authorize remission of the legal consequences of (a crime or conviction); forgive. LME.
†**2** Refrain from exacting (a duty, debt, penalty, etc.). LME–M17.
3 Make courteous allowance for, excuse, (a person, fact, or action). E16.

📖 **1** D. HUME Her father would never have pardoned such obstinacy. E. WILSON The royalists .. had all been pardoned and set free. **2** SHAKES. *Merch. V.* I pardon thee thy life before thou ask it. **3** E. M. FORSTER Whether he droned trivialities .. or sprang kisses on her .. she could pardon him. A. S. NEILL Compromise I can pardon, but not gush. **pardon me**: I beg your pardon.

pardonable /ˈpɑːd(ə)nəb(ə)l/ *adjective.* LME.
[Old & mod. French *pardonnable*, from *pardoner*: see prec., -ABLE.]
Able to be pardoned; excusable.

📖 C. TOMALIN It was an unkind but pardonable act of self-preservation.

■ **pardonableness** *noun* M17. **pardonably** *adverb* L17.

pardoner /ˈpɑːd(ə)nə/ *noun*[1]. ME.
[Anglo-Norman, formed as PARDON *noun*: see -ER[2].]
Hist. A person licensed to sell papal indulgences.

pardoner /ˈpɑːd(ə)nə/ *noun*[2]. L16.
[from PARDON *verb* + -ER[1].]
A person who pardons an offence, offender, etc.

pare /ˈpɑːriː/ *noun*[1]. *NZ.* L19.
[Maori.]
A lintel in a Maori building.

pare /pɛː/ *verb & noun*[2]. ME.
[Old & mod. French *parer* adorn, arrange, peel (fruit) from Latin *parare* prepare.]
► **A** *verb trans.* **I** Cut.
1 Trim by cutting off projecting or irregular parts. Also, cut away or shave (*off*) the outer edge or surface of (a thing); *spec.* peel (fruit or vegetables). ME. ►**b** Cut away or shave *off* (the outer part of a thing). LME. ►**c** Orig., prune by cutting off superfluous shoots. Later, reduce the thickness of (a hedge etc.). LME.
2 Slice off the turf etc. from the surface of (the ground); slice off (turf) from the ground. Chiefly in ***pare and burn*** below. M16.
3 Reduce (a thing) by or as by cutting or shaving *away*; bring or cut *down* in size, amount, etc.; make gradual reductions in (a thing). M16.

📖 **1** K. MANSFIELD Taking a pearl penknife out of his pocket he began to pare his nails. **b** DELIA SMITH Using a sharp knife, pare the rind .. from both the bacon and the pork. *fig.*: A. THOMAS I did not see how it was possible .. to pare .. any more of our expenses. **3** A. DAVIS I did want to pare down my political involvements to a minimum. A. BELL Discursive footnotes abandoned, and references pared to a minimum. C. ANGIER As she grew older she pared more and more away in her writing.

►†**II 4** Get ready, prepare; adorn. LME–E17.
Phrases & comb.: ***cheese-pare***: see CHEESE *noun*[1]. **pare and burn** cut the turf of (land) two or three inches deep and burn it, to use the ashes as manure. **pare to the bone** reduce to a minimum. **pare to the quick** cut deeply, esp. so as to hurt.
► **B** *noun.* Something pared (off). Long *obsolete* exc. *Scot.* LME.
■ **pared** *ppl adjective* that has been pared (*down*) LME. **parer** *noun* an instrument for paring something; a person who pares something: L16.

paregoric /parɪˈgɒrɪk/ *adjective & noun.* L17.
[Late Latin *paregoricus* from Greek *parēgorikos* encouraging, soothing, from *parēgorein* console, soothe.]
► **A** *adjective.* Of a medicine: relieving pain, soothing. L17.
paregoric elixir a camphorated (or formerly, ammoniated) tincture of opium flavoured with aniseed and benzoic acid, formerly used to treat diarrhoea and coughing in children.
► **B** *noun.* **1** A soothing or pain-relieving medicine. L17.
2 *spec.* = ***paregoric elixir*** above. L19.

pareiasaur /pəˈrʌɪəsɔː/ *noun.* E20.
[mod. Latin *Pareiasaurus* genus name, from Greek. *pareia* cheek: see -SAUR.]
PALAEONTOLOGY. Any of a group of herbivorous reptiles of the Permian period.
■ **pareia'saurian** *noun & adjective* (**a**) *adjective* of, pertaining to, or characteristic of a pareiasaur; (**b**) *noun* a pareiasaur: E20.

pareia'saurus *noun*. pl. **-ruses**, **-ri** /-rʌɪ, -riː/, a pareiasaur; *spec.* one of the genus *Pareiasaurus*: L19.

pareira /pəˈrɛːrə/ *noun*. E18.
[Portuguese *parreira* vine trained against a wall.]
In full ***pareira brava*** /ˈbrɑːvə/ [= wild]. A drug, formerly much used as a diuretic, made from the root of any of several Brazilian climbing plants; any of the plants yielding this drug, esp. *Chondrodendron tomentosum* (family Menispermaceae) and (more fully ***false pareira***) the related velvet-leaf, *Cissampelos pareira*.

†**parel** *noun*. ME.
[Aphet. from APPAREL *noun*. Cf. PARREL.]
1 Physical or moral stature, bearing; quality, workmanship. Cf. APPAREL *noun* 2. ME–E16.
2 A body of troops. LME–E16.
3 Apparatus, equipment; furniture. Cf. APPAREL *noun* 1. LME–M16. ▸**b** = APPAREL *noun* 3. LME–M17.
4 Ornament, decoration. M16–L17. ▸**b** A mantelpiece. M16–M19.
5 A preparation of eggs etc. for fining wine. L16–E18.

†**parel** *verb trans.* Infl. **-ll-**. ME.
[Aphet. from APPAREL *verb*.]
1 = APPAREL *verb* 3. Only in ME.
2 Fine (wine). Only in E17.

†**parelion** *noun* var. of PARHELION.

paren /pəˈrɛn/ *noun*. E20.
[Abbreviation of PARENTHESIS.]
Chiefly TYPOGRAPHY. A round bracket. Usu. in *pl.*

parencephalon /parɛnˈsɛf(ə)lɒn, -ˈkɛf-/ *noun*. E18.
[from PARA-¹ + ENCEPHALON.]
ANATOMY. The cerebellum.

parenchyma /pəˈrɛŋkɪmə/ *noun*. Pl. **parenchymata** /parɛŋˈkɪmətə/. Also **-chym(e)** /-kɪm/. M17.
[Greek *paregkhuma* something poured in besides, formed as PARA-¹ + *egkhuma* infusion.]
1 ANATOMY & ZOOLOGY. **a** The functional tissue of a gland or other organ, as distinguished from connective tissue or stroma, and from muscular tissue. M17. ▸**b** Cellular tissue composing the main bulk of the body in acoelomate invertebrates, esp. flatworms. M17.
2 BOTANY. Soft succulent tissue, consisting of isodiametric thin-walled cells, and freq. intercellular spaces, found esp. in the softer parts of leaves, the pulp of fruits, the bark and pith of stems, etc. Cf. PROSENCHYMA. M17.
■ **parenchymal**, **parenchy'matic** *adjectives* of, pertaining to, or consisting of parenchyma, parenchymatous M19.

parenchymatous /parɛŋˈkɪmətəs/ *adjective*. M17.
[formed as prec. + -OUS.]
1 a ANATOMY & ZOOLOGY. Consisting of or of the nature of parenchyma; *spec.* designating flatworms whose bodies are composed of solid parenchyma with no visceral cavity. M17. ▸**b** MEDICINE. Of or belonging to the parenchyma of an organ; occurring in or affecting the parenchyma. E19.
2 BOTANY. Consisting of or of the nature of parenchyma; of or belonging to the parenchyma. L18.

parenchymous /pəˈrɛŋkɪməs/ *adjective*. Now *rare*. M17.
[from *parenchym* var. of PARENCHYMA + -OUS.]
= prec.

parenesis *noun* var. of PARAENESIS.

parens patriae /parɛnz ˈpatriiː/ *noun phr.* M18.
[mod. Latin, lit. 'parent of the country'.]
LAW. The monarch, or any other authority, regarded as the legal protector of citizens unable to protect themselves.

parent /ˈpɛːr(ə)nt/ *noun*, *adjective*, & *verb*. LME.
[Old & mod. French from Latin *parent-*, *parens* father or mother (pl. *parentes* parents, progenitors, kinsfolk), use as noun of pres. pple of *parere* bring forth: see -ENT.]
▸ **A** *noun*. **1** A person who has fathered or given birth to a child; a biological father or mother; a person who holds the position or exercises the functions of such a parent, a protector, a guardian. LME. ▸**b** An animal or plant considered in relation to its offspring. L18.
2 a An ancestor, a forefather. LME. ▸†**b** A relative; a kinsman, a kinswoman. LME–L18.
3 *fig.* **a** A thing from which another is derived or has its existence; a source, a cause, an origin. L16. ▸**b** NUCLEAR PHYSICS. A nuclide that becomes transformed into another (daughter) nuclide by radioactive decay. E20. ▸**c** = ***parent company*** below. L20.

> 🕮 **1** C. TOMALIN Most of her childhood meals were eaten with Granny and not with her parents. ***adoptive parent***, ***biological parent***, ***birth parent***, ***natural parent***, etc. ***single parent***: see SINGLE *adjective & adverb*. **2a our first parents** *arch.* Adam and Eve. **3c** *Accountancy* It is quite usual . . that a subsidiary's sole asset is a debt owed by its parent.

▸ **B** *attrib.* or as *adjective*. (Freq. with hyphen.) That is a parent. M17.
Special collocations & comb.: **parent cell** = ***mother cell*** s.v. MOTHER *noun*¹ & *adjective*. **parent–child** *attrib. adjective* of or pertaining to both a parent and a child. **parent company** a company of which other companies are subsidiaries. **parentcraft** (knowledge of or skill in) the rearing of children. **parent-figure** a person regarded or treated as a parent. **parent-in-law**, pl. **parents-in-law**, a father-in-law or mother-in-law. **parents' day** a day on which parents can visit their children's school. **parent ship** a ship which protects smaller vessels or which acts as a base for ships or aircraft. **parents' meeting** a meeting of parents with their children's teachers at a school. **parent–teacher** *attrib. adjective* of or pertaining to parents and the teachers of their children; ***parent–teacher association***, a local organization of parents and teachers established to promote closer relations and improve educational facilities.
▸ **C** *verb*. **1** *verb trans.* **a** Beget, produce. M17. ▸**b** Be or act as a parent to (*lit. & fig.*); rear (a child). L19.
2 *verb intrans.* Be a parent; take care of one's children. M20.

> 🕮 **1b** *Times* The Suez Canal Company, with its position and its money, . . wanting to parent the idea. *Listener* Many . . are most suitable candidates to parent the child in question. **2** *Redbook* Young men and women can parent . . who have had no experience with small children.

■ †**parentation** *noun* the performance of the funeral rites of a parent or relative; a memorial service for the dead: E17–E19. **parented** *adjective* (*rare*) having parents E20. **parenting** *verbal noun* the action of the verb; *spec.* taking care of one's children: M20. **parentless** *adjective* M16. **parentship** *noun* = PARENTHOOD M19.

parentage /ˈpɛːr(ə)ntɪdʒ/ *noun*. L15.
[Old & mod. French, formed as PARENT *noun*: see -AGE.]
1 a Exercise of the functions of a parent; parental conduct or treatment. *rare*. L15. ▸**b** The condition or status of a parent; parenthood. L19.
2 Derivation or descent from parents; hereditary status or quality; lineage, birth. L15.
†**3** One's parents. *rare*. Only in 16.
†**4** Relationship, kinship; relations collectively, kindred. E16–M18.

> 🕮 **1b** W. M. CLARKE 'My two children' (his first acknowledgement of parentage in print). **2** SHAKES. *2 Hen. VI* The elder . . ignorant of his birth and parentage, Became a bricklayer when he came to age. V. NABOKOV Annabel was . . of mixed parentage: half-English, half-Dutch. *fig.*: F. W. FARRAR Sin . . shows by ethical likeness its Satanic parentage. **3** SPENSER He . . Inquyrd, which of them most did love her parentage?

parental /pəˈrɛnt(ə)l/ *adjective*. M16.
[Latin *parentalis*, from *parent-*: see PARENT, -AL¹.]
Of, pertaining to, or of the nature of a parent; characteristic of or resembling a parent.

> 🕮 M. STOTT At sixteen youngsters cannot be forced to live in the parental home. J. UGLOW Godfrey's parental right must imply Eppie's filial duty.

■ **parentalism** *noun* (the assumption of) the attitude of a parent; paternalism: L19. **parentality** /par(ə)nˈtalɪti/ *noun* parenthood L18. **parentally** *adverb* in the manner of a parent L18.

parentalia /par(ə)nˈteɪlɪə/ *noun pl.* E18.
[Latin, use as noun of neut. pl. of *parentalis*: see PARENTAL, -IA².]
ROMAN HISTORY. Periodical observances in honour of dead parents or relations.

parentela /par(ə)nˈtiːlə/ *noun*. E20.
[Late Latin = relationship, from Latin *parent-*: see PARENT.]
BIOLOGY. The set of all descendants of a particular pair of individuals.
■ **parentelic** /-ˈtɛlɪk/ *adjective* of or pertaining to relationship deriving from common progenitors L19.

†**parentele** *noun*. LME.
[French *parentèle* from late Latin PARENTELA.]
1 Kinship; kindred. LME–M16.
2 = PARENTAGE 2. L15–M18.

parenteral /pəˈrɛnt(ə)r(ə)l/ *adjective*. E20.
[from PARA-¹ + Greek *enteron* intestine + -AL¹.]
MEDICINE. ▸**A** *adjective*. Involving or designating the introduction of a substance into the body other than by the mouth or gut, esp. by injection. E20.
▸ **B** *noun*. A preparation for parenteral administration. M20.
■ **parenterally** *adverb* otherwise than by or into the gut E20.

parenthesis /pəˈrɛnθɪsɪs/ *noun*. Pl. **-theses** /-θɪsiːz/. M16.
[Late Latin from Greek, from *parentithenai* place in besides, formed as PARA-¹ + EN-² + *tithenai* to place: see THESIS.]
1 A word, clause, sentence, etc., inserted (as an explanation, qualification, aside, or afterthought) into a passage which is already grammatically complete, and usu. marked off by brackets, dashes, or commas. Also, the use of such insertions, esp. as a rhetorical figure. M16. ▸†**b** A rhetorical digression. M16–M18. ▸**c** *transf.* An interval; an interlude; a hiatus. L16.
2 (Inclusion of words within) a pair of round brackets. L16. ▸**b** Either of a pair of (esp. round) brackets used to include words inserted parenthetically (usu. in *pl.*). E18. ▸**c** LOGIC & COMPUTING. A left-hand or right-hand bracket, esp. used in pairs to disambiguate a complex expression by grouping the symbols occurring within the scope of an operator. E20.

> 🕮 **1** J. MUIRHEAD What is illegible . . but . . obvious from the context . . is in italics, within marks of parenthesis ( ). **b** T. GATAKER But let this go for a Parenthesis; return we to our task. **c** JOYCE The years . . of allotted human life formed a parenthesis of infinitesimal brevity.

Phrases: **in parenthesis** by way of explanation or digression.
Comb.: **parenthesis-free notation** = ***Polish notation*** s.v. POLISH *adjective*.

parenthesize /pəˈrɛnθɪsʌɪz/ *verb trans.* Also **-ise**. M19.
[from prec. + -IZE.]
1 Insert or express (a statement, idea, etc.) parenthetically. M19.
2 Put (a word, expression, etc.) between parentheses; bracket. M19.

parenthetic /par(ə)nˈθɛtɪk/ *adjective*. L18.
[from PARENTHESIS after *antithesis*, *antithetic*, etc.]
= PARENTHETICAL 1.

parenthetical /par(ə)nˈθɛtɪk(ə)l/ *adjective*. E17.
[formed as prec. + -AL¹.]
1 Of, pertaining to, or of the nature of a parenthesis; inserted as a parenthesis. E17.
2 Characterized by, addicted to, or using parenthesis. M19.
3 Of legs: bandy. *joc.* M19.

> 🕮 **1** R. D. WALSHE Parenthetical material can be marked off . . by commas, by dashes, by round brackets . . and by square brackets.

■ **parenthetically** *adverb* in a parenthetical manner; in parentheses; by way of parenthesis: M17.

parenthood /ˈpɛːr(ə)nthʊd/ *noun*. M19.
[from PARENT *noun* + -HOOD.]
The state or condition of being a parent.

parenticide /pəˈrɛntɪsʌɪd/ *noun*. *rare*. M17.
[from Latin *parent-* (see PARENT *noun*) + -I- + -CIDE.]
A person who murders his or her parent.

pareoean /parɪˈiːən/ *adjective & noun*. E20.
[from PARA-¹ + Greek *eōios* dawn, eastern + -AN.]
ANTHROPOLOGY. ▸**A** *adjective*. Designating the southern Mongol people in and near China. E20.
▸ **B** *noun*. A member of this people. E20.

parepididymis /parɛpɪˈdɪdɪmɪs/ *noun*. Pl. **-didymides** /-dɪˈdɪmɪdiːz/. M19.
[from PARA-¹ + EPIDIDYMIS.]
= PARADIDYMIS.
■ **parepididymal** *adjective* paradidymal L19.

parera /ˈparɛːrə/ *noun*. NZ. M19.
[Maori.]
The grey duck, *Anas superciliosa*.

parergon /pəˈrəːgɒn/ *noun*. Pl. **-ga** /-gə/. E17.
[Latin from Greek, formed as PARA-¹ + *ergon* work.]
†**1** An ornamental accessory or addition, esp. in a painting; an embellishment. E17–E18.
2 Subsidiary work or business, apart from one's ordinary employment. Also, a work, composition, etc., that is supplementary to or a by-product of a larger work. E17.

pareschatology /ˌparɛskəˈtɒlədʒi/ *noun*. L20.
[from Greek *pareskhatos* penultimate, formed as PARA-¹ + *eskhatos* last + -OLOGY.]
THEOLOGY. The doctrine of or a theory about human life between physical death and its final state. Cf. ESCHATOLOGY.

paresis /ˈparɪsɪs/ *noun*. L17.
[mod. Latin from Greek = letting go, paralysis, from *parienai*, formed as PARA-¹ + *hienai* let go.]
MEDICINE. **1** Partial or incomplete paralysis. L17.
2 In full ***general paresis***. Chronic inflammation of the brain and meninges, occurring in tertiary syphilis and causing progressive dementia and general paralysis. Also called ***general paralysis (of the insane)***. M19.

paresthesia *noun* see PARAESTHESIA.

Paretan /pəˈreɪt(ə)n, -ˈriːt(ə)n/ *adjective*. M20.
[from PARETO + -AN.]
Of or pertaining to Vilfredo Pareto or his economic or sociological theories or methods.
■ Also **Paretian** /-ʃ(ə)n/ *adjective* M20.

paretic /pəˈrɛtɪk/ *adjective & noun*. E19.
[from PARESIS: see -ETIC.]
MEDICINE. ▸**A** *adjective*. Of or pertaining to paresis; affected with or characterized by paresis. E19.
▸ **B** *noun*. A person affected with paresis. L19.
■ **paretically** *adverb* L19.

Pareto /pəˈreɪtəʊ, -ˈriːtəʊ/ *noun*. E20.
[Vilfredo *Pareto* (1848–1923), Italian economist and sociologist.]
Used *attrib.* and in *possess.* with ref. to the theories or methods of Pareto, esp. the law or formula by which he claimed to be able to express the income distribution of any society.
Comb.: **Pareto-optimal** *adjective* pertaining to or designating a distribution of wealth etc. such that any redistribution beneficial to one individual is detrimental to one or more others.

pareu /ˈpɑːreɪuː/ *noun.* M19.
[Tahitian.]
A sarong worn by Polynesian men and women, made of a single straight piece of cloth, usu. of printed cotton.

pareve /ˈpɑːrəvə/ *adjective.* Also **parev** /ˈpɑːrəv/, **parve** /ˈpɑːvə/. M20.
[Yiddish *parev(e)*.]
JUDAISM. Made without milk, meat, or their derivatives, and therefore permissible to eat with both meat and dairy dishes according to dietary laws.

par excellence /par ɛkslɑ̃ːs, pɑːr ˈɛks(ə)ləns/ *adverbial & adjectival phr.* L17.
[French from Latin *per excellentiam* by virtue of excellence.]
Pre-eminent(ly); supreme(ly), above all. Now usu. as *postpositive adjective.*
A. CARTER Saskia . . started that cookery series; now she's the TV chef *par excellence.* D. MORGAN Pentecostalism . . was emerging as the religion par excellence of the media age.

parfait /ˈpɑːfeɪ/ *noun.* L19.
[French, lit. 'perfect'.]
A rich iced pudding of whipped cream, eggs, etc. Also, a sweet consisting of layers of ice-cream, fruit, syrup, whipped cream, etc., served in a tall glass.

Parfait Amour /ˌpɑːfeɪ(t) aˈmʊə/ *noun phr.* E19.
[French, lit. 'perfect love'.]
A kind of sweet spiced liqueur.

parfilage /ˈpɑːfɪlɑːʒ, *foreign* parfilaːʒ/ *noun.* L19.
[French, from *parfiler* unravel thread by thread from Old French *pourfiler*, from *pour* for + *fil* thread.]
Hist. The unravelling of gold or silver thread from embroidery, fashionable as a pastime esp. among ladies in 18th-cent. France.

†**parfit** *adjective, adverb, & noun* see PERFECT *adjective* etc.

parfleche /ˈpɑːflɛʃ/ *noun & adjective. N. Amer.* E19.
[Canad. French *parflèche*, from French *parer* (see PARRY *verb*) + *flèche* arrow.]
▶**A** *noun.* (A) depilated (esp. buffalo's) hide dried by stretching on a frame; an article made from this. E19.
▶**B** *attrib.* or as *adjective.* Made of parfleche. M19.

parfocal /pɑːˈfəʊk(ə)l/ *adjective.* L19.
[from PAR *noun*[1] + FOCAL *adjective.*]
OPTICS. Designating or pertaining to two or more lenses (esp. in a microscope) the focal points of which lie in the same plane, so that they may be interchanged without adjusting the focus (foll. by *with*).
■ **parfoˈcality** *noun* the property of being parfocal M20. **parfocaliˈzation** *noun* the action or result of parfocalizing something M20. **parfocalize** *verb trans.* make parfocal M20. **parfocally** *adverb* L20.

parfumerie /parfymri/ *noun.* Pl. pronounced same. M19.
[French.]
A shop or department which sells perfume. Also, a perfume factory.

pargana /pəˈɡʌnə/ *noun.* Also (earlier) **pergana**, **pergunnah**. E17.
[Persian & Urdu *parganah* district.]
In the Indian subcontinent, a division of territory comprising a number of villages.

pargasite /ˈpɑːɡəsʌɪt/ *noun.* E19.
[from *Pargas*, a town in Finland + -ITE[1].]
MINERALOGY. A green or greenish-blue variety of hornblende.

parge /pɑːdʒ/ *verb trans.* M17.
[App. from next.]
= PARGET *verb* 1.
Comb.: **parge-work** = PARGETING *noun* 2.
■ **parging** *noun* = PARGETING L19.

parget /ˈpɑːdʒɪt/ *verb & noun.* LME.
[Old French *pargeter* fill up joints in masonry, from *par* through, all over + *jeter* cast (see JET *verb*[2]).]
▶**A** *verb trans.* Infl. **-t-**, **-tt-**.
1 Cover or daub with parget; plaster (a wall etc.); decorate with pargeting. LME.
†**2** *transf.* Cover or decorate (a surface) with or *with* ornamental work, as gilding, precious stones, etc. Also (*rare*), cover (the face or body) thickly with paint etc. LME–L19.
3 *fig.* Cover or disguise with an attractive appearance. Now *rare* or *obsolete.* L16.
▶**B** *noun.* **1** Plaster spread on a wall, ceiling, etc.; whitewash; roughcast. LME.
2 *spec.* Ornamental work in plaster; a facing of plaster etc. with ornamental designs in relief or indented, formerly used for decorating walls. LME.
3 Gypsum used for making plaster. Now *rare* or *obsolete.* M17.
■ **pargeter**, **-tt-** *noun* a plasterer; a whitewasher: M16. **pargetry** *noun* = PARGETING 2 E20.

pargeting /ˈpɑːdʒɪtɪŋ/ *noun.* Also **-tt-**. LME.
[from prec. + -ING[1].]
1 The action of PARGET *verb.* LME.
2 Plaster; (ornamental) plasterwork; *spec.* = PARGET *noun* 2. LME.

pargo /ˈpɑːɡəʊ/ *noun.* Now *US.* Also †**porgo**. Pl. **-os**. M16.
[Spanish & Portuguese, app. from Latin *phager*. Cf. PORGY.]
= *sea bream* s.v. SEA.

parhelion /pɑːˈhiːlɪən/ *noun.* Pl. **-ia** /-ɪə/, **-ions**. Also †**parelion**. M17.
[Latin *parelion*, Greek *parēlion*, *-os*, from *para-* PARA-[1] + *hēlios* sun.]
1 A bright spot on a solar halo or parhelic circle, freq. occurring in pairs on either side of the sun and sometimes prismatically coloured; a mock sun, a sun-dog. M17.
2 *fig.* An image or reflection of something. M17.
■ **parhelic** *adjective* pertaining to or resembling a parhelion; ***parhelic circle***, ***parhelic ring***, a band of light parallel to the horizon and passing through the sun, caused by reflection of light by atmospheric ice crystals, seen esp. around sunset: L19.

parhypate /pɑːˈhɪpətiː/ *noun.* Also **paryp-** /pəˈrɪp-/. E17.
[Greek, formed as PARA-[1] + HYPATE.]
In ancient Greek music, the second note up in a lower tetrachord, immediately above the hypate.

pariah /pəˈrʌɪə/ *noun.* E17.
[Tamil *paraiyar* pl. of *paraiyan* lit. 'hereditary drummer', from *parai* drum.]
1 Orig., a member of a very extensive low caste in southern India, especially numerous at Madras. Later, a member of a low caste or of no Hindu caste. *obsolete* exc. *Hist.* E17.
2 *transf.* A member of a despised social class; a social outcast. E19.
3 = ***pariah-dog*** below. E19.
2 JOHN BROOKE They treated Bute as if he were a pariah . . with whom no contact should be made.
Comb.: **pariah brig** a deep-sea vessel in use in waters around the Indian subcontinent; **pariah-dog** (chiefly in the Indian subcontinent) a half-wild stray dog; also called ***pye-dog***.
■ **pariahdom** *noun* the condition of a pariah L19.

Parian /ˈpɛːrɪən/ *noun & adjective.* M16.
[from Latin *Parius* of *Paros* (see below): see -AN.]
▶**A** *noun.* **1** A native or inhabitant of the island of Paros in the Aegean Sea, in antiquity a source of white marble. M16.
2 *ellipt.* **a** = ***Parian ware*** below. M19. ▸**b** = ***Parian cement*** below. L19.
▶**B** *adjective.* **1** Of or pertaining to the island of Paros. E17.
2 Made of or designating Parian ware. L19.
Special collocations: **Parian cement** a plaster similar to Keene's cement but prepared with borax in place of alum. **Parian marble** a fine white marble obtained in antiquity from the island of Paros. **Parian ware** a hard-paste fine white unglazed porcelain resembling parian marble.

paribuntal /parɪˈbʌnt(ə)l/ *noun.* E20.
[from *Par(acale*, *Par(añaque*, *Par(ang*, or *Par(asang*, places in the Philippines + BUNTAL.]
A fine straw used for hats.

parichnos /pəˈrɪknɒs/ *noun.* L19.
[from PAR(A-[1] + Greek *ikhnos* track, trace.]
BOTANY. A strand of tissue found beside the leaf traces in fossil plants of the family Lepidodendraceae.

paries /ˈpɛːriːz/ *noun.* Pl. **parietes** /pəˈrʌɪtiːz/. E18.
[Latin *paries*, *pariet-* wall, partition.]
ANATOMY & BIOLOGY. A part or structure enclosing or forming the boundary of an organ; the wall or outer lining of a cavity. Usu. in *pl.*

parietal /pəˈrʌɪt(ə)l/ *noun & adjective.* E16.
[French *pariétal* or late Latin *parietalis*, from *pariet-*: see PARIES, -AL[1].]
▶**A** *noun.* A parietal bone (see sense B.1a below). E16.
▶**B** *adjective.* **1 a** ANATOMY & ZOOLOGY. Belonging to or connected with the wall of the body or the lining of a body cavity; *spec.* designating, pertaining to, or situated near a pair of bones, right and left, forming part of the sides and top of the skull, between the frontal and occipital bones. L16. ▸**b** BOTANY. Belonging to or attached to the wall of a hollow organ, esp. an ovary. E19.
2 Of or pertaining to residence within a college. *US.* M19.
3 *gen.* Of or belonging to a wall; mural. *rare* exc. with ref. to prehistoric art. M19.
1a parietal bone either of a pair of bones, right and left, forming part of the sides and top of the skull, between the frontal and occipital bones. **parietal cell** an acid-secreting cell of the stomach wall, an oxyntic cell. **parietal eye** a pineal eye. **parietal lobe** a lobe in each cerebral hemisphere lying below the crown of the skull. ***parietal pleura***: see PLEURA *noun*[1] 1. **2** A. ULAM At Harvard, the formerly idiotically strict parietal rules had been eroded . . to sensibly hypocritical proportions. **3** H. F. OSBORN This Art . . is also mural or parietal . . consisting of drawings . . on the walls of caverns.

†**parietary** *noun.* LME–L16
[Anglo-Norman *paritarie*, Old French *paritaire* (mod. *pariétaire*) from late Latin *parietaria*, from Latin *pariet-*: see PARIES.]
= PELLITORY 2.

parietes *noun* pl. of PARIES.

parietin /pəˈrʌɪɪtɪn/ *noun.* M19.
[from mod. Latin (*Xanthoria*) *parietina*, the lichen from which it was first obtained, from Latin *parietinus* of walls, from *pariet-*: see PARIES, -IN[1].]
CHEMISTRY. An anthraquinone derivative present as an orange-yellow pigment in some lichens.

parieto- /pəˈrʌɪɪtəʊ/ *combining form.* L19.
[from *pariet-* (see PARIES), PARIETAL *adjective*: see -O-.]
1 ANATOMY & ZOOLOGY. Forming adjectives with the sense 'belonging to or connected with the parietal bone or lobe and —', as ***parieto-frontal***, ***parieto-occipital***, ***parieto-temporal***, etc.
2 Chiefly ZOOLOGY. Forming adjectives with the sense 'belonging to or connected with the wall of a cavity or of the body, and —'.

pari-mutuel /parimytɥɛl (*pl. same*); pɑːrɪˈmjuːtʃʊəl, -tjʊəl/ *noun.* L19.
[French = mutual stake or wager. Cf. MUTUEL.]
1 A form of betting in which those backing the first three places divide the losers' stakes. L19.
2 A booth for placing bets under this system; a totalizator. E20.

paring /ˈpɛːrɪŋ/ *noun.* LME.
[from PARE *verb* + -ING[1].]
1 The action of PARE *verb.* LME.
2 A thin portion cut or peeled from the surface of a thing; a shaving. Freq. in *pl.* LME.
2 ***apple parings***, ***nail parings***, etc.
Attrib. & comb.: In the sense 'used for paring', as ***paring-chisel***, ***paring gouge***, ***paring-knife***, etc. Special combs., as **paring bee** *N. Amer.* a gathering for peeling apples etc.

pari passu /pɑːriː ˈpasuː, ˈpari/ *adverbial phr.* M16.
[Latin, lit. 'with equal step'.]
With equal speed; side by side; simultaneously and equally. Also, on an equal footing, without preference.

paripinnate /parɪˈpɪnət/ *adjective.* M19.
[from Latin *pari-*, *par* equal + PINNATE.]
BOTANY. Pinnate with an even number of leaflets, i.e. without a terminal leaflet.

Paris /ˈparɪs/ *noun.* L15.
[The capital of France.]
Used *attrib.* to designate things made or designed in, or associated with, Paris.
†**Paris ball** a tennis ball. **Paris blue** Prussian blue. **Paris club** a group of the major creditor nations of the International Monetary Fund, meeting informally in Paris to discuss the financial relations of the IMF member nations. ***Paris commune***: see COMMUNE *noun*[1] 2. **Paris daisy** a bushy plant of the Canary Islands, *Argyranthemum frutescens* of the composite family, with white-rayed flowers and greyish foliage. **Paris embroidery** a fine white cord embroidery worked in satin stitch on piqué. **Paris green** a vivid green toxic pigment which is a double salt of copper arsenite and acetate used as an insecticide.
¶ See also ***tout Paris*** s.v. TOUT *adjective*, ***plaster of Paris*** s.v. PLASTER *noun* 2a.

parisa *noun* pl. of PARISON *noun*[1].

parish /ˈparɪʃ/ *noun.* Also †**-roch(e)**. ME.
[Anglo-Norman, Old French *paroche* and Old & mod. French *paroisse* from ecclesiastical Latin *parochia* alt. (after *parochus* public purveyor from Greek *parokhos*) of *paroechia* from Greek *paroikia* sojourning, formed as PARA-[1] + *oikos* dwelling, house.]
1 ECCLESIASTICAL. Orig., a subdivision of a county, consisting of a township or cluster of townships having its own church and a priest to whom its tithes etc. were paid. Later, an area within such a subdivision having its own church. Now also, a subdivision of a diocese, usu. having its own church and a priest or pastor with spiritual responsibility for the people living in the area. ME.
2 A district, often identical with an original parish, constituted for various purposes of local civil administration or government, as (**a**) *Hist.* the administration of the Poor Law, (**b**) the maintenance of highways. Also ***civil parish***. ME. ▸**b** A subdivision of a US county made for purposes of local self-government (*obsolete* exc. *Hist.*); in Louisiana, a territorial division corresponding to a county in other States. *US.* M17.
3 The inhabitants of a parish, *esp.* those who belong to or attend a particular church. ME. ▸†**b** As many people as would fill a parish. *rare* (Shakes.). Only in E17. ▸**c** A congregation. *US.* M19.
4 CURLING. = HOUSE *noun*[1] 10b. L19.
2 on the parish (**a**) *Hist.* receiving parish relief (freq. in ***go on the parish***); (**b**) *colloq.* = ***on the dole*** s.v. DOLE *noun*[1].
Attrib. & comb.: In the senses 'of, pertaining to, or belonging to a parish, parochial', as ***parish altar***, ***parish bounds***, ***parish living***, ***parish meeting***, ***parish school***, etc.; 'intended for the service or use of the parish', as ***parish magazine***, ***parish room***, etc.; *Hist.* 'maintained or provided by the parish as the agency for poor relief' as ***parish poor***, ***parish relief***, ***parish workhouse***, etc. Special combs., as **parish church** the (principal or original) church of a parish; **parish clerk** (**a**) *Hist.* an official performing various duties concerned with the church in a parish; (**b**) an official in charge of the public records of a parish; **parish communion**, **parish Eucharist**: held for parishioners as the principal service of the day (usu. Sunday); ***parish*** CONSTABLE; **parish council** the council of a parish; *spec.* a local administrative body in rural civil parishes; **parish councillor** a member of

a parish council; ***parish Eucharist***: see ***parish communion*** above; ***parish lantern***: see LANTERN *noun*; **parish mass**: celebrated in a parish church; **parish priest**: in charge of a parish; **parish pump** a pump provided for the use of parishioners (used allusively to indicate (esp. political) limitation of scope, outlook, or knowledge); **parish pumpery** parochialism; **parish register**: recording the baptisms, marriages, and funerals in a parish; **parish-rigged** *adjective* (*Nautical slang*) poorly or cheaply equipped or clothed; †**parish-top** a spinning-top for the use of parishioners; **parish work** pastoral work in a parish, esp. helping the poor and the sick.

■ †**parishional** *adjective* of or pertaining to a parish; parochial: E17–E19. **pa'rishioner** *noun* an inhabitant or member of a parish LME. **pa'rishionership** *noun* (*rare*) the status of a parishioner M19.

parishad /'pʌrɪʃad, pʌrɪ'ʃad/ *noun.* E20.
[Sanskrit *pariṣad*, from *pari* around + *sad-* sit.]
In the Indian subcontinent, an assembly, a council.
ZILLAH ***parishad***.

Parisian /pə'rɪzɪən/ *noun & adjective.* LME.
[Old & mod. French *parisien*, formed as PARIS: see -IAN.]
▶ **A** *noun.* **1** A native or inhabitant of Paris, the capital city of France. LME.
2 The French spoken in or associated with Paris. M19.
▶ **B** *adjective.* Of or pertaining to Paris; resembling Paris or that of Paris. E17.
Parisian cloth: of cotton warp and worsted weft, made in England. **Parisian matins** the massacre of Huguenots throughout France begun without warning in Paris about 2 a.m. on the feast of St Bartholomew in Paris (24 August), 1572 (cf. ***Sicilian Vespers*** s.v. SICILIAN *adjective*.). **Parisian stitch** an upright stitch worked alternately over one and three horizontal threads of canvas.
■ **Parisianism** *noun* (a) Parisian character, habit, or practice L19. **Parisianize** *verb trans.* make Parisian M19.

Parisienne /parizjɛn/ *noun.* Pl. pronounced same. M17.
[French, fem. of *Parisien* PARISIAN.]
A Parisian girl or woman.

parisis /'parɪzɪs/ *noun & adjective.* Long *obsolete* exc. *Hist.* LME.
[from French = minted at Paris.]
(Designating) a coin minted at Paris, esp. a denier (worth one-fourth more than one minted at Tours).

parison /'parɪs(ə)n/ *noun*[1]. Pl. **-sa** /-sə/. L16.
[Greek, use as noun of neut. of *parisos* exactly balanced, formed as PARA-[1] + *isos* equal.]
RHETORIC. An even balance of clauses, syllables, etc., in a sentence.
■ **parisonic** /-'sɒnɪk/ *adjective* characterized by parison L19.

parison /'parɪs(ə)n/ *noun*[2]. M19.
[French *paraison*, from *parer* from Latin *parare* prepare: see -ISON.]
A rounded mass of glass formed by rolling immediately after removal from the furnace.

paristhmitis /parɪs'θmʌɪtɪs/ *noun.* Now *rare* or *obsolete.* E19.
[from Greek *paristhmion* tonsil (from *para-* by + *isthmos* neck, narrow passage) + -ITIS.]
MEDICINE. Tonsillitis.

parisyllabic /ˌparɪsɪ'labɪk/ *adjective & noun.* M17.
[from Latin *par*, *pari-* equal + *syllaba* SYLLABLE *noun* + -IC. Cf. IMPARISYLLABIC.]
GRAMMAR. ▶**A** *adjective.* Of a Greek or Latin noun: having the same number of syllables in all cases of the singular. M17.
▶ **B** *noun.* A parisyllabic noun. L19.

†**paritor** *noun.* L15–L19.
[Aphet.]
= APPARITOR 1.

parity /'parɪti/ *noun*[1]. L16.
[Old & mod. French *parité* or late Latin *paritas*, from *par*: see PAR *noun*[1], -ITY.]
1 The state or condition of being equal; equality of rank, status, or pay. L16.
2 Equality of nature, character, or tendency; likeness, similarity, analogy; parallelism. E17.
3 †**a** The property of an integer of being an even not an odd number. E–M17. ▸**b** MATH. & COMPUTING. The property of an integer by virtue of which it is odd or even; the property of employing odd or even numbers. E20. ▸**c** COMPUTING. In full ***parity bit***. A bit that is automatically made 1 or 0 so as to make the parity of the word or set containing it either odd or even, as previously determined. M20. ▸**d** PHYSICS. The property of a spatial wave function that either remains the same or changes sign when all the coordinates change sign; also (with specifying word), a similar property with respect to certain other symmetry operations; the value +1 or −1 of the quantum number (eigenvalue) corresponding to such a property. M20.
4 COMMERCE. Equivalence between a commodity's prices in different currencies, between the nominal and the market value of stocks etc., or between different legally specified forms of a national currency. L19. ▸**b** The value of one currency in terms of another or others at an established exchange rate. M20. ▸**c** An agreed price for agricultural produce relative to other commodities. M20. ▸**d** Equivalence of pay for jobs or categories of work perceived as being comparable or analogous; the practice or system of setting pay levels according to such perceived comparability. M20.

📖 **1** I. D'ISRAELI With the disciples of parity, a free election . . was a first state principle. JAN MORRIS The Italians demanded parity with the French. *Daily Telegraph* The principle of parity between the sexes. **parity of esteem** the state or condition of (*spec.* administratively comparable educational institutions) being regarded as equal. **2** G. BERKELEY There is . . no parity of case between Spirit and Matter. **d even parity**: for which a wave function remains the same. **odd parity**: for which a wave function changes sign. **4b** *Economist* The pound's previous parity with the dollar. G. BROWN Whether to devalue or . . try to hold the parity of sterling. ***PURCHASING power parity***. **d** *New Yorker* The practice of paying policemen and firemen at the same level, known as parity.

Comb.: ***parity bit***: see sense 3c above; **parity check** COMPUTING a check on the correctness of a set of binary digits that involves ascertaining the parity of a number derived from the set in a predetermined way; **parity checking** COMPUTING the action of performing a parity check; **parity digit** COMPUTING = ***parity bit*** above.

parity /'parɪti/ *noun*[2]. L19.
[from PAROUS + -ITY.]
MEDICINE. **1** The fact or condition of having borne children. L19.
2 The number of times a particular woman has conceived or (occas.) given birth. E20.

park /pɑːk/ *noun.* ME.
[Old & mod. French *parc* from medieval Latin *parricus*, from Germanic base repr. by Old High German *pfarrih*, *pferrih* (German *Pferch*) pen, fold, corresp. to Old English *pearruc* (see PADDOCK *noun*[2], PARROCK).]
1 An enclosed tract of land reserved for hunting, held by royal grant or prescription and stocked with deer etc. Now chiefly *Hist.* exc. in proper names. ME. ▸**b** A large ornamentally landscaped area, usu. with woodland and pasture, attached to a country house, and used for recreation and occas. for keeping deer, cattle, or sheep. Freq. in names of estates. E18.
2 An enclosed piece of land for pasture or tillage; a paddock. *dial.* LME. ▸†**b** An enclosure into which animals are driven for slaughter; a corral. *US.* L18–M19.
3 An enclosed area for public recreation, usu. large and ornamentally landscaped, esp. in or adjoining a city or town. Freq. in proper names. M17. ▸**b** A large area of land set apart as national property to be kept in its natural state for public benefit and enjoyment and for the conservation of wildlife; = ***national park*** s.v. NATIONAL *adjective*. Also, a large enclosed area where animals are exhibited to the public. M19. ▸**c** A sports ground, esp. for football or (*N. Amer.*) baseball (cf. ***ballpark*** s.v. BALL *noun*[1]). M19.
4 (An area reserved for) the artillery, tools, stores, etc., in a military encampment. L17. ▸**b** An area in or near a city or town, for parking cars and other vehicles. Freq. with specifying word. E20.
5 A high valley among mountains. *US.* E19.
6 An oyster-farm. M19.
7 [from the verb.] The gear position in which an automatic transmission is locked, preventing a motor vehicle from moving. M20.
8 An estate set aside for industrial development. Freq. with specifying word. M20.

📖 **1b** ***Buscot Park, Mansfield Park, Stonor Park***, etc. **3** B. BAINBRIDGE Mary . . preferred streets to parks. ***Central Park, Hyde Park, Phoenix Park, Regent's Park***, etc. **c** *Football Monthly* Influence . . exerted on the Luton team . . in the dressing-room and out on the park. **4b *car park, caravan park, lorry park***, etc. **8 *science park*** etc.

Phrases: ***industrial park***: see INDUSTRIAL *adjective*. ***national park***: see NATIONAL *adjective*. ***safari park***: see SAFARI *noun*. ***WILDLIFE park***. ***ZOOLOGICAL park***.
Comb.: **park cattle** (also ***white park cattle***) (animals of) a breed of primitive cattle, typically white in colour with dark ears and muzzles, maintained in a semi-wild state in several parks in Britain; **park course** an enclosed racecourse; **park-keeper** the caretaker of a park; **parkland** (*a*) open grassland scattered with clumps of trees; (*b*) an area landscaped as a park; (*c*) a piece of land set aside by the national government for public recreation and wildlife conservation; **park-leaves** (*obsolete* exc. *dial.*) (*a*) the tutsan, *Hypericum androsaemum*; †(*b*) the chaste-tree, *Vitex agnus-castus*; **parkway** (*a*) a highway, esp. a dual carriageway, with trees, grass, etc., planted alongside; (*b*) a railway station with extensive parking facilities, serving as an interchange between the road and rail systems (freq. in proper names).
■ **parkish** *adjective* resembling or pertaining to a park E19. **parklet** *noun* a small park M19. **parklike** *adjective* resembling a park E19. **parkly** *adjective* (*rare*) parklike M16. **parkward(s)** *adverb* towards the park L16.

park /pɑːk/ *verb.* E16.
[from the noun.]
1 *verb trans.* Enclose (as) in a park. Long *rare.* E16.
2 *verb trans.* Arrange (artillery, tools, stores, etc.) in a military encampment. Usu. in *pass.* M16.
3 *verb trans.* Bring (a vehicle) to a halt in a stationary position intended to be clear of the flow of traffic, esp. in a car park or at the roadside; manoeuvre (a vehicle) into a particular position of this kind. M19. ▸**b** *verb intrans.* Park a vehicle; (of a vehicle) be parked. M19.
4 *verb trans.* Leave (a person or thing) in a convenient place until required; put aside for a while. E20.
5 *verb intrans.* Kiss and embrace in a parked car. *N. Amer. slang.* M20.

📖 **3** J. T. STORY I . . parked the car and went into a call-box. J. FOWLES I . . parked where I could see the cinema. **4** B. BEHAN I've no chairs but park yourselves on the floor. A. TYLER Parked the kids with a neighbour. *Banker* Lots of investors like to park money there.

Comb.: **park-and-ride** *adjective & noun* (designating or pertaining to) a system whereby commuters, shoppers, etc., travel by private car to car parks on the outskirts of a city and continue their journey to the city centre by public transport.

parka /'pɑːkə/ *noun.* L18.
[Aleut from Russian = skin jacket.]
A long hooded skin jacket worn by Eskimos; a similar garment, usu. of windproof fabric, worn esp. by mountaineers.

parkade /pɑː'keɪd/ *noun.* Chiefly *N. Amer.* M20.
[from PARK *noun*, *verb* + -ADE, prob. after *arcade*.]
A building designed and constructed for the parking of vehicles; a multi-storey car park.

parker /'pɑːkə/ *noun*[1]. *obsolete* exc. *Hist.* ME.
[Anglo-Norman = medieval Latin *parcarius*, from *parc* PARK *noun*: see -ER[2].]
A caretaker of a park, a park-keeper.

parker /'pɑːkə/ *noun*[2]. M20.
[from PARK *verb* + -ER[1].]
1 A person who parks a vehicle. M20.
2 In *pl.* = PARKING ***light***. *Austral. colloq.* M20.

Parkerize /'pɑːkərʌɪz/ *verb trans.* E20.
[from the *Parker* Rust-Proof Co. of America, which introduced the process, + -IZE.]
Give (iron or steel) a protective rustproof coating by brief immersion in a hot acidic solution of a metal phosphate (usu. manganese dihydrogen phosphate). Chiefly as ***Parkerizing*** *verbal noun.*
¶ *Parkerized* and *Parkerizing* are proprietary terms in the UK and US respectively.

Parker's cement /pɑːkəz sɪ'mɛnt/ *noun phr. obsolete* exc. *Hist.* E19.
[from James *Parker*, who patented it in England in 1796.]
A hydraulic cement made with burnt marl, sand, and lime, largely superseded in the 19th cent. by Portland cement. Also called ***Roman cement***.

Parkes /'pɑːks/ *noun.* M19.
[Alexander *Parkes* (1813–90), English chemist.]
METALLURGY. ***Parkes process***, †***Parkes' process***, (erron.) ***Parke's process***, a process for removing silver and gold from molten lead by adding zinc, which forms an alloy with them that collects on the surface.

Parkesine /'pɑːksiːn/ *noun. obsolete* exc. *Hist.* M19.
[formed as prec. + -INE[5].]
An early type of celluloid.

parkie /'pɑːki/ *noun. colloq.* (chiefly *Scot.* & *north.*). Also **parky**. M20.
[from PARK *noun*: see -IE, -Y[6].]
A park-keeper.

parkin /'pɑːkɪn/ *noun.* Chiefly *north.* E19.
[Perh. from surname *Parkin*, *Perkin*, dim. of male forename *Per Peter*.]
A kind of bread or cake made with treacle, (usu.) oatmeal, and (occas.) ginger.

parking /'pɑːkɪŋ/ *noun.* E16.
[from PARK *verb* + -ING[1].]
1 The action of PARK *verb*. E16.
2 Ground landscaped as (in) a park. Also (*US*), a strip of grass, with or without trees, in the centre of a street or between the footpath and the curb. L19.
3 Space reserved or used for parking motor vehicles. M20.
Comb.: **parking bay** a space, esp. a recess at the side of a road or in a car park, allocated for parking; **parking brake**: for holding a motor vehicle or trailer at rest; **parking deck** (*a*) a floor of a building used for parking; (*b*) a multi-storey car park; **parking disc** a small circular permit for display in the window of a parked vehicle; **parking lamp**, **parking light** a small (often detachable) light on a vehicle to indicate position while parked; **parking lot** (chiefly *US*) a plot of land used as a car park; **parking meter** a coin-operated meter receiving fees and registering the time a vehicle is allowed to park; **parking orbit** an orbit around the earth or some other planet in which a space vehicle is temporarily placed; **parking tag**, **parking ticket** a notice of a fine etc. imposed for illegal parking.

Parkinsonian /pɑːkɪn'səʊnɪən/ *noun*[1] *& adjective*[1]. L19.
[from J. *Parkinson* (see PARKINSON'S DISEASE) + -IAN.]
MEDICINE. ▶**A** *noun.* A person affected with Parkinsonism. L19.
▶ **B** *adjective.* Characteristic of or affected with Parkinsonism. E20.

Parkinsonian /pɑːkɪnˈsəʊnɪən/ *noun*[2] & *adjective*[2]. M20.
[from C. N. *Parkinson* (see PARKINSON'S LAW) + -IAN.]
▶ **A** *noun.* A believer in Parkinson's law. M20.
▶ **B** *adjective.* Of or pertaining to C. N. Parkinson or Parkinson's law. M20.

Parkinsonism /ˈpɑːkɪns(ə)nɪz(ə)m/ *noun*[1]. Also **p-**. E20.
[formed as PARKINSONIAN *noun*[1] & *adjective*[1] + -ISM.]
MEDICINE. = PARKINSON'S DISEASE. Also, the group of symptoms typical of this disease but occurring in other cerebral disorders.

Parkinsonism /ˈpɑːkɪns(ə)nɪz(ə)m/ *noun*[2]. M20.
[formed as PARKINSONIAN *noun*[2] & *adjective*[2] + -ISM.]
(An instance of) the principle expressed in Parkinson's law.

Parkinson's disease /ˈpɑːkɪns(ə)nz dɪˌziːz/ *noun phr.* L19.
[James *Parkinson* (1755–1824), English surgeon and palaeontologist.]
MEDICINE. A chronic, slowly progressive disorder of the central nervous system that occurs chiefly in later life as a result of degenerative changes in the brain and produces tremor, rigidity of the limbs, and slowness and imprecision of movement. Also ***Parkinson's***. Also called ***Parkinsonism***.

Parkinson's law /ˈpɑːkɪns(ə)nz ˌlɔː/ *noun phr.* M20.
[from *Parkinson* (see below) + -'S[1] + LAW *noun*[1].]
The theory expounded by the English historian and journalist Cyril Northcote Parkinson (1909–93), that work expands to fill the time available for its completion.

parky *noun* var. of PARKIE.

parky /ˈpɑːki/ *adjective*[1]. M19.
[from PARK *noun* + -Y[1].]
Resembling a park. Also, having many parks.

parky /ˈpɑːki/ *adjective*[2]. *colloq.* L19.
[Origin unkn.]
Cold, chilly.
R. LEHMANN Oo, it's parky in here. I'll . . fetch the stove.

Parl. *abbreviation.*
Parliament; Parliamentary.

parlance /ˈpɑːl(ə)ns/ *noun.* L16.
[Old French, from *parler* speak from Proto-Romance from Latin *parabola* PARABLE *noun*: see -ANCE.]
1 Speaking, speech; *esp.* debate, parley. *arch.* L16.
2 A particular way of speaking, esp. as regards vocabulary, idiom, etc. Usu. with specifying word. L18.
2 D. CARNEGIE In the parlance of newspaper men, I had a scoop. N. F. DIXON In Freudian parlance the company man might be described as having a weak ego. ***academic parlance***, ***common parlance***, ***legal parlance***, ***vulgar parlance***, etc.

parlando /pɑːˈlandəʊ/ *adverb, adjective, & noun.* L19.
[Italian.]
MUSIC. ▶**A** *adverb & adjective.* A direction: in an expressive or declamatory manner, as if speaking. L19.
▶ **B** *noun.* Pl. **-dos**, **-di** /-di/. An expressive or declamatory passage or piece. M20.

parlatory /ˈpɑːlət(ə)ri/ *noun.* M17.
[medieval Latin *parlatorium*, from *parlare* PARLE *verb*: see -ORY[1].]
A room in a convent for reception or conversation.

parlay /ˈpɑːleɪ/ *verb & noun. N. Amer.* L19.
[Alt. of PAROLI.]
▶ **A** *verb trans. & intrans.* **1** Use (winnings accruing from a bet or a cumulative series of bets) as a stake for a further bet. L19.
2 Increase (capital) by gambling; *fig.* exploit (a circumstance); transform (an advantage, asset, etc.) *into* something greater or more valuable. *colloq.* M20.
2 *Globe & Mail (Toronto)* To parlay critical acclaim for his first feature film into big bucks.
▶ **B** *noun.* A cumulative series of bets in which winnings accruing from each transaction are used as a stake for a further bet. E20.

parle /pɑːl/ *verb & noun.* Now *arch. & dial.* LME.
[Old & mod. French *parler*: see PARLANCE. Cf. PAROLE.]
▶ **A** *verb.* **1** *verb intrans.* Speak; converse; hold conference. LME.
2 *verb intrans.* Treat, discuss terms, parley (*with*). M16. ▸**b** *verb trans.* Treat with, parley with. *rare.* M17.
▶ **B** *noun.* **1** Speech, language, parlance. L16. ▸**b** Talk; conversation. L16.
2 A conference, a debate; *spec.* a discussion of terms between enemies under truce (cf. PARLEY *noun* 2). Also, a truce. L16.

parlementaire /pɑːləmɛnˈtɛː/ *noun.* E20.
[French, from *parlementer* discuss terms, parley.]
A person deputed to parley with an enemy.

parley /ˈpɑːli/ *noun & verb.* LME.
[Perh. from Old French *parlée* use as noun of fem. pa. pple of *parler* speak: see PARLANCE, -Y[5]. Cf. BARLEY *interjection*.]
▶ **A** *noun.* **1** Speech, talk; conversation, discourse, conference; debate, argument. *arch.* LME.
2 An informal conference with an enemy, under truce, for discussing the mutual arrangement of matters such as terms of armistice, the exchange of prisoners, etc. L16.
1 H. G. WELLS The schoolmaster without further parley . . administered a sound thrashing. **2** G. F. KENNAN Parleys began . . which soon led to a cessation of hostilities.
▶ **B** *verb.* **1** *verb intrans.* Speak, talk; converse, discourse, confer, (*with*). *arch.* L16. ▸**b** *verb trans.* Use in speech, speak (esp. a foreign language). L16.
2 *verb intrans.* Discuss terms; *esp.* hold a parley (*with*). E17. ▸**b** *verb trans.* Speak to, address; hold discussion or parley with. Now *rare.* E17.
1 F. O'BRIEN The two of them parleyed together. **2** E. BOWEN She had parleyed, and made an alliance. V. CRONIN To persuade proud Maria Theresa to parley with the king.

parleyvoo /pɑːlɪˈvuː/ *noun, verb, & adjective. joc. colloq.* M18.
[from French *parlez-vous (français)?* do you speak (French)?]
▶ **A** *noun.* **1** The French language; a French word or idiom; the study of French. M18.
2 A French person. L18.
▶ **B** *verb intrans.* Speak French; *loosely* speak a foreign language. M18.
▶ **C** *adjective.* French; *loosely* foreign. *rare.* E19.

parliament /ˈpɑːləm(ə)nt/ *noun.* Also **P-**. ME.
[Old & mod. French *parlement*, from *parler*: see PARLANCE, -MENT; spelling *-ia-* infl. by Anglo-Latin *parliamentum*.]
1 The action of speaking; a speech; a conversation, a conference; a discussion, a debate. Long *obsolete* exc. *Scot. dial.* ME. ▸†**b** = PARLEY *noun* 2. ME–E17.
2 The supreme executive legislature of the United Kingdom, consisting of the House of Commons, and the House of Lords; any of the antecedents of this legislature, orig. a council called by an English monarch to discuss some matter of general or national importance. Also, an assembly of the members of any of these legislatures for a particular period, esp. between one dissolution and the next; the members of any of these legislatures collectively. ME.
3 Any corresponding consultative or legislative assembly in another country, *spec.* (*a*) *Hist.* in Scotland before the union of 1707 or Ireland before the union of 1801; (*b*) in any of various former British colonies, as Australia or Canada. Also, an assembly of the members of any of these legislatures; the members of any of these legislatures collectively. LME.
4 Each of the twelve supreme courts of justice in which the edicts, declarations, and ordinances of the king were registered in pre-revolutionary France. *obsolete* exc. *Hist.* M16.
5 a A representative assembly of Devon and Cornwall tinners, held for the redress of grievances and the general regulation of the stannaries. *obsolete* exc. *Hist.* L16. ▸**b** A consultative assembly of the members of the Middle or the Inner Temple. L16.
6 The place where a parliament meets; *spec.* = ***Houses of Parliament*** (b) below. E17.
7 A thin crisp rectangular gingerbread. Also ***parliament-cake***. E19.
2 C. V. WEDGWOOD The significance of Parliament as the ultimate court of justice for the realm. A. PRICE When the Civil War broke out Monson naturally sided with the King . . and Steyning declared for Parliament. *Parliamentary Affairs* A bill calling for fixed-term Parliaments at five year intervals. **3** *BBC Wildlife* The first new party to enter the Swedish Parliament since 1918.

Phrases: **Act of Parliament** (*a*) *Hist.* a law made by the British monarch with the advice of Parliament; (*b*) a statute passed by both Houses of Parliament and ratified by royal assent; (*c*) ***Act of Parliament clock***, an 18th-cent. wall clock used in inns etc. and characterized by gold numerals on a black or green dial not covered by glass. ***High Court of Parliament***: see COURT *noun*[1]. **Houses of Parliament** (*a*) the House of Commons and the House of Lords regarded together; (*b*) buildings in Westminster, London where they meet. **Little Parliament** the assembly of 120 members, nominated by Cromwell and his Council, which sat from 4 July to 12 December 1653. **Long Parliament** *Hist.* the second of two Parliaments summoned by Charles I in 1640, which sat from November 1640 through the Civil War to March 1653, was briefly restored in 1659, and finally dissolved in 1660 (cf. ***Rump Parliament*** below). ***Member of Parliament***: see MEMBER *noun* 2. ***Portuguese parliament***: see PORTUGUESE *adjective*. **Rump Parliament** *Hist.* that part of the Long Parliament which continued to sit after the exclusion or arrest in 1648 of about 140 Members of Parliament thought likely to oppose the trial of Charles I, by soldiers under the command of Colonel Thomas Pride. **Short Parliament** *Hist.* the first of two Parliaments summoned by Charles I in 1640, which sat from 13 April to 5 May, and was dismissed owing to its insistence on seeking a general redress of grievances before granting the King the money he required. ***Speaker of Parliament***, ***Speaker of the Parliament***: see SPEAKER 2a.

Comb.: ***parliament-cake***: see sense 7 above; **Parliament-chamber** the room in which a parliament meets, *spec.* that in the Old Palace of Westminster; **Parliament clock** = ***Act of Parliament clock*** above; **parliament heel** NAUTICAL a list deliberately created for careening or repairs; **Parliament House** the building in which a parliament meets; **parliament man** *arch.* a Member of Parliament.

■ †**parliamental** *adjective* of or pertaining to Parliament; parliamentary: L16–L18. **parliamenˈteer** *noun* (*Hist.*) = PARLIAMENTARIAN *noun* 2 M17. **parliamenˈteering** *noun* engagement in parliamentary affairs; electioneering: E18.

parliament /pɑːləm(ə)nt/ *verb. obsolete* exc. *dial.* L15.
[Old French *parlementer*, formed as prec.]
1 *verb intrans.* Talk, converse; confer, parley. L15.
2 *verb intrans.* & †*trans.* (with *it*). Attend Parliament; discharge the duties of a Member of Parliament. M17.

parliamentarian /pɑːləm(ə)nˈtɛːrɪən/ *noun & adjective.* Also **P-**. E17.
[from PARLIAMENT *noun* + -ARIAN.]
▶ **A** *noun.* †**1** A person accepting religious prescription by parliament. Only in E17.
2 *Hist.* An adherent or supporter of the cause of Parliament during the English Civil War of the 17th cent. M17.
3 A member of a parliament, *esp.* one well-versed in parliamentary practice and procedure; a skilled or experienced parliamentary debater. M19.
2 A. PRICE The unfortunate Parliamentarians wouldn't have stood a chance, caught deploying in the open by the Royalist horsemen. **3** A. F. DOUGLAS-HOME He came through the debates with a greatly enhanced reputation as a Parliamentarian.
▶ **B** *adjective.* Of or pertaining to a parliamentarian or parliamentarians, parliamentary. L17.
■ **parliamentarianism** *noun* the parliamentary principle or system M19.

parliamentary /pɑːləˈmɛnt(ə)ri/ *adjective & noun.* Also **P-**. E17.
[from PARLIAMENT *noun* + -ARY[1].]
▶ **A** *adjective.* **1** Of, pertaining to, or resembling a parliament; belonging to a parliament. E17. ▸**b** *spec.* Of or adhering to the cause of Parliament in the English Civil War of the 17th cent. M18.
2 Enacted, ratified, or established by a parliament. E17.
3 Consonant with or agreeable to the practice of a parliament; according to the constitution of a parliament. E17. ▸**b** Of language: permissible in a parliament; admissible in polite conversation; civil, courteous. E19.
1 C. P. LUCAS The . . Bermudian Assembly is . . the oldest Parliamentary institution in the British Empire outside the United Kingdom. *Listener* Heads of governments . . in the parliamentary democracies. **b** A. PRICE An up-and-coming Parliamentary officer, one of Cromwell's trusted lieutenants. **2** *Times* They draft the Government's Parliamentary bills. **3** *Time* James Allen, a master of parliamentary tactics. **b** *Liverpool Daily Post* Politely and in strictly Parliamentary language calling one another incompetent administrators.

Special collocations: **Parliamentary Commissioner for Administration** the ombudsman in the UK. **Parliamentary Counsel** a group of barristers employed as civil servants to draft government bills and amendments. **parliamentary party** (the elected members of) a political party in Parliament, as distinguished from the party in the country as a whole. **parliamentary private secretary** a Member of Parliament assisting a government minister. **parliamentary train** *Hist.* a train carrying passengers at a rate not exceeding one penny a mile, which every railway company was formerly obliged by Act of Parliament to run daily each way over its system. **parliamentary under-secretary** a Member of Parliament in a department of State, ranking below a minister.
▶ **B** *noun.* **I 1** A member of Parliament. E17.
2 *Hist. ellipt.* = ***parliamentary train*** above. M19.
▶ **II 3** = PARLEMENTAIRE *noun.* M19.
■ **parliamenˈtarily** *adverb* in a parliamentary way; in accordance with parliamentary procedure: M18. **parliamentarism** *noun* a parliamentary system of government L19. **parliamentariˈzation** *noun* the act or process of becoming parliamentary in character or in means of government E20. **parliamentaryism** *noun* = PARLIAMENTARISM M19.

parloir /parlwaːr/ *noun.* Pl. pronounced same. E18.
[French: see next.]
A conversation room in a monastery or convent; = PARLOUR *noun* 1. Also, a similar room in a prison.

parlour /ˈpɑːlə/ *noun & adjective.* Also ***-or**. ME.
[Anglo-Norman *parlur*, Old French *parleor*, *parleur* (mod. *parloir*), from Proto-Romance antecedent also of *parler*: see PARLANCE, -OUR.]
▶ **A** *noun.* **1** A room for conversation in a monastery or convent. ME.
2 Orig., a private room set apart for conversation or conference in any large or public building. Later, a sitting-room in a private house. LME.
3 A shop or business providing goods or services of a particular kind. Freq. with specifying word. Orig. *US.* L19.
4 A room or building equipped for milking cows. M20.

📖 1 J. T. FOWLER The..outer Parlour..was usually on the western side of the cloister. 2 P. AUSTER The downstairs parlour—which featured a number of..easy chairs.
3 *beauty parlour, ice-cream parlour, massage parlour*, etc. banking parlour the head office of a bank.

▶**B** *attrib.* or as *adjective*. **1** Of, pertaining to, or resembling a parlour; suited or adapted for (use in) a parlour. L18.

2 Designating a person who professes but does not actively give support for a specified (esp. radical) political view; designating a political view professed but not actively supported. *derog.* L18.

📖 2 A. BOYLE One of those Parlour Pinks..so often ridiculed for playing at Communism.

Special collocations & comb.: **parlour-boarder** *Hist.* a boarding-school pupil living with the family of the principal and having privileges not shared by the other boarders. **parlour-car** *US* a luxuriously fitted railway carriage. **parlour game** an indoor game, *esp.* a word game. **parlour-house** (*a*) a house with a parlour; (*b*) *US slang* an expensive brothel. **parlour-maid** a female domestic servant who waits at table. **parlour palm** a Central American dwarf fan palm, *Chamaedorea elegans*, grown as a house-plant.

parlous /ˈpɑːləs/ *adjective & adverb.* Now *arch. & dial.* LME.
[Syncopated form of PERILOUS.]
▶**A** *adjective*. **1** Perilous, dangerous. LME. ▸**b** Awkward, precarious; risky to deal with. M17.
2 Keen, shrewd; cunning; malicious; wicked. Also, extraordinary, excessive. LME.

📖 **1b** GEO. ELIOT Chapman's business affairs were in such a parlous state..he could pay her nothing.

▶**B** *adverb*. In a parlous manner, *esp.* excessively. L16.
▪ **parlously** *adverb* LME. **parlousness** *noun* M16.

parlyaree /pɑːlɪˈɑːriː/ *noun*. M20.
[formed as PALARIE.]
A variety of (orig. theatrical, later homosexual) slang characterized by Italianate vocabulary.

parm /pɑːm/ *interjection & verb*. M20.
[Repr. a pronunc.]
Pardon. Freq. in ***parm me***.

Parma /ˈpɑːmə/ *noun*[1]. M19.
[A city and province in northern Italy. Cf. PEARMAIN.]
▶**I 1** Used *attrib.* to designate things from or associated with Parma. M19.
1 Parma ham a type of ham which is eaten uncooked. **Parma violet** (*a*) any of various cultivated violets with double, scented, usu. light purple flowers, prob. cultivars of *Viola odorata*, often crystallized for food decoration or used in perfume; (*b*) (of) a medium or deep shade of purple.
▶**II 2** *ellipt.* A Parma violet; a medium or deep shade of purple. E20.

parma /ˈpɑːmə/ *noun*[2]. Now *rare*. L19.
[Russian = wooded ridge (esp. in the northern Urals), from Komi.]
GEOLOGY. A low dome or anticline.

parmacetty /pɑːməˈsɛti/ *noun*. *obsolete* exc. *dial.* Also **-citty** /-ˈsɪti/. M16.
[Alt. of SPERMACETI.]
1 = SPERMACETI. M16.
†**2** In full ***parmacetty whale***. A sperm whale. M18–M19.
1 *poor man's parmacetty*: see POOR MAN.

Parmenidean /pɑːˌmɛnɪˈdiːən/ *adjective & noun*. *rare*. L17.
[from Greek *Parmenidēs* (see below) + -AN.]
▶**A** *adjective*. Of or pertaining to the Greek philosopher Parmenides of Elea of the 5th cent. BC, or his philosophy. L17.
▶**B** *noun*. A follower or adherent of Parmenides. L17.

Parmentier /parmɑ̃tje/ *adjective*. E20.
[Antoine A. *Parmentier* (1737–1813), French agriculturist, who popularized the potato in France.]
COOKERY. Made or served with potatoes.

Parmesan /pɑːmɪˈzan/ *adjective & noun*. E16.
[French from Italian *parmigiano*, formed as PARMA *noun*[1].]
▶**A** *adjective*. Of or pertaining to the Italian city and province of Parma. E16.
Parmesan cheese a hard dry cheese made orig. at Parma and used esp. in grated form.
▶**B** *noun*. = ***Parmesan cheese*** above. M16.

parmigiana /pɑːmɪˈdʒɑːnə/ *adjective* (chiefly *postpositive*). L19.
[Italian, fem. of *parmigiano*: see prec.]
COOKERY. Made or served with Parmesan cheese.

parnas /pɑːˈnas/ *noun*. Also **-nass**. Pl. **-nassim** /-nəˈsɪm/. M19.
[Hebrew, from Greek *pronous* provident.]
The lay leader of the congregation of a synagogue.

parnassia /pɑːˈnasɪə/ *noun*. L18.
[mod. Latin (see below), from PARNASS(US + -IA[1].]
Any of several marsh plants of the genus *Parnassia*, which includes grass of Parnassus.

Parnassian /pɑːˈnasɪən/ *adjective & noun*. M17.
[from Latin *Parnas(s)ius*, *-eus*, formed as PARNASSUS: see -AN, -IAN.]
▶**A** *adjective*. **1** Of or pertaining to Parnassus; of or pertaining to poetry, poetic. M17.
2 *spec.* Of or pertaining to a group of French poets in the latter half of the 19th cent., emphasizing strictness of form, (named from the anthology *Le Parnasse contemporain* (1866)). E20.
▶**B** *noun*. **1** A poet. M17.
2 *spec.* A French poet of the Parnassian group. L19.
3 *ENTOMOLOGY*. A papilionid butterfly of the holarctic alpine genus *Parnassius* or the subfamily Parnassiinae containing it, related to the swallowtails. E20.
▪ **Parnassianism** *noun* the Parnassian style in poetry E20.

parnassim *noun* pl. of PARNAS.

Parnassus /pɑːˈnasəs/ *noun*. LME.
[Latin *Parnas(s)us* from Greek *Parnas(s)os* (see below).]
1 A mountain in central Greece, sacred in antiquity to Apollo and the Muses. Also used allusively with ref. to literary, esp. poetic, inspiration. LME.
2 *grass of Parnassus*, a marsh plant, *Parnassia palustris*, of (or closely allied to) the saxifrage family, with solitary white flowers and mostly radical cordate leaves. L16.

Parnate /ˈpɑːneɪt/ *noun*. M20.
[Origin unkn.]
PHARMACOLOGY. (Proprietary name for) the drug tranylcypromine.

†**parnel** *noun* see PANEL *noun*[2].

Parnellite /ˈpɑːnɛlʌɪt/ *noun & adjective*. L19.
[from *Parnell* (see below) + -ITE[1].]
▶**A** *noun*. A follower or supporter of the politician Charles Stewart Parnell (1846–91), Irish Nationalist leader and advocate of Home Rule for Ireland. L19.
▶**B** *adjective*. Of or pertaining to Parnell or the Parnellites. L19.
▪ **Parnellism** *noun* Parnellite principles or policies L19.

paroccipital /parɒkˈsɪpɪt(ə)l/ *adjective & noun*. M19.
[from PAR(A-[1] + OCCIPITAL.]
ANATOMY & ZOOLOGY. ▶**A** *adjective*. Situated at the side of the occiput, or beside the occipital bone; *spec.* designating certain bones or bony processes. M19.
▶**B** *noun*. A paroccipital bone or process. M19.

†**paroch(e)** *noun* var. of PARISH.

parochet /paˈroxet/ *noun*. Also ***parocheth*** & other vars. Pl. ***-chot*** /-xɒt/. L19.
[Hebrew *pārōḵeṯ* curtain. Cf. Akkadian *parāku* shut off.]
A richly decorated curtain which hangs in front of the Ark in a synagogue.

parochial /pəˈrəʊkɪəl/ *adjective*. LME.
[Anglo-Norman *parochiel*, Old French *parochial* from ecclesiastical Latin *parochialis*, from *parochia*: see PARISH, -AL[1].]
1 Of or pertaining to an ecclesiastical parish. LME. ▸**b** Of or pertaining to a civil parish. M18.
2 *fig.* Merely local or provincial; restricted or narrow in scope. M19.

📖 **1** A. KENNY Much..parochial work was connected with the marriages of..parishioners. **parochial church council** the ruling body of a parish in the Anglican Church. **parochial school** *Scot. & N. Amer.* a school established and maintained by a religious body. **2** ISAIAH BERLIN Historians ..warn us..against setting up our parochial values as universally valid. C. SAGAN Many branches of science where ..knowledge is similarly provincial and parochial.

▪ **parochialism** *noun* narrow limitation of perspective or interests M19. **parochiˈality** *noun* (*a*) the quality or state of being parochial; (*b*) in *pl.*, parochial matters: M18. **parochialiˈzation** *noun* the action or process of making something parochial or of becoming parochial L19. **parochialize** *verb* (*a*) *verb trans.* make parochial; (*b*) *verb intrans.* do parish work: L19. **parochially** *adverb* L17.

†**parochian** *noun & adjective*. LME.
[Old French *parochien* from medieval Latin *parochianus*, from *parochia*: see PARISH, -AN.]
▶**A** *adjective*. Of or pertaining to a parish, parochial. LME–M17.
▶**B** *noun*. **1** A parishioner. LME–M18.
2 A parish clergyman. *rare*. E17–E18.

†**parochin** *noun*. *Scot.* Also **-ine**. E16–E19.
[from late Latin *parochia* or Old French *paroche*, from *parochia* (see PARISH): origin of suffix unkn.]
= PARISH.

parochot *noun* pl. of PAROCHET.

parode /ˈparəʊd/ *noun*. M19.
[Greek *parodos* entrance from the side, formed as PARA-[1] + *odos* way.]
In Greek drama, the first ode sung by the chorus after its entrance.

parody /ˈparədi/ *noun & verb*. L16.
[Late Latin *parodia* or Greek *parōidia* burlesque song or poem, formed as PARA-[1] + *ōidē* ODE: see -Y[3].]
▶**A** *noun*. **1** A prose, verse, or (occas.) other artistic composition in which the characteristic themes and the style of a particular work, author, etc., are exaggerated or applied to an inappropriate subject, esp. for the purposes of ridicule; in *MUSIC* also, a composition that employs reworked material from another piece or passage, with serious intent. Also, the composition of parodies, parodies as a genre. L16.
2 *fig.* A poor or feeble imitation, a travesty. M19.

📖 2 L. BLUE A terrible grin,..like an awful parody of the smile on the face of my kind hostess.

▶**B** *verb*. **1** *verb trans.* Compose a parody of; be a parody of. M18. ▸**b** *verb intrans.* Parody a composition. *rare*. L19.
2 *verb trans. fig.* Imitate in a poor or feeble manner, travesty. M18.

📖 1 LEIGH HUNT He parodied music as well as words. H. CARPENTER 'Tis the voice of the Lobster' parodies Isaac Watts's 'Tis the voice of the Sluggard'. 2 V. WOOLF These young men parodied her husband, she reflected.

▪ **parodiable** *adjective* L19. **parodial** /pəˈrəʊdɪəl/ *adjective* pertaining to or resembling (a) parody E19. **parodic** /pəˈrɒdɪk/ *adjective* resembling (a) parody E19. **parodical** /pəˈrɒdɪk(ə)l/ *adjective* = PARODIC L18. **parodically** /pəˈrɒdɪk(ə)li/ *adverb* L19. **parodist** *noun* the author of a parody M18. **paroˈdistic** *adjective* resembling (a) parody; that parodies something: L19. **paroˈdistically** *adverb* M19. **parodize** *verb trans. & intrans.* parody M17.

paroecious /pəˈriːʃəs/ *adjective*. Also **paroicous** /pəˈrɔɪkəs/. L19.
[from PARA-[1] + -*oecious*, Latin after *dioecious*, *monoecious*.]
BOTANY. Of a bryophyte: having the antheridia on the same branch as the archegonia and immediately below them.
▪ **paroecism** /-sɪz(ə)m/ *noun* the condition of being paroecious L19.

paroemia /pəˈriːmɪə/ *noun*. Now *rare*. M16.
[Latin from Greek *paroimia* by-word, proverb, from *paroimos* by the way, formed as PARA-[1] + *oimos* way: see -IA[1].]
RHETORIC. A proverb, an adage.
▪ †**paroemial** *adjective* M17–E18. **paroemiˈographer** *noun* a writer or collector of proverbs E19. **paroemiˈography** *noun* (*a*) the writing of proverbs; (*b*) a collection of proverbs: E19. **paroemiˈologist** *noun* an expert in or student of paroemiology M19. **paroemiˈology** *noun* the branch of knowledge that deals with proverbs M19.

paroemiac /pəˈriːmɪak/ *adjective & noun*. *rare*. L17.
[Greek *paroimiakos*, from *paroimia*: see prec., -AC.]
GREEK PROSODY. (Designating or pertaining to) the short line with which an anapaestic verse usually ends.

paroicous *adjective* var. of PAROECIOUS.

parol /pəˈrəʊl, ˈpar(ə)l/ *noun & adjective*. Also †**-ole**. L15.
[(Law French var. of) Old & mod. French PAROLE *noun*.]
▶**A** *noun*. **1** Chiefly *LAW*. Something said or spoken; an utterance, a word. Now only in ***by parol***, by word of mouth or in a writing not sealed. L15.
2 *LAW* (now *Hist.*). The pleadings filed in an action. E17.
▶**B** *adjective*. **1** *LAW*. Of a contract or lease: made by word of mouth or in a writing not sealed. Usu. *postpositive*. L16.
2 Expressed or given orally; verbal; not in writing. Now only in legal use. E17.

parole /pəˈrəʊl, *in sense A.4 usu. foreign* parɒl/ *noun, adjective, & verb*. L15.
[Old & mod. French from Proto-Romance, from Latin *parabola* PARABLE *noun*. Cf. prec.]
▶**A** *noun & adjective*. †**I** *noun & adjective*. **1** Var. of PAROL. L15.
▶**II** *noun*. **2** A person's word of honour; *spec.* (*a*) a prisoner of war's promise to abide by the specific terms of a conditional release (also more fully ***parole of honour***); (*b*) a prisoner's promise of good behaviour in return for release before the expiry of a custodial sentence. Also, the granting to or acceptance by a prisoner of war or (now esp.) a convicted prisoner of a conditional release on the basis of such a promise; the system or practice of granting or accepting such a conditional release. L15.
3 *MILITARY*. The password used by an officer or inspector of the guard. L18.
4 *LINGUISTICS*. The actual linguistic behaviour or performance of an individual, in contrast to the linguistic system. Opp. LANGUE 3. M20.

📖 2 A. FRASER The King..had given his parole, his word of honour. E. LEONARD I'd be left facing fifty to life, no chance of parole. ***parole board***, ***parole officer***, etc.

Phrases: **on parole** in the position of being conditionally released (now esp. from a custodial sentence) on promising to abide by specific terms. ***parole of honour***: see sense 2 above.
▶**B** *verb*. Infl. **-l-**, **-ll-**.
1 *verb trans.* Put on parole; release on parole. M17.
†**2** *verb intrans.* Pledge one's word. L17–E18.
▪ **paroˈlee** *noun* (orig. & chiefly *US*) a prisoner released on parole E20.

parolein /ˈparəliːn/ *noun*. Also **-leine**. L19.
[from PAR(AFFIN + Latin *oleum* oil + -IN[1], -INE[5].]
PHARMACOLOGY. Liquid paraffin.

paroli /ˈpɑːrəli/ *noun*. E18.
[French from Italian, from *paro* like from Latin *par* PAR *noun*[1]. Cf. PARLAY.]
In a gambling card-game (esp. faro), the staking of double the sum previously staked.

paromoeon /parəˈmiːɒn/ *noun*. *rare*. L16.
[mod. Latin from Greek *paromoion* neut. of *paromoios* closely resembling, formed as PARA-[1] + *homoios* like.]
(An instance of) alliteration.

paromomycin /ˌparəʊməˈmʌɪsɪn/ *noun*. M20.
[from Greek *paromoios* closely resembling: see prec., -MYCIN.]
PHARMACOLOGY. (Any of) a mixture of broad-spectrum antibiotics related to neomycin which are produced by strains of the bacterium *Streptomyces rimosus*.

paronomasia /parənəˈmeɪzɪə/ *noun*. L16.
[Latin from Greek, formed as PARA-[1] + *onomasia* naming.]
A play on words, a pun; punning.
▪ **paronomastic** /-ˈmastɪk/ *adjective* characterized by or employing paronomasia E19.

paronychia /parəˈnɪkɪə/ *noun*. L16.
[Latin from Greek *paronykhia*, formed as PARA-[1] + *onukh-*, *onux* nail.]
1 MEDICINE. An inflammation around a toenail or fingernail. L16.
2 BOTANY. Any of various small plants of the genus *Paronychia* (family Caryophyllaceae), with conspicuous silvery stipules usually concealing the minute apetalous flowers. M17.

paronym /ˈparənɪm/ *noun*. M19.
[Greek *parōnumon* use as noun of neut. of *parōnumos* adjective, formed as PARA-[1] + *onuma* name: see -NYM.]
1 A word which is a derivative or cognate of another. M19.
2 A word formed by partial translation of a foreign word. Opp. HETERONYM 2. L19.
▪ **paronymous** /pəˈrɒnɪməs/ *adjective* (*a*) derived from the same root; cognate; (*b*) formed by partial translation of a foreign word: M17. **paronymy** /pəˈrɒnəmi/ *noun* †(*a*) *rare* = PARONOMASIA; (*b*) the formation of a word by partial translation of a foreign word: E17.

paroophoron /parəʊˈɒf(ə)rɒn/ *noun*. L19.
[from PARA-[1] + OOPHORON.]
ANATOMY. A group of vestigial tubules in the female behind each ovary, derived from the lower mesonephros and corresponding to the male parepididymis. Cf. EPOOPHORON.

paroquet *noun* var. of PARAKEET.

parore /pəˈrɔːreɪ/ *noun*. *NZ*. M20.
[Maori.] = LUDERICK.

parosmia /pəˈrɒzmɪə/ *noun*. E19.
[from PARA-[1] + Greek *osmē* smell: see -IA[1].]
MEDICINE. Disorder of the sense of smell.

parosteal /pəˈrɒstɪəl/ *adjective*. M19.
[from PARA-[1] + Greek *osteon* bone + -AL[1].]
MEDICINE. Designating or pertaining to (a tumour of) the periosteum.

parotic /pəˈrɒtɪk/ *adjective*. M19.
[formed as next + -IC.]
ANATOMY & ZOOLOGY. Situated near the ear.

parotid /pəˈrɒtɪd/ *adjective* & *noun*. L17.
[French *parotide* from Latin *parotid-*, PAROTIS from Greek *parōtid-*, *-tis*, formed as PARA-[1] + *ōt-*, *ous* ear: see -ID[2].]
ANATOMY, MEDICINE, & ZOOLOGY. ▶**A** *adjective*. Situated beside or near the ear; *spec.* designating either of a pair of large salivary glands situated just in front of each ear; of or pertaining to these glands or the surrounding region. Also, pertaining to or designating a similarly situated venom gland in snakes. L17.
parotid duct a duct from the parotid gland opening into the mouth opposite the second upper molar tooth; also called ***Stensen's duct***.
▶**B** *noun*. †**1** A parotid tumour or swelling. M18–E19.
2 A parotid gland. L18.
¶ Earlier examples in *-ides* have been regarded as repr. the pl. of PAROTIS.
▪ **parotiˈdectomy** *noun* (an instance of) surgical removal of a parotid gland L19. **parotiˈditis** *noun* = PAROTITIS L19.

†**parotis** *noun*. Pl. **parotides**. M16.
[mod. Latin from Latin: see prec.]
1 A parotid tumour or swelling. M16–L19.
2 A parotid gland. E17–M18.

parotitis /parəˈtʌɪtɪs/ *noun*. L18.
[from PAROTID *noun* + -ITIS.]
MEDICINE. Inflammation of a parotid gland.
infectious parotitis mumps.
▪ **parotitic** /-ˈtɪtɪk/ *adjective* pertaining to or affected with parotitis M19.

parotoid /pəˈrəʊtɔɪd/ *adjective* & *noun*. L19.
[formed as PAROTID + -OID.]
ZOOLOGY. (Designating or pertaining to) any of various glands which form warty excrescences behind the eyes in some amphibians, esp. toads.

parous /ˈparəs/ *adjective*. L19.
[Back-form. from derivs. of next.]
MEDICINE. Having borne offspring.

-parous /ˈparəs/ *suffix*.
[from Latin *-parus* bearing, from *parere* bring forth: see -OUS.]
Forming adjectives with the sense 'bearing, producing', as ***biparous***, ***multiparous***, ***oviparous***, ***viviparous***.

Parousia /pəˈruːzɪə/ *noun*. L19.
[Greek = presence (of persons), from *pareinai* be present.]
CHRISTIAN THEOLOGY. = ***second coming*** s.v. SECOND *adjective*.

parovarium /parəˈvɛːrɪəm/ *noun*. Now *rare*. M19.
[from PARA-[1] + OVARIUM.]
ANATOMY. The epoophoron; the epoophoron and paroophoron together, representing the vestigial remnants of the mesonephros in the female. Also called ***organ of Rosenmüller***.
▪ **parovarian** *adjective* L19.

paroxysm /ˈparəksɪz(ə)m/ *noun*. LME.
[medieval Latin *paroxysmus* irritation, exasperation from Greek *paroxusmos*, from *paroxunein* goad, exasperate, formed as PARA-[1] + *oxunein* sharpen.]
1 MEDICINE. An episode of increased acuteness or severity of a disease; a sudden recurrence or attack, a sudden worsening of symptoms. LME.
2 A violent attack or outburst of a (specified) emotion or activity; a fit, a convulsion. Also, a natural disturbance, as an earthquake, volcanic eruption, etc. M17. ▸**b** The extreme stage of a violent action or episode. Now *rare* or *obsolete*. M17. ▸†**c** An open quarrel. M17–E18.

> 🕮 **2** R. P. WARREN Her face was contorted in a paroxysm of laughter. D. MURPHY Flinging it across my mother's room in a paroxysm of frustrated rage.

▪ **paroˈxysmal** *adjective* of or pertaining to a paroxysm or paroxysms; violent, convulsive; GEOLOGY catastrophic: M17. **paroˈxysmic** *adjective* (*rare*) = PAROXYSMAL M19.

paroxytone /pəˈrɒksɪtəʊn/ *noun* & *adjective*. M18.
[mod. Latin *paroxytonus* from Greek *paroxutonos*, formed as PARA-[1], OXYTONE.]
GRAMMAR (esp. GREEK GRAMMAR). ▶**A** *noun*. A word having an acute accent or stress on the penultimate syllable. M18.
▶**B** *adjective*. Of or pertaining to a paroxytone or paroxytones. L19.
▪ **paroxyˈtonic** *adjective* characterized by or employing paroxytone accent or stress L19.

parp /pɑːp/ *noun*, *interjection*, & *verb*. M20.
[Imit.]
▶**A** *noun* & *interjection*. (Repr.) the honking sound produced by a car horn. M20.
▶**B** *verb trans.* & *intrans.* (Cause to) produce such a noise. M20.

parpen /ˈpɑːp(ə)n/ *noun*. Also **parpend** /ˈpɑːp(ə)nd/. ME.
[Old French *parpain*, *per-* (mod. *parpaing*), medieval Latin *parpanus*, prob. from Proto-Romance, from Latin *per* through + *pannus* (see PANE *noun*[1]).]
1 A stone running through a wall from side to side, with two smooth vertical faces; a bondstone. Also, a stone squared or dressed for this purpose. Also ***parpen stone***. ME.
2 In full ***parpen wall***. A thin wall built of parpen stones or of single bricks; *esp.* an interior partition-wall. LME.

parquet /ˈpɑːki, ˈpɑːkeɪ, *in sense 3 foreign* parkɛ/ *noun*. E19.
[Old & mod. French = small marked-off space etc., dim. of *parc* PARK *noun*: see -ET[1].]
1 A flooring, *esp.* one composed of blocks of various woods arranged in a geometric pattern. Also ***parquet floor***. E19.
2 (The front part of) the ground floor of a theatre or auditorium. Chiefly *US*. M19.
3 In France and French-speaking countries, the branch of the administration of the law that deals with the prosecution of crime. L19.
Comb.: ***parquet floor***: see sense 1 above; **parquet work** = PARQUETRY.

parquet /ˈpɑːki, ˈpɑːkeɪ/ *verb trans*. L17.
[from (the same root as) prec.]
Provide with a parquet floor; construct of parquetry. Chiefly as ***parqueted*** /-keɪd/ *ppl adjective*.

parquetry /ˈpɑːkɪtri/ *noun*. M19.
[French *parqueterie*, formed as PARQUET *noun*: see -ERY.]
Inlaid work of blocks of various woods arranged in a geometric pattern, esp. for furniture or flooring.

parr /pɑː/ *noun*. Also **par**. Pl. same, **-s**. E18.
[Origin unkn.]
A young salmon between the stages of fry and smolt, distinguished by dark rounded patches evenly spaced along its sides. Also, a young trout.
Comb.: **parr marks** the marks on the sides of a parr.

parrakeet *noun* see PARAKEET.

parramatta /parəˈmatə/ *noun* & *adjective*. Orig. *Austral*. Also **para-**. E19.
[*Parramatta*, settlement (now a city) in New South Wales, Australia.]
(Made of) a light but coarse dress fabric with a weft of wool and a warp of cotton (or silk).

parrel /ˈpar(ə)l/ *noun*. ME.
[App. var. of PAREL *noun*.]
NAUTICAL. A sliding band of rope or metal attaching a yard or boom to a mast while allowing it vertical movement.

parrhesia /pəˈriːzɪə, -sɪə/ *noun*. L16.
[medieval Latin from Greek *parrēsia* free-spokenness, formed as PARA-[1] + *rhēsis* speech.]
Chiefly RHETORIC. Frankness or boldness of speech.

parricide /ˈparɪsʌɪd/ *noun*. M16.
[Old & mod. French, or (in sense 1) Latin *par(r)icida*, (in sense 2) Latin *par(r)icidium*, assoc. with Latin *pater* FATHER *noun*, *parens* PARENT *noun* & *verb*: see -CIDE. Cf. PATRICIDE.]
1 A person who kills a near relative, esp. either parent. Also *transf.*, a person who kills the ruler of, or commits treason against, his or her country. M16.
2 The action of killing a near relative, esp. either parent. Also *transf.*, the action of killing the ruler of, or committing treason against, one's country. L16.
▪ **parriˈcidal** *adjective* of or pertaining to (a) parricide; guilty of parricide: E17. †**parricidious** *adjective* = PARRICIDAL E17–E19.

parrock /ˈparək/ *noun* & *verb*. Now *Scot.* & *dial.*
[Old English *pearruc*: see PARK *noun*. Cf. PADDOCK *noun*[2] & *verb*.]
▶**A** *noun*. **1** Orig., a fence or a set of hurdles for enclosing a space of ground. Later, a small enclosure or field; a paddock. OE.
2 A small apartment or narrow cell in a building; a stall, coop, etc., for animals. LME.
▶**B** *verb trans.* Enclose or confine in a parrock or small field. LME.

parroco /ˈparɒkəʊ/ *noun*. Pl. **-os**. M19.
[Italian *parroco*, Spanish *párroco* = parish priest.]
In Italian- and Spanish-speaking countries, a priest, *esp.* a parish priest.

parrot /ˈparət/ *noun* & *verb*. E16.
[Prob. from French (now dial.) *perrot* parrot, dim. of *Pierre* Peter: see -OT[1]. Cf. PARAKEET, PIERROT.]
▶**A** *noun*. **1** Any of numerous birds of the order Psittaciformes or family Psittacidae of the tropics and southern hemisphere, with a powerful short hooked bill, typically scansorial and often brightly coloured, many being kept as cage-birds and some being able to mimic speech and other sounds. Cf. LORY, MACAW *noun*[1], PARAKEET. E16.
2 *transf.* A person who mindlessly and mechanically repeats the words or actions of another. L16.
3 More fully ***sea-parrot***. A puffin. L17.

> 🕮 **1** ***ground parrot***, ***night parrot***, etc. ***sick as a parrot***: see SICK *adjective*. **2** H. WILLIAMSON Jargon, to be repeated until one was a parrot.

Comb.: **parrotbill** (*a*) a type of cutting tool with blades resembling a parrot's beak; (*b*) any small short-billed gregarious bird of the subfamily Paradoxornithinae (family Timaliidae), including the reedling and several eastern Asian species; **parrot-crossbill** a crossbill, *Loxia pytyopsittacus*, of northern Eurasia, having a large heavy bill; **parrot-coal** *Scot.* & *north.* cannel coal; **parrot disease** = PSITTACOSIS; **parrot-fashion** *adverb* with mindless and mechanical repetition, by rote; **parrot fever** = ***parrot disease*** above; **parrot-finch** any weaver-bird of the genus *Erythrura*; **parrot-fish** any of several labroid fishes with vivid colouring, or a strong hard beaklike mouth adapted for grazing on coral reefs; *esp.* (*a*) any beaked fish of the tropical family Scaridae; (*b*) any brightly coloured fish of the wrasse family; **parrot-house** a building in a zoo for housing parrots; *fig.* a room etc. filled with loud or raucous conversation; **parrot mouth** a malformation of a horse's mouth in which the upper incisors project beyond the lower, preventing grazing; **parrot-pea** any of several Australian leguminous shrubs of the genus *Dillwynia*, resembling heathers; **parrot's bill** *NZ* = ***kaka-beak***; **parrot snake** a S. American green tree snake, *Leptophis occidentalis*; **parrot's-perch** an instrument of torture on which the victim is hung upside down, the weight of the body pressing upon the forearms; **parrot tulip** any of various cultivated tulips with jagged petals, often of variegated colours.
▶**B** *verb*. **1** *verb intrans.* & †*trans.* with *it*. Chatter like a parrot; repeat words or phrases mindlessly and mechanically. Freq. foll. by *away*, *on*. L16.
2 *verb trans.* Repeat (words, an idea, etc) mindlessly and mechanically. M17.
3 *verb trans.* In *pass.* Be taught by rote or mechanical repetition. Now *rare* or *obsolete*. L18.

> 🕮 **1** R. CHRISTIANSEN Another voice parroting away from behind the mask of classroom decorum. **2** A. CARTER 'I see, I see', said Victoria, parroting a grown-up. *Listener* We don't need television programmes to parrot what the papers say.

▪ **parroter** *noun* (*rare*) = PARROT *noun* 2 M19. **parrotism** *noun* (*rare*) = PARROTRY L18. **parrotize** *verb intrans.* (*rare*) = PARROT *verb* 1 M17. **parrotlet** *noun* any of several tiny tropical American parrots esp. of the genera *Forpus* or *Touit*, with mainly green plumage and a short tail E20. **parrot-like** *adjective* resembling (that of) a parrot; *spec.* characterized by mindless and mechanical repetition M17. **parrotry** *noun* mindless and mechanical repetition of the words or actions of another L18. **parroty** *adjective (rare)* resembling or characteristic of a parrot E19.

parry /ˈpari/ *verb & noun.* L17.
[Prob. repr. French *parez* imper. of *parer* from Italian *parare* ward off (orig. 'make ready, prepare'). Cf. PARA-², PARADE *noun & verb.*]
▶ **A** *verb.* **1** *verb intrans. & trans.* Stop, avert, or ward off (a weapon, a blow, etc.), esp. with a countermove; FENCING block or turn aside (an opponent's blade). L17.
2 *verb intrans. & trans. fig.* Avert (a threat to oneself); deal skilfully with (an awkward question or demand). E18. ▶**b** *verb trans.* Counter by saying. E20.

📖 **1** J. CLAVELL She attacked again but he parried the onslaught. **2** A. BROOKNER Her daughters must . . laugh & parry even when the proposals are sincere. R. DEACON A question . . the Home Secretary had to parry . . with a . . piece of disinformation.

▶ **B** *noun.* An act of parrying or warding off a weapon, threat, etc., esp. with a countermove. E18.

📖 P. O'DONNELL You defend with a simple parry. ***thrust and parry***: see THRUST *noun* 5a.

†**pars** *noun*¹ *pl.* Only in ME.
[Old French pl. of *part* PART *noun* infl. by Latin *pars* part.]
Parts of speech, grammar.
¶ Perh. the source of PARSE *verb & noun.*

pars /pɑːz/ *noun*². L19.
[Latin.]
ANATOMY. A part (of an organ or structure). Only in mod. Latin phrs. with specifying adjective.
pars intermedia /ɪntəˈmiːdɪə/ a layer of tissue between the anterior and posterior lobes of the pituitary gland.

parse /pɑːz/ *verb & noun.* M16.
[Origin uncertain: perh. from PARS *noun*¹.]
▶ **A** *verb.* **1** *verb trans. & intrans.* Describe (a word in context) grammatically, by stating the relevant part of speech, inflection, and place within the sentence structure; resolve (a sentence, phrase, etc.) into component parts of speech for grammatical description. M16. ▶**b** COMPUTING. Analyse (a string) into syntactic components, esp. to test conformability to a given grammar. M20.
2 *verb trans. transf.* Examine or analyse minutely. L18.
▶ **B** *noun.* COMPUTING. The action or result of parsing a string. M20.
Comb.: **parse-tree** a diagrammatic or abstract representation of the parsed structure of a sentence or string.
■ **parser** *noun* (*a*) a person who parses; a book on parsing; (*b*) COMPUTING a program for parsing: M19.

parsec /ˈpɑːsɛk/ *noun.* E20.
[from PAR(ALLAX + SEC(OND *noun*¹.]
ASTRONOMY. A unit of length equal to the distance at which a star would have a heliocentric parallax of one second of arc, approx. equal to 3.09 × 10^{16} metres (19.2 × 10^{12} miles, 3.26 light-years).

Parsee /pɑːˈsiː, ˈpɑːsiː/ *noun & adjective.* Also **Parsi**. E17.
[Persian *Pārsī* Persian, from *Pārs* Persia.]
▶ **A** *noun.* **1** An adherent of Zoroastrianism; *spec.* a descendant of a group of Zoroastrian Persians who fled to India in the 7th and 8th cents. to escape Muslim persecution. Also called ***Guebre***. E17.
2 = PAHLAVI *noun.* L18.
▶ **B** *adjective.* That is a Parsee; of or pertaining to the Parsees or their religion. Also = PAHLAVI *adjective.* L17.
■ **Parseeism** *noun* the religion of the Parsees, Zoroastrianism M19. ˈ**Parsism** *noun* (now *US*) = PARSEEISM M19.

parsemé /parsəme, ˈpɑːsəmeɪ/ *adjective.* E19.
[French, pa. pple of *parsemer* sprinkle, strew.]
Esp. of a fabric, garment, etc.: decorated with embroidered motifs, beads, etc., sprinkled over a background. Usu. *postpositive.*

Parseval /ˈpɑːsɪv(ə)l/ *noun.* E20.
[from August von *Parseval* (1861–1942), the inventor.]
Hist. A type of non-rigid German airship.

Parsi *noun & adjective* var. of PARSEE.

parsimonious /pɑːsɪˈməʊnɪəs/ *adjective.* L16.
[formed as next + -OUS.]
1 Of a person: characterized by or employing parsimony; sparing; niggardly. L16.
2 Of a thing: yielding sparingly, unproductive; meagre. E18.
3 a PSYCHOLOGY. Exhibiting economy of action. M20. ▶**b** BIOLOGY etc. Of a scientific (esp. phylogenetic) hypothesis: assuming the simplest state, process, evolutionary pathway, etc., in accordance with the law or principle of parsimony. L20.

📖 **1** A. POWELL Always keen on economy . . occasionally a trifle parsimonious. N. LOWNDES A parsimonious man whose chief pleasure in life had been watching their money grow. **2** E. MUIR The parsimonious ground That at its best will bear A few thin blades.

■ **parsimoniously** *adverb* M18. **parsimoniousness** *noun* L17.

parsimony /ˈpɑːsɪməni/ *noun.* LME.
[Latin *parsimonia*, *parci-*, from *pars-* pa. ppl stem of *parcere* refrain, spare: see -MONY.]
1 The careful or sparing use of money or other material resources. LME. ▶**b** Stinginess, niggardliness. M16.
2 *fig.* Economy in the use of immaterial things; *spec.* in PSYCHOLOGY, the principle that organisms tend towards economy of action in learning or in fulfilling their needs. M17. ▶**b** In full ***law of parsimony***. = OCCAM'S ***razor***. M19.

parsley /ˈpɑːsli/ *noun.*
[Old English *petersilie*, corresp. to Middle Dutch *petersilie* (mod. *-selie*), Old High German *petersilia* (German *Petersilie*), and Old French *peresil* (mod. *persil*), from Proto-Romance var. of Latin *petroselinum* from Greek *petroselinon*, from *petra* rock + *selinon* parsley.]
1 An umbelliferous plant, *Petroselinum crispum*, much grown for its finely divided, usu. curled, aromatic leaves, which are used to flavour or garnish dishes; the leaves of this plant. Also, any other plant of the genus *Petroselinum*. OE.
2 With specifying words: any of various umbelliferous plants related to parsley or resembling it in their finely divided leaves. E16.
2 ***cow parsley***, ***fool's parsley***, ***hedge parsley***, ***milk parsley***, ***stone parsley***, etc.
Comb.: **parsley-bed** a bed of parsley, esp. as a supposed place where babies are born (cf. GOOSEBERRY-*bush*); †**parsley breakstone** = PARSLEY-PIERT; **parsley caterpillar** the larva of the anise swallowtail butterfly, *Papilio zelicaon*, which is a pest of umbelliferous plants in western N. America; **parsley fern** a fern of mountain screes, *Cryptogramma crispa*, with finely divided fronds like parsley leaves; **parsley frog** a western European spade-foot toad, *Pelodytes punctatus*, with green spots on its back; **parsley-leaved elder** a cultivated variety of elder with laciniate leaves, *Sambucus nigra* 'laciniata'; **parsley sauce** a white sauce flavoured with parsley; **parsleyworm** the larva of the black swallowtail butterfly, *Papilio polyxenes asterius*, which is a pest of umbelliferous plants in eastern N. America.
■ **parsleyed** *adjective* (of food) cooked or served with parsley E20.

parsley-piert /pɑːslɪˈpɪət/ *noun.* L16.
[App. popular alt. of French *perce-pierre* lit. 'pierce-stone' (cf. ***breakstone*** s.v. BREAK-), infl. by prec. See also PERCEPIER.]
Either of two dwarf plants of the rose family, *Aphanes arvensis* and *A. inexspectata*, of dry or stony ground, cornfields, etc., with fan-shaped trifid leaves and minute green axillary flowers. Formerly also (by confusion), the knawel, *Scleranthus annuus*.

parsnip /ˈpɑːsnɪp/ *noun.* LME.
[Old French *pasnaie* (mod. *panais*), with assim. to NEEP: cf. TURNIP.]
1 An umbelliferous plant, *Pastinaca sativa*, with pinnate leaves and yellow flowers, grown for its pale yellow sweet fleshy root; this root, eaten as a vegetable. LME.
2 With specifying word: any of various umbellifers allied to or resembling the common parsnip. M16.
1 before you can say parsnips *colloq.* very rapidly. **2 *cow parsnip***, ***meadow parsnip***, ***water-parsnip***, ***wild parsnip***, etc.

parson /ˈpɑːs(ə)n/ *noun.* Also †**person**. See also PERSON *noun.* ME.
[Law French *parsone* var. of Old French *persone*: see PERSON *noun.*]
▶ **I 1** ECCLESIASTICAL (now *Hist.*). A holder of a parochial benefice in full possession of its rights and dues. ME.
2 *gen.* Any beneficed member of the clergy, a rector, a vicar; *colloq.* any (esp. Protestant) member of the clergy. L16.
3 *fig.* A signpost. Chiefly *dial.* L18.
4 [From the black dress of a clergyman.] ▶**a** An animal or bird which is black or partly black in colour, as a black lamb, a black rabbit, a puffin, or a cormorant. E19. ▶**b** *spec.* In full ***parson-bird***. = TUI. M19.
1 *parson* IMPARSONEE.
▶†**II** See PERSON *noun*
Comb.: ***parson-bird***: see sense 4b above; **parson-in-the-pulpit** *dial.* [from the shape of the flowers] cuckoo-pint, *Arum maculatum*; **Parson Jack Russell (terrier)**, **Parson Russell (terrier)** (an animal of) a breed of fox terrier, usu. white with black or brown markings, similar to the smaller Jack Russell; **parson's freehold** *Hist.* the life tenure of a parson in his benefice; **parson's nose** the fatty extremity of a fowl's rump; **parson's table** *US* a simple square-topped wooden table; **parson's-week** a holiday period (usu. of 13 days) calculated to include only one Sunday.
■ **parsondom** *noun* (*joc.*) = PARSONRY M19. **parsoness** *noun* (*colloq.*, now *rare* or *obsolete*) the wife of a parson L18. **parsonhood** *noun* the state or condition of a parson L18. **parˈsonic** *adjective* of, pertaining to, or characteristic of a parson or parsons L18. **parˈsonical** *adjective* = PARSONIC M19. **parˈsonically** *adverb* M18. **parsoning** *noun* acting as or doing the work of a parson L18. **parsonish** *adjective* resembling or characteristic of a parson or parsons E19. **parsonly** *adjective* belonging to or befitting a parson or parsons L18. **parsonry** *noun* parsons collectively L19.

parsonage /ˈpɑːs(ə)nɪdʒ/ *noun.* LME.
[Anglo-Norman & Old French *personage* from medieval Latin *personaticum*, from Latin *persona*: see PARSON, PERSON *noun*, -AGE.]
1 *Hist.* The benefice or living of a parson. LME.
2 The church-house provided for a parson. Later also, the house of any (esp. beneficed) member of the clergy. Also ***parsonage-house***. L15.
3 SCOTTISH HISTORY. The proportion of a parish tithe formerly due to a parson. Also ***parsonage teinds***. L16.

Parsonian /pɑːˈsəʊnɪən/ *adjective.* M20.
[from Talcott *Parsons* (1902–1979), Amer. sociologist + -IAN.]
SOCIOLOGY. Of, pertaining to, or designating Parsons' theories of action and change within a society or culture, or his structural-functional method of analysing a social system.
■ **Parsonianism** *noun* L20.

pars pro toto /pɑːz prəʊ ˈtəʊtəʊ/ *noun phr.* E18.
[Latin.]
A part taken as representative of the whole. Freq. *attrib.*

part /pɑːt/ *noun & adverb.* OE.
[Orig. from Latin *part-*, *pars*; in Middle English reinforced by Old & mod. French *part* (= Provençal *part*, Spanish, Italian *parte*) from Latin.]
▶ **A** *noun.* **I** Portion or division of a whole.
†**1** = ***part of speech*** below. OE–M17.
2 A quantity which together with others makes up a whole (whether actually separate from the rest or not); an amount, but not all, of a thing or a number of things; a portion. When denoting a number of items also treated as *pl.* Also without article. OE. ▶**b** A division of a book usu. larger than a chapter; *spec.* each of the portions of a book issued at intervals in paper covers with a view to being subsequently bound together. Also, a division of a poem or other literary or musical work; an episode of a television or radio serial. LME. ▶**c** A portion of a human or animal body; *spec.* in *pl.*, the genitals (freq. with specifying word). LME. ▶**d** Any of the manufactured objects that are assembled together to make a machine or instrument, esp. a motor vehicle; a component. L19.
3 (With numeral.) Any of a number of equal portions into which a thing is or may be divided; an exact divisor, a submultiple; *spec.* (*a*) *arch.* with preceding ordinal numeral, denoting the number of equal portions as would make up a whole; (*b*) with preceding cardinal numeral, denoting the proportionate division of a whole, the remainder being specified or contextually implied. ME. ▶†**b** With preceding cardinal numeral, expr. multiplication: times. LME–E17.
4 †**a** A constituent of a quality or action; a point, a particular, a respect. M16–E18. ▶**b** An essential or integral constituent. Also without article. M18.
†**5** A particle of matter. E18–E19.

📖 **2** ROBERT JOHNSON The greater part of his men . . were idle. J. WAIN I'll do part of it myself. ANNE STEVENSON Erect, steaming chimneys, / part of the steel works. W. RAEPER The sum of his works is greater than its . . parts. **b** *Gramophone* Part Two—a massive setting of the Te Deum—requires four soloists. **c** G. ALLEN All parts which are seldom . . exercised tend to atrophy. S. A. GRAU The young girls giggled and felt a hot touch in their parts. ***natural parts***, ***private parts***, ***privy parts***, ***secret parts***, ***shameful parts***, etc. **d** G. W. STUBBINGS A. C. transformers . . have no moving parts. *Scientific American* Industry mass-produces parts in great variety. *Nature* It was built entirely from used parts. **3** P. HEYLIN Retaining a third part of the profits to himself. L. STRACHEY He was one part blackguard . . and three parts buffoon. R. B. PARKER I put five *parts* of vodka . . into a pitcher. ***eighth part***, ***fifth part***, ***twelfth part***, etc. **4b** F. A. KEMBLE That formed no part of our discussion. J. B. MOZLEY Affection is part of insight. G. VIDAL He felt himself to be a part of something large and opulent.

▶ **II** Allotted portion, share.
6 A portion of something that is allotted or belongs to a particular person; a share; (without article) involvement, interest, concern. ME.
7 a A person's share in some action; what one has to do; a person's function, business, or duty; a function performed by a thing. LME. ▶**b** A character sustained or assumed or feigned by a person, esp. for a special purpose; THEATRICAL a character assigned to or represented by an actor in a play, etc.; the words assigned to or spoken by an actor in such a character; a written or printed copy of these. Freq. in ***play a part*** below. LME.
8 MUSIC. The sequence of notes to be sung by a particular voice or played by a particular instrument in music for two or more performers; the voice or instrument itself; a written or printed copy of this for the use of a particular performer. E16.
†**9** A piece of conduct, an act. Usu. with qualification expr. praise or blame. M16–E18.
10 A personal quality or attribute, esp. of an intellectual kind; an ability. Usu. in *pl.* M16.

📖 **6** S. DOBELL Death can have no part in Beauty. **7a** A. TROLLOPE Was it not a brother's part to go to a sister in affliction? **b** J. GAY The man of . . simple heart Thro' life disdains a double part. P. SCOTT One day at rehearsals . . I had to speak her part. **8** *Crescendo* Many drummers . . never see a drum part. **10** LD MACAULAY Some of them were indeed . . men of parts.

▶ **III** Region; side.
11 †**a** A party, a body of adherents; a faction. ME–L16. ▶**b** A side in a contract, contest, question, or any relation of opposite people or groups of people. LME.

12 In *pl.* A portion of a country or of the world; a region, an area. LME.

†**13** A (physical) side; a direction in space. LME–L18.

> **11b** S. LEACOCK Are they degenerate enough to bring an action . . indicting the express company as a party of the second part? **12** R. HILL Do you come from these parts? **13** T. HUTCHINSON [Norwich] is on every part walled in.

▶ **IV** [from the verb.] Parting.

†**14** Parting, leave-taking. *rare*. Only in E17.

15 = PARTING *noun* 2b. *US*. L19.

> **15** R. MACDONALD The part in her hair was white and straight.

Phrases: ***act a part***: see ACT *verb*. ***art and part***, ***art or part***: see ART *noun*¹. ***bear a part***: see BEAR *verb*¹. **for my part**, etc., as regards my etc. share in the matter; as far as I etc. am concerned. ***for the most part***: see MOST *adjective*. ***have no part nor lot in***, ***have neither part nor lot in***: see LOT *noun*. **in good part** favourably, without offence; chiefly in ***take in good part***. **in ill part** unfavourably, with offence; chiefly in ***take in ill part***. **integration by parts** MATH. integration using the formula $\int u(dv/dx)dx = uv - \int v(du/dx)dx$, where u and v are functions of the same variable x. **look the part** have the appearance befitting a particular character in a play etc. NAMING ***of parts***. †**of the part of**, †**of my part** etc. = ***on the part of*** below. **on the other part** (now *rare*) = ***on the other hand*** s.v. HAND *noun*. **on the part of** (*a*) as regards (a person), as far as (a specified person) is concerned; (*b*) (of behaviour) proceeding from (a specified person or party). **part and parcel** an essential part *of*. **part of speech** each of the several categories to which words are assigned in accordance with their grammatical and semantic functions (in English usually reckoned as noun, adjective, pronoun, verb, adverb, preposition, conjunction, and interjection). **play a part** (*a*) participate in, have an assigned or expected function to perform; (*b*) represent a character in a play etc.; (*c*) dissemble. **play one's part** perform an assigned or expected function (*in*). **play the part of** represent the character of in a play etc. ***principal parts***: see PRINCIPAL *adjective*. ***quantal part***: see QUANTAL 1. ***spare part***: see SPARE *adjective*. ***standing part***: see STANDING *adjective*. **take part** (*a*) have a share in or *in* an activity, participate (*in*); (*b*) ***take part with***, side with, range oneself on the side of. **take the part of** support, back up, (a contestant). ***the more part***: see MORE *adjective* 1a. ***top one's part***: see TOP *verb*¹.

▶ **B** *adverb*. In part, partly, to some extent. E16.

> J. TRAPP The ship that is part in the water, and part in the mud. W. MOTHERWELL I watched those cold part-opened lips. *Mind* The culture-hero has a vague complex status, part man, part demi-god.

Comb.: **part-book** a book containing one part (or a number of parts printed separately) of a harmonized musical composition; **part-bred** (of a horse) having an unspecified but authenticated proportion of pure-bred stock in its ancestry; **part-exchange** *noun & verb* (*a*) *noun* a transaction in which the owner of an article exchanges it for another one (usu. new) and pays a sum of money to cover the difference between the value of the two; (*b*) *verb trans.* exchange in this way; **part-load** a load that is carried as part of a larger load; **part-own** *verb trans.* own jointly with another or others; **part-owner** a person who owns something jointly with another or others; **part-payment** payment in part; **part-playing** playing of music in parts; **part-singing** singing in parts; **part-song** a song for three or more voice-parts, often without accompaniment, in simple harmony (not with the parts independent as in the glee, or contrapuntally treated as in the madrigal); **part-time** *adjective & adverb* (employed, occurring, lasting, etc.) for less than the customary number of working hours in a week; **part-timer** a part-time worker, student, etc.; **part-way** *adverb* (*a*) of the part of the way; (*b*) partly; **part-work** *adjective & noun* (*a*) *adjective* designating a system of part-time work; (*b*) *noun* a book etc. published in parts; **part-writing** composition of music in parts; the combination of parts in musical composition.

part /pɑːt/ *verb*. Pa. pple **parted**, (*obsolete* exc. HERALDRY) **part**. ME.

[Old & mod. French *partir* from Proto-Romance from Latin *partire* *partiri*, from *part-*: see prec.]

▶ **I 1** *verb trans.* **a** Divide into parts (by physical separation, by assigning boundaries, or merely in thought); break, sever. Now *rare*. ME. ▸**b** Divide (the hair) along a parting with a comb etc. E17. ▸**c** NAUTICAL. Break, or allow the breaking of, (a rope, cable, etc.) so as to come loose from an anchor, mooring, etc. M18.

2 *verb trans.* Make a separation between (two or more persons or things); separate (one) *from* another; keep separate (*from*), form a boundary between; *techn.* separate (gold and silver) from each other by means of an acid. ME. ▸**b** Break up (a gathering). *rare*. LME.

3 *verb intrans.* Become or be separated or detached *from*; come off. Also, proceed *from*. *rare*. ME.

4 *verb intrans.* (Of two or more persons or things) go away from each other, separate; (of one) depart. ME.

5 a *verb intrans.* Take one's leave; set out; (usu. with *hence* or other qualification) die. *arch*. ME. ▸†**b** *verb trans.* Depart from, leave. E16–E19.

6 *verb intrans.* Undergo division; break in two or in pieces. LME.

7 *verb intrans.* Make or cause separation, division, or distinction. *arch*. E17.

8 *verb trans.* Give up, part with. *dial*. E19. ▸**b** *verb intrans.* Give or pay money. *slang*. Also (*Austral. & NZ colloq.*) foll. by *up*. M19.

> **1a** AV *Lev.* 2:6 Thou shalt part it in pieces. **b** W. BOYD His pale brown hair was cut short and parted neatly in the middle. **2** J. HOWELL A fool and his money is soon parted. C. KINGSLEY The women shrieked to their lovers to part the combatants. J. R. GREEN The peninsula which parts the Baltic from the Northern seas. W. MARCH An odd, hesitant smile that parted her lips. **3** POPE Ev'n thought meets thought, ere from the lips it part. **4** T. GRAY The curfew tolls the knell of parting day. B. MONTGOMERY We parted good friends. B. NEIL Do you remember the day we parted . . ? **5** H. F. CARY Aged and poor he parted thence. **6** L. URIS In reflex his lips parted . . but he stopped the words. I. MURDOCH As the clouds were parting, small puddles . . were being touched by the . . sun. **7** AV *Prov.* 18:18 The lot causeth contentions to cease, and parteth betweene the mighty. **8b** P. G. WODEHOUSE He has the stuff in sackfuls, but he hates to part.

▶ **II 9** *verb trans.* Divide among a number of recipients (foll. by *between*); apportion; share (*out*, *with*). Now *arch.*, *Scot.*, *& dial.* ME.

†**10** *verb intrans.* Make division into shares; give, take, or have a share; participate, partake. ME–L17.

†**11** *verb trans.* Give a part of; give away, bestow. LME–E16.

▶†**III 12** *verb trans.* Side with, take the side of. *rare*. M17–E18.

Phrases, & with adverbs & prepositions in specialized senses: ***part brass rags***: see BRASS *adjective*. **part company** break an association or relationship (*with*). ***part fair***: see FAIR *adverb*. **part from** (*a*) go away from, leave; (*b*) (now *rare*) = ***part with*** (a). ***part hence***: see sense 5a above. **part off** separate (a piece) from a block in wood or metal turning. **part with** (*a*) cease to keep possession of, give up; (of a body or substance) give off (heat, a constituent part); (*b*) (now *rare*) = ***part from*** (a) above.

Partaga /pɑːˈtɑːɡə/ *noun*. Also **p-**. M19.

[Origin unkn.]

(Proprietary name for) a Havana cigar.

partage /partaːʒ/ *noun*. Pl. pronounced same. LME.

[French, from *partir* PART *verb*: see -AGE.]

1 A part, a portion, a share. LME.

2 The action of dividing something; division, partition. M16.

¶ Formerly fully naturalized.

partake /pɑːˈteɪk/ *verb*. Pa. t. **-took** /-ˈtʊk/; pa. pple **-taken** /-ˈteɪk(ə)n/. M16.

[Back-form. from PARTAKER, PARTAKING.]

▶ **I** *verb trans.* †**1** Give a part of (a thing) *to* another; share *with*; impart; make known. M16–E17.

†**2** Make (a person) a sharer *of* information or news; inform *of*. M–L16.

3 Take a part or share in, participate in. L16. ▸†**b** Share in (information, news), be informed of. L16–M17. ▸**c** Consume (a meal); eat, drink. Now *rare* or *obsolete*. E17.

> **3** A. W. KINGLAKE Adventurers who were willing to partake his fortunes. A. E. HOUSMAN It partakes the solidity of its indestructible foundations, the sloth . . of man.

▶ **II** *verb intrans.* **4** Take a part or share in an action or condition; have a portion or lot in common with others. Cf. PARTICIPATE 4. (Foll. by *in*, *of* a thing.) L16. ▸**b** Receive or get a part or portion of something, esp. food or drink; eat, drink. Freq. foll. by *of*. E17.

5 Have some of the qualities or characteristics of a person or thing; possess a certain amount of a quality or attribute. Formerly also, have an admixture of a substance. (Chiefly & now only foll. by *of*.) L16.

†**6** Take part *with* a person, take sides. Only in L16.

> **4** *Nature* Leptons . . do not partake in the strong interactions. L. GORDON Eliot was a solitary who yet saw it as his duty to partake of the world. **b** J. P. SMITH Chris could not touch anything, but the widow partook with . . relish. E. BOWEN Vast meals were spread and partaken of. Jo GRIMOND It was customary to partake of a high tea. **5** P. KAVANAGH His farm . . partook of some of the qualities of a Louth farm.

■ **partakable** *adjective* †(*a*) capable of partaking; (*b*) *rare* able to be partaken of: M17.

partaker /pɑːˈteɪkə/ *noun*. Also (earlier) †**part taker**. LME.

[from PART *noun* + TAKER, after Latin *particeps*.]

1 A person who takes a part or share, a participator, a sharer. (Foll. by *of*, *in*.) LME.

†**2** A person who takes another's part or side; a supporter. L15–M18.

> **1** H. BINNING Let be a spirit who is a partaker of a divine nature. D. H. LAWRENCE She was . . an onlooker, whilst Ursula was a partaker.

partaking /pɑːˈteɪkɪŋ/ *noun*. LME.

[from PART *noun* + TAKING *noun*, after late Latin *participatio(n-)* PARTICIPATION.]

1 Sharing, participation. LME.

†**2** The action or an act of taking sides in a dispute or contest. M16–M17.

partan /ˈpɑːt(ə)n/ *noun*. *Scot.* & *north*. LME.

[App. Celtic (Gaelic, Manx *partan*, Irish *partón*, *partán*), perh. ult. from Old Irish *partaing* red.]

1 A crab; *esp.* the edible crab, *Cancer pagurus*. LME.

2 An ugly or bad-tempered person. L19.

parted /ˈpɑːtɪd/ *adjective*¹. LME.

[from PART *verb* + -ED¹.]

1 †**a** Variegated, pied. LME–L16. ▸**b** Chiefly HERALDRY. = PARTY *adjective* 2. LME.

2 That has parted or been parted; divided; separated. LME. ▸**b** Dead. *arch*. L16.

> **2** E. BOWEN Lulu's hands hung between his parted knees.

parted /ˈpɑːtɪd/ *adjective*². L16.

[from PART *noun* + -ED².]

†**1** Having abilities or talents of a specified kind; talented, accomplished. L16–L17.

2 Given a dramatic part or character. *rare* exc. in ***overparted***. E17.

†**parter** *noun*¹. LME–M17.

[from PART *verb* + -ER¹.]

A person who or thing which parts something, a divider, a separator.

parter /ˈpɑːtə/ *noun*². M20.

[from PART *noun* + -ER¹.]

Something having a specified number of parts, *spec.* a radio or television production in a specified number of episodes. Only as 2nd elem. of comb.

four-parter, ***two-parter***, etc.

parterre /pɑːˈtɛː/ *noun*. E17.

[French, use as noun of *par terre* on or along the ground.]

1 A level space in a garden occupied by an ornamental arrangement of flower-beds. E17.

2 A level space on which a house or village stands. L17.

3 The part of the ground-floor of the auditorium of a theatre behind the orchestra; *US* the part beneath the galleries; the occupants of this. E18.

parthenian /pɑːˈθiːnɪən/ *adjective*. *rare*. M17.

[from Greek *parthenios*, formed as PARTHENO-: see -IAN.]

Of or pertaining to a virgin.

■ **parthenic** /-ˈθɛn-/ *adjective* (*rare*) [Greek *parthenikos*] = PARTHENIAN; *fig.* unviolated: M19.

partheno- /ˈpɑːθɪnəʊ/ *combining form*.

[from Greek *parthenos* virgin: see -O-.]

Chiefly BIOLOGY. Forming nouns (and derived adjectives & adverbs) denoting an absence of fertilization or conjugation in reproduction, as ***parthenocarpy***, ***parthenogenesis***, etc.

parthenocarpy /ˈpɑːθɪnəkɑːpi/ *noun*. E20.

[German *Parthenocarpie*, formed as PARTHENO- + Greek *karpos* fruit + -Y³.]

BOTANY. The development of a fruit without prior fertilization.

■ **partheno'carpic** *adjective* (of a fruit) produced without prior fertilization E20. **partheno'carpically** *adverb* M20.

parthenogenesis /ˌpɑːθɪnəˈdʒɛnɪsɪs/ *noun*. M19.

[from PARTHENO- + -GENESIS.]

BIOLOGY. Reproduction from a gamete without fertilization, esp. as a normal process in invertebrates and lower plants. Formerly also, asexual reproduction, as by fission or budding.

■ **'parthenogen** *noun* (*a*) a parthenogenone; (*b*) a parthenogenetic individual: M20. **parthenoge'netic** *adjective* pertaining to, of the nature of, or characterized by parthenogenesis; reproducing by parthenogenesis: L19. **parthenoge'netically** *adverb* in a parthenogenetic manner; in the way of or by means of parthenogenesis: L19. **parthenogenic** *adjective* (*rare*) parthenogenetic L19. **parthenogenone** *noun* an organism of parthenogenetic origin, with only one parent M20.

Parthenopean /ˌpɑːθɪnəˈpiːən/ *adjective*. L18.

[from Italian *Partenopea*, from Latin *Parthenopeius*, from *Parthenope* Naples: see -AN.]

= NEAPOLITAN *adjective*; *spec.* (*Hist.*) designating the short-lived republic established in Naples by French revolutionary forces in 1799.

parthenospore /ˈpɑːθɪnəˌspɔː/ *noun*. L19.

[from PARTHENO- + SPORE.]

BOTANY. A thick-walled spore resembling a zygospore, but produced without conjugation by certain primitive algae and fungi.

Parthian /ˈpɑːθɪən/ *noun & adjective*. ME.

[from *Parthia* (see below) + -AN.]

▶ **A** *noun*. **1** A native or inhabitant of Parthia, an ancient kingdom in the north-east of present-day Iran. ME.

2 The Iranian language or script of the Parthians. M20.

▶ **B** *adjective*. **1** Of or pertaining to Parthia or the Parthians. L16.

2 [After the custom of Parthian horsemen of firing missiles backward while in real or pretended retreat.] Designating a glance, remark, etc., delivered by a person at the moment of departure. Cf. PARTING ***shot***. L19.

> **2** C. HARE And with this Parthian shot the historian withdrew.

parti /parti (*pl. same*)/ *noun*. L18.

[French = choice, formed as PARTY *adjective*. Cf. PARTIE.]

A person (esp. a man) considered in terms of eligibility for marriage on grounds of wealth, social status, etc.

parti- /ˈpɑːti/ *combining form*. Now *rare*. **E16**.
[from PARTI(COLOURED).]
1 Particoloured, as ***parti-coat***.
2 Partly in one way and partly in another, diversely, as ***parti-decorated***.

partial /ˈpɑːʃ(ə)l/ *adjective & noun*. **LME**.
[Old French *parcial* (mod. *partial* in the senses of branch I, *partiel* in those of branch II) from late Latin *partialis*, from Latin *part-*, *pars* PART *noun*: see -IAL.]
▶**A** *adjective*. **I 1 a** Inclined beforehand to favour one party in a cause, or one side of a question, more than the other, prejudiced, biased. Opp. IMPARTIAL 1. **LME**. ▸**b** Favouring a particular person or thing excessively, favourably disposed. Foll. by *to*. *obsolete* exc. as passing into other senses. **L16**. ▸**c** Foll. by *to*: having a liking for, fond of, (esp. something inanimate). *colloq.* **L17**.

> **1a** S. JOHNSON The duty of criticism is neither to depreciate nor dignify by partial representations. G. M. TREVELYAN He proceeded to reply with a feeble and partial argument. **b** J. GAY By partial fondness shown, Like you, we doat upon our own. **c** C. MCCULLERS Mick was very partial to hot chocolate.

▶**II 2** Pertaining to or involving a part, not the whole; constituting only a part; incomplete. **LME**. ▸**b** Constituent, component. **L15**. ▸†**c** Particular, individual, personal. **L15–L16**.
3 *ASTRONOMY*. Of an eclipse: in which only part of the disc of the eclipsed object is covered or darkened. **E18**.

> **2** D. LODGE After the weekend's partial thaw, the weather has turned bitterly cold again.

Special collocations: **partial counsel** *SCOTS LAW* (now *Hist.*) advice or communication to any of the parties in a cause which excluded the party giving it from being a witness in that cause; ***purge of partial counsel***: see PURGE *verb* 4. **partial denture**: that replaces some but not all of a person's natural teeth. **partial derivative** *MATH*. a derivative of a function of two or more variables with respect to one of the variables, the other(s) being treated as constant. **partial differentiation** *MATH*. the process of obtaining a partial derivative. **partial dislocation** *CRYSTALLOGRAPHY* a dislocation in which the displacement is not an integral multiple of the lattice spacing (*SHOCKLEY* ***partial dislocation***). **partial fraction** *MATH*. each of two or more simpler fractions as the sum of which a compound fraction can be expressed. **partial involucre** *BOTANY* the involucre of a partial umbel. **partial order**, **partial ordering** *MATH*. a transitive antisymmetric relation among the elements of a set, which does not necessarily apply to each pair of elements. **partial pressure** the pressure that would be exerted by a constituent gas of a mixture if it alone occupied the space. **partial product** *MATH*. (*a*) the product of one term of a multiplicand and one term of its multiplier; (*b*) the product of the first *n* terms of a series, where *n* is a finite integer (including 1). **partial sum** *MATH*. the sum of the first *n* terms of a series. **partial tone** = sense B.1 below. ***partial umbel***: see UMBEL 1. **partial valency** *CHEMISTRY* (now *Hist.*) a partially unsatisfied valency formerly attributed to some atoms in unsaturated compounds to account for the addition reactions of olefins and the stability of the benzene ring. ***partial veil***: see VEIL *noun* 7. **partial verdict** a verdict finding a person guilty of part of a charge.
▶**B** *noun*. **1** *ACOUSTICS*. Each of the simple or sinusoidal components of a complex musical sound. **L19**.
2 *CRYSTALLOGRAPHY*. A partial dislocation. **M20**.
2 *SHOCKLEY* ***partial***.
■ **partialism** *noun* (*a*) (the holding of) a partial theory or view, which does not take into account all the facts; (*b*) *THEOLOGY* (*rare*) particularism: **M19**. **partialist** *noun* (*a*) a partial person; (*b*) a person who holds a partial theory or view; (*c*) *THEOLOGY* (*rare*) a particularist: **L16**.

partial /ˈpɑːʃ(ə)l/ *verb trans*. Infl. **-ll-**. **M20**.
[from prec.]
Foll. by *out*: eliminate or remove the influence of (a factor or variable) during statistical analysis when considering the relationship between other variables.

partialise *verb* var. of PARTIALIZE.

partiality /pɑːʃɪˈalɪti/ *noun*. **LME**.
[Old & mod. French *parcial(i)té* from medieval Latin *partialitas*, from late Latin *partialis*: see PARTIAL *adjective & noun*, -ITY.]
1 The quality or character in a person of being partial; prejudice, bias, unfairness; an instance of this. **LME**. ▸**b** Fondness; a predilection. **L16**.
†**2** Party-spirit, rivalry; factiousness. **L15–M18**. ▸**b** A party, a faction. **M16–E17**.

> **1** A. FRANCE A personal view, with all the partiality that that implies. **b** N. ANNAN He developed a partiality for dried figs.

partialize /ˈpɑːʃ(ə)lʌɪz/ *verb*. Also **-ise**. **L16**.
[French *partialiser*, from *partial* PARTIAL *adjective & noun*: see -IZE.]
1 *verb trans*. Make partial or one-sided; bias. **L16**.
†**2** *verb intrans*. Favour one side unduly or unjustly. **L16–M17**.
3 *verb trans*. Make partial as opp. to universal. **L19**.

partially /ˈpɑːʃ(ə)li/ *adverb*. **L15**.
[from PARTIAL *adjective & noun* + -LY[2].]
1 To some extent; in part, partly; incompletely. **L15**.
2 †**a** In a biased manner, with partiality; unfairly, unjustly. **L15–M18**. ▸**b** With special favour or affection. Now *rare*. **M17**.

> **1** L. DUNCAN The door stood partially open. *Which?* Registered blind or partially-sighted people. **partially ordered set** *MATH*. a set whose members exhibit partial ordering.

partialness /ˈpɑːʃ(ə)lnɪs/ *noun*. **E18**.
[formed as prec. + -NESS.]
The quality of being partial as opp. to total; incompleteness.

partiary /ˈpɑːʃ(ə)ri/ *noun & adjective*. *rare*. **E17**.
[Partly from French *partie* PARTY *noun*; partly from Latin *partiarius* sharer, from *part-*, *pars* PART *noun*: see -ARY[1].]
▶†**A** *noun*. **1** A person who supports a particular side or party, esp. in a narrow or prejudiced way. Only in **E17**.
2 A partaker. Only in **M17**.
▶**B** *adjective*. Taking or having a share; that is so only in part. **M17**.

partible /ˈpɑːtɪb(ə)l/ *adjective*. **LME**.
[Late Latin *partibilis*, from Latin *partire*, *-iri* PART *verb*: see -IBLE.]
1 Able to be parted, divided, or distributed; subject to partition. **LME**.
2 Involving or designating a system of inheritance in which the estate of a deceased person is divided equally among the heirs. **M17**.
■ **partiˈbility** *noun* **M17**.

particeps criminis /ˌpɑːtɪsɛps ˈkrɪmɪnɪs/ *noun & adjectival phr*. Pl. of noun ***participes criminis*** /pɑːˌtɪsɪpiːs ˈkrɪmɪnɪs/. **M17**.
[Latin.]
Chiefly *LAW*. (That is) a partner in crime or accomplice.

participable /pɑːˈtɪsɪpəb(ə)l/ *adjective*. **L15**.
[In sense 1 from Old French, from *participer*, in sense 2 from medieval Latin *participabilis*, from Latin *participare*: see PARTICIPATE *verb*, -ABLE.]
†**1** Liable or entitled to participate. Only in **L15**.
2 Able to be participated in or shared. **E17**.

participant /pɑːˈtɪsɪp(ə)nt/ *adjective & noun*. **LME**.
[Old & mod. French, pres. pple of *participer* from Latin *participare*; see PARTICIPATE *verb*, -ANT[1].]
▶**A** *adjective*. **1** Participating, partaking, sharing. **LME**. ▸†**b** Sharing the nature of something. **LME–M17**.
†**2** Cognizant, informed, *of*. **E–M16**.
▶**B** *noun*. **1** A person who participates in something; a participator. **M16**.
†**2** With possess. pronoun A person who takes part with another; a collaborator. **M16–L17**.
Comb.: **participant observer** a research worker (esp. in the social sciences) who, while appearing as a member of the group under observation, is gathering information about it.

participate /pɑːˈtɪsɪpeɪt/ *verb*. Pa. pple & ppl adjective **-ated**, (earlier) †**-ate**. **L15**.
[Latin *participat-* pa. ppl stem of *participare*, from *particip-*, *particeps* taking part, from *part-*, *pars* PART *noun* + *cip-* weakened form of *cap-* stem of *capere* take: see -ATE[3].]
▶**I** *verb trans*. †**1** Make (a person) a sharer. **L15–M17**.
2 Take a part or share in; possess in common *with* others. Now *rare*. **M16**.
†**3** Give a part of (a thing) *to* another; share (a thing) *with* others, communicate, impart; make known. **M16–M19**.

> **2** C. M. YONGE She found him the only person who could thoroughly participate her feeling.

▶**II** *verb intrans*. **4** Take a part or share in an action or condition, or (formerly) a material thing. Cf. PARTAKE 4. (Foll. by *in*, †*of*, †*with* a thing, *with* a person.) **L15**. ▸**b** Orig., have some of the qualities or characteristics of a person or thing. Now (*literary*), possess a specified quality. (Chiefly & now only foll. by *of*.) Cf. PARTAKE 5. **M16**.

> **4** A. HUTSCHNECKER The patient can continue to be active and participate in work and social activities. JAN MORRIS A group of singers is performing a children's song, and encouraging its audience to participate.

■ **participator** *noun* **L18**.

participation /pɑːˌtɪsɪˈpeɪʃ(ə)n/ *noun*. **LME**.
[Old & mod. French from late Latin *participatio(n-)*, formed as prec.: see -ATION.]
1 The action or fact of having or forming part *of*. **LME**.
2 The fact or condition of sharing in common; association as partners. **LME**.
3 The action or an act of taking part with others (*in* an action or matter), *spec.* the active involvement of members of a community or organization in decisions which affect them. **M17**.

> **1** T. NORTON This Sacrament being instituted for the participation of Christ by faith. **2** STEELE Their satisfations are doubled, their Sorrows lessen'd by Participation. **3** A. TOFFLER Goals set without the participation of those affected will be increasingly hard to execute. E. YOUNG-BRUEHL Her father's illness . . dictated his withdrawal from active participation in meetings and conferences.

Comb.: **participation mystique** *ANTHROPOLOGY* imaginative identification with people and objects outside oneself, regarded as an attribute of primitive peoples; **participation sport**: regarded as affording entertainment primarily to participants rather than spectators (cf. *SPECTATOR* ***sport***).

■ **participational** *adjective* involving or requiring participation **M20**.

participative /pɑːˈtɪsɪpeɪtɪv/ *adjective*. **M17**.
[medieval Latin *participitativus*, formed as PARTICIPATE: see -ATIVE.]
1 Having the quality of participating. *rare*. **M17**.
2 Pertaining to or characterized by participation, esp. in decision-making. **M20**.

> **2** *Christian Science Monitor* Employees enjoy . . a sense of ownership stemming from participative management.

participatory /pɑːˈtɪsɪpət(ə)ri/ *adjective*. **L19**.
[from PARTICIPATE + -ORY[2].]
Characterized by participation, esp. in decision-making in an organization, community, or society; (esp. of forms of entertainment or art) allowing members of the general public to take part.

> J. DIDION The hearing lasted from two until 7:15 p.m., five hours of participatory democracy. *Listener* Participatory broadcasting could be . . a threat to the impartial provision of facts.

participes criminis *noun phr*. pl. of PARTICEPS CRIMINIS.

participial /pɑːtɪˈsɪpɪəl/ *adjective & noun*. **L16**.
[Latin *participialis*, from *participium* PARTICIPLE: see -AL[1].]
GRAMMAR. ▶**A** *adjective*. Of the nature of a participle; of, pertaining to, or involving a participle. **L16**.
past participial, ***present participial***, etc. **participial adjective** an adjective that is a participle in origin and form, as English ***burnt***, ***cutting***, ***engaged***.
▶**B** *noun*. A verbal derivative of the nature of or similar to a participle. **L16**.

participle /ˈpɑːtɪsɪp(ə)l/ *noun*. **LME**.
[Old French, by-form of *participe* from Latin *participium*, from *particeps* (see PARTICIPATE), after Greek *metokhē*, from *metekhein* partake. For the intrusive *l* cf. *principle*, *treacle*.]
†**1** A person, animal, or thing that partakes of the nature of two or more different classes. **LME–L17**.
2 *GRAMMAR*. A non-finite part of a verb used with an auxiliary verb in expressing tense and voice, as in English (*has*) *gone*, (*had been*) *kicked*, (*will be*) *working*, and which may be used adjectivally (cf. ***participial adjective*** s.v. PARTICIPIAL *adjective*). **LME**.
2 ***past participle***, ***present participle***, etc. *DANGLING* ***participle***. ***fused participle***: see FUSE *verb*[1] 2. ***suspended participle***: see SUSPENDED *ppl adjective*.

particle /ˈpɑːtɪk(ə)l/ *noun*. **LME**.
[Latin *particula* dim. of *part-*, *pars* PART *noun*: see -CLE.]
1 A small part of a whole. Now *rare* or *obsolete* in *gen.* sense. **LME**. ▸**b** A very small part of a proposition, statement, or text; a clause; an article of a formula. Now *rare* or *obsolete*. **M16**. ▸**c** A small piece of ground. *local*. **M19**.
2 A minute portion of matter; the smallest perceptible part of an aggregation or mass; *MATH*. a hypothetical thing having mass concentrated at a point but no physical size; *PHYSICS* any of numerous subatomic constituents of the physical world that interact with each other and include electrons, neutrinos, photons, and alpha particles; formerly, an atom, a molecule. **LME**. ▸**b** A very small or the smallest conceivable amount of something immaterial. **E17**. ▸**c** *ROMAN CATHOLIC CHURCH*. The portion of the Host given to each lay communicant. **E18**.
3 *GRAMMAR*. **a** A minor part of speech, *esp.* one that is short and indeclinable, a function word. Also, a prefix, a suffix, as in English *un-*, *-ly*, *-ness*. **M16**. ▸**b** The adverb or preposition used with, and in certain constructions separated from, the verb in a phrasal verb. **E20**.

> **2** B. SPOCK The fat droplets have been broken up into much smaller particles. A. HARDY Mud . . formed from the still finer particles of material carried out from the coast. E. FIGES In the shafts of light . . she could see particles moving. ***elementary particle***, ***lambda particle***, ***tau particle***, etc. **b** J. GALSWORTHY Without a particle of shame. **3a** J. L. AUSTIN The special verbal device of the connecting particle.

Comb.: **particle accelerator** = ACCELERATOR 4; **particle board** (a sheet of) a building material made by compressing and heating small pieces of wood, usu. with a binding material; **particle physics** the branch of physics that deals with the properties, relationships, and interactions of subatomic particles.

particoloured /ˈpɑːtɪkʌləd/ *adjective*. Also **party-**, ***-lored**. **M16**.
[from PARTY *adjective* + COLOURED.]
Partly of one colour and partly of another or others; variegated; *fig.* varied, diversified.
■ **particolour** *noun, adjective, & verb* (*a*) *noun* a particoloured thing, *esp.* a dog with a particoloured coat; (*b*) *adjective* particoloured; (*c*) *verb trans*. (*rare*) make particoloured: **E17**.

particular /pəˈtɪkjʊlə/ *adjective & noun*. **LME**.
[Old French *particuler* (mod. *-ier*) from Latin *particularis*, from *particula* PARTICLE: see -AR[1].]
▶**A** *adjective*. **1** †**a** Belonging to or affecting a part, not the whole, of something; not universal. **LME–M17**. ▸**b** *LOGIC*. Designating a proposition in which something is predicated of some but not all of a class. Opp. UNIVERSAL *adjective* 1b. **M16**.

2 Pertaining to a single definite thing or person, or set of things or persons, as distinguished from others; of one's (its etc.) own; special; not general. Freq. with possess. pronoun LME. ▸†**b** Belonging only *to* a specified person or thing; restricted *to*. L16–E18.
3 Belonging to, concerning, or known to an individual person or set of people and no other; private, personal, not public; (of a person) not occupying a public position. *obsolete* exc. *Scot.* LME.
4 Relating to or concerned with the separate parts or details of a whole; describing something in detail. LME. ▸**b** Attentive to details; specially careful; precise; exacting with regard to details; fastidious, scrupulous. E17.
5 That is a unit or definite one among a number; considered by itself, apart from the rest; individual. LME. ▸†**b** Existing by itself apart from others; actually separate or distinct. LME–M17.
6 Distinguished in some way among others of the kind; more than ordinary; especially good or enjoyable; (now *Scot.*) strange, odd; remarkable. L15. ▸**b** Designating certain modifications of ordinary iambic metres used for hymns. Chiefly *US*. L19.
7 †**a** Specially attentive to a person. E17–E19. ▸**b** Closely acquainted, intimate. *obsolete* exc. as passing into sense 6. E18.

📖 **1b** ***particular negative*** etc. **2** E. BLUNDEN In the trenches a subaltern's business was rather general than particular. K. CLARK Painters with different aims can find in him inspiration . . for their own particular endeavours. *Times* Everyone should receive the training appropriate to his particular aptitude. **4b** J. GALSWORTHY So long as a Forsyte got what he was after, he was not too particular about the means. **5** T. HARDY Winterborne . . had mentioned no particular hour in his invitation to the Melburys. L. DURRELL This particular night was full of a rare summer lightning. **6** U. BENTLEY The one with the mole had a particular charm.

Special collocations: ***particular average***: see AVERAGE *noun*² 3. **Particular Baptist** CHRISTIAN CHURCH a member of a Baptist denomination holding the doctrine of the election and redemption of some but not all people (cf. PARTICULARISM 2). **particular estate** LAW (now *Hist.*) an estate in actual possession, as opp. to any remainder. **particular integral** MATH. (*a*) a solution of a differential equation obtained by assigning values to the arbitrary constants of the complete primitive of the equation; †(*b*) a singular solution of a differential equation. ***particular*** INTENTION. ***particular rule***: see RULE *noun*. **particular solution** = *particular integral* (a) above.

▸ **B** *noun*. †**1** A part or section of a whole; *spec.* a division of a discourse or argument. LME–M19.
2 A minute or subordinate part of a thing considered apart from the rest; a detail, an item; a feature, a factor; in *pl.*, items or details of information; information as to details; a detailed account. LME. ▸†**b** A statement giving the details of a thing; a detailed description or enumeration. E17–L18.
3 a LOGIC. A particular proposition. M16. ▸**b** A particular case or instance; an individual thing in relation to the whole class. Chiefly in ***the particular*** or in *pl.* L16. ▸†**c** A single thing among a number, considered by itself; an individual thing or person; a person not holding a public position. L16–M18.
†**4 a** (One's) individual case; (one's) personal interest, concern, profit, or advantage; a private matter. Freq. in ***for one's particular***, ***for particular***, in (one's) own case, as far as (oneself) is concerned. M16–L18. ▸**b** Personal relation, close acquaintance; personal regard. *rare*. E–M17.
5 a A special friend, a favourite. *slang*. M18. ▸**b** A thing specially characteristic of a place or person; one's special choice or favourite. E19.

📖 **2** P. ROTH That one knew exactly . . down to the smallest particular. *Which?* There's no legal obligation for estate agents to produce accurate particulars. **3b** F. L. WRIGHT Proceeding from generals to particulars in the field of work. E. H. GOMBRICH Endowed with the gift of seeing the universal in the particular.

Phrases: ***for one's particular***, ***for particular***: see sense 4a above. **in particular** (*a*) as one of a number distinguished from the rest; especially; †(*b*) one by one, individually; †(*c*) privately. †**in the particular** in the particular case. **London particular** †(*a*) a kind of madeira imported through London; (*b*) (chiefly *Hist.*) a dense fog affecting London.

▪ **particularness** *noun* (*rare*) E18.

particularise *verb* var. of PARTICULARIZE.

particularism /pəˈtɪkjʊlərɪz(ə)m/ *noun*. E19.
[French *particularisme*, mod. Latin *particularismus*, German *Partikularismus*, all ult. from Latin *particularis* PARTICULAR: see -ISM.]
1 Exclusive attachment to one's own party, sect, nation, etc.; exclusiveness; exclusive attention to a particular subject; specialism. E19.
2 CHRISTIAN THEOLOGY. The doctrine that some but not all people are elected and redeemed. M19.
3 POLITICS. The principle of leaving each State in an empire or federation free to govern itself and promote its own interests, without reference to those of the whole. M19.
4 PHILOSOPHY. Concern with elements which have a particular rather than a universal application, or to which no general standard is applicable. M20.
5 SOCIOLOGY & ECONOMICS. The state or fact of having a particular or fixed nature rather than a universal, general, or mobile nature. Cf. UNIVERSALISM 4. M20.

▪ **particularist** *noun & adjective* (*a*) *noun* an advocate or adherent of particularism; (*b*) *adjective* of or pertaining to particularists or particularism: E18. **particulaˈristic** *adjective* particularist L19. **particulaˈristically** *adverb* M20.

particularity /pətɪkjʊˈlarɪti/ *noun*. E16.
[Old & mod. French *particularité* or late Latin *particularitas*, from Latin *particularis* PARTICULAR: see -ITY.]
1 A particular point or circumstance, a detail. E16. ▸**b** A special or distinctive quality or feature; a peculiarity. Now *rare*. L16.
†**2** (A) personal interest or advantage; regard to personal or private interest; an act dictated by this. *Scot.* M16–E17.
3 The quality or fact of being particular; CHRISTIAN THEOLOGY the doctrine of God's incarnation as Jesus as a particular person at a particular time and place. L16. ▸†**b** A particular or individual matter or affair; a particular instance. Only in L16.

📖 **1** *Times Lit. Suppl.* Sociologists are notorious for . . generalizing terms that ride roughshod over the particularities of history. **3** GLADSTONE Charges which . . are so deficient in particularity. G. GORER Two groups of people identified themselves with more particularity than was called for. ***scandal of particularity***: see SCANDAL 1b.

particularize /pəˈtɪkjʊlərʌɪz/ *verb*. Also **-ise**. L16.
[French *particulariser*, formed as PARTICULAR: see -IZE.]
1 *verb trans.* Make particular as opp. to general; apply or restrict to a particular thing. *rare*. L16.
2 *verb trans.* Mention or describe particularly; state specially or one by one; treat individually or in detail. L16. ▸**b** *verb intrans.* Attend to details; go into detail. E17.
3 *verb trans.* Represent as an individual thing; distinguish, differentiate. *rare*. L16.

📖 **1** V. WOOLF The general question which was apt to particularize itself at such moments as these. **2** JOHN BOYLE In mentioning your friends, I must particularize Mr. Pope.

▪ **particulariˈzation** *noun* M17.

particularly /pəˈtɪkjʊləli/ *adverb*. LME.
[from PARTICULAR *adjective* + -LY².]
1 a In the case of or in respect of each one of a number; one by one, individually. Now *rare* or *obsolete*. LME. ▸**b** In relation to or in the case of one thing or person, or set of things or persons, as distinguished from another or others; specifically. M16. ▸**c** LOGIC. In relation to some but not all of a class. L16.
2 In relation to particulars or details; minutely, in detail. L15.
3 In a special degree; more than others, more than in other cases; especially; more than usual, very. E17.
†**4** Personally, intimately. L17–M18.

📖 **1b** N. YOUNG The CND leadership particularly condemned those actions which had a disruptive . . flavour. **2** C. U. SHEPARD A mineral which . . I shall more particularly describe. **3** J. M. COETZEE There were times, particularly in the mornings, when a fit of exultation would pass through him. D. LEAVITT She is now talking to a particularly large woman.

particulate /pɑːˈtɪkjʊlət, -eɪt, pə-/ *adjective & noun*. L19.
[from Latin *particula* PARTICLE + -ATE².]
▸ **A** *adjective*. Existing in the form of minute separate particles; of or pertaining to minute separate particles. L19.
particulate inheritance GENETICS the manifestation in offspring of discrete characters each inherited from one or other of the parents.
▸ **B** *noun*. A particulate substance; particulate material. M20.

particule /partikyl/ *noun*. Pl. pronounced same. LME.
[(French from) Latin *particula* PARTICLE.]
†**1** A small part; a particle. LME–M18.
2 The French preposition *de* as a prefix of nobility in personal names. L19.

partie /parti/ *noun*. Pl. pronounced same. L17.
[French: see PARTY *noun*. Cf. PARTI.]
A match in a game; a game.

partie carrée /parti kare/ *noun phr.* Pl. ***parties carrées*** (pronounced same). M18.
[French, formed as prec. + *carrée* square.]
A party of four, esp. comprising two men and two women.

partier /ˈpɑːtɪə/ *noun*. *colloq.* M20.
[from PARTY *noun* + -ER¹.]
A person who likes to give or attend parties; a person at a party.

parties carrées *noun phr.* pl. of PARTIE CARRÉE.

partified /ˈpɑːtɪfʌɪd/ *adjective*. *colloq.* E20.
[from PARTY *noun* + -FY + -ED¹.]
Dressed up for a party, made ready for a party.

partify /ˈpɑːtɪfʌɪ/ *verb trans.* *rare*. E18.
[from PARTY *noun* + -FY.]
Make partisan; imbue with party spirit.

partigiano /partiˈdʒiano/ *noun*. Also **P-**. Pl. **-ni** /-ni/. M20.
[Italian (Tuscan): see PARTISAN *noun*¹.]
Hist. A member of the Italian resistance during the war of 1939–45, an Italian partisan.

partile /ˈpɑːtʌɪl, -tɪl/ *adjective*. L16.
[Late Latin *partilis* divisible, from Latin *partire*, *partiri* PART *verb*: see -ILE.]
†**1** = PARTIAL *adjective* II. L16–L17.
2 ASTROLOGY. Of an aspect: exact, within a degree of exactness. Opp. PLATIC. E17.

parting /ˈpɑːtɪŋ/ *noun*. LME.
[from PART *verb* + -ING¹.]
1 The action of PART *verb*; an instance of this; *spec.* (a) leave-taking; (a) departure. LME.
2 A place where things part or are parted. Freq. in ***the parting of the ways***. LME. ▸**b** A line of scalp revealed in a person's hair by combing the hair away in opposite directions on either side. Cf. PART *noun* 15. L17.
3 A thing which separates things or keeps them separate. Chiefly *techn.* E18.

📖 **1** B. JOWETT I said . . a few words to the boys at parting. F. RAPHAEL There were painful partings with his devoted . . servants. ***attrib.***: D. LEAVITT He casts a parting glance at Elaine. **3** *Nature* The dominant rock . . is . . a thick-bedded lithia greywacke with thin silty or shaly partings.

Comb.: **parting shot** a remark delivered by a person at the moment of departure (cf. PARTHIAN *adjective* 2); **parting tool** any of various tools used for separating pieces of material or for trimming, cutting fine outlines, etc.

parti pris /parti pri, pɑːti ˈpriː/ *noun & adjectival phr.* M19.
[French, lit. 'side taken', formed as PARTI + *pris* pa. pple of *prendre* take.]
▸ **A** *noun phr.* Pl. ***partis pris*** (pronounced same). A preconceived view, a prejudice; bias. M19.
▸ **B** *adjectival phr.* Prejudiced, biased; on the side of a particular party. E20.

partisan /ˈpɑːtɪzan, pɑːtɪˈzan/ *noun*¹ & *adjective*. Also **-zan**. M16.
[French from Italian dial. *partisano*, *parteźan*, (Tuscan) *partigiano*, from Italian *parte* from Latin *part-*, *pars* PART *noun*. Cf. PARTIGIANO.]
▸ **A** *noun*. **1** An adherent or supporter of a party, person, or cause; *esp.* a zealous supporter; a prejudiced, unreasoning, or fanatical adherent. M16.
2 MILITARY. **a** A member of a party of light or irregular troops employed in making surprise attacks; a guerrilla, *spec.* (also **P-**) one operating in enemy-occupied Yugoslavia, Italy, and parts of eastern Europe in the war of 1939–45. L17. ▸**b** A commander of such a body of light or irregular troops; a guerrilla leader. E18.

📖 **1** P. GAY He appointed himself Freud's heated partisan, energetically defending psychoanalytic innovations. **2a** *New Left Review* The struggle . . between the Yugoslav Partisans and the Nazi occupation forces.

▸ **B** *adjective*. **1** Of or pertaining to military partisans; pertaining to irregular or guerrilla warfare. E18.
2 Of, pertaining to, or characteristic of a partisan; supporting a party, esp. zealously; prejudiced, one-sided. M19.

📖 **2** F. SMYTH He is not partisan; . . his evidence is available to prosecution and defence counsel. WILLY RUSSELL Criticism is never subjective and should not be confused with partisan interpretation.

▪ **partisanly** *adverb* M19. **partisanship** *noun* zealous support for a party, person, or cause; lack of impartiality: M19.

partisan /ˈpɑːtɪzan/ *noun*². Also **-zan**. M16.
[French †*partizane* (now *pertuisane*, after *pertuiser* bore through) from Italian †*partesana* dial. var. of *partigiana* use as noun (sc. *arma* weapon) of fem. of *partigiano*: see prec.]
Chiefly *Hist.* **1** A military weapon used by infantrymen in the 16th and 17th cents., consisting of a long-handled spear with a blade having one or more lateral cutting projections; such a weapon borne ceremonially by civic and other guards. M16.
2 A soldier or civic guard armed with a partisan. M17.
¶ Obsolete after E18 until revived by Sir Walter Scott in E19.

partis pris *noun phr.* pl. of PARTI PRIS *noun phr.*

partita /pɑːˈtiːtə/ *noun*. Pl. **-te** /-ti/, **-tas**. L19.
[Italian, fem. pa. pple of *partire* divide from Latin *partiri* PART *verb*.]
MUSIC. A suite for a solo instrument, chamber ensemble, or (in modern use) orchestra. Also, in baroque music: a set of variations.

partite /ˈpɑːtʌɪt/ *adjective*. L16.
[from Latin *partitus* divided, pa. pple of *partiri* PART *verb*: see -ITE¹.]
Divided into parts; (of a leaf, insect's wing, etc.) divided to or nearly to the base.

partition /pɑːˈtɪʃ(ə)n/ *noun & verb.* LME.
[Old & mod. French from Latin *partitio(n-)*, from *partit-* pa. ppl stem of *partiri*: see PART *verb*, -ION.]
▶ **A** *noun.* **I 1** The action of dividing something into parts or shares; the fact of being so divided; division; POLITICS the division of a country into two or more States or areas of government; *spec.* (*a*) the division of Ireland into Northern Ireland and Eire; (*b*) the division of the Indian subcontinent into India and Pakistan. LME.
2 The action of separating two or more persons or things; the fact or condition of being separated; separation. LME.
3 A thing whose presence divides something into two; *esp.* a light interior wall or screen; a septum in a plant or animal structure. LME.
4 Each of a number of spaces into which an object is divided; *gen.* (now *rare*) a part, a portion. M16.

📖 **1** J. COLVILLE The Germans and Russians have consecrated their Unholy Alliance by a formal partition of Poland. **3** SLOAN WILSON An inner office . . separated from the rest of the room by a partition of . . brick. **4** C. V. WEDGWOOD A number of Courts sat there, in partitions roughly boarded off one from another.

▶ **II** *techn.* **5** LAW. A division of real property between joint-tenants, tenants in common, or coparceners, by which their co-tenancy or co-ownership is abolished and their individual interests in the land are separated; a division into severalty. L15.
6 LOGIC. Analysis by systematic enumeration of the constituent parts of a thing. M16.
7 MATH. †**a** = DIVISION 5. L16–E18. ▸**b** Any of the ways of expressing a number as a sum of positive integers. M19. ▸**c** A collection of non-empty subsets of a given set such that each element of the latter is a member of exactly one of the subsets; a way of dividing a set thus. E20.
8 MUSIC. An arrangement of the several parts of a composition one above another on the same stave or set of staves; a score. Now *rare* or *obsolete.* L16.
9 PHYSICAL CHEMISTRY. The distribution of a solute between two immiscible or slightly miscible solvents in contact with one another, in accordance with its differing solubility in each. M19.
10 COMPUTING. **a** A self-contained part of a program; a group of programs within a program library. M20. ▸**b** Each of a number of portions into which some operating systems divide memory. L20.
Comb.: **partition chromatography** a method of chromatography which utilizes the differing solubilities of the components of a mixture in a liquid sorbent; *spec.* that in which the sorbent is a polar liquid and the carrier a less polar liquid; **partition coefficient** PHYSICAL CHEMISTRY the ratio of the concentrations of a solute in either of two immiscible or slightly miscible liquids, or in two solids, when it is in equilibrium across the interface between them; **partition function** PHYSICS a function which enters into the expression for the distribution of the particles of a system among different energy states (symbol *Z*); **partition wall** a wall forming a partition, *esp.* a light internal wall separating one room from another.
▶ **B** *verb trans.* **1** Divide into parts; divide by a partition; divide and share *out* or *between*; LAW divide (land) into severalty. M18.
2 Make separate (*from*) by a partition. Also foll. by *off.* M19.

📖 **1** B. HINES Packed into the aisles between the rows of pegs, their hanging clothes partitioning the room into corridors. H. WOUK Hitler partitioned Yugoslavia up among Germany, Italy and the Balkan allies. L. GORDON The chorus, partitioned between various individual voices, represents all who confront the mystery of corruption. **2** M. CHABON They had partitioned the dining room from the living room.

■ **partitional** *adjective* (now *rare*) M17. **partitioned** *adjective* having a partition; divided or formed by a partition (also foll. by *off*): E17. **partitioner** *noun* a person who partitions something, esp. land E19. **partitioning** *noun* (*a*) partitions, esp. of a house, collectively; material for partitions; (*b*) the action of the verb: M17. **partitionism** *noun* (POLITICS) belief in or advocacy of partition M20. **partitionist** *noun & adjective* (POLITICS) (*a*) *noun* a believer in or advocate of partition; (*b*) *adjective* of or pertaining to partition or partitionists: E20. **partitionment** *noun* (*a*) the action of partitioning something; (*b*) *rare* a partition; a compartment: M19.

partitive /ˈpɑːtɪtɪv/ *adjective & noun.* LME
[French *partitif* or medieval Latin *partitivus*, from Latin *partit-*: see prec., -IVE.]
GRAMMAR. ▶**A** *adjective.* Of a word or form: denoting or indicating that only a part of a whole is referred to. LME.
partitive genitive: used to indicate a whole divided into or regarded in parts.
▶ **B** *noun.* A partitive word or form. M16.
■ **partitively** *adverb* E16.

partizan *noun*[1] *& adjective, noun*[2] vars. of PARTISAN *noun*[1] *& adjective, noun*[2].

partless /ˈpɑːtlɪs/ *adjective.* Now *rare.* ME.
[from PART *noun* + -LESS.]
†**1** Having no part or share (*of, in*). ME–L16.
2 Having no parts; indivisible. L17.

Partlet /ˈpɑːtlɪt/ *noun*[1]. *arch.* Orig. †**Pertelot(e)**. LME.
[Old French *Pertelote*, the hen in *Reynard the Fox* and Chaucer's *Nun's Priest's Tale.* Cf. CHANTICLEER.]
More fully ***Dame Partlet*** (A personal name for) a hen.

partlet /ˈpɑːtlɪt/ *noun*[2]. Also †**pat-**. L15.
[Old French *patelette* dim. of *patte* paw, band of material: see -LET.]
Hist. An item of clothing formerly worn over the neck and upper part of the chest.

partly /ˈpɑːtli/ *adverb.* E16.
[from PART *noun* + -LY[2].]
With respect to a part; in part; to some extent, not wholly. (Usu. repeated in ref. to each of the parts mentioned.)

📖 J. PAYN A partly-heard conversation. J. C. POWYS Barter always won favour, partly by reason of his being a gentleman. E. BOWEN This back room was partly store, partly office. J. KOSINSKI Chance's last words were partly lost in the excited murmuring of the audience.

partner /ˈpɑːtnə/ *noun & verb.* ME.
[Alt. of PARCENER by assoc. with PART *noun*: cf. PARDNER. See also next.]
▶ **A** *noun.* **1** A person who possesses something jointly with another or others. Now *rare.* ME. ▸†**b** A participant, a partaker. ME–M16.
2 *gen.* A person who takes part with another or others in doing something; an associate, a colleague; (now only in ***partner in crime***) an accomplice. Also (chiefly *US*) as *voc.* as a familiar form of address. ME. ▸**b** A person who is associated with another or others in the carrying on of a business with shared risks and profits. LME. ▸**c** A companion in dancing; a person accompanying another to a party or other entertainment. E17. ▸**d** A player (esp. one of two) on the same side in a game. L17. ▸**e** A spouse; a member of a couple who live together or are habitual companions; a lover. M18.
3 BIOLOGY. Either of a pair or group of symbiotically associated organisms. E20.

📖 **2** E. LEONARD How you doing, partner? ***sparring partner***: see SPAR *verb*[1]. **b** G. SWIFT He was a partner in a successful firm of consultant engineers. ***junior partner, senior partner***, etc. ***dormant partner***: see DORMANT *adjective.* ***latent partner***: see LATENT *adjective.* ***limited partner***: see LIMITED *adjective.* ***silent partner***: see SILENT *adjective.* ***sleeping partner***: see SLEEPING *ppl adjective.* ***special partner***: see SPECIAL *adjective.* **c** *Beano* Right, gentlemen—take your partners for the waltz! **e** V. BRAMWELL Partners who snore or move around when they're asleep are a problem.

Comb.: **partners desk, partners' desk** a large flat-topped pedestal desk at which two people may sit opposite each other.
▶ **B** *verb.* **1** *verb trans.* Make a partner, join, *with.* ME.
2 *verb trans.* Be or act as the partner of. L19.
3 *verb intrans.* Associate as partners; join *with* as a partner. M20.

📖 **2** *Daily Telegraph* The Colonials had scored 192 for the loss of four wickets . . . On resuming Bonnor partnered Giffen. **3** L. MCMURTRY It's odd I partnered with a man like you.

■ **partnering** *noun* association as partners; the action, work, or style of a partner, esp. in dancing: L19. **partnerless** *adjective* M19.

partners /ˈpɑːtnəz/ *noun.* Also (earlier) †**paut-**. ME.
[Pl. of Old French *pautonier* servant, camp-follower, perh. also infl. by prec.]
A timber framework secured to and strengthening the deck of a wooden ship round the holes for the masts.

partnership /ˈpɑːtnəʃɪp/ *noun.* L16.
[from PARTNER *noun* + -SHIP.]
1 The fact or condition of being a partner; association or participation as a partner. L16.
2 An association of two or more people as partners; a joint business. E17. ▸**b** The partners of a business collectively. E19.
3 MATH. = FELLOWSHIP 9. E18.

📖 **1** *Times Lit. Suppl.* Men living in partnership with women. ***limited partnership***: see LIMITED *adjective.* **2** *World of Cricket Monthly* Repairing the damage with a fourth-wicket partnership of 90 in 85 minutes. *Times* A deeper partnership between Japan and Europe.

partness /ˈpɑːtnɪs/ *noun.* E20.
[from PART *noun* + -NESS.]
The fact or quality of being partial or incomplete.

partocracy /pɑːˈtɒkrəsi/ *noun.* M20.
[from PART *noun*: see -CRACY.]
POLITICS. Government by a single party, without any right of opposition; the body of people forming such a government.

partogram /ˈpɑːtəgram/ *noun.* M20.
[from Latin *partus* birth + -O- + -GRAM.]
MEDICINE. A graphical record of the progress of a confinement from the onset of contractions.

parton /ˈpɑːtɒn/ *noun.* M20.
[from PART(ICLE + -ON.]
PARTICLE PHYSICS. Each of the hypothetical pointlike constituents of the nucleon that have been invoked to explain the way the nucleon inelastically scatters electrons of very high energy.

partook *verb pa. t.* of PARTAKE.

partouse /partuz/ *noun.* Also **-ze**. Pl. pronounced same. M20.
[French, formed as PARTY *noun* + *-ouse* pejorative slang suffix.]
1 A party at which there is indiscriminate and collective sexual activity. M20.
2 A nightclub etc. noted for the licentiousness of its entertainment. L20.

partridge /ˈpɑːtrɪdʒ/ *noun & verb.* ME.
[Old French *pertriz*, *-driz* (mod. *perdrix*) alt. of *perdiz* from Latin *perdix*, *-dic-*: for the final consonant cf. CABBAGE *noun*[1].]
▶ **A** *noun.* **1** Any of numerous Old World gallinaceous birds which together with pheasants and quails constitute the subfamily Phasianinae (family Phasianidae), being generally smaller than pheasants but larger than quails; *spec.* any of the genus *Perdix* of Europe and Asia, esp. (more fully ***grey partridge***) *Perdix perdix*, a game-bird native to Britain and central Europe and also introduced in N. America. ME. ▸**b** Any of several similar birds, mainly American gallinaceous birds of the family Phasianidae or Tetraonidae. M17.
†**2** MILITARY. A kind of charge for cannons consisting of a number of missiles fired together. Also ***partridge-shot***. L17–M19.
1 ***Barbary partridge, chukar partridge, French partridge, red-legged partridge, seesee partridge, snow partridge***, etc. ***b birch partridge, mountain partridge, spruce partridge***, etc.
Phrases: SEA ***partridge***.
Comb.: **partridge-berry** either of two N. American plants with edible red berries eaten by game, the mitchella, *Mitchella repens*, and the checkerberry, *Gaultheria procumbens*; the fruit of either of these plants; **partridge pea** (*a*) a variety of field pea with speckled seeds; (*b*) *US* a yellow-flowered leguminous plant, *Cassia fasciculata*, with sensitive leaves; ***partridge shot***: see sense 2 above; **partridge-wood** the wood of the angelin, *Andira inermis*, a reddish-brown timber with darker parallel stripes.
▶ **B** *verb intrans.* Catch, hunt, shoot, or snare partridges. *rare.* M18.

†**part taker** *noun* see PARTAKER.

parturiate /pɑːˈtjʊərɪeɪt/ *verb intrans. rare.* M17.
[Irreg. from Latin *parturire*: see next, -ATE[3].]
Produce young, give birth; (of a plant) bear fruit.

parturient /pɑːˈtjʊərɪənt/ *adjective & noun.* L16.
[Latin *parturient-* pres. ppl stem of *parturire* be in labour (from *part-* pa. ppl stem of *parere*: see PARENT): see -ENT.]
▶ **A** *adjective.* **1** About to give birth; in labour; (of a plant) bearing fruit; *fig.* ready to produce something; productive *of*, big *with.* L16.
2 Of or pertaining to parturition. M18.
▶ **B** *noun.* A parturient woman. M20.
■ **parturiency** *noun* the state of being parturient; productiveness (of ideas etc.): M17.

parturition /pɑːtjʊəˈrɪʃ(ə)n/ *noun.* M17.
[Late Latin *parturitio(n-)*, from Latin *parturit-* pa. ppl stem of *parturire*: see prec., -ITION.]
The action of giving birth to young; childbirth.

party /ˈpɑːti/ *noun.* ME.
[Old & mod. French *partie* part, share, side in a contest, litigant from Proto-Romance use as noun of Latin *partita* fem. pa. pple of *partiri* PART *verb*: cf. next. See also PARTIE.]
▶ **I** A part, a side.
†**1** A part, a portion; a part of the body. ME–M17.
†**2 a** = PART *noun* 12. Usu. in *pl.* ME–L16. ▸**b** = PART *noun* 13. LME–L16.
3 = PART *noun* 11b. *obsolete* exc. as passing into sense 5 below. ME.
†**4** A point, a particular; (part of) a matter. ME–E16.
▶ **II** A body of people.
5 A body of people united in a cause, opinion, etc., in opposition to others who maintain a different one; *spec.* (*a*) *Hist.* either of the two bodies of combatants in a battle, tournament, etc.; (*b*) a political group organized on a national basis. ME. ▸**b** The system of taking sides on public questions; attachment to or zeal for a group united in pursuit of common (esp. political) aims. E18.
6 MILITARY. A detachment of troops selected for a particular service or duty. LME.
†**7** A game, esp. at piquet. LME–L18.
8 A gathering for social pleasure or amusement; a social gathering or entertainment, esp. of invited guests in a person's home. E18. ▸**b** An attack, a battle; a military operation; a unit engaged in a military operation. *Military slang.* M20.
9 A group of people, *esp.* one gathered together for a temporary purpose; a group of people travelling together or engaged in a common activity. L18.

📖 **5** H. WILSON Neither of the two major parties could have reached a majority. ***Conservative Party, Labour Party, Nazi Party, Republican Party***, etc. **b** J. W. CROKER Party is in England a stronger passion than love, avarice, or ambition. **8** J. OSBORNE Let's make it a party . . let's just whoop it up! ***dinner party, garden party, tea party, wine-party***, etc. **9** R. V. JONES The party that was assembled to conduct the interrogation numbered four. A. PRICE A party of police was sent to arrest them. ***fishing party, hunting party, walking party, working party***, etc.

▶ **III** A single person.

10 A person or group of people forming one side in a contract, dispute, law case, etc. **ME.** ▸†**b** An opponent, an antagonist. **L15–M17.**

11 A person who takes part or is implicated in a specified deed, event, or matter. Foll. by *to*, †*in*. **LME.**

12 The individual person concerned or in question; the person referred to; a person. Now *colloq.* **LME.**

†**13** A colleague, a partner; a (good or bad) match in marriage. Chiefly *Scot.* **L15–M19.**

14 A telephone subscriber; a person using a telephone (orig., one on a party line). **E20.**

📖 **10** A. J. AYER He was not allowed to become a party to the suit. **11** H. JAMES Nothing against the validity of a friendship that the parties to it have not a mutual resemblance. L. DEIGHTON Was her secretary a party to whatever was going on, I wondered. E. YOUNG-BRUEHL He saw his defeat coming and preferred not to be party to it. **12** E. LANGLEY The elderly party . . took the violin from Blue's hand. S. BELLOW What I literally am: a basically unimportant old party.

▶ **IV** Senses of doubtful affinity.

†**15** A decision. **L16–M18.**

†**16** A proposal, an offer. **M17–M18.**

Phrases: ***collapse of a stout party***: see STOUT *adjective*. ***Grand Old Party***: see GRAND *adjective*[1]. ***innocent party***: see INNOCENT *adjective*. **keep the party clean** act responsibly to conform to accepted patterns of behaviour. **make one's party good** make good one's cause or position. ***maroon party***: see MAROON *noun*[1] 2. ***parliamentary party***: see PARLIAMENTARY *adjective*. ***pyjama party***: see PYJAMAS. ***raiding party***: see RAID *verb* 1. ***stag party***: see STAG *noun* etc. ***stout party***: see STOUT *adjective*. ***third party***: see THIRD *adjective & noun*.

Comb.: **party animal** a particularly energetic and gregarious person, esp. on social occasions; a person who enjoys habitually attending parties and other social occasions; **party boat** *N. Amer.*: for hiring by people who want to go fishing; **party game**: such as might be played at a party; **party line** (*a*) a policy, or the policies collectively, adopted by a political party; (*b*) a telephone line number shared by two or more subscribers; **party-liner** a person who follows a party line in politics; **party list** a voting system used with proportional representation, in which people vote for a party rather than a candidate and each party is assigned a number of seats which reflects its share of the vote and which are filled from a list of candidates; **party man** (*a*) a man belonging to or (loyally) supporting a particular party, esp. in politics; (*b*) a man who often goes to or gives parties; †(*c*) a soldier belonging to, or an officer commanding, a party of troops; **party manners** good manners, best behaviour; **party piano** a boogie-woogie or barrel-house style of piano-playing; **party piece** a poem, song, trick, etc., regularly performed by someone in order to entertain others; **party plan** a sales strategy by which goods are displayed or demonstrated at parties in people's homes; **party politics** politics as it relates to political parties; **party-political** *adjective & noun* (*a*) *adjective* of or pertaining to party politics; (*b*) *noun* a party-political broadcast, a television or radio programme in which a representative of a political party presents material intended to foster support for it; **party poop**, **party pooper** *N. Amer. slang* a person who throws a gloom over social enjoyment; **party popper** a device which rapidly ejects a long thin strip of paper, used as an amusement at parties; **party spirit** (*a*) a feeling of solidarity with and support for one's political party; (*b*) a feeling or atmosphere of festivity; **party ticket** = ***party line*** (a) above; †**party verdict** a person's share in a joint verdict; **party wall**: between two adjoining properties or pieces of land occupied by different parties, each of whom has a right in it; **party wire** *US* = ***party line*** (b) above.

▪ **partyism** *noun* the system of political parties; party spirit: **M19.** **partyless** *adjective* not having or not belonging to a political party **L19.** **partyness** *noun* (POLITICS) the state of being thoroughly imbued with party spirit **M20.**

party /ˈpɑːti/ *adjective.* **LME.**
[Old & mod. French *parti* from Proto-Romance from Latin *partitus* pa. pple of *partiri* PART *verb*: cf. prec. See also PARTI.]

†**1** Particoloured. **LME–E18.**

2 HERALDRY. Of a shield: divided into parts of different tinctures, usually by a line in the direction of an ordinary (indicated by *per*). **L15.**

2 ***party per pale, party per pile***, etc.

party /ˈpɑːti/ *verb.* **L16.**
[from the noun.]

†**1** *verb trans. & intrans.* Take the part of; side with or *with*. *Scot.* **L16–L18.**

2 a *verb intrans.* Give a party; attend a party, *esp.* go to parties frequently. **E20.** ▸**b** *verb trans.* Entertain at a party; accompany to a party. **M20.**

📖 **2c** *TV Times* He's never been one for partying and nightclubbing.

partycolored, **partycoloured** *adjectives* see PARTI-COLOURED.

parula /ˈparʊlə/ *noun.* **L19.**
[medieval Latin = coal tit (adopted as mod. Latin genus name), dim. of Latin *parus* titmouse.]

Any bird of the American genus *Parula* of small wood warblers, typically having a bluish back and yellow breast. Also ***parula warbler***.

parure /pəˈrʊə/ *noun.* **ME.**
[Old & mod. French, from *parer*: see PARE *verb*, -URE.]

†**1** An ornament for an alb or amice. **ME–E16.**

†**2** A paring, a peeling. **LME–L16.**

3 A set of jewels or other ornaments intended to be worn together. **E19.**

parvalbumin /pɑːˈvalbjʊmɪn/ *noun.* **M20.**
[from Latin *parvus* small + ALBUMIN.]

BIOCHEMISTRY. A calcium-binding muscle protein of low molecular weight found in some vertebrates.

parvanimity /pɑːvəˈnɪmɪti/ *noun. literary.* **L17.**
[from Latin *parvus* small after MAGNANIMITY.]

Littleness of mind, lack of magnanimity; an instance of this.

parve *adjective* var. of PAREVE.

parvenu /ˈpɑːvənuː, -njuː/ *noun & adjective.* **E19.**
[French, use as noun of pa. pple of *parvenir* arrive from Latin *pervenire*, formed as PER-[1] + *venire* come.]

▶ **A** *noun.* Fem. **-ue.** A person of humble origin who has gained wealth or position and risen in society, *esp.* one regarded as unfitted for the position achieved in this way, or as lacking the accomplishments appropriate to it; an upstart. **E19.**

📖 *fig.*: P. USTINOV Napoleon . . had now re-established France's reputation among the other crowned heads as a parvenu.

▶ **B** *adjective.* That has recently risen to wealth or position; resembling or characteristic of a parvenu. **E19.**

📖 D. COUPLAND Parvenu wealth always treats the help like dirt. G. HANCOCK Parvenu peoples . . hanker after ancestors.

▪ **parveˈnudom** *noun* the world of parvenus **L19.** **parveˈnuism** *noun* the habits or practices of parvenus, parvenu character **M19.**

parvis /ˈpɑːvɪs/ *noun.* **LME.**
[Old & mod. French (also †*parevis*) from Proto-Romance from late Latin *paradisus* PARADISE (in the Middle Ages denoting the area in front of St Peter's, Rome).]

1 An enclosed area, often surrounded with colonnades or porticoes, in front of a building, esp. a cathedral or church; a single colonnade in front of a church. **LME.** ▸**b** *Hist.* A room over a church porch. **M19.**

2 A public or academic conference or disputation. Long *obsolete* exc. *Hist.* **LME.**

parvitude /ˈpɑːvɪtjuːd/ *noun. rare.* **M17.**
[from Latin *parvus* small, after MAGNITUDE.]

1 Littleness, smallness. **M17.**

†**2** An absolutely minute thing, an atom. **M–L17.**

parvovirus /ˈpɑːvəʊvʌɪrəs/ *noun.* **M20.**
[from Latin *parvus* small + -O- + VIRUS.]

MICROBIOLOGY. Any of a group of very small animal viruses consisting of single-stranded DNA in an icosahedral capsid without an envelope and occurring in a wide variety of vertebrates. Also *spec.* in VETERINARY MEDICINE, one of these (more fully ***canine parvovirus***) which causes contagious disease in dogs.

parwanah /pəːˈwɑːnə/ *noun.* Also **pur-**. **L17.**
[Urdu from Persian *parwāna* a royal patent or diploma, a warrant.]

In the Indian subcontinent: a letter of authority; an order, a licence, a pass.

parylene /ˈparɪliːn/ *noun.* **M20.**
[from PAR(AX)YLENE.]

Any of several transparent thermoplastic polymers made as thin films or particles by condensation of paraxylene or its derivatives.

parypate *noun* var. of PARHYPATE.

pas /pa, pɑː/ *noun.* Pl. same. **E18.**
[French.]

1 The right of going first; precedence. **E18.**

2 A step in dancing; a kind of dance, esp. in classical ballet. Chiefly with qualifying phr. **L18.**

2 ***pas ciseaux***: see ***pas de ciseaux*** below. ***pas d'action*** /daksjɔ̃/ a dance expressing a theme or narrative. ***pas de basque*** /də bask/ a step in three beats, similar to a waltz step but with a circular movement of the right leg on the second beat. ***pas de bourrée*** /də bure/ = ***BOURRÉE step***. ***pas de chat*** /də ʃa/ [lit. 'of cat'] a jump in which each foot in turn is raised to the opposite knee. ***pas de cheval*** /də ʃəval/ [lit. 'of horse'] a step in which a pawing movement is executed with one foot. ***pas de ciseaux***, ***pas ciseaux*** /(də) sizo/ [lit. 'of scissors'] a jump in which the legs are opened wide apart in the air. ***pas de deux*** /də ˈdəː, də dø/ a dance for two people. ***pas GLISSÉ***. ***pas de quatre*** /də ˈkatr(ə), *foreign* katʁ/ a dance for four people. ***pas de trois*** /də ˈtrwʌ, *foreign* tʁwa/ a dance for three people. ***pas seul*** /sœl/ [sole, alone] a dance for one person.

pasan /ˈpɑːz(ə)n/ *noun.* Now *rare* or *obsolete*. Also **-ang** /aŋ/. **L18.**
[Persian †*pāzan*, Pahlavi *pāchin*.]

A wild goat, a bezoar goat.

¶ Erron. identified by Buffon with the gemsbok.

Pascal /paˈskɑːl, ˈpaskɑːl, -al; *esp. in sense* 2 ˈpask(ə)l/ *noun.* Also **p-**, (in sense 3) **PASCAL**. **L19.**
[from *Pascal*: see next.]

1 a MATH. ***Pascal's triangle***, a triangular array of numbers in which those at the ends of the rows are 1 and each of the others is the sum of the nearest two numbers in the row above (the apex, 1, being at the top). **L19.** ▸**b** PHILOSOPHY. ***Pascal's wager***, the argument that it is in one's own best interest to behave as if God exists, since the risk of eternal punishment in hell outweighs any advantage in believing otherwise. **L19.**

2 (Usu. **p-**.) The SI unit of pressure, equal to one newton per square metre (approx. 0.000 145 pound per square inch, 9.9×10^{-6} atmosphere). (Symbol Pa.) **M20.**

3 COMPUTING. A high-level structured programming language used for teaching and general programming. **L20.**

Pascalian /paˈskɑːlɪən/ *noun & adjective.* **E20.**
[from *Pascal* (see below) + -IAN.]

▶ **A** *noun.* An admirer or student of the French scholar and scientist Blaise Pascal (1623–62), or his ideas and work. **E20.**

▶ **B** *adjective.* Of or pertaining to Pascal or his ideas and work. **M20.**

Pasch /pask, pɑːsk/ *noun. arch.* **LOE.**
[Old French *pasches*, *paskes* (mod. *Pâques*) from ecclesiastical Latin *pascha* from Greek *paskha* from Aramaic *pasha* from Hebrew *pesaḥ* PASSOVER. Cf. PACE *noun*[2].]

1 The Christian festival of Easter. **LOE.**

2 The Jewish festival of Passover. **ME.**

paschal /ˈpask(ə)l, ˈpɑːs-/ *adjective & noun.* **LME.**
[Old & mod. French *pascal* from ecclesiastical Latin *paschalis*, from *pascha*: see prec., -AL[1].]

▶ **A** *adjective.* **1** Of or pertaining to Passover. **LME.**

2 Of or pertaining to Easter; used in Easter celebrations. **LME.**

Special collocations: **paschal candle** CHRISTIAN CHURCH a large candle blessed and lighted in the service of Holy Saturday and placed by the altar until Pentecost or (formerly) Ascension Day. **paschal lamb** (*a*) a lamb killed and eaten at Passover; (*b*) Jesus Christ. **Paschaltide** = ***Eastertide*** s.v. EASTER *noun*.

▶ **B** *noun.* **1** A paschal candle; a candlestick to hold this. **LME.**

2 Passover; a Passover lamb. **L16.**

1 ***Judas of the paschal***: see JUDAS 2.

pasch-egg /ˈpaskɛg/ *noun.* Now *Scot.* & *north.* **L16.**
[from PASCH + EGG *noun*.]

A hard-boiled egg dyed in various colours, as an Easter gift; an Easter egg.

Paschen–Back effect /ˈpaʃ(ə)nbak ɪˌfɛkt/ *noun phr.* **E20.**
[formed as PASCHEN SERIES + E. E. A. *Back* (1881–1959), German physicist.]

PHYSICS. The splitting of spectral lines that occurs when the source is in a magnetic field so strong that the extent of the splitting is comparable to the separation of the components of a multiplet.

Paschen body /ˈpaʃ(ə)n bɒdi/ *noun phr.* **M20.**
[Enrique *Paschen* (1860–1936), Mexican-born bacteriologist.]

MEDICINE. Each of the numerous small, possibly viral particles found in epithelial cells in cases of smallpox and cowpox. Usu. in *pl.*

Paschen series /ˈpaʃ(ə)n sɪəriːz/ *noun phr.* **E20.**
[L. C. H. Friedrich *Paschen* (1865–1947), German physicist.]

A series of lines in the infrared spectrum of atomic hydrogen, between 1.88 and 0.82 micrometre.

pascual /ˈpaskjʊəl/ *adjective.* **M17.**
[Old French from medieval Latin *pascualis*, from Latin *pascum* pasture, grazing: see -AL[1].]

Of or pertaining to pasture-land; *esp.* (of a plant) growing in pasture-land.

pascuant /ˈpaskjʊənt/ *adjective.* **E19.**
[from Latin *pascum*: see prec., -ANT[1].]

HERALDRY. Of an animal: grazing.

pas d'âne /padan/ *noun.* **L19.**
[French, lit. 'donkey's step'.]

FENCING. Two rings below the cross-guard of some old swords for protecting the fingers.

Pasdar /pɑːsˈdɑː/ *noun.* Pl. **Pasdaran** /pɑːsˈdɑːrən/, **Pasdars**. **L20**
[Persian *pāsdār* guard.]

A member of the Iranian revolutionary guard responsible for the suppression of political dissent.

pas devant /pɑ dəvɑ̃/ *adjectival phr.* **M20.**
[French = not in front (of the children).]

In full ***pas devant les enfants*** /lez ɑ̃fɑ̃/. Of a statement, action, etc.: not appropriate or proper for the present company.

📖 N. MITFORD 'Adultery is for when you're older, darling.' 'Oh I see. A sort of pas devant thing?'

pasear /paseɪ'ɑː/ *verb intrans. & noun. US dial. & slang.* M19.
[Spanish = take a walk. Cf. next.]
(Take) a walk.

paseo /pa'seɪəʊ, *foreign* pa'seo/ *noun.* Pl. **-os** /-əʊz, *foreign* -ɔs/. M19.
[Spanish.]
In Spain, Spanish-speaking parts of America, and the south-western US: a leisurely walk or stroll; a parade or procession, *esp.* at a bullfight; also, a road, an avenue.

pash /paʃ/ *noun*[1]. *obsolete* exc. *dial.* E17.
[Origin unkn.]
The head.
¶ First recorded in Shakes.

pash /paʃ/ *noun*[2]. Now chiefly *dial.* E17.
[from PASH *verb.*]
†**1** A smashing or crushing blow. *rare.* Only in E17.
2 (The noise of) a crashing fall. L17.
3 A heavy fall of rain or snow. *dial.* L18.
4 *transf.* A great quantity or number, a disordered heap. L18.

pash /paʃ/ *noun*[3] *& adjective. slang.* E20.
[Abbreviation of PASSION *noun.*]
▶**A** *noun.* Passion; (a person who is the object of) an infatuation. E20.

📖 I. RANKIN Maybe he's whisked her off to Tenerife for a bit of pash under the sun. A. LURIE Miranda likes you . . . I think she has quite a pash on you.

▶**B** *adjective.* Passionate. E20.

pash /paʃ/ *verb.* Now chiefly *dial.* LME.
[Prob. imit.: cf. *bash, dash, smash,* etc.]
1 *verb trans.* Hurl or throw violently so as to cause breakage. LME.
2 *verb trans.* Strike or knock violently, esp. so as to bruise or smash. LME.
3 *verb trans.* Break in pieces; smash by blows. LME.
4 *verb trans.* Drive *out* by a violent blow. M16.
5 *verb intrans.* Of rain, a wave, etc.: fall or beat violently *against, down,* etc. L16.

pasha /'pɑːʃə/ *noun.* Also **pacha**. See also BASHAW. M17.
[Turkish *paşa,* formed as PADISHAH.]
Hist. (The title of) a Turkish officer of high rank, as a military commander, a provincial governor, etc.
■ **pashadom** *noun* (now *rare*) the realm of pashas L19.

pashalic /'pɑːʃəlɪk, pə'ʃɑːlɪk/ *noun & adjective.* Also **pachalic**, (earlier) †**bashalik**. L17.
[Turkish *paşalık,* formed as prec. + *-lık* suffix indicating quality or condition.]
Hist. ▶**A** *noun.* The jurisdiction of a pasha; the district governed by a pasha. L17.
▶**B** *adjective.* Of or pertaining to a pasha. M19.

pashm /'paʃ(ə)m/ *noun.* L19.
[Persian *pašm* wool.]
The underfur of some Tibetan animals, esp. that of the goat, as used for cashmere shawls.

pashmina /pʌʃ'miːnə/ *noun.* L19.
[Persian *pašmīn* woollen, formed as prec.]
1 = prec. L19.
2 A garment, esp. a shawl, made from pashmina or from a blend of pashmina and silk. L20.

Pashto /'pʌʃtəʊ/ *noun & adjective.* Also **-tu** /-tuː/. L18.
[Pashto *pəkhtō, pəstō.*]
▶**A** *noun.* The Iranian official language of Afghanistan, also used in some areas of Pakistan. L18.
▶**B** *attrib.* or as *adjective.* Of or designating this language. L18.

Pashtun *noun & adjective* var. of PAKHTUN.

pasigraphy /pə'sɪgrəfi/ *noun.* L18.
[from Greek *pasi* for all + -GRAPHY.]
A system of writing for universal use and understanding, with characters representing ideas instead of words.
■ **pasi'graphic** *adjective* L18.

pasilaly /'pasɪlali/ *noun. rare.* E19.
[from Greek *pasi* for all + *lalia*: see -LALIA, -Y³.]
A spoken language for universal use.

Pasionaria /,pasɪə'nɑːrɪə/ *noun.* Also **-nara** /-nɑːrə/. M20.
[Spanish (lit. 'passion-flower'), nickname for the Spanish Communist leader Dolores Ibarruri (1895–1975).]
A popular female leader or figurehead of a political or other cause.

📖 *Times* Henry Fonda's little girl . . grew up to be not only a gifted actress but the Pasionaria of the antiwar movement.

paskha /'pasxə, 'paskə/ *noun.* Also ***paska***. E20.
[Russian = Easter.]
A rich Russian dessert made with curd cheese, dried fruit, nuts, spices, etc., set in a mould and traditionally eaten at Easter.

pasmo /'pazməʊ/ *noun.* E20.
[Amer. Spanish, from Spanish *pasmo* spasm.]
AGRICULTURE. A disease of flax caused by the fungus *Mycosphaerella linorum,* distinguished by circular brown or yellowish lesions on affected plants. Also ***pasmo disease***.

paso /'paso, 'pasəʊ/ *noun.* Pl. **-os** /-ɔs, -əʊz/. E20.
[Spanish.]
An image or group of images representing Passion scenes, carried in procession as part of Holy Week observances in Spain.

paso doble /,pasə(ʊ) 'dəʊbleɪ/ *noun phr.* Pl. **paso dobles**. E20.
[Spanish = double step.]
A quick ballroom dance based on a Latin American style of marching; a piece of music for this dance, usu. in 2/4 time.

paspalum /'pasp(ə)ləm/ *noun.* L18.
[mod. Latin (see below) from Greek *paspalos* a kind of millet.]
Any of various chiefly S. American grasses constituting the genus *Paspalum,* cultivated in the US and Australasia for fodder.

†**paspy** *noun* see PASSEPIED.

pasque-flower /'pɑːskflaʊə/ *noun.* Orig. †**passeflower**. L16.
[French *passe-fleur* a variety of anemone, alt. after *pasque* PASCH, on account of its early flowering.]
A spring-flowering plant related to the anemones, *Pulsatilla vulgaris,* of calcareous grassland in Europe, with bell-shaped purple flowers clothed with hairs. Also, a related N. American plant, *P. nuttalliana,* with violet or white flowers.

pasquil /'paskwɪl/ *noun & verb.* M16.
[medieval Latin *Pasquillus* from Italian *Pasquillo* dim. of *Pasquino*: see PASQUIN.]
▶**A** *noun.* †**1** = PASQUIN 1. M16–M17.
2 = PASQUINADE *noun.* M16.
▶†**B** *verb trans.* Infl. **-ll-**. Libel or satirize in a pasquil; lampoon. E–M17.
■ †**pasquiller** *noun* a composer of pasquils L16–M17.

Pasquin /'paskwɪn/ *noun.* M16.
[Italian *Pasquino* name of the statue: see sense 1.]
Hist. **1** A statue in Rome on which abusive Latin verses were annually posted in the 16th cent.; *transf.* an imaginary person to whom anonymous lampoons were conventionally ascribed. M16.
†**2** = PASQUINADE *noun.* E17–M18.

pasquinade /paskwɪ'neɪd/ *noun & verb.* Orig. †**-ata**. L16.
[Italian *pasquinata,* French *pasquinade,* formed as prec.: see -ADE.]
▶**A** *noun.* A lampoon, a satire, orig. one exhibited in a public place. L16.
▶**B** *verb trans.* Satirize or libel in a pasquinade. L18.

pass /pɑːs/ *noun*[1]. ME.
[Var. of PACE *noun*¹, infl. by French *pas* and PASS *verb.*]
▶**I** †**1** A step, a stride, a pace. ME–M18.
†**2** = PASSUS. ME–M17.
▶**II** A passage.
3 a Orig., a road or path through a wood etc., exposed to ambush or robbery. Now, a narrow and difficult or dangerous passage through a mountainous region or over a mountain range; *spec.* (MILITARY) one viewed as a strategic entrance to a country or place. ME. ▶**b** *gen.* A way by which to pass or get through; a road, a route. E17. ▶**c** A place at which a river can be crossed by ford, ferry, or (*occas.*) a bridge. Now *rare.* M17. ▶**d** A navigable channel, esp. at the mouth of a river or in a delta. L17. ▶**e** A passage for fish over or past a weir. M19. ▶**f** A passage in a church. *Scot. dial.* L19.

📖 **3a** SIR W. SCOTT The guide . . Led slowly through the pass's jaws.

Phrases: **sell the pass** betray a cause.

pass /pɑːs/ *noun*[2]. L15.
[Partly from French *passe,* from *passer* to pass; partly from the verb.]
▶**I** The condition to or through which a thing passes.
†**1** Realization, completion; end, outcome. *obsolete* exc. in ***bring to pass***, ***come to pass*** below or as passing into sense 2. L15.
2 A situation or point in the course of any affair; *esp.* a critical position, a predicament. M16.

📖 **1** SHAKES. *Sonn.* To no other pass my verses tend Than of your graces and your gifts to tell. **2** M. KEANE Things must have come to a pass for the girls to leave their whole life . . behind. N. BAWDEN She believed . . the masculine principle . . had brought the world to the pass it was in.

▶**II** †**3 a** Behaviour. *rare.* Only in M16. ▶**b** An action. *rare* (Shakes.). Only in E17.
†**4** The fact of passing as approved; reputation, estimation. L16–E17.
5 The action or an act of passing or moving from one place to another; passage. Now chiefly *spec.* as in sense 11 below. L16. ▶**b** Departure from life, death. *arch.* M17.
6 The changing of the position of a thing by sleight of hand etc.; a juggling or conjuring trick. L16.
7 a FENCING. A lunge, a thrust; a round of fencing. L16. ▶†**b** *fig.* A witty remark, a sally. *rare.* E17–E19. ▶**c** BULLFIGHTING. A movement of the cape made by a bullfighter to attract the bull and regulate the direction of its attack; = QUITE *noun.* M19.
8 The passing of an examination or course of study; *esp.* the attainment of such a standard in a degree course as satisfies the examiners without entitling the candidate to honours; a mark or certificate awarded for this. M19.
9 An act of passing the hands over something, esp. in hypnotism. M19.
10 a FOOTBALL & HOCKEY etc. A transference of the ball to another player in the same team. L19. ▶**b** In REAL TENNIS, a service which drops in the pass-court; in TENNIS, a shot which succeeds in going beyond the reach of the racket of an opponent. L19.
11 *spec.* **a** An act of passing something through or over a piece of equipment in order to subject it to a mechanical, chemical, or other process. Also, a series of back-and-forth or cyclic movements forming a single operation in a mechanical process. L19. ▶**b** SPORT. A single run over a course or lap of a circuit, esp. as one of several. M20. ▶**c** An act of flying past; a short sweeping movement or dive made by an aircraft. M20.
12 An action, gesture, or remark intended as a sexual advance. Chiefly in ***make a pass at***. *colloq.* E20.
13 An act of declining to make a bid in a game of bridge etc. Also *gen.*, any act of declining or being unable to act in one's turn in a game etc. E20.
14 In full ***food-pass***. The passing of food from one bird of prey to another while in flight. M20.

📖 **3b** SHAKES. *Meas. for M.* When I perceive your Grace, like pow'r divine, Hath looked upon my passes. **5** D. WELCH How dread must be the pass from . . this earthly state to those abodes. **6** R. DAVIES Making some showy passes with cards. **8** *Observer* To aim at two A level passes . . with the view to going to a university. **12** A. WILSON He made a . . grossly physical pass at her.

▶**III** Permission or authorization to pass.
15 A document authorizing the holder to pass into, out of, or through a place, or into a zone of restricted access; *spec.* (MILITARY) a document authorizing the holder to be absent from quarters, esp. for a specified length of time. L16. ▶†**b** An order sending a pauper or vagrant back to his or her parish. M17–L18. ▶**c** An identity document formerly issued to non-white people in South Africa and Rhodesia, restricting movement and residence in particular areas. E19. ▶**d** A document or ticket authorizing the holder to travel free or at a reduced rate on a train, bus, etc., or giving free admission to a theatre etc. Also, a season ticket. M19.

📖 **15** A. EDEN Nicholas came home . . for his final leave . . and I was given a pass for forty-eight hours to join him.

▶**IV** †**16** An iron ring through which the ball was driven in the game of pall-mall. E17–E18.
17 In full ***pass-hemp***. The third quality of Russian hemp. M18.
18 The aperture formed by the grooves in a rolling-mill, which gives the metal the requisite shape. L19.

Phrases: **bring to pass** [*to pass* usu. regarded as inf. of verb] accomplish, realize; bring about. **come to a pretty pass** reach a regrettable state of affairs. **come to pass** [*to pass* usu. regarded as inf. of verb] happen, come about. ***free pass***: see FREE *adjective.* ***slow pass***: see SLOW *adjective & adverb.*

Comb.: **passband** a frequency band within which signals are transmitted by a filter without attenuation; **pass check** a pass allowing a ticket-holder readmission to a theatrical performance etc.; **pass-court** REAL TENNIS the area in front of the grille on the hazard side enclosed by the end wall, the main wall, the service line, and the pass line; **pass door** a communicating door between the backstage area and the auditorium in a theatre; ***pass-hemp***: see sense 17 above; **passkey** (*a*) a private key to a gate, door, etc., for special purposes; (*b*) a master-key; **pass law** *Hist.* a law formerly current in South Africa regulating the carrying of passes; **pass line** REAL TENNIS the line between the pass-court and the service court; **passmark** the lowest mark that must be obtained in order to pass an examination; **pass play** AMER. FOOTBALL a sequence of passes between members of the same team; **pass rusher** AMER. FOOTBALL a defensive lineman who rushes opposing players in an attempt to prevent them from passing the ball.

†**pass** *noun*[3]. *rare.* LME–M19.
[Latin *passum* neut. of *passus* pa. pple of *pandere* spread; as reintroduced in US prob. after Spanish *pasa* raisin.]
More fully ***pass wine***. Wine made from raisins.
¶ Rare after L17 until reintroduced in US in 19.

pass /pɑːs/ *verb*. Pa. pple **passed**, †**past**. ME.
[Old & mod. French *passer* from Proto-Romance (repr. in medieval Latin *passare*), from Latin *passus* PACE *noun*[1]. See also PAST *adjective & noun*, PAST *preposition & adverb*.]

▶ **I** (Cause to) go, proceed, or move onward.
1 *verb intrans. & trans.* with *adverbial obj.* Go on, move onward, proceed. Usu. with preposition or adverbial adjunct. ME. ▸**b** *verb intrans.* Go on or proceed in narration, consideration, etc. Now usu. foll. by *on*. LME. ▸**c** *verb intrans.* Of a line, string, etc.: extend, run. E18.
2 *verb trans.* Cause or enable to go on, move onward, or proceed; convey, send. Usu. with preposition or adverbial adjunct. LME.
3 *verb trans.* Move; cause to go *round*, *over*, etc. Formerly also *spec.*, push through a sieve. M16.
4 *verb intrans.* Thrust or lunge with a sword. Foll. by *on*, *upon*. L16. ▸†**b** *verb trans.* Make (a thrust). *rare* (Shakes.). Only in L16.

📖 **1** E. BOWEN A servant with a lighted taper passed from gas-bracket to gas-bracket. TOLKIEN He rose . . and drawing the curtain passed out into the cave. G. GREENE He passed into one of the offices of the inner court. **2** T. WASHINGTON The way whereby Xerxes passed his army. I. ALLEN A canal . . sufficient to pass boats of 25 tons. **3** E. H. YATES He had passed the wet sponge over the slate. I. MURDOCH A sense of constriction as if a wire . . had been passed round his chest.

▶ **II** Go away; depart.
5 *verb intrans.* Go away; depart or remove oneself *from*. Also, (of a thing) be taken away or removed *from*. *arch.* ME. ▸**b** *fig.* Depart *from* or forsake a course, practice, principle, etc. LME.
6 Die. Now usu. foll. by *away*, *on*. ME.

📖 **5** AV *Matt.* 26:39 Let this cup passe from me. E. ARNOLD The holy man . . made The eight prostrations . . Then turned and passed. **6** *Evening Post (Nottingham)* Ernest . . passed away December 12th after much suffering. B. EMECHETA A dying old man eager to tell it all . . before he passed to the other side. P. ANGADI As soon as the old Queen passed on . . there seemed an almost audible sigh of relief.

▶ **III** †**7** *verb intrans.* Go or move about, travel; be active. ME–L16.

▶ **IV** (Cause to) go from one to another; transfer, be transferred.
8 *verb intrans.* Go or be transported or transferred from a place, condition, state, etc. ME. ▸**b** Of letters, words, etc.: be exchanged. M16.
9 *verb intrans.* LAW. Of property, a title, etc.: be conveyed *to* a person; come by inheritance *into*, *to*. LME. ▸**b** *verb trans.* Convey in legal form or with legal effect. L16.
†**10** *verb trans.* Send forth or out, emit. *rare*. LME–E17.
11 *verb trans.* Give in pledge (one's word or promise). *arch.* LME.
12 a *verb intrans.* Be handed or put about; (esp. of money) be in circulation, have currency. *arch.* L15. ▸**b** *verb trans.* Put about; put (esp. money) into circulation, give currency to. L16.
13 *verb trans.* Cause to go from one to another; hand, transfer. Also foll. by *down*, *over*, *round*, etc. L16. ▸**b** *verb trans. & intrans.* SPORT. Send (the ball) to another player in one's own team. M19.
14 *verb trans.* Discharge from the body as or with excreta. L17. ▸**b** *verb intrans.* Be discharged in this way. *arch.* M18.

📖 **8** B. STEWART A substance passes from the solid to the liquid state. D. H. LAWRENCE Both men passed into perfect unconsciousness. J. C. OATES A cold that passed into bronchitis and then into pnuemonia. A. J. AYER The Cambridge chair passed into the . . hands of John Wisdom. **b** P. ACKROYD Queries and corrections passed between them. **9** LD MACAULAY The time when the crown passed from Charles the second to his brother. E. LONGFORD The Mornington title would pass to the second Wellesley brother. **13** J. BUCHAN One of the flankers . . passed the word to the others. L. R. BANKS He used to pass me notes. R. INGALLS The food . . started to be passed around. G. SWIFT Jenny passes up the cameras. **14** A. DESAI He stood waiting . . locked into a terrible urgency to pass water.

▶ **V** (Cause to) go by; move past.
15 *verb trans. & intrans.* Go by, proceed past, (a person or thing); leave (a thing etc.) on one side or behind in proceeding; *spec.* overtake, esp. in a vehicle. ME. ▸**b** *verb trans.* Cause to go by; *spec.* have (troops etc.) march by for inspection. E16.
16 *verb intrans.* Of time, things in time, etc.: elapse, go by; come to an end. ME. ▸**b** *verb intrans.* Of an event, occurrence, etc.: proceed in the course of things; take place, happen. ME. ▸**c** *verb trans.* Spend or use up (a period of time), esp. engaged in a particular activity. Also foll. by *away*. LME.
17 *verb trans.* †**a** Go by without attending to; neglect, omit. LME–M17. ▸**b** Omit in narration, leave unmentioned. L16. ▸**c** Omit payment of (a dividend etc.). L19.
18 *verb intrans.* **a** POKER etc. Retire from the game. L16. ▸**b** In BRIDGE etc.: decline to make a bid; *gen.* decline or be unable to act in one's turn in a game etc. M19.

📖 **15** G. GREENE He passed the lit windows of the restaurant-car. V. SCANNELL This grave procession passed. I. MURDOCH They must have passed the turning. J. GARDNER Watching cars and trucks and buses pass on the highway. **16** V. BRITTAIN A fortnight passed in which no letter came. JULIETTE HUXLEY Marriages crack but some survive; the storm passes. S. JOHNSON Morton knew that the opportunity for protest had passed. **b** M. EDGEWORTH Reflect coolly upon what has passed. A. SCHLEE What had passed between them might prove irreversible. **c** B. PYM That territory in which a vast number of people pass their lives. F. FORSYTH He dawdled, passing the time staring into lighted shop windows.

▶ **VI** (Cause to) go or get through.
19 *verb intrans.* Go or get through, esp. in the face of obstruction or difficulty; have or effect passage. ME. ▸†**b** *verb trans.* Of a weapon: pierce, penetrate. L16–E18.
20 *verb trans.* Go across (a sea, frontier, mountain range, etc.), go through (a barrier). Also (*rare*), go through or traverse (a forest, street, etc.). ME. ▸†**b** *verb intrans.* Go across a sea etc. L16–M17. ▸**c** *verb trans.* Cause or allow to go through a barrier or obstruction. E17.
21 *verb intrans.* Go without check or challenge; be tolerated or allowed to serve the purpose; be accepted as adequate, go uncensured. ME. ▸**b** Foll. by *as*, *for*: be accepted or currently known as; be taken for (esp. someone or something else). L16. ▸**c** Foll. by *on*, *upon*: deceive, impose on. *arch.* L17. ▸**d** Foll. by *by*: be currently known by (a name or appellation). M18. ▸**e** Be held or accepted as a member of a religious or ethnic group other than one's own; *spec.* (of a person with some black ancestry) be accepted as white. Chiefly *US*. M20.
22 a *verb trans. & intrans.* Go or get through (a trial or test) successfully; *spec.* achieve a satisfactory or required standard in (an examination); *arch.* endure or experience (an event, suffering, etc.). ME. ▸**b** *verb trans.* Of an examiner: judge the performance or condition of (a candidate) in an examination to be satisfactory. M19.
23 a *verb trans. & intrans.* Of a proposal, *spec.* a bill: be examined and approved by (a legislative or deliberative body). LME. ▸**b** *verb trans.* Examine and cause or allow (a proposal) to proceed, esp. to further legislative or parliamentary processes. M16. ▸†**c** *verb trans.* Allow to go unchecked or without notice; overlook. E17–E19.

📖 **19** E. ARNOLD He set A triple guard, and bade no man should pass. W. GOLDING Flint roads where a wagon might pass. **20** MILTON These Gates for ever shut, which none can pass. **21** C. M. YONGE Very little is required. You will easily pass in a crowd. J. BRAINE 'He's a lovely little boy.' 'He'll pass'. **b** BETTY SMITH Although she was only fourteen, she . . could pass for sixteen easily. P. V. WHITE The skirting of sand and detritus which passed for a beach. V. S. PRITCHETT In London literary circles he passed as the . . Romantic Slav. **22a** R. WEST In . . the usual local examinations . . we had always passed with honours. *Oxford Star* He has passed two life-saving awards. **23** J. MCCARTHY The bill passed without substantial alteration. G. GREENE Their conversation was like a letter which has to pass a censorship. **b** E. LONGFORD A Corn Law had been passed early in 1815.

▶ **VII** Give or pronounce judgement etc. (on); consider.
24 *verb intrans.* Of a jury, judge, court, etc.: hear and decide *on* a case or point; *arch.* adjudicate *between* parties. Formerly also, give a verdict *for* or *against*. ME. ▸**b** Serve *on* a jury. *arch.* L16.
25 *verb intrans.* Of a verdict, sentence, or judgement: be given or pronounced. LME.
†**26** *verb trans.* Process, execute, accomplish, (a matter or business). LME–M18.
†**27** *verb intrans.* Take account of, consider, care. Foll. by *for*, *how*, *of*, *on*, *to do*. Usu. in neg. contexts. M16–L17.
28 *verb trans.* **a** Utter or pronounce (a judicial sentence). L16. ▸**b** Express (esp. a criticism) in speech. E17.

📖 **28b** C. STORR He passed remarks about her figure. A. HARDING Passing audible comment upon the family.

▶ **VIII** Go beyond, exceed.
29 *verb trans.* Go beyond or outside of; overstep (bounds). *arch.* ME.
30 *verb trans.* Go beyond (a point, place, or stage in life etc.). *arch.* ME.
31 *verb trans. & †intrans.* Surpass or excel (a person or thing) in some quality. *arch.* ME. ▸**b** *verb trans.* Exceed in number, measurement, or amount. Now *rare*. ME. ▸†**c** *verb intrans. impers.* Exceed all ordinary limits, be beyond description. M16–L17.
32 *verb trans.* Exceed or be beyond the compass or range of (a faculty); be too great for. LME.

📖 **29** W. COWPER He marks the bounds which Winter may not pass. **30** AV 1 *Cor.* 7:36 If she passe the floure of her age. **32** AV *Phil.* 4:7 The peace of God which passeth all vnderstanding. ALDOUS HUXLEY This given reality is an infinite which passes all understanding.

Phrases: **let pass** allow to go unchecked or uncensored. **pass a person's lips** be eaten or uttered by a person. **pass a remark** make an observation, esp. a disparaging one. ***pass as sterling***: see STERLING *adjective* 2a **passed ball** BASEBALL a pitch that the catcher fails to stop or control, enabling a base runner to advance. **passed pawn** CHESS: that has advanced beyond the pawns on the other side. ***pass for sterling***: see STERLING *adjective* 2a. ***pass in one's checks***: see CHECK *noun*[1]. **pass in one's marble** *Austral. slang* die. ***pass muster***: see MUSTER *noun*. **pass one's eye over** read cursorily. **pass one's lips** be spoken or uttered by one. ***pass round the hat***: see HAT *noun*. ***pass the buck***: see BUCK *noun*[9]. ***pass the pikes***: see PIKE *noun*[4]. **pass the time of day** *colloq.* exchange greetings, chat idly. ***pass to one's reward***: see REWARD *noun* 3. **pass water** urinate. ***ships that pass in the night***: see SHIP *noun* 1. ***well to pass***: see WELL *adjective*. ***will pass in a crowd***, ***would pass in a crowd***: see CROWD *noun*[2].

With adverbs in specialized senses: **pass away** (*a*) *arch.* (of a person) depart, leave; (*b*) (of a thing) come to an end, cease to be; (of time) elapse; †(*c*) relinquish, surrender, (rights etc.); (see also senses 6, 16c above). **pass by** (*a*) *verb phr. intrans.* go or proceed past a person or thing without stopping; (*b*) *verb phr. trans.* go or proceed past (a person or thing) without stopping or without taking notice; overlook; take no notice of, ignore. **pass off** (*a*) (of a feeling, condition, etc.) disappear gradually; (*b*) (of a proceeding) be carried through in a specified way; (*c*) misrepresent (a person or thing) as something else; (*d*) evade or lightly dismiss (an awkward remark etc.). **pass on** (*a*) proceed on one's way; continue; (*b*) transmit (a thing, esp. a message) to the next person in a series (***pass on the torch***: see TORCH *noun*); (see also senses 1b, 4, 6, 21c, 24, 27 above). **pass out** (*a*) faint, become unconscious; (*b*) (chiefly *dial.*) die; (*c*) successfully complete a course of instruction, esp. (MILITARY) a cadet training course etc.; (*d*) distribute; (*e*) BRIDGE (of the players) make three consecutive passes following (a bid), this bid becoming the contract, or make no positive bid at all in (a hand), (usu. in *pass.*). **pass over** (*a*) go across; CHEMISTRY (of a substance) vaporize during distillation and condense in a receiving vessel; (*b*) (of a period of time) elapse, come to an end; (*c*) hand over, transfer; (*d*) omit, disregard, ignore; *spec.* ignore the claims of (a person) to promotion or advancement; (*e*) die; (see also sense 13 above). **pass through** be in a place temporarily while on the way to somewhere else; chiefly as ***passing through***. **pass up** *colloq.* refuse, reject, or forgo (an opportunity etc.).

With prepositions in specialized senses: **pass by** — †(*a*) go through or by way of; (*b*) go past; (see also sense 21d above). **pass over** — cross above or on the surface of; traverse; (see also sense 3 above). **pass through** — (*a*) go from side to side of; cross (a city etc.), esp. without stopping; (*b*) experience; (*c*) make or force a passage through; penetrate; (*d*) cause to pass or go through; ***pass through one's hands***: see THROUGH *preposition & adverb*; ***pass through the mill***: see MILL *noun*[1]; ***pass through the pikes***: see PIKE *noun*[5].

passable /ˈpɑːsəb(ə)l/ *adjective & adverb*. LME.
[Old & mod. French, from *passer*: see PASS *verb*, -ABLE.]
▶ **A** *adjective*. **1** Of a road, river, pass, etc.: that may be passed or traversed. LME.
2 Tolerable; satisfactory; adequate. L15.
†**3** Able to pass or have passage. M16–M18.
4 Of money: that may be circulated, that has valid currency. Now *rare*. L16.

📖 **1** G. L. HARDING The road is fairly smooth and passable in all weathers now. **2** C. P. SNOW *Jean Santeuil* was a passable work, maybe a good one. *Daily Telegraph* Britain had a passable end to a disastrous year.

▸†**B** *adverb*. = PASSABLY. L16–E18.
■ **passableness** *noun* the quality of being passable E18. **passably** *adverb* tolerably, adequately E17.

passacaglia /pasəˈkɑːlɪə/ *noun*. M17.
[Italian from Spanish *pasacalle*, from *pasar* pass + *calle* street (orig. often played in the streets).]
A slow musical composition usu. with a ground bass and in triple time; an early kind of dance to this music.

passacaille /pasəˈkʌɪ/ *noun*. Also **passe-**. E18.
[French from Spanish *pasacalle*: see prec.]
= prec.

passade /pəˈseɪd/; *in sense 2* paˈsɑːd, *foreign* pasad (*pl. same*)/ *noun*. M17.
[French from Italian *passata* or Provençal *passada*, from medieval Latin *passare* PASS *verb*: see -ADE.]
1 HORSEMANSHIP. A forwards or backwards turn performed on the spot. *rare*. M17.
2 A transitory love affair; a passing romance. E19.

passado /pəˈsɑːdəʊ/ *noun*. Pl. **-os**. L16.
[Alt. of Spanish *pasada* = French *passade*: see prec., -ADO.]
1 FENCING. A forward thrust with the sword, the rear foot being moved at the same time. L16.
2 An amorous interchange. Now *rare*. E17.

passage /ˈpasɪdʒ, *in sense 11 freq.* paˈsɑːʒ/ *noun*. ME.
[Old & mod. French, formed as PASS *verb*: see -AGE.]
▶ **I** The action of passing.
1 The action of going or moving onward, across, or past; movement from one place or point to another, or over or through a space or medium; transit. ME. ▸**b** The passing by of people. Also, passers-by. *rare*. L16. ▸**c** The extension of a line, string, etc., from one point to another. *rare*. E17. ▸**d** The migratory flight of a bird. Chiefly in **on passage**, **passage migrant** below. L18.
2 Possibility of passing through; liberty, leave, or right to pass through. ME.
3 An act of travelling from one place to another, a journey, (now usu. by sea). ME. ▸**b** The right of conveyance as a passenger, esp. by sea; accommodation as a passenger. M17.
4 *fig.* Transition from one state or condition to another; *spec.* (now *rare*) death. ME.

†**5** A charge levied upon passengers, a toll. L15–L19.
†**6** The fact of a coin, custom, etc., being generally accepted; currency. L15–M17.
7 The passing into law of a legislative measure. L16.
8 An act of defecation; in *pl.*, motions, faeces. L17.
9 HORSEMANSHIP. A slow collected trot in which the feet are momentarily held high before striking the ground. E18.
10 The action of causing something to pass or go through. M19.
11 MEDICINE & BIOLOGY. The process of propagating micro-organisms or cells in a series of host organisms or culture media, so as to maintain them or modify their virulence; a stage in this process. L19.

> **1** G. B. SHAW He snatches the curtain from her and bars her passage. *Practical Boat Owner* The Red Sea has . . political troubles affecting the passage of small craft. M. WARNOCK The past is a paradise from which we have been excluded by the passage of time. **b** SHAKES. *Oth.* What, ho! No watch? No passage? Murder! Murder! **2** J. D. WHITNEY The depression in the ridge is not sufficiently deep to give passage to a water-course. **3** W. M. CLARKE They . . sailed across to Boulogne . . and had a remarkably smooth passage. **b** A. MASON He had barely enough money to buy his passage to the next port. P. AUSTER Booking passage on some ship and sailing to China. **10** *Pediatrics* The passage of urine with an odor . . similar to that of maple syrup.

► **II** A means of passing.
12 That by which a person or thing may pass; a road, a path, a route, a channel, etc.; a duct, vessel, etc., in the body. ME. ▸**b** A place at which a river or strait may be crossed by means of a ford, ferry, or bridge. Now *rare* or *obsolete*. ME.
13 *spec.* A (narrow) way giving access, esp. to various rooms in a building; a corridor; an alley. E17.

> **12** SOUTHEY Was it the toil of human hands Had hewn a passage in the rock? S. LEACOCK 'Oh, well,' the Cave-man went on, 'there are lots of ways and passages through.' **13** R. L. STEVENSON The servant led us down a matted passage. *Beano* This stone moves—it must be a secret passage. *fig.*: J. L. WATEN Soft light that cleaved silvery passages through the darkness.

► **III** **14** *Hist.* An obsolete game for two players using three dice, in which the aim was to throw doublets over ten. LME.
► **IV** **15** A thing that passes or takes place; an occurrence, an event; a proceeding. Now chiefly *spec.* an (esp. amorous) interchange of words, actions, etc. (usu. in *pl.*). M16. ▸**b** An exchange of blows, a (now only armed) fight; *fig.* a verbal dispute. Now only in ***passage of arms***, ***passage at arms***. L16.
16 A usu. short part or section of a book, speech, etc., considered by itself, esp. for a specific reason. M16. ▸†**b** A remark, an observation. Only in M17. ▸**c** MUSIC. Orig., a progression from one note to another by means of intermediate notes; a short series of such notes, a phrase. Now, a usu. short part or section of a musical composition, *esp.* one forming an identifiable unit. L17. ▸**d** ART. A particular part of a picture; *spec.* a part where one tone merges into another; the technique of achieving this effect. M19. ▸**e** *gen.* An episode in a course of action. *rare.* M19.

> **15** W. BESANT Certain passages and rumours of passages between Will Stephen and this simple country maid. E. F. BENSON There had been that little passage before dinner . . a shade of friction about her smoking. **16** DAY LEWIS His voice would choke at an affecting passage in one of his own sermons. L. C. KNIGHTS The clarity of the analysis mark the passage as unmistakably post-Restoration. H. R. LANDON Nissen suppressed certain letters and passages within letters.

Phrases: **bird of passage** (*a*) a migrant bird; *esp.* = *passage-migrant* below; (*b*) a transient visitor. †**in passage** in passing, by the way. *middle passage*: see MIDDLE *adjective*. *north-east passage*: see NORTH-EAST *adjective*. *north-west passage*: see NORTH-WEST *adjective*. **on passage** (of a bird) on a flight of migration. *purple passage*: see PURPLE *adjective & noun*. RITE *of passage*.
Comb.: **passage-bird** = *bird of passage* above; **passage-boat** a boat for carrying passengers, plying regularly between two places; **passage grave** ARCHAEOLOGY a usu. megalithic burial chamber inside a man-made mound and with a passage connecting it to the outside; **passage-hawk** a full-grown falcon taken during its migration for the purpose of training; **passage-migrant** a bird that stays for a short time in an area on its seasonal migration route; **passage-money** money charged for a journey, fare; **passage-room** *rare* a room through which one passes to another; **passage tomb** ARCHAEOLOGY = *passage grave* above; **passageway** = sense 13 above; **passage-work** (the execution of) music of interest chiefly for the scope it gives for virtuosic display.

passage /ˈpasɪdʒ/ *verb*[1] *intrans. & trans.* L18.
[French *passager* alt. of *passéger* from Italian *passeggiare* walk, pace, from Latin *passus* PACE *noun*[1].]
HORSEMANSHIP. Move or cause to move sideways in riding (by pressure of the rein on the horse's neck and of the rider's leg on the opposite side). Chiefly as ***passaging*** *verbal noun*.

passage /ˈpasɪdʒ, *in sense 3 also* paˈsɑːʒ/ *verb*[2]. L18.
[from the noun.]
1 *verb intrans.* Carry on a passage of arms; *fig.* fence with words etc., argue. L18.
2 *verb intrans.* Make a passage or journey in a ship etc. E19.
3 *verb trans.* MEDICINE & BIOLOGY. Subject a strain of (micro-organisms or cells) to a passage. E20.

passalid /ˈpas(ə)lɪd/ *adjective & noun*. E20.
[from mod. Latin *Passalus* genus name from Greek *passalos* peg: see -ID[3].]
ENTOMOLOGY. ►**A** *adjective*. Of or pertaining to the family Passalidae of somewhat rounded black or brown beetles, found in decaying wood in warm forest regions and noted for the way they tend their young. E20.
►**B** *noun*. A beetle of this family. E20.

Passamaquoddy /pasəməˈkwɒdi/ *noun & adjective*. Pl. of noun same, **-ies**. E18.
[Micmac *pestəmo:kwatik* Passamaquoddy Bay, lit. 'place where pollack are plentiful'.]
Designating or pertaining to, a member of, an Algonquian people inhabiting parts of SE Maine and (formerly) SW New Brunswick; (of) the language of this people.

passament *noun* var. of PASSEMENT *noun*.

passant /ˈpas(ə)nt/ *adjective*. ME.
[Old & mod. French, pres. pple of *passer* PASS *verb*: see -ANT[1].]
†**1** Passing, transitory, transient. ME–E18.
2 HERALDRY. Of an animal: walking towards the dexter side and looking ahead, with three paws on the ground and the dexter forepaw raised. Freq. *postpositive*. LME.
†**3** Surpassing; exceeding. LME–L15.
†**4** Passing, proceeding. E17–E18.
†**5** Current, in vogue. E17–M19.
†**6** Cursory, done in passing. Only in L17.

†**passarado** *noun. rare.* E17–M19.
[Origin unkn. Cf. next.]
NAUTICAL. = next.

†**passaree** *noun. rare.* M17–M19.
[Origin unkn. Cf. prec.]
NAUTICAL. A rope or tackle used to spread the clews and haul down the sheet-blocks of the foresail and mainsail, or a studding-sail, when sailing large before the wind.

passata /pəˈsɑːtə/ *noun*. L20.
[Italian, use as noun of fem. of *passato* puréed.]
A thick paste made from sieved tomatoes and used esp. in Italian cooking.

passback /ˈpɑːsbak/ *noun*. M20.
[from PASS *verb* + BACK *adverb*.]
1 AMER. FOOTBALL. = SNAP-BACK 1b. M20.
2 FOOTBALL. A defensive pass directed backwards to a team-mate, usu. the goalkeeper. L20.

passbook /ˈpɑːsbʊk/ *noun*. Also (esp. in sense 3) **pass book**. E19.
[from PASS *noun*[2] + BOOK *noun*.]
1 A book issued by a bank or (now usu.) building society to an account-holder, recording sums deposited and withdrawn. E19.
2 A book compiled by a trader for a customer, recording goods sold on credit. M19.
3 = PASS *noun*[2] 15c. *S. Afr.* M20.

pass-by /ˈpɑːsbʌɪ/ *noun*. Pl. **-bys**. M16.
[from PASS *verb* + BY *adverb*.]
1 The action of passing by. *rare.* M16.
2 MINING. A siding or a place on a track in a working where vehicles can pass. L19.

passe /pɑs/ *noun*. M19.
[French, from *passer* PASS *verb*.]
In roulette: the section of the cloth covering the numbers 19 to 36; a bet placed on this section.

passé /ˈpaseɪ, *foreign* pɑse/ *adjective & noun*. L18.
[French, pa. ppl adjective of *passer* PASS *verb*.]
►**A** *adjective*. Also (fem.) **-ée**.
1 Past one's prime. *arch.* L18.
2 No longer fashionable; out of date, behind the times. E19.
►**B** *noun*. BALLET. The transitional movement of the leg from one position to the next. M20.

passecaille *noun* var. of PASSACAILLE.

Passe Colmar /pas ˈkɒlmə/ *noun phr.* M19.
[Origin unkn.]
A variety of pear ripening in November and December.

†**passed** *adjective* see PAST *adjective & noun*.

passed-master /pɑːstˈmɑːstə/ *noun*. M16.
[from *passed* pa. pple of PASS *verb* + MASTER *noun*[1].]
A person who has passed as a master; a person qualified or accomplished in some subject. Cf. PAST MASTER.

passée *adjective & noun* see PASSÉ.

†**passeflower** *noun* see PASQUE-FLOWER.

passeggiata /passedˈdʒiata/ *noun*. Pl. **-te** /-te/. M20.
[Italian.]
A stroll, a promenade.

passéisme /pɑseism/ *noun*. M20.
[French.]
Adherence to and regard for the traditions and values of the past, esp. in the arts.
■ ***passéist***, (fem.) **-iste** /-ist (*pl. same*)/ *noun & adjective* (a person who is) traditionalist E20.

passel /ˈpas(ə)l/ *noun*. *US colloq.* M19.
[Repr. a pronunc. of PARCEL *noun*.]
An indeterminate number or quantity, a group, a pack.

> W. WHARTON I found myself . . with a passel of guys who wanted to kill people.

†**passemeasure** *noun*. M16–L19.
[Alt. of Italian *passe-mezzo*, *passa-*, of unkn. origin.]
A slow dance in 2/4 time of Italian origin, related to the pavane and popular in the 16th cent.; a piece of music for this dance.

passement /ˈpasm(ə)nt/ *noun & verb*. As noun also **passa-** /ˈpasə-/. M16.
[French, from *passer* PASS *verb*: see -MENT.]
►**A** *noun*. = PASSEMENTERIE. M16.
►**B** *verb trans.* Adorn with *passementerie*; edge with decorative braiding. M16.

passementerie /pasmɑ̃tri, ˈpasm(ə)ntri/ *noun*. E17.
[French, formed as prec.: see -ERY.]
Decorative trimming consisting of gold or silver lace, gimp, or braid.

passenger /ˈpasɪndʒə/ *noun & adjective*. ME.
[Old & mod. French *passager* use as noun of adjective meaning 'passing', formed as PASSAGE *noun*: see -ER[2]. For the intrusive *n* cf. *harbinger*, *messenger*, etc.]
►**A** *noun*. **1** A traveller (usually on foot). Now *rare* exc. in ***foot-passenger*** or as in sense 3. ME.
†**2** A vessel carrying passengers; a ferry. ME–M17. ▸**b** The operator of a ferry. ME–L16
3 A traveller in or on a public or private conveyance; any occupant of such a conveyance other than the driver, pilot, crew, etc. E16. ▸**b** A member of a team, crew, etc., who does no effective work and is consequently a burden on the other members. *colloq.* M19. ▸**c** A passenger train. *colloq.* L19. ▸**d** MEDICINE. A passenger cell. L20.
†**4** A bird of passage; *spec.* a passage-hawk. L16–L17.

> **1** POPE The snappish cur (the passenger's annoy) Close at my heel. **3** G. GREENE The purser . . watched the passengers cross the . . quay. DAY LEWIS I enjoy . . flying in an air-liner, where the passengers are snugly enclosed. P. THEROUX Most of the passengers got out here and stumbled across the tracks. **b** L. P. DAVIES The scheme was really yours . . Jack Latham wasn't much more than a passenger.

Comb.: **passenger-mile** a unit of traffic measurement representing one passenger travelling a distance of one mile; **passenger-pigeon** a N. American pigeon, *Ectopistes migratorius*, noted for its long migrations in huge flocks, and hunted to extinction by 1914.
►**B** *attrib.* or as *adjective*. **1** Of or pertaining to passengers; *spec.* for the use of a passenger or passengers. E17.
2 MEDICINE & BIOLOGY. Designating a cell, gene, etc., which is transported by, or carried within, another organism, tissue, etc., in the manner of a passenger within a vehicle. M20.

> **1** A. PRICE He was on the passenger list. A. MUNRO Catherine . . slides out of the car on the passenger side. **2** *Science News* The hypothesis that 'passenger' white blood cells in the transplant are . . responsible for the recipient's immune response.

■ **passengered** *adjective* (*rare*) (of a conveyance) carrying or occupied by passengers E20.

passe-partout /paspɑːˈtuː, pɑːs-/ *noun & verb*. L17.
[French, from *passer* PASS *verb* + *partout* everywhere.]
►**A** *noun*. **1** A thing which goes or provides a means of going everywhere; *spec.* a master-key. L17.
2 A frame or border into which a picture of suitable size may be inserted for display; a frame for displaying mounted photographs etc., consisting of two sheets of transparent material (or one sheet with a card backing) stuck together at the edges with adhesive tape. Also, adhesive tape used in such framing. M19.
►**B** *verb trans.* Frame (a picture) using passe-partout. L17.

passepied /paspjeɪ, *foreign* pɑspje (*pl. same*)/ *noun*. Also Anglicized as †**paspy**. L17.
[French, from *passer* PASS *verb* + *pied* foot.]
A dance of Breton origin resembling a quick minuet, popular in the 17th and 18th cents.; a piece of music for this dance, in triple time.

passer /ˈpɑːsə/ *noun*. LME.
[from PASS *verb* + -ER[1].]
1 A person who or thing which passes. LME.
2 *spec.* **a** SPORT. A player who passes the ball to another player. E20. ▸**b** A person who receives and passes on counterfeit money. *slang.* E20.

passer-by /pɑːsəˈbʌɪ/ *noun*. Pl. **passers-by**. M16.
[from *pass by* s.v. PASS *verb*: see -ER[1].]
A person who passes or goes by (on foot), esp. by chance.

Passeres /ˈpasəriːz/ *noun pl.* L19.
[mod. Latin order name (now usu. *Passeriformes*), pl. of Latin *passer* sparrow.]
ORNITHOLOGY. Passerine birds collectively.

passerine /ˈpasərʌɪn/ *adjective & noun*. L18.
[formed as prec. + -INE[1].]
ORNITHOLOGY. ▶**A** *adjective*. **1** Of or pertaining to the large cosmopolitan order Passeriformes of birds with feet adapted for perching, including crows, finches, swallows, thrushes, warblers, etc. L18.
2 Of about the size of a sparrow. *rare*. L19.
▶**B** *noun*. A passerine bird. M19.

passers-by *noun* pl. of PASSER-BY.

passe-temps /pastɑ̃/ *noun*. Now *rare* or *obsolete*. Pl. same. M16.
[French *passetemps*, from *passer* PASS *verb* + *temps* time.]
A pastime.

pass–fail /pɑːsˈfeɪl/ *adjective*. M20.
[from PASS *verb* + FAIL *verb*.]
Of, pertaining to, or designating a scoring system in which performance is assessed simply in terms of success or failure, without further divisions of standard.

passglas /ˈpasglaːs/ *noun*. Pl. **-gläser** /-glɛːzər/. L19.
[German.]
A tall cylindrical drinking-glass graduated with parallel rings or a spiral, made chiefly in Germany in the 17th cent.

pass-guard /ˈpɑːsgɑːd/ *noun*. *obsolete* exc. *Hist.* M16.
[App. from PASS *noun*[2] + GUARD *noun*.]
A piece of armour worn to protect the left elbow when fighting a joust or tournament.

passibility /pasɪˈbɪlɪti/ *noun*. ME.
[Christian Latin *passibilitas*, from *passibilis*: see next, -ITY.]
1 The quality of being passible. ME.
†**2** Passiveness; inaction; sloth. *rare*. LME–M16.

passible /ˈpasɪb(ə)l/ *adjective*. ME.
[Old & mod. French, or Christian Latin *passibilis*, from Latin *pass*- pa. ppl stem of *pati* suffer: see -IBLE.]
1 Chiefly THEOLOGY. Capable of suffering or feeling; susceptible of sensation or emotion. ME.
†**2** Liable to suffer change or decay. LME–L17.
†**3** Able to be suffered or felt. M16–E17.
■ **passibleness** *noun* (*rare*) = PASSIBILITY 1 E17.

passiflora /pasɪˈflɔːrə/ *noun*. M18.
[mod. Latin (see below), from Latin *pass*- (see PASSION *noun*) + -I- + *-florus* flowering.]
= ***passion-flower*** s.v. PASSION *noun*.

passim /ˈpasɪm/ *adverb & adjective*. E19.
[Latin, lit. 'scatteredly', from *passus* scattered, pa. pple of *pandere* spread out.]
Of an allusion or reference in a published work: (to be found) at various places throughout the text.

passimeter /pəˈsɪmɪtə/ *noun*. E20.
[from PASS *verb* or PASS(ENGER + -IMETER.]
Hist. A machine for issuing tickets to train and bus passengers and recording the number of them.

passing /ˈpɑːsɪŋ/ *noun*. ME.
[from PASS *verb* + -ING[1].]
1 The action of PASS *verb*; *spec.* dying, death. Also foll. by adverb or preposition. ME.
2 A type of thread made by winding a thin strip of gold or silver about a core of silk. M19.

> 📖 **1** N. STREATFEILD There was a good deal of passing down of clothes. R. P. GRAVES Alfred's . . tribute to his father was a poem full of grief at his passing. G. LORD The black tom fled at her passing. **in passing** (*a*) by the way; (*b*) in the course of speech, conversation, etc.

Comb.: **passing-bell** (*a*) a bell (now rarely) rung immediately after death as a signal for prayers; (*b*) *fig.* a thing foreboding or signalling the passing away of something; **passing note** MUSIC: not belonging to the harmony but interposed between two notes essential to it to achieve a smooth transition; **passing place** a place where people or things may pass; *spec.* a widened section on a narrow or single-track road.

passing /ˈpɑːsɪŋ/ *adjective, adverb, & preposition*. ME.
[from PASS *verb* + -ING[2].]
▶**A** *adjective*. **1** That passes. ME.
2a That passes away or elapses; transient, fleeting. ME. ▶**b** Done or made in passing; cursory. M18.
†**3** Surpassing; extreme. ME–M17.

> 📖 **1** D. MACKENZIE The noise of a passing car. B. BREYTENBACH He had been abandoned by some passing fugitives. **2a** R. NIEBUHR Conflict between the national units remains as a permanent rather than a passing characteristic. G. DURRELL This . . transformed the coconut from being a passing fancy to being Pooh's favourite toy. **b** M. R. D. FOOT These armed bodies deserve passing mention at least.

Special collocations: **passing shot** TENNIS a shot in which the ball is aimed beyond and out of reach of an opponent. **passing show** an entertainment using as material current events and interests, a revue.
▶**B** *adverb*. Surpassingly, in the highest degree, exceedingly. *arch*. ME.

> 📖 T. HARDY It would be passing mean to enrich herself by a legal title . . which was not essentially hers.

▶†**C** *preposition*. **1** Beyond a specified measure or number; more than. Chiefly in ***not passing***. LME–M18.
2 To a greater degree than, more or better than. LME–M16.
3 Beyond the limit or range of. LME–M19.

> 📖 **1** HENRY MORE He was not passing fifty nine years when he died.

■ **passingly** *adverb* (*a*) in passing, cursorily; (*b*) *arch.* surpassingly; exceedingly: ME. **passingness** *noun* transitoriness M19.

passion /ˈpaʃ(ə)n/ *noun*. ME.
[Old & mod. French from Christian Latin *passio(n-)* suffering, affection, from Latin *pass*- pa. ppl stem of *pati* suffer: see -ION.]
▶**I** The suffering of pain.
1 CHRISTIAN THEOLOGY. (Now usu. **P-**.) *sing.* & †in *pl.* The suffering of Jesus on the Cross (freq. including that in Gethsemane). Formerly also in asseverations. ME. ▶**b** The narrative of the suffering of Jesus from the Gospels; *esp.* a musical or dramatic setting of this. ME.
2 a The sufferings of a martyr; martyrdom. *arch.* ME. ▶**b** A narrative account of a martyrdom. E20.
3 *gen.* Any form of suffering or affliction. Long *rare*. ME.
4 A painful disorder or affliction of a (specified) part of the body. Now *rare* or *obsolete*. LME. ▶†**b** A violent attack of disease. LME–M17.
4 ***cardiac passion***, ***hysteric passion***, ***iliac passion***, etc.
▶**II** (An) emotion, (a) mental state.
5 (A) strong barely controllable emotion. ME. ▶**b** A fit or outburst of such an emotion. L16. ▶**c** A literary composition or passage marked by strong emotion; an emotional speech. *arch.* L16.
6 (A) strong sexual feeling; a person who is the object of such feeling. LME.
7 (An outburst of) anger or rage. M16.
8 A strong enthusiasm for a (specified) thing; an aim or object pursued with strong enthusiasm. M17.

> 📖 **5** S. HAZZARD Paul's face no more expressed loathing . . than Carol's expressed love; yet those were their prevailing passions. R. THOMAS She was shaking with passion, anger and resentment. **b** H. H. MILMAN Henry fell on his knees and in a passion of grief entreated her merciful interference. **6** J. WILKINS Which set a man at liberty from his lusts and passions. W. H. AUDEN The lips so apt for deeds of passion. W. STYRON Her continuing, unflagging passion for Nathan struck me with awe. **7** DAY LEWIS Climbing into the pulpit, he rapidly fell into a passion, stamping and thundering. **8** V. WOOLF His passion was for the law. W. RAEPER Riding was more than a joy to him, it was a passion.

▶**III 9** The fact or condition of being affected or acted upon by external agency; subjection to external force. Opp. ***action***. Now *rare* or *obsolete*. LME. ▶†**b** A way in which a thing is or may be affected by external agency; a property, an attribute. L16–E18.
Phrases: ***crime of passion***: see CRIME *noun*. ***grande passion***. ***grand passion***: see GRAND *adjective*[1]. ***the tender passion***: see TENDER *adjective*.
Comb.: **Passion cross** = ***Calvary cross*** s.v. CALVARY 1; **passion-flower** any of numerous mostly tropical climbing plants of the genus *Passiflora* (family Passifloraceae), with a complex flower whose parts were thought to resemble or correspond to the things associated with the Crucifixion of Jesus; *esp.* that of the S. American *P. caerulea*, often grown for ornament; **passion-fruit** the edible fruit of several kinds of passion-flower, *esp.* that of the Brazilian *Passiflora edulis*, an egg-shaped berry with purple wrinkled skin and sweet yellow pulp surrounding small black seeds; **passion killer** *sing* & (usu.) in *pl.* (*slang*) an unattractive, esp. unrevealing, pair of knickers or other undergarment; **passion-play** a miracle play representing the Passion of Jesus; **Passion Sunday** the fifth Sunday in Lent; **Passion-tide** the last two weeks of Lent, including Passion Week and Holy Week; **passion vine** = ***passion-flower*** above; **Passion Week** (*a*) the fifth week of Lent, beginning with Passion Sunday and ending with Palm Sunday; (*b*) Holy Week.
■ **passionful** *adjective* (*rare*) full of suffering, passion, or anger E17.

passion /ˈpaʃ(ə)n/ *verb*. *arch.* LME.
[Old & mod. French *passionner*, formed as prec.]
1 *verb trans.* Excite or imbue with (a) passion. LME.
†**2** *verb trans.* Affect with suffering, afflict. L15–E17.
3 *verb intrans.* Express or be affected by passion or a strong emotion, formerly esp. sorrow. L16.

passional /ˈpaʃ(ə)n(ə)l/ *adjective & noun*. LME.
[Latin *passionalis*, from *passio(n-)*: see PASSION *noun*, -AL[1].]
▶**A** *adjective*. Of or pertaining to passion; inspired or characterized by passion. LME.

> 📖 M. INNES The original murder . . seemed to be a passional crime; one . . of revenge or retribution.

▶**B** *noun*. †**1** *gen.* A story of suffering. *rare*. Only in L15.
2 *spec.* A book containing accounts of the sufferings of saints and martyrs, for reading on their feast days. Cf. PASSIONARY. M17.

passionary /ˈpaʃ(ə)n(ə)ri/ *noun*. LME.
[medieval Latin *passionarium*, from Latin *passio(n-)*: see PASSION *noun*, -ARY[1].]
= PASSIONAL *noun* 2.

passionate /ˈpaʃ(ə)nət/ *adjective & noun*. LME.
[medieval Latin *passionatus*, from Latin *passio(n-)*: see PASSION *noun*, -ATE[2].]
▶**A** *adjective*. **1** Of a person: affected with or easily moved to passion or strong emotion, *spec.* intense sexual love or desire. LME. ▶**b** Of an emotion: intense. M16. ▶**c** Of an action, speech, etc.: marked by such emotion; expressive of such emotion. L16.
2 Easily moved to anger or rage; hot-tempered, irascible. LME. ▶†**b** Of a person: angry, enraged. L15–E19. ▶**c** Of an action, speech, etc.: marked by anger. L16.
3 †**a** Affected with sorrow; sad. L16–M17. ▶**b** Inclined to pity, compassionate. *obsolete* exc. *dial.* L16.
†**4** Infatuated, in love. M17–E18.

> 📖 **1** S. AUSTIN Her husband's house and garden were daily thronged with her passionate admirers. D. MACDONALD He's about as passionate as a bowl of oatmeal. WILLY RUSSELL They're young, and they're passionate about things that matter. **b** T. FULLER He made a passionate speech, to exhort them to unite. J. F. LEHMANN Glimpses of passionate devotion to his art. **2** W. COWPER A temper passionate and fierce May suddenly your joys disperse. **c** J. MCCARTHY The debates were long, fierce and often passionate.

▶**B** *ellipt.* as *noun*. A person affected with passion or strong emotion, formerly *spec.* love. *arch.* M17.
■ **passionately** *adverb* L16. **passionateness** *noun* M17.

†**passionate** *verb trans.* M16.
[formed as PASSION *verb*: see -ATE[3].]
1 = PASSION *verb* 1. M16–M17.
2 Express or perform with passion. M16–E17.

> 📖 **2** SHAKES. *Tit. A.* Thy niece and I . . cannot passionate our tenfold grief.

passion-dock /ˈpaʃ(ə)ndɒk/ *noun*. Chiefly *north.* E19.
[Alt. of ***patience-dock*** (b) s.v. PATIENCE *noun*, by assoc. with PASSION *noun*, the leaves being eaten at Passion-tide.]
The plant bistort, *Polygonum bistorta*.

passioned /ˈpaʃ(ə)nd/ *adjective*. *arch.* E16.
[from PASSION *verb*, *noun*: see -ED[1], -ED[2].]
1 Affected with passion; marked by passion. E16.
†**2** = PASSIONATE *adjective* 3. E16–M17.

Passionist /ˈpaʃ(ə)nɪst/ *noun & adjective*. E19.
[from PASSION *noun* + -IST. Cf. French *passioniste*.]
ROMAN CATHOLIC CHURCH. ▶**A** *noun*. A member of a religious order founded in Italy in the 18th cent., stressing the contemplative life and vowing to keep alive the memory of Christ's Passion. E19.
▶**B** *adjective*. Of or pertaining to a Passionist or the Passionists. M19.

passionless /ˈpaʃ(ə)nlɪs/ *adjective*. E17.
[from PASSION *noun* + -LESS.]
Lacking passion, without passion.

> 📖 A. LIVINGSTONE The ideal cohabitation: a close but passionless intellectual friendship.

■ **passionlessly** *adverb* L19. **passionlessness** *noun* M19.

passival /paˈsʌɪv(ə)l/ *adjective*. L19.
[from Latin *passivus* PASSIVE + -AL[1].]
GRAMMAR. Designating an intransitive verb with a passive meaning.

passivate /ˈpasɪveɪt/ *verb trans.* E20.
[from PASSIVE + -ATE[3].]
1 Make (metal) passive or inert, esp. by altering the surface layer, in order to prevent corrosion etc. E20.
2 Coat (a semiconductor) with inert material to protect it from contamination. M20.
■ **passiˈvation** *noun* E20. **passivator** *noun* a passivating agent M20.

passive /ˈpasɪv/ *adjective & noun*. LME.
[Old & mod. French *passif*, *-ive* or Latin *passivus*, from *pass*-: see PASSION *noun*, -IVE.]
▶**A** *adjective*. **I** †**1** Suffering; exposed to suffering. LME–M17.
2 That is the object of action; acted on or produced by an external agency. LME.
3 GRAMMAR. Designating, being in, involving, or pertaining to a voice comprising those forms of transitive verbs that attribute the action to the person or thing to whom it is directed (the logical object). Opp. ***active***. LME.
4 Not active; not participating, affecting, or influencing in some way; inert. LME. ▶**b** (Of vocabulary etc.) that is understood but not used by a person (LINGUISTICS); latent, existing but not manifest. M20.

5 *SCOTS LAW*. (Of a title to an estate) under a liability; (of an heir or executor) liable for the debts of an estate. **L16.**

6 Offering no resistance or opposition; submissive. **E17.**

📖 **2** LD MONBODDO The mind is . . merely passive, receiving like wax the impressions of external objects. BOSWELL The most common distinction was between active and passive male prostitutes. **4** H. READ A situation to which he cannot be a passive onlooker, but in which he must participate. D. LEAVITT He was merely the passive victim of a broken home. **6** A. LURIE Polly had acted falsely . . playing the passive, admiring female.

▶ **II** *techn.* **7** *MEDICINE*. Orig., characterized by sluggish or diminished flow of blood. Later, (of congestion) not directly due to local inflammation. **E19.**

8 *CHEMISTRY*. Not readily entering into chemical combination; *esp.* (of a metal) having a thin inert surface layer of oxide which prevents reaction. **M19.**

9 *LAW & COMMERCE*. (Of a debt, bond, or share) incurring no interest; (of a trust) on which the trustees have no duty to perform, nominal; (of a trade balance) unfavourable. **M19.**

10 *ELECTRONICS*. Containing no source of electromotive force. **E20.**

11 Of radar, a satellite, etc.: not generating its own signal; receiving or reflecting radiation from a transmitter, target, etc. **M20.**

12 (Of heating systems) making use of incident sunlight as an energy source; (of buildings) having such a heating system. **L20.**

Special collocations: **passive-aggressive** *adjective* (*PSYCHIATRY*) of or denoting a personality disorder in which aggression is expressed by indirect resistance to the demands of others but with avoidance of direct confrontation. **passive immunity** *MEDICINE*: resulting from antibodies that have been introduced into the body from outside. **passive matrix** *ELECTRONICS* a display system in which individual pixels are selected using two control voltages for the row and column. **passive obedience** (*a*) surrender to another's will without cooperation; (*b*) compliance with commands irrespective of their nature. **passive resistance** a non-violent refusal to cooperate, esp. with legal requirements. **passive-resister** a person who practises passive resistance. **passive sacrifice** *CHESS* (*a*) a sacrifice in which a piece attacked by an opponent's move is left to be captured; (*b*) a sacrifice that an opponent need not accept. **passive smoker** a person who suffers passive smoking. **passive smoking** the involuntary inhalation, esp. by a non-smoker, of smoke from others' cigarettes etc.

▶ **B** *noun*. **1 a** That which is acted on; a passive quality or property. **LME.** ▸**b** *LACE-MAKING*. In *pl.* The bobbins holding the threads which correspond to the warp threads in weaving. **E20.**

2 *GRAMMAR*. *The* passive voice; a passive form of a verb. **LME.**

3 A passive, unresisting, or submissive person or thing. Now *rare*. **LME.**

2 *INDIRECT passive*. *neuter passive*: see NEUTER *adjective* 1b.

■ **passively** *adverb* **LME.** **passiveness** *noun* **M17.**

passivise *verb* var. of PASSIVIZE.

passivism /ˈpasɪvɪz(ə)m/ *noun*. **E20.**
[from PASSIVE + -ISM.]
The quality or condition of being passive; *spec.* the principle or practice of using passive resistance.

passivist /ˈpasɪvɪst/ *noun*. **L19.**
[from PASSIVE + -IST.]
A person who or thing which is passive; *spec.* an adherent or practitioner of passive resistance, esp. in wartime.

passivity /paˈsɪvɪti/ *noun*. **M17.**
[from PASSIVE + -ITY.]
†**1** Ability to suffer; passibility. **M–L17.**

2 The quality or state of being acted on by an external agent; an instance of this, a passive quality. **M17.** ▸**b** *GRAMMAR*. Passive meaning or construction. **L19.**

3 Absence of activity or participation; inertness; *CHEMISTRY* the state of inactivity of a passive substance, esp. a metal. **M17.**

4 Absence of resistance or opposition; submissiveness. **L17.**

📖 **3** P. BROOK Whatever life there was on-stage was offset by the passivity . . of the audience.

passivize /ˈpasɪvʌɪz/ *verb*. Also **-ise**. **E20.**
[from PASSIVE + -IZE.]
†**1** *verb trans.* = PASSIVATE 1. Only in **E20.**

2 *verb trans.* & *intrans.* *GRAMMAR*. Convert or be convertible into the passive form. **M20.**

■ **passivizable** *adjective* (*GRAMMAR*) **L20.** **passiviˈzation** *noun* (*GRAMMAR*) **M20.**

passless /ˈpɑːslɪs/ *adjective*. **M17.**
[from PASS *noun*² + -LESS.]
1 Impassable. *poet.* **M17.**

2 Without a pass or authorization document. **E20.**

passman /ˈpɑːsmən/ *noun*. Pl. **-men**. **M19.**
[from PASS *noun*² + MAN *noun*.]
1 In some universities: a male student who reads for and takes a pass degree. *arch.* **M19.**

2 A male prisoner who is allowed to leave his cell. *slang*. **M20.**

pass-out /ˈpɑːsaʊt/ *noun*. **L19.**
[from *pass out* s.v. PASS *verb*.]
1 (A document giving) permission to leave and re-enter a theatre etc. **L19.**

2 An act of fainting or becoming unconscious; a person who has become unconscious. **M20.**

Passover /ˈpɑːsəʊvə/ *noun*. **M16.**
[In branch I from *pass over* pass without touching or affecting, translating Hebrew *pesah* (cf. PASCH); in branch II from *pass over* s.v. PASS *verb*.]
▶ **I 1** The Jewish spring festival held from the 14th to the 21st day of the month Nisan, commemorating the sparing of the Israelites from the death of their first-born and the liberation of the Israelites from Egyptian bondage (*Exodus* 12). **M16.**

2 = ***paschal lamb*** s.v. PASCHAL *adjective*. **M16.**

▶ **II** (**p-**.)

3 An act of passing over or going from one place to another. *arch.* **M17.**

4 An act of passing over or ignoring something in speech or writing; an intentional omission. *Scot. arch.* **E19.**

passport /ˈpɑːspɔːt/ *noun*. **L15.**
[French *passeport*, from *passer* PASS *verb* + *port* PORT *noun*¹.]
†**1** Authorization to pass from a port or leave a country, or to enter or pass through a country; *gen.* authorization to do anything. **L15–E17.**

2 Orig., an official document authorizing a person to travel to, from, or through a (specified) foreign country usu. under defined restrictions of time and purpose. Now, an official document issued by a government certifying the holder's identity and citizenship, and entitling the holder to travel under its protection to and from foreign countries. **M16.** ▸†**b** A permit for a pauper etc. to proceed to a specified destination and ask alms on the way. **M16–E17.** ▸**c** *NAUTICAL*. A document granted by a State to a neutral merchant ship, esp. in time of war, authorizing it to proceed without molestation in certain waters. **L16.**

3 *fig.* An authorization to pass or go anywhere; *spec.* a thing giving the right, privilege, or opportunity to enter into some state, sphere of action, etc. **L16.** ▸**b** A certificate intended to introduce or secure a person's admission; a voucher. *arch.* **L16.**

📖 **2** ***Nansen passport***: see NANSEN 1. **3** B. EMECHETA The fact that one had been to a university was the passport to a successful life. M. FORSTER He held that magic passport into the Barrett household: he was *family*.

Comb.: **passport control** (*a*) the issue or inspection of passports; (*b*) the department at a port, airport, etc., where passports are checked; **passport photo**, **passport photograph** (*a*) the identification photograph in a passport; (*b*) a photograph of the size required for passports.

■ **passportless** *adjective* **L16.**

pass-through /ˈpɑːsθruː/ *adjective* & *noun*. **M20.**
[from *pass through* s.v. PASS *verb*.]
▶ **A** *adjective*. **1** Through which something may be passed. **M20.**

2 Of costs etc.: chargeable to the customer. *US*. **L20.**

▶ **B** *noun*. **1** A passage; a means of passing through; *spec.* a hatch through which food etc. is passed. **M20.**

2 An act of passing through. **L20.**

passus /ˈpasəs/ *noun*. Pl. same. **L16.**
[Latin = step, pace.]
A section, division, or canto of a (medieval) story or poem.

passway /ˈpɑːsweɪ/ *noun*. *arch.* **E19.**
[from PASS *noun*¹ + WAY *noun*.]
A means of passing; *spec.* a (mountain) pass.

password /ˈpɑːswəːd/ *noun*. **E19.**
[from PASS *noun*² + WORD *noun*.]
1 A selected word or phrase securing admission, recognition, etc., when used by those to whom it is disclosed. **E19.**

2 *COMPUTING*. A confidential sequence of characters that has to be typed in order to gain access to a particular computer, network, etc. **M20.**

past /pɑːst, past/ *adjective* & *noun*. As adjective also †**passed**. **ME.**
[Obsolete pa. pple of PASS *verb*.]
▶ **A** *adjective*. **1** Gone by in time; elapsed, over; that existed or occurred prior to the current time. **ME.**

2 Of a period of time or a thing in a sequence: recently completed or gone by; that has just passed. **ME.**

3 Of or pertaining to a former time; *spec.* in *GRAMMAR* (of a participle or tense) expressing an action that has happened or a state that existed (cf. PRETERITE *adjective* 2). **ME.**

📖 **1** *Gentleman's Magazine* Time was; Time is: but . . lay hold on the Opportunity before the Time is past. A. HARDING Whatever . . caused her past distress, . . had no power to cloud her pleasure now. M. WARNOCK We can remember some things clearly, others, perhaps less long past, not at all. **2** J. G. BALLARD Over the past week they have excavated a rectangular pit. *Antiquity* This past October it was planned to remove one celebrated figure. **3** *Nature* A past-president of the Royal Meteorological Society. A. LURIE A few past artists whose work she might look at.

▶ **B** *noun*. **1** *The* time that has gone by, *the* time before the present. **M16.**

2 What has happened in past time. **M17.**

3 *GRAMMAR*. The past tense; a verb in the past tense. **L18.**

4 The past life or condition of a person or thing; *spec.* a discreditable one. **M19.**

📖 **1** R. MACAULAY He looked back seven years into the past. D. EDEN In the past he had had more tenacity. A. C. CLARKE This technique had never worked well in the past. **2** B. F. WESTCOTT No repentance on earth can undo the past. DAY LEWIS When I was younger . . I wished to travel light, unencumbered by the past. **4** R. LEHMANN She had a past: twice married, twice divorced. P. H. JOHNSON A dull, old-fashioned hotel that lived on its past.

Comb. & special collocations: **past definite** = ***past historic*** below; **past future** *GRAMMAR* a tense expressing an action viewed as future in relation to a given time in the past; **past historic** *GRAMMAR* a tense expressing completed action in the past; ***past perfect***: see PERFECT *adjective* 9(b), *noun* 3.

†**past** *verb pa. pple*: see PASS *verb*.

past /pɑːst/ *preposition* & *adverb*. **ME.**
[Obsolete pa. pple of PASS *verb*.]
▶ **A** *preposition*. **1** Beyond in time; beyond the age for or the time of; after; (in stating the time of day) so many minutes, or a quarter or half an hour, after a particular hour (specified or *ellipt.* understood). **ME.** ▸**b** Older than (a specified age). Also (*arch.*) *postpositive*. **M16.**

2 a Beyond in place; at or on the further side of. **ME.** ▸**b** Of (actual or implicit) motion: by, so as to pass. **M16.**

3 †**a** More than, above (in number or quantity). **LME–M17.** ▸**b** Beyond in manner or degree. Now *rare*. **E17.**

4 Beyond the reach, range, or limits of. Also (*arch.*), without. **LME.** ▸**b** Beyond the ability or power of. Chiefly in ***not put it past a person***, think (a person) quite capable of doing a specified action or behaving in a specified way. *colloq.* **E17.**

📖 **1** G. GREENE The clock said five past ten. R. RENDELL You should have been . . at home by eleven. But you didn't get in till quarter past. D. ABSE It was past two o'clock. J. WAIN A fine handsome woman, only a little past her first youth. B. PYM The bowl of hyacinths, now a little past their best. **b** O. SACKS Ninety-three—and he doesn't look a day past seventy. **2a** E. BOWEN She looked . . past him into the study. P. LARKIN For past these doors are rooms. **b** D. ABSE The sandbanks would swerve and curve past Jack Peterson's house. I. MCEWAN Caroline gathered up the tray and edged past him. G. SWIFT After leaving the churchyard, I take the minor road past Hyfield. **4** C. HARE I'm past caring. G. W. TARGET This is getting past a joke.

▶ **B** *adverb*. **1** So as to pass or go by. **E19.**

2 On one side, aside. *Scot. & N. Irish*. **M19.**

📖 **1** W. C. SMITH The tread of time as it hastens past. L. BRUCE They just nip at your heels when you ride past on your bike. **2** R. L. STEVENSON I'm prood to think ye're layin' past siller.

Phrases & comb.: ***march past***: see MARCH *noun*³. ***not to put it past a person***: see sense A.4b above. **past it** *colloq.* incompetent, incapable, or unusable by reason of age. **past oneself** (*obsolete exc. dial.*) beside oneself (with rage etc.). **past-pointing** *MEDICINE* an inability to point straight at an object or locate it accurately with the eyes closed, indicating malfunction in the cerebellum or in the labyrinth of the ear. ***past REDEMPTION***. ***past redress***: see REDRESS *noun* 2.

pasta /ˈpastə/ *noun*. **L19.**
[Italian, from late Latin: see PASTE *noun*.]
1 A type of dough made from durum wheat flour and water and extruded or stamped into particular shapes (and often dried if not for immediate use). Also, an Italian dish consisting largely of this and usu. a sauce. **L19.**

2 Marijuana. *slang*. **L20.**

pastance /ˈpast(ə)ns/ *noun*. *arch.* **L15.**
[Anglicized from French PASSE-TEMPS.]
Recreation.

paste /peɪst/ *noun* & *adjective*. **ME.**
[Old French (mod. *pâte*) from late Latin *pasta* small square piece of a medicinal preparation from Greek *pastē*, also in pl. *pasta*, *pastai* barley porridge, uses as noun of *pastos* sprinkled, from *passein* sprinkle.]
▶ **A** *noun*. **1** Flour moistened and kneaded; dough. Now only *spec.*, = PASTRY 1. Now usu. somewhat *arch.* exc. *US*. **ME.** ▸**b** Any of various soft sweet mixtures made from powdered or ground ingredients and liquid. **LME.** ▸**c** A spreadable mixture of seasoned finely ground meat, fish, etc. **E19.**

2 *gen.* Any moist but fairly stiff mixture, made esp. from a powder and liquid; *spec.* (*arch.*) a poultice. **LME.**

3 A mixture of flour, water, etc., used as an adhesive for sticking esp. wallpaper and other light materials. LME. ▸†**b** = PASTEBOARD *noun* 1. Also, a head-dress made of this. Only in 16.

4 Heavy, very clear flint glass used for making imitation gems; an imitation gem or (*collect.*) imitation gems made of this. M17.

5 *fig.* The material of which a person is said to be made. *arch.* M17.

6 A mixture of clay, water, etc., used for making pottery; *esp.* one based on kaolin for making porcelain. M18.

📖 **1c** ***anchovy-paste, meat-paste, shrimp-paste***, etc. ***Italian paste***: see ITALIAN *adjective*. **2** L. CHAMBERLAIN Cream together the egg yolk and the mustard to make a smooth paste. ***Vienna paste***: see VIENNA 1. **3** *Which?* Hang new wallpaper using a paste which incorporates a fungicide. ***scissors and paste***: see SCISSORS 1. **4** LYTTON The diamonds went to the jeweller's, and Lady Frances wore paste. T. H. WHITE The combs and brushes sparkled with ornaments in cut paste. **6** ***hard paste***: see HARD *adjective*. ***soft paste***: see SOFT *adjective*.

Comb.: **paste-bodied** *adjective* (of Chinese porcelain) made of a fine white clay; **paste grain** BOOKBINDING split sheepskin coated with paste or glue to harden it and improve the grain; **paste-wash** *noun & verb* (BOOKBINDING) (*a*) *noun* a coating of paste diluted with water, used to improve the grain of the leather; (*b*) *verb trans.* apply paste-wash to (leather) prior to decoration; **paste-water** = *paste-wash noun* above.

▶ **B** *attrib.* or as *adjective*. Made of paste; adorned with a gem or gems of paste. L18.

📖 W. IRVING High-heeled shoes . . with paste or diamond buckles.

paste /peɪst/ *verb*. M16.
[from the noun.]

1 *verb trans.* Cause to adhere (as) by means of paste; stick or fasten with paste. Also foll. by *down, on, over, together*, etc. M16. ▸**b** COMPUTING. Insert or reproduce at a new location (already existing text). Freq. assoc. with *cut*. L20.

2 *verb trans.* Cover (*over*) with material pasted on. E17.

3 *verb trans.* Beat, thrash; strike hard; CRICKET hit (a ball) hard. *slang*. M19.

📖 **1** V. WOOLF Her husband read the placards pasted on the brick. **3** *K.O.* Canizales cleaned up, pasting him with vicious shots.

Comb.: **paste-down** orig., a piece of paper used as a lining inside the cover of a book; now, the part of the endpaper which is pasted to the inside of the cover; **paste-in** a correction or illustration printed separately from the main text of a book and pasted to the margin of the relevant page by its inner edge; **paste-over** a piece of paper pasted over text to cancel it; the use of a paste-over or paste-overs; **paste-up** (*a*) a plan of a page with sections of text etc. either pasted on or represented by outlines; a document prepared for copying in this way; (*b*) *gen.* any piece of paper or card with a newspaper etc. clipping pasted on it.
■ **paster** *noun* (*a*) a person who pastes something; (*b*) a piece of adhesive paper; *spec.* an adhesive label: M18.

pasteboard /ˈpeɪs(t)bɔːd/ *noun & adjective*. E16.
[from PASTE *noun* or *verb* + BOARD *noun*.]

▶ **A** *noun*. **I 1** Stiff material made by pasting sheets of paper together (and, now, compressing them). Also (now *rare*), a piece of this, *spec.* a board or cover of a book. E16. ▸**b** *fig.* This as the type of something flimsy, unsubstantial, or counterfeit (cf. sense B.2 below). E19.

2 *slang*. **a** A visiting-card. M19. ▸**b** A playing-card. M19. ▸**c** A train ticket. M19.

▸**II 3** (Usu. with hyphen.) A board on which paste or dough is rolled out. M19.

▶ **B** *attrib.* or as *adjective*. **1** Made of pasteboard. L16.

2 *fig.* Unsubstantial; unreal, counterfeit. M17.

pastel /ˈpast(ə)l/ *noun & adjective*. L16.
[(French from) Italian *pastello* dim. of *pasta* paste from late Latin: see PASTE *noun & adjective*, -EL². In sense 1 of the noun partly from Provençal *pastel*.]

▶ **A** *noun*. **1** The plant woad, *Isatis tinctoria*; the blue dye obtained from it. L16.

2 (A crayon made of) a dry paste made from ground pigments and gum-water. L16.

3 A drawing made with a pastel or pastels. Also, the art of drawing with pastels. M19.

4 A pale and subdued shade of a colour. L19.

📖 **2 *in pastel*** drawn with a pastel or pastels.
3 M. MOORCOCK On the eggshell walls hang more pastels of the seaside.

▶ **B** *adjective*. Of a pale or subdued shade or colour. L19.

📖 P. SCOTT Pastel colours such as salmon pink.

pastellist /ˈpastəlɪst/ *noun*. Also **pastelist**. L19.
[from prec. + -IST.]
An artist who works with pastels.

pastern /ˈpast(ə)n/ *noun*. Orig. †**pastron**. ME.
[Old French *pasturon* (mod. *pâturon*), from *pasture* (dial. *pâture*) hobble, ult. from medieval Latin *pastoria*, *-orium* use as noun of fem. and neut. of Latin *pastorius* pertaining to a shepherd, formed as PASTOR.]

†**1** A shackle fixed on the foot of a horse (esp. one not broken in) or other pastured animal. ME–E17.

2 The part of a horse's foot between the fetlock and the hoof. LME. ▸**b** The corresponding part in other quadrupeds; *transf.* the human ankle. M16. ▸**c** In full ***pastern-bone***. Either of the two phalangeal bones in the foot of a horse (***upper pastern*** or ***great pastern*** and ***lower pastern*** or ***small pastern***) between the cannon-bone and the coffin-bone. E17.

Comb.: **pastern-joint** the joint or articulation between the cannon-bone and the great pastern-bone.
■ **pasterned** *adjective* having pasterns of a specified kind E17.

Pasteur /paˈstəː, *foreign* pastœːr/ *noun*. M19.
[Louis *Pasteur* (1822–95), French scientist.]
BIOCHEMISTRY & MEDICINE etc. Used *attrib.* and (formerly) in *possess.* to designate apparatus and methods devised by Pasteur and effects discovered by him.
Pasteur effect the inhibition of fermentation by oxygen, in favour of respiration. **Pasteur flask** a glass flask with an elongated neck bent downwards to reduce the entry of microorganisms from the air. **Pasteur pipette** a glass pipette which at one end has a rubber bulb and at the other terminates as a capillary tube; orig. *spec.* a sterilized pipette of this kind. **Pasteur treatment** = PASTEURISM.

pasteurella /pɑːstəˈrɛlə, -stjə-, pa-/ *noun*. Pl. **-llae** /-liː/, **-llas**. E20.
[mod. Latin, from prec. + -ELLA after *salmonella*.]
BACTERIOLOGY. A small rodlike Gram-negative bacterium of the genus *Pasteurella*, which includes those causing plague and other acute infectious diseases in people and warm-blooded animals.

pasteurellosis /ˌpɑːstərɛˈləʊsɪs, pa-/ *noun*. Pl. **-lloses** /-ˈləʊsiːz/. E20.
[from prec. + -OSIS.]
MEDICINE & VETERINARY MEDICINE. An infection produced by a bacterium of the genus *Pasteurella*.

pasteurise *verb* var. of PASTEURIZE.

Pasteurism /ˈpastərɪz(ə)m, -stjə-, ˈpɑː-/ *noun*. L19.
[from PASTEUR + -ISM.]
MEDICINE. A therapeutic method, esp. for rabies, involving successive inoculations with attenuated virus gradually increasing in virulence. Also called ***Pasteur treatment***.

pasteurize /ˈpɑːstʃəraɪz, -stjə-, ˈpas-/ *verb trans.* Also **-ise**. L19.
[from PASTEUR + -IZE.]
Subject (milk, wine, etc.) to a process of partial sterilization, usu. involving heat treatment or irradiation, so as to kill most of the micro-organisms present, making it safe for consumption and improving its keeping quality. Freq. as ***pasteurized*** *ppl adjective*.
■ **pasteuriˈzation** *noun* L19. **pasteurizer** *noun* an apparatus for pasteurizing milk L19.

pasticcio /paˈstɪtʃəʊ/ *noun*. Pl. **-os**. M18.
[Italian = pie, pasty, from Proto-Romance, from late Latin *pasta* PASTE *noun*.]
= PASTICHE *noun*.

pastiche /paˈstiːʃ/ *noun & verb*. L19.
[French formed as prec.]

▶ **A** *noun*. A medley of various things; *spec.* (*a*) a picture or a musical composition made up of pieces derived from or imitating various sources; (*b*) a literary or other work of art composed in the style of a well-known author, artist, etc. L19.

📖 R. GITTINGS Nearly every poem . . was a pastiche of a different poet. *Ashmolean* A 17th century pastiche made up from . . two different Roman statues.

▶ **B** *verb trans. & intrans.* Copy or imitate the style of (an artist, author, etc.). M20.

pasticheur /pastiːˈʃəː/ *noun*. E20.
[French, from prec. + *-eur* -OR.]
An artist who imitates the style of another artist.

pastie /ˈpeɪsti/ *noun*. *slang*. M20.
[from PASTE *verb* + -IE.]
A decorative covering for the nipple worn by a stripper. Usu. in *pl.*

pastiglia /paˈstiːʎa, paˈstiːlɪə/ *noun*. E20.
[Italian = paste.]
Intricately moulded gesso used in the decoration of furniture, caskets, etc., in Renaissance Italy.

pastil *noun* var. of PASTILLE.

pastillage /ˈpastɪlɪdʒ, *foreign* pastijaːʒ/ *noun*. E20.
[French, lit. 'compression of paste into blocks'.]
CERAMICS. Decoration consisting of slip dribbled from a thin tube or a spouted vessel.

pastille /ˈpast(ə)l, -tɪl/ *noun*. Also **pastil**. M17.
[French from Latin *pastillus* little loaf or roll, lozenge, dim. of *panis* loaf.]

1 A small pellet of aromatic paste burnt as a perfume or as a fumigator, deodorizer, or disinfectant. M17.

2 A small flat, usually round, sweet, often coated with sugar and sometimes medicated; a lozenge. M17. ▸**b** MEDICINE. A small disc of barium platinocyanide whose gradual change of colour when exposed to X-rays was formerly used as an indication of the dose delivered. E20.

Comb.: **pastille burner** an ornamental ceramic container in which to burn aromatic pastilles.

pastime /ˈpɑːstʌɪm/ *noun & verb*. L15.
[from PASS *verb* + TIME *noun*.]

▶ **A** *noun*. **1** That which serves to pass the time agreeably; recreation. *arch.* L15.

2 A particular form of (enjoyable) recreation; a hobby; a sport, a game. L15.

†**3** A passing or elapsing of time; a space of time. L15–E16.

📖 **1** T. HARDY The children had been given this Friday afternoon for pastime. **2** K. CLARK Generations of amateurs have indulged in the civilised pastime of book collecting. A. HARDING I should like to . . make drawing or painting the means of supporting myself, rather than mere pastimes.

▶ **B** *verb*. †**1** *verb intrans.* Pass one's time pleasantly; amuse oneself. Only in 16. ▸†**b** *verb trans.* Divert, amuse. Only in L16.

2 *verb trans.* Amuse oneself with. *rare*. M19.

†**pastinate** *verb trans.* LME–M18.
[Latin *pastinat-* pa. ppl stem of *pastinare* dig: see -ATE³.]
Dig, esp. in preparation for planting.

pastiness /ˈpeɪstɪnɪs/ *noun*. E17.
[from PASTY *adjective* + -NESS.]
The quality or condition of being pasty.

pasting /ˈpeɪstɪŋ/ *noun*. L16.
[from PASTE *verb* + -ING¹.]

1 The action of PASTE *verb*. L16.

2 A beating, a thrashing. *slang*. M19.

pastis /ˈpastɪs, paˈstiːs/ *noun*. E20.
[French.]
(A drink of) a liqueur flavoured with aniseed.

pastless /ˈpɑːstlɪs/ *adjective*. M20.
[from PAST *noun* + -LESS.]
Having no past or no history.

past master /pɑːst ˈmɑːstə/ *noun phr.* Also **past-master**. M18.
[In sense 1 from PAST *adjective* + MASTER *noun*¹; in sense 2 later spelling of PASSED-MASTER.]

1 A person who has filled the office of master in a guild, Freemasons' lodge, etc. M18.

2 A person who is especially adept or expert in a (specified) subject or activity. Cf. next. L19.

📖 **2** L. P. HARTLEY Harold . . proved himself a past-master of intrigue.

past mistress /pɑːst ˈmɪstrɪs/ *noun*. M19.
[Cf. PAST MASTER 2.]
A woman who is especially adept or expert in a (specified) subject or activity.

pastness /ˈpɑːstnɪs/ *noun*. E19.
[from PAST *adjective* + -NESS.]
The state or condition of being past; the quality or fact of being (connected with) the past.

📖 T. S. ELIOT The historical sense involves a perception, not only of the pastness of the past, but of its presence. M. WARNOCK To be a memory . . an image must be accompanied by . . a feeling of pastness.

pastophorus /paˈstɒf(ə)rəs/ *noun*. Pl. **-ri** /-rʌɪ, -riː/. Also Anglicized as **pastophor** /ˈpastə(ʊ)fɔː/. M17.
[Latin from Greek *pastophoros*, from *pastos* shrine + *-phoros* carrying.]
Hist. In ancient Egypt, a priest of an order responsible for carrying the shrines of gods in procession.
■ **pastophorium** /pastə(ʊ)ˈfɔːrɪəm/ *noun*, pl. **-ia** /-ɪə/, the apartment of the pastophori in a temple M18.

pastor /ˈpɑːstə/ *noun & verb*. ME.
[Anglo-Norman, Old French *pastour* (mod. *pasteur*) accus. of *pastre* (mod. *pâtre* shepherd) from Latin *pastor*, from *past-* pa. ppl stem of *pascere* feed, graze: see -OR. In sense 1 later infl. in US by Spanish *pastor*.]

▶ **A** *noun*. **1** A herdsman, a shepherd. Now *rare* exc. *US*. ME.

2 A person who has the spiritual care of a body of Christians, as a bishop, priest, minister, etc.; *spec.* a minister in charge of a church or congregation, esp. in some non-episcopal Churches. ME.

3 *gen.* Any person exercising protective care or guidance over a group of people. ME.

4 ORNITHOLOGY. In full ***rose-coloured pastor***. A pink and black Eurasian starling, *Sturnus roseus*. E19.

▶ **B** *verb*. †**1** *verb trans.* Look after as a herdsman or shepherd. *rare*. Only in L16.

2 *verb trans. & intrans.* Have the spiritual care of (a congregation) as pastor; be minister of (a church). E17.
■ **pastorage** *noun* (*rare*) †(*a*) spiritual care, oversight, or guidance; (*b*) a pastor's house: M17. **pastorly** *adjective* of, pertaining to, or befitting a pastor E17. **pastorship** *noun* the position of pastor; the function or tenure of a pastor: M16.

pastoral /ˈpɑːst(ə)r(ə)l/ *adjective & noun*. LME.
[Latin *pastoralis*, from PASTOR: see -AL[1].]
▶ **A** *adjective*. **I 1** Of or pertaining to shepherds or their occupation; pertaining to or occupied in sheep or cattle farming. LME. ▸**b** (Of land) used for pasture; (of scenery, a landscape, etc.) having the simplicity or natural charm associated with pastureland. L18.
2 Of literature, music, or works of art: portraying rural life or the life of shepherds, esp. in an idealized or romantic form. L16.

1 C. S. LEWIS The change from . . a pastoral to an agricultural economy. *Auckland Star* Criticized the Government . . when it . . refused pastoral farmers shortterm help. **b** M. GIROUARD A setting of woods . . and gently swelling hills, a pastoral landscape. **2** R. CHRISTIANSEN The idyllic blue-skied world of classical pastoral poetry.

▶ **II 3** Of or pertaining to a pastor or the spiritual care of a congregation. LME. ▸**b** Of or pertaining to a teacher's responsibility for giving moral care or guidance. M20.

3 W. RAEPER He had no pastoral duties . . but only appeared on Sunday to preach. **b** *Times Educ. Suppl.* A clear separation between the academic and the pastoral sides of school life.

Special collocations: **pastoral epistles** CHRISTIAN CHURCH the books of the New Testament comprising the letter of Paul to Timothy and that to Titus. **pastoral lease** *Austral. & NZ* a lease of land for sheep or cattle farming. **pastoral letter** CHRISTIAN CHURCH an official letter from a bishop to all the clergy or members of his or her diocese. **pastoral staff** ECCLESIASTICAL a bishop's crosier. **pastoral theology** CHRISTIAN CHURCH: considering religious truth in relation to spiritual needs.

▶ **B** *noun*. **I 1** A book on the cure of souls. LME.
2 ECCLESIASTICAL. A pastoral staff. M17.
3 CHRISTIAN CHURCH. A pastoral letter. M19.
4 CHRISTIAN CHURCH. In *pl*. The pastoral epistles. E20.
▶ **II** †**5** A pastoral game or pastime. *rare*. L16–E17.
6 A pastoral poem, play, picture, etc. L16. ▸**b** MUSIC. = PASTORALE. M18.
7 Pastoral poetry as a form or style of literary composition. L16.

■ **pastoˈrality** *noun* (now *rare*) (*a*) the quality of being pastoral; (*b*) a ceramic pastoral figure: E19. **pastoraliˈzation** *noun* the fact or process of pastoralizing land, esp. industrial land M20. **pastoralize** *verb trans.* (*a*) make (land) rural or agricultural; (*b*) celebrate in a pastoral poem etc.: E19. **pastorally** *adverb* M18. **pastoralness** *noun* L19.

pastorale /pastəˈrɑːl, -ˈrɑːli/ *noun*. Pl. **-les**, **-li** /-li/. E18.
[Italian, use as noun of *pastorale* adjective 'pastoral'.]
MUSIC. **1** A slow instrumental composition in compound time, often with drone notes in the bass suggestive of a shepherd's bagpipes. E18.
2 A simple musical play with a rural subject. L19.

pastoralia /pɑːstəˈreɪlɪə/ *noun pl.* E18.
[Latin, neut. pl. of *pastoralis* PASTORAL: see -IA[2].]
Spiritual care or guidance as a subject of theological study; the duties of a pastor.

M. SULLIVAN The new Warden . . gave . . a full course in Pastoralia.

pastoralism /ˈpɑːst(ə)r(ə)lɪz(ə)m/ *noun*. M19.
[from PASTORAL *adjective* + -ISM.]
1 The pastoral style in literature etc. M19.
2 The practice of tending animals, *esp.* sheep or cattle. M20.

pastoralist /ˈpɑːst(ə)r(ə)lɪst/ *noun*. L18.
[formed as prec. + -IST.]
1 A writer of pastorals. L18.
2 A person whose occupation is tending animals; *spec.* (*Austral. & NZ*) a sheep or cattle farmer. L19.

pastorate /ˈpɑːst(ə)rət/ *noun*. L18.
[from PASTOR *noun* + -ATE[1].]
1 The position or office of pastor; the tenure of a pastor. L18.
2 A body of pastors; pastors collectively. M19. ▸**b** An organization in some university cities, esp. Oxford and Cambridge, based on an Anglican church and devoted to the spiritual care and guidance of undergraduates. L19.

pastorela /pastəˈrɛlə/ *noun*. L19.
[Provençal, Portuguese, ult. formed as PASTORAL.]
= PASTOURELLE.

pastorie /pɑːstʊˈriː/ *noun*. *S. Afr.* M20.
[Afrikaans from Dutch from medieval Latin *pastoria*.]
The residence of a pastor of one of the Dutch Reformed Churches.

†**pastoritial** *adjective*. *rare*. M17–E18.
[from Latin *pastoritius*, *-icius* (from PASTOR) + -AL[1].]
= PASTORAL *adjective*.

pastose /paˈstəʊs/ *adjective*. E20.
[Italian *pastoso* doughy, formed as PASTA: see -OSE[1].]
ART. Thickly painted.
■ **pastosity** /-ˈstɒs-/ *noun* L18.

pastourelle /pasturɛl (*pl. same*), pastʊˈrɛl/ *noun*. L19.
[French, fem. of *pastoureau* shepherd.]
A medieval lyric whose theme is love for a shepherdess.

pastrami /paˈstrɑːmi/ *noun*. M20.
[Yiddish from Romanian *pastramă*, prob. of Turkish origin.]
Highly seasoned smoked beef, usu. served in thin slices.

attrib.: D. BARTHELME He . . buys a pastrami sandwich at the deli.

†**pastron** *noun* see PASTERN.

pastry /ˈpeɪstri/ *noun*. LME.
[from PASTE *noun* after Old French *pastaierie*, from *pastaier* pastry-cook: see -RY.]
1 Flour mixed with fat and water (and occas. other ingredients) to form a dough used as a base and covering for pies etc; this substance after having been baked. (*rare* before 19.) LME.
2 a *collect.* Articles of food, esp. cakes, made wholly or partly of pastry. M16. ▸**b** A small confection made wholly or partly of pastry. E20.
3 A place where pastry is made. *obsolete* exc. *Hist.* L16.
†**4** The art or skill of a person who makes pastry. E–M18.

1 DICKENS Tarts wherein the raspberry jam coyly withdrew itself . . behind a lattice-work of pastry. F. DALE Roll out the pastry thinly. ***puff pastry***, ***shortcrust pastry***, etc. **2b** E. FEINSTEIN The . . almond pastries at Gerbo's café. ***Danish pastry***: see DANISH *adjective*.

Comb.: **pastry-cook** a person whose occupation is the making of pastry or pastries, esp. for public sale; **pastry cream** a thick, creamy custard used as a filling for cakes or flans.

pasturable /ˈpɑːstʃərəb(ə)l/ *adjective*. LME.
[from PASTURE *noun* or *verb* + -ABLE.]
That may be pastured; fit for or affording pasture.

pasturage /ˈpɑːstʃərɪdʒ/ *noun*. E16.
[Old French (mod. *pâturage*), formed as PASTURE *noun* + -AGE.]
1 The action or occupation of pasturing animals. E16.
2 = PASTURE *noun* 1. E16.
3 Pasture-land; a piece of grazing land. E16.
4 SCOTS LAW. The servitude right of pasture. L16.

1 H. MARTINEAU This soil was not . . fit for pasturage. **2** J. RUSKIN A waste of barren rock, with pasturage only for a few goats. **3** *Environment Now* Woody country . . intermixed with patches of pasturage.

pasture /ˈpɑːstʃə/ *noun*. ME.
[Old French (mod. *pâture*) from late Latin *pastura*, from Latin *past-* pa. ppl stem of *pascere* feed, pasture: see -URE.]
1 The grass or herbage eaten by grazing animals, esp. cattle or sheep. ME.
2 A piece of land covered with grass used or suitable for the grazing of animals, esp. cattle or sheep; pasture-land. ME.
3 The action of an animal feeding. *rare*. ME.
†**4** Food; nourishment, sustenance. *lit. & fig.* LME–L18.

1 *Maclean's Magazine* Lighter spring run-offs . . cause dry pasturelands. That means less pasture for livestock. **2** *Times* Sheep that were rapidly transferred back from good pasture to poorer hill grazing. M. MOORCOCK The . . pig herd was rumoured to be moving back to its old pastures. *fig.*: *Age (Melbourne)* Money would pour out of the country to find greener pastures elsewhere. ***permanent pasture***: see PERMANENT *adjective*. **put out to pasture** *fig.* retire.

Comb.: **pasture-land** grassland used or suitable for the grazing of animals.
■ **pastural** *adjective* M16.

pasture /ˈpɑːstʃə/ *verb*. LME.
[Old French *pasturer* (mod. *pâturer*), formed as prec.]
1 *verb intrans.* = GRAZE *verb*[1] 1. LME.
2 *verb trans.* = GRAZE *verb*[1] 2. LME.
3 *verb trans.* = GRAZE *verb*[1] 3. Also, use (land) as pasture. LME.

3 *National Observer (US)* It's a pleasant drive over rolling hills and through pastured valleys.

■ **pasturer** *noun* (*rare*) a person who pastures animals LME. **pasturing** *noun* (*a*) the action of the verb; (*b*) pasturage, pasture-land: M16.

pasty /ˈpasti, ˈpeɪsti/ *noun*. ME.
[Old French *pastée*, *pasté* (mod. *pâté(e)*), ult. from late Latin *pasta* PASTE *noun*: see -Y[5].]
Orig., a pie made of seasoned meat, esp. game, in a pastry crust, baked without a dish. Now, a small pastry parcel containing a sweet or esp. savoury filling, baked without a dish to shape it.
cheese pasty, ***meat pasty***, etc. ***Cornish pasty***: see CORNISH *adjective*.

pasty /ˈpeɪsti/ *adjective*. E17.
[from PASTE *noun* + -Y[1].]
Of, like, or covered with paste or pastry; *esp.* of the colour of pastry, pale and dull; having a complexion that is unhealthily pale.

M. SPARK Gardnor's face . . looked pasty, as if he had eaten something that disagreed with him. P. DICKINSON He . . stood looking at her, a pasty pudgy kid in specs.

pat /pat/ *noun*[1]. LME.
[Orig. prob. imit.; later from the verb.]
▶ **I** A noise or action.
1 A blow with a flat or blunt surface. *obsolete* exc. *dial.* LME.
2 The sound made by striking something lightly with a flat object; *spec.* the sound of a light footstep or footsteps. L17.
3 A light stroke or tap with a flat object, esp. to flatten or smooth something, or with the hand or fingers as a sign of affection, approbation, etc. E19.

2 M. O. W. OLIPHANT The pat of those footsteps which scarcely touched the ground. **3** A. FRANCE Very reassuring to have the occasional friendly pat on the arm. **pat on the back** a gesture, word, etc., of approval or congratulation.

▶ **II** A physical object.
4 A small flattish mass of a soft substance (esp. butter) shaped (as) by patting it. M18. ▸**b** *transf.* A thing resembling a pat of butter etc. in shape and size or appearance; *spec.* a roundish patch of dung. M19.
4b ***cow-pat***: see COW *noun*[1].

Pat /pat/ *noun*[2]. *slang*. In sense 2 usu. **p-**. E19.
[Abbreviation of male forename *Patrick*.]
1 (A nickname for) an Irishman. Cf. PADDY *noun*[2]. E19.
2 [Abbreviation of PAT MALONE.] ***one*** ***one's Pat***, on one's own, alone. Chiefly *Austral.* E20.

pat /pat/ *verb & adverb*[1]. M16.
[from or rel. to PAT *noun*[1].]
▶ **A** *verb*. Infl. **-tt-**.
†**1** *verb trans.* Throw or drop (an object) *upon* a surface. *rare*. Only in M16.
2 *verb trans.* Hit or strike with a flat or blunt implement. Also, set in motion in this way. Now chiefly *dial.* L16.
3 *verb trans. & intrans.* Tap or beat lightly on (a surface), esp. so as to produce a gentle sound. E17. ▸**b** *verb intrans.* Walk or run with light footsteps. Cf. PAD *verb*[1] 2b. E17.
4 *verb trans.* Strike lightly and repeatedly with the hand or a flat surface so as to shape or make flat or smooth; tap gently with a piece of absorbent material so as to make dry. E17.
5 *verb trans.* Gently strike or tap (a person etc.) with the open hand or the fingertips, esp. as a sign of affection, sympathy, congratulation, etc. Also, lightly strike (a pocket, clothing, etc.) in this way in order to feel what may be inside. E18.

3 M. SPARK A light rain had started to pat the windows. **4** M. WARNER You mix the dough, then you pat it into shape. **5** W. CATHER As she bent forward . . she patted his cheek. R. K. NARAYAN Gajapathi put his arm round Chandrau's shoulders and patted him. R. WARNER As one might pat, somewhat absent-mindedly, a dog. JULIAN GLOAG He . . patted his pockets in search of matches. P. FARMER She had a stomach problem, Frau Seyffertitz told us, patting her plump belly. **pat on the back** *fig.* congratulate, express approval of the actions of.

Comb.: **pat-a-cake** [the first words of a nursery rhyme chanted to accompany the action] a children's game of gently clapping the hands together; **pat-ball** (*a*) a simple ball game played between two players; (*b*) *derog.* (esp. slow or tactical) lawn tennis.
▶ **B** *adverb*. With a patting sound. Usu. redupl. L17.

R. BLOOMFIELD Still on, pat, pat, the Goblin went.

pat /pat/ *adverb*[2] *& adjective*. L16.
[App. rel. to PAT *noun*[1], *verb & adverb*.]
▶ **A** *adverb*. In a manner that exactly fits the purpose or occasion; appositely, opportunely. Also, too readily, too promptly; glibly, facilely. L16.

E. FIGES It has all come so pat, been accepted so passively. **have pat**, **have down pat**, **have off pat** know or have memorized perfectly. **stand pat** (chiefly *N. Amer.*) (*a*) abide stubbornly by one's decision or opinion; (*b*) POKER retain one's hand as dealt.

▶ **B** *adjective*. That comes exactly to the purpose; apposite, opportune; (of words etc.) known thoroughly, memorized. Also, glib, facile. M17.

THACKERAY Backing his opinion with a score of pat sentences from Greek and Roman authorities. G. SAYER Cooke considered his apparent logicality as pat oversimplification. **pat hand** POKER a hand which is of sufficient value to play as it is dealt.

¶ In some uses the part of speech is indeterminate.

Pat. *abbreviation*.
Patent.

pata /ˈpʌtə/ *noun*. M20.
[Sanskrit *paṭa*.]
Cloth, canvas; *esp.* (an example of) an ancient form of Indian painting typically executed on a strip of cloth or scroll of canvas.

pataca /pəˈtɑːkə/ *noun*. L19.
[Spanish & Portuguese.]
1 *Hist.* = PATACOON. L19.
2 The basic monetary unit of Macao (and formerly of Timor). E20.

patache /pəˈtɑːtʃeɪ, *in sense 2* pəˈtɑːʃ/ *noun*. L16.
[French or Spanish from Arab. *baṭāš* large two-masted ship.]
Hist. **1** A small Spanish ship for communicating between the vessels of a fleet. L16.
2 A small public conveyance formerly used in France. M19.

patacoon /patəˈkuːn/ *noun*. L16.
[Spanish *patacon* from Portuguese *patacão* augm. of *pataca* piece of eight, dollar: see -OON.]
Hist. A Portuguese and Spanish silver coin, current in the 17th and 18th cents.

patagium /pəˈteɪdʒɪəm/ *noun*. Pl. **-ia** /-ɪə/. E19.
[Latin = gold edging on a tunic.]
1 ENTOMOLOGY. Either of a pair of lateral processes on the prothorax of certain insects. Also called ***shoulder-lappet***. E19.
2 ZOOLOGY. A fold of skin along the side of the body of a gliding mammal which can be extended to act as a parachute; the wing-membrane of a bat; the fold of skin enclosing the upper wing muscles of a bird. L19.
■ **patagial** *adjective* L19.

Patagonian /patəˈgəʊnɪən/ *noun & adjective*. M18.
[from *Patagonia* (see below) + -IAN.]
▶ **A** *noun*. Orig., a member of a S. American Indian people inhabiting the region of Patagonia in southern Argentina, said to be the tallest known people. Later, any native or inhabitant of this region. Formerly also *fig.*, a giant, a gigantic example of a thing. M18.
▶ **B** *adjective*. Of or pertaining to Patagonia or its inhabitants. Formerly also, gigantic, immense. M18.
Patagonian cavy, **Patagonian hare** either of two large cavies, *Dolichotis patagonum* and *D. salinicola*, of central S. America; also called *mara*.
■ †**Patagon** *noun* = PATAGONIAN *noun* L16–L18.

pataka /ˈpɑːtʌkə/ *noun*. M19.
[Maori.]
A Maori storehouse for food, raised on posts.

patamar *noun* var. of PATTAMAR.

patana /ˈpat(ə)nə/ *noun*. M19.
[Sinhalese.]
In Sri Lanka: an area of grassland occurring at high elevation.

pataphysics /patəˈfɪzɪks/ *noun*. M20.
[from Greek *ta epi ta metaphusika* lit. 'the (works) imposed on the Metaphysics'.]
The notional branch of knowledge that deals with a realm additional to metaphysics, a concept introduced by Alfred Jarry (1873–1907), French writer and dramatist of the absurd.
■ **pataphysical** *adjective* M20.

Patarin /ˈpatərɪn, -iːn/ *noun & adjective*. Also **-ene** /-iːn/. E18.
[French, or medieval Latin pl. *Patarini*, prob. from *Pattaria*, the ragmen's quarter of Milan.]
ECCLESIASTICAL HISTORY. ▶**A** *noun*. A member of a group of craftsmen, peasants, etc., in 11th-cent. Milan who opposed clerical concubinage and marriage. E18.
▶ **B** *adjective*. Designating or pertaining to the Patarins or their beliefs. E20.

patart /ˈpatɑːt/ *noun*. L16.
[Old French.]
Hist. A copper coin formerly used in Flanders and Picardy, current from the 16th to the 18th cents.

patas /pəˈtɑː/ *noun*. M18.
[Senegalese French from Wolof *pata*.]
More fully ***patas monkey***. A monkey, *Erythrocebus patas*, of grassland and savannahs in sub-Saharan Africa. Also called ***red monkey***.

Patau's syndrome /ˈpataʊz ˌsɪndrəʊm/ *noun phr*. Also **Patau syndrome**. M20.
[K. *Patau*, 20th-cent. German physician.]
MEDICINE. A congenital condition due to trisomy of chromosome 13, 14, or 15, marked by malformations of the brain and other parts and usu. fatal soon after birth.

Patavinian /patəˈvɪnɪən/ *noun*. L18.
[from Latin *Patavinus* of Patavinium + -IAN.]
Hist. A native or inhabitant of the Roman town of Patavium (now Padua); *esp.* the Roman historian Livy.
■ Also †**Patavin** *noun*: only in E17.

Patavinity /patəˈvɪnɪti/ *noun*. E17.
[Latin *patavinitas*, formed as prec.: see -ITY.]
The dialectal characteristics of the Latin of Patavium (now Padua), esp. as found in Livy's writings; *gen.* (a) provincialism in style.

patch /patʃ/ *noun*¹. LME.
[Perh. from Anglo-Norman var. of Old French *pieche* dial. var. of *piece* PIECE *noun*.]
1 *gen.* A piece of some material put or fastened on to repair, strengthen, or protect a weak or damaged area. LME. ▶**b** A piece of plaster etc. put over a wound or scar. LME. ▶**c** A pad or piece of material worn to shield or protect an injured eye. L16. ▶**d** A piece of cloth sewn on a uniform as a badge. L19. ▶**e** An adhesive piece of drug-impregnated material worn on the skin so that the drug may be absorbed gradually over a period of time. L20.
2 A small scrap, piece, or remnant of something; *spec.* any of the pieces of cloth used to make up a patchwork. E16.
3 *Hist.* A small piece of black silk worn for adornment on the face in the 17th and 18th cents. L16.
4 A portion of a surface of recognizably different appearance or character from the rest; *spec.* (the contents of) a small piece or area of ground. L16. ▶**b** A roughly circular area of floating pieces of ice. E19. ▶**c** An area assigned to a police officer or patrolled by a particular person or group, esp. a police officer or social worker; *fig.* an area of responsibility. *colloq.* M20.
5 A piece of greased cloth or leather used as wadding for a rifle-ball or to clean the bore. M19.
6 A temporary electrical connection. M19. ▶**b** COMPUTING. A small piece of code inserted into a program to improve its functioning or to correct a fault. M20. ▶**c** MUSIC. A (usu. pre-set) configuration of the controls of a synthesizer. L20.
7 A period of time having a specified characteristic or quality. E20.

> 📖 **1** R. KIPLING A paper patch was slapped over the bullet hole. R. DAHL He wore . . a brown tweed jacket with patches all over it. **c** C. POTOK He wore a thick bandage over his . . eye in place of the black patch. **d** R. B. PARKER A fatigue jacket with . . a Seventh Division patch. **2** T. ARNOLD Much of ancient history consists . . of patches put together . . without any redaction. **4** E. WAUGH He . . gazed towards the patch of deepening shadow. J. GARDAM Never been farther than the rhubarb patch in ten years. P. AUSTER The university housing project with its patches of green grass. U. HOLDEN Damp patches showed under her armpits. **c** M. EDWARDES The management . . said that things were not so bad in their patch. **7** C. CONNOLLY Poetry has gone through a bad patch. S. BRETT I had a long patch out of work.

Phrases: **not a patch on** *colloq.* in no way comparable to. ***of shreds and patches***: see SHRED *noun*. **PEYER'S PATCH**. ***purple patch***: see PURPLE *adjective & noun*.
Comb.: **patch-board** a plugboard, *esp.* one in an analogue computer; **patch-box** *Hist.* a usu. highly decorated box for holding patches for the face; **patch cord** an insulated lead with a plug at each end, used to connect the sockets of a patch-board or different pieces of electronic apparatus; **patch fox** a yellowish N. American variety of the red fox with a cross-shaped patch across the shoulders; **patch lead** = ***patch cord*** above; **patch panel** = ***patch-board*** above; **patch-plug** = ***patch cord*** above; **patch pocket** a pocket which is sewn on to the outside of a garment; **patch reef** a small isolated platform of coral; **patch test** MEDICINE a test for determining sensitivity to a substance by applying it as a patch to a patient's skin and noting whether erythema is produced; **patch-test** *verb trans.* (MEDICINE) subject to a patch test.

patch /patʃ/ *noun*². *obsolete* exc. *dial.* M16.
[Perh. Anglicized from Italian *pazzo*.]
Orig., a foolish person, a simpleton; a jester, a clown. Later, an ill-tempered person, esp. a child (cf. CROSSPATCH).
■ †**patchery** *noun*¹ foolish conduct; roguery, knavery: M16–E17.

patch /patʃ/ *verb*. LME.
[from PATCH *noun*¹.]
1 *verb trans.* Apply a patch or patches to, in order to repair, strengthen, protect, etc. Also, (of a thing) serve as a patch to. Freq. foll. by *up*. LME. ▶**b** *fig.* Repair or make whole, esp. hastily or in a makeshift manner; settle (a quarrel). Usu. foll. by *up*. L16.
2 *verb trans.* Make up by joining pieces together as in patchwork; *esp.* put together hastily or insecurely. Freq. foll. by *together, up*. E16. ▶**b** Join, piece together. Now *rare* or *obsolete*. M17.
3 *verb trans.* **a** Apply as a patch to something; *fig.* incorporate clumsily or badly. M16. ▶**b** Diversify or variegate with contrasting patches. Usu. in *pass.* L16.
4 *verb trans. & intrans. Hist.* Adorn (the face) with patches. Usu. in *pass.* L17.
5 ELECTRICITY. **a** *verb trans. & intrans.* Connect or be connected by a temporary electrical connection. Also foll. by *in, into*. E20. ▶**b** *verb trans.* Represent or simulate by means of temporary connections. M20.
6 *verb trans.* COMPUTING. Correct or improve (a program, routine, etc.) by inserting patches. M20.

> 📖 **1** B. MALAMUD He repaired his socks and patched his old shirts. N. GORDIMER Two pairs of windows with cardboard patching broken panes. **b** E. BOWEN It was up to him to . . patch things up. J. BARNES They sent men off to fight, then they patched them up. **2** R. P. JHABVALA Huts patched together out of mud and old boards. A. N. WILSON Styles . . found in village churches: real Gothic . . patched up with Tractarian Gothic. **3a** *Independent* The builders simply patched the new domestic system into the one that already served the farmyard. **b** K. MANSFIELD Tussock grass patched with purple orchids. **5a** T. PYNCHON Wagner and . . Wolf were patched into speakers from . . the radio shack.

Comb.: **patch-up** *noun & adjective* (an action) executed in a hasty or makeshift manner.
■ **patcher** *noun* a person who patches something, esp. to repair clothes etc. E16. **patchery** *noun*² (*a*) the action of the verb; (*b*) a thing put together from pieces or fragments, a patchwork (*lit.* & *fig.*): L16. **patching** *noun* (*a*) the action of the verb; an instance of this; (*b*) patchers collectively: LME.

patchouli /ˈpatʃʊli, pəˈtʃuːli/ *noun*. Also **-ouly**. M19.
[Tamil *paccuḷi*.]
1 Either of two Indo-Malayan labiate shrubs, *Pogostemon cablin* and *P. heyneanus*, whose leaves yield an essential oil much used in perfumery. M19.
2 Perfume prepared from this plant. M19.
■ **patchoulied** *adjective* (*poet.*) perfumed with patchouli E20.

patchwork /ˈpatʃwəːk/ *noun, adjective, & verb*. L17.
[from PATCH *noun*¹ or *verb* + WORK *noun*.]
▶ **A** *noun*. **1** A thing composed of pieces or fragments put together, esp. in a makeshift or incongruous manner; a medley, a jumble. Now usu. taken as *fig.* use of sense A.2. L17.
2 A piece of needlework consisting of small pieces of various fabrics, differing in colour and pattern, and sometimes size and shape, sewn together to form one article, esp. a quilt, cushion, etc. E18.

> 📖 **1** M. SEYMOUR Crane's stories . . were an impenetrable patchwork of truth and fantasy.

▶ **B** *adjective*. **1** Composed of miscellaneous pieces or fragments. Now usu. taken as *fig.* use of sense B.2. E18.
2 Of a quilt etc.: formed out of patchwork; put together from patches. M19.

> 📖 **1** W. TAYLOR Second-hand minds and patchwork intellects. **2** A. UTTLEY A patchwork quilt for Joshua's bed. *fig.*: H. WOUK Yellow-and-green patchwork fields.

▶ **C** *verb*. **1** *verb trans.* Assemble (pieces) haphazardly; make by haphazardly putting together items; cobble together. M20.
2 *verb trans.* In *pass.* Be scattered with areas of contrasting colour or appearance. L20.
3 *verb intrans.* Make patchworks. L20.

> 📖 **1** A. S. BYATT Texts from which Simmonds had patchworked his theory of the universe. **2** *Guardian* The fields . . are patchworked with buttercups. **3** R. GODDEN Lots of our mothers patchworked to make the quilts.

■ **patchworker** *noun* a maker of patchwork M19. **patchworky** *adjective* resembling or suggestive of patchwork L19.

patchy /ˈpatʃi/ *adjective*. L18.
[from PATCH *noun*¹ + -Y¹.]
Consisting of or having many patches; uneven in quality. Also, occurring only in patches; irregular, inconsistent.

> 📖 E. NESBIT I will write a paper all by myself. It won't be patchy. *Listener* The dispute . . has been settled, buses are running but they're patchy in places.

■ **patchily** *adverb* E20. **patchiness** *noun* E19.

pate /ˈpeɪt/ *noun*¹. ME.
[Origin unkn.]
1 The head, the skull; *spec.* the crown of the head, now *esp.* a bald one. Now *arch.* & *joc.* ME.
2 The head as the seat of the intellect; a person's mind or intellectual power. Formerly also, a person with a mind of a specified quality. Now *arch.* & *joc.* L16.
3 The skin of a calf's head. L17.

> 📖 **1** SHAKES. *2 Hen. VI* Let him to the Tower, And chop away that factious pate of his. W. BOYD The afternoon sun warmed the pates of the . . mourners. **2** M. MCLUHAN May my pate become a glue-pot if I don't . . get that book reprinted.

■ **pated** *adjective* having a pate of a specified kind (***knotty-pated***) L16.

pate /paˈteɪ/ *noun*². M19.
[Maori.]
An evergreen shrub or small tree of New Zealand, *Schefflera digitata* (family Araliaceae), with large glossy digitate leaves.

pâte /pɑːt/ *noun*. M19.
[French = PASTE *noun*.]
1 ***pâte brisée*** /brize/ [= broken], a type of sweet shortcrust pastry. M19.
2 The clay from which porcelain is made. Only in phrs. below. M19.
3 ***pâte de verre*** /də vɛːr/ [= of glass], powdered glass that has been fired a second time. E20.
2 ***pâte dure*** /dyr/ (porcelain made from) hard clay. ***pâte-sur-pâte*** /-syrpɑt/ [lit. '*pâte* on *pâte*'] a method of relief decoration formed by applying layers of white slip upon unfired porcelain. ***pâte tendre*** /tɑ̃dr/ [= tender] (porcelain made from) soft clay.

pâté /ˈpateɪ/ *noun*. E18.
[French from Old French *pasté*: see PASTY *noun*. Cf. PATTY *noun*.]
1 A pie, a pasty. Now *rare*. E18.
2 A rich paste or spread made from finely minced or pounded meat, fish, herbs, etc. L19.
Phrases: **pâté de campagne** /də kɒmˈpɑːnjə/ a coarse pork and liver pâté. **pâté de foie gras** /də fwɑː grɑː/ (orig. a pie or pasty filled with) a smooth rich paste of fatted goose liver. **pâté en croûte** /ɑ̃ kruːt/ a pâté baked in a pastry surround. **pâté maison** /ˈmɛzɔ̃/ a pâté prepared according to the recipe of a particular restaurant. ***rough pâté***: see ROUGH *adjective*. ***Strasbourg pâté***: see STRASBOURG 1.

patée *adjective* var. of PATTÉE.

†patefy *verb trans*. M16–L18.
[Latin *patefacere* disclose, from *patere* be open + *facere* make: see -FY.]
Reveal to the eye or mind; disclose.
■ **†patefaction** *noun* [-FACTION] the action of revealing something; a revelation, a disclosure: M16–L19.

patel /pəˈtɛl, ˈpɑːtɪl/ *noun*. Also **patil**. L18.
[Hindi *patel*, Marathi *pāṭīl*, from Sanskrit *paṭṭakila*, from *paṭṭaka* copperplate, land grant.]
In central and southern India, the head of a village.

patella /pəˈtɛlə/ *noun*. Pl. **-llae** /-liː/. Orig. Anglicized as **†patel**. L15.
[Latin, dim. of *patina*: see PATEN.]
1 **†a** *gen*. A pan. Only in L15. ▸**b** ARCHAEOLOGY. A small pan or shallow vessel, *esp*. a Roman one. M19.
2 ANATOMY. A small flattened convex bone covering the front of the knee-joint; the kneecap. L16.
3 A natural structure in the form of a shallow cup or pan. L17.
4 ZOOLOGY. A univalve mollusc of the genus *Patella*, which includes the common limpet. Chiefly as mod. Latin genus name. L17.
■ **patellar** *adjective* of, pertaining to, or joined to the patella; ***patellar reflex***, a reflex movement in response to a sharp tap on the patellar tendon: L19. **patellate** /-lət/ *adjective* shaped like a patella E19. **pateˈllectomy** *noun* (an instance of) surgical removal of the patella M20. **patelliform** *adjective* having the form of a patella; shaped like a shallow pan or a limpet shell: E19.

patellofemoral /pəˌtɛləʊˈfɛm(ə)r(ə)l/ *adjective*. M20.
[from PATELLA + -O- + FEMORAL.]
ANATOMY. Of, pertaining to, or connecting the patella and the femur.

paten /ˈpat(ə)n/ *noun*. Also **†-ine**. ME.
[Anglo-Norman var. of Old & mod. French *patène* or Latin *patena*, *-ina* shallow dish or pan from Greek *patanē* plate.]
1 CHRISTIAN CHURCH. A (usu. gold or silver) plate on which the host is laid during the Eucharist and which may serve as a cover for the chalice at the time of communion. ME. ▸**b** *gen*. A shallow dish or plate. Now chiefly *Hist*. LME.
2 A thin metal disc. L16.
■ **patener** *noun* (*Hist*.) an acolyte who held up the empty paten during a part of high mass in medieval times M19.

patency /ˈpeɪt(ə)nsi/ *noun*. M17.
[from PATENT *noun*, *adjective*: see -ENCY.]
1 The state or condition of being open or exposed to view; manifestness, obviousness. M17.
2 ANATOMY & MEDICINE. The condition of being open, expanded, or unobstructed. M19.

patent /ˈpeɪt(ə)nt, ˈpat-/ *noun*. LME.
[Ellipt. for *letters patent*: see next.]
1 A document constituting letters patent; *esp*. a licence from a government to an individual or organization conferring for a set period the sole right to make, use, or sell some process or invention; a right conferred in this way. LME. ▸**†b** A papal licence or indulgence. Only in LME. ▸**†c** *gen*. An official certificate or licence; *esp*. a health certificate. E–M17.
2 *fig*. A sign of entitlement or possession; licence, permission, title. L16.
3 An area of land conferred by letters patent. *US*. M17.
4 A process, invention, or commodity for which a patent has been taken out. M19.

> 📖 **1** G. BURNET They thought fit to take out a patent, which constituted them a body, by the name of the Royal Society. *Scientific American* The first patent on a living organism became the cornerstone of the biotechnology industry. **2** M. O. W. OLIPHANT That hand . . was a patent of gentility.

Comb.: **patent office** an office which issues patents and where claims to patents are examined; **patent-right** the exclusive right conferred by letters patent; **patent roll** in Britain, a parchment roll containing the letters patent issued in any one year.
■ **†patenter** *noun* (*rare*) = PATENTEE M17–L19.

patent /ˈpeɪt(ə)nt, *esp. in branch I* ˈpat-/ *adjective*. LME.
[In branch I from Old & mod. French *patent*, *patente* from Latin *patent-* pres. ppl stem of *patere* lie open (see -ENT); orig. from Old & mod. French *lettres patentes*, medieval Latin *litterae patentes* letters patent (see below). In branch II directly from Latin.]
▸**I** **1** ***letters patent***, an open document issued by a monarch or government in order to record a contract, authorize or command an action, or confer a right, privilege, title, etc. LME.
2 Established or conferred by letters patent. Chiefly in ***patent house***, ***patent theatre*** below. L16.
3 Of an invention etc.: protected by a patent; made and marketed under a patent. Also *fig*., special for its purpose; ingenious, well-contrived. L18.
▸**II** **4** Of a place, building, etc.: not shut in or enclosed, readily accessible. Now *rare*. LME. ▸**b** Of a door, outlet, etc.: allowing free passage, open. L15.
5 Esp. of a fact, quality, etc.: open to view, exposed; manifest, evident, obvious. Opp. ***latent***. LME. ▸**b** MEDICINE & VETERINARY MEDICINE. Of (a stage in) a parasitic infection: characterized by detectable parasitic organisms or cysts in the tissues or faeces of the host. E20.
6 Spreading, expanded; *spec*. †(***a***) HERALDRY. = PATTÉE; (***b***) BOTANY (of branches, teeth, etc.) widely divergent; (***c***) ZOOLOGY having a wide aperture or a shallow cavity. LME.
7 Generally accessible or available for use; public. Now *rare*. L15.

> 📖 **5** R. D. LAING Intensification of the being through . . making patent the latent self. K. M. E. MURRAY It was now patent to him that the Dictionary could not be completed in . . the time named. P. FARMER Her patent joy in things seemed sometimes so fragile.

Special collocations & phrases: **joined patent**, **†joint patent** sharing by letters patent in some privilege or office. ***letters patent***: see sense 1 above. **patent house** = ***patent theatre*** below. **patent insides** inside pages of a newspaper which are bought by a publisher already printed with syndicated articles etc. **patent leather** leather with a glossy varnished surface, used esp. for shoes and belts. **patent log** a mechanical device for measuring the speed of a ship. **patent medicine** a proprietary medicine manufactured under a patent and available without prescription. ***Patent Safety***: see SAFETY *noun* 5. **patent still** a type of still using steam heating to produce alcohol of greater strength and purity than a pot still. **patent theatre** *Hist*. any of several London theatres established by Royal Patent between the 17th and 19th cents. and holding a monopoly on legitimate dramatic productions.
■ **patently** *adverb* in a patent manner; openly; plainly, obviously: LME.

patent /ˈpeɪt(ə)nt, ˈpat-/ *verb trans*. L17.
[from PATENT *noun*, *adjective*.]
1 Obtain a patent right to (land). *US*. L17.
2 Admit to a privilege, right, office, etc., by letters patent. Now *rare* or *obsolete*. L18.
3 Take out or obtain a patent for (an invention etc.); obtain by patent the sole right to make, use, or sell. E19.
4 METALLURGY. Subject (wire) to a process similar to normalizing to improve the ductility. Chiefly as ***patenting*** *verbal noun*. L19.
■ **patentaˈbility** *noun* ability to be patented L19. **patentable** *adjective* able to be patented E19. **patentor** *noun* (***a***) a person, department, etc., that grants or approves the granting of a patent; (***b***) = PATENTEE 2: L19.

patentee /peɪt(ə)nˈtiː, pat-/ *noun*. LME.
[from PATENT *noun* + -EE¹.]
1 A person who has been granted a privilege etc. by letters patent. LME.
2 A person or organization holding a patent for an invention etc. or entitled for the time being to its benefit. L17.

pater /ˈpeɪtə, *in sense 1 also* ˈpɑːtə/ *noun*. ME.
[Latin.]
1 = PATERNOSTER *noun* 1. ME.
†2 An ecclesiastical or spiritual father. E17–M19.
3 Father. Cf. MATER 2. Chiefly *joc*. & *School slang*. E18. ▸**b** ANTHROPOLOGY. A person's legal as opp. to biological father. Cf. GENITOR *noun*¹ 2. M20.

patera /ˈpat(ə)rə/ *noun*. Pl. **-rae** /-riː/. M17.
[Latin, from *patere* be open.]
1 ROMAN ANTIQUITIES. A broad shallow dish used esp. for pouring libations. M17.
2 ARCHITECTURE. An ornament resembling a shallow dish; any flat round ornament in bas-relief. L18.
3 ASTRONOMY. A broad, shallow, bowl-shaped feature on a planet's surface. L20.

†paterero, **pateraro** *nouns* vars. of PEDRERO.

Pateresque /peɪtəˈrɛsk/ *adjective*. E20.
[from *Pater* (see below) + -ESQUE.]
Resembling the writing style or method of criticism of the English essayist and critic Walter Horatio Pater (1839–94).

paterfamilias /peɪtəfəˈmɪlɪas, patə-/ *noun*. Pl. **patres-** /ˌpeɪtriːz-, ˌpatriːz-/. L15.
[Latin, formed as PATER + archaic genit. of *familia* family.]
1 A male head of a family or household. L15.
2 ROMAN LAW. The male head of a family or household having authority over its members. Also, any male legally independent and free from parental control. M19.

> 📖 **1** R. P. GRAVES Edward Housman . . accompanied by his six eldest children, the outward picture of a . . Victorian paterfamilias.

Paterian /peɪˈtɪərɪən/ *adjective*. M20.
[formed as PATERESQUE + -IAN.]
= PATERESQUE.

paternal /pəˈtəːn(ə)l/ *adjective*. LME.
[Late Latin *paternalis*, from Latin *paternus*, formed as PATER: see -AL¹.]
1 a Of, pertaining to, or characteristic of a (real or spiritual) father or fathers; fatherly. LME. ▸**b** Of or belonging to one's father. E17. ▸**c** That is a (real or spiritual) father. Now *rare* or *obsolete*. M17.
2 Inherited from a father; related through a father or the father's side. E17.

> 📖 **1a** M. LANE He began his paternal career with the usual prejudice in favour of sons. **paternal government** government as by a father, paternalism. **b** J. GALSWORTHY Following in a hansom from the paternal mansion where they had dined. **2** M. MEYER His paternal ancestors had for over two hundred years been sea-captains.

■ **paterˈnality** *noun* (*rare*) paternal quality, condition, or personality M19. **paternally** *adverb* E17.

paternalism /pəˈtəːn(ə)lɪz(ə)m/ *noun*. L19.
[from prec. + -ISM.]
The principle or practice of behaving in a paternal manner towards others; *spec*. the claim or attempt by a government, company, etc., to take responsibility for the welfare of its people or to regulate their life for their benefit.
■ **paternalist** *adjective* & *noun* (***a***) *adjective* = PATERNALISTIC; (***b***) *noun* a person who advocates or practises paternalism: E20. **paternaˈlistic** *adjective* of, pertaining to, or of the nature of paternalism L19. **paternaˈlistically** *adverb* E20.

paternity /pəˈtəːnɪti/ *noun*. Also (as a title) **P-**. LME.
[Old & mod. French *paternité* or late Latin *paternitas*, from *paternus*: see PATERNAL, -ITY.]
1 The quality or condition of being a father; fatherhood. LME. ▸**†b** Government (as) by a father; patriarchy. E17–E18.
2 With possess. adjective (as ***his paternity*** etc.): a title of respect given to an ecclesiastical father. Formerly also, an ecclesiastical father, *esp*. a bishop. LME.
3 Paternal origin or descent; *fig*. source, origin, authorship. E19.
Comb.: **paternity test** a blood test to determine the possibility of a particular individual being the father of a particular child.

paternoster /patəˈnɒstə, pɑːt-/ *noun*. OE.
[Latin *pater noster* lit. 'our father', the first two words of the Lord's Prayer in Latin.]
1 The Lord's Prayer, esp. in the Latin version. OE. ▸**b** A repetition or recital of this as an act of worship. ME. ▸**c** *transf*. A form of words repeated as or like a prayer, imprecation, or charm. Also, a nonsensical or tedious recital. LME.
2 Any of several special beads occurring at regular intervals in a rosary to indicate that a paternoster is to be said. Also, the whole rosary. ME.
3 = ***paternoster line*** below. M19.
4 A lift consisting of a series of doorless compartments moving continuously on an endless belt. Also more fully ***paternoster elevator***, ***paternoster lift***. E20.
1c **devil's paternoster** a muttered imprecation, esp. to oneself.
Comb.: ***paternoster elevator***: see sense 4 above; **paternoster lake** PHYSICAL GEOGRAPHY each of a line of lakes in a glaciated valley; ***paternoster lift***: see sense 4 above; **paternoster line** a fishing-line to which hooks or weights are attached at intervals; **paternoster-while** a length of time sufficient to say a paternoster.

paternoster /patəˈnɒstə/ *verb intrans*. M19.
[from the noun.]
Fish with a paternoster line.

Paterson's curse /ˌpatəs(ə)nz ˈkəːs/ *noun phr*. *Austral*. & *NZ*. Also **Patt-**. E20.
[Prob. from Richard Eyre *Paterson* (1844–1918), Australian grazier.]
Any of several European kinds of viper's bugloss, esp. *Echium plantagineum*, naturalized locally in Australia and New Zealand and regarded as weeds. Also called ***Salvation Jane***.

patesi /pəˈteɪsi/ *noun*. L19.
[Erron. transliteration of Sumerian *ensi*.]
Hist. In ancient Sumer: the ruler of a city-state; a priest-king.

path /pɑːθ/ *noun*¹. Pl. **paths** /pɑːðz, pɑːθs/. In sense 2 also (*Scot*. & *north*.) **peth** /pɛθ/.
[Old English *pæþ* = Old Frisian *path*, *pad*, Old Low German (Dutch) *pad*, Old & mod. High German *pfad*, from West Germanic, of unkn. origin.]
1 A way or track formed by continued treading, *esp*. a narrow (usu. unenclosed) one across open country, through a wood or field, over a mountain, etc.; a specially made way for pedestrians in a garden, park, wood, etc., or alongside a road; a footpath. OE. ▸**b** A specially laid track for cyclists or for machinery to run on. L19. ▸**c** PHYSIOLOGY. A pathway in the nervous system. L19. ▸**d** BIOCHEMISTRY. A metabolic pathway. E20. ▸**e** A schedule

available for allocation to an individual railway train over a given route. M20.

2 a A hollow or deep cutting in a road. *north.* OE. ▸**b** A steep road or ascent. Freq. in street-names and place-names. *Scot. & north.* LME.

3 The (usu. unmarked) course along which a person or thing moves or travels. OE.

4 *fig.* A course of action, procedure, or conduct. Also, a succession of movements made or operations undergone by something. OE.

5 MATH. A continuous mapping of a real interval into a space; a single continuous unbranched series of nodes and lines in a graph. M20.

> 📖 **1** M. LOWRY Half-cultivated fields bordered by narrow grass paths. L. R. BANKS I almost ran up the path to her house. ***INDIAN path.*** **3** A. GRAY She . . drew him onto the pavement out of the path of a lorry. B. CHATWIN Two lonely people . . would cross paths on their afternoon walk. **4** F. HOYLE Go straight to the President. I'll try to smooth your path there. A. STORR There is a danger that love is being idealised as the only path to salvation.

Phrases: ***a lion in the path***: see LION *noun*. CRITICAL ***path***. ***free path***: see FREE *adjective, noun, & adverb*. ***lead up the garden path***: see LEAD *verb*[1]. ***mean free path***: see MEAN *adjective*[2]. ***shining path***: see SHINING *adjective*. ***strike a path***: see STRIKE *verb*.

Comb.: **path-breaker** a person who or thing which opens a way for others to follow in a particular subject etc.; a pioneer; **path-breaking** *adjective* (of a person, invention, etc.) pioneering in some subject; **path difference** PHYSICS difference in path length; **path length** PHYSICS the overall length of the path followed by a light ray, sound wave, etc.; **path-master** N. AMER. HISTORY a public official in charge of supervising local road construction and repair; **pathname** COMPUTING a description of where a file or other item is to be found in a hierarchy of directories.

■ **pathless** *adjective* having no path; trackless, untrodden: L16. **pathlessness** *noun* M19. **pathlet** *noun* (*rare*) a small path L18.

path /paθ/ *noun*[2]. Also **path.** (point). M20.
[Abbreviation.]
= PATHOLOGY.

†**path** *verb*. Chiefly *poet.* OE.
[from PATH *noun*[1].]
▸ **I 1** *verb trans.* Go upon or along (a way, course, etc.). *lit. & fig.* OE–E19.
2 *verb trans.* Make or beat down by treading. E16–L18.
3 *verb intrans.* Follow a path; pursue a course. L16–E17.
▸ **II 4** *verb trans.* Pave. LME–L18.

Pathan /pəˈtɑːn/ *noun & adjective*. M17.
[Hindi *Paṭhān* from Pashto *Paṣtāna* pl. of *Paṣtūn* PAKHTUN.]
▸ **A** *noun*. A member of a Pashto-speaking people of SE Afghanistan and NW Pakistan. M17.
▸ **B** *attrib.* or as *adjective*. Of or pertaining to the Pathans. L18.

patha patha /ˈpatə ˈpatə/ *noun phr. S. Afr.* M20.
[from Xhosa *phathphatha* feel with the hands.]
1 A sensuous African dance; music for this dance. M20.
2 Sexual intercourse. *slang.* L20.

pathematic /paθɪˈmatɪk/ *adjective*. Now *rare* or *obsolete*. E19.
[Greek *pathēmatikos* liable to passions, from *pathēma* what a person suffers, suffering emotion, formed as PATHOS: see -IC.]
Of or pertaining to the emotions; caused or characterized by emotion.

pathetic /pəˈθɛtɪk/ *adjective & noun*. L16.
[French *pathétique* from late Latin *patheticus* from Greek *pathētikos* sensitive, from *pathētos* liable to suffer, formed as PATHOS: see -ETIC.]
▸ **A** *adjective*. **1** †**a** Producing an effect upon the emotions; moving, stirring. L16–M18. ▸**b** *spec.* Exciting pity or sadness; full of pathos. M18.
†**2** Expressing or arising from strong emotion; passionate, earnest. M17–M18.
3 Of or pertaining to the emotions. *arch.* exc. in ***pathetic fallacy*** below. M17.
4 ANATOMY. Designating the trochlear nerve, and the superior oblique muscle of the eyeball which it supplies. Now *rare* or *obsolete*. L17.
5 Miserably inadequate, feeble, useless. *colloq.* M20.

> 📖 **1b** E. BOWEN She . . turned pathetic eyes on Penelope and made appeal with soundless moving lips. N. FRYE It is pathetic to . . see how buoyant is his hope of being understood. **3 pathetic fallacy** the attribution of human emotion or responses to inanimate things or animals, esp. in art and literature. **5** G. F. KENNAN It was a rather pathetic affair, attended by only thirty-five persons.

▸ **B** *absol.* as *noun*. **1** In *pl.* & †*sing.* Pathetic expressions or feelings. Now *rare* or *obsolete*. M17.
2 ***the pathetic***, that which is pathetic; pathetic quality, expression, or feeling; people who arouse pity in others, as a class. E18.
3 In *pl.* The branch of knowledge that deals with human emotions. *rare*. L19.

> 📖 **2** M. BRADBURY A deep regard for the pathetic, the sad people of this world.

■ **pathetical** *adjective* (now *rare*) = PATHETIC *adjective* L16. **pathetically** *adverb* (*a*) so as to excite pity or sadness; (*b*) with strong emotion, passionately, earnestly; (*c*) *colloq.* inadequately, feebly: L16.

pathfinder /ˈpɑːθfʌɪndə/ *noun*. Orig. *US*. M19.
[from PATH *noun*[1] + FINDER.]
1 A person who discovers a path or way, an explorer; *spec.* any of the pioneers who settled in and explored the American West in the 19th cent. M19. ▸**b** In full ***pathfinder badge***. A badge awarded to a Scout or Guide for knowledge of local geography. E20. ▸**c** (The pilot of) an aircraft sent ahead to locate and mark the target area for bombing etc. M20. ▸**d** A member of an Anglican organization for secondary schoolchildren or any similar youth organization; in *pl.* (**P-**), this organization. M20.
2 *fig.* A person who seeks out or promulgates a new idea; an experimental or novel plan, device, etc., which is seen as preparatory in some way. L19.

> 📖 **2** *Nuclear Energy* Despite being pathfinders, the . . Magnox stations . . saved the UK Central Electricity Generating Board some $230 million. *attrib.*: *New Age* 'Music from the Hearts of Space' was the pathfinder 'space music' program.

Comb.: **pathfinder prospectus** COMMERCE a prospectus containing information relating to the proposed flotation of a company issued prior to the official prospectus.

pathic /ˈpaθɪk/ *noun & adjective*. E17.
[Latin *pathicus* from Greek *pathikos*, formed as PATHOS: see -IC.]
▸ **A** *noun*. **1** A man or boy who is the passive partner in anal intercourse. Now *rare*. E17.
2 A person who suffers or undergoes something. Now *rare* or *obsolete*. M17.
▸ **B** *adjective*. **1** Pertaining to or designating the passive partner in homosexual anal intercourse. Now *rare*. M17.
2 Passive; suffering. M19.

patho- /ˈpaθəʊ/ *combining form*.
[from Greek *pathos* suffering, disease: see -O-.]
Disease.

■ **pathobiˈology** *noun* the branch of biology that deals with the processes associated with disease or injury, general pathology L20. **pathophysioˈlogic**, **pathophysioˈlogical** *adjectives* of, involving, or pertaining to abnormal physiological processes: M20. **pathophysioˈlogically** *adverb* as regards pathophysiology L20. **pathophysiˈology** *noun* (the branch of medicine that deals with) the disordered physiological processes associated with disease or injury M20. **pathoˈtoxin** *noun* a toxin whose presence causes or helps to cause a disease M20. **pathotype** *noun* (MICROBIOLOGY) a pathogenically distinct variety of a micro-organism M20.

pathogen /ˈpaθədʒ(ə)n/ *noun*. L19.
[from PATHO- + -GEN.]
MEDICINE & BIOLOGY. An agent that causes disease, *esp.* a micro-organism.

■ **pathoˈgenesis** *noun* the production and development of disease; the manner of development of a disease: L19. **pathoˈgenesy** *noun* (now *rare* or *obsolete*) = PATHOGENESIS L19. **pathogeˈnetic** *adjective* of or pertaining to the production of disease; pathogenic: M19. **pathogeˈnetically** *adverb* as regards pathogenesis E20. **paˈthogeny** *noun* (now *rare* or *obsolete*) = PATHOGENESIS M19.

pathogenic /paθəˈdʒɛnɪk/ *adjective*. M19.
[from PATHO- + -GENIC.]
1 MEDICINE & BIOLOGY. Producing physical disease; pathogenetic. M19. ▸**b** PSYCHOLOGY. Causing or tending to cause mental illness; (potentially) psychologically disturbing. M20.
2 *fig.* Morally or spiritually unhealthy; having a deleterious effect on society. L20.

■ **pathoˈgenically** *adverb* as regards pathogenic behaviour or properties E20. **pathogenicity** /-ˈnɪsɪti/ *noun* the state of being pathogenic; the degree to which something is pathogenic: L19.

pathognomonic /paθəgnə(ʊ)ˈmɒnɪk/ *adjective & noun*. E17.
[Greek *pathognōmonikos* skilled in diagnosis, formed as PATHO- + *gnōmonikos*, from *gnōmōn* judge: see -IC.]
MEDICINE. ▸**A** *adjective*. Of a sign or symptom: specifically characteristic or indicative of a particular disease or condition. E17.
▸ **B** *noun*. A pathognomonic sign or symptom. E18.

pathognomy /pəˈθɒgnəmi/ *noun*. L18.
[formed as prec. after *physiognomy*.]
The branch of knowledge that deals with the passions or emotions or their manifestations.

■ **pathogˈnomic** *adjective* (*a*) of or pertaining to pathognomy; (*b*) = PATHOGNOMONIC: L17. **pathogˈnomical** *adjective* (*rare*) = PATHOGNOMIC M17.

pathography /pəˈθɒgrəfi/ *noun*. M19.
[from PATHO- + -GRAPHY.]
†**1** The, or a, description of disease. Only in M19.
2 A study of the life of an individual or the history of a community as influenced by a disease or a psychological condition; the writing of such studies, as a branch of literature. E20.

■ **pathographer** *noun* a person who writes a pathography L20.

pathologic /paθəˈlɒdʒɪk/ *adjective*. Chiefly *US*. M17.
[Greek *pathologikos*, formed as PATHO- + -LOGIC.]
= PATHOLOGICAL *adjective*
¶ Rare before L19.

pathological /paθəˈlɒdʒɪk(ə)l/ *adjective & noun*. L17.
[formed as prec.: see -ICAL.]
▸ **A** *adjective*. **1 a** Pertaining to pathology. L17. ▸**b** Involving, caused by, or of the nature of disease or illness; *hyperbol.* compulsive, obsessive, extreme. M19.
2 Pertaining to the passions or emotions. *rare*. L18.
3 MATH. Grossly abnormal in properties or behaviour, as compared with functions normally encountered in classical applications. M20.

> 📖 **1a** J. FORBES Noticed by almost every pathological anatomist. *Brain* Pathological examination of the excised tissue. **b** A. BRODAL In chronic encephalitis the pathological changes are found in the same regions as in the acute stages. V. NABOKOV Age had developed in her a pathological stinginess.

▸ **B** *noun*. A person whose psychological disposition or state is pathological. M20.

pathologically /paθəˈlɒdʒɪk(ə)li/ *adverb*. E19.
[from PATHOLOGIC or prec.: see -ICALLY.]
1 In terms of pathology. E19. ▸**b** *colloq.* Abnormally. M20.
2 In relation to the passions or emotions. *rare*. E19.

pathologist /pəˈθɒlədʒɪst/ *noun*. M17.
[from next + -IST.]
An expert in or student of pathology; *esp.* a specialist in the laboratory examination of samples of body tissue, usu. for diagnostic or forensic purposes.
speech pathologist: see SPEECH *noun*.

pathology /pəˈθɒlədʒi/ *noun*. L16.
[French *pathologie* or mod. Latin *pathologia*, from (the same root as) PATHO-: see -LOGY.]
†**1** In *pl.* Sorrows. Only in L16.
2 The science of the causes and effects of diseases; *esp.* the branch of medicine that deals with the laboratory examination of samples of body tissue for diagnostic or forensic purposes. E17. ▸**b** Pathological features considered collectively; the typical behaviour of a disease; a pathological condition. L17. ▸**c** *transf. & fig.* (The science of) mental, social, or linguistic, etc., abnormality or malfunction. Usu. with specifying word. M19.
3 The branch of knowledge that deals with the passions or emotions. *rare*. L17.
4 MATH. A pathological feature of a mathematical system, esp. of a surface or field in the neighbourhood of a particular point. M20.

> 📖 **2** A. MACLEAN I'm not a specialist in pathology—and you require one for an autopsy. ***plant pathology***: see PLANT *noun*. **b** *Scientific American* For every pathology there is an underlying biochemical defect. **c** D. M. SMITH The major metropolitan states . . experience high levels of social pathology. ***speech pathology***: see SPEECH *noun*.

patholopolis /paθəˈlɒp(ə)lɪs/ *noun*. *rare*. E20.
[from PATHOLO(GICAL + -POLIS.]
A diseased or morally degenerate city.

pathos /ˈpeɪθɒs/ *noun*. L16.
[Greek = suffering, feeling, rel. to *paskhein* suffer, *penthos* grief.]
1 A pathetic expression or utterance. *rare*. L16.
2 A quality in speech, writing, events, persons, etc., which excites pity or sadness; the power of stirring tender or melancholy emotion. M17.
3 Physical or mental suffering. *rare*. L17.

> 📖 **2** V. SACKVILLE-WEST His death held no pathos, since it was in accordance with what he had chosen. A. LIVINGSTONE The war had a special pathos for Lou, since fighting on each side was a country she felt to be her own.

pathway /ˈpɑːθweɪ/ *noun*. M16.
[from PATH *noun*[1] + WAY *noun*.]
1 A way that constitutes or serves as a path; the course of a path or track. M16.
2 a PHYSIOLOGY. A route, formed by a chain of nerve cells, along which impulses of a particular kind usually travel. E20. ▸**b** A sequence of chemical reactions undergone by a compound or class of compounds, esp. in a living organism. E20.

> 📖 **1** M. MOORCOCK The procession moved along gravel pathways. *fig.*: *Scientific American* The flow diagram shows the pathways of the energy that drives machines. **2a** H. L. HOLLINGWORTH The course of the various sensory pathways in the spinal cord. **b** *Nature* The pathways and interactions of mercury in the estuarine and marine environment. ***metabolic pathway***: see METABOLIC 2.

-pathy /pəθi/ *suffix*.
[Greek *-patheia* suffering, feeling: see -Y[3]. In sense 2 extracted from HOMOEOPATHY.]
Forming nouns with the senses (*a*) a disease or disorder in a particular part, as ***encephalopathy***, ***neuropathy***, or

of a particular kind, as ***idiopathy***; (***b***) a method of cure, curative treatment, as ***allopathy***, ***hydropathy***, etc.

†**patible** *noun*. LME–M18.
[Latin *patibulum* fork-shaped yoke or gibbet, from *patere* lie open + *-bulum* instr. suffix.]
A gibbet, a cross; the horizontal bar of a cross.

†**patible** *adjective*. E17.
[Latin *patibilis*, from *pati* suffer: see -IBLE.]
1 Capable of or liable to suffering; passible. Only in 17.
2 Capable of undergoing something; subject to something. E17–M19.

patibulary /pəˈtɪbjʊləri/ *adjective*. *rare*. Chiefly *joc*. M17.
[formed as PATIBLE *noun* + -ARY[1].]
Of or pertaining to the gallows; suggesting or resembling the gallows.
■ **patibulate** *verb trans*. kill by hanging M17.

patience /ˈpeɪʃ(ə)ns/ *noun*. ME.
[Old & mod. French from Latin *patientia*, from *patient-* pres. ppl stem of *pati* suffer: see -ENCE.]
▶ **I** Being patient.
1 a (The capacity for) calm endurance of pain, trouble, inconvenience, etc. Formerly also foll. by *of* pain etc. ME. ▸**b** Forbearance under provocation, *esp*. tolerance of the faults or limitations of other people. LME. ▸**c** (The capacity for) calm self-possessed waiting. LME. ▸**d** Constancy in exertion or effort; perseverance. E16.
†**2** Indulgence; permission. LME–E17.

> **1a** SHAKES. *Rich. III* How hath your lordship brook'd imprisonment?.. With patience, noble lord, as prisoners must. *Blackwood's Magazine* Queues of workers formed to wait in patience for the.. trams. **b** H. KELLER I had made many mistakes, and Miss Sullivan had pointed them out again and again with gentle patience. **c** H. HUNTER Behold the fruits of eleven years patience. **d** W. HARTE He learnt with patience and with meekness taught. **2** SHAKES. *1 Hen. VI* Nor other satisfaction do I crave But only, with your patience, that we may Taste of your wine.

▶ **II** Special senses.
3 BOTANY. = ***patience-dock*** (a) below. LME.
4 A card-game for one player in which the object is to arrange cards turned up at random into a specified order (also called ***solitaire***); an adaptation of such a game for more than one person. E19.
Phrases: **have no patience with** (*a*) be unable to tolerate; (*b*) be irritated by. **lose patience** become impatient (*with*).
Comb.: **patience-dock** (*a*) a kind of dock, *Rumex patientia*, formerly grown as a pot-herb; (*b*) *north*. = PASSION-DOCK.

patience /ˈpeɪʃ(ə)ns/ *verb intrans*. *rare*. L16.
[from the noun.]
Have or exercise patience.

patiency /ˈpeɪʃ(ə)nsi/ *noun*. *rare*. L17.
[from PATIENT after *agency*: see -ENCY.]
The quality or condition of being patient or passive.

patient /ˈpeɪʃ(ə)nt/ *adjective*, *noun*, & *verb*. ME.
[Old & mod. French from Latin *patient-*: see PATIENCE *noun*, -ENT.]
▶ **A** *adjective*. **1** Having or exercising patience (*with*, *to*, or *towards* a person, fault, etc.). ME.
2 Foll. by *of*: ▸**a** Enduring or capable of enduring (evil, suffering, etc); tolerant of. *arch*. or *poet*. LME. ▸**b** Of a word, statement, etc.: capable of bearing (a particular interpretation). M17.

> **1** AV *1 Thess*. 5:14 Now we exhort you, brethren.. be patient toward all men. R. M. BENSON We must form a habit of patient expectation. A. CROSS You've been very patient with my bad temper. P. GAY His search.. helped to school Freud in patient and precise observation. **2a** EVELYN Plants least patient of Cold. WORDSWORTH Streams that April could not check Are patient of thy rule. **b** *Church Times* It is a carefully worded motion and.. patient of many interpretations.

Special collocations: **patient Lucy** = *busy Lizzie* s.v. LIZZIE 4.
▶ **B** *noun*. **1** A person receiving or registered to receive medical treatment; a sick person, *esp*. one staying in a hospital. LME. ▸**b** A person who suffers (patiently). Now *rare* or *obsolete*. LME.
†**2** A person subject to supervision or correction by another. LME–M17.
3 A person who or thing which undergoes an action (*arch*.). Now chiefly GRAMMAR, the entity affected by the action of a verb. Opp. ***agent***. L15.

> **1** D. CARNEGIE More patients suffering from mental diseases in the hospitals. ***private patient***: see PRIVATE *adjective*. ***voluntary patient***: see VOLUNTARY *adjective*. **3** E. UNDERHILL Baptism is a crucial act of surrender performed by the baptised, who is agent, not patient.

▶†**C** *verb trans*. & *intrans*. Make or be patient; *refl*. calm oneself. M16–M17.
■ **patienthood** *noun* the state or condition of being a patient L20. **patientless** *adjective* having no patients E19. **patiently** *adverb* ME. **patientness** *noun* LME.

patiki /ˈpɑːtɪki/ *noun*. *NZ*. M19.
[Maori.]
Any of several flatfishes found in New Zealand waters.

patil *noun* var. of PATEL.

patina /ˈpatɪnə/ *noun*. M18.
[Italian from Latin = shallow dish or pan.]
A usu. green film or incrustation produced by oxidation on the surface of old bronze; a similar alteration of the surface of coins, flint, etc. Also, a gloss or sheen on wooden furniture produced by age, polishing, etc; an acquired change in the appearance of a surface, *esp*. one suggestive of age.

> R. FRAME A mahogany dining-table shows its patina best by candlelight. *fig*.: R. HOGGART He develops a strong patina of resistance, a thick.. skin for not taking notice.

■ **patinaed** /ˈpatɪnəd/ *adjective* covered with a patina, patinated M20.

patinate /ˈpatɪneɪt/ *verb trans*. L19.
[from prec. + -ATE[3].]
Cause to develop a patina; cover with a patina.

> D. WELCH Console tables charmingly patinated with dust and furniture polish. L. R. ROGERS Most sculptors today.. use acids.. to patinate their work.

■ **patiˈnation** *noun* the formation or production of a patina; the condition of having a patina: L19.

patine /pəˈtiːn/ *noun*[1] & *verb*. L19.
[French formed as PATINA.]
▶ **A** *noun*. = PATINA. L19.
▶ **B** *verb trans*. = PATINATE. L19.

†**patine** *noun*[2] var. of PATEN.

patio /ˈpatɪəʊ/ *noun*. Pl. **-os**. E19.
[Spanish = court of a house.]
1 Orig., an inner court, open to the sky, in a Spanish or Spanish-American house. Now also, a usu. roofless paved area adjoining and belonging to a house. E19.
2 MINING. A yard or floor where ores are cleaned, sorted, or amalgamated. Also *ellipt*., the patio process. M19.
Comb.: **patio door** a large glass sliding door leading to a patio, garden, or balcony; **patio process** an orig. Mexican process of amalgamating silver ores on an open floor.

patisserie /pəˈtiːs(ə)ri/ *noun*. Also **pât-**. L16.
[French *pâtisserie* from medieval Latin *pasticium*, from *pasta* PASTE *noun*.]
1 *sing*. & in *pl*. Articles of food made by a pastry-cook, pastries collectively. L16.
2 A shop which sells pastries. E20.

patissier /pəˈtiːsɪə, *foreign* patisje/ *noun*. Fem. **-iere**, **-ière** /-ɪɛː, *foreign* -jɛːr/. Also **pât-**. E20.
[French.]
A pastry-cook.

Patjitanian /padʒɪˈtɑːnɪən/ *adjective*. M20.
[from *Pajitan* (see below) + -IAN.]
Of or pertaining to Pajitan, a town on the south coast of Java in Indonesia; *spec*. (ARCHAEOLOGY) designating or pertaining to an early palaeolithic industry discovered near there.

patka /ˈpʌtkɑː, -kə/ *noun*. L19.
[Panjabi *paṭkā* from Sanskrit *paṭṭikā* turban-cloth.]
A kind of light head-covering worn by people of the Indian subcontinent, esp. Sikhs.

patlander /ˈpatlandə/ *noun*. *slang*. Now *rare* or *obsolete*. E19.
[from PAT *noun*[2] + LAND *noun*[1] + -ER[1].]
An Irishman.

†**patlet** *noun* var. of PARTLET *noun*[2].

Pat Malone /pat məˈləʊn/ *noun*. *slang* (chiefly *Austral*.). E20.
[Rhyming slang, from personal name.]
on one's Pat Malone, on one's own, alone. Cf. PAT *noun*[2] 2, TOD *noun*[4].

Patmorean /patˈmɔːrɪən/ *adjective*. M19.
[from *Patmore* (see below) + -AN.]
Of, pertaining to, or characteristic of the English poet Coventry K. D. Patmore (1823–96) or his writing.

Patna /ˈpatnə/ *noun*. M19.
[A district in north central Bihar, India.]
In full ***Patna rice***. A variety of long-grained rice, used chiefly in curries and other savoury dishes.

patness /ˈpatnɪs/ *noun*. M17.
[from PAT *adjective* + -NESS.]
The quality or condition of being pat; contrived neatness; glibness.

patois /ˈpatwɑː/ *noun* & *adjective*. M17.
[Old & mod. French = rough speech, perh. from Old French *patoier* handle roughly, trample, from *patte* paw, of unkn. origin.]
▶ **A** *noun*. Pl. same /-wɑːz/.
1 A dialect (orig. in France) of the common people in a particular area, differing fundamentally from the literary language; any non-standard local dialect. M17.
2 *transf*. A social dialect; jargon. L18.
3 The creole of the English-speaking Caribbean, esp. Jamaica. M20.
▶ **B** *attrib*. or as *adjective*. Of, pertaining to, or of the nature of a patois. L18.

patonce /pəˈtɒns/ *adjective*. M16.
[Perh. rel. to POTENCÉ.]
HERALDRY. Of a cross: having limbs usu. expanding in a curved form from the centre, with ends resembling those of the cross flory. Usu. *postpositive*.

patootie /pəˈtuːti/ *noun*. *US slang*. E20.
[Perh. alt. of POTATO.]
A sweetheart, a girlfriend; a pretty girl.

patresfamilias *noun* pl. of PATERFAMILIAS.

patri- /ˈpatri, ˈpeɪtri/ *combining form*.
[from Latin *patr-*, *pater* FATHER *noun*: see -I-.]
Forming nouns and adjectives, esp. in ANTHROPOLOGY & SOCIOLOGY, with the sense '(of or pertaining to) social organization defined by male dominance or relationship through the male line'.
■ **patriclan** *noun* a patrilineal clan M20. **patriˈlateral** *adjective* (esp. of marriage between cousins) pertaining to or designating a relationship in which a father and one of his siblings or other relatives are both involved as parents M20. **patripoˈtestal** *adjective* (SOCIOLOGY) characterized by the exercise of authority in a household by a father E20.

patria /ˈpatrɪə, ˈpeɪtrɪə/ *noun*. E20.
[Latin: see next.]
One's native country; one's homeland. Also, heaven, regarded as the true home from which the soul is exiled while on earth.

patrial /ˈpeɪtrɪəl/ *adjective* & *noun*. E17.
[French, or medieval Latin *patrialis*, from Latin *patria* fatherland, from *patr-*, *pater* father: see -AL[1].]
▶ **A** *adjective*. **1** Of or pertaining to one's native country. *rare*. E17.
2 *Hist*. Having or pertaining to the right of abode in the UK as conferred on citizens of the UK, its colonies, and the Commonwealth by the Immigration Act 1971 until its emendation by the British Nationality Act 1981 (British birth being a qualifying criterion). L20.
▶ **B** *noun*. *Hist*. A person with patrial status. L20.
■ **patriˈality** *noun* (eligibility for) patrial status L20.

patriarch /ˈpeɪtrɪɑːk/ *noun*. ME.
[Old & mod. French *patriarche* from ecclesiastical Latin *patriarcha* from Greek *patriarkhēs*, from *patria* family, clan + *-arkhēs* -ARCH.]
1 The male head or ruler of a family or tribe; *spec*. in biblical use, (***a***) each of the twelve sons of Jacob, from whom the tribes of Israel were descended (usu. in *pl*.); (***b***) in *pl*., Abraham, Isaac, and Jacob, and their forefathers. ME.
2 (**P-**.) ECCLESIASTICAL. An honorific or official title given to a bishop of high rank, esp. (***a***) a bishop of one of the ancient sees of Antioch, Alexandria, Rome, Constantinople, and Jerusalem; (***b***) a head of any of various autocephalous or Uniate Eastern Churches; (***c***) ROMAN CATHOLIC CHURCH a bishop next above primates and metropolitans and immediately below the Pope in rank. ME. ▸**b** *transf*. Any high dignitary of a Church which does not have the patriarchate or of a religion other than Christianity. Now *rare*. L15.
3 (A person regarded as) the father or founder of an institution, tradition, science, school of thought, etc. M16.
4 A man who or thing which is the oldest or most venerable of a group, *esp*. the oldest man in a village or neighbourhood; a veteran, a grand old man. E18.

> **4** *New Yorker* Lew Wasserman,.. at seventy-seven, Hollywood's reigning patriarch, rose to toast his companions.

■ **patriarchess** *noun* (*rare*) the wife of a patriarch; a female patriarch; the oldest woman in a community: M17. **patriarchism** *noun* the patriarchal system of social or ecclesiastical organization, government, etc. M17. **Patriarchist** *noun* (*Hist*.) a supporter of the Patriarch of Constantinople against the Exarch of Bulgaria during the schism of 1872–1945 E20. †**patriarchship** *noun* (*rare*) the (ecclesiastical) position or office of a patriarch; a patriarchate: M16–E18.

patriarchal /peɪtrɪˈɑːk(ə)l/ *adjective*. LME.
[Late Latin *patriarchalis*, from ecclesiastical Latin *patriarcha*: see prec., -AL[1].]
1 Of, belonging to, or ruled by an ecclesiastical patriarch; of the nature or rank of a patriarch of a Church. LME.
2 Of, pertaining to, or characteristic of the biblical patriarchs or their times. M17.
3 Of, pertaining to, or of the nature of a patriarchy. E19.
4 Venerable, ancient; (the) oldest. Cf. PATRIARCH *noun* 4. M19.

> **1 Patriarchal church** each of the five great basilicas of Rome (St John Lateran, St Peter's, St Paul's outside the Walls, Santa Maria Maggiore, and St Laurence outside the Walls). **patriarchal cross** a cross with two transverse pieces, the upper being the shorter, as an emblem of the patriarchs of the Greek Orthodox Church. **2** J. NORRIS Who could to Patriarchal years live on.

■ **patriarchalism** *noun* patriarchal rule or government M19. **patriarchally** *adverb* M19. **patriarchic** *adjective* (*rare*) = PATRIARCHAL L18. **patriarchical** *adjective* (now *rare*) = PATRIARCHAL E17.

patriarchate /ˈpeɪtrɪɑːkət/ *noun*. **E17.**
[medieval Latin *patriarchatus*, formed as prec.: see -ATE¹.]
1 *CHRISTIAN CHURCH*. **a** The position or office of patriarch; the jurisdiction of a patriarch. **E17.** ▸**b** The province or see of a patriarch. **M17.** ▸**c** The residence of a patriarch. **M19.**
2 The rank or authority of a tribal patriarch; a patriarchal system. **M17.**

patriarchy /ˈpeɪtrɪɑːki/ *noun*. **M16.**
[medieval Latin *patriarchia* from Greek *patriarkhia*, from *patriarkhēs* PATRIARCH: see -Y³.]
†**1** = PATRIARCHATE 1a. **M16–L17.**
2 A patriarchal system of society or government; rule by the eldest male of a family; a family, tribe, or community so organized. **M17.**

patriate /ˈpatrɪeɪt, ˈpeɪ-/ *verb trans.* Orig. *Canad.* **M20.**
[from RE)PATRIATE *verb*.]
Transfer control over (a constitution) from a mother country to its former dependency.
■ **patriˈation** *noun* **L20.**

patricentric /patrɪˈsɛntrɪk/ *adjective*. **M20.**
[from PATRI- + -CENTRIC.]
Centred on the father or the male line.

patrices *noun pl.* see PATRIX.

patrician /pəˈtrɪʃ(ə)n/ *noun*¹ & *adjective*¹. **LME.**
[Old & mod. French *patricien*, from use as noun of Latin *patricius* of a noble father, from *patr-*, *pater* father: see -ICIAN.]
▶**A** *noun*. **1** *Hist.* A member of a noble class or order; *spec.* (*a*) a person belonging to one of the original citizen families of ancient Rome (cf. PLEBEIAN); (*b*) a member of an order founded by, or a class of officer representing, the Byzantine Emperor; (*c*) a member of the hereditary noble citizenry in various medieval Italian republics. **LME.**
2 *gen.* A person of noble birth or rank; an aristocrat. **M17.**
▶**B** *adjective*. Of or pertaining to a patrician; composed of patricians; noble, aristocratic. **E17.**

📖 W. SPALDING The power .. vested in the senate truly belonged to the patrician order. P. FARMER Amid the drawling consciously patrician tones, a hint of suburban vowels.

■ **patricianism** *noun* patrician quality, style, or spirit; patricians collectively: **E19.** **patricianly** *adverb* in a patrician manner, aristocratically **L19.** **patricianship** *noun* the condition or rank of a patrician; patricians collectively: **E19.**

Patrician /pəˈtrɪʃ(ə)n/ *noun*². **M17.**
[Latin *Patriciani* (pl.), from *Patricius* the presumed father of the sect: see -IAN.]
ECCLESIASTICAL HISTORY. A member of a heretical sect which arose in the 4th cent. and held that the flesh was created by the Devil, not by God.

Patrician /pəˈtrɪʃ(ə)n/ *adjective*². **L19.**
[from Latin *Patricius* Patrick (see below) + -AN.]
Pertaining to or founded by St Patrick, 5th-cent. apostle to, and patron saint of, Ireland.

patriciate /pəˈtrɪʃɪət/ *noun*. **M17.**
[Latin *patriciatus*, from *patricius*: see PATRICIAN *noun*¹, -ATE¹.]
1 *Hist.* The position or rank of patrician. **M17.**
2 A patrician order or class; the aristocracy. **L18.**

patricide /ˈpatrɪsʌɪd/ *noun*. **L16.**
[Late Latin *patricida* (sense 1), *patricidium* (sense 2) alts. (after *pater* father and *fratricida* FRATRICIDE) of *par(r)icida*, *-idium*: see PARRICIDE.]
1 A person who kills his or her father. **L16.**
2 The action of killing one's father. **E17.**
■ **patriˈcidal** *adjective* of or pertaining to (a) patricide; guilty of patricide: **E19.**

patrico /ˈpatrɪkəʊ/ *noun*. *slang*. Now *rare* or *obsolete*. Pl. **-oes**. **M16.**
[Perh. contr. of *pattering* ppl adjective from PATTER *verb*¹ + COVE *noun*².]
A priest, *esp.* an illiterate one of low standing; a parson.

patrilineal /patrɪˈlɪnɪəl/ *adjective*. **E20.**
[from PATRI- + LINEAL *adjective*.]
Of, pertaining to, or based on (kinship with) the father or the male line; recognizing kinship with and descent through males.
■ **ˈpatriline** /ˈpatrɪlʌɪn/ *noun* a patrilineal line of descent **M20.** **patrilineage** *noun* patrilineal lineage **M20.** ˌ**patrilineˈality** *noun* **M20.** **patrilineally** *adverb* **M20.** **patrilinear** *adjective* = PATRILINEAL **E20.** **ˈpatriliny** *noun* the observance of patrilineal descent and kinship **E20.**

patrilocal /patrɪˈləʊk(ə)l/ *adjective*. **E20.**
[from PATRI- + LOCAL *adjective*.]
Designating or pertaining to a pattern of marriage in which the couple settles in the husband's home or community.
■ **patriloˈcality** *noun* the custom of patrilocal residence **M20.** **patrilocally** *adverb* **M20.**

patrimonial /patrɪˈməʊnɪəl/ *adjective*. **M16.**
[Latin *patrimonialis*, from *patrimonium*: see next, -AL¹.]
1 Pertaining to or constituting a patrimony; hereditary. **M16.**
2 *SOCIOLOGY*. Designating or pertaining to a traditional type of social structure in which a (male) ruler maintains authority through officials, an army, etc., retained by him and having loyalty to him personally. **M20.**
Special collocations: **patrimonial seas**, **patrimonial waters** an area extending beyond territorial waters, the natural resources of which belong to the coastal nation though vessels of other countries have freedom of passage through it.
■ **patrimonialism** *noun* a system of patrimonial authority **M20.** **patrimonially** *adverb* in the way of patrimony, hereditarily **M17.**

patrimony /ˈpatrɪməni/ *noun*. **ME.**
[Old & mod. French *patrimoine* from Latin *patrimonium*, from *patr-*, *pater* father: see -MONY.]
1 a The estate or property belonging by ancient right to an institution etc.; *spec.* the ancient endowment of a church. **ME.** ▸**b** Property or an estate inherited from one's father or ancestors; a heritage, an inheritance. **LME.**
†**2** The fact of inheriting from an ancestor; inheritance. **L15–L16.**

📖 **1a patrimony of St Peter** *Hist.* the Papal States. **b** H. JAMES The modest patrimony which, on his father's death, he had shared with his brothers.

patrin /ˈpatrɪn/ *noun*. *slang*. **M19.**
[Romany.]
A trail left by Gypsies, using arrangements of grass, leaves, twigs, etc., to indicate the direction taken.

patriot /ˈpatrɪət, ˈpeɪt-/ *noun & adjective*. **L16.**
[French *patriote* from late Latin *patriota* fellow-countryman from Greek *patriōtēs*, from *patrios* of one's fathers, from *patris* fatherland: see -OT².]
▶**A** *noun*. †**1** A fellow-countryman, a compatriot. *rare*. **L16–E17.**
2 A person devoted to his or her country; a person (claiming to be) ready to support or defend his or her country's freedom and rights. **E17.** ▸**b** *spec.* A member of a resistance movement or patriotic front. **M20.**
3 A devotee, a supporter (*of* a person, cause, etc.). *rare*. **M17.**
Phrases: **Patriots' Day** *US* the anniversary of the Battle of Lexington and Concord in the American Revolution, 19 April 1775, observed as a legal holiday in Maine and Massachusetts.
▶**B** *attrib.* or as *adjective*. = PATRIOTIC 2. **M18.**
■ **patrioˈteer** *noun* a person who makes a public display of patriotism, esp. insincerely **E20.** **patriotess** *noun* (*rare*) a female patriot **M19.**

patriotic /patrɪˈɒtɪk, peɪt-/ *adjective*. **M17.**
[Late Latin *patrioticus* from Greek *patriōtikos*, from *patriōtēs* PATRIOT: see -IC.]
†**1** Of or belonging to one's country. Only in **M17.**
2 Of, pertaining to, or characteristic of a patriot; devoted to the well-being or interests of one's country. **M18.**
2 patriotic front a militant nationalist political organization.
■ **patriotical** *adjective* (*rare*) patriotic **L17.** **patriotically** *adverb* **L18.**

patriotism /ˈpatrɪətɪz(ə)m, ˈpeɪt-/ *noun*. **E18.**
[from PATRIOT + -ISM.]
The quality of being patriotic; devotion to one's country.

Patripassian /patrɪˈpasɪən/ *noun & adjective*. **L16.**
[ecclesiastical Latin *patripassianus*, from *patr-*, *pater* father + *passus* having suffered: see PASSION *noun*, -IAN.]
ECCLESIASTICAL HISTORY. ▶**A** *noun*. A person who believes that God the Father suffered on the Cross in the person of the Son (a heresy of the 3rd cent.). **L16.**
▶**B** *adjective*. Belonging to, or involving the doctrine of, the Patripassians. **E18.**
■ **patripassianism** *noun* the doctrine of the Patripassians **M19.**

patrist /ˈpatrɪst/ *noun*. **M20.**
[from PATR(I- + -IST.]
PSYCHOLOGY. A person whose behaviour or attitude is modelled on or dominated by his or her father.

patristic /pəˈtrɪstɪk/ *adjective*. **M19.**
[German *patristisch*, from Latin *patr-*: see next, -ISTIC.]
Of or pertaining to the Fathers of the Church or patristics.
■ **patristical** *adjective* = PATRISTIC **M19.** **patristicism** /-sɪz(ə)m/ *noun* (*rare*) (a theological system based on) the doctrine or mode of thought of the Fathers of the Church **M19.**

patristics /pəˈtrɪstɪks/ *noun*. **M19.**
[German *Patristik*, from Latin *patr-*, *pater* father: see -ICS.]
CHRISTIAN CHURCH. The branch of theology that deals with the lives, writings, and doctrines of the Fathers of the Church.

patrix /ˈpeɪtrɪks/ *noun*. Pl. **-trixes**, **-trices** /-trɪsiːz/. **L19.**
[from Latin *patr-*, *pater* father after MATRIX *noun*.]
In type-founding, pottery, etc.: a punch, pattern, or model from which a mould or matrix is formed.

†**patrocinate** *verb trans.* **L16–E19.**
[Latin *patrocinat-* pa. ppl stem of *patrocinari* rel. to *patronus* PATRON *noun*: see -ATE³.]
Defend, champion, patronize, (a cause etc.).

patroclinous /patrəˈklʌɪnəs/ *adjective*. **E20.**
[from Greek *patr-*, *patēr* father + -O- + *klinein* to lean, slope + -OUS.]
GENETICS. Resembling the male more closely than the female parent; involving or possessing a tendency to inherit a character or characters from the male parent only.
■ **ˈpatrocliny** *noun* patroclinous inheritance **E20.**

patrol /pəˈtrəʊl/ *noun*. Also †**-ole**. **M17.**
[German *Patrolle* from French *patrouille*, from *patrouiller*: see next.]
1 The action or an act of patrolling a place, esp. at regular intervals; a reconnaissance flight by military aircraft. **M17.**
2 A person, group, vehicle, etc., that goes on a patrol. **L17.**
3 An advance detachment of troops sent to reconnoitre the country and gain information about enemy numbers, movements, etc. **E18.** ▸**b** A unit of scouts or guides forming part of a troop. **E20.**
4 An official controlling traffic where children cross the road. **L20.**

📖 **1** A. J. P. TAYLOR Fighter aeroplanes .. could not be on patrol in the air all the time. M. DEWAR Four members of the guard, returning from a patrol of the barrack perimeter. **2** *Independent* Twelve policemen died near Santa Marta on the north coast when a narcotics patrol was hit with claymore mines. ***shore patrol***: see SHORE *noun*¹.

Comb.: **patrol car** a police car used in patrolling roads; **patrolman** (orig. *US*) a man who is on patrol, *esp.* a policeman assigned to patrol a particular beat or district; **patrol wagon** *N. Amer.* a police van for transporting prisoners.
■ **patroˈlette** *noun* a woman or girl on patrol duty **M20.**

patrol /pəˈtrəʊl/ *verb*. Also †**-ole**. Infl. **-ll-**. **L17.**
[French *patrouiller* paddle about in mud (cf. Old French *patoier*), from *patte* paw, foot + dial. *gad)rouille* mud, dirty water.]
1 *verb intrans.* Go on patrol, act as a patrol. **L17.**
2 *verb trans.* Go over, round, or along (a building, area, border, etc.) for the purpose of watching, guarding, or protecting people or things. **M18.**

📖 **1** W. IRVING Numbers of armed guards patrolled around them. B. W. ALDISS Dispatch riders patrol up and down the convoy, seeing to it that the trucks keep even distance. **2** A. MACLEAN A sentry with slung gun patrolling the battlements. *fig.*: J. HARVEY From face to face, his glower patrolled the table.

■ **patroller** *noun* a person on patrol duty **E18.**

patrology /pəˈtrɒlədʒi/ *noun*. **E17.**
[from Greek *patr-*, *patēr* father + -OLOGY. Cf. mod. Latin *patrologia*.]
Patristics; a treatise on or collection of the writings of the Fathers of the Church.
■ **patroˈlogical** *adjective* **E18.** **patrologist** *noun* **E18.**

patron /ˈpeɪtr(ə)n; *in branch III* paˈtrɒn, *foreign* patrɔ̃, *foreign* paˈtrɒn/ *noun*. Also †**pattern**. See also PATTERN *noun*. **ME.**
[Old & mod. French from Latin *patronus* protector of clients, advocate, defender, from *patr-*, *pater* father. In branch III repr. mod. French and Spanish uses: cf. PADRONE.]
▶**I** Senses arising in medieval Latin.
1 A holder of the right of presentation to an ecclesiastical benefice. **ME.**
2 More fully ***patron saint***. A saint to whose intercession and protection a person, place, occupation, etc., is specially entrusted. **LME.** ▸**b** A tutelary (pagan) divinity. Now only *attrib.* **LME.**

📖 **1** W. BLACKSTONE The right of presentation to a church accrues to the ordinary by neglect of the patron to present. **2b** *Independent* The reincarnation of Ptah, patron god of the capital city of ancient Egypt.

▶**II** Senses from classical Latin *patronus*.
3 A lord, a master; a protector. **LME.**
4 *ROMAN HISTORY*. **a** A defender before a court of justice; an advocate, a pleader. **LME.** ▸**b** A former owner of a manumitted slave. **M16.** ▸**c** A patrician in relation to his client (see CLIENT 2). **M16.**
5 a A person who uses money or influence to advance or defend the interests of a person, cause, institution, art, etc.; a distinguished person invited to hold an office of honour in a charity etc. so that it might benefit from his or her position and influence; *Hist.* the person to whom a book was dedicated. **LME.** ▸†**b** A supporter or champion of a theory or doctrine. **L16–L18.** ▸**c** A person who supports or frequents a business, sport, etc.; *esp.* a regular customer at a shop, public house, etc.; **E17.**
6 (**P-**.) A member of either of two political associations (the Patrons of Husbandry and the Patrons of Industry) founded respectively in the US in 1867 and in Canada in 1891 to promote farming interests. *N. Amer.* (now chiefly *Hist.*). **L19.**

📖 **5a** A. C. GRAYLING Vienna, where he and his wife established themselves as patrons of the arts. *Independent* The Duchess of Kent, as Patron of Age Concern, opens a new Day Centre. **c** G. BORDMAN An audience of a mere thirty patrons had its money refunded.

▶ **III** Repr. mod. Romance uses.
7 The captain or master of a Mediterranean galley or coaster (now *rare* or *obsolete*); in N. American waters, the captain or steersman of a longboat, barge, etc. **LME.**
8 [French.] A case for pistol cartridges; a cartridge. *obsolete* exc. *Hist.* **M16.**
†**9** A master or owner of slaves in countries bordering the eastern and southern Mediterranean. **E17–E18.**
10 [Spanish.] A manager or boss of a hacienda; in New Mexico, the master or head of a family. **M19.**
11 [French & Spanish *patron*, Italian *padrone*.] The proprietor of an inn or restaurant, esp. in Continental Europe. **L19.**

📖 **11** T. ALLBEURY In the warmth of a small restaurant . . The *patron* moved among his customers.

■ **patronate** /ˈpatr(ə)nət, ˈpeɪt-/ *noun* (*rare*) the position of patron; the jurisdiction or right of a patron: **L17.** **patroˈnee** *noun* (*rare*) a recipient of patronage **E19.** **patronless** *adjective* having no patron **M17.** **patronly** *adjective* of, pertaining to, or befitting a patron **M19.** **patronship** *noun* the position or office of patron **M16.**

patron /ˈpeɪtr(ə)n/ *verb trans. rare.* **E17.**
[from the noun.]
Act as patron to, favour, (a person etc.).

patronage /ˈpatr(ə)nɪdʒ, ˈpeɪt-/ *noun & verb.* **LME.**
[Old & mod. French, from *patron*: see **PATRON** *noun*, **-AGE**.]
▶ **A** *noun.* **1** *ECCLESIASTICAL.* = **ADVOWSON. LME.**
2 The action of a patron in giving support, protection, custom, etc. **M16.** ▸**b** (Favour shown with) a patronizing manner. **E19.**
3 *ROMAN HISTORY.* The body of patrons; the relation of patron to client. **L17.**
4 The control of appointments to offices, privileges, etc., in public service. **M18.**
Phrases: **Arms of Patronage** *HERALDRY* arms derived from those of a patron or superior.
Comb.: **Patronage Secretary** the member of the British Government through whom patronage is administered.
▶†**B** *verb trans.* = **PATRONIZE. L16–M17.**

patronal /pəˈtrəʊn(ə)l/ *adjective.* **E17.**
[French from Latin *patronalis*, from *patronus* **PATRON** *noun*: see **-AL**¹.]
Of or pertaining to a patron or patron saint; of the nature of a patron.
patronal festival *ECCLESIASTICAL* a feast observed on the feast day of the patron saint or dedication of a church, town, etc.

patronat /patrɔna/ *noun.* **M20.**
[French.]
An organization of industrial employers in France; French employers collectively.

patroness /ˈpeɪtr(ə)nɪs, ˈpat-/ *noun & verb.* **LME.**
[from **PATRON** *noun* + **-ESS**¹.]
▶ **A** *noun.* A female patron or patron saint; a tutelary goddess. **LME.**
▶ **B** *verb intrans. & trans.* Act as patroness (to). **M19.**

patronise *verb* var. of **PATRONIZE.**

patronite /paˈtrəʊnʌɪt/ *noun.* **E20.**
[from A. R. *Patron* (fl. 1906), Peruvian metallurgist + **-ITE**¹.]
MINERALOGY. A lustrous black fine-grained mixture of vanadium sulphides occurring in Peru and mined as an ore of vanadium.

patronize /ˈpatrənʌɪz/ *verb trans.* Also **-ise. L16.**
[French †*patroniser* or medieval Latin *patronizare*, from Latin *patronus*: see **PATRON** *noun*, **-IZE**.]
1 Act as a patron towards, extend patronage to, (a person, cause, etc.); support, encourage. **L16.** ▸†**b** Defend, justify; advocate; countenance. **L16–L18.**
2 Treat or speak about (a person etc.) condescendingly. **L18.**
3 Frequent (a shop etc.), esp. as a customer. **E19.**
■ **patroniˈzation** *noun* **L18.** **patronizer** *noun* **L16.** **patronizing** *ppl adjective* that takes the part of a patron; *esp.* showing an attitude of conscious superiority towards another: **E18.** **patronizingly** *adverb* **M19.**

patronne /patrɔn/ *noun.* Pl. pronounced same. **L18.**
[French: cf. **PATRON** *noun*.]
A woman who is the owner, or the wife of the owner, of a business, esp. a café, hotel, or restaurant.

patronymic /patrəˈnɪmɪk/ *noun & adjective.* **E17.**
[Late Latin *patronymicus* from Greek *patrōnumikos*, from *patrōnumos*, from *patr-*, *patēr* father + *onuma* name: see **-NYM**, **-IC**.]
▶ **A** *noun.* A name derived from that of a father or ancestor, esp. by addition of an affix indicating such descent; a family name. **E17.**
▶ **B** *adjective.* Designating such a name or such an affix. **M17.**
■ **ˈpatronym** *noun* a patronymic **E19.** **patronymical** *adjective* patronymic **E17.** **patronymically** *adverb*, by, or in relation to, a patronymic. **M18.**

patroon /pəˈtruːn/ *noun.* **M17.**
[In senses 1 & 2 app. alt. of **PATRON** *noun*. In sense 3 from Dutch.]
†**1** = **PATRON** *noun* 4, 5. **M17–E18.**
2 The captain, master, or officer in charge of a ship or boat. Now *rare.* **M18.**
3 *US HISTORY.* A landowner with certain manorial privileges granted under the former Dutch governments of New York and New Jersey. **M18.**
■ **patroonship** *noun* (chiefly *Hist.*) the position of patroon; the estate of a patroon: **E19.**

patsy /ˈpatsi/ *noun. slang* (chiefly *N. Amer.*). **L19.**
[Origin unkn.]
A person who is ridiculed, deceived, blamed, or victimized.

patsy /ˈpatsi/ *adjective. US slang.* **M20.**
[Origin unkn.]
Satisfactory, all right.

pattable /ˈpatəb(ə)l/ *adjective. rare.* **L19.**
[from **PAT** *verb* + **-ABLE**.]
That invites patting.

pattamar /ˈpatəmɑː/ *noun.* Also **pata-. L16.**
[Portuguese *patamar* from Malay *pattamari* from Marathi *phattemarī*, from *pattā* dispatch + *mār-* to strike.]
†**1** In India: a person who carried messages, a courier. **L16–L18.**
2 An Indian dispatch-boat; *spec.* a lateen-rigged sailing vessel, with up to three masts, used on the west coast of India. **E18.**

pattawalla /ˈpatəwɒlə/ *noun.* **L19.**
[Hindi *paṭṭa-ūālā* person wearing a belt, from Sanskrit *paṭṭaka* band: cf. **WALLAH**.]
In India: a messenger, a servant.

patte /pat/ *noun.* **L18.**
[French, of unkn. origin.]
1 A paw; *joc.* a hand. Chiefly & now only in phr. below. **L18.**
2 A short band or strap sewn on a dress as a trimming, or used to fasten a coat, hold a belt in place, etc. **M19.**
1 ***patte de velours*** /də vlur/ [lit. 'velvet paw'] a cat's paw with the claws held in, as a symbol of resolution or inflexibility combined with apparent gentleness.

pattée /ˈpateɪ, -ti/ *adjective.* Also **patée. L15.**
[French, formed as prec.]
HERALDRY. Of a cross: having limbs which are nearly triangular, being very narrow where they meet and widening out towards the extremities. Usu. *postpositive.*

patten /ˈpat(ə)n/ *noun & verb.* **LME.**
[Old & mod. French *patin*, formed as **PATTE**: cf. **-INE**¹.]
▶ **A** *noun.* **I** Chiefly *Hist.*
1 Any of various former kinds of shoe, *esp.* one into which the foot was slipped or one made of wood. **LME.**
2 *spec.* A snowshoe; a skate. **M16.**
3 A kind of overshoe with a usu. wooden sole set on an iron ring etc., worn to raise the feet above mud or wet. **L16.**
4 A round plate of wood fastened under the hoof of a horse to prevent it from sinking in boggy ground. **E19.**
▶ **II 5** *ARCHITECTURE.* A base, a foot, as (*a*) the base of a column; (*b*) a bottom sill of a partition etc. **M17.**
Comb.: **patten-shoe**: designed for a lame horse.
▶ **B** *verb intrans.* Go (about) on pattens. **M19.**
■ **pattened** *adjective* wearing pattens **L18.** †**pattener** *noun* a maker of pattens **LME–M17.**

patter /ˈpatə/ *verb*¹ & *noun*¹. **LME.**
[from **PATER** *noun*, **PATERNOSTER** *noun*.]
▶ **A** *verb.* **1** *verb trans. & (now rare) intrans.* Recite (a prayer, charm, etc.) rapidly, mechanically, or indistinctly. **LME.**
2 *verb intrans.* **a** Talk rapidly and continuously without regard to sense or matter, prattle; talk rapidly and persuasively to attract or maintain interest. **LME.** ▸**b** Speak the slang or coded language of criminals, or the jargon of a profession or class. **E19.**
3 *verb trans.* Speak (a language). *slang.* **E19.**

📖 **1** H. ALLEN Old women . . pattering and murmuring their morning prayers. **2a** J. BUCHAN He . . pattered about his duchesses till the snobbery of the creature turned me sick. **3 patter flash** speak (a particular) slang.

▶ **B** *noun.* **1** The slang or coded language used by criminals; the jargon of a profession or class; any language not generally understood. **M18.**
2 a The rapid persuasive talk used by a street trader, magician, etc., to attract or maintain interest. Also, speech-making, oratory. **L18.** ▸**b** Rapid speech introduced into a song; the words of a song. **L19.**
3 Mere talk; chatter, babble. *colloq.* **M19.**

📖 **2a** P. AUSTER His patter about the brushes . . with that rapid salesman's pitch.

Comb. & phrases: ***gammon and patter***: see **GAMMON** *noun*³; **patter-song** a humorous song in which many words are fitted to a few notes and sung rapidly.
■ **patterer** *noun* **E16.**

patter /ˈpatə/ *verb*² & *noun*². **E17.**
[Dim. and frequentative of **PAT** *verb*: see **-ER**⁵. Cf. **PITTER** *verb*, **PITTER-PATTER**.]
▶ **A** *verb.* **1** *verb intrans.* Make a rapid succession of light sounds or taps. **E17.** ▸**b** Run with quick short steps. **E19.**
2 *verb trans.* Cause to fall or strike with a rapid succession of short soft strokes. **E19.**

📖 **1** W. H. AUDEN The rain comes pattering out of the sky.

▶ **B** *noun.* The action or fact of pattering; a rapid succession of light taps. **M19.**
the patter of little feet, **the patter of tiny feet** (with allus. to the sound of young children running etc.) the presence of a young child, the expectation of the birth of a child.

†**patter** *verb*³ & *noun*³. *Austral.* **L18.**
[Aboriginal.]
▶ **A** *verb trans.* Eat. **L18–L19.**
▶ **B** *noun.* Food. **E19–E20.**

†**patterero**, **patteraro** *nouns* vars. of **PEDRERO.**

pattern /ˈpat(ə)n/ *noun & verb.* Orig. †**patron**. See also **PATRON** *noun.* **ME.**
[Alt. of **PATRON** *noun*.]
▶ **A** *noun.* **1** A design, plan, model, etc., from which a thing is to be made. **ME.** ▸**b** *spec.* A paper plan used in making a garment. **L18.** ▸**c** *ANGLING.* A design on which an artificial fly is modelled. Also, a fly of a particular design. **L19.**
2 An original to be imitated; an exemplar, a model. **LME.** ▸**b** An example, an instance, *esp.* a typical one. **M16.**
†**3** A copy of something; a likeness. *rare.* **L15–E18.**
4 *FOUNDING.* †**a** A matrix, a mould. Only in **E16.** ▸**b** A model in wood etc. of a casting, used to shape the mould in which the casting is to be made. **E19.**
†**5** A precedent. **L16–L17.**
6 A (repeated) decorative design, esp. on or in china, carpets, cloth, wallpaper, etc.; a style or type of decoration. **L16.** ▸**b** Decorative figures or markings occurring naturally or by chance. **M19.** ▸**c** The arrangement of marks made on a target by the shot from a gun. **M19.** ▸**d** An arrangement or order discernible in objects, actions, ideas, situations, etc. **E20.** ▸**e** *SPORT.* A set sequence of tactical movements in a game; a positional formation or style of play adopted. **M20.**
7 A specimen, *esp.* one presented as a sample of a larger group; *spec.* a model of a proposed coin, not subsequently adopted for the currency. **M17.**
8 A sufficient quantity of material for making a garment, esp. a dress; a dress-length. *US.* Now *rare.* **L17.**
9 In Ireland: (the festivities marking) the festival of a patron saint. **M18.**

📖 **1** W. S. JEVONS Common things . . are made by machinery, and are copies of an original pattern. **2** JO GRIMOND There is no pattern for success. **b** C. LAMB The only pattern of consistent gallantry I have met with. A. PRICE A luxuriant frame of hair, . . side-whiskers and beard, the very pattern of the late Victorian clergyman. **6** *Ashmolean* There are dragons in the pattern of his brocaded sleeves. **b** J. LINGARD Rectangles of light broke the . . larger rectangle of the terrace into patterns. **d** R. D. LAING He may set out . . to disrupt old patterns of experience and behaviour. L. R. BANKS Lights flashed on and off . . in patterns. W. M. CLARKE Ill health . . settled the pattern of his life. ***BEHAVIOUR pattern.***

Comb.: **pattern baldness** genetically determined baldness in which hair is gradually lost according to a characteristic pattern; **pattern-bomb** *verb trans. & intrans.* bomb (a target) from a number of aircraft according to a prescribed pattern intended to produce the maximum effect; **pattern book** a book of cloth, wallpaper, etc., patterns or designs; **pattern card** a sample of cloth, wallpaper, etc., fixed to a card; a book of such cards; **pattern congruity** *LINGUISTICS* conformity to the phonological structure of a language; **pattern darning** a type of embroidery in which darning stitches form a design, freq. as a geometric background; **pattern-paper**: from which a garment pattern is made; **pattern practice** in learning a foreign language, intensive repetition of its distinctive constructions and patterns; **pattern room**, **pattern shop** the part of a factory, foundry, etc., in which patterns for castings are prepared; **pattern-welded** *adjective* (*ARCHAEOLOGY*) made by pattern-welding; **pattern-welding** *ARCHAEOLOGY* a technique in which metal bars and strips of different type and colour were welded together and hammered out to give a patterned artefact; a piece of pattern-welded metal.
▶ **B** *verb.* **I** †**1** *verb trans.* Be a pattern, example, or precedent for. **L16–M17.**
2 *verb trans.* †**a** Work *out* according to a pattern or model. **L16–M17** ▸**b** Make or shape in accordance with a pattern or model. Foll. by *after, on,* †*to,* †*from.* **E17.**
3 *verb trans.* Match, parallel, equal; compare to. *arch.* **L16.**
4 *verb trans.* Take as a pattern; imitate, copy. *rare.* **E17.**
5 *verb intrans.* Foll. by *by, after*: take as a model for oneself. *US.* Now *rare.* **L17.**

📖 **2** *Cassell's Family Magazine* He has patterned his conduct on the example of his father. *Computing Review* PASCAL is a simple algorithmic language patterned after ALGOL 60. **5** J. H. BEADLE A nice family for us Americans to pattern after.

▶ **II 6** *verb trans.* Decorate with a pattern. **M19.**
7 *verb trans.* Arrange into a pattern; design or organize for a specific purpose. **M20.**
8 *verb intrans. LINGUISTICS.* Make or form part of a pattern. **M20.**

📖 **6** E. JOLLEY Pale blue stuff, patterned all over with roses.

■ **patter'nation** *noun* the action or fact of forming a pattern; *spec.* non-uniformity in the distribution of spray from a jet: M20. **patterner** *noun* a person who designs patterns L19. **patterny** *adjective* (*rare*) characterized by the (obtrusive) presence of a pattern L19.

patterned /ˈpat(ə)nd/ *adjective.* E19.
[from prec.]
Having or decorated with a pattern or patterns; forming a pattern.
patterned ground ground showing a definite pattern of stones, fissures, vegetation, etc. (commonly polygons, rings, or stripes), typical of periglacial regions.

patterning /ˈpat(ə)nɪŋ/ *noun.* M19.
[from PATTERN + -ING¹.]
1 The style or arrangement of patterns; patterns collectively. M19.
2 The action of arranging things into a pattern; the fact of forming a pattern. E20.
📖 **1** G. RAWLINSON The patterning of the pillars with chevrons. **2** I. WATT The narrator's patterning of the ideas.

patternise *verb* var. of PATTERNIZE.

patternism /ˈpat(ə)nɪz(ə)m/ *noun.* M20.
[from PATTERN *noun* + -ISM.]
The description or classification of religions or literature according to recurrent patterns rather than historical development.
■ **patternist** *noun & adjective* (*a*) *noun* a proponent of patternism; (*b*) *adjective* of or pertaining to patternism: M20.

patternize /ˈpat(ə)nʌɪz/ *verb trans. rare.* Also **-ise.** E17.
[from PATTERN *verb* + -IZE.]
†**1** = PATTERN *verb* 2. Only in E17.
†**2** = PATTERN *verb* 1. Only in M17.
3 Reduce to or arrange in a pattern. M19.
■ **patterni'zation** *noun* arrangement in a pattern, patternation M20.

patternless /ˈpat(ə)nlɪs/ *adjective.* E17.
[from PATTERN *noun* + -LESS.]
†**1** Unmatched, peerless. Only in E17.
2 Having no pattern; plain, undecorated. M19.
3 Forming no discernible pattern. M20.

patteroller /ˈpatərəʊlə/ *noun.* M19.
[Repr. southern US pronunc. of PATROLLER.]
US HISTORY. A person who watched and restricted the movements of black people at night in the southern US.

Patterson's curse *noun phr.* var. of PATERSON'S CURSE.

Pattinson's process /ˈpatɪns(ə)nz ˌprəʊsɛs/ *noun phr.* M19.
[H. L. *Pattinson* (1796–1858), English metallurgical chemist.]
A process formerly used for desilverizing and purifying lead.
■ **pattinsonize** *verb trans.* extract silver from by the Pattinson process L19.

pattle /ˈpat(ə)l/ *noun. Scot. & north.* Also **pett-** /ˈpɛt-/. LME.
[Origin uncertain: cf. PADDLE *noun*¹.]
A small spade with a long handle, used chiefly to remove earth adhering to a plough.

pattress /ˈpatrɪs/ *noun.* L19.
[Alt. of *pateras* pl. of PATERA.]
A block fixed to a surface to receive a gas bracket, electric light switch, ceiling rose, etc.; the base of a wall socket. Also *pattress block*, *pattress box*.

patty /ˈpati/ *noun.* M17.
[Alt. of French PÂTÉ by assoc. with PASTY *noun*.]
1 A little pie or pasty. M17.
2 A small flattened cake of chopped or minced food, esp. meat. E20.
3 A sweet in the form of a thin disc, freq. peppermint-flavoured. Chiefly *N. Amer.* E20.
4 *transf.* A quantity of any substance formed into a disc shape. M20.
📖 **4** G. PRIESTLAND Watching the poor of India making cowdung patties for fuel.
Comb.: **patty-cake** (*a*) = sense 1 above; (*b*) *N. Amer.* = *pat-a-cake* s.v. PAT *verb*; *play patty-cake* (fig.), cooperate; deal (with); **pattypan** (*a*) a small tin pan in which patties are baked; †(*b*) a patty baked in this way; (*c*) (more fully *pattypan squash*) (chiefly *N. Amer.*) a squash of a saucer-shaped variety with a scalloped rim and creamy white flesh.

patu /ˈpatuː/ *noun. NZ.* M18.
[Maori.]
A short clublike weapon of stone or whalebone with sharpened edges, used for striking.

patulous /ˈpatjʊləs/ *adjective.* E17.
[from Latin *patulus* spreading, from *patere* be open: see -ULOUS.]
1 Open; expanded; gaping. E17.
2 Esp. of the boughs of a tree: spreading. L17.
3 *BOTANY.* Of a calyx etc.: outwardly divergent. M18.
■ **patulent** *adjective* (*rare*) = PATULOUS 1 E18. **patulously** *adverb* L19. **patulousness** *noun* L19.

paturon /ˈpatjʊrɒn/ *noun.* E20.
[from Greek *patein* to tread + *oura* tail + *-on*.]
ZOOLOGY. The basal segment of a chelicera.

patwari /patˈwɑːri/ *noun.* Also **putwary** /pʌtˈwɑːri/ & other vars. E19.
[Hindi *paṭwārī*, from Sanskrit *paṭṭa* document + *pāla* keeper.]
In the Indian subcontinent: a village registrar or treasurer under a zemindar.

patzer /ˈpɑːtsə, ˈpat-/ *noun. slang.* Also **pot-** /ˈpɒt-/. M20.
[Origin unkn. Cf. German *patzen* bungle.]
A poor player at chess.

paua /ˈpɑːwə/ *noun. NZ.* Also **pawa.** M19.
[Maori.]
1 A large gastropod mollusc of the genus *Haliotis*, esp. *H. iris*, native to New Zealand, which attaches itself to rocks by suction and is sometimes used as food. Cf. ABALONE, ORMER. M19.
2 In full ***paua shell***. The large oval shell of this mollusc, which has a row of holes along the back and a nacreous lining and is used to make jewellery and ornaments. L19.

paucal /ˈpɔːk(ə)l/ *adjective & noun.* M20.
[from Latin *paucus* few + -AL¹.]
GRAMMAR. (An inflected form) denoting more than two entities but fewer than the number denoted by the plural.
■ **pau'cality** *noun* the state or condition of being paucal M20.

pauchty *adjective* var. of PAUGHTY.

pauci- /ˈpɔːsi/ *combining form.*
[from Latin *paucus*: see -I-.]
Few, little.
■ **pauciar'thritis** *noun* (*MEDICINE*) arthritis affecting a few joints M20. **pauciar'ticular** *adjective* (*MEDICINE*) (designating arthritis) affecting few joints M20. **pauciba'cillary** *adjective* (*MEDICINE*) (designating a disease) characterized by a low incidence of bacteria M20. **pauci'spiral** *adjective* (*ZOOLOGY*) having few whorls M19.

†**paucify** *verb trans. rare.* M17–L18.
[from Latin *pauci-*, *paucus* few: see next, -FY.]
Make few or fewer.

paucity /ˈpɔːsɪti/ *noun.* LME.
[Old & mod. French *paucité* or Latin *paucitas*, from *pauci-*, *paucus* few: see -ITY.]
Smallness of number or quantity; fewness, scantiness.
📖 N. MANDELA Electing such representatives to Parliament is made ridiculous by their paucity of numbers. M. SAWYER The place was spectacular only in the paucity of its ambitions.

paughty /ˈpɔːti/ *adjective. Scot. & north.* Also **pauch-.** L16.
[Origin unkn.]
Haughty, proud; insolent, impertinent.

Paul /pɔːl/ *noun*¹. M16.
[Male forename from Latin *Paulus*.]
1 *Paul's betony* [believed to be a plant described by Paulus Aegineta as betony], heath speedwell, *Veronica officinalis*; also, thyme-leaved speedwell, *V. serpyllifolia*. M16.
2 = PAOLO. M18.
3 *Paul Pry* [a character in a US song], an impertinent prying person. E19.
4 *Paul Jones* [John *Paul Jones* (1747–92), Scot. naval officer noted for his victories in the American War of Independence], a ballroom dance in which the dancers change partners after circling in concentric rings. E20.
Comb.: **Paul-Pry** *verb intrans.* be inquisitive, pry.
¶ See also *rob Peter to pay Paul* s.v. PETER *noun*¹.

†**paul** *noun*² & *verb* var. of PAWL.

Paul–Bunnell /pɔːlbʌˈnɛl/ *noun.* M20.
[J. R. *Paul* (1893–1936) and W. W. *Bunnell* (1902–1965), US physicians.]
MEDICINE. Used *attrib.* to designate a test in which an antibody reaction to sheep red blood cells confirms a diagnosis of infectious mononucleosis (glandular fever).

pauldron /ˈpɔːldr(ə)n/ *noun. obsolete* exc. *Hist.* Also **poul-** /ˈpəʊl-/. L16.
[Aphet. from Old French *espauleron*, from *espaule* (mod. *épaule*) shoulder from Latin *spatula* (in late Latin shoulder-blade), with intrusive *d*.]
A piece of armour covering the shoulder.

Pauli /ˈpaʊli/ *noun.* E20.
[Wolfgang *Pauli* (1900–58), Austrian-born physicist.]
Pauli exclusion principle, ***Pauli's exclusion principle***, = EXCLUSION ***principle***.

Paulian /ˈpɔːlɪən/ *noun.* LME.
[ecclesiastical Latin *Paulianus*, from Latin *Paulus* Paul: see -IAN.]
ECCLESIASTICAL HISTORY. A member of a sect founded by Paul of Samosata in the 3rd cent. AD, which rejected the separate personalities of the Logos and the Holy Spirit and denied Christ's pre-existence.
■ Also **Paulianist** *noun* L17.

Paulician /pɔːˈlɪʃ(ə)n/ *noun & adjective.* E18.
[medieval Latin *Pauliciani*, Greek *Paulikianoi*, of unkn. origin: see -ICIAN.]
ECCLESIASTICAL HISTORY. ▶**A** *noun.* A member of a sect which arose in Armenia in the 7th cent., having affinities with the Paulians and professing modified Manichaeism. E18.
▶**B** *adjective.* Of or belonging to the Paulicians. M18.
■ **Paulicianism** *noun* the doctrine of the Paulicians M19.

paulin /ˈpɔːlɪn/ *noun.* M19.
[Aphet. from TARPAULIN.]
A waterproof covering such as tarpaulin.

Pauline /ˈpɔːlʌɪn/ *noun & adjective.* LME.
[medieval Latin *Paulinus*, from *Paulus*: see PAUL *noun*¹, -INE¹.]
▶**A** *noun.* †**1** *CHRISTIAN CHURCH.* A member of any of various religious orders named after St Paul. LME–L17.
2 A present or past member of St Paul's School, London, or of any other school named after the saint. M19.
▶**B** *adjective.* **1** Of, pertaining to, or characteristic of St Paul, his writings, or his doctrines; of or pertaining to a school named after St Paul. E19.
2 *CHRISTIAN CHURCH.* Of or pertaining to Pope Paul VI or the liturgical and doctrinal reforms pursued during his pontificate (1963–78) as a result of the Second Vatican Council. M20.
📖 **1** *Observer* Sir Keith Joseph, whose Pauline conversion had just occurred. **Pauline privilege**: conceded by St Paul (1 *Corinthians* 7:15) to allow a newly converted Christian to contract a new marriage should the current non-Christian spouse wish to separate or seriously impede his or her Christian observance.
■ **Paulinism** /-lɪn-/ *noun* (*CHRISTIAN CHURCH*) (*a*) the doctrine of St Paul; Pauline theology; (*b*) an expression or feature characteristic of St Paul: M19. **Paulinist** /-lɪn-/ *noun* (*CHRISTIAN CHURCH*) an adherent of St Paul or his doctrine L19. **Paulinistic** /-lɪˈnɪs-/ *adjective* (*CHRISTIAN CHURCH*) of or pertaining to a Paulinist or Paulinism M19. **Paulinize** /-lɪn-/ *verb trans.* (*CHRISTIAN CHURCH*) imbue with Paulinism M19.

Paulist /ˈpɔːlɪst/ *noun.* M17.
[from PAUL *noun*¹ + -IST.]
ECCLESIASTICAL. **1** In the Indian subcontinent, a Jesuit. M17.
2 A member of the Missionary Society of St Paul the Apostle, founded in New York in 1858 as a Roman Catholic order. L19.

Paulista /paʊˈliːstə/ *noun.* E19.
[Portuguese, from *São Paulo* (see below) + *-ista* -IST.]
Orig. (now *Hist.*), a person of mixed Portuguese and Brazilian Indian descent, *esp.* one who was among the explorers or settlers of the hinterlands of southern Brazil. Now, a native or inhabitant of the city of São Paulo in southern Brazil.

paulo-post-future /ˌpɔːləʊpəʊstˈfjuːtʃə/ *adjective & noun.* E19.
[mod. Latin *paulo post futurum* translating Greek *ho met oligon mellōn* the future after a little.]
1 *GRAMMAR.* (Designating) a tense of the passive of Greek verbs, chiefly used to indicate that an event will take place immediately. E19.
2 *fig.* (Of or pertaining to) an immediate or proximate future. M19.

paulownia /pɔːˈləʊnɪə, -ˈlɒvnɪə/ *noun.* M19.
[mod. Latin (see below), from Anna *Paulowna* (1795–1865), daughter of Tsar Paul I and wife of William II of the Netherlands.]
BOTANY. Any of several east Asian deciduous trees of the genus *Paulownia*, of the figwort family, with blue or lilac bell-shaped flowers and large, often hairy leaves; *esp.* the ***kiri***, *P. tomentosa*.

Paul Revere /pɔːl rəˈvɪə/ *adjective.* Chiefly *US.* E20.
[N. Amer. silversmith (1735–1818), best known for warning of the British approach in 1775. See also REVERE *adjective*.]
Designating or pertaining to silverware of a style characteristic of the colonial period in N. America.

paunch /pɔːn(t)ʃ/ *noun*¹ & *verb.* LME.
[Anglo-Norman *pa(u)nche*, Old Northern French *panche* var. of Old French *pance* (mod. *panse*) from Proto-Romance, from Latin *pantex*, *pantic-* (usu. in pl.) bowels, intestines.]
▶**A** *noun.* **1** The abdomen; the stomach; the front of the body between the waist and the groin, esp. when large or protruding. LME.
2 The rumen or first and largest stomach of a ruminant. Now *rare* exc. *dial.* LME. ▸**b** An animal's entrails used as food; tripe. LME. ▸**c** In *pl.* Entrails, viscera. Now *Scot. & north.* M16.
📖 **1** F. KING His trousers, pushed out by a small, rounded paunch.
▶**B** *verb.* **1** *verb trans.* Stab, esp. in the paunch. Also, puncture the paunch of (an animal) to allow the escape of harmful gases. Now *rare* exc. *dial.* M16. ▸**b** Disembowel, eviscerate, (an animal). L16.
2 a *verb intrans.* Stuff the stomach with food; glut. *obsolete* exc. *Scot.* M16. ▸**b** *verb trans.* Swallow hastily or greedily. *rare.* L16.

■ **punched** *adjective* paunchy; having a paunch of a specified kind: M17. **paunchiness** *noun* the state or condition of being paunchy L19. **paunchy** *adjective* having a large paunch L16.

paunch /pɔːn(t)ʃ/ *noun*². Also **pan-** /pɑːn-/. E17.
[Prob. identical with prec., through use of Old French *pance* for stomach armour.]
NAUTICAL. A thick strong mat of yarn, cordage, or rope, or a wooden covering or shield, used to give protection from chafing, esp. on a mast or spar.

pauper /ˈpɔːpə/ *noun*. L15.
[Latin = poor.]
1 A poor person; a person having no property or means of livelihood; a person dependent on the charity of others; *Hist.* a person in receipt of poor law relief. Also, a beggar. L15.
2 LAW (now *Hist.*). A person allowed, because of poverty, to bring a legal action without payment. Cf. FORMA PAUPERIS. M17.

1 RACHEL ANDERSON We don't need the rector's money, we're not paupers. ***casual pauper***: see CASUAL.

■ **pauperage** *noun* = PAUPERDOM M19. **pauperdom** *noun* (*a*) destitution; (*b*) the realm of paupers, paupers collectively: L19. **pauperism** *noun* (*a*) poverty; the presence of people dependent on public relief as an established fact or condition in a society; (*b*) paupers collectively: E19. **pauperiˈzation** *noun* the action of pauperizing someone; the condition of being pauperized: M19. **pauperize** *verb trans.* make a pauper of M19. **pauperous** *adjective* (*a*) (long *rare* or *obsolete*) pertaining to the poor; (*b*) poor: E17.

paupiette /pɔːpˈjɛt/ *noun*. Orig. †**poupiet**. E18.
[French, prob. from Italian *polpetta*, from Latin *pulpa* PULP *noun*: see -ETTE. Cf. PUPTON.]
COOKERY. A long thin slice of fish, meat, etc., esp. rolled and stuffed with a filling. Usu. in *pl.*

pauraque /paʊˈrɑːkeɪ/ *noun*. M20.
[Prob. a Hispanicized form of a local word.]
A long-tailed nightjar, *Nyctidromus albicollis*, found mainly in Central and S. America.

paurometabolous /ˌpɔːrəʊmɪˈtabələs/ *adjective*. L19.
[from Greek *pauros* small, little + *metabolos* changeable: see -OUS.]
ENTOMOLOGY. Of an insect: that undergoes some slight or imperfect metamorphosis, as insects of the orders Orthoptera and Hemiptera.

pauropod /ˈpɔːrəpɒd/ *noun*. L19.
[mod. Latin *Pauropoda* (see below), from Greek *pauros* small, little + *-podos* footed, formed as -POD.]
ZOOLOGY. A myriapod of the order Pauropoda, resembling a minute pale centipede.

pause /pɔːz/ *noun*. LME.
[Old & mod. French, or Latin *pausa* from Greek *pausis*, from *pausein* stop, cease. In sense 3 from Italian *pausa*.]
1 An act of stopping or ceasing for a short time; a short interval of inaction or silence; a hesitation. LME. ▸**b** Intermission, delay, hesitation, waiting. L16. ▸**c** The facility to temporarily interrupt a mechanical or electronic process, esp. sound or video recording or reproduction. Also (in full ***pause button*** etc.), a device controlling this. M20.
2 *spec.* A break or rest in speaking or reading, esp. at the end of a phrase, clause, or sentence; PROSODY a break occurring at a fixed point in a poetic line and having a specific metrical value, a caesura. LME.
3 MUSIC. †**a** A character denoting an interval of silence; a rest. M16–M18. ▸**b** The character 𝄐 or 𝄑 placed over or under a note, rest, or silent bar, indicating that it is to be lengthened for an unspecified duration. E19.
4 HEBREW GRAMMAR. The form of a word or vowel preceding any of the chief stops. Chiefly in ***in pause***, ***into pause***. Cf. PAUSAL. L19.

1 J. BALDWIN There was a short pause before morning service began. **b** L. GRANT-ADAMSON The kicks had left it . . puffy and it throbbed without pause. **c** *Q* The system has . . direct CD track access, . . pause and play. **2** R. P. WARREN They talked slowly, with little pauses.

Phrases: **at pause** = *in a pause* below. **give a person pause** cause a person to stop, hesitate, or doubt. **in a pause**, **in pause** pausing, hesitating; in suspense.
■ **pausal** *adjective* of or pertaining to a pause; *spec.* (HEBREW GRAMMAR) designating the form of a word in pause, in which a vowel is changed (usu. lengthened): L19. **pauseless** *adjective* M19. **pauslessly** *adverb* M19.

pause /pɔːz/ *verb*. LME.
[from prec. or Old & mod. French *pauser* or Latin *pausare*.]
1 *verb intrans.* Make a pause; cease or interrupt movement, speech, etc., for a short time; wait, *esp.* hesitate. LME. ▸†**b** *verb refl.* Hold (oneself) back. *rare* (Shakes.). Only in L16.
2 *verb intrans.* Dwell, linger. Usu. foll. by *on*. M16.
3 *verb trans.* Cause to hesitate or pause. *rare*. M16.

1 M. FRAYN Everyone paused in mid-handshake. E. WELTY There was one window, and she paused now and then, . . looking out at the rain.

■ †**pauser** *noun* (*rare*) a person who pauses E–M17.

†**pautners** *noun* see PARTNERS.

pauxi /ˈpɔːksi/ *noun*. M18.
[from Spanish (now *paují*), perh. a local deriv. of Spanish *pavo* turkey.]
ORNITHOLOGY. = ***helmeted* CURASSOW**.

pav /pav/ *noun*¹. *colloq.* M19.
[Abbreviation of PAVILION *noun*.]
1 *Hist.* The London Pavilion, a music hall and theatre, later a cinema. M19.
2 A cricket pavilion. E20.

pav /pav/ *noun*². *Austral. & NZ colloq.* M20.
[Abbreviation.]
= PAVLOVA.

pavage /ˈpeɪvɪdʒ/ *noun*. L15.
[Old & mod. French, from *paver* PAVE *verb*: see -AGE.]
1 *Hist.* (The right to levy) a tax or toll towards the paving of roads. L15.
2 The action of paving a road; the laying of a pavement. M16.

pavane /pəˈvan, -ˈvɑːn/ *noun*. Also **pavan**, /ˈpav(ə)n/. M16.
[French, prob. from Italian dial. *pavana* fem. of *pavano* of Padua, from *Pavo* dial. name of Padua (Italian *Padova*): see PADUAN.]
1 *Hist.* A grave and stately dance in slow duple time, performed in elaborate clothing and popular in the 16th cent. M16.
2 A piece of music for this dance or in its rhythm. M16.

pave /peɪv/ *noun*¹. Chiefly *US*. M19.
[Abbreviation.]
= PAVEMENT.

pave *noun*² see PAVÉ.

pave /peɪv/ *verb trans.* ME.
[Old & mod. French *paver*, prob. back-form. formed as PAVEMENT.]
1 Lay paving or a pavement on (a road, yard, etc.). ME.
2 Cover or overlay as with a pavement. LME. ▸**b** Write interlinear or marginal translations in (a Latin or Greek textbook). *School slang*. L19.

1 R. P. JHABVALA The courtyard was paved in black and white marble squares. P. CUTTING The paths were not paved and . . the ways were very muddy. **2** *Times* Thousands . . simply walk to the city to see if the streets are paved with gold.

Phrases: **pave the way** make things ready (*for*); facilitate or lead on to an event etc.
■ **paven** *ppl adjective* (chiefly *poet.*) [irreg., after *shaven* etc.] having a pavement, paved M17.

pavé /ˈpaveɪ, *foreign* pave (*pl. same*)/ *noun*. Also (earlier) Anglicized as **pave** /peɪv/. LME.
[French, use as noun of pa. pple of *paver* PAVE *verb*.]
1 A paved road or path. LME.
2 A setting of jewels placed close together so that no metal is visible. L19.

1 G. NICHOLSON This was a typical little Flanders climb over heavily cambered *pavé*. **2** *Maclean's Magazine* Thirty-two thousand diamonds set in pavé.

pavement /ˈpeɪvm(ə)nt/ *noun & verb*. Also (*dial. & techn.*) **pamment** /ˈpam(ə)nt/. ME.
[Old French from Latin *pavimentum* beaten floor, from *pavire* beat, tread down: see -MENT.]
▸ **A** *noun*. **1** A paved surface; the top covering or layer of a floor, courtyard, road, etc., made of pieces of a hard material fitted closely together or of an undivided hard coating so as to give a compact, uniform, and smooth surface. Also, paving, material of which a pavement is made. ME.
2 The paved part of a public thoroughfare; *spec.* (*a*) (now *N. Amer. & techn.*) a paved roadway (as opp. to an adjacent footpath); (*b*) a paved footpath beside a roadway and at a slightly higher level. ME. ▸**b** The level part of the sanctuary of a church, between the lowest altar step and the altar rail. L19.
3 A tile, brick, etc., suitable for use in paving. *dial. & techn.* L18.
4 a GEOLOGY. A horizontal or gently sloping expanse of bare rock, esp. of deeply fissured limestone. E19. ▸**b** ANATOMY & ZOOLOGY. A structure or formation resembling a pavement; *esp.* a hard flat surface formed by close-set teeth, as in certain sharks. M19.

1 *Omni* Those endless expanses of pavement in Paris's metro system. **2** J. FRAME As she walked she sidestepped the many cracks in the pavement. T. HILLERMAN Chee pulled his patrol car off the dirt and onto the pavement of Route 33.

Phrases: ***moving pavement***: see MOVING *adjective*. **on the pavement** (*a*) without accommodation; (*b*) abandoned.
Comb.: **pavement artist** (*a*) a person who draws with coloured chalks or pastels on paving-stones in order to earn money from passers-by; (*b*) *US* an artist who displays his or her work for sale on a pavement. **pavement-pounder** *slang* a police officer; **pavement-tooth** each of the broad flat teeth forming the pavement of an animal; **pavement-toothed** *adjective* having teeth arranged in a pavement.

▸ **B** *verb trans.* Lay with a pavement; pave. Usu. in *pass.* L16.

paver /ˈpeɪvə/ *noun*. L15.
[from PAVE *verb* + -ER¹.]
1 A person who paves a road etc. L15. ▸**b** A machine for depositing and spreading material for a road etc. M20.
2 A paving-stone, a paving-tile. L17.

pavia /ˈpeɪvɪə/ *noun*. Now chiefly HORTICULTURE. M18.
[mod. Latin (see below), from Peter Paaw, (*Pavius*) (1589–1617), professor of botany at Leiden.]
Any of various buckeyes of the former genus *Pavia* (now a section of the genus *Aesculus*) characterized by having a smooth, not prickly, capsule; *esp.* the red buckeye, *Aesculus pavia*.

Pavian /ˈpɑːvɪən, pəˈviːən/ *noun & adjective*. M19.
[from *Pavia* (see below) + -AN.]
▸ **A** *adjective*. Of, pertaining to, or characteristic of Pavia, a city in northern Italy, or its people. M19.
▸ **B** *noun*. A native or inhabitant of Pavia. L19.

pavid /ˈpavɪd/ *adjective*. *rare*. M17.
[Latin *pavidus*, from *pavere* quake with fear: see -ID¹.]
Fearful, timid.

†**pavier** *noun* see PAVIOR.

pavilion /pəˈvɪljən/ *noun & verb*. ME.
[Old & mod. French *pavillon* tent, canopy from Latin *papilio(n-)* butterfly, tent.]
▸ **A** *noun*. **1** A tent, *esp.* one that is large and decorated and rises to a central peak (as now used at shows, fairs, etc.). ME. ▸**b** HERALDRY. A charge representing a tent. E18.
2 *fig.* A thing shaped like or used as a pavilion; a thing which covers, conceals, protects, etc. LME.
†**3** A covering, a canopy. LME–L16.
†**4** A flag, an ensign, *esp.* one indicating a ship's nationality. L16–L18.
5 An ornamental building or summer-house, *esp.* one in a park or large garden, or at a resort. L17. ▸**b** A building at a cricket or other sports ground used for changing, refreshments, etc. L18. ▸**c** A temporary stand at an exhibition. L20.
6 a A usu. elaborately decorated projecting subdivision of a building or façade. L17. ▸**b** A detached or semi-detached block or building in a hospital complex. M19.
7 *Hist.* A French gold coin struck by Philip VI of Valois in 1329, the obverse of which represented the king seated under a canopy. Also, an imitation of this struck by the Black Prince for use in France. M18.
8 The part of a gem cut as a brilliant that lies between the girdle and the point or culet. M18.

1 T. H. WHITE The tent was . . shabby, compared with the splendid pavilions of the . . knights. **5** R. W. EMERSON We . . came down into the Italian garden and . . a French pavilion. *Independent* Music that would sit well in the Palm Court or the pier pavilion. **b** *Milton Keynes Express* Stony Stratford Football Club . . pavilion was destroyed by fire.

▸ **B** *verb trans.* **1** Shelter, enclose, or house (as) in a pavilion; canopy. ME.
2 Provide with a pavilion. M17.

1 R. GRANT Pavilioned in splendour And girded with praise.

pavillon /pavijɔ̃/ *noun*. L19.
[French, lit. 'pavilion'.]
1 The bell-shaped mouth of a trumpet or similar musical instrument. L19.
2 *pavillon chinois* /ʃinwa/ [= Chinese], a percussion instrument similar to a Turkish crescent, consisting of a stick having transverse brass plates from which hang a number of small bells which jingle. Also called ***jingling Johnny***. L19.

paving /ˈpeɪvɪŋ/ *noun*. LME.
[from PAVE *verb* + -ING¹.]
1 The action of PAVE *verb*. LME.
2 (The material of) a pavement. LME.
Comb.: **paving-stone** a stone for paving; **paving-tile** a tile for paving a floor, yard, path, etc., freq. glazed and sometimes ornamentally patterned.

pavior /ˈpeɪvɪə/ *noun*. Also **-iour**, (earlier) †**-ier**. ME.
[Old & mod. French *paveur*, from *paver* PAVE *verb* + *-eur* -ER²: see -IER, -OR.]
1 A person who paves roads etc. ME.
2 A paving-stone. Formerly also, paving. E17.

pavis /ˈpavɪs/ *noun & verb*. Also **-ise**. LME.
[Old & mod. French *pavais* (mod. *pavois*) from Italian *pavese* from medieval Latin *pavense*, from *Pavia*, a city in northern Italy where pavises were orig. made.]
Hist. ▸ **A** *noun*. **1** A large convex shield for protecting the whole body against arrows, used esp. in sieges; any large shield. LME.
2 A screen of pavises; a pavisade; any screen used in fighting. LME.
▸ **B** *verb trans.* Cover, shelter, or defend with a pavis. LME.
■ **paviser**, **-or** *noun* a soldier armed with or bearing a pavis LME.

pavisade /pavɪˈseɪd/ *noun.* E17.
[French *pavesade* from Italian *pavesata*, from *pavese* PAVIS: see -ADE.]
Hist. A defence or screen of pavises joined in a continuous line. Also, a canvas screen placed around a ship's deck as a defence against enemy fire and to conceal the crew's operations.

pavisand /ˈpavɪsand/ *verb intrans.* E20.
[from prec.]
Display a formidable array of clothing and ornament; flaunt one's appearance.

pavise *noun & verb* var. of PAVIS.

Pavlov /ˈpavlɒv/ *noun.* E20.
[Ivan Petrovich *Pavlov* (1849–1936), Russian physiologist.]
Used *attrib.* and in *possess.* with ref. to Pavlov's work, esp. the conditioning of the salivary reflexes of a dog to the mental stimulus of the sound of a bell.

pavlova /ˈpavləvə, pavˈləʊvə/ *noun.* Orig. *Austral. & NZ.* E20.
[from Anna *Pavlova* (1881–1931), Russian ballerina.]
A dessert consisting of a meringue base or shell filled with whipped cream and fruit, and sometimes marshmallow.

Pavlovian /pavˈləʊvɪən/ *adjective.* M20.
[from PAVLOV + -IAN.]
Of, pertaining to, or derived from Pavlov's work on conditioned reflexes; of the nature of a reaction or response made unthinkingly or under the influence of others.

📖 *Daily Telegraph* The report . . will inevitably touch off a Pavlovian response from Leftist circles.

Pavo /ˈpɑːvəʊ/ *noun.* E18.
[Latin = peacock.]
(The name of) a constellation of the southern hemisphere between Grus and Triangulum Australe; the Peacock.

pavonazzo /pavoˈnaddzo/ *adjective & noun.* E19.
[Italian from Latin *pavonaceum*, formed as next: see -ACEOUS.]
(Designating) a red or purplish marble or breccia, freq. veined with a variety of colours.
▪ ***pavonazzetto*** /pavonatˈtzetto/ *noun* (a) stone similar to *pavonazzo* L19.

†**pavone** *noun. rare* (Spenser). Only in L16.
[Italian from Latin *pavo(n-)*.]
A peacock.

pavonian /pəˈvəʊnɪən/ *adjective.* L18.
[from Latin *pavo(n-)*: see next, -IAN.]
Of, pertaining to, or resembling a peacock.

pavonine /ˈpavənʌɪn/ *adjective & noun.* M17.
[Latin *pavoninus*, from *pavo(n-)* peacock: see -INE[1].]
▶ **A** *adjective.* **1** Of, pertaining to, resembling, or characteristic of a peacock. M17.
2 Resembling the neck or tail of a peacock in colouring. L17.

📖 **2** *New Yorker* A tall goblet . . embellished with pavonine designs.

▶ **B** *noun.* An iridescent tarnish found on some ores and metals. *rare.* E19.

pavor /ˈpavɔːr/ *noun.* M17.
[Latin.]
†**1** Fear, terror, dread. *rare* (only in Dicts.). Only in M17.
2 A sudden inexplicable terror striking a sleeping person, esp. a child. Only in phrs. below. L19.
2 ***pavor diurnus*** /dʌɪˈəːnəs/ [= diurnal] such a terror occurring during the day. ***pavor nocturnus*** /nɒkˈtəːnəs/ [= nocturnal] such a terror occurring during the night (cf. ***night-terrors*** s.v. NIGHT *noun*.).

Pavulon /ˈpavjʊlɒn/ *noun.* Also **p-**. M20.
[Origin unkn.]
PHARMACOLOGY. (Proprietary name for) the drug pancuronium.

pavvy /ˈpavi/ *noun. slang.* Also **pavy.** L19.
[Abbreviation: see -Y[6].]
= PAVILION.

pavy /ˈpeɪvi/ *noun*[1]. L17.
[French *pavie*, from *Pavie* Pavia (see PAVIAN).]
A hard clingstone peach or nectarine.

pavy *noun*[2] var. of PAVVY.

paw /pɔː/ *noun*[1] *& verb.* ME.
[Old French *powe, poue, poe* from Proto-Romance, from Frankish (repr. in Middle Dutch *pôte*, Dutch *poot*).]
▶ **A** *noun.* **1** The foot of an animal, having claws and pads. ME. ▸**b** The foot of any animal; *esp.* the claw of a bird. *rare.* LME.
2 A person's hand, esp. when clumsy, awkwardly used, or (formerly) brutal. *colloq.* LME. ▸**b** *transf.* Handwriting; signature; (artistic) style; handiwork. Cf. FIST *noun*[1] 3, HAND *noun* 16, 17. E17.
3 [from the verb.] The action or an act of pawing. E17.

📖 **2** A. BURGESS Workers soon had rifles . . in their unhandy paws.

▶ **B** *verb.* **1** *verb trans. & intrans.* Touch or strike (a person or thing) with a paw. LME.
2 *verb intrans. & trans.* Of a horse etc.: strike or scrape (the ground) with a hoof. E17.
3 *verb trans.* Touch or handle awkwardly or roughly; *esp.* (*colloq.*) fondle (a person) awkwardly or lasciviously. Also foll. by *about.* E17. ▸**b** *verb intrans.* Pass a hand awkwardly or clumsily (*over, through*, etc.). M19.

📖 **3** C. ISHERWOOD He kept stroking . . Sally's arm and pawing her hand. **b** D. RUNYON Butch starts pawing through her satchel looking for something.

With prepositions in specialized senses: **paw at** (*a*) touch or strike with a paw; (*b*) *colloq.* attempt to fondle, fondle awkwardly or lasciviously.

paw /pɔː/ *noun*[2]. *colloq. & dial.* (chiefly *US*). E20.
[Repr. a pronunc. of PA *noun*[2]: cf. MAW *noun*[5].]
= PA *noun*[2].

†**paw** *adjective. slang.* M17–M18.
[App. from PAH *interjection.* Cf. PAW-PAW.]
Improper; obscene.

pawa *noun* var. of PAUA.

pawang /ˈpɑːwaŋ/ *noun.* E19.
[Malay.]
In Malaysia and Indonesia: a medicine man, a sorcerer; a wise man, an expert.

pawk /pɔːk/ *noun. Scot. & north.* E16.
[Origin unkn.]
A trick, a cunning device; (an) artifice.

pawky /ˈpɔːki/ *adjective.* Orig. *Scot. & north.* M17.
[from PAWK + -Y[1].]
Crafty, artful; cunning, shrewd; drily humorous, arch.
▪ **pawkily** *adverb* E18. **pawkiness** *noun* L19.

pawl /pɔːl/ *noun & verb.* Also †**pall**, †**paul**. E17.
[Perh. from Low German, Dutch *pal* rel. to *pal* adjective, immobile, fixed: ult. origin unkn.]
▶ **A** *noun.* **1** NAUTICAL. Each of a set of short stout bars that engage with the whelps and prevent a capstan, windlass, or winch from recoiling. E17.
2 A pivoted, usu. curved, bar or lever whose free end engages with the teeth of a cog-wheel or ratchet so that it can only turn or move one way. E18.
Comb.: **pawl-bitt**, **pawl-post** NAUTICAL a strong vertical post in which the pawls of a windlass are fixed; **pawl-rim** NAUTICAL a notched cast-iron ring for a pawl to catch in.
▶ **B** *verb.* **1** *verb trans.* Stop or secure by means of a pawl. E18.
2 *verb trans. & intrans. fig.* (Cause to) stop or cease. *colloq.* E19.

pawn /pɔːn/ *noun*[1]. LME.
[Anglo-Norman *poun*, Old French *poön, peon* from medieval Latin *pedo(n-)* foot-soldier, from Latin *ped-*, *pes* foot. Cf. PEON.]
1 CHESS. Any of the sixteen chessmen (eight per player) of smallest size, capability, and value. LME.
2 *fig.* A person or thing used by another for his or her own purposes. L16.

📖 **2** B. CASTLE Inexcusable to use these refugees as political pawns.

Phrases: ***hanging pawn***: see HANGING *adjective.* ISOLATED ***pawn***. ***passed pawn***: see PASS *verb.*
Comb.: **pawn chain** an unbroken diagonal line of pawns crossing several adjacent files; **pawn skeleton** the structure of the pawns at the end of a chess opening; **pawn storm** an attack of pawns against a castled king.

pawn /paʊn/ *noun*[2]. Formerly *Scot.*, now only HERALDRY. Also **-e.** LME.
[Old French *poun, poon* (mod. *paon*) from Latin *pavo(n-)*.]
A peacock.

pawn /pɔːn/ *noun*[3] *& verb.* L15.
[Old French *pan, pand, pant* pledge, security, plunder from West Germanic word repr. by Old Frisian *pand*, Old Saxon, Middle Dutch *pant* (Dutch *pand*), Old High German *pfant* (German *Pfand*).]
▶ **A** *noun.* **1** A thing or person given, or left in another's keeping, as security for a debt or for the performance of some action; a pledge, a surety. Now *rare.* L15. ▸**b** *fig.* (A sign or symbol of) a promise. L16. ▸**c** A person held as a security for debt and used as a slave. M19.
2 The state or condition of being given or held as a pledge or as security for the repayment of a loan. Chiefly in ***at pawn***, ***in pawn***. M16 ▸**b** The action of pawning or pledging something. E19.
3 A pawnbroker, a pawnshop. Chiefly *Scot.* M19.

📖 **2** *Blackwood's Magazine* Redeem one of the innumerable suits . . he has in pawn.

Comb.: **pawnbroker** a person who lends money on the security of an article pawned; **pawnbrokery** (*a*) a pawnbroker's shop; (*b*) pawnbroking; **pawnbroking** the occupation or action of lending money on the security of pawned articles; **pawnshop** a pawnbroker's shop or place of business; **pawn-ticket**: issued by a pawnbroker in exchange for an article pawned, bearing particulars of the loan.
▶ **B** *verb trans.* Give (a thing) as security for the payment of a debt or the performance of an action; *spec.* deposit with a person, esp. a pawnbroker, as security for the repayment of a loan. Also *fig.*, pledge, wager, (one's honour, life, word, etc.). M16.

📖 G. GREENE I've pawned a lot . . and dropped the ticket in the nearest dustbin. A. N. WILSON Eladie . . had to pawn her diamond cross for £4.

▪ **pawnable** *adjective* M18. †**pawnage** *noun* (*rare*) the action of pawning something; a pawned object: E17–M19. **pawner** *noun* M18.

†**pawn** *noun*[4]. L16–L19.
[Dutch *pand* from French *pan*: see PANE *noun*[1].]
A gallery, a covered walk; *esp.* one in a bazaar, exchange, or arcade along which goods were displayed for sale.

pawne *noun* var. of PAWN *noun*[2].

pawnee /pɔːˈniː/ *noun*[1]. L17.
[from PAWN *verb* + -EE[1].]
A person with whom something is pawned.

Pawnee /pɔːˈniː/ *noun*[2] *& adjective.* Also †**Pane.** Pl. of noun same, **-s.** L18.
[Canad. French *Pani* from a N. Amer. Indian language.]
1 Of or pertaining to, a member of, a confederacy of N. American Indians formerly inhabiting the valleys of the Loup, Platte, and Republican Rivers in Nebraska. L18. ▸**b** (Of or pertaining to) the language of these people. E19.
†**2** Of or pertaining to, a member of, the Wichita Indians, esp. bands formerly inhabiting the Red River valley of Oklahoma and Texas. L18–E20.

pawnee /pɔːˈniː/ *noun*[3]. E19.
[Hindi *pānī* from Sanskrit *pānīya*.]
Esp. in the Indian subcontinent: a drink; water as taken in drinks.

pawpaw /ˈpɔːpɔː/ *noun*[1]. Also **papaw** /pəˈpɔː/; in sense 1 now freq. **papaya** /pəˈpʌɪə/. L16.
[Spanish & Portuguese *papaya, papayo* (the tree) from Carib or Arawak: the subsequent change to *pa(w)paw* is unexpl.]
1 a The melon-shaped fruit of the tree *Carica papaya* (see below), much eaten in tropical countries, which has pinkish or orange flesh enclosing a mass of dark grey seeds. L16. ▸**b** A tropical American tree, *Carica papaya* (family Caricaceae), commonly cultivated throughout the tropics, with palmate leaves on an unbranched stem and an acrid milky juice which has the property of tenderizing meat (see PAPAIN). E17.
2 A small N. American tree, *Asimina triloba* (family Annonaceae), with dull purple flowers and ovate leaves (also ***pawpaw tree***); the oblong edible fruit of this tree, with seeds like beans embedded in a sweet pulp. M18.

Pawpaw /ˈpɔːpɔː/ *noun*[2]. Also **Papaw.** E18.
[A region on the coast of Benin, W. Africa.]
Hist. A Jamaican slave who came from the coastal region of what is now Benin.

paw-paw /ˈpɔːpɔː/ *adjective. slang* (now *rare*). L18.
[Redupl. of PAW *adjective.*]
Improper, naughty; nasty; indecent, obscene, immoral.

PAX *abbreviation.*
Private automatic exchange.

pax /paks/ *noun.* LME.
[Latin = peace.]
1 ECCLESIASTICAL. (Also **P-**.) = PEACE *noun* 4C. LME.
2 ECCLESIASTICAL HISTORY. A tablet of gold, silver, ivory, glass, etc., with a projecting handle, depicting the Crucifixion or other sacred subject, which was kissed by all participants at mass. Also called ***osculatory***. LME.
3 Peace, tranquillity, concord; *esp.* peace between nations. Chiefly (after ***pax Romana*** below) in phrs. with Latin or mod. Latin adjective referring to the dominant influence of a State, empire, etc. L15.
4 A friend; good friends. *School slang.* L18.
5 As *interjection.* A call for quiet or (a) truce. *School slang.* M19.

📖 **1** *Church Times* At the Pax the Italian matron . . warmly shook me by the hand. **3** R. RAINE The whole Western world . . is living under . . a Pax Americana. ***pax Romana*** /rəʊˈmɑːnə/ the peace which existed between nationalities within the Roman Empire.

Paxarete /paxaˈrete/ *noun.* Also ***Paja-***. E19.
[A town in the Jerez district of Spain.]
A mixture of fortified wine and boiled-down grape juice, formerly drunk as a sherry, now used primarily for colouring or sweetening sherry or whisky.

paxilla /pakˈsɪlə/ *noun.* Pl. **-llae** /-liː/. L19.
[mod. Latin, from Latin *paxillus* small stake, peg.]
ZOOLOGY. A raised ossicle in some starfishes bearing hinged spines which may be lowered to create a cavity next to the aboral surface.
▪ **paxillar** *adjective* of or pertaining to paxillae E20. **paxiˈlliferous** *adjective* = PAXILLOSE M19. **paxilliform** *adjective*

having the shape of a paxilla L19. **paxillose** *adjective* bearing paxillae E20.

Paxolin /ˈpaksəlɪn/ *noun*. E20.
[Prob. invented word.]
(Proprietary name for) a type of laminated plastic widely used as an electrical insulating material.

paxwax /ˈpakswaks/ *noun*. Now *dial*. LME.
[Prob. alt. of FAX *noun*¹ + base of WAX *verb*¹. See also TAXWAX.]
The nuchal ligament, esp. in a domestic quadruped.

pay /peɪ/ *noun*. ME.
[Old & mod. French *paie*, formed as next.]
†**1** Satisfaction, pleasure, liking. Chiefly in ***to pay***, acceptably. ME–E17.
2 Money paid for labour or service; wages, salary, stipend. ME.
3 *fig*. Retaliation, penalty, retribution; punishment. Also, recompense, compensation. Long *obsolete* exc. *dial*. ME.
4 a The action of paying, payment, esp. of wages or salary. LME. ▸**b** The condition of being (regularly) paid. Chiefly in ***in pay, in the pay of***, below. L16.
5 A (good, bad, etc.) person at repaying debts. E18.
6 *MINING*. A remunerative yield of metal, oil, or natural gas. Also, a bed of ore etc. yielding this. M19.
7 = PAYMASTER. *slang*. L19.

🕮 **2** B. CASTLE With statutory incomes controls abolished, both consultants and GPs were getting restive about their pay. *Jazz & Blues* Jones certainly earned his pay. **3** SHAKES. *Ven. & Ad.* When her lips were ready for his pay. **4a** *Guardian* At Boots, the highest rate of pay rose by 58 per cent.

Phrases: ***dead pay***: see DEAD *adjective & adverb*. ***equal pay***: see EQUAL *adjective*. ***full pay***: see FULL *adjective*. **in pay** in receipt of a wage or salary. **in the pay of** in the paid employment of. ***RETIRED pay***. ***sick pay***: see SICK *adjective*. ***to pay***: see sense 1 above.

pay /peɪ/ *verb*¹. Pa. t. & pple **paid** /peɪd/. ME.
[Old & mod. French *payer* from Latin *pacare* appease, pacify, (in medieval Latin) pay, from *pac-*, *pax* PEACE *noun*; the sense 'give money for' was developed through that of pacifying a creditor.]
†**1** *verb trans*. Appease, pacify; satisfy; please, gratify; be acceptable to, meet with the approval of. Usu. in *pass*. ME–E16.
2 *verb trans*. **a** Give (a person) money etc. that is due for goods received, a service done, or a debt incurred; remunerate. Also, hand over or transfer (money etc.) in return for something (foll. by *to* the recipient). Also with double obj. (***pay a person money*** etc.). ME. ▸**b** Hand over or transfer money in discharge of (a debt, fee, wage, etc.); hand over or transfer the amount of (a price). LME.
3 *verb trans*. *fig*. Give (a thing owed, due, or deserved); discharge (an obligation, promise, etc.); give in retribution or retaliation (*arch*.); experience (pain or trouble) as punishment or in exchange for some advantage. Also with double obj., as in sense 2a. ME.
4 *verb trans*. Give what is due for (a deed) or to (a person); reward, recompense; punish. ME. ▸**b** *spec*. Beat, flog. Now *dial*. L16.
5 *verb intrans*. Give money in return for something; *esp*. discharge a debt; *fig*. make amends, give restitution. ME.
6 *verb trans*. Give or bestow (attention, respect, a compliment, a visit, etc.). Usu. with *to* or indirect obj. LME.
7 *verb trans*. = ***pay for*** (a) below; *fig*. compensate, make up for. Now *rare* or *obsolete*. L16.
8 *verb trans*. Chiefly *NAUTICAL*. Let out (a rope, chain, anchor, etc.) gradually. Now only foll. by *out*. E17.
9 *NAUTICAL verb trans. & intrans*. (Cause to) turn to leeward. Now only foll. by *off*. E17.
10 a *verb trans*. Of a thing: yield money sufficient for (= ***pay for*** (b) below); yield (an amount, return, etc.). M17. ▸**b** *verb intrans. & trans*. Yield an adequate return (to); be profitable or advantageous (to). L18.

🕮 **2a** G. GREENE She must have been receiving wages from some source for he paid her none. B. TRAPIDO 'Have them on me,' she said, when we tried to pay her. *Sporting News* A three-year contract that will pay him $16.25 million. **b** W. RAEPER Mr Powell had paid the last quarter's rent. **3** I. WATTS Praise, everlasting praise, be paid To him that earth's foundation laid. R. SOUTH Inflaming themselves with Wine, till they come to pay the Reckoning with their Blood. J. WAIN Society agreed that I should pay the price, and I've paid it. **4** G. MACDONALD Enough he labours for his hire; . . nought can pay his pain. **5** *Omni* It's the person who cheated . . who should pay. *Economist* Contracts normally give customers 30 days to pay. **6** E. WAUGH He decided to pay one of his rare . . visits to his mother. G. GREENE She was . . paying him the half-attention a parent pays a child. **10a** A. CARNEGIE This was my first investment . . and Adams Express paid a monthly dividend. **b** *Dress* It will pay you to consult me as to your plans. J. CONRAD Answering back, as a general rule, does not pay. R. HARLING It pays to advertise.

Phrases, & with prepositions in specialized senses: ***hell to pay***: see HELL *noun*. **not if you paid me, not if you paid him**, etc., under no circumstances; not at all. **paid holidays** an agreed holiday period for which wages are paid as normal. ***pay a call***: see CALL *noun*. ***pay a person in his or her own coin***: see COIN *noun*. **pay dearly** pay a lot (*for*); suffer greatly (*for*). **pay for** (*a*) give money etc. for (goods, a service, etc.); (***pay for one's whistle, pay too dear for one's whistle***: see WHISTLE *noun*); (*b*) be sufficient to buy or to cover the cost of; (*c*) *fig*. make amends for, atone for; suffer or be punished for; (***pay for one's scot***: see SCOT *noun*²). ***paying guest***: see GUEST *noun* 1. **pay its way, pay one's way** cover its or one's cost or expenses. ***pay one's attentions to***: see ATTENTION *noun* 3. ***pay one's last respects, pay one's respects***: see RESPECT *noun*. ***pay one's scot***: see SCOT *noun*². ***pay on the line***: see LINE *noun*². ***pay reverence to***: see REVERENCE *noun*. ***pay sauce***: see SAUCE *noun*. **pay the piper (and call the tune)** pay the cost of (and so have the right to control) an activity or undertaking. ***pay through the nose***: see NOSE *noun*. **pay with the fore-topsail** *Nautical slang* leave port without paying debts or creditors. ***pitch and pay***: see PITCH *verb*² 7a. **put paid to** *colloq*. (*a*) deal effectively with (a person); (*b*) put an end to (a hope etc.). ***rob Peter to pay Paul***: see PETER *noun*¹. ***the devil to pay***: see DEVIL *noun*.
With adverbs in specialized senses: **pay back** (*a*) repay (a loan etc.); (*b*) punish, be revenged on. **pay down** (*a*) lay (money) down in payment, pay immediately; (*b*) reduce (debt) by repayment. **pay in** pay (money) into a bank account or a fund. **pay off** (*a*) pay (a debt) in full (***pay off old scores***: see SCORE *noun*); (*b*) settle accounts (with); (*c*) dismiss (a worker) with a final payment; (*d*) (of a ship) have its crew discharged at the end of a voyage; (*e*) *colloq*. be profitable or advantageous; succeed, show results; (see also sense 9 above). **pay out** (*a*) pay (money) from funds under one's control or in one's possession; disburse, spend; (*b*) = ***pay back*** above; (*c*) get rid of by paying; (see also sense 8 above). **pay over** hand over or transfer in payment; pay (*to*). **pay up** pay (a debt) in full; ***paid-up member***, a member of an organization who is up to date with his or her subscriptions.
■ **pay'ee** *noun* a person to whom a sum of money is (to be) paid; *esp*. the person to whom a cheque is made payable: M18. **payer** *noun* a person who pays (esp. a sum of money) ME. **payor** *noun* = PAYER L19.

pay /peɪ/ *verb*² *trans*. Pa. t. & pple **payed**, **paid** /peɪd/. E17.
[Old French *peier* from Latin *picare*, from *pic-*, *pix*, PITCH *noun*¹.]
Chiefly *NAUTICAL*. Smear or cover with pitch, resin, tallow, etc., to protect against water etc.

pay- /peɪ/ *combining form*. M16.
[Repr. PAY *noun*, *verb*¹.]
1 Forming nouns and adjectives with the senses 'of or pertaining to payment', 'that pays', 'for (the use of) which payment is charged'.
2 Forming nouns and adjectives of the type ***pay-as-you-——***.
pay-and-display *adjective & noun* (designating) a parking system in which a motorist buys a temporary permit from a coin-operated machine and displays it in the window of the vehicle. **pay-as-you-earn** a system by which an employer deducts income tax from an employee's wages before paying them to the employee and sends the deduction to the Inland Revenue; abbreviation *PAYE*. **pay-as-you-go** *adjective* designating a system or practice of paying debts and meeting costs as they arise. **pay-bed** a hospital bed for private patients. **paybob** *slang* = PAYMASTER. **pay-book**: containing a record of payments (esp. wages) made. **pay channel** a television channel for which viewers pay a subscription fee (esp. in contrast to those channels provided at no extra cost on the payment of a basic subscription fee to a cable or satellite television service). **pay-claim** a request for a higher rate of pay made by an employee, trade union, etc., to an employer. **pay dirt** (*a*) ground containing ore in sufficient quantity to be profitably extracted; (*b*) *fig*. (a source of) profit or reward. **pay envelope** *N. Amer*. = ***pay-packet*** below. **pay freeze** a prohibition on wage and salary increases. **pay gravel** = ***pay dirt*** above. **paymistress** a woman responsible for payment of people or services; *fig*. a thing (personified as female) that pays or rewards. **payout** an act or the action of paying out; an amount of money paid out. **pay-packet** a packet containing an employee's wages or notification of them; *fig*. a salary, an income. **pay-per-view** a system of television broadcasting in which viewers pay a fee to watch a particular programme (usually a film or a sporting event). **pay phone** a coin-operated telephone. **pay rise** an increase in a person's rate of pay. **payroll** *noun & verb* (*a*) *noun* (a list of) employees receiving regular pay; the personnel costs of a company etc.; (*b*) *verb trans*. (*colloq*.) finance (a person, activity, etc.). **pay slip** a note given to an employee when payment of a wage or salary is made, showing details of the amount and usu. deductions made by the employer. **pay station** *US* a public pay phone. **pay toilet** a public toilet which one has to pay to use. **pay-tone** an audible telephone signal indicating when a caller using a pay phone should insert a coin. **pay-television**, **pay-TV** television broadcasting for which payment by subscription (or by coin in the slot) gives the ability to watch a particular channel.

payable /ˈpeɪəb(ə)l/ *adjective & noun*. LME.
[from PAY *verb*¹ + -ABLE.]
▶ **A** *adjective*. **1** Of a sum of money, a bill, etc.: that is to be paid; falling due (usu. *at* or *on* a specified date or *to* a specified person). LME.
2 Able to be paid. *rare*. E18.
3 Esp. of a mine etc.: capable of yielding profit, profitable. M19.
▶ **B** *noun*. In *pl*. Debts owed by a business; liabilities. Cf. RECEIVABLE *noun*. L20.
■ **paya'bility** *noun* ability or willingness to pay; profitability: E19.

payas *noun pl*. var. of PAYESS.

payback /ˈpeɪbak/ *noun*. M20.
[from ***pay back*** s.v. PAY *verb*¹.]
1 Reward, return; *spec*. profit from an investment, esp. when equal to the initial outlay. M20.
2 (An act of) revenge or retaliation. L20.
Comb.: **payback period** the time required for an investment to pay for itself in terms of profit or savings.

pay-day /ˈpeɪdeɪ/ *noun*. E16.
[from PAY- + DAY *noun*.]
1 The day on which payment is made or due to be made; *esp*. a specified day each week, month, etc., on which wages are regularly paid; *STOCK EXCHANGE* the day on which a transfer of stock must be paid for. E16.
2 *NAUTICAL*. Wages; the amount paid to a person on pay-day. E20.

PAYE *abbreviation*.
Pay as you earn.

payed *verb pa. t. & pple*: see PAY *verb*².

payess /ˈpeɪɛs/ *noun pl*. Chiefly *N. Amer*. Also **payas** & other vars. M20.
[Yiddish from Hebrew *pē'ōṯ* pl. of *pē'āh* corner (cf. *Leviticus* 19:27).]
Uncut ear-locks worn by male Orthodox Jews.

payload /ˈpeɪləʊd/ *noun*. M20.
[from PAY- + LOAD *noun*.]
1 The part of a vehicle's load, esp. an aircraft's, from which revenue is derived; cargo, passengers, etc. M20.
2 An explosive charge carried by an aircraft or missile. M20.
3 Equipment, personnel, etc., carried by a spacecraft to monitor operations, conduct experiments, etc. M20.
■ **Payloader** *noun* (proprietary name for) a heavy mobile machine for lifting and loading cargo etc. M20.

paymaster /ˈpeɪmɑːstə/ *noun*. M16.
[from PAY- + MASTER *noun*¹.]
1 An official responsible for paying troops, workers, etc. M16.
2 *transf*. A person, organization, etc., requiring service or loyalty in return for (esp. previously given) pay. L20.
Comb.: **Paymaster-General** the head of the office of the British Government that acts as the government's paying agent.

payment /ˈpeɪm(ə)nt/ *noun*. ME.
[Old & mod. French *paiement*, from *payer* PAY *verb*¹: see -MENT.]
1 An act, or the action or process, of paying. (Foll. by *of* the money etc. paid, the debt discharged, the payee; *for* the thing bought or recompensed.) ME.
2 (A sum of) money etc. paid. LME.

🕮 **1** H. CARPENTER She . . demanded a husband in payment for her father's death. JOAN SMITH She made out a cheque in payment of the forgotten parking ticket. R. INGALLS It takes me everything I earn just to keep up the payments on my apartment. B. VINE Released on payment of a ransom. *Money Management* Pensions already in payment would be unaffected. **2** *Financial Times* They pay no VAT at all until they receive payment from their customers.

Phrases: ***balance of payments***: see BALANCE *noun*. ***deferred payment***: see DEFER *verb*¹ 2. ***stop payment***: see STOP *verb*. ***suspend payment***: see SUSPEND 2. ***token payment***: see TOKEN *noun & adjective*.

Payne's grey /peɪnz ˈgreɪ/ *noun phr*. M19.
[William *Payne* (fl. 1800), English artist.]
A composite pigment composed of blue, red, black, and white permanent pigments, used esp. for watercolours.

paynim /ˈpeɪnɪm/ *noun & adjective*. Now *arch. & poet*. ME.
[Old French *pai(e)nime* from ecclesiastical Latin *paganismus* heathenism, from Latin *paganus* PAGAN: see -ISM.]
▶ **A** *noun*. †**1** Pagan or non-Christian lands collectively. Only in ME.
2 A pagan, a heathen; a non-Christian, *esp*. a Muslim, a Saracen. ME.
▶ **B** *adjective*. Pagan, heathen; non-Christian, *esp*. Muslim, Saracen. ME.
■ **paynimry** *noun* pagans or heathens collectively LME.

paynize /ˈpeɪnʌɪz/ *verb trans*. Also **-ise**. M19.
[from *Payne*, the inventor of the process.]
Impregnate (wood) with a solution of calcium or barium sulphide followed by one of calcium sulphate, as a hardener and preservative.

pay-off /ˈpeɪɒf/ *noun*. E20.
[from ***pay off*** s.v. PAY *verb*¹.]
1 (The paying of) the amount of money that goes to a winner in a gamble. E20. ▸**b** A confidence trick in which the victim is encouraged by the secretly arranged success of a small bet, investment, etc., to venture a large sum which will be lost. *Criminals' slang*. E20. ▸**c** The return on an investment; profit. Also, the point at which an investment begins to become profitable. M20.
2 A result, a conclusion, an outcome; a recompense, *esp*. a financial one; a retributory act. E20. ▸**b** A climax, a denouement. M20.
3 A bribe; bribery. *colloq*. M20.

🕮 **1** E. LEONARD He liked the sound of quarter-slot payoffs better; it sounded more like real money. **2** G. F. NEWMAN All the inconvenience and suffering, and this was the pay-off. *New Musical Express* The ex-manager has reportedly left with a multi-million pound compensation payoff. **3** S. BELLOW Even to get to talk to the director, a payoff was necessary.

Comb.: **pay-off line** the point or punch-line of a story etc.; **pay-off man** *Criminals' slang* (*a*) a confidence trickster; (*b*) the cashier of a gang of criminals; **pay-off matrix**, **pay-off table** *MATH*. in game theory, an array specifying the utilities to the players of all the possible outcomes of a game, conflict, etc.

payola /peɪˈəʊlə/ *noun. slang* (orig. *US*). **M20.**
[from PAY *noun* or *verb*[1] + -OLA.]
Bribery aimed at getting a person to use his or her position, influence, etc., to promote a particular commercial interest, product, etc.; *spec.* bribery of a disc jockey for promoting a record or song. Also, a bribe of this kind.

paysage /peizaːʒ/ *noun.* Pl. pronounced same. **E17.**
[French, from *pays* country: see -AGE.]
(A representation of) a rural scene or landscape.
¶ Formerly naturalized.
▪ ***paysagist*** /peizaːʒɪst/ *noun* a landscape-painter **E19.**

paysan /peizɑ̃/ *noun & adjective.* **E19.**
[French: see PEASANT. Cf. next.]
▶ **A** *noun.* Pl. pronounced same. A peasant, a countryman, esp. in France. **E19.**
▶ **B** *adjective.* **1** Resembling that of a peasant, rustic. *rare.* **L19.**
2 = PEASANT *adjective* 2. **L19.**

paysanne /peizan/ *noun.* Pl. pronounced same. **M18.**
[French, fem. of PAYSAN.]
A peasant-woman, a countrywoman, esp. in France.

Pazand /ˈpɑːzand/ *noun & adjective.* Also **-end** /-ɛnd/. **L18.**
[Persian *pā-zand* interpretation of the Zend, from *Zend*: see ZEND-AVESTA.]
(Pertaining to or designating) a transcription of or the method of transcribing Persian sacred texts from the Pahlavi into the Avesta script.

pazazz *noun* var. of PIZZAZZ.

PB *abbreviation. slang.*
Poor bloody.

Pb *symbol.*
[Latin *plumbum.*]
CHEMISTRY. Lead.

PBI *abbreviation. slang.*
Poor bloody infantry(man).

PBS *abbreviation. US.*
Public Broadcasting Service.

PBX *abbreviation.*
Private branch exchange.

PC *abbreviation*[1].
1 Personal computer.
2 Police Constable.
3 Political correctness, politically correct.
4 Postcard.
5 Privy Counsellor.
1 PC card a printed circuit board for a personal computer, esp. one built to the PCMCIA standard.

pc *abbreviation*[2].
1 Per cent.
2 (Freq. as *pl.* **pcs.**) Piece.
3 Postcard.

PCB *abbreviation.*
1 Polychlorinated biphenyl.
2 Printed circuit board.

PCC *abbreviation.*
1 Parochial church council
2 *Hist.* Prerogative Court of Canterbury.

PCI *abbreviation.*
COMPUTING. Peripheral Component Interconnect, a standard for connecting computers and their peripherals.

PCM *abbreviation.*
Pulse code modulation.

PCMCIA *abbreviation.*
COMPUTING. Personal Computer Memory Card International Association, denoting a standard specification for memory cards and interfaces in personal computers.

PCN *abbreviation.*
Personal communications network, a digital mobile telephony system.

p-code *abbreviation.*
COMPUTING. Pseudocode.

PCP *abbreviation.*
1 PHARMACOLOGY. Phencyclidine.
2 MEDICINE. *Pneumocystis carinii* pneumonia.

PCR *abbreviation.*
BIOCHEMISTRY. Polymerase chain reaction (esp. as a means of detecting and reproducing nucleic acid).

PCS *abbreviation.*
Personal communications services, a digital mobile telephony system.

pct. *abbreviation. US.*
Per cent.

PCV *abbreviation.*
Passenger-carrying vehicle.

PCY *abbreviation.*
Hist. Prerogative Court of York.

PD *abbreviation*[1].
1 Police Department. *US.*
2 ELECTRICITY. Potential difference.
3 Pretty damn quick. *slang.*
4 Preventive detention or detainee.

pd *abbreviation*[2].
ELECTRICITY. Potential difference.

Pd *symbol.*
CHEMISTRY. Palladium.

pd. *abbreviation.*
Paid.

PDA *abbreviation.*
COMPUTING. Personal digital assistant, a palmtop computer used to store information such as addresses and telephone numbers, and for simple word processing and spreadsheeting.

PDC *abbreviation.*
Programme delivery control, a system for broadcasting a coded signal at the beginning and end of a television programme which can be recognized by a video recorder and used to begin and end recording.

PDP *abbreviation.*
Parallel distributed processing.

pdq *abbreviation. slang.*
Pretty damn quick.

PDS *abbreviation.*
1 Party of Democratic Socialism (in Germany, successor to the E. German Communist Party).
2 COMPUTING. Processor direct slot.

PDT *abbreviation. N. Amer.*
Pacific Daylight Time.

PE *abbreviation.*
1 Physical education.
2 Also **pe.** Plastic explosive.

pea /piː/ *noun*[1]. **M17.**
[Back-form. from PEASE, taken as pl. only.]
▶ **I 1** Any of the round seeds of the plant *Pisum sativum*, which grow in elongated pods, and are eaten as a vegetable when green or as a pulse when dried. **M17.** ▸**b** The hardy annual leguminous climbing plant, *Pisum sativum*, which produces these seeds and bears papilionaceous flowers. Also ***pea-plant.*** **L17.**
2 Any of the edible seeds of several other leguminous plants, esp. (in the New World) cowpea, *Vigna unguiculata*, and pigeon-pea, *Cajanus cajan.* Also (with specifying word), any of numerous leguminous plants, wild or cultivated, more or less resembling the pea-plant. **E18.**
3 [With allus. to the pea used by a thimble-rigger.] A competitor, esp. a horse, generally expected to win; a favourite. *slang* (*obsolete* exc. *Austral.*). **L19.**
1 *garden pea, mangetout pea, marrowfat pea,* etc. **as like as two peas** indistinguishable. **2 *butterfly pea, chick-pea, everlasting pea, glory pea, meadow pea, Sturt's desert pea, sweet pea,*** etc. **field pea, grey pea** a variety of pea, *Pisum sativum* var. *arvense*, grown as fodder.
▶ **II** Something small and round like a pea.
4 The roe or spawn of certain fishes. *obsolete* exc. *dial.* **M18.**
5 A very small size of coal; in *pl.*, coals of a very small size. **L19.**
Comb.: **pea-bean** a variety of kidney bean, *Phaseolus vulgaris*, with small rounded seeds; **pea-beetle** = ***pea-bug*** below; **peaberry** a coffee berry containing one seed instead of the usual two, through non-fertilization of one ovule or subsequent abortion; **pea-bone** the pisiform bone of the wrist; **pea-brain** *colloq.* (***a***) a stupid person, a dunce, a fool; (***b***) the (supposedly small) brain of such a person; **pea-brained** *adjective* (*colloq.*) stupid, foolish; having a (supposedly) small brain; **pea-bug** a small N. American beetle, *Bruchus pisorum*, now found also in southern Europe and Britain, whose larvae infest and destroy pea-plants; **pea-bulb** a very small round electric light bulb, freq. used as an indicator light; **pea-bush** any of various Australian leguminous shrubs, esp. of the genus *Sesbania*; **pea-chafer** = ***pea-bug*** above; **pea-cod** (*obsolete* exc. *dial.*) = PEASECOD; **pea-comb** a triple comb occurring in some varieties of domestic fowl (from its fancied resemblance to a pea-blossom); **pea-combed** *adjective* (of a fowl) having a pea-comb; **pea-crab** any of several small crabs of the genus *Pinnotheres*, which live commensally in the shells of bivalve molluscs such as mussels or oysters; **pea-dove** a dove, *Zenaida aurita*, of the W. Indies; **pea-flour** flour made from dried split peas, pease-meal; **pea-flower** any large papilionaceous flower resembling that of the pea, *Pisum sativum*; **pea-flowered** *adjective* having pea-flowers; **pea gravel** gravel consisting of particles similar in size to peas; **pea-green** *adjective & noun* (of) a bright green; **pea-grit** GEOLOGY pisolitic limestone; **pea-gun** = ***peashooter*** below; **pea-lamp** = ***pea-bulb*** above; **pea-meal** = ***PEASE-meal***; **pea-moth** a noctuid moth, *Laspeyresia nigricana*, whose larvae infest pea-plants; ***pea-plant***: see sense 1b above; **pea-shell** = PEA-POD; **peashooter** (***a***) a toy weapon consisting of a tube through which peas are propelled by blowing; (***b***) a person who shoots with this; **pea-stake**, **pea-stick**: for supporting a garden pea-plant; **pea tree** any of several leguminous trees or shrubs with flowers like those of the pea, *esp.* (more fully ***Siberian pea tree***) *Caragana arborescens*; **pea-urchin** a very small round sea urchin, *Echinocyamus pusillus*; **pea-vine** *US* (***a***) the climbing stem and leaves of the pea, esp. when dried as hay; (***b***) a N. American meadow vetch, *Vicia americana*; **pea-viner** a machine for picking, washing, and grading peas; **pea-weevil** = ***pea-bug*** above.
¶ Ambiguous early examples of the pl. *peas* have been regarded as belonging at PEASE.

pea /piː/ *noun*[2]. **M19.**
[Abbreviation.] = PEAK *noun*[1] 3c.

Peabody /ˈpiːbɒdi/ *noun. US.* **M19.**
[Imit. (see below).]
In full ***Peabody bird***. A N. American whitethroated sparrow, *Zonotrichia albicollis*, whose call ends with three triple notes supposed to resemble repetition of the surname 'Peabody' (or 'Canada'). Also called ***Canada bird***.

peace /piːs/ *noun.* **ME.**
[Anglo-Norman *pes*, Old French *pais* (mod. *paix*) from Latin *pax*, *pac-*.]
1 Freedom from, or cessation of, war or hostilities; the or a state of a nation or community in which it is not at war with another. **ME.** ▸†**b** With *possess.* or *of*: a state or relation of concord and amity with a specified person, esp. a monarch or lord; recognition of the person's authority and acceptance of his or her protection. **ME–L16.** ▸**c** A ratification or treaty of peace between two nations or communities previously at war. Formerly also, an agreement or treaty effecting truce. **LME.**
2 Freedom from civil disorder; public order and security, esp. (usu. ***the peace***) as maintained by law. **ME.**
3 Freedom from disturbance or perturbation, esp. as a condition of an individual; quiet, tranquillity. **ME.**
4 Freedom from quarrels or dissension between individuals; a state of friendliness. **ME.** ▸†**b** *transf.* An author or maintainer of concord. **LME–M16.** ▸**c** Eccl. ***the peace***: a ceremonial greeting (as a handshake or kiss) exchanged during a service in some Churches (now usu. only in the Eucharist), symbolizing Christian love and unity; *spec.* = ***kiss of peace*** s.v. KISS *noun.* **M16.**
5 Freedom from mental, spiritual, or emotional disturbance; calm. **ME.**
6 Absence of noise, movement, or activity; stillness. **ME.**

🕮 **1** *USA Today* Neutrality is essential if we are to .. play a constructive role in achieving peace. **c** V. CRONIN The peace of Kutchuk Kainanji, signed in August 1774. **2** G. GORER The emphasis of the British Police .. has been on the preservation of peace, on the prevention of crime and violence. **3** AV *1 Chron.* 12:18 Peace be unto thee and .. to thine helpers. T. GRAY Let him sleep in peace. M. DICKENS A place where she could get some peace and quiet. **4** H. B. STOWE One of the greatest destroyers of domestic peace is Discourtesy. **5** V. BROME To preserve Freud's peace of mind, Jones went to great trouble to conceal his quarrel. **6** *Independent* The early morning sound of Tornado F3 fighters is about to disturb the rural peace.

Phrases: **at peace** (***a***) in a state of concord or friendliness, not at variance; (***b***) in a state of quiet, serene; (***c***) *euphem.* dead. ***breach of the peace***: see BREACH *noun* 2. CARTHAGINIAN ***peace***. ***declaration of peace***: see DECLARATION 4. **hold one's peace**, (*arch.*) **keep one's peace** remain silent, refrain from speaking. ***Justice of the Peace***: see JUSTICE *noun.* ***keep one's peace***: see ***hold one's peace*** above. **keep the peace** refrain, or prevent others, from disturbing the public peace; maintain public order. ***kiss of peace***: see KISS *noun.* **make one's peace** effect reconciliation for oneself, (*with* another). **make peace** bring about a state of peace. ***no peace for the wicked***: see WICKED *noun* 1. ***pipe of peace***: see PIPE *noun*[1]. ***Prince of Peace***: see PRINCE *noun.* ***sessions of the peace***: see SESSION *noun* 3b. ***surety of peace, surety of the peace***: see SURETY *noun.* **the King's peace, the Queen's peace** (***a***) *Hist.* the protection given to certain people by the monarch, as those employed on royal business, travelling on the king's highway, etc.; (***b***) the general peace of the kingdom under the monarch's authority; civil order. ***wand of peace***: see WAND *noun* 6. ***win the peace***: see WIN *verb*[1].
Comb.: **peace-breaker** a person who breaks or violates peace; a violator of public order and security; **peace camp** an informal encampment, usu. near a military establishment, set up as a public protest against that establishment or against some aspect of military policy; **Peace Corps** *US* (the name of) an organization that sends young people to work as volunteers in developing countries; **peace dividend** a financial benefit from reduced defence spending; a sum of money available for other purposes when spending on defence is reduced; **peace economy** an economy characteristic of peacetime, in which defence expenditure is relatively low and only a small part of the labour force is engaged in arms production etc.; **peace-keeper** a person who keeps or maintains peace; (a member of) a peace-keeping organization or force; **peace-keeping** the active maintenance of a truce between nations or communities, esp. by international military forces; (freq. *attrib.*); **peace-man** †(***a***) a man at peace with the king, or under the king's peace; (***b***) a man who favours or advocates peace; **peace-offering** (***a***) (in biblical translations) an offering or sacrifice presented as an expression of thanksgiving to God; (***b***) an offering made to make or obtain peace; a propitiatory sacrifice or gift; **peace-officer** a civil officer appointed to preserve the public peace; †**peace-parted** *adjective* (*rare*, Shakes.) that has departed this life in peace; ***peace-pipe***: see PIPE

noun¹; **peace pledge** (*a*) = FRANK-PLEDGE 2; (*b*) an undertaking to abstain from fighting or to promote peace; **peace prize**: presented for a contribution to the prevention of war; **peace sign** a sign of peace made by holding up the hand with palm outturned and the first two fingers extended in a V shape; **peace talk** conversation or discussion about peace or the ending of hostilities; *spec.* in *pl.*, a conference or series of discussions aimed at achieving peace; **peacetime** the time or (*US*) a period when a country is not at war.

peace /piːs/ *verb. arch.* ME.
[from the noun, prob. from use as interjection.]
1 *verb intrans.* In *imper.*: be silent, keep quiet. ME.
†**2** *verb intrans.* Be or become still or silent; refrain from or cease speaking. LME–M17.
†**3** *verb trans.* Reduce to peace; calm, appease. E–M16.

peaceable /ˈpiːsəb(ə)l/ *adjective, noun, & adverb.* Also †**-cible**. ME.
[Old French *peisible* (mod. *paisible*) alt. of *plaisible* from late Latin *placibilis* pleasing, from Latin *placere* please: see -IBLE. Later conformed to PEACE *noun* and words in -ABLE.]
▶ **A** *adjective.* **1** Disposed to or in favour of peace; avoiding, or inclined to avoid, strife; not argumentative, quarrelsome, or pugnacious. ME. ▶†**b** Not talkative or noisy, taciturn; quiet in behaviour. L15–E19.
2 Characterized by peace; peaceful. ME. ▶†**b** Free from physical commotion or disturbance. LME–E17.

> 🕮 **1** SCOTT FITZGERALD An adult conflict, to which there was no peaceable solution. **2** JER. TAYLOR For kings . . we may . . pray for peaceable reign.

▶†**B** *noun.* A peaceable or friendly person; *collect.* the people who are peaceable. ME–E17.
▶†**C** *adverb.* Peaceably. ME–M18.
■ **peacea'bility** *noun* (long *rare*) LME. **peaceableness** *noun* ME. **peaceably** *adverb* ME.

peaceful /ˈpiːsfʊl, -f(ə)l/ *adjective.* ME.
[from PEACE *noun* + -FUL.]
1 = PEACEABLE *adjective* 1. Now *rare.* ME.
2 Full of or characterized by peace; free from strife or commotion; undisturbed, untroubled, calm, quiet. ME.
3 Pertaining to a time or state of peace. L16.
4 Not violating or infringing peace; *esp.* designating a method for effecting some end for which force, violence, or war, is an alternative or more obvious means. L19.

> 🕮 **2** *Holiday Which?* Ambleside is . . peaceful except for the traffic. **3** M. HOWITT An unarmed population, accustomed only to peaceful occupations. **4** G. HOWELL Peaceful picketing is no longer prohibited. *peaceful coexistence*: see COEXISTENCE 2.

■ **peacefully** *adverb* so as to make for peace, peaceably; in peace, tranquilly: ME. **peacefulness** *noun* M17.

peaceless /ˈpiːslɪs/ *adjective.* E16.
[from PEACE *noun* + -LESS.]
Devoid of peace; not peaceful.
■ **peacelessness** *noun* M19.

peacemaker /ˈpiːsmeɪkə/ *noun.* LME.
[from PEACE *noun* + MAKER, translating Latin *pacificus*.]
1 A person who makes or brings about peace; a person who allays strife or reconciles opponents. LME.
2 A revolver, a gun; a warship. *joc.* M19.
■ **peacemaking** *noun & adjective* M16.

peacemonger /ˈpiːsmʌŋgə/ *noun. derog.* E19.
[from PEACE *noun* + MONGER.]
A peacemaker; a person who aims at or advocates peace by reprehensible means.

peacenik /ˈpiːsnɪk/ *noun.* M20.
[from PEACE *noun* + -NIK.]
A member of a pacifist movement, esp. in the 1960s and 1970s.

peach /piːtʃ/ *noun¹ & adjective.* ME.
[Old French *pe(s)che* (mod. *pêche*) from medieval Latin *persica* (*pessica*) from classical Latin *persicum* (*malum*) lit. 'Persian (apple)'.]
▶ **A** *noun.* **1** The round sweet juicy stone-fruit of the peach tree, usu. having a downy yellow and red-tinged skin (cf. NECTARINE *noun*); (also ***peach tree***) the tree of the rose family, *Prunus persica*, bearing this fruit, cultivated in warm-temperate countries. ME. ▶**b** *fig.* A person or thing of exceptional worth or quality; a particularly suitable or desirable person or thing, *esp.* an attractive young woman. *colloq.* M18.
2 Any of various other edible fruits resembling the peach, or of the plants producing them; *esp.* (*a*) (in full ***African peach***, ***Guinea peach***, ***Sierra Leone peach***) (the large juicy berry of) *Sarcocephalus latifolius*, a climbing W. African shrub of the madder family; (*b*) (more fully ***native peach***) (the fruit of) the quandong, *Eucarya acuminata*; also, (the fruit of) the emu-apple, *Owenia acidula*. Usu. with specifying word. M18.
3 = ***peach brandy*** below. *US.* E19.
4 A soft pinkish-orange colour. L19.

> 🕮 **1b** P. DICKINSON A history essay, a real peach for which she'd only needed to look up a few dates. *Yankee* He's a peach of a husband.

Phrases: ***African peach***: see sense 2(a) above. ***clingstone peach***: see CLING *verb*. ***freestone peach***: see FREESTONE 2. ***Guinea peach***: see sense 2(a) above. ***native peach***: see sense 2(b) above. **peaches and cream** (designating) a fair complexion characterized by creamy skin and pink cheeks. ***Sierra Leone peach***: see sense 2(a) above.

Comb.: **peach aphid**, **peach aphis** an aphid infesting peach trees; *esp.* = ***peach-potato aphid*** below; **peach-black** a black pigment made from calcined peach-stones; **peach-bloom** *noun & adjective* (*a*) (of) the delicate powdery deposit on the surface of a ripe peach; (having) a soft pink flush on the face; (*b*) = ***peach-blow*** (a), (b) below; **peach-blossom** (*a*) the purplish-pink blossom of the peach tree; (*b*) (in full ***peach-blossom moth***) a woodland moth, *Thyatira batis*, with pinkish-white spots on its wings; **peach-blow** *noun & adjective* (*a*) (of) a delicate purplish-pink colour; (*b*) (designating oriental porcelain with) a glaze of purplish-pink, usu. with green markings; (*c*) (designating) a type of glass of a similar colour; **peach brandy** brandy made from the juice of peaches; a drink of this; **peach fuzz** *N. Amer. slang* the down on the chin of an adolescent boy whose beard has not yet developed; ***peach leaf curl***: see ***leaf curl*** s.v. LEAF *noun*¹; ***peach Melba***: see MELBA 1; **peach-palm** a palm, *Bactris gasipaes*, widely cultivated in tropical S. America for its large red and orange fruit which becomes mealy and edible when cooked; **peach-pip**, **peach-pit** a peach-stone; **peach-potato aphid**, **peach-potato aphis** an aphid, *Myzus persicae*, which transmits many plant virus diseases; **peach-stone** the hard oval stone of the peach, covered with irregular cavities; ***peach tree***: see sense 1 above; **peach yellows** a fatal disease of cultivated peach trees, esp. in the US, which causes stunting, distortion, and yellowing of the leaves, caused by a mycoplasma-like organism.

▶ **B** *adjective.* Of a soft pinkish-orange colour. M19.
■ **peachery** *noun* a place where peaches are grown; a collection of growing peach trees: E19.

†**peach** *noun².* L16–L18.
[Russian *pech'*.]
In Russia, a stove.

peach /piːtʃ/ *verb.* LME.
[Aphet. from APPEACH.]
†**1** *verb trans.* Accuse formally; impeach, indict. LME–E18.
2 *verb intrans.* Inform *on* or give accusatory information *against* an accomplice or associate. Now *slang.* L16. ▶**b** *verb trans.* Give accusatory information against (an accomplice or associate). Now *rare.* L16.
3 *verb trans.* Divulge. *colloq.* M19.

peacherino /piːtʃəˈriːnəʊ/ *noun. slang* (chiefly *US*). Pl. **-os**. E20.
[Fanciful alt. of PEACH *noun*¹.]
= PEACH *noun*¹ 1b.
■ Also **peache'roo** *noun* M20.

pea-chick /ˈpiːtʃɪk/ *noun.* M16.
[from *pea* in PEACOCK, PEAHEN + CHICK *noun*¹.]
1 A young peafowl. M16.
2 *fig.* A young and vain person. M18.

peachy /ˈpiːtʃi/ *adjective.* L16.
[from PEACH *noun*¹ + -Y¹.]
1 Of the nature or appearance of a peach, esp. in colour or texture; (of a person's cheeks) round, soft, and with a delicate pink flush like a peach; (of a person) having a peaches and cream complexion. L16.
2 Attractive, outstanding, marvellous. *slang.* E20.
Comb.: **peachy-keen** *adjective* (*N. Amer. slang*) = sense 2 above.
■ **peachiness** *noun* E19.

†**peacible** *adjective, noun, & adverb* see PEACEABLE.

pea-coat /ˈpiːkəʊt/ *noun.* L18.
[from PEA(-JACKET + COAT *noun*.]
= PEA-JACKET.

peacock /ˈpiːkɒk/ *noun & verb.* Also †**po-**. ME.
[from var. of PO *noun*¹ + COCK *noun*¹.]
▶ **A** *noun.* **1** A male peafowl, *esp.* one of the common species *Pavo cristatus*, having a strutting gait, brilliant plumage and a tail (with eyelike markings) that can be expanded erect in display like a fan. Also *gen.*, = PEAFOWL. ME. ▶**b** *fig.* A proud, vain. or ostentatious person. LME.
2 (Usu. **P-**.) *The* constellation Pavo. M17.
3 *ellipt.* A peacock butterfly; a peacock moth. E19.
4 *ellipt.* Peacock blue. L19.

> 🕮 **1b** GEO. ELIOT To have such a nice-stepping long-necked peacock for his daughter.

Comb.: **Peacock Alley** *US* [the main corridor of the original Waldorf-Astoria Hotel in New York] the main corridor of a hotel; **peacock blue** (of) a lustrous greenish-blue colour, the colour of a peacock's neck; **peacock butterfly** an Old World nymphalid butterfly, *Inachis io*, with ocellated wings; **peacock copper** iridescent copper ore, *esp.* chalcopyrite or bornite; **peacock-eye** the ocellus on a peacock's feather; **peacock-flower** (*a*) either of two leguminous trees with flamboyant red flowers, *Delonix regia*, of Madagascar, and the W. Indian *Caesalpinia pulcherrima*, both widely planted in the tropics; (*b*) = ***peacock tiger-flower*** below; **peacock-iris** any of various ornamental southern African bulbous plants of the genus *Moraea*, related to and resembling irises; **peacock moth** a pale geometrid moth, *Semiothisa notata*, with brown markings; also (in full ***sharp-angled peacock moth***), the related moth *S. alternaria*; **peacock ore** = ***peacock copper*** above; **peacock pheasant** any of several small pheasants of the SE Asian genus *Polyplectron*, with markings like those of a peacock; **peacock's feather** a feather of a peacock, *esp.* one of the long feathers forming the tail coverts; *fig.* = ***borrowed plumage*** s.v. BORROW *verb*¹; **peacock's tail** a seaweed, *Padina pavonia*, which has fan-shaped fronds marked with concentric fringed lines; **peacock throne** the former throne of the Kings of Delhi, later that of the Shahs of Iran (Persia), adorned with precious stones forming an expanded peacock's tail; *transf.* (chiefly *Hist.*) the office of the Shah of Iran (Persia); **peacock tiger-flower** a tiger-flower, *Tigridia pavonia*, grown for its flamboyant flowers; **peacock worm** a colourful fan worm, *Sabella pavonina*, of shallow European seas.

▶ **B** *verb.* **1** *verb intrans. & refl.* Strut about or pose in order to display one's beauty, elegance, or accomplishments. L16.
2 *verb trans.* Puff *up*; dress *up*. L19.
3 *verb trans.* AUSTRAL. HISTORY Choose or buy the best parts of (an area or property). L19.

> 🕮 **1** D. LESSING I went into the workroom and peacocked around, and the girls all clapped.

■ **peacockery** *noun* foppery, ostentatious display L19. **peacockish** *adjective* like (that of) a peacock; peacocky: M16. **peacockishly** *adverb* M19. **peacockishness** *noun* L19. **peacockly** *adjective & adverb* (*arch.*) (*a*) *adjective* peacocky; (*b*) *adverb* with vainglorious display: LME. **peacockry** *noun* peacockery E20. **peacocky** *adjective* suggesting a peacock in bearing; assuming airs; ostentatious; showy: M19.

Peacockian /piːˈkɒkɪən/ *adjective & noun.* L19.
[from *Peacock* (see below) + -IAN.]
▶ **A** *adjective.* Of, pertaining to, or characteristic of the English novelist and poet Thomas Love Peacock (1785–1866) or his writing. L19.
▶ **B** *noun.* An admirer or student of Peacock or his writing. L19.

peafowl /ˈpiːfaʊl/ *noun.* E19.
[from PEA(COCK + FOWL *noun*.]
Either of two pheasants, *Pavo cristatus* (also ***common peafowl***, ***blue peafowl***, ***Indian peafowl***), orig. native to the Indian subcontinent and widely kept for the plumage of the male, and (more fully ***green peafowl***) *P. muticus* of SE Asia. Also (in full ***Congo peafowl***), the pheasant *Afropavo congensis* of rainforests in the Democratic Republic of Congo (Zaire). Cf. PEACOCK, PEAHEN.

peag /piːg/ *noun.* Also **peak** /piːk/. M17.
[Amer. Indian: see WAMPUM.]
= WAMPUM.

péage /ˈpeɪɑːʒ, *in sense 2 also foreign* peaʒ (*pl. same*)/ *noun.* In sense 1 also †**payage**. LME.
[Old & mod. French from medieval Latin *pedaticum*, from Latin *ped-*, *pes* foot: see -AGE: cf. PEDAGE. In sense 2 from mod. French.]
1 Toll paid for passing through a place or country. *obsolete* in *gen.* sense. LME.
2 Toll paid to travel on a French motorway; a gate or barrier where this is paid. L20.

peagle *noun* var. of PAIGLE.

†**pea-goose** *noun.* Also **peak-**. M16–E19.
[from unkn. 1st elem. + GOOSE *noun*.]
A dolt, a fool.

peahen /ˈpiːhɛn/ *noun.* Also †**po-**. ME.
[formed as PEACOCK + HEN *noun*.]
A female peafowl.

peai /piːˈʌɪ/ *noun & verb.* Also **piai**. E17.
[Carib *piai*.]
▶ **A** *noun.* More fully ***peai-man***. A medicine man or witch-doctor among the Indians of Guiana and other parts of S. America. E17.
▶ **B** *verb trans.* Practise the arts of a peai-man on; treat by witch-doctoring. L19.

pea-jacket /ˈpiːdʒakɪt/ *noun.* E18.
[Prob. from Dutch *pijjakker*, *-jekker*, from *pij* (Middle Dutch *pīe*, of unkn. origin) + *jekker* jacket, with assim. to JACKET *noun*.]
A short double-breasted overcoat of coarse woollen cloth, worn esp. by sailors.

peak /piːk/ *noun¹ & adjective.* M16.
[Rel. to PIKE *noun*¹, *noun*²; in branch II prob. partly var. of back-form. from PICKED *adjective*¹. Cf. PIC *noun*², PIQUE *noun*⁴.]
▶ **A** *noun.* **I 1 a** A projecting part of a garment, formerly esp. of a widow's hood. M16. ▶**b** A pointed or tapering extremity. Now *rare* or *obsolete* exc. as below. L16. ▶**c** The point of a beard. Formerly also, a pointed beard. L16. ▶**d** The stiff projecting part at the front of a cap. M17. ▶**e** A pointed part in the hairline on the forehead. Chiefly in ***widow's peak***, such a part in the middle of the forehead. M19.
2 Lace; a lace ruff. Long *obsolete* exc. *Scot. dial.* L16.
3 NAUTICAL **a** The narrow part of a ship's hold at the bow (***forepeak***) or stern (***after-peak***). L17. ▶**b** The upper end of a gaff; the upper aftermost corner of a sail extended by a gaff. E18. ▶**c** = BILL *noun*² 3. Cf. PEA *noun*². L18.
▶ **II 4** The pointed top or summit of a mountain; a mountain or hill with a more or less pointed summit, or of a conical form; *transf.* a pointed top of something, *spec.* one on a graph. M17.
5 A point in a period at which a varying quantity, (as traffic flow, prices, demand for electric power, etc.) is at its greatest; the time when this occurs; a culminating point or climax; a time of greatest success, achievement, etc. E20.

6 *PHONETICS.* The most prominent sound in a syllable with regard to sonority. **M20.**
7 The highest point of a wave. **M20.**

> 📖 **4** C. FRANCIS In the far distance . . were the peaks of the Himalayas. **5** T. WILLIAMS They are men at the peak of their physical manhood. M. STOTT Whenever your own energy is at its peak. *Buses Extra* These services run outward in the evening peak.

▶ **B** *attrib.* or as *adjective.* Characterized by or pertaining to a greatest value or quantity; greatest; that is a maximum. **E20.**

> 📖 *Times Review of Industry* Processes used to produce for peak loads. *Holiday Which?* At peak times . . one aircraft takes off every 40 seconds.

Comb. & special collocations: **peak cap**: with a peak at the front; **peak experience** *PSYCHOLOGY* a momentary awareness of joy or fulfilment akin to ecstasy; **peak factor** *ELECTRICITY* the ratio of the maximum value (or the difference between the maximum and minimum values) of a wave to the r.m.s. value; **peak flowmeter** *MEDICINE* a device used to measure lung capacity in monitoring breathing disorders such as asthma; **peak hour** a time of day when traffic is heaviest, television audiences are greatest, etc.; **peak shaving** storage of part of the gas produced when demand is low so that it can be used to increase the supply at times of peak demand; **peak-to-peak** *adjective & adverb* (measured or expressed as the difference) between extreme values of a periodically varying quantity; **peak voltmeter** *ELECTRICITY*: that measures the peak value of an alternating voltage.

peak *noun*[2] var. of PEAG.

peak /piːk/ *verb*[1] *intrans.* **LME.**
[Origin unkn.]
†**1** Move about dejectedly or silently; mope; slink; shrink. **LME–E17.**
2 Droop in health and spirits, waste away; look sickly or emaciated. Chiefly in ***peak and pine***. Cf. PEAKED 2, PEAKY *adjective*[1]. **M17.**

> 📖 **2** SHAKES. *Macb.* Weary sev'nights, nine times nine, Shall he dwindle, peak, and pine.

peak /piːk/ *verb*[2]. **L16.**
[from PEAK *noun*[1].]
▶ **I** *verb intrans.* **1** Project or rise in a peak. Also foll. by *up*. **L16.**
2 Reach maximum value, activity, etc.; reach the peak of one's condition. **M20.**
3 Level *out* after reaching a peak. **M20.**

> 📖 **2** *Times* Interest rates have yet to peak. J. LE CARRÉ Paul had peaked early in life. *Running* He . . peaked just in time for . . last year's indoor championship.

▶ **II** *verb trans.* **4** Bring to a head; bring to a peak or maximum; *fig.* accentuate. Also foll. by *up*. **L19.**

peak /piːk/ *verb*[3]. **E17.**
[Prob. aphet. from APEAK.]
NAUTICAL. **1** *verb trans.* Raise or tilt up (esp. a yard, oars) vertically. **E17.**
2 *verb intrans.* Of a whale: raise its tail or flukes straight up in diving vertically. **L19.**

peaked /piːkt/ *adjective.* **LME.**
[from PEAK *noun*[1] + -ED[2].]
1 Having a peak, rising into a peak; pointed; cut, trimmed, or brought to a peak or point. Cf. PICKED *adjective*[1], PIKED *adjective*[1]. **LME.**
2 Sharp-featured, thin, pinched, as from illness or hunger; sickly-looking. Cf. PEAK *verb*[1], PEAKY *adjective*[1]. **M19.**
■ **peakedness** *noun* **M19.**

†**peak-goose** *noun* var. of PEA-GOOSE.

peaking /ˈpiːkɪŋ/ *adjective.* Now *dial.* **L16.**
[from PEAK *verb*[1] + -ING[2].]
1 Sneaking, skulking; mean-spirited. **L16.**
2 = PEAKY *adjective*[1]. **L17.**

peakish /ˈpiːkɪʃ/ *adjective.* **M19.**
[from PEAKY *adjective*[1] + -ISH[1].]
Somewhat peaky.

Peakrel /ˈpiːkr(ə)l/ *noun.* **L17.**
[from *Peak* (see below) + *-rel* (cf. *cockerel*, *mongrel*).]
A native or inhabitant of the Peak District in Derbyshire, England.

peaky /ˈpiːki/ *adjective*[1]. *colloq.* **E19.**
[Rel. to PEAK *verb*[1], PEAKED 2: see -Y[1].]
Sickly, feeble; tired, slightly unwell.

> 📖 G. LORD You all right? You look a bit peaky.

peaky /ˈpiːki/ *adjective*[2]. **M19.**
[from PEAK *noun*[1] + -Y[1].]
1 Having many peaks; characterized by peaks or sharp variations. **M19.**
2 = PEAKED *adjective* 1. **M19.**

> 📖 **1** G. J. KING The frequency response of a cartridge with a peaky treble resonance.

■ **peakiness** *noun* **E20.**

peal /piːl/ *noun*[1]. **ME.**
[Aphet. from APPEAL *noun*.]
†**1** A stroke on or ringing of a bell as a call or summons, esp. to prayer or church. **ME–L17.**
2 A long loud reverberating sound made by the ringing of a bell or set of bells; *spec.* a series of changes rung on a set of bells. **LME.** ▸**b** A set of bells tuned to one another. **L18.**
3 *transf.* A sound resembling the peal of a bell, esp. made in laughing, by thunder, etc. **E16.** ▸**b** A loud discharge of a gun, cannon, etc., as a salute, signal, etc. *obsolete* exc. *Hist.* **L16.**

> 📖 **2** JOYCE The belfry of George's Church sent out constant peals. **3** L. M. MONTGOMERY She . . burst into such a hearty and unusual peal of laughter. **b** LD MACAULAY The peal of a musket . . was the signal.

peal /piːl/ *noun*[2]. Also **peel**. **M16.**
[Origin unkn.]
A young salmon or trout; a grilse. Also more fully ***salmon peal***.

peal /piːl/ *verb*[1]. *obsolete* exc. *dial.* **LOE.**
[Origin unkn. Cf. PELL *verb*.]
1 *verb trans.* Strike or pound with repeated blows. **LOE.**
2 *verb intrans.* Pound, beat, hammer, *at*, *on*, etc.; *fig.* work hard, work *away*. **LME.**

peal /piːl/ *verb*[2] *trans. & intrans. obsolete* exc. *dial.* **LME.**
[Aphet.]
= APPEAL *verb.*

peal /piːl/ *verb*[3]. **M17.**
[from PEAL *noun*[1].]
1 *verb intrans. & trans.* Sound (a peal); produce (a sound etc.) with loud reverberation. **M17.**
†**2** *verb trans.* Assail (a person, the ears, etc.) *with* loud noise, entreaty, etc. **M17–E18.**
3 *verb trans.* Cause (a bell) to ring loudly or in peals. *rare.* **E19.**

> 📖 **1** N. MONSARRAT All round us . . the bells began to peal, filling the air with . . clanging thunder. U. LE GUIN Shevek was wakened by the bells in the Chapel tower pealing . . for morning religious service.

pealer /ˈpiːlə/ *noun. obsolete* exc. *dial.* **LME.**
[Aphet. Cf. PEAL *verb*[2].]
= APPEALER.

pean /piːn/ *noun.* **M16.**
[Origin unkn.]
HERALDRY. A fur resembling ermine but having gold markings on a black field.

Peano /peɪˈɑːnəʊ/ *noun.* **E20.**
[Giuseppe *Peano* (1858–1932), Italian mathematician.]
MATH. Used **attrib.** and in **possess.** to designate concepts introduced by or arising from the work of Peano.
Peano axioms, **Peano's axioms** a set of axioms from which the properties of the natural numbers may be deduced. **Peano curve** any curve which passes through all points of the unit square in two dimensions, esp. when the limit of a series of modifications to a simple curve; an analogous space-filling curve in a higher dimension. **Peano postulates**, **Peano's postulates** = *Peano axioms* above.

peanut /ˈpiːnʌt/ *noun & adjective.* **E19.**
[from PEA *noun*[1] + NUT *noun*.]
▶ **A** *noun.* **1** A S. American leguminous plant, *Arachis hypogaea*, widely grown in the tropics, bearing underground pods which contain nutlike seeds valuable as a food and a source of oil (also called ***groundnut***); a seed of this plant. Also, (the seed of) any of several legumes with similar seeds, *esp.* (more fully ***hog peanut***) *Amphicarpaea bracteata* of N. America. **E19.**
2 *ELECTRICITY.* In full ***peanut valve***. A kind of small thermionic valve. **E20.**
3 a *sing.* & in *pl.* A small or unimportant person or thing. *colloq.* **M20.** ▸**b** *spec.* In *pl.* A small or inadequate sum of money. *colloq.* **M20.**

> 📖 **3a** S. BELLOW Never, you bloody little peanut! J. M. COETZEE This isn't a life sentence. This is just a labour gang. It's peanuts. **b** *Sunday Times* I've worked very hard . . and now I realise that I've been earning peanuts.

Comb.: **peanut brittle** a brittle toffee containing whole roasted peanuts; **peanut butter** a paste of ground roasted peanuts; **peanut gallery** *N. Amer. slang* the top gallery in a theatre; ***peanut valve***: see sense 3 above; **peanut worm** = SIPUNCULID *noun*.
▶ **B** *attrib.* or as *adjective.* Unimportant; worthless. *slang.* **M19.**

pea-pod /ˈpiːpɒd/ *noun.* **L19.**
[from PEA *noun*[1] + POD *noun*[2].]
The pod or legume of the pea-plant. Cf. earlier PEASECOD.

pear /pɛː/ *noun.* Also (*Scot.*) **peer** /pɪə/.
[Old English *pere*, *peru*, corresp. to Middle Low German, Middle Dutch *pere* (Dutch *peer*), from popular Latin fem. sing. var. of Latin *pirum*, whence also Old & mod. French *poire*.]
1 A large usu. yellowish or brownish-green dessert fruit borne by the pear tree, a pome broadest at the base and tapering towards the stalk. **OE.**
2 The tree of the rose family, *Pyrus communis*, which bears this fruit (in full ***pear tree***); (usu. with specifying word) any of several other trees of the genus *Pyrus*. Also, the wood of such a tree. **LME.**
3 *transf.* A thing shaped like a pear; *esp.* a pear-shaped pearl or gem. **L16.**
4 With specifying word: any of various other fruits or plants in some way resembling the pear; *spec.* (*W. Indies*) (the fruit of) the avocado pear, *Persea americana*. **M18.**

> 📖 **1** ***apples and pears***: see APPLE *noun*. ***Bartlett pear***, ***pear warden***, ***Virgouleuse pear***, ***William pear***, etc. **3** A. HAMILTON Some beautiful Pearls . . among them a Pair of Pears. **4** ***alligator pear***, ***anchovy pear***, ***avocado pear***, ***balsam pear***, ***garlic pear***, ***prickly pear***, ***wooden pear***, etc.

Comb.: **pear-blight** either of two destructive diseases of pear trees, one caused by a bacterium, *Micrococcus amylovorus*, which turns the leaves rapidly brown (also called ***fire-blight***), and one caused by any of several beetles which bore into the bark; **pear-drop** a thing shaped like a pear; *spec.* (***a***) a pear-shaped sweet, *esp.* one flavoured with pear essence; (***b***) a pear-shaped jewel, *esp.* a pendent one in an earring etc.; **pear-louse** a plant-louse (esp. of the genus *Psylla*) which infests the leaves and young shoots of the pear tree; **pear midge** a small gall midge, *Contarinia pyrivora*, whose larvae damage the fruit of pear trees; **pearmonger** *arch.* a seller of pears; **pear-sucker** = ***pear-louse*** above; ***pear tree***: see sense 2 above; **pearwood** (***a***) the wood of the pear tree; (***b***) ***Nigerian pearwood***, the wood of the W. African tree *Guarea cedrata* (family Meliaceae), used as a substitute for mahogany.

pear /pɪə/ *verb intrans. obsolete* exc. *dial.* **LME.**
[Aphet.]
= APPEAR.

pearl /pəːl/ *noun*[1] *& adjective.* **LME.**
[Old & mod. French *perle* prob. from Proto-Romance, from Latin dim. of *perna* leg, ham, leg-of-mutton shaped bivalve.]
▶ **A** *noun.* **I 1** A hard smooth round iridescent mass, usu. white or bluish grey, formed of layers of calcium carbonate deposited around a foreign body in the shell of certain bivalve molluscs and valued as a gem for its lustre; the substance of which this is composed. Now also, an artificial imitation of this; in *pl.*, a necklace of pearls. **LME.**
2 *fig.* A precious, noble, or fine thing; a fine or the finest example. **LME.**
3 *HERALDRY* (now *Hist.*). The tincture argent in the fanciful blazon of arms of peers. **L16.**

> 📖 **1** P. O'DONNELL They have found . . four button pearls, two drop pearls, and perhaps a dozen . . seed pearls. S. BELLOW She would wear pearls on her throat. ***pearl of orient***: see ORIENT *noun*. **2** *Milton Keynes Express* Rodney Henson . . as stand in wicket keeper played a pearl of a match. **cast pearls before swine** offer a good or valuable thing to a person incapable of appreciating it.

▶ **II** *transf.* **4** †**a** The pupil or lens of the eye. **LME–E17.** ▸**b** A thin white film over the eye; a kind of cataract. *obsolete* exc. *dial.* **LME.**
5 A small round drop resembling a pearl in shape, colour, or lustre. **LME.** ▸**b** A small amount or size of something; *spec.* (***a***) a small piece of clean coal; (***b***) a small gelatinous capsule used to administer liquid medicine in pill form. **M19.**
6 *collect. sing.* & in *pl.* Teeth. **L16.**
7 Any of the bony protuberances encircling the base of a deer's antler. **L16.**
8 A size of type equal to about 5 points, formerly the smallest, later intermediate between ruby and diamond. **M17.**
9 Any of several small white or silver balls set on a coronet, *spec.* as represented on a heraldic charge; *PHILATELY* a small white circle on a coloured ground. **L17.**
10 The colour of a pearl, a clear pale bluish grey. **L17.**

> 📖 **5** E. BLISHEN A pearl of rain hung at his nose. **10** *Westminster Gazette* He watched the . . dawn change from a thin grey line of pearl into . . pink and amethyst.

▶ **B** *attrib.* or as *adjective.* Resembling a pearl in shape, colour, or lustre; made or consisting of pearl; set or provided with a pearl or pearls. **L16.**
Comb. & special collocations: **pearl-ash** commercial potassium carbonate; **pearl barley**: reduced to small rounded grains by grinding; **pearl-berry** (the pearl-like fruit of) an ornamental S. American rock-plant, *Margyricarpus pinnatus*, of the rose family; **pearl-bordered** *adjective* edged with (spots resembling) pearls; ***pearl-bordered fritillary***, either of two European woodland fritillaries (butterflies) of the genus *Boloria*, with whitish spots on the underedge of the hindwings; **pearl bulb** an electric light bulb that is translucent rather than transparent; **pearl-bush** any of several Chinese shrubs of the genus *Exochorda*, related to *Spiraea* and bearing showy white flowers; **pearl button** a button made of pearl, mother-of-pearl, or an imitation of this; **pearl-diver** (***a***) a person who dives for pearl-oysters; (***b***) *slang* a person who washes crockery in a café or restaurant; **pearlessence** an imitation of mother-of-pearl, orig. made from fish-scales; ***pearl everlasting***: see EVERLASTING *noun* 4; **pearleye** any of several long-bodied ocean fishes of the family Scopelarchidae, with tubular eyes which are directed upward and bear a glistening white spot that may be a light organ; **pearlfish** †(***a***) a shellfish producing pearls; (***b***) any of various small slender fishes constituting the family Carapidae, which live in the shell or body cavities of marine bivalves, tunicates, and echinoderms; also called

fierasfer; (*c*) any of several other fishes with pearly scales or pale spots (usu. with specifying word); **pearl-fisher** a person who fishes for pearls; **pearl-fishery** (*a*) = *pearl-fishing* below; (*b*) (an establishment in) a place or district where pearls are fished; **pearl-fishing** the occupation or industry of fishing for pearls; **pearl-fruit** = *pearl-berry* above; **pearl-hen** the domestic guinea-fowl; **pearl millet** a white-seeded form of bulrush millet, *Pennisetum americanum*; **pearl mussel** a mussel, esp. a freshwater one, from which pearls may be obtained; **pearl onion** a very small onion, used esp. for pickling; **pearl-opal** = CACHOLONG; **pearl oyster** any bivalve mollusc of the tropical genus *Pinctada* (family Pteriidae), esp. *Pinctada margaritifera*, a major commercial source of pearls; **pearl-perch** an edible marine percoid fish, *Glaucosoma scapulare* (family Glaucosomidae), of the east coast of Australia; **pearl-powder** a cosmetic powder for whitening the skin; **pearl-shell** mother-of-pearl; a shell which produces pearls or nacre; **pearlside(s)** a small cosmopolitan marine fish, *Maurolicus muelleri* (family Gonostomatidae), with a row of rounded pale blue light-organs along its belly and tail; **pearl-sinter** = FIORITE; **pearl spar** MINERALOGY dolomite occurring as clusters of white or pinkish pearly rhombohedral crystals; **pearl-stone** = PERLITE; **pearlware** *adjective & noun* (designating) fine white glazed pottery, orig. manufactured by Josiah Wedgwood; **pearl-white** *adjective & noun* (*a*) *adjective* pearly white; (*b*) *noun* pearl-powder; pearlware; **pearlwort** any of various small plants of the genus *Sagina*, of the pink family, with inconspicuous white or apetalous flowers.

■ **pear'lescence** *noun* a pearlescent effect or material M20. **pear'lescent** *noun & adjective* (a material or finish) resembling mother-of-pearl in colour, lustre, etc. M20. **pearlet** *noun* (*rare*) a little pearl M16. **pearlish** *adjective* slightly pearly L19. **pearlized** *adjective* treated so as to resemble mother-of-pearl M20. **pearl-like** *adjective* resembling (that of) a pearl E19.

†pearl *noun*[2]. Pl. same. Chiefly *dial.* L17–E19.
[Perh. alt. of BRILL *noun*, infl. by prec.]
= BRILL *noun*.

pearl *noun*[3] see PURL *noun*[1].

pearl /pəːl/ *verb*[1]. LME.
[from PEARL *noun*[1] or Old & mod. French *perler*, formed as PEARL *noun*[1].]
1 *verb trans.* Adorn or set (as) with pearls or mother-of-pearl. Usu. in *pass.* LME.
2 *verb trans.* Sprinkle with dew, tears, etc.; cover with pearl-like drops. Chiefly *poet.* L16.
3 *verb intrans.* Form pearl-like drops or beads. L16.
4 *verb intrans.* Dive or fish for pearls. M17.
5 *verb trans.* Reduce (barley etc.) to small rounded grains. Cf. earlier PEARLED *adjective* 3. M19.
6 *verb trans.* Make pearly in colour or lustre. *poet.* M19.

📖 **1** P. J. BAILEY The pictured moon Pearled round with stars. **2** F. KING Orange juice in a slender glass pearled with moisture from the ice cubes in it.

pearl *verb*[2] see PURL *verb*[1].

pearled /pəːld/ *adjective.* LME.
[from PEARL *noun*[1], *verb*[1]: see -ED[2], -ED[1].]
1 Set or adorned with pearls or mother-of-pearl; made of pearl or mother-of-pearl. Chiefly *poet.* LME.
2 Sprinkled with dew, tears, etc. *poet.* L16.
3 Formed into drops or small rounded grains. E17.
4 Resembling a pearl in colour or lustre. E18.

pearler /ˈpəːlə/ *noun*[1]. L19.
[from PEARL *verb*[1] + -ER[1].]
A pearl-fisher; an employer of pearl-divers. Also, a small boat used for pearl-fishing.

pearler *noun*[2] see PURLER.

pearling /ˈpəːlɪŋ/ *noun*[1]. *Scot. & north.* E17.
[from *pearl* var. of PURL *verb*[1] + -ING[1].]
A type of lace for trimming the edges of garments; picot lace; in *pl.*, clothes trimmed with pearling.

pearling /ˈpəːlɪŋ/ *noun*[2]. M17.
[from PEARL *verb*[1] + -ING[1].]
1 The action of PEARL *verb*[1]. M17.
2 Carved decoration resembling pearls. L19.

pearlite /ˈpəːlʌɪt/ *noun.* L19.
[from PEARL *noun*[1] + -ITE[1].]
METALLURGY. A finely laminated mixture of ferrite and cementite formed in cast iron and steel by the cooling of austenite containing more than 0.8 per cent carbon.
■ **pearlitic** /-ˈlɪtɪk/ *adjective* E20.

pearly /ˈpəːli/ *adjective, adverb, & noun.* LME.
[from PEARL *noun*[1] + -Y[1].]
► **A** *adjective.* **1** Resembling a pearl in shape, lustre, or colour. LME. ►**b** *spec.* Of a clear pale bluish grey. L18.
2 Having or producing (many) pearls or (much) mother-of-pearl. E17.
3 Made of pearl; set with a pearl or pearls. M18.
4 *fig.* Exceedingly precious; of supreme (spiritual) purity or worth. L18.

📖 **1** *Daily Telegraph* The flash of pearly teeth between smiling lips. J. BETJEMAN Waves of pearly light . . along the shafted stone.

Special collocations: **pearly everlasting**: see EVERLASTING *noun* 4. **Pearly Gates** the gates of Heaven (with allus. to *Revelation* 21: 21). **Pearly King**, **Pearly Queen** a London costermonger or his wife dressed in traditional ceremonial clothes covered with pearl buttons. **pearly** NAUTILUS. **Pearly Queen**: see **Pearly King** above. **pearly whites** *slang* teeth.
► **B** *adverb.* With respect to pearls (*rare*); with a pearly tinge. E19.
► **C** *noun.* **1** In *pl.* (Clothes decorated with) pearl buttons. L19. ►**b** A costermonger. E20.
2 *ellipt.* In *pl.* = ***pearly whites*** above. *slang.* E20.
3 [Perh. a different word.] In *pl.* *The* uncontrollable shaking of the bowing arm sometimes experienced by a violinist etc. as a result of nervousness before a performance. *slang.* L20.
■ **pearliness** *noun* M19.

pearmain /ˈpɛːmeɪn, ˈpəː-, pəˈmeɪn/ *noun.* Also (now *rare*) **per-**. ME.
[Old French *parmaine*, *per-* (in Anglo-Latin *permanus*, *pirum parmennorum* pearmain, pearmain pear) prob. from Proto-Romance alt. of Latin *Parmensis* of Parma: see PARMA *noun*[1].]
†**1** An old variety of baking pear, = WARDEN *noun*[2]. ME–E17.
2 Any of several varieties of apple with firm white flesh; *esp.* = WORCESTER 3. L16.

pear-shaped /ˈpɛːʃeɪpt/ *adjective.* M18.
[from PEAR *noun* + SHAPED *adjective.*]
1 Shaped like a pear; tapering towards the top; (of a person) plump and wide-hipped. M18.
2 Of a musical or (usu.) vocal tone: rich, mellow, sonorous. M20.
1 go pear-shaped (*colloq.*, orig. *RAF slang*) go wrong, become disordered.

Pearson /ˈpɪəs(ə)n/ *noun.* E20.
[Karl *Pearson* (1857–1936), English mathematician.]
STATISTICS. Used *attrib.* and in *possess.* with ref. to various statistical formulae and techniques devised or described by Pearson, esp. (*a*) members of a family of curves including many probability distribution functions; (*b*) a measure of the skewness of statistical distributions; (*c*) the product-moment correlation coefficient; (*d*) the chi-square test; (*e*) a set of formulae used to estimate human stature from the length of limb bones.
■ **Pear'sonian** *adjective* of or originated by Karl Pearson E20.

peart *adjective, noun, adverb, & verb* see PERT.

peasant /ˈpɛz(ə)nt/ *noun & adjective.* LME.
[Anglo-Norman *paisant*, Old French *païsant*, *paisent* (also mod.) PAYSAN alt. (with *-ant*) of earlier *païsenc*, from *païs* (mod. *pays*) country from Proto-Romance alt. of Latin *pagus* country district: see -ANT[2].]
► **A** *noun.* **1** Chiefly *Hist.* & SOCIOLOGY. A person who lives in the country and works on the land, esp. as a smallholder or a labourer; *spec.* a member of an agricultural class dependent on subsistence farming. LME. ►†**b** A serf; a bonded labourer or servant. M–L16.
2 A person of low social status; an ignorant, stupid, or unsophisticated person; a boor, a lout. Now *colloq.* (freq. *derog.*). M16.

📖 **1** N. MANDELA I moved up and down my country and spoke to peasants in the countryside. B. CHATWIN The peasants . . believed that the new ideology allowed them to divide the landlord's property. **2** GODFREY SMITH Laura took me out riding . . . I'm a complete peasant in this, but she's an expert. G. LYALL Of course I'm not alone, you—you peasant D'you think I drive myself?

► **B** *attrib.* or as *adjective.* **1** Of, pertaining to, or of the nature or character of a peasant or peasants; that is a peasant. M16.
2 Of a style of art, dress, etc.: resembling that of peasants. Cf. PAYSAN *adjective* 2. E20.

📖 **1** T. C. WOLFE His peasant suspicion . . of any life that differed from that of his village. H. ARENDT The Boers had lost . . their peasant relationship to the soil. ***peasant class***, ***peasant family***, ***peasant revolution***, ***peasant society***, etc. **peasant economy** an agricultural economy in which the family is the basic unit of production. ***peasant proprietor***: see PROPRIETOR 1. **2** ***peasant blouse***, ***peasant skirt***, ***peasant tapestry***, ***peasant weave***, etc.

■ **peasantess** *noun* a female peasant M19. **peasantism** *noun* (*a*) the political doctrine that power should be vested in the peasant class; (*b*) the political doctrine that the peasant class and the intelligentsia are the only true revolutionary forces: L19. **peasantist** *noun & adjective* (*a*) *noun* an adherent of peasantism; (*b*) *adjective* of or pertaining to pesantists or peasantism: L19. **peasantry** *noun* (*a*) peasants collectively; (*b*) the condition of being a peasant; the legal position or rank of a peasant; (*c*) the conduct or quality of a peasant, rusticity: L16. **peasanty** *adjective* characteristic of peasants M20.

peascod *noun* var. of PEASECOD.

pease /piːz/ *noun.* Now *arch. & dial.* exc. in comb. below. Pl. same; **-sen**, **-son**, /-z(ə)n/.
[Old English *pise*, pl. *pisan* from late Latin *pisa*, pl. *pisae*, for earlier *pisum*, pl. *pisa*, from Greek *pison*, pl. *pisa*. See also PEA *noun*[1].]
1 = PEA *noun*[1] 1, 2. OE.
†**2** A thing of very small value or importance. LME–L16.
†**3** In *pl.* The eggs of certain fishes. Cf. PEA *noun*[1] 4. Only in LME.

Comb.: **pease-brose** *Scot.* a dish made of pease-meal mixed with boiling water; **pease-meal**: made from dried split peas; **pease pudding** a dish of dried split peas boiled to a pulp.

peasecod /ˈpiːzkɒd/ *noun.* Now *arch. & dial.* Also **peascod**. LME.
[from PEASE + COD *noun*[1].]
A pea-pod.

peasen, **peason** *nouns pl.* see PEASE.

pea-soup /piːˈsuːp/ *noun.* E18.
[from PEA *noun*[1] + SOUP *noun.*]
1 Soup made from peas; *spec.* a thick, dull yellow soup made from dried split peas. E18.
2 *fig.* More fully ***pea-soup fog***. A dense fog. M19.
■ **pea-souper** *noun* (*colloq.*) †(*a*) *Austral.* a recently arrived immigrant from Britain; (*b*) = PEA-SOUP 2: M19.

peasy /ˈpiːzi/ *adjective.* L18.
[from PEASE + -Y[1].]
1 Of the small size of a pea; of the appearance, colour, etc., of peas or pease-meal. Chiefly *dial.* L18.
2 Made of peas or pease-meal. *Scot.* E19.

peat /piːt/ *noun*[1]. ME.
[Anglo-Latin *peta*, perh. from Celtic (cf. Old Irish *pit* portion) & rel. to PIECE *noun.*]
1 Vegetable matter partly decomposed in wet acid conditions in bogs and fens to form a firm brown deposit resembling soil, freq. cut out and dried for use as fuel and in gardening; (chiefly *Scot. & north.*) a cut (usu. brick-shaped) piece of peat, for use as fuel. ME.
2 A dark brown resembling the colour of peat. L20.

📖 **1** R. S. THOMAS This is the land where they burn peat. *Undercurrents* Next month we will cut our first peats. *Garden News* Always plant in . . plenty of garden compost or peat.

Comb.: **peat-ash** the ash of burnt peat; **peatbog**: composed of peat; **peat-coal** a soft earthy lignite; **peat-hag** a piece of unbroken ground from which peats have been cut; **peat-house** an outbuilding for storing peats; **peatman** a person who cuts, dries, or sells peats for fuel; **peatmoss** (*a*) (chiefly *Scot. & north.*) a peatbog; (*b*) peat; (*c*) any of various mosses of the genus *Sphagnum*, which grow in damp conditions and form peat as they decay; **peat-reek** (*a*) the smoke of a peat-fire; (*b*) *colloq.* Highland whisky, *esp.* that (illicitly) distilled over a peat-fire and supposedly flavoured with peat-smoke; **peat-spade**: for cutting peats, having a triangular blade and a cutting wing on the right side.
■ **peatery** *noun* a place from which peats are cut; a peatbog: E19. **peaty** *adjective* of the nature or character of peat; having much peat: M18.

peat /piːt/ *noun*[2]. Now *arch. & Scot. dial.* M16.
[Origin unkn. Cf. PET *noun*[1] & *adjective.*]
1 (A term of endearment for) a girl or woman. M16.
2 A proud or arrogant person. *derog.* L16.
3 A lawyer allegedly under the patronage of a particular judge. *rare.* L17.
¶ Obsolete by L17, but revived in E19 by Sir Walter Scott.
■ **peatship** *noun* L17.

peau-de-soie /pəʊdəˈswɑː, *foreign* podəswa/ *noun.* M19.
[French, lit. 'silk skin'.]
A close-woven heavy satin silk; an (esp. rayon) imitation of this.

peau d'Espagne /po dɛspaɲ/ *noun phr.* Also **P-**. M19.
[French, lit. 'skin of Spain'.]
1 Perfumed leather. M19.
2 A scent suggestive of the aroma of this leather. L19.

peau d'orange /po dɔrɑ̃ʒ, pəʊ dɒˈrɑːnʒ/ *noun phr.* L19.
[French, lit. 'orange peel'.]
MEDICINE. A characteristic pitted appearance of the skin of the breast in some cases of breast cancer.

peavey /ˈpiːvi/ *noun.* *N. Amer.* Also **peavy**. L19.
[from *Peavey*, surname of the inventor.]
A lumberer's cant-hook with a spike at the end.

peb /pɛb/ *noun.* *Austral. slang.* E20.
[Abbreviation.]
= PEBBLE *noun* 4.

peba /ˈpiːbə/ *noun.* M19.
[from Tupi *tatu-peba*, from *tatu* armadillo + *peba* low.]
ZOOLOGY. A long-nosed armadillo of the genus *Dasypus*, *esp.* the nine-banded *D. novemcinctus*. Also ***peba armadillo***.

pebble /ˈpɛb(ə)l/ *noun & verb.* Also †**pi-**, †**-pp-**. LOE.
[Origin unkn.]
► **A** *noun.* **1** A small smooth rounded stone, worn by the action of water, ice, sand, etc. Also more fully ***pebble stone***. LOE.
2a An agate or other gem, esp. when found as a pebble in a stream. L16. ►**b** A type of colourless transparent rock-crystal, formerly used in spectacle lenses; a lens made of this. Now *rare*. L17.
3 *ellipt.* = ***pebble-ware*** below. M18.
4 *fig.* A high-spirited person or animal, *esp.* one hard to control. Occas. used as a term of endearment. *slang* (chiefly *Austral.*). E19.
5 Any of several moths having wavy markings resembling those of agate; *esp.* (*a*) (in full ***pebble prominent***)

Notodonta ziczac; (**b**) (in full ***pebble hook-tip***) *Drepana falcataria*. M19.

📖 **1** *attrib.*: W. BOYD On one side of the pool was a . . pebble beach. **the only pebble on the beach** a unique or irreplaceable person or thing (chiefly in neg. contexts, esp. with ref. to a (former) lover). **2** ***Scotch pebble***: see SCOTCH *adjective*.

Comb.: **pebble-beached** *adjective* (*slang*) (**a**) penniless, destitute; (**b**) dazed, absent-minded; **pebble-bed** (**a**) GEOLOGY a conglomerate that contains pebbles, *esp.* one from which they readily work loose with weathering; (**b**) NUCLEAR PHYSICS a nuclear reactor in which the fuel elements are in the form of pellets, freq. with a coating of moderator (usu. *attrib.*); **pebble chopper** ARCHAEOLOGY a simple tool with a cutting edge made by striking a few flakes from a pebble (cf. ***pebble tool*** below); **pebble culture** ARCHAEOLOGY: characterized by the use of pebble tools; **pebble-dash** mortar with pebbles in it, used as a coating for external walls; **pebble-dashed** *adjective* coated with pebble-dash; **pebble-dashing** = ***pebble-dash*** above; **pebble glasses**, **pebble spectacles**, etc.: having very thick convex lenses (cf. sense 2b above); **pebble grain** a patterned grain produced by pebbling leather (see sense B.2 below); **pebble-grained** *adjective* having a pebble grain; ***pebble hook-tip***: see sense 5 above; **pebble lens** a very thick convex spectacle lens (cf. sense 2b above); **pebble-lensed** *adjective* having a pebble lens; ***pebble prominent***: see sense 5 above; ***pebble spectacles***: see ***pebble glasses*** above; ***pebble stone***: see sense 1 above; **pebble tool** ARCHAEOLOGY a simple tool made by chipping and shaping a pebble; **pebble-ware** a speckled or mottled variety of Wedgwood pottery made by incorporating clays of different colours in the paste; **pebble weave**: producing a rough surface.

▶ **B** *verb trans.* **1** Pelt (as) with pebbles. E17.

2 Treat (leather) with a patterned roller to produce a rough or indented surface, as if pelted by pebbles. Chiefly as ***pebbling*** *verbal noun*. L19.

¶ Earliest in *comb.* Not recorded as noun in isolation until ME.

■ **pebbled** *adjective* (**a**) (chiefly *poet.*) covered with pebbles, pebbly; (**b**) (of spectacles etc.) having or resembling pebble lenses: L16. **pebbly** *adjective* (**a**) having many pebbles; covered with pebbles; (**b**) *fig.* resembling pebbles; uneven: E17.

pébrine /ˈpeɪbrɪn/ *noun*. L19.
[French from Provençal *pebrino*, from *pebre* pepper.]
A disease of silkworms caused by the microsporidian parasite *Nosema bombycis* and characterized by the appearance of dark spots and the stunting of growth. Also ***pébrine disease***. Cf. NOSEMA.

pec /pɛk/ *noun*. *slang* (chiefly *N. Amer.*). M20.
[Abbreviation.]
A pectoral muscle. Usu. in *pl.* Cf. PECT.

pecan /ˈpiːk(ə)n, pɪˈkan, pɪˈkɑːn/ *noun*. L18.
[French *pacane* from Illinois *pakani*.]
A pinkish-brown smooth nut having a rich-flavoured oily kernel resembling a walnut; the tree producing this, *Carya illinoinensis*, a very tall hickory of the southern US.
bitter pecan a smaller, bitter-seeded hickory, *Carya aquatica*, of the southern US.

peccable /ˈpɛkəb(ə)l/ *adjective*. E17.
[Old & mod. French from medieval Latin *peccabilis*, from Latin *peccare* to sin: see -ABLE.]
1 Capable of sinning, liable to sin. E17.
2 Sinful, wrong. *rare*. M17.
■ **peccaˈbility** *noun* M17.

peccadillo /pɛkəˈdɪləʊ/ *noun*. Pl. **-oes**, **-os**. L16.
[Spanish *pecadillo* dim. of *pecado* sin.]
A small fault, a venial sin; a trifling offence.

📖 R. L. STEVENSON What the boy does . . as a manly peccadillo, the girl will shudder at . . as vice. W. GOLDING There had been in him . . a natural goodness . . so that even his sins were peccadilloes.

peccaminous /pɛˈkamɪnəs/ *adjective*. *rare*. M17.
[from late Latin *peccamin-*, *-men* (from Latin *peccare* to sin) + -OUS.]
Sinful.

peccant /ˈpɛk(ə)nt/ *adjective & noun*. L16.
[Latin *peccant-* pres. ppl stem of *peccare* sin; in sense 1 from Old & mod. French *peccant*: see -ANT¹.]
▶ **A** *adjective*. **1** Causing disease; (formerly esp. of a bodily humour) unhealthy, corrupt. Now *rare*. L16. ▸**b** *fig.* Disordered; disruptive. E17.
2 That commits or has committed an offence or sin; sinning, offending; blameworthy. E17.
3 Violating a rule or principle; faulty, incorrect. *rare*. E17.
▶ **B** *noun*. A sinner; an offender. *rare*. L16.
■ **peccancy** *noun* (**a**) unhealthiness; (**b**) faultiness; sinfulness; (**c**) an offence; a sin: E17.

peccary /ˈpɛk(ə)ri/ *noun*. E17.
[Carib *pakira*.]
Any of several dark-furred gregarious piglike artiodactyl mammals of the family Tayassuidae, which inhabit forest and forest scrub in Central and S. America; the skin of a peccary, tanned and used esp. for making gloves.
collared peccary *Tayassu tajacu*, whose range extends north to Texas. ***white-lipped peccary***: see WHITE *adjective*.

peccavi /pɛˈkɑːviː/ *interjection & noun*. E16.
[Latin = I have sinned.]
▶ **A** *interjection*. Acknowledging guilt. E16.
▶ **B** *noun*. An acknowledgement or confession of guilt. L16.

pech /pɛk, pɛx/ *verb & noun*. *Scot., Ir., & north. dial.* M16.
[App. imit.]
▶ **A** *verb intrans.* Breathe hard, as from exertion, or with difficulty; puff, pant; become short of breath. M16.

📖 I. RANKIN By the time he reached the second floor, he was peching.

▶ **B** *noun*. A gasping or laboured breath; a pant. Also, a sigh. M16.

pechan /ˈpɛk(ə)n/ *noun*. *Scot.* L18.
[Origin unkn.]
The stomach.

pecia /ˈpiːsɪə/ *noun*. Pl. **-iae** /-ɪiː/, **-ie** /-ɪiː/, **-ias**. E20.
[medieval Latin = PIECE *noun*.]
A gathering, usu. of four leaves, of a manuscript.

peck /pɛk/ *noun*¹. ME.
[Anglo-Norman *pek* (whence Anglo-Latin *pecca*, *peccum*), of unkn. origin.]
1 A unit of capacity for dry goods equal to a quarter of a bushel, equivalent (in Britain) to two imperial gallons (approx. 9.09 litres) or (in the US) to eight quarts (approx. 8.81 litres), formerly also varying according to place and to the commodity measured. ME. ▸**b** A liquid measure equal to two gallons. *dial.* L19.
2 A vessel of this capacity. ME.
†**3** A measure of land equal to three acres (approx. 1.214 hectares). LME–M18.
4 *transf.* A great quantity or number. Chiefly in ***a peck of trouble(s)***. M16.

peck /pɛk/ *noun*². *obsolete* exc. *dial.* L15.
[Var. of PICK *noun*¹.]
= PICK *noun*¹ 1. Also, a tool for gathering peas, beans, etc.
¶ Perh. also the 1st elem. of PECK HORN.

peck /pɛk/ *noun*³. M16.
[from PECK *verb*¹.]
1 Food. *slang* (orig. *Criminals'*). M16.
2 An impression or mark made by pecking; a hole; a dot. L16.
3 An act of pecking; a blow struck by a bird with the beak; a hasty or perfunctory kiss. E17.

📖 **3** S. HASTINGS Far too busy to give her more than an absent-minded peck on the cheek.

Comb.: **peck order** = PECKING *order*; **peck-right** the precedence which allows a bird of a higher status within a group to attack those of a lower status without retaliation.

peck /pɛk/ *noun*⁴. *US Black slang*. M20.
[Abbreviation.]
= PECKERWOOD *noun* 2.

peck /pɛk/ *verb*¹. ME.
[Prob. from Middle Low German *pekken* peck with the beak, of unkn. origin.]
▶ **I** †**1** ***peck mood***, become angry. Only in ME.
▶ **II** **2** *verb trans.* Of a bird: strike or strike at with the beak; indent or pierce by striking with the beak; take or pluck *off*, put or pluck *out*, by striking with the beak. LME. ▸**b** Make (a hole etc.) by striking with the beak. M18. ▸**c** Kiss perfunctorily or hastily, give a peck to. M20.
3 *verb intrans.* Of a bird: strike or *at* something or someone with the beak. LME. ▸**b** *fig.* Carp, cavil, or nag *at*. M17.
4 *verb trans.* Of a bird: take (food) with the beak, esp. in small amounts at a time. Freq. foll. by *up*. LME.
5 *verb trans. & intrans.* Of a person: eat, feed. Now chiefly *spec.*, eat or pick at (food) daintily or listlessly. *colloq.* M16.
6 a *verb intrans.* Type slowly and laboriously (*at* a typewriter). *colloq.* E20. ▸**b** *verb trans.* Type *out* slowly and laboriously. *colloq.* M20.

📖 **2** *Monitor (Texas)* Never *peck* the hand that throws you the crumbs. **b** I. WEDDE This rain! pecks neat holes. **c** D. LODGE Morris pecked her awkwardly on the cheek. **3** R. FRAME Thrushes pecked—and snails in shells . . surrendered. **4** S. C. HALL The fowls were left to peck up anything they might find.

▶ **III** [Infl. by PICK *verb*¹.]
7 *verb trans.* Strike with a pick or other pointed tool, so as to pierce, break, etc. (freq. foll. by *down*, *up*, etc.); mark with short strokes. E16. ▸**b** *verb intrans.* Strike with a pick (*at*). *obsolete* exc. *dial.* M17.
8 *verb trans.* Dig up or *up* with a sharp implement. *obsolete* exc. *dial.* E18.

peck /pɛk/ *verb*². E17.
[Var. of PICK *verb*².]
1 *verb trans.* Pitch, fling, throw; jerk. *obsolete* exc. *dial.* E17.
†**2** *verb intrans.* Incline *towards*. M–L17.
3 *verb intrans.* Pitch forward; *esp.* (of a horse) stumble as a result of striking the ground with the front rather than the flat of the hoof. *colloq.* M18.

pecked /pɛkt/ *adjective*. M19.
[from PECK *verb*¹ + -ED¹.]
That has been pecked; *spec.* (ARCHAEOLOGY) consisting of or characterized by indentations.
pecked line: formed by short dashes (- - - - - -).

pecker /ˈpɛkə/ *noun*. L16.
[from PECK *verb*¹ + -ER¹.]
1 A kind of hoe. L16. ▸**b** WEAVING. A shuttle-driver. M19.
2 A bird that pecks. Chiefly as 2nd elem. in bird-names, as ***flower-pecker***. Earlier in WOODPECKER. L17.
3 Courage, resolution. Chiefly in ***keep one's pecker up***, remain cheerful. M19.
4 The penis. *coarse slang* (chiefly *N. Amer.*). E20.
Comb.: **pecker-head** *N. Amer. coarse slang* an aggressive objectionable person.

peckerwood /ˈpɛkəwʊd/ *noun & adjective*. *US*. M19.
[from WOODPECKER with reversal of the elems.]
▶ **A** *noun*. **1** A woodpecker. *dial.* M19.
2 A white person, *esp.* a poor one. *Black slang*. E20.
▶ **B** *adjective*. Small, insignificant; inferior. Chiefly *dial.* M19.

📖 *Newsweek* Conditions encourage not the efficient experienced producers but the peckerwood . . operators.

pecket /ˈpɛkɪt/ *verb trans. & intrans.* Now *dial.* Infl. **-t-**, **-tt-**. M19.
[Frequentative of PECK *verb*¹.]
Peck repeatedly.

peck horn /ˈpɛk hɔːn/ *noun phr.* *Jazz slang*. M20.
[Perh. from PECK *noun*² + HORN *noun*.]
A mellophone; a saxophone.

pecking /ˈpɛkɪŋ/ *noun*. LME.
[from PECK *verb*¹ + -ING¹.]
1 The action of PECK *verb*¹; an instance of this. LME.
2 BUILDING. In *pl.* Misshapen and underburnt bricks used only for non-visible or temporary work. L19.
Comb.: **pecking order** (**a**) a social hierarchy amongst a group of animals (orig. observed in hens) in which those of higher rank are able to attack or threaten those of lower rank without retaliation; (**b**) *transf.* any hierarchy based on rank or status.

peckish /ˈpɛkɪʃ/ *adjective*. *colloq.* L18.
[from PECK *verb*¹ + -ISH¹.]
1 Hungry. L18.
2 Irritable, touchy. *US*. L19.

📖 **1** O. MANNING Having had no tea, he was . . a trifle peckish.

■ **peckishness** *noun* E19.

peckle /ˈpɛk(ə)l/ *noun & verb*¹. *obsolete* exc. *dial.* L16.
[Reduced form.]
▶ **A** *noun*. A speckle. L16.
▶ **B** *verb trans.* Speckle. L16.
■ **peckled** *adjective* speckled, variegated M16.

peckle /ˈpɛk(ə)l/ *verb*² *trans.* *rare*. E19.
[from PECK *verb*¹ + -LE³.]
Peck slightly or repeatedly.

Peck's bad boy /pɛks bad ˈbɔɪ/ *noun phr.* *US slang*. L19.
[A character created by George Wilbur *Peck* (1840–1916), US newspaper writer.]
An unruly or recalcitrant person.

Pecksniff /ˈpɛksnɪf/ *noun*. E20.
[Surname of a character in Dickens's *Martin Chuzzlewit*.]
A hypocrite professing benevolence etc.
■ **Peckˈsniffery** *noun* L19. **Peckˈsniffian** *adjective* M19.

pecky /ˈpɛki/ *adjective*. *US*. M19.
[App. from PECK *noun*³ + -Y¹.]
Of timber: showing signs of decay caused by various fungi.

📖 *Detroit Free Press* It's paneled in pecky wood.

Peclet number /ˈpɛkleɪ nʌmbə/ *noun phr.* M20.
[J. C. E. *Peclet* (1793–1857), French physicist.]
PHYSICS. A dimensionless parameter used in calculations of heat transfer between a moving fluid and a solid body, representing the ratio of the convected to the conducted heat and equal to the product of the Reynolds number and the Prandtl number.

pecorino /pɛkəˈriːnəʊ/ *noun*. M20.
[Italian, from *pecora* sheep.]
A hard Italian cheese made from ewe's milk.

pect /pɛkt/ *noun*. *N. Amer. slang*. L20.
[Abbreviation.]
A pectoral muscle. Usu. in *pl.* Cf. PEC.

pectase /ˈpɛkteɪz/ *noun*. M19.
[from PECT(IN + -ASE.]
BIOCHEMISTRY. = PECTINESTERASE.

pectate /ˈpɛkteɪt/ *noun*. M19.
[from PECT(IC + -ATE¹.]
CHEMISTRY. A salt or ester of pectic acid.

pecten /ˈpɛktɛn/ *noun.* Pl. **pectines** /ˈpɛktɪniːz/, **pectens**. LME.
[Latin = comb, wool-card, pubic hair; rel. to *pectere*, Greek *pek(t)ein* to comb.]
†**1** *ANATOMY.* The bones in the hand between the wrist and fingers; the metacarpus. In early use also, the bones of the foot, the metatarsus. LME–M16.
2 *ANATOMY.* The pubic region; the pubis. Now only in ***pecten pubis***, the anterior edge of the upper pubis. LME.
3 (The shell of) a bivalve mollusc of the genus *Pecten* or a similar genus; a scallop. L17.
4 *ZOOLOGY.* Any of various comblike structures, *esp.* (*a*) a pigmented vascular projection from the choroid in the eye of a bird; (*b*) an appendage in an arthropod consisting of or bearing a row of bristles or chitinous teeth, e.g. on the feet of pollen-gathering bees and in the breathing apparatus of mosquito larvae. E18.

pectic /ˈpɛktɪk/ *adjective.* M19.
[Greek *pektikos*, from *pektos* fixed, congealed, curdled, from stem of *pēgnuein* make firm or solid: see -IC.]
CHEMISTRY. **1** ***pectic acid***, any of a class of colloidal polymers of galacturonic acid derived from natural pectins by hydrolysis. M19.
2 Containing, consisting of, or producing pectic acid or pectins. L19.

pectin /ˈpɛktɪn/ *noun.* M19.
[from Greek *pektos* (see prec.) + -IN¹.]
BIOCHEMISTRY. Any of a group of neutral colloidal polymers occurring naturally in plant tissues, esp. in the cell walls of fruits, which mainly consist of partially esterified galacturonic acid, and are extracted or synthesized for use as emulsifying and gelling agents.
Comb.: **pectinmethylesterase** = PECTINESTERASE.
■ **pectiˈnaceous** *adjective* (*rare*) = PECTIC 2 M19.

pectinase /ˈpɛktɪneɪz/ *noun.* L19.
[from prec. + -ASE.]
BIOCHEMISTRY. An enzyme found in plants and in certain bacteria and fungi which hydrolyses pectin to its constituent monosaccharides.

pectinate /ˈpɛktɪnət/ *adjective.* LME.
[Latin *pectinatus* pa. pple of *pectinare* to comb, formed as PECTEN: see -ATE².]
†**1** Of hemp: dressed, combed. Only in LME.
2 Chiefly *BOTANY & ZOOLOGY.* Shaped like a comb; having straight narrow closely-set projections or divisions like the teeth of a comb. L18.
■ **pectinately** *adverb* M19.

pectinate /ˈpɛktɪneɪt/ *verb. rare.* E17.
[Latin *pectinat-* pa. ppl stem of *pectinare*: see prec., -ATE³.]
†**1** *verb trans.* Comb. E–M17.
2 *verb trans. & intrans.* Interlock (*with*) like the teeth of two combs. M17.

pectinated /ˈpɛktɪneɪtɪd/ *adjective.* L17.
[formed as PECTINATE *adjective*: see -ED¹.]
Chiefly *BOTANY & ZOOLOGY.* = PECTINATE *adjective* 2.

pectination /pɛktɪˈneɪʃ(ə)n/ *noun.* M17.
[formed as PECTINATE *verb* + -ATION.]
†**1** The action of interlocking or the condition of being interlocked like the teeth of two combs. *rare.* Only in M17.
2 The condition of being pectinate; a pectinate or comblike structure. E19.

pectineal /pɛkˈtɪnɪəl/ *adjective.* M19.
[from PECTINEUS + -AL¹.]
ANATOMY & ZOOLOGY. Pertaining to or connected with the pectineus or with the pubic bone, esp. its upper anterior surface.

pectines *noun pl.* see PECTEN.

pectinesterase /pɛktɪˈnɛstəreɪz/ *noun.* M20.
[from PECTIN + ESTERASE.]
BIOCHEMISTRY. An enzyme found in plants and in certain bacteria and fungi, which hydrolyses pectin to pectic acid and methanol. Also called ***pectase***, ***pectinmethylesterase***.

pectineus /pɛkˈtɪnɪəs/ *noun.* E18.
[mod. Latin, from Latin *pectin-*, PECTEN.]
ANATOMY. A flat muscle arising from the front of the pubis and inserted into the femur just behind the small trochanter.

pectini- /ˈpɛktɪni/ *combining form.*
[from Latin *pectin-*, PECTEN: see -I-.]
Comb, comb-shaped, comblike.
■ **pectiniˈbranchiate** *adjective* of, pertaining to, or designating a gastropod mollusc with comblike gills, of the order Mesogastropoda (formerly Pectinibranchiata) M19.

pectinite /ˈpɛktɪnʌɪt/ *noun.* L17.
[formed as prec. + -ITE¹.]
PALAEONTOLOGY. A fossil pecten or scallop.

pectinous /ˈpɛktɪnəs/ *adjective.* Now *rare* or *obsolete.* M19.
[from PECTIN + -OUS.]
BIOCHEMISTRY. = PECTIC 2.

pectize /ˈpɛktʌɪz/ *verb trans. & intrans.* Also **-ise**. L19.
[from Greek *pektos* (see PECTIC) + -IZE.]
Change into a gelatinous mass; congeal.
■ **pectiˈzation** *noun* the process of congealing or forming a gel M20.

pectolite /ˈpɛktəlʌɪt/ *noun.* E19.
[formed as prec. + -LITE.]
MINERALOGY. A whitish or greyish hydrous silicate of calcium and sodium, occurring in aggregates of needle-like monoclinic crystals in igneous rocks.

pectora *noun* pl. of PECTUS.

pectoral /ˈpɛkt(ə)r(ə)l/ *noun & adjective.* LME.
[Old & mod. French from Latin *pectorale* breastplate, *pectoralis* (adjective), from *pector-*, *pectus* breast, chest: see -AL¹. Cf. PEC, PECT.]
▶ **A** *noun.* **1 a** An ornamental cloth or breastplate worn over the chest, *spec.* by a Jewish high priest or by a Roman Catholic bishop in celebrating mass. LME. ▶**b** A piece of armour for the chest. L16. ▶**c** An ornamental cloth or a piece of armour for the chest of a horse. *obsolete* exc. *Hist.* E17.
2 A medicine, food, or drink good for digestive or esp. respiratory complaints. Now *rare.* E17.
3 = ***pectoral muscle***, ***pectoral fin*** below. Usu. in *pl.* M18.
▶ **B** *adjective.* **1** Chiefly *ANATOMY.* Of, pertaining to, situated or occurring in or upon the chest; thoracic. L15.
2 Of a medicine, food, or drink: good for digestive or esp. respiratory complaints. Now *rare.* L16.
3 Worn on the chest. E17.
4 *fig.* Proceeding from the heart, emotional. *arch.* M17.
Special collocations: **pectoral arch** the bones which support the forelimbs, the pectoral or shoulder girdle. **pectoral cross** *CHRISTIAN CHURCH* a cross or crucifix worn on a long chain around the neck so that it rests on the chest, worn esp. by bishops, abbots, and priests. **pectoral fin** each of the paired lateral fins attached to the pectoral arch in fishes, corresponding to the forelimbs of other vertebrates. ***pectoral girdle***: see GIRDLE *noun*¹ 4a. **pectoral muscle** any of the four large paired muscles which cover the front of the ribcage and serve to draw the forelimbs towards the chest (freq. in *pl.*). **pectoral quail** a stubble-quail. **pectoral sandpiper** a migratory Arctic-breeding sandpiper, *Calidris melanotos*, which often has dark streaked markings on the breast.

pectoriloquy /pɛktəˈrɪləkwi/ *noun.* M19.
[from Latin *pector-* (see prec.) + *loqui* speak: see -Y⁴.]
MEDICINE. Transmission of the voice through the chest wall, heard with the stethoscope and indicating either a cavity or consolidation in the lung.

pectose /ˈpɛktəʊs, -z/ *noun.* M19.
[from PECTIN + -OSE².]
BIOCHEMISTRY. An insoluble precursor of pectin. Also called ***protopectin***.

pectous /ˈpɛktəs/ *adjective.* Now *rare.* M19.
[from Greek *pektos* (see PECTIN) + -OUS.]
CHEMISTRY & BIOCHEMISTRY. **1** Congealed, turned into a gel. M19.
2 = PECTIC 2. M19.

pectus /ˈpɛktəs/ *noun. rare.* Pl. **pectora** /ˈpɛkt(ə)rə/. L17.
[Latin = breast, chest.]
ANATOMY & ZOOLOGY. The front of the thorax; *esp.* (*a*) the breast of a bird; (*b*) the lower surface of the thorax or prothorax of an insect.

†**peculate** *noun.* E17–M18.
[Latin *peculatus*, formed as next: see -ATE¹.]
= PECULATION.

peculate /ˈpɛkjʊleɪt/ *verb.* M18.
[Latin *peculat-* pa. ppl stem of *peculari* rel. to *peculium*: see PECULIAR, -ATE³.]
†**1** *verb trans.* Rob (a State or country) by peculation. M18–E19.
2 *verb trans.* Embezzle (money). E19.
3 *verb intrans.* Practise peculation. M19.

> 🕮 **2** SOUTHEY The people . . accused them of having peculated the public money. **3** B. MALAMUD He was arrested for peculating from official funds.

■ **peculative** *adjective* that practises embezzlement or peculation E20.

peculation /pɛkjʊˈleɪʃ(ə)n/ *noun.* M17.
[formed as prec. + -ATION, for Latin *peculatus* PECULATE *noun.*]
Embezzlement, esp. of public money or property by an official; an instance of this.

> 🕮 W. S. MAUGHAM He accuses him of oppressing the people, of peculation, and of maltreating various persons. A. LURIE The peculations of small Italian businessmen lack charm.

peculator /ˈpɛkjʊleɪtə/ *noun.* M17.
[Latin, formed as PECULATE *verb* + -OR.]
An embezzler, esp. of public money or property.

peculiar /pɪˈkjuːlɪə/ *adjective & noun.* LME.
[Latin *peculiaris* not held in common with others, from *peculium* property in cattle, private property, from *pecu* cattle, money. Cf. PECUNIARY.]
▶ **A** *adjective.* **1** Distinguished in nature or character; particular, special. LME.
2 That exclusively belongs or pertains to or is characteristic of an individual person or thing, or group of persons or things. Now only of a quality, feature, etc., (formerly also of property, possessions, etc.). Foll. by *to* or (formerly) with possess. L15. ▶**b** *ASTRONOMY.* Designating or pertaining to the motion of an individual star etc. relative to a system of which it is part, esp. that component of its proper motion which is not due to parallax. E20.
†**3** Separate, independent; single. E16–L18.
4 Unlike others, singular, unusual, strange, odd. E17. ▶**b** *ASTRONOMY.* (Of a galaxy) not belonging to any of the common types; (of a star) showing features uncharacteristic of the spectral class to which it belongs. M20.

> 🕮 **1** HENRY MILLER The communion loaf . . which each one receives only according to his peculiar state of grace. A. N. WILSON Tolstoy's ability to get along . . with young men . . was . . a source of peculiar annoyance to his wife. **2** R. MACAULAY As for flowers, there is a ruby-coloured pink peculiar to this place. D. M. FRAME Self-contempt is a malady peculiar to man. J. WAINWRIGHT Police stations have an aura peculiar to themselves. **3** W. TOOKE The Khanate of Kazan subsisted as a peculiar state till the year 1552. **4** G. CHARLES An eccentric aunt . . , usually unmarried . . , fond of peculiar clothes and hair styles. R. WEST A touch of silver gave her golden hair a peculiar etherealized burnish. ***funny peculiar***: see FUNNY *adjective.*

Special collocations: **peculiar institution** *US HISTORY* the system of black slavery in the Southern States of the US. **peculiar jurisdiction** *ECCLESIASTICAL LAW*: exempt from the jurisdiction of the bishop of the diocese. **peculiar people** (*a*) the Jews as God's chosen people; (*b*) *THEOLOGY* those chosen by God for salvation; (*c*) (with caps.) an evangelical fundamental Christian denomination founded in 1838 and relying on divine healing of disease.
▶ **B** *noun.* **1** *ECCLESIASTICAL.* A parish or church exempt from the jurisdiction of the diocese in which it lies. M16. ▶†**b** *transf.* Any place exempt from ordinary jurisdiction. L16–M17. ▶†**c** In the former colonies and provinces of New England: a district or piece of land not (yet) incorporated in a town. E18–E19.
2 Something which is the property of or belongs exclusively to an individual or group of individuals. *arch.* L16. ▶†**b** *spec.* = ***peculiar people*** (a), (b) above. E–M17.
†**3** A feature or quality exclusive to or characteristic of a thing. L16–M18.
†**4** An individual member of a group or collective whole; an item. E17–E18.
5 (**P-**.) A member of the fundamentalist Peculiar People. L19.
Phrases: **court of peculiars** *Hist.*: having jurisdiction over the peculiars of the archbishop of Canterbury. **Dean of peculiars** a member of the clergy invested with the charge of a church or parish exempt from the jurisdiction of the diocese in which it lies. †**one's own peculiar**, †**one's peculiar** one's private interest or special concern. **royal peculiar** a church or parish subject to the jurisdiction of the monarch only.
■ **peculiarism** *noun* (now *rare*) the fundamentalist doctrine or practices of the Peculiar People M19. **peculiarize** *verb trans.* †(*a*) appropriate exclusively *to*; (*b*) give peculiarity or singularity to: E17.

peculiarity /pɪˌkjuːlɪˈarɪti/ *noun.* E17.
[from prec. + -ITY.]
†**1** The condition or fact of belonging exclusively to an individual or group of individuals; exclusive possession. Only in E17. ▶**b** *spec.* (*THEOLOGY*) The condition of being God's chosen people. M17–L18.
2 The quality of being peculiar to or characteristic of an individual person or thing; an instance of this, a distinguishing characteristic. E17.
†**3** A particular liking or regard; a partiality. L17–M19.
4 The quality of being unusual or unlike others; singularity, strangeness, oddity; an instance of this, an odd trait or characteristic. M18.

> 🕮 **2** J. WAIN It is an architectural peculiarity of Paddington Station that it does not have . . a main entrance. **4** M. R. MITFORD Another very singular peculiarity about Mr. Talfourd; he can't spell.

peculiarly /pɪˈkjuːlɪəli/ *adverb.* LME.
[from PECULIAR *adjective* + -LY².]
1 Particularly, especially; *colloq.* more than usually. LME.
2 As regards an individual or group of individuals alone; individually. M16.
3 Unusually, singularly, strangely, oddly. M19.

> 🕮 **1** J. BUCHAN Black George had smoked a peculiarly evil type of Greek tobacco. A. S. BYATT I've never understood why people find it so peculiarly distasteful. **2** C. THUBRON The place was pervaded by an indefinable but peculiarly Chinese smell. F. WYNDHAM The gruff bravado that I had come to regard as peculiarly hers. **3** C. BRONTË You are peculiarly situated: very near happiness; yes; within reach of it.

peculium /pɪˈkjuːlɪəm/ *noun.* L17.
[Latin: see PECULIAR.]
1 A private or exclusive possession or property. L17.
2 *ROMAN LAW.* The property which a father allowed his child, or a master allowed his slave, to treat as if it were his or her own. E18.

†**pecunial** *adjective.* LME.
[Late Latin *pecunialis*, from Latin *pecunia* money: see PECUNIARY, -AL¹.]
1 = PECUNIARY *adjective* 1. LME–E18.
2 = PECUNIARY *adjective* 2. E–M16.

†**pecuniar** *adjective & noun. rare.* LME.
[Old & mod. French *pécuniaire*, formed as next: see -AR¹.]
▶ **A** *adjective.* = PECUNIARY *adjective* 1. LME–M17.
▶ **B** *noun.* In *pl.* Money matters. Only in E19.

pecuniary /pɪˈkjuːnɪəri/ *adjective & noun.* E16.
[Latin *pecuniarius*, from *pecunia* money, orig. 'riches in cattle', from *pecu* cattle, money: see -ARY¹. Cf. prec., PECULIAR.]
▶ **A** *adjective.* **1** Consisting of money; exacted in money. E16. ▸**b** Of an offence: entailing a money penalty or fine. E17.
2 Of or pertaining to money. E17.

📖 **1** *Morecambe Guardian* He had admitted obtaining pecuniary advantage at a previous hearing. **2** W. M. CLARKE Not a princely sum, but enough to ward off any pecuniary anxieties.

▶†**B** *noun.* Money; in *pl.*, money matters. E17–E19.
■ **pecuniarily** *adverb* in respect of money E17.

pecunious /pɪˈkjuːnɪəs/ *adjective.* LME.
[Latin *pecuniosus*, from *pecunia*: see prec., -OUS.]
Well provided with money; wealthy.
■ **pecuniˈosity** *noun* the state of being pecunious M19.

ped /pɛd/ *noun¹.* Now *dial.* See also PAD *noun⁴.* LME.
[Origin unkn. Cf. PEDLAR.]
A wicker pannier; a hamper with a lid.

ped /pɛd/ *noun².* *slang* (now chiefly *US*). M19.
[Abbreviation.]
= PEDESTRIAN *noun.*

ped /pɛd/ *noun³.* M20.
[Greek *pedon* ground, earth.]
SOIL SCIENCE. An individual aggregate of material or a structural unit in an undisturbed soil.

ped- *combining form¹* see PAEDO-.

ped- *combining form²* see PEDO-².

pedage /ˈpɛdɪdʒ/ *noun.* *obsolete* exc. *Hist.* LME.
[medieval Latin *pedagium*, earlier *pedaticum*: see PÉAGE.]
Toll paid for passing through a place or country; = PÉAGE 1.

pedagog *noun & verb* see PEDAGOGUE.

pedagogal /ˈpɛdəgɒg(ə)l/ *adjective. rare.* L18.
[from PEDAGOGUE + -AL¹.]
Of or pertaining to a pedagogue.

pedagogic /pɛdəˈgɒgɪk, -ˈgɒdʒ-/ *adjective & noun.* L18.
[French *pédagogique* from Greek *paidagōgikos* or directly from *pédagogie*: see PEDAGOGUE, -IC.]
▶ **A** *adjective.* Of, pertaining to, or characteristic of a pedagogue or pedagogy. L18.

📖 M. COX He was not an educator in a narrow pedagogic sense.

▶ **B** *noun sing.* & (usu.) in *pl.* (treated as *sing.*). The art or science of teaching. E19.
■ **pedagogical** *adjective* = PEDAGOGIC *adjective* E17. **pedagogically** *adverb* in the manner of a pedagogue; in relation to pedagogy: L19.

pedagogism *noun* var. of PEDAGOGUISM.

pedagogist /ˈpɛdəgɒgɪst, -ˈgɒdʒ-/ *noun.* L19.
[from PEDAGOGY + -IST.]
An expert in or student of pedagogy.

pedagogue /ˈpɛdəgɒg/ *noun & verb.* Also ***-gog**. LME.
[Latin *paedagogus* from Greek *paidagōgos* slave who took a child to and from school, from *paid-*, *pais* boy (cf. PAEDO-) + *agōgos* leading.]
▶ **A** *noun.* **1** A schoolmaster, a teacher, now *esp.* a strict, dogmatic, or pedantic one. LME. ▸†**b** An assistant teacher. M16–E17.
2 A man, esp. a slave, who took a child to and from school and supervised the child's behaviour generally. *obsolete* exc. CLASSICAL HISTORY. L15.
†**3** A schoolroom; a school building. *rare.* L15–M18.

📖 **1** S. CONRAN Monsieur Sardean was a boring little pedagogue, but he had long ago stopped lecturing . . Lili.

▶ **B** *verb trans.* Instruct as a pedagogue. Now *rare.* L17.
■ **pedagoguery** *noun* (*a*) *rare* a school; (*b*) the occupation of a pedagogue: E19. **pedagoguish** *adjective* characteristic of a pedagogue M19.

pedagoguism /ˈpɛdəgɒgɪz(ə)m, -gɒdʒ-/ *noun.* Also **-gogism**. M17.
[from prec. + -ISM.]
The character, methods, or function of a pedagogue; pedagogy.

pedagogy /ˈpɛdəgɒgi, -gɒdʒi/ *noun.* Also (*arch.*) **paed-**. M16.
[In sense 1 from Latin *paedagogium*; in sense 2 from French *pédagogie* from Greek *paidagōgia* office of a pedagogue, from *paidagōgos*: see PEDAGOGUE, -Y³.]
1 A place of instruction; a school, a college. *obsolete* exc. *Hist.* M16.
2 The art or science of teaching; teaching; *transf.* discipline, training. L16.

pedal /ˈpɛd(ə)l/ *noun¹.* E17.
[French *pédale* from Italian *pedale* footstalk, tree-trunk (*pedale d'organo* organ pedal) from Latin *pedalis*, from *ped-*, *pes* foot: see -AL¹. Cf. next.]
1 a A foot-operated lever in an organ; *spec.* (*a*) each of the (wooden) keys for operating a (usu. separate) set of bass pipes; (*b*) a lever for drawing a number of stops out or in at once. Also = ***pedalboard*** below. E17. ▸**b** Each of the set of (usu. seven) foot-operated levers on a harp for altering the pitch of the strings. L18. ▸**c** A foot-operated lever on a piano, usu. one of two or three, for making the tone fuller or softer; *esp.* the sustaining pedal. E19. ▸**d** Any foot-operated lever on various other musical instruments, as a harpsichord, kettledrum, etc. Now also, a foot-operated device for producing a sound effect on an electric guitar etc. (also ***effects pedal***). L19.
2 A foot-operated lever on a machine, as a loom etc.; *spec.* (*a*) either of a pair of levers for transmitting power to a bicycle or tricycle wheel; (*b*) any of the foot-operated controls in a motor vehicle. L18
3 MUSIC. **a** A note (regularly either tonic or dominant) sustained (or reiterated) in one part, usu. the bass, through a succession of harmonies, some of which are independent of it. M19. ▸**b** The lowest or fundamental note of a harmonic series in some brass and wind instruments. M19.
4 GEOMETRY. A curve or surface which is the locus of the feet of the perpendiculars let fall from a fixed point upon the tangents to a given curve or surface. M19.
5 A foot. Usu. in *pl. joc.* M19.
1c ***damper pedal***, ***loud pedal***, ***shifting pedal***, ***soft pedal***, ***sustaining pedal***. **4** **negative pedal** GEOMETRY that curve or surface of which a given one is the pedal. **oblique pedal** a curve or surface constructed like a pedal but with the lines meeting the tangents at a constant angle not a right angle. **second pedal** the pedal of the pedal (of a curve or surface).
Comb.: **pedal bin** a bin for rubbish with a lid which is opened by means of a pedal; **pedalboard** the keyboard of pedals on an organ; **pedal boat** a small boat, esp. a pleasure-boat, propelled by means of pedals, a pedalo; **pedal car** a toy car propelled by means of pedals; **pedal clarinet**: sounding an octave below a bass clarinet; **pedal cycle** a bicycle; **pedal keyboard** = *pedalboard* above; **pedal note** = sense 3b above; **pedal point** = sense 3a above; **pedal power** *colloq.* bicycling as a means of transport; **pedal-pusher** (*a*) *colloq.* a cyclist; (*b*) in *pl.*, knee-length or calf-length trousers, suitable for wearing when cycling; **pedal steel (guitar)** an electric guitar fixed on a stand and connected to pedals for altering the string tension so as to produce glissando effects; **pedal wireless** a small radio transceiver with a generator powered by a person pedalling, used in the Australian outback.

pedal /ˈpɛd(ə)l/ *noun².* L19.
[Italian *pedale*: see prec.]
Straw consisting of the thicker part at the foot of the stalk, used for weaving and plaiting. Also ***pedal straw***.

pedal /ˈpɛd(ə)l, *in sense 1 also* ˈpiː-/ *adjective.* E17.
[Latin *pedalis*, from *ped-*, *pes* foot: see -AL¹. Cf. PEDAL *noun²*.]
1 Chiefly ANATOMY & ZOOLOGY. Of or pertaining to the foot or feet (now chiefly *joc.* in *gen.* use). E17.
2 GEOMETRY. Pertaining to or designating a curve or surface which is the pedal of another curve or surface (see PEDAL *noun¹* 4). M19.
1 **pedal bone** the coffin-bone of a horse. **2** **pedal origin**, **pedal pole** the fixed point from which a pedal curve or surface is constructed.
¶ Not always clearly distinguishable from attrib. uses of PEDAL *noun¹*.

pedal /ˈpɛd(ə)l/ *verb.* Infl. **-ll-**, ***-l-**. L19.
[from PEDAL *noun¹*.]
1 *verb intrans. & trans.* Work the pedals of (a bicycle etc.), propel (a bicycle etc.) by working the pedals. L19.
2 *verb trans. & intrans.* Use the pedals in playing (a piece of music) on an organ etc. L19.

📖 **1** B. HINES A little boy, pedalling a tricycle round in tight circles. W. MAXWELL He pedals for dear life over the final stretch of road. **2** A. FOLDES Pedalling is one of the most complicated processes in piano playing.

■ **pedaller** *noun* a person who pedals; *spec.* a cyclist: L19.

pedalfer /pɪˈdalfə/ *noun.* E20.
[from PED(O-² + AL(UMINIUM + Latin *ferrum* iron.]
SOIL SCIENCE. A soil without a layer of accumulated calcium carbonate, but in which iron and aluminium oxides have tended to accumulate (usu. acidic and characteristic of humid climates).
■ **pedalferic** *adjective* E20.

pedalier /pɛdəˈlɪə/ *noun.* L19.
[French *pédalier*, from *pédale* PEDAL *noun¹*.]
The pedalboard of an organ.

pedalo /ˈpɛdələʊ/ *noun.* Pl. **-o(e)s**. M20.
[from PEDAL *noun¹* + -O.]
A small pedal-operated pleasure-boat, usu. with paddle-wheels.

pedanda /pɛˈdandə/ *noun.* E19.
[Balinese.]
In Bali, a brahmin priest.

pedant /ˈpɛd(ə)nt/ *noun & adjective.* L16.
[French *pédant* from Italian *pedante*, perh. from 1st elem. of Latin *paedagogus* PEDAGOGUE.]
▶ **A** *noun.* †**1** A schoolmaster, a teacher; a pedagogue. L16–E18.
2 A person who parades or reveres excessively academic learning or technical knowledge; a person excessively concerned with trifling details or insisting on strict adherence to formal rules or literal meaning. Also, a person obsessed by a theory, a doctrinaire. L16.

📖 **2** A. S. NEILL Only pedants claim that learning from books is education. E. S. PERSON A third-rate pedant masquerading as a scholarly genius.

▶ **B** *attrib.* or as *adjective.* Pedantic. *arch.* E17.

pedantic /pɪˈdantɪk/ *adjective.* L16.
[from prec. + -IC.]
Having the character of a pedant; characterized by or exhibiting pedantry. Formerly also, characteristic of a teacher.

📖 J. GALSWORTHY Twirling their partners at great pace, without pedantic attention to the rhythm. C. PRIEST To choose too carefully is to become pedantic, closing the imagination to wider visions.

■ **pedantical** *adjective* (now *rare*) = PEDANTIC L16. **pedantically** *adverb* in a pedantic manner M17. **pedanticly** *adverb* (now *rare*) = PEDANTICALLY M17.

pedanticism /pɪˈdantɪsɪz(ə)m/ *noun.* L19.
[from PEDANTIC + -ISM.]
A pedantic expression or idea; (a piece of) pedantry.

📖 *Verbatim* In most contexts . . *data* used as a plural strikes me as a pedanticism.

pedantise *verb* var. of PEDANTIZE.

pedantism /ˈpɛd(ə)ntɪz(ə)m/ *noun.* Now *rare.* L16.
[from PEDANT + -ISM.]
1 The character or style of a pedant; pedantry. Also, a piece of pedantry. L16.
†**2** The office or authority of a teacher; the state of being under such authority. E–M17.

pedantize /ˈpɛd(ə)ntʌɪz/ *verb.* Also **-ise**. E17.
[from PEDANT + -IZE.]
1 *verb intrans. & trans.* (with *it*). Speak or write pedantically. E17.
2 *verb trans.* Make pedantic. M18.

pedantocracy /pɛd(ə)nˈtɒkrəsi/ *noun.* M19.
[from PEDANT: see -CRACY.]
A system of government by pedants; a governing body of pedants.
■ **pedantocrat** /pɪˈdantəkrat/ *noun* L19. **peˌdantoˈcratic** *adjective* L19.

pedantry /ˈpɛd(ə)ntri/ *noun.* L16.
[from PEDANT + -RY, after French *pédanterie* or Italian *pedanteria*.]
The manner or behaviour characteristic of a pedant; excessive reverence for academic learning or technical knowledge; excessive concern for trifling details or strict adherence to formal rules or literal meaning; an instance or example of this.

📖 S. J. GOULD Natural history sank into a mire of unproductive pedantry. A. ROBERTS Criticism of the King's conduct is not mere pedantry.

pedate /ˈpɛdeɪt/ *adjective.* M18.
[Latin *pedatus* having feet, from *ped-*, *pes* foot: see -ATE².]
1 Having divisions like the claws of a bird's foot; *spec.* in BOTANY, (of a leaf etc.) palmately divided with the outer leaflets or lobes stalked and freq. further subdivided. M18.
2 ZOOLOGY. Having feet, footed. *rare.* E19.
■ **pedately** *adverb* E19.

pedatifid /pɪˈdeɪtɪfɪd/ *adjective.* L18.
[formed as prec. + -I- + -FID.]
BOTANY. Pedately divided at least halfway to the base.

pedder /ˈpɛdə/ *noun.* Now *Scot. & dial.* ME.
[App. from PED *noun¹*. Cf. medieval Latin *pedarius* a person who goes on foot, PEDLAR.]
A pedlar.

peddle /ˈpɛd(ə)l/ *verb.* M16.
[In branch I back-form. from PEDLAR; in branch II prob. var. of PIDDLE *verb* by assoc. in form and sense with branch I.]
▶ **I 1** *verb intrans.* Follow the occupation of a pedlar; go about carrying small goods for sale. M16.
2 *verb trans.* Sell (esp. small goods or goods in small quantities) as a pedlar. E19. ▸**b** *fig.* Advocate or promote

(a philosophy, way of life, etc.). M19. ▸c Sell (esp. drugs) illicitly. *colloq.* M20.

> 1 J. ARBUTHNOT To go hawking and peddling about the streets, selling knives, scissars, and shoe-buckles. 2 S. BELLOW During the depression . . she went out and peddled stuff from door to door. H. CARPENTER A travelling salesman, peddling fancy goods around his native Connecticut. b D. LODGE It's a very crude kind of historicism he's peddling.

▸**II 3** *verb intrans.* Busy oneself with trifling matters; work at something in a trifling or petty way. L16.

■ **peddling** *adjective* (*a*) that peddles; (*b*) (of a thing) trifling, insignificant, petty: M16.

peddler *noun & verb* see PEDLAR.

pede /piːd/ *noun.* M16.
[Latin *ped-*, *pes* foot: cf. Italian *piede*.]
A foot, a base. Only in *comb.* as below.
Comb.: **pede-cloth** an altar carpet; **pede-window** *Hist.* a window at the west end of a cruciform church.

pedee /ˈpiːdiː/ *noun. obsolete* exc. *dial.* M17.
[Origin unkn.]
A boy attendant, a groom; (in 19th cent., on the River Tyne) the boy at the keel of a boat.

†**pedelion** *noun.* ME–M19.
[Old French *pié* (mod. *pied*) *de lion* lit. 'lion's foot'.]
Any of several plants having fruits, leaves, etc., supposed to resemble clawed feet, *esp.* (*a*) lady's mantle, *Alchemilla vulgaris*; (*b*) Christmas rose, *Helleborus niger*.

pederasty /ˈpɛdərasti/ *noun.* Also **paed-** /ˈpiːd-, ˈpɛd-/. E17.
[mod. Latin *paederastia* from Greek, from *paiderastēs*, from *paid-*, *pais* boy + *erastēs* lover.]
Sexual relations between a man and a boy; anal intercourse with a boy as a passive partner.
■ **pederast** *noun* [Greek *paiderastēs*] a man who performs or practises pederasty M17. **pedeˈrastic** *adjective* [Greek *paiderastikos*] of, pertaining to, or practising pederasty E18.

pedes *noun* pl. of PES.

pedestal /ˈpɛdɪst(ə)l/ *noun & verb.* M16.
[French *piédestal* (†*pied d'estel*) from Italian *piedestallo*, from *piè* foot + *di* of + *stallo* STALL *noun*¹; the 1st syll. was conformed to Latin *ped-*, *pes* foot.]
▸**A** *noun.* **1** The part of a column below the base, comprising the plinth(s) and the dado if present; the base on which an obelisk, statue, vase, etc., is erected. Also, either of two supports at either end of the writing-surface of a desk, usually containing drawers. M16. ▸**b** *fig.* A position of being admired or exalted to an exaggerated or unwarranted degree. Freq. in ***put on a pedestal***. M19.
2 A base, a foundation, (material or immaterial). L16.
3 The foot; the leg. *joc.* L17. ▸†**b** = CHAIR *noun*¹ 6; a base to support the chair. E–M19.
4 An upright support of a machine or apparatus; the column supporting a wash-basin; (the base of) a lavatory pan. L18. ▸**b** ENGINEERING. The lower upright member of a journal-bearing; a metal frame attached to the lower part of a railway vehicle in which a journal-box is supported while free to move up and down. L19.
5 TELEVISION. The level of the video signal voltage during line blanking; this part of the signal. M20.

> 1b J. HILTON Now the games-captain was tottering if not already fallen from the pedestal. A. S. DALE Women before marriage were princesses on pedestals. 4 D. STOREY On a wooden pedestal, stood a massive globe.

Comb.: ***pedestal basin***: see ***pedestal wash-basin*** below; **pedestal desk** a desk with a writing-surface supported at either end by a pedestal; **pedestal mat**: which fits around the base of a lavatory or wash-basin pedestal; **pedestal table**: with one heavy central support; **pedestal wash-basin**, **pedestal basin**: on a single columnar support.
▸**B** *verb trans.* Infl. **-ll-**, ***-l-**. Set on a pedestal; provide with a pedestal. M17.
■ **pedestalled** *adjective* L19.

pedestrial /pɪˈdɛstrɪəl/ *adjective.* Long *rare.* E17.
[from Latin *pedestr-* (see next) + -IAL.]
†**1** = PEDESTRIAN *adjective.* E–M17.
2 Of or pertaining to the foot; (of archery) performed with the bow drawn against the foot. L18.
3 Adapted for walking. L19.

pedestrian /pɪˈdɛstrɪən/ *adjective & noun.* E18.
[from French *pédestre* or its source Latin *pedestr-*, *pedester* going on foot (after Greek *pezos*), written in prose, from *ped-*, *pes* foot: see -IAN.]
▸**A** *adjective.* **1** Esp. of writing: prosaic, dull, uninspired. E18.
2 a Going on foot; performed on foot. L18. ▸**b** [Partly the noun used attrib.] Of, pertaining to, or adapted for walking or walkers; (of a portrait or statue) representing a person on foot. M19.

> 1 A. G. GARDINER In conversation I am naturally rather a pedestrian person. S. NAIPAUL Despite the pedestrian and factual style, his response to Jonestown was . . enthusiastic. 2 H. R. LANDON Pedestrian traffic was hampered by . . carriages and wagons. b Z. TOMIN The ancient bridge, recently made strictly pedestrian. **pedestrian crossing** a marked section of the roadway on which pedestrians are given precedence over vehicular traffic when crossing there. **pedestrian precinct** a paved area reserved for pedestrians only, usu. in a town centre or shopping centre.

▸**B** *noun.* A person who walks, esp. as a physical exercise or athletic performance; a person on foot rather than in a vehicle. L18.
■ **pedestrianate** *verb intrans.* (now *rare*) go on foot, walk M19. **pedestrianism** *noun* the practice of walking; walking as an exercise or athletic performance: L19. **pedestrianly** *adverb* in a prosaic or dull manner M19.

pedestrianize /pɪˈdɛstrɪənʌɪz/ *verb.* Also **-ise**. E19.
[from prec. + -IZE.]
1 a *verb intrans. & trans.* (with *it*.). Go on foot, walk. E19. ▸**b** *verb trans.* Close to vehicular traffic and make accessible only to pedestrians; make into a pedestrian precinct. M20.
2 a *verb intrans.* Produce something prosaic or dull. M19. ▸**b** *verb trans.* Make prosaic or dull. M20.
■ **pedestrianiˈzation** *noun* the action of pedestrianizing a place; the state of being pedestrianized: M20.

†**pedestrious** *adjective.* M17–E19.
[from Latin *pedestr-* (see PEDESTRIAN) + -IOUS.]
Going on foot, esp. as opp. to flying or swimming.

pedi- /ˈpɛdi/ *combining form.*
[from Latin *ped-*, *pes* foot: see -I-.]
Of the foot. Also repr. PEDAL *noun*¹
■ **pedicab** *noun* a small pedal-operated vehicle, usu. a tricycle, serving as a taxi in countries of the Far East M20. **pediform** *adjective* (ZOOLOGY) having the form of a foot E19. **peˈdigerous** *adjective* (ZOOLOGY) bearing feet or legs E19.

pedia *noun* pl. of PEDION.

pediatric *adjective*, **pediatrics** *noun* see PAEDIATRIC, PAEDIATRICS.

pedication /pɛdɪˈkeɪʃ(ə)n/ *noun.* Also **paed-** /piːd-, pɛd-/. L19.
[mod. Latin *paedicatio(n-)*, from Latin *paedicat-* pa. ppl stem of *paedicare* have anal intercourse with: see -ATION.]
Anal intercourse.
■ **pedicate** *verb intrans. & trans.* [back-form.] perform or practise pedication (on) M20.

pedicator /ˈpɛdɪkeɪtə/ *noun.* Also **paed-** /ˈpiːd-, ˈpɛd-/. M17.
[Latin *paedicator*, from *paedicat-*: see prec., -OR.]
A person who performs or practises pedication.
¶ Rare before M20.
■ **pedicatory** *adjective* of or pertaining to pedication L20.

pedicel /ˈpɛdɪs(ə)l/ *noun.* L17.
[mod. Latin *pedicellus* dim. of *pediculus* PEDICLE.]
1 BOTANY. A small stalk or stalklike structure in a plant. Orig., the filament of a stamen; now, each of the stalks which bear the individual flowers in a branched inflorescence (cf. PEDUNCLE 1). Also, a main flower-stalk when short or slender. L17.
2 ZOOLOGY. A small stalklike structure in an animal; *spec.* (*a*) the second joint of an insect's antenna; (*b*) an eye-stalk of a crustacean; (*c*) a tube-foot of an echinoderm; (*d*) the bony process on the skull of a deer from which an antler grows. E19.
■ **pediˈcellar** *adjective* pertaining to or of the nature of a pedicel E20. **pedicelled** *adjective* having a pedicel, pedicellate E19.

pedicellaria /ˌpɛdɪsəˈlɛːrɪə/ *noun.* Pl. **-iae** /-iiː/. L19.
[mod. Latin, formed as prec. + Latin *-aria* -ARY¹.]
ZOOLOGY. Each of numerous organs like small pincers on the outside of an echinoderm.

pedicellate /ˈpɛdɪs(ə)leɪt/ *adjective.* E19.
[formed as PEDICEL + -ATE².]
BOTANY & ZOOLOGY. Having a pedicel or pedicels.
■ Also **pedicellated** *adjective* M19.

pedicle /ˈpɛdɪk(ə)l/ *noun.* E17.
[Latin *pediculus* dim. of *ped-*, *pes* foot: see -CLE.]
1 BOTANY. Formerly, the petiole of a leaf; the pedicel of a flower or fruit. Later, a minute stalklike support, as of a seed, gland, etc. Now *rare.* E17.
2 A stalk by which a tumour is attached to the body; SURGERY a narrow strip of skin and subcutaneous tissue attaching a piece of tissue used for grafting to its original site. M18. ▸**b** ANATOMY. Either of the two narrow thickened parts of a vertebra connecting the centrum with the lamina, and forming part of the neural arch. M19.
3 ZOOLOGY. = PEDICEL 2. E19.

pedicular /pɪˈdɪkjʊlə/ *adjective.* M16.
[(French *pédiculaire* from) Latin *pedicularis*, from *pediculus* louse, from *pedis* louse: see -CULE, -AR¹.]
Of or pertaining to a louse or lice; lousy.

pediculated /pɪˈdɪkjʊleɪtɪd/ *adjective.* E19.
[formed as PEDICLE + -ATE³ + -ED².]
MEDICINE. Having a pedicle, borne on a pedicle; stalked.

pediculicide /pɛdɪˈkjuːlɪsʌɪd/ *noun.* E20.
[formed as next + -I- + -CIDE.]
An agent that kills lice.
■ **ˌpediculiˈcidal** *adjective & noun* (*a*) *adjective* fatal to lice; (*b*) *noun* a pediculicidal substance: E20.

pediculosis /pɪˌdɪkjʊˈləʊsɪs/ *noun.* Pl. **-loses** /-ˈləʊsiːz/. E19.
[from Latin *pediculus* louse + -OSIS.]
Infestation of the body or skin with lice.

pediculous /pɪˈdɪkjʊləs/ *adjective.* M16.
[from late Latin *pediculosus*, formed as prec.: see -ULOUS.]
Infested with lice, lousy; of or pertaining to a louse or lice.

pedicure /ˈpɛdɪkjʊə/ *noun & verb.* M19.
[French *pédicure*, from Latin *ped-*, *pes* foot + *curare* CURE *verb*.]
▸**A** *noun.* **1** A person whose business is the treatment of feet; a chiropodist. M19.
2 Treatment of the feet, either remedial, as in the removal of corns and bunions, or cosmetic; a session of such treatment. L19.
▸**B** *verb trans.* Give (a) pedicure to. L19.
■ **pedicurist** *noun* = PEDICURE *noun* 1 L19.

pedigree /ˈpɛdɪgriː/ *noun & adjective.* LME.
[Anglo-Norman *pé de grue* (lit. 'foot of a crane'), from *pé* (Old French *pie*, mod. *pied*) foot + *grue* crane (from a mark used to denote succession in a genealogical tree).]
▸**A** *noun.* **1** A genealogical table or tree; a genealogy presented in tabular form. LME.
2 The ancestry or descent of a person, family, or domestic animal. LME. ▸**b** *transf.* Origin and succession, derivation. M16. ▸**c** The history of an individual person or thing; a list of achievements; a criminal record. *colloq.* E20.
3 Descent in the abstract, *esp.* distinguished or ancient descent. LME.
4 A family, a line of succession; a long series of people. Now *rare.* M16.

> 2 C. DARWIN The pedigree of a race-horse is of more value . . than its appearance. E. WAUGH Few Englishmen . . could not assume a mediaeval name if they chose to pick about in their pedigree. b A. N. WILSON Manning's view of 'Catholic society' had an equally hybrid pedigree. c *Daily Telegraph* Candidates should have a good product management pedigree. 3 S. HASTINGS Countess Costa de Beauregard, an old lady of distinguished pedigree.

▸**B** *attrib.* or as *adjective.* Esp. of an animal: having a recorded line of descent from known progenitors; of pure stock. M19.
■ **pedigreed** *adjective* (*a*) = PEDIGREE *adjective*; (*b*) *slang* having a criminal record: E19.

pediluvium /pɛdɪˈluːvɪəm, -ˈljuː-/ *noun.* Pl. **-ia** /-ɪə/. L17.
[mod. Latin, from PEDI- + Latin *-luvium* washing, from *luere* to wash.]
A foot-bath; a washing of the feet.

pediment /ˈpɛdɪm(ə)nt/ *noun.* Orig. †**peri-**. L16.
[Origin uncertain: perh. alt. of PYRAMID *noun*.]
▸**I 1** The triangular part crowning the front of a building in the classical style, usu. situated over a portico and consisting of a flat recessed field framed by a cornice and often ornamented with sculptures; a similarly placed part of a building in mannerist or baroque style (irrespective of shape); a similar feature surmounting and abutting on a niche, door, screen, etc. L16.
2 PHYSICAL GEOGRAPHY. A broad gently sloping rock surface that extends outwards from the abrupt foot of a mountain in arid and semi-arid regions and is usu. covered with a layer of alluvium. L19.
▸**II** [Referred to Latin *ped-*, *pes* foot.]
3 A (physical) base. E18.
■ **pediˈmental** *adjective* of, pertaining to, or shaped like a pediment M19. **pedimenˈtation** *noun* (PHYSICAL GEOGRAPHY) the formation of a pediment M20. **pedimented** *adjective* having or characterized by a pediment or pediments; shaped or placed like a pediment: M19.

pediocratic /pɛdɪəˈkratɪk/ *adjective.* E20.
[from Greek *pedion* plain + *kratos* strength + -IC.]
GEOLOGY. Designating a period when erosion predominates over crustal upheaval, leading to an overall lessening of relief.

pedion /ˈpɛdɪɒn/ *noun.* Pl. **-ia** /-ɪə/. L19.
[Greek: see prec.]
CRYSTALLOGRAPHY. A crystal form consisting of a single face, without any symmetrically equivalent face.

pedipalp /ˈpɛdɪpalp, ˈpiː-/ *noun.* Also in Latin form **pedipalpus** /pɛdɪˈpalpəs, piː-/, pl. **-pi** /-pʌɪ, -piː/. E19.
[mod. Latin *pedipalpi* pl., from PEDI- + Latin *palpus* PALP *noun*.]
ZOOLOGY. **1** Each of the second pair of appendages attached to the cephalothorax of most arachnids, variously specialized as pincers in scorpions, sensory organs in spiders, and locomotory organs in horseshoe crabs. E19.
2 = ***whip scorpion*** s.v. WHIP *noun.* E19.

pediplain /ˈpɛdɪpleɪn/ *noun.* M20.
[from PEDI(MENT + PLAIN *noun*[1].]
PHYSICAL GEOGRAPHY. An extensive plain formed in a desert by the coalescence of neighbouring pediments.

pediplanation /ˌpɛdɪpləˈneɪʃ(ə)n/ *noun.* M20.
[from PEDI(MENT + PLANATION.]
PHYSICAL GEOGRAPHY. Erosion to, or the formation of, a pediplain or a pediplane.

pediplane /ˈpɛdɪpleɪn/ *noun.* M20.
[from PEDI(MENT + PLANE *noun*[3].]
A piedmont slope in arid and semi-arid regions comprising in general a pediment and a peripediment.

pediunker /pɛdɪˈʌŋkə/ *noun.* E20.
[Origin unkn. Orig. used in Tristan da Cunha in the S. Atlantic.]
A grey shearwater, *Procellaria cinerea*, of southern oceans.

pedlar /ˈpɛdlə/ *noun & verb.* Also (esp. *US* & in sense A.3) **peddler**. ME.
[Alt. of PEDDER: for the ending *-ler* cf. TINKLER *noun*[1], TINKER *noun*.]
► **A** *noun.* **1** A person who goes about carrying small goods for sale, *esp.* one who goes from door to door with the goods in a pack; *fig.* a person who deals in something in a small way; a retailer *of* gossip etc. ME.
2 A person who works in a petty, incompetent, or ineffective way. *derog.* L16.
3 A person who sells goods illicitly, esp. on a person-to-person basis; *esp.* a person who sells drugs illegally. Orig. *US.* L19.

> 📖 **3** W. S. BURROUGHS The peddler sometimes slips a hot shot to an addict.

Phrases: **pedlar's French** the cant of criminals; unintelligible jargon.
► **B** *verb.* †**1** *verb trans.* Make a pedlar of. Only in M17.
2 *verb intrans.* Act as a pedlar. M19.
■ **pedlarism** *noun* (*rare*) = PEDLARY *noun* 3 L17.

pedlary /ˈpɛdləri/ *noun & adjective.* M16.
[from prec. + -Y[3]: cf. BEGGARY.]
► **A** *noun.* **1** Trifling or contemptible practices or things; trash, rubbish. M16.
2 Goods sold by pedlars. L16.
3 The occupation of a pedlar. E17.
► **B** *attrib.* or as *adjective.* **1** Belonging to a pedlar or a pedlar's occupation. M16.
†**2** *fig.* Fit for a pedlar; trashy. M16–L17.

pedo- /ˈpɛdəʊ/ *combining form*[1].
[formed as PEDI-: see -O-.]
= PEDI-.
■ **pedomancy** *noun* (*rare*) divination by inspection of the soles of the feet L16. **pedomotive** *adjective & noun* (a vehicle) worked by the foot or feet E19. **pedoscope** *noun* an X-ray machine for showing the fitting and movement of the feet inside shoes (formerly common in shoe shops) E20.

pedo- /ˈpɛdəʊ/ *combining form*[2]. Before a vowel also **ped-**.
[from Greek *pedon* ground: see -O-.]
Of or pertaining to soil or types of soil.
■ **pedocal** *noun* a soil that contains a layer of accumulated calcium carbonate (generally characteristic of dry climates) E20. **pedoˈcalic** *adjective* of, pertaining to, or of the nature of a pedocal E20. **pedosphere** *noun* the earth's soil layer M20.

pedo- *combining form*[3] see PAEDO-.

pedogenic /pɛdə(ʊ)ˈdʒɛnɪk/ *adjective.* E20.
[from PEDO-[2] + -GENIC.]
Soil-forming.
■ **pedogenesis** *noun* soil formation M20. **pedogeˈnetic** *adjective* M20. **pedogeˈnetical** *adjective* L20. **pedogeˈnetically** *adverb* M20. **pedogenically** *adverb* L20.

pedology /pɪˈdɒlədʒi, pɛ-/ *noun.* E20.
[from PEDO-[2] + -OLOGY.]
The branch of science that deals with soil, esp. its formation, nature, and classification; soil science.
■ **pedoˈlogic**, **pedoˈlogical** *adjectives* of or pertaining to pedology or soil E20. **pedoˈlogically** *adverb* in pedological terms; as regards pedology: M20. **pedologist** *noun* E20.

pedometer /pɪˈdɒmɪtə, pɛ-/ *noun.* E18.
[French *pédomètre*, formed as PEDO-[1] -METER.]
An instrument for estimating the distance travelled on foot by recording the number of steps taken.

pedon /ˈpɛdɒn/ *noun.* M20.
[Greek = ground, earth.]
SOIL SCIENCE. A notional column of soil extending vertically from the surface to the underlying parent material, taken as representative of the surrounding soil and its horizons.

pedophile *noun & adjective*, **pedophilia** *noun* vars. of PAEDOPHILE, PAEDOPHILIA.

pedotribe *noun* var. of PAEDOTRIBE.

pedotrophy *noun* var. of PAEDOTROPHY.

Pedrail /ˈpɛdreɪl/ *noun. obsolete* exc. *Hist.* E20.
[from Latin *ped-*, *pes* foot + RAIL *noun*[2].]
A vehicle that travels by means of wheels with spring-loaded pads or feet attached round the circumference, enabling it to pass over obstacles and rough ground.

†**pedraro** *noun* var. of PEDRERO.

pedregal /pɛdrɪˈgɑːl, ˈpɛdrɪg(ə)l/ *noun.* M19.
[Spanish, from *piedra* stone from Latin *petra*.]
In Mexico and the south-western US: a rocky tract, esp. in a volcanic region; an old lava-field.

pedrero /pɛˈdrɛːrəʊ/ *noun.* Pl. **-os**. Also †**peterero**, †**pater-**, †**-eraro**, & other vars., pl. **-oes**. L16.
[Spanish = Old French PERRIER *noun*[1]. Cf. PETRARY.]
Hist. A weapon for discharging stones, broken iron, partridge-shot, etc., and for firing salutes.

pedro /ˈpɛdrəʊ/ *noun.* L19.
[from SANCHO PEDRO.]
A card-game like Sancho Pedro but in which the sancho, or nine of trumps, does not count; the five of trumps in such games.

Pedro Ximenez /ˌpɛdrəʊ hɪˈmeɪnɛθ/ *noun.* M19.
[Name of its Spanish introducer.]
A sweet white Spanish grape used esp. in making sherry and sweet wine.

peduncle /pɪˈdʌŋk(ə)l/ *noun.* M18.
[mod. Latin *pedunculus*, from Latin *ped-*, *pes* foot: see -UNCLE.]
1 BOTANY. The main stalk of an inflorescence or infructescence to which the pedicels are attached. M18.
2 ZOOLOGY & MEDICINE. A stalk or stalklike projection in an animal; *spec.* (*a*) a pedicel (eye-stalk) of a crustacean; (*b*) the stalk by which a cirripede, brachiopod, etc., is attached to a foreign body; (*c*) the pedicle of a tumour; (*d*) any of several bundles of nerve fibres connecting two parts of the brain; (*e*) the narrowed fleshy base of the pectoral or caudal fin in certain fish, before the rays commence. L18.
■ **peduncled** *adjective* having a peduncle or peduncles L18. **peduncular** *adjective* of, pertaining to, or of the nature of a peduncle E19. **pedunculate** *adjective* having a peduncle or peduncles; ***pedunculate oak***, the common oak, *Quercus robur*, in which each group of acorns is borne on a long peduncle: M18. **pedunculated** *adjective* = PEDUNCULATE M18. **peduncuˈlation** *noun* the condition of being pedunculate M19.

pedway /ˈpɛdweɪ/ *noun.* M20.
[from PED(ESTRIAN + WAY *noun*.]
A footway built for pedestrians in an urban environment.

ped-xing /pɛdˈɛksɪŋ/ *noun. N. Amer.* L20.
[Repr. an abbreviation of ***pedestrian crossing*** s.v. PEDESTRIAN *noun*, with *x* repr. the word 'cross': cf. X, X.]
(Abbreviation on N. American road signs for) a pedestrian crossing.

pee /piː/ *noun*[1]. M17.
[Origin unkn.]
MINING. The portion common to two veins which intersect.

pee /piː/ *noun*[2]. M18.
[Origin unkn.]
MINING. A small piece of ore.

pee /piː/ *noun*[3]. *colloq.* L19.
[from PEE *verb*. See also PEE-PEE *noun*[2].]
1 An act of urinating. L19.
2 Urine. M20.

> 📖 **1** K. AMIS He went and had a pee.

pee /piː/ *noun*[4]. *colloq.* Pl. same. L20.
[Repr. pronunc. of abbreviation *p.*]
A penny of the decimal currency introduced in Britain in 1971.

pee /piː/ *verb. colloq.* Pa. t. & pple **peed**. L18.
[Euphem. for PISS *verb*, from its first letter.]
1 *verb trans.* Wet by urinating; *refl.* urinate into one's clothes. L18.
2 *verb intrans.* Urinate. L19.
3 *verb trans.* Pass (urine, blood, etc.) from the bladder. L20.

> 📖 **1** G. KERSH Even the Sarn-Major peed 'imself laughing.

pee em /piː ˈɛm/ *noun & adverb. informal.* Also **peeyem** /piːˈɛm/. M20.
[Repr. pronunc. of *p.m.* s.v. P, P.]
(In) the afternoon.

peek /piːk/ *verb*[1] *& noun*[1]. Also (earlier) †**pike**. LME.
[Origin unkn.: cf. KEEK.]
► **A** *verb.* **1** *verb intrans.* Look through a crevice, or out of or into a recess etc.; peer, peep; look quickly or furtively. Also, glance *at*. Usu. foll. by adverb or preposition. LME.
2 COMPUTING. (Usu. **PEEK**.) ►**a** *verb intrans.* Use PEEK to read a memory location. Foll. by adverb or preposition (as sense 1), also *to*. L20. ►**b** *verb trans.* Use PEEK to ascertain the contents of (a memory or memory location). L20.

> 📖 **1** W. C. WILLIAMS We kids all took turns peeking through a hole in the wall. B. MALAMUD He retreated behind a massive column and peeked out at short intervals. G. PALEY Livid yawned, stretched, peeked at the clock. A. S. DALE William put a ladder up to the garden wall to peek over.

► **B** *noun.* **1** A quick or furtive look, a peep. M19.
2 COMPUTING. (Usu. **PEEK**.) A statement or function in BASIC for reading the contents of a specified memory location. Cf. POKE *noun*[4] 5. L20.

peek /piːk/ *verb*[2] *& noun*[2]. *dial.* E19.
[Imit.]
► **A** *verb intrans.* Utter a faint high-pitched sound (*dial.*); *Scot.* speak in a thin, piping voice; whine, complain. E19.
► **B** *noun.* The shrill sound of a small bird. M19.

peekaboo /piːkəˈbuː/ *noun & adjective.* Also **peek-bo** /ˈpiːkbəʊ/. L16.
[from PEEK *verb*[1] + BOO *interjection*.]
► **A** *noun.* The game of hiding one's face and suddenly revealing it, as played by an older person with a young child. L16.
► **B** *adjective.* **1** Of (part of) a garment: having a pattern of small holes so as to reveal the skin beneath. L19.
2 Of a hairstyle: hanging in front so as to cover an eye and part of the face. M20.
¶ Rare before L19.

peekapoo /piːkəˈpuː/ *noun. US.* L20.
[from PEKE + POODLE *noun*, conformed to prec.]
A dog that is a cross between a Pekingese and a poodle.

peek-bo *noun & adjective* var. of PEEKABOO.

peel /piːl/ *noun*[1]. Also **pele**. ME.
[Anglo-Norman, Old French *pel* (mod. *pieu*) from Latin *palus* stake: cf. PALE *noun*[1], PALLET *noun*[3].]
†**1** A stake. *rare.* Only in ME.
2 A fence formed of stakes; a stockade; a stockaded (and moated) enclosure. Long *obsolete* exc. SCOTTISH HISTORY. ME.
†**3** A castle; *esp.* a small castle or tower. ME–L17.
4 [Prob. from ***peel-house*** below.] A small square tower or fortified dwelling built in the 16th cent. as a defence against raids in the border country of England and Scotland, with the ground floor used for cattle and the upper part (reached by an external ladder or movable stair) as living quarters. E18.
Comb.: **peel-house**, **peel-tower** = sense 4 above.

peel /piːl/ *noun*[2]. LME.
[Old French *pele* (mod. *pelle*) from Latin *pala*, from base of *pangere* fix, plant.]
1 A shovel or shovel-shaped implement; *esp.* a baker's shovel, a pole with a broad flat disc at the end for putting loaves etc. into the oven and bringing them out. Now *dial.* & *techn.* LME.
2 PRINTING (now *Hist.*). A T-shaped instrument used to hang up damp freshly printed sheets to dry. L17.
3 The blade of an oar. *US.* L19.

peel /piːl/ *noun*[3]. M16.
[Alt. of PILL *noun*[2].]
1 The rind or outer layer of a fruit, vegetable, prawn, etc. Formerly, a layer of an onion. M16.
2 RUGBY FOOTBALL. The action of peeling from a set formation. L20.
1 ***candied peel***: see CANDIED 1.

peel /piːl/ *noun*[4]. *Scot.* & CURLING. E18.
[Origin unkn.: rel. to PEEL *verb*[2].]
A match, an equal; a drawn match.

peel /piːl/ *noun*[5]. E20.
[from PEEL *verb*[3].]
An act of peeling in croquet.

peel *noun*[6] var. of PEAL *noun*[2].

peel /piːl/ *verb*[1]. ME.
[Collateral form of PILL *verb*[1]; their differentiation may have been assisted by Old & mod. French *peler* to peel, *piller* to pillage.]
► **I** Pillage.
†**1** *verb trans.* = PILL *verb*[1] 5. ME–M18.
2 *verb trans.* Take by violence, plunder; cheat. Long only *Scot.* (now *rare*). LME.
► **II** Strip.
3 *verb trans.* **a** Strip (a thing) of its natural outer layer; remove the peel, skin, bark, etc., of. LME. ►**b** Remove (peel, skin, bark, etc.) from the outside of a fruit, vegetable, etc.; remove or separate (a label, banknote, etc.) from the outside or top of something, strip away; usu. foll. by *off*. Also, turn *back* (a bed-sheet, bedclothes) so as to expose the undersheet. L16.
4 *verb intrans.* Of an outer layer or coating: become detached, come *off* or *away*; *spec.* (of skin or paint) come off in flakes, become loose so as to be easily pulled off. Of a surface or object: lose (part of) its outer layer or coating; *spec.* (of the body or part of it) shed skin in flakes, have skin that is dead and easily stripped off. L16.
5 a *verb intrans.* Take off one's outer clothes (orig., in preparation for a fight) or all one's clothes. Also foll. by

off. colloq. L18. ▸**b** *verb trans.* Strip of clothing; take *off* (a garment). *colloq.* E19.

6 *verb intrans.* Move *off* or *away*; separate from a body of people, vehicles, etc., or (SURFING) of waves; RUGBY FOOTBALL leave a scrum or set formation (also foll. by *off*). M20.

📖 **3a** G. LORD She wanted to . . help Elvira peel the potatoes. **b** A. BLEASDALE Pulls out the other money, peels off three five-pound notes and hands her the rest. G. NAYLOR She . . bought a kiwi and walked along peeling the skin with her thumbnails. **4** *McCall's* Too many women continue to burn, blister, peel . . every summer. J. HERRIOT The skin had peeled off Meg's nose. N. RANKIN The long drive . . lined by . . trees with peeling bark. M. CHABON The greenish paint was . . peeling from the side of the first wooden house. **5a** *Variety* The gals are peelin' in 23 clubs. **b** A. LURIE She peeled off her sodden coat. **6** C. RYAN Escorting fighters began peeling out of formation. *Surfing World* The outside banks were peeling so fast they were unrideable. M. ANGELOU The line of marchers was exhausted. People had begun to peel away.

Phrases: ***keep an eye peeled, keep one's eye(s) peeled***: see EYE *noun*. †**pack and peel**, †**pack or peel** *Scot.* deal *in* as a merchant; have dealings *with*. **peel one's eyes** keep one's eyes peeled, watch carefully, *(for)*.

peel /piːl/ *verb*^{2} *trans. Scot.* & CURLING. L17.
[Origin unkn.: rel to PEEL *noun*^{4}.]
Equal, match.

peel /piːl/ *verb*^{3} *trans. & intrans.* L19.
[Walter H. *Peel* (fl. 1868), noted croquet player.]
CROQUET. Send (a ball other than one's own) through a hoop.

peelable /ˈpiːləb(ə)l/ *adjective.* M20.
[from PEEL *verb*^{1} + -ABLE.]
Suitable for peeling, able to be peeled.
■ **peelaˈbility** *noun* M20.

peeled /piːld/ *adjective.* LME.
[from PEEL *verb*^{1} + -ED^1.]
1 Bald; tonsured. Long *rare* or *obsolete*. LME.
2 Plundered, reduced to destitution. *obsolete* exc. as passing into *fig.* use of sense 3 or 4. E16.
3 Without the usual or natural covering; bare; *transf.* beggarly, wretched. E16.
4 Stripped of peel, skin, bark, etc. E18.
Phrases: ***keep an eye peeled, keep one's eye(s) peeled***: see EYE *noun*. **scattered and peeled** [*Isaiah* 18:2 (AV)] dispersed, destroyed.

peeler /ˈpiːlə/ *noun*^{1}. LME.
[from PEEL *verb*^{1} + -ER^1.]
†**1 a** A plunderer, a thief. LME–E17. ▸**b** A plant that impoverishes the soil. L16–M18.
2 a A person who or thing which peels fruit, trees, etc. L16. ▸**b** A crab when it casts its shell. Also ***peeler crab***. M19.
3 An exceptional or noteworthy instance of a thing; *spec.* (*a*) a violent storm; (*b*) *US* a person of exceptional or unusual qualities; a lively or energetic person. E19.
4 A person who removes his or her clothing; *spec.* (*a*) a pugilist ready to strip for a fight; (*b*) a striptease artist. M19.
5 A cowboy. *US.* L19.
6 In full ***peeler log***. The trunk of a tree, esp. a softwood tree, suitable for the manufacture of veneer by the use of a rotary lathe, which peels thin sheets of wood from the log. M20.

peeler /ˈpiːlə/ *noun*^{2}. *colloq.* E19.
[from Sir Robert *Peel* (see BOBBY *noun*^{1}) + -ER^1.]
A member of the Irish constabulary (founded under the secretaryship of Sir Robert Peel) (now *Hist.*); *arch.* a (British) policeman, = BOBBY *noun*^{1}.

peeling /ˈpiːlɪŋ/ *noun.* M16.
[from PEEL *verb*^{1} + -ING^1. In sense 3 prob. alt. of a Chinese word.]
1 The action of PEEL *verb*^{1}. M16.
2 That which is peeled off; *esp.* a strip or piece of peel or skin removed from a fruit or vegetable (usu. in *pl.*). L16.
†**3** A silk satin fabric, orig. imported from China. L17–E19.

📖 **2** *Sunday Times* Posting old tomatoes and potato peelings down the waste disposal. P. BENSON My mother came into the yard with a saucepan of peeling and crusts.

Peelite /ˈpiːlʌɪt/ *noun & adjective.* M19.
[formed as PEELER *noun*^{2} + -ITE^1.]
Hist. ▸**A** *noun.* A member of the group of Conservatives who supported Sir Robert Peel's measure for the repeal of the Corn Laws in 1846, and who continued to form an identifiable group for some years afterwards. M19.
▸**B** *adjective.* Of or pertaining to the Peelites. M19.

peel-off /ˈpiːlɒf/ *noun & adjective.* M20.
[from PEEL *verb*^{1} + OFF *adverb*.]
▸**A** *noun.* The action of peeling off. M20.
▸**B** *adjective.* Readily peeled off. L20.

📖 *Marketing* Special peel-off labels on the backs of bottles.

peely-wally /ˈpiːlɪwɒli, piːlɪˈwali/ *adjective. Scot.* M19.
[Prob. imit. of a whining sound.]
Pale, feeble, sickly, ill-looking.

peen /piːn/ *noun.* Also **pein**. L17.
[Origin uncertain: cf. next, PANE *noun*^{2}.]
The end of a hammer head opposite to the face, esp. when sharp.

peen /piːn/ *verb trans.* E16.
[App. of Norse origin: cf. Swedish dial. *pena*, *päne*, Danish dial. *pene*, *paene*, Norwegian dial *penna*, *paenna*.]
Beat thin with a hammer, hammer *out*; strike with the peen of a hammer.

peenge /piːn(d)ʒ/ *verb intrans. Scot. & north.* L16.
[Symbolic: perh. from WHINGE after *peek*, *peevish*, etc.]
Whine, complain; mope.

peent /piːnt/ *noun & verb. N. Amer.* L19.
[Imit.]
▸**A** *noun.* A nasal piping sound made by a woodcock before or after a flight. L19.
▸**B** *verb intrans. & trans.* Of a woodcock: emit (a peent). L19.

peeoy /ˈpiːɔɪ, pɪˈɔɪ/ *noun. Scot.* E19.
[Imit.]
A child's squib consisting of a small cone of damp gunpowder which is lighted at the top.

peep /piːp/ *noun*^{1}. *US.* M20.
[Alt. of JEEP.]
A small sturdy motor vehicle with four-wheel drive, orig. designed for military use.

peep *noun*^{2} see PIP *noun*^{3}.

peep /piːp/ *verb*^{1} & *noun*^{3}. LME.
[Imit.: cf. CHEEP.]
▸**A** *verb intrans.* **1** Cheep, chirp; beep. LME.
2 Speak in a weak, querulous, shrill tone. *arch.* exc. *local.* M16.
3 Betray a confidence; inform. *slang.* E20.
▸**B** *noun.* **1 a** (Repr.) a cheep. LME. ▸**b** A single or slight sound; a single piece of information. Usu. in neg. contexts. E20. ▸**c** A short high-pitched sound produced electronically and lasting longer than a pip; a bleep. M20.
†**2** A brood *of* chickens. Only in L15.
3 a A young chicken. L17. ▸**b** Any of several sandpipers. *US.* L18.

📖 **1b** D. ADAMS We haven't heard a peep out of them since we left. L. CODY If there's one peep out of her, belt her.

peep /piːp/ *verb*^{2} & *noun*^{4}. LME.
[Symbolic: cf. PEEK *verb*^{1}, PEER *verb*^{2}.]
▸**A** *verb.* **1** *verb intrans.* Look through a narrow opening into a larger space; look furtively, slyly, or pryingly. LME.
2 *verb intrans. fig.* Emerge or protrude a very short distance into view; begin to appear or show itself; appear as if looking out or over something; (of a mental characteristic etc.) show itself a little unintendedly. Freq. foll. by *out*. L16.
3 *verb trans.* Cause to appear slightly; protrude (the head etc.) *out* from a hiding place. L16.

📖 **1** E. BOWEN Miss Fitzgerald, standing on tiptoe, peeped over the lace blind. A. PATON Her children hid behind her skirts and peeped out at the visitors. **2** WILKIE COLLINS The stem of a pipe peeped out of the breast-pocket of his coat. E. GERARD Between the stones . . the maidenhair and spleenwort were beginning to peep.

▸**B** *noun.* **1** The first appearance *of* daylight or morning. Chiefly in ***peep of day***. M16.
2 = PEEKABOO *noun*. Cf. PEEP-BO. *obsolete* exc. *dial.* L17.
3 An act of peeping; a furtive or surreptitious glance. M18.
Comb. (of verb & noun): **peep-hole** a small hole that may be looked through; **peep-show** a small display of pictures etc. viewed through a lens or hole set in a box or machine; **peep-sight** a backsight for rifles with a slit for bringing the foresight into line with the object aimed at; **peep-toe** *adjective & noun* (designating) a kind of shoe whose tip is cut away allowing the toes to be seen; **peep-toed** *adjective* having a peep-toe.

peep-bo /ˈpiːpbəʊ/ *noun.* E19.
[Inversion of BO-PEEP.]
= PEEKABOO *noun*.

pee-pee /ˈpiːpiː/ *noun*^{1}. *US dial. & Jamaican.* L19.
[Perh. imit. of the bird's call.]
A young chicken; (esp. in Jamaica) a young turkey.

pee-pee /ˈpiːpiː/ *noun*^{2}. *nursery & colloq.* E20.
[Redupl.]
= PEE *noun*^{3}.

peeper /ˈpiːpə/ *noun*^{1}. L16.
[from PEEP *verb*^{1} + -ER^1.]
1 A young chicken or pigeon. Now *rare* or *obsolete*. L16.
2 A small tree frog of the genus *Hyla*, esp. *H. crucifer* of eastern N. America. *US.* M19.

peeper /ˈpiːpə/ *noun*^{2}. M17.
[from PEEP *verb*^{2} + -ER^1.]
1 A person who peeps or peers; *esp.* one who looks or pries furtively. M17. ▸**b** A private detective or investigator; a police officer. *US slang.* M20.
2 An eye. Usu. in *pl. slang.* L17.
3 In *pl.*, a pair of spectacles. Formerly also, a mirror; a small telescope. *slang.* L17.

peeping /ˈpiːpɪŋ/ *ppl adjective.* L16.
[from PEEP *verb*^{2} + -ING^2.]
That peeps or peers; that looks or pries furtively.
peeping Tom [in the story of Lady Godiva, the only person who looked out as she rode by naked] a prying person, *spec.* a voyeur. **peeping Tommery** the activity of a peeping Tom, voyeurism.

peepul /ˈpiːp(ə)l/ *noun.* Also **pipal**. L18.
[Hindi *pīpal* from Sanskrit *pippala*.]
= BO-TREE. Also ***peepul-tree***.

peepy /ˈpiːpi/ *adjective. dial. & colloq.* M19.
[from PEEP *verb*^{2} & *noun*^{4} + -Y^1.]
Drowsy, sleepy.

peer /pɪə/ *noun*^{1} & *adjective.* ME.
[Anglo-Norman, Old French *per*, *peer* (mod. *pair*) from Latin *par*, *par-* equal: cf. PAIR *noun*^{1}.]
▸**A** *noun.* **1** A person of the same standing or rank as the person(s) in question; a person or thing of the same effectiveness or ability as the one(s) in question; an equal. ME. ▸**b** A person of the same age-group or social set as the person(s) in question. M20.
†**2** A person who is associated with another; a companion; a rival. ME–E19
3 A person of high rank; a noble. ME.
4 *spec.* A member of one of the degrees of nobility in the UK or its constituent countries, comprising the ranks of duke, marquess, earl, viscount, and baron. Cf. PEERESS. LME.
5 GREEK HISTORY. A citizen of Sparta who had equal right to hold State offices. M19.

📖 **1** J. BRYCE Some of those men were the peers of the best European statesmen of the time. **have no peer** be unequalled, be unrivalled. **b** J. FOWLES He was not like the great majority of his peers and contemporaries. *Scientific American* The major difference between U.S. babies and their age peers in other countries is that U.S. babies are smaller. **4** ***life peer***: see LIFE *noun*. **peer of the realm** any of the category of hereditary peers who (when of age and not otherwise disqualified) are entitled to a seat in the House of Lords. **peer of the United Kingdom**, (*Hist.*) **peer of England**, **peer of Great Britain** = ***peer of the realm*** above.

Comb.: **peer group** a group of people, freq. a group of adolescents, having the same age, social status, interests, etc.; **peer pressure** pressure or influence arising from members of a person's peer group; **peer review** the evaluation by (other) experts of a research project for which a grant is sought, a paper received for publication in a learned journal, etc.; *gen.* a review of commercial, professional, or academic efficiency, competence, etc., by others in the same occupation; **peer-review** *verb trans.* subject to peer review; **peer-to-peer** *adjective* denoting computer networks in which each computer can act as a server for the others, allowing shared access to files and peripherals without the need for a central server.

▸**B** *adjective.* Equal (*to*). Long *rare*. ME.
■ **peerdom** *noun* (*a*) = PEERAGE 2; †(*b*) the territory of a French peer; (*c*) equality: E17. **peership** *noun* (*a*) = PEERAGE 2; †(*b*) = PEERDOM (b); (*c*) equality: L16.

peer *noun*^{2} see PEAR *noun*.

peer /pɪə/ *verb*^{1}. LME.
[Old French *perer* var. of *pairier*, *parer* from late Latin *pariare* make or be equal, from Latin *par*, *par-* equal.]
†**1** *verb trans.* Class as equal; put in the same category or on an equal footing *with*. LME–M17.
2 *verb trans.* Equal, rank with, match. LME.
3 *verb intrans.* Be equal, rank *with*. LME.
4 *verb trans.* [from PEER *noun*^{1}.] Make a peer; raise to the peerage. *colloq.* M18.

peer /pɪə/ *verb*^{2}. L16.
[Var. of PIRE; perh. partly aphet. from APPEAR. Cf. also PORE *verb*.]
1 *verb intrans.* Look keenly, esp. in order to discern something indistinct or obscured. L16.
2 *verb intrans. fig.* = PEEP *verb*^{2} 2. L16.
3 *verb intrans.* Come in sight; be seen, appear. *arch.* L16.
†**4** *verb trans.* Cause to appear or peep out. *rare* (Shakes.). Only in L16.

📖 **1** L. M. MONTGOMERY Curious faces peered from the windows. I. MURDOCH He peered, trying to discern the shadowy intruders. P. DICKINSON Leaning into the shaft, peering down into the darkness. **2** CARLYLE Already streaks of blue peer through our clouds.

■ **peeringly** *adverb* in a peering manner M19.

peerage /ˈpɪərɪdʒ/ *noun.* LME.
[from PEER *noun*^{1} + -AGE.]
1 *The* body or class of peers (and peeresses), *the* nobility. LME.
2 The rank or status of a peer or peeress; a title of nobility. L17.
3 A book containing a list of the peers (and peeresses), with their genealogy, history, etc. M18.

📖 **1** J. MCCARTHY Mr. Bruce was raised to the Peerage as Lord Aberdare. **2** A. PRYCE-JONES He refused a peerage because he disapproved of heriditary honours.

peeress /ˈpɪərɪs/ *noun*. L17.
[from PEER *noun*¹ + -ESS¹.]
The wife or widow of a peer. Also (more fully ***peeress in her own right***), a woman having the rank of a peer by creation or descent.

peerie /ˈpiːri/ *adjective & noun*. *Scot*. (now *dial*.). E19.
[Origin unkn.]
▶ **A** *adjective*. Small, diminutive. E19.
peerie folk fairies. **peerie pinkie**, **peerie winkie** the little finger.
▶ **B** *noun*. A Shetland sheepdog. M20.

peerless /ˈpɪəlɪs/ *adjective*. ME.
[from PEER *noun*¹ + -LESS.]
Having no peer; matchless.
peerless primrose: see PRIMROSE *noun*.
■ **peerlessly** *adverb* L16. **peerlessness** *noun* E17.

peery /ˈpɪəri/ *noun*. *Scot*. & *north*. M17.
[from PEER *noun*² + -Y⁶.]
A child's spinning-top.

peery /ˈpɪəri/ *adjective*. L17.
[from PEER *verb*² + -Y¹.]
1 Inclined to peer; prying, inquisitive, suspicious. L17.
2 Knowing, sly. *slang*. Now *rare* or *obsolete*. M18.

peesweep /ˈpiːzwiːp/ *noun*. *Scot*. & *dial*. L18.
[Imit. of the bird's call. Cf. PEEWIT.]
The lapwing, *Vanellus vanellus*.

peetweet /ˈpiːtwiːt/ *noun*. *US*. M19.
[Imit. of the bird's call.]
The spotted sandpiper of N. and S. America, *Actitis macularia*.

peeve /piːv/ *verb & noun*. Orig. *US*. E20.
[Back-form. from PEEVISH.]
▶ **A** *verb*. **1** *verb trans*. Irritate, annoy; vex. Freq. as ***peeved*** *ppl adjective*. E20.
2 *verb intrans*. Grumble, complain petulantly. E20.

📖 **1** R. MACAULAY She's . . rather peeved that David doesn't cut more ice.

▶ **B** *noun*. A grumble, a cause of complaint or irritation; a peevish mood. E20.

peever /ˈpiːvə/ *noun*. *Scot*. M19.
[Origin unkn.]
The stone, piece of pottery, etc., used in hopscotch. Also (usu. in *pl*.), hopscotch.

peevish /ˈpiːvɪʃ/ *adjective*. LME.
[Origin unkn.]
†**1** Silly, foolish; beside oneself; out of one's senses. LME–L17.
2 †**a** Spiteful, malignant, mischievous, harmful. LME–E17. ▸**b** Of the wind: piercing. *dial*. E19.
†**3** Wretched, damned. *colloq*. E–M16.
4 Querulous, irritable, childishly fretful; spiteful; (of a quality, action, etc.) characterized by or exhibiting petty vexation or spite. M16.
†**5** Perverse, obstinate; self-willed, skittish; capricious, coy. M16–L17.

📖 **4** J. JOHNSTON His voice was peevish At any moment . . he might stop speaking to her.

■ **peevishly** *adverb* M16. **peevishness** *noun* LME.

peewee /ˈpiːwiː/ *noun & adjective*. In sense 3 also (*dial*.) **peeweep** /ˈpiːwiːp/. M19.
[In branch I of the noun, redupl. of WEE *adjective*; in branch II, imit. of the birds' calls. Cf. PEWEE, next.]
▶ **A** *noun*. **I 1** A small marble. M19.
2 A small child. L19.
▶ **II 3** The lapwing, *Vanellus vanellus*. *Scot*. L19.
4 The magpie lark, *Grallina cyanoleuca*. *Austral*. L19.
▶ **B** *adjective*. (Esp. of a person) small, short; composed of small people or children. *N. Amer*. L19.

📖 E. BIRNEY The surprisingly large feet of the peewee doorman.

peewit /ˈpiːwɪt/ *noun*. Also **pewit**. E16.
[Imit. of the bird's calls.]
1 The lapwing, *Vanellus vanellus*; its cry. E16.
2 More fully ***peewit gull***. The black-headed gull, *Larus ridibundus*. L17.
3 Any of various tyrant flycatchers. *US*. M19.

PEG *abbreviation*.
Polyethylene glycol.

peg /pɛg/ *noun*¹. LME.
[Prob. from Low Dutch: cf. Middle Dutch *pegge*, Dutch dial. *peg* plug, peg, Low German *pigge* peg. Cf. also Middle Low German, Middle Dutch *pegel* peg, pin, bolt.]
1 A pin or bolt of wood, metal, plastic, etc., usu. cylindrical and freq. tapered at one end, used to hold two things together or to stop up a hole, or which may be driven partly into or fastened on to a wall, the ground, etc., to hang a garment etc. from, attach a rope etc. to, or to serve as a marker in a game etc. Also, a clothes-peg (see CLOTHES). LME.
2 *fig*. The interval between two successive pegs; a step, a degree. Chiefly in ***bring down a peg (or two)***, ***take down a peg (or two)***, etc., humble (a person), lower the status of (a person). L16.
3 *spec*. **a** A tooth, *esp*. a child's tooth. Now *dial*. L16. ▸**b** Any of the wooden or metal pins used to tighten or loosen (and so tune) the strings of a musical instrument. E17. ▸**c** The pin on which a pegtop spins. M18. ▸**d** Any of the pins used as markers in a peg-tankard (see below); a measure of beer or other alcoholic drink. Now *rare*. L18. ▸**e** A wooden, brass, or leather pin used in shoemaking to fasten the uppers to the sole etc. Now chiefly *Hist*. E19. ▸**f** A cricket stump. M19. ▸**g** = ***peg-leg*** below. Also *joc*., a leg. M19. ▸**h** ANGLING & SHOOTING. A place or area (usu. marked by a peg) allotted to a competitor from or within which to fish, shoot, etc. L19. ▸**i** MOUNTAINEERING. A piton. E20. ▸**j** COMMERCE. A limit set on an exchange rate, share price, etc. Cf. PEG *verb* 6b below. M20.
4 An implement with a pin or hook for tearing, harpooning, husking corn, etc. Also, the hook itself. Now chiefly *Hist*. E18.
5 a A thrusting blow. *obsolete* exc. *dial*. M18. ▸**b** A long low throw at a base in baseball. *US colloq*. E20.
†**6** (Pl. same.) A shilling. *slang*. L18–E20.
7 A drink of brandy or whisky and soda-water. *Anglo-Indian*. M19.
8 A segment of a citrus fruit. Cf. PIG *noun*¹ 7. *W. Indies*. E20.
9 A short blunt structure or outgrowth in a plant, an animal, etc. M20.

📖 **1** F. NORRIS The little peg holding down the cover slipped. B. HINES Billy found an empty peg and hung his jacket on it. ***puzzle-peg***, ***tent-peg***, etc. **3d** W. OWEN When he'd drunk a peg. **g** *Healthy Living* A good pair of pegs is . . one of the most popular features of the top players. **h** *Angler's Mail* Sean Ashby . . was runner-up at the next peg with an almost identical net of fish. **j** *Economist* Indexing of oil prices and severing the dollar peg.

Phrases: **a peg to hang an idea on** etc., an occasion, pretext, excuse, or theme for an idea etc. **a round peg in a square hole**, **a square peg in a round hole** a person in a situation unsuited to his or her capacities or disposition, a misfit. ***bring down a peg (or two)***: see sense 2 above. ***CHOTA peg***. ***crawling peg***: see CRAWL *verb* 3. **move a peg** make a move, stir. **off the peg** (of a garment etc.) available for immediate purchase or use; ready-made. **on the peg** *Military slang* on a charge, under arrest. ***Scotch peg***: see SCOTCH *adjective*. ***take down a peg (or two)***: see sense 2 above.
Comb.: **peg-bag**: for holding clothes-pegs; **pegboard** a type of perforated board used to hold pegs in some games, or for commercial displays etc. (proprietary name in the US); **pegbox** a structure at the head of a stringed instrument where the strings are attached to the tuning-pegs; **peg doll**: made from a clothes-peg or similar piece of wood; **peg-house** *slang* (*a*) a public-house; (*b*) *US* a brothel for male homosexuals; **peg-leg** *colloq*. (a person having) an artificial leg; **peg-legged** *adjective* having a peg-leg; *transf*. pegtopped; **peg-tankard** *Hist*. a tankard having pegs inserted at regular intervals to mark the quantity each person should drink.
■ **peglike** *adjective* resembling a peg E20.

Peg /pɛg/ *noun*². L17.
[Alt. of MEG *noun*¹. Cf. PEGGY.]
†**1** ***gone to Peg Trantum's***, dead. *slang*. L17–E19.
2 ***Old Peg***, skimmed-milk cheese. *dial*. L18.

peg /pɛg/ *verb*. Infl. **-gg-**. LME.
[from PEG *noun*¹.]
†**1** *verb trans*. Gorge, stuff, (oneself). *rare*. Only in LME.
2 *verb trans*. Drive or insert a peg or pegs into; fasten, attach, or block up with a peg or pegs; insert or fasten as a peg; *spec*. †(*a*) thrust a peg into the nose of (a pig etc.) to stop it from rooting; (*b*) insert small wooden pegs into (a stalk of tobacco); (*c*) CRICKET drive pegs into (the face of a bat) to try and level the grain. Freq. foll. by *down*, *in*, *out*, etc. M16. ▸**b** Fasten a sole on to (a shoe etc.) with wooden pegs. M19.
3 †**a** *verb trans*. Drive (a thought, idea, etc.) *into* a person by repetition. E–M17. ▸**b** *verb intrans*. Work persistently, toil. Foll. by *along*, *away (at)*, *on*, etc. *colloq*. E19.
4 a *verb intrans*. & *trans*. Aim (a missile, weapon, etc.) *at*. L17. ▸**b** *verb trans*. BASEBALL. Throw (the ball) long and low; stop (a base-runner) with such a throw. *US colloq*. L19. ▸**c** *verb trans*. Of a pointer or setter: point at, set, (a game-bird). L19.
5 *verb trans*. Strike or pierce with a peg or sharp implement; harpoon. Now *rare* or *obsolete*. M18.
6 *verb trans*. *fig*. ▸**a** Confine; restrict. (Foll. by *down*.) E19. ▸**b** COMMERCE. Prevent the price of (stock etc.) from falling or rising by buying or selling freely at a given price; fix (a price, wage, exchange rate, etc.) at or *at* a certain level or in line with a certain standard (also foll. by *to*). L19. ▸**c** Categorize; form a fixed opinion of; identify (*as*). Freq. in ***have pegged***. Chiefly *N. Amer. colloq*. E20.
7 *verb intrans*. Walk vigorously or quickly. Foll. by *along*, *away*, *off*, etc. *dial*. & *colloq*. E19.
8 a *verb trans*. & *intrans*. Mark (the score) in cribbage with pegs on a cribbage-board. E19. ▸**b** *verb intrans*. Foll. by *out*: (*a*) score the winning point in cribbage; (*b*) hit the peg in croquet as one's final stroke of a game. L19. ▸**c** *verb trans*. Foll. by *back*: (esp. in horse-racing) reduce (an opponent's lead) by a specified distance, gain on; overtake. E20.
9 *verb trans*. Mark out with pegs; *esp*. mark out the boundaries of (a mining claim etc.) with pegs. Usu. foll. by *out*. M19. ▸**b** *spec*. (ANGLING). Mark *out* (a stretch of river-bank etc.) with pegs; allot a position or peg to (an angler). E20.
10 *verb intrans*. Foll. by *out*: die. *slang*. M19.
11 *verb trans*. Hang (washing) out or *out* with pegs on a clothes-line. E20.

📖 **2** D. H. LAWRENCE They were pegging down carnations. B. HINES He pegged the stick into the soil. *High Magazine* The tent . . thrashed and groaned as I began pegging it. J. Cox His baggy white trousers . . pegged at the ankles. **3b** M. TWAIN I still lack about 30,000 words . . I shall peg along day by day. *People* I have just kept pegging away year after year. **6b** *Daily Telegraph* British Rail is to peg prices for a year. *Which?* Increases in farm spending will be pegged to a maximum. **c** J. LUDWIG: Mitchell has her pegged. *TV Guide (Canada)* The man Jack pegged as the passer of a counterfeit bill. **8c** *fig*.: *Times* The Government was pegging back Labour's lead in the opinion polls. **9** *Daily Telegraph* Regulations will have to be interpreted by the prospectors before they start pegging their claims. **10** M. KINGTON Many of them seem to suffer from . . oxygen starvation . . and peg out. **11** S. NAIPAUL Neighbours saw her . . pegging the sodden clothes out. V. S. PRITCHETT Picks up the washing and pegs it back on the line.

■ **pegged** *ppl adjective* (*a*) secured or fastened together with a peg or pegs; (*b*) *N. Amer*. = PEGTOP *adjective*: E17. **pegger** *noun* E17.

pegall /pɛˈgɔːl/ *noun*. E19.
[Carib *pagāla*.]
In Guyana, a kind of basket woven from palm-tree bark.

pegasse /pəˈgas/ *noun*. E20.
[Origin unkn.]
A kind of peaty soil found in the Caribbean and northern S. America.

Pegasus /ˈpɛgəsəs/ *noun*. LME.
[Latin from Greek *Pēgasos*, the winged horse fabled to have sprung from the blood of the slain Medusa and later represented as the favourite horse of the Muses, from *pēgē* spring, fount.]
1 (The name of) a conspicuous constellation of the northern hemisphere, joined by one star to Andromeda. LME.
2 HERALDRY. A charge representing a winged horse. M16.
3 *fig*. A flight of (esp. poetic) inspiration or genius. E17.
4 ZOOLOGY. A fish of the genus *Pegasus* or the family Pegasidae; = ***sea-moth*** s.v. SEA *noun*. Now only as mod. Latin genus name. M19.

📖 **3** SHAFTESBURY I will allow you the Pegasus of the poets.

■ **Peˈgasean** *adjective* of, pertaining to, or resembling the mythological Pegasus; swift; *fig*. poetic: L16.

peggotty /ˈpɛgəti/ *noun*. Also (earlier & as US proprietary name) **Pegity**. E20.
[Extension of PEG *noun*¹.]
A children's board game in which players aim to make a row of five pegs in a pegboard.

peggy /ˈpɛgi/ *noun*. E19.
[from PEG *noun*² + -Y⁶.]
1 In full ***peggy tub***. A washtub. *arch*. *colloq*. E19.
2 Any of various warblers. Also, a pied wagtail. Also ***peggy wagtail***, ***peggy warbler***, ***peggy whitethroat***, etc. *dial*. M19.
3 A steward in a ship's mess. *Nautical slang*. E20.
Comb.: **peggy bag** a type of handbag having side handles and outside pockets; ***peggy tub***: see sense 1 above; **Peggy-with-her-lantern**, **Peggy-with-lantern** = JACK-O'-LANTERN 2.

Pegity *noun* see PEGGOTTY.

pegmatite /ˈpɛgmətʌɪt/ *noun*. M19.
[Greek *pēgmat-*, *pēgma* thing joined together + -ITE¹.]
GEOLOGY. A coarsely crystallized rock commonly occurring in igneous intrusions, esp. dykes, and consisting mainly of feldspar and quartz.
■ **pegmatitic** /-ˈtɪtɪk/ *adjective* resembling, consisting of, or having the structure of pegmatite L19. **pegmatoid** *noun* & *adjective* (a rock) resembling or similar in structure to pegmatite L19.

pego /ˈpiːgəʊ/ *noun*. *slang*. Pl. **-os**. L17.
[Origin unkn.]
The penis.

pegomancy /ˈpiːgəmansi, ˈpɛg-/ *noun*. *rare*. E18.
[from Greek *pēgē* spring, fount + -MANCY.]
Divination by the examination of springs or fountains.

pegtop /ˈpɛgtɒp/ *noun & adjective*. Also **peg-top**. L18.
[from PEG *noun*¹ + TOP *noun*².]
▶ **A** *noun*. **1** A spinning-top which is spun by the rapid uncoiling of a string wound around a central pin or peg. L18. ▸**b** A game consisting of spinning pegtops. E19.
2 In *pl*. Pegtop trousers. M19.
▶ **B** *attrib*. or as *adjective*. Of a garment: having the shape of a pegtop; wide at the top and narrow at the bottom. M19.

📖 *Punch* This Autumn Collection . . emphasizing . . peg-top skirts.

■ **pegtopped** *adjective* (*a*) wearing pegtop trousers; (*b*) = PEGTOP *adjective*: M19.

Pegu /ˈpɛɡjuː/ *noun & adjective*. L16.
[See below.]
▶ **A** *noun*. Pl. **Pegues**. = PEGUAN *noun*. L16.
▶ **B** *adjective*. = PEGUAN *adjective*. E19.

Peguan /ˈpɛɡjʊən/ *noun & adjective*. M17.
[from *Pegu* (see below) + -AN, -ER¹.]
▶ **A** *noun*. **1** A native or inhabitant of the city or district of Pegu in Myanmar (Burma); *esp*. a Mon. M17.
2 The language of the Peguans, a form of Mon. E20.
▶ **B** *adjective*. Of or pertaining to the Peguans or their language. L19.
■ **Peguer** /ˈpɛɡjʊə/ *noun* (now *rare*) = PEGUAN *noun* 1 E18.

PEI *abbreviation*.
Prince Edward Island (Canada).

Peierls /ˈpʌɪəlz/ *noun*. L20.
[Rudolf *Peierls* (1907–95), German-born physicist.]
PHYSICS. Used *attrib*. with ref. to a spatially periodic distortion of a linear chain of atoms or molecules in certain solids, which is proposed as the cause of their change from a conducting to a semiconducting or insulating state at low temperatures.
Peierls distortion, ***Peierls transition***.

Peigan *adjective & noun* var. of PIEGAN.

peignoir /ˈpeɪnwɑː/ *noun*. M19.
[French, from *peigner* to comb + *-oir*, -ORY¹.]
A woman's loose dressing-gown or bathrobe.

pein *noun* var. of PEEN *noun*.

peine /pɛn, peɪn/ *noun*. M16.
[French.]
Pain, punishment.
peine forte et dure /fɔːr e dyːr/ [= strong and hard] *Hist*. a form of torture used on a prisoner who refused to accept jury trial in which the body was pressed, to death if necessary, with heavy weights; *transf*. severe punishment, suffering.

peineta /pɛiˈneta/ *noun*. M20.
[Spanish.]
A woman's ornamental comb traditionally worn with a mantilla.

peirastic /pʌɪˈrastɪk/ *adjective*. *rare*. Also (earlier) **pir-**. M17.
[Greek *peirastikos* tentative, from *peiran* to try.]
Experimental, provisional, speculative.

Peirce /pəːs/ *noun*. E20.
[C. S. *Peirce* (1839–1914), US pragmatic philosopher and logician.]
Used in *possess*. with ref. to the theories or methods of Peirce.
Peirce's Law a logical formula relating to implication, which can be expressed as $[(P \supset Q) \supset P] \supset P$.
■ **Peircian** *adjective* of or relating to the theories or methods of Peirce E20.

peise /peɪz, piːz/ *noun*. ME.
[Anglo-Norman, Old French *peis*, later *pois*: see POISE *noun*¹.]
†**1** = POISE *noun*¹ 1. ME–E17.
2 A piece of some heavy substance used as a weight; *spec*. (*a*) a standard weight for goods; (*b*) a weight in the mechanism of a clock. Now *Scot. & dial*. ME.
†**3** = POISE *noun*¹ 2. LME–E17.
4 Balance, poise, equilibrium. Cf. POISE *noun*¹ 5. Now *dial*. LME.
†**5** = POISE *noun*¹ 3. L15–E17.

peise /peɪz, piːz/ *verb*. LME.
[Old & mod. French *peis-*, later *pois-*, tonic stem of *peser*: see POISE *verb*.]
†**1** *verb trans*. Weigh, measure the weight of. LME–E17.
2 *verb trans*. Estimate esp. the weight of by touch or feel. Long *obsolete* exc. *Scot. & dial*. LME. ▸†**b** *fig*. Weigh in the mind; consider, ponder. LME–M17.
3 *verb trans*. **a** = POISE *verb* 4c. Long *obsolete* exc. *Scot*. LME. ▸†**b** = POISE *verb* 4a. LME–E17.
†**4** *verb trans*. = POISE *verb* 3a. LME–E17.
5 *verb trans*. †**a** Drive down by force of weight. LME–L16. ▸**b** Force (*loose*, *up*, etc.) by weight or pressure. *dial*. E19.
6 *verb intrans*. Weigh a specified amount. Chiefly with compl. Now *dial*. LME.

pejorate /ˈpiːdʒəreɪt/ *verb trans*. M17.
[Late Latin *pejorat-* pa. ppl stem of *pejorare* make worse, from Latin *pejor* worse: see -ATE³.]
Make worse, cause to deteriorate.

pejoration /piːdʒəˈreɪʃ(ə)n/ *noun*. M17.
[medieval Latin *pejoratio(n-)*, formed as prec.: see -ATION.]
1 Worsening, deterioration; an instance of this; *spec*. (a) depreciation in value. M17.
2 *LINGUISTICS*. Development of a less favourable meaning or connotation. Opp. ***amelioration***, ***melioration***. L19.

pejorative /pɪˈdʒɒrətɪv/ *adjective & noun*. L19.
[French *péjoratif*, *-ive*, formed as PEJORATE: see -ATIVE.]
▶ **A** *adjective*. Depreciatory, contemptuous; *esp*. (*LINGUISTICS*) giving or acquiring a less favourable meaning or connotation (opp. ***ameliorative***, ***meliorative***). L19.

📖 *Guardian* Formerly pejorative words like dyke . . and even male chauvinist pig are now sported proudly.

▶ **B** *noun*. *LINGUISTICS*. A pejorative word, affix, etc. L19.

📖 *India Today* Secretaries mumbling pejoratives . . began walking out.

■ **pejoratively** *adverb* L19.

pejorism /ˈpiːdʒərɪz(ə)m, ˈpɛ-/ *noun*. L19.
[Latin *pejor* worse + -ISM, after *pessimism*.]
The belief that the world is becoming worse.
■ **pejorist** *noun* E20.

pekan /ˈpɛk(ə)n/ *noun*. M18.
[Canad. French from Eastern Abnaki *pékané*.]
= FISHER 2b.

peke /piːk/ *noun*. *colloq*. E20.
[Abbreviation.]
= PEKINGESE *noun* 3.

pekea /pɪˈkiːə/ *noun*. Also **pikia**, **piqui** /pɪˈkiː/, & other vars. E17.
[Portuguese *piquiá* from Tupi *peki*.]
Either of two trees of tropical S. America, *Caryocar brasiliense* and *C. villosum* (family Caryocaraceae), valued for their edible oily nuts.

Pekin, ***pékin*** *nouns* see PEKING.

Pekinese *noun & adjective* var. of PEKINGESE.

Peking /piːˈkɪŋ/ *noun*. Also **-kin** /-ˈkɪn/; in sense 2 ***pékin*** /pekɛ̃ (*pl. same*)/. L18.
[French *pékin* from *Peking* (Beijing), the capital of China.]
1 a A type of silk. L18. ▸**b** = ***Peking duck*** (a) below. L19. ▸**c** A type of Chinese rug or carpet. E20.
2 Among French soldiers: a civilian. *slang* (*derog*.). *obsolete* exc. *Hist*. E19.
Comb.: **Peking duck** (*a*) (a bird of) a breed of large white duck with yellow bill and legs, imported from China to Britain and the US in 1873; (*b*) a Chinese dish consisting of strips of roast duck served with shredded vegetables, sauce, etc.; **Peking man** a fossil hominid described in 1926 from remains found in caves in China and now usu. classed as *Homo erectus*; **Peking opera** a stylized form of opera dating from the late 18th cent. in China, in which speech, singing, mime, and acrobatics are performed to an instrumental accompaniment. **Peking robin** an Asian babbler, *Leiothrix lutea*, with grey upperparts and red and yellow underparts, which has a loud melodious song and is popular as a cage-bird (esp. in China).
■ **Pekingˈology** *noun* the study of Chinese politics or current affairs M20.

Pekingese /piːkɪˈniːz/ *noun & adjective*. Also **Pekinese**. M19.
[from prec. + -ESE.]
▶ **A** *noun*. Pl. same, (in sense 3 also) **-s**.
1 A native or inhabitant of Peking (Beijing). M19.
2 The form of Mandarin spoken in Peking. M19.
3 A Pekingese dog. E20.
▶ **B** *adjective*. Of, pertaining to, or associated with the city of Peking (Beijing) or its inhabitants; *spec*. designating (an animal of) a small breed of dog with long hair and a snub nose, orig. from Peking. L19.
Pekingese stitch an embroidery stitch formed by looping a second thread through a base of back stitch.

pekoe /ˈpiːkəʊ, ˈpɛ-/ *noun*. E18.
[Chinese (Amoy) *pekho*, from *pek* white + *ho* down, hair.]
A high-quality black tea, made from leaves picked young with the down still on.
orange pekoe: see ORANGE *adjective*¹.

pelade /pɪˈlɑːd/ *noun*. Also (earlier) **pelada** /pɪˈlɑːdə/. M18.
[French, from *peler* deprive of hair.]
MEDICINE. Alopecia, esp. in a locally inflammatory form.
■ **peladic** /pɪˈladɪk/ *adjective* L19.

pelage /ˈpɛlɪdʒ/ *noun*. E19.
[French, from Old French *peil*, *pel* (mod. *poil*) hair, down + -AGE.]
The fur, hair, wool, etc., of a mammal.

Pelagian /pɪˈleɪdʒɪən/ *noun*¹ & *adjective*¹. LME.
[ecclesiastical Latin *Pelagianus*, from *Pelagius* (see below): see -AN.]
CHRISTIAN CHURCH. ▶**A** *noun*. A follower of the doctrines of the British lay monk Pelagius, of the 4th and 5th cents., esp. of his view that the human will is capable of good without the assistance of divine grace. LME.
▶ **B** *adjective*. Of, pertaining to, or associated with Pelagius or his doctrines. LME.
■ **Pelagianism** *noun* L16. **Pelagianize** *verb intrans*. (*rare*) hold or express Pelagian views E17.

pelagian /pɪˈleɪdʒɪən/ *adjective*² & *noun*². E17.
[Latin *pelagius* from Greek *pelagios* of the sea (cf. next): see -AN.]
▶ **A** *adjective*. †**1** Of or pertaining to the sea shells from which Tyrian purple dye was obtained. *rare*. Only in E17.
2 Of, pertaining to, or inhabiting the open sea or ocean; pelagic. Now *rare* or *obsolete*. M18.
▶ **B** *noun*. An inhabitant of the open sea. *rare*. M19.

pelagic /pɪˈladʒɪk/ *adjective*. M17.
[Latin *pelagicus* from Greek *pelagikos*, from *pelagos* level surface of the sea: see -IC.]
1 Of or pertaining to the open sea, as distinguished from the shallow water near the coast; oceanic. Now chiefly *spec*., living on or near the surface of the open sea or ocean, as distinguished from its depths; designating or inhabiting a part of the sea away from or independent of the littoral and benthic regions. M17.
2 Of sealing or whaling: performed on the open sea. L19.
3 Of seabed material: formed within the sea, not transported from the land. L19.
4 = LIMNETIC *adjective*. L19.
5 Of a (species of) bird: inhabiting the open sea beyond the continental shelf and returning to shore only to breed. M20.
■ **pelagically** *adverb* in pelagic regions M20.

pelamyd /ˈpɛləmɪd/ *noun*. Also **-mid**. Pl. **-ds**, **pelamides** /pɛˈlamɪdiːz/. L16.
[Latin *pelamyd-*, *-mys*, *-mis* from Greek *pēlamud-*, *-mus*.]
A young or small bonito or tunny.

pelandok /pəlanˈdɒk/ *noun*. E19.
[Malay.]
= KANCHIL.

pelargonic /pɛlɑːˈɡɒnɪk/ *adjective*. M19.
[from PELARGONIUM + -IC.]
CHEMISTRY. = NONANOIC.

pelargonin /pɛləˈɡəʊnɪn/ *noun*. E20.
[from PELARGONIUM + -IN¹.]
CHEMISTRY. An anthocyanin (usu. isolated as the red chloride, $C_{27}H_{31}O_{15}Cl$) that is the colouring matter of zonal pelargoniums.
■ **pelargonidin** *noun* an anthocyanidin of which pelargonin and many other red plant pigments are glycosides E20.

pelargonium /pɛləˈɡəʊnɪəm/ *noun*. E19.
[mod. Latin (see below), from Greek *pelargos* stork, app. after earlier *geranion* GERANIUM: see -IUM.]
Any of various plants of the mostly southern African genus *Pelargonium* (family Geraniaceae), many of which are grown as garden plants (popularly called geraniums); a flowering stem of such a plant.
regal pelargonium, ***zonal pelargonium***, etc.

Pelasgian /pɪˈlazɡɪən, -dʒɪən/ *noun & adjective*. L15.
[from Latin *Pelasgus* (from Greek *Pelasgos*, *Pelasgios*) + -IAN.]
Hist. ▶**A** *noun*. **1** A member of a pre-Hellenic people inhabiting the coasts and islands of the eastern Mediterranean and Aegean. L15.
2 The Indo-European language attributed to this people. M20.
▶ **B** *adjective*. Designating or pertaining to this people or their language. M19.

Pelasgic /pɪˈlazɡɪk, -dʒɪk/ *adjective & noun*. L18.
[Latin *Pelasgicus* from Greek *Pelasgikos*: see -IC. Cf. prec.]
▶ **A** *adjective*. Of, pertaining to, or characteristic of the Pelasgians. L18.
▶ **B** *noun*. The Pelasgian language. *rare*. M20.

Pele /ˈpɛleɪ/ *noun*¹. M19.
[*Pele*, goddess of volcanoes in Hawaiian mythol.]
GEOLOGY. **1** ***Pele's hair*** [translating Hawaiian *lauoho o Pele*], volcanic glass in the form of spun threads of rapidly solidified lava, orig. found near the volcano Kilauea. M19.
2 ***Pele's tears*** [translating Hawaiian *waimaka o Pele*], small drops of volcanic glass, usu. spheroidal or tear-shaped and with strands of Pele's hair attached. M20.

pele *noun*² var. of PEEL *noun*¹.

Peléan /pɪˈleɪən/ *adjective*. Also **Pelean**, **Peléean**, **p-**. E20.
[from Mount *Pelée*, a volcano on the island of Martinique + -AN.]
GEOLOGY. Pertaining to, or designating a type of volcanic eruption characterized by the lateral emission of *nuées ardentes* and the vertical extrusion of very viscous lava which tends to form a solid plug.

pelecypod /pɪˈlɛsɪpɒd/ *adjective & noun*. L19.
[mod. Latin *Pelecypoda* (alternative name of the class Bivalvia), from Greek *pelekus* hatchet + *-podos* footed.]
ZOOLOGY & PALAEONTOLOGY. ▶**A** *adjective*. Designating or pertaining to a bivalve mollusc. L19.
▶ **B** *noun*. A pelecypod mollusc, a bivalve. L19.
■ **peleˈcypodous** *adjective* (*rare*) = PELECYPOD *adjective* M19.

Peléean *adjective* var. of PELÉAN.

pelerine /ˈpɛlərɪn, -iːn/ *noun*. M18.
[French *pèlerine* transf. use of fem. of *pèlerin* pilgrim.]
Hist. A woman's mantle or cape; *esp*. a long narrow cape, usu. of lace or silk, with ends meeting at a point in front, popular in the 19th cent.

†**peletre** *noun* see PELLITORY.

pelf /pɛlf/ *noun*. LME.
[Old Northern French var. of Old French *pelfre*, *peufre* spoil, rel. to *pelf(r)er* pillage, rob (cf. Anglo-Latin *pelf(r)are*): ult. origin unkn. See PILFER *noun*, *verb*.]
†**1** Stolen goods; booty. LME–L15.
†**2** Property; possessions. LME–M19.
3 Money, riches. Now *esp*., dishonestly acquired wealth. L15.

4 †**a** Trumpery, trash, rubbish. M16–E17. ▸**b** A worthless person. *obsolete* exc. *dial.* M16. ▸**c** Refuse. Now only (*dial.*), vegetable refuse, weeds. L16.

📖 **3** W. C. WILLIAMS I think you cheat or lie for pelf.

■ †**pelfry** *noun* (*a*) booty, spoil; (*b*) trumpery, trash: LME–E17.

Pelham /ˈpɛləm/ *noun.* M19.
[from the surname *Pelham.*]
A horse's bit combining a snaffle and a curb. Also more fully ***Pelham bit***.

pelican /ˈpɛlɪk(ə)n/ *noun.* LOE.
[Late Latin *pelicanus* from Greek *pelekan*, prob. from *pelekus* axe, *pelekan* hew with an axe, with ref. to the appearance or action of the bird's bill.]
1 Any of various large gregarious fish-eating water-birds, constituting the family Pelecanidae and genus *Pelecanus*, having a long hooked bill with a greatly distensible pouch hanging below it, used to store fish when caught. In early and biblical use [after late Latin (Vulgate) *pelicano solitudinis* pelican of the wilderness], a bird of uncertain identity. LOE. ▸**b** The pelican as fabled to revive or feed its young with its own blood. LME. ▸†**c** *fig.* Christ as reviver of the dead in spirit by his blood. E16–E19.
2 A representation of a pelican in art, heraldry, etc. LME.
3 *Hist.* An alembic having two curved tubes which pass down from the head and re-enter at the body of the vessel. M16.
4 *Hist.* A pronged instrument formerly used for extracting teeth. M17.
5 *Hist.* A type of cannon carrying a six-pound shot. M17.
6 (**P-**.) (Proprietary name for) any of a range of books published under the name 'Pelican'. M20.
7 [from *Pedestrian Light Controlled*, with alt.] More fully ***pelican crossing***. In Britain, a pedestrian crossing with traffic lights operated by pedestrians. M20.

📖 **1** ***white pelican***: see WHITE *adjective*. **b** W. CONGREVE Would'st thou have me turn Pelican, and feed thee out of my own Vitals? **2** B. CHATWIN White porcelain sculptures—a pelican, a turkeycock. **6** CLIVE JAMES He wrote a Pelican about Buddha.

Comb.: ***pelican crossing***: see sense 7 above; **Pelican flag** *US* the State flag of Louisiana; **pelican-flower** a W. Indian birthwort, *Aristolochia grandiflora*, with a very long floral tube; **pelican's foot** a European marine gastropod mollusc, *Aporrhais pespelecani*, with long digitate processes on the lip of the full-grown shell; the shell of this mollusc; **Pelican State** *US* the State of Louisiana.

Pelignian *noun & adjective* see PAELIGNIAN.

pelike /ˈpɛlɪki, pɛˈliːki/ *noun.* Pl. **-kai** /-kʌɪ/. L19.
[Greek *pelikа.*]
GREEK ANTIQUITIES. A type of wide-mouthed amphora with a broad base, used for holding wine or water.

Pelion /ˈpiːlɪən/ *noun.* L16.
[See below.]
pile Pelion (up)on Ossa, ***pile Ossa (up)on Pelion***, ***heap Pelion (up)on Ossa***, ***heap Ossa (up)on Pelion*** [Mounts *Pelion* and *Ossa* in Thessaly, Greece (translating Latin (Virgil) *imponere Pelio Ossam*)], add to what is already great, *esp.* add difficulty to difficulty.

peliosis /pɛlɪˈəʊsɪs/ *noun.* Pl. **-oses** /-ˈəʊsiːz/. M19.
[mod. Latin from Greek *peliōsis*, from *pelios* livid: see -OSIS.]
MEDICINE. The extravasation of blood, esp. in purpura.
peliosis rheumatica /ruˈmatɪkə/ = *SCHÖNLEIN's disease.*

pelisse /pəˈliːs/ *noun.* E18.
[Old & mod. French from medieval Latin *pellicia*: see PILCH *noun.*]
Hist. **1** A long fur-lined mantle or cloak, esp. as part of a hussar's uniform. Formerly also *gen.*, a fur garment. E18.
2 a A woman's long fitted coat, or long cloak with armholes or sleeves, usu. of a rich fabric. M18. ▸**b** A child's outer garment. E19.

pelite /ˈpiːlʌɪt/ *noun.* L19.
[from Greek *pēlos* clay, earth, mud + -ITE¹.]
GEOLOGY. A sediment or sedimentary rock composed of very fine clay or mud particles, esp. of hydrated aluminium silicates; lutite.
■ **pelitic** /pɪˈlɪtɪk/ *adjective* of the nature of, pertaining to, or derived from pelite, lutaceous L19.

pell /pɛl/ *noun*¹. *obsolete* exc. *Hist.* ME.
[Anglo-Norman *pell*, *peal*, Old French *pel* (mod. *peau*) from Latin *pellis* skin, leather, parchment.]
†**1** An animal skin or hide; *esp.* a furred skin used to make, line, or trim a cloak. ME–L16.
2 *Hist.* Either of two rolls of parchment for recording receipts and disbursements, formerly kept at the Exchequer; ***the Pells***, the Office of the Exchequer in which these rolls were kept. LME.
2 Clerk of the Pells *Hist.* an officer formerly charged with the entry of receipts and disbursements on the pells.

Pell /pɛl/ *noun*². E20.
[from John *Pell*: see PELLIAN.]
MATH. In full ***Pell equation***, ***Pell's equation***. A Diophantine equation of the form $x^2 - ay^2 = 1$ (where *a*, *x*, and *y* are integers).

pell /pɛl/ *verb.* ME.
[Origin uncertain: perh. rel. to Latin *pellere* drive. Cf. PEAL *verb*¹.]
1 *verb intrans.* Move hurriedly, rush. Long *obsolete* exc. *Scot. & dial.* ME.
2 *verb trans. & intrans.* Beat or knock (a person) down or *down* violently. Now *Scot.* LME.

pellack *noun* var. of PELLOCK.

pellagra /pɛˈlagrə, -ˈleɪgrə/ *noun.* E19.
[Italian, from *pelle* skin (from Latin *pellis* PELL *noun*¹) + *-agra* after PODAGRA.]
MEDICINE. A condition caused by nicotinic acid (niacin) deficiency, characterized by dermatitis, diarrhoea, and mental disturbance and common where maize is the staple food.
Comb.: **pellagra-preventive factor** niacin, nicotinic acid.
■ **pellagraˈgenic** *adjective* causing pellagra E20. **pellagrin** *noun* a person affected with pellagra M19. **pellagrose** *adjective* affected with pellagra M19. **pellagrous** *adjective* of or pertaining to pellagra M19.

pellet /ˈpɛlɪt/ *noun*¹ & *verb.* LME.
[Old & mod. French *pelote* from Proto-Romance dim. of Latin *pila* ball: see -ET¹.]
▶ **A** *noun.* **1** A small usu. rounded mass of something; *spec.* a hard compressed ball or pill of animal feed, medicine, pesticide, etc. LME.
2 *spec.* **a** Orig., a (usu. stone) missile shot from a mortar etc.; a cannon-ball. Later, a bullet or piece of small shot. LME. ▸**b** An imitation bullet, now esp. of compressed paper, used in a toy gun etc. M16. ▸**c** A small mass of bones, feathers, etc., regurgitated by a bird of prey; a cast. E19. ▸**d** A small round piece of animal excreta, esp. produced by a rabbit. E20.
3 HERALDRY. A black spot representing a cannon-ball; an ogress. LME.
4 A rounded or flat circular boss found in coins, architectural mouldings, etc. M19.

📖 **1** W. H. AUDEN Doctor Thomas sat over his dinner . . Rolling his bread into pellets. S. PLATH I twisted a kleenex to small, pill-sized pellets. *Stock & Land (Melbourne)* When a sheep's diet shifts from grass to pellets, it is eating a more nutritious food. *Which?* Protect . . plants like *Helleborus niger* . . from slugs using pellets. **2a** G. LORD He fired . . into the cave mouth. Pellets flew around. *fig.*: J. MARK Sagging clouds, out of which fell leaden pellets of water.

Comb.: **pellet bell** *Hist.* a small bell sounded by a loose pellet in its cavity, and attached to a dancer's clothing, a tambourine, etc., esp. in the Middle Ages; **pellet bomb** a type of small anti-personnel bomb; **pellet bow** *Hist.* a type of bow firing clay pellets for shooting game; **pellet mill** a machine for pelleting powders.
▶ **B** *verb trans.* **1** Orig., send in the form of a pellet or pellets. Later, form or shape into pellets, pelletize; *spec.* coat (seed) with soluble nutritive and protective substances to facilitate handling and promote growth. L16.
2 Hit with (esp. paper) pellets, small shot, etc. L19.

📖 **1** *Times* Low seed rates can be achieved . . by using seed pelleted with basic slag.

■ **pelletable** *adjective* able to be formed into pellets L20. **pelleted** *adjective* (*a*) HERALDRY marked or charged with pellets; (*b*) formed into or supplied as pellets: E17. **pellety** *adjective* (HERALDRY) pelleted L16.

pellet /ˈpɛlɪt/ *noun*². LME.
[Old French *pelet(t)e* dim. of *pel*: see PELL *noun*¹, -ET¹. Cf. PELT *noun*¹.]
†**1** A thin skin or membrane; a pellicle. *rare.* Only in LME.
2 An animal pelt; *esp.* a sheepskin. Long *obsolete* exc. *Scot.* LME.

pelleter /ˈpɛlɪtə/ *noun*¹. M20.
[from PELLET *noun*¹ + -ER¹.]
A machine for forming pellets, *esp.* one for coating or pelleting plant seed.

†**pelleter** *noun*² see PELLITORY.

pelletize /ˈpɛlɪtʌɪz/ *verb trans.* Also **-ise**. M20.
[from PELLET *noun*¹ + -IZE.]
Form or shape into pellets.
■ **pelletiˈzation** *noun* M20. **pelletizer** *noun* = PELLETER *noun*¹ M20.

Pellian /ˈpɛlɪən/ *adjective.* M19.
[from John *Pell* (1610–85), English mathematician + -IAN.]
MATH. ***Pellian equation***, = ***Pell's equation*** s.v. PELL *noun*².

pellicle /ˈpɛlɪk(ə)l/ *noun.* M16.
[French *pellicule* from Latin *pellicula* dim. of *pellis* skin: see -CLE.]
Chiefly SCIENCE. A small or thin skin; a fine sheet or layer covering a surface or (occas.) enclosing a cavity; a membrane, a cuticle, a film.
■ **peˈllicular** *adjective* of, pertaining to, or of the nature of a pellicle; having or characterized by a pellicle; membranous, filmy: M19. **pellicule** *noun* (*rare*) = PELLICLE LME.

pellitory /ˈpɛlɪtəri/ *noun.* In sense 1 orig. †**peletre** †**pelleter**. LME.
[In sense 1 Old French *peletre* alt. of *peretre* from Latin PYRETHRUM, in sense 2 alt. of PARIETARY. For change of ending cf. FUMITORY *noun*¹.]
1 More fully ***pellitory of Spain***. A N. African daisy-like plant, *Anacyclus pyrethrum*, of the composite family; its pungent root, used as a remedy for toothache. LME. ▸†**b** Either of two plants resembling this in the pungency of their root or leaf: (*a*) (more fully ***false pellitory of Spain***) masterwort, *Peucedanum ostruthium*; (*b*) (more fully ***bastard pellitory***) sneezewort, *Achillea ptarmica*. L16–M18.
2 More fully ***pellitory of the wall***. A plant of the nettle family, *Parietaria judaica*, with ovate leaves and inconspicuous greenish flowers, often found on old walls and steep banks. M16.

pell-mell /pɛlˈmɛl/ *adverb, adjective, noun, & verb.* L16.
[French *pêle-mêle* from Old French *pesle mesle*, *mesle pesle*, etc., redupl. of *mesle* stem of *mesler* (mod. *mêler*) mix, MEDDLE.]
▶ **A** *adverb.* **1** In a confused medley or disorderly mingling; together without any order (esp. in flight or pursuit). L16. ▸**b** *spec.* With ref. to fighting or combat: without keeping ranks, hand to hand, in a mêlée. Now *rare* or *obsolete.* L16.
†**2** Indiscriminately; in a mass, as a whole. L16–M17.
3 Esp. with ref. to action by an individual: in a disorderly rush; headlong, recklessly. L16.

📖 **1** W. HEATH ROBINSON The giants . . fled pell-mell to the mountains. M. WARNER Her compliments, in disjointed phrases falling pell-mell. **3** D. WIGODER I was desperate to rush pell-mell into the unknown future.

▶ **B** *adjective.* Disorderly and rushed; confused; indiscriminate. L16.

📖 H. KELLER The mechanical process . . of putting words on paper at pell-mell speed.

▶ **C** *noun.* Confusion, disorder; a confused or disorderly mixture or crowd; *spec.* a hand-to-hand fight, a mêlée. L16.
▶ **D** *verb trans.* Orig. (*rare*), mix up in disorder. Now, run or flee in hurried confusion or disorder. E17.

📖 *Time* Eavesdropping reporters pell-melled off to another hill.

†**pell mell** *noun phr.* var. of PALL-MALL.

pellock /ˈpɛlək/ *noun. Scot.* Also **-ack**. ME.
[Origin unkn.]
A porpoise.

pellotine /ˈpɛlətiːn/ *noun.* L19.
[from Mexican Spanish *pellote* PEYOTE + -INE⁵.]
CHEMISTRY. An alkaloid, $C_{13}H_{19}NO_3$, obtained from peyote and formerly used as a hypnotic.

pellucid /pɪˈluːsɪd, pɛ-, -ˈljuːsɪd/ *adjective.* E17.
[Latin *pellucidus*, from *pellucere*, *perlucere* shine through: see PER-¹, LUCID.]
1 Transmitting, or allowing the passage of, light; translucent, transparent. E17.
2 *fig.* (Of a person, the mind, etc.) not confused, perceiving clearly; (of a sound, piece of writing, etc.) clear, distinct. Formerly also, (of a quality etc.) easily detectable. M17.

📖 **1** J. C. OATES The pellucid water, though agitated . . did not turn cloudy. C. BRAYFIELD The late afternoon sky was growing pale . . and taking on a pellucid apricot tint. **pellucid zone** = *ZONA pellucida.* **2** C. LAMB To muddle their faculties, perhaps never very pellucid. H. E. BATES The nightingale gave a startling pellucid whistle. C. RYCROFT His elegant and pellucid literary style.

■ **pelluˈcidity** *noun* the quality or condition of being pellucid; translucence, transparency: M17. **pellucidly** *adverb* E19. **pellucidness** *noun* (*rare*) = PELLUCIDITY L17.

Pelman /ˈpɛlmən/ *adjective.* E20.
[Christopher Louis *Pelman*, founder (in 1899) of the Pelman Institute for the Scientific Development of Mind, Memory and Personality in London.]
Designating a system of memory training devised and taught by the Pelman Institute.

Pelmanism /ˈpɛlmənɪz(ə)m/ *noun.* E20.
[from prec. + -ISM.]
The Pelman system of memory training. Also (*transf.*), a card-game in which matching pairs must be selected from cards laid face down on a table.
■ **Pelmanist**, **Pelmanite** *nouns* a student or advocate of Pelmanism E20. **Pelmanize** *verb* (*a*) *verb intrans.* practise Pelmanism; (*b*) *verb trans.* train (a person, one's memory, etc.) in the techniques of Pelmanism: E20.

pelmatozoan /pɛlmətəˈzəʊən/ *adjective & noun.* E20.
[from mod. Latin *Pelmatozoa* (see below), from Greek *pelmat-*, *pelma* sole of the foot + *zōion* animal: see -AN.]
ZOOLOGY & PALAEONTOLOGY. ▶ **A** *adjective.* Of, pertaining to, or belonging to the former division Pelmatozoa, comprising echinoderms which are fixed to the substrate by a stalk and including crinoids, blastoids, and cystoids. E20.
▶ **B** *noun.* A stalked echinoderm. E20.

pelmeny /pɛlˈmɛni/ *noun pl.* **M20.**
[Russian *pel'meni.*]
Small pasta cases stuffed with seasoned meat etc. as a Russian dish.

pelmet /ˈpɛlmɪt/ *noun.* **E20.**
[Prob. alt. of French **PALMETTE.**]
A narrow border of fabric, wood, etc., fitted across the top of a door or window to conceal curtain fittings.

pelo- /ˈpiːləʊ, ˈpɛləʊ/ *combining form* of Greek *pēlos* clay, mud: see **-O-**.
■ **pelo'batid** *noun* an amphibian of the family Pelobatidae, which includes spade-foot toads **M20. pelophile** *noun* (ECOLOGY) a plant which grows or thrives on mud or clay **E20. pelophilous** /-ˈlɒfɪləs/ *adjective* clay-loving **L19.**

peloid /ˈpiːlɔɪd/ *noun.* **M20.**
[formed as **PELO-** + **-OID.**]
1 Any semi-solid substance used in pelotherapy. **M20.**
2 GEOLOGY. A minute particle of microcrystalline or cryptocrystalline carbonate. **M20.**
■ **pe'loidal** *adjective* **M20.**

pelon /peˈlon/ *adjective & noun.* Pl. of noun ***-es*** /-ɛs/. **L19.**
[Spanish *pelón* bald, hairless.]
In Latin America: (an animal, esp. a dog) having almost no hair.

pelong /piːˈlɒŋ/ *noun & adjective.* **L17.**
[Perh. from Malay *pelang* striped.]
(Made of) a kind of silk formerly used in southern India, esp. for formal robes.

Peloponnesian /pɛləpəˈniːzj(ə)n, -ʒ(ə)n/ *noun & adjective.* **L15.**
[from Greek *Peloponnēsos*, Latin *Peloponnesus* Peloponnese (see below) + **-IAN.**]
▶ **A** *noun.* A native or inhabitant of the Peloponnese, the peninsula forming the southernmost part of the Greek mainland. **L15.**
▶ **B** *adjective.* Of or pertaining to the Peloponnese or its inhabitants. **L16.**
Peloponnesian war GREEK HISTORY the war of 431–404 BC, fought and won by Sparta and its Peloponnesian allies against Athens.

peloria /pɪˈlɔːrɪə/ *noun.* **M19.**
[mod. Latin from Greek *pelōros* monstrous, from *pelōr* monster: see **-IA**[1].]
BOTANY. Abnormal symmetry of structure in flowers normally zygomorphic (e.g. toadflax).
■ **peloriate** *adjective* = **PELORIC L19. peloric** *adjective* affected by or exhibiting peloria **M19. 'pelorism** *noun* = **PELORIA M19. 'pelorize** *verb trans.* affect with peloria **M19.**

pelorus /pɪˈlɔːrəs/ *noun.* **M19.**
[*Pelorus*, reputed name of Hannibal's pilot.]
A sighting device resembling a mariner's compass for taking the bearings of a distant object.

pelota /pɪˈlɒtə, -ˈləʊtə/ *noun.* **E19.**
[Spanish = ball, augm. of *pella* from Latin *pila* ball.]
1 A Basque or Spanish ball game played in a walled court using basket-like wicker rackets attached to gloves. **E19.**
2 The ball used in pelota. **E20.**
■ ***pelotari*** /peloˈtari/ *noun* a pelota player **E20.**

pelotherapy /piːləʊˈθɛrəpi/ *noun.* **M20.**
[from **PELO-** + **THERAPY.**]
MEDICINE. The therapeutic application of mud to the body.

peloton /ˈpɛlətɒn/ *noun.* **E18.**
[French, from *pelote*: see **PELLET** *noun*[1].]
†**1** A small ball or pellet. *rare.* Only in **E18.**
2 a = **PLATOON** *noun* 1. Now *rare* or *obsolete.* **E18.** ▸**b** CYCLING. The main field or group of cyclists in a race. **M20.**

pelouse /pəluz/ *noun.* Pl. pronounced same. **E20.**
[French.]
Esp. in France: an area of grass; *spec.* a public enclosure at a racecourse.

pelt /pɛlt/ *noun*[1]. **ME.**
[Perh. var. of **PELLET** *noun*[2] or shortened form of **PELTRY** *noun*[1].]
1 The dressed or undressed skin of an animal with the wool, hair, etc., still on; a fell. **ME.**
2 *spec.* The raw skin of an animal (esp. a sheep) stripped ready for tanning. **M16.**
†**3** A garment made of an animal pelt or animal pelts. **M16–M17.**
4 The human skin, esp. when bare. Now *joc.* **E17.**
5 The dead quarry of a hawk. **E17.**

> **1** J. CLAVELL He . . worked the pelt around to bring the naked back legs out through the belly slit. *fig.*: N. GORDIMER The long white pelt of a carpet with the feel of soft grass. **4 in one's pelt** naked.

Comb.: **peltmonger** *arch.* a dealer in pelts; **pelt-wool** wool pulled from the skin of a dead sheep.

pelt /pɛlt/ *noun*[2]. **LME.**
[from **PELT** *verb*[1].]
1 A vigorous blow or stroke (as) with a missile. **LME.** ▸**b** The torrential falling of rain, snow, etc.; a pelting storm. **E19.**
2 An outburst of temper; a rage. *obsolete* exc. *dial.* **L16.**
3 The action of pelting, *esp.* the action of running fast; an instance of this. **E19.**

> **1** SMOLLETT The cripple . . gave him . . a good pelt on the head with his crutch. **b** ANTHONY HOPE The rush of the wind and the pelt of the rain. **3 at full pelt, full pelt** as fast as possible.

pelt /ˈpɛlt/ *noun*[3]. Now *Scot. & dial.* **M16.**
[App. formed as **PALTRY** *noun.*]
Trash, rubbish; *esp.* rags. Also, refuse, waste.

†**pelt** *noun*[4] see **PELTA.**

pelt /pɛlt/ *verb*[1]. **L15.**
[Perh. contr. of **PELLET** *noun*[1] *& verb.*]
1 *verb trans.* Deliver repeated blows to (now only *Scot. & north.*); strike repeatedly with (esp. many small) missiles. **L15.** ▸**b** *fig.* Assail with insults, abuse, etc. **M17.**
2 *verb intrans.* Deliver repeated strokes or blows; fire missiles. Freq. foll. by *at.* **M16.** ▸**b** Of rain, hail, etc.: beat (down) heavily; fall torrentially; drive, lash. **E17.**
3 *verb trans.* Drive by force of blows, missiles, etc. Now *rare* or *obsolete.* **L16.**
†**4** *verb intrans.* Throw out angry words. **L16–E18.**
5 *verb trans.* Hurl (missiles etc.) with intent to strike. Freq. foll. by *at.* **L17.**
6 *verb intrans.* Move or run fast and vigorously. Freq. foll. by *along, away, down*, etc. **M19.**

> **1** W. C. WILLIAMS He was pelted with stones. J. HOWKER Pelting the phone box with snowballs. **b** S. JOHNSON If they had wit, they should have kept pelting me with pamphlets. **2** P. V. WHITE He pelted slowly and viciously . . and the stones made a slow, dead noise on the horse's hide. **b** J. CLARE The storm pelted down. **5** B. CHATWIN The storm broke, and pelted hailstones. *fig.*: HUGH WALPOLE All the young Pitts . . were pelting oratory at my father. **6** STEVIE SMITH Oh never was happiness like mine as I pelt along on my cloud. TOECKEY JONES I pelted down the drive and out of the gate.

pelt /pɛlt/ *verb*[2] *trans.* **L16.**
[from **PELT** *noun*[1].]
Strip the pelt from (an animal), skin, fleece. Also, strip (the skin or pelt) *from.*

pelta /ˈpɛltə/ *noun.* Pl. **-tae** /-tiː/. Also Anglicized as †**pelt.** **E17.**
[Latin from Greek *peltē* a small light leather shield.]
1 CLASSICAL ANTIQUITIES. A small light shield; a buckler. **E17.**
2 BOTANY. Any of various shieldlike structures; *spec.* (in a lichen) a flat apothecium without an excipulum. **M18.**
3 An ornamental motif resembling a shield in architecture, metalwork, etc. **E20.**
■ **peltate** *adjective* (*a*) BOTANY shield-shaped; *spec.* (of a leaf etc.) more or less circular and having the stalk attached at a point on the underside; (*b*) (of architecture, metalwork, etc.) ornamented with a pelta or peltae: **M18. peltately** *adverb* **E19.**

peltast /ˈpɛltast/ *noun.* **E17.**
[Latin *peltasta* from Greek *peltastēs*, from *peltē* **PELTA.**]
GREEK HISTORY. A foot-soldier armed with a pelta and javelin.

pelter /ˈpɛltə/ *noun.* **L18.**
[from **PELT** *verb*[1] + **-ER**[1].]
1 a A pelting shower. *colloq.* **L18.** ▸**b** A person who pelts or hurls missiles. **E19.**
2 Something exceptionally large. *dial.* **L18.**
3 An old or slow horse. *US colloq.* **M19.**
4 A rage, a temper. *Scot. & dial.* **M19.**
5 A person who or thing which pelts or moves fast and vigorously. *colloq.* **L19.**

> **1** J. B. PRIESTLEY Something more than a mere shower . . a downright pelter. F. B. YOUNG A pelter of flying turf shed from hoofs thudding past him. **5 in a pelter** in a hurry, at speed.

pelter /ˈpɛltə/ *verb.* Chiefly *dial.* **E18.**
[from **PELT** *verb*[1] + **-ER**[5].]
1 *verb trans.* = **PELT** *verb*[1] 1. **E18.**
2 *verb intrans.* = **PELT** *verb*[1] 2b. **E19.**
3 *verb intrans.* = **PELT** *verb*[1] 6. **E20.**

Peltier /ˈpɛltɪeɪ/ *noun.* **M19.**
[J. C. A. *Peltier* (1785–1845), French amateur scientist.]
PHYSICS. Used *attrib.* with ref. to an effect whereby heat is given out or absorbed when an electric current passes across a junction between two materials.
Peltier cooling, ***Peltier effect***, ***Peltier heating***, etc. **Peltier coefficient** the quantity of heat liberated or absorbed at a junction between two conductors, or between a given material and a reference conductor, when a unit of charge passes between them.

pelting /ˈpɛltɪŋ/ *adjective*[1]. *arch.* **M16.**
[App. rel. to **PELTRY** *noun*[2], **PALTRY.**]
Paltry, petty; insignificant; worthless.

pelting /ˈpɛltɪŋ/ *adjective*[2]. **L16.**
[from **PELT** *verb*[1] + **-ING**[2].]
1 Violent, passionate, hot. *obsolete* exc. *dial.* **L16.**
2 That pelts; *esp.* (of rain etc.) beating, driving, lashing. **E18.**

Pelton wheel /ˈpɛltən wiːl/ *noun phr.* **L19.**
[L. A. *Pelton* (1829–1908), US engineer and inventor.]
A type of undershot water-wheel driven by a jet of water directed at buckets fixed to the rim.

peltry /ˈpɛltri/ *noun*[1]. **LME.**
[Anglo-Norman *pelterie*, Old French *peleterie* (mod. *pelleterie*), from *peletier* furrier, from *pel*: see **PELL** *noun*[1], **-RY.**]
1 Undressed skins, esp. of animals valuable for their furs; pelts collectively. **LME.**
2 In *pl.* Kinds or varieties of pelts. **E19.**

peltry /ˈpɛltri/ *noun*[2] *& adjective.* **M16.**
[App. var. of **PALTRY** *noun & adjective.* Cf. **PELT** *noun*[3].]
▶†**A** *noun.* (A piece of) rubbish; a worthless thing. Chiefly *Scot.* **M16–M19.**
▶ **B** *adjective.* Rubbishy; worthless. *Scot.* **L16.**

peludo /pɛˈluːdəʊ/ *noun.* Pl. **-os.** **M19.**
[Spanish, lit. 'hairy', from *pelo* from Latin *pilus* hair.]
A South American hairy armadillo of the genus *Chaetophractus.*

pelure /pəˈlʊə/ *noun*[1]. Now *rare* or *obsolete.* **ME.**
[Anglo-Norman *pellure*, Old French *peleure*, *pelure*, from *pel*: see **PELL** *noun*[1], **-URE.**]
Orig., animal fur; *esp.* a fur lining or trimming on a garment. Later, a fur coat.

pelure /ˈpɛljʊə/ *noun*[2]. **L19.**
[French, lit. 'peeling', from *peler* to peel: see **-URE.**]
Esp. PHILATELY. A kind of very thin paper. Also ***pelure-paper.***

pelure d'oignon /p(ə)lyːr dɔɲɔ̃/ *noun & adjectival phr.* **M20.**
[French, lit. 'onion peel': see prec.]
▶ **A** *noun phr.* Pl. ***-s -s*** (pronounced same). A tawny colour characteristic of some aged red wines; a wine of this colour. **M20.**
▶ **B** *adjectival phr.* (Designating a wine) of this colour. **M20.**

pelves *noun* pl. of **PELVIS.**

pelvi- /ˈpɛlvi/ *combining form.*
[Latin **PELVIS.**]
Chiefly ANATOMY & MEDICINE. Of or pertaining to a pelvis; of the pelvis and —, as ***pelvi-rectal***, ***pelvi-ureteric***, etc.
■ **pel'vimeter** *noun* an instrument for measuring the internal diameters of the pelvis **E19. pel'vimetry** *noun* measurement of the dimensions of the pelvis **M19.**

pelvic /ˈpɛlvɪk/ *adjective.* **M19.**
[from next + **-IC.**]
Of, pertaining to, or contained in the pelvis.
pelvic arch = ***pelvic girdle*** below. **pelvic fin** in a fish, a ventral fin supported by the pelvic girdle. **pelvic floor** the muscular base of the abdomen, attached to the pelvis. **pelvic girdle** the framework formed by the bones of the pelvis which supports the hind limbs. **pelvic inflammatory disease** an inflammation of the female genital tract, accompanied by fever. **pelvic thrust** a repeated thrusting movement of the pelvis, esp. during sexual intercourse.

pelvis /ˈpɛlvɪs/ *noun.* Pl. **pelves** /ˈpɛlviːz/, **pelvises.** **E17.**
[Latin = basin, laver.]
1 The basin-shaped cavity formed (in most vertebrates) by the fused right and left innominate or hip-bones, consisting of the ilium, ischium, and pubis on each side, together with the sacrum and coccyx; these bones collectively, constituting the pelvic girdle. Also, the part of the abdomen containing the pelvis. **E17.**
2 ANATOMY. The expanded portion at the top of the ureter, into which the kidney tubules open. Also ***pelvis of the kidney***, ***renal pelvis.*** **L17.**
3 ZOOLOGY. The basal part of the calyx of a crinoid. **M19.**

pelycosaur /ˈpɛlɪkəsɔː/ *noun.* **M20.**
[from Greek *peluk-*, *pelux* bowl + **-O-** + **-SAUR.**]
A fossil synapsid reptile of the order Pelycosauria, known from late Carboniferous and Permian remains, and often having some of the vertebrae extended into long bony spines.
■ **pelyco'saurian** *adjective & noun* (*a*) *adjective* of, pertaining to, or characteristic of a pelycosaur; (*b*) *noun* a pelycosaur: **L19.**

pembina /ˈpɛmb(ə)nə/ *noun.* Chiefly *Canad.* **M18.**
[Canad. French *pimbina*: cf. Cree *ni:pimina:na.*]
The bush cranberry, *Viburnum trilobum.*

Pembroke /ˈpɛmbrʊk/ *noun.* **L18.**
[A town in SW Wales.]
In full ***Pembroke table.*** A small table with fixed legs, having a drop-leaf on each side.

pemmican /ˈpɛmɪk(ə)n/ *noun.* **L18.**
[Cree *pimihka:n*, from *pimiy* grease.]
1 A pressed cake consisting of pounded dried meat mixed to a paste with melted fat, berries, etc., orig. made by N. American Indians and later adapted by explorers, travellers, etc. **L18.**
2 *fig.* Extremely condensed thought, writing, etc. **L19.**

pemoline /ˈpɛməliːn/ *noun.* **M20.**
[App. from elems. of the systematic chemical name 2-*imino*-4-*oxo*-5-*phenyloxazolidine.*]
PHARMACOLOGY. A crystalline heterocyclic compound, $C_9H_8N_2O_2$, that is a stimulant of the central nervous

system used to treat fatigue, amphetamine addiction, etc.

pemphigus /ˈpɛmfɪɡəs/ *noun*. L18.
[mod. Latin, from Greek *pemphig-*, *pemphix* bubble.]
MEDICINE. Any of several skin diseases characterized by the formation of blisters.
■ **pemphigoid** *adjective* of the nature of or (esp. of a group of skin disorders) resembling pemphigus E19. **pemphigous** *adjective* of the nature of or affected with pemphigus M19.

pemphis /ˈpɛmfɪs/ *noun*. E20.
[mod. Latin (see below) from Greek = cloud.]
Either of two small trees of the genus *Pemphis*, of the purple loosestrife family; esp. *Pemphis acidula*, of coastal areas in the tropics of Africa and southern Asia.

pemphix /ˈpɛmfɪks/ *noun*. *rare*. M19.
[Greek: see PEMPHIGUS.]
MEDICINE. = PEMPHIGUS.

pempidine /ˈpɛmpɪdiːn/ *noun*. M20.
[from the systematic chemical name, 1,2,2,6,6-*pentamethylpiperidine*.]
PHARMACOLOGY. An alkaline liquid, $C_{10}H_{21}N$, which has been used as a ganglion-blocking agent to treat severe hypertension.

PEN *abbreviation*.
International Association of Poets, Playwrights, Editors, Essayists, and Novelists.

pen /pɛn/ *noun*[1].
[Old English *penn*, of unkn. origin. Cf. PEND *noun*[2].]
1 A small enclosure for cows, sheep, poultry, etc.; a fold, a coop, etc. OE. ▸**b** A number of animals in a pen or sufficient to fill a pen. L19. ▸**c** A division in a sheep-shearing shed. Also, a job as a sheep-shearer. *Austral. & NZ*. L19.
2 *transf.* **a** A device for confining the water in a river or canal, so as to form a head of water; a weir, a dam. L16. ▸**b** Any small place of confinement; *spec.* (*slang*, chiefly *US*) a prison cell (cf. PEN *noun*[5]). E17. ▸**c** A farm, a plantation, a country park. *W. Indies*. M18. ▸**d** A covered dock for a naval vessel, esp. a submarine. E20.

📖 **1** J. T. STORY Across the empty pens, the wet, rusty rails of the cattle market. **b** *Stock & Land (Melbourne)* A pen of 150 . . ewes. **2b** *New York Evening Journal* Prisoners in the pen of the . . jail.

Comb.: **penfold** a pen, an enclosure; **pen-mate** *Austral. & NZ slang* a shearer who catches sheep out of the same pen as another shearer; **pen-pond** a pond formed by a pen or dam.

pen /pɛn/ *noun*[2]. ME.
[Old & mod. French *penne* from Latin *penna* feather, (pl.) pinions, wings, (in late Latin) pen.]
▸ **I** A writing tool.
1 Orig., a feather with its quill sharpened and split to form a nib, used for writing or drawing by being traced over a surface after being dipped in ink. Now, a small instrument consisting of a metal nib fitted into a holder, used for writing or drawing with ink; the nib of such an instrument; *gen.* any instrument for writing or drawing with ink. ME. ▸**b** *transf.* The practice of writing; a particular style of writing; a writer, an author, (now *rare*). LME.
2 An instrument resembling a pen in form or function; *spec.* †(*a*) an engraver's tool; (*b*) a pencil (now *dial.*); (*c*) a light-pen or similar device used to enter commands or data into a computer. LME.

📖 **1** P. AUSTER Quinn did all his writing with a pen, using a typewriter only for final drafts. ***cartridge-pen***, ***drawing-pen***, ***fountain-pen***, ***marker-pen***, ***quill pen***, ***stylographic pen***, etc. **b** B. MONTGOMERY The old adage was probably correct: the pen was mightier than the sword. R. DEACON Aphra Behn was forced to support herself . . not only by the pen, but as a . . secret agent.

▸ **II** A feather, a quill.
3 a A feather of a bird. *obsolete* exc. *dial.* LME. ▸**b** In *pl.* The flight-feathers or pinions of birds regarded as the organs of flight; wings. Now *poet. & arch.* LME. ▸**c** A short rudimentary feather. Chiefly *dial.* E19.
4 *spec.* The quill of a feather. *obsolete* exc. *dial.* LME.
5 *transf.* †**a** A pipe or tube resembling a quill. *rare*. LME–L16. ▸**b** A spoon, orig. one made out of a quill, used for taking snuff. *Scot. & dial.* L18. ▸**c** The rigid petiole or midrib of a leaf. *dial.* E19. ▸**d** = GLADIUS 2. L19.

Phrases: **put pen to paper** begin writing. ***slip of the pen***: see SLIP *noun*[3] 8.
Comb.: **pencraft** *rare* the skill or occupation of writing; **pen-feather** (*a*) a quill-feather of a bird's wing; (*b*) an undeveloped feather; **pen-feathered** *adjective* (*a*) (of a young bird) having undeveloped feathers, not fully fledged; *fig.* immature; (*b*) (of a horse or its coat) rough and bristly; **pen-friend** a friend communicated with only (and usu. regularly) by letter; **pen-gun** (*a*) *Scot.* (*arch.*) a pop-gun made from a quill; (*b*) (**P-**) (US proprietary name for) a small cylindrical gas bomb; **penholder** (*a*) a small cylindrical rod or tube of wood, metal, plastic, etc., to which the nib of a pen may be fixed, forming the handle of the pen; (*b*) a similar tube, often on its own base, into which (part of) a pen may be inserted; (*c*) ***penholder grip***, in table tennis, a grip in which the bat is held between thumb and forefinger; **pen-light** a small electric torch shaped like a fountain-pen; **pen-name** a literary pseudonym; **pen-pal** *colloq.* = ***pen-friend*** above; **pen recorder** an instrument for producing a continuous graphical record of a variable measured quantity by means of a pen; **pen recording**: made by a pen recorder; **pen shell** = ***fan mussel*** s.v. FAN *noun*[1]; **penwiper** (*a*) a usu. small piece of cloth etc. for cleaning a pen by wiping the ink from it; (*b*) *slang* a handkerchief; **penwoman** a woman skilled in using a pen; a female writer; **penwork** work done with a pen, *esp.* the decoration and ornamental lettering of illuminated books and manuscripts.
■ **penful** *noun* (now *rare*) the quantity (of ink) taken up by a pen at one dip M16. **penlike** *adjective* resembling a pen L16.

pen /pɛn/ *noun*[3]. M16.
[Origin unkn.]
A female swan.

pen /pɛn/ *noun*[4]. E18.
[Brittonic.]
A head, a promontory; a hill. Only in place-names.

pen /pɛn/ *noun*[5]. *N. Amer.* L19.
[Abbreviation.]
= PENITENTIARY *noun* 3. Cf. PEN *noun*[1] 2b.

pen /pɛn/ *verb*[1] *trans.* Infl. **-nn-**. Pa. t. & pple **penned** /pɛnd/, †**pent**.
[Old English (in *onpennad* unpenned, opened), from PEN *noun*[1]. Cf. PEND *verb*[1], PENT *adjective*.]
1 Enclose so as to prevent from escaping; shut in, confine. Freq. foll. by *in*, *up*. OE.
2 *spec.* **a** Confine (the water) in a river or canal by means of a pen; dam up. Now *rare*. L16. ▸**b** Confine (cattle, poultry, etc.) in a pen; put into or keep in a pen. E17.

📖 **1** P. H. JOHNSON They had somehow penned me into a corner. **2b** G. CRABBE Drive that stout pig and pen him in thy yard.

pen /pɛn/ *verb*[2]. Infl. **-nn-**. L15.
[from PEN *noun*[2].]
1 *verb trans.* Set down in writing; compose and write; write. L15. ▸**b** *verb intrans.* Write. E20.
†**2** *verb trans.* Write of or about, describe in writing. M16–M17.

📖 **1** A. BRIGGS Edmund Spenser penned the immortal line. P. USTINOV The astonishing document was penned by Alexander, alone at his desk.

Pen. *abbreviation*.
Peninsular.

penacute /piːnəˈkjuːt/ *adjective & noun*. M18.
[from Latin *pene*, *paene* almost + ACUTE after *penultimate*.]
HEBREW & GREEK GRAMMAR. (A word) having an acute accent on the penultimate syllable.

penaeid /pɪˈniːɪd/ *adjective & noun*. Also **peneid**. L19.
[mod. Latin *Penaeidae* (see below), from *Penaeus* genus name: see -ID[3].]
ZOOLOGY. ▸**A** *adjective*. Of, pertaining to, or designating the widespread family Penaeidae of marine decapod crustaceans resembling shrimps. L19.
▸ **B** *noun*. A crustacean of this family. E20.

penal /ˈpiːn(ə)l/ *adjective & noun*. LME.
[Old & mod. French *pénal* or Latin *penalis*, *poen-*, from *poena* PAIN *noun*[1]: see -AL[1].]
▸ **A** *adjective*. **1 a** Having as its object the infliction of punishment, punitive; prescribing the punishment to be inflicted for an offence. LME. ▸**b** Of an act or offence: liable to punishment; punishable, esp. by law. L15. ▸**c** Constituting punishment; inflicted as punishment; (of a sum of money) payable as a penalty or fine. E17. ▸**d** Involving, pertaining to, or characterized by (a) legal punishment. M17. ▸**e** Used or appointed as a place of punishment. M19.
2 Extremely severe, esp. in the way of punishment. Now usu. of taxation etc. LME.

📖 **1a** H. J. STEPHEN Penal provisions intended for the better preservation of game. *Independent* Mandatory life sentences for murder would be abolished . . under changes in penal law. **c penal servitude** *Hist.* (*a*) imprisonment with hard labour; (*b*) transportation. **e** *New York Review of Books* Several conducted tours of the penal colony on Buru Islands. **2** *Spectator* We have had to struggle with . . a penal Bank rate.

▸ **B** *noun*. (A sentence or period of) imprisonment. Also, a school punishment. *slang*. M19.
■ **penally** *adverb* †(*a*) severely, painfully; (*b*) by way of punishment: LME.

penalise *verb* var. of PENALIZE.

penality /pɪˈnalɪti/ *noun*. Now *rare*. L15.
[Old & mod. French *pénalité* from medieval Latin *penalitas*, from Latin *poenalis*: see prec., -ITY.]
†**1** Pain, suffering; = PENALTY 2. L15–E16.
†**2** = PENALTY 1. Only in M16.
3 The character or fact of being penal. M17.

penalize /ˈpiːn(ə)lʌɪz/ *verb trans*. Also **-ise**. M19.
[from PENAL + -IZE.]
1 Subject to a penalty; subject to some comparative disadvantage. M19.
2 Make or declare (an action) penal or legally punishable. L19.

📖 **1** *Kansas City Star* Kansas was penalized five yards for offside.

■ **penaliˈzation** *noun* L19.

penalty /ˈpɛn(ə)lti/ *noun*. L15.
[from unrecorded legal Anglo-Norman from Old & mod. French *pénalité* PENALITY: see -TY[1].]
1 a A punishment imposed for breach of a law, rule, or contract; a loss or disadvantage of some kind, either prescribed by law for some offence, or agreed on in case of breach of contract; *spec.* a fine. L15. ▸**b** *fig.* A disadvantage or loss resulting from an action, quality, etc., esp. of one's own. M17. ▸**c** SPORT. A disadvantage imposed on a competitor or a side, usu. in the form of an advantage given to the opponent(s), as punishment for a breach of rules, esp. a foul; *spec.* (the award of) a free kick at goal. Also, a handicap. L19. ▸**d** BRIDGE. A number of points awarded to opponents on a declarer's failing to make a contract, or to a declarer on successfully making a doubled contract. E20.
†**2** Pain, suffering. *rare*. E16–M17.

📖 **1a** *Headlight* Seven drivers . . escaped without financial penalty, when they were convicted . . by the town's magistrates. R. CHRISTIANSEN An earthquake . . saves two innocent young lovers from the death penalty exacted for adultery. **b** F. WELDON I . . discovered the penalties of success. **c** *Independent* Two minutes from half-time Poole brought down Cross and the referee awarded a penalty.

Phrases: **on penalty of**, **under penalty of** under the threat of.
Attrib. & comb.: With ref. to an advantage given to an opponent as punishment for a foul etc., as ***penalty bully***, ***penalty corner***, ***penalty kick***, ***penalty shot***, ***penalty try***, etc. Special combs., as **penalty area**: in front of the goal on esp. a football pitch, within which offences can incur the award of a penalty; **penalty bench** esp. in ice hockey, a bench in a penalty box for match officials and penalized players; **penalty box** esp. in ice hockey, an area of seating for players temporarily withdrawn from play as a penalty and for match officials; **penalty card** BRIDGE a card exposed illegally and which must be left face up until it can be legally played or picked up; **penalty clause** a clause in a contract stipulating a penalty for failure to fulfil any of its obligations; **penalty double** BRIDGE a double made to increase a score if an opponent's contract is defeated; **penalty goal**: scored as a result of a penalty; **penalty killer** ICE HOCKEY a player responsible for preventing the opposing side from scoring while his or her own team's strength is reduced through penalties; **penalty killing** the activity of a penalty killer; **penalty line**: marking a penalty area on a football pitch; **penalty pass** BRIDGE a pass of one's partner's take-out double, made with the intention of gaining a penalty; **penalty point** a point awarded or deducted as a punishment; *spec.* one imposed for a driving offence, such points being recorded cumulatively on a person's driving licence; **penalty rate** *Austral.* an increased rate of pay for overtime; **penalty spot** SPORT the spot from which a penalty is taken.

penance /ˈpɛnəns/ *noun & verb*. ME.
[Old French from Latin *poenitentia* PENITENCE: see -ANCE.]
▸ **A** *noun*. †**1** Repentance, penitence. ME–L17.
2 In the Roman Catholic and Orthodox Churches, a sacrament including confession of and contrition and absolution for a sin or sins. ME.
3 The performance of a punishment or discipline, either voluntary or imposed by ecclesiastical authority, as an outward expression of repentance for and expiation of a sin; *spec.* (ECCLESIASTICAL) such a punishment or discipline officially imposed by a priest on a penitent after confession, as an integral part of the sacrament of penance. Freq. in ***do penance***, undergo such punishment or discipline. ME. ▸**b** Sufferings after death as a punishment for sins; the sufferings of purgatory. Long *rare* or *obsolete*. LME.
4 *transf.* An unpleasant task or situation, *spec.* one regarded as a punishment for something. ME. ▸†**b** Poor or scanty fare. *rare*. LME–L16.
†**5** Pain, suffering, distress, sorrow. ME–E16
†**6** A punishment. ME–M18.

📖 **3** P. KAVANAGH 'And now for your penance' the priest said. 'Say the litany of the Saints.' B. MOORE I offered up prayers at Benediction in penance for shouting at you. **4** DEFOE We . . made our horses do penance for that little rest.

▸ **B** *verb trans.* Subject to penance; impose or inflict penance on; chastise. L16.

pen and ink /pɛn ən(d) ˈɪŋk/ *noun*, *adjectival*, & *verb phr.* Also (the usual form as adjective) **pen-and-ink**. LME.
[from PEN *noun*[2] + AND *conjunction*[1] + INK *noun*[1].]
▸ **A** *noun phr.* **1** The instruments of writing; writing. LME.
2 A drawing made using pen and ink. M19.
3 A stink. *rhyming slang*. M19.
▸ **B** *adjective*. **1** Occupied in writing; clerkly. L17.
2 Esp. of a drawing: done or made with pen and ink. Also, done or described in writing. E19.
▸ **C** *verb intrans.* **1** Write. *rare*. E19.
2 Stink. *rhyming slang*. L19.

penanggalan /pəˈnaŋɡələn/ *noun*. M19.
[Malay.]
In Malaysian folklore: a female vampire.

Penang lawyer /pɪˈnaŋ ˈlɔːjə/ *noun phr.* E19.
[from *Penang*, an island and State of Malaysia + either LAWYER, app. with ref. to its supposed use as a weapon to settle disputes, or perh. *lawyer* from *loyar*, *-ak* Malayan aboriginal term for the species of licuala used.]
A walking stick made from the stem of a dwarf palm, *Licuala acutifolia*. Also, a Malacca cane.

penannular /pɛˈnanjʊlə/ *adjective.* M19.
[formed as PENE- + ANNULAR.]
Nearly annular; of the form of an almost complete ring.

penates /pɪˈnɑːtiːz, -ˈneɪt-/ *noun pl.* E16.
[Latin *Penates* (pl.), from *penus* provision of food, rel. to *penes* within.]
ROMAN HISTORY. The protective gods of a house, esp. of its storeroom; household gods.
lares and penates: see LAR *noun* 1.

penatin /ˈpɛnətɪn/ *noun.* Now *rare* or *obsolete.* M20.
[from mod. Latin *Penicillium notatum* (now *chrysogenum*) + -IN[1]. Cf. NOTATIN.]
BIOCHEMISTRY. = NOTATIN.

penbard /ˈpɛnbɑːd/ *noun.* L18.
[Welsh *penbardd*, from *pen* head, chief + *bardd* BARD *noun*[1].]
A head or chief bard.

Penbritin /pɛnˈbrɪtɪn, ˈpɛnbrɪtɪn/ *noun.* M20.
[from PEN(ICILLIN + *-brit-* + -IN[1].]
PHARMACOLOGY. (Proprietary name for) the drug ampicillin.

pence /pɛns/ *noun.* ME.
[Syncopated form of *pennies*: see PENNY.]
1 Pl. of PENNY *noun.* Now chiefly following numerals. ME.
2 (*erron.*) *sing.* A penny, esp. in British decimal currency. Usu. in ***one pence***. *colloq.* L20.
1 ***Peter's pence***: see PETER *noun*[1]. ***pounds, shillings, and pence***: see POUND *noun*[1].
■ **penceless** *adjective* (*rare*) lacking money, penniless M17.

pencel /ˈpɛns(ə)l/ *noun.* *obsolete* exc. *Hist.* & HERALDRY. Also **pensil**. ME.
[Anglo-Norman, reduced form of PENNONCEL.]
1 A small pennon or streamer. ME.
†**2** A lady's token worn or carried by a knight. LME–L15.

penchant /ˈpɒ̃ʃɒ̃/ *noun.* L17.
[French, use as noun of pres. pple of *pencher* incline, lean.]
An inclination, a (strong or habitual) liking.

> 🕮 B. MACDONALD Daddy had a penchant for inviting people to stay with us. F. SPALDING She revealed a penchant for drawing.

penchée /pɑ̃ʃe, ˈpɒnʃeɪ/ *adjective.* M20.
[French, fem. of *penché* pa. pple of *pencher* lean, incline.]
BALLET. Esp. of an arabesque: performed while leaning forward. Usu. *postpositive*.

pencil /ˈpɛns(ə)l, -sɪl/ *noun.* ME.
[Old French *pincel* (mod. *pinceau*) from Proto-Gallo-Romance alt. of Latin *penicillus* paintbrush, dim. of *peniculus* brush, dim. of *penis* tail.]
▶ **I 1** A paintbrush made with fine hair, tapered to a point, *esp.* a small one suitable for delicate work. *arch.* ME. ▸**b** The art or skill of painting or writing; a particular style of painting or writing. LME.
2 An instrument for marking, drawing, or writing, consisting of a thin rod of a substance (esp. graphite) which leaves a (usu. delible) mark on a surface, enclosed in a wooden cylinder sharpened to a tapering end from which the substance is applied; a similar instrument consisting of a retractable lead enclosed in a metal or plastic case. L16. ▸**b** A cosmetic in the form of a pencil for easy application. Chiefly with specifying word. L19.

> 🕮 **2** C. BRAYFIELD She snatched up a pencil . . and scribbled on the top of the title page. *attrib.*: *Antiquaries Journal* The artist had made two pencil drawings of him. ***lead pencil, propelling pencil, slate-pencil***, etc. **b** ***eyebrow pencil, lip pencil, styptic pencil***, etc.

▶ **II** Something resembling a pencil.
3 A small tuft of hairs, feathers, etc., springing from or close to a point on a surface. Now only in ZOOLOGY & BOTANY. L16.
4 The penis. *slang.* L16.
5 PHYSICS etc. A group of rays converging to or diverging from a single point. L17.
6 GEOMETRY. A figure formed by a set of straight lines meeting in a point. Also, a set of curves of a given order, passing through a number of points corresponding to that order; a set of planes or curved surfaces passing through one line or curve. M19.
Phrases: ***lead in one's pencil***: see LEAD *noun*[1]. **optic pencil** the double cone of rays that pass from a single point through the lens of the eye and are focused on the retina. ***sharpen one's pencil***: see SHARPEN 1.
Comb.: **pencil-and-paper** *adjective* (esp. of a game) requiring (only) pencil and paper; **pencil beam** a narrow beam of light or other radiation in which the individual rays (or paths of particles) are nearly parallel, esp. one having an approximately circular cross-section; **pencil-box**: for holding pencils, pens, etc.; **pencil-case** a (freq. decorative) container for holding pencils, pens, etc.; **pencil cedar** any of several N. American junipers, esp. *Juniperus virginiana*, the wood of which is used for making pencils; any of several Australian trees resembling these or yielding similar wood, as *Dysoxylum mollissimum* (family Meliaceae); **pencil flower** any of several leguminous plants of the genus *Stylosanthes*; **pencil-line** a line (resembling one) drawn with a pencil; ***pencil-line moustache***, a very thin moustache; **pencil mark** *spec.* a natural mark on an animal, esp. on a dog's toes, resembling that made by a pencil; **pencil moustache** = ***pencil-line moustache*** above; **pencil pusher** *US slang* (*derog.*) a clerk, an office-worker of low status; **pencil-sharpener** an instrument for sharpening a pencil by rotating it against a cutting edge; **pencil skirt** a very narrow straight skirt; **pencil-stone** compact pyrophyllite, used for slate-pencils.

pencil /ˈpɛns(ə)l, -sɪl/ *verb.* Infl. **-ll-**, ***-l-**. L15.
[from the noun.]
1 *verb trans.* **a** Paint with a fine brush (*arch.*); mark (as) with a pencil; *spec.* fill (an area) with thin or delicate pencil lines. Freq. as ***pencilled*** *ppl adjective.* L15. ▸**b** In early use, depict or represent in a painting or esp. in writing. Later, sketch, draw, or outline in pencil. E17. ▸**c** MEDICINE. Treat (a wound etc.) *with* something applied with a fine brush. Now *rare*. E19.
2 *verb trans.* Write or jot down with a pencil. Also foll. by adverb. M18. ▸**b** Enter (a horse's name) in a betting book. RACING *slang.* L19. ▸**c** *fig.* Foll. by *in*: note down or arrange provisionally or tentatively. E20.
3 *verb intrans.* Of light: form into pencil beams. *rare.* L18.

> 🕮 **1a** A. DJOLETO The minister . . pencilled his eyebrows and used women's face powder. **b** D. C. PEATTIE They are like frail tulips delicately pencilled and painted. **2** P. ACKROYD His method of editing manuscripts was to pencil alterations . . in the margin. **c** *Daily Telegraph* The French had pencilled in a launch shot for Skynet. **3** W. SOYINKA The sunlight pencilled thinly along the floor.

■ **pencilling** *noun* (*a*) the action of the verb; (*b*) (a) natural marking on an animal, esp. on a dog's toes, resembling that made by pencil; (*c*) a drawing, sketch, or note made in pencil: E18.

penciller /ˈpɛns(ə)lə, -sɪl-/ *noun.* Also ***-iler**. L18.
[from prec. + -ER[1].]
1 A person who draws; a draughtsman, a writer. Formerly also *spec.*, an artist who painted in part of the design in calico printing. L18.
2 A bookmaker's clerk. RACING *slang.* L19.

pend /pɛnd/ *noun*[1]. *Scot.* LME.
[French *pendre* or Latin *pendere* hang.]
1 An arch; an arched or vaulted roof, passage, or entrance. LME.
2 *fig.* The vault of heaven, the sky. M17.
3 An arched conduit; a covered sewer. E19.

pend /pɛnd/ *noun*[2]. M16.
[Alt. of PEN *noun*[1]. Cf. next.]
†**1** = PEN *noun*[1] 1. Only in M16.
2 Pressure; *fig.* an emergency, a pinch. *dial.* E19.

pend /pɛnd/ *verb*[1] *trans.* LME.
[Alt. of PEN *verb*[1]. Cf. prec.]
†**1** Pen or shut in; confine. Freq. foll. by *up*. LME–L18.
2 Pinch. *dial.* E19.

pend /pɛnd/ *verb*[2] *trans. Scot.* LME.
[from PEND *noun*[1].]
Arch, vault.

pend /pɛnd/ *verb*[3]. L15.
[App. from French *pendre* hang from late Latin from Latin *pendere*, or aphet. from APPEND *verb* or DEPEND.]
1 *verb intrans.* & *trans.* Hang; be attached or attach to. Now *literary.* L15.
2 *verb intrans.* Depend *on*. Now *dial.* M16.
3 *verb intrans.* Hang over, incline, lean. *obsolete* exc. *dial.* L17.

pend /pɛnd/ *verb*[4] *trans. colloq.* M20.
[Back-form. from PENDING.]
Treat as pending; postpone deciding on or attending to.

pendant /ˈpɛnd(ə)nt, *in sense 5b* ˈpɛnənt, *in sense 9 usu. foreign* pɑ̃dɑ̃ (*pl. same*)/ *noun.* Also **-ent**. ME.
[Old & mod. French, use as noun of pres. pple of *pendre* hang, from Latin *pendere*: see -ANT[1].]
▶ **I** Something that hangs or is suspended.
1 ARCHITECTURE. **a** An ornamental projection, *spec.* a boss, carved with a stem so as to hang down esp. from a vault or ceiling or (in a staircase) from the bottom of a projecting newel. ME. ▸**b** In an open timber roof, a supporting wooden post placed against a wall, usu. resting on a corbel and attached to the hammerbeam or the principal rafter. Also ***pendant post***. LME.
†**2 a** In *pl.* The testicles. ME–M17. ▸**b** BOTANY. An anther. M17–L18.
3 A loosely hanging jewel, bead, etc., attached to clothing etc. as an ornament; *spec.* a dangling earring, the jewel etc. in such an earring. Now chiefly, a loosely hanging jewel etc. attached to a chain and forming a necklace. LME. ▸†**b** The ornamented end of a belt or girdle designed to hang down from the buckle. LME–L16.
4 †**a** A plumb-line. *rare.* LME–M16. ▸†**b** A pendulum. Only in M17. ▸**c** A hanging light, *esp.* one designed to hang from the ceiling. M19.
5 NAUTICAL. **a** A short line hanging from the head of a mast, yard-arm, or clew of a sail, having a block or a thimble spliced in the end for attaching tackles. LME. ▸**b** = PENNANT *noun*[1] 1b. L15.
†**6** = PENNON 1. M16–M17.

> 🕮 **3** E. F. BENSON I want to wear the moon as a pendant round my neck. **4c** A. AYCKBOURN She switches out the pendant, depriving Annie of . . her reading light. P. FITZGERALD The pendants of Lalique glass glimmering from the high ceilings.

▶†**II 7** Slope, inclination. ME–M17.
▶ **III 8** A thing by which something is hung or suspended. Now *spec.* the shank and ring of a pocket-watch. L16.
9 a A parallel, match, or companion to a thing, esp. in a picture. L18. ▸**b** An additional or supplementary statement, piece of writing, etc., forming a complement. M19.

> 🕮 **9a** *Independent* Portrait of the Painter Hendrick Martensz Sorgh and its pendant, a portrait of Sorgh's wife. **b** B. MAGEE *Conjectures and Refutations* . . can be seen as a pendant to *The Logic of Scientific Discovery*.

■ **pendanted** *adjective* (ARCHITECTURE) having pendants M17.

pendant *adjective* var. of PENDENT *adjective.*

pendeloque /ˈpɒnd(ə)lɒk, *foreign* pɑ̃dlɔk (*pl. of noun same*)/ *adjective* & *noun.* M19.
[French, from Old French *pendeler* dangle.]
(A gem, esp. a diamond) cut in the shape of a drop.

pendency /ˈpɛnd(ə)nsi/ *noun.* M17.
[from PENDENT *adjective* + -ENCY.]
1 The state or condition of being pending or undecided. M17.
2 Pendent position; droop. *rare.* L18.

pendent *noun* var. of PENDANT *noun.*

pendent /ˈpɛnd(ə)nt/ *adjective.* Also **-ant**. LME.
[formed as PENDANT *noun*; later infl. by Latin *pendent-* pres. ppl stem of *pendere* hang: see -ENT.]
1 Hanging downwards. LME.
2 Overhanging; jutting out. Also, slanting. LME. ▸**b** *fig.* Impending. *rare.* E19.
3 Hanging or floating unsupported in the air or in space; supported above the ground on arches, columns, etc. (now *rare* or *obsolete*). L16.
4 Hanging in the balance, undecided, unsettled, pending. M17.
5 GRAMMAR. Of a construction, esp. a sentence: incomplete; having no verb. M19.

> 🕮 **1** LYTTON The boat gently brushed aside their pendant boughs. *Holiday Which?* Mackintosh's library, with its pendant light fittings. **3** E. BOWEN A full moon pendent over the river.

■ **pendently** *adverb* (*rare*) M17.

pendente lite /pɛnˌdɛnti ˈlʌɪti/ *adverbial phr.* E18.
[Latin, lit. 'with the lawsuit pending'.]
LAW. During the progress of a suit; during litigation.

pendentive /pɛnˈdɛntɪv/ *noun* & *adjective.* E18.
[French *pendentif*, *-ive* (adjective), from Latin *pendent-*, *-ens*: see PENDENT *adjective*, -IVE.]
ARCHITECTURE. ▶**A** *noun.* **1** Each of the concave triangles formed by the intersection of a dome with its rectangular base (usu. formed from four supporting arches). E18.
2 = PENDANT *noun* 1. *rare.* M19.
▶ **B** *adjective.* Of or pertaining to pendentives; of the form of a pendentive; having pendentives. L18.

pendicle /ˈpɛndɪk(ə)l/ *noun.* Chiefly *Scot.* LME.
[medieval Latin *pendiculum*, from Latin *pendere* hang + *-culum* -CULE.]
1 A thing dependent on another, a subsidiary, an appurtenance; *spec.* a piece of land or other property forming a subsidiary part of an estate; *esp.* such a part separately sublet. LME.
2 A hanging ornament, a pendant. Now *rare.* L15.
■ **pendicler** *noun* the holder of a pendicle, a tenant L18.

pending /ˈpɛndɪŋ/ *preposition* & *adjective.* M17.
[Anglicized from Old & mod. French *pendant*: see PENDANT *noun*, -ING[2].]
▶ **A** *preposition.* **1** During, throughout the continuance of. M17.
2 While awaiting, until. M19.

> 🕮 **1** J. L. MOTLEY Pending the peace negotiations, Philip had been called upon to mourn for his wife and father. **2** T. CAPOTE The Kansas Supreme Court having granted them a stay pending the outcome of appeals. R. C. A. WHITE The person may be . . bailed pending further enquiries.

▶ **B** *adjective.* **1 a** Hanging, overhanging. *rare.* M18. ▸**b** Impending, imminent. E19.
2 Remaining undecided, awaiting decision or settlement. L18.

📖 **1b** *Family Practice* The patient admitted to depression and fear of pending death. **2** TOECKEY JONES The disturbing details of a pending divorce case. *Business Traveller* A useful middleman who could help move your file from its pending status to one of action. **pending basket**, **pending tray**: a basket or tray in an office for correspondence etc. awaiting attention.

pendle /ˈpɛnd(ə)l/ *noun. obsolete* exc. *dial.* E16.
[(from French *pendre*) from Latin *pendere* hang: see -LE[1].]
†**1** An altarcloth. Only in E16.
†**2** A hanging ornament, a pendant. M16–E19.
†**3** A natural or artificial overhanging part. M16–E18.
4 A pendulum. M18.

Pendleton /ˈpɛnd(ə)lt(ə)n/ *noun. Chiefly US.* M20.
[*Pendleton* Woolen Mills in Pendleton, Oregon, USA.]
A brightly coloured checked sports shirt.
¶ Proprietary name in the US.

Pendragon /pɛnˈdrag(ə)n/ *noun.* LME.
[Welsh = chief leader in war, from *pen* head, chief + *dragon* dragon, from Latin *dracon-* dragon, the standard of a cohort.]
Hist. (A title for) an ancient British or Welsh prince holding or claiming supreme power, a chief leader or ruler.
■ **Pendragonship** *noun* the rank or position of Pendragon M19.

pendulant /ˈpɛndjʊl(ə)nt/ *adjective.* M17.
[from PENDULUM *noun* + -ANT[1].]
Pendulous, pendent.

pendular /ˈpɛndjʊlə/ *adjective.* L19.
[formed as prec. + -AR[1].]
Esp. of a vibration: of, pertaining to, or resembling that of a pendulum.

pendulate /ˈpɛndjʊleɪt/ *verb intrans.* L17.
[from PENDULUM *noun* + -ATE[3].]
1 Swing like a pendulum, sway to and fro, oscillate. L17.
2 *fig.* Be undecided; vacillate. M19.

pendule /ˈpɛndjuːl/ *noun.* Now *rare.* L16.
[In sense 1 app. formed as PENDULOUS; in senses 2, 3 from French.]
1 A pendulous or hanging object; *spec.* a hanging ornament, a pendant. Now *rare* or *obsolete.* L16.
†**2** = PENDULUM *noun* 1. M17–L18.
3 A (usu. small and ornamental) clock with a pendulum. Now *rare* or *obsolete.* M17.
4 MOUNTAINEERING. = PENDULUM *noun* 3. M20.

pendule /ˈpɛndjuːl/ *verb intrans. & refl.* L19.
[from the noun.]
MOUNTAINEERING. = PENDULUM *verb.*

penduline /ˈpɛndjʊlʌɪn/ *adjective & noun.* E19.
[French, from mod. Latin *pendulinus*, from Latin *pendulus* PENDULOUS: see -INE[1].]
ORNITHOLOGY. ▶**A** *adjective.* (Of a bird's nest) pendulous, hanging; (of a bird) building a hanging nest; *spec.* designating a tit of the family Remizidae, esp. the Eurasian *Remiz pendulinus.* E19.
▶**B** *noun.* A penduline tit. L19.

pendulous /ˈpɛndjʊləs/ *adjective.* E17.
[from Latin *pendulus* pendent (from *pendere* hang down) + -OUS: see -ULOUS.]
1 †**a** Placed so as to project or overhang; overhanging. E17–E18. ▸**b** Hanging down, pendent; *esp.* drooping, sagging. M17. ▸**c** Hanging or floating in the air or in space. Now *rare* or *obsolete.* M17.
2 *fig.* Vacillating, wavering, undecided. Now *rare.* E17. ▸†**b** Dependent, contingent, *on.* M–L17.
3 (Of a thing) suspended so as to swing, oscillating; (of movement) oscillatory. E18.

📖 **1b** F. WELDON She thought . . she would have pendulous breasts and a flabby belly. T. GUNN An Elizabethan ceiling with great pendulous decorations like stalactites. DENNIS POTTER The street light . . had the pendulous droop of a flower.

■ **penduˈlosity** *noun* (*rare*) M17. **pendulously** *adverb* M17. **pendulousness** *noun* M17.

pendulum /ˈpɛndjʊləm/ *noun.* M17.
[mod. Latin from medieval Latin = anything pendent, perh. after Italian *pendolo* use as noun of neut. of Latin *pendulus* PENDULOUS.]
1 A rod, cord, wire, etc., with a weight or bob at or near one end, suspended from a fixed point so as to swing or oscillate freely under the influence of gravity; *esp.* a weighted rod used to regulate and control the movement of the works of a clock by the regularity of its motion. M17.
†**2** A clock controlled by a pendulum. M17–E18.
3 MOUNTAINEERING. A move in which a climber uses his or her momentum to swing to a new position. M20.
Phrases etc.: **compound pendulum** (*a*) a pendulum having a number of weights at fixed distances; (*b*) = **gridiron pendulum** s.v. GRIDIRON *noun* 2b; (*c*) an actual pendulum regarded theoretically (opp. *simple pendulum* (a) below). **conical pendulum** a pendulum the bob of which revolves in a circle, the rod thus describing a cone. ***Foucault pendulum***, ***Foucault's pendulum***: see FOUCAULT. **horizontal pendulum** a horizontal rod pivoted at one end so as to swing freely in a horizontal plane, and weighted at the other end, supported by a thread or wire passing to a fixed point above the pivot; **inverted pendulum** a vertical rod with a heavy weight at its upper end and resting on a bearing at the other, held in position by springs which allow it to oscillate in a vertical plane; **simple pendulum** (*a*) a theoretical or ideal pendulum consisting of a particle having weight but no magnitude, suspended by a weightless inextensible rod, and moving without friction; (*b*) a pendulum consisting simply of a single bob suspended by a cord or wire; (*c*) a pendulum not connected to any mechanism. **spherical pendulum** = ***conical pendulum*** above.
Comb.: **pendulum-ball**, **pendulum-bob** the heavy weight forming the lower end of a pendulum; **pendulum-clock** a clock controlled by a pendulum; **pendulum governor**: having two equal pendulums operating by centrifugal force to lift a weighted sleeve and so gradually close a valve; **pendulum saw** a machine saw that cuts stationary wood as it swings across it like a pendulum; **pendulum-spring** the spring from which the pendulum of a clock is suspended; **pendulum swing** a swinging movement like that of a pendulum; **pendulum-wheel** (*a*) the escape wheel of a clock; (*b*) the balance-wheel of a watch; **pendulum-wire** flat steel wire used for pendulum-springs.

pendulum /ˈpɛndjʊləm/ *verb intrans.* L19.
[from the noun.]
Chiefly MOUNTAINEERING. Swing like a pendulum, esp. in order to move across a rock face.

pene- /ˈpiːni/ *prefix.*
[Latin *paene.*]
Nearly, almost.
■ **penecontempoˈraneous** *adjective* (GEOLOGY) almost contemporaneous; *esp.* occurring immediately after deposition: E20. **penecontemporaˈneity** *noun* (GEOLOGY) the condition of being penecontemporaneous M20. **penecontempoˈraneously** *adverb* (GEOLOGY) almost contemporaneously, immediately after deposition M20.

penectomy /pɛˈnɛktəmi/ *noun.* L20.
[from PEN(IS *noun* + -ECTOMY.]
Surgical amputation of the penis.

peneid *adjective & noun* var. of PENAEID.

Penelope /pəˈnɛləpi/ *noun.* L16.
[Greek *Pēnelopē*, wife of Odysseus in Greek mythol., who, during his absence, put off her suitors by saying she would marry only when her weaving was finished, which she then unravelled each night.]
1 A faithful wife. L16.
2 ORNITHOLOGY. A guan of the genus *Penelope.* *rare.* M19.
3 In full ***Penelope canvas***. A double-thread canvas used for tapestry work. L19.
■ **Peneloˈpean** *adjective* of or resembling the time-gaining tactics of Penelope M19. **Penelopize** *verb intrans.* play for time like Penelope M19.

peneplain /ˈpiːnɪpleɪn/ *noun & verb.* Also **-plane**. L19.
[from PENE- + PLAIN *noun*[1].]
PHYSICAL GEOGRAPHY. ▶**A** *noun.* A low, nearly featureless tract of land of undulating relief, *esp.* one formed by long subaerial erosion of land undisturbed by crustal movement, representing the penultimate stage in the cycle of erosion in a humid climate; a former surface of this kind subsequently uplifted, dissected, buried, etc. L19.
▶**B** *verb trans.* Erode to a peneplain. E20.
■ **peneplanation** /-pləˈneɪʃ(ə)n/ *noun* erosion to a peneplain L19.

penes *noun* pl. of PENIS.

Penest /pɪˈnɛst/ *noun.* M19.
[Greek *penestēs.*]
GREEK HISTORY. A Thessalian serf.

penetrability /ˌpɛnɪtrəˈbɪlɪti/ *noun.* E17.
[medieval Latin *penetrabilitas*, from Latin *penetrabilis*: see next, -ITY.]
1 Capacity of penetrating. E17.
2 Ability to be penetrated; *spec.* that (supposed) property of matter by which two bodies can occupy the same space at the same time. M17.

penetrable /ˈpɛnɪtrəb(ə)l/ *adjective.* LME.
[Old & mod. French *pénétrable* from Latin *penetrabilis*, from *penetrare*: see PENETRATE, -ABLE.]
†**1** Capable of penetrating; penetrative, penetrating. LME–M17.
2 Able to be penetrated or pierced; into or through which access may be gained. M16.
3 *fig.* Able to be penetrated by intellectual or moral reasoning; susceptible to impressions or ideas. L16.

📖 **1** HENRY MORE A Substance . . most perfectly penetrable, which entirely passeth through every thing. **2** M. R. D. FOOT The five great German submarine bases . . were too carefully guarded to be penetrable. **3** SHAKES. *Rich. III* I am not made of stones, But penetrable to your kind entreaties.

penetral /ˈpɛnɪtr(ə)l/ *noun.* Now *rare.* Also **-trale** /-trɑːl/ L16.
[Latin *penetral(e)* (usu. in pl. *penetralia*: see next), from *penetrālis* interior, innermost, from stem of *penetrare* PENETRATE.]
sing. & in *pl.* The innermost parts of a building etc.; the penetralia.

penetralia /pɛnɪˈtreɪlɪə/ *noun pl.* M17.
[Latin *penetralia*: see prec.]
The innermost parts of a building etc.; *esp.* the sanctuary or innermost shrine of a temple; *fig.* secret parts, mysteries.
■ Also **penetralium** *noun* (*rare*) E19.

penetrameter /pɛnɪˈtramɪtə/ *noun.* E20.
[from PENETRA(TION + -METER.]
An instrument for determining the wavelength, intensity, or total received dose of X-rays by measuring photographically their transmission through layers of metal of known thickness.

penetrance /ˈpɛnɪtr(ə)ns/ *noun.* M17.
[In sense 1 from next + -ANCE: in sense 2 from German *Penetranz.*]
†**1** The action of penetrating; penetration. *rare.* Only in M17.
2 GENETICS. The extent to which a particular gene or set of genes is expressed in the phenotypes of individuals possessing it, measured by the proportion of carriers of the gene showing the characteristic phenotype. M20.

penetrant /ˈpɛnɪtr(ə)nt/ *adjective & noun.* M16.
[Latin *penetrant-* pres. ppl stem of *penetrare*: see next, -ANT[1].]
▶**A** *adjective.* **1** Having the property of penetrating or piercing. *arch.* M16.
2 *fig.* Having or showing mental penetration or insight; acute. *arch.* L16.
3 GENETICS. Producing in the phenotype the characteristic effect of a gene or combination of genes. M20.
▶**B** *noun.* †**1** A person of penetration or insight. *rare.* Only in M18.
2 A coloured or fluorescent liquid used to penetrate cracks, pores, and other surface defects to facilitate their detection. M20.

penetrate /ˈpɛnɪtreɪt/ *verb.* M16.
[Latin *penetrat-* pa. ppl stem of *penetrare* place or enter within, from *penitus* inner, inmost, rel. to *penes* within, in the power of. Cf. Old & mod. French *pénétrer.*]
1 *verb trans.* Get into or through, gain entrance or access into, esp. with force, effort, or difficulty; pierce; *spec.* see through (darkness, fog, etc.). M16. ▸**b** Of a male: insert the penis into the vagina or anus of (a sexual partner). (*rare* (Shakes.) before M20.) E17. ▸**c** Permeate; cause to be permeated, imbue *with.* L17. ▸**d** Infiltrate (an organization) as a spy. M20.
2 *verb intrans.* Get in or through, gain entrance or access, esp. with force, effort, or difficulty. Usu. foll. by *into, through, to.* M16.
3 *verb trans. fig.* Get or have insight into; see mentally into or through; attain knowledge of; discern. M16. ▸**b** *verb intrans.* Gain insight or knowledge (*into*). Also, be understood or fully realized. M16.
4 *verb trans. fig.* Affect deeply; touch emotionally. *arch.* L16.

📖 **1** H. KELLER The afternoon sun penetrated the mass of honeysuckle. J. WYNDHAM Her mouth moved, but not a word penetrated the clatter of the engine. P. THEROUX The ground was hardened clay: they needed a pneumatic drill to penetrate it. S. HASTINGS The underfloor heating . . never penetrated the upper floors. **c** J. C. POWYS The soul of this man . . penetrated his . . flesh and blood. G. ORWELL Mists . . seemed to penetrate your bones. **d** S. ROSENBERG The Young Communist League were instructed to penetrate the socialist ranks. **2** E. M. FORSTER She penetrated to the inner depths. J. GALSWORTHY The warm air . . penetrated into the very heart of the house. R. C. HUTCHINSON The east wind penetrated through the heaviest clothing. J. MARK No sound could possibly have penetrated. **3** J. ROSENBERG He wished to penetrate the problem of man's inner life. F. HERBERT We penetrated the disguise quite easily. A. N. WILSON Happiness . . is so much harder to penetrate than sorrow. **b** E. M. FORSTER It is impossible to penetrate into the minds of elderly people. G. MOFFAT The gates were open . . it wasn't till we came back hours later that it really penetrated.

■ **penetrator** *noun* a person who or device which penetrates E19.

penetrating /ˈpɛnɪtreɪtɪŋ/ *ppl adjective.* L16.
[from prec. + -ING[2].]
1 That gets or forces a way into or through something; that permeates something; *esp.* (of a smell) sharp, pungent, (of a sound) shrill, piercing, easily heard through or above other sounds. L16.
2 *fig.* Deeply affecting; emotionally touching. *arch.* M17.
3 *fig.* Having or showing insight; acute, discerning. L17.

📖 **1** W. ABISH One cannot escape the penetrating smell of fresh paint. RACHEL ANDERSON There was a mean penetrating wind blowing from the north east. A. LIVELY She . . put two fingers in her mouth and let forth a penetrating whistle. **3** P. AUSTER He asks very penetrating questions. J. BAYLEY The story is remarkable for its . . penetrating understanding of . . the young woman's mind.

■ **penetratingly** *adverb* L17. **penetratingness** *noun* M17.

penetration /pɛnɪˈtreɪʃ(ə)n/ *noun.* LME.
[Latin *penetratio(n-)*, formed as PENETRATE: see -ATION.]
1 The action or an act of penetrating or getting into or through something; the ability to do this; MILITARY an

attack, an incursion; the action or an act of permeating. Formerly also, a puncture, a wound. LME. ▸**b** The insertion by a male of his penis into the vagina or anus of a sexual partner. E17. ▸**c** The supposed occupation of the same space by two bodies at the same time. M17. ▸**d** The infiltration of an organization by spies. M20. ▸**e** *COMMERCE.* The extent to which a product is known or bought by consumers. M20.

2 *fig.* The action or capacity of penetrating something with the mind; the ability to see mentally into or through a thing; insight, discernment. E17.

3 a Orig., the power of a telescope. Now usu., depth of focus. L18. ▸**b** *GUNNERY.* The depth to which a bullet or other projectile will penetrate a material. E19.

1 A. MOOREHEAD This wilderness protected Australia from penetration by the peoples of SE Asia. **d** J. HIGGINS The extraordinarily successful penetration by the KGB of the French intelligence service. **e** *Marxism Today* Video recorders will still attain a 40% penetration of UK households in the course of 1985.

Comb.: **penetration agent** a spy sent to penetrate an enemy organization; **penetration aid** an object released from a missile as a decoy to draw off any attacking missiles; **penetration twin** *CRYSTALLOGRAPHY* a twin crystal that presents the appearance of two interpenetrating crystals; **penetration twinning** the formation of penetration twins.

penetrative /ˈpɛnɪtrətɪv, -treɪt-/ *adjective.* LME.
[medieval Latin *penetrativus*, formed as PENETRATE: see -IVE.]
1 Having the quality of penetrating or getting into or through something; *esp.* (of a smell or sound) penetrating. LME.
2 *fig.* That affects emotionally. *rare.* E17.
3 *fig.* = PENETRATING *ppl adjective* 3. E18.
■ **penetratively** *adverb* L17. **penetrativeness** *noun* M17.

penetrometer /pɛnɪˈtrɒmɪtə/ *noun.* E20.
[from PENETR(ATION + -OMETER.]
An instrument for determining the consistency or hardness of a substance (as soil or snow) by measuring the depth or rate of penetration of a rod or needle driven by a known force.

penghulu /pɒŋˈhuːluː/ *noun.* E19.
[Malay.]
In Malaysia and Indonesia, a headman, a chief.

pengö /ˈpɛŋgə, -gəʊ/ *noun.* Pl. same, **-ös**. Also **-go** (pl. **-go(e)s**). E20.
[Hungarian, lit. 'ringing'.]
The chief monetary unit of Hungary from 1927 to 1946, when it was replaced by the forint.

penguin /ˈpɛŋgwɪn/ *noun.* L16.
[Origin uncertain: doubtfully from Welsh *pen* head + *gwyn* white.]
†**1** The great auk. L16–L18.
2 Any member of the family Spheniscidae of gregarious diving birds of coasts around the southern oceans, having an upright stance, a long bill, mainly black and white plumage, and wings reduced to scaly flippers or paddles for swimming under water. L16.
3 A machine like an aeroplane but incapable of flight, used in the early stages of an airman's training. Also, a non-flying member of an air force. *Air Force slang.* E20.
4 (**P-**.) (Proprietary name for) any of a range of paperback books published under the name 'Penguin'. M20.
2 *emperor penguin, fairy penguin, gentoo penguin, jackass penguin, king penguin, rockhopper penguin*, etc.
Comb.: **penguin suit** a dinner jacket.
■ **penguinery** *noun* a colony of penguins; a place where penguins congregate and breed: M19.

-penia /ˈpiːnɪə/ *suffix.*
[Greek *penia* poverty, need.]
MEDICINE. Deficiency, esp. of a constituent of the blood, as ***granulocytopenia***, ***leucopenia***, ***lymphopenia***.

penial /ˈpiːnɪəl/ *adjective.* L19.
[from PENIS + -AL[1].]
= PENILE *adjective.*

†**penible** *adjective.* LME.
[Old & mod. French *pénible*, from *peine*: see PAIN *noun*[1], -IBLE.]
1 Painstaking, careful. LME–L15.
2 Causing or involving pain or trouble. (*rare* after M17.) LME–L19.

penicillamine /pɛnɪˈsɪləmiːn/ *noun.* M20.
[from PENICILLIN + AMINE.]
CHEMISTRY & PHARMACOLOGY. An amino acid, $(CH_3)_2C(SH)CH(NH_2)COOH$, produced by the hydrolysis of penicillins and used as a pharmacological chelating agent.

penicillanic /ˌpɛnɪsɪˈlanɪk/ *adjective.* M20.
[from PENICILL(IN + *-an-* + -IC.]
CHEMISTRY. ***penicillanic acid***, a heterocyclic acid, $C_8H_{11}NO_3S$, whose molecular structure is the nucleus of the penicillins.

penicillate /ˈpɛnɪsɪlət/ *adjective.* E19.
[from PENICILLUS + -ATE[2].]
1 *ZOOLOGY & BOTANY.* Bearing or forming a penicillus or penicilli. E19.
2 Marked with streaks as of a pencil or brush. *rare.* L19.
■ **penicillately** *adverb* L19. **peniciˈllation** *noun* (a) penicillate structure or form M19. **peniˈcilliform** *adjective* (*ANATOMY, ZOOLOGY, & BOTANY*) of the form of or resembling a brush or pencil E19.

penicilli *noun* pl. of PENICILLUS.

penicillia *noun* pl. of PENICILLIUM.

penicillin /pɛnɪˈsɪlɪn/ *noun.* E20.
[from PENICILLIUM + -IN[1].]
1 Orig., an antibiotic agent obtained from cultures of the mould *Penicillium chrysogenum*. Now, any of a group of antibiotics that are amino-substituted derivatives of 6-aminopenicillanic acid, produced naturally by certain moulds of the genera *Penicillium* and *Aspergillus* or prepared synthetically, and active against many kinds of bacteria. Also with distinguishing letter, as ***penicillin G***. E20.
†**2** In full ***penicillin A***, ***penicillin B***. = NOTATIN. Only in M20.
Comb.: **penicillin unit** a unit of penicillin having the same antibiotic activity as a certain quantity (almost exactly 0.6 microgram) of a standard preparation of the sodium salt of benzylpenicillin (penicillin G).
■ **penicillinase** *noun* any of several bacterial enzymes (lactamases) which can inactivate penicillins M20.

penicillium /pɛnɪˈsɪlɪəm/ *noun.* Pl. **-ia** /-ɪə/. M19.
[mod. Latin, formed as PENICILLUS + -IUM, from the brushlike fruiting bodies.]
1 *MICROBIOLOGY.* Any ascomycetous fungus of the genus *Penicillium*, including several moulds common on foodstuffs. Chiefly as mod. Latin genus name. M19.
2 = PENICILLUS. *rare.* L19.

penicilloic /ˌpɛnɪsɪˈləʊɪk/ *adjective.* M20.
[from PENICILLIN + -OIC.]
BIOCHEMISTRY. ***penicilloic acid***, any of the acids produced when a penicillin is hydrolysed (as by a penicillinase) and the C–N bond of the lactam ring broken.
■ **peniˈcilloate** *noun* a salt or ester of a penicilloic acid M20.

penicillus /pɛnɪˈsɪləs/ *noun.* Pl. **-lli** /-lʌɪ/. E19.
[mod. Latin from Latin: see PENCIL *noun*.]
ANATOMY, ZOOLOGY, & BOTANY. A brushlike bundle of slightly divergent hairs or other structures; a tuft of minute branching vessels.

penide /ˈpɛnɪd/ *noun.* Now *rare* or *obsolete.* LME.
[Old French *penide*, *-ite* from medieval Latin *penidium*, usu. in pl. *-ia*, from medieval Greek *penidion*. Cf. PENNET.]
A piece or stick of barley sugar, or other boiled sweet, esp. as a remedy for a cold. Usu. in *pl.*

†**penile** *noun.* Also **-isle**. E17–E18.
[from Latin *paene* almost + obsolete form of ISLE *noun*[1].]
= PENINSULA.

penile /ˈpiːnʌɪl/ *adjective.* M19.
[mod. Latin *penilis*, formed as PENIS + -ILE.]
Of or pertaining to the penis.

penillion *noun pl.* see PENNILL.

peninsula /pɪˈnɪnsjʊlə/ *noun.* M16.
[Latin *paeninsula*, formed as PENE- + *insula* island.]
A piece of land that is almost an island, being nearly surrounded by water; a piece of land projecting into the sea, a lake, etc., so that the greater part of its boundary is coastline.
Malay peninsula: see MALAY *adjective* 1. **the Peninsula** Spain and Portugal.

peninsular /pɪˈnɪnsjʊlə/ *adjective & noun.* E17.
[from prec. + -AR[1], after French *péninsulaire*.]
▸ **A** *adjective.* **1** Of, pertaining to, or of the nature of a peninsula. E17.
2 *spec.* (**P-**.) Of or pertaining to the peninsula of Spain and Portugal, or esp. the war carried on there between 1808 and 1814. E19.
▸ **B** *noun.* An inhabitant of a peninsula. L19.
■ **peninsuˈlarity** *noun* (*rare*) (*a*) the narrow-minded character or outlook supposed to result from living in a peninsula and having limited contact with other peoples etc.; (*b*) the condition of being a peninsula: L19.

peninsulate /pɪˈnɪnsjʊleɪt/ *verb trans.* M16.
[from PENINSULA + -ATE[3].]
Esp. of a river: make (a piece of land) into a peninsula.
■ **peninsuˈlation** *noun* E20.

penis /ˈpiːnɪs/ *noun.* Pl. **penises**, **penes** /ˈpiːniːz/. L17.
[Latin = tail, penis.]
ANATOMY & ZOOLOGY. The male genital organ which carries the duct for the emission of sperm, in mammals consisting largely of erectile tissue and serving also for the elimination of urine.
Comb.: **penis-bone** = *os penis* s.v. OS *noun*[1]; **penis-envy** *PSYCHOLOGY* envy of the male's possession of a penis, postulated by Freud to account for various behavioural characteristics or problems in women.

†**penisle** *noun* var. of PENILE *noun*.

penistone /ˈpɛnɪstən/ *noun & adjective.* M16.
[A town in South Yorkshire.]
†**1** (Made of) a kind of coarse woollen cloth formerly used for garments, linings, etc. M16–M19.
2 (Designating) sandstone flags quarried around Penistone, used for paving-stones. L17.

penitence /ˈpɛnɪt(ə)ns/ *noun.* ME.
[Old & mod. French *pénitence* from Latin *paenitentia*, *poen-*, from *paenitens*, *-tent-*: see PENITENT, -ENCE.]
1 = PENANCE *noun* 3. Now *rare.* ME.
2 The fact or state of being penitent; contrition for sin committed, with desire and intention of amendment; repentance. L15.
■ **penitency** *noun* (now *rare*) (*a*) = PENITENCE 2; †(*b*) *rare* = PENITENCE 1: L15.

penitent /ˈpɛnɪt(ə)nt/ *adjective & noun.* ME.
[Old & mod. French *pénitent* from Latin *paenitent-* pres. ppl stem of *paenitere* cause want or discontent to, make sorry: see -ENT.]
▸ **A** *adjective.* **1** That repents, with serious desire and intention to amend the sin or wrongdoing; repentant, contrite. ME. ▸**b** Expressive of repentance. E18.
2 Undergoing penance. Now *rare.* LME.
†**3** Grieved, vexed; relenting. *rare.* M16–E17.

1 J. H. NEWMAN A penitent prodigal who has squandered God's gifts. **b** DEFOE She wrote me several penitent letters, acknowledging her crime, and begging me to forgive her.

▸ **B** *noun.* **1** A person who repents; a repentant sinner. LME.
2 A person performing (ecclesiastical) penance; a person under the direction of a confessor. LME.
3 In *pl.* The members of any of various Roman Catholic congregations or orders, associated for mutual discipline, the giving of religious aid to criminals, etc. L15.
4 [from the resemblance to a white-cowled penitent figure.] A spike or pinnacle of compact snow or ice, freq. occurring in large groups and resulting from differential ablation of a snow or ice field by the sun. Freq. *attrib.* E20.

1 V. S. REID Crying is for penitents who can wash the page clean and start over again. **2** S. O'FAOLÁIN The canon, barely glancing at his two waiting penitents, entered the confessional.

Comb.: **penitent-form** a form or bench for penitents.
■ **penitently** *adverb* M16. **penitentness** *noun* (*rare*) E18.

penitential /pɛnɪˈtɛnʃ(ə)l/ *adjective & noun.* LME.
[Old & mod. French *pénitencial* (also mod. *-ciel*) from late Latin *paenitentialis*, from Latin *paenitentia*: see PENITENCE, -IAL.]
▸ **A** *adjective.* **1** Pertaining to, expressive of, or constituting ecclesiastical penance; of the nature of a penance. LME.
2 Of, pertaining to, or expressive of penitence or repentance. L16.

1 W. COWPER My penitential stripes, my streaming blood, Have purchas'd Heaven **2 penitential psalms** seven psalms (6, 32 (31 in the Vulgate), 38 (37), 51 (50), 102 (101), 130 (129), and 143 (142)) expressing penitence.

▸ **B** *noun.* **1** A book containing in codified form the canons of the Church on the eliciting of confessions and the imposition of appropriate penances. LME.
2 A person performing or undergoing penance, a penitent. *rare.* E17.
3 In *pl.* = ***penitential psalms*** above. M17.
4 In *pl.* The signs, utterances, or behaviour of a penitent; expressions of penitence. Now *rare* or *obsolete.* E18.
■ **penitentially** *adverb* M17.

penitentiary /pɛnɪˈtɛnʃ(ə)ri/ *noun & adjective.* LME.
[medieval Latin *paenitentiarius*, from *paenitentia*: see PENITENCE, -ARY[1].]
▸ **A** *noun.* **I** †**1** A place of penitential discipline or punishment for ecclesiastical offences. LME–M17.
2 *Hist.* A refuge for prostitutes resolving to change their way of life. E19.
3 A reformatory prison; *spec.* a State or federal prison. *N. Amer.* E19.
▸ **II 4 a** A priest appointed to administer penance, *spec.* one vested with power to deal with extraordinary cases. LME. ▸**b** An office or congregation in the papal court, forming a tribunal for deciding on questions relating to penance, dispensations, etc. M17.
†**5** = PENITENT *noun* 1, 2. M16–M17.
†**6** A member of a religious order encouraging personal discipline etc. Cf. PENITENT *noun* 3. M–L17.
Phrases: **grand penitentiary** a cardinal who presides over the penitentiary of the papal court and has the granting of absolution in cases reserved for the papal authority.
▸ **B** *adjective.* **1** Of or pertaining to penance; administering or undergoing penance. L16.
2 Expressive of penitence; repentant. *rare.* L18.
3 Intended for or pertaining to the penal and reformatory treatment of criminals. L18.
4 Of an offence: punishable by imprisonment in a penitentiary. *US.* M19.
■ †**penitentiaryship** *noun* the office or position of an ecclesiastical penitentiary or confessor L16–E18.

penk *noun* see PINK *noun*[2].

penknife /ˈpɛnnʌɪf/ *noun.* Pl. **-knives** /-nʌɪvz/. LME.
[from PEN *noun*² + KNIFE *noun*.]
A small pocket knife, orig. used for making and mending quill pens, now made with one or more blades (also occas. other tools) which fold inside the handle.

penman /ˈpɛnmən/ *noun*¹. Pl. **-men**. L16.
[from PEN *noun*² + MAN *noun*.]
1 A person who writes or uses a pen with a specified degree of skill. L16.
2 A writer, an author. L16.
3 A man who is employed to write or copy documents etc.; a clerk, a secretary, a notary. Now *rare*. L16. ▸**b** A forger. *Criminals' slang*. M19.
■ **penmanship** *noun* (*a*) the art of using a pen, calligraphy; (*b*) the action of composing a document etc: L17.

Penman /ˈpɛnmən/ *noun*². M20.
[H. L. *Penman*, 20th-cent. Brit. agriculturist.]
Used *attrib.* and in *possess.* to designate a formula for calculating the rate of evaporation of water from an area esp. of agricultural land under given conditions.

penmen *noun* pl. of PENMAN *noun*¹.

Penn. *abbreviation.* Also **Penna.**
Pennsylvania.

†**pennage** *noun. rare.* E17–M19.
[French, from *penne* plume + -AGE.]
Plumage.

pennant /ˈpɛnənt/ *noun*¹. LME.
[Blend of PENNON and PENDANT *noun*.]
1 a = PENNON 1. (*rare* before E19.) LME. ▸**b** *NAUTICAL.* A sharply tapering flag; *spec.* one flown at the masthead of a ship in commission. Cf. earlier PENDANT *noun* 5b. L17. ▸**c** *SPORT.* A flag symbolizing a league championship or identifying a team; the championship itself. *N. Amer.* L19.
2 *NAUTICAL.* = PENDANT *noun* 5a. E17.

📖 **1a** R. RENDELL The pennants on the turrets streamed in the wind, taut and fluttering. **b** R. TRAVERS *Swanhilda* . . ran up her signal flag, a pennant which gave her number and port of registration. **broad pennant** a short swallow-tailed pennant marking a commodore's ship in a squadron. **c** G. ADAIR A Bob Dylan poster and a college football team pennant were pinned to the walls. *attrib.*: *New York Times* The Red Sox . . a pennant contender, did not lose more than 4 games in . . the entire season.

■ **pennanted** *adjective* having or decorated with a pennant or pennants M19.

pennant /ˈpɛnənt, *foreign* -ant/ *noun*². M18.
[Welsh, from *pen* head + *nant* brook, stream, valley; also a common Welsh place-name.]
More fully ***pennant grit***. Any of a series of grit and sandstone strata lying between the upper and lower coal measures in the S. Wales and Bristol Coalfields, used for paving etc. Also ***pennant flag***, ***pennant rock***, ***pennant stone***, etc.

pennate /ˈpɛnət/ *adjective.* M19.
[Latin *pennatus* winged, feathered, from *penna* feather: see -ATE².]
Winged, wing-shaped, feather-shaped; penniform; *BOTANY* (of a diatom) bilaterally symmetrical.

pennated /ˈpɛneɪtɪd/ *adjective.* Now *rare* or *obsolete*. E18.
[formed as prec. + -ED².]
†**1** *BOTANY.* Pinnate. E18–E19.
2 *ZOOLOGY.* Having slender lateral ribs like the veins of a feather. Also, penniform. E19.

pennatulacean /pɛˌnatjʊˈleɪʃ(ə)n, -ʃɪən/ *adjective & noun.* L19.
[mod. Latin *Pennatulacea* noun pl. (see below), from *Pennatula* genus name, formed as PENNATE + *-ula* dim. ending: see -ACEAN.]
ZOOLOGY. ▶**A** *adjective.* Of or pertaining to the order Pennatulacea of alcyonarian coelenterates, which have polyps arranged in rows along an axial skeletal rod set in the seabed. L19.
▶**B** *noun.* A member of this order; a sea-pen. L19.
■ **peˈnnatulid** *noun* a pennatulacean; now usu. *spec.*, one of the family Pennatulidae (freq. *attrib.*): L19.

penne /ˈpɛneɪ/ *noun pl.* M20.
[Italian, pl. of *penna* feather, quill, pen.]
Pasta in the form of short wide tubes, cut diagonally at the ends like an old-fashioned quill pen; an Italian dish consisting of this, served with a sauce.

penned /pɛnd/ *adjective.* LME.
[from PEN *noun*² + -ED².]
Having wing-feathers or quills. Now chiefly (esp. of a hawk) having feathers of a specified type.

penner /ˈpɛnə/ *noun*¹. *obsolete* exc. *dial.* LME.
[medieval Latin *pennarium*, from Latin *penna* PEN *noun*²: see -ER².]
A case of metal, leather, etc., for holding pens. Later also, a writing-case.

penner /ˈpɛnə/ *noun*². M16.
[from PEN *verb*² + -ER¹.]
The writer *of* a document, statement, etc.

penner /ˈpɛnə/ *noun*³. L19.
[from PEN *verb*¹ + -ER¹.]
1 ***penner-up***, a person who pens sheep ready to be sheared. *Austral. & NZ.* L19.
2 A person who pens cattle. E20.

pennet /ˈpɛnɪt/ *noun. obsolete* exc. *dial.* ME.
[Old French *penite*: see PENIDE.]
= PENIDE.

penni /ˈpɛni/ *noun.* Pl. **-iä** /-ɪɑː/, same. L19.
[Finnish.]
A former monetary unit of Finland, equal to one-hundredth of a markka.

penni- /ˈpɛni/ *combining form* of Latin *penna* feather: see -I-.
■ **peˈnniferous** *adjective* (*rare*) feathered E19. **penniform** *adjective* (*ANATOMY & BIOLOGY*) resembling a feather; *esp.* (of a muscle) having oblique fibres on either side of a central axis: E18. **penninerved** *adjective* (*BOTANY*) pinnately nerved L19. **penniveined** *adjective* (*BOTANY*) = PENNINERVED M19.

penniä *noun pl.* see PENNI.

pennies *noun* pl. of PENNY *noun*.

penniless /ˈpɛnɪlɪs/ *adjective.* ME.
[from PENNY + -LESS.]
Having no money; poor, destitute.
■ **pennilessly** *adverb* L19. **pennilessness** *noun* L19.

pennill /ˈpɛnɪl/ *noun.* Pl. **pen(n)illion** /pɛˈnɪ(θ)lɪən/. L18.
[Welsh = verse, stanza, from *pen* head.]
An improvised stanza sung to the accompaniment of a harp at an eisteddfod etc. Usu. in *pl.*

pennine /ˈpɛnʌɪn/ *noun.* M19.
[from the *Pennine* Alps: see -INE⁵.]
MINERALOGY. = PENNINITE.

penninite /ˈpɛnɪnʌɪt/ *noun.* M19.
[from PENNINE + -ITE¹.]
MINERALOGY. A green or greenish-blue variety of chlorite, forming rhombohedral crystals.

pennon /ˈpɛnən/ *noun.* LME.
[Old & mod. French *pen(n)on* from Proto-Romance deriv. of Latin *penna* PEN *noun*².]
1 A long narrow triangular or swallow-tailed flag, usu. attached to the head of a lance, formerly the ensign of a knight under the rank of banneret, now the military ensign of lancer regiments. LME. ▸**b** *fig.* A thing shaped like a pennon. E17.
2 *gen.* Any flag or banner. LME.
†**3** A knight-bachelor; an ensign-bearer. LME–M17.
4 *NAUTICAL.* = PENNANT *noun*¹ 1b. E17.
5 A wing, a pinion. *poet.* M17.
■ **pennoned** *adjective* having or bearing a pennon M19.

pennoncel /ˈpɛnənsɛl/ *noun. obsolete* exc. *Hist.* LME.
[Old French *penoncel* (in medieval Latin *penuncellus*) dim. of *penon* PENNON: see -EL².]
A small pennon.

penn'orth *noun & adverb* var. of PENNYWORTH.

Pennsylvania /pɛnsɪlˈveɪnɪə/ *noun.* M18.
[from Admiral Sir William *Penn* (1621–70), founder of the State (see below) + SYLVAN + -IA¹.]
Used *attrib.* to designate a native or inhabitant of, or things originating in or associated with, the mid-Atlantic State of Pennsylvania, USA.
Comb.: **Pennsylvania Dutch**, **Pennsylvania German** *nouns & adjectives* (*a*) *nouns* (*pl.*) the descendants of the German and Swiss settlers of Pennsylvania in the 17th and 18th cents.; (*sing.*) the High German dialect of these settlers or their descendants; (*b*) *adjectives* of or pertaining to these people or their dialect.

Pennsylvanian /pɛnsɪlˈveɪnɪən/ *noun & adjective.* L17.
[from prec. + -AN.]
▶**A** *noun.* **1** A native or inhabitant of Pennsylvania. L17.
2 *GEOLOGY.* The Pennsylvanian period; the system of rocks dating from this time. E20.
▶**B** *adjective.* **1** Of, pertaining to, or characteristic of Pennsylvania or its people. L17.
2 *GEOLOGY.* Designating or pertaining to the period of the Palaeozoic era in N. America following the Mississippian and preceding the Permian, and corresponding to the Upper Carboniferous in Europe. L19.

penny /ˈpɛni/ *noun & adjective.*
[Old English *peniġ*, *pæniġ*, earlier *pen(n)ing*, *pending* = Old Frisian *penning*, *panning*, Old Saxon (Dutch) *penning*, Old High German *pfenning* (German *Pfennig*), Old Norse *penningr*, from Germanic.]
▶**A** *noun.* Pl. **pennies** /ˈpɛnɪz/, PENCE.
▶**I 1** Orig. (*Hist.*), a monetary unit and coin of the old English (later British) currency, equal to 1⁄240 pound (abbreviation ***d.***). Now, a British monetary unit and coin equal to one-hundredth of a pound (abbreviation ***p.***). OE. ▸**b** Any of various monetary units or coins of equal or similar value used in other countries of former British rule or in parts of Britain having some degree of autonomy. Usu. with specifying word. M16.
2 A denarius. Chiefly in biblical translations. OE. ▸**b** Any of various European coins of small denomination (chiefly *Hist.*). Also (*N. Amer. colloq.*), a cent. E18.
†**3** With *the* and ordinal numeral: a specified proportion of a sum of money. OE–M19.
4 a A piece of money. Also, a sum of money, money (now *rare* exc. in ***pretty penny*** s.v. PRETTY *adjective*). ME. ▸**b** In *pl.* Money, a (now usu. small) sum of money. ME. ▸**c** The sum required by a particular tax, customary payment, etc. With specifying word. ME.
5 A very little or the least amount of money, wealth, etc. Usu. in neg. contexts. ME.
6 A coin of a specified material as ***gold penny***, ***silver penny***, etc. Now *Hist.* LME.

📖 **1** BETTY SMITH Small . . marbles made of clay which cost a penny. A. DJOLETO Torto's mother gave Mensa threepence and Torto a penny. *Coin Monthly* No pennies were issued in 1950. **4b** B. CHATWIN She earned a few pennies doing chores. **5** *Independent* The union . . has spent 11 months negotiating with vice-chancellors . . and 'so far they have not offered a penny'.

▶**II** *transf.* †**7** = ***pennyweight*** below. OE–L16.
8 = ***pennyland*** below. *obsolete* exc. *dial.* L18.
Phrases: ***a penny more and up goes the*** DONKEY. **bad penny** an unwanted thing that reappears or reoccurs repeatedly. ***earn an honest penny***: see HONEST *adjective*. ***every penny***: see EVERY *adjective* 1. **in for a penny (in for a pound)** expr. the intention of completing an enterprise, once undertaken, whatever the cost. ***not have a penny to bless oneself with***: see BLESS *verb*¹. ***not have two pennies to rub together***: see RUB *verb*. **pennies from heaven** unexpected (financial) benefits. **penny for the guy** used by children to ask for money toward celebrations of Guy Fawkes night. **penny for your thoughts** used to ask a person lost in thought to tell what he or she is thinking about. ***penny wise and pound foolish***: see *penny wise* below. ***Peter's penny***: see PETER *noun*¹. ***pretty penny***: see PRETTY *adjective*. ***Saturday penny***: see SATURDAY *adjective*. **spend a penny** visit a lavatory, urinate (with allus. to the former price of admission to public lavatories). ***ten a penny***: see *two a penny* below. **the penny drops** understanding dawns. ***turn an honest penny***: see HONEST *adjective*. **two a penny**, **ten a penny** commonplace, easily obtainable; of little value.
▶**B** *attrib.* or as *adjective*. **1** Costing a penny; inexpensive. ME.
2 Of little worth or value; cheap; paltry. M16.

📖 **1** *North American Review* Scattered all over the country by the penny press. B. DUFFY To think of all the poor waifs . . without even shoes or a penny pie.

Comb. & special collocations: **penny ante** *noun & adjective* (*N. Amer.*) (*a*) *noun* poker played for small (esp. penny) stakes; (*b*) *adjective* contemptible, trivial; **penny arcade** = ***AMUSEMENT arcade***; **penny black** (a specimen of) the first adhesive postage stamp in the UK, issued in 1840, costing one penny; **penny cress** a cruciferous weed, *Thlaspi arvense*, with flat round pods; **penny dreadful** a cheap sensational novelette or comic; **penny-farthing** *adjective & noun* (*a*) *adjective* ineffective; insignificant; (*b*) *noun* an early form of bicycle having a large front wheel and a small rear one; **penny-fee** *Scot.* (esp. low) wages; ***penny gaff***: see GAFF *noun*² 2; **penny-grass** (chiefly *dial.*) yellow rattle, *Rhinanthus minor*; **penny-in-the-slot** *adjective* (*a*) (of a machine) activated by a coin inserted into a slot; (*b*) *fig.* automatic; **pennyland** (*obsolete* exc. *dial.*) a variable measure of land formerly having a rental value of a penny a year; **penny loafer** *N. Amer.* a casual shoe with a slot in which coins can be placed; **penny pies** (the round fleshy leaves of) the navelwort *Umbilicus rupestris*; **penny-pincher** a parsimonious person; **penny-pinching** *adjective & noun* (*colloq.*) (*a*) *adjective* parsimonious, mean; (*b*) *noun* extreme frugality, meanness; **penny plain** *adjective* plain and unpretentious; **penny-post** *noun & adjective* (now *Hist.*) (designating) a system for carrying letters or packets at a penny each, orig. within a 10 mile radius of London and later throughout the British Empire; **penny-postage** (now *Hist.*) the postage of letters at a penny each; †**penny-rent** rent paid in money; periodic payment in cash; revenue; **penny share** a low-priced share in a small company; **penny stock** (chiefly *N. Amer.*) common stock valued at less than one dollar a share, and therefore highly speculative; **penny-stone** *Scot. & north.* a disc-shaped stone used as a quoit; a game played with a number of these; **pennyweight** a unit of weight equal to 24 grains (1⁄20 troy ounce); **pennyweighter** *US Criminals' slang* a thief who steals jewellery or precious stones or metals; **penny whistle** a tin pipe with six holes, which may be variously covered to give different notes; **penny-wisdom** the quality of being penny wise; **penny wise** *adjective* (overly) careful in small expenditures; ***penny wise and pound foolish***, thrifty in small matters while careless or wasteful in large ones; **pennywort** any of several round-leaved plants; *esp.* (*a*) (more fully ***wall pennywort***) navelwort, *Umbilicus rupestris*; (*b*) (more fully ***marsh pennywort***) a small creeping marsh plant with round undivided leaves, *Hydrocotyle vulgaris* (family Hydrocotylaceae), allied to the umbellifers.
¶ The pl. *pennies* is now used only of a number of individual coins. See PENCE.

penny-a-line /pɛnɪəˈlʌɪn/ *adjective & verb.* M19.
[from (*a*) *penny a line*.]
▶**A** *adjective.* Of writing or a writer: paid at the rate of a penny a line (now *Hist.*). Also, (of writing) superficial, of little literary value. M19.
▶**B** *verb trans. & intrans.* Write (material) for a penny a line or in the style of a penny-a-liner. Chiefly as ***penny-a-lining*** *verbal noun & ppl adjective*. M19.
■ **penny-a-liner** *noun* a person, esp. a journalist, who practises penny-a-line writing M19.

pennyroyal /pɛnɪˈrɔɪəl/ *noun.* **M16.**
[Alt. of Anglo-Norman *puliol real*, i.e. Old French *pouliol* (mod. *pouliot*) and *real* ROYAL.]
1 A small procumbent mint of damp heaths, *Mentha pulegium*, formerly much used medicinally. **M16.**
2 In N. America: any of several similar aromatic labiate plants, *esp.* (more fully ***American pennyroyal***) *Hedeoma pulegioides.* **M16.**

pennyworth /ˈpɛnɪwəːθ/ *noun & adverb.* Also **penn'orth** /ˈpɛnəθ/. **OE.**
[from PENNY + WORTH *noun*¹.]
▶ **A** *noun.* **1** As much as can be bought or sold for a penny. **OE.** ▸**b** *fig.* A very small or the least amount. Freq. in neg. contexts. **LME.**
†**2** A thing or things which can be bought or sold for a given sum, as opp. to the money itself. **ME–M17.**
3 Profit; money's-worth. Also, a bargain of a specified kind. **ME.**

1 E. NESBIT Oswald got a pennyworth of alum, because it is so cheap. **b** *New York Review of Books* There was . . never a pennyworth of truth in this story. **3** SIR W. SCOTT The armour, which I have no doubt is a great pennyworth. ***a lumping pennyworth***.

▶†**B** *adverb.* Preceded by *a* (rarely *the*): for a small amount of money; as a bargain; cheaply. **LME–L18.**

Penobscot /pɛˈnɒbskɒt/ *noun & adjective.* **E17.**
[Abnaki name.]
▶ **A** *noun.* Pl. same, **-s**.
1 A member of an Algonquian people of the Penobscot River valley in Maine. **E17.**
2 The language of this people, a dialect of Eastern Abnaki. **L19.**
▶ **B** *attrib.* or as *adjective.* Of or pertaining to the Penobscot or their language. **E18.**

penology /piːˈnɒlədʒi/ *noun.* **M19.**
[from Latin *poena* penalty + -LOGY.]
The branch of knowledge that deals with the prevention and punishment of crime and with the penal system.
■ **penoˈlogical** *adjective* **M19.** **penologist** *noun* **M19.**

pen-pusher /ˈpɛnpʊʃə/ *noun. colloq.* Freq. *derog.* **E20.**
[from PEN *noun*² + PUSHER.]
A clerk; a low-level bureaucrat. Also, a writer, *esp.* a literary hack.

A. S. BYATT She writes hilarious parodies of the ridiculous plots employed by female pen-pushers.

■ **pen-pushing** *noun* the writing of inferior literature, bureaucratic reports, etc. **M20.**

Penrose /ˈpɛnrəʊz/ *noun.* **L20.**
[Roger *Penrose* (b. 1931), Brit. mathematical physicist.]
MATH. & PHYSICS. Used *attrib.* to designate concepts and techniques arising from Penrose's work.
Penrose diagram a two dimensional representation of space–time in which two spatial dimensions are suppressed. **Penrose process** a postulated mechanism whereby energy can under certain circumstances escape from a black hole. **Penrose tile** each of the elements used in a Penrose tiling. **Penrose tiling** any spatially nonperiodic tiling of the plane using tiles of a finite number of shapes; a three-dimensional analogue of this.

†**pensee** *noun*¹ var. of PENSÉE.

†**pensee** *noun*², *adjective, & verb* see PANSY.

pensée /pɑ̃se/ *noun.* Also (in sense 1) †***pensee***. Pl. pronounced same. **LME.**
[Old French *pensee*; in sense 2 reintroduced from French.]
†**1** Thoughtfulness, anxiety, care; a thought, an idea. **LME–L15.**
2 A poem or prose composition expressing a single thought or reflection. Also, an aphorism. **L19.**

penseful *adjective* var. of PENSIFUL.

penseroso /pɛnsəˈrəʊzəʊ, *foreign* penseˈroːzo/ *noun & adjective.* **L18.**
[Italian, obsolete form of *pensieroso*, from †*pensiere* thought, from Provençal *pensier*, from Proto-Romance var. of Latin *pensare* weigh, ponder, consider: see POISE *verb*.]
▶ **A** *noun.* Pl. **-sos** /-zəʊz/, **-si** /-zi/. (A person having) a brooding or melancholy character. **L18.**
▶ **B** *adjective.* Pensive, brooding, melancholy. **E19.**

pensiero /penˈsjɛːro/ *noun.* Pl. **-ri** /-ri/. **E20.**
[Italian.]
1 A thought, an idea; an anxiety. **E20.**
2 ART. A sketch. **M20.**

pensiful /ˈpɛnsɪfʊl, -f(ə)l/ *adjective. obsolete* exc. *Scot. & north.* Also **pense-** /ˈpɛnsɪ-, ˈpɛns-/. **LME.**
[Perh. from (the same root as) PENSIVE or from PENSÉE: see -FUL.]
Thoughtful, pensive; brooding, melancholy; anxious.
■ **pensifulness** *noun* **LME.**

pensil *noun* var. of PENCEL.

pensile /ˈpɛnsʌɪl/ *adjective.* **E17.**
[Latin *pensilis*, from *pens-* pa. ppl stem of *pendere* hang: see -ILE.]
1 Suspended, hanging down, pendent. **E17.** ▸**b** Overhanging; situated on a steep slope. **M18.**
2 Supported on arches over an empty space; vaulted. **E17.**
3 That constructs a hanging nest; penduline. **E19.**

pension /ˈpɛnʃ(ə)n, *in sense A.6b also foreign* pɑ̃sjɔ̃ (*pl. same*)/ *noun & verb.* **LME.**
[Old & mod. French from Latin *pensio(n-)* payment, rent, from *pens-* pa. ppl stem of *pendere* weigh, pay: see prec., -ION.]
▶ **A** *noun.* †**1** A payment; a tribute, a tax; a contribution; a price paid or received; an expenditure, an expense. **LME–M17.**
2 ECCLESIASTICAL HISTORY. A fixed payment made out of or charged to the revenues of a benefice. **LME.**
3 †**a** A regular payment made to a person for present services or to retain allegiance, goodwill, etc.; a salary, a stipend, a fee. **LME–M19.** ▸**b** A regular payment made to a person of rank or a royal favourite to enable him or her to live to an expected standard. Also, a regular payment made to an artist or scholar for services to the State or to fund work. **E16.**
4 **a** A periodic (esp. annual) payment made by each member of a guild, college, or society, esp. an Inn of Court, towards its general expenses. *obsolete* exc. *Hist.* **LME.** ▸**b** A consultative assembly of the members of Gray's Inn, one of the Inns of Court in London. Now *rare.* **L16.**
5 A regular payment made to a person or to a deceased person's dependants, esp. by a government or an employer, in consideration of past services or for disability, poverty, or other charitable reasons; *spec.* (*a*) a regular payment made esp. by the State to enable a person (usu. of State retirement age or above) to subsist without working; (*b*) a regular payment from a fund etc. to which the recipient has contributed (freq. with an employer) as an investment during his or her working life in order to realize a return upon retirement (freq. *attrib.*). **E16.**
6 †**a** Payment for board and lodging, or for the board and education of a child. **M16–E19.** ▸**b** A usu. fixed-rate boarding-house or (formerly) a boarding-school in France or another country in Continental Europe. **M17.**

3b JAS. HARRIS These professors were maintained with liberal pensions. **5** S. UNWIN The married man . . completed over fifty years' service with the firm, and eventually retired on a pension. R. P. JHABVALA When my father died, my mother was promised a pension from his office. M. ATWOOD He got the limp in the war and it was typical of the government that they wouldn't give him a pension. M. WESLEY She has her old age pension, hasn't she? *Which?* The basic pension is paid to everyone who has sufficient National Insurance . . contributions. ***old age pension***, ***State pension***, ***war pension***, etc. ***personal pension***: see PERSONAL *adjective*. **6b** E. HEATH The young officer dropped us near a small *pension* which . . had a couple of rooms. EN PENSION. †**in pension** = EN PENSION.

Comb.: **pension book**: supplied by the government, in which a record of pension payments received is kept; **pension fund** the funds invested by a company etc. for the payment of pensions to former employees or (occas.) their dependants; **pension mortgage**: in which the borrower repays interest only and also contributes to a pension plan, part of the proceeds of which is used to repay the capital at the end of the mortgage period; **pension plan** an arrangement or system for contributions into and payments from a pension fund.

▶ **B** *verb.* **1** *verb trans.* Grant a pension to. Also, retain or bribe with a pension. Now *rare.* **L16.** ▸**b** Foll. by *off*: dismiss with a pension, esp. on retirement; cease to employ or use. **M19.**
2 *verb intrans.* Live or stay in a pension or boarding-house. Now *rare.* **M17.**

1 WELLINGTON A plan for pensioning public officers incapable of service is required. *Daily Telegraph* In his last, invalid years the Spain of Don Juan Carlos honoured and pensioned him. **b** M. FORSTER Even now, when she was old and pensioned off, Miss Arabel visited her faithfully.

¶ Formerly fully naturalized in sense A.6b.
■ **pensionless** *adjective* **M19.**

pensionable /ˈpɛnʃ(ə)nəb(ə)l/ *adjective.* **L19.**
[from PENSION *verb* + -ABLE.]
1 Entitled to a pension; (of a job, service, etc.) entitling a person to a pension. **L19.**
2 Of, pertaining to, or affecting a person's pension. **E20.**

1 *Times* The Civil Service is to offer pensionable jobs to men and women . . between 40 and 60.

■ **pensionaˈbility** *noun* entitlement to a pension **M20.** **pensionably** *adverb* **L19.**

pensionary /ˈpɛnʃ(ə)n(ə)ri/ *noun*¹. Now *rare.* **M16.**
[medieval Latin *pensionarius* receiver or payer of a pension, from Latin *pensio(n-)*: see PENSION, -ARY¹.]
1 A person receiving a pension; *spec.* a person in the pay or hire of another, a hireling. **M16.**
2 The chief municipal magistrate of a Dutch city; *esp.* (also ***Grand Pensionary***) the first minister and magistrate of the former Dutch province of Holland and Zeeland. *obsolete* exc. *Hist.* **L16.**

pensionary /ˈpɛnʃ(ə)n(ə)ri/ *noun*². **L16.**
[from PENSION + -ARY¹, prob. after medieval Latin *pensionarius* (see prec.).]
A residence for pensioners. Formerly also *spec.*, a residence at Cambridge University for undergraduates not financially supported by their college.

Server A pensionary for retired seamen.

pensionary /ˈpɛnʃ(ə)n(ə)ri/ *adjective.* Now *rare.* **L15.**
[formed as PENSIONARY *noun*¹.]
†**1** Providing an ecclesiastical pension or endowment. **L15–M16.**
2 Receiving a pension; in the pay of a person or persons; *fig.* mercenary. **M16.**
3 Consisting, or of the nature, of a pension. **M16.**

pensione /penˈsjoːne/ *noun.* Pl. **-ni** /-ni/. **M20.**
[Italian.]
In Italy, a small hotel or boarding house.

pensioneer /ˌpɛnʃəˈnɪə/ *verb intrans.* **M20.**
[from PENSION *noun* + -EER, after ELECTIONEER.]
Seek votes in an election by promising higher pensions. Chiefly as ***pensioneering*** *verbal noun*

pensioner /ˈpɛnʃ(ə)nə/ *noun.* **LME.**
[Anglo-Norman, or Old French *pensionier* from medieval Latin *pensionarius*: see PENSIONARY *noun*¹, -ER².]
▶ **I** **1** An officer in the Inns of Court who collected the pensions and kept the relevant accounts. *obsolete* exc. *Hist.* **LME.**
2 A person receiving a pension or regular pay for services performed; (freq. *derog.*) a mercenary soldier, a hireling. *obsolete* exc. *Hist.* **L15.** ▸**b** A person receiving a pension in consideration of past services or because of age, disability, or other circumstance preventing or limiting ability to work. **E17.** ▸**c** A pimp. *derog.* **M19.**
†**3** *spec.* An attendant, a retainer, a member of a bodyguard, esp. of the British monarch within the royal palace; a gentleman-at-arms. *obsolete* exc. *Hist.* **M16.**
†**4** = PENSIONARY *noun*¹ 2. **E17–M18.**

2b R. RENDELL The anxiety of a disabled pensioner expecting an ambulance. ***old age pensioner***: see OLD *adjective*.

▶ **II** **5** At Cambridge University, an undergraduate without financial support from his or her college, a student without a college scholarship. Cf. COMMONER *noun* 7. **LME.**
†**6** A person who lives in a boarding-house; a boarder; *esp.* a female boarder in a convent or school in France and French-speaking countries. **M17–E19.**

pensioni *noun* pl. of PENSIONE.

pensionnaire /pɑ̃sjɔnɛːr/ *noun.* Pl. pronounced same. **L16.**
[French from medieval Latin *pensionarius*: see PENSIONARY *noun*¹.]
1 A person receiving a pension; a pensioner, a paid retainer. *rare.* **L16.**
2 A person who boards in a French lodging-house or institution, or with a French family. **L18.**

pensionnat /pɑ̃sjɔna/ *noun.* Pl. pronounced same. **M19.**
[French.]
In France and other European countries: a boarding-house, a boarding-school.

pensive /ˈpɛnsɪv/ *adjective & noun.* **LME.**
[Old & mod. French *pensif*, *-ive*, from *penser* think from Latin *pensare* weigh, balance, consider: see POISE *verb*, -IVE.]
▶ **A** *adjective.* **1** Thoughtful, meditative, musing; reflective. **LME.** ▸**b** *spec.* Sadly or sorrowfully thoughtful; gloomy, brooding, melancholy. Formerly also, repentant *of*, sorry *for*. **LME.**
†**2** Thoughtful about plans or future events; *spec.* anxious, apprehensive. **LME–M17.**
3 Associated with or implying thought, anxiety, or melancholy. **M16.**

1 P. ACKROYD She was wrapped in so pensive a mood that she neither saw nor heard me. S. ROSENBERG Pensive, preoccupied, he rarely looked up at you. **b** C. JACKSON The peculiarly pensive way . . of resting her chin on her palm as if in melancholy thought. **3** J. G. FARRELL He had taken care to position himself in a nobly pensive attitude.

▶ **B** *absol.* as *noun.* (A) pensive manner or mood. *rare.* **L18.**
■ †**pensived** *adjective* (*rare*, Shakes.) made pensive, saddened: only in **L16.** **pensively** *adverb* **M16.** **pensiveness** *noun* **LME.**

penstemon *noun* var. of PENTSTEMON.

penster /ˈpɛnstə/ *noun. rare.* **E17.**
[from PEN *noun*², *verb*² + -STER.]
A writer; *esp.* a literary hack.

penstock /ˈpɛnstɒk/ *noun.* **E17.**
[from PEN *noun*¹ + STOCK *noun*¹.]
1 A sluice or floodgate regulating the flow from a pent body of water, as in a water-mill. **E17.**
2 A channel, trough, or tube for conveying water from a lake, dam, etc., esp. to a water-wheel or turbine. Orig. *US.* **L18.**

pensum /ˈpɛnsəm/ *noun. rare.* **E18.**
[Latin = weight, charge, duty, from *pendere* weigh.]
A duty, an allotted task. Also, a school-task or lesson to be prepared; (*US*) this as a punishment.

†pensy *noun, adjective*[2], *& verb* see **PANSY.**

pensy /ˈpɛnsi/ *adjective*[1]. Now *Scot. & dial.* **LME.**
[formed as **PENSIVE**: see **-Y**[7].]
1 = **PENSIVE. LME.**
2 Conceited. **E18.**
3 Fretful; peevish. Also, fastidious in appetite. **E19.**

†pent *noun*[1]. **L16–E18.**
[App. from **PENT** *adjective*. Cf. **BENT** *noun*[2], *adjective*.]
A place in which water is pent up; a reservoir, an enclosed pool. Cf. **PEN** *noun*[1] 2a.

pent /pɛnt/ *noun*[2]. **M18.**
[Abbreviation of **PENTHOUSE** *noun*.]
A sloping roof or covering, a penthouse.

pent /pɛnt/ *adjective.* **L16.**
[from †*pent* pa. pple of **PEN** *verb*[1].]
1 Of a place, room, etc.: enclosed, shut *up*, sealed. **L16.**
2 Confined within narrow limits; restricted; imprisoned. Also foll. by *in*, *up*. **E17.**

📖 **1** LONGFELLOW All left at once the pent-up room, And rushed into the open air. **2** G. GREENE There has never been any hint of shy pent passions . . among the co-eds. *Independent* Her pent up aggression, her sour violent spirit.

†pent *verb pa. t. & pple* of **PEN** *verb*[1].

penta- /ˈpɛntə/ *combining form.* Before a vowel usu. **pent-**.
[Greek *penta-*, combining form of *pente* five.]
Having five, fivefold.
■ **penta'chloride** *noun* (CHEMISTRY) a chloride containing five atoms of chlorine in its molecule **M19.** **pentachloro'ethane** *noun* (CHEMISTRY) a colourless liquid, $Cl_3C{\cdot}CHCl_2$, that is used as a solvent and in the synthesis of other chlorinated hydrocarbons **L19.** **pentachloro'phenate** *noun* (CHEMISTRY) a salt of pentachlorophenol, *esp.* the sodium salt **M20.** **pentachloro'phenol** *noun* (CHEMISTRY) a colourless crystalline acidic solid, C_6Cl_5OH, used in insecticides, fungicides, weedkillers, wood preservatives, etc. **L19.** **penta'cyclic** *adjective* (***a***) BOTANY (of a flower) having the parts in five whorls; (***b***) CHEMISTRY containing five rings in the molecule: **L19.** **penta'dactyl**, (now *rare*) **-yle** *adjective* having five fingers, toes, or finger-like processes; *spec.* in ZOOLOGY, designating the ancestral limb-bone pattern of land vertebrates: **E19.** **†pentadactylous** *adjective* = **PENTADACTYL L17–L19.** **penta'decane** *noun* (CHEMISTRY) any of a series of saturated hydrocarbons (alkanes) with the formula $C_{15}H_{32}$, *spec.* (also ***n*-pentadecane**) the unbranched isomer, $CH_3(CH_2)_{13}CH_3$ **L19.** **penta'delphous** *adjective* (BOTANY) (of stamens) united by the filaments so as to form five groups; (of a plant) having the stamens so united **M19.** **pentaerythritol** /ˌpɛntæˈrɪθrɪtɒl/ *noun* (***a***) CHEMISTRY a crystalline alcohol, $C(CH_2OH)_4$, used in the manufacture of paints and varnishes; (***b***) CHEMISTRY & PHARMACOLOGY (more fully ***pentaerythritol tetranitrate***) a crystalline solid, $C(CH_2NO_3)_4$, used as an explosive and as a vasodilator in the treatment of heart conditions: **L19.** **pen'tagamist** *noun* a person who has been married five times **M17.** **penta'gastrin** *noun* (MEDICINE) a synthetic pentapeptide having the same action as the hormone gastrin **M20.** **pentagrid** *noun* (ELECTRONICS) a thermionic valve having five grids, a heptode **M20.** **pen'tagynous** *adjective* (BOTANY) having five styles **E19.** **penta'hydrate** *noun* (CHEMISTRY) a hydrate containing five moles of water per mole of the compound **E20.** **pentahy'drated** *adjective* (CHEMISTRY) hydrated with five moles of water per mole of the compound **M19.** **penta'hydric** *adjective* (CHEMISTRY) containing five hydroxyl groups in the molecule **L19.** **pentalogue** *noun* a set of five rules or laws **L18.** **pen'talogy** *noun* a combination of five mutually connected parts; a pentad: **E20.** **pen'talpha** *noun* = **PENTAGRAM E19.** **pentamer** *noun* (CHEMISTRY) a compound whose molecule is composed of five molecules of monomer **E20.** **pen'tameral** *adjective* = **PENTAMEROUS L19.** **penta'meric** *adjective* (CHEMISTRY) of the nature of a pentamer, consisting of a pentamer or pentamers **M20.** **pen'tamerism** *noun* (BIOLOGY) the condition or character of being pentamerous **E20.** **pen'tamerous** *adjective* (BIOLOGY) having parts arranged in groups of five **E19.** **pen'tamery** *noun* = **PENTAMERISM E20.** **penta'methylene** *noun* (CHEMISTRY) †(***a***) cyclopentane; (***b***) the divalent straight-chain radical $-(CH_2)_5-$: **L19.** **pentamethylene'diamine** *noun* (CHEMISTRY) = **CADAVERINE L19.** **pen'tandrous** *adjective* (BOTANY) having five stamens **E19.** **penta'nucleotide** *noun* (BIOCHEMISTRY) an oligonucleotide containing five nucleotides **M20.** **penta'peptide** *noun* (BIOCHEMISTRY) an oligopeptide containing five amino acid residues **E20.** **penta'petalous** *adjective* (BOTANY) having five petals **E18.** **pen'tapolis** *noun* (*Hist.*) a confederacy or group of five towns **LME.** **penta'politan** *adjective* (*Hist.*) of or pertaining to a pentapolis **M18.** **pen'tarsic** *adjective* (PROSODY) having five stresses **L19.** **penta'sepalous** *adjective* (BOTANY) having five sepals **M19.** **pentastyle** *noun & adjective* (ARCHITECTURE, *rare*) (a building or portico) having five columns **E18.** **penta'tonic** *adjective & noun* (MUSIC) (***a***) *adjective* consisting of five notes or sounds; (***b***) *noun* a five-note scale, *esp.* one without semitones, equivalent to an ordinary major scale with the fourth and seventh omitted: **M19.** **penta'tonically** *adverb* (MUSIC) according to a pentatonic scale **M20.** **penta'tonicism**, **penta'tonism** *nouns* (MUSIC) the property of consisting (mostly) of notes from a pentatonic scale; the practice of writing pentatonic music: **M20.** **penta'valent** *adjective* (CHEMISTRY) having a valency of five **L19.**

pentachord /ˈpɛntəkɔːd/ *noun.* **L17.**
[from **PENTA-** + **CHORD** *noun*[1].]
MUSIC. **1** †**a** The interval of a fifth. *rare.* Only in **L17.** ▸**b** A series of five musical notes. **E19.**
2 A musical instrument with five strings. **E18.**

pentacle /ˈpɛntək(ə)l/ *noun.* **L16.**
[medieval Latin *pentaculum*, formed as **PENTA-** + Latin *-culum* **-CLE**.]
A pentagram, esp. as a magical symbol. Also *occas.*, a hexagram or other magical symbol.

pentad /ˈpɛntad/ *noun.* **M17.**
[Greek *pentad*, *-as* from *pente* five: see **-AD**[1].]
1 The number five in the Pythagorean system. **M17.**
2 CHEMISTRY. Orig., a pentavalent element or group. Now, a pentameric unit within a polymer. **M19.**
3 A group of five; *spec.* (***a***) a period of five years (cf. **DECADE** 3); (***b***) METEOROLOGY a period of five days. **L19.**

pentagon /ˈpɛntəg(ə)n/ *noun.* **L16.**
[French *pentagone* or late Latin *pentagonum* from Greek *pentagōnon* use as noun of neut. of adjective *pentagōnos*, formed as **PENTA-**: see **-GON**.]
1 A plane figure with five straight sides and five angles. Also, a fort with five bastions. **L16.**
2 ***the Pentagon***, a pentagonal building in Washington, D.C., used as the headquarters of the US Department of Defense; *allus.* the leadership of the US military. **M20.**

📖 **2** J. BARTH I can't stop the Pentagon from making and deploying the neutron bomb.

■ **Pentagon'ese** *noun* the style of language supposedly characteristic of the leadership of the US military **M20.** **Penta'gonian** *noun* a person who works in the Pentagon **M20.**

pentagonal /pɛnˈtag(ə)n(ə)l/ *adjective.* **L16.**
[French, or medieval Latin *pentagonalis*, from *pentagonum*: see prec., **-AL**[1].]
1 Of, pertaining to, or having the form of a pentagon. **L16.**
2 Of a solid: having a pentagonal base or section. Also, contained by pentagons. **L16.**
■ **pentagonally** *adverb* in a pentagonal form **M17.** **pentagonoid** *adjective* resembling a pentagon, somewhat pentagonal **L19.**

pentagram /ˈpɛntəgram/ *noun.* **M19.**
[Greek *pentagrammon* use as noun of neut. of *pentagrammos* of five lines: see **PENTA-**, **-GRAM**.]
1 A five-pointed star, formerly used as a mystic or magical symbol, formed by extending the sides of a pentagon both ways to their points of intersection, or by drawing a continuous line in five straight segments, each of which ultimately crosses two others, until the end of the fifth meets the beginning of the first. **M19.**
2 A series of five letters or characters. **L20.**

pentahedron /pɛntəˈhiːdr(ə)n, -ˈhɛd-/ *noun.* Pl. **-dra** /-drə/, **-drons**. **L18.**
[from **PENTA-** + **-HEDRON**.]
A solid figure or object with five plane faces.
■ **pentahedral** *adjective* having the form of a pentahedron; having five faces: **E19.** **†pentahedrical** = **PENTAHEDRAL**: only in **M17.**

pen-tail /ˈpɛnteɪl/ *noun.* **L19.**
[from **PEN** *noun*[2] + **TAIL** *noun*[1].]
More fully ***pen-tail shrew***, ***pen-tail tree shrew***. A very small rare tree shrew, *Ptilocercus lowii*, of Malaysia, Sumatra, and Borneo, with a fringe of long, stiff hairs at the end of its tail.
■ **pen-tailed** *adjective*: ***pen-tailed shrew***, ***pen-tailed tree shrew*** = **PEN-TAIL E20.**

pentameter /pɛnˈtamɪtə/ *noun & adjective.* **E16.**
[Latin from Greek *pentametros*, *-on* uses as noun of masc. and neut. of adjective, formed as **PENTA-** + **-METER**.]
PROSODY. ▸**A** *noun.* A line of five metrical feet; *spec.* (***a***) in Greek and Latin prosody, a dactylic line having two halves, each consisting of two feet and a long syllable, freq. alternated with hexameters in elegiac verse; (***b***) in English verse, a ten-syllable line made up of five iambs. **E16.**
▸**B** *adjective.* Consisting of five metrical feet. **M16.**
■ **pentametrize** *verb trans.* make into, or like, a pentameter **M19.**

pentamidine /pɛnˈtamɪdiːn/ *noun.* **M20.**
[from **PENTANE** + **AMIDINE** *noun*[2].]
PHARMACOLOGY. A diamidine that is used in the prevention and treatment of certain tropical diseases, esp. sleeping sickness.

pentane /ˈpɛnteɪn/ *noun.* **L19.**
[from **PENTA-** + **-ANE**.]
CHEMISTRY. Each of three isomeric liquid alkanes with the formula C_5H_{12}; *esp.* (also ***n*-pentane**) the unbranched isomer, $CH_3(CH_2)_3CH_3$.
■ **penta'noic** *adjective*: ***pentanoic acid***, a fatty acid, $CH_3(CH_2)_3COOH$, that is an oily liquid present in various plant oils (also called ***valeric acid***) **E20.** **pentanol** *noun* each of the isomeric alcohols of the formula $C_5H_{11}OH$; *esp.* (more fully ***pentan-1-ol***) the unbranched primary alcohol, $CH_3(CH_2)_3CH_2OH$ (*n*-amyl alcohol): **M20.**

pentangle /ˈpɛntaŋg(ə)l/ *noun.* **LME.**
[In sense 1 perh. from medieval Latin alt. of *pentaculum* **PENTACLE**, after Latin *angulus* **ANGLE** *noun*[3]; in sense 2 from **PENTA-** + **ANGLE** *noun*[3].]
1 = **PENTAGRAM. LME.**
2 = **PENTAGON.** *rare.* **M17.**

pentangular /pɛnˈtaŋgjʊlə/ *adjective.* **M17.**
[from **PENTANGLE** 2 + **-AR**[1].]
Having five angles or angular points; pentagonal.

pentapedal /pɛntəˈpiːd(ə)l/ *adjective.* **L20.**
[from **PENTA-** + **PEDAL** *adjective*, after *bipedal*, *quadrupedal*.]
ZOOLOGY. Five-legged; *spec.* designating a slow gait in kangaroos in which the forelegs and tail together alternate with the hind legs.

pentaploid /ˈpɛntəplɔɪd/ *adjective & noun.* **E20.**
[from **PENTA-** + **-PLOID**.]
BIOLOGY. ▸**A** *adjective.* (Of a cell) containing five homologous sets of chromosomes; (of an individual) composed of pentaploid cells. **E20.**
▸**B** *noun.* A pentaploid individual. **E20.**

pentapody /pɛnˈtapədi/ *noun.* **M19.**
[Greek *pentapous* of five feet, formed as **PENTA-** + *pous*, *pod-* foot.]
PROSODY. A line of verse consisting of five feet; a sequence of five feet in a verse.

pentaprism /ˈpɛntəprɪz(ə)m/ *noun.* **M20.**
[from **PENTA-** + **PRISM**.]
A prism whose cross-section is a pentagon with one right angle and three angles of 112½ degrees, so that any ray entering through one of the faces forming the right angle is deflected through 90 degrees.

pentarch /ˈpɛntɑːk/ *noun.* **M17.**
[Late Greek *pentarkhos*, formed as **PENTA-** + **-ARCH**.]
The ruler of any of a group of five districts or kingdoms; a member of a governing body of five people. Formerly also, a leader of a group of five people.

pentarch /ˈpɛntɑːk/ *adjective.* **L19.**
[from **PENTA-** + Greek *arkhē* beginning.]
BOTANY. Of a vascular bundle: having five strands of xylem, formed from five points of origin.

pentarchy /ˈpɛntɑːki/ *noun.* **L16.**
[Greek *pentarkhia* a rule of five, formed as **PENTA-** + **-ARCHY**.]
Government by five rulers; a group of five districts or kingdoms each under its own ruler; a governing body of five.

pentastich /ˈpɛntəstɪk/ *noun.* **M17.**
[mod. Latin *pentastichus* from Greek *pentastikhos*, formed as **PENTA-** + *stikhos* row, line of verse.]
PROSODY. A group of five lines of verse.

pentastomid /pɛntəˈstəʊmɪd/ *noun & adjective.* **E20.**
[mod. Latin *Pentastomida* (see below), from *Pentastoma* genus name, formed as **PENTA-** + Greek *stoma* mouth (from the appearance of the mouth and adjacent two pairs of chitinous hooks): see **-ID**[3].]
ZOOLOGY. ▸**A** *noun.* Any of various parasitic wormlike animals of the class Pentastomida (or Pentastoma), which infest the lungs and nasal passages of vertebrates and are allied to the arthropods. Also called ***linguatulid***, ***tongue-worm***. **E20.**
▸**B** *adjective.* Of, pertaining to, or designating this phylum. **M20.**
■ **'pentastome** *noun* = **PENTASTOMID** *noun* **L19.**

pentasyllabic /pɛntəsɪˈlabɪk/ *adjective.* **L18.**
[from **PENTA-** + **SYLLABIC**. Cf. late Latin *pentasyllabus* from Greek *pentasullabos* adjectives.]
Having five syllables.

Pentateuch /ˈpɛntətjuːk/ *noun.* **LME.**
[ecclesiastical Latin *pentateuchus* from ecclesiastical Greek *pentateukhos* use as noun of adjective, formed as **PENTA-** + *teukhos* implement, vessel, (later) book.]
1 The first five books of the Old Testament and Hebrew Scriptures, Genesis, Exodus, Leviticus, Numbers, and Deuteronomy, traditionally ascribed to Moses, taken together as a group. **LME.**
2 *transf.* A volume consisting of five books or sections. *rare.* **M17.**
1 ***Samaritan Pentateuch***: see **SAMARITAN** *adjective*.
■ **Penta'teuchal** *adjective* of, pertaining to, or contained in the Pentateuch **M19.**

pentathlon /pɛnˈtaθlɒn, -lən/ *noun.* Also in Latin form **†-athlum**. **E17.**
[Greek *pentathlon*, formed as **PENTA-** + *athlon* contest.]
1 CLASSICAL HISTORY. An athletic contest in which competitors engaged in five different events (leaping, running, discus-throwing, spear-throwing, and wrestling), to be performed in a single day. **E17.**
2 An athletic or sporting contest in which competitors engage in five different events (esp. (in full ***modern pentathlon***) fencing, shooting, swimming, riding, and cross-country running), to be performed usu. in a single day or over two consecutive days. **E20.**
■ **pentathlete** *noun* a competitor in a pentathlon **E19.**

pentathol /ˈpɛntəθal/ *noun.* **M20.**
[Alt. of **PENTOTHAL**: cf. **-OL**.]
PHARMACOLOGY. = **THIOPENTONE.**

pentatomid /pɛnˈtatəmɪd/ *adjective & noun*. L19.
[mod. Latin *Pentatomidae* (see below), from *Pentatoma* genus name, formed as PENTA- + Greek *tomos* cut (from the five joints in the antennae): see -ID[3].]
ENTOMOLOGY. ►**A** *adjective*. Of, pertaining to, or designating the family Pentatomidae of plant-feeding heteropteran bugs, mostly of warm climates, and often brilliantly coloured. L19.
►**B** *noun*. A pentatomid bug; a shieldbug, a stink-bug. M20.

pentazocine /pɛnˈtazə(ʊ)siːn/ *noun*. M20.
[from PENTANE + AZO- + OC(TA- + -INE[5].]
PHARMACOLOGY. A tricyclic heterocyclic compound, $C_{19}H_{27}NO$, that is a potent non-addictive analgesic given esp. during childbirth.

penteconta- /ˈpɛntɪkɒntə/ *combining form*. Before a vowel **-cont-**.
[Repr. Greek *pentēkonta* fifty.]
Having or consisting of fifty.
■ †**pentecontarch** *noun* a commander of fifty men LME–M17. **penteconta'glossal** *adjective* written in fifty languages M19.

penteconter /ˈpɛntɪkɒntə/ *noun*[1]. E17.
[Greek *pentēkontēr*.]
GREEK HISTORY. A commander of a troop of fifty men.

penteconter /ˈpɛntɪkɒntə/ *noun*[2]. M19.
[Greek *pentēkontērēs*.]
GREEK ANTIQUITIES. A cargo ship with fifty oars.

Pentecost /ˈpɛntɪkɒst/ *noun*.
[Old English *pentecosten* from accus. of ecclesiastical Latin *Pentecoste* from Greek *Pentēkostē* use as noun of fem. ordinal adjective of *pentēkonta*, from *pente* five + *-konta*; re-adopted in Middle English from Old French *pentecoste* (mod.-*côte*).]
1 (The day of) the Jewish harvest festival, observed on the fiftieth day after the second day of Passover (*Leviticus* 23: 15–16). Also, a synagogue ceremony held on the same day to mark the giving of the Torah on Mount Sinai. OE.
2 A Christian festival observed on the seventh Sunday after Easter, commemorating the descent of the Holy Spirit on the disciples (as recorded in *Acts* 2); the day of this festival, Whit Sunday. Also, the season of this festival, Whitsuntide. OE. ►**b** The actual day and event that this festival commemorates. L19.
3 *fig*. The descent of the Holy Spirit on the Christian believer. M18.

pentecostal /pɛntɪˈkɒst(ə)l/ *noun & adjective*. M16.
[Latin *pentecostalis* from *Pentecoste*: see PENTECOST, -AL[1].]
►**A** *noun*. **1** Usu. in *pl*. Offerings formerly made in the Church of England at Whitsuntide by the parishioners to the priest, or by one church to another greater or older church to which it is related. *obsolete* exc. *Hist*. M16.
2 (**P-**.) A member of a Pentecostal sect; an adherent of Pentecostalism. E20.

> 📖 **2** *New Yorker* Bible-study groups among Wyndal's Pentecostals stress divination and prophecy.

►**B** *adjective*. **1** Of or pertaining to Pentecost. M17. ►**b** *fig*. Of or pertaining to the many nationalities present at Pentecost, or to the speaking in many languages which occurred at that event. L19.
2 (Usu. **P-**.) Designating or pertaining to a Christian sect or movement which, or individual who, emphasizes the gifts of the Holy Spirit (e.g. speaking in tongues, prophecy, etc.), expresses religious feeling through uninhibited or enthusiastic acts (e.g. clapping, shouting, etc.), and is freq. fundamentalist in outlook and not attached to any of the main denominations. E20.
■ **Pentecostalism** *noun* the beliefs and practices of Pentecostal movements or sects M20. **Pentecostalist** *noun & adjective* (*a*) *noun* = PENTECOSTAL *noun* 2; (*b*) *adjective* of or pertaining to Pentecostalism: E20.

pentecostys /pɛntɪˈkɒstɪs/ *noun*. Pl. **-styes** /-stiːz/. E19.
[Greek *pentekostus*, from *pentēkostos* fiftieth.]
GREEK HISTORY. A troop of fifty soldiers as a division of the Spartan army.

Pentel /ˈpɛntɛl/ *noun*. M20.
[Arbitrary formation: perh. from PEN *noun*[2].]
(Proprietary name for) a type of ball-point pen with a free flow like a felt-tip pen.

Pentelic /pənˈtɛlɪk/ *adjective*. L16.
[Latin *Pentelicus* from Greek *Pentelikos*, from *Pentelē* a deme of Attica: see -IC.]
Pentelic marble, a white marble quarried on Mount Pentelicus, near Athens.

pentene /ˈpɛntiːn/ *noun*. L19.
[from PENTA- + -ENE.]
CHEMISTRY. Any acyclic alkene with the formula C_5H_{10}; *esp*. any of the unbranched isomers.

†**pentereme** *noun*. *rare*. M17–M19.
[from Greek *pente* five + Latin *remus* oar.]
GREEK ANTIQUITIES. = QUINQUEREME *noun*.

penthemimer /pɛnθɪˈmɪmə/ *noun*. L16.
[Late Latin *penthemimeres* from Greek *penthēmimerēs* consisting of five halves, from *pente* five + *hēmimerēs* halved (formed as HEMI- + *meros* part).]
CLASSICAL PROSODY. A group of five half-feet; *spec*. (*a*) either half of a pentameter; (*b*) the first part of a hexameter as far as a caesura in the middle of the third foot.
■ **penthemimeral** *adjective* designating a caesura occurring in the middle of the third foot in a line M19.

penthouse /ˈpɛnthaʊs/ *noun & adjective*. Orig. (*arch*.) **pentice** /ˈpɛntɪs/, †**pentis**, & other vars. ME.
[Anglo-Norman, aphet. from Old French *apentis*, *apendis*, from medieval Latin use of late Latin *appendicium* appendage, from Latin *appendere* (see APPEND); refash. in 16 by assoc. with French *pente* slope + HOUSE *noun*[1], as if 'sloping house'.]
►**A** *noun*. **1** A subsidiary structure attached to the wall of a main building, having a sloping (or, formerly, horizontal) roof, and serving as a shelter, a covered walk or arcade, a porch, an outhouse, etc. Also, a sloping roof or ledge projecting from the wall of a building for shelter from the weather; *rare* the eaves of a roof when projecting greatly. ME. ►**b** A free-standing shed with a sloping roof. E19.
2 *transf*. & *fig*. Any of various structures or projections of the nature of or resembling a penthouse, as (*a*) an awning, a canopy; (*b*) in REAL TENNIS, the sloping roof of the corridor or galleries running around three sides of the court. M16.
3 A separate flat, apartment, etc., situated on the roof or the top floor of a tall building. L19.
►**B** *attrib*. or as *adjective*. **1** Of, pertaining to, or resembling a penthouse. E17.
2 (**P-**.) [The Penthouse Theatre at Washington University, Seattle.] Designating or pertaining to theatre-in-the-round. M20.

> 📖 **1** A. FRATER In the lift, ascending to the penthouse suite.

penthouse /ˈpɛnthaʊs/ *verb trans*. E17.
[from prec.]
Provide with a penthouse; *fig*. cover or shelter as with a penthouse. Usu. in *pass*.

pentice *noun & adjective* see PENTHOUSE *noun & adjective*.

pentimento /pɛntɪˈmɛntəʊ/ *noun*. Pl. **-ti** /-ti/. E20.
[Italian, lit. 'repentance'.]
ART. A visible trace of (an) earlier painting beneath a layer or layers of paint; (a) painting revealed by such traces.

†**pentis** *noun & adjective* see PENTHOUSE *noun & adjective*.

pentitol /ˈpɛntɪtɒl/ *noun*. E20.
[from PENTA- + -ITOL.]
CHEMISTRY. Any pentahydric alcohol.

Pentland /ˈpɛntlənd/ *noun*. M20.
[*Pentland* Hills, Midlothian, Scotland, site of the Scottish Plant Breeding Station.]
Used *attrib*. in the names of varieties of potato developed at the Scottish Plant Breeding Station.
Pentland Crown, ***Pentland Dell***, etc.

pentlandite /ˈpɛntləndʌɪt/ *noun*. M19.
[from J. B. *Pentland* (1797–1873), Irish traveller + -ITE[1].]
MINERALOGY. A bronze-yellow sulphide of iron and nickel which crystallizes in the cubic system and is the principal ore of nickel.

pentobarbitone /pɛntəˈbɑːbɪtəʊn/ *noun*. M20.
[from PENT(ANE + -O- + BARBITONE.]
PHARMACOLOGY. A sedative-hypnotic and anticonvulsant barbiturate drug, 5-ethyl-5-(1-methylbutyl)-barbituric acid. Cf. NEMBUTAL.
■ Also **pentobarbital** *noun* (*US*) M20.

pentode /ˈpɛntəʊd/ *noun*. E20.
[from PENTA- + -ODE[2].]
ELECTRONICS. A thermionic valve having five electrodes. Also ***pentode valve***.

pentograph *noun* var. of PANTOGRAPH.

Pentomic /pɛnˈtɒmɪk/ *adjective*. Also **p-**. M20.
[from PENTA- + ATOMIC.]
MILITARY. Divided into five battle groups armed with nuclear weapons.

pentomino /pɛnˈtɒmɪnəʊ/ *noun*. Pl. **-oes**. M20.
[from PENT(A- + D)OMINO.]
1 Each of the twelve distinct planar shapes that can be formed by joining five identical squares by their edges. M20.
2 (**P-**.) In *pl*. (Proprietary name for) a board game involving these shapes. M20.

penton /ˈpɛntɒn/ *noun*. M20.
[from PENTA- + -ON.]
BIOLOGY. A capsomere which occupies each of the twelve vertices of the icosahedral capsid of an adenovirus.

pentosan /ˈpɛntəsan/ *noun*. L19.
[from PENTOSE + -AN.]
BIOCHEMISTRY. A polysaccharide whose constituent monosaccharides are pentoses.

pentose /ˈpɛntəʊz, -s/ *noun*. L19.
[from PENTA- + -OSE[2].]
CHEMISTRY. Any monosaccharide sugar with five carbon atoms in its molecule (e.g. ribose, xylose).
Comb.: **pentose cycle**, **pentose phosphate cycle**, **pentose phosphate shunt**, **pentose shunt** BIOCHEMISTRY a cyclic metabolic pathway in animals and higher plants by which glucose phosphate is converted to a pentose phosphate, which is afterwards converted into hexose and triose phosphates that can be recycled.

pentosuria /pɛntəˈsjʊərɪə/ *noun*. E20.
[from PENTOSE + -URIA.]
MEDICINE. (A congenital defect causing) abnormal excretion of pentoses in the urine.
■ **pentosuric** *adjective & noun* (*a*) *adjective* of, pertaining to, or having pentosuria; (*b*) *noun* an individual with pentosuria: E20.

Pentothal /ˈpɛntəθal/ *noun*. Also **p-**. M20.
[Alt. of THIOPENTAL.]
PHARMACOLOGY. (Proprietary name for) the drug thiopentone.

pentoxide /pɛnˈtɒksʌɪd/ *noun*. M19.
[from PENTA- + OXIDE.]
CHEMISTRY. Any oxide containing five atoms of oxygen in its molecule or empirical formula.

pent-roof /ˈpɛntruːf/ *noun*. M19.
[from PENT(HOUSE *noun* + ROOF *noun*.]
A roof sloping in one direction only, like that of a penthouse; = ***shed roof*** s.v. SHED *noun*[2].

pentrough /ˈpɛntrɒf/ *noun*. L18.
[from PEN *noun*[1] + TROUGH.]
A trough or channel, usu. of planks or boards, for conveying water from a weir, dam, etc., to the place where its force is applied, as in a water-mill.

pentryl /ˈpɛntrɪl/ *noun*. M20.
[from PENTA- after TETRYL.]
A crystalline explosive with similar properties to tetryl, but with five nitro groups in its molecule.

pentstemon /pɛntˈstiːmən, -ˈstɛmən, ˈpɛn(t)stɪmən/ *noun*. Also **penstemon** /pɛnˈstiːmən, -ˈstɛm-, ˈpɛnstɪmən/. M18.
[mod. Latin (see below), irreg. formed as PENTA- + Greek *stēmōn*, taken as = stamen.]
Any of various N. American plants constituting the genus *Penstemon*, of the figwort family, cultivated for their showy tubular two-lipped flowers, and having five stamens of which one is sterile.

pentyl /ˈpɛntʌɪl, -tɪl/ *noun*. L19.
[from PENTA- + -YL.]
CHEMISTRY. A radical, $C_5H_{11}\cdot$, derived from a pentane. Cf. AMYL. Usu. in *comb*.

penuche /pɛˈnuːtʃi/ *noun*. Also **panocha** /paˈnɒtʃə/, **panoche** /paˈnɒtʃi/, & other vars. M19.
[Amer. Spanish *panoche*.]
1 A kind of coarse brown sugar used in Mexico. M19.
2 A kind of sweet resembling fudge, made with brown sugar, butter, milk or cream, and often nuts. *N. Amer*. L19.

penult /pɪˈnʌlt, ˈpɛnʌlt/ *adjective & noun*. L15.
[Abbreviation of PENULTIMA, PENULTIMATE.]
►**A** *adjective*. = PENULTIMATE *adjective*. *arch*. L15.
►**B** *noun*. †**1** The penultimate day (of a month). *Scot*. M16–M17.
2 LINGUISTICS. A penultimate syllable. E19.

penultima /pɪˈnʌltɪmə/ *noun*. Long *rare* or *obsolete*. Pl. **-mae** /-miː/, **-mas**. LME.
[Latin *paenultima* fem. of *paenultimus* PENULTIMATE.]
The penultimate syllable (of a word or verse).

penultimate /pɪˈnʌltɪmət/ *adjective & noun*. L17.
[Latin *paenultimus* (from *paene* almost + *ultimus* last), after ULTIMATE *adjective & noun*.]
►**A** *adjective*. Second last, last but one, (of a series). Also, occurring on the second last syllable. L17.
►**B** *noun*. The last but one; *spec*. the last syllable but one of a word. E19.
■ Also †**penultim** *adjective & noun* LME–E18.

penumbra /pɪˈnʌmbrə/ *noun*. Pl. **-brae** /-briː/, **-bras**. M17.
[mod. Latin, from Latin *paene* almost + *umbra* shadow.]
1 The partially shaded outer region of a shadow (contrasted with the umbra) when the light comes from a source of some size; *esp*. (ASTRONOMY) that of the shadow cast by the moon or the earth in an eclipse. M17. ►**b** ASTRONOMY. The lighter periphery of a sunspot, surrounding the dark core or umbra. M19.
2 *transf*. Any partial shade or shadow round a thing; a surrounding area of uncertain extent (*lit*. & *fig*.). E19.

> 📖 **2** E. FIGES Round the lightswitch, a dark penumbra caused by the many hands . . rubbed against the wall. E. J. HOBSBAWM The vast penumbra of semi-dependent artisans and outworkers. P. MEDAWAR Almost all chronic illness is surrounded by a penumbra of gloomy imaginings.

■ **penumbral** *adjective* M18. **penumbrous** *adjective* (*rare*) L19.

penurious /pɪˈnjʊərɪəs/ *adjective*. L16.
[medieval Latin *penuriosus*, from Latin *penuria* PENURY: see -OUS.]
1 (Of a person) destitute, needy, poor; (of a thing, circumstance, etc.) characterized by want or scarcity; poor, scanty. L16.
2 Parsimonious, grudging; mean. E17.
3 Fastidious. Long *obsolete* exc. *Scot.* E18.
■ **penuriously** *adverb* L16. **penuriousness** *noun* M17.

penury /ˈpɛnjʊri/ *noun*. LME.
[Latin *penuria*, *paenuria* perh. rel. to *paene* almost: see -Y³.]
1 Destitution, indigence; poverty. LME.
2 A lack, a dearth, a scarcity, (*of* something). LME.
3 Miserliness, parsimoniousness. Now *rare*. M17.

Penutian /pəˈnuːʃ(ə)n, -ˈnuːtɪən/ *noun & adjective*. E20.
[from Yokuts (and related langs.) *pen* two + Miwok (and related langs.) *uti* two + -AN.]
(Of or pertaining to) a N. American Indian language family of California and (in some classifications) areas to the north. Also, designating or pertaining to (any of) the peoples speaking a Penutian language.

Penzance brier /pɛnˈzans ˈbrʌɪə/ *noun phr*. E20.
[James Plaisted Wilde, Lord *Penzance* (1816–99), English lawyer and amateur horticulturist.]
Any of various hybrid roses derived from the sweet-brier, *Rosa rubiginosa*, first developed by Lord Penzance.

peola /piːˈəʊlə/ *noun*. *US Black slang*. M20.
[Origin unkn.]
A light-skinned black person, esp. a girl.

peon /ˈpiːən, *in branch I also* pjuːn, *in branch II also* peɪˈɒn, *foreign* peˈon/ *noun*. Pl. **-s**, (in sense 3 also) **-es** /-ɪz, *foreign* -ɛs/. E17.
[In sense 1 from Portuguese *peão*, in senses 2 and 3 from Spanish *peón* peasant, from medieval Latin *pedo(n-)* foot-soldier: see PAWN *noun*¹.]
▶ **I 1** In the Indian subcontinent and SE Asia: a person of low rank; *spec.* (*a*) a foot-soldier; (*b*) an orderly; (*c*) an office boy. E17.
▶ **II 2** A Spanish-American day labourer or farmworker, *esp.* one in poor circumstances. Also (*Hist.*), a debtor held in servitude by a creditor, esp. in the southern US and Mexico. E19.
3 = BANDERILLERO. M20.
■ **peonage**, **peonism** *nouns* (*a*) the state of being a peon; (*b*) the system of having or using peons: M19.

peonin /ˈpiːənɪn/ *noun*. E20.
[from PEONY + -IN¹.]
CHEMISTRY. An anthocyanin that is the colouring matter of red peonies.
■ **peonidin** /pɪˈɒnɪdɪn/ *noun* [-IDIN] an anthocyanidin of which peonin is a glycoside E20.

peony /ˈpiːəni/ *noun & adjective*. OE.
[Latin *peonia*, *paeonia* from Greek *paiōnia*, from *Paiōn* the physician of the gods: see -Y³.]
▶ **A** *noun*. **1** Any of various stout perennial herbaceous plants and shrubs constituting the genus *Paeonia* (family Paeoniaceae), much grown for their showy globular flowers, freq. double, and esp. crimson, pink, or white in colour; a flower or flowering stem of such a plant. OE.
2 The colour especially associated with peonies, a dark pink or crimson. E20.
1 *tree peony*.
▶ **B** *adjective*. Resembling a peony in colour, dark pink or crimson; (of the cheeks) plump and rosy. E19.

people /ˈpiːp(ə)l/ *noun*. Pl. same, (now only in sense 1) **-s**. ME.
[Anglo-Norman *poeple*, *people*, from Old French *pople* (also mod. *peuple*), from Latin *populus*.]
1 A body of persons composing a community, nation, ethnic group, etc.; = FOLK 1. Treated as *sing.* (with pl. **-s**) or *pl.* ME.
2 a *pl.* The persons belonging to a particular place, congregation, company, or class. ME. ▶†**b** A company, a multitude. ME–M17.
3 *pl.* **a** Persons in relation to a superior; *spec.* (*a*) the subjects of a ruler; (*b*) the attendants, followers, servants, etc., of a master, employer, etc. ME. ▶**b** Persons in relation to an individual, the members of a person's family, community, etc., collectively. LME.
4 *pl.* Human beings; persons in general. Freq. with specifying word. ME. ▶**b** *pl.* Living creatures, animals. *literary*. M17. ▶**c** *be people*, be a person of a specified (*good*, *fine*, etc.) kind. *US colloq.* E20.
5 *pl.* **a** The common people; the mass of the community as opp. to the ruling or official classes; *spec.* (*ECCLESIASTICAL*) the laity. LME. ▶**b** The whole body of citizens, regarded as the source of political power; *spec.* the electorate. M17. ▶**c** (Usu. **P-**.) The State prosecution in a law case. *US*. E19.

> 🕮 **1** G. BROWN Peoples in the World whom he liked—he had a particular love of the Poles. J. BARNES The Kamchatkans, a people of eastern Siberia. **2a** *Star (Sheffield)* The people of England should not bury their heads in the sand. **3a** QUEEN VICTORIA From my heart I thank my beloved people. **b** J. AGATE Promises to invite me home to lunch with his people. **4** OED There were some sheep in the field, but no people. P. CAMPBELL Unexpectedly we had seven people to lunch. ***country people***, ***poor people***, ***townspeople***, ***working people***, etc. **5a** T. F. SIMMONS Separate devotions for the priest and people. **b** T. BENN Regarding government as the people's instrument for shaping their own destiny. **c** *New York Law Journal* Pre-trial statements made by the People's witnesses.

Phrases: ***beautiful people***: see BEAUTIFUL *adjective*. ***be gathered to one's people***: see GATHER *verb*. CHOSEN ***people***. ***enemy of the people***: see ENEMY *noun*. ***gentle people***: see GENTLE *adjective*. ***little people***: see LITTLE *adjective*. ***man of the people***: see MAN *noun*. ***of all people***: see OF *preposition*. ***peculiar people***: see PECULIAR *adjective*. ***people of the Book***: see BOOK *noun*. **Peoples of the Sea** the seafaring migrant peoples who invaded and settled parts of ancient Egypt, Syria, and Palestine. ***plain people***: see PLAIN *adjective*¹ & *adverb*. ***the good people***: see GOOD *adjective*. ***tribune of the people***: see TRIBUNE *noun*¹ 1.

Comb.: **people carrier** a motor vehicle with three rows of seats, enabling the transport of more passengers than the average car; **people-king** *arch.* a sovereign people; **people meter** (in N. America) an electronic device which records the television viewing habits of a household, for use in compiling ratings; **people person** *colloq.* a person who enjoys or is particularly good at interacting with others; **people power** (*a*) physical effort exerted by people as opp. to machines etc.; (*b*) political or other pressure applied by the people, esp. through the public demonstration of popular opinion; **people's army** (*a*) an army organized on egalitarian or Communist principles; (*b*) an army composed of the common people; **People's Bureau** a foreign embassy of the Libyan Arab Republic; **people's car** an inexpensive motor car designed for popular sale; ***People's Charter***: see CHARTER *noun*; **people's choice** a popular favourite; **People's Court** (*a*) *Hist.* a court set up by the Nazi regime in Germany to deal with political offences; (*b*) a court in the Soviet and similar legal systems; **people's democracy** a political system in which power is regarded as being invested in the people, *spec.* a Communist State; **People's front** = ***popular front*** s.v. POPULAR *adjective*; **People's Palace** a recreation and entertainment centre for the people in a locality; **people's park**: for the use of all members of a community; **People's Power** = ***people power*** above; **people's republic** (a designation of) any of various left-wing or Communist States; **people's theatre**: run on socialist lines for the use of the community; **people's war** (*a*) a war in which the people are regarded as fighting against oppressive rulers or foreign aggression; (*b*) a war involving all members of the community, a total war.

■ †**peopledom** *noun* (*a*) a province or deme in ancient Greece; (*b*) a democracy: M17–E18. **peoplehood** *noun* the condition, state, or awareness of being a people E20. **peopleless** /-l-l-/ *adjective* without people, uninhabited E17. †**peopleship** *noun* (*rare*) citizenship M17–L19.

people /ˈpiːp(ə)l/ *verb*. LME.
[Old & mod. French *peupler*, from *peuple*: see prec.]
1 *verb trans.* Fill with people or inhabitants; populate. LME.
2 *verb trans.* Occupy as inhabitants; inhabit. Freq. as ***peopled*** *ppl adjective*. L15.
3 *verb intrans.* Become populated; grow populous. M17.

> 🕮 **1** *Landscape* Robins . . has peopled the garden with . . nymphs and satyrs. **2** R. WEST Treetops . . thickly peopled with birds. *fig.*: C. KINGSLEY The heroes of Troy . . peopled her imagination.

■ **peopler** *noun* (*a*) a person who populates a country, colony, etc.; (*b*) an inhabitant: E17.

PEP *abbreviation*.
1 (Also /pɛp/.) Personal equity plan, an investment scheme whereby investors may acquire shares or unit trusts in British companies without liability for tax on dividends or capital gains.
2 Political and Economic Planning.
3 Project Employment Programme.

pep /pɛp/ *noun & verb*. *colloq.* (orig. *US*). E20.
[Abbreviation of PEPPER *noun*.]
▶ **A** *noun*. Energy, animation, spirit. E20.

> 🕮 *Punch* Send me a subject with a bit more pep in it.

▶ **B** *verb trans.* Infl. **-pp-**. Foll. by *up*: fill or inspire with energy, invigorate, enliven; cheer up. E20.

> 🕮 P. FUSSELL Glen Miller's pepped-up version of the St. Louis Blues.

Comb.: **pep pill**: containing a stimulant drug; **pep rally** *N. Amer.* a meeting to inspire enthusiasm, esp. before a sporting event; **pep talk** a usu. short talk to revive the morale of or encourage its hearers.
■ **pepful** *adjective* full of life or energy E20. **pepless** *adjective* E20. **pepper-up** (pl. **peppers-up**), **pepper-upper** *nouns* a person who or thing which enlivens or stimulates M20.

peperino /pɛpəˈriːnəʊ/ *noun*. L18.
[Italian, from *peper-* (see PEPPERONI) + dim. suffix *-ino* (because it consists of small grains).]
GEOLOGY. A light porous grey tuff containing fragments of leucite etc., found in the Albano hills, Italy; any pyroclastic deposit containing varied fragments.

peperite /ˈpɛpərʌɪt/ *noun*. M19.
[French *pépérite*, prob. from *pépérino*, formed as prec.: see -ITE¹.]
GEOLOGY. A brecciated volcanic material in marine sedimentary rock, formed by the intrusion of lava or magma into wet sediment.

peperomia /pɛpəˈrəʊmɪə/ *noun*. L19.
[mod. Latin (see below), from Greek *peperi* pepper: see -IA¹.]
Any of numerous succulent plants, chiefly of tropical America, constituting the genus *Peperomia* of the pepper family, including a number grown as house-plants for their ornamental foliage.

peperoni *noun* var. of PEPPERONI.

pepino /pɛˈpiːnəʊ/ *noun*. Pl. **-os**. M19.
[Spanish = cucumber.]
1 In Spain and Spanish-speaking countries, a cucumber. *rare*. M19.
2 *PHYSICAL GEOGRAPHY*. A steep conical hill characteristic of karst topography, esp. in Puerto Rico. Cf. HUM *noun*³, MOGOTE. M19.
3 A spiny plant of the Andes, *Solanum muricatum*, of the nightshade family, sometimes grown for its fruit; the elongated fruit of this plant, which is yellow with purple streaks and tastes like a melon. L19.

peplos /ˈpɛplɒs/ *noun*. Pl. **-ploi** /-plɔɪ/, **-ploses**. L18.
[Greek.]
GREEK ANTIQUITIES. A (usu. rich) outer robe or shawl worn by women in ancient Greece, hanging in loose folds and sometimes drawn over the head; *spec.* the one woven for the statue of the goddess Athene at Athens, and carried in procession to her temple at the greater Panathenaea.

peplum /ˈpɛpləm/ *noun*. L17.
[Latin, formed as prec.]
1 = PEPLOS. L17.
2 Formerly, a kind of overskirt, in supposed imitation of the ancient peplum. Now also, a usu. short flounce on a jacket, blouse, or tunic, hanging from the waist over a skirt; a jacket etc. incorporating this. M19.
■ **peplumed** *adjective* (of a garment) made with a peplum L20.

pepo /ˈpiːpəʊ/ *noun*. In sense 1 also (earlier) †**pepon**. Pl. **-s**, **pepones** /pɪˈpəʊniːz/. LME.
[Latin *pepo(n-)* pumpkin, from Greek *pepōn*: see POMPION.]
†**1** A pumpkin, a gourd; = POMPION 1. LME–E18.
2 *BOTANY*. A many-seeded fleshy fruit, with parietal placentae and a hard rind chiefly derived from the receptacle of the flower, esp. characteristic of the gourd family. M19.

pepper /ˈpɛpə/ *noun*.
[Old English *piper*, *-or* = Old Frisian *piper*, Old Saxon *pipari*, *pepar* (Dutch *peper*), Old High German *pfeffar* (German *Pfeffer*), from West Germanic, from Latin *piper* from Greek *peperi* from Sanskrit *pippalī* berry, peppercorn. Cf. PEP *noun & verb*.]
1 A pungent condiment prepared from the whole or ground dried berries (peppercorns) of the plant *Piper nigrum* (see sense 2 below), either unripe (more fully ***black pepper***, the stronger form), or ripe or unripe but husked (more fully ***white pepper***). Also, any similar condiment prepared from other plants, esp. forms of *Capsicum annuum* (e.g. chillis). OE. ▶**b** *fig.* Pungency, sharpness; indignation, anger. Freq. in proverbial expressions. OE.
2 The chief plant yielding pepper, *Piper nigrum* (family Piperaceae), a climbing shrub indigenous to southern India and Sri Lanka, having alternate stalked entire leaves, flowers in pendulous spikes, and small berries which turn red when ripe. Also, any other plant of the genus *Piper* or of the family Piperaceae. OE.
3 The bell-shaped, smooth-skinned, mildly pungent fruit of certain varieties of the plant *Capsicum annuum*, eaten in salads or as a vegetable either unripe (more fully ***green pepper***) or ripe (more fully ***orange pepper***, ***red pepper***, ***yellow pepper***); the plant of the nightshade family bearing this fruit. Also ***sweet pepper***. Also called ***capsicum***. L19.
4 A pepper tree. L19.
5 *ellipt.* = PEPPER-POT 1. L19.
6 In skipping, a rapid rate of turning the rope. E20.

Phrases: **African pepper** = ***Guinea pepper*** (a) below. ***black pepper***: see sense 1 above. CAYENNE ***pepper***. ***chilli pepper***: see CHILLI *noun*. ***green pepper***: see sense 3 above. **Guinea pepper** (*a*) a W. African tree, *Xylopia aethiopica* (family Annonaceae); the spicy fruit of this tree, used as a condiment and medicinally; (*b*) = ***grains of Paradise*** s.v. GRAIN *noun*¹ 3a. ***Jamaica pepper***: see JAMAICA 1. **Japan pepper** a Japanese tree, *Zanthoxylum piperitum*, of the rue family; its spicy fruit, used as a condiment. **Java pepper** the cubeb, *Piper cubeba*. **long pepper** the dried fruit-spikes of the Indian plant *Piper longum*, used as a seasoning or medicinally. **red pepper** (*a*) = CAYENNE ***pepper***; (*b*) see sense 3 above. STUFFED ***pepper***. **sweet pepper** (*a*) see sense 3 above; (*b*) *US* = ***pepperbush*** below. ***white pepper***: see sense 1 above.

Comb.: **pepperbush** any of several N. American shrubs of the genus *Clethra* (family Clethraceae), esp. *C. alnifolia* and *C. acuminata*, with dense spikelike racemes of fragrant white flowers; **pepper-caster** = PEPPER-POT 1; **pepper dulse** *Scot.* a pungent edible seaweed, *Laurencia pinnatifida*; **pepper gas** an anti-personnel gas that irritates the throat and nasal passages; **pepper-grass** †(*a*) pillwort, *Pilularia globulifera* (whose sporangia resemble peppercorns); (**b**) *US* = **pepperwort** (a) below; **pepper-mill** a hand-mill for grinding pepper; †**pepper-quern** a quern or hand-mill for grinding pepper; **pepper-root** any of several N. American cruciferous plants of the genus *Dentaria* (or *Cardamine*), esp. *D. diphylla*, with a pungent root; **pepper-sauce** any of various pungent sauces or condiments made with pepper(s); **pepper saxifrage** an umbelliferous plant of damp pastures, *Silaum silaus*, with yellowish flowers and a fetid smell; **pepper shaker** *N. Amer.* = PEPPER-POT 1; **pepper shrike** a tropical American songbird of the genus *Cyclarhis*, of the vireo family, with mainly green and yellow plumage and a heavy, hooked bill; **pepper soup** a W. African soup made with red pepper and other hot spices; **pepper spray** an aerosol spray containing oils derived from cayenne pepper, irritant to the eyes and respiratory passages and used as a disabling weapon; **pepper steak**: coated liberally with crushed peppercorns before cooking; **pepper tree** (*a*) a Peruvian evergreen tree, *Schinus molle* (family Anacardiaceae), with an aromatic fruit, widely grown as a shade tree in hot countries; (**b**) either of two Australasian trees of the family Winteraceae, *Drimys lanceolata* of Tasmania, with fruits that were used as a substitute for pepper, and *Pseudowintera colorata* of New Zealand, with peppery fernlike leaves; (**c**) = KAWAKAWA *noun*[1] 1; **pepper-vine** (*a*) the climbing plant *Piper nigrum*, from which black pepper and white pepper are prepared; (**b**) a N. American plant, *Ampelopsis arborea*, allied to the Virginia creeper, with pungent black berries; **pepperwood** (the timber of) any of several trees having aromatic wood or bark, esp. the Hercules' club, *Zanthoxylum clava-herculis*; **pepperwort** (*a*) any of various peppery-tasting cruciferous plants constituting the genus *Lepidium* (orig. *esp.* dittander, *L. latifolium*; (**b**) *N. Amer.* = ***pepper-root*** above.

■ **pepperette** /pɛpəˈrɛt/ *noun* (*rare*) a pepper-pot E20.

pepper /ˈpɛpə/ *verb.*

[Old English (*ge*)*pip*(*o*)*rian* (corresp. to Old Norse *pipra*, Old High German *pheffarōn*, Middle High German, German *pfeffer*(*e*)*n*, Dutch *peperen*), from the noun.]

1 *verb trans.* **a** Sprinkle, season, or treat with pepper. OE. ▸**b** Sprinkle (a surface) as with pepper; cover, dot, or stud with numerous small objects, spots, etc. Usu. in *pass.* E17. ▸**c** Give pungency, spice, or flavour to (speech or writing). E17. ▸†**d** Praise, flatter. M17–L18.

2 *verb trans.* Inflict severe punishment or suffering on; beat severely, trounce. Formerly also, destroy, ruin. L15.

†**3** *verb trans.* [translating French *poivrer*.] Infect with venereal disease. E17–E18.

4 a *verb trans.* Pelt (a person) with missiles; fire shot, bullets, etc., at. Freq. *fig.* M17. ▸**b** *verb intrans.* Fire *away* (*at* a person etc.). L19.

5 *verb trans. & intrans.* Pour or scatter like pepper. E19.

🕮 **1a** H. GLASSE Dried salmon . . should be moderately peppered. **b** C. SAGAN Thousands of stars . . are peppered across the canopy of night. ANTHONY SMITH Scientific papers are . . peppered with references. A. BROOKNER His hair . . is peppered with grey. **4a** V. WOOLF Her words peppered the audience as with a shower of . . little stones. A. CARTER The Czech . . peppered them with a hail of bullets. *Times* Spokesmen . . were peppered with reporters' questions. **b** W. A. WALLACE He could not possibly be peppering away at the pheasants. **5** J. CLARE Grinning north-winds . . pepper'd round my head their hail and snow. C. MANN The driven sand and salt peppering into their eyes.

¶ Not recorded in ME; re-formed L15.

pepper-and-salt /pɛp(ə)r(ə)ndˈsɔːlt, -ˈsɒlt/ *noun & adjective.* L18.

[from PEPPER *noun* + AND *conjunction*[1] + SALT *noun*[1] & *adjective*[1].]

▸ **A** *noun.* **1** A kind of cloth made of interwoven dark and light threads, presenting a flecked or speckled appearance. L18.

2 The plant harbinger-of-spring, *Erigenia bulbosa*, so called from the colour-contrast of its white petals and dark anthers. *US.* M19.

▸ **B** *attrib.* or as *adjective.* Of, characteristic of, or resembling pepper-and-salt; *esp.* (of hair) being flecked with grey. Cf. SALT-AND-PEPPER. M19.

🕮 J. GASKELL My hair is nearly white. Last time I looked it was only pepper-and-salt. W. S. MAUGHAM Very neat in his black coat and pepper-and-salt trousers. **pepper-and-salt fundus** MEDICINE a symptom of congenital syphilis, the fundus of the eye having a speckled appearance.

pepperbox /ˈpɛpəbɒks/ *noun.* M16.

[from PEPPER *noun* + BOX *noun*[2].]

1 A pepper-pot. Now *rare.* M16.

2 *transf.* **a** A small cylindrical turret or cupola. *rare.* E19. ▸**b** An early type of revolver with five or six barrels revolving round a central axis. Usu. *attrib.* M19.

3 In Eton fives, an irregular buttress protruding into the court. M19.

peppercorn /ˈpɛpəkɔːn/ *noun & adjective.* OE.

[from PEPPER *noun* + CORN *noun*[1].]

▸ **A** *noun.* **1** The dried berry of the pepper plant, *Piper nigrum*. OE.

2 A rent of one peppercorn; *fig.* an insignificant amount. E17.

3 A tuft of peppercorn hair. Usu. in *pl. S. Afr.* M20.

Comb.: **peppercorn hair** *S. Afr.* hair growing in sparse tight curls, characteristic of Nama; **peppercorn tree** *Austral.* = ***pepper tree*** (a) s.v. PEPPER *noun.*

▸ **B** *attrib.* or as *adjective.* (Of a rent) of or consisting of a peppercorn, nominal; *fig.* very small, insignificant. L18.

peppered /ˈpɛpəd/ *adjective.* L16.

[from PEPPER *noun, verb*: see -ED[2], -ED[1].]

That has been peppered, provided with pepper.

peppered moth the geometrid moth *Biston betularia*, which is usu. white speckled with black, and is noted for the melanic forms which predominate in industrial areas. **peppered steak** = ***pepper steak*** s.v. PEPPER *noun.*

pepperer /ˈpɛp(ə)rə/ *noun.* ME.

[Sense 1 from PEPPER *noun* + -ER[2]; sense 2 from PEPPER *verb* + -ER[1].]

1 A dealer in pepper and spices; a grocer. *obsolete* exc. *Hist.* ME.

2 A person who or thing which peppers something. Chiefly *fig.* E18.

pepperidge /ˈpɛp(ə)rɪdʒ/ *noun. US.* L17.

[Alt. of PIPPERIDGE.]

= ***black gum*** s.v. BLACK *adjective.*

pepperina /pɛpəˈriːnə/ *noun. Austral.* M20.

[from PEPPER *noun* + *-ina*, after *casuarina*.]

= ***pepper tree*** (a) s.v. PEPPER *noun.*

peppering /ˈpɛp(ə)rɪŋ/ *adjective.* E18.

[from PEPPER *verb* + -ING[2].]

That peppers; pungent, angry; (of rain) falling heavily.

peppermint /ˈpɛpəmɪnt/ *noun.* L17.

[from PEPPER *noun* + MINT *noun*[2].]

1 A pungent hybrid mint, *Mentha* × *piperita*, with lanceolate, often red-tinged leaves and spikes of lilac flowers, cultivated for its essential oil. L17.

2 a The essential oil of peppermint; any of various preparations made from this oil, characteristically having a pungent aromatic flavour leaving an after-sensation of coolness, and chiefly used as a flavouring or for various medical purposes (also ***oil of peppermint***, ***peppermint oil***). Also, a cordial or liqueur flavoured with peppermint. M18. ▸**b** A sweet flavoured with peppermint; *spec.* = ***peppermint cream***, ***peppermint-drop*** below. E19. ▸**c** Any of various colours, esp. pale green, associated with peppermint-flavoured drinks or sweets. M19.

3 More fully ***peppermint-gum***, ***peppermint-tree***. Any of several Australian eucalypts, esp. *Eucalyptus amygdalina* and *E. piperita*, which yield an aromatic oil like that of peppermint. L18.

Comb.: **peppermint cordial** a cordial flavoured with peppermint; **peppermint cream** a cream sweet flavoured with peppermint and often covered with chocolate; **peppermint-drop** a type of boiled sweet flavoured with peppermint; **peppermint-flavoured** *adjective* flavoured with peppermint; **peppermint geranium** a white-flowered pelargonium, *Pelargonium tomentosum*, with leaves which give off a peppermint smell when bruised; ***peppermint gum***: see sense 3 above; **peppermint lump** a type of sweet flavoured with peppermint; ***peppermint oil***: see sense 2a above; **peppermint-tea** an infusion of the leaves of the peppermint; ***peppermint-tree***: see sense 3 above; **peppermint-water** a cordial distilled from peppermint.

■ **pepperminty** *adjective* of, pertaining to, or resembling peppermint; that tastes or smells of peppermint: M20.

pepperoni /pɛpəˈrəʊni/ *noun.* Also **pepe-**. M20.

[Italian *peperone* chilli, from *peper-*, *pepe* pepper from Latin *piper* (see PEPPER *noun*) + augm. suffix *-one*.]

Beef and pork sausage seasoned with pepper.

pepper-pot /ˈpɛpəpɒt/ *noun.* L17.

[from PEPPER *noun* + POT *noun*[1].]

1 A small usu. round container with a perforated lid for sprinkling pepper; anything resembling or held to resemble this. L17.

2 a A West Indian dish of meat (or fish, game, etc.) and vegetables stewed with cassareep and red pepper or other hot spices. Also more fully ***pepper-pot soup***. L17. ▸**b** In Pennsylvania, a stew of tripe and dumplings highly seasoned with pepper. L18.

🕮 **1** G. MACDONALD One house with the pepper-pot turrets.

peppery /ˈpɛp(ə)ri/ *adjective.* L17.

[from PEPPER *noun* + -Y[1].]

1 Having much pepper; of the nature of or resembling pepper, pungent. L17.

2 *fig.* Of a person, mood, etc.: irritable, testy; (of a thing) irritating, objectionable; strong, powerful. E19.

■ **pepperiness** *noun* L19.

peppy /ˈpɛpi/ *adjective.* Orig. *US.* E20.

[from PEP *noun* + -Y[1].]

Full of pep or vigour; spirited, energetic, lively, forceful.

■ **peppiness** *noun* E20.

Pepsi-Cola /pɛpsɪˈkəʊlə/ *noun.* E20.

[from arbitrary formation + COLA *noun*[1].]

(Proprietary name for) an American aerated soft drink and the syrup preparations from which it is made.

■ Also **Pepsi** *noun* (proprietary name) E20.

pepsin /ˈpɛpsɪn/ *noun.* M19.

[from Greek *pepsis* digestion + -IN[1].]

BIOCHEMISTRY. The chief digestive enzyme of the stomach, an endopeptidase which splits proteins into polypeptides able to be absorbed, and was formerly used medicinally.

■ **pepsinate** *verb trans.* mix or treat with pepsin L19. **pepˈsinogen** *noun* the proenzyme form of pepsin L19.

peptic /ˈpɛptɪk/ *adjective & noun.* M17.

[Greek *peptikos* capable of digesting, from *peptos* cooked, digested: see -IC. Cf. DYSPEPTIC.]

▸ **A** *adjective.* **1** Orig., having the quality of digesting. Now, belonging or pertaining to digestion, *spec.* that in which pepsin is concerned. M17.

†**2** Having the quality of promoting or assisting digestion; = DIGESTIVE *adjective* 2. M17–E19.

†**3** Capable of digesting; having good digestion; = EUPEPTIC 2. Only in E19.

1 peptic digestion gastric digestion. **peptic gland**: that secretes the pepsin-containing gastric juice. **peptic ulcer** an ulcer in the gastric mucosa due to its partial digestion by pepsin and acid.

▸ **B** *noun.* †**1** = DIGESTIVE *noun* 1. Only in M19.

2 In *pl.* The digestive organs. *joc.* Now *rare* or *obsolete.* M19.

peptide /ˈpɛptʌɪd/ *noun.* E20.

[German *Peptid* back-form. from *Polypeptid* POLYPEPTIDE.]

BIOCHEMISTRY. Any compound in which two or more amino acids are linked together in a linear sequence, the carboxyl group of each acid being joined to the amino group of the next.

VASOACTIVE ***intestinal peptide***.

Comb.: **peptide bond** a carbon–nitrogen bond of the type ·OC·NH·, such as those linking the amino-acid residues in a peptide chain; **peptide chain** a linear sequence of amino-acid residues joined by peptide bonds; **peptide linkage** = ***peptide bond*** above.

■ **peptidase** /ˈpɛptɪdeɪz/ *noun* an enzyme which hydrolyses peptides E20. **peptidic** /pɛpˈtɪdɪk/ *adjective* M20. **peptidyl** /ˈpɛptɪdʌɪl, -dɪl/ *noun* a radical formed by a peptide, esp. by the removal of an NH_2 group from an amide group M20.

peptidergic /pɛptʌɪˈdəːdʒɪk/ *adjective.* M20.

[from PEPTIDE + -ERGIC.]

PHYSIOLOGY. Releasing or involving a neuropeptide as a neurotransmitter; *spec.* designating a neurone which releases one or more particular neuropeptides when stimulated.

peptidoglycan /pɛpˌtʌɪdəˈɡlʌɪkan/ *noun.* M20.

[from PEPTIDE + -O- + GLYCAN.]

BIOCHEMISTRY. = MUREIN. Also, the glycosaminoglycan which forms the strands of this.

peptidolysis /pɛptʌɪˈdɒlɪsɪs/ *noun.* L20.

[from PEPTIDE + -O- + -LYSIS.]

BIOCHEMISTRY. The breakdown of a polypeptide into smaller peptides or amino acids by hydrolysis of peptide bonds.

■ **peptidoˈlytic** *adjective* L20.

peptize /ˈpɛptʌɪz/ *verb trans.* Also **-ise**. M19.

[from PEPTONE + -IZE.]

CHEMISTRY. Convert (a solid or semi-solid colloid) into a sol by chemical means.

■ **peptizaˈbility** *noun* the quality of being peptizable M20. **peptizable** *adjective* able to be peptized E20. **peptiˈzation** *noun* M19. **peptizer** *noun* a substance which causes peptization or serves to prevent the coagulation of a colloidal suspension; *spec.* a catalyst used to facilitate the vulcanization of rubber: M20.

peptogen /ˈpɛptədʒ(ə)n/ *noun.* L19.

[from Greek *peptos* (see PEPTIC) + -GEN.]

Any of various substances which stimulate the secretion of pepsin by the gastric mucosa.

peptolysis /pɛpˈtɒlɪsɪs/ *noun.* E20.

[from PEPTONE + -LYSIS.]

BIOCHEMISTRY. = PEPTIDOLYSIS.

■ **peptoˈlytic** *adjective* E20.

peptone /ˈpɛptəʊn/ *noun.* Now *rare.* M19.

[Greek *pepton* neut. of *peptos*: see PEPTIC, -ONE.]

BIOCHEMISTRY. A protein made soluble by partial digestion.

■ **peptoniˈzation** *noun* the action or process of peptonizing something L19. **peptonize** *verb trans.* make (a protein) soluble by partial predigestion, esp. in the treatment of food L19. **peptonizer** *noun* a peptonizing agent L19. **peptoˈnuria** *noun* (MEDICINE) the presence of peptones in the urine L19.

Pepuzian /pɪˈpjuːzɪən/ *noun.* M16.

[medieval Latin *Pepuziani*, from *Pepuzia* Pepuza (see below): see -IAN.]

ECCLESIASTICAL HISTORY. A member of a 2nd-cent. sect of Montanists originating in Pepuza in Phrygia, an ancient country of Asia Minor.

Pepysian /ˈpiːpsɪən/ *adjective.* L18.

[from *Pepys* (see below) + -IAN.]

Of, pertaining to, or characteristic of the English diarist Samuel Pepys (1633–1703), his writings, his library, or the age in which he lived.

■ **Pepysiˈana** *noun pl.* [-ANA] publications or other items concerning or associated with Pepys L19.

Pequot /ˈpiːkwɒt/ *noun & adjective.* M17.

[Narragansett *Pequttôog* pl.]

▸ **A** *noun.* Pl. same, **-s**.

1 A member of an Algonquian people of southern New England. M17.

2 The language of this people. E20.

▶**B** *attrib.* or as *adjective.* Of or pertaining to the Pequot or their language. **M17.**

per /pəː/ *preposition.* **LME.**
[Latin (whence Old French & Italian *per*, French **PAR** *preposition.*).]
1 Through, by; by means of: (*a*) in Latin and mod. Latin (also medieval Latin & Italian) phrs., as ***per annum***, ***per se***; (*b*) in Old French phrs. and words derived therefrom, as ***trial per pais*** (cf. **PAR** *preposition*, **PER-**[2]). **LME.**
2 *HERALDRY.* In the direction of (a specified ordinary). **M16.**
3 By means of, by the instrumentality of; in accordance with (usu. ***as per***: see below); *LAW* as laid down by (a judge) in a specified case. **L16.**
4 For each, for every, as ***per cent***, ***per mil***, etc. Cf. **A** *adjective* 4. **L16.** ▸**b** With ellipsis of following noun: per hour, per cent, etc. Chiefly *US.* **L19.**

> 📖 **2** C. BOUTELL A shield . . may be divided . . by lines drawn per pale and per fesse. **3** *Modern Law Review* It cannot make a bare declaration (see *per* Lord Hailsham L.C., H.L.Deb., Vol. 318). J. JOHNSTON Arrivals at Kingstown per Royal Mail steamers. *Times* Per Edmund Burke, you cannot draw up an indictment against a whole nation. **4** J. W. REDWAY Hurricane winds . . estimated to have a velocity of 125 miles per hour. J. HERRIOT Twelve tablets per calf. *Scientific American* Per-kilogram allowances are not sufficient . . for children whose growth has been stunted. **b** D. G. PHILLIPS We'll get married as soon as he has a raise to twelve per.

Phrases (chiefly with Latin words in the accus.): **as per** in accordance with; (in full ***as per usual***) as usual. ***per aliud*** /ˈalɪʊd/ [*alius* another person or thing] with reference to something else; extrinsically. ***per anum*** /ˈeɪnəm/ by the anus (esp. with ref. to sexual intercourse). **per arsin** /ˈɑːsɪn/ [**ARSIS**] *MUSIC* by descent from higher to lower pitch; ***per arsin et thesin*** /ɛt ˈθiːsɪn/ [**THESIS**] by inversion (in a canon etc.). ***per consequens*** /ˈkɒnsɪkwɛnz/ (long *rare* or *obsolete*) consequently. **per curiam** /ˈkjʊərɪam/ *LAW* by decision of a judge, or of a court with none dissenting. ***per impossibile*** /ɪmpɒˈsɪbɪli/ as is impossible. ***per incuriam*** /ɪnˈkjʊərɪam/ *LAW* through lack of due regard to the law or the facts. **per primam (intentionem)** /ˌpriːmam ɪntɛnsɪˈəʊnɛm/ *MEDICINE* by first intention (see **INTENTION** 6). **per pro** [abbreviation of Latin ***per procurationem*** below] (*a*) by the agency of (esp. a person who signs in place of another) (the correct formal use); (*b*) on behalf of (esp. a person who does not sign himself or herself); abbreviation ***pp.*** ***per procurationem*** /ˌprɒkjʊrɑːtɪˈəʊnɛm/ *rare* per pro. ***per SALTIRE.*** ***per saltum*** /ˈsaltʊm/ [= jump] without intermediate steps, all at once.

per- /pəː, *unstressed* pə/ *prefix*[1].
1 Repr. Latin *per-* (formed as prec.) in words derived from Latin (directly or through French) or formed in English on Latin models: (*a*) in verbs and their derivs. with the senses 'through', as ***perforate***, ***pervade***; 'thoroughly, completely', as ***perfect*** *verb*; 'away entirely, to destruction', as ***perish***, ***pervert*** *verb*; (*b*) in adjectives & adverbs with the sense 'extremely, very', as ***perfervid***.
2 *CHEMISTRY.* Forming nouns and adjectives denoting the maximum proportion of some element in a compound; esp. (*a*) in names of oxides, acids, etc., in *-ic*, denoting the compound which contains the greatest proportion of oxygen (now largely superseded by **PEROXY-**, **PEROXO-**, or unrelated names), as ***perbromic***, ***pernitric***; also in names of salts of these acids, and related compounds, as ***permanganate***; (*b*) in names of binary compounds in *-ide* (formerly *-uret*), designating that in which the element or radical combines in the largest proportion with another element, as ***peroxide***.
■ **per'acetate** *noun* (*CHEMISTRY*) †(*a*) an acetate containing a maximum proportion of the acid radical; (*b*) an ester or related derivative of peracetic acid: **M19.** **pera'cetic** *adjective* (*CHEMISTRY*): ***peracetic acid***, $CH_3CO{\cdot}O{\cdot}OH$, a colourless corrosive pungent liquid that is explosive when hot and is used as an oxidizing agent, bleach, sterilizing agent, etc. **E20.** **per'acid** *noun* (*CHEMISTRY*) an acid containing a peroxide group, esp. the group ·CO·O·OH **E20.** **peral'kalic**, **per'alkaline** *adjectives* (*GEOLOGY*) designating rocks containing a high proportion of soda and potash (now, a proportion greater than that of alumina) **E20.** **peralka'linity** *noun* (*GEOLOGY*) the state of being peralkaline **M20.** **pera'luminous** *adjective* (*GEOLOGY*) designating rocks containing a higher proportion of alumina than of soda and potash combined **E20.** **per'borate** *noun* (*CHEMISTRY*) any of the derivatives of boric acid containing a peroxo anion, which are strongly oxidizing; *esp.* the sodium salt, used in washing powders: **L19.** **per'boric** *adjective* (*CHEMISTRY*): ***perboric acid***, the supposed parent acid of the perborates, to which the formula HBO_3 was formerly ascribed **L19.** **per'ester** *noun* (*CHEMISTRY*) an ester of a peracid **M20.**

per- /pəː/ *prefix*[2] (not productive).
Repr. Old French *per* or French *par* (see **PAR** *preposition*, **PER** *preposition*) in phrs which have coalesced into single English words, as ***peradventure***, ***perchance***; also (with 2nd elem. English) ***perhaps***.

peracarid /pɛrəˈkarɪd/ *noun & adjective.* **M20.**
[mod. Latin *Peracarida* (see below), from Greek *pēra* pouch + *karis* small crustacean: see **-ID**[3].]
▶**A** *noun.* A crustacean belonging to the superorder Peracarida of the class Malacostraca, characterized by a brood pouch in the female and including sand-hoppers (amphipods) and woodlice (isopods). **M20.**
▶**B** *adjective.* Of, pertaining to, or designating this superorder. **M20.**
■ **peracaridan** *noun* = **PERACARID** *noun* **M20.**

per accidens /pəːr ˈaksɪdɛnz/ *adverbial phr.* **E16.**
[mod. Latin, formed as **PER** + Latin *accidens, accident-*: see **ACCIDENT.**]
1 By virtue of some non-essential circumstance; contingently, indirectly. Opp. **PER SE. E16.**
2 *LOGIC.* By which the quantity of the proposition is changed from universal to particular in a conversion. Opp. **SIMPLY** 2c. **L16.**

peract /pəːˈrakt/ *verb trans.* Now *rare.* **E17.**
[Latin *peract-* pa. ppl stem of *peragere*, formed as **PER-**[1] + *agere* drive, do.]
Practise, perform; accomplish, carry out.
■ †**peractor** *noun* a kind of theodolite **L17–M18.**

peracute /pəːrəˈkjuːt/ *adjective.* **LME.**
[Latin *peracutus* very sharp, formed as **PER-**[1] + **ACUTE.**]
Now chiefly *VETERINARY MEDICINE.* Of a disease: very severe; accompanied by much inflammation.

peradventure /p(ə)rədˈvɛntʃə, pəːr-/ *adverb & noun. arch.* exc. *joc.* **ME.**
[Old French *per* or *par auenture* (see **PAR** *preposition*, **PER** *preposition*, **ADVENTURE** *noun*); in 15–16 assim. to Latin.]
▶**A** *adverb.* †**1** = **PERCHANCE** *adverb* 1. **ME–E17.**
2 = **PERHAPS** *adverb* 2. **ME.**
3 = **PERHAPS** *adverb* 1. **ME.**

> 📖 **2** LYTTON Unless, peradventure, their wives were comely. **if peradventure** if it should chance that. **3** HOBBES It may peradventure be thought, there was never such a time. B. BREYTENBACH Peradventure they were the only two windows in the house.

▶**B** *noun.* The possibility of a thing being so or not; (an) uncertainty, (a) doubt; a chance. Freq. in ***beyond peradventure***, ***beyond all peradventure***, ***past peradventure***, ***past all peradventure***. **M16.**

> 📖 W. COWPER Some to be saved . . others to be left to a peradventure. J. L. MOTLEY This was now proved beyond peradventure. H. B. FORMAN The poem . . ends with shadowiness and peradventure.

¶ Cf. **PERCASE**, **PERCHANCE**, **PERHAPS.**

peragrate /ˈpɛrəgreɪt/ *verb trans.* Long *rare.* **M16.**
[Latin *peragrat-* pa. ppl stem of *peragrare*, formed as **PER-**[1] + *ager* field, country: see **-ATE**[3].]
Travel or pass through (*lit.* & *fig.*).
■ †**peragration** *noun* **M16–L17.**

perahera /pɛrəˈhɛrə/ *noun.* **L17.**
[Sinhalese *perahära.*]
In Sri Lanka: a religious procession.

perai /pɪˈrʌɪ, piː-/ *noun.* **M18.**
[Portuguese *piraí* from Tupi, from *pirá* fish + *i* small. Cf. **PIRANHA.**]
= **PIRANHA.**

peramble /pəˈramb(ə)l/ *verb & noun.* Long *obsolete* exc. *dial.* **E16.**
[Latin *perambulare* (see **PERAMBULATE**), conformed to **AMBLE.**]
▶**A** *verb.* †**1** *verb trans.* & *intrans.* Perambulate. **E16–M17.**
2 *verb intrans.* Wander, ramble, (in speech or writing). **M17.**
▶**B** *noun.* **1** †**a** = **AMBULATORY** *noun* Only in **M16.** ▸**b** A walk, an amble. *rare.* **M20.**
2 A long rambling statement. **E19.**

perambulate /pəˈrambjʊleɪt/ *verb.* **LME.**
[Latin *perambulat-* pa. ppl stem of *perambulare*, formed as **PER-**[1], **AMBULATE.**]
1 *verb trans.* Walk through, over, or about (a place or space). Formerly also, travel or pass through, traverse. **LME.** ▸**b** *spec.* Travel through and inspect (a territory) for surveying purposes. **E17.** ▸**c** Walk round the boundaries of (a parish, forest, etc.) in the course of a perambulation; beat the bounds of. **E17.**
2 *verb intrans.* Walk from place to place, walk about. **E17.**
3 *verb trans.* Wheel or convey (*about*) in a pram. **M19.**

> 📖 **2** J. I. M. STEWART Guests like placid penguins perambulated. *fig.*: *Sunday Express* Perambulating . . through the sexy, self-assured middle years of the Mediterranean woman.

perambulation /pərambjʊˈleɪʃ(ə)n/ *noun.* **LME.**
[Anglo-Norman, Latin or medieval Latin *perambulatio(n-)*, formed as prec.: see **-ATION.**]
1 The action or an act of perambulating; a walk; a survey on foot. (Foll. by *of* the place.) **LME.** ▸**b** The action or ceremony of walking officially round a parish, forest, etc., for the purpose of asserting and recording its boundaries and preserving the rights of possession; beating the bounds. **L15.**
†**2** *fig.* Comprehensive description; in *pl.*, ramblings. **E16–M17.**
3 A written account of a survey or tour of inspection. **L16.**
4 The boundary traced or the space enclosed by perambulating; a circuit, a circumference; an extent (*lit.* & *fig.*). **E17.**

> 📖 **4** *Natural World* Within the perambulation there are 30,900 acres of heathland.

perambulator /pəˈrambjʊleɪtə/ *noun.* **E17.**
[from (the same root as) **PERAMBULATE** + **-OR.** Cf. **PRAM** *noun*[2].]
1 A person who perambulates; a traveller; a pedestrian. **E17.**
2 A machine for measuring distances by means of a large wheel trundled by a handle along the ground, with a mechanism for recording the revolutions; an odometer. **L17.**
3 A pram. **M19.**

†**perambulatory** *noun.* **M17–M19.**
[formed as prec. + **-ORY**[1].]
A place for walking about in; a walk.

perambulatory /pəˈrambjʊlət(ə)ri/ *adjective.* **E17.**
[formed as prec. + **-ORY**[2].]
Given to perambulating; vagrant, wandering, itinerant; pertaining to or characterized by perambulation.

per annum /pər ˈanəm/ *adverbial phr.* **E17.**
[mod. Latin, formed as **PER** + accus. of Latin *annus* year.]
For or in each year. Abbreviation ***p.a.***

> 📖 M. J. COE The main peak area has a rainfall of between 30" and 40" per annum.

p/e ratio *abbreviation.*
Price-earnings ratio.

Perbunan /pəˈbjuːnən/ *noun.* **M20.**
[German, from *per-* of unkn. origin + **BUNA** + *N*, chemical symbol for nitrogen.]
(Proprietary name for) a nitrile rubber first made in Germany.

perc *noun*, *verb* vars. of **PERK** *noun*[3], *verb*[2].

Percaine /ˈpəːkeɪn/ *noun.* **M20.**
[from **PER-**[1] + **-CAINE.**]
PHARMACOLOGY (now *Hist.*). A preparation of cinchocaine.

percale /pəˈkeɪl, *foreign* pɛrkal/ *noun.* **E17.**
[Origin unkn.; in mod. use from French (= Spanish *percal*, Italian *percalle*).]
Orig., a fabric imported from India in the 17th and 18th cents. Later, a light fine cotton fabric without gloss.
■ **percaline** /ˈpəːkəliːn, -ɪn/ *noun* [French] a lustrous cotton fabric **M19.**

per capita /pə ˈkapɪtə/ *adverbial & adjectival phr.* **L17.**
[mod. Latin, formed as **PER** + accus. pl. of Latin *caput* head.]
▶**A** *adverbial phr.* **1** *LAW.* (Divided, shared, etc.) equally among or by individuals, on an individual basis. Opp. **PER STIRPES. L17.**
2 For each person or head of population. **E20.**

> 📖 **2** *Scientific American* The ratio of the explosive yield to the . . population is . . 10 tons per capita.

▶**B** *adjectival phr.* Possessed, performed, etc., by each person when averaged over a population etc. **M20.**

> 📖 *New Statesman* For the bulk of humanity per capita consumption remains the same.

■ **per caput** /ˈkapʊt/ *adverbial & adjectival phr.* (*a*) *adverbial phr.* = **PER CAPITA** *adverbial phr.* 2; (*b*) *adjectival phr.* = **PER CAPITA** *adjectival phr.*: **E20.**

percase /pəˈkeɪs/ *adverb.* Long *obsolete* exc. *dial.* **LME.**
[Anglo-Norman *per cas*, *par cas*, Old French *par cas*, from Old French **PER** + *cas* (see **CASE** *noun*[1]).]
= **PERHAPS** *adverb* 1. Formerly also = **PERHAPS** *adverb* 2, **PERCHANCE** 1.
¶ Cf. **PERADVENTURE**, **PERCHANCE**, **PERHAPS.**

perceant /ˈpəːs(ə)nt/ *adjective.* Now *rare* or *obsolete.* **LME.**
[Old & mod. French *perçant* pres. pple of *percer* **PIERCE** *verb*: see **-ANT**[1].]
Keen, piercing, (*lit.* & *fig.*).

perceivance /pəˈsiːv(ə)ns/ *noun.* Long *obsolete* exc. *dial.* **M16.**
[Old French *percevance*, from *percevoir*: see **PERCEIVE**, **-ANCE.**]
Discernment, wisdom; perception (mental or physical).

perceive /pəˈsiːv/ *verb.* **ME.**
[Anglo-Norman & Old French vars. of Old French *perçoivre* (now repl. by *percevoir*) from Latin *percipere*, seize, obtain, collect, understand, formed as **PER-**[1] + *capere* seize, take.]
▶**I** Take in with the mind or senses.
1 *verb trans.* & (occas.) *intrans.* Become aware or conscious of (a thing); apprehend with the mind. Formerly also *refl.* & in *pass.* in same sense. (Foll. by a thing (*to be*), *that*, subord. clause) **ME.** ▸**b** Foll. by *as*: look on as being, regard as. **E19.**
†**2** *verb trans.* Grasp the meaning of, comprehend. **ME–L16.**
3 *verb trans.* Become aware of (an object) through one of the senses, esp. sight. (With constructions as sense 1.) **ME.**
†**4** *verb trans.* Apprehend what is not manifest or present; see through, see into. **LME–M17.**

📖 **1** P. MACDONALD She perceived No. 14 to be a 'converted' house . . that . . was now the warren of retired grocers. N. ALGREN It took a cardinal to perceive that the country's economic collapse was . . a piece of luck. D. HALBERSTAM As politicians perceived television's force they . . put more . . pressure on the networks. **b** B. TRAPIDO Roger . . must have perceived it as a reproach. **3** J. CONRAD I perceived he had not shaved himself.

▶†**II** Take into possession.

5 *verb trans.* Receive, get, obtain. **L15–M18.**

■ **perceivable** *adjective* (earlier in UNPERCEIVABLE) **L15.** †**perceivably** *adverb* (earlier in UNPERCEIVABLY) perceptibly, appreciably **M17–L18.** †**perceivedly** *adverb* perceptibly: only in **E17. perceivedness** *noun* the fact or condition of being perceived **L19. perceiver** *noun* **LME.**

per cent /pə 'sɛnt/ *adverbial & noun phr.* Also ***percent** & with final point (see note below). **M16.**

[from PER + CENT *noun*¹.]

▶ **A** *adverbial phr.* With preceding numeral, expr. a proportion (of a part to the whole, of a change to the original, or of interest to principal): by the hundred; for, in, or to every hundred. Repr. % **M16.**

📖 *Listener* The French national product rose at a rate of no less than 8 per cent a year. *Guardian* The tampon market is worth about £14 millions a year. Tampax has 62 per cent. P. GAY Electing the . . spokesman remained the privilege of a mere 6 percent of adult males. ***a hundred per cent, one hundred per cent***: see HUNDRED *noun* 1.

▶ **B** *noun.* **1** In *pl.* With preceding numeral: stocks or securities, esp. British Government stocks, paying the specified rate of interest. **L18.**

2 Percentage. **M19.**

3 One part in every hundred; one per cent. **M20.**

📖 **1** ***three per cents, four per cents***, etc. **3** *Daily Telegraph* The retail price index has risen by only three-quarters of a per cent.

¶ With a final point taken as abbreviation of PER CENTUM.

percentage /pə'sɛntɪdʒ/ *noun.* **L18.**

[from prec. + -AGE.]

1 A rate or proportion per cent; a quantity or amount reckoned as so many hundredth parts of another, esp. of the whole of which it is a part; a part considered in its quantitative relation to the whole, a proportion (*of* something). **L18.**

2 *fig.* Personal benefit or advantage; probability of a successful outcome (*in* a situation, course of action, etc.). *colloq.* **M19.**

📖 **1** *Theatre Research International* A slightly higher percentage of his plays appear to reach the stage. **2** J. PORTER There was no percentage in hanging around the airport.

Phrases: **play the percentages** *slang* play safely or methodically with regard to the odds in favour of success.

Comb.: **percentage point** a unit used in expr. the numerical difference between two percentages.

■ **percentage-wise** *adverb* as a percentage; relatively: **E20.**

percenter /pə'sɛntə/ *noun.* **M19.**

[from PER CENT + -ER¹.]

With preceding numeral: that on (or from) which the percentage specified by the number is reckoned; a thing whose value is reckoned as the specified percentage; a person who deals in money involving interest or commission at the specified rate.

percentile /pə'sɛntʌɪl/ *noun.* **L19.**

[from PER CENT + -ILE.]

Each of the 99 intermediate values of a variate which divide a frequency distribution into 100 groups each containing one per cent of the total population (so that e.g. 50 per cent have values below the 50th percentile); each of the 100 groups so formed.

percentual /pə'sɛntjʊəl/ *adjective.* **M20.**

[from PER CENT + -UAL, after *accentual*, *eventual*, etc.]

Expressed as a percentage; proportional.

per centum /pə 'sɛntəm/ *adverbial phr.* **M17.**

[Latinized form of PER CENT.]

= PER CENT *adverbial phr.* Freq. in legal contexts.

†**percepier** *noun.* **L16–M18.**

[French *perce-pierre* lit. 'pierce-stone': cf. PARSLEY-PIERT.]

The plant parsley-piert, *Aphanes arvensis*.

percept /'pəːsɛpt/ *noun.* **M19.**

[from Latin *perceptum* neut. of pa. pple of *percipere* PERCEIVE, after *concept*.]

1 An object of perception. **M19.**

2 The mental product or result of perceiving (as distinguished from the action). **L19.**

percepta *noun* pl. of PERCEPTUM.

perceptible /pə'sɛptɪb(ə)l/ *adjective.* **LME.**

[(Old French from) late Latin *perceptibilis*, from *percept-*: see PERCEPTION, -IBLE.]

†**1** Perceptive *of*. **LME–L18.**

2 Able to be perceived by the senses or intellect. **E17.**

📖 **2** J. CARY Not a silence, but a perceptible drop in the volume of noise.

■ **percepti'bility** *noun* †(*a*) the faculty of or capacity for perceiving; (*b*) the state or property of being perceptible: **M17. perceptibly** *adverb* in or to a perceptible degree; in a perceptible manner: **E18.**

perception /pə'sɛpʃ(ə)n/ *noun.* **LME.**

[Branch II from Old & mod. French from Latin *perceptio(n-)*, from *percept-* pa. ppl stem of *percipere* PERCEIVE: see -ION. Branch I directly from Latin.]

▶ **I** Corresp. to PERCEIVE I.

1 The state of being or process of becoming aware or conscious of a thing, *spec.* through any of the senses. **LME.** ▸**b** The intuitive or direct recognition of a moral, aesthetic, or personal quality, e.g. the truth of a remark, the beauty of an object; an instance of this. **E19.**

2 A result of perceiving; a mental image, a conception, (*of* a person or thing). **L17.**

3 The faculty of perceiving; an ability to perceive. **E18.**

4 *PHILOSOPHY.* The action of the mind by which it refers its sensations to an external object as their cause. **M18.**

5 *PSYCHOLOGY.* The neurophysiological processes, including memory, by which an organism becomes aware of and interprets external stimuli. **L19.**

📖 **1** J. LOCKE Having Ideas and Perception being the same thing. A. TOFFLER Man's perception of time is closely linked with his internal rhythms. **b** G. VIDAL Someone had told him that, thought Caroline, delighted with her perception. **2** A. FRANCE A perception of the analyst as cold . . leads to minimal progress. **3** S. HASTINGS Her perceptions heightened by emotion, the capital . . was . . beautiful. A. HARDING Her sharp perceptions might have detected my increasing intimacy with him.

▶ **II** Corresp. to PERCEIVE II.

6 The collection or receiving of rents etc. *obsolete* exc. *LAW.* **LME.**

†**7** *CHRISTIAN CHURCH.* The receiving or partaking of the elements in the Eucharist. **LME–L17.**

■ **perceptional** *adjective* of, pertaining to, or of the nature of, perception **M19.**

perceptive /pə'sɛptɪv/ *noun & adjective.* **LME.**

[medieval Latin *perceptivus*, from *percept-*: see prec., -IVE.]

▶ **A** *noun.* †**1** An optical instrument of some kind. Only in **LME.**

2 In *pl.* The perceptive faculties or organs. **M19.**

▶ **B** *adjective.* **1** Characterized by or capable of perceiving; pertaining to or having perception; instrumental to perception. **M17.** ▸**b** Of ready perception, discerning; exhibiting discernment. **M19.**

†**2** Perceptible, cognizable. **M18–E19.**

📖 **1b** G. GREENE The author of the most perceptive life of Stevenson.

■ **perceptively** *adverb* in a perceptive manner; in respect of perception: **L18. perceptiveness** *noun* **M19. percep'tivity** *noun* **L17.**

perceptron /pə'sɛptrɒn/ *noun.* **M20.**

[from PERCEPT + -TRON.]

A model or machine devised to represent or simulate the ability of the brain to recognize and discriminate.

perceptual /pə'sɛptjʊəl/ *adjective.* **L19.**

[from *percept-* in PERCEPTION etc. + -UAL, after *conceptual*.]

Of or pertaining to perception; of the nature of percepts.

perceptual defence a raising of the threshold of perception when the stimulus is emotionally charged in an unfavourable way.

Comb.: **perceptual-motor** *adjective* involving motor behaviour as guided by or dependent on perception.

■ **perceptuali'zation** *noun* the action or result of perceptualizing something **M20. perceptualize** *verb trans.* express in perceptual terms **L19. perceptually** *adverb* **L19.**

perceptum /pə'sɛptəm/ *noun.* Pl. **-ta** /-tə/. **L19.**

[Latin, neut. of *perceptus* pa. pple of *percipere* PERCEIVE.]

= PERCEPT 1.

perceptuo-motor /pə'sɛptjʊəʊ,məʊtə/ *adjective.* **M20.**

[from Latin *perceptus* (see prec.) + -O- + MOTOR *adjective*.]

= *PERCEPTUAL-motor*.

perch /pəːtʃ/ *noun*¹. Pl. usu. same. **ME.**

[Old & mod. French *perche* from Latin *perca* from Greek *perkē*.]

1 A small European spiny-finned freshwater fish, *Perca fluviatilis*, which has two distinctive dorsal fins and is caught for food and game; any fish of the genus *Perca* or the family Percidae, *esp.* (more fully ***yellow perch***) *P. flavescens* of N. America. **ME.**

2 Any of various teleost fishes resembling the common perch or taking its place as food. **E17.**

Phrases: **climbing perch** a southern Asian freshwater fish, *Anabas testudineus*, which is able to breathe air and migrate between bodies of water. **dusky perch** the mero, *Epinephelus guaza*. ***GOLDEN perch. Nile perch***: see NILE 1. ***pirate-perch***: see PIRATE *noun* 4. ***red perch***: see RED *adjective*. ***RINGED perch. silver perch***: see SILVER *noun & adjective*. ***white perch***: see WHITE *adjective*. ***yellow perch***: see sense 1 above.

perch /pəːtʃ/ *noun*². **ME.**

[Old & mod. French *perche* from Latin *pertica* pole, measuring rod. Cf. PERK *noun*¹.]

▶ **I 1** A pole, a rod, a stick. Long *obsolete* exc. *dial.* in *gen.* sense. **ME.** ▸**b** A pole set up in the bed of a river etc. to aid navigation. **LME.** ▸**c** The centre pole by which the hinder carriage is connected to the forecarriage in some horse-drawn vehicles. **M17.**

▶ **II 2** Orig., a rod of a definite length used for measuring land etc. Later, a measure of length, esp. for land, walls, etc., standardized at 5½ yards (approx. 5.029 m). Also called ***pole, rod***. Now *rare* exc. *Hist.* **ME.** ▸**b** More fully ***square perch***. A measure of area (of land, brickwork, etc.), equal to the 160th part of an acre or 30¼ sq. yards (approx. 25.29 sq. metres). Also called ***pole, rod, square pole, square rod***. Now *rare* exc. *Hist.* **ME.** ▸**c** A solid measure used for stone, usually containing 24.75 cu. ft (approx. 0.7008 cu. metre) but varying locally. **E19.**

▶ **III 3 a** A horizontal bar used as a peg. *obsolete* exc. *Hist.* **LME.** ▸**b** A horizontal bar for a hawk or tame bird to rest on; anything on which a bird alights or rests. **LME.** ▸†**c** A bar to support a candle or candles, esp. as an altar-light. **L15–M16.** ▸**d** A thing or place where a person alights or on which a person rests, *esp.* one that is high or precarious; *colloq.* a small high seat on a vehicle for the driver or a servant. **E16.** ▸**e** *THEATRICAL.* A platform from which lights are directed on to the front of the stage; in *pl.*, the lights placed on this. **M20.**

4 Orig., a wooden bar, or frame of two parallel bars, over which pieces of cloth were pulled for examination or dressing. Now, a horizontal bar used in softening leather. **M16.**

📖 **3b** *Birder's World* A tall spike of common mullein makes an attractive perch for an Indigo Bunting. **d** H. E. BATES 'Take a perch'. Forrester sat down. W. J. BURLEY You keep this perch warm for a while, I'm doing a walkabout.

Phrases: **come off one's perch**, **get off one's perch** *slang* climb down, adopt a less arrogant or condescending manner. **hop the perch** *slang & dial.*, *arch.* be ruined or vanquished; die. **knock off one's perch** *slang* upset, vanquish, or ruin a person; disconcert, humiliate, or snub a person. ***square perch***: see sense 4b above. **tip over the perch**, **tip the perch** *arch. slang & dial.* = ***hop the perch*** above.

Comb.: **perch-bolt**: on which the perch of a carriage turns.

■ **perchery** *noun & adjective* (*a*) *noun* a series of cages with perches, in which hens are confined for intensive laying; (*b*) *adjective* kept or produced in a perchery: **L20**

perch /pəːtʃ/ *verb.* **LME.**

[Old & mod. French *percher*, formed as PERCH *noun*². Cf. PERK *verb*¹.]

1 *verb intrans.* (Esp. of a bird) alight or settle on a perch; (of a person or thing) sit or rest on something that is raised up or affords little room. **LME.**

2 *verb trans.* Set or place on a place that is raised up or affords little room. Chiefly *refl.* or in *pass.* **LME.**

3 *verb trans.* Provide with a perch or perches. *rare.* **LME.**

4 *verb trans.* Stretch (cloth) on a perch for examination or dressing; soften (leather) using a perch. Chiefly as ***perching*** *verbal noun.* **M16.**

📖 **1** C. RAINE The seagull perches on the roof. E. FEINSTEIN I took to perching on the window seat. *Holiday Which?* Chateau ruins perch high above the . . Loire. **2** R. P. JHABVALA He would take out his spectacles and perch them on . . his nose. P. DE VRIES A pink . . hat perched at an angle. G. SWIFT He . . perched himself on the edge of his desk.

perchance /pə'tʃɑːns/ *adverb. arch. & literary.* **ME.**

[Anglo-Norman *par cheanse*, Old French *par cheance*, formed as PAR *preposition* + CHANCE *noun*, with later assim. to PER-². Cf. PERCASE.]

1 In a statement of fact: as it chances or chanced, as it happens or happened. **ME.**

2 = PERHAPS *adverb* 1. **LME.**

3 = PERHAPS *adverb* 2. **LME.**

📖 **2** SHAKES. *Haml.* To die, to sleep; To sleep, perchance to dream. G. GISSING Did *she*, perchance, understand him. **3** H. JAMES Pinnie looked at him askance . . as if perchance he were joking.

¶ Cf. PERADVENTURE, PERCASE, PERHAPS.

perched /pəːtʃt/ *adjective.* **L17.**

[from PERCH *noun*², *verb*: see -ED², -ED¹.]

1 Provided with a perch or perches. **L17.**

2 *GEOLOGY.* Designating a block or boulder left resting on a pinnacle or other narrow support, e.g. by the melting of the ice which carried it there; having an elevation that is exceptionally high in relation to the immediate locality; (of groundwater) separated from an underlying saturated zone by an intervening unsaturated zone. **M19.**

percher /'pəːtʃə/ *noun.* **E18.**

[from PERCH *verb* + -ER¹.]

1 [Cf. *hop the perch* s.v. PERCH *noun*².] A dying person. *slang.* **E18.**

2 A bird that perches; *spec.* one with feet adapted for perching; a member of the order Passeriformes. **L18.**

3 *CRICKET.* A ball that seems to hang in the air; *spec.* = BOUNCER 4. **E20.**

percheron /'pəːʃ(ə)rɒn/ *noun.* **L19.**

[French adjective, from *le Perche*, a region of northern France where orig. bred.]

(An animal of) a breed of heavy draught horse combining strength with agility and speed.

perchloric /pəˈklɔːrɪk/ *adjective.* E19.
[from PER-¹ + CHLORIC.]
CHEMISTRY. **perchloric acid**, a colourless fuming toxic liquid, $HClO_4$, that contains chlorine in its highest oxidation state and is a powerful oxidizing agent.
■ **perchlorate** *noun* a salt or ester of perchloric acid E19. **perchloride** *noun* (arch.) a chloride containing the highest possible proportion of chlorine E19. **perchloro-** *combining form* [-O-] involving or resulting from the maximum possible replacement of hydrogen by chlorine M19. ˌ**perchloroˈethylene** *noun* = TETRACHLOROETHYLENE L19.

percid /ˈpəːkɪd, ˈpəːsɪd/ *adjective & noun.* L19.
[mod. Latin *Percidae* (see below), from Latin *Perca* perch: see -ID³.]
▶ **A** *adjective.* Of or pertaining to the family Percidae of freshwater fishes with a spiny first dorsal fin, native to the northern hemisphere and including the common perches. L19.
▶ **B** *noun.* A percid fish. L19.

perciform /ˈpəːsɪfɔːm/ *adjective & noun.* L19.
[mod. Latin *Perciformes* noun pl. (see below), from Latin *perca* PERCH *noun*¹: see -FORM.]
▶ **A** *adjective.* Of the form of or resembling a perch; *spec.* belonging to or characteristic of the large order Perciformes of teleost fishes, characterized in general by fins (including two dorsal fins) containing spines. L19.
▶ **B** *noun.* A perciform fish. L19.

percipient /pəˈsɪpɪənt/ *noun & adjective.* M17.
[Latin *percipient-* pres. ppl stem of *percipere* PERCEIVE: see -ENT.]
▶ **A** *noun.* A person who or thing which perceives; *spec.* one who perceives something outside the range of the senses, a person with extrasensory perception. M17.
▶ **B** *adjective.* That perceives or is capable of perceiving, conscious; perceptive, discerning. L17.
■ **percipience** *noun* the action or condition of perceiving, perception M18. **percipiency** *noun* (rare) †(*a*) percipience; (*b*) the quality of being percipient: M17. **percipiently** *adverb* E20.

†**percoct** *verb trans. rare.* M17–L19.
[Latin *percoct-* pa. ppl stem of *percoquere*, formed as PER-¹ + *coquere* COOK *verb*.]
Boil or heat through or thoroughly; *fig.* overdo.

percoid /ˈpəːkɔɪd/ *adjective & noun.* M19.
[mod. Latin *Percoides* noun pl., from Latin *perca* PERCH *noun*¹ + -OID.]
▶ **A** *adjective.* Of or pertaining to the suborder or superfamily Percoidei or Percoidea of perciform fishes, including perches, basses, jacks, snappers, grunts, sea breams, and drums. M19.
▶ **B** *noun.* A percoid fish. M19.

percolate /ˈpəːkələt/ *noun.* L19.
[from the verb: see -ATE².]
A product of percolation.

percolate /ˈpəːkəleɪt/ *verb.* E17.
[Latin *percolat-* pa. ppl stem of *percolare*, formed as PER-¹ + *colare* to strain, from *colum* sieve, strainer: see -ATE³. Cf. PERK *verb*².]
1 *verb trans.* Cause (a liquid) to pass through a porous body or substance; cause (a finely divided solid) to trickle or pass through pores or minute apertures, sift. Now *rare.* E17. ▸**b** *fig.* Cause to pass as through a filter; cause to pass by degrees or to diffuse. L17.
2 *verb intrans.* (Of a liquid) pass through a porous body or substance; filter, ooze, or trickle (*through, down*) (*lit. & fig.*). L17.
3 *verb trans.* (Of a liquid) ooze or filter through (a porous body or substance); permeate (*lit. & fig.*). L18.
4 *verb intrans.* Walk, stroll. *US slang.* M20.
5 a *verb trans.* Make (coffee) in a percolator. M20. ▸**b** *verb intrans.* Of coffee: be prepared in a percolator, bubble in a percolator. M20.

> 📖 **2** D. ACHESON It took time for report of the events to percolate . . through Tokyo to Washington. **3** *New Statesman* This has . . slowly percolated British consciousness.

■ **percolative** *adjective* (rare) allowing or involving percolation M19.

percolation /pəːkəˈleɪʃ(ə)n/ *noun.* E17.
[Latin *percolatio(n-)*, formed as prec.: see -ATION.]
1 The action of causing a liquid to percolate; *spec.* (PHARMACOLOGY) the process of obtaining an extract by passing successive quantities of a solvent through a pulverized substance until all the soluble material has been dissolved. E17.
2 The action or an act of percolating through something; filtering, oozing. E17.
†**3** PHONETICS. The emission of the breath through a narrow opening in producing a speech sound. M17–E18.

percolator /ˈpəːkəleɪtə/ *noun.* M19.
[from PERCOLATE *verb* + -OR. Cf. PERK *noun*³.]
1 An apparatus or substance which percolates liquid; *spec.* a device for making coffee in which boiling water is passed downwards through coffee grounds; now, an electric coffee-pot in which this is done automatically. M19.
2 A carburettor. *US slang.* M20.
3 A party, esp. = ***house-rent party*** s.v. HOUSE *noun*¹ & *adjective. US slang.* M20.

percontation /pəːkɒnˈteɪʃ(ə)n/ *noun. rare.* E17.
[Latin *percontatio(n-)*, from *percontat-* pa. ppl stem of *percontare, -ari* enquire, interrogate: see -ATION.]
A question, an enquiry.
■ **percontatorial** /pəkɒntəˈtɔːrɪəl/ *adjective* given to or pertaining to questioning M19.

per contra /pəː ˈkɒntrə/ *adverbial & noun phr.* M16.
[Italian.]
▶ **A** *adverbial phr.* On the opposite side (of an account, assessment, etc.); on the other hand. M16.

> 📖 R. FRY The article won't do . . much good, but *per contra* it won't do . . any harm.

▶ **B** *noun phr.* The opposite side. E19.

perculsion /pəˈkʌlʃ(ə)n/ *noun. rare.* M17.
[from Latin *perculs-* pa. ppl stem of *percellere* upset + -ION.]
Orig., a mental shock. Later, a physical shock or blow.

percur /pəˈkəː/ *verb trans. rare.* Infl. **-rr-**. M17.
[Latin *percurrere*, formed as PER-¹ + *currere* to run.]
Run through, traverse, (by movement or extension).
■ **percurrent** /-ˈkʌr(ə)nt/ *adjective* extending throughout something L16. **percursory** *adjective* running, or running through something, quickly M19.

percuss /pəˈkʌs/ *verb.* M16.
[Latin *percuss-* pa. ppl stem of *percutere* strike or thrust through, formed as PER-¹ + *quatere* shake, strike, dash.]
†**1** *verb trans.* Strike so as to shake or give a shock to; hit, knock. M16–L17.
2 *verb trans. & intrans.* MEDICINE. Gently tap or strike (a part of the body) with the finger or an instrument, esp. for diagnostic purposes. M19.
■ **percussive** *noun & adjective* †(*a*) *noun* = REPERCUSSIVE *noun*; (*b*) *adjective* of, pertaining to, or characterized by percussion; (of an instrument) producing sound by percussion; (of a sound) such as is produced by percussion, sharp, abrupt: LME. **percussively** *adverb* L19. **percussiveness** *noun* M19. **percussor** *noun* an instrument or device for medical percussion L19.

percussion /pəˈkʌʃ(ə)n/ *noun.* LME.
[(Old & mod. French from) Latin *percussio(n-)*, formed as prec.: see -ION.]
1 The action of coming forcibly into contact with an object so as to give a shock; an instance of this, a blow, a knock. LME.
2 The playing of a musical instrument by striking it or striking two parts together (chiefly in ***instrument of percussion***, ***percussion instrument***); *collect.* the percussion instruments of an orchestra etc.; the players of these. L18.
3 The striking of an explosive powder so as to produce a spark and explode the charge in a firearm. E19.
4 MEDICINE. The action of percussing a part of the body. M19.

> 📖 **2** *Listener* BBC Northern Orchestra . . requires: Timpani and Percussion . . Salary £3,876 per annum.

Comb.: ***percussion cap***: see CAP *noun*¹ 10; **percussion drill**: that works by delivering a rapid succession of heavy blows; **percussion gun**: that uses percussion to explode the charge; ***percussion instrument***: see sense 2 above; **percussion lock** a gunlock in which the charge is exploded by means of a percussion cap; **percussion welding** a form of resistance welding in which momentary pressure is applied to the parts to be joined.
■ **percussionist** *noun* †(*a*) a person who uses a percussion gun; (*b*) a person who plays a percussion instrument: E19.

percutaneous /pəːkjuːˈteɪnɪəs/ *adjective.* L19.
[from Latin *per cutem* through the skin + -ANEOUS, after *cutaneous*.]
Made, done, or effected through the skin.
■ **percutaneously** *adverb* through the skin L19.

Percy /ˈpəːsi/ *noun. slang. derog.* E20.
[Male forename.]
A conscientious objector, a coward; an effeminate man; (in the armed services) an officer, an educated man.

perdie *interjection & adverb* see PARDI.

per diem /pəː ˈdiːɛm, ˈdʌɪɛm/ *adverbial, noun, & adjectival phr.* E16.
[mod. Latin, formed as PER + accus. of Latin DIES.]
▶ **A** *adverbial phr.* For or in each day. E16.
▶ **B** *noun phr.* An amount or allowance of so much each day. Chiefly *N. Amer.* E19.
▶ **C** *adjectival phr.* Daily. Chiefly *N. Amer.* E19.

perdition /pəˈdɪʃ(ə)n/ *noun.* ME.
[Old French *perdiciun* (mod. *-tion*) or ecclesiastical Latin *perditio(n-)*, from Latin *perdit-* pa. ppl stem of *perdere* destroy, formed as PER-¹ + *dare* give, put: see -ITION.]
1 CHRISTIAN THEOLOGY. The condition of final spiritual ruin or damnation, the future condition of the wicked and finally impenitent or unredeemed; the fate of those in hell, eternal death. ME. ▸†**b** The place of destruction or damnation, hell. LME–M17.
2 *gen.* The fact or condition of being destroyed or ruined; utter destruction. Now *rare.* LME.
†**3** Loss, diminution, lessening. E16–E17.
†**4** A thing that causes destruction, the ruin of something. E17–E18.

> 📖 **1** SHAKES. *Oth.* Excellent wretch! Perdition catch my soul But I do love thee.

perdricide /ˈpəːdrɪsʌɪd/ *adjective. joc.* E19.
[from French *perdrix* partridge from Latin *perdix, -ic-*: see -CIDE.]
That kills partridges, esp. for sport.

†**perdrigon** *noun.* L16–L19.
[French, lit. 'young partridge', app. with ref. to its colour.]
A variety of plum formerly highly valued for its flavour.

perdu /pəːˈdjuː, *foreign* pɛrdy/ *adjective & noun.* Also **-due**. L16.
[Old & mod. French, pa. pple of *perdre* lose from Latin *perdere*: see PERDITION.]
▶ **A** *adjective.* †**1** Posted in, or designating, a sentinel's position that is so dangerous that death is almost inevitable. Only in ***sentinel perdue***, ***perdue sentinel***. L16–L17. ▸**b** Placed in a very hazardous situation; (of a case) desperate. E–M17.
2 Hidden and on the watch; lying in ambush. Chiefly in ***lie perdu***, ***set perdu***, ***stand perdu***, etc. E17.
3 Concealed, hidden; out of sight; disguised. E18.

> 📖 **2** E. A. BARTLETT Plenty of Greeks lying *perdu* about . . the wood. **3** W. IRVING Honest, good-fellow qualities . . which had lain perdue. BARONESS ORCZY This untenanted cottage . . lay perdu, off both the main and the secondary roads.

▶†**B** *noun.* **1** A soldier in a very hazardous situation; a body of such soldiers, a forlorn hope; a soldier on watch or on guard; a spy. E17–M18.
2 A morally abandoned person; a profligate. E–M17.
¶ Orig. introduced from the French military phr. *sentinelle perdue*, and so spelt as fem. *perdue*; now usu. spelt according to gender.

perduellion /pəːdjʊˈɛlɪən/ *noun.* M16.
[Latin *perduellio(n-)*, from *perduellis* public enemy, formed as PER-¹ + *duellis* warrior: see -ION.]
Rom. & SCOTS LAW (now *Hist.*). Hostility against the State; treason.

perdurable /pəˈdjʊərəb(ə)l/ *adjective.* LME.
[Old French (also *par-*) from late Latin *perdurabilis*, from Latin *perdurare* endure, formed as PER-¹ + *durare* harden, endure, from *durus* hard: see -ABLE.]
1 Enduring continuously, permanent; everlasting, eternal. LME.
2 Of a material thing: able to withstand wear or decay; imperishable; lasting indefinitely. LME.
¶ Rare or obsolete M17–L18.
■ **perduraˈbility** *noun* (now chiefly PHILOSOPHY) LME. **perdurableness** *noun* (rare) E17. **perdurably** *adverb* ME.

perdure /pəˈdjʊə/ *verb intrans.* L15.
[Old French *perdurer*, *par-* from Latin *perdurare*: see prec.]
Continue in time, endure.
■ **perdurance** *noun* (now *rare*) permanence, duration E16. **perduˈration** *noun* (arch.) continuous duration, continuance LME.

père /pɛːr, pɛː/ *noun.* E17.
[French = father.]
1 Father: used in France and French-speaking countries as a title preceding the name of a priest. Cf. FATHER *noun* 3C. E17.
2 The father, senior: appended to a name to distinguish between a father and son of the same name. Cf. FILS *noun*¹. E19.
3 ***père de famille*** /də famiːj, də fəˈmiː/, a father of a family, a family man. E19.
2 *père et fils* /ɛ fis, eɪ ˈfiːs/ father and son.

Père David /pɛː ˈdeɪvɪd, pɛː daˈviːd/ *noun.* L19.
[Armand *David* (1826–1900), French missionary and naturalist.]
In full ***Père David deer***, ***Père David's deer***. A large long-tailed deer, *Elaphurus davidianus*, discovered in China but now extinct in the wild, though surviving in captivity.

peregrinate /ˈpɛrɪɡrɪnət/ *adjective. rare.* L16.
[Latin *peregrinatus* pa. pple, formed as next: see -ATE².]
Having the air of a person who has lived or travelled abroad.

peregrinate /ˈpɛrɪɡrɪneɪt/ *verb. literary & joc.* L16.
[Latin *peregrinat-* pa. ppl stem of *peregrinari* travel or stay abroad, from *peregrinus*: see PEREGRINE, -ATE³.]
1 *verb intrans.* Travel, journey. L16.
2 *verb trans.* Travel along or across; traverse. M19.
■ **peregrinator** *noun* a traveller; a pilgrim; a wanderer: E17. **peregrinatory** *adjective* (rare) characteristic of a peregrinator; travelling: L18.

peregrination /ˌpɛrɪɡrɪˈneɪʃ(ə)n/ *noun.* LME.
[(Old & mod. French *pérégrination* from) Latin *peregrinatio(n-)*, formed as prec.: see -ATION.]
†**1** A journey through life, esp. viewed as a temporary precursor of eternal life in heaven. LME–M18.
2 †**a** A pilgrimage. E16–M17. ▸**b** *gen.* The action or an act of travelling abroad or from place to place; a course of travel, esp. abroad; a journey, esp. on foot; in *pl.*, travels.

M16. ▸†**c** An act, or the condition, of living as a sojourner in a foreign land; sojourn. M–L17.
†**3** *fig.* A systematic going through a subject, writing, course of study, etc. E17–E18.

📖 **2b** S. JOHNSON In this dismal gloom of nocturnal peregrination. M. SCAMMELL A first-class library . . miraculously preserved throughout all her peregrinations.

peregrine /ˈpɛrɪɡrɪn/ *adjective & noun.* LME.
[Old & mod. French *pérégrin* from Latin *peregrinus* foreign, travelling, from *pereger* that is abroad or on a journey, *peregre* (adverb) abroad, formed as PER-¹ + *ager* field: see -INE¹. Cf. PILGRIM.]
▸ **A** *adjective.* **1** ***peregrine falcon***, †***falcon peregrine*** [translating medieval Latin *falco peregrinus* pilgrim falcon, so called because the bird was caught full-grown as a passage-hawk, not taken from the nest], a falcon, *Falco peregrinus*, of cosmopolitan distribution and much valued for hawking on account of its fast and accurate flying. LME.
2 Foreign; outlandish, strange; imported from abroad. Formerly also, extraneous to the matter in hand. E16.
3 ASTROLOGY. Of a planet: situated in a part of the zodiac where it has none of its essential dignities. L16.
4 Travelling; wandering. Formerly also, on a pilgrimage. M17.

📖 **4** G. M. BROWN A single stroke took him . . on the forehead; and, a peregrine spirit, he shook this world from him.

Special collocations: ***peregrine falcon***: see sense 1 above. **peregrine praetor** ROMAN HISTORY a second praetor appointed at Rome to administer justice between Roman and non-Roman citizens and between non-Roman citizens themselves. **peregrine tone** one of the tones used in plainsong, in which the reciting note changes halfway through.
▸ **B** *noun.* **1** A person who lives or travels in a foreign land; an immigrant; a pilgrim. Long *rare.* M16. ▸**b** ROMAN HISTORY. A resident in ancient Rome who was not a Roman citizen. L19.
2 A peregrine falcon. L16.
■ **pereˈgrinity** *noun* (*a*) the condition of being a foreigner or alien; †(*b*) foreignness, strangeness: L16.

pereion /pəˈrʌɪən, -ˈriː-/ *noun.* M19.
[Greek *peraioōn*, *peraiōn* pres. pple of *peraioun* to transport.]
ZOOLOGY. The thorax of a crustacean.
■ **pereiopod** *noun* a locomotory appendage of a pereion L19.

peremptory /pəˈrɛm(p)t(ə)ri, ˈpɛrɪm-/ *adjective, adverb, & noun.* LME.
[Anglo-Norman *peremptorie* = Old & mod. French *peremptoire* from Latin *peremptorius* deadly, mortal, decisive, from *perempt-* pa. ppl stem of *perimere* take away entirely, destroy, formed as PER-¹ + *emere* buy: see -ORY².]
▸ **A** *adjective.* **I 1** Orig. LAW. (Of a command, order, decree, etc.) admitting no refusal, absolute, imperative; (of a plea, defence, etc.) that if upheld ends an action. LME. ▸†**b** Of a statement or conclusion: incontrovertible, decisive. M16–E18.
2 †**a** Of a day or time: definitely fixed for the performance of some act, esp. in a court of law. E16–M18. ▸**b** Positively fixed; absolutely settled; essential. L16.
†**3** Of a person: resolute; resolved, determined, (*to do* a thing, *that* a thing be done); obstinate, self-willed. L16–M18.
4 Of people, their words, actions, etc.: positive in opinion or assertion, fully assured; *esp.* not admitting or intolerant of disagreement or refusal; overconfident, dogmatic; imperious, dictatorial. L16.

📖 **1 peremptory challenge** LAW an objection to a proposed juror made by counsel without the obligation to give a reason. **2b** R. W. EMERSON It is a peremptory point of virtue that a man's independence be secured. **4** G. GISSING The dinner-bell came with its peremptory interruption. A. S. BYATT She had said, peremptory as always, that he was to go straight to Room III.

▸†**II 5** Deadly, destructive. M16–E17.
▸†**B** *adverb.* Peremptorily; by a peremptory order, without fail. LME–M17.
▸ **C** *noun.* LAW. A peremptory challenge, writ, etc. Now *US.* E17.
■ **peremptorily** *adverb* (*a*) so as to settle a matter; conclusively, definitely; (*b*) LAW by way of peremptory challenge; without giving a reason for the objection; †(*c*) determinedly; obstinately; †(*d*) without exception or question; (*e*) with the air of a command; imperiously, abruptly: LME. **peremptoriness** *noun* L16.

perennate /pəˈrɛneɪt/ *verb intrans.* E17.
[Latin *perennat-* pa. ppl stem of *perennare* (formed as PER-¹ + *annus* year), or formed as next: see -ATE³.]
Last or live through a number of years, as a perennial plant.
■ **pereˈnnation** *noun* L19.

perennial /pəˈrɛnɪəl/ *adjective & noun.* M17.
[from Latin *perennis*, formed as PER-¹ + *annus* year: see -IAL.]
▸ **A** *adjective.* **1** †**a** Remaining green or leafy throughout the year, evergreen. M17–M18. ▸**b** Of a spring, stream, etc.: lasting or continuing throughout the year. E18.
2 Of plants, their roots, etc., and invertebrate animals: remaining alive through a number of years; *spec.* designating herbaceous plants which die down to the root and shoot up afresh every year. L17.
3 Lasting through a succession of years, or through a long, indefinite, or infinite time; continual, perpetual; enduring, never-failing; everlasting. M18.

📖 **3** A. STORR Man's perennial capacity to imagine Utopia.

▸ **B** *noun.* **1** A perennial plant. M18.
2 Something that lasts, or remains fresh, through a succession of years. L18.

📖 **1** ***hardy perennial***: see HARDY *adjective* 2. **2** C. LAMB His jokes . . were old trusty perennials.

■ **perenniˈality** *noun* the quality of being perennial; something that is perennial: M19. **perennially** *adverb* throughout the year; continually, perpetually; always: L18.

perennibranchiate /pərɛnɪˈbraŋkɪət/ *adjective.* M19.
[from mod. Latin *Perennibranchia* nounpl., formed as PERENNIAL + BRANCHIA: see -ATE².]
ZOOLOGY. Of an amphibian: retaining gills throughout life.
■ **peˈrennibranch** *noun* a perennibranchiate organism L19.

†**perennity** *noun.* L16–E18.
[Latin *perennitas*, formed as PERENNIAL: see -ITY.]
The quality of being perennial; permanence, perpetuity.

perentie /pəˈrɛnti/ *noun. Austral.* E20.
[Aboriginal.]
A large burrowing monitor lizard, *Varanus giganteus*, found in desert areas of central and western Australia.

perequation /pɛrɪˈkweɪʃ(ə)n/ *noun.* E17.
[French *péréquation* from Latin *peraequatio(n-)*, from *peraequare* make quite equal, formed as PER-¹ + *aequare*: see EQUATE, -ATION.]
The action of making equal; *spec.* the addition of an amount to one price or cost to make it equal to another.
¶ Rare before E20.

perequitate /pəˈrɛkwɪteɪt/ *verb trans. rare.* L18.
[Latin *perequitat-* pa. ppl stem of *perequitare*, formed as PER-¹ + *equitare*: see EQUITATION, -ATE³.]
Ride through on horseback.

perestroika /pɛrɪˈstrɔɪkə/ *noun.* L20.
[Russian *perestroĭka* restructuring.]
The reform of the economic and political system of the former USSR, first proposed by Leonid Brezhnev in 1979 and actively promoted under the leadership of Mikhail Gorbachev from 1985.
■ **perestroikan** *adjective* L20.

perfay /pəˈfeɪ/ *interjection.* Long *arch.* ME.
[Old French *per fei*, *par fei*, formed as PER + FAY *noun*¹.]
By my faith; truly.

perfect /ˈpəːfɪkt/ *adjective, adverb, & noun.* Orig. †**parfit**. ME.
[Old & mod. French *parfit(e)* from Latin *perfectus* pa. pple of *perficere* accomplish, formed as PER-¹ + *facere* make. Present spelling assim. to Latin *perfectus*. Cf. PUFFICK.]
▸ **A** *adjective.* **I** †**1 a** Of a legal act: duly completed. ME–M16. ▸**b** Of a foetus: fully formed. LME–M16. ▸**c** Grown up, adult (esp. legally). LME–L18.
2 Fully accomplished; thoroughly versed or trained *in*, or conversant *with. arch.* ME. ▸†**b** Prepared, made ready. LME–M16. ▸**c** Thoroughly learned, esp. by heart or by rote; (of a person) having learned a lesson or part thoroughly. L16.
3 Having all the essential elements, qualities, or characteristics; not deficient in any particular; being an ideal example of. ME. ▸†**b** Of sound mind, sane. LME–E17. ▸**c** Of a geometrical figure, a point in time, etc.: exact, precise. LME. ▸**d** Of a copy, representation, etc.: accurately reproducing or reflecting the original. M16. ▸**e** Unqualified; pure; absolute, complete, utter. Also (chiefly *colloq. & dial.*) mere, sheer; unmitigated. L16.
4 Free from any flaw or defect of quality; faultless; in a state of supreme or (occas.) near excellence. ME. ▸**b** *spec.* Of or marked by supreme moral excellence; holy; immaculate. ME.
†**5** Of a statement or speaker: definite, certain. *rare.* M16–E17.
†**6** In a state of complete satisfaction; contented. *rare* (Shakes.). Only in E17.

📖 **2** W. WHEWELL The other persons . . not being very perfect in their duties. **c** SHAKES. *Ven. & Ad.* The lesson is but plain, And once made perfect never lost again. **3** G. GREENE If he had wanted to hide, here was the perfect hiding-place. R. C. HUTCHINSON No good sending a perfect gentleman to bargain with politicians. S. HASTINGS During a period of perfect Indian summer, the Blitz began. A. C. CLARKE They rode in perfect silence. **c** J. TYNDALL Heavy hail had fallen . . the stones being perfect spheres. L. DEIGHTON Leaned back in his chair and blew a perfect smoke ring. **d** *Which?* You could . . make perfect copies with no loss of quality. **e** T. H. HUXLEY To a perfect stranger . . such a method of description would be unintelligible. G. B. SHAW You are a perfect baby in the things I . . understand. I. MURDOCH My life's been a perfect chaos for nearly a year. **4** T. HARDY You must be deemed perfect to-day at least. I. MCEWAN My English is not perfect. V. BRAMWELL Most adults over 45 won't have perfect vision and may need glasses.

▸ **II** *techn.* **7** MATH. Of a number: equal to the sum of its factors. LME.
8 MUSIC. Of an interval: belonging to the group comprising the fourth, the fifth, and the octave. Formerly also, (of a note) three times the length of a note of the next lower denomination. LME.
9 GRAMMAR. Designating or pertaining to a verbal aspect or tense denoting a completed action or a state or habitual action which began in past time, (*a*) in time regarded as present (also ***present perfect***) (in English usu. *has* or *have done*, *has* or *have been doing*), (*b*) ***past perfect***, in time regarded as past or preceding a particular past point in time (in English usu. *had done*, *had been doing*), (*c*) ***future perfect***, in time regarded as future or following a particular future point in time (in English usu. *shall* or *will have done*, *shall* or *will have been doing*). L15.
10 PHYSIOLOGY, ANATOMY, etc. Having characteristics developed to the fullest or most advanced degree; typical. L17.
11 BOTANY. Of a flower: having all parts present; *esp.* having both male and female organs present and functional. E18.
12 ENTOMOLOGY. Of or in the finally developed or adult state. M19.
13 PHYSICS. Ideal, theoretical; obeying mathematical laws exactly. M19.
14 PRINTING. (Of a sheet) printed on both sides; (of a ream) comprising 516 sheets. M19.
15 MYCOLOGY. (Of a state or stage in the fungal life cycle) marked by the production of sexual spores; (of a fungus) in the sexual state. L19.
16 Designating a form of bookbinding in which the leaves are attached to the spine by gluing rather than folding and sewing. L19.
17 ECONOMICS. Designating (notional or actual) ideal market conditions in which adverse factors such as restricted information and dominant market shares are absent. L19.
18 MATH. **a** Of a group: such that the subgroup generated by the set of commutators of the group is the group itself. L19. ▸**b** Of a set of points: closed, and such that every neighbourhood of each point of the set contains at least one other point of the set. E20.
Special collocations: **perfect cadence** MUSIC a cadence consisting of the direct chord of the tonic preceded by a dominant or subdominant chord, and forming a full close. **perfect crime** an ingenious crime that cannot be detected or solved. **perfect gas** = ***ideal gas*** s.v. IDEAL *adjective.* **perfect pitch** the ability to recognize or reproduce the exact pitch of a note; absolute pitch.
▸ **B** *adverb.* = PERFECTLY. *obsolete* exc. *poet. & dial.* LME.
▸ **C** *noun.* **1** That which is perfect, perfection. *rare.* LME.
2 ECCLESIASTICAL HISTORY. A Catharist who had received the spiritual baptism and thereby accepted all the precepts of Albigensian doctrine. M18.
3 GRAMMAR. (A word or form in) the perfect aspect or tense or (***present perfect***, ***past perfect***, ***future perfect***) one of the perfect aspects or tenses. M19.
3 ***prophetic perfect***: see PROPHETIC 1.

perfect /pəˈfɛkt/ *verb trans.* LME.
[from the adjective.]
†**1** Bring to full development. LME–E17.
2 Make perfect or faultless; *loosely* bring nearer to perfection, improve. LME. ▸**b** Make (a person) accomplished at or perfect in or *in* some activity. E17.
3 Complete (successfully); finish. L15. ▸**b** PRINTING. Complete the printing of a sheet of a book etc. by printing the second side. E19.

📖 **2** G. VIDAL Stokharin has perfected a painless death by poison. A. EDEN He had . . the opportunity and resources to perfect his prowess. S. BIKO The power-based society of the Westerner . . ever concerned with perfecting their technological know-how. **b** H. JAMES Perfecting herself in French, which she already knows very well. **3** L. STEFFENS They have perfected a plan to keep the citizens informed. S. QUINN He had perfected a little magic show. **b perfecting machine**, (*US*) **perfecting press** a printing machine, on which the sheet, as it passes through, is printed first on one side and then on the other.

■ **perfecˈtation** *noun* (*rare*) the action or process of making or becoming perfect M19. **perfectedly** *adverb* (*rare*) perfectly, completely L17. **perfecter** *noun* a person who or thing which perfects something LME. **perfectionize** *verb trans.* (*rare*) perfect E19. **perfector** *noun* (*a*) a perfecter; (*b*) PRINTING a perfecting machine: L16.

perfecta /pəˈfɛktə/ *noun.* Chiefly *US.* L20.
[Amer. Spanish *quiniela perfecta* perfect quinella.]
A form of betting in which the first and second finishers of a race must be predicted in the correct order.

perfectibilism /pəːfɪkˈtɪbɪlɪz(ə)m/ *noun.* M19.
[from PERFECTIBLE + -ISM.]
The doctrine of the perfectibility of human nature.
■ **perfectibilist** *noun* a person who holds the doctrine of perfectibilism L18.

For other words beginning with *per-* see the entry for **per-**¹

perfectibility /pəfɛktɪˈbɪlɪti/ *noun*. **L18**.
[from next + -ILITY.]
1 Ability to be perfected or brought to a state of perfection; *spec.* the capacity of human nature to progress indefinitely towards physical, mental, and moral perfection; the doctrine of this capacity. **L18**.
2 A state of perfection. *rare*. **E19**.

📖 **1** E. GELLNER The nineteenth century, the age of belief in progress and the perfectibility of man.

■ **perˌfectibiliˈtarian** *noun* = PERFECTIBILIST **L19**.

perfectible /pəˈfɛktɪb(ə)l/ *adjective*. **M17**.
[medieval Latin *perfectibilis*, from Latin *perfectus*: see PERFECT *adjective, adverb, & noun*, -IBLE; later referred to PERFECT *verb*.]
Able to be perfected or brought to a state of perfection.

📖 C. P. SNOW Societies are no more perfectible than individual men.

■ **perfectiˈbilarian** *noun* (*rare*) = PERFECTIBILIST **M19**. **perfectiˈbilian** *noun* (*rare*) = PERFECTIBILIST **E19**.

perfection /pəˈfɛkʃ(ə)n/ *noun & verb*. **ME**.
[Old & mod. French from Latin *perfectio(n-)*, from *perfectus*: see PERFECT *adjective, adverb, & noun*.]
▶ **A** *noun*. †**1** The fact or condition of being perfected or completed; completion. **ME–L17**. ▸**b** The full growth or development of a thing. **M16–M19**. ▸**c** MUSIC. The condition of being perfect. **E17–L19**.
2 The condition, state, or quality of being perfect or free from all defect; supreme or near excellence; flawlessness, faultlessness. **ME**. ▸**b** An embodiment of this; a perfect person or thing. **L15**.
3 The condition or state of being morally perfect; holiness. Formerly *spec.*, monastic discipline. **ME**.
4 The most perfect degree or the height *of* a quality, condition, etc. **ME**.
5 The action, process, or fact of making perfect or bringing to (successful) completion. **LME**.
6 A quality, feature, or accomplishment of great excellence. *arch*. **L15**.
7 Proficiency in some activity. **M16**.

📖 **2** D. MADDEN Bunches of Tiger Lilies, magnificent in their beauty and perfection. **4** M. R. MITFORD The perfection of cunning is to conceal its own quality. **5** J. MORLEY For this process of perfection, we need . . the meditative, doubting, critical type. **6** J. POTTER I constantly discover new graces, new perfections, and new merits.

Phrases: **counsel of perfection**: see COUNSEL *noun*. **to perfection** perfectly.
▶ **B** *verb trans*. *rare*. Bring to perfection, perfect. **M16**.
■ **perfectionment** *noun* the action of perfecting something **E19**.

perfectionate /pəˈfɛkʃ(ə)neɪt/ *verb trans*. Now *rare*. **L16**.
[from prec. + -ATE^{3}.]
Bring to perfection; perfect.
■ **perfectioˈnation** *noun* (*rare*) **E19**.

perfectionism /pəˈfɛkʃ(ə)nɪz(ə)m/ *noun*. **M19**.
[from (the same root as) next: see -ISM.]
1 A doctrine holding that religious, moral, social, or political perfection is attainable; *esp.* the theory that human moral or spiritual perfection can be or has been attained; *spec.* (**P-**) the doctrine of the Perfectionists of Oneida Creek in New York. **M19**.
2 Refusal to accept any standard short of perfection. **M20**.

📖 **2** *Radio Times* His unusual rigorous perfectionism—undergoing five hours of vocal training every day for five months.

perfectionist /pəˈfɛkʃ(ə)nɪst/ *noun & adjective*. **M17**.
[from PERFECTION + -IST.]
▶ **A** *noun*. **1** A person who holds a doctrine maintaining the attainability of religious, moral, social, or political perfection; *esp.* a person or *spec.* (**P-**) a member of a sect holding that human moral or spiritual perfection can be or has been attained. **M17**. ▸**b** *spec.* (**P-**.) A member of the communistic community of Oneida Creek in New York. **M19**.
2 A person who is only satisfied with the highest standards. Freq. *derog*. **M20**.

📖 **2** M. FORSTER A perfectionist who had spent days organising the order of her poems for best effect.

▶ **B** *adjective*. Demanding perfection. **M20**.

📖 J. MALCOLM An unbelievably perfectionist mother . . obsessed with taking care of Simone.

■ **perfectioˈnistic** *adjective* (**a**) of or pertaining to Perfectionists; (**b**) = PERFECTIONIST *adjective*: **L19**.

Perfectist /ˈpəːfɪktɪst/ *noun*. *obsolete* exc. *Hist*. **E17**.
[from PERFECT *adjective* + -IST.]
= PERFECTIONIST 1; *esp.* a Perfectionist of the 17th cent.

perfective /pəˈfɛktɪv/ *adjective & noun*. Now *rare* exc. GRAMMAR. **E17**.
[medieval Latin *perfectivus*, from *perfectus*: see PERFECT *adjective*, -IVE.]
▶ **A** *adjective*. **1** Tending to make perfect or complete; conducive to the perfecting *of* a thing. **E17**.
2 In the process of being perfected. **M19**.
3 GRAMMAR. Designating or pertaining to a verbal aspect expressing completed action. **M19**.
▶ **B** *noun*. †**1** A perfectionist. *rare*. Only in **E17**.
2 GRAMMAR. A perfective aspect or form of a verb. **E20**.
■ **perfectiˈvation** *noun* the action of making a verb perfective **E20**. **perfectively** *adverb* **E18**. **perfectiveness** *noun* **E18**. **perfecˈtivity** *noun* the quality of being perfective **E20**. **perfectivize** *verb trans.* make perfective **E20**.

perfectly /ˈpəːfɪk(t)li/ *adverb*. **ME**.
[from PERFECT *adjective* + -LY^{2}.]
1 Completely, thoroughly; to the fullest extent; absolutely. **ME**.
2 In a manner or way that is perfect or faultless; with supreme excellence. Formerly also *spec.*, in a manner morally or religiously perfect. **ME**.
3 Entirely, quite. **M16**. ▸**b** PHYSICS. To a theoretically ideal or maximum degree. **L18**.

📖 **1** GEO. ELIOT I understand the difficulty perfectly, mother. **2** R. LYND A perfectly judged long kick into touch would regain . . all the ground that Cambridge had won. D. M. THOMAS One may love the crippled child more than the perfectly formed one. **3** D. H. LAWRENCE She was perfectly happy to do just nothing. G. VIDAL You know perfectly well that I seldom play cards.

perfectness /ˈpəːfɪk(t)nɪs/ *noun*. **ME**.
[from PERFECT *adjective* + -NESS.]
The quality or condition of being perfect; perfection.

perfecto /pəˈfɛktəʊ/ *noun*. Pl. **-os**. **L19**.
[Spanish = perfect.]
A large thick cigar tapered at each end.

perfervid /pəˈfəːvɪd/ *adjective*. **M19**.
[mod. Latin *perfervidus*, formed as PER-^{1} + FERVID.]
Very fervid; burning; impassioned.

📖 R. FIRBANK Her perfervid, soul-tossed eyes. C. P. SNOW Pamphlets expressing perfervid devotion to the Bourbon monarchy.

■ **perfervidly** *adverb* **E20**. **perfervidness** *noun* **L19**. **perfervour** *noun* the quality of being perfervid **M19**.

perficient /pəˈfɪʃ(ə)nt/ *adjective*. *rare*. **M17**.
[Latin *perficient-* pres. ppl stem of *perficere* complete: see -ENT.]
That accomplishes or achieves something; effectual, actual.

perfide Albion /pɛrfid albjɔ̃/ *noun phr.* **M19**.
[French.]
= ***perfidious* ALBION**.

perfidious /pəˈfɪdɪəs/ *adjective*. **L16**.
[from Latin *perfidiosus*, from *perfidia* PERFIDY: see -OUS.]
Characterized by perfidy; guilty of breaking faith; basely treacherous.

📖 D. M. FRAME If he is perfidious, he must be a thoroughgoing fraud. ***perfidious* ALBION**.

■ **perfidiously** *adverb* **L16**. **perfidiousness** *noun* **L16**.

perfidy /ˈpəːfɪdi/ *noun*. **L16**.
[Latin *perfidia*, from *perfidus* treacherous, formed as PER-^{1} + *fides* FAITH: see -Y^{3}.]
Deceitful breach of faith or betrayal of trust; *esp.* the profession of faith or friendship in order to deceive or betray.
■ Also **perˈfidity** *noun* (*rare*) **E17**.

perfin /ˈpəːfɪn/ *noun*. **M20**.
[from PERF(ORATED + IN(ITIAL *noun*.]
PHILATELY. A postage stamp perforated with the initials or other insignia of an organization, esp. to prevent misuse.

†**perfix** *verb trans*. **E16–L18**.
[from PER-^{1} + FIX *verb*.]
Fix firmly or definitely.

perflate /pəˈfleɪt/ *verb trans*. Now *rare*. **M16**.
[Latin *perflat-* pa. ppl stem of *perflare*, formed as PER-^{1} + *flare* blow: see -ATE^{3}.]
Blow through, ventilate.
■ **perflation** *noun* **M17**.

perfluent /pəˈfluːənt/ *adjective*. Now *rare*. **L17**.
[Latin *perfluent-* pres. ppl stem of *perfluere*, formed as PER-^{1} + *fluere* flow: see -ENT.]
(Having the quality of) flowing through.

perfluoro- /pəˈfluːərəʊ/ *combining form*.
[from PER-^{1} + FLUORO-.]
CHEMISTRY. Involving or resulting from the maximum possible replacement of hydrogen by fluorine.
■ **perfluoroˈcarbon** *noun* any binary compound of carbon and fluorine, analogous to a hydrocarbon **M20**.

perfoliate /pəˈfəʊlɪət/ *adjective*. **L17**.
[mod. Latin *perfoliatus*, formed as PER-^{1} + FOLIATE *adjective*.]
1 BOTANY. (Of a sessile leaf or bract) extended at the base to encircle the node, so that the stem apparently passes through it; (of a plant) having such leaves. Formerly, (of a stem) apparently passing through the leaf. **L17**.
2 ENTOMOLOGY. Of (part of) an antenna: resembling one or more round plates pierced by a shaft. **E19**.
■ **perfoliated** *adjective* (ENTOMOLOGY) = PERFOLIATE 2 **M18**. **perfoliˈation** *noun* perfoliate condition **M19**.

perforable /ˈpəːf(ə)rəb(ə)l/ *adjective*. *rare*. **L19**.
[from PERFORATE *verb* + -ABLE.]
Able to be perforated.

perforant /ˈpəːf(ə)r(ə)nt/ *adjective*. **M19**.
[Latin *perforant-* pres. ppl stem of *perforare*: see PERFORATE *verb*, -ANT^{1}.]
Perforating.
perforant path ANATOMY a tract of nerve fibres leading to the hippocampus.

perforate /ˈpəːf(ə)rət/ *adjective*. **LME**.
[Latin *perforatus* pa. pple of *perforare*: see next, -ATE^{2}.]
= PERFORATED. Chiefly BOTANY, having translucent glandular dots.

perforate /ˈpəːfəreɪt/ *verb*. **M16**.
[Latin *perforat-* pa. ppl stem of *perforare*, formed as PER-^{1} + *forare* bore, pierce: see -ATE^{3}. Cf. earlier PERFORATED.]
1 *verb trans*. Make a hole or holes through; pierce with a pointed instrument etc.; *spec.* make a row of small holes in (paper etc.) so that a part may be torn off easily. **M16**. ▸**b** Make a hole or holes into the interior of (a thing); bore into. **E18**. ▸**c** Pass through; extend through the substance of. **E19**.
2 *verb intrans*. **a** Penetrate; make a perforation. (Foll. by *into*.) **L18**. ▸**b** Become perforated. **L19**.
■ **perforator** *noun* an instrument or machine used for perforating **M18**.

perforated /ˈpəːfəreɪtɪd/ *ppl adjective*. **L15**.
[from PERFORATE *adjective* or *verb* + -ED^{1}.]
1 Pierced with a hole or holes. **L15**.
2 Made or outlined by perforations. *rare*. **L18**.
1 perforated tape: in which data are recorded by means of the pattern of holes punched in it.

perforation /pəːfəˈreɪʃ(ə)n/ *noun*. **LME**.
[Old & mod. French from medieval Latin *perforatio(n-)*, formed as PERFORATE *verb*: see -ATION.]
1 The action of perforating; the fact or condition of being perforated. **LME**.
2 A hole made by boring, punching, or piercing; an aperture passing through or into anything; *spec.* each of a row of small holes punched in a sheet of paper, allowing for a part to be torn off easily. **LME**.
Comb.: **perforation plate** BOTANY (in a xylem vessel) a perforated area in the common wall of adjacent vessel members, allowing the free passage of sap.

perforative /ˈpəːf(ə)rətɪv/ *adjective & noun*. **LME**.
[Old & mod. French *perforatif*, *-ive* or medieval Latin *perforativus*, formed as PERFORATE *verb* + -IVE.]
▶ **A** *adjective*. Having the quality of perforating. **LME**.
▶†**B** *noun*. **1** A penetrating medicine. Only in **LME**.
2 An instrument used for perforating. Only in **M18**.

perforce /pəˈfɔːs/ *adverb, noun, & adjective*. **ME**.
[Old French *par force* assim. to PER-^{2}, FORCE *noun*^{1}.]
▶ **A** *adverb*. †**1** By violence; forcibly. **ME–L17**.
2 By constraint of circumstance; of necessity, unavoidably. **M16**.

📖 **2** P. L. FERMOR On a temporary footing which perforce grew longer, I remained. *Scientific American* One may be, perforce or by intention, an astrophysicist one day and a high-energy physicist the next.

▶ **B** *noun*. Force; necessity. Chiefly in ***by perforce***, ***of perforce***. **E16**.
▶ **C** *adjective*. Necessitated, forced. *rare*. **L16**.
Phrases: **perforce of** by dint of.

perforin /ˈpəːfərɪn/ *noun*. **L20**.
[from PERFORATE *verb* + -IN^{1}.]
BIOCHEMISTRY. A protein, released by killer cells of the immune system, which destroys targeted cells by creating lesions like pores in their membranes.

perform /pəˈfɔːm/ *verb*. **ME**.
[Anglo-Norman *parfourmer*, *per-* (in Anglo-Latin *performare*) alt. (after *forme* FORM *noun*) of Old French *parfornir*, *-furnir* (in medieval Latin *perfurnire*), from *par* PER-^{1} + *furnir* FURNISH *verb*.]
1 *verb trans*. Carry out, fulfil (a command, promise, undertaking, etc.). **ME**.
2 a *verb trans*. Execute, accomplish, do, (any action, operation, or process undertaken or ordered). **LME**. ▸**b** *verb intrans*. Do or carry out any action, operation, or process undertaken or ordered; do (*badly*, *well*, etc.). **LME**. ▸†**c** *verb trans*. Grant or give (something promised). **M16–M17**. ▸**d** *verb intrans*. Have sexual intercourse with a person, esp. satisfactorily. *slang*. **E20**. ▸**e** *verb intrans*. Of an investment: yield a (high or low) profit (foll. by *well*, *badly*, etc.); *esp.* be profitable. (Earlier in PERFORMER 1b.) **M20**.
†**3** *verb trans*. Make or construct (an object); execute (a literary or artistic work). **LME–L18**.
†**4** *verb trans*. **a** Complete or finish (an action, process, etc.). **LME–E17**. ▸**b** Complete or make up by addition of what is wanting. **LME–M16**.
†**5** *verb trans*. Complete the construction of (an object or structure); *esp.* complete by the addition of trimming or decoration. **LME–E17**.

For other words beginning with *per-* see the entry for **per-**^{1}

†**6** *verb trans.* Bring about, effect, produce, (a result). LME–E18.

7 a *verb trans.* Carry out formally or solemnly (a public function, ceremony, or rite); present (a play, ballet, etc.) on stage or to an audience; play or sing (a piece of music) for an audience. E17. ▸**b** *verb trans.* Represent (a part in a play, a role in a ballet, etc.) on stage or to an audience; act or play (a part). E17. ▸**c** *verb intrans.* Act in a play; play music; sing; dance. M19. ▸**d** *verb intrans.* Show extreme anger; make a great fuss. *Austral. slang.* L19.

> **1** E. YOUNG Our Fleet, if war, or commerce, call, His will performs. **2** T. HARDY She performed her duties in her father's house. F. TUOHY They fluttered down . . performing on the way a complete back-somersault in the air. P. BARKER She began the sequence of actions that she would perform hundreds of times that day. J. IRVING Larch performed a Caesarean section. **b** *Daily Telegraph* The engine warms up rapidly and performs eagerly. *Tennis* He performed well . . reaching the quarterfinals. **7a** J. L. SANFORD The mass performed by the priest at the altar. A. C. BOULT A private performance of a Requiem that had never been performed in public. V. CRONIN The private theatre, where two short comedies and two ballets were performed. **b** SHAKES. *Temp.* Bravely the figure of this harpy hast thou Perform'd, my Ariel. **c** F. ASTAIRE He did not long to perform himself, he had never acted or danced. C. ACHEBE Five or six dancing groups were performing.

Phrases: ***performing arts***: see ART *noun*[1]. ***performing rights***: for the performance of a piece of music etc. ***perform one's stations, perform the stations***: see STATION *noun*.

■ **performaˈbility** *noun* the quality of being performable M20. **performable** *adjective* able to be performed M16. **performatory** *adjective* = PERFORMATIVE *adjective* M20. **performing** *ppl adjective* (*a*) that performs; (*b*) *spec.* designating an animal trained to perform tricks to entertain the public: L16.

performance /pəˈfɔːm(ə)ns/ *noun.* L15.
[from prec. + -ANCE.]
1 The execution or accomplishment of an action, operation, or process undertaken or ordered; the doing of any action or work; the quality of this, esp. as observable under particular conditions; *spec.* the capabilities of a machine, esp. a motor vehicle or aircraft, measured under test. L15. ▸**b** Something performed or done; an action, a deed; *esp.* a notable deed or achievement; *spec.* a literary or artistic work (now *rare*). L16. ▸**c** *spec.* The extent to which an investment is profitable, esp. in relation to other commodities; an instance of this. E20.
2 The carrying out or fulfilment of a command, duty, purpose, promise, etc. M16.
3 The action of performing a play, a part in a play, a piece of music, etc.; an instance of this, a public exhibition or production of a play, piece of music, etc. E17. ▸†**b** A ceremony, a rite. L17–M18. ▸**c** A display of anger or exaggerated behaviour; a fuss, a scene. Also, a difficult or annoying procedure. *colloq.* M20.

> **1** A. PATON They worked and sang together in the performance of the daily tasks. J. BRONOWSKI To . . step up the performance of the water wheel as a machine. *Which?* Philips gave the best blend of price and performance. **b** P. GAY Freud's lecture was a lively, highly skilful forensic performance. **2** H. F. CARY To fair request Silent performance maketh best return. **3** F. FERGUSSON An Easter performance of the *Mattias Passion.* L. HELLMAN Tallulah, in the first months of the play, gave a fine performance. **c** R. INGALLS She put on a performance, talked loudly, looking round at the other people in the restaurant.

Phrases: ***specific performance***: see SPECIFIC *adjective*.
Comb.: **performance art** a form of visual art combining static elements with dramatic performance; **performance artist** a person engaged or taking part in performance art; **performance bond**: issued by a bank etc. guaranteeing the fulfilment of a particular contract; **performance car**: with very good performance; **performance poetry**: intended to be performed as a dramatic monologue or exchange and freq. involving extemporization; **performance practice** the body of codes or standards dictating the style of performance of a piece of music, based on assumptions about the notation, instruments, etc., of the period concerned; **performance test** (*a*) PSYCHOLOGY a non-verbal test of ability or intelligence based on the performance of certain manual tasks; (*b*) the measurement of weight gain, food conversion, and other heritable characteristics, as a guide to selective breeding of farm animals; **performance-tested** *adjective* (of a farm animal) having had heritable qualities evaluated; **performance testing** the evaluation of a farm animal's heritable characteristics.

performative /pəˈfɔːmətɪv/ *adjective & noun.* M20.
[from PERFORM + -ATIVE, after *imperative.*]
▶ **A** *adjective.* Of or pertaining to performance; *spec.* (PHILOSOPHY & LINGUISTICS) designating or pertaining to an utterance that effects an action by being spoken or by means of which the speaker performs a particular act. M20.
▶ **B** *noun.* A performative utterance. M20.
■ **performatively** *adverb* L20. **performativeness** *noun* M20.

performer /pəˈfɔːmə/ *noun.* L16.
[from PERFORM + -ER[1].]
1 A person who carries out or executes an undertaking, action, etc., esp. in a specified manner. L16. ▸**b** An investment which yields a (high or low) return; *esp.* one which is profitable. Cf. PERFORM 2e. E20.
2 A person who performs a part in a play, a piece of music, etc., as a public exhibition of art or skill; a person who takes part in a public entertainment. E18. ▸**b** A person who tends to make a great fuss or show extreme anger. *slang* (chiefly NAUTICAL). M20.

> **1** R. GREENE A fit performer of our enterprise. **b** *Times* The shares have still easily been the poorest performers of any domestic bank this year. **2** C. TOMALIN Katherine was always a performer She needed to enchant an audience. S. ROSENBERG Intourist arranged gala concerts with top performers.

†**perfricate** *verb trans.* L16–M17.
[Latin *perfricat-* pa. ppl stem of *perfricare*, formed as PER-[1] + *fricare* rub: see -ATE[3].]
Rub thoroughly or all over.

perfrication /pəːfrɪˈkeɪʃ(ə)n/ *noun.* Now *rare* or *obsolete.* E17.
[from prec. + -ATION.]
The action of rubbing thoroughly or all over; vigorous friction.

perfume /ˈpəːfjuːm/ *noun.* M16.
[French *parfum*, from *parfumer*, †*per-*: see next.]
1 Orig., the esp. pleasantly odorous fumes or vapour given off by the burning of a substance. Later, the odour emitted by any sweet-smelling substance. M16. ▸**b** *fig.* (Good) repute. L16.
2 Orig., a substance emitting a sweet smell when burned. Later, a sweet-smelling fluid (esp. for applying to the body) containing the essence of flowers, spices, etc. M16.

> **1** E. LANGLEY The orange blossoms . . hurt my heart with the wildness of their perfume. **2** *Looks* A bottle of perfume and some tights.

■ **perfumeless** *adjective* L19. **perfumy** *adjective* having or emitting a perfume; like perfume: M19.

perfume /ˈpəːfjuːm, pəˈfjuːm/ *verb trans.* M16.
[French *parfumer*, †*perfumer* from Italian †*parfumare*, †*per-* (now *pro-*) lit. 'smoke through': see PER-[1], FUME *verb*.]
1 Fill or impregnate with the fumes or vapour of a burning substance for the purpose of imparting a sweet smell to or (formerly) fumigating. *obsolete* exc. as in sense 2. M16.
2 Impregnate with a sweet smell; impart a sweet smell to. M16.

> **2** P. GALLICO Perfuming the district with the scent of lemon and orange trees.

perfumed /ˈpəːfjuːmd, pəˈfjuːmd/ *adjective.* M16.
[from PERFUME *noun, verb*: see -ED[2], -ED[1].]
1 Impregnated with a sweet smell. M16.
2 Having a natural perfume; sweet-smelling. E17.

perfumer /pəˈfjuːmə/ *noun.* M16.
[from PERFUME *noun, verb* + -ER[1].]
1 A person engaged in making or selling perfumes. M16.
†**2** A person employed to fumigate or perfume rooms. *rare* (Shakes.). Only in L16.

perfumery /pəˈfjuːm(ə)ri/ *noun.* E19.
[from PERFUME *noun* + -ERY. Cf. also PARFUMERIE.]
The preparation of perfumes; *collect.* perfumes. Also, a perfumer's place of business.

perfunction /pəˈfʌŋ(k)ʃ(ə)n/ *noun. rare.* M17.
[Latin *perfunctio(n-)*, from *perfunct-*: see PERFUNCTORY, -ION.]
The action of finishing or accomplishing something.

perfunctionary /pəˈfʌŋ(k)ʃ(ə)n(ə)ri/ *adjective. rare.* M19.
[formed as prec. + -ARY[2].]
= PERFUNCTORY.

†**perfunctorious** *adjective.* E17–E19.
[formed as next + -OUS.]
= PERFUNCTORY.
■ †**perfunctoriously** *adverb* E17–E19.

perfunctory /pəˈfʌŋ(k)t(ə)ri/ *adjective.* L16.
[Late Latin *perfunctorius* careless, negligent, from *perfunct-* pa. ppl stem of *perfungi* perform, discharge, get rid of, formed as PER-[1] + *fungi*: see FUNCTION *noun*, -ORY[2].]
1 Done as a piece of routine or duty; done for form's sake only and so without interest or enthusiasm; formal, mechanical. L16.
2 Of a person: acting merely by way of duty; (qualifying an agent-noun) doing the act specified mechanically and without interest or enthusiasm. E17.

> **1** J. LONDON The question was perfunctory, and she knew what the answer would be. A. CROSS No one . . much noticed her departure, though there were a few perfunctory waves. C. THUBRON Her smile was perfunctory, meaningless. **2** J. NORRIS How many perfunctory inquirers there are that carelessly interrogate this Divine oracle.

■ **perfunctorily** *adverb* L16. **perfunctoriness** *noun* M17.

†**perfurnish** *verb trans.* Chiefly *Scot. & north.* LME.
[Old & mod. French *parfourniss-*, *-furniss-* stem of *parfornir*, *-furnir*: see PERFORM.]
1 = PERFORM 1, 2. LME–L16.
2 = PERFORM 4b. Also, supply. LME–E19.
3 = PERFORM 4a. LME–M16.

perfusate /pəˈfjuːzeɪt/ *noun.* E20.
[from PERFUSE + *-ate* after *filtrate*, *precipitate*, etc.]
PHYSIOLOGY. A fluid used in perfusion.

perfuse /pəˈfjuːz/ *verb trans.* LME.
[Latin *perfus-* pa. ppl stem of *perfundere*, formed as PER-[1] + *fundere* pour out.]
1 Pour or diffuse through; cause to flow through or (formerly) away (*lit.* & *fig.*). LME.
2 Cover or sprinkle with something wet; *esp.* (*fig.*) suffuse with colour, a quality, etc. M16.
3 MEDICINE & PHYSIOLOGY. Supply (an organ, tissue, or body) with a fluid artificially by circulating it through blood-vessels or other natural channels; pass a fluid through (a hollow organ). E20.
■ **perfusive** *adjective* having the quality of being diffused all through (chiefly *fig.*) E19.

perfusion /pəˈfjuːʒ(ə)n/ *noun.* L16.
[Latin *perfusio(n-)*, formed as prec.: see -ION.]
1 The action of pouring a fluid on, over, or through something; *spec.* the pouring of water over a person in baptism. L16.
2 MEDICINE. The process of passing a fluid, esp. treated blood or a substitute for blood, through an organ or tissue; treatment of a patient by continuous transfusion of prepared blood. E20.

pergameneous /pəːgəˈmiːnɪəs/ *adjective.* E19.
[from Latin *pergamena*: see PARCHMENT *noun*, -EOUS.]
Of the nature or texture of parchment.

Pergamenian /pəːgəˈmiːnɪən/ *noun & adjective.* L16.
[from Latin *Pergamenus* adjective, from Latin *Pergamum* (see below), Greek *Pergamos*: see -IAN.]
▶ **A** *noun.* A native or inhabitant of Pergamum, the capital of an ancient kingdom in Asia Minor (now Bergama in Turkey). L16.
▶ **B** *adjective.* Of or pertaining to Pergamum, the school of sculpture that flourished there in the 3rd and 2nd cents. BC, or the early Christian Church founded there. L18.
■ Also **Pergamene** *noun & adjective* M19.

pergamentaceous /pəːgəmɛnˈteɪʃəs/ *adjective.* M19.
[from medieval Latin *pergamentum*, formed as PERGAMENEOUS: see -ACEOUS.]
= PERGAMENEOUS.

pergana *noun* see PARGANA.

pergelisol /pəːˈdʒɛlɪsɒl/ *noun.* M20.
[from PER-[1] + Latin *gelare* freeze + -I- + -SOL.]
PHYSICAL GEOGRAPHY. = PERMAFROST.

pergola /ˈpəːgələ/ *noun.* M17.
[Italian from Latin *pergula* projecting roof, vine arbour, from *pergere* come or go forward.]
†**1** An elevated stand or balcony. *rare.* Only in M17.
2 An arbour or covered walk, formed of growing plants trained over trellis-work. L17.

Pergonal /pəːˈgəʊnal/ *noun.* M20.
[from PER-[1] + GON(ADOTROPHIN + *-al* after *Nembutal*, *veronal*, etc.]
MEDICINE. (Proprietary name for) any of various hormonal preparations, *esp.* a preparation of human menopausal gonadotrophin used to treat infertility arising from gonadotrophin deficiency.

pergunnah *noun* see PARGANA.

†**perhap** *adverb.* LME–M17.
[from PER + HAP *noun.*]
Perhaps.

perhaps /pəˈhaps/ *adverb & noun.* L15.
[from PER + HAP *noun* + -S[1]. Cf. P'RAPS.]
▶ **A** *adverb.* **1** Qualifying a statement, or by ellipsis a word or phr., so as to express possibility with uncertainty: it may be that; maybe, possibly. L15.
2 In a conditional clause expr. hypothesis: as may happen or be the case; as is possible; by any chance. Now *rare* exc. in ***unless perhaps***. L16.

> **1** B. PYM Must we always like everybody? . . Perhaps not. J. CANNAN Perhaps you would be good enough to withdraw. E. WAUGH There is the Drowned Sailor motif—an echo of the *Waste Land* perhaps? A. S. BYATT I don't know how to start, and perhaps I ought not to try. F. SWINNERTON Not, perhaps, an atheist, he was proud of his command of medieval history. H. SECOMBE Perhaps I'll die of pneumonia. **2** AV 2 *Cor.* 2:7 Lest perhaps, such a one should be swallowed vp with ouermuch sorrow.

▶ **B** *noun.* **1** A statement qualified by 'perhaps'; an expression of possibility combined with uncertainty, suspicion, or doubt. M16.
2 Something that may or may not happen or exist; a mere possibility. Chiefly in ***the great perhaps***. M19.

> **1** P. HENISSART Perhaps you're telling the truth; it's a big perhaps.

¶ Cf. PERADVENTURE, PERCASE, PERCHANCE.

perhexiline /pəˈhɛksɪliːn/ *noun*. M20.
[Blend of PIPERIDINE and HEXYL.]
PHARMACOLOGY. A derivative of piperidine which is a vasodilator whose maleate is given to relieve angina pectoris; 2-(2,2-dicyclohexylethyl)piperidine, $C_{19}H_{35}N$.

peri /ˈpɪəri/ *noun*. L18.
[Persian *perī*.]
In *IRANIAN MYTHOLOGY*, one of a race of superhuman beings, originally represented as evil but subsequently as good and graceful; *transf.* a graceful or beautiful person.

peri- /ˈpɛri/ *prefix*.
[from Greek *peri* (preposition & adverb) round, around, round about, about.]
Used with the sense 'encircling, around, in the vicinity of, near' to form adjectives (& derived adverbs) & nouns, esp. (*a*) *MEDICINE* referring to a region or structure lying around or near a specified part; (*b*) *ASTRONOMY* referring to the point in the orbit of a body at which it is nearest to the primary about which it revolves (opp. APO-).
■ **periˈanal** *adjective* situated or occurring around the anus L19. **periˈapical** *adjective* situated or occurring around the apex of the root of a tooth E20. **periˈapsis** *noun*, pl. **-apses** /-ˈapsiːz/, *ASTRONOMY* the point in the path of an orbiting body at which it is nearest to the primary M20. **periarˈterial** *adjective* (*ANATOMY*) situated or occurring around an artery L19. **periarˈticular** *adjective* (*MEDICINE*) situated or occurring around a joint of the body L19. **periblem** *noun* [Greek *periblēa* garment, covering] *BOTANY* (according to the histogen theory) the intermediate layer of an apical meristem, which develops into the cortical tissue (cf. DERMATOGEN, PLEROME) L19. **periˈbronchial** *adjective* (*MEDICINE*) situated or occurring around the bronchi L19. **pericaˈpillary** *adjective* (*ANATOMY*) situated or occurring around a capillary vessel E20. **periˈcellular** *adjective* (*BIOLOGY*) situated or occurring around a living cell or cells L19. **pericemental** *adjective* (*ANATOMY*) of or pertaining to the pericementum of a tooth L19. **pericemenˈtitis** *noun* (*MEDICINE*) inflammation of the pericementum of a tooth L19. **pericementum** *noun* (*ANATOMY*) the layer of connective tissue between the root of a tooth and the alveolar bone L19. **pericentre** *noun* the point in the path of a body revolving round a centre at which it is nearest to the centre E20. **perichoˈresis** *noun* [Greek *perikhōrēsis* going round] *CHRISTIAN THEOLOGY* = CIRCUMINCESSION L18. **periˈcolic** *adjective* (*MEDICINE*) situated or occurring around the colon E20. **periˈcynthion** *noun* [Greek *Kunthios* adjective designating Mount Cynthus: see CYNTHIA] *ASTRONOMY* the point at which a spacecraft in lunar orbit is nearest to the moon's centre, after having been launched from the earth (cf. PERILUNE) M20. **periˈcystic** *adjective* (*MEDICINE*) situated or occurring around the bladder or around a cyst L19. **pericyte** *noun* (*ANATOMY*) any of various branching cells found within the walls of capillary blood-vessels E20. **periˈdental** *adjective* (*ANATOMY*) periodontal M19. **periˈdiastole** *noun* (*PHYSIOLOGY*) the short interval of time between the diastole of the heartbeat and the following systole M19. **peridiaˈstolic** *adjective* (*PHYSIOLOGY*) of or pertaining to the peridiastole L19. **periˈfovea** *noun* (*ANATOMY*) the perifoveal region M20. **periˈfoveal** *adjective* (*ANATOMY*) designating the part of the retina regarded as the periphery of its central region, surrounding the parafovea E20. **periˈgenital** *adjective* (*ANATOMY*) situated or occurring around the genitals M20. **periˈglacial** *adjective* (*PHYSICAL GEOGRAPHY*) characteristic of or designating a region where an adjacent ice sheet or glacier, or frost action, has modified the landscape E20. **periˈglacially** *adverb* (*PHYSICAL GEOGRAPHY*) in or by a periglacial environment M20. **periglaciˈation** *noun* (*PHYSICAL GEOGRAPHY*) the state of being subject to a periglacial climate; periglacial processes collectively: M20. **perigon** *noun* [-GON] *MATH.* an angle of 360 degrees M19. **perigoˈnadial** *adjective* (*BIOLOGY*) situated or occurring around a gonad L19. **periˈhaemal** *adjective* (*ZOOLOGY*) designating a system of circular and radial channels in echinoderms L19. **perijove** *noun* (*ASTRONOMY*) the point nearest to Jupiter in the orbit of any of Jupiter's satellites M19. **periˈkaryal** *adjective* (*ANATOMY*) of, pertaining to, or occurring in a perikaryon M20. **perikaryon** /-ˈkarɪən/, pl. **-karya** /-ˈkarɪə/, *noun* [KARYO-] *ANATOMY* the part of a nerve cell that contains the nucleus L19. **perilune** *noun* (*ASTRONOMY*) the point at which a spacecraft in lunar orbit (esp. one launched from the moon) is nearest to the moon's centre (cf. PERICYNTHION) M20. **perilymph** *noun* (*ANATOMY*) the fluid within the bony labyrinth of the ear, surrounding the membranous labyrinth M19. **perilymˈphatic** *adjective* (*ANATOMY*) of or pertaining to the perilymph L19. **perimenoˈpausal** *adjective* occurring at around the time of the menopause M20. **periˈmenopause** *noun* the perimenopausal period of life M20. **perimorph** *noun* a mineral or crystal that encloses another L19. **perimysium** /-ˈmɪsɪəm/ *noun* [Greek *mus* muscle] *ANATOMY* the connective tissue that forms sheaths around bundles of muscle fibres in a muscle and around the muscles themselves M19. **periˈnephric** *adjective* (*ANATOMY*) situated or occurring around the kidney L19. **periˈneural** *adjective* (*ANATOMY*) situated or occurring around a nerve or a bundle of nerve fibres L19. **periˈneurium** *noun* (*ANATOMY*) the sheath of connective tissue surrounding a bundle of nerve fibres M19. **periˈnuclear** *adjective* (*a*) *BIOLOGY* situated or occurring around a cell nucleus; (*b*) *MEDICINE* situated or occurring around the eyeball: L19. **periˈocular** *adjective* situated or occurring around the eye or the eyeball L19. **perioesophageal** /ˌpɛriɪːsɒfəˈdʒiːəl/ *adjective* (*ANATOMY*) situated or occurring around the oesophagus L19. **perionychia** /-ˈnɪk-/ *noun* (*MEDICINE*) = PARONYCHIA 1 L19. **periˈoperative** *adjective* (*MEDICINE*) occurring or performed around the time of an operation; pertaining to such a time: M20. **periˈoperatively** *adverb* (*MEDICINE*) during a perioperative period L20. **periˈoral** *adjective* (*ANATOMY*) situated or occurring around the mouth L19. **periˈotic** *adjective* (*ANATOMY*) surrounding the inner ear M19. **peripaˈpillary** *adjective* (*ANATOMY*) situated or occurring around the optic papilla L19. **periˈpediment** *noun* (*PHYSICAL GEOGRAPHY*) a broad gently sloping surface that tops a thickness of detrital alluvium and either extends outward from a mountain foot in an arid or semi-arid region or else continues the line of an intervening pediment M20. **periˈphonic** *adjective* (of sound reproduction) involving speakers at different heights so as to add a vertical distribution of sound to the horizontal one of stereophony L20. **peˈriphony** *noun* periphonic sound reproduction L20. **periˈphyton** *noun* (*ECOLOGY*) a community of organisms living upon the surfaces of submerged objects in water; *spec.* submerged microflora: M20. **periˈportal** *adjective* (*ANATOMY*) situated or occurring around the portal vein L19. **periproct** *noun* [formed as PROCTO-] *ZOOLOGY* the part of the body surface surrounding the anus in echinoderms and some other invertebrates L19. **periˈrenal** *adjective* (*ANATOMY*) perinephric L19. **perisarc** *noun* [Greek *sark-*, *sarx* flesh] *ZOOLOGY* an outer horny layer secreted by some colonial coelenterates L19. **perisaˈturnium** *noun* (*ASTRONOMY*) the point nearest to Saturn in the orbit of any of Saturn's satellites M19. **perisperm** *noun* (*BOTANY*) (*a*) a thin outer layer, the remains of the nucellus, which surrounds the endosperm in some seeds; †(*b*) the endosperm generally; (*c*) the testa of a seed: E19. **perispleˈnitis** *noun* (*MEDICINE*) inflammation of the peritoneal tissue forming the capsule of the spleen L19. **perispore** *noun* (*BOTANY*) an outer layer surrounding the spore in certain ferns M19. **periˈsystole** *noun* (*PHYSIOLOGY*) the short interval of time between the systole of the heartbeat and the following diastole M17. **perisyˈstolic** *adjective* (*PHYSIOLOGY*) of or pertaining to the perisystole M19. **periˈtelevision** *adjective* pertaining to the connection of other equipment to a television (*peritelevision socket*, a SCART socket) L20. **peritenˈdineum** *noun* (*ANATOMY*) the sheath of connective tissue round a tendon L19. **peˈritomy** *noun* (an instance of) surgical removal of a ring of the conjunctiva from around the cornea, performed to relieve pannus L19. **peritreme** /-triːm/ *noun* [Greek *trēma* perforation, hole] *ZOOLOGY* a small chitinous ring surrounding a spiracle in an insect M19. **peritrich** /-trɪk/ *noun* (*ZOOLOGY*) a peritrichous organism E20. **peˈritrichate** *adjective* (*ZOOLOGY*) (of a bacterium) peritrichous M20. **peˈritrichous** *adjective* [Greek *trikh-*, *thrix* hair] *ZOOLOGY* (of a ciliate) having no cilia except for a ring of them around the mouth; (of a bacterium) having flagella over the whole body surface: L19. **peˈritrichously** *adverb* (*ZOOLOGY*) in the manner of a peritrichous organism E20. **peritrophic** /-ˈtrəʊfɪk, -ˈtrɒfɪk/ *adjective* (*ZOOLOGY*) designating a chitinous tube or membrane that lines the gut of many insects and some crustaceans and is wrapped round faeces when they are expelled E20. **periˈtubular** *adjective* (*ANATOMY*) situated or occurring around a tubule, esp. of the urogenital system L20. **perityˈphlitis** *noun* [Greek *tuphlon* caecum, from *tuphlos* blind] *MEDICINE* (now *Hist.*) inflammation of (a part near) the caecum, as in appendicitis and typhlitis M19. **periˈungual** *adjective* (*MEDICINE*) situated or occurring around the nails L19. **peri-ˈurban** *adjective* (esp. in Africa) immediately adjoining a city or conurbation M20. **periureˈteric** *adjective* (*MEDICINE*) situated or occurring around one ureter or both E20. **periuˈrethral** *adjective* (*MEDICINE*) situated or occurring around the urethra L19. **periˈvascular** *adjective* (*ANATOMY*) situated or occurring around a blood-vessel L19. **perivenˈtricular** *adjective* (*ANATOMY*) situated or occurring around a ventricle, esp. a ventricle of the brain L19. **periˈvisceral** *adjective* (*ANATOMY*) situated or occurring around the viscera M19. **periviˈtelline** *adjective* (*BIOLOGY*) situated or occurring around the vitellus of an ovum L19.

periagua *noun* var. of PIRAGUA.

perianth /ˈpɛrɪanθ/ *noun*. Orig. in Latin form **perianthium** /pɛrɪˈanθɪəm/. E18.
[French *périanthe* from mod. Latin *perianthium*, formed as PERI- + Greek *anthos* flower, after *pericarpium* PERICARP.]
BOTANY. †**1** A calyx; (in plants of the composite family) the involucre. Only in 18.
2 The protective outer whorl(s) of a flower, *esp.* one in which corolla and calyx are not differentiated. E19.
3 The fused uppermost perichaetial bracts surrounding the calyptra of a liverwort. M19.
Comb.: **perianth segment** one of the distinct leaves forming a perianth, esp. when they are not differentiated into petals and sepals.

periapt /ˈpɛrɪapt/ *noun*. L16.
[French *périapte* from Greek *periapton*, formed as PERI- + *haptos* fastened, from *haptein* fasten.]
An amulet.

periarteritis /ˌpɛrɪɑːtəˈrʌɪtɪs/ *noun*. L19.
[from PERI- + ARTERY + -ITIS.]
Inflammation of the outer layer of an artery.
periarteritis nodosa /nəˈdəʊsə/ [Latin, fem. of *nodosus* NODOSE] an often fatal form of periarteritis characterized by the formation of aneurysms.

periastron /pɛrɪˈastrən/ *noun*. Also **-aster** /-ˈastə/. M19.
[from PERI- + Greek *astron* star, after *perigee*, *perihelion*.]
ASTRONOMY. The point nearest to a star in the path of a body orbiting that star.
■ **periastral** *adjective* L19.

periblem /ˈpɛrɪblɛm/ *noun*. L19.
[Greek *periblēma* something thrown round, from *periballein* throw round, formed as PERI- + *ballein* to throw.]
BOTANY. In the histogen theory, the intermediate layer of an apical meristem, which gives rise to the cortex. Cf. DERMATOGEN, PLEROME.

peribolus /pəˈrɪb(ə)ləs/ *noun*. Pl. **-li** /-lʌɪ/. Also **-los** /-lɒs/, pl. **-loi** /-lɔɪ/. E18.
[Greek *peribolos*, formed as PERI- + *bol-*, from *ballein* to throw.]
(The wall bounding) an enclosure around a Greek temple or an early Christian church.

†**pericard** *noun* & *adjective*. M17.
[French *péricarde* formed as next.]
▶ **A** *noun*. = PERICARDIUM. M–L17.
▶ **B** *adjective*. Surrounding or enveloping the heart. Only in E18.

pericardium /pɛrɪˈkɑːdɪəm/ *noun*. Pl. **-dia** /-dɪə/. LME.
[medieval Latin from Greek *perikardion*, formed as PERI- + *kardia* heart: see -IUM.]
ANATOMY & *ZOOLOGY*. The membranous sac which encloses the heart and the beginning of the major blood-vessels in vertebrates; the cavity or sinus enclosing or constituting the heart in certain invertebrates.
■ **pericarˈdectomy** *noun* (*a*) pericardiectomy E20. **pericardiac** *adjective* pericardial M19. **pericardial** *adjective* of, pertaining to, or occurring in the pericardium M17. **pericardic** *adjective* (*rare*) pericardial M17. **pericardiˈectomy** *noun* (an instance of) surgical removal of all or part of the pericardium E20. **pericardiocentesis** /-sɛnˈtiːsɪs/, pl. **-teses** /-ˈtiːsiːz/, *noun* [Greek *kentēsis* pricking, from *kentein* to prick] surgical puncturing of the pericardium M20. **pericardiˈotomy** *noun* (an instance of) surgical incision into the pericardium E20. **pericarˈditis** *noun* inflammation of the pericardium L18. **pericarˈdotomy** *noun* (*a*) pericardiotomy E20.

pericarp /ˈpɛrɪkɑːp/ *noun*. Orig. in Latin form **pericarpium** /pɛrɪˈkɑːpɪəm/. L17.
[French *péricarpe* from mod. Latin *pericarpium* from Greek *perikarpion* pod, husk, shell, formed as PERI- + *karpos* fruit: see -IUM.]
BOTANY. The wall of a ripened ovary or fruit. Also, a seed-vessel.
■ **periˈcarpial** *adjective* M19.

†**pericarpium** *noun*[1]. M17–E18.
[mod. Latin from Greek *perikarpion* bracelet, formed as PERI- + *karpos* wrist.]
A plaster applied to the wrist to serve as a cure for something.

pericarpium *noun*[2] see PERICARP.

pericentric /pɛrɪˈsɛntrɪk/ *adjective*. M19.
[from PERI- + -CENTRIC.]
1 Arranged or situated around a centre or central body. M19.
2 *CYTOLOGY*. Involving parts of a chromosome at both sides of the centromere. Freq. in ***pericentric inversion***. Opp. PARACENTRIC *adjective* 2. M20.

perichaetia *noun* pl. of PERICHAETIUM.

perichaetial /pɛrɪˈkiːtɪəl/ *adjective*. E19.
[from next + -AL[1].]
BOTANY. Belonging to or constituting the perichaetium.

perichaetium /pɛrɪˈkiːtɪəm/ *noun*. Pl. **-tia** /-tɪə/. L18.
[mod. Latin, formed as PERI- + Greek *khaitē* long hair.]
BOTANY. A group of modified leaves surrounding the archegonium of a moss or foliose liverwort (in the latter case fused into a tubular sheath).

perichaetous /pɛrɪˈkiːtəs/ *adjective*. L19.
[from mod. Latin *Perichaeta* genus name, formed as PERI- + Greek *khaitē* long hair, + -OUS.]
ZOOLOGY. Of an earthworm: having segments surrounded by setae.

perichondrium /pɛrɪˈkɒndrɪəm/ *noun*. Pl. **-dria** /-drɪə/. M18.
[mod. Latin, formed as PERI- + Greek *khondros* cartilage: see -IUM.]
ANATOMY. The layer of fibrous connective tissue that envelopes cartilages (other than at the joints).
■ **perichondrial** *adjective* surrounding or enveloping a cartilage; of or pertaining to the perichondrium: M19. **perichonˈdritis** *noun* inflammation of the perichondrium M19.

periclase /ˈpɛrɪkleɪz/ *noun*. M19.
[mod. Latin *periclasia*, formed as PERI- + Greek *klasis* breaking (with allus. to its perfect cleavage).]
MINERALOGY. Magnesium oxide crystallizing in the cubic system and occurring in marble and limestone.

Periclean /pɛrɪˈkliːən/ *adjective*. E19.
[from *Pericles* (see below) + -AN.]
Of or pertaining to Pericles (*c* 495–429 BC), Athenian statesman, and his age in Athenian history, when Athens was intellectually and materially pre-eminent among the Greek city-states.

periclinal /pɛrɪˈklʌɪn(ə)l/ *adjective* & *noun*. L19.
[from Greek *periklinēs* sloping on all sides, formed as PERI- + *klinēs* sloping, from *klinein* to lean, slope: see -AL[1].]
▶ **A** *adjective*. **1** *GEOLOGY*. Sloping in all directions from a central point. L19.
2 *BOTANY*. Of a cell wall etc.: parallel to the surface of the meristem. Of growth: taking place by the formation of periclinal walls. Opp. ***anticlinal***. L19.
3 Designating a plant chimera in which genetically different tissues are in distinct layers. E20.
▶ **B** *noun*. A periclinal surface or layer; a periclinal chimera. L19.
■ **periclinally** *adverb* L19.

pericline /ˈpɛrɪklʌɪn/ *noun*[1]. Now *rare* or *obsolete*. Orig. in Latin form **periclinium** /pɛrɪˈklʌɪnɪəm/, pl. **-nia** /-nɪə/. E19.
[mod. Latin *periclinium*, formed as PERI- + Greek *klinē* couch.]
BOTANY. In plants of the composite family: the involucre.

pericline /ˈpɛrɪklʌɪn/ *noun*[2]. **M19.**
[formed as **PERICLINAL.**]
1 *MINERALOGY.* A variety of albite occurring as large elongated white crystals, often twinned. **M19.**
2 *GEOLOGY.* A periclinal dome or basin. **M20.**

periclinia *noun pl.* see **PERICLINE** *noun*[1].

periclinium *noun* see **PERICLINE** *noun*[1].

†periclitate *verb.* **E16.**
[Latin *periclitat-* pa. ppl stem of *periclitari*, from *peric(u)lum*: see **PERIL, -ATE**[3].]
1 *verb trans.* Imperil, endanger. **E16–M18.**
2 *verb intrans.* Cause danger, take risks. **L17–M19.**
■ **†periclitation** *noun* (*a*) the action of imperilling someone or something; peril, danger, hazard; (*b*) an experiment, a venture: **E16–L19.**

pericope /pəˈrɪkəpi/ *noun.* **M17.**
[Late Latin from Greek *perikopē* section, formed as **PERI-** + *kopē* cutting, from *koptein* to cut.]
A short passage or paragraph of a text, *esp.* (*CHRISTIAN CHURCH*) a portion of Scripture appointed for reading in public worship.

pericranium /pɛrɪˈkreɪnɪəm/ *noun.* Pl. **-nia** /-nɪə/, **-niums**. Also (esp. in sense 2) **†-crane, †-crany**. **LME.**
[medieval Latin from Greek *perikranion* use as noun of *perikranios* round the skull, formed as **PERI-** + *kranion* skull.]
1 *ANATOMY.* The membrane enveloping the skull; the external periosteum of the cranial bones. **LME.**
2 The skull; the brain, esp. as the seat of mind or thought. Chiefly *joc.* (now *rare*). **L16.**

periculous /pəˈrɪkjʊləs/ *adjective.* **M16.**
[from Latin *periculosus*, from *periculum*: see **PERIL, -ULOUS.**]
= **PERILOUS.**

pericycle /ˈpɛrɪsʌɪk(ə)l/ *noun.* **L19.**
[Greek *perikuklos* all round, spherical, *perikukloun* encircle.]
BOTANY. The outermost part of the stele in a root or stem.

pericyclic /pɛrɪˈsʌɪklɪk, -ˈsɪk-/ *adjective.* **M20.**
[from **PERI-** + **CYCLIC.**]
CHEMISTRY. Designating or pertaining to a reaction that involves a concerted rearrangement of bonding in which all the bonds broken or formed in the reaction lie on a closed ring, whether or not a cyclic molecule is involved.

periderm /ˈpɛrɪdəːm/ *noun.* **M19.**
[from **PERI-** + Greek *derma* skin.]
BOTANY. The corky layer of a plant stem; *spec.* a secondary protective tissue, formed from cork cambium and its derivatives, which replaces the epidermis of a stem or root after injury or when it is thickened by secondary growth.
■ **periˈdermal** *adjective* **L19.**

peridia *noun* pl. of **PERIDIUM.**

peridinian /pɛrɪˈdɪnɪən/ *noun & adjective.* **E20.**
[from mod. Latin *Peridinium* genus name, from Greek *peridinēs* whirling round, formed as **PERI-** + *dinos* a whirling, from *dinein* spin round: see **-IAN.**]
BIOLOGY. (Designating, of, or pertaining to) a dinoflagellate, usually from a marine habitat, belonging to the order Peridinales.

peridium /pɪˈrɪdɪəm/ *noun.* Pl. **-dia** /-dɪə/. **E19.**
[Greek *pēridion* dim. of *pēra* wallet.]
BOTANY. The outer coat of a sporangium or other fruiting body of a fungus.
■ **peridial** *adjective* **L19.**

peridot /ˈpɛrɪdɒt/ *noun.* **ME.**
[Old French *peritot* (mod. *-dot*) = medieval Latin *peridotus*, of unkn. origin. In sense 2 readopted from French.]
†1 A green gemstone. Only in **ME.**
2 Olivine (chrysolite), esp. as used as gem. **E18.**
■ **peridotite** *noun* (*GEOLOGY*) any of the group of plutonic rocks containing little or no feldspar but much olivine **L19. peridotitic** /-ˈtɪt-/ *adjective* containing, consisting of, or resembling peridotite **L19.**

periegesis /ˌpɛrɪiːˈdʒiːsɪs/ *noun.* Pl. **-geses** /-ˈdʒiːsiːz/. **E17.**
[Greek *periēgēsis*, formed as **PERI-** + *hēgēsis* leading, from *hēgeisthai* to lead, guide.]
A description of a place or region.

periergy /ˈpɛrɪəːdʒi/ *noun. rare.* **M16.**
[Greek *periergia*, from *periergos* overcareful, formed as **PERI-** + *ergon* work.]
RHETORIC. Excessive elaborateness of style.

perifuse /ˈpɛrɪfjuːz/ *verb trans.* **M20.**
[from **PERI-** after **PERFUSE.**]
MEDICINE. Subject to an enveloping flow of liquid.
■ **periˈfusate** *noun* the liquid that results from perifusion **M20. periˈfusion** *noun* the action or process of perifusing something **M20.**

perigee /ˈpɛrɪdʒiː/ *noun.* Formerly also in Latin & Greek forms. **L16.**
[French *périgée* from mod. Latin *perig(a)eum* from late Greek *perigeion* use as noun (sc. *diastēma* distance) of neut. of *perigeios* close round the earth, formed as **PERI-** + *gaia, gē* earth.]
(Opp. **APOGEE.**)
1 *ASTRONOMY.* The point nearest to the earth in the path of a body orbiting the earth. (Orig. also used with ref. to the sun and planets, viewed geocentrically). **L16.**
†2 The point in the sky at which the sun has the lowest altitude at noon (i.e. at the winter solstice). Only in **M17.**
3 *fig.* A lowest point, a nadir. *rare.* **M17.**
■ **periˈgean** *adjective* of or pertaining to perigee **E19.**

perigonium /pɛrɪˈgəʊnɪəm/ *noun.* Pl. **-nia** /-nɪə/. Also **perigone** /ˈpɛrɪgəʊn/. **E19.**
[(French *périgone* from) mod. Latin *perigonium*, formed as **PERI-** + Greek *gonos* offspring, seed.]
BOTANY. **1** = **PERIANTH** 2. **E19.**
2 The modified leaves surrounding the antheridia of a bryophyte. **M19.**
■ **perigonial** *adjective* **L19.**

Périgord /ˈpɛrɪgɔː, ˈpeɪ-/ *noun.* **M18.**
[A region of SW France.]
Used *attrib.* to designate things obtained from or associated with Périgord.
Périgord pie a meat pie flavoured with truffles; any rich or highly seasoned pie. ***Périgord truffle***: see **TRUFFLE** *noun* 1.

Périgordian /pɛrɪˈgɔːdɪən/ *adjective & noun.* **M20.**
[French *Périgordien*, formed as prec.: see **-IAN.**]
ARCHAEOLOGY. (Designating or pertaining to) an upper palaeolithic culture or series of industries represented by flint tools of the kind found at Laugerie-Haute in the Périgord region of SW France.

Perigordine *noun & adjective* var. of **PERIGOURDINE.**

Perigourdine /pɛrɪˈgɔːdiːn/ *noun & adjective.* Also **-gord-, pé-**. **L19.**
[French *périgordine* (fem.), from *Périgord* (see below): see **-INE**[1].]
▶ **A** *noun.* A country dance of the Périgord region in SW France, usually in triple time, sometimes accompanied by singing; a piece of music for this dance. **L19.**
▶ **B** *adjective.* Of or pertaining to the Périgord region; *esp.* pertaining to the gastronomic specialities of the region. **M20.**

Périgueux /ˈpɛrɪgəː, ˈpeɪ-/ *noun.* **M19.**
[A city in the Périgord region of SW France.]
Périgueux sauce, sauce Périgueux, a kind of sauce made from truffles.

perigynium /pɛrɪˈdʒɪnɪəm/ *noun.* Pl. **-nia** /-nɪə/. **E19.**
[mod. Latin, formed as **PERI-** + Greek *gunē* woman (used for 'pistil'): see **-IUM.**]
BOTANY. **1** The inflated membranous sac surrounding the ovary of a sedge; the utricle. **E19.**
2 The modified leaves surrounding the archegonium in mosses; the membrane enclosing the archegonium in some liverworts. **M19**

perigynous /pəˈrɪdʒɪnəs/ *adjective.* **E19.**
[from mod. Latin *perigynus* (formed as prec.) + **-OUS.**]
BOTANY. (Of stamens) situated at the same level as the ovary, being inserted (together with the petals and sepals) at the edge of a cup-shaped receptacle; (of a flower) having the stamens so placed. Cf. **EPIGYNOUS, HYPOGYNOUS.**
■ **perigyny** *noun* perigynous condition **L19.**

perihelion /pɛrɪˈhiːlɪən/ *noun.* Also **†-lium**. Pl. **-lia** /-lɪə/. **M17.**
[Graecized form of mod. Latin *perihelium*, formed as **PERI-** + Greek *hēlios* sun.]
1 *ASTRONOMY.* The point in the orbit of a planet, comet, etc., at which the closest distance from the sun is reached. **M17.**
2 *fig.* The highest point, the zenith. **E19.**

peril /ˈpɛrɪl, -r(ə)l/ *noun & verb.* **ME.**
[Old & mod. French *péril* from Latin *peric(u)lum* experiment, risk, danger, from base of *experiri* to try + *-culum* **-CLE.**]
▶ **A** *noun.* **1** Liability or exposure to the possibility of imminent injury or destruction; jeopardy, danger. **ME.**
2 A case or cause of peril; a danger; (usu. with prec. adjective) a threat regarded as emanating from a particular people, race, or country. **ME.**
3 A perilous or dangerous matter. Chiefly in ***it is peril to do***. Long *rare.* **ME.**

> 🕮 **1** H. BELLOC In peril, as in battle or shipwreck, each man will save himself. R. MACAULAY The fish he had angled for had seen their peril and eluded it. **2** P. G. WODEHOUSE He seemed . . like a man gazing down an unknown path full of unknown perils. C. ALLEN Fear of the 'Russian peril' led to increased British activity.

Phrases: **at one's peril** taking the risk or responsibility of the consequences; esp. in warnings, referring to the risk incurred by disregard. **at peril of** = ***in peril of*** below. **in peril of** liable or exposed to (an imminent fate, *arch.* a cause of danger). **in peril of doing** liable to incur loss or injury by doing. **in peril of one's life** liable to imminent risk of death. **†in peril to do** = ***in peril of doing*** above. **†on one's peril, †to one's peril** = ***at one's peril*** above. ***yellow peril***: see **YELLOW** *adjective.*
Comb.: **peril point** *ECONOMICS* (chiefly *US*) a critical threshold below which a tariff may not be reduced without harming the domestic economy.
▶ **B** *verb trans.* Infl. **-ll-, *-l-.** = **IMPERIL. M16.**

perilla /pəˈrɪlə/ *noun.* **L18.**
[mod. Latin (see below), of unkn. origin.]
Any of several labiate plants of the genus *Perilla*, natives of eastern Asia; esp. *P. frutescens*, grown as a half-hardy ornamental plant on account of its deep-purple leaves.
Comb.: **perilla oil** a drying oil obtained from the seeds of *Perilla frutescens*, used as a substitute for linseed oil and in Asia as an edible oil.

perilous /ˈpɛrɪləs/ *adjective & adverb.* **ME.**
[Old French *perillous, -eus* (mod. *périlleux*) from Latin *periculosus*, from *periculum*: see **PERIL, -OUS.** See also **PARLOUS.**]
▶ **A** *adjective.* **1** Fraught with peril; dangerous; hazardous; full of risk. **ME.**
†2 Capable of inflicting or doing serious harm; arousing a feeling of peril; dreadful, terrible. **LME–E17.**

> 🕮 **1** KEATS Magic casements, opening on the foam Of perilous seas. ***the Siege Perilous***: see **SIEGE** *noun* 1a.

▶**†B** *adverb.* Dangerously, severely; extremely, very. **LME–M19.**
■ **perilously** *adverb* in a manner involving peril; dangerously: **ME. perilousness** *noun* **L16.**

†periment *noun* see **PEDIMENT.**

perimeter /pəˈrɪmɪtə/ *noun.* **LME.**
[Latin *perimetros* from Greek, formed as **PERI-** + *metron* measure: see **-METER.**]
1 The continuous line or lines forming the boundary of a closed geometrical figure or of any area or surface; a circumference, a periphery; the length of this. **LME.** ▸**b** A defended boundary of a military position; the boundary of an airfield or civil airport. **M20.**
2 An instrument for measuring the extent and characteristics of a person's field of vision. **L19.**

> 🕮 **1b** *attrib.*: *Punch* Families of the astronauts living outside the perimeter fence of the Manned Spacecraft Centre.

Comb.: **perimeter track** a taxiway round an airfield; a track round the edge of a sports ground etc.

perimetral /pəˈrɪmɪtr(ə)l/ *adjective. rare.* **L17.**
[formed as prec. + **-AL**[1]: cf. **DIAMETRAL.**]
= **PERIMETRIC** 1.

perimetric /pɛrɪˈmɛtrɪk/ *adjective.* **L19.**
[from **PERIMETER** + **-IC**, after *meter, metric.*]
1 Of or pertaining to a perimeter. **L19.**
2 Pertaining to or obtained by perimetry. **L19.**
■ **perimetrical** *adjective* perimetric **L19. perimetrically** *adverb* by means of a perimeter or perimetry **L19.**

perimetry /pəˈrɪmɪtri/ *noun.* **L16.**
[formed as **PERIMETER** + **-Y**[3].]
†1 = **PERIMETER** 1. Only in **L16.**
2 Measurement of a perimeter or circumference. *rare.* **L19.**
3 Measurement of a person's field of vision by means of a perimeter. **L19.**

†perinaeum *noun* var. of **PERINEUM.**

perinatal /pɛrɪˈneɪt(ə)l/ *adjective.* **M20.**
[from **PERI-** + **NATAL** *adjective*[1].]
MEDICINE. Of or pertaining to the period comprising the latter part of foetal life and the early postnatal period (commonly taken as ending either one week or four weeks after birth).
■ **perinatally** *adverb* in the perinatal period **M20. perinaˈtologist** *noun* an expert or specialist in perinatology **L20. perinaˈtology** *noun* the branch of obstetrics that deals with the perinatal period **L20.**

perineum /pɛrɪˈniːəm/ *noun.* Also **†-naeum**. **LME.**
[Late Latin *perin(a)eum* from Greek *perinaion, -neos.*]
The part of the body between the anus and the scrotum or vulva.
■ **perineal** *adjective* of, pertaining to, or situated in the perineum **M18. perineo-** *combining form* [**-O-**] of the perineum and — **M19.**

period /ˈpɪərɪəd/ *noun & adjective.* **LME.**
[Old & mod. French *période* from Latin *periodus* cycle, sentence from Greek *periodos* circuit, revolution, recurrence, course, orbit, rounded sentence, formed as **PERI-** + *hodos* way, course.]
▶ **A** *noun.* **I** A course or extent of time.
1 The time during which a disease runs its course; the time occupied by each attack of intermittent fever from its accession to its remission; each of the successive stages in the progress of a disease. **LME.** ▸**†b** *gen.* The time during which anything runs its course; time of duration. **LME–L17.**
2 A length of time marked by the recurrence of the times of astronomical events (e.g. the changes of the moon falling on the same days of the year), used as a unit in chronology; any length of time occupied by a recurring process or marked by the regular recurrence of a phenomenon. **E17.** ▸**b** *ASTRONOMY.* The time in which a planet or satellite performs one revolution about its primary or rotates once on its axis. **E18.** ▸**c** *SCIENCE.* The interval of time between successive occurrences of the same state in an oscillatory or cyclic phenomenon (e.g. a mechanical vibration, an alternating current, a variable star, or an electromagnetic wave); the time taken by one

complete cycle; *MATH.* the interval between successive equal values of a periodic function. **M19.**

3 A portion of time characterized by the same prevalent features or conditions; a distinct portion of history or of an artist's life; *the* portion of time in question; (with possess. adjective) the particular historical or cultural portion of time with which one is concerned. **E18.** ▸**b** *GEOLOGY.* A major division of geological time; *spec.* one that is a subdivision of an era and is itself divided into epochs. **M19.** ▸**c** An occurrence of menstruation. **L19.** ▸**d** A portion of time allocated to a lesson or other activity in a school. **L19.** ▸**e** Each of the intervals into which the playing time of a sporting event is divided. **L19.**

📖 **1** *latent period*: see LATENT *adjective.* **2b** *Aeroplane* Lunar gravity should draw the probe into an orbit which has a period of about 10 hr. C. SAGAN A planet with . . the same period of rotation . . as Earth. **3** R. FRY Lady Cunard . . wanted a Picasso of the blue period. M. KELLY The battle of Agincourt . . was outside his period. N. CHOMSKY During the period of its industrial dominance Britain advocated economic liberalism. P. GASKELL Lithographic cylinder machines . . had a productivity comparable with . . the letterpress machinery of the period. M. KLINE The second great period of Greek history. A. N. WILSON Like all aristocratic children of the period, they saw very little of their father. **b** N. CALDER Every geologic period from the Precambrian to the Quaternary. **c** I. MCEWAN My period has started and I need to get something. *Daily Mirror* We can stimulate the return of periods with an ovulatory drug.

▸ **II** Completion, end of any course.

4 The final stage or point of completion of a process or course of action; an end, a finish, a conclusion; an outcome; a consummation. Esp. in ***put a period to***, ***come to a period***. *arch.* **E16.**

†**5** An acme, a zenith. **L16–E17.**

†**6** A limit in space, an appointed end (of a journey or course); *fig.* an end to be attained, a goal. **L16–L18.**

†**7** A stage in the progress of a thing; a point in time, a moment, an occasion. **E17–L18.**

📖 **6** SHAKES. *Merry W.* This is the period of my ambition.

▸ **III 8 a** A grammatically complete sentence, *esp.* one consisting of several clauses. In *pl.*, rhetorical or formal language. **L16.** ▸**b** *CLASSICAL PROSODY.* A group of two or more cola; a metrical group of verses each containing two or more cola. **M19.**

9 a A full pause such as is properly made at the end of a sentence. Long *rare* or *obsolete.* **L16.** ▸**b** = ***full stop*** (a) s.v. FULL *adjective.* **L16.** ▸**c** As *interjection.* Added to a statement to emphasize a place where there is or should be a full stop, freq. (*colloq.*) implying finality, absoluteness, etc. Chiefly *N. Amer.* **M20.**

10 A set of digits in a long number marked off by commas or spaces to assist reading, or by dots placed over the first and last to indicate the repeating digits of a recurring decimal. **L17.**

11 *MUSIC.* = SENTENCE *noun* 7b. **M19.**

12 *CHEMISTRY.* A horizontal row in the periodic table of the elements; the set of elements occupying such a row, usu. comprising an alkali metal and those elements of greater atomic number up to and including the next noble gas. Cf. GROUP *noun* 3c (b). **L19.**

📖 **8a** W. S. MAUGHAM The liquid, exquisitely balanced periods fell from his lips like music. **9c** R. CARVER Gone and never coming back. Period.

Phrases: ***Dionysian period***: see DIONYSIAN *adjective* 3. ***free period***: see FREE *adjective.* ***LUNISOLAR period***. ***METONIC period***. ***middle period***: see MIDDLE *adjective.* **out of period** anachronistic. ***PAYBACK period***. ***refractory period***: see REFRACTORY *adjective* 5. ***safe period***: see SAFE *adjective.* ***Sothic period***: see SOTHIC 1. ***Victorian period***: see VICTORIAN *adjective*[1].

Comb.: **period-luminosity** *adjective* (*ASTRONOMY*) relating the period of a variable star, esp. a cepheid, to its luminosity.

▸ **B** *attrib.* or as *adjective.* Belonging to, characteristic of, or representative of a particular period of the past, esp. in style or design. **E20.**

📖 K. MOORE It was apparently quite period enough for them and they enthused over its 'art nouveau' alcoves. **period piece** a work of art, furniture, literature, etc., considered in relation to its associations with or evocativeness of a past period; *derog.* such a work possessing interest only from such associations or evocativeness.

†**period** *verb trans. & intrans.* **L16–L17.**
[from the noun.]
Bring or come to an end, conclude.

periodic /pɪərɪˈɒdɪk/ *adjective*[1]. **M17.**
[French *périodique* or Latin *periodicus* from Greek *periodikos* coming round at certain intervals, from *periodos*: see PERIOD *noun & adjective*, -IC.]

1 Of or pertaining to the revolution of a celestial object in its orbit. **M17.**

2 Characterized by periods; recurring or reappearing at regular or any intervals (of time or space); intermittent; *MEDICINE* having regularly recurring symptoms. **M17.**

3 Of or pertaining to a rhetorical or grammatical period; characterized by or expressed in periods. **E18.**

4 = PERIODICAL *adjective* 4. *rare.* **M19.**

📖 **2** E. BOWEN Her periodic sallies to the shops became more frequent. **periodic classification** *CHEMISTRY* the classification of the elements in accordance with the periodic law. **periodic function** *MATH.*: whose dependent variable returns to the same value at constant intervals of the independent variable. **periodic law** *CHEMISTRY*: that the elements, when listed in order of their atomic numbers (orig., atomic weights), fall into recurring groups, so that elements with similar properties occur at regular intervals. **periodic system** *CHEMISTRY* = ***periodic classification*** above. **periodic table** *CHEMISTRY* a table of the elements arranged according to the periodic law; *spec.* one in which they are arranged in order of atomic number, usu. in rows, such that groups of elements with analogous electronic structures and similar properties form vertical columns of the table.

periodic /pəːrʌɪˈɒdɪk/ *adjective*[2]. **M19.**
[from PER-[1] + IODIC.]
CHEMISTRY. ***periodic acid***, any of several oxoacids of iodine that contain a higher proportion of oxygen than iodic acid and differ from one another in their degree of hydration; *spec.* the acid H_5IO_6.

periodic acid–Schiff *adjective & noun* (designating) a procedure for detecting carbohydrates by oxidizing them with periodic acid and then staining them with Schiff's reagent.

■ **periodate** /pəˈrʌɪədeɪt/ *noun* a salt of periodic acid **M19.**

periodical /pɪərɪˈɒdɪk(ə)l/ *adjective & noun.* **E17.**
[from Latin *periodicus*: see PERIODIC *adjective*[1], -ICAL.]
▸ **A** *adjective.* **1** = PERIODIC *adjective*[1] 1. **E17.**
2 = PERIODIC *adjective*[1] 2. **E17.**
†**3** = PERIODIC *adjective*[1] 3. **L17–L18.**
4 (Of literary publications, magazines, etc.) published at regular intervals longer than a day but shorter than a year, as weekly, monthly, etc.; written in, characteristic of, or pertaining to such publications. **E18.**

📖 **2** J. GROSS There was no adequate established platform for advanced opinion in the periodical press. **periodical cicada** the seventeen-year cicada.

▸ **B** *noun.* A magazine etc. whose successive issues are published at regular intervals longer than a day but shorter than a year. Also, a newspaper. **L18.**

periodically /pɪərɪˈɒdɪk(ə)li/ *adverb.* **M17.**
[from PERIODIC *adjective*[1] or PERIODICAL: see -ICALLY.]
At regularly recurring intervals; from time to time, every now and then.

📖 N. SEDAKA Periodically, we had to give concerts . . in front of our parents. N. SYMINGTON Freud read Latin and quotes in it periodically through his writings.

periodicity /ˌpɪərɪəˈdɪsɪti/ *noun.* **M19.**
[French *périodicité*, from Latin *periodicus*: see PERIODIC *adjective*[1], -ITY.]
1 a Esp. *SCIENCE.* The quality or character of being periodic; tendency to recur at (esp. regular) intervals. **M19.** ▸**b** *CHEMISTRY.* The complex periodic variation of the properties of the chemical elements with increasing atomic number. **L19.** ▸**c** The frequency of a periodic phenomenon, esp. an alternating current. **E20.**
2 Recurrence of a woman's periods; menstruation. **M19.**

periodize /ˈpɪərɪədʌɪz/ *verb trans.* Also **-ise.** **E17.**
[from PERIOD *noun* + -IZE.]
†**1** Bring to an end, conclude. Only in **17.**
2 Divide (a portion of time) into periods; assign (historical and cultural events) to specified periods. **M20.**
■ **periodiˈzation** *noun* the action or an act of periodizing something; the grouping of historical and cultural events in distinct periods for the purposes of discussion and evaluation: **M20.**

periodogram /pɪərɪˈɒdəgram/ *noun.* **L19.**
[from PERIOD *noun* + -O- + -GRAM.]
A diagram or method of graphical representation designed to detect or display any periodicity in a set of measurements; *spec.* one in which the results of harmonic analysis of the data, performed on the assumption in turn of different periods of variation, are plotted as a function of the period.

periodograph /pɪərɪˈɒdəgrɑːf/ *noun.* **L19.**
[formed as prec. + -GRAPH.]
1 = PERIODOGRAM. Now *rare.* **L19.**
2 An instrument for automatically making a periodogram analysis or Fourier analysis of a curve by optical means. **M20.**

periodontal /pɛrɪəˈdɒnt(ə)l/ *adjective.* **M19.**
[from PERI- + Greek *odont-*, *odous* tooth + -AL[1].]
ANATOMY. Situated or occurring around a tooth; pertaining to the tissues that surround and support the teeth.
■ **periodontally** *adverb* in the periodontal area **M20.** **periodontia** *noun* periodontics **E20.** **periodontic** *adjective* = PERIODONTAL **E20.** **periodontics** *noun* the branch of dentistry that deals with periodontal tissue, disorders, etc. **M20.** **periodontist** *noun* an expert or specialist in periodontics **E20.** ˌ**periodonˈtitis** *noun* inflammation of periodontal tissue **L19.** **periodontium** *noun* †(*a*) the periodontal membrane, which invests the root of a tooth; (*b*) all the tissues surrounding and supporting the teeth: **L19.** **periodontoclasia** /ˌpɛrɪədɒntə(ʊ)ˈkleɪzjə/ *noun* [Greek *klasis* breaking] destruction or degeneration of periodontal tissue **E20.** ˌ**periodonˈtology** *noun* periodontics **E20.** ˌ**periodonˈtosis** *noun*, pl. **-toses** /-ˈtəʊsiːz/, periodontal disease; *spec.* loss of alveolar bone without inflammation, causing displacement or loosening of the teeth: **M20.**

perioeci /pɛrɪˈiːsʌɪ/ *noun pl.* In sense 2 usu. ***perioikoi*** /pɛrɪˈɔɪkɔɪ/. **L16.**
[(Latinized from) Greek *perioikoi* pl. of *perioikos* dwelling around or near, neighbouring, formed as PERI- + *-oikos* dwelling.]
†**1** People living on the same parallel of latitude but on opposite meridians. Cf. ANTOECI. **L16–L18.**
2 *GREEK HISTORY.* People living in the country around Sparta but not subjugated to it. **M19.**
■ ***perioecic*** *adjective* (*GREEK HISTORY*) **M19.**

periost /ˈpɛrɪɒst/ *noun.* **E20.**
[Abbreviation.]
ANATOMY. = PERIOSTEUM.

periosteum /pɛrɪˈɒstɪəm/ *noun.* Pl. **-stea** /-stɪə/. **L16.**
[mod. Latin from Greek *periosteon*, formed as PERI- + *osteon* bone.]
ANATOMY. The thin layer of connective tissue which envelops the bones (except where they are covered by cartilage), and from the inner part of which the bone substance is produced.
■ **periosteal** *adjective* surrounding or occurring around a bone; of or pertaining to the periosteum: **M19.** ˌ**periosˈtitis**, **-osteˈitis** *noun* inflammation of the periosteum **M19.**

periostracum /pɛrɪˈɒstrəkəm/ *noun.* Pl. **-ca** /-kə/. **M19.**
[mod. Latin, formed as PERI- + Greek *ostrakon* shell of a mussel etc.]
ZOOLOGY. The outer horny covering of the shell of a mollusc or brachiopod.

†**peripatetian** *noun.* **M16–M18.**
[Contr. of French *péripatéticien*, formed as next: see -ICIAN.]
A philosopher of the Peripatetic school.

peripatetic /ˌpɛrɪpəˈtɛtɪk/ *noun & adjective.* **LME.**
[Old & mod. French *péripatétique* or Latin *peripateticus* from Greek *peripatētikos*, from *peripatein* walk up and down, formed as PERI- + *patein* to tread: see -ETIC. In senses A.1, B.1 with reference to Aristotle's practice of walking about while teaching.]
▸ **A** *noun.* **1** (**P-.**) A member of the sect of philosophers who held the doctrines of Aristotle. **LME.**
2 A person who walks or travels about; (chiefly *joc.*) an itinerant dealer or trader; a peripatetic teacher. **E17.**
3 In *pl.* Journeyings to and fro; movements hither and thither. *joc.* **M18.**
▸ **B** *adjective.* **1** (**P-.**) Of or belonging to the school or system of philosophy founded by Aristotle, or the Aristotelian sect of philosophers; held or believed by this sect. **M16.**
2 Walking about or travelling from place to place, esp. in connection with an occupation; characterized by this; (of a teacher) working in more than one institution. **M17.**

📖 **2** *Observer* He leads a peripatetic life, rarely sleeping in the same bed two nights running.

■ **peripatetical** *adjective* (now *rare*) †(*a*) (**P-**) of or pertaining to the Peripatetics; = PERIPATETIC *adjective* 1; (*b*) (chiefly *joc.*) = PERIPATETIC *adjective* 2: **M16.** **peripatetically** *adverb* in the course of walking about or moving on **M19.** **peripateticism** /-sɪz(ə)m/ *noun* (*a*) (**P-**) the Peripatetic system of philosophy; (*b*) (chiefly *joc.*) the habit or practice of being peripatetic: **M17.**

peripatize /ˈpɛrɪpətʌɪz/ *verb intrans. rare.* Also **-ise.** **M17.**
[from Greek *peripatein*: see prec., -IZE.]
Be peripatetic; walk about.

peripatos *noun* see PERIPATUS.

peripatus /pəˈrɪpətəs/ *noun.* In sense 1 also **-os** /-ɒs/. **L17.**
[Late & (sense 2) mod. Latin from Greek *peripatos*, formed as PERI- + *patos* way, path.]
1 The walk in the Lyceum where Aristotle taught; *transf.* the school of Aristotle, the Peripatetic school of philosophy. **L17.**
2 *ZOOLOGY.* An equatorial animal of the genus *Peripatus*, with a soft wormlike body and stumpy legs, sometimes classed as an arthropod but having both arthropod and annelid characteristics. **M19.**

peripeteia /ˌpɛrɪpɪˈtʌɪə, -ˈtiːə/ *noun.* Also **-tia** /-ˈtiːə/. **L16.**
[Greek, ult. formed as PERI- + stem *pet-* of *piptein* to fall.]
A sudden change of fortune or reverse of circumstances (fictional or real).

peripherad /pəˈrɪf(ə)rad/ *adverb.* **E19.**
[from PERIPHERY + -AD[3].]
ANATOMY. To or towards the periphery.

peripheral /pəˈrɪf(ə)r(ə)l/ *adjective & noun.* **E19.**
[from PERIPHERY + -AL[1].]
▸ **A** *adjective.* **1** Of, pertaining to, or situated in or on the periphery; constituting or characteristic of the circumference or external surface; *ANATOMY* of the surface or outward part of the body (esp. with ref. to the circulation and nervous system), distal. **E19.**
2 *fig.* Marginal, superficial, of minor importance; not essential or relevant (*to*), subordinate (*to*). **M20.**

3 COMPUTING. Designating equipment used in conjunction with a computer without being an integral or necessary part of one; designating operations involving such equipment. M20.

> 📖 **1 peripheral neuritis** a disorder of the peripheral nerves, esp. when involving weakness and numbness of the limbs. **peripheral nervous system** all the nervous system other than the central nervous system. **2** *Vancouver Province* Canadian cultural expression will remain peripheral to Canadians. L. GORDON To Eliot, war, as a historical event, was peripheral to its private moral meaning. *Antiquaries Journal* A widespread impression that the study of costume is a peripheral . . domain.

▶ **B** *noun.* COMPUTING. A peripheral device. M20.

■ **periphe'rality** *noun* the quality of being peripheral L20. **peripheralize** *verb trans.* make peripheral; chiefly *fig.*, marginalize: L20. **peripherally** *adverb* in a peripheral way or position; at or with regard to the periphery: M19.

peripherial /pɛrɪˈfɪərɪəl/ *adjective. rare.* L17.
[formed as PERIPHERY + -AL[1].]
= PERIPHERAL *adjective* 1.

peripheric /pɛrɪˈfɛrɪk/ *adjective.* E19.
[formed as PERIPHERY + -IC.]
= PERIPHERAL *adjective* 1.
■ **peripherical** *adjective* L17. **peripherically** *adverb* M19.

periphery /pəˈrɪf(ə)ri/ *noun.* LME.
[Late Latin *peripheria* from Greek *periphereia*, from *peripherēs* revolving round, formed as PERI- + *pherein* BEAR *verb*[1].]
†**1** Each of three atmospheric layers formerly regarded as enveloping the earth. Only in LME.
2 A line that forms the boundary of something, esp. of a round or rounded surface; the circumference of a closed curvilinear figure; the sum of the sides of a polygon; (a thing forming) the external boundary or surface of a space or object. M17.
3 A borderline region, space, or area; an edge, a border. M18.

> 📖 **3** F. WELDON On the periphery of her consciousness, a cluster of others waiting for admission. H. KISSINGER Alarm and insecurity in countries around the Soviet periphery.

periphrase /ˈpɛrɪfreɪz/ *noun.* L16.
[French *périphrase* formed as PERIPHRASIS.]
= PERIPHRASIS.

periphrase /ˈpɛrɪfreɪz/ *verb.* E17.
[French *périphraser*, formed as prec.]
1 *verb trans.* Express by periphrasis. E17.
2 *verb intrans.* Use circumlocution; speak or write periphrastically. M17.

periphrasis /pəˈrɪfrəsɪs/ *noun.* Pl. **-ases** /-əsiːz/. M16.
[Latin from Greek, from *periphrazein*, formed as PERI- + *phrazein* declare.]
The figure of speech which consists in expressing a meaning by many or several words instead of by few or one; a roundabout way of speaking or writing; (a) circumlocution.

periphrastic /pɛrɪˈfrastɪk/ *adjective.* E19.
[Greek *periphrastikos*, from *periphrazein*: see prec., -IC.]
1 Of the nature of, characterized by, or involving periphrasis; circumlocutory. E19.
2 GRAMMAR. Of a case, tense, etc.: formed by the combination of words rather than by inflection (e.g. English *did go*, *of the people* as against *went*, *the people's*). L19.
■ **periphrastical** *adjective* (long *rare*) M17. **periphrastically** *adverb* M17.

periplasm /ˈpɛrɪplaz(ə)m/ *noun.* L19.
[from PERI- + Greek PLASMA.]
1 BOTANY. The outer (non-functional) portion of the protoplasm in the oogonium or antheridium of certain fungi. L19.
2 MICROBIOLOGY. The region of a bacterial or other cell immediately within the cell wall, outside the plasma membrane. M20.
■ **peri'plasmic** *adjective* M20.

†**peripleumony** *noun* var. of PERIPNEUMONY.

periplus /ˈpɛrɪplʌs/ *noun.* Pl. ***-pli*** /-plʌɪ, -pliː/. L18.
[Latin from Greek *periplous*, formed as PERI- + *plous* voyage.]
(A) circumnavigation; a voyage (or journey) round a coastline etc.; a narrative of such a voyage.

†**peripneumony** *noun.* Also **-nia**, **-pleu-**. LME–L19.
[Late Latin *peripneumonia*, *-pleu-* from Greek, formed as PERI- + Greek *pneumōn*, *pleumōn* lung: see -IA[1].]
Pneumonia.
■ †**peripneumonic** *adjective* L17–M19.

†**peripter** *noun.* Also **-ere**. L17–E19.
[French *périptère* from Latin *peripteros*, *-on* from Greek *peripteros* adjective, formed as PERI- + *pteron* wing.]
ARCHITECTURE. A peripteral building.

peripteral /pəˈrɪpt(ə)r(ə)l/ *adjective.* E19.
[from prec. + -AL[1].]
ARCHITECTURE. Having a single row of pillars surrounding it, like an ancient Greek temple.

perique /pɛˈriːk/ *noun.* L19.
[Louisiana French, app. from *Perique* nickname of P. Chenet, who first grew it.]
In full ***perique tobacco***. A strong dark tobacco from Louisiana.

Periscian /pɛˈrɪsɪən, -ʃɪən/ *noun & adjective.* Long *rare.* L16.
[from Latin *Periscii* from Greek *Periskioi*, from *periskios* throwing a shadow all round, formed as PERI- + *skia* shadow: see -AN.]
(Designating or pertaining to) a person who lives within one of the polar circles.

periscope /ˈpɛrɪskəʊp/ *noun.* E19.
[from PERI- + -SCOPE.]
†**1** A general view, a survey. *rare.* Only in E19.
2 *Hist.* A kind of photographic objective lens. M19.
3 A tubular device containing prisms or mirrors and enabling a person in a trench, a crowd, a submerged submarine, etc., to look into one end and see things visible from the other end. L19.
Comb.: **periscope depth**: at which a submarine's periscope will just break the surface of the water.
■ **periscopic** /-ˈskɒp-/ *adjective* (*a*) (of a lens or eyeglass) giving a wide field of view; (*b*) of, pertaining to, or involving a periscope: E19. **periscopically** *adverb* L20. **periscopism** *noun* the capacity of seeing over a wide field of view without moving the eyes L19.

perish /ˈpɛrɪʃ/ *verb & noun.* ME.
[Old & mod. French *périss-* lengthened stem of *périr* from Latin *perire* pass away, come to nothing, die, formed as PER-[1] + *ire* go.]
▶ **A** *verb.* **1** *verb intrans.* Come to a violent, sudden, or untimely end; be destroyed; cease to exist, come to an end; die; incur spiritual death, suffer moral or spiritual ruin. Also in imprecations (now chiefly in ***perish the thought***). ME. ▸**b** Of a substance or object, esp. rubber: deteriorate, rot; lose its normal qualities. LME.
2 *verb intrans.* ***be perished***, have perished (now *rare*); (also ***be perishing***) (of a person) be very cold or very hungry or very thirsty. ME.
3 *verb trans.* †**a** Put an end to (an immaterial thing). ME–M17. ▸**b** Kill (a person etc.); wreck (a ship, building, etc.). *arch.* LME. ▸†**c** Destroy spiritually; ruin morally. LME–M18. ▸**d** Lose (a possession); waste, squander. Now *dial.* LME. ▸**e** Cause (a substance or object) to deteriorate or rot, esp. as the result of exposure to injurious conditions or substances; (now *dial.*) affect (a person, a part of the body) severely with cold, hunger, etc. M16.

> 📖 **1** J. BUCHAN His two sons had both perished at sea. E. BOWEN The breath of raw air . . perished on the steady warmth of the hall. PUBLISH *or perish*. **b** D. LODGE A long chain . . with a sponge-rubber ball, slightly perished, at the end. **2** N. STREATFEILD She told her she was perished and poked the fire.

▶ **B** *noun.* †**1** ***upon the perish***, on the point or in process of perishing. *rare.* Only in E19.
2 A state of near starvation, great thirst, or any kind of deprivation or destitution. Chiefly in ***do a perish***, come to such a state. *Austral. colloq.* L19.
■ **perishless** *adjective* imperishable E17. **perishment** *noun* (now *dial.*) †(*a*) destruction, damage, loss; (*b*) the state of being very cold: M16.

perishable /ˈpɛrɪʃəb(ə)l/ *adjective & noun.* L15.
[from prec. + -ABLE.]
▶ **A** *adjective.* Liable to perish; subject to destruction, decay, or death; *esp.* naturally subject to speedy decay. L15.
▶ **B** *noun.* **1** In *pl.* Perishable things, *esp.* perishable foodstuffs. M18.
2 ***the perishable***, that which is perishable or transitory. E19.
■ **perisha'bility** *noun* E19. **perishableness** *noun* L17. **perishably** *adverb* in a perishable manner, by being perishable L19.

perisher /ˈpɛrɪʃə/ *noun.* M19.
[from PERISH *verb* + -ER[1].]
1 A vigorous or extreme course of action. Only in ***go in a perisher***. *Austral. slang.* Now *rare.* M19.
2 = PERISH *noun* 2. *Austral. colloq.* L19.
3 An annoying, contemptible, or pitiable person. *slang.* L19.
4 A periscope; (the course of training for) an officer training to become a submarine commander. *Nautical slang.* E20.

perishing /ˈpɛrɪʃɪŋ/ *adjective & adverb.* LME.
[from PERISH *verb* + -ING[2].]
▶ **A** *adjective.* **1** That perishes. LME.
2 That causes the perishing of something; *spec.* (*colloq.*) very cold. LME.
3 Troublesome; confounded. *colloq.* M19.

> 📖 **2** W. S. MAUGHAM Isn't it awful, the weather? You must be perishing. D. LODGE Let's get on with it. It's perishing in here. **3** M. ALLINGHAM These perishing crooks, who do they think they are?

▶ **B** *adverb.* Excessively, very. Chiefly with ref. to cold or hunger. *colloq.* E19.
■ **perishingly** *adverb* so as to cause to perish; = PERISHING *adverb*: L17.

perispomenon /pɛrɪˈspəʊmɪnən/ *adjective & noun.* Pl. **-mena** /-mɪnə/. Also Anglicized as **perispome** /ˈpɛrɪspəʊm/. E19.
[Greek *perispōmenon* neut. of pres. pple pass. of *perispan* draw around, mark with a circumflex, formed as PERI- + *span* draw, pull.]
GREEK GRAMMAR. (A word) having a circumflex accent on the last syllable.

perissodactyl /pərɪsə(ʊ)ˈdaktɪl/ *adjective & noun.* M19.
[mod. Latin *Perissodactyla* (see below), from Greek *perissos* uneven + *daktulos* finger, toe.]
ZOOLOGY. (Designating or pertaining to) any living or extinct mammal belonging to the order Perissodactyla of odd-toed ungulates, including horses, zebras, rhinoceroses, and tapirs.

†**perissology** *noun.* M16–L18.
[Late Latin *perissologia* from Greek, from *perissos* redundant + *logos* saying, speech: see LOGOS, -OLOGY.]
RHETORIC. (A) pleonasm.

peristalith /pəˈrɪstəlɪθ/ *noun.* L19.
[from Greek *peristatos* standing round + -LITH.]
ARCHAEOLOGY. A ring or row of standing stones surrounding a grave-mound etc.

peristalsis /pɛrɪˈstalsɪs/ *noun.* M19.
[Back-form. from next.]
The involuntary muscular movement of the intestines and some other tubular organs by which their contents are propelled along, consisting of waves of alternate circular constrictions and relaxations.

peristaltic /pɛrɪˈstaltɪk/ *adjective.* M17.
[Greek *peristaltikos* clasping and compressing, from *peristallein* wrap up or round, formed as PERI- + *stallein* to place: see -IC.]
Of the nature of or involving peristalsis.
peristaltic pump: operating by means of a constriction that moves along a tube.
■ **peristaltically** *adverb* by or with peristaltic motion M19.

peristome /ˈpɛrɪstəʊm/ *noun.* Also **peristomium** /pɛrɪˈstəʊmɪəm/, pl. **-mia** /-mɪə/. L18.
[mod. Latin *peristoma*, formed as PERI- + Greek *stoma* mouth.]
1 BOTANY. The fringe of small teeth around the mouth of the capsule in mosses. L18.
2 ZOOLOGY. The part of the body or body surface surrounding the mouth in various invertebrates, e.g. insects, crustaceans, and hydrozoans; the somite of an earthworm bearing the mouth. M19.
■ **peri'stomal**, **peri'stomial** *adjectives* surrounding the mouth; pertaining to, of the nature of, or having a peristome: L19.

peristrephic /pɛrɪˈstrɛfɪk/ *adjective.* M19.
[from Greek *peristrephein* turn round, formed as PERI- + *strephein* turn: see -IC.]
Panoramic, unfolding.
■ **peristrephical** *adjective* E19.

peristyle /ˈpɛrɪstʌɪl/ *noun.* E17.
[French *péristyle* from Latin *peristylum* from Greek *peristulon* use as noun of neut. of *peristulos* having pillars all round, formed as PERI- + *stulos* column.]
ARCHITECTURE. **1** A row of columns surrounding a building, court, cloister, etc.; the court etc. surrounded by the columns. E17.
2 The columned porch of a church or other large building; a pillared verandah. L17.
■ **peri'stylar** *adjective* pertaining to, having, or of the nature of a peristyle L19.

†**perit** *noun.* M16–M19.
[Origin unkn.]
A unit of weight equal to 1/9600 grain.

†**perite** *adjective.* E16–E19.
[(French †*perit*, *-ite*) formed as PERITUS.]
Experienced, expert, skilled.

peritectic /pɛrɪˈtɛktɪk/ *adjective & noun.* E20.
[from PERI- after EUTECTIC.]
▶ **A** *adjective.* Of, pertaining to, or designating a reaction that occurs between the solid phase and the liquid phase during the cooling of a mixture, with the formation of a second solid phase. E20.
peritectic point a state where two solid phases and one liquid phase coexist in equilibrium, the composition being such that a fall in temperature results in the disappearance of the two phases that exist at higher temperatures; the point representing this state in a phase diagram.
▶ **B** *noun.* A peritectic point or temperature. E20.
■ **peritectically** *adverb* by a peritectic reaction M20. **peritectoid** *adjective* of, pertaining to, or designating a reaction analogous to a peritectic reaction but involving three solid phases M20.

perithecium /pɛrɪˈθiːsɪəm/ *noun.* Pl. **-cia** /-sɪə/. M19.
[mod. Latin, formed as PERI- + Greek *thēkē* case: see -IUM.]
BOTANY. A flask-shaped or spherical ascocarp usu. with a narrow opening.

periti *noun* pl. of PERITUS.

For other words beginning with *peri-* see the entry for **peri-**

peritoneum /ˌpɛrɪtəˈniːəm/ *noun*. Pl. **-neums**, **-nea** /-ˈniːə/. Also †**-aeum**. LME.
[Late Latin *peritoneum*, *-naeum* from Greek *peritonaion*, *-neion* use as noun of neut. of *peritonaios*, from *peritonos* stretched around, formed as PERI- + *-tonos* stretched.]
ANATOMY. **1** The thin serous membrane which lines the inside of the abdominal cavity and is folded over the surfaces of the abdominal viscera, which it keeps in place; in vertebrates below mammals, and some invertebrates, the membrane lining the whole body-cavity. LME.
†**2** The perineum. Only in LME.
■ **peritoneal** *adjective* of, pertaining to, situated in, or affecting the peritoneum M18. **peritoneoscopy** /ˌpɛrɪtəˈniːɒskəpi, ˌpɛrɪtəʊnɪˈɒskəpi/ *noun* visual examination of the peritoneal contents by means of a narrow instrument passed through a small incision in the peritoneum M20. **peritonitic** /-ˈnɪtɪk/ *adjective* pertaining to or affected with peritonitis L19. **perito'nitis** *noun* inflammation of the peritoneum L18.

peritrack /ˈpɛrɪtrak/ *noun*. L20.
[from PERI(METER + TRACK *noun*.]
A perimeter track.

peritrochium /pɛrɪˈtrəʊkɪəm/ *noun*. E18.
[mod. Latin from Greek *peritrokhion* wheel, from *peritrokhos* circular, formed as PERI- + *trokhos* hoop, round thing.]
MECHANICS. A wheel, as part of the machine called the wheel and axle.

peritus /pəˈrʌɪtəs/ *noun*. Pl. **-ti** /-tʌɪ, -tiː/. M20.
[Latin, rel. to *expertus* EXPERT *adjective*.]
CHRISTIAN CHURCH. An expert in theology, a theologian.

periwig /ˈpɛrɪwɪg/ *noun & verb*. E16.
[Var. of PERUKE, with *-wi-* repr. /y/ of French *perruque*. Cf. WIG *noun*³.]
▶ **A** *noun*. **1** *Hist.* A wig. E16.
†**2** Some marine animal. M–L17.
▶ **B** *verb trans.* Infl. **-gg-**. Put a periwig on; dress, cover, or conceal with or as with a periwig. Freq. *fig. arch.* L16.
■ **periwigged** *adjective* E17.

periwinkle /ˈpɛrɪwɪŋk(ə)l/ *noun*¹ & *adjective*. Also (earlier) †**perwynke**, †**perwinkle**. LOE.
[Late Latin *pervinca* (readopted in Middle English from Anglo-Norman *pervenke* var. of Old & mod. French *pervenche* from late Latin) for earlier *vicapervica*, *vincapervinca*.]
▶ **A** *noun*. **1** Any of several evergreen trailing shrubby plants of the genus *Vinca* (family Apocynaceae), with salver-shaped chiefly purple-blue flowers; *esp.* (more fully ***lesser periwinkle***) *V. minor* and (more fully ***greater periwinkle***) *V. major*, long cultivated and freq. naturalized in Britain. LOE.
†**2** *fig.* **a** A person who excels; the fairest, the choicest. LOE–LME. ▸**b** A girl, a woman. E–M17.
3 †**a** HERALDRY. The tincture azure in the fanciful blazon of arms of peers. Only in E18. ▸**b** A purple-blue colour like that of the periwinkle flower. E20.
1 Madagascar periwinkle a related pink-flowered plant, *Catharanthus roseus*, widely grown in the tropics.
▶ **B** *attrib.* or as *adjective*. Of the colour periwinkle. L20.

periwinkle /ˈpɛrɪwɪŋk(ə)l/ *noun*². M16.
[Origin unkn.]
(The shell of) any of numerous small rounded gastropod molluscs of the family Littorinidae, which are abundant in the intertidal zone of rocky coasts; *esp.* (more fully ***common periwinkle***) the edible *Litorina littorea*, which is common around NW Europe. Also called ***winkle***.

†**perjure** *noun & adjective*. ME.
[Anglo-Norman *perjur* = Old & mod. French *parjur(e* or Latin *perjurus* adjective, from *perjurare*: see next.]
▶ **A** *noun*. A person who commits perjury; a perjurer. ME–E17.
▶ **B** *adjective*. Perjurious; perjured. LME–L16.

perjure /ˈpəːdʒə/ *verb*. L15.
[Old & mod. French *parjurer*, †*per-* from Latin *perjurare*, refash. of *pe(r)ierare* swear falsely, formed as PER-¹ + *jurare* swear.]
1 *verb trans.* In *pass.* Be guilty of perjury. Cf. earlier PERJURED 1. L15. ▸†**b** *verb trans.* Cause to commit perjury. *rare* (Shakes.). Only in E17.
†**2** *verb trans.* Break (an oath, vow, promise, etc.). L15–E19.
3 *verb intrans.* (now *rare*) & *refl.* Swear falsely, commit perjury; break an oath, promise, etc. M17.
> 🕮 **1** B. UNSWORTH She was not present . . so . . she is perjured because she has said on oath that she witnessed this scene. **3** R. BOLT Evidence is given on oath, and he will not perjure himself.

■ †**perjuration** *noun* the action or an act of perjuring oneself; perjury: L16–E18. **perjurer** *noun* a person who commits perjury, *spec.* (in LAW) when under oath; a person who breaks an oath or promise: M16.

perjured /ˈpəːdʒəd/ *adjective & noun*. LME.
[pa. pple of prec. (see -ED¹) after Anglo-Norman *perjuré*, Old French *par-* pa. pple of verb intrans.]
▶ **A** *adjective*. **1** Guilty of perjury; deliberately breaking an oath, promise, etc. LME.
†**2** False, lying; perjurious. L16–E19.
†**3** Falsely sworn. *rare*. L16–L17.
▶ **B** *absol.* as *noun*. A perjured person; *collect.* perjured people. Long *rare*. E16.

perjury /ˈpəːdʒ(ə)ri/ *noun*. LME.
[Anglo-Norman *perjurie*, Old French *parjurie* (mod. *parjure*) from Latin *perjurium* false oath, oath-breaking, from *perjurare*: see PERJURE *verb*, -Y³.]
The action or an act of solemnly affirming the truth of a statement that one knows to be false, *spec.* (LAW) of wilfully giving false evidence or testimony while under oath. Also, the action or an act of taking an oath which one does not intend to keep; the violation of a promise, vow, or solemn undertaking; a breach of oath.
> 🕮 A. MILLER Lying now, or . . lying in the court . . in either case you have committed perjury. R. BOLT Society . . proffers an oath and with it the opportunity for perjury.

■ **per'jurious** *adjective* †(*a*) (of a person) guilty of perjury; false to an oath, promise, etc.; (*b*) (of an action etc.) characterized by or resulting from perjury: LME. **per'juriously** *adverb* M16. †**perjurous** *adjective* = PERJURIOUS L16–M19.

perk /pəːk/ *noun*¹. LME.
[from dial. var. of Old & mod. French *perche*: see PERCH *noun*².]
1 A pole, a rod, a stick. Now *dial.* LME.
2 A perch for a (tame) bird. Now *dial.* LME.
3 A (horizontal) bar or bracket on or against which to hang or support something, esp. a candle, an icon, etc. (now *dial. & Hist.*). Also (now *dial.*), a rope fixed horizontally to support or hang something on; *spec.* (*dial.*) a clothes-line. LME.
4 A variable linear measure; = PERCH *noun*² 4. *dial.* E19.

perk /pəːk/ *noun*². *colloq.* E19.
[Abbreviation.]
= PERQUISITE. Usu. in *pl.*
> 🕮 *Sunday Times* The main perks are expenses, particularly while on location. T. K. WOLFE Free lunch . . . This pathetic little perk of the office was taken very seriously.

perk /pəːk/ *noun*³. Also **perc**. M20.
[Abbreviation of PERCOLATOR.]
A coffee percolator; coffee made in a percolator.

perk /pəːk/ *adjective*. Long *dial.* L16.
[Origin unkn. Cf. PERK *verb*¹.]
Assertive, assured; conceited; saucy, pert; lively, in good spirits; neat, attractive.

perk /pəːk/ *verb*¹. LME.
[Perh. from PERK *noun*¹ or Old & mod. French dial. var. of *percher*: cf. PERCH *verb*.]
1 *verb intrans.* Of a bird: alight, perch. Also *transf.* (of a person) take an elevated position (occas. *refl.*). LME.
2 *verb intrans. & trans.* (with *it*). Assume or have a brisk, lively, jaunty, assertive, or conceited attitude or manner. LME. ▸**b** Thrust oneself forward presumptuously, insolently or ambitiously; *fig.* exalt oneself. Freq. foll. by *up*. E16. ▸**c** *fig.* Of a thing: project or stick *up*, *out*, *into*, etc. L16.
3 *verb trans.* Make neat or attractive; preen, as a bird does its plumage. Also foll. by *up*, *out*. L15.
4 *verb trans. & intrans.* Raise (one's head etc.) briskly, assertively, interestedly, etc. Also foll. by *up*, *out*. L16.
5 a *verb intrans.* Become lively; recover health, liveliness, confidence, courage, etc. Usu. foll. by *up*. *colloq.* M17. ▸**b** *verb trans.* Rejuvenate or enliven (a person, process, thing, etc.); restore health, liveliness, confidence, courage, etc., in (a person). Usu. foll. by *up*. *colloq.* M20.
> 🕮 **3** M. DIBDIN The male was off again, perking up his feathers. **5a** J. LINGARD Susan and Jane perked up when the boys came in. *Investors Chronicle* The gilt market perked up on Monday, heartened by a strong US bond market. **b** *Publishers Weekly* Sufficiently pragmatic to perk the interest of . . readers concerned with change.

perk /pəːk/ *verb*². *colloq.* (orig. *US*). Also **perc**. Infl. **-k-**. M20.
[Abbreviation of PERCOLATE *verb*.]
1 *verb trans.* Make (coffee) in a percolator. Also foll. by *up*. M20.
2 *verb intrans.* Of (coffee in) a percolator: bubble, boil. Also *fig.*, be or become active, stimulated, etc. M20.
> 🕮 **1** R. MACDONALD I just perked some coffee . . . Would you like a cup? **2** *Newsweek* By summer . . the economy will be perking quite nicely.

Perkin /ˈpəːkɪn/ *noun*. M19.
[Sir William *Perkin* (1838–1907), English chemist.]
1 ***Perkin's mauve***, †***Perkin's purple***, ***Perkin's violet***, = MAUVEINE. Now *Hist.* M19.
2 CHEMISTRY. ***Perkin reaction***, ***Perkin synthesis***, ***Perkin's reaction***, ***Perkin's synthesis***, any of various reactions discovered by Perkin, *esp.* the condensation of an aromatic aldehyde with the anhydride of an aliphatic acid. L19.

Perkinism /ˈpəːkɪnɪz(ə)m/ *noun*. *obsolete* exc. *Hist.* L18.
[from Elisha *Perkins* (1741–99), Amer. physician, who invented the method, + -ISM.]
= TRACTORATION.

perky /ˈpəːki/ *adjective*. E19.
[from PERK *verb*¹ or *adjective* + -Y¹.]
Assertive, forward; jaunty; cheerful; lively; bright, fresh; neat, attractive.
> 🕮 A. JESSOPP They give utterance to perky platitudes about the clergy. J. M. FLEMING Between her attacks she seemed perky enough and she was quite cheery. P. ROSE Jane was attractive, with perky good looks. *Detroit Free Press* Girls' topper sets and perky dresses.

■ **perkily** *adverb* L19. **perkiness** *noun* L19.

perlaceous /pəːˈleɪʃəs/ *adjective*. L18.
[formed as PEARL *noun*¹ + -ACEOUS.]
Resembling pearl; pearly, nacreous.

perlative /ˈpəːlətɪv/ *adjective & noun*. M20.
[from Latin *perlatus* pa. pple of *perferre* carry through, convey, + -IVE.]
GRAMMAR. ▶**A** *adjective*. Designating, being in, or pertaining to a case in some inflected languages expressing movement alongside or means of transportation. M20.
▶ **B** *noun*. The perlative case; a word, form, etc., in the perlative case. M20.

perle /pəːl/ *noun*. L19.
[French: see PEARL *noun*¹.]
PHARMACOLOGY. A round or oval gelatin capsule containing a (volatile or unpleasant) medicine.

perlection /pəˈlɛkʃ(ə)n/ *noun*. *rare*. L15.
[Latin *perlectio(n-)*, from *perlect-* pa. ppl stem of *perlegere* read through, formed as PER-¹ + *legere* read: see -ION.]
The action of reading through something.

perlemoen /pəːləˈmʊn/ *noun*. *S. Afr.* M19.
[Afrikaans *perelemoer*, from Dutch *paarlmoer* mother-of-pearl.]
= ABALONE.

perlite /ˈpəːlʌɪt/ *noun*. M19.
[French, from *perle* PEARL *noun*¹ + -ITE¹.]
A form of obsidian consisting of vitreous globules expandable by heating and used for insulation, plant growth media, etc.
■ **perlitic** /-ˈlɪtɪk/ *adjective* pertaining to or characteristic of perlite; *spec.* of or designating a cracked structure in natural glasses caused by contraction during cooling: L19.

perlocution /pəːləˈkjuːʃ(ə)n/ *noun*. L16.
[medieval or mod. Latin *perlocutio(n-)*, formed as PER-¹ + *locutio(n-)* speaking, LOCUTION.]
†**1** The action of speaking; utterance, elocution. *rare*. Only in L16.
2 PHILOSOPHY & LINGUISTICS. An act of speaking or writing which aims to effect an action but which in itself does not effect or constitute the action, as persuading, convincing. Cf. ILLOCUTION. M20.
■ **perlocutionary** *adjective* of, pertaining to, or of the nature of a perlocution (cf. LOCUTIONARY, ILLOCUTIONARY) M20.

Perlon /ˈpəːlɒn/ *noun*. Also **p-**. M20.
[Arbitrary, after *nylon*.]
(Proprietary name for) nylon 6, a type of nylon produced by the polymerization of caprolactam.

perlustrate /pəˈlʌstreɪt/ *verb trans.* Now *rare*. M16.
[Latin *perlustrat-* pa. ppl stem of *perlustrare*, formed as PER-¹ + *lustrare* wander through, from *lustrum*: see LUSTRATE.]
Travel through and view all over; survey thoroughly.

perlustration /pəːlʌˈstreɪʃ(ə)n/ *noun*. M17.
[from prec.: see -ATION.]
1 The action of perlustrating. M17.
2 *transf.* The action of going through and examining a document; *esp.* the inspection of correspondence passing through the post. L19.

perm /pəːm/ *noun*¹ & *verb*¹. *colloq.* E20.
[Abbreviation.]
▶ **A** *noun*. = ***permanent wave*** s.v. PERMANENT *adjective*. E20.
▶ **B** *verb trans.* Give a permanent wave to (the hair). E20.

perm /pəːm/ *noun*². *colloq.* M20.
[Abbreviation.]
= PERMUTATION 3b.

perm /pəːm/ *verb*² *trans. colloq.* M20.
[Abbreviation of PERMUTE or from prec.]
Make a selection of (so many) *from* a larger number; make a permutation of.

permaculture /ˈpəːməkʌltʃə/ *noun*. L20.
[from PERMA(NENT *adjective* + CULTURE *noun*.]
ECOLOGY. The development of agricultural ecosystems intended to be complete and self-sustaining.

permafrost /ˈpəːməfrɒst/ *noun*. M20.
[from PERMA(NENT *adjective* + FROST *noun*.]
Subsoil or other underground material that is at a temperature of less than 0°C throughout the year, as in Arctic regions; permanently frozen ground.

permain *noun* see PEARMAIN.

permalloy /ˈpəːməlɔɪ/ *noun*. E20.
[from PERM(EABLE + ALLOY *noun*.]
Any of a series of nickel–iron alloys which have very high magnetic permeability and are used in electrical equipment, esp. in telecommunications.

For other words beginning with *peri-* see the entry for **peri-**

permanence /ˈpəːm(ə)nəns/ *noun.* LME.
[Old & mod. French, or medieval Latin *permanentia*, from *permanent-*: see PERMANENT, -ENCE.]
1 The fact, condition, or state of being permanent; continued existence or duration; continuance, abiding. LME.
2 The quality of being permanent. L17.
■ **permanency** *noun* (*a*) the quality of being permanent; (*b*) an example of something permanent; a permanent person, thing, position, etc.: M16.

permanent /ˈpəːm(ə)nənt/ *adjective & noun.* LME.
[Old & mod. French, or Latin *permanent-* pres. ppl stem of *permanere* remain to the end, from PER-[1] + *manere* stay: see -ENT.]
▶ **A** *adjective.* Continuing or designed to continue indefinitely without change; abiding, lasting, enduring; persistent. Opp. ***temporary***. LME.

V. BRITTAIN Nothing was permanent; everyone and everything was always on the move. A. EDEN It all seemed so permanent; the same family . . established at this same site for four centuries. D. LODGE If it wasn't for the cuts, I'd have had a permanent job by now.

Special collocations: **permanent blue** (the colour of) artificial ultramarine. **permanent hardness** water hardness which is not removed by boiling. **permanent magnet** a magnet which retains its magnetic properties in the absence of an inducing electric field or current. **permanent magnetism**: which persists in the absence of an inducing field or current. **permanent pasture**: left unploughed for a long period and used for growing grass. **permanent press** (of, pertaining to, or designating) a process for producing materials which retain their crease, press, shape, etc.; (of, pertaining to, or designating) a fabric treated by this process. **permanent revolution** the state or condition, envisaged by L. D. Trotsky (1879–1940), of a country's continuing revolution being dependent on a continuing process of revolution in other (esp. neighbouring) countries. **Permanent Secretary** a senior civil servant, now usu. a permanent adviser to a minister. **permanent set** (the amount of) irreversible deformation of a substance after being subjected to stress. **permanent tooth**: replacing a milk tooth and lasting most of a mammal's life. **Permanent Under-Secretary** (*a*) a senior permanent adviser to a Secretary of State; (*b*) = ***Permanent Secretary*** above. **permanent wave** an artificial wave or curl in the hair, intended to last for several months. **permanent way** the finished roadbed of a railway. **permanent white** a paint or tint of bright white which does not discolour.
▶ **B** *absol.* as *noun.* **1** ***the permanent***, that which endures or persists. M18.
2 A permanent person or thing. E19. ▸**b** = ***permanent wave*** above. E20.
■ **permanentize** *verb trans.* make permanent M20. **permanently** *adverb* in a permanent manner; so as to last or continue: L15.

permanganate /pəˈmaŋgənət, -eɪt/ *noun.* M19.
[from PER-[1] + MANGAN(ESE + -ATE[1].]
CHEMISTRY. A salt of the manganese oxyanion MnO_4^-. Cf. MANGANATE.
■ **permanganic** /pəːmaŋˈganɪk/ *adjective* containing manganese in its highest oxidation state (7); ***permanganic acid***, a strong acid, $HMnO_4$, known only as a purple aqueous solution: M19.

permansive /pəˈmansɪv/ *adjective.* M19.
[Latin *permans-* pa. ppl stem of *permanere* remain (see PERMANENT) + -IVE.]
GRAMMAR. Of a tense: denoting a permanent state.

permeabilise *verb* var. of PERMEABILIZE.

permeability /pəːmɪəˈbɪlɪti/ *noun.* M18.
[formed as PERMEABLE + -ITY.]
1 The quality or condition of being permeable; ability to be permeated; the degree to which a solid allows the passage of fluid through it. M18.
2 PHYSICS. One of the physical parameters of a medium, equal to the ratio of the magnetic induction to the magnetic field strength at any point (also ***magnetic permeability***); (in full ***relative permeability***) the ratio of the magnetic permeability of a medium to that of free space (see ***permeability of free space*** below). L19.
Phrases: **coefficient of permeability** the volume of fluid flowing through a unit cross-section of a solid in unit time under a unit (pressure or concentration) gradient. ***magnetic permeability***: see sense 2 above. **permeability of free space** a constant μ_0 which in the cgs electromagnetic system of units is unity and in the International System of Units is defined as being $4\pi \times 10^{-7}$ henry per metre. ***relative permeability***: see sense 2 above.
Comb.: **permeability coefficient** = ***coefficient of permeability*** above; **permeability tuning** ELECTRONICS tuning in which the resonant frequency of a circuit is changed by moving a magnetic core into or out of a coil forming part of the circuit, so as to change the inductance.

permeabilize /ˈpəːmɪəbɪlʌɪz/ *verb trans.* Also **-ise**. L20.
[formed as next + -IZE.]
BIOLOGY. Make permeable. Freq. as ***permeabilized*** *ppl adjective.*
■ **permeabiliˈzation** *noun* L20.

permeable /ˈpəːmɪəb(ə)l/ *adjective.* LME.
[Late Latin *permeabilis*, from Latin *permeare* PERMEATE: see -ABLE.]
1 Able to be permeated or passed through; permitting the passage or diffusion of something; penetrable. Foll. by *by*, *to*. LME.
†**2** Capable of permeating; penetrative. M17–M18.

1 *Which?* Traditional gloss paints . . aren't permeable to water vapour.

■ **permeableness** *noun* = PERMEABILITY 1 L17.

permeameter /pəːmɪˈamɪtə/ *noun.* L19.
[from PERMEA(BILITY + -METER.]
1 An instrument for measuring the magnetic permeability of a substance or object. L19.
2 An instrument for measuring the permeability of a substance, esp. soil, to fluids. E20.

permeance /ˈpəːmɪəns/ *noun.* M19.
[formed as next + -ANCE.]
1 Something that permeates. M19.
2 The fact of permeating. M19.
3 PHYSICS. (A measure of) the property of a magnetic circuit of allowing the passage of magnetic flux lines, equal to the ratio of the total flux produced to the magnetomotive force producing it (i.e. the reciprocal of the reluctance). L19.

permeant /ˈpəːmɪənt/ *adjective.* M17.
[Latin *permeant-* pres. ppl stem of *permeare* PERMEATE: see -ANT[1].]
Permeating; passing or diffusing through something.

permease /ˈpəːmɪeɪz/ *noun.* M20.
[from PERMEATE + -ASE.]
BIOCHEMISTRY. An enzyme which assists the passage of a substrate into a cell through the cell membrane.

permeate /ˈpəːmɪeɪt/ *verb.* M17.
[Latin *permeat-* pa. ppl stem of *permeare* pass through, formed as PER-[1] + *meare* go, pass: see -ATE[3].]
1 *verb trans.* Spread throughout; penetrate; pervade, saturate. M17.
2 *verb intrans.* Diffuse itself; spread *among*, *through*, etc.; penetrate *into*. M17.

1 R. BRADBURY There were no windows; the light seemed to permeate the walls. J. UGLOW Her letters are permeated by protests. E. YOUNG-BRUEHL The prose pieces . . are also permeated with questions about time.

■ **permeˈation** *noun* E17. **permeative** *adjective* (*rare*) pervasive M17. **permeator** *noun* (*a*) a person who or thing which permeates; (*b*) a vessel divided into two by a semipermeable membrane, used in the large-scale removal of solutes from a liquid by reverse osmosis: M20.

per mensem /pəː ˈmɛnsɛm/ *adverbial phr.* M17.
[mod. Latin, formed as PER + accus. sing. of Latin *mensis* month.]
For or in each month.

permethrin /pəːˈmɛθrɪn/ *noun.* L20.
[from PER-[1] + RES)METHRIN.]
A synthetic pyrethroid, $C_{21}H_{20}Cl_2O_3$, used in insecticidal sprays.

Permian /ˈpəːmɪən/ *noun & adjective.* L16.
[from *Perm*, a city and province in the west of the Urals + -IAN.]
▶ **A** *noun.* **1** (A person who speaks) any of the Permic languages. L16.
2 GEOLOGY. The Permian period; the system of rocks dating from this time. L16.
▶ **B** *adjective.* **1** GEOLOGY. Designating or pertaining to the last period of the Palaeozoic era, following the Carboniferous and preceding the Triassic, in which amphibians, and reptiles resembling mammals, flourished and many sandstones were deposited. M19.
2 Designating (people who speak any of) the Permic languages. L19.

Permic /ˈpəːmɪk/ *adjective.* E20.
[formed as prec. + -IC.]
Designating or pertaining to a group of Finno-Ugric languages spoken by certain peoples living west of the Urals, including Komi (Zyrian) and Udmurt (Votyak).

per mil /pə ˈmɪl/ *adverbial phr.* Also (earlier) **per mille** /pə ˈmɪli/. L17.
[from PER + Latin *mille* thousand.]
Per thousand. Cf. PER CENT.

A. GRIMBLE Five or six per mil of his parishioners at most.

permillage /pəˈmɪlɪdʒ/ *noun.* L19.
[from PER + French or Latin *mille* thousand + -AGE, after PERCENTAGE. Cf. prec.]
Rate per thousand; an amount reckoned as so much in the thousand.

per mille *adverbial phr.* see PER MIL.

permineralization /pəˌmɪn(ə)rəlʌɪˈzeɪʃ(ə)n/ *noun.* Also **-isation**. L19.
[from PER-[1] + MINERALIZATION.]
GEOLOGY. The action or result of fossilization by the precipitation of dissolved minerals in the interstices of hard tissue.
■ **perˈmineralize** *verb trans.* subject to permineralization E20.

perminvar /ˈpəːmɪnvɑː/ *noun.* E20.
[from PERM(EABILITY + INVAR(IABLE.]
Any of a series of alloys containing nickel, iron, and cobalt which have an approximately constant magnetic permeability over a range of field strengths.
¶ Proprietary name in the US.

For other words beginning with *per-* see the entry for **per-**[1]

permirific /pəːmʌɪˈrɪfɪk/ *adjective.* M19.
[medieval Latin *permirificus*: see PER-[1], MIRIFIC.]
Very wonderful or marvellous.

permis de séjour /pɛrmi də seʒuːr/ *noun phr.* Pl. same. L19.
[French.]
Permission to stay in a country; a residence permit.

permissible /pəˈmɪsɪb(ə)l/ *adjective.* LME.
[Old & mod. French, or medieval Latin *permissibilis*, formed as next: see -IBLE.]
That can or ought to be permitted; allowable.

E. WAUGH When very drunk it is permissible to fall into a light doze. **permissible dose** the amount of ionizing radiation above which damage to health is thought to occur.

■ **permissiˈbility** *noun* L19. **permissibly** *adverb* M19.

permission /pəˈmɪʃ(ə)n/ *noun.* LME.
[Old & mod. French, or Latin *permissio(n-)*, from *permiss-* pa. ppl stem of *permittere* PERMIT *verb*: see -ION.]
1 The action of permitting, allowing, or giving consent; liberty or licence to do something; leave. LME.
2 A (formal) consent or authorization; *esp.* a document giving this, = PERMIT *noun* 2. E18.
3 *spec.* An authorization given to a publisher to quote from a copyright work; the formal acknowledgement of this. M20.

1 I. COMPTON-BURNETT I have . . been granted permission to call Miss Fellowes by her Christian name. *Physics Bulletin* The article is published by permission of the Director of the Physics and Engineering Laboratory. V. BROME Jones had been forced to apologise for absenting himself from duty without permission. ***PLANNING permission***. **2** C. LASSALLE Queue . . outside the office of the principal's secretary for a signed permission.

permissive /pəˈmɪsɪv/ *adjective & noun.* L15.
[French, or medieval Latin *permissivus*, from Latin *permiss-*; see prec., -IVE.]
▶ **A** *adjective.* **1** Permitted, allowed; done or acting with permission; optional. L15.
2 Having the quality of permitting or giving permission; that allows something to be done or to happen. Now freq., tolerant, liberal, allowing freedom, esp. in sexual matters. L15.
3 GRAMMAR. Of a verbal mood: expressing permission or a wish. M19.

1 *Modern Law Review* Advising about perpetuities, permissive waste and the principal mansion house. **2** *Time* A permissive parent like mild-mannered Mike Mansfield. B. BAINBRIDGE He dated the onset of the permissive society as preceding the Profumo Affair.

▶ **B** *ellipt.* as *noun.* **1** GRAMMAR. The permissive mood; a word, form, etc., in the permissive mood. M19.
2 A permissive person. M20.
■ **permissively** *adverb* in a permissive way; by permission: L16. **permissiveness** *noun* M19. **permissivism** *noun* tolerant or permissive beliefs or attitudes M20. **permissivist** *noun* a tolerant or permissive person M20.

permit /ˈpəːmɪt/ *noun*[1]. E16.
[from the verb.]
1 (Formal) permission. E16.
2 A document giving permission to do a specified thing; a warrant, a licence. L17.

2 R. C. HUTCHINSON No one's allowed to move . . five kilometres without a permit. D. ATHILL Unable to get a permit to work in England. ***residence permit***, ***travel permit***, ***work permit***, etc.

permit /ˈpəːmɪt/ *noun*[2]. L19.
[Alt. of Spanish *palometa* little dove.]
Any of several deep-bodied carangid fishes of the genus *Trachinotus*; esp. *T. falcatus*, found in warm waters of the western Atlantic and Caribbean and caught for food and sport.

permit /pəˈmɪt/ *verb.* Infl. **-tt-**. LME.
[Latin *permittere* surrender, allow, formed as PER-[1] + *mittere* let go.]
▶ **I** *verb trans.* †**1** Commit, submit, resign, hand over, (a person or thing) *to* another person, force, influence, etc. LME–E19.
2 Allow the doing or occurrence of; give permission or opportunity for. L15.
3 Allow or give consent to (a person or thing) to do or experience something. Usu. foll. by *to do*. L15. ▸**b** *refl.* Allow (oneself) to indulge *in* an activity, a condition or state, etc. L17.
†**4** Let pass, pass by, pass over, omit. M16–L17.

2 R. LYND The condition on which I should permit the exercise of their art. D. MURPHY Even in our Spartan household bronchitic patients were permitted a fire in their bedroom. **3** J. LONDON If he will . . permit you to accept a wedding present from me. J. HELLER He was under house arrest for months before he was permitted to leave.

▶ **II 5** *verb intrans.* Give an opportunity; allow something. M16. ▸**b** Foll. by *of*: allow for, admit of. M19.

5 *weather permitting*: see WEATHER noun.
b B. BETTELHEIM The concentration camp permits of no really successful defence.

■ †**permittable** *adjective* = PERMISSIBLE L16–M18. †**permittance** *noun* (*a*) = PERMISSION 1; (*b*) *PHYSICS* = CAPACITANCE: L16–E20. **permi'ttee** *noun* a person to whom something is (formally) permitted; the recipient or holder of a permit: M19. **per'mitter** *noun* M17.

permittivity /pəːmɪˈtɪvɪti/ *noun*. L19.
[from PERMIT *verb* + -IVITY.]
PHYSICS. One of the physical parameters of a medium, determining its ability to store electrical energy in an electric field and equal to the ratio of the electric flux density to the electric field strength at any point (also ***absolute permittivity***); (in full ***relative permittivity***) the ratio of the absolute permittivity of a medium to that of free space. Also called ***dielectric constant***.
permittivity of free space a constant ε_0 which in the cgs electrostatic system of units is unity and in the International System of Units is $1/\mu_0c^2$ (= 8.854×10^{-12}) farad per metre, where μ_0 is the permeability of free space and *c* is the speed of light.

Permo-Carboniferous /ˌpəːməʊkɑːbəˈnɪf(ə)rəs/ *adjective & noun*. L19.
[from PERMIAN + -O- + CARBONIFEROUS.]
GEOLOGY. (Of, pertaining to, including, or linking) the Permian and Carboniferous systems or periods together.

Permo-Triassic /ˌpəːməʊtrʌɪˈasɪk/ *adjective & noun*. L19.
[from PERMIAN + -O- + TRIASSIC.]
GEOLOGY. (Of, pertaining to, including, or linking) the Permian and Triassic systems or periods together.
■ **Permo-'Trias** *noun* the Permo-Triassic system or period E20.

permsec /ˈpəːmsɛk/ *noun*. M20.
[from PERM(ANENT *adjective* + SEC(RETARY) *noun*.]
Esp. in an African country, = ***Permanent Secretary*** s.v. PERMANENT *adjective*.

permselective /pəːmsɪˈlɛktɪv/ *adjective*. M20.
[from PERM(EABLE + SELECTIVE.]
CHEMISTRY. Of a membrane: selectively permeable to certain molecules or ions, esp. to either cations or anions.
■ ˌ**permselec'tivity** *noun* the property or degree of being permselective M20.

permutable /pəˈmjuːtəb(ə)l/ *adjective*. LME.
[Late Latin *permutabilis*, formed as PERMUTE: see -ABLE.]
1 Liable to change; inconstant. LME.
2 (Esp. of mathematical functions) able to be exchanged; interchangeable. L18.
■ **permuta'bility** *noun* M17.

permutate /ˈpəːmjʊteɪt/ *verb trans*. L16.
[Latin *permutat-* pa. ppl stem of *permutare*: see PERMUTE, -ATE³.]
†**1** Change, alter. Only in L16.
2 Exchange; change the order of. L19.

permutation /pəːmjʊˈteɪʃ(ə)n/ *noun*. LME.
[Old & mod. French, or Latin *permutatio(n-)*, from *permutat-* pa. ppl stem of *permutare*: see next, -ATION. Cf. PERM *noun*².]
†**1** Exchange; interchange; barter. LME–L19.
2 (A) change of state, position, form, etc.; transmutation. Also, a changed form, a transmutation. Now *rare*. LME. ▸**b** *LOGIC*. = OBVERSION 2. M19.
3 a Orig. (*MATH*.), transposition of the two middle terms of a proportion. Now, the action of changing the arrangement, esp. the linear order, of a set of items; each of the possible different arrangements or orders which result. L16. ▸**b** A selection of a specified number of things from a larger set, esp. matches in a football pool. M20.

3 I. ASIMOV Even the best gene analysis of parents can't assure that all gene permutations . . will be favourable. Y. MENUHIN Basic exercises . . have been put together in ways susceptible of infinite permutation.

Comb.: **permutation group** *MATH*. a group of elements that are permutations of a set; also called ***substitution group***.
■ **permutational** *adjective* pertaining to permutation or permutations L19.

permute /pəˈmjuːt/ *verb*. LME.
[Latin *permutare*, formed as PER-¹ + *mutare* change. Perh. partly from Old & mod. French *permuter*. Cf. PERM *verb*².]
†**1** *verb trans. & intrans*. Exchange or interchange (things, situations, etc., esp. benefices). LME–E18.
2 *verb trans*. Change the position, state, form, etc., of; transmute. Now *rare* or *obsolete*. LME.
3 *verb trans*. *MATH. & LINGUISTICS*. Alter the order, sequence, or arrangement of. L19.
■ **permuter** *noun* M16.

permutite /ˈpəːmjʊtʌɪt, pəˈmjuːtʌɪt/ *noun*. In sense 2 **Permutit** /-tɪt/. E20.
[German *Permutit*, from Latin *permutare* (see prec.) + German *-it* -ITE¹.]
1 Any of a class of artificial zeolites which are widely employed as ion-exchangers, esp. for the softening of water. Freq. *attrib*., as ***permutite process***. E20.
2 (Proprietary name for) materials and equipment for softening water by using such substances. E20.

pern /pəːn/ *noun*¹. M19.
[mod. Latin *Pernis* (see below) from Greek *ptemis* a kind of hawk.]
A bird of the genus *Pernis*, *esp*. a honey-buzzard.

pern *noun*² var. of PIRN *noun*.

Pernambuco /pəːnamˈbuːkəʊ/ *noun*. L16.
[A State of Brazil.]
Used *attrib*. to designate the hard reddish timber of the leguminous tree *Caesalpinia echinata*, used for making violin bows and as the source of a red dye.

pernancy /ˈpəːnənsi/ *noun*. M17.
[Anglo-Norman *pernance* = Old French *prenance* the action of taking into possession, from *pren-* stem of *prendre* take: see -ANCE, -ANCY.]
LAW (now *Hist*.). The taking or receiving of something; taking into possession; receipt, as of a tithe, rent, etc.

pernavigate /pəˈnavɪɡeɪt/ *verb trans*. M17.
[from PER-¹ + NAVIGATE, orig. as pa. pple after Latin *pernavigatus* sailed through.]
Sail through; steer a course through.

pernettya /pəˈnɛtɪə/ *noun*. M19.
[mod. Latin (see below), from A. J. *Pernetty* (1716–1801), French explorer.]
Any of several small evergreen shrubs of the genus *Pernettya* (now often included in the genus *Gaultheria*), of the heath family, of southern temperate regions; esp. *P. mucronata*, grown for its coloured berries and sometimes planted as cover for game.

†**pernicion** *noun*. E16–M18.
[Late Latin *pernicio(n-)* var. of *pernicies* destruction: see next, -ION.]
Total destruction; perdition; ruin.

pernicious /pəˈnɪʃəs/ *adjective*¹. LME.
[from Latin *perniciosus*, from *pernicies* destruction, formed as PER-¹ + *nec-*, *nex* death, destruction: see -IOUS.]
1 Tending to destroy, kill, or injure; destructive, ruinous; (rapidly) fatal. LME.
2 Orig. esp. of a person: wicked; villainous. Now *gen*., damaging, harmful; undesirable. LME.

2 P. G. WODEHOUSE But for her pernicious influence, Ruth would have been an ordinary sweet American girl. J. UGLOW She condemns the power of fiction to embody fantasy as straightforwardly pernicious. *Journal of Navigation* Garlic was thought to have a particularly pernicious effect.

Special collocations: **pernicious anaemia** a form of anaemia, formerly always fatal, resulting from vitamin B_{12} deficiency, esp. caused by lack of the intrinsic factor which enables its absorption. **pernicious contrary** a substance, difficult to detect in the raw material, which inhibits the pulping of waste paper or cardboard.
■ **perniciously** *adverb* M16. **perniciousness** *noun* L16.

pernicious /pəˈnɪʃəs/ *adjective*². *rare*. M17.
[from Latin *pernic-*, *pernix* swift + -IOUS.]
Rapid; swift.

†**pernicity** *noun*. L16–E18.
[Latin *pernicitas*, formed as prec.: see -ITY.]
Swiftness; quickness.

pernickety /pəˈnɪkəti/ *adjective*. Orig. *Scot*. E19.
[Origin unkn. Cf. PERSNICKETY.]
Of a person, attribute, or action: particular about details or trifles; fastidious, punctilious. Also, of a thing or an activity: requiring precise or special handling or care; intricate.

J. GATHORNE-HARDY Such pernickety table manners . . seem to me absurd. E. FIGES They became pernickety about small things, always fussing about trifles. *Notes & Queries* A vast number of substantiating references . . at once persuasive and pernickety.

■ **pernicketiness** *noun* L19.

pernio /ˈpəːnɪəʊ/ *noun*. Pl. **perniones** /pəːnɪˈəʊniːz/. L17.
[Latin.]
MEDICINE. A chilblain; *collect*. chilblains.

perniosis /pəːnɪˈəʊsɪs/ *noun*. Pl. **-oses** /-ˈəʊsiːz/. L19.
[from prec. + -OSIS.]
MEDICINE. Any of a group of conditions caused by the effect of cold on blood-vessels in the skin, including chilblains and Raynaud's disease.

pernoctate /ˈpəːnɒkteɪt/ *verb intrans*. E17.
[Latin *pernoctat-* pa. ppl stem of *pernoctare*, formed as PER-¹ + *noct-*, *nox* night: see -ATE³.]
Stay all night; pass the night.

pernoctation /pəːnɒkˈteɪʃ(ə)n/ *noun*. M17.
[Latin *pernoctatio(n-)*, formed as prec.: see -ION.]
The action of passing or spending the night, esp. (*ECCLESIASTICAL*) in prayer. Also, an all-night vigil.

Pernod /ˈpəːnəʊ, *foreign* pɛrno/ *noun*. E20.
[*Pernod* Fils, the manufacturing firm.]
(Proprietary name for) a clear yellow-green aniseed-flavoured aperitif, orig. *spec*. a brand of absinthe; a drink of this.

peroba /pəˈrəʊbə/ *noun*. E19.
[Portuguese from Tupi *iperoba*, from *ipe* bark + *roba* bitter.]
(The wood of) any of several Brazilian hardwood trees, esp. (more fully ***red peroba***) *Aspidosperma polyneuron* (family Apocynaceae) and (more fully ***white peroba***) *Paratecoma peroba* (family Bignoniaceae).

perofskite *noun* var. of PEROVSKITE.

perogi *noun* var. of PIEROGI.

†**perone** *noun*. L17–M18.
[mod. Latin from Greek *peronē* pin, buckle, fibula.]
ANATOMY. = FIBULA 1.

peroneal /pɛrəʊˈniːəl/ *adjective*. M19.
[from prec. + -AL¹.]
ANATOMY. Pertaining to or connected with the outer side of the leg.

peroneus /pɛrəʊˈniːəs/ *noun*. E18.
[mod. Latin, from PERONE.]
ANATOMY. Any of several muscles arising from the fibula and acting to turn the foot. Usu. with mod. Latin specifying word.

Peronism /ˈpɛrɒnɪz(ə)m/ *noun*. M20.
[Spanish *Peronismo*, or from the name *Perón* (see below) + -ISM.]
The political ideology of Juan Domingo Perón (1895–1974), president of Argentina 1946–55 and 1973–4, advocating nationalism and the organization of labour in the interests of social progress; the political movement supporting Perón or his policies. Cf. JUSTICIALISM.
■ **Peronist** *adjective & noun* (*a*) *adjective* of, pertaining to, or advocating Peronism; (*b*) *noun* a supporter of Perón or Peronism: M20.

peroperative /pərˈɒp(ə)rətɪv/ *adjective*. L20.
[from PER-¹ + OPERATIVE.]
SURGERY. Given, performed, or occurring during an operation.

†**peropus** *noun*. E17–E18.
[Origin unkn.]
A type of double camlet used in the early part of the 17th cent. Cf. PARAGON *noun* 5.

peroral /pəːrˈɔːr(ə)l/ *adjective*. E20.
[from PER-¹ + ORAL.]
Occurring or carried out by the mouth.
■ **perorally** *adverb* M20.

perorate /ˈpɛrəreɪt/ *verb*. E17.
[Latin *perorat-* pa. ppl stem of *perorare* speak at length or to the close, formed as PER-¹ + *orare* speak: see -ATE³.]
1 *verb intrans. & (rare) trans*. Speak, deliver, declaim, (a speech or oration). E17.
2 *verb intrans*. Sum up or conclude a speech or oration. E19.
■ **perorator** *noun* (*rare*) M16. **pe'roratory** *adjective & noun* (*a*) *adjective* of or pertaining to peroration; (*b*) *noun* (a) peroration: L19.

peroration /pɛrəˈreɪʃ(ə)n/ *noun*. LME.
[Old & mod. French *péroration* or Latin *peroratio(n-)*, formed as prec.: see -ATION.]
1 The conclusion of an oration, speech, or written discourse, which forcefully or earnestly sums up the content for the hearers or readers; any rhetorical conclusion to a speech. LME.
2 A rhetorical passage. Also, (a) discourse; rhetoric. L16.

1 D. CECIL A . . general meditation . . which rises gradually to an impassioned peroration. **2** E. NORTH He was planning a further peroration on . . the worth of things.

■ **perorational** *adjective* M19.

perosis /pəˈrəʊsɪs/ *noun*. Pl. **-roses** /-ˈrəʊsiːz/. M20.
[Greek *pērōsis* maiming, from *pēroun* maim: see -OSIS.]
VETERINARY MEDICINE. A deformity of the leg in poultry, involving dislocation of the gastrocnemius tendon.

perosmate /pəˈrɒzmeɪt/ *noun*. L19.
[from PER-¹ + OSM(IUM + -ATE¹.]
CHEMISTRY. A salt of osmium containing the anion $[OsO_4(OH)_2]^{2-}$, in which osmium has an oxidation state of 8. Cf. OSMATE.

perovskia /pɛˈrɒvskɪə/ *noun*. E20.
[mod. Latin (see below), from V. A. *Perovski* (1794–1857), governor of the Russian province of Orenburg + -IA¹.]
Any of various shrubby labiate plants of the genus *Perovskia*, of west and central Asia; esp. *P. atriplicifolia*, grown for its long panicles of deep-blue flowers.

perovskite /pəˈrɒfskʌɪt/ *noun*. Also **-of-**. M19.
[from L. A. *Perovski* (1792–1856), Russian mineralogist + -ITE¹.]
Calcium titanate, occurring as yellow, brown, or black pseudocubic crystals and usu. containing lanthanides or alkali metals in place of much of the calcium and often niobium in place of some titanium. Also, any of a group of related minerals and ceramics having the same crystal structure. Freq. *attrib*.

For other words beginning with *per-* see the entry for **per-**¹

peroxidase /pəˈrɒksɪdeɪz/ *noun.* **E20.**
[from PEROXIDE + -ASE.]
BIOCHEMISTRY. An enzyme which catalyses the oxidation of a substrate by a peroxide, usu. hydrogen peroxide.
■ **peroxiˈdatic** *adjective* characteristic of a peroxidase **M20.**

peroxide /pəˈrɒksʌɪd/ *noun.* **E19.**
[from PER-¹ + OXIDE.]
1 *CHEMISTRY.* Orig., the compound of oxygen with another element which contains the greatest possible proportion of oxygen. Now usu., a compound having at least one pair of oxygen atoms bonded to each other in its molecule, or containing the anion O_2^{2-}. Also *spec.*, hydrogen peroxide, used as a bleach, disinfectant, etc. **E19.**
2 = ***peroxide blond*** below. *colloq.* **E20.**

> 📖 **1** *HYDROGEN peroxide.* **2** *Independent* Drug bosses, peroxide blondes and the rest of the local smart set.

Comb.: **peroxide blond, peroxide blonde** *colloq.* a woman with peroxided or bleached hair; **peroxide bond** a single bond between two oxygen atoms in a molecule; **peroxide group** the divalent group ·O·O·; **peroxide ion** the anion O_2^{2-}.
■ **peroxiˈdation** *noun* conversion into a peroxide **M19.** **peroxided** *adjective* (*a*) treated with (hydrogen) peroxide; (*b*) having bleached hair: **E20.** **peroxidic** /-ɒkˈsɪdɪk/ *adjective* having the properties of a peroxide; containing or forming part of a peroxide group: **M20.** **peroxidize** *verb trans. & intrans.* change into a peroxide **E19.**

peroxisome /pəˈrɒksɪsəʊm/ *noun.* **M20.**
[from PEROXIDE + -SOME³.]
CYTOLOGY. A cytoplasmic organelle present in many kinds of cell, which contains the reducing enzyme catalase and usu. some oxidases that produce hydrogen peroxide.
■ **peroxiˈsomal** *adjective* **M20.**

peroxo- /pəˈrɒksəʊ/ *combining form.* Also as attrib. adjective **peroxo.**
[from PER-¹ + OXO-.]
INORGANIC CHEMISTRY. Designating or containing a peroxide group.
¶ PEROXY- is the usual form in organic chemistry.
■ **peroxoˈsulphate** *noun* a salt of a peroxosulphuric acid **L20.** **peroxosulˈphuric** *adjective*: ***peroxosulphuric acid***, either of two solid hygroscopic oxyacids of sulphur, H_2SO_5 and $H_2S_2O_8$: **L20.**

peroxy- /pəˈrɒksi/ *combining form.* Also as attrib. adjective **peroxy. L19.**
[from PER-¹ + OXY-.]
CHEMISTRY. Forming the names of compounds, radicals, etc., containing a larger proportion of oxygen than the parent compound, and now *spec.* containing a peroxide group.
¶ PEROXO- is now the usual form in inorganic chemistry.

perp /pəːp/ *noun. US Police slang.* **L20.**
[Abbreviation.]
The perpetrator of a crime.

Perp /pəːp/ *adjective. colloq.* Also **Perp., p-. M19.**
[Abbreviation.]
= PERPENDICULAR *adjective* 3.

perpend /pəˈpɛnd/ *verb trans. & intrans. arch.* **LME.**
[Latin *perpendere* weigh exactly, consider, formed as PER-¹ + *pendere* weigh.]
Weigh (a thing) mentally, ponder, consider (a thing).

> 📖 J. BUCHAN He retired to the inn . . to . . perpend the situation. R. ADAMS I should have to perpend before lashing out on something . . much dearer.

perpendicular /pəːp(ə)nˈdɪkjʊlə/ *adverb, adjective, & noun.* **LME.**
[Latin *perpendicularis*, from *perpendiculum* plummet, plumb-line, formed as PER-¹ + *pendere* hang: see -CULE, -AR¹.]
▶ **A** *adverb.* At right angles; vertically. Now *rare.* **LME.**
▶ **B** *adjective.* **1** *GEOMETRY.* Of a line or plane: situated at right angles *to* a given line, plane, or surface. **L15.**
2 Situated at right angles to the plane of the horizon; vertical. **M16.** ▸†**b** Directly dependent. **M16–L17.** ▸**c** Of a hill, cliff, etc.: nearly vertical; precipitous. **L16.** ▸†**d** Directly leading *to*. Only in **M17.** ▸**e** Of a person: in an erect position; upright. **M18.**
3 *ARCHITECTURE.* (**P-.**) Designating or in the style of architecture representing the third stage of English Gothic, prevalent during the 15th and 16th cents. and characterized by vertical tracery in large windows. **E19.**

> 📖 **1** *Scientific American* The needle is held perpendicular to the skin and 15 quick punctures are made. **2** A. MACLEAN Sheer, perpendicular walls of rock.

▶ **C** *noun.* **1** *GEOMETRY.* A straight line at right angles to a given line, plane, or surface. **L16.**
2 An instrument for indicating the vertical line from any point, as a spirit-level, a plumb-line, etc. **E17.**
3 A line at right angles to the plane of the horizon; a vertical line, plane, or face. Also, a very steep or precipitous face. **M17.** ▸**b** Upright or erect position; *fig.* moral uprightness. **M19.** ▸**c** A party at which most of the guests remain standing. *arch. slang.* **L19.**

■ ˌ**perpendicuˈlarity** *noun* (*a*) vertical or upright position; (*b*) *GEOMETRY* position or direction at right angles *to* a given line, plane, or surface: **L16.** **perpendicularly** *adverb* (*a*) directly up or down, vertically; (*b*) *GEOMETRY* at right angles *to* a given line, plane, or surface: **M16.**

perpension /pəˈpɛnʃ(ə)n/ *noun. arch.* **E17.**
[Late Latin *perpensio(n-)*, from *perpens-* pa. ppl stem of *perpendere* PERPEND: see -ION.]
Mental weighing; thorough consideration.

perpetrate /ˈpəːpɪtreɪt/ *verb trans.* **M16.**
[Latin *perpetrat-* pa. ppl stem of *perpetrare* perform, formed as PER-¹ + *patrare* bring about: see -ATE³.]
1 Commit or perform as a crime or evil act. **M16.**
2 In weakened sense: commit or perform as an error, a shocking or outrageous deed, etc. Freq. *joc.* **M17.**

> 📖 **1** R. D. LAING Outrageous violence perpetrated by human beings on human beings. B. MAGEE The most horrific excesses have been perpetrated with sincere moral conviction. **2** H. JAMES To sit there . . and accept the horrors they would perpetrate in the house. R. MACAULAY They've got to undo all the follies the last government perpetrated. M. MEYER The usual faults perpetrated by young playwrights.

■ **perpeˈtration** *noun* (*a*) the action of perpetrating a crime, error, etc.; (*b*) an evil deed: **LME.** **perpetrator** *noun* **L16.**

perpetual /pəˈpɛtʃʊəl, -tjʊəl/ *adjective, adverb, & noun.* **ME.**
[Old & mod. French *perpétuel* from Latin *perpetualis*, *perpetuus*, from *perpet-*, *perpes* continuous, uninterrupted, formed as PER-¹ + *petere* be directed towards: see -AL¹.]
▶ **A** *adjective.* **1** Lasting or destined to last for ever; eternal; (of a position, office, etc.) permanent (during life). **ME.** ▸**b** That serves or remains valid for ever or for an unlimited time. **LME.** ▸**c** Of an investment: irredeemable. **M19.**
2 Continuing or continued in time without interruption; incessant; continuous; constant; frequent, much repeated. **LME.** ▸**b** Continuous in spatial extent. **M17.** ▸**c** *HORTICULTURE.* Blooming or fruiting several times in one season. Also, lasting for more than one season. **M19.**

> 📖 **1** P. H. GIBBS A new and beautiful world in which there would be perpetual peace. N. GORDIMER The river . . was perpetual, fed by an underground source. L. LAWRENCE A meaning that was vast and perpetual beyond space or time. **2** DAY LEWIS The summers . . seem perpetual sunshine. E. L. DOCTOROW The perpetual dusk of the cavernous prison. A. STORR He . . when his friends were ill, became very disturbed about them, making perpetual enquiries. M. LANE Her later childhood was a perpetual struggle to subdue her impulsive nature.

Special collocations: **perpetual calendar** (*a*) a calendar which can be adjusted to show any combination of day, date, and month; (*b*) a set of tables from which the day of the week can be reckoned for any date. **perpetual check** (*CHESS* etc.) a position of play, resulting in a draw, in which one player cannot prevent the other from making an unlimited sequence of checking moves. **perpetual curate** *Hist.* a clergyman in charge of a new church or appointed at the request of a lay rector to execute the spiritual duties of a benefice; a vicar. **perpetual motion** motion that goes on for ever; *spec.* that of a hypothetical machine running for ever unless subject to external forces or to wear. **perpetual spinach** = *SPINACH beet.* **perpetual student** a person who stays on as a student at a university etc. far beyond the normal period.
▶ **B** *adverb.* Perpetually. **LME.**

> 📖 *Garden News* Perpetual . . fruiting strawberries will be at the height of their season now. **perpetual-flowering carnation** a variety of carnation with a long flowering season.

▶ **C** *noun.* †**1** A hereditary or heritable office. Only in **M16.**
2 *HORTICULTURE.* A type of rose that flowers several times in one season; a remontant strawberry. Also, a perennial plant. **E18.**
2 ***hybrid perpetual***: see HYBRID *adjective.*
■ **perpetualism** *noun* the quality of being perpetual; *spec.* a (political or religious) doctrine based on the belief in or advocacy of the perpetuity of something: **L19.** **perpetualist** *noun* an advocate of or believer in the perpetuity of something **M19.** **perpetuˈality** *noun* the quality, state, or condition of being perpetual **M16.** **perpetually** *adverb* (*a*) *arch.* eternally, for ever; (*b*) incessantly; continually, constantly: **LME.** **perpetualness** *noun* = PERPETUALITY **E17.**

perpetuana /pəpɛtʃʊˈɑːnə, -tjʊ-/ *noun.* **L16.**
[Arbitrary formation from PERPETUAL.]
Hist. A durable woollen fabric made in England from the 16th cent.

perpetuance /pəˈpɛtʃʊəns, -tjʊ-/ *noun.* **M16.**
[Old French *perpétuance*, from *perpétuer* perpetuate: see -ANCE.]
The action of perpetuating something; the fact or condition of being perpetuated.

perpetuate /pəˈpɛtʃʊeɪt, -tjʊeɪt/ *verb trans.* Pa. pple & ppl adjective **-ated**, (earlier) †**-ate. E16.**
[Latin *perpetuat-* pa. ppl stem of *perpetuare*, from *perpetuus*: see PERPETUAL, -ATE³.]
1 Make perpetual; cause to endure or continue indefinitely. **E16.**
†**2** Continue or extend without interruption. **E17–L18.**

> 📖 **1** E. BOWEN His unconscious nature perpetuated itself in stone as the house went up. J. C. RANSOM They would tend to perpetuate a system in which the power . . belonged to them. *Christian Science Monitor* Ideas expressed in the news media . . were seen as perpetuating women's inferior role.

■ **perpetuative** *adjective* having a tendency to perpetuate something **M20.** **perpetuator** *noun* **M19.**

perpetuation /pəpɛtʃʊˈeɪʃ(ə)n, -tjʊ-/ *noun.* **LME.**
[medieval Latin *perpetuatio(n-)*, formed as prec. + -ATION.]
The action of perpetuating something.

perpetuity /pəːpɪˈtjuːɪti/ *noun.* **LME.**
[Old & mod. French *perpétuité* from Latin *perpetuitas*, from *perpetuus*: see PERPETUAL, -ITY.]
1 The quality or state of being perpetual. **LME.**
2 A perpetual possession, tenure, or position. **LME.** ▸**b** *LAW.* A restriction making an estate inalienable perpetually or for a period beyond certain limits fixed by law; an estate so restricted. **E17.**
3 A perpetual annuity. **E19.**
1 for perpetuity, in perpetuity for ever; for an indefinitely long period.

perpetuum mobile /pəːˌpɛtjʊəm ˈməʊbɪli, pəːˌpɛtjʊʊm ˈməʊbɪleɪ/ *noun phr.* **L17.**
[from Latin *perpetuus* PERPETUAL + *mobilis* movable, MOBILE *adjective*, after *primum mobile*.]
1 = ***perpetual motion*** s.v. PERPETUAL *adjective.* **L17.**
2 *MUSIC.* = ***moto perpetuo*** s.v. MOTO *noun*¹. **L19.**

perphenazine /pəˈfɛnəziːn/ *noun.* **M20.**
[from PI)PER(IDINE + PHEN(YL + AZINE.]
PHARMACOLOGY. A phenothiazine derivative similar to but stronger than chlorpromazine, used as a sedative, antiemetic, and antidepressant.

†**perplex** *noun. rare.* **M17–M18.**
[from the verb.]
Perplexity.

†**perplex** *adjective.* **LME.**
[Old & mod. French *perplexe* or Latin *perplexus* involved, intricate, formed as PER-¹ + *plexus* pa. pple of *plectere* plait, interweave, involve.]
1 = PERPLEXED 1. **LME–L16.**
2 = PERPLEXED 2. **M16–L17.**

perplex /pəˈplɛks/ *verb trans.* **L16.**
[Back-form. from PERPLEXED.]
1 Confuse or bewilder (a person). **L16.** ▸†**b** Torment, trouble. **L16–E18.**
2 Make (a thing) intricate or complicated; confuse, muddle. **E17.**
3 Cause to become tangled; entangle, intertwine. *arch.* **E17.**

> 📖 **1** A. CARTER An obscure . . dialect just about to perplex three generations of philologists. **2** J. WESLEY Perplexing a subject plain in itself. **3** T. T. STODDART Some trout . . attempt to cut or perplex the tackle among stones or weeds.

■ **perplexing** *adjective* causing perplexity **M17.** **perplexingly** *adverb* in a perplexing manner **M19.**

perplexed /pəˈplɛkst/ *adjective.* **L15.**
[from PERPLEX *adjective* + -ED²; in mod. use from PERPLEX *verb* + -ED¹.]
1 Of a person: confused or bewildered by some intricate or complicated matter. Formerly also *gen.*, troubled. **L15.**
2 Of a thing: intricate, involved, complicated. **E16.**
3 Of an object: having the parts intricately intertwined. *arch.* **E17.**

> 📖 **1** ALDOUS HUXLEY 'A most peculiar way of talking' . . said Bernard, staring . . in perplexed astonishment. P. L. FERMOR Anglia? They had never heard of it and went on their way perplexed. **2** T. REID His style is disagreeable, being full of perplexed sentences. M. INNES This has been a perplexed business.

■ **perplexedly** /-ksɪdli/ *adverb* (*a*) (now *rare* or *obsolete*) in an intricate, involved, or complicated manner; (*b*) with perplexity or bewilderment: **L16.** **perplexedness** /-ksɪdnɪs/ *noun* **E17.**

†**perplexitive** *noun & adjective. rare.* **LME.**
[from next + -IVE.]
▶ **A** *noun.* An uncertain or perplexing situation. **LME–M16.**
▶ **B** *adjective.* Perplexing. **M17–E18.**

perplexity /pəˈplɛksɪti/ *noun.* **ME.**
[Old & mod. French *perplexité* or late Latin *perplexitas*, from *perplexus*: see PERPLEX *adjective*, -ITY.]
1 Inability to deal with or understand a thing owing to its intricate nature; confusion, bewilderment; an instance of this. **ME.** ▸†**b** Torment, trouble. **LME–M17.**
2 An intricately involved or confused state *of* a thing. **M16.**
3 A thing causing confusion or bewilderment; an intricate or complicated matter. **L16.**

For other words beginning with *per-* see the entry for **per-**¹

📖 1 W. GERHARDIE He hesitated what to do. His mind was in a state of perplexity. *Literature & Theology* Note 6.. comments with perplexity on.. critical-historical and linguistic-literary approaches. JULIETTE HUXLEY He.. was at a loss, in strange perplexity. **2** W. G. PALGRAVE The dense perplexity of dwarf palm, garlanded creepers, glossy undergrowth. **3** J. A. FROUDE The condition of the clergy was a pressing and practical perplexity.

perquisite /ˈpəːkwɪzɪt/ *noun.* LME.
[medieval Latin *perquisitum* acquisition, use as noun of neut. pa. pple of Latin *perquirere* search diligently for, formed as PER-[1] + *quaerere* seek. Cf. PERK *noun*[2].]
†**1** *LAW.* Property acquired otherwise than by inheritance. LME–E18.
2 *LAW* (now *Hist.*). Casual profits coming to the lord of a manor, in addition to the regular annual revenue. M16.
3 Any casual fee or remuneration additional to the normal salary or revenue of an office or position; a benefit incidental to a particular employment. M16. ▸**b** *spec.* A thing that has served its primary use and to which a subordinate or employee then has a customary right. E18. ▸**c** A gratuity expected or claimed by a waiter, porter, etc.; a customary tip. E18. ▸**d** The income from any office. E18.
4 *fig.* A thing to which a person has the sole right. L18.

📖 **3** G. GORER The extra perquisites of housing and clothing allowances, security of tenure.. and a pension. S. WEINTRAUB The Queen.. quickly learned.. to enjoy the perquisites of her position. L. M. MONTGOMERY The apple lay untouched on her desk until.. Timothy.. annexed it as one of his perquisites.

perquisition /pəːkwɪˈzɪʃ(ə)n/ *noun.* LME.
[Late Latin *perquisitio(n-)* investigation, research, from Latin *perquisit-* pa. ppl stem of *perquirere*: see prec., -ION.]
†**1** *LAW.* The acquiring of something otherwise than by inheritance. *rare.* Only in LME.
2 A thorough or diligent search, *esp.* one undertaken officially. E17.

perradial /pəˈreɪdɪəl/ *adjective.* L19.
[from mod. Latin *perradius* (formed as PER-[1] + RADIUS) + -AL[1].]
ZOOLOGY. Pertaining to the primary rays or axes in certain coelenterates; primarily radial.

perrhenic /pəˈriːnɪk/ *adjective.* E20.
[from PER-[1] + RHENIUM + -IC.]
CHEMISTRY. ***perrhenic acid***, a strong oxidizing acid, $HReO_4$, known only in aqueous solution.
■ **perrhenate** *noun* a salt of this acid E20.

perrier /ˈpɛrɪə/ *noun*[1]. LME.
[Old French (mod. *pierrier*) formed as PETRARY.]
Hist. = PEDRERO.

Perrier /ˈpɛrɪeɪ/ *noun*[2]. E20.
[Source *Perrier*, a spring at Vergèze, France, where this water comes from.]
(Proprietary name for) a sparkling natural mineral water; a drink of this.

perron /ˈpɛrən; *foreign* pɛrɔ̃ (*pl. same*)/ *noun.* LME.
[Old & mod. French from Proto-Romance augm. of Latin *petra* stone: see -OON.]
Orig., a large block of stone, with or without steps, used as a platform, monument, etc. Now only *spec.*, a platform with one or two flights of steps in front of the entrance to a church or other (large) building; the flight or flights of steps leading to such a platform.

perrotine /pɛrə(ʊ)ˈtiːn/ *noun.* M19.
[French, from *Perrot*, surname of the inventor: see -INE[4].]
A machine for printing calico using wooden blocks.

perruquier /pɛˈruːkɪeɪ/ *noun.* M18.
[French, from *perruque* PERUKE: see -IER.]
A person who makes, dresses, or sells wigs.

perry /ˈpɛri/ *noun.* ME.
[Old French *peré*, from Proto-Romance alt. of Latin *pirum* PEAR *noun*: see -Y[5].]
A drink resembling cider, made from the juice of pears.

persalt /ˈpəːsɒlt/ *noun.* Now *rare.* E19.
[from PER-[1] + SALT *noun.*]
CHEMISTRY. A salt formed by a peroxo anion.

perscrutation /pəːskruːˈteɪʃ(ə)n/ *noun.* LME.
[Old French from Latin *perscrutatio(n-)*, from *perscrutat-* pa. ppl stem of *perscrutare*, formed as PER-[1] + *scrutare*, *scrutari* search closely: see -ATION.]
A thorough investigation; careful scrutiny.

perse /pəːs/ *adjective & noun. arch.* LME.
[Old & mod. French *pers* from medieval Latin *persus* dusky, of unkn. origin.]
Orig., (of) a bluish or bluish-grey colour. Later, (of) a dark blue or purplish black.

per se /pəː ˈseɪ/ *adverbial phr.* L16.
[Latin.]
By or in itself; intrinsically, essentially. Opp. PER ACCIDENS 1.

📖 *Brain* Whether the determinant factor is actually the size of the external load per se. ***A per se***: see A, A 1.

¶ Cf. AMPERSAND.

persea /ˈpəːsɪə/ *noun.* E17.
[Latin from Greek.]
Orig., an Egyptian fruit-bearing tree described by the ancients, perh. *Mimusops schimperi* (family Sapotaceae). Now, any fruit of various tropical trees and shrubs of the genus *Persea* of the laurel family, which includes the avocado pear, ***Persea americana***.

persecute /ˈpəːsɪkjuːt/ *verb trans.* ME.
[Old & mod. French *persécuter* back-form. from *persécuteur* PERSECUTOR.]
†**1** Pursue or hunt with intent to catch, injure, or kill; *fig.* follow up or pursue (a subject etc.). ME–L17.
2 (Seek out and) subject to hostility or ill treatment, esp. on the grounds of political, religious, or other beliefs regarded as unacceptable; oppress. L15.
3 Prosecute (a person) at law. *obsolete* exc. *dial.* L15.
4 Harass, trouble; annoy persistently. M16.

📖 **1** DRYDEN With Balearick Slings or Gnossian Bow, To persecute from far the flying Doe. **2** G. GREENE The Roman Catholic Syrians are claiming they are a persecuted minority. A. BRINK For the state to persecute and try to break a man. ROSEMARY MANNING Lesbians were not actively persecuted when I was a young woman. **4** G. MEREDITH Your persecuting me to become your wife. I. MURDOCH I'm being persecuted by the most frightful man.

■ **persecuˈtee** *noun* a person who is persecuted L19. **persecutive** *adjective* (*rare*) of a persecuting nature; given to persecution: M17.

persecution /pəːsɪˈkjuːʃ(ə)n/ *noun.* ME.
[Old & mod. French *persécution* from Latin *persecutio(n-)*, from *persecut-*: see PERSECUTOR, -ION.]
1 The action of persecuting someone or subjecting someone to hostility or ill treatment; the fact of being persecuted; an instance, esp. a particular course or period, of this. ME. ▸**b** Harassment; persistent annoyance. L16.
†**2** The action of pursuing with intent to catch, injure, or kill; *fig.* pursuit of a subject etc. LME–M17.
†**3** Legal prosecution. LME–M16.

📖 **1** H. CARPENTER The defender of the Catholic Church against Communist persecution. R. DEACON Argentinian Intelligence was used as a major weapon of.. persecution.

Comb.: **persecution complex**, **persecution mania** a delusion that one is being persecuted.
■ **persecutional** *adjective* of or pertaining to persecution L19.

persecutor /ˈpəːsɪkjuːtə/ *noun.* LME.
[Old & mod. French *persécuteur* or late Latin *persecutor*, from Latin *persecut-* pa. ppl stem of *persequi*, formed as PER-[1] + *sequi* follow: see -OR.]
A person who persecutes someone.
■ **persecutress** *noun*, pl. **-trices** /-trɪsiːz/, a female persecutor M17. **perseˈcutrix** *noun* (*rare*) = PERSECUTRESS L16.

persecutory /ˈpəːsɪkjuːt(ə)ri/ *adjective.* M17.
[from PERSECUTE + -ORY[2].]
Of or pertaining to persecution; given to persecution.

📖 *Times Lit. Suppl.* The Elizabethans.. were not persecutory and did not approve the hounding of this.. minority.

Perseid /ˈpəːsɪɪd/ *noun & adjective.* L19.
[from PERSEUS + -ID[3].]
ASTRONOMY. (Designating) any of an annual shower of meteors seeming to radiate from the constellation Perseus in early August.

perseity /pəˈsiːɪti/ *noun. rare.* L16.
[medieval Latin *perseitas*, from Latin PER SE: see -ITY.]
The quality or condition of existing independently.

Perseus /ˈpəːsɪəs, -sjuːs/ *noun.* M16.
[Latin & Greek, name of rescuer of Andromeda in Greek mythol.]
(The name of) a conspicuous constellation of the northern hemisphere, lying in the Milky Way between Andromeda and Auriga.

†**persever** *verb* var. of PERSEVERE.

perseverance /pəːsɪˈvɪər(ə)ns/ *noun.* ME.
[Old & mod. French *persévérance* from Latin *perseverantia*, from *perseverant-* pres. ppl stem of *perseverare*: see PERSEVERE, -ANCE.]
1 The fact, process, condition, or quality of persevering; constant or steadfast persistence in a course of action or in pursuit of an aim. ME.
2 *THEOLOGY.* Continuance in a state of grace leading finally to a state of glory. LME.

📖 **1** L. APPIGNANESI All striving and perseverance.. she considered contemptible.

perseverant /pəːsɪˈvɪər(ə)nt/ *adjective.* Now *rare.* LME.
[Old & mod. French *persévérant* pres. pple of *persévérer*: see PERSEVERE, -ANT[1].]
1 Steadfast, persistent. LME.
†**2** *transf.* Lasting, enduring. LME–E16.

■ **perseverantly** *adverb* ME.

perseverate /pəˈsɛvəreɪt/ *verb intrans.* E20.
[Back-form. from next.]
PSYCHOLOGY. Repeat a response after the cessation of the original stimulus.
■ **perseverative** *adjective* of, pertaining to, or of the nature of (a) perseveration E20. **perseverator** *noun* E20.

perseveration /pəsɛvəˈreɪʃ(ə)n/ *noun.* LME.
[Old & mod. French *persévération* from Latin *perseveratio(n-)*, from *perseverat-* pa. ppl stem of *perseverare*: see next, -ATION.]
1 Perseverance. LME.
2 *PSYCHOLOGY.* The prolonged and sometimes pathological repetition of an action, thought, or utterance. E20.

persevere /pəːsɪˈvɪə/ *verb.* Also †**persever**. LME.
[Old & mod. French *persévérer* from Latin *perseverare* abide by strictly, persist, from *perseverus* very strict: see PER-[1], SEVERE.]
1 *verb intrans.* Continue steadfastly or determinedly in a course of action or (formerly) a condition or state, esp. in the face of difficulty. (Foll. by *in*, *with*.) LME. ▸†**b** With adjective or noun compl.: remain, continue to be. E16–M17. ▸†**c** Proceed steadily on one's way. Only in 16. ▸†**d** Continue *to do*. L16–L18.
†**2** *verb intrans.* Continue or remain *in* a place or *in* a state or condition; (of a thing) continue, last, endure. LME–L18.
†**3** *verb trans.* Maintain or support continuously; cause to continue; preserve. E16–M17.
4 *verb trans.* With direct speech as obj.: continue an argument etc. by saying, persist. M19.

📖 **1** C. P. SNOW Luria persevered in searching for.. the rewards. R. WHELAN Parks persevered and eventually went on to a long and distinguished career. ROSEMARY MANNING My.. sense of duty.. makes me persevere with a book I don't really enjoy. **4b** *Listener* 'What about full frontals?' George persevered.

■ **perseveringly** *adverb* in a persevering manner E17.

Pershing /ˈpəːʃɪŋ/ *noun.* M20.
[J. J. *Pershing* (1860–1948), US general.]
A type of short-range surface-to-surface ballistic missile. Also ***Pershing missile***.

Persian /ˈpəːʒ(ə)n, -ʃ(ə)n/ *adjective & noun.* ME.
[Old French *persien*, from Latin *Persia* from Greek *Persis* from Old Persian *pārsa*, (mod. *pārs*, Arab. *fārs*): see -AN.]
▶ **A** *adjective.* **1** Of or pertaining to Persia (now Iran), a country in the Middle East, its inhabitants, or their language. ME.
2 *spec.* Of a thing: native to, made in, or attributed to Persia. E17. ▸†**b** Made of the material called 'Persian' (see sense B.3 below). E18–M19. ▸**c** Of or pertaining to a Persian cat (see below). L19.
Special collocations: **Persian berry** the unripe fruit of a Persian buckthorn, *Rhamnus infectorius*, formerly the source of a yellow dye. **Persian blinds** = PERSIENNES. **Persian blue** a bright pale blue. **Persian carpet**, **Persian rug**: woven esp. in Persia in a traditional brightly coloured pattern of animals, plants, figures, geometric shapes, etc. **Persian cat** (an animal of) a breed of cat, orig. from Persia, with long hair, a broad round head, and a stocky body. **Persian green** a bright dark green. **Persian greyhound** = SALUKI. **Persian insect-powder** pyrethrum powder. **Persian lamb** = KARAKUL 2. ***Persian lilac***: see LILAC *noun.* **Persian morocco**: made from the skin of a hairy variety of sheep. **Persian red** = *INDIAN red*. ***Persian rug***: see ***Persian carpet*** above. **Persian sheep** (an animal of) a southern African breed of sheep, bred for its meat. †**Persian silk** = sense B.3 below. ***Persian walnut***: see WALNUT 1. **Persian wheel** (*a*) = ***bucket-wheel*** s.v. BUCKET *noun*[1]; (*b*) a type of water-wheel with radial compartments, used for raising water. **Persian Yellow (rose)** a variety of the Austrian briar with fragrant double yellow flowers, *Rosa foetida* var. *persiana*.
▶ **B** *noun.* **1** A native or inhabitant of Persia (now Iran). ME.
2 The language of Persia, a member of the Iranian group of languages. Cf. FARSI, PAHLAVI. M16.
†**3** A thin soft silk, chiefly used for linings. L17–L19.
4 = ***Persian cat*** above. L19.
5 *ellipt.* A traditional Persian pattern; a Persian carpet or rug. L19.
4 ***smoke Persian***: see SMOKE *noun* 8.
¶ Cf. IRANIAN.
■ **Persianist** *noun* an expert in or student of Persian language, history, art, etc. E20. **Persianiˈzation** *noun* the process of making or becoming Persian in appearance, character, etc. E20. **Persianize** *verb trans. & intrans.* make or become Persian in customs, character, etc. E19.

Persic /ˈpəːsɪk/ *noun & adjective. arch.* L16.
[In sense A.1 from Latin *persicum* (see PEACH *noun*[1]); in other senses from Latin *Persicus*, from *Persae* Persians: see -IC.]
▶ **A** *noun.* †**1** A peach. Only in L16.
2 = PERSIAN *noun* 2. M18.
▶ **B** *adjective.* = PERSIAN *adjective* 1. E17.

persicaria /pəːsɪˈkɛːrɪə/ *noun.* Also (earlier) Anglicized as **persicary** /ˈpəːsɪk(ə)ri/. LME.
[medieval Latin, from Latin *persicum* PEACH *noun*[1] (from the resemblance of the leaves to those of the peach) + *-aria* -ARY[1].]
Any of various knotweeds now or formerly included in the genus *Persicaria*; *esp.* redshank, *P. maculosa*.

For other words beginning with *per-* see the entry for **per-**[1]

persico /ˈpəːsɪkəʊ/ *noun.* E18.
[French, dim. of Savoy dial. *perse* peach from Latin *persicum*.]
A cordial prepared by macerating the kernels of peaches, apricots, etc., in spirit.

persiennes /pəːsɪˈɛnz/ *noun pl.* M19.
[French, use as noun of fem. pl. of †*persien*: see PERSIAN.]
Window-shutters or outside blinds made of light movable slats fastened horizontally in a frame.

persiflage /ˈpəːsɪflɑːʒ/ *noun.* M18.
[French, from *persifler* to banter, formed as PER-[2] + *siffler* to whistle: see -AGE.]
Light banter or raillery; frivolous talk.
▪ **persifleur** /ˈpəːsɪfləː/ *noun* a person who indulges in persiflage M19.

persimmon /pəˈsɪmən/ *noun & adjective.* E17.
[Alt. of Virginia Algonquian *pessemmins*.]
▶**A** *noun.* **1** The plumlike orange edible fruit of a N. American tree, *Diospyros virginiana*, of the ebony family, which is very astringent until fully soft; the similar but larger fruit of the Chinese and Japanese tree *D. kaki*, widely grown in warm countries. Also, as the type of something desirable (*US colloq.*). E17.
2 Any of the trees producing this fruit or related to them. Also ***persimmon tree***. M17.
3 The colour of persimmon fruit, reddish orange; the colour of persimmon wood, reddish brown. *US*. L20.
▶**B** *adjective.* Of the colour of persimmon fruit or wood. *US*. E20.

persist /pəˈsɪst/ *verb.* M16.
[Latin *persistere*, formed as PER-[1] + *sistere* stand.]
1 *verb intrans.* Continue firmly or obstinately in or *in* a state, opinion, course of action, etc., esp. against opposition. Also foll. by †*to do*, *with*. M16. ▸**b** *verb intrans.* Be insistent in or *in* a statement or question. L17. ▸**c** *verb trans.* With direct speech as obj.: continue an argument etc. by saying. M19.
†**2** *verb intrans.* With adjective or noun compl.: remain, continue to be. M16–E18.
3 *verb intrans.* Continue in existence; last, endure. M18.

> 📖 **1** J. LONDON Why do you persist in writing such things? A. PATON The dogs were fierce . . but he persisted. L. NAMIER Rutland . . had already once refused, and did so again; still Pulteney persisted. M. BRADBURY Having bound themselves by marriage, they persist with it. **b** GOLDSMITH [Callisthenes] persisted in his innocence to the last. **c** A. BROOKNER 'But what about your boyfriend?' Caroline persisted. **2** MILTON But they persisted deaf, and would not seem To count them things worth notice. **3** T. IRELAND Her private sense of alienation from her father still persisted. A. BISHOP The . . financial worry, though now less pressing, persisted.

▪ **persister** *noun* †(*a*) *rare* a person who persists; (*b*) BIOLOGY a bacterium which continues to live in the presence of enough antibiotic to kill most members of its species: M18. **persistingly** *adverb* in a persisting manner M19. **persistive** *adjective* having the quality of persisting E17.

persistence /pəˈsɪst(ə)ns/ *noun.* Also (earlier) †**-ance**. M16.
[French *persistance*, from *persister*, formed as prec.; later refash. after late Latin *persistentia*: see -ANCE, -ENCE.]
1 a The action or fact of persisting; firm or obstinate continuance in a particular course in spite of opposition; an instance of this. M16. ▸**b** = PERSISTENCY 1a. M19.
2 Continued existence in time; endurance. E17. ▸**b** The continuance of a sensation, esp. of a visual impression on the retina, after the stimulus which caused it is removed. M19. ▸**c** (The duration of) the emission of light by a luminescent substance or screen after the external source of energy is removed. E20.

> 📖 **1** RACHEL ANDERSON Thanks to Alice's persistence in getting me to school . . I scraped by. N. SAHGAL Dogs lost their common sense and barked with a stupid persistence, on and on. **2** S. O'FAOLÁIN One of the more surprising things about . . primitive societies is their persistence. E. YOUNG-BRUEHL How can anti-Semitism's strange persistence through the centuries be explained?

persistency /pəˈsɪst(ə)nsi/ *noun.* L16.
[from prec. + -ENCY.]
1 a The quality of persisting; firmness or obstinacy in adhering to a course, purpose, or opinion. L16. ▸**b** = PERSISTENCE 1a. M19.
2 = PERSISTENCE 2. M19.

> 📖 **1a** L. M. MONTGOMERY Take a whim into his head and cling to it with . . amazing silent persistency.

persistent /pəˈsɪst(ə)nt/ *adjective.* E19.
[from PERSISTENCE or PERSIST: see -ENT.]
1 ZOOLOGY & BOTANY. Of a part of an animal or plant (as a horn, a leaf, a calyx, etc.): remaining attached; not falling off. Opp. DECIDUOUS, CADUCOUS. E19.
2 Persisting in an action etc.; having or characterized by persistency. M19.
3 Enduring. M19.
4 Of an action: continuous; constantly repeated. M19.
5 GEOLOGY. Of a stratum: extending continuously over the whole area occupied by the formation. M19.
6 ECOLOGY. Of a chemical, or (occas.) radioactivity: remaining within the environment for a long time after its introduction. M20.

> 📖 **2** H. JAMES The good lady continued, with a persistent candour. ROSEMARY MANNING She succumbed to his persistent wooing. W. RAEPER A tireless and persistent campaigner for women's education. **3** A. C. BOULT A persistent cough refused to yield to treatment. A. SILLITOE The persistent rain of one autumn. **4** I. MURDOCH There were the persistent rumours about German arms. RACHEL ANDERSON My dog, keeping up her persistent whine by the door.

▪ **persistently** *adverb* M19.

persnickety /pəˈsnɪkɪti/ *adjective. N. Amer. colloq.* E20.
[Alt.]
= PERNICKETY.

person /ˈpəːs(ə)n/ *noun.* Also †**parson**. ME.
[Old French *persone* (mod. *personne*) from Latin *persona* mask used by an actor, a person who plays a part (also in senses 2, 6, 7 below). Cf. PARSON.]
▶**I 1** A part played in a drama or in actual life; a character (in a play or story); a persona; a guise. Now chiefly in ***persons of the drama***, = DRAMATIS PERSONAE. ME.

> 📖 **1** *Look Now* I take on a different person with every song I sing.

▶**II 2** An individual human being; *spec.* a human being as opp. to a thing or an animal. ME. ▸**b** Any individual, one. *colloq.* L18. ▸**c** An individual of inferior status. L18. ▸**d** As 2nd elem. of comb. (replacing *man* or *woman* in order to avoid sexual distinction): a man or woman having a specified profession, occupation, or office. L20. ▸**e** An individual characterized by a preference or liking for a specified thing. L20.
3 a With specifying word: an individual regarded in terms of his or her appearance or figure. Now *rare* or *obsolete*. ME. ▸**b** The living body of an individual, regarded either together with its clothing and adornments or simply as the physical form or figure. LME.
4 The actual self or being of an individual. Chiefly with possess. ME. ▸**b** Bodily presence. *obsolete* exc. in ***in person*** below. L15.
5 LAW. An individual (also ***natural person***) or a group of individuals as a corporation (also ***artificial person***), regarded as having rights and duties recognized by the law. LME. ▸**b** *euphem.* The genitals; *spec.* the penis. E19.

> 📖 **2** M. L. KING It was necessary to employ an office staff of ten persons. M. SARTON Women are at last becoming persons first and wives second. M. FLANAGAN You're just the nicest, smartest person. G. BODDY The person to whom Kathleen turned . . for love and understanding. A. PHILLIPS The infant sought contact with a person, not . . gratification from an object. **b** YEATS It makes a person be thinking of . . death and judgement. **c** F. BURNEY This person wishes for a longer conference with you. **d** ***chairperson***, ***salesperson***, etc. **e** T. HEALD I should say you're more of a cat person. **3a** L. STERNE A pale thin person of a man. **b** *Notes & Queries* These they put in their hats, or anywhere about their persons. L. DURRELL As for money . . he . . would never carry it on his person. Q. BELL His person was pleasing, his manners courtly. JOAN SMITH Her long blonde hair tumbled artistically about her person. **4** E. FEINSTEIN She still saw God and the State united in the Tsar's person.

▶**III 6** CHRISTIAN THEOLOGY. (Usu. **P-**.) ▸**a** Each of the three modes of being of the Godhead, the Father (***First Person***), the Son (***Second Person***), or the Holy Spirit (***Third Person***), who together constitute the Trinity. ME. ▸**b** The personality of Christ, esp. as uniting his divine and human natures. M16.
7 GRAMMAR. Each of the classes of personal pronouns and corresponding verbal forms (of which there are three in modern English) denoting or indicating the participant(s) or individual(s) referred to in speech or writing. E16.
8 PHILOSOPHY. A self-conscious or rational (esp. embodied) being. M17.

> 📖 **7** M. GEE He . . had practised his French . . always forgetting the persons, always forgetting the Mademoiselle.

Phrases: †**accept persons**, †**accept the person of** show favouritism (to). ***displaced person***: see DISPLACE *verb*. **first person** (*a*) GRAMMAR the person denoting or indicating the individual etc. speaking or writing; (*b*) (*F- P-*) see sense 6a above. **in one's own person** †(*a*) = ***in person*** below; (*b*) as oneself. **in person** with one's own bodily presence; personally. **in the person of** (*a*) in the character of, representing; (*b*) (as) represented by. ***legal person***: see LEGAL *adjective*. NETHER ***person***. ***person of confidence***: see CONFIDENCE *noun* 6. ***purse and person***: see PURSE *noun*. †**respect persons**, †**respect the person of** show favouritism (to). **second person** (*a*) GRAMMAR the person denoting or indicating the individual etc. addressed; (*b*) (*S- P-*) see sense 6a above. **third person** (*a*) = ***third party*** s.v. THIRD *adjective & noun*; (*b*) GRAMMAR the person denoting or indicating the individual etc. referred to; (*c*) (*T- P-*) see sense 6a above.
Comb.: **person-day**, **person-hour**, etc., a day, hour, etc., of one person's work etc., as a unit of measure; **person-object** PSYCHOLOGY a person as the object of one's thoughts etc.; **person-to-person** (*a*) between individuals; (*b*) (of a telephone call) booked through the operator to a specific person.

person /ˈpəːs(ə)n/ *verb trans.* Infl. **-n-**, **-nn-**. M17.
[from the noun.]
†**1** = PERSONATE *verb* 2. *rare* (Milton). Only in M17.
2 = MAN *verb* 1. (Used to avoid sexual distinction.) Freq. *joc.* L20.

> 📖 **2** *Washington Post* 'That was Ron,' said Linda Willis, who was personing the phone.

persona /pəˈsəʊnə, pəː-/ *noun.* Pl. **-nas**, **-nae** /-niː/. E20.
[Latin: see PERSON *noun*.]
1 A character assumed by an author, performer, etc., in his or her writing, work, etc. E20.
2 An aspect of the personality as displayed to others. Cf. ANIMA. E20.

> 📖 **1** *Dance Theatre Journal* He often disguised himself as one of several personas. *Tennis* When he speaks on the subject, you can hear all three of his personas. **2** ROSEMARY MANNING The portrait on the jacket of my 1983 novel . . shows me in my serious, thoughtful persona. A. STORR Civilised life demands that we all develop a persona.

personable /ˈpəːs(ə)nəb(ə)l/ *adjective.* LME.
[from PERSON *noun* + -ABLE.]
1 Pleasing in appearance. Now chiefly, pleasing in manner or behaviour; agreeable, likeable. LME.
†**2** LAW. Having the status of a legal person, and so competent to maintain a plea etc. M16–M17.

> 📖 **1** *Leicester Mercury* Personable lady wanted as housekeeper to three children.

▪ **personableness** *noun* E17.

personably /ˈpəːs(ə)nəbli/ *adverb.* L15.
[from prec. + -LY[2].]
†**1** Personally, in person. L15–M16.
2 In a personable manner; pleasantly, agreeably. L20.

persona designata /pəˌsəʊnə dɛsɪɡˈnɑːtə/ *noun phr.* Pl. ***personae designatae*** /pəˌsəʊniː dɛsɪɡˈnɑːtiː/. L19.
[Law Latin, formed as PERSONA + Latin *designata* fem. of *designatus*: see DESIGNATE *adjective*.]
A person individually specified in a legal action, as opp. to one included in a category.

personae *noun pl.* see PERSONA.

personae designatae, ***personae gratae***, ***personae non gratae*** *noun phrs. pl.* see PERSONA DESIGNATA etc.

personage /ˈpəːs(ə)nɪdʒ/ *noun.* LME.
[Partly from Old French (mod. *personnage*), partly from medieval Latin *personagium*: see -AGE.]
†**1** = PERSON *noun* 3b. LME–L18. ▸**b** = PERSON *noun* 3a. M16–E19.
2 A person, an individual; *esp.* a person of high rank, distinction, or importance. LME.
†**3** A representation of a person; a statue, a portrait. L15–E17.
†**4** One's individual self. M16–M17.
†**5** Rank or character as an attribute of a person, esp. of a particular type. M–L16.
6 A character in a play, story, etc.; a part in a play. M16.

> 📖 **2** L. M. MONTGOMERY He was an odd-looking personage with an ungainly figure. C. CHAPLIN No longer was I a nondescript . . ; now I was a personage of the theatre. A. LIVINGSTONE It was a grand . . home life, with coming and going of high military personages. **6** W. STYRON The characters are Sophie and her father and a personage new to this narrative.

Phrases: **in the personage of** as represented by, in the person of.

persona grata /pəˌsəʊnə ˈɡrɑːtə/ *noun phr.* Pl. ***personae gratae*** /pəˌsəʊniː ˈɡrɑːtiː/. L19.
[Late Latin, formed as PERSONA + Latin *grata* fem. of *gratus* pleasing.]
A person, esp. a diplomat, acceptable to certain others.

> 📖 *Listener* Gandhi was . . always *persona grata* with the high-ups.

personal /ˈpəːs(ə)n(ə)l/ *adjective & noun.* LME.
[Old French (also *personel*, mod. *personnel*) from Latin *personalis*, from *persona*: see PERSON *noun*, -AL[1].]
▶**A** *adjective.* **I 1** Of, pertaining to, concerning, or affecting a person as an individual (rather than as a member of a group or of the public, or in a professional capacity etc.); individual; private; one's own. LME. ▸**b** Applicable or belonging only *to*. M18.
2 Done, made, etc., in person; involving the actual presence or action of the individual. LME. ▸†**b** Present or engaged in person. L16–E17.
3 Of or pertaining to one's person or body. LME.
4 Of, referring or tending to refer to, a person's character, private concerns, etc., esp. in a disparaging or offensive way. E17. ▸**b** Having oneself as object; directed to oneself. L18. ▸**c** Directed to or intended for a particular individual. M19.

1 J. T. STORY A doorbell makes every visitor sound the same—a knock is very personal. T. BENN Records about individuals relating to their own personal affairs. V. BROME Freud and Jung were . . trying to prevent personal differences from interfering with professional relations. D. LODGE He drives to his personal parking space. *Voice of the Arab World* Arafat's driver and personal bodyguard. **2** A. J. CRONIN Some . . disinclined for the personal encounter even sent their wives. I. MURDOCH Rosa decided to open her campaign by a personal visit, rather than by a letter. **3** ADDISON A Princess whose Personal Charms . . were now become the least part of her Character. D. ATTENBOROUGH The sloth . . pays . . little attention to its personal hygiene. **4** *Medical & Physical Journal* A dispute which . . has degenerated into personal abuse. C. ODETS How much, if I'm not getting too personal, did such a violin cost you? *Rugby World* It was nothing personal against the young man himself. **b** O. MANNING Times being what they were, personal pride was out of place. **c** J. SYMONS The rectangular package was . . marked *Personal*

▶ **II 5** *GRAMMAR.* **a** Designating a verb used in all persons (PERSON *noun* 7). Opp. ***impersonal***. Now *rare*. **M16.** ▸**b** Designating each of the pronouns corresponding to the grammatical persons (e.g. *I, you, them*). **M17.**

†**6** *CHRISTIAN THEOLOGY.* = HYPOSTATIC 1. **M16–E17.**

7 *PHILOSOPHY.* **a** Of, pertaining to, or characteristic of a self-conscious or rational being. **M17.** ▸**b** Existing as a person, not a thing or abstraction. **M19.**

▶ **III 8** Personable. *rare.* **M17.**

Special collocations & phrases: ***chattels personal***: see CHATTEL 2. **personal action** *LAW*: brought for compensation or damages for loss of a thing from the person responsible, rather than for recovery of the (movable) thing itself. **personal bar** *LAW* = ESTOPPEL 1. **personal column** a section of a newspaper devoted to private advertisements or messages. **personal computer**: designed for use by an individual esp. in an office, business, or home environment. **personal diligence** *SCOTS LAW* (now *Hist.*) the process for enforcing payments, recovering debts, etc., by imprisonment of the debtor. ***personal effects***: see EFFECT *noun*. ***personal equation***: see EQUATION 4. **personal equity plan** = *PEP* s.v. P, P. **personal estate** = *personal property* below. ***personal identification number***: see PIN *noun*². **personal information manager** a computer program functioning as an address book, organizer, diary, etc. **personal injury** *LAW*: to a person's body rather than his or her property or reputation. **personal law**: applicable to a person or class of people (e.g. one distinguished by religion) irrespective of where situated. **personal organizer** (*a*) a loose-leaf notebook with sections for various kinds of information, including a diary; (*b*) a hand-held microcomputer serving the same purpose. **personal pension** a pension scheme that is independent of the contributor's employer. **personal property** *LAW* all property (including debts etc.) except land and those interests in land passing to the heir on the owner's death. **personal representative** *LAW* an executor or administrator of the estate of a deceased person. ***personal servitude***: see SERVITUDE 3. **personal shopper** an individual who is paid to assist another to purchase goods, either by accompanying them while shopping or by shopping on their behalf. **personal space** *SOCIOLOGY* the area around an individual where encroachment by others causes anxiety or uneasiness. **personal stereo** a small portable cassette player and/or radio used with lightweight headphones. **personal touch** a personal element added to something otherwise impersonal. ***personal watercraft***: see *watercraft* s.v. WATER *noun*.

▶ **B** *noun*. **1** In *pl.* Personal belongings; personal matters. Formerly also *spec.*, personal property. Now *rare*. **E18.** ▸**b** In *pl.* Personal remarks. **M18.** ▸**c** An advertisement or notice in the personal column of a newspaper. Chiefly *N. Amer.* **M19.**

2 *BASKETBALL.* A foul involving bodily contact with an opponent. **M20.**

personalia /pəːsəˈneɪlɪə/ *noun pl.* **E20.**
[Latin, neut. pl. of *personalis* PERSONAL: see -IA².]
Personal matters; personal mementoes.

personalise *verb* var. of PERSONALIZE.

personalism /ˈpəːs(ə)n(ə)lɪz(ə)m/ *noun*. **M19.**
[from PERSONAL + -ISM.]
1 The quality of being personal; *spec.* a theory or system based on personal ideas or applications. **M19.**
2 *PHILOSOPHY.* Any of various systems of thought which maintain the primacy of the (human or divine) person on the basis that reality has meaning only through the conscious minds of people. **E20.**
3 *POLITICS.* Allegiance to a person, esp. a political leader, rather than to a party or ideology. **M20.**

personalist /ˈpəːs(ə)n(ə)lɪst/ *noun & adjective*. **L19.**
[from PERSONAL + -IST: cf. prec.]
▶ **A** *noun*. **1** A writer of personal anecdotes etc. *rare*. **L19.**
2 An adherent of personalism. **E20.**
▶ **B** *adjective*. Of, characterized by, or in accordance with personalism. **M20.**
■ **personaˈlistic** *adjective* (*a*) individual, idiosyncratic; (*b*) *PSYCHOLOGY* of or based on an individual and his or her personal experiences: **M20.**

personality /pəːsəˈnalɪti/ *noun*. **LME.**
[Old French *personalité* (mod. -nn-) from late Latin *personalitas*, from Latin *personalis*: see PERSONAL, -ITY.]
1 The quality or fact of being a person as distinct from a thing or animal; the quality which makes a being a person. **LME.** ▸**b** *CHRISTIAN THEOLOGY.* The condition of the Godhead of existing as three persons. **L15.** ▸**c** Actual existence as a person. **M19.**
2 †**a** The fact of being done in person. *rare*. Only in **M17.** ▸**b** The fact of relating or referring to an individual person or persons, esp. in a disparaging or offensive way; a disparaging or offensive remark (usu. in *pl.*). **M18.**
3 *LAW.* †**a** = PERSONALTY 1. **M17–E18.** ▸**b** = PERSONALTY 2. *rare*. **M18.**
4 †**a** A personal quality or characteristic. *rare*. Only in **M18.** ▸**b** The assemblage of qualities or characteristics which makes a person a distinctive individual; the (esp. notable or appealing) distinctive character of a person. **L18.**
5 A person, *esp.* one of unusual character. Now chiefly *spec.*, an important or famous person; a celebrity. **M19.** ▸**b** The body. *rare*. **M19.**

1 W. PALEY These capacities constitute personality, for they imply consciousness and thought. **2b** A. TROLLOPE Never referring with clear personality to those . . nearest to her when . . a child. *Nineteenth Century* The Court . . will not stand . . journalistic personalities about its members. **4b** DAY LEWIS For the autobiographer, his personality is . . the foundation . . of what he tries to build. *New York Times* The chief thing about Sally . . is that she has personality. L. APPIGNANESI The sheer force of his exuberant personality and charm. *transf.*: P. V. PRICE Unexpected weather conditions can cause infinite variations in the personality of a wine. ***MINNESOTA Multiphasic Personality Inventory***. ***modal personality***: see MODAL *adjective* 6b. ***multiple personality***: see MULTIPLE *adjective*. ***split personality***: see SPLIT *adjective*. **5** N. MAILER I was a personality on television. A. TOFFLER Twiggy, the Beatles . . —thousands of 'personalities' parade across the stage of contemporary history.

Comb.: **personality cult** excessive devotion to a single (political) leader based on certain aspects of his or her personality; **personality disorder** *PSYCHIATRY* a deeply ingrained and maladaptive pattern of behaviour of a specified kind, usu. apparent by the time of adolescence and causing long-term difficulties in personal relationships or in functioning in society; **personality inventory** a questionnaire designed to assess traits of personality.

personalize /ˈpəːs(ə)n(ə)lʌɪz/ *verb trans*. Also **-ise**. **M18.**
[from PERSONAL *adjective* + -IZE.]
Personify; embody in a person; make (an object) more obviously related to, or identifiable as belonging to, a particular individual, esp. by marking with a name etc.

Times Educ. Suppl. This has the benefit of personalizing the software because the pupils' favourite pictures can be used.

■ **personaˈlization** *noun* **L19.**

personally /ˈpəːs(ə)n(ə)li/ *adverb*. **LME.**
[from PERSONAL *adjective* + -LY².]
1 With the personal presence or action of the individual specified; in person. **LME.** ▸**b** In relation to the actual person specified (as the object of an action etc.). **L15.**
2 As a person; in the form or character of a person. **LME.**
3 In one's personal capacity; as an individual; as regards oneself. **M19.**

1 DYLAN THOMAS The cheque came from Lady Clark. Should I thank her personally? H. ACTON An old gentleman whom she did not meet personally but who remained a . . pen-pal. **2** G. W. H. LAMPE The Logos . . personally subsisting as the Son. **3** B. PYM 'Those exquisite drawings.' Personally, I thought them disgusting. P. BENSON I'll hold you personally responsible.

personalness /ˈpəːs(ə)n(ə)lnɪs/ *noun*. **L19.**
[from PERSONAL *adjective* + -NESS.]
The quality of being personal.

personalty /ˈpəːs(ə)n(ə)lti/ *noun*. **M16.**
[Legal Anglo-Norman *personalté*, from Old French *personal*: see PERSONAL, -TY¹.]
LAW. **1** ***in the personalty***, (of an action) brought for compensation or damages for the loss, rather than the recovery, of a thing. *obsolete* exc. *Hist.* **M16.**
2 Personal property; *gen.* personal belongings. **M18.**

persona non grata /pəˌsəʊnə nɒn ˈɡrɑːtə, nəʊn/ *noun phr.* Pl. ***personae non gratae*** /pəˌsəʊniː, ˈɡrɑːtiː/. **E20.**
[formed as PERSONA GRATA + Latin *non* not.]
An unacceptable or unwelcome person.

personate /ˈpəːs(ə)nət/ *adjective*. **L16.**
[Latin *personatus* masked, feigned, from *persona* mask: see PERSON *noun*, -ATE².]
†**1** Personated, feigned, pretended. **L16–E19.**
†**2** Of the nature of a person; embodied in or as a person. Only in **17.**
3 *BOTANY.* Of a two-lipped corolla (as in an antirrhinum): having the opening between the lips closed by an upward projection of the lower lip. Opp. ***ringent***. **M18.**

personate /ˈpəːs(ə)neɪt/ *verb*. **L16.**
[Late Latin *personat-* pa. ppl stem of *personare*, from *persona*: see PERSON *noun*, -ATE³.]
1 *verb trans. & intrans.* Act or play the part of (a character in a drama etc.). **L16.**
†**2** *verb trans.* Represent or describe in writing; symbolize. **L16–L17.**
3 *verb trans.* Pretend to be (another person), esp. for the purpose of fraud; *spec.* (*POLITICS*) cast a vote in the name of (another person); impersonate. **E17.**
4 *verb trans.* Stand for, represent, symbolize; personify, embody. Now *rare* or *obsolete*. **E17.**
†**5** *verb trans.* Feign (a quality). **E–M17.**
■ **persoˈnation** *noun* (*a*) the action or an act of personating; (*b*) a person as a personification of a quality etc.: **L16.** **personative** /ˈpəːs(ə)neɪtɪv/ *adjective* (of poetry) involving dramatic representation **L18.** **personator** *noun* **E17.**

personeity /pəːsəˈniːɪti, -ˈneɪɪti/ *noun*. *rare*. **E19.**
[from PERSON *noun* after CORPOREITY.]
That which constitutes a person; a being of the nature of a person.

personhood /ˈpəːs(ə)nhʊd/ *noun*. **M20.**
[from PERSON *noun* + -HOOD.]
The quality or condition of being a person.

personification /pəˌsɒnɪfɪˈkeɪʃ(ə)n/ *noun*. **M18.**
[from PERSONIFY + -FICATION.]
1 The representation of a thing or abstraction as a person; *ART* the symbolic representation of a thing or abstraction by a human figure. **M18.** ▸**b** An imaginary person or thing regarded as representing a thing or abstraction. **M19.**
2 A person or thing as a striking example or the embodiment of a quality etc. **E19.**
3 A dramatic representation or literary description of a person or character. *rare*. **E19.**

1a B. JOWETT The personifications of church and country as females. H. F. TOZER Scylla, who is the personification of the whirlpool. **2** SAKI Courtenay Youghal . . youthfully elegant, the personification of decorative repose.

■ **personificator** *noun* = PERSONIFIER **M19.**

personifier /pəˈsɒnɪfʌɪə/ *noun*. **L18.**
[from next + -ER¹.]
1 A speaker or writer who uses personification. **L18.**
2 A person who personates or acts the part of another. **L19.**

personify /pəˈsɒnɪfʌɪ/ *verb trans*. **E18.**
[French *personnifier*, from *personne*: see PERSON *noun*, -FY.]
1 Represent (a thing or abstraction) as a person; attribute a personal nature or personal characteristics to; *ART* symbolize by a figure in human form. **E18.**
2 Make or turn into a person; give a human form to. *rare*. **M18.**
3 Be an embodiment of (a quality etc.); exemplify in a typical manner. **E19.**
4 Pretend to be, impersonate. Now *rare*. **E19.**

1 A. STORR Boethius . . personifies Philosophy as a woman. **3** E. BOWEN The wild cats in the kitchen . . seemed to be chaos personified.

personize /ˈpəːs(ə)nʌɪz/ *verb*. Now *rare* or *obsolete*. Also **-ise**. **L16.**
[from PERSON *noun* + -IZE.]
†**1** *verb intrans.* Act a part. Only in **L16.**
2 *verb trans.* Represent as a person, personify. **M18.**

personkind /pəːs(ə)nˈkʌɪnd/ *noun*. Freq. *joc.* **L20.**
[from PERSON *noun* + MAN)KIND.]
The human race; humankind. (Used in order to avoid sexual distinction.)

personnel /pəːsəˈnɛl/ *noun*. **E19.**
[French, use as noun of adjective (see PERSONAL), as contrasted with MATÉRIEL.]
1 The body of people employed in an organization etc. or engaged in a service or undertaking, esp. a military one. Opp. ***matériel***. **E19.** ▸**b** *spec.* The members of an orchestra or band. **M20.** ▸**c** The department in an organization etc. concerned with the appointment, welfare, records, etc., of employees. Also more fully ***personnel department***. **M20.**
2 Personal appearance. *rare*. **M19.**
Comb.: **personnel carrier** an armoured vehicle for transporting troops etc. ***personnel department***: see sense 1c above.

personology /pəːsəˈnɒlədʒi/ *noun*. **E20.**
[from PERSON *noun* + -OLOGY.]
PSYCHOLOGY. The branch of science that deals with personality.
■ **personoˈlogical** *adjective* **M20.** **personologist** *noun* **M20.**

persorption /pəˈsɔːpʃ(ə)n/ *noun*. **M20.**
[from PER(MEATION + SORPTION.]
CHEMISTRY. Sorption in which gas molecules enter pores in a solid which are little larger than themselves.

perspective /pəˈspɛktɪv/ *noun & verb*. **LME.**
[medieval Latin *perspectiva* use as noun (sc. *ars* art) of fem. of late Latin *perspectivus*, from Latin *perspect-* pa. ppl stem of *perspicere* look at closely, formed as PER-¹ + *specere* look: see -IVE.]

For other words beginning with *per-* see the entry for **per-**¹

▶**A** *noun*. †**I 1** *sing.* & in *pl.* The science of sight; optics. LME–M17.

2 An optical instrument, as a magnifying glass, telescope, etc. LME–L18.

▶**II 3** The art of drawing solid objects on a plane surface so as to give the same impression of relative position, size, or distance, as the actual objects do when viewed from a particular point. L16. ▸**b** *fig.* A mental view of the relative importance of the relationships or aspects of a subject or matter; a point of view, a way of regarding a matter. E17. ▸**c** *transf.* The appearance of objects with regard to relative position, distance from the viewer, etc. E19. ▸**d** GEOMETRY. The relation of two figures in the same plane, such that pairs of corresponding points lie on concurrent lines, and corresponding lines meet in collinear points. M19. ▸**e** An apparent spatial distribution in perceived sound. Freq. ***auditory perspective***, ***sound perspective***, etc. M20.

4 †**a** A picture or figure designed to appear distorted or confused except when viewed from one position, or presenting totally different aspects from different positions. Freq. in ***piece of perspective***. L16–L17. ▸**b** A picture done according to the rules of perspective; *spec.* a picture appearing to enlarge or extend the actual space, or to give the effect of distance. M17.

5 A view, a prospect, *esp.* an extensive one. E17. ▸**b** *fig.* A mental prospect; expectation. M18.

> 📖 **3** C. HAYES Rules of colour, proportion and perspective. R. COBB The . . painter had looked . . on this scene, as viewed from a height—an interesting exercise in perspective. **b** R. MAY A historical perspective gives us new light on the present. M. SCHORER The perspectives which define the form and theme of her book. **5** I. MCEWAN At this distance, the perspective distorted by a bluish early morning mist. **b** R. THOMAS She had had the sense of wider avenues opening, giving new perspectives.

▶**III** †**6** Close inspection; insight. L16–M17.

Phrases: ***aerial perspective***: see AERIAL *adjective* 3. **in perspective** (*a*) drawn or viewed in accordance with the rules of perspective; (*b*) correctly regarded as to relative importance; (*c*) in prospect; expected. ***oblique perspective***: see OBLIQUE *adjective*. **out of perspective** (*a*) drawn or viewed contrary to the rules of perspective; (*b*) not correctly regarded as to relative importance.

▶**B** *verb trans.* Draw or put in perspective. *rare*. E19.

■ **perspectival** *adjective* of or pertaining to perspective M19. **perspectivism** *noun* (*a*) PHILOSOPHY the theory that knowledge of a subject is inevitably partial and limited by the individual perspective from which it is viewed; (*b*) the (esp. literary) practice of regarding and analysing a situation, work of art, etc., from different points of view: E20. **perspectivist** *noun* (*a*) an artist who specializes in perspective effects; (*b*) a person who studies the principles of perspective: M20. **perspecti'vistic** *adjective* of or pertaining to perspectivism M20. **perspec'tivity** *noun* (PHILOSOPHY) the condition of being limited by a particular point of view E20.

perspective /pəˈspɛktɪv/ *adjective*. LME.
[Late Latin *perspectivus*: see prec., -IVE.]

▶**I** †**1** Relating to sight; optical. LME–L16.

†**2** Of an optical instrument: magnifying, assisting the sight. L16–M19.

▶**II 3** Of or pertaining to perspective; drawn in perspective. E17.

†**4** Prospective. Only in 18.

■ **perspectively** *adverb* †(*a*) as through an optical instrument; †(*b*) clearly, evidently; (*c*) in perspective; (*d*) GEOMETRY so as to be in perspective: M16.

Perspex /ˈpəːspɛks/ *noun*. Also **p-**. M20.
[Irreg. from Latin *perspect-* pa. ppl stem of *perspicere* look through, formed as PER-[1] + *specere* look (at).]

(Proprietary name for) polymerized methyl methacrylate, a tough transparent thermoplastic that is much lighter than glass and does not splinter. Freq. *attrib.*

¶ Other proprietary names for this substance are PLEXIGLAS, LUCITE.

perspicacious /pəːspɪˈkeɪʃəs/ *adjective*. E17.
[from Latin *perspicac-*, *-ax*, from *perspicere*: see PERSPECTIVE *noun* & *verb*, -ACIOUS.]

1 Seeing clearly; keen, sharp. *arch.* E17.

2 Having a clear understanding; perceptive, discerning. M17.

> 📖 **1** S. JOHNSON So thick a mist, that the most perspicacious eye could see but a little way. **2** E. WAUGH Lord Curzon was more perspicacious . . and discerned the great talents.

■ **perspicaciously** *adverb* M18. **perspicaciousness** *noun* E18.

perspicacity /pəːspɪˈkasɪti/ *noun*. M16.
[French *perspicacité* or late Latin *perspicacitas*, formed as prec.: see -ACITY.]

1 Clearness of understanding; great perception, discernment. M16.

2 Keenness of sight. *arch.* E17.

> 📖 **1** M. WESLEY Envied for his perspicacity in avoiding the problem. A. FRANCE This view of an all-seeing therapist with almost supernatural powers of . . perspicacity.

†**perspicience** *noun*. LME–M18.
[Latin *perspicientia*, from *perspicient-* pres. ppl stem of *perspicere*: see PERSPECTIVE *noun* & *verb*, -ENCE.]
= PERSPICACITY 1.

perspicuity /pəːspɪˈkjuːɪti/ *noun*. L15.
[Latin *perspicuitas*, from *perspicuus* transparent, clear, from *perspicere*: see PERSPECTIVE *noun* & *verb*, -ITY.]

†**1** Transparency, translucence. L15–M18.

2 Clearness of statement or exposition; lucidity. M16.

†**3** Distinctness to the sight; conspicuousness. *rare*. L16–M17.

4 Discernment, perspicacity. Formerly also, keenness of sight. M17.

perspicuous /pəˈspɪkjʊəs/ *adjective*. L15.
[from Latin *perspicuus*: see prec., -OUS.]

†**1** Transparent, translucent. L15–M18.

2 Easily understood; clearly expressed; lucid. L16.

3 Easily seen, conspicuous. Now *rare* or *obsolete*. L16.

4 Discerning, perspicacious. Formerly also, having keen sight. L16.

■ **perspicuously** *adverb* L16. **perspicuousness** *noun* E18.

perspirable /pəˈspʌɪərəb(ə)l/ *adjective*. E17.
[from PERSPIRE + -ABLE.]

1 Capable of perspiring; liable to perspire. E17. ▸**b** Of, pertaining to, or involving perspiration. E19.

†**2** Exposed to air or the wind, airy. Only in 17.

†**3** Able to be secreted in or as perspiration. M17–M19.

■ **perspira'bility** *noun* M18.

perspiration /pəːspɪˈreɪʃ(ə)n/ *noun*. E17.
[French, from *perspirer* from Latin *perspirare*: see next, -ATION.]

†**1** Breathing or blowing through. E17–E18.

2 Excretion of moisture through the pores of the skin, orig. only imperceptibly as water vapour, now also tangibly as fluid droplets; sweating. E17. ▸†**b** = TRANSPIRATION. M17–L18. ▸†**c** Evaporation. M17–E18.

3 Something which is perspired; sweat. E18.

> 📖 **2** J. GALSWORTHY He . . broke into a gentle perspiration. **3** R. P. JHABVALA His face . . was glistening with perspiration. D. LODGE It was very hot. She felt perspiration trickling down her breastbone. ***sensible perspiration***: see SENSIBLE *adjective* 1.

perspire /pəˈspʌɪə/ *verb*. M17.
[French †*perspirer* from Latin *perspirare* breathe everywhere, formed as PER-[1] + *spirare* breathe.]

†**1** *verb intrans.* Of the wind: breathe or blow gently. *rare*. Only in M17.

†**2** *verb intrans.* Of a volatile substance: pass out through pores in the form of vapour; escape by evaporation; evaporate. M17–L18.

3 *verb trans.* †**a** Emit, give off, (gas, vapour, etc.). L17–M19. ▸**b** Give off (moisture) through pores, either imperceptibly as vapour, or tangibly as liquid, esp. in mammalian skin. L17.

4 *verb intrans.* Of a person or animal: give out watery fluid through the pores of the skin, orig. as imperceptible perspiration, now also as tangible perspiration or sweating. E18.

■ **'perspirative** *adjective* (*rare*) promoting perspiration M18. **perspiratory** *adjective* (*a*) producing or promoting perspiration; (*b*) of, pertaining to, or of the nature of perspiration: E18. **perspiry** *adjective* (*colloq.*) full of perspiration M19.

per stirpes /pəː ˈstəːpiːz/ *adverbial phr*. L17.
[mod. Latin, formed as PER + accus. pl. of Latin *stirps* family.]
LAW.

(Divided, shared, etc.) equally among the branches of a family (and then each share among the members of one branch). Opp. PER CAPITA *adverbial phr.* 1.

perstringe /pəˈstrɪn(d)ʒ/ *verb trans*. M16.
[Latin *perstringere*, from *per* PER-[1] + *stringere* tie, bind.]

1 Censure; pass strictures on; criticize adversely. M16.

†**2** Touch on; hint at. E17–L18.

†**3** Dazzle; make dim. E–M17.

■ †**perstriction** *noun* (*rare*) [Latin *perstrictio(n-)*: cf. STRICTION] the action or an instance of perstringing someone: only in L17.

persuadable /pəˈsweɪdəb(ə)l/ *adjective*. Also †**-sw-**. E16.
[from PERSUADE + -ABLE.]

†**1** Persuasive. *rare*. Only in E16.

2 Able to be persuaded; easy to persuade; persuasible. L16.

■ **persuada'bility** *noun* L18. **persuadableness** *noun* M18.

persuade /pəˈsweɪd/ *verb*. Also †**-sw-**. L15.
[Latin *persuadere*, formed as PER-[1] + *suadere* advise, recommend.]

▶**I** *verb trans.* With a person as obj.

1 Successfully urge *to do*; talk *into* or *out of* an action; attract, lure, or entice to something or in a particular direction. L15.

2 Cause, lead, or bring to believe a statement, doctrine, etc., or the truth *that* or *of*; talk *into* or *out of* a belief. E16.

3 Try to lead *to do*, urge or advise strongly; try to convince (a person) *that*. *obsolete* exc. *dial.* E16.

> 📖 **1** DICKENS Be persuaded into being respectable. M. SHADBOLT I've been trying to persuade Izzy down to the city for the last five years. S. UNWIN Nothing would persuade many . . important publishers to disclose their turnover figures. **2** W. CATHER She talked nervously . . as if she were trying to persuade herself. G. B. SHAW Nothing will persuade me that any boy . . likes . . the drudgery of the professional footballer. *Theological Studies* Persuade him . . of the pathological element in his personality. **3** ANTHONY WOOD I persuaded the society to set it above the arches, but I was not then heard.

▶**II** *verb trans.* With an idea as obj.

†**4** Urge or recommend the acceptance of (a statement, opinion, etc.); inculcate. L15–L17.

†**5** Advocate or recommend (an act, course of action, etc.). L15–L18.

†**6** Lead a person to believe (*that*, a proposition, etc.); prove, demonstrate. E16–E18.

7 Lead a person to the performance or practice of (an act, course of action, etc.) by argument, pleading, etc. *arch.* M16.

▶**III** *verb intrans.* †**8** Talk earnestly *with* a person in order to secure agreement or compliance; expostulate *with*, plead *with*. L15–L17.

9 Use persuasion or pleading; be successful in persuasion, carry conviction; be convincing. L15.

> 📖 **9** G. F. GRAHAM In order to persuade, we address the feelings and the imagination.

■ **persuading** *adjective* (now *rare*) that persuades; persuasive: L16. **persuadingly** *adverb* (long *rare*) M16.

persuader /pəˈsweɪdə/ *noun*. Also †**-sw-**. M16.
[from prec. + -ER[1].]

1 A person who or thing which persuades someone. M16.

2 A thing used to compel submission or obedience, *esp.* a gun or other weapon. *slang*. L18.

3 TELEVISION. An electrode in an image orthicon camera tube which deflects the returning beam of scanning electrons into the electron multiplier. Freq. *attrib.* M20.

persuasible /pəˈsweɪsɪb(ə)l/ *adjective*. Also †**-sw-**. LME.
[Latin *persuasibilis*, from *persuas-*: see next, -IBLE.]

†**1** Having the power to persuade; persuasive. LME–M17.

2 Able or ready to be persuaded; open to persuasion. E16.

■ **persuasi'bility** *noun* ability or readiness to be persuaded E17.

persuasion /pəˈsweɪʒ(ə)n/ *noun*. Also †**-sw-**. LME.
[Latin *persuasio(n-)*, from *persuas-* pa. ppl stem of *persuadere* PERSUADE: see -ION.]

1 The action or an act of persuading or trying to persuade; something tending or intended to induce belief or action; an argument, an inducement. LME. ▸**b** Persuasiveness. E17.

2 The fact or condition of being persuaded or convinced of something, assurance; something of which one is persuaded, a belief, a conviction. E16.

3 *spec.* A religious belief, opinion, or creed. Now also, a political opinion or standpoint. E17. ▸**b** A body of people holding a particular religious belief; a sect, a denomination. E18. ▸**c** A kind, a sort, a nationality. *joc.* M19.

> 📖 **1** E. A. FREEMAN By force or persuasion, he gained over to his side the Princes of Aquitaine. *Times* The full cogency of their persuasions. *Times Lit. Suppl.* Backgrounding the intellectual propositions and foregrounding the moral persuasions of religion. *Scots Magazine* His is always the voice of persuasion, not strident condemnation. **b** LYTTON The persuasion of his silvery tongue. **2** J. PRIESTLEY My doubts were . . converted into a full persuasion. D. BREWSTER His persuasion of Flamsteed's fitness for the work. **3** W. LIPPMANN Totalitarian states . . of the fascist or the communist persuasion. E. SAINTSBURY Sincere in their religious beliefs though not of the same persuasion. **b** J. I. M. STEWART Uncle Norman . . a cleric, although of the presbyterian persuasion. **c** G. H. LEWES Homer—*not* I believe a gentleman of the Caledonian persuasion. OED No one of the male persuasion was present.

persuasive /pəˈsweɪsɪv/ *adjective* & *noun*. Also †**-sw-**. L15.
[French *persuasif*, *-ive* or medieval Latin *persuasivus*, from Latin *persuas-*: see prec., -IVE.]

▶**A** *adjective*. Capable of or skilled in persuading; tending or fitted to persuade. L15.

▶**B** *noun*. Something adapted or intended to persuade; a motive, an inducement. L15.

■ **persuasively** *adverb* M17. **persuasiveness** *noun* E17. †**persuasory** *adjective* = PERSUASIVE *adjective* L16–M19.

†**persue** *noun*. Orig. **parcy**. M16–M17.
[App. orig. from French *percée* act of piercing, later confused with PURSUE.]
HUNTING. The track of blood left by a wounded animal, esp. a deer.

persulphate /pəˈsʌlfeɪt/ *noun*. Also **-sulf-**. E19.
[from PER-[1] + SULPHATE.]
CHEMISTRY. Orig., a sulphate containing a high proportion of sulphate ions (i.e. containing a metal in a high valency state). Now usu. = PEROXOSULPHATE.

For other words beginning with *per-* see the entry for **per-**[1]

persulphuric /pəːsʌlˈfjʊərɪk/ *adjective*. Also **-sulf-**. L19.
[from PER-¹ + SULPHURIC.]
CHEMISTRY. = PEROXOSULPHURIC.

†**perswade** *verb*, †**perswasion** *noun* vars. of PERSUADE, PERSUASION.

PERT /pəːt/ *abbreviation*.
Programme evaluation and review technique (orig., programme evaluation research task), a form of network analysis used esp. to deal with events of uncertain duration.

pert /pəːt/ *adjective, noun, adverb, & verb*. Also (now *US & dial.*; the usual form in senses A.2b, 4a) **peart** /pɪət/. ME.
[Old French *apert*, from Latin *apertus* pa. pple of *aperire* open; partly blended with Old French *aspert*, *espert* from Latin *expertus* expert. Cf. APERT.]
▶ **A** *adjective*. **I** †**1 a** Open, unconcealed; manifest, evident. ME–L16. ▸**b** Of personal appearance: (formerly) beautiful, attractive; (now) neat and suggestive of jauntiness. ME.

> **1b** T. OTWAY He's so very little, pert and dapper. W. G. HARDY Slim young body and pert young breasts.

▶ **II 2** †**a** Expert, skilled. ME–E16. ▸**b** Quick to see and act, sharp; clever. *obsolete* exc. *dial.* LME.

> **2b** MILTON The pertest operations of wit. H. B. STOWE She's such a peart young un, she won't take no lookin' arter.

▶ **III 3** Of a person, esp. a young one: forward, presumptuous, or impudent in speech and behaviour. Later also (of speech, behaviour, etc.), impertinent, cheeky. LME.
4 a Lively; sprightly; cheerful. *obsolete* exc. *US & dial.* E16. ▸**b** Of plants: fresh, verdant. Now *dial.* E18.

> **3** S. RICHARDSON Pamela, don't be pert to his Honour. G. W. TARGET He seemed rather too pert about the whole business.

▶ **B** *noun*. A pert person or thing. Long *rare*. LME.
▶ **C** *adverb*. In a pert manner. LME.
▶ **D** *verb intrans*. Behave pertly. Long *rare*. M17.
■ **pertish** *adjective* somewhat pert, inclined to be pert E19. †**pertlike** *adjective* pert-looking, pert L16–M18. **pertly** *adverb* ME. **pertness** *noun* LME.

pertain /pəˈteɪn/ *verb intrans*. LME.
[from tonic stem of Old French *partenir* from Latin *pertinere* extend, tend or belong (to), formed as PER-¹ + *tenere* hold.]
1 Belong or be attached *to*, *spec.* (**a**) as a part, (**b**) as an appendage or accessory, †(**c**) as a possession, legal right, or privilege. Formerly also foll. by indirect obj. LME. ▸**b** Be appropriate *to*. LME.
2 Have reference or relation *to*; relate *to*. Formerly also foll. by indirect obj. LME.

> **1** C. BARKER Scenes which pertain to an age happily passed away. W. C. BRYANT The cares of war Pertain to all men born in Troy. E. S. PERSON However unique . . the . . experience of falling in love, certain general characteristics pertain to it. **2** P. LIVELY Most of what he said pertained to himself.

■ **pertainings** *noun pl.* belongings, appurtenances M19. **pertainment** *noun* (*rare*) a piece of property, an appurtenance L19.

pertechnetic /pəːtɛkˈniːtɪk/ *adjective*. M20.
[from PER-¹ + TECHNET(IUM + -IC.]
CHEMISTRY. ***pertechnetic acid***, the acid $HTcO_4$, obtainable as dark red crystals.
■ **perˈtechnetate** *noun* a salt of this acid, esp. as used in medical scanning as a radioactive tracer M20.

Pertelot *noun* see PARTLET *noun*¹.

Pertelote *noun* see PARTLET *noun*¹.

Pertelot(e) *nouns* see PARTLET *noun*¹.

Pertex /ˈpəːtɛks/ *noun*. L20.
[from *Per-* (perh. from PERMEABLE) + TEX(TILE.]
(Proprietary name for) a lightweight breathable fabric used to make clothing and equipment for camping, climbing, and other outdoor pursuits.

Perthes disease /ˈpəːtəz dɪˌziːz/ *noun phr.* Also **Perthes' disease**. E20.
[G. C. *Perthes* (1869–1927), German surgeon.]
MEDICINE. Degeneration of the head of the femur in children owing to an impaired blood supply, sometimes leading to necrosis and progressive deformity of the hip-joint.

perthite /ˈpəːθʌɪt/ *noun*. M19.
[from *Perth*, Ontario, Canada + -ITE¹.]
MINERALOGY. A variety of alkali feldspar usu. consisting of roughly parallel intergrowths of an exsolved sodium-rich phase (as albite) and a potassium-rich phase (as microcline).
■ **perthitic** /pəːˈθɪtɪk/ *adjective* of or pertaining to (the texture of) perthite E20. **perˈthitically** *adverb* in the manner of perthite M20.

pertinacious /pəːtɪˈneɪʃəs/ *adjective*. E17.
[Latin *pertinac-*, *pertinax*, formed as PER-¹ + *tenax* holding fast: see TENACIOUS.]
1 Of a person: persistent or stubborn in adhering to an opinion, intention, etc.; resolute; obstinate. Chiefly *derog.* E17.
2 Of a thing or state: persistent, continuing. M17.
■ **pertinaciously** *adverb* E17. **pertinaciousness** *noun* M17.

pertinacity /pəːtɪˈnasɪti/ *noun*. L15.
[French *pertinacité* or medieval Latin *pertinacitas*, formed as prec.: see -ITY.]
The quality of being pertinacious; persistency; perverse obstinacy.
■ Earlier †**pertinacy** *noun* LME–M18.

pertinence /ˈpəːtɪnəns/ *noun*. M17.
[from PERTINENT *adjective* + -ENCE.]
The fact of being pertinent to the matter in hand.

pertinency /ˈpəːtɪnənsi/ *noun*. L16.
[Latin *pertinent-*: see next, -ENCY.]
The quality of being pertinent to the matter in hand; relevance; appositeness.

pertinent /ˈpəːtɪnənt/ *adjective & noun*. LME.
[Old & mod. French, or Latin *pertinent-* pres. ppl stem of *pertinere*: see PERTAIN, -ENT.]
▶ **A** *adjective*. †**1** Belonging (*to*). LME–M17.
2 Appropriate, suitable in nature or character; relating to the matter in hand, relevant; to the point; apposite. LME.

> **2** B. JOWETT Good judges who make pertinent remarks on the case. D. ROWE Lao Tsu, whose wisdom is as pertinent today as it was two . . thousand years ago. M. M. R. KHAN His typically . . pertinent usage of language.

▶ **B** *noun*. **1** *LAW* (chiefly *Scot.*). A thing belonging to an estate, the ownership of which it follows. Usu. in *pl.* LME.
2 In *pl.* Belongings; appurtenances. *obsolete* exc. *Scot.* E16.
■ **pertinently** *adverb* LME.

†**pertrouble** *verb trans*. Chiefly *Scot.* Also (earlier) **perturble**. LME–E19.
[Old French *pertrubler*, formed as PER-² + *trubler*: see TROUBLE *verb*.]
Perturb, trouble greatly.

perturb /pəˈtəːb/ *verb trans*. LME.
[Old French *pertourber* from Latin *perturbare*, formed as PER-¹ + *turbare* disturb, confuse.]
1 Disturb greatly (physically or mentally); cause disorder or irregularity in; unsettle, disquiet; agitate, throw into confusion. LME.
2 Subject (a system, a moving object, a process) to an influence tending to alter the normal or regular state or path; *PHYSICS* subject (a set of equations or its solution) to a perturbation. L19.
■ **perturbable** *adjective* E19. †**perturbance** *noun* great disturbance, perturbation LME–E18. **perturbancy** *noun* (*rare*) perturbation M17. **perturbant** *noun* (*rare*) a perturbing agent; *PHYSICS* a perturber: L19. **perturbed** *adjective* (**a**) disquieted, agitated, restless; confused, deranged; (**b**) *PHYSICS* subjected to a perturbation; (earlier in UNPERTURBED): E16. **perturbedly** /-bɪdli/ *adverb* M19. **perturber** *noun* (**a**) a disturber, a troubler; (**b**) *PHYSICS* a particle which interacts with a radiating atom or ion, affecting the wavelength of the emitted radiation: LME. **perturbingly** *adverb* so as to perturb M20.

perturbate /pəˈtəːbət/ *adjective*. L15.
[Latin *perturbatus* pa. pple of *perturbare*: see prec., -ATE².]
Confused, unclear; perturbed, out of order; irregular.

perturbate /ˈpəːtəbeɪt/ *verb trans. rare*. M16.
[Latin *perturbat-*: see next, -ATE³.]
Perturb.
■ **perturbator** *noun* a disturber, a troubler, a perturber M16.

perturbation /pəːtəˈbeɪʃ(ə)n/ *noun*. LME.
[Old French *perturbacion* from Latin *perturbatio(n-)* from *perturbat-* pa. ppl stem of *perturbare* PERTURB: see -ATION.]
1 The action or an instance of perturbing someone; the fact or condition of being perturbed; disturbance, disorder, commotion; mental agitation or disquietude; irregular variation. LME. ▸**b** A cause of disturbance or agitation. L16.
2 The deviation of a system, process, etc., from its regular or normal state or path, caused by an outside influence; *esp.* in *ASTRONOMY*, the deflection of a body from a theoretically regular orbit by the attraction of other bodies, or by the deviation of its primary from spherical form; an instance of this. E19. ▸**b** *PHYSICS*. A slight alteration of (a set of equations representing) a physical, esp. a quantum, system (as an atom) from a relatively simple or directly soluble form to one which may be studied by comparison with it. Freq. *attrib.*, as ***perturbation calculation***, ***perturbation expansion***, ***perturbation theory***, etc. L19.
■ **perturbational** *adjective* of, pertaining to, or of the nature of perturbation M19.

perturbative /pəˈtəːbətɪv, ˈpəːtəbeɪtɪv/ *adjective*. M17.
[Late Latin *perturbativus*, from Latin *perturbat-*: see prec., -IVE.]
Causing or apt to cause perturbation or disturbance; pertaining to or involving (physical or mathematical) perturbation.
■ **perturbatively** *adverb* L20.

†**perturble** *verb* see PERTROUBLE.

†**pertusion** *noun*. E17.
[Latin *pertusio(n-)*, from *pertus-* pa. ppl stem of *pertundere* punch or bore into a hole, formed as PER-¹ + *tundere* beat: see -ION.]
1 A hole punched or bored. E–M17.
2 The action of punching or boring a hole. Only in M18.

pertussis /pəˈtʌsɪs/ *noun*. L18.
[mod. Latin, formed as PER-¹ + *tussis* cough.]
MEDICINE. Whooping cough.
■ **pertussal** *adjective* L19.

Perugian /pəˈruːdʒɪən/ *noun & adjective*. M18.
[from *Perugia* (see below) + -AN.]
▶ **A** *noun*. A native or inhabitant of Perugia, a city and province in central Italy. M18.
▶ **B** *adjective*. Of or pertaining to Perugia; *spec.* of or designating a division of the Umbrian school of painting having Perugia as its centre. M19.

Peruginesque /pəruːdʒɪˈnɛsk/ *adjective*. M19.
[from *Perugino* (see below), from *Perugia*: see prec., -INE¹, -ESQUE.]
Resembling the style of the Italian painter Pietro Vannucci (*c* 1450–1523), known as Pietro Perugino.

peruke /pəˈruːk/ *noun*. M16.
[French *perruque* from Italian *perrucca*, *parrucca*, of unkn. origin. See also PERIWIG.]
†**1** A head of hair. M16–E17.
2 *Hist.* A skullcap covered with hair to imitate the natural hair of the head; a wig. E17.
■ **peruked** *adjective* wearing a peruke M17. **perukier** /pɛrəˈkɪə/ *noun* (*rare*) [alt. of PERRUQUIER] a wig-maker E19.

peruse /pəˈruːz/ *verb trans*. L15.
[Prob. from unrecorded Anglo-Latin verb, formed as PER-¹ + Proto-Romance base of USE *verb*.]
†**1** Use up; wear out by use. L15–L16.
2 †**a** Go through, deal with, or examine one by one. L15–E18. ▸**b** Travel through observantly or exploringly. *obsolete* exc. *dial.* E16.
†**3** Go over (something written etc.) again; revise. E16–M17.
4 Read through or over; examine, survey, read, or study, esp. thoroughly or carefully. M16.

> **4** G. MACDONALD I had perused his person, his dress and his countenance. M. DE LA ROCHE 'Read,' she commanded . . and they perused the letter together. A. CROSS Janet waited for Kate to peruse the menu.

■ **perusable** *adjective* E19. **perusal** *noun* (**a**) a survey, an examination; (**b**) an act of reading something through or over: L16. **peruser** *noun* M16.

Peruvian /pəˈruːvɪən/ *noun & adjective*. E17.
[mod. Latin *Peruvia* Peru + -AN.]
▶ **A** *noun*. **1** A native or inhabitant of Peru, a country in S. America. E17.
2 [Prob. based on Polish and Russian Union.] A Jew, *esp.* one from central or eastern Europe (*derog.* & *racially offensive*); (among Jews) a crude or dishonest person, a boor. *S. Afr. slang*. L19.
▶ **B** *adjective*. Of, native to, or produced in Peru. E17.
Peruvian bark cinchona bark. ***Peruvian*** IPECACUANHA. **Peruvian lily** = ALSTROEMERIA.

perv /pəːv/ *noun & verb*. *slang* (chiefly *Austral.*). Also **perve**. M20.
[Abbreviation of PERVERT *noun*.]
▶ **A** *noun*. **1** A sexual pervert. M20.
2 A lustful or erotic gaze. M20.
▶ **B** *verb intrans*. Act like a sexual pervert; gaze *at* or *on* with sexual or erotic interest. M20.
■ **pervy** *adjective* sexually perverted M20.

pervade /pəˈveɪd/ *verb*. M17.
[Latin *pervadere*, formed as PER-¹ + *vadere* go, walk.]
1 *verb trans*. Pass or flow through; traverse. Now *rare*. M17.
2 *verb trans*. Extend throughout; spread through or into every part of; permeate, saturate. M17.
3 *verb intrans*. Become diffused. Now *rare*. M17.
■ **pervadingly** *adverb* in a pervading manner M19.

pervagate /ˈpəːvəgeɪt/ *verb trans*. L19.
[Latin *pervagat-* pa. ppl stem of *pervagari*, formed as PER-¹ + *vagari* wander: see -ATE³.]
Wander through.
■ **pervaˈgation** *noun* M17.

pervaporation /pəvapəˈreɪʃ(ə)n/ *noun*. E20.
[from PER(MEATION + E)VAPORATION.]
CHEMISTRY. The evaporation of a liquid through a semi-permeable membrane with which it is in contact.

For other words beginning with *per-* see the entry for **per-**¹

■ **per'vaporate** *verb trans. & intrans.* evaporate through a semi-permeable membrane **E20.**

pervasion /pə'veɪʒ(ə)n/ *noun.* **M17.**
[Latin *pervasio(n-)*, formed as next: see **-ION.**]
The action of pervading something; pervasiveness.

pervasive /pə'veɪsɪv/ *adjective.* **M18.**
[from Latin *pervas-* pa. ppl stem of *pervadere* **PERVADE** + **-IVE.**]
(Capable of) pervading.
■ **pervasively** *adverb* **L19. pervasiveness** *noun* **L19.**

perve *noun & verb* var. of **PERV** *noun & verb.*

perveance /'pəːvɪəns/ *noun.* **E20.**
[Perh. from **PERVIOUS** + **-ANCE**, after *permeance* etc.]
ELECTRONICS. A constant relating current to voltage in some thermionic diodes (as in an electron gun).

pervenche /pɛː'vɑːnʃ/ *noun.* **L19.**
[French = **PERIWINKLE** *noun*[1].]
More fully ***pervenche blue***. A shade of light blue resembling the colour of the flowers of the periwinkle.

†**pervene** *verb. rare.* Orig. & chiefly *Scot.* **L16.**
[Latin *pervenire*, formed as **PER-**[1] + *venire* come. Cf. French *parvenir* arrive.]
1 *verb intrans.* Attain or get *to*. **L16–L17.**
2 *verb trans.* Gain access to, haunt. Only in **L18.**

perverse /pə'vəːs/ *adjective.* **LME.**
[Old & mod. French *pervers(e)* from Latin *perversus* pa. pple of *pervertere*: see **PERVERT** *verb.*]
1 Turned away from or against what is right or good; wicked. **LME.** ▸**b** Obstinate or persistent in error or wrongdoing. **L16.**
2 Of a person, action, etc.: going against or departing from what is reasonable or required; wayward, petulant, peevish, untoward. **LME.** ▸†**b** Of a thing or event: adverse, unpropitious. **LME–E18.**
3 a Contrary to the accepted standard or practice; incorrect; wrong. **M16.** ▸**b** Of a verdict: against the weight of evidence or the direction of the judge on a point of law. **M19.**
■ **perversely** *adverb* **M16. perverseness** *noun* **M16. perversity** *noun* the quality or character of being perverse; an instance of this, a perverse characteristic or act: **LME.**

perversion /pə'vəːʃ(ə)n/ *noun.* **LME.**
[Latin *perversio(n-)*, from *pervers-* pa. ppl stem of *pervertere*: see **PERVERT** *verb*, **-ION.**]
1 The action of perverting someone or something; the state of being perverted; turning aside from truth or right; diversion to an improper use; (a) corruption, (a) distortion; a perverted or corrupted form *of* something. **LME.**
2 Preference for an abnormal form of sexual activity; sexual deviance. Also, (an) abnormal or deviant sexual activity or behaviour. **L19.**

pervert /'pəːvəːt/ *noun.* **M17.**
[App. absol. use of next.]
A perverted person; *spec.* (***a***) *arch.* an apostate; (***b***) a sexually perverted person.

†**pervert** *adjective.* **LME–M16.**
[Perh. abbreviation of **PERVERTED.**]
Perverted, perverse; wicked.

pervert /pə'vəːt/ *verb.* **LME.**
[Old French *pervertir* or Latin *pervertere* turn round or the wrong way, overturn, ruin, corrupt, formed as **PER-**[1] + *vertere* turn.]
▶ **I** *verb trans.* †**1** Turn upside down; upset, overthrow; ruin. **LME–M17.**
2 Divert from the proper course, use, aim, etc.; misuse, misapply; wilfully misconstrue. **LME.**
3 *spec.* Turn (a person, the mind, etc.) away from right belief, opinion, or action; lead astray; corrupt. **LME.**
†**4** Turn aside, deflect. *rare* (Shakes.). Only in **E17.**
▶ **II** *verb intrans.* **5** Deviate from the right path; apostatize. **LME.**
■ **perversive** *adjective* (***a***) *rare* tending to turn awry or distort; (***b***) having the character or quality of perverting someone or something in nature, character, or use: **L17. perverted** *adjective* (***a***) that has been perverted; (***b***) exhibiting or practising perversion: **LME. pervertedly** *adverb* **E19. pervertedness** *noun* **E19. perverter** *noun* **L15. pervertible** *adjective* **L15.**

†**pervestigation** *noun.* **E17–E18.**
[Latin *pervestigatio(n-)*, from *pervestigat-* pa. ppl stem of *pervestigare* trace out, formed as **PER-**[1] + *vestigare* track, trace: see **-ATION.**]
Diligent investigation.

pervicacious /pəːvɪ'keɪʃəs/ *adjective.* **M17.**
[Latin *pervicac-*, *pervicax*, from *pervic-* base of *pervincere*, formed as **PER-**[1] + *vincere* conquer, prevail against: see **-IOUS.**]
Very obstinate or stubborn; headstrong, wilful; refractory.
■ **pervicaciously** *adverb* **M16. pervicaciousness** *noun* the quality or state of being pervicacious **L16. pervicacity** /-'kasɪti/ *noun* (now *rare*) pervicaciousness **E17.** †**pervicacy** *noun* pervicaciousness **M16–M18.**

pervious /'pəːvɪəs/ *adjective.* **E17.**
[from Latin *pervius*, formed as **PER-**[1] + *via* way: see **-OUS.**]
1 Allowing passage through; affording passage or entrance; permeable. **E17.** ▸**b** *fig.* Readily intelligible; (of a person or the mind) open to influence or argument. **E17.**
2 Penetrating, permeating; pervasive. Now *rare.* **L17.**
■ **perviousness** *noun* **M17.**

†**perwinkle**, †**perwynke** *nouns* see **PERIWINKLE** *noun*[1].

perylene /'pɛrɪliːn/ *noun.* **E20.**
[from *per(idinaphth)ylene* (indicating the structure, with two naphthalene molecules fused to a central ring): see **-ENE.**]
CHEMISTRY. A yellow solid hydrocarbon, $C_{20}H_{12}$, whose molecule consists of five fused aromatic rings and from which certain pigments are derived.

pes /peɪz, piːz/ *noun.* Pl. **pedes** /'pɛdeɪz, -iːz/. **LME.**
[Latin = foot.]
1 *MUSIC.* A short repeating bass or tenor part in a song, *spec.* that in 'Sumer is icumen in'. **LME.**
2 *ANATOMY & ZOOLOGY.* The terminal segment of the hind limb of a vertebrate animal; the foot. Cf. **MANUS** 2. **M19.**
2 pes cavus /'keɪvəs, 'kɑːvəs/ [Latin *cavus* hollow] claw foot. **pes planus** /'pleɪnəs, 'plɑːnəs/ [Latin *planus* flat] flat foot.

Pesach /'pɛsak, *foreign* -x/ *noun.* **E17.**
[Hebrew *pesaḥ*.]
= **PASSOVER** 1.

pesade /pəzad (*pl. same*), pə'zɑːd/ *noun.* **E18.**
[French, alt. of *posade* from Italian *posata* lit. 'pause, resting', from *posare* to pause, from Latin *pausare*: see **-ADE.**]
A dressage movement (now superseded by the levade) in which the horse raises its forequarters high and balances on its hind legs which are deeply bent.

pesage /'pɛsɪdʒ/ *noun.* **LME.**
[Old French, from *peser*: see next, **-AGE.**]
Hist. A duty imposed in the Middle Ages for the service of weighing goods.

pesanteur /pəzɑ̃tœːr/ *noun. rare.* **L15.**
[French, from *pesant* pres. pple of *peser* weigh: see **POISE** *verb*, **-ANT**[1], **-OR.**]
Heaviness; weight.
¶ Formerly naturalized.

Pesaro /pɛ'sɑːrəʊ/ *adjective.* **M19.**
[A city in N. Italy.]
Designating majolica made in the 15th and 16th cents. at Pesaro.

peseta /pə'seɪtə/ *noun.* **E19.**
[Spanish, dim. of *pesa* weight from Latin *pensa* pl. of *pensum* neut. pa. pple of *pendere* weigh: cf. **PESO.** See also **PISTAREEN.**]
Orig., a Spanish silver coin. Now, the basic monetary unit of Spain, equal to 100 céntimos (replaced by the euro in 2002).

pesewa /pɛ'siːwə/ *noun.* **M20.**
[Fante *pesewa*, Twi *pέsewa* = penny.]
A monetary unit of Ghana, equal to one-hundredth of a cedi.

peshcush /'pɛʃkʊʃ/ *noun.* **M17.**
[Persian *pēškaš* first drawn, first-fruits, tribute, from *pēš* before, in front + *kā* drawing.]
Hist. In Eastern countries: an offering, a present, a tribute.

Peshitta /pə'ʃiːtə/ *noun.* Also **Peshito** /pə'ʃiːtəʊ/. **L18.**
[Syriac *pšīṭtā* lit. 'the simple or plain'.]
The principal ancient Syriac version of the Bible.

peshmerga /pɛʃ'məːgə/ *noun.* Pl. **-s**, same. **M20.**
[from Kurdish *pêshmerge* from *pêsh* before, in front of + *merg* death.]
A member of a Kurdish nationalist guerrilla organization.

peshwa /'pɛʃwɑː/ *noun.* **L17.**
[Persian *pišwā* chief.]
INDIAN HISTORY. The chief minister of the Maratha princes from *c* 1660. Also, the hereditary monarch of the Maratha State from 1749 to 1818.
■ **peshwaship** *noun* the rule or office of peshwa **L18.**

pesky /'pɛski/ *adjective & adverb. colloq.* (orig. *US*). **L18.**
[Perh. rel. to **PEST.**]
▶ **A** *adjective.* Confounded; annoying, tiresome; troublesome. **L18.**
▶ **B** *adverb.* Peskily. **M19.**
■ **peskily** *adverb* confoundedly **M19. peskiness** *noun* irksomeness, tiresomeness, disagreeableness **M20.**

peso /'peɪsəʊ/ *noun.* Pl. **-os.** **M16.**
[Spanish = weight, (a coin of) a certain weight of precious metal, from Latin *pensum*: see **PESETA.**]
Orig., a gold or silver coin current in Spain and its colonies. Now, (a note or coin representing) the basic monetary unit of Chile, Colombia, Cuba, the Dominican Republic, Mexico, Uruguay, Argentina, Guinea-Bissau and the Philippines, equal to 100 centésimos in Uruguay and 100 centavos elsewhere.

pess /pɛs/ *noun.* Long *obsolete* exc. *dial.* **L16.**
[Origin unkn.]
= **HASSOCK** 2.

For other words beginning with *per-* see the entry for **per-**[1]

pessary /'pɛs(ə)ri/ *noun.* **LME.**
[Late Latin *pessarium*, repl. *pessulum* dim. of *pessum*, from Greek *pessos*, *-on* pessary, oval stone used in board games: see **-ARY**[1].]
MEDICINE. **1** A medicated plug (orig. of wool, lint, etc.,) to be inserted in an opening in the body. Now only *spec.* a vaginal suppository, used to treat infection or as a contraceptive. **LME.**
2 An elastic or rigid device, freq. ring-shaped, placed in the vagina to support the uterus, or as a contraceptive. **M18.**

pessimal /'pɛsɪm(ə)l/ *adjective.* **M20.**
[from Latin *pessimus* worst + **-AL**[1].]
Worst, least favourable; at the worst possible extreme. Opp. **OPTIMAL.**

pessimise *verb* var. of **PESSIMIZE.**

pessimism /'pɛsɪmɪz(ə)m/ *noun.* **L18.**
[from Latin *pessimus* worst + **-ISM**, after **OPTIMISM.**]
†**1** The worst possible state, condition, or degree. **L18–E19.**
2 The tendency to take a gloomy view of circumstances or prospects; hopelessness about the future. **E19.**
3 The doctrine that this world is the worst of all possible worlds; the belief that everything naturally tends to evil. **L19.**
■ **pessimize** *verb trans.* (*rare*) make the worst of; take a pessimistic view of: **M19.**

pessimist /'pɛsɪmɪst/ *noun & adjective.* **M19.**
[formed as prec. + **-IST**: cf. French *pessimiste*.]
▶ **A** *noun.* A person inclined to pessimism. **M19.**
▶ **B** *attrib.* or as *adjective.* Pessimistic. **M19.**
■ **pessi'mistic** *adjective* pertaining to, of the nature of, or characterized by pessimism **M19. pessi'mistically** *adverb* **L19.**

pessimum /'pɛsɪməm/ *noun.* **M20.**
[Latin, neut. sing. of *pessimus* worst.]
The most unfavourable condition (orig. esp., in the habitat of an animal or plant). Freq. *attrib.* Opp. **OPTIMUM** *noun.*

pest /pɛst/ *noun.* **L15.**
[French *peste* or Latin *pestis* plague, contagious disease.]
1 A fatal epidemic disease; *spec.* bubonic plague. Now *rare.* **L15.**
2 A troublesome, annoying, or destructive person, animal, or thing; *spec.* an insect which attacks crops, livestock, etc. **E16.**
2 pest of society (a member of) a group of people regarded as behaving objectionably. ***tin pest***: see **TIN** *noun & adjective.*
Comb.: †**pest-cart**: for carrying away corpses during a plague; **pest-house** *Hist.* a hospital for people with an infectious disease, esp. the plague. **pest officer**: responsible for the control or extermination of animal pests; **pest-ship** *Hist.* a ship having a contagious disease, esp. the plague, on board.
■ †**pestful** *adjective* pestiferous, pestilential **E17–L18. pesty** *adjective* (*US colloq.*) obnoxious, troublesome, annoying **M20.**

pesta /'pɛstə/ *noun.* **M20.**
[Malay & Indonesian from Portuguese *festa*.]
In Malaysia: a festive gathering, a festival.

Pestalozzian /pɛstə'lɒtsɪən/ *adjective.* **E19.**
[from *Pestalozzi* (1746–1827), Swiss educational reformer + **-AN.**]
Of or pertaining to the system of elementary education devised by Jean Henri Pestalozzi in order to develop children's faculties in natural order, beginning with the perceptual powers.
■ **Pestalozzi** *adjective* designating any of several village communities for refugee and homeless children established on Pestalozzian principles in Switzerland and elsewhere in Europe after the war of 1939–45 **M20.**

peste /pɛst/ *interjection & verb.* **M18.**
[As interjection from French *peste* (see **PEST**); as verb from French *pester*.]
▶ **A** *interjection.* Expr. annoyance. *arch.* **M18.**
▶ **B** *verb trans.* Invoke a plague on. Now *rare* or *obsolete.* **E19.**

pester /'pɛstə/ *noun.* **L16.**
[from next.]
†**1** (An) obstruction; (an) encumbrance. **L16–E17.**
2 (An) annoyance; a nuisance. Long *rare.* **E17.**

pester /'pɛstə/ *verb trans.* **M16.**
[French *empestrer*, later infl. by **PEST.** Cf. **IMPEST.**]
1 a Clog, entangle; obstruct, encumber; impede (a person); overcrowd (a place). Long *obsolete* exc. *Scot.* **M16.** ▸†**b** Crowd or huddle (persons or things *in* or *into*). **L16–L17.**
2 Orig. (of vermin, wild beasts, etc.), infest. Now, plague, annoy, trouble, esp. with frequent or persistent questions or requests. **M16.**
■ †**pesterable** *adjective* (esp. of wares) cumbersome, bulky, obstructive **M16–E17. pesterer** *noun* **E17. pesterment** *noun* (*obsolete* exc. *dial.*) the action of pestering; the fact of being pestered; annoyance, worry: **L16. pesterous** *adjective* (*rare*) having the quality of pestering, troublesome **M16. pestersome** *adjective* annoying, troublesome **M19.**

pesticide /'pɛstɪsʌɪd/ *noun.* **M20.**
[from **PEST** + **-I-** + **-CIDE.**]
A substance for destroying pests, esp. insects; occas., a herbicide.

■ **pestiˈcidal** *adjective* M20.

pestiferous /pɛˈstɪf(ə)rəs/ *adjective.* LME.
[In branch I from Latin *pestifer*, from *pestis* plague + *-fer*: see -FEROUS. In branch II from French *pestiféré*.]
▶ **I 1** Bringing or producing plague, pestilent; harmful, noxious, deadly. LME.
2 *fig.* Bearing moral contagion; pernicious. Now also (*colloq.*), irritating, annoying, constituting a pest or nuisance. LME.
▶ **II 3** Afflicted with a contagious disease, esp. the plague. M17.
■ **pestiferously** *adverb* M19.

pestilence /ˈpɛstɪl(ə)ns/ *noun.* ME.
[Old & mod. French from Latin *pestilentia*, formed as next: see -ENCE.]
1 A fatal epidemic disease affecting people or animals. ME. ▸**b** *spec.* (Bubonic) plague. LME.
2 *fig.* Something morally pernicious; evil conduct, wickedness. Now *rare.* ME.
†**3** A cause of trouble or injury. LME–M16.
Phrases: †**a pestilence on —!**, †**a pestilence upon —!** may a plague strike —!
Comb.: †**pestilence-wort** the plant butterbur, *Petasites hybridus*, formerly regarded as a specific against plague.

pestilent /ˈpɛstɪl(ə)nt/ *adjective, noun, & adverb.* LME.
[Latin *pestilent-*, *-ens*, from *pestis* plague: see -ENT.]
▶ **A** *adjective.* **1** Destructive to life; deadly; poisonous. LME.
2 Carrying, producing, or tending to produce infectious disease. Long *rare* or *obsolete.* E16.
3 *fig.* Harmful or dangerous to morals or public order; noxious; pernicious. E16.
4 Of the nature of a nuisance; troublesome, annoying. *colloq.* L16.
▶†**B** *noun.* A pestilent thing or person; a pestilence. LME–L16.
▶†**C** *adverb.* Confoundedly. M16–L17.
■ **pestilently** *adverb* E16.

pestilential /pɛstɪˈlɛnʃ(ə)l/ *adjective.* LME.
[medieval Latin *pestilentialis*, from Latin *pestilentia* PESTILENCE: see -AL[1].]
1 Of the nature of or pertaining to pestilence or epidemic disease, esp. bubonic plague. LME.
2 Producing or tending to produce pestilence or epidemic; infectious, unhealthy. LME.
3 Morally harmful or pernicious. M16.
4 = PESTILENT 4. *colloq.* L19.
1 †**pestilential fever** typhus.
■ **pestilentially** *adverb* M17. †**pestilentious** *adjective* = PESTILENTIAL LME–M18.

pestle /ˈpɛs(ə)l/ *noun.* ME.
[Old French *pestel* from Latin *pistillum*, from *pist-* pa. ppl stem of *pinsere* pound: see -LE[2].]
1 The leg of any of various animals, esp. the pig, used as food. *obsolete* exc. *dial.* ME.
2 A usu. club-shaped instrument for crushing or pounding substances (as herbs, spices, drugs, chemicals, etc.) in a mortar (taken with the mortar as the symbol of the apothecary's profession). ME.
†**3** The thickened spadix of plants of the arum family. L16–L17.
4 Any of various mechanical devices for pounding, stamping, pressing, etc., esp. in a mill. E17.

pestle /ˈpɛs(ə)l/ *verb.* LME.
[Old French *pesteler*, from *pestel*: see prec.]
1 *verb trans.* Beat, pound, or triturate (as) with a pestle. Also *fig.* LME.
2 *verb intrans.* Work *away* at something with a pestle. M19.

pesto /ˈpɛstəʊ/ *noun.* M20.
[Italian, contr. of *pestato* pa. pple of *pestare* pound, crush.]
A sauce of crushed basil, nuts (esp. pine nuts), cheese, garlic, and olive oil, served with pasta and other foods. Cf. PISTOU.

pestology /pɛˈstɒlədʒi/ *noun.* E20.
[from PEST + -OLOGY.]
The branch of science that deals with pests and methods of dealing with them.
■ **pestoˈlogical** *adjective* E20. **pestologist** *noun* E20.

PET *abbreviation.*
1 Polyethylene terephthalate.
2 Positron emission tomography.

pet /pɛt/ *noun*[1] *& adjective.* Orig. *Scot. & north.* E16.
[Origin unkn.]
▶ **A** *noun.* **1** An indulged or spoiled child; any person indulged or treated as a favourite; an obedient or obliging person (freq. as a term of endearment). Formerly also, (a name for) a person who is a favourite boxer. E16. ▸**b** In full *pet-day*. A fine sunny day in the middle of a period of bad weather. *Scot., Anglo-Irish, & Canad.* E19.
2 An animal domesticated or tamed and kept for pleasure or companionship; *spec.* (*Scot. & north.*) a lamb brought up by hand. M16.

> 🕮 **1** P. G. WODEHOUSE Do be a pet and . . talk to Jane Hubbard . . . She must be feeling lonely. N. PODHORETZ I was the special pet of numerous relatives. W. TREVOR 'Are you rested, pet?' her mother inquired. ***TEACHER's pet.***

▶ **B** *adjective.* **1** Of an animal: kept as a pet. L16.
2 Favourite, particular. E19. ▸**b** That causes or involves especial dislike. *joc.* L19.

> 🕮 **1** *Beano* I need the services of Joe, my pet crow! **2** C. BROOKE-ROSE I mustn't bore you with my pet theories. S. NAIPAUL Ralph had . . succeeded in establishing himself as his pet architect. **b** ***pet aversion, pet hate, pet peeve***, etc.

Comb. & special collocations: **pet-day**: see sense A.1b above; **pet-food**: for pet animals; **pet-form** an alteration of a name used as a pet name; **pet name** a name expressing fondness or familiarity; **pet-name** *verb trans.* call by a pet name; **pets' corner** a part of a zoo etc. for animals normally kept as pets; **pet-shop**: selling animals to be kept as pets; **pet-sitter** a person who takes care of someone's pet(s) whilst they are away.

pet /pɛt/ *noun*[2]. L16.
[Origin unkn.]
Offence at being or feeling slighted; a fit of esp. childish sulking or peevishness from this cause.

pet /pɛt/ *verb*[1]. Orig. *Scot. & north.* Infl. **-tt-**. E17.
[from PET *noun*[1].]
1 *verb trans.* Treat as a pet or with favouritism; indulge; fondle. E17.
2 *verb trans.* Stroke (an animal). E19.
3 *verb intrans.* Engage in erotic caressing and other esp. genital stimulation with or *with* another person. E20.

> 🕮 **1** H. T. LANE He realized she was in pain . . and he began . . to pet and comfort her. L. APPIGNANESI Petted and pampered . . she . . developed a sense of her own specialness. **2** S. BELLOW The cats . . came to be petted. **petting zoo** *N. Amer.*: at which visitors (esp. children) may handle and feed the animals. **3** N. MAILER To play the bobby-soxer who petted with a date in the living room. N. SEDAKA Sat in the back seat kissing and petting. ***heavy petting***: see HEAVY *adjective*.

pet /pɛt/ *verb*[2]. *obsolete* exc. *Scot.* Infl. **-tt-**. E17.
[from PET *noun*[2].]
1 *verb intrans.* Take offence at the way one is treated; sulk. E17.
2 *verb trans.* Cause to take offence. E19.

Pet. *abbreviation.*
Peter (New Testament).

PETA /ˈpiːtə/ *abbreviation.*
People for the Ethical Treatment of Animals.

peta- /ˈpɛtə/ *combining form.* L20.
[from PE(N)TA-, 10^{15} being $(10^3)^5$, suggested by the supposed analogy of *tera-*, *tetra-*: cf. EXA-.]
Used in names of units of measurement to denote a factor of 10^{15}, as ***petabyte***, ***petaelectronvolt***, etc. Abbreviation ***P***.

Pétainism /ˈpɛtanɪz(ə)m/ *noun.* M20.
[French *pétainisme*, from *Pétain* (see below): see -ISM.]
Hist. The policy pursued by the French military commander and head of government Henri Philippe Pétain (1856–1951) of collaborating with the German occupying forces in France during the war of 1939–45; *transf.* any policy of political collaboration.
■ **Pétainist** *adjective & noun* (*a*) *adjective* of, pertaining to, or supporting Pétainism; (*b*) *noun* a supporter of Pétainism: M20.

petal /ˈpɛt(ə)l/ *noun & verb.* E18.
[mod. Latin *petalum* from late Latin = metal plate from Greek *petalon* lamina, leaf, use as noun of neut. of *petalos* outspread, from base *pet-* as in *petannusthai* unfold.]
▶ **A** *noun.* **1** BOTANY. Each of the individual divisions (modified leaves) of the corolla, typically coloured and differentiated from the green sepals. E18.
2 ZOOLOGY. (The dilated end of) a petaloid ambulacrum. L19.
Comb.: **petal collar** a collar cut in the shape of petals; **petal ware** a type of Byzantine pottery characterized by petal-shaped decorations.
▶ **B** *verb trans.* Infl. **-ll-**, **-l-**. Provide or scatter with petals. *poet.* E20.
■ **petalled**, **petaled** *adjective* (*a*) adorned (as) with petals; resembling a petal or petals; (*b*) having petals of a specified kind or number: L18. **petalless** /-l-l-/ *adjective* E19. **petal-like** *adjective* resembling a petal E19.

petala *noun* pl. of PETALON.

petaliferous /pɛtəˈlɪf(ə)rəs/ *adjective.* M19.
[formed as PETAL *noun* + -I- + -FEROUS.]
Having petals.

petaline /ˈpɛt(ə)lʌɪn/ *adjective.* L18.
[mod. Latin *petalinus*, from *petalum* PETAL *noun*: see -INE[1].]
Pertaining to a petal; consisting of petals.

petalism /ˈpɛt(ə)lɪz(ə)m/ *noun.* E17.
[Greek *petalismos*, from *petalon* leaf: see PETAL *noun*, -ISM.]
Hist. The custom of temporary banishment practised in ancient Syracuse, similar to the ostracism of ancient Greece, but using olive-leaves rather than potsherds.

petalite /ˈpɛt(ə)lʌɪt/ *noun.* E19.
[from Greek *petalon* leaf + -ITE[1].]
MINERALOGY. A lithium aluminosilicate, occurring as whitish or greyish masses with a leaflike cleavage and used in some ceramics.

petalody /ˈpɛt(ə)ləʊdi/ *noun.* M19.
[from Greek *petalōdēs* leaflike, from *petalon* leaf (see PETAL, -ODE[1]) + -Y[3].]
BOTANY. An abnormal condition in which the reproductive organs or other parts of a flower are transformed into petals.
■ **petaˈlodic** *adjective* M19.

petaloid /ˈpɛt(ə)lɔɪd/ *adjective.* M18.
[mod. Latin *petaloideus*, from *petalum* PETAL *noun*: see -OID.]
Of the form of or resembling a petal, esp. (BOTANY) in being of a colour other than green, and leaflike; ZOOLOGY designating the curved paired ambulacra of some irregular echinoids.
■ Also **petaloidal** *adjective* L19.

petalon /ˈpɛtəlɒn/ *noun.* Pl. ***-la*** /-lə/. L17.
[Greek: see PETAL.]
The gold plate worn on the mitre of a Jewish high priest.

pétanque /petɑ̃k, pəˈtaŋk/ *noun.* M20.
[French.]
A game similar to boules.

petard /pɪˈtɑːd/ *noun.* M16.
[French *pétard*, from *péter* break wind: see -ARD.]
Hist. **1** A small bomb made of a metal or wooden box filled with powder, used to blow in a door etc. or to make a hole in a wall. M16.
2 A kind of firework that explodes with a sharp report, a cracker. M17.
1 ***hoist with one's own petard***: see HOIST.
■ **petarˈdeer**, **-ier** *noun* a soldier in charge of firing a petard M17.

petasma /pɛˈtazmə/ *noun.* L19.
[mod. Latin from Greek = something spread out, from *pet-*: see PETAL.]
ZOOLOGY. A membranous appendage attached to the first pair of pleopods in male penaeid prawns.

petasus /ˈpɛtəsəs/ *noun.* L16.
[Latin from Greek *petasos*, from *pet-*: see PETAL.]
A hat with a low crown and broad brim, worn in ancient Greece; *spec.* (GREEK MYTHOLOGY) such a hat, or a brimless hat with wings, represented as worn by the god Hermes.

petaurist /pɪˈtɔːrɪst/ *noun.* M17.
[Greek *petauristēs* springboard performer, from *petauron* springboard: see -IST.]
†**1** An acrobat, a tumbler. *rare.* Only in M17.
2 ZOOLOGY. = ***flying phalanger*** s.v. FLYING *ppl adjective.* Now *rare.* M19.

petchary /ˈpɛtʃəri/ *noun.* M19.
[Imit. of its cry.]
The grey kingbird, *Tyrannus dominicensis*, of the W. Indies and the Florida coast.

pet-cock /ˈpɛtkɒk/ *noun.* M19.
[App. from PET *noun*[1] + COCK *noun*[1].]
A small plug-cock fastened in a pipe or cylinder for drainage or testing.

Pete /piːt/ *noun.* In senses 2, 3 also **p-**. E20.
[Dim. of PETER *noun*[1].]
1 Used in various exclamatory phrs. expr. exasperation or annoyance. E20.
2 (Usu. **p-**.) ▸**a** A safe. *slang.* E20. ▸**b** Nitroglycerine as used for safe-breaking. *slang.* M20.
3 ***sneaky Pete***, illicit or cheap intoxicating drink. *slang* (chiefly *US*). M20.
1 ***for Pete's sake***: see SAKE *noun*[1].

petechia /pɪˈtiːkɪə/ *noun.* Pl. **-iae** /-ɪiː/. L18.
[mod. Latin from Italian *petecchie* (pl.) skin eruption, from popular Latin dim. of Latin *petigo* scab, eruption.]
MEDICINE. A small flat red or purple spot caused by bleeding into the skin, on the surface of an organ, etc. Usu. in *pl.*
■ **petechial** *adjective* of, pertaining to, or characterized by petechiae E18. **petechiate** *adjective* marked or affected by petechiae L19.

peter /ˈpiːtə/ *noun*[1]. In sense 1 & many combs. **P-**. LME.
[Male forename from ecclesiastical Latin *Petrus* from ecclesiastical Greek *Petros* lit. 'stone', translating Palestinian Aramaic *kēpā* the rock, surname of Simon given by Jesus (*Matthew* 16:18).]
†**1** The name of one of the Apostles, used in asseverations. Only in LME.
2 *slang.* **a** A trunk, a suitcase; a bundle. M17. ▸**b** A safe, a cash-box; a till. M19. ▸**c** A prison cell; a prison. L19. ▸**d** A stupefying drug. *US.* L19. ▸**e** The penis. E20.
3 BRIDGE & WHIST. = ECHO *noun* 6. L19.
Comb. & phrases: ***Blue Peter***: see BLUE *adjective*; **peter-boat** *dial.* [with allus. to St Peter's occupation as a fisherman] (*a*) a small decked fishing boat; (*b*) a dredger's reversible boat; **Peter-fish** = ***St Peter's fish*** s.v. SAINT *adjective & noun*; **Peter Grievous** *noun &*

adjective (*dial.*) (designating) a person who complains or whines; **Peternet** a kind of fishing net stretched from the shore with the other end anchored in the sea; **Peter-penny** = ***Peter's pence*** below; **Peter's fish** = ***St Peter's fish*** s.v. SAINT *adjective & noun*; **Peter's pence**, **Peter's penny** (*a*) *Hist.* an annual tax of one penny from each householder having land of a certain value, paid until the Reformation to the papal see; (*b*) since 1860, a voluntary payment to the papal treasury; **Petertide** (the period around) 29 June, the feast of St Peter in the Church of England and of St Peter and St Paul in the Roman Catholic and Orthodox Churches; **rob Peter to pay Paul** take away from one person to pay another; discharge one debt by incurring another; ***St Peter's fish***, ***St Peter's wort***: see SAINT *noun & adjective*.

peter *noun*[2] var. of PETRE.

peter /ˈpiːtə/ *verb*. E19.
[Origin uncertain. In senses 3, 4 cf. prec.]
1 *verb trans.* Cease, stop doing. *slang*. E19.
2 *verb intrans.* (Orig. of a vein of ore) diminish or come to an end gradually. Usu. foll. by *out*. E19. ▸**b** *verb trans.* Exhaust (foll. by *out*); squander (foll. by *away*). Freq. as ***petered*** *ppl adjective*. M19.
3 *verb intrans.* WHIST & BRIDGE. = ECHO *verb* 5. L19.
4 *verb trans.* Blow open (a safe). *slang*. E20.

📖 **2** V. WOOLF The music petered out on the last word. H. CARPENTER Where the lane petered out into a mere path.

Peterborough /ˈpiːtəbʌrə/ *noun & adjective*[1]. *N. Amer.* Also **Peterboro**, pl. **-os**. L19.
[A city in Ontario, Canada.]
(Designating) a type of all-wood canoe originally built at Peterborough in Canada.

Peterborough /ˈpiːtəbʌrə/ *adjective*[2]. E20.
[A city in eastern England, the location of certain sites of the neolithic age.]
Designating or belonging to a type of neolithic pottery decorated with impressed patterns; formerly also designating a culture regarded as characterized by this pottery.

†**peterero** *noun* var. of PEDRERO.

peterman /ˈpiːtəmən/ *noun*. Pl. **-men**. LME.
[from PETER *noun*[1], in sense 1 with allus. to St Peter's occupation as a fisherman.]
1 A fisherman. Formerly *spec.*, one engaged in some particular kind of fishing. LME.
2 *slang*. **a** A person who steals trunks or cases from vehicles. Now *rare*. E19. ▸**b** A robber who drugs his or her victim. L19. ▸**c** A safe-blower. E20.

Peter Pan /piːtə ˈpan/ *noun*. E20.
[The hero of J. M. Barrie's play *Peter Pan, the boy who wouldn't grow up* (1904).]
A person who retains youthful features or who is immature.
Comb.: **Peter Pan collar** a flat collar with rounded points.
■ **Peter Pannish**, **Peter Panish** *adjective* childish, immature E20. **Peter Pannishness**, **Peter Panishness** *noun* E20.

Peter principle /ˈpiːtə ˌprɪnsɪp(ə)l/ *noun phr.* M20.
[Laurence Johnston *Peter* (1919–90), US educationalist and author, who propounded it.]
The principle that members of a hierarchy are promoted until they reach a level at which they are no longer competent.

Peters /ˈpiːtəz/ *noun*. L20.
[Arno *Peters* (b. 1916), German historian.]
Peters projection, ***Peters' projection***, a world map projection in which areas are shown in correct proportion at the expense of distorted shape, using a rectangular decimal grid to replace latitude and longitude.
¶ Devised to be a fairer representation of equatorial countries (i.e. most developing countries), whose area is under-represented by the usual projections such as Mercator's.

Petersen grab /ˈpiːtəs(ə)n ˈgrab/ *noun phr.* E20.
[C. G. J. *Petersen* (1860–1928), Danish marine biologist.]
A kind of grab for obtaining a sample of the bed of a body of water, consisting of two semicircular hinged jaws which close automatically on contact with the bottom.

Petersen graph /ˈpiːtəs(ə)n ˈgrɑːf/ *noun phr.* M20.
[Julius *Petersen* (1839–1910), Danish mathematician.]
MATH. A graph having ten vertices and fifteen lines, which may be drawn as a pentagram within a pentagon, each vertex of the latter being joined by a line to the nearest vertex of the former.

petersham /ˈpiːtəʃ(ə)m/ *noun*. E19.
[Viscount *Petersham* (1790–1851), English army officer.]
1 *Hist.* **a** In *pl.* Wide trousers gathered at the ankle to form a flounce, fashionable during the Regency period in Britain. Also ***Petersham trousers***. E19. ▸**b** A kind of heavy overcoat with a short shoulder cape, fashionable during the Regency period in Britain; a thick woollen fabric used to make such coats. M19.
2 A narrow heavy ribbed cotton or silk used for strengthening, esp. of belts and hatbands. L19.

Peterson /ˈpiːtəs(ə)n/ *noun*. M20.
[Manufacturer's name.]
In full ***Peterson pipe***. (Proprietary name for) a type of tobacco-pipe.

peth *noun* see PATH *noun*[1].

pethidine /ˈpɛθɪdiːn/ *noun*. M20.
[from P(IPER)IDINE with insertion of ETH(YL).]
PHARMACOLOGY. A painkilling drug given esp. during childbirth which has actions similar to those of morphine but of shorter duration.
¶ A proprietary name for this drug is DEMEROL.

pétillant /petijɑ̃, ˈpeɪtɪjɒ̃/ *adjective*. L19.
[French, formed as next: see -ANT[1].]
Sparkling, lively. Of wine: slightly sparkling.
■ ***pétillance*** *noun* M20.

petillate /ˈpɛtɪleɪt/ *verb intrans. rare*. M19.
[French *pétiller* dim. of *péter* break wind: see -ATE[3].]
Effervesce.

petiole /ˈpɛtɪəʊl/ *noun*. M18.
[mod. Latin *petiolus* from Latin var. of *peciolus* little foot, fruit-stalk: see -OLE[1].]
1 BOTANY. The stalk of a leaf, by which it is attached to the stem. M18.
2 ZOOLOGY. A slender stalk between two structures, as the eye-stalk of some crustaceans, the stalk connecting the abdomen and thorax in wasps, ants, and other insects, etc. L18.
■ **petiolar** *adjective* pertaining to or of the nature of a petiole M18. **petiolate**, **petiolated** *adjectives* having a petiole, stalked (opp. *sessile*) M18. **petioled** *adjective* = PETIOLATE L18.

petiolule /ˈpɛtɪəljuːl/ *noun*. M19.
[mod. Latin *petiolulus* dim. of *petiolus*: see PETIOLE, -ULE.]
BOTANY. The stalk of a leaflet in a compound leaf.
■ **petiˈolulate** *adjective* having a petiolule L19.

petit /ˈpɛti/ *adjective*[1] & *noun*. *obsolete* exc. in phrs. ME.
[formed as PETTY *adjective*. Cf. next.]
▶ **A** *adjective*. †**1** Of small size; small in number. ME–L17.
†**2** = PETTY *adjective* 3. LME–M18.
3 = PETTY *adjective* 2. L15.
Special collocations: ***petit jury*** = ***petty jury*** s.v. PETTY *adjective*. ***petit treason***: see TREASON *noun* 2b.
▶ **B** *noun*. †**1** = PETTY *noun*[1] 1a. LME–L17.
†**2** A variety of the domestic pigeon. *rare*. Only in E18.

petit /pəti, pəˈtiː, ˈpɛti; same in pl. collocations/ *adjective*[2]. E18.
[French: see PETTY *adjective* and cf. prec. Cf. PETITE.]
The French (masc.) for 'little, small', occurring in various phrases used in English.
■ ***petit battement*** /batmɑ̃/, pl. **-s -s** (pronounced same), a battement executed with the moving leg bent E20. ***petit beurre*** /bœːr/, pl. **-s -s** (pronounced same), a sweet butter biscuit E20. ***petit bleu*** /blø/, pl. **-s -s** (pronounced same), (in France) a telegram E20. ***petit déjeuner*** /deʒøne (*pl. same*), ˈdeɪʒəneɪ/, pl. **-s -s** (pronounced same), breakfast in France or elsewhere L19. ***petit grain*** /grɛ̃ (*pl. same*), greɪn/, pl. **-s -s** (pronounced same) [lit. 'little grain', from the small green fruits originally used], any of various essential oils with a floral scent, distilled from parts of the orange tree and other citrus plants, and used in perfumery M19. ***petit-maître*** /pətimɛtr/, pl. ***petits-maîtres*** (pronounced same), [lit. 'little master'] (*a*) a dandy, a fop, a coxcomb; (*b*) a musician, writer, etc., of minor importance: E18. ***petit pain*** /pɛ̃/, pl. **-s -s** (pronounced same), a small bread roll M18. ***petit point*** /pwɛ̃, pwã, pɔɪnt/ (*a*) embroidery on canvas using small stitches; (*b*) tent-stitch: L19. ***petit poussin*** /pusɛ̃/ (now *rare*) (pl. **-s -s**, pronounced same) = POUSSIN E20. ***petits chevaux*** /pəti ʃəvo/ a gambling game in which bets are placed on mechanical horses made to spin round a flag at the centre of a special table L19. ***petits soins*** /swɛ̃/ small attentions or services E19. ***petit souper*** /pəti supe/ (now *rare*), pl. **-s -s** (pronounced same), a small informal dinner party M18. ***petit suisse*** /sɥis, swiːs/ a small round cream cheese E20. ***petit tranchet*** /trɑ̃ʃɛ, trɑːnʃɪt/ ARCHAEOLOGY a small stone artefact of mesolithic and neolithic cultures with the end made into a broad cutting edge M20. ***petit verre*** /vɛːr/, pl. **-s -s** (pronounced same), a glass of liqueur M19.

petit bourgeois /pɛtɪ ˈbʊəʒwɑː, pəˌtiː; *foreign* pəti burʒwa/ *noun & adjectival phr.* Pl. **petits bourgeois** (pronounced same). Fem. **petite bourgeoise** /pəˌtiːt ˈbʊəʒwɑːz, *foreign* pətit burʒwaːz/, pl. **-s -s** (pronounced same). M19.
[French, lit. 'little citizen': see prec., BOURGEOIS *adjective & noun*[2].]
▶ **A** *noun phr.* A member of the lower middle classes; *derog.* a person judged to have conventional or conservative attitudes. M19.
▶ **B** *adjectival phr.* Pertaining to or characteristic of the petite bourgeoisie; lower middle class; conventional. L19.

📖 G. CLARE From *petit bourgeois* backgrounds, the sons of shopkeepers and minor employees.

petite /pəˈtiːt, *foreign* pətit/ *adjective & noun*. M16.
[French, fem. of *petit*: see PETIT *adjective*[2].]
▶ **A** *adjective*. **1** †**a** Of a small size or importance. M16–L17. ▸**b** Of small stature. Now chiefly of a woman or girl. L18. ▸**c** Designating a small size in women's clothing. E20.
2 The French (fem.) for 'little, small', occurring in various phrases used in English E18.
3 MICROBIOLOGY. Designating mutant strains of yeast that are characterized by defective mitochondrial DNA and tend to form small colonies. M20.
2 ***petite amie*** /ami/, pl. **-s -s** /pətits ami/, the usu. young female lover of a man, a mistress. ***petite marmite*** /marmit/, pl. **-s -s** (pronounced same), soup served in a marmite. ***petite morale*** /mɔral/ minor social conventions or morals. ***petite noblesse*** /nɔblɛs/ the lesser nobility in France. ***petite pièce*** /pjɛs/, pl. **-s -s** (pronounced same), a minor work by an author.
▶ **B** *noun*. **1** A petite woman or girl. M20.
2 A petite size in women's clothing. M20.
3 A petite strain of yeast. M20.
■ **petiteness** *noun* the quality of being petite L17.

petite bourgeoise *noun & adjectival phr.* see PETIT BOURGEOIS.

petite bourgeoisie /pəˌtiːt bʊəʒwɑːˈziː, *foreign* pətit burʒwazi/ *noun phr.* E20.
[French, formed as PETITE + BOURGEOISIE.]
The lower middle classes collectively.

petit four /pɛti ˈfɔː; *foreign* pəti fuːr/ *noun phr.* Pl. **petits fours** /pɛti ˈfɔːz; *foreign* pəti fuːr/. L19.
[French, lit. 'little oven': see PETIT *adjective*[2].]
A small cake or biscuit usu. served with the coffee after a meal.

petition /pɪˈtɪʃ(ə)n/ *noun*. ME.
[Old & mod. French *pétition* from Latin *petitio(n-)*, from *petit-* pa. ppl stem of *petere* aim at, lay claim to, ask, seek: see -ION.]
1 The action of formally asking or humbly requesting; an entreaty, a supplication; a solemn prayer, *spec.* any of the clauses of such a prayer. ME. ▸**b** The subject of a formal or humble request, the thing asked or entreated. LME.
2 A formal written request, *esp.* one signed by many people appealing to a person or body in authority in some cause. LME. ▸**b** *spec.* The form in which the Houses of Parliament formerly presented a measure to the monarch for assent. *obsolete* exc. *Hist.* LME.
†**3** MATH. A postulate; an axiom. E16–L18.
4 LAW. A formal written application made to a court for a writ, judicial action in a suit, etc. M18.
Phrases: ***millenary petition***: see MILLENARY *adjective*. **Petition and Advice** ENGLISH HISTORY the Remonstrance presented by Parliament to Cromwell in 1657. **petition of right** (*a*) *Hist.* a common-law remedy against the Crown for the recovery of property; (*b*) ***Petition of Right***, the parliamentary declaration of the people's rights and liberties, presented in the form of a petition in 1627 and assented to by Charles I.
■ **petitional** *adjective* (*rare*) E17. **petitionary** *adjective* (*a*) of the nature of, constituting, or containing a petition; (*b*) *arch.* (of a person) entreating, petitioning: L16.

petition /pɪˈtɪʃ(ə)n/ *verb*. E17.
[from the noun.]
1 *verb trans.* Make or present a petition to. E17. ▸**b** Ask or beg for (a thing). M17.
2 *verb intrans.* Make or present a petition *for* a thing or *to* an authority. M17.

📖 **1** W. RAEPER MacDonald petitioned his father to send another cask. **2** LYTTON The Colonel petitioned for three days consideration.

■ **petitionable** *adjective* L19. **petitioˈnee** *noun* (*US LAW*) the party against whom a petition is filed M18.

petitioner /pɪˈtɪʃ(ə)nə/ *noun*. LME.
[from PETITION *noun* + -ER[2] (cf. Anglo-Latin *petitionarius*); later regarded as from PETITION *verb* + -ER[1].]
1 A person who makes or presents a petition. LME. ▸**b** ENGLISH HISTORY. A person who signed an address to Charles II in 1680 petitioning for the summoning of Parliament. M18.
2 LAW. A plaintiff petitioning in a suit or action. E16.

petitio principii /pɪˌtɪʃɪəʊ prɪnˈsɪpɪʌɪ, prɪŋˈkɪp-/ *noun phr.* M16.
[Latin = assuming a principle, from *petitio* (see PETITION *noun*) + genit. of PRINCIPIUM.]
LOGIC. A fallacy in which a conclusion is taken for granted in a premiss; begging the question.

petitive /ˈpɛtɪtɪv/ *adjective*. E20.
[from Latin *petit-* pa. ppl stem of *petere* (see PETITION *noun*) + -IVE.]
Of, pertaining to, or expressing a prayer or request.

petit mal /pəti ˈmal/ *noun phr.* L19.
[French, lit. 'little sickness'.]
Mild epilepsy, with only momentary loss of consciousness. Cf. GRAND MAL.

petitory /ˈpɛtɪt(ə)ri/ *adjective*. LME.
[Late Latin *petitorius*, from Latin *petitor* candidate, from *petit-*: see PETITION *noun*, -ORY[2].]
1 LAW. Orig., (of a claim) made or established by means of a petition to a court etc. Now (*Scot.*), (of a writ etc.) characterized by laying claim to something, esp. a right of ownership. LME.
2 Characterized by asking, entreating; petitionary. Now *rare*. L16.

petits bourgeois *noun phr.* pl. of PETIT BOURGEOIS.

petits pois /pəti 'pwɑː, *foreign* pəti pwa/ *noun phr. pl.* E19.
[French, lit. 'small peas': see PETIT *adjective*².]
Small young green peas.

peto /'peto/ *noun*. Pl. **-os** /-ɔs/. M20.
[Spanish.]
A padded protective covering for a picador's horse.

Petrarchan /pɪ'trɑːk(ə)n/ *adjective*. E19.
[from *Petrarch* (Italian *Petrarca*): see below, -AN.]
Of, pertaining to, characteristic of, or in the style of the Italian poet Petrarch (1304–74); *spec.* designating a sonnet with an octave rhyming *abbaabba* and a sestet usu. rhyming *cdcdcd* or *cdecde*.
■ '**Petrarchism** *noun* imitation of the style of Petrarch L19. '**Petrarchist** *noun* an imitator of Petrarch E19. '**Petrarchize** *verb intrans.* (*rare*) imitate the style of Petrarch. L16.

petrary /'pɛtrəri/ *noun*. *obsolete* exc. *Hist.* E17.
[medieval Latin *petraria*, from Latin *petra* stone: see -ARY¹. Cf. PEDRERO, PERRIER *noun*¹.]
= PEDRERO.

petre /'piːtə/ *noun*. Also **peter**. L16.
[from Latin, Greek *petra* rock; in sense 1 abbreviation of SALTPETRE.]
1 = SALTPETRE. Also †*petre-salt*. Now *rare* or *obsolete*. L16.
†**2** *oil of petre*, petroleum. M17–M18.

Petrean /pɪ'triːən/ *adjective & noun*. M17.
[from Latin *petraeus* from Greek *petraios* rocky, of the city of Petra (see below), from *petra* rock: see -EAN.]
▶ **A** *adjective*. **1** (**p-**.) Rocky; of or pertaining to rocks or stones. *rare*. M17.
2 Of or pertaining to Petra, a city in Jordan. M19.
▶ **B** *noun*. A native or inhabitant of Petra. E20.

petrefact /'pɛtrɪfakt/ *noun*. E20.
[from Latin *petra* stone, after *artefact*.]
An object made of stone.

petrel /'pɛtr(ə)l/ *noun*. E17.
[Perh. from PETER *noun*¹, with allus. to St Peter's walking on the water (see *Matthew* 14:29), + *-el* by analogy with *cockerel*, *dotterel*, etc.]
Any of a number of sea birds with mainly black (or brown) and white plumage and usu. a hooked bill, of the families Procellariidae, Pelecanoididae, and Hydrobatidae, some of which feed while seeming to walk on the sea. Freq. with specifying word.
diving petrel, ***pintado petrel***, ***snowy petrel***, ***storm petrel***, etc.

petrescent /pɪ'trɛs(ə)nt/ *adjective*. Now *rare* or *obsolete*. M17.
[from Latin *petra* stone + -ESCENT.]
Having the quality of petrifying, petrifactive.
■ **petrescence** *noun* the process of petrifying something M17.

Petri dish /'pɛtri dɪʃ, 'piːtri/ *noun phr.* Also **p-**. L19.
[R. J. *Petri* (1852–1922), German bacteriologist.]
A shallow, circular, flat-bottomed glass or plastic dish with vertical sides and a cover used to hold media for the culture of micro-organisms.

petrifaction /pɛtrɪ'fakʃ(ə)n/ *noun*. LME.
[from PETRIFY: see -FACTION.]
1 a The action of petrifying something; the condition of being petrified; conversion into stone; MEDICINE the formation of a calculus. LME. ▸**b** *fig.* A state of extreme fear or terror. E18.
2 A thing formed by being petrified; a stony mass. L17.
■ **petrifactive** *adjective* having the quality of petrifying; causing petrifaction. M17.

petrific /pɪ'trɪfɪk/ *adjective*. Now *rare*. M17.
[medieval Latin *petrificus*, from Latin *petra* stone: see PETRIFY, -FIC.]
1 Having the quality of petrifying or turning into stone; MEDICINE causing the formation of a calculus. M17.
2 Petrified, stony. E19.

petrification /ˌpɛtrɪfɪ'keɪʃ(ə)n/ *noun*. Now *rare*. E17.
[French *pétrification* or medieval Latin *petrificatio(n-)*, from *petrificat-* pa. ppl stem of *petrificare*: see next, -FICATION.]
1 a = PETRIFACTION 1a. E17. ▸**b** *fig.* = PETRIFACTION 1b. L17.
2 = PETRIFACTION 2. L17.

petrify /'pɛtrɪfʌɪ/ *verb*. LME.
[medieval Latin *petrificare*, from Latin *petra* stone: see -FY.]
1 *verb trans.* Convert into stone or a stony substance; *spec.* turn (an organic body) into a stony concretion by encrusting or more usu. replacing its original substance with a calcareous, siliceous, or other mineral deposit. LME. ▸**b** *verb intrans.* Become converted into stone or a stony substance. M17.
2 *verb trans. & intrans.* Deprive (the mind, a faculty, etc.) of feeling, vitality, or capacity for change; harden, deaden. E17.
3 *verb trans.* Make motionless or rigid with fear, astonishment, etc.; *esp.* terrify. L18.
📖 **3** P. THEROUX Large barking dogs petrify me.
■ **petrified** *adjective* that has been petrified; rigid with fear, terrified: L16.

Petrine /'piːtrʌɪn/ *adjective*. M19.
[from ecclesiastical Latin *Petrus* Peter (see PETER *noun*¹) + -INE¹.]
1 Of, pertaining to, or characteristic of St Peter. M19.
2 Of, pertaining to, or characteristic of Peter I the Great (1672–1725), tsar of Russia. E20.
■ **Petrinism** *noun* the doctrine of or attributed to St Peter, Petrine theology M19.

pétrissage /petrisaːʒ/ *noun*. L19.
[French, from *pétriss-*, *pétrir* knead: see -AGE.]
A kneading process used in massage.

petro- /'pɛtrəʊ/ *combining form*¹.
[from Greek *petros* stone, *petra* rock: see -O-.]
1 Rock.
2 ANATOMY. The petrous portion of the temporal bone, as ***petrosphenoidal***, ***petrotympanic***.
■ **petro'fabric** *adjective* of or pertaining to petrofabrics M20. **petro'fabrics** *noun* the texture and microscopic structure of a rock or rocks; the branch of geology that deals with these, esp. as guides to their past movements: M20. **petro'silex** *noun* a hard rock rich in silica L18. **petrosi'liceous** *adjective* consisting of or containing petrosilex L18. **petrotec'tonic** *adjective* of or pertaining to petrotectonics M20. **petrotec'tonics** *noun* the branch of geology that deals with the structure of rocks, esp. as a guide to their past movements M20.

petro- /'pɛtrəʊ/ *combining form*².
[Abbreviation.]
Petroleum, oil.
■ **petro-currency** *noun* the currency of a petroleum-exporting country, of which the exchange rate varies chiefly with the fluctuations of the petroleum market L20. **petrodollar** *noun* a notional monetary unit earned by a petroleum-exporting country L20.

Petrobrusian /pɛtrə(ʊ)'bruːsɪən/ *noun*. M16.
[Latin *Petrobrusiani* pl., from *Pierre de Bruys* (Latinized as *Petrus Brusianus*): see below, -IAN.]
ECCLESIASTICAL HISTORY. A follower of Pierre de Bruys, who in southern France in the early 12th cent. rejected infant baptism, transubstantiation, and the authority of the Church, and opposed the building of churches and the observance of fasts.

petrochemical /pɛtrə(ʊ)'kɛmɪk(ə)l/ *adjective & noun*. E20.
[from PETRO-¹, PETRO-² + CHEMICAL.]
▶ **A** *adjective*. Of or pertaining to petrochemistry or petrochemicals. E20.
▶ **B** *noun*. A compound or element obtained from petroleum or natural gas. Freq. ***attrib.*** in *pl.* M20.
■ **petrochemically** *adverb* M20.

petrochemistry /pɛtrə(ʊ)'kɛmɪstri/ *noun*. M20.
[from PETRO-¹, PETRO-² + CHEMISTRY.]
1 GEOLOGY. The branch of chemistry that deals with the composition and formation of rocks (as distinct from minerals, ore deposits, etc.), esp. igneous and metamorphic ones. M20.
2 The branch of chemistry that deals with petroleum and natural gas, and with their refining and processing. M20.

petrogenesis /pɛtrə(ʊ)'dʒɛnɪsɪs/ *noun*. E20.
[from PETRO-¹ + -GENESIS.]
The formation of rocks, esp. igneous and metamorphic rocks; the branch of science that deals with this.
■ **petroge'netic** *adjective* E20. **petroge'netically** *adverb* as regards petrogenesis L20. **petrogenic** *adjective* E20. **petrogeny** /pɪ'trɒdʒɪni/ *noun* petrogenesis L19.

petroglyph /'pɛtrə(ʊ)glɪf/ *noun*. L19.
[French *pétroglyphe*, formed as PETRO-¹ + Greek *glyphē* carving.]
A rock-carving, *esp.* a prehistoric one.

petrograph /'pɛtrə(ʊ)grɑːf/ *noun*. E19.
[from PETRO-¹ + -GRAPH.]
= PETROGLYPH.

petrography /pɛ'trɒgrəfi/ *noun*. M17.
[from PETRO-¹ + -GRAPHY.]
The branch of science that deals with the description, composition, and classification of rocks.
■ **petrographer** *noun* L19. **petro'graphic** *adjective* (***petrographic province***: see PROVINCE 6b) M19. **petro'graphical** *adjective* M17. **petro'graphically** *adverb* as regards petrography M19.

petroil /'pɛtrɔɪl/ *noun*. E20.
[from PETROL + OIL *noun*.]
= MIXTURE 7b.

petrol /'pɛtr(ə)l/ *noun*. M16.
[French *pétrole* from medieval Latin PETROLEUM. In sense 2 reintroduced from French.]
†**1** = PETROLEUM. M16–E19.
2 Refined petroleum as used as a fuel in motor vehicles. L19.
3 A shade of blue likened to the colour of petrol. E20.
Comb.: **petrol blue** = sense 3 above; **petrol bomb** a simple bomb consisting of a petrol-filled bottle and a wick; **petrol-bomb** *verb trans.* attack or destroy with a petrol bomb; **petrol cap** a cap covering the inlet to the petrol tank of a motor vehicle; **petrol coupon** a petrol rationing coupon; **petrol-electric** *adjective* (*a*) driven by electric motors powered by current from a generator which is driven by a petrol engine; (*b*) (of an electricity generator) driven by petrol; **petrol gauge** a meter indicating the quantity of petrol in a tank; **petrol head** *Austral. slang* a car enthusiast; **petrol lighter** a cigarette-lighter employing petrol; **petrol pump** (*a*) a pump at a filling station for supplying motor vehicles with petrol; (*b*) a pump which delivers petrol from the petrol tank of a motor vehicle or aircraft to the engine; **petrol station** = ***filling station*** s.v. FILLING *noun*.
■ **petrolless** /-l-l-/ *adjective* having no petrol E20.

For other words beginning with *petro-* see the entry for **petro-**¹

petrolatum /pɛtrə'leɪtəm/ *noun*. *US*. L19.
[mod. Latin, from PETROL + Latin *-atum* -ATE¹.]
Petroleum jelly.

petroleum /pɪ'trəʊlɪəm/ *noun*. E16.
[medieval Latin, from Latin *petra* rock + *oleum* oil.]
A dark viscous liquid consisting chiefly of hydrocarbons that is present in some rocks and is refined for use as a fuel for heating and in internal-combustion engines, for lighting, as a solvent, etc.
liquid petroleum: see LIQUID *adjective & noun*.
Comb.: **petroleum coke** the solid non-volatile residue left after the distillation and cracking of petroleum; **petroleum ether** a volatile oil distilled from petroleum, consisting chiefly of pentane and hexane; **petroleum geology** the branch of geology that deals with the formation, occurrence, and exploitation of oil and natural gas; **petroleum jelly** a soft greasy semi-solid mixture of hydrocarbons obtained from petroleum, used as an ointment and lubricant.
■ **petroleous** *adjective* containing petroleum, rich in petroleum M18.

pétroleur /pɛtrɔlœːr/ *noun*. Fem. **-euse** /-øːz/. Pl. pronounced same. L19.
[French, from *pétrole* PETROL + *-eur* -OR.]
An arsonist who uses petrol.

petrolic /pɪ'trɒlɪk/ *adjective*. L19.
[from PETROL + -IC.]
Of or pertaining to petrol or petroleum; pertaining to the use of petrol-driven motor vehicles.

petroliferous /pɛtrə'lɪf(ə)rəs/ *adjective*. L19.
[from PETROLEUM + -I- + -FEROUS.]
Yielding or containing petroleum.

petrolize /'pɛtrəlʌɪz/ *verb trans.* Also **-ise**. L19.
[from PETROL, PETROLEUM + -IZE.]
1 Set on fire by means of petrol. L19.
2 Cover (water) with a surface film of oil to kill mosquito larvae. E20.
■ **petroli'zation** *noun* E20.

petrology /pɪ'trɒlədʒi/ *noun*. E19.
[from PETRO-¹ + -OLOGY.]
1 The branch of geology that deals with the origin, structure, and composition of rocks. Cf. LITHOLOGY 1. E19.
2 The petrological features *of* a thing or place. L19.
■ **petro'logic** *adjective* (chiefly *US*) L19. **petro'logical** *adjective* E19. **petro'logically** *adverb* as regards petrology M19. **petrologist** *noun* E19.

petronel /'pɛtrən(ə)l/ *noun*. L16.
[French *petrinal* var. of *poitrinal* use as noun of adjective meaning 'pertaining to the breast or chest', from *poitrine* breast, chest from Proto-Romance alt. of Latin *pector-*, *pectus*. So called because in firing it the butt-end rested against the chest.]
Hist. **1** A carbine or large pistol used in the 16th and early 17th cents., esp. by cavalry. L16.
2 A soldier armed with a petronel. L16.

Petronella /pɛtrə'nɛlə/ *noun*. L19.
[Perh. from female forename.]
A Scottish country dance.

petrophysics /pɛtrə(ʊ)'fɪzɪks/ *noun*. M20.
[from PETRO-¹ + PHYSICS.]
The branch of geology that deals with the physical properties and behaviour of rocks.
■ **petrophysical** *adjective* M20. **petrophysicist** *noun* L20.

petrosal /pɪ'trəʊs(ə)l/ *adjective & noun*. M18.
[from Latin *petrosus* stony, rocky, from *petra* stone: see -OSE¹, -AL¹.]
ANATOMY. ▶**A** *adjective*. Designating, belonging to, or connected with the petrous portion of the temporal bone; designating nerves derived from the facial and glossopharyngeal nerves that pass through the petrosal bone or are situated in a notch in it. M18.
▶ **B** *noun*. The petrosal bone. M19.

petrous /'pɛtrəs/ *adjective*. M16.
[formed as prec. + -OUS.]
ANATOMY. Designating a very hard part of the temporal bone (in some animals a separate bone) which contains the inner ear.

pe-tsai /peɪ'tsʌɪ/ *noun*. L18.
[Chinese (Pekingese) *báicài* (Wade–Giles *pê ts'ai*) lit. 'white vegetable': cf. PAK-CHOI.]
A kind of Chinese cabbage, *Brassica pekinensis*, with leaves in a loose head, grown as a winter vegetable.

pettable /ˈpɛtəb(ə)l/ *adjective.* M20.
[from PET *verb*¹ + -ABLE.]
Suitable for petting.
■ **petta'bility** *noun* M20.

pettah /ˈpɛtə/ *noun.* M18.
[Tamil *pēṭṭai*, app. ult. from Sanskrit *pratiṣṭhā* establishment.]
In the southern part of the Indian subcontinent: a town or village lying outside or around a fort, and itself sometimes partly fortified.

petted /ˈpɛtɪd/ *adjective*¹. E18.
[from PET *verb*¹ + -ED¹.]
Treated as a pet, made a pet of; indulged, spoiled by indulgence.

petted /ˈpɛtɪd/ *adjective*². M18.
[from PET *noun*² + -ED².]
In a pet; offended or sulky at feeling slighted; piqued; pettish.
■ **pettedly** *adverb* M19. **pettedness** *noun* L19.

petter /ˈpɛtə/ *noun.* M19.
[from PET *verb*¹ + -ER¹.]
1 A person who pets or indulges someone. M19.
2 A person who engages in petting. E20.

petti- /ˈpɛti/ *combining form.* E20.
[from PETTICOAT.]
Forming nouns denoting a garment with some of the characteristics or functions of a petticoat, as ***petti-blouse***, ***pettipants***.

pettichaps /ˈpɛtɪtʃaps/ *noun.* L17.
[from PETTY *adjective* + *chaps* pl. of CHAP *noun*² or *noun*³.]
ORNITHOLOGY. Any of several warblers, *esp.* the garden warbler, ***Sylvia borin***.

petticoat /ˈpɛtɪkəʊt/ *noun.* Orig. two words. LME.
[from PETTY *adjective* + COAT *noun.*]
1 †**a** A small coat worn by men under the doublet. LME–M16. ▸**b** A waistcoat. *dial.* L17.
2 An undergarment worn by women and girls, consisting of a skirt or a skirt and bodice; a similar outer garment worn by females in ancient Greece and Rome or in non-Western tropical countries. Also (now *rare*), a skirt as distinguished from a bodice, worn for show externally or under a dress. LME. ▸†**b** The skirt of a woman's riding-habit. M17–E19.
3 A woman, a girl; the female sex. E17.
4 In *pl.* Skirts collectively. Formerly also, skirts worn by children, including young boys (chiefly in ***in petticoats***). E17.
5 The skirts of a scholar's or clergyman's gown (*joc.* or *derog.*); the kilt of a Scotsman; a fustanella. E18.
6 The outer circle of an archery target. M19.
7 A sheet hung round a yacht to conceal the design during launching. L19.
Phrases: **a — in petticoats** a female counterpart of —. **be in petticoats** (*a*) be or behave like a woman; (*b*) *arch.* be very young. **wear the petticoat** = ***be in petticoats*** (a).
Comb.: **petticoat bodice**, †**petticoat body**: attached to or worn with a petticoat; **petticoat breeches** *Hist.* loose wide breeches with legs resembling skirts, fashionable during the reign of Charles II; **petticoat government** (undue) rule or predominance of women in the home, or in politics; **petticoat tail** a thin triangular piece of shortbread.
■ **petticoated** *adjective* having or wearing a petticoat; female: M18. **petticoatless** *adjective* L19. **petticoaty** *adjective* resembling a petticoat L19.

pettifog /ˈpɛtɪfɒg/ *verb intrans.* Infl. **-gg-**. E17.
[Back-form. from next. Cf. earlier PETTIFOGGING *noun.*]
Act as a pettifogger; conduct a petty case in a minor court; practise legal chicanery; *transf.* quibble.

pettifogger /ˈpɛtɪfɒgə/ *noun.* M16.
[from PETTY *adjective* + FOGGER.]
An inferior legal practitioner; *esp.* one who employs mean or dubious practices; a rascally lawyer; *transf.* any petty practitioner; a tyro.
■ **pettifoggery** *noun* pettifogging practice; legal chicanery: M17.

pettifogging /ˈpɛtɪfɒgɪŋ/ *noun.* L16.
[formed as PETTIFOG + -ING¹.]
The action of a pettifogger; pettifoggery.

pettifogging /ˈpɛtɪfɒgɪŋ/ *adjective.* E17.
[formed as PETTIFOG + -ING².]
Acting as a pettifogger; pertaining to or characteristic of pettifoggers; mean, shifty; quibbling, petty; trivial.

> 🕮 DICKENS You are . . a well-matched pair of mean, rascally, pettifogging robbers. F. SWINNERTON The face of a poor, damned pettifogging actor.

pettish /ˈpɛtɪʃ/ *adjective.* L16.
[from PET *noun*² + -ISH¹.]
Subject to fits of offended ill humour; peevish, petulant; in a pet, irritable; proceeding from, pertaining to, or of the nature of a pet.

> 🕮 S. WEYMAN With a pettish exclamation [she] turned away. H. DUNMORE A spoiled, stupid, pettish woman who thought less of her children than the cat does.

■ **pettishly** *adverb* E17. **pettishness** *noun* M17.

pettitoe /ˈpɛtɪtəʊ/ *noun.* M16.
[Origin uncertain: in form and sense corresp. to French *petite oie* lit. 'little goose', with early assim. to PETTY *adjective* and TOE *noun.*]
1 A pig's foot, esp. as an article of food. Formerly also (in *pl.*), edible entrails of various animals. Usu. in *pl.* M16.
2 The foot of a person, esp. a child. Usu. in *pl.* L16.

pettle *noun* var. of PATTLE.

pettle /ˈpɛt(ə)l/ *verb. Scot. & north.* E18.
[Frequentative of PET *verb*¹: see -LE³.]
1 *verb trans.* Pet, fondle; indulge. E18.
2 *verb intrans.* Nestle; cuddle up. M19.

petty /ˈpɛti/ *noun*¹. L16.
[from PETTY *adjective.*]
1 †**a** A small boy at school; a boy in a lower form. L16–M19. ▸**b** A school or class for small boys. *obsolete* exc. *Hist.* E19.
2 A privy, a lavatory. Cf. ***little house*** s.v. LITTLE *adjective.* Now *dial.* M19.

petty /ˈpɛti/ *noun*². *colloq.* E20.
[Abbreviation.]
A petticoat.

petty /ˈpɛti/ *adjective.* LME.
[Old & mod. French *petit* from Proto-Romance word repr. in late Latin *pitinnus*, *pitulus* 'very small' and regarded as a symbolic word of children's speech. See also PETIT *adjective*¹ & *noun*, *adjective*².]
1 Small in size or stature. *obsolete* exc. in special collocations. LME.
2 Minor, of secondary rank, of lesser importance. LME.
3 Of little importance; insignificant, trivial; small-minded. L16.

> 🕮 **2** J. A. FROUDE Mithridates was once more a petty Asiatic prince existing upon sufferance. G. GREENE It isn't a gang which would usually get further than an occasional petty theft. G. L. HARDING Details of history in this period are details of petty events, leaving no permanent effects. **3** P. SCOTT How petty to get one's own back for little humiliations suffered. A. THWAITE Collins belonged to the school of petty carping and fault-finding.

Special collocations & comb.: **petty apartheid** apartheid as applied in everyday life; racial segregation in its trivial applications. ***petty average***: see AVERAGE *noun*² 1. **Petty Bag** *Hist.* an office of the common-law jurisdiction of the Court of Chancery, which issued writs and commissions of various kinds. **petty bourgeois** = PETIT BOURGEOIS. **petty bourgeoisie** = PETITE BOURGEOISIE. ***petty canon***: see CANON *noun*² 2. **petty cash** small cash items of receipt or expenditure. ***petty constable***: see CONSTABLE 4. †**petty god** a demigod. **petty jury** (now *US*): which tries the final issue of fact in civil or criminal proceedings and pronounces its verdict. ***petty larceny***. **petty-minded** *adjective* having or characteristic of a mind that dwells on the trivial and ignores what is important. ***petty morel***: see MOREL *noun*¹. **petty officer** †(*a*) a minor or inferior officer; (*b*) a naval rating corresponding in rank to a corporal or sergeant in the army. **petty pan** (now *dial.*) a small pan. †**petty school** a school for small boys; a junior or preparatory school. ***petty serjeanty***: see SERJEANTY 2. ***petty sessions***: see SESSION *noun.* **petty spurge** a small spurge, *Euphorbia peplus*, common as a garden weed. ***petty treason***: see TREASON *noun* 2b. **petty whin** a dwarf spiny yellow-flowered leguminous shrub of heaths, *Genista anglica*.
■ **pettily** *adverb* M19. **pettiness** *noun* L16.

petulant /ˈpɛtjʊl(ə)nt/ *adjective & noun.* L16.
[Old & mod. French *pétulant* from Latin *petulant-*, *-lans* rel. to *petere* seek, aim at: see -ANT¹.]
▶ **A** *adjective.* **1** Immodest; wanton, lascivious. Now *rare.* L16.
2 Pert; insolent; rude. Now *rare.* E17.
3 Exhibiting peevish impatience and irritation, esp. over trivial matters. M18.
▶ **B** *noun.* A petulant person. L17.
■ **petulance** *noun* (*a*) the fact or quality of being petulant; (*b*) (now *rare*) a pert or insolent remark: M16. **petulancy** *noun* = PETULANCE (a) M16. **petulantly** *adverb* E17.

†**petun** *noun.* L16–L19.
[French from Tupi *pety.*]
Tobacco.

petunia /pɪˈtjuːnɪə/ *noun.* E19.
[mod. Latin (see below), from French PETUN + -IA¹.]
Any of various ornamental herbaceous plants of the genus *Petunia*, allied to the tobacco plant, which are mostly hybrid derivatives of the S. American *P. axillaris* and *P. integrifolia* and bear white, pink, violet, or variegated funnel-shaped blooms; a flowering stem of such a plant.

petuntse /peɪˈtʊntsə, pɪˈtʌntsə/ *noun.* E18.
[Chinese *báidūnzi* (Wade–Giles *pe-* (Pekingese), *pai-tun tzŭ*), from *bái* white + *dūnzi* block of stone.]
A white earth prepared (orig. in China) by pulverizing a kaolinized granite, used with kaolin in the manufacture of porcelain to obtain transparency.

Petzval /ˈpɛtsvɑːl, -v(ə)l/ *noun.* L19.
[J. M. *Petzval* (1807–91), Hungarian mathematician.]
OPTICS. Used ***attrib.*** to designate concepts relating to compound lenses.
Petzval condition the condition for freedom from astigmatism in a compound lens, that the sum of the ratios of the power of each element to its refractive index be zero. **Petzval lens**: consisting of two widely-spaced colour-corrected compound lenses whose negative elements are on the inner sides. **Petzval sum** a number representing the degree of curvature of the field of a compound lens, derived from the refractive indices and surface radii of its elements.

Peulh /pəːl/ *noun & adjective.* Pl. of noun same, **-s**. L18.
[French from Wolof.]
= FULAH.

peulvan /pølvɑ̃/ *noun.* Also **-ven**. Pl. pronounced same. M19.
[French from Breton *peulvan*, from *peul* stake, pillar + *van* mutated form of *man* appearance.]
ARCHAEOLOGY. An upright megalithic stone, *esp.* one in Brittany.

Peutingerian /pjuːtɪnˈdʒɪərɪən/ *adjective.* L18.
[from K. *Peutinger* (1465–1547), of Augsburg, whose family owned the map until 1714: see -IAN.]
Peutingerian table, a map on parchment of the military roads of the ancient Roman Empire, supposed to be a copy of one constructed about AD 226.

Peutz–Jeghers syndrome /pəːtsˈjeɪgəz ˌsɪndrəʊm/ *noun phr.* M20.
[from J. L. A. *Peutz* (1886–1957), Dutch physician + H. *Jeghers* (1904–90), US physician.]
MEDICINE. A familial syndrome appearing in adolescence, characterized by gastro-intestinal polyposis and pigmentation of the lips, mouth, and fingers.

pew /pjuː/ *noun*¹. LME.
[Old French *puye*, *puie* from Latin *podia* pl. of PODIUM.]
1 ECCLESIASTICAL. Orig., a place in a church with a seat (often raised and enclosed) for a particular worshipper or group of worshippers. Later, a bench with a back, of a type placed in the main part of some churches to seat the congregation. LME. ▸**b** *sing.* & in *pl.* The people who occupy pews, the congregation; lay people as opp. to clergy. L19.
†**2** Station, situation; allotted place. LME–L17.
†**3** A raised standing-place or desk in a church to enable a preacher, reader, etc., to be seen and heard. L15–L17.
†**4** A raised seat or bench for people sitting in an official capacity; a rostrum used by public speakers, academic disputants, etc.; a stand for people doing business in a public place; a box in a theatre. M16–L17.
5 *gen.* A seat. Chiefly in ***take a pew***, ***have a pew*** (usu. in *imper.*). *colloq.* L19.

> 🕮 **1** A. TROLLOPE The squire was once more seen in the old family pew at church. **5** E. WAUGH It's been another scorcher, eh? Mind if I take a pew?

Comb.: **pew group** POTTERY a representation of people seated on a high-backed bench, usu. in salt-glazed stoneware. **pew-rent**: paid for the exclusive use of a particular pew or seat in a church.
■ **pewage** *noun* the arrangement or provision of pews; rent paid for a pew or pews: L17. **pewdom** *noun* the system or prevalence of pews in churches; M19. **pewful** *noun* as many people as will fill a pew M17. **pewless** *adjective* M19.

pew /pjuː/ *noun*². *Scot.* LME.
[Imit.]
†**1** The thin cry of a bird, esp. the kite. LME–M16.
2 A fine current of breath forced through the slightly parted lips; a thin stream of air or smoke. E18.
3 A small quantity. E19.
Phrases: **play pew** make the slightest sound or exertion (in expressed or implied neg. contexts).

pew /pjuː/ *noun*³. M18.
[French *pieu* from Old French *peu* var. of *pel* from Latin *palus* post, stake.]
A long-handled pointed implement for handling fish, blubber, etc.

pew /pjuː/ *verb*¹ *trans.* LME.
[from PEW *noun*¹.]
1 Provide with pews. LME.
2 Shut up in or as in a pew. E17.
■ **pewing** *noun* (*a*) the action of the verb; (*b*) pews collectively: LME.

pew /pjuː/ *verb*² *intrans.* Chiefly (long only) *Scot.* LME.
[Imit.: cf. PEW *noun*².]
†**1** Cry in a plaintive manner. LME–L16.
2 Rise or come out like smoke. E19.

pew /pjuː/ *interjection. arch.* L16.
[Natural exclam.]
= POOH *interjection.*

pewee /ˈpiːwiː/ *noun. N. Amer.* L18.
[Imit. Cf. PEEWEE.]
Formerly = FLYCATCHER 1C. Now *spec.* a flycatcher of the genus *Contopus*.

pewl *verb & noun* see PULE *verb & noun.*

pewter /ˈpjuːtə/ *noun & adjective.* ME.
[Old French *peutre*, *peaultre* = medieval Latin *peltrum* from Proto-Romance, of unkn. origin.]
▶ **A** *noun.* **1** A grey alloy of tin, antimony, and copper (formerly, tin and lead) used for domestic utensils. ME.

2 a Pewter utensils collectively; pewter ware. L16. **b** A pewter mug. M19.
3 A cup given as a prize; prize-money; money. *slang.* E19.
4 The colour of the alloy, a bluish or silver grey. L20.
Comb.: **pewterwort** = *rough horsetail* s.v. ROUGH *adjective.*
▶ **B** *adjective.* Of the colour pewter. E20.
■ **pewterer** *noun* a person who makes pewter utensils ME. **pewtery** *noun* (*rare*) (**a**) pewter utensils collectively; (**b**) a room in which the pewter of a house is kept: M17. **pewtery** *adjective* (*rare*) of the nature of or resembling pewter M19.

pewy /ˈpjuːi/ *adjective. Hunting slang.* E19.
[from PEW *noun*[1] (with ref. to enclosed pews) + -Y[1].]
Of countryside: divided into enclosures by fences.

-pexy /ˈpɛksi/ *suffix.*
[Greek -*pēxia*, *pēxis* fixing or putting together, from *pēgnunai* join, fix: see -Y[3].]
Forming nouns denoting (an instance of) a surgical operation for fixing an organ in position, as ***nephropexy***, ***orchidopexy***.

Peyer's patch /ˈpʌɪəz patʃ/ *noun phr.* M19.
[from J. K. *Peyer* (1653–1712), Swiss anatomist.]
ANATOMY. Any of numerous areas of lymphoid tissue in the wall of the small intestine which are involved in the development of immunity to antigens present there. Usu. in *pl.*
■ **Peyerian** /pʌɪˈɪərɪən/ *adjective* (now *rare*) M19.

peyote /peɪˈəʊti/ *noun.* M19.
[Amer. Spanish from Nahuatl *peyotl.*]
= MESCAL 3.
Comb.: **peyote button** = *MESCAL button.*
■ **peyotism** /ˈpeɪətɪz(ə)m/ *noun* a religious cult of American Indians in which peyote is taken sacramentally M20. **peyotist** /ˈpeɪətɪst/ *noun* a person who practises peyotism M20.

Peyronie's disease /ˈpɛrəniːz dɪˌziːz/ *noun phr.* E20.
[F. de la *Peyronie* (1678–1747), French physician.]
MEDICINE. Induration of the corpora cavernosa of the penis, causing pain and curvature during erection.

peytral /ˈpeɪtr(ə)l/ *noun.* ME.
[Anglo-Norman *peitral*, Old French *peitral* (mod. *poitrail*) from Latin *pectorale* breastplate, use as noun of neut. sing. of *pectoralis* PECTORAL. Cf. POITREL.]
Hist. A piece of armour to protect the breast of a horse, often richly ornamented. Also, a breast collar.

peziza /pɪˈzʌɪzə/ *noun.* M19.
[mod. Latin (see below): cf. Latin *pezica*, *pezita*, from Greek *pezis* stalkless mushroom.]
A cup fungus of the genus *Peziza*, growing on the ground or on decaying wood etc.

PF *abbreviation*[1].
Patriotic Front.

pf *abbreviation*[2].
[Italian.]
MUSIC. *Pianoforte*: soft then loud, more loudly.

pf. *abbreviation.*
Pfennig.

PFA *abbreviation.*
1 Professional Footballers' Association.
2 Pulverized fuel ash.

Pfalzian /ˈpfaltsɪən/ *adjective & noun.* M20.
[from German *Pfalz* the Palatinate, from Latin *palatium*: see PALACE, -IAN.]
GEOLOGY. (Designating or pertaining to) a minor orogenic episode in Europe which is believed to have occurred in the Permian period.

Pfannkuchen /ˈpfankuːxən/ *noun.* Pl. same. L19.
[German, from *Pfanne* PAN *noun*[1] + *Kuchen* cake.]
In Germany and German-speaking countries: a pancake.

PFC *abbreviation. US.*
1 Poor foolish (forlorn, etc.) civilian.
2 Private First Class.

PFD *abbreviation.*
Personal flotation device (a life jacket or similar buoyancy aid).

Pfefferkuchen /ˈpfɛfərkuːxən/ *noun.* Pl. same. L19.
[German, from *Pfeffer* PEPPER *noun* + *Kuchen* cake.]
In Germany and German-speaking countries: a spiced cake, gingerbread.

Pfeiffer /ˈpfʌɪfə/ *noun.* L19.
[Richard *Pfeiffer* (1858–1945), German bacteriologist.]
BACTERIOLOGY. **1** Used in *possess.* and *attrib.* to designate the specific lysis of the cholera vibrio in the presence of antibody and complement. L19.
2 ***Pfeiffer's bacillus***, ***Pfeiffer bacillus***, a bacterium, *Haemophilus influenzae*, formerly thought to be the causal agent of influenza. E20.

pfella /ˈ(p)fɛlə/ *noun.* Also **-ller** /-lə/. E20.
[Repr. Aboriginal pronunc. of FELLOW *noun.*]
Used as a marker of an adjective, demonstrative, or numeral in Australian pidgin.
📖 M. FRANKLIN A superman, a big pfella chief.

pfennig /ˈ(p)fɛnɪɡ/ *noun.* Pl. **-s**, same. M16.
[German: see PENNY.]
A monetary unit of Germany until the introduction of the euro in 2002, equal to one-hundredth of a mark.

pfft /ft, pft/ *noun, interjection, & verb.* E20.
[Imit.]
▶ **A** *noun.* = PHUT *noun.* E20.
▶ **B** *interjection.* = PHUT *interjection.* M20.
▶ **C** *verb intrans.* Pa. t. & pple **pfft**. Come to an end, collapse; (of a couple) separate, divorce. *Journalists' slang. US.* M20.

PFI *abbreviation.*
Private Finance Initiative, a scheme whereby public services such as the National Health Service raise funds for capital projects from commercial organizations.

pfui /ˈfuːi, *foreign* pfʊɪ/ *interjection.* M19.
[German: cf. PHOOEY.]
Expr. contempt or disgust, orig. among German-speakers.

Pfund series /fʊnt ˈsɪəriːz/ *noun phr.* M20.
[A. Herman *Pfund* (1879–1949), US physicist.]
PHYSICS. A series of lines in the infra-red spectrum of atomic hydrogen, between 7.46 and 2.28 micrometres.

PG *abbreviation.*
Parental guidance (a cinema film classification).

pg /piːˈdʒiː/ *noun & verb. colloq.* Also **PG**. E20.
[Abbreviation.]
▶ **A** *noun.* Pl. **-'s**. A paying guest. E20.
▶ **B** *verb intrans.* Pa. t. & pple **-'d** pres. pple **-'ing**. Reside as a paying guest. E20.

PGCE *abbreviation.*
Postgraduate Certificate of Education.

PGR *abbreviation.*
Psychogalvanic reflex or response.

ph.
A consonantal digraph, pronounced /f/, used in classical Latin to repr. the Greek letter ϕ (cogn. with Sanskrit *bh*, Germanic *b*), and occurring in English words derived from Latin or Greek words or elements. In late popular and medieval Latin and in Romance langs. *f* was often substituted for *ph*, as now regularly in Spanish, Italian, and some French words, whence the spelling of English ***fancy***, ***fantasy***. In ***phantom*** and ***pheasant*** (French *fantôme*, *faisan*) there has been etymological reversion to *ph*.

pH /piːˈeɪtʃ/ *noun.* E20.
[from *p* repr. German *Potenz* power + H·, symbol for the hydrogen ion.]
CHEMISTRY. Acidity or alkalinity of a solution, soil, etc., expressed numerically as the logarithm to the base 10 of the reciprocal of the activity of hydrogen ions (in moles per litre).
¶ A pH of 7 corresponds to a neutral solution, one less than 7 to an acidic solution, and one greater than 7 to an alkaline solution.
■ **pH-stat** *noun* a device for automatically maintaining a solution at constant pH M20.

phacelia /fəˈsiːlɪə/ *noun.* E19.
[mod. Latin (see below), from Greek *phakelos* cluster + -IA[1], with ref. to the clustered flowers.]
Any of various chiefly annual N. American plants constituting the genus *Phacelia* (family Hydrophyllaceae), with clustered blue, violet, or white flowers, freq. grown for ornament.

phaco- /ˈfakəʊ/ *combining form.*
[from Greek *phakos* lentil, wart: see -O-.]
Lens; lenticular.
■ **phacoanaphyˈlactic** *adjective* (MEDICINE) of, pertaining to, or involving phacoanaphylaxis E20. **phacoanaphyˈlaxis** *noun* (MEDICINE) allergic reaction to protein released from the crystalline lens of the eye M20. **phacolite** *noun* (**a**) MINERALOGY a colourless variety of chabazite occurring as crystals of lenticular form; (**b**) GEOLOGY a phacolith: M19. **phacolith** *noun* (GEOLOGY) an intrusive mass of igneous rock situated between strata at the top of an anticline or the bottom of a syncline E20.

phacoidal /faˈkɔɪd(ə)l/ *adjective.* E20.
[from PHACO- + -OID + -AL[1].]
GEOLOGY. Lens-shaped, lenticular; (of rock) characterized by the presence of lenticular inclusions.

phacopid /fəˈkəʊpɪd, ˈfakəpɪd/ *adjective & noun.* E20.
[mod. Latin *Phacopidae* (see below), from *Phacops* genus name, formed as PHACO- + Greek *ōps* eye, face: see -ID[3].]
PALAEONTOLOGY. ▶**A** *adjective.* Of, pertaining to, or designating the family Phacopidae of trilobites, the members of which were characterized by large compound eyes and a rounded glabella which widened frontwards. E20.
▶ **B** *noun.* A trilobite of this family. E20.

Phaeacian /fiːˈeɪʃ(ə)n/ *noun.* M17.
[from Latin *Phaeacia*, Greek *Phaiakia* + -AN.]
An inhabitant of Scheria in the story of Odysseus, whose people were noted for their luxury; a gourmand.

phaenogam /ˈfiːnəgam/ *noun.* Now *rare* or *obsolete.* Also **phe-**. M19.
[mod. Latin *phaenogama* (sc. *vegetabilia*), from Greek *phaino-* showing + *gamos* marriage, sexual union.]
BOTANY. A flowering plant; a phanerogam.
■ **phaenoˈgamic**, **phaeˈnogamous** *adjectives* phanerogamic E19.

†**phaenomenon** *noun* var. of PHENOMENON.

phaeochrome /ˈfiːəkrəʊm/ *adjective.* E20.
[from Greek *phaios* dusky + *khrōma* colour.]
HISTOLOGY. = CHROMAFFIN.

phaeochromocyte /fiːə(ʊ)ˈkrəʊmə(ʊ)sʌɪt/ *noun.* E20.
[from prec. + -O- + -CYTE.]
MEDICINE. A chromaffin cell, *esp.* one in the adrenal medulla.
■ **phaeochromocyˈtoma** *noun*, pl. **-mas**, **-mata** /-mətə/, a tumour arising from chromaffin cells of the adrenal medulla E20.

phaeophorbide /fiːəˈfɔːbʌɪd/ *noun.* E20.
[from Greek *phaios* dusky + *phorbē* pasture, food + -IDE.]
BIOCHEMISTRY. Either of two compounds formed by the action of a strong acid on chlorophyll or phaeophytin; an ester of either of these compounds.

phaeophytin /fiːəˈfʌɪtɪn/ *noun.* E20.
[from Greek *phaios* dusky + *phuton* plant + -IN[1].]
BIOCHEMISTRY. Either of two compounds formed by the action of a weak acid on chlorophyll; a phytyl ester of a phaeophorbide.

phaeton /ˈfeɪt(ə)n/ *noun.* L16.
[French *phaéton* from Latin *Phaethon* from Greek *Phaethōn* (*phaethōn* shining), in Greek mythol. the son of Helios and Clymene, who was allowed to drive the sun's chariot for a day, with disastrous results.]
†**1** A rash or adventurous charioteer like Phaethon; any charioteer; a thing that, like Phaethon, sets the world on fire. L16–M18.
2 Chiefly *Hist.* A light four-wheeled open carriage, usually drawn by a pair of horses, and with one or two forward-facing seats. M18.
3 A touring car. *US.* E20.
■ **phaeˈthontic** *adjective* belonging to, characteristic of, or resembling Phaethon M17.

phage /feɪdʒ/ *noun.* E20.
[Abbreviation.]
BIOLOGY. A bacteriophage; bacteriophages collectively.
Comb.: **phage display** a technique for producing and studying novel proteins and polypeptides by inserting a gene fragment into a gene responsible for the surface protein of a bacteriophage, the new protein appearing in the surface coating of the phage, in which it can be manipulated and tested for biological activity; **phage type** a division of a bacterial species characterized by a common susceptibility to a particular group of phages; **phage-type** *verb trans.* determine the phage type of.

phagedaena /fadʒɪˈdiːnə, fag-/ *noun.* Also (earlier) ***-dena**. L16.
[Latin from Greek *phagedaina*, from *phagein* eat.]
An ulcer resulting from spreading necrosis or gangrene of surrounding tissue.
■ **phagedaenic** *adjective & noun* (**a**) *adjective* of the nature of, characterized by, or affected with phagedaena; †(**b**) *adjective & noun* (designating) a corrosive liquid preparation used for destroying proud flesh or for cleansing ulcers: M17. **phagedaenous** *adjective* = PHAGEDAENIC (a) M17.

-phagia /ˈfeɪdʒɪə, -dʒə/ *suffix.*
[Greek: see -PHAGY, -IA[1].]
Forming nouns with the sense 'eating, feeding, swallowing', as ***coprophagia***, ***dysphagia***; = -PHAGY.

phagocyte /ˈfagə(ʊ)sʌɪt/ *noun & verb.* L19.
[from Greek *phago-* eating (from *phagein* eat) + -CYTE: see -O-.]
▶ **A** *noun.* A leucocyte or other cell in the body that phagocytoses bacteria or foreign particles. L19.
▶ **B** *verb trans.* Phagocytose. E20.
■ **phagocytaˈbility** *noun* ability to undergo phagocytosis E20. **phagocytable** *adjective* susceptible to phagocytosis E20. **phagocytic** /-ˈsɪt-/ *adjective* pertaining to, or having the nature or function of, a phagocyte L19. **phagocytically** /-ˈsɪt-/ *adverb* as regards phagocytosis E20. **phagocyˈtizable** *adjective* phagocytable M20. **phagoˈcytize** *verb trans.* phagocytose E20. **phagocytose** /-ˈsʌɪtəʊz/ *verb trans.* engulf or absorb (a cell or particle) so as to cause isolation or destruction E20. **phagocyˈtosis** *noun* the process by which a cell engulfs or absorbs bacteria or foreign particles so as to isolate or destroy them L19.

phagolysosome /fagəʊˈlʌɪsə(ʊ)səʊm/ *noun.* M20.
[from PHAGO(SOME + LYSOSOME.]
A structure formed in the cytoplasm of a cell by the fusion of a phagosome and a lysosome, in which a foreign particle is digested.
■ **phagolysoˈsomal** *adjective* L20.

phagosome /ˈfagə(ʊ)səʊm/ *noun.* M20.
[from PHAGO(CYTE + -SOME[3].]
BIOLOGY. A vacuole formed in the cytoplasm of a cell when a particle is phagocytosed and enclosed within a part of the cell membrane.
■ **phagoˈsomal** *adjective* L20.

-phagous /fəgəs/ *suffix.*
[from Latin *-phagus*, Greek *-phagos*, from Greek *phagein* eat: see -OUS.]
Forming adjectives with the sense 'that eats or feeds on (what is indicated by the 1st elem.)', as ***coprophagous***, ***polyphagous***.

-phagy /fədʒi/ *suffix.*
[Greek *-phagia*, from *phagein* eat: see -Y³.]
Forming nouns with the sense 'eating, feeding, or swallowing', as ***coprophagy***, ***monophagy***; = -PHAGIA.

†**phainomenon** *noun* var. of PHENOMENON.

phainopepla /fʌɪnə(ʊ)'pɛplə/ *noun.* L19.
[mod. Latin *Phainopepla* (see below), from Greek *phaeinos* shining + *pepla* robes.]
A crested silky flycatcher, *Phainopepla niteus*, of south-western N. America.

phakic /'feɪkɪk/ *adjective.* E20.
[from Greek *phakos* lentil (cf. PHACO-) + -IC.]
Of the eye: having a crystalline lens (as is normal). Opp. APHAKIC.

phalaena /fə'liːnə/ *noun.* Pl. **-nae** /-niː/. M17.
[mod. Latin from Greek *phalaina* var. of *phallaina* moth.]
ENTOMOLOGY (now *Hist.*). A moth of the former genus *Phalaena*, which orig. included all moths other than hawkmoths and was later restricted to a group including geometrids and some pyralids.

phalaenopsid /falɪ'nɒpsɪd/ *noun.* L19.
[from mod. Latin *Phalaenopsis* genus name, from Greek *phalaina* moth + *opsis* appearance: see -ID².]
BOTANY. = ***moth orchid*** s.v. MOTH *noun*¹.

phalange /'falan(d)ʒ/ *noun*¹. LME.
[French from Latin *phalang-*, PHALANX. In sense 2 partly back-form. from *phalanges* pl. of PHALANX.]
†**1** = PHALANX 1. LME–L17.
2 = PHALANX 3, 4. M19.

phalange /'falan(d)ʒ/ *noun*². M16.
[French from Greek *phalaggion*: see PHALANGIUM.]
†**1** = PHALANGIUM 1a. M16–L17.
2 = OPILIONID *noun.* L19.

Phalange *noun*³ & *adjective* var. of FALANGE *noun* & *adjective.*

phalangeal /fə'lan(d)ʒɪəl/ *adjective.* M19.
[from PHALANGE *noun*¹ + -AL¹.]
ANATOMY & ZOOLOGY. Pertaining to or of the nature of a phalanx or phalanges.

phalanger /fə'lan(d)ʒə/ *noun.* L18.
[French, mod. Latin from Greek *phalaggion* venomous spider (with allus. to the webbed toes of the hind feet).]
A marsupial of the family Phalangeridae, native to Australia and New Guinea and comprising cuscuses and some possums; *spec.* a cuscus. Also, any of various other marsupials that can make gliding leaps.
flying phalanger: see FLYING *ppl adjective.* ***vulpine phalanger***: see VULPINE 1.

phalanges *noun pl.* see PHALANX.

†**phalangia** *noun* pl. of PHALANGIUM.

phalangid /fə'lan(d)ʒɪd/ *noun.* L19.
[mod. Latin *Phalangidae* former order name, formed as PHALANGIUM: see -ID³.]
ZOOLOGY. = OPILIONID *noun.*

phalangist /fə'lan(d)ʒɪst, 'falən(d)ʒɪst/ *noun*¹. M19.
[mod. Latin genus name *Phalangista* substituted for *Phalanger*: see PHALANGER, -IST.]
= PHALANGER.

Phalangist *noun*² & *adjective* var. of FALANGIST.

phalangite /'falən(d)ʒʌɪt/ *noun.* M19.
[Latin *phalangita* or *-ites* from Greek *phalagx*: see PHALANX, -ITE¹.]
A soldier belonging to a phalanx.

phalangitis /falan'dʒʌɪtɪs/ *noun.* L19.
[from *phalanges* pl. of PHALANX + -ITIS.]
MEDICINE. Inflammation of one or more of the phalanges.

phalangium /fə'lan(d)ʒɪəm/ *noun.* Pl. †**-ia**. L16.
[Latin from Greek *phalaggion* venomous spider, spiderwort.]
1 †**a** A venomous spider. L16–E19. ▸**b** = OPILIONID *noun.* Now only as mod. Latin genus name. M19.
†**2** Any of several plants of the lily family, esp. of the genus *Anthericum*, formerly reputed to cure the bites of spiders. E17–M18.

phalanstery /'falanst(ə)ri/ *noun.* Also in French form ***phalanstère*** /falɑ̃stɛːr/ (pl. same). M19.
[French *phalanstère*, from PHALANX + *mona*)*stère* formed as MONASTERY.]
A building or set of buildings occupied by a Fourierist phalanx; a Fourierist phalanx; *gen.* any voluntary community; a place where such a community lives.
■ **phalan'sterian** *adjective & noun* (*a*) *adjective* of or pertaining to a phalanstery or the system of phalansteries; (*b*) *noun* a member of a phalanstery; an advocate of phalansteries, a Fourierist: M19.

phalanx /'falaŋks/ *noun.* Pl. **phalanxes** (chiefly in senses 1, 2), **phalanges** /fə'landʒiːz/ (chiefly in senses 3, 4). M16.
[Latin *phalanx*, *phalang-* from Greek *phalagx*.]
1 A line or array of battle (*GREEK HISTORY*); *spec.* a body of heavy-armed infantry drawn up in close order, with shields touching and long spears overlapping (famous in the Macedonian army); any compact body of troops or police officers. M16.
2 A number of people banded together for a common purpose, esp. in support of or in opposition to some cause; a union so formed; a compact body of people or animals (or things) massed in order, e.g. for attack or defence. E17. ▸**b** A group of people living together in community, free of external regulation and holding property in common. M19.
3 *ANATOMY & ZOOLOGY.* Each of the bones of the fingers and toes. Usu. in *pl.* L17.
4 *BOTANY.* A group of stamens united by fusion of their filaments. *rare.* L18.

📖 **1** *Western Morning News* I had to run bent double past a police phalanx protected by their riot shields.
2 M. EDWARDES His phalanx of officials sat on one side . . and our six-man Board . . on the other. R. THOMAS The tables were separated by clumps of . . palms in pots, and phalanxes of gliding waiters. **3** ***ungual phalanx***: see UNGUAL *adjective* 1.

■ **phalanxed** *adjective* drawn up or ranged in a phalanx M18.

phalaris /'falərɪs/ *noun.* E20.
[mod. Latin (see below), from Latin from Greek.]
Any grass of the genus *Phalaris*; esp. *P. aquatica*, grown as a fodder grass.
Comb.: **phalaris staggers** a disease of sheep and cattle caused by the occasional toxicity of canary-grass, *Phalaris aquatica.*

phalarope /'falərəʊp/ *noun.* L18.
[French from mod. Latin *Phalaropus* genus name, from Greek *phalaris* coot + -O- + *pous* foot.]
Each of three small swimming sandpipers constituting the genus *Phalaropus* and the subfamily Phalaropodinae, which have lobed feet and are notable for their reversal of the sexual roles.
grey phalarope, ***red phalarope***, ***red-necked phalarope***, etc.

phalera /'falərə/ *noun.* Pl. **-rae** /-riː/. E17.
[Latin (pl. *-rae*) from Greek *phalara* pl.]
CLASSICAL ANTIQUITIES. A bright metal disc worn on the chest as an ornament by men, or used to adorn the harness of horses.

Phaleucian /fə'l(j)uːsɪən/ *adjective.* L16.
[from Latin *Phaleucius* (for *Phalaecius*), from *Phalaecus* a poet of ancient Greece: see -IAN.]
CLASSICAL PROSODY. Designating (a verse in) an ancient metre consisting of a spondee, a dactyl, and three trochees.

phalli *noun pl.* see PHALLUS.

phallic /'falɪk/ *adjective.* L18.
[Greek *phallikos*, from *phallos*: see PHALLUS, -IC.]
Of or pertaining to a phallus or phallism; representing or suggestive of a phallus; *PSYCHOANALYSIS* designating a stage of (esp. male) development characterized by a preoccupation with the genitals.

📖 C. SHORT I switched my mind to . . the Eiffel Tower. It too was a phallic symbol.

■ **phallically** *adverb* M20. **phallicism** /-sɪz(ə)m/ *noun* veneration of the phallus or the sexual organs as symbolic of the generative power in nature L19. **phallism** *noun* phallicism L19.

phallin /'falɪn/ *noun.* L19.
[from mod. Latin *phalloides*: see PHALLOIDIN, -IN¹.]
CHEMISTRY. A haemolytic substance present in the death cap, *Amanita phalloides*, and formerly thought to be its poisonous principle.

phallo- /'faləʊ/ *combining form* of PHALLUS (also repr. Greek *phallos* and words derived from it): see -O-.
■ **pha'llocracy** *noun* (belief in) dominance by or the superiority of men L20. **phallocrat** *noun* a person who advocates or assumes the existence of a male-dominated society; a man who argues that because he is male he is superior to women: L20. **phallo'cratic** *adjective* of, pertaining to, or designating a phallocrat L20. **phallophoria** /-'fɔːrɪə/ *noun* [Greek *phallēphoria* pl.] the carrying of a phallus, esp. as part of a festival of Dionysus in ancient Greece E20. **phallophoric** /-'fɒrɪk/ *adjective* characterized by phallophoria M20. **phallophorus** /-'lɒf(ə)rəs/ *noun*, pl. **-ri** /-rʌɪ, -riː/, a person who carries a phallus, esp. as part of a festival of Dionysus in ancient Greece M19. **phalloplasty** *noun* plastic surgery of the penis; (an instance of) the making of a penis by plastic surgery: L19. **phallo'toxin** *noun* any of several poisonous peptides present in the death cap toadstool, *Amanita phalloides*, all of which have a similar ring structure of seven amino acids bridged by a sulphur atom M20.

phallocentric /falə(ʊ)'sɛntrɪk/ *adjective.* E20.
[from prec. + -CENTRIC.]
Centred on the phallus, esp. as a symbol of male superiority or dominance.
■ **phallocentricity** /-'trɪsɪti/ *noun* L20. **phallocentrism** *noun* L20.

phalloi *noun* pl. of PHALLOS.

phalloid /'falɔɪd/ *adjective.* M19.
[from PHALLUS + -OID.]
Resembling a phallus.

phalloidin /fa'lɔɪdɪn/ *noun.* Also **-ine** /-iːn/. M20.
[from mod. Latin *phalloides*, specific epithet of the death cap, *Amanita phalloides*, from Greek *phallos* PHALLUS: see -OID, -IN¹, -INE⁵.]
CHEMISTRY. The principal phallotoxin.

phallos /'faləs/ *noun.* Pl. **-lloi** /-lɔɪ/. E20.
[Greek.]
= PHALLUS.

phallus /'faləs/ *noun.* Pl. **-lli** /-lʌɪ, -liː/, **-lluses**. E17.
[Late Latin from Greek *phallos*.]
1 An image of the erect penis, symbolizing the generative power in nature; *spec.* that carried in solemn procession in the Dionysiac festivals in ancient Greece. E17.
2 The penis, esp. as an organ of symbolic significance; an erect penis. E20.
■ **phallism** *noun* phallicism L19.

phanal *noun* var. of FANAL.

Phanar /'fanɑː/ *noun.* Also **F-**. E19.
[Turkish *fener* from Greek *phanarion* (mod. *phanari*) lighthouse, lantern, dim. of *phanos* torch, lamp, lantern. So called from a lighthouse formerly in the Phanar.]
Hist. The area of Istanbul which became the chief Greek quarter after the Ottoman conquest; the Greek official class under the Turks, through whom the affairs of the Christian population in the Ottoman Empire were largely administered; the seat of the Patriarch of Constantinople after the Ottoman conquest.
■ **phanariot** /fə'narɪət/ *noun & adjective* [mod. Greek *phanariōtēs*] a resident in the Phanar; (designating) a Greek official under the Ottoman Empire: E19.

phanero- /'fanərəʊ/ *combining form* of Greek *phaneros* visible, evident: see -O-.
■ **phanero'crystalline** *adjective* (of rock) having a crystalline structure in which the crystals can be seen with the naked eye M19. **phanerophyte** *noun* (*BOTANY*) a plant (esp. a tree or shrub) which bears its perennating buds at least 25 cm (approx. 9.8 inches) above the surface of the ground E20.

phanerogam /'fan(ə)rə(ʊ)gam/ *noun.* M19.
[French *phanérogame*, mod. Latin *phanerogamus*, formed as PHANERO- + Greek *gamos* marriage, sexual union: so called because the reproductive organs were easily seen.]
Any plant of the division Phanerogamia (now disused), which embraced both angiosperms or true flowering plants and gymnosperms, together now more usu. known as spermatophytes or seed plants. Opp. CRYPTOGAM.
■ **phanero'gamic** *adjective* belonging to the Phanerogamia M19. **phane'rogamous** *adjective* = PHANEROGAMIC E19.

phanerozoic /fan(ə)rə(ʊ)zəʊɪk/ *adjective & noun.* L19.
[from PHANERO- + -ZOIC.]
▸ **A** *adjective.* **1** *ZOOLOGY.* Living in exposed conditions above the surface of the ground. Opp. CRYPTOZOIC 1. L19.
2 *GEOLOGY* (**P-**). Designating or pertaining to the whole of geological time since the beginning of the Cambrian, as contrasted with the Precambrian (Cryptozoic). M20.
▸ **B** *noun. GEOLOGY.* The Phanerozoic eon. M20.

phanotron /'fanətrɒn/ *noun.* M20.
[from *phano-* (perh. from Greek *phainein* bring to light, cause to appear) + -TRON.]
ELECTRONICS. A thermionic diode rectifier which uses an arc discharge in mercury vapour or gas at very low pressure.

phansigar /'fɑːnsɪgə/ *noun.* Also **-gur**. L18.
[Hindi *phā̃sigār* strangler, from *phā̃sī* noose + Persian *-gār* agent-suffix.]
Hist. In the Indian subcontinent: a professional robber and assassin of travellers and others; a Thug.

Phantasiast /fan'teɪzɪast/ *noun.* L17.
[ecclesiastical Greek *phantasiastēs*, from Greek *phantasia*: see FANTASY *noun.*]
ECCLESIASTICAL HISTORY. A Docetist who held that Christ's body was only a phantasm.

phantasied *adjective* var. of FANTASIED.

†**phantasim** *noun. rare* (Shakes.). Only in L16.
[Cf. Italian *fantasima*.]
A fantastic being.

phantasise *verb*, **phantasist** *noun*, **phantasize** *verb* see FANTASIZE, FANTASIST.

phantasm /'fantaz(ə)m/ *noun.* ME.
[Old & mod. French *fantasme* from Latin PHANTASMA.]
▸ **I** †**1** Illusion, deceptive appearance. ME–M19.
2 An illusion, an appearance that has no reality; a figment of the imagination; an unreal or imaginary being; an apparition, a ghost. LME.
†**3** An impostor. L16–M17.
4 An illusory likeness (*of* something). M17.
▸ **II** †**5** Imagination, fancy. L15–L17.
†**6** *PHILOSOPHY.* A mental image, appearance, or representation, considered as the immediate object of sense-perception. L16–E20.

7 A fancy, a mental image or illusion. L17.

■ **phan'tasmal** *adjective* of the nature of a phantasm; spectral; unreal, imaginary: E19. **phantas'mality** *noun* the quality of being phantasmal L19. **phan'tasmally** *adverb* in a phantasmal manner or form; as a phantasm: M19. **phan'tasmic** *adjective* phantasmal E19.

phantasma /fan'tazmə/ *noun*. Pl. **-mas**, **-mata** /-mətə/. L16.
[Italian *fantasma* from Latin *phantasma* from Greek, from *phantazein*: see FANTASTIC.]
An illusion, a vision, a dream; an apparition, a ghost.

phantasmagoria /ˌfantazmə'gɒrɪə, -gɔːr-/ *noun*. Also **phantasmagory** /fan'tazməgɒri/. E19.
[Prob. from French *fantasmagorie*, from *fantasme* PHANTASM with fanciful ending.]
1 An exhibition of optical illusions produced chiefly by means of the magic lantern, first exhibited in London in 1802 (*Hist.*); any optical exhibition; an apparatus for rapidly changing the size or nature of images on a screen. E19.
2 A shifting series or succession of phantasms or imaginary figures, e.g. as seen in a dream or as created by literary description; a state of mind characterized by this. E19.
3 A shifting and changing external scene consisting of many elements. E19.

📖 **2** M. LOWRY The mescal-inspired phantasmagoria, or heebie-jeebies, to which Geoffrey has succumbed. **3** E. K. KANE An opium-eater's revery is nothing to the phantasmagoria of the sky tonight.

■ **phantasmagorian** /-'gɔː-/, **phantasmagoric** /-'gɒrɪk/ *adjectives* of, pertaining to, or of the nature of a phantasmagoria; visionary, phantasmal: E19. **phantasmagorical** *adjective* phantasmagoric M19.

phantasmata *noun pl.* see PHANTASMA.

phantast *noun*, **phantastic** *adjective & noun* see FANTAST, FANTASTIC.

phantastica /fan'tastɪkə/ *noun pl.* M20.
[from *phantastic* var. of FANTASTIC + -A³.]
Hallucinogenic drugs collectively.

phantastical *adjective & noun* see FANTASTICAL.

phantastry *noun* var. of FANTASTRY.

phantasy *noun, verb* vars. of FANTASY *noun, verb*.

phantom /'fantəm/ *noun & adjective*. ME.
[Old French *fantosme*, *-ome* (mod. *fantôme*) from popular Latin word from Latin *phantasma* from Greek, from *phantazein*: see FANTASTIC. The spelling *ph-* by etymological reversion.]
▶**A** *noun*. †**1** (An) illusion, (a) delusion, (a) deception; a figment of the imagination, a lie; falsity, unreality. ME–L17.
2 A thing that appears to the sight or other sense but has no material substance; an apparition, a ghost. ME. ▸**b** A person who or thing which has the name and show of power but none of the substance; a weak, diminished, or faint version *of* something. M17. ▸**c** A thing having the form or appearance but not the substance of something; a (material or optical) image *of* something. E18.
3 A mental illusion; an image in a dream or in the mind; the mental image of an external object; the thought or apprehension of something that haunts the imagination. ME.
4 A model of a baby used in obstetric demonstrations; a life-size model of part of the body made of material which absorbs radiation in a similar way to that part, used in radiological investigations. L19.
5 ANGLING. An artificial bait made to resemble live bait. L19.

📖 **2** TENNYSON Hark the Phantom of the house That ever shrieks before a death. **b** P. DE VRIES I had been drained of identity and become a phantom of myself. **c** T. B. BUTLER The thirsty wanderer is deluded by the phantom of a moving, undulating, watery, surface. **3** R. FRAME Keeping up a steady pace . . helps to keep the phantom of the past at bay.

▶**B** *attrib.* or as *adjective*. That is a phantom; merely apparent, illusory; imaginary; false; devised by way of pretence, imitation, or deceit. LME.

📖 *Daily Express* The eleven men, playing a phantom team, swept down the pitch to the unguarded goal. M. MCLUHAN A blind drive toward the phantom security of subrational collectivism.

Comb. & special collocations: **phantom circuit** an additional circuit obtained by using one line from each of two other circuits; **phantom limb** a continuing sensation of the presence of a limb after it has been amputated; **phantom pain**: perceived as in a phantom limb; **phantom pregnancy** = PSEUDOPREGNANCY.

■ **phantomship** *noun* (with possess. adjective, as ***his phantomship*** etc.) a mock title of respect given to a phantom E18.

Pharaoh /'fɛːrəʊ/ *noun*¹. ME.
[ecclesiastical Latin *Pharao*, *-aon-* (whence earlier PHARAON) from Greek *Pharaō* from Hebrew *parʿōh* from Egyptian *pr-ʿo* great house. The English final *h* is from Hebrew.]
1 (The title of) a king of ancient Egypt; *spec.* any of the ones mentioned in the Old Testament and Hebrew Scriptures, under whom Joseph flourished and in whose time the oppression and Exodus of Israel took place; *fig.* a tyrant, a taskmaster. ME.
2 In full ***Old Pharaoh***. A kind of strong beer. *obsolete* exc. *dial.* L17.

Comb.: **Pharaoh hound** a short-coated tan-coloured hunting dog with large, pointed ears; **Pharaoh's ant** the little red ant, *Monomorium pharaonis*, native to warm regions and a pest of heated buildings in temperate regions; **Pharaoh's rat** the ichneumon; **Pharaoh's serpent** [cf. *Exodus* 7:9] an indoor firework which burns and uncoils in serpentine form.

†**pharaoh** *noun*² see FARO *noun*¹.

†**pharaon** *noun*. Also **P-**. OE.
[ecclesiastical Latin *Pharaon-*: see PHARAOH *noun*¹. In sense 2 from French (cf. FARO *noun*¹).]
1 = PHARAOH 1. OE–E16.
2 = FARO *noun*¹. Only in 18.

Pharaonic /fɛː'rɒnɪk, fɛːreɪ'ɒnɪk/ *adjective*. M19.
[from ecclesiastical Latin *Pharaon-* (see PHARAOH *noun*¹) + -IC.]
Of or pertaining to a Pharaoh or the Pharaohs; resembling that of the Pharaohs.

pharate /'fareɪt/ *adjective*. M20.
[from Greek *pharos* cloak + -ATE².]
ENTOMOLOGY. Of an insect: confined within the cuticle of the previous instar.

phare /fɛː/ *noun*. LME.
[Latin *pharus* from Greek PHAROS.]
†**1** A synagogue light. Only in LME.
2 A lighthouse. M16.
†**3** A strait or channel lit by a lighthouse; the Strait of Messina. Cf. FARE *noun*². E17–E18.

†**Pharian** *adjective & noun*. L16.
[from Latin *Pharius*, from *Pharos*: see PHAROS, -IAN.]
▶**A** *adjective*. Of or pertaining to the island of Pharos; *poet.* Egyptian, Nilotic. L16–E18.
▶**B** *noun*. An Egyptian. Only in E18.

Pharisaean /farɪ'siːən/ *adjective*. M17.
[from Latin *pharisaeus* PHARISEE + -AN.]
= PHARISAIC 2.

Pharisaic /farɪ'seɪk/ *adjective*. E17.
[ecclesiastical Latin *pharisaicus* from Greek *pharisaikos*, from *pharisaios* PHARISEE: see -IC. In sense 1 from the manner in which the Pharisees are described by the Gospels.]
1 Strict in doctrine and ritual without the spirit of piety; laying great stress upon the external observances of religion and outward show of morality, and assuming superiority on that account; hypocritical; self-righteous. E17.
2 Of or pertaining to the Pharisees. M17.
■ **Pharisaical** *adjective* (*a*) = PHARISAIC 1; †(*b*) = PHARISAIC 2: M16. **Pharisaically** *adverb* L16.

Pharisaism /'farɪseɪɪz(ə)m/ *noun*. L16.
[French *pharisaïsme*, from *pharisaïque* formed as PHARISAIC: see -ISM.]
The doctrine and practice of the Pharisees; the fact of being a Pharisee. Also, hypocrisy, self-righteousness.

Pharisee /'farɪsiː/ *noun*. OE.
[ecclesiastical Latin *pharisaeus*, *-seus* from Greek *pharisaios* from Aramaic *prīšayyā* emphatic pl. of *prīš* = Hebrew *pārūš* separated, separatist.]
1 A member of a sect within Judaism between the 2nd cent. BC and the time of Jesus who observed strictly the tradition of the elders as well as the written Mosaic law as they interpreted it. OE.
2 A person of the spirit or disposition attributed to the Pharisees in the New Testament; a hypocrite, a self-righteous person. M16.
3 A fairy. Usu. in *pl.* Chiefly *dial.* M19.
■ **Phariseeism** *noun* = PHARISAISM L16.

pharmacal /'fɑːmək(ə)l/ *adjective*. Long *rare*. M17.
[from Latin *pharmacum* from Greek *pharmakon*: see PHARMACO-, -AL¹.]
Pharmaceutical.

pharmaceutic /fɑːmə'sjuːtɪk/ *noun & adjective*. M16.
[Late Latin *pharmaceuticus* from Greek *pharmakeutikos*, from *pharmakeutēs* = *pharmakeus* druggist, from *pharmakon*: see PHARMACY, -IC.]
▶**A** *noun*. **1** In *pl.* (treated as *sing.*) & †*sing.* The science of pharmacy. M16.
2 = PHARMACEUTICAL *noun*. L17.
▶**B** *adjective*. = PHARMACEUTICAL *adjective*. Now *rare*. M17.

pharmaceutical /fɑːmə'sjuːtɪk(ə)l/ *adjective & noun*. M17.
[formed as prec. + -AL¹.]
▶**A** *adjective*. Pertaining to or engaged in pharmacy; pertaining to the preparation, use, or sale of medicinal drugs. M17.

📖 N. G. CLARK Widely used in the pharmaceutical industry for ointments, cosmetics, etc.

▶**B** *noun*. A pharmaceutical preparation; a medicinal drug. L19.

■ **pharmaceutically** *adverb* in relation to, or from the point of view of, pharmacy L18.

pharmaceutist /fɑːmə'sjuːtɪst/ *noun*. L18.
[from Greek *pharmakeutēs*: see PHARMACEUTIC, -IST.]
A pharmacist.

pharmacist /'fɑːməsɪst/ *noun*. M19.
[from PHARMACY + -IST.]
A person skilled or engaged in pharmacy; a person who prepares or dispenses medicines.

📖 P. PARISH The patient who takes over-the-counter drugs . . , without telling the . . doctor what he buys from the pharmacist, may be at risk.

pharmaco- /'fɑːməkəʊ/ *combining form*.
[Greek *pharmako-* combining form of *pharmakon* drug, medicine, poison: see -O-.]
Forming nouns and adjectives, with the sense 'drugs'.
■ **pharmacody'namic** *adjective* of or pertaining to pharmacodynamics L19. **pharmacody'namically** *adverb* as regards pharmacodynamics E20. **pharmacody'namics** *noun* the branch of pharmacology that deals with the effects of drugs and the mechanism of their action M19. **pharmacoge'netic** *adjective* of or pertaining to pharmacogenetics M20. **pharmacoge'neticist** *noun* an expert or specialist in pharmacogenetics L20. **pharmacoge'netics** *noun* the branch of pharmacology that deals with the effect of genetic factors on reactions to drugs M20. **pharmacoge'nomics** *noun* the branch of genetics concerned with determining the likely response of an individual to therapeutic drugs L20. **pharmacoki'netic** *adjective* of or pertaining to pharmacokinetics M20. **pharmacoki'netically** *adverb* as regards pharmacokinetics L20. **pharmacoki'netics** *noun* the branch of pharmacology that deals with the movement of drugs within the body M20. **pharmaco'therapy** *noun* medical treatment by means of drugs E20.

pharmacognosy /fɑːmə'kɒgnəsi/ *noun*. Also in Latin form **-cognosia** /-kɒg'nəʊsɪə/ & in Greek form **-cognosis** /-kɒg'nəʊsɪs/. M19.
[from PHARMACO- + Greek *gnōsis* investigation, knowledge.]
The branch of science that deals with drugs, esp. natural drugs in their unprepared state.
■ **pharmacognosist** *noun* an expert in or student of pharmacognosy E20. **pharmacog'nostic** *adjective* M20. **pharmacog'nostical** *adjective* L19. **pharmacog'nostically** *adverb* from the point of view of pharmacognosy L19. **pharmacog'nostics** *noun* pharmacognosy M19.

pharmacology /fɑːmə'kɒlədʒi/ *noun*. E18.
[mod. Latin *pharmacologia*, from PHARMACO-: see -OLOGY.]
The branch of medicine that deals with the uses, effects, and modes of action of drugs. Formerly also = PHARMACY 2.
■ **pharmaco'logic** *adjective* (chiefly *US*) E20. **pharmaco'logical** *adjective* M19. **pharmaco'logically** *adverb* E20. **pharmacologist** *noun* E18.

pharmacopoeia /fɑːməkə'piːə/ *noun*. Also ***-peia**. E17.
[mod. Latin from Greek *pharmakopoiia* art of preparing drugs, from *pharmakopoios* preparer of drugs, formed as PHARMACO- + *-poios* making, maker.]
1 A book containing a list of drugs with their effects and directions for their use (and, formerly, their preparation and identification); *spec.* such a book officially published and revised periodically. E17.
2 A collection or stock of drugs. E18.
■ **pharmacopoeial** *adjective* pertaining to a pharmacopoeia; (of a drug) recognized in, or prepared, administered, etc., according to the directions of, an official pharmacopoeia: M19. **pharmacopoean** *noun & adjective* (*rare*) †(*a*) *noun* a person knowledgeable about a pharmacopoeia; (*b*) *adjective* pharmacopoeial; formerly, knowledgeable about a pharmacopoeia: M17.

pharmacopolist /fɑːmə'kɒp(ə)lɪst/ *noun*. Now *rare*. M17.
[from Latin *pharmacopola* from Greek *pharmakopōlēs*, formed as PHARMACO- + *pōlēs* seller: see -IST.]
A person who sells medicines.
■ Also †**pharmacopole** *noun* M16–L18.

pharmacy /'fɑːməsi/ *noun*. LME.
[Old French *farmacie* (mod. *ph-*) from medieval Latin *pharmacia* from Greek *pharmakeia* practice of a druggist, from *pharmakon* drug, medicine: see -Y³.]
1 The use or administration of drugs or medicines. Now *poet.* or *rhet.* LME.
2 The preparation and dispensing of drugs, esp. for medicinal purposes; the occupation of a druggist or pharmaceutical chemist. M17.
3 A place where medicines are prepared or dispensed; a dispensary. M19.

pharmakos /'fɑːmakɒs/ *noun*. Pl. ***-koi*** /-kɔɪ/. E20.
[Greek.]
A scapegoat; *spec.* one chosen in ancient Greece in atonement for a crime or misfortune.

†**pharo** *noun* var. of FARO *noun*¹.

pharos /'fɛːrɒs/ *noun*. Pl. **-roi** /-rɔɪ/, **-roses**. M16.
[Appellative use of Latin & Greek place-name.]
1 A lighthouse, a beacon for sailors; *spec.* (**P-**) that built *c* 280 BC on the island of Pharos off Alexandria in Egypt (now a peninsula forming part of the city). M16.

2 Any conspicuous light; a ship's lantern; a candelabrum; a lamp. M18.

Pharsalia /fɑːˈseɪlɪə/ *noun*. E19.
[The region Pharsalus in N. Greece, site of a battle (see PHARSALIAN).]
A resounding defeat; a monumental failure.
■ **Pharsalian** *adjective* of or pertaining to Pharsalia or the battle fought there in 48 BC, in which Pompey was defeated by Caesar E17.

pharyng- *combining form* see PHARYNGO-.

pharyngal /fəˈrɪŋg(ə)l/ *adjective & noun*. M19.
[from mod. Latin *pharyng-*, PHARYNX + -AL¹.]
▶ **A** *adjective*. = PHARYNGEAL *adjective*. M19.
▶ **B** *noun*. = PHARYNGEAL *noun* 2. L19.
■ **pharyngaliˈzation** *noun* pharyngealization M20. **pharyngalized** *adjective* pharyngealized M20.

pharyngeal /fəˈrɪn(d)ʒɪəl, far(ə)nˈdʒiːəl/ *adjective & noun*. E19.
[from mod. Latin *pharyngeus*, formed as prec. + -AL¹.]
▶ **A** *adjective*. Of, pertaining to, or involving the pharynx; *spec*. (PHONETICS) designating (*a*) vowel sounds produced by resonance in the pharynx; (*b*) consonantal sounds articulated with obstruction of the air-stream at the pharynx. E19.
▶ **B** *noun*. **1** A pharyngeal bone, *esp*. one in a fish. M19.
2 PHONETICS. A pharyngeal speech sound. M20.
■ **pharyngealiˈzation** *noun* obstruction of the air-stream at the pharynx; modification into a pharyngeal sound: M20. **pharyngealized** *adjective* produced by pharyngealization M20.

pharynges *noun pl*. see PHARYNX.

pharyngitis /far(ə)nˈdʒʌɪtɪs/ *noun*. M19.
[formed as PHARYNGAL + -ITIS.]
Inflammation of the pharynx.

pharyngo- /fəˈrɪŋgəʊ/ *combining form* of mod. Latin PHARYNX: see -O-. Before a vowel also **pharyng-**.
■ **pharyngectomy** /-r(ə)nˈdʒɛk-/ *noun* (an instance of) surgical removal of the pharynx L19. **pharyngoconjunctival** *adjective* designating a syndrome characterized by conjunctivitis, pharyngitis, and fever that occurs chiefly in epidemics among children M20. **pharyngo-ˈpalatine** *adjective* pertaining to the pharynx and the palate M19. **pharyngoscope** *noun* an instrument for visual examination of the pharynx M19. **pharynˈgotomy** *noun* (an instance of) surgical incision into the pharynx M18.

pharynx /ˈfarɪŋks/ *noun*. Pl. **pharynges** /fəˈrɪndʒiːz/, **pharynxes**. L17.
[mod. Latin *pharynx*, *pharyng-* from Greek *pharugx* throat.]
ANATOMY & ZOOLOGY. In humans, the cavity (with its enclosing muscles and mucous membrane) situated behind the nose, mouth, and larynx and connecting them with the oesophagus; in vertebrates in general, the part of the alimentary canal between the mouth cavity and the oesophagus; in invertebrates, the part of the alimentary canal immediately posterior to the buccal cavity.

phascogale /faˈskɒgəliː/ *noun*. M19.
[mod. Latin genus name, from Greek *phaskō(los* purse + *galē* weasel.]
A small insectivorous mouselike marsupial of the family Dasyuridae, native to Australia and New Guinea.

phase /feɪz/ *noun*. E19.
[Partly from French from mod. Latin PHASIS, partly back-form. from *phases* pl. of PHASIS.]
1 Each of the aspects presented by the moon or a planet, according to the shape of its illuminated portion as seen from the earth; *spec*. each of the stages new moon, first quarter, full moon, and last quarter. E19.
2 A distinct period or stage in a process of change or development; any one aspect of a thing of varying aspects; ZOOLOGY a genetic or seasonal variety of an animal's coloration, form, or behaviour. M19. ▸**b** A temporarily difficult or unhappy period or stage of development, esp. of an adolescent. Freq. in ***go through a phase***, ***pass through a phase***. E20.
3 PHYSICS. A particular stage or point in the cycle of a periodic phenomenon (esp. an alternating current or a light wave), or in a sequence of changes or operations, relative to a particular reference position or time. M19. ▸**b** ELECTRICAL ENGINEERING. Each of the windings of a polyphase machine. E20.
4 A physically distinct and homogeneous form of a substance characterized by its composition and state and separated by a bounding surface from other forms. L19.

> 📖 **1** D. BREWSTER Venus had the same crescent phases as the waxing and the waning moon. **2** LYTTON He saw her in the most attractive phase of her character. *Times* A contract for phase one of a new district hospital. V. BROME Jones' emotional life had entered a new phase. **3** ***in phase*** in the same phase; having the same phase or in the same stage of variation at the same time; (foll. by *with*). ***out of phase*** not in phase.

Comb.: **phase angle** (*a*) an angle representing a difference in phase, 360 degrees (2π radians) corresponding to one complete cycle; (*b*) ASTRONOMY the angle between the lines joining a given planet to the sun and to the earth; **phase-array** an array of radio aerials that is made to transmit or receive at a variable angle by delaying the signals to or from each one by an amount depending on its position relative to the others; **phase change** a change in the phase of a wave or of a substance; **phase contrast** the technique in microscopy of introducing a phase difference between parts of the light supplied by the condenser so as to enhance the outlines of the sample, or the boundaries between parts differing in optical density; usu. *attrib*.; **phase converter** ELECTRICAL ENGINEERING a device which converts an alternating current into one having a different number of phases but the same frequency; **phase diagram** CHEMISTRY a diagram representing the limits of stability of the various phases in a chemical system at equilibrium, with respect to variables such as composition and temperature; **phase distortion** distortion of a waveform caused by a difference in the speed of propagation for components with different frequencies, so that their phase relations are altered; **phase inverter** ELECTRICAL ENGINEERING a phase-splitter which produces two signals 180 degrees out of phase; **phase-lock** *verb trans*. (ELECTRONICS) fix the frequency of (an oscillator or a laser) relative to a stable oscillator of lower frequency by a method that utilizes a correction signal derived from the phase difference generated by any shift in the frequency; **phasemeter** ELECTRICITY an instrument which measures the phase difference between two oscillations having the same frequency, esp. that between an alternating current and the corresponding voltage; **phase modulation** variation of the phase of a radio or other wave as a means of carrying information such as an audio signal; **phase rule** CHEMISTRY: relating the numbers of phases, constituents, and degrees of freedom in a system; **phase shift** PHYSICS a change in the phase of a waveform; **phase space** PHYSICS a multidimensional space in which each axis corresponds to one of the coordinates required to specify the state of a physical system, all the coordinates being thus represented so that a point in the space corresponds to a state of the system; **phase-splitter** ELECTRICAL ENGINEERING a circuit or device which splits a single-phase voltage into two or more voltages differing in phase; **phase velocity** PHYSICS the speed of propagation of a sine wave or a sinusoidal component of a complex wave, equal to the product of its wavelength and frequency.
¶ See note s.v. PHASIS.
■ **phaseless** *adjective* (*rare*) having no phases, of unchanging aspect or state M19.

phase /feɪz/ *verb*¹. E20.
[from the noun.]
1 *verb trans*. Adjust the phase of; bring into phase, synchronize. E20.
2 *verb trans*. Organize or carry out gradually in planned stages or instalments. E20.

> 📖 **2** *Daily Telegraph* To end imprisonment without trial by a phased programme of releases of every detainee and internee.

With adverbs in specialized senses: **phase down** *verb phr. trans*. reduce or decrease gradually or in planned stages. **phase in** *verb phr. trans*. introduce or incorporate gradually or in planned stages. **phase out** (*a*) *verb phr. trans*. remove, eliminate, or take out of gradually or in planned stages; (*b*) *verb phr. intrans*. disappear gradually.
Comb.: **phase-down** a gradual reduction or planned decrease; **phase-in** a gradual introduction; **phase-out** a gradual removal or planned elimination.
■ **phaser** *noun* (*a*) a device that alters the phase of something; MUSIC an instrument that alters a sound signal by phasing; (*b*) SCIENCE FICTION a weapon that delivers a beam that can stun or annihilate: M20.

phase *verb*² var. of FAZE *verb*¹.

phaseolin /fəˈsiːəlɪn/ *noun*. L19.
[from Latin *phaseolus* bean + -IN¹.]
BIOCHEMISTRY. A crystalline globulin found in the seeds of the kidney bean.

phaseollin /fəˈsiːəlɪn/ *noun*. M20.
[Alt. of prec.]
BIOCHEMISTRY. A fungitoxic phytoalexin produced by the kidney bean plant.

phases *noun* pl. of PHASE *noun*, PHASIS.

phasic /ˈfeɪzɪk, -s-/ *adjective*. L19.
[from PHASE *noun* + -IC.]
1 Of, pertaining to, or of the nature of a phase or phases; presenting phases. L19.
2 PHYSIOLOGY. Responding to a varying stimulus or environment rather than to a constant one. E20.
■ **phasically** *adverb* L20.

phasing /ˈfeɪzɪŋ/ *noun*. L19.
[from PHASE *noun*, *verb*¹ + -ING¹.]
1 The action of adjusting or eliminating a phase difference. L19.
2 The relationship between the phases of two or more periodic phenomena having the same frequency. E20.
3 The action of gradually introducing, bringing *in*, or taking *out* something. M20.
4 MUSIC. The modification of the sound signal from an electric guitar etc. by introducing a phase shift into either of two copies of it and then recombining them. Also, a technique in which two parts of an ensemble play the same rhythmic pattern at different speeds. L20.

> 📖 **1** *Times* Pedestrians are ignored in the phasing of traffic lights at many T-junctions. **3** *Guardian* The French . . want to discuss the phasing out of sterling as a reserve currency.

phasis /ˈfeɪsɪs, -sɪs/ *noun*. Pl. **phases** /ˈfeɪsiːz, -siːz/. M17.
[mod. Latin from Greek, from base *pha-*, *phan-* of *phainein* show, appear.]
1 = PHASE *noun* 1. M17. ▸**b** The first appearance of the new moon. L19.
2 = PHASE *noun* 2. M17.
¶ The pl. is not distinguishable in form from that of PHASE *noun*. All instances of the pl. before 19 have been regarded as belonging here.

phasitron /ˈfeɪzɪtrɒn/ *noun*. M20.
[from PHASE *noun* + -I- + -TRON.]
ELECTRONICS. An electron tube suitable for phase modulation of a wave by large amounts, consisting of a central cathode inside a slotted cylindrical anode inside a coaxial second anode, the pattern of electrons being rotated and modulated to alter the phase of the current at the second anode.

phasm /ˈfaz(ə)m/ *noun*. Also in Latin form **phasma** /ˈfazmə/, pl. **-mata** /-mətə/. M17.
[Latin from Greek, from *phaō* shine or *phainein* show, appear.]
1 An extraordinary appearance, esp. of brilliant light in the air. Long *obsolete* exc. *poet*. M17.
2 A phantom, an apparition. *arch*. M17.

phasmid /ˈfazmɪd/ *noun*. L19.
[from prec. + -ID³.]
An insect of the order Phasmida; a leaf insect, a stick insect.

phason /ˈfeɪzɒn/ *noun*. L20.
[from PHASE *noun* + -ON.]
PHYSICS. A quantum or quasiparticle associated with modulation of the phase of the distortion of a crystal lattice.

phasor /ˈfeɪzə/ *noun*. M20.
[from PHASE *noun* + -OR, after *vector*.]
ELECTRICITY. A line whose length and direction represent a complex electrical quantity with no spatial extension.

phat /fat/ *adjective*. *Black slang*. M20.
[Orig. uncertain: perh. a respelling of FAT *adjective*.]
Esp. of a woman: sexy, attractive. Also (chiefly of music): excellent, fashionable.

phatic /ˈfatɪk/ *adjective*. E20.
[from Greek *phatos* spoken or *phatikos* assertory: see -IC.]
Of speech or speech sounds: serving to establish or maintain social relationships rather than to impart information.

Ph.D. *abbreviation*.
Latin *Philosophiae Doctor* Doctor of Philosophy, Doctorate of Philosophy.

pheasant /ˈfɛz(ə)nt/ *noun*. ME.
[Anglo-Norman *fesaunt*, Old & mod. French *faisan* from Latin *phasianus* from Greek *phasianos* (sc. *ornis* bird) of Phasis, ancient name of the River Rioni in Georgia, whence the bird is said to have spread westwards. *Ph-* by etymological reversion; for *t* see -ANT².]
Any of numerous Old World gallinaceous birds which together with partridges and quails constitute the family Phasianidae, being generally large birds with long tails and (in the male) bright, sometimes iridescent colouring; *spec*. any bird of the genus *Phasianus*, *esp*. the game-bird *P. colchicus*; (usu. with specifying word) any of various similar birds of other families. Also, the flesh of any of these birds as food.
golden pheasant, ***Impeyan pheasant***, ***koklass pheasant***, ***ring pheasant***, etc.
Comb.: **pheasant coucal** a coucal, *Centropus phasianus*, which resembles a pheasant, found in Australia and New Guinea; **pheasant-eye narcissus**, **pheasant-eyed narcissus** = ***pheasant's eye*** (c) below; **pheasant's eye** any of several plants having flowers with a darker centre; *esp*. (*a*) a scarlet-flowered ornamental plant, *Adonis annua*, of the buttercup family, sometimes found as a cornfield weed; (*b*) (more fully ***pheasant's eye pink***) a variety of the garden pink *Dianthus plumarius*; (*c*) = ***pheasant's eye narcissus*** s.v. NARCISSUS 1.
■ **pheasantry** *noun* a place where pheasants are reared or kept E18.

pheer *verb* var. of FEER.

†**pheeze** *verb* var. of FEEZE *verb*.

phellem /ˈfɛləm/ *noun*. L19.
[from Greek *phellos* cork + *-em* as in PHLOEM.]
BOTANY. = CORK *noun*¹ 1b.

phello- /ˈfɛləʊ/ *combining form* of Greek *phellos* cork: see -O-.
■ **phelloderm** *noun* (BOTANY) a layer of parenchymatous cells containing chlorophyll, formed by the cork cambium on the inner surface of the periderm L19. **phelloˈdermal** *adjective* of or pertaining to the phelloderm L19. **phellogen** *noun* (BOTANY) = ***cork cambium*** s.v. CORK *noun*¹ L19. **phelloˈgenic** *adjective* of the nature of or pertaining to the cork cambium L19.

pheme /fiːm/ *noun*. *rare*. E20.
[Greek *phēmē* words, speech.]
LINGUISTICS. An inflected or compound word, or a sequence of words, as a unit having grammatical (as opp. to semantic) meaning.

phememe /ˈfiːmiːm/ *noun. rare.* M20.
[from prec. + -EME.]
LINGUISTICS. The smallest linguistic unit.

phen- *combining form* see PHENO-.

phenacaine /ˈfɛnəkeɪn/ *noun.* E20.
[from PHEN- + -*a*- + -CAINE.]
PHARMACOLOGY. A synthetic derivative of phenetidine resembling cocaine in its action and used as an eye anaesthetic. Also called ***holocaine***.

phenacetin /fɪˈnasɪtɪn/ *noun.* L19.
[from PHEN- + ACET(YL + -IN¹.]
PHARMACOLOGY. The acyl derivative of phenetidine, formerly used as an antipyretic.

phenacite *noun* var. of PHENAKITE.

phenagle *verb* var. of FINAGLE.

phenakistoscope /fɛnəˈkɪstəskəʊp/ *noun.* M19.
[from Greek *phenakistēs* cheat, from *phenakizein* to cheat + -SCOPE.]
A toy consisting of a disc or drum with figures representing a moving object in successive positions arranged radially on it, to be viewed in such a way that an impression of actual motion is obtained when the disc or drum is rapidly rotated.
■ **phenakistoˈscopic** *adjective* resembling or reminiscent of a phenakistoscope M20.

phenakite /ˈfɛnəkʌɪt/ *noun.* Also **-cite** /-kʌɪt, -sʌɪt/. M19.
[from Greek *phenak-*, *phenax* cheat (as having been mistaken for quartz) + -ITE¹.]
MINERALOGY. A rare trigonal silicate of beryllium that is a rock-forming mineral occurring as colourless or white scales and prisms.

phenanthrene /fɪˈnanθriːn/ *noun.* L19.
[from PHEN- + ANTHRA(C)ENE.]
CHEMISTRY. A crystalline tricyclic saturated hydrocarbon, $C_{14}H_{10}$, obtained from coal tar oil.

phenanthridine /fɪˈnanθrɪdiːn/ *noun.* L19.
[formed as next + -IDINE.]
CHEMISTRY & PHARMACOLOGY. A white crystalline tricyclic compound, $C_{13}H_9N$, an isomer of acridine, used as a trypanocide; any of various derivatives of this.

phenanthroline /fɪˈnanθrəliːn/ *noun.* L19.
[from PHENANTHR(ENE + QUIN)OLINE.]
CHEMISTRY. A heteroaromatic organic compound, $C_{12}H_8N_2$, whose molecule is based on a phenanthrene ring system, used as an indicator for iron.

phenazine /ˈfɛnəziːn/ *noun.* E20.
[from PHEN- + AZINE.]
CHEMISTRY. A tricyclic compound, $(C_6H_4)_2N_2$, used in organic synthesis.

phencyclidine /fɛnˈsʌɪklɪdiːn/ *noun.* M20.
[from PHEN- + CYCLO- + PIPER)IDINE.]
PHARMACOLOGY & VETERINARY MEDICINE. A powerful analgesic and anaesthetic derived from piperidine whose use is now chiefly restricted to veterinary medicine on account of its hallucinogenic effects. Also called ***PCP***. Cf. ***angel dust*** s.v. ANGEL *noun*.
¶ A proprietary name for this drug is SERNYL.

phene /fiːn/ *noun.* Now *rare.* M19.
[French *phène* from Greek *phaino-* shining: see PHENYL.]
CHEMISTRY. = BENZENE.

phenelzine /fəˈnɛlziːn/ *noun.* M20.
[from PHEN- + E(THY)L + HYDRA)ZINE.]
PHARMACOLOGY. A monoamine oxidase inhibitor that is used as an antidepressant.

Phenergan /ˈfɛnəg(ə)n/ *noun.* M20.
[from PHEN- + *-ergan*, of unkn. origin.]
PHARMACOLOGY. (Proprietary name for) the drug promethazine.

phenethicillin /fɪˌnɛθɪˈsɪlɪn/ *noun.* M20.
[from PHEN- + ETH(YL + PEN)ICILLIN.]
PHARMACOLOGY. A semisynthetic penicillin used to treat penicillin-sensitive infections.

phenetic /fəˈnɛtɪk/ *adjective.* M20.
[from Greek *phainein* appear + *-etic*, after PHYLETIC.]
BIOLOGY. Of or pertaining to phenetics; based on observed similarities and differences without reference to evolutionary relationships.
■ **phenetically** *adverb* as regards showing similar characteristics M20.

phenetics /fəˈnɛtɪks/ *noun.* M20.
[from prec. + -ICS.]
BIOLOGY. The systematic classification of groups of organisms on the basis of observed similarities and differences, without reference to evolutionary relationships.
■ **pheneticist** *noun* M20.

phenetidine /fɪˈnɛtɪdiːn/ *noun.* M19.
[from PHENET(OLE + -IDINE.]
CHEMISTRY. Each of three amino derivatives of phenetole which are oily liquids used esp. in making dyes.

phenetole /ˈfɛnɪtəʊl/ *noun.* M19.
[from PHEN- + ET(HYL + -OLE².]
CHEMISTRY. Ethyl phenyl ether, $C_2H_5{\cdot}O{\cdot}C_6H_5$, a volatile liquid with an aromatic smell.

phenformin /fɛnˈfɔːmɪn/ *noun.* M20.
[from PHEN- + FORM(ALDEHYDE + IM)IN(O-.]
PHARMACOLOGY. A biguanide derivative, $C_{10}H_{15}N_5.HCl$, formerly used in the oral treatment of diabetes.

phengite /ˈfɛn(d)ʒʌɪt/ *noun.* E17.
[Latin *phengites* from Greek *pheggitēs*, from *pheggos* light, lustre: see -ITE¹.]
MINERALOGY. **1** A transparent or translucent kind of stone known to the ancients, probably crystallized gypsum. E17.
2 A variety of muscovite with more silica and less aluminium. M19.

phenic /ˈfiːnɪk, ˈfɛ-/ *adjective.* Now *rare* or *obsolete.* M19.
[French *phénique*, formed as PHENE: see -IC.]
CHEMISTRY. = PHENYLIC.
■ **phenate** *noun* a phenoxide M19.

Phenidone /ˈfɛnɪdəʊn/ *noun.* M20.
[from PHEN- + -IDE + -ONE.]
(Proprietary name for) a photographic developer similar to metol; 1-phenyl-3-pyrazolidone, $C_9H_{10}N_2O$.

phenindione /fɛnɪnˈdʌɪəʊn/ *noun.* M20.
[from PHEN- + INDO-² + -ONE.]
PHARMACOLOGY. A vitamin K analogue, $C_{15}H_{10}O_2$, used as an anticoagulant, esp. in the treatment of thrombosis.

phenix *noun* var. of PHOENIX.

phenmetrazine /fɛnˈmɛtrəziːn/ *noun.* M20.
[from PHEN- + *-metr-* (from MET(HYL + HYD)R(O-) + AZINE.]
PHARMACOLOGY. A compound related to amphetamine which has been used as an appetite suppressant; 3-methyl-2-phenylmorpholine, $C_{11}H_{15}NO$.
¶ A proprietary name for this drug is PRELUDIN.

pheno /ˈfiːnəʊ/ *noun. colloq.* Pl. **-os**. M20.
[Abbreviation.]
(A tablet of) phenobarbitone.

pheno- /ˈfiːnəʊ, ˈfɛnəʊ/ *combining form.* Before a vowel also **phen-**.
[In sense 1 from French *phényle* PHENYL, in sense 2 from Greek *phainein* to show: see -O-.]
1 CHEMISTRY. Phenyl.
2 Showing, manifesting, as ***phenocopy***, ***phenotype***.
■ **phenocopy** *noun* (BIOLOGY) an individual showing features characteristic of a genotype other than its own, but produced environmentally rather than genetically M20. **phenogram** /ˈfɛn-/ *noun* (TAXONOMY) a dendrogram showing phenetic relationships M20. **phenoˈsafranine** *noun* a synthetic red dye which is used in photography as a desensitizer L19.

phenobarb /fiːnə(ʊ)ˈbɑːb, fɛn-/ *noun. colloq.* M20.
[Abbreviation.]
Phenobarbitone.

phenobarbital /fiːnə(ʊ)ˈbɑːbɪt(ə)l, -tal, fɛn-/ *noun. N. Amer.* E20.
[from PHENO- + BARBITAL.]
PHARMACOLOGY. Phenobarbitone.

phenobarbitone /fiːnə(ʊ)ˈbɑːbɪtəʊn, fɛn-/ *noun.* M20.
[from PHENO- + BARBITONE.]
PHARMACOLOGY. A barbiturate widely used as a sedative, hypnotic, and anticonvulsant, 5-ethyl-5-phenylbarbituric acid, $C_{12}H_{12}N_2O_3$.
¶ A proprietary name for this drug is LUMINAL.

phenocryst /ˈfiːnə(ʊ)krɪst, ˈfɛn-/ *noun.* L19.
[French *phénocryste*, formed as PHENO- + Greek *krustallos*: see CRYSTAL *noun*.]
GEOLOGY. Each of the large or conspicuous crystals in a porphyritic rock.

phenogam *noun* var. of PHAENOGAM.

phenol /ˈfiːnɒl/ *noun.* M19.
[French *phénole*, from *phène* PHENE, *phényle* PHENYL: see -OL.]
CHEMISTRY. **1** A hygroscopic crystalline compound, C_6H_5OH, that is a hydroxyl derivative of benzene widely used in making plastics, pharmaceuticals, dyes, etc., and in a weak solution as a household disinfectant. Also called ***carbolic acid***, ***phenylic acid***. M19.
2 Any derivative of an aromatic hydrocarbon in which a hydroxyl group is attached to the ring; a derivative of phenol in which one or more of the hydrogen atoms are replaced by other radicals. M19.
Comb.: **phenolcarboxylic** *adjective*: ***phenolcarboxylic acid***, any acid which contains a carboxyl group and a hydroxyl group bonded to the same benzene ring; **phenol-formaldehyde** *noun & adjective* (designating) any of a class of plastics, resins, etc., made by condensation of phenols with formaldehyde; **phenol oxidase** BIOLOGY = PHENOLASE; **phenol red** a red crystalline solid which is used as a pH indicator in the range 6.7 (yellow) to 8.3 (red) and in medicine is given as a test of kidney function; **phenol resin** a phenolic resin; **phenolsulphonphthalein** = ***phenol red*** above.
■ **phenolase** *noun* (BIOLOGY) any of a class of copper-containing enzymes, found esp. in plants and arthropods, which oxidize phenols to quinones (also called ***phenol oxidase***) E20. **phenolate** *noun* (CHEMISTRY) a phenoxide L19. **phenoliˈzation** *noun* treatment with phenol E20. **phenolized** *adjective* treated with phenol; *spec.* (of a vaccine, cell sample, etc.) suspended in a dilute solution of phenol: E20. **phenoloid** *adjective & noun* (now *rare* or *obsolete*) (a substance) containing phenolic compounds (***phenoloid oil***, a form of creosote) E20.

phenolic /fɪˈnɒlɪk/ *adjective & noun.* L19.
[from prec. + -IC.]
► **A** *adjective.* **1** CHEMISTRY. Of the nature of, belonging to, derived from, or containing a phenol; *esp.* containing or designating a hydroxyl group bonded directly to a benzene ring. L19.
2 Designating a large class of usu. thermosetting polymeric materials that have wide industrial applications as plastics or resins and are prepared from phenols by condensation with aldehydes; made of such a material. E20.

📖 **1** N. G. CLARK The crude oily phenolic layer is separated from the aqueous liquor. **2** *House & Garden* Mural panel in . . black phenolic resin. *Sunday Express* The set has . . stainless steel lids and black phenolic handles.

► **B** *noun.* **1** A phenolic plastic or resin. M20.
2 Any compound containing a hydroxyl group bonded directly to a benzene ring, *esp.* one that occurs in plants. M20.

phenology /fɪˈnɒlədʒi/ *noun.* L19.
[from PHEN(OMENON + -OLOGY.]
The field of study that deals with cyclic and seasonal natural phenomena, esp. in relation to climate and plant and animal life.
■ **phenoˈlogic** *adjective* M20. **phenoˈlogical** *adjective* L19.

phenolphthalein /fiːnɒlˈ(f)θaliːn, -ˈ(f)θeɪl-/ *noun.* L19.
[from PHENOL + PHTHALIC + -EIN.]
A whitish or yellowish crystalline solid, $C_{20}H_{14}O_4$, which is used as an indicator in the pH range 8 (colourless) to 10 (red), and medicinally as a laxative.

phenom /fɪˈnɒm/ *noun. N. Amer. colloq.* L19.
[Abbreviation.]
= PHENOMENON 3; *esp.* an exceptionally gifted person.

phenomena *noun* see PHENOMENON.

phenomenal /fɪˈnɒmɪn(ə)l/ *adjective & noun.* E19.
[from PHENOMENON + -AL¹.]
► **A** *adjective.* **1 a** Of the nature of a phenomenon; consisting of phenomena; perceptible by the senses or through immediate experience. E19. ►**b** Of or pertaining to phenomena, esp. those of a science. M19.
2 Very notable or remarkable; extraordinary, exceptional. M19.

📖 **1** A. J. AYER A reality which transcended the phenomenal world. **2** DAY LEWIS A singer whose breath-control was phenomenal.

► **B** *noun.* ***the phenomenal***, that which is perceptible by the senses or through immediate experience. M19.
■ **phenomeˈnality** *noun* the quality of being phenomenal; something that is phenomenal, a phenomenon: L19. **phenomenaliˈzation** *noun* (PHILOSOPHY) the action or result of phenomenalizing something L19. **phenomenalize** *verb trans.* (PHILOSOPHY) conceive or represent as phenomenal L19. **phenomenally** *adverb* (**a**) remarkably, extraordinarily, exceedingly; (**b**) *rare* in relation to phenomena: E19.

phenomenalism /fɪˈnɒmɪn(ə)lɪz(ə)m/ *noun.* M19.
[from prec. + -ISM.]
PHILOSOPHY. The manner of thinking which considers things from the point of view of phenomena only; the metaphysical doctrine that (actual or possible) phenomena are the only objects of knowledge, or the only realities.
■ **phenomenalist** *noun & adjective* (**a**) *noun* an advocate of phenomenalism; (**b**) *adjective* of or pertaining to phenomenalism or phenomenalists: M19. **phenomenaˈlistic** *adjective* M19. **phenomenaˈlistically** *adverb* as regards or in terms of phenomenalism E20.

†**phenomenas** *noun pl.* see PHENOMENON.

phenomenism /fɪˈnɒmɪnɪz(ə)m/ *noun.* M19.
[from PHENOMENON + -ISM.]
PHILOSOPHY. The metaphysical doctrine of phenomenalism.
■ **phenomenist** *adjective & noun* (**a**) *adjective* of or pertaining to phenomenism or phenomenists; (**b**) *noun* a person who advocates phenomenism: L19. **phenomeˈnistic** *adjective* L19.

phenomenology /fɪˌnɒmɪˈnɒlədʒi/ *noun.* L18.
[from PHENOMENON + -OLOGY.]
1 The branch of knowledge that deals with phenomena as opp. to existence. L18.
2 The branch of a science which describes and classifies its phenomena. M19.
3 PHILOSOPHY. The theory that the pure and transcendental nature and meaning of phenomena, and hence their real and ultimate significance, can only be apprehended subjectively; the method of reduction whereby all factual knowledge and reasoned assumptions about a phenomenon are set aside so that pure intuition of its essence may be analysed. E20.
4 PSYCHOLOGY. The methods of description and analysis developed from philosophical phenomenology applied

to the subjective experiencing of phenomena and to consciousness. **M20.**

■ **pheˌnomeno'logical** *adjective* of or pertaining to phenomenology; dealing with the description and classification of phenomena, not with their explanation or cause: **M19. pheˌnomeno'logically** *adverb* in terms of, or as regards, phenomena or phenomenology **L19. phenomenologist** *noun* a person who makes a study of or adheres to the doctrines of phenomenology **M19.**

phenomenon /fɪ'nɒmɪnən/ *noun.* Also **†phaen-, †phain-.** Pl. **-mena** /-mɪnə/, also (*non-standard*) used as sing., **†-menas. L16.**

[Late Latin *phaenomenon* from Greek *phainomenon* use as noun of neut. pres. pple pass. of *phainein* to show, (in pass.) be seen, appear.]

1 A fact or event that appears or is perceived by one of the senses or by the mind; *esp.* one whose cause or explanation is in question. **L16.**

2 *PHILOSOPHY.* An immediate object of perception (as distinguished from substance, or a thing in itself). **L17.**

3 A very notable, extraordinary, or exceptional fact or occurrence; *colloq.* a thing, person, or animal remarkable for some unusual quality. **E18.**

> **1** H. KISSINGER The curious phenomenon that success seemed to unsettle Nixon. P. DAVIES More phenomena came to be explained on the basis of scientific principles. M. WARNOCK Decision-making, or imagination, or . . humour, all of them in some sense mental phenomena. ***Purkinje phenomenon, Purkinje's phenomenon***: see PURKINJE. ***RAYNAUD's phenomenon. Trousseau's phenomenon***: see TROUSSEAU *noun*².

Phrases: **†salve the phenomena, †save the phenomena** reconcile observed facts with a theory or doctrine with which they appear to disagree.

phenon /'fɛnɒn/ *noun.* **M20.**

[from PHEN- + -ON.]

1 *BIOLOGY.* A group of apparently similar plants or animals. **M20.**

2 *TAXONOMY.* A grouping of organisms established by techniques of numerical analysis. **M20.**

-phenone /'fiːnəʊn, 'fɛ-/ *suffix.*

[from PHEN(YL + KET)ONE.]

Used in *CHEMISTRY* to form names of ketones containing phenyl, with or without substitutions, as ***butyrophenone***.

phenothiazine /fiːnəʊ'θʌɪəziːn, fɛn-/ *noun.* **L19.**

[from PHENO- + THIAZINE.]

1 A heterocyclic compound, $C_{12}H_9NS$, which is used to treat parasitic infestations of animals. **L19.**

2 Any of various derivatives of this, which constitute an important class of tranquillizing drugs used esp. in the treatment of mental illnesses. **M20.**

phenotype /'fiːnə(ʊ)tʌɪp/ *noun.* **E20.**

[German *Phenotypus*, formed as PHENO-: see TYPE *noun*.]

BIOLOGY. An organism distinguishable from others by observable features; the sum of the attributes of an individual, regarded as resulting from the interaction of its genotype with its environment.

■ **phenotypic** /-'tɪp-/, **phenotypical** /-'tɪp-/ *adjectives* of or pertaining to the observable features of, or differences between, organisms (often used with the implication 'not genotypic') **E20. phenotypically** /-'tɪp-/ *adverb* **E20. phenotyping** *noun* allocation to a phenotype **M20.**

phenox- *combining form* see PHENOXY-.

phenoxide /fɪ'nɒksʌɪd/ *noun.* **L19.**

[from PHEN- + OXIDE.]

CHEMISTRY. A salt of phenol, containing the anion $C_6H_5O^-$.

phenoxy /fɪ'nɒksi/ *noun.* **M20.**

[from next as adjective.]

A phenoxy plastic.

phenoxy- /fɪ'nɒksi/ *combining form.* Before a vowel also **phenox-**. Also as attrib. adjective **phenoxy**.

[from PHEN- + OXY-.]

1 *CHEMISTRY.* Designating or containing the group $\cdot O \cdot C_6H_5$.

2 (Only as adjective.) Designating thermoplastics characterized by a linear molecule containing recurring phenoxy groups.

■ **phenoxazine** *noun* a violet-red heterocyclic compound, $C_{12}H_9NO$, used in making oxazine dyes; any compound whose molecule contains the same skeleton as this compound: **L19. phenoxya'cetic** *adjective*: ***phenoxyacetic acid***, the crystalline acid $C_6H_5O \cdot CH_2COOH$; any of the chlorinated derivatives of this, widely used as weedkillers: **L19. phenoxymethylpeni'cillin** *noun* a semisynthetic penicillin, $C_{16}H_{18}N_2O_5S$ **M20.**

phentolamine /fɛn'tɒləmiːn/ *noun.* **M20.**

[from PHEN- + TOL(YL + AMINE.]

PHARMACOLOGY. A tricyclic compound, $C_{17}H_{19}N_3O$, which is used as a vasodilator, esp. in certain cases of hypertension.

phenyl /'fiːnʌɪl, 'fɛnɪl/ *noun.* **M19.**

[French *phényle*, from Greek *phaino-* shining, *phainein* to show, *phainesthai* appear: see -YL. From its being first used in the names of compounds that were by-products of the manufacture of gas used for illumination.]

CHEMISTRY. The cyclic radical $C_6H_5\cdot$ derived from benzene by the loss of one hydrogen atom. Usu. in *comb.*

Comb.: **phenylacetic** *adjective*: ***phenylacetic acid***, $C_6H_5CH_2COOH$, a crystalline acid used in making perfumes, flavourings, penicillin, etc.; **phenylarsonic** *adjective*: ***phenylarsonic acid***, a crystalline solid, $C_6H_5AsO(OH)_2$, used as a trypanocide; **phenylephrine** *PHARMACOLOGY* a compound related to adrenalin used as a vasoconstrictor and nasal decongestant; **phenylhydrazine** a colourless liquid, $C_6H_5NHNH_2$, used as a reagent and in organic synthesis; **phenylhydrazone** any of a class of compounds formed by condensation of an aldehyde or ketone with phenylhydrazine; **phenylmercury** *adjective & noun* (designating) a compound containing a phenyl group bonded directly to a mercury atom; **phenylpropanolamine** *PHARMACOLOGY* a compound, $C_9H_{13}NO$, related to ephedrine and used as a decongestant; also called ***norephedrine***; **phenylpyruvate** a salt of phenylpyruvic acid; **phenylpyruvic** *adjective*: ***phenylpyruvic acid***, a crystalline solid, $C_6H_5CH_2CO \cdot COOH$, which occurs in the urine of a person with phenylketonuria; **phenylthiocarbamide** a crystalline solid, $NH_2 \cdot CS \cdot NH \cdot C_6H_5$, which has a bitter taste to people possessing a certain dominant gene and is tasteless to those lacking it; **phenylthiourea** phenylthiocarbamide.

■ **phenylate** *noun* a phenoxide **L19. phenylic** /fɪ'nɪlɪk/ *adjective*: ***phenylic acid***, phenol **M19.**

phenylalanine /fiːnʌɪl'alənіːn, fɛnɪl-/ *noun.* **L19.**

[from PHENYL + ALANINE.]

BIOCHEMISTRY. A hydrophobic amino acid, $C_6H_5CH_2CH(NH_2)COOH$, which occurs in proteins and is essential in the human diet; 2-amino-3-phenylpropionic acid.

phenylbutazone /fiːnʌɪl'bjuːtəzəʊn, -nɪl-, fɛnɪl-/ *noun.* **M20.**

[from PHENYL + BUT(YL + AZO- + -ONE.]

PHARMACOLOGY & VETERINARY MEDICINE. A drug formerly used as an analgesic, esp. for the relief of rheumatic pain and inflammation, but now largely restricted to veterinary use.

¶ A proprietary name for this drug is BUTAZOLIDIN.

phenylene /'fɛnɪliːn/ *noun.* **M19.**

[from PHENYL + -ENE.]

Orig., a compound assigned the formula C_6H_4. Now, each of three radicals $C_6H_4=$ derived from benzene by the loss of two hydrogen atoms. Usu. in *comb.*

Comb.: **phenylene blue** the dye indamine; **phenylene brown** a brown substance derived from phenylenediamine and used as a dye and histological stain; **phenylenediamine** each of three isomeric solids, $C_6H_4(NH_2)_2$, or any of their alkylated derivatives, which are widely used in the dye industry, as photographic developers, and (the *para* isomer) as an additive in rubber to prevent oxidation.

phenylketonuria /ˌfiːnʌɪlkiːtə'njʊərɪə, -nɪl-, ˌfɛnɪl-/ *noun.* **M20.**

[from PHENYL + KETONURIA.]

MEDICINE. An inherited inability to metabolize phenylalanine normally, which if untreated in children leads to mental handicap.

■ **phenylketonuric** *noun & adjective* (**a**) *noun* an individual with phenylketonuria; (**b**) *adjective* affected with or pertaining to this disorder: **M20.**

phenytoin /fɛ'nɪtəʊɪn/ *noun.* **M20.**

[from PHENY(L + HYDAN)TOIN.]

PHARMACOLOGY. An anticonvulsant used to treat epilepsy; 5,5-diphenylhydantoin, $C_{15}H_{12}N_2O_2$.

pheon /'fiːɒn/ *noun.* **L15.**

[Origin unkn.]

A heraldic charge in the form of a broad arrowhead, *esp.* one engrailed on the inner edge of each barb.

pheran /'feɪrən, 'peɪrən/ *noun.* **M19.**

[Kashmiri, prob. from Persian *pīrāhan* shirt.]

A loose shirt or robe worn by men and women in Kashmir.

Pherecratean /ˌfɛrɪkrə'tiːən/ *adjective & noun.* **M19.**

[from Latin *Pherecratius* from Greek *pherekrateios*, from *Pherekratēs* a Greek poet of the 5th cent. BC: see -EAN.]

CLASSICAL PROSODY. (Designating) a measure consisting of three feet, normally spondee, dactyl, and spondee (or trochee).

■ Also **Pherecratian** /fɛrɪ'kreɪʃ(ə)n/ *adjective* **L18.**

pheromone /'fɛrəməʊn/ *noun.* **M20.**

[from Greek *pherein* convey + -O- + *-mone*, after *hormone*.]

BIOLOGY. A chemical secreted and released by an organism which causes a specific response when detected by another organism of the same (or a closely related) species.

■ **phero'monal** *adjective* of, pertaining to, or of the nature of a pheromone or pheromones **M20.**

phew /fjuː, fjʊ/ *interjection & verb.* **E17.**

[Imit. of puffing.]

► **A** *interjection.* Expr. relief, disgust, discomfort, weariness, or impatience. **E17.**

> S. A. GRAU He does smell. . . phew. M. RUSSELL 'Phew!' he said . . 'After that I need a drink.'

► **B** *verb intrans.* Say 'phew'. **M19.**

phi /fʌɪ/ *noun.* **LME.**

[Greek.]

1 The twenty-first letter (Φ, ϕ) of the Greek alphabet. **LME.**

2 *PETROGRAPHY.* An index of particle size, defined as the negative of the logarithm to the base 2 of the diameter in millimetres. Freq. *attrib.*, as ***phi scale***, ***phi value***, and written as ϕ. **M20.**

3 *STATISTICS.* ***phi coefficient***, the product-moment coefficient of correlation in a case where each of the observed variables has only two possible values. **M20.**

4 *PARTICLE PHYSICS.* In full ***phi meson***. Any of a group of mesons which have the same quantum numbers as the omega meson but a mass of 1019 MeV, and on decaying usu. produce two kaons or three pions. Freq. written ϕ. **M20.**

¶ Rare before **M19.**

phial /'fʌɪəl/ *noun.* Also **†f-. ME.**

[Old & mod. French *fiole* from Latin *phiola*, *phiala* saucer, censer from Greek *phialē* broad flat vessel. See also VIAL.]

A vessel for holding liquids. Now usu. a small glass bottle, esp. for liquid medicine.

■ **phialine** *adjective* (*rare*) resembling that of (a phial) **L19.**

Phi Beta Kappa /ˌfʌɪ ˌbiːtə 'kapə/ *noun phr. US.* **M19.**

[from the initial letters *phi*, *beta*, *kappa*, of Greek *philosophia biou kubernētēs* philosophy the guide of life.]

(A member of) an intercollegiate society to which distinguished (usu. undergraduate) scholars may be elected as an honour. Freq. *attrib.*

Phidian /'fʌɪdɪən/ *adjective.* **M18.**

[from *Phidias* (see below) + -AN.]

Of, pertaining to, or like the work of Phidias (5th cent. BC), the most famous sculptor of ancient Greece.

Phil /fɪl/ *noun. colloq.* **M20.**

[Abbreviation.]

= PHILHARMONIC *noun* 2.

phil- *combining form* see PHILO-.

Phil. *abbreviation.*

1 Philadelphia.

2 Philharmonic.

3 Philippians (New Testament).

4 Philosophy.

-phil *suffix* var. of -PHILE.

philabeg *noun* var. of FILIBEG.

Philadelphia /fɪlə'dɛlfɪə/ *noun.* **L18.**

[A city in Pennsylvania, USA.]

Used *attrib.* to designate persons or things originating in or associated with Philadelphia.

Philadelphia chromosome *MEDICINE* an abnormal small chromosome sometimes found in the leucocytes of leukaemia patients. **Philadelphia lawyer** a very able lawyer, *esp.* one expert in the exploitation of legal technicalities; a shrewd or unscrupulous lawyer.

Philadelphian /fɪlə'dɛlfɪən/ *adjective & noun.* **E17.**

[In senses A.1, 2, B.1, 2 from Greek *philadelphia* brotherly love, formed as PHILO- + *adelphos* brother; in senses A.3, B.3 from Greek *Philadelpheia* the ancient city of Philadelphia in Asia Minor, founded by Attalus II Philadelphus (220–138 BC): see -AN.]

► **A** *adjective.* **1** (**p-.**) Loving one's fellow people; loving humankind. **E17.**

2 Of or pertaining to the 17th-cent.Philadelphians. **L17.**

3 Of or pertaining to the ancient city of Philadelphia in Asia Minor or Philadelphia in Pennsylvania, USA. **L18.**

► **B** *noun.* **1** (**p-.**) A person who loves his or her fellows. **M17.**

2 In *pl.* (The members of) the Philadelphian Society, a religious society organized in England in the late 17th cent. **L17.**

3 A native or inhabitant of the ancient city of Philadelphia in Asia Minor, or of Philadelphia in Pennsylvania, USA. **E18.**

philadelphus /fɪlə'dɛlfəs/ *noun.* **L18.**

[mod. Latin (see below), from Greek *philadelphos* loving one's brother (formed as PHILO- + *adelphos* brother), used as a plant-name.]

Any of various European or N. American shrubs constituting the genus *Philadelphus*, of the hydrangea family, with white flowers having the scent of orange blossom (also called ***mock orange***); *esp.* (any of the hybrids of) *P. coronarius*, grown in gardens (also called ***syringa***).

†philander *noun.* Also (in sense 1) **P-**; (in sense 2) **f-. L17.**

[In sense 1 from Greek *philandros* adjective, fond of men, loving one's husband, formed as PHILO- + *andr-*, *anēr* man, male, husband; in sense 2 from K. *Philander* de Bruyn, 18th-cent. Dutch naturalist.]

1 (A name for) a lover. Cf. PHILLIS. **L17–E19.**

2 Any of various unrelated marsupial mammals, esp. S. American opossums of the genus *Philander* (also ***philander opossum***). **M18–L19.**

philander /fɪ'landə/ *verb intrans.* **M18.**

[from prec.]

Flirt; engage in casual sexual encounters.

■ **philanderer** *noun* **M19.**

philanthrope /ˈfɪlənθrəʊp/ *noun*. **M18.**
[from Greek *philanthrōpos* (adjective) philanthropic, formed as PHILO- + *anthrōpos* man.]
= PHILANTHROPIST.

philanthropic /fɪlənˈθrɒpɪk/ *adjective*. **L18.**
[French *philanthropique*, formed as prec.: see -IC.]
Characterized or motivated by philanthropy; benevolent; humane.

📖 E. F. BENSON She would be . . philanthropic, ready to place herself and her time at the service of suffering. M. MOORCOCK Uncle Semya and his associates were responsible for more philanthropic acts than many public charities.

■ **philanthropical** *adjective* (now *rare* or *obsolete*) = PHILANTHROPIC **E19.** **philanthropically** *adverb* **L18.**

philanthropine /fɪˈlanθrəpɪn/ *noun*. *rare* (now *Hist.*). Also **P-**. **E19.**
[Anglicized from German *Philanthropin* from Greek *philanthrōpinon*, neut. of vars. of *philanthrōpos* adjective: see PHILANTHROPE.]
A school founded in Germany in 1774 by John Bernhard Bassedau (1723–90) to educate children in the principles of philanthropy, natural religion, and cosmopolitanism; any similar institution.
■ **philanˈthropinism** *noun* the educational system of the philanthropine **M19.** **philanˈthropinist** *noun* & *adjective* (*a*) *noun* an advocate of philanthropinism; a pupil at a philanthropine; (*b*) *adjective* of or pertaining to philanthropinism: **M19.**

philanthropy /fɪˈlanθrəpi/ *noun*. **E17.**
[Late Latin *philanthropia* from Greek *philanthrōpia*, formed as PHILANTHROPE: see -Y[3].]
1 Love of humankind; the disposition or effort to promote the happiness and well-being of one's fellow people; practical benevolence. **E17.**
†**2** *spec.* God's love of humans. **M17–E18.**

📖 1 JAN MORRIS His first . . act of philanthropy was a gift of £1,000 to the infant orthopaedic hospital.

■ **philanthropism** *noun* the profession or practice of philanthropy; (a) philanthropic theory or practice: **M19.** **philanthropist** *noun* (*a*) a person who practises philanthropy; †(*b*) *gen.* a friend or lover of humankind: **M18.** **philanthropize** *verb* (*a*) *verb intrans.* be philanthropic, practise philanthropy; (*b*) *verb trans.* treat (a person) philanthropically: **E19.** **philanthropoid** *noun* [*joc.* after ANTHROPOID] a professional philanthropist; a person who dispenses funds from or for a charitable institution: **M20.**

philately /fɪˈlat(ə)li/ *noun*. **M19.**
[French *philatélie*, from Greek PHILO- + *atelēs* free of charge, *ateleia* exemption from payment: see -Y[3]. Greek *atelēs* was taken as 'postage stamp'.]
1 The collecting and study of postage stamps or other devices used for prepayment of postal charges; stamp-collecting. **M19.**
2 Postage stamps collectively. **M20.**
■ **philaˈtelic** *adjective* pertaining to or engaged in philately **M19.** **philaˈtelical** *adjective* = PHILATELIC **L19.** **philaˈtelically** *adverb* **L19.** **philatelism** *noun* = PHILATELY 1 **L19.** **philatelist** *noun* a person devoted to philately, a stamp-collector **L19.**

†**philauty** *noun*. Also in Greek form **philautia**. **E16–E19.**
[Greek *philautia*, from *philautos* loving oneself, formed as PHILO- + *auton* oneself: see -Y[3].]
Self-love; undue regard for oneself or one's own interests.

-phile /fʌɪl/ *suffix*. Also **-phil** /fɪl/.
[Repr. Greek *philos* loving, dear.]
Forming nouns & adjectives in and after Latin and French with the sense 'lover, that loves', as ***Anglophile***, ***bibliophile***, ***logophile***, ***paedophile***, etc.; in BIOLOGY & CHEMISTRY etc., with the sense '(thing) having an affinity for a substance, stain, etc.', as ***eosinophil***, ***hydrophile***, ***nucleophile***, etc. Cf. -PHILOUS.

Philem. *abbreviation*.
Philemon (New Testament).

philharmonic /fɪlhɑːˈmɒnɪk/ *noun* & *adjective*. **M18.**
[French *philharmonique* from Italian *filarmonico*, formed as PHILO-, HARMONIC.]
▶**A** *noun*. **1** A lover of harmony; a person devoted to music. **M18.**
2 *ellipt.* A Philharmonic Society, Orchestra, concert, etc. *colloq.* **M19.**
▶**B** *adjective*. Loving harmony; fond of or devoted to music. Freq. in names of symphony orchestras. **E19.**
Philharmonic Society any of various musical societies, *esp.* that founded in London in 1813 for the promotion of instrumental music.

philhellene /ˈfɪlhɛliːn, fɪlˈhɛliːn/ *adjective* & *noun*. **E19.**
[Greek *philellēn* loving the Greeks, formed as PHILO-, HELLENE.]
▶**A** *adjective*. = PHILHELLENIC. **E19.**
▶**B** *noun*. A lover of Greece or Greek language, art, culture, etc.; *Hist.* an advocate or supporter of Greek national independence. **E19.**

philhellenic /fɪlhɛˈliːnɪk, -ˈlɛnɪk/ *adjective*. **M19.**
[from prec. + -IC: cf. HELLENIC.]
Loving Greece or Greek culture; *Hist.* advocating or supporting Greek national independence.
■ **philˈhellenism** *noun* love of Greece or Greek culture; *Hist.* advocacy or support of Greek national independence: **M19.** **philˈhellenist** *noun* = PHILHELLENE *noun* **E19.**

philia /ˈfɪlɪə/ *noun*. **M20.**
[Greek.]
Amity, friendship, liking.

-philia /ˈfɪlɪə/ *suffix*. Also Anglicized as **-phily** /fɪli/.
[Repr. Greek *philia* friendship, fondness.]
Forming abstract nouns (usu. corresp. to adjectives in -PHIL, -PHILE, -PHILIC, -PHILOUS), with the senses (*a*) affinity for, as ***argyrophilia***; (*b*) undue tendency towards, as ***scopophilia***, ***spasmophilia***, ***thanatophilia***; (*c*) (freq. excessive or abnormal) love of or liking for, as ***Anglophilia***, ***bibliophily***, ***necrophilia***; (*d*) the hobby of collecting, as ***cartophily***, ***notaphily***.

-philic /ˈfɪlɪk/ *suffix*.
[from -PHILE + -IC.]
Forming adjectives with the sense 'having an affinity for, attracted by, liking', as in ***acidophilic***, ***hydrophilic***, ***mesophilic***, ***oenophilic***, etc. Cf. -PHILE, -PHILOUS.

Philip /ˈfɪlɪp/ *noun*. Long *obsolete* exc. *dial.* **LME.**
[Male forename from Greek *Philippos* lit. 'lover of horses', formed as PHILO- + *hippos* horse.]
1 (A name for) the house sparrow. **LME.**
†**2** Any of various former French, Spanish, or Burgundian gold or silver coins issued by kings and dukes named Philip. **L15–M18.**
¶ See also ***appeal from Philip drunk to Philip sober*** s.v. DRUNK *adjective*.

Philippian /fɪˈlɪpɪən/ *noun* & *adjective*. **L16.**
[from *Philippi* (see below) + -AN.]
▶**A** *noun*. A native or inhabitant of Philippi, an ancient city of Macedonia. In *pl.* (treated as *sing.*), St Paul's epistle to the Philippians, a book of the New Testament. **L16.**
▶**B** *adjective*. Of or pertaining to Philippi or the Philippians. **E17.**

Philippic /fɪˈlɪpɪk/ *adjective* & *noun*. Also **p-**. **M16.**
[Latin *philippicus* from Greek *philippikos*, from *Philippos*: see prec., -IC.]
▶**A** *adjective*. Of the character of a philippic; of or pertaining to any person called Philip; of the ancient city of Philippi in Macedonia. **M16.**
▶**B** *noun*. **1** Any of the orations of Demosthenes against Philip of Macedon in defence of Athenian liberty; any of Cicero's orations against Antony; *gen.* a bitter attack, invective, or denunciation. **L16.**
†**2** [Greek *philippeion*.] A gold coin of low value, struck by Philip of Macedon. **M17–L18.**

📖 1 HARPER LEE We were followed up the sidewalk by a Philippic on our family's moral degeneration.

philippina /fɪlɪˈpiːnə/ *noun*. Also **philopoena** /fɪləˈ-/. **M19.**
[Repr. German *Vielliebchen* dim. from *viellieb* very dear, alt. to *Philippchen* little or darling Philip.]
A nut with two kernels. Also, a custom of German origin in which a gift may be claimed by the first of two people who have shared a nut with two kernels to say 'philippina' at their next meeting; a gift claimed in this way.

Philippine /ˈfɪlɪpiːn/ *adjective*[1] & *noun*. **L18.**
[from St *Philip* Neri (1515–95), founder of the Congregation of the Fathers of the Oratory at Rome + -INE[1].]
▶**A** *noun*. Pl. **-ines**, **-ini** /-iːniː/. An Oratorian father or priest. Also (*Hist.*), a member of a religious society of young unmarried poor women whose patron was St Philip Neri. **L18.**
▶**B** *adjective*. Of, pertaining to, or characteristic of the Oratorians or the Oratory of St Philip Neri. **M19.**

Philippine /ˈfɪlɪpiːn/ *adjective*[2]. **E19.**
[from Spanish FILIPINO.]
Of or pertaining to the Philippines, a country in SE Asia consisting of a chain of over 7,000 islands; of or pertaining to Filipinos.

Philippini *noun pl.* see PHILIPPINE *noun*.

philippinite /fɪlɪˈpiːnʌɪt/ *noun*. **M20.**
[from PHILIPPINE *adjective*[2] + -ITE[1].]
GEOLOGY. A tektite from the strewn field of the Philippines.

Philippise *verb* var. of PHILIPPIZE.

Philippist /ˈfɪlɪpɪst/ *noun*. **E18.**
[from *Philip* (see below) + -IST.]
ECCLESIASTICAL HISTORY. A follower of the moderate Protestant reformer Philip Melanchthon (1497–1560); an adiaphorist.

Philippize /ˈfɪlɪpʌɪz/ *verb*. Also **-ise**. **M17.**
[Greek *philippizein*, from *Philippos* PHILIP: see -IZE.]
1 *verb intrans. Hist.* Act in support of Philip of Macedon. **M17.** ▸**b** *gen.* Speak or write as if influenced, esp. corruptly. **L18.**
2 *verb intrans.* & *trans.* Utter a philippic (against). **E19.**

†**Philistean** *adjective*. **E–M17.**
[from late Latin *Philist(h)aeus* from Greek *Philistiaios*: see -EAN. Cf. PHILISTIAN, PHILISTINE.]
= PHILISTINE *adjective*.

philister /fɪˈlɪstə/ *noun*. *arch.* Also **P-**. **E19.**
[German, translating late Latin *Philistaeus* or Hebrew *pĕlištī*. Cf. PHILISTINE.]
An outsider; an unenlightened or uncultured person. Also (orig.) in German universities, a townsperson, a non-student. Cf. PHILISTINE *noun*.

Philistia /fɪˈlɪstɪə/ *noun*. **M16.**
[medieval Latin = late Latin *Philist(h)aea* = Greek *Philistia*.]
1 (The region in ancient Palestine occupied by) the Philistines. **M16.**
2 Uneducated or unenlightened people as a class or group; a place populated by such people; the culture or lifestyle of such people. Cf. PHILISTINE *noun* 4. **M19.**

Philistian /fɪˈlɪstɪən/ *noun* & *adjective*. **ME.**
[Old French *Philistien* from medieval Latin *Philistianus*, formed as prec.: see -AN. Cf. PHILISTEAN.]
▶**A** *noun*. = PHILISTINE *noun* 1, 2. Long *rare* or *obsolete*. **ME.**
▶**B** *adjective*. Of or pertaining to Philistia or the Philistines. **L17.**

Philistine /ˈfɪlɪstʌɪn/ *noun* & *adjective*. Also **p-**. **ME.**
[French *Philistin* or late Latin *Philistinus* (also *Palaestinus*) from late Greek *Philistinoi* (*Palaistinoi*), from Hebrew *pĕlištī*, rel. to *pĕlešeṯ* Philistia, Palestine.]
▶**A** *noun*. Pl. **-stines**, †**-stim(s)**.
1 A member of a foreign militaristic people who in biblical times occupied the southern coast of Palestine and were hostile to the Israelites. **ME.**
2 *fig.* An antagonist, an enemy; a debauched or drunken person. **E17.**
3 In German universities, a townsperson, a non-student; = PHILISTER. Now *rare* or *obsolete*. **E19.**
4 An uneducated or unenlightened person; a person indifferent or hostile to culture, or whose interests and tastes are commonplace and material. **E19.**

📖 4 G. SAYER The students were philistines who neither appreciated . . music . . nor . . read his sort of books.

▶**B** *adjective*. **1** Of or pertaining to the ancient Philistines. **L16.**
2 Uneducated, unenlightened; indifferent or hostile to culture; aesthetically unsophisticated. **M19.**
■ **Philistinian** /fɪlɪˈstɪnɪən/ *adjective* = PHILISTINE *adjective* 1 **L18.** **philistinish** *adjective* = PHILISTINE *adjective* 2 **L19.** **philistinism** *noun* the culture or lifestyle of a social Philistine; the condition of being a social Philistine: **M19.** **Philistinize** *verb trans.* make into a social Philistine **L19.**

Phillips /ˈfɪlɪps/ *noun*. **M20.**
[Henry F. *Phillips*, Amer. manufacturer.]
(Proprietary name) used ***attrib.*** to designate a screw with a cross-shaped slot or a screwdriver with a corresponding shape.

Phillips curve /ˈfɪlɪps kəːv/ *noun phr.* **M20.**
[from A. W. H. *Phillips* (1914–75), New Zealand economist.]
A supposed inverse relationship between the level of unemployment and the rate of inflation.

phillipsite /ˈfɪlɪpsʌɪt/ *noun*. **E19.**
[from W. *Phillips* (1775–1828), English mineralogist + -ITE[1].]
MINERALOGY. A white or reddish zeolite containing aluminium, calcium, and potassium, found in cruciform fibrous twinned crystals.

Phillis /ˈfɪlɪs/ *noun*. Chiefly *poet.* **M16.**
[Latin *Phyllis* female name, from Greek *Phullis* female name (= foliage), from *phullon* leaf; the substitution of *i* for Latin *y* is perh. due to association with Greek *philos* dear, beloved.]
(A name for) a pretty country girl or a sweetheart (cf. PHILANDER *noun* 1). Also (after Milton), a pretty, neat, or dexterous female servant.

phillumenist /fɪˈluːmənɪst, -ˈljuː-/ *noun*. **M20.**
[from PHIL- + Latin *lumen* light + -IST.]
A collector of matchbox or matchbook labels.
■ **phillumeny** *noun* the collecting of matchbox or matchbook labels **M20.**

phillyrea /fɪˈlɪrɪə, fɪlɪˈriːə/ *noun*. **M17.**
[mod. Latin (see below) from Latin *philyrea* from Greek *philurea*, app. from *philura* lime tree.]
Any of several evergreen shrubs constituting the genus *Phillyrea*, of the olive family, *esp.* the Mediterranean *P. latifolia* and *P. angustifolia*, with opposite leaves and greenish-white flowers in axillary clusters. Also called ***mock privet***.

philo- /ˈfɪləʊ/ *combining form*. Before a vowel or *h* also **phil-**.
[Greek, from *philein* to love, *philos* dear, friend: see -O-.]
Used in (esp.) adjectives and nouns formed in and after Greek, and as a freely productive element, with the sense 'loving, inclining towards, having an affinity for'. Cf. MISO-.
■ **philathˈletic** *adjective* fond of athletics; of or pertaining to fondness for athletics: **M19.** **philobat** *noun* [after *acrobat*] PSYCHOLOGY a (type of) person whose emotional security does not depend on other people or on external objects (opp. OCNOPHIL)

M20. **philo'biblian** *adjective* (*rare*) = PHILOBIBLICAL (a) M18. **philo'biblical** *adjective* (*a*) fond of books and literature; (*b*) devoted to study of the Bible: L19. **philo'biblist** *noun* a book-lover E19. **philo'cynic** *adjective & noun* [Greek *kun-*, *kuōn* dog] (*a*) *adjective* fond of dogs; (*b*) *noun* a dog-lover: E19. **philo'despot** *noun* †(*a*) a person who loves his or her master; (*b*) a person favouring or inclining towards despotism: M17. **philodox** *noun* (*rare*) a person who loves his or her own opinion; an argumentative or dogmatic person: E17. **philomath** *noun* a lover of learning; a student, esp. of mathematics, natural philosophy, astrology, etc.: M17. **philo'mathic** *adjective* = PHILOMATHICAL L18. **philo'mathical** *adjective* devoted to learning; of or pertaining to a philomath: E18. **phi'lomathy** *noun* love of learning E17. **philo'patric** *adjective* [Greek *patra* fatherland] ZOOLOGY (of an animal or species) tending to return to or remain near a particular site, esp. the birthplace M20. **philo'patry** *noun* (ZOOLOGY) philopatric behaviour, esp. a tendency to return to the birthplace to breed; the extent of this: M20. **philoproge'neity** *noun* (*rare*) love of (one's) offspring L19. **philopro'genitive** *adjective* (*a*) prolific; (*b*) loving (one's) offspring: M19. **philopro'genitiveness** *noun* (the instinct or faculty of) love for (one's) offspring E19. **philo'semite** *noun* a person who favours or supports the Jews M20. **philo'technic** *adjective* fond of or devoted to the (esp. industrial) arts E19. **philo'therian** *noun & adjective* (a person) fond of wild animals E20.

philodendron /fɪlə'dɛndrən/ *noun*. Also **-drum** /-drəm/. Pl. **-drons**, **-dra** /-drə/. L19.
[mod. Latin (see below) from Greek, neut. of *philodendros* fond of trees (formed as PHILO- + *dendron* tree), with ref. to its climbing on trees.]
Any of various tropical American climbing aroids constituting the genus *Philodendron*, some species of which are cultivated as house-plants.

philogynist /fɪ'lɒdʒɪnɪst/ *noun*. M19.
[Greek *philogunēs* fond of (a) woman, from *philogunia* love of women, formed as PHILO- + *gunē* woman.]
A person who likes or admires women.
■ **phi'logyny** *noun* liking or admiration for women E17.

philology /fɪ'lɒlədʒi/ *noun*. LME.
[French *philologie* from Latin *philologia* from Greek = love of learning, literature, dialectic, or language, from *philologos* fond of talking or learning, studying words: see PHILO-, LOGOS.]
1 Love of learning and literature; the branch of knowledge that deals with (the linguistic, historical, interpretative, and critical aspects of) literature; literary or classical scholarship. Now chiefly *US*. LME.
2 *spec*. The branch of knowledge that deals with the structure, historical development, and relationships of a language or languages. L17.

> **2** F. TUOHY The professor of Comparative Philology thinks that no one should learn English without . . having mastered Anglo-Saxon.

■ **philologer** *noun* (now *rare*) = PHILOLOGIST L16. **philo'logian** *noun* = PHILOLOGIST M19. **philo'logic** *adjective* = PHILOLOGICAL M17. **philo'logical** *adjective* of, pertaining to, concerned with, or devoted to philology E17. **philo'logically** *adverb* E17. **philologist** *noun* an expert in or student of philology M17. **philologize** *verb intrans*. (*rare*) engage in philology M17. **'philologue** *noun* (*rare*) = PHILOLOGIST L16.

Philomel /'fɪləʊmɛl/ *noun*. *poet*. Also **-mela** /-'miːlə/, †**-mene**. LME.
[Latin *philomela* from Greek *philomēla* nightingale from *Philomēla*, Procne's sister in Greek mythol., who was transformed into a nightingale (or, in some accounts, a swallow). Var. with *-n-* from medieval Latin *philomena*, alt. of Latin (perh. by assoc. with Greek *Melpomenē* the muse of tragedy). Cf. PROGNE.]
The nightingale.

Philonic /fʌɪ'lɒnɪk/ *adjective*. L19.
[from Latin *Philon-*, *Philo*, from Greek *Philōn* male name borne by Philo (see below) + -IC.]
Of or pertaining to the Jewish philosopher Philo, who wrote and taught in Alexandria *c* 20 BC–AD 40.
■ **Philonian** /-'ləʊn-/ *adjective* = PHILONIC *adjective* L19. **'Philonize** *verb intrans*. imitate Philo E17.

philopoena *noun* var. of PHILIPPINA.

philosoph *noun* see PHILOSOPHE.

philosophaster /fɪ,lɒsə'fastə/ *noun*. E17.
[Late Latin, from Latin *philosophus*: see PHILOSOPHER, -ASTER.]
A petty, shallow, or inferior philosopher.

†**philosophate** *verb intrans*. E17–E19.
[Latin *philosophat-*, pa. ppl. stem of *philosophari* philosophize, from *philosophus*: see PHILOSOPHER, -ATE[3].]
Reason as a philosopher; philosophize.

philosophe /fɪlə(ʊ)'zɒf/ *noun*. Also Anglicized as **philosoph** /'fɪlə(ʊ)sɒf/. OE.
[Latin *philosophus*: see PHILOSOPHER. Reinforced in Middle English by Old French *filosofe*, *philosophe*.]
= PHILOSOPHER 1. Also PHILOSOPHIST 2.

philosopheme /fɪ'lɒsəfiːm/ *noun*. L17.
[Late Latin *philosophema* from Greek *philosophēma*, from *philosophein* philosophize, from *philosophos*: see next.]
A philosophical statement, theorem, or axiom; a demonstration or conclusion in philosophy.

philosopher /fɪ'lɒsəfə/ *noun*. ME.
[Anglo-Norman *filosofre*, *philosophre* var. of Old & mod. French *philosophe* from Latin *philosophus* from Greek *philosophos* lover of wisdom, formed as PHILO- + *sophos* wise. Cf. PHILOSOPHE.]
1 A lover of wisdom; an expert in or student of philosophy, a person skilled or engaged in philosophy. ME. ▸**b** A Jesuit in the first stage of his scholastic training. E18.
†**2** An adept in the occult; an alchemist, a magician, an interpreter of dreams. ME–L15.
3 A person who lives by philosophy and reason; a person who speaks or behaves philosophically. L16.
Phrases & comb.: ***natural philosopher***: see NATURAL *adjective*. **philosopher king** (esp. with ref. to the political theory of Plato) a member of an elite whose knowledge enables them to rule justly. **philosophers' egg** (*obsolete* exc. *Hist*.) a medicine made of egg-yolk and saffron, formerly thought to cure the plague. †**philosophers' game**: played with round, triangular, and square numbered pieces on a board resembling two chessboards united. **philosopher's stone**, **philosophers' stone** (*a*) the supreme object of alchemy, a substance supposed to change any metal into gold or silver and (according to some) to cure all diseases and prolong life indefinitely; (*b*) *transf*. a universal cure or solution. ***philosopher's wool***: see WOOL *noun*. **the Philosopher** (now *rare*) Aristotle.
¶ In Middle English, senses 1 & 2 are often inseparable.
■ **philosopheress** *noun* a female philosopher M17. **philosophership** *noun* the practice or character of a philosopher M16.

philosophess /fɪ'lɒsəfɪs/ *noun*. M17.
[French *philosophesse* from *philosophe*: see PHILOSOPHER, -ESS[1].]
A female philosopher.

philosophia perennis /fɪlə,sɒfɪə pə'rɛnɪs/ *noun phr*. M19.
[Latin = perennial philosophy.]
A posited core of philosophical truths independent of and unaffected by time or place, freq. taken to be exemplified in the writings of Aristotle and St Thomas Aquinas.

philosophia prima /fɪlə,sɒfɪə 'priːmə/ *noun phr*. E17.
[Latin = first philosophy.]
(The branch of inquiry that deals with) the most general truths of philosophy; *spec*. (the branch of inquiry that deals with) the divine and the eternal.

philosophic /fɪlə'sɒfɪk/ *adjective & noun*. LME.
[Late Latin *philosophicus*, from Latin *philosophia* PHILOSOPHY: see -IC.]
▸**A** *adjective*. **1** = PHILOSOPHICAL 2b. LME. ▸**b** = PHILOSOPHICAL 2a. Now *rare*. L17.
2 = PHILOSOPHICAL 3. L17.
3 = PHILOSOPHICAL 1. E18.
Special collocations: **philosophic radical** = ***philosophical radical*** S.V. PHILOSOPHICAL *adjective*. ***philosophic wool***: see WOOL *noun*.
▸**B** *noun*. In *pl*. Studies, works, or arguments pertaining to philosophy. M18.

philosophical /fɪlə'sɒfɪk(ə)l/ *adjective & noun*. LME.
[formed as prec.: see -ICAL.]
▸**A** *adjective*. **1** Knowledgeable about, skilled in, or devoted to philosophy or learning (formerly including science); learned. LME.
2 a Of or pertaining to physical science (natural philosophy); scientific. Now *rare*. L15. ▸**b** Of or pertaining to philosophers or philosophy; of the character of, consonant with, or proceeding from philosophy or learning. E16.
3 Befitting or characteristic of a philosopher; wise; temperate; calm esp. in adverse circumstances; stoical, resigned. M17.

> **2b** *Paragraph* It dodges the essential philosophical question of the nature of intelligence. **3** L. BLUE Having lived out of a suitcase for many years, I have grown philosophical about it.

Special collocations: ***philosophical analysis***: see ANALYSIS 4. **philosophical grammar** = ***universal grammar*** S.V. UNIVERSAL *adjective*. **philosophical radical** a member of a group of 19th-cent. radicals advocating political reform based on Benthamite utilitarian philosophy. **philosophical radicalism** the opinions and beliefs of and the reforms advocated by the philosophical radicals.
▸†**B** *noun*. In *pl*. The subjects of study in a course of philosophy. L17–E18.
■ **philosophically** *adverb* LME.

philosophico- /fɪlə'sɒfɪkəʊ/ *combining form* of PHILOSOPHIC, PHILOSOPHICAL: see -O-.

philosophise *verb* var. of PHILOSOPHIZE.

philosophism /fɪ'lɒsəfɪz(ə)m/ *noun*. Chiefly *derog*. L18.
[French *philosophisme*, from PHILOSOPHE philosopher, after *sophisme* SOPHISM.]
(Shallow or affected) philosophizing; a (shallow or affected) philosophical system.

philosophist /fɪ'lɒsəfɪst/ *noun*. Now *rare*. L16.
[In sense 1, app. from Latin *philosophia* PHILOSOPHY + -IST; in sense 2 from French *philosophiste*.]
†**1** = PHILOSOPHER 1. Only in L16.
2 An adherent or practitioner of what is held to be erroneous speculation or philosophy. Also, a rationalist, a sceptic; *spec*. a French Encyclopedist. *derog*. L18.
■ **philoso'phistic**, **philoso'phistical** *adjectives* (now *rare* or *obsolete*) of the character of or pertaining to a speculative philosopher; rationalistic, sceptical: E19.

philosophize /fɪ'lɒsəfʌɪz/ *verb*. Also **-ise**. L16.
[App. after French *philosopher*, from *philosophe*: see PHILOSOPHER, -IZE. Cf. PHILOSOPHY.]
1 *verb intrans*. Reason or argue philosophically; speculate, theorize; moralize. L16. ▸**b** *verb trans*. Bring (a person) *into* a state or condition by philosophical reasoning or argument. M18.
2 *verb trans*. Make philosophical; explain, treat, or argue (a point, idea, etc.) philosophically. E19.
■ **philosophi'zation** *noun* the action of philosophizing; philosophical treatment: E19. **philosophizer** *noun* L17.

philosophy /fɪ'lɒsəfi/ *noun*. ME.
[Old French *filosofie*, (also mod.) *philosophie* from Latin *philosophia* from Greek, from *philosophos* PHILOSOPHER: see -Y[3].]
1 Love, study, or pursuit (through argument and reason) of wisdom, truth, or knowledge. ME.
2 a Now only more fully ***natural philosophy***. The branch of knowledge that deals with the principles governing the material universe and perception of physical phenomena; natural science. Now *arch*. or *Hist*. ME. ▸**b** In full ***moral philosophy***. The branch of knowledge that deals with the principles of human behaviour; ethics. ME. ▸**c** More fully ***metaphysical philosophy***. The branch of knowledge that deals with ultimate reality or with the nature and causes of things and of existence. L18.
3 Advanced knowledge or study; advanced learning. Now chiefly in ***Doctor of Philosophy***. ME.
4 A set or system of ideas, opinions, beliefs, or principles of behaviour based on an overall understanding of existence and the universe; a philosophical system or theory; *gen*. a view, an outlook. ME. ▸**b** Mental or emotional equilibrium; calmness (esp. in adverse circumstances); stoicism, resignation. L18.
†**5** *spec*. The branch of knowledge that deals with the occult; magic; alchemy. LME–L18.
6 The branch of knowledge that deals with the principles of a particular field or subject, as art, politics, science, etc. Foll. by *of*. E18.
†**7** Sceptical or rationalist philosophy, current (esp. in France) in the 18th cent. M–L18.

> **1** R. G. COLLINGWOOD That which lures us onward in the path of philosophy, the quest of truth. ***mathematical philosophy***: see MATHEMATICAL *adjective*. **4** S. BIKO A philosophy that satisfies the black world and gives preferential treatment to certain groups. M. HUGHES It would be a denial of our philosophy to take life. *Observer* My philosophy in racing was always to let the mind rule the heart.

-philous /'fɪləs/ *suffix*.
[from medieval Latin *-philus* from Greek *-philos* (see -PHILE) + -OUS.]
Forming adjectives (often with counterparts in -PHIL, -PHILE) with the sense 'having an affinity for, attracted by, liking' as ***acidophilous***, ***dendrophilous***, ***hydrophilous***, etc. Cf. -PHILIC.

philtre /'fɪltə/ *noun & verb*. Also **-ter**. L16.
[French, from Latin *philtrum* from Greek *philtron* love-potion, from *phil-* stem of *philein* to love, *philos* loving + *-tron* instr. suffix.]
▸**A** *noun*. A potion, drug, or (occas.) charm, supposed to excite sexual attraction, esp. to a particular person; a love-potion. Also *gen*., any allegedly magic potion or drug. L16.
▸**B** *verb trans*. Charm with a philtre; *fig*. bewitch. L17.

philtrum /'fɪltrəm/ *noun*. E17.
[Latin: see PHILTRE *noun*.]
†**1** = prec. E17–M18.
2 ANATOMY. The hollow on the upper lip. M17.

-phily *suffix* see -PHILIA.

phimosis /fʌɪ'məʊsɪs/ *noun*. Pl. **-moses** /-'məʊsiːz/. L17.
[mod. Latin from Greek *phimōsis* muzzling.]
MEDICINE. A congenital narrowing of the opening of the foreskin so that it cannot be retracted.

phinnoc *noun* var. of FINNOC.

phit /fɪt/ *noun & interjection*. L19.
[Imit.]
(Repr.) a brief muted sound of the exhalation or displacement of air, esp. as made by a travelling arrow, bullet, etc.

phiz /fɪz/ *noun*. *joc. colloq*. L17.
[Abbreviation of PHYSIOGNOMY. Cf. PHIZOG, PHYSIOG.]
A person's face; a facial expression.

phizgig *noun* see FIZGIG *noun*[1].

phizog /'fɪzɒg/ *noun*. *joc. colloq*. E19.
[Abbreviation of PHYSIOGNOMY. Cf. PHYSIOG.]
= PHIZ.

phlebo- /'flɛbəʊ/ *combining form* of Greek *phleb-*, *phleps* vein: see -O-. Before a vowel **phleb-**.
■ **phlebec'tasia** *noun* [Greek. *ektasis* extension] abnormal dilatation of a vein M19. **phlebitic** /-'bɪt-/ *adjective* pertaining to or affected with phlebitis L19. **phlebitis** /-'bʌɪt-/ *noun* inflammation

of a vein E19. phle'bology noun the branch of medicine that deals with veins M19. phlebothrom'bosis noun a venous thrombosis in which inflammation of the vein is absent or of only secondary significance L19.

phlebography /flɪ'bɒgrəfi/ noun. M19.
[from PHLEBO- + -GRAPHY.]
MEDICINE. †1 A description of the veins. Only in M19.
2 The recording of the pulse in a vein. rare. E20.
3 Radiography of veins, carried out after the injection of a radio-opaque substance. M20.
■ **phlebogram** /'flɛb-/ noun (a) (now rare) a diagram of the pulsations of a vein; (b) = PHLEBOGRAPH (b): L19. **phlebograph** /'flɛbəgrɑːf/ noun (a) an instrument for recording diagrammatically the pulsations of a vein; (b) a radiograph made by phlebography: L19. **phlebographic** /flɛbə'grafɪk/ adjective pertaining to or involving phlebography M20.

phlebotomy /flɪ'bɒtəmi/ noun. LME.
[Old French *flebothomi* (mod. *phlébotomie*) from late Latin *phlebotomia* from Greek, from *phlebotomos* that opens a vein, formed as PHLEBO-: see -TOMY.]
1 The action or practice of cutting open a vein so as to withdraw blood or (Hist.) let blood flow, as a therapeutic operation; venesection; an instance of this. LME.
2 transf. & fig. Bloodshed; slaughter; extortion of money. L16.
■ **phlebotomist** noun a person trained to take blood from a patient for examination or transfusion; Hist. a person who bled patients: M17. **phlebotomi'zation** noun the action of phlebotomizing L16. **phlebotomize** verb (a) verb intrans. & trans. perform phlebotomy (on); (b) verb intrans. undergo phlebotomy: L16.

Phlegethontic /flɛgɪ'θɒntɪk, flɛdʒ-/ adjective. E17.
[from Greek *Phlegethont-*, *Phlegethōn*: see below, -IC.]
Of, pertaining to, or characteristic of the Phlegethon, a river of fire in Hades in classical mythology.

phlegm /flɛm/ noun. Also (earlier) †fl-. ME.
[Old French *fleume* (mod. *flegme*) from late Latin *phlegma* clammy moisture of the body from Greek = inflammation, morbid state as the result of heat, from *phlegein* to burn.]
1 Orig. (now Hist.), one of the four bodily humours, believed to cause indolence or apathy. Later, the thick viscous fluid secreted by the mucous membranes of the respiratory passages, esp. when excessive or abnormal; spec. that of the throat and bronchi, brought up by coughing; sputum. ME. ▸†b A mass of phlegm, or other mucous secretion. M16–E18.
†2 ALCHEMY & CHEMISTRY. Water as a principle of matter; any watery odourless and tasteless substance obtained by distillation. L15–E19.
3 Phlegmatic temperament or disposition; absence of excitability or enthusiasm; dullness, sluggishness, apathy; calmness, self-possession, evenness of temper. (Formerly believed to result from a predominance of phlegm in the constitution.) L16.
🕮 1 M. WESLEY Rose wheezed, coughed .. her mouth full of phlegm. 3 R. MACAULAY Clare was always restless; she had none of Jane's phlegm and stolidity.
■ **phlegmless** adjective (rare) M17.

phlegmagogue /'flɛgməgɒg/ noun. Now rare. LME.
[Old French *fleumagogue* (mod. *phlegmagogue*) from medieval Latin *fleumagogus* from Greek. *phlegmagōgos*, from *phlegma* PHLEGM + *agōgos* leading, eliciting.]
A medicine for expelling phlegm.

phlegmasia /flɛg'meɪzɪə/ noun. Pl. -iae /-ɪiː/. E18.
[mod. Latin from Greek.]
MEDICINE. Orig., inflammation, esp. inflammation accompanied by fever. Now spec. (a) (in full ***phlegmasia alba dolens*** /ˌalbə 'dəʊlɛnz/, also ***phlegmasia dolens*** [Latin *alba* (fem.) white, *dolens* painful]), inflammation of veins of the leg with swelling and whiteness, caused by thrombophlebitis; (b) (in full ***phlegmasia cerulea dolens*** /sɛˌruːlɪə 'dəʊlɛnz/ [Latin *caerulea* (fem.) blue]), inflammation of veins of the leg with swelling and cyanosis.

phlegmatic /flɛg'matɪk/ adjective & noun. ME.
[Old French *fleumatique* (mod. *flegmatique*) from Latin *phlegmaticus* from Greek *phlegmatikos*, from *phlegmat-*, *phlegma* PHLEGM: see -IC.]
▸A adjective. 1 a Of the nature of phlegm; (of a disease etc.) characterized or caused by excess of phlegm. Formerly also (of the human body), having a predominance of phlegm in the constitution. Now rare or obsolete. ME. ▸†b Of the nature of water, as a principle of matter; rich in this and hence producing sputum when taken as food etc.; watery and insipid. E16–M18.
2 Having or showing the temperament formerly attributed to phlegm as a predominant bodily humour; not easily excited to feeling or action; dull, sluggish, apathetic; stolidly calm, self-possessed. L16.
▸†B noun. A phlegmatic person. rare. ME–E17.
■ **†phlegmatical** adjective phlegmatic L16–L17. **phlegmatically** adverb E19. **†phlegmaticly** adverb L17–E18. **phlegmaticness** noun (rare) L16. **'phlegmatism** noun phlegmatic character L18.

phlegmon /'flɛgmən/ noun. Now rare. LME.
[Latin *phlegmon*, *phlegmona* from Greek. *phlegmonē* inflammation, a boil, from *phlegein* to burn.]
Severe inflammation of cellular tissue, tending to or producing suppuration; an acute local inflammation with redness and swelling; a boil, a carbuncle.
■ **phleg'monic** adjective pertaining to or of the nature of (a) phlegmon M18. **phlegmonoid** adjective resembling (a) phlegmon M18. **phlegmonous** adjective = PHLEGMONIC L17.

phlegmy /'flɛmi/ adjective. LME.
[from PHLEGM + -Y[1].]
1 Of the nature of, consisting of, or characterized by phlegm; affected by phlegm. LME. ▸†b Watery; moist. L16–L17.
2 = PHLEGMATIC adjective 2. LME.
🕮 1 *Guardian* A phlegmy old bronchitic wheezing to the pub.

phloem /'fləʊɛm/ noun. L19.
[from Greek. *phloos* bark + *-ēma* pass. suffix.]
BOTANY. One of the two chief components of a vascular bundle, which conducts synthesized food downwards from the leaves. Cf. XYLEM.

phlogistic /flə'dʒɪstɪk, -'gɪst-/ adjective. M18.
[In sense 1 from PHLOGISTON, in senses 2 and 3 from Greek *phlogistos* flammable: see -IC.]
1 HISTORY OF SCIENCE. Of the nature of or consisting of phlogiston; pertaining to phlogiston. Formerly also, containing phlogiston, combustible. M18.
2 Inflammatory. Now rare or obsolete. M18.
†3 Burning, fiery, heated, inflamed, (lit. & fig.). Chiefly rhet. L18–M19.

phlogisticate /flə'dʒɪstɪkeɪt, -'gɪst-/ verb trans. L18.
[from prec. + -ATE[3].]
HISTORY OF SCIENCE. Make phlogistic; cause to combine with phlogiston. Chiefly as ***phlogisticated*** ppl adjective.
phlogisticated air Hist. nitrogen.
■ **†phlogistication** noun combination with phlogiston; (the name in the phlogistic theory for) deoxidation: L18–E19.

phlogiston /flə'dʒɪstən, -'gɪst-/ noun. M18.
[Greek, from *phlogizein* set on fire, from *phlog-*, *phlox* flame, deriv. of ablaut var. of *phleg-* base of *phlegein* to burn.]
HISTORY OF SCIENCE. A hypothetical substance formerly supposed to exist in combination in all combustible materials and to be released in the process of combustion; the element fire, conceived as fixed in flammable substances.

phlogopite /'flɒgəpʌɪt/ noun. M19.
[from Greek *phlogōpos* fiery, from *phlog-* (see prec.) + *ōp-*, *ōps* face: see -ITE[1].]
MINERALOGY. A brown mica containing magnesium that is a constituent of limestones and dolomites.

phlogosis /flə'gəʊsɪs/ noun. Now rare or obsolete. Pl. -goses /-'gəʊsiːz/. L17.
[mod. Latin from Greek. *phlogōsis*, from *phlog-*: see PHLOGISTON, -OSIS.]
(An) inflammation.

phlomis /'fləʊmɪs, 'flɒmɪs/ noun. E18.
[mod. Latin (see below) from Greek.]
Any of various labiate plants constituting the genus *Phlomis*, sometimes grown for their showy yellow or purple flowers; esp. Jerusalem sage, *P. fruticosa*.

phloretin /flə'rɛtɪn/ noun. M19.
[from next + -ETIN.]
A bicyclic compound, $C_{15}H_{14}O_5$, that is the aglycone of phlorizin.

phlorizin /flə'rʌɪzɪn/ noun. Also -ridz- /-'rɪdz-/, -rrhiz-. M19.
[from Greek. *phloos* bark + *rhiza* root + -IN[1].]
CHEMISTRY. A glucoside, $C_{21}H_{24}O_{10}$, obtained from the bark of the root of apple, pear, plum, and cherry trees.
■ **phlorizini'zation** noun treatment with phlorizin; the state of being phlorizinized: E20. **phlorizinize** verb trans. administer phlorizin to (an animal) to induce glycosuria E20.

phloroglucinol /flɒrəʊ'gluːsɪnɒl/ noun. L19.
[from PHLOR(IZIN + -O- + Greek *glukus* sweet + -IN[1] + -OL.]
A sweet-tasting compound used as a preservative for cut flowers, in making pharmaceuticals, etc.; 1,3,5,-trihydroxybenzene, $C_6H_3(OH)_3$.

phlorrhizin noun var. of PHLORIZIN.

phlox /flɒks/ noun. E18.
[mod. Latin (see below) from Latin = a flame-coloured flower, from Greek, lit. 'flame': see PHLOGISTON.]
Any plant of the N. American genus *Phlox*, of the Jacob's ladder family, with clusters of pink, red, purple, or white salver-shaped flowers, many cultivated forms of which are found in gardens.

phloxine /'flɒksiːn/ noun. Also -in /-ɪn/. L19.
[formed as prec. + -INE[5].]
CHEMISTRY. A red coal tar dyestuff resembling eosin.

phlyctena /flɪk'tiːnə/ noun. Pl. -nae /-niː/. Also Anglicized as **phlycten** /'flɪktən/. L17.
[mod. Latin from Greek *phluktaina* blister, from *phluein*, *phluzein* swell.]
MEDICINE. A small inflamed nodule or vesicle on the conjunctiva or cornea. Formerly also, a pimple or boil on the skin.
■ **phlyctenular** /-'tɛn-/ adjective pertaining to, of the nature of, or characterized by phlyctenae M19.

pho /fəʊ/ interjection. rare. E17.
[Natural exclam. Cf. FAUGH.]
Expr. contemptuous rejection or dismissal.

-phobe /fəʊb/ suffix.
[French from Latin *-phobus* from Greek *-phobos* fearing, adjective ending from *phobos* fear.]
Forming adjectives and nouns with the sense '(a person) fearing, disliking, or antipathetic to', as ***agoraphobe***, ***ailurophobe***, ***Francophobe***, ***hydrophobe***.

phobia /'fəʊbɪə/ noun. L18.
[Independent use of next.]
(A) fear, (a) horror, (an) aversion; esp. an abnormal and irrational fear or dread aroused by a particular object or circumstance.
🕮 D. M. THOMAS The patient developed a mild phobia about looking into mirrors.

-phobia /'fəʊbɪə/ suffix.
[Latin from Greek, from *-phobos*: see -PHOBE, -IA[1].]
Forming abstract nouns denoting (esp. irrational) fear, dislike, antipathy, as ***agoraphobia***, ***Anglophobia***, ***logophobia***.

phobic /'fəʊbɪk/ adjective & noun. L19.
[from PHOBIA + -IC.]
▸A adjective. Pertaining to, characterized by, or symptomatic of a phobia. L19.
▸B noun. A person with a phobia. M20.

phoca /'fəʊkə/ noun. Pl. -cae /-siː, -kiː/, -cas. L16.
[Latin from Greek *phōkē*.]
A seal of the genus *Phoca*. Formerly any seal.

Phocaean /fəʊ'siːən/ noun & adjective. E17.
[from Greek *Phōkaia* Phocaea or Latin *Phocaei* Phocaeans + -AN.]
▸A noun. A native or inhabitant of the ancient city of Phocaea, the most northern of the Ionian cities on the west coast of Asia Minor. E17.
▸B adjective. Of or pertaining to Phocaea or its inhabitants. E17.

Phocian /'fəʊsɪən/ noun & adjective. L15.
[from Greek *Phōkis* Phocis or Latin *Phocii* Phocians + -AN.]
▸A noun. A native or inhabitant of the ancient region of Phocis in central Greece. L15.
▸B adjective. Of or pertaining to Phocis or its inhabitants. E17.

phocid /'fəʊsɪd/ noun & adjective. L19.
[mod. Latin *Phocidae* (see below), from Latin PHOCA (also a mod. Latin genus name): see -ID[3].]
ZOOLOGY. ▸A noun. A seal of the family Phocidae, comprising the true seals. L19.
▸B adjective. Of, pertaining to, or designating this family. M20.
■ **phocine** /-ʌɪn/ adjective of, pertaining to, or designating the subfamily Phocinae, comprising the northern phocids M19.

phocomelia /fəʊkəʊ'miːlɪə/ noun. L19.
[from Greek *phōkē* seal + -O- + Greek *melos* limb + -IA[1].]
A congenital deformity in which the hands or feet are attached close to the trunk, the limbs being grossly underdeveloped or absent.
■ **phocomelic** adjective & noun (a) adjective exhibiting or characteristic of phocomelia; (b) noun a person with phocomelia: M20.

Phoebe /'fiːbi/ noun[1]. poet. LME.
[Latin from Greek *Phoibē*, name of Artemis or Diana as goddess of the moon, fem. of *phoibos* bright.]
The moon personified.

phoebe /'fiːbi/ noun[2]. E18.
[Imit. of the bird's call, with spelling assim. to prec.]
Any small N. American tyrant flycatcher of the genus *Sayornis*, esp. *S. phoebe*, common in the eastern part of the continent.

Phoebean /fɪ'biːən/ adjective. E17.
[from Latin *Phoebeus* from Greek *Phoibeios*, from *Phoibos* PHOEBUS: see -AN.]
Of, pertaining to, or characteristic of Phoebus or Apollo as the god of poetry.

Phoebus /'fiːbəs/ noun. Chiefly poet. LME.
[Latin from Greek *Phoibos*, name of Apollo as the sun-god, lit. 'bright, shining'.]
The sun personified.

Phoenician /fə'nɪʃ(ə)n, -'niː-/ noun & adjective. LME.
[from *Phoenicia* (see below) + -AN.]
▸A noun. 1 A native or inhabitant of Phoenicia, an ancient maritime country approximately corresponding to modern Lebanon. LME.
2 The Semitic language of the Phoenicians. M19.

▶ **B** *adjective.* Of or pertaining to ancient Phoenicia or its inhabitants or colonists; Punic, Carthaginian. **M16.**

phoenicopter /ˈfiːnɪkɒptə/ *noun.* **L16.**
[Latin *phoenicopterus* from Greek *phoinikopteros* (as noun) flamingo, (as adjective) red-feathered, from *phoinik-*, *phoinix* crimson + *pteron* feather.]
The greater flamingo, *Phoenicopterus ruber.*

phoenix /ˈfiːnɪks/ *noun.* Also **phenix.** **OE.**
[(Old French *fenix* (mod. *phénix*) from) Latin *phoenix* from Greek *phoinix* phoenix, date-palm. Assim. to Latin in 16.]
▶ **I 1** A mythical bird with gorgeous plumage, fabled to be the only one of its kind and to live five or six hundred years in the Arabian desert, after which it burnt itself to ashes on a funeral pyre ignited by the sun and fanned by its own wings, rising from its ashes with renewed youth to live through another cycle. **OE.**
2 *transf. & fig.* **a** A person or thing of unique excellence or of matchless beauty; a paragon. **LME.** ▸**b** A thing which rises from the ashes of its predecessor or is renewed after apparent destruction. **L16.**
3 The figure of the phoenix in heraldry or as an ornament. **LME.**
4 (Usu. **P-**.) (The name of) a constellation of the southern hemisphere, west of Grus. Also ***the Phoenix.*** **L17.**

📖 **2a** D. LESSING I'm that phoenix the old-fashioned family doctor. **b** *Your Business* The company is the phoenix from the ashes of the former BL bus building subsidiary.

▶ **II 5** *BOTANY.* Any of the palm trees constituting the genus *Phoenix*, which have pinnate leaves and include the date-palm, *P. dactylifera.* **OE.**
■ **phoenix-like** *adjective & adverb* resembling or in the manner of a phoenix **E17.**

pholas /ˈfəʊləs/ *noun.* Pl. **pholades** /ˈfəʊlədiːz/. **M17.**
[mod. Latin (later adopted as a genus name) from Greek *phōlas* that lurks in a hole, from *phōleos* hole.]
ZOOLOGY. A burrowing bivalve mollusc of the genus *Pholas*, a piddock.

pholcodine /ˈfɒlkədiːn/ *noun.* **M20.**
[from MOR)PHOL(INE + COD(E)INE.]
PHARMACOLOGY. A crystalline alkaloid, $C_{23}H_{30}N_2O_4$, related to codeine and used in some cough linctuses.

phon /fɒn/ *noun.* **M20.**
[Greek *phōnē* sound, voice.]
A unit of perceived loudness such that the loudness in phons of a sound is equal to the intensity in decibels of a pure 1000 Hz tone judged to be equally loud. Formerly, a decibel.

phon- *combining form* see PHONO-.

phonaestheme /ˈfəʊnɪsθiːm/ *noun.* Also ***-nes-**. **M20.**
[from PHONE *noun*[1] + AESTH(ETIC + -EME.]
LINGUISTICS. A phoneme or group of phonemes with semantic associations as a result of its recurrent appearance in words of similar meaning.
■ **phonaesˈthesia**, **phonaesˈthesis** *nouns* sound symbolism; the use of phonaesthemes: **M20.** **phonaesthetic** /-ˈθɛt-/ *adjective* of or pertaining to phonaesthemes **M20.** **phonaesthetically** /-ˈθɛt-/ *adverb* **L20.**

phonation /fə(ʊ)ˈneɪʃ(ə)n/ *noun.* **M19.**
[from Greek *phōnē* sound, voice + -ATION.]
The production of sound by the voice or *esp.* with the vocal cords, esp. as distinguished from articulation; *gen.* vocal utterance.
■ **ˈphonate** *verb* (*a*) *verb intrans.* make a sound with the voice or vocal cords; (*b*) *verb trans.* sound in this way: **L19.** **phonational** *adjective* phonatory **M20.** **ˈphonatory** *adjective* of or pertaining to phonation **L19.**

phonautograph /fəˈnɔːtəgrɑːf/ *noun.* **M19.**
[French *phonautographe*, formed as PHONO- + AUTO-[1] + -GRAPH.]
Hist. An apparatus for automatically recording sound vibrations in the form of a tracing on a revolving cylinder.
■ **phonautoˈgraphic** *adjective* **L19.** **phonautoˈgraphically** *adverb* by means of a phonautograph **L19.**

phone /fəʊn/ *noun*[1]. **M19.**
[Greek *phōnē* sound, voice.]
PHONETICS. An elementary sound of spoken language; a simple vowel or consonant sound. Also, an allophone.

phone /fəʊn/ *noun*[2]. *colloq.* Also **'phone.** **L19.**
[Abbreviation.]
1 A telephone. **L19.**
2 An earphone; a headphone. Usu. in *pl.* **E20.**
1 ***mobile phone, pay phone,*** etc.
Comb.: **phone bank** *US* a systematic telephoning of a large number of people as an electioneering practice; **phone book** a telephone directory; **phone booth**, **phone box** a kiosk in which a public telephone is installed; **phonecard** a prepaid card that allows a person to make calls from a cardphone up to a certain cost; ***phone number***: see NUMBER *noun* 4a; **phone patch** a temporary radio link made to establish communication between a radio operator and a telephone user; ***phone phreak***: see PHREAK *noun*; **phone sex** (a commercial service providing) sexually explicit telephone conversation.

phone /fəʊn/ *verb trans. & intrans. colloq.* Also **'phone.** **L19.**
[Abbreviation.]
= TELEPHONE *verb.*
Comb.: **phone-in** (*a*) a radio or television programme during which members of the public telephone the broadcasting studio to participate in the programme; (*b*) a protest in the form of mass telephone calls of complaint; (*c*) a facility enabling members of the public to telephone a particular organization or service in large numbers.
■ **phoner** *noun* **M20.**

-phone /fəʊn/ *suffix.*
[Greek *phōnē* sound, voice, *phōnos* sounding.]
Forming (*a*) nouns with the sense 'making sound, pertaining to sound', as ***gramophone***, ***megaphone***, ***microphone***, ***saxophone***, ***telephone***; (*b*) adjectives & nouns with the senses 'that speaks', 'speaker of', as ***anglophone***, ***francophone***.

phonematic /fəʊnɪˈmatɪk/ *adjective.* **M20.**
[from Greek *phōnēmat-*, *phōnēma*: see PHONEME, -ATIC.]
LINGUISTICS. **1** = PHONEMIC. **M20.**
2 In prosodic analysis, designating a segmental element of vowel or consonant features which combines with prosodies. **M20.**
■ **phonematically** *adverb* in relation to phonemes or phonematic units; according to the theory of phonemes or phonematic units: **M20.** ˌ**phonematiˈzation** *noun* advancement from allophonic to phonemic status **M20.** ˌ**phonemaˈtology** *noun* phonemics **M20.**

phonematics /fəʊnɪˈmatɪks/ *noun.* **M20.**
[from prec.: see -ICS.]
LINGUISTICS. **1** Phonemics. **M20.**
2 The part of prosodic analysis that deals with phonematic units. **L20.**

phoneme /ˈfəʊniːm/ *noun.* **L19.**
[French *phonème* from Greek *phōnēma* sound, speech, from *phōnein* speak.]
1 *LINGUISTICS.* **a** = PHONE *noun*[1]. *rare.* **L19.** ▸**b** A unit of sound in a language that cannot be analysed into smaller linear units and can distinguish one word from another (e.g. /p/ and /b/ in English *pat, bat*). **L19.**
2 A hallucination in which voices are heard. *arch.* **E20.**

📖 **1b** E. H. GOMBRICH The foreigner imitates the . . new language as far as the phonemes of his native tongue allow. ***pitch phoneme***, ***segmental phoneme***, ***stress phoneme***, etc.

¶ Formerly stressed on 2nd syll.
■ **phonemiˈzation** *noun* phonemicization **M20.**

phonemic /fə(ʊ)ˈniːmɪk/ *adjective.* **M20.**
[from prec. + -IC.]
LINGUISTICS. Of or pertaining to phonemes or analysis using them; analysable in terms of phonemes.
■ **phonemically** *adverb* with regard to phonemes; in terms of phonemes: **M20.** **phonemicity** /fəʊnɪˈmɪsɪti/ *noun* the fact of being phonemic **M20.**

phonemicize /fə(ʊ)ˈniːmɪsʌɪz/ *verb.* Also **-ise.** **M20.**
[from prec. + -IZE.]
LINGUISTICS. **1 a** *verb intrans.* Employ analysis in terms of phonemes. *rare.* **M20.** ▸**b** *verb trans.* Classify, analyse, or describe in terms of phonemes. **M20.**
2 *verb trans. & intrans.* Change from allophonic to phonemic status. **L20.**
■ **phonemiciˈzation** *noun* **M20.**

phonemics /fə(ʊ)ˈniːmɪks/ *noun.* **M20.**
[from PHONEMIC: see -ICS.]
The branch of linguistics that deals with phonemes and phoneme systems; phonemic analysis.
■ **phonemicist** /fə(ʊ)ˈniːmɪsɪst/ *noun* an expert in or student of phonemics **M20.**

phonendoscope /fə(ʊ)ˈnɛndəskəʊp/ *noun.* **L19.**
[from PHON- + ENDO- + -SCOPE.]
An apparatus for making faint sounds, esp. in the human body, more audible.

phonestheme *noun* see PHONAESTHEME.

phonetic /fəˈnɛtɪk/ *adjective & noun.* **E19.**
[mod. Latin *phoneticus* from Greek *phōnētikos*, from *phōnētos* to be spoken, pa. ppl formation from *phōnein* speak, from *phōnē* sound, voice: see -ETIC.]
▶ **A** *adjective.* **1 a** Designating characters in ancient writing that represent sounds rather than ideas or objects. **E19.** ▸**b** Designating (a) spelling in which each letter represents invariably the same spoken sound; designating a symbol used in such spelling. **M19.**
2 Of or pertaining to speech sounds or phonetics; consisting of speech sounds. **M19.**

📖 **1b** ***phonetic alphabet***: see ALPHABET *noun* 2.
2 O. JESPERSEN The greatest revolution . . in the phonetic system of English is the vowel-shift.

▶ **B** *noun.* **1** A Chinese character used to form part of another character having the same or a similar sound. Cf. RADICAL *noun* 1b. **M19.**
2 In *pl.* (treated as *pl.* or, now usu., *sing.*). The branch of linguistics that deals with speech sounds, esp. as physical rather than semantic phenomena. **M19.**
■ **phonetically** *adverb* in a phonetic manner; in relation to speech sound; according to sound or pronunciation: **E19.** **phonetician** /fəʊnɪˈtɪʃ(ə)n, fɒn-/ *noun* an expert in or student of phonetics **M19.** **phoneticism** /-sɪz(ə)m/ *noun* (*a*) phonetic quality; the phonetic system of writing or spelling; (an instance of) phonetic spelling; (*b*) use of the criterion of phonetic similarity to determine the phonemes of a language: **L19.** **phoneticist** /-sɪst/ *noun* (*a*) an advocate of phonetic spelling; (*b*) a phonetician: **M19.** **phoneticization** /fəˌnɛtɪsʌɪˈzeɪʃ(ə)n/ *noun* (*a*) (an instance of) phonetic spelling; (*b*) (greater) correlation of symbol and sound in a writing system: **E20.** **phoneticize** /-sʌɪz/ *verb trans.* make phonetic, write phonetically **M19.**

phonetise *verb* var. of PHONETIZE.

phonetist /ˈfəʊnɪtɪst/ *noun.* **M19.**
[Contr. of PHONETICIST.]
A phoneticist.
■ **phonetism** *noun* phonetic representation; reduction to a phonetic system of writing or spelling: **L19**

phonetize /ˈfəʊnɪtʌɪz/ *verb trans.* Also **-ise.** **L19.**
[from PHONET(IC + -IZE.]
Write (words, sounds) phonetically.
■ **phonetiˈzation** *noun* **M19.**

phoney /ˈfəʊni/ *adjective & noun. colloq.* (orig. *US*). Also **phony.** **L19.**
[Origin unkn.]
▶ **A** *adjective.* (Of a thing) fake, sham, counterfeit; (of a person) insincere, pretentious. **L19.**
phoney war the period of comparative inaction at the beginning of the war of 1939–45.
▶ **B** *noun.* A fake or counterfeit thing; an insincere or pretentious person. **L19.**
Comb.: **phoney-boloney** *N. Amer. slang* = PHONUS-BOLONUS.
■ **phonily** *adverb* falsely, insincerely **M20.**

phoney /ˈfəʊni/ *verb trans. slang* (chiefly *US*). Also **phony.** **M20.**
[from prec.]
Counterfeit, falsify; make *up.*

phoneyness /ˈfəʊnɪnɪs/ *noun. colloq.* (orig. *US*). Also **phoniness.** **M20.**
[from PHONEY *adjective* + -NESS.]
The state or quality of being fake or counterfeit; insincerity, deceitfulness.

-phonia /ˈfəʊnɪə/ *suffix.*
[formed as -PHONY: see -IA[1].]
Forming nouns relating to sound or its perception, as ***paraphonia***; = -PHONY.

phonic /ˈfəʊnɪk, ˈfɒnɪk/ *adjective.* **E19.**
[from Greek *phōnē* sound, voice + -IC.]
1 Of or pertaining to sound; acoustic. **E19.**
2 Of or pertaining to speech sounds; phonetic; *spec.* designating a method of teaching reading by associating letters or groups of letters with particular sounds. **M19.**
1 phonic motor, **phonic wheel** [orig. derived from a tuning-fork] a toothed disc or rotor of magnetic material which is caused to rotate at a constant speed by an electromagnet energized by alternating or interrupted current.
■ **phonically** *adverb* in respect of speech sound; in the form of speech sounds: **M20.**

phonics /ˈfəʊnɪks, ˈfɒnɪks/ *noun.* **L17.**
[formed as prec.: see -ICS.]
†**1** The branch of science that deals with sound, esp. directly transmitted sound. **L17–M19.**
2 The branch of science that deals with spoken sounds; phonetics. **M19.**
3 The correlation between sound and symbol in an alphabetic writing system; the phonic method of teaching reading. **E20.**

phoniness *noun* var. of PHONEYNESS.

phono /ˈfəʊnəʊ/ *noun & adjective.* **M20.**
[Abbreviation.]
▶ **A** *noun.* Pl. **-os.** = PHONOGRAPH *noun* 3. *N. Amer. colloq.* **M20.**
▶ **B** *attrib. adjective.* Designating a type of plug (and the corresponding socket) used with audio and video equipment, in which one conductor is cylindrical and the other is a central part that extends beyond it. **M20.**

phono- /ˈfəʊnəʊ, ˈfɒn-/ *combining form* of Greek *phōnē* sound, voice: see -O-. Before a vowel occas. **phon-**.
■ **phonocamptic** *adjective* (now *rare* or *obsolete*) [Greek *kamptein* to bend] pertaining to (the perception of) reflected sound **L17.** **phonoˈcentrism** *noun* (*LINGUISTICS*) the tendency to regard speech as more fundamental than writing **L20.** **phonodisc** *noun* (*US*) a disc on which sound has been recorded **M20.** **phonofiddle** *noun* a type of violin in which the usual body of the instrument is replaced by a mechanism connected with an amplifying horn **E20.** **phonofilm** *noun* (*Hist.*) a cinema film with a soundtrack **E20.** **phonoˈphobia** *noun* †(*a*) fear of speaking aloud; (*b*) intolerance of or excessive sensitivity to sound: **E20.** **phonophotoˈgraphic** *adjective* of or pertaining to phonophotography **E20.** **phonophotoˈgraphically** *adverb* by means of phonophotography **M20.** **phonophoˈtography** *noun* photographic recording of the physical parameters of speech or singing **E20.** **phonoreception** *noun* (*BIOLOGY*) perception of sound by a living organism; hearing: **M20.** **phonoreceptor** *noun* (*BIOLOGY*) a sensory receptor for sound **M20.** **phonotype** *noun* (a character of) printing type for a phonetic alphabet **M19.** **phonoˈtypic**, **phonoˈtypical** *adjectives* of, pertaining to, or using phonotypes **M19.** **phonotypy** *noun* the use of phonotypes **M19.**

For other words beginning with *phono-* see the main alphabetic sequence of entries

phonocardiogram /fəʊnəʊˈkɑːdɪəgram/ *noun.* E20.
[from PHONO- + CARDIOGRAM.]
MEDICINE. A chart or record of the sounds made by the heart.
▪ **phonocardiograph** *noun* an instrument that records or displays phonocardiograms E20. **phonocardiˈographer** *noun* M20. **phonocardioˈgraphic**, **phonocardioˈgraphical** *adjectives* M20. **phonocardioˈgraphically** *adverb* by means of phonocardiography L20. **phonocardiˈography** *noun* the practice or technique of using a phonocardiograph or phonocardiograms E20.

phonogenic /fəʊnəʊˈdʒɛnɪk/ *adjective.* M20.
[from PHONO- + -GENIC, after *photogenic*.]
Well suited to electrical or mechanical sound reproduction; of or pertaining to pleasing recorded sound.

phonogram /ˈfəʊnəgram/ *noun.* M19.
[from PHONO- + -GRAM; in sense 3 after *telegram*.]
1 A written character representing a spoken sound; *spec.* one in Pitman's phonography. M19.
2 A sound recording; *spec.* one made by a phonograph. L19.
3 A telegram that the sender dictates over the telephone. E20.

phonograph /ˈfəʊnəgrɑːf/ *noun & verb.* M19.
[from PHONO- + -GRAPH.]
▶ **A** *noun.* †**1** = PHONOGRAM 1. *rare.* Only in M19.
†**2** = PHONAUTOGRAPH. Only in M19.
3 The original form of the gramophone, using a cylinder, not a disc, and able to record sound as well as reproduce it (*Hist.*); *N. Amer.* any instrument for playing gramophone records. M19.
▶ **B** *verb trans.* **1** Write down (spoken words) in phonography. *rare.* M19.
2 Record or reproduce by or as by a phonograph. *rare.* L19.
Comb.: ***phonograph record***: see RECORD *noun* 5a.

phonography /fəˈnɒgrəfi/ *noun.* E18.
[from PHONO- + -GRAPHY.]
1 Phonetic spelling; *spec.* the system of phonetic shorthand invented by Isaac Pitman in 1837. E18.
2 The automatic recording or reproduction of sound; the construction and use of phonographs. M19.
▪ **phonographer** *noun* a person who uses phonography M19. **phonoˈgraphic**, **phonoˈgraphical** *adjectives* (*a*) phonetic; of or pertaining to phonography; (*b*) of, pertaining to, or produced by a phonograph: M19. **phonoˈgraphically** *adverb* by means of phonography or a phonograph M19. **phonographist** *noun* (now *rare*) a phonographer M19.

phonolite /ˈfəʊnəlʌɪt/ *noun.* E19.
[from PHONO- + -LITE, with allus. to its resonance when struck with a hammer.]
GEOLOGY. Any of a group of extrusive igneous rocks composed of alkali feldspars and nepheline or other feldspathoid.
▪ **phonolitic** /-ˈlɪtɪk/ *adjective* pertaining to or consisting of phonolite M19.

phonology /fəˈnɒlədʒi/ *noun.* L18.
[from PHONO- + -OLOGY.]
Orig., the branch of science that deals with speech sounds and pronunciation, esp. in a particular language. Now, the branch of linguistics that deals with systems of sounds (including or excluding phonetics), esp. in a particular language; this system for a particular language.
▪ **phonoˈlogic** *adjective* M19. **phonoˈlogical** *adjective* E19. **phonoˈlogically** *adverb* in respect of phonology M19. **phonologist** *noun* E19. **phonologiˈzation** *noun* (*a*) a change to phonemic status; (*b*) development of a phonetic feature to a point where it is a distinguishing feature in a phonemic contrast: M20.

phonometer /fə(ʊ)ˈnɒmɪtə/ *noun.* E19.
[from PHONO- + -METER.]
An instrument for measuring the intensity of sound.
▪ **phonoˈmetric** *adjective* L19. **phonoˈmetrically** *adverb* by means of phonometry M20.

phonometry /fə(ʊ)ˈnɒmɪtri/ *noun.* M20.
[from PHONO- + -METRY.]
A method of investigating language by the statistical analysis of instrumentally measured speech sounds and different informants' responses to the same data.
▪ Also **phonoˈmetrics** *noun* M20.

phonon /ˈfəʊnɒn/ *noun.* M20.
[from PHONO- + -ON.]
1 PHYSICS. A quantum or quasiparticle associated with compressional waves, such as sound or those in a crystal lattice. M20.
2 LINGUISTICS. In stratificational grammar, a phonetic feature which is capable of distinguishing phonemes, a distinctive feature. M20.
▪ **phoˈnonic** *adjective* M20.

phonotactics /fəʊnə(ʊ)ˈtaktɪks/ *noun.* M20.
[from PHONO- + TACTICS.]
LINGUISTICS. The branch of linguistics that deals with the rules governing the possible phoneme sequences in a language; these rules for a particular language etc. Cf. LEXOTACTICS, MORPHOTACTICS.
▪ **phonotactic**, **phonotactical** *adjectives* M20. **phonotactically** *adverb* as regards phonotactics L20.

phonus-bolonus /ˈfəʊnəsbəˈləʊnəs/ *noun. US slang.* E20.
[from alt. of PHONEY *adjective & noun* + alt. of BOLONEY.]
Nonsense, exaggeration; insincerity, pretentiousness; mischief, improper behaviour.

phony *adjective & noun, verb* var. of PHONEY *adjective & noun, verb.*

-phony /fəni/ *suffix.*
[from Greek *-phōnia* from *phōnē* sound, voice: see -Y³.]
Forming nouns relating to sound or its perception, as ***euphony***, ***polyphony***, ***symphony***.

phoo /fuː/ *interjection.* L17.
[Natural exclam.]
Expr. contemptuous rejection, cursory dismissal, reproach, or discomfort or weariness.

phooey /ˈfuːi/ *adjective, interjection, & noun.* Orig. *US.* E20.
[from prec. + -Y¹; partly alt. of PFUI.]
▶ **A** *adjective.* Mad, crazy. *rare.* E20.
▶ **B** *interjection.* Expr. strong disagreement or disapproval. M20.
▶ **C** *noun.* Nonsense, rubbish. Also, an utterance of 'phooey'. M20.

-phor *suffix* see -PHORE.

phorate /ˈfɔːreɪt/ *noun.* M20.
[from PHOS)PHOR(US + -ATE¹.]
An organophosphorus systemic and soil insecticide that is also poisonous to humans.

phorbol /ˈfɔːbɒl/ *noun.* M20.
[from Greek *phorbē* fodder, forage, from *pherbein* feed: see -OL.]
CHEMISTRY. A tetracyclic compound, $C_{20}H_{28}O_6$, some of whose esters are present in croton oil.

-phore /fɔː/ *suffix.* Also in Latin form **-phorus** /ˈfɔːrəs/; (occas.) **-phor**.
[mod. Latin *-phorus* from Greek *-phoros*, *-phoron* bearing, bearer, from *pherein* bear.]
Forming nouns denoting a thing that possesses, contains, transports, or produces what is indicated by the 1st elem., as ***cryophorus***, ***iodophor***, ***ionophore***, ***luminophore***, ***scotophor***, ***semaphore***.

phoresis /fəˈriːsɪs/ *noun.* Now *rare* or *obsolete.* E20.
[formed as next.]
MEDICINE. = CATAPHORESIS 1.

-phoresis /fəˈriːsɪs/ *suffix.* Pl. **-phoreses** /-fəˈriːsiːz/.
[Greek *phorēsis* being carried.]
Forming nouns denoting the movement of small particles by some agency, as ***cataphoresis***, ***electrophoresis***.

phoresy /fəˈriːsi, ˈfɒrəsi/ *noun.* E20.
[French *phorésie*, formed as prec.: see -Y³.]
ZOOLOGY. An association in which one organism is carried by another, without being a parasite on it.
▪ **phoretic** /fəˈrɛt-/ *adjective* M20.

phoria /ˈfɔːrɪə/ *noun.* L19.
[from next.]
MEDICINE. A tendency for the visual axes to be directed towards different points in the absence of a visual stimulus.

-phoria /ˈfɔːrɪə/ *suffix.*
[from Greek *-phoros*: see -PHORE, -IA¹.]
MEDICINE. Forming nouns denoting a tendency to strabismus, as ***esophoria***, ***heterophoria***.

phorminx /ˈfɔːmɪŋks/ *noun.* L18.
[Greek *phormigx*.]
A kind of cithara or lyre used in ancient Greece as an accompaniment to the voice.

phormium /ˈfɔːmɪəm/ *noun.* E19.
[mod. Latin (see below), from Greek *phormion* dim. of *phormos* mat, basket, in ref. to the use made of the fibres.]
Either of two tall New Zealand evergreen plants constituting the genus *Phormium*, of the agave family, which have tough sword-shaped leaves in tufts at the base and panicles of dull red or yellow flowers; *esp.* New Zealand flax, *P. tenax*.

phorometer /fəˈrɒmɪtə/ *noun.* L19.
[from Greek *-phoros* (see -PHORE) + -OMETER.]
An instrument for measuring the degree to which the eyes tend to be differently directed.

phoronid /ˈfɒrənɪd/ *noun & adjective.* E20.
[mod. Latin *Phoronida* (see below), from Latin *Phoronid-*, *Phoronis* a character in Greek mythology: see -ID³.]
ZOOLOGY. (Designating, of, or pertaining to) any worm of the phylum Phoronida, comprising marine coelomates with a horseshoe-shaped lophophore.

phoronomy /fəˈrɒnəmi/ *noun.* L19.
[mod. Latin *phoronomia*, from Greek *phora* motion, from *pherein* bear, carry: see -NOMY.]
= KINEMATICS 1.
▪ **phoroˈnomic** *adjective* M19. **phoroˈnomically** *adverb* L19.

-phorous /ˈfərəs/ *suffix.*
[from (the same root as) -PHORE + -OUS.]
Forming adjectives corresp. to nouns in -PHORE, with the sense '-bearing, having' (the Greek-derived analogue of -FEROUS), as ***mastigophorous***.

-phorus *suffix* see -PHORE.

phos /fɒs/ *noun. arch. slang.* Also **phoss**. E19.
[Abbreviation.]
= PHOSPHORUS 2, 3. Also = ***PHOSSY jaw***.

phosgene /ˈfɒzdʒiːn/ *noun.* E19.
[from Greek *phōs* light + -GENE.]
A colourless gas, $COCl_2$, used as a poison gas and as an intermediate in the manufacture of some synthetic resins and organic chemicals; carbonyl chloride.

phosgenite /ˈfɒzdʒɪnʌɪt/ *noun.* M19.
[from prec. + -ITE¹.]
MINERALOGY. A rare colourless or pale yellow carbonate and chloride of lead formed by the weathering of lead ores and occurring as fluorescent tetragonal crystals.

phosph- *combining form* see PHOSPHO-.

phosphagen /ˈfɒsfədʒ(ə)n/ *noun.* E20.
[from PHOSPHA(TE *noun* + -GEN.]
BIOCHEMISTRY. An organic phosphate in muscle tissue whose phosphate group is readily released and transferred to adenosine diphosphate, so forming the triphosphate needed for muscular contraction.

phosphataemia /fɒsfəˈtiːmɪə/ *noun.* Also ***-temia**. E20.
[formed as next + -AEMIA.]
MEDICINE. The concentration of phosphates (and other compounds of phosphorus) in the blood. Also = HYPERPHOSPHATAEMIA.

phosphatase /ˈfɒsfəteɪz/ *noun.* E20.
[from next + -ASE.]
BIOCHEMISTRY. An enzyme which catalyses the synthesis or hydrolysis of an ester of phosphoric acid.
Comb.: **phosphatase test** a test applied to dairy products to find whether they have been adequately pasteurized.

phosphate /ˈfɒsfeɪt/ *noun & verb.* L18.
[French, formed as PHOSPHO- + -ATE¹.]
▶ **A** *noun.* **1** A salt, ester, or organic derivative of a phosphoric acid; *spec.* (*a*) any such compound of calcium or of iron and aluminium, as a constituent of cereals, minerals, etc.; (*b*) BIOCHEMISTRY any such derivative of a sugar, nucleoside, etc., in a living organism. Also, a radical or group derived from a phosphoric acid. L18.
2 An aerated soft drink containing phosphoric acid, soda water, and flavouring. Chiefly *US.* L19.

📖 **1** ANTHONY HUXLEY Phosphates such as those released by fertilisers, livestock manure and detergents. *Scientific American* Phosphate . . is an essential nutrient of both plants and animals.

Comb.: **phosphate bond** BIOCHEMISTRY a bond between a phosphate group and another part of a molecule, *esp.* such a bond in an adenosine phosphate which is hydrolysed to provide energy in living organisms; **phosphate glass**: of which the major constituent is phosphorus pentoxide or a phosphate; **phosphate island**: consisting largely of phosphate rock; **phosphate rock**: containing a substantial amount of calcium phosphate (usu. in the form of apatite).
▶ **B** *verb trans.* = PHOSPHATIZE 2. M20.
▪ **phosphated** *adjective* (*a*) MINERALOGY converted into a phosphate; (*b*) CHEMISTRY combined with or containing phosphoric acid: E19. **phosphatic** /-ˈfatɪk/ *adjective* of the nature of or containing a phosphate E19.

phosphatemia *noun* see PHOSPHATAEMIA.

phosphatide /ˈfɒsfətʌɪd/ *noun.* L19.
[from prec. + -IDE.]
BIOCHEMISTRY. Orig., any phospholipid. Now *esp.* a fatty acid ester of glycerol phosphate in which a nitrogen base is linked to the phosphate group.
▪ **phosphatidic** /-ˈtɪdɪk, -ˈtʌɪd-/ *adjective*: ***phosphatidic acid***, any of the esterified derivatives of glycerol phosphate in which the hydrogen atoms in both hydroxyl groups are replaced by fatty acid radicals E20. **phosphatidyl** /fɒsfəˈtʌɪdʌɪl, fɒsˈfatɪdʌɪl, -dɪl/ *noun* the radical of phosphatidic acid formed by the loss of a hydrogen atom from the phosphate group; ***phosphatidylcholine***, a substance widely distributed in animal tissues, egg yolk, and some higher plants, consisting of phospholipids linked to choline: M20.

phosphatize /ˈfɒsfətʌɪz/ *verb trans.* Also **-ise**. L19.
[formed as prec. + -IZE.]
1 Convert into a phosphate. Chiefly as ***phosphatized*** *ppl adjective.* L19.
2 Treat with a phosphate; coat (metal) with a phosphate for protection against corrosion. M20.
▪ **phosphatiˈzation** *noun* the action of phosphatizing something; the fact or condition of being phosphatized: L19.

phosphaturia /fɒsfəˈtjʊərɪə/ *noun.* L19.
[formed as prec. + -URIA.]
MEDICINE. The presence of an abnormally large amount of phosphates in the urine.
▪ **phosphaturic** *adjective* L19.

For other words beginning with *phono-* see the entry for **phono-**

phosphazene /ˈfɒsfəziːn/ *noun.* Also (earlier) **-ine**. E20.
[from PHOSPH(INE + AZINE: see -ENE.]
CHEMISTRY. Any compound containing the group ·N=P⁝, esp. as a repeating unit of a ring or chain in which two substituents are attached to each phosphorus atom.

phosphene /ˈfɒsfiːn/ *noun.* L19.
[from Greek *phōs* light + *phainein* to show.]
A visual sensation produced by mechanical stimulation of the retina, as by pressure on the eyeball.

phosphide /ˈfɒsfʌɪd/ *noun.* M19.
[from PHOSPHO- + -IDE.]
CHEMISTRY. A binary compound of phosphorus with another element or radical. Also, a substituted derivative of phosphine, PH_3, in which one of the substituents is a metal or a more electropositive element.

phosphine /ˈfɒsfiːn/ *noun.* L19.
[from PHOSPHO- + -INE⁵, after *amine*.]
CHEMISTRY. **1** A colourless malodorous poisonous gas, PH_3, that is sometimes spontaneously flammable when impure. L19.
2 A substituted derivative of this compound analogous to an amine, in which the substituent is an alkyl or aryl group. L19.
■ **phosphinic** /fɒsˈfɪnɪk/ *adjective*: ***phosphinic acid***, an acid derived from phosphine, *spec.* the acid $H_2PO(OH)$; a substituted derivative of this in which the substituent is an alkyl or aryl group: L19.

phosphite /ˈfɒsfʌɪt/ *noun.* L18.
[French, formed as PHOSPHO- + -ITE¹.]
CHEMISTRY. A salt or ester of phosphorous acid.

phospho- /ˈfɒsfəʊ/ *combining form* of PHOSPHORUS used esp. in BIOCHEMISTRY & CHEMISTRY: see -O-. Before a vowel also **phosph-**.
■ **phosphoˈcreatine** *noun* creatine phosphate, the phosphagen of vertebrate muscle E20. **phosphodiester** /-dʌɪˈɛstə/ *attrib. adjective* designating a bond of the kind joining successive sugar molecules in a polynucleotide M20. **phosphodiesterase** /-dʌɪˈɛstəreɪz/ *noun* an enzyme which breaks a phosphodiester bond in an oligonucleotide M20. **phosphoenolpyˈruvate** *noun* the anion $CH_2{=}C(O\cdot PO(OH)_2)\cdot COO^-$ derived from the phosphate ester of the enol of pyruvic acid M20. **phosphofructoˈkinase** *noun* an enzyme which catalyses the phosphorylation of fructose phosphate to fructose diphosphate M20. **phosphoglucoˈmutase** *noun* an enzyme which catalyses the transfer of a phosphate group between the first and the sixth carbon atoms of a molecule of glucose phosphate M20. **phosphoˈglycerate** *noun* = GLYCEROPHOSPHATE E20. **phosphoˈglyceric** *adjective* = GLYCEROPHOSPHORIC M19. **phosphoˈglyceride** *noun* any phospholipid with a structure based on glycerol phosphate M20. **phosphoˈgypsum** *noun* a form of gypsum containing phosphates, obtained as a by-product in the manufacture of phosphoric acid from phosphate rock M20. **phosphoinositide** /-ʌɪˈnəʊsɪtʌɪd/ *noun* a phospholipid in which inositol is linked to the phosphate group M20. **phosphoˈkinase** *noun* = KINASE 2 M20. **phosphoˈlipase** *noun* an enzyme which hydrolyses lecithin (phosphatidyl choline) and similar phospholipids M20. **phosphoˈlipid** *noun* a compound whose products of hydrolysis include fatty acids and phosphoric acid; any lipid containing phosphoric acid, *esp.* one with a structure based on glycerol phosphate: E20. †**phospholipin** *noun* = PHOSPHOLIPID E–M20. **phosphomonoesterase** /-ˌmɒnəʊˈɛstəreɪz/ *noun* an enzyme which removes a terminal phosphate group from an oligonucleotide or mononucleotide M20. **phosphoˈnitrile** *noun* = PHOSPHAZENE E20. **phosphonitrilic** /-ˈtrɪlɪk/ *adjective* containing the group ·N:P⁝ characteristic of phosphazenes L19. **phosphoˈprotein** *noun* any protein that contains phosphorus other than in a nucleic acid or a phospholipid E20. **phosphoˈsilicate** *noun* any substance which contains phosphate and silicate anions or consists largely of the corresponding oxides M20.

phosphonic /fɒsˈfɒnɪk/ *adjective.* L19.
[from PHOSPHO- after SULPHONIC.]
CHEMISTRY. ***phosphonic acid***, the crystalline acid $HPO(OH)_2$; a substituted derivative of this in which the substituent is an alkyl or aryl group. Also called ***phosphorous acid***.
■ ˈ**phosphonate** *noun* a salt or ester of phosphonic acid M20.

phosphonium /fɒsˈfəʊnɪəm/ *noun.* L19.
[from PHOSPHO- + -ONIUM.]
CHEMISTRY. The ion PH_4^+, analogous to ammonium. Usu. in *comb.*

phosphor /ˈfɒsfə/ *noun.* E17.
[Latin PHOSPHORUS.]
1 (**P-**.) = LUCIFER 1. Now *poet.* E17.
2 A phosphorescent or fluorescent substance, *esp.* a synthetic solid one. E18.
3 The element phosphorus. Only in *comb.* L19.

> 📖 **2** *Fiction Magazine* I watch my thoughts appear .. in the green dancing of the phosphor on the monitor screen.

Comb.: **phosphor bronze** a strong, easily worked bronze containing added phosphorus as a deoxidizer.

phosphorane /ˈfɒsfəreɪn/ *noun.* E19.
[from PHOSPHORUS + -ANE (in sense 1 an arbitrary ending).]
CHEMISTRY. †**1** A compound of one atom of phosphorus with one of chlorine. Only in E19.
2 The (imagined) hydride of phosphorus PH_5; any compound regarded as a derivative of this. M20.

phosphorate /ˈfɒsfəreɪt/ *verb trans. rare.* L18.
[from PHOSPHORUS + -ATE³.]
= PHOSPHORIZE. Chiefly as ***phosphorated*** *ppl adjective.*

phosphoreal /fɒsˈfɔːrɪəl/ *adjective.* Also **-ial**. M18.
[from PHOSPHORUS after *corporeal* etc.: see also -IAL.]
Of or pertaining to phosphorus; resembling that of phosphorus.

phosphoresce /fɒsfəˈrɛs/ *verb intrans.* L18.
[formed as next + -ESCE.]
Exhibit phosphorescence; shine in the dark.

phosphorescence /fɒsfəˈrɛs(ə)ns/ *noun.* L18.
[formed as next + -ESCENCE.]
The emission of light without any perceptible heat; the light so emitted; *techn.* luminescence similar to fluorescence but continuing after the exciting radiation has ceased, or in which the atoms concerned have a relatively long lifetime (e.g. more than 10^{-8} second) in the excited state.

> 📖 *Tarzan Monthly* A vast cavern, eerily lit by the phosphorescence in the rock walls.

phosphorescent /fɒsfəˈrɛs(ə)nt/ *adjective & noun.* M18.
[from PHOSPHORUS + -ESCENT.]
▶ **A** *adjective.* Exhibiting phosphorescence; capable of phosphorescing. M18.
▶ **B** *noun.* A phosphorescent substance. M19.
■ **phosphorescently** *adverb* M19.

phosphoret(t)ed *adjectives* vars. of PHOSPHURETTED.

phosphori *noun pl.* see PHOSPHORUS.

phosphorial *adjective* var. of PHOSPHOREAL.

phosphoric /fɒsˈfɒrɪk/ *adjective.* L18.
[French *phosphorique*, from *phosphore* phosphor, phosphorus from Latin: see PHOSPHORUS, -IC.]
1 Pertaining to or of the nature of a phosphor; phosphorescent. L18.
2 CHEMISTRY. Containing phosphorus in its higher valency (5). Cf. PHOSPHOROUS. L18.

> 📖 **1** DISRAELI A phosphoric light glittered in her Hellenic eyes. **2 phosphoric acid** (**a**) = ***ORTHOPHOSPHORIC acid***; (**b**) any of various oxoacids of phosphorus.

phosphorise *verb* var. of PHOSPHORIZE.

phosphorite /ˈfɒsfərʌɪt/ *noun.* L18.
[from PHOSPHORUS + -ITE¹.]
Orig. = APATITE. Now, any sedimentary rock containing a high proportion of calcium phosphate.
■ **phosphoritic** /fɒsfəˈrɪtɪk/ *adjective* M19.

phosphorize /ˈfɒsfərʌɪz/ *verb trans.* Also **-ise**. L18.
[French *phosphoriser*, from *phosphore*: see PHOSPHORIC, -IZE.]
1 Combine or impregnate with phosphorus. Chiefly as ***phosphorized*** *ppl adjective.* L18.
2 Make phosphorescent; cause to phosphoresce. M19.

phosphorolysis /fɒsfəˈrɒlɪsɪs/ *noun.* M20.
[from PHOSPHOR(US or PHOSPHOR(YLATION + HYDR)OLYSIS.]
BIOCHEMISTRY. A form of hydrolysis in which a bond in an organic molecule is broken and an inorganic phosphate group becomes attached to one of the atoms previously linked.
■ **phosphoroˈlytic** *adjective* M20. **phosphoroˈlytically** *adverb* by means of phosphorolysis M20.

phosphoroscope /ˈfɒsf(ə)rəskəʊp/ *noun.* M19.
[from PHOSPHOR(ESCENCE + -O- + -SCOPE.]
A device for observing and measuring the duration of phosphorescence.

phosphorous /ˈfɒsf(ə)rəs/ *adjective.* L18.
[from next + -OUS.]
1 Phosphorescent. L18.
2 CHEMISTRY. Containing phosphorus in its lower valency (3). Cf. PHOSPHORIC. L18.
2 phosphorous acid the crystalline acid $HPO(OH)_2$.

phosphorus /ˈfɒsf(ə)rəs/ *noun.* Pl. **-ri** /-rʌɪ/, †**-ruses**. E17.
[Latin from Greek *phōsphoros* light-bringing, from *phōs* light + *-phoros* -PHORE.]
1 (**P-**.) = LUCIFER 1. Now *rare.* E17.
2 Any substance or organism that emits light (naturally, or when heated etc.); *esp.* a phosphorescent substance. Now *rare.* E17.
3 A non-metallic allotropic chemical element, atomic no. 15, which is widespread in living organisms and minerals (chiefly in phosphates) and in its commonest form is a waxy whitish solid which undergoes spontaneous oxidation (with chemiluminescence) or ignition in air. (Symbol P.) L17.
3 *red phosphorus*: see RED *adjective.* ***white phosphorus***: see WHITE *adjective.* ***yellow phosphorus***: see YELLOW *adjective.*
Comb.: †**phosphorus box** a box of matches tipped with potassium chlorate and phosphorus; **phosphorus necrosis** necrosis of the jaw caused by exposure to the fumes of phosphorus.

phosphoryl /ˈfɒsfərʌɪl, -rɪl/ *noun.* L19.
[from PHOSPHORUS + -YL.]
CHEMISTRY. The usu. trivalent group ⁝PO. Also, the monovalent phosphate group $\cdot PO(OH)_2$. Usu. in *comb.*

phosphorylase /fɒsˈfɒrɪleɪz/ *noun.* M20.
[from prec. + -ASE.]
BIOCHEMISTRY. An enzyme which introduces a phosphate group into an organic molecule.

phosphorylation /ˌfɒsfɒrɪˈleɪʃ(ə)n/ *noun.* E20.
[formed as prec. + -ATION.]
BIOCHEMISTRY. The introduction of a phosphate group into an organic molecule.
■ **phosˈphorylate** *verb trans.* introduce a phosphate group into M20.

phosphuranylite /fɒsfjʊˈranɪlʌɪt/ *noun.* L19.
[from PHOSPHO- + URANYL + -ITE¹.]
MINERALOGY. A hydrous phosphate of calcium and uranium that occurs as a secondary mineral forming yellow incrustations and seams on uraniferous rocks.

†**phosphuret** *noun.* L18–L19.
[mod. Latin *phosphoretum*, after French *phosphore*: see PHOSPHORIC, *phosphure* phosphide, from -URET.]
CHEMISTRY. A phosphide.

phosphuretted /ˈfɒsfjʊrɛtɪd/ *adjective. obsolete exc. Hist.* Also **-eted**, **-phor-** /-fər-/. E19.
[from prec. + -ED².]
CHEMISTRY. Combined chemically with phosphorus.
phosphuretted hydrogen the gas phosphine.

phoss *noun* var. of PHOS.

phossy /ˈfɒsi/ *noun. arch. colloq.* L19.
[from PHOS + -Y¹.]
= PHOSPHORUS 3. Only in ***phossy jaw***, = PHOSPHORUS ***necrosis***.

phot /fəʊt/ *noun.* L19.
[French from Greek *phōt-*, *phōs* light.]
PHYSICS. †**1** A unit of the product of illumination and duration, equal to one lux maintained for one second. Only in L19.
2 A unit of illumination equal to 10,000 lux (one lumen per square centimetre). E20.

†**phota** *noun.* E17–E19.
[Persian *futa* from Arab. = loincloth.]
An Indian cotton fabric.

Photian /ˈfəʊʃ(ə)n/ *adjective & noun.* M19.
[from *Photius* (see below) + -AN.]
ECCLESIASTICAL HISTORY. ▶**A** *adjective.* Of or pertaining to Photius, a 9th-cent. Patriarch of Constantinople anathematized by the Pope, or the schism involving him. M19.
▶ **B** *noun.* A follower or adherent of Photius. M19.
■ **Photianism** *noun* the doctrine of Photius M19. **Photianist** *adjective & noun* Photian M20.

photic /ˈfəʊtɪk/ *adjective.* M19.
[from Greek *phōt-*, *phōs* light + -IC.]
1 Of or pertaining to light. M19.
2 Designating parts of the oceans penetrated by sufficient sunlight for the growth of plants. E20.
■ **photically** *adverb* by light M20.

Photinian /fəˈtɪnɪən/ *noun & adjective.* M17.
[from late Latin *Photiniani* (pl.), from *Photinus*: see below, -IAN.]
ECCLESIASTICAL HISTORY. ▶**A** *noun.* A follower of Photinus, a heretical 4th-cent. Bishop of Sirmium who maintained a form of Sabellianism. M17.
▶ **B** *adjective.* Of or pertaining to Photinus or the heresy he espoused. E18.
■ **Photinianism** *noun* the doctrine or heresy of the Photinians M17.

photino /fə(ʊ)ˈtiːnəʊ/ *noun.* Pl. **-os**. L20.
[from PHOTON + -INO.]
PARTICLE PHYSICS. The (hypothetical) supersymmetric counterpart of the photon, with spin −½.

photism /ˈfəʊtɪz(ə)m/ *noun.* L19.
[Greek *phōtismos* illumination, from *phōtizein* shine, illuminate, formed as PHOTIC: see -ISM.]
A hallucinatory sensation of light; a visual synaesthesia.

photo /ˈfəʊtəʊ/ *noun & adjective. colloq.* M19.
[Abbreviation.]
▶ **A** *noun.* Pl. **-os**.
1 A photograph. M19.
2 A photo finish. M20.
▶ **B** *adjective.* Photographic. L19.
Comb. & special collocations (see also PHOTO-): **photo call** an occasion at which actors, celebrities, etc., pose for press photographers by arrangement; **photo CD** a compact disc from which still photographs can be displayed on a television screen, and the technology for storing and reproducing photographs in this way; **photo finish** a close finish of a race, *esp.* one in which the winner can be determined only from a photograph; *fig.* a close finish of any contest; **photo lab** a commercial establishment for developing films and printing photographs taken by members of the public; **photo op** (*colloq.*), **photo opportunity** an opportunity provided for press and television photographers to take photographs of a celebrity or celebrities; **photo session** a prearranged session in which a photographer takes photographs of a person for use in advertising.

photo /ˈfəʊtəʊ/ *verb trans.* M19.
[Abbreviation.]
Photograph.

photo- /ˈfəʊtəʊ/ *combining form.*
[Partly from Greek *phōto-* combining form of *phōt-*, *phōs* light: see -O-; partly from PHOTO(GRAPHIC, PHOTO(GRAPHY.]
1 Light.
2 Photography; photographic.

■ **photoabˈsorbing** *adjective* that absorbs light; capable of absorbing a photon: M20. **photoabˈsorption** *noun* absorption of a photon M20. **photoaˈcoustic** *adjective* = OPTOACOUSTIC L20. **photoact** *noun* (BIOCHEMISTRY) a photoaction L20. **photoaction** *noun* (BIOCHEMISTRY) a molecular event caused by light M20. **photoˈactivate** *verb trans.* induce a change in or activate by means of light E20. **photoactiˈvation** *noun* activation by means of light E20. **photoˈactive** *adjective* capable of or involving a chemical or physical change in response to illumination E20. **photoacˈtivity** *noun* the degree to which a substance or system is photoactive E20. **photoaˈffinity** *adjective* (BIOCHEMISTRY) designating a technique of labelling large molecules (esp. proteins) at specific sites by means of smaller molecules which initially form loose complexes at the sites and are then photochemically converted to reactive forms which bond more permanently L20. **photoaˈllergic** *adjective* of or of the nature of a photoallergy M20. **photoˈallergy** *noun* an allergy brought about by light M20. **photoautotroph** /-ˈɔːtə(ʊ)trəʊf/ *noun* (BIOLOGY) a photoautotrophic organism, a green plant M20. **photoautotrophic** /-ˈtrəʊfɪk, -ˈtrɒfɪk/ *adjective* (BIOLOGY) autotrophic and obtaining energy from light M20. **photobioˈlogical** *adjective* of or pertaining to photobiology E20. **photobiˈologist** *noun* an expert in or student of photobiology M20. **photobiˈology** *noun* the branch of biology that deals with the effects of light on living organisms M20. **photoˈbleaching** *noun* a loss of colour when illuminated M20. **photoˈcathode** *noun* a cathode which emits electrons when illuminated, thereby causing an electric current M20. **photochemoˈtherapy** *noun* the use of both drugs and (usu. ultraviolet) light in a course of treatment L20. **photoˈchromoscope** *noun* (*Hist.*) a device for viewing a set of monochrome photographs stereoscopically through differently coloured filters so that they are seen as a single appropriately coloured image L19. **photocliˈnometry** *noun* the process of deriving topographical information about a region from measurements of the brightness distribution in aerial photographs M20. **photocoˈagulate** *verb trans.* (SURGERY) treat by photocoagulation M20. **photocoaguˈlation** *noun* (SURGERY) the use of an intense beam of light to coagulate small areas of tissue, esp. of the retina M20. **photocoˈagulator** *noun* (SURGERY) an apparatus which produces the light beam used for photocoagulation M20. **photocoˈllage** *noun* (a) collage using photographs L20. **photoconˈtrol** *noun* (**a**) control by light; (**b**) (SURVEYING) a system of precisely surveyed reference points that can be identified on aerial photographs: M20. **photoconˈversion** *noun* (BIOCHEMISTRY) a reversible chemical change effected by light, *esp.* that of one form of phytochrome to the other M20. **photoconˈvert** *verb trans.* (BIOCHEMISTRY) change by photoconversion M20. **photocurrent** *noun* an electric current induced by illumination E20. **photodecomˈpose** *verb trans.* & *intrans.* (cause to) undergo photodecomposition L20. **photodecompoˈsition** *noun* decomposition caused by the action of light L19. **photodeˈgradable** *adjective* susceptible to photodegradation L20. **photodegraˈdation** *noun* degradation of a substance caused by light L20. **photodensiˈtometer** *noun* an instrument for measuring the density of a photographic negative or the opacity of a fluid E20. **photodeˈtachment** *noun* (PHYSICS) detachment of an electron from an atom by an incident photon M20. **photodeˈtection** *noun* the detection of light with a photodetector M20. **photodetector** *noun* a device that responds to incident light, *esp.* one whose operation depends on the electrical effect of individual photons M20. **photoˈdimer** *noun* (CHEMISTRY) a dimer formed by photochemical action M20. **photodiˈmeric** *adjective* (CHEMISTRY) designating, of, or pertaining to a photodimer M20. **photodimeriˈzation** *noun* (CHEMISTRY) formation of or conversion into a photodimer M20. **photoˈdimerize** *verb trans.* & *intrans.* (CHEMISTRY) dimerize by the action of light M20. **photoˈdiode** *noun* a semiconductor diode whose resistance depends on the degree of illumination M20. **photodisinteˈgration** *noun* (NUCLEAR PHYSICS) the breaking up of an atomic nucleus by the action of a gamma ray M20. **photodiˈssociate** *verb trans.* (CHEMISTRY) dissociate by means of light M20. **photodissociˈation** *noun* (CHEMISTRY) dissociation of a chemical compound by the action of light E20. **photoˈduplicate** *noun* a photographically made copy of a document M20. **photoˈduplicate** *verb trans.* photocopy M20. **photodupliˈcation** *noun* photographic copying of a document, photocopying E20. **photoeffect** *noun* (PHYSICS) a photoelectric effect, *esp.* the emission of an electron from an atom, or a nucleon from a nucleus, caused by the action of a photon E20. **photoeˈjection** *noun* (PHYSICS) ejection (of an electron from an atom) as a result of the absorption of a photon M20. **photoelectroˈchemical** *adjective* designating, of, or pertaining to an electrochemical cell in which the potential or current depends on the degree of illumination of the cell L20. **photoenzyˈmatic** *adjective* (BIOLOGY) pertaining to or involving a photoenzyme M20. **photoenzyˈmatically** *adverb* by a photoenzyme M20. **photoenzyme** *noun* (BIOLOGY) an enzyme which catalyses a photochemical reaction M20. **photo-essay** *noun* an essay or short biography consisting of text matter and numerous photographs L20. **photo-ˈetch** *verb trans.* etch by a photographic process L19. **photo-exciˈtation** *noun* (PHYSICS) excitation caused by light or by a photon E20. **photofabriˈcation** *noun* the manufacture of integrated circuits by photolithography M20. **photofacˈsimile** *noun* facsimile in which the likeness is reproduced in photographic form M20. **photoˈfinisher** *noun* an organization or machine that produces finished photographs from film or negatives L20. **photofission** *noun* (NUCLEAR PHYSICS) fission of an atomic nucleus caused by a gamma-ray photon M20. **photoflash** *noun* (a flash produced by) a photographic flash bulb or flashlight M20. **photoflood** *noun* a floodlight used in photography and cinematography M20. **photoˈfluorogram** *noun* a photograph of a fluoroscopic X-ray image M20. **photoˈfluorograph** *noun* & *verb* (**a**) *noun* a photofluorogram; (**b**) *verb trans.* examine by photofluorography: M20. **photofluoroˈgraphic** *adjective* of or pertaining to photofluorography M20. **photofluoroˈgraphically** *adverb* by means of photofluorography M20. **photofluoˈrography** *noun* photography of a fluoroscopic X-ray image M20. **photoˈfluoroscope** *noun* an instrument for taking photofluorograms L19. **photofluoˈroscopy** *noun* = PHOTOFLUOROGRAPHY M20. **photogoniˈometer** *noun* (**a**) an instrument for measuring angles indirectly from photographs of an area; (**b**) an instrument for photographically recording the X-rays diffracted at known angles by a crystal or substance: E20. **photogonioˈmetric** *adjective* of or pertaining to photogoniometry M20. **photogoniˈometry** *noun* the practice or technique of using a photogoniometer M20. **photoˈheliograph** *noun* = HELIOGRAPH *noun* 2 M19. **photohelioˈgraphic** *adjective* of or pertaining to a photoheliograph or photoheliography L19. **photoheliˈography** *noun* photography of the sun M19. **photoheterotroph** /-ˈhɛt(ə)rətrəʊf/ *noun* (BIOLOGY) a photoheterotrophic organism M20. **photoheterotrophic** /-ˈtrəʊfɪk, -ˈtrɒfɪk/ *adjective* (BOTANY) heterotrophic and obtaining energy from light M20. **photoheteroˈtrophically** *adverb* (BIOLOGY) in a photoheterotrophic manner L20. **photoinactiˈvation** *noun* (BIOCHEMISTRY) destruction by light of the biological activity of an enzyme etc. M20. **photoinˈduce** *verb trans.* induce by the action of light; BOTANY induce reproductive behaviour in (a plant) by an appropriate sequence of light and darkness: M20. **photoinˈducible** *adjective* able to be photoinduced L20. **photoinˈduction** *noun* the action or process of induction by light, esp. of reproductive behaviour in plants M20. **photoinˈductive** *adjective* (BOTANY) tending to induce flowering or other activity in plants by means of a regime of alternating periods of light and darkness M20. **photoiˈnitiated** *adjective* (of a chemical reaction) initiated by light M20. **photo-interpreˈtation** *noun* the interpretation of aerial photographs E20. **photoinˈterpreter** *noun* a person who interprets aerial photographs M20. **photoioniˈzation** *noun* (PHYSICS) ionization produced by electromagnetic radiation E20. **photoˈionize** *verb trans.* ionize by means of electromagnetic radiation M20. **photokiˈnesis** *noun* (BIOLOGY) (an) undirected movement of an organism in response to light E20. **photokiˈnetic** *adjective* pertaining to or exhibiting photokinesis E20. **photokiˈnetically** *adverb* as regards photokinesis L20. **photoˈlabile** *adjective* unstable in the presence of light M20. **photolaˈbility** *noun* the property of being photolabile M20. **photolithotroph** /-ˈlɪθətrəʊf/ *noun* (BIOLOGY) a photolithotrophic organism M20. **photolithotrophic** /-ˈtrəʊfɪk, -ˈtrɒfɪk/ *adjective* (BIOLOGY) characterized by photolithotrophy M20. **photoliˈthotrophy** *noun* (BIOLOGY) a form of nutrition in which energy is obtained photosynthetically from inorganic compounds M20. **photolumiˈnescence** *noun* luminescence caused by visible light or by infrared or ultraviolet radiation L19. **photolumiˈnescent** *adjective* exhibiting or pertaining to photoluminescence E20. **photomagˈnetic** *adjective* †(**a**) designating electromagnetic rays supposed to have a magnetic effect; (**b**) photomagnetoelectric: M19. **photomagnetoeˈlectric** *adjective* (PHYSICS) designating, of, or pertaining to an effect whereby illumination of a solid subjected to a magnetic field parallel to the surface gives rise to a voltage at right angles to both the direction of the field and that of the illumination M20. **photomap** *noun* a map consisting of or drawn on a photograph or photomosaic of the area concerned M20. **photomask** *noun* in the manufacture of microcircuits, a photographic pattern through which a photoresist is irradiated with ultraviolet light in order to transfer the pattern to it M20. **photomatrix** *noun* (any of) a set of photographic images of characters used in filmsetting M20. **photoˈmesic** *adjective* (NUCLEAR PHYSICS) of or involving a photomeson M20. **photoˈmeson** *noun* (NUCLEAR PHYSICS) a meson emitted from a nucleus as a result of interaction with a gamma-ray photon M20. **photomixer** *noun* (PHYSICS) a device that acts for light waves as a mixer does for electric signals M20. **photomonˈtage** *noun* (a) montage using photographs M20. **photomoˈsaic** *noun* a photographic mosaic M20. **photoˈmural** *noun* a mural consisting of a photograph or photographs M20. **photoˈneutron** *noun* (NUCLEAR PHYSICS) a neutron released from a nucleus by the action of a gamma-ray photon M20. **photonovel** *noun* a story presented as a series of photographs with added dialogue, usu. in a serial publication L20. **photoˈnuclear** *adjective* (NUCLEAR PHYSICS) of or pertaining to the interaction of a photon with an atomic nucleus M20. **photonymograph** /-ˈnɪm-/ *noun* [Greek *onuma* name] an instrument used for producing printed names photographically on maps M20. **photoorganotroph** /-ɔːˈganətrəʊf/ *noun* (BIOLOGY) a photoorganotrophic organism M20. **photoorganotrophic** /-ˈtrəʊfɪk, -ˈtrɒfɪk/ *adjective* (BIOLOGY) characterized by photoorganotrophy M20. **photoorganotrophically** /-ˈtrəʊfɪk-, -ˈtrɒfɪk-/ *adverb* (BIOLOGY) in a photoorganotrophic manner L20. **photoorgaˈnotrophy** *noun* (BIOLOGY) a form of nutrition in which energy is obtained photosynthetically from organic compounds M20. **photo-oxiˈdation** *noun* oxidation caused by the action of light L19. **photo-ˈoxidative** *adjective* involving or characterized by photo-oxidation M20. **photo-ˈoxidizable** *adjective* susceptible to photo-oxidation M20. **photo-ˈoxidize** *verb trans.* oxidize photochemically M20. **photoˈpathic** *adjective* of or pertaining to photopathy L19. **phoˈtopathy** *noun* the behaviour of an organism towards light, in moving towards or away from an illuminated region L19. **photophil(e)** *adjective* tending towards a lighted region; photophilous; *spec.* designating a phase of the circadian cycle of a plant or animal during which light tends to stimulate reproductive activity (cf. SCOTOPHIL): L19. **photoˈphilic**, **phoˈtophilous** *adjectives* (BIOLOGY) thriving best in abundant light: E20. **phoˈtophily** *noun* (BIOLOGY) the state of being photophilous M20. **photophoˈresis** *noun* the motion of small particles under the influence of light E20. **photophoˈretic** *adjective* of or pertaining to photophoresis E20. **photophosphoryˈlation** *noun* (BIOCHEMISTRY) the process by which light energy is utilized by a plant or micro-organism to convert ADP to ATP without the reduction of oxygen to water that occurs in oxidative phosphorylation M20. **photophˈthalmia** *noun* (MEDICINE) inflammation of the cornea produced by strong ultraviolet light, causing blindness or defective vision E20. **photophˈthalmic** *adjective* (MEDICINE) of or pertaining to photophthalmia E20. **photoˈphysical** *adjective* of or pertaining to the physical effect of light L19. **photopigment** *noun* a pigment (e.g. in the eye) whose chemical state depends on its degree of illumination M20. **photopolaˈrimeter** *noun* †(**a**) *rare* an apparatus for measuring the proportion of polarized light in a given beam; (**b**) a telescopic apparatus for photographing distant objects (as planets) and measuring the polarization of light from them: L19. **photopolariˈmetric** *adjective* of or pertaining to photopolarimetry L20. **photopolaˈrimetry** *noun* the practice or technique of using a photopolarimeter L20. **photoˈpolymer** *noun* a polymer produced photochemically M20. **photopolymerizaˈbility** *noun* the property of being photopolymerizable M20. **photoˈpolymerizable** *adjective* able to be photopolymerized M20. **photopolymeriˈzation** *noun* polymerization brought about by the action of light E20. **photoˈpolymerize** *verb trans.* polymerize photochemically E20. **photo-potential** *noun* an electric potential generated by light E20. **photo-print** *noun* a print produced by a photomechanical process; a photographic print: L19. **photoprocess** *noun* (**a**) a printing process involving photography; (**b**) a (biological or chemical) process involving light: L19. **photoproˈduced** *adjective* produced by light or by a single incident photon M20. **photoproduct** *noun* a product of the chemical action of light E20. **photoproduction** *noun* production by light or by a single incident photon M20. **photoproˈtection** *noun* (BIOLOGY) the process whereby illumination of living matter can protect it from being harmed by subsequent ultraviolet irradiation M20. **photoproˈtective** *adjective* (BIOLOGY & MEDICINE) (**a**) of or pertaining to protection conferred by light (as in photoprotection); (**b**) of or pertaining to protection against harmful effects of light: M20. **photoˈprotein** *noun* any protein active in the emission of light by a living creature M20. **photoˈproton** *noun* (NUCLEAR PHYSICS) a proton released from a nucleus by the action of a gamma-ray photon M20. **photoˈradiogram** *noun* a picture, diagram, or the like transmitted by radio E20. **photoreaction** *noun* a photochemical reaction E20. **photo-ˈrecce** *noun* (*colloq.*) photoreconnaissance M20. **photoreˈconnaissance** *noun* (a) reconnaissance by means of aerial photography M20. **photoreˈcovery** *noun* (BIOLOGY) = PHOTOREACTIVATION M20. **photoˈregulate** *verb trans.* regulate (a biological process) by means of light M20. **photoreguˈlation** *noun* the action of photoregulating something M20. **photoˈregulator** *noun* a biological mechanism that regulates a process according to the duration, intensity, etc., of the light which it detects M20. **photo-reporˈtage** *noun* photojournalism; a report that uses photographs: M20. **photoreproˈduce** *verb trans.* reproduce (text) photographically, esp. from typescript L20. **photoreˈsistance** *noun* (PHYSICS) (an) electrical resistance that is dependent on the degree of illumination; a photoresistor: E20. **photoreˈsistive** *adjective* (PHYSICS) exhibiting photoresistance M20. **photoresistor** *noun* (PHYSICS) a resistor whose resistance varies according to the degree of illumination M20. **photoresponse** *noun* a response to light; *esp.* a response of a plant mediated otherwise than through photosynthesis: M20. **photoreˈsponsive** *adjective* responsive to light M20. **photoreˈversal** *noun* reversal of a (biological) process by the action of light M20. **photoreversiˈbility** *noun* (BIOLOGY) the property or an instance of being photoreversible M20. **photoreˈversible** *adjective* (BIOLOGY) able to be reversed by the action of light; (of a substance) changing from one form into another and back again as the degree of illumination increases and decreases: M20. **photoscan** *noun* (MEDICINE) a photograph obtained by photoscanning M20. **photoscanner** *noun* (MEDICINE) an apparatus for taking photoscans M20. **photoscanning** *noun* (MEDICINE) photography of the pattern of radiation from the body following the internal administration of a radioisotope, e.g. to locate tumours M20. **photosensor** *noun* a sensor that responds to light M20. **photoˈsensory** *adjective* (BIOLOGY) pertaining to or involving the perception of light E20. **photo-shock** *noun* a flash or series of flashes of light used as part of shock therapy M20. **photostaˈbility** *noun* the property of being photostable M20. **photostable** *adjective* stable in the presence of light E20. **photoˈstationary** *adjective* (CHEMISTRY) designating a state of equilibrium in a photochemical reaction in which the rate of dissociation of the reactants equals their rate of recombination E20. **photoˈstereograph** *noun* an instrument for the observation, measurement, and interpretation of pairs of stereophotographs for surveying purposes M20. **photoˈstimulate** *verb trans.* stimulate by means of light M20. **photostimuˈlation** *noun* stimulation by means of light M20. **photostory** *noun* a story with accompanying photographs; a strip cartoon with photographs in place of drawings, a photonovel: M20. **photosurface** *noun* a surface which emits electrons when illuminated M20. **photosystem** *noun* either of the two biochemical mechanisms in plants by which light is converted into useful energy M20. **photoˈtelegram** *noun* a telegram sent by phototelegraphy E20. **photoˈtelegraph** *noun* an apparatus used for phototelegraphy E20. **phototeleˈgraphic** *adjective* of or pertaining to phototelegraphy E20. **phototeˈlegraphy** *noun* the telegraphic transmission of pictures; *spec.* facsimile telegraphy in which variations of tone are preserved L19. **photo-theˈodolite** *noun* a theodolite incorporating a camera L19. **phototheraˈpeutic** *adjective* pertaining to or involving phototherapy E20. **photoˈtherapy** *noun* the therapeutic use of light L19. **photoˈtopographer** *noun* an expert in or student of phototopography E20. **phototopoˈgraphic** *adjective* of, pertaining to, or using phototopography L19. **phototopoˈgraphical** *adjective* phototopographic E20. **phototoˈpography** *noun* photogrammetric surveying L19. **photoˈtoxic** *adjective* pertaining to or possessing phototoxicity M20. **phototoˈxicity** *noun* the property of causing a harmful reaction to sunlight M20. **phototransforˈmation** *noun* (a) transformation (of a chemical compound) effected by light M20. **phototranˈsistor** *noun* (ELECTRONICS) a junction transistor which responds to incident light by generating and amplifying an electric current M20. **phototroph** /-trəʊf/ *noun* (BIOLOGY) a phototrophic organism M20. **phototrophic** /-ˈtrəʊfɪk, -ˈtrɒfɪk/ *adjective* (BIOLOGY) characterized by phototrophy M20. **phototrophically** /-ˈtrəʊfɪk-, -ˈtrɒfɪk-/ *adverb* in a phototrophic manner L20. **phototrophy** *noun* (BIOLOGY) nutrition in which sunlight is utilized as a source of energy M20. **phototube** *noun* a photocell in the form of an electron tube with a photoemissive cathode M20. **phototype** *noun* a printing plate or block produced photographically; the process by which such a plate is produced; a picture printed by it: M19. **photovolˈtaic** *adjective* pertaining to, exhibiting, or utilizing the generation of an electromotive force by light incident on an interface between certain pairs of substances E20. **photovolˈtaically** *adverb* in a photovoltaic manner M20. **photovoltaics** *noun* the branch of science and technology that deals with photovoltaic effects and devices L20. **photoˈzincograph** *noun & verb* (**a**) *noun* a plate or picture produced by photozincography; (**b**) *verb trans.* print, produce, or portray by photozincography: M19. **photozincoˈgraphic** *adjective* of or pertaining to photozincography M19. **photozinˈcography** *noun* photolithography using a zinc plate M19.

photoblepharon /fəʊtəʊˈblɛf(ə)rɒn/ *noun.* E20.
[from PHOTO- + Greek *blepharon* eyelid.]
A small luminous fish of the genus *Photoblepharon*, found in the Red Sea and the Indian Ocean.

photocatalysis /ˌfəʊtəʊkəˈtalɪsɪs/ *noun.* Pl. **-lyses** /-lɪsiːz/. E20.
[from PHOTO- + CATALYSIS.]
CHEMISTRY. The acceleration of a reaction by light; the catalysis of a photochemical reaction.
■ **photoˈcatalyse** *verb trans.* subject to photocatalysis E20. **photoˈcatalyst** *noun* a substance that acts as a catalyst in a photochemical reaction E20. **photocataˈlytic** *adjective* pertaining to or exhibiting photocatalysis E20. **photocataˈlytically** *adverb* by photocatalysis E20.

photocell /ˈfəʊtəʊsɛl/ *noun.* L19.
[from PHOTO- + CELL *noun*[1].]
A device which generates an electric current or voltage dependent on the degree of illumination.

photochemical /fəʊtəʊˈkɛmɪk(ə)l/ *adjective.* M19.
[from PHOTO- + CHEMICAL.]
Of or pertaining to the chemical action of light.
photochemical smog a condition of the atmosphere attributed to the action of sunlight on hydrocarbons and nitrogen in it, characterized by increased content of ozone and nitrogen oxides, irritation of eyes, damage to plants, and visibility reduced to a mile (1.6 km) or less.
■ **photochemically** *adverb* in a photochemical manner; by photochemical action: L19.

photochemistry /fəʊtəʊˈkɛmɪstri/ *noun.* M19.
[from PHOTO- + CHEMISTRY.]
The branch of chemistry that deals with the chemical effects of light.
■ **photochemist** *noun* an expert in or student of photochemistry E20.

photochromic /fəʊtə(ʊ)ˈkrəʊmɪk/ *adjective & noun.* M20.
[from PHOTO- + Greek *khrōma* colour + -IC.]
► **A** *adjective.* Of, pertaining to, or displaying photochromism. M20.

Fortune Photochromic glasses that darken when light hits them.

► **B** *noun.* A photochromic substance. M20.
■ **photochromism** *noun* the phenomenon of undergoing a reversible change of colour or shade when illuminated with light of appropriate wavelength M20.

photocompose /ˌfəʊtəʊkəmˈpəʊz/ *verb trans.* E20.
[from PHOTO- + COMPOSE.]
= ***filmset*** s.v. FILM *noun*; make (a printing plate) directly from a photographic image. Freq. as ***photocomposing*** *verbal noun*.
■ **photocomposer** *noun* a machine for carrying out photocomposition E20. ˌ**photocompoˈsition** *noun* photocomposing E20.

photoconducting /ˌfəʊtəʊkənˈdʌktɪŋ/ *adjective.* E20.
[from PHOTO- + CONDUCTING *ppl adjective*.]
PHYSICS. Exhibiting or utilizing a decrease in electrical resistance on illumination.
■ **photoconductance** *noun* photoconductivity M20. **photoconduction** *noun* photoconductivity E20. **photoconductive** *adjective* photoconducting; of or pertaining to the property of being photoconducting: E20. ˌ**photoconducˈtivity** *noun* (a measure of) the property of being photoconductive E20. **photoconductor** *noun* a photoconducting substance or device E20.

photocopier /ˈfəʊtəʊkɒpɪə/ *noun.* E20.
[from PHOTO- + COPIER.]
1 An electrical machine for producing immediate, often full-size, paper copies of text or graphic matter by a process usu. involving the electrical or chemical action of light. E20.
2 A person who operates such a machine. L20.

photocopy /ˈfəʊtəʊkɒpi/ *verb & noun.* E20.
[from PHOTO- + COPY *verb*[1], *noun*[1].]
► **A** *verb trans.* Make a photocopy of. E20.
► **B** *noun.* A copy made by a photocopier. M20.
■ **photocopiable** *adjective* L20.

photodynamic /ˌfəʊtəʊdʌɪˈnamɪk/ *adjective.* L19.
[from PHOTO- + DYNAMIC.]
1 Pertaining to the energy of light. *rare.* L19.
2 Involving or causing a toxic response to light, esp. ultraviolet light. E20.
■ **photodynamically** *adverb* E20.

photoelastic /ˌfəʊtəʊɪˈlastɪk/ *adjective.* E20.
[from PHOTO- + ELASTIC.]
Employing or exhibiting the property of becoming birefringent when mechanically stressed, so that stress patterns in such a substance can be determined from the interference fringes formed by transmitted polarized light.
■ **photoelasticity** /-ˈtɪsɪti/ *noun* the photoelastic method of stress analysis E20.

photoelectric /ˌfəʊtəʊɪˈlɛktrɪk/ *adjective.* M19.
[from PHOTO- + ELECTRIC.]
†**1** Designating or pertaining to a method for obtaining a relief printing plate from a photograph which at different stages involved the action of light and electrodeposition. M19–E20.
2 Providing or employing electric light. Now *rare* or *obsolete.* M19.
3 Of, pertaining to, or employing photoelectricity; involving the emission of electrons from a surface under the action of incident light. M19.
3 photoelectric absorption the absorption of light by an atom which then emits an electron. **photoelectric cell** = PHOTOCELL.
■ **photoelectrical** *adjective* L19. **photoelectrically** *adverb* E20. ˌ**photoelecˈtricity** *noun* electricity produced by light; photoelectric properties: L19.

photoelectron /ˈfəʊtəʊɪlɛktrɒn/ *noun.* E20.
[from PHOTO- + ELECTRON *noun*[2].]
PHYSICS. An electron released from an atom by the action of a photon; *esp.* one emitted from a solid surface under the action of light.
■ **photoelecˈtronic** *adjective* of or pertaining to a photoelectron, or the interaction of light with electrons E20. **photoelecˈtronics** *noun* the branch of science and technology that deals with photoelectronic phenomena M20.

photoemission /ˈfəʊtəʊɪmɪʃ(ə)n/ *noun.* E20.
[from PHOTO- + EMISSION.]
PHYSICS. The emission of electrons from a surface under the action of incident light.
■ **photoeˈmissive** *adjective* exhibiting, employing, or pertaining to photoemission M20. **photoemit** *verb trans. & intrans.* emit (an electron) under the action of incident light M20. **photoemitter** *noun* a photoemissive body or substance M20.

photo-engraving /ˌfəʊtəʊɪnˈgreɪvɪŋ/ *noun.* L19.
[from PHOTO- + ENGRAVING.]
A process by which an image is photographically transferred to a plate for relief printing, the non-printing areas being etched; a plate or print made in this way.
■ **photo-enˈgrave** *verb trans.* engrave in the course of photo-engraving L19. **photo-enˈgraver** *noun* E20.

photofit /ˈfəʊtə(ʊ)fɪt/ *noun & adjective.* L20.
[from PHOTO- + FIT *noun*[3].]
(Designating) a method of building up a picture of a person by assembling a number of photographs of individual facial features; (designating) a picture so formed.

Oxford Times Thames Valley Police have issued a photofit picture and . . description of a man.

photog /fəˈtɒg/ *noun.* *N. Amer. colloq.* E20.
[Abbreviation.]
A photographer.

photogalvanic /ˌfəʊtəʊgalˈvanɪk/ *adjective.* M19.
[from PHOTO- + GALVANIC.]
†**1** = PHOTOELECTRIC 1. Only in M19.
2 PHYSICS. Designating or utilizing the generation of a potential difference between two electrodes by a photochemical reaction in the electrolyte containing them. M20.

photogen /ˈfəʊtədʒ(ə)n/ *noun.* Now *rare.* E19.
[from PHOTO- + -GEN.]
1 A thing that produces light. E19.
2 A kind of paraffin oil. M19.

photogenic /fəʊtə(ʊ)ˈdʒɛnɪk, -ˈdʒiːn-/ *adjective.* M19.
[from PHOTO- + -GENIC.]
1 Photographic. *obsolete* exc. *Hist.* M19.
2 MEDICINE. Produced or caused by light. M19.
3 BIOLOGY. Producing or emitting light. M19.
4 That is a good subject for photography; that shows to good advantage in a photograph or film. E20.

2 *Brain* Clinical descriptions of photogenic epilepsy are few. **3** *Nature* Each dermal photophore consists of a mass of innervated photogenic tissue. **4** *Daily Express* Her perfect oval face and high, photogenic forehead.

■ **photogenically** *adverb* (**a**) by means of light; (**b**) in a manner that lends itself to being photographed or filmed; as regards the appearance in a photograph or film: M19.

photogeology /ˌfəʊtəʊdʒɪˈɒlədʒi/ *noun.* M20.
[from PHOTO- + GEOLOGY.]
The field of study that deals with the geological interpretation of aerial photographs.
■ **photogeoˈlogic**, **photogeoˈlogical** *adjectives* M20. ˌ**photogeoˈlogically** *adverb* by photogeological means M20. **photogeologist** *noun* M20.

photogram /ˈfəʊtəgram/ *noun.* M19.
[Alt. of PHOTOGRAPH after *telegram*.]
1 A photograph. Now *rare.* M19.
2 A picture produced with photographic materials but without a camera. M20.

photogrammetry /fəʊtə(ʊ)ˈgramɪtri/ *noun.* L19.
[from PHOTO- + -GRAM + -METRY.]
The technique of using photographs to obtain measurements of what is photographed, esp. in surveying and mapping.
■ **photograˈmmetric** *adjective* E20. **photograˈmmetrical** *adjective* L19. **photograˈmmetrically** *adverb* by means of photogrammetry; in a photogrammetric manner: E20. **photogrammetrist** *noun* M20.

photograph /ˈfəʊtəgrɑːf/ *noun & verb.* M19.
[from PHOTO- + -GRAPH.]
► **A** *noun.* A picture or other image obtained by the chemical action of light or other radiation on specially sensitized material such as film or glass. M19.

Discovery X-ray photographs of culture pearls. R. THOMAS There were photographs on the piano. *Which?* Flare tends to be a problem when taking photographs against the light. *attrib.*: E. JOLLEY Memories came back . . as vividly as if she was looking at an old photograph album.

► **B** *verb.* **1** *verb trans.* Take a photograph of. M19.
2 *verb intrans.* Practise photography, take photographs. *rare.* M19.
3 *verb intrans.* Be photographed; appear (in a particular way) when in a photograph. L19.

1 M. WARNER They were photographed . . to commemorate their wedding. **3** *Listener* Wales photographs beautifully.

■ **photographable** *adjective* L19. **photograˈphee** *noun* a person who is photographed M19. **phoˈtographer** *noun* a person who takes photographs; *esp.* a person who practises photography as a profession or business: M19.

photographic /fəʊtəˈgrafɪk/ *adjective.* M19.
[formed as PHOTOGRAPHY + -IC.]
Of, pertaining to, used in, or produced by photography; engaged or skilled in photography; *fig.* reproducing with accuracy like that of a photograph.

Creative Camera Who is to blame for bad photographic books? J. G. BALLARD Dental and photographic evidence . . established that the girl was Marion Miller. **photographic memory**: that records visual perceptions with the accuracy of a photograph. **photographic paper** paper with a special coating on which a photographic image can be either recorded (as on film) or developed.

■ **photographically** *adverb* in a photographic manner; by means of or in reference to photography; from a photographic point of view: M19.

photographica /fəʊtəˈgrafɪkə/ *noun pl.* L20.
[from prec. + -A[3].]
Books, albums, or collections of photographs; items connected with photography.

photography /fəˈtɒgrəfi/ *noun.* M19.
[from PHOTO- + -GRAPHY.]
The process or art of taking photographs; the business of producing and printing photographs.
■ **photographist** *noun* (now *rare*) a photographer M19.

photogravure /ˌfəʊtəʊgrəˈvjʊə/ *noun.* L19.
[French, formed as PHOTO- + *gravure* engraving, from *graver* engrave: see -URE.]
A process by which an image is photographically transferred to a plate for intaglio printing, on which the printing areas are etched; a plate or print made in this way.

Stamps The stamps, printed in photogravure . . in sheets of 100.

photoisomer /fəʊtəʊˈʌɪsəmə/ *noun.* M20.
[from PHOTO- + ISOMER.]
CHEMISTRY. An isomer formed by irradiation of another, often more stable, form of a compound.
■ **photoisoˈmeric** *adjective* M20. **photoiˈsomerism** *noun* the fact or property of being or having a photoisomer M20. ˌ**photoisomeriˈzation** *noun* the formation of a photoisomer E20. **photoiˈsomerize** *verb intrans. & trans.* (cause to) undergo photoisomerization M20.

photojournalism /fəʊtəʊˈdʒəːn(ə)lɪz(ə)m/ *noun.* M20.
[from PHOTO- + JOURNALISM.]
The art or practice of presenting news in print through the use of photographs, with or without an accompanying text.
■ **photojournalist** *noun* M20.

photolitho /fəʊtəʊˈlʌɪθəʊ/ *adjective & noun.* M19.
[Abbreviation.]
► **A** *adjective.* Photolithographic. M19.
► **B** *noun.* Pl. **-os.** Photolithography; a photolithograph. L19.

Special collocations & comb.: **photolitho offset** photolithography by an offset process.

photolithography /ˌfəʊtəʊlɪˈθɒɡrəfi/ *noun*. M19.
[from PHOTO- + LITHOGRAPHY.]
1 Lithography in which the image is photographically transferred to the printing surface. M19.
2 *ELECTRONICS*. An analogous process for making integrated circuits and printed circuit boards, in which a semiconductor surface is selectively etched after coating it with a photoresist and using a reduced photograph as a mask during exposure to ultraviolet light. L20.
■ **photoˈlithograph** *noun & verb* (*a*) *noun* a print or picture produced by photolithography; (*b*) *verb trans.* print, produce, or portray by photolithography: M19. **photolithographer** *noun* M19. **ˌphotolithoˈgraphic** *adjective* pertaining to or produced by photolithography M19. **ˌphotolithoˈgraphically** *adverb* by means of photolithography M20.

photolyse /ˈfəʊtəlʌɪz/ *verb*. Also ***-lyze**. M20.
[from next after HYDROLYSE.]
1 *verb trans.* Subject to or decompose by photolysis. M20.
2 *verb intrans.* Undergo photolysis. L20.

photolysis /fə(ʊ)ˈtɒlɪsɪs/ *noun*. Pl. **-lyses** /-lɪsiːz/. E20.
[from PHOTO- + -LYSIS.]
CHEMISTRY. Decomposition or dissociation of molecules by the action of light; an instance of this.
flash photolysis: see FLASH *noun*[2].
■ **photoˈlytic** *adjective* produced by or involving photolysis M20. **photoˈlytically** *adverb* by means of or as regards photolysis M20.

photolyze *verb* see PHOTOLYSE.

photomacrography /ˌfəʊtəʊmaˈkrɒɡrəfi/ *noun*. M20.
[from PHOTO- + MACRO- + PHOTO)GRAPHY.]
= MACROPHOTOGRAPHY.
■ **photoˈmacrograph** *noun* = MACROPHOTOGRAPH M20. **ˌphotomacroˈgraphic** *adjective* M20.

Photomaton /fəʊˈtɒmətən/ *noun*. E20.
[from PHOTO- + AUTO)MATON.]
(Proprietary name for) a machine that takes photographs automatically. Also, a photograph taken by such a machine.
■ Also **Photomat** /ˈfəʊtəʊmat/ *noun* (proprietary name in US) M20.

photomechanical /ˌfəʊtəʊmɪˈkanɪk(ə)l/ *adjective*. L19.
[from PHOTO- + MECHANICAL.]
Designating any process in which photography is involved in the making of a printing plate.
■ **photomechanically** *adverb* E20.

photometer /fə(ʊ)ˈtɒmɪtə/ *noun & verb*. L18.
[from PHOTO- + -METER.]
▶ **A** *noun*. An instrument for measuring the intensity of light or for comparing the intensities of light from different sources. L18.
▶ **B** *verb trans.* Measure the brightness of (a light source or an illuminated surface) by means of a photometer. E20.
■ **photoˈmetric**, **photoˈmetrical** *adjectives* M19. **photoˈmetrically** *adverb* by means of a photometer M19. **photoˈmetrician** /-ˈtrɪʃ(ə)n/ *noun* L19. **photometrist** *noun* M19. **photometry** *noun* measurement of light; the use of a photometer: E19.

photomicrograph /fəʊtəʊˈmʌɪkrəɡrɑːf/ *noun*. M19.
[from PHOTO- + MICRO- + PHOTO)GRAPH.]
A photograph of an image produced by a microscope.
■ **photomiˈcrographer** *noun* L19. **ˌphotomicroˈgraphic** *adjective* pertaining to photomicrography; used for taking photomicrographs: M19. **ˌphotomiˈcrography** *noun* the technique of producing photomicrographs or of studying objects by means of them M19.

photomorphogenesis /ˌfəʊtəʊmɔːfəˈdʒɛnɪsɪs/ *noun*. M20.
[from PHOTO- + MORPHOGENESIS.]
BOTANY. Plant morphogenesis affected by light other than through photosynthesis.
■ **ˌphotomorphogeˈnetic**, **ˌphotomorphoˈgenic** *adjectives* of or pertaining to the effects of light on plants M20. **ˌphotomorphogeˈnetically**, **ˌphotomorphoˈgenically** *adverbs* M20.

photomultiplier /fəʊtəʊˈmʌltɪplʌɪə/ *noun*. M20.
[from PHOTO- + MULTIPLIER.]
A phototube in which the current from the photocathode is multiplied by a succession of secondary electrodes, so that very faint light can be detected. Also *photomultiplier tube*.

photon /ˈfəʊtɒn/ *noun*. E20.
[from PHOTO- + -ON.]
PHYSICS. †**1** = TROLAND. E–M20.
2 A quantum of light or other electromagnetic radiation, the energy of which is proportional to the frequency of the radiation. E20.
■ **phoˈtonic** *adjective* M20. **phoˈtonics** *noun* the branch of technology that deals with the applications of the particle properties of light M20.

photonegative /fəʊtəʊˈnɛɡətɪv/ *adjective*. E20.
[from PHOTO- + NEGATIVE *adjective*.]
1 *ZOOLOGY*. Of an animal: tending to move away from light. E20.
2 *PHYSICS*. Pertaining to or exhibiting a decrease in electrical conductivity under illumination. E20.
■ **ˌphotonegaˈtivity** *noun* M20.

photo-offset /fəʊtəʊˈɒfsɛt/ *noun*. E20.
[from PHOTO- + OFFSET *noun*.]
= PHOTOLITHO *offset*.

photoperiod /ˈfəʊtəʊpɪərɪəd/ *noun*. E20.
[from PHOTO- + PERIOD *noun*.]
BIOLOGY. The period of daily illumination which an organism receives; the length of this period which is most effective in stimulating reproduction or some other function.
■ **photoperiˈodic** *adjective* of, pertaining to, or influenced by photoperiods E20. **photoperiˈodically** *adverb* by means of or with regard to photoperiods M20. **photoperioˈdicity** *noun* photoperiodism M20. **photoˈperiodism** *noun* the phenomenon whereby many plants and animals are stimulated or inhibited in reproduction and other functions by the lengths of the daily periods of light and darkness to which they are subjected E20.

photophobia /fəʊtə(ʊ)ˈfəʊbɪə/ *noun*. L18.
[from PHOTO- + -PHOBIA.]
MEDICINE. Abnormal sensitivity of the eyes to light; abnormal fear of light, esp. as the result of such sensitivity.
■ **photophobic** *adjective* pertaining to or affected with photophobia M19.

photophore /ˈfəʊtəfɔː/ *noun*. L19.
[from Greek *phōtophoros* light-bearing, formed as PHOTO-: see -PHORE.]
A luminiferous organ in certain animals.

photopic /fəʊˈtɒpɪk, -ˈtəʊ-/ *adjective*. E20.
[from PHOTO- + -OPIA + -IC.]
PHYSIOLOGY. Of, pertaining to, or designating vision in illumination similar to daylight, believed to involve chiefly the cones of the retina. Cf. SCOTOPIC.

photoplay /ˈfəʊtəʊpleɪ/ *noun*. Chiefly *N. Amer.* E20.
[from PHOTO- + PLAY *noun*.]
A cinematic representation of a play or drama; a cinema film.

photopositive /fəʊtəʊˈpɒzɪtɪv/ *adjective*. E20.
[from PHOTO- + POSITIVE.]
1 *ZOOLOGY*. Of an animal: tending to move towards light. E20.
2 *PHYSICS*. Pertaining to or exhibiting an increase in electrical conductivity under illumination. E20.
■ **photopositively** *adverb* M20. **ˌphotopoṡiˈtivity** *noun* M20.

photoreactivation /ˌfəʊtəʊrɪaktɪˈveɪʃ(ə)n/ *noun*. M20.
[from PHOTO- + REACTIVATION.]
BIOLOGY. The process whereby illumination of living matter with visible light can counteract the destructive effects on genetic material of previous ultraviolet irradiation.
■ **ˌphotoreactivaˈbility** *noun* the potential for photoreactivation M20. **ˌphotoreˈactivable** *adjective* (of a biological system) capable of displaying photoreactivation; (of damage caused by ultraviolet irradiation) able to be photoreactivated: L20. **ˌphotoreˈactivate** *verb trans.* repair by photoreactivation M20.

photorealism /fəʊtəʊˈrɪəlɪz(ə)m/ *noun*. M20.
[from PHOTO- + REALISM.]
Detailed and not idealized representation in art, characteristically of the banal, vulgar, or sordid aspects of life.
■ **photorealist** *adjective & noun* (*a*) *adjective* pertaining to or characteristic of photorealism; (*b*) *noun* a person who practises photorealism: L20. **photoreaˈlistic** *adjective* = PHOTOREALIST *adjective* L20.

photoreceptor /ˈfəʊtəʊrɪˌsɛptə/ *noun*. E20.
[from PHOTO- + RECEPTOR.]
BIOLOGY. A structure of a living organism which responds to incident light, *esp.* a cell in which light is converted to a nervous or other signal.
■ **photoreception** *noun* the process of absorption, and esp. detection, of light by an animal or plant E20. **photoreˈceptive** *adjective* capable of responding to light; of or pertaining to photoreception: E20.

photoreduction /ˌfəʊtəʊrɪˈdʌkʃ(ə)n/ *noun*. L19.
[from PHOTO- + REDUCTION.]
1 Chemical reduction effected by light; *BOTANY* such a reduction of carbon dioxide with formation of water (rather than oxygen, as in ordinary photosynthesis). L19.
2 Reduction in size effected photographically. M20.
■ **photoreduce** *verb trans.* reduce photochemically or photographically M20.

photoresist /ˌfəʊtəʊrɪˈzɪst/ *noun*. M20.
[from PHOTO- + RESIST *noun*.]
A photosensitive resist which when exposed to light (usu. ultraviolet) loses its resistance or susceptibility to attack by an etchant or solvent.

photorespiration /ˌfəʊtəʊrɛspɪˈreɪʃ(ə)n/ *noun*. M20.
[from PHOTO- + RESPIRATION.]
BOTANY. A respiratory process in many higher plants by which they take up oxygen in the light and give out some carbon dioxide, contrary to the general pattern of photosynthesis.
■ **ˌphotoreˈspiratory** *adjective* of, pertaining to, or evolved by photorespiration M20. **ˌphotoreˈspire** *verb intrans.* carry out photorespiration M20.

photosensitise *verb* var. of PHOTOSENSITIZE.

photosensitive /fəʊtəʊˈsɛnsɪtɪv/ *adjective*. L19.
[from PHOTO- + SENSITIVE.]
Reacting to light in some way (biologically, chemically, electrically, etc.).

> 🕮 D. LODGE The Southerner's spectacles are the photosensitive sort.

■ **ˌphotosensiˈtivity** *noun* E20.

photosensitize /fəʊtəʊˈsɛnsɪtʌɪz/ *verb trans.* Also **-ise**. E20.
[from PHOTO- + SENSITIZE.]
1 *CHEMISTRY*. Of a substance: initiate (a chemical change) by absorbing light energy and transferring it to a reactant. E20.
2 Make photosensitive. M20.
■ **ˌphotosensitiˈzation** *noun* E20. **photosensitizer** *noun* (*a*) a substance capable of photosensitizing a reaction; (*b*) a photodynamic substance: E20.

photoset /ˈfəʊtə(ʊ)sɛt/ *verb trans.* Infl. **-tt-**. Pa. t. & pple **-set**. M20.
[from PHOTO- + SET *verb*[1].]
Compose (matter) by projecting film from which a printing plate is made. Freq. as ***photosetting*** *verbal noun*.
■ **photosetter** *noun* a machine for photosetting L20.

photo-set /ˈfəʊtəʊsɛt/ *noun*. L20.
[from PHOTO- + SET *noun*[2].]
A collection of photographs of a person or on a particular theme.

photosphere /ˈfəʊtəsfɪə/ *noun*. M17.
[from PHOTO- + -SPHERE.]
1 A sphere or orb of light, radiance, or glory. Now only as *fig.* use of sense 2. M17.
2 *ASTRONOMY*. The luminous surface layer of the sun or another star, below the chromosphere. M19.
■ **photospheric** /fəʊtə(ʊ)ˈsfɛrɪk/ *adjective* M19.

Photostat /ˈfəʊtə(ʊ)stat/ *noun & verb*. E20.
[from PHOTO- + -STAT. Cf. STAT *noun*[1].]
▶ **A** *noun*. (Proprietary name for) a photographic copying machine; (**p-**) a photocopy. E20.
▶ **B** *verb trans.* (**p-**.) Infl. **-tt-**. Photocopy. E20.
■ **photoˈstatic** *adjective* designating a photocopy or a photocopier E20.

photosynthate /fəʊtəʊˈsɪnθeɪt/ *noun*. E20.
[from next + -ATE[1].]
A substance formed by photosynthesis.

photosynthesis /fəʊtəʊˈsɪnθɪsɪs/ *noun*. Pl. **-theses** /-θɪsiːz/. L19.
[from PHOTO- + SYNTHESIS.]
The process in plants by which carbon dioxide is converted into organic compounds using the energy of light absorbed by chlorophyll, which in all plants except some bacteria involves the production of oxygen from water; any photochemical synthesis of a chemical compound.
■ **photosynthesize** *verb* (*a*) *verb trans.* create by photosynthesis; (*b*) *verb intrans.* carry out photosynthesis: E20. **photosynthesizer** *noun* an organism which carries out photosynthesis M20. **ˌphotosynˈthetic** *adjective* of, pertaining to, produced by, or involved in photosynthesis E20. **ˌphotosynˈthetically** *adverb* by photosynthesis; as regards photosynthesis: E20.

phototaxis /fəʊtəʊˈtaksɪs/ *noun*. Pl. **-taxes** /-ˈtaksiːz/. L19.
[from PHOTO- + -TAXIS.]
BIOLOGY. The bodily movement or orientation of a motile organism in response to light; an instance of this. Also = PHOTOTROPISM 1.
■ **phototactic** *adjective* exhibiting or characterized by phototaxis L19. **phototactically** *adverb* E20.

phototropic /fəʊtə(ʊ)ˈtrəʊpɪk, -ˈtrɒp-/ *adjective*. L19.
[from PHOTO- + -TROPIC.]
BIOLOGY. **1** Exhibiting or characterized by phototropism. L19.
2 = PHOTOCHROMIC *adjective*. E20.
■ **phototropically** *adverb* L19.

phototropism /fəʊtə(ʊ)ˈtrəʊpɪz(ə)m, fəʊˈtɒtrəpɪz(ə)m/ *noun*. L19.
[from PHOTO- + -TROPISM.]
1 *BIOLOGY*. The directional bending or growth of a plant or a sessile animal in response to light; an instance of this. Also = PHOTOTAXIS. L19.
2 = PHOTOCHROMISM. E20.
■ Also **phototropy** /fəʊˈtɒtrəpi/ *noun* E20.

phototypeset /fəʊtəʊˈtʌɪpsɛt/ *verb trans.* M20.
[from PHOTO- + *typeset* s.v. TYPE *noun*.]
= ***filmset*** s.v. FILM *noun*. Only as ***phototypeset*** *ppl adjective*, ***phototypesetting*** *verbal noun*.
■ **phototypesetter** *noun* a machine for filmsetting M20.

photovisual /fəʊtəʊˈvɪzjʊəl, -ʒʊəl/ *adjective*. E20.
[from PHOTO- + VISUAL.]
1 Of a lens or optical instrument: bringing to the same focus both visible light and rays that can be detected only photographically. E20.
2 ASTRONOMY. Designating a stellar magnitude determined in terms of the spectral response of the eye by photographic or photoelectric means. E20.

phragma /ˈfragmə/ *noun*. Pl. **-mata** /-mətə/. E19.
[Greek = fence, hedge.]
1 A transverse partition between segments of the thorax or between the metathorax and the abdomen in some insects. E19.
2 BOTANY. A false dissepiment in a fruit. M19.

phragmites /fragˈmʌɪtiːz/ *noun*. Pl. same. E20.
[mod. Latin (see below), from Greek *phragmitēs* growing in hedges, formed as prec.]
Any reed of the genus *Phragmites*; *esp*. the common reed, *P. australis*.

phragmoplast /ˈfragmə(ʊ)plast, -plɑːst/ *noun*. E20.
[from (the same root as) PHRAGMA + -O- + -PLAST.]
BIOLOGY. A set of microtubules which forms during mitosis in some plant cells as a barrel-shaped structure joining the two sets of chromosomes after their separation to the poles.
■ **phragmoˈplastic** *adjective* M20.

phragmosome /ˈfragməsəʊm/ *noun*. M20.
[formed as prec. + -SOME[3].]
BIOLOGY. A layer of darker cytoplasm which forms during mitosis in some plant cells at the site of the future cell plate; any of the large number of small particles that form this layer.

phrasal /ˈfreɪz(ə)l/ *adjective*. L19.
[from PHRASE *noun* + -AL[1].]
GRAMMAR. Of the nature of or consisting of a phrase.
phrasal verb an idiomatic verbal phrase consisting of a verb and adverb (e.g. ***break down***) or a verb and preposition (e.g. ***see to***).
■ **phrasally** *adverb* in or by phrases; as a phrase: M20.

phrase /freɪz/ *noun*. Orig. also †**phrasis**. M16.
[Latin *phrasis* from Greek = speech, manner of speaking, from *phrazein* indicate, declare, tell.]
1 Manner or style of expression, *esp*. that characteristic of a language, author, work, etc.; phraseology, language. M16.
2 A small group of words expressing a single concept or entering with some degree of unity into the structure of a sentence, without itself being a sentence; GRAMMAR (*a*) such a group of words that does not contain a predicate or finite verb; (*b*) any syntactic unit larger than a word and smaller than a sentence. Also, a characteristic or idiomatic expression; a pithy or telling expression. M16. ▸†**b** A single word. L16–L17.
3 Exclamatory or exaggerated talk, overeffusive language; an outburst of words. *Scot. & north*. M17.
4 MUSIC. A group of notes forming a more or less distinct unit in a passage or piece. L18.

📖 **1** A. W. WARD The supreme felicity of phrase in which he has no equal. B. FOSTER A very typically American turn of phrase. **2** A. HELPS 'If I were you' is a phrase often on our lips. M. FRAYN 'Exciting new voice'—that was a pretty striking phrase. G. VIDAL A magazine . . called *avant garde* before that phrase became old-fashioned. M. M. R. KHAN He had 'wrapped it up' (his phrase) in neat items of fantasies. **4** A. HOPKINS The woodwind . . plays a little three-note phrase.

Comb.: **phrase book** a book for foreign visitors to a country listing useful expressions in the visitors' language with their equivalent in the language of that country; **phrase-maker** a maker of telling or fine-sounding phrases; **phrase-marker** LINGUISTICS a diagrammatic or formulaic representation of the phrase-structure of a sentence; **phrase name** a name, esp. a surname, derived from a phrase; **phrase-structure** LINGUISTICS the structure of a sentence in terms of constituent phrases.
■ **phraseless** *adjective* (*rare*, Shakes.) which there is no phrase to describe L16. **phrasy** *adjective* (*colloq*.) having many phrases; characterized by great use of phrases: M19.

phrase /freɪz/ *verb*. M16.
[from the noun.]
1 *verb trans*. Put into words, express in words, esp. in a distinctive or telling phraseology; divide (a sentence) into parts when speaking so as to convey better the meaning of the whole. M16.
2 *verb intrans*. Use a phrase or phrases. M16.
3 *verb trans*. Describe (a person or thing) by a designation or descriptive phrase. L16.
4 *verb trans. & intrans*. Talk exaggeratedly (about); make much of, flatter. *Scot*. M17.
5 *verb trans. & intrans*. Divide (music) into phrases when playing; play so as to give due expression to phrasing. L18.

📖 **1** E. M. FORSTER She was got up smart, as she phrased it. A. N. WILSON He phrased his accusations in hysterical anti-Jewish language.

■ **phraser** *noun* a person who uses phrases, or expresses himself or herself in a characteristic or striking manner M17.

phraseogram /ˈfreɪzɪəgram/ *noun*. M19.
[from PHRASE *noun* + -O- + -GRAM.]
A written symbol representing a phrase, esp. in shorthand.

phraseograph /ˈfreɪzɪəgrɑːf/ *noun*. M19.
[formed as prec. + -GRAPH.]
A phrase for which there is a phraseogram.
■ **phraseoˈgraphic** *adjective* of the nature of a phraseogram, written with phraseograms L19. **phraseˈography** *noun* the use of phraseograms M19.

phraseology /freɪzɪˈɒlədʒi/ *noun*. M17.
[mod. Latin *phraseologia*, from Greek *phraseōn* genit. pl. of *phrasis* PHRASE *noun*: see -OLOGY.]
(A) choice or arrangement of words and phrases; style of expression; the particular form of this which characterizes a language, author, work, etc.

📖 W. CROOKES Röntgen suggests a convenient phraseology; he calls a low vacuum tube . . a 'soft' tube. *Oxford Magazine* Some benefactor willing to give '£100,000 plus' (to use modern phraseology).

■ ˌ**phraseoˈlogical** *adjective* (*a*) using characteristic expressions; expressed in a special phrase; (*b*) of or pertaining to phraseology: M17. ˌ**phraseoˈlogically** *adverb* in a phraseological manner; with the use of a phrase: M19. **phraseologist** *noun* a user of phrases; a person who uses striking phrases, esp. in an indiscriminate manner: E18.

phrasing /ˈfreɪzɪŋ/ *noun*. E17.
[from PHRASE *verb* + -ING[1].]
1 The action of PHRASE *verb*; phraseology. E17.
2 The rendering of musical phrases; the manner in which a passage is phrased. L19.

†**phrasis** *noun* see PHRASE *noun*.

phratry /ˈfreɪtri/ *noun*. M19.
[Greek *phratria*, from *phratēr* clansman: cf. BROTHER *noun*.]
1 GREEK HISTORY. A kinship group with corporate identity composed of families with a notional common ancestor; a subdivision of a phyle. M19.
2 ANTHROPOLOGY. A descent group or kinship group in some societies. L19.
■ **phrator** *noun* [Greek *phratōr*] a member of a phratry M19. **phratric** *adjective* M19.

phreak /friːk/ *noun & verb*. L20.
[Alt. of FREAK *noun*, *verb* after *phone*.]
▸ **A** *noun*. More fully ***phone phreak***. A person who makes fraudulent use of a telephone system by electronic means. L20.
▸ **B** *verb trans. & intrans*. Use an electronic device to obtain (a telephone call) without payment. L20.
■ **phreaker** *noun* L20.

phreatic /frɪˈatɪk/ *adjective*. L19.
[from Greek *phreat-*, *phrear* well, cistern + -IC.]
1 PHYSICAL GEOGRAPHY. Pertaining to or designating water below the water-table, esp. that which is capable of movement. Cf. VADOSE. L19.
2 GEOLOGY. Designating or pertaining to a volcanic eruption in which steam or mud is expelled as a result of the sudden heating of underground water when it comes into contact with hot magma or rock. E20.

📖 **1** *Caves & Caving* Bisa Passage . . enters 150ft . . of phreatic passage which could possibly re-enter the main streamway.

■ **phreatomagˈmatic** *adjective* designating or pertaining to a volcanic eruption in which both steam and magmatic gases are expelled M20.

phreatophyte /frɪˈatəfʌɪt/ *noun*. E20.
[formed as prec. + -O- + -PHYTE.]
A plant with a deep root system that draws its water supply from near the water-table.

phren- *combining form* see PHRENO-.

†**phrenesis** *noun*. M16–E19.
[Latin from late Greek *phrenēsis*, from Greek *phren-*, *phrēn*: see PHRENIC.]
= PHRENITIS.

phrenetic *adjective & noun* see FRENETIC.

phrenic /ˈfrɛnɪk/ *adjective & noun*. E18.
[French *phrénique*, from Greek *phren-*, *phrēn* diaphragm, mind (once thought to be located in the diaphragm): see -IC.]
▸ **A** *adjective*. **1** ANATOMY. Diaphragmatic. E18.
†**2** Mental. Only in M19.
1 phrenic nerve the nerve supplying the muscles of the diaphragm.
▸ **B** *noun*. ANATOMY. The phrenic nerve. L18.
■ **phrenicectomy** /-ˈsɛktəmi/ *noun* (an instance of) surgical removal or destruction of a section of the phrenic nerve, formerly carried out as an alternative to phrenicotomy E20. **phreniˈcotomy** *noun* (an instance of) surgical cutting of the phrenic nerve so as to paralyse the diaphragm on one side E20.

phrenitis /frɪˈnʌɪtɪs/ *noun*. Now *rare*. E17.
[Greek *phrenitis* delirium, from *phren-*: see PHRENIC, -ITIS.]
MEDICINE. Encephalitis; brain fever, delirium.
■ **phrenitic** /-ˈnɪt-/ *adjective* affected with or suffering from phrenitis; subject to fits of delirium: L18.

phreno- /ˈfrɛnəʊ/ *combining form* of Greek *phren-*, *phrēn* diaphragm, mind: see PHRENIC, -O-. Before a vowel **phren-**.
■ **phreno-ˈmagnetism** *noun* (*Hist*.) the supposed influence of magnetism on phrenological organs M19.

phrenology /frɪˈnɒlədʒi/ *noun*. E19.
[from prec. + -OLOGY.]
The branch of inquiry that deals with the shape and size of the cranium as supposed indicators of character and mental faculties. Formerly also, the science of mental faculties in general, or the theory that each mental faculty is mediated by an organ in a particular part of the brain.
■ **phrenoˈlogical** *adjective* E19. **phrenoˈlogically** *adverb* in terms of phrenology E19. **phrenologist** *noun* E19. **phrenologize** *verb trans*. examine or analyse phrenologically M19.

†**phrentic** *adjective, noun, & adverb* var. of FRANTIC.

†**phrenzical** *adjective* var. of FRENZICAL.

phrenzy *noun & adjective* see FRENZY *noun & adjective*.

phrontistery /ˈfrɒntɪst(ə)ri/ *noun*. Also in Greek & Latin forms **phrontisterion** /frɒntɪˈstɛrɪɒn/, **-ium** /-ɪəm/, pl. **-ia** /-ɪə/. E17.
[Greek *phrontistērion*, from *phrontistēs* deep thinker, from *phrontizein* be thoughtful, from *phrontis* thought.]
A place for thinking or studying; an educational institution.

Phrygian /ˈfrɪdʒɪən/ *noun & adjective*. L15.
[Latin *Phrygianus*, from *Phrygia*: see below, -IAN.]
▸ **A** *noun*. **1** A native or inhabitant of Phrygia, an ancient country of Asia Minor. L15.
2 The Indo-European language of the ancient Phrygians. L18.
▸ **B** *adjective*. **1** Of or pertaining to Phrygia or Phrygians. L16.
2 Designating a conical cap or bonnet with the top turned over in front, worn by the ancient Phrygians, and in modern times identified with the cap of liberty. L18.
1 Phrygian mode MUSIC (*a*) an ancient Greek mode, reputedly warlike in character; (*b*) a church mode with E as the final and C as the dominant.

phthalazine /ˈθaləziːn/ *noun*. L19.
[from PHTHALIC + AZINE.]
CHEMISTRY. A crystalline heterocyclic base, $C_8H_6N_2$; any derivative of this.

phthalic /ˈθalɪk/ *adjective*. M19.
[from NA)PHTHALIC.]
CHEMISTRY. Having a chemical structure that is formally related to that of naphthalene; of or pertaining to phthalene.
phthalic acid each of three isomeric crystalline dicarboxylic acids, $C_6H_4(COOH)_2$, derived from benzene. **phthalic anhydride** a bicyclic crystalline solid, $C_6H_4(CO)_2O$, used in the manufacture of plastics, resins, dyes, etc.
■ **phthalate** *noun* a salt or ester of phthalic acid M19.

phthalocyanine /θaləʊˈsʌɪəniːn/ *noun*. M20.
[from prec. + -O- + CYANINE.]
CHEMISTRY. **1** A greenish-blue crystalline porphyrin, $C_{32}H_{18}N_8$; any of its substituted derivatives. M20.
2 Any of the metal chelate complexes of such porphyrins, which form a large class of pigments and dyes ranging in colour from green to blue. M20.
2 phthalocyanine blue copper phthalocyanine, a blue pigment. **phthalocyanine green** a chlorinated or brominated derivative of copper phthalocyanine, a green pigment.

phthiocol /ˈθʌɪəkɒl/ *noun*. M20.
[from PHTHI(SIS (because orig. isolated from tuberculosis bacilli) + -O- + *-col* (perh. from ALCOHOL).]
BIOCHEMISTRY. A yellow pigment, $C_{11}H_8O_3$, which has the action of vitamin K.

phthiriasis /(f)θɪˈrʌɪəsɪs/ *noun*. Pl. **-ases** /-əsiːz/. L16.
[Latin from Greek *phtheiriasis*, from *phtheirian* be infested with lice, from *phtheir* louse: see -IASIS.]
MEDICINE. Infestation of the body or skin with lice, esp. crab-lice.

phthises *noun* pl. of PHTHISIS.

phthisic /ˈ(f)θʌɪzɪk, ˈtʌɪ-/ *noun & adjective*. Now *rare*. Also (earlier) †**(p)ti-**. ME.
[Old French *tisike*, *-ique*, later *ptisique*, *thisique* (repl. by mod. French *phthisie*) from Proto-Romance use as noun of fem. of Latin *phthisicus* from Greek *phthisikos* consumptive, from *phthisis*: see PHTHISIS, -IC.]
▸ **A** *noun*. **1** Pulmonary tuberculosis. ME.
†**2** Any of various lung or throat affections; a severe cough; asthma. LME–M18.
▸ **B** *adjective*. = PHTHISICAL. LME.

■ **phthisical** *adjective* of the nature of or pertaining to phthisis; (of a person) consumptive: **E17. phthisicky** /ˈ(f)θɪ-, ˈtɪ-/ *adjective* consumptive; asthmatic; wheezy: **L17.**

phthisio- /ˈ(f)θɪzɪəʊ, ˈtɪ-/ *combining form* of **PHTHISIS**: see **-O-**. Now *rare*.

■ **phthisioˈphobia** *noun* irrational or exaggerated fear of tuberculosis **E20.** †**phthisiotherapist** *noun* a specialist in the treatment of tuberculosis **E–M20.** †**phthisiotherapy** *noun* the medical treatment of tuberculosis **E–M20.**

phthisiology /(f)θɪzɪˈɒlədʒi, tɪ-/ *noun.* Now *rare.* **M19.**
[from **PHTHISIO-** + **-OLOGY**.]
The branch of medicine that deals with tuberculosis.
■ **phthisioˈlogical** *adjective* **E20. phthisiologist** *noun* **M20.**

phthisis /ˈ(f)θʌɪsɪs, ˈtʌɪ-/ *noun.* Now *rare.* Pl. **phthises** /-siːz/. **M16.**
[Latin from Greek, from *phthinein* waste away.]
A progressive wasting disease; *spec.* pulmonary tuberculosis.

phugoid /ˈfjuːɡɔɪd/ *adjective & noun.* **E20.**
[from Greek *phugē* fleeing, flight (misinterpreted as = flying) + **-OID**.]
▶ **A** *adjective.* Of or pertaining to the longitudinal stability of an aircraft flying a nominally horizontal course in a vertical plane; *spec.* designating a slow fore-and-aft oscillation in which the flight path assumes the form of a series of shallow waves and the aircraft undergoes increases and decreases of speed. **E20.**
▶ **B** *noun.* A phugoid oscillation. **E20.**

phulkari /fuːlˈkɑːri/ *noun.* **L19.**
[Hindi *phūlkārī*, from *phūl* flower + *-kār* agent-suffix.]
In NW India: a kind of flower-pattern embroidery; a cloth or shawl so embroidered.

phut /fʌt/ *adverb, interjection, noun, & verb.* **L19.**
[Imit., or from Hindi, Sanskrit *phat* a crack, the sound of a slap.]
▶ **A** *adverb.* **go phut**, come to a sudden end; break down, cease to function. *colloq.* **L19.**
▶ **B** *interjection & noun.* (An exclamation) repr. a dull abrupt sound like that of some impacts. **L19.**
▶ **C** *verb intrans.* Infl. **-tt-**. Land with a phut; come to a sudden end. **E20.**

phut-phut /ˈfʌtfʌt/ *noun & verb.* Verb infl. **-tt-**. **M20.**
[Redupl. of prec.]
= **PUT-PUT** *noun & verb.*

phwat /hwɒt/ *adjective, pronoun, & adverb. Anglo-Irish non-standard.* **L19.**
[Repr. an Anglo-Irish pronunc.]
= **WHAT**.

phwoah /ˈfwɔːə/ *interjection.* Also **-oar**, **-oor**. **L20.**
[Imit.]
Expr. enthusiastic (and esp. sexual) desire.

phyco- /ˈfʌɪkəʊ/ *combining form* of Greek *phukos* seaweed: see **-O-**.

■ **phycobilin** /-ˈbʌɪlɪn/ *noun* [***bile pigment*** s.v. **BILE** *noun*[1]] any of a group of compounds present in some algae as prosthetic groups of phycocyanins and phycoerythrins; (also ***phycobilin pigment***) a phycocyanin, a phycoerythrin: **M20. phycobiliprotein** /-bʌɪlɪˈprəʊ-/ *noun* a protein in which a phycobilin is the prosthetic group; a phycocyanin, a phycoerythrin: **M20. phycobilisome** /-ˈbʌɪ-/ *noun* [**-SOME**[3]] in certain algae, a photosynthetic granule containing phycobiliprotein **M20. phycoˈbiont** *noun* [**-BIONT**] the algal component of a lichen (cf. **MYCOBIONT**) **M20. phycoˈcyanin** *noun* any of various blue photosynthetic pigments in blue-green algae **L19. phycoˈerythrin** *noun* any of various red photosynthetic pigments in red algae and some blue-green algae **L19.**

phycology /fʌɪˈkɒlədʒi/ *noun.* **M19.**
[from prec. + **-LOGY**.]
The branch of botany that deals with seaweeds and other algae.
■ **phycoˈlogical** *adjective* of, pertaining to, or dealing with phycology **L19. phycologist** *noun* **L19.**

phycomycete /fʌɪkəʊˈmʌɪsiːt/ *noun.* Pl. **-mycetes** /-ˈmʌɪsiːts, -mʌɪˈsiːtiːz/. **M20.**
[Anglicized sing. of mod. Latin *Phycomycetes*, formed as **PHYCO-** + Greek *mukētes* pl. of *mukēs* fungus, from their supposed resemblance to algae.]
Any of the various, freq. parasitic and sometimes aquatic, lower fungi, usually having mycelia with no septa, and making up the former class Phycomycetes (now divided into several classes).

phycomycosis /ˌfʌɪkəʊmʌɪˈkəʊsɪs/ *noun.* Pl. **-coses** /-ˈkəʊsiːz/. **M20.**
[from prec. + **-OSIS**.]
Infection with, or a disease caused by, phycomycetes, esp. of the genera *Mucor*, *Rhizopus*, and *Absidia*.

phylactery /fɪˈlakt(ə)ri/ *noun.* **LME.**
[(Old French *filatiere* from) late Latin *fylacterium*, *phyl-* safeguard, amulet from Greek *phulaktērion*, from *phulaktēr* guard, from *phulassein* to guard.]
1 Either of two small leather boxes containing biblical texts written in Hebrew, worn by Jewish men during morning prayer on all days except the Sabbath as a reminder of the obligation to keep the law. **LME.** ▸**b** The fringe which the Israelites were commanded to wear as a reminder (*Numbers* 15:38, 39); any fringe or border. **L16.** ▸**c** *fig.* A reminder; a religious observance, *esp.* an ostentatious or hypocritical one; a burdensome traditional observance. **M17.**
2 A container for a holy relic. **LME.**
3 An amulet; a charm, a safeguard. **E19.**
1 make broad the phylactery [*Matthew* 23:5] boast of one's righteousness.

phylae, **phylai** *noun pl.* see **PHYLE**.

phylarch /ˈfʌɪlɑːk/ *noun.* **M16.**
[Latin *phylarchus* from Greek *phularkhos*, formed as **PHYLE**: see **-ARCH**.]
1 (The title of) any of certain magistrates in the ideal commonwealths of Plato, More, and others. **M16.**
2 The ruler or leader of a phyle in ancient Greece; any tribal chief. **M17.**
■ **phyˈlarchic** *adjective* **E19. phyˈlarchical** *adjective* **M19. phylarchy** *noun* the position of a phylarch; tribal government: **E18.**

phyle /ˈfʌɪli/ *noun.* Pl. **-lai** /-lʌɪ/, **-lae** /-liː/. **M19.**
[Greek *phulē*.]
GREEK HISTORY. Any of the large clans or tribes of ancient Greece, orig. based on supposed kinship and later forming political, administrative, and military units; the cavalry brigade furnished by an Attic tribe.
■ **phylic** *adjective* **L19.**

phyletic /fʌɪˈlɛtɪk/ *adjective.* **L19.**
[Greek *phuletikos*, from *phuletēs* tribesman, formed as prec.: see **-ETIC**.]
BIOLOGY. Of or pertaining to the evolutionary development of a species or other taxonomic grouping.
■ **phyletically** *adverb* as regards the phylum **L19.**

phyletism /ˈfʌɪlɪtɪz(ə)m/ *noun.* **E20.**
[from Greek *phuletēs*: see prec., **-ISM**.]
ORTHODOX CHURCH. An excessive emphasis on the principle of nationalism in the organization of church affairs; a policy which attaches greater importance to ethnic identity than to bonds of faith and worship. Chiefly *Hist.*, with ref. to the schism of the Bulgarian Church between 1872 and 1945.

phyllary /ˈfɪləri/ *noun.* **M19.**
[mod. Latin *phyllarium* from Greek *phullarion* dim. of *phullon* leaf.]
BOTANY. Each of the small bracts making up the involucre of a composite flower.

phyllite /ˈfɪlʌɪt/ *noun.* **E19.**
[from Greek *phullon* leaf + **-ITE**[1].]
1 *MINERALOGY.* An aluminosilicate of iron, magnesium, and potassium. *obsolete* exc. *Hist.* **E19.**
2 *GEOLOGY.* A fine-grained metamorphic rock with a well-developed schistosity, intermediate between slate and schist. **L19.**
■ **phyllitic** /fɪˈlɪtɪk/ *adjective* consisting of or having the character of phyllite **L19.**

phyllo *noun* var. of **FILO**.

phyllo- /ˈfɪləʊ/ *combining form* of Greek *phullon* leaf: see **-O-**.

■ **phyllocarid** /-ˈkarɪd/ *noun & adjective* [Greek *karis* shrimp, prawn] *ZOOLOGY* (designating) any of various branchiopods possessing phyllopodia **L19. phylloˈmania** *noun* excessive or abnormal development of leaves **L17. phyˈllophagous** *adjective* feeding on leaves **M19. phylloplane** *noun* (*ECOLOGY*) the leaf surface of a plant or plants, esp. as an environment for micro-organisms **M20. phyllopod** *noun & adjective* (*ZOOLOGY*) (designating) an entomostracan crustacean with lamellate swimming feet **M19. phyllopodium** /-ˈpəʊ-/ *noun*, pl. **-ia**, (*a*) *BOTANY* the base of a leaf-stalk; the main axis of a leaf; (*b*) *ZOOLOGY* a broad flat limb in some crustaceans: **L19. phylloˈquinone** *noun* (*BIOCHEMISTRY*) vitamin K_1, a yellow fat-soluble oil that is present in green leafy vegetables and is important in blood clotting **M20. phylloˈsilicate** *noun* (*MINERALOGY*) any of the group of silicates characterized by SiO_4 tetrahedra linked in sheets of indefinite extent in which the ratio of silicon and aluminium to oxygen is 2:5 **M20. phyllosome** *noun* [**-SOME**[3]] *ZOOLOGY* the larval form of certain macrurous crustaceans; a glass crab: **M19. phyllosphere** *noun* (*ECOLOGY*) the surface area of leaves, or of all the parts of a plant above ground **M20.**

phylloclade /ˈfɪləʊkleɪd/ *noun.* Also (earlier) in Latin form **-cladium** /-ˈkleɪdɪəm/, pl. **-ia** /-ɪə/. **M19.**
[mod. Latin *phyllocladium*, from **PHYLLO-** + Greek *klados* a shoot.]
BOTANY. A flattened branch or stem-joint (as in butcher's broom, *Ruscus aculeatus*, and in cacti) resembling and functioning as a leaf.
■ **phyˈllocladous** *adjective* having phylloclades **L19.**

phyllode /ˈfɪləʊd/ *noun.* Also in Latin form **phyllodium** /fɪˈləʊdɪəm/, pl. **-dia** /-dɪə/. **M19.**
[mod. Latin *phyllodium* from Greek *phullōdēs* leaflike, from *phullon* leaf: see **-ODE**[1].]
BOTANY. A flat expanded petiole resembling and functioning as a leaf-blade.
■ **phyˈllodial** *adjective* pertaining to or of the nature of a phyllode **M19. phyˈllodinous** *adjective* bearing phyllodes **L19.**

phyllody /ˈfɪləʊdi/ *noun.* **M19.**
[formed as prec. + **-Y**[3].]
BOTANY. An abnormal condition in which parts of a flower, esp. the petals or sepals, are changed into leaves.

phylloid /ˈfɪlɔɪd/ *adjective & noun.* **M19.**
[mod. Latin *phylloides*, from Greek *phullon* leaf: see **-OID**.]
BOTANY. ▶ **A** *adjective.* Resembling a leaf; foliaceous. **M19.**
▶ **B** *noun.* A leaflike assimilatory organ in brown algae. **M19.**

phyllome /ˈfɪləʊm/ *noun.* **L19.**
[mod. Latin *phylloma* from Greek *phullōma* foliage, from *phulloun* clothe with leaves, from *phullon* leaf: see **-OME**.]
BOTANY. Any leaf or organ regarded as a modified leaf (as a petal, stamen, etc.).
■ **phyˈllomic** *adjective* **L19.**

phyllotaxis /fɪlə(ʊ)ˈtaksɪs/ *noun.* Also **-taxy** /-ˈtaksi/. **M19.**
[from **PHYLLO-** + **-TAXIS**, **-TAXY**.]
BOTANY. The arrangement of leaves or other lateral members on an axis or stem; the geometrical principles of such arrangement.
■ **phyllotactic** *adjective* **M19.**

phylloxera /fɪlɒkˈsɪərə, fɪˈlɒksərə/ *noun.* **M19.**
[mod. Latin *Phylloxera* (see below), from **PHYLLO-** + Greek *xēros* dry.]
An insect now or formerly included in the homopteran gall-forming genus *Phylloxera* (family Phylloxeridae); *esp.* (more fully ***grape phylloxera***, ***vine phylloxera***) *Viteus vitifolii*, a destructive pest of vines.

phylogenesis /fʌɪlə(ʊ)ˈdʒɛnɪsɪs/ *noun.* **L19.**
[from Greek *phulon*, *phulē* tribe, race + **-O-** + **-GENESIS**.]
BIOLOGY. The evolutionary development of a species or other group of organisms through a succession of forms. Also, the evolutionary development of a particular (esp. anatomical) feature of an organism. Cf. **ONTOGENESIS**.
■ **phylogeˈnetic** *adjective* **L19. phylogeˈnetical** *adjective* (*rare*) **L19. phylogeˈnetically** *adverb* with reference to or as regards phylogenesis **L19. phylogeˈnetics** *noun* the branch of biology that deals with phylogenesis, esp. the factors influencing its course **M20.**

phylogeny /fʌɪˈlɒdʒ(ə)ni/ *noun.* **L19.**
[formed as prec. + **-GENY**.]
BIOLOGY. **1 a** = **PHYLOGENESIS**. **L19.** ▸**b** A diagram representing phylogenesis. **L19.**
2 = **PHYLOGENETICS**. **L19.**
■ **phyloˈgenic** *adjective* **L19. phyloˈgenically** *adverb* **L20.**

phylum /ˈfʌɪləm/ *noun.* Pl. **-la** /-lə/. **L19.**
[Greek *phulon* tribe, race.]
1 *BIOLOGY.* A basic taxonomic grouping (used esp. in the animal kingdom) ranking above class and below kingdom, in *BOTANY* equivalent to a division. **L19.**
2 *LINGUISTICS.* A group of languages related, or believed to be related, less closely than those of a family or stock. **M20.**

📖 **1** *Scientific American* A rather primitive arthropod (a phylum that includes insects, arachnids and crustaceans).

†**phyma** *noun.* Pl. **-mata**. **L17–M18.**
[Latin from Greek *phuma*, *phumat-*.]
MEDICINE. An inflamed swelling; an external tubercle.

physalis /ˈfʌɪsəlɪs, ˈfɪs-, fʌɪˈseɪlɪs/ *noun.* **E19.**
[mod. Latin (see below), from Greek *phusallis* bladder.]
Any of the various chiefly American plants constituting the genus *Physalis*, of the nightshade family, with a calyx which becomes inflated in the fruit and freq. with edible berries; *esp.* the Cape gooseberry, *P. peruviana*, and the alkekengi, *P. alkekengi*.

Phys. Ed. *abbreviation.*
Physical education.

Physeptone /fʌɪˈsɛptəʊn/ *noun.* **M20.**
[Origin unkn.]
(Proprietary name for) methadone.

physeter /fʌɪˈsiːtə/ *noun.* **L16.**
[Latin from Greek *phusētēr*, from *phusan* to blow.]
†**1** A large whale. **L16–L18.**
2 A sperm whale. Now only as mod. Latin genus name. **M18.**

physiatric /fɪzɪˈatrɪk/ *noun.* **M19.**
[from Greek *phusis* nature + *iatrikos* medical: see **-IC**.]
sing. & (usu.) in *pl.* (treated as *sing.*). The use of natural agents such as heat and light in medicine.
■ **physiatrist** /fɪˈzʌɪətrɪst/ *noun* **M20.**

physic /ˈfɪzɪk/ *noun. arch.* Also (earlier) †**fi-**. **ME.**
[Old French *fisique* medicine (mod. *physique* †natural science, physics) from Latin *physica* from Greek *phusikē* use as noun (sc. *epistēmē* knowledge) of fem. of *phusikos* natural, from *phusis* nature: see **-IC**.]
†**1** Natural science. **ME–L19.**
2 The art or practice of healing. **ME.** ▸**b** Medical people collectively. Now *rare* or *obsolete*. **LME.**
†**3** Medical treatment; *fig.* a healthy practice or habit; a mental, moral, or spiritual remedy. **ME–E18.**
4 (A) medicine; *spec.* a cathartic. **ME.**

5 Medical science; the physician's art. LME.

> 📖 **4** R. GRAVES A wild beast falling sick Will find its own best physic—Herb, berry, root. ***Indian physic***: see INDIAN *adjective*.

Comb.: **physic-ball** a bolus for administration to an animal; **physic garden** a garden for the cultivation of medicinal plants; a botanical garden.

physic /ˈfɪzɪk/ *adjective*. Now *rare* or *obsolete*. LME.
[(Old & mod. French *physique* from) Latin *physicus* from Greek *phusikos*: see prec.]
†**1** Medical; medicinal. LME–M18.
2 Physical; natural. M16.

physic /ˈfɪzɪk/ *verb trans*. Now *colloq*. Infl. **-ck-**. LME.
[from PHYSIC *noun*.]
Dose or treat with medicine, esp. a purgative; *fig.* relieve, alleviate.

physical /ˈfɪzɪk(ə)l/ *adjective & noun*. LME.
[medieval Latin *physicalis*, from Latin *physica*: see PHYSIC *noun*, -ICAL.]
▶ **A** *adjective*. **I** Pertaining to medicine.
1 Medical. Now *rare*. LME. ▸†**b** Of a person: practising medicine. M–L18.
†**2** Medicinal; curative, therapeutic. LME–E19.
†**3** Like medicine in taste, smell, etc. M17–E18.
†**4** Needing or receiving medical treatment. M17–M18.
▶ **II** Pertaining to matter.
5 Of or pertaining to matter, or the world as perceived by the senses; material as opp. to mental or spiritual. L16. ▸**b** Of or pertaining to physics or natural science; in accordance with the laws of nature. L16. ▸**c** Of a person: dealing with or devoted to natural science or the material world. L17. ▸**d** COMMERCE. (Of a commodity) actually existing and deliverable; (of a market) involving the immediate delivery of a commodity rather than notional or future delivery. M20.
6 a Of an attribute, action, or faculty: bodily rather than mental; involving the body; carnal. L18. ▸**b** Characterized by or suggestive of bodily (as distinct from mental or psychological) activities or attributes. Of a person or action: inclined to be bodily aggressive or violent; making frequent use of gesture and bodily contact. L20.

> 📖 **5** T. BIRCH On physical maps layer colours . . show lowlands in greens. A. TOFFLER Image formation . . is . . a physical process, dependent upon finite characteristics of nerve cells. **b** *Nature* Of the physical . . nature of the coronal matter we know very little. **c** J. DISKI Mo was a physical rather than a social anthropologist. **6a** L. WOOLF The physical attraction which he was . . feeling for Katharine. W. GOLDING As if the grief were a physical pain. G. GORDON Down a coal mine . . doing physical labour, which would have exhausted his body. P. COSGRAVE He had exceptional physical charm. M. STOTT Women usually have less physical strength than men. V. BRAMWELL Take plenty of physical exercise. **b** *Rugby World* Rugby is a physical game. A. THWAITE The poems are indeed very physical, full of clasping and embracing. S. BELLOW He was very physical with people. He dropped a hand on your knee.

Special collocations: *physical* ANTHROPOLOGY. **physical chemistry** the application of the techniques and theories of physics to the study of chemical systems; the branch of chemistry that deals with this. **physical culture** the development of the body by exercise. **physical culturist** an advocate or exponent of physical culture. **physical education** regular instruction in bodily exercise and games, esp. in schools. **physical force** material as opp. to moral force; the use of armed power to effect or repress political changes. **physical geography** the branch of geography that deals with the natural features of the earth's surface. ***physical jerks***: see JERK *noun*[1]. **physical object** PHILOSOPHY an object that exists in space and time and that can be perceived. **physical optics** the branch of optics that deals with the properties of light itself (as opp. to the function of sight); *esp.* the part dealing with wave theory and the phenomena explained by it (e.g. interference and diffraction). **physical science** (any branch of) the science that deals with inanimate matter and energy (e.g. astronomy, physics, chemistry, geology). **physical theatre** a form of theatre which emphasizes the use of physical movement (as in dance and mime) for expression. **physical therapy** physiotherapy. **physical torture** *slang* physical training. **physical training** the systematic use of exercises to promote physical fitness.

▶ **B** *noun*. **1** In *pl.* Physical powers, physical strength. *rare*. E19.
2 *The* physical world. M19.
3 = MEDICAL *noun* 2. M20.
4 COMMERCE. In *pl.* (Contracts for) physical commodities. L20.
■ **physiˈcality** *noun* †(*a*) *joc.* (used as a title for) a medical man; (*b*) physical condition; (*c*) the quality that pertains to physical sensation or to the body as opp. to the mind: L16. **physicaliˈzation** *noun* (a) representation of an idea by physical means M20. **physicalize** *verb trans.* express or represent by physical means or in physical terms M19. **physicalness** *noun* E18.

physicalist /ˈfɪzɪk(ə)lɪst/ *noun & adjective*. M19.
[from prec. + -IST.]
PHILOSOPHY. ▶**A** *noun*. **1** A person who maintains that human behaviour and ethics are determined by or explicable in terms of physical properties and laws. M19.
2 An adherent of physicalism. M20.
▶ **B** *adjective*. Of or pertaining to physicalism. M20.
■ **physicalism** *noun* the theory that all reality must eventually be expressible in the language of physics M20. **physicaˈlistic** *adjective* pertaining to or characterized by physicalism M20. **physicaˈlistically** *adverb* M20.

physically /ˈfɪzɪk(ə)li/ *adverb*. L16.
[from PHYSIC *adjective* or prec.: see -ICALLY.]
1 According to nature or to physics; not intellectually, morally, or spiritually. L16. ▸†**b** Intrinsically. E17–L18. ▸†**c** Practically, almost. L17–M18.
2 As regards the body, in bodily terms; in shape, size, and other material properties. L16.
†**3** Medically; medicinally. L16–E18.

> 📖 **1** W. R. GROVE An atom or molecule physically indivisible. LD MACAULAY It would be physically impossible for . . them to surrender themselves in time. **2** J. P. HENNESSY Physically, Mrs Trollope was a small woman. *Science* Artificial aids for the physically handicapped. I. MURDOCH The tempest which raged in Bogdan's soul rarely expressed itself physically. *Which?* A DAT cassette is physically smaller than an ordinary tape.

physician /fɪˈzɪʃ(ə)n/ *noun*. ME.
[Old French *fisicien* (mod. *physicien* physicist), formed as PHYSIC *noun*: see -ICIAN.]
1 A person who practises medicine, esp. non-surgical medicine; a specialist in medical diagnosis and treatment; *spec.* one with a legal qualification to practise. ME.
†**2** A natural philosopher, a physicist. LME–E17.
3 *transf.* & *fig.* A healer; a person who cures moral, spiritual, or political ills. LME.

> 📖 **1** J. BARTH I was unhealthy and . . didn't care to consult a physician about it. CONSULTING ***physician***.

■ **physicianer** *noun* (*dial.*) = PHYSICIAN 1 E19. **physicianess** *noun* a female physician M17. **physicianly** *adjective* L19. **physicianship** *noun* the position or office of physician; (with possess. adjective, as ***his physicianship*** etc.) a mock title of respect given to a physician: M18.

physicism /ˈfɪzɪsɪz(ə)m/ *noun*. M19.
[from PHYSICS + -ISM.]
The doctrine which refers all phenomena to physical or material forces; materialism.

physicist /ˈfɪzɪsɪst/ *noun*. E18.
[from PHYSIC *noun*, PHYSICS + -IST.]
†**1** An expert in medical science. *rare*. Only in E18.
2 An expert in or student of physics; a natural scientist. M19.
3 An adherent of physicism. L19.

physicky /ˈfɪzɪki/ *adjective*. M18.
[from PHYSIC *noun* + -Y[1].]
Having the taste, smell, or other qualities of medicine; affected by medicine.

physic-nut /ˈfɪzɪknʌt/ *noun*. M17.
[from PHYSIC *noun* + NUT *noun*.]
A tropical American shrub, *Jatropha curcas*, of the spurge family (also ***physic-nut bush***, ***physic-nut tree***); the fruit or seed of this shrub, yielding pulza-oil and used as a purgative.

physico- /ˈfɪzɪkəʊ/ *combining form*.
[from PHYSIC *noun*, PHYSICS + -O-.]
1 Of or pertaining to physics and (the subject implied or denoted by the 2nd elem.); of or pertaining to the physical branch of (that subject); as ***physico-geographical***, †***physico-medical***.
2 Physical and —, as ***physico-mental***.

physico-chemical /ˌfɪzɪkəʊˈkɛmɪk(ə)l/ *adjective*. M17.
[from prec. + CHEMICAL.]
Of or pertaining to physical chemistry; of or pertaining to physics and chemistry.
■ **physico-chemically** *adverb* L19. **physico-chemist** *noun* an expert in or student of physical chemistry, or physics and chemistry. M19. **physico-chemistry** *noun* physical chemistry; physics and chemistry: M20.

physico-mathematical /ˌfɪzɪkəʊmaθ(ə)ˈmatɪk(ə)l/ *adjective*. M17.
[from PHYSICO- + MATHEMATICAL.]
Of or pertaining to the application of mathematics to physics.

physico-mechanical /ˌfɪzɪkəʊmɪˈkanɪk(ə)l/ *adjective*. Now *rare*. M17.
[from PHYSICO- + MECHANICAL.]
Of or pertaining to the dynamics of physical forces, or the branch of science that deals with mechanical phenomena.

physico-theology /ˌfɪzɪkəʊθɪˈɒlədʒi/ *noun*. E18.
[from PHYSICO- + THEOLOGY.]
Hist. A theology founded on the facts of nature and the evidence of design found there; natural theology.
■ **ˌphysico-theoˈlogical** *adjective* L17. **physico-theologian** *noun* M19.

physics /ˈfɪzɪks/ *noun*. L15.
[Pl. of PHYSIC *adjective* used as noun, translating Latin *physica* neut. pl. from Greek *ta phusika* the natural (*sc.* things), collective title of Aristotle's physical treatises, from *phusis* nature: see -ICS.]
1 a *Hist.* Natural science in general, *esp.* the Aristotelian system of natural science. L15. ▸**b** The branch of science that deals with the nature and properties of matter and energy, in so far as they are not dealt with by chemistry or biology; the science whose subject-matter includes mechanics, heat, light and other radiation, sound, electricity, magnetism, and the structure of atoms. Also, the physical properties and phenomena of a thing. E18.
†**2** The science of, or a treatise on, medicine. *rare*. E17–L18.

> 📖 **1b** *Science Survey* Astrophysicists—those who apply physics to astronomical problems. *Nature* The physics underlying this calculation is . . childishly simple.

physio /ˈfɪzɪəʊ/ *noun*. *colloq*. Pl. **-os**. M20.
[Abbreviation.]
A physiotherapist; physiotherapy.

physio- /ˈfɪzɪəʊ/ *combining form*.
[Partly from Greek *phusio-*, from *phusis* nature, partly from PHYSIO(LOGY: see -O-.]
1 Nature.
2 Physiology, physiological.
■ **physioˈchemical** *adjective* pertaining to physiological chemistry L19. **physiognosy** *noun* [Greek *gnōsis* knowledge] natural history; natural science: E19. **physiopathoˈlogic** *adjective* (MEDICINE, chiefly *US*) physiopathological M20. **physiopathoˈlogical** *adjective* (MEDICINE) of or pertaining to physiopathology M19. **physiopaˈthology** *noun* (MEDICINE) the disordered physiology of disease or a diseased organism E20. **physiophiˈlosophy** *noun* a philosophical system in which an attempt is made to construct all knowledge a priori M19. **physioˈplastic** *adjective* formed by nature E19. **physio-psychoˈlogic** *adjective* physio-psychological M20. **physio-psychoˈlogical** *adjective* of or pertaining to physio-psychology L19. **physio-psyˈchology** *noun* physiological psychology L19.

physiocrat /ˈfɪzɪəkrat/ *noun*. L18.
[French *physiocrate*, from *physiocratie* physiocracy, formed as PHYSIO-: see -CRACY, -CRAT.]
Hist. An 18th-cent. French economist, = ECONOMIST 3a.
■ **physiˈocracy** *noun* government according to a supposed natural order; *spec.* the doctrine of the physiocrats: M19. **physioˈcratic** *adjective* E19.

physiog /ˈfɪzɪɒɡ/ *noun*. *joc. colloq*. M19.
[Abbreviation of PHYSIOGNOMY. Cf. PHIZ, PHIZOG.]
A person's face; a facial expression.

physiognomonical /fɪzɪˌɒɡnəˈmɒnɪk(ə)l/ *adjective*. Now *rare* or *obsolete*. M17.
[from medieval Latin *physiognomonicus* from Greek *phusiognōmonikos*, from *phusiognōmonia*: see next, -ICAL.]
Physiognomic.

physiognomy /fɪzɪˈɒ(ɡ)nəmi/ *noun*. LME.
[Old French *phisonomie* (mod. *physionomie*) from medieval Latin *phisonomia*, *physionomia*, late Latin *physiognomia* from late Greek *phusiognōmia* contr. of Greek *phūsiognōmonia*, from *phusis* nature + *gnōmon-*, *gnōmōn* interpreter: see -Y[3]. The *g* occurs from 16.]
1 The art of judging character from the features of the face or the form of the body generally. LME.
2 A person's face or expression, esp. viewed as indicative of the mind and character; the general cast of features of a race; *transf.* the general appearance or external features of a thing, *spec.* (ECOLOGY) of a plant community. LME. ▸†**b** A portrait. L15–E17.
†**3** Prediction of the future from the features of the face etc.; a fortune so foretold. Also, fortune foretold or character divined by astrology. M16–M17.
4 *fig.* The ideal, mental, moral, or political aspect of anything as an indication of its character; characteristic aspect. L17.

> 📖 **2** N. HAWTHORNE The old highways . . adapted themselves . . to the physiognomy of the country. F. TOMLIN Friends had begun to notice a change in Eliot's physiognomy.

■ †**physiognomer** *noun* a physiognomist L15–E18. **physioˈgnomic** /fɪzɪə(ɡ)ˈnɒmɪk/ *adjective* of the nature of or pertaining to physiognomy; pertaining to the face as indicative of character; skilled in physiognomy: E18. **physioˈgnomical** *adjective* physiognomic L16. **physioˈgnomically** *adverb* in a physiognomic manner; according to the rules of physiognomy; as regards characteristic features: E17. **physiognomist** *noun* [French *physiognomiste*] a person skilled in physiognomy; a person who reads character (or, formerly, professed to predict the future) from a person's face: L16. **physiognomize** *verb trans.* examine or study physiognomically; infer the character of from physiognomy: M17.

physiography /fɪzɪˈɒɡrəfi/ *noun*. E19.
[from PHYSIO- + -GRAPHY.]
1 The branch of knowledge that deals with natural objects and natural phenomena. Now *rare* or *obsolete*. E19.
2 Physical geography; geomorphology; the physiographic features *of* a region. L19.
■ **physiographer** *noun* L19. **physioˈgraphic** *adjective* (***physiographic province***: see PROVINCE 6c) M19. **physioˈgraphical** *adjective* L18. **physioˈgraphically** *adverb* from a physiographical point of view E20.

physiolater /fɪzɪˈɒlətə/ *noun*. *rare*. L19.
[from PHYSIO- + -LATER.]
A worshipper of nature.
■ **physiolatry** *noun* M19.

physiologer /fɪzɪˈɒlədʒə/ *noun.* Now *rare* or *obsolete.* L16.
[from late Latin *physiologus* from Greek *phusiologos*, from *phusiologia*: see PHYSIOLOGY, -LOGER.]
= PHYSIOLOGIST. L17.

physiological /ˌfɪzɪəˈlɒdʒɪk(ə)l/ *adjective.* E17.
[formed as next + -ICAL.]
†**1** Pertaining to the material universe or to natural science; physical. E17–E19.
2 Pertaining to physiology or its subject-matter. E19.
2 physiological psychology the branch of psychology that deals with the interrelation between physiological events, esp. in the brain, and mental ones. ***physiological saline***: see SALINE *noun* 3.
■ **physioˈlogic** *adjective* M17. **physiologically** *adverb* in a physiological manner; according to the principles of physiology; from a physiological point of view: E17.

physiologist /fɪzɪˈɒlədʒɪst/ *noun.* M17.
[from next + -IST.]
†**1** A natural philosopher; *spec.* (*Hist.*) a philosopher of the Ionic school. M17–E19.
2 An expert in or student of physiology. L18.
■ **physiologize** *verb* †(*a*) *verb intrans.* inquire into natural causes and phenomena; †(*b*) *verb trans.* explain in accordance with natural philosophy; (*c*) *verb intrans.* (*rare*) form physiological conclusions or theories: L17.

physiology /fɪzɪˈɒlədʒi/ *noun.* M16.
[French *physiologie* or Latin *physiologia* from Greek *phusiologia* natural philosophy, formed as PHYSIO-: see -OLOGY.]
†**1** Natural philosophy, natural science; a particular system or doctrine of natural science. M16–L18.
2 The branch of science that deals with the normal functioning of living organisms and their parts, in so far as it is not dealt with by more recent sciences such as biochemistry and immunology. Also, the physiological features of a thing. E17.

> **2** C. DARWIN Elucidating the physiology of the muscles of the hand. I. BANKS In some strange inversion of physiology, my hands were moist while my mouth was dry.

physiotherapy /ˌfɪzɪə(ʊ)ˈθɛrəpi/ *noun.* E20.
[from PHYSIO- + THERAPY.]
The treatment of disease, injury, or deformity by physical methods such as manipulation, massage, infrared heat treatment, and exercise, rather than by drugs.
■ ˌ**physiotheraˈpeutic** *adjective* of, pertaining to, or involving physiotherapy E20. **physiotherapist** *noun* a person skilled or trained in physiotherapy E20.

physique /fɪˈziːk/ *noun.* E19.
[French, use as noun of adjective = physical: see PHYSIC *adjective.*]
The form, size, and development of a person's body.

> CONAN DOYLE He was clearly a professional acrobat, a man of magnificent physique. R. BERTHOUD His shortish, stocky physique.

physisorption /fɪzɪˈsɔːpʃ(ə)n/ *noun.* M20.
[from PHYSI(CAL + AD)SORPTION.]
CHEMISTRY. Adsorption which does not involve the formation of chemical bonds.
■ **physiˈsorb** *verb trans. & intrans.* [back-form.] collect by physisorption M20.

physo- /ˈfʌɪsəʊ/ *combining form* of Greek *phusa* bladder: see -O-.
■ **physoˈclistous** *adjective* [Greek *kleistos* closed] designating a teleost fish in which there is no opening between the swim-bladder and the gut L19. **physoˈgastric** *adjective* exhibiting physogastry E20. **physogastry** *noun* [Greek *gastr-*, *gastēr* abdomen] a condition in which the abdomen of certain insects becomes distended by the growth of fat bodies or other organs E20. **physoˈstomous** *adjective* [Greek *stoma* mouth] designating a teleost fish in which there is an opening between the swim-bladder and the gut L19.

physostegia /fʌɪsəʊˈstiːdʒə/ *noun.* M19.
[mod. Latin (see below), from Greek *phusa* bladder + *stegē* roof, with ref. to the inflated calyx of the fruiting plant.]
Any of various N. American labiate plants constituting the genus *Physostegia*, with spikes of pink or white flowers; *esp.* the obedient plant, *P. virginiana.*

physostigma /fʌɪsəʊˈstɪgmə/ *noun.* M19.
[mod. Latin (see below), from Greek *phusa* bladder + STIGMA, with ref. to the hooded extension of the style.]
Any of several African leguminous vines of the genus *Physostigma*, esp. *P. venenosum*; (a medicinal extract of) the poisonous seed of *P. venenosum*, the Calabar bean.

physostigmine /fʌɪsəʊˈstɪgmiːn/ *noun.* M19.
[from prec. + -INE[5].]
CHEMISTRY & PHARMACOLOGY. A tricyclic alkaloid, $C_{15}H_{21}N_3O_2$, which is the active principle of the Calabar bean and is used medicinally (esp. as a miotic) on account of its anticholinesterase activity.

phyt- *combining form* see PHYTO-.

phytal /ˈfʌɪt(ə)l/ *adjective.* E20.
[from PHYTO- + -AL[1].]
ECOLOGY. Designating, of, or pertaining to the parts of a lake etc. which are shallow enough to permit the growth of rooted green plants; littoral.

phytane /ˈfʌɪteɪn/ *noun.* E20.
[from PHYTO- + -ANE.]
CHEMISTRY. A colourless liquid isoprenoid hydrocarbon, $C_{20}H_{42}$, that is the paraffin corresponding to phytol and occurs in petroleum and some rocks, probably as a breakdown product of chlorophyll.

phytase /ˈfʌɪteɪz/ *noun.* E20.
[from PHYTO- + -ASE.]
BIOLOGY. Any of a class of enzymes found esp. in cereals and yeast which convert phytic acid to myo-inositol and phosphoric acid.

-phyte /fʌɪt/ *suffix.*
[formed as PHYTO-.]
Forming nouns denoting a plant or plantlike organism, as ***bryophyte***, ***dermatophyte***, ***saprophyte***.

phytic /ˈfʌɪtɪk/ *adjective.* E20.
[from PHYTIN + -IC.]
BIOCHEMISTRY. ***phytic acid***, a phosphoric acid ester, $C_6H_6(OPO_3H_2)_6$, of myo-inositol which is found in plants, esp. in the seeds of cereals, and readily binds with metals to form salts.
■ **phytate** *noun* a salt or ester of phytic acid E20.

phytin /ˈfʌɪtɪn/ *noun.* E20.
[from PHYTO- + -IN[1].]
BIOCHEMISTRY. An insoluble salt of phytic acid with calcium and magnesium, found in plants; *loosely* phytic acid.

†**phytivorous** *adjective.* M17–M19.
[from PHYTO- + -I- + -VOROUS.]
= HERBIVOROUS.

phyto- /ˈfʌɪtəʊ/ *combining form.* Before a vowel also **phyt-**.
[from Greek *phuton* plant, from *phu-* BE, grow: see -O-.]
Forming nouns and adjectives, and derived adverbs, with the sense 'plant, plants'.
■ **phytoaˈgglutinin** *noun* a plant protein that is an agglutinin M20. **phytoaˈlexin** *noun* (*BOTANY*) a substance that is produced by plant tissues in response to contact with a parasite and specifically inhibits the growth of that parasite M20. **phytoˈbenthos** *noun* the aquatic flora of the region at or near the bottom of the sea M20. **phytoˈbezoar** *noun* (*MEDICINE & VETERINARY MEDICINE*) a pathological concretion of vegetable matter in the gastro-intestinal tract L19. **phytoˈchemical** *adjective* of or pertaining to phytochemistry M19. **phytoˈchemically** *adverb* by phytochemical methods L20. **phytoˈchemist** *noun* an expert in or student of phytochemistry M20. **phytoˈchemistry** *noun* the chemistry of plants and plant products M19. **phytoˈcidal** *adjective* lethal or injurious to plants M20. **phytocide** *noun* a phytocidal agent M20. **phytoˈecdysone** *noun* (*BIOLOGY*) any ecdysone that occurs in a plant M20. **phytoˈflagellate** *noun* (*ZOOLOGY*) a plantlike flagellate belonging to a class most of whose members possess chromatophores and perform photosynthesis M20. **phytogeˈnetic** of or relating to the origin and evolution of plants L19. **phytohaemaˈgglutinin** *noun* a plant protein that is a haemagglutinin, *spec.* that extracted from the French bean M20. **phytoˈhormone** *noun* = HORMONE 2 M20. **phyˈtometer** *noun* a plant or group of plants used to indicate, by its health and rate of growth, the physical properties of its surroundings E20. **phytoˈmonad** *noun* (*ZOOLOGY*) a phytoflagellate belonging to the order Phytomonadina E20. **phytoˈsanitary** *adjective* pertaining to the health of plants; *spec.* designating a certificate stating that a plant is free from infectious diseases: M20. **phytosaur** *noun* an extinct aquatic reptile of the suborder Phytosauria, chiefly of the Triassic period, which resembled a crocodile E20. **phytoˈsaurian** *adjective* of, pertaining to, or characteristic of a phytosaur E20. **phytoˈsterol** *noun* (*BIOCHEMISTRY*) any of a large class of sterols found in plants L19. **phyˈtotomy** *noun* (now *rare*) plant anatomy M19. **phytoˈtoxic** *adjective* poisonous or injurious to plants M20. **phytoˈtoxicant** *noun* a substance poisonous or injurious to plants; *esp.* one present in the air: M20. **phytotoˈxicity** *noun* the property of being phytotoxic M20. **phytoˈtoxin** *noun* (*a*) a toxin derived from a plant; (*b*) a substance poisonous or injurious to plants, *esp.* one produced by a parasite: E20. **phytotron** *noun* [-TRON] a laboratory where plants can be maintained and studied under a wide range of controlled conditions M20.

phytochrome /ˈfʌɪtəkrəʊm/ *noun.* L19.
[from PHYTO- + Greek *khrōma* colour.]
†**1** Xanthophyll; chlorophyll. *rare.* L19–E20.
2 *BOTANY.* A blue-green compound which has two forms interconvertible by the absorption of light, and which regulates many aspects of development in higher plants according to the nature and timing of the light which it absorbs. M20.

phytogenic /fʌɪtə(ʊ)ˈdʒɛnɪk/ *adjective.* *rare.* L19.
[from PHYTO- + -GENIC.]
GEOLOGY & MINERALOGY. Formed by or derived from plants.

phytogeography /ˌfʌɪtəʊdʒɪˈɒgrəfi/ *noun.* M19.
[from PHYTO- + GEOGRAPHY.]
The branch of science that deals with the geographical distribution of plants.
■ **phytogeographer** *noun* M19. **phytogeoˈgraphic** *adjective* phytogeographical L19. **phytogeoˈgraphical** *adjective* pertaining to phytogeography, dealing with the geographical distribution of plants M19.

phytography /fʌɪˈtɒgrəfi/ *noun.* L17.
[from PHYTO- + -GRAPHY.]
A description of plants; descriptive botany.
■ **phytoˈgraphic** *adjective* L17.

phytol /ˈfʌɪtɒl/ *noun.* E20.
[from PHYTO- + -OL.]
BIOCHEMISTRY. An acyclic terpenoid alcohol, $C_{20}H_{40}O$, whose molecule forms part of those of chlorophyll and vitamins E and K.
■ **phytyl** *noun* the radical $C_{20}H_{39}O-$ E20.

phytolacca /fʌɪtəʊˈlakə, fɪtəʊ-/ *noun.* M18.
[mod. Latin (see below), formed as PHYTO- + *lacca* crimson lake, the juice of the berries being used as a dye.]
Any of various chiefly tropical or subtropical American plants constituting the genus *Phytolacca* (family Phytolaccaceae), with long racemes of small white flowers succeeded by black berries; *esp.* the Virginian poke, *P. americana.* Also, a preparation of such a plant used medicinally.

phytolith /ˈfʌɪtəlɪθ/ *noun.* Also (earlier) †**-lithus**, pl. **-thi**. E19.
[from PHYTO- + -LITH.]
†**1** A fossil plant. E19–E20.
2 A minute mineral particle formed inside a plant. M20.
■ †**phytolite** *noun* = PHYTOLITH 1 L18–M19.

phytology /fʌɪˈtɒlədʒi/ *noun.* Now *rare.* M17.
[from PHYTO- + -OLOGY.]
Botany.
■ **phytoˈlogical** *adjective* M17. **phytologist** *noun* E18.

phyton /ˈfʌɪtɒn/ *noun.* M19.
[French from Greek *phuton*: see PHYTO-, -ON.]
BOTANY. The smallest part of a plant which will reproduce when separated; a unit of plant structure or morphology.

phytopathogenic /ˌfʌɪtəʊpaθə(ʊ)ˈdʒɛnɪk/ *adjective.* E20.
[from PHYTO- + PATHOGENIC.]
BIOLOGY. Producing disease in plants.
■ **phytoˈpathogen** *noun* a micro-organism which produces disease in plants M20. **phytopathogenicity** /-ˈnɪsɪti/ *noun* the property of being phytopathogenic E20.

phytopathology /ˌfʌɪtəʊpəˈθɒlədʒi/ *noun.* M19.
[from PHYTO- + PATHOLOGY.]
The branch of science that deals with diseases of plants. Also called ***plant pathology***.
■ ˌ**phytopathoˈlogical** *adjective* L19. **phytopathologist** *noun* L19.

phytophagous /fʌɪˈtɒfəgəs/ *adjective.* E19.
[from PHYTO- + -PHAGOUS.]
ZOOLOGY. Esp. of an insect or other invertebrate: feeding on plants.
■ **phytophagy** *noun* the state or habit of being phytophagous L19.

phytophthora /fʌɪˈtɒfθ(ə)rə/ *noun.* E20.
[mod. Latin *Phytophthora* (see below), from PHYTO- + Greek *phthora* destruction.]
A fungus of the genus *Phytophthora* (order Peronosporales), which includes several parasitic species that damage plants; esp. *P. infestans*, the cause of potato blight.

phytoplankton /ˈfʌɪtəʊplaŋkt(ə)n/ *noun.* L19.
[from PHYTO- + PLANKTON.]
BIOLOGY. Plankton consisting of microscopic plants.
■ **phytoplankter** *noun* a phytoplanktonic individual or species M20. **phytoplankˈtonic** *adjective* pertaining or belonging to phytoplankton M20.

phytosociology /ˌfʌɪtəʊsəʊʃɪˈɒlədʒi, -səʊsɪ-/ *noun.* E20.
[from PHYTO- + SOCIOLOGY.]
The science of plant communities and their composition and structure.
■ ˌ**phytosocioˈlogical** *adjective* E20. ˌ**phytosocioˈlogically** *adverb* from a phytosociological point of view M20. **phytosociologist** *noun* E20.

PI *abbreviation.*
Private investigator.

pi /pʌɪ/ *noun*[1]. LME.
[Greek: in sense 2 repr. initial letter of Greek *periphereia*, English *periphery*, etc.; in sense 3 from the shape; in sense 4 after *pi-orbital* etc. (see P, P III).]
1 The sixteenth letter (Π, π) of the Greek alphabet. LME.
2 *MATH.* The ratio of the circumference of a circle to its diameter, an irrational number equal to 3.14159 . . . (approximated by 22/7). Usu. written π. E18.
3 *ELECTRICITY.* A four-terminal set of three circuit elements in which one element is in series between two in parallel. Usu. *attrib.*, as ***pi-network*** etc. Usu. written π or Π. E20.
4 *PHYSICS & CHEMISTRY.* Used *attrib.* to designate an electron, orbital, molecular state, etc., possessing one unit of angular momentum about an internuclear axis. (Usu. written π with ref. to one electron or orbital, Π with ref. to a molecule as a whole.) E20.
Comb.: **pi-bond** *CHEMISTRY* a bond formed by a pi-orbital.

pi /pʌɪ/ *noun*[2]. E20.
[Chinese *bi* (Wade–Giles *pi*).]
ARCHAEOLOGY. A jade disc with a hole in the middle, used in ancient China for symbolic or ritual purposes.

pi noun3 see PIE noun4.

pi /pʌɪ/ *adjective*. Chiefly *School slang*. Also **pie**. M19.
[Abbreviation.]
Pious, sanctimonious.

pia /ˈpʌɪə/ *noun1*. L19.
[Abbreviation.]
ANATOMY. **1** = PIA MATER. L19.
2 In full *pia-arachnoid*. The pia mater and the arachnoid, considered as one structure. L19.

pia /ˈpʌɪə/ *noun2*. M19.
[Polynesian.]
Any of several Polynesian plants of the monocotyledonous genus *Tacca* (family Taccaceae), esp. *T. leontopetaloides*; the starch (Tahiti arrowroot) produced from the tubers of these plants.

piache /pɪˈɑːtʃi/ *noun*. M16.
[Of S. Amer. Indian origin: = Carib *piai* PEAI.]
An Indian witch-doctor in Central and S. America.

piacle /ˈpʌɪək(ə)l/ *noun*. Now *rare*. LME.
[Old French, or Latin *piaculum*, from *piare* appease: see -CLE.]
†**1** An expiatory offering; expiation. LME–E18.
2 †**a** Offence, guilt. E–M17. ▸**b** A crime or sin requiring expiation. M17.

piacular /pʌɪˈakjʊlə/ *adjective*. E17.
[Latin *piacularis*, from *piaculum*: see prec., -AR1.]
1 Requiring expiation; sinful, wicked. E17.
2 Making expiation; expiatory. M17.

> **2** A. BURGESS He was . . penitent . . but he brought few piacular gifts.

■ **piacuˈlarity** *noun* the quality of being piacular E19.

piaffe /pɪˈaf/ *verb & noun*. M18.
[French *piaffer* strut, make a show.]
HORSEMANSHIP. ▶**A** *verb intrans.* Move (esp. on the spot) with a high slow trotting step. M18.
▶**B** *noun*. An act of piaffing. L19.

piaffer /pɪˈafə/ *verb & noun*. M18.
[formed as prec.]
▶†**A** *verb intrans.* = PIAFFE *verb*. M–L18.
▶**B** *noun*. = PIAFFE *noun*. M19.

Piagetian /pɪəˈʒɛtɪən, -ˈʒeɪən/ *adjective*. M20.
[from *Piaget* (see below) + -IAN.]
Of or pertaining to the theories or methods of the Swiss educational child psychologist Jean Piaget (1896–1980).

piai *noun & verb* var. of PEAI.

pial /ˈpʌɪəl/ *adjective*. L19.
[from PIA *noun1* + -AL1.]
ANATOMY. Of or pertaining to the pia mater or the pia-arachnoid.

pia mater /pʌɪə ˈmeɪtə/ *noun phr.* LME.
[medieval Latin = tender mother, translating Arab. *al-'umm ar-raḳīḳa* thin mother, tender mother: see DURA MATER.]
ANATOMY. A delicate, fibrous, highly vascular membrane which forms the innermost of the three meninges enveloping the brain and spinal cord. Cf. PIA *noun1*.
■ **pia-ˈmatral** *adjective* of or pertaining to the pia mater M19.

pian /pɪˈan, *foreign* pjɑ̃/ *noun*. Also **pians** /pɪˈanz/. E17.
[Spanish, Portuguese *(e)pian*, French *pian*, from a S. Amer. Indian language.]
The disease yaws.

Pian /ˈpʌɪən/ *adjective*. E20.
[from Latin *Pius* (see below) + -AN.]
Of or pertaining to any of the Popes named Pius; *spec.* of or pertaining to the pontificate or the liturgical reforms of Pope Pius V (1504–72) or Pope Pius X (1835–1914).

pianette /pɪəˈnɛt/ *noun*. L19.
[from PIANO *noun2* + -ETTE.]
A small piano.

piani *noun* pl. of PIANO *noun1*.

pianino /pɪəˈniːnəʊ/ *noun*. Pl. **-os**. M19.
[Italian, dim. of *piano*: see PIANO *noun2*.]
An upright piano, *esp.* a cottage piano.

pianism /ˈpɪənɪz(ə)m/ *noun*. M19.
[from PIANO *noun2* + -ISM.]
1 The art of composing or arranging for the piano; *spec.* the style of a particular composer in doing this. M19.
2 The art or technique of playing the piano. L19.

pianissimo /pɪəˈnɪsɪməʊ/ *adverb, adjective, & noun*. E18.
[Italian, superl. of PIANO *adverb & adjective*.]
MUSIC. ▶**A** *adverb & adjective*. A direction: very soft(ly). (Abbreviation ***pp*** or ***ppp***.) E18.
▶**B** *noun*. Pl. **-mos**, **-mi** /-mi/. A very soft passage. L19.

pianist /ˈpɪənɪst/ *noun*. M19.
[French *pianiste*, from *piano*: see -IST.]
1 A player on a piano. M19.
2 A radio operator. *slang*. M20.
■ **pianiste** /pɪəˈniːst/ *noun* (*arch.*) = PIANIST 1 E19.

pianistic /pɪəˈnɪstɪk/ *adjective*. L19.
[from PIANISM or PIANIST: see -ISTIC.]
Of, pertaining to, or characteristic of a pianist or pianism; suitable for performance on a piano.
■ **pianistically** *adverb* E20.

piannet /ˈpʌɪənɛt/ *noun*. Now *dial.* L16.
[from PIE *noun1* + 2nd elem. prob. from *Annette*, female forename.]
A magpie. Cf. PIET *noun* 1.

piano /ˈpjɑːnəʊ/ *noun1*. Pl. **-nos**, **-ni** /-ni/. M18.
[formed as PIANO *adverb & adjective*.]
1 MUSIC. A soft or quiet passage. M18.
2 A flat or storey in an Italian building. M19.

piano /pɪˈanəʊ/ *noun2*. Pl. **-os**. E19.
[Italian, abbreviation of PIANOFORTE or aphet. from FORTE-PIANO.]
1 A large keyboard musical instrument having metal strings struck by hammers and stopped by dampers, with two or three pedals to regulate the volume or length of the notes. E19.
2 The playing of this instrument. M20.

> **1** *cottage piano*, *grand piano*, *player-piano*, *upright piano*, etc. **2** *Gramophone* He then went on to study piano.

Comb.: **piano accordion**: with the melody played on a small upright keyboard, instead of on buttons; **piano-action** the mechanism by which the impulse of the fingers on piano keys is communicated to the strings; **piano concerto**: in which a piano is the solo instrument; **piano-organ** a mechanical piano constructed like a barrel-organ; **piano quartet** a quartet written for violin, viola, cello, and piano; an ensemble for playing such a quartet; **piano quintet** a quintet written for piano and four string instruments; an ensemble for playing such a quintet; **piano reduction** an arrangement of orchestral music for performance on the piano; **piano roll** a roll of perforated paper which controls the movement of the keys in a Pianola or similar instrument; **piano score** a reduced version of an orchestral or chamber score for performance on the piano; **piano stool** a stool for a pianist to sit on, often with a space inside for music; **piano trio** a trio written for a piano and two string instruments, usu. violin and cello; an ensemble for playing such a trio; **piano wire** strong steel wire used for piano strings.
■ **pianoless** *adjective* (of a group of musicians) without a piano or pianist M20.

piano /ˈpjɑːnəʊ/ *adverb & adjective*. L17.
[Italian from Latin *planus* flat, later (of sound) soft, low.]
1 *adverb & adjective*. MUSIC. A direction: soft(ly), quiet(ly). (Abbreviation ***p***.) L17.
2 *adjective*. Of a person: quiet, subdued. E19.

pianoforte /pɪˌanəʊˈfɔːti/ *noun*. M18.
[Italian, earlier *pian(o) e forte* lit. 'soft and loud' (with ref. to its capacity for gradation of tone). Cf. FORTE-PIANO.]
= PIANO *noun2* 1.
■ **pianofortist** *noun* (*rare*) a pianist M19.

Pianola /pɪəˈnəʊlə/ *noun*. Also **p-**. L19.
[App. dim. of PIANO *noun2*: see -OLA.]
1 (Proprietary name for) a mechanical device for attachment to a piano, enabling it to be played automatically using a piano roll, and a piano incorporating such a device. Cf. ***PLAYER-piano***. L19.
2 (**p-**.) An easy bridge hand needing no skill (more fully ***Pianola hand***); an easy task. E20.
■ **pianolist** *noun* a person who plays a Pianola E20.

piano nobile /ˌpjano ˈnoːbile/ *noun phr.* L19.
[Italian, from *piano* floor, storey (see PIANO *noun1*) + *nobile* noble, great.]
ARCHITECTURE. The main (usu. first-floor) storey of a large house, containing the principal rooms.

piano piano /ˈpjano ˈpjano/ *adverbial phr.* Also (earlier) †***pian piano***. E17.
[Italian = softly, softly.]
In a quiet leisurely manner; little by little.

pians *noun* var. of PIAN.

Piarist /ˈpʌɪərɪst/ *noun*. M19.
[Italian *Piaristi* (masc. pl.), from mod. Latin *patres scholarum piarum* fathers of the religious schools: see -IST.]
A member of a Roman Catholic secular order, founded in Rome *c* 1600 and devoted to teaching the young.

piassava /piːəˈsɑːvə/ *noun*. Also **-ba** /-bə/. M19.
[Portuguese from Tupi *piaçába*.]
A stout fibre from the leaf-stalks of various tropical palm trees, esp. the S. American *Attalea funifera* and *Leopoldinia piassaba* and the African *Raphia hookeri*, used for brooms, brushes, etc. (also ***piassava fibre***). Also, a palm producing this fibre.

Piast /pjɑːst/ *noun*. M18.
[Polish, from name of a peasant reputed to be the ancestor of the Polish kings.]
Hist. A native Pole of regal or ducal rank.

piaster *noun* see PIASTRE.

Piastraccia /pɪəˈstrɑːtʃə/ *noun*. E20.
[A quarry near Seravezza, northern Italy.]
A variety of white marble with thin grey veins.

piastre /pɪˈastə/ *noun*. Also *-**ter**. L16.
[French from Italian *piastra (d'argento)* plate (of silver), from Latin *emplastra*, *emplastrum* PLASTER *noun*. See also PLASTRON.]
1 A small coin and monetary unit, orig. in Turkey, now in various countries of the Middle East. L16.
2 *Hist.* A Spanish or Spanish-American peso or dollar. Also, a similar coin in other countries. E17.
3 *Hist.* A note and monetary unit formerly used in Indo-China. E20.

Piat /ˈpiːət/ *noun*. M20.
[Acronym, from projector infantry anti-tank.]
An anti-tank weapon used in the war of 1939–45.

piazza /pɪˈatsə/ *noun*. L16.
[Italian = French *place* PLACE *noun2*.]
1 A public square or market-place, *esp.* one in an Italian town. Formerly also, any open space surrounded by buildings. L16.
2 a A covered gallery or walk surrounding an open square; a single such gallery or walk in front of a building. Now *rare*. M17. ▸**b** The veranda of a house. Chiefly *US*. E18.

> **2b** W. KENNEDY She descended the five steps of the back piazza.

■ **piazzaed** /-əd/ *adjective* having a piazza or piazzas L17. **piazzetta** /pɪətˈsɛtə/ *noun* a small piazza E19.

†**pibble** *noun & verb* var. of PEBBLE.

pibble-pabble /ˈpɪb(ə)lpab(ə)l/ *noun*. *rare*. Also **-babble** /-bab(ə)l/. L16.
[Alt.]
= BIBBLE-BABBLE.

pibcorn /ˈpɪbkɔːn/ *noun*. *obsolete* exc. *Hist.* L18.
[Welsh *pibgorn*, *pib gorn* lit. 'pipe of horn'.]
A Welsh form of the hornpipe (the instrument).

piblokto /pɪˈblɒktəʊ/ *noun*. Also **-ockto**. L19.
[Inupiaq *pibloktoq*.]
Among Eskimos, a condition characterized by episodes of hysterical excitement or frenzy followed by depression or stupor, affecting esp. women in winter; hysteria in a dog or other animal.

pibroch /ˈpiːbrɒk, -brɒx/ *noun*. E18.
[Gaelic *piobaireachd* the art of playing the bagpipe, from *piobair* piper (from *piob* pipe from English *pipe*) + *-achd* suffix of function.]
A series of variations on a theme for the bagpipes, usu. of a martial or funerary character.

PIBS /pɪbz/ *abbreviation*.
Permanent interest-bearing share (of a building society).

pic /piːk/ *noun1*. Also **pik**, **pike** /pʌɪk/. L16.
[(French from) Turkish *pik* from Greek *pekhus* ell, cubit.]
A measure of length used in the eastern Mediterranean region, varying from about 46 to 78 cm (18 to 31 inches).

†**pic** *noun2*. M17–E19.
[French, or Spanish *pico*. Cf. PEAK *noun1*, PICO, PIKE *noun5*.]
A peak. Chiefly in ***Pic of Tenerife***.

pic /pɪk/ *noun3*. *colloq.* L19.
[Abbreviation. Cf. earlier PICCY.]
1 A picture; a painting, a photograph. L19.
2 A cinema film. M20.

pic /pɪk/ *noun4 & verb*. *colloq.* E20.
[Abbreviation of PICADOR or from Spanish *pica* lance.]
▶**A** *noun*. **1** A picador. E20.
2 A picador's lance; a thrust made with this. E20.
▶**B** *verb trans. & intrans.* Pa. t. & pple **pic'd**. Spear (a bull) with a lance. E20.

pica /ˈpʌɪkə/ *noun1*. L15.
[Anglo-Latin: see PIE *noun3* and cf. BREVIER.]
†**1** ECCLESIASTICAL HISTORY. = PIE *noun3* 1. L15–M16.
2 A size of type equal to 12 points; a typographic unit of measurement of this size (approx. ⅙ inch). Also, a size of letters in typewriting with 10 characters to the inch. L16.

pica /ˈpʌɪkə, ˈpiːkə/ *noun2*. M16.
[Latin = magpie, prob. translating Greek *kissa*, *kitta* magpie, false appetite.]
MEDICINE & VETERINARY MEDICINE. A tendency or craving to eat substances other than normal food, occurring during childhood or pregnancy, or as a symptom of disease.

picador /ˈpɪkədɔː/ *noun*. L18.
[Spanish, from *picar* prick, pierce.]
In a bullfight, a person mounted on horseback who goads the bull with a lance.

picante /pɪˈkanteɪ/ *adjective*. L20.
[Spanish, lit. 'pricking, biting'.]
Of food: hot, spicy.

Picard /ˈpɪkɑːd/ *noun & adjective*. ME.
[French.]
▶**A** *noun*. A native or inhabitant of Picardy, a region and former province in northern France; the dialect of French spoken there. ME.

▶ **B** *adjective.* Of or pertaining to Picardy, its inhabitants, or their dialect. **M17.**

picarel /ˈpɪkərɛl/ *noun.* **E20.**
[French: cf. PICKEREL *noun*[1].]
Any small fish of the genus *Maena*; *spec.* (more fully ***blotched picarel***) the Mediterranean *M. maena*, a brightly coloured protogynous hermaphrodite with a black patch on the side.

picaresque /pɪkəˈrɛsk/ *adjective & noun.* **E19.**
[French from Spanish *picaresco*, from *pícaro* roguish, knavish, (noun) rogue: see -ESQUE and cf. next.]
▶ **A** *adjective.* **1** Of or pertaining to rogues, knaves, or urchins; *esp.* (of a style of esp. Spanish fiction) dealing with the episodic adventures of such characters. **E19.**
2 Drifting; wandering. **M20.**

📖 **1** F. RAPHAEL The picaresque narrative combined an apology for . . debaucheries with a spicy enumeration of them.

▶ **B** *absol.* as *noun.* The picaresque style. **L19.**

picaro /ˈpɪkərəʊ/ *noun.* Pl. **-os.** **E17.**
[Spanish: see PICARESQUE.]
A rogue, a scoundrel.

📖 *New Yorker* Her function is that of all picaros: to infiltrate a society at every level.

picaroon /pɪkəˈruːn/ *noun*[1] *& verb.* **E17.**
[Spanish *picarón* augm. of *pícaro*: see PICARESQUE, -OON.]
▶ **A** *noun.* **1** A rogue, a scoundrel; a thief. **E17.**
2 A pirate. **E17.**
3 A small pirate ship. **E17.**
▶ **B** *verb intrans.* Practise piracy; loiter in wait for a target. **E17.**

picaroon /pɪkəˈruːn/ *noun*[2]. *N. Amer.* **M19.**
[Perh. from French *piqueron* little pike, dart, goad, from *pique* pike: see -OON.]
A long pole fitted with a spike or hook, used in logging and fishing.

Picassian /pɪˈkasɪən/ *adjective.* **M20.**
[from *Picasso* (see below) + -IAN.]
Of, pertaining to, or characteristic of the Spanish painter Pablo Picasso (1881–1973) or his style of painting.
■ Also **Picasso'esque** *adjective* **M20.**

picayune /pɪkəˈjuːn/ *noun & adjective. N. Amer.* **E19.**
[French *picaillon* old copper coin of Piedmont, halfpence, cash from Provençal *picaioun*, of unkn. origin.]
▶ **A** *noun.* Orig. (in the southern US), a Spanish half-real, worth 6¼ cents. Now, a five-cent piece or other coin of small value; *colloq.* an insignificant or mean person or thing. **E19.**

📖 M. G. EBERHART His life wouldn't be worth a picayune.

▶ **B** *adjective.* Mean, contemptible, insignificant. *colloq.* **E19.**

📖 A. HUTSCHNECKER To get lost in picayune trifles was interfering with his performance.

■ **picayunish** *adjective* (*colloq.*) = PICAYUNE *adjective* **M19.**

†**piccadill** *noun.* Also **pick-.** **E17.**
[French *pic(c)adille* any of the sections making up a ruff or collar, app. from Spanish dim. of *picado* pricked, pierced, slashed.]
1 A decorative edging of cutwork or vandyking, esp. on a collar or ruff; a wide collar or ruff so decorated. **E17–E19.**
2 A stiff band of covered board or wire for supporting a wide collar or ruff. Only in **17.**
3 A halter; a noose. *joc.* Only in **17.**

Piccadilly /pɪkəˈdɪli/ *noun.* **L19.**
[*Piccadilly Circus*, a street and area in London where several roads converge.]
1 ***Piccadilly weepers***, long side whiskers worn without a beard. Cf. DUNDREARY. **L19.**
2 ***Piccadilly window***, a monocle. *arch. slang.* **L19.**

piccalilli /ˈpɪkəlɪli, pɪkəˈlɪli/ *noun.* **M18.**
[Prob. from PICKLE *noun*[1] + CHILLI.]
A pickle of chopped vegetables, mustard, and hot spices.

piccaninny /ˈpɪkənɪni/ *noun & adjective.* Chiefly *W. Indies, S. Afr., & Austral.* Also **-nin** /-nɪn/, ***picka-**, **pickney** /ˈpɪkni/. **M17.**
[W. Indian creole from Spanish *pequeño* or Portuguese *pequeno* little, small, *pequenino* very small, tiny.]
▶ **A** *noun.* A small black or Australian Aboriginal child. **M17.**
▶ **B** *adjective.* Very small; tiny. **E18.**
piccaninny dawn, piccaninny daylight (chiefly *Austral.*) earliest dawn, first light.
¶ Considered *offensive* as used by white people.

piccata /pɪˈkɑːtə/ *adjective.* **L20.**
[Italian, fem. of *piccato* larded, pa. pple of *piccarsi* prick oneself.]
Sliced, sautéed, and served in a sauce of lemon, parsley, and butter. Chiefly in ***veal piccata***.

piccolo /ˈpɪkələʊ/ *noun & adjective.* **M19.**
[Italian = small.]
▶ **A** *noun.* Pl. **-os.**
1 A small flute sounding an octave higher than the ordinary flute; a player on this in an orchestra etc. **M19.** ▸**b** An organ-stop having the tone of a piccolo. **L19.**
2 A small upright piano. **M19.**
3 A waiter's assistant in a hotel, restaurant, etc.; a page at a hotel. **E20.**
4 A jukebox. *US slang.* **M20.**
▶ **B** *adjective.* Designating the highest-pitched member of a family of musical instruments. **M19.**
■ **piccoloist** *noun* a person who plays on the piccolo **L19.**

Picco pipe /ˈpɪkəʊ pʌɪp/ *noun phr.* Also **p-.** **L19.**
[from surname of Sardinian musician who played on the instrument in London in 1856.]
A very small flute with a flared lower end and two finger-holes and one thumb-hole.

piccy /ˈpɪki/ *noun. colloq.* **M19.**
[Abbreviation: see -Y[6]. Cf. PIC *noun*[3].]
A picture; a painting, a photograph.

pice /pʌɪs/ *noun.* **E17.**
[Hindi *paisā*. Cf. PAISA.]
Hist. A former monetary unit in the Indian subcontinent, equal to a quarter of an anna.
■ **piceworth** *noun* as much as could be bought for a pice **M19.**

picein /ˈpʌɪsiːn, -sɪɪn/ *noun.* **L19.**
[from Latin *piceus* pitchy, from *pic-, pix* PITCH *noun*[1]: see -IN[1].]
1 CHEMISTRY. A glucoside, $CH_3CO{\cdot}C_6H_4{\cdot}O{\cdot}C_6H_{11}O_5$, present in various trees, esp. willows and conifers. **L19.**
2 An inert thermoplastic substance composed of hydrocarbons from rubber, shellac, and bitumen, used to make joints airtight. Also ***picein wax***. **E20.**

Picene /ˈpʌɪsiːn/ *adjective & noun.* **E17.**
[Latin *Picenus*, from *Picenum* (see below).]
Hist. ▶**A** *adjective.* Of or pertaining to Picenum, an ancient region of central Italy, or the pre-Roman iron-age culture associated with it. **E17.**
▶ **B** *noun.* A native or inhabitant of Picenum; the language attested there. **E17.**
■ Also **Pi'cenian** *adjective & noun* **M19.**

Picentine /pɪˈkɛntʌɪn, -ˈsɛnt-/ *adjective & noun.* **E18.**
[Latin *Picentinus*, from *Picenum*: see prec., -INE[1].]
▶ **A** *adjective.* = PICENE *adjective.* **E18.**
▶ **B** *noun.* = PICENE *noun.* **M19.**

piceous /ˈpɪsɪəs/ *adjective.* **M17.**
[formed as PICEIN: see -EOUS.]
1 Flammable, combustible. *rare.* **M17.**
2 Pitch-black. **E19.**

pichi /ˈpɪtʃi/ *noun.* Also **pichey** & other vars. **E19.**
[Amer. Spanish, from Araucanian = small.]
A small armadillo, *Zaedyus pichiy*, of the pampas of Argentina and Chile.

pichiciago /pɪtʃɪˈsjeɪgəʊ/ *noun.* Pl. **-os.** **E19.**
[Spanish *pichiciego*, formed as prec. + *ciego* blind (from Latin *caecus*).]
A fairy armadillo, *esp.* the lesser or pink fairy armadillo, *Chlamyphorus truncatus*.

pichurim /ˈpɪtʃərɪm/ *noun.* **M19.**
[Of S. Amer. Indian origin.]
A S. American tree, *Nectandra pichurim*, of the laurel family; (in full ***pichurim bean***) the aromatic cotyledon of the seed of this tree, used in cookery and medicine.

piciform /ˈpʌɪsɪfɔːm, ˈpɪkɪ-/ *adjective.* **L19.**
[from mod. Latin *Piciformes* (see below), from Latin *picus* woodpecker: see -FORM.]
ORNITHOLOGY. Belonging or pertaining to the order Piciformes, which includes woodpeckers, toucans, barbets, and honeyguides.

pick /pɪk/ *noun*[1]. **ME.**
[Var. of PIKE *noun*[1]. See also PECK *noun*[2].]
▶ **I 1** A tool consisting of a long shaft set at right angles in the middle of a curved iron or steel bar with a point at one end and a chisel-edge or point at the other, used for breaking up hard ground, rock, etc. **ME.** ▸**b** A pointed or edged hammer used for dressing millstones. **L15.**

📖 **1** J. A. MICHENER Small picks . . used by modern archaeologists. J. G. FARRELL A short-handled pick . . to loosen the earth. J. GARDAM The picks of the miners long ago.

▶ **II 2** = PIKE *noun*[1] 3. Long *obsolete* exc. *Scot.* **ME.**
3 †**a** A tool for gathering peas, beans, etc. Only in **LME.** ▸**b** A pitchfork; = PIKE *noun*[1] 3b. *dial.* **L18.** ▸**c** An instrument for detaching limpets etc. *Scot. dial.* **L19.**
†**4** = PIKE *noun*[1] 2. **L15–L17.**
5 An instrument for picking. Chiefly as 2nd elem. of comb., as ***ear-pick***, ***toothpick***. Cf. earlier PIKE *noun*[1] 2c. **E17.** ▸**b** A plectrum. *colloq.* **L19.**
▶ **III 6** = PIKE *noun*[1] 5. *obsolete* exc. *dial.* **L16.**
▶ **IV 7** A diamond in playing-cards. *obsolete* exc. *north.* **L16.**

Comb.: **pickman** a labourer who works with a pick; **pick-pole** *US* = PICAROON *noun*[2].

pick /pɪk/ *noun*[2] *& adjective.* **E16.**
[from PICK *verb*[1].]
▶ **A** *noun.* **1** An act of picking; a stroke with something pointed. **E16.**
2 A mouthful of food; a sparing meal; *transf.* a very small part (*of* something), a particle, a jot, (freq. in neg. contexts). Now *dial.* **L17.**
3 PRINTING. A speck of hardened ink or dirt on type in forme, causing a blot; an intrusive piece of metal on an electrotype or stereotype plate. **L17.**
4 An act of choosing or selecting something; the right of selection; that which is selected, a choice; *spec.* (***a***) *N. Amer. colloq.* a person chosen as a member of a team etc.; (***b***) *colloq.* the favourite to win a contest or race; the best part or example of a thing. **M18.**
5 ART. An area filled in with dots. **M19.**
6 The quantity or part of a crop picked or gathered at a particular time. **L19.**
7 BASKETBALL. A permissible block. **M20.**

📖 **2** AUSTIN CLARKE A pick of meat on Feastdays. W. TREVOR They didn't take a pick of notice. **4** CLIVE JAMES Take your pick from . . baklava . . and almond triangles. K. GIBBONS Foster is not the right pick. M. SCAMMELL The pick of the best jobs available. M. MOORCOCK To have his pick of the ladies.

▶ **B** *adjective.* Best. Cf. PICKLOCK *noun*[2] *& adjective*[2]. *colloq.* **E19.**

pick /pɪk/ *noun*[3]. *Scot. & north.* **E17.**
[from PICK *verb*[2].]
1 An act of throwing or pitching; a throw, a pitch. **E17.** ▸**b** A stone etc. pitched or thrown in a game. **L19.**
2 An emetic. *dial.* **E19.**
3 WEAVING. A throw of the shuttle, esp. as a unit of measurement in calculating the speed of the loom; *transf.* a single thread of the weft (produced by one pick of the shuttle), esp. as a unit of measurement for expressing the fineness of a fabric. **M19.**

†**pick** *noun*[4] see PIKE *noun*[5].

pick /pɪk/ *verb*[1]. Also (earlier, now *dial.*) **pike** /pʌɪk/. **ME.**
[Origin uncertain: cf. French *piquer*, Middle Low German, Middle Dutch *picken* (Dutch *pikken*), PICK *noun*[1], PIKE *noun*[1].]
▶ **I 1** *verb trans.* **a** Pierce, indent, or dig into the surface of (a thing) by striking with a pick or other pointed instrument. (Earlier as PICKING *noun*[1] 1a.) Now *rare.* **ME.** ▸†**b** Of a bird: strike with the beak, peck. **M16–M17.** ▸**c** Make (a hole) by piercing or probing with a pointed instrument. **M17.**
2 *verb trans.* Probe (part of the body, a pimple, etc.) with the finger, a pointed instrument, etc., to remove unwanted matter. **ME.**
3 *verb trans.* Remove unwanted matter from (a thing), esp. in preparing food prior to cooking; pluck (a fowl etc.); remove the stalks etc. from (esp. soft fruit), hull. **ME.** ▸**b** Remove adhering flesh from (a bone, carcass, etc.), esp bit by bit. **L15.**
†**4** *verb trans.* Make (a person) clean, trim, or neat; (of a bird) preen (itself). **ME–L17.**
5 *verb trans.* Pull apart the strands of (wool etc.) with a pointed instrument; card. **M16.**
6 *verb trans.* Pluck (the strings) in guitar-playing etc.; play (a guitar etc.). Chiefly *N. Amer.* **M19.**

📖 **2** M. COKE He picked his Nose, which . . is neither graceful nor royal. G. NAYLOR You were picking your teeth with a . . straw. **3** MOLLIE HARRIS The art of picking ducks. **b** R. HODGSON Left him for the birds to pick, Left him there for carrion. S. COOPER He picked the fish clean.

▶ **II 7** *verb trans.* Detach and take (something) from its place of attachment, esp. with the fingers; *spec.* pluck (a flower or fruit) from a stem, tree, etc. Also foll. by *off.* **ME.** ▸†**b** *fig.* Infer, deduce. **M16–E17.**
8 *verb intrans.* (with *at*) & *trans.* (Of a bird) take up (small bits of food) with the beak; (of a person or animal) eat (food or a meal) fastidiously, in small mouthfuls, or without interest. **ME.**
9 *verb trans.* Choose or select carefully from among a group. **ME.** ▸**b** *verb trans. & intrans.* Make (one's way) by treading carefully or fastidiously. **E18.** ▸**c** *verb intrans.* Search with some selection. **E19.** ▸**d** *verb trans.* Guess; predict. *Austral. & NZ colloq.* **E20.**
10 Seek and find an opportunity for (esp. a quarrel or fight). **LME.**

📖 **7** R. BRAUTIGAN Pick the . . cherries on the tree. M. LEITCH He . . picked a piece of fluff from his sleeve. S. HASTINGS They strolled across the fields . . picking cowslips. **8** R. L. STEVENSON We'll pick a bit of dinner. A. LURIE Jeanne sat . . picking at the angel-food cake. **9** P. HENISSART 'She really picks them,' muttered McGuire. 'Does she know who he is?' L. DUNCAN He said I picked nice adjectives. P. AUSTER He looked through the pile, trying to decide which one to pick. P. LIVELY I was the form outcast . . who was never picked for teams. **b** G. GREENE Like a Victorian lady picking her way across a muddy street. **10** C. PETERS She picked quarrels with him constantly.

▶ **III 11** *verb trans.* Rob; steal. Now only in ***pick a pocket***, ***pick a wallet***, etc., or (fig.) ***pick a person's brains*** below. ME. ▶†**b** *verb intrans.* Practise petty theft. LME–M16.

12 *verb trans.* Open (a lock) with an instrument other than the key, esp. with intent to steal. LME.

📖 **11** R. P. JHABVALA The young man's pocket was picked. J. CHEEVER I picked his wallet of fifty dollars.

Phrases: ***a crow to pick***: see CROW *noun*[1] 1. ***have a bone to pick with someone***: see BONE *noun*. **pick and choose** select carefully or fastidiously. **pick a person's brains** elicit ideas, information, etc., from a person for one's own use. ***pick a salad***. †**pick a thank** curry favour. ***pick holes in***: see HOLE *noun*[1]. **pick one's feet up** walk without stumbling. ***pick out of a hat***: see HAT *noun*. ***pick to pieces***: see PIECE *noun*.

With adverbs in specialized senses: **pick in** ART fill in (an area) with dots or small marks. **pick off** (*a*) aim at and shoot one by one without haste; *fig.* eliminate (opposition etc.) singly; (*b*) BASEBALL put out (a runner) at a base; (see also sense 7 above). **pick out** (*a*) extract by picking; dig out; (*b*) select from a group with care or deliberation; (*c*) distinguish by sight or hearing from surrounding objects etc.; (*d*) make out (the meaning of a passage etc.); ascertain (the facts of a matter); (*e*) play (a tune) by ear on the piano etc.; (*f*) highlight (a painting etc.) with touches of another colour; *esp.* (freq. foll. by *in*, *with*) accentuate (decoration etc.) with a contrasting colour. **pick over** sort, select the best from (esp. soft fruit). **pick up** (*a*) take hold of and raise or lift from the ground or any low position; take up (a stitch) with a knitting-needle; *refl.* recover from a fall, setback, etc; ***pick up one's crumbs***: see CRUMB *noun*; ***pick up stakes***: see STAKE *noun*[1]; (*b*) *verb phr. intrans.* collect unretrieved game after a shooting party; (*c*) acquire or gain by chance or without effort; (*d*) (now *rare*) capture (a ship); (*e*) fetch (a person, animal, or thing) from the charge of another person; stop for and take along with one, esp. in a vehicle; (*f*) make the acquaintance of (a person) casually, esp. with the intention of having a sexual relationship; (*g*) (of the police etc.) arrest, apprehend; (*h*) *slang* rob; steal; (*i*) find fault with, call to account (*for*); (*j*) CRICKET succeed in hitting (a ball, esp. a low one); (*k*) detect by scrutiny or with a telescope, radio, searchlight, etc.; regain sight of or contact with (a track, trail, etc.); (*l*) resume or continue (an activity); renew (a friendship); (*m*) (cause to) revive, improve, or recover; (*n*) *verb phr. intrans. & trans.* (of a vehicle, aircraft, etc.) recover (speed); (*o*) **pick up on**, catch up with; become aware of, appreciate; (*p*) undertake to pay (a bill etc.); cf. ***pick up the tab*** s.v. TAB *noun*[1] 4; (*q*) *verb phr. trans. & intrans.* (*colloq.*, chiefly *N. Amer.*) tidy or clean up (a room); (*r*) GOLF pick up one's ball, esp. when conceding a hole.

With prepositions in specialized senses: **pick at** — (*a*) make a movement to pick; (*b*) (now *dial.*, *US*, & *Austral.*) = ***pick on*** (a) below; (see also sense 8 above). **pick on** — (*a*) find fault with, nag at; *esp.* single out for adverse criticism, victimize; (*b*) select, choose.

Comb.: **pick-and-mix** (also **pick'n'mix**) *noun & adjective* (*a*) *noun* sweets or other items chosen from a selection of different kinds and purchased together; (*b*) *adjective* denoting a method of assembling something by choosing elements or items from among a large variety of different possibilities; **pick-and-roll** BASKETBALL a manoeuvre in which an offensive player frees a teammate holding the ball using a pick on an opposing defender, and then moves towards the basket for a pass. **pick-a-tree** (chiefly *north.*) the green woodpecker; **pick-cheese** *dial.* the great tit, the blue tit; **pick-me-up** *colloq.* (*a*) a restorative drink etc., a tonic; (*b*) a cheering experience, piece of news, etc.; **pick-proof** *adjective* (of a lock) secure against picking; **pickthank** *noun & adjective* (now *arch.* & *dial.*) (*a*) *noun* a flatterer, a sycophant; (*b*) *adjective* flattering, sycophantic; **pick-your-own** *adjective* (of a farm etc.) operating a system whereby the customer picks his or her own produce for purchase; (of such produce) sold under this system.

■ **pickable** *adjective* able to be picked (earlier in UNPICKABLE) L19.

pick /pɪk/ *verb*[2]. See also PECK *verb*[2]. ME.
[Var. of PITCH *verb*[2].]
†**1** *verb trans.* Fix or stick (something pointed) in the ground etc.; pitch (a tent etc.). *rare*. ME–L16.
2 *verb trans. & intrans.* Thrust; throw; pitch. Now *dial.* L15.
3 *verb trans.* Vomit, throw *up*. Now only *north.* M16.
4 *verb trans.* Of an animal: give birth to (young) prematurely. *dial.* L18.

pickaback *adverb, adjective, noun, & verb* var. of PIGGYBACK.

†**pickadill** *noun* var. of PICCADILL.

pickage /ˈpɪkɪdʒ/ *noun*. LME.
[Anglo-Norman *picage*, from Old & mod. French *piquer*: see -AGE.]
A toll paid for breaking the ground in setting up stalls etc. at fairs. Cf. TERRAGE.

pickaninny *noun & adjective* see PICCANINNY.

†**pickard** *noun*. M16–E19.
[from PICK *noun*[1] or *verb*[1] + CARD *noun*[1].]
A card with spikes or teeth for raising a nap on cloth.

pickaxe /ˈpɪkaks/ *noun*. Also ***-ax**; (earlier) †**pikoys**. ME.
[Old French *picois*, later alt. by assoc. with AXE *noun*[1]. Cf. PIKE *noun*[1].]
▶ **A** *noun*. = PICK *noun*[1] 1. Formerly also, a mattock. ME.
▶ **B** *verb*. **1** *verb trans.* Break (the ground etc.) with a pickaxe. E19.
2 *verb intrans.* Work with a pickaxe. M19.

picked /ˈpɪkɪd/ *adjective*[1]. LME.
[from PICK *noun*[1] + -ED[2].]
1 Having a sharp point or spine; = PIKED *adjective*[1] 1. Now *arch.* & *dial.* LME. ▶**b** In names of animals: spiny. Chiefly in ***picked dogfish*** below. M18.
†**2** = PIKED *adjective*[1] 2. M16–M18.

Special collocations: **picked dogfish** = *spur-dog* s.v. SPUR *noun*[1]. †**picked-hatch** a hatch with a row of spikes at the top; *transf.* a brothel.

picked /pɪkt/, *poet.* ˈpɪkɪd/ *adjective*[2]. LME.
[from PICK *verb*[1] + -ED[1].]
1 That has been picked. LME.
†**2** Adorned, ornate; refined; particular, fastidious. LME–M17.

📖 **2** SHAKES. *Haml.* The age is grown so picked.

pickeer /pɪˈkɪə/ *verb intrans. arch.* M17.
[App. from Dutch *pickeren* prick, spur, from French *piquer*.]
†**1** Maraud, pillage, plunder; practise piracy. M17–E18.
2 Skirmish; scout around. M17.
†**3** *fig.* **a** Flirt. M17–E18. ▶**b** Bicker. L17–M19.
■ **pickeerer** *noun* M17.

pickelhaube /ˈpɪk(ə)l(h)aʊbə/ *noun*. Pl. **-haubes**, **-hauben** /-(h)aʊbən/. L19.
[German.]
Hist. A spiked helmet worn by German soldiers, esp. before and during the war of 1914–18.

picker /ˈpɪkə/ *noun*[1]. Also (earlier, now *dial.*) **piker** /ˈpʌɪkə/. ME.
[from PICK *verb*[1] + -ER[1].]
1 A person who picks; *spec.* (*a*) a thief; (*b*) a person who picks or gathers, esp. a specified type of produce. ME.
2 Any of various tools or machines used for picking. E17.
3 A young cod. *Scot. & US dial.* L19.
4 A person who plucks the strings of a guitar, banjo, etc. Orig. *US*. E20.
1 ***fruit-picker***, ***hop-picker***, ***potato-picker***, etc.
Comb.: **picker-up** *Austral. & NZ* an assistant in a shearing shed who gathers up the fleece as it is shorn.

picker /ˈpɪkə/ *noun*[2]. E19.
[from PICK *verb*[2] + -ER[1].]
WEAVING. A small instrument in the shuttle-box of a loom which drives the shuttle to and fro through the warp.

pickerel /ˈpɪk(ə)r(ə)l/ *noun*[1]. ME.
[Dim. of PIKE *noun*[3]: see -REL and cf. Anglo-Latin *pikerellus*. Cf. PICAREL.]
1 A young pike. ME.
2 Any of several (esp. smaller) kinds of American pike, as *Esox americanus* and *E. niger*. Chiefly *N. Amer.* M18.
Comb.: **pickerel frog** *US* a common N. American frog, *Rana palustris*; **pickerel-weed** any of several freshwater plants; *esp.* (*a*) *dial.* any of various pondweeds (genus *Potamogeton*); (*b*) the N. American plant *Pontederia cordata* (family Pontederiaceae), with heart-shaped leaves and spikes of blue flowers.

pickerel /ˈpɪk(ə)r(ə)l/ *noun*[2]. *Scot.* M19.
[Prob. from PICK *verb*[1] + -REL (cf. DOTTEREL).]
A small wading bird; *esp.* the dunlin.

Pickering series /ˈpɪk(ə)rɪŋ sɪəriːz/ *noun phr.* E20.
[Edward Charles *Pickering* (1846–1919), US astronomer.]
PHYSICS. A series of lines in the spectrum of ionized helium, between 1.01 and 0.36 micrometre.

pickery /ˈpɪkəri/ *noun*. E16.
[from PICKER *noun*[1] + -ERY.]
SCOTS LAW (now *Hist.*). Petty theft.

picket /ˈpɪkɪt/ *noun*[1]. Also (esp. in sense 4) **pi(c)quet**. L17.
[Old & mod. French *piquet*, from *piquer* prick, pierce, from *pic* pike: see -ET[1].]
▶ **I 1** A stake with a pointed top on which a soldier was required to stand on one foot as a form of punishment; this punishment. *obsolete* exc. *Hist.* L17.
2 *gen.* A pointed stake, post, or peg driven into the ground for use in fences or (*Hist.*) fortifications, or to mark a position in surveying, secure a tent, tether a horse, etc. E18.
3 An elongated rifle bullet with a conical front. M19.

📖 **2** *Sun (Baltimore)* The fence pickets protrude . . out of the sand. *attrib.*: G. NAYLOR It was the smallest house . . with iron picket fences. **b** J. McDOUGALL Tamarack logs to make a strong, high picket.

▶ **II 4** MILITARY. **a** A small body of troops or a single soldier sent out to watch for the enemy or held in quarters in readiness for such duty. M18. ▶**b** A camp guard on police duty in a garrison town etc.; a group of sentries. L18. ▶**c** Duty as a picket. Chiefly in ***on picket***. L18.
5 A person or group of people stationed outside a place of work with the aim of persuading people, esp. workers, not to enter during a strike etc.; an act of picketing. M19.

📖 **4** *Saturday Review* The Imperial Guard . . attacked our picquets, but were repulsed. **b** J. G. FARRELL We'll establish pickets every few yards. **5** *Oxford Star* The incident happened during a . . picket at Gate 16. *Building Today* Leading . . figures formed a picket to keep contractors off the site.

Comb.: **picket-boat** a vessel employed for reconnoitring or scouting in advance of the fleet etc.; **picket-house** MILITARY the building where a picket is stationed in a garrison; **picket line** a boundary established by workers on strike, esp. at an entrance to a place of work, which others are asked not to cross; **picket-pin (gopher)** *US* a ground squirrel of western N. America, esp. *Spermophilus richardsoni*.

picket *noun*[2] var. of PIQUET *noun*[1].

picket /ˈpɪkɪt/ *verb*. M18.
[from PICKET *noun*[1].]
1 *verb trans.* **a** Enclose with pickets or stakes; fence. M18. ▶**b** Tether (a horse etc.) to a picket. E19.
2 *verb trans.* Punish or torture with the picket. *obsolete* exc. *Hist.* M18.
3 *verb trans. & intrans.* MILITARY. Post (soldiers) as a picket. L18.
4 a *verb trans.* Establish a picket at (a place of work etc.). M19. ▶**b** *verb intrans.* Demonstrate as a picket. M19.

📖 **1b** *Horse & Hound* A Cavalry Regiment must . . be able to picket its horses. **4a** R. BRAUTIGAN A more valid protest than picketing missile bases. **b** *Times* Strikers . . were picketing near the main gates.

■ **picketer** *noun* M19.

picketing /ˈpɪkɪtɪŋ/ *noun*. M18.
[from PICKET *verb*, *noun*[1] + -ING[1].]
1 The action of PICKET *verb*. M18.
2 A fence made of pickets. *US*. M18.
1 ***secondary picketing***: see SECONDARY *adjective*.

pickfork /ˈpɪkfɔːk/ *noun. obsolete* exc. *dial.* ME.
[from PICK *noun*[1] or PICK *noun*[3] + FORK *noun*. Cf. PITCHFORK *noun*[1].]
A pitchfork.

pickie /ˈpɪki/ *noun. Scot. & Anglo-Irish local.* L19.
[from PICK *noun*[3] + -IE.]
Hopscotch.

picking /ˈpɪkɪŋ/ *noun*[1]. Also (now *dial.*) **piking** /ˈpʌɪkɪŋ/. OE.
[from PICK *verb*[1] + -ING[1].]
1 †**a** A mark produced by piercing or pricking; a prick. Only in OE. ▶**b** That which is or may be picked or picked up; an amount picked; in *pl.*, remaining scraps, leftovers, gleanings. M17. ▶**c** A gain, a profit, *esp.* one acquired fortuitously or without effort. Usu. in *pl.* M18.
2 The action of PICK *verb*[1]; an instance of this. ME.
3 *spec.* Theft; *esp.* petty theft, pilfering. LME.

📖 **1b** P. AUSTER Pickings for scavengers were slim in this neighbourhood. M. SPARK Carrion crow descended on Martin for the last-minute pickings. **c** *Times* The City is expecting rich pickings from the privatization of the . . industry. M. MOORCOCK The foxes . . had discovered the city to be congenial, with easy pickings. **2** H. WILLIAMSON Germans had been digging, when all sound of picking had stopped. B. MASON The nagging and picking went on in Bo's honey-smooth voice. J. GARDAM There was a great blackberry picking going on.

Comb.: **picking-belt** a conveyor belt on which coal is picked or sorted.

picking /ˈpɪkɪŋ/ *verbal noun*[2]. E19.
[from PICK *verb*[2] + -ING[1].]
The action of PICK *verb*[2].
Comb.: **picking-fork** a pitchfork; **picking-hole** *north.* a window or door in a barn through which bales are thrown; **picking peg** = PICKER *noun*[2].

pickle /ˈpɪk(ə)l/ *noun*[1]. LME.
[Middle Low German, Middle Dutch *pekel* (whence also German *Pökel*), of unkn. origin.]
1 Orig., a spicy sauce served with meat. Later, a salty or acid liquor (usu. brine or vinegar, freq. seasoned or spiced) in which food, esp. vegetables or fruit, is preserved. LME. ▶**b** *transf.* An acid or other chemical solution for cleaning or bleaching metal, wood, etc. L18.
2 *fig.* A plight, a predicament. Now *colloq.* M16. ▶**b** Condition. *rare*. E18. ▶**c** A person, esp. a boy, who is always causing trouble; a mischievous child. *colloq.* L18. ▶†**d** In *pl.* Nonsense, rubbish. *slang*. M–L19.
3 A particular type of food preserved in a pickle and eaten as a relish. E18.

📖 **1** ***a rod in pickle***: see ROD *noun*. **in pickle** *fig.* kept in readiness for use. **2** S. PLATH Getting stuck with a baby, and then you'd . . be in a pickle. *Waterski International* Casso got into a terrible pickle when missing a buoy. **3** R. WEST Some cold beef and pickles in the bar. ***cauliflower pickle***, ***lime pickle***, ***mango pickle***, etc.

pickle /ˈpɪk(ə)l/ *noun*[2] & *adjective*. *Scot. & north.* M16.
[Origin unkn.]
▶ **A** *noun*. **1** A grain of wheat, barley, or oats. M16. ▶**b** A grain or particle of sand, dust, etc. E17.
2 A small quantity or amount. M17.
▶ **B** *adjective*. A small quantity or amount of. M17.

pickle /ˈpɪk(ə)l/ *verb*[1] *trans.* M16.
[from PICKLE *noun*[1].]
1 Steep in pickle; preserve in pickle. Also, preserve in salt. M16.
2 NAUTICAL HISTORY. Rub salt or vinegar on the back of (a person) after whipping or flogging. E18.
3 Steep in or treat with an acid or other chemical solution for cleaning, bleaching, etc. M19.

📖 **1** MOLLIE HARRIS Hams . . pickled . . in a mixture of old beer, brown sugar, juniper berries and salt. R. DAHL The only way to get the body home . . was to pickle it.

■ **pickled** *adjective* (*a*) that has been pickled; (*b*) (of wooden furniture etc.) artificially aged; (*c*) *slang* drunk; †(*d*) mischievous, roguish: **M16.**

pickle /ˈpɪk(ə)l/ *verb*². *obsolete* exc. *dial.* **LME.**
[from PICK *verb*¹ + -LE³.]
1 *verb trans.* Clean or clear by minute picking. *rare.* **LME.**
2 Eat sparingly or fastidiously; pick at (food). **E16.**

pickle-herring /ˈpɪk(ə)lhɛrɪŋ/ *noun.* Now *rare.* **L16.**
[In sense 1 from Middle Dutch *peeckel-harinck*; sense 2 of unkn. origin.]
†**1** A pickled herring. **L16–L18.**
2 A clown, a buffoon. **E18.**

pickler /ˈpɪklə/ *noun.* **M18.**
[from PICKLE *verb*¹ + -ER¹.]
1 A vegetable grown or suitable for pickling. **M18.**
2 A person who pickles vegetables etc. **M19.**

picklock /ˈpɪklɒk/ *noun*¹ & *adjective*¹. **M16.**
[from PICK *verb*¹ + LOCK *noun*².]
▸ **A** *noun.* **1** A person, esp. a thief, who picks locks. **M16.**
2 An instrument for picking locks. **L16.**
▸ **B** *attrib. adjective.* Used for picking a lock. **E17.**

picklock /ˈpɪklɒk/ *noun*² & *adjective*². **L18.**
[from PICK *adjective* or PICK *verb*¹ + LOCK *noun*¹.]
(Designating) English wool of the highest quality.

pickney *noun & adjective* var. of PICCANINNY.

pick-off /ˈpɪkɒf/ *noun.* **M20.**
[from *pick off* s.v. PICK *verb*¹.]
1 Chiefly AERONAUTICS. A device in a control or guidance system which produces or alters a pneumatic or electrical output in response to a change in motion. **M20.**
2 BASEBALL. An act of catching a runner off base by means of the pitcher or catcher suddenly throwing the ball to that base. **M20.**

📖 **2** *attrib.*: *Washington Post* Ryan's attempted pickoff throw went wide.

pickpocket /ˈpɪkpɒkɪt/ *noun & verb.* **L16.**
[from PICK *verb*¹ + POCKET *noun.*]
▸ **A** *noun.* **1** A person who steals from the pockets of others. **L16.**
2 Any of various weeds which impoverish the land, *esp.* shepherd's purse, *Capsella bursa-pastoris*, and corn spurrey, *Spergula arvensis*. *dial.* **L19.**
▸ **B** *verb intrans. & trans.* Steal from the pockets of (a person). Chiefly as ***pickpocketing*** *verbal noun.* **L17.**

pickpurse /ˈpɪkpəːs/ *noun. arch.* **LME.**
[from PICK *verb*¹ + PURSE *noun.*]
†**1** = PICKPOCKET *noun* 1. **LME–E18.**
2 = PICKPOCKET *noun* 2. *dial.* **L16.**

Pick's disease /ˈpɪks dɪˌziːz/ *noun phr.* **E20.**
[In sense 1 from Friedel *Pick* (1867–1926), Bohemian physician; in sense 2 from Arnold *Pick* (1851–1924), Bohemian neurologist.]
1 A form of polyserositis involving constrictive pericarditis, hepatomegaly, and ascites. **E20.**
2 A rare form of progressive dementia, usu. arising in late middle age and often familial, which is caused by localized atrophy of the brain. **M20.**

picksome /ˈpɪks(ə)m/ *adjective. arch.* **M19.**
[from PICK *verb*¹ + -SOME¹.]
Fastidious; particular.

picktooth /ˈpɪktuːθ/ *noun & adjective.* Now *rare.* Pl. **-s.** **M16.**
[from PICK *verb*¹ + TOOTH *noun.*]
▸ **A** *noun.* A toothpick. **M16.**
▸ **B** *adjective.* Idle, indolent; leisurely. **E18.**

pick-up /ˈpɪkʌp/ *noun & adjective.* **M19.**
[from *pick up* s.v. PICK *verb*¹.]
▸ **A** *noun.* **I 1** A thing picked up; *spec.* a person met casually, *esp.* one with whom a person aims to establish a sexual relationship. **M19.**
2 The action or an act of picking up. **L19.**
3 The quantity of unretrieved game collected after a shoot. **L19.**
4 The capacity for increasing speed; acceleration. **E20.**
5 Reception of signals by electrical apparatus; *spec.* interference. **E20.**
6 NUCLEAR PHYSICS. A nuclear reaction in which an incident particle such as a proton captures a nucleon from a target atom. Also ***pick-up reaction***. **M20.**
7 MUSIC. A series of introductory notes leading into the opening part of a tune; an anacrusis. **M20.**
8 Tendency to pick up or absorb a substance. **M20.**

📖 **2** W. G. GRACE Pick-up and return must be one action. *Daily Telegraph* Sales showed their expected pick-up. *Arizona Daily Star* Pick-up of trash will be subject to a . . charge. *Soldier* An internal rescue hoist . . for pick ups in inaccessible areas. **4** *Athletics Weekly* It was . . his pick-up which gave him the . . lead.

▸ **II 9** A thing which picks up something; a passenger or goods vehicle, *esp.* a slow or last train. **L19.**

10 a = *pick-me-up* s.v. PICK *verb*¹. **L19.** ▸**b** A current collector on an electric tram etc. **L19.** ▸**c** A sensor, a transducer; a device that produces an electrical signal in response to some other kind of signal or charge; *esp.* (*a*) the part of a record-player carrying the stylus, a cartridge; an analogous part of a compact-disc player; (*b*) a device attached to or forming part of a musical instrument which picks up sound vibrations to be amplified electrically. **E20.**
11 ANGLING. A semicircular loop of metal for guiding the line back on to the spool as it is reeled in. **M20.**
12 A small truck or van with an open body, used for carrying light loads. **M20.**

📖 **10c** *Canberra Times* Features . . 3-beam laser pick-up for improved tracking accuracy. **12** R. THOMAS Elfed the Milk . . in his pick-up loaded with crates.

▸ **B** *attrib.* or as *adjective.* **1** Impromptu; done or formed on the spur of the moment or with whatever components etc. are to hand. **M19.**
2 That picks up or is used in picking up. **L19.**

📖 **1** D. BAKER He . . made records with . . many pick-up bands.

Special collocations: **pick-up arm** in a record-player, the arm carrying the pick-up. **pick-up truck** = sense A.12 above. **pick-up tube** TELEVISION a vacuum tube that produces an electrical signal corresponding to an optical image formed in it or on it; a camera tube.

pickwick /ˈpɪkwɪk/ *noun*¹. **M19.**
[formed as PICKWICKIAN.]
Hist. A cheap kind of cigar.

pickwick /ˈpɪkwɪk/ *noun*². **M19.**
[from PICK *verb*¹ + WICK *noun*¹.]
Hist. A piece of wire used to pull up the wick of an oil-lamp.

Pickwickian /pɪkˈwɪkɪən/ *adjective & noun.* **M19.**
[from *Pickwick* (see below) + -IAN.]
▸ **A** *adjective.* **1** Of, pertaining to, or resembling Mr Pickwick, a character in Dickens's *Pickwick Papers* (1837), and founder of the Pickwick Club described in the novel, esp. in being generous, jovial, and plump; (of a word or sense of a word) not literally meant, misused so as to avoid offence. **M19.**
2 MEDICINE. (Also **p-**.) Having or designating a syndrome occurring in some obese people which is characterized by somnolence, respiratory abnormalities, and bulimia. **M20.**
▸ **B** *noun.* **1** A member of the Pickwick Club. **M19.**
2 MEDICINE. A person with the Pickwickian syndrome. **M20.**
■ **Pickwickianly** *adverb* **L19.**

picky /ˈpɪki/ *adjective. colloq.* **M19.**
[from PICK *verb*¹ + -Y¹.]
Excessively fastidious; fussy, finicky.

📖 *Practical Parenting* Some children are picky eaters. A. TYLER It's just growing pains that make her so picky and critical.

■ **pickily** *adverb* **L20.** **pickiness** *noun* **L20.**

picloram /ˈpɪklərəm/ *noun.* **M20.**
[from PIC(OLINE + CH)LOR-¹ + AM(INE.]
A derivative of picolinic acid used as a herbicide and defoliant; 4-amino-3,5,6-trichloropicolinic acid, $C_5NCl_3 \cdot NH_2 \cdot COOH$.

picnic /ˈpɪknɪk/ *noun & verb.* **M18.**
[French *pique-nique*, of unkn. origin.]
▸ **A** *noun.* **1** Orig., a social event for which each guest provided a share of the food. Later, an excursion to the country, seaside, etc., taking food to be eaten outside. Now also, any informal meal eaten out of doors. **M18.**
2 *fig.* Orig., an assemblage, an anthology. Later, an agreeable experience; a straightforward task (freq. in neg. contexts). *colloq.* **E19.** ▸**b** A disagreeable task or experience; a fuss. *Austral. & NZ colloq.* (*iron.*) **L19.**
3 *Hist.* A member of the Picnic Society (see below). **E19.**
4 In full ***picnic ham***. A cut of shoulder bacon in the form of a ham. *N. Amer.* **E20.**

📖 **1** attrib.: ***picnic basket***, ***picnic hamper***, ***picnic lunch***, ***picnic site***, etc. ***teddy bears' picnic***: see TEDDY BEAR 1. **2** M. MITCHELL Dazzled by these tales, freedom became a never-ending picnic, a barbecue . . a carnival. *Scientific American* Compared with introducing genetically engineered crops, it has been a picnic. **no picnic**, **not a picnic** not an easy task, a formidable undertaking.

Comb.: **picnic area** a piece of ground set aside for picnics; **picnic blanket** a thick blanket for spreading on the ground at a picnic; **picnic chair** a usu. collapsible chair for use at a picnic; **picnic ground** = *picnic area* above; *picnic ham*: see sense 4 above; **picnic lunch** a packed lunch; **picnic meal** (*a*) a meal eaten as a picnic; (*b*) a quick meal eaten indoors; **picnic plate** a plastic or paper plate; **picnic races** *Austral. & NZ* a race meeting for amateurs held in a rural area; **Picnic Society** *Hist.* a fashionable society in London in the early 19th cent. whose members contributed to mutual social events and entertainments; **picnic table** a usu. collapsible table for use at a picnic.

▸ **B** *verb.* Infl. **-ck-**.
1 *verb intrans.* Hold or take part in a picnic. **E19.**
2 *verb trans.* Provide or constitute a picnic for. *rare.* **M19.**

📖 **1** P. CHAPLIN They played poker, swam, picnicked.

■ **picnicker** *noun* a person who takes part in a picnic **M19.** **picˈnickery** *noun* (*a*) an assemblage of various items; (*b*) *sing.* & in *pl.*, the requisites for a picnic: **E19.** †**Picnickian** *noun* (*rare*) (*a*) = PICNIC *noun* 3; (*b*) = PICNICKER: **E–M19.** **picnicky** *adjective* (*colloq.*) of, pertaining to, or characteristic of a picnic **L19.**

†**pico** *noun.* **L17–M18.**
[Spanish Cf. PIC *noun*².]
A peak, a conical mountain; *spec.* the Peak of Tenerife.

pico- /ˈpiːkəʊ, ˈpʌɪkəʊ/ *combining form.* **E20.**
[from Spanish *pico* beak, peak, little bit: see -O-.]
1 Used in names of units of measurement to denote a factor of one million-millionth (10^{-12}), as ***picofarad***, ***picogram***, ***picosecond***, etc. Abbreviation ***p***.
2 With the sense 'extremely small', as ***picornavirus***.

picoline /ˈpɪkəliːn/ *noun.* **M19.**
[from Latin *pic-*, *pix* pitch + *oleum* oil + -INE⁵.]
CHEMISTRY. A colourless liquid heteroaromatic base with a pungent smell, obtained from coal tar, bone-oil, etc.; 2-methylpyridine, $C_5H_4N \cdot CH_3$.
■ **picoˈlinic** *adjective*: ***picolinic acid***, a crystalline acid, $C_5H_4N \cdot COOH$, derived from picoline **L19.**

picong /ˈpiːkɒŋ/ *noun. W. Indies.* **M20.**
[Spanish *picón*.]
Verbal taunting or ridicule; banter.

picoplankton /ˈpiːkəʊplaŋkt(ə)n/ *noun.* **L20.**
[from PICO- + PLANKTON.]
BIOLOGY. Plankton consisting of organisms between 0.2 and 2.0 micrometres in diameter, or with a wet weight of the order of a picogram.
■ **picoplankˈtonic** *adjective* **L20.**

picornavirus /pɪˈkɔːnəvʌɪrəs/ *noun.* **M20.**
[from PICO- + RNA + VIRUS.]
MICROBIOLOGY. Any of a group of very small animal viruses consisting of single-stranded RNA in an icosahedral capsid with no envelope, including enteroviruses, rhinoviruses, and the virus of foot-and-mouth disease.

picory /ˈpɪk(ə)ri/ *noun.* Long *arch.* **L16.**
[French *picorée* from Spanish *pecoreá*, from *pecorear* steal or carry off cattle.]
Pillage; looting.

picot /ˈpiːkəʊ/ *noun & verb.* **E17.**
[French, dim. of *pic* peak, point, prick: see -OT¹.]
▸ **A** *noun.* Any of a series of small loops worked in lace or embroidery, used to form an ornamental edging, buttonhole, etc. Also called ***pearl***. **E17.**
▸ **B** *verb trans.* Ornament (cloth etc.) with picots. **E20.**

picotah /pɪˈkɒtə/ *noun.* **E19.**
[Portuguese = ship's pump-brake.]
In southern India, a counterpoised device for raising water.

picotee /pɪkəˈtiː/ *noun & adjective.* **E18.**
[French *picoté(e)* pa. pple of *picoter* mark with points, prick, formed as PICOT.]
▸ **A** *noun.* A variety of carnation, having light petals marked or edged with a darker colour. **E18.**
▸ **B** *adjective.* Of a colour, pattern, etc.: resembling that of the picotee. **L19.**

picquet *noun*¹ var. of PIQUET *noun*¹.

picquet *noun*² see PICKET *noun*¹.

picr- *combining form* see PICRO-.

picral /ˈpɪkral/ *noun.* **E20.**
[from PICRIC + AL(COHOL.]
METALLURGY. An etchant consisting of a solution of picric acid in ethyl alcohol.

picric /ˈpɪkrɪk/ *adjective.* **M19.**
[from Greek *pikros* bitter + -IC.]
CHEMISTRY. ***picric acid***, a crystalline acid obtained by nitrating phenol, used in dyeing and in the manufacture of explosives; 2,4,6-trinitrophenol, $C_6H_2(NO_2)_3OH$.
■ **picrate** *noun* a salt or ester of picric acid **M19.** **picryl** *noun* the radical $C_6H_2(NO_2)_3 \cdot$ **M19.**

picrite /ˈpɪkrʌɪt/ *noun.* **E19.**
[from Greek *pikros* bitter + -ITE¹.]
†**1** MINERALOGY. = DOLOMITE. *rare.* Only in **19.**
2 GEOLOGY. A dark ultrabasic igneous rock, generally hypabyssal, containing abundant olivine together with other esp. ferromagnesian minerals. **M19.**
■ **picritic** /pɪˈkrɪtɪk/ *adjective* **M20.**

picro- /ˈpɪkrəʊ/ *combining form.* Before a vowel also **picr-**. **M19.**
[from Greek *pikros* bitter, or from PICRIC: see -O-.]
1 Used with the sense 'bitter', *esp.* (MINERALOGY) forming names of magnesium minerals (noted for often having a bitter taste).
2 CHEMISTRY. Forming names of derivatives of picric acid.
■ **picroˈchromite** *noun* (MINERALOGY) a chromite of magnesium, $MgCr_2O_4$, belonging to the spinel group, known as a synthetic

product or (with impurities) as a brittle black mineral E20. **picrolichenic** /pɪkrə(ʊ)ˈlʌɪkənɪk/ *adjective*: **picrolichenic acid**, a bitter crystalline polycyclic acid isolated from the lichen *Pertusaria amara* E20. **picrolichenin** /-ˈlʌɪk-/ *noun* picrolichenic acid M19. **picrolite** *noun* (MINERALOGY) a fibrous variety of serpentine E19. **picroˈtoxin** *noun* (CHEMISTRY) a bitter toxin obtained from the seeds of the shrub *Anamirta cocculus* and related plants of the family Menispermaceae, used as a respiratory and central nervous system stimulant (now only in veterinary medicine) (cf. COCCULUS INDICUS) M19.

Pict /pɪkt/ *noun*. OE.
[Late Latin *Picti* (pl.), prob. from Latin *picti* painted or tattooed people, formed as next.]
Hist. A member of an ancient people of disputed origin and ethnological affinities, formerly inhabiting Scotland north of the Forth and Clyde, and eventually amalgamated with the Scots before the Middle Ages.
Comb.: **Pictland** *Hist.* the area of ancient Scotland formerly inhabited by the Picts; **Picts' house** any of several underground structures attributed to the Picts, found in NE Scotland and Orkney.
■ **Pictish** *noun & adjective* (*a*) *noun* the language of the Picts, found in inscriptions etc.; (*b*) *adjective* of or pertaining to the Picts or their language: L16.

pict /ˈpɪkt/ *verb trans. rare*. L15.
[Latin *pict-*: see PICTURE *noun*.]
Paint, decorate; depict.
¶ Not recorded between L15 and M19.

pictogram /ˈpɪktə(ʊ)gram/ *noun*. E20.
[formed as next + -O- + -GRAM.]
= next.

pictograph /ˈpɪktə(ʊ)grɑːf/ *noun*. M19.
[from Latin *pictus* painted + -O- + -GRAPH.]
1 A pictorial symbol or sign; *esp.* a symbol representing a word or group of words in a writing system. Also, a piece of writing consisting of pictographs. M19.
2 A chart using pictures to represent statistical data. M20.
■ **pictoˈgraphic** *adjective* consisting of or using pictographs M19. **picˈtography** *noun* the art or practice of using pictographs M19.

Pictor /ˈpɪktə/ *noun*. L19.
[Latin: see next.]
(The name of) an inconspicuous constellation of the southern hemisphere, next to the star Canopus in the constellation Puppis.

pictorial /pɪkˈtɔːrɪəl/ *adjective & noun*. M17.
[from late Latin *pictorius*, from Latin *pictor* painter, from *pict-*: see PICTURE *noun*, -IAL.]
► **A** *adjective*. **1** Of or pertaining to a painter or painting, drawing, etc., in general. Now *literary*. M17.
2 Consisting of or expressed in a picture or pictures. E19.
3 Containing or illustrated by a picture or pictures. E19.
4 *fig.* Picturesque; graphic. E19.

> 🕮 **1** J. ROSENBERG Massing and contrasting lights and darks to gain pictorial animation. *Artist* Deals . . with what is around him . . for his pictorial purposes. **2** *Asian Art* Another level of meaning in Chinese pictorial art. *Times Lit. Suppl.* A drawing . . which remains our only pictorial evidence of a playhouse of Shakespeare's time. **3** *Discovery* Sets of pictorial postcards of the park.

► **B** *noun*. **1 a** A periodical having pictures as the main feature. M19. ►**b** A magazine article consisting chiefly of photographs. L20.
2 A (usu. commemorative) postage stamp printed with a picture or scene. M20.
■ **pictorialism** *noun* the practice of pictorial representation; the use of a pictorial style; *spec.* photography in which the aim is to create pictures of intrinsic merit rather than to record events, scenes, etc.: M19. **pictorialist** *noun* a person who uses a pictorial style; an advocate or practitioner of pictorialism: M19. **pictoriaˈlization** *noun* the action of pictorializing something E20. **pictorialize** *verb trans.* represent in or illustrate by pictures L19. **pictorially** *adverb* (*a*) by means of a picture or pictures; (*b*) in the manner of or as the subject of a picture: M19.

pictorical /pɪkˈtɒrɪk(ə)l/ *adjective. rare*. L16.
[from Latin *pictor* (see prec.) + -ICAL.]
= PICTORIAL *adjective*.

picturable /ˈpɪktʃ(ə)rəb(ə)l/ *adjective*. L18.
[from PICTURE *verb* + -ABLE.]
Able to be represented in a picture; imaginable, conceivable; picturesque.
■ **picturaˈbility** *noun* E19.

picture /ˈpɪktʃə/ *noun*. LME.
[Latin *pictura*, from *pict-* pa. ppl stem of *pingere* to paint.]
†**1** The art or process of pictorial representation; painting and drawing. LME–M19.
†**2** Paintings and drawings collectively. LME–L16.
3 A flat or surface representation of something that visually resembles it or is meant to evoke it; a painting, a drawing, a photograph. L15. ►**b** A portrait, now esp. a photograph, of a person or group. Formerly also, a sculpted likeness. L15. ►**c** A person strongly resembling another; the image *of* a person. E18. ►**d** A tableau formed by actors in a play etc. Now *rare*. E19. ►**e** *fig.* A beautiful or picturesque person or thing. Also *iron.*, a striking expression, pose, etc. *colloq.* E19.
4 A mental image or impression of something; a concrete illustration; MEDICINE the sum of the clinical or other features present in a particular case. M16. ►**b** A state of affairs, a situation; the observable scene, the outlook. E20.
5 A vivid written or spoken description. L16.
6 A person or thing seen as the embodiment *of* some quality. L16.
7 A visible image produced by an optical or electronic system; *esp.* the image on a radar or television screen. M17.
8 A cinematographic scene or film; in *pl.*, films collectively, the cinema industry. Now *colloq.* L19. ►**b** *the pictures*, a showing of films at a cinema; the cinema. *colloq.* E20.

> 🕮 **1** LEIGH HUNT That subtler spirit . . which picture cannot express. **3** M. MOORCOCK The pictures on the wall were fine. A. DESAI She had been visiting her favourite pictures in the museum. *Proverb*: A picture is worth a thousand words. **b** T. HEGGEN The girl friend . . who got her picture in *True Detective* for shooting her husband. P. CUTTING I was confronted by a photographer. Before I could say anything he had taken my picture. **c** J. AUSTEN 'How excessively like her brother . .' 'The very picture of him, indeed!' **e** E. M. BRENT-DYER Her face when she saw them was a picture! W. TREVOR He'd told her . . about his house by the sea, a perfect picture it sounded. **4** N. TINBERGEN We had to build up our picture from many partial case-histories. J. LINGARD He could not get a clear picture in his mind of his father. D. D'SOUZA Factors that are central to an accurate picture of her identity as an American black. **b** *Observer* Such flotations are only a small part of the picture worldwide. **5** *Scotsman* The picture he painted . . was in gloomy terms. **6** I. MURDOCH He remained . . looking the picture of health. **b** K. AMIS Picture of a thoroughly . . contented housewife, she thought. **8** B. SCHULBERG I've got Dorothy Lamour for a South Sea picture. I. SHAW The picture was not scheduled to start for another ten minutes. **b** P. GRACE I went to the pictures . . with my cousins.

Phrases: ***as pretty as a picture***: see PRETTY *adjective*. ***devil's picture-books***: see DEVIL *noun*. **get the picture** *colloq.* grasp or become aware of a particuar situation. **in the picture** fully informed or involved. **out of the picture** no longer involved, irrelevant. ***pretty as a picture***: see PRETTY *adjective*. **put a person in the picture** inform him or her of a particular situation, brief him or her. ***steal the picture***: see STEAL *verb*. ***talking picture***: see TALKING *ppl adjective*.
Comb.: **picture black** TELEVISION (the signal voltage corresponding to) the light level of the darkest element of a television picture; **picture-book** *noun & adjective* (*a*) *noun* a book containing many illustrations, usu. for children; (*b*) *adjective* characteristic of a picture-book; excessively or sentimentally pretty; **picture-card** (*a*) a court-card; (*b*) = ***picture postcard*** below; †**picture-drawer** an artist, *esp.* a portrait-painter; **picture element** TELEVISION = PIXEL; **picture-frame** (*a*) frame made to hold a picture; (*b*) THEATRICAL the stage or stage setting as a composition; **picture frequency** TELEVISION the number of times per second a complete television image is scanned or transmitted; **picture gallery** a room or building exhibiting or containing a collection of pictures; **picture-goer** *colloq.* a frequenter of the cinema; **picture hat** [after depictions of such a hat in the paintings of Reynolds and Gainsborough] a woman's wide-brimmed decorated hat; **picture library**: containing a collection of prints, photographs, etc.; **picture magazine** = PICTORIAL *noun* 1a; **picture monitor** TELEVISION a screen for displaying the immediate image received by a television camera; **picture-moulding** (*a*) woodwork etc. used for framing pictures; (*b*) = ***picture-rail*** below; **picture palace** *arch.* a cinema; **picture-plane** an imaginary plane lying at the front edge of a painting where its perspective meets that of the viewer; **picture postcard** a postcard with a picture or view on one side and space for both a message and the address on the other; **picture-postcard** *adjective* (of a view etc.) conventionally attractive or pretty; **picture-rail**, **picture-rod** a horizontal rail on a wall for hanging pictures from; **picture researcher** a person who finds prints, photographs, etc., to illustrate a book, programme, etc.; **picture search** *noun & adjective* (designating) a facility on a video recorder enabling a picture to be seen while advancing or rewinding a tape; **picture show** (*a*) an exhibition of pictures; (*b*) a film show at a cinema; **picture signal** TELEVISION the component of the video signal which determines the brightness of individual pixels; **picture-space** the apparent space behind the picture-plane of a painting, created by perspective etc.; **picture stage** = ***picture-frame*** (b) above; **picture telegraphy** = FACSIMILE ***telegraphy***; **picture-telephone** = ***videophone*** s.v. VIDEO *adjective & noun*; ***picture theatre***: see THEATRE *noun* 5c; **picture tube** the cathode-ray tube of a television set; **picture window** a large window consisting of a single pane of glass; **picture-wire** strong thin wire used for hanging pictures; **picture-writing** (*a*) writing in which pictures or pictorial symbols are used, rather than words and letters; (*b*) a record in picture-writing.
■ **pictural** *noun & adjective* (*rare*) (*a*) *noun* a painting; (*b*) *adjective* = PICTORIAL *adjective* 1: L16. **picturedom** *noun* the realm of pictures, esp. films E20. **picturedrome** *noun* (now *rare* or *obsolete*) a cinema E20. **picturegraph** *noun* = PICTOGRAPH E20. **pictureless** *adjective* E19. **Picturephone** *noun* (US proprietary name for) a videophone M20.

picture /ˈpɪktʃə/ *verb trans*. L15.
[from the noun.]
1 Represent in a picture or in pictorial form; give an illustration of. Now also, take a photograph of. L15. ►**b** Represent or express symbolically. Now *rare*. E16.
2 Describe graphically in words. L16.
3 Form a mental picture of, imagine. M18.

> 🕮 **1** DAY LEWIS Madly exuberant herbaceous borders pictured in a seedsman's catalogue. **2** R. CHRISTIANSEN A satirical magazine . . pictured her as the toothless hag Madame Coco. **3** J. AUSTEN She . . could not seriously picture to herself a more . . estimable man. E. NORTH She . . pictured how he would look at his father's age. A. LIVELY I picture you . . winding the family clock.

■ **picturing** *noun* (*a*) pictorial representation; a picture; (*b*) the formation or description of a mental picture: M16.

pictured /ˈpɪktʃəd/ *adjective*. E17.
[from PICTURE *noun*, *verb*: see -ED[2], -ED[1].]
1 Adorned with a picture or pictures. Chiefly *poet.* E17.
2 Represented in or illustrated by a picture. M18.

picturesque /pɪktʃəˈrɛsk/ *adjective, noun, & verb*. E18.
[French *pittoresque* from Italian *pittoresco*, from *pittore* painter from Latin *pictor*: see PICTORIAL, -ESQUE. Assim. to PICTURE *noun*.]
► **A** *adjective*. **1** Possessing the elements or qualities of a picture; fit to be the subject of a picture; *esp.* (of a landscape etc.) pleasing or striking in composition or colour. Also, (of a route etc.) affording views of this kind. E18.
2 Of language etc.: strikingly graphic or vivid; colourful; *iron.* profane. M18.
†**3** Of a person: perceptive of or liking picturesque scenes etc. L18–M19.

> 🕮 **1** J. ROSENBERG The artist's . . delight in picturesque attire. *Sunday Express* Take time to explore the picturesque coves, the narrow lanes. **picturesque gardening** the picturesque arrangement of a garden, landscape gardening. **2** *New York Times* Byproducts with picturesque names like putrescine and cadaverine. *Weekend Australian* Criticism is put in more picturesque language than we normally hear.

► **B** *absol.* as *noun*. That which is picturesque; picturesque elements, qualities, etc., collectively. M18.

> 🕮 *American Quarterly* His fondness for local history or for the picturesque.

► **C** *verb trans.* Make picturesque in appearance etc. *rare*. L18.
■ **picturesquely** *adverb* L18. **picturesqueness** *noun* the quality or condition of being picturesque L18. **picturesquerie** *noun* the picturesque; (an example of) picturesqueness: M20.

picturize /ˈpɪktʃərʌɪz/ *verb trans.* Also **-ise**. M19.
[from PICTURE *noun* + -IZE.]
Represent by or illustrate with a picture or pictures.
■ **picturiˈzation** *noun* E20.

†**picucule** *noun*. Only in 19.
[from Latin *picus* woodpecker + *cuculus* cuckoo.]
ORNITHOLOGY. = ***woodcreeper*** s.v. WOOD *noun*[1] & *adjective*[1].

picuda /pɪˈkuːdə/ *noun*. M20.
[Amer. Spanish, from Spanish *picudo* pointed, sharp.]
= ***great barracuda*** s.v. BARRACUDA 1.

picul /ˈpɪkʌl/ *noun*. L16.
[Malay, Javanese *pikul* a load.]
A unit of weight used in China and SE Asia, equal to about 100 catties (about 60 kg).

piculet /ˈpɪkjʊlɪt/ *noun*. M19.
[App. double dim. of Latin *picus* woodpecker: see -ULE, -ET[1].]
Any of various very small soft-tailed tropical woodpeckers of the genus *Picumnus* and some related genera.

PID *abbreviation*.
Pelvic inflammatory disease.

piddle /ˈpɪd(ə)l/ *verb & noun*. M16.
[In branch I of the verb perh. alt. of PEDDLE by assoc. with Low German *piddeln*; in branch II perh. based on PISS *verb* or PEE *verb*, after PUDDLE *noun*, *verb*.]
► **A** *verb*. **I 1** *verb intrans.* Work at something in a trifling or petty way; busy oneself with trifling matters. Now freq. foll. by *about*, *around*. M16.
2 *verb intrans.* Of a bird: move the bill about in search of food. Now *rare*. L16.
3 *verb intrans.* Pick at or toy with one's food. E17.
4 *verb trans.* While *away* (time); fritter *away*. M18.
► **II 5** *verb intrans.* Urinate. *colloq.* L18.
► **B** *noun*. Urine; an act of urinating. *colloq.* L19.
■ **piddler** *noun* a person who piddles; a poor worker, a dabbler, a trifler: E17. **piddling** *adjective* (*colloq.*) trifling, petty M16. **piddly** *adjective* (*colloq.*) = PIDDLING M20.

piddock /ˈpɪdək/ *noun*. M19.
[Origin unkn.]
Any of various marine bivalve molluscs of the genus *Pholas* or the family Pholadidae containing it, which burrow in softer rocks; *esp.* the common species, *P.*

dactylus, with a long ovate shell, which along with others is used for bait.

pidgin /ˈpɪdʒɪn/ *noun & adjective*. Also (now the usual form in sense A.1) **pigeon**. E19.
[Chinese alt. of English *business*.]
▸**A** *noun*. **1** Business. Chiefly in ***be a person's pidgin***, be a person's concern or affair. E19.
2 A form of a language as spoken in a simplified or altered form by non-native speakers, esp. as a means of communication between people not sharing a common language. L19.

📖 **2** *American Speech* The Angolan slaves . . have carried . . Portuguese pidgin with them.

▸**B** *attrib. adjective*. Of the nature of a pidgin; *spec.* designating a language as altered in a pidgin. M19.
pidgin English a pidgin in which the chief language is English, orig. that used between Chinese and Europeans.
■ **pidginist** *noun* an expert in or student of pidgin languages L20. **pidginiˈzation** *noun* the fact or process of pidginizing something; a pidginized language: M20. **pidginize** *verb trans.* produce a simplified or pidgin form of (a language, word, etc.) M20.

pi-dog *noun* var. of PYE-DOG.

Pidyon Haben /ˈpɪdjən hɑːˈben/ *noun phr.* L19.
[Hebrew *pidyōn habbēn* redemption of the son.]
A Jewish ceremony performed thirty days after the birth of a first-born male child to redeem him from being nominally committed to the service of the priesthood.

pie /pʌɪ/ *noun*¹. ME.
[Old & mod. French from Latin *pica* magpie, rel. to *picus* green woodpecker. See also MAGPIE.]
1 a The magpie. Now *rare*. ME. ▸**b** With specifying word: any of various other birds resembling the magpie, esp. in having black and white (pied) plumage. L19.
2 *transf.* †**a** A cunning or wily person. LME–L16. ▸**b** A chattering or saucy person. M16.
1b *SEA-pie*. *tree pie*: see TREE *noun*.

pie /pʌɪ/ *noun*². ME.
[Prob. identical with prec., perh. because the miscellaneous contents of a pie are comparable with the miscellaneous objects collected by magpies.]
1 A baked dish of meat, fish, fruit, or vegetables enclosed in (and often covered with) a layer of pastry. Also, such a dish with just a top layer of pastry. ME.
2 A collection of things made into a heap; *spec.* a pit or heap of potatoes or other roots covered with straw and earth for storage and protection. *local*. E16.
3 A thing resembling a pie in shape, variety of content, etc. M19.
4 a A highly desirable thing; a prize, a treat. Also, a bribe. M19. ▸**b** A thing easily accomplished or dealt with. L19. ▸**c** Political favour or patronage. *US slang*. L19.
5 Wealth, market share, etc., considered as something to be shared out M20.
6 A group of wool buyers who share the wool they buy at a sale and so do not bid against one another. *Austral.* M20.

📖 **1** ***apple-pie***, ***cottage-pie***, ***mince-pie***, ***pork-pie***, ***pumpkin-pie***, ***raised pie***, ***rhubarb-pie***, etc. **3** ***bran-pie***, ***dirt-pie***, ***mud-pie***. **4a** E. M. BRENT-DYER I wouldn't have missed it for pie! **5** *Wall Street Journal* National Broadcasting Co . . . gets 30% . . of the total television advertising pie.

Phrases etc.: ***have a finger in the pie***: see FINGER *noun*. ***Nesselrode pie***. *PENNY pies*. **pie in the sky** *colloq.* an unrealistic prospect of future happiness, esp. after present suffering; an extravagant promise unlikely to be fulfilled. ***porky-pie***: see PORKY *noun*². ***sweetie-pie***: see SWEETIE 2.
Comb.: **pie-biter** (*a*) *US* a person who is fond of eating pies; *fig.* a person who takes part in political patronage; (*b*) *Austral. slang* = ***pie-eater*** (b) below; **pie-card** *US slang* (*a*) a meal-ticket; (*b*) (the holder of) a union-card; **pie-cart** *NZ* a stall, van, etc., from which hot food or drink is sold; **pie chart** a circle divided into sectors with areas representing the relative quantities or frequencies of a set of items; **pie-counter** *US* a counter from which pies are sold; *fig.* a source of political favour or patronage; **pie diagram** = ***pie chart*** above; **pie-eater** (*a*) a person who eats pies; (*b*) *Austral. slang* a person of no importance, a fool; **pie-eyed** *adjective* (*slang*) intoxicated to such an extent that vision is affected; very drunk; **pie-face** a person with a round or blank face; a stupid person; **pie-faced** *adjective* having a round face or a blank facial expression; stupid; **pie-funnel** a support for a piecrust during cooking; **pie graph** = ***pie chart*** above; **pieman** a man who makes pies for sale; **pie-melon** *Austral.* a variety of watermelon, *Citrullus lanatus*; **pie-plant** a plant providing fruit etc. for pies; *spec.* (*US*) rhubarb; **pie-wagon** *US slang* a police van used to carry prisoners.
■ **pieless** *adjective* (*rare*) M19. **pielet** *noun* (*rare*) a small pie L19.

pie /pʌɪ/ *noun*³. Also (esp. in sense 2) **pye**. L15.
[Origin uncertain: corresponded to Anglo-Latin *pica*, showing that the name was commonly identified with Latin *pica* PIE *noun*¹: cf. PICA *noun*¹.]
1 *ECCLESIASTICAL HISTORY.* A collection of rules in the pre-Reformation Church to show how to deal with the concurrence of more than one service or office on the same day. L15.
2 *Hist.* More fully ***pie book***. An alphabetical index to rolls and records. Now *rare*. L18.

pie /pʌɪ/ *noun*⁴. Also ***pi**, †**pye**. M17.
[Perh. translating French PÂTÉ pie, patty.]
1 *PRINTING.* Type in a confused mass, such as results from the accidental breaking up of a forme. M17.
2 *transf.* Confusion, chaos. M19.

pie /pʌɪ/ *noun*⁵. M19.
[Hindi *pāī* from Sanskrit *pādikā*, from *pāda* quarter: cf. PICE.]
Hist. A small copper coin formerly used in India, worth one-twelfth of an anna (orig., a quarter of an anna, = PICE).

pie *adjective* var. of PI *adjective*.

pie /pʌɪ/ *verb trans.* Pres. pple & verbal noun **pieing**. L19.
[from PIE *noun*⁴.]
PRINTING. Make (type) into pie; mix up, muddle.

piebald /ˈpʌɪbɔːld/ *adjective & noun*. L16.
[from PIE *noun*¹ + BALD.]
▸**A** *adjective*. **1** Esp. of a horse or other animal: having irregular patches of two different colours, esp. black and white; pied. L16.
2 Composed of dissimilar parts or contrasting elements; of mixed qualities; motley, mongrel. Freq. *derog.* L16.

📖 **1** W. VAN T. CLARK The shadowy mountains . . piebald with lingering snow. **2** CARLYLE This piebald, entangled . . style of writing.

▸**B** *noun*. **1** A person or thing of mixed character, a mongrel. Freq. *derog.* M18.
2 An animal, esp. a horse, of two different colours, esp. black and white. M19.
■ **piebaldness** *noun* (*rare*) L19.

piece /piːs/ *noun*. ME.
[Anglo-Norman *pece*, Old French *piece* (mod. *pièce*) from Proto-Romance (cf. medieval Latin *petia*, *pecia*, *pet(t)ium*), prob. of Gaulish origin: cf. PEAT *noun*¹.]
1 A separate part of a material thing; any of the distinct portions or objects of which a material thing is composed. ME. ▸**b** *spec.* Any of the irregular sections of a jigsaw or similar puzzle. E20.
2 A portion *of* land, a distinct or enclosed area. ME.
3 A single, usu. small quantity *of* a substance or a non-material thing. ME.
4 A single item of a group or class of similar objects; an article of furniture, luggage, ordnance, etc. ME. ▸**b** A musician with his or her instrument, as part of an orchestra or band. E20.
5 A person, an individual. Now usu. *spec.*, a young woman, esp. regarded as a sexual object. ME.
6 a A period of time; a while. Now *dial.* ME. ▸**b** A short distance; a part of the way. *N. Amer. & dial.* LME.
†**7** A part or portion of a non-material thing. LME–M18.
8 An instance or specimen *of* a (material or non-material) thing. LME. ▸†**b** A person regarded as an exemplar *of* some quality. E17–L18.
9 A cask *of* wine or brandy. LME.
10 A specific length of cloth or wallpaper. LME.
11 a An article of armour; a part of a suit of armour. LME. ▸†**b** A fortress, a stronghold. E16–E18. ▸**c** A cannon, a large gun. E16. ▸**d** A portable firearm, a handgun. Now chiefly *N. Amer. slang*. L16.
12 A coin (freq. with specifying word). Formerly *spec.* an English gold coin. LME.
13 Any of the objects used to make moves in a board game such as chess, draughts, backgammon, etc.; *spec.* (*CHESS*) a chessman other than a pawn. M16.
14 a More fully ***piece of work***. A specimen of workmanship; a work of art; *spec.* (*a*) a painting; (*b*) a statue; (*c*) a play. M16. ▸**b** A (usu. short) literary or musical composition, as a poem, sonata, newspaper article, etc. M16. ▸**c** A short discourse; a passage for recitation. *dial. & N. Amer.* M19.
†**15** A boat. M16–L17.
16 A separate article of property in transit, a package; *spec.* (*Hist.*) in the N. American fur trade, a package weighing about ninety pounds. Chiefly *N. Amer.* L18.
17 A slice of bread and butter, a sandwich; a snack. *Scot. & dial.* L18.
18 In *pl.* ▸**a** In the malting process, grain spread out for steeping. M19. ▸**b** Sugar of a poorer quality obtained from a later boiling of the sugar liquor. M19. ▸**c** Oddments of wool which are detached from the skirtings of a fleece. Also, the skirtings themselves. Chiefly *Austral. & NZ*. L19.
19 Foll. by *of*: a share in, involvement in; a financial interest in (a business, project, etc.). Freq. in ***a piece of the action*** below. *slang*. E20.
20 A quantity of a drug, esp. morphine or heroin, approximately equal to one ounce. *N. Amer. slang*. M20.
21 [from *masterpiece*.] A particularly elaborate graffito. *slang*. L20.

📖 **1** G. K. CHESTERTON He slit the paper into about five pieces. *Daily Telegraph* Still wearing dated, conventional two-piece outfits. ***base-piece***, ***ear-piece***, ***eyepiece***, etc. *fig.*: W. G. HARDY Suddenly the pieces seemed to fit together. **3a** J. MOYNAHAN A piece of music like Wagner's *Liebestod*. G. VIDAL Sawing a piece of bacon in half. **4** *Times* Many vital pieces of equipment. R. RENDELL She'd got some beautiful furniture in her place—valuable pieces. **b** *Washington Post* Asha's songs were . . played . . by the eight-piece orchestra. **5** J. HELLER There was Mary Slocum . . a short sexy piece. **6b** *New Yorker* He lives down the road a piece. **7** H. WOTTON One of the most fastidious pieces of my life. **8** A. C. DUCAREL The . . screen at the west end of the choir is a beautiful piece of architecture. DAY LEWIS I do not use the hyphen in my surname—a piece of inverted snobbery. **11a** ***head-piece***, ***shoulder-piece***, ***thigh-piece***, etc. **d** E. LEONARD Vincent . . went for his piece yelling . . halt or he'd fire. **12** R. BRAUTIGAN The sun was like a huge fifty-cent piece. **14b** K. CLARK He wrote . . over one hundred symphonies and many hundreds of occasional pieces. G. KEILLOR I got $6000 . . for writing a piece about the Grand Ole Opry.

Phrases: **all of a piece**, **of a piece** consisting of a single piece or mass; *fig.* (all) of the same kind; uniform, consistent; (foll. by *with*). **all to pieces** (*a*) into many pieces, asunder (***go all to pieces*** = ***go to pieces*** below); (*b*) in many pieces or fragments; (*c*) *dial. & N. Amer.* (with appreciative connotation) thoroughly, very well. **a piece of the action** *slang* a share of the profits accruing from something; a share in the excitement. ***bits and pieces***: see BIT *noun*². ***blanket-piece***: see BLANKET *noun* 5. **by the piece** at a rate of so much per fixed amount; (paid) according to the amount of work done. ***come to pieces***: see ***to pieces*** below. ***fall to pieces***: see ***to pieces*** below. ***give a piece of one's mind to***: see MIND *noun*¹. ***go to pieces***: see ***to pieces*** below. **into pieces** into fragments, asunder; to pieces. **in one piece** consisting of a single piece or mass; *fig.* whole, without injury or loss. **in pieces** (*a*) broken, in fragments; (*b*) into fragments, asunder; to pieces. *LETTERING piece*. **love to pieces** *colloq.* love very much. ***of a piece***: see ***all of a piece*** above. **of one piece** = ***in one piece*** above. **on piece**, **on the piece** doing piece-work. ***pick to pieces***: see ***to pieces*** below. **piece by piece** with one piece or part after another in succession; gradually. **piece of arse**, **piece of ass** *coarse slang* (chiefly *N. Amer.*) a woman regarded as an object of sexual gratification; sexual intercourse with a woman. ***piece of cake***: see CAKE *noun*. ***piece of crumpet***: see CRUMPET 5. ***piece of eight***: see EIGHT *noun* 1. **piece of flesh** *arch.* a human being. **piece of gold**, **piece of silver**, etc., a gold, silver, etc., coin. ***piece of goods***: see GOOD *noun*. ***piece of meat***: see MEAT *noun*. **piece of tail** *coarse slang* (chiefly *N. Amer.* = ***piece of arse*** above. ***piece of water*** a small lake, a pond. **piece of work** (*a*) a task, a difficult thing; *colloq.* a commotion, a to-do; (*b*) a person of a specified (usu. unpleasant) kind; freq. in ***nasty piece of work***; (see also sense 14a above). ***pull to pieces***: see ***to pieces*** below. **to pieces** into fragments, asunder; to a state of distraction or confusion; ***come to pieces***, ***go to pieces***, break up, lose cohesion; *fig.* break down emotionally or mentally; ***fall to pieces***, disintegrate, collapse; *dial. & Austral. slang* give birth to a child; ***pick to pieces***, ***pull to pieces***, = ***take to pieces*** (b) below; ***take to pieces***, (*a*) separate into component parts, take apart; (*b*) *fig.* criticize unfavourably or harshly; refute (an argument etc.) strongly; (see also ***all to pieces***, ***love to pieces*** above).
Comb.: **piece-bag** *N. Amer.* a bag or box for holding pieces of cloth; **piece-broker** *arch.* a dealer in cloth remnants; **piece-dye** *verb trans.* dye (cloth) after weaving; **piece-goods** cloth woven in fixed lengths for sale; **piece-mould** a sculptor's mould which can be removed in pieces; **piece-payment** payment by the piece or item produced; **piece-price** a price paid for piece-work; **piece-rate** rate of payment for piece-work; **piece-work** (*a*) work paid for by the amount produced; (*b*) = PATCHWORK *noun* 2; **piece-worker**: who is paid according to the amount done.
■ **piecewise** *adverb* by pieces; *spec.* in *MATH.*, throughout each of a finite number of pieces but not necessarily throughout the whole: L17.

piece /piːs/ *verb*. LME.
[from the noun.]
1 *verb trans.* Mend, make whole, or complete by adding a piece; patch. LME.
2 *verb trans.* **a** Join together to form one thing; mend (something broken) by joining the pieces; make by putting pieces together; *fig.* infer or construct from previously unrelated facts. Now usu. foll. by *together*. L15. ▸**b** Unite (*with*), join (*to*). Now *rare*. L16.
†**3** *verb intrans.* Come together, assemble; agree. Only in 17.

📖 **1** *fig.*: SHAKES. *Ant. & Cl.* I will piece her opulant throne with kingdoms. **2a** A. P. HERBERT Piecing the jagged fragments of canvas together. J. FIELD I gradually pieced together the hints and clues. H. G. WELLS She never succeeded in piecing together a consecutive story of his experiences.

With adverbs in specialized senses: **piece down** increase the length or width of (a garment) by inserting a piece of material. **piece on** fit on, esp. as the corresponding piece. **piece out** complete or enlarge by the addition of a piece; eke out. ***piece together***: see sense 2a above. **piece up** repair or make up by joining pieces or parts; patch up.
■ **piecer** *noun* a person who pieces things, a patcher; *spec.* (*Hist.*) a child employed in a spinning-mill to join the ends of broken threads: E19.

pièce à thèse /pjɛs a tɛːz/ *noun phr.* Pl. ***pièces à thèse*** (pronounced same). M20.
[French.]
A play written with the aim of supporting a thesis or proposition. Also called ***thesis-play***.

pièce de circonstance /pjɛs də sirkɔ̃stɑ̃:s/ *noun phr.* Pl. ***pièces de circonstance*** (pronounced same). **M19.**
[French.]
A literary composition, theory, etc., arising out of a particular situation.

pièce de conviction /pjɛs də kɔ̃viksjɔ̃/ *noun phr.* Pl. ***pièces de conviction*** (pronounced same). **L19.**
[French.]
An object produced as evidence in a criminal case, an exhibit; *fig.* the conclusive argument which decides a question.

pièce de résistance /pjɛs də rezistɑ̃:s/ *noun phr.* Pl. ***pièces de résistance*** (pronounced same). **L18.**
[French.]
1 The most important or outstanding item. **L18.**
2 The main dish of a meal. **M19.**

📖 *Musical Quarterly* After a fantasy for flute . . came the *pièce de résistance*, *El Sitio de Zaragoza*.

pièce d'occasion /pjɛs dɔkazjɔ̃/ *noun phr.* Pl. ***pièces d'occasion*** (pronounced same). **L19.**
[French.]
A literary or musical work written for a special occasion.

pièce justificative /pjɛs ʒystifikati:v/ *noun phr.* Pl. ***-s -s*** (pronounced same). **L18.**
[French.]
A document serving as proof of an allegation; a justification of an assertion.

piecemeal /ˈpi:smi:l/ *verb trans.* Now *rare*. **E17.**
[from next.]
Divide or distribute piecemeal; dismember.

piecemeal /ˈpi:smi:l/ *adverb, noun, & adjective.* **ME.**
[from PIECE *noun* + -MEAL.]
▶ **A** *adverb.* **1** One part or piece at a time; piece by piece, gradually; separately. **ME.**
2 Into or in pieces or fragments. **L16.**

📖 **1** E. H. GOMBRICH Invention can only progress piecemeal . . through gradual improvement. K. TYNAN Planning to break up the collection and resell it piecemeal. **2** *Country Companion* If the prey is too heavy . . they will tear it . . and carry it away piecemeal.

▶†**B** *noun.* A small piece, portion, or fragment. Chiefly in ***by piecemeals***. **L16–E19.**
by piecemeal = sense A.1 above.
▶ **C** *adjective.* Consisting of pieces; done bit by bit; gradual **E17.**

📖 *Design Week* A series of piecemeal refurbishments by different consultancies.

piecen /ˈpi:s(ə)n/ *verb trans. techn.* **M19.**
[from PIECE *noun* + -EN[5].]
Join the broken ends of (a thread) during spinning.
■ **piecener** *noun* **M19.**

pièce noire /pjɛs nwa:r/ *noun phr.* Pl. ***-s -s*** (pronounced same). **M20.**
[French, lit. 'black play '.]
A play or film with a tragic or macabre theme.

pièce rose /pjɛs ro:z/ *noun phr.* Pl. ***-s -s*** (pronounced same). **M20.**
[French, lit. 'pink play'.]
A play or film with a pleasantly entertaining theme; a comedy.

pièces à thèse, ***pièces de circonstance***, ***pièces de conviction***, ***pièces de résistance***, ***pièces d'occasion*** *noun phrs.* pls. of PIÈCE À THÈSE etc.

pièces justificatives, ***pièces noires***, ***pièces roses*** *noun phrs.* pls. of PIÈCE NOIRE etc.

piecrust /ˈpʌɪkrʌst/ *noun & adjective.* **L16.**
[from PIE *noun*[2] + CRUST *noun*.]
▶ **A** *noun.* Baked pastry forming the crust of a pie. **L16.**
▶ **B** *attrib.* or as *adjective.* Resembling piecrust in appearance, texture, etc.; *spec.* (of a table or garment) having an ornamental edge. **M18.**

📖 *Times* Pie crust frills on Valentino's pink evening dress.

pied /pʌɪd/ *adjective.* **ME.**
[from PIE *noun*[1] + -ED[2].]
1 Orig., black and white, like a magpie. Later, of any different colours in patches, *esp.* of white with patches of one other colour; particoloured. **ME.**
2 Variegated (*with*). **M17.**

📖 **2** T. PYNCHON He comes in speckled, pied with rain.

Special collocations & comb.: **pied-billed grebe** a New World grebe, *Podilymbus podiceps*. **pied crow** a black and white crow, *Corvus albus*, found in sub-Saharan Africa. **pied duck** = ***Labrador duck*** s.v. LABRADOR 1. **pied flycatcher** a black and white flycatcher, *Ficedula hypoleuca*, found from Europe and SW Asia to central Africa. **Pied Friars** *Hist.* a small order of friars in Norwich who dressed in brown and white. **pied goose** = ***MAGPIE goose***. **pied hornbill** either of two Asiatic hornbills of the genus *Anthracoceros*. **pied kingfisher** either of two kingfishers of the genus *Ceryle* found in Asia and Africa. **Pied Monk** [from the white tunic and black scapular] a Bernardine monk, a Cistercian monk. **Pied Piper (of Hamelin)** in a German legend, a piper in particoloured dress who rid Hamelin of rats by charming them into the river, and who, when refused the promised reward, led away the children of the town; *transf.* a person enticing followers, esp. to their doom. **pied wagtail** a western European wagtail that is a black-backed subspecies of the Eurasian *Motacilla alba* (cf. ***white wagtail*** s.v. WHITE *adjective*). **pied woodpecker** the great spotted woodpecker, *Dendrocopos major*, found in Eurasia and N. Africa.
■ **piedness** *noun* **E17.**

pied-à-terre /pjeɪdɑːˈtɛː/ *noun.* Pl. **pieds-à-terre** (pronounced same). **E19.**
[French, lit. 'foot to earth'.]
A small town house, flat, or room used for short periods of residence; a home base.

📖 B. VINE These cousins had a pied-à-terre in London, a studio in Chelsea.

pied d'éléphant /pje delefɑ̃/ *noun phr.* Pl. ***pieds d'éléphant*** (pronounced same). **M20.**
[French, lit. 'elephant's foot'.]
A padded sack used to protect the lower part of the body on a bivouac when mountaineering etc.

Piedfort /ˈpjeɪfɔ:t/ *noun.* **M20.**
[from French *pied* foot + *fort* strong.]
NUMISMATICS. A coin that is thicker than a normal issue, made as a collector's item.

piedmont /ˈpi:dmɒnt/ *noun & adjective.* **M19.**
[*Piedmont*, a region of the north-eastern US, after Italian *Piemonte*, a region in NW Italy, from *piede* foot + *monte* mountain.]
GEOLOGY. ▶**A** *noun.* A region at the foot of a mountain or mountain range. **M19.**
▶ **B** *attrib.* or as *adjective.* That is a piedmont; situated or occurring at the foot of a mountain or mountain range. **L19.**

Piedmontese /pi:dmɒnˈti:z/ *noun & adjective.* **M17.**
[formed as prec. + -ESE.]
▶ **A** *noun.* Pl. same.
1 A native or inhabitant of Piedmont in NW Italy. **M17.**
2 The dialect of this region. **M17.**
▶ **B** *adjective.* Of or pertaining to this region, its inhabitants, or the Italian dialect spoken by them. **M18.**

piedmontite *noun* var. of PIEMONTITE.

pied noir /pje nwa:r/ *noun phr.* Pl. ***-s -s*** (pronounced same). **M20.**
[French lit. 'black foot'.]
A person of European origin who lived in Algeria during French rule.

pie-dog *noun* var. of PYE-DOG.

piedra /ˈpjɛdrə/ *noun.* **L19.**
[Spanish = stone from Latin *petra*.]
MEDICINE. Any of various fungal diseases of the hair, characterized by the presence on the hairs of small hard waxy nodules. Usu. with qualifying adjective.
black piedra, ***white piedra***, etc.

piedroit /pjedrwa/ *noun.* Pl. pronounced same. **L17.**
[French *pied droit* lit. 'straight foot'.]
ARCHITECTURE. A square pillar attached to a wall, having neither base nor capital.

pieds-à-terre *noun* pl. of PIED-À-TERRE.

pieds d'éléphant *noun phr.* pl. of PIED D'ÉLÉPHANT.

pieds noirs *noun phr.* pl. of PIED NOIR.

Piegan /ˈpi:g(ə)n/ *adjective & noun.* Also **Peigan**. **L18.**
[Blackfoot *Piikániwa*.]
▶ **A** *adjective.* Of or pertaining to a N. American Indian people of the Blackfoot confederacy, inhabiting the Rocky Mountain regions of Alberta and Montana. **L18.**
▶ **B** *noun.* Pl. **-s**, same. A member of this people. **M19.**

piemontite /ˈpi:mɒntʌɪt/ *noun.* Also **pied-** /ˈpi:d-/. **L19.**
[from Italian *Piemonte* (see PIEDMONT) + -ITE[1].]
MINERALOGY. A monoclinic silicate of the epidote group containing calcium, aluminium, iron, and manganese, and occurring as brown or black crystals.

piepowder /ˈpʌɪpaʊdə/ *adjective & noun.* **ME.**
[Anglo-Norman *piepuldrus* from Anglo-Latin *pedepulverosus* dusty-footed, from Latin *pede* abl. sing. of *pes* foot + *pulver-*, *pulvis* dust (see POWDER *noun*[1]) + *-osus* -OSE[1].]
▶†**A** *adjective.* Travelling, itinerant. *rare.* **ME–E17.**
▶ **B** *noun.* **1** A traveller, *esp.* an itinerant merchant or trader. Chiefly in ***court of piepowders*** below. Long *obsolete* exc. *Hist.* **ME.**
†**2** A court of piepowders; a plea in such a court. Only in **ME.**
1 court of piepowders a summary court formerly held at fairs and markets to administer justice among itinerant dealers.

pier /pɪə/ *noun.* **ME.**
[Anglo-Latin *pera*, of unkn. origin.]
1 A support of one of the spans of a bridge. (*rare* before **17.**) **ME.**
2a A solid structure extending into the sea or a river to protect a harbour and form a landing-stage for vessels; a breakwater, a mole. Also, a similar structure in the form of a platform supported on pillars or girders for use as a pleasure promenade or landing-stage. **LME.** ▸†**b** *transf.* A haven, a harbour. **M16–E18.** ▸**c** A long narrow structure projecting from the main body of an airport terminal along which passengers walk to and from their aircraft. **M20.**
3 BUILDING. A solid support designed to sustain vertical pressure; *spec.* (***a***) an extent of wall between adjacent openings; (***b***) a doorpost, a gatepost; (***c***) a pillar from which an arch springs. **E17.**

📖 **2a** M. FORSTER There is a steamer leaves the pier at ten in the morning. *Guardian* He fell 50 ft into the sea from a funfair ride on Palace Pier, Brighton. **c** *New Scientist* A moving walkway along the pier to the two terminals. **3** E. WAUGH The park gates . . swung on rusticated stone piers. E. H. GOMBRICH In Romanesque . . churches we . . find round arches resting on massive piers.

Comb.: **pier-glass** a large tall mirror, used orig. to fill the wall between two windows; **pier-master** the officer in charge of a pier; **pier-mirror** = ***pier-glass*** above; **pier-stake** any of the pillars on which a pier is supported; **pier-table** a low table or bracket in the space between two windows, often under a pier-glass.
■ **pierage** *noun* (***a***) the use of a pier or wharf; (***b***) the fee paid for this: **L16.** **pierless** *adjective* **M19.**

pierce /pɪəs/ *noun. rare.* **E17.**
[from the verb.]
The act or process of piercing; a hole made by piercing.

pierce /pɪəs/ *verb.* **ME.**
[Old & mod. French *percer* from Proto-Romance, from Latin *pertusus* pa. pple of *pertundere* bore through, from *per* PER-[1] + *tundere* to thrust.]
▶ **I** *verb trans.* **1** Penetrate (a substance) as a sharp-pointed instrument does; prick or stab *with* a sharp-pointed instrument. **ME.**
2 Make a hole, opening, or tunnel into or through (something); bore through, perforate. **ME.** ▸**b** Make (a hole etc.) by pricking or stabbing with a sharp-pointed instrument. **LME.**
3 Force one's way through or into; break through or into. **ME.**
4 Reach or penetrate with the sight or the mind; see into, discern. Now only with non-material obj. **LME.**
5 Penetrate with pain, grief, or other emotion; hurt or affect deeply. **LME.**

📖 **1** E. FERBER The tools of the workmen . . pierced the rocklike clay walls. B. HINES She . . pierced the skin with her beak. *fig.*: H. MARTINEAU Gusts of wind . . piercing her with cold. G. LORD The . . flash of their torch as its light pierced the dark. **2** D. HAMMETT The fourth wall . . was pierced by two windows. R. RENDELL Mummy thought it . . vulgar to have your ears pierced. **3** A. J. P. TAYLOR This attack pierced the German line. **5** *Classical Quarterly* Leto was pierced by hopeless birth-pangs.

▶ **II** *verb intrans.* **6** Enter or penetrate (*into*, *through*, etc.) in the manner of something with a sharp point; project or jut sharply. **ME.**
7 Penetrate with the mind or the sight *into* or *through*; see *into*. **M16.**

📖 **7** D. LEAVITT I . . try to pierce through her with a stare.

■ **pierceable** *adjective* (earlier in IMPIERCEABLE, UNPIERCEABLE) **M16.**

pierced /pɪəst/ *adjective.* **ME.**
[from prec. + -ED[1].]
1 *gen.* That has been pierced; punctured, perforated, penetrated. **ME.**
2a HERALDRY. (Of a charge) perforated with a circular hole so that the tincture of the field appears through; (of an animal) having an arrow, spear, etc., fixed in but not passing through the body. **E17.** ▸**b** Of silver, china, porcelain, etc.: ornamented with perforations. **M18.**
Special collocations: **pierced earring**: designed to be worn in a pierced ear. **Pierced Nose** = NEZ PERCÉ.

piercement /ˈpɪəsm(ə)nt/ *noun.* **E20.**
[from PIERCE *verb* + -MENT.]
GEOLOGY. The penetration of overlying strata by a mobile rock core, often of salt. Usu. *attrib.*
Comb.: **piercement dome** = DIAPIR.

piercer /ˈpɪəsə/ *noun.* **ME.**
[Anglo-Norman *persour*, from Old & mod. French *percer*: see PIERCE *verb*, -ER[1].]
1 A person who pierces; *spec.* a person employed or skilled in perforating wood or metal. **ME.**
2 A thing which pierces; *spec.* a pointed tool for boring holes, as an auger, awl, gimlet, etc. **ME.** ▸**b** A bodily organ used in piercing, as the sting or ovipositor of an insect. **L17.** ▸**c** An eye with a keen or penetrating glance. Usu. in *pl. colloq.* **M18.**

piercing /ˈpɪəsɪŋ/ *noun.* **LME.**
[from PIERCE *verb* + -ING[1].]
1 The action of PIERCE *verb.* **LME.**
2 A hole, a perforation. **L19.**

piercing /ˈpɪəsɪŋ/ *adjective*. LME.
[from PIERCE *verb* + -ING².]
1 That pierces or penetrates like a sharp-pointed instrument or weapon. LME.
2 Esp. of cold, sound, or light: having a physical effect suggestive of the action of a pointed instrument; sharp, keen, penetrating. LME.
3 Having a keen or painful effect on the feelings or mind; deeply distressing. LME.
4 (Of the eyes, an expression, etc.) penetrating, very perceptive; (of intelligence) sharp. LME.

🕮 **2** S. COOPER Cally.. blew a piercing whistle. JULIETTE HUXLEY Stars of fabulous brilliance: piercing in so dark a sky. **3** I. MURDOCH A genuine piercing shame. M. M. R. KHAN The blinding piercing headaches. **4** J. R. ACKERLEY My fine blue eyes can emit a piercing stare.

■ **piercingly** *adverb* LME. **piercingness** *noun* M17.

pier-head /pɪəˈhɛd/ *noun & adjective*. L17.
[from PIER *noun* + HEAD *noun*.]
▶ **A** *noun*. The outward or seaward end of a pier. L17.
Comb.: **pier-head jump** (*a*) an act of leaving a ship as it is about to sail; (*b*) a person who joins a ship as it is leaving the dock.
▶ **B** *adjective*. Designating or pertaining to entertainment associated with summer shows on piers in seaside resorts. M20.

Pierian /pʌɪˈɛrɪən, -ˈɪər-/ *adjective*. L16.
[from Latin *Pierius*, from *Pieria*: see below, -AN.]
Belonging to Pieria, a district in northern Thessaly, that in classical mythology was reputed home of the Muses and the location of a spring sacred to them.

🕮 POPE Drink deep, or taste not the Pierian spring.

pierid /ˈpʌɪərɪd/ *noun & adjective*. L19.
[mod. Latin *Pieridae* (see below), from PIERIS: see -ID³.]
ENTOMOLOGY. ▶**A** *noun*. A butterfly of the family Pieridae, the members of which are mainly white, yellow, or orange and include the whites, brimstones, and sulphurs. L19.
▶ **B** *adjective*. Of, pertaining to, or designating this family. E20.

pierine /ˈpʌɪəriːn, -ʌɪn/ *noun & adjective*. L19.
[mod. Latin *Pierinae* (see below), from next: see -INE¹.]
ENTOMOLOGY. ▶**A** *adjective*. Of, pertaining to, or designating the subfamily Pierinae of pierids, which includes cabbage whites and orange-tips. L19.
▶ **B** *noun*. A butterfly of this subfamily. M20.

pieris /ˈpʌɪərɪs/ *noun*. Pl. same. M19.
[mod. Latin (see below) from Latin = a muse, from *Pieria*: see PIERIAN.]
1 Any of various evergreen shrubs of the genus *Pieris*, of the heath family, native to N. America and Asia and bearing ornamental panicles of waxy white bell-shaped flowers. M19.
2 ENTOMOLOGY. A butterfly of the genus *Pieris*, the members of which are white and include the common cabbage whites. Chiefly as mod. Latin genus name. M19.

pierogi /pəˈrəʊgi/ *noun*. *N. Amer.* Also **per-**, **pir-**. Pl. **-ies**. E20.
[Polish, pl. of *pieróg*.]
A dish consisting of dough dumplings stuffed with a filling such as potato or cheese, boiled and then optionally fried, and typically served with onions or sour cream; an individual dumpling.

pierrette /pɪəˈrɛt, pjɛˈrɛt/ *noun*. L19.
[French, fem. dim. of *Pierre* Peter, corresp. to next: see -ETTE.]
A female member of a company of pierrots.

pierrot /ˈpɪərəʊ, ˈpjɛrəʊ/ *noun*. Also **P-**. M18.
[French, appellative use of pet-form of *Pierre* Peter: see -OT¹. Cf. PARROT.]
A typical character in French pantomime. Now also, a musical entertainer with a whitened face and a loose white costume.

🕮 *attrib.*: R. COLLIER The concert party.. in pierrot costumes.

■ **pierrotic** /-ˈrɒtɪk/ *adjective* of, pertaining to, or characteristic of pierrots E20.

Piesporter /ˈpiːzpɔːtə/ *noun*. L19.
[German, from *Piesport* (see below): see -ER¹.]
A Moselle wine produced at Piesport, a village near Trier in Germany.

piet /ˈpʌɪət/ *noun & adjective*. Chiefly & now only *Scot. & north.* Also **pyet**, **pyot**. ME.
[from PIE *noun*¹ + -OT¹ (later -ET¹).]
▶ **A** *noun*. **1** A magpie. Cf. PIANNET. ME. ▶**b** A water ouzel. Also *water-piet*. M19.
2 A talkative or saucy person. L16.
▶ **B** *attrib.* or as *adjective*. Like a magpie, esp. in appearance; piebald. E16.

Pietà /pɪeɪˈtɑː, *foreign* pjeˈta/ *noun*. M17.
[Italian, from Latin *pietas* PIETY.]
A painting or sculpture representing the Virgin Mary holding the dead body of Jesus on her lap or in her arms.

pietas /piːˈeɪtɑːs/ *noun*. E20.
[Latin: see PIETY.]
An attitude of respect towards an ancestor, institution, etc.

pietism /ˈpʌɪətɪz(ə)m/ *noun*. L17.
[German *Pietismus* from mod. Latin, formed after next: see -ISM.]
1 ECCLESIASTICAL HISTORY. (Also **P-**.) A movement originated by P. J. Spener (1635–1705) in Frankfurt in the late 17th cent. for the revival of piety in the Lutheran Church; the principles or practices of this movement. Now also, any similar movement within Protestantism. L17.
2 Devotion to strict religious practice; pious sentiment, esp. of an affected or exaggerated nature. E19.

pietist /ˈpʌɪətɪst/ *noun*. L17.
[German, from Latin *pietas*: see PIETY, -IST.]
1 ECCLESIASTICAL HISTORY. (Also **P-**.) A follower of pietism. L17.
2 A person characterized by or professing (often affected or exaggerated) piety; a person devoted to strict religious practice, esp. as opp. to intellectual belief. M18.
■ **pieˈtistic** *adjective* pertaining to pietists or pietism; characterized by pietism: M19. **pieˈtistical** *adjective* (*rare*) = PIETISTIC E19. **pieˈtistically** *adverb* (*rare*) L19.

piet-my-vrou /ˈpɪtmeɪfrəʊ/ *noun*. *S. Afr.* M19.
[Afrikaans, lit. 'Peter my wife', in imit. of the bird's call.]
= ***red-chested cuckoo*** s.v. RED *adjective*. Also, the robin-chat *Cossypha dichroa*, which imitates the call of this cuckoo and is parasitized by it.

pietra commessa /pi,eːtra komˈmessa/ *noun phr*. Pl. ***pietre commesse*** /pi,eːtre komˈmesse/. M17.
[Italian, lit. 'stone fitted together'.]
(An example of) mosaic work.

pietra dura /pi,eːtra ˈduːra/ *noun phr*. Pl. ***pietre dure*** /pi,eːtre ˈduːre/. E19.
[Italian, lit. 'hard stone'.]
Semiprecious stones; *sing.* & in *pl.*, mosaic work of such stones.

pietra serena /pi,eːtra seˈreːna/ *noun phr*. L19.
[Italian, lit. 'clear stone'.]
Bluish sandstone much used for building in Florence and throughout Tuscany.

pietre commesse, ***pietre dure*** *noun phrs*. pls. of PIETRA COMMESSA, PIETRA DURA.

piety /ˈpʌɪəti/ *noun*. ME.
[Old French *piete* (mod. *piété*) from Latin *pietas* dutifulness, from *pius* PIOUS. See also PITY *noun*.]
▶†**I 1** = PITY *noun* I. ME–E17.
▶ **II 2** Habitual reverence and obedience to God; devotion to religious duties and observances; godliness, devoutness. LME.
3 Dutifulness to parents, superiors, etc.; affectionate loyalty and respect. E16.
4 An instance of religious devotion or affectionate loyalty; a pious act, observance, or characteristic. M17.

🕮 **2** LD MACAULAY He was a man of.. fervent piety.. and an exemplary parish priest. **3** M. LANE In the excess of her filial piety she had revised what he had written. **4** P. ROSE His complex portrait of.. socialism was replaced by bland pieties in its favour.

Phrases: ***mount of piety***: see MOUNT *noun*¹.
¶ See note s.v. PITY *noun*.

piezo /pʌɪˈiːzəʊ, ˈpiːzəʊ/ *adjective*. E20.
[Abbreviation.]
= PIEZOELECTRIC *adjective*.

piezo- /pʌɪˈiːzəʊ, ˈpiːzəʊ/ *combining form*.
[from Greek *piezein* press, squeeze: see -O-.]
PHYSICS. Forming nouns and adjectives with the sense 'pressure, stress'.
■ **piezo-crystal** *noun* a piezoelectric crystal used in an electric circuit E20. **piezomagˈnetic** *adjective* of, pertaining to, or exhibiting piezomagnetism E20. **piezoˈmagnetism** *noun* magnetism induced in a crystal by the application of mechanical stress E20. **piezoreˈsistance** *noun* change in the electrical resistance of a solid when subjected to mechanical stress M20. **piezoreˈsistive** *adjective* of, pertaining to, or utilizing piezoresistance or piezoresistivity M20. **piezoresisˈtivity** *noun* change in the electrical resistivity of a solid when subjected to mechanical stress M20.

piezoelectric /pʌɪ,iːzəʊɪˈlɛktrɪk, ,piːzəʊ-/ *adjective & noun*. L19.
[from prec. + ELECTRIC.]
PHYSICS. ▶**A** *adjective*. Of, pertaining to, exhibiting, or utilizing piezoelectricity. L19.
▶ **B** *noun*. A piezoelectric substance or body. E20.
■ **piezoelectrical** *adjective* M20. **piezoelectrically** *adverb* E20.

piezoelectricity /pʌɪ,iːzəʊɪlɛkˈtrɪsɪti, ,piːzəʊ-/ *noun*. L19.
[from PIEZO- + ELECTRICITY.]
PHYSICS. Electric polarization in a substance resulting from the application of mechanical stress. Cf. ELECTROSTRICTION.

piezometer /pʌɪˈzɒmɪtə/ *noun*. E19.
[from PIEZO- + -METER.]
Any of various instruments for measuring the pressure of a liquid or gas, or something connected with pressure (as the compressibility of liquid or the depth of water).
■ **piezoˈmetric** *adjective* of or pertaining to the measurement of hydrostatic pressure in an aquifer E20.

piff /pɪf/ *interjection*. L18.
[Imit.]
Repr. the sound made by a bullet as it travels through the air. Also ***piff-paff***.

Piffer /ˈpɪfə/ *noun*. *slang* (now *Hist.*). L19.
[from *PFF*, initials of the name of the force + -ER¹.]
A member of the Punjab Frontier Force (a military unit raised in 1849 and employed esp. to police the North-West Frontier of India) or of one of the regiments that succeeded it.

pifferaro /pifeˈraːro/ *noun*. Pl. **-ri** /-ri/. M19.
[Italian, from next.]
A performer on the *piffero*.

piffero /ˈpiffero/ *noun*. Pl. **-ri** /-ri/. E18.
[Italian = Spanish *pifaro*, French *fifre*: see FIFE.]
In Italy: a type of oboe, a shawm; also, a bagpipe with an inflated sheepskin for the reservoir.

piffle /ˈpɪf(ə)l/ *verb & noun*. *colloq.* (orig. *dial.*). M19.
[App. imit., with dim. ending -LE³.]
▶ **A** *verb intrans*. Talk or act in a feeble or trifling way. M19.

🕮 R. KIPLING They piddled and piffled with iron; I'd given my orders for steel!

▶ **B** *noun*. Foolish or empty talk; nonsense, drivel. L19.

🕮 J. HIGGINS 'You are as radiant as the morning, Countess.' .. 'What piffle!'

■ **piffler** *noun* L19. **piffling** *adjective* that piffles; trivial, worthless: M19.

piff-paff *interjection* see PIFF.

pig /pɪg/ *noun*¹. ME.
[Origin uncertain: perh. repr. unrecorded Old English form found only in *picbrēd* acorns (lit. 'swine-bread').]
▶ **I 1** A domesticated even-toed ungulate derived from the wild boar *Sus scrofa*, with a large head, a broad flat snout, and a stout often almost hairless body, kept as a source of bacon, ham, pork, etc. Orig. (now *US*), the young of this animal. ME. ▶**b** Any of various other ungulates of the genus *Sus* or the family Suidae, with bristly hair and tusklike canines; *esp.* the wild boar; any of various other animals thought to resemble the pig in appearance or behaviour. Usu. with specifying word. M17.
2 The flesh of this animal (esp. a young one) used as food. Chiefly *non-standard* or *joc.* LME.
3 a Chiefly as a term of abuse: a person regarded as having the qualities or characteristics associated with pigs; *esp.* (*a*) a glutton (freq. in ***make a pig of oneself***); (*b*) a disagreeable, obstinate, or unpleasant person; (*c*) *US* a promiscuous, esp. dirty or unattractive, woman. M16. ▶**b** An unpleasant or awkward thing, task, etc. *colloq.* E20.
4 A police officer. *slang. derog.* E19.
5 Any of various forms of transport; *esp.* (in Northern Ireland) an armoured personnel carrier. *slang.* L19.

🕮 **1b** *bush-pig*, *Guinea-pig*, *sea-pig*, etc. **3a** *Wanted* They didn't buy me any chips.. the mean pigs. **b** *Times* A pig of a year for a seller of domestic appliances. *Footloose* With sore feet, the next stretch was a pig, being a hard, very stony track. **4** N. LUARD The police Rover and some motorcycle pigs.

▶ **II 6** An oblong ingot of metal (now usu. iron or lead) from a smelting-furnace. Also = ***pig-iron*** below. Cf. SOW *noun*¹ 5. L16. ▶**b** Any of the smaller channels in a smelting-furnace. Cf. SOW *noun*¹ 5b. E19.
7 A segment of a citrus fruit or (formerly) an apple. Cf. PEG *noun*¹ 8. L19.
8 A device which fits snugly inside an oil or gas pipeline and is sent through it to clean or inspect the inside, or to act as a barrier between fluids either side of it. M20.

🕮 **7** D. WELCH I squeezed my pig of lemon over the sliver of salmon.

Phrases: **bleed like a pig**, **bleed like a stuck pig** bleed profusely. ***blind pig***: see BLIND *adjective & adverb*. **bring one's pigs to market**, **drive one's pigs to market** succeed in realizing one's potential. **draw pig on pork**, **draw pig on bacon** COMMERCE (*arch. slang*) (of a firm) draw an accommodation bill on another branch of a firm so that drawer and drawee are one and the same. ***grease the fat pig***: see GREASE *verb* 3. **in a pig's eye** *interjection* (chiefly *US & Austral. slang*): expr. derisive incredulity (freq. preceding a statement emphatically repudiated). **in pig** (of a sow or (*colloq.*, usu. *derog.*) a woman) pregnant. ***long pig***: see LONG *adjective*¹. **make a**

pig's ear *colloq.* make a mess *of*. ***male chauvinist pig***: see **MALE** *adjective & noun*. **on the pig's back** *Irish, Austral., & NZ slang* in a fortunate position. **pig in a blanket** *US* (*a*) oysters etc. cooked in strips of bacon; (*b*) a kind of hot dog. **pig in a poke** a thing bought or accepted without opportunity for prior inspection (esp. in ***buy a pig in a poke***). **pig in the middle** (the middle player in) a children's ball game for three, in which the middle player has to intercept the ball as it passes between the other two; *fig.* a person placed awkwardly between opposing forces. **pigs might fly**: expr. ironical disbelief. **please the pigs** *colloq.* if circumstances permit. ***stick pigs***: see **STICK** *verb*[1].

Comb.: **pig-bed** the bed of sand in which pigs of iron are cast; **pig-boat** *US slang* a submarine; **pig-boiling** *METALLURGY* a stage in the puddling of unrefined pig-iron, characterized by the rapid bubbling of gas from the molten metal; **pig-cote** (now *rare*) a pigsty; **pig-dog** *Austral. & NZ* a dog used in hunting wild pigs in Australia and New Zealand; **pig-face** any of several Australasian mesembryanthemums, esp. *Disphyma australe*, which has pink or purplish-red flowers and edible berries; **pigfish** (*a*) any of several wrasses and grunts (fishes), esp. *Orthopristis chrysoptera* of the Western Atlantic and (more fully ***giant pig***) the blue groper, *Achoerodus gouldii*; (*b*) any of various fishes of southern oceans of the family Congiopodidae, typically having a protuberant snout; **pig-herd** a keeper of a herd of pigs; **pig-hunting** (chiefly *NZ HISTORY*) hunting for wild pigs; **pig-ignorant** *adjective* (*colloq.*) extremely ignorant; **pig-iron** cast iron as first obtained from the smelting-furnace, in the form of oblong blocks; **Pig Island** *Austral. & NZ slang* New Zealand [from the pigs introduced there by Captain Cook]; **Pig Islander** *Austral. & NZ slang* a New Zealander; **pig-jump** *noun & verb* (*Austral. slang*) (*a*) *noun* a jump made by a horse from all four legs without bringing them together; (*b*) *verb intrans.* (of a horse) jump in this way; **pig Latin** a secret language formed from English by transferring the initial consonant or consonant cluster of each word to the end of the word and adding a vocalic syllable (usually /eɪ/); **pig-lead** lead in the form of pigs, as it comes from the smelting furnace; **pig-lily** *S. Afr.* the arum lily, *Zantedeschia aethiopica*; **pig louse** †(*a*) a woodlouse; (*b*) a large louse, *Haematopinus suis*, parasitic on pigs; **pigman** a person who looks after pigs on a farm; **pigmeater** *Austral. slang* a bullock fit only for pig's food; **pig-metal** metal, usu. iron, in the form of pigs; **pig-mould** any of the channels in a pig-bed; **pignut** (*a*) (the edible tuber of) an umbelliferous plant, *Conopodium majus*, of acid pastures and woods; also called ***earth-nut***, ***hognut***; (*b*) *N. Amer.* the small pear-shaped nut of the broom hickory, *Carya glabra*; (more fully ***pignut hickory***) this tree; **pig-out** [from *pig out* (see **PIG** *verb* 3)] *colloq.* a bout of eating a large amount of food; **pigpen** *US* a pigsty; **pig-root** *verb intrans.* (*Austral. & NZ slang*) (of a horse) buck; **pig's breakfast** *colloq.* an unappetizing or messy thing; **pig's ear** *rhyming slang* beer; (see also ***make a pig's ear*** above); **pigsty** (*a*) a pen for pigs, consisting of a shed and an open yard; (*b*) *transf.* a dirty or disorganized place; **pig's wash** (*a*) = ***pigswill*** below; (*b*) *derog.* weak inferior liquor; **pig's whisper** (*a*) *dial.* a low whisper; (*b*) *slang* a very brief space of time; **pigswill** kitchen refuse and scraps fed to pigs; **pigwash** pigswill; **pig-washing** *METALLURGY* the refining of molten pig-iron by treatment with iron oxide etc.; **pigweed** any of various plants used as animal fodder, esp. fat-hen, *Chenopodium album*, various weedy amaranths (genus *Amaranthus*), and (*Austral.*) the purslane, *Portulaca oleracea*.

■ **piglike** *adjective & adverb* like (that of) a pig **E17**.

pig /pɪɡ/ *noun*[2]. Now *Scot. & north.* **LME**.
[Origin unkn.: cf. **PIGGIN**, **PRIG** *noun*[1].]
1 An earthenware pitcher, jar, or other vessel. **LME**.
2 *spec.* An earthenware or stone hot-water bottle. **M19**.

pig /pɪɡ/ *verb*. Infl. **-gg-**. **LME**.
[from **PIG** *noun*[1].]
1 *verb intrans. & trans.* Of a sow: give birth to (piglets), farrow. **LME**.
2 a *verb intrans. & trans.* (with *it*). Live or sleep together in crowded, disorderly, or dirty conditions. **L17**. ▸**b** *verb trans.* Crowd (people) together like pigs. *rare*. **L19**.
3 a *verb intrans.* With *out*: gorge oneself (*on* a food). **L20**. ▸**b** *verb trans.* Eat greedily. **L20**.

> 🕮 **2** J. BUCHAN They would have to pig it in a moorland inn. **pig along** live from day to day like an animal.

pig-bel /pɪɡˈbɛl/ *noun*. **M20**.
[Pidgin English *pig-belly*.]
MEDICINE. A severe necrotizing enterocolitis found in Papua New Guinea, caused by *Clostridium welchii* and associated with feasting on pork.

pigeon /ˈpɪdʒɪn, ˈpɪdʒ(ə)n/ *noun*[1]. **LME**.
[Old French *pijon* young bird, esp. young pigeon (mod. *pigeon* pigeon) from Proto-Romance alt. of late Latin *pipio(n-)*, from imit. base.]
1 Any of the granivorous or fruit-eating birds of the family Columbidae, esp. those that are relatively large; *esp.* a bird descended from the rock dove, *Columba livia*, domesticated and trained to carry messages etc., and now widespread as a feral species. Formerly *spec.*, a young bird of this kind. Cf. **DOVE** *noun*. **LME**.
2 *fig.* **a** (A term of endearment for) a young woman, a girl. **L16**. ▸**b** A person easily swindled or tricked, esp. in gaming. *slang*. **L16**. ▸**c** A stool-pigeon. **M19**. ▸**d** A person who carries a journalist's report from one country to another in order to evade censorship. *slang*. **L20**.
1 ***carrier pigeon***, ***homing pigeon***, ***passenger pigeon***, ***poulter pigeon***, ***woodpigeon***, etc.
Phrases etc.: **Cape pigeon** = **PINTADO** 2. ***clay pigeon***: see **CLAY** *noun* 5. ***put a cat among the pigeons***, ***put the cat among the pigeons***: see **CAT** *noun*[1]. ***stool-pigeon***: see **STOOL** *noun* 13b.
Comb.: **pigeon-berry** (the berry of) any of several plants whose fruit is attractive to birds; *esp.* (*a*) *N. Amer.* the pokeweed, *Phytolacca americana*; (*b*) *W. Indies* the sky-flower, *Duranta erecta*; (*c*) *Austral.* (in full ***pigeon-berry ash***, ***pigeon-berry tree***) any of several trees of eastern Australian rainforest, esp. *Cryptocarya erythroxylon*, of the laurel family, and *Elaeocarpus obovatus* (family Elaeocarpaceae); **pigeon breast** a laterally constricted chest, resulting in forward protrusion of the sternum; **pigeon-breasted** *adjective* having a pigeon breast; **pigeon chest** = ***pigeon breast*** above; **pigeon-chested** *adjective* = ***pigeon-breasted*** above; **pigeon drop** *US Criminals' slang* a confidence trick which begins with the dropping of a wallet in front of the victim; **pigeon-fancier** a person who keeps and breeds fancy pigeons; **pigeon-fancying** the keeping and breeding of fancy pigeons; **pigeon grass** *US* any of several panic-grasses, esp. *Setaria pumila*; **pigeon guillemot** a mainly black guillemot, *Cepphus columba*, of the N. Pacific; **pigeon-hawk** (*a*) *US* = **MERLIN**; †(*b*) any of various hawks of the family Accipitridae; **pigeon-hearted** *adjective* faint-hearted, timid; **pigeon-house** a dovecot; †**pigeon-livered** *adjective* (*rare*, Shakes.) meek, gentle; ***pigeon-loft***: see **LOFT** *noun* 8; **pigeon-pair** a set of twins, or any pair of children, consisting of one boy and one girl; **pigeon-pea** (the edible seed of) the cajan, *Cajanus cajan*; **pigeon-plum** (the edible grapelike fruit of) a tree of the W. Indies and Florida, *Coccoloba diversifolia*, of the knotgrass family; **pigeon-post** the conveyance of letters or dispatches by homing pigeons; **pigeon's blood** *adjectival phr.* (of a ruby) dark red; **pigeon's milk** (*a*) an imaginary article for which children are sent on a fool's errand; (*b*) a curdlike secretion from a pigeon's crop, with which it feeds its young; **pigeon tick** a tick, *Argas reflexus*, occurring mainly on pigeons; **pigeon-toed** *adjective* (of a person or horse) having toes or feet that turn inwards; **pigeon-weed** *US* corn gromwell, *Lithospermum arvense*; **pigeon-wing** *US* (*a*) a dance step performed by jumping up and striking the legs together; (*b*) a figure in skating outlining the open wings of a pigeon; **pigeon-wood** the wood of various tropical or subtropical trees or shrubs used in cabinet-work, so called from the marking or colouring; any of these trees, esp. (*W. Indies*) *Dipholis salicifolia* (family Sapotaceae) and (*NZ*) *Hedycarya arborea* (family Monimiaceae); **pigeon-woodpecker** *US* = ***common flicker*** s.v. **FLICKER** *noun*[1].

■ **pigeoˈneer** *noun* (*US*) a person who trains or breeds homing pigeons, formerly esp. in the US Army Signal Corps **E20**. **pigeonry** *noun* a place where pigeons are kept **M19**.

pigeon *noun*[2] see **PIDGIN**.

pigeon /ˈpɪdʒɪn, ˈpɪdʒ(ə)n/ *verb trans. arch.* **L17**.
[from **PIGEON** *noun*[1].]
Make a dupe of; trick, swindle, esp. at cards or in gaming.

pigeongram /ˈpɪdʒɪnɡram, ˈpɪdʒ(ə)n-/ *noun*. **L19**.
[from **PIGEON** *noun*[1] + **-GRAM**.]
A message conveyed by a homing pigeon.

pigeon-hole /ˈpɪdʒɪnhəʊl, ˈpɪdʒ(ə)n-/ *noun & verb*. **L16**.
[from **PIGEON** *noun*[1] + **HOLE** *noun*[1].]
▶ **A** *noun*. **1** A small recess (usu. one of a series) for a domestic pigeon to nest in; *transf.* a small room, apartment, etc. Formerly also (*Criminals' slang*) the stocks; an instrument in which the hands of culprits were confined, when being flogged. **L16–L17**.
†**2** In *pl.* An old outdoor game, probably in which balls were bowled at small arched apertures. Only in **17**.
3 A hole in a wall or door for the passage of pigeons; *transf.* any of a series of holes for the passage of liquids, escape of gases, etc. **L17**.
†**4** *TYPOGRAPHY*. An excessively wide space between words. *slang*. **L17–E20**.
5 Any of a series of compartments in a desk or on a wall, open in front, for keeping and sorting papers, letters, etc. **L17**. ▸**b** *fig.* Any of a series of categories for the classification of facts, ideas, people, etc. **M19**.
†**6** A seat in the top row of the gallery of a theatre. *rare*. **M18–M19**.

> 🕮 **5b** R. H. MORRIESON I had privately consigned Len Ramsbottom to the pigeon-hole 'lousiest typist ever'.

▶ **B** *verb trans*. **1** Deposit in a pigeon-hole for later reference; *fig.* shelve (a matter) for, or on pretext of, future consideration. **M19**.
2 Furnish with or divide into a set of pigeon-holes. **M19**.
3 Assign to a definite place in the memory, or in an ordered group of ideas; categorize mentally. **L19**.

> 🕮 **1** B. T. BRADFORD She pigeon-holed her worry about him, deciding she must concentrate on Francesca. **3** *National Times* He was labelled schizophrenic . . a diagnosis flung . . around . . to pigeon-hole misfits.

■ **pigeon-holer** *noun* **L19**.

pigeonite /ˈpɪdʒ(ə)nʌɪt/ *noun*. **E20**.
[from *Pigeon* Point, Minnesota + **-ITE**[1].]
MINERALOGY. A clinopyroxene of magnesium, ferrous iron, and calcium, occurring chiefly in basic igneous rocks.
■ **pigeonitic** /pɪdʒəˈnɪtɪk/ *adjective* **M20**.

piggery /ˈpɪɡ(ə)ri/ *noun*. **L18**.
[from **PIG** *noun*[1] + **-ERY**.]
1 A pig-breeding establishment; a pigsty. **L18**.
2 Piggishness. **M19**.

> 🕮 **1** *fig.*: J. L. STEPHENS The interior was a perfect piggery full of fleas and children.

piggie *noun* var. of **PIGGY** *noun*.

piggin /ˈpɪɡɪn/ *noun*. Chiefly *Scot. & dial.* **M16**.
[Perh. from **PIG** *noun*[2].]
A small pail or cylindrical vessel, *esp.* a wooden one with one stave longer than the rest serving as a handle.

pigging /ˈpɪɡɪŋ/ *noun*. **E17**.
[from **PIG** *noun*[1], *verb* + **-ING**[1].]
1 The action of **PIG** *verb*. **E17**.
2 ***pigging back*** (*METALLURGY*), the addition of more pig-iron to the charge in an open-hearth furnace in order to raise its carbon content. **E20**.
3 Hog-tying. Chiefly in ***pigging string*** below. **E20**.
4 The use of a snugly fitting device to clean or inspect the inside of an oil or gas pipeline. **L20**.
Comb.: **pigging string** a short rope used for hog-tying.

piggish /ˈpɪɡɪʃ/ *adjective*. **L18**.
[from **PIG** *noun*[1] + **-ISH**[1].]
Pertaining to or characteristic of a pig; resembling a pig; having a quality or attribute associated with pigs; stubborn, greedy, selfish, dirty, etc.
■ **piggishly** *adverb* **L18**. **piggishness** *noun* **L18**.

piggle /ˈpɪɡ(ə)l/ *verb*. *dial.* **M19**.
[Origin unkn.: cf. **PIDDLE** *verb*.]
1 *verb trans.* Uproot, pick out, esp. with a pointed instrument. **M19**.
2 *verb intrans.* Trifle *with*. **E20**.
■ **piggling** *ppl adjective* paltry, niggling **E20**.

piggy /ˈpɪɡi/ *noun*. Also **piggie**. **E17**.
[from **PIG** *noun*[1] + **-Y**[6], **-IE**.]
1 A little pig; (a pet name for) a pig or other animal. **E17**. ▸**b** A toe. *colloq.* (esp. *nursery*). **L20**.
2 The game of tip-cat; the piece of wood used in this game. **M19**.
Comb.: **piggy bank** a pig-shaped money box, often of pottery; *transf.* any supply of savings; **piggy in the middle** = ***pig in the middle*** s.v. **PIG** *noun*[1].
¶ Sense 1b derives from the nursery game 'This little piggy (or pig) went to market,' etc., which is usu. counted out on a child's toes.

piggy /ˈpɪɡi/ *adjective*. **M19**.
[from **PIG** *noun*[1] + **-Y**[1].]
Resembling a pig; dirty, greedy, stubborn, etc., in a way usu. associated with pigs; piggish. Of the eyes: small and sunken.

piggyback /ˈpɪɡɪbak/ *adverb, adjective, noun, & verb*. Also **pickaback** /ˈpɪkəbak/. **M16**.
[Origin unkn.]
▶ **A** *adverb*. Also (earlier) †**a pick-pack**, †**on pick-pack**, (now *dial.*) **pick-a-pack**, & other vars. On the back and shoulders of another person like a pack or bundle; *transf.* on top of another vehicle etc. Freq. in ***carry piggyback***, ***ride piggyback***. **M16**.
▶ **B** *adjective*. **1** Involving carrying or being carried on a person's back and shoulders. **E19**.
2 *transf.* Involving the carrying or mounting of one object on top of another, esp. one vehicle on top of another (freq. a loaded truck on a flat railway car). **M20**.

> 🕮 **2** *Times* Piggyback transplants, in which a patient given a new heart did not have his old heart taken away. **piggyback plant** a N. American plant, *Tolmiea menziesii*, of the saxifrage family, with cordate leaves that produce plantlets at the junction with the petiole.

▶ **C** *noun*. **1** A piggyback ride given to a child etc. **E20**.
2 A vehicle carried on top of another. **M20**.
▶ **D** *verb*. **1** *verb intrans.* Ride (as if) on a person's back and shoulders. **M20**.
2 *verb trans.* Give a piggyback to; *transf.* carry or mount on top of another thing, *esp.* carry or mount (a loaded truck) on a flat railway car. **M20**.

> 🕮 **2** *Times* The . . piggy-backing of the craft on a jumbo jet to take it from California to Florida. *Weekend Australian* A 190-litre freezer that piggybacks a microwave oven.

piggy-wiggy /pɪɡɪˈwɪɡi/ *noun*. *joc. & nursery*. Also **-wig** /-wɪɡ/. **M19**.
[Fanciful extension of **PIGGY** *noun*.]
(A pet name for) a pig.

> 🕮 *fig.*: E. BOWEN Scrumptious Irish teas make a perfect piggy-wiggy of me.

pigheaded /pɪɡˈhɛdɪd/ *adjective*. **E17**.
[from **PIG** *noun*[1] + **HEADED**.]
Having a head like that of a pig. Chiefly *fig.*, stubborn, perverse.
■ **pigheadedly** *adverb* **L19**. **pigheadedness** *noun* **E19**.

pight /pʌɪt/ *verb*[1] *trans.* Now *arch. rare*. **L16**.
[pa. t. & pple of **PITCH** *verb*[2] used as a present tense.]
Pitch; set in place or in order.

pight *verb*[2] *pa. t. & pple*: see **PITCH** *verb*[2].

pightle /ˈpʌɪt(ə)l/ *noun*. Chiefly *dial.* **ME**.
[Origin unkn.: in Anglo-Latin *pitellum* etc. Cf. **PINGLE** *noun*.]
A small field or enclosure.

piglet /ˈpɪglɪt/ *noun.* L19.
[from PIG *noun*[1] + -LET.]
A little pig; a young pig.

pigling /ˈpɪglɪŋ/ *noun.* E18.
[from PIG *noun*[1] + -LING[1].]
= PIGLET.

pigment /ˈpɪgm(ə)nt/ *noun & verb.* LOE.
[Latin *pigmentum*, from base of *pingere* PAINT *verb* + -MENT. Cf. PIMENT.]
▶ **A** *noun.* **1** A spice. Long *arch.* LOE.
2 Any substance (usu. artificially prepared) used for colouring or painting; *spec.* a dry substance, usu. in the form of powder, which, when mixed with oil, water, etc., constitutes a paint. LOE. ▸**b** The natural colouring matter in the tissues of an animal or plant. M19.

📖 **2** E. H. GOMBRICH Painters . . had to prepare their own pigments mostly from . . plants and minerals. **b** P. PARISH White patches on the skin due to loss of pigment may occur. PHYCOBILIN *pigment*. RESPIRATORY *pigment*.

Comb.: **pigment epithelium**, **pigment layer** ANATOMY a layer of pigmented cells in the retina overlying the choroid; **pigment printing** (*a*) a method of printing textiles with water-insoluble pigments, using a resin to bind the pigment to the cloth; (*b*) PHOTOGRAPHY any of various methods of making prints using certain sensitized organic colloids.
▶ **B** *verb trans.* Colour (as) with a pigment. E20.
■ **pigˈmental** *adjective* = PIGMENTARY *adjective* 2 M19. **pigmented** *adjective* coloured with pigment L19. **pigmentless** *adjective* L19.

pigmentary /ˈpɪgm(ə)nt(ə)ri/ *adjective & noun.* LME.
[Latin *pigmentarius* of paints or unguents, (as noun) a dealer in these, from *pigmentum*: see PIGMENT, -ARY[1].]
▶ **A** *adjective.* †**1** Of or pertaining to an apothecary. Only in LME.
2 Of, pertaining to, or consisting of (natural) pigment. M19.
▶†**B** *noun.* A maker or seller of ointments, drugs, etc.; an apothecary. Only in LME.

pigmentation /pɪgm(ə)nˈteɪʃ(ə)n/ *noun.* M19.
[from PIGMENT + -ATION, after *coloration*.]
Coloration or (MEDICINE) discoloration by formation or deposition of pigment in the tissues; the presence of pigment.

pigmentocracy /pɪgm(ə)nˈtɒkrəsi/ *noun. rare.* M20.
[from PIGMENT *noun*: see -CRACY.]
A society based on the predominance of people of a particular (esp. white or lighter) skin-colour; the predominating class in such a society.

pigmy *noun, adjective, & verb* var. of PYGMY.

pignerate *verb* var. of PIGNORATE.

pignon /pinjɔ̃/ *noun.* Pl. pronounced same. E17.
[French = Spanish *piñon*, Portuguese *pinhão*, all from late Latin deriv. of Latin *pinea* pine cone.]
The edible seed of the stone pine, *Pinus pinea*, of southern Europe.

pignorate /ˈpɪgnəreɪt/ *verb trans.* Now *arch. rare.* Also **pignerate**. E17.
[Latin *pignerat-* (medieval Latin *-or-*) pa. ppl stem of *pignerare*, from *pigner-* (medieval Latin *-or-*), *pignus* a pledge: see -ATE[3].]
Give or take as a pledge; pledge, pawn.
■ **pignoˈration** *noun* M16.

pigskin /ˈpɪgskɪn/ *noun & adjective.* M19.
[from PIG *noun*[1] + SKIN *noun*.]
▶ **A** *noun.* **1** (Leather made from) the skin of a pig; *slang* an article made of such leather, esp. a saddle or (*N. Amer.*) a football. M19.
2 MEDICINE. = PEAU D'ORANGE. L19.
▶ **B** *adjective.* Made of pigskin. L19.

pigsney /ˈpɪgsni/ *noun. arch. & dial.* Also **-ny**. LME.
[from PIG *noun*[1] + -'S[1] + EYE *noun*, with prosthetic *n*.]
1 A specially cherished or darling girl or woman (formerly also boy or man). Chiefly as a term of endearment. LME.
†**2** A (little) eye. M17–L18.

pigsticking /ˈpɪgstɪkɪŋ/ *noun.* M19.
[from PIG *noun*[1] + STICKING *noun*.]
1 The hunting of wild boar with a spear. M19.
2 The butchering of pigs. L19.
■ **pigsticker** *noun* (*a*) a person who participates in the sport of pigsticking; a horse trained for this; (*b*) *slang* a lance, knife, or similar sharp weapon; (*c*) *dial. & slang* a pork-butcher: M19.

pigtail /ˈpɪgteɪl/ *noun.* L17.
[from PIG *noun*[1] + TAIL *noun*[1].]
1 Tobacco twisted into a thin coil. L17.
2 A plait of hair hanging down from the back of the head, *esp.* one worn by soldiers and sailors in the late 18th and early 19th cents., and formerly customary among the Chinese. Now chiefly, either of a pair of such plaits worn at the sides of the head, esp. by schoolgirls. M18. ▸**b** A Chinese. *slang. derog.* M19.
3 A small candle. *dial.* E19.
4 ELECTRICITY. A short length of flexible braided wire connecting a stationary part to a moving part. E20.
■ **pigtailed** *adjective* (*a*) having a tail like a pig's; ***pigtailed macaque***, a macaque, *Macaca nemestrina*, native from eastern India to Indonesia; (*b*) wearing or plaited in a pigtail: M18.

pi-jaw /ˈpʌɪdʒɔː/ *verb & noun. arch. slang.* L19.
[from PI *adjective* + JAW *noun*[1].]
▶ **A** *verb trans.* Give a moralizing lecture to. L19.
▶ **B** *noun.* A moralizing lecture or exhortation, *esp.* one given to children by a teacher or parent. E20.

pik *noun* var. of PIC *noun*[1].

pika /ˈpʌɪkə, ˈpiːkə/ *noun.* E19.
[Tungus *piika*.]
Any of various small lagomorph mammals constituting the genus *Ochotona* and family Ochotonidae, having short rounded ears, short legs, and a very small tail, and found in the mountains and deserts of western N. America and north-east and central Asia. Also called ***calling hare***, ***mouse-hare***, ***rock rabbit***, etc.

pikau /ˈpiːkaʊ/ *noun & verb. NZ.* M19.
[Maori.]
▶ **A** *noun.* A pack for carrying on the back, a knapsack. M19.
▶ **B** *verb trans.* Carry (a load or pack) on the back. L19.

pike /pʌɪk/ *noun*[1]. See also PICK *noun*[1]. OE.
[Origin unkn. Cf. PEAK *noun & adjective*, PICK *verb*[1]. In some senses assoc. with PIKE *noun*[4].]
▶ **I 1** = PICK *noun*[1] 1. *obsolete* exc. *dial.* OE.
▶ **II 2** A sharp point, a spike; the pointed tip of something. ME. ▸†**b** A hedgehog's prickle; a thorn, a spine. Chiefly *Scot.* ME–L18. ▸†**c** = PICK *noun*[1] 5. Only in L16.
3 A staff or stick with an iron point, a pikestaff. Formerly also *spec.*, a pilgrim's staff. Now *dial.* ME. ▸**b** A pitchfork. Now *dial.* LME.

📖 **2** *New Yorker* The metal pike of the turnstile.

▶ **III** Earlier form of *peak*.
4 a The long pointed toe of a shoe, fashionable in the 14th cent. *obsolete* exc. *Hist.* LME. ▸**b** The pointed end of an anvil. Cf. BICK. Now *dial.* L17.
5 A narrow pointed piece of land at the side of a field of irregular shape. Cf. PICK *noun*[1] 6. *dial.* L16.
Comb.: **pike-pole** *N. Amer.* a pole with a spike and a hook, used for driving and guiding floating logs.

pike /pʌɪk/ *noun*[2]. *north.* ME.
[App. specialized use of PIKE *noun*[1] or of Scandinavian origin: cf. Norwegian dial. *pīk* pointed mountain, *piktind* peaked summit.]
1 A pointed summit; a mountain or hill with a pointed summit. Now chiefly in proper names. Cf. PEAK *noun*[1] 4. ME. ▸**b** A cairn, beacon, or tower erected on the highest point of a mountain or hill. M18.
2 A small circular pointed stack of hay or corn erected temporarily in a field. M17.

pike /pʌɪk/ *noun*[3]. Pl. same, -**s**. ME.
[from PIKE *noun*[1], after the shape of the fish's jaw.]
Any of various large predatory freshwater fishes of the genus *Esox* and family Esocidae, occurring in the northern temperate zone, and having a long slender snout; *esp.* (more fully ***northern pike***) *E. lucius*. Also (usu. with specifying word), any of various other fishes resembling the true pikes, *esp.* a pikeperch (see below), garpike, or squawfish.
Comb.: **pikehead** a freshwater perciform fish, *Luciocephalus pulcher* (family Luciocephalidae), of Malaysia; **pikeperch** any of various predatory percid fishes of the genus *Stizostedion*, found in European and N. American rivers; *esp.* the zander, the sauger, or the walleye.

pike /pʌɪk/ *noun*[4]. E16.
[French *pique* back-form. from *piquer* pierce, puncture, from *pic* pike, pick. Sometimes assoc. with PIKE *noun*[1].]
1 Chiefly *Hist.* An infantry weapon consisting of a long wooden shaft with a pointed iron or steel head. E16.
†**2** A soldier armed with a pike, a pikeman. M16–M17.

📖 **1** R. CHRISTIANSEN The governor's . . head . . on the end of a pike.

Phrases: **pass the pikes**, **pass through the pikes** *arch.* run the gauntlet (*of*). †**push of pike** fighting at close quarters. **run the pikes**, **run through the pikes** *arch.* = ***pass the pikes*** above. ***stand of pikes***: see STAND *noun*[1] 16. ***trail a pike***: see TRAIL *verb*.

pike /pʌɪk/ *noun*[5]. Also (earlier) †**pick**. M16.
[formed as PIC *noun*[2].]
1 = PEAK *noun*[1] 4. Long *obsolete* exc. in a few proper names. M16.
†**2** NAUTICAL. ***on pike***, ***on the pike***, in a vertical position, straight up and down. Cf. APEAK. L16–E17.

pike /pʌɪk/ *noun*[6]. Now chiefly *US.* E19.
[Abbreviation of TURNPIKE.]
1 A turnpike road. Freq. in ***come down the pike***, appear on the scene; come to notice. E19. ▸**b** A railway line or system. M20.
2 A toll-bar, a toll-gate; the toll paid at this. M19.

📖 **1** W. A. PERCY The winding dirt pike we took.

pike /pʌɪk/ *noun*[7]. E20.
[Origin unkn.]
A position in diving, trampolining, and gymnastics in which the body is bent over at the waist whilst the legs are kept straight and the feet pointed. Also ***pike position***.

pike *noun*[8] var. of PIC *noun*[1].

†**pike** *adjective.* E16–E18.
[Perh. from French PIQUANT.]
Seasoned, spiced, hot.

pike /pʌɪk/ *verb*[1]. Long *obsolete* exc. *Scot.* LME.
[from PIKE *noun*[1].]
Provide with a pike or spike; *spec.* shoe (a horse) with spiked horseshoes for additional grip.

pike /pʌɪk/ *verb*[2]. Now *slang.* LME.
[Origin uncertain: cf. Old Danish *pikke af* hasten off, French *piquer* spur.]
†**1** *verb refl.* Hasten off; go *away* quickly. LME–L16.
2 *verb intrans.* Go; proceed; *fig.* die. Freq. with adverbs. E16.
3 *verb intrans.* Back out; hold oneself back. L19.

📖 **3** *Numbers* You wouldn't be piking, would you?

pike /pʌɪk/ *verb*[3] *trans.* L18.
[from PIKE *noun*[4].]
Wound or kill with a pike.

📖 S. HEANEY Pike / and spit him.

pike /pʌɪk/ *verb*[4] *trans. dial.* M19.
[from PIKE *noun*[2].]
Heap or pile up (hay or corn) into pikes.

pike /pʌɪk/ *verb*[5] *intrans.* M20.
[from PIKE *noun*[7].]
Go into a pike position in diving, gymnastics, etc.

pike *verb*[6] see PICK *verb*[1].

piked /pʌɪkt, ˈpʌɪkɪd/ *adjective*[1]. ME.
[from PIKE *noun*[1], *verb*[1]: see -ED[2], -ED[1].]
1 Having a sharp point or spike. Cf. PICKED *adjective*[1] 1. ME. ▸**b** Of an animal or plant: having a sharp point, spines, or prickles. Now *rare.* E17.
2 Tapering to a point. LME.
Special collocations: **piked dogfish** = ***spur-dog*** s.v. SPUR *noun*[1]. **piked horn** a woman's tall conical head-dress fashionable in the 14th and 15th cents. **piked shoe** a shoe with a long pointed toe, a poulaine. **piked whale** the minke whale.

piked /pʌɪkt/ *adjective*[2]. M20.
[from PIKE *noun*[7] + -ED[2].]
In a pike position; performed with the body in a pike position.

pikel /ˈpʌɪk(ə)l/ *noun.* Long *arch. & dial.* E17.
[Dim. of PIKE *noun*[1].]
A hay-fork, a pitchfork.

pikelet /ˈpʌɪklɪt/ *noun*[1]. L18.
[Welsh (*bara*) *pyglyd* pitchy (bread).]
1 A thin kind of crumpet. Orig. *dial.* L18.
2 A drop-scone. Chiefly *Austral. & NZ.* M20.

pikelet /ˈpʌɪklɪt/ *noun*[2]. L19.
[from PIKE *noun*[3] + -LET.]
A young or small pike.

pikeman /ˈpʌɪkmən/ *noun*[1]. Pl. **-men**. E16.
[from PIKE *noun*[1] + MAN *noun*.]
1 A person in charge of picking millstones and keeping them in order. *Scot.* E16.
2 A person who works with a pickaxe; a miner. L16.

pikeman /ˈpʌɪkmən/ *noun*[2]. *obsolete* exc. *Hist.* Pl. **-men**. M16.
[from PIKE *noun*[4] + MAN *noun*.]
A soldier armed with a pike.

pikeman /ˈpʌɪkmən/ *noun*[3]. Pl. **-men**. M19.
[from PIKE *noun*[6] + MAN *noun*.]
The keeper of a turnpike.

piker /ˈpʌɪkə/ *noun*[1]. *slang.* M19.
[App. from PIKE *noun*[6] + -ER[1].]
1 A vagrant, a tramp; a Gypsy. M19.
2 A bullock living wild in the bush. *Austral.* L19.

piker /ˈpʌɪkə/ *noun*[2]. *slang.* L19.
[from PIKE *verb*[2] + -ER[1].]
1 A cautious or timid gambler who makes only small bets; a person who takes no chances; a person who avoids doing his or her share of work, a shirker. L19.
2 A person who speculates in stocks, esp. with only small sums. L19.

piker *noun*[3] see PICKER *noun*[1].

pikestaff /ˈpʌɪkstɑːf/ *noun.* LME.
[In sense 1 prob. from Old Norse *pikstafr*; in sense 2 from PIKE *noun*[4].]
1 A staff or walking-stick with a metal point or tip at the lower end. Now only *Scot.* LME.
2 The wooden shaft of a pike or similar weapon. L16.

Phrases: **as plain as a pikestaff** [alt. of *as plain as a packstaff*] (*a*) very obvious, quite plain; (*b*) of ordinary or unattractive appearance, ugly.

pikey /ˈpʌɪki/ *noun. dial. & slang.* **M19.**
[from **PIKE** *noun*[6] + **-Y**[6].]
= **PIKER** *noun*[1] 1.

piki /ˈpiːki/ *noun.* **L19.**
[Hopi *piːki*.]
Maize-meal bread in the form of very thin sheets, made by the Hopi Indians of the south-western US.

pikia *noun* var. of **PEKEA.**

piking *noun* see **PICKING** *noun*[1].

†**pikoys** *noun* see **PICKAXE.**

piky /ˈpʌɪki/ *adjective.* **L19.**
[from **PIKE** *noun*[3] + **-Y**[1].]
Of the nature of pike (the fish), containing many pike.

pilaff *noun* var. of **PILAU.**

pilage /ˈpʌɪlɪdʒ/ *noun.* **E19.**
[from **PILE** *noun*[3] + **-AGE.**]
= **PELAGE.**

pilaster /pɪˈlastə/ *noun.* **L16.**
[French *pilastre* from Italian *pilastro* or medieval Latin *pilastrum*, from Latin *pila* pillar, **PILE** *noun*[3]: see **-ASTER.**]
ARCHITECTURE. 1 A rectangular column or pillar, *esp.* one projecting from a wall. Formerly also, the square pier of an arch, bridge, etc. **L16.**
†**2** A cylindrical shape. **L16–E17.**
■ **pilastered** *adjective* having or supported on pilasters **L17.**

pilastrade /pɪləˈstreɪd/ *noun.* **E19.**
[Italian *pilastrata*, from *pilastrare* adorn with pilasters, from *pilastro*: see prec., **-ADE.**]
ARCHITECTURE. A row of pilasters.

Pilate /ˈpʌɪlət/ *noun.* **LME.**
[Pontius *Pilate*, the Roman governor of Judaea (AD 26–36) who was involved in the trial of Jesus.]
1 Orig. (*derog.*), a corrupt or lax person, esp. a prelate. Now, a person who evades responsibility for his or her actions. **LME.**
†**2** ***Pilate's voice***, a loud magisterial voice (resembling that of the character of Pilate in a mystery play). **LME–M16.**

Pilates /pɪˈlɑːtiːz/ *noun.* **M20.**
[The name of Joseph *Pilates* (1880–1967), German physical fitness specialist, who developed the exercises and apparatus.]
(Proprietary name for) a system of exercises using special apparatus, designed to improve physical strength, flexibility, and posture, and enhance mental awareness. Also *attrib.*
¶ Pilates' own name for the system was *contrology*.

pilau /pɪˈlaʊ, ˈpiːlaʊ/ *noun.* Also **pilaff** /pɪˈlaːf/, **pilaw** /pɪˈlɔː/, **pulao** /pəˈlaʊ/, & other vars. **E17.**
[Turkish *pilâv* cooked rice = Persian *pilaw* boiled rice and meat.]
An Indian or Middle Eastern dish of rice (or occas. other grain) cooked in stock with spices and often meat, fish, vegetables, etc.
Comb.: **pilau rice** an Indian or Middle Eastern dish of rice cooked in stock with spices eaten as an accompaniment to a main meal.

pilch /pɪltʃ/ *noun.*
[Late Old English *pyl(e)ċe* = Old High German *pelliz* (German *Pelz* fur), from late Latin *pellicia* cloak, from Latin *pellicea* fem. of *pelliceus* made of skins, from *pellis* skin, **FELL** *noun*[1]. Cf. **PELISSE.**]
1 A garment lined with fur. Later, a leather or coarse woollen garment. *obsolete* exc. *Hist. & Scot. dial.* **LOE.**
2 †**a** A rug laid over a saddle. **M16–E18.** ▸**b** A child's light frameless saddle; = **PAD** *noun*[3] 2a. **M19.**
3 A triangular piece of (usu. waterproof) material worn over a baby's nappy. *arch.* **L17.**

pilch /pɪltʃ/ *verb intrans.* Now *Scot. & dial.* **ME.**
[Origin uncertain: cf. Low German *pl(e)ken*, Norwegian *pilka*, Old French *peluchier* pick.]
Pick; pluck; pilfer.

pilchard /ˈpɪltʃəd/ *noun.* Also †**-cher.** **M16.**
[Origin unkn.: ending assim. to **-ARD.**]
A small clupeid marine fish, *Sardina pilchardus*, which is an important food fish of European waters, the young often being marketed as sardines. Also (usu. with specifying word), any of various related food fishes, esp. of the genus *Sardinops*.

pilcher /ˈpɪltʃə/ *noun*[1]. *rare.* **L16.**
[Prob. from **PILCH** *noun* + **-ER**[1].]
†**1** A scabbard. *rare.* (Shakes.). Only in **L16.**
†**2** = **PILCH** *noun* 1. Only in **M17.**
3 = **PILCH** *noun* 3. *Canad. dial. rare.* **E20.**

†**pilcher** *noun*[2] var. of **PILCHARD.**

pilcorn /ˈpɪlkɔːn/ *noun. obsolete* exc. *Hist.* **ME.**
[from *pilled* ppl adjective of **PILL** *verb*[1] + **CORN** *noun*[1]. Cf. **PILGARLIC.**]
A kind of oat formerly cultivated, *Avena nuda*, in which the husk does not adhere to the grain. Also called ***naked oat***.

pilcrow /ˈpɪlkrəʊ/ *noun. arch.* Also (earlier) †**pilcraft.** **LME.**
[Perh. alt.]
= **PARAGRAPH** *noun* 2.

pile /pʌɪl/ *noun*[1].
[Old English *pīl* = Middle Low German, Middle Dutch *pīl* (Dutch *pijl*), Old High German *pfīl* (German *Pfeil*), from Latin *pilum* javelin. Cf. **SPILE** *noun*[2].]
1 †**a** A dart; an arrow. **OE–LME.** ▸**b** The pointed head of a dart, lance, or arrow. **L16.** ▸**c** *Hist.* A heavy javelin carried by a Roman foot-soldier. **E17.**
2 †**a** A spike, a nail; a prickle, a spine. **OE–ME.** ▸**b** A blade or leaf (of grass). **E16.**
3 A pointed stake or post; *esp.* a large heavy beam driven vertically into the bed of a river, soft ground, etc., to support a superstructure, as a bridge, pier, wall, the foundations of a house, etc. **OE.**
4 **HERALDRY.** A triangular charge or subordinary consisting of a figure formed by two lines meeting in an acute angle and pointing downwards. **L15.**

📖 **3** C. McCullough The piles upon which the house was poised. J. Mark Two piles . . supported the central span. *Construction News* Deep piles . . to reach through the silt. **4 in pile** arranged in the form of a pile. **party per pile** divided by lines in the form of a pile.

Comb.: **pile-building** = *pile-dwelling* below; **pile-drive** *verb* (*a*) *verb trans.* construct using a pile-driver; push or hit like a pile-driver; (*b*) *verb intrans.* (of a vessel) advance with difficulty in heavy seas; **pile-driver** (*a*) a machine for driving piles into the ground, either by the repeated dropping of a weight on the head of the pile or by using a steam hammer; (*b*) *colloq.* a very strong or powerful blow or kick; **pile-dwelling** a dwelling built on piles, esp. in a lake; **pile-shoe** an iron point fixed to the lower end of a pile; **pile-work** (a) construction consisting of piles; *spec.* a (prehistoric) structure on piles in a lake.

†**pile** *noun*[2]. **ME.**
[Origin unkn.]
1 A small castle or tower; = **PEEL** *noun*[1] 3. **ME–E17.**
2 *spec.* = **PEEL** *noun*[1] 4. **L15–L18.**

pile /pʌɪl/ *noun*[3]. **ME.**
[Prob. from Anglo-Norman *peile*, *pil*, Old French *poil* from Latin *pilus* hair.]
1 **a** A downy feather or part of a feather. *rare.* **ME.** ▸**b** Red or yellow markings on white or pale-coloured fowls; a fowl with this coloration. **M19.**
2 Hair; *esp.* fine soft hair, down; the fine undercoat of certain dogs; *rare* a single downy hair. **L15.**
3 The projecting surface on a fabric (such as velvet, plush, etc., or esp. a carpet), formed by weaving a secondary warp in loops which are either cut or left intact. Cf. **NAP** *noun*[2] 1. **M16.** ▸**b** Any of the projecting threads forming such a surface on a fabric. **L18.** ▸**c** A fabric with a pile, *esp.* velvet. **M19.**

📖 **3** A. Brink The thick . . pile of Susan's new carpet.

■ **piled** *adjective* †(*a*) covered with pile or hair; (*b*) (of fabric) having a pile, esp. of a specified type or thickness: **LME.** **pileless** /-l-l-/ *adjective* having no pile **M20.**

pile /pʌɪl/ *noun*[4]. **LME.**
[Old & mod. French = heap, pyramid, mass of masonry from Latin *pila* pillar, pier, mole.]
†**1** A pillar; a support, esp. of a bridge. **LME–M18.**
2 A heap of things (of considerable height) laid or lying on one another. **LME.**
3 *spec.* **a** A series of weights fitting one within or on another, so as to form a solid cone or other figure. Now *rare.* **LME.** ▸**b** A heap of wood or faggots on which a sacrifice, person, or dead body is burnt; a pyre. **L16.** ▸**c** Any large group or collection of things (without reference to height). Now *colloq.* (*sing.* & in *pl.*), a large quantity, amount, or number. **E17.** ▸**d** A large amount of money; a fortune. **M18.** ▸**e** **FOUNDING.** A number of metal rods laid on each other in rows, to be rolled after reheating. **M19.**
4 A large imposing building; a large group of tall buildings. **E17.**
5 A series of plates arranged so as to produce a potential difference or voltage; *spec.* = ***GALVANIC pile***. **E19.**
6 A nuclear reactor. Now *rare.* **M20.**

📖 **2** E. Hemingway The huge pile of sawdust. A. Schlee The pile of luggage. *Holiday Which?* Piles of green slate stacked by the road. R. Christiansen A . . pile of . . exam papers. **3c** *New Yorker* We trained a pile of those girls. *Star (Tarrytown, USA)* Piles of hate mail. **d** I. Hamilton A Boston boy had made his . . pile as a mining engineer. N. Mailer To the money she was born with, Jessica had added her own pile. A. Brien He is making a pile selling insurance. **4** B. Mason A handsome pile designed by John Nash. S. Hastings A . . gaunt, baronial pile.

pile /pʌɪl/ *noun*[5]. **LME.**
[Old & mod. French, or medieval Latin *pila*.]
1 The reverse side of a coin, opposite to the face. *arch.* **LME.**
2 The under iron of a minting apparatus, bearing the die for the impression of the reverse side of a coin. *obsolete* exc. *Hist.* **M16.**
1 ***cross and/or pile***: see **CROSS** *noun* 10.

pile /pʌɪl/ *noun*[6]. **LME.**
[Prob. from Latin *pila* ball, from the shape of an external pile.]
A haemorrhoid. Usu. in *pl.*

pile /pʌɪl/ *verb*[1] *trans.* **LME.**
[from **PILE** *noun*[1]. Cf. **SPILE** *verb*[2].]
1 Provide, strengthen, or support with piles; drive piles into. **LME.**
2 Drive in (a pile). *rare.* **E16.**
■ **piling** *noun* (*a*) the action of the verb; (*b*) piles collectively; a structure made of piles; wood for piles: **LME.**

pile /pʌɪl/ *verb*[2]. **LME.**
[from **PILE** *noun*[4].]
1 *verb trans.* Form into a pile or heap; heap up. Usu. foll. by *on*, *up*. **LME.** ▸**b** = **FAGGOT** *verb* 4. **M19.** ▸**c** **TANNING.** Form (hides) into a pile in order to sweat them and cause the hair to come off. Chiefly as ***piling*** *verbal noun.* **L19.**
2 **a** *verb intrans.* Form a pile or large mass, amass. Now usu. foll. by *up*. **E17.** ▸**b** *verb trans.* Amass, accumulate. Usu. foll. by *up*. **M19.** ▸**c** *verb intrans.* Enter or leave (a place, vehicle, etc.) or move in a hurried, tightly packed, or disorderly crowd. Foll. by *in*, *into*, *on*, *off*, *out of*, etc. **M19.**
3 *verb trans.* Cover or load *with* things to form a heap. **M17.**
4 **a** *verb trans.* Crash (a vehicle). Usu. foll. by *up*. **L19.** ▸**b** *verb intrans.* Of a vehicle: crash (*into*). Also foll. by *up*. **M20.**

📖 **1** P. Gallico Piled up blocks of masonry to form a wall. Toeckey Jones Mother . . piled a second helping of vegetables on Helen's plate. E. North Julia piled up the plates. **2a** R. Burns Chill o'er his slumbers, piles the drifty heap! E. Bowen Traffic . . piled up at intersections. J. Irving Wilbur Larch let the mail pile up unanswered. C. Tomalin The *Blue Review*'s debts piled up. **b** J. A. Gibbs The cricketer goes on . . piling up runs. **c** H. L. Foster The tourists piled towards the exits. R. Graves There were about three thousand prisoners . . and more piled in every day. N. West All six . . piled into one cab. G. Greene His fellow guests piled out of cars. **3** L. Black Piling his plate with meat. **4a** N. Shute The fellow was so drunk that he'd probably have piled his car up anyway. **b** *Oxford Mail* Nine cars . . piled up on the M25. *Sailplane & Gliding* Another helicopter has piled into the trees.

Phrases: **pile arms** position (usu. three) rifles with the butts on the ground and the muzzles together, for easy access. **pile it on**, **pile on the agony** *colloq.* exaggerate for effect or to gain sympathy. ***pile Pelion (up)on Ossa***, ***pile Ossa (up)on Pelion***: see **PELION.**
Comb.: **pile-up** *colloq.* (*a*) a crash involving several road vehicles; (the wreckage at) the scene of such a crash; (*b*) an accumulation of things, tasks, etc; (*c*) **ELECTRONICS** a lack of linearity or resolution in a pulse circuit caused by the pulses arriving too rapidly.
■ **piler** *noun* **E17.**

pilea /ˈpʌɪlɪə/ *noun.* **E20.**
[mod. Latin (see below), from Latin **PILEUS.**]
Any of various tropical plants constituting the genus *Pilea* of the nettle family, several of which are grown as house-plants for their ornamental leaves; *esp.* the artillery plant, *P. microphylla*.

pileated /ˈpʌɪlɪeɪtɪd/ *adjective.* **E18.**
[from Latin *pileatus* capped, formed as **PILEUS**: see **-ATE**[2], **-ED**[1].]
Chiefly **ZOOLOGY.** Having a cap; *esp.* (of a bird) having a conspicuous cap or crest.
pileated woodpecker a N. American woodpecker, *Dryocopus pileatus*, with a prominent red cap.
■ **pileate** *adjective* (esp. **BOTANY**, of fungi) having a pileus or cap **E19.**

pilei *noun* pl. of **PILEUS.**

pilentum /pɪˈlɛntəm/ *noun.* **M19.**
[Latin = a luxurious chariot used by women.]
Hist. A one- or two-horse open carriage.

pileus /ˈpʌɪlɪəs/ *noun.* Pl. **-lei** /-lɪʌɪ/. **M18.**
[Latin = felt cap.]
1 **BOTANY.** The spore-bearing circular structure surmounting the stipe in a mushroom or toadstool, which has an undersurface composed of radiating plates or gills. Also called ***cap***. **M18.**
2 **CLASSICAL ANTIQUITIES.** A felt cap without a brim. **L18.**

pilewort /ˈpʌɪlwəːt/ *noun.* **LME.**
[from **PILE** *noun*[6] + **WORT** *noun*[1].]
The lesser celandine, *Ranunculus ficaria*, formerly a reputed remedy for piles.

pilfer /ˈpɪlfə/ *noun.* **LME.**
[Anglo-Norman, Old French *pelfre*, from *pelfrer*: see next, and cf. **PELF.**]
1 The action of pilfering. Now only in ***pilfer-proof*** below. **LME.**
2 That which is pilfered; plunder, booty. Now *rare.* **LME.**
Comb.: **pilfer-proof** *adjective* resistant to or protected against being broken into or stolen.
¶ Sense 1 in isolated use after **LME** until *pilfer-proof* used in **M20.**

pilfer /ˈpɪlfə/ *verb.* **M16.**
[Anglo-Norman, Old French *pelfrer* pillage, rob, of unkn. origin. Cf. prec., (earlier) **PILFERY.**]
1 *verb trans.* Plunder, steal. Later *spec.*, steal in small quantities. **M16.** ▸**b** Rob (a person or place). *rare.* **M19.**

2 *verb intrans.* Pillage, plunder. Later *spec.*, steal on a small scale. M16.

1 DICKENS Old palings mended with stakes pilfered from the . . hedges. 2 H. SPENCER A servant . . who pilfers may have to suffer pain when being discharged.

■ **pilferer** *noun* L16.

pilferage /ˈpɪlf(ə)rɪdʒ/ *noun*. E17.
[from prec. + -AGE.]
†**1** Stolen goods. *rare*. Only in E17.
2 The action or practice of pilfering; stealing on a small scale. E19.

†**pilfery** *noun*. L15.
[from PILFER *verb* + -Y[3].]
1 (A) robbery. L15–L16.
2 = PILFERAGE 2. L16–E18.
3 The product of pilfering; stolen property. L16–E17.

pilgarlic /pɪlˈgɑːlɪk/ *noun*. E16.
[from *pilled* pa. pple & ppl adjective of PILL *verb*[1] + GARLIC. Cf. PILCORN.]
1 A bald head; a bald-headed man; *derog*. a weak or pitiable person. Now chiefly *dial*. E16.
2 Oneself, I, me (esp. as an object of pity). *dial. & US slang*. L17.

pilger /ˈpɪlgə/ *noun & verb*. E20.
[German = pilgrim, with allus. to the alternate feeding in and partial withdrawal of the billet during the operation of the mill, said to resemble the steps of pilgrims approaching a shrine.]
METALLURGY. ▶**A** *noun*. Used *attrib*. to designate a rolling-mill or process for reducing the outside diameter of a tube without changing the inside diameter. E20.
▶**B** *verb trans*. Make in a pilger mill. Chiefly as ***pilgering*** *verbal noun*. E20.

pilgrim /ˈpɪlgrɪm/ *noun & verb*. ME.
[Provençal *pelegrin* = Italian *pellegrino*, Old & mod. French *pèlerin*, from Latin *peregrinus* foreign: see PEREGRINE. For the change of final *n* to *m* cf. *buckram*, *grogram*.]
▶**A** *noun*. **1** A person who travels from place to place; a traveller; a wanderer. Now chiefly *poet*. ME.
2 *spec*. A person who journeys to a sacred place as an act of religious devotion. ME.
3 A person regarded as journeying through life etc.; a person who travels in quest of something, or for respectful or sentimental reasons. ME.
4 *Hist*. In full ***Pilgrim Father***. A member of the group of English Puritans who founded the colony of Plymouth, Massachusetts, in 1620. Now usu. in *pl*. L18. ▸**b** An original settler of any region of the US or New Zealand (*Hist*.); a newcomer, a recent immigrant. *US & NZ*. M19.

2 A. MASON Pilgrims . . traditionally gathered in Jerusalem. 3 *Life* Elvis's Memphis estate . . draws 500,000 pilgrims a year.

Attrib. & comb.: In the senses of 'that is a pilgrim, of or pertaining to a pilgrim or pilgrims', as ***pilgrim city***, ***pilgrim cloak***, ***pilgrim monk***, ***pilgrim staff***, etc. Special combs., as **pilgrim-bottle** a flat bottle with a ring on each side of the neck by which it may be hung from the waist etc.; ***Pilgrim Father***: see sense 4 above; **pilgrim's bottle** = *pilgrim-bottle* above; **pilgrim's shell** *Hist*. (a representation of) a scallop shell carried by a pilgrim as a sign of having visited a shrine, *spec*. that of St James at Compostela in Spain.

▶**B** *verb intrans*. Make a pilgrimage; travel or wander like a pilgrim. M16.
■ **pilgrimer** *noun* (*rare*) a pilgrim M16. **pilgrimess** *noun* (*rare*) a female pilgrim L16. **pilgrimize** *verb intrans. & †trans*. (with *it*) make a pilgrimage (*to*) L16.

pilgrimage /ˈpɪlgrɪmɪdʒ/ *noun & verb*. ME.
[Provençal *pelegrinatge*, formed as prec.: see -AGE.]
▶**A** *noun*. **1** A journey made by a pilgrim; a journey made to a sacred place as an act of religious devotion. ME. ▸**b** *fig*. Life regarded as a journey, esp. to a future state of rest or blessedness. ME.
2 *gen*. Any journey. Now (with allus. to sense 1), a journey made for respectful, nostalgic, or sentimental reasons. LME.
3 *transf*. A sacred place to which pilgrims journey. Now *rare*. LME.

1 JAN MORRIS The holy pilgrimage to Mecca. 2 W. ABISH His annual pilgrimage to the city of Balzac.

Phrases: **Pilgrimage of Grace** *Hist*. the movement in 1536 in northern England opposing the dissolution of the monasteries etc. during the Reformation.
▶**B** *verb intrans*. †**1** Live among strangers. LME–M17.
2 Orig. *gen*., travel. Later *spec*., make a (holy) pilgrimage. LME.

pili /ˈpiːliː/ *noun*[1]. L19.
[Hawaiian, lit. 'adhere', in ref. to the clinging awns.]
In Hawaii: the tropical grass *Heteropogon contortus*, formerly used as a thatching material.

pili *noun*[2] pl. of PILUS.

piliated /ˈpɪlɪeɪtɪd, ˈpʌɪ-/ *adjective*. M20.
[from PILUS + -I- + -ATE[2] + -ED[1], or directly from PILUS after *fimbriated*.]
BACTERIOLOGY. Bearing pili.

pilidium /pʌɪˈlɪdɪəm/ *noun*. Pl. **-dia** /-dɪə/. M19.
[mod. Latin from Greek *pilidion* dim. of *pilos* felt cap: see -IUM.]
†**1** BOTANY. The hemispherical apothecium of certain lichens. Only in M19.
2 ZOOLOGY. The early free-swimming cap-shaped larva of nemertean worms of the order Heteronemertea. L19.

piliferous /pʌɪˈlɪf(ə)rəs/ *adjective*. M19.
[from Latin PILUS + -I- + -FEROUS.]
BOTANY & ZOOLOGY. Bearing or having hair; tipped with a hair.
piliferous layer the part of the epidermis of a root which bears root-hairs.

piliform /ˈpʌɪlɪfɔːm/ *adjective*. E19.
[formed as prec. + -FORM.]
Shaped like a hair, in the form of a hair, hairlike.

piligerous /pʌɪˈlɪdʒ(ə)rəs/ *adjective*. M19.
[from Latin PILUS + -I- + -GEROUS.]
Chiefly ZOOLOGY. Bearing hair, clothed with hair.

Pilipino /pɪlɪˈpiːnəʊ/ *noun & adjective*. M20.
[Tagalog from Spanish FILIPINO.]
(Designating or pertaining to) the language now usu. called Filipino.

pill /pɪl/ *noun*[1]. *local*. OE.
[Collateral form of POOL *noun*[1].]
A tidal creek or pool.
¶ Not recorded in ME.

pill /pɪl/ *noun*[2]. Now *dial*. ME.
[App. rel. to PILL *verb*[1].]
1 An outer covering or skin; *esp*. the peel of a fruit, tuber, etc. Also, tree bark. ME.
†**2** = PELT *noun*[1] 5. Only in 17.

pill /pɪl/ *noun*[3]. LME.
[Middle Low German, Middle Dutch *pille* (Dutch *pil*), prob. from Latin *pilula* PILULE.]
1 Orig., a small ball of compacted medicine for swallowing whole. Now, a compressed tablet of, or a capsule containing, medicine. LME. ▸**b** *fig*. An unpleasant or painful necessity; a humiliation. M16. ▸**c** An oral contraceptive containing one or more synthetic female hormones. Chiefly ***the pill***. M20. ▸**d** A barbiturate or amphetamine tablet. *slang*. M20.
2 *gen*. A small ball of any substance; a pellet. LME. ▸**b** Orig., a cannon-ball. Later, a bullet, a shell, a bomb, etc. Now *Military slang* or *joc*. E17. ▸**c** A ball, *esp*. a football; in *pl*., billiards. *joc. & colloq*. L19. ▸**d** A pellet of opium prepared for smoking. *slang*. L19. ▸**e** A cigarette. *slang*. E20. ▸**f** In *pl*. The testicles; *fig*. nonsense. *slang*. M20. ▸**g** A small ball of fluff formed by rubbing or wear on the surface of (esp. knitted) fabric. M20.
3 (Usu. ***Pills***.) (A nickname for) a doctor; a medical officer. Chiefly *Nautical slang*. M19.
4 An objectionable person; a bore. *slang*. L19.

1 D. M. THOMAS The mild sleeping pill isn't working. **b** *bitter pill*: see BITTER *adjective*. *blue pill*: see BLUE *adjective*. *happy pill*: see HAPPY *adjective*. **sugar the pill**, **sweeten the pill** make an unpleasant necessity acceptable. **c** COMBINED *pill*. **come off the pill** stop taking a course of contraceptive pills. *male pill*: see MALE *adjective & noun*. *mini pill*: see MINI-. *morning-after pill*: see MORNING. **on the pill** taking a course of contraceptive pills. 4 M. ATWOOD He's a pill . . What a creep.

Comb.: **pill-bag** *US* a doctor's bag for carrying large amounts of pills; **pill-beetle** any of various small rounded beetles of the family Byrrhidae, esp. *Byrrhus pilula*, which are able to retract the head and appendages; **pillbox** (*a*) a small shallow cylindrical box for holding pills; (*b*) (more fully ***pillbox hat***) a hat resembling this in shape; (*c*) MILITARY a small enclosed concrete fort, partly underground and used as an outpost; **pill-bug** any of various woodlice of the family Armadillidae, esp. *Armadillidium vulgare*, which are able to roll into a ball; **pill head** *slang* a drug addict; **pill-millipede** any of various millipedes of the order Glomerida, esp. *Glomeris marginata*, which are able to roll into a ball; **pill peddler** *slang* a doctor; a pharmacist; **pill popper** *colloq*. a barbiturate or amphetamine addict; *transf*. a person who regularly takes large amounts of any sort of pill; **pill-popping** *noun & adjective* (*a*) *noun* the action of regularly taking large amounts of pills, esp. addictive drugs; an act of taking a large amount of pills; (*b*) *adjective* of, pertaining to, or characterized by such action; **pill pusher**, **pill roller**, **pill shooter** *slang* = *pill peddler* above; **pill slab** *Hist*.: used in rolling medicine into pills; **pill-woodlouse** = *pill-bug* above; **pillwort** any of several aquatic plants of the genus *Pilularia*, allied to the ferns, with slender tapering leaves and sporangia borne in globular sporocarps at the leaf-bases; *esp*. the European species, *Pilularia globulifera*.

pill /pɪl/ *verb*[1]. LOE.
[Latin *pilare* deprive of hair, pillage, from PILUS hair. See also PEEL *verb*[1].]
▶**I 1** *verb intrans*. **a** Of an outer layer or coating, esp. skin or bark: peel *off* or *away*. Now *dial*. LOE. ▸**b** Of (esp. knitted) fabric: form balls of fluff on the surface. M20.
2 *verb trans*. **a** = PEEL *verb*[1] 3a. Now *arch. & dial*. ME. ▸**b** Peel or pare (skin, bark, etc.), esp. from a fruit or vegetable. Freq. foll. by *off*. Now *dial*. LME.
3 a *verb trans*. Pull or tug (hair etc.); remove or pluck out (hair); remove the hair from. Now *dial*. ME. ▸†**b** *verb intrans*. Lose hair; (of an animal) shed the coat. E16–M17.
4 *verb trans*. Orig., clear (land) of vegetation. Now (*dial*.), graze (land) closely. M16.
▶**II 5** *verb trans*. Plunder or pillage (a city, building, etc.); rob (a person). Formerly also *spec*., impoverish (soil). *arch. & dial*. ME.
†**6** *verb intrans*. Commit pillage; rob, plunder. ME–L17.
†**7** *verb trans*. Take (goods etc.) as plunder. LME–E17.
Phrases: **pill and poll** *arch*. ruin by depredations or extortions; strip bare.
■ **piller** *noun* †(*a*) = PEELER *noun*[1] 1; (*b*) (now *dial*.) = PEELER *noun*[1] 2: LME. **pilling** *noun* (*a*) the action of the verb; (*b*) (now *dial*.) = PEELING *noun* 2: LME.

pill /pɪl/ *verb*[2] *trans*. M18.
[from PILL *noun*[3]. Cf. PIP *verb*[2].]
1 Dose with pills; drug. Now chiefly as ***pilled (up)*** *ppl adjective*. M18.
2 a Reject by ballot; *fig*. ostracize, blackball. *colloq*. M19. ▸**b** Fail (a candidate) in an examination. *colloq. rare*. E20.

pillage /ˈpɪlɪdʒ/ *noun & verb*. LME.
[Old & mod. French, from *piller* from Latin *pilare*: see PILL *verb*[1], -AGE.]
▶**A** *noun*. **1** The action or an act of plundering or sacking a city, building, etc., esp. in war; looting; *transf*. extortion. LME.
2 Goods plundered, esp. from an enemy in war; booty, spoil; *spec*. in LAW, the right for the captors of a ship taken as booty to keep for themselves everything above the main deck apart from the guns and fittings. *obsolete* exc. *Hist*. LME.

1 H. H. WILSON The object of the incursion being pillage, not fighting. *Asian Art* In the pillage . . many bronze vessels were . . carried off and sold.

▶**B** *verb*. **1** *verb trans. & intrans*. Plunder, sack, or rob (a city, building, person, etc.), esp. in war; loot. L16.
2 *verb trans*. Carry off as booty; spoil or destroy (goods). E17.

1 A. DUGGAN A gang of . . legionaires had pillaged our valley. J. M. MCPHERSON Soldiers have pillaged civilian property since the beginning of time. *fig*.: A. RIDLER To a painter's pillaging eye. 2 G. GREENE The doors were all off, . . the furniture pillaged . . and smashed. *fig*.: LD MACAULAY Every thing . . given to others seemed to him to be pillaged from himself.

■ **pillager** *noun* E17.

pillaloo /ˈpɪlaluː/ *noun & interjection*. *dial*. L18.
[Natural exclam.]
(A cry) expr. grief or anger.

pillar /ˈpɪlə/ *noun & verb*. ME.
[Anglo-Norman *piler*, Old & mod. French *pilier* from Proto-Romance, from Latin *pila* PILE *noun*[4].]
▶**A** *noun*. **1** ARCHITECTURE. A detached usu. narrow vertical structure of stone, wood, brick, etc., used to support a superstructure, as a fixed point of attachment, or for ornamentation. Also, a natural column of sheer rock resembling this. ME. ▸**b** A platform or stand for public penance. Also, a whipping post. *obsolete* exc. *Hist*. M16. ▸**c** = ***pillar-box*** below. Now *rare* or *obsolete*. M19.
2 *transf*. A vertical column of air, vapour, water, etc. ME.
3 *fig*. A person who or thing which is regarded as a mainstay or support of something; *esp*. a person who is a prominent supporter *of* some institution or principle. ME.
4 Any vertical support or post, as in a piece of furniture, a machine, etc.; a pedestal. LME. ▸**b** A piece of metal separating the movements of a watch. L17. ▸**c** A post of metal etc. forming part of the bodywork of a motor vehicle situated between the front and rear doors or between the front doors and the windscreen. E20.
5 A portable pillar carried as a symbol of office. *obsolete* exc. *Hist*. E16.
†**6** A column of printed matter. M16–E17.
7 MINING. A solid mass of coal etc. left to support the roof of a mine. E18.
8 ANATOMY. Any of various supporting structures within the body, usu. occurring in pairs. E19.
9 CONCHOLOGY. = COLUMELLA (c). Now *rare*. M19.

2 JAN MORRIS I saw, issuing from a squat chimney . . a pillar of black smoke. 3 J. BALDWIN She was one of the pillars of the church, a powerful evangelist. H. EVANS Parliament, law and obituaries were three pillars of *The Times*. M. DIBDIN A man above suspicion, a pillar of the community.

Phrases: BORD *and pillar*. **from pillar to post**, †**from post to pillar** [orig. with ref. to a real-tennis court] from one place (of appeal etc.) to another. ***Hercules' Pillars***, ***Pillars of Hercules***: see HERCULES. **pillars of the fauces** ANATOMY the folds of mucous membrane on either side of the opening from the mouth into the pharynx. ***standing pillar***: see STANDING *adjective*.
Comb.: **pillar-and-claw** *adjective* (of a piece of furniture) having a central pedestal with a divided base; **pillar and room** = BORD *and pillar*; **pillar and scroll clock** *US* a mantel clock in a rectangular cage with a scrolled top and ornamental pillars at the sides; **pillar and stall** = *pillar and room* above; **pillar apostle** each of the Apostles Peter, James, and John (with allus. to *Galatians* 2:9); **pillar-box** a public postbox shaped like a pillar; ***pillar-box red***, a bright shade of red, the colour of a pillar-box;

pillar-buoy a cylindrical buoy; **pillar clock** (*a*) a clock with a round movement resting on ornamental pillars; (*b*) a clock, esp. a Japanese one, designed to be attached to a pillar or upright; **pillar drill** ENGINEERING a drilling machine with a work table attached to a column at its base; **pillar-file** a small flat file; **pillar plate** the plate of a watch movement next behind the dial; **pillar rose** a climbing rose suitable for training on an upright; **pillar-stone** ARCHAEOLOGY a standing stone, a menhir.

▶**B** *verb trans.* **1** Provide with a pillar or pillars, esp. for support or ornamentation. **E17.**

2 Embody in the form of a pillar. *literary. rare.* **E19.**

■ **pillared** *adjective* (*a*) provided with a pillar or pillars, esp. for support or ornamentation; (*b*) (chiefly *literary*) shaped into or of the form of a pillar: **LME. pillaret** *noun* a small pillar **M17. pillarist** *noun* a stylite **M17. pillarless** *adjective* **L19.**

pillicock /ˈpɪlɪkɒk/ *noun.* **ME.**

[from 1st elem. perh. of Scandinavian origin (cf. Norwegian dial. *pill*) + COCK *noun*[1]. See also PILLOCK.]

1 The penis. *arch. coarse slang.* **ME.**

†**2** Used as a term of endearment, esp. for a young boy. **L16–M17.**

pillion /ˈpɪljən/ *noun & verb.* **L15.**

[Gaelic *pillean*, *pillin*, Irish *pillín*, dim. of *pell* couch, pallet, cushion, from Latin *pellis* skin.]

▶**A** *noun.* Orig. (now *Hist.*), a light saddle, esp. for a woman; a pad attached to the back of a saddle for an additional rider or luggage. Now, a seat for a passenger behind the rider of a motorcycle (also ***pillion seat***). **L15.**

pillion passenger, ***pillion rider***, ***pillion riding***, etc. **go pillion**, **ride pillion**, **sit pillion** travel on a pillion.

Comb.: **pillion cloth** a saddle-cloth for placing under a pillion.

▶**B** *verb trans.* Chiefly as ***pillioned*** *ppl adjective.*

1 Equip (a horse etc.) with a pillion. **M19.**

2 Place or seat on a pillion. **E20.**

pilliver /ˈpɪlɪvə/ *noun.* Now *north.* **LOE.**

[App. from PILLOW *noun* + Old Norse *ver* case, cover.]

Orig., a pillow. Later, a pillowcase.

pilliwinks /ˈpɪlɪwɪŋks/ *noun. obsolete* exc. *Hist.* Also †**pyrewinks**, (earlier) **pinnywinkles** /ˈpɪnɪwɪŋk(ə)lz/, & other vars. **LME.**

[Origin unkn.]

An instrument of torture used for squeezing the fingers. Usu. ***the pilliwinks***.

pillock /ˈpɪlək/ *noun.* **M16.**

[Contr. of PILLICOCK.]

1 = PILLICOCK 1. *north.* **M16.**

2 *transf.* A stupid person; a fool. Freq. as a term of mild abuse. *slang.* **M20.**

pillory /ˈpɪləri/ *noun & verb.* **ME.**

[Anglo-Latin *pillorium* from Old French *pillorie*, *pellorie*, (also mod.) *pilori*, prob. from Provençal *espilori*, of unkn. origin.]

▶**A** *noun. Hist.* A device for punishment, usu. consisting of a wooden framework mounted on a post, with holes for trapping the head and hands, and in which an offender was confined and exposed to public assault and ridicule. Cf. STOCK *noun*[1] 5. **ME.**

finger-pillory a device in which the fingers were held with the first joint bent.

▶**B** *verb trans.* **1** *Hist.* Put in a pillory; punish by putting in a pillory. **L16.**

2 *fig.* Expose to public ridicule or contempt. **L17.**

📖 **2** *Independent* The . . document publicly pillories and prejudices two of the officers.

■ †**pillor** *verb trans.* [back-formation] = PILLORY *verb* 1 **M17–E19. pillorize** *verb trans.* = PILLORY *verb* 1 **M17.**

pillow /ˈpɪləʊ/ *noun.*

[Old English *pyle*, *pylu*, corresp. to Middle Low German *pöle*, Middle Dutch *pöluwe*, *pēl-* (Dutch *peluw*), Old High German *pfuliwi*, *pfulwo* (German *Pfühl*), from West Germanic, from Latin *pulvinus*.]

1 A support for the head in sleeping or reclining; *esp.* a (usu. oblong) cloth cushion stuffed with feathers, flock, synthetic material, etc., used for this purpose in a bed. **OE.**

2 A cushion, a pad; *spec.* (*a*) (now *rare*) the pad of a saddle; (*b*) a lace-pillow. **OE.**

3 *transf.* **a** A piece of wood, metal, etc., used as a support; a block, a bearing. **LME.** ▸**b** ARCHITECTURE. The return part of an Ionic volute. **M17.**

4 GEOLOGY. A body of lava resembling a pillow in shape, characteristic of eruption under water. **L19.**

📖 **1** SHAKES. *Tit. A.* Sung thee asleep, his loving breast thy pillow. R. WEST *Rosamund* . . still lay back on her pillows.

Phrases: **sew pillows under a person's elbows** (now *rare* or *obsolete*) give a person a sense of false security.

Comb.: **pillow-bere**: see BERE *noun*[2]; **pillow-block** a cradle supporting the bearing of an axle, roller, etc.; **pillow-book** (*a*) a book, esp. a romantic or erotic one, suitable for reading in bed; (*b*) in Japanese classical literature, a type of private journal or diary; **pillowcase** a washable cotton etc. cover for a pillow; **pillow cover**, †**pillow coat** = *pillowcase* above; **pillow-fight** a mock fight with pillows, esp. by children; **pillow-lace** lace worked on a lace-pillow; **pillow lava**: exhibiting pillow structure; **pillow mound** ARCHAEOLOGY a low oblong mound freq. surrounded by a ditch; **pillow-sham** *N. Amer.* a decorative cover for a bed pillow when not in use; **pillowslip** = *pillowcase* above; **pillow sofa** a sofa-bed with large heavily-stuffed cushions; **pillow structure** GEOLOGY a rock structure in which numerous closely fitting pillows are fused together; **pillow talk** romantic or intimate conversation in bed; **pillow tank** a collapsible rubber container for storing large quantities of liquid; **pillow-word** in classical Japanese poetry, a meaningless word prefixed to another for euphony.

■ **pillowed** *adjective* (GEOLOGY) having a pillow structure **M20. pillowy** *adjective* resembling the shape or texture of a pillow; *esp.* soft, yielding: **L18.**

pillow /ˈpɪləʊ/ *verb.* **E17.**

[from the noun.]

1 *verb trans.* & (*poet., rare*) *intrans.* Rest or lay (one's head etc.) (as) on a pillow. **E17.**

2 *verb trans.* Serve as a pillow for. *poet. rare.* **E19.**

📖 **1** I. MCEWAN Colin had dozed off . . , his head pillowed on his forearm. J. MAY The old man . . pillowed his back against one of the boat seats.

pilo- /ˈpʌɪləʊ/ *combining form* of Latin *pilus* hair: see **-O-**.

■ **pilo'cystic** *adjective* (MEDICINE) (of a dermoid cyst) containing hair **L19. piloe'rection** *noun* the erection or bristling of hair or fur **M20. piloe'rector** *noun* a hormone or neurotransmitter that causes piloerection (freq. *attrib.*) **M20. pilo'motor** *noun & adjective* (a nerve, muscle, etc.) involved in producing movement of the hairs **L19. pilo'nidal** *adjective* (MEDICINE) pertaining to or designating an abnormal sinus containing hair, esp. near the coccyx **L19. pilose'baceous** *adjective* pertaining to or designating sebaceous glands that open into hair follicles **L19.**

pilocarpine /pʌɪlə(ʊ)ˈkɑːpiːn/ *noun.* **L19.**

[from mod. Latin *Pilocarpus* (see below) + -INE[5].]

CHEMISTRY & PHARMACOLOGY. A volatile alkaloid obtained esp. from the leaves of jaborandi (genus *Pilocarpus*), and used to contract the pupils.

pilón /piˈlon, piːˈləʊn/ *noun. US.* Pl. ***-lones*** /-ˈlonɛs, -ˈləʊnɪz/. **L19.**

[Mexican Spanish from Spanish = sugar loaf, pillar, post.]

In Mexico and the south-western US, a small gift given to a customer making a purchase etc.

pilose /ˈpʌɪləʊz/ *adjective.* **M18.**

[from Latin *pilosus*, from *pilus* hair: see -OSE[1].]

BOTANY & ZOOLOGY. Covered with long soft hairs. Cf. PUBESCENT *adjective* 2.

■ **pi'losity** *noun* **E17.**

pilot /ˈpʌɪlət/ *noun.* **E16.**

[French *pilote* from medieval Latin *pilotus* var. of *pedo(t)ta*, from Greek *pēdon* oar, pl. rudder: see -OT[2].]

1 a A person who steers a ship; *esp.* a qualified coastal navigator taken on board at a particular place to steer a ship into or out of a port, or through a channel etc. **E16.** ▸**b** (Also **P-**.) A navigational handbook for use at sea. **L17.** ▸**c** A person who operates the flying controls of an aircraft, balloon, spacecraft, etc., *esp.* a person qualified to do this as a profession. See also ***automatic pilot*** s.v. AUTOMATIC *adjective.* **M19.** ▸**d** A jockey. **L20.**

2 *transf.* A leader or guide, esp. through an unknown area of land; a scout; *spec.* the leader of a pack of hounds. **L16.** ▸**b** In full ***pilot engine***. A locomotive coupled in front of another at the head of a train. **M19.**

3 In full ***pilot-fish***. A small carangid fish of warm seas, *Naucrates ductor*, which frequently accompanies sharks, turtles, etc., and has dark vertical bars along the sides; any of various other fishes which accompany sharks, boats, etc. **M17.** ▸**b** More fully ***pilot snake***. The northern race of the copperhead snake. **L18.**

4 = ***cow-catcher*** s.v. COW *noun*[1]. *US.* **M19.**

5 In full ***pilot wire***, ***pilot cable***. An auxiliary wire or cable for conveying information about an associated power line etc. or for operating apparatus connected with one. **L19.**

6 An experimental undertaking carried out prior to some full-scale project or activity; *esp.* a test episode of a television series used to assess audience reaction etc. Freq. *attrib.* **E20.**

7 TELECOMMUNICATIONS. An unmodulated reference signal transmitted with another signal for purposes of control or synchronization. Freq. *attrib.*, as ***pilot carrier***, ***pilot tone***, etc. **M20.**

📖 **1a** DEFOE Like a ship without a pilot, that could only run before the wind. I. MCEWAN A quick exchange of shouts between . . pilot and . . crew, and the boat moved on. **drop the pilot** *fig.* abandon a trustworthy adviser. **b** *Practical Boat Owner* Every abnormal wave documented in the pilot. **c** S. BELLOW The pilot announced that we had reached our cruising altitude. *Air Enthusiast* Impossible for pilots to fly the 20 hours per month stipulated by NATO. ***test pilot***: see TEST *noun*[1]. **2** I. L. IDRIESS He needed a pilot to show him the waterholes. **6** *Nature* It could be the pilot for future investments . . in industrial research. *TV Times* The second pilot to an unrealised series. ***pilot episode***, ***pilot film***, ***pilot plant***, ***pilot programme***, ***pilot project***, ***pilot scheme***, ***pilot study***, etc.

Comb.: **pilot balloon** a small balloon used to track air currents etc.; **pilot-bird** (*a*) (now *rare*) any of various sea birds which accompany ships; (*b*) a small Australian warbler, *Pycnoptilus floccosus*, of the family Acanthizidae; **pilot biscuit** *US* hard tack; **pilot-boat** a boat used by a pilot to meet an incoming ship etc.; **pilot-bread** = ***pilot biscuit*** above; **pilot burner** *US* = ***pilot light*** (*a*) below; ***pilot cable***: see sense 5 above; ***pilot carrier***: see sense 7 above; **pilot chute** a small parachute used to bring a main one into operation; **pilot-cloth** thick blue woollen cloth for seamen's coats etc.; **pilot-coat** = PEA-JACKET; **pilot driver** an engine-driver who accompanies another over a route with which the latter is unfamiliar; ***pilot engine***: see sense 2b above; ***pilot-fish***: see sense 3 above; **pilot-flame** = ***pilot-light*** (a) below; **pilot hole** a small hole drilled ahead of a full-sized hole as a guide; **pilot-house** (*a*) a ship's wheel-house; (*b*) a house on land belonging to a sea pilot; **pilot jet** a narrow-bored jet in a motorcycle carburettor delivering petrol at a low rate when the engine is idling; **pilot lamp** = ***pilot light*** (b) below; **pilot light** (*a*) a small gas burner kept alight for lighting a larger burner; (*b*) an electric indicator light or control light; **pilot-major** *Hist.* the chief pilot of a fleet etc.; **pilot-man** a railway official who directs the movement of trains over a single-track line; **pilot officer**: holding the lowest commissioned rank in the Royal Air Force; **pilot parachute** = ***pilot chute*** above; ***pilot snake***: see sense 3b above; ***pilot tone***: see sense 7 above; **pilot valve** ENGINEERING a small auxiliary valve that is operated in association with a larger valve; **pilot whale** either of two delphinoid whales, *Globicephala melas*, of temperate Atlantic and southern waters, and *G. macrorhynchus*, of mainly subtropical waters; also called ***blackfish***; ***pilot wire***: see sense 5 above.

■ **pilotism** *noun* (now *rare* or *obsolete*) = PILOTAGE 1 **E17. pilotless** *adjective* (*a*) (esp. of an aircraft) without a human pilot; (*b*) without a pilot-light: **E17. pilotry** *noun* (now *rare* or *obsolete*) = PILOTAGE 1 **M18. pilotship** *noun* (now *rare* or *obsolete*) the office or function of pilot **M17.**

pilot /ˈpʌɪlət/ *verb trans.* **L16.**

[from the noun, after French *piloter*.]

1 Act as a pilot on (a ship, an aircraft, etc.); conduct (passengers) as a pilot. **L16.** ▸**b** Act as a pilot in the course of or during (a journey etc.). Chiefly *poet.* **E18.**

2 *transf.* Act as a leader or guide for; conduct, direct. **L16.** ▸**b** *spec.* Secure the passage of (a bill) *through* a legislative body. Orig. *US.* **E20.**

3 Produce a pilot or test for (an idea, scheme, etc.); try out. **M20.**

📖 **1** *Times* A fly-past of aircraft piloted by men of the R.A.F. *Daily Telegraph* The first woman to pilot a hot air balloon across the English Channel. S. QUINN He . . was piloting steamships out of Hamburg. **2** H. STURGIS She deftly piloted the discussion to other projects. *Discovery* Mechanical equipment is required to pilot the call through each successive stage. E. SIMPSON Piloted by a matron through two locked doors. **3** *Daily Telegraph* The debit card . . piloted in petrol stations will become widely available.

pilotage /ˈpʌɪlətɪdʒ/ *noun.* **E17.**

[French, from *piloter*: see prec., -AGE.]

1 The action of piloting something or someone; the function or office of pilot. **E17.**

2 Payment for the services of a pilot. **E17.**

pilotaxitic /ˌpʌɪləʊtakˈsɪtɪk/ *adjective.* **L19.**

[from Greek *pilos* felt + *taxis* arrangement: see -ITIC.]

PETROGRAPHY. Having or designating a texture formed by a felted mass of acicular or lath-shaped crystals in a holocrystalline igneous rock.

pilotis /piləti/ *noun pl.* **M20.**

[French.]

ARCHITECTURE. A series of columns or piles, used to raise the base of a building above ground level.

pilous /ˈpʌɪləs/ *adjective.* **M17.**

[formed as PILOSE: see -OUS.]

ZOOLOGY. = PILOSE.

pilpul /ˈpɪlp(ə)l/ *noun.* **L19.**

[Hebrew, from *pilpēl* search, debate hotly.]

(An instance of) subtle or keen rabbinical disputation; *transf.* unprofitable argument, hair-splitting.

■ **pilpulist** *noun* a subtle or keen disputant, esp. in rabbinical argument **M19. pilpu'listic** *adjective* of or pertaining to pilpul or pilpulists; characterized by subtle or keen disputation: **L19.**

Pils /pɪlz, -s/ *noun.* **M20.**

[Abbreviation of PILSNER.]

A type of lager beer similar to Pilsner.

Pilsner /ˈpɪlznə, ˈpɪls-/ *noun.* Also **Pilsen** /ˈpɪlz(ə)n, ˈpɪls-/, **Pilsener** /ˈpɪlz(ə)nə, ˈpɪls-/. **L19.**

[German, from *Pilsen* (Czech *Plzeň*) province and city in Bohemia.]

A type of pale lager with a strong hop flavour, orig. produced in Plzeň. Also more fully ***Pilsner beer***.

Comb.: **Pilsner glass** a tall beer glass tapered at the bottom.

Piltdown /ˈpɪltdaʊn/ *attrib. adjective.* **E20.**

[A village in Sussex, England.]

Designating or pertaining to a fraudulent fossil composed of a human cranium and an ape jaw and found near Piltdown, or the supposed primitive hominid *Eoanthropus dawsoni*, to which these remains were ascribed.

📖 *transf.*: N. FLEMING So there is a brain underneath that thatch-covered Piltdown skull of yours.

■ **Piltdowner** *noun* a Piltdown man; a person having the supposed appearance, intelligence, or behaviour of primitive man: **M20.**

pilule /ˈpɪljuːl/ *noun*. LME.
[Old & mod. French from Latin *pilula* dim. of *pila* ball: see -ULE. Cf. PILL *noun*[3].]
A small pill.
■ **pilular** *adjective* of, pertaining to, or resembling a pill or pills E19. **pilulous** *adjective* (*rare*) of the size of a pill, minute L19.

pilus /ˈpʌɪləs/ *noun*. Pl. **pili** /ˈpʌɪlʌɪ/. M20.
[Latin = hair.]
BACTERIOLOGY. Any of several types of ultramicroscopic filamentous appendages that are produced by some bacterial cells.

pily /ˈpʌɪli/ *adjective*[1]. E16.
[from PILE *noun*[5] + -Y[1].]
(Of a fabric) having a pile or nap; (of an animal's coat) comprising a mixture of short soft hairs and longer harder ones.

pily /ˈpʌɪli/ *adjective*[2]. M17.
[from PILE *noun*[1] + -Y[5].]
HERALDRY. Of a field: divided into a (usu. specified) number of piles.

PIM *abbreviation*.
COMPUTING. Personal information manager.

Pima /ˈpiːmə/ *noun*[1] & *adjective*[1]. E19.
[Spanish, shortening of *Pimahito*, from Pima *pimahaitu* nothing.]
► **A** *noun*. Pl. same, **-s**. A member of a N. American Indian people living chiefly along the Gila and Salt rivers in Arizona. Also, the Uto-Aztecan language of the Pima and Papago, *esp.* the dialect of the Pima. E19.
► **B** *attrib*. or as *adjective*. Of or pertaining to the Pima or their language. E20.

Pima /ˈpiːmə/ *noun*[2] & *adjective*[2]. M20.
[from *Pima* County, Arizona, USA.]
In full ***Pima cotton***. (Made of) a fine quality cotton developed from Egyptian cotton.

Piman /ˈpiːmən/ *adjective* & *noun*. L19.
[from prec. + -AN.]
► **A** *adjective*. Of or pertaining to the Pima or Papago Indians or their language. L19.
► **B** *noun*. A Pima or Papago Indian; a member of any of several peoples ethnically and linguistically related to the Pima and Papago. Also, an Uto-Aztecan language group comprising Pima, Papago, and some closely related languages. M20.

pimelea /pɪˈmiːlɪə/ *noun*. L18.
[mod. Latin (see below), from Greek *pimelē* soft fat, with allus. to the oily seeds.]
Any of various Australasian evergreen shrubs constituting the genus *Pimelea* (family Thymelaeaceae) with small terminal clusters of white or pink flowers freq. surrounded by coloured bracts.

pimelic /pɪˈmiːlɪk/ *adjective*. M19.
[from Greek *pimelē* soft fat + -IC.]
CHEMISTRY. ***pimelic acid***, a solid saturated fatty acid, $HOOC(CH_2)_5COOH$, used in biochemical research and the plastic industry; 1, 7-heptanedioic acid.

piment /pɪˈmɛnt/ *noun*. Long *arch*. ME.
[Old French from Latin *pigmentum* pigment, paint, (scented) unguent, (in medieval Latin) scented or spiced confection or drink. Cf. PIGMENT.]
1 A drink made with wine, honey, and spices. ME.
†**2** A scented or perfumed unguent. Only in ME.

pimento /pɪˈmɛntəʊ/ *noun* & *adjective*. L17.
[Spanish PIMIENTO.]
► **A** *noun*. Pl. **-os**.
†**1** Cayenne pepper. Only in L17.
2 The spice allspice; (more fully ***pimento tree***) the W. Indian tree, *Pimenta dioica*, of the myrtle family, from which allspice is obtained. Now *W. Indies*. L17.
3 A sweet (esp. a red) pepper. E20.
Comb.: **pimento dram** a Jamaican liqueur made with pimento berries steeped in rum etc.; **pimento red** (of) an orange-red colour; ***pimento tree***: see sense 2 above.
► **B** *adjective*. Pimento red. M20.

pi-meson /pʌɪˈmiːzɒn, -ˈmɛzɒn/ *noun*. M20.
[from PI *noun*[1] + MESON *noun*[3].]
PARTICLE PHYSICS. = PION *noun*. Freq. written ***π-meson***.
■ **pi-mesic**, **pi-meˈsonic** *adjectives* = PIONIC *adjective* M20.

†**pimgenet** *noun*. *slang* or *dial*. L17–M19.
[Origin unkn.]
A small red pimple.

pimiento /pɪmɪˈɛntəʊ, pɪmˈjɛn-/ *noun*. Pl. **-os**. Also **-ta** /-tə/. M17.
[Spanish from Latin *pigmentum*: see PIMENT. Cf. PIMENTO.]
1 = PIMENTO *noun* 2. *W. Indies*. M17.
2 = PIMENTO *noun* 3. M19.

pimp /pɪmp/ *noun* & *verb*. L16.
[Origin unkn.]
► **A** *noun*. **1** A person who provides opportunities for illicit sexual intercourse; now *esp*. a man who takes a percentage of a prostitute's earnings, freq. in return for arranging clients etc.; a pander. L16.
2 *transf*. & *fig*. A person who ministers or panders to an undesirable, despicable, or immoral impulse or thing; *gen*. a despicable person. E18.
3 An informer, a tell-tale. *Austral*. & *NZ slang*. L19.
4 A male prostitute. *US slang*. M20.

> 📖 **1** S. ROSENBERG A couple of pimps who provided visitors . . with prostitutes.

Comb.: **pimpmobile** *US slang* a large flashy car, *esp*. one used by a pimp.
► **B 1** *verb intrans*. Act as a pimp; pander. Freq. foll. by *for*, *to*. M17.
2 *verb trans*. Provide (a person) as a prostitute. M18.
3 *verb intrans*. Tell tales; inform *on* someone. *Austral*. & *NZ slang*. M20.
■ **pimpish** *adjective* M20.

pimpernel /ˈpɪmpənɛl/ *noun*. LME.
[Old French *pimpernelle* (mod. *pimprenelle*), earlier *piprenelle* from Proto-Romance, from adjective derived from Latin *piper* PEPPER *noun*, the fruit of the burnet resembling a peppercorn.]
†**1** Either of two plants of the rose family, the great burnet, *Sanguisorba officinalis*, and the salad burnet, *S. minor*. Also, burnet saxifrage. LME–M19.
2 More fully ***scarlet pimpernel***. A small low-growing weed, *Anagallis arvensis*, of the primrose family, with smooth ovate leaves and usu. bright scarlet (rarely blue, flesh-coloured, or white) flowers which close in cloudy or rainy weather. LME. ▸**b** With specifying word: any of various plants related to or resembling the scarlet pimpernel. L16.
3 (Usu. **P-**.) A person whose exploits resemble those of the elusive and daring hero of Baroness Orczy's novel *The Scarlet Pimpernel* (1905), who smuggled aristocrats and their supporters out of revolutionary France. Also *transf*., a thing that is elusive or evades capture. M20.
2b bog pimpernel a creeping plant of wet places, *Anagallis tenella*, with delicate pink flowers. **water pimpernel** = ***brookweed*** s.v. BROOK *noun*. **wood pimpernel**, **yellow pimpernel** a procumbent loosestrife of woodland, *Lysimachia nemorum*, with ovate leaves and yellow flowers.

pimping /ˈpɪmpɪŋ/ *adjective*. L17.
[Origin unkn.]
Small, insignificant, mean; in poor health or condition, sickly.

pimple /ˈpɪmp(ə)l/ *noun* & *verb*. ME.
[Nasalized form rel. to Old English *piplian* break out in pustules, ult. also to Latin *papula* pustule, Lithuanian *pāpas* nipple.]
► **A** *noun*. **1** A small hard inflamed (occas. suppurated) spot on the skin; a papule, a pustule. ME.
2 *transf*. Anything resembling a pimple; a small rounded swelling or lump. L16. ▸**b** The head. *slang*. E19.

> 📖 **1** G. LORD Two pieces of chocolate mean two pimples on my chin.

► **B** *verb*. **1** *verb trans*. Raise pimples on; spot or cover (as) with pimples. E17.
2 *verb intrans*. Become pimply; develop small swellings, spots, etc. M17.

> 📖 **1** L. MACNEICE The rain comes pimpling The paving stones with white.

■ **pimpled** *adjective* having or characterized by pimples E16. **pimpling** *noun* the presence of pimples; the fact of being covered with pimples: L16. **pimply** *adjective* covered or spotted with pimples M18.

pin /pɪn/ *noun*[1].
[Late Old English *pinn* corresp. to Middle Low German *pin*, Middle & mod. Low German, Middle & mod. Dutch *pinne* (mod. also *pin*), Old High German *pfinn* (Middle High German *pfinne*), Old Norse *pinni*, all from Latin *pinna* any of various objects likened to a wing or feather, but assoc. in use with *penna* PEN *noun*[2].]
► **I 1** A small piece of wood, metal, plastic, etc., usu. cylindrical and freq. tapered or pointed at one end, used for fastening or holding together parts of a structure, for conveying or checking motion in part of a mechanism, as a marker, indicator, or guide, etc.; a peg; a bolt. LOE.
2 *spec*. **a** The latch of a door. Chiefly *dial*. ME. ▸**b** MUSIC. = PEG *noun*[1] 3b. L15. ▸**c** = PEG *noun*[1] 3d. Now *rare*. L16. ▸**d** MEDICINE. A steel rod used to join the ends of fractured bones during healing. L19. ▸**e** Each of the metal projections of a plug which make the electrical connections when inserted into a socket. L19. ▸**f** GOLF. A pole bearing a small flag, used to mark the position of a hole. E20. ▸**g** A metal peg holding down the activating lever of a hand-grenade, preventing its explosion. E20.
3 A small thin sharply pointed piece of esp. steel wire with a round or flattened head, used (esp. in sewing) for holding things together or in place; (usu. with specifying word) any similar fastener having a pointed or penetrating part or used for personal ornamentation; (chiefly *N. Amer.*) a badge fastened with a pin. ME.

> 📖 **1** ***belaying pin***, ***coupling pin***, ***linchpin***, etc. **3** J. FOWLES Ernestina stared . . at his dark blue cravat with its pearl pin. N. LOWNDES Fingering her hair and fastening a stray piece with a pin. ***drawing pin***, ***dressmaker pin***, ***hairpin***, ***safety pin***, ***split pin***, etc.

► **II** *fig*. **4** A type of something very small, insignificant, or of little worth. ME.
†**5** That on which something depends. LME–M18.
6 A mood, a frame of mind. Chiefly in ***in a merry pin***, ***on a merry pin***. Now *arch*. & *dial*. LME.
†**7** A degree, a step. L16–L18.

> 📖 **4** ROSEMARY MANNING I don't think I cared a pin. P. FARMER For two pins I'd have . . tipped that bowl and all its contents over Becky.

► **III** *transf*. **8** †**a** (A disease characterized by) a spot on the surface of the eyeball (chiefly in ***pin and web***). Formerly also, (a disease characterized by) a hard swelling on the underside of a hawk's foot. LME–E18. ▸†**b** A knot in wood. M–L16. ▸**c** A hard spot occurring in steel during manufacture. M19.
9 a A point, a peak. *obsolete* exc. *dial*. L15. ▸**b** In full ***pin-bone***. A projecting hip-bone esp. of a horse or cow. Now *dial*. M17.
10 A leg. Usu. in *pl*. *colloq*. E16.
11 A skittle; a skittle knocked down, as a scoring point; in *pl*., the game of skittles. Cf. *ninepin* (a) s.v. NINE, ***tenpin*** s.v. TEN. L16. ▸†**b** A piece in chess or merrills. L17–L18.
12 A small keg for beer, holding half a firkin or about 20.5 litres or 4.5 gallons. L16.
13 *ellipt*. **a** = ***KNITTING-pin***. L19. ▸**b** = ***rolling-pin*** s.v. ROLLING *noun*. L19.
► **IV** [from the verb.]
14 CHESS. An act of pinning; a position in which a piece is pinned. M19.
Phrases: **hear a pin drop** be surrounded by absolute silence or stillness. **pins and needles** a pricking or tingling sensation, esp. in a limb recovering from numbness; ***on pins and needles***, in a state of agitated suspense. **pull the pin** *N. Amer. slang* (cause to) cease or resign. **put in the pin** *slang* check or stop an activity, esp. drinking alcohol. ***tirl at the pin***: see TIRL *verb*[3] 3.
Comb.: **pinball** (*a*) a pincushion; (*b*) a game in which a small metal ball is propelled across a sloping table and repeatedly redirected by various mechanisms controlled by the player towards targets which indicate the score when they are hit (freq. *attrib.*); **pinboard** (*a*) ELECTRICITY a panel having an array of identical sockets each connected to part of a set of wires, so that inserting a pin into a socket makes a connection between a specific pair or group of wires; (*b*) a board on which messages, pictures, etc., can be pinned for display; ***pin-bone***: see sense 9b above. **pin-boy** *Hist.*: who retrieves balls and resets pins in bowling etc.; **pin-cherry** a N. American wild cherry, *Prunus pensylvanica*; **pin clover** *US* the common stork's-bill, *Erodium cicutarium*, a naturalized European plant used as fodder; **pin connection**: of the parts of an iron or steel bridge by pins (instead of rivets, etc.); **pincord** *adjective* & *noun* = ***needlecord*** s.v. NEEDLE *noun*; **pin-curl** (*a*) *Hist*. an artificial curl of hair held in place by a hairpin; (*b*) a curl held in place during setting by a hairpin etc.; **pin-dropping** *adjective* (of silence) absolute, total; **pin-dust**: from filings of metal produced in the making of pins; **pin-eyed** *adjective* (of a heterostylous plant, esp. a primula, or its flowers) having the style as long as the mouth of the corolla-tube, with the stamens inserted at the base of the tube (opp. ***thrum-eyed***); **pin-feather** an immature feather, before the vanes have expanded, and while the barrel is full of fluid, a pen-feather; **pin-fit** *verb trans*. & *intrans*. pin and adjust the shape or fit of (a garment) on a person, before stitching; **pin-grass** = ***pin clover*** above; **pin-high** *adjective* (GOLF) (of a ball) at the same distance ahead as the pin; **pin hinge**: in which the two leaves are pivoted on a pin passing through a sheath in each; **pinholder** a support for cut flowers etc., comprising a base with projecting pins; **pin-hook** a small weak hook made from a pin; **pin-hooker** *US slang* a person who buys a small item and resells at a higher price in the same market; **pin joint**: in which two parts are connected by a pin passing through an eye in each; **pin-jointed** *adjective* fixed with a pin joint; **pin-leg** (*a*) a thin spindly leg; (*b*) an artificial leg; **pin lever** *noun* & *adjective* (designating) a pin-pallet watch or escapement; **pin-man** (*a*) a person who sells pins; (*b*) a figure of a person drawn in short straight lines without breadth, a matchstick figure; **pin-mark** a circular impression on the side of a piece of type, made by the ejection mechanism of the casting mould; **pin oak** a N. American oak, *Quercus palustris*, with persistent dead branches resembling pegs fixed in the trunk; **pin pallet**: in the form of a metal pin or a semi-circular jewel in the escapement of a watch; **pin-paper** a piece of paper stuck with many pins; *fig*. a collection of samples; **pin-patch** *dial*. a periwinkle; **pin plate** ENGINEERING: with a hole for the pin in a pin joint; **pin-pool**: played with three balls and five small pins; **pin-rack** NAUTICAL a rack or frame on the deck of a ship, in which belaying-pins are fixed; **pin seal** the treated skin of a young seal, used as leather; **pin-setter** a person who or machine which rearranges fallen pins in bowling etc.; **pin-spot** (*a*) a small round spot like a pin's head; any of a number of these forming a textile pattern; (*b*) THEATRICAL a small powerful spotlight for illuminating a very small object or area; **pin-stitch** an openwork stitch used esp. to fill in motifs in broderie anglaise or cut-work; **pin-table** a table used in playing pinball; **pin-tuck** a very narrow tuck, esp. for decoration; **pin-tucked** *adjective* having pin-tucks; **pin valve** = ***needle valve*** s.v. NEEDLE *noun*; **pinweed** any of various N. American plants constituting the genus *Lechea*, of the rockrose family, with axillary racemes of inconspicuous flowers; **pin-work** *noun* & *verb* (*a*) *noun* fine raised stiches shaped like crescents or points, used in needle-lace to lighten the effect of a raised design; (*b*) *verb trans*. work (flax yarn) on a wooden pin to make the yarn supple; **pinworm** (*a*) any parasitic nematode worm of the genus *Oxyuris* or a related genus, e.g. the human parasite *Enterobius vermicularis*, a threadworm; the disease caused by this, enterobiasis, threadworm; (*b*) (in full ***tomato pinworm***) the larva of a moth, *Keiferia lycopersicella*, which bores into the buds and fruits of tomato plants.

PIN /pɪn/ *noun*². L20.
[Acronym.]
A personal identification number as issued by a bank etc. for the validation of electronic transactions. Also ***PIN number***.

pin /pɪn/ *verb trans.* Infl. **-nn-**. ME.
[from PIN *noun*¹. In branch II perh. reduced form of PIND *verb*.]
▸ **I** Fix, attach, or confine with a pin.
1 Join or hold together with a pin or pins; construct or repair using a pin or pins. (Foll. by *to*, *together*.) ME.
2 Fasten with a pin or pins; attach or transfix with a pin or other sharp-pointed instrument. LME. ▸**b** Fasten together the clothes or parts of a garment of (a person) with pins. *obsolete* exc. DRESSMAKING. L15.
3 BUILDING. Fill in the joints or interstices of masonry with small stones or chips. Formerly also, face with stone, marble, etc.; underpin. *obsolete* exc. *Scot.* LME.
4 *fig.* **a** Attach firmly to (foll. by *on*, *to*). Now chiefly *spec.*, fix (blame, responsibility, etc.) *on*, blame or hold a person responsible for (a mistake, crime, etc.). L16. ▸**b** Make dependent or contingent *on*. Now *rare* exc. in ***pin one's faith on***, ***pin one's faith to***, ***pin one's hopes on*** below. L16.
5 *transf.* **a** Hold fast in an inescapable position. Freq. foll. by *against*, *down*, *on*. E18. ▸**b** CHESS. Prevent (an opposing piece) from moving except by exposing a more valuable piece to capture. M18.

> 📖 **1** P. MORTIMER Pinning a ten shilling note to the letter. J. D. HAMILTON Where there is more than one ticket they are pinned together. **2** G. P. R. JAMES She had a shawl . . pinned across her shoulders. C. A. MURRAY Pinning out his entomological specimens. L. MCMURTRY Since pinning on the sheriff's badge . . his sense of responsibility . . had grown. D. MADDEN Her hair is pinned up in heavy coils. **4a** F. WARNER He wants to find a group he can pin the blame for the fire on. P. LOMAS Our tendency is to pin a degrading label on him. **5** B. ENGLAND Trying to pin the man down by weight alone. C. RYCROFT A lorry . . pinned her against a wall. L. ERDRICH Trees . . fell . . pinning beneath their branches the roaring men.

▸ **II 6** Enclose, confine; hem in; shut *up*; *spec.* impound (an animal). Now *rare*. LME.
Phrases, & with adverbs in specialized senses: **pin a person's ears back** chastise or rebuke him or her. **pin down** (*a*) restrict the actions or movement of (an enemy etc.); (*b*) bind (a person) to or *to* a promise, arrangement, etc.; (*c*) force (a person) to declare his or her intentions; (*d*) specify or define precisely; (see also sense 5a above). **pin one's ears back** listen attentively. **pin one's faith on**, **pin one's faith to**, **pin one's hopes on** rely on absolutely, believe implicitly. ***pin the rap on***: see RAP *noun*¹.
Comb.: **pin-down** the action or policy of putting children in care into solitary confinement for long periods of time; **pinout** ELECTRONICS a diagram showing the arrangement of pins on an integrated circuit and their functions.

piña /ˈpiːnjə, *foreign* ˈpiɲa/ *noun*. Also Anglicized as **pina** /ˈpiːnə/, the usual form in sense 1b. L16.
[S. Amer. Spanish, Portuguese *pinha* pineapple, (orig.) pine cone, from Latin *pinea* pine cone.]
1 †**a** A pineapple. L16–E17. ▸**b** ***piña colada*** /kəˈlɑːdə/ [lit. 'strained pineapple'], a drink made with pineapple juice, rum, and coconut (milk). E20.
2 A spongy mass of silver produced by partial expulsion of mercury from an amalgam. Now *rare* or *obsolete*. E17.

pinaceous /pʌɪˈneɪʃəs/ *adjective*. *rare*. M19.
[from mod. Latin *Pinaceae* (see below), from Latin *pinus* PINE *noun*²: see -ACEOUS.]
Of or pertaining to the Pinaceae or pine family.

pinaces *noun* pl. of PINAX.

pinacocyte /ˈpɪnəkəsʌɪt/ *noun*. L19.
[from Greek *pinak-*, *pinax* slab, tablet + -O- + -CYTE.]
ZOOLOGY. Each of the flattened cells which form the outermost cell-layer in sponges.

pinacoid /ˈpɪnəkɔɪd/ *adjective & noun*. Also **-koid**. L19.
[formed as prec. + -OID.]
CRYSTALLOGRAPHY. ▸**A** *adjective*. Of a plane: intersecting one of the three coordinate axes and parallel to the other two. L19.
▸ **B** *noun*. A pinacoid plane; a crystal form consisting of two (or more) parallel planes or faces. L19.
■ **pinacoidal** *adjective* of, pertaining to, or characteristic of a pinacoid; *spec.* designating a triclinic crystal form having a centre of symmetry: L19.

pinacol /ˈpɪnəkɒl/ *noun*. E20.
[from PINAC(ONE + -OL.]
CHEMISTRY. An alcohol having two hydroxyl groups bonded to adjacent tertiary carbon atoms; *spec.* the simplest alcohol of this kind, 1,4-dimethylpropan-2,3-diol, $(CH_3)_2C(OH)C(OH)(CH_3)_2$ (also called ***tetramethyl ethylene glycol***).
Comb.: **pinacol rearrangement** a reaction (as the conversion of pinacol into pinacolone) in which a 1,2-glycol loses water on heating with acid to form a ketone.

pinacolone /ˈpɪnəkələʊn/ *noun*. E20.
[from PINACOL + -ONE.]
CHEMISTRY. A colourless oily ketone, $CH_3COC(CH_3)_3$, having an odour of peppermint; 3,3-dimethyl-2-butanone. Also, any other ketone in which the carbonyl group is bonded to at least one tertiary carbon atom.
■ Also **pinacoline** *noun* M19.

pinacone /ˈpɪnəkəʊn/ *noun*. M19.
[German *Pinakon*, from Greek *pinak-*, *pinax* tablet + *-on* -ONE.]
CHEMISTRY. = PINACOL.

pinacotheca /pɪnəkə(ʊ)ˈθiːkə/ *noun*. E17.
[Latin from Greek *pinakothēkē*, from *pinak-*, *pinax* tablet, picture + *thēkē* repository.]
A place for storing and exhibiting works of art.

pinafore /ˈpɪnəfɔː/ *noun*. L18.
[from PIN *verb* + AFORE.]
1 An apron, *esp.* one with a bib, orig. pinned to the front of a dress; a sleeveless wraparound garment tied at the back, worn to protect the clothes. L18.
2 A collarless sleeveless girl's garment worn over a dress and fastened at the back (*Hist.*); (in full ***pinafore dress***) a collarless sleeveless dress worn over a blouse or jumper. L19.
■ **pinafored** *adjective* wearing a pinafore E19.

pinakoid *adjective & noun* var. of PINACOID.

pinang /pɪˈnaŋ/ *noun*. M17.
[Malay.]
The areca tree, *Areca catechu*; its seed, the areca nut.

pinard /pinar/ *noun*. Also **P-**. Pl. pronounced same. E20.
[French.]
Rough red wine; *gen.* any wine; a glass of this.

pinarette /pɪnəˈrɛt/ *noun*. M20.
[from PINA(FO)RE + -ETTE.]
A short pinafore.

pinaster /pʌɪˈnastə/ *noun*. M16.
[Latin, from *pinus* PINE *noun*²: see -ASTER.]
The maritime pine, *Pinus pinaster*.

piñata /pɪˈnjɑːtə/ *noun*. L19.
[Spanish = jug, pot.]
In Mexico and the south-western US: a decorated container filled with sweets or small gifts, which is opened (esp. by breaking) by a blindfolded person at a festive celebration.

pinate /ˈpʌɪneɪt/ *noun*. M19.
[from PINIC + -ATE¹.]
CHEMISTRY. A salt or ester of pinic acid.

pinax /ˈpɪnaks/ *noun*. Pl. **pinaces** /ˈpɪnəsiːz/. L17.
[Latin from Greek = board, plank, tablet, picture.]
1 A tablet; a list inscribed on this; a catalogue, an index. Now *rare* or *obsolete*. L17.
2 ANTIQUITIES. A (painted or engraved) plate, platter, or dish. M19.

PINC /pɪŋk/ *abbreviation*.
Property income certificate.

pince-nez /pansˈneɪ, *foreign* pɛ̃sne/ *noun* (treated as *sing.* or *pl.*). L19.
[French, from *pincer* PINCH + *nez* nose.]
A pair of eyeglasses kept in position by a spring clipping the nose rather than by earpieces.
■ **pince-nezed** *adjective* wearing a pince-nez E20.

pincer /ˈpɪnsə/ *noun sing.* LME.
[from (the same root as) PINCERS.]
1 = PINCERS 1. Usu. *attrib.* LME.
2 ZOOLOGY. A claw of a crab, scorpion, etc. E19.
3 = ***pincer movement*** below. M20.

> 📖 **3** L. ADAMIC To prevent Germany and Japan from closing the pincer . . around Russia.

Comb.: **pincer movement** MILITARY designating an operation involving the convergence of two forces from opposite directions on an enemy position.
■ **pincer-like** *adjective* resembling pincers or claws in shape E17.

pincer /ˈpɪnsə/ *verb trans.* E18.
[from the noun.]
Grip, compress, or torture (as) with pincers.

> 📖 B. HINES He pincered it . . between his forefinger and thumb.

pincers /ˈpɪnsəz/ *noun pl.* (also treated as *sing.*). ME.
[Anglo-Norman, = Old French *pincier* PINCH *verb*: see -ER². See also PINCER *noun*.]
1 Treated as *pl.* & (occas.) *sing.* A pair of blunt usu. concave pivoting jaws attached to handles, resembling scissors but used as a gripping tool. Also ***pair of pincers***. ME.
2 ZOOLOGY. Treated as *pl.* A grasping or gripping organ formed by two opposed hinged claws, mandibles, etc.; a structure resembling such an organ. M17.
3 Treated as *sing.* = ***pincer movement*** s.v. PINCER *noun*. M20.

> 📖 **1** *Essentials* Use pincers to remove the old . . nails. **3** J. A. MICHENER A stupendous march north in an effort to create a pincers.

¶ In attrib. use & in comb. usu. in sing. PINCER.

pincette /pɪnˈsɛt/ *noun*. M16.
[French, dim. of *pince* a pair of pincers.]
A small pair of pincers.

pinch /pɪn(t)ʃ/ *verb & noun*. ME.
[Anglo-Norman *pincher* (only recorded as *pinché*) var. of Old French *pincier* (mod. *pincer*) from Proto-Romance word meaning 'prick, punch'.]
▸ **A** *verb*. **I 1** *verb trans. & intrans.* Grip or compress (something) tightly and sharply; *esp.* grip the skin of (a person or part of the body) tightly and sharply between the tips of a finger and thumb; nip; squeeze. Also, crush (usu. in *pass.*). ME. ▸†**b** *verb trans.* Pleat, gather, crimp. LME–E16.
2 *verb trans. & intrans.* Constrict (the body or a part of the body) painfully. LME.
3 *verb trans.* Bring into a state or condition by nipping or squeezing. LME.
4 *verb trans. & intrans.* Foll. by *off*: constrict or become constricted at a particular (esp. connecting) point until separation into two parts occurs; detach or become detached in this way. L17. ▸**b** *verb trans.* HORTICULTURE. Remove (a bud, leaf, shoot, etc.) with the fingers to encourage growth. Usu. foll. by adverb. L17.

> 📖 **1** J. K. JEROME Avoid getting your fingers pinched between . . the spokes of the wheel. C. CHAPLIN If some of us looked a little pale . . he would tell us to pinch our cheeks. L. R. BANKS The copper had hold of me as if he wanted to pinch my arm in half. **2** E. FIGES My shoes pinch, making my feet ache. A. DESAI The spectacles . . pinched the top of her nose. ***where the shoe pinches***: see SHOE *noun*. **4** E. L. ORTIZ Pinch off pieces of the dough. **b** *Gardening Which?* Pinching back the growing tips will also encourage the plants. A. LURIE Pinching off a half-dead bloom.

▸ **II** *transf. & fig.* **5** †**a** *verb trans.* Hurt, torment, torture, (as) with a pinch. ME–E17. ▸**b** *verb trans.* Afflict, trouble; (of physical or emotional distress) pain, exhaust, waste; (of a person, problem, etc.) harass, distress. ME. ▸†**c** *verb intrans. & trans.* Carp or cavil (at); find fault (with); object (to). LME–L16. ▸**d** *verb trans.* RACING. Urge or press (a horse), esp. to exhaustion. M18.
6 †**a** *verb intrans.* Move, stay, or press close to, encroach *on*. ME–M18. ▸**b** *verb trans.* NAUTICAL. Sail (a vessel) too close to the wind. L19.
7 a *verb intrans.* Give or spend sparingly; be mean or parsimonious. *obsolete* exc. *dial.* ME. ▸**b** *verb trans.* Limit or restrict the supply of (a thing). Now *dial.* exc. in ***pinch pennies***, ***pinch a penny***. M16. ▸**c** *verb intrans.* Be straitened in means, suffer from penury. M16. ▸**d** *verb trans.* Restrict or stint (a person, oneself, etc.), esp. *in*, *for*, or *of* (a thing). L16.
8 *verb trans.* Confine (esp. a person); restrict (an idea, liberty, etc.); trap or pin down in argument. Now *rare*. LME.
9 *verb trans.* **a** Steal (a thing); rob (a person). *slang*. L16. ▸**b** Extract or extort (money) *from* or *out of*. Now *rare*. L18. ▸**c** Arrest, take into custody. M19.
10 *verb trans.* Move (a heavy object) with a succession of small heaves with a crowbar. Now *Scot.* L18.
11 *verb intrans.* GEOLOGY & MINING. Of a stratum or a vein or deposit of ore: contract in volume, become gradually thinner; *spec.* (foll. by *out*) become thinner to the point of extinction, run out. M19.

> 📖 **5b** DEFOE The king finding his affairs pinch him at home. MRS H. WOOD Debt pinches the mind, more than hunger pinches the body. *Fortnightly Review* The labouring classes . . have been pinched . . by hard times. **7d** F. TROLLOPE She wasn't used to be pinched for money herself. H. JAMES We have to . . provide and pinch, to meet all the necessities. **9a** JULIETTE HUXLEY Parrain . . knew all my wrong-doings: my pinching of sugar.

▸ **B** *noun*. **1** †**a** A fold, pleat, or gather in a garment etc. LME–M19. ▸**b** GEOLOGY & MINING. A thin or compressed point of a stratum or vein. Freq. in ***pinch and swell***. Cf. ***pinch-out*** below. L19. ▸**c** ELECTRONICS. A fused glass seal at the base of a valve through which the electrode contacts pass. M20. ▸**d** PHYSICS. A contraction in a cylindrical or toroidal plasma produced by the pinch effect. M20.
2 An instance, occasion, or time of special difficulty; a critical juncture; a crisis, an emergency. Chiefly in ***at a pinch***, ***in a pinch***. L15. ▸**b** The crucial point of an argument, theory, etc. Now *rare*. M17. ▸**c** A steep or difficult part of a road; a steep hill. Now chiefly *dial.*, *Austral.*, & *NZ*. M18.
3 †**a** (An) emotional pain caused esp. by fear, grief, remorse, shame, etc. M16–L17. ▸**b** Stress caused esp. by poverty, cold, hunger, etc.; difficulty, hardship. Freq. in ***feel the pinch***. E17.
4 The action or an act of pinching; a nip, a squeeze. L16.
5 An amount (esp. of a powdered or crystallized substance) that may be taken up between a finger and thumb; *fig.* a very small quantity. L16.

6 A pointed or beaked iron lever for prising, moving heavy objects, etc.; a crowbar. L17.
7 a An act of stealing, a theft; a stolen thing. *slang*. M18. **▸b** An arrest, a charge; imprisonment. *slang*. E20.

1d THETA *pinch*. **2** R. L. STEVENSON The coxwain.. could be trusted at a pinch with almost anything. *Motorboats Monthly* Seating for four people, or five at a pinch. *Commercials* The pinch is likely to come at the end of the year. **3b** BOSW. SMITH Those who were rendered keener by the pinch of hunger. A. JESSOPP He never knew what the pinch of poverty was. **4** ISAAC TAYLOR Feeling the pinch of a tight shoe. **5** *Guardian* Grate some Cheddar cheese into a bowl, add a pinch of curry powder. ***take with a pinch of salt***: see SALT *noun*[1].

Comb.: **pinch-bar** = sense B.6 above; **pinch-bottle** *US* (*a*) a bottle with indented sides, *spec.* a whiskey bottle; (*b*) whiskey; **pinch-bug** *US* a stag beetle; **pinch effect** (*a*) the constriction of a fluid (as a toroidal plasma) through which a large electric current is flowing, caused by the attractive force of the current's own magnetic field; (*b*) the slight narrowing of a record groove caused by a sideways movement of the cutting stylus, resulting in a vertical movement of the playing stylus at that point; **pinch-fist** a mean or miserly person; **pinch-gut** *noun & adjective* (*obsolete* exc. *dial.*) (*a*) *noun* a person who stints on food; (*b*) *adjective* niggardly, scanty; **pinch-hit** *verb intrans.* (*a*) BASEBALL substitute for another batter, esp. at a critical point in a game; (*b*) *US* act as a substitute (*for*), esp. in an emergency; **pinch-hitter** (*a*) BASEBALL a substitute batter; (*b*) *US* a person acting as a substitute; **pinch-off** ELECTRONICS in a field-effect transistor, the cutting off of the channel current at the gate region; ***pinch-off voltage***, the reverse bias that must be applied to a gate to achieve pinch-off; **pinch-out** GEOLOGY & MINING the gradual thinning of a vein or stratum to extinction; **pinch-point** a narrow, difficult, or congested point; **pinch-roll** (*a*) either of a pair of (usu. hydraulic) rollers which grip material passing between them; (*b*) = ***pinch roller*** below; **pinch-roller** a spring-loaded roller in a tape recorder or tape deck, which presses the tape against the capstan; **pinch-run** *verb intrans.* (BASEBALL) substitute for another base-runner, esp. at a critical point in a game; **pinch-runner** BASEBALL a substitute base-runner; **pinch-waist** *noun & adjective* (having) a tightly fitted waist; **pinch-wheel** = ***pinch roller*** above.
■ **pinchable** *adjective* that may be pinched; that invites pinching: E20. **pincher** *noun* a person who or thing which pinches LME. **pinching** *noun* an act or the action of pinching; the (painful) sensation caused by a pinch: ME. **pinchingly** *adverb* in a pinching manner L16.

pinchbeck /ˈpɪn(t)ʃbɛk/ *noun & adjective*. M18.
[Christopher *Pinchbeck* (d. 1732), English watchmaker and inventor.]
▸ A *noun*. **1** An alloy of copper and zinc, resembling gold and used in cheap jewellery etc. M18.
2 *fig.* A false, counterfeit, cheap, or worthless thing. M19.
▸ B *attrib.* or as *adjective*. **1** Made of pinchbeck. M18.
2 *fig.* False, counterfeit; cheap, worthless. M19.

pinche /pɪn(t)ʃ/ *noun*. L18.
[French, from Spanish *pincho*.]
A tamarin; *spec.* the cotton-top tamarin, *Saguinas oedipus*. Also ***pinche monkey***.

pinched /pɪn(t)ʃt/ *adjective*. E16.
[from PINCH *verb* + -ED[1].]
1 Gripped or compressed tightly, esp. between a finger and thumb, the teeth, the jaws of a pincers, etc.; squeezed. Also, shaped as if compressed tightly; contracted at one part. (Foll. by *in*, *up*.) E16. **▸b** PHYSICS. Confined by the pinch effect. E20.
2 Of the features or appearance: drawn or wasted (as) with cold, hunger, pain, worry, etc. E17.
3 Confined or restricted in space, scope, etc.; small, narrow; scanty. M17. **▸b** Of paper: slightly smaller than a regular size. L19.
4 Straitened; deprived; restricted in means or circumstances. E18.

2 J. MARK Her face was pinched.. as if the life were being sucked out of it. G. HARRIS A smile transformed her pale, pinched features. **3** *New Yorker* Small towns and pinched minds hold room enough for her. **4** DICKENS Do you know how pinched and destitute I am?

pinchpenny /ˈpɪn(t)ʃpɛni/ *noun*. LME.
[from PINCH *verb* + PENNY *noun*.]
A mean person, a miser.

pincushion /ˈpɪnkʊʃ(ə)n/ *noun*. E17.
[from PIN *noun* + CUSHION *noun*.]
1 A small cushion in which pins may be stuck in readiness for use. E17.
2 Any of several plants with flower-heads resembling a pincushion; *spec.* (*a*) any of several scabiouses, *esp.* sweet scabious, *Scabiosa atropurpurea*; (*b*) *Austral.* (more fully ***blue pincushion***) an Australian plant, *Brunonia australis* (family Brunoniaceae), with rounded heads of blue flowers. M19.
Comb.: **pincushion distortion** a form of optical distortion in which straight lines along the edge of a screen, lens, etc., bulge towards the centre.

pind /pɪnd/ *verb trans. obsolete* exc. *dial.* See also POIND.
[Old English *ġepyndan*, from base repr. also by PINFOLD, POND *noun*, POUND *noun*[2]. Cf. PIN *verb*.]
†**1** Enclose; imprison; dam up (water). OE–L17.
2 *spec.* Impound (an animal). ME.
†**3** Distrain. *Scot.* LME–E18.

pinda /ˈpɪndə/ *noun*[1]. L18.
[Sanskrit *piṇḍa* lump.]
HINDUISM. A cake or ball of rice offered to the memory of one's ancestors, esp. as part of funerary rites.

pinda *noun*[2] var. of PINDAR.

pindan /ˈpɪndan/ *noun*. *Austral.* L19.
[Aboriginal.]
A tract of arid sandy country characteristic of parts of western Australia; the low scrubby vegetation occurring in such tracts.

pindar /ˈpɪndə/ *noun*. *W. Indies & US*. Also **-da**, **-der**. L17.
[Portuguese *pinda* from Kikongo *mpinda*, Mpongwe *mbenda*.]
(The fruit of) the peanut, *Arachis hypogaea*.

Pindari /pɪnˈdɑːri/ *noun*. Also **-darry**. L18.
[Marathi *peṇḍhār(ā)* marauding band, Hindi *piṇḍārā*, Marathi *peṇḍhārī* marauder.]
Hist. A member of a body of mounted raiders active in Central India in the 17th and 18th cents.

Pindaric /pɪnˈdarɪk/ *adjective & noun*. M17.
[Latin *Pindaricus* from Greek *Pindarikos*, from *Pindaros* Pindar: see below, -IC.]
▸ A *adjective*. Of, pertaining to, or characteristic of the style of, the ancient Greek lyric poet Pindar (*c* 518–*c* 438 BC). M17.
▸ B *noun*. A poem (esp. an ode) or a poetic form (esp. a metre) in the style of Pindar. Usu. in *pl.* L17.
■ **Pindarism** *noun* Pindaric style E18.

Pindarry *noun* var. of PINDARI.

pinder /ˈpɪndə/ *noun*[1]. *obsolete* exc. *Hist.* ME.
[from PIND *verb* + -ER[1].]
An officer of a manor, in charge of impounding stray animals.

pinder *noun*[2] var. of PINDAR.

pine /pʌɪn/ *noun*[1]. Now *arch. & dial.*
[Old English *pīne* = Old Saxon, Old High German *pīna* (Dutch *pijn(e)*, German *Pein*), Old Norse *pína*, all from medieval Latin *pena* from Latin *poena*. Cf. PINE *verb*. Superseded by PAIN *noun*[1].]
1 Punishment; suffering or loss inflicted as punishment; *spec.* the sufferings of hell or purgatory. *obsolete* exc. *dial.* OE.
2 †**a** Bodily suffering. ME–E17. **▸b** Mental distress or trouble; grief, sorrow; anguish. Now *arch. & dial.* ME.
†**3** Trouble taken in accomplishing or attempting something. ME–L17.
4 Complaint, lament. *rare*. LME.
5 †**a** Hunger; starvation; *fig.* intense desire or longing. Cf. PINE *verb* 3, 4. M16–E18. **▸b** A wasting disease of sheep. E19.

pine /pʌɪn/ *noun*[2] & *adjective*. OE.
[Latin *pinus*, reinforced in Middle English by Old & mod. French *pin* from Latin.]
▸ A *noun*. **1** Any coniferous tree of the genus *Pinus*, comprising usu. large trees with evergreen needle-shaped leaves growing in clusters, native to northern temperate regions, and valued esp. as a source of timber, tar, and turpentine (also ***pine tree***); the soft wood of these trees, often used to make furniture. OE. **▸b** Any coniferous tree of certain other genera, *esp.* (*Austral. & NZ*) any tree of the genus *Callitris* (also ***pine tree***); the wood of these trees. L18.
†**2** In *pl.* The edible seeds of certain pines, esp. the stone pine, *Pinus pinea*. ME–L16.
3 With specifying word: any of various trees or herbaceous plants of other families, resembling the true pines in foliage or some other respect. M16.
4 *transf.* A thing made of pine, as a mast. Chiefly *poet.* L16.
5 (The fruit of) the pineapple, *Ananas comosus*. M17.
1 ***lodge-pole pine***, ***maritime pine***, ***Norway pine***, ***Scots pine***, ***stone pine***, ***umbrella pine***, ***Weymouth pine***, etc. **b** ***celery-top pine***, ***Chile pine***, ***cypress pine***, ***dammar pine***, ***Murray pine***, ***Norfolk Island pine***, etc. **3** ***ground-pine***, ***Leichhardt pine***, ***prince's pine***, ***screw-pine***, etc. **5** ***wild pine*** *W. Indies* any of various epiphytic bromeliads of the genus *Tillandsia*.
▸ B *adjective*. **1** Made of pine. M17.
2 Having the scent of pine-needles. L19.
Comb. & special collocations: **pine-barren** *N. Amer.* a level sandy tract of land, covered scantily with pines; ***pine-barren beauty***, the pixie moss, *Pyxidanthera barbulata*; **pine beauty** a cryptically coloured moth, *Panolis flammea*, whose larvae feed on pines; **pine-bud moth** a tortricid moth, *Blastesthia turionella*, whose larvae feed on pine buds; **pine carpet (moth)** either of two geometrids, *Thera obeliscata* and *T. firmata*, whose larvae feed on pines; **pine cone** the cone-shaped fruit of a pine or fir; **pine-drops** a saprophytic N. American plant, *Pterospora andromedea* (family Monotropaceae); **pine grosbeak** a large finch, *Pinicola enucleator*, of pinewoods in Europe and N. America; **pine gum** *US* resin or turpentine obtained from any of several kinds of pine, esp. the slash pine, *Pinus caribaea*, and southern pine, *Pinus echinata*; **pine hawkmoth** a hawkmoth, *Hyloicus pinastri*, whose larvae feed on the pine; **pine-kernel** a seed of a pine, esp. an edible one; **pine-knot** (*a*) a knot of pinewood, esp. for use as fuel; (*b*) *transf.* a very hard or tough thing; (*c*) *fig.* hardness, toughness; **pine land** *US* land on which pine trees are the characteristic growth; **pine lander** a person who lives off pine land; **pine lappet (moth)** a large brown European moth, *Dendrolimus pini*, whose caterpillar is a pest of pines; **pine linnet** *rare* = ***pine*** SISKIN; **pine-lizard** = ***fence lizard*** s.v. FENCE *noun*; **pine marten** a N. Eurasian marten, *Martes martes*, which is brown with a yellowish throat; **pine-mouse** a pine vole, *Pitymys pinetorum*, usu. inhabiting pine-barrens in the eastern US; **pine-needle** the needle-shaped leaf of a pine; **pine nut** a pine cone, *esp.* one containing edible seeds; an edible seed of any of several pines, esp. the European stone pine, *Pinus pinea*, and the Mexican stone pine, *Pinus cembroides*; **pine-oil** any of various oils obtained from the leaves, twigs, wood, or resin of pines; **pine overcoat** *US slang* a coffin; **pinesap** *US* either of two saprophytic plants, yellow bird's nest, *Monotropa hypopitys*, or (more fully ***sweet pinesap***) the allied *Monotropsis odorata*, which smells of violets; ***pine*** SISKIN; **pine-snake** a variety of bullsnake of N. American pinewoods; ***pine straw***: see STRAW *noun* 2b; **pine tag** *US* a pine needle; **pine-top** (*a*) the top of a pine; (*b*) *US slang* cheap or illicit whiskey; **pine tree** (*a*) see senses 1, 1b above; (*b*) ***pine-tree money***, silver coins bearing the figure of a pine, struck in Massachusetts in the late 17th cent.; (*c*) ***pine-Tree State***, (*US*) Maine; **pine vole** a vole of the holarctic genus *Pitymys*; **pine warbler** a small warbler, *Dendroica pinus*, of N. American pinewoods; **pineweed** *N. Amer.* nitweed, *Hypericum gentianoides*; **pinewood** (*a*) a forest of pines; (*b*) the timber of the pine.
■ **pinery** *noun* (*a*) a plantation or grove of pines; (*b*) a place where pineapples are grown: M18.

pine /pʌɪn/ *verb*.
[Old English *pīnian* corresp. to Middle Low German, Middle Dutch *pīnen* (Dutch *pijnen*), Old High German *pīnōn* (German *peinen*), Old Norse *pína*: rel. to PINE *noun*[1].]
1 *verb trans.* & (*rare*) *intrans.* (Cause to) suffer; (cause to) experience pain or distress. Cf. PAIN *verb* 2, 3a. Long *obsolete* exc. *Scot.* OE.
2 *verb trans.* Put to work; exert (oneself). Long *obsolete* exc. *Scot.* ME.
3 *verb trans.* Exhaust or waste with physical or emotional suffering, esp. hunger, disease, or grief; starve; wear out. Also foll. by *away*, *out*. Now *rare* exc. *dial.* ME.
4 *verb intrans.* Become exhausted or wasted from physical or emotional suffering, esp. hunger, disease, or grief; languish. LME. **▸b** *transf.* Of a thing: lose vigour or intensity; decrease. E18.
5 a *verb trans.* Dry or cure (fish) by exposure to the weather. Now *Scot. dial.* M16. **▸b** *verb intrans.* Of fish: shrink in the process of curing. *rare*. L17.
6 *verb intrans.* Yearn; have an intense longing; languish with desire. Foll. by *after*, *for*, *to do*. L16.
7 *verb trans. & intrans.* Lament or repine at (a loss etc.). *arch.* M17.

4 S. JOHNSON You must get a place, or pine in penury. **6** E. WAUGH I feel you will pine for cosmopolitan dishes. S. RUSHDIE She pines for her late mother. S. CHITTY She pined to be Rodin's wife. E. PAWEL The prisoner pining away for his freedom. **7** *Times* We pine the passing of.. red telephone kiosks.

■ **pining** *noun* (*a*) the action of the verb; (*b*) a wasting disease of sheep: OE.

pineal /ˈpɪnɪəl, ˈpʌɪ-/ *adjective & noun*. L17.
[French *pinéal*, from Latin *pinea* pine cone (from the organ's shape in humans): see -AL[1].]
ANATOMY. **▸A** *adjective*. **1** ***pineal gland***, ***pineal organ***, ***pineal body***, a small outgrowth behind and above the third ventricle of the brain, which has an endocrine function, in some vertebrates forming a light-sensitive median eye (***pineal eye***) involved in control of circadian rhythms, and in others secreting melatonin. L17.
2 Pertaining to, connected with, or forming part of the pineal gland. L19.
▸ B *noun*. The pineal gland. E20.
■ **pineaˈlectomize** *verb trans.* perform pinealectomy on E20. **pineaˈlectomy** *noun* (an instance of) surgical removal of the pineal gland E20. **pineˈalocyte** *noun* an epithelioid cell characteristic of the pineal gland, which secretes melatonin and other hormones M20. **pineaˈloma** *noun*, pl. **-mas**, **-mata** /-mətə/, MEDICINE a tumour of the pineal gland, thought to arise from the parenchymal cells E20.

pineapple /ˈpʌɪnap(ə)l/ *noun*. LME.
[from PINE *noun*[2] + APPLE.]
1 a The fruit of the pine; a pine cone. *obsolete* exc. *dial.* LME. **▸b** A representation of a pine cone, used for decoration. Now *rare*. L15.
2 [From its resemblance to a pine cone.] The large juicy edible fruit of a tropical American bromeliad, *Ananas comosus*, a collective fruit developed from a conical spike of flowers and having yellow flesh surrounded by a tough segmented skin and topped with a tuft of stiff leaves; the plant which bears this fruit. M17. **▸b** A bomb; a hand-grenade; a light trench mortar. Also more fully ***pineapple bomb***. *slang*. E20. **▸c** ***the pineapple***, unemployment benefit, the dole. *slang*. M20.
Comb.: ***pineapple bomb***: see sense 2b above; **pineapple fibre**: of the leaves of the pineapple; **pineapple lily** the plant eucomis (genus *Eucomis*), in which the cluster of flowers is surmounted by a tuft of sterile leafy bracts; **pineapple rum**: flavoured with pineapple; **pineapple weed** a small mayweed, *Matricaria discoidea*, native to N. America, with rayless flower-heads which smell like pineapple when crushed.

Pineau /ˈpiːnəʊ, *foreign* pino/ *noun.* Also **p-**. Pl. **-eaux** /-əʊ, *foreign* -o/. **M18.**
[French, from *pin* pine + dim. suffix *-eau* (from the form of the grape cluster).]
1 = PINOT. Now *rare.* **M18.**
2 An aperitif made from unfermented grape juice and brandy. **M20.**

pinene /ˈpʌɪniːn/ *noun.* **L19.**
[from Latin *pinus* PINE *noun*² + -ENE.]
CHEMISTRY. A bicyclic terpene, $C_{10}H_{16}$, of which there are several isomers; *esp.* either of two (α-*pinene* and β-*pinene*) which are colourless flammable liquids occurring in turpentine and used as solvents and in chemical syntheses.

piner /ˈpʌɪnə/ *noun*¹. **OE.**
[from PINE *verb* + -ER¹.]
†**1** A tormentor. **OE–L16.**
2 A person who or thing which pines; *spec.* an animal suffering from a wasting disease. **E17.**

piner /ˈpʌɪnə/ *noun*². *obsolete* exc. *Scot. dial.* **ME.**
[Origin uncertain: perh. from Middle Dutch *piner* (Dutch *pijner*), from *pinen* (Dutch *pijnen*) labour, or directly from PINE *noun*¹, *verb*: see -ER¹.]
A labourer. Now *esp.*, a peat or turf cutter.

pinetum /pʌɪˈniːtəm/ *noun.* Pl. **-ta** /-tə/. **M19.**
[Latin, from *pinus* PINE *noun*².]
A plantation or collection of pines or other conifers, for scientific or ornamental purposes.

piney /ˈpʌɪni/ *noun.* **M19.**
[Malayalam *payani*.]
A resinous tree of southern India, *Vateria indica* (family Dipterocarpaceae). Chiefly in combs. (see below).
Comb.: **piney resin** the oleoresin obtained from the trunk of *Vateria indica*; **piney tallow** a fatty substance obtained from the fruit of *Vateria indica*; **piney varnish** = *piney resin* above.

piney *adjective* var. of PINY.

piney wood /ˈpʌɪni wʊd/ *noun phr. US.* **L18.**
[from *piney* var. of PINY *adjective*.]
A pinewood; a region of pinewoods; *spec.* (in *pl.*) tracts of poor land in the southern US on which pines are the characteristic growth.

pin-fire /ˈpɪnfʌɪə/ *adjective*¹ & *noun*¹. **L19.**
[from PIN *noun*¹ + FIRE *verb*.]
(Designating) a form of cartridge for a breech-loading gun, fired by a pin thrust by the hammer of the lock into the fulminate; (designating) a gun having such a cartridge.

pin-fire /ˈpɪnfʌɪə/ *adjective*² & *noun*². **E20.**
[from PIN *noun*¹ + FIRE *noun*.]
(Designating) an opal characterized by closely spaced specks of colour.

pinfold /ˈpɪnfəʊld/ *noun* & *verb.*
[Late Old English *pundfald*, from base repr. also by POND *verb*, POND *noun*, POUND *noun*² + FOLD *noun*¹.]
▶ **A** *noun.* **1** A pen or enclosure for cattle, horses, sheep, etc.; a pound, a fold. **LOE.**
2 *transf.* & *fig.* A place of confinement; a prison; a trap. **LME.**
▶ **B** *verb trans.* Shut up or enclose in a pinfold; *fig.* confine within narrow limits. **E17.**

ping /pɪŋ/ *noun.* **M19.**
[Imit.]
1 An abrupt high-pitched ringing sound. **M19.**
2 = PINK *noun*⁷ 3. Chiefly *US & Austral.* **E20.**
3 A very short pulse of high-pitched, usu. ultrasonic, sound, as emitted by sonar; an audible signal by which this is represented to a user of such equipment. **M20.**

🕮 **1** *Sunday Express* Shows of low fashion no longer led to the pleasuring ping of cash tills.

ping /pɪŋ/ *verb*¹ *trans.* & *intrans. obsolete* exc. *dial.* **OE.**
[Latin *pungere* prick.]
Prick; poke, push; urge.

ping /pɪŋ/ *verb*². **M18.**
[Imit.]
1 *verb trans.* Cause (a thing) to make an abrupt high-pitched ringing sound. **M18.** ▸**b** Fire or discharge (a missile) with such a sound. **M20.** ▸**c** *RACING.* Of a horse: jump (a fence) well; leave (the starting stalls) swiftly. Chiefly with *it. colloq.* **L20.**
2 *verb intrans.* Make an abrupt high-pitched ringing sound; fly with such a sound. **M19.** ▸**b** Of a sonar etc.: emit a very short pulse of high-pitched sound. **M20.** ▸**c** = PINK *verb*³ 2. **M20.**

🕮 **1** J. LE CARRÉ He lightly pinged the edge of his Drambuie glass. **2** *fig.*: *Listener* Words and concepts heard nowhere else pinged out on Third Programme drama.

pinga /ˈpiŋa/ *noun.* **M20.**
[Portuguese, lit. 'drop (of water)'.]
A raw white rum distilled from sugar cane in Brazil; a drink of this.

pingao /ˈpiːŋaʊ/ *noun.* **M19.**
[Maori.]
A club-rush, *Desmoschoenus spiralis*, of New Zealand, which is a sand-binder with bronzy leaves.

pinger /ˈpɪŋə/ *noun.* **M20.**
[from PING *verb*² + -ER¹.]
1 A device that transmits short high-pitched signals at brief intervals for purposes of detection, measurement, or identification. **M20.**
2 A timer used esp. in cooking that pings after a pre-set period of time elapses. **M20.**

🕮 **2** P. DICKINSON Two eggs . . boiled for two minutes . . . The pinger pinged.

pingle /ˈpɪŋg(ə)l/ *noun. obsolete* exc. *dial.* **M16.**
[Origin unkn. Cf. PIGHTLE.]
A small enclosed piece of land; a paddock, a close.

pingle /ˈpɪŋg(ə)l/ *verb.* **E16.**
[Origin uncertain. In branch II, cf. Swedish dial. *pyngla* be busy about small matters, work in a trifling way.]
▶ **I 1** *verb intrans.* Strive, contend, vie. *Scot.* **E16.**
2 *verb trans.* Press (someone) hard in a contest, vie with; trouble. *obsolete* exc. *Scot.* **E16.**
3 *verb intrans.* Struggle against difficulties; labour, exert oneself; toil for a living. *Scot.* **E16.**
▶ **II 4** *verb intrans.* Work in a trifling or ineffectual way; meddle *with* in a petty way; dally. Now *Scot. & north.* **L16.**
5 *verb intrans.* Pick *at* one's food; eat with little appetite, nibble. Now *dial.* **E17.**

pingo /ˈpɪŋgəʊ/ *noun.* Pl. **-o(e)s.** **M20.**
[Inupiaq *pinguq* nunatak.]
PHYSICAL GEOGRAPHY. A persistent low conical or dome-shaped mound, often with a crater on top, formed in regions with thin or discontinuous permafrost and consisting of a layer of soil over a large core of ice; a round depression in temperate regions thought to be the remains of such a mound.

ping-pong /ˈpɪŋpɒŋ/ *noun.* **E20.**
[Imit., from the sound emitted on contact between bat and ball or ball and table.]
1 An indoor game based on lawn tennis, played with small rubber- or plastic-covered bats and a ball bounced on a table divided by a net; table tennis. **E20.** ▸**b** *fig.* A series of swift (usu. verbal) exchanges between two parties, esp. of a diplomatic or political nature. **E20.**
2 A type of drum in a West Indian steel band; a melody played on such a drum. **M20.**

🕮 **1** *attrib.*: *Listener* Those ping-pong balls at a fair that rise and fall on spurts of water. ***aerial ping-pong***: see AERIAL *adjective* 4. **b** J. CLEARY Two hours of diplomatic ping-pong hadn't touched her; she looked . . poised.

¶ Proprietary name (**P-**) in the US.

ping-pong /ˈpɪŋpɒŋ/ *verb.* **E20.**
[from the noun.]
1 *verb intrans.* Play ping-pong. Also, move back and forth in the manner of a ping-pong ball. **E20.**
2 *verb trans. fig.* Send back and forth, pass or send around aimlessly or unnecessarily. **L20.**

🕮 **1** *fig.*: *Daily Telegraph* Funny lines . . that . . ping-pong back and forth in long sustained volleys with the audience's laughter. **2** *Washington Post* The administration 'ping-ponged' the proposal back and forth.

pinguecula /pɪŋˈgwɛkjʊlə/ *noun.* Pl. **-lae** /-liː/. **M19.**
[formed as PINGUICULA.]
MEDICINE. A small yellow region of degeneration of the conjunctiva near the edge of the cornea.

pinguedinous /pɪŋˈgwɛdɪnəs/ *adjective.* **L16.**
[from Latin *pinguedin-*, *pinguedo* fatness (from *pinguis* fat) + -OUS.]
Of the nature of or resembling fat; fatty, greasy.

pinguefy /ˈpɪŋgwɪfʌɪ/ *verb.* Now *rare.* **L16.**
[Latin *pinguefacere*, from *pinguis* fat: see -FY.]
1 *verb trans.* Fatten; make fat or greasy; make (soil) fertile. **L16.**
†**2** *verb intrans.* Become fat. **L16–E19.**

pinguescence /pɪŋˈgwɛs(ə)ns/ *noun. rare.* **E19.**
[formed as next: see -ESCENCE.]
The process of becoming or growing fat; obesity.

pinguescent /pɪŋˈgwɛs(ə)nt/ *adjective.* **L18.**
[Latin *pinguescent-* pres. ppl stem of *pinguescere* grow fat, from *pinguis* fat: see -ESCENT.]
Becoming or growing fat, fattening; flourishing.

pinguicula /pɪŋˈgwɪkjʊlə/ *noun.* **L16.**
[Latin, fem. (in sense 1 sc. *planta*) of *pinguiculus* dim. of *pinguis* fat: see -CULE.]
1 *BOTANY.* An insectivorous bog plant of the genus *Pinguicula*; a butterwort. **L16.**
2 *MEDICINE.* = PINGUECULA. *rare.* **L19.**

pinguid /ˈpɪŋgwɪd/ *adjective.* Now chiefly *joc.* **M17.**
[from Latin *pinguis* fat: see -ID¹.]
Of the nature of or resembling fat; unctuous, greasy; (of soil) fertile.

🕮 C. MACKENZIE A wig as dark and curly and pinguid as Perique tobacco. A. CRAIG He held my hand too long in pinguid fingers.

▪ **pinˈguidity** *noun* fatness; fatty matter: **L16.**

pinguin /ˈpɪŋgwɪn/ *noun.* Also **ping-wing** /ˈpɪŋwɪŋ/. **L17.**
[Origin unkn.]
A large prickly W. Indian plant, *Bromelia pinguin*, allied to the pineapple; the edible fruit of this.

pinguitude /ˈpɪŋgwɪtjuːd/ *noun. rare.* **E17.**
[Latin *pinguitudo*, from *pinguis* fat: see -TUDE.]
Fatness.

ping-wing *noun* var. of PINGUIN.

pinhead /ˈpɪnhɛd/ *noun* & *adjective.* **L16.**
[from PIN *noun*¹ + HEAD *noun*.]
▶ **A** *noun.* **1 a** The head of a pin; (the type of) something of very small size or value; an object (usu. rounded in form) resembling a pin's head, as a small grain etc. **L16.** ▸**b** A woven pattern of small dots on cloth; cloth having such a pattern; *ellipt.* a garment made of such cloth. **L19.**
2 A small minnow. **M19.**
3 The top of the pin or peg in the game of quoits. **L19.**
4 A person with a small head; *esp.* (*fig.*) a stupid person, a fool. **L19.**

🕮 **1a** J. CLEARY The street lights are on, yellow pin-heads climbing the hill. **b** L. A. G. STRONG Those chaps . . so successfully turned his blue pinhead that several people . . thought it was brand new. **4** *Times* The clubs . . follow the line of that pinhead, Ken Bates.

▶ **B** *attrib.* or as *adjective.* **1** Of the nature of or resembling the head of a pin; very small and usu. round; *spec.* designating a fine grade of oatmeal. **M19.**
2 Made of cloth with a woven pattern of small dots. **E20.**

▪ **pinheaded** *adjective* (*a*) (of a flower) pin-eyed; (*b*) (of a person) having a small head like that of a pin; *esp.* (*fig.*) stupid, foolish: **M19.** **pinheadedness** *noun* **E20.**

pinhole /ˈpɪnhəʊl/ *noun* & *adjective.* **L17.**
[from PIN *noun*¹ + HOLE *noun*¹.]
▶ **A** *noun.* **1** A hole into which a pin or peg fits. **L17.**
2 a A hole made by a pin; any very small aperture or perforation resembling a pin-prick. **L17.** ▸**b** A small hole in timber caused by a wood-boring beetle or its larva. **L19.** ▸**c** A very small cavity in a solid, esp. a casting; a very small area from which a coating such as gold plating is absent. **E20.** ▸**d** *ellipt.* A pinhole camera. **L20.**

🕮 **1** *Rally Car* The tyre . . comes with pin holes to fit studs in ice . . conditions.

▶ **B** *attrib.* or as *adjective.* Pertaining to, involving, or of the nature of a very small aperture or perforation; *spec.* (*PHOTOGRAPHY*) having or pertaining to the use of a pinhole aperture in place of a lens. **M19.**

🕮 G. J. DAVIES Pinhole cavities in a sand-cast aluminium alloy, the result of hydrogen evolution. ***pinhole camera***, ***pinhole photography***, etc.

Comb.: **pinhole borer** the larva of any of various small brown or black beetles (ambrosia beetles) of the families Scolytidae (esp. the genus *Xyleborus*) or Platypodidae (esp. the genus *Platypus*), which bore tunnels into trees or felled timber; also called ***shot-borer***, ***shot-hole borer***.

▪ **pinholing** *noun* the presence or formation of pinholes in a solid or on a surface **E20.**

pinic /ˈpʌɪnɪk/ *adjective.* **M19.**
[French *pinique*, from Latin *pinus* PINE *noun*²: see -IC.]
CHEMISTRY. ***pinic acid***, a dicarboxylic acid, $C_9H_{14}O_4$, obtained from pine resin, whose molecule contains a four-membered ring.

pinion /ˈpɪnjən/ *noun*¹. **ME.**
[Old & mod. French *pignon* wing-feather, wing, pinnacle, battlement, (now only) gable from Proto-Romance augm. of Latin *pinna* PIN *noun*¹. Cf. PENNON.]
1 A battlement, a pinnacle; a gable. Long *dial. obsolete* exc. in ***pinion-end***, a gable-end. **ME.**
2 The terminal segment of a (bird's) wing usu. including the flight feathers; (chiefly *poet.* & *rhet.*) a bird's wing as used in flight. **LME.** ▸**b** Orig., the whole wing of a cooked or dressed fowl. Now *spec.* the terminal segment of the wing. **M17.**
3 Any of the primary flight feathers of a bird's wing, esp. the outermost one. **M16.**
†**4** A winglike adornment or style of cut of the shoulder or sleeve of a garment, fashionable in the 16th and 17th cents. **L16–M17.**
5 The anterior border of an insect's wing. Usu. in *comb.* in collectors' names of moths. **E18.**

🕮 **2** *fig.*: E. DARWIN When light clouds on airy pinions sail.

▪ **pinioned** *adjective* (*a*) having a pinion or pinions; winged; (*b*) (of a bird) subjected to pinioning: **LME.**

pinion /ˈpɪnjən/ *noun*². **L16.**
[Anglicized from Spanish PIÑON.]
1 The seed of the physic-nut, *Jatropha curcas*. **L16.**
2 = PIÑON. **M19.**

pinion /ˈpɪnjən/ *noun*³. M17.
[Old & mod. French *pignon* alt. of †*pignol*, from Proto-Romance from Latin *pinea* pine cone, from *pinus* PINE *noun*².]
A small cog-wheel which engages with a larger one; a cogged spindle or axle which engages with a wheel.
rack and pinion: see RACK *noun*².

pinion /ˈpɪnjən/ *verb trans.* M16.
[from PINION *noun*¹.]
1 Bind together (the arms) of a person; deprive (a person) of the use of the arms in this way. M16. ▸**b** Bind (a person, the arms) securely *to* something. M17.
2 Cut off the pinion of (a bird's wing) to prevent flight; cut off a pinion or bind the wings of (a bird) to prevent flight. L16.
🕮 **1** R. LINDNER The fight . . was over, with the boy pinioned face down. *fig.*: F. SPALDING She pinioned a young clergyman in a corner. **b** BARONESS ORCZY They were pinioned to one another back to back.

pinions /ˈpɪnjənz/ *noun pl.* Chiefly *dial.* L18.
[French *peignon* combings, from *peigner* to comb.]
Short pieces and knots of wool combed out of the long staple; noils.

pinite /ˈpʌɪnʌɪt, ˈpɪn-/ *noun.* E19.
[German *Pinit*, from *Pini* name of mine at Schneeburg, Saxony: see -ITE¹.]
MINERALOGY. A grey-green or brownish mica formed as a pseudomorph by the alteration of other minerals such as spodumene or cordierite.

pinjrapol /ˈpɪndʒrəpəʊl/ *noun.* E19.
[Marathi *piñjrā-pol*, Gujarati *pā̃jrā-pol*, from *piñjrā*, *pā̃jrā* (Sanskrit *pañjara*, *piñjara*) cage + *pol* (Sanskrit *paura*) enclosed yard.]
In the Indian subcontinent, an enclosure or reserve where old or sick animals are kept and tended.

pink /pɪŋk/ *noun*¹. L15.
[Middle Dutch *pin(c)ke* small seagoing vessel, fishing boat (whence also French *pinque*, Spanish *pinque*, Italian *pinco*), of unkn. origin.]
Chiefly *Hist.* A small sailing vessel with a narrow stern; *spec.* †(*a*) a flat-bottomed boat used for fishing etc.; (*b*) a small warship (esp. in the Danish Navy) in which the stern was broadened out at the level of the upper deck while remaining narrow below.
Comb.: **pink-stern** (*a*) a narrow stern like that of a pink; (*b*) a small vessel having such a stern; **pink-sterned** *adjective* having a stern like that of a pink.

pink /pɪŋk/ *noun*². Also (earlier) **penk** /pɛŋk/. L15.
[Origin unkn.]
1 A minnow. Now *dial.* L15.
2 a A young salmon before it becomes a smolt; a samlet, a parr. Cf. PINK *noun*⁴. E19. ▸**b** A one-year-old grayling. E20.

pink /pɪŋk/ *noun*³. E16.
[from PINK *verb*¹.]
†**1** A decorative hole or eyelet punched in a garment; decorative scalloping. Cf. PINKING *noun*¹. E16–M17.
†**2** A stab with a dagger, rapier, etc. E–M17. ▸**b** A slight gunshot wound. *rare.* L19.

pink /pɪŋk/ *noun*⁴. L16.
[Perh. short for *pink eye* s.v. PINK *adjective*¹: cf. synon. French *œillet* dim. of *œil* eye.]
▸**I 1** Any of numerous plants with narrow leaves, tubular calyces, and petals usu. with jagged edges, constituting the genus *Dianthus* (family Caryophyllaceae); *spec.* any of the garden forms or hybrids of *D. plumarius*, with fragrant white or pink flowers, sometimes with a dark centre. Also, a flower or flowering stem of such a plant. Cf. CARNATION *noun*³. L16. ▸**b** With specifying word: (a flower of) any of various plants allied to or resembling the pink. L16.
2 *fig.* **a** *The* finest example *of* excellence; *the* embodied perfection *of* a particular quality. L16. ▸**b** A beauty; a smart person, a dandy. *arch.* E17. ▸**c** *The* most perfect condition or degree of something; *the* height, *the* extreme. Freq. in ***in the pink*** (*colloq.*), in very good health or condition. M18.
🕮 **1** ***Cheddar pink***, ***clove pink***, ***Deptford pink***, ***maiden pink***, etc. **b** ***Carolina pink***, ***fire-pink***, ***moss-pink***, ***rose-pink***, ***sea-pink***, etc. **2a** M. M. SHERWOOD I have been admiring your cupboards; they are the very pink of elegance.
▸**II 3** More fully ***hunting-pink***. Scarlet when worn by fox-hunters; a scarlet hunting-coat; the cloth of which it is made; *transf.* a fox-hunter. E19.
4 A pale red colour. Freq. with specifying word. M19. ▸**b** Chiefly *Hist.* This colour formerly used to represent a British colony or dominion on a map. Cf. RED *noun* 1C. E20.
5 A pink variety of potato; a potato of this variety. Cf. PINK-EYE *noun*¹ 1. M19.
6 *ellipt.* Anything distinguished by pink colour, as the pink ball in snooker, rosé wine, pink clothing, pink gin, pink salmon, etc. E20.
7 A white person. *Black slang.* E20.
8 A person whose politics are left of centre; a liberal or moderate socialist. Cf. RED *noun* 5b. *colloq.* (freq. *derog.*). E20.
🕮 **3** W. HOLTBY Superb in his pink, on his great black horse. **4** L. BROMFIELD Shades of . . violet and candy pink. **6** *Snooker Scene* Struggling home on the pink in the seventh frame. **8** R. CASSILIS The pompous Pinks who had once been the backbone of the . . Labour Party.
Comb.: **pink chaser** *Black slang* a black person regarded as excessively friendly towards white people; **pink-coloured** *adjective* of the colour of the pink; having a pink colour; **pink spot** the spot on which the pink ball is placed in snooker.

pink /pɪŋk/ *noun*⁵. *Scot.* L16.
[from PINK *adjective*¹.]
A very small thing.

pink /pɪŋk/ *noun*⁶. M17.
[Origin unkn.]
A yellowish or greenish-yellow lake pigment made by combining vegetable colouring matter with a white base, as a metallic oxide.
brown pink, ***Dutch pink***, ***French pink***, etc.

pink /pɪŋk/ *noun*⁷. L17.
[Imit.]
†**1** A sea bird. Only in L17.
2 The chaffinch. *dial. rare.* E19.
3 A metallic rattle; pinking of an engine. E20.

Pink /pɪŋk/ *noun*⁸. *US slang.* E20.
[Abbreviation of PINKERTON.]
A Pinkerton employee; a detective.

pink /pɪŋk/ *adjective*¹. *obsolete* exc. *dial.* E16.
[Origin uncertain: perh. rel. to early Dutch *pinck* small, Dutch *pink* the little finger. Cf. PINK *noun*⁵.]
Small, contracted. Chiefly in ***pink eye***, a small eye, a winking or half-shut eye.

pink /pɪŋk/ *adjective*². M17.
[from PINK *noun*⁴.]
1 Of the colour of the pink (PINK *noun*⁴ 1); of a pale red colour (freq. with specifying word). M17. ▸**b** Designating a sporting edition of a newspaper, printed on pink paper. L19. ▸**c** Chiefly *Hist.* Designating or pertaining to a British colony or dominion on a map, conventionally coloured pink. M20.
2 Of a coat worn for fox-hunting: scarlet. M19.
3 Politically left of centre; tending to socialism. Cf. RED *adjective* 8b. *colloq.* (freq. *derog.*). M19.
4 Extreme, utter, absolute. Also used as mere intensifier. *slang.* L19.
5 Slightly indecent or vulgar. *slang.* L19.
6 Of a plan, process, etc.: that must be kept secret. *Military slang.* E20.
7 Of a person: white. M20.
8 Of or associated with homosexuals. L20.
🕮 **1** W. GOLDING The pink flush on my mother's cheeks. ***coral-pink***, ***rose-pink***, ***salmon-pink***, ***shocking pink***, ***shrimp-pink***, etc. **3** A. F. DOUGLAS-HOME Pink bourgeois Socialism . . just as much a target as blue Conservatism. **4** B. MARSHALL These rotten new kids really are the pink limit.
Phrases: **strike me pink!** *slang*: expr. astonishment or indignation. **swear pink** *colloq.* make vehement protestations; swear blind. ***tickle pink***: see TICKLE *verb*.
Comb. & special collocations: **pink bollworm** the pinkish larva of a small brown moth, *Pectinophora gossypiella* (family Gelechiidae), which is a destructive pest feeding on the flowers, lint, or seeds of cotton plants; **pink button** *STOCK EXCHANGE* a jobber's clerk; **pink champagne** rosé champagne; champagne to which a small quantity of still red wine has been added; **pink cockatoo** a white Australian cockatoo, *Cacatua leadbeateri*, with a pink head and breast; also called ***Leadbeater's cockatoo***; **pink-collar** *adjective* [after *blue-collar*, *white-collar*] (of a profession etc.) traditionally associated with women; **pink disease** a disease of children associated with mercury poisoning, characterized by pinkness of parts of the body, restlessness, and photophobia; **pink elephant** *colloq.* a type of something extraordinary or impossible; in *pl.*, hallucinations experienced by a drunk or delirious person; **pink fir apple** a potato of a pink-skinned knobbly variety; **pink-foot** *adjective & noun* (*a*) *adjective* (*poet.*) = ***pink-footed*** below; (*b*) *noun*, pl. **-feet**, occas. **-foots**, the pink-footed goose; **pink-footed** *adjective* having pink feet; ***pink-footed goose***, a short-necked pinkish-grey migrating goose, *Anser brachyrhynchus*, of northern Europe; **pink gilding**, **pink gold**: with a pink tinge resulting from a combination of gold, silver, and copper; **pink gin** gin flavoured with Angostura bitters; a drink of this; ***pink gold***: see ***pink gilding*** above; **pink lady** (*a*) a cocktail consisting of gin, egg-white, and grenadine; (*b*) *US slang* a barbiturate; (*c*) *US & Austral.* a voluntary hospital helper; **pink noise** *PHYSICS* random noise having equal energy per octave, and so having more low-frequency components than white noise; **pink paper** a parliamentary paper or schedule issued regularly, giving details of all papers presented to Parliament or printed since the date of the last such schedule; **pink pound** the perceived buying power of homosexuals as a group; **pink purslane** a succulent plant with small pink flowers, *Montia sibirica*, of the purslane family, which is native to N. America and Siberia and is sometimes grown for ornament; **pinkroot** the root of any of several plants of the genus *Spigelia* (family Loganiaceae), used as an anthelmintic; any of these plants, esp. *S. marilandica* of the southern US, and *S. anthelmia* of the W. Indies and S. America, having showy red funnel-shaped flowers; **pink salmon** the humpback salmon or gorbuscha; also, the pink flesh of any salmon, as food; **pink slip** (chiefly *N. Amer.*) a notice of dismissal from employment; **pink-slip** *verb trans.* dismiss, fire; **pink tea** *N. Amer.* a formal tea party or other social engagement; a type of something polite or genteel; **pink triangle** a triangular piece of pink cloth sewn on to clothing to identify homosexual men in Nazi concentration camps; *gen.* a similar emblem indicating support for homosexual freedom and rights; **Pink 'Un** *colloq.* (*a*) a newspaper printed on pink paper, *esp.* the *Sporting Times* or the *Financial Times*; (*b*) a member of staff of such a newspaper; **pinkwash** a pink liquid composition used for coating walls etc. (cf. WHITEWASH *noun*); **pink-washed** *adjective* having a coating of pinkwash; **pink wine** a rosé wine; **pinkwood** (the ornamental wood of) any of various trees, *esp.* (*Austral.*) the wallaby-bush, *Beyeria viscosa*, and (*US*) Brazilian tulip-wood, *Dalbergia frutescens*.
■ **pinkish** *adjective* somewhat pink L18. **pinkly** *adverb* with a pink colour; *fig.* embarrassedly: M19. **pinkness** *noun* the quality or state of being pink L19.

pink /pɪŋk/ *verb*¹. ME.
[Perh. of Low Dutch origin: cf. Low German *pinken* strike, peck.]
1 *verb intrans.* Make a hole or holes; prick, stab. *rare.* ME.
2 *verb trans.* Ornament (cloth, leather, etc.) by cutting or punching eyelet-holes, slits, etc., esp. to display a contrasting lining or undergarment. Now also, cut a scalloped or zigzag pattern on (a raw fabric edge). Freq. as ***pinked*** *ppl adjective.* E16.
3 *verb trans.* Adorn, beautify. M16.
4 *verb trans.* Pierce slightly with a sword, bullet, etc.; nick. L16. ▸**b** *BOXING.* Strike (a person) with the fist so as to cause a visible mark. *arch.* E19.
†**5** *verb trans. & intrans.* Cut or puncture (the skin) as a decoration; tattoo. E17–L18.
🕮 **2** S. PEPYS A long cassocke . . of black cloth, and pinked with white silke under. **4** R. LOWELL Hoydens with air-guns . . pink the pigeons.
■ **pinker** *noun* †(*a*) *rare* a person who stabs someone; (*b*) a person who cuts or punches designs in cloth, leather, etc.: E16.

pink /pɪŋk/ *verb*² *intrans. obsolete* exc. *dial.* M16.
[Origin uncertain: cf. Dutch *pinken* shut the eyes, wink, leer.]
1 a Of the eyes: be half shut; blink; peer. M16. ▸**b** Of a person: peer with half-shut eyes; blink, wink, esp. in a sleepy or sly manner. L16. ▸†**c** *transf.* Of a candle etc.: shine with a glimmer of light; twinkle. L16–L17.
2 Of a day, night, etc.: draw *in*. L19.

pink /pɪŋk/ *verb*³ *intrans.* M18.
[Imit.]
1 Trickle, drip; make a tinkling sound in dripping. *Scot.* M18.
2 Of an internal-combustion engine: emit a series of metallic rattling sounds caused by overrapid combustion of the mixture in the cylinder. E20.
🕮 **2** *Drive* Driving on . . 2-star petrol caused the engine to 'pink' noisily.

pink /pɪŋk/ *verb*⁴. L18.
[from PINK *adjective*².]
1 *verb intrans.* Blush, become pink. Freq. foll. by *up*. L18.
2 *verb trans.* Shear (a sheep) closely so that the colour of the animal's skin shows through. Chiefly in ***pink 'em***. *Austral. & NZ colloq.* L19.
3 *verb trans.* Make or colour pink. E20.
🕮 **1** I. EDWARDS-JONES She positively pinks up with pleasure at the mere mention of his name. **3** *fig.*: D. H. LAWRENCE The pretty . . bourgeois pinks his language just as pink If not pinker.

pinkeen /pɪŋˈkiːn/ *noun. Anglo-Irish.* M19.
[from PINK *noun*² + -EEN².]
A little fish, a minnow.

pinken /ˈpɪŋkən/ *verb.* L19.
[from PINK *adjective*² + -EN⁵.]
1 *verb intrans.* Become pink. L19.
2 *verb trans.* Make pink. M20.
🕮 **1** J. COE His cheeks pinkened with vexation.

pinkers /pɪŋkəz/ *noun.* Chiefly *Nautical slang.* M20.
[from PINK *noun*⁴, *adjective*²: see -ER⁶.]
Pink gin; a drink of this.

Pinkerton /ˈpɪŋkət(ə)n/ *noun & adjective.* L19.
[Allan *Pinkerton* (1819–84), founder of a semi-official detective force in the US in 1850.]
▸**A** *noun.* A detective, *esp.* one who is armed. L19.
▸**B** *attrib.* or as *adjective.* Of or pertaining to a detective; that is a detective. L19.

pink-eye /ˈpɪŋkʌɪ/ *noun*¹. L18.
[from PINK *adjective*² + EYE *noun*.]
1 More fully ***pink-eye potato***. A variety of potato having pink eyes or buds; a potato of this variety. L18.
2 Conjunctivitis (in humans or livestock); *esp.* a bacterial infection in cattle causing severe conjunctivitis and corneal ulceration. L19.
3 Cheap whisky or red wine; alcoholic drink mixed with methylated spirits. Cf. PINKIE *noun*². *slang* (chiefly *Austral. & Canad.*). E20.

pink-eye /ˈpɪŋkʌɪ/ *noun*². *Austral.* L19.
[Aboriginal.]
A festival, a holiday.

pinkie /ˈpɪŋki/ *noun*¹. Also **pinky**. M19.
[from PINK *noun*¹ + -IE, -Y⁶.]
Chiefly *Hist.* A narrow-sterned fishing and trading vessel resembling a Danish pink (PINK *noun*¹).

pinkie /ˈpɪŋki/ *noun*². Also **pinky**. L19.
[from PINK *noun*⁴ + -IE, -Y⁶.]
1 Cheap red wine; alcoholic drink mixed with methylated spirits. *slang* (chiefly *Austral.*). L19.
2 A white person. *Black slang.* M20.
3 Either of two marine fishes, the pink-coloured red grunter, *Pagellus natalensis*, an edible sparid, and (perh. by confusion) the small greenish rock grunter, *Pomadasys olivaceum*, often used as live bait. *S. Afr.* M20.
4 ANGLING. The maggot of a greenbottle fly. M20.
5 = PINK *noun*⁴ 8. Cf. PINKO *noun*. *colloq.* (freq. *derog.*). L20.

pinkie /ˈpɪŋki/ *adjective & noun*³. Also **pinky**. L16.
[Partly from PINK *adjective*¹, partly from Dutch *pink* the little finger: see -IE, -Y⁶.]
▸**A** *adjective.* Small, diminutive, tiny. Freq. in ***pinkie-eyed***, having small eyes. Chiefly *Scot.* L16.
▸**B** *noun.* A small object; *nursery & colloq.* the little finger. E19.

F. FORSYTH Raised his glass, Russian style, between fore-finger and thumb, pinkie extended. ***attrib.***: S. BRILL All the steps . . were blocked by the guys with the pinky rings.

pinking /ˈpɪŋkɪŋ/ *noun*¹. E16.
[from PINK *verb*¹ + -ING¹.]
The action of PINK *verb*¹; *esp.* the decoration of cloth etc. with holes or scalloped or zigzag edges; an example of such decoration, an ornamental edging.
Comb.: **pinking-iron** a sharp instrument for cutting out pinked borders. **pinking scissors**, **pinking shears** a dressmaker's serrated scissors used for cutting a zigzag edge.

pinking /ˈpɪŋkɪŋ/ *verbal noun*². E20.
[from PINK *verb*³ + -ING¹.]
The action of PINK *verb*³; *esp.* the production of metallic rattling in an engine by faulty combustion; an instance of this.

pinko /ˈpɪŋkəʊ/ *adjective & noun. slang.* Pl. **-o(e)s**. E20.
[from PINK *adjective*² + -O.]
▸**A** *adjective.* **1** Intoxicated. Chiefly *Austral.* E20.
2 Somewhat pink in colour, pinkish. Only in ***pinko-grey*** below. E20.
3 Tending to socialism; = PINK *adjective*² 3. Chiefly *N. Amer.* Freq. *derog.* E20.

2 pinko-grey *adjective & noun* (**a**) *adjective* of a pinkish-grey colour; *spec.* (of a person) white; (**b**) *noun* a white person. **3** P. ZIEGLER You were slightly pinko or at least a Leftist Liberal.

▸**B** *noun.* = PINK *noun*⁴ 8. Chiefly *N. Amer.* Freq. *derog.* M20.

City Limits That Jesus will lead the righteous . . against Satanic Communism . . caused . . queasiness amongst pinkoes, liberals and subversives.

Pinkster /ˈpɪŋkstə/ *noun. US.* Also **Pinxter**, (esp. in comb.) **P-**. M18.
[Dutch = Pentecost.]
Whitsuntide, esp. as celebrated in areas of former Dutch influence, as New York.
Comb.: **Pinkster flower** a pink azalea, *Rhododendron periclymenoides*, which flowers about Whitsuntide.

pinky *noun*¹, *noun*², *adjective*² & *noun*³ vars. of PINKIE *noun*¹, *noun*², *adjective & noun*³.

pinky /ˈpɪŋki/ *adjective*¹. L18.
[from PINK *adjective*² + -Y¹.]
Tinged with pink, somewhat pink.
▪ **pinkily** *adverb* L19. **pinkiness** *noun* E19.

pinlay /ˈpɪnleɪ/ *noun.* E20.
[Blend of PIN *noun*¹ and INLAY *noun.*]
DENTISTRY. An inlay or onlay held in place partly by a pin or pins inserted in the tooth.

pinledge /ˈpɪnlɛdʒ/ *noun.* E20.
[from PIN *noun*¹ + LEDGE *noun.*]
DENTISTRY. A pinlay, *esp.* one fixed to ledges cut in the lingual surface of a tooth.

†**pinlock** *noun. rare.* L17–L19.
[App. from PIND *verb* + LOCK *noun*².]
A poundmaster's fee for impounding beasts.

pin-money /ˈpɪnmʌni/ *noun.* L17.
[from PIN *noun*¹ + MONEY *noun.*]
1 *Hist.* A sum allotted to a woman for clothing and other personal expenses; *esp.* such an allowance provided for a wife's private expenditure. L17.
2 *transf.* Spending money, esp. for incidental expenses; a trivial sum of money. M19.

2 B. T. BRADFORD Katherine's millions are pin money in comparison to his billions.

pinna /ˈpɪnə/ *noun*¹. E16.
[mod. Latin from Latin, Greek *pina, pinna.*]
ZOOLOGY. A bivalve mollusc of the genus *Pinna*, having a large silky byssus; a fan mussel. Now chiefly as mod. Latin genus name.

pinna /ˈpɪnə/ *noun*². Pl. **pinnae** /ˈpɪniː/, †**pinnas**. L18.
[mod. Latin from Latin var. of *penna* feather, wing, fin.]
1 BOTANY. Each primary division of a pinnate or pinnatifid leaf, esp. of a fern. L18.
2 ANATOMY & ZOOLOGY. The broad flap of skin-covered cartilage which forms the external ear in humans and other mammals; the auricle. M19.
3 ZOOLOGY. Any of various structures in animals resembling fins or wings. M19.

pinnace /ˈpɪnɪs/ *noun.* M16.
[French *pinace*, †*pinasse* (cf. medieval Latin (Gascon) *pinacia, pinassa*) = Italian *pinaccia*, Spanish *pinaza*, prob. ult. from Proto-Romance from Latin *pinus* PINE *noun*².]
1 a A small light vessel, usu. two-masted and schooner-rigged, often used for communicating between a senior officer's ship and other vessels under his command. Now *Hist. & poet.* M16. ▸**b** A small boat (orig. eight-oared, now usu. motor-driven) forming part of the equipment of a warship or other larger vessel. L17.
†**2** *fig.* A woman; *spec.* a mistress; a prostitute. M16–L17.

pinnacle /ˈpɪnək(ə)l/ *noun.* ME.
[Old French *pin(n)acle* (mod. *pinacle*) from late Latin *pinnaculum* dim. of Latin *pinna* feather, wing, pinnacle: see PIN *noun*¹, -CULE.]
1 A small ornamental turret, usu. culminating in a pyramid or cone, crowning a buttress, roof, etc. ME. ▸†**b** *transf.* A vertical pointed structure resembling this; a pyramid. LME–E18.
2 A natural feature forming a peak; *esp.* a pointed or projecting rock or outcrop. ME.
3 *fig.* A high place or situation; the highest point or pitch; the culmination or climax (of success, ambition, etc.); a person who has attained this. LME.

1 C. BROOKS Points of roofs and pinnacles along the skyline. **2** ***attrib.***: *Scotsman* The 200ft-high . . pinnacle rock near Lochinver. **3** *Bella* Butlers . . regard working at the Palace as the pinnacle of their careers.

pinnacle /ˈpɪnək(ə)l/ *verb.* M17.
[from the noun.]
1 *verb trans.* Set (as) on a pinnacle. Chiefly *poet.* M17. ▸**b** *fig.* Form the highest point or culmination of, crown. *rare.* E19.
2 *verb intrans.* = RAFT *verb*¹ 5. *N. Amer.* M19.

pinnacled /ˈpɪnək(ə)ld/ *adjective.* LME.
[from PINNACLE *noun, verb*: see -ED², -ED¹.]
1 Having a pinnacle or pinnacles; provided with pinnacles or peaks. LME.
2 Elevated (as) on a pinnacle. M19.

1 ROSEMARY MANNING A huge . . Victorian house, turreted and pinnacled in Scottish-baronial style.

pinnae *noun pl.* see PINNA *noun*².

pinnate /ˈpɪneɪt/ *adjective.* E18.
[Latin *pinnatus*, from *pinna, penna*: see PINNA *noun*², -ATE².]
1 BOTANY & ZOOLOGY. Resembling a feather; having lateral parts or branches on each side of a common axis, like the vanes of a feather; having feather-like markings; (of a compound leaf) composed of a series of (usu. opposite) leaflets arranged on each side of a common petiole. E18.
2 PHYSICAL GEOGRAPHY. Of a drainage pattern: marked by closely-spaced tributaries meeting a stream at an acute angle. M20.
1 ***odd-pinnate***: see ODD *adjective.*
▪ **pinnately** *adverb* M19.

pinnated /ˈpɪneɪtɪd/ *adjective.* M18.
[formed as prec. + -ED¹.]
1 Chiefly BOTANY & ZOOLOGY. = PINNATE 1. M18.
2 ZOOLOGY. Having parts like wings or like fins. M18.
2 pinnated grouse any of various grouse of the genus *Tympanuchus*, having winglike tufts of feathers on the neck; *esp.* the prairie chicken, *T. cupido.*

pinnati- /pɪˈneɪti, pɪˈnati/ *combining form* of Latin *pinnatus* PINNATE: see -I-.
▪ **pinnatifid** *adjective* (BOTANY) (of a leaf etc.) pinnately cleft at least halfway to the middle M18. **pinnatifidly** *adverb* in a pinnatifid manner L19. **pinnatiˈpartite** *adjective* pinnately divided nearly to the midrib M19. **pinnatisect** *adjective* pinnately divided to the midrib, but not so as to form separate leaflets M19.

pinnation /pɪˈneɪʃ(ə)n/ *noun.* L19.
[formed as PINNATE: see -ATION.]
BOTANY. Pinnate formation; (manner of) division into pinnae.

pinnay /ˈpɪneɪ/ *noun. rare.* E20.
[Tamil *pinnai, punnai*. Cf. POON *noun*¹.]
= POON *noun*¹.
Comb.: **pinnay oil** = ***poon oil*** s.v. POON *noun*¹.

pinned /pɪnd/ *adjective.* LME.
[from PIN *noun*¹, *verb*: see -ED², -ED¹.]
†**1** Enclosed, confined. Only in LME.
2 Provided or decorated with pins. L17. ▸**b** Of a college student: presented with or wearing a fraternity or sorority pin as a pledge of affection; informally engaged. *US colloq.* M20.
3 Fastened with a pin or pins. E20.

pinner /ˈpɪnə/ *noun*¹. *obsolete* exc. *Hist.* ME.
[from PIN *noun*¹ + -ER¹.]
A maker of pins.

pinner /ˈpɪnə/ *noun*². *obsolete* exc. *dial.* L15.
[Var.]
= PINDER *noun*¹.

pinner /ˈpɪnə/ *noun*³. M17.
[from PIN *verb* + -ER¹.]
1 *Hist.* A woman's close-fitting cap of the 17th and 18th cents., having a long flap or lappet on either side, sometimes pinned up on the head. Also, either of these flaps. M17.
2 A person who fastens, attaches, or transfixes something with a pin or pins. E19.
3 A pinafore, an apron with a bib. *dial.* M19.

pinnet /ˈpɪnɪt/ *noun. Scot. rare.* M18.
[In sense 1 var. of PENNANT *noun*¹; in sense 2 perh. dim. of PINNACLE *noun*: see -ET¹.]
1 A streamer, a pennant. M18.
†**2** A pinnacle. Only in E19.

pinni- /ˈpɪni/ *combining form.*
[Repr. Latin *pinna, penna* wing, fin: see -I-.]
Chiefly ZOOLOGY & BOTANY. Of or pertaining to a fin or fins; pinnate, pinnately.
▪ **pinniform** *adjective* of the form of or resembling a fin or a feather; pinnate: M18.

pinning /ˈpɪnɪŋ/ *noun.* LME.
[from PIN *verb* + -ING¹.]
1 The action of PIN *verb.* LME.
2 a In *pl.* Small stones used for filling the joints or interstices of masonry. Now *rare.* L16. ▸**b** A pin or peg, used for fastening masonry. Now *rare.* M17.
3 An informal type of engagement or a pledge of affection between two young people, marked by an exchange of fraternity or sorority pins; the exchange of such pins. *US colloq.* M20.

pinniped /ˈpɪnɪpɛd/ *adjective & noun.* Also **-pede** /-piːd/. M19.
[from mod. Latin *Pinnipedia* noun pl., from Latin *pinna* fin, wing + *ped-, pes* foot (cf. Latin *pinnipes* wing-footed).]
ZOOLOGY. ▸**A** *adjective.* Having feet resembling fins. Now *spec.* designating or pertaining to a mammalian pinniped (see sense B. below). M19.
▸**B** *noun.* A pinniped animal; *spec.* any of a group of mammals of the order Carnivora which have the digits fused to form flippers adapted for swimming (i.e. seals, sea lions, and walruses). Cf. FISSIPED. M19.

†**pinno** *verb trans. rare* (Spenser). Only in L16.
[Alt.]
= PINION *verb* 1.

pinnock /ˈpɪnək/ *noun.* Now *local.* ME.
[1st elem. app. imit.: see -OCK.]
Any of various small hedge-birds; *esp.* the hedge sparrow or dunnock.

pinnothere /ˈpɪnəθɪə/ *noun.* Also **pinnote(e)r** /ˈpɪnətɪə/. E17.
[Latin *pinoteres* (mod. Latin *pinnotheres*), formed as PINNA *noun*¹ + Greek *terein* to guard.]
A crab of the genus *Pinnotheres*; = ***pea-crab*** s.v. PEA *noun*¹. Now *rare* or *obsolete* exc. as mod. Latin genus name ***Pinnotheres***.

pinnule /ˈpɪnjuːl/ *noun.* In sense 1 also (earlier) **pinule**. In senses 2, 3 also **pinnula** /ˈpɪnjʊlə/, pl. **-lae** /-liː/. L16.
[Latin *pinnula* dim. of PINNA *noun*²: see -ULE.]
1 Either of two sights (usu. small perforated metal plates) at the ends of the alidade or index of an astrolabe, quadrant, or similar instrument. *obsolete* exc. *Hist.* L16.
2 ZOOLOGY. A part or organ resembling a small wing or fin, or a barb of a feather; *spec.* any of the jointed lateral branches along the arms of a crinoid. M18.
3 BOTANY. A subdivision of the pinna of a leaf, esp. of a fern; a leaflet; a lobe. L18.
▪ **pinnular** *adjective* of or pertaining to a pinnule L19. **pinnulate** *adjective* having pinnules E19.

pinny /ˈpɪni/ *noun. colloq.* M19.
[Abbreviation.]
A pinafore; an apron, *esp.* one with a bib.

pinnywinkle *noun* var. of PILLIWINKS.

pinochle /ˈpiːnɒk(ə)l/ *noun. N. Amer.* Also (now *rare*) **pinocle**. M19.
[Origin unkn.]
A card-game resembling bezique and played with a double pack of 48 cards (from nine to ace only); the com-

bination of the queen of spades and jack of diamonds in this game.

pinocytosis /ˌpiːnəʊsʌɪˈtəʊsɪs, ˌpɪnəʊ-, ˌpʌɪnəʊ-/ *noun*. L19.
[from Greek *pinein* to drink + *-cytosis* after *phagocytosis*.]
BIOLOGY. A process by which droplets of liquid are taken into a cell in small vesicles pinched off from the cell membrane.
¶ Rare until recoined in M20.
▪ **pinocytic** /-ˈsɪtɪk/ *adjective* = PINOCYTOTIC M20. **pinocytose** *verb trans. & intrans.* absorb (liquid etc.) by pinocytosis M20. **pinocytotic** /-sʌɪˈtɒtɪk/ *adjective* of or pertaining to pinocytosis M20.

pinole /piːˈnəʊleɪ/ *noun*. US. M19.
[Amer. Spanish from Aztec *pinolli*.]
Parched cornflour mixed with the flour of mesquite beans, sugar, and spice.

pinoleum /pɪˈnəʊlɪəm/ *noun*. L19.
[from Latin *pinus* PINE *noun*² + *oleum* OIL *noun*.]
A material used for blinds, consisting of thin strips of pine-wood coated with oil-paint and threaded close together to form a flat flexible sheet which can be rolled up.

piñon /pɪˈnjɒn, ˈpɪnjən/ *noun*. Pl. **-ons**, **-ones** /-əʊnɪz/. M19.
[Spanish: cf. French PIGNON.]
(The edible seed of) any of a group of small pines of south-western N. America, esp. *Pinus edulis*, *P. monophylla*, and *P. quadrifolia*. Also, the wood of these trees.

pinosylvin /pʌɪnəʊˈsɪlvɪn/ *noun*. M20.
[from mod. Latin *Pin(us) sylv(estris* taxonomic name of Scots pine, from Latin *pinus* PINE *noun*², *sylvestris* of woods (see SYLVESTRIAN *adjective*¹): see -O-, -IN¹.]
BIOLOGY. Any of a group of related toxic compounds occurring in pines and conferring resistance to fungal and insect attack; *spec.* 3,5-dihydroxystilbene, $C_{14}H_{12}O_2$.

Pinot /ˈpiːnəʊ/ *noun*. M19.
[French, var. of PINEAU.]
(Any of several varieties of vine yielding) a black or white grape used in wine-making; wine made from these grapes.
Pinot Noir /nwɑː/, **Pinot Blanc** /blɒŋk/: two of the chief varieties.

pinotage /ˈpɪnə(ʊ)tɑːʒ/ *noun*. M20.
[Blend of PINOT and *Hermitage* (see HERMITAGE 3), former name in S. Africa for Cinsaut.]
A variety of red wine grape grown in South Africa, produced by crossing Pinot Noir and Cinsaut; wine made from these grapes.

pinpoint /ˈpɪnpɔɪnt/ *noun*¹ & *adjective*. M19.
[from PIN *noun*¹ + POINT *noun*¹.]
▸**A** *noun*. **1** The point of a pin; *esp.* (*fig.*) something extremely small or sharp. M19.
2 AERONAUTICS. A landmark seen and identified from an aircraft; the ground position of an aircraft as determined from such a sighting. M20.

📖 **1** V. GORNICK His eyes were pinpoints of rage. R. RENDELL No longer were any pinpoints of light visible.

▸**B** *attrib.* or as *adjective*. **1** Of the nature of the point of a pin, extremely small or sharp. M19.
2 Characterized by very small points; (of a textile etc.) very fine in texture. L19.
3 Performed with or characterized by great positional accuracy; very precise, highly detailed. M20.

📖 **1** J. WAIN A roadside café at a pinpoint village in the Alpes Vaudoises. **2** *Guardian* A seam-free, pinpoint mesh stocking. **3** *Motorboats Monthly* The race-bred hull . . ensures . . pinpoint handling that was a joy.

▪ **pinpointed** *adjective* having a small or sharp point E20.

Pinpoint /ˈpɪnpɔɪnt/ *noun*². L20.
[from PIN *noun*² + POINT *noun*¹.]
(Proprietary name for) a service whereby a customer can use a credit or similar card in conjunction with his or her PIN number to obtain goods (esp. petrol or train tickets) from an automatic dispenser. Chiefly *attrib.*

pinpoint /ˈpɪnpɔɪnt/ *verb trans*. E20.
[from PINPOINT *noun*¹.]
1 Locate with great accuracy; *esp.* identify (an objective) as a target for bombing. E20.
2 Bring into prominence, emphasize, highlight; identify precisely. M20.

📖 **1** *Allure* Wine critic Harriet Lembeck . . can pinpoint a vineyard and vintage with uncanny accuracy. **2** M. M. KAYE Something glinted brightly in the . . sun pinpointing an insignificant hill-top. L. DEIGHTON The evidence I'm providing for you to pinpoint the traitor there.

▪ **pinpointable** *adjective* M20.

pinprick /ˈpɪnprɪk/ *verb & noun*. M18.
[from PIN *noun*¹ + PRICK *noun*.]
▸**A** *verb trans.* **1** Prick with or as with a pin. M18.
2 *fig.* Irritate; annoy by petty actions. L19.

📖 **1** R. GODDEN Pinpricked all over with fear, I tiptoed away. **2** *Times* Such pinpricking gestures as refusing to cooperate . . in the extradition of . . terrorists.

▸**B** *noun*. **1** A prick caused by a pin; a minor puncture. M19.
2 *fig.* A petty annoyance, a minor irritation. L19.

📖 **1** *fig.*: J. E. GORDON A pinprick of light . . trembled on the horizon. **2** *attrib.*: *Time* After . . a few pinprick air raids . . the intruders were in retreat. **policy of pinpricks** a series of petty hostile acts pursued as a national or party strategy.

Comb.: **pinprick picture** a coloured print perforated with pinholes to give an illuminated effect when held to the light.

pinsapo /pɪnˈsapəʊ/ *noun*. Pl. **-os**. M19.
[Spanish.]
The Spanish fir, *Abies pinsapo*, which is characterized by radially arranged leaves.

pinscher /ˈpɪnʃə/ *noun*. E20.
[German.]
(A dog of) a breed of short-coated terrier, usu. having pricked ears and a docked tail; (a dog of) a breed of miniature terrier with either pricked or drop ears.
DOBERMANN *pinscher*.

pinson /ˈpɪns(ə)n/ *noun*. Long *obsolete* exc. *Hist.* LME.
[Perh. rel. to next, or from Old & mod. French *pincer* to pinch.]
A type of thin shoe or slipper worn until the early 17th cent. Usu. in *pl.*

pinsons /ˈpɪns(ə)nz/ *noun pl.* Long *obsolete* exc. *dial.* LME.
[Old French *pinçon* from *pince* pincers.]
Pincers, forceps. Also ***pair of pinsons***.

pinstripe /ˈpɪnstrʌɪp/ *noun & adjective*. L19.
[from PIN *noun*¹ + STRIPE *noun*².]
▸**A** *noun*. **1** A very narrow stripe, *spec.* one repeated as a pattern woven into or printed on (esp. serge or worsted) cloth. L19.
2 *ellipt.* A (man's) pinstripe suit, conventionally worn by a businessman. M20.
3 A person who wears pinstriped clothing; = PINSTRIPER. L20.
▸**B** *attrib.* or as *adjective*. Designating cloth with very narrow woven or printed stripes; (of a garment) made of such cloth. L19.
▪ **pinstriped** *adjective* having very narrow stripes; wearing a garment of pinstripe cloth; *fig.* characteristic of a businessman or businesswoman: L19.

pinstriper /ˈpɪnstrʌɪpə/ *noun*. Chiefly *US*. L20.
[from prec. + -ER¹.]
A person who wears pinstriped clothing; *spec.* (*a*) a player in the New York Yankees baseball team; (*b*) a businessman or businesswoman.

pinswell /ˈpɪnzwɪl/ *noun*. Long *obsolete* exc. *dial.* L16.
[Origin unkn.]
A boil; an ulcer; a pimple; a large blister.

pint /pʌɪnt/ *noun*¹. LME.
[Old & mod. French *pinte*, of unkn. origin.]
1 A unit of liquid or dry capacity equal to one-eighth of a gallon (in Britain 20 fluid ounces); in Britain (more fully ***imperial pint***) equivalent to 34.68 cu. in. (0.5683 litre); in the US (more fully ***US pint***) equivalent to 28.87 cu. in. (0.4731 litre) for liquid measure, 33.60 cu. in. (0.5506 litre) for dry measure. Also, a measure of shellfish, being the amount containable in a mug etc. having a capacity of one pint. LME.
2 A container having a capacity of such a measure; a pint-pot. L15.
3 *ellipt.* A pint of a liquid, esp. milk; *colloq.* a pint of beer. M18.

📖 **1** attrib.: **pint glass**, **pint measure**, **pint mug**, etc. **3** W. MCILVANNEY He was just coming out for a quiet pint.

Comb.: **pint-pot** (*a*) *colloq.* a seller of beer; (*b*) a mug having the capacity of a pint; *esp.* a pewter pot of this size for beer; **pint-size**, **pint-sized** *adjectives* (*a*) having a capacity of one pint; (*b*) *colloq.* small.

pint /pʌɪnt/ *noun*². Chiefly *US colloq.* & *dial.* M19.
[Repr. a pronunc.]
= POINT *noun*¹.

pinta /ˈpɪntə/ *noun*¹. E19.
[Spanish, lit. 'coloured spot' from late Latin *pincta* from Latin *picta* use as noun of fem. pa. pple of *pingere* to paint.]
A skin disease widespread in tropical America, caused by the spirochaete *Treponema carateum* and characterized by rough blotchy skin.

pinta /ˈpʌɪntə/ *noun*². *colloq.* M20.
[Repr. *pint of* as spoken, orig. in an advertising slogan. Cf. CUPPA.]
A pint of milk.

pintadera /pɪntəˈdɛːrə/ *noun*. E20.
[Spanish = instrument used to decorate bread, from *pintado* mottled, from *pintar* to paint.]
ARCHAEOLOGY. A small patterned usu. terracotta stamp for creating decorations, found in neolithic cultures in the eastern Mediterranean and in America.

pintado /pɪnˈtɑːdəʊ/ *noun*. Pl. **-o(e)s**. E17.
[Portuguese, Spanish = guinea-fowl, use as noun of pa. pple of *pintar* to paint, from Proto-Romance var. of Latin *pictus* pa. pple of *pingere* to paint. Cf. PINTO.]
†**1** A painted or printed cotton cloth imported from the East Indies. E17–E18.
2 More fully ***pintado bird***, ***pintado petrel***. A black and white petrel, *Daption capense*, of southern oceans. Also called ***Cape pigeon***. E17.
3 A guinea-fowl. M17.
4 Any of several spotted fishes of S. American waters, *esp.* the cero. L19.

pintail /ˈpɪnteɪl/ *noun*. ME.
[from PIN *noun*¹ + TAIL *noun*¹.]
†**1** A hare. *rare*. Only in ME.
2 A migratory duck, *Anas acuta*, of the northern hemisphere, the male of which has two long pointed feathers in the tail. Also more fully ***pintail duck***. M18. ▸**b** Any of various other birds with a pointed tail, *esp.*: (*a*) a pintailed sandgrouse; (*b*) *N. Amer.* a sharp-tailed grouse; (*c*) *US local* a ruddy duck; (*d*) *Austral.* a rainbow bird. L19.
3 A woman, *esp.* one with narrow hips. Chiefly *dial.* L18.
4 A surfboard or sailboard with a back which tapers to a point. M20.
▪ **pintailed** *adjective* having a pointed tail; ***pintailed sandgrouse***, a sandgrouse, *Pterocles alchata*, of central Asia and Mediterranean countries: L19.

Pinteresque /pɪntəˈrɛsk/ *adjective*. M20.
[from *Pinter* (see below) + -ESQUE.]
Of, pertaining to, or characteristic of the British playwright Harold Pinter (b. 1930) or his works.

📖 *Listener* Everyone . . talked like overheard conversations . . . They invented a word for it—Pinteresque.

▪ Also **Pinterish** *adjective* M20.

pintid /ˈpɪntɪd/ *noun*. Also (earlier) **-ide**. M20.
[Spanish *pintide*, formed as PINTA *noun*¹ + *id*(*e*: cf. SYPHILIDE.]
MEDICINE. A skin lesion of the type characteristic of pinta.

pintle /ˈpɪnt(ə)l/ *noun*.
[Old English *pintel* dim. of a base repr. by Old Frisian, Low German, Dutch, German *pint*: see -LE¹. Cf. CUCKOO-PINT.]
1 The penis. *obsolete* exc. *dial.* OE.
2 A pin, a bolt, *esp.* one on which some other part turns, as the pivot of a hinge etc. L15.
Phrases: ***priest's pintle***: see PRIEST *noun*.

pinto /ˈpɪntəʊ/ *adjective & noun*. Chiefly *N. Amer.* Pl. **-os**. M19.
[Spanish = painted, mottled, from Proto-Romance. Cf. PINTADO.]
▸**A** *adjective*. **1** Of a horse: piebald; skewbald. M19.
2 ***pinto bean***, a variety of kidney bean with mottled seeds, widely cultivated in Central America and the south-western US; the seed of this. E20.
▸**B** *noun*. A piebald horse. M19.

Pintsch gas /ˈpɪntʃ gas/ *noun phr.* L19.
[from Richard *Pintsch* (1840–1919), German inventor.]
An oil-gas made chiefly from shale oil, formerly much used for lighting railway carriages, lighthouses, buoys, etc.

Pintupi /ˈpɪntuːpiː/ *noun & adjective*. Also **-tubi** /-tuːbiː/. M20.
[Aboriginal.]
▸**A** *noun*. Pl. same.
1 A member of an Aboriginal people inhabiting the desert regions of Central Australia. M20.
2 The language of this people. M20.
▸**B** *attrib.* or as *adjective*. Of or pertaining to the Pintupi or their language. M20.

pinule *noun* see PINNULE.

pin-up /ˈpɪnʌp/ *adjective & noun*. L17.
[from PIN *verb* + UP *adverb*¹.]
▸**A** *adjective*. †**1** Adapted for being pinned up. Only in L17.
2 (Of a photograph, poster, etc.) intended for display on a wall etc.; (of a person) sexually attractive, popular. Also, pertaining to or characteristic of such a picture or person. M20.

📖 **2** E. CRISPIN She had a figure like the quintessence of all pin-up girls. *Year's Work in English Studies* A folder . . with genealogical chart, four pin-up illustrations and a list.

▸**B** *noun*. A pin-up photograph, poster, etc.; the subject of such a picture, esp. a sexually attractive person, celebrity, etc. M20.

📖 D. ABSE He was charismatic, / yet without side. He was their pin-up.

pin-wheel /ˈpɪnwiːl/ *noun & verb*. E18.
[from PIN *noun*¹ + WHEEL *noun*.]
▸**A** *noun*. **1** A wheel in the striking train of a clock in which pins are set to lift the hammer; a cog-wheel whose teeth are small pins set into the rim of the wheel. E18.
2 A small Catherine-wheel firework. M19. ▸**b** *transf.* Something shaped or operating like a Catherine-wheel (firework). Freq. *attrib.* E20.
▸**B** *verb intrans.* Rotate in the manner of a Catherine-wheel (firework). M20.

Pinxter *noun* var. of PINKSTER.

Pinxton /ˈpɪŋkst(ə)n/ *noun & adjective.* E19.
[See below.]
(Designating) a soft-paste porcelain made at the town of Pinxton in Derbyshire from 1796 to 1813.

piny /ˈpʌɪni/ *adjective.* Also **piney**. E17.
[from PINE *noun*² + -Y¹.]
Having many pines, covered with pines, consisting of pines; of or pertaining to a pine; *spec.* characterized by the fresh or aromatic smell of pine needles.

Pinyin /pɪnˈjɪn/ *noun.* M20.
[Chinese *pīnyīn* lit. 'spell sound'.]
A system of romanized spelling for transliterating the Chinese language, adopted officially by the People's Republic of China in 1979.

piob mhor /piːp ˈvɔːr, piːəb/ *noun phr.* M19.
[Gaelic *pìob mhòr* lit. 'big pipe'.]
A kind of bagpipes traditionally played in the Scottish Highlands.

piolet /pjəʊˈleɪ/ *noun.* M19.
[French (Savoy dial.), dim. of *piolo*, app. cogn. with *pioche*, *pic*.]
A two-headed ice-axe used by mountaineers.

pion /ˈpʌɪɒn/ *noun.* M20.
[from PI-(MESON + -ON.]
NUCLEAR PHYSICS. Any of a group of mesons that have masses of approximately 140 MeV (270 times that of the electron), zero spin, zero hypercharge, and isospin of 1, and on decay usu. produce a muon and a neutrino (if charged) or two photons (if neutral); a pi-meson.
■ **piˈonic** *adjective* of, pertaining to, or involving a pion, or an atom having a negative pion orbiting the nucleus M20.

†**pion** *verb trans. & intrans.* L16–M17.
[Old French *pio(u)ner* dig, from *pion* foot-soldier: see next, PEON.]
Dig or excavate (earth, a ditch, etc.).

pioneer /pʌɪəˈnɪə/ *noun.* In sense 3c also **P-**. E16.
[French *pionnier*, Old French *paonier*, *peon(n)ier* from *paon*, *peon*, *pion*: see PAWN *noun*¹, PEON, -EER.]
1 MILITARY. A member of an infantry group going with or ahead of an army or regiment to prepare roads, terrain, etc., for the main body of troops. E16.
†**2** A digger, an excavator; a miner. L16–M17.
3 An originator or initiator of a new enterprise etc.; a founder of or early worker in a particular field or subject; an innovator; a forerunner. Also, an explorer, a settler, a colonist. E17. ▸**b** ECOLOGY. A plant or animal which establishes itself in an unoccupied area. Also ***pioneer species***. E20. ▸**c** A member of any of various organizations claiming a pioneering function in some field; *spec.* (*a*) in the former USSR and some other Communist countries, a member of a movement for children below the age of sixteen; (*b*) in Ireland, a member of the Pioneer Total Abstinence Association; *transf.* a teetotaller. E20.

> 📖 **3** *Daily Chronicle* The pioneer of modern experiments in gliding flight. W. C. HANDY Wilbur Sweatman—a . . jazz pioneer. N. SHERRY Nicoll . . was becoming well known as a pioneer in psychological medicine. *attrib.*: W. IRVING He . . felt a throb of his old pioneer spirit, impelling him to . . join the adventurous band.

■ **pioneerdom** *noun* (*rare*) (*a*) the condition or state of a pioneer; (*b*) pioneers collectively: L19. **pioneership** *noun* the function or action of a pioneer M19.

pioneer /pʌɪəˈnɪə/ *verb.* L18.
[from the noun.]
1 *verb intrans.* Act as pioneer, prepare the way as a pioneer. Freq. as ***pioneering*** *ppl adjective.* L18.
2 *verb trans.* Prepare or open up (a way, road, etc.) as a pioneer. L18.
3 *verb trans.* Be a pioneer of; initiate or originate (an enterprise etc.), lead the way or innovate in; lead or guide (a person). E19.
4 *verb trans. & intrans.* ECOLOGY. Of a plant: colonize (new territory). M20.

> 📖 **1** *Time* The leader in state judicial innovation . . California . . pioneered in halting the death penalty. E. SHOWALTER The pioneering English women doctors who worked in mental institutions. **2** SEBASTIAN EVANS In pioneering the way for future research. **3** J. BRIGGS He pioneered the use of artificial fertilizers . . in agriculture.

pionization /ˌpʌɪənʌɪˈzeɪʃ(ə)n/ *noun.* Also **-isation**. M20.
[from PION *noun* + -IZATION.]
NUCLEAR PHYSICS. The production of numerous low-energy pions by the collision of two high-energy nucleons.

piopio /ˈpjuːpjuː, *foreign* piɔpiɔ/ *noun.* L19.
[Maori, of imit. origin.]
A small rare thrushlike bird of New Zealand, *Turnagra capensis*, of the whistler family Pachycephalidae. Also called ***native thrush***, ***New Zealand thrush***.

piosity /pʌɪˈɒsɪti/ *noun.* E20.
[from PIOUS + -ITY, after *religiosity*.]
Affected or excessive piousness, sanctimoniousness; an instance of this.

piou-piou /pjupju/ *noun.* Pl. pronounced same. M19.
[French.]
(A name for) a French private soldier.

pious /ˈpʌɪəs/ *adjective.* LME.
[from Latin *pius* dutiful, pious: see -OUS.]
1 Characterized by, having, or showing reverence to God or gods; devout, godly, religious; sacred as opp. to secular; earnest, heartfelt. Now also, hypocritically virtuous, self-righteous, sanctimonious. LME.
2 Dutiful or loyal to relatives, friends, superiors, etc. *arch.* E17.

> 📖 **1** A. WILSON The rot had begun . . with a growing distaste for accuracy . . a life of conferences and pious platitudes. V. S. PRITCHETT I was a pious little boy, packed with the Ten Commandments and spotless on Sundays. K. AMIS As a pious man . . he'll have in mind his duty to God. F. SPALDING She . . led assembly, giving the school a pious quotation to reflect on. **pious fraud** deception intended to benefit those deceived and esp. to strengthen religious belief. **pious hope** an extravagant or unrealistic hope expressed to preserve an appearance of optimism.

■ **piously** *adverb* E17. **piousness** *noun* E17.

pip /pɪp/ *noun*¹. LME.
[Middle Low German *pip*, Middle Dutch *pippe*, *pipse* (German *Pips*), corresp. to Old High German *pfiffiz*, prob. ult. alt. of Latin *pituita* slime (see PITUITARY).]
1 A scale or horny patch on the tip of the tongue of a bird, associated with infectious coryza, esp. in poultry. LME.
2 a An unspecified illness in humans, an ailment, a malaise. Freq. with *the*. *joc. & colloq.* LME. ▸**b** Ill humour, bad temper; poor health. Chiefly in phrs. below. *colloq.* M18.

> 📖 **2a** T. H. HUXLEY We are all well, barring . . various forms of infantile pip. **b get the pip** become depressed, despondent, or unwell. **give a person the pip** make a person bad-tempered or dispirited, annoy, irritate. **have the pip** be depressed, despondent, or unwell.

pip /pɪp/ *noun*². LME.
[Abbreviation of PIPPIN.]
†**1** A pippin. LME–E17.
2 Any of the seeds in certain edible fruits (as an apple, orange, grape, etc.). L18.
3 An excellent thing or person, a fine example *of* a thing. Cf. PIPPIN 3b. *slang* (chiefly *US*). E20.
2 squeeze until the pips squeak exact the maximum payment from (a person).
■ **pipless** *adjective* M19.

pip /pɪp/ *noun*³. Orig. (now *dial.*) **peep** /piːp/. L16.
[Origin unkn.]
1 Each of the dots or symbols on playing-cards, dice, and dominoes; *transf.* a numeral card as opp. to a court-card. Formerly also (*fig.*), a small amount, a degree. L16.
2 A spot, as on the skin or on a spotted fabric. Now *dial.* L17.
3 HORTICULTURE. An individual flower or corolla in the umbel of a cowslip, polyanthus, etc. Chiefly *dial.* M18.
4 Each of the rhomboidal segments of the skin of a pineapple, corresponding to one blossom of the compound inflorescence from which the fruit is developed. M19.
5 MILITARY. Each of a maximum of three stars worn on the shoulders of an officer's uniform to denote rank. E20.
6 a A sharp, narrow, usu. small spike or deflection in a line displayed on a cathode-ray screen. M20. ▸**b** A voltage pulse. M20.

> 📖 **5** L. DURRELL An extra pip on his shoulder, betokening heaven knows what increase of rank and power.

pip /pɪp/ *noun*⁴. E20.
[Imit.]
A short high-pitched sound, usu. electronically produced; *spec.* one broadcast over the radio as a time signal or transmitted over a telephone line as a signal. Freq. in *pl.*

> 📖 R. THOMAS It was Audrey's voice. The pips cut into it and Martin pushed in the coin.

pip /pɪp/ *noun*⁵. E20.
Arbitrary syllable used for *p* in telephone communications and in the oral spelling of code messages.
pip emma [= *p.m.*] post meridiem.

pip /pɪp/ *verb*¹. Infl. **-pp-**. L16.
[Sense 1 app. var. of PEEP *verb*¹ (cf. CHIP *verb*²); sense 2 perh. a different word of imit. origin (cf. CHIP *verb*¹).]
1 *verb intrans.* Esp. of a young bird: chirp. L16.
2 *verb trans.* Of a young bird: crack (the shell of the egg) when hatching. M19.

pip /pɪp/ *verb*². Infl. **-pp-**. L19.
[from PIP *noun*² or *noun*³. Cf. PILL *verb*².]
1 *verb trans.* Defeat, beat, esp. narrowly; hit with a shot; blackball. Freq. in ***pip at the post***, ***pip on the post***, ***pip to the post***, defeat or forestall narrowly at the last moment. *colloq.* L19. ▸**b** Reject, disqualify; fail (a candidate) in an examination; (of a candidate) fail (an examination). *slang.* E20.
2 *verb intrans.* Die. Also foll. by *out*. *slang.* E20.

> 📖 **1** A. GILBERT You won't be able to buy . . that ring. Someone's pipped you on the post. *Athletics Weekly* Closest ever finish when . . Doherty just pipped . . Cunningham on the line.

pip /pɪp/ *verb*³ *intrans.* Infl. **-pp-**. M20.
[from PIP *noun*⁴.]
Make a short high-pitched sound; *spec.* (of a radio, telephone, etc.) emit such sounds as a signal.

pipa /pɪˈpɑː, ˈpʌɪpə/ *noun*¹. Also **pipal**. E18.
[Prob. from Galibi.]
The Suriname toad. Now chiefly as mod. Latin genus name.

pipa /piːˈpɑː/ *noun*². M19.
[Chinese *pípa*.]
A Chinese type of lute.

pipage /ˈpʌɪpɪdʒ/ *noun.* Also **pipeage**. E17.
[from PIPE *noun*¹ + -AGE.]
The conveyance or distribution of liquid or gas by pipes; the making or laying down of pipes; pipes collectively.

pipal *noun* var. of PEEPUL.

pipe /pʌɪp/ *noun*¹.
[Old English *pipe* = Old Frisian, Middle Low German, Middle Dutch *pipe* (Dutch *pijp*), Old High German *pfīfa* (German *Pfeife*), Old Norse *pípa*, ult. from Latin *pipare* peep, chirp, of imit. origin; reinforced in Middle English by Old & mod. French *pipe*. Cf. next.]
▸**I 1** A simple wind instrument consisting of a single tube, freq. with holes for varying the pitch but without keys; *arch.* any woodwind instrument. OE. ▸**b** = ORGAN-PIPE 1. LME. ▸**c** NAUTICAL. A boatswain's whistle; the sounding of this as a call to the crew; in *pl.* (*slang*), (a nickname for) a boatswain. M17. ▸**d** *sing.* & (usu.) in *pl.* A wind instrument consisting of or having as a part a set of tubes (with or without holes); *spec.* (*a*) pan-pipes; (*b*) bagpipes. E18.
2 A high-pitched, esp. thin or shrill, song or note, esp. of a bird; *sing.* & (now usu.) in *pl.*, the voice, esp. as used in singing, the vocal cords. L16.

> 📖 **1** P. FARMER He brought a pipe cut out of a reed on which he taught me to play. **2** R. JEFFERIES The thin pipe of a gnat. *New Musical Express* Cave wrapped his pipes round the . . slow, wrenching blues.

▸**II 3** A hollow cylinder or tube of metal, plastic, wood, etc., used to convey water, gas, etc. OE. ▸**b** In *pl.* Top-boots. *arch. slang.* E19. ▸**c** A piece of tubular confectionery or icing. M19. ▸**d** A tubular part of something, e.g. of a key. M19. ▸**e** Something easy to accomplish. *US slang.* E20.
4 *Hist.* (**P-**.) The department of the Exchequer responsible for drawing up the pipe rolls (see below). LME.
5 a A tubular organ, passage, canal, or vessel in an animal body. Usu. in *pl.*, the blood-vessels, the gut, or *esp.* the respiratory passages. Now *colloq.* or *dial.* LME. ▸**b** A tubular or pipelike natural formation, *esp.* the stem of a plant, etc. E16.
6 a MINING & GEOLOGY. A more or less cylindrical, usu. vertical, cavity; a tubular mass of rock, ore, sediment, etc.; *spec.* (*a*) a vertical cylindrical cavity in a calcareous rock such as chalk, freq. filled with sand or gravel; (*b*) a vertical eruptive channel opening into the crater of a volcano; (*c*) a vertical cylindrical mass of intrusive volcanic rock, such as those in which diamonds are found. M17. ▸**b** METALLURGY. A funnel-shaped cavity on the surface of an ingot caused by shrinkage of the metal during cooling; a condition characterized by such cavities. M19.
7 Each of the channels of a decoy for wildfowl. M17.
3 *overflow pipe*, ***service-pipe***, etc.
▸**III 8** A device for smoking tobacco etc., consisting essentially of a narrow tube with a bowl at one end for containing the burning tobacco etc., the smoke from which is drawn into the mouth through the tube; *rare* a quantity *of* tobacco sufficient to fill the bowl of a pipe, a pipeful. L16. ▸**b** A rest period during which a pipe may be smoked; the distance covered or time taken in travelling between two rest periods; the distance covered while smoking a pipeful of tobacco. *N. Amer. colloq.* (*obsolete* exc. *Hist.*). L18.

> 📖 **8** A. DJOLETO Father was relaxing in a deck-chair, pipe in mouth, quite contented.

Phrases: **hit the pipe**: see HIT *verb*. **lay pipe(s)** *fig.* (*US slang*) (*a*) cheat, manipulate; *spec.* engage in political corruption; (*b*) (of a man) have sexual intercourse. **peace-pipe** a tobacco-pipe traditionally smoked as a token of peace amongst N. American Indians. **pipe of peace** = ***peace-pipe*** above. **put a person's pipe out** *colloq.* foil, thwart, or frustrate a person.
Comb.: **pipe band** a (freq. military) band consisting of bagpipe players with drummers and a drum major; **pipe berth** a collapsible or otherwise easily stored canvas etc. bed with a frame of metal pipes used on small vessels; **pipe bomb** a home-made bomb contained in a pipe; **pipeclay** *noun & verb* (*a*) *noun* a fine white clay forming a ductile paste with water, used esp. for making tobacco-pipes and whitening leather etc.; *slang* (chiefly

MILITARY) excessive attention to dress and appearance; (**b**) *verb trans.* whiten (leather etc.) with pipeclay; *slang* (chiefly MILITARY) put in good order; **pipe-cleaner** something used for cleaning a tobacco-pipe, *spec.* a piece of flexible wire covered with tufted material; **pipe cot** = *pipe berth* above; **pipedream** [perh. with ref. to dreams produced by smoking opium] a fantastic or impracticable notion or plan; a castle in the air; **pipedreaming** fantastic speculation, wishful thinking; **pipe-fiend** *US slang* an opium smoker or addict; **pipefish** any of numerous fishes having a long slender armoured body and a tubular snout, chiefly of the family Syngnathidae, of warm waters worldwide, which also includes sea horses; **pipe-gun** (**a**) *dial.* a pop-gun; (**b**) a gun made out of a pipe; **pipe-lay** *noun & verb* (**a**) *noun* the laying of pipes for water, gas, etc.; an instance of this; (**b**) *verb intrans.* (*US slang*) = *lay pipe(s)* (a) above; **pipe-layer** a person or thing which lays pipes for water, gas, etc.; *US slang* a person engaging in political corruption; **pipe-light** a strip of paper folded or twisted for lighting a pipe, a spill; **pipe major** the leader of or NCO commanding a (regimental) pipe band; **pipeman** a pipe-smoker; a worker attending to a pipe; **pipe-metal** an alloy of tin and lead, with or without zinc, used for organ-pipes; **Pipe-Office** *Hist.* the office of the Clerk of the Pipe in the Exchequer; **pipe-opener** *colloq.* a spell of exercise taken to clear the respiratory passages and fill the lungs with fresh air; *fig.* a preliminary event; **pipe-organ** an organ using pipes instead of or as well as reeds; **pipe-rack** (**a**) a perforated shelf by which the pipes in an organ are supported; (**b**) a rack for tobacco-pipes; (**c**) a rack or support for a set of pipelines above the ground; **pipe roll** *Hist.* [prob. from the pipe form into which subsidiary documents were rolled] the annual accounts of sheriffs etc. kept by the British Exchequer from the 12th cent. to the 19th cent.; **pipesnake** any of various mainly red and black tropical snakes of the family Aniliidae; **pipe-stapple** *Scot. & north.* a pipe-stem; **pipe-stem** the shaft of a tobacco-pipe; **pipe-still** a still in which crude oil is heated by passing it through a series of tubes inside a furnace; **pipe-stone** a hard red clay or soft stone used by N. American Indians for tobacco-pipes (cf. CATLINITE); **pipe tobacco** tobacco specially cut and dried for smoking in a pipe; **pipe tree** any of several shrubs whose stems were formerly used to make pipe stems, *esp.* (**a**) (more fully ***blue pipe tree***) lilac, *Syringa vulgaris*; (**b**) (more fully ***white pipe tree***) mock orange, *Philadelphus coronarius*; **pipe-vine** = DUTCHMAN'S *pipe*; **pipework** pipes collectively; piping as part of a structure; **pipewort** an aquatic and marsh plant, *Eriocaulon aquaticum* (family Eriocaulaceae), of western Ireland, the Hebrides, and N. America, with leafless stems bearing heads of inconspicuous flowers; **pipe wrench** a wrench with one fixed and one movable jaw, designed so as to grip a pipe etc. when turned in one direction only.

■ **pipeful** *noun* a quantity of tobacco etc. sufficient to fill the bowl of a pipe E17. **pipeless** *adjective* L19. **pipelike** *adjective* resembling a pipe in shape or form, tubular E17.

pipe /pʌɪp/ *noun*[2]. LME.
[Anglo-Norman *pipe*, Anglo-Latin *pipa*, from prec.]
A large cask, now esp. for wine; this as a measure of two hogsheads, usu. equivalent to 105 gallons (approx. 477 litres); the quantity of wine etc. held by such a cask. Cf. BUTT *noun*[3].
Comb.: †**pipe-wine** wine drawn directly from the pipe or wood.

pipe /pʌɪp/ *verb*[1]. OE.
[Latin *pipare* in medieval Latin sense 'blow a pipe', from *pipa* PIPE *noun*[1], reinforced in Middle English by Old French *piper* chirp, squeak from Latin *pipare*. In branch III directly from PIPE *noun*[1].]
▶ **I 1** *verb intrans.* Play on or blow a pipe or pipes; play shrill plaintive music. OE.
2 *verb trans.* Play (music or a tune) on a pipe or pipes. LME.
3 *verb trans.* Bring or lead (a person or thing) into a place or condition by playing a pipe. M16. ▸**b** NAUTICAL. Summon (a crew) to a meal, duty, etc., by a boatswain's pipe; signal or mark the arrival of (an officer etc.) by playing a pipe or pipes. Foll. by adverb. E18.

📖 **1** J. THOMSON The Shepherd . . Sits piping to his Flocks. **2** KEATS Happy melodist, unwearied, For ever piping songs for ever new. **3** BROWNING They pipe us free from rats or mice. **b** *Times* The Duke was piped on board.

▶ **II 4** *verb intrans.* †**a** Utter a shrill weak sound; talk or sing weakly and shrilly; cheep, squeak, peep. ME–L15. ▸**b** Make a high-pitched clear sound, whistle; talk or sing loudly and shrilly; (of a bird) sing. E16. ▸**c** Weep, cry. Also (orig. NAUTICAL) ***pipe one's eye(s)***, ***pipe the eye(s)***. *slang.* L18.
5 *verb trans.* Utter or sing (words, a song, etc.) in a weak and shrill or a clear and high-pitched voice. LME.
6 *verb intrans.* Breathe hard, pant from exertion. *slang.* E19.

📖 **4b** *Daily Telegraph* The wind piping in the rigging. **5** T. H. WHITE The curlew . . had been piping their mournful plaints. A. GUINNESS 'Ah, beauty! Beauty!' piped Eddie Marsh, whose voice was . . astonishingly high.

▶ **III** †**7** *verb trans.* Drink (a liquid). *rare.* Only in L16.
†**8** *verb intrans.* Flow or be conveyed as through a pipe. *rare.* Only in M17.
9 *verb intrans.* Smoke a pipe. *N. Amer. colloq.* M17.
10 *verb trans.* HORTICULTURE. Propagate (a pink etc.) by taking a cutting at a joint of the stem. L18.
11 *verb trans.* **a** Trim or ornament (a garment etc.) with piping. Usu. in *pass.* M19. ▸**b** Arrange (icing, cream, etc.) in decorative lines or twists on a cake etc.; ornament (a cake etc.) in this way. L19.
12 *verb trans. & intrans.* Watch, notice, look (at); follow or observe (a person), esp. stealthily. Also foll. by *off*. *slang & dial.* M19.
13 *verb trans.* Provide or supply (a place) with pipes for gas, water, etc. L19.
14 *verb trans.* Convey (water, gas, etc.) through or by means of pipes. L19. ▸**b** Transmit (music, television signals, etc.) over wire or cable. M20.
With adverbs in specialized senses, & phrases: **pipe away** NAUTICAL dismiss (a crew) from duty by piping; give a signal for (a boat) to start. **pipe down** (**a**) *verb phr. trans. & intrans.* (NAUTICAL) dismiss (a crew) from duty by piping; (**b**) *verb phr. intrans.* (*colloq.*) stop talking, be quiet or less insistent (freq. in. *imper.*). **pipe in** bring or welcome (a person or thing) in to the accompaniment of bagpipes. ***pipe one's eye(s)***, ***pipe the eye(s)***: see sense 4c above. **pipe the side** NAUTICAL pipe a salute given to certain officers and dignitaries when boarding or leaving a ship. **pipe up** (**a**) *verb phr. trans.* strike up (music); (**b**) *verb phr. intrans.* make an interjection, speak up (in a piping voice); (of a wind) rise, increase.
Comb.: **pipe-down** NAUTICAL the action or time of piping down a crew; a call on the boatswain's pipe signalling sailors to retire for the night.

†**pipe** *verb*[2] *trans.* LME–M18.
[from PIPE *noun*[2].]
Put (wine etc.) in a pipe or cask.

piped /pʌɪpt/ *adjective.* E16.
[from PIPE *noun*[1], *verb*[1]: see -ED[2], -ED[1].]
1 Having a pipe or pipes; having the form of a pipe, tubular. E16.
2 Formed into or ornamented with decorative piping. L19.
3 Conveyed by pipes. L19. ▸**b** Received over wire or cable rather than directly from broadcast signals. M20.
4 Drunk, intoxicated; under the influence of drugs. *US slang.* E20.

📖 **3** E. NORTH Her cottage had no piped water. **b piped music** pre-recorded background music played through loudspeakers in a public place.

pipeline /ˈpʌɪplʌɪn/ *noun & verb.* M19.
[from PIPE *noun*[1] + LINE *noun*[2].]
▶ **A** *noun.* **1** A continuous line of pipes; a long pipe for conveying oil, gas, etc., long distances, esp. underground; a (usu. flexible) tube for carrying liquid in machinery etc. M19.
2 *transf. & fig.* A channel of supply, information, communication, etc. Freq. in ***in the pipeline***, being planned, worked on, or produced. E20.
3 SURFING. (The hollow formed by the breaking of) a very large wave; a place where such waves are formed. M20.
4 COMPUTING. A linear sequence of specialized modules used for pipelining. Freq. *attrib.* M20.
▶ **B** *verb trans.* **1** Provide with or convey by a pipeline. L19.
2 COMPUTING. Design or execute using the technique of pipelining. Freq. as ***pipelined*** *ppl adjective.* M20.
■ **pipeliner** *noun* a worker on an oil, gas, etc., pipeline E20. **pipelining** *noun* (**a**) the laying of pipelines; (**b**) transportation by means of pipelines; (**c**) COMPUTING a form of computer organization in which successive steps of a process are executed in turn by a sequence of modules able to operate concurrently, so that another process can be begun before the previous one is finished: M20.

piper /ˈpʌɪpə/ *noun.* OE.
[from PIPE *noun*[1], *verb*[1] + -ER[1].]
▶ **I 1** A person who plays a pipe, esp. as an itinerant musician; *spec.* a person who plays the bagpipes. OE.
2 Any of several fishes; *spec.* (**a**) a gurnard, *Trigla lyra* (from the sound it makes when caught); (**b**) *NZ* a halfbeak, *Hemirhamphus intermedius*. E17.
3 A broken-winded horse. *slang & dial.* M19.
4 A young pigeon, a squab. L19.
1 pay the piper (and call the tune): see PAY *verb*[1]. ***Pied Piper (of Hamelin)***: see PIED *adjective.*
▶ **II** †**5** A worker who lays or repairs pipes. Only in LME.
6 A person who smokes a pipe. Now *rare.* M17.
7 A kind of caddis-fly larva which uses a piece of reed as a case. Long *rare* or *obsolete.* M17.
8 A dog used to lure wildfowl into the pipe of a decoy. M19.
9 = BLOWER *noun*[1] 3. L19.
10 A person who ornaments cakes with decorative piping. *rare.* E20.
■ **piperly** *adjective* (now *rare*) resembling or characteristic of a piper or itinerant musician; paltry, beggarly: L16.

piperaceous /pɪpəˈreɪʃəs/ *adjective.* L17.
[from Latin *piper* pepper + -ACEOUS.]
†**1** Of the nature of pepper; pungent. Only in L17.
2 BOTANY. Of or pertaining to the Piperaceae or pepper family. M19.

piperade /pɪpəˈrɑːd; *foreign* piparad (*pl. same*)/ *noun.* M20.
[French.]
A dish originating in the Basque country, consisting of eggs scrambled with tomatoes and peppers.

piperazine /pɪˈpɛrəziːn, pʌɪ-/ *noun.* L19.
[from PIPER(IDINE + AZINE.]
CHEMISTRY & PHARMACOLOGY. A crystalline heterocyclic compound, $C_4H_{10}N_2$, used as an anthelmintic, insecticide, etc.

piperic /pɪˈpɛrɪk/ *adjective.* M19.
[formed as PIPERINE + -IC.]
CHEMISTRY. ***piperic acid***, a bicyclic carboxylic acid, $C_{12}H_{10}O_4$, derived from piperine.

piperidine /pɪˈpɛrɪdiːn, pʌɪ-/ *noun.* M19.
[formed as next + -IDINE.]
CHEMISTRY. A colourless, strongly basic liquid with an unpleasant odour, whose molecule is a saturated six-membered ring, $(CH_2)_5NH$.

piperine /ˈpɪpəriːn/ *noun.* E19.
[from Latin *piper* pepper + -INE[5].]
CHEMISTRY. A crystalline alkaloid, $C_{17}H_{19}NO_3$, obtained from pepper plants and yielding piperic acid and piperidine.

piperitious /pɪpəˈrɪʃəs/ *adjective. joc. rare.* L19.
[from Latin *piper* pepper + -ITIOUS[1].]
Peppery, biting, pungent.

piperonal /pɪˈpɛrənal/ *noun.* M19.
[German, formed as PIPERINE + *-on* -ONE + -AL[2].]
CHEMISTRY. A crystalline bicyclic aldehyde, $(OCH_2O)C_6H_3{\cdot}CHO$, obtained synthetically and from certain flowers and used in perfumery. Also called ***heliotropin***.
■ **piperonyl** *noun* (CHEMISTRY) a radical derived from piperonal; ***piperonyl butoxide***, a yellow oily liquid, $C_{19}H_{30}O_5$, used in insecticides as a synergist for pyrethrins: L19.

piperoxan /pɪpəˈrɒksan/ *noun.* Also **-ane** /-eɪn/. M20.
[from the semi-systematic name 2-*piper*idinomethyl-1,4-benzodi*oxan*.]
PHARMACOLOGY. An experimental antipsychotic drug, $C_{14}H_{19}NO_2$, with alpha-adrenergic blocking properties.

pipery /ˈpɪp(ə)ri/ *noun.* L17.
[French *piperie*: cf. Spanish *pipero* cooper, from *pipa* barrel.]
A raft or boat resembling a catamaran, used in the W. Indies and S. America.

pipette /pɪˈpɛt/ *noun & verb.* Also ***-et**. M19.
[French, dim. of *pipe* PIPE *noun*[1]: see -ETTE.]
▶ **A** *noun.* A freq. tubular device for transferring or measuring small quantities of a liquid or gas by means of aspiration and dispensation, used esp. in scientific laboratories. M19.
▶ **B** *verb trans.* Infl. **-tt-**, ***-t-**. Transfer, measure, draw *off* or *out* (a liquid or gas) with a pipette. M19.
■ **pipetting** *verbal noun* the action of the verb; an instance of this: E20.

pipi /ˈpɪpi/ *noun.* Also **pippi(e)**, **pippy**. M19.
[Maori.]
1 An edible bivalve mollusc, *Amphidesma australe*, of sandy beaches in New Zealand; any of several other edible bivalves, esp. *Chione stutchburyi*. *NZ.* M19.
2 An edible bivalve mollusc of southern Australia, *Plebidonax deltoides*. *Austral.* L19.

piping /ˈpʌɪpɪŋ/ *noun.* ME.
[from PIPE *verb*[1] + -ING[1].]
1 The action of PIPE *verb*[1]. ME.
2 HORTICULTURE. A cutting of a pink etc. taken at a joint. M19.
3 Pipes for conveying water etc. collectively; a system of pipes, esp. in a building. M19.
4 Edging for a garment, a seam on upholstery, etc., consisting of a thin pipelike length of folded cloth, often enclosing a fine cord. M19.
5 Ornamentation for a cake etc., consisting of lines or twists of icing, cream, etc. M19.
6 METALLURGY. = PIPE *noun*[1] 6b. M19.
7 An assault using a length of pipe as a weapon. *US.* L20.

📖 **1** SHELLEY Far and wide rebounded The echo of his pipings. P. SCOTT A shrill piping of birds.

piping /ˈpʌɪpɪŋ/ *adjective & adverb.* LME.
[from PIPE *verb*[1] + -ING[2].]
▶ **A** *adjective.* **1** Shrill and weak in sound; high-pitched and clear; whistling. LME. ▸**b** Of a bird: having a piping cry. Now only in names. L18.
2 Playing a pipe; *fig.* characterized by the sound of pipes (associated with peace rather than martial instruments). L16.
3 Piping hot. *colloq.* L19.

📖 **1** A. HALEY He could . . hear Kizzy's piping voice among the others. W. BOYD The piping shouts of tally-ho. **b piping crow** = ***piping shrike*** below. **piping plover** a small buff-coloured bird, *Charadrius melodus*, of coastal areas in eastern N. America. **piping shrike** a white-backed form of the Australian magpie *Gymnorhina tibicen*, a State emblem of S. Australia. **2** SHAKES. *Rich. III* In this weak piping time of peace. SWIFT Lowing herds and piping swains. **3** *Globe & Mail (Toronto)* Piping flavorful soup . . rated a full five stars.

▶ **B** *adverb.* ***piping hot***, (of food, water, etc.) so hot as to make a whistling or hissing sound, very or suitably hot. LME.

L. BLUE Sprinkle the bananas with .. sugar .. and lemon juice, and eat them piping hot.

pipistrelle /pɪpɪˈstrɛl, ˈpɪp-/ *noun.* Also **-el**. L18.
[French from Italian *pipistrello* alt. of *vipistrello* repr. Latin *vespertilio* bat, from *vesper* evening.]
A small bat of the widespread genus *Pipistrellus*, *esp.* one of the common Eurasian species *Pipistrellus pipistrellus*.

pipit /ˈpɪpɪt/ *noun.* M18.
[Prob. imit.]
Any of numerous small, typically ground-dwelling birds with brown-streaked plumage, of the widespread genus *Anthus* or related genera of the family Motacillidae.
meadow pipit, ***rock pipit***, ***tawny pipit***, ***tree pipit***, etc.

pipkin /ˈpɪpkɪn/ *noun.* M16.
[Origin unkn.]
1 A small usu. earthenware pot or pan. M16.
2 = PIGGIN. *dial.* (chiefly *US*). M19.

pipkrake /ˈpɪpkreɪk, -krɑːkə/ *noun.* Pl. **-krakes**, **-kraker** /-krɑːkə/. M20.
[Swedish dial., from *pip* PIPE *noun*[1] + *krake* var. of *klake* frozen ground.]
PHYSICAL GEOGRAPHY. An ice-needle; needle ice.

pipped /pɪpt/ *adjective*[1]. *slang.* L18.
[from PIP *noun*[1] + -ED[2].]
1 Unwell, depressed. L18.
2 Annoyed, irritated. E20.

pipped /pɪpt/ *adjective*[2]. *slang.* E20.
[Origin uncertain: perh. from PIP *verb*[2].]
Tipsy, drunk.

pipperidge /ˈpɪp(ə)rɪdʒ/ *noun.* See also PEPPERIDGE. M16.
[Origin unkn.]
1 The fruit of the barberry, *Berberis vulgaris*; (more fully ***pipperidge-bush***) the bush bearing this. Now *dial.* M16.
2 = PEPPERIDGE. *US.* E19.

pippi(e) *nouns* vars. of PIPI *noun.*

pippin /ˈpɪpɪn/ *noun.* ME.
[Old & mod. French *pepin* (mod. also *pépin*) rel. to synon. Spanish *pepita*, Italian *pippolo*, *pipporo*, from Proto-Romance. Cf. PIP *noun*[2].]
1 The seed of a fruit; *esp.* a pip. *obsolete* exc. *north.* ME.
2 Any of numerous varieties of fine-flavoured eating apple. LME.
3 a Orig., a fool. Later, as a term of endearment: dear. *slang.* Now *rare.* M17. ▸**b** An excellent person or thing, a beauty. Cf. PIP *noun*[2] 3. *slang* (orig. *US*). L19.
2 ***Cox's orange pippin***, ***Newtown pippin***, ***Ribston pippin***, etc. ***sound as a pippin*** very sound.

pip-pip /pɪpˈpɪp/ *noun & interjection.* E20.
[Imit.]
1 (Repr.) a repeated short high-pitched sound, *spec.* that made by a motor car horn. E20.
2 (An utterance of) goodbye. Cf. TOODLE-PIP. *arch. slang.* E20.

2 F. DONALDSON Well, pip pip and good-bye-ee and so forth.

†**pipple** *noun & verb* var. of PEBBLE.

pippy *noun* var. of PIPI *noun.*

pippy /ˈpɪpi/ *adjective.* L19.
[from PIP *noun*[2], *noun*[1] + -Y[1].]
1 Full of pips. L19.
2 Depressed; annoyed; ailing. *slang.* L19.

pipradrol /ˈpɪprədrɒl/ *noun.* M20.
[from PIP(E)R(IDINE + -*a*- + HY)DROL.]
PHARMACOLOGY. An antidepressant drug, $(C_6H_5)_2$-$C_5H_8N{\cdot}CH_2OH.HCl$, which acts as a central nervous system stimulant. Also ***pipradrol hydrochloride***.

pipsissewa /pɪpˈsɪsɪwə/ *noun.* N. *Amer.* L18.
[Abnaki *kpi-pskʷáhsawe* flower of the woods.]
A kind of wintergreen with whorled leaves, *Chimaphila umbellata* (also called ***prince's pine***); the leaves of this plant, used as a diuretic and tonic.

pipsqueak /ˈpɪpskwiːk/ *noun.* E20.
[Symbolic and imit.]
1 (A name for) an insignificant or contemptible person or thing. *colloq.* E20.
2 a A small high velocity shell distinguished by the sound of its flight. *slang.* E20. ▸**b** A short high-pitched sound; something making such a sound. *slang.* E20.

1 M. ATWOOD Among the boys are a few pipsqueaks whose voices have not yet changed. *attrib.*: F. POHL He'd get smashed .. because he's just a pipsqueak tyrant.

pipsyl /ˈpɪpsʌɪl, -sɪl/ *noun.* M20.
[from the chemical name *p-iodophenylsulphonyl*: see -YL.]
CHEMISTRY. The radical $I{\cdot}C_6H_4{\cdot}SO_2{\cdot}$, compounds of which are used as radioactive labels. Usu. in *comb.*

pipy /ˈpʌɪpi/ *adjective.* E18.
[from PIPE *noun*[1] + -Y[1].]
1 Containing pipes or tubes; shaped like a pipe, tubular. E18.
2 Given to crying or weeping. *slang.* M19.
3 Piping, shrill. L19.

piquancy /ˈpiːk(ə)nsi/ *noun.* M17.
[from next: see -ANCY.]
The quality of being piquant.

E. SIMPSON The prohibition gave a certain piquancy to our clandestine rendezvous.

■ Also **piquance** *noun* (*rare*) L19.

piquant /ˈpiːk(ə)nt, -kɑːnt/ *adjective & noun.* In senses A.2 & 3 also **piquante** /pɪˈkɑːnt/. E16.
[French, pres. ppl adjective of *piquer*: see PIQUE *verb*[1], -ANT[1].]
▶ **A** *adjective.* **1** Sharp or stinging to the feelings; severe, bitter. Long *arch.* E16.
2 Of food etc.: agreeably pungent, sharp-tasting, spicy; savoury, appetizing. M17.
3 Pleasantly stimulating to the mind; racy, spicy; fascinating, charming. M17.

2 *Listener* A piquant *guacamole*, .. avocado pear seasoned with tomatoes, onions, coriander, and chilli peppers. **3** *Athenaeum* Valentine is both handsome and piquant in her gipsyish way. V. S. PRITCHETT Piquant asides relieve the long chronicle.

▶ **B** *noun.* **1** Something sharp or pointed, as a hedgehog's prickle. *rare.* M19.
2 A piquant dish. *rare.* M19.
■ **piquantly** *adverb* L17. **piquantness** *noun* (*rare*) E18.

pique /piːk/ *noun*[1]. M16.
[French, formed as PIQUE *verb*[1].]
1 A quarrel or feeling of enmity between two or more people; ill feeling, animosity. M16.
2 (A feeling of) anger or resentment resulting from a slight or injury, esp. to one's pride; offence taken. L16.

2 V. BROME The industrialist's son did not .. care for her, and partly out of pique she decided to marry another. D. ARKELL Henri's jealous pique about .. Yvonne's men friends.

pique /piːk/ *noun*[2]. M17.
[French *pic*, of unkn. origin.]
PIQUET. The winning of thirty points on cards and play before one's opponent begins to count, entitling one's score to begin at sixty. Cf. REPIQUE.

pique /ˈpiːkeɪ, piːk/ *noun*[3]. M18.
[Amer. Spanish from Quechua *piqui*, *piki*.]
= JIGGER *noun*[2] 1.

pique /piːk/ *noun*[4]. Now *rare* or *obsolete.* L18.
[Alt. of PEAK *noun*[1].]
The pointed extremity of a collar, saddle, etc.

pique *noun*[5] var. of PIQUÉ.

pique /piːk/ *verb*[1]. M17.
[French *piquer* prick, pierce, sting, irritate, *se piquer* take offence, from Proto-Romance. Cf. PICK *verb*[1].]
1 *verb trans.* Stimulate or provoke (a person) to action or emotion, esp. by arousing jealousy etc.; arouse (curiosity, interest, etc.). M17.
2 *verb trans.* Wound the pride of, irritate, or offend (a person); make resentful. L17.
3 *verb refl.* & (*rare*) *intrans.* Pride or congratulate oneself *on*, take pride *in.* L17.

2 E. F. BENSON Lucia had been just a little piqued by Maud's apparent indifference. M. M. R. KHAN 'I never realised you were not only mean .. but also lazy!' This piqued me. **3** E. B. BROWNING He piqued himself on being very like the pictures .. of Shakespeare!

■ **piquable** *adjective* (*rare*) able or inclined to be piqued M19.

pique /piːk/ *verb*[2]. M17.
[from PIQUE *noun*[2].]
PIQUET. **1** *verb trans.* Score a pique against (one's opponent). M17.
2 *verb intrans.* Score a pique. M17.

piqué /ˈpiːkeɪ/ *noun, adjective, & verb.* Also **pique**. M19.
[French, use as noun of pa. pple of *piquer* backstitch, PIQUE *verb*[1].]
▶ **A** *noun.* **1** A stiff fabric woven in a strongly ribbed or raised pattern (orig. in imitation of hand quilting); the raised pattern (characteristic) of such a fabric. M19.
2 Work inlaid with gold etc. dots. L19.
3 BALLET. A step directly on to the point of the leading foot without bending the knee. M20.
▶ **B** *adjective.* **1** COOKERY. Larded. *rare.* M19.
2 Made of piqué; having the pattern of piqué. L19.
3 Inlaid with gold etc. dots. L19.
4 BALLET. Stepping directly on to the point of the leading foot without bending the knee. E20.
▶ **C** *verb trans.* COOKERY. Lard. M19.

piquet /pɪˈkɛt/ *noun*[1]. Also †**picket**, †**picquet**. M17.
[French, of unkn. origin.]
A card-game for two players with a pack of 32 cards, the cards from the two to the six being excluded.

■ **piquetist** *noun* a piquet player L19.

piquet *noun*[2] see PICKET *noun*[1].

piqueur /pikœːr/ *noun.* Pl. pronounced same. M19.
[French, from *piquer* PIQUE *verb*[1] + -*eur* -OR.]
In France, an attendant on a hunt, *spec.* one directing hounds.

piqui *noun* var. of PEKEA.

piqûre /pikyːr/ *noun.* Also **piqure**. Pl. pronounced same. E20.
[French, from *piquer*: see PIQUE *verb*[1], -URE.]
A hypodermic injection; a puncture made in the skin by such an injection.

PIR *abbreviation.*
Passive infrared (denoting a type of sensor).

pir /pɪə/ *noun.* L17.
[Persian *pīr* = old man.]
A Muslim saint or holy man. Formerly also (*rare*), the tomb or shrine of such a person.

piracy /ˈpʌɪrəsi/ *noun.* M16.
[Anglo-Latin *piratia*, from Latin *pirata* PIRATE *noun* + -*ia* -Y[3]: see -ACY.]
1 Robbery, kidnapping, or violence committed at sea or from the sea without lawful authority, esp. by one vessel against another; similar behaviour in other forms, *esp.* hijacking; an instance of this. M16. ▸**b** PHYSICAL GEOGRAPHY. = CAPTURE *noun* 3. E20.
2 Unauthorized reproduction or use of something, as a book, recording, computer program, or idea, esp. when in contravention of patent or copyright; plagiarism; an instance of this. L18.

1 C. FRANCIS Because the admiral was Drake, the crew assumed .. piracy would bring .. plenty of prize-money. **2** *Time* The cabal of Paris designers who tried to prevent style piracy.

piragua /pɪˈragwə/ *noun.* Also **periagua** /pɛrɪˈagwə/. E17.
[Spanish from Carib = dugout. Cf. PIROGUE.]
1 A long narrow canoe hollowed from the trunk of a single tree or from the trunks of two trees fastened together. E17.
2 An open flat-bottomed schooner-rigged vessel; a kind of two-masted sailing barge. M17.

Pirandellian /pɪr(ə)nˈdɛlɪən/ *adjective.* E20.
[from *Pirandello* (see below) + -IAN.]
Of, pertaining to, or characteristic of the Italian playwright Luigi Pirandello (1867–1936) or his style.
■ **Pirandellism** *noun* the style or method of Pirandello; a characteristic example of this: M20.

Piranesian /pɪrəˈneɪzɪən/ *adjective.* E20.
[from *Piranesi* (see below) + -AN.]
Of, pertaining to, or characteristic of the Italian architect and artist Giovanni Battista Piranesi (1720–78), his style, or his theories.

piranha /pɪˈrɑːnə, -njə/ *noun.* Also (earlier, now *rare*) **piraya** /pɪˈrɑːjə/. M18.
[Portuguese from Tupi *pirán*ʸ*e*, *piráya*, from *pirá* fish + *sainha* tooth. Cf. PERAI.]
Any of several gregarious predatory freshwater fishes of S. America, of the genus *Serrasalmus* and related genera of the characin family, noted for their aggressiveness and voracity.

fig.: *Literary Review* Those Fifth Avenue piranhas who would eventually lead him .. towards his ruin.

Pirani gauge /pɪˈrɑːni geɪdʒ/ *noun phr.* E20.
[M. S. von *Pirani*, 20th-cent. German physicist.]
PHYSICS. A gauge which measures very low pressures in gases by their cooling effect on the resistance of a heated metal filament.

pirarucú /pɪrərʊˈkuː/ *noun.* M19.
[Portuguese from Tupi, from *pirá* fish + *urucú* annatto, red.]
= ARAPAIMA.

pirastic *adjective* see PEIRASTIC.

pirate /ˈpʌɪrət/ *noun & adjective.* ME.
[Latin *pirata* from Greek *peiratēs*, from *peiran* to attempt or attack, *peira* attempt, trial: see -ATE[1].]
▶ **A** *noun.* **1** A person who commits piracy; a person who robs and plunders on or from the sea; *gen.* a plunderer, a despoiler, a bandit. ME.
2 A vessel used for piracy or manned by pirates. M16.
3 A person who reproduces or uses something, as a book, recording, idea, etc., without authority and esp. in contravention of patent or copyright; a plagiarist. Also, a thing reproduced or used in this way. E17.
4 An animal the habits of which suggest piracy, as (***a***) a hermit crab; (***b***) a small voracious freshwater fish, *Aphredoderus sayanus*, common in the eastern US. L18.
5 PHYSICAL GEOGRAPHY. A river that captures the headwaters of another. Also ***river-pirate***. L19.
6 An unlicensed bus, taxi, etc. L19.

7 A person, organization, etc., broadcasting or (formerly) receiving radio etc. programmes without official authorization. **E20.**

📖 **1** G. GREENE Pirates . . sailing the seven seas in search of gold. **3** *New Scientist* The video-pirates, who have cashed in by selling illegal copies.

▶**B** *attrib.* or as *adjective.* Of, pertaining to, or characteristic of a pirate or pirates; of the nature of a pirate; reproduced without authorization, pirated; broadcasting etc. without licence. **E18.**

📖 *Sunday Times* Shady East End companies, copying foreign garments for pirate versions. M. FLANAGAN She had a radio and . . would listen . . to forbidden pirate stations. A. MACRAE His striped pirate T-shirt.

Special collocations & comb.: **pirate-perch** = sense A.4b above. **pirate radio ship**: used to transmit radio programmes from outside the territorial waters of the receiving country. **pirate-stream** = sense A.5 above.
■ **piratess** *noun* (*rare*) a female pirate **M19.** **piratedom** *noun* (*rare*) pirates collectively; the world of pirates: **E20.**

pirate /ˈpʌɪrət/ *verb.* **E16.**
[from the noun.]
1 *verb trans.* Practise piracy on, rob, plunder, (a person, place, etc.); obtain (goods etc.) through piracy. **E16.**
2 *verb intrans.* Act as a pirate, practise piracy. **L17.**
3 *verb trans.* Reproduce or use (another's work, idea, etc.) without authority, esp. in contravention of patent or copyright. Freq. as ***pirated*** *ppl adjective.* **E18.**

📖 **3** *Times Lit. Suppl.* Efforts to . . protect British books against the importation of foreign pirated editions.

piratical /pʌɪˈratɪk(ə)l/ *adjective.* **M16.**
[from Latin *piraticus* from Greek *peiratikos*, from *peiratēs* pirate: see -ICAL.]
1 Obtained by piracy, pirated. **M16.**
2 Of, pertaining to, or characteristic of a pirate or piracy; of the nature of, given to, or engaged in piracy; *fig.* rakish, dashing. **L16.**
■ **piratic** *adjective* = PIRATICAL **M17.** **piratically** *adverb* **M16.**

piraya *noun* see PIRANHA.

pire /pɪə/ *verb intrans.* Long *obsolete* exc. *dial.* **LME.**
[Low German *piren*, East Frisian *piren*, of unkn. origin.]
= PEER *verb*[2] 1.

piriform *adjective* var. of PYRIFORM.

pirimicarb /pɪˈrɪmɪkɑːb/ *noun.* **L20.**
[from *pirimi-* alt. of PYRIMI(DINE + CARB(AMATE.]
A heterocyclic insecticide, $C_{11}H_{18}N_4O_2$, that is used specifically against aphids.

piripiri /ˈpɪrɪpɪri/ *noun. NZ.* **M19.**
[Maori.]
1 A fragrant wiry marsh plant, *Haloragis micrantha* (family Haloragaceae), of eastern and southern Asia, Australasia, etc. **M19.**
2 More fully ***piripiri bur***. Any of various small prostrate plants of the genus *Acaena*, of the rose family, with pinnate leaves, heads of inconspicuous flowers, and fruits in the form of burs, widespread in the southern hemisphere. Also called ***biddy-bid***. **M19.**

piri-piri /ˈpɪrɪpɪri/ *noun.* **M20.**
[Ronga = pepper.]
A sauce made with red peppers. Also ***piri-piri sauce***.

pirk /pəːk/ *noun.* **L20.**
[Perh. a var. of PERK *noun*[1] or PERCH *noun*[2].]
A metal weight fitted with a hook, used as a lure for sea fishing.

pirl /pəːl/ *verb & noun. Scot. & dial.* **LME.**
[Prob. imit.: cf. PURL *noun*[1], *noun*[2], *verb*[2].]
▶**A** *verb.* **1** *verb trans. & intrans.* Whirl, revolve. **LME.**
2 *verb trans.* Twist or spin (threads or fibres) into cord, braid, etc. **E16.**
3 *verb intrans.* Of water, smoke, etc.: curl, ripple. **L18.**
▶**B** *noun.* A ripple on water; a twist, a curl. **L15.**

pirn /pəːn/ *noun & verb.* Now *Scot. & dial.* As noun also **pern**. **LME.**
[Origin unkn.: cf. prec.]
▶**A** *noun.* **1** A small cylinder on which thread etc. is wound; a bobbin, a spool, a reel; this wound with thread etc. **LME.**
†**2** An imperfection in cloth; a stripe, a mark. *rare.* **L17–M18.**
3 Thread wound on a bobbin etc.; the amount able to be wound on a bobbin etc. *rare.* **E18.**
▶**B** *verb trans.* Wind or reel (thread etc.) on to a bobbin etc. *Scot.* **E19.**
■ **pirned** *adjective* (*Scot.*) striped, variegated **L15.** **pirnie** *adjective & noun* (*Scot.*) (*a*) *adjective* (of cloth) striped; (*b*) *noun* a nightcap (usu. striped): **L17.**

pirog /pɪˈrɒɡ/ *noun.* Pl. **-i** /-i/, **-en** /-ən/. **M19.**
[Russian.]
In Russian or E. European cookery: a large pie. Cf. PIROSHKI.

pirogi *noun* var. of PIEROGI.

pirogue /pɪˈrəʊɡ/ *noun.* **E17.**
[French, prob. from Carib.]
= PIRAGUA 1. Also, any canoe or open boat.

piroplasm /ˈpʌɪrə(ʊ)plaz(ə)m/ *noun.* **E20.**
[from Latin *pirum* pear (from the shape) + -O- + -PLASM.]
A protozoan of the sporozoan subclass Piroplasmea, which comprises species parasitic in red blood cells and transmitted by ticks.
■ **piroplasˈmosis** *noun*, pl. **-moses** /-ˈməʊsiːz/, any of a group of diseases of mammals, esp. red-water of cattle, caused by infestation of the blood with piroplasms **E20.**

piroshki /pɪˈrɒʃki/ *noun pl.* Also **-tchki** /-tʃki/, **-zhki** /-ʒki/. **E20.**
[Russian *pirozhki* pl. of *pirozhok* dim. of PIROG.]
In Russian, E. European, or Jewish cookery: small pastries or patties filled with meat, fish, rice, etc.

pirouette /pɪrʊˈɛt/ *noun & verb.* **M17.**
[French: ult. origin unkn.]
▶**A** *noun.* **1** HORSEMANSHIP. A full circle made by pivoting on a hind leg while walking or cantering. **M17.**
2 An act of spinning round on one foot or on the points of the toes by a ballet dancer etc.; *gen.* a rapid whirl of the body. **E18.**
3 MUSIC. A form of mouthpiece used with a shawm, rackett, etc. **L19.**

📖 **2** P. LIVELY Sandra . . performed a little pirouette, as though warming up for Swan Lake.

▶**B** *verb intrans.* Perform a pirouette; move with a whirling motion, spin, whirl. **E19.**

📖 O. MANNING She pirouetted across the studio floor.

■ **pirouetter** *noun* **E19.** **pirouettist** *noun* **L19.**

pirozhki *noun pl.* var. of PIROSHKI.

Pirquet /ˈpɪəkeɪ/ *noun.* **E20.**
[Baron C. P. *Pirquet* von Cesenatico (1874–1929), Viennese paediatrician.]
MEDICINE. Used **attrib.** to designate a skin test for an immune reaction to tuberculin.

pirr /pəː/ *noun.* Chiefly *Scot. & N. Irish.* Also **pirre**. **M18.**
[Imit., from the bird's cry.]
A black-headed sea bird, *esp.* a tern. Earliest (*rare*) in ***pirrmaw*** [MAW *noun*[3]].

pirrie /ˈpɪri/ *noun.* Now *dial.* Also **pirry**. **LME.**
[App. imit.: see -IE, -Y[6].]
A (sudden) blast of wind, a squall.

piśācī *noun* see PISHASHI.

pis aller /pizale (*pl. same*), piːzˈaleɪ/ *noun.* **L17.**
[French, from *pis* worse + *aller* go.]
The worst that can be or happen; a last resort.

Pisan /ˈpiːz(ə)n/ *noun & adjective.* **E17.**
[Italian *Pisano* from Latin *Pisanus*, from *Pisa*: see below, -AN.]
▶**A** *noun.* A native or inhabitant of Pisa, a city in central Italy on the River Arno. **E17.**
▶**B** *adjective.* Of, pertaining to, or characteristic of Pisa. **E19.**

†**pisang** *noun.* Latterly chiefly *S. Afr.* **M17–E20.**
[Malay.]
= BANANA 1, 2.

pisanite /pɪˈzɑːnʌɪt/ *noun.* **M19.**
[from Felix *Pisani* (d. 1920), French mineralogist + -ITE[1].]
MINERALOGY. A blue variety of melanterite, containing copper in place of some iron.

pisatin /ˈpʌɪsətɪn, ˈpɪs-, -z-/ *noun.* **M20.**
[from mod. Latin taxonomic name of the pea, *Pisum sativum* (from Latin *pisum* pea + *sativus* SATIVE) + -IN[1].]
BIOCHEMISTRY. A heterocyclic compound, $C_{17}H_{14}O_6$, produced by the pea plant as a fungitoxic phytoalexin.

piscary /ˈpɪskəri/ *noun & adjective.* **L15.**
[medieval Latin *piscaria* fishing rights, use as noun of neut. pl. of Latin *piscarius* pertaining to fishing, from *piscis* fish: see -ARY[1].]
▶**A** *noun.* **1** The right of fishing (as a thing owned). Now chiefly in ***common of piscary***, the right of fishing in another's water in common with the owner and others. **L15.**
2 A place where fish may be caught; a fishing-ground, a fishery. **E17.**
▶**B** *attrib.* or as *adjective.* Of or pertaining to fishing. *rare.* **M19.**

piscation /pɪˈskeɪʃ(ə)n/ *noun. rare.* **E17.**
[Late Latin *piscatio(n-)*, from Latin *piscat-* pa. ppl stem of *piscari* to fish, from *piscis* fish: see -ATION.]
Fishing.

piscatology /pɪskəˈtɒlədʒi/ *noun. rare.* **M19.**
[from Latin *piscat-* (see prec.) + -OLOGY.]
The science of fish or fishing.

piscator /pɪˈskeɪtə/ *noun. rare.* **M17.**
[Latin, formed as prec.: see -OR.]
A fisherman, an angler.

piscatorial /pɪskəˈtɔːrɪəl/ *adjective.* **E19.**
[formed as next + -IAL.]
= PISCATORY 1.
■ **piscatorially** *adverb* **E19.**

piscatory /ˈpɪskət(ə)ri/ *adjective.* **M17.**
[Latin *piscatorius*, from PISCATOR: see -ORY[2].]
1 Of or pertaining to fishing; engaged in or enthusiastic about fishing. **M17.**
2 = PISCINE *adjective. rare.* **M18.**

Pisces /ˈpʌɪsiːz, ˈpɪskiːz/ *noun.* Pl. same. **OE.**
[Latin, pl. of *piscis* fish.]
1 (The name of) an inconspicuous constellation on the ecliptic just north of the celestial equator, between Aquarius and Aries; ASTROLOGY (the name of) the twelfth zodiacal sign, usu. associated with the period 19 February to 20 March (see note s.v. ZODIAC); the Fishes. **OE.**
2 A person born under the sign Pisces. **E20.**

📖 **1** *attrib.*: D. BLOODWORTH The lucky things for Pisces people are silver, bloodstone, and number seven. **2** V. PACKER Would a Pisces get along with a Capricorn?

■ **Piscean** /ˈpʌɪsɪən, -ˈsiːən/ *adjective & noun* (*a*) *adjective* of or pertaining to Pisces; (characteristic of a person) born under the sign Pisces; (*b*) *noun* = PISCES 2: **E20.**

†**Pisces Austrina** *noun phr.* see PISCIS AUSTRINUS.

piscicapture /ˈpɪsɪkaptʃə/ *noun. joc. rare.* **M19.**
[from Latin *piscis* fish + *captura* capture.]
The catching of fish.
■ **piscicapturist** *noun* a catcher of fish **L19.**

piscicide /ˈpɪsɪsʌɪd/ *noun.* **M20.**
[from Latin *piscis* fish + -CIDE.]
1 The killing of fish. **M20.**
2 A person who or thing which kills fish. **M20.**

pisciculture /ˈpɪsɪkʌltʃə/ *noun.* **M19.**
[from Latin *piscis* fish after *agriculture* etc.]
The artificial breeding and rearing of fish.
■ **pisciˈcultural** *adjective* **M19.** **pisciˈculturally** *adverb* **L19.** **pisciˈculturist** *noun* a person engaged or interested in pisciculture **M19.**

piscifauna /ˈpɪsɪfɔːnə/ *noun.* **L19.**
[from Latin *piscis* fish + FAUNA.]
The native fishes of a district or country collectively.

pisciform /ˈpɪsɪfɔːm/ *adjective.* **E19.**
[formed as prec. + -FORM.]
Shaped like a fish.

piscina /pɪˈsiːnə, pɪˈsʌɪnə/ *noun.* Pl. **-nas**, **-nae** /-niː/. **L16.**
[Latin = fish-pond, in medieval Latin in sense 2, from *piscis* fish.]
1 A fish-pond. Also (*Hist.*), a pool or pond for bathing or swimming. **L16.**
2 ECCLESIASTICAL. A stone basin for draining water used in the Mass, found chiefly in Roman Catholic and pre-Reformation churches, usu. on the south side of the altar. **L18.**

piscine /pɪˈsiːn/ *noun.* **ME.**
[Old & mod. French formed as prec.: see -INE[4].]
1 A pool, a pond, *esp.* one for bathing or swimming. **ME.**
2 = PISCINA 2. *rare.* **L15.**
¶ Sense 1 obsolete from 16 until L19.

piscine /ˈpɪsʌɪn/ *adjective.* **L18.**
[from Latin *piscis* fish + -INE[1].]
Of, pertaining to, of the nature of, or characteristic of a fish or fishes.
■ **piˈscinity** *noun* (*joc., rare*) the quality or condition of being a fish **M19.**

Piscis Austrinus /ˌpʌɪsɪs ɒˈstrʌɪnəs, ˌpɪ-/ *noun phr.* Also (earlier) †**Pisces Austrina**. **L17.**
[mod. Latin, from Latin *piscis* fish + *austrinus* southern.]
(The name of) a constellation of the southern hemisphere south of Aquarius and Capricorn; the Southern Fish.

Piscis Volans /ˌpʌɪsɪs ˈvəʊlənz, ˌpɪ-/ *noun phr.* **M18.**
[mod. Latin, from Latin *piscis* fish + *volans* flying.]
= VOLANS.

piscivorous /pɪˈsɪv(ə)rəs/ *adjective.* **M17.**
[from Latin *piscis* fish + -VOROUS.]
Fish-eating, ichthyophagous.

pisco /ˈpɪskəʊ/ *noun.* Pl. **-os**. **M19.**
[A port in Peru.]
A white brandy made in Peru from muscat grapes; a drink of this.

pisé /pize, ˈpiːzeɪ/ *noun & adjective.* Also ***pisée***. **L18.**
[French, use as noun of pa. ppl adjective of *piser* beat, pound, (earth) from Latin *pinsare*.]
▶**A** *noun.* A building material of stiff clay or earth, sometimes mixed with gravel, forced between boards which are removed as it hardens; building with this material. Also ***pisé de terre*** /də tɛːr, tɛː/ [= of earth]. Also called ***terre pisée***. **L18.**
▶**B** *attrib.* or as *adjective.* Made with or using *pisé*. **M19.**

Pisgah /ˈpɪzgə/ *noun.* **M17.**
[A mountain range east of the River Jordan, from where Moses was allowed to view the promised land (*Deuteronomy* 3:27).]
Pisgah sight, ***Pisgah view***, a faint view or glimpse of something unobtainable or distant.

pish /pɪʃ/ *verb.* **L16.**
[from next.]
1 *verb intrans.* Say 'pish!'; sneer, scoff. Freq. foll. by *at.* **L16.**
2 *verb trans.* Say 'pish' to; reject or deprecate by saying 'pish!'. (Foll. by *away, down.*) **E17.**

📖 **1** V. WOOLF He sat . . frowning and fidgeting, and pishing and pshawing and muttering things to himself.

pish /pɪʃ; *as interjection also* pʃ/ *interjection & noun.* **L16.**
[Natural exclam. Cf. **PSHAW**, **TUSH** *interjection.*]
▶ **A** *interjection.* Expr. contempt, impatience, or disgust. **L16.**
▶ **B** *noun.* An utterance of 'pish'; nonsense, rubbish. **L16.**

pisha paysha /pɪʃə ˈpeɪʃə/ *noun phr.* **E20.**
[App. alt. of *pitch* (or *peace*) *and patience.*]
A Jewish card-game for two players, resembling beggar-my-neighbour.

pishashi /pɪˈʃɑːʃi/ *noun.* Also ***piśācī*** & other vars. **E19.**
[Sanskrit *piśācī* (fem.) from *piśāca* devil, ghoul.]
In the Indian subcontinent: a she-devil, *spec.* as a spring whirlwind.

pisher /ˈpɪʃə/ *noun*¹. *rare.* **E20.**
[from **PISH** *verb* + **-ER**¹.]
A person who says 'pish!', a scoffer.

pisher /ˈpɪʃə/ *noun*². *US slang.* **M20.**
[Yiddish = **PISSER**, from German *pissen*: see **-ER**¹.]
A bedwetter; a young, insignificant, or contemptible person or thing.

pishogue /pɪˈʃəʊg/ *noun.* *Anglo-Irish.* Also **pishrogue** /pɪˈʃrəʊg/. **E19.**
[Irish *piseog*, *pisreog* witchcraft from Middle Irish *piseóc*, *pisóc.*]
1 Sorcery, witchcraft; a spell, an incantation, a charm. Also, a fairy, a witch. **E19.**
2 An incredible or invented story; a folk tale. **M20.**

pish-pash /ˈpɪʃpaʃ/ *noun.* Also **-posh** /-pɒʃ/. **M19.**
[Origin unkn.]
An Indian soup or stew of rice with small pieces of meat.

pishrogue *noun* var. of **PISHOGUE.**

pisiform /ˈpʌɪsɪfɔːm, ˈpɪzɪ-/ *adjective & noun.* **M18.**
[mod. Latin *pisiformis*, from *pisum* **PEA** *noun*¹: see **-FORM.**]
▶ **A** *adjective.* Shaped like a pea; of small globular form. **M18.**
pisiform bone ANATOMY a small globular bone of the upper row of the carpus.
▶ **B** *noun.* A pisiform bone. **E19.**

piskun /ˈpɪskən/ *noun.* **L19.**
[Blackfoot *pisskani.*]
A N. American Indian trap for buffalo, consisting of a run along which buffalo were stampeded into a V-shaped natural or artificial canyon, into an enclosure, or over a steep drop.

pismire /ˈpɪsmʌɪə/ *noun.* *obsolete* exc. *dial.* **ME.**
[from **PISS** *noun* + **MIRE** *noun*²: so called from the urinous smell of an anthill. Cf. **PISSANT.**]
An ant.

Pismo clam /ˈpɪzməʊ klam/ *noun phr.* **E20.**
[*Pismo* Beach, California.]
A large thick-shelled edible clam, *Tivela stultorum* (family Veneridae), of the SW coast of the US.

pisolite /ˈpɪzəlʌɪt, ˈpʌɪsə-/ *noun.* **E18.**
[mod. Latin *pisolithus*, from Greek *pisos* pea: see **-LITE.** Cf. next.]
GEOLOGY. **1** = **PISOLITH.** Also, a small rounded accretion of volcanic ash. **E18.**
2 A sedimentary rock, esp. a limestone, consisting chiefly of pisoliths; peastone. **E19.**
■ **pisoˈlitic** *adjective* of, consisting of, or resembling pisolite or pisolites **M19.**

pisolith /ˈpɪzəlɪθ, ˈpʌɪsə-/ *noun.* **L18.**
[formed as prec.: see **-LITH.**]
GEOLOGY. Each of the small rounded accretions resembling peas which are cemented together to make up a pisolitic rock, similar to but larger than ooliths. Cf. prec.
■ **pisoˈlithic** *adjective* **M19.**

piss /pɪs/ *noun.* Now *coarse slang.* **ME.**
[from the verb.]
Urine; *transf.* unpalatable drink. Also, the action or an act of urinating.

📖 JOYCE Horse piss and rotted straw . . . It is a good odour to breathe. A. FUGARD Just hang on for a second I want to have a piss. E. LEONARD In the mountains . . take a piss in a stream. **on the piss** engaged in a bout of heavy drinking. **piss and vinegar** energy, aggression. **piss and wind** empty talk, bombast. **take the piss (out of)** make fun (of), mock, deride.

Comb.: With certain adjectives in sense 'very, extremely, excessively', as ***piss-elegant***, ***piss-poor***. Special combs., as **piss artist** a glib unreliable person; a person who fools about; a drunkard; **piss-cutter** *N. Amer.* someone or something excellent, a clever or crafty person; **pisshead** a drunkard; **piss-hole** (*a*) a hole made by urine; (*b*) an unpleasant place; **piss-house** a privy, a lavatory; **piss-pot** a chamber-pot; **piss-proud** *adjective* having an erection attributed to a full bladder, esp. upon awakening; **piss-take** a parody; **piss-taker** a person who mocks; **piss-taking** mockery; **piss-up** (*a*) = **COCK-UP** 2; (*b*) a session of heavy drinking.
¶ Often considered taboo, and seldom recorded in 18th and 19th cents.

piss /pɪs/ *verb.* Now *slang.* **ME.**
[Old & mod. French *pisser* from Proto-Romance, of imit. origin.]
1 *verb intrans.* Discharge urine, urinate. **ME.**
2 *verb trans.* Discharge as or with urine. **ME.**
3 *verb trans.* Urinate on or in, wet with urine; put *out* or extinguish (fire) by urination. **LME.** ▶**b** *refl.* Wet one's clothing with urine; be very frightened, amused, or excited. **M20.**

📖 **1** M. HERR Some troops were pissing on the ground. **piss in a person's pocket** *Austral.* ingratiate oneself or be on very familiar terms with a person. **piss in the wind** act ineffectually, waste one's time. †**pissing-while** a very short time. **2** H. ROTH Does he piss water as mortals do, or only the purest of vegetable oil?

With adverbs in specialized senses: **piss about**, **piss around** fool or mess about; potter about. **piss away** squander, waste, (money etc.). **piss down** rain heavily, pour (*with* rain). **piss off** (*a*) *verb phr. trans.* annoy, irritate, make depressed; (*b*) *verb phr. intrans.* go away, make off, (freq. in *imper.*). **piss on** *fig.* defeat heavily, surpass easily, humiliate. **piss up** spoil, ruin, mess up.
¶ Often considered taboo, and seldom recorded in 18th and 19th cents.: cf. **PEE** *verb.*

pissabed /ˈpɪsəbɛd/ *noun.* **L16.**
[from **PISS** *verb* + **ABED**, after French *pissenlit.*]
1 The dandelion (so called from its diuretic property). Chiefly *dial.* **L16.**
2 A bedwetter. *slang.* **M17.**

pissaladière /pisaladjɛːr/ *noun.* Also **-iera** /-jera/. **M20.**
[French from Provençal *pissaladiero*, from *pissala* salt fish.]
A Provençal open tart similar to pizza, usu. with onions, anchovies, and black olives.

pissant /ˈpɪsant/ *noun, verb, & adjective.* **M17.**
[from **PISS** *noun* + **ANT.** Cf. **PISMIRE.**]
▶ **A** *noun.* An ant; *fig.* an insignificant or contemptible person or thing. Chiefly *dial. & US.* **M17.**
▶ **B** *verb intrans.* Mess *around.* *Austral. slang.* **M20.**
▶ **C** *attrib.* or as *adjective.* Insignificant, worthless, contemptible. *US slang.* **L20.**

pissasphalt /ˈpɪsasfalt/ *noun.* **E17.**
[Latin *pissasphaltus* from Greek *pissasphaltos*, from *pissa* pitch + *asphaltos* **ASPHALT.**]
Hist. A semi-liquid bituminous substance mentioned by ancient writers. Cf. **MUMMY** *noun*¹ 4.

pissed /pɪst/ *adjective.* *slang.* **E20.**
[from **PISS** *noun, verb*: see **-ED**², **-ED**¹.]
1 Drunk, intoxicated. Also foll. by *up.* **E20.**
2 Angry, irritated, annoyed; fed up, depressed. Exc. N. Amer. usu. foll. by *off.* **M20.**

📖 **1** R. MASON I'm pissed as a newt. D. BOGARDE Rooke . . took his glass. 'I think . . I'd better get pissed'. **2** A. LURIE She was pissed at being turned out of Her Own Living-Room. L. R. BANKS He was pissed off but I didn't know why, if it was something I'd done or just a mood.

pisser /ˈpɪsə/ *noun.* Now *slang.* **LME.**
[from **PISS** *verb* + **-ER**¹.]
1 A person who urinates. **LME.**
2 The penis; the female genitals. **E20.**
3 An extraordinary person or thing; a difficult or distasteful event, an annoying or disappointing thing; an unpleasant person; (in weakened sense) a fellow, a chap. Orig. *US.* **M20.**
4 A lavatory. *N. Amer.* **M20.**
2 pull a person's pisser = ***pull a person's leg*** s.v. **LEG** *noun.*

pissing /ˈpɪsɪŋ/ *adjective & adverb.* *slang.* **M20.**
[from **PISS** *verb* + **-ING**².]
▶ **A** *adjective.* Paltry, insignificant; brief. **M20.**
▶ **B** *adverb.* Exceedingly, very, abominably. **L20.**

📖 P. WAY 'Pissing awful weather', said Don.

■ **pissingly** *adverb* **L20.**

pissoir /piswaːr/ (*pl. same*); piːˈswɑː, ˈpɪswɑː/ *noun.* **E20.**
[French.]
A public urinal, esp. in France.

pissy /ˈpɪsi/ *adjective.* *slang.* **E20.**
[from **PISS** *noun* + **-Y**¹.]
Of, pertaining to, or redolent of urine; *fig.* rubbishy, inferior; disagreeable.

pistachio /pɪˈstɑːʃɪəʊ, pɪˈstatʃəʊ/ *noun & adjective.* Also (earlier) †**-ace**; (now *rare*) **-ache.** **LME.**
[Old French *pistace* (mod. *pistache*), superseded by forms from Italian *pistacchio*, both from Latin *pistacium* from Greek *pistakion*, *pistakē*: cf. Persian *pista*. Cf. **FISTIC** *noun.*]
▶ **A** *noun.* Pl. **-os.**
1 The tree *Pistacia vera* (family Anacardiaceae), a native of western Asia much cultivated in southern Europe. Also ***pistachio tree.*** **LME.**
2 The fruit of *Pistacia vera*, a nutlike drupe; its edible greenish kernel. Also ***pistachio nut.*** **LME.**
3 A green colour resembling that of the kernel of the pistachio nut. Also ***pistachio green.*** **L18.**
▶ **B** *attrib.* or as *adjective.* Of the colour or flavour of the kernels of the pistachio nut; containing pistachios. **E18.**

pistacia /pɪˈsteɪʃə/ *noun.* **LME.**
[Late Latin from Greek *pistakē*: see prec.]
The pistachio tree, *Pistacia vera.* Also, any other tree of the genus *Pistacia*, including the mastic tree, *P. lentiscus*, and the turpentine tree, *P. terebinthus.*

pistacite /ˈpɪstəsʌɪt/ *noun.* **E19.**
[German *Pistazit*, formed as prec. + **-ITE**¹.]
MINERALOGY. Epidote, esp. in a green ferric variety.

pistareen /pɪstəˈriːn/ *noun.* **L18.**
[App. alt. of **PESETA.**]
Hist. A small Spanish silver coin formerly used in Central and southern North America and the W. Indies.

piste /piːst/ *noun.* **E18.**
[French = track from Latin *pista* (sc. *via*) beaten track from fem. pa. pple of *pinsere* pound, stamp.]
1 A trail or track beaten by a horse or other animal; the track of a racecourse or training ground. **E18.**
2 The specially marked-out rectangular playing area in fencing. **E20.**
3 A specially prepared or marked slope or trail of compacted snow used as a ski-run. **E20.**
Comb.: **piste-basher** *colloq.* (*a*) a machine which compacts and levels the snow on ski runs; (*b*) a person who enjoys skiing on pistes.
■ **pisteur** /piːˈstəː/ *noun* a person employed to prepare the snow on a skiing piste **M20.**

pistia /ˈpɪstɪə/ *noun.* **M18.**
[mod. Latin (see below), from Greek *pistos* drinkable, liquid (perh. alluding to its deriving its nutriment from water).]
A floating water-plant, *Pistia stratiotes* (family Araceae), allied to the duckweeds, which covers the surface of ponds and reservoirs in warm countries. Also called ***water lettuce.***

pistic /ˈpɪstɪk/ *adjective & noun.* **M17.**
[Late Latin *pisticus* (Vulgate) from Greek *pistikos*, of disputed origin and meaning: see **-IC.**]
▶ **A** *adjective.* **1** ***nard pistic***, ***pistic nard***, (in biblical translations and allusions) = **SPIKENARD** 1. **M17.**
2 Pertaining to faith or trust rather than to reason. *rare.* **E20.**
▶ **B** *noun.* A person who accepts things simply on trust. *rare.* **M20.**

pistil /ˈpɪstɪl/ *noun.* Also (earlier) in Latin form **pistillum** /pɪsˈtɪləm/, pl. **-lla** /-lə/. **E18.**
[French *pistile* or Latin *pistillum* **PESTLE** *noun.*]
BOTANY. The unit of the gynoecium, equivalent to either a single carpel (more fully ***simple pistil***), where the carpels are free, or to the whole gynoecium (more fully ***compound pistil***), where the carpels are fused.
■ **pistillary** *adjective* of, pertaining to, or of the nature of a pistil **M19.** **pistillate** *adjective* (of a flower) having one or more carpels but no stamens (opp. ***staminate***) **E19.** **pistiˈlliferous** *adjective* = **PISTILLATE** **L18.** **pistilline** *adjective* (*a*) = **PISTILLATE**; (*b*) = **PISTILLARY**: **M19.** **pistillode** *noun* a rudimentary pistil **E20.** **pistillody** *noun* metamorphosis of floral organs into pistils **M19.** **pistilloid** *adjective* resembling a pistil **L19.**

†**pistle** *noun.* **OE.**
[Aphet. from (the same root as) **EPISTLE** *noun.*]
1 = **EPISTLE** *noun* 1. **OE–L18.**
2 = **EPISTLE** *noun* 2. **OE–L16.**
3 A (spoken) story or discourse. **LME–M16.**

pistol /ˈpɪst(ə)l/ *noun & verb.* **M16.**
[French †*pistole* from German *Pistole* from Czech *pišťala.*]
▶ **A** *noun.* **1** A small firearm to be held in one hand; a similar small handgun discharged without an explosive, as one using compressed air. **M16.**
2 *transf.* A person armed with or skilled in the use of a pistol, a pistoleer. **L16.**
3 a A swaggering or peculiar person; a fellow, a chap. Chiefly *derog. dial.* **M19.** ▶**b** A remarkable person, *esp.* a reliable person of strong character, a stalwart. *US slang.* **L20.**

📖 **1** J. THURBER The murders had been done with an automatic pistol, not a revolver. ***air pistol***, ***duelling pistol***, ***machine pistol***, ***starting pistol***, ***muff pistol***, ***water-pistol***, etc. **beat the pistol** = ***jump the gun*** s.v. **GUN** *noun.* ***put a pistol to one's head***, ***put a pistol to someone's head***: see **HEAD** *noun.* ***smoking pistol***: see **SMOKING** *ppl adjective.* **with a pistol at one's head** under pressure, while being threatened.

Comb.: **pistol-grip** a handle or grip shaped like the butt of a pistol, *spec.* on the underside of a gun-stock; **pistol-hand** (*a*) the hand in which a pistol is held; (*b*) = ***pistol-grip*** above; **pistol-packer** *colloq.* a person armed with a pistol; **pistol-packing** *adjective* (*colloq.*) carrying or armed with a pistol; **pistol-shot** (*a*) a shot fired from a pistol; (*b*) the range of a pistol; (*c*) a person who shoots (*well, badly*, etc.) with a pistol; **pistol shrimp** = ***snapping*** *shrimp* s.v. SNAPPING *ppl adjective*; **pistol-whip** *verb trans.* (orig. *US*) strike or beat (a person) with the butt of a pistol; **pistol-whipping** a beating with the butt of a pistol.

▶**B** *verb trans.* Infl. **-ll-**, ***-l-**. Shoot (esp. a person) with a pistol. **L16.**

■ †**pistolade** *noun & verb* (*a*) *noun* (a wound inflicted by) a pistol shot; (*b*) *verb trans.* attack or fire on with pistols: **L16–E19.**

pistole /pɪˈstəʊl/ *noun.* **L16.**

[French, shortening of PISTOLET *noun*².]

Hist. Any of various gold coins of the 17th and 18th cents.; *spec.* (*a*) a Spanish two-escudo piece; (*b*) = LOUIS *noun*¹; (*c*) a Scottish £12 (= £1 English) piece of William III.

pistoleer /pɪstəˈlɪə/ *noun.* **M19.**

[from PISTOL *noun* + -EER.]

A person (skilled in) using a pistol; a soldier armed with a pistol.

■ Also †**pistolier** *noun* **L16–E17.**

pistolero /pistoˈlero, pɪstəˈlɛːrəʊ/ *noun.* Pl. **-os** /-ɔs, -əʊz/. **M20.**

[Spanish.]

In Spain and Spanish-speaking countries: a gunman, a gangster.

pistolet /ˈpɪstəlɛt; *foreign* pistɔlɛ (*pl. same*)/ *noun*¹. **M16.**

[French = small dagger, pistol, from Italian *pistoletto* app. dim. of *pistolese* use as noun of adjective from *Pistoia* a town in Tuscany, western Italy, known for weapon-making: see -ET¹.]

†**1** = PISTOL *noun* 1. Latterly *Scot.* **M16–L19.**

2 Esp. in Belgium: a small bread roll (so called because of its shape). **M19.**

†**pistolet** *noun*². **M16–M17.**

[French, of unkn. origin.]

= PISTOLE.

pistolgraph /ˈpɪst(ə)lɡrɑːf/ *noun. obsolete* exc. *Hist.* **M19.**

[from PISTOL *noun* after *photograph*.]

A camera for taking instantaneous photographs. Also = PISTOLGRAM.

■ **pistolgram** *noun* an instantaneous photograph **M19.**

piston /ˈpɪst(ə)n/ *noun & verb.* **E18.**

[French from Italian *pistone* var. of *pestone* pestle, rammer, augm. from *pest-* in *pestello* from Latin *pistillum*: see PESTLE *noun*.]

▶**A** *noun.* **1** A mechanical device consisting of a disc attached to the end of a rod and fitting closely within a tube in which it can move back and forth, so that it can impart motion to a fluid (as in a pump) or derive motion from the expansion of a fluid (as in an internal-combustion engine). **E18.**

2 *MUSIC.* **a** A sliding valve in a brass instrument, used to alter the pitch of the note. **L19.** ▶**b** A button in an organ pushed in to combine a number of stops. Also ***thumb-piston***. **L19.**

Comb.: **piston corer**, **piston core sampler** an underwater core sampler consisting of a weighted cylinder containing a piston so arranged that as the cylinder sinks into the bottom sediments a partial vacuum arises inside, allowing the pressure of water to force it further in; **piston drill** a percussion drill in which the bit is attached to the rod of a piston; **piston engine** an engine, esp. in an aircraft, in which motion is derived from a piston (rather than a turbine); a reciprocating engine; **piston-engined** *adjective* powered by a piston engine; **piston-head** the disc forming the end of a piston; **pistonphone** *ACOUSTICS* a device for producing precise known sound pressures with a vibrating piston, used mainly for calibrating microphones; **piston pin** a pin securing a piston to its connecting rod in an internal-combustion engine; **piston ring** a ring on a piston sealing the gap between the piston and the cylinder wall; **piston-rod** the rod forming part of a piston; **piston slap** (the sound of) the rocking of a loosely fitting piston against the cylinder wall; **piston-valve** (*a*) a valve in a piston, as in that of a pump; (*b*) a valve formed by a small piston, as in the cylinder of a steam engine.

▶**B** *verb intrans.* Move like a piston. **M20.**

pistou /pistu, ˈpiːstuː/ *noun.* **M20.**

[Provençal, = Italian PESTO.]

A sauce or paste made from crushed basil, garlic, cheese, etc., used esp. in Provençal dishes; a thick vegetable soup made with this. Cf. PESTO.

pit /pɪt/ *noun*¹.

[Old English *pytt* (whence Old Norse *pyttr*) = Old Frisian *pelt*, Old Saxon *putti* (Middle Dutch *pulte*, Dutch *put*), Old High German *pfuzzi* (German *Pfütze* pool, puddle), from West Germanic.]

▶**I 1** A usu. large or deep hole or cavity in the ground, made by digging or natural occurring or produced. **OE.**

2 A hole or excavation made in digging for a mineral deposit or for use in a particular (esp. industrial) process (freq. with specifying word); *spec.* a coal-pit, (the shaft of) a coalmine. **OE.**

3 A hole dug or sunk in the ground for water; a well, a water-hole; a pond, a pool. Long *obsolete* exc. as passing into sense 1. **OE.**

4 A hole dug in the ground for a dead body; a grave. Now chiefly *arch. & dial.* **ME.**

5 A covered or concealed excavation serving as a trap for a wild animal or (esp. in biblical allusions) for an enemy; a pitfall. Freq. *fig.* **ME.**

6 A deep hole for the confinement of prisoners, a dungeon. *obsolete* exc. *Hist.* **ME.**

7 The abode of evil spirits and lost souls; hell. Freq. in ***the pit of hell***. **ME.**

8 A hole or excavation made for the storage and protection of roots, vegetables, etc. Also, a sunken area (usu. covered with a glazed frame) where young or tender plants are grown without artificial heat. **L15.**

9 A sunken area in a workshop floor giving access to the underside of a motor vehicle. Also, an area at the side of a motor-racing track where racing-cars are serviced and refuelled, esp. during a race (freq. in *pl.*). **M19.**

1 AV *Jer.* 2:6 A land of deserts and of pittes. J. REED We looked down into two massive pits, ten or fifteen feet deep. *fig.*: C. ANGIER Jean was in a deep pit of depression. **2** DISRAELI He had never been down a pit in all his life. ***chalk-pit***, ***coal-pit***, ***gravel-pit***, etc. ***saw-pit***, ***tan-pit***, etc. **3** AV *Lev.* 11:36 A fountaine or pit, wherein there is plenty of water, shalbe cleane. **4** SHAKES. *Rich. II* And soon lie Richard in an earthy pit. *Spectator* The bodies were thrown into an unmarked pit below the gallows. **5** AV *Ps.* 57:6 They haue digged a pit before me, into the midst whereof they are fallen themselves. *Beano* Dig a pit and animals will fall into it! **6** SIR W. SCOTT Look for the key of our pit, or principal dungeon. **7** BUNYAN The Hobgoblins, Satyrs, and Dragons of the Pit. B. STOKER They are devils of the Pit! **9** M. GILBERT He climbed out of the pit . . and said . . 'You've come to buy a car.' *Kart & Superkart* Terry's motor began to misfire . . and he pulled into the pits.

▶**II 10** A natural hollow or indentation in an animal or plant body or in any surface. **ME.** ▶**b** An armpit. *slang.* **M20.**

11 A small indentation left on the skin after smallpox, acne, etc.; a similar minute depression or spot on a surface resembling this. **L17.**

12 A pocket in a garment. *slang.* **E19.**

13 *BOTANY.* A cavity or discontinuity in a secondary cell wall where the primary wall is not covered by the secondary wall. **M19.**

14 A bed, a bunk. *slang* (orig. *MILITARY*). **M20.**

10 H. MCMURTRIE A little round indentation or pit behind each nostril. **b** *Rolling Stone* Simmons answers by spraying his pits with a can of Royal Copenhagen. **11** *London Gazette* A short thick man . . some few pits of the Small Pox. T. HOOPER The surface of the royal jelly will be covered in tiny pits.

▶**III 15** An enclosure in which an animal (esp. a cock or a dog) may be set to fight against another for sport; *esp.* = COCKPIT 1. Also, a sunken enclosure in which animals of a particular kind are kept (freq. with specifying word). **M16.**

16 That part of the auditorium of a theatre on the floor of the house, esp. the part behind the stalls; the people occupying this area (cf. COCKPIT 3). **M17.** ▶**b** = ***orchestra pit*** s.v. ORCHESTRA 3. **M20.**

17 A part of the floor of an exchange allotted to special trading. (Freq. with specifying word.) *N. Amer.* **E20.**

15 ***bear-pit***, ***cock-pit***, ***lion-pit***, ***snake-pit***, etc. **16** W. S. MAUGHAM Declaiming the blank verse of Sheridan Knowles with an emphasis to rouse the pit to frenzy. N. STREATFEILD In the pit, Cook and Clare enjoyed themselves enormously. **17** ***grain-pit***, ***wheat-pit***, etc.

Phrases: **bordered pit** *BOTANY*: in which the pit cavity is overarched by an extension of the secondary cell wall. **pit and gallows**, **gallows and pit** *SCOTS LAW* (*obsolete* exc. *Hist.*) the privilege, formerly conferred on barons, of executing male thieves or other felons by hanging on a gallows and female thieves or other felons by drowning in a pond or pool. **pit of the stomach** (*a*) the bottom or floor of the stomach; (*b*) the depression below the bottom of the breastbone. ***the BOTTOMLESS pit***. **the pits** (*slang*, orig. *US*) the worst or most despicable example of something; *esp.* a particularly obnoxious or contemptible person.

Comb.: **pit aperture** *BOTANY* an opening on the inner surface of a secondary cell wall, forming the entrance to a pit cavity; **pit-bank** the raised ground or platforms at the surface of a coalmine on which the coals are sorted and screened; **pit-bing** (chiefly *Scot.*) a heap of waste from a pit or mine; **pit boss** *US slang* an employee in a casino in charge of gaming-tables; **pit-bottom** the bottom of a pit; *spec.* the bottom of the shaft in a coalmine or the adjacent part of the mine; **pit-bottomer** a collier employed at the pit-bottom; **pit-brow** the edge of a pit; *spec.* = ***pit-bank*** above; **pit bull terrier** (a dog of) an American variety of bull terrier, usu. fawn or brindled with white markings; **pit canal** *BOTANY* a channel in the secondary cell wall of a bordered pit, leading to the pit cavity; **pit cavity** *BOTANY* the space within a simple pit, extending from the primary cell wall to the aperture bordering the cell lumen; **pit-coal** (now *arch. rare*) coal obtained from a pit or mine; **pit-comb** *adjective* (*ARCHAEOLOGY*) designating pottery decorated with rows of indentations and patterns like the impression of a comb; **pit dog** = ***pit bull terrier*** above; **pit-head** the top of a pit or shaft in a coalmine; the area immediately surrounding this; **pit-headman** a workman employed at a pit-head; **pit-heap** a heap of excavated material near the mouth of a pit or shaft in a coalmine; the whole of the surface works of a coalmine; **pit-hole** a hole forming a pit; *spec.* a grave; **pit-lamp** *noun* (chiefly *Canad.*) a miner's lamp; *transf.* a lamp used in hunting or fishing at night, = ***jack-light*** s.v. JACK *noun*¹; **pit-lamp** *verb trans. & intrans.* (*Canad.*) hunt (deer etc.) using a pit-lamp; **pit membrane** *BOTANY* the part of a primary cell wall dividing the two pits of a pit pair; **pit-mirk** *adjective* (*Scot. & north.*) as dark as a pit, pitch-dark; **pit organ** a sensory receptor sensitive to changes in temperature, present in a small depression in front of each eye of a pit viper; **pit pair** *BOTANY* a pair of pits in adjacent cell walls, sharing the same pit membrane; **pit-planting** a method of planting trees in which a hole is dug, and the roots settled over a mound of earth in the bottom of the hole before it is refilled; the planting of trees in small depressions in order to conserve moisture; **pit pony** *Hist.* a pony kept underground for haulage in a coalmine; **pit-prop** a baulk of wood used to support the roof of a mine; **pit-saw** *noun & verb* (*a*) *noun* a large saw for cutting timber, working in a saw-pit, with handles at the top and bottom; (*b*) *verb trans. & intrans.* cut (timber) with a pit-saw; **pit-sawn** *adjective* (of timber) cut with a pit-saw; **pit-sawyer** the person standing in a saw-pit and working the lower handle of a pit-saw (opp. ***top-sawyer***); **pit silage** silage made in a pit silo; **pit silo** a silo in the form of a pit instead of a tower; **pit stop** in motor racing, a stop at a pit for servicing and refuelling, esp. during a race; **pit tip** a mass of waste material deposited near the mouth of a pit or coalmine; ***pit viper***: see VIPER 1b; **pit-wood** timber used for frames, props, etc., in a coalmine.

■ **pitless** *adjective* (*rare*) **L19.**

pit /pɪt/ *noun*². Chiefly *N. Amer.* & *S. Afr.* **M19.**

[App. from Dutch *pit*, Middle Dutch *pitte* (fem.), Middle Low German, Low German, West Frisian, East Frisian *pit* pith, kernel, pip, ult. rel. to PITH *noun*.]

The stone of a fruit. Also, a pip.

J. MAY Bryan ate a cherry, putting the large pit neatly into an empty dish.

pit /pɪt/ *verb*¹. Infl. **-tt-**. **LME.**

[from PIT *noun*¹.]

▶**I 1** *verb trans.* Put or throw into a pit, esp. for storage. **LME.**

2 *verb trans.* Set (an animal, esp. a cock or a dog) to fight against another animal for sport, orig. in a pit or enclosure. **M18.**

3 *verb trans. fig.* Set (people or things) in opposition or rivalry (freq. foll. by *against*); match (one's skill, strength, etc.) *against* an opponent (freq. in ***pit one's wits against***). **M18.**

1 T. GRANGER They . . were pitted like beasts, tumbled into the graue. S. G. OSBORNE He dug and pitted the potatoes. **2** C. KNIGHT The collier pitted his cock against that of the sporting farmer. **3** R. P. GRAVES He pitted himself against the scholars. *Tennis* The draw pits Becker vs. McEnroe in the first match.

▶**II 4** Make a pit or pits in or on; *esp.* mark or disfigure with pock-marks. Usu. in *pass.* **L15.** ▶**b** *verb intrans.* Produce small hollows or pits in a surface. *rare.* **E18.** ▶**c** *verb trans.* Provide with pits or holes; dig pits in. **M19.**

5 *verb intrans.* Sink in or contract so as to form a pit or hollow; become marked with pits or small depressions. **M18.**

6 *verb intrans.* Of a racing-driver: make a pit stop. **M20.**

4 J. CARY A long tobacco-coloured face, deeply pitted by smallpox. A. CARTER The walls . . were pitted with bullet holes. **6** *Autocar* Mike Spence . . pitted . . with sudden engine trouble.

pit /pɪt/ *verb*² *trans.* Orig. *US.* Infl. **-tt-**. **E20.**

[from PIT *noun*².]

Remove the pit or stone from (fruit); = STONE *verb* 5.

pita /ˈpiːtə/ *noun*¹. Also **pito** /ˈpiːtəʊ/. **L17.**

[Amer. Spanish from Taino.]

A tough fibre obtained from any of several tropical American plants, esp. the bromeliad *Aechmea magdalenae*, used for cordage etc. Also, any of the plants yielding this fibre.

pita *noun*² var. of PITTA *noun*².

pitahaya /pɪtəˈhʌɪə/ *noun.* **L18.**

[Spanish, prob. from Taino.]

Any of several tall cacti of Mexico and the south-western US with edible fruit, esp. *Carnegiea gigantea*.

pit-a-pat /ˈpɪtəpat/ *adverb, noun, verb, & adjective.* Also **pit-pat** /ˈpɪtpat/. **E16.**

[Imit. Cf. PITTER-PATTER.]

▶**A** *adverb.* With a series of quick light alternating or reiterated sounds; palpitatingly; patteringly. Freq. in ***go pit-a-pat***. **E16.**

▶**B** *noun.* A series of quick light alternating or reiterated sounds; the action producing this; palpitation, pattering. **L16.**

▶**C** *verb intrans.* Infl. **-tt-**. Go pit-a-pat, palpitate, patter. **E17.**

▶**D** *adjective.* Of the nature of, or characterized by, such a series of sounds; palpitating; pattering. **M17.**

pitarah /pɪˈtɑːrə/ *noun.* **E19.**

[Hindi *pitārā*, *peṭārā*.]

In the Indian subcontinent, a basket or box used to carry clothes when travelling by palanquin.

Pitcairner /ˈpɪtkɛːnə/ *noun.* **M19.**

[from *Pitcairn* (see below) + -ER¹.]

A native or inhabitant of the Pitcairn Islands in the central S. Pacific, *spec.* of Pitcairn Island, the chief of the group, settled with a mixed European and Polynesian population by mutineers from HMS *Bounty* in 1790.

Pitcairnese /pɪtkɛːˈniːz/ *noun & adjective*. **M20.**
[formed as prec. + -ESE.]
▶ **A** *noun*. The language of Pitcairn Island, a mixture of English and Polynesian (mainly Tahitian) elements. **M20.**
▶ **B** *attrib*. or as *adjective*. Of or pertaining to the people of Pitcairn Island or the Pitcairn Islands or their language. **M20.**

pitch /pɪtʃ/ *noun*¹.
[Old English *pić* corresp. to Old Saxon *pik* (Dutch *pek*), Old High German *peh* (German *Pech*), Old Norse *bik*, from Germanic, from Latin *pic-*, *pix*.]
1 A black or dark brown tenacious resinous substance, hard when cold, semi-liquid when hot, obtained as a residue from the distillation of wood tar or turpentine and used for caulking the seams of ships, to protect wood from moisture, etc. **OE.**
2 Any of various similar dark viscous substances of mineral origin; asphalt, bitumen. **LME.**
3 a The resin or crude turpentine which exudes from pine and fir trees. **LME.** ▶†**b** = ***pitch tree*** below. Only in **L17.**
2 ***glance pitch***, ***mineral pitch***, etc. **3a** ***Burgundy pitch***: see BURGUNDY *noun*.
Comb.: **pitch-black** *adjective* of the brownish-black colour of pitch; intensely black; **pitch-brand** a mark of ownership made with pitch on a sheep etc.; *fig.* a mark or characteristic of infamy, a stigma; **pitch-cap** *noun & verb* (chiefly *Hist.*) (*a*) *noun* a cap lined with hot pitch, *esp.* one used as an instrument of torture by the soldiery during the Irish rebellion of 1798; (*b*) *verb trans.* torture (a person) with a pitch-cap; **pitch-dark** *adjective* as dark as pitch, intensely or completely dark; **pitch-darkness** the state of being pitch-dark; **pitch-fibre** a black waterproof material consisting of compressed cellulose or asbestos fibre impregnated with pitch and used for making pipes; **pitch-kettle** a large vessel for boiling or heating pitch, esp. for use on board ship; †**pitch-kettled** *adjective* (*slang*) utterly puzzled, nonplussed; **pitch-knot** a knot of a pine or other tree burned as a light; **pitch-mark** = ***pitch-brand*** above; **pitch-oil** *W. Indies* a kind of fuel, esp. for domestic use; **pitch-opal** an inferior variety of common opal with a resinous lustre; **pitch-ore** (*a*) a dark brown ore of copper, containing chrysocolla and limonite; also called ***pitchy copper ore***; (*b*) = PITCHBLENDE; **pitch pine** (the timber of) any of several pine trees with notably resinous wood, esp. *Pinus rigida* and *Pinus palustris* of N. America; **pitch-plaster** *Hist.* a curative or stimulant plaster made with pitch; **pitch tree** any of various coniferous trees containing much resin; *esp.* the Norway spruce, *Picea abies*.
■ **pitchlike** *adjective* resembling (that of) pitch, dark and viscous **L17.**

pitch /pɪtʃ/ *noun*². **L15.**
[from PITCH *verb*².]
▶ **I** †**1** An act of setting down or paying monies owed; a payment. Also, an act of pitching on or selecting something. *rare*. **L15–L18.**
2 An act of plunging head foremost; *NAUTICAL* the forward plunge of a ship's head in a longitudinal direction. **M18.** ▶**b** The action or an act of pitching (on the part of an aircraft or spacecraft about a lateral axis); the extent of such motion. **E20.**
3 a = ***pitch-farthing*** s.v. PITCH *verb*². Now *dial. rare*. **M18.** ▶**b** A card-game derived from all fours. **E20.**
4 The action or an act of pitching or throwing something; *spec.* (*a*) *CRICKET* the manner of delivery of the ball in bowling, esp. so as to strike the ground at a specified point or from a specified direction (freq. in ***pitch of the ball***); the spot at which the ball bounces; (*b*) *BASEBALL* the action or an act of pitching the ball to a batter; a player's right or turn to do this; (*c*) *GOLF* the action of hitting a lofted approach-shot with the ball running only a short distance on striking the ground; (more fully ***pitch shot***) an instance of this. **M19.**
5 a A talk, a chat. *arch. slang*. **L19.** ▶**b** Behaviour or speech intended to influence or persuade, esp. for the purpose of sales or advertising; an instance of this, a line (freq. in ***sales pitch***). *colloq.* **L19.**

> 🕮 **2** G. MACDONALD Every roll and pitch of the vessel. **b** *Scientific American* Shifting his weight to control the craft in pitch, roll and yaw. **angle of pitch** the angle between the direction of the wind relative to an aircraft and the plane containing its horizontal axes. **4** A. G. STEEL The high-dropping full-pitch is an excellent ball. E. BAKER It was the fastest pitch Chester had ever thrown. *Times* As a golfer . . she can . . play delightful little pitches. **5a** R. BOLDREWOOD Starlight and Jim were having a pitch about the best way to get aboard. **b** *Observer* Actor Charlton Heston makes a recorded pitch for cable television.

▶ **II 6** A net set for catching fish. Now *rare* or *obsolete*. **E16.**
7 †**a** = PITCHER *noun*² 3. Only in **L17.** ▶**b** = PITCHER *noun*² 4. *local*. **L17.**
8 A quantity of something pitched or thrown; *spec.* (*a*) the quantity of hay etc. thrown up by a pitchfork; (*b*) the quantity of a particular commodity placed for sale in a market or other similar place. **M19.**
9 = PITCHER *noun*² 5. *rare*. **L19.**
▶ **III 10** *gen.* The place or point at which something is pitched or placed. *rare*. **M16.**
†**11** *fig.* A position taken up and maintained; a fixed opinion or resolution. Only in **E17.**
12 a A place at which a person stations himself or herself or is stationed; a portion of ground selected by or allotted temporarily or permanently to a person, a camp-site; *esp.* a spot in a street or other public place where a street vendor sells wares or has a stall or at which a street performer, bookmaker, charity collector, etc., stations himself or herself. Also, the part of a market, stock exchange, etc., where particular commodities are bought and sold. Orig. *US*. **L17.** ▶**b** A place or spot in a river where an angler takes his or her stand. **M19.**
13 A particular portion of a field or of a mine allotted to an individual workman. *local*. **L18.**
14 a *CRICKET*. The place where the wickets are pitched; the area of ground between the creases. **L19.** ▶**b** The area of play in a field-game; the field, the ground. **E20.**

> 🕮 **12a** P. SCOTT A naked holy man occupying a pitch . . to the right of the main entrance. *Times* The insurance pitch had another busy, nervous day. B. GELDOF My pitch was Dean Street. **b** *Coarse Fishing* The angler is only as good as the pitch he is fishing. **14b** *Times* A goalless tie . . on a snow-covered slippery pitch.

▶ **IV 15** †**a** The highest or most extreme point, the top, the summit. **M16–M17.** ▶†**b** A projecting point of some part of the body. Also, the shoulders. **L16–E17.** ▶**c** The extreme point of a cape or headland, where it projects furthest into the sea. Chiefly *US*. **L17.**
16 a The height to which a falcon or other bird of prey soars before swooping down on its prey. Freq. in ***fly a pitch***. **L16.** ▶†**b** The height to which anything rises; altitude, elevation. **L16–L18.**
†**17** The height (of a person or animal), stature. **L16–E19.**
18 *fig.* The highest point or degree of something; the acme, the climax. Now *rare* exc. in ***at the pitch of one's voice***. **E17.**
19 The height of a roof (esp. an arched roof) or ceiling above the floor, or of the vertex of an arch above the springing line. **E17.**

> 🕮 **15** MILTON Down they fell Driv'n headlong from the Pitch of Heaven. **16** SHAKES. *2 Hen. VI* And bears his thoughts above his falcon's pitch. **b** J. TRAPP Blazing comets . . when they begin to decline from their pitch, they fall to the earth. **17** J. MOXON Makes the work fall too low for the pitch of the Workman. **18** W. BLACK When the general hilarity was at its pitch.

▶ **V 20 a** The comparative degree or intensity of a quality or attribute; point or position on an ideal scale; elevation, status, level. **M16.** ▶**b** *spec.* In copper-smelting, the degree of malleability of the metal. **M19.**
21 The quality of the sound of a musical instrument or voice which is governed by the rate of the vibrations producing it; the degree of highness or lowness of tone. Also, a particular standard of pitch for voices and instruments, as ***concert pitch*** etc. **L16.**

> 🕮 **20** J. VENEER They arrive at such a pitch, as they cannot think of without horror and astonishment. E. A. FREEMAN The family which . . has risen from obscurity to the highest pitch of greatness. **21** *Early Music* Performances on modern instruments at present-day pitch are lively. M. WARNER His natural pitch was baritone.

▶ **VI 22** The degree of inclination to the horizon; a sloping part or place; *spec.* (*a*) (chiefly *MOUNTAINEERING*) a downward inclination or slope; a steep place, a declivity; a descent, esp. a steep one; a section of a climb; (*b*) *MINING & GEOLOGY* the inclination of a vein of ore or seam of coal from the horizontal; a dip, a rise; (*c*) *ARCHITECTURE* the inclination of a sloping roof or of rafters to the horizontal; the steepness of slope of a roof; the proportion of the height of a roof to its span; (*d*) (the slope of) a flight of steps; (*e*) the setting or inclination of the cutting or biting part of a device, permitting penetration to a required depth. **M16.**
▶ **VII 23** Chiefly *MECHANICS*. The distance between successive corresponding points or lines; *spec.* (*a*) the distance between the centres of any two successive teeth of a cog-wheel or links of a gear-chain; (*b*) the distance between the successive convolutions of the thread of a screw; (*c*) a measure of the angle of the blades of a screw propeller, equal to the distance forward a blade would move in one revolution if it exerted no thrust on the medium. **E19.**
24 The density of typed or printed characters on a line, usu. expressed as the number of characters per inch. **M20.**
Phrases: ***absolute pitch***: see ABSOLUTE *adjective* 10. ***full pitch***: see FULL *adjective*. ***perfect pitch***: see PERFECT *adjective*. ***queer someone's pitch***: see QUEER *verb* 2. ***relative pitch***: see RELATIVE *adjective*. ***wild pitch***: see WILD *adjective, noun, & adverb*.
Comb.: **pitch accent** *PHONETICS* a stress placed on a word or syllable by its differing in pitch from its immediate surroundings; **pitch-accented** *adjective* having a pitch accent; **pitch-and-putt** a type of miniature golf course in which the green can be reached in one; the form of golf played on such a course; *fig.* an insignificant distance; **pitch-and-run** *GOLF* a chip shot with a short forward run; **pitch-and-toss** a game of combined skill and chance in which coins are pitched at a mark and then tossed; *Scot.* a manoeuvre in the game of knifey; **pitch axis** = ***PITCHING axis***; **pitch bend** *MUSIC* a facility in a synthesizer that enables the player to change the pitch of the note played by a small amount; **pitch-circle** a circular pitch-line; **pitch contour** *PHONETICS* the pattern of continuous variation in pitch; **pitch control** *AERONAUTICS* (equipment for) control of the pitch of an aircraft's propellers or (esp.) a helicopter's rotors; control of the pitching motion of an aircraft; **pitch curve** *PHONETICS* = ***pitch contour*** above; **pitch-hole** (*a*) a hole into which something pitches or is pitched; an opening in the wall of a barn etc. through which corn or hay is pitched; (*b*) *N. Amer.* a defect in a road or trail; a pothole; **pitch length** *GEOLOGY* the length of an ore shoot in the direction of greatest dimension; **pitch-line** an imaginary line, usually a circle, passing through the teeth of a cog wheel, pinion, rack, etc., so as to touch the corresponding line in another cog-wheel etc. when the two are geared together; **pitchman** *N. Amer.* a person selling gadgets or novelties at a fair or in the street; *transf. & fig.* an advertiser, a person delivering a sales pitch; **pitchmeter** (*a*) a device in an aeroplane for detecting or measuring pitching; (*b*) an instrument for measuring the pitch of sound; **pitch phoneme** *LINGUISTICS* each of a set of phonemes distinguished by different levels of pitch; **pitch-pipe** *MUSIC* a small pipe used to set the pitch for singing or tuning an instrument; ***pitch shot***: see sense 4 above. See also combs. s.v. PITCH *verb*².

pitch /pɪtʃ/ *verb*¹ *trans.* **OE.**
[from PITCH *noun*¹.]
1 Cover, coat, or smear with pitch; mark or brand (a sheep etc.) with pitch; soil or stain with pitch. **OE.**
2 *fig.* Make as dark as pitch; envelop in pitchy darkness. **M17.**

pitch /pɪtʃ/ *verb*². Pa. t. & pple **pitched**, (earlier, now *arch. rare*) **pight** /pʌɪt/. **ME.**
[Origin uncertain: perh. rel. to Old English *pićung* stigmata, ult. origin unkn. See also PICK *verb*².]
▶ **I** †**1** *verb trans.* Thrust or drive (a pointed instrument) firmly into the ground; drive into a solid body and make fast (a nail, stake, etc.); fix (an object) on a pole, spear, etc.; plant, implant; stick, fasten. **ME–L18.**
†**2** *verb trans.* Thrust a pointed instrument into or through (a solid body); stab, pierce, transfix. Only in **ME.**
3 *verb trans.* Fix and erect (a tent), establish (a camp), as a temporary place of abode, esp. *in* a specified place. **ME.** ▶**b** *verb intrans.* Encamp. **LME.**
4 *verb trans.* **a** Put (a thing) in a fixed or definite place or position; set, place, situate. Usu. in *pass.* **ME.** ▶**b** *spec.* Set *up* (a stone etc.) on end; set (a stone) on edge for paving. Now *rare* or *obsolete*. **E17.**
5 *verb trans.* †**a** Set about or stud with gems. Also *gen.*, fill, provide, (a thing) *with* things stuck or placed in or on it. **ME–M17.** ▶**b** Pave (a road, path, or street) with stones (orig. with pebbles or cobbles) set on end. Also, make a foundation for (a macadamized road) with larger stones placed on edge by hand. **M16.**
†**6** *verb trans. fig.* Set, fix (one's trust, purpose, attention, etc.) *in* or *on* an object or *in* a state. **LME–E19.**
7 †**a** *verb intrans.* ***pitch and pay***, pay down at once, pay ready money. **LME–E17.** ▶**b** *verb trans.* Place or lay out (wares) in a fixed place for sale, esp. in a market or other similar place. **M16.**
†**8** *verb trans.* Put together; construct by fastening the parts together. Usu. in *pass.* **LME–E17.**
9 *verb trans.* Place and make fast (a net or snare) with stakes, poles, or pegs. Long *arch. rare*. **M16.**
10 a *verb intrans.* Place or locate oneself; take up one's abode; settle, alight. **E17.** ▶**b** *verb refl. & intrans.* Seat oneself, sit down. Now *dial. & colloq.* **L18.**

> 🕮 **1** J. DYKE A stake, or a post is pitched in the ground. **3** SHAKES. *Rich. III* Here pitch our tent, even here on Bosworth field. H. BELLOC The army had marched ten miles, and there the second camp was pitched. **b** G. GROTE The succeeding troops . . pitched as they could without any order. **4a** W. BLACK The abrupt hill, on which the town of Bridgenorth is pitched. V. WOOLF The man . . had pitched the house in a hollow. **5a** H. HOLCROFT Pitching the top with multitude of stakes. **6** T. FULLER He pitched his thoughts on the holy war. BUNYAN She thought He pitched His innocent eyes just upon her. **10** E. F. BENSON It pitched among the cabbages, and had to be instantly recovered.

▶ **II 11** *verb intrans.* Fall headlong heavily, land on the head or strike forcibly against something as a result of being thrown. **ME.** ▶**b** *CRICKET*. Of a bowled ball: strike the ground at a specified length or travel in a specified direction. **E19.**
12 *verb trans. gen.* Cast, throw, or fling forward; hurl or throw (a thing) esp. underhand and aimed to land at a specified point. **LME.** ▶**b** *verb trans.* Throw (sheaves, hay, etc.) with a pitchfork, esp. on to a cart or stack. **LME.** ▶**c** *verb trans. & intrans.* In *CRICKET*, bowl and cause (a ball) to strike the ground at a specified length or to travel in a specified direction; in *BASEBALL* etc., deliver or throw (the ball) to the batter; in *GOLF*, play (a ball) with a pitch shot; in various games, throw (a flat object) towards a mark or so as to fall in or near a specified place. **M18.** ▶**d** *verb trans.* Utter, tell, esp. untruthfully or with exaggeration; praise extravagantly. *slang*. **M19.** ▶**e** *verb intrans.* Esp. of a man: make sexual advances to. Also foll. by (*up*) *to*. *slang* (chiefly *US*). **E20.** ▶**f** *verb intrans. COMMERCE*. Make a bid or offer for business, esp. for a client's account. Freq. foll. by *for*. **L20.** ▶**g** *verb trans.* Discard or throw away (an object) as

unwanted. *N. Amer. colloq.* L20. ▸**h** *verb trans.* Drive (a motor vehicle) at speed, esp. into a bend or round a racetrack. *colloq.* L20.

13 *verb intrans.* **a** Incline or slope forwards and downwards; dip; *N. Amer.* (of a roof or other structure) slope downwards; (esp. of a linear feature) have a pitch of a given angle and direction; drop *down* or descend abruptly to a lower level. E16. ▸**b** (Of a swelling) subside, (of loose soil) settle; *fig.* lose ground. Now *dial.* L18.

14 †**a** *verb trans.* Of a ship: plunge (its head) forwards in a longitudinal direction. Only in E17. ▸**b** *verb intrans.* Of a ship: plunge with its head forwards in a longitudinal direction, rise and fall alternately at bow and stern; progress with pitching. L17. ▸**c** *verb trans.* Of a ship: have (a mast or other part of the structure) cast *away*, *overboard*, etc., by a pitching movement. E18. ▸**d** *verb intrans.* Of a person, animal, or vehicle: progress or move *about* with a vigorous jogging motion, lurch. M19. ▸**e** *verb intrans.* Of an aircraft or spacecraft: rotate or rock about a lateral axis. L19. ▸**f** *verb trans.* Cause (an aircraft or spacecraft) to rotate or rock about a lateral axis. M20.

📖 **11** J. MORSE A large pine has been seen . . to pitch over endwise. G. JONES Ahab, a heavy man, had pitched into the yard off the roof of the stable. **b** N. CARDUS I was certain the ball had pitched off the wicket. *Times* Patel received the perfect ball . . which pitched on his middle stump. **12** SIR W. SCOTT As far as one might pitch a lance. B. MALAMUD Pitched balls of clay at each other. M. IGNATIEFF The sleigh overturned and pitched his . . baggage into a ravine. **c** *Times of India* The ball was pitched short. **d** *Saturday Evening Post* Louie . . pitches kitchen gadgets. **13a** A. K. LOBECK The convergence being in the direction toward which the anticline pitches. W. VAN T. CLARK The ravine pitches down to the creek. **14b** K. MANSFIELD The little steamer pressed on, pitching gently, over the grey . . water. R. DAHL The ship . . pitched and rolled in the most alarming manner. **d** H. B. STOWE The lumbering Newfoundland, who came pitching tumultuously toward them. B. ENGLAND Ansell ran blindly, . . pitching and staggering over the pitted earth.

▸**III 15** *verb trans.* Set in order for fighting, prepare (a battle or battlefield); draw up (troops) in array. *obsolete* exc. in ***pitched battle*** s.v. PITCHED *adjective*¹ 1. LME.

16 *verb trans.* †**a** Determine (a future event); fix, settle, arrange. M16–M17. ▸**b** In all fours and similar card-games: establish (a suit) as trumps by leading a card of that suit. L19.

†**17** *verb trans.* Establish (a fact); ascertain; come to a conclusion about. Only in 17.

18 *verb trans.* **a** Set at a particular rate or degree, esp. as adjusted to a specified level. Formerly also, set or fix *at* a price or rate. E17. ▸**b** Set at a particular musical pitch, determine the pitch of (a tune, the voice, an instrument); *fig.* express in a particular style or at a particular level. L17.

19 *verb trans.* Set (a competitor) *against* another in a contest or competition; pit. *rare.* E19.

📖 **16** T. KYD Between us theres a price already pitcht. **17** S. CHARNOCK Who can pitch a time and person that originated this notion? **18** R. S. BALL Our second assumption regarding the mass of the Earth was pitched too low. *Optima* The pitching of issue rates . . in the money market. **b** I. MCEWAN When she spoke her tone was . . pitched a little higher than before. **19** *Observer* The Schneider Trophy . . pitched sea planes against each other.

▸**IV 20** *verb trans. & intrans.* MECHANICS. Fit (*into*); interlock, engage, (*with*). Now *rare.* M17.

21 *verb trans.* BREWING. Add yeast to (wort) for the purpose of inducing fermentation. M19.

Phrases, & with adverbs & prepositions in specialized senses: **in there pitching** *N. Amer. colloq.* making a vigorous and continuous effort, actively taking part. ***pitch and pay***: see sense 7a above. **pitch for** COMMERCE forecast or estimate (a share price etc.); aim at (a particular result). **pitch in** *colloq.* set to work vigorously or determinedly; turn (aside) to a particular objective; begin; add one's contribution to a general effort. **pitch into** *colloq.* attack or assail forcibly with blows or with words; rebuke or criticize strongly. **pitch it strong** speak forcefully; state a case with feeling or enthusiasm, exaggerate. **pitch on** decide on; make choice of, choose; now *esp.* select more or less casually, let one's choice fall on. **pitch the wickets** CRICKET stick or fix the stumps in the ground and place the bails. **pitch the woo**, **pitch woo** (orig. & chiefly *US*) court, make love to.

Comb.: **pitch-farthing** = ***chuck-farthing*** s.v. CHUCK *verb*²; **pitch-in** *US colloq.* a communal meal to which each participant contributes food or drink; **pitch-out** *N. Amer.* (*a*) BASEBALL a pitch served by the pitcher intentionally beyond the reach of the batter; (*b*) AMER. FOOTBALL a lateral pass behind the scrimmage line between two backs; **pitch-penny** *US* a variety of pitch-and-toss; **pitchpole** *noun* (*a*) *dial.* a somersault; (*b*) AGRICULTURE a kind of harrow; **pitchpole** *verb trans. & intrans.* (*dial.*) (*a*) (cause to) somersault; (*b*) NAUTICAL cause to capsize head foremost; (*c*) WHALING throw (a harpoon); **pitch-up** a sudden uncontrolled upward pitch of an aircraft, esp. as experienced during a climb or descent; (a tendency towards) deviation of this nature. See also combs. s.v. PITCH *noun*².

pitchblende /ˈpɪtʃblɛnd/ *noun.* L18.
[German *Pechblende*, from *pech* PITCH *noun*¹ + BLENDE.]
MINERALOGY. Native uranium oxide, occurring as an amorphous or microcrystalline variety of uraninite in brown to black masses, and containing radium from the decay of uranium.

pitched /pɪtʃt/ *adjective*¹. LME.
[from PITCH *noun*², *verb*²: see -ED², -ED¹.]
1 That has been pitched. Chiefly in ***pitched battle*** below. LME.
2 a That has a pitch of a particular kind or magnitude. (Freq. with specifying word.). L16. ▸**b** Of a roof: sloping. E17.
1 pitched battle a battle planned beforehand and fought on chosen ground, as opp. to a casual skirmish. **2** ***high-pitched***, ***low-pitched***, etc.

pitched /pɪtʃt/ *adjective*². LME.
[from PITCH *noun*¹, *verb*¹: see -ED², -ED¹.]
Smeared, covered, saturated, or otherwise treated with pitch.

pitcher /ˈpɪtʃə/ *noun*¹. ME.
[Old French *pichier*, *pechier* pot (mod. *pichet*) from Frankish, rel. to BEAKER.]
1 A large usu. earthenware vessel with a handle and usu. a lip, for holding and pouring out liquids; a jug; a jug-shaped or vase-shaped vessel. ME.
2 BOTANY. The pitcher-like structure of a pitcher-plant (see below). M19.
3 In *pl.* Fragments of broken pottery crushed and reused in the manufacturing process. M20.

📖 **1** W. STYRON I circle the table with the china pitcher of foaming cider.

Comb.: †**pitcher-house** a room for the storage of wine and ale; **pitcher-plant** any of certain carnivorous plants bearing deep lidded pitcher-like structures with a liquid secretion at the bottom, in which insects are trapped and drowned; *esp.* (*a*) any plant of the N. American genus *Sarracenia* (family Sarraceniaceae), in which the pitchers take the form of modified leaves; (*b*) any plant of the chiefly SE Asian genus *Nepenthes* (family Nepenthaceae), in which the pitchers are at the end of the leaf tendrils.
■ **pitcherful** *noun* as much as a pitcher will hold; the contents of a pitcher: LME. **pitcher-like** *adjective* resembling a pitcher in shape or function M19.

pitcher /ˈpɪtʃə/ *noun*². E18.
[from PITCH *verb*² + -ER¹.]
▸**I 1** *gen.* A person who pitches something. E18.
2 The player in baseball who delivers the ball to the batter. M19.
▸**II 3** An iron bar for making holes in the ground, as for setting stakes or hop-poles. E18.
4 A cutting, rod, or stake planted in the ground in order to take root. Chiefly *local.* L18.
5 A stone used for paving, esp. one set on edge; a set. M19.
6 The flat stone or piece of wood pitched in hop-scotch, or at a mark or hole in various games. *Scot. & dial.* M19.

pitchfork /ˈpɪtʃfɔːk/ *noun*¹ & *verb.* ME.
[Alt. of PICKFORK, later infl. by PITCH *verb*².]
▸**A** *noun.* A long-handled fork with two sharp prongs, for lifting and pitching hay, straw, or sheaves. ME.
rain pitchforks rain very hard.
▸**B** *verb trans.* **1** Throw or cast (as) with a pitchfork; *fig.* thrust (a person) forcibly or unsuitably into a position or office (freq. as ***pitchforked*** *ppl adjective*). M19.
2 Stab or attack with a pitchfork. M19.

📖 **1** D. DELILLO I watch him pitchfork the spaghetti down his gullet. J. WAIN I was pitchforked into Oxford at seventeen.

pitchfork /ˈpɪtʃfɔːk/ *noun*². L19.
[from PITCH *noun*² + FORK *noun*, after *pitch-pipe*.]
A tuning-fork, used for setting the pitch of a tune or instrument.

pitchi /ˈpɪtʃi/ *noun. Austral.* L19.
[Aboriginal.]
A dish or container hollowed out of a solid log.

pitching /ˈpɪtʃɪŋ/ *noun.* LME.
[from PITCH *verb*² + -ING¹.]
1 The action of PITCH *verb*²; an instance of this. LME.
2 The result of pitching; pavement composed of paving-stones that have been pitched. L17.
Comb.: **pitching axis** AERONAUTICS a lateral axis of an aircraft or spacecraft about which pitching takes place, usu. specified to be perpendicular to its longitudinal axis or to its direction of flight; a pitch axis; **pitching moment** AERONAUTICS a moment tending to turn an aircraft or spacecraft about its pitching axis; **pitching-temperature** BREWING the temperature at which the wort is pitched; **pitching-yeast** BREWING yeast used or prepared for use in pitching wort.

pitchstone /ˈpɪtʃstəʊn/ *noun.* L18.
[from PITCH *noun*¹ + STONE *noun*.]
GEOLOGY. A dull vitreous rock resembling hardened pitch, formed by partial hydration of obsidian.

pitchy /ˈpɪtʃi/ *adjective.* E16.
[from PITCH *noun*¹ + -Y¹.]
1 Full of pitch, having much pitch; coated, smeared, soiled, or sticky with pitch. E16.
2 Of the consistency of pitch; viscid; bituminous. M16.
3 As dark as pitch; pitch-black; intensely dark; (of darkness) intense, thick; *fig.* morally black or defiling, grossly wicked. L16.
3 pitchy copper ore = ***pitch-ore*** (a) s.v. PITCH *noun*¹.
■ **pitchiness** *noun* L16.

piteous /ˈpɪtɪəs/ *adjective.* ME.
[Anglo-Norman *pitous*, Old French *pitos*, *piteus* from Proto-Romance, from Latin *pietas* PIETY, PITY *noun*: see -EOUS.]
1 Deserving of or arousing pity; lamentable, mournful. ME.
2 Full of pity; compassionate, merciful. *arch.* ME.
†**3** Full of piety; pious, godly, devout. LME–L16.
†**4** Paltry, mean. *rare* (Milton). Only in M17.

📖 **1** M. BINCHY 'What did I do this time?' Helen looked piteous.

¶ Cf. partly synonymous PITIABLE, PITIFUL.
■ **piteously** *adverb* ME. **piteousness** *noun* LME.

pitfall /ˈpɪtfɔːl/ *noun.* ME.
[App. from PIT *noun*¹ + FALL *noun*¹, now usu. taken as FALL *noun*² or *verb*.]
†**1** An ambush. Only in ME.
2 A concealed pit into which animals etc. may fall and be captured. Formerly also *spec.*, a trap for catching birds in which a trapdoor falls over a hollow. LME.
3 A cunning device designed to catch someone unawares. Now *rare.* L16.
4 A hidden or unsuspected danger, drawback, difficulty or opportunity for error. M18.

📖 **4** *Science News Letter* The road to conquest of poliomyelitis . . has been long and full of pitfalls. N. SEDAKA My life too has had . . its brief summits and sudden pitfalls.

■ **pitfalled** *adjective* full of pitfalls E19.

pith /pɪθ/ *noun.*
[Old English *piþa* corresp. to Middle Low German, Middle Dutch *pitte*, *pit*, from West Germanic, repr. only in the Low German group, of unkn. origin.]
1 The central column of spongy parenchymatous tissue in the stems and branches of dicotyledonous plants, the stems of rushes, etc.; the medulla. Also, a similar tissue occurring in other parts of plants, as that lining the rind in certain fruits (e.g. the orange). OE.
2 *fig.* The innermost or central part; the essential or vital part (*of*); the spirit, the essence. OE.
3 a Physical strength; vigour, toughness. ME. ▸**b** Force, vigour, energy, esp. of words or speech. E16.
4 The spongy inner part or core of a horn, bone, feather-shaft, etc.; the inner part of a loaf of bread. *obsolete* exc. *dial.* LME.
5 Importance, weight. Esp. in ***of great pith***. LME.
†**6** The spinal cord; the brain substance. E17–M19.

📖 **2** *New Scientist* The pith of the argument. B. MASON The very pith and essence of our relationship. **3a** S. COLVIL We'll both defend with all our pith. **b** R. L. STEVENSON His speech full of pith.

Comb.: **pith fleck** a discoloured streak in wood, formed of parenchyma embedded in xylem, usu. due to injury, as by the burrowing of fly larvae; **pith hat**, **pith helmet** a lightweight sun-helmet made of the dried pith of the sola or a similar tropical plant; **pith ray** BOTANY a medullary ray; ***pith-ray fleck***, = ***pith fleck*** above; **pith-tree** a leguminous tree, *Aeschynomene elaphroxylon*, of tropical Africa, having soft white pithlike wood.
■ **pithful** *adjective* (*rare*) full of pith; pithy: M16. **pithless** *adjective* M16. **pithlike** *adjective* resembling (that of) pith M19.

pith /pɪθ/ *verb trans.* L15.
[from the noun.]
†**1** Provide with pith, give pith or vigour to. *rare.* Only in L15.
2 Pierce or sever the spinal cord of (an animal) so as to kill or cause insensibility; *spec.* slaughter (cattle) in this way. E19.
3 Remove or extract the pith from. M19.

†**pithanology** *noun.* E17–M18.
[Greek *pithanologia*, from *pithanos* persuasive + *-logia* speech etc.: see -LOGY.]
Persuasiveness of speech; the use of specious or plausible arguments.

Pithecanthropus /pɪθɪˈkanθrəpəs/ *noun.* Also **p-**. L19.
[mod. Latin (former genus name), from Greek *pithēkos* ape + *anthrōpos* man.]
†**1** A hypothetical evolutionary intermediate between apes and man. Only in L19.
2 = ***Java man*** s.v. JAVA 1. L19.
■ **pithecanˈthropic** *adjective* of or pertaining to Pithecanthropus; *fig.* apelike, clumsy: L19. **pithecanthropine** *adjective & noun* (a being) resembling or closely related to Pithecanthropus E20. **pithecanthropoid** *adjective* = PITHECANTHROPIC, PITHECANTHROPINE L19.

pitheciine /pɪˈθiːsɪʌɪn/ *adjective.* Also **-cine** /-sʌɪn/. L19.
[from mod. Latin *Pitheciinae* (see below), from *Pithecia* genus name, from Greek *pithēkos* ape: see -INE¹.]
ZOOLOGY. Of, pertaining to, or characteristic of the subfamily Pitheciinae of S. American cebid monkeys, which includes the sakis, uakaris, night monkeys, and titis.
■ Also **pithecian** *adjective* L19.

pithecoid /pɪˈθiːkɔɪd/ *adjective & noun.* M19.
[from Greek *pithēkos* ape + -OID.]
▶ **A** *adjective.* Resembling or pertaining to the apes, esp. the higher or anthropoid apes; apelike. M19.
▶ **B** *noun.* An anthropoid ape. L19.

pithiatism /pɪˈθʌɪətɪz(ə)m/ *noun.* E20.
[from Greek *peithō* persuasion + *iatos* curable: see -ISM.]
PSYCHOLOGY (now chiefly *Hist.*). A form of hysteria or hysterical symptom which is curable by suggestion; the treatment of hysteria by this means.
■ **pithiˈatic** *adjective* E20.

Pithiviers /pɪˈtiːvjeɪ/ *noun.* L20.
[A town in northern France.]
In full ***Pithiviers cake***. A French cake made of puff pastry with a rich almond filling.

pithos /ˈpɪθɒs/ *noun.* Pl. **-thoi** /-θɔɪ/. L19.
[Greek.]
ARCHAEOLOGY. A large spherical wide-mouthed earthenware jar used for holding wine, oil, food, etc.

pithy /ˈpɪθi/ *adjective.* ME.
[from PITH *noun* + -Y¹.]
1 Full of strength or vigour; *spec.* (of liquor) strong, very alcoholic. Now *dial.* ME.
2 Full of substance or significance; *esp.* (of speech or writing) containing much matter in few words; concise, condensed, forcible; terse. E16.
3 Consisting or of the nature of pith; full of pith. M16.
📖 **2** GEO. ELIOT He was a pithy talker. N. SHERRY His style is pithy and controlled.
■ **pithily** *adverb* LME. **pithiness** *noun* M16.

pitiable /ˈpɪtɪəb(ə)l/ *adjective.* LME.
[Old French *piteable*, *pitoi-* (mod. *pitoyable*), from *piteer*, *pitier*: see PITY *verb*, -ABLE.]
1 Deserving of or arousing pity; lamentable, mournful. LME.
2 Despicable, contemptible, miserable. L18.
📖 **1** V. S. PRITCHETT A pitiable portrait of an ailing little boy. **2** J. B. PRIESTLEY A pitiable record of . . stupidity.
¶ Cf. partly synonymous PITEOUS, PITIFUL.
■ **pitiableness** *noun* L17. **pitiably** *adverb* E19.

pitiful /ˈpɪtɪfʊl, -f(ə)l/ *adjective & adverb.* ME.
[from PITY *noun* + -FUL.]
▶ **A** *adjective.* **1** Full of pity; compassionate, merciful. ME.
2 Deserving of or arousing pity; lamentable, mournful. LME.
†**3** Characterized by piety; pious. *rare.* LME–L16.
4 Despicable, contemptible, miserable. L16.
📖 **1** H. SPURLING Pitiful . . to the maltreated. **2** M. FORSTER His blindness now struck her as utterly pitiful. **4** H. JAMES A pitiful surrender to agitation.
▶†**B** *adverb.* Pitifully. Only in L16.
📖 SHAKES. *Much Ado* How pitiful I deserve.
¶ Cf. partly synonymous PITEOUS, PITIABLE.
■ **pitifully** *adverb* ME. **pitifulness** *noun* M16.

pitiless /ˈpɪtɪlɪs/ *adjective.* LME.
[from PITY *noun* + -LESS.]
Without compassion; showing no pity; merciless.
📖 W. DE LA MARE Age takes in pitiless hands All one loves most.
■ **pitilessly** *adverb* E17. **pitilessness** *noun* M18.

pitman /ˈpɪtmən/ *noun*¹. Pl. in branch I **-men**, in branch II **-mans**. E17.
[from PIT *noun*¹ + MAN *noun*.]
▶ **I** †**1** The digger of a pit or common grave. Only in E17.
2 A man who works the lower end of the saw in a sawpit; a pit-sawyer. E18.
3 A man who works in a pit or mine, esp. a coalmine; a collier. M18.
4 A mechanic working in a motor-racing pit. E20.
5 A musician in an orchestra pit. *US colloq.* M20.
▶ **II** **6** A connecting-rod, esp. in a sawmill. Chiefly *US.* E19.

Pitman /ˈpɪtmən/ *noun*². Also **Pitman's** /ˈpɪtmənz/. L19.
[Sir Isaac *Pitman* (1813–97), who devised this system.]
In full (proprietary) ***Pitman's Shorthand***, also ***Pitman shorthand*** etc. A system of shorthand notation first published in 1837.
■ **Pitˈmanic** *adjective* resembling or suggestive of Pitman's Shorthand E20.

pitmans *noun pl.* see PITMAN *noun*¹.

Pitman's *noun* var. of PITMAN *noun*².

pitmatic /pɪtˈmatɪk/ *noun.* L19.
[from PIT *noun*¹ after MATHEMATIC *noun & adjective*.]
sing. & in *pl.* (treated as *sing.*). A local patois used by miners in NE England.

pitmen *noun pl.* see PITMAN *noun*¹.

pito *noun* var. of PITA *noun*¹.

Pitocin /pɪˈtəʊsɪn/ *noun.* E20.
[from PIT(UITARY *adjective* + OXYT)OCIN.]
PHARMACOLOGY. (Proprietary name for) an aqueous solution of oxytocin.

pitometer /pɪˈtɒmɪtə/ *noun.* E20.
[from PITOT + -METER.]
= PITOT *meter*.

piton /ˈpiːtɒn/ *noun.* L19.
[French = eye-bolt.]
1 MOUNTAINEERING. A metal spike which is hammered into rock or ice and used to secure a rope through an eye at one end. L19.
2 A (steep-sided) volcanic peak, esp. in the W. Indies. E20.
Comb.: **piton hammer** a hammer designed for fixing and extracting pitons.

pitot /ˈpiːtəʊ/ *noun.* Also **P-**. L19.
[Henri *Pitot* (1695–1771), French scientist.]
PHYSICS & AERONAUTICS. Used *attrib.* to designate devices for measuring the relative velocity of air or other fluid, used esp. to determine the airspeed of an aircraft.
pitot head a pitot-static tube. **pitot meter** a flowmeter having one pressure opening facing upstream and the other downstream. **pitot-static** *adjective* designating a device consisting of a pitot tube inside or adjacent to a parallel tube closed at the end but with holes along its length, the pressure difference between them being a measure of the relative velocity of the fluid. **pitot tube** an open-ended right-angled tube pointing in opposition to the flow of a fluid and used to measure pressure; also, a pitot-static tube.

pitpan /ˈpɪtpan/ *noun.* L18.
[Miskito *pitban* boat.]
A flat-bottomed boat made from a hollowed tree-trunk, used in Central America; a dugout.

pit-pat *adverb, noun, verb, & adjective* var. of PIT-A-PAT.

Pitressin /pɪˈtrɛsɪn/ *noun.* E20.
[from PIT(UITARY *adjective* + VASOP)RESSIN.]
PHARMACOLOGY. (Proprietary name for) an aqueous solution of vasopressin.

pitso /ˈpiːtsəʊ/ *noun.* Pl. **-os**. E19.
[Sesotho.]
A Sotho tribal assembly.

pitta /ˈpɪtə/ *noun*¹. M19.
[mod. Latin (see below) from Telugu *pitta* (young) bird.]
Any of several Old World passerines constituting the genus *Pitta* and the family Pittidae, noted for their vivid colouring, strong bill, short tail, and long legs. Also called ***ant-thrush***.

pitta /ˈpɪtə/ *noun*². Also **pita**. M20.
[mod. Greek *pētta*, *pit(t)a* bread, cake, pie. Cf. Turkish *pide*, Aramaic *pittā* in similar sense.]
A flat unleavened bread of Mediterranean and Arab countries, which can be cut open to receive a filling.

pittance /ˈpɪt(ə)ns/ *noun.* ME.
[Old French *pi(e)tance* from medieval Latin *pitantia*, *pietantia*, from Latin *pietas* PITY *noun*: see -ANCE.]
1 a *Hist.* A pious bequest to a religious house to provide an allowance of food, wine, etc., at particular festivals or on the anniversary of the benefactor's death; such an allowance. ME. ▶**b** A charitable gift of food or money; an alms. LME.
2 a A small allowance or portion of food and drink; a scanty meal. Now *rare.* ME. ▶**b** An (esp. meagre) allowance of money, wages, etc., as a means of livelihood. E17.
3 *gen.* A small portion or amount (*of*); a small or sparing allowance or share. LME.
📖 **1b** E. H. GOMBRICH He was granted a small pittance. **2b** C. THUBRON Women clattered at sewing-machines . . for a pittance. **3** J. LOCKE A small pittance of Reason and Truth.

pittancer /ˈpɪt(ə)nsə/ *noun. obsolete* exc. *Hist.* LME.
[Old French *pitancier* from medieval Latin *pitantiarius*, from *pitantia*: see prec., -ER².]
An officer in a religious house responsible for distributing pittances.

pitted /ˈpɪtɪd/ *adjective*¹. LOE.
[from PIT *verb*¹, *noun*¹: see -ED¹, -ED².]
Having pits or small depressions on or in the surface; marked with pits. Also, scarred by smallpox, acne, etc.
📖 H. WOUK His . . face was pitted, as though he had . . been a bad acne sufferer. P. BENSON The silencer was pitted with holes.

pitted /ˈpɪtɪd/ *adjective*². E20.
[from PIT *verb*², *noun*²: see -ED¹, -ED².]
Of a fruit: having the pit or stone removed.

pitter /ˈpɪtə/ *noun. N. Amer.* L19.
[from PIT *noun*² + -ER¹.]
A mechanical device for removing the pits or stones from fruit.

pitter /ˈpɪtə/ *verb intrans.* Now *rare* or *obsolete.* L16.
[Imit.: cf. PATTER *verb*², TWITTER *verb*.]
Make a rapid succession of light short sounds.

pitter-patter /pɪtəˈpatə, ˈpɪtəpatə/ *noun, verb, & adverb.* LME.
[Redupl. of PATTER *verb*¹, *verb*². Cf. PIT-A-PAT.]
▶ **A** *noun.* **1** Rapid repetition of words; *spec.* rapid mechanical repetition of prayers. LME.
2 A rapid succession of light beating sounds, as those made by rain, light footsteps, etc. M19.
▶ **B** *verb.* **1** *verb trans. & intrans.* Patter or repeat (words) in a rapid mechanical way. L15.
2 *verb intrans.* Beat with a rapid succession of light taps or pats, as rain; palpitate. L18.
▶ **C** *adverb.* With a rapid succession of light beating sounds. L17.

pitticite /ˈpɪtɪsʌɪt/ *noun.* E19.
[German *Pittizit*, from Greek *pitta* pitch + *-iz* -IC + *-it* -ITE¹.]
MINERALOGY. An amorphous hydrated sulphate and arsenate of iron occurring as kidney-shaped masses.

pitting /ˈpɪtɪŋ/ *noun.* M17.
[from PIT *verb*¹ + -ING¹.]
1 A pit or small depression in a surface, as on the skin by smallpox, on metal by corrosion, etc.; a series or mass of such depressions or spots. M17.
2 The action of PIT *verb*¹; *spec.* (*a*) the digging of a pit or pits; (*b*) the formation of a pit by soil subsidence; (*c*) the action of setting cocks to fight, dogs to kill rats, etc., in a pit for sport; (*d*) the action of putting something into a pit, or of storing vegetables etc. in pits; (*e*) MEDICINE the formation of a temporary impression in soft tissue when pressed with a finger, as in fluid oedema; (*f*) BOTANY the formation of pits on the wall of a cell or vessel. M18. ▶**b** = ***pit-planting*** s.v. PIT *noun*¹. M19.

Pittite /ˈpɪtʌɪt/ *noun*¹ *& adjective.* L18.
[from W. *Pitt* (see below) + -ITE¹.]
Hist. ▶**A** *noun.* A political supporter of the British statesman William Pitt 'the Younger' (1759–1806), or of his policies. L18.
▶ **B** *adjective.* Of or pertaining to Pitt or the Pittites. E19.
■ **Pittism** *noun* the policies of William Pitt E19.

pittite /ˈpɪtʌɪt/ *noun*². *arch.* E19.
[from PIT *noun*¹ + -ITE¹.]
A person occupying a seat in the pit of a theatre.

pitto /ˈpɪtəʊ/ *noun.* L17.
[Fon *kpitu*.]
A W. African beer made from fermented maize or rice.

pittosporum /pɪˈtɒsp(ə)rəm/ *noun.* L18.
[mod. Latin (see below), from Greek *pitta* pitch + *sporos* seed, from the resinous pulp surrounding the seeds.]
Any of numerous chiefly subtropical evergreen shrubs or small trees constituting the genus *Pittosporum* (family Pittosporaceae), native esp. to Australasia and China, which bear small often fragrant flowers and are cultivated for ornament in warm climates.

pituicyte /pɪˈtjuːɪsʌɪt/ *noun.* M20.
[from PITUITARY + -CYTE.]
ANATOMY. A specialized cell with branching processes, resembling a glial cell and characteristic of the neurohypophysis.

pituita /pɪtjʊˈʌɪtə/ *noun.* Long *rare* or *obsolete.* Also †**-uit**. L17.
[Latin = gum, slime. Cf. French *pituite*.]
PHYSIOLOGY. Phlegm, mucus.

pituitary /pɪˈtjuːɪt(ə)ri/ *adjective & noun.* E17.
[Latin *pituitarius*, formed as prec.: see -ARY¹.]
ANATOMY & PHYSIOLOGY. ▶**A** *adjective.* Orig., of, pertaining to, or secreting phlegm or mucus. Now, of, pertaining to, or designating the major endocrine gland (see ***pituitary gland*** below). E17.
pituitary body = ***pituitary gland*** below. **pituitary extract** a preparation of the pituitary gland for therapeutic use. **pituitary gland** the major endocrine gland, a small bilobed body attached to the base of the brain that is important in controlling growth and development and the functioning of the other endocrine glands; also called ***hypophysis***.
▶ **B** *ellipt.* as *noun.* †**1** A mucous membrane. Only in M19.
2 The pituitary gland. L19.

pituitous /pɪˈtjuːɪtəs/ *adjective.* Now *rare.* L16.
[from Latin *pituitosus*, formed as PITUITA: see -OUS.]
1 Of, pertaining to, or of the nature of mucus. L16.
2 = PHLEGMATIC *adjective* 1a, 2. M17.

Pituitrin /pɪˈtjuːɪtrɪn/ *noun.* Also **p-**. E20.
[from PITUITARY + -IN¹.]
PHARMACOLOGY. (Proprietary name for) an extract of the posterior lobe of the pituitary gland containing the hormones oxytocin and vasopressin.

pituri /ˈpɪtjʊəri/ *noun.* M19.
[Aboriginal.]
An Australian shrub of the nightshade family, *Duboisia hopwoodii*, containing nicotine, the leaves and twigs of which are chewed by Aborigines as a narcotic; a drug prepared from this.

pity /ˈpɪti/ *noun*. ME.
[Old French *pité* (mod. *pitié*) from Latin *pietas*, *-tat-* PIETY. See note below. See also PIETY.]
▶ **I** †**1** The quality of being pitiful or merciful; clemency, mildness. ME–E17.
2 Tenderness and concern aroused by the suffering or misfortune of another; compassion, sympathy. ME.
3 A reason or cause for pity; a regrettable fact or circumstance. ME.
†**4** Grief, distress; remorse, repentance. ME–L16.
†**5 a** A condition deserving pity; a pitiable state. LME–E17. ▸**b** An object of pity. *rare*. L16–E18.

📖 **2** P. AUSTER Pity for that forlorn figure. P. GROSSKURTH The humiliation Klein experienced . . was so intense that other members were moved to pity. **3** SHAKES. *Oth.* The pity of it, Iago! E. BOWEN Pity it rained. L. R. BANKS It was a pity we were too late. JULIETTE HUXLEY The book is forgotten: a pity.

▶ † **II 6** = PIETY II. ME–L17.
Phrases: **for pity's sake**, †**for pity** for goodness' sake. **have pity**, **take pity** feel or show pity, be merciful or compassionate, (foll. by *on*, *upon*, †*of*). **the more's the pity**, **more's the pity** so much the worse.
¶ In ME both *pity* and *piety* appear in the sense 'compassion', later both appear also in the sense 'piety'; they are not completely differentiated before E17.

pity /ˈpɪti/ *verb*. L15.
[from the noun, perh. after Old French *piteer*, *pitier* (mod. *pitoyer*).]
1 *verb trans.* Feel pity for; be sorry for. Now also, feel or show slight contempt for (a person) as inferior or immoral. L15.
†**2** *verb trans.* Move to pity; grieve. E16–M19.
†**3** *verb intrans.* Be moved to pity; grieve, be sorry. M16–M19.
4 *verb trans.* Grieve for, regret. Now *arch. rare*. M17.

📖 **1** S. HASTINGS Her sisters were to be pitied for the awfulness of their lives. U. HOLDEN I must not pity myself.

■ **pitier** *noun* E17. **pitying** *adjective* †(*a*) grieving; (*b*) feeling or showing pity, expressive of pity: L16. **pityingly** *adverb* (earlier in UNPITYINGLY) M19.

pityriasis /pɪtɪˈrʌɪəsɪs/ *noun*. Pl. **-ases** /-əsiːz/. L17.
[mod. Latin from Greek *pituriasis* scurf, from *pituron* bran: see -IASIS.]
MEDICINE. Formerly, any of various skin conditions characterized by the development of fine flaky scales. Now only in mod. Latin phrs.
pityriasis capitis /ˈkapɪtɪs/ [Latin = of the head] dandruff.

più /pjuː/ *adverb*. E18.
[Italian.]
MUSIC. More: used in directions, as ***più mosso*** more animated(ly).

pium /ˈpiːʌm/ *noun*. M19.
[Portuguese from Tupi *piũ*.]
A S. American buffalo gnat, *Simulium pertinax*. Also ***pium fly***.

piupiu /ˈpjuːpjuː/ *noun*. *NZ*. L19.
[Maori.]
Dressed flax; a Maori skirt made of this worn by men and women performing action songs and dances.

piuri *noun* var. of PURREE.

pivo /ˈpiːvəʊ/ *noun*. Pl. **-os**. Also **piva** /ˈpiːvə/. M20.
[Russian = beer.]
In Russia and some countries to the west: a beer made from barley malt and hops.

pivot /ˈpɪvət/ *noun*. LME.
[Old & mod. French, prob. from Proto-Romance base repr. by French dial. *pue* tooth of a comb, harrow, etc., Provençal *pua* (mod. *pivo*), Spanish *pu(y)a* point, of unkn. origin.]
1 A short shaft or pin on which something turns or oscillates, as the pin of a hinge, the end of an axle, etc.; a fulcrum. Also (*gen.*), a part of anything on which another part turns. LME.
2 MILITARY. The person about whom a body of troops wheels. Also, that flank by which the alignment of troops is corrected. L18.
3 *transf.* & *fig.* **a** A crucial or central point, person, etc., on which everything depends. E19. ▸**b** *spec.* A device in classical Japanese poetry involving the use of a pun which implies one meaning with the words preceding it and another with those following. L19. ▸**c** In football and other games, (the position of) a centre-back or other central player. E20. ▸**d** BASKETBALL. A move in which the player with the ball takes a step while keeping one foot in contact with the floor. E20. ▸**e** MATH. A non-zero element of a determinant or matrix used in a special way in the numerical evaluation of the determinant, or in the numerical solution of simultaneous linear equations. Cf. PIVOTING 2. M20. ▸**f** LINGUISTICS. = ***pivot word*** below. M20.

📖 **1** E. BRUTON One pivot of each wheel. J. C. POWYS He turned his . . head on the pivot of his neck. **3a** S. HASTINGS The Colonel . . was the pivot of her existence. M. FORSTER Mary Barrett had been . . a pivot upon which the . . family turned. **3c** *attrib.*: *Rebound* Front-court forward . . the pivot position.

Comb.: **pivot bearing** = FOOTSTEP 3c; **pivot class** LINGUISTICS the class of pivot words; **pivot foot** BASKETBALL the foot kept in contact with the floor in a pivot; **pivot grammar** LINGUISTICS a grammar of an early stage in children's speech in which two word classes are postulated, pivot words and a larger open class; **pivot-hole**: into which the ends of the spindle of a wheel in a watch or clock are run; **pivot-joint** ANATOMY a joint in which the articular movement is that of a pivot; **pivotman** a player in a centre-back or other central position; **pivot word** LINGUISTICS any of a set of words used at an early stage of a child's acquisition of language as central items to which other words are attached.

pivot /ˈpɪvət/ *verb*. M19.
[from the noun, partly after French *pivoter*.]
1 *verb trans.* Provide with or attach by means of a pivot or pivots; hinge. Usu. in *pass.* M19.
2 *verb intrans.* Turn as on a pivot; hinge; *spec.* (MILITARY) swing round a central point. Also (*fig.*), depend *on*, hinge *on*. M19.

📖 **1** R. H. HUTTON Scott's romances . . are pivoted on . . public interests. **2** W. S. CHURCHILL To pivot on Spion Kop mountain. G. STEINER Part of western literature pivots on . . personal identity. R. FRAME She pivoted round on her heels.

■ **pivotaˈbility** *noun* the extent to which an object can be turned as if on a pivot M20. **pivotable** *adjective* able to be turned as if on a pivot M20.

pivotal /ˈpɪvət(ə)l/ *adjective*. M19.
[from PIVOT *noun* + -AL¹.]
1 Of, pertaining to, or acting as a pivot; central, crucial, vital. M19.
2 MATH. Constituting or involving the pivot of a determinant or matrix. E20.
3 LINGUISTICS. Of, pertaining to, or based on pivot grammar or pivot words. M20.

📖 **1** L. APPIGNANESI The pivotal commitment in his life. C. HEILBRUN Montaigne, whose essay . . is pivotal in any study. **pivotal man** *Hist.* a man considered to have an important role in the re-establishment of industry and commerce after the war of 1914–18, and hence eligible for early demobilization.

■ **pivotalism** *noun* (*Hist.*) the policy of releasing pivotal men from active service before others E20. **pivotally** *adverb* in a pivotal manner; as on a pivot: L19.

pivoting /ˈpɪvətɪŋ/ *verbal noun*. M19.
[from PIVOT *verb* + -ING¹.]
1 The action of PIVOT *verb*. M19.
2 MATH. The use of a pivot in making a column of a determinant or matrix consist entirely of zeros except for one unit element, as a step in evaluating the determinant, or in the numerical solution of simultaneous linear equations. M20.

pix /pɪks/ *noun*¹ *pl. informal*. E20.
[Pluralized abbreviation of PICTURE *noun*.]
Pictures, *esp.* photographs.

📖 *Ritz* Brooke Shields posed for pix.

pix *noun*² & *verb* var. of PYX *noun* & *verb*.

pixel /ˈpɪks(ə)l, -sɛl/ *noun*. M20.
[from PIX *noun*¹ + ELEMENT *noun*.]
ELECTRONICS. Each of the small areas of uniform illumination of which the image is formed on a television or computer screen etc.
Comb.: **Pixelvision** (proprietary name for) a film-making system (orig. designed for children) which uses a low-resolution video camera to record images L20.

pixelate /ˈpɪksəleɪt/ *verb trans.* Also **pixell-**, **pixil-** /ˈpɪksɪl-/. L20.
[from prec. + -ATE³.]
ELECTRONICS. **1** Divide (an image) into pixels, usu. for display or storage in a digital format. L20.
2 Display an image of (someone or something) on television as a small number of large pixels, usu. in order to disguise someone's identity. L20.
■ **pixeˈlation** *noun* L20.

pixie /ˈpɪksi/ *noun*. Also **pixy**. M17.
[Origin unkn.]
In folklore, a supernatural being with magical powers; a fairy, an elf. Earliest in ***pixie-path*** below.
Comb.: **pixie cap**, **pixie hat** a pointed hat resembling that in which pixies are traditionally depicted; **pixie hood** a pointed hood; **pixie-led** *adjective* led astray by pixies; lost, bewildered, confused; **pixie-path** a path by which those who follow it become bewildered and lost; **pixie-pear** (chiefly *dial.*) the fruit of the hawthorn.
■ **pixie-like** *adjective* = PIXYISH M20. **pixyish** *adjective* of the nature of or resembling a pixie M20.

pixilate *verb* var. of PIXELATE.

pixilated /ˈpɪksɪleɪtɪd/ *adjective*. Also **-ll-**. M19.
[from PIXIE + *-lated* as in *elated*, *emulated*, etc., or var. of *PIXIE-led*.]
1 Crazy, whimsical; bewildered, confused; intoxicated. Orig. *US dial.* M19.
2 Having or pertaining to movements animated by the pixilation technique. M20.

pixilation /pɪksɪˈleɪʃ(ə)n/ *noun*. Also **-ll-**. M20.
[from prec.: see -ATION.]
1 A theatrical and cinematographic technique whereby human characters move or appear to move as if artificially animated. Also ***pixilation technique***. M20.
2 The state or condition of being pixilated or crazy, confused, intoxicated, etc. M20.

pixillated *adjective*, **pixillation** *noun* vars. of PIXILATED, PIXILATION.

pixy *noun* var. of PIXIE.

Piyut /piːˈjuːt/ *noun*. Also **Piyyut**. Pl. **-im** /-ɪm/. L19.
[Hebrew *piyyūṭ* poem, poetry from Greek *poiētēs*: see POET.]
A poem recited in a synagogue in addition to the standard liturgy.

pizazz *noun* var. of PIZZAZZ.

pize /pʌɪz/ *noun*. *obsolete* exc. *dial*. E17.
[Origin unkn.]
In exclamatory or imprecatory phrs., as ***a pize on*** —, ***pize on*** —, ***pize take*** —, etc.

pize /pʌɪz/ *verb*. *dial*. L18.
[Origin unkn.]
1 *verb trans.* Strike; *spec.* hit (a ball) with the hand in the game of pize-ball (see below). L18.
2 *verb intrans.* & *trans.* Throw (a ball) in pize-ball. M19.
Comb.: **pize-ball** a game similar to rounders, played mainly in Yorkshire, in which the ball is hit with the flat of the hand.
■ **pizer** *noun* a bowler in pize-ball M19.

pizotifen /pɪˈzəʊtɪfɛn/ *noun*. M20.
[from PI(PERIDINE + BEN)ZO- + *-tifen* from alt. of THIOPHENE.]
PHARMACOLOGY. A tricyclic drug, $C_{19}H_{21}NS$, with serotonin receptor blocking properties, used as a prophylactic for migraine.

pizza /ˈpiːtsə/ *noun*. L19.
[Italian = pie. Cf. ZA.]
A flat usu. round base of dough baked with a topping of tomatoes, cheese, meat, olives, etc.

📖 *attrib.*: *Sunday Times* Washing dishes in a pizza parlour.

Comb.: **pizza box** (*a*) a square, shallow cardboard box for a takeaway or precooked pizza; (*b*) a computer casing which is not very tall and has a square cross section.

pizzazz /pɪˈzaz/ *noun*. *slang* (orig. *US*). Also **pazazz**, **pizazz**, **pzazz**, & other vars. M20.
[Perh. invented by Diana Vreeland, fashion editor in the 1930s of *Harper's Bazaar*.]
Vitality, attractive lively style; sparkle, flashiness.

📖 *American Speech* The catchy phrases, . . smart sayings, the pizzazz. *Hairdo Ideas* Asymmetrical pizzazz.

pizzeria /piːtsəˈriːə/ *noun*. M20.
[Italian, formed as PIZZA + *-eria* -ERY.]
A place where pizzas are made or sold.

pizzicato /pɪtsɪˈkɑːtəʊ/ *noun*, *adjective* & *adverb*. M19.
[Italian, pa. pple of *pizzicare* pinch, twitch, from *pizzare*, from Old & mod. Italian *pizza* point, edge.]
MUSIC. ▶ **A** *noun*. Pl. **-ti** /-ti/, **-tos**. A note or passage played on a violin, cello, etc., by plucking a string with the finger instead of bowing. M19.
▶ **B** *adjective* & *adverb*. (Played) by plucking a string instead of bowing. L19.

pizzle /ˈpɪz(ə)l/ *noun*. Now chiefly *Austral*. L15.
[Low German *pēsel*, Flemish *pēzel*, dim. of Middle Low German *pēse*, Middle Dutch *pēze* (Dutch *pees* sinew, string, penis), whence also synon. Middle Low German, Middle Dutch *pēserik* (Dutch *pezerik*). Cf. -LE¹.]
The penis of an animal, esp. a bull (formerly used as a whip).

p-j *abbreviation*. *colloq.* Also **PJ**.
Usu. in *pl.* Pyjama.

PK *abbreviation*.
1 MEDICINE. Prausnitz–Küstner.
2 Psychokinesis, psychokinetic.

pk. *abbreviation*.
1 Park.
2 Peak.
3 Peck(s).

PKU *abbreviation*.
MEDICINE. Phenylketonuria.

pl. *abbreviation*.
1 Place.
2 Plate.
3 Chiefly MILITARY. Platoon.
4 Plural.

PLA *abbreviation*.
1 People's Liberation Army.
2 Port of London Authority.

placable /ˈplakəb(ə)l/ *adjective*. LME.
[Old French, or Latin *placabilis*, from *placare*: see PLACATE, -ABLE.]
†**1** Pleasing, agreeable. LME–M16.
2 Able to be (easily) placated or pacified; mild, forgiving. L16.
3 Peaceable, quiet. *rare*. E17.
■ **placaˈbility** *noun* M16. **placableness** *noun* M17. **placably** *adverb* M19.

placage /plaˈkɑːʒ/ *noun*. L18.
[French, from *plaquer* to plaster or veneer, formed as PLAQUE: see -AGE.]
The action or an act of facing a wall with a thin layer of plaster, marble, etc.

placard /ˈplakɑːd/ *noun*. Also (earlier) †**-art**. L15.
[French †*placquart*, *-ard* (now *placard*), from Old French *plaquier* (mod. *plaquer*) lay flat, plaster from Middle Dutch *placken*: see -ARD. See also PLACCATE, PLACKET.]
▶ **I 1** †**a** An official document giving authority or permission for something; a warrant, a licence. L15–E18. ▶**b** An official announcement or decree, an edict, a proclamation. *obsolete* exc. *Hist.* E16.
2 A printed or handwritten poster or notice advertising or announcing something. Now also, a sign bearing a slogan or image, used by a demonstrator etc. to attract public attention. M16.

> **2** G. B. SHAW I saw by the placards that a Christmas pantomime was going on inside. *Daily Chronicle* Anti-militarist placards. *Times* Demonstrators . . chanting and waving placards.

▶ **II 3 a** A piece of armour, *esp.* a breast- or backplate; *spec.* an additional plate worn over or under the cuirass. Cf. PLACCATE 1. *obsolete* exc. *Hist.* L15. ▶**b** A garment or front panel, freq. decorated, worn under an open coat or gown. *obsolete* exc. *Hist.* L15.

placard /ˈplakɑːd, plaˈkɑːd/ *verb trans.* L17.
[from the noun.]
1 Make known or advertise (a thing) by means of placards; post or display (a notice etc.) as a placard. L17.
2 Set up or affix placards on or in (a wall, town, etc.), cover with placards. E19.

> **1** O. SITWELL Notices about the dangers of fire were suddenly placarded all over the ship. **2** *Daily Telegraph* Theatres . . placarded with pictures of actresses in their underclothes.

■ **placarder** *noun* E19.

†**placart** *noun* see PLACARD *noun*.

placate /pləˈkeɪt, ˈplakeɪt, ˈpleɪ-/ *verb trans.* L17.
[Latin *placat-* pa. ppl stem of *placare* please, appease: see -ATE³.]
Overcome the hostility or resentment of; pacify, appease, propitiate.

> V. BROME Something must be done to placate the rebellious Viennese. A. BROOKNER All wives are discontented and can be placated with gifts of jewellery.

■ **placater** *noun* L19. **plaˈcating** *ppl adjective* that placates or is intended to placate a person, conciliatory E20. **plaˈcatingly** *adverb* E20. **plaˈcation** *noun* the action or an act of placating a person; conciliation, appeasement; a propitiatory act: L16.

placatory /pləˈkeɪt(ə)ri/ *adjective*. M17.
[Latin *placatorius*, formed as prec.: see -ORY².]
Tending or intended to placate or appease a person, conciliatory, propitiatory.

placcate /ˈplakət/ *noun*. *obsolete* exc. *Hist.* L16.
[App. var. of PLACARD *noun*. Cf. PLACKET, Anglo-Latin *placatum*.]
†**1** = PLACKET 1. Only in L16.
2 A piece of armour consisting of a plate worn over the cuirass. Also, a leather jacket or doublet lined with metal strips and worn under the outer armour. Cf. PLACARD *noun* 3a. M17.

place /pleɪs/ *noun*¹. OE.
[Old & mod. French from Proto-Romance alt. of Latin *platea* broad way, open space from Greek *plateia* (sc. *hodos*) broad way, fem. of *platus* broad. Superseded STEAD *noun*, STOW *noun*¹ in gen. use.]
▶ **I 1** Orig., an open space in a town, a market-place. Now, a small square or a side-street, esp. a cul-de-sac, lined with houses (freq. in proper names). OE.
2 a Available room or space. *arch.* ME. ▶**b** Space as opp. to time. Chiefly *poet.* & *rhet.* M17.
3 A particular part or portion of space or of a surface, whether occupied or not; a position or situation in space or with reference to other bodies. ME. ▶†**b** *ellipt.* A place of battle, a battlefield. ME–E18.
4 a A residence, a dwelling, a house; a person's home. Formerly *spec.* a religious house, a convent; a country house with its surrounding lands. ME. ▶**b** A particular spot or area inhabited or frequented by people, as a city, a town, a village, etc. LME. ▶**c** A building, establishment, or area devoted to a specific purpose. Freq. with specification, as *place of amusement*, *bathing-place*, etc. M16. ▶†**d** A fortress, a citadel; a fortified city. L16–M19. ▶**e** *euphem.* A lavatory. E20.
5 A point reached in reading or working on a book or document; a particular passage in or extract from a book etc. ME. ▶†**b** A subject, a topic. Cf. LOCUS *noun*¹ 3. E16–L17.
6 A particular part or spot on a body or surface, esp. on the skin. LME.
7 a The point or pitch to which a falcon etc. rises before swooping down on the quarry. Now chiefly *fig.* in ***pride of place***, the most prominent or important position. E17. ▶**b** ASTRONOMY. The apparent position of a celestial object on the celestial sphere. M17.

> **1** JOYCE First he shot down Raglan Road and then he tore up Marlborough Place. **2b** T. GRAY He pass'd the flaming bounds of Place and Time. **3** J. PORTER A damned silly place to have traffic lights. G. VIDAL The Park was the most peaceful place in the city. J. IRVING Stay in one place so I can find you. **4a** S. MOSTYN I called at your place . . but . . you had been gone half an hour. E. WELTY The cherry trees on the McKelva place. **b** JAN MORRIS Oxford is an edgy and exhausting place. J. BARZUN The year is 1890 and the place Cambridge, Massachusetts. E. WAUGH The pub. Not such a bad little place. **c** L. SPALDING There were pizza places and a Korean restaurant. **5** J. CARY She picked up her book and looked for her place. **6** B. GOOLDEN She . . examined a pink place on her wrist. **7a** SHAKES. *Macb.* A falcon tow'ring in her pride of place. N. TAKATSUKUSA Pride of place among the native songbirds is . . given to the *uguisu*.

▶ **II 8** Position or standing in an order or scale of estimation or merit; *spec.* a person's rank or status; the duties and rights appropriate to a rank etc. Formerly also *spec.*, high rank or position. ME. ▶**b** MATH. The position of a figure in a series, in decimal or similar notation, as indicating its value or denomination. Freq. in *pl.* with numeral, expr. the number of figures, esp. after a decimal point. LME. ▶**c** A step or point in an order of progression or consideration. Usu. in ***in the first place***. M17. ▶**d** RACING. Any of the first three or sometimes four final positions in a race, esp. other than the winner's; *US* second position. M19.
9 A proper or appropriate position; *fig.* a fitting time or occasion, reasonable opportunity or grounds. ME.
10 A position occupied by habit, allotment, or right; a space, esp. a seat, for a person in a public building, conveyance, etc., or at a dining-table; a position as a member of a team, a student at an educational establishment, etc. LME. ▶**b** The space previously or customarily occupied by another person or thing. Freq. in ***in place of***, ***in the place of***, ***take the place of*** below. M16.
11 A job, a situation, esp. in government employment; *spec.* high office, esp. as a government minister. LME. ▶**b** The duties or rights of an office or position; one's duty or business. M17.

> **8** D. FRANCIS The chestnut colt was beaten into fourth place. **b** *Biometrika* It was necessary to calculate a τ, to eight places. **9** O. W. HOLMES The ludicrous has its place in the universe. H. PAYNE This is no place for a history of Daedalic sculpture. J. J. CONNINGTON A tidy person with a place for everything, and everything in its place. E. S. PERSON The father gives the bride away, acknowledging that her place is now beside her husband. **10** E. HEMINGWAY The train was full and I knew there was no chance of a place. V. GLENDINNING At the dinner party there is a spare place at the table. D. WILLIAMS Too many students chasing too few university places. M. AMIS I take my place in the slouching queue. **11** G. STEIN She found a place for her as nursemaid to a little girl.

Phrases: **all over the place** in disorder, chaotic. ***ANOTHER place***. ***between a rock and a hard place***: see ROCK *noun*¹. ***DECIMAL place***. **fall into place** begin to make sense or cohere. ***free place***: see FREE *adjective*. ***friends in high places***: see FRIEND *noun*. **give place to** to make room for, yield precedence to, be succeeded by. **go places** *colloq.* be successful. ***go to a better place***: see GO *verb*. ***have one's heart in the right place***: see HEART *noun*. ***HOLY place***. **in a person's place** (*a*) in a person's situation or circumstances; (*b*) = *in place of* below. **in place** in the original or proper position, in position; suitable, appropriate. ***in place of***: see ***in the place of*** below. **in places** in some parts or places but not others. **in place of**, **in the place of** instead of; in exchange for. **keep a person in his or her place** suppress a person's aspirations or pretensions. **know one's place** know how to behave in a manner appropriate to one's situation, social status, etc. **out of place** in the wrong position, misplaced; unsuitable, inappropriate. ***place in the sun***: see SUN *noun*¹. **place of arms** = PLACE D'ARMES. ***place of OBSERVATION***. ***place of vantage***: see VANTAGE *noun*. **place of worship** a place where religious worship is performed; *spec.* a building designed for this purpose, as a church, chapel, synagogue, mosque, etc. **put a person in his or her place** remind a person of his or her failings, lowly status, etc.; rebuff, humiliate. **put oneself in another's place** imagine oneself in another's situation. **take one's place** go to or take up one's correct or legitimate place; *spec.* be seated. **take place** happen, occur, come to pass. **take the place of** replace, be substituted for. ***the other place***: see OTHER *adjective*. ***unity of place***: see UNITY *noun*¹ 8. ***USURP the place of***.

Comb.: **Place Act** *Hist.* an Act of Parliament excluding people holding office under the Crown from sitting in the House of Commons; **place-bet** a bet on a horse etc. to finish a race in any of the first three, four, or (*US*) two positions, esp. other than the winner's; **place-betting** the action of making a place-bet; **place-book** = *COMMONPLACE-book*; **place-brick** a brick imperfectly fired through being on the outward or windward side of the kiln or clamp; **place card** a card marking the place allocated to a person at a table etc.; **place-holder** (*a*) a person holding a place or office, *spec.* in government service; (*b*) MATH. any symbol occupying a position in an expression, esp. a symbol for a variable, or a significant zero in a representation of a number; **place horse** a horse etc. finishing a race in any of the first three, four, or (*US*) two positions, esp. other than the winner's; **place-hunter** a person persistently attempting to secure a job in government service, esp. through motives of self-interest; **place-kick** *noun* & *verb* (RUGBY FOOTBALL) (*a*) *noun* a kick made when the ball is previously placed on the ground; a place-kicker; (*b*) *verb intrans.* make a place-kick; **place-kicker** RUGBY FOOTBALL a player specializing in taking place-kicks; **placeman** a person appointed to a job, esp. in government service, for political reasons; **place-mat** a small mat placed on a table underneath a person's plate; **place-money** money bet on or won by a horse etc. finishing a race in any of the first three, four, or (*US*) second positions, esp. other than the winner's; **place-name** the name of a town, village, hill, field, lake, etc.; ***place-setting***: see SETTING *noun* 6; **place-value** the numerical value that a digit has by virtue of its position in a number.

place /plas/ *noun*². Pl. pronounced same. L17.
[French: see prec.]
In France, a square in a town etc. Freq. in proper names.

place /pleɪs/ *verb*. LME.
[from PLACE *noun*¹. Cf. French *placer*.]
1 *verb trans.* Set or position in a particular place or spot; put or bring into a particular state or situation. LME. ▶**b** Arrange or dispose (a number of things) in proper or appropriate relative places. M16. ▶**c** SPORT. Guide (a ball) with careful control; RUGBY FOOTBALL score (a goal) from a place-kick. E19.
2 *verb trans.* **a** Appoint (a person) to a post, esp. as a member of the clergy. M16. ▶**b** Arrange for the employment, accommodation, marriage, etc., of; settle (a person), put into the care of. Also foll. by †*forth*, *out*. L16. ▶**c** Put (a thing) into a suitable or desirable place for a certain purpose; *spec.* (*a*) invest (money) (also foll. by *out*); (*b*) make or give out (an order) in order to be supplied with something; (*c*) dispose of or deliver (goods) to a customer; (*d*) arrange for the performance or publication of (a play, piece of writing, etc.); (*e*) order or obtain a connection for (a telephone call), esp. through an operator. E18.
3 a *verb trans.* Assign rank, importance, or worth to; rank, classify; assign to a particular place, setting, or date, locate. M16. ▶**b** *verb trans.* State the final position of (a horse etc.) in a race, among the first three or sometimes four, esp. other than the winner's; in *pass.*, finish a race in any of the first three, four, or (*US*) two positions, esp. other than the winner's. E19. ▶**c** *verb trans.* Identify, recognize, or remember correctly; classify superficially or by guesswork. Orig. *US*. M19. ▶**d** *verb intrans.* Achieve a certain final position in a race etc., *spec.* among the first three, four, or (*US*) two, esp. other than the winner's. E20.
4 *verb trans.* Put or repose (confidence, trust, importance, etc.) *in* or *on* a person or thing. E17.
5 *verb trans.* Believe or assert (a quality, attribute, etc.) to consist or be found *in* something. Formerly also, ascribe (a fact, circumstance, etc.) *to* something as a cause. E17.

> **1** J. A. FROUDE Lord Russell was . . placed under arrest. T. HARDY Vine had placed Margery in front of him. J. STEINBECK Placed a flower in a vase. A. BLEASDALE Take the coffin . . and place it on the trestles. **2b** J. BUCHAN He placed his child in an English school. **c** C. ANGIER The novel was hard to place, because publishers were afraid. **3a** A. S. NEILL I see that I place politics before everything in education. G. GREENE Forced to place her stories in the Edwardian . . past. P. GAY Darwin had undertaken to place man . . in the animal kingdom. **b** T. FITZGEORGE-PARKER Canardeau . . won twenty-five races . . and had been placed fifty-five times. **c** T. COLLINS I had met him before, but couldn't place him. P. H. JOHNSON Three or four couples . . , anonymous, hard to place by class or even by race. **d** *Arena* In the Miss World contest . . she places third. **4** A. HARDING The trust which once I placed in Philip.

■ **placeable** *adjective* able or liable to be placed M16.

placea *noun* var. of PLATEA.

placebo /pləˈsiːbəʊ/ *noun*. Pl. **-o(e)s**. ME.
[Latin = I shall please or be acceptable (1st word of *Psalms* 114:9), 1st person sing. future indic. of *placere* please.]
1 ROMAN CATHOLIC CHURCH. The vespers for the dead, from the initial word of the antiphon formerly used to open the office. ME.
†**2** A flatterer, a sycophant. LME–L18.
3 A pill, medicine, procedure, etc., prescribed more for the psychological benefit to the patient of being given a prescription than for any physiological effect. Also, a substance with no therapeutic effect used as a control in testing new drugs etc.; a blank sample in a test. L18.

> **3** A. HAILEY Complaining of a cold, I give them placebos—harmless . . sugar pills.

Comb.: **placebo effect** a beneficial or adverse effect produced by a placebo which cannot be attributed to the placebo itself.

place d'armes /plas darm/ *noun phr.* Pl. ***places d'armes*** (pronounced same). **E18.**
[French = place of arms.]
An assembly point for troops, weapons, or ammunition; a parade ground; an arsenal.

placee /pleɪˈsiː/ *noun.* Orig. *US.* **M20.**
[from PLACE *verb* + -EE¹.]
COMMERCE. An investor to whom shares etc. are sold by direct or private placement.

placeless /ˈpleɪslɪs/ *adjective.* **LME.**
[from PLACE *noun*¹ + -LESS.]
†**1** Without a fixed place or home. *rare.* Only in **LME.**
2 Not confined to place; not having a specific location, not bounded or defined. Also, not distinguishable from other places, devoid of local character. **L16.**
3 Having no stated place or locality. **M17.**
4 Having no job or post; out of office, unemployed. **E19.**
■ **placelessly** *adverb* **M19.** **placelessness** *noun* **L20.**

placement /ˈpleɪsm(ə)nt, *in sense (b) also foreign* plasmɑ̃/ *noun.* **M19.**
[from PLACE *verb* + -MENT. Cf. French *placement.*]
The action or an act of placing or arranging a thing or person; the fact of being placed; placing, arrangement, position; *spec.* (*a*) (a period of) attachment to a workplace or educational establishment other than one's own, in order to gain experience etc.; (*b*) the allocation of places to people at a dining-table etc.

🕮 *Times* Placement of orders is tailing off. P. AUSTER The story takes on special meaning when its placement in the book is considered. *EuroBusiness* Students . . have to complete a two-month industrial placement in each country.

placenta /pləˈsɛntə/ *noun.* Pl. **-tas**, (in sense 2 usu.) **-tae** /-tiː/. **L17.**
[Latin = cake, from Greek *plakount-*, *plakous* flat cake, from base *plak-* of *plax* flat object.]
1 ANATOMY & ZOOLOGY. Orig. †***placenta uterina***. A round flat spongy vascular organ to which the foetus of most mammals is attached by the umbilical cord, through which oxygen and nutrients pass from the maternal blood, and which is expelled as the afterbirth (cf. PLACENTAL *adjective* 2). Also, a structure having a similar function in other animals, as some viviparous fishes, ascidians, etc. **L17.**
2 BOTANY. An area of tissue to which the ovules are attached in the ovary. Also, a projecting mound of tissue from which the sporangia of ferns arise. **L17.**
1 ABRUPTIO PLACENTAE. **placenta praevia** /ˈpriːvɪə/, **placenta previa** [Latin = going before] MEDICINE (a condition involving) a placenta which partially or wholly blocks the neck of the uterus, so interfering with normal delivery of a baby.
■ **placenˈtiferous** *adjective* (ZOOLOGY & BOTANY) bearing or having a placenta **M17.** **placenˈtitis** *noun* (MEDICINE) inflammation of the placenta **M19.** **placenˈtophagy** *noun* the eating of the placenta after giving birth **E20.**

placental /pləˈsɛnt(ə)l/ *adjective & noun.* **L18.**
[from prec. + -AL¹.]
▶ **A** *adjective.* **1** ANATOMY, BOTANY, & ZOOLOGY. Of or pertaining to a placenta. **L18.**
2 ZOOLOGY. Designating a mammal characterized by the development of a true placenta (i.e. not a monotreme or a marsupial). **M19.**
▶ **B** *noun.* ZOOLOGY. A placental mammal, a eutherian. **M19.**

placentary /ˈplas(ə)nt(ə)ri, pləˈsɛnt(ə)ri/ *adjective. rare.* **M19.**
[from PLACENTA + -ARY¹.]
ANATOMY, BOTANY, & ZOOLOGY. Of, pertaining, or relating to a placenta or placentas.

placentation /plas(ə)nˈteɪʃ(ə)n/ *noun.* **M18.**
[from PLACENTA + -ATION.]
1 BOTANY. The disposition or arrangement of the placenta or placentae in the ovary. **M18.**
2 ZOOLOGY. The formation and arrangement of the placenta in the uterus. **L19.**

placentography /plas(ə)nˈtɒɡrəfi/ *noun.* **M20.**
[from PLACENTA + -O- + -GRAPHY.]
MEDICINE. Examination of the placenta using radiography or ultrasound.
■ **plaˈcentogram** *noun* a radiographic examination or image of the placenta **M20.**

placentology /plas(ə)nˈtɒlədʒi/ *noun.* **M20.**
[from PLACENTA + -OLOGY.]
The branch of anatomy or zoology that deals with the placenta.
■ **placentologist** *noun* **M20.**

placer /ˈpleɪsə/ *noun*¹. **M16.**
[from PLACE *verb* + -ER¹.]
1 A person who places, sets, or arranges something. Chiefly *techn.* **M16.**
2 A dealer in stolen goods, a fence. *slang.* **M20.**
3 A person awarded a (usu. specified) place in a competition, race, etc. Chiefly *US.* **M20.**

placer /ˈpleɪsə, ˈplasə/ *noun*². Chiefly *N. Amer.* **E19.**
[Amer. Spanish = deposit, shoal, rel. to *placel* sandbank from *plaza* place.]
MINING. A deposit of sand, gravel, or earth, esp. in the bed of a stream, containing particles of gold or other valuable minerals; a place where this detritus is washed for gold etc.

placer /ˈpleɪsə/ *noun*³. *Austral. & NZ slang.* **E20.**
[from PLACE *noun*¹ + -ER¹.]
1 A gold-digger working on the same spot year after year. **E20.**
2 A sheep which attaches itself to a particular spot or object. Also ***placer sheep***. **E20.**

places d'armes *noun phr.* pl. of PLACE D'ARMES.

†**placet** *noun*¹ var. of PLACIT.

placet /ˈpleɪsɛt, ˈplakɛt/ *interjection & noun*². **L16.**
[Latin = it pleases, 3rd person sing. pres. indic. of *placere* please.]
▶ **A** *interjection.* Expr. assent to a vote in a council or assembly of a university, Church, etc. **L16.**
▶ **B** *noun.* Assent or sanction (as) by an utterance of '*placet*'; *spec.* †(*a*) assent of a monarch or government to an ecclesiastical ordinance; (*b*) an affirmative vote in a council or assembly of a university, Church, etc. **L16.**

placid /ˈplasɪd/ *adjective.* **E17.**
[French *placide* or Latin *placidus* pleasing, favourable, gentle, from *placere* please: see -ID¹.]
Mild, calm, peaceful; unruffled, tranquil, serene; (of a person) not easily disturbed or aroused.

🕮 P. S. BUCK Except for the slight . . wind . . , the waters lay placid and unmoved. J. MARK Disturbed by Cleaver's placid acceptance of the fact that his home was disintegrating over his head. D. CECIL Over-excited—this was an ominous symptom in a woman who was ordinarily placid.

■ **plaˈcidity** *noun* the quality of being placid, calmness, tranquillity, peacefulness **E17.** **placidly** *adverb* **E17.** **placidness** *noun* **E18.**

Placidyl /ˈplasɪdɪl/ *noun.* **M20.**
[from PLACID + -YL.]
PHARMACOLOGY. The drug ethchlorvynol.
¶ Proprietary name in the US and Canada.

placing /ˈpleɪsɪŋ/ *noun.* **LME.**
[from PLACE *verb* + -ING¹.]
The action of PLACE *verb*; the fact or condition of being placed; an act or instance of this; setting, location, arrangement; *spec.* (*a*) (a) sale of a large quantity of stocks or shares, esp. a new issue; (*b*) a position or ranking in a race, contest, etc.

🕮 *Bicycle Action* If you can't win . . get the best placing you can.

†**placit** *noun.* Also **-et**. **E17.**
[formed as PLACITUM. Cf. Italian *placito.*]
1 An opinion, a judgement; a decision, a decree, an ordinance. **E17–M19.**
2 A plea, a petition. *rare.* Only in **E19.**

placita *noun* pl. of PLACITUM.

†**placitory** *adjective. rare.* **M17–M19.**
[formed as next + -ORY².]
LAW. Of or pertaining to pleas or pleading.

placitum /ˈplasɪtəm/ *noun. obsolete* exc. *Hist.* Pl. **-ta** /-tə/. **M17.**
[Latin, neut. pa. pple of *placere* please, in medieval Latin = sentence of a court, trial, plea.]
A decree, decision, or verdict of a judge, court, assembly, etc.; in *pl.*, proceedings of a court, assembly, etc.

plack /plak/ *noun.* Chiefly *Scot. & north.* **LME.**
[Prob. from Flemish *placke*, *plecke* small coin, French *plaque*, *plecque*, medieval Latin *plac(c)a*, *plaka*: see PLAQUE.]
Hist. Any of various small coins current in Scotland or the Netherlands in the 15th and 16th cents.

🕮 J. BUCHAN I don't care a plack for politics.

■ **plackless** *adjective* (*Scot.*) without a plack, penniless **L18.**

placket /ˈplakɪt/ *noun.* **E17.**
[Alt. of PLACARD *noun*. Cf. earlier PLACCATE.]
1 An apron, a petticoat; *transf.* a woman. *arch.* **E17.**
2 An opening or slit in a garment, for fastenings or access to a pocket; a flap of fabric under such an opening. **E17.** ▸†**b** The vagina. *coarse slang.* **E17–E18.**
3 A pocket, esp. in a woman's skirt. **M17.**
Comb.: **placket-hole** an opening in a garment to give access to a pocket.

placode /ˈplakəʊd/ *noun.* **E20.**
[German *Plakode*, from Greek *plakōdēs* laminated, flaky, formed as next: see -ODE¹.]
EMBRYOLOGY. A localized thickening of the ectoderm in a vertebrate embryo which contributes to the formation of a sensory organ, ganglion, feather or scale, etc.

placoderm /ˈplakədəːm/ *noun & adjective.* **M19.**
[from Greek *plak-*, *plax* tablet, flat plate + -O- + Greek *derma* skin.]
PALAEONTOLOGY. ▶ **A** *noun.* A (fossil) fish of the Palaeozoic order Placodermata or Placodermi, having the skin of head and pectoral region encased in broad flat bony plates. **M19.**
▶ **B** *adjective.* Of or pertaining to the order Placodermata or Placodermi. **E20.**

placodioid /pləˈkəʊdɪɔɪd/ *adjective.* **E20.**
[from mod. Latin *Placodium* genus name (formed as Greek *plakōdēs*: see PLACODE) + -OID.]
BOTANY. Of a lichen thallus: more or less disc-shaped, crustose at the centre with lobes around the edge.

placodont /ˈplakədɒnt/ *noun.* **L19.**
[formed as next + -ODONT.]
PALAEONTOLOGY. Any of a group of fossil aquatic reptiles of the Triassic period having short flat grinding palatal teeth.

placoid /ˈplakɔɪd/ *adjective & noun.* **M19.**
[from Greek *plak-*, *plax* flat plate, tablet + -OID.]
ZOOLOGY. ▶ **A** *adjective.* **1** Designating a toothlike fish-scale of dentine and enamel with a flat base, as forming the dermal armour of cartilaginous fishes. **M19.**
2 Having placoid scales. Formerly *spec.*, of or designating an order of cartilaginous fishes ('Placoidei') including sharks and rays. **M19.**
▶ **B** *noun.* A placoid fish. **M19.**

placula /ˈplakjʊlə/ *noun.* Pl. **-lae** /-liː/. **L19.**
[mod. Latin, formed as prec.: see -CULE.]
BIOLOGY. A disc-shaped embryonic stage (as in some sponges). Also, a hypothetical primitive metazoan resembling this.
■ **placulate** *adjective* having the form of a placula **L19.**

plafond /plafɔ̃ (*pl. same*), plaˈfɔ̃(d)/ *noun.* **M17.**
[French, from *plat* flat + *fond* bottom.]
1 ARCHITECTURE. An ornately decorated ceiling, either flat or vaulted; painting or decoration on a ceiling. Also, a soffit. **M17.**
2 CARDS. An early form of contract bridge. **M20.**

plagal /ˈpleɪɡ(ə)l/ *adjective.* **L16.**
[medieval Latin *plagalis*, from *plaga* plagal mode, from Latin *plagius* from medieval Greek *plagios* (in *plagios hēchos* plagal mode), in classical Greek = oblique, from *plagos* side: see -AL¹.]
MUSIC. Of a church mode: having sounds comprised between the dominant note and its octave, the final being near the middle of the compass. Cf. AUTHENTIC *adjective* 6.
plagal cadence, **plagal close** a cadence in which the chord of the subdominant (major or minor) immediately precedes that of the tonic.

plage /plɑːʒ, *in sense 4* pleɪdʒ/ *noun.* **LME.**
[Old French = region, (mod.) beach (from Italian *piaggia*) from medieval Latin *plaga* open space.]
†**1** A region, a district; a zone. **LME–E17.**
†**2** Each of the four principal directions or quarters of the compass; a direction, a side. **LME–M17.**
3 A beach or promenade at a seaside resort, esp. at a fashionable one; a seaside resort. **L19.**
4 ASTRONOMY. A bright region of the sun's chromosphere, usually associated with sunspots. Also ***plage region***. **M20.**

plagi- *combining form* see PLAGIO-.

plagiarise *verb* var. of PLAGIARIZE.

plagiarism /ˈpleɪdʒərɪz(ə)m/ *noun.* **E17.**
[formed as PLAGIARY + -ISM.]
1 The action or fact of plagiarizing a work, idea, author, etc.; literary theft; an act or instance of this. **E17.**
2 A plagiarized idea, passage, work, etc. **L18.**

🕮 **1** R. ELLMANN Plagiarism is the worst of his crimes. He brazenly takes over the best known passages. **2** H. CRICHTON-MILLER Jung uses the term Analytical psychology (. . a plagiarism from Stout).

plagiarist /ˈpleɪdʒərɪst/ *noun.* **L17.**
[from PLAGIARY + -IST.]
A person who plagiarizes a work, idea, author, etc. (Foll. by *of*.)
■ **plagiaˈristic** *adjective* characteristic of a plagiarist, pertaining to or characterized by plagiarism **E19.** **plagiaˈristically** *adverb* **E19.**

plagiarize /ˈpleɪdʒərʌɪz/ *verb.* Also **-ise**. **E18.**
[from next + -IZE.]
1 *verb trans.* Take and use as one's own (the thoughts, writings, inventions, etc., of another person); copy (literary work, ideas, etc.) improperly or without acknowledgement; pass off the thoughts, work, etc., of (another person) as one's own. **E18.**
2 *verb intrans.* Practise or commit plagiarism. **M19.**

1 S. T. FELSTEAD Anyone could take a story from a book and plagiarize it. 2 P. GAY Did Freud plagiarize and then excuse his illicit borrowings?

■ **plagiariˈzation** *noun* = PLAGIARISM 1 L19. **plagiarizer** *noun* = PLAGIARIST M19.

plagiary /ˈpleɪdʒəri/ *adjective & noun*. Now *rare*. L16.
[from Latin *plagiarius* kidnapper, literary from thief, from *plagium* kidnapping from Greek *plagion*: see -ARY[1].]
▶ **A** *adjective*. †**1** That plagiarizes, plagiarizing. L16–M17.
†**2** That kidnaps, kidnapping. *rare*. Only in L17.
†**3** Obtained by plagiarism, plagiarized. L17–E19.
▶ **B** *noun*. †**1** A kidnapper. Only in 17.
2 A plagiarist. E17.
3 Plagiarism. M17. ▸**b** A plagiarism. L17.

plagio- /ˈpleɪdʒɪəʊ, ˈplagɪəʊ/ *combining form*. Before a vowel or *h* also **plagi-**.
[from Greek *plagios* oblique, slanting, from *plagos* side: see -O-.]
Oblique, slanted, offset from the straight or direct line.
■ **plagioceˈphalic** *adjective* (MEDICINE) characterized by plagiocephaly L19. **plagioˈcephaly** *noun* (MEDICINE) oblique deformity of the skull, with greater development of the anterior part on one side and the posterior part on the other L19. **plagioˈclastic** *adjective* (MINERALOGY) having cleavages at an oblique angle to each other (cf. PLAGIOCLASE) M19. **plagioclimax** *noun* (ECOLOGY) in a plant community, a climax produced or affected by some disturbance of the natural conditions M20. **plagioˈgranite** *noun* (GEOLOGY) any of a range of plagioclase-rich (potassium-poor) ophiolitic granites M20. **plagiosere** *noun* [SERE *noun*[2]] ECOLOGY a series of plant communities whose development is affected by some disturbance of the natural conditions M20. **plagiotropic** /-ˈtrəʊpɪk, -ˈtrɒpɪk/ *adjective* (BOTANY) designating or pertaining to a part or organ of a plant whose two halves react differently to the influences of light, gravity, or other external influences, and which therefore takes up an oblique or horizontal position L19. **plagiotropically** /-ˈtrəʊp-, -ˈtrɒp-/ *adverb* (BOTANY) in a plagiotropic manner E20. **plagiotropism** /-ˈtrəʊp-/ *noun* (BOTANY) plagiotropic condition or character L19. **plagiotropous** /-ˈɒtrəpəs, -əˈtrəʊpəs/ *adjective* (BOTANY) = PLAGIOTROPIC *adjective* E20. **plagiotropously** *adverb* (BOTANY) = PLAGIOTROPICALLY E20. **plagiˈotropy** *noun* (BOTANY) = PLAGIOTROPISM E20.

plagioclase /ˈpleɪdʒɪəkleɪz/ *noun*. M19.
[from PLAGIO- + Greek *klasis* breaking, cleavage.]
MINERALOGY. Any of a series of triclinic feldspars (sodium or calcium aluminosilicates) which occur widely in rocks and as free crystals (orig. characterized as having two cleavages at an oblique angle).

plagiostome /ˈpleɪdʒɪəstəʊm/ *noun*. M19.
[from PLAGIO- + Greek *stoma* mouth.]
ZOOLOGY. A cartilaginous fish of the group Plagiostomi, having the mouth placed transversely beneath the snout; a shark, a ray.
■ **plagiˈostomous** *adjective* having the mouth placed transversely beneath the snout M19.

plagium /ˈpleɪdʒɪəm/ *noun*. Now *rare* or *obsolete*. L16.
[Latin: see PLAGIARY.]
1 CIVIL LAW. Kidnapping. L16.
†**2** = PLAGIARISM. Only in 17.

plague /pleɪg/ *noun*. LME.
[Latin *plaga* stroke, wound, pestilence, infection, prob. from Greek (Doric) *plaga*, (Attic) *plēgē*, from verb meaning 'strike' rel. to Latin *plangere*.]
†**1** A blow, a stroke; a wound. LME–M16.
2 a An affliction, a calamity, a scourge, esp. when regarded as a divine punishment; *spec.* an unusual infestation of vermin, a pest, etc. LME. ▸**b** A thing causing trouble or irritation; a nuisance, a trouble; an annoying person, animal, etc. (Foll. by *of*, *to*.) Now *colloq.* M16.
3 †**a** An illness, a disease. LME–L17. ▸**b** *spec.* An infectious, esp. contagious, disease spreading rapidly over a wide area with great mortality; a pestilence; *spec.* (freq. ***the plague***) bubonic plague. M16.

2a *Beano* A plague of moths in the castle! 3b *Daily Telegraph* Plague has broken out in . . northern China and is spreading. **a plague on** —, **a plague upon** —, **a plague take** — (*joc.* or *arch.*) expr. impatience, anger, or dismissiveness towards someone or something. **avoid like the plague** avoid at all costs, shun completely. BUBONIC ***plague***. ***white plague***: see WHITE *adjective*.

Comb.: **plague-flea** any of several fleas, esp. *Xenopsylla cheopsis*, which transmit the plague bacillus, *Yersinia pestis*, from rats to humans; **plague-house** a house marked as having inmates infected with the plague; **plague pipe** *Hist.* a small clay pipe in which tobacco etc. was smoked as a supposed disinfectant against the plague; **plague pit** a deep pit for the common burial of plague victims; **plague-rat** a rat carrying plague; **plague spot** (*a*) a spot on the skin caused by or characteristic of the plague; (*b*) a spot or locality infected with plague; †**plague-water** an infusion of various herbs and roots in purified alcohol, giving supposed protection against the plague.
■ **plagueless** *adjective* (*rare*) M19. **plaguesome** *adjective* (*colloq.*, now *rare*) troublesome, annoying, confounded E19. **plaguesomeness** *noun* M19.

plague /pleɪg/ *verb trans*. L15.
[from the noun.]
1 Affect as with plague; afflict, trouble, torment. L15.
2 Pester or harass continually; annoy, irritate; tease. *colloq.* L16.

1 H. A. L. FISHER The country was plagued for five generations by useless civil war. 2 E. O'BRIEN I won't plague you . . , I'll leave you alone. *Motor Sport* An Australian friend . . continually plagued me to sell it to him. **plague the life out of** tease or torment excessively.

■ **plagued** *adjective* (*a*) afflicted, tormented; infected with plague; (*b*) *colloq.* confounded, cursed, damnable: L16. **plaguer** *noun* (*rare*) M17.

plaguey *adjective & adverb* var. of PLAGUY.

plaguily /ˈpleɪgɪli/ *adverb*. L16.
[from next + -LY[2].]
In a plaguy manner; *colloq.* annoyingly, excessively, exceedingly, extremely.

J. BUCHAN I am plaguily hungry.

plaguy /ˈpleɪgi/ *adjective & adverb*. Also **plaguey**. L16.
[from PLAGUE *noun* + -Y[1].]
▶ **A** *adjective*. **1** Of the nature of or pertaining to a plague or the plague. *arch.* L16. ▸**b** Infected or afflicted with the plague, plague-stricken. Now *rare* or *obsolete*. E17.
2 a Causing severe affliction or trouble. L16. ▸**b** Troublesome, annoying, harassing; confounded, damnable, cursed; excessive, exceeding, very great. *colloq.* E17.

2b E. R. EDDISON For all your idle plaguy ways.

▶ **B** *adverb*. = PLAGUILY. *colloq.* L16.

D. CROCKETT I was plaguy well pleased with her.

plaice /pleɪs/ *noun*. Pl. same, (now *rare*) **-s**. ME.
[Old French *plaiz*, *plaïs*, later *plaise*, *pleisse* from late Latin *platessa*, from Greek *platus* broad.]
1 A European flatfish, *Pleuronectes platessa*, which is brown with orange spots and a white underside, and is an important food fish; (freq. with specifying word) any of various related flatfishes, as (more fully ***American plaice***) the long rough dab, *Hippoglossoides platessoides*. Also, the flesh of any of these as food. ME.
2 = FLUKE *noun*[1] 2. Also more fully ***plaice-worm***. *dial.* E18.

plaid /plad, pleɪd/ *noun*[1] *& adjective*[1]. E16.
[Gaelic *plaide* from Middle Irish (cf. mod. Irish *pluid*, *plaid* blanket), of unkn. origin.]
▶ **A** *noun*. **1** A long piece of twilled woollen cloth, usu. with a chequered or tartan pattern, worn over the shoulder as the outer article of the traditional Highland dress. E16.
2 The twilled woollen cloth used for a plaid. Also, any of various other fabrics with a tartan pattern. M16.
3 A man wearing a plaid; a Highlandman. Long *rare* or *obsolete*. L18.
4 A plaid or tartan pattern; a pattern of bars or stripes crossing each other at right angles. L19.

1 EVELYN Painted . . as . . a Scotch highlander in his plaid. L. G. GIBBON She took little Ewan . . and a plaid to wrap him in for sleep. 2 GEORGIANA HILL Plaids . . were made in large and small checks, in woollen cloth, in Irish poplin. 3 SIR W. SCOTT He was hanged . . with his lieutenant, and four plaids besides.

▶ **B** *attrib.* or as *adjective*. Made of plaid, having a pattern like plaid. E18.
■ **plaided** *adjective* (*a*) dressed in or wearing a plaid; (*b*) made of plaid; having a plaid pattern: E19. **plaiding** *noun* (chiefly *Scot.*) (*a*) = PLAID *noun*[1] 2; (*b*) = PLAID *noun*[1] 1; (*c*) = PLAID *noun*[1] 4: M16.

Plaid /plʌɪd/ *noun*[2] *& adjective*[2]. M20.
[Welsh = party.]
▶ **A** *noun*. In full ***Plaid Cymru*** /ˈkʌmri/ [= of Wales]. A Welsh political party founded in 1925 and dedicated to seeking autonomy for Wales. M20.
▶ **B** *attrib.* or as *adjective*. Of, pertaining, or belonging to this party. M20.

plaidie /ˈpladi, ˈpleɪdi/ *noun*. *Scot.* Also **-y**. E18.
[from PLAID *noun*[1]: see -IE, -Y[6].]
A small plaid; *colloq.* & *poet.* a plaid.

plaidoyer /plɛdwaje/ *noun*. *rare*. Pl. pronounced same. M17.
[French, lit. 'a pleading', use as noun of inf. of verb 'to plead', from *plaid* PLEA *noun*.]
An advocate's speech. Also *gen.*, a pleading, a plea.

R. CROSSMAN Harold made a very long and not very persuasive *plaidoyer*.

plaidy *noun* var. of PLAIDIE.

plain /pleɪn/ *noun*[1]. ME.
[Old French (mod. *plaine*) from Latin *planum* use as noun of neut. of *planus* PLAIN *adjective*[1] (cf. PLANE *noun*[3]); later directly from PLAIN *adjective*[1].]
▶ **I 1 a** A level tract of country; an extent of level ground or flat meadowland. ME. ▸**b** *transf.* A level expanse of sea or sky. M16. ▸**c** In *pl.* Level treeless tracts of country; prairie. Chiefly *US* & *Austral.* L18.
2 An open space on which a battle is fought; *the* battlefield. *poet.* LME.
3 A (real or imaginary) level or flat surface, a plane; *spec.* †(*a*) a geometrical plane; (*b*) *arch.* a smooth usu. flat material surface, *esp.* the flat or broad side of a thin object (as opp. to the *edge*); †(*c*) a flat horizontal area. Cf. PLANE *noun*[3] 1. LME.
4 Plain cloth. Also, a kind of flannel. Usu. in *pl.* *arch.* LME.
†**5** A design, a plan. M16–M17.
6 The horizontal surface of a billiard-table. Now *rare* or *obsolete*. L18.
7 FRENCH HISTORY. ***the Plain***, a moderate party in the National Convention during the French Revolution, so called because its members occupied seats on the floor of the hall. Cf. MOUNTAIN 4. E19.
8 An open space surrounded by houses. *local*. M19.
9 A plain knitting stitch, plain knitting, (see PLAIN *adjective*[1] 7b). L19.

1 DAY LEWIS Beyond . . the White Mountain rising up from the Wexford plain. C. THUBRON From the foothills to . . the coastal plain. **Cities of the Plain** Sodom and Gomorrah (on the plain of Jordan in ancient Palestine) before their destruction, by fire from heaven, for the wickedness of their inhabitants (*Genesis* 19:24). ***cock-of-the-plains***: see COCK *noun*[1] 1. **the plains** *Anglo-Indian* the river valleys of the northern part of the Indian subcontinent (cf. ***the hills*** s.v. HILL *noun*). **b** E. K. KANE On the east we have the drift plain of Wellington Channel. **c** K. S. PRICHARD She had decided to watch the plains for first sight of the horses. *Arizona Daily Star* Snow fell . . in the northern Plains. **2** SHAKES. *Rich. III* I will lead forth my soldiers to the plain. **3** P. S. WORSLEY The silver plains Of two huge valves, embossed with graven gold.

▶†**II** [absol. use of PLAIN *adjective*[1].]
10 *The* plain fact, *the* plain state. LME–L17.
Comb.: **plain buffalo**, **plains buffalo** a N. American buffalo (bison) of a variety, smaller and of a lighter colour than the wood buffalo, which formerly inhabited the central and western prairies; **plainsman** a native or inhabitant of a flat country or the wide open plains of a particular region, esp. in N. America; **plains turkey** (*a*) the Australian bustard, *Choriotis australis*, of the family Otididae; (*b*) *Austral. slang* a bush tramp; ***plains viscacha***: see VISCACHA (b); **plains-wanderer** a ground-dwelling bird of SE Australia, *Pedionomus torquatus*, resembling a quail; **plain turkey** = ***plains turkey*** above; **plain-wanderer** = ***plains-wanderer*** above. See also PLAINS CREE, PLAINS INDIAN.

plain /pleɪn/ *noun*[2]. Now *arch.*, *Scot.*, & *dial.* M16.
[from PLAIN *verb*.]
An expression of pain, grief, or discontent; lamentation, plaint.

plain /pleɪn/ *adjective*[1] *& adverb*. ME.
[Old French *plain*, *plaine* from Latin *planus*, *plana* from base meaning 'flat'. See also PLANE *adjective*.]
▶ **A** *adjective*. **I 1** Esp. of a horizontal surface: flat, level, even; free from elevations and depressions. Now *rare* or *obsolete*. ME. ▸†**b** GEOMETRY. = PLANE *adjective* 2a. L16–E18.
2 Free from obstructions or interruptions; (of a tract of land) open, clear *of* woods, buildings, or occupants; (of the sea) open. *obsolete* exc. *dial.* ME. ▸**b** Of one's line of sight: unobstructed, clear. E17.
3 Smooth, even; free from roughness or unevenness of surface. Long *obsolete* exc. in ***plain-work*** (b) below. LME.

1 SHAKES. *Mids. N. D.* Follow me then to plainer ground. **2** G. FENTON Able to give him battell in the plaine sea. A. MUNDAY There were two woods . . but now they are both made plaine of wood. **b** J. HAYWARD Slew them or tooke them prisoners, in the plaine view of their King. **3** J. PITTS Smooth'd over the Meal, and made it plain.

▶ **II 4** Clear to the senses or mind; evident, obvious; easily distinguishable or recognizable. ME.
5 That is clearly as designated; manifest, direct; downright, absolute. ME.
6 Of which the meaning is evident; simple, intelligible, readily understood. LME.
7 Not intricate or complicated; simple. M17. ▸**b** Designating a knitting stitch made by putting a needle through the front of the corresponding stitch of the previous row and in front of the needle on which this row is held, and passing the yarn from the back round the front of the first needle; designating knitting using this stitch. Cf. PLAIN *noun*[1] 9. M19.

4 B. JOWETT Let me make my meaning plainer in this way. R. HUGHES It was plain their quarry was a merchant brig. **5** C. LAMB He reaped plain unequivocal hatred. **6** J. CARLYLE Tell her distinctly what you want . . in few plain words. **7** F. BURNEY She determined . . to place them in some cheap school, where they might be taught plain work. **b** *Guardian* Cable stitch jacket, plain knit pants.

▶ **III 8** †**a** Without armour or weapons; unarmed. Only in ME. ▸**b** Unembellished, without addition or decoration; not ornate; (of a drawing, lithograph, etc.) not coloured. Also (of a person's name) without addition or title. LME. ▸**c** Of a playing-card: not a court-card or a trump. M19. ▸**d** (Of an envelope, wrapper, etc.) not marked outside with information as to its sender or contents (freq. in ***under plain cover***); (of a motor vehicle, esp. a

van) not displaying information as to its owner or purpose. E20.
9 MUSIC. Monophonic (opp. *polyphonic*). LME.
10 Esp. of food: made or prepared simply; made with few ingredients; not rich or elaborate or highly seasoned. M17.

> **8b** A. P. HERBERT The frock's plain, and a bit of ornament helps. G. VIDAL He had worn coloured shirts but now plain white ones seemed more sound. *Truck & Driver* For just plain egg and bacon, the charge is 78p. **d** N. BALCHIN I expect they'll send a plain van to collect the old boy. **10** R. WEST We will find you some plain biscuits for tea. S. HASTINGS The food was of the nursery variety, plain and wholesome.

▶**IV 11** Open in behaviour; guileless, candid, frank. Now only, outspoken, straightforward, blunt. LME.
12 Free from ambiguity, evasion, or subterfuge; direct. L15.

> **11** I. WALTON To be plain with you, I wil sing none. **12** W. CONGREVE Tell me in plain Terms what the Matter is. A. CHRISTIE He had, in plain language, 'run away'.

▶**V 13** Ordinary, not outstanding; not distinguished by special qualities or abilities, or by rank or position. LME.
14 Simple and unpretentious in dress or manners; unaffected; dressed or living without luxury or ostentation. LME.
15 Of ordinary appearance; (esp. of a girl or woman) not beautiful or pretty; homely; ugly. M18.

> **13** BURKE To me, who am but a plain man, the proceeding looks a little too refined. J. K. HOSMER The admission . . of . . the plain people to a share in the government. **14** A. COWLEY The old plain way, ye Gods, let me be Poor. J. S. BLACKIE His habits . . were remarkably plain and frugal. **15** V. S. PRITCHETT I dared not look . . at the pretty girls and my eyes sought out plain and ugly ones.

Phrases: ***as plain as a*** PIKESTAFF. ***as plain as the nose on your face***: see NOSE *noun*. **be plain with** speak bluntly to. ***plain living and high thinking***: see LIVING *noun*^{1}.
▶**B** *adverb*. **I 1** Clearly, distinctly; openly. ME.
†**2** Levelly; evenly. LME–M17.
3 Simply, unequivocally, absolutely. M16.
▶**II** [Partly from PLAIN *adjective*^{2}.]
†**4** Entirely; fully. ME–M16.
†**5** Directly, due. LME–E18.
Special collocations & comb.: **plain bearing** ENGINEERING a bearing consisting of a cylindrical hole in a block. **plain bob** CAMPANOLOGY a method of change-ringing in which the treble works in continuous plain hunt. **plainchant** = *plainsong* below. **plain chocolate** (a) dark chocolate for eating made without added milk (opp. *milk chocolate*). **plain clothes** civilian clothes as opp. to uniform, esp. as worn by a member of a police detective force while on duty. **plain-clothes** *adjective* wearing plain clothes; ***plainclothesman***, ***plainclothes man***, a plain-clothes policeman, a detective. **plain cook** a person capable (only) of doing plain cooking. **plain-cook** *verb intrans.* do plain cooking. **plain cooking** the preparation of simple dishes; food prepared in a simple way. **plain dealer** (now *rare*) a person who practises plain dealing. **plain dealing** (*a*) openness and sincerity of conduct; candour, straightforwardness; †(*b*) a kind of card-game. **plain-dealing** *adjective* that practises plain dealing; open, sincere, straightforward. ***plain Dunstable***: see DUNSTABLE *noun*. ***plain English***: see ENGLISH *noun*. **plain flour**: without a self-raising agent. **plain-headed** *adjective* †(*a*) ignorant, simple; (*b*) having a smooth or unornamented head. **plain-hearted** *adjective* (now *rare*) having a sincere and open heart; without deceit; ingenuous, innocent. **plain-heartedly** *adverb* (*rare*) in a sincere or open manner, ingenuously. **plain-heartedness** *rare* the state or condition of being sincere or open, ingenuousness. **plain hunt** CAMPANOLOGY in change-ringing, a regular path taken by a bell from first position to last and back again. **plain hunting** CAMPANOLOGY the action of ringing a bell in plain hunt. ***plain Jane***: see JANE *noun*^{2} 1. **plain language** (*a*) the manner of speech used by the Society of Friends; (*b*) = *plain text* (b) below. **plain man** an ordinary or average man, *esp.* one not given to complex reasoning or philosophical speculation. **Plain People** *US* the Amish, the Mennonites, the Dunkers. **plain sailing** †(*a*) = *plane sailing* (a) s.v. PLANE *adjective*; (*b*) sailing a straightforward course; (*c*) *fig.* an uncomplicated situation or course of action. **plain-sailing** *adjective* straightforward in action. **plain-saw** *verb trans.* saw (timber), produce (a board), by plain sawing. **plain sawing** the method or action of sawing timber tangential to the growth rings, so that the rings make angles of less than 45° with the faces of the boards produced; the production of boards by this method. **plain service** a church service without music. **plain sewing** (*a*) needlework that does not involve embroidery or ornamental work; (*b*) *slang* homosexual behaviour involving (mutual) masturbation. **plainsong** [translating Latin *cantus planus*] MUSIC (*a*) unaccompanied music of a form developed in the early Church, sung in unison in the medieval modes and in free rhythm corresponding to the accentuation of the words (cf. GREGORIAN *adjective* 2); (*b*) (obsolete exc. *Hist.*) a simple melody or theme, often accompanied by a running melody or descant. ***plain Spanish***: see SPANISH *noun* 3a. **plain-speaking** *noun & adjective* (*a*) *noun* plainness of speech, candour, frankness; (*b*) *adjective* plain-spoken. **plain-spoken** *adjective* (*a*) given to speaking plainly; outspoken, unreserved; (*b*) plainly spoken; clearly or frankly expressed. **plain-spokenness** the action or fact of being plain-spoken. ***plain*** SURMULLET. **plain text** (*a*) a text not in cipher or code; (*b*) uncoded language. **plaintile** a kind of flat roofing-tile. **plain tripe** the first stomach or rumen of a ruminant, esp. as an article of food. **plain weave**: woven by plain weaving. **plain weaving**: with the weft alternately over and under the warp. **plain-work** (*a*) work of a plain or simple kind without ornamentation or embellishment; *spec.* = *plain sewing* (a) above; (*b*) *rare* an even surface produced on stone etc. by the light action of a chisel.
■ **plainish** *adverb & adjective* (*a*) *adverb* in a somewhat plain manner; (*b*) *adjective* somewhat plain, rather plain: M19. **plainly** *adverb* ME. **plainness** /-n-n-/ *noun* ME.

†plain *adjective*^{2}. ME.
[Old & mod. French *plein* from Latin *plenus* full. Cf. PLAIN *adverb* II.]
1 Full, plenary, entire, perfect; (esp. of a council, assembly, or court) full or complete in number or extent. ME–L17.
2 Of battle etc.: regular, open. Chiefly in ***in plain battle***. ME–E18.
3 Full *of*. *rare*. Only in L15.

plain /pleɪn/ *verb*. ME.
[Old & mod. French *plaign-* pres. stem of *plaindre* from Latin *plangere* lament. Cf. COMPLAIN.]
1 *verb trans.* = COMPLAIN *verb* 1. Long *obsolete* exc. *Scot.* ME.
2 *verb intrans.* & †*refl.* Utter lamentations, give expression to sorrow. Now *poet.* & *dial.* ME. ▸**b** = COMPLAIN *verb* 5. *dial.* M19.
3 *verb intrans.* & †*refl.* = COMPLAIN *verb* 3. (Foll. by *of*, *against*, *on*, *that*.) Now *arch.* & *dial.* ME. ▸**b** *verb intrans.* Tell tales, inform (*against*, *on*). *dial.* L18. ▸**c** *verb trans.* = COMPLAIN *verb* 4. *dial.* M19.
4 *transf.* & *fig.* **a** *verb intrans.* Emit a plaintive or mournful sound. M17. ▸**b** *verb trans.* Say in a querulous tone. E20.

> **2** A. PHILIPS Small Cause, I ween, has lusty Youth to plain. **3** T. KYD I will go plaine me to my Lord the King. SIR W. SCOTT Though something I might plain . . Of cold respect to stranger guest. **4a** M. LINSKILL The wind went on . . sobbing, raging, plaining over the barren moor.

■ **plainer** *noun* †(*a*) LAW = COMPLAINANT *noun* 1; (*b*) (now *dial.*) a complainer, a grumbler: ME. **plaining** *noun* (*arch.*) the action of the verb; an instance of this; (a) lamentation; (a) complaint: ME. **plaining** *adjective* (*arch.*) that plains; plaintive, mourning; complaining: L15.

plainful /ˈpleɪnfʊl, -f(ə)l/ *adjective*. *arch.* M16.
[from PLAIN *noun*^{2}, *verb* + -FUL.]
Distressing, pitiful, grievous. Also, that mourns or emits a mournful sound.

Plains Cree /pleɪnz ˈkriː/ *noun & adjective*. M19.
[from PLAIN *noun*^{1} + -S^{1} + CREE *noun & adjective*.]
▶**A** *noun*. Pl. **-s**, same. A member of a Cree people inhabiting the more northerly areas of the N. American plains; the language of this people. M19.
▶**B** *attrib.* or as *adjective*. Of or pertaining to this people or their language. E20.

Plains Indian /pleɪnz ˈɪndɪən/ *noun & adjective*. L17.
[from PLAIN *noun*^{1} + -S^{1} + INDIAN.]
▶**A** *noun*. A member of any of various N. American Indian peoples formerly inhabiting the plains. L17.
▶**B** *adjective*. Of or pertaining to (any of) these peoples. E20.

plaint /pleɪnt/ *noun*. ME.
[from Old & mod. French *plainte* use as noun of pa. pple fem. of *plaindre*, or from Old French *plaint*, *pleint* from Latin *planctus*, from *plangere* PLAIN *verb*.]
1 The action or an act of plaining; (a) lamentation. Now chiefly *literary*. ME.
2 A statement or representation of wrong, injury, or injustice suffered; a complaint. Formerly also, cause or matter of complaint. *arch.* ME.
3 LAW. An oral or written statement of grievance made to a court for the purpose of obtaining redress; an accusation, a charge. ME.

> **1** L. DURRELL Professional mourners . . with their plaints for the dead. *transf.*: F. NORRIS A jangling of bells and a moaning plaint of gearing. **2** J. BAILLIE They graciously, His plaint and plea receiv'd. A. STORR Emptiness is a characteristic plaint of depressives.

■ **plaintful** *adjective* (long *rare*) †(*a*) grievous; (*b*) full of mourning or complaint, mournful: ME.

plaint /pleɪnt/ *verb*. Long *obsolete* exc. *Scot.* Now *rare*. ME.
[from PLAINT *noun*.]
1 *verb intrans.* Make complaint, complain; *rare* lament, wail. ME.
†**2** *verb trans.* Cover or fill with complaints. *rare*. Only in LME.

plaintiff /ˈpleɪntɪf/ *noun*. LME.
[Law French *plaintif* use as noun of Old & mod. French *plaintif*: see PLAINTIVE *adjective*.]
LAW. A person or body suing a defendant in a court of law. Formerly also *gen.*, a person who complains, a complainer.

> J. R. ACKERLEY My father was the plaintiff and must therefore have brought the action.

plaintive /ˈpleɪntɪv/ *adjective*. LME.
[Old & mod. French *plaintif*, *-ive*, from *plaint(e* PLAINT *noun*: see -IVE.]
1 Grieving, lamenting. Formerly also, suffering. Now *rare*. LME.
†**2** Being or pertaining to the plaintiff in a suit. LME–L16.
3 Expressing sorrow; mournful, sad. L16.

> **1** DRYDEN To sooth the sorrows of her plaintive son. **3** ALDOUS HUXLEY The words awoke a plaintive echo in Bernard's mind. E. BOWEN Peter was glad to have Emmeline home, and was plaintive with her for her absence. *Face* A plaintive song of lost love.

■ **plaintively** *adverb* L18. **plaintiveness** *noun* L18.

plaisanterie /plɛzɑ̃tri/ *noun*. Pl. pronounced same. E18.
[French: see PLEASANTRY.]
A pleasantry.

plaister *noun*, *verb* see PLASTER *noun*, *verb*.

plait /plat/ *noun & verb*. LME.
[Old French *pleit* from Proto-Romance use as noun of neut. of Latin *plicitus* pa. pple of *plicare* to fold: see PLY *verb*^{1}. Cf. PLAT *noun*^{3}, *verb*^{2}, PLEAT *noun*, *verb*, PLET *noun*^{1} & *verb*.]
▶**A** *noun*. **1** A fold, wrinkle, or crease, esp. in a fabric or natural structure; *spec.* = PLEAT *noun* 2. *arch.* LME. ▸**b** *fig.* A twist of character; a quirk, a dodge, a trick; a hidden recess in the mind etc. *arch.* L16.
2 An interlaced length of three or more strands of hair, ribbon, straw, or any cordlike substance; *esp.* a tress of interwoven strands of hair. LME.

> **1** S. RICHARDSON A grave formal young man, his prim mouth set in plaits. D. G. MITCHELL And then smoothed down the plaits of her apron. **b** LD MACAULAY Two characters . . of which he knew all the plaits and windings. **2** SIAN EVANS Her dark hair, braided in two plaits, hung outside the bedclothes. C. LASSALLE Along the walls, garlic plaits and heavy baskets. ***Grecian plait***: see GRECIAN *adjective*.

Comb.: **plait-dance**: in which the participants hold ribbons which are plaited and unplaited in the course of the dance; **plait-stitch** = *PLAITED stitch*; **plait-work** a decorative pattern, common in ancient and medieval art, in the form of interlacing or plaited bands.
▶**B** *verb*. **1** *verb trans.* = PLEAT *verb* 1. *arch.* LME. ▸†**b** Fold, double up; knit (the brows). LME–M17.
2 *verb trans.* Interweave; interlace three or more strands of (hair, ribbon, straw, or any cordlike substance) so as to form a plait. LME. ▸**b** Make (a braid, garland, mat, etc.) by plaiting. E19.
3 *verb trans.* & *intrans.* Twist, cross (esp. the feet). Long *rare*. E17.

> **2** SIR W. SCOTT The little wild boy . . who used to run about and plait rushes. RACHEL ANDERSON Alice . . taught her how to plait her hair. **b** KEATS And with her finger old and brown she plaited Mats o' Rushes.

■ **plaiter** *noun* M18. **plaiting** *noun* the action of the verb; something plaited: LME. **plaitless** *adjective* (*rare*) L19.

plaited /ˈplatɪd/ *adjective*. LME.
[from prec.: see -ED^{2}, -ED^{1}.]
1 Having or formed into a plait or plaits. LME. ▸**b** Wrinkled, corrugated, fluted, striated. E16.
†**2** *fig.* Involved, complicated, complex. LME–M17.

> **1** ADDISON Tho' barks or plaited willows make your hive. G. HARRIS Two had the plaited hair and swarthy faces of Jorgan Islanders. **b plaited stitch** a kind of herring-bone stitch used in worsted work or Berlin work.

plan /plan/ *noun*. L17.
[French = plane surface, ground-plan, alt. (after *plan* PLANE *adjective*) of †*plant*, from *planter* PLANT *verb*, with sense after Italian *pianta* plan of a building.]
▶**I 1** In a perspective drawing, any of several imaginary planes perpendicular to the line of vision forming a grid within which the objects represented appear to diminish in size according to the distance between the viewer and the planes. L17.
†**2** An imaginary flat surface or plane; a surface on which something stands. Cf. PLANE *noun*^{3} 2. Only in E18.
▶**II 3 a** A drawing or diagram made by projection on a horizontal plane, *esp.* one showing the layout of a building or one floor of a building. Cf. ELEVATION 5. E18. ▸**b** A detailed map of a town, district, etc., drawn on a relatively large scale. L18. ▸**c** A diagram, table, or programme indicating the times, places, etc., of forthcoming events or proceedings; *spec.* in the Methodist Church, a document listing the preachers for all the services in a circuit during a given period. L18.
4 a An organized and esp. detailed method according to which something is to be done; a scheme of action, a design; an intention; a proposed proceeding. Also *loosely*, a way of proceeding. E18. ▸**b** A scheme for the economic development of a country, *esp.* one running for a specified period (***five-year plan***, ***four-year plan***, etc.). M20. ▸**c** A scheme for the regular payment of contributions towards a pension, insurance policy, etc. Freq. with specifying word. M20.
5 A design according to which things are, or are intended to be, arranged; an arrangement. M18.

3a P. BROOK He builds his model from a plan, prepared with compass and ruler. 4a A. BROOKNER She must write to Toto, asking him about his plans for the future. R. RAYNER My mind was on the plan I'd cooked up. **according to plan** in a prearranged manner, on schedule (esp. satisfactorily so). **plan of campaign** an organized course of action targeted towards achieving a specific objective or purpose. **c** ***pension plan, savings plan***, etc. **5** D. FRANCIS Fiona looked at the seating plan and said to meet at table six. ***open plan***: see OPEN *adjective*.

Comb.: **planholder** a person contributing to a pension plan etc.; **plan-position indicator** an instrument giving a display on a cathode-ray tube of the positions of objects detected by a rotating radar scanner; **plansifter** (US proprietary name for) a machine consisting of a set of superimposed flat sieves of differing mesh, used in flour milling to separate and grade broken grain; **plan view** a view of an object as projected on a horizontal plane (see sense 3a above).

■ **planful** *adjective* (*rare*) full of plans or schemes L19. **planless** *adjective* without a plan; unplanned; unsystematic: E19. **planlessly** *adverb* L19. **planlessness** *noun* E20. **planster** *noun* (*chiefly derog.*) a planner M20.

plan /plan/ *verb*. Infl. **-nn-**. E18.
[from the noun.]
1 *verb trans.* Design, make a plan of (a proposed building, a new town, etc.) as a basis for building etc. E18.
2 *verb trans.* Make a plan or diagram of (a piece of ground, an existing building, etc.); plot. M18.
3 *verb trans.* **a** Arrange in advance (an action or proposed proceeding); devise, contrive. Also foll. by *out*. M18. ▸**b** Include (esp. a Methodist preacher) in a plan. Usu. in *pass.* E19.
4 *verb intrans.* Make a plan or plans (*for*). L18. ▸**b** Foll. by *on*: intend (a thing, *doing*). *colloq.* E20.

1 W. P. COURTNEY The gardens were planned by the best landscape gardeners of the day. **3a** E. A. FREEMAN Never was a campaign more ably planned. ALAN BENNETT I had my life planned out. **4** M. PUZO He planned for the future of his empire. **b** A. TYLER Do you plan on staying with Muriel forever?

plan- *combining form* see PLANO-².

planar /ˈpleɪnə/ *adjective & noun*. M19.
[from PLANE *noun*³ + -AR¹, after *linear*.]
▸ **A** *adjective*. **1** Of or pertaining to a plane; (having parts) situated in or forming a plane or (esp. parallel) planes; flat, two-dimensional. M19.
2 ELECTRONICS. Designating or pertaining to a solid-state device having boundaries of a number of different *n*- and *p*-type regions lying in a single plane. Also, designating a process in which such devices are made by the diffusion of impurities into a semiconductor through holes etched in a thin silicon oxide layer. M20.
▸ **B** *noun*. COMPUTING. A horizontal motherboard. L20.
■ **plaˈnarity** *noun* the quality or condition of being planar M19.

planarian /pləˈnɛːrɪən/ *noun & adjective*. M19.
[from mod. Latin *Planaria* genus name, from Latin *planarius* on level ground (used as = flat): see -AN.]
ZOOLOGY. ▸**A** *noun*. Any of numerous free-living turbellarian flatworms of the division Tricladida, found in fresh or salt water or in moist earth, having flattened bodies and great powers of regeneration. M19.
▸ **B** *adjective*. Of, pertaining to, or characteristic of a planarian or planarians. L19.
■ **planarioid** *adjective* of the form of or resembling a planarian M19.

planation /pləˈneɪʃ(ə)n/ *noun*. L19.
[from PLANE *noun*¹ + -ATION.]
PHYSICAL GEOGRAPHY. The levelling of a landscape by erosion.
■ **planate** *verb trans.* make level by erosion (orig. & chiefly as ***planated*** *ppl adjective*.) E20.

planch /plɑːn(t)ʃ/ *noun*. ME.
[Old & mod. French *planche*: see PLANK *noun*. Cf. PLANCHE.]
1 A plank or board of wood; *dial.* a floor. *obsolete* exc. *dial.* ME.
2 A slab or flat plate of metal, stone, baked clay, etc.; *spec.* in enamelling, a slab of baked fireclay used to support the work during baking. L16.

planch /plɑːn(t)ʃ/ *verb trans. obsolete* exc. *dial.* E16.
[from prec. or French †*plancher* to plank, floor with planks.]
Make from planks, floor or cover with planks or boards. Chiefly as ***planched*** *ppl adjective*.
■ **planching** *noun* (*a*) the action of the verb; (*b*) planks collectively, boarding; *esp.* flooring: LME.

planche /plɑːnʃ/ *noun*. E20.
[French = plank, slab: see PLANK *noun*. Cf. PLANCH *noun*.]
GYMNASTICS. A position in which the body is held parallel with the ground, esp. by the arms (as on the parallel bars, rings, etc.).

plancher /ˈplɑːnʃə, *in sense 4 foreign* plɑ̃ʃe (*pl. same*)/ *noun*. ME.
[French (Old French *planchier*) = planking, floor, from *planche*: see PLANK *noun*, -ER².]
1 **a** A floor. Formerly also, a platform of planks or boards. *obsolete* exc. *dial.* ME. ▸†**b** An upper storey; a wooden inner roof, a ceiling, etc. E16–E17.
2 A wooden plank, a board; planking, boarding. *obsolete* exc. *dial.* LME.
†**3** ARCHITECTURE. = PLANCIER. M16–E18.
4 In France, the minimum of Treasury bills which banks are obliged to hold. Cf. FLOOR *noun* 1b. M20.

planchet /ˈplɑn(t)ʃɪt/ *noun*. E17.
[Dim. of PLANCH *noun*: see -ET¹.]
1 A plain metal disc from which a coin is made. E17.
2 A small shallow dish used to contain a specimen while its radioactivity is measured. M20.

planchette /plɑːnˈʃɛt/ *noun*. M19.
[French, dim. of *planche*: see PLANK *noun*, -ETTE.]
1 A small usu. heart-shaped board, supported by two castors and a vertical pencil, which, when one or more people rest their fingers lightly on the board, supposedly writes automatic messages under spirit guidance. M19.
2 = PLANCHET 2. M20.

1 *attrib.*: D. BLOODWORTH The planchette board circled wildly, both men keeping their fingers hard down upon it.

plancier /planˈsɪə/ *noun*. M17.
[Old & mod. French †*plancier*, cogn. with *planchier*: see PLANCHER *noun*.]
ARCHITECTURE. A soffit or underside, esp. of the corona of a cornice.

Planck /plaŋk/ *noun*. E20.
[Max K. E. L. *Planck* (1858–1947), German physicist.]
PHYSICS. Used in *possess.* and *attrib.* to designate various concepts developed or discovered by Planck.
Planck constant = ***Planck's constant*** below. **Planck equation**, **Planck formula**: stating Planck's law. **Planck law** = ***Planck's law*** below. **Planck radiation formula**, **Planck radiation law**: stating Planck's law. **Planck's constant** one of the fundamental physical constants (symbol *h*), relating the energy *E* of a quantum of electromagnetic radiation to its frequency ν according to the equation $E = h\nu$; approximately 6.626 × 10^{-34} joule-second. **Planck's equation**, **Planck's formula**: stating Planck's law. **Planck's law** a law, forming the basis of quantum theory, which states that the energy radiated by a black body per unit time, area, and wavelength range is given by $E_\lambda = 2\pi hc^2\lambda^{-5}/[\exp(hc/\lambda kT) - 1]$ (where *h* is Planck's constant, *c* is the speed of light, *k* is Boltzmann's constant, T is temperature in kelvins). **Planck's radiation formula**, **Planck's radiation law**: stating Planck's law.
■ **Planckian** *adjective* of, pertaining to, or being a black body E20.

planctus /ˈplaŋktəs/ *noun*. Pl. *same* /-tuːs/. E20.
[Latin = beating of the breast, lamentation.]
A medieval poem or song of lament. Cf. PLANH.

plane /pleɪn/ *noun*¹. ME.
[Old & mod. French, var. (infl. by *planer* verb) of †*plaine* from late Latin *plana* planing instrument, from *planare*: see PLANE *verb*¹.]
1 A flat tool used by plumbers, bricklayers, etc., to smooth the surface of sand, clay in a mould, etc. ME.
2 A tool, consisting of a wooden or metal block with an adjustable metal blade projecting at an angle, used to level down and smooth a wooden surface by paring shavings from it. Also, a similar tool for smoothing the surface of soft metal. Freq. with specifying word. LME.
2 ***compass plane, jack plane, jointer-plane, panel plane, smoothing-plane***, etc.
Comb.: **plane-bit**, **plane-iron** the cutting blade of a plane; **plane stock** the stock or body of a plane.

plane /pleɪn/ *noun*². LME.
[Old & mod. French from Latin *platanus* from Greek *platanos*, from *platus* broad.]
1 Any of various lofty trees constituting the genus *Platanus* (family Platanaceae), with palmately-lobed leaves and flowers in pendulous ball-like heads; *esp.* (*a*) (more fully ***oriental plane***) *Platanus orientalis* of eastern Europe and western Asia; (*b*) (more fully ***London plane***) *Platanus* × *hispanica*, a hybrid or cultivar of the oriental plane with peeling bark, much planted as a street tree; (*c*) (more fully ***American plane***) *Platanus occidentalis* of south-western N. America. Also ***plane tree***. LME.
2 The sycamore, *Acer pseudoplatanus*, which has leaves like those of *Platanus*. Also ***plane tree***. *Scot. & north.* L16.

plane /pleɪn/ *noun*³. E17.
[Latin *planum* flat surface, use as noun of neut. of *planus* PLAIN *adjective*¹, introduced in 17 as refash. of PLAIN *noun*¹ to express the geometrical and allied uses (cf. French *plan* which similarly replaced *plain*).]
▸ **I 1** A geometrical surface which has the property that every straight line joining any two points in it lies wholly in it, the intersection of two such surfaces being a straight line; a two-dimensional continuum of zero curvature. Also, an imaginary flat surface in space or in a material object, in which lie certain points, lines, structures, paths of rays, etc., or about which some relation (esp. of symmetry) is present; *esp.* a horizontal level. E17.
2 A flat or level surface of a material object, a body of water, etc. L17.
3 *spec.* **a** In a perspective drawing, any of several imaginary flat surfaces which may be parallel or perpendicular to the horizon, forming a hypothetical framework within which objects may be represented according to their relative size (freq. with specifying word). E18. ▸**b** Each of the natural faces of a crystal; (an imaginary plane corresponding to) a planar array of structures, esp. atoms, within a crystalline solid. E19. ▸**c** A relatively thin, flat or slightly curved, usu. movable structure used to produce an upwards, downwards, or occas. lateral force by the flow of the surrounding air or water over its surface; an aerofoil, a hydrofoil; *spec.* a hydroplane on a submarine. Cf. AEROPLANE *noun* 1. E19. ▸**d** ANATOMY. With specifying word: any of various imaginary plane surfaces used as standards of reference for the positions of bodily organs, parts of the skull, etc. M19. ▸**e** A main road in a mine, inclined or level, along which coal etc. is conveyed. L19. ▸**f** COMPUTING. A flat usu. square array of magnetic cores or other elements in a memory. M20. ▸**g** The level at which a speedboat, surfboard, etc., is able to hydroplane. Chiefly in ***on the plane***, ***on to the plane***. Cf. PLANE *verb*² 3. L20.
4 *fig.* A level or standard of thought, knowledge, attainment, existence, etc. M19.

1 H. HUNTER The mists . . repeated on different planes the lustre of his rays. *Scientific American* The planes of the orbits . . are considerably inclined to that of the orbit of Jupiter. ***bedding plane, focal plane, glide-plane, vertical plane***, etc. ***plane of the ecliptic, plane of flotation, plane of polarization, plane of projection, plane of symmetry***, etc. **2** N. SAHGAL He seemed to have the planes and angles of my father's face printed on his subconscious. *INCLINED* ***plane***. **3a** **picture plane** (*a*) the actual surface of a painting etc.; (*b*) an imaginary plane at the front edge of a painting where its perspective meets that of the viewer. **b** ***cleavage plane, lattice plane***, etc. **d** ***coronal plane, medial plane, sagittal plane***, etc. **g** *Motorboats Monthly* Large seas . . may prevent a motor cruiser getting on to the plane. **4** N. MANDELA The . . major races are on . . different planes of achievement in the Civilisation of the West. R. P. JHABVALA We are too mundane for her. She wants to get onto a higher plane.

▸†**II 5** = PLAN *noun* 3. M17–E18.
Comb.: **planesman** [after *helmsman*] a person who operates the hydroplanes on a submarine.

plane /pleɪn/ *noun*⁴. Also **'plane**. E20.
[Abbreviation.]
= AEROPLANE *noun* 2.
Attrib. & comb.: In the sense 'of or pertaining to an aeroplane or aeroplane travel', as ***plane crash, plane fare, plane ticket***, etc. Special combs., as **planeload** as much or as many as can be carried in an aeroplane; **planeside** *US* an area beside an aeroplane; **plane time** the time of departure of an aeroplane on a scheduled flight.
■ **planeful** *noun* as much or as many as an aeroplane will hold M20.

plane /pleɪn/ *adjective*. M17.
[Refash. of PLAIN *adjective*¹ (after French *plan*, *plane* which similarly replaced *plain*, *plaine*) from Latin *planus*. Cf. PLANE *noun*³.]
1 Of a material surface: flat, level. M17.
2 **a** GEOMETRY. Of a surface: perfectly flat or level, without curvature, so that every straight line joining any two points in it lies wholly in it. Of an angle, figure, curve, etc.: lying wholly in such a surface. E18. ▸**b** Pertaining to or involving only plane or two-dimensional surfaces or magnitudes E18.
Comb. & special collocations: **plane chart**: on which the meridians and parallels of latitude are represented by equidistant straight lines (cf. ***plane sailing*** (a) below); **plane-parallel** *adjective* both plane and parallel; **plane-polarized** *adjective* (of light etc.) consisting of electromagnetic oscillations that remain in the same two (mutually perpendicular) planes; **plane sailing** (*a*) the practice of determining a ship's position on the theory that she is moving on a plane; navigation by a plane chart; (*b*) *fig.* = ***plain sailing*** (c) s.v. PLAIN *adjective*¹; **plane-table** *noun & verb* (*a*) *noun* a surveying instrument used for direct plotting in the field, consisting of a circular drawing board mounted horizontally on a tripod, and having an alidade pivoted over its centre; (*b*) *verb trans.* survey with the plane-table; **plane-tabler** a surveyor who uses a plane-table; ***plane*** TRIGONOMETRY.
■ **planeness** *noun* M17.

plane /pleɪn/ *verb*¹. ME.
[Old & mod. French *planer* from late Latin *planare* plane, make smooth, from *planus* PLAIN *adjective*¹.]
▸ **I 1** *verb trans.* Make (a surface) even or smooth; level, smooth. Formerly also, spread out evenly or smoothly. Now chiefly in ***plane the way*** below. ME. ▸†**b** Put on a level *with* or raze *to* the ground. M16–E17.
†**2** *verb trans. fig.* Make plain or intelligible; show or state plainly. LME–M17.
1 **plane the way** *arch.* clear a path; make a person's passage, progress, etc., trouble-free.
▸ **II 3** *verb trans.* Smooth the surface of (wood, metal, etc.) with or as with a plane or planing-machine. LME.
4 *verb intrans.* Use or work with a plane or planing-machine. E18.

3 P. FITZGERALD It just needs taking off its hinges and planing a little. **plane away**, **plane off** remove (as) by planing.

plane /pleɪn/ *verb*² *intrans.* LME.
[French *planer*, from *plan* PLANE *noun*³ (because a soaring bird extends its wings in a plane).]
1 Of a bird: soar on outspread motionless wings. LME.

2 Travel, glide. Freq. foll. by *down*, *out*, etc. E20.
3 Of a speedboat, surfboard, etc.: skim along the surface of the water as a result of lift produced hydrodynamically. E20.

1 J. BETJEMAN The seagulls plane and circle out of sight. 2 J. P. CARSTAIRS I had planed into the large air terminal at Los Angeles. 3 *Windsurf* It will plane in conditions where other hulls will wallow.

planer /ˈpleɪnə/ *noun.* LME.
[from PLANE *verb*¹ + -ER¹.]
1 Orig., a tool or instrument for smoothing. Later, a tool for planing wood; a plane; a planing-machine. LME.
2 A person who makes something level; a worker who uses a plane or planing-machine. M16.
3 PRINTING. A flat block which is struck with a mallet to level type in a forme before locking it up. M19.

planer-tree /ˈpleɪnətriː/ *noun.* E19.
[I. J. *Planer* (1743–89), German botanist.]
A small swamp tree of the south-eastern US, *Planera aquatica*, allied to the elm but with warty fruits. Also called ***water elm***.

planeshear *noun* var. of PLANK SHEER.

planet /ˈplanɪt/ *noun*¹. ME.
[Old & mod. French *planète* from late Latin *planeta*, *planetes* (only in pl. *planetae* for older Latin *stellae errantes* wandering stars) from Greek *planētēs* wanderer, from *planan* wander rel. to *plazein* cause to wander.]
1 Each of the seven major celestial bodies which move independently of the fixed stars (in order of supposed distance from the earth in the Ptolemaic system, the moon, Mercury, Venus, the sun, Mars, Jupiter, and Saturn). *obsolete* exc. *Hist.*, ASTROLOGY, and as in sense 4 below. ME.
2 ASTROLOGY. The supposed influence or quality of a moving celestial body (including the moon and sun) in affecting people and events. Later *gen.*, an occult controlling fateful power. ME.
3 *fig.* A source of influence; a prominent or influential person. LME.
4 ASTRONOMY. Any of various rocky or gaseous bodies that revolve in elliptical orbits around the sun and are visible by its reflected light; *esp.* each of the nine major planets (see below); any of various smaller bodies that revolve around these; a similar body revolving around another star. Also, the earth (cf. ***Planet Earth*** below). M17.
5 In full ***planet-wheel***. A wheel which revolves around a central wheel with a fixed axis in an epicyclic or planetary gear. E20.

2 L. MACNEICE There is more than one way of . . being 'born under' any planet. 3 J. ADAMS What the conjunctions and oppositions of two such political planets may produce, I know not. 4 *Independent* The 'geological' features it shows on Venus should tell us how the planet has evolved. *New York Review of Books* The whole planet thinks of you as a complete bastard.

Phrases: ***joy of a planet***: see JOY *noun*. **major planet** each of the larger bodies which orbit the sun (in order of increasing distance from the sun, Mercury, Venus, the earth, Mars, Jupiter, Saturn, Uranus, Neptune, Pluto). **minor planet** = ASTEROID *noun* 1. **primary planet** a planet which orbits the sun. ***red planet***: see RED *adjective*. **secondary planet** a planet which orbits another planet, a satellite, a moon.
Comb.: **planet cage** a cylindrical form of planet carrier; **planet carrier** a frame on which planet-wheels are mounted in a planetary gear; **Planet Earth** (a name for) the earth, esp. as the planet on which humans live, as distinct from outer space; **planetfall** [after *landfall*] a landing or arrival on a planet after a journey through space; **planet-gear** (a) planetary or epicyclic gear; a planet-wheel; **planet pinion** a planet-wheel, *esp.* one smaller than the sun wheel; **planet-stricken**, **planet-struck** *adjectives* (*arch.*) afflicted by the supposed malign influence of an adverse planet; stricken with paralysis or another sudden physical disorder; stricken with sudden fear or amazement; ***planet-wheel***: see sense 5 above; **planet-wide** *adjective* occurring all over a planet.
■ **planetal** *adjective* (*rare*) of or belonging to the planets, planetary E17.

planet /ˈplanɪt/ *noun*². Now *rare*. Also **planeta** /plәˈniːtә/. LME.
[medieval Latin *planeta* chasuble, perh. abbreviation of late Latin *planetica* (*vestis*) traveller's cloak, use as noun of fem. of *planeticus* wandering: cf. prec.]
An early kind of chasuble consisting of a large loose mantle covering the whole body.

planetaria *noun pl.* see PLANETARIUM.

planetarian /planɪˈtɛːrɪәn/ *adjective & noun. rare.* M17.
[formed as PLANETARY: see -ARIAN.]
▶ **A** *adjective.* Of or pertaining to a planet or planets; planetary. M17.
▶ **B** *noun.* †**1** An astrologer. Only in M17.
2 An (imaginary or hypothetical) inhabitant of a planet. E19.

planetarium /planɪˈtɛːrɪәm/ *noun.* Pl. **-iums**, **-ia** /-ɪә/. M18.
[mod. Latin, formed as next: see -ARIUM.]
1 A mechanized model representing the movements of the planets around the sun; an orrery. M18.
2 A plan or model of the planetary system. M19.
3 A device for projecting images of the planets, constellations, etc., and their movements on to the interior of a darkened dome for public viewing; a building housing such a device. E20.

3 L. DEIGHTON Pin-pointed like stars on a planetarium were the lights of the city.

planetary /ˈplanɪt(ә)ri/ *adjective & noun.* L16.
[from late Latin *planetarius* astrologer (use as noun of adjective = of a planet or planets), from *planeta*: see PLANET *noun*¹, -ARY¹.]
▶ **A** *adjective.* **1** Of or pertaining to a planet or planets; of the nature of or resembling a planet; having some characteristic quality of a planet. L16. ▸**b** ASTROLOGY. Under or resulting from the supposed influence of a planet. E17.
2 *fig.* Wandering like a planet; erratic. E17.
3 Of or pertaining to the planet Earth; worldwide, terrestrial, mundane. M19.
4 MECHANICS. Characterized by the circular motion of a part about a point outside itself; *spec.* (*a*) of, pertaining to, or involving epicyclic gearing; (*b*) designating a heavy rolling-mill in which a hot metal strip is forced between two large rolls, each surrounded by a number of smaller work rolls which rotate against the direction of feed; (*c*) designating a mixer or stirrer in which paddles are rotated about an axis which itself is moved in a circular path. E20.

1 *Sciences* Mars became the major objective of NASA's planetary explorations. *Esquire* From far away she looks like a sprite . . or maybe a planetary alien. 2 J. NORRIS Such wandring, unprincipled, Planetary men as these. 3 *Blackwood's Magazine* The Latin language has a planetary importance; it belongs . . to all lands.

Special collocations: **planetary electron** an electron bound to an atomic nucleus. **planetary engineering** modification of an extraterrestrial planet for human occupation. **planetary gear** (*a*) an epicyclic gear; (*b*) any gear-wheel whose axis revolves around another wheel. **planetary hour** (*a*) see HOUR 1; (*b*) ASTROLOGY any of twelve equal divisions of the period from sunrise to sunset, or from sunset to sunrise, each believed to be ruled by a planet. **planetary nebula** ASTRONOMY an expanding shell of gaseous material surrounding a star. ***planetary precession***: see PRECESSION 2a. **planetary system** a system comprising a star and its planets; the solar system. ***planetary year***: see YEAR *noun*¹.
▶ **B** *noun.* †**1** An astrologer, a star-gazer. E17–E18.
2 A planetary body. E19.
3 A planetary nebula. E20.
4 A planetary gear or wheel (= ***planet-gear***, ***planet-wheel*** s.v. PLANET *noun*¹). M20.

planetesimal /planɪˈtɛsɪm(ә)l/ *noun & adjective.* E20.
[from PLANET *noun*¹ + INFINIT)ESIMAL *adjective*.]
ASTRONOMY. ▶**A** *noun.* A small solid body following a planetary orbit; a miniature planet. E20.
▶ **B** *adjective.* Pertaining to, involving, or composed of planetesimals; *esp.* designating the hypothesis that the planets were formed by the accretion of a vast number of planetesimals in a cold state. E20.

planetic /plәˈnɛtɪk/ *adjective.* Now *rare* or *obsolete*. M17.
[Late Latin *planeticus* from Greek *planētikos* wandering, from *planētēs*: see PLANET *noun*¹, -IC.]
Erratic, erring.

planetismal /planɪˈtɪzm(ә)l/ *noun & adjective.* E20.
[Alt. of PLANETESIMAL.]
ASTRONOMY. = PLANETESIMAL *noun & adjective*.

planetocentric /ˌplanɪtәʊˈsɛntrɪk/ *adjective.* E20.
[from PLANET *noun*¹ + -O- + -CENTRIC.]
ASTRONOMY & ASTRONAUTICS. Referred to, measured from, or having a planet as centre (usu. a planet other than the earth).

planetography /planɪˈtɒɡrәfi/ *noun. rare.* M18.
[from PLANET *noun*¹ + -OGRAPHY.]
The branch of knowledge that deals with the planets; a treatise on or description of the planets.

planetoid /ˈplanɪtɔɪd/ *noun & adjective.* E19.
[from PLANET *noun*¹ + -OID.]
▶ **A** *noun.* A celestial object resembling a planet; a minor planet, an asteroid. E19.
▶ **B** *attrib.* or as *adjective.* Of or pertaining to a minor planet or an asteroid. M19.
■ **planetoidal** *adjective* = PLANETOID *adjective* L19.

planetology /planɪˈtɒlәdʒi/ *noun.* E20.
[from PLANET *noun*¹ + -OLOGY.]
ASTRONOMY. The branch of science that deals with the planets and their evolution.
■ **planetoˈlogic** *adjective* E20. **planetoˈlogical** *adjective* L20. **planetologist** *noun* M20.

planform /ˈplanfɔːm/ *noun.* E20.
[from PLAN *noun* + FORM *noun*.]
The shape or outline of an aircraft wing as projected upon a horizontal plane.

plangency /ˈplandʒ(ә)nsi/ *noun.* M19.
[from next + -CY.]
The quality of being plangent.

plangent /ˈplandʒ(ә)nt/ *adjective.* E19.
[Latin *plangent-* pres. ppl stem of *plangere* beat (the breast), strike noisily: see -ENT.]
Esp. of the sound of the sea, waves, etc.: reverberating, mournfully resonant. Also *gen.*, loud-sounding, strident; plaintive, sad.

F. W. FARRAR The mingled scream of weltering tempest and plangent wave. P. FARMER Stan stood improvising for me alone his plangent, melancholy music. P. LARKIN Poem after poem begins in her peculiarly plangent way, like a hand swept across strings.

■ **plangently** *adverb* E20.

plangorous /ˈplaŋɡ(ә)rәs/ *adjective.* L16.
[from Latin *plangor* noisy beating, loud lamenting, from *plangere*: see prec., -OUS.]
Characterized by loud lamentation.

planh /plɑ̃/ *noun.* Pl. pronounced same. M19.
[Provençal from Latin PLANCTUS.]
A mournful troubadour song.

plani- /ˈpleɪni/ *combining form* of PLANE *noun*³, *adjective*, or of Latin *planus* flat, smooth, level: see -I-.
■ **planiform** *adjective* having a flattened shape; *spec.* (of a joint) arthrodial: M19. **planiˈspiral** *adjective* of a flat spiral form; forming a flat coil: L19.

planification /ˌplanɪfɪˈkeɪʃ(ә)n/ *noun.* Orig. *US.* M20.
[French, from *planifier* plan: see -FICATION.]
Systematic planning or organization; the management of resources according to a plan, esp. of economic or political development; an instance of this.

planigale /ˈplanɪɡeɪl, planɪˈɡeɪliː/ *noun.* M20.
[mod. Latin, formed as PLANI- after *phascogale*.]
Any of several flat-skulled mouselike carnivorous marsupials of the genus *Planigale* (family Dasyuridae), native to Australia and New Guinea.

planigram /ˈplanɪɡram, ˈpleɪn-/ *noun.* M20.
[from PLANI(GRAPHY + -GRAM.]
MEDICINE. An image obtained by planigraphy; a cross-sectional image.

planigraphy /plәˈnɪɡrәfi/ *noun.* M20.
[from PLANI- + -GRAPHY.]
The process of obtaining a visual representation of a plane section through living tissue, as by tomography, ultrasonography, etc.
■ **planiˈgraphic** *adjective* of, pertaining to, designating, or produced by planigraphy M20.

planimeter /plәˈnɪmɪtә/ *noun.* M19.
[French *planimètre*, formed as PLANI-: see -METER.]
An instrument with a movable pointer used for mechanical measurement of the area of an irregular plane figure.

planimetric /pleɪnɪˈmɛtrɪk/ *adjective.* E19.
[formed as prec. + -IC.]
Of or pertaining to planimetry; *spec.* in CARTOGRAPHY etc., pertaining to or designating features other than relief or contours.
■ **planimetrical** *adjective* = PLANIMETRIC E18. **planimetrically** *adverb* by means of or with regard to planimetry or planimetric features M20.

planimetry /plәˈnɪmɪtri/ *noun.* LME.
[formed as prec.: see -METRY.]
The measurement of plane surfaces, esp. by means of a planimeter; the geometry of plane surfaces, plane geometry.

planing /ˈpleɪnɪŋ/ *noun*¹. LME.
[from PLANE *verb*¹ + -ING¹.]
1 The action of PLANE *verb*¹. LME.
†2 A piece planed off; a shaving. L16–E18.
Comb.: **planing-machine**, **planing-mill** a machine for planing wood or metal.

planing /ˈpleɪnɪŋ/ *noun*². E20.
[from PLANE *verb*² + -ING¹.]
The action of PLANE *verb*², *esp.* the action of hydroplaning.

planish /ˈplanɪʃ/ *verb trans.* LME.
[Old French *planiss-* lengthened stem of *planir* to smooth (mod. *aplanir*) from *plain* PLAIN *adjective*¹, PLANE *adjective*: see -ISH².]
1 Make level or smooth; level. LME.
2 *spec.* Flatten (sheet metal, a metal object) with a smooth-faced hammer, or by rubbing a flat-ended tool over the surface; flatten and reduce (metal for making coins etc.) to a required thickness by passing between rollers; polish (paper etc.) by means of a roller. L17.
Comb.: **planishing hammer** a hammer with polished slightly convex faces, used for planishing sheet-metal; **planishing**

roller a roller used in planishing something; *esp.* (in *pl.*) the second pair of polished iron rollers between which metal for making coins is passed.

■ **planisher** *noun* (*a*) a person who planishes something; (*b*) a tool or instrument used for planishing something: **M19.**

planisphere /ˈplanɪsfɪə/ *noun.* **LME.**
[medieval Latin *planisphaerium*, from Latin *planus* **PLAIN** *adjective*¹ + *sphaera*, Greek *sphaira* **SPHERE** *noun*, in form infl. by French *planisphère*.]
A map, chart, or graduated scale formed by the projection of a sphere, or part of one, on a plane; *esp.* a polar projection of half (or more) of the celestial sphere, as in one form of astrolabe.

■ **planispheric** *adjective* of the nature of or pertaining to a planisphere **M19.**

plank /plaŋk/ *noun.* **ME.**
[Old Northern French *planke* (mod. dial. *planque*) = Old & mod. French *planche* from late Latin *planca* plank, slab, use as noun of fem. of *plancus* flat, flat-footed, used as a cognomen *Planc(i)us*, *Plancianus*.]
1 A long flat relatively thick piece of sawn timber; *spec.* a piece at least 2 inches or 50 mm thick as used for building, flooring, etc.; **ME.** ▸**b** Such timber; planking. **M16.** ▸**c** *fig.* A means of extricating a person from a dangerous or difficult situation (with ref. to the use of a plank to save a shipwrecked person from drowning). **M17.**
2 A flat slab of wood having a particular purpose; *spec.* (*a*) a narrow footbridge; (*b*) a table, a board; (*c*) a surfboard. **ME.**
†**3** A flat slab of stone, *esp.* a gravestone. **LME–L17.**
4 A long, comparatively narrow piece of cultivated land; *spec.* a clear-cut division or single plot of land, as distinct from a number of irregular scattered strips of runrig land. Chiefly *Scot. dial.* **M17.**
5 *fig.* An item, esp. an important point of policy, of a political or other programme. Orig. *US.* **M19.**

> 🕮 **1a** D. Francis The weathered old grey beams . . holding up the planks of the floor above. *transf.*: J. Montague We drank brown tea, bit buttered planks of soda bread. **c** J. G. Whittier God grant . . We still may keep the good old plank, of simple faith in Him! **2** *Surf Scene* It is often difficult for a surfer to justify the purchase of a custom plank. **5** *Guardian* The control of dogs . . will stand alongside private roads as a plank in the next manifesto.

Phrases: ***thick as two planks***, ***thick as two short planks***: see **THICK** *adjective*. **walk the plank** (of a pirate's captive) be made to walk blindfold along a plank jutting out over the side of a ship to one's death in the sea; *fig.* take a potentially dangerous course of action.

Comb.: **plank-bed** a bed of boards without a mattress, used as part of the discipline of convents, prisons, etc.; †**plank-board** a thick board suitable for flooring etc.; **plank-buttress** a buttress-root forming a broad flat growth at the base of the trunk in certain tropical trees; **plank-owner** *Nautical slang* (chiefly *US*) (*a*) a member of the original crew of a ship; a marine with long service with his ship or unit; (*b*) a marine with a light task; **plank-road** (chiefly *N. Amer.*) a road made of adjoining planks laid transversely on longitudinal bearing timbers; **plank steak** steak served on a wooden board; **plank-way** the narrow section of deck between the side and frame of the hatch in a wherry etc.

■ **plankless** *adjective* **M19.** **plankways** *adverb* in the manner or direction of a plank; lengthways: **L19.** **plankwise** *adverb* = **PLANKWAYS E19.**

plank /plaŋk/ *verb.* **LME.**
[from the noun.]
1 *verb trans.* **a** Provide, floor, or cover with planks. Also foll. by *over*. **LME.** ▸**b** Fasten *together* or *down* with planks. **M19.**
2 *verb trans.* Reallocate or exchange (land) so as to replace scattered runrig strips with a single compact plot of equal size. Usu. in *pass.* Chiefly *Scot. dial.* **L16.**
3 *verb trans.* Place, put, or set down or *down*, esp. in an abrupt or undignified manner. Also *spec.*, lay (money) *down*, pay (*out* or *up*) abruptly or on the spot. *colloq.* **E19.**
4 *verb trans.* with *it*. Sleep (as) on a plank; lie on the floor or the ground. **E19.**
5 *verb trans.* Fix (fish, steak, etc.) on a wooden board and cook over a hot fire. Also, serve on a wooden board. Chiefly as ***planked*** *ppl adjective*. *N. Amer.* **M19.**

> 🕮 **1a** *Scientific American* Once the hull was entirely planked, deck beams were inserted. **3** K. S. Prichard She planked down all the money they had saved. J. T. Farrell He . . planked himself down at the enamel-topped kitchen table.

planking /ˈplaŋkɪŋ/ *noun.* **LME.**
[from **PLANK** *verb* + **-ING**¹.]
1 Planks collectively, esp. used for flooring or some other surface; *spec.* the planks forming the outer shell and inner lining of a ship. **LME.**
2 The action of **PLANK** *verb*. **L15.**

> 🕮 **1** D. Profumo They clattered over the wooden planking of a bridge.

plank sheer /ˈplaŋk ʃɪə/ *noun.* Also **planeshear** /ˈpleɪnʃɪə/. **E18.**
[Alt. of **PLANCHER.**]
The outermost deck planking of a wooden ship, in men-of-war forming a shelf above the gunwale; the gunwale.

■ Also †**plank-sheering** *noun*: only in **L17.**

plankter /ˈplaŋ(k)tə/ *noun.* **M20.**
[German, from Greek *plagktēr* wanderer, from stem also of **PLANKTON.**]
BIOLOGY. A planktonic organism; = **PLANKTONT.**

planktic /ˈplaŋ(k)tɪk/ *adjective.* **M20.**
[from stem of **PLANKTON** + **-IC**, after German *planktisch*.]
= **PLANKTONIC** *adjective*.

planktology /plaŋ(k)ˈtɒlədʒi/ *noun.* **L19.**
[formed as prec. + **-OLOGY**, after German *Planktologie*.]
The branch of science that deals with plankton.

■ **plankto'logical** *adjective* **E20.** **planktologist** *noun* **L19.**

plankton /ˈplaŋ(k)t(ə)n, -tɒn/ *noun.* **L19.**
[German, from Greek *plagkton* neut. of *plagktos* wandering, drifting, from base of *plazein*: see **PLANET** *noun*¹.]
collect. Floating or drifting organisms, esp. very small ones, found at various depths in the ocean and fresh water, and (more fully ***aerial plankton***) in the atmosphere. Cf. **NEKTON.**

microplankton, ***phytoplankton***, ***zooplankton***, etc.

Comb.: **plankton feeder** an animal whose diet includes plankton; **plankton indicator** an apparatus including a filter that is towed behind a ship to allow estimation of plankton density; **plankton net** a very fine net used to collect samples of plankton or other very small organisms; **plankton recorder** a modified type of plankton indicator in which the filter is in the form of a continuously moving roll.

■ **planktono'logical** *adjective* = **PLANKTOLOGICAL M20.** **plankto'nology** *noun* = **PLANKTOLOGY L19.** **planktotrophic** /-ˈtrəʊfɪk, -ˈtrɒfɪk/ *adjective* (*ECOLOGY*) feeding on plankton **M20.**

planktonic /plaŋ(k)ˈtɒnɪk/ *adjective & noun.* **L19.**
[from prec. + **-IC.**]
▸ **A** *adjective.* Of, pertaining to, characteristic of, or found in plankton. **L19.**
▸ **B** *noun.* (A fossil of) a planktonic organism, esp. a foraminiferan. **M20.**

planktont /ˈplaŋ(k)tɒnt/ *noun.* **L19.**
[formed as **PLANKTON** + **-ONT.**]
BIOLOGY. An individual planktonic organism.

planned /pland/ *ppl adjective.* **L18.**
[from **PLAN** *verb* + **-ED**¹.]
Designed, projected, arranged, etc., (as) in accordance with a plan; that is the result of planning or a plan.

> 🕮 J. Aiken Dru had been a planned child, whereas I was an unexpected . . afterthought. **planned economy** an economy in which industrial production and development etc. are determined by an overall national plan. **planned obsolescence** a systematic policy of obsolescence of consumer goods due to deliberate changes in design, cessation of the supply of spare parts, use of poor-quality materials, etc.

planner /ˈplanə/ *noun.* **E18.**
[from **PLAN** *verb* + **-ER**¹.]
1 A person who plans or makes a plan; a deviser, an arranger; *spec.* a person who plans or controls the development or reconstruction of an urban area, or who engages in economic planning. **E18.**
2 A list, chart, table, etc., giving information which enables a person to organize his or her commitments, plan a course of action, etc. **L20.**

> 🕮 **1** L. Mumford Washington . . might have been a miracle of the solo town planner's art. D. Rowe No strategic planner, no matter how intelligent, perceptive and powerful, can guard against every contingency.

planning /ˈplanɪŋ/ *noun.* **M18.**
[from **PLAN** *verb* + **-ING**¹.]
The action of **PLAN** *verb*; the action or work of a planner, *esp.* the designing or controlling of urban or economic development; the making or delineation of a plan or diagram.

planning application, ***planning blight***, ***planning committee***, ***planning officer***, etc. ***town and country planning***: see **TOWN** *noun*.

Comb.: **planning gain** provision by a developer to include projects beneficial to a community (shops, sports grounds, etc.) in a proposal in return for permission for a commercially viable but potentially unacceptable development; **planning permission** formal permission for a building development, alteration to an existing structure, etc., esp. from a local authority.

plano /ˈpleɪnəʊ/ *adjective.* **M20.**
[from **PLANO-**¹.]
Of a surface of a lens: plane, flat.

plano- /ˈpleɪnəʊ/ *combining form*¹.
[from Latin *planus* flat, smooth, level: see **-O-**. Cf. **PLANI-**.]
Of or pertaining to a plane or flat surface or position; *spec.* (with adjectives of shape) denoting modification of a form towards a plane, as ***plano-conical*** etc., or combination of a plane with another surface, 'plane and —', as ***plano-cylindrical*** etc.

■ **plano'concave** *adjective* having one surface plane and the opposite one concave **L17.** **plano'convex** *adjective* (*a*) having one surface plane and the opposite one convex; (*b*) having a flattened convex form: **M17.** **plano-'miller** *noun* a milling machine with a flat bed and a sliding crosspiece carrying rotating cutters, used esp. for heavy planing work **E20.** **plano'spiral** *adjective* = **PLANISPIRAL M19.**

plano- /ˈplanəʊ/ *combining form*². Before a vowel **plan-**.
[from Greek *planos*, wandering, from *planan* wander: see **PLANET** *noun*¹, **-O-**.]
BIOLOGY. Forming nouns and adjectives with the sense 'free-living, motile', as ***planont***.

■ **planogamete** *noun* (*BIOLOGY*) a motile gamete or conjugating cell, a zoogamete **L19.** **planoga'metic** *adjective* of or pertaining to planogametes **L20.** **planospore** *noun* (*MYCOLOGY*) a motile spore, a zoospore **M20.**

planography /pləˈnɒɡrəfi/ *noun.* **M19.**
[from **PLANO-**¹ + **-GRAPHY.**]
1 The art of drawing plans; *spec.* a method used in hydraulic engineering to delineate drainage systems. *rare.* **M19.**
2 The art or process of printing from a plane surface, in contrast to processes in which the matter to be printed is in relief or intaglio. **E20.**

■ **plano'graphic** *adjective* **L19.**

planometer /pləˈnɒmɪtə/ *noun.* **M19.**
[from **PLANO-**¹ + **-METER.**]
A flat plate, usually of cast iron, used in metalwork as a standard gauge for plane surfaces.

planont /ˈplanənt/ *noun.* **E20.**
[from **PLANO-**² + **-ONT.**]
BIOLOGY. A motile spore, gamete, or zygote in certain protozoans and fungi.

Planorbis /pləˈnɔːbɪs/ *noun.* Pl. **-bes** /-biːz/. **L18.**
[mod. Latin, from Latin *planus* **PLANE** *adjective* + *orbis* **ORB** *noun*¹.]
ZOOLOGY. A freshwater snail (pond snail) of the genus *Planorbis*, characterized by a rounded shell in the form of a flat spiral. Now only as mod. Latin genus name.

■ **planorbiform** *adjective* resembling a Planorbis; of a rounded planispiral shape: **M19.**

planosol /ˈpleɪnə(ʊ)sɒl, ˈplanə(ʊ)-/ *noun.* **M20.**
[from **PLANO-**¹ + **-SOL.**]
SOIL SCIENCE. An intrazonal soil with a thin, strongly leached surface horizon overlying a compacted hardpan or clay-pan, occurring on flat uplands with poor drainage.

■ **plano'solic** *adjective* **M20.**

plant /plɑːnt/ *noun.* **OE.**
[Latin *planta*. In later senses infl. by medieval or mod. uses of Latin *planta*, and French *plante*, or by **PLANT** *verb*.]
1 A young tree, shrub, vegetable, or flower newly planted or intended for planting; a set, a cutting. Now *dial.* **OE.** ▸**b** A young tree or sapling used as a pole, staff, or cudgel. Now chiefly *dial.* **LME.** ▸**c** *fig.* A thing planted or springing up; a young person; a novice. Now *rare.* **LME.**
2 *gen.* & *BIOLOGY.* A living organism other than an animal, typically fixed to a substrate, able to subsist wholly on inorganic substances, and moving chiefly by growth; *esp.* (more fully ***green plant***) such an organism having cellulose cell walls and capable of photosynthesis by means of chlorophyll (i.e. excluding bacteria and fungi). Freq., a small (esp. herbaceous) organism of this kind, as opp. to a tree or shrub. **M16.**
3 Machinery, fixtures, and apparatus used in an industrial or engineering process; a single machine or large piece of apparatus. Also, the premises, fittings, and equipment of a business or (chiefly *N. Amer.*) institution; a factory. **L18.** ▸**b** The equipment, stock, vehicles, etc., of a drover, farm, etc. *Austral.* **M19.**
4 **a** A hiding place, esp. for stolen or illicit goods; hidden goods or people; a hoard, *spec.* a drug-user's supply or equipment. *slang.* **L18.** ▸**b** A spy, a detective; a group or cordon of detectives, hidden police officers, etc. *slang.* **E19.** ▸**c** A person or thing planted or introduced surreptitiously or incriminatingly. *colloq.* **E20.**
5 A person's stance, footing, or foothold. **E19.**
6 A scheme or plot to swindle or defraud a person; an elaborately planned burglary or other illegal act. *slang.* **E19.**
7 A growth of something planted or sown, a crop. Also, the action of growing, growth. **M19.**
8 A deposit of fish spawn or fry etc.; a bedded as opp. to a native oyster. *US.* **M19.**
9 *BILLIARDS & SNOOKER* etc. A shot whereby the cue-ball strikes either one of two touching or nearly touching (usu. red) balls with the result that the other is potted. **L19.**

> 🕮 **2** M. Armstrong An attractive . . plant, with stout, smooth, hollow flower-stems. *Garden News* The plant should thrive if given the same conditions as rhododendrons. ***caustic plant***, ***pitcher-plant***, ***rubber plant***, ***sensitive plant***, ***spider plant***, ***vascular plant***, ***woody plant***, etc. **3** H. Wilson Industry tends to defer the ordering of new plant during a depression. N. Gordimer The metal box factory and the potato crisp plant. *Ships Monthly* An elaborate air-conditioning plant which included 106 . . ventilating systems. **4c** *Newsweek* FBI 'plants' who infiltrated the Communist Party. **7** Rider Haggard There was a very full plant of swedes, which would have produced a fine crop. **miss plant** fail to spring from seed.

For other words beginning with *plani-* see the entry for **plani-**

Comb.: **plant-animal** (now *rare*) a zoophyte; *fig.* a dull or stupid person; **plant-beetle** a leaf-beetle; **plant-bug** any hemipteran that infests and feeds on plants, *esp.* a mirid, an aphid; **plant-cane** a sugar cane of one year's growth; **plant-cutter** (*a*) a S. American passerine bird of the genus *Phytotoma*, which habitually bites off the shoots of plants; (*b*) in *pl.* (*US HISTORY*), rioters in Virginia who systematically cut down tobacco plants; **plant-feeder** any animal that feeds on plants; **plant geographer** = PHYTOGEOGRAPHER; **plant geography** = PHYTOGEOGRAPHY; **planthopper** a small, leaping, plant-sucking bug of the family Delphacidae, which includes some pests of rice and sugar cane; **plant hormone** = HORMONE 2, PHYTOHORMONE; **plant kingdom** plants collectively, as one of the major divisions of the natural world (now in *BIOLOGY* usu. excluding bacteria, fungi, and often protists); **plant-louse** a small hemipteran that infests plants, *esp.* an aphid; **plantmilk** a synthetic milk substitute prepared from vegetable matter; **plant pathology** = PHYTOPATHOLOGY; **plantsman** an expert gardener, a connoisseur of plants; **plantsmanship** expert knowledge of gardening, esp. with an interest in unusual or rare plants; **plantswoman** a female plantsman.

■ **plantless** *adjective* M19. **plantlet** *noun* an undeveloped or diminutive plant E19. **plantlike** *adjective* resembling (that of) a plant M16. **plantling** *noun* a young or small plant, a plantlet M18.

plant /plɑːnt/ *verb trans.* OE.
[Latin *plantare*, reinforced in Middle English by Old & mod. French *planter* from Latin.]
1 Place (a seed, bulb, or growing thing) in the ground so that it may take root and grow; establish (a garden, orchard, etc.) by doing this. OE. ▸**b** Introduce into an area or country as a new breed; deposit (young fish, spawn, oysters, etc.) in a river or lake to live or grow; naturalize. L19.
2 Found, establish (a colony, city, church, etc.). OE. ▸**b** Settle (a person) in a place, establish as a settler or colonist. ME. ▸**c** *refl.* Establish oneself, settle. M16.
3 Set, insert, or place firmly *in*, *on*, *up*, or *down*; put or fix in position; situate, locate; post, station. LME. ▸**b** Put or place (artillery) in position. M16. ▸**c** *refl.* Place or station oneself, take up a position, esp. heavily or obstructively. E18. ▸**d** Deliver (a blow, kiss, ball, etc.) with deliberate aim. *colloq.* E19.
4 Implant or introduce (an idea etc.) *in* another's mind; cause (a doctrine etc.) to become established. LME. ▸**b** Establish or set up (a person or thing) in a particular condition or situation. Now *rare*. M16.
5 Provide or intersperse *with* a number of usu. scattered objects. LME. ▸**b** Stock or supply (a piece of land) *with* growing plants etc. Also foll. by *to*, *in*. L16. ▸**c** Provide (a vacant church) *with* a minister. Now *rare* or *obsolete* *Scot.* L16. ▸**d** Colonize, settle, or people (a place) *with* inhabitants, cattle, etc. E17.
6 a Hide, conceal, (esp. stolen goods). *slang* (now chiefly *Austral.*). E17. ▸**b** Surreptitiously post or infiltrate (a person), esp. as a spy or agent; conceal or introduce (a thing) for a specified purpose, esp. so as to incriminate, compromise, or mislead on discovery. *colloq.* L17.
7 Abandon (a person), esp. at a social function; terminate one's relationship with. *slang* (now *rare*). M18.
8 Bury (a dead person). *slang* (orig. *US*). M19.

📖 **1** JO GRIMOND The few dozen trees I planted round my house. E. WELTY She planted every kind of flower. A. N. WILSON The English garden, planted long since by old Volkonsky. **plant out** transfer from a pot or frame to the open ground; set out (seedlings) at intervals to give room for growth; arrange plants or trees in a piece of ground. **b** R. BRAUTIGAN Some fish and game people were planting trout in the streams. **2b** E. A. FREEMAN Teutonic soldiers planted as colonists by the Roman government. **3** R. L. STEVENSON A low, brown cottage, planted close against the hill. G. NAYLOR One hand . . firmly planted on the bride's shoulder. DENNIS POTTER Times to fly, and times to plant your feet. **c** H. JAMES She planted herself there . . guarding a treasure. **d** J. WAIN The kick he would plant . . in the dog's mouth as it yelped at him. **5** ADDISON A vast Ocean planted with innumerable Islands. **b** S. CHITTY The valley . . is closely planted with fruit trees. **6b** R. G. COLLINGWOOD He might have planted treasonable correspondence in his coat. *Guardian* Activists . . planted a bomb on board the . . airliner. S. BRILL Investigators . . had planted an informant among organized-crime figures.

■ **plantable** *adjective* able to be planted; fit for planting or cultivation: L17. **planting** *noun* (*a*) the action of the verb; (*b*) (chiefly *Scot. & north.*) a clump or bed of things (esp. trees) planted, a plantation: OE. **planting** *ppl adjective* that grows plants; owning or cultivating a plantation or estate: E19.

†**plantage** *noun.* E17.
[French, from *planter*: see prec., -AGE.]
1 Vegetation, herbage. E17–E19.
2 The cultivation of plants, planting. M–L17.

Plantagenet /plan'tadʒɪnɪt/ *noun & adjective.* L16.
[Latin *planta genista* lit. 'sprig of broom', said to have been worn as a crest by the Plantagenets and the origin of their name.]
▸**A** *noun.* Any of the kings of England from Henry II to Richard III. L16.
▸**B** *adjective.* Designating or pertaining to (any of) these kings. M19.

plantain /'plantɪn, -teɪn/ *noun*¹. LME.
[Old & mod. French *plantain* from Latin *plantagin-*, *plantago*, from *planta* sole of the foot, from its broad prostrate leaves.]
Any of various low-growing plants constituting the genus *Plantago* (family Plantaginaceae), with dense cylindrical spikes of inconspicuous flowers and leaves in a basal rosette usu. pressed closely to the ground; *esp.* (*a*) (in full ***greater plantain***) *P. major*, with long tapering spikes and broadly ovate leaves, (*b*) = RIBWORT ***plantain***. Also (with specifying word), any of various plants resembling the plantain, esp. in their broad leaves.
Indian plantain, ***rattlesnake plantain***, ***rose plantain***, ***water plantain***, etc.
Comb.: **plantain lily** = HOSTA.

plantain /'plantɪn, -teɪn/ *noun*². Now *rare* or *obsolete*. M16.
[French †*plantain*, *plantoine*, used beside *platane*, from Latin PLATANUS.]
A plane tree (genus *Platanus*).

plantain /'plantɪn, -teɪn/ *noun*³. Also (earlier) †**platan**. M16.
[Spanish *plátano*, *plántano*, prob. assim. of Central or S. Amer. name (e.g. Galibi *palatana*, Carib *balatana*, Arawak *pratane*) to Spanish *plátano*, *plántano* plane tree.]
A banana (the fruit); *spec.* (esp. *N. Amer. & W. Indies*) any of the varieties of this fruit with a high starch content, which are picked when not yet ripe and cooked as a vegetable in tropical countries. Also, a plant producing this fruit, esp. *Musa paradisiaca*.
Comb.: **plantain-eater** = TURACO.

plantal /'plɑːnt(ə)l/ *adjective.* Now *rare*. M17.
[from PLANT *noun* + -AL¹ after *animal*: translating Greek *phutikos*.]
Of or pertaining to a plant, vegetable; *PHILOSOPHY* belonging to the lowest and simplest kind of life.

plantar /'plantə/ *adjective.* E18.
[Latin *plantaris*, from *planta* sole of the foot: see -AR¹.]
ANATOMY & MEDICINE. Of or pertaining to the sole of the foot.

plantation /plan'teɪʃ(ə)n, plɑːn-/ *noun.* LME.
[French, or Latin *plantatio(n-)*, from *plantat-* pa. ppl stem of *plantare*: see PLANT *verb*, -ATION.]
1 a The action of planting seeds or plants in the ground. Now *rare*. LME. ▸**b** The settling of people, esp. in a conquered or dominated country; (an instance of) the planting or establishing of a colony, colonization. L16. ▸**c** The founding of something, as an institution, a religion, etc. E17.
†**2** Something which has been founded or established, as an institution, a church, etc. LME–E18.
3 A bed or clump of growing plants; an area planted with trees etc. M16.
4 A settlement in a conquered or dominated country, a colony. *Hist.* E17. ▸†**b** A company of settlers. M17–E18.
5 An estate or large farm, esp. in a former British colony, on which cotton, tobacco, etc., are cultivated, formerly chiefly by slave labour. M17.

📖 **3** A. BURGESS It was a mansion . . and it had wide grounds and a beech plantation. **5** ANTHONY HUXLEY The establishment of rubber and coffee plantations in the Far East.

Comb.: **plantation creole** a creolized language arising amongst a transplanted and largely isolated black community, as slaves in the US; **plantation crêpe** *adjectival phr.* (*US*) designating a kind of crêpe rubber sole on footwear; **plantation song** a song of the kind formerly sung by black slaves on American plantations.

Planté /'plɑːnteɪ/ *noun.* L19.
[R. L. Gaston *Planté* (1834–89), French physicist.]
ELECTRICITY. Used *attrib.* to designate a type of lead-acid accumulator plate, a cell containing such plates, and the process by which they are formed.

planter /'plɑːntə/ *noun.* LME.
[from PLANT *verb* + -ER¹.]
1 A person who plants seeds, bulbs, etc.; a cultivator of the soil, a farmer. LME.
2 A settler in or founder of a colony, a colonist; *spec.* (*Hist.*), in Ireland, (*a*) any of the English or Scottish settlers planted on forfeited lands in the 17th cent.; (*b*) a person settled in the holding of an evicted tenant in the 19th cent. E17.
3 The founder or popularizer of a church, religion, etc. M17.
4 The manager or occupier of a cotton, tobacco, etc., plantation or estate, orig. in the W. Indies or the southern US. M17.
5 A snag formed by a tree-trunk embedded in a more or less erect position in a river. *US. arch.* L18.
6 a An implement or machine for planting or sowing seeds. M19. ▸**b** A pot, tub, etc., for growing or displaying plants. M20.
Comb.: **planter's punch**, **planters' punch** a cocktail containing rum.
■ **planterdom** *noun* the class of planters, planters collectively M19. **plantership** *noun* the position or condition of a planter E17.

plantigrade /'plantɪgreɪd/ *adjective & noun.* M19.
[French from mod. Latin *plantigradus*, from Latin *planta* sole of the foot + -I- + *-gradus* walking.]
ZOOLOGY. ▸**A** *adjective.* **1** Walking upon the soles of the feet, like a human; designating or adapted for such a manner of walking. Formerly *spec.*, designating or pertaining to a member of a former tribe Plantigrada of carnivorous mammals, including bears, badgers, and racoons. M19.
2 Of a human: having flat feet. M19.
▸**B** *noun.* A plantigrade animal. M19.

Plantin /'plantɪn/ *noun.* E20.
[Christophe *Plantin* (1514–89), printer of Antwerp.]
TYPOGRAPHY. Any of a class of old-face types based on a 16th-cent. Flemish original.

plantocracy /plɑː'nɒkrəsi/ *noun.* M19.
[from PLANT(ER: see -O-, -CRACY.]
A body of planters, esp. (in the W. Indies) regarded as a ruling or dominant class. Usu. ***the plantocracy***.

plantula /'plantjʊlə/ *noun.* Pl. **-lae** /-liː/. E19.
[mod. Latin, dim. of *planta* sole of the foot: cf. -ULE.]
ENTOMOLOGY. A lobe on an insect's foot which assists in gripping surfaces; *spec.* a lobe on the tarsus of a dipteran fly.

plantule /'plantjuːl/ *noun.* Now *rare* or *obsolete*. M18.
[mod. Latin *plantula* dim. of Latin *planta* a shoot, slip: see -ULE.]
BOTANY. An embryonic or rudimentary plant.

planula /'planjʊlə/ *noun.* Pl. **-lae** /-liː/. L19.
[mod. Latin, dim. of Latin *planus* PLANE *adjective*: see -ULE.]
ZOOLOGY. A free-swimming coelenterate larva with a flattened ciliated solid body. Also ***planula larva***.
■ **planuloid** *adjective* resembling a planula L19.

planxty /'plaŋ(k)sti/ *noun.* *Anglo-Irish.* L18.
[Origin unkn.]
A lively tune in triplets for harp, fiddle, etc., slower than a jig; a dance to this.

plap /plap/ *verb intrans.* Infl. **-pp-**. M19.
[Imit.: cf. *flap*, *slap*.]
Come down or fall with (the sound of) a flat impact; make a flapping sound, flap.

plapper /'plapə/ *verb intrans.* M19.
[Imit.]
Make sounds with the lips; (of liquid) make the sound of boiling or bubbling.

plaque /plak, plɑːk/ *noun.* M19.
[French from Dutch *plak* tablet, from *plakken* to stick: cf. PLACARD *noun*.]
1 An ornamental plate or tablet of metal, porcelain, etc., hung up as a wall decoration, inserted in a piece of furniture, or esp. affixed to a monument or building and containing identifying or commemorative details. M19. ▸**b** A small ornamental tablet worn as a badge of high rank in an honorary order. M19.
2 a *MEDICINE.* A flat raised patch, growth, or deposit. L19. ▸**b** *MEDICINE.* (A patch of) fibrous tissue or fatty matter (atheroma) on the wall of an artery. L19. ▸**c** (A patch of) sticky or hard material containing bacteria deposited on the surface of a tooth. Also ***dental plaque***. L19.
3 *BIOLOGY.* A relatively clear area in a culture of micro-organisms or other cells produced by the inhibitory or lethal effect of a virus or other agent. E20.
4 *MEDICINE.* A flat applicator formerly used in the application of radium or radium salts to the skin as a treatment for underlying cancer. Also more fully ***radium plaque***. E20.
5 A counter used in gambling. E20.
6 *MUSIC.* A thin metal plate inserted into the separated tip of the double reed of certain wind instruments while the reed is being scraped. M20.

📖 **1** P. THEROUX The brass plaque on the landing . . said *Borges*. J. BERGER There is a plaque with an inscription which pays tribute to Chavez' heroism. **2a *senile plaque***: see PLAQUE *adjective* 1. **b** *Time* His left main coronary artery was clogged with cholesterol-laden plaque. **c** *Daily Telegraph* Plaque produces the harmful acids . . that cause tooth decay.

■ **pla'quette** *noun* a small plaque or ornamental tablet E19.

plash /plaʃ/ *noun*¹. Also (*dial.*) **plosh** /plɒʃ/.
[Old English *plæsc* corresp. to Middle Dutch *plasch* pool, of imit. origin. Cf. PLASH *verb*².]
A shallow piece of standing water, a marshy pool, a puddle; marsh, mire.
■ **plashet** *noun* (now *dial.*) a little plash or marshy pool L16.

plash /plaʃ/ *noun*². *obsolete* exc. *dial.* LME.
[Prob. from PLASH *verb*¹.]
A plashed branch, bush, or thicket.

plash /plaʃ/ *noun*³ *& adverb.* Also **plosh** /plɒʃ/. E16.
[Prob. from PLASH *verb*².]
▸**A** *noun.* The sound produced by water or other liquid striking something or being struck; a splash, (gentle) splashing; *Scot. & north.* a heavy fall of rain. E16.

📖 H. JAMES The plash of the oars was the only sound.

▸**B** *adverb.* With a plash. M19.

plash /plaʃ/ *verb*[1] *trans.* L15.
[Old French *plassier, plaissier* from Proto-Romance from Latin *plectere* weave, plait. Cf. PLEACH *verb*, SPLASH *verb*[1].]
1 Bend down and interweave (stems, branches, and twigs) to form a hedge or fence. L15. ▸†**b** Interlace or train (growing branches etc.) in or against a trellis etc.; intertwine, interweave. L16–M18. ▸†**c** *gen.* Bend or break down (a plant etc.). E17–E18.
2 Make or renew (a hedge) by cutting stems partly through, bending them down, and interlacing them with growing branches and twigs. E16. ▸†**b** Defend or enclose (esp. a wood) by forming a hedge in this way. L16–L18.
■ **plashing** *noun*[1] (*a*) the action of the verb; (*b*) a piece of plashed hedge or thicket: L15.

plash /plaʃ/ *verb*[2]. M16.
[Imit.: rel. to PLASH *noun*[3]. Cf. Middle & mod. Low German *plaschen*, Middle & mod. Dutch *plassen*, PLASH *noun*[1], SPLASH *verb*[1].]
1 *verb trans.* Strike or stir up the surface of (water or other liquid). M16. ▸**b** Dash with breaking water or other liquid so as to wet. L16.
2 *verb intrans.* Move, tumble, strike, or be struck with a (gentle) splashing sound. M17.
2 J. BUCHAN The echo of a plashing stream descended the steeps.
■ **plashing** *noun*[2] the action of the verb; the sound of dashing or falling water M16. **plashingly** *adverb* with plashing L19.

plashy /ˈplaʃi/ *adjective*[1]. M16.
[from PLASH *noun*[1] + -Y[1].]
Covered in or characteristic of shallow pools or puddles; marshy, swampy, boggy.

plashy /ˈplaʃi/ *adjective*[2]. L16.
[from PLASH *noun*[3] + -Y[1].]
That plashes or splashes, splashy; *transf.* splashed with colour.
■ **plashily** *adverb* (*rare*) with a plashing noise, in a plashy manner E20.

-plasia /ˈpleɪzɪə/ *suffix.*
[from Greek *plasis* moulding, conformation (from *plassein* form, mould) + -IA[1].]
MEDICINE & BIOLOGY. Forming nouns denoting or relating to (types of) growth or development (of tissue), as ***dysplasia***, ***fibroplasia***.

plasm /ˈplaz(ə)m/ *noun.* E17.
[Late Latin PLASMA.]
†**1** A mould or matrix in which something is cast or formed; a cast of a fossil. Also (*rare*), something moulded. E17–L19.
†**2** = PLASMA 2. *rare.* Only in M18.
3 = PLASMA 4. Now *rare.* M19.
4 = PLASMA 3. L19.

-plasm /ˈplaz(ə)m/ *suffix.*
[Extracted from PROTOPLASM.]
Forming nouns denoting shapeless or mouldable substances, esp. (BIOLOGY) kinds of protoplasm or intracellular ground substance, as ***cytoplasm***, ***ectoplasm***, ***idioplasm***, ***sarcoplasm***.

plasma /ˈplazmə/ *noun.* E18.
[Late Latin from Greek *plasma, plasmat-* mould, image, (also) formation, from *plassein* to mould, to form. Cf. PLASTIC *adjective*.]
†**1** Form, mould, shape. *rare.* E18–E19.
2 A subtranslucent green variety of chalcedony, valued as a semiprecious stone. L18.
3 PHYSIOLOGY. The pale yellowish protein-rich liquid in which the cells of the blood are suspended. Also, (the liquid component of) lymph. Freq. *attrib.* with ref. to (the concentration of) substances dissolved in the blood, as ***plasma protein***. M19.
4 BIOLOGY. Protoplasm, cytoplasm. Now *rare.* M19.
5 PHYSICS. An ionized gas containing electrons and free positive ions, formed usu. at high temperatures; *esp.* an electrically neutral one exhibiting certain phenomena due to the collective interaction of charges. Also, an analogous collection of charged particles in which one or both kinds are mobile, as the conduction electrons in a metal, the ions in a salt solution. E20.
6 SOIL SCIENCE. The colloidal or relatively soluble material between grains of a soil. M20.
Comb. (see also PLASMA-): **plasma arc** a very hot plasma jet produced by passing a noble gas through a nozzle that is one electrode of an electric arc, used in plasma torches; **plasma cell** PHYSIOLOGY †(*a*) a type of cell found in connective tissue; (*b*) a fully differentiated lymphocyte, a plasmacyte; **plasma diagnostics** PHYSICS the determination of the characteristics of gaseous plasmas by methods which do not significantly alter them; **plasma-dynamic**, **plasma-dynamical** *adjectives* of or pertaining to plasma dynamics; **plasma dynamics** the branch of physics that deals with the dynamical properties and behaviour of gaseous plasmas; **plasma engine** a jet engine that produces and ejects gaseous plasma; **plasma frequency** the natural resonant frequency of a plasma oscillation, equal to the minimum frequency of electromagnetic waves that can travel through the plasma without attenuation; **plasma jet** a high-speed stream of plasma (ionized gas) ejected from a plasma engine or plasma torch; **plasma membrane** BIOLOGY a membrane which forms the external boundary of the cytoplasm of a cell or encloses a vacuole and regulates the passage of molecules in and out of the cytoplasm; **plasma oscillation** a collective oscillation of the charged particles in a plasma; **plasma probe** a device that is inserted or immersed in an ionized gas to investigate its physical properties; **plasma propulsion**: by means of a plasma engine; **plasma sheath** a thin charged layer covering a surface in an ionized gas; **plasma sheet** a layer of plasma in the earth's magnetotail, lying in the equatorial plane beyond the plasmapause, with two divergent branches that reach the earth in polar latitudes; **plasma torch** a small device that produces a very hot plasma jet for use in cutting solids or coating them with refractory material.

plasma- /ˈplazmə/ *combining form.*
[from prec.]
Chiefly BIOLOGY & PHYSICS. Of, pertaining to, or consisting of plasma. Cf. PLASMO-.
■ **plasmablast** *noun* = PLASMOBLAST L20. **plasmaˈcellular** *adjective* (PHYSIOLOGY) of or pertaining to plasma cells M20. **plasmagel** *noun* (BIOLOGY) cytoplasm in the form of a gel, esp. surrounding the plasmasol in an amoeboid cell E20. **plasmagene** *noun* (BIOLOGY) a cytoplasmic entity having some properties of a gene M20. **plasmapause** *noun* (PHYSICS) the outer limit of a plasmasphere, marked by a sudden change in plasma density M20. **plasmasol** *noun* (BIOLOGY) cytoplasm in the form of a sol, such as forms the central regions of an amoeboid cell, within the plasmagel E20. **plasmasphere** *noun* (PHYSICS) the roughly toroidal region surrounding and thought to rotate with the earth (or another planet) at latitudes away from the poles, containing a relatively dense plasma of low-energy electrons and protons M20. **plasmaˈspheric** *adjective* of or pertaining to a plasmasphere L20.

plasmacyte /ˈplazməsʌɪt/ *noun.* M20.
[from PLASMA- + -CYTE.]
PHYSIOLOGY & MEDICINE. A fully differentiated lymphocyte which produces a single type of antibody, a plasma cell.
■ **plasmacytic** /-ˈsɪtɪk/ *adjective* of, pertaining to, or composed of plasmacytes M20. **plasmaˈcytoid** *adjective* resembling (that of) a plasmacyte M20. **plasmacyˈtoma** *noun*, pl. **-mas**, **-mata** /-mətə/, a myeloma composed largely of plasma cells, multiple myeloma M20. **plasmacyˈtosis** *noun*, pl. **-toses** /-ˈtəʊsiːz/, (a condition characterized by) abnormal proliferation of plasma cells M20.

plasmal /ˈplazmal, -m(ə)l/ *noun.* E20.
[German, formed as PLASMA + -AL[2].]
BIOCHEMISTRY. An aldehyde resulting from the hydrolysis of a plasmalogen.
Comb.: **plasmal reaction** a chemical test for detecting plasmalogens and aldehydes in tissue.

plasmalemma /ˈplazmələmə/ *noun.* Pl. **-mmas**, **-mmae** /-miː/. E20.
[from PLASMA- + Greek *lemma* rind: see LEMMA *noun*[2].]
BIOLOGY. A plasma membrane which bounds a cell, esp. one immediately within the wall of a plant cell.
■ **plasmalemmal** *adjective* of, pertaining to, or formed from a plasmalemma M20. **plasmaˈlemmasome** *noun* (CYTOLOGY) a plant or microbial cell organelle formed by invagination of the plasmalemma M20.

plasmalogen /plazˈmaləd͡ʒ(ə)n/ *noun.* E20.
[formed as PLASMAL + -OGEN.]
BIOCHEMISTRY. Any of a class of phospholipids having an unsaturated ether linkage in place of one of the fatty acid ester linkages.
■ **plasmaloˈgenic** *adjective* M20.

plasmapheresis /plazməˈfɛrɪsɪs, -fəˈriːsɪs/ *noun.* E20.
[from PLASMA- + Greek *aphairesis* APHAERESIS.]
MEDICINE. The removal of blood plasma from the body by the withdrawal of blood, its separation into plasma and cells, and the reintroduction of the cells in an appropriate medium (performed esp. to remove antibodies in treating autoimmune conditions).

plasmaphoresis /plazməˈfɒrɪsɪs, -fəˈriːsɪs/ *noun.* M20.
[Alt. of prec. after -PHORESIS.]
MEDICINE. = prec.

plasmatic /plazˈmatɪk/ *adjective.* E19.
[from PLASMA + -ATIC.]
Of or pertaining to plasma, esp. that of the blood.

plasmatocyte /plazˈmatəsʌɪt/ *noun.* M20.
[from Greek *plasmat-, plasma* PLASMA + -O- + -CYTE.]
ZOOLOGY. A large basophilic phagocytic cell of variable shape and with a large nucleus, of a type common in the haemolymph of many insects.

plasmic /ˈplazmɪk/ *adjective. rare.* L19.
[from PLASM + -IC.]
Pertaining to or consisting of plasm; protoplasmic.

plasmid /ˈplazmɪd/ *noun.* M20.
[from PLASM + -ID[2].]
BIOLOGY. A genetic structure in a cell that can replicate independently of the chromosomes; *spec.* a small circular strand of DNA in the cytoplasm of a bacterium or protozoan.

plasmin /ˈplazmɪn/ *noun.* M19.
[French *plasmine*, formed as PLASM + -IN[1].]
BIOCHEMISTRY. †**1** An extract of blood plasma containing soluble proteins including fibrinogen. M–L19.
2 A proteolytic enzyme which destroys blood clots by attacking fibrin. M20.
■ **plasˈminogen** *noun* the inactive precursor, present in blood, of the enzyme plasmin (also called ***profibrinolysin***) M20.

plasmo- /ˈplazməʊ/ *combining form.*
[from PLASMA + -O-.]
Chiefly BIOLOGY. Of, pertaining to, or consisting of plasma or protoplasm. Cf. PLASMA-.
■ **plasmoblast** *noun* an immature plasmocyte L19. **plasmoˈblastic** *adjective* of or pertaining to plasmoblasts L20. **plasmocyte** *noun* †(*a*) ZOOLOGY a type of anucleate blood cell in amphibians; (*b*) = PLASMACYTE: L19. **plasmocytoma** *noun*, pl. **-mas**, **-mata** /-mətə/, = PLASMACYTOMA E20. **plasmosome** *noun* (now *rare*) a nucleolus L19.

Plasmochin /ˈplazməkɪn/ *noun.* Now *rare.* E20.
[from PLASMODIUM + German *Chinin* quinine.]
PHARMACOLOGY. (Proprietary name for) the drug pamaquin.

plasmodesma /plazmə(ʊ)ˈdɛzmə/ *noun.* Pl. **-mata** /-mətə/, **-men** /-mən/. Also **plasmodesm** /ˈplazmə(ʊ)dɛz(ə)m/, pl. **-s**. E20.
[German *Plasmodesma*, pl. *-desmen*, formed as PLASMO- + Greek *desma, desmos* bond, chain.]
BOTANY. A narrow thread of cytoplasm that passes through cell walls and allows communication between plant cells.
■ **plasmodesmatal** *adjective* of, pertaining to, or of the nature of plasmodesmata M20.

plasmodia *noun* pl. of PLASMODIUM.

plasmodiophorid /ˌplazmə(ʊ)dɪə(ʊ)ˈfɔːrɪd, -ˈfɒrɪd/ *noun.* L20.
[from PLASMODI(UM + -O- + -PHOR(E + -ID[3].]
MYCOLOGY. A fungus which produces a plasmodial stage.

plasmodium /plazˈməʊdɪəm/ *noun.* Pl. **-ia** /-ɪə/. L19.
[from PLASMA- + -ODE[1] + -IUM.]
BIOLOGY. **1** A multinucleate amoeboid mass or sheet of naked protoplasm, formed by the fusion of the cytoplasm of a number of amoeboid cells, esp. as forming the vegetative stage of a slime mould. L19.
2 Any of various parasitic sporozoans of the genus *Plasmodium*, several of which invade human liver and blood cells and cause malaria. L19.
■ **plasmodial** *adjective* pertaining to, of the nature of, or arising from a plasmodium L19.

plasmogamy /plazˈmɒgəmi/ *noun.* E20.
[from PLASMO- + -GAMY.]
BIOLOGY. The fusion of the cytoplasm of two or more cells, *spec.* without fusion of the nuclei.

plasmoid /ˈplazmɔɪd/ *noun.* M20.
[from PLASMA + -OID.]
PHYSICS & ASTRONOMY. A coherent mass of plasma (ionized gas).

plasmolysis /plazˈmɒlɪsɪs/ *noun.* L19.
[from PLASMO- + -LYSIS.]
BIOLOGY. Contraction of the cytoplasm of a plant cell with separation of the plasma membrane from the cell wall, due to the osmotic withdrawal of liquid into a medium of high concentration.
■ **ˈplasmolysable** *adjective* able to be plasmolysed L19. **ˈplasmolyse** *verb trans.* subject to plasmolysis, cause plasmolysis in (freq. as ***plasmolysed***, ***plasmolysing*** *ppl adjectives*) L19. **plasmoˈlytic** *adjective* pertaining to, exhibiting, or causing plasmolysis L19. **plasmoˈlytically** *adverb* by means of plasmolysis E20.

plasmolyticum /plazmə(ʊ)ˈlɪtɪkəm/ *noun.* Pl. **-ca** /-kə/. M20.
[mod. Latin, formed as PLASMO- + Greek *lutikos* able to loosen (from *luein* loosen).]
BOTANY. A substance or solution used to produce plasmolysis.
■ Also **plasmolyte** *noun* E20.

plasmoma /plazˈməʊmə/ *noun.* Pl. **-mata** /-mətə/, **-mas**. E20.
[from PLASMA + -OMA.]
MEDICINE. = PLASMACYTOMA.

plasmon /ˈplazmɒn/ *noun.* In sense 2 also **-one** /-əʊn/. E20.
[from PLASMA + -ON (arbitrary ending in sense 1).]
1 (Usu. **P-**.) (Proprietary name for) an extract of soluble milk proteins. *obsolete* exc. *Hist.* E20.
2 GENETICS. The totality of cytoplasmic or extranuclear genetic factors. M20.
3 ASTRONOMY & PHYSICS. = PLASMOID. M20.
4 PHYSICS. The quantum or quasiparticle associated with a collective oscillation of charge density. M20.

Plasmoquine /ˈplazməkwɪn, -kwiːn/ *noun.* Now *rare.* E20.
[from PLASMODIUM + QUIN(IN)E.]
PHARMACOLOGY. (Proprietary name for) the drug pamaquin.

plasmotomy /plazˈmɒtəmi/ *noun.* E20.
[from PLASMO- + -TOMY.]
BIOLOGY. A mode of reproduction in certain protozoans, in which the organism divides into two or more multinucleate daughter cells.

■ **plasmo'tomic** *adjective* M20.

-plast /plast, plɑːst/ *suffix.*
[Greek *plastos* formed, moulded: see PLASTIC *adjective*.]
BIOLOGY. Forming nouns denoting cellular constituents, esp. plastids, as ***chloroplast***, ***leucoplast***, etc.

plaster /ˈplɑːstə/ *noun.* Also (now *Scot.* & *north.*) **plaister** /ˈpleɪstə/.
[Old English *plaster*, corresp. to Old Saxon *plāstar*, Old High German *pflastar* (German *Pflaster*), Old Norse *plástr*, from medieval Latin *plastrum* for Latin *emplastrum* (prob. infl. by Latin *plasticus* PLASTIC *adjective*) from Greek *emplastron*, from *emplastos* daubed, plastered, from *emplassein* (cf. PLASTIC *adjective*): see -ER². In Middle English reinforced (in senses 2 and 3) by Old French *plastre* (mod. *plâtre*).]
1 Orig., a bandage or dressing spread with a curative or protective substance, which usu. becomes adhesive at body temperature, applied to the body. Now usu., adhesive material used to cover and close superficial wounds, or to fix larger bandages or dressings in place; a piece or strip of this; (also more fully ***sticking-plaster***). OE. ▸**b** *fig.* A healing or soothing means or measure, now *esp.* a temporary or inadequate one. ME.
2 a In full ***plaster of Paris***. Partly dehydrated gypsum, which when mixed with water swells to form a pliable paste which rapidly hardens and is used esp. for casts and moulds. ME. ▸**b** In full ***plaster cast***. A bandage stiffened with plaster of Paris and applied when wet to a broken limb etc. to provide a protective casing; the material of this. L19.
3 A soft pliable mixture, *spec.* of lime, sand, water, and freq. fibre, spread on walls, ceilings, etc., to form a hard surface when dry. LME. ▸**b** *transf.* A sticky mass. Now *rare.* L16.

📖 **1** ***court-plaster***, ***lead-plaster***, ***mustard plaster***, etc. **poor man's plaster** a plaster composed of tar, resin, and yellow wax. **2a** *attrib.*: R. BERTHOUD Make a plaster model and use the . . machine to translate it into marble. D. HIGHSMITH Frankie knew every gilded swirl and cherub, every plaster rose, every painted bulb. **b** *Independent* He arrived on crutches with his left foot in plaster. C. BRAYFIELD Keith . . left hospital with his arm and half his chest in a plaster cast. **3** A. DILLARD The workmen . . found brick walls under the plaster and oak planks under the brick.

Comb.: **plasterboard** a lightweight building board with a filling of plaster, used to form or line the inner walls of houses etc.; **plaster-bronze** a plaster cast covered with bronze dust to resemble a bronze; **plaster cast** (*a*) a statue or mould made of plaster; (*b*) see sense 2b above; **plaster casting** the making of a plaster cast; **plaster jacket** a body casing or bandage stiffened with plaster to correct curvature of the spine etc.; **plaster saint** a person claiming to be or regarded as being without moral faults or human frailty; a sanctimonious person, a hypocrite; **plasterwork** the plaster-covered surface of a wall etc.; decorative plastered surfaces collectively; work executed in plaster; **plasterworker** a person who works with plaster, a plasterer.
■ **plasterless** *adjective* M19. **plaster-like** *adjective* resembling (that of) plaster E17. †**plasterwise** *adverb* in the manner or of the consistency of a plaster M16–M18. **plastery** *adjective* of the nature of or like plaster; built with or as with plaster: LME.

plaster /ˈplɑːstə/ *verb trans.* Also (now *Scot.* & *north.*) **plaister** /ˈpleɪstə/. ME.
[from the noun or French *plastrer*, *plâtrer* plaster (a wall).]
1 Cover (a wall etc.) with plaster or a similar substance. Also foll. by *over*. ME. ▸**b** *transf.* Coat or daub thickly and unevenly with or *with* an adhesive substance; cover extensively or to excess. Also foll. by *over*. LME. ▸**c** *fig.* Load or heap to excess, e.g. with praise. Also, patch or mend superficially or provisionally, gloss over or *over*, cover *up*. M16.
2 Treat medically with (a) plaster; apply a plaster or plaster cast to; *fig.* soothe, alleviate. LME.
3 Mix or pound into a soft sticky mass. Later *spec.* (*a*) *slang* (now *rare*) shatter (a bird) with shot; (*b*) *slang* defeat heavily or utterly in a sports contest. LME. ▸**b** Shell or bomb (a target) extensively or heavily. *slang.* E20.
4 Apply or stick (something), esp. thickly or extensively, like (a) plaster; make (esp. hair) smooth with water, lotion, etc., fix *down*. E17.
5 Treat with plaster; *spec.* (*a*) treat (wine) with gypsum or potassium sulphate to neutralize excessive acidity etc.; (*b*) dust (a vine) with gypsum to prevent rot or mildew; (*c*) treat and improve (land or a crop) with plaster of Paris. E19.

📖 **1** *Century Magazine* The chimneys were usually . . well plastered on the inside with clay. **b** C. MORGAN She liked the . . friendly advertisements with which the shelter was plastered. *Independent* The same jokes mainly involving our heroes being plastered in slime. **c** G. B. SHAW Telling my father what a fine boy I was and plastering him with compliments. *Guardian* Social workers . . describe their work as plastering up the cracks of the welfare state. **2** *Cambrian News* My daughter was fast asleep . . the bones reset and plastered. **4** K. GRAHAME He dipped his hairbrush in the water-jug, parted his hair . . and plastered it down. J. BUCHAN Stamps and . . the smell of gum, with which I plastered them in an album. P. KAVANAGH He plastered on the black grease with a table knife.

■ **plastered** *adjective* (*a*) covered with, treated with, or made of plaster; (*b*) *slang* drunk, intoxicated: LME. **plasterer** *noun* (*a*) a person who works with plaster, *spec.* a person who plasters buildings; (*b*) a hymenopteran insect, esp. of the family Colletidae, which constructs cells of a plaster-like substance: LME. **plastering** *noun* (*a*) the action of the verb; (*b*) plastered work, a coating of plaster or of anything plastered or daubed on: LME.

plastic /ˈplastɪk/ *noun*¹. Now *rare* or *obsolete*. L16.
[French *plastique* from Latin (*ars*) *plastica* from Greek *plastikē* (sc. *tekhnē* art) fem. of *plastikos* PLASTIC *adjective*.]
In *pl.* & †*sing.* The art of modelling or sculpting figures etc.

†**plastic** *noun*². M17–M19.
[Late Latin *plasticus*, from Greek *plastikos*: see next.]
A modeller, a sculptor; *fig.* a creator.

plastic /ˈplastɪk/ *adjective* & *noun*³. M17.
[French *plastique* or Latin *plasticus* from Greek *plastikos*, from *plastos* pa. pple of *plassein* to mould, to form: see -IC. Cf. PLASMA.]
▸ **A** *adjective.* **1** Characterized by or capable of moulding or shaping clay, wax, etc. M17. ▸**b** Concerned with the surgical reconstruction or repair of parts of the body, freq. by transfer of tissue. Chiefly in ***plastic surgeon***, ***plastic surgery*** below. M19.
2 Esp. PHILOSOPHY. Of a natural force or principle: causing the growth or production of natural, esp. living, things; *fig.* forming or adapting immaterial things or concepts; formative, creative. M17.
3 That can be (easily) moulded or shaped; pliant, pliable; *fig.* susceptible, impressionable, flexible. M17. ▸**b** BIOLOGY. Pertaining to or (of an organism) exhibiting an adaptability to environmental changes. E20.
4 Pertaining to, characteristic of, or produced by moulding, modelling, or sculpture. E18. ▸**b** Pertaining to or involving the production of a permanent change in shape, without fracture or rupture, by the temporary application of pressure or tension. Chiefly in ***plastic deformation***, ***plastic flow***. L19.
5 BIOLOGY & MEDICINE. Capable of forming or being organized into tissue. Chiefly in ***plastic lymph***, fluid in which new structures form during healing. M19.
6 [Partly from attrib. use of PLASTIC *noun*³.] Made of or containing plastic; of the nature of a plastic. E20. ▸**b** *fig.* Artificial; superficial, insincere. M20.

📖 **1** POPE So watchful Bruin forms, with plastic care, Each growing lump, and brings it to a bear. **2** E. DOWDEN The plastic energy of the imagination. **3** A. T. THOMSON Kneading the coating material, so as to render it very plastic. D. GRAYSON Is not the prime struggle . . to keep the mind plastic? To see and . . hear things newly? **6** *New Yorker* The armchairs are protected by plastic covers. L. GRANT-ADAMSON Carrying a very large plastic . . bag holding everything he had brought. T. K. WOLFE They were unusually vulgar, even for plastic toys. **b** *Observer* Hawaii, that plastic paradise.

▸ **B** *noun.* **1** ***the plastic***, †(*a*) plastic or creative principle; (*b*) plastic art, plastic beauty. M17.
2 A solid substance that is easily moulded or shaped. (*rare* before E20.) E19. ▸**b** A plastic explosive. M20.
3 Any of a large class of substances which are polymers based on synthetic resins or modified natural polymers, and may be moulded, extruded, or cast while soft or liquid, and then set into a rigid or slightly elastic form, usu. by heating or cooling; material of this kind, esp. when not in fibrous form. E20.
4 Credit cards; a credit card. *colloq.* L20.

📖 **3** J. BRAINE He owned a plastics factory. *Amateur Photographer* Black cases of plastic with simulated textured panelling. ***expanded plastic***, ***laminated plastic***, ***reinforced plastic***, ***thermoplastic***, etc. **4** *Which?* She opened accounts and applied for plastic in ten shops.

Special collocations & comb.: ***plastic arts***: see ART *noun*¹. **plastic bomb**: containing plastic explosive. **plastic-bomb** *verb trans.* attack or destroy with a plastic bomb or plastic explosives. **plastic bronze** soft bronze containing a high proportion of lead, used for bearings. **plastic bullet** a projectile made of PVC or similar material and used by security and police forces esp. for riot control. **plastic clay** GEOLOGY any of a group of Eocene clay beds immediately below the London clay. **plastic crystal** a soft substance in which the molecules occupy the points of a regular crystal lattice but have freedom of rotation about those points. **plastic explosive** a putty-like explosive able to be shaped by hand. ***plastic lymph***: see sense A.5 above. **plastic money** *colloq.* (orig. *US*) credit cards considered as a form of money. **plastic paint** paint thick and coarse enough to retain a texture given by a brush etc. **plastic surgeon** a qualified practitioner of plastic surgery. **plastic surgery** the process of reconstructing or repairing parts of the body esp. by the transfer of tissue, either after injury or for cosmetic purposes. **plasticware** articles, esp. kitchen equipment or utensils, made of plastic. **plastic wood** a mouldable material which hardens to resemble wood and used for filling crevices etc.
■ **plastically** *adverb* in a plastic manner; by moulding or modelling; as a plastic substance: M19. **plasticism** /-sɪz(ə)m/ *noun* the theory or practice of the plastic arts M19. **plasticity** /plaˈstɪsɪti/ *noun* (*a*) the quality of being plastic, *spec.* ability to be moulded or to undergo a permanent change in shape; (*b*) BIOLOGY adaptability of (part of) an organism to changes in its environment: L18. **plasticly** *adverb* (*rare*) = PLASTICALLY L17.

-plastic /ˈplastɪk/ *suffix.*
[from -PLASTY or Greek *plastos* formed + -IC.]
Forming adjectives, usu. corresp. to nouns in ***-plasty*** or ***-plasia***.

plasticate /ˈplastɪkeɪt/ *verb trans.* E20.
[from PLASTIC *adjective* + -ATE³. In sense 2 from French *plastiquer*.]
1 Change (particles of rubber or thermoplastic) into a homogeneous plastic (mouldable) mass by passing through a suitable extruder, usu. with simultaneous heating. Also *fig.*, make artificial or plastic. E20.
2 Attack or destroy with a plastic bomb or plastic explosives. M20.
■ **plasti'cation** *noun* M20. **plasticator** *noun* an extruder for plasticating rubber or thermoplastic particles, usu. by subjecting them simultaneously to pressure and heat M20.

plastician /plaˈstɪʃ(ə)n/ *noun.* E20.
[from PLASTIC *adjective* + -ICIAN.]
An expert or specialist in plastic art, plastic surgery, or the use of plastics.

Plasticine /ˈplastɪsiːn/ *noun.* L19.
[from PLASTIC *adjective* + -INE⁴.]
(Proprietary name for) a soft plastic claylike substance, used esp. by children for modelling.

plasticize /ˈplastɪsʌɪz/ *verb trans.* Also **-ise**. E20.
[from PLASTIC *adjective* + -IZE.]
1 Make plastic or mouldable, produce or promote plasticity in, e.g. by adding a solvent or by plastication. E20.
2 Treat or make with plastic. M20.
■ **plastici'zation** *noun* the process of making something (more) plastic or mouldable; *spec.* (*a*) the addition of a plasticizer to a synthetic resin; (*b*) = PLASTICATION: E20. **plasticized** *adjective* (*a*) made (more) plastic, treated with a plasticizer; (*b*) treated or made with plastic; (*c*) *fig.* artificial, superficial: M20. **plasticizer** *noun* a substance which plasticizes something, *spec.* one (usu. a solvent) added to a synthetic resin to produce or promote plasticity and flexibility and to reduce brittleness E20.

plasticky /ˈplastɪki/ *adjective. colloq.* Also **-icy**. L20.
[from PLASTIC *noun*³ + -Y¹.]
Suggestive of or resembling plastic.

📖 R. RENDELL The gun . . was a toy, as you could tell really by the plasticky look of it.

plastid /ˈplastɪd/ *noun* & *adjective.* L19.
[German, from Greek *plastos* (see -PLAST) + -ID².]
▸ **A** *noun.* †**1** BIOLOGY. A unit of protoplasm, a cell. Only in L19.
2 BOTANY. An organelle in the cytoplasm of a plant cell bound by a double membrane and usu. containing pigment or food substances, as a chloroplast. L19.
▸ **B** *adjective.* Having the character of a plastid. *rare.* L19.
■ **plastidome** *noun* the plastids of a cell collectively E20.

plastidule /ˈplastɪdjuːl/ *noun. obsolete* exc. *Hist.* L19.
[German *Plastidul*, formed as PLASTID + -ULE.]
BIOLOGY. A hypothetical ultimate particle of protoplasm.

plastify /ˈplastɪfʌɪ/ *verb trans.* E20.
[from PLASTIC *adjective* + -FY.]
= PLASTICIZE.
■ **plastifier** *noun* = PLASTICIZER E20.

plastigel /ˈplastɪdʒɛl/ *noun.* M20.
[formed as prec. + GEL *noun*.]
A plastisol thickened to a putty-like consistency so that it retains its shape when heated.

plastimeter *noun* var. of PLASTOMETER.

plastique /plaˈstiːk, *foreign* plastik (*pl. same*)/ *noun.* L19.
[French, use as noun of adjective = plastic.]
1 Statuesque poses or slow graceful movements in dancing; the art or technique of performing these. L19.
2 A plastic substance used for modelling. E20.
3 Plastic explosive; a plastic bomb. M20.

plastiqueur /ˈplastɪkə, *foreign* plastikœːr (*pl. same*)/ *noun.* M20.
[French, formed as PLASTIC *adjective* & *noun*³ + *-eur* -OR.]
A person who plants or detonates a plastic bomb.

plastisol /ˈplastɪsɒl/ *noun.* M20.
[from PLASTIC *noun*³ + SOL *noun*⁵.]
A dispersion of particles of a synthetic resin in a non-volatile liquid consisting chiefly or entirely of plasticizer, which can be converted into a solid plastic simply by heating. Cf. ORGANOSOL.

plastochron /ˈplastəkrɒn/ *noun.* Also **-chrone** /-krəʊn/. E20.
[German, from Greek *plastos* (see -PLAST) + *khronos* time.]
BOTANY. The interval of time between the initiation of leaf growth at two consecutive nodes in a growing shoot apex.
■ **plasto'chronic** *adjective* M20.

plastocyanin /plastə(ʊ)ˈsʌɪənɪn/ *noun.* M20.
[from CHLORO)PLAST + -O- + CYAN- + -IN¹.]
BIOCHEMISTRY. A blue copper-containing protein found in the chloroplasts of green plants and in certain bacteria,

and involved in electron transfer during photosynthesis.

plastogamy /plaˈstɒɡəmi/ *noun.* **L19.**
[from Greek *plastos* (see **-PLAST**) + **-O-** + **-GAMY**.]
BIOLOGY. = **PLASMOGAMY**.
■ **plastoˈgamic** *adjective* **E20.**

plastome /ˈplastəʊm/ *noun.* **M20.**
[from **PLASTID** after **GENOME**.]
GENETICS. The total genetic information in the plastids of a cell.

plastometer /plaˈstɒmɪtə/ *noun.* Also **plastimeter** /plaˈstɪmɪtə/. **E20.**
[from **PLAST**(**ICITY** + **-OMETER**.]
An instrument for measuring the plasticity of a substance.
■ **plastometry** *noun* **E20.**

plastoquinone /plastə(ʊ)ˈkwɪnəʊn/ *noun.* **M20.**
[from **CHLORO**)**PLAST** + **-O-** + **QUINONE**.]
BIOCHEMISTRY. Any of a homologous series of compounds which have a quinone nucleus with a terpenoid sidechain, *esp.* one of these involved in electron transfer during photosynthesis in the chloroplasts of plants.

plastron /ˈplastrən/ *noun.* **E16.**
[French from Italian *piastrone* augm. of *piastra* breastplate from Latin *emplastrum* **PLASTER** *noun*. See also **PIASTRE**.]
1 a *Hist.* A steel breastplate worn beneath a hauberk. **E16.** ▸**b** A fencer's padded and freq. leather-covered breastplate. Also, a lancer's ornamental covering for the breast, made from facings material. **M17.**
2 *ZOOLOGY.* **a** The ventral part of the shell of a tortoise or turtle; an analogous ventral plate in other animals. **M19.** ▸**b** *ENTOMOLOGY.* A patch of cuticle in an aquatic insect covered with hairs which retain a thin layer of air for breathing under water. **M20.**
3 a A kind of ornamental front on a woman's bodice. **L19.** ▸**b** A man's starched shirt-front. **L19.**
4 *ORNITHOLOGY.* A coloured area on the breast or belly of a bird, resembling a shield. **L19.**
■ **plastral** *adjective* of or pertaining to a plastron **L19.**

-plasty /plasti/ *suffix.*
[Greek *plastos*: see **-PLAST**, **-Y**³.]
Forming nouns, chiefly in surgery, with the sense 'moulding, grafting, formation', as ***dermatoplasty***, ***heteroplasty***.

plat /plat/ *noun*¹. Now *arch. & dial.* **LME.**
[Old & mod. French = flat surface or thing, (mod.) dish, use as noun of adjective: see **PLAT** *adjective*.]
1 A flat thing, part, or surface; any of various flat objects; the flat part or side of something. *obsolete* exc. *Scot.* **LME.**
2 A thing placed in a flat or horizontal position; a platform; a foot bridge. *obsolete* exc. *Scot. & dial.* **LME.**
†**3** Any surface. **M–L16.**
4 A place, a spot; a locality, a situation. *obsolete* exc. *dial.* **M16.**
5 A flat country, a plateau, a tableland. *US & dial.* **L18.**
6 A widened space in a mine, near the shaft, where trucks may pass, ore be collected, etc. Chiefly *Austral.* **M19.**
¶ Recorded earlier in **ME** in surnames and place-names.

plat /plat/ *noun*². **LME.**
[Var. of **PLOT** *noun*, infl. by prec.]
▸**I 1** A plot of ground. Now *arch. & dial.* **LME.**
▸**II** (Earlier than corresp. uses of **PLOT** *noun*.)
2 A plan or diagram of something; *esp.* a ground-plan of a building or of an area of land; a map, a chart. Now *US.* **E16.**
†**3** *fig.* A plan of the actual or proposed arrangement of something; an outline, a sketch; a plan of action or proceeding; a scheme. **E16–E18.**
†**4** The plot of a literary work. **L16–E17.**
▸**III 5** *SCOTTISH ECCLESIASTICAL HISTORY.* The late 16th-cent. scheme for the reorganization of the Church in Scotland on a presbyterian system; the body in charge of this. **L16.**

plat /plat/ *noun*³. *obsolete* exc. *dial.* **E16.**
[Var. of **PLAIT** *noun*.]
†**1** A fold; a pleat. *rare.* **E–M16.**
2 A plait of hair, straw, etc. **M16.**
3 *NAUTICAL.* A braided rope used to protect cables. **L17.**

plat /pla/ *noun*⁴. Pl. pronounced same. **M18.**
[French: see **PLAT** *noun*¹.]
A dish of food.
plat du jour /dy ʒuːr/ = ***dish of the day*** s.v. **DISH** *noun* 3a.

plat /plat/ *adjective & adverb. obsolete* exc. *Scot. dial.* **ME.**
[Old & mod. French from popular Latin from Greek *platus* broad, flat.]
▸**A** *adjective.* **1** Flat, level; plane; plain. **ME.**
2 *fig.* Forthright, blunt, straightforward, unqualified. **LME.**
▸**B** *adverb.* **1** In or into a flat or horizontal position; level or even with the ground or a surface. **ME.**
2 Entirely, quite, absolutely. **LME.**
3 Forthrightly, bluntly, straightforwardly, without circumlocution or qualification. **LME.**
4 Exactly, due, or straight in direction. **LME.**

plat /plat/ *verb*¹. *obsolete* exc. *dial.* Infl. **-tt-**. **ME.**
[from **PLAT** *adjective*.]
†**1** *verb intrans.* Lie, sink, or fall down flat. Chiefly *Scot.* **ME–E19.**
2 *verb trans.* Lay, throw, or cause to fall down flat; spread or press flat. **LME.**
3 *verb trans.* Put or place quickly, energetically, or unceremoniously (*into*). *obsolete* exc. *Scot.* **E16.**

plat /plat/ *verb*² *trans.* Infl. **-tt-**. **ME.**
[Var. of **PLAIT** *verb*.]
Intertwine, intertwist, plait (hair, straw, etc.); form by plaiting.
■ **platting** *noun* (**a**) the action of the verb, plaiting; (**b**) plaited straw, palmetto, etc., in ribbon-like strips, for making hats, bonnets, etc.: **LME.**

plat /plat/ *verb*³ *trans.* Infl. **-tt-**. **M16.**
[Var. of **PLOT** *verb*¹.]
†**1** Plan; sketch. **M16–E17.**
2 Make a plan of, plot on a plan or chart; plot to calculate distances, area, etc. Now *US.* **E18.**

platan *noun*¹ see **PLATANUS**.

†**platan** *noun*² see **PLANTAIN** *noun*³.

platanna /plaˈtanə/ *noun. S. Afr.* **L19.**
[Afrikaans, app. from Dutch *plat* flat + *-hander* lit. 'handed one'.]
= ***clawed toad*** s.v. **CLAWED** *adjective* (a).

platanus /ˈplat(ə)nəs/ *noun.* Also (*arch.*) Anglicized as **platan** /ˈplat(ə)n/. **LME.**
[Latin from Greek *platanos* **PLANE** *noun*².]
Any tree of the genus *Platanus*; = **PLANE** *noun*² 1.

platband /ˈplatband/ *noun.* **L17.**
[French *platebande*, from *plate* fem. of *plat* (see **PLAT** *adjective*) + *bande* **BAND** *noun*².]
1 *ARCHITECTURE.* A flat rectangular moulding or fascia, the projection of which is less than its breadth. **L17.**
2 *HORTICULTURE.* A narrow bed of flowers or strip of turf forming a border. **E18.**

plate /pleɪt/ *noun.* **ME.**
[Old French = thin sheet of metal from medieval Latin *plata* plate armour, use as noun of *platus* adjective, app. var. of popular Latin source of **PLAT** *adjective*.]
▸**I 1** A flat, comparatively thin, usu. rigid sheet, slice, leaf, or lamina of metal or other substance, of more or less uniform thickness and even surface, freq. adapted to form part of a mechanism. **ME.**
2 a *Hist.* A thin piece of steel or iron formed as armour for a part of the body, either as a separate piece or to overlap with others in composing a piece of armour; armour composed of such a piece or pieces. **ME.** ▸**b** A piece of metal (esp. steel) cladding formed as armour for a warship, armoured vehicle, etc.; armour composed of such cladding. Also ***armour-plate***. **M19.**
3 Metal beaten, rolled, or cast into sheets. **LME.**
4 *ARCHITECTURE.* A horizontal timber at the top or bottom of a framing, often supporting other portions of a structure. Usu. with specifying word, as ***ground-plate***, ***roof-plate***, ***wall-plate***, ***window-plate***, etc. **LME.**
†**5** A confection or sweet made in a flat cake. **LME–M17.**
6 A smooth or polished piece of metal etc. for writing or engraving on. **LME.**
7 a A polished sheet of copper or steel engraved to print from; an impression from such a sheet, an engraving; an illustration separate from the text and usu. on special paper in a book; *loosely* a full-page illustration. **M17.** ▸**b** A stereotype, electrotype, or plastic cast of a page of composed movable types, or a metal or plastic copy of filmset matter, from which sheets are printed. **E19.**
8 A piece or strip of metal, wood, plastic, etc., bearing a name or inscription, for affixing to something. **M17.** ▸**b** *spec.* Such a plate bearing the registration number of a vehicle, a number plate. Usu. in *pl.* **M20.**
9 *ANATOMY & BIOLOGY.* A thin flat organic structure or formation. **M17.**
10 a *ELECTRICITY.* A thin piece of metal that acts as a charge-storing electrode in a capacitor. **L18.** ▸**b** *ELECTRICITY.* A metal electrode in a cell or battery, *esp.* one in the form of a flat sheet or grid. **E19.** ▸**c** *ELECTRONICS.* The anode of a thermionic valve. **E20.**
11 An early form of rail for a tramway or railway consisting of a flat strip of iron or steel with a projecting flange to retain the wheels; *gen.* a rail (now only in ***platelayer*** below). **E19.**
12 *DENTISTRY.* The portion of a denture which is moulded to the shape of the mouth and gums and holds the artificial teeth; a similar portion of any orthodontic appliance; *colloq.* a whole denture or orthodontic appliance. **M19.**
13 A thin sheet of metal, porcelain, or (now usu.) glass, coated with a light-sensitive film on which single photographs are taken in larger or older types of camera. Also (with specifying word, as ***half-plate***, ***quarter-plate***), a standard size of photographic print or negative. **M19.**
14 A light shoe for a racehorse. Cf. earlier **PLATE** *verb* 4. **M19.**
15 *BASEBALL & SOFTBALL.* A flat piece of metal, stone, or (now usu.) whitened rubber marking the station of a batter (also ***home plate***) or pitcher. **M19.**
16 A number of animal skins sewn together, for making up into fur coats or for linings, trimmings, etc. **E20.**
17 *GEOLOGY.* Each of the several nearly rigid pieces of lithosphere thought to make up the earth's surface and to be moving slowly relative to one another, their boundaries being identified with belts of seismic, volcanic, and tectonic activity. **M20.**

📖 **1** ***face-plate***, ***heel-plate***, ***jig plate***, ***keel-plate***, ***kicking plate***, ***mirror-plate***, etc. **2a** ***breastplate*** etc. **7a** *Horse & Hound* The plates were destroyed after 750 signed . . prints had been produced. **8** ***bookplate***, ***brass plate***, ***coffin-plate***, ***letter-plate***, ***licence plate***, ***name-plate***, etc. **9** ***end-plate***, ***gill plate***, ***metaphase plate***, ***neural plate***, etc. **10b** ***X-plate***: see X, x 6. ***Y-plate***: see Y, y 5. **12** L. Erdrich Delicate biters, because their teeth hurt or plates did not fit well. **13** ***wet plate***: see **WET** *adjective*. **15** R. Angell An instant . . throw that nailed the runner at the plate.

▸**II** †**18** A piece of (silver) money, a silver coin, (usu. more fully ***plate of silver***). Latterly *spec.* a Spanish coin worth an eighth of a piastre or dollar. **ME–E17.**
19 *collect. pl.* Utensils for table and domestic use, orig. of silver or gold, later also of other metals. Also, objects of one metal plated with another. **ME.**
20 *HERALDRY.* A roundel representing a flat piece of silver with a plain surface; a roundel argent. **LME.**
†**21 a** Precious metal; bullion; *esp.* silver. **LME–M18.** ▸**b** Standard of value of Spanish silver coins. **L17–E19.**
22 A prize of a silver or gold cup etc. given to the winner of a horse-race or (later) other contest; a race or contest in which the prize is such a plate. **M17.**
23 Silver or gold thread used in embroidery etc. **M18.**
24 A thin coating of metal, *esp.* one applied electrolytically. **E20.**
19 ***gold plate***, ***silver plate***. **22** ***selling plate***: see **SELLING** *verbal noun*.
▸**III 25** A shallow, usu. circular vessel, orig. of metal or wood, now commonly of earthenware or china, from which food may be eaten or served. **LME.** ▸**b** A similar vessel of metal or wood etc. used esp. for taking the collection at a place of worship. **L18.** ▸**c** In *pl.* In full ***plates of meat***. Feet. *rhyming slang.* **L19.**
26 The food placed on a plate; a plateful; a dish or course of food; *US* a main course of a meal served on one plate. Formerly also, a supply of food; eating and drinking. **L16.**
27 *BIOLOGY & MEDICINE.* A shallow vessel, usu. a Petri dish, containing or used to contain a medium for the culture of micro-organisms. **L19.**
28 A place at a formal meal or banquet, for which a person subscribes. *US.* **E20.**
29 A plate of cakes, sandwiches, etc., contributed towards the catering at a social gathering. *Austral. & NZ.* **M20.**

📖 **25** W. Perriam He's . . wolfing down his salad while I push mine round the plate. ***dessert-plate***, ***dinner-plate***, ***fruit-plate***, ***soup-plate***, etc. ***paper plate***, ***plastic plate***, etc. **a lot on one's plate**, **enough on one's plate**, **plenty on one's plate** a lot etc. to worry about or cope with. **on a plate** *fig.* without having been asked or sought for, without requiring any effort or return from the recipient, in ready-to-use form. ***plenty on one's plate***: see ***a lot on one's plate*** above. **26** D. E. Westlake The man . . recommended the roast beef plate.

Comb.: **plate armour** armour of metal plates, for a man, ship, etc. **plate camera** a camera designed to take photographs on coated glass plates rather than film; **plate-clutch** a form of clutch in which the engaging surfaces are flat metal plates; **plate count** an estimate of cell density in milk, soil, etc., made by inoculating a culture plate with a dilute sample and counting the colonies that appear; **plate cylinder** in a rotary printing-press, the cylinder to which printing plates are attached; **plate girder** a girder formed of a plate or plates of iron or steel; **plate glass** *noun & adjective* (made of) thick fine-quality glass, used for mirrors, shop windows, etc., orig. cast in plates; ***plate-glass university***, any of the new British universities founded in the 1960s; **platelayer** orig., a person employed in laying, repairing, and renewing plates on a tramway or railway; now, a person employed in fixing and repairing the rails of a railway; **plate line** a line left on the margin of an engraving by the pressure of the plate; **plate-mark** (**a**) = **HALLMARK** 1; (**b**) an impression left on the margin of an engraving by the pressure of the plate; **plate metal** iron run off from a refinery and allowed to set in moulds, to be broken up and remelted etc.; **plate mill** a rolling-mill for metal plates; **plate number** (**a**) a serial number in the margin of a plate from which postage stamps are printed; (**b**) a serial number on the pages of some engraved music, which can indicate the chronological place of the score in the publisher's output; (**c**) the registration number of a motor vehicle, exhibited on a plate; **plate paper** paper of fine quality on which engravings are printed; **plate pewter** the hardest variety of pewter, used for plates and dishes; **plate pie** a pie with pastry above and below the filling; **plate-powder** a polishing powder for silver plate and silverware generally; **plate-printer** a printer who prints from plates; **plate-rack** a rack or frame in which plates are placed to drain, or in which plates are stored; **plate-rail** = sense 11 above; **plate-roll** a smooth roller for rolling metal plate or sheet; **plate tectonic** *adjective* of, pertaining to, or relating to plate tectonics; **plate tectonics** GEOLOGY a theory according to which large-scale phenomena of the earth's surface are explained in terms of moving lithospheric plates (see sense 17 above) and sea floor spreading; **plate tracery** ARCHITECTURE tracery formed by perforations in otherwise continuous stone; **plateworker** †(*a*) a person who works in gold or silver; (*b*) a worker in sheet metal.

■ **plateful** *noun* as much or as many as will fill a plate L16. **plateless** *adjective* L19. **platelike** *adjective* resembling a plate M19.

plate /pleɪt/ *verb trans.* LME.

[from the noun.]

1 a Cover or overlay with plates of metal, for ornament, protection, or strength; cover (esp. a ship) with armour-plates. LME. ▸**b** SURGERY. Treat (a fracture) by fixing the fractured parts together with a metal plate; attach a plate to (a bone). E20.

2 a Cover with a thin coating or film of metal; *esp.* cover (an article of a baser metal) with gold or silver. L17. ▸**b** Apply (gold, silver, etc.) as a thin covering or coating (*on, upon*), deposit as a coating, esp. electrolytically. L18.

3 Make or beat (metal) into plates. L17.

4 Shoe (a racehorse) with plates. L17.

5 BIOLOGY & MEDICINE. Inoculate (cells or infective material) *into* or *on to* a culture plate, esp. with the object of purifying a particular strain or estimating viable cell numbers. Freq. foll. by *out*. L19.

6 Make a plate of (type) for printing. E20.

7 Provide (a book) with a bookplate. E20.

8 Practise fellatio or cunnilingus on. *slang*. M20.

9 Provide (a goods vehicle) with a plate recording particulars of weight etc. according to government regulations. M20.

10 Put on a plate; serve ready on a plate. M20.

platea /plə'tiːə/ *noun*. Also ***placea*** /plə'siːə/. Pl. ***-eae*** /-iːiː, -iːʌɪ/. M19.

[Latin = street, (in late Latin) courtyard, square, from Greek.]

Hist. In medieval drama, an area before a raised stage, providing additional acting space as well as accommodation for the audience.

plateau /'platəʊ, plə'təʊ/ *noun*¹ & *adjective*. Pl. **-x** /-z/, **-s**. L18.

[French, Old French *platel*, from *plat* PLAT *adjective*: see -EL².]

▸ **A** *noun*. **1 a** PHYSICAL GEOGRAPHY. An elevated tract of comparatively flat or level land; a tableland. L18. ▸**b** *transf.* A more or less level portion of a graph or trace (orig., of the pulse) adjacent to a lower sloping portion; a stage, condition, or period when there is neither an increase nor a decrease in something. L19.

2 An ornamented tray or dish for table-service. L18.

> 📖 **1a** *Independent* A rocky plateau . . surrounded by jagged and hostile mountains. **b** *Country Living* The first incline of a learning curve that . . would reach a plateau several months hence.

▸ **B** *attrib.* or as *adjective*. Of the nature of or pertaining to a plateau; *spec.* in MEDICINE, (of the pulse) having an abnormally prolonged period of constant blood pressure, esp. due to stenosis. E20.

Comb.: **plateau basalt** basaltic lava extruded from fissures and forming sheets that cover many square miles; **plateau gravel** gravel occurring as a sheet on hilltops or a plateau, at a height that suggests it has been raised by earth movement since its deposition.

Plateau /'platəʊ/ *noun*². E20.

[J. A. F. *Plateau* (1801–83), Belgian physicist.]

MATH. ***Plateau's problem***, ***Plateau problem***, ***problem of Plateau***, the problem of finding the surface of smallest area bounded by any given closed curve.

plateau /'platəʊ, plə'təʊ/ *verb intrans.* M20.

[from PLATEAU *noun*¹.]

Enter a period of stability or stagnation; cease increasing or progressing, level *out*.

> 📖 *Times* The downward trend . . has itself plateaued and in some districts has begun to rise.

plateaux *noun pl.* see PLATEAU *noun*¹.

plated /'pleɪtɪd/ *adjective*. L15.

[from PLATE *verb, noun*: see -ED¹, -ED².]

1 That has been plated; wearing plate armour; protected by armour-plate; covered with a thin coating or film of metal. L15.

2 Of a garment etc.: having an outer surface or nap of finer material than the body. M19.

1 plated wire a wire of a non-magnetic metal such as copper having a thin coating of a magnetic alloy, used as an element in some computer memories.

platelet /'pleɪtlɪt/ *noun*. L19.

[from PLATE *noun* + -LET.]

A small or minute plate; *spec.* (more fully ***blood platelet***) a minute colourless disc-shaped corpuscle, large numbers of which are found in the blood of mammals and aid coagulation; a thrombocyte.

Comb.: **platelet count** (a calculation of) the number of platelets in a stated volume of blood.

platen /'plat(ə)n/ *noun*. Also (now *rare*) **-tt-**. LME.

[Old & mod. French *platine*, from *plat* (see PLAT *adjective*, -INE⁴), partly also popular alt. of *patène* PATEN.]

†**1** ECCLESIASTICAL. = PATEN 1. LME–E17.

†**2** A flat plate of metal for any of various purposes. M16–E19.

3 PRINTING. An iron (formerly wooden) plate in a printing-press, which presses paper against inked type to secure an impression; a flat metal surface by means of which pressure is applied in a press. L16.

4 In a typewriter or computer printer, the surface (usu. a cylindrical roller) against which paper is held and characters are typed or printed. L19.

5 ENGINEERING. The movable table of a planing- or milling-machine. E20.

Comb.: **platen press** a printing-press or other machine having a platen.

plater /'pleɪtə/ *noun*. ME.

[from PLATE *verb* or *noun* + -ER¹.]

1 A person who plates something; a person who coats or plates articles with a film of metal, esp. of silver or gold; a person engaged in the manufacture or application of metal plates, formerly esp. in iron shipbuilding. ME.

2 An inferior racehorse. Cf. ***selling plater*** s.v. SELLING *verbal noun*. *arch. slang*. M19.

¶ Before 18 recorded in surnames only.

plateresque /platə'rɛsk/ *adjective*. L19.

[Spanish *plateresco*, from *platero* silversmith etc., from *plata* silver: see -ESQUE.]

Resembling silver work; rich and grotesque in decorative style.

†**plate-vein** *noun*. E17–M19.

[Origin unkn.]

The cephalic vein in the horse.

platform /'platfɔːm/ *noun*. M16.

[French *plateforme* plan, from *plate* fem. of *plat* (see PLAT *adjective*) + *forme* FORM *noun*.]

▸†**I 1** GEOMETRY. A plane figure; a surface, esp. a plane surface. M16–L17.

2 An architectural plan; a draughtsman's drawing; a chart, a map; *fig.* a plan of action, government, administration, etc.; a scheme, a design, a description; a thing intended or taken as a pattern, a model. M16–L19.

▸ **II 3** A raised level surface or area; a natural or man-made terrace, a flat elevated piece of ground, a tableland, a plateau; *spec.* (*a*) a level place constructed for mounting guns in a fort or battery; †(*b*) an open walk or terrace on the top of a building or on a wall; (*c*) PHYSICAL GEOGRAPHY a level or nearly level strip of land at the base of a cliff close to the water-level; a similar terrace elsewhere thought to have been originally formed by the sea; a former erosion surface or plateau represented by a common surface or summit level of adjacent hills etc.; (*d*) GEOLOGY a part of a craton where the basement complex, elsewhere exposed as a shield, is overlain by more recent undisturbed, mainly sedimentary, strata. M16.

†**4 a** The area occupied by a structure; the site of a group of buildings, a fort, camp, etc. L16–L18. ▸**b** *fig.* The ground, foundation, or basis *of* an action, event, calculation, condition, etc. E17–M19.

5 NAUTICAL. †**a** A division of the orlop of a man-of-war, between the cockpit and the mainmast. M17–E18. ▸**b** A light deck in a small boat or yacht. M20.

6 *gen.* A raised level surface formed with planks, boards, etc., used for standing, sitting, walking, for seeing or being seen, or for any purpose for which such an arrangement is useful. E18.

7 *spec.* **a** A piece of raised flooring in a hall, or in the open air, from which a speaker addresses an audience, on which an artist gives a performance, or on which officials or promoters of a meeting sit; the people appearing on a platform; *fig.* an opportunity to make a speech or express an opinion; a situation from which to proceed or make progress. E19. ▸**b** A basis on which a united stand is taken or a public appeal made; *spec.* (orig. *US*) a public declaration of the principles and policy of a political party, *esp.* such a declaration issued by the representatives of a US political party assembled in convention to nominate candidates for an election. E19.

8 A horizontal stage or piece of flooring resting on wheels, as in a railway carriage, truck, or tramcar; the horizontal base of a motor vehicle; the open portion of the floor at the end of a railway car of a type used esp. in the US; the floor area at the entrance to a bus. M19.

9 A raised walk, floor, or other elevated structure along the side of the track at a railway station, for convenience in getting on and off a train. M19.

10 A structure designed to stand on the bed of the sea (or a lake) to provide a stable base above water-level from which several oil or gas wells can be drilled or regulated. M20.

11 AERONAUTICS etc. A gyroscopically stabilized mounting isolated from the angular motion of the craft carrying it and providing an inertial frame for the accelerometers of an inertial guidance system; the apparatus associated with this. M20.

12 *ellipt.* A platform sole; a platform shoe. M20.

13 A rigid diving-board, *esp.* one at any of several fixed heights above the water used in diving competitions. L20.

14 COMPUTING. A standard system architecture; a (type of) machine and/or operating system, regarded as the base on which software applications are run. L20.

> 📖 **6** P. AUSTER Armed police guards stood on platforms surveying the workers. **7a** J. S. BLACKIE To go to the pulpit or platform with a thorough command of his subject. E. B. WHITE He can't use one of my books as a platform. *Offshore Engineer* The experience gained . . will serve as a respectable platform to penetrate further into a wider market place. **b** H. G. WELLS I adopted Votes for Women as the first plank of my political platform. *Survey* The Communist Party . . has held conventions to . . discuss its strategy and approve a platform. **8** H. ALLEN The cart was nothing more than a strong, framed platform resting on a high axle. M. MOORCOCK He leaps to the platform just as the bus moves forward.

Comb.: **platform body** a vehicle body having a floor but no sides or roof; **platform game** a type of video game featuring two-dimensional graphics with horizontally scrolling levels on which the action takes place and between which the animated characters must move to proceed through the stages of the game; **platform machine** = ***platform scale*** below; **platform paddle tennis** = ***platform tennis*** below; **platform party** the group of officials or other people who sit on the platform at a ceremony or meeting; **platform plank** *US* a particular principle or policy in the declared platform of a political party; **platform rocker** (orig. *US*) a rocking-chair constructed with a fixed stationary base; **platform sandal** a sandal with a platform sole; **platform scale** a weighing-machine with a platform on which the object to be weighed is placed; **platform shoe** a shoe with a platform sole; **platform sole** a very thick outer sole on a shoe; **platform-soled** *adjective* having a platform sole; **platform stage** THEATRICAL a stage consisting of a simple raised platform projecting into the area for the audience (without a proscenium arch or curtain); **platform tennis** a form of paddle tennis played on a platform, usu. of wood, enclosed by a wire fence; **platform ticket** a ticket admitting a non-traveller to a station platform; **platform truck** a road transport vehicle having a platform body.

platform /'platfɔːm/ *verb*. M16.

[from the noun.]

†**1** *verb trans.* Provide (a building) with an open walk or terrace on the top. M16–L18.

†**2** *verb trans.* Plan, outline, sketch, draw up a scheme of, (*lit.* & *fig.*). L16–M17.

3 *verb trans.* Place (as) on a platform. L18.

4 *verb intrans.* **a** Speak *for* something to be part of a political platform. *rare*. M19. ▸**b** Speak on a public platform. Now *rare*. L19.

platformed /'platfɔːmd/ *adjective*. M17.

[from PLATFORM *noun, verb*: see -ED², -ED¹.]

Formed as a platform, level-topped; elevated as on a platform or plateau; provided with a platform.

platformer /'platfɔːmə/ *noun*¹. L16.

[from PLATFORM *verb* or *noun* + -ER¹.]

†**1** A schemer, a contriver, a plotter. L16–E17.

2 A person who speaks on a public platform. L19.

3 COMPUTING. A platform game. L20.

Platformer /'platfɔːmə/ *noun*². M20.

[from next + -ER¹.]

An installation for Platforming.

Platforming /'platfɔːmɪŋ/ *verbal noun*. M20.

[from PLAT(INUM + *re*)*forming* verbal noun (see REFORM *verb*¹ 8).]

(Proprietary name for) a process for reforming petroleum using a platinum catalyst.

attrib.: ***Platforming process***, ***Platforming unit***, etc.

■ **platformate** *noun* the end product of the Platforming process M20.

platic /'platɪk/ *adjective*. E17.

[Late Latin *platicus* broad, general from Greek *platikos* broad, diffuse, from *platus* broad: see -IC.]

ASTROLOGY. Of an aspect: not exact or within a degree, but within half the sum of the orbs of the (usu. two) planets concerned. Opp. PARTILE 2.

platin- *combining form* see PLATINO-.

platina /'platɪnə, plə'tiːnə/ *noun*. *obsolete* exc. *Hist.* M18.

[Spanish, dim. of *plata* silver: see -INE⁴.]

= PLATINUM.

platinate /'platɪneɪt/ *noun*. M19.

[from PLATINUM + -ATE¹.]

CHEMISTRY. A salt containing tetravalent platinum in the anion; *esp.* a salt containing the $[Pt(OH)_6]^{2-}$ ion.

platinate /ˈplatɪneɪt/ *verb trans.* L19.
[from PLATINUM + -ATE[3].]
= PLATINIZE.

plating /ˈpleɪtɪŋ/ *noun.* E19.
[from PLATE *verb* + -ING[1].]
▶ **I 1** The action of PLATE *verb.* E19.
▶ **II 2** An external layer or sheath of plates, cladding of (metal) plates. M19.
3 The surface of precious metal plating copper etc.; any metal coating. M19.
4 BIOLOGY & MEDICINE. A culture on a plate. E20.
Comb.: **plating certificate** a certificate stating that a goods vehicle has had a plating examination; **plating examination** a legally-required inspection of a goods vehicle to establish weight, roadworthiness, etc.

platini- /ˈplatɪni/ *combining form.* L19.
[from PLATINUM: see -I-.]
Of or containing platinum, esp. in the platinic (tetravalent) state, as ***platinichloride***. Cf. PLATINO-.

platinic /pləˈtɪnɪk/ *adjective.* M19.
[from PLATINUM + -IC, after *ferric* etc.]
CHEMISTRY. Of or containing platinum in the tetravalent state. Cf. PLATINOUS.

platiniferous /platɪˈnɪf(ə)rəs/ *adjective.* E19.
[from PLATINUM + -FEROUS.]
Bearing or yielding platinum.

platiniridium /ˌplatɪnɪˈrɪdɪəm/ *noun.* M19.
[from PLATIN(O- + IRIDIUM.]
MINERALOGY. A native alloy of platinum and iridium, occurring as small white grains or cubes with truncated angles.

platinise *verb* var. of PLATINIZE.

platinite /ˈplatɪnʌɪt/ *noun.* In sense 2 also **P-**. M19.
[from PLATINUM + -ITE[1].]
1 CHEMISTRY. A salt containing divalent platinum in the anion. M19.
2 METALLURGY. An alloy of iron and nickel which has the same coefficient of expansion as platinum, used esp. in metal-to-glass contacts in lamps. E20.

platinize /ˈplatɪnʌɪz/ *verb trans.* Also **-ise**. E19.
[from PLATINUM + -IZE.]
Coat or plate with platinum.
■ **platiniˈzation** *noun* E20.

platino- /ˈplatɪnəʊ/ *combining form.* Before a vowel also **platin-**.
[from PLATINUM: see -O-.]
Of or containing platinum, esp. in the platinous (divalent) state. Cf. PLATINI-.
■ **platinoˈcyanide** *noun* any of a series of fluorescent salts containing the anion $[Pt(CN)_4]^{2-}$ M19. **platino-iˈridium** *noun* = PLATINIRIDIUM L19.

platinode /ˈplatɪnəʊd/ *noun. obsolete* exc. *Hist.* M19.
[from PLATINUM + -ODE[2].]
ELECTRICITY. The negative plate or cathode of a voltaic cell (orig. made of platinum). Opp. ZINCODE.

platinoid /ˈplatɪnɔɪd/ *noun.* L19.
[from PLATINUM + -OID.]
1 Any of the platinum metals. Usu. in *pl.* L19.
2 An alloy of copper, zinc, nickel, and tungsten, resembling platinum and resistant to tarnishing. L19.

platinotype /ˈplatɪnə(ʊ)tʌɪp/ *noun.* L19.
[from PLATINO- + -TYPE.]
(A photograph taken by) an early photographic process using paper coated with potassium chloroplatinite and ferric oxalate, and developed in hot potassic oxalate solution.

platinous /ˈplatɪnəs/ *adjective.* M19.
[from PLATINUM + -OUS, after *ferrous* etc.]
Of or containing platinum in the divalent state. Cf. PLATINIC.

platinum /ˈplatɪnəm/ *noun & adjective.* E19.
[Alt. of PLATINA after other metals in *-um*.]
▶ **A** *noun.* **1** A rare silvery heavy metal which is a chemical element of the transition series, atomic no. 78, is relatively inert with a very high melting point, and is used in jewellery, as a catalyst, etc. (Symbol Pt.) E19.
2 A greyish-white or silvery colour like that of platinum. E20.
Phrases: **go platinum** (of a recording) achieve sales meriting a platinum disc.
▶ **B** *attrib.* or as *adjective.* **1** Made of platinum, consisting of platinum. M19.
2 Of the colour of platinum, greyish-white, silvery. M20.
Comb. & special collocations: **platinum-black** a black powder consisting of finely divided platinum; **platinum blond**, **platinum blonde** *adjective & noun* (**a**) *adjective* (of the hair) silvery-blond in colour; (of a person) having silvery-blond hair; (**b**) *noun* a person, esp. a woman, with platinum-blond hair; **platinum-blue** any of a class of dark blue polymeric complexes formed by divalent platinum with amide ligands; **platinum disc** a framed platinum disc awarded to a recording artist or group for sales of a recording of at least a million; **platinum group**: comprising the platinum metals; **platinum metals** a group of similar metallic elements of the transition series often associated in ores, comprising platinum, iridium, palladium, osmium, rhodium, and ruthenium; **platinum sponge** a grey spongy amorphous form of platinum obtained on heating ammonium chloroplatinate and used as a catalyst.

platitude /ˈplatɪtjuːd/ *noun.* E19.
[French, from *plat* (see PLAT *adjective*), after *certitude*, *exactitude*, etc.: see -TUDE.]
1 Flatness, dullness, insipidity, commonplaceness (as a quality of speech or writing). E19.
2 A flat, dull, or commonplace remark or statement, *esp.* one spoken or written with an air of importance or solemnity. E19.

📖 **2** *Independent* Trotting out old platitudes about adopting a step-by-step approach.

■ **platiˈtudinal** *adjective* (*rare*) = PLATITUDINOUS L19.

platitudinarian /ˌplatɪtjuːdɪˈnɛːrɪən/ *noun & adjective.* M19.
[from prec., after *latitude*, *latitudinarian*, etc.: see -ARIAN.]
▶ **A** *noun.* A person who speaks or writes platitudes. M19.
▶ **B** *adjective.* Characterized by platitude; given to delivering platitudes. M19.
■ **platitudinarianism** *noun* L19.

platitudinary /platɪˈtjuːdɪn(ə)ri/ *adjective.* E20.
[from PLATITUDE, after *latitude*, *latitudinary*, etc.: see -ARY[1].]
= PLATITUDINARIAN *adjective.*

platitudinize /platɪˈtjuːdɪnʌɪz/ *verb intrans.* Also **-ise**. L19.
[from PLATITUDIN(OUS etc. + -IZE.]
Speak or write platitudes.
■ **platitudinizer** *noun* L19.

platitudinous /platɪˈtjuːdɪnəs/ *adjective.* M19.
[from PLATITUDE, after *multitude*, *multitudinous*, etc.: see -OUS.]
Characterized by or of the nature of a platitude; full of platitudes; (of a person) speaking or writing platitudes, given to delivering platitudes.

📖 P. TOYNBEE What a fearful, platitudinous old bore Gurdjieff seems when one reads his quoted words.

■ **platitudinously** *adverb* L19. **platitudinousness** *noun* M19.

Platonian /pləˈtəʊnɪən/ *noun & adjective. rare.* M16.
[from Greek *Platōn* Plato + -IAN.]
▶ †**A** *noun.* A Platonist. M16–E17.
▶ **B** *adjective.* = PLATONIC *adjective* 1. M20.

Platonic /pləˈtɒnɪk/ *adjective & noun.* In senses A.2, 3, B.2 now usu. **p-**. M16.
[Latin *Platonicus* from Greek *Platōnikos*, from *Platōn* Plato: see -IC.]
▶ **A** *adjective.* **1** Of, pertaining to, or associated with the Greek philosopher Plato (*c* 429–347 BC) or his doctrines; conceived or composed after the manner of Plato. M16. ▸**b** Of a person: holding or maintaining the doctrines of Plato; that is a follower of Plato. M17.
2 a Of love, a relationship, etc.: of a purely spiritual character, not sexual. M17. ▸**b** Feeling or professing platonic love. M17.
3 Confined to words or theory, not leading to action, harmless. M19.

📖 **1 Platonic body, Platonic solid** each of the five regular polyhedra (tetrahedron, cube, octahedron, dodecahedron, icosahedron). **Platonic year** *Hist.* a cycle in which the heavenly bodies were supposed to go through all their possible movements and return to their original positions, after which, according to some, all history would then repeat itself (sometimes identified with the period of precession of the equinoxes, about 25,800 years).
2a S. QUINN She is . . ready for the heat of love and tired of Platonic crushes.

▶ **B** *noun.* †**1** A follower of Plato, a Platonist. E17–M18.
2 †**a** A platonic lover. M17–M18. ▸**b** In *pl.* The acts or doings of a platonic lover, non-sexual attitudes. E19.

📖 **2b** R. MACAULAY To Vicky a young man *was* a young man and no platonics about it.

■ **Platonical** *adjective* (now *rare* or *obsolete*) = PLATONIC *adjective* M16. **platonically** *adverb* in a Platonic or (usu.) platonic manner M17. †**Platonician** *noun* [French *platonicien*] a Platonist M18–M19. **Platonicism** /-sɪz(ə)m/ *noun* (*rare*) = PLATONISM 3 L17.

Platonise *verb* var. of PLATONIZE.

Platonism /ˈpleɪt(ə)nɪz(ə)m/ *noun.* In sense 3 usu. **p-**. L16.
[mod. Latin *platonismus*, from Greek *Platōn* Plato: see -ISM.]
1 The philosophy or doctrine of Plato, or of his followers. L16.
2 A doctrine or tenet of Platonic philosophy; a saying of, or like those of, Plato. E17.
3 Belief in or practice of platonic love. L18.

Platonist /ˈpleɪt(ə)nɪst/ *noun & adjective.* M16.
[medieval Latin *platonista*, from Greek *Platōn* Plato: see -IST.]
▶ **A** *noun.* **1** A follower of Plato; a person who holds the doctrines or philosophy of Plato. M16.
2 A platonic lover. M18.
▶ **B** *attrib.* or as *adjective.* Of or pertaining to Platonists or Platonism or platonic love. L19.
■ **Platoˈnistic** *adjective* pertaining to or characteristic of Platonists or Platonism M19. **Platoˈnistically** *adverb* L20.

Platonize /ˈpleɪt(ə)nʌɪz/ *verb.* Also **-ise**. E17.
[Greek *platōnizein*, from *Platōn* Plato: see -IZE.]
1 *verb intrans.* Follow the philosophy or doctrine of Plato; philosophize after the manner of Plato; be a Platonist. E17.
2 *verb trans.* Give a Platonic character to; make Platonic. M19.

platoon /pləˈtuːn/ *noun & verb.* M17.
[French *peloton* little ball, platoon, dim. of *pelote*: see PELLET *noun*[1], -OON.]
▶ **A** *noun.* **1** MILITARY. Orig., a small body of foot-soldiers, detached from a larger body and operating as an organized unit. Now, a subdivision (usu. a quarter) of a company, a tactical unit commanded by a lieutenant and usu. divided into three sections. M17.
2 MILITARY. A number of shots fired simultaneously by a platoon or body of men; a volley. *obsolete* exc. *Hist.* E18.
3 Any group of people acting together; *spec.* (**a**) AMER. FOOTBALL a group of players trained to act together as a single unit of attack or defence and usu. sent into or withdrawn from the game as a body; (**b**) US SPORT a group of players who alternate in the same position in a team. E18.
4 A group of vehicles moving together as if in convoy owing to the constraints of the traffic system. L20.

📖 **3** *Baseball Illustrated* Shane Mack began the season as a platoon right fielder, but ended up as a regular. *Time* A platoon of media advisers . . oversaw his every move.

▶ **B** *verb.* †**1** *verb intrans.* Fire a volley. Only in 18.
2 *verb trans.* Dispose in platoons. *rare.* M20.
3 US SPORT. **a** *verb trans.* Alternate (a player) with another in the same position. M20. ▸**b** *verb intrans.* Interchange with or *with* another player in the same position. M20.

Platt /plat/ *noun & adjective.* E19.
[Abbreviation formed as next.]
= PLATTDEUTSCH.

Plattdeutsch /platˈdɔɪtʃ/ *noun & adjective.* M19.
[German from Dutch *Platduitsch* Low German, from *plat* flat, low + *Duitsch* German.]
(Of or pertaining to) the German of those dialects of Germany which are not High German; Low German.

platteland /ˈplatəland, *foreign* ˈplatəlant/ *noun. S. Afr.* M20.
[Afrikaans, from Dutch *plat* flat + *land* country.]
The remote rural part of South Africa.
■ **plattelander** /ˈplatəlandə, *foreign* ˈplatəlandər/ *noun* a native or inhabitant of the platteland M20.

platten *noun* see PLATEN.

platter /ˈplatə/ *noun.* ME.
[Anglo-Norman *plater*, from *plat* dish, use as noun of Old & mod. French *plat*: see PLAT *adjective*, -ER[2].]
1 A large flat dish or plate, esp. for food; the food placed on a platter, a platterful; *N. Amer.* a main course of a meal, served on a platter. ME.
2 A gramophone record. *slang.* M20.
3 The metal disc of a turntable unit, on which the record is placed for playing. L20.
4 COMPUTING. A rigid metal disk coated, usually on both sides, with magnetic material on which information is stored inside a disk file. L20.
1 on a platter, **on a silver platter** *fig.* = ***on a plate*** s.v. PLATE *noun* 25.
Comb.: **platter-face** *arch.* a broad, round, flat face; **platter-faced** *adjective* (*arch.*) having a broad, round, flat face.
■ **platterful** *noun* as much or as many as will fill a platter E17.

platy /ˈplati/ *noun.* E20.
[Colloq. abbreviation of mod. Latin *Platypoecilus* former genus name (formed as PLATY- + Greek *poikilos* variegated).]
Any ornamental freshwater fish of the genus *Xiphophorus*, native to SE Mexico, esp. *X. maculatus*. Also ***platy-fish***.

platy /ˈpleɪti/ *adjective.* M16.
[from PLATE *noun* + -Y[1].]
†**1** Consisting or formed of plates; platelike. M16–E17.
2 MINERALOGY & PETROGRAPHY. Consisting of or easily separating into plates; flaky. E19.

platy- /ˈplati/ *combining form.*
[Greek *platu-*, combining form of *platus*.]
Broad, flat.
■ **platyceˈphalic**, **platyˈcephalous** *adjectives* having a flat or broad head M19. **platyˈcephaly** *noun* platycephalic condition E20. **platyˈpellic** *adjective* [Greek *pella* bowl] having or designating a pelvis whose transverse diameter is much greater than its anteroposterior diameter L19. **platyˈscopic** *adjective* designating a lens or combination of lenses giving a wide field of view L19.

platycodon /platɪˈkəʊd(ə)n/ *noun.* M19.
[mod. Latin (see below), from PLATY- + Greek *kōdōn* bell.]
A Chinese and Japanese plant of the bellflower family, *Platycodon grandiflorus*, grown for its light blue saucer-shaped flowers (balloon-shaped when in bud). Also called ***balloon-flower***.

platyhelminth /platɪˈhɛlmɪnθ/ *noun.* Pl. **-helminths**, in Latin form **-helminthes** /-hɛlˈmɪnθiːz/. L19.
[mod. Latin *Platyhelminthes* pl. (see below), formed as PLATY- + HELMINTH.]
ZOOLOGY. A worm of the phylum Platyhelminthes; = FLATWORM.

platykurtic /platɪˈkəːtɪk/ *adjective.* E20.
[from PLATY- + Greek *kurtos* bulging + -IC.]
STATISTICS. Of a frequency distribution or its graphical representation: having less kurtosis than the normal distribution.
▪ **platykurˈtosis** *noun* the property of being platykurtic M20.

platymeria /platɪˈmɪərɪə/ *noun.* Also Anglicized as **platymery** /ˈplatɪmɪəri/. L19.
[from PLATY- + Greek *mēria* thigh-bones: see -IA[1], -Y[3].]
ANTHROPOLOGY. The condition of a (usu. fossil) femur of which the anteroposterior diameter of its shaft is unusually small relative to the corresponding transverse diameter.
▪ **platymeric** *adjective* of, pertaining to, or exhibiting platymeria L19. **platymerism** *noun* = PLATYMERIA M20.

platypus /ˈplatɪpəs/ *noun.* L18.
[mod. Latin *Platypus* (orig. genus name, but already in use for a genus of beetle), from Greek *platupous* flat-footed, from *platus* flat + *pous* foot.]
In full ***duck-billed platypus***. A semi-aquatic burrowing monotreme mammal, *Ornithorhynchus anatinus*, of Tasmania and E. Australia, which has brown fur, webbed feet, a bony beak shaped like that of a duck, and a flattened tail, and lays leathery eggs.
▪ **platypussary** *noun* (*Austral.*) an enclosure or building in which platypuses are kept M20.

platyrrhine /ˈplatɪrʌɪn/ *noun & adjective.* Also **platyrhine**. M19.
[from Greek *platus* flat + *rhin-*, *rhis* nose: see -INE[1].]
▶ **A** *noun. ZOOLOGY.* A platyrrhine primate. M19.
▶ **B** *adjective.* **1** *ZOOLOGY.* Of, pertaining to, or designating a primate having a flattened nose with widely separated nostrils directed outwards (as in most of the New World monkeys). M19.
2 *ANTHROPOLOGY.* Of a person or skull: having the nose or the nasal bones flat or broad. L19.
▪ **platyrrhiny** *noun* platyrrhine condition L19.

platysma /pləˈtɪzmə/ *noun.* Pl. **-mas**, **-mata** /-mətə/. L17.
[mod. Latin, from Greek *platusma* flat piece, plate, from *platunein* widen, from *platus* broad, flat.]
ANATOMY. A thin broad layer of muscle fibres extending from the collar-bone to the angle of the jaw.

platytera /platɪˈtɛːrə/ *noun.* E20.
[Greek *platutera* lit. 'she who is wider', compar. of *platus* wide.]
ECCLESIASTICAL. A type of icon of the Incarnation depicting the Mother of God in an attitude of prayer, and in front of her the Christ-child, each usu. surrounded by a mandorla.

platzel /ˈplats(ə)l/ *noun.* M20.
[Yiddish, perh. rel. to German *Plätzchen* fancy biscuit.]
A flat crisp bread roll.

†**plaud** *verb & noun.* L16.
[Latin *plaudere* clap.]
▶ **A** *verb trans.* Applaud; praise. L16–E19.
▶ **B** *noun.* Applause; praise. L16–M19.

plaudit /ˈplɔːdɪt/ *noun.* E17.
[Abbreviation of next.]
An act of applauding; a round of applause; *gen.* any emphatic expression of approval. Now usu. in *pl.*

plaudite /ˈplɔːdɪti/ *noun.* Now *rare.* M16.
[from Latin, 2nd person pl. imper. of *plaudere* clap.]
1 An appeal for applause at the conclusion of a play or other performance. M16.
†**2** A round of applause. L16–E18.

plauditory /ˈplɔːdɪt(ə)ri/ *adjective. rare.* M19.
[Irreg. from PLAUDIT after *auditory* etc.: see -ORY[2].]
Applauding, laudatory, expressive of approval.

plaur /ˈplaʊə/ *noun.* Also ***plav*** /plav/. E20.
[Romanian.]
Any of the floating mats of reeds in the delta of the Danube; the material of which such mats are composed.

plausibility /plɔːzɪˈbɪlɪti/ *noun.* L16.
[formed as next: see -ITY.]
†**1** Readiness to applaud or approve. L16–M17.
†**2** The quality of deserving applause or approval; agreeableness, affability. Also, an instance of this, a praiseworthy quality or trait, an agreeable or courteous act. L16–L17.
3 a The quality of seeming reasonable or probable (though speculative), apparent worthiness of acceptance; appearance of reasonableness; speciousness. Also, an instance of this, a plausible argument or statement. M17. ▸**b** The capacity to sound plausible, (deceptive) convincingness or persuasiveness. M18.

> 🕮 **3a** *Spectator* Not to be taken in by plausibilities that 'wouldn't wash'. *Scientific American* These facts . . add up to the overall plausibility of the outlined evolutionary picture. S. QUINN She expressed some doubts about the plausibility of the death instinct. **b** J. A. FROUDE His plausibility long enabled him to explain away his conduct.

plausible /ˈplɔːzɪb(ə)l/ *adjective & noun.* M16.
[Latin *plausibilis*, from *plaus-* pa. ppl stem of *plaudere* clap: see -IBLE.]
▶ **A** *adjective.* †**1** Deserving applause or approval; praiseworthy, commendable. M16–E18.
†**2 a** Acceptable, agreeable, pleasing, gratifying; winning public approval, popular. M16–E19. ▸**b** Of a person, a person's manners, etc.: affable, ingratiating, winning. L16–M19.
3 a Of an argument, statement, etc.: seeming reasonable or probable (though speculative); apparently acceptable or trustworthy (sometimes with the implication of mere appearance); specious. M16. ▸**b** Of a person: convincing or persuasive but deceptive. M19.
†**4** Expressive of applause or approval. M16–E17.

> 🕮 **3a** H. E. BATES Nothing plausible or logical . . emerged in anything that anybody said. P. H. NEWBY The information . . is plausible, but it is not accurate. G. VIDAL He was always able to express himself in the most plausible way. **b** W. MARCH She had been so innocent, so plausible in her denials.

▶ **B** *noun.* A plausible argument or statement. M17.
▪ **plausibleness** *noun* (now *rare*) plausibility L16. **plausibly** *adverb* L16.

plausive /ˈplɔːsɪv/ *adjective.* Now *rare.* E17.
[from Latin *plaus-* (see prec.) + -IVE.]
1 Expressive of applause or approval. E17.
2 Plausible. E17.

plaustral /ˈplɔːstr(ə)l/ *adjective. literary. rare.* M18.
[from Latin *plaustrum* wagon + -AL[1].]
Of or pertaining to a cart or wagon.

Plautine /ˈplɔːtʌɪn/ *adjective.* L19.
[Latin *Plautinus*, from *Plautus* (see below): see -INE[1].]
Pertaining to, characteristic of, or in the style of the Roman comic playwright Titus Maccius Plautus (*c* 250–184 BC).

plav *noun* var. of PLAUR.

play /pleɪ/ *noun.* OE.
[from the verb.]
▶ **I 1** Active bodily exercise; brisk and vigorous action of the body or limbs, as in fencing, dancing, leaping, etc. *obsolete* exc. as passing into other senses. OE.
2 The action of lightly and briskly wielding or plying a weapon etc. Chiefly as 2nd elem. of comb., as ***cudgel-play***, ***swordplay***, etc. OE.
3 *fig. & gen.* Action, activity, operation, working, esp. with rapid movement or change, or variety. (Now almost always of abstract things, as fancy, thought, etc.) M16.
4 Rapid, brisk, or light movement, esp. when alternating or fitful; elusive change or transition (of light or colour); light motion about or impact on something. E17. ▸**b** *ellipt.* Play of light, play of colour. Now *rare.* L17.
5 a Free or unimpeded movement, esp. from or about a fixed point; the possible or proper motion of a piece of mechanism or of a part of the living body; freedom or room for movement; the space in or through which a piece of mechanism etc. can or does move. M17. ▸**b** *fig. & gen.* Free action; freedom, opportunity, or room for action; scope for activity. M17. ▸**c** Attention, patronage; a show of interest; publicity. *slang* (orig. *US*). E20.

> 🕮 **3** DISRAELI That enchanting play of fancy which had once characterized her. **4** S. BELLOW He could not restrain the play of muscles in his throat. E. H. GOMBRICH The play of sunlight on the green pastures. A. J. TOYNBEE The fishermen . . knitting new nets with an unconscious play of their deft fingers. *House & Garden* Mirrored panels bounce light reflections back and forth in never-ending play. **5a** D. BLOODWORTH Just look at the play on this steering wheel. *Practical Householder* To make the tool completely rigid . . modifications were needed . . to eliminate play between various components. **b** R. DAVIES She was too stupid to give her nastiness serious play.

▶ **II 6** Exercise or action by way of recreation or amusement, now esp. as a spontaneous activity of children or young animals; *colloq.* an instance or period of such activity. Formerly also *spec.*, sexual dalliance, sexual activity. OE. ▸†**b** (A source of) enjoyment or pleasure; a joy, a delight. ME–E16. ▸**c** The condition of not being at work, the condition of being on strike, out of work, ill, etc., (now *dial.*); *Scot.* a holiday or break from school. E17.
7 A particular amusement or diversion; a game, a sport, a pastime. *obsolete* exc. *Scot.* OE. ▸**b** A country fair or gala, a festival. *Scot. & dial.* L18.
8 Jest, fun, sport; trifling. Chiefly in ***in play***. ME.
9 An act or proceeding, esp. of a crafty or underhand kind; manner of action, method of proceeding; a trick. *obsolete* exc. as passing into sense 10. ME.
10 The carrying on or playing of a game or games; manner or style of playing a game; skill in playing a game. ME. ▸**b** The status of the ball etc. in a game in respect of being playable within the rules (chiefly in ***in play***, ***out of play***); the part of a pitch etc. in which the ball is in play. L18.
11 *spec.* The playing of a game or games for money or other valuable stakes; gaming, gambling. ME.
12 An attempt to achieve or gain something; a move, a manoeuvre, a venture; *spec.* (***a***) *N. Amer. SPORT* an attacking move in a team game, an action that advances a team's interest; (***b***) *slang* an attempt to attract or impress a person sexually (esp. in ***make a play (for)***); (***c***) *COMMERCE* an opportunity for investment, a business deal, a commercial venture. M19.

> 🕮 **6** MILTON Wearied with their amorous play. R. S. THOMAS His work was play after the dull school. A. STORR Rough-and-tumble play, which is important in learning. **7** R. W. EMERSON The plays of children are nonsense, but very educative nonsense. **10** G. A. MACDONNELL Eliciting his opponent's best play. *Club Cricketer* In spite of . . interruptions with rain, play did start.

▶ **III 13** A mimic representation of an action or story as a spectacle on the stage, on film, etc.; a dramatic performance; a composition in the form of dialogue, intended for performance on the stage usu. with appropriate movement, costume, etc. OE. ▸**b** A performance, proceeding, or piece of action in real life. Now *rare.* L16.
13 ***acting play***, ***closet play***, ***costume play***, ***dumb play***, ***morality play***, ***mystery play***, ***passion play***, etc.
▶ **IV 14** Performance on a musical instrument. *obsolete* exc. *Scot.* ME.
15 The act of playing a disc, tape, etc. *colloq.* M20.
Phrases: **a play within a play** a play acted as part of the action of another play. **as good as a play** *colloq.* very entertaining or amusing. **at play** (***a***) engaged in playing by way of recreation or amusement; (***b***) in the course of gambling. ***boys' play***: see BOY *noun.* **bring into play**, **call into play** begin to exercise, bring into action, give scope for. ***child's play***: see CHILD *noun.* **come into play** come into action or operation, become active or relevant. ***double play***: see DOUBLE *adjective & adverb.* ***fair play***: see FAIR *adjective.* ***foul play***: see FOUL *adjective.* **hold in play** = ***keep in play*** below. **in full play** in full action or operation, acting with full force. **in play** †(***a***) actively engaged or employed; (***b***) *COMMERCE* (of a company etc.) in a position where a takeover bid can be made or is invited; (see also senses 8, 10b above). **into play** *COMMERCE* (of a company etc.) into a position where a takeover bid can be made or is invited. **keep in play** keep (a person etc.) exercised, occupied, or engaged; give (a person) something to do, esp. in the way of self-defence in a contest etc. **make play** (***a***) *RACING & HUNTING* tax the powers of pursuers or followers; (***b***) keep an adversary engaged; (***c***) ***make play with***, ***make great play with***, etc., use freely and with a view to advantage, make much of. **out of play** †(***a***) unoccupied, out of employment or office; (***b***) see sense 10b above. **play of words** the use of words merely or mainly for the purpose of producing a rhetorical or fantastic effect. **play on words**, **play upon words** a playful use of words to convey a double meaning or produce a fantastic or humorous effect by similarity of sound with difference of meaning; a pun. ***POSITIONAL play***. ***secular plays***: see SECULAR *adjective* 6. ***set play***: see SET *adjective.* ***state of play***: see STATE *noun.* ***triple play***: see TRIPLE *adjective & adverb.*
Comb.: **play-act** *verb* (***a***) *verb intrans.* act in a play; pretend, make believe; behave theatrically or insincerely; (***b***) *verb trans.* act (a scene, part, etc.) in a play, pretend to be; **play-acting** the acting of a play or plays, dramatic performance; theatrical or insincere behaviour; **play-actor** an actor of plays, a dramatic performer; a person who play-acts; **play-actress** (now *rare*) a female actor of plays; **playbill** (***a***) a poster or placard announcing a play and usu. giving the names of the actors; (***b***) *US* a theatre programme; **playbook** (***a***) a book of plays or dramatic compositions; (***b***) a book of games and pastimes for children; (***c***) *AMER. FOOTBALL* a book containing various strategies and systems of play; **playbox** a box in which a child, esp. at a boarding-school, keeps toys, books, and other personal possessions; **playbroker** an agent who serves as an intermediary between playwrights and managers or actors; **play-by-play** *adjective & noun* (designating) a running commentary on a game; **play-centre** a place where children can play under supervision outside school; (chiefly *NZ*) a preschool playgroup; **play clothes**: used only for playing in; **play-day** (***a***) a day given up to play; a day exempted from work; *esp.* a school holiday; (***b***) *THEATRICAL* a day on which a play is performed; **play-debt** *arch.* a gambling debt; **play-doctor** a professional improver of other people's plays; **Play-Doh** (proprietary), **play-dough** a child's modelling clay; **play face** an expression seen in apes or monkeys at play, in which the mouth is open but the teeth are hidden; **playfellow** a child's companion in play, a playmate; **playfere** (long *obsolete* exc. *Scot.*) a child's companion in play, a playmate; **playfight** a fight in play; **playfighting** fighting in play; **playgame** a game not taken seriously; an amusement; a plaything; **playgoer** a person who (habitually) goes to see plays, a frequenter of the theatre; **playgoing** (habitual) going to see plays, frequenting of the theatre; **playhour** an hour set aside for play; **playland** an area suitable for recreation; **playleader** an adult who leads or helps with children's play; the leader of, or a helper at, a playgroup; **playleadership** the status or function of a playleader; **play-lunch** *Austral. & NZ* a snack taken by children to school for eating at playtime; **playmake** *verb intrans.* lead attacks in a team game, bring other players on one's side into a position to score, (chiefly as ***playmaking*** *verbal noun*); **playmaker** (***a***) now *rare* a writer of plays; (***b***) a player in a team game who leads attacks or brings other players on his or her side into a position to score; **playmate** (***a***) a child's companion in play; (***b***) (orig. *US*) a companion in amorous (esp. sexual) play, a lover; **play-material** (***a***) material used by children at play; (***b***) relatively unimportant classified information passed on by a

double agent; **playmonger** *derog.* a writer of plays; **play-pen** a portable enclosure for a young child to play in; **playroom** a room used for children to play in; **playscheme** a local project or scheme providing recreational facilities and activities for children for a certain period of time, typically during the school holidays; **play school** a nursery-school, a kindergarten; **playstreet** a street closed to traffic so that children can play in it; **play-suit** (*a*) a light casual outfit; (*b*) a set of clothes for a young child to play in; **play-table** a gaming-table; **play therapist** a practitioner of play therapy; **play therapy** PSYCHOLOGY therapy in which emotionally disturbed children are encouraged to act out and express their fantasies and feelings through play, aided by the therapist's interpretations; **play-way** an educational method which seeks to utilize play; **playwriter** = PLAYWRIGHT; **playwriting** = PLAYWRIGHTING.

■ **playless** *adjective* M19. **playlet** *noun* a slight or short dramatic play L19.

play /pleɪ/ *verb.*

[Old English *pleg(i)an*, *plægian* = Middle Dutch *pleien* dance, leap for joy, rejoice.]

▶ **I 1** *verb intrans.* **a** Exercise or occupy oneself, be busily engaged; act, operate, work. *obsolete* exc. as passing into other senses. OE. ▸†**b** Clap the hands. OE–ME. ▸**c** Strut, dance, or otherwise make a display, as a cock bird before hens. Also foll. by *up*. M18.

2 *verb intrans.* Of a living being: move about swiftly with a lively, irregular, or capricious motion; spring, fly, or dart to and fro; gambol, frisk; flit, flutter. OE.

3 *verb intrans. & trans.* (Cause to) bubble and roll about as a boiling liquid; boil. *obsolete* exc. *dial.* LME.

4 *verb trans.* Carry out or practise (an action), perform or execute (a movement); *esp.* (infl. by branch II), perform or practise (a trick, joke, etc.) in the way of sport, deceit, etc. Formerly also, exercise (a craft). LME.

5 *verb trans.* †**a** Deal with; treat. L15–L16. ▸**b** Wield or ply (something) lightly and briskly; keep in motion or use; actuate, operate, (an instrument). L16. ▸**c** ANGLING. Allow (a fish) to become exhausted by pulling against a line. E18.

6 a *verb intrans.* Keep moving to and fro. *rare.* E16. ▸**b** *verb intrans.* Of a thing: move briskly or lightly, esp. with alternating or irregular motion; change or alternate rapidly; strike lightly on or *on* a surface; flutter, flicker, glitter, ripple. L16. ▸**c** *verb trans.* Cause to move briskly or lightly, esp. with alternating or irregular motion; exhibit with brilliant effect; strike lightly on a surface. E18.

7 *verb intrans.* Move, revolve, or oscillate freely, esp. within a definite space; have proper unimpeded movement, have free play. L16.

8 a *verb intrans.* Operate artillery, fire (*on*, *upon*). Of artillery, a mine, a firework, etc.: be discharged or fired, go *off*. L16. ▸**b** *verb trans.* Discharge, fire, or let *off* (artillery, fireworks, etc.). (Foll. by *on*, *upon*.) L16. ▸†**c** *verb trans.* Finish drinking (liquor), toss *off*. *slang.* L16–E17.

9 a *verb intrans.* Emit a jet of water; cause or allow a jet of water to be emitted; spout. M17. ▸**b** *verb trans.* Cause to emit a jet of water, cause to spout. *rare.* E18.

📖 **1a** SIR T. BROWNE There is an invisible Agent . . who plays in the dark upon us. **2** MILTON The Seale And bended Dolphins play. C. THIRLWALL He played about them like a bee. **4** M. DICKENS I would have felt worse . . for playing her such a dirty trick. **5b** STEELE Playing the razor, with a nimble wrist, mighty near the nose. C. A. LINDBERGH I pulled the flashlight from my belt and was playing it down towards the . . fog. **c** *Coarse Fishing* This match . . saw me play and land a pike. *fig.*: I. MURDOCH I felt that I was playing a big fish. Hugo was communicative. **6b** DRYDEN When Western Winds on curling Waters play. N. P. WILLIS The breaking waves play'd low upon the beach. M. REID The tempest still played around us. F. M. FORD Over her throat there played the reflection from a little pool. J. B. MORTON A shy smile played about his lips. **9a** DICKENS The fire-engine maker . . having brought out . . his stock to play upon its last smouldering ashes. G. SWIFT The fountain was playing on the ornamental pond. A. BROOKNER The gardener's hosepipe is playing on the . . orange-trees.

▶ **II 10 a** *verb intrans.* & (long *obsolete* exc. *Scot.*) *refl.* (Now esp. of a child or young animal) employ or exercise oneself or itself in the way of amusement or recreation; amuse or divert oneself; sport, frolic; engage in or take part in a game or games; *spec.* (now *rare*) engage in sexual dalliance or activity, have sexual intercourse. OE. ▸†**b** *verb intrans.* Be joyful or merry, rejoice, esp. as in heaven. Only in ME. ▸**c** *verb intrans.* Abstain from or be off work; take a holiday; be on strike, be out of work. *obsolete* exc. *dial.* LME.

11 *verb trans. & intrans.* with *at*. Exercise or employ oneself in (a game etc.) by way of amusement or recreation or as a sport; pretend to be or act out for amusement or recreation; make believe *that*. OE.

12 *verb intrans.* Make sport or jest at another's expense; mock. (Foll. by *with*, †*at*, †*on*, †*upon* the person mocked.) *obsolete* exc. as passing into sense 13. OE.

13 *verb intrans.* Foll. by *with*: amuse oneself with, sport with; touch or finger lightly by way of amusement; treat or do lightly or frivolously; trifle or toy with; *colloq.* masturbate (chiefly in ***play with oneself***). ME.

14 a *verb intrans.* Act, behave, conduct oneself (in a specified way). Chiefly in phrs. below. LME. ▸**b** *verb trans.* with *it* as obj. Behave or act in a particular manner; proceed in a specified way. Chiefly in phrs. below. L19.

15 *verb trans.* **a** Compete with or contend against in a game, be on the team or side opposing. LME. ▸**b** Choose or employ (a person) to take part in a match; include in a team. M18. ▸**c** Occupy as one's position in a team, typically take up the position of in a game. L19.

16 *verb trans.* **a** Stake or wager in a game; hazard or bet in gambling. L15. ▸**b** Bet or gamble at or on (races, cards, etc.); take chances with. *colloq.* (orig. *US*). M19.

17 *verb intrans.* Engage in or take part in a game for money or other valuable stakes; gamble. E16.

18 *verb trans.* **a** Move or throw (a piece etc.) as an item in the playing of a game; in CHESS etc., move (a piece) to another square on the board; in CARDS, lay face upwards or otherwise display (a card), take and display cards from (a hand). M16. ▸**b** In ball games: strike and direct (the ball) with a bat, racket, cue, etc., deliver (the ball) with the hand in a particular direction or to a particular position. M18.

19 *verb trans. fig.* ▸**a** Use or treat as a counter or plaything, manage or use for one's own ends. Also, fool, swindle. M17. ▸**b** Set in opposition, oppose, pit (one person, thing, or party *against* another), esp. for one's own advantage. Also foll. by *off (against)*. M17.

20 *verb trans.* Bring into a condition by playing. Chiefly in ***play oneself in***, get into form for play, adapt oneself to the conditions of play; spend time becoming accustomed to or familiar with a situation. M19.

21 *verb intrans.* Of a sports pitch, wicket, etc.: be in such condition as to have a specified effect on play. Of a hand at cards etc.: be constituted so as to have a specified effect on play. M19.

22 *verb intrans.* Cooperate, comply, agree; do what is required of one. Usu. in neg. contexts. *colloq.* M20.

📖 **10a** MILTON And young and old com forth to play On a Sunshine Holyday. CHESTERFIELD A man may play with decency; but if he games he is disgraced. A. S. NEILL Ma father says that we just play ourselves at this school. W. MAXWELL Up and down Ninth Street there were children I could play with. P. CUTTING The alleyways were thronged with children playing. G. BODDY She played in the school croquet tournament. **11** E. GASKELL He taught young ladies to play billiards. J. R. LOWELL Children who play that everything is something else. W. CATHER The Captain still played whist as well as ever. *Observer* The team . . play attractive football. J. BETJEMAN They played at Auction Bridge. *Times* As many people . . like playing soldiers as like playing trains. W. BOYD He had behaved like an excited schoolboy playing at spies. V. BRAMWELL Try to play tennis or go swimming in the early evening. **13** W. COWPER I play with syllables, and sport in song. G. GREENE One hand was playing with his moustache. V. CANNING I like a girl who doesn't play with her food. *Lancashire Life* How could they . . build docks when they had merely £60,000 to play with. J. WAINWRIGHT She was playing with me like a cat teasing a trapped mouse. **15b** *Times* Surrey played the eleven which has done so well for them. **c** *play centre forward*, *play half-back*, etc. **16b** P. G. WODEHOUSE I was a rich man . . . But unfortunately I played the Market. **19b** *Manchester Examiner* The Sultan likes to play off one Power against another. O. NASH The wise child handles father and mother By playing one against the other. **22** E. WAUGH The Air Force aren't playing until they know what's going on.

▶ **III 23** *verb intrans.* **a** Perform on a musical instrument, produce music from an instrument. Foll. by *on*, *upon*. OE. ▸**b** Of music: sound. Of an instrument: produce music. E16. ▸**c** Of a disc, tape, etc.: reproduce (esp. musical) sound, esp. *for* a specified time. Of a radio etc.: transmit or give out (esp. musical) sound. E20.

24 *verb trans.* **a** Perform (music, a piece of music) on an instrument, produce (music) from an instrument. L15. ▸**b** Express or represent by music performed on an instrument. Chiefly *poet.* E17. ▸**c** Perform the musical compositions of (a particular composer). L19.

25 *verb trans.* Accompany (a person or persons) *in*, *out*, *off*, etc., with instrumental music. Also, pass *away* (time) in playing music. L17.

26 *verb trans.* **a** Produce musical sound from, perform music on, (a musical instrument). E18. ▸**b** Cause recorded sound to be reproduced from (a disc, tape, record-player, radio, etc.). E20.

📖 **23a** T. S. ELIOT You need a good piano. You'll play all the better. **b** OED Just then the music began to play. M. BRADBURY Somewhere . . in the house a guitar is playing. **c** G. GREENE Somewhere in another room a gramophone began to play. A. BRINK On the sideboard the transistor was playing. **24a** G. VIDAL Joe Bailey flung himself upon the piano and played romantic ballads. **c** E. LANGLEY Blue took out the violin, and . . played Dvorak. **25** J. HATTON It is customary in American theatres for the orchestra to play the audience out. **26a** E. MCBAIN My kid sister plays piano. J. WAINWRIGHT Played a certain way a violin string is capable of cracking a wine glass. **b** J. GRENFELL He isn't allowed to play the gramophone . . after ten o'clock. G. NAYLOR I thought we'd . . play some tapes.

▶ **IV** †**27 a** *verb intrans.* Exercise oneself with weapons, fight, *spec.* for exercise or as a pastime with swords or sticks; joust, tourney; fence. ME–L18. ▸**b** *verb trans.* Esp. with cognate obj.: fight in (a bout or contest). LME–L16.

▶ **V 28** *verb intrans.* Perform a drama, act a part in a drama; perform. In early use also, gesture. ME.

29 a *verb trans.* Represent (an action or story) in mimic action; perform as a spectacle on the stage, on film, etc.; give a dramatic performance of (a work). ME. ▸**b** *verb intrans.* Be performed as a spectacle on the stage etc.; (of a film) be shown in a cinema etc. (Foll. by *for* a specified time.) E16.

30 *verb trans.* Represent (a person or character) in a dramatic performance; act the part of. LME.

31 *verb trans.* Sustain the character of in real life; perform the duties or characteristic actions of; act as if one were, act or behave as or like, act the part of. Chiefly with *the* before the obj. & in various standard phrs. LME.

32 Foll. by *out*: ▸**a** *verb trans.* Perform to the end; *fig.* bring to an end; *refl.* come to an end, become exhausted, worn out, or obsolete. Freq. as ***played out*** *ppl adjective.* L16. ▸**b** *verb intrans.* Be performed to the end, reach the end; become exhausted, worn out, or obsolete. M19.

33 *verb trans.* Perform a play etc. in (a specified town, theatre, etc.); appear as a performer or entertainer at (a particular place). L19.

📖 **28** J. TEY 'Is he playing just now?' . . 'He had a part in that silly Comedy at the Savoy'. J. AGATE She played in *La Belle Hélène*. **29a** J. VAN DRUTEN Olive plays this scene with all the conviction possible. S. BRETT Charles kept feeling that he was back in rep, playing some antiquated thriller. **b** *New Yorker* Mr Zeffirelli watched the action . . and he told us that . . the scene was playing well. G. BORDMAN It played continuously from its opening night until the end of 1881. **31** B. EARNSHAW I played the young freethinker Who doesn't give a damn. **32a** J. QUINCY This burlesque . . gradually played itself out, and came to an end. E. BOWEN When she feels played out she goes to bed with a book. P. ROTH No . . chance for a . . revival of the drama we would seem very nearly to have played out. **b** LADY BIRD JOHNSON Past one my enthusiasm played out and I put my head in the pillow. **33** *Guardian* Gielgud . . played sixty towns and gave 81 performances. L. CODY The band was playing Clarkestead Leisure Centre that night.

Phrases: ***play a good game of***: see GAME *noun*. ***play a part***: see PART *noun*. ***play a person foul***: see FOUL *adverb* 7. ***play a person's game***: see GAME *noun*. ***play a poor game of***: see GAME *noun*. ***play at fast and loose***: see FAST *adjective*. ***play ball (with)***: see BALL *noun*[1] 2b. ***play* BOOTY. play both ends against the middle** *colloq.* keep one's options open, try to keep favour with opposing sides. ***play both sides of the street***: see STREET *noun*. **play by ear** (*a*) perform (music) without having seen a score; (*b*) = ***play it by ear*** below. ***play cat and mouse***: see CAT *noun*[1]. ***play ducks and drakes with***: see DUCK *noun*[1]. **play fair** play according to the rules of the game, without cheating; act justly or honourably. **play false** (*a*) *verb intrans.* cheat in a game or contest; be deceitful; (*b*) *verb trans.* deceive, betray, (a person). ***play fast and loose***: see FAST *adjective*. **play favourites** *colloq.* show favouritism. ***play first fiddle***: see FIDDLE *noun*. **play for a fool**, **play for a sucker**, etc., treat (a person) as a dupe, make a fool of, cheat. **play for laughs** try to arouse laughter in one's audience. **play for safety** (*a*) = ***play safe*** below; (*b*) (BILLIARDS & SNOOKER etc.) engage in safety play, play with the aim of leaving one's opponent unable to score. ***play for the gallery***: see GALLERY *noun* 5. **play for time** try to gain more time for oneself; postpone an action or decision. ***play games with***: see GAME *noun*. ***play God***: see GOD *noun*. ***play havoc (with)***: see HAVOC *noun* 2. ***play hell with***: see HELL *noun*. ***play high***: see HIGH *adjective, adverb, & noun*. ***play hob***: see HOB *noun*[1]. ***play hookey***: see HOOKEY 1. ***play house***: see HOUSE *noun*[1]. **play into the hands of** act so as to give an advantage to (another, either partner or opponent). **play it by ear** proceed instinctively or step by step according to results or circumstances, improvise. **play it cool** *colloq.* behave in a relaxed or assured manner; affect indifference. ***play it straight***: see STRAIGHT *adjective*[1]. **play it for laughs** = ***play for laughs*** above. ***play merry hell (with)***: see HELL *noun*. **play off the stage** act much better than (another actor); dominate the stage at the expense of (another person). ***play old gooseberry***: see GOOSEBERRY 3. **play on** (*a*) make use of, take advantage of, (a quality or disposition of another person); (*b*) ***play on a word***, ***play on words***, make playful use of a double meaning of a word or words, pun. ***play one's ace***: see ACE *noun* 1. ***play one's cards right***, ***play one's cards well***: see CARD *noun*[2] 1. ***play one's part***: see PART *noun*. ***play opposite***: see OPPOSITE *preposition*. ***play* POLITICS. *play* POSSUM. *play propriety***: see PROPRIETY 5. **play safe** act in such a way as to avoid risks. ***play second fiddle***: see FIDDLE *noun*. ***play silly buggers***: see BUGGER *noun*[1] 3. **play straight** = ***play it straight*** above. ***play the ape***: see APE *noun* 1. ***play the bear with***: see BEAR *noun*[1]. ***play the — card***: see CARD *noun*[2] 1. ***play the devil with***: see DEVIL *noun*. ***play the* DICKENS. *play the field***: see FIELD *noun*. ***play the fool***: see FOOL *noun*[1]. ***play the fox***: see FOX *noun* 1. ***play the game***: see GAME *noun*. ***play the giddy goat***, ***play the giddy goat***: see GOAT *noun*. ***play the giddy ox***. ***play the hop***: see HOP *noun*[2]. ***play the jack***: see JACK *noun*[1]. ***play the man***: see MAN *noun*. **play the market** speculate in stocks etc. ***play the part of***: see PART *noun*. ***play the percentages***: see PERCENTAGE. ***play third fiddle***: see FIDDLE *noun*. ***play to the gallery***: see GALLERY *noun* 5. ***play truant***: see TRUANT *noun*. **play upon** = ***play on*** above. ***play with fire***: see FIRE *noun*. **what is X playing at?** *colloq.* what is X really doing? what are X's real intentions or motives?

With adverbs in specialized senses: **play along** *colloq.* (*a*) cooperate, comply, agree (= sense 22 above), pretend to agree or cooperate, (freq. foll. by *with*); (*b*) deceive or tease (a person). **play around** *colloq.* amuse oneself; behave in a playful or irresponsible manner; *spec.* have a sexual relationship *with* (a person or persons), esp. casually or extramaritally. **play away** (*a*) lose in gambling; waste, squander, throw away recklessly; (*b*) *SPORT* play on an opponent's ground; *transf.* conduct an illicit sexual liaison or relationship; see also sense 25 above. **play back** (*a*) *CRICKET* step back to play a stroke, esp. defensively; (*b*) reproduce or play (sounds) shortly after recording, esp. to monitor quality etc.; *fig.* repeat, think about again. **play down** (*a*) ***play down to***, lower one's standard, quality, etc., to suit the tastes or demands of (one's public); bring oneself down to (a low standard, level, etc.); (*b*) minimize; try to make (something) appear smaller or less important than in reality; make little of. **play forward** *CRICKET* step or reach forward to play a good (or full length) delivery. **play off** (*a*) cause (a person) to appear in a disadvantageous light; (*b*) pass off as something else, palm off; (see also senses 5c, 8a, b, c, 19b, 25 above); **play on** (*a*) *CRICKET* (of a batsman) play the ball on to the wicket, putting himself or herself out; (*b*) continue playing. **play through** *GOLF* continue playing, overtaking other players on the course who have agreed to suspend their game to allow this. **play up** (*a*) behave in a boisterous, unruly, or troublesome manner; misbehave; *spec.* (of a horse) jump or frisk about; (*b*) behave manfully or heroically; act in a helpful or cooperative manner; (*c*) make the most of; emphasize; exploit or trade on, esp. in journalism and advertising; (*d*) tease, annoy, irritate, (a person); make sport with; give trouble to; (*e*) ***play up to*** (orig. *Theatrical slang*), act in a drama so as to support or assist another actor; support, back up; flatter, toady.

Comb.: **play-the-ball** *RUGBY LEAGUE* a move restarting play after a tackle, in which the tackled player kicks or heels the ball from the ground.

playa /ˈplʌɪə/ *noun.* Orig. *US.* **M19.**
[Spanish = shore, beach, coast, from late Latin *plagia*: see PLACE.]
1 A flat area of silt or sand, free of vegetation and usu. salty, lying at the bottom of a desert basin and dry except after rain; (more fully ***playa lake***) a temporary lake formed after rain in such an area. **M19.**
2 In Spain and Spanish-speaking countries: a beach. **M19.**
3 *GEOGRAPHY.* Flat alluvial coastland. **L19.**

playable /ˈpleɪəb(ə)l/ *adjective.* **L15.**
[from PLAY *verb* + -ABLE.]
†**1** Given to play, playful, sportive. *rare.* Only in **L15.**
2 Able to be played. **M19.** ▸**b** Of a cricket or football ground etc.: in a suitable condition for playing on. **L19.**
■ **playaˈbility** *noun* **L19.**

playback /ˈpleɪbak/ *noun.* **E20.**
[from PLAY *verb* + BACK *adverb.*]
1 The reproduction or playing of a recording, usu. shortly after it has been made, esp. to monitor quality etc. **E20.**
2 An apparatus for playing recordings. **E20.**
3 *CINEMATOGRAPHY.* A technique of recording the voice of a singer for the soundtrack of a film as a substitute for that of an actor or actress when songs are called for. Chiefly in ***playback singer***, a singer whose voice is so used. **M20.**

playboy /ˈpleɪbɔɪ/ *noun. colloq.* **E19.**
[from PLAY *noun* + BOY *noun.*]
An irresponsible pleasure-seeking man, *esp.* a wealthy one.
■ **playboyish** *adjective* **M20.**

play-down /ˈpleɪdaʊn/ *noun.* Orig. *Canad.* **M20.**
[from PLAY *verb* + DOWN *adverb.*]
A game or match in a series of play-offs.

player /ˈpleɪə/ *noun.* **LOE.**
[from PLAY *verb* + -ER[1].]
▶ **I** A person.
1 *gen.* A person who plays or who plays something. **LOE.**
2 a A person who plays for money or other valuable stakes; a gambler. **ME.** ▸**b** A person who engages in some game, usu. specified in the context; a person practised or skilful in some game. **LME.** ▸**c** *spec.* A professional player at cricket (opp. GENTLEMAN 5c) or golf (now *Hist.*); *transf.* any professional. **E19.** ▸**d** A speculator or dealer in stocks etc.; a company etc. competing in a market or participating in a business venture. **M20.**
†**3** A person who performs tricks to amuse others; a juggler; an acrobat. **LME–M16.**
4 A person who acts a character on the stage; a dramatic performer, an actor. **LME.**
5 A person who plays a musical instrument. **LME.**
2a ***card-player***, ***football player***, ***tennis player***, etc. **4** ***bit-part player***, ***strolling player***, etc. **5** ***flute player***, ***piano player***, etc.
▶ **II** A thing.
6 A metal pendant to a horse's bit. **L16.**
7 A machine for playing back recordings. **M20.**
7 ***cassette player***, ***record-player***, etc.

Comb.: **player-coach** a person who both plays in a team and acts as coach to it; **player-manager** a person who both plays in a team and manages it; **player-piano** a piano having a mechanical apparatus by which it can be played automatically.

Playfair /ˈpleɪfɛː/ *noun.* **E20.**
[Lyon *Playfair*, 1st Lord Playfair (1818–98), Brit. chemist and administrator.]
A code or cipher in which successive pairs of letters are replaced by pairs chosen in a prescribed manner from a matrix of 25 letters, usu. arranged in accordance with a keyword. Usu. more fully ***Playfair cipher***, ***Playfair code***, etc.

playful /ˈpleɪfʊl, -f(ə)l/ *adjective.* **ME.**
[from PLAY *noun* + -FUL.]
Full of play, fond of play, inclined to play; done in fun; pleasantly humorous or jocular.

> 🕮 W. J. LOCKE Pontifex—Pontifex something . . a playful title given him by her mother. *Village Voice* Handsome male cat . . great purrer, playful. A. CHAMBERS I think he intended only to be playful, to tease, not to wound. B. CHATWIN The Rococo style in porcelain—an art of playful curves.

■ **playfully** *adverb* **L18.** **playfulness** *noun* **L18.**

playgirl /ˈpleɪɡəːl/ *noun. colloq.* **M20.**
[from PLAY *noun* + GIRL *noun*, after PLAYBOY.]
An irresponsible pleasure-seeking woman, *esp.* a wealthy one.

playground /ˈpleɪɡraʊnd/ *noun.* **L18.**
[from PLAY *noun* + GROUND *noun.*]
A piece of ground used for playing on, *esp.* one attached to a school; *transf.* any place of recreation.

> 🕮 H. NIELSEN European playgrounds where Jack Keith might be holidaying. G. SWIFT Our classroom . . with a view of a dim, walled-round asphalt playground. *fig.*: F. RAPHAEL Only in the world of imagination was there a playground for impossible dreams. ***adventure playground***, ***junk playground***.

playgroup /ˈpleɪɡruːp/ *noun.* **E20.**
[from PLAY *noun* + GROUP *noun.*]
1 *SOCIOLOGY.* A group formed naturally by young children in a neighbourhood for play and companionship. **E20.**
2 A group of preschool children brought together on a regular basis to play together under supervision; an establishment where such a group plays. **M20.**

playhouse /ˈpleɪhaʊs/ *noun.* Also (esp. in sense 2) **play-house**. **LOE.**
[from PLAY *noun* + HOUSE *noun*[1].]
1 A house or building in which plays are acted; a theatre. **LOE.**
2 A toy house in or with which children may play. **L18.**
¶ In isolated use before **L16.**

playing /ˈpleɪɪŋ/ *verbal noun.* **ME.**
[from PLAY *verb* + -ING[1].]
The action of PLAY *verb*

Comb.: **playing-card** any of a set or pack of 52 cards (see CARD *noun*[2] 1) used in playing various games; **playing field** a field or piece of ground for playing on, *esp.* one attached or belonging to a school; ***level playing field*** (fig.), a situation in which no one is favoured or handicapped and all participate on equal terms; ***playing-marble***: see MARBLE *noun* 4.

playlist /ˈpleɪlɪst/ *noun & verb.* **M20.**
[from PLAY *noun* + LIST *noun*[3].]
▶ **A** *noun.* **1** A list of theatrical plays to be performed. **M20.**
2 A shortlist of musical recordings chosen to be broadcast by a radio station in a given period. **L20.**
▶ **B** *verb trans.* Place (a recording) on a playlist. **L20.**

play-off /ˈpleɪɒf/ *noun.* **L19.**
[from PLAY *verb* + OFF *adverb.*]
An additional game or match played to decide a draw or tie; a replay. Also, (each of) a series of games or matches played to decide a championship etc.

playsome /ˈpleɪs(ə)m/ *adjective.* Now chiefly *dial.* **E17.**
[from PLAY *noun* + -SOME[1].]
Inclined to play; playful.
■ **playsomely** *adverb* **M17.** **playsomeness** *noun* **L17.**

plaything /ˈpleɪθɪŋ/ *noun.* **L17.**
[from PLAY *noun* + THING *noun*[1].]
A thing to play with, a toy; a person, animal, or thing treated as a thing to be played or trifled with.

> 🕮 A. R. WALLACE Among our favourite playthings were popguns . . and pistols. I. MURDOCH She was the helpless plaything of great mechanical forces. A. S. DALE Chesterton's women do not yearn to own property . . . Neither are they the . . playthings of husbands.

playtime /ˈpleɪtʌɪm/ *noun.* **E17.**
[from PLAY *noun* + TIME *noun.*]
1 a The time during which a play is being performed. *rare.* **E17.** ▸**b** The time for the performance of a play. *rare.* **M18.**
2 A time for play or recreation; *spec.* a short break between classes at a school. **M17.**

playwright /ˈpleɪrʌɪt/ *noun.* **E17.**
[from PLAY *noun* + WRIGHT.]
A writer of plays, a dramatist, *esp.* a professional one.
■ **playwrighting** *noun* the writing of plays, the occupation of a playwright **L19.**

plaza /ˈplɑːzə/ *noun.* **L17.**
[Spanish from Proto-Romance source of PLACE *noun*[1].]
A market-place, square, or open public space, orig. in Spain and Spanish-speaking countries; (chiefly *N. Amer.*) a large paved area surrounded by or adjacent to buildings, esp. as a feature of a shopping complex.

plaza de toros /ˌplaθa dɛ ˈtoros, ˌplaza/ *noun phr.* Pl. ***plazas de toros*** /ˌplaθas, ˌplazas/. **E19.**
[Spanish.]
In Spain and Spanish-speaking countries: a bullring.

plc *abbreviation.*
Public limited company.

plea /pliː/ *noun.* **ME.**
[Anglo-Norman *ple*, *plai*, Old French *plait*, Old & mod. French *plaid* agreement, talk, lawsuit, discussion from Latin *placitum* decision, decree, use as noun of neut. pa. pple of *placere* PLEASE. Cf. PLEAD.]
▶ **I** *LAW.* **1** A suit or action at law; the presentation of an action in court. Now *Hist. & Scot.* **ME.**
2 a A pleading; an allegation or statement formally made by a party to the court in support of his or her case. Now chiefly *SCOTS LAW.* **LME.** ▸**b** A formal statement by or on behalf of a prisoner or defendant, alleging facts either in answer to the indictment or to a plaintiff's declaration or bill or showing cause why the prisoner or defendant should not be compelled to answer. Freq. with specifying word. **LME.** ▸**c** *ellipt.* A plea of guilty. Freq. in ***cop a plea*** (*US slang*), plead guilty, usu. as part of a bargain or agreement with the prosecution. **E20.**

> 🕮 **1** J. ARBUTHNOT A plea between two country esquires about a barren acre. **2b** B. BAINBRIDGE Exercising extreme caution in dealing with pleas of insanity. ***defence plea***, ***declinatory plea***, ***peremptory plea***, etc.

▶ **II** *gen.* **3** Controversy, debate, strife; a quarrel. Now *Scot.* **ME.**
4 That which is pleaded or maintained, esp. in justification; an appeal, an argument; an apology, an excuse; a demand, a request, an entreaty. **M16.**
†**5** *transf.* That which is demanded by pleading; a claim. *rare* (Shakes.). Only in **L16.**

> 🕮 **4** MILTON So spoke the Fiend, and with necessity, The tyrant's plea excused his devilish deeds. D. JACOBSON Tears in their eyes, and pleas for forgiveness falling from their lips. P. GROSSKURTH Jones was to make a plea . . to Freud to give . . Klein a fair hearing.

Phrases: **common pleas** (*obsolete* exc. *Hist.*) (*a*) civil actions at law brought by one subject against another (cf. ***Pleas of the Crown*** below); (*b*) (more fully ***Court of Common Pleas***) the court where such actions were heard. **hold a plea** try an action. **hold pleas** try actions at law, have jurisdiction. **plea-in-bar** = ***special plea(-in-bar)*** below. **plea-in-law** *Scot.* a statement of the legal grounds of a civil action. ***plea of tender***: see TENDER *noun*[2] 1. **Pleas of the Crown** (*obsolete* exc. *Hist.*) (*a*) legal proceedings in which the Crown had a financial interest, as by exacting a fine, as distinct from those involving claims between subjects (cf. ***common pleas*** above); (*b*) legal proceedings including all criminal proceedings, as involving conduct held to be committed against the Crown (in Scotland, limited to proceedings concerned with murder, rape, robbery, and arson). **special plea(-in-bar)** *LAW* a plea either in abatement or in bar of an action or prosecution, alleging a new fact, and not merely disputing the ground of action or charge.

Comb.: **plea bargain** (orig. *US*) an arrangement entered into by plea-bargaining; **plea-bargaining** (orig. *US*) a practice whereby a defendant pleads guilty to a reduced charge in exchange for the prosecution's cooperation in securing a more lenient sentence or an agreement to drop other charges; **plea-house** *rare* a court of law.

plea /pliː/ *verb intrans. & trans. Scot. & north.* **LME.**
[from prec.]
Plead.

pleach /pliːtʃ/ *verb & noun.* **LME.**
[Old French (mod. dial. *plêcher*), var. of *ple(i)ssier*, *pla(i)ssier* PLASH *verb*[1].]
▶ **A** *verb trans.* **1** Interlace (bent-down or partly cut stems and branches of young trees and brushwood) to form a fence or hedge. Cf. PLASH *verb*[1] 1. **LME.**
2 Make or renew (a hedge or fence) by the above process. Cf. PLASH *verb*[1] 2. **E16.**
3 *transf.* Entwine, interlace, tangle, plait. **M19.**

> 🕮 **3** A. C. SWINBURNE Poppied hair of gold Persephone . . pleached . . about her brows.

▶ **B** *noun.* Interlacing or intertwining of boughs; a flexible branch or stem; an intertwined arrangement of these, forming a hedge. **E19.**
■ **pleached** *adjective* (*a*) (esp. of a walk or arbour) formed by pleaching of boughs and twigs, fenced or overarched with pleached boughs; (*b*) interlaced, intertwined, tangled: **L16.**

plead /pliːd/ *verb.* Pa. t. & pple **pleaded**; (now chiefly *Scot., dial., & N. Amer.*) **pled** /plɛd/; ***plead.** **ME.**
[Anglo-Norman *pleder*, Old French *plaidier* (mod. *plaider*), from *plaid* PLEA *noun.*]
†**1 a** *verb intrans. & trans.* (with *it*). Contend in debate; wrangle, argue *with* or *against*. **ME–L16.** ▸**b** *verb intrans.* Raise or prosecute a suit or action, litigate. **LME–M16.**
2 *verb intrans.* **a** Address a court as an advocate on behalf of a party; urge the claim or state the case of a party to a suit. **ME.** ▸**b** *fig.* Make an earnest appeal or supplication, make entreaties; beg, implore. (Foll. by *with* a person (*to do* something), *for* a thing, a person on whose behalf one speaks; *against*). **ME.**
3 *verb intrans.* *LAW.* Put forward an allegation or formal statement to a court as part of an action at law; *esp.* put

forward an answer or objection on behalf of a defendant to a plaintiff's bill. LME.

4 *verb trans.* Petition for in a court of law. Formerly also (*transf.*), beg, entreat for. *obsolete* exc. *Scot.* LME.

†**5** *verb trans.* Go to law with, sue, (a person). *rare.* LME–L15.

6 *verb trans.* Maintain (a plea or cause) by argument in a court of law. LME.

7 *LAW.* **a** *verb trans. & intrans.* Allege formally in the course of the pleadings; declare formally as a plea. Chiefly in ***plead guilty***, ***plead not guilty*** below. LME. ▸**b** *verb trans. fig.* Allege, offer, or maintain as a plea, esp. in defence, apology, or excuse or as extenuating an offence; beg, implore, entreat. Freq. with direct speech as obj. E17. ▸**c** *verb trans. LAW.* Enter a plea on behalf of (a person). Chiefly in ***plead a person guilty***, ***plead a person not guilty***. Chiefly *US.* E20. ▸**d** *verb intrans.* Plead guilty. *colloq.* M20.

†**8** *verb trans.* Argue or dispute on in a court of law; practise (law). LME–L16.

> **1a** AV *Job* 16:21 O that one might plead for a man with God. **2a** GIBBON He had pleaded with distinction in the tribunals of Rome. **b** F. WELDON Godfrey . . begged and pleaded with me to have his child. A. PRYCE-JONES I should . . have gone to camp . . but I pled successfully for leave. **3** DRYDEN He will not hear me out! . . Was ever criminal forbid to plead? **6** R. LYND The conventional forms under which divorce cases are pled. **7a** A. HIGGINS The . . welder who had killed his girl friend was pleading insanity. **plead guilty** enter a plea of guilty; *fig.* admit responsibility for an action etc. **plead innocent** *colloq.* = ***plead not guilty*** below. **plead not guilty** enter a plea of not guilty; *fig.* deny responsibility for an action etc. **b** A. DJOLETO 'Please don't!' Torto pleaded, about to cry. A. S. DALE He . . managed by pleading ill health . . to enjoy its income yet extricate himself.

pleadable /ˈpliːdəb(ə)l/ *adjective.* LME.
[Anglo-Norman *pledable* = Old French *plaidable*, from *plaidier* PLEAD: see -ABLE.]
1 That may be alleged formally in the course of the pleadings in a court of law. LME.
2 *gen.* That may be pleaded, claimed, or alleged on behalf of a cause. M16.
3 Of a cause: that may legally be maintained or defended in a court of law. L16.

pleader /ˈpliːdə/ *noun.* ME.
[Old French *plaideor* (mod. *plaideur*), from *plaidier* PLEAD: see -ER².]
1 A person who pleads in a court of law; an advocate. ME.
2 *gen.* A person who pleads, entreats, or implores. E17.
Phrases: ***special pleader***: see SPECIAL *adjective.*

pleading /ˈpliːdɪŋ/ *noun.* ME.
[from PLEAD + -ING¹.]
†**1** Litigation; an instance of this, a lawsuit, an action; a controversy. ME–M16.
2 The advocating of a cause in a court of law; the art of composing formal statements; the body of rules relating to this art. LME.
3 *gen.* Intercession, advocacy; supplication, earnest entreaty; an instance of this. LME.
4 A formal written (formerly oral) statement in a civil action prepared by each side and setting out the cause of action or the defence. Usu. in *pl.* M16.

> **3** A. LIVELY With many pleadings . . that I should take great care of his clothes. **4** *Times* The judge intimated that . . the matters raised . . were not relevant to the pleadings.

Phrases: ***special pleading***: see SPECIAL *adjective.*

pleading /ˈpliːdɪŋ/ *ppl adjective.* L16.
[from PLEAD + -ING².]
Entreating, beseeching, imploring.
■ **pleadingly** *adverb* M19.

pleasable /ˈpliːzəb(ə)l/ *adjective.* Now *rare.* LME.
[Old French *pleisable*, *plaisable* agreeable, from †*plaisir* (mod. *plaire*) PLEASE: see -ABLE.]
1 Able to be pleased; even-tempered, mild. LME.
†**2** Acceptable, pleasing, agreeable. LME–M16.

pleasance /ˈplɛz(ə)ns/ *noun*¹. Now *arch. & poet.* Also **-aunce.** ME.
[Old & mod. French *plaisance*, from *plaisant* pres. pple of †*plaisir* PLEASE: see -ANCE.]
†**1** That which pleases one; pleasure, desire; wish, will. ME–M16.
2 The condition or feeling of being pleased; enjoyment, delight. LME.
3 †**a** The action of pleasing someone; agreeable manners or behaviour, courtesy. LME–L16. ▸**b** A lively or pleasing trick; a pleasantry. L17.
4 Pleasure-giving quality; pleasantness. Also, something which causes pleasure; that in which one delights. LME.
5 A secluded enclosure or part of a garden, esp. as attached to a large house, laid out with pleasant walks, trees, garden ornaments, etc. (Repr. in some Scottish street-names etc.) LME.

> **2** TENNYSON When my passion seeks Pleasance in love-sighs. **4** J. SPEED Deseruedly for the pleasance of the place named Beaulieu. BYRON How Vain are the pleasaunces on earth supplied. **5** JAN MORRIS Outside the Governor's Palace, in what was His Excellency's private pleasance.

†**pleasance** *noun*². LME–E19.
[Perh. from French *Plaisance* from Latin *Placentia* whence Italian *Piacenza* a city in northern Italy known for textile manufacture.]
A fine gauzelike fabric.

†**pleasancy** *noun.* M16–E18.
[formed as PLEASANCE *noun*¹: see -ANCY.]
Pleasantness; gaiety.

pleasant /ˈplɛz(ə)nt/ *adjective & adverb.* ME.
[Old & mod. French *plaisant* pres. pple of †*plaisir* (mod. *plaire*) PLEASE: see -ANT¹.]
▸ **A** *adjective.* **1** Having the quality of giving pleasure; agreeable to the mind, feelings, or senses. ME.
2 Esp. of a person: having pleasing manners, bearing, or appearance; agreeable, cheerful, good-humoured. Freq. in *comb.*, as ***pleasant-looking***, ***pleasant-faced***, etc. LME.
3 a Humorous, jocular; merry, gay. *obsolete* exc. *Scot.* M16. ▸**b** Boisterous or excited from drinking alcohol; tipsy. Now *rare* or *obsolete.* L16.
†**4** Amusing, ridiculous. L16–M18.

> **1** H. JAMES The pleasantest incident of her life . . was coming to an end. E. M. FORSTER The vine and the wych-elm had no pleasant connexions for her. **2** L. P. HARTLEY He had a pleasant musical voice. J. DISKI He had been pleasant enough, listening politely. **3a make pleasant** be festive, make merry.

▸ **B** *adverb.* Pleasantly. Now *non-standard.* M16.

> M. R. WALKER [My husband] scarce spoke pleasant all day.

■ **pleasantly** *adverb* LME. **pleasantness** *noun* LME.

pleasant /ˈplɛz(ə)nt/ *verb. rare.* E17.
[In sense 1 from PLEASANT *adjective*, in sense 2 from French *plaisanter* to jest, formed as PLEASANT *adjective.*]
†**1** *verb trans.* Please by indulgence, indulge; spend in pleasure. E–M17.
2 *verb intrans.* Joke, make humorous remarks. M19.

pleasantry /ˈplɛz(ə)ntri/ *noun.* L16.
[French *plaisanterie*, formed as PLEASANT *adjective*: see -RY.]
1 a A humorous speech, action, or exchange; *esp.* a joke, an amusing remark. Freq. in *pl.* L16. ▸**b** Pleasant and lively humour in conversation; jocularity, fun; good-humoured ridicule. M17.
2 †**a** Pleasure, enjoyment. *rare.* M–L18. ▸**b** A pleasurable circumstance; an instance of enjoyment. L18.
3 A courteous or polite remark, *esp.* one made in casual conversation. Usu. in *pl.* M20.

> **1a** R. WEST The slap of . . cold air . . was like a pleasantry and we laughed as we ran. **b** C. JOHNSTON Pumping his brain for pleasantry and labouring for wit. **2a** S. RICHARDSON To take up the . . Company's Attention . . will spoil their Pleasantry. **3** A. HARDING His words . . were double-edged—far different from the easy pleasantries of Charles.

pleasaunce *noun* var. of PLEASANCE *noun*¹.

please /pliːz/ *verb.* ME.
[Old French *plaisir* (mod. *plaire*) from Latin *placere* be pleasing.]
▸ **I 1** *verb intrans.* Be agreeable; give pleasure or satisfaction. (Foll. by *to*, *with*.) ME.
2 *verb trans.* (orig. with dat. obj.). Be agreeable to; satisfy, delight. ME. ▸**b** *refl.* Gratify or satisfy oneself; *colloq.* do as one likes. L16.
3 *verb trans. impers.* (usu. with *it* as subj. & orig. with dat. obj.). Be agreeable or acceptable to; be the will or inclination of. Freq. in ***may it please you***, ***please God*** below, and as passing into sense 8. Also foll. by †*to*, *to do*. ME.
4 *verb trans.* In *pass.* Be gratified, delighted, or satisfied *with*; be glad or have the will *to do*; think proper or be so obliging as *to do*. LME.
5 *verb trans.* Appease, pacify, satisfy. *obsolete* exc. *dial.* LME.

> **1** F. J. FURNIVALL That the main object of poetry is to please, seems to me too contemptible. **2a** G. GREENE She did all she could to please them. J. FRAME He wanted . . to please his customers. **b** S. UNWIN In England people pleased themselves. **3** J. BUTLER It pleased God to unite Christians in communities. W. HAMILTON It pleased Mr Buchanan . . to stigmatise The Germ as an unwholesome publication. **4** E. A. FREEMAN A noble and powerful city, inhabited by rich, daring, and he is pleased to add faithless, citizens. *Time* He was not pleased with the . . wagon's seats.

▸ **II** †**6** *verb trans.* Like, take pleasure in. *Scot.* LME–E18.
7 *verb intrans.* Think fit; have the will or desire; be satisfied. E16.

> **7** *Law Reports* The plaintiff . . has a right to . . trial where he pleases. A. DUGGAN The Emperor did as he pleased without worrying.

▸ **III 8** *verb trans. & intrans.* In imper. or optative form: be agreeable, be acceptable; be willing or kind enough to do (arch. *to do*). Now freq. used in making a polite request or indicating acceptance: if you please. M17.

> **8** S. HYLAND 'Shall I tell him you're coming?' 'Yes please'. *Beano* P-Please stop fighting, chaps—just for m-me! V. BRAMWELL *Please remember*: If a pain is sharp . . see your doctor. *New York Times* If you go to all this effort, facts please.

Phrases: †**and you please** = ***if you please*** below. **as you please** as you like, as you could wish for. **if you please** with your permission, if you like, if you are willing: esp. as a courteous qualification to a request etc.; *iron.* (as an indignant intensifier) if I may be allowed to say so and be believed. **may it please you** *arch.* may it be agreeable or acceptable to you. ***pleased as Punch***: see PUNCH *noun*⁴ 3. **pleased to meet you** I am glad to make your acquaintance (usu. as a formal response to an introduction). **please God** God willing. †**please it you** = ***may it please you*** above. ***please the pigs***: see PIG *noun*¹. †**please you** = ***may it please you*** above. ***pretty please***: see PRETTY *adjective.* †**so please you** = ***may it please you*** above.
Comb.: †**please-man** *rare* a person who tries to please men.
■ **pleasedly** *adverb* in a pleased manner M17. **pleasedness** *noun* the condition of being pleased M17. **pleaser** *noun* a person who or thing which pleases or tries to please someone (foll. by *of*) E16.

pleasing /ˈpliːzɪŋ/ *noun.* LME.
[from prec. + -ING¹.]
1 The action of PLEASE; the giving of pleasure or satisfaction; the fact of being pleased or satisfied. LME. ▸†**b** Appeasing, pacification. Only in LME.
†**2** A person's liking, pleasure, or will. Formerly also (*rare*), a source of pleasure; an object of delight. LME–E16.
†**3** Pleasingness. Only in L16.

pleasing /ˈpliːzɪŋ/ *adjective.* LME.
[formed as prec. + -ING².]
That pleases or is likely to please someone; that gives pleasure, pleasant, agreeable.
■ **pleasingly** *adverb* (*a*) in a pleasing manner; so as to please someone; †(*b*) with pleasure; pleasedly: LME. **pleasingness** *noun* (*a*) the quality of being pleasing, pleasantness; †(*b*) the quality of being pleased, pleasure: L16.

pleasurable /ˈplɛʒ(ə)rəb(ə)l/ *adjective.* L16.
[from next + -ABLE, after *comfortable*. Cf. LEISURABLE.]
1 (Capable of) giving pleasure; agreeable, pleasant. L16.
†**2** Devoted to or engaged in pleasure; pleasure-seeking. L16–E18.

> **1** A. DESAI Baumgartner . . found the drink . . fiery in a pleasurable way. **2** S. WARD Idle pleasurable gentlemen.

■ **pleasuraˈbility** *noun* (*rare*) E19. **pleasurableness** *noun* M17. **pleasurably** *adverb* M17.

pleasure /ˈplɛʒə/ *noun.* LME.
[Old French *plesir*, (also mod.) *plaisir*, use as noun of *plaisir* PLEASE, with final syll. assim. to -URE.]
1 The condition or sensation induced by the experience or anticipation of what is felt or viewed as good or desirable; enjoyment, delight. Opp. ***pain***. LME. ▸**b** The indulgence of physical (esp. sexual) desires or appetites; sexual gratification. LME. ▸**c** The pursuit of sensuous enjoyment as a chief object of life or end in itself. Freq. in ***business before pleasure***. E16.
2 A person's will, desire, or choice; that which is agreeable to one or in conformity with one's wish or will. Chiefly with possess. pronoun LME.
3 a A source or object of pleasure or delight. Freq. in ***it is my pleasure***, ***it was my pleasure*** below. LME. ▸†**b** A pleasure-ground. L15–M17. ▸**c** A particular locality (esp. as a place-name). *rare.* L16.
4 The quality which gives enjoyment; pleasurableness. L15.

> **1** M. GEE A little girl . . laughing wildly . . shrieking with pleasure. **c** SHAFTESBURY When we follow Pleasure merely, we are disgusted. *personified*: W. COWPER Where Pleasure is adored, That reeling goddess with the zoneless waist. **2** LD MACAULAY They would . . till his pleasure should be known, keep their men together. **3a** C. MILNE Few greater pleasures than lying in bed. **4** H. F. TOZER What I had never felt before—the pleasure of pale colours.

Phrases: **at Her Majesty's pleasure**, **at His Majesty's pleasure** detained in a British prison (for life, or an unspecified period). **at one's pleasure**, **at pleasure** as or when one pleases, at will. **do a person a pleasure**, **do a person pleasure** perform an acceptable service, do a person a favour, please or gratify (foll. by *of* the favour done). **during a person's pleasure** while a person pleases. ***gold of pleasure***: see GOLD *noun*¹ & *adjective.* **it is my pleasure**, **it was my pleasure**, etc., an acknowledgement or dismissal of thanks; don't mention it. ***lady of pleasure***: see LADY *noun & adjective.* **man of pleasure**: devoted to the pursuit of sensual or sexual pleasure. **may I have the pleasure?** will you dance with me? **my pleasure** = ***it is my pleasure*** above. ***pleasures of the table***: see TABLE *noun.* **take a pleasure**, **take pleasure** gain satisfaction or enjoyment, delight, (*in*). **with pleasure** gladly, certainly. **woman of pleasure** (*a*) a woman devoted to the pursuit of sensual or sexual pleasure; (*b*) = ***lady of pleasure*** s.v. LADY *noun & adjective.*
Attrib. & comb.: In the sense 'of or for pleasure, devoted to or used for pleasure', as ***pleasure-cruiser***, ***pleasure-dome***, ***pleasure-garden***, ***pleasure-steamer***, ***pleasure-trip***, etc. Special combs., as

pleasuredrome an amusement centre; **pleasure-ground** an area or piece of land laid out or adapted and ornamented for recreation or enjoyment; **pleasure-house** a house used for enjoyment or recreation; a summer-house; **pleasuremonger** a person who makes a living by providing pleasure to others; a person devoted to pleasure; **pleasure-pain** *PSYCHOLOGY* (a feeling or stimulus of) pleasure or pain as relating to the pleasure principle (usu. *attrib.*); **pleasure principle** *PSYCHOLOGY* (the theory which proposes) the instinctive drive to gain pleasure and avoid pain as the basic motivating force in human life; **pleasure-seeker** a person who seeks enjoyment or amusement; *spec.* a holiday-maker; **pleasure-seeking** *noun* the seeking of amusement or enjoyment; **pleasure-seeking** *adjective* that seeks amusement or enjoyment.

▪ **pleasureful** *adjective* full of pleasure, pleasing, delightful **M16**. **pleasureless** *adjective* devoid of pleasure, joyless **E19**. **pleasurer** *noun* a pleasure-seeker; a holiday-maker: **M19**. **pleasurist** *noun* (*rare*) (*a*) a devotee of (esp. sensual) pleasure; (*b*) a pleasure-seeker: **L17**.

pleasure /ˈplɛʒə/ *verb*. **M16**.
[from the noun.]
1 *verb trans.* **a** Give (esp. sexual) pleasure to; please. **M16**. ▸**b** *refl.* Take one's pleasure; *esp.* gain sexual satisfaction. **E17**. ▸**c** *impers.* with *it* as subj. Be enjoyable or satisfying to. Cf. **PLEASE** 3. **M20**.
2 *verb intrans.* **a** Take pleasure, delight. Foll. by *in*, *to do*. **M16**. ▸**b** Go out for recreation; go on an excursion, take a holiday. Chiefly as ***pleasuring*** *verbal noun*. *colloq.* **L16**.

> 🕮 **1a** K. AMIS He was grateful to have been given the chance of pleasuring her. **b** J. CRITCHLEY Parliamentary scene-writers—pleasuring themselves in the Press Gallery. **c** *New Yorker* It pleasured him to see the smoke. **2a** A. WICKHAM I will pleasure in the faultless way My flesh dissolves. **b** D. M. MULOCK Refused, year after year, to take her autumn pleasuring.

▪ **pleasured** *ppl adjective* filled with pleasure; that has been pleasured: **E17**.

pleat /pliːt/ *noun*. **LME**.
[By-form of **PLAIT** *noun*.]
1 = **PLAIT** *noun* 2. *obsolete* exc. *Scot.* and in ***French pleat*** s.v. **FRENCH** *adjective*. **LME**.
2 A fold of cloth or drapery. Now *esp.* any of a series of folds held in place along one edge by pressing, stitching, etc., by which part of a garment or piece of fabric is regularly and symmetrically taken in. Freq. with specifying word, as ***box pleat***, ***knife pleat***, etc. Cf. **PLAIT** *noun* 1. **LME**.

pleat /pliːt/ *verb trans.* **LME**.
[By-form of **PLAIT** *verb*.]
1 Fold (cloth etc.). Now *esp.* gather (part of a garment or a piece of fabric) into regular folds held in place along one edge. Freq. as ***pleated*** *ppl adjective*. **LME**.
2 = **PLAIT** *verb* 2. *obsolete* exc. *dial.* **LME**.
▪ **pleater** *noun* a person who or thing which pleats fabric etc. **E20**.

pleather /ˈplɛðə/ *noun*. **L20**.
[from *p* (for **POLYURETHANE**) + **LEATHER** *noun*.]
Imitation leather made from polyurethane.

pleb /plɛb/ *noun & adjective*. **M17**.
[Orig. in pl. from Latin *plebs* (earlier *plebes*). Later in sense 1 abbreviation of **PLEBEIAN**. Cf. **PLEBE**.]
▸**A** *noun*. **1** **a** A member of the common people or working classes; = **PLEBEIAN** *noun* 2. *colloq.* (usu. *derog.*). **M17**. ▸**b** = **PLEBE** 2. *US colloq.* **L19**.
2 *ROMAN HISTORY.* In *pl.* The common people, orig. comprising all citizens who were not patricians, senators, or knights. **M19**.

> 🕮 **1a** D. LESSING The poor bloody plebs have to put up with modern medicine.

▸**B** *attrib.* or as *adjective*. = **PLEBEIAN** *adjective* 3. **L20**.

> 🕮 *Face* Diana places terrible pleb emphasis on poetry.

¶ In isolated use before **M20**.
▪ **plebbish** *adjective* (*colloq.*, usu. *derog.*) = **PLEBBY** **E20**. **plebbishness** *noun* (*colloq.*, usu. *derog.*) **M19**. **plebby** *adjective* (*colloq.*, usu. *derog.*) = **PLEBEIAN** *adjective* 3 **M20**. **plebifiˈcation** *noun* (*rare*, *colloq.*, usu. *derog.*) the action of making something plebeian **E19**. **plebify** *verb trans.* (*rare*, *colloq.*, usu. *derog.*) make plebeian; vulgarize: **L19**.

plebania /plɪˈbeɪnɪə/ *noun*. *rare*. **E18**.
[medieval Latin, from *plebanus* rural dean, from *plebs*, *plebes* diocese, parish, parish church.]
ECCLESIASTICAL HISTORY. A parish church whose parish includes one or more subordinate chapels.
▪ Also †**plebanian** *noun*: only in **M17**.

plebe /pliːb/ *noun*. **E17**.
[In sense 1 perh. from Old & mod. French *plèbe* from Latin *plebs* (see **PLEB**); in sense 2 perh. abbreviation of **PLEBEIAN**.]
†**1** *ROMAN HISTORY.* The plebs. **E–M17**.
2 A newly entered cadet at a military or naval academy; a freshman. Cf. **PLEB** *noun*. *US colloq.* **M19**.

> 🕮 **2** *attrib.*: N. ARMSTRONG Number one in his class at the end of his plebe year.

plebeian /plɪˈbiːən/ *noun & adjective*. **M16**.
[from Latin *plebeius*, from *plebs*: see **PLEB**, **-IAN**.]
▸**A** *noun*. **1** *ROMAN HISTORY.* A commoner, a member of the plebs, as opp. to a patrician, senator, or knight. **M16**.
2 *gen.* A person of undistinguished birth or rank, a member of the common people. **L16**.

> 🕮 **2** B. BREYTENBACH Where the plebeians . . peek at the aristocrats. *fig.*: LYTTON But one sort of plebeian, and that is the coward.

▸**B** *adjective*. **1** *ROMAN HISTORY.* Of or belonging to the plebs. **M16**.
2 Of undistinguished birth or rank; of or pertaining to the common people. **E17**.
3 Commonplace, undistinguished; uncultured, vulgar, coarse; ignoble. **E17**.

> 🕮 **2** G. M. TREVELYAN Harrow, founded under Elizabeth to meet local and plebeian needs, began to rise. **3** *Melody Maker* Unswervingly plebeian in his dress sense.

▪ **plebeiance** *noun* (*rare*) plebeian condition or action **E17**. **plebeianism** *noun* plebeian character or style **L18**. **plebeianize** *verb trans.* make plebeian, reduce to plebeian rank **M19**. **plebeianly** *adverb* (*rare*) **M17**. **plebeianness** /-n-n-/ *noun* (*rare*) **M19**.

plebiscita *noun* pl. of **PLEBISCITUM**.

plebiscitarian /plɪˌbɪsɪˈtɛːrɪən/ *adjective & noun*. **L19**.
[formed as **PLEBISCITARY** + **-IAN**.]
▸**A** *adjective*. = **PLEBISCITARY**. **L19**.
▸**B** *noun*. An advocate or supporter of a plebiscite. *rare*. **L19**.

plebiscitary /plɪˈbɪsɪt(ə)ri/ *adjective*. **L19**.
[French *plébiscitaire*, formed as next + **-ARY**[1].]
Of, pertaining to, or of the nature of a plebiscite; advocating or supporting a plebiscite.

plebiscite /ˈplɛbɪsʌɪt, -sɪt/ *noun*. **M16**.
[French *plébiscite* from Latin *plebiscitum*, from *plebs*, (see **PLEB**) + *scitum* ordinance, decree use as noun of neut. pa. pple of *sciscere* approve, vote for: see **-ITE**[1].]
1 *ROMAN HISTORY.* A law enacted by the plebeians' assembly. **M16**.
2 A direct vote of the whole electorate of a State etc. to decide a question of public importance, e.g. a proposed change in the constitution, union with another State, acceptance of a government programme, etc. (cf. **REFERENDUM**). Also, a public expression (with or without binding force) of the wishes or opinion of a community. **M19**.

> 🕮 **2** V. BROME Hitler ordered the Austrian Chancellor . . to call off his plebiscite. *Japan Times* The election widely regarded as a plebiscite on Noriega's rule.

plebiscitum /plɛbɪˈsʌɪtəm/ *noun*. Pl. **-ta** /-tə/. **L16**.
[Latin: see prec.]
1 = **PLEBISCITE** 1. Now *rare*. **L16**.
2 = **PLEBISCITE** 2. **M19**.

pleck /plɛk/ *noun*. *obsolete* exc. *dial.* **ME**.
[Cogn. with Middle & mod. Dutch *plecke* piece of ground, spot, stain, blemish, Dutch *plek* spot, Low German *plek* piece of ground, place: prob. already in Old English. Perh. also rel. to Middle Low German *plack*, Low German *plak(ke)*, patch, spot, rag, Dutch *plak* slice, flat piece.]
1 A small piece of ground; a plot; a small enclosure. **ME**.
†**2** A (discoloured) patch; a stain, a blemish. **ME–M16**.
3 A square bed of hay. *dial.* **L17**.
4 A place; a town, a village. *dial.* **L17**.

plecopterous /plɪˈkɒpt(ə)rəs/ *adjective*. **M19**.
[from mod. Latin *Plecoptera* noun pl., from Greek *plekos* wickerwork, from *plekein* plait, twist + *pteron* wing: see **-OUS**.]
†**1** *ZOOLOGY.* Of or pertaining to the family Plecoptera of cartilaginous fishes. *rare*. Only in **M19**.
2 *ENTOMOLOGY.* Of or pertaining to the Plecoptera, a small order of insects comprising the stoneflies. **L19**.
▪ **plecopteran** *noun & adjective* (*a*) *noun* an insect of the order Plecoptera; (*b*) *adjective* of or pertaining to this order: **L19**.

plectognath /ˈplɛktəgnaθ/ *adjective & noun*. **L19**.
[from mod. Latin *Plectognathi*, from Greek *plektos* twisted, plaited + *gnathos* jaw.]
ZOOLOGY. ▸**A** *adjective*. Of or pertaining to the order Plectognathi (or Tetraodontiformes) of teleost fishes having beaklike mouths and thick or spiny skins, including puffer-fishes. **L19**.
▸**B** *noun*. A fish of this order. **L19**.
▪ **plectoˈgnathic** *adjective* = **PLECTOGNATH** *adjective* **M19**.

plectonemic /plɛktə(ʊ)ˈniːmɪk/ *adjective*. **M20**.
[from Greek *plektos* twisted + *nēma* thread + **-IC**.]
Chiefly *BIOCHEMISTRY.* Pertaining to or designating two or more similar helices coiled together side by side in such a way that they cannot be fully separated unless they are unwound. Opp. **PARANEMIC**.
▪ **plectonemically** *adverb* **M20**.

plectra *noun pl.* see **PLECTRUM**.

plectre /ˈplɛktə/ *noun*. *obsolete* exc. *poet.* **E17**.
[French from Latin **PLECTRUM**.]
= **PLECTRUM** 1.

plectrum /ˈplɛktrəm/ *noun*. Pl. **-trums**, **-tra** /-trə/. **LME**.
[Latin from Greek *plēktron* anything to strike with, from *plēssein* strike.]
1 Orig. (*rare*), a device for tightening the strings of a harp. Now, a thin flat piece of horn, metal, plastic, etc., held in the hand and used to pluck the strings of a guitar, lyre, etc. Also, the corresponding mechanical part of a harpsichord etc. **LME**.
2 *ANATOMY & ZOOLOGY.* A small process, a single thick bristle; *esp.* a ridge forming part of some insect stridulating organs. **E19**.

pled *verb pa. t. & pple*: see **PLEAD**.

pledge /plɛdʒ/ *noun*. **ME**.
[Old French *plege* (mod. *pleige*) from Frankish Latin *plebium* corresp. to *plebire* warrant, assure, engage, perh. from Germanic base of **PLIGHT** *noun*[1] infl. by Latin *praebere* furnish, supply.]
1 **a** *LAW* (now *Hist.*). A person acting as surety for another; a bail, a surety; a member of a frank-pledge. **ME**. ▸†**b** A hostage. **LME–M17**.
2 The condition of being given or held as a pledge; the state of being pledged. Chiefly in ***lay in pledge***, ***lay to pledge***, ***put in pledge***, ***put to pledge*** below. **LME**.
3 A solemn commitment to do or refrain from doing something; a promise, a vow; *spec.* (***the pledge***), a solemn undertaking to abstain from alcohol. **LME**. ▸**b** A student who has promised to join a fraternity or sorority. *US*. **E20**. ▸**c** The promise of a donation to a charity, cause, etc., in response to an appeal for funds; such a donation. **E20**.
4 A thing deposited as security for the fulfilment of a contract, payment of a debt, etc., and liable to forfeiture in case of failure. **L15**. ▸**b** A symbol of challenge to do battle; a gage. *rare*. **L16**. ▸**c** *fig.* A child considered as a token of mutual love and duty between parents or as a hostage given to fortune. **L16**. ▸**d** A thing put in pawn. **E19**.
5 A thing given or taken as a sign of favour, love, etc., or as a token of something to come. **E16**.
6 An assurance of allegiance or goodwill to a person, cause, etc., confirmed by drinking; the drinking of a health to a person etc., a toast. **L16**.

> 🕮 **1a** N. BACON Each one being pledge for others good abearing. **3** *Times* The . . Tories must stick by their election pledge. P. MONETTE His own pledge to fight . . was unswerving. **c** *Keyboard Player* The money was raised by listeners telephoning pledges. **4** C. THIRLWALL They . . sent seven galleys . . as a pledge of their loyalty. **c** *Household Words* Little pledges of affection had to be christened. **d** GEO. ELIOT Hold the ring . . as a pledge for a small sum.

Phrases: **keep the pledge** abide by one's undertaking to abstain from alcohol. †**lay in pledge**, **lay to pledge** give (a person or thing) as a pledge or guarantee. **put in pledge**, **put to pledge** pawn, hand (a thing) over as a pledge. **sign the pledge**, **take the pledge** make a solemn undertaking to abstain from alcohol.

Comb.: **pledge card** (*a*) a card on which to sign a temperance pledge; (*b*) *N. Amer.* a card on which a person undertakes to contribute to a fund, sponsor a charity event, etc.

pledge /plɛdʒ/ *verb*. **LME**.
[from the noun: cf. Old French *plegier* (mod. *pleiger*).]
†**1** **a** *verb trans.* Become surety for, make oneself responsible for, (a person or thing). **LME–L15**. ▸**b** *verb intrans.* Become surety. *rare*. Only in **L16**.
2 *verb trans.* Deposit or assign as security for the repayment of a loan or the performance of an action; pawn. **L15**. ▸**b** *fig.* Promise solemnly by the pledge of, stake, (one's life, honour, word, etc.). (Foll. by *that*, *to*.) **L18**.
3 *verb trans. & intrans.* Give assurance of allegiance, fidelity, etc., to (a person) by the act of drinking; toast. Formerly also, drink (wine, a health, etc.) as confirmation of allegiance, goodwill, etc. *arch.* **M16**.
4 *verb trans.* Bind (a person) (as) by a solemn promise. Freq. *refl.* **L16**. ▸**b** Enrol (a new student) in a fraternity or sorority; (of a student) promise to join (a fraternity or sorority). *US*. **M19**.
5 *verb trans.* **a** Guarantee the performance of; undertake to give. **L16**. ▸**b** Promise solemnly (*to do* something). **E20**.

> 🕮 **2** E. HUXLEY He's sold and pledged and mortgaged everything. **b** R. DINNAGE I'd really pledged my life and soul to her. **3** JONSON Drink to me, only with thine eyes, And I will pledge with mine. **4** A. UTTLEY Becky discovered it and had to be pledged to secrecy. P. KAVANAGH Patrick pledged himself . . that he would not compromise. **5b** LYNDON B. JOHNSON Nations . . pledged to work toward . . disarmament.

Phrases: ***pledge one's troth***: see **TROTH** *noun*. †**pledge out** redeem (a thing) from pawn or pledge; ransom or bail (a person) out of prison etc.

▪ **pledgeable** *adjective* able to be pledged or pawned **M19**. **pleˈdgee** *noun* (*a*) a person with whom a pledge or pawn is deposited; (*b*) a person who takes a pledge, *spec.* (*US*) = **PLEDGE** *noun* 3b: **M18**. **pledger** *noun* †(*a*) a person who drinks to the health of another; (*b*) a person who pledges himself or herself; a person who takes a pledge; (*c*) = **PLEDGOR**: **L16**. **pledgor** *noun* (*LAW*) a person who deposits something as a pledge or pawn **M18**.

pledget /ˈplɛdʒɪt/ *noun.* M16.
[Origin unkn.]
A small compress or wad of cotton wool, lint, or other soft absorbent material for applying over a wound, sore, etc.

-plegia /ˈpliːdʒə/ *suffix.*
[from Greek *plēgē* blow, stroke (from *plēssein* to strike) + -IA¹.]
MEDICINE. Forming nouns denoting a kind of paralysis, as ***hemiplegia***, ***paraplegia***, etc.

Pleiad /ˈplʌɪəd/ *noun.* Also (in sense 2) **p-**. Pl. **-s**, **-es** /-iːz/. LME.
[Latin *Pleias*, pl. *Pleiades* from Greek *Pleias*, pl. *Pleiades* (each of) the seven mythical daughters of Atlas and Pleione: see -AD¹.]
1 ASTRONOMY. In *pl.* A cluster of small stars in the constellation Taurus (usu. spoken of as seven, though there are several hundred, of which only six are easily visible to the naked eye). LME.
2 *fig.* A brilliant cluster or group of (usu. seven) persons or things, *esp.* a group of poets. Cf. CONSTELLATION 3. E17.

plein-air /plɛnɛːr/ *adjective.* L19.
[from French EN PLEIN AIR.]
Designating a style or school of impressionist painting originating in France during the late 1860s, which sought to represent the transient effects of atmosphere and light by direct observation from nature. Also, designating a work painted out of doors or representing an outdoor scene and painted with a spontaneous technique.
■ ***plein-airisme*** /-ism/ *noun* the theories and practices of the *plein-airistes* M20. ***plein-airiste*** /-ist/ *noun* a painter of the *plein-air* school L19.

plein jeu /plɛ̃ ʒø/ *adverbial, adjectival, & noun phr.* M19.
[French = full play.]
MUSIC. ▶**A** *adverbial & adjectival phr.* A direction: with full power; *spec.* without reeds in organ playing. M19.
▶**B** *noun phr.* A type of mixture stop in an organ; music written for the full organ. M19.

pleio- /ˈplʌɪəʊ/ *combining form.*
[Greek, combining form of *pleiōn*, *-ion* more, compar. of *polus* much (see POLY-): see -O-. See also PLEO-, PLIO-.]
Having more than a certain or the usual number.
■ **pleiochasium** /-ˈkeɪz-/ *noun*, pl. **-ia**, [Greek *khasis* chasm, separation] BOTANY a cyme in which the branching is continued by more than two branches of the same order L19. **pleio'mazia** *noun* (ANATOMY) pleomastia M19. **plei'omerous** *adjective* (BOTANY) (of a floral whorl) having more than the normal number of parts L19. **plei'omery** *noun* (BOTANY) pleiomerous condition L19. **pleio'phyllous** *adjective* (BOTANY) exhibiting an abnormal increase in the number of leaves at a given point or of leaflets in a compound leaf M19. **pleiophylly** *noun* (BOTANY) pleiophyllous condition M19. **pleiotaxy** *noun* (BOTANY) an abnormal increase in the number of whorls in a perianth M19.

†**Pleiocene** *adjective & noun* var. of PLIOCENE.

pleiomorphic *adjective* var. of PLEOMORPHIC.

pleione /plʌɪˈəʊni/ *noun.* M19.
[mod. Latin (see below), from Greek *Pleionē* the mother of the Pleiades.]
Any of various orchids constituting the genus *Pleione*, of northern India, Nepal, China, etc., with fleshy pseudobulbs and ornamental white, pink, or purple flowers.

pleiotropy /plʌɪˈɒtrəpi/ *noun.* M20.
[from PLEIO- + Greek *tropē* turn, turning: see -Y³.]
GENETICS. The production by a single gene of two or more apparently unrelated phenotypic effects; an instance of this.
■ **pleiotropic** /-ˈtrəʊpɪk, -ˈtrɒpɪk/ *adjective* pertaining to, exhibiting, or of the nature of pleiotropy M20. **pleiotropically** /-ˈtrəʊp-, -ˈtrɒp-/ *adverb* M20. **pleiotropism** *noun* = PLEIOTROPY E20.

Pleistocene /ˈplʌɪstəsiːn/ *adjective & noun.* M19.
[from Greek *pleistos* most + *kainos* new, recent (as containing remains of the greatest number of modern species).]
GEOLOGY. ▶**A** *adjective.* Of, pertaining to, or designating the earliest epoch of the Quaternary period, after the Pliocene and before the Holocene. M19.
▶**B** *noun.* The Pleistocene epoch; the series of rocks dating from this time, dominated in the northern hemisphere by widespread glaciation. M19.
¶ Orig. applied to the latter part of the Pliocene epoch.

plenar /ˈpliːnə/ *adjective.* Long *arch. rare.* Also **plener**. ME.
[Anglo-Norman *plener* = Old French *plen(i)er*, *planier* (mod. *plénier*) from late Latin *plenarius* complete, from Latin *plenus* full: see -AR¹.]
†**1** = PLENARY *adjective* 2. Also, (of a place of assembly) filled, full. ME–L15.
2 = PLENARY *adjective* 1. ME.

plenarium /plɪˈnɛːrɪəm/ *noun.* Pl. **-ia** /-ɪə/. E20.
[medieval Latin, from late Latin *plenarius* complete. Cf. PLENARY.]
A book or manuscript containing a complete set of sacred writings, e.g. all the Gospels or all the Epistles.

plenarty /ˈpliːnəti/ *noun.* LME.
[Anglo-Norman *plenerte*, Old French *plenierete* fullness, from *plen(i)er* complete: see -TY¹.]
1 ECCLESIASTICAL LAW. The fact of a church living's being occupied; the state of having an incumbent. LME.
†**2** Completeness, fullness. *rare.* M17–E18.

plenary /ˈpliːnəri/ *adjective & noun.* LME.
[Late Latin *plenarius*, from Latin *plenus* full; in sense B.2 from PLENARIUM: see -ARY¹. Cf. earlier PLENAR.]
▶**A** *adjective.* **1** Complete, entire, perfect, not deficient in any element or respect; absolute, unqualified. LME.
2 Having all the members of an assembly etc. present; fully constituted, fully attended. M16. ▶**b** Of, presented to, or taking place at a full session of a conference etc. L20.
3 LAW. Of an ordinary proceeding: complete, with all its formal steps. Opp. ***summary***. E18.
4 Possessing full powers or authority. *rare.* M19.

> 🕮 **1** J. A. FROUDE A legate . . sent with plenary powers to hear the cause. **plenary indulgence** ROMAN CATHOLIC CHURCH a complete remission of temporal punishment for sin. ***plenary inspiration***: see INSPIRATION *noun*. **2 plenary session** a full meeting of a conference etc., the participants in which otherwise meet in smaller groups.

▶**B** *noun.* **1** *ellipt.* **a** = ***plenary indulgence*** above. *rare.* E19. ▶**b** = ***plenary session*** above; ***in plenary***, (of an assembly, conference, etc.) fully constituted or attended in plenary session. M20.
2 = PLENARIUM. E20.

> 🕮 **1b** *New Yorker* In his speech to the conference plenary he appeared to be struggling.

■ **plenarily** *adverb* L16.

plene /pliːn/ *adjective.* L19.
[Latin *plenus* full. Cf. PLAIN *adjective*².]
Of or pertaining to a system of full orthographic notation in Hebrew, whereby vowel sounds are indicated by certain vocalic signs; of or pertaining to similar conventions in other Middle Eastern and oriental languages.

plene administravit /ˌpliːnɪ ədmɪnɪˈstreɪvɪt/ *noun phr.* E18.
[Latin = he has fully administered.]
LAW. A plea in defence of an executor, administrator, etc., of a deceased person's estate that all the estate's assets have been exhausted in the payment of debts.

plener *noun* var. of PLENAR.

plenilune /ˈpliːnɪluːn, ˈplɛn-/ *noun.* Chiefly *poet.* LME.
[Latin *plenilunium* full moon, use as noun of adjective (sc. *tempus* time), from *plenus* full + *luna* moon.]
The time of full moon; a full moon.
■ **plenilunal** *adjective* (*rare*) = PLENILUNAR L19. **plenilunar** *adjective* belonging to or resembling the full moon M18. **plenilunary** *adjective* (*rare*) = PLENILUNAR M17.

plenipo /ˈplɛnɪpəʊ/ *noun. colloq.* Pl. **-oes**. L17.
[Abbreviation.]
= PLENIPOTENTIARY *noun.*

plenipotent /plɛˈnɪpət(ə)nt/ *adjective. rare.* M17.
[Late Latin *plenipotent-*, formed as next after *omnipotent-* OMNIPOTENT.]
Invested with or possessing full power or authority.
■ **plenipotence** *noun* full power or authority M17. **plenipotency** *noun* the quality of being plenipotent; full authority: E17. **plenipo'tential** *adjective* of or belonging to a plenipotentiary; possessing full authority: M17.

plenipotentiary /ˌplɛnɪpəˈtɛnʃ(ə)ri/ *adjective & noun.* M17.
[medieval Latin *plenipotentiarius*, from Latin *plenus* full + *potentia* power: see -ARY¹.]
▶**A** *adjective.* **1** Invested with full power, esp. as the deputy, ambassador, or envoy of a sovereign ruler; exercising absolute or discretionary power or authority. Freq. *postpositive.* M17.
2 Of or belonging to a plenipotentiary; absolute, full, unlimited. M17.

> 🕮 **1** S. HASTINGS He . . had been . . Minister Plenipotentiary to Sweden. AMBASSADOR ***plenipotentiary***. **2** S. RUSHDIE A third party who would have plenipotentiary authority over the property.

▶**B** *noun.* A person invested with plenipotentiary power or authority, esp. with regard to a particular transaction, as the conclusion of a treaty. M17.

> 🕮 L. OLIPHANT Mr Wade . . delivered the *ultimata* to the French and English plenipotentiaries.

plenish /ˈplɛnɪʃ/ *verb.* Now chiefly *Scot. & north.* LME.
[Old French *pleniss-* lengthened stem of *plenir* fill, from *plein* from Latin *plenus* full: see -ISH².]
1 *verb trans.* Fill up, supply, stock; replenish. LME. ▶**b** *spec.* Furnish (a house etc.). L16.
†**2** *verb intrans.* Spread widely; fill a vacant space. LME–M16.
■ **plenishing** *noun* (**a**) the action of the verb; (**b**) equipment, stock, (household) furniture; *spec.* a bride's contribution to setting up house; ***outsight plenishing***: see OUTSIGHT *noun*¹: L15.

plenist /ˈpliːnɪst/ *noun. obsolete* exc. *Hist.* M17.
[from Latin PLENUM + -IST.]
An adherent of the theory that all space is full of matter and that there is no such thing as a vacuum. Opp. VACUIST.

plenitude /ˈplɛnɪtjuːd/ *noun.* LME.
[Old French from late Latin *plenitudo*, from Latin *plenus* full: see -TUDE.]
1 The condition of being absolutely full in quantity, measure, or degree; completeness, perfection. LME. ▶**b** Comparative fullness; plentifulness, abundance. M17. ▶**c** HERALDRY. Fullness of the moon. Cf. COMPLEMENT *noun* 1b. M19.
†**2** MEDICINE. Abundance or excess of blood or of humours. Cf. PLETHORA 1. M16–E19.
3 The condition of being filled or full of something; fullness. Formerly also = PLENUM *noun* 1. M17.
†**4** The condition of being fully supplied with everything; affluence. M17–L18.

> 🕮 **1** P. E. DOVE God in the full plenitude of majesty. **b** R. WHELAN He . . was delighted with the plenitude of oranges.

■ **pleni'tudinous** *adjective* (*rare*) well-filled; stout, portly: E19.

plenteous /ˈplɛntɪəs/ *adjective.* Now chiefly *poet.* ME.
[Old French *plentivous*, *-evous*, from *plentif*, *-ive*, from (also mod. dial.) *plenté* PLENTY + *-if*, *-ive* -IVE. Cf. BOUNTEOUS.]
1 Present or existing in plenty or in full supply; plentiful, copious. ME.
2 Bearing or yielding abundantly; fertile, prolific, productive. Freq. foll. by *in*, †*of*. Now *rare* or *obsolete.* ME.
†**3** Possessing abundance; rich. ME–M17.
†**4** Giving abundantly; generous, bountiful. ME–L17.

> 🕮 **1** COLERIDGE A plenteous crop of . . philosophers. **2** SHAKES. *Meas. for M.* Her plenteous womb Expresseth his full tilth.

■ **plenteously** *adverb* ME. **plenteousness** *noun* LME.

plentiful /ˈplɛntɪfʊl, -f(ə)l/ *adjective.* LME.
[from PLENTY *noun* + -FUL.]
1 Present or existing in great plenty; abundant; copious. LME.
2 Provided with or yielding abundance; copiously supplied; opulent. Now *rare.* L15.
†**3** Generous, profuse, lavish. M16–E17.

> 🕮 **1** M. MOORCOCK Those who remembered when it was plentiful were puritanical about food. ***as plentiful as blackberries***: see BLACKBERRY *noun* 1. **2** LYTTON His table plentiful but plain.

■ **plentifully** *adverb* (**a**) in plentiful measure or number; copiously; with abundance; †(**b**) *rare* with fullness of treatment or expression; in detail: LME. **plentifulness** *noun* (**a**) (now *rare*) the state or condition of having or yielding abundance; abundant productiveness; (**b**) abundance, copiousness, plenty: M16.

plentify /ˈplɛntɪfʌɪ/ *verb.* Long *dial. rare.* M16.
[formed as prec. + -FY.]
†**1** *verb trans.* Make plentiful; enrich; fertilize (soil). M16–E17.
2 *verb intrans.* Become plentiful. *dial.* E20.

plentitude /ˈplɛntɪtjuːd/ *noun.* E17.
[Alt. of PLENITUDE, infl. by PLENTY *adjective.*]
Plenitude.

plenty /ˈplɛnti/ *noun, adjective, & adverb.* ME.
[Old French *plentet*, (also mod. dial.) *plenté* from Latin *plenitas*, *-tat-* fullness: see -TY¹.]
▶**A** *noun.* **1** †**a** The state of having abundance. *rare.* Only in ME. ▶†**b** Full or complete state; fullness, completeness, perfection. Only in ME. ▶**c** The state of having much or being in abundance; plentifulness. Freq. in ***in plenty***, plentiful, in abundance. LME.
2 a A full or abundant supply; a large or sufficient amount or number (*of*); abundance *of* something. Also, a great deal. ME. ▶**b** A large number (of). Cf. sense B.1b below. Now *rare* or *obsolete.* ME. ▶**c** A large quantity, *a* plentiful supply (*of*). Now chiefly *US.* E17.
3 a Abundance of the necessaries and comforts of life; a condition or time of general abundance. ME. ▶†**b** In *pl.* Provisions; things constituting the necessaries and comforts of life; possessions. L16–E18.

> 🕮 **1c** P. S. BUCK The general feeling of plenty in this rich land. **2a** D. M. DAVIN In plenty of time to prepare for . . Christmas. *Studio News* There's . . plenty happening in the . . field. ***plenty on one's plate***: see PLATE *noun* 25. **c** Z. N. HURSTON Ah . . collect . . tales and Ah know y'all know a plenty. **3a** LD MACAULAY A plenty unknown in . . Munster. ***horn of plenty***: see HORN *noun.*

▶**B** *adjective.* **1 a** *pred.* Existing or present in ample quantity or number; present in abundance; plentiful, numerous. Now chiefly *colloq.* ME. ▶**b** *postpositive.* Numerous, many. Cf. sense A.2b above. *rare* exc. *dial.* ME. ▶**c** *attrib.* Abundant, many. *colloq. & dial.* M19.
†**2** Characterized by or having abundance; abundantly supplied. *rare.* Only in L16.
3 Excellent. *slang.* M20.

📖 **1a** R. L. STEVENSON Quartz and . . cinnabar. Both were plenty in our Silverado. **c** B. GILROY Plenty snake hidin' in the grass. *New Yorker* There's plenty more . . where that came from.

▶ **C** *adverb.* Abundantly; exceedingly. *colloq.* M19.

📖 B. SCHULBERG You got Irving Thalberg plenty worried.

plenum /ˈpliːnəm/ *noun & adjective.* L17.
[Latin, neut. of *plenus* full (sc. *spatium* space): cf. VACUUM. In sense 2 later infl. by Russian *plenum* plenary session.]
▶ **A** *noun.* **1** *PHYSICS.* A space completely filled with matter; *spec.* the whole of space regarded as being so filled. Opp. VACUUM *noun* 3a. L17. ▸**b** *transf.* A condition of fullness; a full place. L18.
2 A full assembly; a meeting of a legislative body, conference, association, etc., at which all the members are expected to be present; *spec.* a meeting of all the members of a Communist Party committee. L18.
3 (The air in) a plenum chamber in a ventilation system etc. M20.

📖 **2** *Daily Telegraph* Elected by secret vote at plenums of the . . party committees.

▶ **B** *attrib.* or as *adjective.* Pertaining to or designating an artificial ventilation system in which fresh air is forced into a building and drives out the stale air. E20.
plenum chamber, **plenum space** an enclosed space in which air pressure is maintained above that of the atmosphere, as in a building's ventilation system, in an air-cooled engine, etc.

pleo- /ˈpliːəʊ/ *combining form.*
[Greek, combining form of *pleōn* poet. var. of *pleiōn*, *-on*: see -O-. See also PLEIO-. Cf. PLIO-.]
Having more than a certain or the usual number.
■ **pleocy'tosis** *noun* (*MEDICINE*) the presence of an abnormally large number of cells (*spec.* of lymphocytes in the cerebrospinal fluid) E20. **pleo'mastia** *noun* (*MEDICINE*) the possession of more than the usual number of mammae or nipples E20.

pleochroic /pliːəˈkrəʊɪk/ *adjective.* M19.
[from prec. + Greek *khrōs* colour + -IC.]
CRYSTALLOGRAPHY & MINERALOGY. Of, pertaining to, or exhibiting pleochroism; showing different colours when viewed in different crystallographic directions; dichroic, trichroic.
pleochroic halo each of a series of concentric dark-coloured circles with a radioactive inclusion at the centre, seen in sections of certain minerals (usu. in *pl.*).

pleochroism /pliːˈɒkrəʊɪz(ə)m/ *noun.* M19.
[formed as prec. + -ISM.]
CRYSTALLOGRAPHY & MINERALOGY. The property of differentially absorbing different wavelengths of light depending on their direction of incidence or state of polarization; *esp.* (in biaxial crystals) dichroism, (in triaxial crystals) trichroism; an instance of this.

pleomorphic /pliːəˈmɔːfɪk/ *adjective.* Also (*rare*) **pleio-** /ˈplʌɪə-/. L19.
[from PLEO- + Greek *morphē* form + -IC.]
Having more than one form; of variable form; *spec.* (*a*) *BIOLOGY* exhibiting different forms at different stages of the life cycle, as certain bacteria, protozoans, parasitic fungi, etc.; (*b*) *CHEMISTRY & MINERALOGY* crystallizing in two or more fundamentally different forms; polymorphic; (*c*) *MEDICINE* designating or pertaining to a tumour of highly variable structure, esp. an adenoma of the salivary gland (usu. benign).
■ **pleomorphism** *noun* the fact or condition of being pleomorphic M19. **'pleomorphy** *noun* = PLEOMORPHISM L19.

pleon /ˈpliːɒn/ *noun.* M19.
[from Greek *plein* swim, sail + -ON.]
ZOOLOGY. The abdomen of a crustacean, as bearing the pleopods (swimming limbs).

pleonasm /ˈpliːənaz(ə)m/ *noun.* Also **pleonasmus** /pliːəˈnazməs/. M16.
[Late Latin *pleonasmus* from Greek *pleonasmos*, from *pleonazein* be superfluous, from *pleiōn* more.]
1 The use of more words than are necessary to convey meaning; redundancy of expression, either as a fault of style or as a figure purposely used for emphasis or clarity; an instance of this; a superfluous word or phrase. M16. ▸†**b** *GRAMMAR.* The addition of a superfluous letter or syllable to a word. *rare.* L17–M18.
2 *gen.* Superfluity, redundancy; something superfluous or redundant. E17. ▸**b** *ANATOMY & MEDICINE.* (A growth showing) excess in size or esp. number of parts. M19.

📖 **2** *New Left Review* The . . clause is mere pleonasm, a repetition.

pleonastic /pliːəˈnastɪk/ *adjective.* L18.
[from Greek *pleonastos* numerous, abundant from *pleonazein*: see prec., -IC.]
1 Characterized by or constituting pleonasm; superfluous, redundant. L18.
2 Done to excess or superfluity. L19.
■ †**pleonastical** *adjective* pleonastic: only in M17. **pleonastically** *adverb* E18.

pleonexia /pliːəˈnɛksɪə/ *noun. rare.* M19.
[Greek, from *pleonektein* be greedy, have or want more, from *pleiōn* more + *ekhein* have: see -IA[1].]
Abnormal covetousness, avarice or greed.
■ **pleonectic** *adjective* M19.

pleophony /pliːˈɒf(ə)ni/ *noun.* M20.
[from PLEO- + -PHONY, after *homophony* etc.]
LINGUISTICS. Vowel duplication; epenthesis of a vowel which harmonizes with that in the preceding syllable.

pleopod /ˈpliːəpɒd/ *noun.* M19.
[formed as PLEON + -O- + -POD.]
ZOOLOGY. Each of the paired biramous swimming limbs attached to the abdomen of a crustacean.

pleoptics /pliːˈɒptɪks/ *noun pl.* (usu. treated as *sing.*). M20.
[from PLEO- + *optics*: see OPTIC *noun.*]
OPHTHALMOLOGY. A method of treating amblyopia, strabismus, etc., by stimulating the use and sensitivity of the fovea, e.g. with bright light.
■ **pleoptic** *adjective* M20.

plereme /ˈplɪəriːm/ *noun.* M20.
[from Greek *plērēs* full + -EME.]
LINGUISTICS. In glossematics: a minimal unit of meaningful expression; a unit of expression with content (as the name of a thing, quality, act, etc.). Opp. CENEME.
■ **plere'matic** *adjective* of or pertaining to pleremes M20. **plere'matics** *noun* the branch of glossematics that deals with pleremes M20.

plerion /ˈplɛrɪən/ *noun.* L20.
[Irreg. from Greek *plērēs* full + *-ion* neut. noun suffix.]
ASTRONOMY. A supernova remnant of a relatively short-lived type with a flat radio emission spectrum originating throughout its volume rather than just from an outer shell, typified by the Crab nebula.
■ **pleri'onic** *adjective* L20.

plerocephalic /plɪərəʊsɪˈfalɪk, -kɛˈfalɪk/ *adjective.* E20.
[from Greek *plēro-*, *plērēs* full + -CEPHALIC.]
MEDICINE. Of oedema: caused by increased intracranial pressure.

plerocercoid /plɪərəʊˈsəːkɔɪd/ *noun.* E20.
[formed as prec. + Greek *kerkos* tail + -OID.]
ZOOLOGY. A larval form in some tapeworms, in which the body is solid, lacking a bladder. Also ***plerocercoid larva***.

pleroma /plɪˈrəʊmə/ *noun.* M18.
[Greek *plērōma* that which fills, from *plēroun* make full, from *plērēs* full.]
THEOLOGY. **1** In Gnosticism, the spiritual universe as the abode of God and of the totality of the divine powers and emanations. M18.
2 The totality of the Godhead which dwells in Christ; completeness, fullness, (with allus. to *Colossians* 2:9). E19.
■ **plero'matic** *adjective* pertaining to the pleroma M19.

plerome /ˈplɪərəʊm/ *noun.* L19.
[German *Plerom* from Greek *plērōma*: see prec., -OME.]
BOTANY. In the histogen theory, the innermost layer of an apical meristem, which gives rise to the central vascular tissue. Cf. DERMATOGEN, PERIBLEM.

plerophory /plɪˈrɒf(ə)ri/ *noun.* Now *rare.* E17.
[Greek *plērophoria* fullness of assurance, ult. from *plērēs* full + *phoros* bearing: see -ORY[1].]
Chiefly *THEOLOGY.* Full assurance or certainty.

plesio- /ˈpliːsɪəʊ, -z-/ *combining form.*
[from Greek *plēsios* near: see -O-.]
Chiefly *SCIENCE.* Near, close to.
■ **plesio'morphous** *adjective* (*CRYSTALLOGRAPHY*) crystallizing in closely similar but not identical forms M19.

plesiosaur /ˈpliːsɪəsɔː, ˈpliːz-/ *noun.* M19.
[mod. Latin *Plesiosaurus* genus name, formed as prec.: see -SAUR.]
Any of a group of extinct marine reptiles of Mesozoic times, having a small head (often on a long neck), a short tail, and four large paddle-like limbs.
■ **plesio'saurian** *adjective & noun* (*a*) *adjective* of, pertaining to, or characteristic of a plesiosaur; (*b*) *noun* a plesiosaur: M19. **plesio'sauroid** *adjective & noun* (designating or characteristic of) a long-necked plesiosaur M19. **plesio'saurus** *noun*, pl. **-ri** /-rʌɪ, -riː/, **-ruses**, a plesiosaur of the genus *Plesiosaurus*, with a long neck M19.

†**plesser** *noun* see PLESSOR.

plessimeter /plɛˈsɪmɪtə/ *noun. obsolete* exc. *Hist.* M19.
[French *plessimètre*, from Greek *plēssein* strike: see -IMETER.]
MEDICINE. = PLEXIMETER.
■ **plessi'metric** *adjective* L19. **plessimetry** *noun* medical percussion L19.

plessor /ˈplɛsə/ *noun.* Also (earlier) †**-er**. M19.
[Irreg. from Greek *plēssein* to strike + -OR, -ER[1].]
MEDICINE. A small hammer used in medical percussion and to test reflexes. Also called ***plexor***.

plet /plɛt/ *noun*[1] *& verb.* Chiefly *Scot. & north.* LME.
[By-form of PLAIT *noun & verb.*]
▶ **A** *noun.* A plait. LME.
▶ **B** *verb trans.* Infl. **-tt-**.
1 Plait. LME.
†**2** Fold; fold in one's arms. LME–E17.

plet /plɛt/ *noun*[2]. M19.
[Russian *plet'*.]
Hist. A three-thonged whip loaded with lead, used for flogging in Russia.

-plet /plɛt/ *suffix.* L20.
[The ending of *triplet*, *multiplet*, etc.]
Chiefly *PARTICLE PHYSICS.* Used with prefixed numeral to denote a multiplet having the specified number of members, as ***15-plet***.

plethora /ˈplɛθ(ə)rə/ *noun.* M16.
[Late Latin from Greek *plēthōrē* fullness, repletion, from *plēthein* be full.]
1 *MEDICINE & BIOLOGY.* Orig., a condition characterized by excess of blood or of a bodily humour (or of juices in a plant). Later, an excess of red cells in the blood. Now *rare* or *obsolete.* M16.
2 Overfullness, oversupply; an excess, a glut. (Foll. by *of.*) E18.

📖 **2** N. F. DIXON With a plethora of spies there are not enough secrets to go round.

†**plethoretic** *adjective. rare.* E18–L19.
[from prec. after *theoretic* etc.]
= PLETHORIC.

plethoric /ˈplɛθ(ə)rɪk, plɪˈθɒrɪk/ *adjective.* LME.
[medieval Latin *plet(h)oricus* from Greek *plethorikos*, from *plēthōrē*: see -IC.]
1 *MEDICINE.* Characterized by an excess of blood or of a bodily humour; having a full fleshy body and ruddy complexion. LME.
2 Full to excess, overloaded; swollen, inflated. M17.
■ †**plethorical** *adjective* = PLETHORIC 1: only in 17. **plethorically** *adverb* E19.

plethory /ˈplɛθ(ə)ri/ *noun.* Now *rare.* E17.
[Prob. from prec. after *allegoric*, *allegory*.]
= PLETHORA 1, 2.

plethron /ˈplɛθrən/ *noun. rare.* Pl. **-ra** /-rə/. E17.
[Greek.]
An ancient Greek measure of length, equal to approx. 100 feet (30.5 m); a square measure with sides of one plethron, equivalent to slightly less than a quarter of an acre (0.1 hectare).

plethysmograph /plɪˈθɪzməgrɑːf/ *noun.* L19.
[from Greek *plēthusmos* enlargement (ult. from *plēthus* fullness) + -GRAPH.]
PHYSIOLOGY. An instrument for recording and measuring variation in the volume of a part of the body, esp. due to changes in blood pressure.
■ **plethysmogram** *noun* the record produced by a plethysmograph L19. **plethysmo'graphic** *adjective* L19. **plethysmo'graphically** *adverb* by means of a plethysmograph L19. ˌ**plethys'mography** *noun* the use of a plethysmograph L19.

pleur- *combining form* see PLEURO-.

pleura /ˈplʊərə/ *noun*[1]. Pl. **-rae** /-riː/. LME.
[medieval Latin from Greek = side, rib.]
ANATOMY & ZOOLOGY. **1** Either of two serous membranes, right and left, which form a closed double-walled sac around each lung in a mammal, one side or layer (in full ***pulmonary pleura***, ***visceral pleura***) being attached to the lung, the other (in full ***costal pleura***, ***parietal pleura***) to the inner wall of the chest. LME.
2 A lateral part in various animal structures; the pleuron of an arthropod. E19.

pleura *noun*[2] pl. of PLEURON.

pleurae *noun* pl. of PLEURA *noun*[1].

pleural /ˈplʊər(ə)l/ *adjective*[1]. M19.
[from PLEURA *noun*[1] + -AL[1].]
ANATOMY & ZOOLOGY. Of or pertaining to a pleura or the pleurae.

pleural /ˈplʊər(ə)l/ *adjective*[2]. L19.
[from PLEURON + -AL[1].]
ZOOLOGY. Of or pertaining to a pleuron or the pleura; costal; lateral.

pleurapophysis /plʊərəˈpɒfɪsɪs/ *noun.* Pl. **-physes** /-fɪsiːz/. M19.
[from PLEUR(O- + APOPHYSIS.]
ANATOMY & ZOOLOGY. Either of a pair of transverse processes of a vertebra, in the thoracic region forming the ribs and otherwise fused to the diapophysis.

pleuric /ˈplʊərɪk/ *adjective. rare.* M19.
[from PLEURA *noun*[1] + -IC.]
ZOOLOGY. = PLEURAL *adjective*[1].

pleurisy /ˈplʊərɪsi/ *noun.* Also †**plu-**. LME.
[Old French *pleurisie* (mod. *pleurésie*) from late Latin *pleurisis* alt. of earlier Latin, Greek PLEURITIS.]
1 *MEDICINE.* Inflammation of the pleurae, with impairment of the lubricating function and pain on breathing, associated with disease of the chest or abdomen, esp. pneumonia. Formerly also, an instance of this. LME.
†**2** *fig.* Unhealthy excess. M16–E18.

Comb.: **pleurisy-root** *N. Amer.* the butterfly-weed, *Asclepias tuberosa*; its root, a reputed remedy for pleurisy.
¶ Sense 2 and forms in *plu-* arise partly from a mistaken derivation from the stem of **PLURAL** *adjective*.

pleurite /ˈplʊərʌɪt/ *noun*. **M19.**
[from Greek **PLEURA** *noun*[1] + **-ITE**[1].]
ZOOLOGY. A sclerite of a pleuron of an arthropod; a section of the lateral exoskeleton. Cf. **STERNITE, TERGITE.**

pleuritic /plʊəˈrɪtɪk/ *adjective*[1] *& noun*. **L16.**
[Old & mod. French *pleurétique* from Latin *pleuriticus* from Greek *pleuritikos*, from Greek **PLEURITIS**: see **-ITIC.**]
► **A** *adjective*. **1** Suffering from pleurisy. **L16.**
2 Of, pertaining to, or characteristic of pleurisy. **M17.**
► **B** *noun*. A person affected with pleurisy. *rare*. **M18.**
■ †**pleuritical** *adjective* = **PLEURITIC** *adjective*[1] **E17–M18.**

pleuritic /plʊəˈrɪtɪk/ *adjective*[2]. **L19.**
[from **PLEURITE** + **-IC.**]
ZOOLOGY. Of or pertaining to a pleurite or the pleurites; lateral. Cf. **PLEURAL** *adjective*[2].

pleuritis /plʊəˈrʌɪtɪs/ *noun*. **L17.**
[Latin from Greek **PLEURA** *noun*[1] + **-ITIS.**]
MEDICINE. = **PLEURISY 1.**

pleuro /ˈplʊərəʊ/ *noun*. *colloq.* Chiefly *Austral.* **M19.**
[Abbreviation.]
Pleuropneumonia.

pleuro- /ˈplʊərəʊ/ *combining form*. Before a vowel also **pleur-.**
[from Greek *pleura* side, *pleuron* rib: see **-O-.**]
Chiefly *SCIENCE & MEDICINE*. Of, pertaining to, or involving the side or pleura.
■ **pleuroˈbranchia** *noun*, pl. **-iae**, *ZOOLOGY* a gill attached directly to the thoracic wall in a crustacean **L19. pleuroˈcarpous** *adjective* (of a moss) bearing the archegonia and capsules on short side-branches (opp. **ACROCARPOUS**) **M19. pleurodont** *noun & adjective* (*ZOOLOGY*) (**a**) *noun* a lizard having teeth fixed to the side of the jawbone; (**b**) *adjective* pertaining to or having such teeth: **M19. pleuroˈdynia** *noun* (*MEDICINE*) severe pain in the muscles between the ribs or in the diaphragm, as caused by rheumatism, in Bornholm disease, etc. **E19. pleuˈrolysis** *noun* (*MEDICINE*) = **PNEUMOLYSIS M20. pleuro-peritoˈneal** *adjective* (*ANATOMY & ZOOLOGY*) of or pertaining to the pleurae and the peritoneum or the pleuro-peritoneum **L19. pleuro-periˈtoneum** *noun* (*ANATOMY*) the pleurae and the peritoneum; *esp.* (*ZOOLOGY*) the serous membrane lining the body-cavity of vertebrates other than mammals: **L19. pleuˈrotomy** *noun* (an instance of) surgical incision into the pleura **L19. pleurotyphoid** *noun* (*MEDICINE*) typhoid fever with pleurisy **E20.**

pleuron /ˈplʊərɒn/ *noun*. Pl. **-ra** /-rə/. **E18.**
[Greek = rib, side.]
ANATOMY & ZOOLOGY. The lateral part of the body wall, the side of the body; *spec.* either of the sclerotized regions forming the lateral part of each segment of the body of an arthropod (cf. **STERNUM, TERGUM**).

pleuronectid /plʊərəˈnɛktɪd/ *noun*. Also (earlier) **pleuronect** /ˈplʊərənɛkt/. **M19.**
[from mod. Latin *Pleuronectidae* (see below), from *Pleuronectes* genus name of the plaice, from Greek **PLEURA** *noun*[1] side + *nēktēs* swimmer: see **-ID**[3].]
ZOOLOGY. A flatfish of the plaice family Pleuronectidae.

pleuropneumonia /ˌplʊərəʊnjuːˈməʊnɪə/ *noun*. **E18.**
[from **PLEURO-** + **PNEUMONIA.**]
MEDICINE & VETERINARY MEDICINE. Inflammation involving the pleurae and the lung; pneumonia complicated with pleurisy; *esp.* a contagious febrile disease of horned cattle, transmitted by a mycoplasma.
■ **pleuropneumonia-like** *adjective*: ***pleuropneumonia-like organism*** = **MYCOPLASMA** (abbreviation *PPLO*) **M20.**

†**plevin** *noun*. **ME–M18.**
[Old French *plevine* pledge from medieval Latin *plevina*, from *plevire* to warrant.]
Chiefly *LAW*. Pledge, assurance, (a) warrant.

plew /pluː/ *noun*. **M19.**
[Canad. French *pêlu* = French *poilu* hairy, from *poil* hair.]
The skin of a beaver.

-plex /plɛks/ *suffix*[1].
[Latin, from *plicare* to fold. Cf. **-FOLD.**]
Forming adjectives from cardinal numerals (and adjectives meaning 'many') with the senses 'multiplied by', 'having so many parts or elements', as ***simplex, duplex, multiplex***, etc., and parallel nouns (esp. *US*) with the senses 'a building or dwelling divided into a specified number of floors, residences, etc.', as ***duplex, triplex***, etc.

-plex /plɛks/ *suffix*[2].
[from **COMPLEX** *noun*.]
Forming nouns with the sense 'an integrated industrial facility or other organization characterized by (the expanded form of) the initial element', as ***metroplex, nuplex, wasteplex***, etc.

plexal /ˈplɛks(ə)l/ *adjective*. *rare*. **L19.**
[from **PLEXUS** + **-AL**[1].]
Of or pertaining to a plexus.

plexiform /ˈplɛksɪfɔːm/ *adjective*. **E19.**
[from **PLEX(US** + **-I-** + **-FORM.**]
ANATOMY. Of the form of a plexus; forming a plexus or plexuses.
plexiform layer either of two layers of the retina separated by the inner nuclear layer, the outer one containing synapses between the rods and cones and the neurones of the nuclear layer, the inner one synapses between these neurones and ganglion cells.

Plexiglas /ˈplɛksɪɡlɑːs/ *noun*. Chiefly *N. Amer.* Also **p-, -glass. M20.**
[formed as next + **GLASS** *noun*.]
(Proprietary name for) a solid transparent plastic that is a methyl methacrylate resin (see **PERSPEX**).

> *attrib.*: *Face* Plexiglas drop earrings by Dinny Hall.

¶ Another proprietary name for this substance is **LUCITE.**

pleximeter /plɛkˈsɪmɪtə/ *noun*. Now *rare*. **M19.**
[from Greek *plēxis* percussion (from *plēssein* strike) + **-METER.**]
MEDICINE. In diagnosis by percussion, an object, esp. a small thin plate of ivory, wood, etc., placed firmly on the body and struck with a small hammer (plessor). Also called ***plessimeter***.
■ Also **plexometer** *noun* **L19.**

plexor /ˈplɛksə/ *noun*. **M19.**
[Irreg. formed as prec. + **-OR.**]
MEDICINE. = **PLESSOR.**

plexure /ˈplɛkʃə/ *noun*. *rare*. **L17.**
[from Latin *plex-* pa. ppl stem of *plectere* plait, interweave + **-URE**, after *flexure*.]
A plaiting or interweaving; something plaited or interwoven; a plexus.

plexus /ˈplɛksəs/ *noun*. Pl. **-uses. L17.**
[Latin, formed as prec.]
1 *ANATOMY & ZOOLOGY.* A structure consisting of a bundle of minute closely interwoven and intercommunicating fibres or tubes; a network of nerve fibres or blood-vessels. Usu. with specifying word, as ***brachial plexus, myenteric plexus***, etc. **L17.**
2 *gen.* Any intertwined or interwoven mass; an intricate arrangement or collection of things; a web, a network. **M18.**
1 ***CHOROID plexus. Meissner's plexus***: see **MEISSNER** *noun* 2. ***solar plexus***: see **SOLAR** *adjective*[1].

pliable /ˈplʌɪəb(ə)l/ *adjective*. **LME.**
[French, from *plier* bend: see **PLY** *verb*[1], **-ABLE.** In sense 3, aphet. from **APPLIABLE.**]
1 Easily bent or folded; flexible, supple, yielding. Formerly also, easily moulded or shaped. **LME.**
2 *fig.* Flexible in disposition or character; easily influenced; compliant, docile; adaptable. **LME.**
†**3** Applicable, pertinent. **L16–M17.**

> **1** *Independent* Thatch . . needs to be damp to be pliable. **2** P. KAVANAGH I was always very pliable I took my father's advice. A. BROOKNER Is there . . something too easy about him, pliable, compliant?

■ **pliaˈbility** *noun* **M18. pliableness** *noun* **M16. pliably** *adverb* **E17.**

pliancy /ˈplʌɪənsi/ *noun*. **L17.**
[from next: see **-ANCY.**]
The quality of being pliant; flexibility.

pliant /ˈplʌɪənt/ *adjective*. **ME.**
[Old & mod. French, pres. pple of *plier* bend: see **PLY** *verb*[1], **-ANT**[1].]
1 Bending; able to be (easily) bent or folded; lithe, flexible. Formerly also, ductile, plastic. **ME.**
2 *fig.* **a** Easily inclined to a particular course; readily influenced; yielding, compliant; accommodating. **LME.** ►**b** That lends itself to some purpose; suitable. *rare*. **E17.** ►**c** Adaptable, versatile. **M17.**

> **1** H. JAMES The pliant slimness of his figure. A. HARDING How to make little boats from pliant reeds. **2a** R. NIEBUHR They . . weakened the authority of the state and made it more pliant. P. GAY A pliant female playing a supporting role.

■ **pliantly** *adverb* **M17. pliantness** *noun* (now *rare*) **ME.**

plica /ˈplɪkə, ˈplʌɪkə/ *noun*. Pl. **-cae** /-kiː/, in sense 3 **-cas. M17.**
[mod. Latin from medieval Latin = fold, from Latin *plicare*: see **PLY** *verb*[1].]
1 *MEDICINE.* In full ***plica polonica*** /pɒˈlɒnɪkə/ [mod. Latin = of Poland]. A densely matted condition in chronically filthy hair. Now *rare* or *obsolete*. **M17.**
2 *ANATOMY & ZOOLOGY.* A fold or ridge of tissue. **E18.**
3 *MEDIEVAL MUSIC.* A notational symbol, variously interpreted but now usu. considered to represent a type of ornament; the ornament indicated. **L18.**
2 plica circularis /sɜːkjʊˈlɑːrɪs/, pl. **plicae circulares** /-ˈlɑːriːz/, any of the circular folds in the mucous membrane of the small intestine; usu. in *pl.*
■ **plical** *adjective* pertaining to or of the nature of a plica **L19.**

plicate /ˈplʌɪkət/ *adjective*. **M18.**
[from prec. + **-ATE**[2].]
Chiefly *BOTANY*. Having parallel folds or ridges; folded, pleated.
■ **plicately** *adverb* **M19.**

plicate /ˈplɪkeɪt, plʌɪˈkeɪt/ *verb trans.* **L17.**
[Latin *plicat-* pa. ppl stem of *plicare* fold: see **-ATE**[3].]
1 Fold, pleat. Usu. in *pass.* **L17.**
2 *MEDIEVAL MUSIC.* Add a plica to. **E20.**
■ **plicated** *ppl adjective* †(**a**) *rare* complicated; (**b**) folded, plicate; (**c**) *MEDIEVAL MUSIC* having a plica: **M17.**

plication /plɪˈkeɪʃ(ə)n, plʌɪ-/ *noun*. **LME.**
[Orig. from medieval Latin *plicatio(n-)*, formed as prec.; in mod. use from Latin *plicare* after *complicate, complication*: see **-ATION.**]
1 The action of folding; a folded condition. **LME.**
2 A fold. **M18.**
3 *GEOLOGY.* The bending or folding of strata; a fold in a stratum. **M19.**

plicature /ˈplɪkətʃə/ *noun*. **LME.**
[Latin *plicatura* folding, formed as **PLICATE** *verb*: see **-URE.**]
= **PLICATION.**

plié /plije/ *noun*. Pl. pronounced same. **L19.**
[French, pa. pple of *plier* bend.]
BALLET. A movement in which the knees are bent outwards in line with the out-turned feet.

plied *verb*[1], *verb*[2] *pa. t. & pple* of **PLY** *verb*[1], *verb*[2].

plier /ˈplʌɪə/ *noun*. **M16.**
[from **PLY** *verb*[1] + **-ER**[1]; in sense 2 partly from **PLY** *verb*[2].]
1 In *pl.* Pincers with gripping jaws usu. having parallel serrated surfaces, used for bending wire, manipulating small objects, etc. Also ***pair of pliers. M16.***
2 A person who plies something. **L17.**

plight /plʌɪt/ *noun*[1]. Now chiefly *arch. & poet.*
[Old English *pliht* = Old Frisian, Middle & mod. Dutch *plicht*, Old High German *pfliht* (German *Pflicht* duty), from Germanic. In sense 3 prob. from the verb, as in ***troth-plight*** s.v. **TROTH.**]
†**1** Peril, danger, risk. **OE–M17.**
†**2** Sin, offence; guilt, blame. Only in **ME.**
3 (An) undertaking of a risk or obligation; a pledge under risk of forfeiture; *spec.* (an) engagement to marry. **ME.**

> **3** G. MEREDITH An engagement, . . a mutual plight of faith.

■ **plightful** *adjective* †(**a**) perilous; sinful, guilty, blameworthy; (**b**) *rare* fraught with suffering: **ME.**

plight /plʌɪt/ *noun*[2]. **ME.**
[Anglo-Norman *plit* var. of Old French *ploit, pleit* fold, **PLAIT** *noun*. In branch I perh. infl. by prec.]
► **I 1** Condition, state. Now *esp.* an unfortunate condition, a predicament. **ME.** ►†**b** Manner, way. *rare*. **LME–L16.**
2 Bodily or physical condition; a healthy state; (good) health, now usu. of an animal. **LME.**
†**3** State of mind, mood, esp. *to do* something. **LME–E18.**
4 State or position in law; the status of an enactment, privilege, etc; a person's legal standing. Now *rare* or *obsolete*. **M16.**
5 Attire, dress. Now *rare* or *obsolete*. **L16.**

> **1** P. HEYLIN The Town remaining in as good plight . . as most Towns . . which want a navigable river. F. RAPHAEL He was sympathetic to the victim's plight. **2** H. MARTINEAU The fine plight of my cows. **5** SPENSER Sunburnt Indians . . Their tawney bodies in their proudest plight.

►†**II 6** A fold of cloth or drapery; a pleat. **LME–L17.** ►**b** A fold in a natural structure; a convolution. **M16–L17.**
7 A unit of measure for lawn or other cloth. **LME–M16.**
8 A plait of hair; an interwoven mass. **E17–E19.**

> **8** COLERIDGE Tricks her hair in lovely plight.

plight /plʌɪt/ *verb*[1] *trans.* Now chiefly *arch. & poet.*
[Old English *plihtan* formed as **PLIGHT** *noun*[1]. Cf. Old High German *pflihten* engage oneself, Middle Dutch *plichten* guarantee.]
†**1** With dat. obj.: cause to incur danger, bring danger on; compromise (life, honour, etc.). Only in **OE.**
2 Orig., put (something) in danger or risk of forfeiture; give (something) in pledge. Now chiefly, pledge (one's faith, love, etc.). **ME.**
†**3** Pledge or commit oneself to do or give (something); promise solemnly. **ME–L16.**
4 Engage or bind *oneself*; in *pass.*, be engaged or bound *to* someone. **ME.**

> **2** LD MACAULAY They came . . to plight faith to William. ***plight one's troth***: see **TROTH** *noun*. **4** E. PEACOCK His daughter was plighted to the very man he would have chosen.

†**plight** *verb*[2] *trans.* **LME.**
[By-form of **PLAIT** *verb*; rel. to **PLIGHT** *noun*[2].]
1 Fold, pleat; contract into folds or wrinkles. **LME–L17.** ►**b** Fold in one's arms, embrace. **LME–L16.**
2 Plait; tie in a knot. **L16–M17.**

plim /plɪm/ *verb*. Chiefly *dial.* Infl. **-mm-. M17.**
[Origin unkn. Cf. **PLUM** *verb*.]
1 *verb intrans.* Swell, fill *out*, grow plump. **M17.**
2 *verb trans.* Spread, distend. *rare*. **L19.**

plimsoll /ˈplɪms(ə)l/ *noun*. In sense 1 also **P-**, in sense 2 also **-sole. L19.**
[S. *Plimsoll* (1824–98), English politician and promoter of the Merchant Shipping Act of 1876. In sense 2, prob. from the resemblance of the side of the sole to a Plimsoll line; also infl. by **SOLE** *noun*[2].]

1 ***Plimsoll line, Plimsoll mark, Plimsoll's mark***, a marking on a ship's side indicating the legal limit of the ship's submersion when loaded with cargo under various sea conditions. **L19.**
2 A rubber-soled canvas leisure or sports shoe. Usu. in *pl.* **L19.**

> **1** *fig.*: A. POWELL Waves of intoxication, lapping against the Plimsoll Line of articulation.

▪ **plimsolled, -soled** *adjective* having or wearing plimsolls **M20.**

Plinian /ˈplɪnɪən/ *adjective.* **M17.**
[Latin *Plinianus*, from Gaius *Plinius* Secundus (Pliny the Elder (AD 23–79), Roman naturalist, and his nephew Pliny the Younger (AD 61/2–113)). In sense 2 after Italian *Pliniano*, with ref. to the eruption of Vesuvius in AD 79, in which Pliny the Elder died.]
1 Belonging to or named after Pliny, esp. the elder. *rare.* **M17.**
2 Designating (a stage of) a volcanic eruption in which a narrow stream of gas and magma is violently ejected from a vent to a height of several miles. **E20.**

plink /plɪŋk/ *verb, noun, interjection, & adverb.* **M20.**
[Imit.]
▶ **A** *verb intrans. & trans.* **1** *verb intrans.* Emit a short sharp metallic or ringing sound; play a musical instrument in this manner. **M20.**
2 *verb intrans. & trans.* Shoot (a gun) *at* a target, esp. casually; hit (something) with a shot from a gun. **M20.**

> **1** P. CAREY In the wet you live amongst plinking buckets. **2** *Air Gunner* Fine for . . paper targets, but not so good for plinking at . . cans.

▶ **B** *noun.* The sound or action of plinking; a sharp metallic noise. **M20.**
▶ **C** *interjection & adverb.* With a plink. **M20.**

> TOLKIEN Plink! a silver drop falls.

▪ **plinker** *noun* (*colloq.*) (*a*) an airgun, a cheap low-calibre firearm; (*b*) a person who shoots with such a gun, esp. casually: **L20.**

plinth /plɪnθ/ *noun.* **L16.**
[French *plinthe* or Latin *plinthus* from Greek *plinthos* tile, brick, stone squared for building.]
1 a ARCHITECTURE. The lower square slab or block at the base of a column or pedestal. **L16.** ▸**b** A block of stone etc. serving as a base or pedestal to a statue, vase, etc.; a supporting foundation or base, *esp.* the squared base of a piece of furniture, item of equipment, etc. **E18.** ▸**c** ARCHITECTURE. The projecting part of a wall immediately above the ground. Also (more fully ***plinth course***), a course of bricks or stones in a wall, above ground level, by which the part of the wall above is made to be set back in relation to the part below. **E19.**
2 ARCHITECTURE. †**a** The abacus of the capital of a column. **E17–E18.** ▸**b** A plain course surmounting a cornice; a flat projecting part of a wall immediately beneath the eaves. Now *rare* exc. *Scot.* **E17.**
3 A shallow wooden, plastic, etc., cabinet in which a record deck is mounted. **M20.**

> **1b** J. RABAN The bronze doctor on his plinth. *Which?* No plinth for the oven . . no shelves for the cupboards. **c** H. BRAUN Castle plinths are . . of great projection. **3** *Gramophone* The unit . . was delivered already mounted in a plinth.

Comb.: **plinth block**: sited on the floor and forming part of the base of the moulding of a door or window; ***plinth course***: see sense 1c above.

plinthite /ˈplɪnθʌɪt/ *noun.* **M19.**
[from Greek *plinthos* (see prec.) + -ITE¹.]
A brick-red kind of clay; now usu. *spec.* (SOIL SCIENCE), a reddish lateritic soil.

plio- /ˈplʌɪəʊ/ *combining form.*
[mod. Latin var. of PLEIO-, orig. in PLIOCENE.]
Having more than a certain or the usual number; PALAEONTOLOGY of, pertaining to, or including the Pliocene epoch.
▪ **Plio-ˈPleistocene** *adjective & noun* (GEOLOGY) (of, pertaining to, or designating) the Pliocene and Pleistocene epochs together or (esp.) the period of transition between them **E20.**

Pliocene /ˈplʌɪə(ʊ)siːn/ *adjective & noun.* Also †**Pleio-**. **M19.**
[from Greek *pleiōn* more + *kainos* new, recent (as containing more remains of modern species than the Miocene).]
GEOLOGY. ▶**A** *adjective.* Of, pertaining to, or designating the latest epoch of the Tertiary period or sub-era, after the Miocene and before the Pleistocene. **M19.**
▶ **B** *noun.* The Pliocene epoch; the series of rocks dating from this time. **M19.**

Pliofilm /ˈplʌɪəʊfɪlm/ *noun.* Also **p-**. **M20.**
[from *Plio-* (origin unkn.) + FILM *noun.*]
(Proprietary name for) a type of transparent waterproof plastic film used esp. for packaging or waterproofing things.

> *attrib.*: H. MCCLOY These furs were . . in dry cleaner's Pliofilm bags.

pliosaur /ˈplʌɪə(ʊ)sɔː/ *noun.* **M19.**
[mod. Latin *Pliosaurus* genus name, from PLIO- (as being more like a lizard than the ichthyosaurs): see -SAUR.]
Any of a group of extinct marine reptiles of Mesozoic times related to plesiosaurs, having a short neck and a large head and jaws.
▪ **plioˈsaurian** *adjective & noun* (*a*) *adjective* of, pertaining to, or characteristic of a pliosaur; (*b*) *noun* a pliosaur: **L19.** **pliosaurus** *noun*, pl. **-ruses**, **-ri** /-rʌɪ, -riː/, a pliosaur of the genus *Pliosaurus* **M19.**

pliotron /ˈplʌɪə(ʊ)trɒn/ *noun.* **E20.**
[from PLIO- + -TRON.]
ELECTRONICS. A high-vacuum thermionic valve with one or more grids between the electrodes.

plip-plop /ˈplɪpplɒp/ *noun, interjection, & verb.* **M20.**
[Imit.]
▶ **A** *noun & interjection.* (Repr.) a rhythmically regular sequence of light sounds. **M20.**
▶ **B** *verb intrans.* Infl. **-pp-**. Make such a sequence of sounds. **L20.**

plique à jour /plik a ʒuːr/ *noun.* **L19.**
[French, lit. 'braid that lets in the daylight'.]
A technique in enamelling in which small areas of translucent enamel are fused into the spaces of a wire framework to give an effect similar to stained glass.

plisky /ˈplɪski/ *noun & adjective. Scot. & north.* **E18.**
[Origin unkn.]
▶ **A** *noun.* **1** A mischievous trick; a frolic. **E18.** ▸**2b** An awkward plight. **E19.**
▶ **B** *adjective.* Tricky, mischievous. *rare.* **L19.**

plissé /ˈpliːseɪ, *foreign* plise, (pl. of noun same)/ *noun & adjective.* **L19.**
[French, pa. pple of *plisser* to pleat.]
▶ **A** *noun.* Orig., a piece of fabric shirred or gathered into narrow pleats; a gathering of pleats. Now usu., fabric with a wrinkled or puckered finish produced by chemical treatment. **L19.**
▶ **B** *adjective.* Formed into small pleats; treated so as to give a wrinkled or puckered effect. **L19.**

> *Times* A train of . . silver tissue, lined with plissé chiffon.

PLM *abbreviation.*
Paris–Lyons–Mediterranean (Railway).

PLO *abbreviation.*
Palestine Liberation Organization.

ploce /ˈplɒsiː/ *noun.* **L16.**
[Late Latin from Greek *plokē* plaiting, from *plekein* to plait.]
RHETORIC. The repetition of a word in an altered or more expressive sense or for the sake of emphasis.

plock /plɒk/ *noun.* **M20.**
[Imit.]
A sharp click or report, as of one hard object striking another.

plod /plɒd/ *noun*¹. **L19.**
[from PLOD *verb.*]
1 The action or an act or spell of plodding; a heavy laborious walk, a trudge. **L19.** ▸**b** The sound of a heavy dull tread; a tramp, a thud. **E20.**
2 [With allus. to Mr *Plod* the policeman in Enid Blyton's 'Noddy' stories for children.] A police officer (also ***PC Plod***); in *pl.*, the police collectively. Chiefly *joc.* or *derog.* **L20.**

plod /plɒd/ *noun*². Now *Austral. colloq.* **E20.**
[Origin uncertain: perh. rel. to PLOT *noun.*]
1 A short story or tale, orig. (*dial.*) esp. a dull one; an untrue story, an excuse. **E20.**
2 A (particular) piece of ground worked by a miner. Also, a work sheet with information relevant to this. **M20.**

plod /plɒd/ *verb.* Infl. **-dd-**. **M16.**
[Prob. symbolic.]
1 *verb intrans.* Walk heavily or without elasticity; move or progress doggedly or laboriously, trudge. Also foll. by *on*, *along*, *up*, etc. **M16.** ▸**b** *verb trans.* Trudge along or over (a road etc.); make (one's way) by plodding. **M18.**
2 *verb intrans.* Work steadily and laboriously; toil, drudge, slave. (Foll. by *at*.) **M16.**
†**3** *verb intrans.* Of a hound: remain behind in one spot giving tongue continuously. **L16–L17.**
†**4** *verb intrans.* Plot. **M17–L18.**

> **1** D. H. LAWRENCE The two women plodded on through the wet world. TOLKIEN Up slope and down dale they plodded. *transf.*: P. FARMER We plod across one desert after another in our . . Chevrolet Chevette. **b** T. GRAY The plowman homeward plods his weary way. **2** G. MEREDITH The secret of good work—to plod on and . . keep the passion fresh.

▪ **plodder** *noun* a person who plods; *esp.* a person who works slowly and laboriously, a persevering toiler, a drudge: **L16.** **ploddingly** *adverb* in a plodding manner **L16.** **ploddingness** *noun* the state or condition of being plodding **L19.**

plodge /plɒdʒ/ *verb intrans.* Chiefly *dial.* **E19.**
[Prob. rel. to PLOD *verb.*]
Wade or walk heavily in water, mud, etc.

-ploid /plɔɪd/ *suffix.*
[The ending of HAPLOID, DIPLOID.]
BIOLOGY. Forming nouns and adjectives with ref. to the number of chromosome sets in a cell or organism, as ***euploid***, ***hexaploid***, etc.; occas. with prefixed numeral, as ***16-ploid***.

ploidy /ˈplɔɪdi/ *noun.* **M20.**
[from HA)PLOIDY, POLY)PLOIDY, etc.]
BIOLOGY. The number of homologous sets of chromosomes in a cell or in each cell of an organism; degree of polyploidy.

ploiter /ˈplɔɪtə/ *verb intrans.* Chiefly *dial.* **M19.**
[Rel. to PLOUTER.]
Work ineffectively; potter; dawdle.

plombe /plɒm/ *noun.* Also **plomb**. **E20.**
[German *Plombe* plombe, filling (of tooth) from French *plomb* lead: see PLUMB *noun.*]
MEDICINE & BIOLOGY. (A mass of) soft inert supporting material or filler inserted into a cavity in the body.
▪ **plombage** /plɒmˈbɑːʒ/ *noun* the introduction of plombe, esp. into the pleural cavity **M20.**

plombière /plɒmbɪˈɛː/ *noun.* **M19.**
[French *Plombières*-les-Bains, a village in the Vosges department of eastern France.]
A kind of dessert made with ice-cream and glacé fruits.

PL/I *abbreviation.* Also **PL/1**.
COMPUTING. Programming Language One, a high-level language designed to replace both Fortran and Cobol in their respective fields.

plongeur /plɔ̃ʒœːr/ *noun.* Pl. pronounced same. **M20.**
[French, from *plonger* plunge, immerse in liquid + *-eur* -OR.]
A person employed as a menial in a restaurant or hotel, esp. to wash dishes.

plonk /plɒŋk/ *noun*¹. *colloq.* (orig. *Austral.*). **M20.**
[Prob. alt. of French *vin blanc* white wine.]
Cheap or inferior wine; an example of this. Also *joc.*, wine of any kind.

> *Sunday Telegraph* Few people swig the . . best claret as if it were common plonk. *Match Fishing* Money . . plus a bottle of plonk changed hands.

▪ **plonko** *noun* (*Austral. slang*), pl. **-os**, an excessive drinker of plonk; an alcoholic: **M20.**

plonk /plɒŋk/ *verb, noun*², *interjection, & adverb. colloq.* (orig. *dial.*). **L19.**
[Imit.: cf. PLUNK *noun, verb, adverb, & interjection.*]
▶ **A** *verb.* **1 a** *verb trans.* Hit or strike with a heavy thud. **L19.** ▸**b** *verb intrans.* Of a musical instrument etc.: emit a heavy inexpressive sound. Of a person etc.: play a musical instrument heavily and inexpressively. Freq. foll. by *away*. **E20.**
2 a *verb trans.* Set or drop (something) in position heavily or clumsily; put *down* firmly or abruptly. Also, place (a person or thing) abruptly or incongruously in a particular position or set of circumstances; seat (someone) hurriedly or unceremoniously. **M20.** ▸**b** *verb intrans. & refl.* Sit down heavily or unceremoniously. **M20.**

> **1b** D. HEFFRON By age three I was plonking away at the piano. **2a** *Woman* An officious nurse plonked down a gas and air mask on my face. TIRESIAS Large advertisements plonked incongruously down in open country. *Daily Telegraph*: *The Merry Wives of Windsor* . . is plonked . . into a Fifties semi-detached. **b** M. SPARK Walter . . plonked himself . . on the sofa.

▶ **B** *noun.* A heavy thud, as of one hard object hitting another. **E20.**

> *Oxford Magazine* The satisfying plonk of *The Observer* falling on the doormat.

▶ **C** *interjection & adverb.* With a plonk, directly, abruptly. **E20.**

> *Punch* A . . Zeppelin laid a couple of bombs plonk into the homestead.

▪ **plonkingly** *adverb* in a plonking manner **M20.**

plonker /ˈplɒŋkə/ *noun.* **M19.**
[from PLONK *verb* + -ER¹.]
1 a Something large or substantial of its kind (*dial.*). Also (*slang*), the penis. **M19.** ▸**b** An artillery shell. *Austral. slang.* **E20.**
2 A foolish or inept person. *slang.* **M20.**

plop /plɒp/ *verb, noun, adverb, & interjection.* Also redupl. **plop-plop**. **E19.**
[Imit.: cf. PLUP.]
▶ **A** *verb.* Infl. **-pp-**.
1 *verb intrans.* Fall (as) with a plop; drop flat *into* or *on*; (of a bubble etc.) rise *up* with a plop. **E19.** ▸**b** *verb trans.* Set or put (a thing or person) *down* or *into* with a plop, cause to emit a plop. **E20.**

2 *verb intrans.* Emit a sound or series of sounds suggestive of plopping. **E20.**

> **1** A. GIBBS He . . startled all the turtles, who plopped into the water. B. MALAMUD The choppy water, plopping against the boats. B. BREYTENBACH Each individual drop I could hear plopping on the rooftiles. **b** A. BERGMAN She plopped herself . . onto the couch. *Sea Angling Quarterly* Plop the fish back in the sea. **2** R. ADAMS The surface of the river was . . plopping in the rain.

▶ **B** *noun.* An abrupt hollow sound as of a smooth object dropping into water without splashing or a bubble bursting in boiling liquid; the act of falling with such a sound. **M19.**

> A. GLYN The gas fire went out with a plop. J. M. COETZEE He could hear the plop of frogs.

▶ **C** *adverb & interjection.* With a plop. **M19.**

> C. KINGSLEY A few great drops of rain fell plop into the water. L. C. DOUGLAS People sometimes come plop up against a challenge. R. INGALLS Something fell from above, just in front of me: plop!

ploration /plə'reɪʃ(ə)n/ *noun. rare.* **E19.**
[Latin *ploratio(n-)*, from *plorat-* pa. ppl stem of *plorare* weep: see -ATION.]
Weeping; an instance of this.

plore /plɔː/ *noun.* **L20.**
[Irreg. from EXPLORE.]
An exhibit in a (science) museum which visitors are encouraged to handle or otherwise explore; a hands-on exhibit.

plosh *noun*[1] var. of PLASH *noun*[1].

plosh *noun*[2] & *adverb* var. of PLASH *noun*[3] & *adverb*.

ploshchadka /plɒʃ'tʃadkə/ *noun.* Pl. **-ki** /-ki/. **E20.**
[Russian = ground, area, platform.]
ARCHAEOLOGY. A raised area or platform, *spec.* one formed of burnt clay from the debris of collapsed buildings, found in Ukrainian sites of the neolithic period.

plosion /'pləʊʒ(ə)n/ *noun.* **E20.**
[from EXPLOSION.]
PHONETICS. The sudden release of air in the pronunciation of a stop consonant.
■ **plosional** *adjective* **M20.**

plosive /'pləʊsɪv, -z-/ *noun & adjective.* **L19.**
[from EXPLOSIVE.]
PHONETICS. ▶ **A** *noun.* A stop consonant pronounced with a sudden release of air. **L19.**
▶ **B** *adjective.* Of, pertaining to, or of the nature of a plosive. **E20.**

plot /plɒt/ *noun & verb*[1]. **LOE.**
[Origin unkn.: cf. PLAT *noun*[2]. In branch II assoc. with COMPLOT *noun*.]
▶ **A** *noun.* **I 1** A small piece of ground, *esp.* one used for a special purpose identified contextually; a place where plants of a specified kind are grown. Cf. PLAT *noun*[2] 1. **LOE.** ▶†**b** The site or situation of a town, city, etc. **M16–E17.** ▶**c** A grave or area of graves, esp. as belonging to a particular family, in a burial ground. Orig. *N. Amer.* **L19.**
†**2** A small portion of a surface differing in character or aspect from the rest of the surface; a patch, a spot, a mark. **LME–E19.**
3 a A ground-plan; a map, a chart; (chiefly *US*) a graph, a diagram, esp. as representing the relative positions of a number of ships, aircraft, etc. Cf. PLAT *noun*[2] 2. **M16.** ▶**b** THEATRICAL. A scheme or plan indicating the disposition and function of lighting and stage property in a particular production. **M19.** ▶**c** The action or an act of plotting something on a graph; the result of this; (a curve on) a graph. **E20.** ▶**d** A group of enemy aircraft as represented on a radar screen. *RAF slang.* **M20.**
†**4** *fig.* A plan of the actual or proposed arrangement of something; a sketch, an outline. Cf. PLAT *noun*[2] 3. **M16–E17.**
5 A plan or scheme for the constitution or accomplishment of something; a design. Cf. PLAT *noun*[2] 3. *obsolete* exc. as passing into sense 7 below. **L16.**
6 The plan or scheme of a literary work; the interrelationship of the main events in a play, novel, film, etc. Cf. PLAT *noun*[2] 4. **M17.**

> **1** *Law Reports* A land company . . sold the . . land in building plots. B. BEHAN Dublin Corporation gave the men plots of one-eighth of an acre. P. PEARCE There was a vegetable plot and . . one flower-bed. **b** W. PATTEN The plot of this Castell standeth so naturally strong. P. HOLLAND They who founded it . . were so blind . . they could not choose it for the plot of Chalcedon. **2** E. TOPSELL The horse will be . . full of scabs and raw plots about the neck. **3a** H. WOUK He saw Captain Hoban staring at the plot, where the destroyer's pencilled course was curving in. **b** T. RATTIGAN The lighting for this scene has gone mad. This isn't our plot. **c** *Scientific American* A plot of the data on a semilog graph. **d** R. COLLIER Every radar station reported a mass plot. **5** R. CUDWORTH A design . . of the Devil . . to counter-work God . . in the plot of christianity. **6** M. WARNOCK Every story needs a central figure and a plot. P. LIVELY Operatic plots are so satisfying. Everyone getting their just desserts.

▶ **II 7** A secret plan, esp. to achieve an unlawful end; a conspiracy; (freq. with specifying word). Also *joc.*, a sly plan, an innocent scheme. **L16.**

> **7** W. ROBERTSON The author of this dangerous plot was Charles, duke of Bourbon. A. CROSS A clever plot, discrediting Janet and me. ***Gunpowder Plot, Popish Plot, Rye House Plot***, etc. ***the Bye Plot***: see BYE *adjective*. ***the Main Plot***: see MAIN *adjective*.

Comb. & phrases: **lose the plot** *colloq.* lose the ability to understand or cope with what is happening, lose touch with reality; **plot-line** the main features of the plot of a play, novel, film, etc.; a summary; **plot-ratio**: representing the density of building in a specified area of land.

▶ **B** *verb.* Infl. **-tt-**.
1 *verb trans.* **a** Make a ground-plan, map, or diagram of (an existing object); (freq. foll. by *out*) make a plan of (something to be laid out, constructed, or made); draw to scale; mark (a point or course) on a chart or diagram. Also, mark out or allocate (points) on a graph, make (a curve etc.) by marking out a number of points on a graph. **L16.** ▶**b** Make or draw (a plan, map, or diagram) by plotting. **M19.** ▶**c** THEATRICAL. Plan or devise (a stage production); arrange lighting and stage property for (a production). **M20.**
2 *verb trans.* Plan, contrive, devise, (something to be carried out or accomplished, esp. a crime or conspiracy); lay plans for. Also foll. by *to do, that.* **L16.**
3 *verb trans.* Devise or plan the plot of (a play, novel, film, etc.). **L16.**
4 *verb intrans.* Form a plan or plot, esp. for a crime or conspiracy; scheme, lay plans, contrive, conspire. **E17.**

> **1** W. C. ROBERTS-AUSTIN The results . . plotted into curves . . form permanent records. E. J. HOWARD He'd plotted . . the shortest course back home. R. V. JONES A track of similar shape to that . . we had plotted from the aerial photographs. **b** DAVID CLARK In plotting the map . . distances and elevations . . must be obtained. **2** HUGH WALPOLE He plotted to dethrone a princess. E. EDWARDS Whatsoever he had . . plotted, he had never plotted treason. **3** F. BROWN A big difference in plotting soap operas and plotting magazine stories. *absol.*: *Daily Telegraph* Mrs Robins plots better but relies a bit much on coincidence. **4** M. L. KING When evil men plot, good men must plan.

■ **plotful** *adjective* (*rare*) full of plots, scheming **M18.** **plotless** *adjective* (*a*) without a plot or story, having no plot; (*b*) ECOLOGY (of a method of sampling) not based on a defined unit of area: **E18.** **plotlessness** *noun* (*rare*) **E19.** **plottable** *adjective* able to be plotted **M20.** **plottage** *noun* (*a*) (chiefly *US*) the size or value of a specified piece of land, regarded in terms of the area accumulated from its constituent plots (freq. in ***plottage increment***); (*b*) ***a mess of plottage***, a theatrical production with a poorly constructed plot (by analogy with ***mess of pottage*** s.v. MESS *noun*): **M20.** **plottingly** *adverb* in a plotting manner **M18.** **plotwise** *adverb* as regards or in terms of the plot of a novel etc. **M20.**

plot *verb*[2] var. of PLOTE.

plotch /plɒtʃ/ *noun.* Long *obsolete* exc. *Scot.* **M16.**
[Origin unkn. Cf. BLOTCH *noun*.]
= BLOTCH *noun* 1.

plotch /plɒtʃ/ *verb trans. rare.* **E20.**
[Perh. from prec., or imit.]
Splash on to, mark.

plote /pləʊt/ *verb trans. Scot. & north.* Also **plot** /plɒt/, infl. **-tt-**. **E18.**
[Origin unkn.]
1 Scald, parboil; plunge into boiling water. **E18.**
2 Scorch, burn. **L18.**

Plotinian /plə'tɪnɪən/ *adjective.* **L18.**
[from *Plotinus* (see below) + -IAN.]
Of or pertaining to the Greek philosopher Plotinus (*c* 205–70), founder and leading exponent of Neoplatonism.
■ '**Plotinism** *noun* the system or teaching of Plotinus **E19.** '**Plotinist** *noun* a follower or adherent of Plotinus **E19.** '**Plotinize** *verb* (*a*) *verb intrans.* philosophize in accordance with the principles of Plotinism; (*b*) *verb trans.* cause to resemble Plotinism: **E19.**

Plott /plɒt/ *noun.* **M20.**
[from Jonathan Plott (fl. 1750–80) and his descendants.]
In full ***Plott hound***. (An animal of) a breed of hunting dog developed from German stock by the Plott family of N. Carolina, having a smooth dark brown coat and large drooping ears.

plotted /'plɒtɪd/ *adjective.* **L16.**
[from PLOT *noun* & *verb*[1]: see -ED[2], -ED[1].]
1 That has been plotted. **L16.**
2 Constructed or provided with a plot. Freq. with qualifying adverb. **E18.**

plotter /'plɒtə/ *noun.* **L16.**
[formed as prec. + -ER[1].]
1 A person who plots something; *spec.* a person who plans or takes part in a plot to achieve an unlawful end, a conspirator. **L16.**
2 A thing which plots something; *spec.* an instrument for automatically plotting a graph; a device capable of drawing with a pen under the control of a computer. **E20.**
3 A person who owns or leases a plot of land. **E20.**

plottie *noun* var. of PLOTTY *noun*.

plotting /'plɒtɪŋ/ *verbal noun.* **L16.**
[from PLOT *verb*[1] + -ING[1].]
The action of PLOT *verb*[1].
Attrib. & comb.: In the sense 'used in plotting or drawing to scale', as ***plotting-book***, ***plotting paper***, etc. Special combs., as **plotting board** (*a*) a form of drawing board on which the positions or courses of objects may be plotted; (*b*) an instrument for automatically plotting a graph; **plotting machine** a machine for automatically plotting a map; **plotting rod** a long rod made for moving the counters on a plotting table; **plotting table** (*a*) a large table bearing a small-scale map of a region on which the positions of enemy aircraft may be represented by movable counters etc.; (*b*) = ***plotting board*** (b) above.

plotting /'plɒtɪŋ/ *ppl adjective.* **M17.**
[formed as prec. + -ING[2].]
That plots something, scheming.
■ **plottingly** *adverb* **M18.**

plotty /'plɒti/ *noun. Scot.* Also **-ie**. **E19.**
[from PLOTE + -Y[6].]
A hot drink made of wine or spirits with hot water and spices.

plotty /'plɒti/ *adjective. colloq.* **L19.**
[from PLOT *noun* + -Y[1].]
Connected with a plot or intrigue. Also, (of a novel, play, or film) having an (excessively) elaborate or complicated plot.

plotz /plɒts/ *verb. US slang.* **M20.**
[Yiddish *platsen* from German *platzen* to burst, in sense 1 also infl. by German *Platz* place, seat.]
1 *verb intrans.* Sit down, flop; slouch, loaf *around*. **M20.** ▶**b** *verb trans.* Cause to sit down; abandon. **M20.**
2 *verb intrans.* Burst. Chiefly *fig.*, be beside oneself with frustration or annoyance, show one's anger. **M20.**
■ **plotzed** *adjective* intoxicated, drunk **M20.**

plough /plaʊ/ *noun.* Also (now *arch. & N. Amer.*) **plow**. **LOE.**
[Old Norse *plógr* = Old Frisian *plōch*, Old Saxon *plōg* (Dutch *ploeg*), Old High German *pfluoc* (German *Pflug*), from Germanic from north. Italic word, repr. by Lombardic Latin *plovus*, Rhaetian *plaumatorum*, and prob. Latin *plaustrum*, *plostrum*, *ploxenum*, *-inum*. The native Old English word was *sulh* (rel. to Latin *sulcus* furrow). In branch II from the verb.]
▶ **I 1 a** = PLOUGH-LAND 1. *obsolete* exc. *Hist.* **LOE.** ▶**b** = PLOUGH-LAND 2. **M19.**
2 a A team of horses, oxen, etc., harnessed to a plough. Chiefly *Scot.* **LOE.** ▶**b** A team of draught animals harnessed to a cart or wagon; such a team with its cart or wagon. Chiefly *dial.* **E16.**
3 An agricultural implement with a cutting blade fixed in a frame drawn by a tractor or by draught animals, used to prepare the soil for sowing or planting by cutting furrows in it and turning it up. Freq. preceded by specifying word. **ME.**
4 (Usu. **P-**.) (The name of) a distinctive group of seven bright stars in Ursa Major, two of which give a line to the polestar; also called ***Charles's Wain***, ***Dipper***, ***Big Dipper***, ***Great Dipper***. Also, Ursa Major. **ME.**
5 Any of various implements or mechanical parts resembling an agricultural plough in structure or function; *spec.* (*a*) BOOKBINDING a device for cutting or trimming the edges of a book; (*b*) a plane for cutting rabbets or grooves; (*c*) an implement for deflecting material against which it moves or which moves against it, *esp.* a snowplough; (*d*) MINING a machine with cutting blades for removing a thin strip of coal when hauled along a coal-face. **L17.**
6 YOGA. A position assumed by lying on one's back and swinging the legs over one's head until the feet approach or touch the floor. **E20.**

> **1a** D. HUME Ecclesiastical revenues which . . contained eighteen thousand four hundred ploughs of land. **b** P. WAYRE The rabbit . . its white scut bouncing across the open plough. **2b** W. BORLASE The driver of a plough . . laden with tin. **3** P. S. BUCK The deep curl of earth turning as the plough went into the soil. M. PYKE The land was tilled by means of a primitive plough. ***breast plough***, ***foot plough***, ***swing plough***, ***wheel plough***, etc. **follow the plough** be a ploughman. **put one's hand to the plough**, **set one's hand to the plough** (in allus. to *Luke* 9:62) undertake a task; enter on a course of life or conduct. **under the plough** (of land) in cultivation. **4** K. GRAHAME Dominant amidst the Population of the Sky . . hangs the great Plough. **5** SNOWPLOUGH *noun*.

▶ **II 7** The action of rejecting a candidate as not reaching the pass standard in an examination; the fact of being thus rejected; an instance of this. *colloq.* **M19.**

> **7** C. READE It is only out of Oxford a plough is thought much of.

Comb.: **plough-alms** *Hist.* a due payable to the Church in Anglo-Saxon and feudal times, consisting of one penny per annum for each plough or plough-land; **plough-beam** the central longitudinal beam or bar of timber or iron in a plough, to which the other principal parts are attached; **ploughbote** *Hist.* wood or timber which a tenant had a right to cut for making and repairing ploughs and other agricultural implements; **plough-boy** a boy who leads the animals drawing a plough; **plough-bullock** (*a*) a bullock used in ploughing; (*b*) (chiefly *Hist.*) a participant in the celebration of Plough Monday; **plough-driver** a person who drives the animals drawing a plough; **plough-foot** (*a*) see FOOT *noun* 9; †(*b*) = *plough-staff* below; **plough-gate** *Scot. & north.* (now *Hist.*) †(*a*) = PLOUGH-LAND 1; (*b*) a much smaller quantity of land; **plough-gear**, (*Scot.*) **plough-graith** *collect.* harness and equipment for a plough; **plough grinding** a method of grinding and sharpening to a bevelled edge wires used in cotton spinning; **plough-ground** *adjective* produced by plough grinding; **plough-handle** the handle, or either of two handles, of a plough; **plough-head** †(*a*) the share-beam of a plough; (*b*) the front part of a plough; **plough-iron** an iron part of a plough; *spec.* in *pl.*, the coulter and share collectively; **plough-jogger** *arch., joc. & derog.* a person who pushes a plough; a ploughman; **plough-line** (*a*) the line marking the limit of ploughed land; (*b*) cord used for the reins of a plough; in *pl.*, the reins of a plough; **Plough Monday** the first Monday after Epiphany, on which the start of the ploughing season was traditionally celebrated by a procession of disguised ploughmen and boys drawing a plough from door to door; **plough pan** a compacted layer in cultivated soil resulting from repeated ploughing; **plough-pattle**, **-pettle** *Scot. & north.* = *plough-staff* below; **plough-point** the (freq. detachable) point of a ploughshare; *US* the first (often detachable) share at the front of a plough; **plough-press** BOOKBINDING a press in which a book is held while the edges are cut; **plough-shoe** any of various appliances for covering, protecting, or supporting a ploughshare; **plough-soil** soil thrown up by ploughing; **plough-staff** a staff, ending in a small spade or shovel, for clearing the coulter and mould-board of earth, roots, weeds, etc.; **plough-stilt** (*obsolete* exc. *Scot. & dial.*) a plough-handle; **plough-stock** (chiefly *US*) the iron or metal frame of a plough; **plough-stot** (chiefly *Hist.*) = *plough-bullock* (b) above; **plough-tail** the rear or handles of a plough; ***at the plough-tail***, following the plough (*lit. & fig.*); **plough-wright** a maker of ploughs.

plough /plaʊ/ *verb.* Also (now *arch. & N. Amer.*) **plow**. LME.
[from the noun.]
1 *verb trans.* Make furrows in and turn up (the earth, a piece of land) with a plough, esp. as a preparation for sowing or planting. Also foll. by *up*. LME. ▸**b** Produce (a furrow, ridge, line) in the earth with a plough. L16. ▸**c** Turn or extract (roots, weeds, etc.) with a plough. Freq. foll. by *out, up, down*. L16.
2 *verb intrans.* Use a plough, work as a ploughman, till the ground with a plough. M16. ▸**b** Of the earth, a piece of land: be easy, hard, etc., to work with a plough. M18.
3 *verb trans.* Furrow, gash, or scratch (a surface) as with a plough; produce (a furrow, gash, or scratch) on a surface thus. Freq. foll. by *up*. L16.
4 *verb trans.* Of a ship etc.: cleave (the surface of the water) (chiefly *poet.*); cut (a course) through the water. E17. ▸**b** *verb intrans.* Of a ship etc.: cleave *through* the surface of the water, cut a course *through* the water. M19.
5 *verb trans.* Furrow (the face or brow) deeply with wrinkles; cause (deep wrinkles) to furrow the face or brow. *arch.* E18.
6 *verb trans.* Cut and remove extraneous material from (a thing) with a plough in any of various processes; *spec.* (*a*) cut or plane (a rabbet or groove); (*b*) BOOKBINDING cut or trim (the edges of a book); (*c*) MINING cut (coal) from a coal-face; clear (coal) from the coalface after cutting; (*d*) clear (a road, runway, etc.) of snow using a snowplough. E19.
7 *verb intrans.* Move, esp. clumsily and laboriously, through soft ground, snow, etc.; (esp. of a motor vehicle, train, or aeroplane) travel or be propelled clumsily and violently *into* or *through* an obstacle. M19. ▸**b** *verb intrans. & trans. fig.* Advance laboriously or doggedly *through*, labour, plod; make (one's way) thus. L19.
8 *verb trans.* Reject (a candidate) as not reaching the required standard, *spec.* the pass standard in an examination; fail to reach the required standard in (an examination etc.). *colloq.* M19.

> 🕮 **1** H. HUNTER As much land as a yoke of oxen could plough in one day. P. FITZGERALD The ground beneath the trees had been ploughed up for potatoes. **2** LEIGH HUNT Twenty-three pair of oxen were ploughing together. A. S. NEILL These boys are going out to the fields to plough. **3** SIR W. SCOTT The course which the river had ploughed for itself down the valley. **4** W. COWPER He and his eight hundred Shall plough the wave no more. W. BLACK The steamer . . ploughed her way across the . . rushing waters of the Minch. **5** BYRON On thy sweet brow is sorrow plough'd by shame. J. G. HOLLAND Pride . . ploughed no furrows across her brow. **6** S. PARETSKY Drifts lining the road. Halstead had not been plowed. **7** G. MANVILLE FENN Deane came ploughing through the snow. *Daily Telegraph* A . . train was derailed . . when it ploughed into a herd of cattle. **b** R. CHURCH I . . ploughed my way through the volumes . . of magazines. **8** V. WOOLF Like people who have been ploughed in some examination. P. LARKIN Not many people plough Greats . . and become a professor of Latin.

Phrases, & with adverbs in specialized senses: **plough a lonely furrow** carry on without help or companionship. **plough back** turn (grass etc.) with a plough into the soil to enrich it; *fig.* invest (income or profit) in the enterprise producing it. **plough in** embed or bury (manure, vegetation, etc.) in the soil by ploughing. **plough the sand(s)** labour uselessly. **plough under** bury in the soil by ploughing.

Comb.: **plough-back** ECONOMICS investment of income or profit in the enterprise producing it; the capital so invested; **plough-in** NAUTICAL the uncontrolled downward pitching of a hovercraft caused by part of the leading edge of the skirt touching the water when the craft is moving at speed; an instance of this; **ploughing engine** a steam traction-engine used for ploughing, *esp.* either of a pair that stand at opposite sides of a field and pull the plough from side to side by cable; **ploughing-match** a competitive exhibition of ploughing.

■ **ploughable** *adjective* able to be ploughed; arable: L16. **ploughed** *adjective* (*a*) *gen.* that has been ploughed; (*b*) (*slang*, chiefly *US*) drunk: M16. **plougher** *noun* LME.

plough-land /ˈplaʊland/ *noun.* Also (now *arch. & N. Amer.*) **plow-**. ME.
[from PLOUGH *noun* + LAND *noun*[1].]
1 *Hist.* A measure of land used in the northern and eastern counties of England after the Norman Conquest, based on the area able to be tilled by one plough-team of eight oxen in the year. Cf. HIDE *noun*[2]. ME.
2 (A piece of) land under cultivation with the plough; arable land. M16.

ploughman /ˈplaʊmən/ *noun.* Also (now *arch. & N. Amer.*) **plow-**. Pl. **-men**. ME.
[formed as prec. + MAN *noun*.]
1 A man who uses a plough; *gen.* a farm labourer. ME.
2 ***ploughman's lunch***, (*ellipt.*) ***ploughman's***, a cold meal of bread and cheese or paté and usu. pickle and salad, freq. served in a public house at lunchtime. L20.
1 ploughman's spikenard a calcicolous plant, *Inula conyzae*, of the composite family, with yellow rayless heads and leaves having a spicy fragrance.
■ **ploughmanship** *noun* the work of a ploughman; skill in ploughing: M17.

ploughshare /ˈplaʊʃɛː/ *noun.* Also (now *arch. & N. Amer.*) **plow-**. LME.
[formed as prec. + SHARE *noun*[1].]
The large pointed blade of a plough, which, following the coulter, cuts a slice of earth and passes it on to the mould-board.

> 🕮 AV *Micah* 4:3 They shall beate their swords into plowshares, and their spears into pruning hookes.

Comb.: **ploughshare bone** ANATOMY = VOMER.

plounce /plaʊns/ *verb trans. & intrans. obsolete* exc. *dial.* M17.
[Perh. from Old French *plonce* 3rd person sing. pres. indic. of *ploncier* by-form of *plonger* PLUNGE *verb*, or perh. of imit. origin, as *bounce, pounce* (cf. FLOUNCE *verb*[1]).]
Plunge in water or liquid mud; duck, souse; flounder.

plout /plaʊt/ *verb & noun. Scot. & north.* E18.
[Perh. imit. Cf. PLOUTER.]
▸ **A** *verb intrans.* Plunge or splash in water or other liquid; fall with a splash, fall heavily and abruptly. E18.
▸ **B** *noun.* A heavy fall of rain. E19.
¶ Earliest in *comb.* Not recorded in isolation until E19.

plouter /ˈplaʊtə/ *verb & noun.* Chiefly *Scot.* E19.
[App. frequentative of prec. Cf. PLOUTER.]
▸ **A** *verb intrans.* Flounder or splash about in water or mud; dabble or work in anything wet or dirty. Also, work ineffectually, potter. E19.
▸ **B** *noun.* The action or an act of ploutering; floundering in water; (the sound of) splashing. E19.

plover /ˈplʌvə/ *noun.* ME.
[Anglo-Norman = Old French *plovier, plouvier* (mod. *pluvier* alt. after *pluie* rain) from Proto-Romance from Latin *pluvia* rain: see -ER[2].]
Any of various small to medium-sized short-billed gregarious birds of the cosmopolitan family Charadriidae, esp. of the genus *Charadrius*, typically feeding beside water; also, any of several similar shorebirds. Freq. with specifying word.
crab plover, Egyptian plover, golden plover, green plover, Kentish plover, mountain plover, ringed plover, snowy plover, etc.
■ **plovery** *adjective* (*a*) having many or frequented by plovers; (*b*) of, characteristic of, or reminiscent of a plover: L19.

plow *noun, verb*, **plow-land** *noun*, etc., see PLOUGH *noun, verb*, PLOUGH-LAND, etc.

ploy /plɔɪ/ *noun.* Orig. *Scot. & north.* L17.
[Origin unkn.]
1 An activity in which one engages; a personal enterprise or undertaking, esp. for amusement; a game, a pastime, an escapade; a trick. L17.
2 A stratagem suggested by particular circumstances and employed to gain a calculated advantage; a cunning device or manoeuvre. M20.

> 🕮 **1** *Blackwood's Magazine* They gathered . . to such ploys as the sheep-shearing or the sheep-washing. JULIETTE HUXLEY The . . cross-stitch I was set to do before I could indulge my own ploys. **2** G. BOYCOTT Gooch . . fell for an old ploy from Roberts. B. CASTLE CPSA has called off the overtime ban. So my ploy has worked.

PLP *abbreviation.*
Parliamentary Labour Party.

PLR *abbreviation.*
Public Lending Right.

pluck /plʌk/ *noun.* ME.
[from the verb.]
▸ **I 1** An act of plucking; a sudden sharp pull, a tug, a twitch, a snatch. ME. ▸†**b** *fig.* A turn; a bout; an attempt. E16–M18. ▸**c** NAUTICAL. A pull, a tow. E20.
2 An act of rejecting a candidate as not reaching the pass standard in an examination; the fact of failing to reach the pass standard in an examination. *arch. colloq.* M19.

> 🕮 **1** F. BURNEY Little dog gave it a pluck; knot slipt. T. WOOLNER Her breath caught with short plucks. **b** BUNYAN They . . have a mind to have a pluck with Gyant Dispair. **c** N. SHUTE I'll get my launch to give you a pluck in later. **2** H. M. SMYTHIES Visions of a pluck danced before the weary eyes of tutor and pupil.

▸ **II 3** The heart, liver, and lungs (and other viscera) of an animal as used for food. E17. ▸**b** *transf.* The entrails of a person. E18.
4 The heart as the seat of courage; courage, boldness, spirit. L18. ▸**b** Boldness or clarity in a photographic print or negative. *colloq.* L19. ▸**c** Wine. *US Black slang.* M20.

> 🕮 **3** J. T. STORY That was pig's pluck—you know, the liver and lights. **b** M. KINGSLEY Unpleasant-looking objects stuck on sticks. They were . . in fact the plucks of witch-doctors. **4** E. NESBIT You've got kids worth having! I wish my Denny had their pluck. *Woman's Own* The little lad showed a lot of pluck . . going to his mother's aid.

▸ **III 5** Something that is plucked. Long *rare* or *obsolete* in *gen.* sense. M17. ▸**b** A fish, esp. a herring, forming part of a catch, damaged during removal from the net. M18.
6 A two-pronged fork with the teeth at right angles to the shaft. Chiefly *Scot.* E19.
Comb.: **pluck side** GEOLOGY = *lee side* (b) s.v. LEE *noun*[1] *& adjective*.
■ **pluckless** *adjective* without pluck; devoid of courage or spirit: E19.

pluck /plʌk/ *verb.*
[Late Old English *ploccian, pluccian* corresp. to Middle Low German *plucken*, Middle Dutch *plocken* (Flemish *plokken*), Old Norse *plokka, plukka*, from Germanic, prob. from Proto-Romance base of Old French (*es*)*peluchier* (mod. *éplucher*) pluck.]
1 *verb trans.* Pull off, pick, (a flower, hair, feather, etc.) from where it grows. LOE. ▸**b** Foll. by *up*: pull (something) out of the place in which it is planted or set; uproot, eradicate; raze, demolish. Now *arch. rare.* L15. ▸**c** GEOLOGY. Chiefly of glacier ice: break loose (pieces of rock) by mechanical force on projections and cavities in a rock; erode (rock) by this process. (Foll. by *out, away*, etc.) L19.
2 Foll. by *up*: ▸**a** *verb trans.* Summon (one's courage, strength, etc.); raise (one's spirits). ME. ▸**b** *verb intrans.* Recover one's strength; summon one's courage, raise one's spirits. *arch.* M19.
3 a *verb trans.* Pull at, esp. abruptly or with a jerk; twitch; sound (the string of a musical instrument) by doing this, twang, play (a musical instrument) in this way. ME. ▸**b** *verb intrans.* Pull *at*, esp. abruptly or with a jerk, twitch something. Formerly also, make a sudden movement in order to grasp something (*lit. & fig.*). LME.
4 a *verb trans.* Pull, drag, snatch, *away, off, out*, etc. *arch.* LME. ▸**b** *verb intrans.* Drag; snatch or take by force, steal. Also, draw a card from a pack. Long *rare* or *obsolete.* LME. ▸**c** *verb trans.* Pull or tear apart, in pieces, etc. Freq. with adverbial compl. Now *rare* or *obsolete.* E16. ▸**d** *verb trans.* Foll. by *down*: demolish (a building). *arch.* M16.
5 *verb trans. fig.* ▸**a** Bring (a person or thing) into or out of a specified state or condition; bring (disaster etc.) *on* a person; now *esp.* rescue (a person) *from* danger etc. Now chiefly *arch.* LME. ▸†**b** Bring down, bring low; humble, humiliate. Foll. by *down.* M16–L17.
6 *verb trans.* **a** Pull off the feathers, hair, etc. from; *esp.* strip (a bird) of feathers. LME. ▸**b** Shape or thin (the eyebrows) by removing hairs. LME.
7 *verb trans. fig.* Plunder; swindle. *arch.* LME.
8 *verb trans.* Reject (a candidate) as not reaching the pass standard in an examination. Usu. in *pass. arch. colloq.* E18.

> 🕮 **1** J. M. BARRIE Tweeny is . . very busily plucking the feathers off a bird. A. UTTLEY Red roses . . she had hastily plucked from the tree. **b** *fig.*: E. B. BROWNING I plucked up her social fictions. **2a** R. B. SHERIDAN I'll pluck up resolution. L. GARFIELD The gentleman had . . plucked up his courage to ask for the mistress's hand. **b** G. B. SHAW He eats another date, and plucks up a little. **3a** GOLDSMITH Children . . pluck'd his gown. M. SPARK A girl was plucking the strings of a guitar. **b** TENNYSON The children pluck'd at him to go. L. GORDON Literally plucking at his sleeve while he talked. **4a** H. FAST Simmons grabbed my arm . . and fairly plucked me out of there. JOAN SMITH She plucked it from the letter-box. **c** J. RAY Take a Rook and plucking it limbe from limbe, cast the . . limbes about your field. **d** R. SIMPSON He ordered the church . . to be plucked down. **5a** DICKENS The grim life out of which she had plucked her brother. *Daily Mirror* Owner John Reed, plucked to safety with his fire crew. **6a** R. C. HUTCHINSON She was plucking a cockerel she had killed. **b** S. GIBBONS You shall not find me plucking my

eyebrows, nor dieting. **7** G. W. LE FEVRE To allow a fair profit to the proprietor without plucking the traveller. **8** G. A. SALA If you had to pass an examination for the post . . you would in all probability be plucked.

*Phrases: **a crow to pluck**:* see CROW noun[1] 1. **pluck a rose** *arch. slang* (of a woman) urinate, defecate.

■ **plucker** *noun* (*a*) *gen.* a person or thing which plucks; (*b*) a machine for disentangling and straightening long wool to make it ready for combing: LME. **plucking** *noun* (*a*) the action of the verb; (*b*) something that is plucked: LME.

plucked /plʌkt/ *adjective*[1]. LME.
[from PLUCK *verb* + -ED[1].]
That has been plucked; *spec.* (*a*) (of a dressed fur) having had some of the longer guard hairs removed by plucking; (*b*) (of the eyebrows) shaped or thinned by plucking; (*c*) (of a stringed instrument) intended to be played by plucking; (*d*) GEOLOGY (of rock) eroded or broken off by plucking.
plucked wool wool from a dead sheep.

plucked /plʌkt/ *adjective*[2]. *arch. colloq.* M19.
[from PLUCK *noun* + -ED[2].]
Having pluck or courage, esp. of a specified kind.

plucky /ˈplʌki/ *adjective.* M19.
[from PLUCK *noun* + -Y[1].]
1 Characterized by pluck; showing determination to fight or struggle; bold, courageous, spirited. M19.
2 Of a photographic print or negative: bold, clear. *colloq.* L19.

1 E. SHOWALTER It was considered plucky and spirited . . to kick a football through No Man's Land.

■ **pluckily** *adverb* M19. **pluckiness** *noun* M19.

plud /plʌd/ *noun.* Long *obsolete* exc. *dial.* ME.
[Origin uncertain: cf. Irish, Gaelic *plod* a pool, standing water; also PUDDLE *noun*.]
A pool, a puddle.

pluff /plʌf/ *noun, adverb, & interjection. Scot.* E16.
[Imit.]
► **A** *noun.* †**1** A kind of handgun. Only in E16.
2 A strong puff or explosive emission of air, gas, smoke, or dust; *colloq.* a shot of a musket or fowling-piece. M17.
3 A powder-puff. *obsolete* exc. *dial.* E19.
► **B** *adverb & interjection.* Repr. the sound of a strong puff or explosive emission of air etc.; with a pluff. *colloq.* M19.
■ **pluffy** *adjective* (*a*) having a puffed-up appearance; puffy, fleshy; (*b*) fluffy, downy: E19.

plug /plʌg/ *noun.* E17.
[Middle Low German, Middle Dutch *plugge* (Dutch *plug*), with by-forms Middle Low German *plügge* (Low German *plüg*), Middle & mod. Low German *plock*, *pluck*, Middle High German *pfloc*, *pflocke* (German *Pflock*): ult. origin unkn.]
1 A piece of solid material fitting tightly into a hole or aperture, used to fill a gap or cavity, or act as a wedge; *transf.* a natural accretion acting in the same way. Also, any of various devices resembling this in form or function, *esp.* one for temporarily stopping the waste pipe leading out of a sink, hand-basin, or bath. E17. ▸**b** The release-mechanism of a water-closet flushing-apparatus. Now *obsolete* exc. *Hist.* and in ***pull the plug*** below. M19. ▸**c** A device, usu. consisting of metal pins in an insulated casing, for inserting into a socket to make an electrical connection, esp. between an appliance and the mains. Also (more fully ***wall plug***), a fixed socket for receiving such a plug. L19. ▸**d** GEOLOGY. A cylindrical mass of solidified lava filling the neck of a volcano. Also, a mass of rock, esp. salt, which has been forced upwards by tectonic pressures, lifting overlying strata into a dome. L19. ▸**e** = ***spark-plug*** s.v. SPARK *noun*[1]. L19. ▸**f** HORTICULTURE. A small piece of turf or pre-planted soil used esp. for filling or seeding a lawn. Orig. & chiefly *US.* M20. ▸**g** MEDICINE. A small area of scalp with strong hair-growth grafted on to a balding area in hair transplantation. L20.
2 A fire hydrant. Also (chiefly *US*), ***fire-plug***. E18.
3 A cake or stick of tobacco (more fully ***plug tobacco***); a piece of this, esp. for chewing. E18.
4 A blow of the fist; a punch, a knock. *arch. slang.* L18.
5 a More fully ***plug horse***. A horse. Freq. with specifying word. *US, Austral., & NZ slang.* M19. ▸**b** An incompetent or undistinguished person. Also, a man, a fellow. *slang.* M19. ▸**c** A book which sells badly, a remainder. *colloq.* L19.
6 More fully ***plug-hat***. A tall silk hat (*US*). Also *Austral.*, a bowler hat. *slang.* M19.
7 A piece of (often free) publicity for an idea, a product, an entertainment, etc. *colloq.* (orig. *US*). E20.
8 ANGLING. A lure with one or more hooks attached. M20.

1 G. BUDD A string of small abscesses . . separated . . by a plug of lymph. A. J. CRONIN The . . oil bottle, corked with a plug of newspaper. **b** C. MACKENZIE The plug in the water-closet seldom worked. **c** H. PINTER There used to be a wall plug for this electrolux. **d** T. KENEALLY He found shelter under a granite plug close to a small stream. *Holiday Which?* The Cathedral of Le Puy is a striking affair, high on a volcanic plug. **e** J. BUCHAN They had flown . . to Egypt without cleaning their plugs! **3** W. STYRON He . . drew out a fresh plug of dark brown tobacco. J. A. HAWGOOD Tobacco fetches ten and fifteen shillings a plug. **5a** M. TWAIN The Kanaka, without spur or whip, sailed by us on the old plug. O. HENRY The grey plugs dashed out . . whickering for oats. **c** *Publishers Weekly* The so-called plugs are weeded out . . making room for new titles. **7** B. T. BRADFORD I'll give the charity a nice fat plug right up front in the story. *New Statesman* BBC 2's . . unadulterated 30 minute plug for George Davies and his . . clothing empire.

*Phrases: **navy plug**:* see NAVY 4b. **pull the plug** (*a*) flush a lavatory; (*b*) (chiefly *fig.*) disconnect suddenly from a source of supply, (foll. by *on*) bring to a sudden conclusion.

Comb.: **plug-bayonet** *Hist.* an early form of bayonet, which was fixed in the muzzle of a gun; **plugboard** a board containing several sockets into which plugs may be inserted to interconnect electric circuits, telephone lines, computer components, etc., by means of short lengths of wire; **plug-cock** a tap with a perforated plug allowing the passage of liquid when the tap is turned on; **plug-compatible** *adjective & noun* (*a*) *adjective* designating or pertaining to computing equipment compatible with a given device or system to the extent that it can be plugged in and operated successfully; (*b*) *noun* a plug-compatible device; **plug-drawer** *Hist.* a person taking part in the plug riots; **plug flow** GEOLOGY & PHYSICS flow of a body of ice or viscous fluid *en bloc*, with no shearing between adjacent layers; idealized flow without mixing of particles of fluid; **plug fuse** ELECTRICITY a fuse that is screwed into a socket; **plug gauge** a gauge in the form of a plug, used for measuring the diameter of a hole; ***plug-hat***: see sense 6 above; **plug-hole** an aperture for a plug, esp. at the top of the waste pipe leading out of a sink, hand-basin, or bath; ***go down the plug-hole*** (*fig.*), be completely lost or wasted; ***plug horse***: see sense 5 above; **plug nozzle** in a rocket or jet engine, a nozzle containing a central plug that widens towards the exit and then narrows, so that gas is expelled in a converging annular stream; **plug riots** *Hist.* a series of riots in 1842, when cotton-mills in Lancashire were stopped from working by the removal of a few bolts or plugs in the boilers to prevent steam from being raised; **plug-switch** ELECTRICITY a switch in which a circuit is completed by inserting a metal plug; **plug-tap** a cylindrical tap for cutting the threads of female screws or of screw-plates; ***plug tobacco*** = sense 3 above.

plug /plʌg/ *verb.* Infl. **-gg-**. M17.
[from the noun.]
1 a *verb trans.* Stop or fill (a hole or aperture) with or (as) with a plug. Also foll. by *up*. M17. ▸**b** *verb trans.* Insert as a plug; drive (something) in. Chiefly *fig.* M19. ▸**c** *verb trans. & intrans.* Cut a cylindrical core (from). *US.* L19. ▸**d** *verb trans. & intrans.* Esp. of a man: copulate (with). *slang.* E20. ▸**e** *verb trans.* Connect (an appliance or apparatus) electrically by inserting a plug *in* or *into* a socket; insert (a plug etc.) *into* a socket. E20. ▸**f** *verb intrans.* Be (able to be) plugged *in* or *into*. M20.
2 *verb intrans.* Work steadily away (*at*); persevere doggedly; plod. Freq. with adverbial compl. *colloq.* M19.
3 *verb trans.* Put a bullet into, shoot. *slang.* L19.
4 *verb trans.* Strike (a person) with the fist or a missile. *slang.* L19.
5 *verb intrans.* Stick or jam; become obstructed; (of a golf ball) become stuck in a hazard during play. E20. ▸**b** *verb trans.* Cause a golf ball to become stuck in a hazard during play. Usu. in *pass.* M20.
6 a *verb trans.* Seek to popularize (an idea, product, etc.) by repeated presentation or recommendation; give (esp. free) publicity to, draw attention to. *colloq.* (orig. *US*). E20. ▸**b** *verb intrans.* Foll. by *for*: act in support of or make favourable statements about (a person or thing). *US colloq.* E20.

1a J. KOSINSKI The people knew their weather and . . plugged any holes in their houses. *Daily Mirror* The Post Office . . had plugged the loophole in the franking machine system. **b** DYLAN THOMAS Its up to me & him to plug in lots more expenses. **c** *Chicago Tribune* The . . best way to tell quality is to 'plug' the melon. **e** *Scribner's Magazine* He wandered in to his radio . . and plugged in the ear phones. *transf.*: *Scientific American* Your car will actually be plugged into a computer. **f** *Physics Bulletin* This assembly plugs into a choice of sockets. **2** P. G. WODEHOUSE I am plugging along with *Hot Water* and have done 60,000 words. *Philadelphia Inquirer* Ronnie's not a quitter. He really plugs. **3** G. GREENE Don't say a word or I'll plug you. **4** P. G. WODEHOUSE Sidcup got a black eye. Somebody plugged him with a potato. **5** M. GOWING The membranes must not 'plug', that is, get blocked. **6a** *Daily Express* I . . thought it would encourage them to plug my songs. CLIVE JAMES She found the concentration of rehearsal More challenging by far than plugging *Persil.* **b** D. RUNYON Miss Missouri Martin keeps plugging for Dave the Dude.

With adverbs in specialized senses: **plug back** = ***plug off*** below. **plug in** connect electrically by inserting a plug in a socket. **plug off** seal off (part of an oil well, a water-bearing rock formation) by inserting a plug.

Comb.: **plug-and-play** *adjective* (of computer hardware and software) capable of being installed or connected to other equipment with minimal adjustment or reconfiguration having to be performed by the user; **plug-in** *adjective & noun* (*a*) *adjective* able to be connected (esp. electrically) by means of a plug; (*b*) *noun* a plug-in device or unit.

■ **pluggable** *adjective* able to be plugged, suitable for plugging M20. **plugging** *noun* (*a*) the action of the verb; (*b*) plugs collectively: E18.

plugged /plʌgd/ *adjective.* L19.
[from PLUG *noun, verb*: see -ED[2], -ED[1].]
1 *gen.* That has been plugged, that has a plug. L19.
2 Of a coin: having a portion removed and the space filled with base material. Freq. in ***plugged nickel*** (esp. ***not worth a plugged nickel***). *US.* L19.
Comb.: **plugged-in** *adjective* (*a*) connected by means of a plug; (*b*) *colloq.* aware of what is happening, in fashion, etc.

plugger /ˈplʌgə/ *noun.* M19.
[from PLUG *noun, verb*: see -ER[1].]
1 A person or thing which plugs something. M19.
2 ANGLING. A person who fishes with a plug. M20.

plugola /plʌˈgəʊlə/ *noun. colloq.* (orig. *US*). M20.
[from PLUG *noun* + -OLA, prob. after PAYOLA.]
Incidental or surreptitious promotion of a person or product, esp. on radio or television; a bribe for this.

plug-ugly /plʌgˈʌgli/ *noun & adjective. slang* (orig. & chiefly *US*). M19.
[from unkn. 1st elem. + UGLY.]
► **A** *noun.* A thug, a ruffian. M19.

Illustrated Weekly of India He was a bull-necked . . pig-eyed, stocky officer, the very picture of the plug-ugly.

► **B** *attrib.* or as *adjective.* Of, pertaining to, or characteristic of a plug-ugly; thuggish; villainous-looking. M19.

S. BELLOW That sooty, plug-ugly town.

plum /plʌm/ *noun & adjective*[1].
[Old English *plūme* corresp. to Middle Low German *plūme*, Middle High German *pflūme* (German *Pflaume*; in Old High German *pflūmo* plum tree), Old Norse *plóma* (perh. from Old English), with by-forms Middle & mod. Low German, Middle Dutch *prūme* (Dutch *pruim*), Old High German *pfrūma*, from medieval Latin *pruna*: see PRUNE *noun*.]
► **A** *noun.* **1** The edible roundish fleshy fruit of the tree *Prunus domestica* (see sense 2 below), usu. purple, red, or yellow when ripe, with a sweet pulp and a flattish pointed stone. OE.
2 The tree bearing this fruit, *Prunus domestica*, of the rose family, allied to the blackthorn. Also, the wood of this tree. OE.
3 Any of various trees allied to the plum or resembling it, esp. in their fruit; the fruit of such a tree. E17.
4 a A dried grape or raisin as used in puddings, cakes, etc. Now *rare* exc. in certain combs. below. M17. ▸**b** = ***sugar-plum*** s.v. SUGAR *noun & adjective. rare.* L17. ▸**c** A stone or mass of rock embedded in a matrix, as in a conglomerate, concrete, etc. *rare.* E19. ▸**d** *fig.* A desirable thing, a coveted prize; one of the best things in a book, piece of music, etc.; the pick of a collection of things, *esp.* a choice job or appointment. E19.
5 a The sum of £100,000. *slang.* Now *rare* or *obsolete.* L17. ▸†**b** A person who has £100,000. *slang.* Only in 18.
6 A deep reddish-purple colour. L19.

3 ***beach plum***, ***cherry-plum***, ***Chickasaw plum***, ***myrobalan plum***, etc. **b** ***date plum***, ***hog plum***, ***Java plum***, ***Kaffir plum***, ***marmalade plum***, ***sebesten plum***, etc. **4d** *Academy* A reviewer who picks all the 'plums' out of a book.

Comb.: †**plum-broth** a thick soup of beef, prunes, raisins, currants, white bread, spices, wine, sugar, and other ingredients, formerly traditionally served at Christmas; **plum cake** a cake containing raisins, currants, and often orange peel and other preserved fruits; **plum-colour** = sense A.6 above; **plum-coloured** *adjective* = sense B.1 below; **plum-duff** a rich boiled suet pudding with raisins, currants, spices, and other ingredients; **plum-fir** a coniferous tree of Chile, *Podocarpus andinus*, so called from the soft flesh surrounding the seed; **plum-in-the-mouth** *adjective* (*colloq.*) = PLUMMY *adjective* 2b; **plum-pie** †(*a*) a pie containing raisins and currants; *esp.* a mince pie; (*b*) a pie containing plums or prunes; **plum-pockets** a fungal disease of plums in which the fruit grows hollow, without a stone; **plum-porridge** (*obsolete* exc. *Hist.*) porridge made with prunes, raisins, currants, etc., formerly traditionally served at Christmas; †**plum-pottage** a thick pottage made with prunes, raisins, currants, broth, bread, etc.; = ***plum-broth*** above; **plum pox** an aphid-borne virus disease of plum trees characterized by yellow blotches on the leaves and pockets of dead tissue in the fruit; also called ***sharka***; **plum pudding** (*a*) a suet pudding with raisins; *spec.* a rich boiled pudding made with flour, breadcrumbs, raisins, currants, spices, etc., sometimes flavoured with brandy or other spirit and traditionally served at Christmas; ***plum-pudding dog***, = DALMATIAN *noun* 2; ***plum-pudding mahogany***, mahogany with a mottled finish; ***plum-pudding stone***, = ***pudding-stone*** s.v. PUDDING *noun*; ***plum-pudding voyage*** (*arch. colloq.*), a short voyage for which a supply of fresh provisions is carried; (*b*) a pudding of fresh plums in a crust; (*c*) *colloq.* part of the muscular flesh of a whale; (*d*) *Military slang* a type of trench mortar bomb; **plum-puddinger** *arch. colloq.* a whaling ship employed in short voyages (cf. ***plum-pudding voyage*** above); a member of the crew of such a ship; **plum tomato** a plum-shaped tomato; **plum tree** = sense A.2 above; ***shake the plum tree*** (*US*), obtain the rewards of political office.
► **B** *attrib.* or as *adjective.* **1** Of a deep reddish-purple colour. E20.
2 Choice, valuable, coveted. M20.

1 V. SACKVILLE-WEST Buttoned into her plum velvet bodice. **2** P. MONETTE Lindsay, who'd just landed a plum job at Paramount.

■ **plumlike** *adjective* (esp. of a fruit) resembling a plum M19.

plum /plʌm/ *adjective*². Now *dial.* L16.
[App. from PLUM *verb*.]
1 = PLUMP *adjective*¹ 3. L16.
2 Soft, light, and springy in texture and consistency. M19.

plum /plʌm/ *verb*. *obsolete* exc. *dial.* Infl. **-mm-**. LME.
[Perh. rel. to PLIM *verb*, PLUMP *verb*².]
1 *verb intrans.* Become plump; become soft, light, and springy in texture and consistency. LME.
2 *verb trans.* **a** Make plump; cause to become soft, light, and springy in texture and consistency. L16. ▸**b** Fill (a person) *up* with false information. E20.

plumach /ˈpluːmaʃ/ *noun*. *obsolete* exc. *Hist.* Also **-sh**. L15.
[French *plumache* (now only dial.) = Italian *piumaccio* a plume or bunch of feathers, from Latin *pluma* feather + suffix repr. *-aceus* -ACEOUS.]
A plume.

plumage /ˈpluːmɪdʒ/ *noun*. LME.
[Old & mod. French, formed as PLUME *noun* + -AGE.]
1 Feathers collectively; the natural covering of a bird. LME. ▸†**b** FALCONRY. Feathers fed to a hawk to be disgorged as a cast. L15–M17.
2 A bunch or tuft of feathers used as an ornament; a plume. Now *rare*. M16.

🕮 **1** *Bird Watching* A noticeably smaller bird with very dark body plumage. *fig.*: A. B. GIAMATTI Teenage boys, in the plumage of scarlet windbreakers. ***borrowed plumage***: see BORROW *verb*¹. **2** CARLYLE Nothing of the soldier but the epaulettes and plumages.

■ **plumaged** *adjective* provided with plumage, feathered, having plumage E19.

plumash *noun* var. of PLUMACH.

plumassier /pluːməˈsɪə/ *noun*. L16.
[French, from †*plumasse* a large plume, formed as PLUME *noun* with augm. suffix *-asse* from Latin *-acea* adjective suffix: see -IER.]
A person who works or trades in ornamental feathers.

plumate /ˈpluːmeɪt/ *adjective*. *rare*. E19.
[from Latin *pluma* PLUME *noun* + -ATE².]
BOTANY & ZOOLOGY. = PLUMOSE.

plumb /plʌm/ *noun*. ME.
[Prob. from Old French (repr. by *plomme* sounding-lead) from Proto-Romance from Latin *plumbum* lead, with later assim. to Old & mod. French *plomb* lead.]
1 A ball of lead or other heavy material, *esp.* one attached to a line for determining the vertical on an upright surface. ME. ▸**b** A sounding-lead, a plummet. LME.
2 Orig. ***plumb jordan***, a deep hole functioning as a privy or lavatory. Later, a deep pool in a river, the sea, etc.; a perpendicular fall. *Scot. & north.* E16.
1 out of plumb out of the perpendicular.
Comb.: **plumb-bob** a (usu. conoidal) bob forming the weight of a plumb-line; ***plumb jordan***: see sense 2 above; **plumb-line** *noun* (*a*) a line or cord with a plumb attached, for determining the vertical; (*b*) *fig.* a means of testing or judging; a standard; †(*c*) GEOMETRY a vertical or perpendicular line; a straight line at right angles to another; (*d*) a sounding-line; *fig.* a means of exploring or experiencing emotional depths; **plumb-line** *verb trans.* measure or determine (as) by a plumb-line; **plumb-rule** a mason's instrument for determining the vertical, consisting of a line or cord with a plumb attached, fastened to and swinging freely on the surface of a narrow straight-edged board marked with a longitudinal line which, when its position is vertical, coincides with the string.

plumb /plʌm/ *adjective & adverb*. LME.
[from PLUMB *noun*. As adverb cf. French *à plomb* straight down.]
▸ **A** *adjective*. **1** Vertical, perpendicular. LME.
2 a Downright, thoroughgoing; sheer. M18. ▸**b** CRICKET. Of a wicket: level, true. E20.

🕮 **1** T. PYNCHON The stairwell doesn't appear plumb, but tilted. **2a** D. RUNYON No guy is going to walk into a sack wide awake unless he is a plumb sucker.

▸ **B** *adverb*. **1** Vertically, perpendicularly; straight *down*. LME.
2 a Completely, entirely, quite. *slang* (chiefly *N. Amer.*). L16. ▸**b** Exactly, directly, precisely. E17.

🕮 **1** MILTON Fluttring his pennons vain plumb down he drops. **2a** L. MACNEICE Carrick, the castle as plumb assured As thirty years ago. O. NASH Us cattle ranchers is shore tired o' you sheepmen plumb ruinin' our water. **b** G. GREENE The helicopter sank . . plumb in the centre of the roped-off space.

plumb /plʌm/ *verb*. LME.
[from PLUMB *noun*, *adjective*, perh. partly also after French *plomber* cover or weight with lead. In branch III also back-form. from PLUMBER.]
▸ **I 1** *verb intrans.* Sink or fall like a plummet; fall vertically. *rare*. LME.

🕮 **1** *Saturday Evening Post* [He] . . rolled down and plumbed into the yard.

▸ **II 2** *verb trans.* Weight (a thing) with lead. LME.
3 *verb trans.* Measure the depth of (water) with a plumb; determine (a depth); *fig.* get to the bottom of; explore or experience the emotional depths of. M16.
4 *verb trans.* Seal (a packet, parcel, etc.) with a leaden seal. Now *rare*. M17.
5 *verb trans.* Make vertical, test (an upright surface) to determine the vertical. E18.
6 a *verb trans.* Place vertically above or below. M19. ▸**b** *verb intrans.* Hang vertically. M19.

🕮 **2** W. TAYLOR The oars are plumbed in the handle, so as to balance on the edge. **3** J. CONRAD He had plumbed . . the depths of horror and despair. E. BIRNEY Eyes too bright black to be plumbed. *Match Fishing* I plumbed the depth and found 12' at about four rod lengths. **plumb a track** *US colloq.* trace or follow out a road. **4** T. JEFFERSON I shall have the whole corded and plumbed by the Custom house. **5** S. J. P. THEARLE Aids in plumbing the frames and keeping the side of the ship fair.

▸ **III 7** *verb intrans.* Work (orig. in lead) as a plumber. L19.
8 *verb trans.* Provide (a building or room) with plumbing. E20. ▸**b** Fit (an appliance) as part of a plumbing system. Freq. foll. by *in*. M20.

🕮 **8** OED The house has been duly plumbed, painted and whitewashed. **b** *Practical Householder* A water filter . . is plumbed into the rising main.

■ **plumbless** *adjective* (chiefly *literary*) unable to be plumbed; fathomless: M17.

plumb- *combining form* see PLUMBO-.

plumbaginous /plʌmˈbadʒɪnəs/ *adjective*. L18.
[from Latin *plumbagin-*, PLUMBAGO: see -OUS.]
Containing or consisting of plumbago or graphite.

plumbago /plʌmˈbeɪɡəʊ/ *noun*. Pl. **-os**. E17.
[Latin, from *plumbum* lead (used to translate Greek *molubdaina*, from *molubdos* lead).]
1 †**a** An ore containing lead; usu. *spec.*, litharge; occas., galena, minium. E–M17. ▸**b** [By confusion with galena: cf. LEAD *noun*¹ 6.] Graphite, black lead. Also in ART. (chiefly *Hist.*), lead pencil (freq. *attrib.*). L18.
2 Any of various shrubs and herbaceous plants constituting the genus *Plumbago* (family Plumbaginaceae), with spikelike racemes of flowers having a tubular calyx and five-lobed corolla; esp. *P. auriculata*, a blue-flowered southern African plant grown for ornament. Also called ***leadwort***. M18.

plumbane /ˈplʌmbeɪn/ *noun*. E19.
[from Latin *plumbum* lead + -ANE.]
CHEMISTRY. †**1** Lead chloride. Only in E19.
2 Any of a partly hypothetical series of saturated lead hydrides analogous to alkanes; *spec.* lead tetrahydride, PbH_4, an extremely unstable gas. Also, an alkyl compound of lead. E20.

plumbate /ˈplʌmbeɪt/ *noun*¹. M19.
[from Latin *plumbum* lead + -ATE¹.]
CHEMISTRY. A salt of lead, esp. tetravalent lead, which contains oxygen or hydroxyl.
plumbate(II) a salt of divalent lead containing oxygen or hydroxyl, a plumbite.

plumbate /ˈplʌmbeɪt/ *adjective & noun*². E20.
[from Latin *plumbum* lead + -ATE².]
▸ **A** *adjective*. Of, pertaining to, or designating a type of glazed and usu. monochrome pottery varying from greyish-black to dark olive in colour made in pre-Columbian Central America. E20.
▸ **B** *ellipt.* as *noun*. Plumbate pottery. M20.

plumbean /ˈplʌmbɪən/ *adjective*. Long *rare*. M17.
[formed as next: see -AN, -EAN.]
Resembling lead; leaden; lead-coloured.

plumbeous /ˈplʌmbɪəs/ *adjective*. L16.
[from Latin *plumbeus* leaden, from *plumbum* lead: see -EOUS, -OUS.]
†**1** Weighing like lead; moving heavily, ponderous. L16–L17.
2 Made of or resembling lead; (chiefly ORNITHOLOGY) lead-coloured. E17. ▸**b** CERAMICS. Lead-glazed. L19.

plumber /ˈplʌmə/ *noun*. LME.
[Old French *plommier* (mod. *plombier*) from Latin *plumbarius*, from *plumbum* lead: see -ER².]
1 Orig., a person who dealt and worked in lead. Now, a person who fits and repairs the apparatus of a water supply, heating, sanitation, etc., in a building. LME.
2 *transf.* **a** An armourer or engineering officer. *Military slang*. M20. ▸**b** During the administration of US President Richard M. Nixon (1969–74), a member of a White House special unit which investigated leaks of government secrets, esp. by illegal means, such as installing concealed microphones. *slang*. M20.
1 plumber's friend a plunger for clearing blocked drains. ***plumber's snake***: see SNAKE *noun* 3.
¶ Recorded from LOE in surnames.

plumbery /ˈplʌm(ə)ri/ *noun*. LME.
[Old French *plommerie*, (also mod.) *plomberie* lead-work, plumber's workshop, formed as prec. + -ERY.]
1 A plumber's workshop. LME.
2 Plumber's work, plumbing. LME.

plumbet /ˈplʌmɪt/ *noun & adjective*. Long *obsolete* exc. *Hist.* M16.
[Origin uncertain: perh. from French *plomb* lead, PLUMB *noun*: see -ET¹. Cf. BLUNKET, PLUNKET *noun & adjective*¹.]
(Of) a coarse woollen fabric of greyish-blue colour; (of) plunket.

plumbian /ˈplʌmbɪən/ *adjective*. M20.
[from Latin *plumbum* lead + -IAN.]
MINERALOGY. Having a constituent element partly replaced by lead.

plumbic /ˈplʌmbɪk/ *adjective*. L18.
[from Latin *plumbum* lead + -IC.]
1 CHEMISTRY. Of or containing lead, esp. in the tetravalent state. Cf. PLUMBOUS. L18.
2 MEDICINE. Due to the presence of lead. L19.

plumbicon /ˈplʌmbɪkɒn/ *noun*. M20.
[from Latin *plumbum* lead, after VIDICON.]
A type of television camera tube in which the photoconductive layer of the signal plate is of lead monoxide.

plumbiferous /plʌmˈbɪf(ə)rəs/ *adjective*. L18.
[from Latin *plumbum* lead + -I- + -FEROUS.]
Containing lead.

plumbing /ˈplʌmɪŋ/ *noun*. LME.
[from PLUMB *verb* + -ING¹.]
1 The action of PLUMB *verb*; now *esp.* the activity or trade of a plumber. LME.
2 The result of this action; plumber's work, the system or apparatus of water supply, heating, sanitation etc., in a building. M18.
3 *transf.* Something resembling a system of water supply in appearance or function; *spec.* (*a*) *colloq.* a system of pipes, tubes, or ducts in an engine or other apparatus or installation; (*b*) *Jazz slang* a trumpet, trombone, or similar wind instrument; (*c*) *colloq.* lavatory installations collectively; *spec.* a water-closet, a lavatory; (*d*) *colloq.* (chiefly *joc.*) the excretory tracts, the urinary system. E20.

plumbism /ˈplʌmbɪz(ə)m/ *noun*. L19.
[from Latin *plumbum* lead + -ISM.]
MEDICINE. Lead poisoning.

plumbite /ˈplʌmbaɪt/ *noun*. M19.
[from Latin *plumbum* lead + -ITE¹.]
CHEMISTRY. A salt of lead containing oxygen or hydroxyl; *esp.* = ***plumbate*(II)** s.v. PLUMBATE *noun*¹.

plumbo- /ˈplʌmbəʊ/ *combining form*. Before a vowel **plumb-**. M19.
[from Latin *plumbum* lead: see -O-.]
Chiefly CHEMISTRY & MINERALOGY. Of, pertaining to, or containing lead, as ***plumbosolvent***.

plumbosolvent /plʌmbəʊˈsɒlv(ə)nt/ *adjective*. L19.
[from PLUMBO- + SOLVENT.]
Of water: capable of dissolving lead.
■ **plumbosolvency** *noun* capacity to dissolve lead L19.

plumbous /ˈplʌmbəs/ *adjective*. L17.
[from Latin *plumbosus* full of lead: see -OUS.]
†**1** Heavy, dull, ponderous; leaden, lead-coloured. L17–M18.
2 CHEMISTRY. Of or containing lead, esp. in the divalent state. Cf. PLUMBIC. M19.

plume /pluːm/ *noun*. LME.
[Old & mod. French from Latin *pluma* small soft feather, down.]
1 A feather, now *esp.* a large or conspicuous one for ornament or display. Also *spec.* in ORNITHOLOGY, a contour feather as distinct from a plumule. LME.
2 a Downy plumage, down; plumage generally. *arch.* E16. ▸**b** The web or vane of a quill; the feathering of an arrow. *rare*. E19.
3 An ornamental feather or bunch of feathers or tuft of horsehair etc., usu. symbolizing dignity or rank, esp. as attached to a helmet, hat, or other head-dress, or worn in the hair. M16.
4 Any of various objects resembling a plume or plumage in form or lightness; *spec.* (*a*) BOTANY a tuft of pappus-hairs; formerly, a plumule; (*b*) ZOOLOGY a plumose or feather-like part, hair, organ, or formation; (*c*) ASTRONOMY a long thin projection from the solar corona near the poles; (*d*) a trail of smoke, vapour, etc., issuing from a localized source and spreading out as the trail travels; (*e*) GEOLOGY a column of magma rising from the lower mantle and spreading out under the lithosphere, proposed to explain the motion of lithospheric plates and the siting of volcanic activity away from plate margins. L16.
5 In full ***plume-moth***. A member of the family Pterophoridae of small long-legged moths with narrow feather-like wings. E19.

📖 **1** T. GRAY With ruffled plumes and flagging wing. A. NEWTON The dorsal plumes of the Egrets. *fig.*: C. KINGSLEY My soul . . in the rapid plumes of song Clothed itself sublime and strong. ***borrowed plumes***: see BORROW *verb*[1]. **2a** J. WILSON Vaunt not, gay bird! thy gorgeous plume. **b** Z. M. PIKE They buried the arrow to the plume in the animal **3** J. REED A plume of ostrich feathers, which he stuck in his hat. A. DUGGAN A . . soldier under a tall plume of stiffened horsehair. **4** G. ORWELL The smoke . . floated straight upwards in still plumes. S. COOPER A plume of dust drifted up from the desolate grey land.

Comb.: **plume-bearing** *adjective* that bears feathers; **plume-moth**: see sense 5 above; †**plume-plucked** *adjective* (*rare*, Shakes.) stripped of plumes, humbled; **plume-thistle** any of various thistles constituting the genus *Cirsium*, with a pappus of plumose (not simple) hairs.

■ **plumeless** *adjective* E17. **plumelet** *noun* †(*a*) BOTANY = PLUMULE 1; (*b*) a small plume: E19. **plumelike** *adjective* resembling (that of) a plume; feathery: M19. **plumery** *noun* (chiefly *literary*) plumes collectively; a mass of plumes: E19. **plumifi'cation** *noun* (*rare*) the action of feathering, the fact of being feathered E19.

plume /pluːm/ *verb*. LME.

[In branch I from Old & mod. French *plumer*, from *plume* PLUME *noun*; in branch II from PLUME *noun* or Latin *plumare* cover with feathers.]

▶ **I** †**1** *verb intrans.* FALCONRY. Of a hawk: pluck the feathers of the prey. Also foll. by *on*. LME–M17.

2 *verb trans.* †**a** Pluck (feathers) from a bird. E16–L17. ▸**b** Pluck feathers from (a bird); strip, bare. Now *rare*. L16.

📖 **1** DRYDEN He peeps about . . like a hawk that will not plume, if she be looked on. **2b** SIR W. SCOTT I will so pluck him as never hawk plumed a partridge. *fig.*: BACON The King cared not to plume his Nobilitie . . to feather himselfe.

▶ **II 3 a** *verb trans.* Provide or cover (as) with feathers; feather; decorate with a plume or plumes. LME. ▸†**b** *verb trans.* Set or place as a plume. *rare* (Milton). Only in M17. ▸**c** *verb intrans.* Of a a trail of smoke, vapour, etc.: form a plume, move in a plume. M20.

4 a *verb refl.* Dress oneself with borrowed plumes. Chiefly *fig.* L16. ▸**b** *verb refl.* & †*intrans. fig.* Take credit to oneself, pride, congratulate oneself, esp. regarding something trivial or to which one has no claim. Freq. foll. by *on*. M17.

5 *verb trans.* **a** *refl.* Of a bird: preen itself. E18. ▸**b** Preen, trim, (feathers, wings, etc.), esp. in preparation for flight. E19.

📖 **3** JOSEPH STRUTT Several arrows . . plumed with feathers. JOYCE Cattle . . smoke pluming their foreheads. *Daily Telegraph* Both sides of the valley were plumed with beechwoods. **c** W. STYRON Smoke was pluming upward from the chimney. **4b** T. JEFFERSON The atheist . . plumes himself on the uselessness of such a God. J. GROSS *The Fortnightly* plumed itself on being the champion of the enlightened. **5b** OUIDA Herons plumed their silvery wings. *fig.*: J. L. MOTLEY Calumny plumed her wings for a fresh attack.

plumeau /plymo/ *noun*. Pl. ***-eaux*** /-o/. L19.

[French, formed as PLUME *noun*.]

A duvet.

plumed /pluːmd, *poet.* 'pluːmɪd/ *adjective*. LME.

[from PLUME *noun*, *verb*: see -ED[2], -ED[1].]

1 Provided or covered (as) with feathers; feathered; ornamented with a plume or plumes. LME.

2 Plucked; stripped of plumes or feathers. Long *rare*. L16.

1 plumed partridge = MOUNTAIN *quail*. **plumed serpent** a mythical creature depicted as part bird, part snake; *spec.* (freq. with cap. initials) any of various ancient Meso-American gods having this form, *esp.* Quetzalcoatl, the Aztec god of vegetation and fertility.

plumeria /pluː'mɪərɪə/ *noun*. E18.

[mod. Latin (see below), from C. Plumier (*Plumerius*), French botanist (1646–1704): see -IA[1].]

Any of various tropical trees constituting the genus *Plumeria* (family Apocynaceae), having large fragrant salver-shaped flowers and including the frangipani, *P. rubra*.

plumet /'pluːmɪt/ *noun*. *rare*. L16.

[French, formed as PLUME *noun* + -ET[1].]

A small plume.

plumetis /'pluːmɪti/ *noun*. M19.

[French, from *plumeté* adjective (HERALDRY) sprinkled with spots like bunches of feathers.]

Embroidery worked on a tambour; feather-stitch. Also, a fine light dress fabric woven with raised dots or tufts.

plumetty /'pluːmɪti/ *adjective*. L15.

[from French *plumeté*: see prec., -Y[1].]

HERALDRY. Of a field: charged with overlapping feathers.

plumigerous /pluː'mɪdʒ(ə)rəs/ *adjective*. Now *arch.* *rare*. M17.

[from Latin *plumiger* feather-bearing, from *pluma* PLUME *noun*: see -I-, -GEROUS.]

Plume-bearing; relating to the wearing of plumes.

plumiped /'pluːmɪpɛd/ *adjective*. Now *arch.* *rare*. E18.

[Latin *plumiped-*, *-pes* feather-footed, from *pluma* PLUME *noun* + *-i-* + *ped-*, *pes* foot.]

Having plumed or winged feet.

plummer-block /'plʌməblɒk/ *noun*. E19.

[from 1st elem. of uncertain origin (perh. from the surname *Plummer*) + BLOCK *noun*.]

MECHANICS. A metal box that supports a revolving shaft, with a movable cover fastened by bolts giving access to the bearings.

plummet /'plʌmɪt/ *noun*. LME.

[Old French *plommet*, *plombet* dim. of *plomb*: see PLUMB *noun*, -ET[1].]

1 A ball of lead or other heavy material, attached to a line and used for determining the vertical; a plumb-bob; a plumb-rule. Also, a similar appliance attached to a quadrant or other scientific instrument. LME. ▸**b** *fig.* A criterion of rectitude or truth. Long *rare*. M16.

2 A piece of lead or other heavy material attached to a line, and used for sounding the depth of water; a sounding-lead. LME.

†**3** The pommel or knob on the hilt of a sword (sometimes weighted with lead). *Scot.* LME–L18.

4 A stick of lead, for writing, ruling lines, etc.; a lead pencil. *obsolete* exc. *Hist.* LME.

†**5** A ball or lump of lead, *esp.* one used as a missile or, fastened to a line, as a weapon or instrument of punishment. Also *fig.*, something oppressive, something which weighs one down. LME–L19.

6 A weight for any of various purposes; *spec.* †(*a*) a leaden weight for a gymnastic exercise; a weight for a cestus; †(*b*) a weight of a clock; *fig.* a motive force, a spring of action; (*c*) ANGLING a weight attached to a fishing-line, used with a float as a sounding-lead, or to keep the float upright. M16.

📖 **2** SHAKES. *Temp.* My son i' th' ooze is bedded; and I'll seek him deeper than e'er plummet sounded. M. F. MAURY The greatest depths . . reached with the plummet are in the North Atlantic. **6** *Coarse Fishing* We took . . a big float and a plummet and we plumbed every part . . we could reach.

■ **plummetless** *adjective* unfathomable L19.

plummet /'plʌmɪt/ *verb*. E17.

[from the noun.]

†**1** *verb trans.* Fathom, sound. *rare*. Only in E17.

†**2** *verb trans.* Let fall or draw (a vertical line) by means of a plummet. *rare*. Only in E18.

3 *verb intrans.* Fish with a line weighted with a plummet. *rare*. L19.

4 *verb intrans.* & *trans.* (Cause to) drop, fall, or plunge rapidly. Also foll. by *down*. M20.

📖 **4** *Sun (Baltimore)* The fatal flight that plummeted her into the sea from lightning-swept skies. D. ADAMS It plummeted fifteen storeys and smashed itself . . on the ground below. R. OWEN Anglo-Soviet relations plummeted from relatively cordial to relatively chilly.

plummy /'plʌmi/ *adjective*. M18.

[from PLUM *noun* + -Y[1].]

1 Consisting of, having many, or rich in plums. Also, resembling a plum or plums, esp. in colour. M18.

2 *fig.* **a** Rich, good, desirable. *colloq.* E19. ▸**b** (Of the voice) rich and thick-sounding, esp. as supposedly characteristic of the British upper classes; mellow and deep but somewhat drawling; (of a person) having or speaking in such a voice, upper-class. *colloq.* L19.

📖 **2a** *Punch* A plummy job . . that should certainly bring promotion. **b** A. BURGESS He had . . a plummy patrician voice.

■ **plummily** *adverb* M20. **plumminess** *noun* E20.

plumose /pluː'məʊs, 'pluːməʊs/ *adjective*. M18.

[Latin *plumosus*, from *pluma* PLUME *noun*: see -OSE[1].]

Chiefly ZOOLOGY, BOTANY, & MINERALOGY. Feathery; having feathers or feather-like structures; resembling a feather, esp. in having two series of fine separated filaments on opposite sides.

plumose anemone a sea anemone of the genus *Metridium*, having feathery tentacles.

plumosite /'pluːməsʌɪt/ *noun*. M19.

[formed as prec. + -ITE[1].]

MINERALOGY. = JAMESONITE.

plumosity /pluː'mɒsɪti/ *noun*. *rare*. M17.

[formed as PLUMOSE + -ITY.]

Feathery or feathered condition.

plumous /'pluːməs/ *adjective*. *rare*. E19.

[formed as prec. + -OUS.]

Feathery, downy.

plump /plʌmp/ *noun*[1]. Now *arch.* & *dial.* LME.

[Origin unkn.]

A compact body of people, animals, or things; a band, a company; a flock; a cluster, a clump.

📖 SIR W. SCOTT Soon appears O'er Horncliff-hill, a plump of spears. *National Observer (US)* The little plump of yachts cast anchor.

plump /plʌmp/ *noun*[2]. LME.

[from PLUMP *verb*[1].]

1 An act of plumping; an abrupt plunge, a heavy fall; a thud. LME.

2 A sudden heavy fall of rain. Chiefly *Scot.* E18.

plump /plʌmp/ *adjective*[1]. L15.

[Middle & mod. Dutch *plomp*, Middle Low German *plomp*, *plump* blunt, obtuse, unshaken, blockish (whence German *plump*), perh. rel. to PLUMP *verb*[1]. In branch II cf. Middle Low German *plumpich* corpulent.]

▶ **I** †**1** Blunt, forthright; dull in intellect, blockish, rude. L15–E17.

†**2** Of an arrowhead: blunt and broad. Only in M16.

▶ **II 3** Esp. of a person, animal, or part of the body: having a full rounded shape; fleshy; chubby; filled out. Also *fig.* (*colloq.*), rich, abundant; full and round in tone; big; complete. M16.

📖 **3** F. QUARLES Will no plump Fee Bribe thy false fists? V. NABOKOV Nice, plump, . . glossy red strawberries positively crying to be bitten into. H. CARPENTER Fanny is . . distinctly plump, if not positively fat. K. LETTE The unmistakably plump vowels of his mother.

■ **plumpen** *verb trans.* & *intrans.* (*rare*) make or become plump L17. **plumpish** *adjective* somewhat plump M18. **plumpishness** *noun* L20. **plumply** *adverb*[1] E17. **plumpness** *noun*[1] M16. **plumpy** *adjective* characterized by plumpness; plump: E17.

plump /plʌmp/ *verb*[1]. ME.

[Middle & mod. Low German *plumpen* = Middle & mod. Dutch *plompen* fall into water (whence German *plumpen*): ult. origin imit. Cf. PLUNK *verb*.]

1 *verb intrans.* Of a solid body: fall or drop heavily and abruptly, land with a thud. Freq. foll. by *down*. ME. ▸**b** *transf.* & *fig.* Come abruptly into a specified place or condition. E19.

2 *verb trans.* Drop, let fall, or throw down abruptly and heavily; set (oneself, a thing) down with a thud. LME.

3 *verb trans.* Utter abruptly, blurt *out*. *colloq.* L16.

4 *verb intrans.* Orig., vote at an election *for* or for a single candidate instead of an optional two or more. Now, opt *for* one of two or more possibilities; (occas.) decide *against*. E19.

📖 **1** H. JAMES It has been like plumping into cold water. A. J. CRONIN He plumped . . upon his knees beside the bed. M. PIERCY She plumped down in the rocking chair. **b** L. CARR With a convulsive gurgle, out plumped the words. T. H. HUXLEY We . . plumped into bitter cold weather. **2** C. MCCULLOUGH Ralph . . plumped them down on the . . table. *refl.*: T. WILLIAMS Mitch plumps himself down on the bed. **3** THOMAS HUGHES I plumped out that St. Paul's was the finest cathedral in England. **4** W. PERRIAM He'd finally plumped for Friday, . . after wrestling with the pros and cons of . . every evening.

plump /plʌmp/ *verb*[2] *trans.* & *intrans.* M16.

[from PLUMP *adjective*[1].]

Make or become plump. Freq. foll. by *out*, *up*.

📖 L. BLACK The cosmetics . . a little too thick, the hips starting to plump. C. CONRAN Dried fruit . . soaked and plumped in water. P. CAREY He plumped up his pillow and made himself comfortable.

■ **plumping** *adjective* (*colloq.*) very large, unusually big E20.

plump /plʌmp/ *verb*[3]. *rare*. M16.

[from PLUMP *noun*[1].]

†**1** *verb intrans.* Form a compact body of people, animals, or things; mass or cluster together. Only in M16.

2 *verb trans.* Sow (seed) in clumps. M19.

plump /plʌmp/ *adverb* & *adjective*[2]. L16.

[from PLUMP *verb*[1].]

▶ **A** *adverb*. **1** With a heavy and abrupt fall or drop; with a thud. L16.

2 *fig.* Directly; without circumlocution or concealment, bluntly, flatly. M18.

📖 **1** R. HUGHES Poor little Jacko . . fell plump on the deck and broke his neck. W. C. WILLIAMS I ran plump into such a window as I had been working on. **2** R. BOLDREWOOD He told us, plump and plain, that he wasn't going to shift. M. SINCLAIR Look me straight in the face and say plump out what I've done.

▶ **B** *adjective*. **1** Descending directly, vertical, sheer. Also, directly facing in position. *rare*. E17.

2 *fig.* Of a statement etc.: direct, blunt, unqualified. *colloq.* L18.

3 Esp. of a sum of money: paid in full, complete. *rare*. M19.

📖 **2** *Fortnightly Review* Neither man nor woman would dare to answer with a plump No.

■ **plumply** *adverb*[2] L18. **plumpness** *noun*[2] (*colloq.*) L18.

plumper /'plʌmpə/ *noun*[1]. L17.

[from PLUMP *verb*[2] + -ER[1].]

A thing which plumps or fills something out; *spec.* in *pl.* (now *Hist.*), small balls or pads carried in the mouth to fill out the cheeks.

plumper /'plʌmpə/ *noun*[2]. M18.

[from PLUMP *verb*[1], *adverb* + -ER[1].]

†**1** A heavy blow; a heavy fall. *slang*. M18–E19.

2 A vote cast at an election for a single candidate instead of an optional two or more. Also, an elector casting such a vote. L18.

3 An unusually large specimen of its kind; *spec.* an untruth told on a large scale, a downright lie. *arch. colloq.* E19.

plumptitude /ˈplʌm(p)tɪtjuːd/ *noun.* Now *arch. rare.* E19.
[from PLUMP *adjective*¹ + -*titude*, after *aptitude*, *gratitude*, etc.: see -TUDE.]
Plumpness.

plumula *noun* see PLUMULE.

plumularian /pluːmjʊˈlɛːrɪən/ *noun & adjective.* M19.
[from mod. Latin *Plumularia* (see below) + -AN.]
ZOOLOGY. (Of, pertaining to, or designating) a hydroid of the genus *Plumularia*, colonies of which have alternating branches bearing polyps along one surface.

plumule /ˈpluːmjuːl/ *noun.* In sense 1 also in Latin form **-ula** /-jʊlə/, pl. **-lae** /-liː/. E18.
[French, or Latin *plumula* dim. of *pluma* PLUME *noun*: see -ULE.]
1 BOTANY. A primordial shoot above the cotyledon(s) in an embryo plant. E18.
2 A little feather; *spec.* in ORNITHOLOGY, a down feather. M19. ▸**b** ENTOMOLOGY. A small plumose organ or structure. L19.
■ **plumuˈlaceous** *adjective* (ORNITHOLOGY) of the nature of a plumule, downy L19. **plumular** *adjective* of or pertaining to a plumule L19.

plumy /ˈpluːmi/ *adjective.* L16.
[from PLUME *noun* + -Y¹.]
†**1** Made of down, downy. L16–E18.
2 Characterized by or having many plumes or feathers; feathered. L16.
3 Plumelike, feathery. E17.
4 Decorated with a plume or plumes. E18.

> 📖 **1** DRYDEN Her head did on a plumy pillow rest. **2** T. R. JONES It causes their plumy covering to repel moisture. **3** YEATS When the live west flashed with surge of plumy fire. S. LESLIE Traveller's Joy encircled the bushes with plumy seed-burst like the feathers of . . Birds of Paradise. **4** J. C. ATKINSON He saw the horses and the plumy black wain.

■ **pluminess** *noun* (*rare*) E19.

plunder /ˈplʌndə/ *noun.* M17.
[from next.]
1 The action of plundering or taking something as spoil, esp. in war; pillage, depredation. Now *rare* or *obsolete.* M17. ▸**b** The acquisition of property by violent, questionable, or dishonest means; spoliation. L17.
2 Goods or valuables taken from an enemy by force, esp. in war; booty, loot. M17. ▸**b** Property acquired by violent, questionable, or dishonest means; *colloq.* profit, gain. L18.
3 Personal belongings or household goods collectively; luggage, baggage. *US local.* E19.

> 📖 **1** J. LEONI After the plunder and spoiling of the Temple. **b** J. A. FROUDE The wretched novice was an object of general plunder. **2** H. H. WILSON The instigator of the depredations . . sharing in the plunder. H. NEWBOLT Take your ill-got plunder, and bury the dead. **b** J. G. HOLLAND Men . . actuated by no higher motive than a love of plunder. **3** J. F. COOPER You seem to have but little plunder . . for one . . so far abroad.

plunder /ˈplʌndə/ *verb.* M17.
[Middle & mod. Low German *plündern* from Middle & mod. Low German *plünderen* lit. 'rob of household effects', from Middle High German *plunder* bedclothes, household effects (mod. German *Plunder* lumber, trash). Cf. Middle Low German, Middle Dutch *plunde*, *plunne* (Low German *plünde*, *plünn* (pl.) rags, old clothes), Dutch *plunje* clothes, baggage.]
1 *verb trans.* Rob (a place or person) of goods or valuables forcibly, esp. as in war; pillage, ransack, spoil. Also, rob systematically. M17.
2 *verb trans.* Take (goods or valuables) by violent, questionable or dishonest means; embezzle; take by robbery, steal, esp. systematically. M17.
3 *verb intrans.* Commit depredations. M17.

> 📖 **1** C. THIRLWALL Royal troops plundered the camp of all that fell in their way. HENRY MILLER Continents had been . . plundered of all that was precious. *fig.*: A. C. GRAYLING His writings are plundered for aphorisms. **2** G. HARRIS Brigands . . paused as they sorted through the plundered goods. *Sun* An investment racket in which they . . made a million by plundering the life savings of clients. **3** S. AUSTIN The Hungarians . . pushed on . . plundering and laying waste by the way. O. HENRY The band would ride into the . . settlements . . plundering for the provisions and ammunition they needed.

■ **plunderage** *noun* (**a**) the action of plundering; pillage, spoliation; LAW the embezzling of goods on shipboard; (**b**) goods or valuables obtained by plundering: L18. **plunderer** *noun* a person who plunders; a pillager, a robber: M17. **plunderous** *adjective* given to or characterized by plundering M19.

plunderbund /ˈplʌndəbʊnd/ *noun. US colloq.* E20.
[from PLUNDER *noun* + BUND *noun*².]
A corrupt alliance of political, commercial, and financial interests engaged in exploiting the public.

plunge /plʌn(d)ʒ/ *noun.* LME.
[from the verb.]
1 A place for plunging; a deep pool, a depth. *obsolete* exc. *dial.* LME. ▸**b** In full *plunge bed.* A flower-bed, often containing peat or other moisture-retaining materials, in which plants in pots can be sunk. M20. ▸**c** In full *plunge pool.* A cold-water pool forming part of the equipment of a sauna. L20.
2 A sudden plunging movement. L15.
3 The point at which a person is plunged into trouble, difficulty, or danger; a critical situation, a strait; a dilemma. *obsolete* exc. *dial.* E16.
4 An act of plunging; a sudden downward movement into or through water etc.; a dive, a dip. E18.
5 The breaking of a wave. Also (*Scot.*), a heavy downpour of rain. L18.
6 A reckless bet. *slang.* L19.
7 GEOLOGY. The angle a fold axis or linear feature makes with the horizontal, measured in a vertical plane. E20.

> 📖 **1c** *Detroit Free Press* A hot sauna and then you're thrown into a cold plunge. **2** R. BADEN-POWELL By directing the animal's plunges judiciously I got him . . on *terra firma*. **3** H. CHOLMLEY I was in the greatest plunge for money. A. LOVELL Demanding payment . . put the Prince to a great plunge. **4** R. L. STEVENSON The plunge of our anchor sent up clouds of birds. *fig.*: A. FRANCE Each plunge into psychotherapy helped me to feel much more positive. **take the plunge** *colloq.* take a decisive first step, commit oneself irrevocably to a course of action. **5** LONGFELLOW The plunge of the implacable seas.

Comb.: **plunge basin** PHYSICAL GEOGRAPHY a deep basin excavated at the foot of a waterfall by the action of the falling water; **plunge bath** a large and deep bath in which the whole body can be immersed; *plunge bed*: see sense 1b above; **plunge-churn** (now *rare*) a churn consisting of an upright wooden cask in which a plunger is worked up and down; **plunge cut** ENGINEERING a cut made by plunge grinding; *plunge-cut grinding* = *plunge grinding* below; **plunge grinding** ENGINEERING grinding by means of a wheel with no traverse of the work; **plunge cutting** the action of making a plunge cut; **plunge neckline** a low-cut neckline; **plunge pool** (**a**) PHYSICAL GEOGRAPHY (the water in) a plunge basin; (**b**) see sense 1c above.

plunge /plʌn(d)ʒ/ *verb.* LME.
[Old French *plungier*, *plongier* (mod. *plonger*) from Latin *plumbum* lead.]
1 *verb trans.* Put, thrust, or throw forcibly or abruptly *into* or *in* water etc. or a deep place; immerse completely. Formerly also, baptize by immersion. LME.
2 *verb trans.* Foll. by *into* or †*in*: cause (a person) to enter a certain condition or embark on a certain course abruptly or impetuously. LME.
3 *verb intrans.* **a** Throw oneself *into* water etc.; dive, esp. head first; fall abruptly and involuntarily, esp. from a great height, *into* a depth. Also, penetrate suddenly *into* a crowd of people or things, esp. so as to be lost to view. LME. ▸**b** Move with a rush *down*, *into*, or *out of*; move or travel *along* or *on* rapidly and clumsily. M19. ▸**c** Descend abruptly and steeply; dip suddenly; GEOLOGY (of a fold) have an axis that slopes or dips downwards; (of an axis) slope or dip downward. M19. ▸**d** Of profit, monetary value, etc.: diminish rapidly, drop suddenly in value. M20.
†**4** *verb trans.* Overwhelm, esp. *with* trouble or difficulty; put in a difficult or awkward position, embarrass. L15–L17.
5 *verb intrans.* (Of a horse) start violently forward and downward; (of a ship) pitch. M16.
6 *verb trans.* Sink (a plant, a pot containing a plant) in the ground. M17.
†**7** *verb trans.* Penetrate and traverse, explore the depths of, by plunging. *rare.* M17–E18.
8 *verb intrans.* Enter *into* a certain condition or embark on a certain course abruptly or impetuously; involve oneself deeply. L17.
9 *verb intrans.* Of artillery: fire downwards from a higher level. Freq. as *plunging ppl adjective. rare.* E19.
10 a *verb intrans.* Spend money or bet recklessly; speculate or gamble deeply; run into debt. *slang.* L19. ▸**b** *verb trans.* Bet or speculate (a sum of money). *colloq. rare.* E20.
11 *verb trans.* Release (signals, points, etc.) on a railway by depressing a plunger. E20.

> 📖 **1** E. K. KANE The lance is plunged into the left side. T. H. HUXLEY You have only to plunge a lighted taper into it. **2** B. JOWETT We are plunged . . into philosophical discussions. D. LODGE Economic recession . . plunged his . . colleagues into deep gloom. D. ROWE His father lost his business and plunged the family into poverty. **3a** DICKENS He plunged into the thickest portion of the little wood. T. CALLENDER He . . plunged head first under the water. *Toronto Sun* A four-year-old . . boy . . plunged almost 200 feet from a high-rise balcony. **b** R. KIPLING He stumbled across the landing and plunged into Torpenhow's room. A. BURGESS Panic caused him to plunge down the path. **c** B. HARTE The stage-road that plunged from the terrace . . into the valley below. M. GEE The cliffs are magnificent, . . the edge of England plunging sheer into the waves. **d** *Time* Inflation was raging . . the lira was plunging. **5** M. EDGEWORTH He taught Sawney to rear and plunge, whenever his legs were touched. **6** *Amateur Gardening* Pot up and plunge spring-flowering bulbs. **8** A. RADCLIFFE It was only to plunge into new errors. B. JOWETT We plunge abruptly into the subject of the dialogue. **10a** M. E. BRADDON She has been plunging rather deeply. **b** JOYCE Boylan plunged two quid on my tip.

■ **plunging** *ppl adjective* that plunges; *plunging neckline* = *plunge neckline* s.v. PLUNGE *noun*: M16. **plungingly** *adverb* L19.

plungeon /ˈplʌn(d)ʒ(ə)n/ *noun.* L15.
[French *plongeon* (Old French *plongon*) diving bird, from *plonger* dive, plunge + -*eon*, after *pigeon*.]
†**1** A diving bird; a diver. L15–M18.
2 A ford across a large open ditch. *dial.* & *Hist.* L17.

plunger /ˈplʌn(d)ʒə/ *noun.* E17.
[from PLUNGE *verb* + -ER¹.]
1 A person who plunges into or through water etc.; a diver. E17.
2 A thing which plunges, esp. an instrument or part of a mechanism which works or is worked with a plunging or thrusting movement; *spec.* (**a**) a piston; (**b**) a knob, button, etc., used to operate signalling mechanisms and points on a railway system; (**c**) a device used in plumbing consisting of a rubber cup on a handle for clearing blocked pipes by a plunging and sucking action; (**d**) JAZZ *slang* (more fully *plunger mute*) a plunging device resembling the type employed in plumbing, used as a mute for a trumpet or trombone. L18.
3 A type of sailing boat used in the Pacific coast oyster fisheries. *N. Amer.* M19.
4 A person who bets or speculates recklessly. *slang.* M19.
2 *landed plunger*: see LANDED *adjective.*
Comb.: *plunger mute*: see sense 2 above; **plunger-pump**: that works using a plunger or plungers; **plunger-valve**: that has a plunging action.

plunk /plʌŋk/ *noun, adverb, & interjection.* M18.
[from PLUNK *verb*.]
▶ **A** *noun.* **1** Orig., a large sum, a fortune. Later (*US slang*), a dollar. M18.
2 The action of PLUNK *verb*; an instance of this; (the sound of) a heavy blow. Also, an abrupt vibratory sound; *esp.* the sound made by the sharply plucked string of a stringed instrument. E19.
▶ **B** *adverb & interjection.* Repr. the sound of a heavy blow or fall, or the sharply plucked string of a stringed instrument; with a plunking noise. M19.

plunk /plʌŋk/ *verb.* L18.
[Prob. imit. Cf. PLONK *verb*, PLUMP *verb*¹.]
1 *verb intrans.* Esp. of a raven: croak, cry. *Scot. rare.* L18.
2 a *verb intrans.* Fall or drop down heavily or abruptly. E19. ▸**b** *verb trans.* Put down or throw heavily or abruptly. L19.
3 a *verb trans.* Cause (a string) to sound with a plunk; play (a note etc.) on a stringed instrument with a plunk. E19. ▸**b** *verb intrans.* Sound with a plunk. E20.
4 *verb intrans. & trans.* Play truant (from); be a truant (from). *Scot. colloq.* E19.
5 *verb trans.* **a** Drive or propel with a sudden push. *colloq.* L19. ▸**b** Hit, wound, shoot. *slang* (orig. *US*). L19.

plunket /ˈplʌŋkɪt/ *noun & adjective*¹. Long *obsolete* exc. *Hist.* LME.
[Prob. from Old French *plunkié*, *plonquié* lead-coloured, lead-grey, a kind of grey cloth, from pa. pple of *plonquier* cover with lead from late Latin, from Latin *plumbum* lead. Cf. BLUNKET, PLUMBET.]
(Of) a woollen fabric of light greyish-blue colour; (of) a light greyish blue.

Plunket /ˈplʌŋkɪt/ *adjective*². *NZ.* E20.
[Lady *Plunket*, wife of the Governor-General of New Zealand 1904–10, used with ref. to the *Plunket Society*, popular name for the Royal New Zealand Society for the Health of Women and Children.]
Designating a nurse trained in the methods of child-feeding and care advocated by the Royal New Zealand society for the Health of Women and Children, a baby reared according to these methods, or a clinic following them. Cf. KARITANE.

plunkety-plunk /ˈplʌŋkɪtɪplʌŋk/ *noun & adjective.* L19.
[Imit. redupl. of PLUNK *noun*.]
(Making) an abrupt vibratory sound.

plunther /ˈplʌnðə/ *verb intrans. rare.* M19.
[App. rel. to BLUNDER *verb*.]
Flounder, as in deep snow (foll. by *on*, *along*).

plup /plʌp/ *noun & interjection.* E20.
[Imit. Cf. PLOP *noun*.]
(Repr.) a soft plopping sound.

pluperfect /pluːˈpəːfɪkt/ *adjective & noun.* L15.
[mod. Latin *plusperfectum* from Latin (*tempus praeteritum*) *plus quam perfectum* (past tense) more than perfect translating Greek. (*khronos*) *hupersuntelikos*: cf. French *plus-que-parfait*.]
▶ **A** *adjective.* **1** GRAMMAR. Of a tense: designating a time or action completed prior to some past point of time specified or implied; past perfect. L15.
2 Orig., superfluous. Later, more than perfect; *colloq.* complete, thorough. E19.

> 📖 **2** *Accountancy* Jones recently described the period . . as 'pluperfect hell' for companies while Europe adjusts to the single market.

▶ **B** *noun.* GRAMMAR. (A word or form in) the pluperfect (past perfect) tense. M19.

plural /ˈplʊər(ə)l/ *adjective & noun.* LME.
[Old French *plurel* (mod. *pluriel*) from Latin *pluralis* adjective (with *numerus, genitivus*) and noun (sc. *numerus* number), from *plur-, plus* more: see PLUS, -AL[1].]

▶ **A** *adjective.* **1** GRAMMAR. Of the form or class of a noun, verb, etc.: denoting more than one (or in languages with duals etc., more than a minimum number). Opp. SINGULAR *adjective* 5a. LME.
2 More than one in number; consisting of, containing, pertaining to, or equivalent to, more than one. L16.

1 R. QUIRK The reanalysis of several plural count nouns. **2** SHAKES. *Two Gent.* Better have none Than plural faith, which is too much by one. ***plural*** MARRIAGE. **plural society** a society composed of different ethnic groups or cultural traditions or in the political structure of which ethnic or cultural differences are reflected. **plural voting** the system or practice of casting more than one vote, or of voting in more than one constituency.

▶ **B** *noun.* **1** GRAMMAR. The plural number; a plural word or form. Opp. SINGULAR *noun* 1. LME.
2 The fact or condition of there being more than one. M17.
1 *royal plural*: see ROYAL *adjective.*
■ **plurally** *adverb* LME.

plurale tantum /plʊəˌreɪli ˈtantəm/ *noun phr.* Pl. ***pluralia tantum*** /plʊˈreɪlɪə/. M20.
[from medieval Latin *plurale* the plural, from Latin *pluralis* PLURAL *adjective* + *tantum* only.]
GRAMMAR. A noun which (in any particular sense) is used only in plural form.

pluralise *verb* var. of PLURALIZE.

pluralism /ˈplʊər(ə)lɪz(ə)m/ *noun.* E19.
[from PLURAL *adjective* + -ISM, after next.]
1 The system or practice of the holding by one person of two or more offices or positions, esp. ecclesiastical offices or benefices, at one time. E19.
2 PHILOSOPHY. A theory or system of thought recognizing more than one ultimate principle (cf. DUALISM 1, MONISM; opp. SINGULARISM). Also, the theory that the knowable world is made up of a plurality of interacting things. L19. ▸**b** PSYCHOLOGY. The theory that behaviour is determined by a number of interacting causal factors. M20.
3 a A theory advocating increased devolution and autonomy for individual bodies in preference to the development of monolithic State power. Also, the belief that power should be shared among a number of political parties. E20. ▸**b** A form of society or State in which ethnic or cultural groups maintain their independent traditions, practices, and attitudes. Also, the toleration or acceptance of a diversity of opinions, values, theories, etc. M20.

pluralist /ˈplʊər(ə)lɪst/ *noun & adjective.* E17.
[from PLURAL *adjective* + -IST. Cf. DUALIST.]
▶ **A** *noun.* **1** A person who holds two or more offices or positions, esp. ecclesiastical offices or benefices, at one time. E17.
2 PHILOSOPHY. An adherent or practitioner of pluralism. L19.
3 A person who favours increasing devolution and autonomy for individual bodies in preference to the development of monolithic State power. Also, an adherent or advocate of a form of society in which ethnic or cultural groups maintain their independent traditions, practices, and attitudes; a person who tolerates or accepts a diversity of opinions, values, theories, etc. E20.
▶ **B** *attrib.* or as *adjective.* Of or pertaining to pluralists or pluralism. E19.

pluralistic /plʊərəˈlɪstɪk/ *adjective.* M19.
[from prec. + -IC.]
Of or belonging to pluralists or pluralism; of the nature of pluralism.
■ **pluralistically** *adverb* L19.

plurality /plʊəˈralɪti/ *noun.* LME.
[Old & mod. French *pluralité* from late Latin *pluralitas*, from Latin *pluralis* PLURAL *adjective*: see -ITY. In branch II senses as if directly from Latin *plur-, plus*. Cf. DUALITY.]
▶ **I 1** The state or fact of being plural. LME. ▸**b** The fact of there being many; numerousness; a large number or quantity; a multitude. LME.
2 The holding by one person of two or more offices or positions, esp. ecclesiastical offices or benefices, at one time. Also, any of two or more offices or positions, esp. ecclesiastical offices or benefices, held by one person at one time. LME.
▶ **II 3** The greater number or part; more than half of the whole; = MAJORITY 3. L16.
4 A political majority which is not absolute. *US.* L18.

pluralize /ˈplʊər(ə)lʌɪz/ *verb.* Also **-ise**. E19.
[from PLURAL *adjective* + -IZE.]
1 a *verb trans.* Make plural; attribute plurality to; express in the plural. E19. ▸**b** *verb intrans.* Become plural; assume plural form; express or form a plural. L19.
2 *verb intrans.* Be or become a pluralist; hold two or more offices or positions, esp. ecclesiastical offices or benefices, at one time. M19.
■ **pluraliˈzation** *noun* L19. **pluralizer** *noun* (*a*) GRAMMAR a pluralizing affix, inflection, or word; a count noun; (*b*) *rare* a pluralist: M19.

plurative /ˈplʊərətɪv/ *adjective.* L16.
[Latin *plurativus* plural, from *plur-, plus* more: see -ATIVE.]
†**1** GRAMMAR. = PLURAL *adjective* 1. *rare.* Only in L16.
2 LOGIC. Of a proposition: involving more than half the subject. M19.

pluri- /ˈplʊəri/ *combining form.*
[from Latin *plur-, plus* more, pl. *plures* several: see -I-.]
Several, more than one.
■ **pluridisciˈplinary** *adjective* having or consisting of several disciplines or branches of learning; interdisciplinary: L20. **pluriform** *adjective* having a variety of forms, views etc.; multiform: L20. **pluriˈformity** *noun* multiformity, variety of form M20. **pluriˈlingual** *adjective & noun* (*a*) *adjective* knowing or using many languages, written in many languages, multilingual; (*b*) a plurilingual person: M20. **pluriˈlingualism** *noun* the state or practice of knowing or using many languages L20. **pluriˈliteral** *adjective & noun* (SEMITIC GRAMMAR) (*a*) *adjective* containing more than three letters in the root; (*b*) *noun* a root consisting of more than three letters: E19. **pluriˈlocular** *adjective* (BIOLOGY) containing many cavities or cells E19. **pluriˈmodal** *adjective* consisting of or involving more than one mode M20. **pluriˈparity** *noun* multiparity L19. **pluˈriparous** *adjective* (*a*) = MULTIPAROUS 1; (*b*) = MULTIPAROUS 2: L15. **pluriˈpresence** *noun* presence in more than one place at the same time L18. **plurisegˈmental** *adjective* (*a*) PHYSIOLOGY involving nerves from more than one segment of the spinal column; (*b*) LINGUISTICS (*rare*) = SUPRASEGMENTAL *adjective*: L19. **pluriˈserial** *adjective* consisting of or arranged in several series or rows L19. **pluriˈseriate** *adjective* pluriserial L19. **pluriˈsyllable** *noun* a word of two or more syllables E20. **plurisyˈllabic** *adjective* having two or more syllables, polysyllabic M20. **pluriˈvalent** *adjective* (esp. in CYTOLOGY) multivalent E20.

pluriarc /ˈplʊərɪɑːk/ *noun.* M20.
[French, from PLURI- + ARC *noun*.]
A musical instrument of W. Africa made of a wooden resonator to which several curved rods holding taut strings are attached.

pluries /ˈplʊərɪiːz/ *noun.* LME.
[Latin = several times, from *plur-, plus* more, several.]
LAW (now *Hist.*). More fully ***pluries capias*** /ˈkeɪpɪəs, ˈkap-/ [= you are to seize: see CAPIAS]. A third writ issued when the first and second have failed.

pluripotency /plʊərɪˈpəʊt(ə)nsi/ *noun.* E20.
[from PLURI- + POTENCY.]
BIOLOGY. The property of being pluripotential.
■ Also **pluripotence** *noun* M20.

pluripotent /plʊərɪˈpəʊt(ə)nt/ *adjective.* M20.
[from PLURI- + POTENT *adjective*[2].]
BIOLOGY. = next.

pluripotential /ˌplʊərɪpəˈtɛnʃ(ə)l/ *adjective.* E20.
[from PLURI- + POTENTIAL *adjective*.]
BIOLOGY & MEDICINE. Of a cell, tissue, or organism: capable of developing or differentiating in any of various ways; multipotential.
■ **pluripotentiˈality** *noun* = PLURIPOTENCY M20.

plurisign /ˈplʊərɪsʌɪn/ *noun.* M20.
[from PLURI- + SIGN *noun*.]
A sign or word used with more than one meaning simultaneously. Opp. MONOSIGN.
■ **pluriˈsignative** *adjective* (of a sign or word) used with more than one meaning simultaneously M20. **pluriˈsignatively** *adverb* M20.

pluris petitio /ˌplʊərɪs pɪˈtɪʃɪəʊ/ *noun phr.* M18.
[Latin = the asking of more.]
SCOTS LAW. The asking more judicially than is truly due.

†**plurisy** *noun* var. of PLEURISY.

pluri-valued /plʊərɪˈvaljuːd/ *adjective.* M20.
[from PLURI- + VALUED.]
LOGIC. Of a system of logic: using truth values in addition to those of true and false; many-valued.

plurry /ˈplʌri/ *adjective & adverb. Austral. & NZ slang.* E20.
[Alt. of BLOODY *adjective & adverb.* Cf. BLERRY.]
Bloody, damn, cursed(ly).

plus /plʌs/ *preposition, noun, adverb, adjective, & conjunction.* M16.
[Latin = more.]
▶ **A** *preposition.* **I 1** Made more by, increased by, with the addition of, (a specified number, amount, or proportion); above zero by (a specified amount); with the addition of, inclusive of, (some specified portion or constituent element of the whole). Also (*colloq.*), having in addition, having gained; with, accompanied by; (following a noun) more than (a specified number), with extra qualities, better than usual. M16.

W. R. GROVE A compound of one equivalent of hydrogen plus two of oxygen. P. MOYES The Second World War, an unbelievable thirty-plus years ago. N. LUARD That meant me plus Billy to drive me. It was a two-part job. *New Musical Express* We've both lost a day's wages plus all that fare money.

▶ **II 2** As the name of the mathematical symbol +, signifying a positive quantity or quality, something added, etc. (part of speech unfixed and ambiguous). L16.
2 *alpha plus, beta plus, gamma plus*: see ALPHA etc.
▶ **B** *noun.* Pl. **-s(s)-**.
1 The mathematical symbol +. Also ***plus sign***. M17.
2 A quantity added; a positive quantity; an additional or extra thing; an addition, a gain; an advantage. M17.

1 *Scientific American* The superscript plus sign denotes a positive ion. **2** *Daily Telegraph* Fiction is not on the wane, but . . registered a plus in the number of books. *Which?* Weigh up the pluses and minuses. E. NORTH Every . . hopeful thing that happens is a plus for me.

▶ **C** *adverb.* (Charged) positively. M18.
▶ **D** *adjective.* **1** Additional, extra. Also (*colloq.*), of superior quality; excellent of its kind. M18. ▸**b** Of a golfer: having an adverse handicap of a specified number of strokes or points. E20.
2 Positively charged. L18.
3 Of a quantity: positive, preceded by the plus sign; of the nature of a positive quantity or an addition. E20.

1 *Publishers Weekly* The material for the plus sale is always at hand in the book business. *Globe & Mail (Toronto)* Living room, 15′ dining room are plus features. *Moneypaper* A tendency to exaggerate plus and minus points.

▶ **E** *conjunction.* And in addition. *colloq.* (chiefly *N. Amer.*). M20.

Black World All the ladies brought pies . . plus they had coffee and tea. *Detroit Free Press* Plus they've added pitchers Rudy May and Ross Grimsley.

Comb.: **plus-foured** *adjective* wearing or dressed in plus-fours; **plus-fours** (a suit having) long wide men's knickerbockers, formerly much worn for golf etc. (so called because the overhang at the knee requires an extra four inches of material); **plus juncture** LINGUISTICS = *open juncture* s.v. OPEN *adjective*; **plus-minus** ICE HOCKEY a running total used as an indication of a player's effectiveness, calculated by adding one for each goal scored by the player's team in even-strength play while the player is on the ice, and subtracting one for each goal conceded; ***plus sign***: see sense B.1 above. **plus-size** *adjective* (*N. Amer.*) of a woman or women's clothing: of a larger size than normal; outsize. **plus-twos** a narrower version of plus-fours.
■ **plusage** *noun* (*rare*) (*a*) a number of pluses collectively; (*b*) something extra or added on; a bonus; a surcharge: M20.

plush /plʌʃ/ *noun & adjective.* L16.
[French †*pluche* contr. of *peluche*, from Old French *peluchier* (see PLUCK *verb*), from Italian *peluzzo* dim. of *pelo* from Latin *pilus* PILE *noun*[3].]
▶ **A** *noun.* **1** A rich fabric of silk, cotton, wool, or other material (or of two of these combined), with a long soft nap. L16. ▸**b** A garment (in *pl.* breeches) made of this fabric. *arch.* M19.
2 *transf.* A substance likened to or resembling this fabric. E17.

1 JOYCE Snug in their spooncase of purple plush, faded, the twelve apostles. **b** J. T. HEWLETT A footman in green plushes and a powdered head. **2** J. FLETCHER O my black swan, sleeker than signet's plush. C. A. JOHNS Eggs, from which emerge . . bodies enveloped in a soft plush of grey yarn.

▶ **B** *attrib.* or as *adjective.* **1** Made of or with plush, resembling plush. E17.
2 Luxurious, expensive, stylish. *colloq.* E20.

1 J. B. PRIESTLEY The . . dress circle had the usual plush chairs. J. R. ACKERLEY He lifted the heavy plush tablecloth. **2** L. DEIGHTON It was a plush office . . : modern-design . . desks and chairs and a sheepskin rug on the floor. *Today* Retires to his plush drawing room with its antiques and works of art.

Comb. & special collocations: **plush-copper** MINERALOGY a fibrous variety of cuprite; **plush-stitch** a kind of stitch in worsted or wool work, forming projecting loops which can be cut so as to make a long nap as in plush; **plush-velvet** a kind of plush with short nap, resembling velvet; **plush-velveteen** a cotton plush made to resemble silk plush.
■ **plushed** *adjective* (*rare*) (*a*) made like plush; (*b*) dressed in plush: L16. **pluˈshette** *noun* a fabric imitating plush L19. **plushly** *adverb* richly, sumptuously, elegantly M20. **plushness** *noun* L20.

plushy /ˈplʌʃi/ *adjective.* E17.
[from prec. + -Y[1].]
1 Of the nature of or resembling plush; covered or decorated with plush. E17.
2 Luxurious, expensive, stylish; sumptuous, elegant. *colloq.* E20.
■ **plushily** *adverb* E20. **plushiness** *noun* M20.

plusquam- /ˈplʌskwam/ *combining form. joc. arch.* M16.
[Latin *plus quam* more than.]
Forming adjectives from adjectives with the sense 'more than'.

Plutarchian /pluːˈtɑːkɪən/ *adjective.* M19.
[from Latin *Plutarchius*, from Lucius Mestrius *Plutarchus* (see below): see -AN, -IAN.]
Of, pertaining to, or characteristic of the Greek Platonist philosopher and biographer Plutarch (*c* AD 46–120) or his work.

plutarchy /ˈpluːtɑːki/ *noun*. **M17.**
[from Greek *ploutos* wealth + -ARCHY.]
Government by wealth or the wealthy; plutocracy.

plute /pluːt/ *noun*¹. *slang* (now chiefly *US*). **L19.**
[Abbreviation.]
= PLUTOCRAT.

†**plute** *noun*² see PLUTEUS.

pluteus /ˈpluːtɪəs/ *noun*. Pl. **-ei** /-ɪʌɪ/. Also (earlier) †**plute**. **LME.**
[Latin.]
1 ROMAN ANTIQUITIES. A movable wooden wall or shed employed as a military engine for besieging a city etc.; ARCHITECTURE a barrier or light wall placed between columns. Also, a shelf for books, small statues, busts, etc. **LME.**
2 ZOOLOGY. A planktonic larva of an echinoid or ophiuroid, somewhat triangular with lateral projections. **L19.**
■ **pluteal** *adjective* (*rare*) of or pertaining to a pluteus **LME.** **pluteiform** *adjective* (ZOOLOGY) of the form of a pluteus **L19.**

Pluto /ˈpluːtəʊ/ *noun*¹. **M20.**
[Latin from Greek *Ploutōn* god of the underworld. In sense 2 see below.]
1 A small planet, the outermost in the solar system, discovered in 1930, having a strongly elliptical orbit lying mainly beyond that of Neptune. **M20.**
2 (A toy dog representing) a cartoon dog named Pluto that made its first appearance in Walt Disney's *Moose Hunt*, 1931. **M20.**

Pluto /ˈpluːtəʊ/ *noun*². **M20.**
[Acronym, from *pipe line under the ocean*.]
Hist. (The code-name for) a system of pipelines laid in 1944 to carry petrol supplies from Britain to Allied forces in France.

plutocracy /pluːˈtɒkrəsi/ *noun*. **M17.**
[Greek *ploutokratia*, from *ploutos* wealth: see -CRACY.]
1 Government by wealth or by the wealthy. Also, a State governed in this way. **M17.**
2 A ruling or influential class of wealthy people; a body of plutocrats. **M19.**

plutocrat /ˈpluːtəkrat/ *noun*. **M19.**
[from (the same root as) prec. after *aristocrat*, *democrat*, etc.: see -CRAT.]
A member of a plutocracy; a person possessing or exercising power or influence over others by right of wealth.
■ **plutoˈcratic** *adjective* of or pertaining to a plutocrat or plutocrats; characterized by plutocracy: **M19.** **plutoˈcratical** *adjective* plutocratic **M19.** **plutoˈcratically** *adverb* **M19.** **plutocratizing** /pluːˈtɒkrətʌɪzɪŋ/ *noun* the action or process of making government, a State, etc., plutocratic **L19.**

pluto-democracy /ˌpluːtəʊdɪˈmɒkrəsi/ *noun*. Chiefly *derog*. **L19.**
[from Greek *ploutos* wealth + -O- + DEMOCRACY.]
Plutocratic government purporting to be democratic. Also, a State which is a plutocracy purporting to be a democracy.

plutogogue /ˈpluːtəgɒg/ *noun*. **L19.**
[formed as prec. + -O- + Greek *agōgos* leading, from *agein* to lead, after *demagogue*.]
A spokesman for plutocrats; a person who justifies or advocates the interests of the wealthy.

plutography /pluːˈtɒgrəfi/ *noun*. *rare*. **L20.**
[formed as prec. + -GRAPHY.]
The graphic depiction of the lives of the wealthy, considered as a literary genre.

plutolatry /pluːˈtɒlətri/ *noun*. *rare*. **L19.**
[formed as prec. + -OLATRY.]
Excessive respect for or worship of wealth.
■ **plutolater** *noun* a person having an excessive respect for or worshipping wealth **M20.**

plutology /pluːˈtɒlədʒi/ *noun*. *rare*. **M19.**
[formed as prec. + -OLOGY.]
= PLUTONOMY.
■ **plutological** *adjective* = PLUTONOMIC **E20.** **plutologist** *noun* = PLUTONOMIST **L19.**

plutomania /pluːtə(ʊ)ˈmeɪnɪə/ *noun*. *rare*. **M17.**
[formed as prec. + -MANIA.]
†**1** A mania for wealth. Only in **M17.**
2 PSYCHIATRY. A delusional belief that one possesses immense wealth. **L19.**
■ **plutomanic** /pluːtə(ʊ)ˈmanɪk/ *adjective* characterized by plutomania **M20.**

pluton /ˈpluːt(ə)n/ *noun*. **M20.**
[German, back-form. from *plutonisch* PLUTONIC *adjective*.]
GEOLOGY. An intrusive body of igneous rock formed beneath the earth's surface, *esp.* a large one.

Plutonian /pluːˈtəʊnɪən/ *adjective & noun*. **M17.**
[from Greek *Ploutōn* PLUTO *noun*¹ + -IAN.]
▶ **A** *adjective*. **1** Of or pertaining to the god Pluto; belonging to or suggestive of the underworld; infernal. **M17.**
2 GEOLOGY. = PLUTONIC *adjective* 1. **E19.**
3 Of or pertaining to the planet Pluto. **L20.**
▶ **B** *noun*. GEOLOGY. = PLUTONIST. **E19.**

plutonic /pluːˈtɒnɪk/ *adjective & noun*. **L18.**
[formed as prec. + -IC.]
▶ **A** *adjective*. **1** GEOLOGY. Pertaining to or involving the formation of rocks at great depths in the earth's crust; abyssal; *spec.* pertaining to or designating igneous rocks formed at great depths by intense heat. Also, designating, pertaining to, or advocating Plutonism. **L18.**
2 Belonging to or resembling Pluto; Plutonian. **E19.**
▶ **B** *noun*. GEOLOGY. In *pl.* Plutonic rocks. **M19.**

plutonism /ˈpluːt(ə)nɪz(ə)m/ *noun*. In sense 1 usu. **P-**. **M19.**
[from prec. + -ISM.]
GEOLOGY. **1** *Hist.* The theory that the rocks of the earth's crust were formed primarily by solidification from magma, rather than by precipitation from the sea. Cf. NEPTUNISM. **M19.**
2 Geological activity associated with the formation of plutons. **M20.**
■ **Plutonist** *noun* (*Hist.*) an advocate of Plutonism **L18.**

plutonium /pluːˈtəʊnɪəm/ *noun*. **L18.**
[Latin *Plutonium*, from Greek *Ploutōn* PLUTO *noun*¹; in sense 2 from PLUTO *noun*¹ + -IUM, after *uranium*, *neptunium*.]
†**1** A place where there are noxious or poisonous vapours. *rare*. Only in **L18.**
2 CHEMISTRY. †**a** = BARIUM. Only in **E19.** ▸**b** A radioactive metallic chemical element of the actinide series, atomic no. 94, which is produced artificially and is chemically similar to uranium, one isotope (plutonium-239) being fissile and used in nuclear weapons and reactors. (Symbol Pu.) **M20.**

plutonomy /pluːˈtɒnəmi/ *noun*. **M19.**
[from Greek *ploutos* wealth + *nomos* law, after *economy*.]
The branch of knowledge that deals with the production and distribution of wealth; economics.
■ **plutoˈnomic** *adjective* of or pertaining to plutonomy, economic **M19.** **plutonomist** *noun* an expert in or student of plutonomy, an economist **M19.**

plutonyl /ˈpluːt(ə)nʌɪl, -nɪl/ *noun*. **M20.**
[from PLUTON(IUM + -YL.]
CHEMISTRY. The ion PuO_2^{2+}. Usu. in *comb.*

pluvial /ˈpluːvɪəl/ *noun*¹. *obsolete* exc. *Hist.* **M17.**
[medieval Latin *pluviale* rain-cloak, use as noun of neut. of Latin *pluvialis*: see next.]
ECCLESIASTICAL. A long cloak worn as a ceremonial vestment; = COPE *noun*¹ 2; a similar garment worn by a monarch as a robe of state.

pluvial /ˈpluːvɪəl/ *adjective & noun*². **M17.**
[Latin *pluvialis* pertaining to rain, from *pluvia* rain, from *pluere* to rain: see -AL¹.]
▶ **A** *adjective*. **1** Of or pertaining to rain; rainy; characterized by much rain; *spec.* designating a period of relatively high average rainfall during the geological past, esp. the Pleistocene, alternating with interpluvial periods. **M17.**
2 PHYSICAL GEOGRAPHY. Caused by rain. **M19.**
▶ **B** *noun*. A pluvial period. **E20.**

pluviculture /ˈpluːvɪkʌltʃə/ *noun*. Chiefly *joc.* **E20.**
[from Latin *pluvia* rain + CULTURE *noun*, after *agriculture* etc.]
The art or branch of knowledge that deals with rain-making; the production and implementation of schemes for producing rain.
■ **pluviˈculturist** *noun* a student or practitioner of or expert in pluviculture **E20.**

pluviograph /ˈpluːvɪəgrɑːf/ *noun*. **L19.**
[from Latin *pluvia* rain + -O- + -GRAPH.]
A recording rain-gauge.

pluviometer /pluːvɪˈɒmɪtə/ *noun*. **L18.**
[formed as prec. + -OMETER.]
An instrument for measuring rainfall; a rain-gauge.
■ **pluviometric** /-əˈmetrɪk/ *adjective* of or pertaining to the measurement of rainfall; ***pluviometric coefficient***, the ratio of the mean daily rainfall of a particular month to that of the whole year: **L19.** **pluviometrical** /-əˈmetrɪk(ə)l/ *adjective* pluviometric **E19.** **pluviometrically** /-əˈmetrɪk(ə)li/ *adverb* **L19.**

Pluviose /ˈpluːvɪəʊs/ *noun*. Also ***Pluviôse*** /plyvjoːz/. **L18.**
[French *Pluviôse*, from Latin *pluviosus*: see next, -OSE¹.]
Hist. The fifth month of the French Republican calendar (introduced 1793), extending from 20 January to 18 February.

pluvious /ˈpluːvɪəs/ *adjective*. **LME.**
[Old French *pluvieus* (mod. *pluvieux*) or Latin *pluviosus*, from *pluvia* rain: see PLUVIAL *adjective*, -IOUS.]
Of, pertaining to, or characterized by rain; full of or carrying rain or moisture; rainy.
■ **pluviosity** /pluːvɪˈɒsɪti/ *noun* (*rare*) the quality of being rainy or of bringing rain; the amount of rainfall: **M19.**

Pluvius /ˈpluːvɪəs/ *adjective*. **E20.**
[Latin = rainy, causing or bringing rain.]
Designating the insurance of holidays, outdoor sports, events, etc., against disruption by bad weather. Freq. in ***Pluvius policy***.

ply /plʌɪ/ *noun*. **LME.**
[Old & mod. French *pli*, from *plier*, †*pleier*: see next.]
1 Plight, condition. Freq. in ***in good ply***, in good condition, fit; ***out of ply***, in bad condition, unfit. *Scot.* **LME.**
2 a A fold, a thickness, esp. as produced by folding cloth etc.; a strand or twist of rope, yarn, or thread; any of the layers composing a multilayer material such as plywood or laminated plastic. Freq. as 2nd elem. of comb. with specifying word indicating the number of strands or layers. **LME.** ▸**b** = PLYWOOD. **E20.**
3 A bend, crook, or curvature, esp. of the elbow or middle joint of a limb or (FALCONRY) of a hawk's wing. Now *rare* or *obsolete*. **L16.**
4 The condition of being bent or turned to one side; a twist, a turn; a bias, inclination, or tendency of mind or character. **E17.**
5 COMPUTING. The number of half-moves ahead investigated by a chess-playing program in planning the next move; a half-move investigated in such a calculation. **M20.**
2 ***three-ply***, ***two-ply***, etc. ***radial-ply***: see RADIAL *adjective* 4c.
Comb.: **ply rating** a number indicative of the strength of a tyre casing (orig. the number of cord plies in it).

ply /plʌɪ/ *verb*¹. Now *dial. rare*. Pa. t. & pple **plied** /plʌɪd/. **LME.**
[Old & mod. French *plier* alt. of Old French *pleier* (mod. *ployer*) from Latin *plicare* fold.]
1 *verb intrans.* Bend or be bent; yield (*to* pressure or movement); be pliable or yielding. *obsolete* exc. *Canad. dial.* **LME.** ▸†**b** Bend in reverence; bow. Also, bend one's body forcibly; twist, writhe. **LME–M19.**
2 *verb intrans. fig.* Yield, give way *to*; tend; comply, consent; be pliant or tractable. Now *rare* or *obsolete*. **LME.**
3 *verb trans.* Bend; fold (cloth etc.); mould or shape (a plastic substance etc.). **LME.** ▸†**b** *fig.* Influence (a person) in will or disposition; alter the sense of (a word); adapt, accommodate. **LME–M17.**

ply /plʌɪ/ *verb*². Pa. t. & pple **plied** /plʌɪd/. **LME.**
[Aphet. from APPLY *verb*.]
▶ **I 1** *verb intrans.* Employ or occupy oneself busily or steadily; work *at*. Now *rare*. **LME.**
2 *verb refl.* Devote oneself assiduously (*to*), exert oneself (*with* a weapon etc.). Also (*rare*), address oneself *to*. Long *obsolete* exc. *dial.* **LME.**
3 *verb trans.* Use or wield (a tool or weapon) vigorously; employ, exert (a faculty). **LME.** ▸**b** Devote one's energy to, practise, work at (esp. one's business or trade). **L15.**
4 *verb trans.* Orig., work away at; attack vigorously or repeatedly (*with*). Now chiefly, offer something to (a person) frequently or persistently; urge (a person) to take; supply persistently *with*. **M16.**
5 *verb trans.* Importune; repeatedly approach (a person) and present *with* something for attention. Formerly also, solicit patronage from. **L16.**

> 🕮 **1** MILTON Ere half these Authors be read (which will soon be with plying hard). *New Monthly Magazine* I plied at Cicero and Demosthenes. **3** J. KEROUAC She plied the broom around the kitchen. ***ply the labouring oar***: see LABOURING *ppl adjective*. **b** A. BROOKNER This market, in which humbler people ply their trades. *Times* They ply competitive national solutions. **4** L. STRACHEY Doctors were plying her with wine. J. LINGARD He enjoyed the coffee . . , was plied with more. **5** SHAKES. *Merch. V.* He plies the Duke at morning and at night. J. AGATE My hosts plied me with embarrassing questions.

▶ **II 6** *verb intrans.* Of a ship: beat up against the wind; tack, work to windward. Also foll. by *off and on*, *up and down*, etc. **M16.** ▸†**b** *verb trans.* Use (a tide etc.) to work a ship up a river, to windward, etc. *rare*. **M16–L17.** ▸**c** *verb intrans. gen.* Direct one's course, steer; move onwards; make *towards*. Now only *poet.* **L16.**
7 a *verb trans.* Cross (a river, ferry, etc.) by rowing, sailing, etc. **E18.** ▸**b** *verb intrans.* Esp. of a ship: travel more or less regularly to and fro *between* specified places. **E19.**
8 *verb intrans.* Of a boatman, taxi-driver, etc.: wait or attend regularly, have one's stand *at* a certain place for hire or custom. **E18.**

> 🕮 **6** MILTON To ply up and down . . with Relief where they saw Need. W. DAMPIER They always go before the Wind, being unable to Ply against it. **c** W. SCORESBY We plied towards the land. A. H. CLOUGH Upsprung the breeze, And all the darkling hours they plied. **7a** *Daily News* Bargemen who ply Father Thames by day and night. **b** V. WOOLF Ships regularly plying between London and Buenos Aires. **8** *Chambers's Journal* I must on no account ply for hire. J. MARQUAND Where the barges of forgotten emperors had plied once.

Plyglass /ˈplʌɪglɑːs/ *noun*. Also **p-**. **M20.**
[from PLY *noun* + GLASS *noun*.]
(Proprietary name for) units consisting of two or more panes of glass enclosing one or more hermetically sealed spaces, which may contain dry air or be filled with a translucent material like glass fibre.

Plym /plɪm/ *noun*. *rare*. **E20.**
[Abbreviation of PLYMOUTH.]
1 A native or inhabitant of Plymouth in SW England. *joc.* **E20.**
2 A member of the Plymouth Brethren. *colloq.* **M20.**

plymetal /ˈplʌɪmɛt(ə)l/ *noun.* E20.
[from PLY *noun* or PLY(WOOD + METAL *noun*.)]
A construction material consisting of plywood faced on both sides with aluminium.

Plymouth /ˈplɪməθ/ *noun.* E19.
[A town and port in the county of Devon in SW England.]
▶ **I** *attrib.* **1** Designating things originating in or associated with Plymouth. E19.
Plymouth Brethren: see BROTHER *noun.* **Plymouth china**, **Plymouth porcelain** a hard-paste porcelain formerly manfactured at Plymouth. **Plymouth cloak** *arch. slang* a cudgel or staff carried for protection by a person without a cloak or upper garment or undressed. **Plymouth earthenware** a coarse, brown and yellow earthenware manufactured at Plymouth in the 18th cent. **Plymouth gin** a variety of gin orig. manufactured in the west of England. ***Plymouth porcelain***: see ***Plymouth china*** above.
▶ **II** *ellipt.* **2** Plymouth porcelain. M19.
3 Plymouth gin. E20.

Plymouth Rock /plɪməθ ˈrɒk/ *noun.* M19.
[A granite boulder at Plymouth, Massachusetts, on which the Pilgrim Fathers are supposed to have stepped from the *Mayflower*.]
(A bird of) a breed of large domestic fowl of American origin, having grey plumage with blackish stripes, and yellow beak, legs, and feet.

plywood /ˈplʌɪwʊd/ *noun & adjective.* E20.
[from PLY *noun* + WOOD *noun*¹.]
▶ **A** *noun.* Board made of two or more thin layers of wood bonded together with the grain of adjacent layers crosswise to give increased strength and resistance to warping; an example of this. E20.
▶ **B** *attrib.* or as *adjective.* Of, pertaining to, or made of plywood. E20.

PM *abbreviation.*
1 Prime Minister.
2 Provost Marshal.

Pm *symbol.*
CHEMISTRY. Promethium.

p.m. *abbreviation.*
1 *Post meridiem.*
2 Post-mortem.

PMBX *abbreviation.*
Private manual branch exchange.

PMG *abbreviation.*
1 Paymaster General.
2 *Hist.* Postmaster General.

PMRAFNS *abbreviation.*
Princess Mary's Royal Air Force Nursing Service.

PMS *abbreviation.*
Premenstrual syndrome.

PMT *abbreviation.*
Premenstrual tension.

PNdB *abbreviation.*
Perceived noise decibel(s).

pneo- /ˈpniːəʊ, niːəʊ/ *combining form. rare.*
[from Greek *pneein*, *pnein* blow, breathe: see -O-.]
MEDICINE. Pertaining to breathing.
■ **pneograph** *noun* an instrument for measuring the force and duration of expiration L19.

PNEU *abbreviation.*
Parents' National Education Union.

pneu /njuː; *in sense 3 also foreign* pnø/ *noun. colloq.* E20.
[Abbreviation.]
1 Pneumonia. E20.
2 A pneumatic tyre. Usu. in *pl.* E20.
3 A letter etc. sent by the Parisian pneumatic dispatch system. E20.

pneuma /ˈnjuːmə/ *noun.* LME.
[Greek = wind, breath, spirit, that which is blown or breathed, from *pneein*, *pnein* blow, breathe.]
1 EARLY MUSIC. **a** = NEUME 1. LME. ▸**b** = NEUME 2. L19.
2 The spirit, the soul. *rare.* L19.
¶ Rare before L19.

pneumat- *combining form* see PNEUMATO-.

pneumatic /njuːˈmatɪk/ *adjective & noun.* M17.
[French *pneumatique* or Latin *pneumaticus* from Greek *pneumatikos*, from *pneumat-*, *pneuma*: see prec., -ATIC. Cf. next.]
▶ **A** *adjective.* **1** Pertaining to or operated by means of wind or (esp. compressed) air; containing compressed air. M17. ▸**b** Of, pertaining to, or characteristic of a woman with a well-rounded figure, esp. a large bosom. *joc.* E20.
2 ZOOLOGY, ANATOMY, & PHYSIOLOGY. **a** Pertaining to breath or breathing; respiratory. *rare.* L17. ▸**b** Containing or connected with air-filled cavities, as those in the bones of birds. M19. ▸**c** *Hist.* Designating or pertaining to a school of (orig. ancient Greek) physicians who held that an invisible fluid or spirit permeating the body formed the vital principle on which health depended. M19.
3 Chiefly CHRISTIAN THEOLOGY. Belonging or relating to the spirit or spiritual existence; spiritual. M18.
4 Of, relating to, or involving gases. Now *rare* exc. in ***pneumatic trough*** below. L18.
Special collocations & comb.: **pneumatic dispatch** the conveyance of letters, parcels, etc., along tubes by compression or exhaustion of air. **pneumatic drill** a heavy mechanical drill for breaking up a road surface etc. and driven by force of compressed air. **pneumatic duct** a tube connecting the swim-bladder of some fishes with the oesophagus. **pneumatic tube**: for pneumatic dispatch. **pneumatic tyre**: inflated with compressed air. **pneumatic-tyred** *adjective* fitted with pneumatic tyres. **pneumatic trough** an apparatus in which gases may be collected in jars over a surface of water or mercury.
▶ **B** *noun.* See also PNEUMATICS.
1 = PNEUMATOLOGY 1. *rare.* M19.
2 GNOSTIC PHILOSOPHY. A spiritual being of a high order. L19.
3 A pneumatic tyre. Also, a vehicle fitted with pneumatic tyres. L19.
■ **pneumatically** *adverb* L17. **pneumaˈticity** *noun* the quality or condition of being pneumatic; *esp.* (degree of) pneumatization in bones: M19.

pneumatical /njuːˈmatɪk(ə)l/ *adjective.* E17.
[formed as prec. + -ICAL.]
†**1** = PNEUMATIC *adjective* 1. E17–E19.
2 = PNEUMATIC *adjective* 4. Long *rare.* E17.
3 = PNEUMATIC *adjective* 3. Now *rare* or *obsolete.* L17.

pneumatics /njuːˈmatɪks/ *noun.* M17.
[from PNEUMATIC *adjective* after *dynamics* etc.: see -ICS.]
1 The branch of physics that deals with the mechanical properties of air and other elastic fluids or gases. M17.
2 = PNEUMATOLOGY 1. *obsolete* exc. *Hist.* L17.

pneumatique /njuːməˈtiːk, *foreign* pnømatik (*pl. same*)/ *noun.* E20.
[French: see PNEUMATIC.]
The pneumatic dispatch system in Paris; a letter etc. sent by this system.

pneumatisation *noun*, **pneumatise** *verb* vars. of PNEUMATIZATION, PNEUMATIZE.

pneumatist /ˈnjuːmətɪst/ *noun. rare.* L18.
[from PNEUMATIC *adjective* + -IST.]
Chiefly *Hist.* An advocate or adherent of the pneumatic theory of physiology.
■ **pneumatism** *noun* the theory or beliefs of the pneumatists M19.

pneumatization /ˌnjuːmətʌɪˈzeɪʃ(ə)n/ *noun.* Also **-isation.** M20.
[formed as next: see -IZATION.]
ANATOMY & BIOLOGY. The development or presence of air-filled cavities in bone or other tissue.

pneumatize /ˈnjuːmətʌɪz/ *verb trans.* Also **-ise.** M19.
[from PNEUMATIC *adjective* + -IZE.]
†**1** Blow air through (molten metal). Only in M19.
2 Provide with air-filled cavities, make pneumatic. Chiefly as ***pneumatized*** *ppl adjective.* L19.

pneumato- /ˈnjuːmətəʊ/ *combining form.* Before a vowel **pneumat-**. Cf. PNEUMO-.
[Greek, combining form of *pneuma*: see PNEUMA, -O-.]
Air, gas; breath, respiration; spirit.
■ **pneumatocele** *noun* (MEDICINE) a cyst containing air or gas; a hernia of the lung: L17. **pneuˈmatocyst** *noun* (ZOOLOGY) an air-sac in an animal body; *esp.* the gas-filled chamber of a pneumatophore: M19. **pneumaˈtometer** *noun* an instrument for measuring the volume or force of inspiration or expiration, a spirometer M19. **pneumatoˈtherapy** *noun* treatment of diseases, esp. of the lungs, by inhalation of compressed or rarefied air L19. **pneumatoˈthorax** *noun* (MEDICINE) = PNEUMOTHORAX E19.

pneumatology /njuːməˈtɒlədʒi/ *noun.* L17.
[mod. Latin *pneumatologia*, formed as PNEUMATO- + -LOGY.]
1 The branch of theology that deals with the Holy Spirit and other spiritual beings. L17. ▸**b** Psychology. *arch.* L18.
2 Any of several branches of science dealing with air and gases, esp. as regards physiological properties; pneumatics. Now *rare* or *obsolete.* M18.
■ **pneumatoˈlogical** *adjective* of or pertaining to pneumatology L18. **pneumatologist** *noun* E19.

pneumatolysis /njuːməˈtɒlɪsɪs/ *noun.* L19.
[from PNEUMATO- + -LYSIS.]
GEOLOGY. The chemical alteration of rock and formation of minerals by the action of hot magmatic gases and vapours.
■ **pneumatolˈytic** *adjective* involving or formed by pneumatolysis L19. **pneumatoˈlytically** *adverb* M20.

Pneumatomachian /njuːmətə(ʊ)ˈmeɪkɪən/ *noun & adjective.* E18.
[ecclesiastical Greek *pneumatomakhos*, formed as PNEUMATO-: see -MACHY, -AN, -IAN.]
ECCLESIASTICAL HISTORY. ▶**A** *noun.* An adversary of the Holy Spirit; *spec.* a member of a 4th-cent. sect who denied the divinity or personality of the Holy Spirit. E18.
▶ **B** *adjective.* Of, pertaining to, or characteristic of a Pneumatomachian or Pneumatomachians. E20.
■ **Pneumatomachist** /-ˈtɒməkɪst/ *noun* a Pneumatomachian M17.

pneumatophore /ˈnjuːmətəfɔː/ *noun.* M19.
[from PNEUMATO- + -PHORE.]
1 ZOOLOGY. A specialized part of a siphonophore colony containing an air-sac and serving as a float. M19.
2 BOTANY. In mangroves and similar plants of waterlogged soils, an aerial root extending from the main root, with numerous lenticels which are thought to promote the passage of oxygen. E20.

pneumatosis /njuːməˈtəʊsɪs/ *noun.* Pl. **-toses** /-ˈtəʊsiːz/. L17.
[mod. Latin from Greek *pneumatōsis* inflation: see PNEUMATO-, -OSIS.]
†**1** PHYSIOLOGY. The supposed generation of the principle of sensation and voluntary motion in the brain. *rare.* L17–E18.
2 MEDICINE. (An) accumulation of air or gas in the body; emphysema. E19.

pneumaturia /njuːməˈtjʊərɪə/ *noun.* L19.
[French *pneumaturie*, formed as PNEUMATO-, -URIA.]
MEDICINE. The passage of gas through the urethra during urination.

pneumectomy /njuːˈmɛktəmi/ *noun.* L19.
[from PNEUM(O- + -ECTOMY.]
MEDICINE. = PNEUMONECTOMY.

pneumic /ˈnjuːmɪk/ *adjective. rare.* M19.
[French *pneumique* for *pneumonique*: see PNEUMO-, -IC.]
Pertaining to the lungs, pulmonary.

pneumo- /ˈnjuːməʊ/ *combining form.*
[In sense 1 from Greek *pneuma* wind, spirit, air (see PNEUMA); in sense 2 contr. of PNEUMONO-, from Greek *pneumōn* lung: see -O-.]
1 Pertaining to or involving air or gas. Cf. PNEUMATO-.
2 Of or pertaining to the lungs. Cf. PNEUMONO-.
■ **pneumocele** *noun* (MEDICINE) (*a*) a pneumatocele; (*b*) the presence of air within the skull: M19. **pneumoconiˈosis** *noun*, pl. **-oses** /-əʊsiːz/, [Greek *konis* dust] MEDICINE a disease of the lungs produced by inhalation of dust L19. **pneumoconiˈotic** *adjective & noun*, (a person) affected with pneumoconiosis M20. **pneumoˈgastric** *adjective & noun* (ANATOMY) (*a*) *adjective* relating to the lungs and the stomach; formerly *spec.*, designating or connected with the vagus nerve; (*b*) *noun* (now *rare* or *obsolete*) the vagus nerve: M19. **pneuˈmolysis** *noun* (MEDICINE) the surgical separation of the parietal pleura from the chest wall to allow a tuberculous lung to collapse and heal E20. **pneumoperiˈcardium** *noun* (MEDICINE) (an instance of) the presence of air or gas in the pericardium M19. **pneumoperitoˈneum** *noun* (MEDICINE) (an instance of) the presence of air or gas in the peritoneal cavity (either accidentally or artificially induced) L19. **pneumoventricuˈlography** *noun* (MEDICINE) = PNEUMOENCEPHALOGRAPHY E20.

pneumococcus /njuːmə(ʊ)ˈkɒkəs/ *noun.* Pl. **-cocci** /-ˈkɒk(s)ʌɪ, -ˈkɒk(s)iː/. L19.
[mod. Latin, from PNEUMO(NIA + COCCUS.]
MEDICINE. A paired bacterium (diplococcus), *Streptococcus pneumoniae*, associated with pneumonia, and sometimes meningitis.
■ **pneumococcal**, **pneumococcic** /-ˈkɒk(s)ɪk/, **pneumococcous** *adjectives* of, pertaining to, or caused by a pneumococcus L19.

pneumocystis /njuːmə(ʊ)ˈsɪstɪs/ *noun.* M20.
[mod. Latin *Pneumocystis* (see below) formed as PNEUMO- + late Latin CYSTIS.]
MEDICINE. A parasitic protozoan, *Pneumocystis carinii*, which may inhabit the lungs. Also (in full ***pneumocystis carinii pneumonia***, ***pneumocystis carinii pneumonitis***, ***pneumocystis pneumonia***, ***pneumocystis pneumonitis***), a fatal form of pneumonia characterized by cysts in the lungs, caused by infection with this organism, esp. in immunosuppressed individuals.

pneumoencephalography /ˌnjuːməʊɛnsɛfəˈlɒgrəfi, -kɛf-/ *noun.* M20.
[from PNEUMO- + ENCEPHALOGRAPHY.]
MEDICINE. Radiography of the brain involving the displacement of cerebrospinal fluid in the ventricles by air or oxygen introduced as a contrast medium, usu. by lumbar puncture. Cf. VENTRICULOGRAPHY.
■ **pneumoenˈcephalogram** *noun* an X-ray taken by pneumoencephalography M20. **pneumoencephaloˈgraphic** *adjective* M20. **pneumoencephaloˈgraphically** *adverb* M20.

pneumogram /ˈnjuːməgram/ *noun.* E20.
[from PNEUMO- + -GRAM.]
MEDICINE. An X-ray photograph made by pneumography.

pneumograph /ˈnjuːməgrɑːf/ *noun.* L19.
[from PNEUMO- + -GRAPH.]
MEDICINE. **1** An instrument for recording the movements of the chest in respiration; a stethograph. L19.
2 = PNEUMOGRAM. M20.

pneumographic /njuːmə(ʊ)ˈgrafɪk/ *adjective.* L19.
[formed as prec. + -IC.]
MEDICINE. **1** Pertaining to or of the nature of a pneumograph or stethograph. *rare.* L19.
2 Pertaining to or involving radiographical pneumography. E20.

▪ **pneumo'graphically** *adverb* by means of pneumography M20.

pneumography /njuːˈmɒɡrəfi/ *noun.* M19.
[from PNEUMO- + -GRAPHY.]
MEDICINE. **1** (An) anatomical description of the lungs. *rare* (only in Dicts.). M19.
2 The radiography of tissues into which air or oxygen has been introduced as a contrast medium. E20.

pneumon- *combining form* see PNEUMONO-.

pneumonectomy /njuːmə(ʊ)ˈnɛktəmi/ *noun.* L19.
[from PNEUMON(O- + -ECTOMY.]
Surgical removal of a lung; an instance of this.
▪ **pneumonectomized** *adjective* that has undergone pneumonectomy M20.

pneumonia /njuːˈməʊnɪə/ *noun.* E17.
[mod. Latin from Greek, from *pneumōn*, *pneumon-* lung: see -IA[1].]
MEDICINE & VETERINARY MEDICINE. Inflammation of the lung caused by bacterial or other infection and characterized by the blocking of the alveoli with pus; a form or case of this.
double pneumonia: affecting both lungs. **single pneumonia**: affecting one lung.
Comb.: **pneumonia blouse** *colloq.* a woman's blouse of thin or light material with a low neckline.

pneumonic /njuːˈmɒnɪk/ *adjective.* L17.
[French *pneumonique* or mod. Latin *pneumonicus* from Greek *pneumonikos* of the lungs, affected with lung disease, from *pneumōn* lung: see -IC.]
MEDICINE. †**1** Pertaining to the lungs; pulmonary. *rare.* L17–E18.
2 Pertaining to, of the nature of, characterized by, or affected with pneumonia. L18.

pneumonitis /njuːməˈnʌɪtɪs/ *noun.* E19.
[mod. Latin, from Greek *pneumōn* lung + -ITIS.]
MEDICINE. Inflammation of the walls of the alveoli in the lung; pneumonia, esp. caused by a viral or unknown agent.
▪ **pneumo'nitic** *adjective* M19.

pneumono- /ˈnjuːmənəʊ, njʊˈməʊnəʊ/ *combining form.* Before a vowel **pneumon-**.
[from Greek *pneumōn*, *pneumon-* lung: see -O-. Cf. PNEUMO-.]
Of or pertaining to the lungs.
▪ **pneumonoconi'osis** *noun*, pl. **-oses** /-ˈəʊsiːz/, = PNEUMOCONIOSIS M19. **pneumonoconi'otic** *adjective & noun* = PNEUMOCONIOTIC M20. **pneumo'nolysis** *noun* = PNEUMOLYSIS M20. **pneumonoultramicro'scopicsilicovolcanoconi'osis**, **-koniosis** *noun* a factitious long word alleged to mean 'a lung disease caused by inhaling very fine ash and sand dust' M20.

pneumotachograph /njuːmə(ʊ)ˈtakəɡrɑːf/ *noun.* E20.
[from PNEUMO- + Greek *takhos* speed + -GRAPH.]
MEDICINE & PHYSIOLOGY. An apparatus for recording the rate of airflow during breathing.
▪ **'pneumotach** *noun* (*colloq.*) a pneumotachograph L20. **pneumotachogram** *noun* a record produced by a pneumotachograph E20. **pneumotacho'graphic** *adjective* of or pertaining to pneumotachography E20. **pneumota'chography** *noun* measurement with a pneumotachograph M20.

pneumothorax /njuːməʊˈθɔːraks/ *noun.* Pl. **-races** /-rəsiːz/, **-raxes**. E19.
[from PNEUMO- + THORAX.]
MEDICINE. The presence of air or gas in the pleural cavity of the thorax, caused by perforation of the chest wall or of the lung; pneumatothorax.
artificial pneumothorax pneumothorax induced diagnostically or, formerly, in the treatment of tuberculosis.

PNG *abbreviation.*
Papua New Guinea.

pnicogen /ˈpnɪkədʒ(ə)n/ *noun.* M20.
[from Greek *pnigein* choke, stifle + -O- + -GEN.]
CHEMISTRY. Any of the elements in group V of the periodic table, comprising nitrogen, phosphorus, arsenic, antimony, and bismuth.
▪ **pnictide** *noun* a binary compound of a pnicogen with a more electropositive element or radical M20.

p-n-p /piːɛnˈpiː/ *adjective.* Also **pnp**, **PNP**. M20.
[from *p*-, *n*- in P-TYPE, N-TYPE, repr. the structure.]
ELECTRONICS. Designating a semiconductor device in which an *n*-type region is sandwiched between two *p*-type regions.

pnyx /pnɪks/ *noun.* E19.
[Greek *pnux*.]
GREEK ANTIQUITIES. The public place of assembly in ancient Athens, a semicircular level cut out of the side of a little hill west of the Acropolis.

PO *abbreviation.*
1 Petty Officer.
2 Pilot Officer.
3 Postal order.
4 Post office.

Po *symbol.*
CHEMISTRY. Polonium.

†**po** *noun*[1]. OE–E16.
[Old English *pāwa*, *pēa* from Latin *pavo* (whence also Middle Low German *pāwe* (Dutch *pauw*), Old High German *pfāwo* (German *Pfau*)).]
A peacock. Also ***pocock*** (see PEACOCK), ***pohen*** (see PEAHEN).
¶ *Pocock* survives as a surname.

po /pəʊ/ *noun*[2]. *colloq.* Pl. **poes**, **pos**. L19.
[French *pot (de chambre)*.]
A chamber-pot.

po *interjection* var. of POH.

po' /pɔː/ *adjective. US dial.* L19.
[Repr. a pronunc.]
= POOR *adjective.*

p'o /pɒ/ *noun.* M19.
[Chinese *pò*.]
In Chinese philosophy: soul, spirit.

POA *abbreviation.*
Prison Officers' Association.

poa /ˈpəʊə/ *noun.* M18.
[mod. Latin from Greek = grass.]
Any grass of the genus *Poa*; meadow-grass. Also ***poa-grass***.

poach /pəʊtʃ/ *verb*[1] *trans.* LME.
[Old French *pochier* (mod. *pocher*) orig. enclose in a bag, from *poche* bag, pocket.]
Cook (an egg) without the shell in simmering, or over boiling, water; *transf.* cook (fish, fruit, etc.) by simmering in water or another liquid. Earliest as ***poached*** *ppl adjective.*
poached-egg flower, **poached-egg plant** a small Californian annual, *Limnanthes douglasii* (family Limnanthaceae), with white and yellow flowers, grown for ornament.

poach /pəʊtʃ/ *verb*[2]. Also (*dial. & techn.*) **potch** /pɒtʃ/. E16.
[Perh. from French *pocher* in spec. use. 'to pocket': see prec.]
▸ **I 1** *verb trans.* **a** Ram or roughly push together, or in a heap. Long *obsolete* exc. *dial.* E16. ▸**b** Poke *out* (the eyes). Long *rare* or *obsolete.* L16. ▸**c** Poke (a thing) with or *with* the point of a stick, a finger, a foot, etc.; stir *up* by poking. *obsolete* exc. *dial.* M17.
2 a *verb intrans.* Poke or probe (as) with a stick etc.; *fig.* intrude. *obsolete* exc. *dial.* M16. ▸**b** *verb trans.* Poke or push (a stick, a finger, a foot, etc.) into a hole etc. *obsolete* exc. *dial.* L17.
†**3 a** *verb trans.* Thrust, stab, pierce. E–M17. ▸†**b** *verb intrans.* Make a stab or thrust *at* as in fencing. *rare.* Only in E17.
▸ **II 4** *verb intrans.* Sink into wet heavy ground in walking; move with difficulty over soft ground, or through mud or mire. E17.
5 *verb trans.* Press or stamp down with the feet; trample (soft or sodden ground) into muddy holes; cut *up* (turf etc.) with hoofs. L17.
6 *verb intrans.* Of land: become sodden, miry, and full of holes by being trampled. E18.
7 *verb trans. techn.* Mix with water and reduce to a uniform consistency. L19.
▸ **III 8** *verb intrans.* **a** Encroach or trespass on the lands or rights of another in order to acquire something unlawfully or unfairly, esp. to steal game; take game or fish illegally or unfairly. Freq. foll. by *on.* E17. ▸**b** *TENNIS* etc. Play a ball in one's partner's portion of the field or court. L19.
9 *verb trans.* Trespass on (land or water), esp. in order to steal game. E18.
10 *verb trans.* Catch and carry off (game or fish) illegally; capture or appropriate illegally or unfairly. M19.

> 🕮 **8** M. E. G. DUFF The politician feels . . he is poaching on the preserves of the geographer. **9** G. CRABBE He poach'd the wood and on the warren snared. **10** R. MACAULAY He poached a . . salmon in a . . stream. H. WILSON The Treasury were trying to poach him to come as . . permanent secretary.

poacher /ˈpəʊtʃə/ *noun*[1]. In sense 3 also **potcher** /ˈpɒtʃə/. M17.
[from POACH *verb*[2] + -ER[1].]
1 A person who poaches on the lands or rights of another; a person who takes game or fish illegally or unfairly. M17.
2 a [Cf. POCHARD.] The wigeon, *Anas americana. US.* L19. ▸**b** A small marine fish covered in bony plates, of the mainly Arctic family Agonidae; a pogge. Also ***sea-poacher***. L19.
3 *PAPER-MAKING.* Each of a series of machines by which rags etc. are comminuted, washed, bleached, and reduced to pulp. L19.
1 poacher turned gamekeeper a person who now preserves the interests he or she previously attacked.
Comb.: **poacher's pocket**, **poacher pocket** a large concealed pocket in a coat.

poacher /ˈpəʊtʃə/ *noun*[2]. M19.
[from POACH *verb*[1] + -ER[1].]
A vessel or pan for poaching eggs, usu. with shallow cuplike compartments; a kettle or pan in which fish etc. can be poached.

poachy /ˈpəʊtʃi/ *adjective.* E18.
[from POACH *verb*[2] + -Y[1].]
Of land: retentive of moisture and so liable to be trampled into muddy holes; sodden, swampy.

pobby /ˈpɒbi/ *adjective.* Orig. *dial.* L19.
[from POBS: see -Y[1].]
1 Swollen, blown. L19.
2 Of food: pulpy, mushy. M20.

poblacion /poblaˈsjon, -ˈθjon/ *noun.* Pl. ***-es*** /-ɛs/. E20.
[Spanish *población* population, town, city, village.]
1 In Spain and Spanish-speaking countries: a community; a district of a town etc. E20.
2 In the Republic of the Philippines: the principal community of a district; a town that is an administrative centre. M20.

poblador /poblaˈdor/ *noun.* Pl. ***-es*** /-ɛs/. M20.
[Spanish.]
In Spanish America: a settler, a colonist; *spec.* a country person who moves to settle or squat in a town.

poblano /pɒˈblɑːnəʊ/ *noun.* Pl. **-os**. E20.
[Spanish, lit. 'of Puebla' (a state of southern Mexico).]
A large dark green chilli pepper of a mild-flavoured variety.

pobs /pɒbz/ *noun pl. dial. & nursery.* E19.
[Origin unkn.]
Porridge; soft or semi-liquid food; bread and milk.

pocan /ˈpəʊk(ə)n/ *noun.* M19.
[Perh. var. of or rel. to PUCCOON.]
Pokeweed, *Phytolacca americana*.

pochade /pɔʃad (*pl. same*), pɒˈʃɑːd/ *noun.* L19.
[French, from *pocher* sketch (roughly), blur: see -ADE.]
A rough, smudgy, or blurred sketch.
Comb.: ***pochade box*** a small portable box of colours for sketching.

pochard /ˈpəʊtʃəd, ˈpɒ-, -kəd/ *noun.* M16.
[Origin uncertain: perh. from var. of POACHER *noun*[1] or POKER *noun*[1] + *-ard* as in *mallard*.]
Any of the tribe Aythyini of diving ducks, with the legs set far back below a heavy body; *esp.* the Eurasian *Aythya ferina* (also called ***dun-bird***), *Netta rufina* (in full ***red-crested pochard***), and the American redhead, *Aythya americana*.
white-eyed pochard = ***ferruginous duck*** s.v. FERRUGINOUS 2.

poché /ˈpɒʃeɪ, *foreign* pɔʃe/ *noun.* E20.
[French, use as noun of pa. pple of *pocher* sketch.]
ARCHITECTURE. Shading on an architectural plan representing the solid parts of a building; the use of such shading.

pochette /pɒˈʃɛt/ *noun.* L19.
[French: see POCKET *noun*.]
1 A small violin, as used by French dancing-masters. Cf. KIT *noun*[2]. L19.
2 A small pocket. E20.
3 A handbag shaped like an envelope. Also ***pochette bag***. E20.

pochismo /poˈtʃizmo/ *noun.* Pl. ***-os*** /-ɔs/. M20.
[Mexican Spanish, formed as next + *-ismo* -ISM.]
A form of slang consisting of English words given a Mexican Spanish form or pronunciation; a word of this sort.

pocho /ˈpotʃo/ *noun & adjective.* Freq. *derog.* Pl. of noun ***-os*** /-ɔs/. M20.
[Mexican Spanish = Spanish *pocho* discoloured, pale, faded.]
(Designating or pertaining to) a citizen of the US of Mexican origin or a culturally Americanized Mexican.

pochoir /pɔʃwaːr/ *noun.* Pl. pronounced same. M20.
[French = stencil.]
A process used in book illustration, esp. for limited editions, in which a monochrome print is coloured by hand, using a series of stencils; a print made by this process.

pock /pɒk/ *noun & verb.*
[Old English *poc*, *pocc-* = Middle Low German, Middle Dutch *pocke* (Dutch *pok*, Low German *pocke* whence German *Pocke*), from Germanic, from base repr. also by Middle High German *pfoch*. See also POX *noun*.]
▸ **A** *noun.* Pl. **pocks**, †**pox**.
1 A small pustule or pus-filled eruption; *esp.* any of the pustules typical of chickenpox and smallpox. OE. ▸**b** A disfiguring spot or mark; a disfiguring pit or scar, a pock-mark. L19.
†**2** = POX *noun* 1. ME–M19.
▸ **B** *verb trans.* Mark with pocks or with disfiguring spots; pock-mark. M19.

> 🕮 A. CARTER The wall . . was pocked with bullet holes. D. NOBBS Lawns . . were pocked with slivers of earth cast up by worms. J. STALLWORTHY Wading shoreward / with . . bullets pocking the sea.

Pockels /ˈpɒk(ə)lz/ *noun*. **M20**.
[F. C. A. *Pockels* (1865–1913), German physicist.]
Used *attrib.* with ref. to an electro-optical effect in certain crystals similar to the Kerr effect, as ***Pockels cell***, ***Pockels effect***.

pocket /ˈpɒkɪt/ *noun & adjective*. **ME**.
[Anglo-Norman *poket(e* dim. of Old Northern French **POKE** *noun*^{1}, corresp. to Old French *pochet*, (also mod.) **POCHETTE** dim. of Old & mod. French *poche* **POUCH** *noun*: see **-ET**^{1}. Cf. **PUCKER** *verb*.]
▶ **A** *noun*. **1** A bag or sack, now esp. for hops or wool and of a particular size according to the commodity. **ME**.
2 A small bag or pouch worn on the person; *spec.* one sewn into or on clothing, or one formed by sewing three sides of a piece of material on to clothing, for carrying a purse or other small articles. **LME**.
3 [From the use of a pocket to carry money.] One's stock of cash; one's financial resources, one's private means. **E18**.
4 Each of the open-mouthed bags or pouches placed at the corners and on each side of a billiard- or snooker-table, into which the balls are driven. **M18**.
5 a *ZOOLOGY & ANATOMY*. A sac or pouchlike cavity in the body of an animal. **L18**. ▸**b** A pouchlike compartment in the cover of a book, in a suitcase, in a car door, etc. **E19**.
6 *MINING & GEOLOGY*. A cavity in a rock or stratum, freq. one filled with foreign material, esp. gold or other ore, or water; an abruptly dilated part of a vein or lode; an isolated accumulation of alluvial gold, opal, etc. **M19**.
7 A wide or deep hollow among hills or mountains; an open area surrounded by higher ground. **M19**.
8 a A position in which a competitor in a race is hemmed in by others and so has no chance of winning. **L19**. ▸**b** *AMER. FOOTBALL*. A shielded area formed by blockers from which a player attempts to pass; the group of blockers forming such a shield. **M20**.
9 A local atmospheric condition; *spec.* = ***air-pocket*** s.v. **AIR** *noun*^{1}. **E20**.
10 An isolated area or group, orig. *spec.* one held by or consisting of troops surrounded by opposing forces; a small area contrasted with or differing from its surroundings; an isolated or local concentration *of*. **E20**.

> 🕮 **2** R. FRAME From the pocket of her coat she took out a notepad. M. M. R. KHAN Not allowed to keep their hands in the pockets of their shorts. *Nursery rhyme*: Lucy Locket lost her pocket, Kitty Fisher found it; Not a penny was there in it, Only ribbon round it. ***breast-pocket***, ***hip-pocket***, etc. ***bellows pocket***, ***patch pocket***, etc. **3** N. MANDELA The cost of milk, meat and vegetables is beyond the pockets of the average family. **10** *Daily Express* Aid . . must wait not only until the . . army is beaten, but until pockets of resistance have been wiped out. T. PYNCHON A . . battle of attrition in a minor pocket developed during the advance on Rome. L. DEIGHTON Pockets of gas in the broken pipes were still blazing fiercely. ***frost pocket*** etc.

Phrases etc.: ***burn a hole in one's pocket***: see **BURN** *verb* 9b. **in a person's pocket** close to or intimate with a person; under the personal control or direction of a person; ***live in each other's pockets***, live in excessively close proximity, live in mutual dependence. **in pocket** (*a*) having money available; in possession of funds; (*b*) (following specifications of an amount of money) having that amount of money left over or as profit. ***line one's pocket***: see **LINE** *verb*^{1} 2. **out of pocket** †(*a*) having no money available; out of funds; (*b*) having lost money by a transaction. **out-of-pocket** *adjective* designating expenses incurred in cash. ***piss in a person's pocket***: see **PISS** *verb* 1. **put in one's pocket** pocket, take or keep to oneself, conceal, suppress. **put one's hand in one's pocket** spend or provide money from one's own resources. ***save one's pocket***: see **SAVE** *verb*.
▶ **B** *attrib.* or as *adjective*. Adapted or intended for carrying in a pocket; small enough to be carried in a pocket; tiny, diminutive. **L16**.
Comb. & special collocations: **pocket battleship** *Hist.* a warship armoured and equipped like, but smaller than, a battleship; **pocket beach** *PHYSICAL GEOGRAPHY* a small, narrow, sheltered beach; **pocket billiards** (*a*) a N. American type of the game pool; (*b*) *colloq.* (orig. *Schoolboys' slang*) manipulation of the male genitals by the hand through a trouser pocket; ***pocket borough***: see **BOROUGH** 3; ***pocket calculator***: see **CALCULATOR** 2b; **pocket expenses** small personal outlays of money; ***pocket gopher***: see **GOPHER** *noun*^{2} 2; **pocket handkerchief** (*a*) a handkerchief for carrying in a pocket; (*b*) a very small area (*of* land etc.); (*c*) a light sail; **pocket-hole** an opening in a garment through which the hand is put into a pocket; **pocket knife** a knife with one or more blades which fold into the handle, for carrying in a pocket; **pocket money** (*a*) money carried in the pocket for occasional expenses; (*b*) money given as an allowance to a person, esp. a child, who has no other significant income; **pocket-mouse** a small N. American rodent of the family Heteromyidae, with large cheek pouches, *esp.* one of the genus *Perognathus* (***SPINY pocket-mouse***); **pocket passer** *AMER. FOOTBALL* a player who passes the ball from a pocket; **pocket-picker** *arch.* a pickpocket; **pocket-picking** *arch.* pickpocketing; **pocket-piece** *arch.* a piece of money carried in the pocket as a lucky charm (freq. an obsolete, damaged, or spurious coin); **pocket-plum(s)** = ***plum-pockets*** s.v. **PLUM** *noun*; **pocket rot** a fungus infection causing localized decay in the trunks or roots of trees (freq. with specifying word); **pocket-size**, **pocket-sized** *adjectives* of a size suitable for carrying in the pocket; petty, small-scale; **pocket valley** *PHYSICAL GEOGRAPHY* a steep-sided usu. flat-floored valley formed by a stream which emerges at the foot of a steep slope; **pocket Venus** a small and beautiful woman; **pocket veto** *US* an indirect veto of a legislative bill by the President, a State governor, etc., by retaining the bill unsigned until it is too late for it to be dealt with during the legislative session; **pocket-watch** a watch intended to be carried in the pocket of a waistcoat, jacket, etc.
■ **pocketful** *noun* as much or as many as a pocket will hold **E17**. **pocketless** *adjective* **L19**. **pocket-like** *adjective* resembling (that of) a pocket **L19**.

pocket /ˈpɒkɪt/ *verb*. **L16**.
[from the noun.]
▶ **I** *verb trans*. **1** Put into one's pocket; confine or enclose in a small space as in a pocket. Also foll. by *up*. **L16**.
2 *fig.* Take or accept (an affront etc.) without showing resentment; submit to, endure meekly; conceal or suppress (pride, anger, or another feeling); *rare* refrain from publishing (a report, letter, etc.). Formerly also foll. by *up*. **L16**.
3 Take possession of for one's own, appropriate, esp. dishonestly. **M17**.
4 Drive (a ball) into one of the pockets of a billiard- or snooker-table. **M18**.
5 Provide with pockets. Usu. in *pass*. **L19**.
6 *MEDICINE*. Form into a pouch or cavity. *rare*. **L19**.
7 Hem in (a competitor) during a race so as to remove the chance of winning. **L19**.

> 🕮 **1** J. M. COETZEE I withdraw, locking the door behind me and pocketing the key. **3** A. DJOLETO He had pocketed two hundred pounds in a day through overpricing. **7** *Sunday Pictorial* This horse was hopelessly pocketed . . and got through too late.

▶ **II** *verb intrans*. **8** Form or pucker into pocket-like folds. Chiefly as ***pocketing*** *ppl adjective*. **E17**.
■ **pocketaˈbility** *noun* the capacity to be put or carried in a pocket **L20**. **pocketable** *adjective* able to be put or carried in a pocket **L17**. **pocketableness** *noun* (*rare*) = **POCKETABILITY** **L19**. **pocketer** *noun* **E19**.

pocketa /ˈpɒkɪtə/ *interjection & adverb*. Usu. redupl. **pocketa-pocketa**. **M20**.
[Imit.]
Repr. the regular sound of a smoothly running internal-combustion engine; with such a sound.

pocketbook /ˈpɒkɪtbʊk/ *noun*. **E17**.
[from **POCKET** *noun* + **BOOK** *noun*.]
1 A small book suitable for carrying in a pocket; *N. Amer.* a book in a cheap edition, *esp.* a paperback. **E17**.
2 A book for notes, memoranda, etc., intended to be carried in a pocket; a notebook. Also, a booklike case with compartments for papers, banknotes, etc., for carrying in a pocket; a handbag or purse for banknotes or coins. Now chiefly *US*. **L17**.
3 The female external genitals. *US slang*. **M20**.

pockety /ˈpɒkɪti/ *adjective*. **L19**.
[from **POCKET** *noun* + **-Y**^{1}.]
1 Of a mineral deposit: having the ore unevenly distributed in pockets. **L19**.
2 Of the nature of a hollow among hills or mountains; characterized by hollows. **L19**.

pockmanty /pɒkˈmanti/ *noun*. *Scot. arch.* Also **-manky** /-ˈmaŋki/. **L16**.
[Alt., after **POKE** *noun*^{1}.]
= **PORTMANTEAU** *noun* 1.

pock-mark /ˈpɒkmɑːk/ *noun & verb*. **L17**.
[from **POCK** *noun* + **MARK** *noun*^{1}.]
▶ **A** *noun*. A scar, mark, or pit left by a pustule (orig. esp. of smallpox); any disfiguring mark or depression. **L17**.

> 🕮 G. DURRELL Clay freckled with pockmarks of the falling rain. T. PYNCHON Red pockmarks on the pure white skin.

▶ **B** *verb trans*. Mark or disfigure with pock-marks (*lit.* & *fig.*). Freq. as ***pock-marked*** *ppl adjective*. **M18**.

> 🕮 V. CANNING A . . shower was pock-marking the surface of the lake. M. SPARK His . . face was pock-marked as if he had had smallpox. P. CUTTING The . . houses were pock-marked with bullet holes.

pockwood /ˈpɒkwʊd/ *noun*. *obsolete* exc. *W. Indies*. **L16**.
[from **POCK** *noun* + **WOOD** *noun*^{1}.]
The lignum-vitae tree, *Guaiacum officinale*, whose wood and gum were formerly used to treat syphilis (also ***pockwood-tree***); the wood of this tree.

pocky /ˈpɒki/ *adjective*. Now *rare*. **LME**.
[from **POCK** *noun* + **-Y**^{1}.]
1 Full of or marked with pocks or pustules; *spec.* infected with the pox (usu. syphilis). **LME**.
2 Pertaining to, or of the nature of, a pock or pustule, or the pox (usu. syphilis, occas. smallpox); syphilitic, variolous. **M16**.
■ †**pockify** *verb trans*. mark with pocks; infect with pox or syphilis: **E17–E18**. **pockiness** *noun* (*rare*) **M16**.

poco /ˈpəʊkəʊ, *foreign* ˈpoːko/ *adverb*. **E18**.
[Italian.]
MUSIC. A direction: a little, rather.

†**pocock** *noun & verb* see **PEACOCK**.

pococurante /ˌpəʊkəʊkjʊˈranti/ *noun & adjective*. Now *rare*. **M18**.
[Italian, from *poco* little + *curante* caring.]
▶ **A** *noun*. A careless, indifferent, or nonchalant person. **M18**.
▶ **B** *adjective*. Caring little; careless, indifferent, nonchalant. **E19**.
■ **pococuranteism**, **-tism** *noun* the character, spirit, or style of a pococurante; indifference; nonchalance: **M19**.

Pocomania /pəʊkə(ʊ)ˈmeɪnɪə/ *noun*. **M20**.
[Prob. Hispanicized form of local name, with 2nd elem. interpreted as **-MANIA**.]
A Jamaican religious rite combining revivalism with ancestor-worship and spirit possession; the cult in which this rite is practised.
■ **pocomaniac** *noun* an adherent of this cult **M20**.

pocosin /pəˈkəʊsɪn/ *noun*. *US*. Also **-quo-**. **M17**.
[Prob. from Algonquian *poquosin*.]
In the southern US: a tract of low swampy ground, usu. wooded; a marsh, a swamp.

poculum /ˈpɒkjʊləm/ *noun*. Pl. **-la** /-lə/. **M19**.
[Latin.]
ROMAN ANTIQUITIES. A cup, a drinking-vessel.

POD *abbreviation*.
1 Pay on delivery.
2 Post Office Department. *US*.

pod /pɒd/ *noun*^{1}. **L16**.
[Origin uncertain: perh. var. of **PAD** *noun*^{3}.]
= **PAD** *noun*^{3} 9.

pod /pɒd/ *noun*^{2}. **L17**.
[Back-form. from **PODWARE**.]
▶ **I 1** A (long) seed-vessel, esp. a dry and dehiscent one; *spec.* that of a leguminous plant, a legume. **L17**.
2 *ZOOLOGY*. A silkworm cocoon; an egg-case, esp. of a locust. **M18**.
3 A large protuberant abdomen. *dial.* **E19**.
4 A purse-net with a narrow neck for catching eels. Also ***pod-net***. **L19**.
5 *GEOLOGY*. A body of ore or rock whose length greatly exceeds its width and height. **M20**.
6 An elongated streamlined compartment attached to an aircraft and containing an engine, fuel tanks, etc.; a detachable compartment in a spacecraft; any protruding or detachable casing on or in a craft or vehicle. **M20**.
▶ **II** Cf. **POT** *noun*^{4}.
7 Marijuana. *slang*. **M20**.
Phrases: **in pod** *colloq.* pregnant.
Comb.: **pod corn**, **pod maize** a primitive variety of maize, *Zea mays* var. *tunicata*, in which the glume lengthens to envelop each kernel; **pod razor** a large razor shell, *Ensis siliqua*; **pod shell** a tellin, *Pharus legumen*, which resembles a razor shell.

pod /pɒd/ *noun*^{3}. Orig. *US*. **M19**.
[Origin unkn.]
A small herd or school of seals or whales, or occas. of other animals; a small flock of birds.

pod /pɒd/ *verb*. Infl. **-dd-**. **M18**.
[from **POD** *noun*^{2}.]
1 *verb intrans*. Bear or produce pods. **M18**.
2 *verb trans*. Gather (peas etc.) in the pod. Cf. earlier **PODDER** *noun*^{1}. **E19**.
3 *verb trans*. Hull or remove (peas etc.) from pods. **E20**.

pod- *combining form* see **PODO-**.

-pod /pɒd/ *suffix*. In some words (also) **-pode** /pəʊd/.
[Greek *pod-*, *pous* foot.]
Chiefly *ZOOLOGY*. Foot, footed, having feet of a specified kind or number, as ***arthropod***, ***cephalopod***, ***mono-pod(e)***, ***tetrapod***, etc.; ***hemipode***, ***megapode***, etc.
¶ Cf. words from **PODIUM**, as ***lamellipodium***, ***pseudopodium*** etc.

podagra /pəˈdagrə, ˈpɒdəgrə/ *noun*. Also †**-agre**. **ME**.
[Latin from Greek, from *pod-*, *pous* foot + *agra* seizure, trap, from a base meaning 'chase', 'catch'.]
MEDICINE. Gout; *spec.* gout in the foot, esp. in the big toe.
■ **podagral** *adjective* of or pertaining to gout, gouty **E19**. **podagric** *adjective & noun* (*a*) *adjective* podagral, gouty; (*b*) *noun* a sufferer from gout: **LME**. **podagrous** *adjective* podagral, gouty **M19**.

podal /ˈpəʊd(ə)l/ *adjective*. **L19**.
[formed as **-POD** + **-AL**^{1}.]
ZOOLOGY. Of or pertaining to a foot or footlike organ; pedal.

podalgia /pə(ʊ)ˈdaldʒə/ *noun*. **M19**.
[mod. Latin, from Greek *pod-*, *pous* foot: see **-ALGIA**.]
Pain in the foot, as from gout, rheumatism, etc.

podalic /pə(ʊ)ˈdalɪk/ *adjective*. **L19**.
[Irreg. from Greek *pod-*, *pous* foot, after *cephalic*.]
Of or pertaining to the feet. Chiefly in ***podalic version*** (*MEDICINE*), the turning of a foetus so as to deliver the feet first.

podargus /pəˈdɑːgəs/ *noun*. M19.
[mod. Latin *Podargus* genus name, from Greek *podargos* swift-footed.]
A greyish-brown nocturnal bird of the Australasian family Podargidae, a frogmouth; *esp.* the tawny frogmouth, *Podargus strigoides*.

podded /ˈpɒdɪd/ *adjective*. M18.
[from POD *noun*² + -ED².]
1 Bearing pods; leguminous; growing (as a seed) in a pod. Freq. as 2nd elem. of comb. M18.
2 Esp. of an aircraft engine: mounted in a pod or pods. M20.

podder /ˈpɒdə/ *noun*¹. L17.
[from POD *noun*², *verb* + -ER¹.]
A person employed in gathering peas etc. in the pod.

podder *noun*² var. of PODWARE.

†**poddinger** *noun*. L15–E19.
[Alt. of POTTINGER, perh. by assoc. with *pudding*.]
= PORRINGER 1.

poddish /ˈpɒdɪʃ/ *noun*. *obsolete* exc. *dial*. E16.
[Alt. of POTTAGE.]
(Oatmeal) porridge.

poddle *verb* see PADDLE *verb*¹.

poddy /ˈpɒdi/ *adjective, noun, & verb*. *colloq*. M19.
[from POD *noun*² + -Y¹.]
► **A** *adjective*. **1** Corpulent, obese. M19.
2 Of a calf, lamb, etc.: fed by hand. *Austral*. L19.
► **B** *noun*. **1** An unbranded calf. *Austral*. L19.
2 A calf (less commonly a lamb or foal) fed by hand. *Austral*. L19.
Comb.: **poddy-dodger** *Austral*. a person who steals unbranded calves; a cattle-rustler; **poddy-dodging** *Austral*. stealing of unbranded calves, cattle-rustling.
► **C** *verb trans*. Feed (a calf, lamb, etc.) by hand. *Austral*. L19.

podeon /ˈpɒdɪən/ *noun*. M19.
[Greek *podeōn* narrow end, from *pod-* PODO-.]
ENTOMOLOGY. The petiole of a petiolate hymenopteran.

podere /poˈdeːre/ *noun*. Pl. **-ri** /-ri/. L19.
[Italian.]
An Italian farm or estate.

podestà /podeˈstaː/ *noun*. M16.
[Italian from Latin *potestas*, *-tat-* power, authority, magistrate.]
Orig. (now *Hist.*), a governor appointed by Frederick I (Holy Roman Emperor 1155–90, and King of Germany 1152–90) over one or more cities of Lombardy; an elected chief magistrate of a medieval Italian town or republic. Later, a subordinate judge or magistrate in an Italian municipality; an administrative head of an Italian commune.

podetium /pə(ʊ)ˈdiːʃɪəm/ *noun*. Pl. **-tia** /-ʃɪə/. M19.
[mod. Latin, from Greek *pod-*, *pous* foot + arbitrary ending: see -IUM.]
BOTANY. In some lichens, a stalklike outgrowth of the thallus, esp. bearing an apothecium.

podex /ˈpəʊdɛks/ *noun*. Now *rare* or *obsolete*. L16.
[Latin.]
Orig., the buttocks. Now only ENTOMOLOGY, the pygidium.

podge /pɒdʒ/ *noun*. *dial*. & *colloq*. M19.
[Origin unkn.: parallel to earlier PUDGE *noun*². Cf. next.]
Something podgy; *spec*. a short fat person; a short thick-set animal; a plump child. Also, excess weight, fat.

podge *verb* see PUDGE *verb*.

podger /ˈpɒdʒə/ *noun*. L19.
[from PODGE *noun* + -ER¹.]
Any of various tools having the form of a short bar.

podgy /ˈpɒdʒi/ *adjective*. M19.
[from PODGE *noun* + -Y¹. Cf. PUDGY.]
Short and fat; squat; plump, fleshy.

> 🕮 J. BERGER Esther's hands are tapered . . Laura's are podgy and squat. J. WAIN A short podgy chap, legs only just long enough to reach the floor from his seat.

■ **podgily** *adverb* (*rare*) in a podgy way, to a podgy degree L19. **podginess** *noun* E20.

podia *noun pl*. see PODIUM.

podiatry /pə(ʊ)ˈdʌɪətri/ *noun*. Chiefly *N. Amer*. E20.
[from PODO- + IATRO- + -Y³.]
= CHIROPODY. Also *spec.*, a branch of chiropody that deals esp. with the bones of the foot and the mechanics of walking.
■ **podiatric** /pɒdɪˈatrɪk/ *adjective* E20. **podiatrist** *noun* E20.

podical /ˈpəʊdɪk(ə)l/ *adjective*. *rare*. L19.
[from Latin *podic-*, *podex* PODEX + -AL¹.]
ZOOLOGY. Pertaining to the podex, anal.

podiform /ˈpɒdɪfɔːm/ *adjective*. M20.
[from POD *noun*² + -I- + -FORM.]
Having the form of a pod; *spec.* designating a thick rod-shaped mineral deposit, esp. of chromite.

podite /ˈpɒdʌɪt, ˈpəʊdʌɪt/ *noun*. L19.
[from Greek *pod-*, *pous* foot + -ITE¹.]
ZOOLOGY. A leg or ambulatory limb of an arthropod, esp. of a crustacean. Usu. in compounds, as ***dactylopodite***, ***exopodite***, etc.
■ **poditic** /-ˈdɪtɪk/ *adjective* L19.

podium /ˈpəʊdɪəm/ *noun*. Pl. **-ia** /-ɪə/, (in branch I also) **-iums**. M18.
[Latin = elevated place, balcony from Greek *podion* dim. of *pod-*, *pous* foot: see -IUM.]
► **I 1** A raised platform surrounding the arena in an ancient amphitheatre. M18.
2 ARCHITECTURE. **a** A continuous projecting base or pedestal, a stylobate. L18. ►**b** A projecting lower structure around the base of a tower block. M20.
3 A raised platform or dais at the front of a hall or stage; *spec.* one occupied by the conductor of an orchestra. M20.
► **II 4** ZOOLOGY. A foot; an organ acting as a foot; *esp.* a tube-foot of an echinoderm. M19.

podley /ˈpəʊdli/ *noun*. *Scot.* Also **-ler** /-lə/, (earlier) †**-lock**. E16.
[Origin uncertain: perh. earlier form of POLLACK.]
A young saithe. Also, the pollack, *Pollachius pollachius*.

podo /ˈpəʊdəʊ, ˈpɒd-/ *noun*. Pl. **-os**. E20.
[Abbreviation of PODOCARP.]
(The timber of) any of several E. African podocarps.

podo- /ˈpɒdəʊ/ *combining form*. Before a vowel **pod-**.
[Greek, combining form of *pod-*, *pous* foot: see -O-.]
Of or pertaining to a foot or feet, or a footlike structure.
■ **podocyte** *noun* (ANATOMY) each of the epithelial cells which envelop the capillaries in a kidney glomerulus, having many irregular processes which interlock with those of the other cells to form the outer layer of the filtering apparatus M20. **podoˈcytic** *adjective* (ANATOMY) of, pertaining to, or designating a podocyte or podocytes M20. **podomere** *noun* (ZOOLOGY) each of the sections of a segmented leg or other appendage of an animal, esp. an arthropod E20. **podoscaph** *noun* (now *rare*) [Greek *skaphos* ship] (*a*) a canoe-shaped float attached to the foot, or a pair of these, for moving on water; (*b*) a boat propelled by treadles: L19. **podoˈtheca** *noun* (ZOOLOGY) the scaly sheath covering the legs and feet of a bird or reptile L19. **podoˈthecal** *adjective* of, pertaining to, or designating a podetheca L19.

podocarp /ˈpəʊdəkɑːp, ˈpɒd-/ *noun*. Also in Latin form **Podocarpus** /pɒdə(ʊ)ˈkɑːpəs/. M19.
[mod. Latin *Podocarpus* (see below), from PODO- + Greek *karpos* fruit.]
Any of various coniferous trees and shrubs, chiefly of the southern hemisphere, which constitute the genus *Podocarpus* (family Podocarpaceae), and in which the seed is surrounded by a fleshy, often brightly coloured, receptacle.

Podolian /pəˈdəʊlɪən/ *adjective*. M19.
[from *Podolia* (see below) + -AN.]
Of or pertaining to Podolia, a region in SW Ukraine.

podophyllum /pɒdəˈfɪləm/ *noun*. M18.
[mod. Latin (see below), formed as PODO- + Greek *phullon* leaf.]
Either of two plants of the genus *Podophyllum*, of the barberry family, the May-apple, *P. peltatum*, and the Himalayan *P. hexandrum*, both having large palmate leaves and a solitary white flower in a fork between them; a drug obtained from the dried rootstock of either of these plants.
■ **podophyllin** /pɒdəˈfɪlɪn/ *noun* (CHEMISTRY) a yellow bitter resin with purgative properties, obtained from the dried rhizome of podophyllum (also ***podophyllin resin***) M19.

Podsnap /ˈpɒdsnap/ *noun*. E20.
[A character in Dickens's *Our Mutual Friend* (1864–5).]
A person embodying insular complacency and self-satisfaction and refusal to face up to unpleasant facts.
■ **Podˈsnappery** *noun* the behaviour or outlook of Dickens's Mr Podsnap or of a Podsnap L19. **Podˈsnappian** *adjective* of, pertaining to, or characteristic of Dickens's Mr Podsnap or a Podsnap E20.

podsol *noun* var. of PODZOL.

podu /ˈpəʊduː/ *noun*. M20.
[Telugu.]
= KUMRI.

Podunk /ˈpəʊdʌŋk/ *adjective & noun*. M17.
[Place-name of southern New England of Algonquian origin.]
► **A** *adjective*. Designating or pertaining to a N. American Indian people formerly inhabiting an area around the Podunk River in Hartford County, Connecticut. M17.
► **B** *noun*. Pl. **-s**, same.
1 A member of this people. M19.
2 (A name for) a fictitious insignificant, out-of-the-way town; a typical small town. *US colloq*. M19.

podura /pəʊˈd(j)ʊərə/ *noun*. M19.
[mod. Latin, from Greek *pod-*, *pous* foot + *oura* tail.]
ENTOMOLOGY. A springtail, a collembolan. Now chiefly as mod. Latin genus name.
■ Also **podurid** *noun* L19.

podware /ˈpɒdwɛː/ *noun*. Long *obsolete* exc. *dial*. Also **podder** /ˈpɒdə/. LME.
[Origin unkn.]
Orig., field crops; fodder for cattle. Later, pulse plants having pods.

podzol /ˈpɒdzɒl/ *noun*. Also **-sol** /-sɒl/. E20.
[Russian, from *pod-* under + *zola* ash. Var. alt. after -SOL.]
SOIL SCIENCE. An acidic, generally infertile soil characterized by a white or grey subsurface layer resembling ash, from which minerals have been leached into a lower dark layer, and occurring esp. under coniferous woods or heaths in moist, usu. temperate climates. Formerly also, the white or grey layer alone.
■ **podˈzolic** *adjective* of the nature of a podzol or resembling one in possessing a leached layer E20. **podzoliˈzation** *noun* the leaching of bases out of the upper parts of a soil and their deposition lower down; the formation of a podzolic soil: E20. **podzolize** *verb trans. & intrans.* (cause to) become podzolic (chiefly as ***podzolized*** *ppl adjective*, ***podzolizing*** *verbal noun*) E20.

POE *abbreviation*.
Port of Entry.

poë-bird /ˈpəʊiːbəːd/ *noun*. Now *rare* or *obsolete*. Also **poy-bird**. L18.
[from Tahitian *poie* earring (with ref. to the tufts of white feathers at the throat).]
= TUI.

†**poecilitic** *adjective* see POIKILITIC.

poecilo- *combining form* see POIKILO-.

Poe-esque /pəʊˈɛsk/ *adjective*. Also **Poesque**. E20.
[from *Poe* (see below) + -ESQUE.]
Of, pertaining to, or characteristic of the American short-story writer, poet, and critic Edgar Allan Poe (1809–49) or his work.

poêlée /pwale/ *noun*. Pl. pronounced same. M19.
[French, lit. 'panful', from *poêler* cook in a pan.]
A broth or stock made with bacon and vegetables.

poem /ˈpəʊɪm/ *noun*. L15.
[Old & mod. French *poème* or Latin *poema* (Plautus) from Greek *poēma* early var. of *poiēma* work, fiction, poem, from *po(i)ein* make, create.]
1 A metrical composition of words expressing facts, thoughts, or feelings in poetical form; a self-contained piece of poetry. L15.
2 A non-metrical composition of words having some quality or qualities in common with poetry. See also ***prose-poem*** s.v. PROSE *noun*. L16.
3 *fig.* A thing (other than a composition of words) having poetic qualities. M17.

> 🕮 **1** G. P. KRAPP The poem opens with the conventional epic formula. Y. WINTERS A poem differs from a work written in prose by virtue of its being composed in verse. ***dream-vision poem***, ***epic poem***, ***love poem***, ***narrative poem***, ***praise poem***, etc. **3** C. KINGSLEY Our life will be a real poem. R. W. EMERSON Names which are poems. SYMPHONIC ***poem***. ***tone poem***: see TONE *noun*.

Comb.: **poemscape** an imaginary world envisaged in a poem.

poena /ˈpiːnə/ *noun*. Pl. **poenae** /ˈpiːniː/. M17.
[Latin.]
1 Chiefly THEOLOGY & ROMAN LAW. A punishment, a penalty. M17.
2 = IMPOSITION 4b. *School slang*. M19.
1 poena damni /ˈdamnʌɪ/ [= of loss] THEOLOGY a feeling of loss, as a punishment; the pain of loss. **poena sensus** /ˈsɛnsəs/ [= of sense] THEOLOGY a feeling of physical torment, as a punishment; the pain of sense.

Poesque *adjective* var. of POE-ESQUE.

poesy /ˈpəʊɪsi, -zi/ *noun*. *arch*. LME.
[Old & mod. French *poésie* from Proto-Romance from Latin *poesis* from Greek *po(i)ēsis* creation, poetry, poem, from *po(i)ein* make, create. See also POSY *noun*.]
1 Poetry. LME.
†**2** A poem. In early use also, any inventive or imaginative composition. LME–M19.
†**3** A motto or short inscription (often metrical, and usu. in patterned or formal language); = POSY *noun* 1. LME–L17.
†**4** A bunch of flowers, a nosegay; = POSY *noun* 2. L16–L17.

> 🕮 **1** P. SIDNEY Not ryming and versing that maketh Poesie. M. PATTISON The high-water mark of English Poesy.

poet /ˈpəʊɪt/ *noun*. ME.
[Old & mod. French *poète* from Latin *poeta* (Plautus) from Greek *po(i)ētes* maker, author, poet, from *po(i)ein* make, create.]
1 A person who composes poetry, a writer of poems, an author who writes in verse, *esp.* one distinguished by special imaginative or creative power, insight, sensibility, and faculty of expression. ME.
†**2** *gen.* An author, a writer. LME–M18.
3 An imaginative practitioner of any of the fine arts; any person possessing special powers of imagination or expression. M19.

> 🕮 **1** H. BELLOC He is a very good writer of verse; he is not exactly a poet. *fig.*: J. THOMSON O nightingale! best poet of the grove. **3** *Daily Chronicle* Schumann is a minor poet among musicians.

Phrases & comb.: **poet laureate** †(*a*) (a title, esp. one conferred by a university, given to) an eminent poet; (*b*) (with cap. initials) (the title of) a poet appointed as a member of the royal household to write poems for State occasions. **poet-laureateship** the office or position of poet laureate. **Poets' Corner** part of the south transept of Westminster Abbey, which contains the graves or monuments of several poets. **poet's narcissus** the pheasant's eye narcissus, *Narcissus poeticus*. **poet's poet** a poet whose poetry is generally considered to appeal chiefly to other poets.

■ **poe'tese** *noun* mannered style of language supposedly characteristic of poets **M20**. **poethood** *noun* (*a*) *rare* poets collectively; (*b*) the position or status of poet: **M19**. **poetless** *adjective* **L19**. **poetling** *noun* (*a*) a young poet; (*b*) a petty or inferior poet, a poetaster: **L18**. **poetship** *noun* the position or function of a poet **L18**.

poetast /ˈpəʊɪtast/ *verb intrans.* **E20**.
[Back-form. from next.]
Compose in the manner of a poetaster; write paltry or inferior verse.

poetaster /pəʊɪˈtastə/ *noun & verb.* **L16**.
[mod. Latin (Erasmus), from Latin *poeta* **POET**: see **-ASTER**.]
▶ **A** *noun.* A paltry or inferior poet; a writer of poor or trashy verse. **L16**.
▶ **B** *verb intrans.* = **POETAST**. Chiefly as ***poetastering*** *ppl adjective & verbal noun* **L17**.
■ **poetastery**, **-try** *noun* the work of a poetaster, paltry or inferior verse or versification **M19**.

poetaz /ˈpəʊɪtaz/ *noun.* Pl. same. **E20**.
[from *poe(ticus* + *taz(etta*, the specific epithets of two species of *Narcissus*.]
In full ***poetaz daffodil***, ***poetaz narcissus***. Any of a group of hybrids between *Narcissus poeticus* and *N. tazetta*, bearing two or more fragrant white or yellow flowers with a short corona.

poète maudit /pɔɛt modi/ *noun phr.* Pl. ***-s -s*** (pronounced same). **M20**.
[French, lit. 'cursed poet'.]
A poet who is insufficiently appreciated by his or her contemporaries.

poetess /ˈpəʊɪtɪs/ *noun.* **M16**.
[from **POET** + **-ESS**[1]. Cf. **POETRESS**.]
A female poet; a woman who composes poetry.

poetic /pəʊˈɛtɪk/ *adjective & noun.* **M16**.
[Old & mod. French *poétique* from Latin *poeticus* from Greek *po(i)ētikos*, from *po(i)ētēs* **POET**: see **-IC**. Cf. next.]
▶ **A** *adjective.* **1** *gen.* Of or pertaining to poets or poetry; characteristic of or appropriate to poets or poetry. **M16**.
2 Orig., that is a poet, that write(s) poetry. Now, having the imagination, sensibility, or faculty of expression of a poet; fond of poetry, able to appreciate poetry. **M17**.
3 a Composed as poetry; consisting of or written in verse. **M17**. ▸**b** Having the style or character proper to poetry as a fine art; elevated or sublime in expression. **M19**.
4 Celebrated in poetry; affording a subject for poetry. *rare*. **M18**.

> 🕮 **1** A. CAMPBELL The wealth of poetic diction at his command. A. BURGESS *The Waves*, whose poetic prose now reads . . awkwardly. *Punch* By no stretch of poetic imagination could the moon be described as companionless. ***poetic justice***: see **JUSTICE** *noun*. ***poetic licence***: see **LICENCE** *noun* 4. **2** J. AUSTEN I am not poetic enough to separate . . poetry entirely from . . Character. D. H. LAWRENCE Gazing at the sea, like a . . poetic person. **3a** *Daily News* The literary output of Félibrism has been mainly poetic. W. R. TRASK The ancients had loaded down their poetic narratives with a superfluity of similes. ***Poetic EDDA***.

▶ **B** *noun.* †**1** A poet. Only in **M17**.
2 *sing.* & in *pl.* The part of literary criticism that deals with poetry; the branch of knowledge that deals with the techniques of poetry. In *pl.* also, a treatise on poetry, *spec.* the one written by Aristotle. **E18**.
3 In *pl.* Poetic composition; the writing of poems. **M19**.
■ **poeticness** *noun* (*rare*) **M17**.

poetical /pəʊˈɛtɪk(ə)l/ *adjective.* **LME**.
[formed as prec.: see **-ICAL**.]
1 = **POETIC** *adjective* 1. Also (long *arch.*) such as is found in poetry, fictitious, imaginary, ideal. **LME**. ▸†**b** *ASTRONOMY.* Designating the rising or setting of a star relative to the position of the sun, acronychal, cosmical, heliacal. **L16–E18**.
2 a = **POETIC** *adjective* 3b. **LME**. ▸**b** = **POETIC** *adjective* 3a. **M16**.
3 = **POETIC** *adjective* 2. **L16**.
4 = **POETIC** *adjective* 4. *rare*. **L19**.

> 🕮 **1** L. STEPHEN It . . cannot be said that an eye for the main chance is inconsistent with the poetical character. E. JONG You . . think my Description is poetical, but 'tis nearer the Truth. ***poetical justice***: see **JUSTICE** *noun*. **2a** *Daily Telegraph* The soloist starts . . with a most poetical . . eleven note row. **b** ***poetical works***.

■ **poeti'cality** *noun* †(*a*) a poetic expression; (*b*) poetic quality or style: **L16**. **poetically** *adverb* (*a*) in a poetic manner, style, or form; in poetry or verse; in a way appropriate to poetry or a poet; (*b*) in relation to poetry; as respects poetry: **LME**. **poeticalness** *noun* = **POETICALITY** (b) **M19**.

poeticise *verb* var. of **POETICIZE**.

poeticism /pəʊˈɛtɪsɪz(ə)m/ *noun.* **M19**.
[from **POETIC** + **-ISM**.]
1 The composing of poetry; poeticality; an instance of this. **M19**.
2 A poetic expression; an example of poetic diction. **E20**.

poeticize /pəʊˈɛtɪsʌɪz/ *verb.* Also **-ise**. **E19**.
[from **POETIC** + **-IZE**.]
1 *verb trans.* Give a poetic character to; treat in (esp. trivial or inferior) poetry. **E19**.
2 *verb intrans.* Write or speak like a poet; compose (esp. trivial or inferior) poetry. **M19**.
¶ Cf. **POETIZE**.
■ **poeticizable** *adjective* **E20**. **poetici'zation** *noun* **E20**. **poeticizer** *noun* **M20**.

poetico- /pəʊˈɛtɪkəʊ/ *combining form.* **E19**.
[from Latin *poeticus* **POETIC**: see **-O-**.]
Forming adjectives with the sense 'poetic and', as ***poetico-metaphysical*** etc.

poeticule /pəʊˈɛtɪkjuːl/ *noun.* **L19**.
[from **POET** + **-I-** + **-CULE**.]
A petty or insignificant poet.

poetise *verb* var. of **POETIZE**.

poetism /ˈpəʊɪtɪz(ə)m/ *noun.* **M19**.
[from **POET** + **-ISM**.]
1 = **POETICISM** 1. **M19**.
2 = **POETICISM** 2. *rare*. **M19**.

poetize /ˈpəʊɪtʌɪz/ *verb.* Also **-ise**. **L16**.
[Old & mod. French *poétiser*, from *poète* **POET**: see **-IZE**.]
1 *verb intrans.* Compose poetry; write or speak in verse, or in poetic style. **L16**.
†**2** *verb trans.* Record or tell in poetry. Only in **E17**.
3 *verb trans.* Make poetic; turn into poetry; compose poetry about; write or speak poetically about. **M18**.
¶ Cf. **POETICIZE**.
■ **poeti'zation** *noun* **L19**. **poetizer** *noun* **L16**.

poetomachia /pəʊˌiːtəˈmeɪkɪə/ *noun. literary.* **E17**.
[Latinized from Greek *po(i)ētēs* **POET** + *-makhia*: see **-MACHY**.]
A quarrel or contest among poets.

†**poetress** *noun.* **LME–M18**.
[Alt. of Latin *poetris* poetess, after **-ESS**[1].]
= **POETESS**.

poetry /ˈpəʊɪtri/ *noun.* **LME**.
[medieval Latin *poetria*, from Latin *poeta* **POET**, prob. after Latin *geometria* **GEOMETRY**.]
†**1** *gen.* Imaginative or creative literature; fable, fiction. **LME–E17**.
2 The art or work of a poet; composition in verse or metrical language, or in some equivalent patterned arrangement of language; the product of this as a form of literature, poems collectively; the expression or embodiment of beautiful or elevated thought, imagination, or feeling, in language and a form adapted to stir the imagination and emotions. **LME**. ▸**b** *fig.* Something resembling or compared to poetry; poetic quality, spirit, or feeling. **M17**.
3 In *pl.* Pieces of poetry; poems collectively. *rare*. **LME**.
4 (Usu. **P-**.) (The name of) a class in a Roman Catholic school, college, or seminary, now only *spec.* the sixth class, immediately above Syntax and below Rhetoric, in certain Jesuit schools. **E17**.
Comb.: **poetry-book** a book containing a collection of poems, *esp.* one for use in schools; **poetry reading** the reading of poetry, esp. to an audience; a poetry recital; **poetry recital** a public performance of poetry; ***poetry slam***: see **SLAM** *noun*[2] 5.
■ **poetryless** *adjective* **M19**.

po-faced /pəʊˈfeɪst/ *adjective.* **M20**.
[Perh. from **POH** *interjection* or **PO** *noun*[2] + **FACED**, infl. by *poker-faced*.]
Having or assuming an expressionless or impassive face, poker-faced; priggish, smug.

poffertje /ˈpɒfətjə/ *noun.* Also ***-tjie*** /-tʃə/. **L19**.
[Dutch *poffertje*, Afrikaans *poffertjie*, from French *pouffer* blow up.]
A small light doughnut or fritter dusted with sugar, as made in the Low Countries and South Africa.

poffle /ˈpɒf(ə)l/ *noun. Scot.* **ME**.
[Origin unkn.]
A small parcel of farmland.
¶ Earliest in place-names.

P. of W. *abbreviation.*
Prince of Wales.

pogamoggan /pɒgəˈmɒg(ə)n/ *noun.* **E19**.
[Ojibwa *pakamākan* lit. 'striking instrument'.]
Hist. A kind of club, usu. a piece of stone or iron attached to a wooden handle, formerly used by some N. American Indians.

poge *noun* var. of **POGUE**.

pogey /ˈpəʊgi/ *noun. N. Amer. slang* (now chiefly *Hist.*). **L19**.
[Origin. unkn. Cf. **POKEY** *noun*[1].]
1 A hostel for the needy or disabled; a local relief centre or welfare office. **L19**.
2 Relief given to the needy from national or local funds; unemployment benefit. **M20**.

pogey bait /ˈpəʊgɪ beɪt/ *noun phr. US slang.* Also **pogie bait**. **E20**.
[Perh. from **POGY** + **BAIT** *noun*[1].]
Candy, sweets.

pogge /pɒg/ *noun.* **L17**.
[Origin unkn.]
Any of various fishes chiefly of the poacher family Agonidae; *esp.* = ***armed bullhead*** s.v. **ARMED** *adjective*[1] 1.

Poggendorff illusion /ˈpɒg(ə)ndɔːf ɪˌl(j)uːʒ(ə)n/ *noun phr.* **L19**.
[J. C. *Poggendorff* (1796–1877), German scientist.]
An optical illusion in which the two ends of a straight line whose central portion is obscured by a strip crossing at an angle seem not to be in line.

poggle *noun & adjective* var. of **PUGGLE** *noun & adjective*.

poggled *adjective* var. of **PUGGLED**.

pogie bait *noun phr.* var. of **POGEY BAIT**.

pogo /ˈpəʊgəʊ/ *noun & verb.* **E20**.
[Origin unkn.]
▶ **A** *noun.* Pl. **-os**.
1 More fully ***pogo stick***. A spring-loaded pole with rests for the feet, on which a person can jump about for amusement. **E20**.
2 In full ***pogo-dancing***. Dancing with movements suggestive of jumping on a pogo stick. **L20**.
▶ **B** *verb intrans.* Jump on or as on a pogo stick; engage in pogo-dancing. **E20**.

pogonion /pəˈgəʊnɪən/ *noun.* Now *rare*. **L19**.
[from Greek *pōgōn* beard, after *inion*.]
ANATOMY. The foremost point on the midline of the chin.

pogonophoran /pəʊgəˈnɒf(ə)r(ə)n/ *noun & adjective.* **L20**.
[from mod. Latin *Pogonophora* (see below), from Greek *pōgōn* beard: see **-PHORE**, **-AN**.]
ZOOLOGY. ▶**A** *noun.* A very long slender tube-dwelling deep-sea invertebrate of the phylum Pogonophora, lacking a mouth and gut, and subsisting mainly on the products of symbiotic bacteria. **L20**.
▶ **B** *adjective.* Of, pertaining to, or designating this phylum. **L20**.
■ **pogonophore** /pəˈgəʊnəfɔː/ *noun* = **POGONOPHORAN** *noun* **M20**. **pogonophorous** *adjective* (*rare*) = **POGONOPHORAN** *adjective* **M20**.

pogonotomy /pəʊgəˈnɒtəmi/ *noun.* **L19**.
[from Greek *pōgōn* beard + **-O-** + **-TOMY**.]
The cutting of a beard; shaving.

pogonotrophy /pəʊgəˈnɒtrəfi/ *noun.* **M19**.
[formed as prec. + **-TROPHY**.]
The cultivation or growing of a beard.

pogrom /ˈpɒgrəm, -grɒm, pəˈgrɒm/ *noun & verb.* **E20**.
[Russian = devastation, from *gromit'* destroy by violent means.]
▶ **A** *noun.* **1** An organized massacre in Russia, orig. and esp. of Jews. **E20**.
2 *gen.* An organized, officially tolerated, attack on any community or group. **E20**.
▶ **B** *verb trans.* Massacre or destroy in a pogrom. **E20**.
■ **pogromist** *noun* an organizer of or participant in a pogrom **E20**.

pogue /pəʊg/ *noun. slang.* Also **poge**. **E19**.
[Perh. rel. to **POUGH** *noun*.]
A bag, a purse, a wallet; money, takings.

pogy /ˈpəʊgi/ *noun.* Chiefly *US local*. **M19**.
[Prob. from Algonquian *pauhaugen*.]
= **MENHADEN**.

poh /pəʊ/ *interjection.* Also **po**, †**pough**. **L17**.
[Natural exclam.]
Rejecting something contemptuously.

†**pohen** *noun* var. of **PEAHEN**.

pohickory /pəʊˈhɪk(ə)ri/ *noun. US.* Long *obsolete* exc. *Hist.* Also **pokahickory** /pəʊkəˈhɪk(ə)ri/. **E17**.
[Virginia Algonquian *pawcohiccora*. Cf. **HICKORY**.]
1 A foodstuff made from pounded hickory nuts. **E17**.
†**2** = **HICKORY** *noun* 1. Only in **M17**.

pohutukawa /pə(ʊ)ˌhuːtəˈkɑːwə/ *noun.* **M19**.
[Maori.]
A New Zealand evergreen tree, *Metrosideros excelsa*, of the myrtle family, which in December and January bears crimson flowers with projecting stamens. Also called ***Christmas tree***, ***fire-tree***.

poi /pɔɪ/ *noun*[1]. **E19**.
[Polynesian: cf. **POIPOI**.]
A Hawaiian dish made from the fermented root of the taro, *Colocasia esculenta*. Also = **POIPOI**.

poi /pɔɪ/ *noun*[2]. *NZ.* **M19**.
[Maori.]
A small light ball swung rhythmically on the end of a string in Maori action songs and dances.

poiesis /pɔɪˈiːsɪs/ *noun.* M20.
[Greek *poiēsis*: see POESY.]
Creative production, esp. of art; PSYCHOLOGY the coining of neologisms, esp. by a schizophrenic.

poietic /pɔɪˈɛtɪk/ *adjective. rare.* E20.
[Greek *poiētikos*: see POETIC.]
Creative, formative, productive, active.

†**poignado** *noun.* Also **poin-**. Pl. **-o(e)s**. M16–E18.
[Alt. of PONIARD: see -ADO.]
A small dagger; a poniard.

poignancy /ˈpɔɪnjənsi/ *noun.* L17.
[from next: see -ANCY.]
The quality or fact of being poignant.
■ Also **poignance** *noun* M18.

poignant /ˈpɔɪnjənt/ *adjective.* LME.
[Old & mod. French, pres. pple of *poindre* from Latin *pungere* prick: see -ANT[1].]
†**1** Of a weapon etc.: sharp-pointed, piercing. LME–L17.
2 Sharp, pungent, or piquant to the taste or smell. LME.
3 Painfully sharp to the emotions or physical feelings; distressing; deeply moving, touching; arousing sympathy. LME.
4 Of words etc.: hurtful, sharp, stinging; severe. Occas., pleasantly pointed. *arch.* L15.
5 Stimulating to the mind or feelings, delightfully piquant. Now *rare.* M17.
†**6** Of an eye, a look: piercing, keen. L18–E19.

2 L. DURRELL By the bed the rich poignant scent of her powder. **3** D. G. ROSSETTI Creature of poignant thirst And exquisite hunger. B. TARKINGTON An unexpected poignant loneliness fell upon his nephew. *Sounds* His . . poignant experience of a broken marriage. **4** DISRAELI Poignant sarcasm. **5** N. HAWTHORNE A more poignant felicity.

■ **poignantly** *adverb* L18.

poikil- *combining form* see POIKILO-.

poikilitic /pɔɪkɪˈlɪtɪk/ *adjective.* Also †**poecilitic**. M19.
[from Greek *poikilos* variegated, various + -ITE[1] + -IC.]
†**1** GEOLOGY. (Usu. **P-**.) Designating or pertaining to the Permo-Triassic system, as mainly composed of variegated rocks. M–L19.
2 PETROGRAPHY. Of or designating the structure or texture of an igneous rock in which small crystals of one mineral are enclosed within crystals of another. L19.
■ **poikilitically** *adverb* E20.

poikilo- /ˈpɔɪkɪləʊ/ *combining form.* Before a vowel **poikil-**. Also (*rare*) in Latin form **poecilo-** /ˈpiːsɪləʊ/.
[from Greek *poikilos* variegated, various: see -O-.]
Variegated, various, variable. Freq. opp. HOMOEO-.
■ **poikiloblast** *noun* †(*a*) = POIKILOCYTE; (*b*) PETROGRAPHY each of the inclusions in a poikiloblastic rock: L19. **poikiloˈblastic** *adjective* (PETROGRAPHY) of or designating the texture of a metamorphic rock in which small crystals of an original mineral occur within crystals of its metamorphic product E20. **poikilocyte** *noun* (MEDICINE) a red blood cell of abnormal irregular shape L19. **poikilocyˈtosis** *noun* (MEDICINE) the presence of poikilocytes in the blood L19. **poikiloˈderma** *noun* (MEDICINE) a condition in which the skin atrophies and develops variegated pigmentation E20. **poikiloˈdermatous** *adjective* of or pertaining to poikiloderma M20. **poikilosˈmosis** *noun* the state or property of being poikilosmotic M20. **poikilosˈmotic** *adjective* (of an animal) that allows the concentration of solute in its body fluids to vary with that of the surrounding medium E20. **poikilosmoˈticity** *noun* = POIKILOSMOSIS M20.

poikilothermic /ˌpɔɪkɪləˈθəːmɪk/ *adjective.* L19.
[from POIKILO- + THERMIC.]
ZOOLOGY & PHYSIOLOGY. Having a body temperature that varies with the temperature of the surroundings. Opp. HOMOIOTHERMIC *adjective*.
■ **ˈpoikilotherm** *noun* a poikilothermic animal M20. **poikilothermal** *adjective* = POIKILOTHERMIC L19. **poikilothermia** *noun* = POIKILOTHERMY E20. **poikilothermous** *adjective* = POIKILOTHERMIC M20. **ˈpoikilothermy** *noun* the state or property of being poikilothermic M20.

poil /pwɑːl, *foreign* pwal/ *noun.* L16.
[French from Latin *pilus* hair.]
Orig., fabric with a nap or pile (*Scot.*); the fine hair or fur of an animal. Later, silk yarn or thread, esp. of inferior quality.
poil de chèvre /də ʃɛɪvrə, *foreign* də ʃɛːvr/ [French = *chèvre* goat, esp. she-goat]: made from goat's hair and silk.

poilu /ˈpwɑːluː, *foreign* pwaly (*pl. same*)/ *noun. slang.* E20.
[French = hairy, virile, formed as prec.]
A soldier in the French army, *esp.* one who fought in the war of 1914–18.

†**poinado** *noun* var. of POIGNADO.

Poincaré /ˈpwankareɪ, *foreign* pwɛ̃kare/ *noun.* M20.
[Jules-Henri *Poincaré* (1854–1912), French mathematician and physicist.]
MATH. & PHYSICS. Used **attrib.** and in **possess.** to designate various concepts introduced by Poincaré or arising out of his work.
Poincaré conjecture = ***Poincaré's conjecture*** below. **Poincaré cycle** (a single circuit of) a simple closed curve in the phase space of a system, representing one possible solution of the governing differential equations. **Poincaré map**, **Poincaré mapping** (*a*) a representation of the phase space of a dynamic system, indicating all possible trajectories; (*b*) = *Poincaré section* below. **Poincaré's conjecture**: that any simply connected compact three-dimensional manifold is topologically equivalent to a sphere. **Poincaré section** the intersection of a Poincaré map (in sense (a)) with a given line, plane, etc.

poinciana /pɔɪnsɪˈɑːnə/ *noun.* M18.
[mod. Latin (see below), from M. de *Poinci*, 17th-cent. French governor of the Antilles.]
Any of various tropical trees and shrubs constituting the former leguminous genus *Poinciana*, now divided between *Delonix* and *Caesalpinia*; *esp.* (more fully ***royal poinciana***) the Madagascan tree *D. regia*, with racemes of scarlet flowers, widely grown for ornament in the tropics.

poind /pɔɪnd, pɪnd/ *verb & noun. Scot.* LME.
[Var. of PIND.]
▶ **A** *verb trans.* **1** Distrain. LME.
2 Impound. M16.
▶ **B** *noun.* An act of poinding, a distraint; an animal or other chattel poinded. LME.
■ **poindable** *adjective* E16. **poinder** *noun* LME.

Poindexter /ˈpɔɪndɛkstə/ *noun. US colloq.* L20.
[Appar. from the name of one of the main characters in the comedy film *Revenge of the Nerds* (1984).]
A boringly studious or socially inept person.

poinsettia /pɔɪnˈsɛtɪə/ *noun.* M19.
[mod. Latin (see below), from J. R. *Poinsett* (1779–1851), US diplomat and amateur botanist: see -IA[1].]
A shrubby Central American spurge, *Euphorbia* (formerly *Poinsettia*) *pulcherrima*, having large scarlet bracts surrounding small greenish-yellow flowers, much cultivated (esp. at Christmas) as a house-plant.

point /pɔɪnt/ *noun*[1]. ME.
[In branch I from Old & mod. French *point* repr. Latin *punctum* use as noun of neut. pa. pple of *pungere* pierce, prick; in branch II from Old & mod. French *pointe* from Proto-Romance (medieval Latin) *puncta* use as noun of corresp. fem. pa. pple; in branch III partly from French *pointe*, partly from POINT *verb*[1]. Cf. PINT *noun*[2].]
▶ **I 1** A separate or single article, item, or clause in an extended (esp. abstract) whole; an individual part, element, or matter, a detail, a particular. ME.
2 A minute part or particle of something; the smallest or basic unit of measurement, counting, or value. ME. ▸†**b** *spec.* The smallest or a very small part *of* something; a jot, a whit; a moment, an instant. ME–E17. ▸**c** MUSIC. A short strain or snatch of melody (*arch.*); an important phrase or subject, esp. in a contrapuntal composition. LME. ▸†**d** The twelfth part of the side or radius of a quadrant etc.; *spec.* in ASTRONOMY, each of 24 (or 12) equal divisions of the diameter of the sun or moon, by which degree of obscuration in an eclipse was measured. LME–L16. ▸**e** In medieval measurement of time: the fourth (or according to some, the fifth) part of an hour. Long *obsolete* exc. *Hist.* LME. ▸**f** A unit of count in scoring in a game; a unit in appraising the qualities of a competitor or of an exhibit in a competitive show; a unit of credit towards an award or benefit; an advantage or success in an argument, discussion, or other less quantifiable context; *spec.* (*a*) PIQUET the number (or, if equal, the aggregate point value) of cards of the most numerous suit in a hand after discarding; the number scored by the player who holds that number or value; (*b*) BRIDGE a unit by which a hand is evaluated. E18. ▸**g** A recognized unit in quoting variations in price or value, as of stocks, shares, interest rates, and exchange rates (one point representing one per cent in regard to interest rates, and one point being one-hundredth of the smallest monetary unit in regard to exchange rates). E19. ▸**h** TYPOGRAPHY. A unit of measurement for type bodies, in the Continental system 0.376 mm (0.0148 inch), in the British and US system 0.351 mm (0.0138 inch). L19. ▸**i** An Australian unit in measuring rainfall, 0.01 inch. L19. ▸**j** A recognized unit of value and exchange in rationing. M20. ▸**k** A unit of weight used for diamonds and other precious stones, one hundredth of a carat (2 mg). M20.
3 A thing having definite position, without extension; a position in space, time, succession, degree, order, etc. ME. ▸†**b** *spec.* A (specified) degree of condition; plight, state. ME–M18. ▸**c** The precise time at which something happens; a particular instant or moment. ME. ▸**d** A place having definite spatial position but no extent, or of which the position alone is considered; a particular place or position, a spot; *spec.* (*a*) the spot at which a police officer or traffic warden is stationed; a rallying place or rendezvous for police, military personnel, etc.; (*b*) HUNTING a spot to which a straight run is made; a straight run from one spot to another, *esp.* a run (of a specified distance) between a find and a check or the kill. LME. ▸**e** MATH. & SCIENCE. That which is conceived as having a position, but no extent, magnitude, or dimension (as the intersection of two lines). LME. ▸**f** HERALDRY. Each of nine particular spots or places on a shield, which serve to determine the position of a charge etc. Also, an area at the base of a shield delineated by a plain or modified line. LME. ▸†**g** Each of the squares of a chessboard. LME–L15. ▸**h** A definite position in a scale; a position reached in a course; a step, stage, or degree in progress or development, or in increase or decrease; a decisive juncture; the critical moment for action. LME. ▸**i** SCULPTURE. Each of a series of holes drilled in a piece of stone or marble or on the model to be copied to the depth to which the material has to be cut away; the position of such a hole. M19. ▸**j** A socket fixed in a wall etc. connected to an electricity supply and designed to receive the plug of an electrical appliance. E20.
†**4 a** A conclusion, a completion, a culmination. ME–M19. ▸**b** The highest part or degree; the summit, the zenith, the acme. LME–E18.
5 A subject for discussion, a topic; *spec.* the essential or most important part of a discourse. ME.
6 A distinguishing mark or quality; a distinctive trait or feature; a characteristic; *spec.* a feature on the basis of which a judgement is made; in *pl.* the good features or advantages of a person or thing (chiefly in ***have one's points***, ***have its points***). LME.
7 a An end aimed at, an aim, an object; the thing a person is trying to communicate. LME. ▸†**b** A determination, a decision, a resolution. L15–M18. ▸**c** Sense, purpose, or advantage (*in* or *of* a course of action, state of affairs, etc.). Usu. in neg. & interrog. contexts. E20.
8 A minute mark on a surface, of the size or appearance of a fine puncture; a dot, a minute spot or speck. LME.
9 A dot or other small mark used in writing or printing; *spec.* (*a*) a punctuation mark; *esp.* a full stop (= ***full point*** s.v. FULL *adjective*); (*b*) in Semitic alphabets, any of various dots or small strokes associated with letters to indicate vowels or stress, to distinguish consonants, etc. (also ***diacritical point***); (*c*) = ***decimal point*** s.v. DECIMAL *adjective*; (*d*) a dot or mark used in medieval music notation. LME.
10 Lace made wholly with a needle, as opp. to bobbin-lace, needle-lace; *loosely* pillow-lace imitating that done with a needle. Also, an example of this. Freq. with specifying word. Cf. POINT *noun*[2]. M17. ▸†**b** A piece of lace used as a kerchief etc. M17–M18.
11 A marking on a Hudson Bay or Mackinaw blanket indicating weight. L18.

1 J. F. KENNEDY Did the Allies follow Germany's example? This is an important point. A. PHILLIPS Three main points of disagreement. *attrib.*: *Time* The CPI . . withheld support from Sanjay's five-point youth program. **2f** N. MAILER Men who did not have enough points to go home were sent to other outfits. *Times* The championship table . . with Wales a point ahead of France. G. BRANDRETH Points are scored for tricks. ***break-point***, ***brownie point***, ***game point***, ***match point***, etc. **3c** E. BLISHEN At a point in the afternoon we . . were told stories. P. GROSSKURTH At this point she supported her mother. **d** R. V. JONES A point . . roughly . . a mile or so south of Retford. *Horse & Hound* Caught their fox . . after a good hunt . . and a four-mile point. ***checkpoint***, etc. **h** ***boiling-point***, ***breaking-point***, ***dew-point***, ***freezing point***, ***melting point***, etc. **5** E. M. FORSTER Mr. Eagar would never come to the point. B. PYM They were getting off the point. ***debating point***. **6** J. K. JEROME Perfect in all points according . . to the Kennel Club. A. CHRISTIE Letter writing has never been one of my strong points. **7a** R. L. STEVENSON We want that treasure . . that's our point! H. JAMES Though . . Lovelock . . made a great outcry, she carried her point. **c** V. SCANNELL There's no point in telling you. N. MOSLEY What was the point of the expedition? **8** I. MCEWAN A number of small red points. **9** L. MURRAY The point of Interrogation,? The point of Exclamation,!. P. EVANS All of point one of a second. ***exclamation point***, ***floating point***, ***interrogation point***, etc. **10** ***Irish point***, ***rosaline point***, ***rose-point***, etc.

▶ **II 12** A sharp end to which something tapers, used for pricking, piercing, pointing, etc. ME.
13 The salient or projecting part of something, of a more or less tapering form, or ending in an acute angle; a tip, an apex; a sharp projection or prominence. LME. ▸**b** *spec.* A promontory, a cape; (chiefly *US*) a tapering extremity of land, rocks, woods, etc., constituting a special topographical feature, a peak of a mountain or hill. M16. ▸**c** MILITARY. A small leading party of an advanced guard. L16. ▸**d** Any of the extremities, esp. as distinguished by contrasting colour, of a dog, cat, horse, etc.; *spec.* (*a*) in *pl.*, the mane, tail, and lower limbs of a horse; (*b*) in *pl.*, the ears, face, feet, and tail-tip of certain breeds of cat, esp. Siamese; *sing.*, (with specifying word) a cat of such a breed; (*c*) *NZ* (the wool that grows on) the hocks of a sheep. M19. ▸**e** The tip of the lower jaw, esp. as a spot on which a knockout blow can be dealt. L19. ▸**f** DANCING. The tip of the toe; = POINTE. Chiefly in ***on points***. E20. ▸**g** The position at the front of a herd of cattle etc.; the position at the head of a column or wedge of troops. Freq. adverbial in ***ride point***, ***walk point***. *US.* E20.
14 a *Hist.* A tagged lace or cord for attaching hose to a doublet, lacing a bodice, and for other fastenings. LME.

▸**b** NAUTICAL. A short piece of cord attached at the lower edge of a sail for tying up a reef. M18.

15 An object or instrument consisting of or characterized by a sharp tapering end, or which pricks or pierces. L15. ▸**b** *spec.* A pointed weapon, a dagger, a pointed sword, (*arch.*); ARCHAEOLOGY a (worked) pointed flake or blade (freq. with specifying word). L15. ▸**c** Each of twelve tapered divisions on each table of a backgammon board. L16. ▸**d** PRINTING (now chiefly *Hist.*). Each of a set of short sharp pins fixed on the tympan of a press so as to perforate the sheet. L17. ▸**e** ELECTRICITY. A metallic point at which electricity is discharged or collected; in an internal-combustion engine, either of the metal pieces on a sparking plug between which the spark jumps, or either of the metal surfaces of a contact-breaker which touch to complete the circuit, (usu. in *pl.*). M18. ▸**f** A tine of a deer's horn. E19. ▸**g** Either of a pair of tapering movable rails forming a junction at which railway vehicles are directed from one set of rails to another. Usu. in *pl.* M19.

16 Each of 32 directions marked at equal distance on the circumference of a compass; the angular interval between two successive points of a compass (one-eighth of a right angle, or 11° 15′); a corresponding direction or position on the horizon. Exc. NAUTICAL usu. more fully ***point of the compass***. L15.

17 a Arresting or convincing quality in speech or writing; effectiveness, pungency. M17. ▸**b** The salient feature or effective or significant part of a story, discourse, joke, etc. Also, a witty or ingenious turn of thought. L17. ▸**c** THEATRICAL. A gesture, vocal inflection, or other piece of theatrical technique used to underline a climactic moment in a speech, characterization, etc., *esp.* one used to gain immediate applause; a moment so underlined. E19.

18 a CRICKET. (The position of) a fielder stationed a short distance on the off side of the batsman (orig. close to the point of the bat). E19. ▸**b** LACROSSE. (The position of) a player stationed a short distance in front of the goalkeeper and behind the cover-point. M19.

> 🕮 **12** R. C. SHERRIFF He . . produces a pencil and . . sharpens it to a point. T. H. WHITE If you managed to put your point through the ring . . you could canter off proudly with the ring round your spear. A. HIGGINS Five pencils with blunt points. *Embroidery* Examine the needle to see if . . the point has turned under. **13** C. GIBBON Calthorpe tapped the points of the fingers . . together. C. S. FORESTER The jagged points of glass. **b** W. IRVING A small bay within point George. M. TWAIN The big raft was . . around the point. **d** F. E. SMEDLEY A particularly fast mare . . bay, with black points. ***blue point, lilac point, seal point***, etc. **g** I. KEMP Goad walked point and I . . took the tail. **15b** ***Gravette point, Levallois point***, etc. **f** T. ROOSEVELT A fine buck of eight points. **16** J. CLAVELL The galley . . swung a few points to port. N. MONSARRAT From three points of the compass . . the guns roared. **17a** BOSWELL Anything . . worth his while to express, with any degree of point. **b** E. M. FORSTER I fail to understand the point of that remark. R. HOGGART The newer style makes my general point even more forcefully.

▸**III †19** A feat, esp. of arms, a valorous exploit; an encounter, a skirmish. LME–E17.

†20 a A hostile charge or accusation. LME–L15. ▸**b** Trial, examination, (in ***put to point***). LME–L16.

21 FALCONRY. A hawk's action in rising to a position directly over the quarry. Esp. in ***make point, make her point***. L16.

22 A pointer's or setter's act of pointing at game; the rigid attitude assumed by a pointer or setter on finding game. Chiefly in ***make a point, come to a point***. L18.

23 An indication; a hint, a suggestion. Chiefly *US*. L19.

Phrases etc.: ALL-**points**. **at all points** in every part, particular, or respect, fully, chiefly in ***armed at all points***. ***at knife-point***: see ***knife-point*** s.v. KNIFE *noun*. **at point** †(*a*) in readiness, prepared; (*b*) *arch.* = ***at the point*** below. ***at swords' points***: see SWORD *noun*. ***at that point in time***: see TIME *noun*. **at the point** on the point *of doing* something; *arch.* ready *to do*. ***at this point in time***: see TIME *noun*. **beside the point** irrelevant(ly). **case in point** a relevant instance; the instance under consideration. ***come to a point***: see COME *verb*. ***cover-point***: see COVER *verb*². CRITICAL ***point***. ***dead point***: see DEAD *adjective* etc. ***decimal point***: see DECIMAL *adjective*. ***false point***: see FALSE *adjective*. FIXED ***point***. †**from point to point** in every particular, in detail. ***full point***: see FULL *adjective*. ***get to a point where, get to the point where***: see GET *verb*. **have a point** have made a convincing or significant remark; be correct or convincing (in a particular contention). ***high point***: see HIGH *adjective*. **in point** apposite, appropriate, relevant. **in point of** in the matter of; with reference or respect to; as regards. ***in point of*** FACT. ***isoelectric point***: see ISOELECTRIC 2. ISOIONIC ***point***. ISOSBESTIC ***point***. ***Lagrangian point***: see LAGRANGIAN *adjective*. LEIDENFROST ***point***. ***low point***: see LOW *adjective*. **make a point** establish a proposition, prove a contention. **make a point of doing (something)** treat or regard the doing of something as essential or indispensable; make a special object of doing (something). ***mathematical point***: see MATHEMATICAL *adjective*. **nine points** nine points out of a supposed ten, nine tenths, nearly all, (chiefly in ***possession is nine points of the law***). ***nocking point***: see NOCK *verb* 2. NODAL ***point***. ***node point***: see NODE 6b. ***not put too fine a point (up)on it***: see FINE *adjective* & *adverb*. OBJECTIVE ***point***. **off the point** not pertinent(ly), irrelevant(ly). **on points** (*a*) BOXING according to or as a result of the points scored in a number of rounds rather than a knockout (esp. in ***beat on points, defeat on points, lose on points, win on points***); (*b*) on the basis of rationing points; (see also sense 13f above). **on the point of doing** about to do (something), on the verge of doing (something). ***peritectic point***: see PERITECTIC *adjective*. ***point of articulation***: see ARTICULATION 5. **point of departure** *fig.* the starting-point of a thought or action; an initial assumption. **point of honour** an action or circumstance affecting personal honour or reputation. ***point of inflection***: see INFLECTION 5. **point of lay** the stage of a hen's life cycle at which it is able to begin laying eggs. **point of no return** a point in a journey or enterprise at which it becomes essential or more practical to continue to the end. **point of order** an objection or query respecting correct procedure in a debate, meeting, etc. **point-of-sale** *noun* & *adjective* (designating, pertaining to, or for use at) the place at which goods are retailed. **point of sight** = ***point of station*** (c) below. **point of station** (*a*) ASTRONOMY = ***stationary point*** s.v. STATIONARY *adjective*; (*b*) SURVEYING = STATION *noun* 5; (*c*) DRAWING the point in space that represents the eye of the observer. ***point of the compass***: see sense 16 above. **point of view** the position from which a thing is viewed or regarded; a particular way of considering a matter. **point-to-point** *adjective* & *noun* (designating) an amateur steeplechase for horses, esp. hunters, over a set cross-country course. **point-to-pointer** a horse ridden or suitable for riding in point-to-points. **point-to-pointing** riding in point-to-points, point-to-point racing. ***press the point***: see PRESS *verb*¹. ***principal point***: see PRINCIPAL *adjective*. ***quarter-point***: see QUARTER *noun* 10. ***radiant point***: see RADIANT *adjective*. ***saddle point***: see SADDLE *noun* 7. ***salient point***: see SALIENT *adjective*. **score points off** get the better of in an argument etc. ***set point***: see SET *adjective*. ***solstitial point***: see SOLSTITIAL *adjective* 1. ***sore point***: see SORE *adjective*¹. †**stand on one's points**, †**stand on points**, †**stand upon (one's) points** be punctilious, be scrupulous. ***stationary point***: see STATIONARY *adjective*. ***strain a point***: see STRAIN *verb*¹. ***stretch a point***: see STRETCH *verb*. ***strong point***: see STRONG *adjective*. **take a person's point** & vars., understand the import or significance of what a person is saying; concede the truth or value of a particular contention. ***thermal death point***: see THERMAL *adjective*. **to point** *arch.* to the smallest detail; exactly, completely. **to the point** relevant(ly), apposite(ly), pertinent(ly). **to the point of** to the stage of; to such a degree or extent as to justify the name of. TRIGONOMETRICAL ***point***. ***triple point***: see TRIPLE *adjective* & *adverb*. **upon the point of doing** = ***on the point of doing*** above. **up to a point**, **up to a certain point** to a certain extent, but by no means absolutely. ***vanishing-point***: see VANISH *verb*. ***vantage-point***: see VANTAGE *noun*. ***vertical point***: see VERTICAL *adjective*. ***visual point***: see VISUAL *adjective*. ***weak point***: see WEAK *adjective*. ***work a point***: see WORK *verb*.

Comb.: **point-action** *adjective* (GRAMMAR) designating an aspect which is not durative, punctual; **point angle** the angle at a vertex of a solid; *spec.* (*a*) the angle between two opposite edges or surfaces at the tip of a tool; (*b*) the re-entrant solid angle at a vertex of an artificial cavity in a tooth; **point bar** PHYSICAL GEOGRAPHY an alluvial deposit that forms by accretion inside an expanding loop of a river; **point blanket** a Hudson Bay or Mackinaw blanket with points to indicate weight; **point block** a high building with flats, offices, etc., built around a central lift or staircase; **point break** SURFING a type of wave characteristic of a coast with a headland; **point charge** ELECTRICITY a charge regarded as concentrated in a mathematical point, without spatial extent; **point contact** the state of touching at a point only; *spec.* in ELECTRONICS, the contact of a metal point with the surface of a semiconductor so as to form a rectifying junction; **point defect** CRYSTALLOGRAPHY a defect in a crystal structure which involves only one lattice site; **point discharge** an electrical discharge in which current flows between an earthed pointed object and another at a different potential, or the surrounding gas; **point discharger** an object with a point on which discharge may occur; **point-duty** the duty of a police officer or traffic warden stationed at a crossroad or other point to control traffic etc.; **point-event** an occurrence conceived of as having a definite position in space and time but no extent or duration; **point focus** PHYSICS a focus (of a beam of light or particles, etc.) which is small enough to be considered as a point; **point ground** in lace-making, a type of plain net ground; **point group** MATH. & CRYSTALLOGRAPHY †(*a*) a set of points; (*b*) any of the 32 sets of symmetry operations which leave the origin unmoved and form the basis of the crystal classes; **point guard** BASKETBALL the back-court player who directs a team's offence; **point-instant** the minimal unit of space–time; a mere position in space–time; **point man** (*a*) *US* = POINTER 1b; (*b*) the soldier at the head of a patrol; **point mass** PHYSICS a mass regarded as concentrated in a mathematical point, without spatial extent; **point mutation** GENETICS a mutation affecting only one or very few nucleotides in a gene sequence; **point net** simple needle-lace; **point number** in a musical, a song which is integral to the action; **point paper** paper marked for making, copying, or transferring a design; **point-policeman** a policeman on point duty; **point rationing** a system of rationing whereby goods are priced in terms of points and a certain number of points are assigned to each consumer; **point shoe** a shoe with a pointed toe; a ballet shoe blocked at the toe for dancing on points; **point source** a source (as of light or sound) of negligible dimensions; **point spread** US SPORT (a forecast of) the number of points constituting the margin by which a stronger team is expected to defeat a weaker one, used for betting purposes; **points rationing** = ***point rationing*** above; **points victory, points win** a victory won on points; **point-work** BALLET dancing on points.

■ **pointage** *noun* points collectively, *spec.* the number of ration points needed to make a particular purchase M20. **pointlike** *adjective* resembling a point, occupying a very small or negligible space L20.

point /pwɛ̃/ *noun*². Pl. pronounced same. M17.
[French: see prec.]

▸**I 1** Needle-lace (cf. POINT *noun*¹ 10). Chiefly in ***point de —, point d'—*** /d(ə)/ [of], specifying a real or supposed place of manufacture, as ***point d'Alençon, point d'Angleterre, point de France, point de Paris, point de Venise***, etc. M17.

1 ***point d'esprit*** (needle-lace characterized by) a pattern of small square or oblong figures diversifying the net ground.

▸**II 2** ***point d'appui*** /dapɥi/ [= of support], a fulcrum; a strategic point. E19.

3 ***point d'orgue*** /dɔrg/, an organ-point, a pedal-point. L19.

4 ***point de repère*** /də rəpɛːr/, a point of reference. L19.

5 ***point de départ*** /də depaːr/, = ***point of departure*** s.v. POINT *noun*¹. E20.

¶ See also À POINT.

point /pɔɪnt/ *verb*¹. ME.
[Partly from Old & mod. French *pointer*, from *point*, *pointe* POINT *noun*¹; partly from POINT *noun*¹.]

▸**I 1** *verb trans.* Provide with a sharp or tapering point or points; work or fashion to a point, sharpen. ME.

2 *verb trans.* †**a** Make pungent or piquant in taste. *rare*. Only in LME. ▸**b** Give point or force to (words, actions, etc.); lend prominence, distinction, or poignancy to. E18. ▸**c** Foll. by *up*: emphasize, draw attention to. M20.

†**3** *verb trans.* Fasten or lace with tagged points or laces; decorate with points. LME–L16.

4 *verb trans.* Fill in the lines of the joints of (brickwork, a brick structure, in early use tiling) with mortar or cement, smoothed with the point of a trowel etc. Cf. earlier POINTER 1(a). LME.

†**5** *verb trans.* Prick with something sharp. LME–L16.

†**6** *verb trans.* Mark with or indicate by pricks or dots; jot down, note. LME–M17.

7 *verb trans.* Orig., make the stops or pauses required by the meaning in reading (something). Later, insert points or punctuation marks in; now chiefly *spec.* (*a*) insert signs to aid chanting in the text of (a psalm etc.); (*b*) insert points indicating vowels etc. in (written Hebrew etc.). LME. ▸**b** Mark *off* with a point or points, esp. a decimal point. E19.

8 *verb trans.* Work or deepen with a point or pointed tool. Long *rare* exc. *Scot.* M17. ▸**b** SCULPTURE. Mark (a block of stone or marble) with a series of points indicating depth to which initial working or roughing-out is to be done. M19.

9 *verb intrans.* Of an abscess: come to a head. L19.

10 *verb trans.* Insert white hairs into (a self-coloured fur) to imitate another fur. Usu. in *pass.* E20.

> 🕮 **2b** W. SANSOM Rather than pointing her . . depression, the picture comforted her. K. AMIS Stabbing at the air . . to point the turns in his argument. **4** T. CONNOR Whose dismal tower / he pointed and painted when a lad.

▸**II 11** *verb intrans.* **a** Indicate position or direction (as) by extending a finger; direct attention in a certain direction. Usu. foll. by *to*, *at*. LME. ▸**b** *fig.* Direct the mind or thought in a certain direction; hint *at*, allude *to*. Freq. foll. by *to*: suggest, be evidence of, indicate. LME.

12 *verb trans.* Indicate the place or direction of (as) by extending a finger; direct attention to, show. Now usu. foll. by *out* (with simple obj., obj. clause). L15.

13 *verb trans.* Direct or level (a finger, weapon, etc., *at*), aim (*at*); direct (a person, a person's attention or course, *to*); turn or guide in a certain direction. M16.

†**14** *verb intrans.* Project or stick *out* in a point. E17–E18.

15 *verb intrans.* **a** Have its point or length directed *to*, *towards*; lie or face in a certain direction. L17. ▸**b** Be aimed *at*, have a motion or tendency *towards*, *to do*. L18.

16 *verb intrans.* & *trans.* Of a dog: indicate the presence and position of (game etc.) by standing rigidly looking towards it; assume a rigid attitude looking towards (something). E18.

17 *verb intrans.* NAUTICAL. Of a sailing vessel: lay a course close to the wind. Also foll. by *up*. L19.

> 🕮 **11a** *Beano* Don't point—it's not nice. I. MURDOCH *Seegard* . . an almost illegible signpost said, pointing away down a muddy track. A. BROOKNER 'A piece of that,' said Yvette, pointing to a cheesecake. **b** D. H. LAWRENCE The tale . . points the other way. R. TRAVERS The cartridges and the burnt pocket-book . . pointed to murder. R. DEACON Some clues which pointed in the direction of 'Cicero'. **12** J. TEY He wrote a . . letter . . pointing out how under-privileged she had been. O. MANNING Her father had pointed out stars to her. *Scientific American* It was pointed out that enforcing such a statute would cost money. *American Poetry Review* A signpost pointing the way. **13** S. GEORGE Someone . . had pointed me in her direction. M. NA GOPALEEN The finger of scorn is pointed at you. *Independent* He was . . pointing a revolver at . . the security van. ***point the bone***: see BONE *noun*. ***point a finger at, point the finger at***: see FINGER *noun*. **15a** J. M. JEPHSON The churches . . were ordinarily built pointing to the east. P. REDGROVE It pointed always towards the sea. **16** P. V. WHITE Dogs were whining and pointing at the smells of baking meats. P. WAYRE She would point a rabbit . . without disturbing it.

Comb.: **point-and-click** *adjective* & *verb* (COMPUTING) (*a*) *adjective* (of an interface) giving the user the ability to initiate tasks by using a mouse to move a cursor over an area of the screen and clicking on it; (*b*) *verb intrans.* use a mouse in such a way; **point-and-shoot** *adjective* (PHOTOGRAPHY) of, relating to, or denoting an automatic camera which, when it is pointed at a subject and the shutter release is pressed, will take a properly exposed and focused photograph.

■ **pointable** *adjective* †(*a*) *rare* able to be pointed out, visible; (*b*) able to be (readily) pointed or aimed in a certain direction: M16.

†**point** *verb*[2] *trans.* LME.
[Aphet. from APPOINT.]
1 Determine; ordain, decree; nominate. LME–E18.
2 *verb trans.* Equip, furnish. LME–E16.

point-blank /pɔɪnt'blaŋk/ *adjective, noun, & adverb.* L16.
[App. from POINT *verb*[1] + BLANK *noun* (in sense 5).]
▶ **A** *adjective.* **1** Of a shooting-distance or range: from or within which a gun may be fired horizontally; very close to a target. Of a shot or shooting: aimed or fired from or within such a range. L16.
2 Straightforward, direct, plain, blunt. M17.

🕮 **1** G. O. TREVELYAN To crush our line with a heavy point-blank musketry fire. **2** J. CHEEVER A point-blank invitation would only get him a point-blank bitter refusal.

▶ **B** *noun.* **1** Point-blank range. L16.
†**2** A point-blank shot; point-blank shooting. E17–L18.

🕮 **1** *fig.*: SHAKES. *2 Hen. VI* Now art thou within point blank of our jurisdiction regal.

▶ **C** *adverb.* **1** With a direct aim; in a direct or horizontal line; from or within point-blank range. L16.
2 Without qualification or circumlocution; directly, bluntly; straightforwardly. L16.
†**3** Exactly (in purport or effect). E17–M18.

🕮 **2** E. WAUGH It is seldom that they are absolutely, point blank wrong. H. J. EYSENCK Fascists . . refuse point-blank any requests for cooperation. R. K. NARAYAN I told him point blank that he was welcome.

point-device /pɔɪntdɪ'vʌɪs/ *noun, adverb, & adjective.* Now *arch. & literary.* LME.
[App. repr. an Old French phr. = (*à*) *point devis* arranged properly or perfectly.]
▶ **A** *noun.* ***at point-device***, (later) ***by point-device***, perfectly; precisely; with extreme nicety or correctness. Long *rare* or *obsolete.* LME.
▶ **B** *adverb.* Completely, perfectly, to perfection; in every point. L15.
▶ **C** *adjective.* Perfectly correct, perfect; overly neat or nice; extremely precise or scrupulous. E16.

pointe /pwɛ̃t/ *noun.* Pl. pronounced same. M19.
[French: see POINT *noun*[1].]
DANCING. The tip of the toe. Also, a dance movement executed on the tips of the toes.

pointed /'pɔɪntɪd/ *adjective.* ME.
[from POINT *verb*[1], *noun*[1]: see -ED[1], -ED[2].]
▶ **I 1** Having a sharp or tapering point or points; tapering to or ending in a point. ME.
2 *Hist.* Provided with or wearing tagged points or laces. E16.
3 a Directed, aimed; marked, emphasized, clearly defined, evident. L16. ▸**b** Exact to a point; precise. E18.
4 Having point or force, penetrating, cutting. M17.
▶ **II 5** *gen.* That has been pointed. LME.
Special collocations & phrases: ***Middle Pointed***: see MIDDLE *adjective.* **pointed arch** ARCHITECTURE an arch with a pointed crown, characteristic of Gothic architecture. **pointed blanket** = ***point blanket*** s.v. POINT *noun*[1]. **pointed fox** fox fur dyed black and pointed with white hairs (to simulate silver fox).
■ **pointedly** *adverb* L17. **pointedness** *noun* M17.

pointel /'pɔɪnt(ə)l/ *noun.* ME.
[Old French = point of a spear, dim. of *pointe*: see POINT *noun*[1], -EL[2].]
1 A small pointed instrument, *spec.* one for writing or engraving. Long *obsolete* exc. *Hist.* ME.
†**2** The pistil of a flower. Orig., a stamen. L16–M19.
†**3** A small pointed or stalked organ, as a snail's tentacle, a fly's haltere. E17–E18.

pointelle /pɔɪn'tɛl/ *noun & adjective.* Also **P-**. M20.
[Prob. from POINT *noun*[1] (sense 10) or POINT *noun*[2] + French dim. suffix *-elle*: see -EL[2].]
(Designating, pertaining to, or in the style of) knitwear with eyelet-holes giving a lacy effect; (a garment or trimming) having such holes.
¶ *Pointelle* is a proprietary name.

pointer /'pɔɪntə/ *noun.* ME.
[from POINT *verb*[1] or (esp. sense 9) POINT *noun*[1] + -ER[1]. In branch II abbreviation of ***point-to-pointer*** s.v. POINT *noun*[1].]
▶ **I 1** A person who points, or who points or points out something, as †(*a*) a tiler; †(*b*) a maker of tagged points or laces for fastening clothes; (*c*) a person who does ornamental work on the backs of gloves; (*d*) a person who points furs. ME. ▸**b** A person riding at the head of a herd of cattle to keep it going in the desired direction. *US.* M19.
2 In *pl.* The two stars α and γ in Ursa Major, which are nearly in a straight line with the polestar. Also occas., the two stars α and γ in the Southern Cross, which are nearly in a line with the south celestial pole. L16.
3 a A thing used to point something out; *spec.* a rod used to point to what is delineated or written on a map, diagram, blackboard, etc. M17. ▸**b** The index hand or indicator of a clock, balance, gauge, or other instrument. M17. ▸**c** A hint, a clue; a piece of information; a suggestion. *colloq.* L19. ▸**d** COMPUTING. A variable whose value is the address of another variable. Also called ***link***. M20.
4 (An animal of) any of several breeds of large gun dog which have the characteristic of pointing at game, esp. birds, with the distinctive flat-topped muzzle while standing rigidly, often with one foot raised. E18.
5 NAUTICAL. In *pl.* Timbers sometimes fixed diagonally across a hold, to support the beams. M18.
6 Either of the two bullocks next to the pole in a team; *fig.* a schemer, a malingerer, a person who takes unfair advantage of another. Chiefly *Austral.* M19. ▸**b** A rowing boat, pointed at both ends and having a shallow draught, used by loggers. *Canad.* E20.
7 Any of various pointed tools or tools used in pointing. L19.
8 Either of two sharks of the family Lamnidae, (in full ***blue pointer***) the mako, *Isurus oxyrinchus* and (in full ***white pointer***) the white shark, *Carcharodon carcharias.* L19.
9 With prefixed numeral: a thing having so many points, a stag having horns with so many points, as ***ten-pointer***, ***fourteen-pointer***, etc. L19.
▶ **II 10** = ***point-to-pointer*** s.v. POINT *noun*[1]. L20.

pointful /'pɔɪntfʊl, -f(ə)l/ *adjective.* L19.
[from POINT *noun*[1] + -FUL.]
Full of point; apposite, relevant, pertinent.
■ **pointfulness** *noun* L19.

pointillé /pwɛ̃tije/ *adjective.* E20.
[French, pa. pple of *pointiller*: see next.]
Ornamented with designs engraved or drawn with a sharp-pointed tool or style.

pointillism /'pwantɪlɪz(ə)m/ *noun.* Also ***pointillisme*** /*also* pwɛ̃tijism/. E20.
[French *pointillisme*, from *pointiller* mark with dots, from *pointille* from Italian *puntiglio* dim. of *punto* point: see -ISM.]
1 A technique of impressionist painting in which luminous effects are produced by tiny dots of various pure colours, which become blended in the viewer's eye. E20.
2 MUSIC. The breaking up of musical texture into thematic, rhythmic, and tonal fragments. M20.

pointillist /'pwantɪlɪst/ *noun & adjective.* Also **pointilliste** /*also* pwɛ̃tijist (pl. of noun same)/. L19.
[French *pointilliste*, from *pointiller*: see prec., -IST.]
▶ **A** *noun.* A painter who uses the technique of pointillism; a composer whose music is characterized by pointillism. L19.
▶ **B** *attrib.* or as *adjective.* Of or pertaining to pointillists or pointillism. E20.
■ **pointillistic** /pwantɪ'lɪstɪk/ *adjective* E20.

pointing /'pɔɪntɪŋ/ *noun.* LME.
[from POINT *verb*[1] + -ING[1]. In branch II abbreviation of ***point-to-pointing*** s.v. POINT *noun*[1].]
▶ **I 1** The action of POINT *verb*[1]; an instance of this. LME.
2 Cement or mortar filling the joints of brickwork; the protecting facing produced by this. L18.
▶ **II 3** Point-to-point racing. L20.
Comb.: **pointing-bone** a bone, or apparatus consisting of bones, used in the Australian Aboriginal ritual of pointing the bone (see BONE *noun*); **pointing-stick** a stick used for the same purpose as a pointing-bone; †**pointing-stock** a person pointed at; an object of scorn, or ridicule.

pointless /'pɔɪntlɪs/ *adjective.* ME.
[from POINT *noun*[1] + -LESS.]
1 Without a sharp or tapering point; having a rounded or blunt end. ME.
2 Without point or force, ineffective, meaningless; without purpose or advantage, having no good effect. E18.
3 Without a point scored (in a game or contest). L19.
■ **pointlessly** *adverb* L19. **pointlessness** *noun* L19.

pointlet /'pɔɪntlɪt/ *noun. rare.* M19.
[from POINT *noun*[1] + -LET.]
A small point.
■ **pointleted** *adjective* (BOTANY) terminating in a minute point, apiculate. M19.

pointrel /'pɔɪntr(ə)l/ *noun. rare.* L17.
[from POINT *noun*[1] + dim. *-rel* as in *scoundrel*, *wastrel*, etc.]
1 = POINTEL 1. L17.
2 The pointed extremity of the lobe of a leaf. L19.

pointsman /'pɔɪntsmən/ *noun.* Pl. **-men**. M19.
[from POINT *noun*[1] + -S[1] + MAN *noun*.]
1 A person in charge of points on a railway. M19.
2 A police officer or traffic warden stationed on point-duty. L19.

pointwise /'pɔɪntwʌɪz/ *adverb & adjective.* M16.
[from POINT *noun*[1] + -WISE.]
▶ **A** *adverb.* **1** In the manner of a point; so as to form a point. M16.
2 MATH. With regard to individual points. M20.
2 pointwise convergent that converges for each individual point in a space (without reference to the space as a whole).
▶ **B** *adjective.* MATH. That is such when regarded pointwise. M20.

pointy /'pɔɪnti/ *adjective.* M17.
[from POINT *noun*[1] + -Y[1].]
Characteristically or noticeably pointed.
Comb.: **pointy-head** *US colloq.* (*derog.*) a supposed expert or intellectual; **pointy-headed** *adjective* (*US colloq., derog.*) supposedly expert or intellectual.

poipoi /'pɔɪpɔɪ/ *noun.* E19.
[Polynesian, redupl. of POI *noun*[1].]
A Polynesian dish made from fermented fruit, esp. breadfruit.

poire /pwɑː/ *noun. Canad.* (now *Hist.*). L18.
[Abbreviation of Canad. French *poire sauvage* lit. 'wild pear'.]
(The blue-black berry of) any of several N. American shrubs of the genus *Amelanchier*, of the rose family, resembling the pear in their white flowers.

poise /pɔɪz/ *noun*[1]. Also †**-ze**. LME.
[Old French *pois* (mod. *poids*), earlier *peis* PEISE *noun*, from Proto-Romance from Latin *pensum* weight, use as noun of neut. pa. pple of *pendere* weigh.]
†**1** Heaviness, weight; *fig.* importance; burdensomeness. LME–M18.
†**2** The amount that a thing weighs. LME–E18. ▸**b** A measure or standard of weight. M16–E17.
†**3** Forcible impact, momentum; a heavy blow or fall. L15–E17.
†**4** A heavy object, a weight; *fig.* a bias. M16–L19.
5 Equality of weight, balance, equilibrium; steadiness, stability; freq. *fig.*, composure, steadiness of manner. Earliest in ***equal poise***, ***even poise***. M17. ▸**b** The condition of being balanced between alternatives; a pause between opposing actions; indecision, suspense. E18. ▸**c** The way in which the body, head, etc., is poised; (elegant) carriage. L18.

🕮 **1** D. HUME To put . . these circumstances in the scale, and assign to each . . its proper poize and influence. **3** SHAKES. *Tr. & Cr.* The ram that batters down the wall, For the great swinge and rudeness of his poise. **4** GEO. ELIOT Such a hint was likely . . to give an adverse poise to Gwendolen's own thought. **5** T. HOOD Panting, at poise, upon a rocky crest! B. JOWETT The chariots of the Gods in even poise. P. G. WODEHOUSE It was not easy to shake Frances Hammond's poise. **b** POPE Stupify'd in a poize of inaction. F. LEIGHTON The poise of the flood-tide . . was only of brief duration. **c** GEO. ELIOT The backward poise of the girl's head. C. THUBRON My gait was impetuous and uncoordinated. I've never had any poise.

poise /pɔɪz/ *noun*[2]. Pl. **-s**, same. E20.
[from POISEUILLE.]
PHYSICS. A unit of dynamic viscosity in the cgs system, such that a tangential force of one dyne per sq. cm causes a velocity change of one cm per second in a liquid flowing between two parallel planes one cm apart (equal to 0.1 pascal second).

poise /pɔɪz/ *verb.* Also †**-ze**. LME.
[Old French *pois-* (earlier *peis-*: see PEISE *verb*) tonic stem of Old & mod. French *peser* from Proto-Romance from Latin *pensare* frequentative of *pendere* weigh.]
†**1** *verb trans.* Amount to in weight. LME–L16.
2 *verb trans.* Measure or estimate the weight of. Latterly *fig.*, weigh in the mind, ponder. LME–M19.
†**3** *verb trans.* **a** Add weight to; load, burden; weigh *down*, oppress; incline as by weight. L16–M18. ▸†**b** Steady or balance (as) by adding weight; ballast. M17–E18.
4 *verb trans.* **a** Weigh or balance (one thing *with* or *against* another, two things against each other). Chiefly *fig.* Now *rare.* L16. ▸†**b** Be of equal weight with (chiefly *fig.*); counterbalance; match. L16–M18. ▸**c** Place or keep in equilibrium; support, suspend; make even; balance. M17.
5 *verb trans.* **a** Hold or carry steadily or evenly; hold balanced in one's hand, on one's head, etc.; hold in position ready for action. L16. ▸**b** In *pass.* Be ready *for*, *to do*; be about *to do*. M20.
6 *verb intrans.* Be balanced or held in equilibrium; hang supported or suspended; hover; pause in readiness for action. M19.

🕮 **2** L. STERNE A thousand resolutions . . weighed, poised, and perpended. **3b** STEELE That Sobriety or Thought which poises the Heart. **4a** I. D'ISRAELI Again was Cartwright poised against Whitgift. **5** W. CHAMBERS Their favourite mode of carrying things is to poise them on the top of the head. C. JACKSON He poised his pencil, ready to write. B. ENGLAND They poised themselves to strike. **b** W. FAULKNER She looked . . like a rock, poised to plunge over a precipice. *Times* The group . . had reached the bottom of the recession . . and was poised for the upturn. **c** A. STORR The ego . . is uneasily poised between three agencies. **6** C. M. SHELDON Events that were evidently poising for a crisis.

poised /pɔɪzd/ *adjective.* M17.
[from POISE *verb*, *noun*[1]: see -ED[2], -ED[1].]
1 That has been poised; balanced, held in equilibrium etc. M17.

2 Of a person, behaviour, etc.: composed, self-assured. E20.

poiser /ˈpɔɪzə/ *noun*. LME.
[Sense 1 from Anglo-Norman *poisour* = Old French *peseor*, *peseur*, from *peser* weigh; sense 2 directly from POISE *verb*: see -ER[1].]
†**1** A person who weighs something; *spec.* an officer appointed to weigh goods. LME–M17. **2** A thing that poises or balances something; an organ used for balancing, as an insect's haltere. E19. **3** A person who holds something poised or balanced. L19.

Poiseuille /pwaˈzɔːɪ, *foreign* pwazœːj/ *noun*. L19.
[J. L. M. *Poiseuille* (1799–1869), French physiologist.]
PHYSICS. Used *attrib.* and in *possess.* to designate concepts and phenomena to do with fluid flow.
Poiseuille equation = *Poiseuille's equation* below. **Poiseuille flow** laminar or streamline flow of an incompressible viscous fluid, esp. through a long narrow cylinder. **Poiseuille's equation**: expressed the relation between the volume *V* of fluid flowing per second through a long cylinder of length *l* and radius *r* under conditions of Poiseuille flow, viz. $V = \pi r^4 p/8\eta l$, where *p* is the pressure drop over the length of the cylinder and η is the viscosity of the fluid. **Poiseuille's law**: expr. by Poiseuille's equation.

poisha /ˈpɔɪʃə/ *noun*. Pl. same. L20.
[Bengali, alt. of PAISA.]
A monetary unit of Bangladesh, equal to one-hundredth of a taka.
¶ Formerly called *paisa*.

poison /ˈpɔɪz(ə)n/ *noun*, *adjective*, & *adverb*. ME.
[Old French *puison*, (also mod.) *poison* (in Old French = magic potion) from Latin *potio(n-)* POTION.]
▸ **A** *noun*. †**1** A medicinal draught, a potion, *esp.* one prepared with a harmful drug or ingredient; an ingredient of a potion etc. Long *obsolete* exc. as below. ME. **2** Matter which causes death or injury when introduced into or absorbed by a living organism, irrespective of mechanical means or direct thermal changes, esp. when able to kill by rapid action and when taken in a small quantity; a particular substance of this kind. ME. ▸**b** Alcoholic liquor; an alcoholic drink. *colloq.* (orig. *US*). E19. **3** *fig.* **a** A doctrine, influence, etc., considered to be harmful to character, morality, or public order. Also, something which is detested. ME. ▸**b** An undesirable or detested person or persons. E20. **4 a** CHEMISTRY. A substance which destroys or reduces the activity of a catalyst. E20. ▸**b** A fission product, impurity, or additive in a nuclear reactor which interacts with neutrons and thus slows the intended reaction. M20.

> 🕮 **2** ANTHONY HUXLEY A Upas Tree . . from which the natives used to obtain a very effective poison for arrows. R. DAHL The poor thing took poison and killed herself. *SURINAME poison*. **b** P. V. WHITE My lunchtime poison is a dry martini. **name one's poison** say what drink one would like. **what's your poison?** what drink would you like? **3a** C. THIRLWALL The poison of incurable suspicion perverted every noble feeling. R. KIPLING Good-will is meat an' drink . . ill-will is poison. **b** R. BARNARD Eaten up with egotism . . . They're complete poison.

▸ **B** *adjective*. **1** Poisonous, poisoned, envenomed. In mod. use regarded as an attrib. use of the noun. M16. **2** Wicked, dangerous; hateful, objectionable. *US dial.* M19.

> 🕮 **1** M. DE LA ROCHE Her hat . . was half full of mushrooms . . . 'Aren't you afraid you will pick poison ones?' G. PALEY He sells poison chemicals.

▸ **C** *adverb*. Intensely, extremely. Chiefly *US dial.* M19.

> 🕮 M. TWAIN The funeral sermon was . . pison long and tiresome.

Comb. & special collocations: **poison-arrow frog** a small, slender, usu. brightly coloured tropical American frog of the family Dendrobatidae, with skin which secretes a virulent poison used by American Indians to coat their arrows; **poison book** = *poison register* below; **poison-bulb** any of several southern African bulbous plants of the family Amaryllidaceae, esp. *Boophane disticha*; **poison-bush** *Austral.* = *poison-plant* below; **poison elder** = *poison sumac* below; **poison gas**: see GAS *noun*[1] 3f; **poison-green** *noun & adjective* (of) a bright lurid shade of green; **poison-hemlock** *US* hemlock, *Conium maculatum*; **poison ivy** any of several trailing, climbing, or erect N. American shrubs of the genus *Rhus* (family Anacardiaceae); spec. *R. radicans*, which bears trifoliate leaves and greenish flowers and produces severe dermatitis in some individuals when touched; **poison-oak** (*a*) either of two N. American shrubs of the genus *Rhus*, *R. toxicodendron*, allied to poison ivy but always erect, and *R. diversiloba*, which has similar properties; (*b*) *loosely*, poison ivy; **poison oracle** a form of divination among the Zande in which poison is given to a fowl and inferences drawn from the effects; **poison pen** a person who writes anonymous letters with malicious, libellous, or abusive intent; *poison-pen letter*, a letter written by such a person; **poison pill** (*a*) a pill containing poison, *esp.* one which kills by rapid action and may be used to commit suicide by a captured secret agent etc.; (*b*) *transf.* any of various ploys adopted by the object of an unwelcome takeover bid to render itself unattractive to the bidder; **poison-plant** *Austral.* any of various leguminous plants poisonous to stock, esp. shrubs of the genus *Gastrolobium*, and the Darling pea, *Swainsona greyana*; **poison register**, **poisons register** a register kept by a pharmacist of the names of people to whom poison has been made available; **poison sumac** a tall N. American shrub, *Rhus vernix*, which causes dermatitis like the allied poison ivy; **poison-tree** any of various trees with poisonous properties; *esp.* the upas-tree, *Antiaris toxicaria*; **poison vine** = *poison ivy* above; **poisonwood** any of various poisonous trees and shrubs; *esp.* (*a*) = *poison sumac* above; (*b*) the related *Metopium toxiferum*, of the southern US and W. Indies.

■ **poisonful** *adjective* (*obsolete* exc. *dial.*) full of or containing poison; poisonous, deadly; corrupting: E16. **poisony** *adjective* (*rare*) containing or of the nature of poison; poisonous: L16.

poison /ˈpɔɪz(ə)n/ *verb trans.* ME.
[Old French *poisonner* give to drink, from *poison*: see the noun.]
1 Administer poison to; introduce poison into the system of; kill or injure by means of poison. ME. ▸**b** Produce deleterious changes in (the blood, a wound, a limb, etc.) by impregnation or infusion of a harmful natural agent, as bacteria, a toxin, etc. E17. **2** Impregnate, taint, or infect (air, water, etc.) with poison so as to make it harmful to life; charge or smear (a weapon) with poison. LME. **3** *fig.* **a** Corrupt, pervert morally; turn to error or evil. LME. ▸**b** Prove harmful or destructive to (an action, state, etc.); spoil (one's pleasure etc.). E17. **4** Make unfit for its purpose by some deleterious addition or application. E16. ▸**b** CHEMISTRY. Of a substance: reduce or destroy the activity of (a catalyst). E20. ▸**c** Act as a poison in (a nuclear reactor or fuel). M20.

> 🕮 **1** DRYDEN The Water-Snake . . lyes poyson'd in his Bed. V. S. PRITCHETT Mashenka had poisoned her husband. **b** *blood-poisoning*: see BLOOD *noun*. **2** B. MALAMUD You're poisoning my food to kill me off. **poisoned chalice** [Shakes. *Macb.*] *fig.* an assignment, award, honour, etc., which is likely to prove a disadvantage or source of problems to the recipient. **3a** P. TOYNBEE Their suppressed guilt poisons their minds. **b** A. KOESTLER Venality and corruption were poisoning public life. *Rugby World & Post* The game was poisoned by a stamping incident. **4** C. G. W. LOCK Their furnaces were . . 'poisoned', and rendered unfit for refining.

■ **poisonable** *adjective* †(*a*) poisonous; (*b*) able to be poisoned; subject to poison: L15. **poisoner** *noun* (*a*) a person who or (less usu.) a thing which poisons someone or something; (*b*) *Austral. & NZ slang* a cook, esp. for large numbers: LME.

poisoning /ˈpɔɪz(ə)nɪŋ/ *noun*. LME.
[from the verb.]
The action or effect of POISON *verb*; an instance of this. *blood-poisoning*, *food-poisoning*, etc.

poisonous /ˈpɔɪz(ə)nəs/ *adjective*. M16.
[from POISON *noun* + -OUS.]
1 Containing or of the nature of poison; having the quality or properties of a poison; venomous. M16. **2** *fig.* Morally destructive or corrupting; conveying an evil influence; malevolent, malignant. Also (*colloq.*), unpleasant, nasty. L16.

> 🕮 **1** *San Francisco Chronicle* Venom from the viper, a poisonous snake of Southeast Asia. P. GAY The threat of war hung . . like a poisonous fog. **2** P. BOWLES The young man smiled with poisonous mock benevolence. *Literary Review* He was, in short, a poisonous little shit.

■ **poisonously** *adverb* M17. **poisonousness** *noun* (*rare*) E18.

poissarde /pwasard/ *noun*. Pl. pronounced same. L18.
[French, fem. of *poissard* pickpocket, from *poix* pitch, tar: see -ARD.]
A Frenchwoman of the lowest social status; *esp.* (*a*) *Hist.* any of the Parisian market-women who led riots during the revolution of 1789; (*b*) a fishwife.

Poisson /ˈpwasɒn, *foreign* pwasɔ̃/ *noun*. E20.
[S. D. *Poisson* (1781–1840), French mathematician and physicist.]
MATH. Used *attrib.* and in *possess.* to designate mathematical and statistical concepts introduced or discussed by Poisson.
Poisson distribution a discrete frequency distribution which gives the probability of *x* independent events occurring in a fixed time and takes the form $e^{-m}m^x/x!$ where *m* is a parameter and $e = 2.718\ldots$ **Poisson law**, **Poisson's law**: expressed by the Poisson distribution. **Poisson's ratio** the ratio of the proportional decrease in a lateral measurement to the proportional increase in length in a sample of material that is elastically stretched.
■ **Poissonian** /pwaˈsəʊnɪən/ *adjective* of, pertaining to, or designating the Poisson distribution E20.

Poitevin /ˈpwatɪvɪn, *foreign* pwatvɛ̃ (*pl. same*)/ *noun & adjective*. M17.
[French.]
▸ **A** *noun*. A native or inhabitant of Poitou, an ancient province of central France roughly corresponding to the modern departments of Vienne, Deux-Sèvres, and Vendée, or of its capital Poitiers (now the capital of Vienne). Also, the French dialect of Poitou or Poitiers. M17.
▸ **B** *adjective*. Of, pertaining to, or characteristic of Poitou or Poitiers or the dialect spoken there. M17.

poitrel /ˈpɔɪtr(ə)l/ *noun*. L15.
[Old French *poitral*, earlier *peitral* PEYTRAL.]
Hist. = PEYTRAL.

poitrinaire /pwatrinɛːr/ *noun*. Pl. pronounced same. M19.
[French, from *poitrine* chest + *-aire*: see -ARY[1].]
A person with a chest or lung disease.

poitrinal /ˈpɔɪtrɪn(ə)l/ *noun*. L18.
[French: see PETRONEL.]
Hist. **1** = PEYTRAL. L18. **2** = PETRONEL. E19.

poivrade /pwavrad/ *noun*. L17.
[French, from *poivre* pepper: see -ADE.]
Pepper sauce. Also *poivrade sauce*.

†**poize** *verb*, *noun* vars. of POISE *noun*[1], *verb*.

pokahickory *noun* var. of POHICKORY.

pokal /pəʊˈkɑːl/ *noun*. M19.
[German from Latin *poculum* drinking-cup.]
A large German glass tankard, often with a lid.

poke /pəʊk/ *noun*[1]. ME.
[Old Northern French *poque*, *poke* (cf. Anglo-Latin *poca*) var. of Old & mod. French *poche* POUCH *noun*: cf. POCKET *noun*. Cf. also PUCKER *verb*.]
1 A bag; a small sack. Now *dial.* exc. in *pig in a poke* s.v. PIG *noun*[1]. ME. ▸**b** A bag holding a definite measure of wool, coal, meal, etc. Long *obsolete* exc. *dial.* ME. ▸**c** A pocket worn on the person. *arch.* E17. ▸**d** A purse, a wallet; a pocketbook. *N. Amer. slang.* M19. ▸**e** A roll of banknotes; money. *slang.* E20. **2** The stomach of a fish. *obsolete* exc. *dial.* ME. †**3** More fully *poke sleeve*. A long full sleeve. LME–E18. †**4** In full *poke-net*. A bag-shaped fishing net. Chiefly *Scot.* LME. **5** (Disease marked by) a baglike swelling on the neck (now only of sheep). *obsolete* exc. *dial.* E17.
Comb.: **poke-boy**: employed to collect scattered branches in hop-picking; *poke-net*: see sense 4 above; **poke-nook** *dial.* a bottom corner of a bag or sack; *one's own poke-nook*, one's own resources; **poke pudding** (*a*) (now *Scot. & dial.*) a pudding made in a poke or bag; (*b*) *Scot.* a corpulent or gluttonous person; (*derog.* or *joc.*) an English person; *poke-sleeve*: see sense 3 above.

poke /pəʊk/ *noun*[2]. M17.
[Algonquian: in sense 1 from *apooke* tobacco; in sense 2 formed as PUCCOON.]
1 Any of several plants smoked by N. American Indians, e.g. wild tobacco, *Nicotiana rustica*. *obsolete* exc. *Hist.* M17. **2 a** In full *Virginian poke*. A large-leaved succulent N. American plant, *Phytolacca americana* (family Phytolaccaceae), with racemes of small white flowers succeeded by purplish-black berries. E18. ▸**b** In full *Indian poke*. The false hellebore of N. America, *Veratrum viride*. M18.
Comb.: **poke-berry** the berry of Virginian poke, which yields a red dye; the plant itself; **poke-greens** the young leaves of Virginian poke used as a vegetable; **poke-root** (the root of) Indian poke; **poke-salad** = *poke-greens* above; **pokeweed** any herbaceous plant of the chiefly tropical genus *Phytolacca*; *spec.* = sense 2a above.

poke /pəʊk/ *noun*[3]. L18.
[Prob. from POKE *verb*[1].]
1 A projecting brim or front of a woman's bonnet or hat. L18. **2** In full *poke-bonnet*. A bonnet with a projecting brim. E19.

poke /pəʊk/ *noun*[4]. L18.
[from POKE *verb*[1].]
1 An act of poking; a thrust, a push, a nudge; *colloq.* a blow with the fist. L18. ▸**b** CRICKET. A stroke made by jabbing at the ball. M19. **2** A contrivance fastened on an animal to prevent it from breaking through fences. E19. **3** An act of sexual intercourse; a woman considered as a sexual partner. *coarse slang.* E20. **4** Power (esp. of a car), horsepower; strength, vigour. *slang.* M20. **5** COMPUTING. (Usu. **POKE**.) A statement or function in BASIC for altering the contents of a specified memory location. Cf. PEEK *noun*[1] 2. L20.

> 🕮 **1** L. ARMSTRONG The captain and some of the crew wanted to take a poke at him. M. WARNER The Civil Guard ordered them down with a poke of their cudgels. R. HILL Let's drop in at your place and have a poke around. **better than a poke in the eye**, **better than a poke in the eye with a sharp stick**, etc., *colloq.* minimally desirable; *iron.* excellent. **3** *Listener* Turning a series of squalid pokes into . . honourable combats. **4** R. T. BICKERS With all that extra poke under the bonnet, Q It delivers its five watts with a stridency and range which . . compensate for lack of poke.

Comb.: **poke-check** ICE HOCKEY a defensive play made by poking the puck off an opposing player's stick; **poke-out** (*a*) an act of poking out; (*b*) *slang* a parcel of food given to a tramp etc.

poke /pəʊk/ *verb*[1]. In senses 8, 15 usu. **POKE**, infl. **POKEing** etc. ME.
[Middle & mod. Low German, Middle & mod. Dutch *poken*, of unkn. origin. Cf. PUCK *verb*.]
▸ **I** *verb trans.* **1** Thrust or push with a hand, an arm, the point of a stick, etc., usu. so as to cause action or move-

ment; stir or jab (a fire) with a poker etc. ME. ▸**b** In CRICKET, hit (the ball) with a jabbing stroke; in BASEBALL, hit (the ball), esp. in a specified direction. M19. ▸**c** Hit or strike (a person). *colloq.* E20.
2 *fig.* Urge, incite, stir *up*; provoke. Now *rare*. LME.
3 With adverbs & adverbial phrs.: thrust or push (a thing) with a sharp movement. LME. ▸**b** Thrust forward (a finger, head, nose, etc.), esp. obtrusively. E18.
4 Crimp, form the folds in (a ruff) with a poking-stick. *obsolete* exc. *Hist.* L16.
5 Make, produce, find *out*, or stir *up*, by poking. M17.
6 Confine, shut *up* in a poky place. *colloq.* M19.
7 Of a man: have sexual intercourse with (esp. a woman). *coarse slang.* M19.
8 COMPUTING. Use a POKE command to put (a value) in a memory location (foll. by *into*); alter (a memory location) in this way. Cf. POKE *noun*⁴ 5. L20.

🕮 **1** E. WELTY On her knees before the fire, she was poking the big log. P. FARMER Jansey chooses to poke her little brother. P. BENSON She . . poked me . . in the ribs. **c** P. G. WODEHOUSE I'm going to poke Beulah Brinkmeyer right in the snoot. **2** J. I. M. STEWART She was . . trying to poke him up, to get some sort of response. **3** J. H. BURTON Montgomery poked out the eye of Henry II in the tilt-yard. A. T. ELLIS These men jeered and poked sticks through the bars. L. ERDRICH Fleur poked bits of sugar between Russell's lips. **b** D. H. LAWRENCE He was now like a big fish poking its nose above water. R. CHANDLER I poked my head cautiously from the horn-like opening. D. LESSING 'Listen,' he said, poking his chin forward and up. **5** L. BLUE Buy a honey cake . . and poke holes in it. **6** C. E. RIDDELL It would break her heart . . to be poked up in a town.

▶ **II** *verb intrans.* **9** Walk with the head thrust forward, stoop. ME.
10 Make a thrust or thrusts with a hand, a stick, the nose, etc. E17. ▸**b** CRICKET. Make a jabbing stroke at the ball; bat indecisively. Also foll. by *about*, *around*. M19. ▸**c** Aim one's gun at a moving target, rather than swinging and firing. L19.
11 Project obtrusively, stick *out*. *colloq.* E17.
12 Poke one's nose (into), go prying into corners, search, look *around* or *about*, investigate out of curiosity. E18.
13 Potter; move *about* or *around*, work in a desultory, ineffective, or dawdling way. L18.
14 Of a man: have sexual intercourse. *coarse slang.* L20.
15 COMPUTING. Use a POKE command to store a new value in a memory location. (Foll. by *into*.) L20.

🕮 **9** J. WOODFORDE Miss Wood is very pretty, but pokes a good deal. **10** DAY LEWIS I poked at a ladybird with a grass stem. M. PIERCY Lorraine . . poking at the word processor. **11** *Nature* Two small but vital Japanese rocks poking . . out of the western Pacific. **12** J. GLASSCO Stanley ran around . . poking into drawers and cupboards. J. M. COETZEE Soldiers . . poke around among the huts of the fisherfolk. U. HOLDEN I went to her bedroom to poke and pry in her things. **13** M. SINCLAIR A garden to poke about in.

Phrases: ***poke fun at***: see FUN *noun*. ***poke mullock (at)***: see MULLOCK *noun*. **poke one's head** = sense 9 above (see also sense 3b). ***poke one's nose in***: see NOSE *noun*.
■ **pokable** *adjective* L19. **poking** *verbal noun* the action of the verb; an instance of this; ***poking-stick*** (*Hist.*), a rod for stiffening the plaits of ruffs, orig. of wood or bone, later of steel so as to be applied hot: L16. **poking** *adjective* (*a*) that pokes; (*b*) poky: M18.

poke /pəʊk/ *verb*² *trans.* Long only *Scot.* ME.
[from POKE *noun*¹.]
1 Put in a poke or bag. ME.
2 Catch (fish) with a poke-net. L16.

poked /pəʊkt/ *adjective*¹. E17.
[from POKE *noun*¹ + -ED².]
Provided with or having a bag or poke; dilated.

poked /pəʊkt/ *adjective*². M19.
[from POKE *noun*³ + -ED².]
Of a woman's bonnet or cap: provided with or having a projecting brim or front.

pokelogan /pəʊk'ləʊg(ə)n/ *noun. US & Canad. dial.* M19.
[Perh. of Algonquian origin.]
A stagnant backwater; a swamp adjacent to a river, lake, etc.

poker /'pəʊkə/ *noun*¹. M16.
[from POKE *verb*¹ + -ER¹.]
1 A stiff straight metal rod, one end of which is fitted with or made into a handle, for poking or stirring a fire. M16.
2 †**a** A poking-stick. Only in E17. ▸**b** The implement with which poker-work is done. Also *ellipt.*, poker-work. E19. ▸**c** The staff or rod of office carried by a verger, bedell, etc.; a university bedell at Oxford and Cambridge. *joc.* or *slang.* M19.
3 A person who pokes; *esp.* a person who pokes or pries into things. E17.

🕮 **1** *fig.*: H. GRANVILLE He . . would be very handsome if he would not stoop . . . Liz is a poker in comparison. ***RED-HOT poker***. **stiff as a poker** (of a person) rigid and unyielding, esp. in manner.

Comb.: **poker back** (*a*) a perfectly straight back; (*b*) MEDICINE an abnormally rigid and straight spine; **poker-work** ornamental work done by burning a design on the surface of wood with a heated pointed implement; the technique of executing this; **poker-worked** *adjective* made or decorated by this technique.

poker /'pəʊkə/ *noun*². Now *rare* or *obsolete*. Latterly *US colloq.* L16.
[Perh. of Scandinavian origin: cf. Danish *pokker*, Swedish *pocker* the Devil. Cf. also PUCK *noun*¹.]
A hobgoblin, a demon.
old poker the Devil.

poker /'pəʊkə/ *noun*³. M19.
[Origin uncertain: perh. rel. to German *Poch(spiel)* lit. 'bragging game', from *pochen* brag.]
A card-game of US origin played by two or more people who bet on the value of the hands dealt to them, one of whom wins the pool either by having the highest combination at the showdown, or by forcing all opponents to concede without a showing of the hand, sometimes by means of bluff.
Comb.: **poker chip** a chip used as a stake in poker; **poker-dice** (*a*) dice with playing-card designs on some or all faces; (*b*) a dice game in which the thrower aims for combinations of several dice similar to winning hands in poker; **poker-face** an inscrutable face appropriate to a poker player; a face in which a person's thoughts or feelings are not revealed; **poker-faced** *adjective* having a poker-face (cf. PO-FACED); **poker-machine** *Austral.* a gaming-machine; **poker patience** a form of patience the object of which is to form winning poker combinations in each row and column.

poker /'pəʊkə/ *verb trans.* L18.
[from POKER *noun*¹.]
1 Poke, stir, or strike with a poker. L18.
2 Decorate in or adorn with poker-work. L19.
3 Of a verger etc.: escort (a church dignitary) ceremoniously. Cf. POKER *noun*¹ 2c. *joc.* E20.

pokerish /'pəʊk(ə)rɪʃ/ *adjective*¹. *US colloq.* E19.
[from POKER *noun*² + -ISH¹.]
Mysterious and frightening; ghostly, uncanny.

pokerish /'pəʊk(ə)rɪʃ/ *adjective*². M19.
[from POKER *noun*¹ + -ISH¹.]
Inclined to be stiff and unyielding, esp. in manner.

pokey /'pəʊki/ *noun*¹. *slang* (chiefly *US*). E20.
[Alt. of POGEY, perh. infl. by POKY.]
Usu. with *the*: prison, jail.

pokey *noun*² var. of POKIE.

pokey *adjective* var. of POKY.

pokie /'pəʊki/ *noun. Austral. slang.* Also **pokey**. M20.
[from POKER *noun*³ + -IE.]
= ***poker-machine*** s.v. POKER *noun*³.

pok-ta-pok /'pɒktapɒk/ *noun.* M20.
[Maya.]
Chiefly *Hist.* = TLACHTLI.

poky /'pəʊki/ *adjective. colloq.* Also **pokey**. M19.
[from POKE *verb*¹ + -Y¹.]
1 Pottering, piffling; given to petty matters or narrow interests. M19.
2 (Now the usual sense.) Of a room, building, etc.: small in size or accommodation; cramped, confined; mean, shabby. M19.

🕮 **1** H. B. STOWE If religion is going to make me so poky, I shall put it off. **2** A. JESSOPP Chichester seemed . . a poky place. P. PEARCE Cooped up for weeks . . in a poky flat.

■ **pokiness** *noun* L19.

pol /pɒl/ *noun. N. Amer. colloq.* M20.
[Abbreviation.]
A politician.

†**pol** *adjective* see POLL *adjective*.

Polab /'pəʊlɑːb/ *noun & adjective.* L19.
[Slavonic: cf. Czech, Polish *po* on, *Labe* Elbe (river).]
▶ **A** *noun.* **1** A member of a Slavonic people formerly inhabiting the region around the lower Elbe. L19.
2 The West Slavonic language of this people, now extinct. E20.
▶ **B** *attrib.* or as *adjective*. Of or pertaining to the Polabs or their language. M20.
■ **Polabian** /pə(ʊ)'leɪbɪən/ *noun & adjective* = POLAB M19. **Polabish** /pə(ʊ)'lɑːbɪʃ/ *noun & adjective* (of or pertaining to) the Polab language L19.

polacca /pə(ʊ)'lakə/ *noun*¹. E19.
[Italian, use as noun of fem. of *polacco* Polish, from German POLACK.]
A Polish dance, a polonaise; a piece of music for this dance, or of supposedly Polish character.

polacca *noun*² var. of POLACRE.

Polack /'pəʊlak/ *noun & adjective. derog.* & *offensive.* L16.
[French *Polaque*, German *Polack* from Polish *Polak*. Cf. next.]
▶ **A** *noun.* **1** A native or inhabitant of Poland; a Pole. L16.
2 A Jew from Poland. M19.
3 A Polish immigrant, a person of Polish descent. *N. Amer.* L19.
▶ **B** *adjective.* Polish; of Polish origin or descent. E17.

polacre /pə(ʊ)'lɑːkə/ *noun.* Also **polacca** /pə(ʊ)'lakə/. E17.
[French *polacre*, *polaque*, Italian *polacra*, *polacca* = Spanish, Portuguese *polacra*, Dutch *polak*, German *Polack(e)*, *Polacker*: perh. obscurely rel. to prec.]
A three- (occas. two-) masted sailing vessel used esp. in the Mediterranean, with masts made from single pieces.

Polander /'pəʊləndə/ *noun.* Now *rare* or *obsolete*. E17.
[from *Poland* country of eastern Europe + -ER¹.]
A native of Poland, a Pole.

Poland water /'pəʊlənd wɔːtə/ *noun phr.* L19.
[See below.]
A variety of mineral water obtained from springs at Poland, Maine, USA.

polar /'pəʊlə/ *adjective & noun.* M16.
[French *polaire* or mod. Latin *polaris* (in medieval Latin = heavenly), formed as POLE *noun*²: see -AR¹.]
▶ **A** *adjective.* **1** ASTRONOMY & GEOGRAPHY. Of or pertaining to the poles of the celestial sphere or of the earth or other celestial object; situated near or connected with either pole. M16.
2 Magnetic; of or pertaining to a magnetic pole or poles. L17.
3 *fig.* **a** Analogous to a pole of the earth, or to the polestar; pertaining to or of the nature of a central or guiding principle. L18. ▸**b** Directly opposite in character, action, or tendency. M19.
4 PHYSICS. Acting or arranged in two opposite directions. E19.
5 GEOMETRY. Relating or referred to a pole (cf. POLE *noun*² 3); of the nature of a polar. E19.
6 Pertaining to electrical poles; having positive and negative electricity; *esp.* in CHEMISTRY, involving or pertaining to the separation of positive and negative electric charge between parts of a molecule etc.; having an electric dipole moment; (esp. of a liquid) consisting of molecules with an electric dipole moment; (esp. of a solid) ionic, electrovalent. M19.
7 BIOLOGY. Of or pertaining to the poles of a cell, organ, etc. L19.

🕮 **1** E. K. KANE Well known to the Polar traveller. A. BURGESS He has three kinds of clothing—temperate, tropical and polar. L. GORDON These strange lands of more than polar darkness. **2** J. TYNDALL I examined the stones . . and found them strongly polar. **3a** CARLYLE A king over men; whose movements were polar. **b** E. A. NIDA The differences between literal and free translating are . . a polar distinction with many grades. H. READ Order and Disorder might be taken as the polar opposites.

Special collocations: **polar axis** ASTRONOMY the axis of rotation of the earth or other celestial object, passing through the poles; an axis of an equatorial telescope that is parallel to the earth's axis, around which the telescope may be turned to keep track of a star throughout the night. **polar bear** a very large white bear of Arctic regions, *Thalarctos maritimus*. **polar body** CYTOLOGY each of the small cells which bud off from an oocyte at the two meiotic divisions and do not develop into ova. **polar cap** a region of ice or other frozen matter surrounding a pole of a planet. **polar circle** either of the Arctic and Antarctic circles. **polar coordinate** GEOMETRY either of a pair of coordinates describing the position of a point in a plane, the first being the length of the straight line connecting the point to the origin, and the second the angle made by this line with a fixed line (usu. in *pl.*). **polar curve** = POLAR *noun* 2. **polar diagram**: in which the length of the radius joining a fixed point to any point of a curve represents the magnitude of something (e.g. the sensitivity of an aerial) measured in the direction of the radius. **polar distance** the angular distance of any point on a sphere from the nearer pole; the complement of declination or latitude. **polar flattening** the extent to which the polar diameter is shorter than the mean equatorial diameter. **polar hare** *N. Amer.* the Arctic hare, *Lepus arcticus*. **polar lights** the aurora borealis or australis. **polar orbit** an orbit that passes over polar regions, *spec.* one whose plane contains the polar axis. **polar plant** the compass-plant *Silphium laciniatum*. **polar star** the polestar. ***polar vector***: see VECTOR *noun* 2a. **polar wandering** the slow erratic movement of the earth's poles relative to the continents throughout geological time, due largely to continental drift.
▶ **B** *noun.* †**1** *ellipt.* A polar circle. *rare.* Only in L17.
2 GEOMETRY. A curve related in a particular way to a given curve and a fixed point; in a conic section, the straight line joining the points at which tangents from the fixed point touch the curve. M19.

polari *verb & noun* var. of PALARIE.

polari- /'pəʊləri/ *combining form* of medieval Latin *polaris* polar: see -I-.
■ **polari-bi'locular** *adjective* (of a lichen spore) of two cells separated by a thick median wall L19. **polari-'locular** *adjective* = POLARI-BILOCULAR E20.

polarimeter /pəʊlə'rɪmɪtə/ *noun.* M19.
[from prec. + -METER.]
An instrument for measuring the polarization of light, and esp. for determining the rotation of the plane of polarization by a substance through which the light passes.
■ **polari'metric** *adjective* of or pertaining to a polarimeter or polarimetry L19. **polari'metrically** *adverb* M20. **polarimetry**

noun the measurement of the polarization of light or other electromagnetic radiation; the use of a polarimeter: **M19.**

Polaris /pə(ʊ)ˈlɑːrɪs/ *noun.* **M19.**
[from medieval Latin: see POLAR.]
1 The polestar. **M19.**
2 A type of submarine-launched ballistic missile orig. developed for the US Navy, having nuclear warheads. **M20.**
2 attrib.: ***Polaris missile***, ***Polaris submarine***, etc.

polarisable *adjective*, **polarisation** *noun* vars. of POLARIZABLE, POLARIZATION.

polariscope /pə(ʊ)ˈlarɪskəʊp/ *noun.* **E19.**
[from POLARI- + -SCOPE.]
An instrument for showing the polarization of light; a polarimeter.
■ **polariˈscopic** *adjective* **M19.**

polarise *verb*, **polarised** *adjective* vars. of POLARIZE, POLARIZED.

polariton /pə(ʊ)ˈlarɪtɒn/ *noun.* **M20.**
[from POLARIZATION after *exciton* etc.]
PHYSICS. A quasiparticle in an ionic crystal consisting of a photon strongly coupled to a quasiparticle such as a phonon or exciton.

polarity /pə(ʊ)ˈlarɪti/ *noun.* **M17.**
[from POLAR + -ITY.]
1 The tendency of a magnet, lodestone, etc., to point with its extremities to the magnetic poles of the earth; the property of possessing magnetic poles. **M17.**
2 *gen.* The quality of being polar; the possession of poles or an axis in respect of certain physical properties; the property of exhibiting opposite properties in opposite directions; tendency to develop in opposite directions in space, time, serial arrangement, etc. **L17.** ▸**b** BIOLOGY. The tendency of living matter to assume a specific form; the property of regenerating several parts. **M19.**
3 *fig.* **a** Direction of feeling, inclination, etc., towards a single point; tendency, trend; attraction towards a particular object. **M18.** ▸**b** Possession or exhibition of opposite or contrasted aspects, tendencies, etc. **M19.**
4 The state of being electrically polar; the relation of a body to electric poles or electrodes; the electrical condition of a body as positive or negative. **M19.**
Comb.: **polarity therapy** a system of treatment used in alternative medicine, intended to restore a balanced distribution of the body's energy and incorporating manipulation, exercise, and dietary restrictions.

polarizable /ˈpəʊlərʌɪzəb(ə)l/ *adjective.* Also **-isable**. **M19.**
[from POLARIZE + -ABLE.]
Able to be polarized.
■ **polarizaˈbility** *noun* the property of being polarizable; *spec.* the degree to which an atom or molecule can be polarized, expressed in terms of the electric dipole moment induced by unit electric field: **E20.**

polarization /pəʊlərʌɪˈzeɪʃ(ə)n/ *noun.* Also **-isation**. **E19.**
[from next + -ATION. Sense 1 from French *polarisation*, from *pôle* POLE *noun*².]
1 The action of polarizing light or other electromagnetic radiation; the property of being polarized; the extent or direction of this. **E19.** ▸**b** Optical activity (esp. of sugar solutions); measurement of this. **M19.**
2 The action of inducing magnetic or electrical polarity; *spec.* the partial separation of positive and negative electric charge produced in a dielectric by an electric field; the electric dipole moment induced per unit volume. **M19.** ▸**b** The production of an opposite electromotive force at the electrodes of a cell due to the presence of electrolytic decomposition products, producing an apparently increased resistance in the circuit. **M19.**
3 The arrangement of molecules etc. in a definite direction; partial or complete alignment of the spin axes of particles; the direction or extent of this. **M19.**
4 *fig.* **a** The interpretation of a word etc. in a particular way (*rare*); the accentuation of a difference between two things or groups; the process or state of division into two groups representing extremes of opinion, wealth, etc. **L19.** ▸**b** COMMERCE. The system or principle requiring specification by a person offering information on investments, insurance, etc., of status as independent adviser or representative of a company. **L20.**

📖 **1** I. ASIMOV The windows . . were black and . . of appropriate polarization. **4** M. L. SAMUELS Further phonetic divergence, ('polarization' of the existing differences). *Chinese Economic Studies* The polarization between the rich and the poor. J. N. ISBISTER There had begun to be a polarization between himself and his senior colleagues.

polarize /ˈpəʊlərʌɪz/ *verb.* Also **-ise**. **E19.**
[from POLAR + -IZE. Sense 1 from French *polariser*, from *pôle* POLE *noun*².]
1 *verb trans. & intrans.* PHYSICS. Cause the vibrations of (light or other electromagnetic radiation) to be restricted, wholly or partially, to a particular direction. **E19.** ▸**b** *verb trans.* Measure the optical activity of (a solution, esp. of a sugar) in order to determine the concentration of solute. **E20.**
2 *verb trans. fig.* ▸**a** Give a single or particular direction to; interpret (a word etc.) in a particular way. **E19.** ▸**b** *verb trans.* Accentuate a division within (a group, system, etc.); separate into two (or occas. more) opposing groups, extremes of opinion, etc. **M20.**
3 *verb trans.* Induce magnetic or electrical polarity in. Also, cause polarization of (an electrical cell). **M19.** ▸**b** PHYSICS. Produce an alignment of the spins of (particles). **M20.**
4 *verb intrans.* Undergo polarization; exhibit polarity or polarization. **M19.**
1 polarizing filter a photographic etc. filter that preferentially passes light having a particular direction of vibration.
■ **polarizer** *noun* a person who or thing which polarizes; *spec.* a plate, prism, etc., that polarizes a ray of light passing through it: **M19.**

polarized /ˈpəʊlərʌɪzd/ *adjective.* Also **-ised**. **E19.**
[from prec. + -ED¹.]
Subjected to or displaying polarization; *esp.* (of light etc.) having vibrations restricted to a particular direction; (of a lens etc.) able to polarize light passing through it.

polarly /ˈpəʊləli/ *adverb.* **M19.**
[from POLAR + -LY².]
In a polar direction, manner, or degree; with reference to poles.

polarogram /pə(ʊ)ˈlɑːrəgram, ˈpəʊlər-/ *noun.* **E20.**
[formed as next + -GRAM.]
CHEMISTRY. A graphical record of current against voltage produced by a polarograph, typically showing a number of steps corresponding to particular anions in the sample.

polarograph /pə(ʊ)ˈlɑːrəgrɑːf, ˈpəʊlər-/ *noun.* Also ***P-**. **E20.**
[from POLAR(IZATION + -O- + -GRAPH.]
CHEMISTRY. (US proprietary name for) an apparatus for automatic chemical analysis in which a sample is electrolysed at successively higher voltages and the resulting current plotted against voltage to give a polarogram (cf. prec.).
■ **polaroˈgraphic** *adjective* **E20. polaroˈgraphically** *adverb* **M20. polarography** /pəʊləˈrɒgrəfi/ *noun* the technique of using a polarograph **M20.**

Polaroid /ˈpəʊlərɔɪd/ *noun & adjective.* Also **p-**. **M20.**
[from POLARIZE + -OID.]
▶ **A** *noun.* **1** A material which in the form of thin sheets produces a high degree of plane polarization in light passing through it. **M20.** ▸**b** A piece of this material. **M20.**
2 In *pl.* Sunglasses containing Polaroid lenses. **M20.**
3 A photograph taken with a Polaroid camera. **M20.**
▶ **B** *attrib.* or as *adjective.* **1** Made of or employing Polaroid. **M20.**
2 Designating (a photograph taken with) a type of camera that develops the negative and produces a positive print within a short time of the picture being taken. **M20.**
¶ Proprietary name.

polaron /ˈpəʊlərɒn/ *noun.* **M20.**
[from POLAR(IZATION + -ON.]
PHYSICS. A quasiparticle in a crystal consisting of a free electron together with an associated distortion of the crystal lattice.

polarward /ˈpəʊləwəd/ *adverb & adjective.* **M19.**
[from POLAR *adjective* + -WARD.]
(Moving or directed) towards polar regions.

polatouche /pɒləˈtuːʃ/ *noun.* **E19.**
[French from Russian *poletusha*.]
A flying squirrel, *Pteromys volans*, inhabiting coniferous forests across northern Eurasia.

poldavy /pɒlˈdeɪvi/ *noun & adjective.* *obsolete* exc. *Hist.* **L15.**
[from *Poldavide*, a town in Brittany, France: prob. orig. collect. pl.]
▶ **A** *noun sing.* & †in *pl.* (treated as *sing.*). A coarse canvas or sacking, originally woven in Brittany, formerly much used for sailcloth. **L15.**
▶ **B** *adjective.* Made of poldavy. **L16.**

polder /ˈpəʊldə/ *noun.* **E17.**
[Dutch from Middle Dutch *polre*.]
A piece of low-lying land reclaimed from the sea, a lake, etc., and protected by dykes, orig. and esp. in the Netherlands.

pole /pəʊl/ *noun*¹.
[Late Old English *pāl* corresp. to Old Frisian, Middle & mod. Low German *pāl*, Middle Dutch *pael* (Dutch *paal*), Old High German *pfāl* (German *Pfahl*), Old Norse *páll*, from Germanic from Latin *palus* stake, prop.]
1 *gen.* Orig., a stake. Now, a long, slender, more or less cylindrical piece of wood, metal, etc., e.g. the straight stem of a slender tree stripped of its branches; *esp.* one placed with one end in the ground as a support for a tent, a flag, climbing plants, scaffolding, telegraph or telephone wires, etc. **LOE.** ▸**b** A long tapering wooden shaft fitted to the front of a cart, carriage, etc., and attached to the yokes or collars of the draught animals. **LME.** ▸**c** NAUTICAL. A ship's mast; *esp.* one with no sail set. Also, the upper end of a mast rising above the rigging. **M17.** ▸**d** ANGLING. A rudimentary fishing-rod. Also, a long rod used in fishing for roach etc. (also ***roach-pole***). **L17.** ▸**e** FORESTRY. A young tree with a slender straight trunk and no lower branches. **M18.** ▸**f** The long upright flowering stem of an agave. **L19.** ▸**g** The rod used by a pole-vaulter. **L19.** ▸**h** A ski pole. **E20.**
2 As a measure of length: = PERCH *noun*² 2. Now *rare* exc. *Hist.* **E16.** ▸**b** More fully ***square pole***. As a measure of area: = PERCH *noun*² 2b. *obsolete* exc. *Hist.* **M17.**
3 a HORSE-RACING. (The starting position closest to) the inside fence surrounding a racecourse. **M19.** ▸**b** MOTOR RACING etc. In full ***pole position***. The position on the grid on the front row and on the inside of the first bend. Also (*fig.*), an advantageous or leading position. **M20.**
4 HUNTING. The tail of an otter, pheasant, or other quarry. **M19.**

📖 **1** E. A. PARKES A conical tent, with a single pole. P. ROTH That flag, fluttering on its pole, being raised . . over bloody Iwo Jima. ***barber's pole***, ***bargepole***, ***beanpole***, ***flag-pole***, etc. GREASY ***pole***. SLIPPERY ***pole***. **up the pole** *slang* (*a*) crazy, eccentric; (*b*) in difficulties, in error; (*c*) drunk; (*d*) pregnant but unmarried. **would not touch with a ten-foot pole**, **would not touch with a forty-foot pole**, etc., *colloq.* would have nothing to do with (cf. ***would not touch with a bargepole*** s.v. BARGE *noun*). **c under bare poles** with no sail set. **e** attrib.: ***pole plantation***, ***pole wood***, etc. **3b** *Autosport* He would gain start from pole, such an important advantage at Mallory. *fig.*: *Listener* Brazil's foreign investment needs . . would . . take Brazil to pole position in the big league of world debtors.

Comb.: **pole barn**: with sides consisting of poles covered with wire mesh; **pole-bean** *N. Amer.* a climbing bean; **pole-boat** a riverboat propelled by means of a pole or poles; **pole-horse** a horse harnessed alongside of the pole of a cart, carriage, etc., a wheeler as opp. to a leader; **pole-jump** *noun & verb intrans.* = ***pole-vault*** below; **pole-jumper** = ***pole-vaulter*** below; **pole-lathe** a lathe in which the work is turned by a cord passing round it, worked by a treadle; **poleman** (*a*) a man who uses, carries, or fights with a pole; (*b*) (MOTOR RACING etc.) a driver or car in pole position; **pole-mast** a mast formed of a single spar; ***pole position***: see sense 3b above; **pole-reed** a phragmites reed; **pole-screen** a fire-screen mounted on an upright pole or rod; **pole-trap** (chiefly *Hist.*) a circular steel trap for birds, fixed on the top of a post; **pole-vault** *noun & verb* (*a*) *noun* the athletic event of vaulting over a horizontal bar with the aid of a long flexible rod held in the hands to give extra spring; a vault so performed; (*b*) *verb intrans.* perform a pole-vault; **pole-vaulter** an athlete who takes part in a pole-vault, a person who pole-vaults.
■ **poleless** /-l-l-/ *adjective*¹ **M17.**

pole /pəʊl/ *noun*². **LME.**
[Latin *polus* end of an axis from Greek *polos* pivot, axis. Cf. Old & mod. French *pôle*.]
1 Either of the two points in the celestial sphere (north and south) about which the stars appear to revolve and which are the points at which the line of the earth's axis meets the celestial sphere (more fully ***celestial pole***). Also occas. = POLESTAR. **LME.**
2 Either of the two locations on the earth's surface (north and south) which represent the points about which the earth rotates (also ***geographical pole***). Also, either extremity of the axis of any rotating spherical or spheroidal body. **LME.** ▸†**b** Either of the two ends of an axle; a peg on which something turns. *rare.* **L17–M18.**
3 GEOMETRY etc. ▸**a** Either of the points at which an axis intersects a spherical surface. **LME.** ▸**b** A fixed point to which other points, lines, etc., are referred, e.g. the origin of polar coordinates, or the point of which a line or curve is a polar. **M19.** ▸**c** CRYSTALLOGRAPHY. The point at which a straight line perpendicular to a face or plane of a crystal meets the (ideal) sphere of projection. **L19.**
4 *fig.* Each of two (or occas. more) opposed or complementary principles to which the parts of a system or group of phenomena, ideas, etc., are referable. **L15.**
†**5** *sing.* & in *pl.* The sky, the heavens. *poet.* **L16–L18.**
6 A point at which magnetic force is concentrated; *esp.* either of two such opposite points or regions of a magnet (when of elongated form, usually at its ends). **L16.**
7 Either of the two terminal points (positive and negative) of an electric cell, battery, or machine. **E19.**
8 BIOLOGY. Either extremity of the main axis of any organ or cell. **M19.**
9 MATH. A point c near which the magnitude of a function $f(z)$ becomes infinite, but in such a way that, were the function multiplied by an appropriate power of $(z - c)$, it would remain finite. **L19.**

📖 **2** G. MEREDITH We're as far apart as the Poles. F. HOYLE The tendency for air to transfer heat . . to the cold poles. **4** *New Statesman* At the opposite pole to Tchaikovsky's introversion stands Verdi. R. BERTHOUD The three agreeable poles of Moore's life were Hampstead, Kent and Chelsea. **5** POPE Stars unnumber'd gild the glowing pole.

Phrases: ***celestial pole***: see sense 1 above. ***geographical pole***: see sense 2 above. **magnetic pole** (*a*) either of the two points of the earth's surface (near to but not corresponding to the geographical poles, and slowly varying in position) where the lines of force of the earth's magnetic field are vertical; (*b*) = sense 6 above. **north pole** (*a*) the northern geographical pole of the earth, situated on the Arctic ice-cap (usu. **N- P-**); the northern celestial or magnetic pole; (*b*) the pole of a magnet that points north when it is allowed to orient itself with the earth's magnetic field; *pedal pole*: see PEDAL *adjective* 2. **poles apart** differing greatly, widely separated, esp. in nature or opinion. *salient pole*: see SALIENT *adjective*. **south pole** (*a*) the southern geographical pole of the earth, situated in central Antarctica (usu. **S- P-**); the southern celestial or magnetic pole; (*b*) the pole of a magnet that points south when it is allowed to orient itself with the earth's magnetic field.

Comb.: **pole-finding** *adjective* designating impregnated paper which can be used to identify the sign of an electric terminal with which it is in contact, using a colour change. **pole-piece** a mass of iron forming the end of an electromagnet, through which the lines of magnetic force are concentrated and directed; **pole strength** (PHYSICS) the strength of a magnetic pole; the degree to which a pole exerts a magnetic force.

■ **poleless** /-l-l-/ *adjective*² E20.

Pole /pəʊl/ *noun*³. L16.
[German from Middle High German *Polān*, pl. *-āne* from Old Polish *Polanie* lit. 'field-dwellers', from *pole* field.]
A native or inhabitant of Poland; a person of Polish descent.

pole /pəʊl/ *noun*⁴. M17.
[Obsolete French.]
A flatfish; = WITCH *noun*³. Also ***pole dab***, ***pole flounder***.

pole /pəʊl/ *verb*¹. L16.
[from POLE *noun*¹.]
1 *verb trans.* Provide with a pole or poles. L16.
2 *verb trans.* †**a** Set on a pole. Only in E17. ▸**b** Convey (hay, reeds, etc.) on poles. *dial.* E19.
3 *verb trans.* Push, poke, pierce, or strike with a pole; stir *up*, push *off*, with a pole. E18. ▸**b** BASEBALL. Hit (the ball, a shot) hard. E20.
4 *verb trans.* & *intrans.* Propel (a boat etc.) with a pole. M18.
5 *verb trans.* Stir (molten metal, glass) in order to remove oxygen, orig. & esp. using poles of green wood. M19.
6 *verb intrans.* Of an agave: put out a pole (flowering stem). L19.
7 *verb intrans.* Foll. by *on*: take advantage of, impose or sponge on. *Austral. colloq.* E20.
■ **poling** *noun* (*a*) the action of the verb; (*b*) poles collectively: L16.

pole /pəʊl/ *verb*² *trans.* M20.
[from POLE *noun*².]
PHYSICS. Make (a ferroelectric material) electrically polar by the temporary application of a strong electric field.

poleaxe /ˈpəʊlaks/ *noun* & *verb*. Also ***-ax**. ME.
[Middle Dutch *pol(l)aex*, Middle Low German *pol(l)exe*, from *pol(le)* POLL *noun*¹ + *aex* AXE *noun*¹; later assoc. with POLE *noun*¹.]
▶ **A** *noun*. **1** Chiefly *Hist.* A battleaxe. Also, a short-handled axe used in naval warfare for boarding, cutting ropes, etc. ME.
2 Chiefly *Hist.* A halberd or similar long-handled weapon carried by a royal bodyguard. M16.
3 A butcher's axe, having a hammer at the back of the head and used to fell animals. E18.
▶ **B** *verb trans.* Fell with or as with a poleaxe. Freq. *fig.* L19.

> 🕮 A. HALEY The man crumpled without a sound as if he had been poleaxed. L. KENNEDY Poleaxed by this nonsense.

polecat /ˈpəʊlkat/ *noun*. ME.
[Origin uncertain: perh. from Old French *pole*, *poule* chicken, fowl: see CAT *noun*¹.]
1 A dark-brown European carnivorous mammal, *Mustela putorius*, of the weasel family, noted for its fetid smell; (freq. with specifying word) any of various other mustelids of the genus *Mustela* or related genera. Also (*US*), a skunk. ME.
2 *fig.* A detested or immoral person, esp. a prostitute. L16.
Comb.: **polecat ferret** a brown variety of the ferret.

poleis *noun* pl. of POLIS *noun*¹.

polemarch /ˈpɒlɪmɑːk/ *noun*. M17.
[Greek *polemarkhos*, from *polemos* war: see -ARCH.]
GREEK HISTORY. An officer in ancient Greece, orig. a military commander-in-chief, later also having civil functions.

polemic /pəˈlɛmɪk/ *adjective* & *noun*. M17.
[medieval Latin *polemicus* from Greek *polemikos*, from *polemos* war: see -IC.]
▶ **A** *adjective*. = POLEMICAL *adjective*. M17.
▶ **B** *noun*. **1** A controversial argument or discussion; argumentation against some opinion, doctrine, etc.; *sing.* & in *pl.*, aggressive controversy; in *pl.* (treated as *sing.*), the practice of this, esp. in theology. M17.
2 A controversialist; esp. in theology. M17.

> 🕮 **1** C. R. ATTLEE A careful exposition of the Labour programme with very little Party polemics in it. M. TIPPETT It would be misrepresenting this book to finish the Introduction on a note of polemic. D. CUPITT His unwearying polemic against the established Church.

■ **polemicist** /-sɪst/ *noun* a writer of polemics M19.

polemical /pəˈlɛmɪk(ə)l/ *adjective* & *noun*. M17.
[from (the same root as) prec. + -AL¹.]
▶ **A** *adjective*. Of, pertaining to, or of the nature of controversy; controversial, disputatious. M17.

> 🕮 P. ZWEIG He had acquired something of a reputation as a polemical journalist with a sharp tongue. KARL MILLER Far from being authorially neutral . . it is overtly polemical.

▶ **B** *noun*. = POLEMIC *noun* 1. *rare*. E19.
■ **polemically** *adverb* E18.

polemicize /pəˈlɛmɪsʌɪz/ *verb intrans*. Also **-ise**. M20.
[formed as prec. + -IZE.]
Argue or write polemically, carry on a controversy.

polemise *verb* var. of POLEMIZE.

polemist /ˈpɒlɪmɪst/ *noun*. E19.
[Greek *polemistēs* warrior, from *polemos* war: see -IST.]
A polemicist.

polemize /ˈpɒlɪmʌɪz/ *verb intrans*. Also **-ise**. E19.
[Greek *polemizein* wage war, from *polemos* war: see -IZE.]
= POLEMICIZE.

polemology /pɒlɪˈmɒlədʒi/ *noun*. M20.
[from Greek *polemos* war + -LOGY.]
The branch of knowledge that deals with war.
■ **polemoˈlogical** *adjective* M20. **polemologist** *noun* L20.

polemonium /pɒlɪˈməʊnɪəm/ *noun*. E20.
[mod. Latin (see below), from Greek *polemōnion* Jacob's ladder (plant), of uncertain origin.]
Any plant of the genus *Polemonium* (family Polemoniaceae), members of which (e.g. Jacob's ladder, *P. caeruleum*) bear single or clustered bell-shaped flowers.

polemoscope /pəˈlɛməskəʊp, ˈpɒlɪmə-/ *noun*. M17.
[mod. Latin *polemoscopium*, from Greek *polemos* war: see -SCOPE.]
A telescope etc. fitted with a mirror for use in viewing objects not directly before the eye.

polenta /pə(ʊ)ˈlɛntə, *foreign* poˈlɛnta/ *noun*. OE.
[Latin, in later use directly from Italian from Latin = pearl barley.]
Orig., pearl barley, (porridge made from) barley meal. Later, maize flour as used in Italian cookery; a paste or dough made from this boiled and then often fried or baked.

poler /ˈpəʊlə/ *noun*. L17.
[from POLE *noun*¹ or *verb*¹ + -ER¹.]
†**1** A pole used for stirring. Only in L17.
2 A person who sets up or fixes hop-poles. M19.
3 The horse or other draught animal harnessed alongside the pole of a cart, carriage, etc.; a wheeler. *Austral.* & *NZ*. M19.
4 A person who propels a barge, boat, etc., by means of a pole. L19.
5 A cadger, a sponger; a shirker. *Austral. slang*. M20.

polestar /ˈpəʊlstɑː/ *noun*. M16.
[from POLE *noun*² + STAR *noun*¹.]
1 *The* first-magnitude star α Ursae Minoris, now within one degree of the north celestial pole. Also called ***Polaris***, ***polar star***. M16.
2 *fig.* A thing that serves as a guide, a lodestar, a governing principle; a centre of attraction; a cynosure. E17.

poleward /ˈpəʊlwəd/ *adverb* & *adjective*. L19.
[from POLE *noun*² + -WARD. Cf. next.]
▶ **A** *adverb*. Towards or in the direction of the (north or south) pole. L19.
▶ **B** *adjective*. Directed or tending towards the (north or south) pole. L19.

polewards /ˈpəʊlwədz/ *noun*, *adverb*, & *adjective*. M17.
[from POLE *noun*² + -WARDS.]
▶†**A** *noun*. The direction of the (north or south) pole. *rare*. Only in M17.
▶ **B** *adverb*. = POLEWARD *adverb*. M19.
▶ **C** *adjective*. = POLEWARD *adjective*. M20.

poley *noun*¹ var. of POLY *noun*¹.

poley /ˈpəʊli/ *adjective* & *noun*². Chiefly *US*, *Austral.*, & *NZ*. Also **polley**. M19.
[from POLL *noun*³ + -Y¹.]
▶ **A** *adjective*. Chiefly of cattle: hornless, polled. M19.
▶ **B** *noun*. **1** A hornless bullock, cow, etc. *Austral.* M19.
2 A kind of saddle without a pommel, or without knee-pads. M20.

polhode /ˈpɒlhəʊd/ *noun*. M19.
[from Greek *polos* pole + *hodos* way.]
GEOMETRY. A non-plane curve traced on the surface of an ellipsoid by the point of contact of the ellipsoid with a fixed plane on which it rolls about an internal axis. Cf. HERPOLHODE.

Polian /ˈpəʊlɪən/ *adjective*. M19.
[from J. X. *Poli* (1746–1825), Neapolitan naturalist + -AN.]
ZOOLOGY. ***Polian vesicle***, each of the sacs or tubes connected with the circular vessel of the water vascular system in many echinoderms.

polianite /ˈpəʊlɪənʌɪt/ *noun*. M19.
[from Greek *polia* greyness + -n- + -ITE¹.]
MINERALOGY. A steel-grey variety of pyrolusite that occurs as large well-formed crystals of the tetragonal system.

police /pəˈliːs/ *noun*. L15.
[French from medieval Latin *politia* from Latin: see POLICY *noun*¹, -ICE¹: cf. POLITY. See also POLIS *noun*².]
▶**I 1** The regulation and control of a community; civil administration; public order. *obsolete* exc. *Hist.* Orig. *Scot.* L15.
†**2** Civil organization; civilization. M16–M19.
3 A government department which is concerned with maintaining public order and safety, and enforcing the law. E18.
4 a The civil force of a State, responsible for maintaining public order, enforcing the law, and detecting crime; (treated as *pl.*), the members of such a force; a constabulary. Also, any force resembling this whose function is to keep order, enforce regulations, etc. E19. ▸**b** A police officer. Chiefly *Scot.* & *US colloq.* M19.
5 The cleansing or cleanliness of a camp or garrison. *US*. E19.

> 🕮 **4a** L. DUNCAN I'm going to the police, and I'm going to tell them everything. ***military police***, ***railway police***, ***secret police***, ***thought police***, etc. ***police boat***, ***police car***, ***police cell***, ***police escort***, ***police patrol***, ***police raid***, etc. ***help the police in their enquiries***, ***help the police with their enquiries***: see HELP *verb*. ***Prefect of Police***: see PREFECT 1.

▶†**II 6** = POLICY *noun*¹ 3, 4a, 4b. M16–M18.
Comb.: **police action** (*a*) the deeds or activity of the police, an instance of this; (*b*) (a) military intervention without a formal declaration of war; **police bail** the release of a person in police custody with a recognizance that he or she will return at an appointed time; **police box** a telephone box specially for the use of police or for members of the public wishing to contact the police; *police constable*: see CONSTABLE 4b; **police court** a magistrates' court; **police dispatcher** *US* a staff-member in a police station who receives information and transmits it to police patrols; **police dog** (*a*) a dog, esp. a German shepherd, used by the police to track criminals, lost people, etc.; (*b*) a German shepherd dog. **police force** an organized body of police officers of various ranks, responsible for maintaining and enforcing law and order in a particular town, country, etc.; **police informer** a person who gives information about crimes committed and offenders to the police, esp. habitually; **police judge** *Scot.* & *US* a police magistrate; **police magistrate** a stipendiary magistrate who presides in a police court; **police matron** a policewoman who takes charge of women or juveniles at a police station or in court; **police message** a message broadcast on radio etc. at the request of the police; **police novel**: describing crime and its detection by police; **police office** the headquarters of a police force; **police officer** †(*a*) an official whose function is to maintain public order; (*b*) a member of a police force; **policeperson** a police officer; **police positive** a type of Colt's pistol; **police procedural** *adjective* & *noun* (*a*) *adjective* of or pertaining to police procedure; (*b*) *noun* a police novel; **police record** a dossier kept by the police on all people convicted of crime; a personal history which includes some conviction for crime; **police reporter** a newspaper reporter who concentrates on stories concerning crime and police activity; **police science** the branch of science that deals with the investigation of crime; **police scientist** an expert in police science; **police State** a totalitarian State controlled by a national police force with secret supervision of citizens' activities; **police station** the headquarters of a local police force; **police trap** a means, used by the police, of detecting speeding motorists or apprehending wanted people; **police wagon** *US* a patrol wagon; **police-witness** a witness whose testimony supports a police prosecution; **policewoman** a female member of a police force.
■ **policedom** *noun* the body of police; police collectively: M19.

police /pəˈliːs/ *verb*. M16.
[Partly from French *policer*, partly from POLICE *noun*.]
†**1** *verb intrans.* Improve or develop land, esp. by cultivation. Cf. POLICY *noun*¹ II. *Scot.* Only in M16.
†**2** *verb trans.* Maintain civil order in (a State or country). Usu. in *pass.* L16–L18.
3 *verb trans.* **a** Control or regulate by means of police etc.; provide or guard with police etc. M19. ▸**b** *fig.* Keep in order, administer, control. L19.
4 *verb trans.* Make or keep clean or orderly; clean up or *up* (a camp or garrison). *US*. M19.

> 🕮 **3a** C. C. TRENCH The Navy's services in policing the sea lanes against pirates. M. M. KAYE It was not possible to police the boy for every minute of every day. **b** *Time* Some new articles that will enable him to police currency rates.

■ **policeable** *adjective* E20. **policing** *verbal noun* the action of the verb; *spec.* the controlling and keeping in order of a crowded event or a large number of people by means of police: L16.

policeman /pəˈliːsmən/ *noun*. Pl. **-men**. E19.
[from POLICE *noun* + MAN *noun*.]
1 a A male member of a police force; a constable. E19. ▸**b** A police informer. *slang*. E20. ▸**c** NAUTICAL. The member of the watch responsible, if necessary, for waking the rest of the crew. M20.
2 *fig.* **a** A person who or thing which maintains law and order, promotes peace-keeping, etc. L19. ▸**b** A person or thing regarded as a deterrent or obstacle. M20.
3 CHEMISTRY. A glass rod or tube with a soft attachment, usu. a short length of rubber tubing, on one end. E20.

2b sleeping policeman a ramp or ridge in a road surface designed to slow down motor vehicles, a speed hump.
Comb.: **policeman-bird** *Austral.* = JABIRU *noun* 2(a); **policeman fly** *Austral.* any of various small, usu. black wasps, esp. of the sphecid subfamily Nyssoninae, which prey on flies; **policeman's helmet** = *Himalayan balsam* s.v. BALSAM *noun* 6(b).
■ **policemanish** *adjective* policemanlike E20. **policemanlike** *adjective* resembling (that of) a policeman L19. **policemanly** *adjective* appropriate to or characteristic of a policeman M20. **policemanship** *noun* the role or action of a policeman L19.

Police Motu /pəliːs ˈməʊtuː/ *noun*. M20.
[from POLICE *noun* + MOTU *noun*.]
A pidgin, based on Motu, used in Papua as a lingua franca by the British and Australian administrations.

policier /pɔlisje/ *noun*. Pl. pronounced same. L20.
[French, lit. 'detective novel'.]
A film based on a police novel.
¶ Cf. also earlier *roman policier* s.v. ROMAN *noun*³.

policlinic *noun* see POLYCLINIC.

policy /ˈpɒlɪsi/ *noun*¹. LME.
[In branch I from Old French *policie* from Latin *politia* from Greek *politeia* citizenship, government, etc., from *politēs*, from *polis* city, state: cf. POLICE *noun*. In branch II from assoc. with Latin *politus* polished, refined. Cf. also POLITY.]
► **I 1** An organized and established form of government or administration; a constitution, a polity. Now *rare* or *obsolete*. LME.
†**2** Government; the conduct of public affairs; political science. LME–L18.
3 Political sagacity or diplomacy; prudence or skill in the conduct of public affairs. Also, political cunning. LME.
4 a Prudent or expedient conduct or action; sagacity, shrewdness. Also, cunning, craftiness. LME. ▸†**b** A contrivance; a crafty device, a trick. LME–M19.
5 A course of action or principle adopted or proposed by a government, party, individual, etc.; any course of action adopted as advantageous or expedient. LME.

📖 **4a** R. L. STEVENSON It was good policy . . and showed our enemies that we despised their cannonade. **5** W. LIPPMANN During that peace . . Britain pursued a policy of free trade. SLOAN WILSON The company had a policy of giving all job applicants an interview. K. AMIS It's official policy not to be . . discreet. *policy of pinpricks*: see PINPRICK *noun* 2.

► **II** *Scot.* **6** †**a** The improvement or embellishment of an estate, building, town, etc. LME–M18. ▸†**b** The improvements so made; the buildings, plantations, etc., used to make improvements. M16–E18. ▸**c** The (usu. enclosed and laid out) park or gardens surrounding a country house. Now usu. in *pl.* L18.
†**7** The polishing or refining of manners; refinement, culture. Only in 16.

📖 **6c** *Scottish Field* Kinellar House . . is set in policies extending to about 37 acres.

Comb.: **policy-making** the devising of esp. government or party policies; **policy science** the branch of knowledge that deals with the making and implementing of policies; **policy wonk**: see WONK *noun*²3.

policy /ˈpɒlɪsi/ *noun*². M16.
[French *police* from Provençal *polissa*, *-issia*, Catalan *-ice*, prob. from medieval Latin *apodissa*, *-ixa*, alt. of Latin *apodixis* from Greek *apodeixis* demonstration, proof, from *apodeiknunai*: see APODICTIC.]
1 A contract of insurance; a document containing this. M16.
2 A conditional promissory note, depending on the result of a bet. Now *rare*. E18.
3 A form of gambling in which bets are made on numbers to be drawn by lottery. *US*. M19.

📖 **1** C. SAGAN Lloyd's of London . . declined to write such a policy. *Which?* Lump sum policies pay out . . cash . . when you die. *INSURANCE* **policy**.

Comb.: **policyholder** a person, organization, etc., in whose name a policy is held; **policy loan** a loan granted to a policyholder using the policy as security; **policy-slip** *US* the ticket given in return for a bet on numbers to be drawn by lottery; **policy wheel** *US* a revolving drum used in the selection of winning numbers drawn by lottery.

†**policy** *verb trans*. M16–E19.
[French †*policier* administer, from Old French *policie*: see POLICY *noun*¹.]
= POLICE *verb* 2.

poligar /ˈpɒlɪgɑː/ *noun*. L17.
[(Marathi *pāḷegār* from) Telugu *pāḷegāḍu*, = Tamil *pāḷaiyakkāran* holder of a pollam.]
1 In southern India: the holder of feudal estate or territory (a pollam); a subordinate feudal chief. L17.
2 *transf.* (A descendant of) any of the followers of such a chief. Usu. in *pl.* L18.

polio /ˈpəʊlɪəʊ/ *noun*. *colloq.* Pl. **-os**. M20.
[Abbreviation of POLIOMYELITIS.]
1 Poliomyelitis, esp. the paralytic form. Freq. *attrib.* M20.
2 A person who has, or has had, polio. *rare*. M20.

polioencephalitis /ˌpəʊlɪəʊɛnsɛfəˈlʌɪtɪs, -kɛf-/ *noun*. L19.
[mod. Latin, from Greek *polios* grey + *egkephalos* brain + -ITIS.]
MEDICINE. Inflammation of the grey matter of the brain due to viral infection.

poliomyelitis /ˌpəʊlɪəʊmʌɪəˈlʌɪtɪs, ˌpɒlɪəʊ-/ *noun*. L19.
[mod. Latin, from Greek *polios* grey + *muelos* marrow + -ITIS.]
MEDICINE. An infectious viral disease of the central nervous system which may give rise to lymphocytic meningitis or a permanent and sometimes fatal paralysis. Also called *polio*, (in children) *infantile paralysis*.
■ **poliomyelitic** /-ˈlɪtɪk/ *adjective* of or affected with poliomyelitis E20.

poliorcetic /ˌpɒlɪɔːˈsɛtɪk/ *adjective*. M19.
[Greek *poliorkētikos*, from *poliorkētēs* besieger, from *poliorkein* besiege a city, from *polis* city + *erkos* fence, enclosure: see -ETIC.]
Hist. Of or pertaining to the besieging of cities or fortresses.

poliorcetics /ˌpɒlɪɔːˈsɛtɪks/ *noun pl*. M16.
[Greek (*ta*) *poliorkētika* things or matters pertaining to sieges, neut. pl. of *poliorkētikos*: see prec.]
Hist. The art of conducting and resisting sieges.

poliosis /pɒlɪˈəʊsɪs/ *noun*. E19.
[mod. Latin, from Greek *polios* grey + -OSIS.]
MEDICINE. Partial or general (esp. premature) greyness or whiteness of the hair.

poliovirus /ˈpəʊlɪəʊvʌɪrəs/ *noun*. M20.
[from POLIO + VIRUS.]
MEDICINE. Any of a group of enteroviruses including those that cause poliomyelitis.
■ **polioviral** *adjective* L20.

polis /ˈpɒlɪs/ *noun*¹. Pl. ***poleis*** /ˈpɒleɪs/. L19.
[Greek = city.]
Hist. A city-State, esp. in ancient Greece; *spec.* such a State considered in its ideal form.

polis /ˈpəʊlɪs, ˈpɒl-/ *noun*². Chiefly *Scot.* & *Anglo-Irish*. Pl. same. L19.
[Repr. regional pronunc. of POLICE *noun*.]
The police; a police officer.

-polis /pəˈlɪs/ *suffix*. M19.
[from Greek *polis* city.]
Forming names or nicknames of cities or towns, as *cosmopolis*, *Cottonopolis*, *Indianapolis*, etc.

Polisario /pɒlɪˈsɑːrɪəʊ/ *noun*. L20.
[Spanish acronym, from Frente *Po*pular para la *Li*beración de *Sa*gnia el-Hamra y *Rí*o de Oro (Popular Front for the Liberation of Sagnia el-Hamra and Rio de Oro).]
An independence movement in Western (formerly Spanish) Sahara, formed in 1973. Also *Polisario Front*.

polish /ˈpɒlɪʃ/ *noun*¹. L16.
[from the verb.]
1 Refinement, culture; elegance of manner. L16.
2 The action of polishing, the condition of being polished; smoothness, and usu. glossiness, of surface produced by friction or the application of a coating. E18.
3 A substance used for polishing *esp.* one applied to a surface to produce a smooth, and usu. glossy, coating. E19. ▸**b** *ellipt.* = *nail-polish* s.v. NAIL *noun*. E20.

📖 **1** L. DEIGHTON The glossy polish that the best English boarding schools can sometimes provide. **2** A. HARDING I watch . . the sunlight play upon the polish of a table. **3** E. JOLLEY Attacked her linoleum with a rag soaked with kerosene and polish. *floor polish*, *furniture polish*, *silver polish*, etc.

Phrases: *French polish*: see FRENCH *adjective*. *spit and polish*: see SPIT *noun*².

Polish /ˈpəʊlɪʃ/ *adjective* & *noun*². E17.
[from POLE *noun*³ + -ISH¹.]
► **A** *adjective*. **1** Of or pertaining to Poland, a country in central Europe, its Slavonic language, or its inhabitants; belonging or attributed to Poles or Poland. E17.
2 Designating or pertaining to any of various logical theories, methods, or systems developed in Poland before the war of 1939–45. M20.
Special collocations & comb.: **Polish-American** *noun* & *adjective* (*a*) *noun* an American of Polish origin; (*b*) *adjective* of or pertaining to Americans of Polish origin. **Polish draughts** a form of draughts in which the board has 100 squares and each side has 20 pieces. *Polish manna*: see MANNA 6. **Polish notation** LOGIC & COMPUTING a system of formula notation without brackets or special punctuation freq. used to represent the order in which arithmetical operations are performed in many computers and calculators; *reverse Polish notation*, the usual form of Polish notation, with operators following rather than preceding their operands.
► **B** *ellipt.* as *noun*. †**1** Polish draughts. *rare*. Only in M18.
2 The Polish language. L18.
■ **Polishness** *noun* M20.

polish /ˈpɒlɪʃ/ *verb*. ME.
[Old & mod. French *polir* from Latin *polire*: see -ISH², POLITE.]
1 a *verb trans.* & *intrans.* Make smooth, and usu. glossy, by friction; apply polish to. (Foll. by *up*.) ME. ▸**b** *verb intrans.* Become smooth, take a smooth, and usu. glossy, surface. Formerly also (*rare*), become bright. LME.
2 *fig.* **a** *verb trans.* Free from roughness, rudeness, or coarseness; make more elegant or cultured; refine, improve. (Foll. by *up*.) ME. ▸**b** *verb trans.* Do *away*, put *out*, bring *into* by polishing. E18. ▸**c** *verb intrans.* Become refined. E18.
3 *verb trans.* Bring to a finished state; put the finishing touches to. Also (now *rare*), deck out, adorn. (Foll. by *out*, *up*.) LME.
4 *verb trans.* With *off*: finish off quickly and easily; get rid of summarily. *colloq.* E19.
5 *verb trans.* Eat every last trace of food from (one's plate, bowl, etc.). *colloq.* E20.

📖 **1a** N. HINTON I polish and oil it all the time. A. DESAI He watched his father's employees polish and dust. **2a** E. F. BENSON She had determined to polish up her French. **3** C. P. SNOW He's just polishing a sermon. **4** L. GOULD He could polish it off on Sunday. R. JAFFE Annabel polished off the rest of the bottle.

■ **polishable** *adjective* E17. **polishedly** *adverb* in a polished manner L16. **polishedness** *noun* (now *rare*) polished quality L16. **polisher** *noun* a person who or thing which polishes M16.

polishing /ˈpɒlɪʃɪŋ/ *noun*. LME.
[from POLISH *verb* + -ING¹.]
1 The action of POLISH *verb*. LME.
2 In *pl.* The particles removed by a polishing process. L19.
3 The filtration of the last traces of suspended solids from a liquid, *spec.* in the brewing of beer or the purification of effluent. M20.

polisson /pɔlisɔ̃/ *noun*. Pl. pronounced same. M19.
[French.]
An urchin, a scamp; an ill-bred and uncouth person.

politarch /ˈpɒlɪtɑːk/ *noun*. M19.
[Greek *politarkhēs*, from *politēs* (see POLITIC *adjective* & *noun*) + *arkhēs*: see -ARCH.]
Hist. A governor of citizens; a civic magistrate in some oriental cities, as Thessalonica, under the Romans.

Politbureau /ˈpɒlɪtˌbjʊərəʊ/ *noun*. Also **-buro**, pl. **-os**. E20.
[Russian *politbyuro*, from *polit*(*icheskiĭ* political + *byuro* bureau.]
The highest policy-making committee of a Communist country or party, esp. of the former USSR.

polite /pəˈlʌɪt/ *adjective* & *noun*. LME.
[Latin *politus* pa. pple of *polire* to smooth, polish.]
► **A** *adjective*. †**1** Smoothed, polished, burnished. LME–M18. ▸**b** Cleansed, neat, orderly. L15–E18.
2 *transf.* Refined, elegant, scholarly; exhibiting a refined taste; well-regulated, cultured, cultivated. L15. ▸**b** Courteous, treating others with respect and consideration; having or displaying good manners. M18.

📖 **2** V. S. PRITCHETT French, the polite language of her class. J. UGLOW Ostracised from polite society because she was living with a married man. **b** M. PAGE We would make polite noises but firmly decline. H. CARPENTER He was punctiliously polite, opening doors . . carrying bags and parcels.

► **B** *absol.* as *noun*. Polite behaviour. *do the polite* (*colloq.*), behave in a courteous manner. M19.
■ **politeful** *adjective* (*rare*) polite M19. **politely** *adverb* L16. **politeness** *noun* E17.

politesse /pɔlitɛs/ *noun*. E18.
[French from Italian *politezza*, *pulitezza*, from *pulito* formed as prec.]
Formal politeness.

†**politian** *noun*. L16–L18.
[French †*policien* a citizen, a politician, formed as POLICE *noun* + *-ien* -IAN.]
An expert in polity; a politician.

politic /ˈpɒlɪtɪk/ *adjective* & *noun*. Also †**-ck**. LME.
[Old & mod. French *politique* from Latin *politicus* from Greek *politikos* civic, civil, political (as noun, politician) from *politēs* citizen, from *polis* city, state: see -IC.]
► **A** *adjective*. **1** = POLITICAL *adjective* 1; *spec.* of or relating to a constitutional State, as opp. to a despotism; constitutional. Long *rare* exc. in *body politic* s.v. BODY *noun*. LME.
2 (Of a person) sagacious, prudent, shrewd; (of an action or thing) judicious, expedient, skilfully contrived. LME. ▸**b** Scheming, sly, cunning. L16.

📖 **1** *body politic*: see BODY *noun*. **2** *Irish Times* It is politic, of course, for the Loyalists to cut sober figures. **b** W. STUBBS As king we found him suspicious, cold-blooded and politic.

▸† **B** *noun sing.* (see also POLITICS).
1 Policy; politics. LME–E18.
2 a A politician. M16–M18. ▸**b** A temporizer, esp. in matters of religion; a worldly-wise person. L16–M17.

politic /ˈpɒlɪtɪk/ *verb intrans.* Infl. **-ck-**. E20.
[from POLITIC *adjective* or POLITICS.]
Engage in political activity, esp. in order to strike political bargains or seek votes.

political /pəˈlɪtɪk(ə)l/ *adjective* & *noun*. M16.
[from Latin *politicus* (see POLITIC *adjective* & *noun*) + -AL¹.]
► **A** *adjective*. **1** Of, belonging to, or concerned with the form, organization, and administration of a State or part of a State, and with the regulation of its relations with

other States; of or pertaining to public life and affairs as involving authority and government; relating to or concerned with the theory and practice of politics. M16. ▸**b** Belonging to or forming part of a civil (esp. as opp. to military) administration. M19.
†**2** Shrewd, judicious; expedient; = POLITIC *adjective* 2. E17–E19.
3 Having an organized form of government or society. M17.
4 Belonging to or taking the side of an individual, organization, etc.; supporting particular ideas, principles, or commitments in politics; relating to, affecting, or acting according to, the interests of status and authority in an organization etc., rather than matters of principle. M18.

📖 **1** V. BRITTAIN Every type of political opinion from . . Toryism to . . Communism. *Times* M.P.s who provide most of Northern Ireland's political representation at Westminster. P. ABRAHAMS The social, economic and political conditions under which black people live. R. M. FRANKLIN The immediate reason for the Montmartre conference was political. **3** C. J. FRIEDRICH Six nations decided to establish . . a Political Community. **4** G. WOODBRIDGE A highly political and very clever speech.

Special collocations: **political animal** [Greek *politikon zōon* (Aristotle)] a person viewed as living and acting with others; a follower of or participant in politics. **political anthropology** the branch of anthropology that deals with community authority as it has evolved in aboriginal or isolated societies. ***political asylum***: see ASYLUM 2. **political commissar** a person responsible for political education and organization in a military unit in China. **political correctness** conformity to a body of liberal or radical opinion, esp. on social matters, in the avoidance of anything, even established vocabulary, that may conceivably be construed as discriminatory or pejorative; advocacy of this. ***political* ECONOMIST.** ***political* ECONOMY.** **political football** a subject of contentious political debate. **political geography**: that deals with the boundaries, divisions, and possessions of States. **political hostess**: at a party or gathering attended principally by politicians. **political novel**: describing politics and politicians. **political offence**: regarded as justifiable or deserving of special consideration because of its political motivation. **political philosopher**: who specializes in political philosophy. **political philosophy** the philosophy of politics or public ethics. **political police** a police force concerned with State offences. **political prisoner** a person imprisoned for a political offence. **political refugee** a refugee from an oppressive government. **political science** the branch of knowledge that deals with the State and systems of government; the scientific analysis of political activity and behaviour. **political scientist** an expert in or student of political science. **political trial** a trial of a defendant charged with a political offence; a trial conducted for political reasons.

► **B** *noun*. †**1** In *pl.* Political matters, politics. E17–M18.
2 a A person engaged in civil (esp. as opp. to military) administration. Also, a politician. M19. ▸**b** A political prisoner. L19.

📖 **2a** C. ALLEN Most administrators—other than the Sudan politicals—regarded themselves as badly paid.

■ **politicali'zation** *noun* the action of making someone or something political E20. **politicalize** *verb* (*a*) *verb trans.* make political; (*b*) *verb intrans.* practise or discourse on politics: M19. **politically** *adverb* in a political manner; from a political point of view; ***politically correct***, exhibiting or marked by political correctness: L16. **politicalness** *noun* L17.

politicaster /pəlɪtɪ'kastə/ *noun. rare.* M17.
[Italian (or Spanish) *politicastro*, ult. from Latin *politicus*: see POLITIC *adjective & noun*, -ASTER.]
A feeble or contemptible politician.

politician /pɒlɪ'tɪʃ(ə)n/ *noun.* L16.
[French *politicien*, or directly from POLITIC *adjective & noun*: see -IAN. Cf. POLLY *noun*[3].]
†**1** A shrewd or sagacious person; a schemer; an intriguer. L16–M18.
2 An expert in politics; a person engaged in or concerned with politics, esp. as a practitioner. Also *derog.* (*US*), a person with self-interested political concerns. E17.

📖 **2** *American Speech* The 'middle-of-the-road' is the sacred path followed by compromising politicians. *Times* Few Westminster politicians believe Mr. Taverne could win.

■ **politicianism** *noun* (*rare*) M19.

politicize /pə'lɪtɪsʌɪz/ *verb.* Also **-ise**. M18.
[formed as POLITIC *adjective & noun*: see -IZE.]
1 *verb intrans.* Act the politician; discourse on or engage in politics. M18.
2 *verb trans.* Make political, give a political character to. M19.
■ **politici'zation** *noun* M20.

†**politick** *adjective & noun*, **politicks** *noun* vars. of POLITIC *adjective & noun*, POLITICS.

politicly /'pɒlɪtɪkli/ *adverb.* L15.
[from POLITIC *adjective* + -LY[2].]
In a politic or (formerly) political manner.

politico /pə'lɪtɪkəʊ/ *noun.* Chiefly *derog.* Pl. **-o(e)s**. M17.
[Italian *politico*, Spanish *político* politic, a politician.]
A politician. Also, a person holding strong political views or acting from political motivation.

📖 T. CLANCY A real politico would have had to field really tough questions.

politico- /pə'lɪtɪkəʊ/ *combining form.*
[from Greek *politikos* (see POLITIC *adjective & noun*) + -O-.]
Forming nouns and adjectives with the senses 'politically' as ***politico-aesthetic***, ***politico-ethical***, etc., or 'political and', as ***politico-legal***, ***politico-philosophical***, etc.
■ **politico-eco'nomic** *adjective* = POLITICO-ECONOMICAL M19. **politico-eco'nomical** *adjective* pertaining or relating to political economy M19. **politico-re'ligious** *adjective* at once political and religious; *spec.* pertaining to religion as influenced by politics: M18.

politics /'pɒlɪtɪks/ *noun pl.* (treated as *sing.* or *pl.*). Also †**-cks**. LME.
[from POLITIC *noun* + -S[1], orig. from Greek *ta politika* affairs of state, politics, title of a treatise by Aristotle.]
1 A treatise on political science, *spec.* the one written by Aristotle. LME.
2 The art or science of government, dealing with the form, organization, and administration of a State or part of a State, and with the regulation of its relations with other States. E16. ▸**b** Public life and affairs involving the authority and government of a State or part of a State. L17.
3 a Activities concerned with the acquisition or exercise of authority or status; management or control of private affairs and interests within an organization, family, etc. M17. ▸**b** The ideas, principles, or commitments of an individual, organization, etc., in political life; the organizational process or principle according to which decisions are made affecting authority, status, etc. M18.

📖 **2** ***domestic politics***, ***foreign politics***, ***national politics***, etc. **b** B. TARKINGTON Politics is a dirty business for a gentleman. *Daily Telegraph* Regan confessed that 'politics are not my bag.' *Law Times* Sugden . . re-entered politics. **3a** H. CAREY Confound their politicks. E. LEONARD Politics, man. Who you know. **b** W. BLACK What are his politics?

Phrases: **play politics** act on an issue for political or personal gain rather than from principle. ***practical politics***: see PRACTICAL *adjective*. *SEXUAL* ***politics***.

politique /pɔlitik/ *noun.* Pl. pronounced same. E17.
[French, use as noun of adjective = political.]
1 *Hist.* A member or supporter of a French opportunist and moderate party, founded in *c* 1573, which regarded peace and reform as more important than the continuing civil war between Catholics and Huguenots. Also, an indifferentist, a temporizer. Cf. POLITIC *noun* 2b. E17.
2 A political concept or doctrine; an expression of political ideas. M20.

📖 **2** *Listener* His analysis of Communist politique had a tension which lent itself to . . dramatization.

†**politure** *noun.* L16.
[Obsolete French from Latin *politura*, from *polit-* pa. ppl stem of *polire*: see POLISH *verb*, -URE.]
1 Polishing; polish, smoothness. L16–L18.
2 *fig.* Elegance, polish, refinement. L16–E18.

polity /'pɒlɪti/ *noun.* M16.
[Latin *politia* from Greek *politeia*: see POLICY *noun*[1]. Cf. also POLICE *noun*.]
1 Civil order or organization. M16. ▸**b** Administration of a State, a process of civil government or constitution. E18.
†**2** Management, administration; method of management. M16–M19.
3 a A particular form of government or political organization. L16. ▸**b** An organized society; a State as a political entity. M17.

📖 **1b** T. JEFFERSON The original constitution of the American colonies, possessing their assemblies with the sole right of directing their internal polity. **3a** R. HOOKER We preferre . . the Spartan before the Athenian politie. **b** H. A. L. FISHER The christianization of the Scandinavian races and their acceptance as members of the polity of Europe.

■ **politied** *adjective* (*rare*) having or provided with a polity E19. **politize** *verb* (*rare*) (*a*) *verb trans.* deal with politicly or diplomatically; (*b*) *verb intrans.* deal politicly; deal in politics: L16.

politzerization /ˌpɒlɪtsərʌɪ'zeɪʃ(ə)n/ *noun.* Also **-isation**. L19.
[from Adam *Politzer* (1835–1920), Hungarian otologist + -IZATION.]
MEDICINE. Alteration of the pressure inside the middle ear by passing a cannula through the Eustachian tube.

polizei /pɒlɪ'tsʌɪ/ *noun.* Also **P-**. M20.
[German.]
In Germany and German-speaking countries: the police; a police officer.

polizia /pɒlɪ'tsiːə/ *noun.* Also **P-**. Pl. **-zie** /-'tsiːeɪ/. M20.
[Italian.]
In Italy and Italian-speaking countries: the police, a police officer.

polje /'pɒljə/ *noun.* L19.
[Serbo-Croat.]
PHYSICAL GEOGRAPHY. An enclosed plain in a karstic region (esp. in Slovenia) that is larger than a uvala and usu. has steep enclosing walls and a covering of alluvium.

polk *noun* var. of PULK *noun*.

polk /pəʊlk/ *verb intrans.* M19.
[French *polker*, from POLKA *noun*.]
Dance the polka.

polka /'pəʊlkə/ *noun & verb.* M19.
[German, French from Czech, perh. rel. to *Polka* fem. of *Polák* a Pole.]
► **A** *noun.* **1** A lively dance of Bohemian origin in duple time. M19.
2 A piece of music for this dance or in its rhythm. M19.
3 A woman's tight-fitting jacket, usu. knitted. Also ***polka-jacket***. Now *rare*. M19.
Comb.: **polka dot** any of many round dots of uniform size and arrangement, forming a pattern esp. on fabric; the pattern so formed; **polka-dotted** *adjective* patterned with or as with polka dots; **polkamania** an uncontrolled enthusiasm for dancing the polka.
► **B** *verb intrans.* Dance the polka. M19.

poll /pəʊl/ *noun*[1]. ME.
[Perh. of Low Dutch origin (cf. obsolete Dutch, Low German *polle*); but in place-names Old English *poll*, perh. meaning 'hill', may orig. have meant 'head'.]
► **I** The head of a person or animal.
1 The human head. Now *Scot. & dial.* ME.
2 a The crown or top of the head. ME. ▸**b** The part of the head, excluding the face, on which the hair grows; the scalp. E17. ▸**c** The nape of the neck. L17.
†**3 a** An individual in a number or list, regarded like a head in a crowd. ME–L18. ▸**b** An individual animal of cattle, game, etc. (usu. as *pl.* following a numeral). Cf. HEAD *noun* 5b. L15–E17.
4 A poll tax. *rare.* L17.

📖 **2** E. BAIRD The horse . . is resisting by tilting his poll or the top of his head. **b** THACKERAY His bald head might be seen alongside of Mr. Quilter's . . grey poll.

► **II** Senses derived from sense 3 above.
†**5 a** Number of people as ascertained by counting heads. Only in E17. ▸**b** Counting of heads or people; a census. M–L17.
6 a The counting of voters or votes cast, esp. in a political or other election. E17. ▸**b** The action or process of voting at an election. M19. ▸**c** The result of voting; the total number of votes recorded. M19.
7 A survey of public opinion taken by questioning a sample intended to be representative of the whole population. Cf. GALLUP POLL. E20.

📖 **6b** H. WILSON Fourteen months before the voters go to the polls. **c** *Manchester Examiner* At Wednesday's election there was a lighter poll. *DECLARATION* ***of the poll***. **7** *New Yorker* Polls . . show that Carter currently has the approval of about two-thirds of the public. ***opinion poll***, ***popularity poll***, etc.

► **III** *transf.* **8** The flat or rounded end of a pick or similar tool. E17.
9 The top or crown of a hat or cap. E18.
Comb.: **poll-book** *Hist.* an official register of votes cast in an election, or of the electorate; **poll card** = ***polling card*** s.v. POLLING *noun*; **poll-clerk**: with official duties at an election; †**poll-money** money levied at a fixed rate for every head; a poll tax; **poll-rating** a person's popularity as indicated by a poll; †**poll-silver** a poll tax; **poll-taker** a newspaper etc. which conducts an opinion poll; **poll tax** (chiefly *Hist.*) (*a*) a tax levied on every individual in a specified class; (*b*) *spec.* the community charge in Britain.
■ **po'llee** *noun* a person who is questioned in a poll M20.

Poll /pɒl/ *noun*[2]. L16.
[Alt. of MOLL *noun*. Cf. POLLY *noun*[1].]
(A name for) a parrot.

poll /pəʊl/ *adjective & noun*[3]. In sense A.1 also †**pol**. LME.
[Short for *polled* ppl adjective of POLL *verb*.]
► **A** *adjective.* †**1** Designating an awnless variety of cereal. LME–E17.
2 Of a sheet of paper etc.: cut evenly at the edge. *obsolete* exc. in ***deed poll*** s.v. DEED *noun*, ***poll deed*** below. E16.
3 Designating an animal without horns. *rare.* M18.
Special collocations: **poll deed** (now *rare*) = ***deed poll*** s.v. DEED *noun*.
► **B** *noun.* An animal of a hornless breed. L18.

poll /pəʊl/ *verb.* ME.
[from POLL *noun*[1].]
► **I** With ref. to cutting.
1 *verb trans.* Cut short the hair of (a person, a person's head, an animal); cut (the hair). Now chiefly *Scot. & US*. ME.
2 *verb trans.* Cut off the top of (a tree or plant); *esp.* top (a tree) so that it may put out branches; pollard. LME. ▸†**b** Cut off the head of; behead. E–M17.
3 *verb trans.* Cut evenly the edge of (a sheet of paper etc.). Cf. POLL *adjective* 2. E17.

4 *verb trans.* Cut off the horns of (cattle); breed (cattle) without horns. Chiefly as ***polled*** *ppl adjective.* E17.

> 📖 **1** J. HELLER He polled his head at every year's end . . for by then the hair was long. **2** A. TUCKER We prune, and poll, and cut our trees into unnatural shapes. **4** G. E. EVANS This breed of polled (hornless) cattle was evolved by Norfolk and Suffolk farmers.

▶ **II** With ref. to exaction.
5 *verb trans.* Plunder by or as by excessive taxation; rob, pillage. Now *rare.* L15. ▸†**b** *verb intrans.* Practise extortion; pillage, plunder. E16–E17.
5 †**poll and pill** = *pill and poll* s.v. PILL *verb*[1].

▶ **III** With ref. to voting.
6 *verb trans.* **a** Take the vote or votes of; ask the opinion of (a person) on a particular matter. Usu. in *pass.* E17. ▸**b** Of a candidate: receive (so many votes) in a poll; *rare* bring (a voter) to the poll. M19.
†**7** *verb trans.* Count (people etc.). M17–E18.
8 *verb intrans.* Vote at a poll; cast one's vote. L17. ▸**b** *verb trans.* Cast or record (a vote) in a poll. E18.
9 *verb trans.* TELECOMMUNICATIONS & COMPUTING. Interrogate (a measuring device, part of a computer, a node in a network, etc.), esp. as part of a repeated cycle of interrogations. M20.

> 📖 **6a** A. TOFFLER The voter may be polled about specific issues. *Economist* Only . . 12% of those polled expect sales to rise during the first quarter. **b** G. SWIFT In the election . . my grandfather polls only eleven hundred votes.

■ **pollable** *adjective* able to be polled; entitled to vote: M19. †**pollage** *noun* (*a*) extortion; (*b*) exaction of a poll tax: M16–L19.

pollack /ˈpɒlək/ *noun & verb.* Also ***-ock**. LME.
[Perh. of Celtic origin.]
▶ **A** *noun.* Pl. same, **-s**. Any of several marine food fishes of the gadid genus *Pollachius*, having a protruding lower jaw, esp. the green-backed *P. pollachius* of European inshore waters, and the saithe, *P. virens*, of the N. Atlantic. LME.
SEY-*pollack*.
▶ **B** *verb intrans.* Fish for pollack. E19.

pollakanthic /pɒləˈkanθɪk/ *adjective.* E20.
[from Greek *pollakis* many times + *anthein* to flower, from *anthos* flower: see -IC.]
BOTANY. Of a plant: flowering and fruiting several times in its life, polycarpous.
■ Also **pollakanthous** *adjective* M20.

pollam /ˈpɒləm/ *noun.* L18.
[Telugu *pālemu*, Tamil *pālaiyam*: cf. POLIGAR.]
In southern India: a feudal estate or territory held by a poligar.

pollan /ˈpɒlən/ *noun.* E18.
[Irish *pollán*, perh. from *poll* pool + *-án* Celtic formative suffix.]
A form of a freshwater whitefish, *Coregonus albula*, found in the inland loughs of Ireland. Cf. VENDACE.

pollard /ˈpɒləd/ *noun*[1]. *obsolete* exc. *Hist.* ME.
[App. from POLL *noun*[1] (with ref. to the head depicted) + -ARD.]
A base coin of foreign origin, current in England in the late 13th cent.

†**pollard** *noun*[2]. L16–M18.
[from POLL *noun*[1] + -ARD, with ref. to the large head.]
The chub.

pollard /ˈpɒləd/ *adjective & noun*[3]. E16.
[from POLL *verb* + -ARD.]
▶ **A** *adjective.* †**1** Of wheat: awnless. E16–M18.
2 Of a tree: polled, lopped, cut back. M17.
▶ **B** *noun.* **1** A hornless animal of a kind naturally horned; an animal, esp. an ox or goat, of a hornless breed. M16.
†**2** Awnless wheat. L16–L17.
3 Bran sifted from flour; a fine grade of bran containing some flour; flour or meal containing fine bran. L16.
4 A tree which has been polled, so as to produce a growth of young branches at the top. E17.

pollard /ˈpɒləd/ *verb trans.* L17.
[from POLLARD *noun*[3].]
Cut off the branches of (a tree) leaving only the main trunk; make a pollard of.

pollen /ˈpɒlən/ *noun & verb.* E16.
[Latin *pollen*, *pollin-* fine flour or powder, rel. to POLENTA, *pulvis* powder, *puls* (see PULSE *noun*[2]).]
▶ **A** *noun.* †**1** Fine flour or meal; fine powder. E16–M18.
2 BOTANY. The male gametes or microspores of a seed plant, produced as a fine granular or powdery substance in the anthers of a flower or the male cone of a gymnosperm and usu. transported by wind or insects. M18.
Comb.: **pollen analysis** the analysis and identification of pollen grains; **pollen analyst** an expert in pollen analysis, a palynologist; **pollen basket** ENTOMOLOGY a flattened area fringed with hairs on the hind leg of a bee, used for carrying pollen; also called *corbicula*; **pollen brush** ENTOMOLOGY a brush or tuft of hairs forming part of a bee's pollen basket; **pollen-cell** (*a*) a cell which develops into a pollen grain, or forms part of one; (*b*) a cell in a honeycomb in which pollen is stored; **pollen-chamber** in some gymnosperms, a cavity at the tip of the ovule in which pollen is stored prior to germination; **pollen count** an index of the quantity of pollen in the air (esp. as affecting sufferers from hay fever), or preserved at an archaeological site; **pollen diagram** a sequence of pollen spectra from one site, showing changes in the frequencies of various types of pollen with depth or time; **pollen fever** = *hay fever* s.v. HAY *noun*[1]; **pollen grain** each of the tough-coated grains of which pollen consists (usu. a single cell); **pollen index** = *pollen count* above; **pollen mother cell** a cell in a seed plant which yields a tetrad of pollen grains after meiosis; **pollen parent** a plant from which pollen is taken to fertilize another plant artificially so as to produce a hybrid; **pollen-plate** a flat or hollow surface fringed with hairs on the legs or body of a bee, used to carry pollen; **pollen profile** = *pollen diagram* above; **pollen-sac** each of the chambers (in angiosperms usu. four in each anther) in which pollen is formed; **pollen spectrum** the relative frequencies of types of pollen in a sample; **pollen-tube** a tube formed by protrusion of the intine of a pollen grain when deposited on the stigma, which penetrates the style and conveys the fertilizing nuclei to the ovule; **pollen zone** GEOLOGY a distinct climate or vegetation zone (in the geological past) as determined by pollen analysis.
▶ **B** *verb trans.* Pollinate; cover or sprinkle with pollen. *poet. rare.* L19.

pollenin /ˈpɒlənɪn/ *noun.* E19.
[from POLLEN *noun* + -IN[1].]
BIOCHEMISTRY. = SPOROPOLLENIN.

†**pollenize** *verb* see POLLINIZE.

poller /ˈpəʊlə/ *noun.* E16.
[from POLL *verb* + -ER[1].]
†**1** A person who plunders or extorts. E16–L17.
2 †**a** A barber. L16–L17. ▸**b** A person who polls trees. *US.* E19.
3 **a** A person who votes, esp. at an election. L18. ▸**b** Orig., a person who registered voters. Now (chiefly *US*), a person who conducts a poll, esp. an opinion poll. L18.

†**pollet** *noun. rare.* Also **-ette**. M16–M19.
[App. aphet. from French *épaulette*: see EPAULETTE.]
= EPAULETTE 2.

poll-evil /pəʊliːv(ə)l, -vɪl/ *noun.* L16.
[from POLL *noun*[1] + EVIL *noun*[1].]
An inflamed or ulcerous sore on a horse's head, esp. between the ligament and the first bone of the neck.

pollex /ˈpɒlɛks/ *noun.* Pl. **pollices** /ˈpɒlɪsiːz/. M19.
[Latin = thumb, big toe.]
1 ANATOMY & ZOOLOGY. The thumb; the first or innermost digit on the forefoot of a tetrapod vertebrate. Also occas., the big toe or hallux. M19.
2 ZOOLOGY. The movable part of the forceps of some crustaceans. L19.

polley *adjective & noun* vars. of POLEY *adjective & noun*[2].

pollical /ˈpɒlɪk(ə)l/ *adjective.* L19.
[from Latin *pollic-*, POLLEX: see -AL[1].]
ANATOMY. Of or pertaining to the thumb.

pollices *noun* pl. of POLLEX.

pollicitation /ˌpɒlɪsɪˈteɪʃ(ə)n/ *noun.* L15.
[French, or Latin *pollicitatio(n)-*, from *pollicitat-* pa. ppl stem of *pollicitari* promise: see -ATION.]
The action of promising; a promise; a document conveying a promise; *spec.* in CIVIL LAW, a promise not yet formally accepted, but nevertheless binding in some cases.

pollinarium /pɒlɪˈnɛːrɪəm/ *noun.* Pl. **-ia** /-ɪə/. L19.
[mod. Latin, from Latin *pollin-*, POLLEN, after *ovarium* ovary.]
BOTANY. A pollination unit consisting of one or more pollinia with their connected parts.

pollinary /ˈpɒlɪn(ə)ri/ *adjective.* L19.
[formed as next + -ARY[1].]
BOTANY. Of or pertaining to pollen; concerned in the production of pollen.

pollinate /ˈpɒlɪneɪt/ *verb trans.* L19.
[from Latin *pollin-*, POLLEN + -ATE[3].]
Convey pollen to or deposit pollen on (a stigma, an ovule, a flower, a plant) and so allow fertilization. Freq. (esp. with specifying word) as ***pollinated*** *ppl adjective.*
■ **polliˈnation** *noun* the action or an act of pollinating a plant; transport or deposition of pollen: L19. **pollinator** *noun* an insect or other agent that pollinates a plant E20.

pollinctor /pɒˈlɪŋktə/ *noun.* Long *rare.* E17.
[Latin, from *pollinct-* pa. ppl stem of *pollingere* wash (a corpse) and prepare it for cremation: see -OR.]
A person who prepares a dead body for cremation or embalming, by washing, anointing, etc.

polling /ˈpəʊlɪŋ/ *noun.* ME.
[from POLL *verb* + -ING[1].]
1 †**a** The cutting of hair; shearing, clipping. ME–M17. ▸**b** The cutting off of the top of a tree. E17.
†**2** Plundering, extortion, robbery; an instance of this. E16–M17.
†**3** In *pl.* The results or proceeds of polling; offcuttings; spoils. M16–M19.
4 **a** The casting or recording of votes. E17. ▸**b** The action or process of conducting a poll. M20.
5 TELECOMMUNICATIONS & COMPUTING. The action or process of polling a device, network, node, etc.; *spec.* repeated interrogation of each node of a network in turn. M20.

> 📖 **4a** *Manchester Examiner* The polling in the election of nine members of the . . School Board. **b** *Public Opinion* Scientific polling on individual issues fills a great gap in the democratic form of government. A. GARVE You go into the streets and do a little polling on the subject.

Comb.: **polling-booth** a compartment in which a voter can privately mark a ballot-paper; **polling card** a card notifying a voter of voting details for an election; **polling clerk** = *poll-clerk* s.v. POLL *noun*[1]; **polling day** a day on which voting in an election takes place; **polling station** a building etc. where voting takes place in an election.

pollinia *noun* pl. of POLLINIUM.

pollinic /pəˈlɪnɪk/ *adjective.* M19.
[from Latin *pollin-*, POLLEN + -IC.]
BOTANY. Of, containing, or relating to pollen.
■ **pollinical** *adjective* L19.

polliniferous /pɒlɪˈnɪf(ə)rəs/ *adjective.* M19.
[from Latin *pollin-*, POLLEN + -I- + -FEROUS.]
BOTANY. Bearing or producing pollen.

pollinigerous /ˌpɒlɪˈnɪdʒ(ə)rəs/ *adjective.* E19.
[from Latin *pollin-*, POLLEN + -I- + -GEROUS.]
ENTOMOLOGY. (Adapted for) carrying pollen.

pollinise *verb* var. of POLLINIZE.

pollinium /pəˈlɪnɪəm/ *noun.* Pl. **-ia** /-ɪə/. M19.
[mod. Latin, from Latin *pollin-*, POLLEN + -IUM.]
BOTANY. A coherent mass of pollen grains in the anther-cells of the Orchidaceae and Asclepiadaceae, carried as a body by pollinating insects.

pollinivorous /pɒlɪˈnɪv(ə)rəs/ *adjective.* M19.
[from Latin *pollin-*, POLLEN + -I- + -VOROUS.]
BIOLOGY. Feeding on pollen.

pollinize /ˈpɒlɪnʌɪz/ *verb trans.* Now *rare.* Also **-ise**, (earlier) †**pollen-**. E19.
[from Latin *pollin-*, POLLEN + -IZE.]
= POLLINATE.
■ **polliniˈzation** *noun* pollination L19.

polliwog /ˈpɒlɪwɒɡ/ *noun. dial. & US.* Also **pollywog**, **-wiggle** /-wɪɡ(ə)l/, & other vars. LME.
[from POLL *noun*[1] + WIG(GLE *verb*, alt. by assim. of the vowels of the initial and final syllables.]
A tadpole.

pollo /ˈpɒləʊ/ *noun.* Pl. **-os**. M19.
[Spanish, Italian = chicken.]
COOKERY. Chicken, a chicken dish, *esp.* one cooked in an Italian or (Mexican-)Spanish fashion.

pollock *noun* see POLLACK.

polloi /pɒˈlɔɪ/ *noun. slang.* M20.
[Greek = many. Cf. HOI POLLOI.]
A crowd, a mob.

Poll-parrot /pɒlˈparət/ *noun & verb.* Also **p-**. M19.
[from POLL *noun*[2] + PARROT *noun.*]
▶ **A** *noun.* **1** = POLL *noun*[2]. M19.
2 Idle talk or repetition. L19.
▶ **B** *verb trans. & intrans.* = PARROT *verb* 1, 2. M19.

pollster /ˈpəʊlstə/ *noun.* Orig. *US.* M20.
[from POLL *noun*[1] + -STER.]
A person who conducts an opinion poll; an analyst of opinion polls, or of voting patterns generally.

pollucite /ˈpɒljʊsʌɪt, pɒˈluːsʌɪt/ *noun.* M19.
[from Latin *Pollux* (from the mineral's being associated with a variety of petalite called *Castor*: see GEMINI *noun* 1) + -ITE[1].]
MINERALOGY. A rare caesium aluminosilicate crystallizing in the cubic system which occurs as transparent colourless crystals, esp. in pegmatites, and is used as a gemstone.

pollute /pəˈluːt/ *ppl adjective. obsolete* exc. *poet.* LME.
[Latin *pollutus* pa. pple of *polluere*: see next.]
= POLLUTED 1.

pollute /pəˈluːt/ *verb trans.* LME.
[Latin *pollut-* pa. ppl stem of *polluere*, from base of PRO-[1] + base of *lutum* mud.]
1 Make morally impure; violate the purity or sanctity of; desecrate, defile, corrupt. LME.
2 Make physically impure, foul, or filthy; dirty, taint. Now *esp.* contaminate (the environment, the atmosphere, etc.) with harmful or unpleasant substances. M16.

> 📖 **1** D. CUSACK She seems to think I'll pollute that class if I'm left alone with them. **2** P. LIVELY Enough crude oil to pollute twenty miles of coastline.

■ **pollutant** *noun* an agent which fouls or contaminates the environment etc. L19. **polluter** *noun* M16. **pollutive** *adjective* causing environmental pollution L20.

polluted /pəˈluːtɪd/ *ppl adjective.* LME.
[from prec. + -ED[1].]
1 Defiled; made foul or impure; (of the environment etc.) contaminated with harmful or unpleasant substances. LME.
2 Intoxicated by drink or drugs. *slang* (orig. *US*). E20.

> 📖 **1** JULIETTE HUXLEY The Swiss lakes are now so polluted that one is no longer allowed to swim in their waters.

■ **pollutedly** *adverb* (*long rare*) E17. **pollutedness** *noun* (*long rare*) E17.

pollution /pəˈluːʃ(ə)n/ *noun*. ME.
[Old & mod. French, or Latin *pollutio(n-)*, formed as POLLUTE *verb*: see -ION.]
1 Ejaculation of semen without sexual intercourse. ME.
2 a The action of polluting; the condition of being polluted. Orig., defilement, corruption; now chiefly, the presence in the environment, or the introduction into it, of substances which have harmful or unpleasant effects. LME. ▸b A thing that pollutes; a polluted thing. E17.
3 Desecration; defilement of what is sacred. Now *rare*. LME.

📖 **2a** N. G. CLARK Pollution of the atmosphere by the emission of smoke. C. FRANCIS Creatures of the deep sea may . . hide the effects of pollution by burying toxic matter. ***thermal pollution***: see THERMAL *adjective*.

■ **pollutional** *adjective* causing or constituting pollution E20.

Polly /ˈpɒli/ *noun*[1]. E19.
[Dim. of POLL *noun*[2]: see -Y[6].]
(A name for) a parrot.

Polly /ˈpɒli/ *noun*[2]. *slang*. M19.
[Abbreviation of APOLLINARIS.]
A bottle or glass of Apollinaris water.

polly /ˈpɒli/ *noun*[3]. *US & Austral. slang*. M20.
[Abbreviation.]
= POLITICIAN 2.

Pollyanna /pɒlɪˈanə/ *noun*. E20.
[The heroine of stories for children written by Eleanor Hodgman Porter (1868–1920), US author.]
A person able to find apparent cause for happiness in the most disastrous situations; a person who is unduly optimistic or achieves spurious happiness through self-delusion.
■ **Pollyannaish** *adjective* like (a) Pollyanna; naively optimistic; unrealistically happy: E20. **Pollyannaism** *noun* behaviour or a statement characteristic of (a) Pollyanna M20.

pollywog *noun* var. of POLLIWOG.

polo /ˈpəʊləʊ/ *noun*[1]. Pl. **-os**. L19.
[Tibetan *pholo*, lit. 'ball game'.]
1 A game of Eastern origin resembling hockey, played on horseback with long-handled mallets. L19.
2 Any of various team games with a ball and goals. L19.
3 a = *polo hat* below. E20. ▸b = *polo-neck* below. M20.
2 *water polo*.
Comb.: **polo coat** a type of camel-hair coat; **polo collar** (*a*) a kind of stiff upright shirt collar; (*b*) = *polo-neck* (a) below; **polo hat** a small round hat worn esp. in the later 19th cent.; **polo-neck** (*a*) a high, close-fitting roll-collar; (*b*) a jersey with such a collar; **polo-necked** *adjective* having a polo-neck; ***polo-pony***: see PONY *noun* 1b; **polo shirt** (*a*) a coloured shirt of the kind worn by players of polo; (*b*) a shirt with a polo-neck; **polo-stick** a mallet used in playing polo.
■ **poloist** *noun* (*rare*) a player of polo L19.

polo /ˈpəʊləʊ/ *noun*[2]. Pl. **-os**. L19.
[Spanish.]
An Andalusian folk-dance; the music which accompanies this dance.

polocrosse /ˈpəʊləʊkrɒs/ *noun*. M20.
[Blend of POLO *noun*[1] and LACROSSE.]
A game played on horseback with sticks having a head like that of a lacrosse-stick.

polocyte /ˈpəʊləʊsʌɪt/ *noun*. E20.
[from POLE *noun*[2] + -O- + -CYTE.]
EMBRYOLOGY. = ***polar body*** s.v. POLAR *adjective*.

poloidal /pəˈlɔɪd(ə)l/ *adjective*. M20.
[from POLAR *adjective* after *toroidal*.]
Of, pertaining to, representing, or designating a magnetic field associated with a toroidal electric field, in which each line of force is confined to a radial or meridian plane; of the shape of such a field.

polonaise /pɒləˈneɪz/ *noun, adjective, & verb*. M18.
[French, use as noun (sc. *robe* dress, *danse* dance) of fem. of *polonais* POLISH *adjective & noun*[2] from medieval Latin *Polonia* Poland.]
▸**A** *noun*. **1** A slow dance of Polish origin, consisting chiefly of an intricate march or procession, in triple time; a piece of music for this dance or in its time or rhythm. M18.
2 A kind of dress or overdress, with the skirt open at the front and looped up at the back, orig. resembling a garment worn by Polish women. L18. ▸**b** A fabric made from a silk and cotton mixture. Cf. POLONESE *noun* 2. L19.
3 COOKERY. A dish cooked in a Polish style. L19.
4 A polonaise rug or carpet. M20.
▸**B** *adjective*. **1** Designating a kind of rug or carpet made in Persia during the 16th and 17th cents., using silver and gold warp threads. E20.
2 COOKERY. Of a dish: cooked in a Polish style. M20.
▸**C** *verb intrans*. Dance a polonaise; move in a stately manner. E19.

polone *noun* var. of PALONE.

†**polonese** *noun*. Pl. same. E18.
[from French *polonais*, Italian *polonese* Polish: see prec., -ESE.]
1 A native of Poland, a Pole. E18–E19.
2 = POLONAISE *noun* 2. Also, the material for this. M–L18.

Polong /pəʊˈlɒŋ/ *noun*. M19.
[Malay.]
In Malay belief, a usu. malicious spirit or imp.

Polonian /pəˈləʊnɪən/ *adjective*[1] *& noun*. *arch*. M16.
[from medieval Latin *Polonia* Poland + -AN.]
▸**A** *adjective*. Of Poland; Polish. M16.
▸**B** *noun*. A native or inhabitant of Poland. L16.
■ †**Polonish** *adjective* Polish L16–M17. **Polonize** /ˈpəʊlənʌɪz/ *verb trans*. make Polish L19.

Polonian /pəˈləʊnɪən/ *adjective*[2]. M20.
[from *Polonius* (see below) + -AN.]
Characteristic of or resembling Polonius, an elderly sententious courtier in Shakespeare's *Hamlet*.

polonium /pəˈləʊnɪəm/ *noun*. L19.
[from medieval Latin *Polonia* Poland, the native country of Marie Curie (see CURIE) + -IUM.]
CHEMISTRY. A rare highly radioactive metallic chemical element, atomic no. 84, present in some uranium ores. (Symbol Po.)

polony /pəˈləʊni/ *noun*[1]. M18.
[App. alt. of BOLOGNA.]
= ***BOLOGNA sausage***. Also more fully ***polony sausage***.

Polony /ˈpəʊləni, pəˈləʊni/ *adjective & noun*[2]. E17.
[formed as POLONIAN *adjective*[1] *& noun*: see -Y[3].]
▸†**A** *adjective*. Polish. Only in 17.
▸**B** *noun*. A kind of long coat or gown for young boys. Also *gen*., a long loose-fitting garment. *Scot*. Now *rare*. E18.

polos /ˈpɒlɒs/ *noun*. M19.
[Late Greek = a head-dress, from Greek = axis.]
A cylindrical head-dress, seen in some representations of Greek and oriental goddesses.

Polovtsy /pəˈlɒvtsi/ *noun pl*. L18.
[Russian.]
The nomad tribes of the Kipchak Turks, which inhabited the steppes between the Danube and the Volga from the 11th to the 13th cent. Also called ***Kipchak***.
■ **Poloˈvetsian** *adjective & noun* (*a*) *adjective* of or pertaining to the Polovtsy; (*b*) *noun* a member or the Turkic language of the Polovtsy: M20. **Polovtsian** *adjective & noun* (*a*) *adjective* of or pertaining to the Polovtsy; (*b*) *noun* a member of the Polovtsy: E19.

polrumptious /pɒlˈrʌm(p)ʃəs/ *adjective*. *dial. & slang*. L18.
[Perh. from POLL *noun*[1] + RUMPTI(ON + -OUS.]
Unruly, restive; overconfident.

polska /ˈpɒlskə/ *noun*. L19.
[Swedish, from *Polsk* Polish.]
A processional Scandinavian folk-dance of Polish origin, usu. in 3/4 time; a piece of music for this dance.

polt /pəʊlt/ *noun & verb*. *obsolete* exc. *dial*. E17.
[Origin unkn.]
▸**A** *noun*. **1** A blow, a hard rap or knock. E17.
†**2 a** A pestle, a club. Cf. POLT-FOOT. Only in E17. ▸**b** The club-shaped stem and bulb of a leek. Only in M17.
▸**B** *verb trans*. Knock, thrash, beat. M17.

Poltalloch /pɒlˈtalək, -x/ *noun*. L19.
[An estate in Scotland, where the breed was developed.]
In full ***Poltalloch terrier***. A West Highland terrier.

poltergeist /ˈpɒltəgʌɪst/ *noun*. M19.
[German, from *poltern* make a noise, create a disturbance + *Geist* ghost.]
A spirit believed to manifest itself by making noises and moving physical objects.

polt-foot /ˈpəʊltfʊt/ *noun & adjective*. *arch*. L16.
[App. from POLT *noun* 2 + FOOT *noun*.]
▸**A** *noun*. Pl. **-feet** /-fiːt/. A club-foot. L16.
▸**B** *attrib*. or as *adjective*. Club-footed. L16.

poltroon /pɒlˈtruːn/ *noun*. E16.
[French *poltron*, †*poultron* from Italian *poltrone* sluggard, coward (cf. medieval Latin *pultro*), perh. from †*poltro* bed (as if 'lie-abed').]
A spiritless coward; a worthless wretch.
■ **poltroonery** *noun* the behaviour of a poltroon; cowardice: L16. **poltroonish** *adjective* M19.

†**polverine** *noun*. M17–E19.
[Italian *polverino*, from Latin *pulver-*, *pulvis* dust, powder + Italian *-ino* -INE[4].]
The calcined ashes of a plant, brought from the eastern Mediterranean region and Syria, and used in glass-making.

Polwarth /ˈpɒlwəθ/ *noun*. *Austral. & NZ*. E20.
[A county in Victoria, Australia, where the breed originated.]
(An animal of) a hardy breed of sheep with long wool, orig. produced by mating a merino ram with a crossbred ewe.

poly /ˈpəʊli/ *noun*[1]. Now *rare* or *obsolete*. Also **poley**. E16.
[Latin *polium* from Greek *polion*, perh. from *polios* hoary.]
1 More fully ***poly-mountain*** [Latin *polium montanum*]. A kind of germander, *Teucrium polium*, an aromatic labiate plant of southern Europe. Also, a related plant, basil thyme, *Clinopodium acinos*. E16.
2 ***grass poly***, a plant of the purple loosestrife family, *Lythrum hyssopifolia*, which grows in seasonally wet fields and has small lilac flowers in the axils of grasslike leaves. E17.

poly /ˈpɒli/ *noun*[2]. *colloq*. Pl. **-s**. M19.
[Abbreviation.]
= POLYTECHNIC *noun*.

poly /ˈpɒli/ *noun*[3]. *colloq*. M20.
[Abbreviation.]
Polythene.
Comb.: **polybag** a bag made of polythene film; **poly-wrapped** *adjective* wrapped in polythene film.

poly- /ˈpɒli/ *combining form*.
[Greek *polu-*, from *polus* much, *polloi* many.]
Used in words adopted from Greek and in English words modelled on these, and as a freely productive prefix, mainly in scientific and technical use, in senses 'many, much', 'having, involving, containing, etc., many' (*many* variously connoting 'two or more', 'three or more', 'several', or 'a large number' in different contexts); in CHEMISTRY signifying the presence of several or many atoms, radicals, etc., of a particular kind in a molecule etc.; *spec*. forming names of polymers (cf. OLIGO-).
■ **polyaˈcrylamide** *noun* (CHEMISTRY) a polymer of acrylamide, *esp*. a water-soluble polymer of a kind used to form or stabilize gels and as a thickening or clarifying agent M20. **polyˈacrylate** *noun* (CHEMISTRY) an ester or salt of a polyacrylic acid; a polymer of an ester of acrylic acid: M20. **polyaˈcrylic** *adjective* (CHEMISTRY) designating polymers of acrylic acid or its esters, or thermoplastic materials made from such polymers M20. **polyacryloˈnitrile** *noun* (CHEMISTRY) any of the polymers of acrylonitrile, many of which are used as man-made fibres M20. **polyˈallomer** *noun* [ALLO- + -MER] CHEMISTRY any of a class of crystalline thermoplastics which are copolymers of two or more different alkenes M20. **polyalphaˈbetic** *adjective* (CRYPTOGRAPHY) employing more than one alphabet, so that each letter of the alphabet may be encoded as any of two or more characters E20. **polyˈamine** *noun* (CHEMISTRY) any organic compound which contains two or more amine groups M19. **polyˈangular** *adjective* (*rare*) multiangular, polygonal L17. **polyˈanion** *noun* (CHEMISTRY) a negatively charged polyion M20. **polyarˈthritic** *adjective* (MEDICINE) pertaining to or affected with polyarthritis E20. **polyarˈthritis** *noun* (MEDICINE) rheumatic disease affecting several joints L19. **polyarˈticular** *adjective* (MEDICINE) affecting several joints L19. **polyblast** *noun* [-BLAST] BIOLOGY (*a*) a mass of many cells, *esp*. = MORULA *noun*[1] 2; (*b*) a wandering macrophage: L19. **polyˈblastic** *adjective* (BIOLOGY) pertaining to or of the nature of a polyblast E20. **polybutaˈdiene** *noun* (CHEMISTRY) any of the polymers of 1,3-butadiene or its derivatives; synthetic rubber consisting of such polymers: M20. **polyˈcation** *noun* (CHEMISTRY) a positively charged polyion M20. **polyˈcentric** *adjective* = MULTICENTRIC; POLITICS characterized by polycentrism: L19. **polyˈcentrism** *noun* (POLITICS) (belief in) the idea that each separate Communist Party should have the right of full national autonomy and not necessarily conform to the Soviet model M20. **polyˈcephalous** *adjective* [Greek *polukephalos*: see -CEPHALOUS] many-headed E19. **polyˈchloroprene** *noun* (CHEMISTRY) any of the polymers of chloroprene; synthetic rubber (esp. neoprene) consisting of such polymers: M20. **polyˈcholia** *noun* (*rare*, MEDICINE) [Greek *kholē* bile] excessive secretion of bile M19. **polyˈchoral** *adjective* (MUSIC) in which the choral ensemble is divided into groups M20. **polycisˈtronic** *adjective* (GENETICS) comprising or derived from more than one cistron and so containing the information for producing more than one gene M20. **polyˈclimax** *noun* (ECOLOGY) the presence of several climaxes in different parts of a given region; usu. *attrib*.: M20. **polycondenˈsation** *noun* (CHEMISTRY) a condensation reaction which yields a polymer M20. **polyˈconic** *adjective* involving or based on a number of cones; *spec*. designating a system of map projection in which each parallel of latitude is represented by developing a strip from a cone touching the earth's surface along that parallel: M19. **polyˈcormic** *adjective* (BOTANY) [Greek *kormos* trunk (of a tree)] (esp. of certain conifers) having lateral stems equal to or coordinate with the main stem (cf. MONOCORMIC) L19. **polycotyˈledonous** *adjective* (BOTANY) (esp. of certain gymnosperms) having more than one cotyledon in the seed E19. **polycratism** /pəˈlɪkrətɪz(ə)m/ *noun* [-CRAT] government by many rulers, polyarchy E20. **polycross** *adjective* (AGRICULTURE) made by or involving the planting together and subsequent natural cross-pollination of two or more mutually fertile varieties of plant M20. **polyculture** *noun* (*a*) the simultaneous cultivation or exploitation of several crops or animals; (*b*) an area in which this is practised: E20. **polyˈcystic** *adjective* (MEDICINE) having or consisting of several cysts M19. **polyˈdentate** *adjective* (CHEMISTRY) (of a ligand) forming two or more bonds, usu. with the same central atom M20. **polydiˈmensional** *adjective* having or relating to more than three dimensions L19. **polydrug** *adjective* (of drug abuse etc.) involving several drugs together L20. **polyelecˈtronic** *adjective* (CHEMISTRY) containing or pertaining to more than one electron E20. **polyˈendocrine** *adjective* (MEDICINE) characterized by the involvement of several endocrine glands M20. **polyene** *noun* [-ENE] CHEMISTRY any organic compound containing two or more carbon–carbon double bonds, esp. in a chain of conjugated single and double bonds E20. **polyˈenergid** *adjective* (BIOLOGY) having many complete sets of chromosomes E20. **polyˈethene** *noun* = POLYETHYLENE L20. **polyˈethnic** *adjective* belonging to or containing many ethnic groups L19. **polyˈfunctional** *adjective* (CHEMISTRY) having two or more different functional groups in the molecule E20. **polyˈglacial** *adjective* designating a theory postulating more than one glacial period

during the Pleistocene E20. poly'**glacialism** *noun* the polyglacial theory L20. poly'**glacialist** *noun & adjective* (*a*) *noun* a supporter of polyglacialism; (*b*) *adjective* of or pertaining to polyglacialism or polyglacialists: M20. poly'**glycol** *noun* (CHEMISTRY) = POLYETHYLENE *glycol* L19. poly'**haploid** *noun* (BOTANY) a plant descended from polyploids that has half of the set of chromosomes normally expected M20. poly'**hedroid** *noun* (MATH.) = POLYTOPE L19. poly'**hybrid** *noun & adjective* (BIOLOGY) (of, pertaining to, or designating) a hybrid that is heterozygous at several genetic loci E20. **polyion** *noun* (CHEMISTRY) (*a*) an ion which contains a number of atoms of its parent element; (*b*) a large ion derived from a polyelectrolyte: M20. **polyi'onic** *adjective* (CHEMISTRY) of, pertaining to, or of the nature of a polyion; containing polyions: E20. **polyiso'butylene** *noun* (CHEMISTRY) any polymer of isobutylene; synthetic rubber made from such polymers: M20. poly'**isoprene** *noun* (CHEMISTRY) a polymer of isoprene, *esp.* any of those forming the major constituents of natural rubber M20. poly'**karyocyte** *noun* (BIOLOGY) an osteoclast, *esp.* a large one with many nuclei L19. **polyketide** /-'kiːtʌɪd/ *noun* [KETO-] CHEMISTRY a compound formed by the condensation of acetate molecules, esp. in a biological system E20. poly'**lectal** *adjective* [-LECT] LINGUISTICS having or recognizing many regional or social varieties (within a language) L20. poly'**lingual** *adjective* = MULTILINGUAL *adjective* M20. poly'**lingualism** *noun* = MULTILINGUALISM M20. poly'**lithic** *adjective* made of several stones or kinds of stone M19. **polyloquent** /pə'lɪləkwənt/ *adjective* (*rare*) speaking much, voluble M17. **polyme'niscous** *adjective* (of an invertebrate eye) having many lenses L19. **polyme'tallic** *adjective* containing (ores of) several metals L19. **polymetre** *noun* (MUSIC) (*a*) the succession of different metrical patterns in 16th-cent. vocal music; (*b*) music using two or more different time-signatures simultaneously: E20. poly'**metric** *adjective* (MUSIC) of or pertaining to polymetre; using different metres simultaneously: M20. poly'**metrical** *adjective* (MUSIC) = POLYMETRIC E20. **polymor'phemic** *adjective* (LINGUISTICS) consisting of two or more morphemes M20. **polyneme** *adjective* [Greek *nēma* thread] CYTOLOGY (of a chromatid) containing more than one duplex of DNA M20. **polyneu'ropathy** *noun* (MEDICINE) a general degeneration of peripheral nerves that starts distally and spreads proximally M20. poly'**nucleotide** *noun* (BIOCHEMISTRY) a polymeric compound whose molecule is composed of many nucleotides E20. poly'**oestrous** *adjective* (ZOOLOGY) ovulating more than once each year E20. **polyol** *noun* (CHEMISTRY) a polyhydric alcohol M20. poly'**olefin** *noun* (CHEMISTRY) (*a*) a polymer of an olefin, esp. a synthetic resin of this type; (*b*) = POLYENE: M20. poly'**ommatous** *adjective* (*rare*) [Greek *ommat-*, *omma* eye] having many eyes M19. **polyo'rama** *noun* an optical apparatus presenting many views, or a view of many objects M19. **polyoxy'ethylene** *noun* (CHEMISTRY) a polymer in which the repeating unit is the group $\cdot(CH_2{\cdot}CH_2{\cdot}O)\cdot$ M20. **polyoxy'methylene** *noun* (CHEMISTRY) any of a number of polymers prepared from formaldehyde and having the repeating unit $\cdot CH_2{\cdot}O\cdot$; *esp.* any of the tough, strong thermoplastics of this type used as moulding materials: E20. **polyped** *adjective & noun* (*rare*) (an animal) having many feet E19. poly'**petalous** *adjective* (BOTANY) having petals free to the base (opp. *gamopetalous*) E18. poly'**phenol** *noun* (CHEMISTRY) any compound containing more than one phenolic hydroxyl group L19. poly'**phenylene** *noun* (CHEMISTRY) any polymer in which the repeating unit is or contains the *para*-phenylene group; ***polyphenylene oxide***, a thermoplastic containing the polymeric group $\cdot(p\text{-}C_6H_4O)_n\cdot$, used as a moulding material: M20. poly'**phosphate** *noun* (CHEMISTRY) a salt or ester of a polyphosphoric acid E20. **polyphos'phoric** *adjective* (CHEMISTRY) ***polyphosphoric acid***, any oxyacid of pentavalent phosphorus which contains two or more phosphorus atoms in the anion; *esp.* a mixture of polymers of orthophosphoric acid used in organic chemistry as a mild dehydrating agent: L19. poly'**phyllous** *adjective* (BOTANY) having perianth segments free to the base (opp. *gamophyllous*) L18. **polypneustic** /-'pnjuːstɪk/ *adjective* [Greek *-pneustos* breathing] ENTOMOLOGY bearing many spiracles E20. **polypnoea** /pɒlɪ'pniːə/ *noun* [cf. DYSPNOEA] BIOLOGY & MEDICINE abnormally rapid breathing L19. **polypnoeic** /-'pniːɪk/ *adjective* (BIOLOGY & MEDICINE) of or pertaining to polypnoea E20. **polypseu'donymous** *adjective* having many pseudonyms or aliases L19. **polyreaction** *noun* (CHEMISTRY) a reaction that yields a polymeric product M20. **polyribo'nucleotide** *noun* (BIOCHEMISTRY) any polymer of a ribonucleotide M20. **polyribo'somal** *adjective* (BIOLOGY) of or pertaining to a polyribosome M20. poly'**ribosome** *noun* (BIOLOGY) = POLYSOME M20. **polysa'probic** *adjective* (ECOLOGY) designating, of, or inhabiting an aquatic environment that is poor in dissolved oxygen and contains much chemically reducing decayed organic matter E20. **polyse'mantic** *adjective* (LINGUISTICS) having several meanings M19. poly'**sensuous** *adjective* = POLYSEMOUS L19. poly'**sepalous** *adjective* (BOTANY) having sepals free to the base (opp. *gamosepalous*) E19. **polysero'sitis** *noun* (MEDICINE) inflammation of serous membranes E20. **polyspike** *noun* (MEDICINE) a group of rhythmic high-amplitude spikes observed in an electroencephalogram in some brain disorders M20. **polyspore** *noun* (BOTANY) a spore-case containing numerous spores; a compound spore: M19. poly'**sporous** *adjective* (BOTANY & ZOOLOGY) having or producing numerous spores M19. **polyspory** *noun* (BOTANY) the production of unusually many spores E20. poly'**sulphide** *noun* (CHEMISTRY) (*a*) a compound containing two or more sulphur atoms bonded together as an anion or group; (*b*) a polymer (esp. any of a class of synthetic rubbers) in which the units are linked through such groups: M19. poly'**sulphone** *noun* (CHEMISTRY) any polymer in which the units contain the sulphone linkage $\cdot SO_2\cdot$, *esp.* a type of thermosetting synthetic resin used esp. as a moulding material for electrical and electronic components M20. poly'**symmetry** *noun* (*a*) the condition of being symmetrical about several axes; (*b*) CRYSTALLOGRAPHY the property of simultaneously displaying both pseudosymmetry and submicroscopic polysynthetic twinning: L19. **polysympto'matic** *adjective* (MEDICINE) involving or exhibiting many symptoms M20. **polysy'naptic** *adjective* (ANATOMY & PHYSIOLOGY) involving several synapses M20. **polysy'stemic** *adjective* (LINGUISTICS) involving several systems of language analysis M20. poly'**terpene** *noun* (CHEMISTRY) (*a*) any of the higher terpenes, $(C_5H_8)_n$; (*b*) a polymer of a terpene: L19. poly'**thalamous** *adjective* [Greek *thalamos* chamber] (chiefly ZOOLOGY) having or consisting of several chambers or cells E19. poly'**tonic** *adjective* using or having several (musical or vocal) tones M20. poly'**topic** *adjective* (BIOLOGY) of, pertaining to, or designating (a theory of) the independent origin of a species in several places E20. poly'**topical** *adjective* dealing with many subjects L19. poly'**voltine** *adjective* [Italian *volta* time] (of silkworm moths) producing several broods in a year L19. poly'**xenic** *adjective* [Greek *xenos* stranger] BIOLOGY (esp. of a culture) containing organisms of more than one species other than that stated or implied M20. **polyyne** *noun* [-YNE] CHEMISTRY any organic compound containing two or more carbon–carbon triple bonds, esp. in a chain of conjugated single and triple bonds M20.

polyacetylene /pɒlɪə'sɛtɪliːn/ *noun.* L19.
[from POLY- + ACETYLENE.]
CHEMISTRY. **1** = POLYYNE. L19.
2 A black solid polymer having the structure $(-CH{=}CH-)_n$, which is a good conductor, especially when doped with metals. L20.

polyacid /pɒlɪ'asɪd/ *adjective & noun.* M19.
[from POLY- + ACID *adjective, noun.*]
CHEMISTRY. ▶**A** *adjective.* **1** Of a base: (composed of molecules) able to combine with more than one monovalent acid radical. Now *rare.* M19.
2 Of the nature of or pertaining to a polyacid. M20.
▶**B** *noun.* A compound with more than one acidic group; *esp.* an acid containing polymeric anions. E20.

polyad /'pɒlɪad/ *noun. rare.* L19.
[from POLY- after *dyad*, *monad*, etc.]
†**1** CHEMISTRY. A polyatomic element or radical. Only in L19.
2 PHILOSOPHY. A relative containing more than two elements. E20.

polyadelphous /ˌpɒlɪə'dɛlfəs/ *adjective.* E19.
[from POLY- + Greek *adelphos* brother + -OUS.]
BOTANY. Of stamens: having the filaments united so as to form three or more bundles. Of a plant: having the stamens so united.

polyadic /pɒlɪ'adɪk/ *adjective.* E20.
[from POLYAD + -IC.]
Involving three or more quantities or elements.
■ **polyadically** *adverb* M20.

polyamide /pɒlɪ'eɪmʌɪd, -'am-/ *noun.* E20.
[from POLY- + AMIDE.]
CHEMISTRY. Any of a large class of polymers in which the units are linked by an amide group ·CO·NH·, including many synthetic resins such as nylon. Freq. *attrib.*

polyandrium /pɒlɪ'andrɪəm/ *noun.* Pl. **-dria** /-drɪə/. M17.
[Late Latin from Greek *poluandrion* use as noun of neut. sing. of *poluandrios* of or relating to many men: see POLY-, ANDRO-.]
GREEK HISTORY. A burying-place for a number of men, esp. men who had fallen in battle.

polyandrous /pɒlɪ'andrəs/ *adjective.* M19.
[from Greek *poluandros* (in sense 2), formed as POLY- + *andros*: see -ANDROUS.]
1 BOTANY. Having numerous stamens. M19.
2 Having several husbands or male mates; practising, pertaining to, or involving polyandry. M19.

polyandry /'pɒlɪandri/ *noun.* L17.
[Greek *poluandria*, formed as POLY- + *andr-*, *anēr* man, husband: see -Y³.]
1 Polygamy in which one woman has two or more husbands at the same time. Cf. POLYGYNY. L17.
2 The fact or state (of a female animal) of having more than one male mate. E19.
3 BOTANY. The state of having numerous stamens. E20.
■ poly'**andrian** *adjective* (*rare*) = POLYANDROUS L18. poly'**andrist** *noun* a person who practises or favours polyandry; a woman who has several husbands at the same time: M19.

polyantha /pɒlɪ'anθə/ *noun.* L19.
[mod. Latin, fem. of POLYANTHUS.]
Any of various small shrub roses or climbing roses belonging to a group of hybrids between *Rosa chinensis* and *R. multiflora*, bearing flowers in clusters. Freq. more fully ***polyantha rose***.

polyanthus /pɒlɪ'anθəs/ *noun.* E18.
[mod. Latin, lit. 'having many flowers', from Greek *poluanthos*, formed as POLY- + *anthos* flower.]
1 A garden primula, prob. derived from hybrids between the oxlip, *Primula elatior*, and the primrose, *P. vulgaris*, which bears flowers of many different colours in an umbel on a leafless stem. E18.
2 ***polyanthus narcissus***, any of various kinds of garden narcissus, e.g. *Narcissus tazetta*, which have the flowers in an umbel. M19.

polyarch /'pɒlɪɑːk/ *adjective.* L19.
[from POLY- + Greek *arkhē* beginning, origin.]
BOTANY. Of primary xylem or woody tissue: proceeding from many points of origin.

polyarchy /'pɒlɪɑːki/ *noun.* Also †**polygarchy**. E17.
[Greek *poluarkhia*, formed as POLY- + -ARCHY. Form with *-g-* arose by assim. to OLIGARCHY.]
1 Rule or government by many people. Also, a State or city ruled by many. E17.
2 BOTANY. The condition of being polyarch. L19.
■ poly'**archic** *adjective* of, pertaining to, or having the characteristics of a polyarchy L19. poly'**archical** *adjective* (long *rare*) = POLYARCHIC M17.

polyarteritis /ˌpɒlɪɑːtə'rʌɪtɪs/ *noun.* E20.
[from POLY- + ARTERITIS.]
MEDICINE. = PERIARTERITIS.
polyarteritis nodosa = PERIARTERITIS *nodosa*.

polyatomic /ˌpɒlɪə'tɒmɪk/ *adjective.* M19.
[from POLY- + ATOMIC.]
CHEMISTRY. Containing three or more atoms; composed of molecules each containing three or more atoms. Also, polybasic, polyvalent.

polyautography /ˌpɒlɪɔː'tɒgrəfi/ *noun. obsolete* exc. *Hist.* E19.
[from POLY- + AUTOGRAPH + -Y³.]
= LITHOGRAPHY.

polybase /'pɒlɪbeɪs/ *noun.* E20.
[from POLY- + BASE *noun*¹.]
CHEMISTRY. A compound with more than one basic group per molecule.

polybasic /pɒlɪ'beɪsɪk/ *adjective.* M19.
[from POLY- + BASIC *adjective.*]
CHEMISTRY. Of an acid: having more than one replaceable hydrogen atom per molecule.
■ **polybasicity** /-beɪ'sɪsɪti/ *noun* L19.

polybasite /pə'lɪbəsʌɪt/ *noun.* M19.
[from POLY- + Greek *basis* BASE *noun*¹ + -ITE¹.]
MINERALOGY. A monoclinic sulphide and antimonide of silver and copper, usu. occurring as grey prisms with a metallic lustre.

polybrominated /pɒlɪ'brəʊmɪneɪtɪd/ *adjective.* M20.
[from POLY- + BROMINATE + -ED¹.]
CHEMISTRY. Having two or more bromine atoms added to or introduced as substituents in each molecule; ***polybrominated biphenyl***, any of a class of such compounds derived from biphenyl, which have various industrial applications and are persistent environmental pollutants.

polycarbonate /pɒlɪ'kɑːbəneɪt/ *noun.* L19.
[from POLY- + CARBONATE *noun.*]
CHEMISTRY. †**1** A carbonate containing several equivalents of the acid radical. Only in L19.
2 Any of a class of polymers in which the units are linked by the group $-O{\cdot}CO{\cdot}O-$, many of which are thermoplastic resins widely used esp. as moulding materials and films. Freq. *attrib.* M20.

polycarpellary /pɒlɪ'kɑːp(ə)l(ə)ri/ *adjective.* M19.
[from POLY- + CARPELLARY.]
BOTANY. Having or consisting of several carpels.

polycarpous /pɒlɪ'kɑːpəs/ *adjective.* M19.
[from Greek *polukarpos* rich in fruit, formed as POLY- + *karpos* fruit: see -OUS.]
BOTANY. Bearing fruit several times, as a perennial plant. Also = POLYCARPELLARY.
■ Also **polycarpic** *adjective* M19.

polychaete /'pɒlɪkiːt/ *noun & adjective.* Also **-chete**, **-chaet**. L19.
[mod. Latin *Polychaeta* (see below), from Greek *polukhaitēs* having much hair, formed as POLY- + *khaitē* mane, taken as meaning 'bristle'.]
ZOOLOGY. ▶**A** *noun.* Any member of the class Polychaeta of aquatic worms (including lugworms and ragworms) having segmented bodies with numerous bristles on the fleshy lobes of each segment. L19.
▶**B** *adjective.* Of or pertaining to the class Polychaeta. L19.
■ poly'**chaetan**, poly'**chaetous** *adjectives* L19.

polychlorinated /pɒlɪ'klɔːrɪneɪtɪd/ *adjective.* M20.
[from POLY- + CHLORINATE + -ED¹.]
CHEMISTRY. Having two or more chlorine atoms added to or introduced as substituents in each molecule.
polychlorinated biphenyl any of a class of such compounds derived from biphenyl, which have various industrial applications and are persistent environmental pollutants.

polychord /'pɒlɪkɔːd/ *adjective.* L17.
[Greek *polukhordos*, formed as POLY- + *khordē* string (see CORD *noun*¹).]
MUSIC. Of an instrument: having many strings.

polychotomous /pɒlɪ'kɒtəməs/ *adjective.* M19.
[from POLY- + DICHOTOMOUS (as if from DI-²).]
Divided, or involving division, into many parts.

polychrest /'pɒlɪkrɛst/ *noun.* M17.
[Late Latin *polychrestus* from Greek *polukhrēstos*, formed as POLY- + *khrēstos* useful.]
A thing adapted to several different uses. Now *esp.* a homoeopathic drug used to treat various diseases.

polychromasia /ˌpɒlɪkrə'meɪzɪə/ *noun.* E20.
[Back-form. from next: see -CHROMASIA.]
MEDICINE. = POLYCHROMATOPHILIA.
■ **polychromasic** *adjective* = POLYCHROMATOPHIL E20.

polychromatic /ˌpɒlɪkrə(ʊ)ˈmatɪk/ *adjective*. M19.
[from POLY- + CHROMATIC.]
1 Characterized by various colours; many-coloured; (of radiation) containing a number of wavelengths, not monochromatic. M19.
2 MEDICINE. = POLYCHROMATOPHIL. L19.
▪ **polyˈchromatism** *noun* the property of having, or being able to perceive, many colours M20.

polychromatophil /pɒlɪˈkrəʊmətə(ʊ)fɪl/ *adjective*. Also **-phile** /-fʌɪl/. L19.
[from Greek *polukhrōmatos* many-coloured: see POLY-, CHROMATIC, -PHIL.]
MEDICINE. Of an erythrocyte: having an affinity for both basic and acidic stains, and so recognizable when a mixed stain is used. Also, of or pertaining to such erythrocytes.
▪ **polychromatoˈphilia** *noun* the presence of polychromatophil erythrocytes in the blood L19. **polychromatoˈphilic** *adjective* = POLYCHROMATOPHIL L19.

polychrome /ˈpɒlɪkrəʊm/ *noun, adjective, & verb*. E19.
[French from Greek *polukhrōmos* many-coloured, formed as POLY- + *khrōma* colour.]
▶ **A** *noun*. **1** A work of art in several colours, *esp.* a coloured statue or sculpture. E19.
2 An association of many colours (*lit. & fig.*); varied colouring. L19.
3 MEDICINE. A polychromatophil erythrocyte. Now *rare*. E20.
▶ **B** *adjective*. **1** Many-coloured, polychromatic; *esp.* painted, decorated, etc., in many colours. M19.
2 BIOLOGY. Of a stain or dye: containing derivatives which differ in colours from the parent compound. Esp. in ***polychrome methylene blue***. L19.
▶ **C** *verb trans*. **1** Execute or decorate (a work of art) in several colours. Chiefly as ***polychromed*** *ppl adjective*. E20.
2 BIOLOGY. Convert (a stain or dye) to a polychrome form. E20.
▪ **polyˈchromic** *adjective* = POLYCHROME *adjective* 1 M19. **polyˈchromism** *noun* = POLYCHROMATISM E20. **polychromy** *noun* the art of painting or decorating in several colours, esp. as anciently used in pottery, architecture, etc. M19.

polyclad /ˈpɒlɪklad/ *noun & adjective*. L19.
[from mod. Latin *Polycladidea*, *-dida* (see below), formed as POLY- + Greek *klados* branch: see -ID³.]
ZOOLOGY. ▶ **A** *noun*. Any member of the order Polycladida of turbellarian flatworms, characterized by having a main intestine with more than four branches. L19.
▶ **B** *adjective*. Of, pertaining to, or designating this order of turbellarians. L19.

polyclinic /pɒlɪˈklɪnɪk/ *noun*. Also (earlier, now *rare*) **poli-**. E19.
[German *Poliklinik*, from Greek *polis* city + German *Klinik* clinic; later assim. to POLY-.]
A clinic (usu. independent of a hospital) where various kinds of examination and treatment are available to outpatients.

polyclonal /pɒlɪˈkləʊn(ə)l/ *adjective*. E20.
[from POLY- + CLONAL.]
BIOLOGY. Consisting of or derived from many clones.

polyclone /ˈpɒlɪkləʊn/ *noun*. L20.
[from POLY- + CLONE.]
BIOLOGY. A group of cells all descended from one or other of an initial small group of cells.

polycrase /ˈpɒlɪkreɪz, -s/ *noun*. M19.
[from POLY- + Greek *krasis* mixture.]
MINERALOGY. An orthorhombic niobate, tantalate, and titanate of uranium, calcium, yttrium, and other elements, usu. occurring as shiny black prisms.

polycrystal /ˈpɒlɪkrɪst(ə)l/ *noun*. E20.
[from POLY- + CRYSTAL *noun*.]
A polycrystalline body of matter.

polycrystalline /pɒlɪˈkrɪstəlʌɪn/ *adjective*. E20.
[from POLY- + CRYSTALLINE.]
Consisting of many crystalline parts differing randomly in their orientation.
▪ ˌ**polycrystaˈllinity** *noun* M20.

polycyclic /pɒlɪˈsʌɪklɪk, -ˈsɪk-/ *adjective & noun*. M19.
[from POLY- + CYCLIC.]
▶ **A** *adjective*. †**1** MATH. Of a function: relating to more than one closed curve. M–L19.
2 Having or consisting of many rounds, turns, or whorls. L19.
3 CHEMISTRY. Having more than one ring of atoms in the molecule. E20.
4 ELECTRICAL ENGINEERING. Involving the simultaneous transmission along one conductor of currents of different frequencies and voltages. E20.
5 GEOLOGY. Produced by or having undergone many cycles, esp. of erosion and deposition. M20.
6 BIOLOGY. Producing several generations during a year by sexual reproduction. M20.
▶ **B** *noun*. CHEMISTRY. A polycyclic compound. M20.

polycythaemia /ˌpɒlɪsʌɪˈθiːmɪə/ *noun*. Also *-**themia**. M19.
[from POLY- + -CYTE + HAEMO- + -IA¹.]
MEDICINE. An abnormally increased concentration of red cells in the blood.
polycythaemia vera /ˈvɪərə/ [Latin = true] polycythaemia that appears to be primary, a disease of unknown aetiology that is typically marked by itching, cyanosis, and disturbances in the head such as dizziness and tinnitus.
▪ **polycythaemic** *adjective* of, pertaining to, or exhibiting polycythaemia E20.

polydactyl /pɒlɪˈdaktɪl/ *adjective*. Also (earlier) †**-yle**. M19.
[French *polydactyle* from Greek *poludaktulos*, formed as POLY- + *daktulos* finger, toe.]
Having more than the normal number of fingers or toes.
▪ **polydactylism** *noun* the condition of being polydactyl M19. **polydactylous** *adjective* = POLYDACTYL M19. **polydactyly** *noun* = POLYDACTYLISM L19.

polydaemonism /pɒlɪˈdiːmənɪz(ə)m/ *noun*. Also **-demonism**. E18.
[from POLY- + Greek *daimōn* a divinity + -ISM.]
A belief in many divinities (esp. evil spirits).
▪ **polydaemoˈnistic** *adjective* pertaining to or characterized by polydaemonism L19.

polydipsia /pɒlɪˈdɪpsɪə/ *noun*. M17.
[from Greek *poludipsios* very thirsty, *poludipsos* causing excessive thirst (*dipsa* thirst): see POLY-, -IA¹.]
Abnormally excessive thirst.

polydisperse /pɒlɪdɪˈspəːs/ *adjective*. E20.
[from POLY- + DISPERSE *adjective*.]
CHEMISTRY. Existing in the form of or containing colloidal particles having a range of sizes; *esp.* designating macromolecular substances having a simple distribution of particle size with one peak.
▪ **polydispersed** *adjective* = POLYDISPERSE M20. **polydispersity** *noun* the condition or property of being polydisperse E20.

polydymite /pəˈlɪdɪmʌɪt/ *noun*. L19.
[from POLY- + Greek *didumos* twin + -ITE¹.]
MINERALOGY. A sulphide of nickel, light grey with a metallic lustre, crystallizing in the cubic system and occurring as polysynthetic twinned crystals.

polyelectrolyte /pɒlɪɪˈlɛktrəlʌɪt/ *noun*. M20.
[from POLY- + ELECTROLYTE.]
CHEMISTRY. A substance which consists of large usu. polymeric molecules containing several ionizable groups.
▪ **polyelectroˈlytic** *adjective* M20.

polyembryony /pɒlɪˈɛmbrɪəni/ *noun*. M19.
[from POLY- + EMBRYON + -Y³.]
BOTANY & ZOOLOGY. The formation (from a single egg) or presence (in a single seed etc.) of more than one embryo.
▪ **polyembryˈonic** *adjective* M19.

polyergus /pɒlɪˈəːgəs/ *noun*. L19.
[mod. Latin from Greek *poluergos* hard-working.]
An amazon ant. Chiefly as mod. Latin genus name.

polyester /pɒlɪˈɛstə/ *noun*. E20.
[from POLY- + ESTER.]
Any polymer in which the units are joined by an ester linkage, ·CO·O·. Also, (***a***) (more fully ***polyester fibre***) a man-made fibre consisting of such a polymer; (***b***) (more fully ***polyester resin***) any of numerous synthetic resins or plastics consisting of or made from such polymers. Freq. *attrib.*

polyether /pɒlɪˈiːθə/ *noun*. E20.
[from POLY- + ETHER *noun*¹.]
Any of a variety of polymers in which the repeating unit contains an ether linkage, ·C·O·C·, including many plastic foams and epoxy resins. Freq. *attrib.*

polyethylene /pɒlɪˈɛθɪliːn/ *noun*. M19.
[from POLY- + ETHYLENE.]
1 CHEMISTRY. A polymer prepared from an ethylene derivative. Usu. in *comb.* M19.
2 = POLYTHENE. Chiefly *N. Amer.* M20.
Comb.: **polyethylene glycol** any polymer of ethylene glycol; *esp.* any of a series of water-soluble oligomers and polymers having the structure H·$(OCH_2CH_2)_n$·OH, of which the lower members are used as solvents and the higher esp. as waxes; **polyethylene oxide** any polymer having the structure ·$(OCH_2CH_2)_n$·; *esp.* any of a class of thermoplastics of high molecular weight used esp. as water-soluble films; **polyethylene terephthalate** a thermoplastic condensation polymer of ethylene glycol and terephthalic acid widely used to make polyester fibres.
▪ **polyethyˈlenic** *adjective* †(***a***) designating polymers prepared from ethylene derivatives; (***b***) polyunsaturated; of the nature of polyunsaturation: M19.

Polyfilla /ˈpɒlɪfɪlə/ *noun*. M20.
[from POLY- + respelling of FILLER *noun*¹.]
(Proprietary name for) a type of plaster-like filler used to make minor building repairs, such as filling small holes.
🕮 *fig.* (*attrib.*): *London Review of Books* Executing 446 pages of narrative . . requires a certain amount of polyfilla prose.

For other words beginning with *poly-* see the entry for **poly-**

Polyfoto /ˈpɒlɪfəʊtəʊ/ *noun*. Pl. **-os**. M20.
[from POLY- + alt. of PHOTO *noun*.]
▶ **1** (Proprietary name for) a photograph of a person that is one of a series taken in quick succession, esp. in an automatic kiosk.

polygala /pəˈlɪgələ/ *noun*. L16.
[mod. Latin (see below), formed as POLY- + Greek *gala* milk.]
Any plant of the genus *Polygala*; = MILKWORT 1.

polygamic /pɒlɪˈgamɪk/ *adjective*. E19.
[from POLYGAMY + -IC.]
Of or pertaining to polygamy; polygamous.
▪ **polygamical** *adjective* E19. **polygamically** *adverb* (*rare*) M19.

polygamist /pəˈlɪgəmɪst/ *noun & adjective*. M17.
[formed as prec. + -IST.]
▶ **A** *noun*. A person (esp. a man) who practises or favours polygamy. M17.
▶ **B** *adjective*. = POLYGAMISTIC. L19.
▪ **polygaˈmistic** *adjective* of or pertaining to polygamists or polygamy; favouring polygamy: L19.

polygamous /pəˈlɪgəməs/ *adjective*. E17.
[from next + -OUS.]
1 Practising polygamy; of, pertaining to, or involving polygamy. E17. ▸**b** ZOOLOGY. Having more than one mate of the opposite sex. M19.
2 BOTANY. Bearing male, female, and hermaphrodite flowers on the same or on different plants. M18.
▪ **polygamously** *adverb* L19.

polygamy /pəˈlɪgəmi/ *noun*. L16.
[French *polygamie* from late Latin *polygamia* from ecclesiastical Greek *polugamia*, from *polugamos* often married, polygamous, formed as POLY- + -GAMY.]
1 Marriage with several spouses, or more than one spouse, at once; the practice or custom by which one man has more than one wife, or one woman has more than one husband, at the same time. L16. ▸**b** ZOOLOGY. The habit of mating with more than one, or several, of the opposite sex. E19.
†**2** BOTANY. The condition of being polygamous. *rare*. Only in L18.
▪ **polygamize** *verb intrans.* (*rare*) practise polygamy L16.

†**polygarchy** *noun* var. of POLYARCHY.

polygene /ˈpɒlɪdʒiːn/ *noun*. M20.
[Back-form. from POLYGENIC: see GENE.]
GENETICS. A gene whose individual effect on a phenotype is too small to be observed, but which can act together with others to produce observable variation.

polygenesis /pɒlɪˈdʒɛnɪsɪs/ *noun*. M19.
[from POLY- + -GENESIS.]
1 Origination from several independent sources; *esp.* the (hypothetical) origination of a race or species from a number of independent stocks. Cf. POLYGENY. M19.
2 LINGUISTICS. (A theory proposing) the origination of languages from a plurality of independent sources. M20.

polygenetic /ˌpɒlɪdʒɪˈnɛtɪk/ *adjective*. M19.
[from prec. after *genetic*.]
1 Of or pertaining to polygenesis; having more than one origin or source; formed in several different ways. M19.
2 GEOLOGY. Of a volcano: that has erupted several times. M20.
▪ **polygenetically** *adverb* E20.

polygenic /pɒlɪˈdʒɛnɪk/ *adjective*. M19.
[from Greek *polugenēs* of many kinds, formed as POLY- + *genos* kind: see -IC.]
1 GEOLOGY. Polygenous. *rare*. M19.
2 GENETICS. Of, pertaining to, or determined by polygenes. M20.
▪ **polygenically** *adverb* by means of or with regard to polygenes M20.

polygenism /pəˈlɪdʒɪnɪz(ə)m/ *noun*. L19.
[from POLYGENY + -ISM.]
(Belief in) the doctrine of polygeny.
▪ **polygenist** *noun & adjective* (***a***) *noun* an adherent of the doctrine of polygeny; (***b***) *adjective* = POLYGENISTIC: M19. **polygeˈnistic** *adjective* of or pertaining to polygenists or polygenism L19.

polygenous /pəˈlɪdʒɪnəs/ *adjective*. L18.
[formed as POLYGENIC + -OUS.]
1 Composed of constituents of different kinds; *spec.* in GEOLOGY, composed of various kinds of rocks. L18.
2 Of, pertaining to, or involving polygeny. M19.

polygeny /pəˈlɪdʒ(ə)ni/ *noun*. M19.
[from POLY- + -GENY.]
The (hypothetical) origination of humankind from several independent sets of ancestors; the theory of such origination. Cf. POLYGENESIS.

polyglot /ˈpɒlɪglɒt/ *adjective & noun*. M17.
[French *polyglotte* from Greek *poluglōttos*, formed as POLY- + *glōtta* tongue.]
▶ **A** *adjective*. **1** That speaks, writes, or understands many or several languages. M17.

2 Of or relating to many languages; written in many or several languages; characterized by the use of (elements derived from) a plurality of languages. L17.
▶ **B** *noun*. **1** A person who knows several languages. M17.
2 a A book (esp. a bible) in several languages. M17.
▸**b** A mixture of several languages. *rare*. E18.
■ **poly'glottal** *adjective* = POLYGLOT *adjective* M19. **poly'glottic** *adjective* = POLYGLOT *adjective* E19. **polyglottism** *noun* polyglot character; use of or acquaintance with many languages: L19. **poly'glottous** *adjective* = POLYGLOT *adjective* M19.

polygon /'pɒlɪg(ə)n/ *noun & adjective*. Also (earlier) in Latin form †**-gonum**, pl. **-gona**. L16.
[Late Latin *polygonum* from Greek *polugōnon* use as noun of neut. of *polugōnos* adjective, formed as POLY- + -GON.]
▶ **A** *noun*. **1** A plane figure with many (usu. more than four) straight sides and angles; a many-sided figure. L16.
2 A material object having the form of a polygon. M17.
▸**b** PHYSICAL GEOGRAPHY. Any of the approximately polygonal figures characteristic of patterned ground. E20.
Phrases: **polygon of forces** a polygonal figure illustrating a theorem relating to a number of forces acting at one point, each of which is represented in magnitude and direction by one of the sides of the figure; cf. PARALLELOGRAM *of forces*, *triangle of forces* s.v. TRIANGLE *noun* 1.
▶†**B** *adjective*. Having many angles; polygonal. L16–L18.
■ **po,lygoni'zation** *noun* (METALLURGY) the formation of smaller grains within the grains of a metal owing to the migration of dislocations during annealing M20. **po'lygonize** *verb intrans*. (METALLURGY) undergo polygonization M20.

polygonaceous /pəlɪgə'neɪʃəs/ *adjective*. M19.
[from mod. Latin *Polygonaceae* (from POLYGONUM *noun*[1]): see -ACEOUS.]
BOTANY. Of or pertaining to the family Polygonaceae, of which the typical genus is *Polygonum*.

polygonal /pə'lɪg(ə)n(ə)l/ *adjective*. E18.
[from POLYGON + -AL[1].]
Having the form of a polygon; having many (usu. more than four) sides and angles; many-sided; (of a solid body) having a prismatic form whose base or section is a polygon. Also, containing or forming figures or objects of this form.
polygonal numbers [so called because each series can be represented according to a certain rule using triangles, squares, or regular polygons] any of several series of numbers, each beginning with unity, obtained by continued summation of the successive terms of arithmetical progressions whose common difference is a whole number.
■ **polygonally** *adverb* L19. †**polygonial** *adjective* = POLYGONAL E—M18. **poly'gonic** *adjective* (*rare*) = POLYGONAL M19. **polygonous** *adjective* (now *rare* or *obsolete*) = POLYGONAL M17.

polygonum /pə'lɪg(ə)nəm/ *noun*[1]. E18.
[mod. Latin (see below), from Greek *polugonon*, formed as POLY- + *gonu* knee, joint.]
BOTANY. Any of various plants (e.g. knotgrass, persicaria, etc.) now or formerly included in the genus *Polygonum* (family Polygonaceae), with swollen joints sheathed by stipules and small pink or white apetalous flowers; *Austral*. a thicket-forming shrub, *Muehlenbeckia cunninghamii*.

†**polygonum** *noun*[2] see POLYGON.

†**polygony** *noun*. LME–E18.
[Latin *polygonium* from Greek *polugonon*: see -Y[3].]
A plant of the genus *Polygonum*; *esp*. bistort, *Persicaria* (formerly *Polygonum*) *bistorta*.

polygram /'pɒlɪgram/ *noun*. L17.
[from POLY- + Greek *gramma* line: cf. -GRAM.]
1 A figure or design consisting of many lines. L17.
2 A recording made with a polygraph. E20.

polygraph /'pɒlɪgrɑːf/ *noun & verb*. L18.
[from POLY- + -GRAPH; sense A.3 from Greek *polugraphos* adjective = writing much.]
▶ **A** *noun*. †**1** A person who imitates or copies another; an imitator. Only in L18.
2 An apparatus for producing two or more identical drawings etc. simultaneously. E19.
3 A writer of many or various works; a voluminous author. M19.
4 An instrument for graphically recording simultaneous measurements of several physiological characteristics (e.g. rates of pulse and respiration, electrical conductivity of the skin), esp. as used as a lie-detector. L19.
5 A group of three or more consecutive letters. M20.
▶ **B** *verb trans*. Examine with a polygraph, esp. for truthfulness. M20.

polygrapher /pə'lɪgrəfə/ *noun*. L16.
[from (the same root as) prec. + -ER[1].]
1 A writer using polygraphy. *rare*. L16.
†**2** = POLYGRAPH *noun* 2. L18–E19.
3 A user of a polygraph. M20.

polygraphic /pɒlɪ'grafɪk/ *adjective*. M18.
[from next + -IC.]
1 Writing much; voluminous, copious; (of a book) dealing with many subjects. *rare*. M18.
2 Pertaining to the copying of pictures etc. with a polygraph; produced using such a device. L18.
†**3** *fig*. That is an exact copy or imitation of another. L18–E19.
†**4** Pertaining to polygraphy as a method of secret writing. Only in E19.
5 Of, pertaining to, or involving a polygraph measuring physiological characteristics. L19.
6 CRYPTOGRAPHY. Designating or pertaining to a code in which letters are enciphered or deciphered two or more at a time. E20.
■ †**polygraphical** *adjective* (*rare*) (*a*) = POLYGRAPHIC 4; (*b*) = POLYGRAPHIC 2: L16–E19. **polygraphically** *adverb* E20.

polygraphy /pə'lɪgrəfi/ *noun*. L16.
[Greek *polugraphia* prolific writing, formed as POLY- + *-graphia* -GRAPHY.]
1 A kind of code or secret writing. *obsolete* exc. *Hist*. L16.
2 Much writing; prolific or wide-ranging literary work. M17.
3 The use of a polygraph or other device for making copies of drawings, writings, etc. L18.
4 The use of a polygraph to record several physiological characteristics simultaneously. E20.

polygynandrous /,pɒlɪdʒʌɪ'nandrəs, -dʒɪ-/ *adjective*. L20.
[Blend of POLYANDROUS and POLYGYNOUS.]
Chiefly ZOOLOGY. Of, pertaining to, or characterized by the practice of mating within a group containing several males and females, or of belonging to a social group in which several husbands share several wives.

polygynous /pə'lɪdʒɪnəs/ *adjective*. M19.
[from mod. Latin *polygynus*, formed as POLY- + -GYNOUS.]
1 BOTANY. Having numerous pistils. M19.
2 Having several wives or female mates; practising, pertaining to, or involving polygyny. L19.
■ **poly'gynic** *adjective* = POLYGYNOUS 2 L19.

polygyny /pə'lɪdʒɪni/ *noun*. L18.
[from POLY- + Greek *gunē* woman: see -Y[3].]
1 Polygamy in which one man has two or more wives at the same time. Cf. POLYANDRY. L18.
2 The fact or state (of a male animal) of having more than one female mate. E20.
1 SORORAL *polygyny*.
■ **polygynist** *noun* a person who practises or favours polygyny; a man who has several wives at the same time: L19.

polyhalite /pɒlɪ'halʌɪt/ *noun*. E19.
[from POLY- + Greek *hals* salt + -ITE[1].]
MINERALOGY. A triclinic hydrated sulphate of calcium, potassium, and magnesium, usu. occurring as red or yellowish fibrous masses.

polyhedra *noun pl*. see POLYHEDRON.

polyhedral /pɒlɪ'hiːdr(ə)l, -'hɛd-/ *adjective*. E19.
[from next + -AL[1].]
Having the form of a polyhedron; having many faces. Also, of or pertaining to a polyhedron or polyhedra.
polyhedral disease = POLYHEDROSIS.
■ **polyhedric** *adjective* polyhedral; many-sided (freq. *fig*.): E19. **polyhedrical** *adjective* (*rare*) M17. **polyhedrous** *adjective* = POLYHEDRAL L17.

polyhedron /pɒlɪ'hiːdrən, -'hɛd-/ *noun*. Pl. **-dra** /-drə/, **-drons**. L16.
[Greek *poluedron* use as noun of neut. of *poluedros* adjective, formed as POLY- + *hedra* base: see -HEDRON.]
A solid figure or object with many (usu. more than six) plane faces.

polyhedrosis /,pɒlɪhiː'drəʊsɪs, -hɛ-/ *noun*. Pl. **-droses** /-'drəʊsiːz/. M20.
[from POLYHEDRAL + -OSIS.]
A disease of caterpillars, characterized by the presence of polyhedral virus particles.

polyhistor /pɒlɪ'hɪstə/ *noun*. L16.
[Greek *poluistōr* very learned, formed as POLY- + *histōr*: see HISTORY *noun*.]
A man of much or varied learning; a great scholar.
■ **polyhi'storian** *noun* = POLYHISTOR M17. **polyhi'storic** *adjective* of or pertaining to a polyhistor; widely erudite: L19. **polyhistory** *noun* the character or quality of a polyhistor; wide or varied learning: E19.

polyhydramnios /,pɒlɪhʌɪ'dramnɪɒs/ *noun*. L19.
[from POLY- + HYDRAMNIOS.]
MEDICINE. = HYDRAMNIOS.

polyhydric /pɒlɪ'hʌɪdrɪk/ *adjective*. L19.
[from POLY- + HYDRIC *adjective*[1].]
CHEMISTRY. (Of a molecule) containing more than one hydroxyl group; (of a substance) consisting of such molecules.

polyhydroxy- /pɒlɪhʌɪ'drɒksi/ *combining form*. Also as attrib. adjective **polyhydroxy**. L19.
[from POLY- + HYDROXY-.]
CHEMISTRY. Used to form nouns designating compounds or groups containing more than one hydroxyl group, as ***polyhydroxystilbene***.

For other words beginning with *poly-* see the entry for **poly-**

polyimide /pɒlɪ'ɪmʌɪd/ *noun*. M20.
[from POLY- + IMIDE.]
CHEMISTRY. Any polymer in which the units contain imide groups, usu. as ·CO·(N·)·CO·; *esp*. any of a class of thermosetting resins used for heat-resistant films and coatings. Freq. *attrib*.

polyisocyanate /,pɒlɪʌɪsə(ʊ)'sʌɪəneɪt/ *noun*. M20.
[from POLY- + ISOCYANATE.]
CHEMISTRY. Any organic compound containing two or more isocyanate groups; a polyurethane or other polymer prepared from such compounds. Freq. *attrib*.

polylithionite /pɒlɪ'lɪθɪənʌɪt/ *noun*. L19.
[from POLY- + LITHION + -ITE[1].]
MINERALOGY. A variety of lepidolite, *spec*. one with lithium and aluminium atoms in the ratio 2:1.

polylogue /'pɒlɪlɒg/ *noun*. M20.
[from POLY- + -LOGUE.]
A discussion involving more than two people.

polylogy /pə'lɪlədʒi/ *noun*. *rare*. E17.
[Greek *polulogia*, from *polulogos* loquacious: see POLY-, -LOGY.]
Much speaking, loquacity.

polymastia /pɒlɪ'mastɪə/ *noun*. L19.
[from POLY- + Greek *mastos* breast: see -IA[1].]
MEDICINE. The condition of having more than two mammae or nipples.
■ **polymastic** *adjective & noun* (a person or animal) characterized by polymastia L19. **polymastism** *noun* = POLYMASTIA L19.

polymath /'pɒlɪmaθ/ *noun & adjective*. E17.
[Greek *polumathēs* adjective, having learned much, formed as POLY- + *math-* stem of *manthanein* learn.]
▶ **A** *noun*. A person of much or varied learning; a person acquainted with various subjects of study; a great scholar. E17.
▶ **B** *attrib*. or as *adjective*. Polymathic. L19.
■ **poly'mathic** *adjective* pertaining to a polymath; characterized by varied learning: E19. **polymathy** /pə'lɪməθi/ *noun* much or varied learning; acquaintance with many branches of knowledge: M17.

polymenorrhoea /,pɒlɪmɛnə'riːə/ *noun*. Also ***-rrhea**. M20.
[from POLY- + MENORRHOEA.]
MEDICINE. Excessively frequent or unduly profuse menstrual bleeding.

polymer /'pɒlɪmə/ *noun*. M19.
[from Greek *polumerēs* that has many parts, formed as POLY- + *meros* part, share.]
CHEMISTRY. Orig., a substance whose formula is an exact multiple of that of another, composed of the same elements in the same proportions. Now usu., any substance which has a molecular structure built up largely or completely from a number (freq. very large) of similar polyatomic units bonded together; *spec*. any of the (mainly synthetic) organic compounds of this kind which form plastics, resins, rubbers, etc.

> 🕮 *Nature* Natural rubber is still the preferred polymer for many high performance applications. *Scientific American* Glass is an inorganic polymer made up of rings and chains of repeating silicate units. ***attrib***.: A. TOFFLER Suburban homes filled with specialists in . . systems engineering, artificial intelligence, or polymer chemistry. ***high polymer***: see HIGH *adjective*.

■ **po'lymeride** *noun* (now *rare*) = POLYMER M19.

polymerase /'pɒlɪməreɪz, pə'lɪməreɪz/ *noun*. M20.
[from prec. + -ASE.]
BIOCHEMISTRY. An enzyme which catalyses the formation of a polymer (esp. a polynucleotide).
Comb.: **polymerase chain reaction** a method of making multiple copies of a DNA sequence, involving repeated reactions with a polymerase.

polymeric /pɒlɪ'mɛrɪk/ *adjective*. M19.
[formed as prec. + -IC.]
1 CHEMISTRY. Orig., of two or more compounds, or of one compound *with* another: composed of the same elements in the same proportions, the formula of one substance being an exact multiple of that of the other. Now usu., of the nature of or characteristic of a polymer; consisting of a polymer or polymers; (of a reaction) giving rise to a polymer. M19.
2 GENETICS. Of, pertaining to, or displaying polymery. M20.

polymerise *verb* var. of POLYMERIZE.

†**polymerism** *noun*. M–L19.
[from POLYMER + -ISM.]
1 CHEMISTRY. The condition of being polymeric. M–L19.
2 BIOLOGY. The condition of being polymerous. M–L19.

polymerize /'pɒlɪmərʌɪz/ *verb*. Also **-ise**. M19.
[from POLYMER + -IZE.]
1 CHEMISTRY. **a** *verb trans*. Make polymeric; convert into a polymer; cause molecules of (one or more compounds) to combine to form a polymer. M19. ▸**b** *verb intrans*. Become polymeric; be converted into a polymer. L19.
2 *verb trans*. BIOLOGY. Make polymerous. *rare*. L19.

■ **polymeriza'bility** *noun* ability to be polymerized E20. **polymerizable** *adjective* able to be polymerized L19. **polymeri'zation** *noun* the action or process of polymerizing; the formation of polymers; the state of being polymeric: L19. **polymerizer** *noun* an apparatus or installation in which polymerization occurs M20.

polymerous /pəˈlɪm(ə)rəs/ *adjective.* M19.
[from Greek *polumerēs*: see POLYMER, -OUS.]
ZOOLOGY & BOTANY. Consisting of many parts or segments.

polymery /pəˈlɪm(ə)ri/ *noun.* E20.
[from Greek *polumereia* state of having many parts, formed as POLY- + *meros* part: see -Y³.]
GENETICS. The phenomenon whereby a number of genes at different loci (which may be polygenes) can act together to produce a single effect.

polymethyl /pɒlɪˈmiːθʌɪl, -ˈmɛθɪl/ *noun.* M20.
[from POLY- + METHYL.]
CHEMISTRY. A polymer of a methyl compound. Usu. in *comb.*
Comb.: **polymethyl methacrylate** a glassy material obtained by polymerizing methyl methacrylate, with proprietary names PERSPEX, PLEXIGLAS, etc.

polymethylene /pɒlɪˈmɛθɪliːn/ *noun.* L19.
[from POLY- + METHYLENE.]
CHEMISTRY. A compound, group, or polymeric structure which consists of or contains a chain of methylene groups, $\cdot(CH_2)_n\cdot$. Usu. *attrib.*

polymicrian /pɒlɪˈmʌɪkrɪən/ *adjective.* E19.
[from POLY- + Greek *mikros* small + -IAN.]
Containing much within a small space.

polymict /ˈpɒlɪmɪkt/ *adjective.* M20.
[from POLY- + Greek *miktos* mixed.]
PETROGRAPHY. = POLYMICTIC 1.

polymictic /pɒlɪˈmɪktɪk/ *adjective.* M20.
[from prec. + -IC.]
1 PETROGRAPHY. Of a conglomerate: consisting of several different constituents. M20.
2 Of a lake: having no stable thermal stratification but exhibiting perennial circulation. M20.

polymignite /pɒlɪˈmɪgnʌɪt/ *noun.* E19.
[from POLY- + Greek *mignunai* mix + -ITE¹.]
MINERALOGY. A rare orthorhombic oxide of titanium, zirconium, yttrium, iron, cerium, calcium, and other metals, usu. occurring as thin slender black crystals.

polymitosis /ˌpɒlɪmʌɪˈtəʊsɪs/ *noun.* Pl. **-toses** /-ˈtəʊsiːz/. M20.
[from POLY- + MITOSIS.]
BIOLOGY. The occurrence of multiple mitotic cell divisions; any of these divisions.
■ **polymitotic** *adjective* M20.

polymodal /pɒlɪˈməʊd(ə)l/ *adjective.* E20.
[from POLY- + MODAL.]
1 MUSIC. Of, pertaining to, or designating music using two or more modes. E20.
2 STATISTICS. = MULTIMODAL 1. *rare.* M20.
■ **polymo'dality** *noun* E20. **polymodally** *adverb* E20.

polymolecular /ˌpɒlɪməˈlɛkjʊlə/ *adjective.* L19.
[from POLY- + MOLECULAR.]
CHEMISTRY. **1** Having an order or a molecularity of more than one. L19.
2 Consisting of or built up from more than one molecule. M20.
3 Of a film or layer: more than one molecule thick. M20.
4 Consisting of macromolecules which have similar polymeric structures but differing molecular weights. M20.
■ **polymolecu'larity** *noun* M20. **poly'molecule** *noun* [back-form.] a polymeric molecule M20.

polymorph /ˈpɒlɪmɔːf/ *noun.* E19.
[from Greek *polumorphos*: see POLYMORPHOUS.]
1 ZOOLOGY & BOTANY. A polymorphous organism; an individual of a polymorphous species. E19.
2 CHEMISTRY & MINERALOGY. Each of a number of substances of identical chemical composition but different crystalline structure. L19.
3 MEDICINE. A polymorphonuclear leucocyte. E20.
■ **polymorphy** *noun* polymorphism M19.

polymorphean /pɒlɪˈmɔːfɪən/ *adjective. rare.* M17.
[formed as prec. + -EAN.]
Polymorphous.

polymorphic /pɒlɪˈmɔːfɪk/ *adjective.* E19.
[formed as prec. + -IC.]
Polymorphous; now *esp.* = POLYMORPHOUS 2.

polymorphism /pɒlɪˈmɔːfɪz(ə)m/ *noun.* M19.
[formed as POLYMORPHOUS + -ISM.]
Polymorphous character or condition; the occurrence of something in several different forms; CHEMISTRY & MINERALOGY the occurrence of polymorphs. Also, an instance of this.

polymorphonuclear /ˌpɒlɪmɔːfə(ʊ)ˈnjuːklɪə/ *adjective.* L19.
[formed as next + -O- + NUCLEAR.]
MEDICINE. Esp. of a leucocyte: having a nucleus with lobules of various shapes.

polymorphous /pɒlɪˈmɔːfəs/ *adjective.* L18.
[from Greek *polumorphos*, formed as POLY- + *morphē* form: see -OUS.]
1 Having, assuming, or occurring in many or various forms; having many varieties; passing through various forms; multiform. L18.
2 CHEMISTRY & MINERALOGY. Crystallizing in two or more forms; chemically identical but crystallographically different. Cf. POLYMORPHIC. M19.
Comb.: **polymorphous-perverse** *adjective* (PSYCHOANALYSIS) characterized by a diffuse sexuality that can be excited and gratified in many ways and is normal in young children but regarded as perverted in adults.
■ **polymorphously** *adverb* in a polymorphous manner; ***polymorphously perverse*** (PSYCHOANALYSIS) = ***polymorphous-perverse*** above: M20.

polymyalgia rheumatica /ˌpɒlɪmʌɪˈaldʒə ruːˈmatɪkə/ *noun phr.* M20.
[from POLY- + MYALGIA + Latin *rheumatica* fem. of *rheumaticus*: see RHEUMATIC.]
MEDICINE. A rheumatic disease, chiefly affecting the elderly, characterized by muscular pain and stiffness.

polymyositis /ˌpɒlɪmʌɪəˈsʌɪtɪs/ *noun.* L19.
[from POLY- + MYOSITIS.]
MEDICINE. A condition marked by inflammation and degeneration of skeletal muscle throughout the body.

polymythy /ˈpɒlɪmɪθi/ *noun. rare.* E18.
[mod. Latin *polymythia*, formed as POLY- + MYTH: see -Y³.]
Combination of a number of stories in one narrative or dramatic work.

polymyxin /pɒlɪˈmɪksɪn/ *noun.* M20.
[from mod. Latin *polymyxa* (see below), formed as POLY- + Greek *muxa* slime: see -IN¹.]
PHARMACOLOGY. A polypeptide antibiotic obtained from the soil bacterium *Bacillus polymyxa* and active esp. against Gram-negative bacteria.

Polynesian /pɒlɪˈniːzj(ə)n, -ʒ(ə)n/ *adjective & noun.* E19.
[from *Polynesia* (see below), from POLY- + Greek *nēsos* island + -IA¹: see -AN.]
► **A** *adjective.* Of or pertaining to Polynesia, a large collection of island-groups in the central and western Pacific Ocean, which includes New Zealand, Hawaii, Samoa, etc. (usu. excluding Melanesia and Micronesia). Also, of, pertaining to, or designating any of the Austronesian languages of Polynesia. E19.
Polynesian rat a small herbivorous rat, *Rattus exulans*, of SE Asia, New Zealand, and the Pacific islands; also called ***kiore***.
► **B** *noun.* A native or inhabitant of Polynesia. Also, the Polynesian languages as a group. E19.

polyneuritis /ˌpɒlɪnjʊəˈrʌɪtɪs/ *noun.* L19.
[from POLY- + NEURITIS.]
MEDICINE. Any (esp. inflammatory) disorder affecting many peripheral nerves.
■ **polyneuritic** /-ˈrɪtɪk/ *adjective* of, pertaining to, or suffering from polyneuritis L19.

polynia *noun* var. of POLYNYA.

polynomial /pɒlɪˈnəʊmɪəl/ *noun & adjective.* L17.
[from POLY- after *binomial*.]
► **A** *noun.* **1** MATH. Orig., an expression consisting of many terms. Now, a sum of one or more terms each consisting of a constant multiplied by one or more variables raised to a positive (or non-negative) integral power (e.g. $3 + 4xy^2$). L17.
2 A taxonomic name consisting of several terms. L19.
► **B** *adjective.* Consisting of many terms or names. E18.
polynomial time COMPUTING the time required for a computer to solve a problem, where this time is a simple polynomial function of the size of the input.

polynuclear /pɒlɪˈnjuːklɪə/ *adjective.* L19.
[from POLY- + NUCLEAR.]
1 BIOLOGY & MEDICINE. Having several nuclei. Also = POLYMORPHONUCLEAR. L19.
2 CHEMISTRY. Of a complex: containing more than one metal atom. Of a compound: polycyclic. E20.

polynucleated /pɒlɪˈnjuːklɪeɪtɪd/ *adjective.* L19.
[from POLY- + NUCLEATED.]
1 BIOLOGY & MEDICINE. = POLYNUCLEAR 1. L19.
2 Of an urban area: planned in the form of a number of self-contained communities. M20.

polynya /pəʊˈlɪnjə/ *noun.* Also **-ia**. M19.
[Russian, from base of *pole*, *polyana* field.]
A space of open water in the midst of ice, esp. in Arctic seas.

polyocracy /pɒlɪˈɒkrəsi/ *noun.* L20.
[from POLY *noun*² + -O- + -CRACY.]
With *the*: a section of the Establishment characterized by left-wing politics and social activism, and supposedly consisting typically of people educated at or associated with polytechnics. Usu. *derog.*

polyoma /pɒlɪˈəʊmə/ *noun.* Pl. **-mas**, **-mata** /-mətə/. M20.
[from POLY- (with ref. to the wide variety of tumours produced + -OMA.]
MICROBIOLOGY. In full ***polyoma virus***. A papovavirus that is endemic in mice without producing tumours but can produce tumours in young rodents into which it is injected.

polyomino /pɒlɪˈɒmɪnəʊ/ *noun.* Pl. **-oes**. M20.
[from POLY- + D)OMINO.]
A planar shape formed by joining a number of identical squares by their edges.

polyonymous /pɒlɪˈɒnɪməs/ *adjective.* L17.
[from Greek *poluōnumos*, formed as POLY- + *onuma* name: see -NYM, -OUS.]
Having many names or titles; called or known by several different names.
■ **polyonymy** *noun* [Greek *poluōnumia*: see -Y³] the use of several different names for the same person or thing; variety of names or titles: L17.

polyopia /pɒlɪˈəʊpɪə/ *noun.* Also (earlier) Anglicized as †**polyopy**. M19.
[mod. Latin, formed as POLY- + -OPIA.]
OPHTHALMOLOGY. An abnormality of the eyes in which one object is seen as two or more; multiple vision.
■ Also **polyopsia** *noun* M19.

polyp /ˈpɒlɪp/ *noun.* Also (now *rare*) **polype**. LME.
[Old French *polipe* (mod. *-ype*) from Latin POLYPUS.]
1 MEDICINE. A growth, usu. benign and with a stalk, protruding from a mucous membrane. LME.
†**2** = POLYPUS 2. L16–M18.
3 An individual coelenterate as a hydra; *esp.* an individual organism in a coelenterate colony such as coral. M18.

> 🕮 **3** *Times* The starfish eat the tiny polyps which build up the coral.

polypary /ˈpɒlɪp(ə)ri/ *noun.* M18.
[mod. Latin *polyparium*, formed as POLYPUS + -ARIUM.]
The common stem or supporting structure of a colony of polyps, to which the individual zooids are attached.

polype *noun* see POLYP.

polypectomy /pɒlɪˈpɛktəmi/ *noun.* M20.
[from POLYP + -ECTOMY.]
Surgical removal of a polyp; an instance of this.

polypeptide /pɒlɪˈpɛptʌɪd/ *noun.* E20.
[from POLY- + PEPTONE + -IDE.]
BIOCHEMISTRY. An organic polymer consisting of a large number of amino acid residues bonded together in a chain.

> 🕮 attrib.: *Scientific American* A hemoglobin molecule is made up of four polypeptide chains. VASOACTIVE ***intestinal polypeptide***.

polyphagia /pɒlɪˈfeɪdʒɪə, -dʒə/ *noun.* Also (esp. in sense 2) Anglicized as **polyphagy** /pəˈlɪfədʒi/. L17.
[Greek *poluphagia*, from *poluphagos*: see -PHAGIA, -PHAGY.]
1 MEDICINE & PSYCHOLOGY. Excessive eating or appetite, esp. as a symptom of disease. L17.
2 ZOOLOGY. The habit of feeding on various kinds of food. L19.
■ **ˈpolyphage** *noun* (***a***) a person who eats to excess; (***b***) an animal feeding on various kinds of food: E17.

polyphagous /pəˈlɪfəgəs/ *adjective.* E19.
[from Greek *poluphagos* eating to excess: see POLY-, -PHAGOUS.]
Eating much, voracious; ZOOLOGY feeding on various kinds of food.

polyphagy *noun* see POLYPHAGIA.

polyphant /ˈpɒlɪf(ə)nt/ *noun*¹. L17.
[Alt. of POLYPHONE.]
MUSIC (now *Hist.*). A wire-stringed musical instrument resembling a lute.

polyphant /ˈpɒlɪf(ə)nt/ *noun*². L19.
[Alt. of *Pollaphant*, a village in Cornwall, England.]
In full ***polyphant stone***. A kind of Cornish potstone, greenish-grey in colour.

polypharmacy /pɒlɪˈfɑːməsi/ *noun.* M18.
[from POLY- + PHARMACY: cf. Greek *polupharmakos* knowing or using many drugs.]
MEDICINE. The use of several drugs or medicines together in the treatment of disease (freq. with the suggestion of indiscriminate, unscientific, or excessive prescription).
■ **polypharmacal** /-k(ə)l/ *adjective* using many drugs or medicines M17. **,polypharma'ceutical** *noun & adjective* (***a***) *noun* a medicinal preparation containing several drugs; (***b***) *adjective* of or relating to polypharmacy: M20.

polyphase /ˈpɒlɪfeɪz/ *adjective.* L19.
[from POLY- + PHASE *noun*.]
1 ELECTRICITY. Using two, three, or more alternating currents that are identical in frequency but differ in phase. L19.

2 Consisting of or occurring in a number of separate stages. M20.
3 Consisting of or involving a number of different phases of matter. M20.
■ **poly'phasic** *adjective* (PHYSIOLOGY) having several successive peaks of activity etc. E20.

Polypheme /ˈpɒlɪfiːm/ *noun.* E17.
[French *Polyphème* formed as next.]
A Cyclops, a one-eyed giant.
■ **Poly'phemic** *adjective* of the nature of, resembling, or relating to a Polypheme L18.

Polyphemus /pɒlɪˈfiːməs/ *noun.* E19.
[Latin from Greek *Poluphēmos*, a one-eyed giant in Homer's *Odyssey*, lit. 'many-voiced, much spoken of'.]
1 = prec. E19.
2 In full ***Polyphemus moth***. A large N. American saturniid moth, *Antheraea polyphemus*, with a large eyespot on each wing. L19.

polyphiloprogenitive /ˌpɒlɪfɪləʊprə(ʊ)ˈdʒɛnɪtɪv/ *adjective.* E20.
[from POLY- + PHILOPROGENITIVE.]
Esp. of a person's talent, imagination, etc.: very prolific.

polyphloisboian /ˌpɒlɪflɔɪsˈbɔɪən/ *adjective.* Chiefly *joc.* E19.
[from Greek (Homer) *poluphloisboio* (*thalassēs*) of the loud-roaring (sea), genit. of *poluphloisbos*, formed as POLY- + *phloisbos* roaring, din: see -AN.]
Loud-roaring, boisterous.

polyphone /ˈpɒlɪfəʊn/ *noun.* Also **-phon** /-fɒn/. M17.
[from Greek *poluphōnos* having many tones, formed as POLY- + *phōnē* voice, sound. See also POLYPHANT *noun*[1].]
1 MUSIC (now *Hist.*). ▸**a** = POLYPHANT *noun*[1]. M17. ▸**b** A clockwork or hand-operated musical box playing a tune when the corresponding perforated disc is inserted. E20.
2 PHILOLOGY. A written character having more than one phonetic value; a letter or other symbol which stands for different sounds. L19.

polyphonic /pɒlɪˈfɒnɪk/ *adjective.* L18.
[formed as prec. + -IC.]
1 MUSIC. **a** Composed or arranged for several voices or parts, each having a melody of its own; consisting of a number of melodies combined; contrapuntal; of or pertaining to polyphonic music. L18. ▸**b** Of an instrument: capable of producing more than one note at a time. L19.
2 Producing many sounds; many-voiced (*lit.* & *fig.*); (of prose) written to sound pleasant and melodious. M19.
3 PHILOLOGY. Of a letter etc.: having more than one phonetic value. L19.
■ **polyphonical** *adjective* (*rare*) M19. **polyphonically** *adverb* M20.

polyphonist /pəˈlɪfənɪst/ *noun.* E19.
[formed as prec. + -IST.]
1 A person who produces a variety of vocal sounds; a ventriloquist. *rare.* E19.
2 MUSIC. A polyphonic composer or theorist; a contrapuntist. M19.

polyphonous /pəˈlɪf(ə)nəs/ *adjective.* L17.
[formed as prec. + -OUS.]
= POLYPHONIC.

polyphony /pəˈlɪf(ə)ni/ *noun.* E19.
[Greek *poluphōnia*, formed as POLYPHONE: see -PHONY.]
1 Multiplicity of sounds. *rare.* E19.
2 MUSIC. The simultaneous combination of a number of parts, each forming an individual melody, and harmonizing with each other; the style of composition in which the parts are so combined; polyphonic composition; counterpoint. M19.
3 PHILOLOGY. The symbolization of different vocal sounds by the same letter etc.; polyphonic character. *rare.* L19.

2 *fig.: New Statesman* A polyphony of death, art and 'incorporeal love'.

polyphylesis /ˌpɒlɪfʌɪˈliːsɪs/ *noun.* L19.
[Back-form. from next after *genesis*.]
BIOLOGY. The polyphyletic development of a species or other taxon.
■ Also **polyphyly** /ˈpɒlɪfʌɪli/ *noun* E20.

polyphyletic /ˌpɒlɪfʌɪˈlɛtɪk/ *adjective.* L19.
[from POLY- + PHYLETIC.]
Chiefly BIOLOGY. (Esp. of a species or other taxon) originating from several independent ancestors or sources; relating to such origination; polygenetic.
■ **polyphyletically** *adverb* L19. **poly'phyletism** *noun* = POLYPHYLESIS M20.

polyphyodont /pəˈlɪfɪədɒnt/ *adjective.* L19.
[from Greek *poluphuēs* manifold (formed as POLY- + *phuē* growth) + -ODONT.]
ZOOLOGY. Having several successive growths or sets of teeth.

polypi *noun* pl. of POLYPUS.

polypide /ˈpɒlɪpʌɪd/ *noun.* M19.
[from POLYP + *-ide*: cf. -ID[3].]
ZOOLOGY. The movable contents of a bryozoan zooid.

polypidom /pəˈlɪpɪdəm/ *noun.* E19.
[from Latin POLYPUS + *domus*, Greek *domos* house.]
ZOOLOGY. = POLYPARY.

polypier /ˈpɒlɪpɪə/ *noun.* Now *rare.* E19.
[French, from *polype* POLYP + *-ier* after *poirier* pear tree etc.]
ZOOLOGY. = POLYPARY.

polypifer /pəˈlɪpɪfə/ *noun.* E19.
[mod. Latin *Polypifera*: see next, -FER.]
ZOOLOGY. A polypary; a compound organism formed of polyps.

polypiferous /pɒlɪˈpɪf(ə)rəs/ *adjective.* L18.
[from mod. Latin *Polypifera* a former division of invertebrates, from POLYPUS: see -I-, -FEROUS.]
Chiefly ZOOLOGY. Bearing polyps.

polypite /ˈpɒlɪpʌɪt/ *noun.* E19.
[from Latin POLYPUS + -ITE[1].]
†**1** PALAEONTOLOGY. A fossil polyp. *rare.* Only in E19.
2 ZOOLOGY. = POLYP 3. M19.

polyplacophoran /ˌpɒlɪpləˈkɒf(ə)rən/ *noun & adjective.* L19.
[from mod. Latin *Polyplacophora* (see below), formed as POLY- + Greek *plak-*, *plax* tablet, plate, etc. + *-phoros* bearing: see -O-, -AN.]
ZOOLOGY. ▸**A** *noun.* Any mollusc of the class Polyplacophora, which comprises the chitons. L19.
▸**B** *adjective.* Of or pertaining to the class Polyplacophora. L19.

polyploid /ˈpɒlɪplɔɪd/ *adjective & noun.* E20.
[from POLY- + -PLOID.]
BIOLOGY. ▸**A** *adjective.* (Of a cell) containing more than two homologous sets of chromosomes; (of an individual) composed of polyploid cells. E20.
▸**B** *noun.* A polyploid organism. E20.
■ **polyploidize** *verb trans.* make polyploid M20. **polyploidy** *noun* polyploid condition E20.

polypod /ˈpɒlɪpɒd/ *noun*[1]. Now *rare.* LME.
[Old French *polipode* (mod. *polypode*) formed as POLYPODY.]
= POLYPODY.

polypod /ˈpɒlɪpɒd/ *noun*[2] *& adjective.* As noun also (earlier) †**-pode**. M18.
[French *polypode* adjective from Greek *polupod-* stem of *polupous* many-footed: see POLYPUS.]
ZOOLOGY. ▸**A** *noun.* Any of various animals having many feet; *esp.* †(*a*) a millipede; (*b*) an octopus, a squid. Now *rare.* M18.
▸**B** *adjective.* Having many feet or footlike organs; *spec.* designating (an insect in) a phase of larval development characterized by a segmented abdomen with rudimentary or functional appendages. E19.

polypodiaceous /ˌpɒlɪpəʊdɪˈeɪʃəs/ *adjective.* M19.
[from mod. Latin *Polypodiaceae*, from *polypodium* (see POLYPODY): see -ACEOUS.]
BOTANY. Of or pertaining to the fern family Polypodiaceae.

polypody /ˈpɒlɪpəʊdi/ *noun.* Also in Latin form **polypodium** /pɒlɪˈpəʊdɪəm/. LME.
[Latin *polypodium* a kind of fern from Greek *polupodion*, formed as POLY- + *pod-*, *pous* foot + *-ion* dim. suffix.]
Any of various ferns of the genus *Polypodium*, with pinnatifid or pinnate fronds; *esp.* any fern of the *P. vulgare* aggregate species, growing on rocks, old walls, banks, and trees.

polypoid /ˈpɒlɪpɔɪd/ *adjective.* M19.
[from POLYP + -OID.]
ZOOLOGY & MEDICINE. Resembling or of the nature of a polyp.
■ Also **poly'poidal** *adjective* L19.

polypore /ˈpɒlɪpɔː/ *noun.* E20.
[from next.]
A bracket fungus of the genus *Polyporus* or the family Polyporaceae.

polyporus /pəˈlɪp(ə)rəs/ *noun.* L19.
[mod. Latin (see prec.), formed as POLY- + Greek *poros* pore.]
1 = prec. L19.
2 A material for mounting insect specimens, consisting of dried strips of *Polyporus betulinus* or a related fungus. E20.

polypose /ˈpɒlɪpəʊs/ *adjective.* M18.
[formed as next + -OSE[1] or from Latin *polyposus*.]
ZOOLOGY & MEDICINE. = POLYPOUS.

polyposis /pɒlɪˈpəʊsɪs/ *noun.* Pl. **-poses** /-ˈpəʊsiːz/. E20.
[formed as next + -OSIS.]
MEDICINE. A condition characterized by the presence of numerous internal polyps, *esp.* (in full ***polyposis coli*** /ˈkəʊlʌɪ/ [Latin = of the colon]) a hereditary disease which affects the colon and in which the polyps may become malignant.

polypous /ˈpɒlɪpəs/ *adjective.* M18.
[from POLYP or POLYPUS + -OUS.]
1 ZOOLOGY. Pertaining to or of the nature of a polyp; resembling (that of) a polyp (esp. with ref. to reproduction by budding, as in hydras). M18.
2 MEDICINE. Pertaining to or of the nature of a polyp; characterized by polyps. M18.

polypragmatic /ˌpɒlɪpragˈmatɪk/ *adjective.* E17.
[from Greek *polupragmatos*, formed as POLY- + *pragmat-*, *pragma* thing done: see -IC.]
Busying oneself about many affairs (that are not one's own); meddlesome, officious.

polypropylene /pɒlɪˈprəʊpɪliːn/ *noun.* M20.
[from POLY- + PROPYLENE.]
A polymer of propylene, *esp.* any of a number of thermoplastic materials used as films, fibres, or moulding materials. Freq. *attrib.*
■ Also **poly'propene** *noun* M20.

polyprotic /pɒlɪˈprəʊtɪk/ *adjective.* M20.
[from POLY- + PROTON + -IC.]
CHEMISTRY. Of an acid: capable of donating more than one proton to a base, polybasic.

polyprotodont /pɒlɪˈprəʊtədɒnt/ *adjective.* L19.
[from POLY- + PROTO- + -ODONT.]
ZOOLOGY. Having more than two incisor teeth in the lower jaw (as the carnivorous and insectivorous marsupials).

polyptych /ˈpɒlɪptɪk/ *noun.* M19.
[from POLY- after *diptych*, *triptych*.]
An altarpiece, painting, etc., consisting of more than three leaves or panels folded or hinged together.

polypus /ˈpɒlɪpəs/ *noun.* Pl. **-pi** /-pʌɪ/. LME.
[Latin from Greek (Doric, Aeolic) *pōlupos*, var. of Attic *polupous*, formed as POLY- + *pous* foot.]
1 MEDICINE. = POLYP 1. LME.
2 A cephalopod having eight or ten tentacles, as an octopus or a squid. Now only in allusion to Latin or Greek. L15.
3 = POLYP 3. Now *rare* or *obsolete.* M18.

polyrhythm /ˈpɒlɪrɪð(ə)m/ *noun.* E20.
[from POLY- + RHYTHM.]
MUSIC. The use of two or more different rhythms simultaneously; music using such rhythms.
■ **poly'rhythmic** *adjective* involving or using two or more different rhythms, esp. at the same time M20. **poly'rhythmical** *adjective* = POLYRHYTHMIC L19. **poly'rhythmically** *adverb* M20.

polyrod /ˈpɒlɪrɒd/ *noun.* M20.
[from POLY(STYRENE + ROD *noun*.]
A radio aerial consisting of a tapering rod of a dielectric material (usu. polystyrene) projecting from a waveguide. Also ***polyrod aerial***, ***polyrod antenna***.

polysaccharide /pɒlɪˈsakərʌɪd/ *noun.* L19.
[from POLY- + SACCHARIDE.]
CHEMISTRY. A carbohydrate whose molecules consist of a number of monosaccharide residues bonded together (usu. in a chain), *esp.* one of high molecular weight.

polysarcia /pɒlɪˈsɑːsɪə/ *noun.* Now *rare.* L17.
[Late Latin from Greek *polusarkia*, from *polusarkos* very fleshy, formed as POLY- + *sark-*, *sarx* flesh: see -IA[1].]
MEDICINE. Corpulence, obesity.

polysemia *noun* see POLYSEMY.

polysemous /pɒlɪˈsiːməs, pəˈlɪsɪməs/ *adjective.* L19.
[from medieval Latin *polysemus* from Greek *polusēmos*, formed as POLY- + *sēma* sign, *sēmainein* signify: see -OUS.]
Having many meanings; LINGUISTICS. = POLYSEMIC.

polysemy /ˈpɒlɪsiːmi, pəˈlɪsɪmi/ *noun.* Also in mod. Latin form **polysemia** /pɒlɪˈsiːmɪə/. E20.
[formed as prec. + -Y[3].]
LINGUISTICS. The fact of having several meanings; the possession of multiple meanings.
■ **'polyseme** *noun* a word having several or multiple meanings M20. **poly'semic** *adjective* of or pertaining to polysemy; having several meanings, exhibiting polysemy: M20.

polysomatic /ˌpɒlɪsəˈmatɪk/ *adjective.* L19.
[from Greek *polusōmatos* with many bodies, formed as POLY- + *sōmat-*, *sōma* body: see -IC.]
1 PETROGRAPHY. Consisting of more than one grain or more than one mineral. L19.
2 BIOLOGY. Of, pertaining to, or exhibiting polysomaty. M20.

polysomaty /pɒlɪˈsəʊməti/ *noun.* M20.
[formed as prec. + -Y[3].]
BIOLOGY. The occurrence of polyploid cells together with diploid cells in the same somatic tissue.

polysome /ˈpɒlɪsəʊm/ *noun.* M20.
[Contr. of POLYRIBOSOME.]
BIOLOGY. A cluster of ribosomes held together by a strand of messenger RNA which each is translating.
■ **poly'somal** *adjective* M20.

polysomic /pɒlɪˈsəʊmɪk/ *adjective.* M20.
[from POLY- + -SOME[3] + -IC.]
CYTOLOGY. Having more of some normal chromosomes than the usual diploid or polyploid complement.
■ **polysomy** /ˈpɒlɪsəʊmi, pəˈlɪsəmi/ *noun* M20.

polysomnogram /pɒlɪˈsɒmnə(ʊ)gram/ *noun.* L20.
[from POLY- + Latin *somnus* sleep + -O- + -GRAM.]
MEDICINE. An electronic record of the activity of a person's brain, eyes, heart, lungs, limbs, etc., during sleep.

For other words beginning with *poly-* see the entry for **poly-**

■ ˌ**polysomnoˈgraphic** *adjective* of or pertaining to polysomnography L20. **polysomˈnography** *noun* the recording of polysomnograms L20.

polyspermous /pɒlɪˈspəːməs/ *adjective*. L17.
[from Greek *poluspermos*, formed as POLY- + *sperma* seed: see -OUS.]
BOTANY. Having, containing, or producing numerous seeds; many-seeded.

polyspermy /ˈpɒlɪspəːmi/ *noun*. L19.
[Greek *poluspermia* abundance of seed, formed as prec.: see -Y[3].]
BIOLOGY. Penetration of an ovum by more than one sperm.
■ **polyspermic** /pɒlɪˈspəːmɪk/ *adjective* involving or exhibiting polyspermy L19.

polystelic /pɒlɪˈstiːlɪk/ *adjective*. L19.
[from POLY- + STELE + -IC.]
BOTANY. Of a stem or root: having more than one stele.
■ ˈ**polystely** *noun* polystelic condition L19.

polystyrene /pɒlɪˈstʌɪriːn/ *noun*. E20.
[from POLY- + STYRENE.]
A polymer of styrene; *esp.* any of various thermoplastic polymers of styrene used as moulding materials, films, and rigid foams.

polysyllabic /ˌpɒlɪsɪˈlabɪk/ *adjective*. L18.
[from POLY- + SYLLABIC.]
(Of a word) consisting of many (usu. more than three) syllables; (of language etc.) consisting of or characterized by polysyllables.
■ **polysyllabical** *adjective* = POLYSYLLABIC M17. **polysyllabically** *adverb* L19. **polysyllabicity** /-sɪləˈbɪsɪti/ *noun* L19. **polyˈsyllabism** *noun* the use of polysyllables (as a stage in the development of language) M19.

polysyllable /ˈpɒlɪsɪləb(ə)l/ *noun & adjective*. L16.
[Alt. (after SYLLABLE *noun*) of medieval Latin *polysyllaba* use as noun of fem. of *polysyllabus* from Greek *polusullabos*, formed as POLY- + *sullabē* SYLLABLE *noun*.]
► **A** *noun*. A word of many (usu. more than three) syllables. L16.
► **B** *adjective*. = POLYSYLLABIC. Now *rare*. L16.

polysyndeton /pɒlɪˈsɪndɪt(ə)n/ *noun*. L16.
[mod. Latin, formed as POLY- after ASYNDETON.]
RHETORIC. The use of several conjunctions or (usu.) the same conjunction several times, in quick succession.

polysynthesis /pɒlɪˈsɪnθɪsɪs/ *noun*. M19.
[from POLY- + SYNTHESIS.]
LINGUISTICS. The combination of several or all syntactic elements of a sentence in one word. Cf. INCORPORATION 1b.

polysynthetic /ˌpɒlɪsɪnˈθɛtɪk/ *adjective*. E19.
[from Greek *polusunthetos* much compounded, formed as POLY- + *sunthetos*: see SYNTHETIC.]
1 CRYSTALLOGRAPHY. Consisting of or characterized by a series of twin crystals united so as to form a laminated structure. E19.
2 LINGUISTICS. Characterized by polysynthesis. E19.
■ **polysynthetically** *adverb* L19.

Polytec /pɒlɪˈtɛk/ *noun*. *colloq*. Also **-tech**. E20.
[Abbreviation.]
= POLYTECHNIC *noun*. Cf. POLY *noun*[2].

polytechnic /pɒlɪˈtɛknɪk/ *adjective & noun*. E19.
[French *polytechnique*, from Greek *polutekhnos* skilled in many arts, formed as POLY- + *tekhnē* art: see -IC.]
► **A** *adjective*. Pertaining to, dealing with, or devoted to various arts; *esp.* (of an educational institution) giving instruction in various technical or vocational subjects; of, pertaining to, or characteristic of a polytechnic or polytechnics. E19.
► **B** *noun*. Orig., a school giving instruction in various technical subjects. Now, an institution of higher education offering courses (at or below degree level) mainly in technical and vocational subjects. Also, without article: (attendance at) some such institution. M19.
■ **polytechnical** *adjective* pertaining to, devoted to, or practising many arts; polytechnic: E19. **polytechnician** /-ˈnɪʃ(ə)n/ *noun* a student or former student of a (French) polytechnic school L19.

polytene /ˈpɒlɪtiːn/ *adjective*. M20.
[from POLY- + as -TENE.]
CYTOLOGY. Designating or pertaining to a giant chromosome, numbers of which are found in certain meiotic interphase nuclei (esp. in dipteran insects), which is composed of many parallel copies of the genetic material.
■ **polyˈtenic** *adjective* = POLYTENE M20. **polyteny** *noun* the state of being polytene M20.

polytetrafluoroethylene /ˌpɒlɪtɛtrəflʊərəʊˈɛθɪliːn/ *noun*. M20.
[from POLY- + TETRAFLUOROETHYLENE.]
CHEMISTRY. A polymer of tetrafluoroethylene, *esp.* a tough crystalline resinous material resistant to chemicals and with a low coefficient of friction, used as a moulding material and as a coating for bearings, non-stick cooking utensils etc. Abbreviation ***PTFE***.
¶ A proprietary name for this substance is TEFLON.

polytheism /ˈpɒlɪθiːɪz(ə)m/ *noun*. E17.
[French *polythéisme*, from Greek *polutheos* of many gods, formed as POLY- + *theos* god: see -ISM.]
The doctrine or belief that there is more than one god; worship of several gods.

polytheist /ˈpɒlɪθiːɪst/ *noun & adjective*. E17.
[formed as prec. + -IST.]
► **A** *noun*. A person who believes in more than one god; an adherent of polytheism. E17.
► **B** *adjective*. = POLYTHEISTIC. L19.
■ **polytheˈistic** *adjective* of, pertaining to, believing in or characterized by polytheism M18. **polytheˈistical** *adjective* (now *rare*) polytheistic; having a polytheistic character or quality: L17. **polytheˈistically** *adverb* M19.

polythelia /pɒlɪˈθiːlɪə/ *noun*. L19.
[French *polythélie*, formed as POLY- + Greek *thēlē* nipple: see -IA[1].]
MEDICINE. = POLYMASTIA.

polythene /ˈpɒlɪθiːn/ *noun*. M20.
[Contr. of POLYETHYLENE.]
A tough, light, translucent thermoplastic polymer of ethylene used esp. for moulded and extruded articles, as film for packaging, and as a coating. Freq. *attrib.*

polythetic /pɒlɪˈθɛtɪk/ *adjective*. M20.
[from POLY- + Greek *thetos* placed, arranged + -IC.]
Relating to or sharing a number of common characteristics of a group or class, none of them essential for membership of the group or class in question.
■ **polythetically** *adverb* M20.

polythionic /ˌpɒlɪθʌɪˈɒnɪk/ *adjective*. M19.
[from POLY- + Greek *theion* sulphur + -IC.]
CHEMISTRY. Designating any of a group of oxyacids containing two or more atoms of sulphur in the anion.

polytocous /pəˈlɪtəkəs/ *adjective*. L19.
[from Greek *polutokos* producing numerous offspring, formed as POLY- + *tok-*, *tiktein* bring forth: see -OUS.]
1 BOTANY. Bearing fruit many times, polycarpous. *rare*. L19.
2 ZOOLOGY. = MULTIPAROUS 1. M20.

polytomous /pəˈlɪtəməs/ *adjective*. M19.
[from mod. Latin *polytomus*, formed as POLY- + Greek *-tomos* cutting: see -OUS.]
Divided, or involving division, into many parts; *spec.* in BOTANY, (of branching) in which the axis is repeatedly divided into more than two branches at the same point (cf. DICHOTOMOUS).
■ **polytomy** *noun* polytomous character or branching M19.

polytonality /ˌpɒlɪtəʊˈnalɪti/ *noun*. E20.
[from POLY- + TONALITY.]
MUSIC. The simultaneous use of two or more keys in a composition.
■ **polyˈtonal** *adjective* containing or pertaining to polytonality E20. **polyˈtonalist** *noun* a person who writes or advocates polytonal music M20. **polyˈtonally** *adverb* L20.

polytope /ˈpɒlɪtəʊp/ *noun*. E20.
[from POLY- + Greek *topos* place.]
MATH. In geometry of more than three dimensions, a figure corresponding to a polygon in plane geometry or a polyhedron in solid geometry.

polytrichum /pəˈlɪtrɪkəm/ *noun*. Also (in sense 1) †**-trikhon**, (Anglicized) †**-trich**. E16.
[mod. Latin from Latin *polytrichon* from Greek *polutrikhon*, formed as POLY- + Greek *trikh-*, *thrix* hair.]
†**1** Either of two ferns, a maidenhair, *Adiantum capillus-veneris*, and a maidenhair spleenwort, *Asplenium trichomanes*. E16–E18.
2 The moss *Polytrichum commune*, common in acid places. Now only in BOTANY, any moss of the genus *Polytrichum*; such mosses collectively. L16.

polytrope /ˈpɒlɪtrəʊp/ *noun*. E20.
[Back-form. from POLYTROPIC.]
PHYSICS & ASTRONOMY. A polytropic body of gas.

polytrophic /pɒlɪˈtrəʊfɪk, -ˈtrɒfɪk/ *adjective*. M17.
[from Greek *polutrophos*, formed as POLY- + *trephein* feed: see -IC.]
†**1** Highly nutritive. *rare*. Only in M17.
2 BIOLOGY. Feeding on several kinds of food; parasitic on more than one host organism. E20.

polytropic /pɒlɪˈtrəʊpɪk, -ˈtrɒpɪk/ *adjective*. M19.
[from Greek *polutropos*, formed as POLY- + -TROPIC.]
1 Capable of turning to various courses or expedients; versatile. Freq. as an epithet of Ulysses, with allus. to the *Odyssey*. M19.
2 Of a bee: collecting nectar from many kinds of flower. L19.
3 PHYSICS & ASTRONOMY. Pertaining to or characterized by the fact that pressure, temperature, entropy, and volume change in such a way that some property remains constant. E20.

For other words beginning with *poly-* see the entry for **poly-**

polytunnel /ˈpɒlɪtʌn(ə)l/ *noun*. L20.
[from POLY(THENE + TUNNEL *noun*.]
An elongated polythene-covered frame under which seedlings or other plants are grown outdoors.

polytype /ˈpɒlɪtʌɪp/ *noun*. M19.
[from POLY- + TYPE *noun*; sense 1 from French.]
1 PRINTING (now *Hist.*). A stereotype made from a matrix obtained by pressing a wood-engraving etc. into semi-fluid type-metal; a copy of an engraving etc. made from such a cast. M19.
2 CRYSTALLOGRAPHY. A polytypic form of a substance. E20.

polytypic /pɒlɪˈtɪpɪk/ *adjective*. L19.
[from POLY- + Greek *tupikos*, from *tupos* TYPE *noun*: see -IC.]
1 Having several variant forms; *esp.* (of a species) including several subspecies. L19.
2 CRYSTALLOGRAPHY. Exhibiting polytypism; of the nature of a polytype. M20.
3 = POLYTHETIC *adjective*. M20.

polytypism /pɒlɪˈtʌɪpɪz(ə)m/ *noun*. M20.
[from prec. + -ISM.]
1 CRYSTALLOGRAPHY. A kind of polymorphism in which a substance occurs in a number of crystalline modifications (polytypes) which differ only in one of the dimensions of the unit cell. M20.
2 BIOLOGY. The occurrence of several variant forms within a single species. M20.
■ ˈ**polytypy** *noun* = POLYTYPISM 2 M20.

polyunsaturated /ˌpɒlɪʌnˈsatʃʊreɪtɪd, -tjʊr-/ *adjective*. M20.
[from POLY- + UNSATURATED.]
CHEMISTRY. Containing more than one double or triple bond between carbon atoms at which addition can normally occur; *esp.* (of a fatty acid) in which the hydrocarbon chain has more than one double or triple bond.
■ **polyunsaturate** *noun & adjective* (**a**) *noun* a polyunsaturated fatty acid; (**b**) *adjective* = POLYUNSATURATED: M20.

polyurethane /pɒlɪˈjʊərɪθeɪn/ *noun & verb*. M20.
[from POLY- + URETHANE.]
► **A** *noun*. CHEMISTRY. Any of a large class of polymers having the units linked by the group ·NH·CO·O·, important commercially as foams and fibres and as constituents of paints, adhesives, etc. M20.
► **B** *verb trans*. Coat or protect with polyurethane paint, varnish, etc. Chiefly as ***polyurethaned*** *ppl adjective*. L20.

polyuria /pɒlɪˈjʊərɪə/ *noun*. M19.
[from POLY- + -URIA.]
MEDICINE. Abnormally excessive production of urine.
■ **polyuric** *adjective* relating to or affected with polyuria L19.

polyvalent /pɒlɪˈveɪl(ə)nt/, (*exc. in Chem.*) pəˈlɪv(ə)l(ə)nt/ *adjective*. L19.
[from POLY- + -VALENT.]
1 a CHEMISTRY. Having more than one state of valency; having a valency of three or more. L19. ►**b** MEDICINE. = MULTIVALENT *adjective* 1b. E20.
2 MEDICINE. Having the property of counteracting various poisons or affording immunity against various micro-organisms. E20.
3 Chiefly LINGUISTICS & LITERARY CRITICISM. = MULTIVALENT *adjective* 3. M20.
■ **polyvalence** *noun* the state or property of being polyvalent E20.

polyversity /pɒlɪˈvəːsɪti/ *noun*. L20.
[Blend of POLYTECHNIC and UNIVERSITY.]
A higher educational institution combining features of both university and polytechnic.

polyvinyl /pɒlɪˈvʌɪn(ə)l/ *noun*. M20.
[from POLY- + VINYL.]
CHEMISTRY. **1** A polymer derived from a vinyl compound. Usu. in *comb.* M20.
2 A plastic or synthetic resin made by polymerizing a compound containing the vinyl group, $CH_2{=}CH\cdot$. Freq. *attrib.* M20.
Comb.: **polyvinyl acetal** any of a class of synthetic resins prepared from polyvinyl alcohol and an aldehyde and used mainly in safety glass and in lacquers and paints; **polyvinyl acetate** a soft plastic with the repeating unit $\cdot CH_2\cdot CH(O\cdot CO\cdot CH_3)\cdot$, made by polymerizing vinyl acetate and used chiefly in paints and adhesives; **polyvinyl alcohol** any of a series of polymers in which the repeating unit is $\cdot CH_2\cdot CHOH\cdot$, used as emulsifiers, adhesives, coatings, films, and fibres; **polyvinyl chloride** any of various tough, chemically resistant, thermoplastic polymers in which the repeating unit is $\cdot CH_2\cdot CHCl\cdot$, made by polymerizing vinyl chloride and produced in rigid and plasticized forms; **polyvinyl pyrrolidone** a water-soluble polymer of vinyl pyrrolidone which is used as a synthetic blood plasma substitute and in the cosmetic, drug, and food-processing industries.

polyvinylidene /ˌpɒlɪvʌɪˈnʌɪlɪdiːn, -ˈnɪl-/ *noun*. M20.
[from POLY- + VINYLIDENE.]
CHEMISTRY. **1** Used in *comb.* in names of substances which are polymers of vinylidene compounds. M20.
2 A synthetic resin prepared from a vinylidene compound. Freq. *attrib.* M20.

Comb.: **polyvinylidene chloride** any of a class of resinous polymers of vinylidene chloride which have the structure $(\cdot CH_2 \cdot CCl_2 \cdot)_n$ and are used esp. as impact- and chemical-resistant films and fibres.

polywater /ˈpɒlɪwɔːtə/ *noun.* M20.
[from POLY- + WATER *noun.*]
CHEMISTRY (now *Hist.*). A supposed polymeric form of water markedly different from ordinary water, reputedly found in fine capillary tubes.

polyzoan /pɒlɪˈzəʊən/ *noun & adjective.* M19.
[from mod. Latin *Polyzoa* (former taxonomic name), formed as POLY- + Greek *zōia* pl. of *zōion* animal: see -AN.]
ZOOLOGY. = BRYOZOAN.
■ **polyzoic** *adjective* (now *rare*) polyzoan M19. **polyzoon** *noun*, pl. **-zoa**, = POLYZOAN *noun* (usu. in *pl.*) M19.

pom /pɒm/ *noun*¹. *colloq.* E20.
[Abbreviation.]
A Pomeranian dog.

pom /pɒm/ *noun*² *& adjective. Austral. & NZ slang* (usu. *derog.*). Also **P-**. E20.
[Abbreviation.]
= POMMY *noun*¹ *& adjective*¹.

Pom /pɒm/ *noun*³. M20.
[Cf. POMME.]
Dried and powdered cooked potato.
¶ Formerly a proprietary name.

Poma /ˈpəʊmə/ *noun. N. Amer.* M20.
[from J. *Pomagalski*, its inventor.]
(Proprietary name for) a type of ski-lift with detachable supports for the passengers.

pomace /ˈpʌmɪs/ *noun.* LME.
[medieval Latin *pomacium* cider, from Latin *pomum* apple.]
1 The mass of crushed apples in cider-making, before or after the juice is pressed out. Formerly also, cider. LME.
2 Some other thing crushed or pounded to a pulp; *esp.* the refuse of fish, castor oil seeds, etc., after the oil has been extracted, freq. used as a fertilizer. LME.
†**3** The head, heart, lights, liver, and windpipe of a sheep or lamb. L17–M18.
Comb.: **pomace-fly** = DROSOPHILA.

pomacentroid /pəʊməˈsentrɔɪd/ *adjective & noun.* L19.
[from mod. Latin *Pomacentrus* genus name, from Greek *pōma* lid + *kentron* sharp spine, + -OID.]
▸ **A** *adjective.* Of, pertaining to, resembling, or belonging to the family Pomacentridae of usu. small, freq. brightly coloured fishes of temperate and tropical seas, including damselfishes. L19.
▸ **B** *noun.* A fish of the family Pomacentridae. L19.

pomaceous /pə(ʊ)ˈmeɪʃəs/ *adjective.* E18.
[from Latin *pomum* apple + -ACEOUS.]
1 Of, pertaining to, or consisting of apples. E18.
2 BOTANY. Of the nature of a pome; of or pertaining to the Pomoideae, a subfamily of the rose family bearing pomes or fruits like pomes. M19.

pomade /pəˈmeɪd, -mɑːd/ *noun & verb.* M16.
[French *pommade* from Italian *pomata* from mod. Latin POMATUM.]
▸ **A** *noun.* A scented ointment (in which apples were perh. orig. an ingredient) for the skin, now esp. for the skin of the head and for the hair. M16.
📖 P. CAREY He got his pomade and slicked down his hair.
▸ **B** *verb trans.* Anoint with pomade. Chiefly as ***pomaded*** *ppl adjective.* L19.

Pomak /ˈpəʊmak/ *noun.* L19.
[Bulgarian.]
A Muslim Bulgarian.

pomander /pəˈmandə, ˈpɒmandə/ *noun.* L15.
[Old French *pome d'embre* from medieval Latin *pomum ambrae*, *pomum de ambra* apple of amber.]
1 Orig., a mixture of aromatic substances, usu. made into a ball and carried in a small box or bag, esp. as a safeguard against infection. Now, a fruit, esp. an orange, stuck with cloves and usu. tied with ribbon, hung or placed in a wardrobe. L15.
2 A case for this perfume, usu. a ball of gold, silver, or ivory. Now, a small perforated container filled with potpourri etc. for hanging in a wardrobe, etc. L15.

pomarine /ˈpɒmərʌɪn/ *adjective.* M19.
[French *pomarin* formed as POMATORHINE.]
ORNITHOLOGY. = POMATORHINE. Only in ***pomarine skua***, (*US*) ***pomarine jaeger***, a large Arctic-breeding skua, *Stercorarius pomarinus.*
¶ All skuas are in fact anatomically pomatorhine.

pomato /pəˈmɑːtəʊ, -ˈmeɪtəʊ/ *noun.* Pl. **-oes**. E20.
[from P(OTATO + T)OMATO.]
Orig., the fruit of a hybrid potato, which resembled a tomato. Later, the product of attempts to hybridize the potato and the tomato, by grafting or other methods.

pomatorhine /ˈpəʊmətərʌɪn/ *adjective.* L19.
[from mod. Latin *pomatorhinus*, from Greek *pōmat-*, *pōma* lid, cover + -O- + *rhin-*, *rhis* nose: see -INE¹.]
ORNITHOLOGY. Having the nostrils partly covered with a cere.
pomatorhine skua = *POMARINE skua.*

pomatum /pə(ʊ)ˈmeɪtəm/ *noun & verb.* M16.
[mod. Latin, from Latin *pomum* apple + *-atum* -ATE¹.]
▸ **A** *noun.* (A) hair ointment, (a) pomade. M16.
▸ **B** *verb trans.* Anoint with pomatum. Chiefly as ***pomatumed*** *ppl adjective.* M17.

pombe /ˈpɒmbeɪ/ *noun.* M19.
[Kiswahili.]
In Central and E. Africa: a fermented drink made from various kinds of grain and fruit.

pome /pəʊm/ *noun*¹. LME.
[Old French (mod. *pomme*) = apple, from Proto-Romance fem. noun, orig. pl. of Latin *pomum* a fruit, esp. an apple.]
1 A fruit of the apple kind or resembling an apple. Now only *poet.*, an apple. LME. ▸**b** BOTANY. A fruit (e.g. an apple, pear, or quince) consisting of a fleshy enlarged receptacle and a tough central core containing the seeds. L18.
2 A ball or globe, esp. of metal; the orb of sovereignty. LME.
Comb.: †**pome-citron** (the fruit of) the citron, *Citrus medica.*

pome /pəʊm/ *noun*². *joc.* M19.
[Alt.]
A poem.

†**pome** *verb intrans.* M17–E18.
[French *pommer*, from *pomme*: see POME *noun*¹.]
Of a cabbage, lettuce, etc.: form a close compact head.

†**pome-apis** *noun* var. of POMME D'APIS.

pomegranate /ˈpɒmɪɡranɪt/ *noun & adjective.* ME.
[Old French *pome grenate*, *pome garnate*, etc., *pome* (see POME *noun*¹) apple, *grenate* (mod. *grenade*) pomegranate, from Proto-Romance var. of Latin (*malum*) *granatum* lit. 'apple having many seeds'.]
▸ **A** *noun.* **1 a** The large roundish fruit of the tree *Punica granatum* (family Punicaceae), with a golden or orange red-tinged leathery rind and numerous seeds, each surrounded by a somewhat acid reddish pulp. ME. ▸**b** The tree which bears this fruit, native to SW Asia and widely naturalized in the Mediterranean area. Also ***pomegranate tree***. LME. ▸**c** The colour of the pomegranate, a yellowish red. L19.
2 A carved or embroidered representation of a pomegranate. LME.
3 [For *Jimmy Grant*, *immigrant*.] = POMMY *noun*¹. *Austral. obsolete* exc. *Hist.* E20.
▸ **B** *adjective.* Of the colour of the pomegranate, yellowish red. M19.

pomeis /ˈpəʊmɪs/ *noun pl.* Also **pomeys**, **pommes**. M16.
[Perh. old spelling of *pommes* pl. of POME *noun*¹.]
HERALDRY. Roundels vert.

pomelled *adjective* var. of POMMELLED.

pomelo /ˈpɒmələʊ, ˈpʌm-/ *noun.* Also **pumm-** /ˈpʌm-/. Pl. **-os**. M19.
[Origin unkn.]
The shaddock; *US* the grapefruit.

Pomeranchuk /pɒməˈrantʃʊk/ *noun.* M20.
[I. Ya. *Pomeranchuk* (1913–66), Russian physicist.]
PHYSICS. **1** Used *attrib.* with ref. to the cooling that a mixture of liquid and solid helium 3 undergoes when solidified by compression. M20.
2 Used (usu. *attrib.*), to designate various concepts relating to the scattering of subatomic particles at high energies. M20.
2 Pomeranchuk theorem, **Pomeranchuk's theorem**: that the reaction cross-sections for a particle and its anti-particle incident on the same target particle should approach the same constant value as the energy of the incident particle is increased.
■ **Pomeranchukon**, **Pomeranchon** *nouns* (NUCLEAR PHYSICS) = POMERON M20.

Pomeranian /pɒməˈreɪnɪən/ *adjective & noun.* Also (chiefly LINGUISTICS) **-mor-**. M18.
[from *Pomerania* (see below) + -AN.]
▸ **A** *adjective.* Of or pertaining to Pomerania, a historical district on the Baltic Sea in Germany and Poland (formerly a province of Prussia). M18.
Pomeranian bream a fish supposed to be a hybrid between the bream and the rudd or the roach. **Pomeranian dog** (an animal of) a variety of small dog characterized by a pointed muzzle, pricked ears, a tail curling over the back, and long silky hair.
▸ **B** *noun.* **1** A native or inhabitant of Pomerania. L19.
2 = ***Pomeranian dog*** above. L19.
3 The Lechitic dialect of Pomerania, now represented only by Kashubian. M20.

pomerium *noun* var. of POMOERIUM.

Pomerol /ˈpɒmərɒl/ *noun.* M20.
[A commune in Gironde, SW France.]
A red wine produced in Pomerol.

pomeron /ˈpɒmərɒn/ *noun.* M20.
[from POMER(ANCHUK + -ON.]
NUCLEAR PHYSICS. A virtual particle regarded as exchanged in a particular type of subatomic scattering.

†**pomeroy** *noun.* E17–E19.
[App. from Old French POME *noun*¹ + *roy* (mod. *roi*) king.]
A variety of apple formerly grown.

†**pomery** *noun* see POMOERIUM.

†**pomet** *adjective* see POMMETTY.

pomewater /ˈpəʊmwɔːtə/ *noun. obsolete* exc. *dial.* LME.
[App. from POME *noun*¹ + WATER *noun.*]
A large juicy kind of apple.

pomeys *noun pl.* var. of POMEIS.

pomfret /ˈpɒmfrɪt/ *noun.* E18.
[App. from Portuguese *pampo* + -LET, assim. to next. Cf. POMPANO.]
1 Any of several Indo-Pacific butterfishes of the genus *Pampus*, much valued for food, esp. (more fully ***black pomfret***) *P. niger*, (more fully ***white pomfret***) *P. chinensis*, and (more fully ***silver pomfret***) *P. argenteus.* E18.
2 Any of several percoid fishes of the family Bramidae. Chiefly *N. Amer.* L19.
2 Atlantic pomfret = RAY'S BREAM.

pomfret-cake /ˈpɒmfrɪtkeɪk, ˈpʌm-/ *noun.* Also **Pontefract cake** /ˈpɒntɪfrakt/. M19.
[from *Pomfret* (now *Pontefract*) a town in West Yorkshire + CAKE *noun.*]
A liquorice cake of a type orig. made at Pontefract.

pomiculture /ˈpəʊmɪkʌltʃə/ *noun.* L19.
[from Latin *pomum* fruit + CULTURE *noun.*]
The art or practice of fruit-growing.
■ **pomiculturist** *noun* L19.

pomiferous /pə(ʊ)ˈmɪf(ə)rəs/ *adjective.* M17.
[from Latin *pomifer*, from *pomum* fruit: see -FEROUS.]
Producing fruit, esp. apples; BOTANY (of a plant) bearing pomes or similar fruits (rather than berries).

pommage /ˈpɒmɪdʒ/ *noun.* L16.
[Cf. French *pommage* cider harvest or production. In sense 2 perh. a var. of POMACE.]
†**1** Cider. *rare.* Only in L16.
2 = POMACE 1. L18.

pomme /pɔm/ *noun.* Chiefly in pl. (pronounced same). E20.
[French, short for POMME DE TERRE.]
COOKERY. A potato. Chiefly in phrs.
pommes allumettes /pɔmz alymɛt/ [= matchsticks: see ALLUMETTE] matchstick-thin potato chips. ***pommes frites*** /frit/ [= fried] potato chips.

pommé /ˈpɒmeɪ/ *adjective.* Also **pommee**, **pommy** /ˈpɒmi/. E18.
[French, pa. pple of *pommer* POME *verb.*]
HERALDRY. = POMMELLÉ.

†**pomme d'apis** *noun.* Also **pome-apis**. M17–M18.
[French: cf. Latin *malus Appiana* an apple named after Appius, who is said to have grafted it on a quince.]
A variety of apple resembling a quince.

pomme de terre /pɔm də tɛːr/ *noun.* Pl. ***pommes de terre*** (pronounced same). E19.
[French, lit. 'apple of the earth'.]
COOKERY. A potato.

pommee *adjective* var. of POMMÉ.

pommel /ˈpʌm(ə)l, ˈpɒm(ə)l/ *noun.* Also **pummel**. ME.
[Old French *pomel* (mod. *pommeau*) from Proto-Romance dim. of Latin *pomum* fruit, apple. In senses 6, 7 perh. from POMMEL *verb.*]
1 A spherical ornament on the summit of a tower, at the corner of an altar, etc.; the ornamental top of a tent-pole or flagstaff. *obsolete* exc. *Hist.* ME.
2 Any ornamental knob; *esp.* (*a*) one terminating the hilt of a sword, dagger, etc.; †(*b*) a knob on a chair etc. ME. ▸†**b** = POMMELION. M–L17.
†**3** A round boss, knob, or button. ME–L17.
†**4** A rounded or hemispherical projecting part; *esp.* (*poet.*) a woman's breast. ME–L17.
5 a The upward projecting front part of a saddle; the crutch of a side-saddle. LME. ▸**b** Either of a pair of removable curved handgrips fitted to a vaulting horse. L19.
6 a A square-faced tool used by stonemasons as a punch. L18. ▸**b** An oblong wooden block with a convex ribbed face for making leather supple. M19.
7 The knobbed stick used in the game of knur and spell. M19.
Comb.: **pommel horse** a vaulting horse having pommels.

pommel /ˈpʌm(ə)l/ *verb trans.* Infl. **-ll-**, ***-l-**. M16.
[from the noun See also PUMMEL *verb.*]
Beat or strike repeatedly, = PUMMEL *verb.*
📖 D. HAMMETT Clumsy. . blows on my back and shoulder brought me around to find Gilbert pommelling me.

pommelé *adjective* var. of POMMELLÉ.

For other words beginning with *poly-* see the entry for **poly-**

†pommelion *noun.* M18–M19.
[Extension of POMMEL *noun*, perh. infl. by *trunnion*.]
NAUTICAL. The knob on the breech of a cannon; a cascabel.

pommellé /ˈpɒməleɪ/ *adjective.* Also **-elé**, **-elly** /-əli/. M16.
[French *pommelé* pa. pple of *pommeler* (in obsolete sense) assume a rounded or knobbed form, from Old French *pomel*: see POMMEL *noun*, -Y[5].]
HERALDRY. Of a cross: having its limbs ending in knobs like the pommels of sword hilts.

pommelled /ˈpʌm(ə)ld, ˈpɒm(ə)ld/ *adjective.* Also **pomelled**. M18.
[from POMMEL *noun* + -ED[2].]
1 *HERALDRY.* Of a sword: having the pommel of a specified tincture. M18.
2 ***pommelled horse*** = ***pommel horse*** s.v. POMMEL *noun.* M20.

pommer /ˈpɒmə/ *noun.* L19.
[German, alt. form of *Bombard*, formed as BOMBARD *noun*.]
MUSIC. = BOMBARD *noun* 2.

pommes *noun pl.* var. of POMEIS.

pommes de terre *noun* pl. of POMME DE TERRE.

pommetty /ˈpɒməti/ *adjective.* Also (earlier) **†pomet**. LME.
[French *pommeté*, *pommetté*, from *pommette* (Old French *pomete*) dim. of *pomme* apple: see -Y[5].]
Having rounded finials. Now only *HERALDRY*, = POMMELLÉ.

pommey /ˈpʌmi/ *noun. dial.* Also **pommy**. M19.
[App. from French *†pom(m)ee*, *†pomeye* cider, apple sauce: but perh. popular alt. of or rel. to POMACE.]
= POMACE *noun* 1.

pommy /ˈpɒmi/ *noun*[1] & *adjective*[1]. *Austral.* & *NZ slang* (usu. *derog.*). Also **-ie**, **P-**. E20.
[Abbreviation of POMEGRANATE *noun* 3.]
▶ **A** *noun.* An immigrant (esp. a recent one) to Australia or New Zealand from Britain, esp. from England; a person living in Britain, esp. in England. E20.
▶ **B** *attrib.* or as *adjective.* Of or pertaining to British, esp. English, immigrants to Australia or New Zealand; British, *esp.* English. E20.

> P. MCCUTCHAN I'm Australian born and bred, not a pommie immigrant.

Comb.: **Pommyland** Britain or England.

pommy *noun*[2] var. of POMMEY.

pommy *adjective*[2] var. of POMMÉ.

Pomo /ˈpəʊməʊ/ *noun* & *adjective.* L19.
[Pomo *pʰó·mo·* at the red earth hole and *pʰóʔmaʔ* dweller at.]
▶ **A** *noun.* Pl. same, **-os**. A member of a N. American Indian people of northern California; any of the languages of this people. L19.
▶ **B** *attrib.* or as *adjective.* Of or pertaining to the Pomo or their languages. E20.
▪ **Poˈmoan** *noun* & *adjective* (belonging to) the group of Pomo languages. M20.

po-mo /ˈpəʊməʊ/ *adjective* & *noun. colloq.* L20.
[Abbreviation.]
▶ **A** *adjective.* Post-modern. L20.
▶ **B** *noun.* Post-modernism. L20.

pomoerium /pəʊˈmɪərɪəm/ *noun.* Also **pomer-**. Pl. **-ia**. Earlier Anglicized as **†pomery**. M16.
[Latin, perh. of Etruscan origin.]
ROMAN HISTORY. The strip of ground marking the formal, religiously constituted boundary of a city (freq. understood as the strip on either side of the city walls).

pomology /pə(ʊ)ˈmɒlədʒi/ *noun.* E19.
[from Latin *pomum* fruit + -OLOGY.]
The science and practice of fruit-culture. Also, a treatise on fruit-culture.
▪ **pomoˈlogical** *adjective* M19. **pomoˈlogically** *adverb* E20. **pomologist** *noun* M19.

Pomona /pə(ʊ)ˈməʊnə/ *noun* & *adjective.* Also **p-**. M17.
[Latin name of the Roman goddess of fruits and fruit trees from *pomum* fruit.]
▶ **A** *noun.* **1** (Usu. **P-**.) (Used as a title for a treatise on) the fruit trees of a country. M17.
2 (**p-**.) In full ***Pomona green***. A green colour in which yellow predominates over blue. M19.
3 ***Pomona-glass***, a type of ornamental glass stained pale amber on one surface and etched on the other. L19.

> **2** J. FOWLES Such an infinity of greens . . from the most intense emerald to the palest Pomona.

▶ **B** *adjective.* Of a pomona green colour. M19.

Pomoranian *adjective* & *noun* see POMERANIAN.

pomp /pɒmp/ *noun.* ME.
[Old & mod. French *pompe* from Latin *pompa* solemn procession, pomp, from Greek *pompē*, from *pempein* send.]
1 Splendid display or celebration, magnificent show; an example of this. Freq. in ***pomp and circumstance***. ME.
2 Ostentatious display, boastful show; an example of this. *obsolete* exc. (in *pl.*) in or with allusion to the baptismal formula ***the pomps and vanities of this wicked world***. ME.
†3 A triumphal or ceremonial procession; a pageant. L15–E19.

> **1** L. STRACHEY Next year was the fiftieth of her reign, and . . the splendid anniversary was celebrated in solemn pomp. **2** G. STANHOPE Deceiving the World with a Pretence and Pomp of Godliness. G. A. POOLE His armorial bearings (the very essential hieroglyphic of the pomps of this world which we renounce at Baptism). **3** *fig.*: MILTON Forth she went; Not unattended, for on her . . A pomp of winning Graces waited still.

▪ **pompal** *adjective* (*rare*) of the nature of a solemn procession; splendid, showy: M17. **pompless** *adjective* without pomp L18.

pomp /pɒmp/ *verb*[1] *intrans.* & *trans.* (with *it*). Now chiefly *poet.* LME.
[from the noun.]
Exhibit pomp or splendour; conduct oneself or move pompously.

> T. HARDY She has cast me As she pomped along the street Court-clad . . A glance from her chariot-seat.

▪ **pomped** /pɒm(p)t/ *ppl adjective* honoured with pomp, celebrated E20.

pomp /pɒmp/ *verb*[2] *trans.* Now *dial.* LME.
[Var. of base of PAMPER *verb*.]
Feed luxuriously, pamper.

pompadour /ˈpɒmpədʊə/ *noun* & *adjective.* M18.
[Jeanne-Antoinette Poisson, Marquise de *Pompadour* (1721–64), mistress of Louis XV of France.]
▶ **A** *noun.* **1** Any of various items of costume (a pelisse, a kind of handbag, etc.) fashionable in the time of the Marquise de Pompadour or resembling these. M18.
2 A shade of crimson or pink; a fabric of this colour. M18.
3 A S. American cotinga, *Xipholena pompadora*, with brilliant crimson-purple plumage. Also ***pompadour cotinga***. M18.
4 a A style of dressing men's hair, in which it is combed back from the forehead without a parting. *US.* L19. ▸**b** A style of arranging women's hair, in which it is turned back off the forehead in a roll, sometimes over a pad. L19.
▶ **B** *attrib.* or as *adjective.* (Of dress, furniture, etc.) in the style prevalent in the time of the Marquise de Pompadour; *spec.* (**a**) of a crimson colour or fabric; (**b**) patterned with sprigs of (usu. pink and blue) flowers on a white ground; (**c**) (of hair) arranged in a pompadour. M18.

pompadour /ˈpɒmpədʊə/ *verb trans.* E20.
[from prec.]
Arrange (hair) in a pompadour. Chiefly as ***pompadoured*** *ppl adjective.*

pompano /ˈpɒmpənəʊ/ *noun.* Also (earlier) **pam-**. Pl. **-os**, (esp. *collect.*) same. L18.
[Spanish *pámpano* butterfish (perh. from *pámpana* vine leaf, with ref. to the shape).]
Any of various tropical carangid fishes having a deep, laterally compressed, angular body, many of which are caught for sport. Also, any of various similar fishes of other families, as (more fully ***Pacific pompano***) the stromateid *Peprilus simillimus*.
African pompano a silvery carangid fish, *Alectis crinitus*, of the tropical Atlantic and E. Pacific. **common pompano**, **Florida pompano** a carangid fish, *Trachinotus carolinus*, of the W. Atlantic. ***Pacific pompano***: see above.
Comb.: **pompano dolphin**, **pompano dolphinfish** a dolphinfish, *Coryphaena equisetis*, similar to and freq. confused with the dorado, *C. hippurus*.

Pompeian /pɒmˈpeɪən, -ˈpiːən/ *noun*[1] & *adjective*[1]. E17.
[Latin *Pompeianus*, from *Pompeius* (see below).]
▶ **A** *noun.* A follower of the Roman statesman Pompey (Gnaeus Pompeius Magnus, 106–48 BC) or of his son. E17.
▶ **B** *adjective.* Of or pertaining to Pompey or his party. E19.

Pompeian /pɒmˈpeɪən, -ˈpiːən/ *noun*[2] & *adjective*[2]. Also **Pompeiian**. E19.
[from *Pompeii* (see below) + -AN.]
▶ **A** *noun.* A native or inhabitant of Pompeii, an Italian town buried in AD 79 by an eruption of Mount Vesuvius and now excavated. E19.
▶ **B** *adjective.* Of or pertaining to Pompeii; characteristic or imitative of its architecture or painting, esp. its frescoes. M19.
Pompeian red a shade of red resembling that found on the walls of houses in Pompeii.

pompelmous /ˈpɒmp(ə)lmuːs/ *noun.* Also **pampelmouse** /ˈpamp-/, **pompelmouse**, (*S. Afr.*) **pampelmoes** /pamp(ə)lˈmuːs/. L17.
[Dutch *pompelmoes*, perh. repr. Dutch *pompoen* pumpkin + Old Javanese *limoes*, borrowed from Portuguese *limões* pl. of *limão* lemon: lit. 'pumpkin-citron'.]
The shaddock, *Citrus maxima*. Also (*S. Afr.*), any kind of grapefruit.

†pomperkin *noun.* Also **-ir-**. M17–M18.
[Origin unkn.]
A weakly alcoholic drink made from refuse pomace and water; ciderkin.

Pompe's disease /ˈpɒmpəz dɪˌziːz/ *noun phr.* M20.
[from J. C. *Pompe* (1901–45), Dutch physician.]
MEDICINE. A fatal disease arising in early infancy, caused by inherited maltase deficiency and characterized by generalized excess storage of glycogen in muscles, leading to paralysis and heart failure.

pompholyx /ˈpɒmfəlɪks/ *noun.* L17.
[Greek *pompholux*, *pompholug-* a bubble, the slag of ore.]
1 *CHEMISTRY.* Crude zinc oxide. Long *obsolete* exc. *Hist.* L17.
2 *MEDICINE.* A vesicle on the skin. Now usu. *spec.*, a form of eczema in which numerous small vesicles develop in the hard skin of the palms of the hands and soles of the feet. E19.
▪ **pomˈpholygous** *adjective* (*rare*) affected with pompholyx; *fig.* puffed up: M19.

pompier /pɔ̃pje (*pl. same*), ˈpɒmpɪə/ *noun.* M19.
[French, from *pompe* PUMP *noun*[1]: see -IER.]
1 In France, a fireman. M19.
2 An artist regarded as painting in an academic, imitative, vulgarly neoclassical style. E20.
Comb.: ***pompier ladder*** a fire-fighter's scaling ladder.

pompilid /ˈpɒmpɪlɪd/ *noun* & *adjective.* E20.
[mod. Latin *Pompilidae* (see below), from *Pompilus* genus name from Greek *pompilos* pilot-fish: see -ID[3].]
ENTOMOLOGY. ▶**A** *noun.* Any of various members of the family Pompilidae of solitary fossorial wasps, which typically prey on spiders. Also called ***spider-hunting wasp***, ***spider-wasp***. E20.
▶ **B** *adjective.* Of, pertaining to, or designating this family. E20.

pompion /ˈpʌmpɪən/ *noun.* Now *rare.* Also **†pompon**, **pumpion**. E16.
[French *†pompon* nasalized form of *†popon* from Latin *pepo(n-)* large melon from Greek *pepōn*, use as noun of *pepōn* ripe.]
1 A pumpkin; the plant bearing pumpkins, *Cucurbita pepo*. E16.
†2 (A contemptuous name for) a (big) man. L16–E17.

> **2** SHAKES. *Merry W.* We'll use this unwholesome humidity, this gross wat'ry pumpion.

†pompirkin *noun* var. of POMPERKIN.

pompoleon /pɒmˈpəʊlɪən/ *noun.* M19.
[French *pompoléon*: app. connected with POMPELMOUS.]
The shaddock.

pompom *noun* see POMPON *noun*[1].

pom-pom /ˈpɒmpɒm/ *noun* & *interjection.* L19.
[Imit., from the sound of the discharge.]
▶ **A** *noun.* **1** Any of various automatic quick-firing guns, orig. a Maxim, now esp. one of a group of anti-aircraft guns on a ship. L19.
2 The repetitive beat of a simple popular tune or poem. M20.
▶ **B** *interjection.* Repr. a repetitive sound, esp. the beat of a simple popular tune or poem. E20.

pompon /ˈpɒmpɒn, *foreign* pɔ̃pɔ̃ (*pl. same*)/ *noun*[1]. Also (in senses 2, 3) **pompom** /ˈpɒmpɒm/, (in sense 1) **†pompoon**. M18.
[French, of unkn. origin.]
1 A bunch of ribbon, feathers, flowers, silk threads, etc., formerly worn by women in the hair, or on the cap or dress. *obsolete* exc. *Hist.* M18.
2 A variety of chrysanthemum, dahlia, or cabbage rose, bearing small globular flowers. M19.
3 An ornamental ball of wool, silk, ribbons, etc., on a woman's hat, a slipper, etc.; the round tuft on a sailor's cap, on the front of a shako, etc. L19.

> **3** S. CRANE The blue sailor bonnets with their red pompoms. D. WELCH There were green baize curtains with little pompoms around the edge.

▪ **pomponed** /ˈpɒmpɒnd/ *adjective* decked with pompons M18.

†pompon *noun*[2] var. of POMPION.

†pompoon *noun* see POMPON *noun*[1].

pomposity /pɒmˈpɒsɪti/ *noun.* LME.
[Late Latin *pompositas*, from *pomposus*: see POMPOUS, -ITY.]
†1 Pomp, solemnity. *rare.* Only in LME.
2 Self-conscious display of dignity or importance in deportment or language; ostentatiousness; an instance of this. E17.

pomposo /pɒmˈpəʊzəʊ/ *adverb* & *noun.* E19.
[Italian from Latin *pomposus*: see next.]
▶ **A** *adverb. MUSIC.* A direction: in a stately manner. E19.
▶ **B** *noun.* Pl. **-os**.
1 An affected, self-important person. M20.
2 *MUSIC.* A stately movement or passage. M20.

pompous /ˈpɒmpəs/ *adjective.* LME.
[Old & mod. French *pompeux* from Latin *pomposus*, from *pompa* POMP *noun*: see -OUS.]
1 Characterized by pomp; magnificent, splendid. Now *rare.* LME.
2 Marked by an exaggerated display of self-importance or dignity; pretentious. Of language: inflated, turgid. LME.

📖 **1** R. WEST Milan was no longer the pompous seat of the Imperial Court. **2** P. H. GIBBS One day you'll be Prime Minister . . or something of the sort . . . You'll become pompous and solemn. V. WOOLF I cannot endure the Doctor's pompous mummery and faked emotions.

■ **pompously** *adverb* E16. **pompousness** *noun* LME.

'pon /pɒn/ *preposition. arch.* Also **pon**. M16.
[Aphet.]
= UPON *preposition*.

ponask /ˈpəʊnɑːsk/ *verb trans. Canad.* Also **poon-** /ˈpuːn-/. E20.
[from Cree *apwa:na:sk* roasting-spit.]
Cook (esp. game or fish) on a spit or stick over an open fire.

ponasterone /pəʊnəˈstɪərəʊn/ *noun.* M20.
[from mod. Latin *Podocarpus nakaii* (see below), formed as PODOCARP: see -STERONE.]
BIOCHEMISTRY. Any of a group of steroids extracted from various plants, esp. the Japanese podocarp *Podocarpus nakaii*, which act as phytoecdysones in various arthropods.

Ponca /ˈpɒŋkə/ *noun & adjective.* L18.
[Ponca *ppą́kka*.]
▶ **A** *noun.* Pl. same, **-s**.
1 A member of a Siouan people formerly inhabiting the NE plains of Nebraska. L18.
2 The Siouan language of this people. L19.
▶ **B** *attrib.* or as *adjective.* Of or pertaining to the Ponca or their language. L18.

ponce /pɒns/ *noun. slang.* L19.
[Perh. from POUNCE *verb*³.]
1 A person who lives off a prostitute's earnings; a pimp. L19.
2 A male homosexual; a lazy or effeminate man. M20.

ponce /pɒns/ *verb. slang.* M20.
[from the noun.]
1 *verb intrans.* Act as a ponce; live *on* a prostitute's earnings. M20.
2 *verb intrans.* Move or behave in an idle or effete manner. Usu. foll. by *about, around.* M20.
3 *verb trans.* Smarten *up* esp. in a flashy manner, tart up. M20.

📖 **2** N. COHN No poncing about, no dressing up or one-shot gimmicking. **3** J. WAINWRIGHT Why must they ponce everything up to suit their own ends?

ponceau /pɔ̃so, ˈpɒnsəʊ/ *noun.* M19.
[French.]
Poppy-colour, bright red. Also, a red coal tar dye.

poncey /ˈpɒnsi/ *adjective. slang.* Also **poncy**. M20.
[from PONCE *noun* + -Y¹.]
Of, pertaining to, or resembling a pimp or male homosexual; effete.

📖 S. FRY His hair was shorter, but not coiffured or poncey. S. MACKAY It was at some poncey gallery in Mayfair. Invitation only.

poncho /ˈpɒntʃəʊ/ *noun.* Pl. **-os**. E18.
[S. Amer. Spanish from Araucanian.]
A S. American cloak made of a piece of cloth like a blanket with a slit in the middle for the head; any garment in this style.
■ **ponchoed** *adjective* wearing a poncho E20.

poncif /pɔ̃sif/ *noun.* E20.
[French, lit. 'pounced design'.]
Stereotyped literary ideas, plot, character, etc.

poncy *adjective* var. of PONCEY.

pond /pɒnd/ *noun.* ME.
[Alt. of POUND *noun*². Cf. PIND *verb*.]
1 A fairly small body of still water, freq. with a specified purpose, formed artificially by hollowing or embanking; formerly *spec.* = ***fish-pond*** s.v. FISH *noun*¹. Also, a natural pool or small lake; *Canad.* a lake of any size. ME. ▶**b** ***the pond***, the sea, *esp.* the Atlantic Ocean. Cf. HERRING-***pond***. Chiefly *joc.* M17.
2 a In full ***cooling-pond***. A pool built for cooling water heated in an industrial process. L19. ▶**b** = LAGOON *noun* 4. M20.

📖 **1** DAY LEWIS At the bottom of the garden lay the lily ponds under their chestnut trees. ***dew-pond, duck-pond, fish-pond, millpond***, etc.

Comb.: **pond-barrow** *ARCHAEOLOGY* a prehistoric burial place marked by a depression in the ground instead of the more usual mound; **pond-culture** the keeping of fish in ponds; **pond dogwood** *N. Amer.* = ***button-bush*** s.v. BUTTON *noun*; **pond-fish** a freshwater fish often reared in ponds, as the carp; *US* any of various freshwater fishes of the sunfish family Centrarchidae; **pond-life** the animals, esp. the invertebrates, that live in ponds or stagnant water; **pond-lily** (chiefly *US*) a water lily, *esp.* the spatterdock *Nuphar advena*; **pond-pine** a pine tree, *Pinus serotina*, of swampy areas in the southern US; **pond scum** *N. Amer.* (**a**) a mass of algae forming a green film on the surface of stagnant water; (**b**) *colloq.* a person or thing perceived as worthless or contemptible; **pond-skater** any of various usu. predatory insects of the heteropteran family Gerridae which stand and run on water, supported by surface tension; **pond slider** a freshwater turtle, *Pseudemys scripta*, which is widespread in N. America; **pond snail** a freshwater snail inhabiting ponds, *esp.* one of the genus *Limnaea*.

pond /pɒnd/ *verb.* L16.
[from the noun.]
†**1** *verb trans.* Keep or place in a pond. *rare.* L16–M17.
2 *verb trans.* **a** Obstruct (a stream etc.), dam *up* or hold *back* (water), so as to form a pond. L17. ▶**b** Form (a pond) by obstructing a stream etc. M20. ▶**c** Block or cause excessive accumulation of liquid above (a sewage filter). Chiefly as ***ponded*** *ppl adjective*, ***ponding*** *verbal noun.* M20.
3 *verb intrans.* Of water etc.: form a pond; be dammed *up* or held *back.* L18.

pondage /ˈpɒndɪdʒ/ *noun.* L19.
[from POND *noun* + -AGE.]
The storage of water; the capacity of a pond.

ponder /ˈpɒndə/ *noun. rare.* L18.
[from the verb.]
An act or period of pondering.

📖 J. GASH I stood indecisively, then walked out . . for a deep ponder.

ponder /ˈpɒndə/ *verb.* ME.
[Old & mod. French *pondérer* consider, (mod.) balance, moderate from Latin *ponderare* weigh, reflect on, from *ponder-*, *pondus* weight, rel. to *pendere* weigh.]
†**1** *verb trans.* Estimate; judge the worth of, appraise. ME–M16.
†**2** *verb trans.* Ascertain the weight of; weigh. LME–M17. ▶**b** Of a thing: amount in weight to. LME–M16.
3 *verb trans.* Weigh (a matter, words, etc.) mentally, consider carefully; think over. LME.
4 *verb intrans.* Think deeply, reflect. (Foll. by *on, over.*) E17.

📖 **3** P. S. BUCK Wang Lu thought of his land and pondered . . how he could get back to it. A. DJOLETO He pondered the problem for some time. *Philadelphia Inquirer* Edward Shaw never pondered Scoleri's guilt or innocence. **4** A. CROSS Kate pondered . . on the mysteries of the human personality. *Independent* Those who receive our letters can ponder over them . . as often as they please.

■ **ponderer** *noun* M16. **ponderment** *noun* M18.

ponderable /ˈpɒnd(ə)rəb(ə)l/ *adjective.* M17.
[Late Latin *ponderabilis*, from *ponderare*: see PONDER *verb*, -ABLE.]
Able to be weighed; having appreciable weight or significance.
■ **ponderaˈbility** *noun* weight, heaviness; significance: M19.

ponderal /ˈpɒnd(ə)r(ə)l/ *adjective.* E17.
[from Latin *ponder-*, *pondus* weight + -AL¹, after Anglo-Latin *ponderalis* determined by weight.]
Of or pertaining to weight; determined by weight.

ponderance /ˈpɒnd(ə)r(ə)ns/ *noun.* E19.
[App. extracted from PREPONDERANCE.]
Weight; gravity, importance.
■ Also **ponderancy** *noun* L17.

ponderate /ˈpɒnd(ə)rət/ *adjective. rare.* E20.
[Latin *ponderatus* pa. pple, formed as next: see -ATE².]
Careful; deliberate.

ponderate /ˈpɒndəreɪt/ *verb.* Pa. pple **-ated**, †**-ate**. LME.
[Latin *ponderat-* pa. ppl stem of *ponderare* PONDER *verb*: see -ATE³.]
†**1** *verb trans.* Weigh in the mind, ponder. LME–M18.
2 *verb intrans.* Have weight; be heavy, weigh. Formerly also, gravitate. M17.
3 *verb trans.* Estimate the value of; appraise. *rare.* M17.

ponderation /pɒndəˈreɪʃ(ə)n/ *noun.* LME.
[Latin *ponderatio(n-)*, from *ponderare* weigh: see PONDER *verb*, -ATION.]
1 Weighing, balancing; adjustment of weight. Formerly also, heaviness, weight. LME.
2 Mental weighing; grave consideration, pondering. Now *rare.* LME.
3 The fact of weighing more; preponderance. *rare.* L19.

ponderomotive /pɒnd(ə)rə(ʊ)ˈməʊtɪv/ *adjective.* L19.
[from Latin *ponder-*, *pondus* weight, after *electromotive*.]
PHYSICS. That tends to move a weight; *spec.* designating a force exerted on a mass by an electric or magnetic field.

ponderosa /pɒndəˈrəʊzə, -sə/ *noun.* L19.
[Specific epithet of mod. Latin *pinus ponderosa*, fem. of Latin *ponderosus* PONDEROUS.]
In full ***ponderosa pine***. A large conifer of western N. America, *Pinus ponderosa*, which is a valuable timber tree; the wood of this tree. Also called ***yellow pine***, ***western yellow pine***.

ponderous /ˈpɒnd(ə)rəs/ *adjective.* LME.
[Latin *ponderosus*, from *ponder-*, *pondus* weight + *-osus*: see -OUS.]
1 Having great weight, heavy; massive; clumsy or unwieldy through weight or size. LME. ▶**b** Of great weight in proportion to bulk; of high relative density. Now *rare* or *obsolete.* M16.
†**2** *fig.* **a** Of grave concern; weighty, important. L15–L18. ▶**b** Laborious, performed with painstaking care; (of style etc.) lacking inspiration or lightness of touch, dull, tedious. E18.

📖 **1** R. L. STEVENSON My knapsack, . . with those six ponderous tomes of Bancroft, weighed me double. **2b** J. PAYN His rather ponderous manner. S. J. PERELMAN She ate with the slow, ponderous concentration of a heifer. A. CROSS I am a rather ponderous expounder of theology.

■ †**ponderose** *adjective* ponderous (*rare*) LME–M18. **pondeˈrosity** *noun* LME. **ponderously** *adverb* L15. **ponderousness** *noun* L15.

Pondo /ˈpɒndəʊ/ *noun & adjective.* Also †**Amapondo**. E19.
[Xhosa: in form *Amapondo* with pl. or collective prefix.]
▶ **A** *noun.* Pl. **-os**, same, **Amapondo** /aməˈpɒndəʊ/. A member of a Nguni people of the eastern part of the Cape Province; the Xhosa dialect of this people. E19.
▶ **B** *attrib.* or as *adjective.* Of or pertaining to the Pondos or the Xhosa dialect spoken by them. M19.

pondok /ˈpɒndɒk/ *noun. S. Afr.* Also **pondokkie** /pɒnˈdɒki/. E19.
[Afrikaans, prob. from Malay, ult. from Arab. *fundug* hotel.]
A shack or shanty made of oddments of wood, corrugated iron, etc.; *transf.* a house etc. in a poor state of repair.

†**pondus** *noun.* L17–E18.
[Latin = weight.]
A weight; *fig.* power to influence.

pondweed /ˈpɒndwiːd/ *noun.* L16.
[from POND *noun* + WEED *noun*¹.]
Any of various aquatic plants of the genus *Potamogeton* (family Potamogetonaceae). With specifying word: any of certain other aquatic plants of related families.
Canadian pondweed, ***Cape pondweed***, ***horned pondweed***, ***tassel pondweed***, etc.

pondy /ˈpɒndi/ *adjective. US.* L17.
[from POND *noun* + -Y¹.]
Having many ponds; swampy.

pone /ˈpəʊni/ *noun*¹. *obsolete* exc. *Hist.* ME.
[Anglo-Latin, Anglo-Norman, sing. imper. of Latin *ponere* to place.]
LAW. **1** A writ by which a suit was removed from an inferior court to the Court of Common Pleas. ME.
2 A writ requiring the sheriff to secure the appearance of the defendant by the attachment of goods or the requirement of sureties. *rare.* E17

pone /pəʊn/ *noun*². E17.
[Virginia Algonquian *pone*, *apone* bread.]
More fully ***corn pone***. Unleavened maize bread, esp. as made by N. American Indians in thin cakes cooked in hot ashes; a fine light bread made with milk, eggs, etc., in flat cakes. Also, a cake or loaf of such bread.

pone /ˈpəʊni/ *noun*³. E19.
[formed as PONE *noun*¹.]
In certain card-games with several players: the player first in turn to bid or play (usu. sitting next to the dealer in order of play). In a two-handed card-game: the non-dealing player.

ponent /ˈpəʊnənt/ *noun & adjective.* M16.
[from Italian *ponente* (= French †*ponent*, *-ant*) repr. Latin *ponent-*, *ponens* pres. pple of *ponere* to place: see -ENT.]
▶ **A** *noun.* The region of the setting sun; the west. Cf. LEVANT *noun*¹ 1. Now *rare* or *obsolete.* M16.
▶ **B** *adjective.* **1** Situated in the west; westerly. Opp. LEVANT *adjective*² 2. *arch.* M17.
2 *LOGIC.* That posits or affirms. Opp. TOLLENT. *rare.* L18.

ponente /poˈnɛnte/ *noun.* E20.
[Italian: see prec.]
A westerly wind in the Mediterranean.

ponerine /ˈpɒnərʌɪn, -iːn/ *adjective & noun.* E20.
[from mod. Latin *Ponera* genus name: see -INE¹.]
ENTOMOLOGY. ▶**A** *adjective.* Of, pertaining to, or designating the subfamily Ponerinae of mainly subtropical ants. E20.
▶ **B** *noun.* A ponerine ant. E20.

ponerology /pɒnərˈɒlədʒi/ *noun.* L19.
[from Greek *ponēros* evil + -OLOGY.]
THEOLOGY. The doctrine of evil.

pong /pɒŋ/ *noun*¹. E19.
[Imit. In sense 2 abbreviation of PING-PONG *noun*.]
1 A ringing blow; a bang. E19.
2 = PING-PONG *noun* 1. Also, an electronic game resembling this, played on a pinball machine or a television screen. M20.

pong /pɒŋ/ *noun*² & *verb*. *colloq.* E20.
[Origin unkn.]
▶ **A** *noun.* A strong smell, *esp.* an unpleasant one; a stink. E20.
▶ **B** *verb intrans.* Smell strongly and esp. unpleasantly, stink (*of*). E20.
📖 R. RENDELL The place . . just pongs of dirty clothes.

Pong /pɒŋ/ *noun*³. Chiefly *Austral. slang.* (*derog.* & *racially offensive*). E20.
[Origin unkn.]
A Chinese person.

ponga /ˈpʌŋə/ *noun*¹. Also **punga**. M19.
[Maori.]
A New Zealand evergreen tree-fern, *Cyathea dealbata.*

ponga *noun*² var. of PANGA *noun*¹.

pongal /ˈpɒŋg(ə)l/ *noun.* L18.
[Tamil *poṅkal* lit. 'swelling, boiling'.]
The Tamil New Year festival, celebrated by the cooking of new rice.

pongee /pʌnˈdʒiː/ *noun* & *adjective.* E18.
[Chinese *běnjī* (Wade–Giles *pen-chi*) lit. 'own loom', or *běnzhì* (Wade–Giles *pen-chih*) lit. 'home-woven'.]
▶ **A** *noun.* A soft usu. unbleached type of Chinese silk fabric woven from uneven threads of raw silk; any cotton etc. fabric resembling this. E18.
▶ **B** *adjective.* Made of pongee. L19.

pongelo /ˈpɒŋgələʊ/ *noun. arch. slang.* M19.
[Origin unkn.]
Beer.

pongid /ˈpɒŋgɪd/ *noun* & *adjective.* M20.
[mod. Latin *Pongidae* (see below), from *Pongo* genus name: see next, -ID³.]
ZOOLOGY. ▶ **A** *noun.* Any anthropoid ape of the family Pongidae, which includes the gorilla, the chimpanzee, and the orang-utan. M20.
▶ **B** *adjective.* Of, pertaining to, or designating this family. M20.

pongo /ˈpɒŋgəʊ/ *noun.* Pl. **-os**. E17.
[Congolese *mpongo, mpongi, impungu*.]
▶ **I 1** Orig., a large anthropoid African ape, variously identified with the chimpanzee or gorilla; later (mistakenly), the orang-utan. Now chiefly as mod. Latin genus name of the orang-utan. Cf. prec. E17.
▶ **II** Applied to a person. Usu. *derog.*
2 a A marine; a soldier. *Nautical slang.* E20. ▸**b** An Englishman. *NZ* & (now *rare*) *Austral. slang.* M20. ▸**c** An army officer. *Military slang.* M20. ▸**d** A black person. *slang* (*racially offensive*). M20.

Pongola /pɒŋˈgəʊlə/ *noun.* M20.
[A S. African river.]
In full ***Pongola grass***. A drought-resistant creeping southern African grass, *Digitaria decumbens*, grown for fodder in the southern US.

pongy /ˈpɒŋi/ *adjective. colloq.* M20.
[from PONG *noun*² + -Y¹.]
Having a strong and usu. unpleasant smell.

pongyi /ˈpəʊndʒiː, -dʒi/ *noun.* Also **poonghie** & other vars. L18.
[Burmese *hpòngyi*, from *hpòn* glory, *kyì* great.]
A Buddhist monk in Myanmar (Burma).

ponhaus /ˈpɒnhɔːs/ *noun. US dial.* M19.
[Amer. German *Panhas*, from German *Pfanne* frying-pan + *Hase* rabbit.]
A dish made from pork scraps etc.; = SCRAPPLE *noun*².

poniard /ˈpɒnjəd/ *noun* & *verb.* M16.
[French *poignard* alt. of Old French *poignal* from medieval Latin *pugnale*, from Latin *pugnus* fist: see -ARD. Cf. POIGNADO.]
Chiefly *Hist.* ▶**A** *noun.* A small slim dagger. M16.
▶ **B** *verb trans.* Stab (esp. to death) with a poniard. L16.

ponor /ˈpəʊnə/ *noun.* E20.
[Serbo-Croat *pònor, pónor.*]
PHYSICAL GEOGRAPHY. In a karstic region, a steep natural shaft which emerges at the surface, freq. as a swallow-hole.

pons /pɒnz/ *noun.* Pl. **pontes** /ˈpɒntiːz/. L17.
[Latin = bridge.]
1 ANATOMY. A portion of tissue joining two parts of an organ; *spec.* a band of nerve fibres in the front part of the brainstem, connecting the medulla oblongata and the thalamus, and also the two hemispheres of the cerebellum. Also more fully ***pons cerebri*** /ˈsɛrɪbrʌɪ/ [= of the cerebrum], ***pons Varolii*** /vəˈrəʊlɪʌɪ/ [= of Varolius (C. Varoli (1543–75), Italian anatomist)]. L17.
2 ***pons asinorum*** /asɪˈnɔːrəm/ [= bridge of asses], the fifth proposition of the first book of Euclid, so called from the difficulty which beginners find in 'getting over' it. M18.

Ponsonby rule /ˈpʌns(ə)nbi ruːl, ˈpɒn-/ *noun phr.* M20.
[Arthur A. W. H. *Ponsonby* (1871–1946), English politician.]
A rule by which the Government may authorize an agreement without parliamentary approval.

pont /pɒnt/ *noun.* M17.
[Dutch from Middle Dutch *ponte* ferryboat (corresp. to Middle Low German *punte*): see PUNT *noun*¹.]
1 Orig., a large flat-bottomed boat or float, a pontoon. Now only *spec.*, in S. Africa, a large flat-bottomed ferryboat. M17.
†**2** = CAISSON 1. E18–M19.

pontac /ˈpɒntak/ *noun.* L17.
[French (see below).]
A sweet wine from Pontac, Basses Pyrénées, southern France. Also (*Hist.*), a South African fortified wine made with grapes from Pontac.

pontage /ˈpɒntɪdʒ/ *noun.* Now chiefly *Hist.* LME.
[Anglo-Norman, Old French from medieval Latin *pontaticum*, from Latin *pont-*, *pons* bridge: see -AGE.]
A toll for the use of a bridge; a tax paid for the maintenance and repair of a bridge or bridges.

Pontefract cake *noun* var. of POMFRET-CAKE.

pontes *noun* pl. of PONS.

Pontiac fever /ˈpɒntɪak ˌfiːvə/ *noun phr.* L20.
[*Pontiac*, Michigan, US, where the first major outbreak occurred.]
A disease with symptoms resembling influenza, caused by infection with legionellae.

pontianak /pɒntɪˈɑːnak/ *noun*¹. M19.
[Malay *puntianak* var. of *patianak* lit. 'child-killer'.]
In Malayan folklore: a vampire, *esp.* one that is the ghost of a still-born child.

pontianak /pɒntɪˈɑːnak/ *noun*². E20.
[*Pontianak*, a city and former sultanate of Borneo.]
A form of jelutong (latex), orig. from Borneo.

Pontic /ˈpɒntɪk/ *adjective*¹ & *noun*¹. LME.
[Latin *Ponticus* from Greek *Pontikos*, from *Pontos* Pontus (see below), the Black Sea, *pontos* sea: see -IC.]
▶ **A** *adjective.* †**1** Tart, astringent, sour, [perh. from a traditional association of wormwood and other bitter-tasting plants with the region of Pontus]. LME–L17.
2 Of or pertaining to Pontus, an ancient region and kingdom of NE Asia Minor on the Black Sea; designating or pertaining to the Greek dialect of the region. M16.
▶ **B** *noun.* The Greek dialect of Pontus. M20.

pontic /ˈpɒntɪk/ *adjective*² & *noun*². L19.
[from Latin *pont-*, *pons* bridge + -IC.]
▶ **A** *adjective.* ANATOMY & MEDICINE. = PONTINE *adjective*¹. *rare.* L19.
▶ **B** *noun.* DENTISTRY. An artificial tooth forming part of a dental bridge, fixed to the neighbouring teeth, not directly to the jaw. E20.

ponticello /pɒntɪˈtʃɛləʊ/ *noun, adverb,* & *adjective.* M18.
[Italian = little bridge.]
MUSIC. ▶**A** *noun.* Pl. **-os**. The bridge of a stringed instrument. M18.
sul ponticello /sʊl/ [SUL] with the bowing close to the bridge.
▶ **B** *adverb* & *adjective.* A direction: with the bowing close to the bridge. M19.

ponticum /ˈpɒntɪkəm/ *noun.* L19.
[mod. Latin use as specific epithet (see below) of neut. of Latin *Ponticus* PONTIC *adjective*¹.]
A purple-flowered evergreen rhododendron, *Rhododendron ponticum*, of Spain, Portugal, and Asia Minor, much grown and widely naturalized in Britain.

pontifex /ˈpɒntɪfɛks/ *noun.* Also **P-**. Pl. **-tifices** /-ˈtɪfɪsiːz/. L16.
[Latin, from *pontis*, *pons* bridge + *-fex* from *facere* make.]
1 ROMAN HISTORY. A member of the principal college of priests in ancient Rome. L16.
2 = PONTIFF 3. M17.
1 Pontifex Maximus /ˈmaksɪməs/ [superl. of *magnus* great] the head of the principal college of priests in ancient Rome.

pontiff /ˈpɒntɪf/ *noun.* Also **P-**. L16.
[French *pontife* from Latin PONTIFEX.]
1 *gen.* A chief priest. L16.
2 = PONTIFEX 1. E17.
3 Orig. (*Hist.*), a bishop of the early Christian Church. Now *spec.* (more fully ***sovereign pontiff***, ***supreme pontiff***) the Pope. L17.

pontifical /pɒnˈtɪfɪk(ə)l/ *adjective* & *noun.* LME.
[French, or Latin *pontificalis*, from PONTIFEX: see -ICAL.]
▶ **A** *adjective.* **I 1** Pertaining to or befitting a bishop; *spec.* papal. LME.
2 *gen.* Of or pertaining to a chief priest; befitting a high priest. LME.
3 ROMAN HISTORY. Of or belonging to a pontifex. L16.
1 pontifical mass ROMAN CATHOLIC CHURCH a high mass, usu. celebrated by a bishop, cardinal, etc. ***Pontifical Zouave***: see ZOUAVE 1b.
▶ **II 4** Having the pomp or dignity characteristic of a pontiff. Also, pompously dogmatic. LME.
5 Of or pertaining to bridge-building. *rare.* M17.
📖 **4** I. WALLACE The pontifical voice of a network editorial philosopher engulfed him. **5** MILTON Now had they brought the work by wondrous Art Pontifical.

▶ **B** *noun.* **1** In *pl.* & †*sing.* The vestments and insignia of a bishop, cardinal, or abbot. LME.
†**2** The office or the duty of a pontiff or pontifex (usu. in *pl.*); a pontifical ceremony. LME–L17.
3 An office-book of the Western Church, containing the forms for rites to be performed by the Pope or a bishop. L16.
■ **pontific** *adjective* (now *rare*) = PONTIFICAL *adjective* M17. **pontifically** *adverb* LME.

pontificalia /ˌpɒntɪfɪˈkeɪlɪə, -ˈkɑːl-/ *noun pl.* L16.
[Latin, use as noun of neut. pl. of *pontificalis* PONTIFICAL: see -IA².]
The vestments and insignia of a bishop, cardinal, or abbot; pontificals.

pontificalibus /ˌpɒntɪfɪˈkeɪlɪbəs, -ˈkɑːl-/ *noun pl. rare.* M16.
[Latin, abl. of PONTIFICALIA, taken from earlier IN PONTIFICALIBUS.]
= prec. Only with *possess.*, as in ***his pontificalibus***.

pontificality /ˌpɒntɪfɪˈkalɪti/ *noun.* Now *rare* or *obsolete.* LME.
[French †*pontificalité*, formed as PONTIFICAL *adjective* + -ITY.]
= PONTIFICATE *noun.*

pontificate /pɒnˈtɪfɪkət/ *noun.* LME.
[Latin *pontificatus*, from PONTIFEX: see -ATE¹.]
The office, state, or dignity of a pontiff or pontifex; the period during which a person holds this office.
📖 A. N. WILSON In the closing years of the pontificate of Leo XIII.
■ Also †**pontificacy** *noun* E16–L18.

pontificate /pɒnˈtɪfɪkeɪt/ *verb.* E19.
[medieval Latin *pontificat-* pa. ppl stem of *pontificare*, from Latin PONTIFEX: see -ATE³.]
1 ROMAN CATHOLIC CHURCH. **a** *verb intrans.* Officiate as a bishop, esp. at mass. E19. ▸**b** *verb trans.* Celebrate (mass) as a bishop. L19.
2 *verb intrans.* Act like a pontiff, claim to be infallible. Also, be pompously dogmatic. E19. ▸**b** *verb trans.* Utter in a pontifical manner. E20.
📖 **2** M. DIBDIN A didactic voice began pontificating about the ecology of the Po delta.
■ **pontificator** *noun* M20.

pontification /ˌpɒntɪfɪˈkeɪʃ(ə)n/ *noun.* E16.
[formed as prec.: see -ATION.]
†**1** A pontiff's period of office. E16–E17.
2 (An instance of) pontificating or dogmatic utterance. E20.

†**pontifice** *noun. rare* (Milton). Only in M17.
[from Latin *pont-*, *pons* bridge, after *edifice*.]
The edifice of a bridge; a bridge. Cf. PONTIFICAL *adjective* 5.

pontifices *noun* pl. of PONTIFEX.

pontificial /pɒntɪˈfɪʃ(ə)l/ *adjective* & *noun.* L16.
[from Latin *pontificius*, from *pontific-*, PONTIFEX + -AL¹.]
▶†**A** *adjective.* **1** = PONTIFICAL *adjective* 1. L16–M18. ▸**b** Popish, papistical. Only in 17.
2 = PONTIFICAL *adjective* 4. E17.
▶ **B** *noun. rare.*
†**1** An adherent or supporter of a pontiff, *spec.* the Pope; a papist. M17–M19.
2 = PONTIFICAL *noun* 3. M17.

†**pontifician** *adjective* & *noun.* E17.
[formed as prec. + -AN.]
▶ **A** *adjective.* = PONTIFICIAL *adjective* 1. E17–E19.
▶ **B** *noun.* = PONTIFICIAL *noun* 1. Only in L17.

pontil /ˈpɒntɪl/ *noun.* M19.
[French, app. from Italian *pontello*, *puntello* dim. of *punto* point: see -IL. Cf. PUNTY.]
GLASS-MAKING. An iron rod used to hold or shape soft glass (also ***pontil rod***). Also called ***punty***.

pontile /ˈpɒntʌɪl/ *adjective. rare.* L19.
[formed as next + -ILE.]
ANATOMY & MEDICINE. = PONTINE *adjective*¹.

pontine /ˈpɒntʌɪn/ *adjective*¹. L19.
[from Latin *pont-*, *pons* bridge + -INE¹.]
ANATOMY & MEDICINE. Of, pertaining to, or affecting the pons of the brain.

Pontine /ˈpɒntʌɪn, -tiːn/ *adjective*². E20.
[from *Pontus* (see PONTIC *adjective*¹ & *noun*¹) + -INE¹.]
Of or pertaining to Pontus in Asia Minor, Pontic.

Pont l'Évêque /pɔ̃ levɛk/ *noun.* L19.
[A town in Normandy, France.]
More fully ***Pont l'Évêque cheese***. A sweet soft cheese made at Pont l'Évêque.

pont-levis /pɔ̃ləvi (*pl. same*), pɒntˈlɛvɪs/ *noun.* L15.
[French, from *pont* bridge + Old French *leveïs* able to be moved up and down.]
A drawbridge.

pontoneer /pɒntəˈnɪə/ *noun*. Also **-ier**. M19.
[Old & mod. French *pontonnier* from medieval Latin *pontonarius* ferryman, from Latin *ponto(n-)* PONTOON *noun*[1]: see -EER.]
Chiefly MILITARY. A person concerned with pontoons or the construction of a pontoon-bridge.

pontoon /pɒnˈtuːn/ *noun*[1] *& verb*. L17.
[Old & mod. French *ponton* from Latin *ponto(n-)* flat-bottomed ferryboat, from *pont-*, *pons* bridge: see -OON. Cf. PONT *noun*, PUNT *noun*[1].]
► **A** *noun*. **1** A flat-bottomed boat used as a lighter, ferryboat, etc. L17.
2 Chiefly MILITARY. A flat-bottomed boat, hollow metal cylinder, etc., used with others to support a temporary bridge over a river or to provide buoyancy in the water for a temporary structure. L17. ▸**b** Now more fully ***pontoon-bridge***. A temporary bridge over a river supported by a number of flat-bottomed boats, hollow metal cylinders, etc. E18.
3 NAUTICAL. A large flat-bottomed barge or lighter furnished with cranes, capstans, and tackle, used for careening ships, raising weights, etc. M18.
4 = CAISSON 1, 1b. L19.
► **B** *verb trans.* Cross (a river) by means of pontoons. M19.
■ **pontooner** *noun* = PONTONEER L18.

pontoon /pɒnˈtuːn/ *noun*[2]. E20.
[Prob. alt. of *vingt-un* obsolete var. of VINGT-ET-UN.]
1 A card-game in which players try to acquire cards with a face value totalling and not exceeding twenty-one (also called ***vingt-et-un***). Also = NATURAL *noun* 6b. E20.
2 A prison sentence or term of twenty-one months or years. *slang*. M20.

ponty *noun* var. of PUNTY.

Pontypool /pɒntɪˈpuːl/ *adjective & noun*. M18.
[A town in Gwent, Wales.]
► **A** *adjective*. Designating a type of japanned metal ware originally produced at Pontypool or items made from it. M18.
► **B** *noun*. Pontypool ware. M20.

pony /ˈpəʊni/ *noun*. M17.
[Prob. from French *poulenet* dim. of Old & mod. French *poulain* foal from late Latin *pullanus* from Latin *pullus* young animal, foal: see -Y[6]. Cf. PULLEN.]
► **I 1** A horse of any small breed or type; *spec.* one not over a certain height (now usu. 15 hands). M17. ▸**b** More fully ***polo-pony***. A horse used for polo. L19. ▸**c** A racehorse. Usu. in *pl. slang* (chiefly *N. Amer.*). E20.
1 ***Connemara pony***, ***Russian pony***, ***Shetland pony***, ***Timor pony***, etc. ***Shanks's pony***, ***Shanks' pony***: see SHANK *noun*.
► **II 2** Twenty-five pounds sterling. *slang*. L18.
3 A literal translation of a text used by students, a crib. *N. Amer. slang*. E19.
4 A small drinking-glass or measure; this with its contents; the drink contained in this. *slang*. M19.
5 A small chorus girl or dancer. *slang*. E20.
Comb.: **pony-engine** a small locomotive for shunting; **pony express** *Hist.* a rapid mail service using relays of ponies, esp. in the western US in the 1860s; **pony report** *N. Amer.* a condensed report supplied to news agencies; **pony service** *N. Amer.*: supplying pony reports; **pony-tail** a hairstyle (esp. of girls or women) in which the hair is drawn back, tied, and made to hang down like a pony's tail; **pony-trekker** a person who goes pony-trekking; **pony-trekking** pony-riding for long distances across country, esp. as a group holiday activity.

pony /ˈpəʊni/ *verb trans. & intrans. US slang*. E19.
[from the noun.]
1 Pay (a sum of money) *up* in settlement of an account. E19.
2 Prepare (a lesson) by means of a pony or crib. M19.

Ponzi scheme /ˈpɒnzi skiːm/ *noun phr. US*. E20.
[Charles *Ponzi* (d. 1949), who perpetrated such a fraud 1919–20.]
A form of fraud in which belief in the success of a non-existent enterprise is fostered by payment of quick returns to the first investors from money invested by others.

Ponzo illusion /ˈpɒnzəʊ ɪˌluːʒ(ə)n, ɪˌljuː-/ *noun phr.* M20.
[Mario *Ponzo* (1882–1960), Italian psychologist.]
An optical illusion in which two parallel straight lines of equal length appear unequal when seen side by side against a background of converging lines.

POO *abbreviation*.
Hist. Post Office Order.

poo *interjection, noun, & verb* var. of POOH.

pooay *noun* var. of PWE.

pooch /puːtʃ/ *noun & adjective. colloq.* E20.
[Origin unkn.]
► **A** *noun*. A dog, *esp.* a mongrel. E20.
► **B** *adjective*. Mongrel. *rare*. E20.

pooch *verb* see POUCH *verb*.

pood /puːd/ *noun*. M16.
[Russian *pud* from Low German or Old Norse *pund* POUND *noun*[1].]
A Russian weight, equal to slightly more than 16 kg (35 lb).

poodle /ˈpuːd(ə)l/ *noun*. E19.
[German *Pudel* short for *Pudelhund*, from Low German *pud(d)eln* splash in water (the poodle being a water-dog).]
1 a (An animal of) a breed of pet dog, of which there are numerous (esp. miniature) varieties, with tightly curling hair, usu. black or white and often ornamentally clipped. E19. ▸**b** *fig.* A lackey, a servile follower. E20.
2 Orig., (a garment made of) a woolly napped fabric. Now (usu. more fully ***poodle cloth***), a woven or knitted fabric with a curly pile resembling the coat of a poodle dog. E19.
Comb.: ***poodle cloth***: see sense 2 above; **poodle-cut** a hairstyle in which the hair is cut short and curled all over; **poodle-dog** = sense 1a above; **poodle-faker** *slang* (*a*) a man who cultivates female society, esp. for professional advancement; a ladies' man; (*b*) a young newly commissioned officer; **poodle-faking** *slang* the conduct of a poodle-faker.
■ **poodledom** *noun* (*rare, joc.*) the world of poodles; the condition of being a poodle: L19.

poodle /ˈpuːd(ə)l/ *verb*. E19.
[from the noun.]
1 *verb trans.* Treat as a poodle; clip and shave the hair of. Also, overdress, dress *up*. E19.
2 *verb intrans.* Move or travel in a leisurely manner. *colloq.* M20.
> 🕮 **2** *Police Review* What will happen to the chap who wants to quietly poodle along the road at 50 m.p.h.?

■ **poodler** *noun* (*colloq.*) a small motor vehicle M20.

pooey /ˈpuːi/ *interjection & adjective. nursery & slang*. M20.
[from POOH + -Y[1].]
► **A** *interjection*. Expr. distaste, revulsion, derision, or contempt. M20.
> 🕮 *New York Times* A hungry crocodile . . takes one taste of her and cries, 'Yecht, pooey'.

► **B** *adjective*. Of, contaminated by, or resembling excrement; nasty, unpleasant, distasteful. M20.

poof /pʊf, puːf/ *noun*[1]. *slang. derog.* Also **poove** /puːv/, **pouf**. M19.
[Perh. alt. of PUFF *noun*.]
An affected or effeminate man; a male homosexual.
> 🕮 R. RENDELL Get your picture in the papers like some poove of a film actor.

■ **poofy** *adjective* (*slang*) of or pertaining to a poof; effeminate, homosexual: M20.

poof /pʊf/ *verb intrans. colloq.* E20.
[from next.]
Blow up; peter *out*.

poof /pʊf/ *interjection & noun*[2]. Also **pouf**. E19.
[Imit. Cf. PUFF *verb*.]
► **A** *interjection*. Expr. contemptuous rejection. E19.
> 🕮 M. DE LA ROCHE Pouf! You don't know anything.

► **B** *noun*. An utterance of 'poof'; a short sharp puff of air, breath, etc. E20.

poofter /ˈpʊftə, ˈpuː-/ *noun. slang. derog.* E20.
[Fanciful extension of POOF *noun*[1].]
A homosexual; an effeminate man.

pooh /puː/ *noun, interjection, & verb*. Also **poo**. L16.
[Natural exclam. Cf. PUFF *verb*.]
► **A** *noun*. **1** An utterance of 'pooh' (see sense B. below). L16.
2 Excrement, faeces. *nursery & slang*. M20.
► **B** *interjection*. Expr. impatience, contempt, or disgust. E17.
> 🕮 OUIDA 'Pooh,' he said, as he read it, and tore it up.

► **C** *verb*. **1** *verb intrans.* Utter 'pooh'. M17.
2 *verb trans.* Say 'pooh' to; express contempt for. M19.
3 *verb intrans.* Defecate. *nursery & slang*. L20.

Pooh-Bah /puːˈbɑː/ *noun*. Also **pooh-bah**. L19.
[A character in *The Mikado* (1885), a light opera by W. S. Gilbert & A. Sullivan (from POOH *interjection*, BAH *interjection*).]
A person who holds many offices at the same time. Also, a person or body with much influence or many functions; a pompous self-important person.

pooh-pooh /ˈpuːpuː, puːˈpuː/ *noun, interjection, & verb*. Also **pooh pooh**, (in sense A.2 usu.) **poo-poo**. L18.
[Redupl. of POOH.]
► **A** *noun*. **1** An utterance of 'pooh-pooh' (see sense B. below). L18. ▸**b** A person who frequently utters 'pooh-pooh'. *rare*. M19.
2 Faeces, excrement. *nursery & slang*. M20.
2 do poo-poo(s), **go poo-poo(s)**, **make poo-poo(s)** defecate.
Comb.: **pooh-pooh theory** the theory that language is a development of natural interjections.
► **B** *interjection*. = POOH *interjection*. E19.
► **C** *verb trans.* Express contempt for; ridicule; dismiss as unworthy of notice. E19.
> 🕮 Q. BELL He expressed his fears. Sir George pooh-poohed them.

■ **pooh-pooher** *noun* a person who pooh-poohs something M19.

Pooh-sticks /ˈpuːstɪks/ *noun*. Also **pooh-sticks**. E20.
[from Winnie-the-*Pooh*, a toy bear in the children's books of A. A. Milne.]
A game in which sticks are thrown over one side of a bridge into a stream, the winner being the person whose stick emerges first on the other side.

pooja *noun* var. of PUJA.

pook *noun* var. of PUCK *noun*[1].

pook /puːk/ *verb trans. Scot.* M17.
[Origin unkn.]
Pluck, pick, or pinch with the thumb and finger, as in plucking a fowl, picking the stalks off fruit, etc.

pooka /ˈpuːkə/ *noun. Anglo-Irish*. E19.
[Irish *púca* = Old English *pūca* PUCK *noun*[1].]
A hobgoblin, a malignant sprite.

pool /puːl/ *noun*[1].
[Old English *pōl* = Old Frisian, Middle & mod. Low German, Middle Dutch *pōl* (Dutch *poel*), Old High German *pfuol* (German *Pfuhl*), from West Germanic.]
1 A small body of standing or still water, *esp.* one of natural formation. OE. ▸**b** A small shallow accumulation of any liquid; a puddle. M19.
2 A deep still place in a river or stream. OE.
3 *transf. & fig.* A thing resembling a pool (senses 1, 2) in shape, stillness, depth, etc. L16.
4 A tank or other artificially constructed receptacle (to be) filled with water for swimming, diving, etc. Freq. with specifying word. E17.
5 An oil-producing area (*rare*). Also (more fully ***oil pool***), an extent of rock which contains an unbroken reservoir of oil. L19.
> 🕮 **1a** J. M. BARRIE I was searching the pools for little fishes. ***rock pool***, ***tide pool***, etc. **b** A. PATON The rain came down through the roof. The pools formed on the floor. **2** *Scotsman* Rescuers . . searched the deep pools of a salmon river. **3** F. HERBERT Hawat's eyes were two pools of alertness in a dark and deeply seamed face. G. HARRIS In the pool of light below the hatchway stood a young man robed in crimson. R. THOMAS She lay in a pool of deepening isolation. **4** ***paddling pool***, ***swimming pool***, etc.

Phrases: ***solar pool***: see SOLAR *adjective*[1]. **the Pool** *spec.* the city of Liverpool.
Comb.: **pool cathode** ELECTRICITY a cathode consisting of a pool of mercury; **pool house** (chiefly *US*) (*a*) a house by a swimming pool, for the use of bathers; (*b*) a building containing a swimming pool; **pool-measure**, **pool-price** the measure or price of coal at the Pool of London on the River Thames; **pool room** *noun*[1] a room with a swimming-pool in it; **poolside** *noun & attrib. adjective* (located at) the side of a swimming-pool.
■ **pooly** *adjective* (*rare*) resembling a pool; having many pools, swampy: E19.

pool /puːl/ *noun*[2]. L17.
[French *poule* stake, (orig.) hen (see PULLET): cf. Spanish *polla* hen, stake at ombre. Assoc. with POOL *noun*[1] was prob. furthered by the identification of *fish* (in the pool) with French *fiche* counter (see FISH *noun*[2]).]
†**1** A game of cards in which there is a pool (sense 2a). L17–M19.
2 a The stakes laid by the players in a card-game and winnable together; the collective amount of these. E18. ▸**b** A container for these. L18.
3 A game played on a billiard-table in which the object is to pocket all the balls with a cue-ball, *esp.* (*a*) a game in which each player has a ball of a different colour for use as a cue-ball to pocket the other balls in fixed order, the winner taking all the stakes; (*b*) *N. Amer.* a game played with balls numbered one to fifteen, the number of each ball pocketed being added to a player's score; (*c*) *N. Amer.* = ***eight ball*** s.v. EIGHT *noun*. M19.
4 A rifle-shooting contest in which each competitor pays a certain sum for every shot he or she fires and the proceeds go to the winners. M19.
5 a The collective stakes laid on the competitors in a contest, the proceeds being divided among the backers of the winner. M19. ▸**b** *spec.* An organized system of gambling on the results of football matches, esp. on a weekly basis, in which (usu. regular) amounts of money are laid, and winnings of various amounts are paid out. Usu. in *pl.* (freq. as ***the pools***). Also ***football pool(s)***. E20.
6 a A common fund into which all contributors pay and from which financial backing is provided; a source of common funding, esp. for speculative operations on financial markets. Also, the contributors involved in this; a combine. L19. ▸**b** A common supply of people, commodities, resources, etc., which may be shared or drawn on; a group of people who share duties. E20.
7 COMMERCE. An arrangement between competing parties to fix rates and share business, in order to eliminate competition and promote high output and prices. Orig. *US*. L19.
8 SPORT. A contest in which each member of a group or team competes either against every other member, or against each member of another group or team. E20.

📖 **2a** W. BLACK They continued the game . . with the addition of a half-a-crown pool to increase the attraction. **3** *Which?* People in Scotland played the most bar billiards, pool or snooker. ***Kelly pool, snooker's pool***, etc. ***pool-ball, pool cue, pool-hall, pool player, pool-table***, etc. **dirty pool** *N. Amer. colloq.* unfair tactics, dishonesty. **5a** M. TWAIN No pools permitted on the run of the comet—no gambling of any kind. **b** P. FITZGERALD They may have won the pools. ***pools coupon, pools winner***, etc. **6a** *New York Times* Often in pools or syndicates, participants would subscribe large sums. **b** G. F. NEWMAN The official pool out of which informants were paid. *Sunday Telegraph* From its pool of some 45 players, each side selects two separate squads. *Railnews* Locomotive 37672 is one of a small pool of locomotives used to haul china clay. ***car pool, gene pool, typing pool***, etc. **7** *Times* The public was shocked by the revelations of stocks manipulations, pools . . and . . other abuses. **8** *Sunday Telegraph* The team flies to Groningen tomorrow, drawn in a tough pool with Poland, Spain, and Hungary. *Black Belt International* He had fought his way through the pools with his customary efficiency.

Comb.: **pool car** (*a*) a freight vehicle shared by several hirers; (*b*) a car available to several drivers; **pool room** *noun*² (*a*) a room with a pool-table or -tables, *esp.* one where a charge is made for playing; (*b*) a betting shop; **pool shark** *N. Amer. colloq.* an expert at pool; a person who makes money by winning at pool; **pools panel**: which decides the results of football matches for the pools when more than a certain number of matches have been cancelled.

pool /pu:l/ *verb*¹. LME.
[from POOL *noun*¹.]
1 *verb intrans.* (Of land) be or become marshy or full of pools; (of liquid) form a pool or pools, stand. LME.
2 *verb trans.* Make (a hole), esp. for the insertion of a wedge in quarrying. Also (MINING), undercut (coal) so that it falls. E18.
3 *verb intrans.* Of blood: accumulate in parts of the venous system. M20.

📖 **1** F. FITZGERALD All . . lay dead . . their blood pooling in the white gravel rocks. L. NIVEN They worked naked, with sweat pooling on their faces and in their armpits.

pool /pu:l/ *verb*² *trans.* L19.
[from POOL *noun*².]
1 Put (resources etc.) into a common stock or fund; share in common, combine for the common benefit. L19. ▸**b** *spec.* Of transport, an organization, etc.: share or divide (traffic or receipts). L19.
2 Implicate; involve (a person) against his or her will; inform on. *Austral. slang.* E20.

📖 **1** C. FREEMAN They had all agreed to pool their resources and live together. A. BRIEN We pooled our information, only to find it did not always agree. *Observer* When you invest in a unit trust, your money is pooled with that of other investors.

Poole /pu:l/ *adjective.* L19.
[A town in Dorset, a county of SW England.]
Designating a type of clay suitable for pottery found near Poole, or a type of pottery made in Poole.

poon /pu:n/ *noun*¹. L17.
[Malayalam *punna*, Kannada *ponne*, Tamil *puṉṉai*. Cf. PINNAY.]
Any of several large Indo-Malayan trees of the genus *Calophyllum* (family Guttiferae), *esp.* (more fully ***poon tree***) the Alexandrian laurel, *C. inophyllum*. Also, the timber of such a tree, used for masts and spars, and for building purposes.
Comb.: **poon oil** a thick bitter strong-smelling oil, obtained from the seeds of *Calophyllum inophyllum* and used in medicine and for burning in lamps.

poon /pu:n/ *noun*². *slang* (chiefly *Austral.*). M20.
[Origin unkn.]
A simple or foolish person. Also, a person living alone in the outback.

poon /pu:n/ *noun*³. *slang.* M20.
[Abbreviation.]
= POONTANG.

poon /pu:n/ *verb intrans. Austral. slang.* M20.
[Origin unkn.]
Dress *up*; dress flashily.

Poona /'pu:nə/ *noun & adjective.* Also **-ah**. E19.
[A city in Maharashatra State in western India.]
▶ **A** *noun.* = ***Poona painting*** below. E19.
▶ **B** *adjective.* Of or pertaining to Poona; (of an attitude, way of life, etc.) held to be characteristic of the Army officers stationed at Poona during British rule. E19.

📖 N. SHUTE They're county people, all frightfully toffee-nosed and Poona. **Poona painting** an artistic process in imitation of oriental work, in which pictures of thick colouring and no background were produced on thin esp. rice paper; a painting of this nature.

poonac /'pu:nak/ *noun.* L19.
[Sinhalese *punakku* from Tamil *puṇṇakku*.]
An oil-cake made from coconut pulp.

Poonah *noun* var. of POONA.

poonask *verb* var. of PONASK.

poonghie *noun* var. of PONGYI.

poontang /'pu:ntaŋ/ *noun. US slang.* E20.
[Alt. of French *putain* prostitute: see PUTANISM.]
Sexual intercourse, sex; a woman or women regarded as a means of sexual gratification.

poop /pu:p/ *noun*¹. LME.
[Old French *pupe*, *pope* (mod. *poupe*) from Proto-Romance var. of Latin *puppis* poop, stern.]
1 The aftermost part of a ship; the stern; the aftermost and highest deck, often forming the roof of a cabin in the stern. LME.
†**2** *transf.* The seat at the back of a coach. Also, the hinder part of a person or animal, the buttocks, the back of the head. *slang.* LME–E18.
3 (Usu. **P-**.) *The* constellation Puppis. E20.
Comb.: **poop deck** the aftermost and highest deck on a ship; **poop-ornament** *Nautical slang* a ship's apprentice.

poop /pu:p/ *noun*². LME.
[from POOP *verb*¹.]
†**1** A hollow stick through which something is blown. Only in LME.
2 A short blast of sound made in a hollow tube, as a wind instrument; a toot; a gulping sound; the report of a gun. M16.
3 An act of breaking wind or of defecation; faeces. *slang* (orig. *nursery*). M18.
Comb.: **poop-scoop** *colloq.* = POOPER-SCOOPER; **poop-stick** a fool, an ineffectual person (cf. POOP *noun*³).

poop /pu:p/ *noun*³. *colloq.* E20.
[Perh. abbreviation of NINCOMPOOP.]
A stupid or ineffectual person; a fool, a bore.

poop /pu:p/ *noun*⁴. *slang* (chiefly *N. Amer.*). M20.
[Origin unkn.]
Up-to-date or inside information; low-down, the facts.

📖 H. WOUK The latest poop is that they're coming in force to invade Alaska.

Comb.: **poop-sheet** a written notice, bulletin, or report.

poop /pu:p/ *verb*¹. LME.
[Imit.: cf. Middle Low German, Low German *pūpen*, Middle Dutch, Dutch *poepen*.]
1 *verb intrans.* †**a** Make a short blast of sound (as) with a horn; blow, toot; gulp in drinking. LME–L16. ▸**b** Break wind, defecate. *nursery & slang.* E18.
2 a *verb trans.* Fire (a bullet etc.) from a gun, fire a bullet etc. from (a gun); shoot (a person or animal) with a firearm. Freq. foll. by *off*. E20. ▸**b** *verb intrans.* (Of a person) fire a gun, shoot; (of a gun etc.) go off, be fired. Freq. foll. by *away*, *off*, etc. E20.

📖 **1b** *Cape Times* Eyes grow round with wonder at the memory of the elephant 'pooping' on the carpet.

†**poop** *verb*² *trans.* E16–M17.
[Origin uncertain: cf. Dutch *poep* clown.]
Deceive, cheat, cozen, befool.

poop /pu:p/ *verb*³ *trans.* M18.
[from POOP *noun*¹.]
1 Of a wave: break over the stern of a vessel. M18.
2 Of a ship: receive (a wave) over the stern. L19.

poop /pu:p/ *verb*⁴. *colloq.* (orig. *US*). M20.
[Origin unkn.]
1 *verb intrans.* Break down, stop working, conk out. M20.
2 *verb trans.* Tire, exhaust. Freq. foll. by *out*. M20.

pooped /pu:pt/ *ppl adjective. colloq.* (orig. *US*). M20.
[from prec. + -ED¹.]
Exhausted, shattered.

📖 *Sunday Express* Bringing up eight kids . . really has me pooped.

pooper-scooper /'pu:pəsku:pə/ *noun. colloq.* L20.
[from POOP *noun*² 3 + SCOOP *noun*: see -ER¹.]
An implement for clearing up (esp. dog) faeces.

poopnoddy /'pu:pnɒdi/ *noun & adjective.* Long *rare* or *obsolete*. E17.
[Perh. from POOP *verb*² + NODDY *noun*¹.]
(Of) a dupe or simpleton.

poo-poo *noun* see POOH-POOH *noun.*

poopsie /'pu:psi/ *noun. US colloq.* Also **-sy**. M20.
[Perh. from POOP *noun*² + -SY. Cf. POPSY.]
(Used as a term of endearment for) a small child or a sweetheart. Also, a girlfriend.

poopy /'pu:pi/ *noun. nursery & slang.* M20.
[from POOP *noun*² + -Y⁶.]
Faeces. Also as *interjection*, expr. annoyance or dismissal. Freq. in *pl.*

poopy /'pu:pi/ *adjective. colloq.* (chiefly *US*). M20.
[from POOP *noun*³ + -Y¹.]
Resembling or characteristic of a stupid or ineffectual person; stuffy, feeble.

poor /pʊə/ *adjective & noun.* Also (earlier) †**pouer**, †**povere**. ME.
[Old French *povre*, (also mod. dial.) *poure* (mod. *pauvre*), from Proto-Romance from Latin *pauper*. Cf. PO'.]
▶ **A** *adjective.* **1 a** Having few, or no, material possessions; lacking the means to procure the comforts or necessities of life; needy, indigent, destitute. Opp. ***rich***. ME. ▸**b** Of, involving, or characterized by poverty. ME.
2 a Small in amount; less than is wanted or expected; scanty, inadequate; low. ME. ▸**b** Of a number or sum: without addition; meagre, paltry. L16.
3 a Less good than is usual or expected; of little excellence or worth; inferior, paltry. ME. ▸**b** Mentally or morally inferior; mean-spirited, despicable, low. LME. ▸**c** Humble, lowly, insignificant. Freq. *iron.* or *joc.* LME. ▸**d** Slight, of little consequence. E17.
4 Deserving of compassion or pity; unfortunate. Also, deceased, late. ME.
5 a Foll. by *in*, †*of*, and as 2nd elem. of comb.: lacking, deficient in, not well provided with, something specified. LME. ▸**b** *spec.* Of soil, ore, etc.: yielding little, unproductive. LME.
6 Lean or feeble from inadequate nourishment. Formerly also (*gen.*), unwell, poorly, in ill health. L15.

📖 **1a** *Westminster Magazine* My parents, though poor, were religious and honest. W. S. CHURCHILL Warren Hastings was poor, but his ancestors had once owned large estates. *Milton Keynes Express* We were as poor as church mice once, but I would have every minute of it again. A. THWAITE The poet was so poor he was in bed, for his clothes were pawned. **2a** LD MACAULAY The crop . . would be thought poor if it did not exceed twelve millions of quarters. P. BROOK Merce Cunningham usually plays to poor houses. **b** KEATS A poor three hours' absence. **3a** G. DURRELL I took one look at her and decided that . . the portrait . . came a very poor second. R. HOGGART The elaborate white dress and veil can only be poor imitations of a real thing. A. MASON It was a poor enough joke, but the Zealot smiled. **b** R. L. STEVENSON He seemed altogether a poor and debile being. **c** SWIFT In my poor opinion. **d** F. W. H. MYERS Each one of those great sciences was in its dim and poor beginning. **4** T. HARDY Poor woman, she seems to have been a sufferer, though uncomplaining. R. BROOKE And they will know—poor fools, they'll know!—One moment, what it is to love. I. MURDOCH Poor old Austin, he hasn't got anyone. **5** *Scientific American* Cereal and vegetable oils are generally poor in carotene. **b** W. STYRON It was poor, eroded land with weed-choked red-clay fields bare of habitation.

Special collocations, phrases, & comb.: ***in poor nick***: see NICK *noun*¹. **poor boy (sandwich)** *US* a large sandwich filled with a range of simple but substantial ingredients. **poor child** *Hist.* a pupil at a charity school. **poor-cod** a small gadid fish, *Trisopterus minutus*, found in coastal and offshore waters of western Europe; **poor do** *US* a dish made up of scraps of food; a hash. **poor fellow** *verb trans.* (*rare*) address sympathetically or commiseratingly as 'poor fellow'. **Poor-Jack** (*obsolete* exc. *Canad. dial.*) = ***Poor John*** below. **Poor John** (*obsolete* exc. *Scot. dial.*) fish, usu. hake, salted and dried for food. **poor little rich boy, poor little rich girl** a wealthy person whose money brings him or her no happiness. ***poor loser***: see LOSER 2. **poor mouth** *noun* (*US*) a claim to be poor; ***talk poor-mouth***, plead poverty; ***make a poor mouth***: see MOUTH *noun*. **poor mouth** *verb intrans. & trans.* (*US*) (*a*) *verb intrans.* claim to be poor; (*b*) *verb trans.* deprecate, belittle. **poor people** the poor as a class (see sense B.1 below). **poor priests** *Hist.* an order of itinerant preaching clergy founded by Wyclif. **poor relation** a relative with very little money; *fig.* an inferior or subordinate member of a group. ***poor show!***: see SHOW *noun*¹. ***poor snake***: see SNAKE *noun* 2. **poor-spirited** *adjective* †(*a*) morally inferior, low-minded; (*b*) timid, cowardly. **poor White** (chiefly *US*) (a member) of a group of white people regarded as socially inferior. ***put on a poor show, put up a poor show***: see SHOW *noun*¹. **take a poor view of** have a low opinion of; regard unfavourably.
▶ **B** *absol.* as *noun.* **1** *collect.* Needy or destitute people, *spec.* those in financially difficult or humble circumstances; *the* class of poor people. ME.
†**2** *sing.* A poor person. ME–E17.

📖 **1** J. OSBORNE He supports the rich against the poor. F. KAPLAN The working poor had to survive without any help . . from government. *Guardian* Many of those . . could properly be described as the deserving poor. ***casual poor***: see CASUAL *adjective*. ***new poor***: see NEW *adjective*. ***nouveau poor***: see NOUVEAU *adjective* 2b. ***overseer of the poor***: see OVERSEER *noun* 3b. ***Protector of the Poor***: see PROTECTOR *noun*.

Comb.: †**poor-book** a book containing a list of the poor receiving parish relief; **poor-box** a money box, esp. in a church, for gifts towards the relief of the poor; **poor-farm** *US* a farm run at public expense to house and support the poor; **poorhouse** *Hist.* a house for poor people living on public charity; a workhouse; **poor law** *Hist.* the law relating to the support of the poor; **poor-rate** *Hist.* a rate or assessment for the relief or support of the poor; **poor relief** *Hist.* financial assistance given to the poor from State or local community funds; **poorshouse** (chiefly SCOTTISH HISTORY) = ***poorhouse*** above.
■ **poorish** *adjective* somewhat poor, rather poor M17.

poor /pʊə/ *verb*¹. ME.
[from POOR *adjective*.]
†**1** *verb intrans. & trans.* Become or make poor. ME–L16.
2 *verb trans.* Call or describe as unfortunate or deserving of compassion. *rare.* M19.

poor *verb*² see POUR *verb.*

poorly /ˈpʊəli/ *adverb & adjective.* ME.
[from POOR *adjective* + -LY².]
▶ **A** *adverb.* **1** Scantily, inadequately, defectively; in an inferior way, with no great success; not highly. ME.
2 In a state of poverty; needily, destitutely. Now *rare.* ME.
†**3** In a manner unworthy of one's position; meanly, shabbily. LME–E18.
4 Piteously, humbly, contemptibly; without courage. Now *rare.* LME.

📖 **1** T. CALLENDER His exhibitions had been poorly attended. D. FRANCIS The poorly-lit back street. M. BINCHY No neighbours who would . . talk poorly of them for not going. M. SPARK All jobs in publishing were greatly sought after, and, perhaps consequently, poorly paid. ***be poorly served***: see SERVE *verb*¹.

▶ **B** *adjective.* In ill health; unwell. Chiefly *pred.* M18.

📖 J. CHEEVER They all agreed that he looked poorly. He was pale.

poor man /pʊə man/ *noun phr.* Pl. **poor men** /mɛn/. ME.
[from POOR *adjective* + MAN *noun.*]
1 A man who is poor; *esp.* a man who is indigent or needy, or who is one of the poor. ME.
2 In full ***poor man's orange***. A coarse variety of grapefruit or pomelo. Chiefly *NZ.* L19.
Phrases: **poor man of mutton** *Scot.* the remains of a shoulder or leg of mutton cooked as food. **poor man's** — an inferior or cheap substitute for —. **poor man's diggings** *US, Austral., & NZ* land where gold may be mined with little investment. ***poor man's orange***: see sense 2 above. **poor man's orchid** any of various annual garden plants of the genus *Schizanthus*, esp. *S. pinnatus*, of the nightshade family, bearing flowers resembling orchids in varied colours. **poor man's parmacetty** *arch.* shepherd's purse, *Capsella bursa-pastoris*. ***poor man's plaster***: see PLASTER *noun* 1. **poor man's treacle** (now *dial.*) garlic, *Allium sativum*. **poor man's weather-glass** the scarlet pimpernel, *Anagallis arvensis*, which closes its flowers before rain.

poorness /ˈpʊənɪs/ *noun.* ME.
[from POOR *adjective* + -NESS.]
1 The quality or condition of being poor; poverty. ME.
2 *spec.* Defectiveness; lack of some good constituent or desirable quality. LME.

poort /pʊət/ *noun. S. Afr.* L18.
[Dutch *poort* gate, port, in South Africa, a pass.]
A narrow mountain pass, *esp.* one cut by a stream or river.

poortith /ˈpʊətɪθ/ *noun. Scot. & north.* E16.
[Repr. Old French *povertet* from Latin *paupertat-* POVERTY.]
The condition of being poor; poverty.

poor-will /ˈpʊəwɪl/ *noun.* L19.
[Imit.: cf. WHIPPOORWILL.]
A small nightjar of western N America, *Phalaenoptilus nuttallii*, which hibernates.

pooter /ˈpuːtə/ *noun*¹. M20.
[Allegedly from Frederick William *Poos* (1891–1987), US entomologist: see -ER¹.]
A suction bottle for collecting small insects, having one tube through which they are drawn into the bottle and another, protected by muslin or gauze, which is sucked.
■ **poot** *verb trans.* (*colloq.*) use a pooter to collect (insects) L20.

Pooter /ˈpuːtə/ *noun*². M20.
[See below.]
A person resembling Charles Pooter, whose mundane and trivial lifestyle is the subject of George and Weedon Grossmith's *Diary of a Nobody* (1892); a narrow, fastidious, or self-important person.
■ **Pooterish** *adjective* resembling, characteristic of, or associated with Charles Pooter M20.

pooter /ˈpuːtə/ *verb intrans.* E20.
[Origin unkn.]
Hasten away, hurry *off.*

pootle /ˈpuːt(ə)l/ *verb intrans. colloq.* L20.
[Blend of POODLE *verb* and TOOTLE *verb.*]
Move or travel (*along, around*, etc.) in a leisurely manner.

📖 B. BRYSON With two hours to kill, I pootled about aimlessly. M. SAWYER Pootling along at 20 m.p.h. in fourth gear.

pooty /ˈpuːti/ *adjective & noun. nursery & affected.* E19.
[Repr. pronunc. of PRETTY *adjective & noun.*]
= PRETTY *adjective & noun.*

poove *noun* var. of POOF *noun*¹.

POP *abbreviation.*
1 (Also **PoP.**) COMPUTING. Point of presence, denoting equipment that acts as access to the Internet.
2 Post Office Preferred (designating certain sizes of envelope etc.).
3 Printing-out paper.

pop /pɒp/ *noun*¹ *& verb.* LME.
[Imit.: cf. POP *adverb.*]
▶ **A** *noun.* **1 a** A blow, a knock, a slap; a slight rap or tap. *obsolete* exc. *dial.* LME. ▸**b** BASEBALL. A ball hit high into the air but close to the batter, providing an easy catch. *N. Amer.* M20. ▸**c** An injection of a narcotic drug. *slang.* M20.
2 A short abrupt explosive sound, as of a cork being drawn. Also (*dial., rare*), the length of time taken by this, a moment, an instant. M16. ▸**b** A turn at doing something; an attempt, a go. M19. ▸**c** The rapid opening of a pop-valve. E20.
3 a A shot with a firearm. M17. ▸**b** *transf.* A pistol. *slang.* E18.
4 A mark made by a slight rapid touch; a dot, a spot; *spec.* the mark made in branding a sheep. E18.
5 An effervescing drink, as ginger beer or champagne, so called from the sound made when a cork is drawn from such a drink. *colloq.* E19.
6 The action of pawning something. *slang.* M19.
7 The ability of a horse to jump fences or other obstacles, esp. with spirit. *colloq.* L20.

📖 **1b** *Philadelphia Inquirer* Don Baylor then hit a routine pop down the third-base line. **2b** T. BARLING The first shots sounded, faint dry pops like bursting cartons. **c** *New Yorker* Blum Helman had sold the show out . . at sixty thousand dollars a pop. **3a** JAYNE PHILLIPS One of the choppers just below us . . took a rocket . . . We were taking pops ourselves. **5** *Beano* Your prize in the lemonade competition . . ten years' supply of pop! ***ginger-pop, soda-pop***, etc.

Phrases: **in pop** in pawn. ***snap, crackle, and pop, snap, crackle, pop***: see SNAP *noun.*
▶ **B** *verb.* Infl. **-pp-**.
1 *verb trans.* Strike, hit; rap, knock. LME.
2 *verb trans.* Put promptly, suddenly, or unexpectedly (*in, on, out*, etc.). Formerly also, push or thrust *up.* L15. ▸**b** *verb trans.* Put or ask (a question) abruptly (chiefly in ***pop the question*** below). E18.
3 *verb intrans.* Pass, move, go, or come promptly, suddenly, or unexpectedly (*down, in, out, over, up*, etc.). M16. ▸**b** Come *on* or *upon* suddenly or unexpectedly; happen *upon.* M18.
4 *verb intrans.* Make a small quick explosive sound; burst or explode with such a sound. L16. ▸**b** Of the ears: make a small popping sound within the head as pressure is equalized between different parts of the auditory canal, esp. during a change of altitude. M20.
5 *verb trans.* Cause to explode with or make a pop; *spec.* heat (maize or Indian corn) until the kernels swell up and burst open with an explosive sound, make (popcorn) in this way. L16. ▸**b** Open (a can of drink etc.) by pulling a tab or ring-pull, making a small explosive sound. *colloq.* (chiefly *N. Amer.*). L20.
6 a *verb intrans.* Shoot, fire a gun. Formerly also, (of a gun) go off. (Foll. by *at, off.*) *colloq.* L16. ▸**b** *verb trans.* Shoot (*down*). M18.
7 *verb intrans.* Of the eye: protrude, bulge *out.* L17.
8 a *verb intrans.* Die. *slang.* Usu. foll. by *off.* M18. ▸**b** *verb trans.* Kill. *slang.* Usu. foll. by *off.* E19.
9 *verb trans.* Pawn. *slang.* M18.
10 a *verb trans. & intrans.* BASEBALL. Hit (a ball) high in the air but close to the batter, providing an easy catch. (Foll. by *out, up.*) *N. Amer.* M19. ▸**b** *verb intrans.* CRICKET. Of a ball: rise sharply off the pitch when bowled. (Foll. by *up.*) L19.
11 Pay (*for*). *slang.* M20.
12 *verb intrans.* Foll. by *off*: speak angrily or hastily; complain loudly; lose one's temper. *US colloq.* M20.
13 *verb trans. & intrans.* Inject or take (a drug, esp. a narcotic drug). *slang.* M20.
14 *verb trans.* COMPUTING. Retrieve (a piece of data, etc.) from the top of a stack. Also (foll. by *up*), remove the top element of (a stack). M20.

📖 **1** *Boxing Scene* In the first round, he popped me with a left hook and knocked me down. **2** T. ROETHKE I had just popped a letter into the box when I got yours. B. BAINBRIDGE Ask him for some more pills and pop them in her morning tea. M. STOTT Anyone can pop a bag of frozen kippers into a saucepan. *Horse & Rider* Pop the horse over a couple of jumps. **pop one's clogs** *slang* die. **b pop the question** *colloq.* propose marriage. **3** S. PLATH The words just popped out of my mouth. *Beano* Pop down to the store and pick up the groceries. C. WILSON Mozart once said that lengthy tunes were always popping into his head. J. HOWKER People started popping round to each other's houses to borrow things. **pop in and out** visit or come and go frequently or casually. **4** V. WOOLF The seaweed which pops when it is pressed. E. WAUGH Another bottle of champagne popped festively in the parlour. **5** G. F. NEWMAN Occasionally Carney popped a flash with his camera, sending more rats scurrying. **6b** N. FREELING He had taken a shotgun and popped three vandals: one died. **7** A. LURIE That's what you were hoping for, wasn't it? Your eyes were positively popping. **8a** F. BURNEY What a pity it would have been had I popped off in my last illness. **9** G. GREENE She . . gave me presents and I popped them when I needed some ready. **13** E. JONG My father was popping Libriums by the minute.

Comb.: **pop-bottle** a bottle for an effervescing drink; **pop-call** *US* a sudden or unexpected visit; **pop-eye** a protruding, prominent eye (usu. in *pl.*) (cf. POP-EYED *adjective*); **pop fly** = sense A.1 above; **pop-hole** a hole in a hedge, fence, etc., through which animals can pass; **pop-off** (*a*) (now *rare*) the discharge of firearms; (*b*) ***pop-off valve***, a safety valve which operates with a pop; **pop-rivet** (*a*) *noun* a tubular rivet, to be inserted into a hole and clinched by the withdrawing of a central mandrel, used where only one side of the work is accessible; (*b*) *verb trans.* secure or fasten with pop-rivets; **pop-shop** *slang* a pawnshop; **pop-top** *N. Amer.* (a can of drink to be opened by) a tab or ring-pull; **pop-valve** in steam engines, a spring-loaded safety valve designed to open or close very rapidly at a predetermined pressure; **pop-visit** a quick or unannounced visit.

pop /pɒp/ *noun*². L18.
[App. short for POPPET or POPLET.]
(Used as a term of endearment for) a girl, a woman. Also, a mistress, a kept woman.

pop /pɒp/ *noun*³. Also **pop.** (point). E19.
[Abbreviation.]
= POPULATION 2, 4a.

Pop /pɒp/ *noun*⁴. M19.
[Perh. from Latin *popina* cookshop, or English *lollipop shop*, the original rooms having been in the house of a Mrs Hatton who kept such a shop.]
A social club and debating society at Eton College, founded in 1811.

pop /pɒp/ *noun*⁵. *colloq.* (chiefly *US*). M19.
[Abbreviation of POPPA.]
Father. Chiefly as a form of address to one's father or to any older man.

pop /pɒp/ *noun*⁶. *colloq.* M19.
[Abbreviation of POPULAR *adjective & noun.* Cf. POP *adjective.*]
1 A popular song or piece of music; pop music, esp. as opp. to rock (ROCK *noun*³ 2b). Cf. POP *adjective* 1. M19. ▸**b** A popular concert. Now *rare.* M19.
2 *ellipt.* Pop art. M20.

📖 **1** *Melody Maker* Kid Thomas . . leads his septet through standards, pops and tangoes. **top of the pops** a chart-topping song or piece of music; *transf.* anything highly successful or popular.

■ **popism** *noun* (*a*) (the characteristic qualities of) popular music; (*b*) (the cultural and artistic attitudes, outlook, etc. associated with) pop art: L20.

pop /pɒp/ *noun*⁷. *slang.* L19.
[Abbreviation.]
= POPPYCOCK.

pop /pɒp/ *noun*⁸. *US colloq.* M20.
[Abbreviation of POPSICLE.]
An ice-lolly.

pop /pɒp/ *adjective. colloq.* L19.
[Abbreviation of POPULAR *adjective & noun.* Cf. POP *noun*⁶.]
1 Of music, esp. song: popular, modern, current; having a wide appeal; *esp.* simple and tuneful, easily appreciated. Cf. POP *noun*⁶ 1. Also, performing, consisting of, or concerned with music of this nature. L19.
2 Appealing or intended to appeal to popular taste; *spec.* (of a technical, scientific, etc., subject) popularized, presented in a popular form. M20.

📖 **1** M. BRADBURY A pop group, called the Haters, were tunelessly celebrating dim proletarian adolescent oestrus. *Listener* Some of the LPs . . are virtually anthologies of pop songs from the previous 20 years. JILLY COOPER During the holidays they . . play pop music too loudly for their parents' liking. **2** *Observer* Pop archaeology books sell like hot cakes.

Special collocations: **pop art** art based on themes drawn from modern popular culture and the mass media, *spec.* an art form that depicts everyday subjects using strong colour and clear-cut images. **pop artist** an artist who specializes in pop art. **pop culture** (widely disseminated) culture based on popular taste. **pop festival** a festival, often held outdoors, at which popular music etc. is performed. **pop star** a famous and successful singer or performer of pop music.

pop /pɒp/ *adverb.* E17.
[Imit.: cf. POP *noun*¹ *& verb.*]
With (the action or sound of) a pop; instantaneously, abruptly; unexpectedly.
go off pop *Austral. & NZ colloq.* break into angry speech; lose one's temper. **pop goes the weasel** a 19th-cent. country dance in which these words were sung or exclaimed while one dancer darted under the arms of the others to his or her partner.

popadam, popadom *nouns* vars. of POPPADAM.

popcorn /ˈpɒpkɔːn/ *noun.* Orig. *US.* E19.
[from POP *verb* 5 + CORN *noun*¹.]
Maize or Indian corn, the kernels of which swell up and burst open with a small explosive sound when heated; the burst kernels of heated maize or Indian corn.

pope /pəʊp/ *noun*¹. Also (esp. in titles) **P-**. OE.
[ecclesiastical Latin *papa* bishop, from the time of Leo the Great (5th cent. AD) used spec. of the Bishop of Rome, from ecclesiastical Greek *papas* bishop, patriarch, later form of *pappas* father: see PAPA *noun*².]
▶ **I 1** (Used as a title preceding the name of) the Bishop of Rome, the head of the Roman Catholic Church. OE. ▸**b** An effigy of the Pope burnt on the anniversary of the Gunpowder Plot (5 November), or at other times. *obsolete* exc. *dial.* L17.
2 a *transf.* The spiritual head of a religion other than Christianity. LME. ▸**b** *fig.* A person who assumes or is credited with a position, authority, or infallibility like that of the Pope. L16.

3 A bishop of the early Christian Church (*Hist.*); *spec.* in the Coptic and Orthodox Churches, (used as the title of) the Bishop or Patriarch of Alexandria. M16.

📖 **2b** *Nation* Burne-Jones . . accepted him as the infallible Pope of Art.

▶ **II 4** A small thick-bodied percid fish, *Gymnocephalus cernua*, of lowland rivers in northern Eurasia. Also called ***ruffe***. M17.

†**5** A weevil which infests malt or grain. M17–M18.

6 Any of several birds with bright, usu. reddish plumage, *esp.* a puffin, a bullfinch. *local.* L17.

7 A hot spiced mulled wine. E20.

Phrases: **Black Pope** the head or General of the Jesuits. ***kiss the pope's toe***: see TOE *noun*.

Comb.: **pope-day** (now *rare*) the anniversary of the Gunpowder Plot (5 November); **Pope Joan** a card-game using a compartmented tray; the nine of diamonds in this game; **Popemobile** a specially designed bulletproof vehicle with a raised viewing area, used by the Pope esp. when on an official visit to a foreign country; **pope's head** (*a*) any of various cacti of the genus *Melocactus*, esp. *M. communis*, of tropical America and the W. Indies, which bear their flowers on a terminal woolly structure; also called ***Turk's cap***, ***Turk's head***; (*b*) a round long-handled brush or broom for cleaning ceilings, pictures, etc. (also called ***Turk's head***); **pope's nose** = ***parson's nose*** s.v. PARSON *noun*.

■ **popeless** *adjective* M19. **popelike** *adjective* (now *rare*) resembling a pope M16. **popeling** †(*a*) a follower or adherent of the Pope; a papist; (*b*) a petty pope; a person who acts like a pope on a small scale: M16. **popely** *adjective* (*rare*) of or pertaining to a pope L16. **popeship** *noun* (*a*) popedom, popehood; (*b*) (with possess. adjective, as ***his popeship*** etc.) a mock title of respect given to a pope: LME. **popess** *noun* a female pope, a papess E16.

pope /pəʊp/ *noun*². M17.

[Russian *pop* from Old Church Slavonic *popŭ* from West Germanic (cf. Old High German *pfaffo*) from ecclesiastical Latin *papa* from ecclesiastical Greek *papas*: see prec.]

A parish priest of the Russian Orthodox Church.

pope /pəʊp/ *verb.* Also **P-**. M16.

[from POPE *noun*¹.]

1 *verb intrans. & trans.* (with *it*). Act as a pope or the Pope. M16.

2 Orig., follow the Pope; accept the papal ecclesiastical system. Later *spec.*, become a Roman Catholic. *colloq.* E17.

Popean /ˈpəʊpɪən/ *adjective.* E19.

[f Alexander *Pope* (see below) + -AN.]

Of or pertaining to the English poet Alexander Pope (1688–1744) or his poetry.

popedom /ˈpəʊpdəm/ *noun.* LOE.

[from POPE *noun*¹ + -DOM.]

1 The office, position, or dignity of the Pope; the tenure of office of a pope; = PAPACY 1. LOE. ▸**b** *transf. & fig.* A position of supreme authority in any religious system or (*iron.*) in other contexts. L16.

2 a An ecclesiastical polity resembling the papacy. LOE. ▸**b** The papal government, esp. as a European State; = PAPACY 2. M17.

popehood /ˈpəʊphʊd/ *noun.* Long *rare.* Also **P-**. OE.

[from POPE *noun*¹ + -HOOD.]

The condition of being Pope; the papal dignity.

popery /ˈpəʊp(ə)ri/ *noun. derog.* M16.

[from POPE *noun*¹ + -ERY.]

The doctrines, practices, and ceremonial associated with the Pope; the papal ecclesiastical system; Roman Catholicism.

📖 *Christian Socialist* Mr. Paisley appeared in his NO Popery vest.

■ **popery'phobia** *noun* dread of Roman Catholicism E19.

Pope's eye /pəʊps ˈʌɪ/ *noun phr.* Also **p-**. L17.

[from POPE *noun*¹ + -'S¹ + EYE *noun*, prob. from the shape, and this perh. being a delicacy orig. meant for a priest.]

The lymph node surrounded with fat in a sheep's thigh, regarded by some as a delicacy.

pop-eyed /pɒpˈʌɪd/ *adjective.* M19.

[from POP *verb* + EYED *adjective*.]

Having bulging or prominent eyes; wide-eyed, esp. with amazement or incredulity.

popgun /ˈpɒpgʌn/ *noun & verb.* Also **pop-gun**. E17.

[from POP *noun*¹, *verb* + GUN *noun*.]

▶ **A** *noun.* **1** A child's toy gun which shoots a tight-fitting pellet with a small sharp explosive sound by compressing the air behind it with a piston. E17.

2 A small, inefficient, or antiquated firearm. *derog.* M19.

▶ **B** *verb trans. & intrans.* Infl. **-nn-**. Discharge a popgun (at). *rare.* E18.

popinac /ˈpɒpɪnak/ *noun. US.* M19.

[Alt. of OPOPANAX.]

The opopanax-tree, *Acacia farnesiana*.

popinjay /ˈpɒpɪndʒeɪ/ *noun & adjective.* ME.

[Anglo-Norman *papeiaye*, Old French *papegay*, *papingay* (mod. *papegai*) from Spanish *papagayo* from Arab. *babbaġā*, *babġā*. The final syll. is assim. to JAY.]

▶ **A** *noun.* **1** A parrot. *arch.* ME.

2 *fig.* †**a** A beautiful or praiseworthy person (with allus. to the beauty and rarity of the bird). *rare.* Only in ME. ▸**b** A type of vanity or empty conceit, a vain or conceited person (with allus. to the bird's gaudy plumage or its empty repetition of words and phrases). E16.

3 A representation of a parrot, esp. as a heraldic charge or an inn sign, or (formerly) in tapestry. LME.

4 ARCHERY. A shooting target consisting of bunches of plumage set at different heights on a perched pole. M16.

†**5** The prevailing colour of the green parrot; a shade of green. L16–E18.

6 The green woodpecker, *Picus viridis*. *local.* M19.

📖 **1** JOHN OWEN An empty insignificant word like the speech of parrots and popinjays. **2b** J. HELLER A vain and convivial popinjay . . who feels he has already come into his estate.

▶†**B** *attrib.* or as *adjective*. Of the colour or shade of a green parrot. M16–M19.

popish /ˈpəʊpɪʃ/ *adjective*¹. *derog.* E16.

[from POPE *noun*¹ + -ISH¹.]

Of or pertaining to popery; of or belonging to the Roman Catholic Church; papistical. Formerly also (*rare*), of or pertaining to the Pope; papal.

■ **popishly** *adverb* M16. **popishness** *noun* (long *rare*) M16.

Popish /ˈpəʊpɪʃ/ *adjective*². E19.

[from Alexander *Pope* (see POPEAN) + -ISH¹.]

= POPEAN.

poplar /ˈpɒplə/ *noun.* ME.

[Anglo-Norman *popler*, Old French *poplier* (mod. *peuplier*), from *pople* (whence POPPLE *noun*²) from Latin *populus* poplar: for termination cf. *cedar*, *medlar*.]

1 Any of various often tall and fast-growing, sometimes narrowly erect, trees of the genus *Populus*, of the willow family, often with triangular-ovate leaves (also ***poplar tree***); the soft light timber of such a tree. ME.

2 Any of various other trees resembling the poplar: *spec.* (*a*) *N. Amer.* the tulip tree, *Liriodendron tulipifera*; (*b*) *Austral.* either of two trees with leaves like those of many poplars, *Homalanthus populifolius*, of the spurge family, and (more fully ***native poplar***) *Codonocarpus cotinifolius* (family Gyrostemonaceae). E18.

1 ***Balsam poplar***, ***Lombardy poplar***, ***silver poplar***, ***trembling poplar***, ***white poplar***, etc.

Comb.: ***poplar beetle***: see ***poplar leaf-beetle*** below; **poplar-borer** (the wood-boring larva of) a N. American longicorn beetle, *Saperda calcarata*; **poplar grey** a greyish European noctuid moth, *Acronicta megacephala*, whose larvae feed and pupate on poplars; **poplar hawk**, **poplar hawkmoth** a large grey hawkmoth, *Laothoe populi*; **poplar kitten** a kitten-moth, *Furcula bifida*; **poplar leaf-beetle**, **poplar beetle** any of several beetles of the family Chrysomelidae, esp. *Chrysomela populi* and *C. lapponica*, whose larvae feed on poplars, causing skeletonization of the leaves; **poplar lutestring** a European moth, *Tethea or*, with brown lines on the forewings.

■ **poplared** *adjective* planted with poplars L19.

Poplarism /ˈpɒpləriz(ə)m/ *noun.* E20.

[from *Poplar* a district (formerly a borough) in the East End of London + -ISM.]

Hist. The policy of giving out-relief on a generous or extravagant scale, as practised by the board of guardians of Poplar in the 1920s.

■ **Poplarist** *noun* a person who practises or advocates Poplarism E20.

†**poplet** *noun.* L16–L17.

[App. from Old French fem. of *poupelet* darling. Cf. POPLOLLY.]

A female favourite; a wench.

poplexy /ˈpɒplɛksi/ *noun.* Chiefly *Scot.* Now *rare* or *obsolete.* LME.

[Aphet.]

= APOPLEXY.

poplin /ˈpɒplɪn/ *noun & adjective.* E18.

[French †*papeline* perh. from Italian *papalina* use as noun of fem. of *papalino* papal, and so called because orig. made at Avignon, a town in southern France which was the residence of the popes during their exile from Rome, 1309–77, and papal property from 1348 to 1791: see -INE¹.]

▶ **A** *noun.* A plain-woven fabric, orig. of silk and worsted but now usu. of very lightweight cotton, with a corded surface; a fabric made to imitate this. E18.

▶ **B** *attrib.* or as *adjective*. Made of poplin. M18.

poplinette /pɒplɪˈnɛt/ *noun & adjective.* M19.

[from prec. + -ETTE.]

(Made of) a woollen or linen fabric made to imitate poplin.

popliteal /pɒˈplɪtɪəl, pɒplɪˈtiːəl/ *adjective.* L18.

[from next + -AL¹.]

ANATOMY. Pertaining to or situated in the hollow at the back of the knee.

popliteus /pɒˈplɪtɪəs, pɒplɪˈtiːəs/ *noun.* E18.

[mod. Latin, from Latin *poplit-*, *poples* ham, hough.]

ANATOMY. A flat triangular flexor muscle at the back of the knee between the femur and tibia. Also ***popliteus muscle***.

poplolly /pɒpˈlɒli/ *noun. obsolete* exc. *Hist.* E19.

[formed as POPLET.]

A mistress.

popocracy /pɒˈpɒkrəsi/ *noun. US. obsolete* exc. *Hist.* Also **P-**. L19.

[from POP(ULIST *noun* 1 + DEM)OCRACY 4.]

The rule or policy of the Populists in the US.

■ **popocrat** /ˈpɒpəkrat/ *noun* [(DEM)OCRAT 2] a member or supporter of the Populists in the US L19. **popocratic** /pɒpəˈkratɪk/ *adjective* of or pertaining to popocrats or popocracy L19.

popote /pɒpɒt/ *noun.* Pl. pronounced same. E20.

[French.]

A French military kitchen or canteen.

pop-out /ˈpɒpaʊt/ *noun & adjective.* M19.

[from POP *verb* + OUT *adverb*.]

▶ **A** *noun.* **1** The action of popping out, as when a cork is drawn. M19.

2 SURFING. A mass-produced surfboard. M20.

▶ **B** *adjective.* Designating something which pops out. M20.

popover /ˈpɒpəʊvə/ *noun.* Chiefly *N. Amer.* L19.

[from POP *verb* + OVER *adverb*.]

1 A very light cake made from a thin batter, which rises to form a hollow shell when baked. L19.

2 A loose casual garment put on by slipping it over the head; a slipover. M20.

Popovets /pɒˈpɒvjɛts/ *noun.* Pl. **Popovtsy** /pɒˈpɒvtsi/. E19.

[Russian, from *pop* priest.]

ECCLESIASTICAL HISTORY. A member of a group of Old Believers who maintained a hierarchy of episcopacy and priesthood. Freq. in *pl.*

poppa /ˈpɒpə/ *noun. US colloq.* L19.

[Alt. of PAPA *noun*². Cf. POP *noun*⁵.]

= PAPA *noun*².

poppadam /ˈpɒpədəm/ *noun.* Also **popa-**, **-dom**, & other vars. E19.

[Tamil *pappatam*, perh. from *paruppa atam* lentil cake.]

A (flat cake of) thin crisp spiced bread usu. eaten with curry or other Indian food.

popper /ˈpɒpə/ *noun.* LME.

[from POP *verb* + -ER¹.]

†**1** A small dagger. *rare.* Only in LME.

2 A person who or thing which makes a popping sound; *spec.* (*a*) *slang* a gun, a pistol; a gunner; (*b*) *US* (the snapper on) a whiplash; (*c*) ANGLING an artificial lure which makes a popping sound when moved over the surface of the water. M18.

3 A person who makes a brief visit or comes or goes *in*, *over*, etc. *rare.* E19.

4 CRICKET. A ball that rises sharply off the pitch when bowled. M19.

5 A utensil for popping corn. Cf. ***corn-popper*** s.v. CORN *noun*¹. *N. Amer.* L19.

6 A press-stud. *colloq.* M20.

7 a A person who takes pills, esp. of stimulant drugs, freely; a drug-taker. *colloq.* M20. ▸**b** A capsule of amyl or (iso)butyl nitrate taken by drug-users for its stimulant effect; a container holding this drug. *colloq.* M20.

Popperian /pɒˈpɪərɪən/ *noun & adjective.* M20.

[from *Popper* (see below) + -IAN.]

▶ **A** *noun.* A person who follows or advocates the theories or methods of the Austrian-born philosopher Sir Karl Raimund Popper (1902–94). M20.

▶ **B** *adjective.* Of or pertaining to Popper's theories or methods, esp. to his dictum that all scientific statements must be in principle falsifiable or to his criticism of Marxism and other ideologies. M20.

■ **Popperism** *noun* the theory or practice of Popper's philosophical ideas M20.

†**poppering** *noun.* L16–M18.

[Flemish *Poperinge*, a town in W. Belgium.]

An old variety of pear. Also ***poppering pear***.

poppet /ˈpɒpɪt/ *noun.* ME.

[Origin uncertain: based ult. on Latin *pupa*, *puppa* girl, doll: cf. PUPPET (its later var.), -ET¹.]

1 a Chiefly *Hist.* A small human figure, used in sorcery or witchcraft. ME. ▸**b** A small figure in the form of human being, esp. a child; a doll; = PUPPET *noun* 1a. Now *rare.* LME. ▸†**c** An idolatrous image; an idol; = PUPPET *noun* 1b. M16–L17.

2 A small or dainty person. Later, a term of endearment, esp. for a pretty child or young girl: darling, pet. *colloq.* LME.

†**3 a** A person whose actions appear to be independent, but are actually controlled by another; = PUPPET *noun* 2b. M16–E17. ▸**b** A human or other figure with jointed limbs, which can be moved by means of strings or wires; a marionette. Cf. PUPPET *noun* 2a. L16–M18.

4 a Either of the upright stocks of a lathe, esp. an adjustable one; a lathe-head; = PUPPET *noun* 5. Now *rare.* M17. ▸**b** = ***poppet-valve*** below. L19.

5 A cylindrical case for pins and needles, pencils, etc. *obsolete* exc. *dial.* M19.

6 NAUTICAL. Any of several short stout pieces of wood placed beneath a ship's hull to support it in launching.

Also, a short piece of wood used as a support on the gunwale of a boat with rowlocks. M19.

> 2 M. R. MITFORD The little girl . . a curly-headed, rosy-cheeked poppet, . . the pet and plaything of a large family. E. H. CLEMENTS Cheer up, poppet, it's going to be all right.

Comb.: **poppet-head** (*a*) (now *rare*) = sense 4a above; (*b*) a frame at the top of a mining-shaft, supporting the pulleys for the ropes used in hoisting; **poppet-leg** *Austral.* an upright timber at the mouth of a mine shaft, supporting the piece from which the cage is suspended; **poppet-valve** a valve consisting of a flat end-piece which is lifted in and out of an opening by an axial rod; **poppet-valved** *adjective* having one or more poppet-valves.

poppied /ˈpɒpɪd/ *adjective*. E19.
[from POPPY *noun* + -ED².]
1 Filled or decorated with poppies. E19.
2 Having the sleep-inducing quality of the poppy; narcotic. Also, affected by this, drowsy. E19.

> 2 B. TAYLOR A land of dreams and sleep, a poppied land!

popping /ˈpɒpɪŋ/ *verbal noun*. M17.
[from POP *verb* + -ING¹.]
The action of POP *verb*
Comb.: **popping crease** CRICKET a line four feet in front of and parallel to the wicket, within which the person batting must keep the bat or at least one foot grounded.

poppish /ˈpɒpɪʃ/ *adjective*. *rare*. L19.
[from POP *noun*¹ 5 + -ISH¹.]
Of the nature of pop; effervescent.

poppit /ˈpɒpɪt/ *noun*. M20.
[from POP *verb* + IT *pers. pronoun*.]
A usu. plastic bead with a hole at one end and a protruding part at the other, by which it may be joined to other similar beads.

popple /ˈpɒp(ə)l/ *noun*¹ & *verb*. ME.
[Prob. from Middle Dutch *popelen* murmur, babble, quiver, throb, of imit. origin.]
▶ **A** *noun*. †**1** A bubble such as rises and breaks in boiling water. ME–M16.
2 An act or condition of poppling; a rolling or tossing of water etc.; a strong ripple. L19. ▸**b** The (sound of the) agitation on the surface of a boiling liquid. L19.
▶ **B** *verb intrans*. Flow in a tumbling manner, as water from a spring or over a pebbly surface; tumble about, as boiling or otherwise agitated liquid; bubble up; ripple, toss to and fro in short waves. LME.

> J. FERGUSON The mother stirred the poppling porridge on the fire. W. GOLDING The grey, poppling water and the occasional barges.

■ **popply** *adjective* L19.

popple /ˈpɒp(ə)l/ *noun*². Now *dial.* & *US*. LME.
[Old French *pople* (mod. dial. *peuple*): see POPLAR.]
A poplar. Also ***popple tree***.

popple /ˈpɒp(ə)l/ *noun*³. Now *dial.* LME.
[Origin unkn.]
The corn-cockle, *Agrostemma githago*. Formerly also [mistranslating Greek *zizania*, Latin *lolium* darnel], an injurious weed of corn, a tare (chiefly in biblical allusions). Cf. COCKLE *noun*¹, POPPY *noun* 2.

poppy /ˈpɒpi/ *noun*.
[Old English *popæg*, *papæg*, later *popig*, ult. from medieval Latin (whence also Old French *pavou*, mod. *pavot*), alt. of Latin *papaver* poppy.]
▶ **I 1** Any of various plants of the genus *Papaver* (family Papaveraceae) with showy papery flowers and milky latex, *esp.* (more fully ***corn poppy***) *Papaver rhoeas*, a weed of arable land with scarlet flowers; (with specifying word) any of various other plants of the genus *Papaver* or allied genera. Also, a flower or flowering stem of such a plant. OE. ▸**b** More fully ***tall poppy***. A tall or striking thing or person; *spec.* a privileged or distinguished person; ***tall poppy syndrome***, a tendency to discredit or disparage those who have achieved success in public life. Now chiefly *Austral.* M17. ▸**c** An artificial red poppy sold on behalf of the ex-service community and worn in Britain on Remembrance Day and the period directly preceding it (cf. ***FLANDERS poppy***). Also, an artificial white poppy worn as an emblem of peace, esp. on Remembrance Day and the week directly preceding it. E20. ▸**d** Money. *slang*. M20.
2 The corn-cockle, *Agrostemma githago* (= POPPLE *noun*³). Also (with specifying word) [by assoc. with POP *verb*], any of several plants (e.g. bladder campion, *Silene vulgaris*) whose corolla or calyx may be inflated and popped, esp. by children in play. *rare* (chiefly *dial.*). LME.
3 *fig.* A thing with narcotic or sleep-inducing qualities (like extracts of the opium poppy). L16.
4 a Formerly, the opium poppy or any of its extracts as used in pharmacy. Now (*slang*), opium. E17. ▸**b** A perfume derived from a poppy. E20.
5 The bright scarlet colour of the corn poppy, *Papaver rhoeas*. L18.
1 ***Californian poppy***, ***horned poppy***, ***Iceland poppy***, ***opium poppy***, ***oriental poppy***, ***sea poppy***, ***Shirley poppy***, etc.
▶ **II 6** [perh. a different word.] = ***poppy-head*** (b) below. LME.
Phrases: ***corn poppy***: see sense 1 above. ***FLANDERS poppy***. ***opium poppy***: see sense 1 above. ***spattling poppy***: see SPATTLE *verb*¹. ***tall poppy***: see sense 1b above.
Comb.: **poppy anemone** a cultivated anemone, *Anemone coronaria*, with often red flowers like those of poppies; **poppy-colour** a bright scarlet; **poppy-coloured** *adjective* of poppy-colour; **Poppy Day** (*a*) = ***Remembrance Day*** s.v. REMEMBRANCE *noun*; (*b*) the Saturday before Remembrance Day, on which artificial red poppies are sold in the street; (cf. sense 1d above); **poppy-head** (*a*) the seed-capsule of a poppy, having small holes through which the seeds are released when mature; (*b*) ARCHITECTURE an ornamental finial on the top of the end of a church pew; **poppy mallow** any of several N. American mallows of the genus *Callirhoe*, having white, red, or purple flowers like those of poppies; **poppy-seed** the seed of a poppy, esp. the opium poppy, used as a flavouring, to garnish bread, etc.

poppy /ˈpɒpi/ *adjective*¹. *colloq.* L19.
[from POP *noun*¹ or *verb* + -Y¹.]
1 That pops or explodes. *rare*. L19.
2 Of the eye or eyes: protuberant. E20.

poppy /ˈpɒpi/ *adjective*². *colloq.* L20.
[from POP *noun*⁶ or *adjective* + -Y¹.]
Popular; having a wide appeal; *spec.* (of music, a group, etc.) having a sound characteristic of pop music.

poppycock /ˈpɒpɪkɒk/ *noun*. *colloq.* M19.
[Dutch dial. *pappekak*, from *pap* soft + *kak* dung.]
Nonsense, rubbish, humbug.

pops /pɒps/ *noun*. E20.
[Extension of POP *noun*⁵.]
= POP *noun*⁵. Also (JAZZ *slang*), a form of address to any man.

Popsicle /ˈpɒpsɪk(ə)l/ *noun*. Chiefly *US*. Also **p-**. E20.
[Fanciful.]
(Proprietary name for) an ice-lolly.

popsie *noun* var. of POPSY.

popskull /ˈpɒpskʌl/ *noun*. *N. Amer. slang*. M19.
[from POP *verb* + SKULL *noun*¹.]
A powerful or unwholesome (esp. home-made) liquor; inferior whiskey.

popster /ˈpɒpstə/ *noun*. *colloq.* M20.
[from POP *noun*⁶ or *adjective* + -STER.]
A pop musician or artist; an enthusiast for pop music, pop art, or pop culture.

popsy /ˈpɒpsi/ *noun*. *colloq.* Also **-sie**. M19.
[App. a nursery formation from POP *noun*² + -SY. Cf. POOPSIE.]
A woman, a girl; a female friend or acquaintance; a girl-friend. Freq. as a term of endearment.

populace /ˈpɒpjʊləs/ *noun*. L16.
[French from Italian *popolaccio*, -*azzo*, from *popolo* PEOPLE *noun* + -*accio* pejorative suffix.]
The ordinary people, as opp. to titled, wealthy, or educated people; the common people. Also (*derog.*), the mob, the rabble.

†**populacy** *noun*. L16.
[Irreg. from prec.: see -ACY.]
1 The common people; the populace. L16–M19.
2 = POPULOUSNESS. E17–E18.

popular /ˈpɒpjʊlə/ *adjective* & *noun*. LME.
[Anglo-Norman *populer*, Old French *populeir* (later and mod. *populaire*) or Latin *popularis*, from *populus* PEOPLE *noun*: see -AR¹.]
▶ **A** *adjective*. **1** Prevalent or current among the general public; commonly known, general. LME.
2 LAW. Affecting, concerning, or open to the people; public. Now *rare* or *obsolete*. LME.
3 a Of, pertaining to, or consisting of ordinary people, or the people as a whole; constituted or carried on by the people. M16. ▸†**b** Of or belonging to the commonalty or populace; plebeian; vulgar. M16–L17.
†**4** Full of people; populous; crowded. L16–E18.
5 Intended for or suited to the taste or means of ordinary people; adapted to the understanding of lay people as opp. to specialists. L16.
†**6** Aware of or cultivating the favour of the common people; supporting the cause of the common people. L16–L18.
7 a Favoured or admired by the people or by a particular group of people; pleasing, liked. E17. ▸**b** Designating forms of art, music, or other culture which appeal to or are favoured by many people; intended primarily to please, amuse, or entertain (freq. opp. ***serious***). M19.

> 1 JER. TAYLOR Does not God plant remedies there where the diseases are most popular? **3a** H. CARPENTER Williams was . . having little popular success with any of his books. **5** LD MACAULAY Every question . . in a popular style which boys and women could comprehend. G. GREENE The world is modelled after the popular magazines nowadays. **7a** J. STEINBECK It is popular to picture a small-town constable as dumb and clumsy. C. FREEMAN Kelly was the most popular, desirable, sought-after girl at college. **b** R. H. WILENSKI The nineteenth century produced . . popular art of the romantic and descriptive kinds.

Special collocations: **popular capitalism** a style of capitalism in which the general public are encouraged to own shares, property, etc.; the theory or practice of this. **popular etymology** = FOLK *etymology*. **popular front** (freq. with cap. initials) a party or coalition representing left-wing or radical elements; *spec.* an international alliance of Communist, radical, and Socialist elements formed and gaining some power in the 1930s. **popular frontism** (freq. with cap. initials) the principles or policies of a popular front. **popular press** newspapers appealing to or read by ordinary people.
▶ **B** *absol.* as *noun*. †**1 a** *collect.* The common people, *the* populace. M16–M17. ▸**b** In *pl.* The common people. L16–E17.
2 A concert of popular music. M19.
3 A newspaper appealing to or read by ordinary people; a tabloid. M20.
■ **popularish** *adjective* (*rare*) tending to be popular, fairly popular E19. **popularism** *noun* (*a*) a word or phrase in common and widespread use; a colloquialism; (*b*) = POPULISM 1: L19. **popularist** *noun* & *adjective* (*a*) *noun* a democrat; a populist; (*b*) *adjective* concerning or appealing to the people; popular; democratic: L19. **popularly** *adverb* L16. **popularness** *noun* (*rare*) E18.

popularise *verb* var. of POPULARIZE.

popularity /pɒpjʊˈlarɪti/ *noun*. M16.
[from prec., or French *popularité* from Latin *popularitas*, from *popularis* (see prec.): see -ITY.]
†**1** Popular or democratic government; the principle of this. M16–E18.
†**2** The action or practice of cultivating popular favour. L16–E18.
3 The fact or condition of being favoured, beloved, or admired by the people, or by a particular group of people. L16.
†**4** = POPULACE. L16–L18.
†**5** Populousness; density of population. *rare*. M17–E18.

> 3 S. ROSENBERG Men were always hovering around her . . . I may have been a little envious of her popularity.

Comb.: **popularity contest** a competition in which the popularity of individuals is judged; *transf.* an assessment of popularity; **popularity poll** a poll or survey taken in order to assess the popularity of a particular person or issue.

popularize /ˈpɒpjʊlərʌɪz/ *verb*. Also **-ise**. L16.
[from POPULAR *adjective* + -IZE.]
†**1** *verb intrans.* Act popularly; court popular favour. *rare*. Only in L16.
2 *verb trans.* Make popular; *spec.* (*a*) cause to be generally known, liked, or admired; (*b*) make (esp. something technical or scientific) intelligible or attractive to a wide or wider audience. L18.

> 2 *Tait's Edinburgh Magazine* He possesses . . the power of seizing upon and popularizing the finer parts of his subject. *Time* Paul Ecke . . who popularized poinsettias as a living symbol of Christmas.

■ **populariˈzation** *noun* L18. **popularizer** *noun* M19.

populate /ˈpɒpjʊleɪt/ *ppl adjective*. *obsolete* exc. *poet.* L16.
[from medieval Latin *populatus*, formed as next: see -ATE².]
Peopled, populated.

populate /ˈpɒpjʊleɪt/ *verb*. L16.
[medieval Latin *populat-* pa. ppl stem of *populare*, from Latin *populus* people: see -ATE³.]
1 *verb trans.* People, inhabit, form the population of (a country etc.). Also, provide or supply (a country etc.) with inhabitants. L16.
2 *verb intrans.* Of people: increase, grow in numbers by propagation. *rare*. E17.
3 *verb intrans.* Become peopled or populous. *US*. *rare*. L18.

> 1 H. A. L. FISHER Northern and southern America are largely populated by colonists from Europe. D. C. PEATTIE The stars were out, populating all heaven with their . . radiance.

population /pɒpjʊˈleɪʃ(ə)n/ *noun*. L16.
[Late Latin *populatio(n-)*, formed as prec.: see -ATION.]
†**1** A peopled or inhabited place. L16–E17.
2 a The extent to which a place is populated or inhabited; the collective inhabitants of a country, town, area, etc.; a body of inhabitants. E17. ▸**b** The general body of inmates in a prison, rehabilitation centre, etc., as distinct from those in special or restricted categories or units. Freq. in ***in population***. Chiefly *US*. M20.
3 The action or process of supplying with inhabitants; increase of inhabitants. L18.
4 a STATISTICS. A (real or hypothetical) totality of objects or individuals under consideration, of which samples are taken for analysis. L19. ▸**b** GENETICS. A group of animals, plants, or humans, among whose members interbreeding occurs. L19. ▸**c** PHYSICS. The (number of) atoms or subatomic particles that occupy any particular energy state. M20.
5 ASTRONOMY. Each of three (orig. two) groups into which stars can be approximately divided on the basis of their manner of formation (see below). M20.

📖 **2a** ANTHONY HUXLEY A world population where life expectancy is continuously increasing. *South African Panorama* By 1986 . . the town of Richards Bay had a population of nearly 20 000. *transf.*: *British Medical Bulletin* The effect of radiation on proliferating cell populations. **5 population I** stars formed from the debris of other stars. **population II** stars coeval with their galaxy. **population III** stars originating before the period of galaxy-formation.

Comb.: **population biology** the branch of science that deals statistically with biological populations; **population curve** a graph showing the variation of population with time; **population explosion** a rapid or sudden marked increase in the size of a population; **population genetics** the branch of science that deals statistically with the genetics of biological populations; ***population inversion***: see INVERSION 16; **population pyramid** a roughly triangular broad-based figure, the width of which indicates numbers and the height of which indicates age.

▪ **populational** *adjective* L19. **populationist** *noun* a person who holds a theory about population, a demographer M19.

populism /ˈpɒpjʊlɪz(ə)m/ *noun*. Also **P-**. L19.
[formed as next + -ISM.]
1 The political principles and practices of populists. L19.
2 The theories and practices of the populist movement in French literature. M20.

📖 **1** T. ALI Mrs. Gandhi's populism undoubtedly excited a mass response.

populist /ˈpɒpjʊlɪst/ *noun & adjective*. Also **P-**. L19.
[from Latin *populus* people + -IST.]
▶ **A** *noun*. **1** An adherent of a political party seeking to represent all the people, orig. that formed in the US in 1892, whose policies included public control of railways, limitation of private ownership of land, and extension of the currency by free coinage of silver. L19.
2 A member of a group of French novelists in the late 1920s and early 1930s who emphasized observation of and sympathy with ordinary people. M20.
3 A person who seeks to represent the views of ordinary people. M20.

📖 **3** N. MCINNES As a populist, he saw historical efficacity in mass ideologies.

▶ **B** *attrib.* or as *adjective*. Of, pertaining to, or characteristic of a populist or populists. L19.

📖 *Time* The very success of Carter's populist appeal may cause him special backlash problems.

▪ **popuˈlistic** *adjective* L19. **popuˈlistically** *adverb* (*rare*) L20.

populous /ˈpɒpjʊləs/ *adjective*. LME.
[from late Latin *populosus*, from *populus* people: see -ULOUS.]
1 Full of people or inhabitants; having many inhabitants; thickly or densely populated. LME. ▸**b** Of a season or period of time: productive, prolific. *rare*. L18.
†**2** Of a body of people: numerous, abundant. M16–M17.
3 Of or pertaining to the populace. *obsolete* exc. *poet.* L16.

📖 **1** S. HAUGHTON The rivers . . running through more populous districts. T. COLLINS I had become conscious of standing on a populous ant-bed.

▪ **populousness** *noun* (*a*) density of population; †(*b*) multitudinousness: E17.

pop-up /ˈpɒpʌp/ *noun & adjective*. E20.
[from POP *verb* + UP *adverb*¹.]
▶ **A** *noun*. **1** BASEBALL. A ball which is hit softly up into the air and is usually easily caught. E20.
2 *ellipt.* A pop-up toaster, book, etc. L20.

📖 **2** *Los Angeles* Picture books, pop-ups, classics . . and children's cookbooks.

▶ **B** *adjective*. Designed to rise up quickly or having a component that rises up quickly or a mechanism which causes something to rise up quickly; *spec.* (*a*) (of a toaster) operating so as to move toasted bread quickly upwards when ready; (*b*) (of a book, greetings card, etc.) containing three-dimensional figures, scenes, etc., which rise up when a page is turned or a cover lifted; (*c*) COMPUTING (of a menu) able to be superimposed on the screen being worked on and rapidly suppressed. M20.

📖 *Popular Photography* Both models have a built-in, pop-up electronic flash.

poquosin *noun* var. of POCOSIN.

poral /ˈpɔːr(ə)l/ *adjective*. L19.
[from Latin *porus* PORE *noun* + -AL¹.]
Of or pertaining to the pores of the body.

porbeagle /ˈpɔːbiːg(ə)l/ *noun*. M18.
[Perh. from Cornish *porth* harbour, cove + *bugel* shepherd.]
A shark of the N. Atlantic and Mediterranean, *Lamna nasus*, with a pointed snout. Also ***porbeagle shark***.

porcelain /ˈpɔːs(ə)lɪn/ *noun & adjective*. M16.
[French *porcelaine* from Italian *porcellana* cowrie shell, polished surface of this, (hence) chinaware, deriv. in fem. adjective form of *porcella* dim. of *porca* sow from Latin, fem. of *porcus* pig.]
▶ **A** *noun*. **1** A white vitrified translucent ceramic material; china. See also ***Réaumur's porcelain*** s.v. RÉAUMUR *noun* 2a. M16.
2 An article made of this (usu. in *pl.*); such articles collectively (freq. with specifying word). E17.
3 A cowrie. Also ***porcelain-shell***. *local*. E17.
1 *artificial porcelain*, ***hard-paste porcelain***, ***soft-paste porcelain***, ***true porcelain***, etc. **2 *Derby porcelain***, ***Lowestoft porcelain***, ***mandarin porcelain***, ***Sèvres porcelain***, etc.
▶ **B** *adjective*. **1** Made of porcelain. L16.
2 *fig.* Resembling porcelain in fragility, delicacy of colouring, etc. M17.

📖 **2** H. SMART The dispensary ball, at which the porcelain portion of the community danced. A. BIRRELL China creeds and delicate porcelain opinions.

Comb. & special collocations: **porcelain clay** kaolin; **porcelain crab** any of various marine crablike crustaceans belonging to *Porcellana* and other genera (family Galatheoidea), with long antennae, related to the hermit crabs; **porcelain enamel** = ENAMEL *noun* 1; **porcelain fungus** a common edible mushroom, *Oudemansiella mucida*, which is white and covered with a slimy fluid and grows in clusters on beech trees; **porcelain jasper** = PORCELLANITE; ***porcelain shell***: see sense 3 above.

▪ **porceˈlainic** *adjective* = PORCELLANEOUS M19. **porcelainist** *noun* a maker or decorator of porcelain; a connoisseur or collector of porcelains: L19. **Porcelainite** *noun* (proprietary name for) any of certain kinds of fine white stoneware L19. **porcelainiˈzation** *noun* conversion into porcelain E20. **porcelainize** *verb trans.* (*a*) convert into porcelain or a similar substance; (*b*) (chiefly *US*) coat (a metal object or surface) with a vitreous substance by firing: M19. **porcelainous** *adjective* = PORCELLANEOUS M19.

porcellaneous /pɔːsɪˈleɪnɪəs/ *adjective*. L18.
[from Italian *porcellana* PORCELAIN + -EOUS.]
Of the nature of or resembling porcelain.
▪ Also **porcellanic** /-ˈlanɪk/ *adjective* E19. **porcellanous** /-ˈsɛlənəs/ *adjective* M19.

porcellanite /pɔːˈsɛlənʌɪt/ *noun*. L18.
[German *Porzellanit*, from *Porzellan* PORCELAIN: see -ITE¹.]
GEOLOGY. Any of various compact siliceous rocks (e.g. tuffs) having an appearance resembling unglazed porcelain.

porch /pɔːtʃ/ *noun*. ME.
[Old & mod. French *porche* from Latin *porticus* colonnade, gallery, from *porta* gate, PORT *noun*³.]
1 An exterior structure forming a covered approach to the entrance of a building. ME. ▸**b** A small platform outside the hatch of a spacecraft. M20.
2 a A colonnade, a portico; in some Eastern countries, such a place used as a court of justice. Long *obsolete* exc. in ***the Porch*** (a) below. LME. ▸**b** A veranda. Chiefly *N. Amer.* M19. ▸**c** A small utility room attached to the back of a house. *N. Amer. dial.* E20.
3 A transept or side chapel in a church. *north*. E16.
4 *the Porch* = STOA 1. Also called ***the Portico***. M17.
5 TELEVISION. In a video signal, a period of line blanking immediately before or after the line-synchronizing pulse. M20.

📖 **1** R. MCCRUM He returned to the porch, unlocked the front door and stepped inside. **2b** JAYNE PHILLIPS My mother and I . . sat on the porch, looking at the street.

▪ **porched** *adjective* having a porch M19. **porchless** *adjective* without a porch L19.

porcine /ˈpɔːsʌɪn/ *adjective*. M17.
[French *porcin*, *-ine* or Latin *porcinus*, from *porcus* (male) pig: see -INE¹.]
Of or pertaining to a pig or pigs; related to or resembling a pig in appearance, character, etc.

📖 A. C. SWINBURNE Sonnets . . noticeable only for their porcine quality of prurience. I. RANKIN Haldayne snorted his porcine laugh.

porcini /pɔːˈtʃiːni/ *noun pl.* L20.
[Italian = little pigs.]
Ceps (wild mushrooms), esp. as an item on a menu. Also ***porcini mushrooms***.

porcupine /ˈpɔːkjʊpʌɪn/ *noun*. Also (*obsolete* exc. *joc.*) **porpentine** /ˈpɔːp(ə)ntʌɪn/. LME.
[Old French *porc espin* (also *porc d'espine*), mod. *porcépic* from Provençal *porc espi(n* from Proto-Romance, from Latin *porcus* pig, PORK + *spina* SPINE.]
1 Any of various rodents of the families Hystricidae (native to Africa, Asia, and SE Europe) and Erethizontidae (native to the Americas) having the body and tail covered with defensive erectile spines or quills. LME.
2 In full ***sea-porcupine***. = ***porcupine-fish*** below. L17.
3 Any of various mechanical devices with numerous projecting spikes; *esp.* an apparatus for heckling flax, cotton, etc. M18.
4 The echidna, *Tachyglossus aculeatus*. *Austral.* L18.
5 In full ***porcupine grass***. Any of various Australian grasses with long stiff sharp leaves, esp. *Triodia irritans*. Also called ***spinifex***. M19.

Comb.: **porcupine fish** any of various tropical marine fishes of the family Diodontidae, which are covered with sharp spines and able to inflate the body; esp. *Diodon hystrix*; ***porcupine grass***: see sense 4 above; **porcupine-wood** the wood of the coconut palm, with markings which resemble the quills of a porcupine.

▪ **porcupinish** *adjective* resembling or suggesting a porcupine E19. **porcupiny** *adjective* = PORCUPINISH L19.

pore /pɔː/ *noun*. LME.
[Old & mod. French from Latin *porus* from Greek *poros* passage, pore.]
1 A minute, usu. microscopic, opening in a surface (the skin of an animal, the epidermis of a plant, etc.), through which fluids or gases can pass. Also (BOTANY), a small opening in an anther or capsule for the discharge of pollen or seeds. LME. ▸**b** A minute interstice in the soil or between particles of matter, esp. through which liquid can penetrate. LME.
†**2** A passage, a duct (esp. in an animal body). *rare*. LME–E17.
3 In a celestial object: a small point or dot resembling a pore. M19.

📖 **1** ANTHONY HUXLEY Plants . . in dry conditions . . have pores sunk well into the leaf surface. J. C. OATES Sweat broke out through every pore of his body. V. BRAMWELL During your bath, the heat will help widen skin pores.

Comb.: **pore pressure** the pressure of pore water; **pore water** water contained in pores in soil or rock.
▪ **pored** *adjective* having pores (of a specified kind) L17.

pore /pɔː/ *verb*. ME.
[Origin uncertain: perh. from base of PEER *verb*², PIRE *verb*.]
1 *verb intrans.* **a** Look fixedly, gaze, stare. Now only with mixture of sense 1b. ME. ▸**b** Be absorbed in the reading or study of a book, document, etc. Now usu. foll. by *over*. LME. ▸**c** Ponder intently. Usu. foll. by *on*, *over*. LME.
2 *verb trans.* Bring or put into some state by poring. Chiefly in ***pore one's eyes out***, ruin one's sight by close reading. Now *rare*. L16.
3 *verb intrans.* Look closely, as a near-sighted person; peer. Now *rare*. L17.

📖 **1a** F. QUARLES All creatures else pore downward to the ground. **b** L. M. MONTGOMERY I've pored over that geometry until I know every proposition . . by heart. C. P. SNOW She pored with anxious concentration through the advertisement columns. J. DISKI He has been poring over scientific papers. **c** DEFOE When he has thought and pored on it.

▪ **porer** *noun* a person who pores over a book etc. L17.

porencephaly /pɔːrɛnˈsɛf(ə)li, -ˈkɛf-/ *noun*. Also in Latin form **-cephalia** /-sɪˈfeɪlɪə, -kɪ-/. L19.
[from Greek *poros* PORE *noun* + *egkephalos* brain + -Y³.]
MEDICINE. The existence (congenital or caused by disease) of a hollow connecting the lateral ventricle to the surface of the brain.
▪ **porenceˈphalic** *adjective* L19.

porge /pɔːdʒ/ *verb trans.* L19.
[Judaeo-Sp. *porgar*, Spanish *purgar* cleanse from Latin *purgare* PURGE *verb*.]
Make (a slaughtered animal) ritually clean in accordance with Jewish religious laws by removing the sinews and veins.
▪ **porger** *noun* a person whose business is to do this L18.

†**porgo** *noun* var. of PARGO.

porgy /ˈpɔːgi/ *noun*. Chiefly *N. Amer.* M17.
[Alt. of *porgo*, PARGO: perh. also infl. by Amer. Indian words.]
Any of numerous fishes found esp. in N. American Atlantic coastal waters; *spec.* a fish of the sea bream family Sparidae, which includes several food fishes.

poria *noun* pl. of PORION.

poriferan /pəˈrɪf(ə)rən/ *noun & adjective*. M19.
[from mod. Latin *Porifera* (see below) neut. pl. of *porifer*, from Latin *porus* PORE *noun* + *-fer* bearing: see -AN.]
ZOOLOGY. ▶**A** *noun*. A member of the phylum Porifera, which comprises the sponges. M19.
▶ **B** *adjective*. Of or pertaining to this phylum. L19.
▪ **porifer** /ˈpɔːrɪfə/ *noun*, pl. **-fers**, **porifera** /pəˈrɪf(ə)rə/, = PORIFERAN *noun* M19.

poriferous /pəˈrɪf(ə)rəs/ *adjective*. M19.
[from Latin *porus* PORE *noun* + -I- + -FEROUS.]
Having pores.

porin /ˈpɔːrɪn/ *noun*. L20.
[from Greek *poros* PORE *noun* + -IN¹.]
BIOCHEMISTRY. Any of a class of proteins having molecules which can form channels (large enough to allow the passage of small ions etc.) through cellular membranes esp. of some bacteria.

porion /ˈpɔːrɪən/ *noun*. Now *rare*. Pl. **-ia** /-ɪə/. E20.
[from Greek *poros* passage, after *inion*.]
ANATOMY. The uppermost point of the margin of the external auditory meatus.

porism /ˈpɔːrɪz(ə)m, ˈpɒ-/ *noun*. LME.
[Late Latin *porisma* from Greek, from *porizein* find, obtain: see -ISM.]
MATH. In ancient Greek mathematics: a kind of geometrical proposition arising during the investigation of some other proposition, either by immediate deduction (= COROLLARY *noun* 1a), or by consideration of some special case in which the first proposition becomes indeterminate.
▪ **porisˈmatic** /pɔːrɪzˈmatɪk/ *adjective* pertaining to or of the nature of a porism L18. **poristic** /pəˈrɪstɪk/ *adjective* (now *rare*) = PORISMATIC E18.

pork /pɔːk/ *noun*. ME.
[Old & mod. French *porc* from Latin *porcus* (male) pig.]
1 The flesh of pig used as food. ME.
2 A hog, a pig; *spec.* a mature pig. *obsolete* exc. *Hist.* LME.
3 = *pork-barrel* below. *US slang*. L19.
Phrases: **draw pig on pork**: see PIG *noun*[1]. **rabbit-and-pork**: see RABBIT *noun* 4.
Comb.: **pork-barrel** (*a*) a barrel in which pork is kept; (*b*) *colloq*. (orig. *N. Amer.*) (the provision of) government funds obtained for particular areas or individuals on the basis of political patronage; **pork-barrelling** *colloq*. (orig. *N. Amer.*) the process of providing government funds for particular areas or individuals on the basis of political patronage; **pork-butcher** (*a*) a person who slaughters pigs for sale; (*b*) a shopkeeper who specializes in pork; **pork-chop** (*a*) a thick slice of pork (usu. including a rib), esp. (to be) grilled; (*b*) *US slang* (*derog*.) a black American who accepts an inferior position in relation to white people; **pork-chopper** *US slang* (usu. *derog*.) a full-time union official; **pork-eater** CANAD. HISTORY (*a*) a canoeist engaged on the run between Montreal and Grand Portage; (*b*) *gen*. any canoeist, *esp*. an inexperienced one; **porkfish** *US & W. Indies* any of several large edible fishes, *esp*. a black and yellow West Indian grunt, *Anisotremus virginicus*; **pork-knocker** (in Guyana) an independent prospector for gold or diamonds; **porkman** a dealer in pork; **pork-pie** (*a*) a raised pie of minced pork; (*b*) *colloq*. (in full *pork pie hat*) a hat with a flat crown and a brim turned up all round; (*c*) *rhyming slang* a lie (cf. PORKY *noun*[2]); **porkwood** a shrub or small tree of southern Africa, *Kigellaria africana* (family Flacourtiaceae), with pink wood.

porker /ˈpɔːkə/ *noun*. M17.
[from prec. + -ER[1].]
1 A pig, esp. a young hog, fattened for pork. M17.
2 *fig*. A fat person. L19.

porkery /ˈpɔːk(ə)ri/ *noun*. *rare*. LME.
[Cf. Old Northern French *porkerie*, Old French *porcherie* stock of pigs, medieval Latin *porcaria* a piggery, from Latin *porcus*: see PORK, -ERY.]
1 A stock of pigs. LME.
2 Stock of pork, bacon, ham, and similar meats. L19.

porket /ˈpɔːkɪt/ *noun*. M16.
[Old Northern French *porket*, Old French *porchet*, dim. of *porc* pig, PORK.]
A young or small pig or hog. Now (*dial*.) = PORKER 1.

porkling /ˈpɔːklɪŋ/ *noun*. M16.
[from PORK + -LING[1].]
A young or small pig. Formerly also applied derisively to a person.

porky /ˈpɔːki/ *noun*[1]. E20.
[Abbreviation.]
A porcupine.

porky /ˈpɔːki/ *adjective & noun*[2]. *colloq*. M19.
[from PORK + -Y[1].]
▶**A** *adjective*. Of or resembling pork; *esp*. fleshy, obese. M19.

> K.O. Murphy . . looked lethargic at a porky 206 pounds.

▶**B** *noun*. [from *pork-pie* (c) s.v. PORK.] A lie. Also *porky-pie*. *slang*. L20.

> *Daily Telegraph* The Speaker . . forbade 'the Minister's telling porkies' in the Commons last week.

porn /pɔːn/ *noun & adjective*. *colloq*. M20.
[Abbreviation.]
▶**A** *noun*. **1** Pornographer. *rare*. M20.
2 Pornography. M20.
3 With preceding noun, prefix, etc.: television programmes, illustrated books, etc., regarded as catering for a voyeuristic or obsessive interest in a particular subject. *derog* or *joc*. L20.

> **2** *New Society* The stuff men pass round in barrack rooms as 'a nice bit of porn'. ***hard porn, soft porn***, etc. **3** *EatSoup* His book . . isn't just gastro-porn, although the pictures are stunning. *Esquire* For a real kick, try weather porn, . . videotapes featuring amateur camcorder footage of tornadoes.

▶**B** *adjective*. Pornographic. L20.

> J. IRVING A porn magazine of . . loathsome crudity.

Comb.: **pornbroker** [joc. after *pawnbroker*] a dealer in pornography; **porn-shop**: specializing in pornographic material.

pornie /ˈpɔːni/ *noun*. *slang*. M20.
[from PORN + -IE.]
A pornographic film.

porno /ˈpɔːnəʊ/ *adjective & noun*. *colloq*. M20.
[Abbreviation.]
▶**A** *adjective*. Pornographic. M20.
▶**B** *noun*. Pl. **-os**. Pornography; a pornographer. *rare*. M20.

porno- /ˈpɔːnəʊ/ *combining form* of PORNOGRAPHY or PORNOGRAPHIC: see -O-.
■ **pornophile** *noun* a lover of pornography M20. **pornoˈphobic** *adjective* having a horror of pornography L20.

pornocracy /pɔːˈnɒkrəsi/ *noun*. M19.
[from Greek *pornē* prostitute: see -CRACY.]
A group of prostitutes or immoral women having dominating influence, esp. in papal Rome during the tenth century; domination by such a group.
■ **ˈpornocrat** *noun* a member of a pornocracy L19.

pornography /pɔːˈnɒgrəfi/ *noun*. M19.
[from Greek *pornographos* (from *pornē* prostitute + *graphein* write) + -Y[3]: see -GRAPHY.]
1 Description of the life, activities, etc., of prostitutes. *rare*. M19.
2 The explicit description or exhibition of sexual subjects or activity in literature, painting, films, etc., in a manner intended to stimulate erotic rather than aesthetic feelings; literature etc. containing this. M19.
2 ***hard-core pornography, soft pornography***, etc. **child pornography**: showing sexual acts involving children.
■ **ˈpornograph** *noun* an example of pornography, a pornographic writing, illustration, etc. L19. **pornographer** *noun* a person who produces or provides pornography, a pornographic writer, publisher, or artist M19. **pornoˈgraphic** *adjective* pertaining to or of the nature of pornography; dealing in the obscene: L19. **pornoˈgraphically** *adverb* E20.

porny /ˈpɔːni/ *adjective*. *slang*. M20.
[from PORN + -Y[1].]
Pornographic.

Poro /ˈpɒrəʊ/ *noun*. L18.
[W. African: cf. Temne, Mende *poro*.]
A secret society for men with rites of initiation, widespread in Sierra Leone and Liberia and exercising social and political power. Cf. SANDE.

porocyte /ˈpɒrəsʌɪt/ *noun*. L19.
[from Greek *poros* PORE *noun* + -CYTE.]
ZOOLOGY. Any of the pore-containing cells which extend through the body wall of a sponge.

porogamy /pəˈrɒgəmi/ *noun*. E20.
[from Greek *poros* PORE *noun* + -GAMY.]
BOTANY. Fertilization in which the pollen-tube enters the ovule by the micropyle.
■ **porogamic** /-ˈgamɪk/ *adjective* L19. **porogamous** *adjective* E20.

porokeratosis /ˌpɒrəʊkɛrəˈtəʊsɪs, ˌpɔː-/ *noun*. Pl. **-toses** /-ˈtəʊsiːz/. L19.
[from Greek *poros* PORE *noun* (the disease was orig. believed to arise in the pores of the skin) + KERATOSIS.]
MEDICINE. A skin disease in which lesions develop as annular horny ridges enclosing an atrophic area.
■ **porokeratotic** *adjective* M20.

poromeric /pɔːrə(ʊ)ˈmɛrɪk, pɒ-/ *adjective & noun*. M20.
[from PORO(US + POLY)MERIC.]
(Of, pertaining to, or designating) any of a class of synthetic leather-like materials (used esp. in making footwear) which are permeable to water vapour.

porometer /pəˈrɒmɪtə/ *noun*. E20.
[from Greek *poros* PORE *noun* + -OMETER.]
An instrument for measuring the degree of porosity; *spec*. one for estimating the sizes of the stomata of leaves.

poroplastic /pɔːrə(ʊ)ˈplastɪk, pɒ-/ *adjective*. L19.
[from Greek *poros* noun + -O- + PLASTIC *adjective*.]
Of felt for surgical splints etc.: both porous and plastic.

poroporo /ˈpɒrəpɒrəʊ/ *noun*. *NZ*. M19.
[Maori.]
A shrub of New Zealand and Australia, *Solanum aviculare*, of the nightshade family, bearing lavender-coloured flowers and yellowish berries.

porose /pəˈrəʊs/ *adjective*. Now *rare*. LME.
[medieval Latin *porosus*: see POROUS, -OSE[1].]
Full of pores, porous.

porosimeter /pɔːrə(ʊ)ˈsɪmɪtə/ *noun*. E20.
[from next + -METER.]
An instrument for measuring the porosity of materials.
■ **porosimetry** *noun* the measurement of porosity M20.

porosity /pɔːˈrɒsɪti/ *noun*. LME.
[medieval Latin *porositas*, from *porosus* POROUS: see -ITY.]
1 Porous consistency; the degree to which a substance is porous. LME.
2 A porous part or structure; an interstice, a pore. Usu. in *pl*. L16.

porous /ˈpɔːrəs/ *adjective*. LME.
[Old & mod. French *poreux* from medieval Latin *porosus*, from Latin *porus* PORE *noun*: see -OUS.]
1 Full of pores; having minute interstices through which water, air, light, etc., may pass. LME.
2 *fig*. Not retentive or secure; *esp*. admitting the passage of people, information, etc. M17.

> **1** J. WAIN Leather's porous, it lets your skin breathe. *Which?* Leaks can occur if the flashing . . becomes porous with age. **2** M. LEE Border jails were notoriously porous.

■ **porously** *adverb* M19. **porousness** *noun* M17.

porpentine *noun* see PORCUPINE.

porphin /ˈpɔːfɪn/ *noun*. E20.
[from PORPHYRIN.]
CHEMISTRY. A synthetic purple crystalline solid, $C_{20}H_{14}N_4$, which has a macrocyclic aromatic molecule consisting of four pyrrole rings linked by methylene groups, from which the porphyrins are formally derived.

porphobilin /pɔːfə(ʊ)ˈbʌɪlɪn/ *noun*. M20.
[from PORPH(YRIA + -O- + Latin *bilis* BILE *noun*[1] + -IN[1].]
BIOCHEMISTRY. Any of a group of red-brown compounds derived from porphobilinogen.

porphobilinogen /ˌpɔːfə(ʊ)bʌɪˈlɪnədʒ(ə)n/ *noun*. M20.
[from prec. + -OGEN.]
BIOCHEMISTRY. A colourless crystalline substituted pyrrole, $C_{10}H_{14}N_2O_4$, which is a metabolic precursor of porphyrins and is excreted in the commoner forms of porphyria.

porphyr- *combining form* see PORPHYRO-.

porphyria /pɔːˈfɪrɪə/ *noun*. E20.
[from PORPHYRIN + -IA[1].]
MEDICINE. Any of a group of hereditary diseases marked by defects of porphyrin metabolism (leading to the excretion of abnormally large quantities of porphyrins in the urine).
■ **porphyric** *adjective* of, pertaining to, or affected with porphyria M20.

Porphyrian /pɔːˈfɪrɪən/ *adjective & noun*. M16.
[from *Porphyry* (see below) from Latin *Porphyrius* from Greek *Porphurios* + -AN.]
▶**A** *adjective*. Of or pertaining to the Neoplatonist philosopher and opponent of Christianity Porphyry, (233–*c* 306), or his teachings. M16.
▶**B** *noun*. A follower of Porphyry. E18.

porphyrin /ˈpɔːfɪrɪn/ *noun*. E20.
[from HAEMATO)PORPHYRIN.]
BIOCHEMISTRY. Any of a large class of deep-red or purple fluorescent crystalline pigments that are substituted derivatives of porphin in which the four pyrrole rings are linked by =CH– groups, occurring widely in nature, e.g. in haem.
■ **porphyˈrinogen** *noun* a colourless, reduced derivative of a porphyrin, in which the four pyrrole rings are linked by methylene groups E20. **porphyriˈnuria** *noun* (MEDICINE) the presence of excessive amounts of porphyrins in the urine E20.

porphyrio /pɔːˈfɪrɪəʊ/ *noun*. Pl. †**-os**. Also (earlier) †**-ion**. LME.
[Latin *porphyrio(n-)* from Greek *porphuriōn*, from *porphuros* purple.]
(An aquatic bird known to the ancients, usu. identified with) the purple gallinule, *Porphyrio porphyrio*. Now only as mod. Latin genus name.

porphyrise *verb* var. of PORPHYRIZE.

porphyrite /ˈpɔːfɪrʌɪt/ *noun*. L16.
[Latin *porphyrites* (of) porphyry from Greek *porphuritēs*, from *porphura* purple dye: see PORPHYRO-, -ITE[1].]
†**1** = PORPHYRY 1. L16–M18.
2 GEOLOGY. = PORPHYRY 2. L18.

porphyritic /pɔːfɪˈrɪtɪk/ *adjective*. LME.
[medieval Latin *porphyriticus* alt. of Latin *porphyreticus*, from Latin *porphyrites*: see prec., -IC.]
1 Of, pertaining to, or of the nature of porphyry. LME.
2 PETROGRAPHY. Of (the texture of) a rock: containing distinct crystals or crystalline particles embedded in a compact groundmass. L18.
■ **porphyritically** *adverb* (PETROGRAPHY) L19.

porphyrize /ˈpɔːfɪrʌɪz/ *verb trans*. Now *rare*. Also **-ise**. M18.
[from PORPHYR- + -IZE, after French *porphyriser*.]
Grind to a fine powder, orig. on a slab of porphyry.
■ **porphyriˈzation** *noun* M19.

porphyro- /ˈpɔːfɪrəʊ/ *combining form* of Greek *porphura* purple dye, *porphuros* purple: see -O-. Before a vowel also **porphyr-**.
■ **porphyroblast** *noun* (GEOLOGY) a larger recrystallized grain occurring in a finer groundmass in a (usu. metamorphic) rock E20. **porphyroˈblastic** *adjective* (GEOLOGY) marked by the presence of porphyroblasts E20. **porphyroclast** *noun* (GEOLOGY) a larger grain remaining in a finer groundmass in a rock which has undergone dynamic metamorphism M20. **porphyroˈclastic** *adjective* (GEOLOGY) marked by the presence of porphyroclasts E20. **porphyˈropsin** *noun* (BIOCHEMISTRY) any of a class of light-sensitive pigments in the retinas of freshwater vertebrates analogous to rhodopsin in humans M20.

porphyrogenite /ˌpɔːfɪˈrɒdʒɪnʌɪt/ *noun*. Also (earlier) in Latin form **porphyrogenitus** /ˌpɔːfɪrə(ʊ)ˈdʒɛnɪtəs/, pl. **-ti** /-tʌɪ/. E17.
[medieval Latin, after late Greek *porphurogennētos*, from *porphuro-* PORPHYRO- + *gennētos* born.]
Orig. *spec*., a member of the imperial family at Constantinople, reputedly born in a purple-hung or porphyry chamber. Later, a child born after his or her father's accession to a throne; *loosely*, a member of an imperial or royal reigning family; belonging to the highest or most privileged ranks of an organization etc.
■ **porphyroˈgenita** *noun*, pl. **-tae** /-tiː/, a female porphyrogenitus M19.

porphyroid /ˈpɔːfɪrɔɪd/ *noun & adjective*. L18.
[from PORPHYRY + -OID.]
PETROGRAPHY. ▶**A** *noun*. A porphyritic rock. L18.
▶**B** *adjective*. Porphyritic. L18.

porphyry /ˈpɔːfɪri/ *noun*. LME.
[Ult. from medieval Latin *porphyreum*, from Latin *porphyrites*: see PORPHYRITE.]
1 A hard rock quarried in ancient Egypt, having crystals of white or red plagioclase feldspar in a fine red groundmass of hornblende, apatite, etc.; *loosely* any attractive red or purple stone taking a high polish. LME. ▸†**b** A slab of porphyry, esp. one used for grinding drugs on. LME–L17.
2 *GEOLOGY*. An unstratified or igneous rock having a homogeneous groundmass containing larger crystals of one or more minerals (orig. *spec.* of feldspar). L18.
2 ***verd-antique porphyry***: see VERD-ANTIQUE 3.

porpoise /ˈpɔːpəs, -pɔɪs/ *noun & verb*. ME.
[Old French *po(u)rpois*, *-peis*, *-pais* from Proto-Romance comb. of Latin *porcus* pig & *piscis* fish, for Latin *porcus marinus* lit. 'sea-hog'.]
▸ **A** *noun*. **1** Any of various small delphinoid whales of the family Phocaenidae, with a blunt rounded snout and usu. low triangular dorsal fin. ME.
2 A sharp dive by an aircraft or submarine. E20.
▸ **B** *verb intrans*. Move like a porpoise; *spec*. (*a*) (of an aircraft, esp. a seaplane) touch the water or ground and rise again; (*b*) (of a submarine etc.) alternately rise to the surface of the water and submerge. E20.

porr /pɔː/ *noun*. Long *obsolete* exc. *Scot. & dial.* Also **purr** /pəː/. LME.
[from the verb.]
1 A poker. LME.
2 A thrust, a poke; a kick. L16.

porr /pɔː/ *verb trans*. Long *obsolete* exc. *Scot. & dial.* Also **purr** /pəː/. LME.
[Middle Dutch *porren* (*purren*), Dutch *porren*, Middle Low German, Low German (whence German) *purren*, Middle High German *phurren*, app. of West Germanic origin.]
1 Thrust or prod as with a spear or stick. Now chiefly, poke (a fire). LME.
2 Stuff or fill (a receptacle, a space). LME.
3 Push with the foot; kick, esp. with heavy boots. E19.

porraceous /pɒˈreɪʃəs/ *adjective*. *arch*. E17.
[from Latin *porraceus*, from *porrum* leek: see -ACEOUS.]
Of or like a leek; leek-green.

†**porray** *noun* see PURRY.

porrect /pəˈrɛkt/ *adjective*. E19.
[Latin *porrectus*, formed as next.]
ZOOLOGY & BOTANY. Extended forward and outwards.

porrect /pəˈrɛkt/ *verb trans*. LME.
[Latin *porrect-* pa. ppl stem of *porrigere*, from *por-* PRO-[1] + *regere* stretch, direct.]
1 Stretch out, extend (usu. a part of the body). Now only *ZOOLOGY*. LME.
†**2** Direct (a prayer or petition). LME–L15.
3 Submit (a document, etc.) for examination or correction. *obsolete* exc. *ECCLESIASTICAL LAW*. LME.
■ **porrected** *adjective* = PORRECT *adjective* M17. **porrection** *noun* †(*a*) *rare* stretching out, extension; (*b*) (now only *ECCLESIASTICAL*) the action of holding out something for acceptance; proffering, presentation: M17.

porret /ˈpɒrɪt/ *noun*. *obsolete* exc. *dial.* LME.
[Old French *poret*, from Latin *porrum* leek: see -ET[1].]
A young leek or onion.

porridge /ˈpɒrɪdʒ/ *noun*. M16.
[Alt. of POTTAGE, PODDISH. In sense 1 perh. infl. by *porray* obsolete var. of PURRY.]
1 A broth of vegetables, meat, etc., often thickened with barley or another cereal. Now chiefly *US*. M16.
2 A dish consisting of oatmeal or another meal or cereal boiled in water or milk to a thick consistency. Also (*Scot.*) treated as *pl*. M17.
3 A conglomeration, a hotchpotch. M17.
4 Something of the consistency of thick soup or porridge. E18.
5 Imprisonment, a prison sentence. *slang*. M20.

> **2** P. CAREY Oscar was sprinkling sugar on his porridge. **3** *Listener* Brazil . . is an unique porridge of races and nationalities—Negroes from Africa, Portuguese . . Japanese and Chinese. **4** *Skiing Today* Conditions may be anything from brittle, icy crust to wet, sticky porridge. **5** R. SCRUTON A client . . was now doing porridge in the Scrubs.

Phrases: ***keep one's breath to cool one's porridge***, ***save one's breath (to cool one's porridge)***: see BREATH *noun*.
Comb.: **porridge ice** broken ice forced into a continuous mass, pack ice.
■ **porridgy** *adjective* resembling porridge M19.

porrigo /pəˈraɪɡəʊ/ *noun*. Now *rare*. E18.
[Latin = scurf.]
MEDICINE. Any of various diseases of the scalp marked by scaly eruptions.
■ **porriginous** /pəˈrɪdʒɪnəs/ *adjective* E19.

porringer /ˈpɒrɪn(d)ʒə/ *noun*. LME.
[Alt. of POTTINGER, PODDINGER.]
1 A small bowl, often with a handle, for soup, broth, porridge, etc. LME.
2 A hat or cap resembling such a bowl. *joc. rare*. E17.

porron /pɒˈrəʊn, *foreign* poˈrron/ *noun*. Pl. **-es** /-eɪz, *foreign* -ɛs/, **-s**. M19.
[Spanish.]
In Spain and Spanish-speaking countries: a wine-flask with a long spout from which to drink the contents.

Porro prism /ˈpɒrəʊ prɪz(ə)m/ *noun phr*. Also **p-**. M20.
[Ignazio *Porro* (1801–75), Italian scientist.]
A reflecting prism in which the light is reflected on two 45 degree surfaces and returned parallel to the incoming beam. Also, (in *pl.*) a pair of binoculars using two such prisms at right angles, resulting in a conventional instrument with objective lenses that are further apart than the eyepieces.

Porson /ˈpɔːs(ə)n/ *noun*. L19.
[Richard *Porson* (1759–1808), English classical scholar who formulated the rule.]
Porson's law, ***Porson's rule***, the metrical rule that in a Greek tragic iambic trimeter where the last word forms a cretic, the preceding syllable is short.
■ **Porsonian** /pɔːˈsəʊnɪən/ *adjective* of or characteristic of Porson, his work, or a font of Greek type named after him M19.

port /pɔːt/ *noun*[1]. OE.
[Latin *portus* haven, harbour, rel. to *porta* (see PORT *noun*[3]). Readopted in Middle English from Old & mod. French from Latin *portus*.]
1 A place by the shore where ships can shelter from storms, or load and unload; a harbour, a haven (*lit.* & *fig.*). OE.
2 A town or place possessing a harbour where ships load or unload, or begin or end their voyages, or at which passengers embark or disembark, esp. on departure from or arrival in a country; *spec.* such a place where charges may be levied under statute on ships making use of the facilities. Also (more fully ***inland port***), any point or place inland recognized or functioning as a port. OE.
3 *ellipt*. An airport. M20.

> **1** *Daily Telegraph* A . . frigate has also been in port. **2** J. N. MCILWRAITH Sailor-like, he had a lass in every port. C. FRANCIS When ports developed, they grew around the needs of ships.

Phrases: **any port in a storm** *fig.* any refuge in difficult or troubled circumstances. **close port**: situated up-river or within a city. ***free port***: see FREE *adjective*. ***home port***: see HOME *adjective*. ***inland port***: see sense 2 above. ***port of call***: see CALL *noun*. **port of entry** a port by which people and goods may enter a country (see also s.v. PORT *noun*[3] 5b).
¶ See also CINQUE PORTS.

port /pɔːt/ *noun*[2]. Long *obsolete* exc. in comb.
[Old English *port* = Middle Flemish, Middle Dutch *port* town, burgh, city; ult. the same word as prec. or next.]
A town, *spec.* a walled town, a market-town.
¶ Cf. PORTMAN, PORTMOTE, PORTREEVE.

port /pɔːt/ *noun*[3]. OE.
[Latin *porta* door, gate, rel. to *portus* (see PORT *noun*[1]), or *porticus* porch. Readopted in Middle English from Old & mod. French *porte* from Latin *porta*.]
1 a A gate, a gateway, *esp.* that of a city or walled town. Now chiefly *Scot.* OE. ▸†**b** An open space near the gate of a town, as the site of a market or fair for hiring labourers; a market or fair for hiring labourers held in such a space. *Scot.* L18–E20.
2 An opening in the side of a ship; *spec.* a doorway for boarding or loading or a square aperture for firing cannon etc. through. Also, a similar aperture in an aircraft, building, etc., for firing through. LME. ▸**b** The cover or shutter of a port. Also ***port-lid***. E17.
3 The upward curve in the mouthpiece of a curb or Pelham bit. Also ***port-mouth***. L16.
4 a *BILLIARDS*. A small ivory arch through which the ball must pass. *obsolete* exc. *Hist.* L17. ▸**b** *BOWLS & CURLING*. A passage remaining open between two stones or bowls. L18.
5 a An aperture in a chamber or container for the passage of air, steam, etc.; *spec.* (*a*) one in the cylinder of an engine or pump, controlled by a valve; (*b*) one in a loudspeaker cabinet. M19. ▸**b** *MEDICINE*. = PORTAL *noun*[1] 1e. More fully ***port of entry***, ***port of exit*** (see also s.v. PORT *noun*[1]). E20. ▸**c** *ELECTRICITY*. A terminal where a signal enters or leaves a network or device, esp. each of a pair or set through which an equal current flows. Freq. with preceding numeral adjective. M20. ▸**d** *COMPUTING*. A socket or aperture in an electronic circuit or computer network where connections can be made to allow passage of information to or from peripheral equipment; an aperture where a disk etc. may be inserted. M20.

> **2** R. H. DANA We were so near as to count the ports on her side. D. M. DESOUTTER Two large gun ports are visible. **3** E. HARTLEY EDWARDS The mouth-piece . . might be fitted with a very high port. V. GRISSOM Before I sank I had not closed the air inlet port in . . my suit.

port /pɔːt/ *noun*[4]. ME.
[Old & mod. French, formed as PORT *verb*[1].]
▸ **I 1 a** The manner in which a person bears himself or herself; external deportment; carriage, bearing, mien. Also (*rare*), dignified or stately bearing. ME. ▸**b** *fig.* Bearing or purport of a matter. *arch.* M16.
2 a Style of living, *esp.* one that is grand or expensive. Also, social position, station. Now *rare* or *obsolete*. L15. ▸†**b** *transf.* A retinue (as indicative of a splendid style of living). M16–E17.

> **1a** WORDSWORTH His port, Which once had been erect and open, now Was stooping and contracted. L. STRACHEY She rose . . advancing upon the platform with regal port.

▸ **II 3** A thing that is used to carry something; *spec.* †(*a*) a socket for the butt of a lance; (*b*) a frame for holding wicks in candle-making. M16.
†**4** The action of carrying something; a fee for this; postage, carriage. Only in 17.
5 *MILITARY*. The position required by the order 'port arms!' (see PORT *verb*[1] 2). M19.

> **6** *Survival Weaponry* Resist the temptation of carrying the gun at high or low port.

port /pɔːt/ *noun*[5] & *adjective*. M16.
[Prob. orig. the side turned towards the port (PORT *noun*[1]) or place of loading cargo.]
▸ **A** *noun*. The left-hand side (looking forward) of a ship or aircraft. Opp. ***starboard***. M16.

> J. CLEARY I eased the rudder to port . . the plane responded.

▸ **B** *attrib.* or as *adjective*. Situated on or turned towards the left-hand side (looking forward) of a ship or aircraft. M19.
bring the port tacks aboard, ***have the port tacks aboard***, ***on the port tack***: see TACK *noun*[1].

port /pɔːt/ *noun*[6]. L17.
[from *Oporto* a city in Portugal, the chief port of shipment for that country's wines.]
A strong sweet dark-red (occas. brown or white) fortified wine of Portugal. Also, a drink of port; a glass used for port.

> R. FRAME We lunched late, on partridge and port. ***ruby port***, ***tawny port***, etc.

¶ See also PORT-WINE.

port /pɔːt/ *noun*[7]. *Scot.* E18.
[Gaelic & Irish = tune.]
A lively tune, a catch, an air.

port /pɔːt/ *noun*[8]. *Austral. colloq.* L19.
[Abbreviation of PORTMANTEAU *noun*.]
A portmanteau, a suitcase, a travelling bag. Also (*gen.*), a bag (freq. with specifying word).

> D. HEWETT In one hand his leather port holding his working clothes.

port /pɔːt/ *verb*[1] *trans*. M16.
[Old & mod. French *porter* from Latin *portare* bear, carry, from *portus* PORT *noun*[1].]
1 Carry, bear, convey, bring. Now *rare* in *gen.* sense. M16.
2 *MILITARY*. Carry or hold (a pike etc.) with both hands; *spec.* carry (a rifle or other weapon) diagonally across and close to the body with the barrel or blade near the left shoulder (freq. in *imper.* in ***port arms!***). E17.
3 *COMPUTING*. Transfer (a piece of software) from one machine or system to another, esp. with little or no alteration. L20.
Comb.: **port arms** (the position required by) a command to port one's rifle etc.

port /pɔːt/ *verb*[2] *trans*. M16.
[from PORT *noun*[3].]
†**1** Provide or shut in with a gate. M16–E17.
2 *CURLING*. Play (a stone) through an opening between other stones. Cf. PORT *noun*[3] 4b. M19.

port /pɔːt/ *verb*[3]. L16.
[from PORT *noun*[5].]
NAUTICAL. **1** *verb trans. & intrans*. Put or turn (the helm of a ship) to the port or left side. L16.
2 *verb intrans*. Of a ship: turn or go to the port or left side. L19.

porta /ˈpɔːtə/ *noun*. LME.
[mod. Latin from Latin = gate.]
ANATOMY. **1** An opening in an organ at which major blood-vessels enter; *spec.* = ***porta hepatis*** below. LME.
2 The portal vein. Now *rare*. LME.
Phrases: ***porta hepatis*** /ˈhɛpətɪs/ [= of the liver] the transverse fissure of the liver, through which pass various major vessels, nerves, and ducts.

porta- /ˈpɔːtə/ *combining form*.
[from PORTABLE.]
Forming names (often proprietary) of movable or portable objects, as ***Portakabin***, ***Portaloo***, etc.

port-a-beul /pɔːʃtəˈbiːəl/ *noun*. *Scot.* Also **puirt-** /puəʃt-/. Pl. **puirt-**. E20.
[Gaelic, lit. 'music from mouth']
A quick lively tune of Lowland Scottish origin to which Gaelic words of a quick repetitive nature have been added.

portable /ˈpɔːtəb(ə)l/ *adjective & noun.* LME.
[Old & mod. French, or late Latin *portabilis*, from *portare* bear, carry: see PORT *verb*[1], -ABLE.]
▶**A** *adjective.* **1** Able to be carried by hand or on the person; easily moved, carried, or conveyed. Also, (of a piece of apparatus, a device, etc.) of a form smaller and lighter than usual, so as to be easily carried about. LME. ▸**b** *spec.* Of a normally gaseous or liquid substance: liquefied or solidified so as to be more conveniently carried or transported. M18. ▸**c** Of a building etc.: temporary, able to be dismantled and rebuilt elsewhere. L18. ▸**d** Of a right, privilege, etc.: able to be transferred or adapted in changed circumstances; *spec.* (of a pension) transferable between or independent of individual employers. M20. ▸**e** COMPUTING. Of software: not restricted to one machine or system; able to be transferred from one machine or system to another. L20.
†**2** Bearable, tolerable, endurable. LME–M17.
†**3** Of a river etc.: capable of carrying ships or boats; navigable. Only in 17.

📖 **1** J. HERSEY Carrying all the portable things from his church. ***portable computer***, ***portable radio***, ***portable television***, ***portable typewriter***, etc.

▶**B** *noun.* That which is portable; a portable object, as a television, typewriter, etc. L19.
■ **portaˈbility** *noun* M17. **portableness** *noun* E18. **portably** *adverb* M20.

portacabin *noun* var. of PORTAKABIN.

portacaval /pɔːtəˈkeɪv(ə)l/ *adjective.* Also **porto-**. M20.
[from PORTAL *adjective* + CAVA + -AL[1].]
MEDICINE. Designating an anastomosis between the portal vein and one of the venae cavae, esp. an artificial one made to relieve portal hypertension.

portage /ˈpɔːtɪdʒ, *in senses 4, 4b also* pɔːˈtɑːʒ/ *noun*[1]. LME.
[French, formed as PORT *verb*[1]: see -AGE. Cf. PORTLEDGE.]
1 The action or work of carrying or transporting something; carriage. LME. ▸†**b** That which is carried or transported; cargo, freight, baggage. LME–M17. ▸**c** The cost of carriage; porterage. *obsolete* exc. *Hist.* L15.
†**2** NAUTICAL. The burden of a vessel; tonnage. LME–E18.
†**3** In full ***mariner portage***, ***mariner's portage***. A mariner's venture, consisting of freight or cargo, which he could carry on board, either instead of or as part of his wages; the space allowed to a mariner for this. E16–M19.
4 The carrying or transporting of boats and goods between two navigable waters. L17. ▸**b** A place where this is necessary. L17.

📖 **4** J. MACAULAY The custom to run the boats down the rapids . . to save . . portage.

†**portage** *noun*[2]. *rare* (Shakes.). Only in L16.
[from PORT *noun*[3] + -AGE.]
Provision of ports or portholes.

portage /ˈpɔːtɪdʒ, pɔːˈtɑːʒ/ *verb trans. & intrans.* M19.
[from PORTAGE *noun*[1].]
Carry or transport (boats, goods, etc.) over land between navigable waters; travel overland with boats, goods, etc., between (navigable waters).

†**portague** *noun.* M16–M17.
[App. a false sing. of PORTUGUESE, taken as a pl.]
A Portuguese gold coin current in the 16th cent.; a cruzado.

portail /ˈpɔːteɪl/ *noun.* L15.
[French, lit. 'façade of a church', alt. of Old French *portal* from medieval Latin *portale* (see PORTAL *noun*[1] with which *portail* has been confused in French and English).]
= PORTAL *noun*[1] 1.

Portainer /pɔːˈteɪnə/ *noun.* M20.
[from PORT *noun*[1] or *verb*[1] + CON)TAINER.]
(Proprietary name for) a kind of crane designed for the movement of freight containers.

Portakabin /ˈpɔːtəkabɪn/ *noun.* Also **portacabin**. M20.
[from PORTA- + CABIN *noun.*]
(Proprietary name for) a portable room or building.

portal /ˈpɔːt(ə)l/ *noun*[1]. LME.
[Old French from medieval Latin *portale* use as noun of neut. of *portalis* (in medieval Latin = janitor), from Latin *porta* gate: see PORT *noun*[3], -AL[1].]
1 A door or gateway, esp. of stately or elaborate construction; an entrance, with surrounding parts, esp. of a large or magnificent building. Also, a natural entrance, as of a cave. LME. ▸†**b** A valve of the heart. Only in M17. ▸**c** ENGINEERING. A rigid structural frame consisting essentially of two uprights connected at the top by a third member; orig., such a frame forming the end of a truss bridge. L19. ▸**d** (The structural frame forming) the entrance to a tunnel. L19. ▸**e** MEDICINE. The place where a micro-organism, drug, etc., enters or leaves the system (chiefly in ***portal of entry***). Also, the area of the body where a beam of radiation enters or leaves it. Also called ***port***, ***port of entry***, ***port of exit***. E20.
†**2** A partitioned space within the doorway of a room, containing an inner door. Also, such a partition (sometimes a movable piece of furniture). E16–E18.
3 A lesser gate; a small gate. E18.
4 COMPUTING. A website providing a directory of links to other sites and often a search engine and other facilities, used as a starting-point for access to the Internet. Also ***portal site***. L20.

📖 **1** MILTON Through Heav'n, That open'd wide her blazing Portals. K. CLARK When we pass through the portal into the interior. *fig.*: J. LONDON Every portal to success in literature is guarded by those watch-dogs.

Comb.: **portal bracing** (*a*) = sense 1c above; (*b*) the technique of using a portal frame; **portal crane** a crane mounted on a portal frame so that vehicles can pass below; **portal frame** = see sense 1c above; **portal strut** a horizontal member joining the tops of two uprights, esp. in a portal frame.
■ **portalled** *adjective* (*rare*) having a portal or portals M17.

portal /pɔːˈtɑːl, *foreign* porˈtal/ *noun*[2]. Pl. **-es** /-eɪz, *foreign* -ɛs/. M19.
[Spanish = porch, portico, piazza.]
sing. & in *pl.* (treated as *sing.*). A veranda, portico, or arcade in a Spanish-American building.

portal /ˈpɔːt(ə)l/ *adjective.* E17.
[mod. Latin *portalis*, from Latin *porta* PORT *noun*[3]: see -AL[1].]
ANATOMY. †**1** Of the nature of a door or gate; *spec.* designating the valves of the heart. Only in E17.
2 Of, pertaining to, or designating the *porta hepatis* or transverse fissure of the liver, or structures associated with it. M19.
2 hepatic portal vein the great vein formed by the union of the veins from the stomach, intestines, and spleen, conveying blood to the liver. **portal system** (*a*) the system of vessels consisting of the hepatic portal vein with its tributaries and branches; (*b*) any system of blood-vessels which has a capillary network at each end. **portal vein** = ***hepatic portal vein*** above. **renal portal vein** in some lower vertebrates, a vein conveying blood from other organs to the kidney.

portales *noun pl.* see PORTAL *noun*[2].

Portaloo /ˈpɔːtəluː/ *noun.* Also **p-**. M20.
[from PORTA- + LOO *noun*[4].]
(Proprietary name for) a portable building containing a water-closet or lavatory.

portamento /pɔːtəˈmɛntəʊ/ *noun.* Pl. **-ti** /-ti/. L18.
[Italian, lit. 'a carrying'.]
MUSIC. Gliding or moving from one note to another without a break in singing or in playing a trombone or a bowed stringed instrument, as a violin. Also, piano-playing of a style between legato and staccato.

portance /ˈpɔːt(ə)ns/ *noun. arch.* L16.
[French †*portance*, formed as PORT *verb*[1]: see -ANCE.]
Bearing, demeanour; behaviour. Cf. PORT *noun*[4].

portantina /portanˈtiːna, pɔːtanˈtiːnə/ *noun. rare.* Pl. ***-ne*** /-ne, -ni/. M18.
[Italian, from *portante* carrying, bearing + *-ina* dim. suffix.]
Chiefly *Hist.* In Italy, a sedan chair.

Porta Potti /ˈpɔːtəpɒti/. Also **Portapotty** & other vars. *noun phr.* M20.
[from PORTA- + POTTY *noun.*]
(Proprietary name for) a portable building containing a toilet. Also, (proprietary name for) a chemical toilet, or one connected to a holding tank, in a vehicle, boat, etc.

portas *noun* var. of PORTEOUS.

Portastudio /ˈpɔːtəstjuːdɪəʊ/ *noun.* Also **p-**. Pl. **-os**. L20.
[from PORTA- + STUDIO.]
AUDIO. (Proprietary name for) a portable multi-track sound recording and mixing desk.

portate /ˈpɔːtət/ *adjective.* M16.
[Latin *portatus* pa. pple of *portare* PORT *verb*[1]: see -ATE[2].]
HERALDRY. Represented in a sloping position, as if carried on the shoulder. Chiefly in ***cross portate***.

portatile /ˈpɔːtətɪl, -tʌɪl/ *adjective.* Now *rare.* L16.
[medieval Latin *portatilis* that may be carried, from Latin *portat-* pa. ppl stem of *portare* PORT *verb*[1]: see -ATILE.]
†**1** HERALDRY. = prec. Only in L16.
2 Esp. of an altar: portable, that can easily be carried. M17.

portative /ˈpɔːtətɪv/ *adjective & noun.* LME.
[Old & mod. French *portatif*, *-ive* app. alt. of *portatil*, formed as prec.: see -IVE.]
▶**A** *adjective.* **1** Portable; *spec.* designating a kind of small pipe-organ (cf. ***positive organ*** s.v. POSITIVE *adjective*). Now chiefly *Hist.* LME.
2 Having the function of carrying or supporting. L19.
▶**B** *noun.* A portative organ. Usu. in *pl.* *obsolete* exc. *Hist.* LME.

†**port-cocher** *noun* see PORTE-COCHÈRE.

port-crayon /pɔːtˈkreɪən/ *noun.* Also ***porte-crayon*** /pɔrt(ə)krɛjɔ̃ (*pl. same*)/. E18.
[French *porte-crayon*, from *porte-* stem of *porter* carry, PORT *verb*[1] + CRAYON *noun.*]
An instrument used to hold a crayon for drawing, usu. a metal tube split at the end with a sliding ring so as to secure the crayon.

portcullis /pɔːtˈkʌlɪs/ *noun & verb.* ME.
[Old French *porte coleice*, from *porte* door + *col(e)ice*, *coulice* fem. of *couleïs* gliding, sliding, from Proto-Romance from Latin *colare* filter. Cf. COULISSE.]
▶**A** *noun.* **1** A strong barrier in the form of a grating of wooden or iron bars, usu. suspended by chains above the gateway of a fortress etc., and able to be quickly released to slide down vertical grooves in the sides of the gateway and secure the entrance. ME.
2 A figure of a portcullis, as an ornament or a heraldic charge. LME.
3 (Usu. **P-**.) Orig., a person whose badge is a portcullis. Now *spec.*, one of the four pursuivants of the English College of Arms. LME.
4 A silver halfpenny issued in the reign of Queen Elizabeth I, with a portcullis on one side. *obsolete* exc. *Hist.* L16.

📖 **1** SIR W. SCOTT Up drawbridge, . . Warder, ho! Let the portcullis fall. A. SETON They went beneath the raised portcullis through massive walls.

▶**B** *verb trans.* Provide with a portcullis; close (as) with a portcullis. L16.
■ **portcullised** *adjective* (*a*) having a portcullis; closed (as) with a portcullis; (*b*) HERALDRY barred vertically and horizontally to create a grid or lattice resembling that of a portcullis: L16.

port de bras /pɔːr də bra/ *noun phr.* Pl. ***ports de bras*** (pronounced same). E20.
[French, lit. 'carriage of the arms'.]
BALLET. The action or manner of moving and posing the arms; any of a series of exercises designed to develop graceful movement and disposition of the arms.

port de voix /pɔːr də vwa/ *noun.* Pl. ***ports de voix*** (pronounced same). M18.
[French, lit. 'carrying of the voice'.]
MUSIC. Orig., a kind of appoggiatura. Now, a vocal portamento.

Port du Salut *noun phr.* var. of PORT SALUT.

Porte /pɔːt/ *noun.* E17.
[French (*la Sublime*) *Porte* (the exalted) gate translating Turkish official title of the central office of the Ottoman Government.]
Hist. More fully ***the Sublime Porte***, ***the Ottoman Porte***. The Ottoman court at Constantinople; *transf.* the Turkish government.

porte-bouquet /ˈpɔːtbʊkeɪ, -bəʊ-/ *noun.* M19.
[French, from *porte-* stem of *porter* carry, PORT *verb*[1] + BOUQUET.]
A device for holding a bouquet.

porte-cochère /pɔːtkəˈʃɛː, *foreign* pɔrtkɔʃɛːr (*pl. same*)/ *noun.* Orig. †**port-cocher**. L17.
[French, from *porte* PORT *noun*[3] + *cochère* fem. adjective from *coche* COACH *noun.*]
1 A gateway for carriages, leading into a courtyard. L17.
2 A covered area at the entrance to a building into which vehicles can be driven. Chiefly *US.* L19.

porte-crayon *noun* var. of PORT-CRAYON.

ported /ˈpɔːtɪd/ *adjective*[1]. E17.
[from PORT *noun*[3] + -ED[2].]
Provided with a port or ports. Freq. as 2nd elem. of comb.
double-ported, ***single-ported***, etc.

ported /ˈpɔːtɪd/ *ppl adjective*[2]. M17.
[from PORT *verb*[1] + -ED[1].]
MILITARY. Of a weapon: that has been ported.

portée /ˈpɔːteɪ, *foreign* pɔrte (*pl. same*)/ *noun.* Also **portee** /ˈpɔːtiː/ L19.
[French, formed as PORT *verb*[1].]
1 The importance or weight of a theory, an argument, etc.; the (far-reaching) consequences of an action or event. L19.
2 In handloom weaving, a specified number of threads grouped together to form the warp. E20.
3 MILITARY. A self-propelled vehicle on which an anti-tank gun can be mounted. M20.

portefeuille /pɔrtfœːj/ *noun.* Pl. pronounced same. L17.
[French, from *porte-* stem of *porter* carry, PORT *verb*[1] + *feuille* leaf, sheet. Cf. PORTFOLIO.]
= PORTFOLIO 1, 2.

porte-monnaie /ˈpɔːtmɒni/ *noun.* M19.
[French, from *porte-* stem of *porter* carry, PORT *verb*[1] + *monnaie* MONEY *noun.*]
A flat purse or pocketbook, esp. of leather.

Porteña *noun* see PORTEÑO.

Porteña *adjective & noun* see PORTEÑO.

portend /pɔːˈtɛnd/ *verb*[1] *trans.* LME.
[Latin *portendere*, from popular Latin *por-* for PRO-[1] + *tendere* stretch, TEND *verb*[2].]
1 Presage or foreshadow as an omen. LME.
2 Point to or indicate in advance; give warning of by natural means. L16.
†**3** Signify, symbolize. L16–L18.
4 Of a person: predict, forecast. *rare.* E17.
📖 **1** W. STYRON These signs in the heavens might portend some great happening. **2** H. KELLER The chill air portended a snowstorm. I. MURDOCH The black points upon his chin portended a dark and vigorous beard.

portend /pɔːˈtɛnd/ *verb*[2] *trans.* Now *rare* or *obsolete*. LME.
[Old French *portendre* stretch out, extend, formed as prec.]
†**1** Put forward or use as an excuse. *rare.* Only in LME.
2 Stretch out, extend (something). M17.

Porteño /porˈteɲo/ *adjective & noun.* Pl. of noun **-os** /-ɔs/. Fem. **-ña** /-ɲa/, pl. of noun **-s** /-s/. L19.
[Spanish, from *porta* PORT *noun*[1] (spec. the port of Buenos Aires): see below.]
(Of) a native or inhabitant of Buenos Aires, the capital of Argentina and (formerly) of the province of Buenos Aires.

portent /ˈpɔːt(ə)nt/ *noun.* L16.
[Latin *portentum*, from *portendere* PORTEND *verb*[1].]
1 That which portends or presages something about to happen, esp. something of a momentous or calamitous nature; an omen; a supernatural sign or revelation. L16. ▸**b** Significance for the future. *rare.* E18.
2 A prodigy, a marvel. E17.
📖 **1** G. LORD A cloud moved across the sun . . and the cave was dimmed. It was like a portent of evil. C. FRANCIS Even after receiving a forecast . . I still search the sky for weather portents. J. UGLOW He will hear the magic rap of the willow wand, portent of death. **b** POPE A mighty dragon shot, of dire portent.
■ †**portentive** *adjective* (*rare*) having the quality of portending L16–L18.

portentous /pɔːˈtɛntəs/ *adjective.* Also **-tuous** /-tjʊəs/, (esp. in sense 3) **-tious** /-ʃəs/. L15.
[Latin *portentosus*, formed as PORTENT: see -OUS, -IOUS, -UOUS.]
1 Of the nature of a portent; presaging an often calamitous event; ominous. L15.
2 Awesome, impressive; amazing, marvellous, extraordinary. M16.
3 [Infl. by PRETENTIOUS *adjective*.] Pompous, pretentious; overly important, significant. M20.
📖 **1** D. ACHESON The solemn and portentous look of an eminent physician about to impart grim news. **3** *Times* A portentious statement containing the whole truth about the meaning . . of life.
■ **portentously** *adverb* L16.

porteous /ˈpɔːtɪəs/ *noun.* Also **portas** /ˈpɔːtəs/, **-tess** /-tɪs/, & other vars. LME.
[Old French *portehors*, from *porte-* stem of *porter* carry, PORT *verb*[1] + *hors* out of doors. Cf. PORTUARY.]
Hist. **1** A portable breviary in the medieval Church. LME. ▸**b** *transf.* A manual (of some subject). E16.
2 SCOTS LAW (now *Hist.*). A list of the names of indicted offenders prepared by the Justice Clerk. Also ***porteous roll***. LME.

porter /ˈpɔːtə/ *noun*[1]. ME.
[Anglo-Norman, Old & mod. French *portier* from late Latin *portarius* from *porta*: see PORT *noun*[3], -ER[2].]
1 A person in charge of a door or gate, esp. at the entrance of a large building, a public institution, a castle, or a fortified town; a gatekeeper, a doorkeeper. Also, such a person who additionally deals with enquiries etc.; a caretaker. ME.
†**2** ANATOMY. The pyloric opening of the stomach. L16–E17.
📖 **1** DONNE Like a porter in a great house, ever nearest the door. *fig.*: E. HOPKINS God hath set that grim porter, Death. ***hall porter***, ***night porter***, etc. **porter's chair** a high-backed winged leather chair, orig. placed in a hallway for a porter or doorkeeper to sit in. **porter's lodge** a lodge for a porter at the gate of a castle, park, college, etc., formerly used as a place of punishment for servants and dependants.
■ **portership** *noun* (*a*) the office or occupation of a porter; (*b*) (with possess. adjective, as ***your portership*** etc.) a mock title of respect given to a porter: LME.

porter /ˈpɔːtə/ *noun*[2] *& verb.* ME.
[Old & mod. French *port(e)our* (mod. *porteur*) from medieval Latin *portator*, from *portat-* pa. ppl stem of *portare* bear, carry: see PORT *verb*[1], -ER[2], -OUR.]
▶ **A** *noun.* **1 a** A person employed to carry luggage etc., now esp. in a railway station, an airport, or a hotel. ME. ▸**b** *gen.* & *fig.* A person who or thing which carries or conveys something; a carrier. L16. ▸**c** *spec.* A person taken on to carry supplies etc. on a mountaineering expedition. M19. ▸**d** A hospital employee who moves equipment, trolleys, etc. Also ***hospital porter***. M20.
2 An appliance for lifting, carrying, or supporting something; *spec.* an iron bar attached to a usu. heavy object to be forged, by which the object may be moved into position. M16.
3 A dark-brown bitter beer brewed from malt partly charred or browned by drying at a high temperature, apparently made orig. for porters; a drink of this. M18.
4 WEAVING. = BEER *noun*[3]. *Scot.* M18.
📖 **1a** E. HEMINGWAY A porter carried Bill's bags in from the consigne. ***porter's knot***: see KNOT *noun*[1] 6.
▶ **B** *verb trans.* Carry, bear, or convey, esp. as a porter. E19.
■ **porterless** *adjective* without a porter or porters L17. **porterlike** *adjective* (*rare*) resembling a porter in manner, appearance, etc. L16. †**porterly** *adjective* of or (supposedly) characteristic of a porter; rude, vulgar, low: E17–M18.

porterage /ˈpɔːt(ə)rɪdʒ/ *noun*[1]. LME.
[from PORTER *noun*[2] + -AGE.]
The action or work of a porter or carrier of luggage etc.; carriage or transportation of goods, parcels, etc. Also, a charge for this; the personnel available for this.

porterage /ˈpɔːt(ə)rɪdʒ/ *noun*[2]. M18.
[from PORTER *noun*[1] + -AGE.]
The duty or occupation of a porter or doorkeeper. Also, the existence of the services of a porter or caretaker.

porteress *noun* var. of PORTRESS.

porterhouse /ˈpɔːtəhaʊs/ *noun.* Chiefly *N. Amer.* M18.
[from PORTER *noun*[2] 3 + HOUSE *noun*[1].]
1 *Hist.* A place where porter and other malt liquors were sold; a place where steaks, chops, etc., were served, a steak-house. M18.
2 In full ***porterhouse steak***. A large choice steak cut from between the sirloin and the tenderloin. E19.

portess *noun* var. of PORTEOUS.

porteur /pɔrtœːr/ *noun.* Pl. pronounced same. M20.
[French, lit. 'a person who carries'.]
BALLET. A male dancer whose role is (only) to lift and support a ballerina when she performs leaping or jumping movements.

portfire /ˈpɔːtfʌɪə/ *noun.* M17.
[Partial Anglicization of French *porte-feu*, from *porte-* stem of *porter* carry, PORT *verb*[1] + *feu* fire.]
A device used orig. for firing artillery, and now for firing rockets, igniting explosives in mining, etc.

portfolio /pɔːtˈfəʊlɪəʊ/ *noun.* Pl. **-os**. E18.
[Italian *portafogli*, from *porta* imper. of *portare* carry + *fogli* leaves, sheets of paper, pl. of *foglio* from Latin *folium* leaf. First elem. assim. to French PORTEFEUILLE.]
1 A case, usu. in the form of a large book-cover, for holding loose sheets of paper, drawings, maps, music, etc. E18.
2 Such a case containing the official documents of a State department. Hence, the office of a minister of State. M19.
3 The range of investments held by a company or an individual; a list of such investments. M20.
📖 **1** F. O'BRIEN I extracted it from the portfolio in which I kept my writings. A. DESAI Ribbon-bound portfolios of their verse. **2** H. WILSON The prime minister has to allocate . . the various ministerial portfolios. ***Minister without Portfolio***: see MINISTER *noun* 4a. **3** *European Investor* Mixed portfolios are popular, since they balance equity risk. *Independent* Stockbrokers would . . encourage their private clients to hold part of their portfolio in gilts.
Comb.: **portfolio investment** the purchase of stocks and shares in a variety of companies.

porthole /ˈpɔːthəʊl/ *noun.* L16.
[from PORT *noun*[3] + HOLE *noun*[1].]
1 a = PORT *noun*[3] 2. L16. ▸**b** A usu. round and glazed aperture in the side of a ship, aircraft, or spacecraft, for the admission of light or air. Also *transf.*, a small round window. L19.
2 a An aperture in the wall of a shearing shed through which a shearer passes a sheep after shearing. *Austral. & NZ.* L19. ▸**b** ARCHAEOLOGY. A hole in a slab or two adjacent slabs of stone, large enough to allow the passage of a body into a chambered tomb. M20.
3 A port in a steam engine. L19.
📖 **1a** W. FALCONER Full ninety brazen guns her port-holes fill. **b** D. WELCH I walked round the deck passing . . the portholes of Mrs Wright's cabin. WILBUR SMITH The Boeing began to roll forward. Manfred . . peered through the Perspex porthole.
■ **portholed** *adjective* having a porthole or portholes M20.

portia /ˈpɔːʃə/ *noun*[1]. M19.
[Tamil *pūvaracu*, from *pū* flower + *aracu* king.]
In the Indian subcontinent, a tropical evergreen tree, *Thespesia populnea*, of the mallow family, bearing yellow flowers which turn purple. Also ***portia tree***.

Portia /ˈpɔːʃə/ *noun*[2]. E20.
[The heroine of Shakespeare's *Merch. V.*]
(The type of) a female advocate or barrister.

portico /ˈpɔːtɪkəʊ/ *noun.* Pl. **-o(e)s**. E17.
[Italian from Latin *porticus* porch.]
1 ARCHITECTURE. A formal entrance to a classical temple, church, or other building, consisting of columns at regular intervals supporting a roof often in the form of a pediment; a covered walkway in this style; a colonnade. E17.
2 ***the Portico*** = STOA 1. Also called ***the Porch***. L18.
📖 **1** W. C. BRYANT A palace built with graceful porticos. *transf.*: J. THOMSON Now to the verdant portico of woods . . they walk.
■ **porticoed** *adjective* having a portico M17.

porticus /ˈpɔːtɪkəs/ *noun.* Pl. same, **-cuses**. E17.
[Latin: see prec.]
1 = prec. E17.
2 *spec.* in ARCHITECTURE. An addition on the north or south side of a church of the Anglo-Saxon period, resembling an aisle or transept and containing a chapel. L19.

portière /pɔrtjɛːr/ *noun.* Pl. pronounced same. M19.
[French, from *porte* door (see PORT *noun*[3]) + *-ière* (from Latin *-aria* -ARY[1]).]
A curtain hung over a door or doorway, as a screen or for ornament, or to prevent draughts.

portiforium /pɔːtɪˈfɔːrɪəm/ *noun.* Pl. **-ria** /-rɪə/. L19.
[medieval Latin = portable breviary.]
= PORTEOUS 1. Cf. PORTUARY.

porting /ˈpɔːtɪŋ/ *noun.* M20.
[from PORT *noun*[3] + -ING[1].]
The arrangement or size of the ports in an internal-combustion engine.

†**Portingale** *noun* see PORTUGAL.

portion /ˈpɔːʃ(ə)n/ *noun.* ME.
[Old French *porcion*, (also mod.) *portion* from Latin *portio(n-)*, attested first in *pro portione* in proportion.]
1 a The part of anything allotted or belonging to one person; a share. ME. ▸**b** A quantity or allowance of food allotted to, or enough for, one person. L15.
2 a The part or share of an estate given or descending by law to an heir. ME. ▸**b** A dowry. Cf. MARRIAGE ***portion***. E16.
3 That which is allotted to a person by providence; one's lot or destiny. ME.
4 A part of any whole; a specified or limited quantity or amount. ME. ▸**b** JUDAISM. The section of the Pentateuch or of the Prophets appointed to be read on a particular Sabbath or festival. L19.
†**5** The action of dividing; division, distribution. *rare.* LME–M17.
📖 **1b** *Which?* A portion of chips will increase the fat and calorie content. **2b** M. PATTISON Edward . . is to give the moderate portion of 10,000 marks. **4** H. JAMES A portion of the first half of the present century. R. FRAME The whole upper portion of the house . . tumbled into the street. S. QUINN Both . . devoted a large portion of their time to lecturing.
■ **portionable** *adjective* (*rare*) (*a*) proportional; (*b*) (of a woman) endowed with a marriage portion or dowry: LME. **portionless** *adjective* without a portion; dowerless: L18.

portion /ˈpɔːʃ(ə)n/ *verb trans.* ME.
[Old French *portionner* (medieval Latin *portionare*), formed as PORTION *noun*.]
1 Divide into portions or shares; apportion, share *out*. ME. ▸**b** Assign (*to*) as a due portion; allot; = APPORTION *verb* 1. M19.
†**2** Mix in due proportion; = APPORTION *verb* 3. *rare.* LME–E19.
3 Give a dowry to. E18.
📖 **1** L. MACNEICE I peel and portion A tangerine. S. ORBACH Laura's mother portioned out the amounts.

portional /ˈpɔːʃ(ə)n(ə)l/ *adjective. rare.* LME.
[Late Latin *portionalis* partial, from Latin *portio(n-)*: see PORTION *noun*, -AL[1].]
Of a portion or part; partial.
■ **portionally** *adverb* E17.

portionary /ˈpɔːʃ(ə)n(ə)ri/ *noun. obsolete* exc. *Hist.* M16.
[medieval Latin *portionarius* a canon's deputy in a cathedral, from *portio(n-)*: see PORTION *noun*, -ARY[1].]
ECCLESIASTICAL. = PORTIONIST 2.

portioner /ˈpɔːʃ(ə)nə/ *noun.* L15.
[from PORTION *noun, verb* + -ER[1].]
1 SCOTS LAW. The proprietor of a small piece of land forming a portion of a larger piece which has been broken up usu. among joint heirs; a petty laird. L15.
†**2** ECCLESIASTICAL. = PORTIONIST 2. L17–M19.
1 heir-portioner (*a*) = ***heiress-portioner*** below; (*b*) the son or other male representative of an heiress-portioner. **heiress-portioner** any of two or more heirs female who inherit equally in default of heirs male.

portionist /ˈpɔːʃ(ə)nɪst/ *noun.* M16.
[medieval Latin *portionista* (in Anglo-Latin postmaster at Merton (see sense 1 below)), from Latin *portio(n-)*: see PORTION *noun*, -IST.]
1 A student in a university college, receiving or entitled to receive a defined portion or allowance of

food, either (*Hist.*, at St Andrews) as a boarder, or (*spec.* at Merton College, Oxford) as the recipient of a benefaction. **M16.**

2 *ECCLESIASTICAL.* Each of two or more incumbents who share the duties and revenues of a benefice. **M18.**

Port Jackson /pɔːt ˈdʒaks(ə)n/ *noun.* **L18.**
[The harbour of Sydney, Australia.]
Used *attrib.* in the names of plants and animals native to SE Australia.
Port Jackson fig a small fig, *Ficus rubiginosa*, with inedible fruits. **Port Jackson pine** a cypress pine, *Callitris rhomboidea*, with pendulous branches. **Port Jackson shark** a small bullhead shark of the genus *Heterodontus*, esp. *H. portusjacksoni*, which is light brown with black markings. **Port Jackson willow** *S. Afr.* a large yellow-flowered leguminous shrub, *Acacia cyanophylla*, introduced into S. Africa from Australia and now naturalized.

Portland /ˈpɔːtlənd/ *noun.* **M19.**
[Isle of *Portland*, a peninsula in Dorset, a county of SW England.]
Used *attrib.* to designate things originating in or associated with the Isle of Portland.
Portland arrowroot *Hist.* arrowroot made from the starchy tubers of *Arum maculatum* or *A. italicum*. **Portland cement** a hydraulic cement manufactured from chalk and clay which when hard resembles Portland stone in colour. **Portland oolite** a limestone of the Upper Jurassic, quarried as Portland stone. **Portland powder** (chiefly *Hist.*) a herbal remedy for gout. **Portland spurge** a spurge of sandy coasts, *Euphorbia portlandica*. **Portland stone** a valuable limestone quarried in the Isle of Portland and used in building.
■ **Portˈlandian** *adjective* (*GEOLOGY*) of, pertaining to, or designating the subdivision of the Upper Jurassic in which Portland oolite occurs **L19.**

portlandite /ˈpɔːtləndʌɪt/ *noun.* **M20.**
[from prec. + -ITE[1].]
MINERALOGY. A form of calcium hydroxide that occurs as minute colourless hexagonal plates, esp. in Portland cement.

Portland Place /pɔːtlənd ˈpleɪs/ *noun.* **M20.**
[A street in London.]
The BBC, whose headquarters are in Portland Place.

port-last /ˈpɔːtlast/ *noun.* Now *rare* or *obsolete.* **E17.**
[Origin unkn. Cf. PORTOISE.]
NAUTICAL. The gunwale of a ship; the level of a ship's gunwale.

†**portledge** *noun. US.* **M17–L18.**
[Alt. of PORTAGE *noun*[1].]
NAUTICAL. = PORTAGE *noun*[1] 3.

portlet /ˈpɔːtlɪt/ *noun.* **L16.**
[from PORT *noun*[1] + -LET.]
A little port; a creek.

portly /ˈpɔːtli/ *adjective.* **L15.**
[from PORT *noun*[4] + -LY[1].]
1 Stately, dignified; handsome, majestic; imposing. **L15.**
2 Stout, corpulent. **L16.**

> 📖 **2** A. S. BYATT A little rounded by age, still this side of portly.

■ **portliness** *noun* **M16.**

portman /ˈpɔːtmən/ *noun.* Pl. **-men. OE.**
[from PORT *noun*[2] + MAN *noun*.]
Hist. **1** Orig., a citizen of a town; a burgess, a burgher. Later, any of a select number of citizens chosen to administer the affairs of any of certain boroughs. **OE.**
2 A citizen or inhabitant of the Cinque Ports. **M17.**

portmanteau /pɔːtˈmantəʊ/ *noun & adjective.* **M16.**
[French *portemanteau* from *porte-* stem of *porter* carry, PORT *verb*[1] + *manteau* MANTLE *noun*. Cf. POCKMANTY.]
▶ **A** *noun.* Pl. **-s**, **-x** /-z/.
1 A case or bag for carrying clothing etc. when travelling, *esp.* one made of stiff leather and hinged at the back so as to open into two equal parts. **M16.**
2 A rack or arrangement of pegs for hanging clothes on. Now *rare.* **E18.**

> 📖 **1** SMOLLETT Their trunks and portmanteaus must be carried to the Custom-house.

▶ **B** *attrib.* or as *adjective.* **1** Of a word, expression, etc.: consisting of a blend, both in spelling and meaning, of two other words. Of a description, expression, etc.: of general or widespread application. **L19.**
2 *LINGUISTICS.* Designating a morph which represents two morphemes simultaneously. **M20.**

> 📖 **1** *Punch* We must 'brunch'. Truly an excellent portmanteau word. *Listener* 'Culture.' This portmanteau word has been indispensable.

portmanteau /pɔːtˈmantəʊ/ *verb trans. & intrans.* **E20.**
[from prec.]
Combine, esp. to form one word.

portmantologism /pɔːtmənˈtɒlədʒɪz(ə)m/ *noun. rare.* **L19.**
[from PORTMANTEAU *adjective* + -OLOG(Y + -ISM.]
A portmanteau word or expression.

portmote /ˈpɔːtməʊt/ *noun. obsolete* exc. *Hist.* **ME.**
[from PORT *noun*[1], *noun*[2] + MOOT *noun*[1].]
1 The court of a borough. **ME.**
†**2** The court of a port (PORT *noun*[1] 2). **L16–M18.**

porto /ˈpɔrto/ *noun.* Pl. **-os** /-ɔs/. **M19.**
[Portuguese *pôrto* port wine.]
= PORT *noun*[6].

portobello /pɔːtəˈbɛləʊ/ *noun.* Pl. **-os. L20.**
[Perh. alt. of Italian *pratarolo* meadow mushroom, from *prato* meadow.]
More fully ***portobello mushroom***. A large mature mushroom with an open flat cap.

portocaval *adjective* var. of PORTACAVAL.

†**portoise** *noun.* **E18–M19.**
[Origin unkn.]
NAUTICAL. = PORT-LAST.

portolan /ˈpɔːtəlan/ *noun.* Also **portolano** /pɔːtəˈlɑːnəʊ/, pl. **-os. M19.**
[Italian *portolano*, from PORT *noun*[1].]
A book of sailing directions, describing harbours, sea-coasts, etc., and illustrated with charts.

portosystemic /ˌpɔːtəʊsɪˈstɛmɪk, -ˈstiːmɪk/ *adjective.* **M20.**
[from PORTAL *adjective* + -O- + SYSTEMIC.]
SURGERY. Designating an anastomosis between the portal vein and a systemic vein.

portrait /ˈpɔːtrɪt/ *noun, adjective, & adverb.* **M16.**
[French, use as noun of pa. pple of Old French *portraire*: see PORTRAY *verb*.]
▶ **A** *noun.* **1 a** A drawing, painting, or other delineation of an object, scene, etc.; *gen.* a picture, a design. Now *rare* or *obsolete.* **M16.** ▸**b** *spec.* A representation or delineation of a person or animal, esp. of the face or head and shoulders, made by drawing, painting, photography, etc.; a likeness. **L16.** ▸†**c** A solid image, a statue, an effigy. **L16–M17.**
2 The action or art of making a portrait; portraiture. **L16.**
3 a A thing which or person who represents, typifies, or resembles another; an image, a representation, a likeness. **L16.** ▸**b** A verbal picture or representation; a graphic or vivid description. **L16.**

> 📖 **1b** M. MUGGERIDGE There were portraits of all the Austrian Emperors.

Comb.: **portrait-bust** a bust giving an exact, as opp. to an idealized, likeness; **portrait-gallery** a gallery containing a collection of portraits, the collection itself; **portrait-lens** a compound photographic lens adapted for taking portraits; **portrait-painter** a painter of portraits; **portrait-stone** a lasque or flat diamond used to cover a miniature portrait.
▶ **B** *adjective & adverb.* Of a page, book, etc., or the manner in which it is set or printed: upright; having or in a rectangular shape with the height greater than the width. Opp. LANDSCAPE *adjective & adverb.* **E20.**

portrait /ˈpɔːtrɪt/ *verb*[1] *trans.* Now *rare* or *obsolete.* **M16.**
[Earliest as pa. pple *portraited*, app. an extended form of †*portrait* pa. pple of PORTRAY *verb*: see prec.]
1 Make a portrait, picture, or image of; = PORTRAY *verb* 1. **M16.**
†**2** Draw or make (a picture, image, or figure); = PORTRAY *verb* 1b. **M16–M17.**
3 *fig.* Represent or describe graphically. Also foll. by *out*. Cf. PORTRAY *verb* 3b, 4. **L16.**

†**portrait** *verb*[2] *pa. t. & pple*: see PORTRAY *verb*.

portraitist /ˈpɔːtrɪtɪst/ *noun.* **M19.**
[from PORTRAIT *noun* + -IST.]
A person who takes or paints portraits; *esp.* a portrait-painter.

portrait parlé /pɔrtrɛ parle/ *noun phr.* Pl. **-s -s** (pronounced same). **E20.**
[French = spoken portrait.]
A detailed chiefly anthropometric description of a person's physical characteristics, esp. of the type invented by Bertillon (see BERTILLONAGE) and used in the identification of criminals.

portraiture /ˈpɔːtrɪtʃə/ *noun & verb.* **LME.**
[Old French, from pa. pple *portrait*: see PORTRAIT *noun*, PORTRAY *verb*, -URE.]
▶ **A** *noun.* **1** The action or art of portraying; delineation; portrayal. **LME.**
2 A figure or delineation of a person or thing; a picture, a drawing, a portrait. Also, portraits collectively. **LME.** ▸†**b** A solid image, a statue. **M16–E18.**
3 An image, a representation; a mental image, an idea. Cf. PORTRAIT *noun* 3a. **LME.**
4 a The action or art of portraying in words; graphic description. **LME.** ▸**b** A verbal picture or representation; a graphic description. **E17.**
5 Form, likeness, appearance. Now *rare* or *obsolete.* **LME.**

> 📖 **1** *Edinburgh Review* Portraiture rose to its highest excellence as . . sculpture faded. **2** J. ROSENBERG Rembrandt's portraiture comprises at least two-thirds of his painted work. **4a** J. R. SEELEY A tempting subject for literary portraiture. **b** C. CLARKE Shakespeare's portraiture of John of Gaunt.

▶ **B** *verb trans.* Make a portraiture or portrait of, portray. Now *rare* or *obsolete.* **L16.**

portray /ˈpɔːtreɪ/ *noun. rare.* **LME.**
[from the verb.]
The action of portraying something or someone; portrayal. Also, a portrait, a picture.

portray /pɔːˈtreɪ/ *verb.* Pa. t. & pple †**portrait**, **portrayed. ME.**
[Old French *portrai-* stem of *portraire*, from *por-* (from Latin PRO-[1]) + *traire* draw (from Proto-Romance alt. of Latin *trahere*). The form †*portrait* is from Old French.]
1 *verb trans.* Represent (an object) by a drawing, painting, carving, etc.; make a portrait, picture, or image of; delineate, picture, depict. **ME.** ▸†**b** Make (a picture, image, or figure) by drawing, painting, carving, etc. **LME–E17.** ▸†**c** *verb intrans.* Make a drawing, picture, or statue. **LME–M16.**
†**2** *verb trans.* Paint or adorn (a surface) *with* a picture or figure. **LME–M17.**
3 *verb trans.* †**a** Form a mental image of; imagine, fancy. **LME–L18.** ▸**b** Represent, esp. dramatically. **L18.**
4 *verb trans.* Represent in words; describe vividly or graphically. **LME.**

> 📖 **1** *Bazaar Exchange & Mart* The painting is . . full . . of the spirit of the scene portrayed. **3b** J. KIRKUP The noble movements . . portrayed a Maranaw warrior. **4** R. C. TRENCH In the Gospels the lively representation of our Lord portrayed for us.

■ **portrayable** *adjective* **M19.** **portrayal** *noun* the action or product of portraying; delineation, picturing; a picture, a portrait: **M19.** **portrayer** *noun* a person who portrays something; a delineator: **ME.** **portrayment** *noun* (*rare*) = PORTRAYAL **E19.**

portreeve /ˈpɔːtriːv/ *noun.*
[Old English *portġerēfa*, from PORT *noun*[2] + *ġerēfa* REEVE *noun*[1].]
1 Orig., the ruler or chief officer of a town or borough, after the Norman Conquest often identified with or of the status of a mayor; a borough-reeve. Later, an officer subordinate to a mayor; a bailiff. **OE.**
2 An official in charge of a port (PORT *noun*[1] 2). **E17.**

portress /ˈpɔːtrɪs/ *noun.* Also **porteress** /ˈpɔːt(ə)rɪs/. **ME.**
[from PORTER *noun*[1] + -ESS[1].]
A female porter; a woman who acts as porter or door-keeper, esp. in a nunnery.

Port-Royalist /pɔːtˈrɔɪəlɪst/ *noun & adjective.* **E18.**
[from *Port-Royal* (see below) + -IST.]
▶ **A** *noun.* A member or adherent of the community of Port-Royal, a lay 17th-cent. community known for its educational work and its connection with Jansenism, housed in a convent near Versailles (Port-Royal des Champs). **E18.**
▶ **B** *adjective.* Of or pertaining to Port-Royal or the Port-Royalists. **M19.**

Port Salut /pɔː səˈluː/ *noun.* Also **Port du Salut** /ˌpɔː dʊ səˈluː/. **L19.**
[See below.]
A pale mild cheese of a type first produced at Port Salut, a Trappist monastery in NW France.

ports de bras, ***ports de voix*** *noun phrs.* pls. of PORT DE BRAS, PORT DE VOIX.

port-sider /ˈpɔːtsʌɪdə/ *noun. N. Amer. colloq.* **E20.**
[from PORT *noun*[5] + SIDER *noun*.]
A left-handed person.

portsman /ˈpɔːtsmən/ *noun.* Pl. **-men. E17.**
[from PORT *noun*[1] + -'S[1] + MAN *noun*.]
A citizen or inhabitant of one of the Cinque Ports. Usu. in *pl.*

portuary /ˈpɔːtjʊəri/ *noun. arch.* **M19.**
[Alt. of PORTEOUS, perh. after *breviary*.]
= PORTEOUS 1. Cf. PORTIFORIUM.

Portugaise /pɔrtygɛːz, ˈpɔːtjʊgeɪz, ˈpɔːtʃʊ- (pl. of noun same)/ *noun & adjective.* **M19.**
[French (fem.) = Portuguese.]
▶ **A** *noun.* **1** *COOKERY.* ***à la Portugaise***, according to Portuguese style, *spec.* with tomato, onion, or garlic. **M19.**
2 = ***Portuguese oyster*** s.v. PORTUGUESE *adjective.* **M20.**
▶ **B** *adjective. COOKERY.* Of food: prepared *à la Portugaise*. **M20.**

Portugal /ˈpɔːtjʊg(ə)l, ˈpɔːtʃʊg(ə)l/ *noun.* Also (earlier) †**Portingale. L15.**
[A country in the western part of the Iberian peninsula in SW Europe, earlier *Portucal* from medieval Latin *Portus Cale* the port of Gaya, Oporto.]
†**1** A native or inhabitant of Portugal; a Portuguese. **L15–E18.**
†**2** The Portuguese language. **L16–L17.**
3 ***Portugal laurel***, an ornamental evergreen shrub, *Prunus lusitanica*, of Spain and Portugal, allied to the cherry laurel but with serrate leaves. **L18.**

Portuguee /pɔːtjʊˈgiː, pɔːtʃʊˈgiː/ *noun. US.* **M19.**
[Repr. a false sing. of PORTUGUESE, taken as a pl.]
= PORTUGUESE *noun* 2.

Portuguese /pɔːtjʊˈgiːz, pɔːtʃʊˈgiːz/ *noun & adjective*. L16.
[Portuguese *Portuguez*, in medieval Latin *Portugalensis* formed as PORTUGAL + -ESE.]
▶ **A** *noun*. Pl. same, †**-gueses**.
†**1** = PORTAGUE. L16–M17.
2 A native or inhabitant of Portugal, a country in the western part of the Iberian peninsula in SW Europe. L16.
3 The Romance language of Portugal and its territories, and of Brazil, related to but clearly distinct from Spanish. E17.
▶ **B** *adjective*. Of or pertaining to Portugal, its people, or its language; originating in or associated with Portugal. M17.
Portuguese man-of-war: see MAN-OF-WAR 5. **Portuguese oyster** an oyster, *Crassostrea angulata*, with an irregular rounded shell, native to Portugal but cultivated elsewhere, esp. in France. **Portuguese parliament** *Nautical slang* a discussion in which many speak at once and few listen; a hubbub.

portulac /ˈpɔːtjʊlak, -tʃʊ-/ *noun*. Now *rare*. Also **-ack**, (earlier) †**-ace**. LME.
[Latin PORTULACA: cf. Old French *portulache*, *-lague*.]
Purslane, *Portulaca oleracea*.

portulaca /pɔːtjʊˈleɪkə, -tʃʊ-, -ˈlakə/ *noun*. M16.
[mod. Latin (see below), use as genus name of Latin = purslane.]
Any of various succulent, bright-flowered, chiefly tropical plants of the genus *Portulaca* (family Portulacaceae), which includes the pot-herb purslane, *P. oleracea*, and the sun plant, *P. grandiflora*.

†**portulace**, **portulack** *nouns* see PORTULAC.

portunal /ˈpɔːtjʊn(ə)l, ˈpɔːtʃʊ-/ *noun*. M19.
[German, app. from Latin *Portunalis* belonging to *Portunus* god of harbours. Cf. OPPORTUNE.]
An organ-stop with a wooden or metal pipe, producing an open flute tone. Also ***portunal-flute***.

port-wine /ˈpɔːtwʌɪn/ *noun*. L17.
[from PORT *noun*[6] + WINE *noun*.]
= PORT *noun*[6].
Comb.: **port-wine birthmark** = *port-wine mark* below; **port-wine magnolia** *Austral.* an Asian evergreen shrub, *Michelia figo*, of the magnolia family, bearing scented reddish-brown or purple flowers; **port-wine mark**, **port-wine spot**, **port-wine stain** a kind of large red birthmark, a persistent haemangioma or naevus, esp. on the face.
■ **port-winer** *noun* a habitual drinker of port E20. **port-winey** *adjective* resembling or reminiscent of port; of the dark red colour of port: L19.

porty /ˈpɔːti/ *adjective*. M19.
[from PORT *noun*[6] + -Y[1].]
Like or relating to port(-wine); affected by or habitually drinking port.

porule /ˈpɒrjuːl/ *noun*. *rare*. M19.
[from PORE *noun* + -ULE.]
BIOLOGY. A minute pore, esp. within a coral.
■ **porulose**, **porulous** *adjectives* having many minute pores M19.

pory /ˈpɔːri/ *adjective*. *obsolete* exc. *dial.* M16.
[from PORE *noun* + -Y[1].]
Full of or containing pores; porous.

POS *abbreviation*.
Point-of-sale.

pos /pɒz/ *adjective*[1]. *colloq.* E18.
[Abbreviation.]
Positive.

> 📖 R. CRAWFORD 'Are you sure you weren't spotted?' 'Pos'

pos *adjective*[2] var. of POSS *adjective*.

posable /ˈpəʊzəb(ə)l/ *adjective*. Also **poseable**. E20.
[from POSE *verb*[1] + -ABLE.]
Able to be posed.

posada /pəˈsɑːdə, *foreign* poˈsaða/ *noun*. M18.
[Spanish, from *posar* to lodge.]
1 In Spain and Spanish-speaking countries: an inn or place of accommodation for travellers. M18.
2 In Mexico: each of a series of visits traditionally paid to different friends before Christmas, representing Mary and Joseph's search for a lodging in Bethlehem. M20.

posaune /pəˈzaʊnə/ *noun*. Pl. **-nen** /-nən/, **-nes** /-nɪz/. E18.
[German, ult. from Old French *buisine* from Latin *buccina* trumpet.]
MUSIC. **1** A trombone. E18.
2 An organ reed-stop resembling a trombone in tone. M19.

posca /ˈpɒskə/ *noun*. *obsolete* exc. *Hist.* M16.
[Latin = a drink, from stem *po-* to drink: cf. *esca* food.]
A drink of vinegar and water, or of wine diluted with this.

†**pose** *noun*[1]. Latterly *dial.* OE–E19.
[Old English *gepos* from Brittonic base of Welsh, Cornish *pas*, *pâz*, Breton *paz*.]
A cold in the head, catarrh.

pose /pəʊz/ *noun*[2]. *obsolete* exc. *Scot.* LME.
[from French *poser* POSE *verb*[1].]
A secret store of money etc.; a hoard, a hidden treasure.

pose /pəʊz/ *noun*[3]. L18.
[French, from *poser* POSE *verb*[1].]
1 A resting-place on a portage; the distance between two such rests. *N. Amer. obsolete* exc. *Hist.* L18.
2 An attitude or posture of (a part of) the body, *esp.* one deliberately adopted for effect, or by a model, performer, etc., for artistic purposes. E19. ▸**b** *fig.* An attitude of mind or conduct, *esp.* one assumed for effect; a pretence. L19.
3 DOMINOES. = DOWN *noun*[3] 5. M19.

> 📖 **2** M. FONTEYN He will end a ballet with the dancers in a uniform pose, all kneeling. P. FITZGERALD Head a little to one side in a pose of marked attention. E. LEONARD She threw her arms out and struck a pose. R. BERTHOUD The model held a pose for an hour or two. **b** G. GREENE She was compelled to . . wear a pose of cheerfulness. M. IGNATIEFF The atheist's serenity was only a pose . . to confound believers.

pose /pəʊz/ *verb*[1]. ME.
[Old & mod. French *poser* from late Latin *pausare* cease, PAUSE *verb*: in Proto-Romance this verb became confused with, and took over the usual senses of, Latin *ponere* to place (pa. t. *posui*, pa. pple *positum*).]
1 *verb trans.* Put forward as a proposal or as information; (foll. by *as*) state to be. Now usu., present for an answer or solution, or as requiring remedial or evasive action; raise (a question or problem), offer (a threat). ME. ▸†**b** Usu. with obj. clause: assume for argument's sake. LME–E16.
†**2** *verb trans.* Place, put in a certain location. Only in LME.
3 *verb trans.* Place in a certain attitude or position, esp. to be painted or photographed; cause to adopt a certain pose. E19.
4 *verb intrans.* **a** Assume a certain pose; place oneself in position, esp. for artistic purposes. M19. ▸**b** Present oneself in a particular (assumed) character, esp. to impress others; attitudinize; (foll. by *as*) set oneself up as, pretend to be. M19.

> 📖 **1** G. F. KENNAN The questions which the war posed for Socialists everywhere. A. DESAI The menu posed a problem, every item on it being unfamiliar. E. S. PERSON Many tentative forays into love are aborted because they pose either real or symbolic threats. **3** T. PYNCHON Oversize photos of John Dillinger, alone or posed with his mother. *SLR Camera* Very difficult indeed to pose a model, unless you're working with a professional. **4a** H. ACTON He longed to paint her portrait in spite of her reluctance to pose for him. P. CUTTING Ben asked him if he could take his photo. 'Of course you can,' he said, posing proudly. **b** J. BRYCE Politicians have . . begun to pose as the special friends of the working man. G. B. SHAW A man may be allowed to be a gentleman without being accused of posing. C. MACKENZIE I don't pose as an authority on the law. A. KENNY One could enter . . by posing as a member of an embassy staff.

■ **posed** *ppl adjective* †(*a*) grave, sedate; (*b*) placed or arranged in a pose; (*c*) assumed as a pose; deliberately adopted: L17. **posing** *verbal noun & ppl adjective* (*a*) *verbal noun* the action of the verb; (*b*) *ppl adjective* that poses; concerned with posing; ***posing pouch***, a man's garment covering only the genitals: L19.

pose /pəʊz/ *verb*[2] *trans.* E16.
[Aphet. from APPOSE *verb*[1].]
†**1** Question, interrogate; = APPOSE *verb*[1] 1. E16–E18.
2 Place in a difficulty with a question or problem; puzzle, perplex, nonplus. L16.

> 📖 **2** DONNE A thing which would have pos'd Adam to name. G. A. BIRMINGHAM He had posed them with his conundrum at lunch.

posé /ˈpəʊzeɪ, *foreign* poze (*pl. same*)/ *adjective & noun*. E18.
[French, pa. pple of *poser* place, POSE *verb*[1].]
▶ **A** *adjective*. **1** HERALDRY. Of an animal: standing still. E18.
2 Composed, poised, self-possessed. M19.
3 BALLET. Of a position: held, prolonged. M20.
4 Adopted as a pose. *rare*. M20.
▶ **B** *noun*. **1** BALLET. A movement in which a dancer steps with a straight leg on to the full or half point. E20.
2 *N. AMER. HISTORY*. = POSE *noun*[3] 1. M20.

poseable *adjective* var. of POSABLE.

pose plastique /poz plastik/ *noun phr.* Pl. **-s -s** (pronounced same). M19.
[French, lit. 'flexible pose'.]
A type of *tableau vivant*, usu. one featuring near-naked women.

poser /ˈpəʊzə/ *noun*[1]. L16.
[Aphet. from APPOSER.]
1 A person who sets testing questions; an examiner. Now *rare*. L16.
2 A question that poses or puzzles; a puzzle; a difficult problem. L16.

> 📖 **2** R. L. STEVENSON You have to solve, by a spasm of mental arithmetic, such posers as . . a hundred half-pence. STEVIE SMITH Of course the blackberries growing closer Make getting in a bit of a poser.

poser /ˈpəʊzə/ *noun*[2]. L19.
[from POSE *verb*[1] + -ER[1].]
A person who poses; *esp.* = POSEUR.

> 📖 *Daily Mirror* A Poser wears the clothes . . but doesn't have the commitment. *Golf World* What I would call a poser's paradise . . where people go to be seen.

poses plastiques *noun phr.* pl. of POSE PLASTIQUE.

poseur /pəʊˈzəː/ *noun*. Also (fem.) **poseuse** /-ˈzəːz/. L19.
[French, from *poser* POSE *verb*[1] + *-eur* -OR.]
A person who poses for effect or attitudinizes; one who adopts an affected style or demeanour. Cf. POSER *noun*[2].

> 📖 *Times* Eleanor Bron's disastrous Elena converts that passive enchantress into an assertive Bloomsbury *poseuse*. P. BOOTH Class enemies, liberal poseurs who had sold out to the dreaded ethnic minorities.

posey /ˈpəʊzi/ *adjective*. *colloq.* Also **posy**. M20.
[from POSE *noun*[3], *verb*[1] + -Y[1].]
Affected; given to attitudinizing; pretentious.

†**posh** *noun*[1]. M19.
[Perh. from Romany, lit. 'half'; sense 2 perh. a different word.]
1 Money; a coin of small value, *spec.* a halfpenny. *dial.* & *slang*. M19–E20.
2 A dandy. *slang*. L19–E20.

posh /pɒʃ/ *noun*[2]. E20.
[Origin unkn.]
Nonsense, rubbish.

posh /pɒʃ/ *adjective, verb, & adverb*. *colloq.* E20.
[Origin uncertain: perh. from POSH *noun*[1]. See note below.]
▶ **A** *adjective*. Smart, stylish; luxurious; (affecting to be) socially superior; genteel, upper-class. E20.

> 📖 *Lancashire Life* The poshest Granada Ghias . . have electric windows. J. HOWKER The *Gazette* office is really a posh stationers. N. HINTON The people were obviously very rich and they talked in an extremely posh way.

▶ **B** *verb trans.* (freq. *refl.*). Smarten *up*. E20.

> 📖 D. L. SAYERS I don't get time to posh myself up of a morning. *Pilot* Piper were building poshed up versions of the pre-war fabric-covered Cub.

▶ **C** *adverb*. In a posh manner. Freq. in ***talk posh***. M20.
¶ There is no evidence to support the popular derivation of this word from the initials of 'port outward, starboard home' (referring to the more desirable accommodation (i.e. avoiding the direct heat of the sun) on ships travelling between England and India).
■ **poshly** *adverb* L20. **poshness** *noun* M20.

posho /ˈpɒʃəʊ/ *noun*[1]. L19.
[Kiswahili, lit. 'daily rations, supply of food, clothes, etc.']
In E. Africa, (a porridge made from) maize flour; daily rations consisting of this, esp. as given to soldiers, labourers, porters on safari, etc.

posho /ˈpɒʃəʊ/ *noun*[2]. *slang*. Pl. **-os**. L20.
[from POSH *adjective* + -O.]
An upper-class person.

poshteen /pɒˈʃtiːn/ *noun*. Also **-tin**; (earlier) **-st-** /-st-/. E19.
[Persian *postīn* leather, from *post* skin, hide.]
An Afghan greatcoat of sheepskin.

posied /ˈpəʊzɪd/ *adjective*. *arch.* & *poet.* L16.
[from POSY *noun* + -ED[2].]
1 Inscribed with a posy or motto. L16.
2 Provided or decorated with posies of flowers; flowery. L18.

posigrade /ˈpɒzɪgreɪd/ *adjective*. M20.
[from POSITIVE after *retrograde*.]
ASTRONAUTICS. Of, pertaining to, or designating a small rocket giving forward thrust to a spacecraft.

posish /pəˈzɪʃ/ *noun*. *colloq.* (orig. *US*). M19.
[Abbreviation.]
A position; a situation; a state of affairs.

> 📖 T. GIFFORD Very odd thing for a man in Aaron's posish to do.

posit /ˈpɒzɪt/ *verb & noun*. M17.
[Latin *posit-* pa. ppl stem of *ponere* to place.]
▶ **A** *verb trans.* **1** Put in position; set, dispose, situate; place. M17.
2 Chiefly LOGIC & PHILOSOPHY. Assume as a fact; put forward as a basis of argument; affirm the existence of; postulate. Opp. SUBLATE 2. L17.

> 📖 **2** H. CARPENTER This fantastic strain of writing . . posited the existence of Arcadian societies. P. GROSSKURTH Freud posited a structural theory of the mind.

▶ **B** *noun*. PHILOSOPHY. A statement made on the assumption that it will prove acceptable. M20.

position /pəˈzɪʃ(ə)n/ *noun*. LME.
[Old & mod. French, or Latin *positio(n-)* a putting, placing; affirmation; state, subject, etc., formed as prec., rendering Greek THESIS, *thema* THEME: see -ITION.]
1 The place occupied by a thing, person, etc., or in which a thing etc. is put; (a) situation, (a) site, (a) station.

LME. ▸**b** *MILITARY.* A strategic site at which soldiers are stationed. L18.

2 Chiefly *LOGIC & PHILOSOPHY.* The action of positing; the putting forward of a proposition; affirmation, postulation. Now *rare.* LME. ▸**b** A proposition laid down or stated; something posited; an assertion, a tenet. L15. ▸**c** *MATH.* A method of finding the value of an unknown. Also ***rule of false position***, ***rule of position***. M16.

3 *PHONOLOGY.* The situation of a vowel in an open or closed syllable, as affecting its length. L16.

†**4** The action of positioning or placing. E17–M18.

5 The way in which a thing or its parts are disposed or arranged; (a) posture, (a) bodily attitude; *spec.* (**a**) the disposition of the pieces and pawns on the board at any point in a game of chess etc.; (**b**) the disposition of the limbs in a dance step; (**c**) the posture adopted during sexual intercourse; (**d**) *MUSIC* the arrangement of the constituent notes of a chord; (**e**) *MUSIC* the location of the hand on the finger-board of a stringed instrument. E18.

6 a The situation which a person metaphorically occupies in relation to others, to circumstances, etc.; condition, a state of affairs; a point of view. E19. ▸**b** Place in the social scale; social state or standing; status; rank. Also ***social position***. M19. ▸**c** A post of (paid) employment. L19.

7 The state of being favourably or advantageously placed; location or disposition (e.g. in chess, snooker) conferring an advantage. L19.

8 *COMMERCE.* (The inventory of) an investor's net holdings in one or more markets at a particular time; the status of an individual or institutional trader's contract(s), esp. as long- or short-term. E20.

> 📖 **1** F. CHICHESTER Position by dead reckoning at 01.00 hours . . 33° 15′S., 171° 35′E. J. WAIN He was in a position to see everyone who came in at the door. K. AMIS Oswald Hart shifted two . . chairs into position. **b** C. RYAN Camouflaged nettings suddenly swung back to reveal hidden enemy positions. **2** SHAKES. *Oth.* I do not in position Distinctly speak of her. **b** D. HUME An edict, which contains many extraordinary positions and pretensions. **5** A. D. PHILIDOR In this position it is a drawn game. C. BRONTË I cannot see you without disturbing my position in this comfortable chair. N. COWARD Little girls in ballet dresses practising 'positions'. *Times* There was actually—this was, maybe, 1938—a chapter on positions. Wow! **6a** I. MURDOCH Madge was in no position to make complaints. S. UNWIN I explained the position and ended by asking them what they would do in my shoes. P. GROSSKURTH Jones tried to maintain a politically independent position as president. **b** L. URIS He thought the position of women intolerable; they were held in absolute bondage, never seen. G. BUTLER I am a young woman of education and social position. **c** A. C. CLARKE Chief engineer of a liner on the Martian run, which . . is a very responsible position. A. S. DALE His hopes of securing a university position had been destroyed. **7** R. BLOUNT Too much energy goes into cutthroat jockeying for position.

Phrases: **angle of position** = *position angle* below. **circle of position** *ASTRONOMY* a circle on the terrestrial globe whose centre is the substellar point of a given star and whose radius corresponds to the angular distance of the star from the zenith. *DEFINE* ***one's position***. ***eastward position***: see EASTWARD *adjective*. ***false position***: see FALSE *adjective*. ***fifth position***: see FIFTH *adjective*. *FIRST* ***position***. ***five positions***: see FIVE *adjective*. ***fourth position***: see FOURTH *adjective*. **in position** in the proper or designated position. ***lotus position***: see LOTUS 4b. ***missionary position***: see MISSIONARY *adjective & noun*. **out of position** in a position other than the proper or designated one. ***pole position***: see POLE *noun*[1] 3b. ***rule of false position***, ***rule of position***: see sense 2c above. ***second position***: see SECOND *adjective*. ***third position***: see THIRD *adjective & noun*. ***westward position***: see WESTWARD *adjective*.

Comb.: **position angle** an angle giving the direction in which a point lies with respect to another point; *esp.* (*ASTRONOMY*) the angle between the hour circle passing through a celestial object and the line joining that object to another object; **position-finding** the process of ascertaining one's position or that of a distant object, esp. automatically by radio or similar means; **position line** a line on which the observer is computed to be after having taken a bearing; **position paper** a written statement of attitude or intentions (in business etc.); **position vector** *MATH.* a vector which defines the position of a point.

position /pəˈzɪʃ(ə)n/ *verb.* L17.

[from the noun.]

†**1** *verb intrans.* Take up one's position; express one's point of view. *rare.* L17–E18.

2 *verb trans.* Put or set in a particular, appropriate, or advantageous position; place. E19. ▸**b** Promote (a product or service) esp. within a chosen sector of a market, or as the fulfilment of that sector's specific requirements or demands. L20.

> 📖 **2** M. FLANAGAN I positioned myself by the driver's side of the car. A. C. GRAYLING Radiators . . had to be exactly positioned in order not to disturb the symmetry of the rooms.

■ **positioner** *noun* a device for moving an object into position and automatically keeping it there M20.

positional /pəˈzɪʃ(ə)n(ə)l/ *adjective.* L16.

[from POSITION *noun* + -AL[1].]

Of, relating to, or determined by position; *spec.* (*LINGUISTICS*) (of a language) isolating.

positional goods *ECONOMICS* things which are in limited supply and which become more sought after (and relatively more expensive) as material prosperity increases, e.g. houses in fashionable areas, tickets for prestigious events, etc. **positional play** those aspects of a game which are concerned with being in an advantageous position; *esp.* (*CHESS*) play dominated by strategic considerations as opp. to the tactical use of combinations.

■ **positionally** *adverb* E20.

positive /ˈpɒzɪtɪv/ *adjective & noun.* ME.

[Old & mod. French *positif*, *-ive* or Latin *positivus*, from *posit-*: see POSIT, -IVE.]

▸ **A** *adjective.* **I 1** Of law or justice: formally laid down or imposed; proceeding from enactment or custom; conventional. Opp. ***natural***. ME.

2 Explicitly laid down; admitting no question; explicit, express, definite, precise; emphatic. L16.

3 Confident in opinion or assertion; convinced, assured, very sure; *occas.* overconfident, cocksure, dogmatic. M17.

> 📖 **2** M. W. MONTAGU Positive orders oblige us to go tomorrow. E. A. FREEMAN A strong presumption, though it does not reach positive proof. **3** M. E. BRADDON Are you sure? . . Pretty positive. J. BUCHAN Neither was any kind of foreigner; on this my young friend was positive. E. CALDWELL Annette was positive that Doan was truly in love with her.

▸ **II 4** *GRAMMAR.* Designating the primary degree of an adjective or adverb, expressing simple quality; not comparative or superlative. LME.

5 a Having no relation to or comparison with other things; not relative; absolute, unconditional, unqualified. E17. ▸**b** That is absolutely what is expressed by the noun; nothing less than, downright, out-and-out. *colloq.* E19. ▸**c** Functioning for the special purpose required; having or being a well-defined and effective action. E20.

> 📖 **5a** R. BRADLEY Such as feed upon raw Flesh are positive in their Ferocity. **b** E. WAUGH Her herbaceous borders were a positive eye-sore. F. RAPHAEL Byron had shipped out a positive library, including fifty volumes of Parliamentary debates. **c** *Scientific American* Instead of depending on splash lubrication alone . . positive oil feeds are led to . . the crankshaft bearings. *Times* The steering, which used to be somewhat indefinite, is now . . pleasantly positive in action.

▸ **III** Opp. NEGATIVE *adjective* II.

6 Consisting in, characterized by, or expressing the presence or possession of features or qualities, rather than their absence or lack; of an affirmative nature. Also, consisting in or characterized by constructive action or attitudes. LME. ▸**b** Of evidence, an experimental result, etc.: tending to support the hypothesis which the experiment was designed to test. Of a test or an experiment, or the subject of one: producing such a result (freq. *postpositive* in comb.). L19.

7 Of a quantity: greater than zero, to be added, not negative. E18. ▸**b** Reckoned, situated, or tending in a direction opposite to the negative and taken as the direction of increase or progress. L19.

8 Orig., designating that form of electricity produced by rubbing glass with silk (also called ***vitreous***). Now, designating electric charge, potential, etc., having the same polarity as that electrode of a voltaic cell from which the current is held to flow (and towards which the actual flow of electrons occurs); possessing such charge. M18. ▸**b** Designating a north-seeking pole of a magnet; having the polarity of the earth's south pole. M19.

9 *OPTICS.* Of, pertaining to, or displaying birefringence in which the refractive index of the extraordinary ray is greater than that of the ordinary ray. M19.

10 Of a visual image, esp. a photograph: showing the lights and shades (and colour values) true to the original. M19.

11 Of, pertaining to, or designating a copy or likeness of an object with the same relief as that of the original, as opp. the reverse relief of a mould. E20.

> 📖 **6** T. HARDY The soundlessness impressed her as a positive entity rather than as the mere negation of noise. R. CHURCH It was this capacity for enjoyment that made her so positive a character. E. ROOSEVELT This country should make a definite and positive effort to preserve the peace. *Times* All the positive rugby after the interval came from Ireland. M. COREN *The Incredulity of Father Brown* appeared, to positive reviews and a grateful readership. **b** *British Medical Journal* A . . greater proportion of married men were positive for hepatitis B virus. ***rhesus positive***: see RHESUS 2. **7** C. HUTTON When a quantity is found without a sign, it is understood to be positive.

▸ **IV 12** Chiefly *PHILOSOPHY.* Dealing only with matters of fact and experience; practical, realistic; not speculative. L16.

13 Actual, real; concrete. *rare.* M19.

> 📖 **13** E. B. BROWNING The skies themselves looked low and positive As almost you could touch them.

▸ **V 14** Adapted to be placed or set down. Only in ***positive organ*** below. E18.

Special collocations & comb.: **positive column** *PHYSICS* a luminous region extending from near the anode of a low-pressure discharge tube and producing most of the light in a conventional neon tube. **positive definite** *adjectival phr.* (*MATH.*) positive in all cases; (of a square matrix) having all its eigenvalues positive. **positive discrimination** the practice of making distinctions in favour of groups considered to be disadvantaged or underprivileged, esp. in the allocation of resources and opportunities; also called ***reverse discrimination***. **positive electron** = POSITRON. **positive eugenics** the practice of encouraging the birth of children to parents having qualities considered desirable to the community. ***positive FEEDBACK***. **positive-going** *adjective* increasing in magnitude in the direction of positive polarity; becoming less negative or more positive. **positive logic** circuit logic in which the larger or most positive signal is taken as representing 1 and the smaller signal 0. **positive organ** a movable church organ which has to be placed on a stand or on the floor for playing. ***positive prescription***: see PRESCRIPTION 1a. **positive pressure** *MEDICINE* pressure greater than that of the atmosphere, used to force air or oxygen into the lungs to assist respiration or to treat hypoxia. **positive rays** *PHYSICS* = ***canal rays*** s.v. CANAL *noun*. **positive reinforcement** *PSYCHOLOGY* (reinforcement achieved by) a pleasurable or satisfying stimulus provided after a desired response to increase the probability of its repetition. **positive sign** = PLUS *noun* 1. **positive thinking** the practice or result of concentrating one's mind on the good and constructive aspects of a matter so as to eliminate destructive attitudes and emotions. **positive transfer** the transfer of effects from the learning of one skill that facilitate the learning of another. **positive transference** *PSYCHOANALYSIS* transference in which the feelings involved are of a positive or affectionate nature. **positive vetting** the practice or an instance of making exhaustive inquiries into the background and character of a candidate for any post in the (British) Civil Service which involves access to secret material.

▸ **B** *noun.* **1** *GRAMMAR.* (An adjective or adverb in) the positive degree. M16.

2 A thing having actual existence or able to be affirmed; a reality. E17.

†**3** Something which arbitrarily or absolutely prescribes or determines. L17–M18.

4 *ellipt.* A positive quantity, impression, etc.; *spec.* (**a**) the positive electrode of a voltaic cell or battery; (**b**) a positive photographic image. E18.

■ **positively** *adverb* (**a**) definitely, expressly, explicitly; absolutely, simply; (**b**) affirmatively; in respect of what is, rather than what is not; constructively; (**c**) actually, really; in truth, truly; *colloq.* yes, indeed; (**d**) with positive electricity; in the direction taken as positive: LME. **positiveness** *noun* M17. **posiˈtivity** *noun* M17.

positivism /ˈpɒzɪtɪvɪz(ə)m/ *noun.* M19.

[French *positivisme*, formed as prec.: see -ISM.]

1 A philosophical system elaborated by Auguste Comte, recognizing only positive facts and observable phenomena and rejecting metaphysics and theism; a humanistic religious system founded on this philosophy. Also, the belief that every intelligible proposition can be scientifically verified or falsified, and that philosophy can only be concerned with the analysis of the language used to express such propositions. M19.

2 Definiteness; certainty, assurance. M19.

3 *LAW.* The view that laws and their operation derive validity from the fact of having been enacted by authority or of conforming to the established system, rather than from any considerations of morality, natural law, etc. E20.

1 ***logical positivism***: see LOGICAL *adjective*.

positivist /ˈpɒzɪtɪvɪst/ *noun & adjective.* M19.

[French *positiviste*, formed as POSITIVE + -IST.]

▸ **A** *noun.* An adherent or student of positivism. M19.

logical positivist: see LOGICAL *adjective*.

▸ **B** *adjective.* Positivistic. M19.

■ **positiˈvistic** *adjective* of or pertaining to positivists; of the nature of positivism: M19. **positiˈvistically** *adverb* L19.

positon /ˈpɒzɪtɒn/ *noun. rare.* E20.

[from POSITIVE + -ON.]

PHYSICS. †**1** = PROTON 2. Only in E20.

2 = next. M20.

positron /ˈpɒzɪtrɒn/ *noun.* M20.

[from POSITIVE after *electron*.]

PHYSICS. An elementary particle having the same mass as an electron and a numerically equal but positive charge.

Comb.: **positron emission tomography** *MEDICINE* a form of tomography which employs positron-emitting isotopes introduced into the body as a source of radiation instead of applying X-rays externally.

■ **posiˈtronic** *adjective* M20.

positronium /pɒzɪˈtrəʊnɪəm/ *noun.* M20.

[from prec. + -IUM.]

PHYSICS. A short-lived neutral system, analogous to an atom, consisting of a positron and an electron bound together.

†**positure** *noun.* E17.

[Obsolete French from Latin *positura*, from *posit-*: see POSIT, -URE.]

1 The fact of being placed; position, situation; place, locality. Only in 17.

2 Posture. E17–E18. ▸**b** *ASTROLOGY.* Relative position of the planets etc. E17–E19.

3 A law, a principle laid down. *rare.* Only in E17.

Posix /ˈpɒsɪks/ *noun*. L20.
[from initial letters of portable operating system + *-ix*, after UNIX.]
COMPUTING. A set of formal descriptions that provide a standard for the design of operating systems, esp. ones compatible with Unix.

posnet /ˈpɒsnɪt/ *noun*. Now *arch. & dial.* ME.
[Old French *poçonnet* dim. of *poçon* vase: see -ET¹.]
A small metal pot or vessel for boiling, with a handle and three feet.

posnjakite /ˈpɒznjəkʌɪt/ *noun*. M20.
[from E. W. *Posnjak* (1888–1949), Russian-born US geochemist + -ITE¹.]
MINERALOGY. A monoclinic hydrated basic copper sulphate usu. occurring as dark blue crystals similar to langite.

posole /pəˈzəʊli/ *noun*. *N. Amer.* Also **pozole**. M20.
[Mexican Spanish, from Nahuatl *pozolli*.]
A Mexican stew of hominy cooked with pork, beans, and red chilli, traditionally served at Christmas; the maize porridge used as a base for this dish.

posology /pəˈsɒlədʒi/ *noun*. *rare*. E19.
[French *posologie*, from Greek *posos* how much: see -LOGY.]
1 The branch of medicine that deals with dosages. E19.
2 In or with ref. to the writings of Bentham (see BENTHAMISM): the science of quantity, mathematics. E19.
■ **posoˈlogical** *adjective* E19.

pospolite /pɒˈspɒlɪteɪ/ *noun*. *obsolete* exc. *Hist.* L17.
[Polish *pospolite (ruszenie)* general (levy).]
The Polish militia, consisting of the nobility and gentry summoned to serve for a limited time.

poss /pɒs/ *adjective*. *colloq.* Also **pos**. L19.
[Abbreviation.]
Possible. Chiefly in ***if poss, as soon as poss***.

poss /pɒs/ *verb*. Long *obsolete* exc. *dial.* ME.
[Origin unkn.]
1 *verb trans. & †intrans.* Thrust or push with a forcible or violent impact; dash, knock. ME.
2 *verb trans.* Pound, beat down flat, squash; *spec.* beat or stamp (clothes etc.) in water in the process of washing. E17.
Comb.: **poss-stick**, **poss tub**: for beating clothes in during washing.
■ **posser** *noun* = ***poss-stick*** above M18.

posse /ˈpɒsi/ *noun*. M17.
[Abbreviation of next.]
1 A force armed with legal authority; a body of constables or other law enforcers; *esp.* a body of men summoned by a US sheriff to enforce the law. Also (*gen.*), a strong force, company, or assemblage (*of*). M17.
2 A gang of black (esp. Jamaican) youths involved in organized or violent (freq. drug-related) crime. *slang* (orig. *US*). L20.

> 🕮 **1** F. RAPHAEL He posed a posse of rhetorical questions. C. TOMALIN Had she been in trouble, there was a whole posse of relations to turn to.

posse comitatus /ˌpɒsi kɒmɪˈteɪtəs/ *noun phr.* E17.
[medieval Latin (Anglo-Latin) = force of the county.]
1 *Hist.* The body of men above the age of fifteen in a county (excluding peers, clergymen, and the infirm), whom the sheriff may summon to repress a riot or for other purposes; a body of men so raised and commanded by the sheriff. E17.
2 A posse. E19.

possess /pəˈzɛs/ *verb trans.* Pa. t. & pple **-ed**, **†possest**. LME.
[Old French *possesser*, from Latin *possess-* pa. ppl stem of *possidere*, from *potis* (see POTENT *adjective*² & *noun*²) + *sedere* sit.]
▸ **I 1** Hold, occupy (a place, territory); reside in, inhabit; take up, be situated in, on, or at. *obsolete* exc. as passing into sense 2 below. LME. ▸**†b** Of a disease etc.: affect, infect. Only in 17. ▸**†c** Take up the time or attention of; occupy, engross. M17–E18.
2 Hold as property; have belonging to one, own; have as a faculty, attribute, quality, etc.; *gen.* have; LAW have possession of as distinct from ownership. LME. ▸**b** [After French *posséder*.] Have knowledge of or acquaintance with; be conversant with (a language, etc.). *arch.* E17.
3 a Take possession of, seize; come into possession of, obtain, gain. *arch.* E16. ▸**b** Have sexual intercourse with (a woman). L16.
4 Of a demon or spirit, esp. an evil one: occupy and have power over (a person, animal, etc.). Freq. in *pass.* (foll. by *with, by, †of*). E16.
5 Of an idea, mental condition, etc.: take or have hold of (a person); affect or influence strongly and persistently, dominate, obsess. Freq. in *pass.*, foll. by *with* (passing into sense 9), *by*. L16.
6 Maintain (oneself, one's soul, etc.) *in* a state or condition (of patience, quiet, etc.). Also (without *in*), maintain control over, keep calm or steady. M17.

> 🕮 **1** MILTON Dominion giv'n Over all other Creatures that possesse Earth, Aire, and Sea. B. MARTIN The Solar System, in which you see the Sun possesses nearly the central Point. **2** T. F. POWYS What estate he had once possessed Farmer Beerfield had taken away from him. W. S. CHURCHILL Washington possessed the gifts of character for which the situation called. A. SILLITOE What power he possessed came from the strength of his working arms. *Times* He was given a further consecutive year for possessing cannabis. **b** M. ARNOLD Every critic should try and possess one great literature . . besides his own. **3** O. CROMWELL Upon Thursday the One-and-thirtieth, I possessed a Castle called Kilkenny. A. GINSBERG In our solitary / fancy tasting artichokes, possessing every frozen delicacy, / and never passing the cashier. **b** JOYCE All the male brutes that have possessed her. **4** J. CONRAD Had I lived in the Middle Ages . . I would have believed that a talking bird must be possessed by the devil. B. MASON As if he were possessed by the Comic Muse herself, who simply used him as a channel. **5** V. WOOLF An exquisite sense of pleasure and relief possessed him. R. C. HUTCHINSON He had been possessed by the single idea of getting outside the walls. E. WAUGH I can't think what possessed the papers to forecast a triumphal advance to Tunis. **6** J. BUCHAN I tried to possess my soul in patience and to forget how hungry I was.

▸ **II** Causative uses.
†7 Put in (esp. legal) possession of (lands, estates, etc.); settle or establish in. Usu. foll. by *in*. LME–E18.
8 Foll. by *of*, *†with*: endow with, put in possession of. Now only (***a***) *refl.*, take possession of; make one's own, obtain; (***b***) in *pass.*, be in possession of, be endowed with, own, have. L15.
9 Foll. by *with*: cause to be preoccupied or inspired by (a feeling, idea, etc.); imbue, inspire, affect strongly or permanently with; cause to feel. (In *pass.*, passing into sense 5.) *arch.* L16. ▸**†b** Without *with*: influence the opinion of, predispose. L16–L17. ▸**†c** W. obj. clause: persuade, convince. E17–E19.
10 Foll. by *of*, *†with*, *†in*: put in possession of (knowledge etc.), acquaint with. *arch.* L16.

> 🕮 **8** SHAKES. *Ant. & Cl.* I will possess you of that ship and treasure. R. H. MOTTRAM In a moment he had . . possessed himself of the telephone. L. NAMIER 'Country gentleman' can be equated with commoners possessed of armorial bearings and landed estates. G. PRIESTLAND George Engle, . . possessed of both real learning and an irrepressible sense of life's absurdities. **9** F. D. MAURICE He had all his life been possessed with one great conviction. GLADSTONE I wish that I could possess the Committee with the . . vital importance of the subject. **10** SHAKES. *Merch. V.* I have possess'd your Grace of what I purpose. B. FRANKLIN Our debates possessed me so fully of the subject, that I wrote a . . pamphlet on it.

■ **possessed** *ppl adjective* (***a***) *rare* held or taken as property, owned, seized; (***b***) inhabited and controlled by a demon or spirit; demoniac, mad; see also SELF-POSSESSED: L15. **possessible** *adjective* (*rare*) able to be possessed L19.

†possesser *noun* var. of POSSESSOR.

possession /pəˈzɛʃ(ə)n/ *noun*. ME.
[Old & mod. French, or Latin *possessio(n-)*, from *possess-*: see POSSESS, -ION.]
1 The action or fact of possessing something; the holding or having something as one's own or in one's control; actual holding or occupancy as distinct from ownership; LAW visible power or control over a thing, esp. land, which is similar to but may exist apart from lawful ownership. ME. ▸**b** FOOTBALL etc. Control of the ball, puck, etc., by a particular player or team; a period of such control. Also, the extent of a team's control of the ball etc. or dominance in a match. Orig. *US*. L19. ▸**c** *ellipt.* Possession of illegal drugs. *colloq.* L20.
2 A thing possessed, a piece of property, something that belongs to one. Now usu. in *pl.*, belongings, property, wealth. ME. ▸**b** A small farm held under lease. *Scot.* L18. ▸**c** A territory subject to a sovereign ruler or State. Now *esp.* any of a country's foreign dominions. E19.
3 The action of a spirit or demon possessing a person etc.; the fact or state of being so possessed. L16.
4 The state, process, or fact of being possessed by an idea, feeling, etc. Also, a dominating idea or impulse. E17.
5 The action or condition of keeping oneself, one's mind, etc., under control. More commonly SELF-POSSESSION. E18.

> 🕮 **1** M. EDGEWORTH Not one of those . . mothers who expect always to have possession of a son's arm. B. JOWETT Philosophy is the possession of knowledge. V. CRONIN Catherine as Empress came into possession of three country palaces. *Proverb*: Possession is nine points (*also* parts, tenths) of the law. **b** *Guardian* Oldham . . lost and then . . regained possession a yard from the Warrington line. **c** L. CODY No one had gone so far as to be arrested for possession. **2** G. P. R. JAMES Beauty is a woman's best possession till she be old. M. MUGGERIDGE We had . . no furniture or possessions apart from clothes and a few books. **3** M. TIPPETT There is a third form of possession or madness, of which the Muses are the source. E. JOHNSON But the demoniac possession that drove him would not let him rest. **4** LONGFELLOW I have worked steadily on it, for it took hold of me—a kind of possession.

Phrases: ***chose in possession***: see CHOSE *noun*. **in possession** (***a***) actually possessing the thing in question; (***b***) possessed by the person etc. in question. **in possession of** actually possessing, holding, or occupying (something); maintaining control over (one's faculties etc.). **in the possession of** owned or possessed by. ***symbolical possession***: see SYMBOLICAL 2. **take possession** become the possessor or owner (*of*). ***vacant possession***: see VACANT *adjective* 2b.
Comb.: **possession order** an order made by a court of law directing that possession of a property be given to the owner.
■ **possessional** *adjective* (*rare*) pertaining to possession; having possessions or property: L19. **possessionary** *adjective* constituted by or relating to possession; having possession: M17. **possessioned** *adjective* endowed with or holding possessions L18. **possessioner** *noun* (*obsolete* exc. *Hist.*) (***a***) a holder, an occupier; an owner of possessions; (***b***) *spec.* a member of a religious order having possessions or endowments; an endowed ecclesiastic: LME. **possessionless** *adjective* L19.

possessive /pəˈzɛsɪv/ *adjective & noun*. LME.
[Latin *possessivus* (translation of Greek *ktētikē* (*ptōsis* case)), from *possess-*: see POSSESS, -IVE.]
▸ **A** *adjective*. **1** GRAMMAR. Denoting or indicating possession; designating the case of nouns and pronouns expressing possession. LME.
2 Of or pertaining to possession; having the quality of possessing; showing a desire to possess or to retain what one possesses; showing jealous and domineering tendencies towards another person. M16.

> 🕮 **1 possessive adjective** an adjective derived from a pronoun and expressing possession (as English *my, your, their*, etc.). **possessive pronoun** a possessive adjective; the absolute form of any of these (as English *mine, yours, theirs*, etc.). **2** A. S. NEILL I am possessive about my car and my typewriter and my workshop tools. R. THOMAS Angharad hugged her father with possessive love. J. HELLER Rembrandt has a hand on her waist with possessive unconcern.

▸ **B** *ellipt.* as *noun*. GRAMMAR. The possessive case; a possessive pronoun or adjective. LME.
■ **possessively** *adverb* L16. **possessiveness** *noun* M19.

possessor /pəˈzɛsə/ *noun*. Also **†-er**. LME.
[Anglo-Norman *possessour* = Old & mod. French *-eur* from Latin *possessor*, from *possess-*: see POSSESS, -OR.]
A person who possesses something; a person who holds something as property or in actual control; a holder; an owner; LAW a person who takes, occupies, or holds something without necessarily having ownership or as distinguished from the owner.

> 🕮 A. T. ELLIS Youth . . even when its possessor is unattractive, has an appeal of its own. A. BROOKNER At Oxford he was the possessor of a proud reputation.

■ **possessorship** *noun* L19.

possessory /pəˈzɛs(ə)ri/ *adjective*. LME.
[Late Latin *possessorius*, from Latin *possessor*: see prec., -ORY².]
1 Chiefly LAW. Pertaining to a possessor; relating to or arising from possession. LME.
2 That is a possessor; of, belonging to, or characterizing a possessor. M17.
■ Also **posseˈssorial** *adjective* (*rare*) L16.

†possest *verb*: see POSSESS.

posset /ˈpɒsɪt/ *noun & verb*. LME.
[Origin unkn.]
▸ **A** *noun*. **1** (A drink of) hot milk curdled with ale, wine, or other liquor, often flavoured with sugar or spices, formerly much drunk as a delicacy or medicinally. LME.
2 A quantity of milk regurgitated by a baby. L20.
▸ **B** *verb intrans.* **†1** Curdle like a posset. *rare* (Shakes.). Only in E17.
2 Make a posset (*rare*); (of a baby) regurgitate curdled milk. M19.

possibilist /ˈpɒsɪbɪlɪst/ *noun & adjective*. L19.
[French *possibiliste* or Spanish *posibilista*, formed as POSSIBLE + -IST.]
▸ **A** *noun*. **1** A politician whose policies are directed to what is immediately possible or practicable. L19.
2 GEOGRAPHY. A person who emphasizes humankind's freedom of action in shaping the environment and minimizes natural effects and restrictions. E20.
▸ **B** *adjective*. Of or pertaining to possibilists; advocating or believing in possibilism. L19.
■ **possibilism** *noun* possibilist theory or belief; a possibilist doctrine or view: E20. **possibiˈlistic** *adjective* M20.

possibility /pɒsɪˈbɪlɪti/ *noun*. LME.
[Old & mod. French *possibilité* or late Latin *possibilitas*, from Latin *possibilis*: see next, -ITY.]
1 The condition or quality of being possible; ability to be done, happen, or exist. Also, contingency, likelihood, chance. LME. ▸**b** The quality or character of representing or relating to something that is possible. M17. ▸**c** MATH. The condition of being a real quantity. Now *rare* or *obsolete*. L17.
2 A possible thing or circumstance; something that may exist or happen. LME. ▸**b** In *pl.* Unspecified attributes of definite promise; favourable prospects. E19.
3 Orig., the fact of something (expressed or implied) being possible to one, whether through circumstance or

power; capacity, capability, power. Now, chance of having or achieving something (passing into sense 1 above), promise, potential. LME. ▸†**b** *spec.* Pecuniary ability, means; (favourable) pecuniary prospects. Freq. in *pl.* M16–M17.

📖 **1** F. TEMPLE Science and Revelation come into . . collision on the possibility of miracles. J. DISKI We often discuss the possibility of his buying a new jacket. **b** DISRAELI To consult on the possibility of certain views . . and the expediency of their adoption. **2** A. TROLLOPE Her clearer intellect saw possibilities which did not occur to him. M. L. KING To listen to the argument for peace, not as a dream, but as a practical possibility. **b** A. LURIE It had been for sale for over a year, but they were the first to see its possibilities. **3** W. PALEY An instance of conformity beyond the possibility . . of random writing to produce. D. LEAVITT Her life seemed quite suddenly enormous with possibility. **b** SHAKES. *Merry W.* Seven hundred pounds, and possibilities.

Phrases: **by any possibility**, **by no possibility** in any (or no) possible way, (not) possibly. †**in a possibility** in such a position that something (expressed or implied) is possible; having a prospect, expectation, or chance (*of*, *to do*). **in possibility** †(*a*) = *in a possibility* above; (*b*) potentially.

possible /ˈpɒsɪb(ə)l/ *adjective, adverb, & noun.* ME.

[Old & mod. French, or Latin *possibilis*, from *posse* be able: see -IBLE.]

▸ **A** *adjective.* **1** Expr. capability: that may or can exist, be done, or happen; that is in a person's power, that one can do, exert, use, etc. ME. ▸**b** That can be or become (what is denoted by the noun); potential. M18.

†**2** Able *to do*. *rare.* LME–E19.

3 Expr. contingency: that may be or may be conjectured to be (though not known not to be); that is perhaps true or a fact; that perhaps exists. L16. ▸**b** PHILOSOPHY. Logically conceivable; not excluded from existence by being logically contradictory or against reason. M18. ▸**c** That perhaps is or will be (what is denoted by the noun). L19.

4 Able to deal with, get on with, or consider; suitable, tolerable, reasonable. Opp. IMPOSSIBLE *adjective* 2. *colloq.* M19.

5 MATH. Of a number: real. Opp. IMPOSSIBLE *adjective* 1b. *rare.* L19.

📖 **1** E. M. FORSTER The only possible place for a house in Shropshire is on a hill. G. GREENE A single feat of daring can alter the whole conception of what is possible. E. FEINSTEIN From the terrace it was possible to see the River Danube. V. BRAMWELL When possible, run cold water over your wrists . . in hot weather. **as — as possible** as — as may or might be (done), as — as one can or could. **if possible** if it is or was possible, if it can or could be (done). **b** A. P. STANLEY Of the three possible harbours . . they made no use. **3** DAY LEWIS If these are the dominant themes . . it is possible that they may provide the clues. P. LOMAS Paranoia describes a state of mind which fails to distinguish between possible and likely harm. **b** B. RUSSELL Respects in which other possible worlds might differ from the actual world. **c** *Japan Times* Police will . . look for possible . . arms caches. **4** ALDOUS HUXLEY A rather primitive but quite possible little hotel.

▸†**B** *adverb.* Possibly. LME–L18.

▸ **C** *noun.* **1** Whatever is possible; that which can be done, can exist, or can happen. Usu. with *the.* M17.

2 a A possible thing; a possibility. Usu. in *pl.* Now *rare* in *gen.* sense. L17. ▸**b** A possible score in a shooting competition; *ellipt.* the highest possible score. Earliest in ***highest possible***. *colloq.* M19. ▸**c** A person who or thing which possibly may have done, may do, or may attain something (specified or implied); a possible candidate, member of a team, etc. E20.

3 In *pl.* Necessaries, means, supplies. *slang* (now *US*). E19.

📖 **1** D. C. HAGUE Management . . is the art of the possible. J. UGLOW Rarely worried by the discrepancy between the possible and the real. **do one's possible** [French *faire son possible*] do all one can, do one's utmost. **2c** *Times Lit. Suppl.* Most of the presidential possibles . . are college graduates. A. MORICE Going to have a look at some boats . . He'd marked one or two possibles in the local paper.

possibly /ˈpɒsɪbli/ *adverb.* LME.

[from prec. + -LY².]

1 In accordance with or within the range of possibility; by any existing power or means. Now usu. as an intensive with *can* or *could.* LME.

2 According to what may be (as far as one knows); perhaps, maybe. Freq. as an intensive with *may* or *might.* E17.

📖 **1** B. PYM Wondering whether such an occasion could possibly arise. I. MURDOCH You couldn't possibly sew by this light. **2** T. HARDY I should like to come, and possibly may. H. C. J. HUNT Over our bacon and, possibly, eggs. *Nature* The few hominoid species . . considered as possibly close to the direct line of human ancestry.

possident /ˈpɒsɪd(ə)nt/ *noun. rare.* E17.

[from Latin *possident-* pres. ppl stem of *possidere* possess: see -ENT.]

A possessor.

possie /ˈpɒzi/ *noun. Austral. & NZ slang.* Also **possy**, **pozzy**. E20.

[from POSITION *noun* + -IE, -Y⁶.]

A position; a location; a place of residence; an appointment; a job.

POSSLQ /ˈpɒs(ə)lkjuː/ *abbreviation.*

Person of the opposite sex sharing living quarters.

possum /ˈpɒsəm/ *noun & verb.* E17.

[Aphet. from OPOSSUM.]

▸ **A** *noun.* **1** = OPOSSUM 1. Now *colloq.* E17.

2 Any of various small or moderate-sized Australasian marsupials of the families Phalangeridae, Burramyidae, Petauridae, and Tarsipedidae. L18.

3 A contemptible person; a fool, a simpleton. *US & Austral. slang.* M19.

2 ***brushtail possum***, ***honey possum***, ***Leadbeater's possum***, ***ringtail possum***, etc.

Phrases: **play possum** *colloq.* (orig. *US*) pretend unconsciousness or ignorance; feign, dissemble. **stir the possum** *Austral. colloq.* stir up controversy, liven things up.

▸ **B** *verb intrans.* **1** Play possum; feign unconsciousness or ignorance; sham. *US colloq.* M19.

2 Hunt opossums. Chiefly as ***possuming*** *verbal noun. colloq.* (chiefly *Austral.*). M19.

possy *noun* var. of POSSIE.

post /pəʊst/ *noun*¹. OE.

[Latin *postis*, prob. reinforced in Middle English from Old French and Middle Low German, Middle Dutch.]

1 A long stout piece of timber, metal, or other solid material, usu. of round or square cross-section, used in a vertical position in building and construction. Also, as a type of stupidity, ignorance, or deafness. OE. ▸†**b** *fig.* A support, a prop; a pillar (*of* a social group etc.). LME–L16.

2 A stake, pole, column, etc., set upright in or on the ground, as a marker, a stand for displaying notices, a support for a fence, a point of attachment, etc. ME.

3 *ellipt.* **a** A doorpost, a gatepost. ME. ▸**b** A post etc. marking the start or finish of a race; a starting post or winning-post. M17. ▸**c** A goalpost. M19.

†**4** The doorpost on which the reckoning at a tavern was kept; (a record of) one's account. L16–E17.

5 a A vertical mass of stratified rock between joints or fissures. M17. ▸**b** A thick compact stratum of sandstone, limestone, etc. L18. ▸**c** A fine-grained sandstone. L18. ▸**d** A pillar of coal left uncut to support the roof of a mine working. E19.

📖 **1** F. BURNEY They . . know no more than the post. ***bedpost***, ***doorpost***, ***heel-post***, ***newel post***, ***stern post***, etc. **2** R. DAHL A blackboard . . nailed to a post stuck in the ground. P. CAREY The butcher-birds . . sang on the fence posts. ***distance post***, ***finger post***, ***goalpost***, ***guide post***, ***milepost***, ***signpost***, etc. **3b** F. O'BRIEN We will feel 'bucked' when this animal flashes past the post. **c** *Rugby World* A penalty try . . with the conversion . . from in front of the posts.

Phrases: **as deaf as a post** stone-deaf. ***first past the post***: see FIRST. ***from pillar to post***, ***from post to pillar***: see PILLAR *noun.* ***knight of the post***: see KNIGHT *noun.* **on the wrong side of the post(s)** on the wrong track, off course. ***pip at the post***: see PIP *verb*² 1.

Comb.: **post-and-beam** *adjective* (of a method of construction or a building) having a framework of upright and horizontal beams; **post-and-pan** *adjective* (of a method of construction or a building) having a timber framework with the spaces filled in with brickwork, plaster, etc.; **post-and-rail** *adjective* (*a*) (of a fence) simply constructed with posts and one or more rails only; (*b*) *Austral. slang* (of tea) strong and roughly made with stalks etc. floating on the top; **post crown** DENTISTRY a prosthetic crown secured by a post or wire sunk into the root of the tooth; **post-hole** a hole made in the ground to receive the foot of a post; ARCHAEOLOGY a hole orig. dug to receive a wooden post and sometimes packed with stones or clay for support; **post-mill** a windmill pivoted on a post, so as to be turned round to catch the wind; **post-oak** an oak, *Quercus stellata*, of the eastern US, having a close-grained durable wood much used for posts, sleepers, etc.

post /pəʊst/ *noun*². E16.

[French *poste* from Italian *posta* from Proto-Romance contr. of Latin *posita* fem. pa. pple of *ponere* to place. Cf. POST *noun*⁴.]

1 *Hist.* Any of a series of riders stationed at (orig. temporary, later fixed) stages located at suitable distances along certain roads, the duty of each rider being to convey mail (orig. from the monarch) speedily to the next stage, as well as to provide fresh horses for other messengers (cf. POSTMASTER *noun*¹ 3). Also ***standing post***. E16.

2 A person travelling express with letters, messages, etc., esp. on a fixed route (also ***thorough post***); a courier, a post-rider; a letter-carrier, a postman. Chiefly *dial. & Hist.* exc. in titles of newspapers. E16.

3 A vehicle or vessel used to carry mail; a mail-coach. *obsolete* exc. *Hist.* L16.

4 A single dispatch of letters etc. from or to a place; letters etc. collectively, as dispatched or conveyed; the mail; the quantity of mail cleared from a postbox etc. at one time, or delivered to one location. L16.

5 A national or regional organization or agency for the collection, transmission, and distribution of letters and other postal matter (= POST OFFICE 1); the official conveyance of letters, parcels, etc. M17. ▸**b** A post office; a postbox. L18.

6 A location where post-horses were kept; a posting-house. Also, the distance between successive posting-houses, a stage. *obsolete* exc. *Hist.* M17.

7 In full ***post-paper***. A size of writing-paper, usu. 19 by 15¼ inches (approx. 48 by 39 cm). Now *rare.* M17.

📖 **2** AV *Job* 9:25 Now my dayes are swifter then a Poste. V. WOOLF When the post knocks and the letter comes. **4** DYLAN THOMAS Walks fourteen miles to deliver the post. I. MURDOCH An air letter . . arrived by the morning's post. **5** SHELLEY You will receive the 'Biblical Extracts' by the two-penny post. **b** DICKENS Having scarce time to get this letter in the Post.

Phrases: **by post** †(*a*) by courier; with relays of post-horses; (*b*) by the postal service, through the post office. ***by return (of post)***: see RETURN *noun.* †**in post** in the manner or capacity of a courier; at express speed, in haste. ***staging post***: see STAGING *adjective.* ***standing post***: see sense 1 above. †**take post** *verb phr*¹. start on a journey with post-horses; travel quickly using relays of horses. ***thorough post***: see sense 2 above.

Comb.: **postbag** (*a*) a bag for carrying letters and other postal matter, a mailbag; (*b*) a quantity of mail delivered to a particular person; such mail considered as expressing the opinion of the senders; **post-boat** a boat or ship engaged in conveying mails, esp. on a regular route at fixed times; a packet-boat, a mail-boat; **postbox** (*a*) a box in which letters are posted or deposited for dispatch, a letter-box; (*b*) a box to which mail, newspapers, etc., are delivered; (*c*) any box where papers etc. are left for collection; **post-boy** (*a*) a boy who delivers mail; *Hist.* a boy or man who rides post; (*b*) a postilion; (*c*) *Austral.* = ***JACKY Winter***; **post-bus** a post-office vehicle which also carries passengers; **post-cart** *Hist.* a cart for carrying local mail; **post-chariot** *Hist.* a light four-wheeled carriage used for carrying mail and passengers, and differing from a post-chaise in having a driver's seat in front; **post-coach** *Hist.* a mail-coach, a stagecoach; **post-day** (now *rare*) the day on which the post or mail is due or departs; **post-free** *adjective & adverb* (carried) without charge for postage, either officially or through prepayment; **post-girl** a girl who delivers mail; **post-horn** a valveless horn of a kind orig. used by a postman or the guard of a mail-coach to announce arrival; **post-horse** *Hist.* a horse kept at a post-house or inn for use by post-riders or for hire by travellers; **post-lady** = ***postwoman*** below; **postmark** *noun & verb* (*a*) *noun* an official mark stamped on a letter or other postal package, *esp.* one giving the place, date, and time of dispatch or arrival and serving also to cancel the postage stamp; (*b*) *verb trans.* mark (an envelope etc.) officially with a postmark (usu. in *pass.*); **post-paid** *adjective* having the postage prepaid; ***post-paper***: see sense 7 above; **post-rider** *Hist.* a person who rides post, a mounted letter-carrier; **post-road** *Hist.* a road on which a series of post-houses was established; **post room** the department in a company that deals with incoming and outgoing mail; **post-runner** a person who carries messages or transports mail along a certain route on foot; **post-town** (*a*) a town having a (head) post office; (*b*) a town with its own postcode; (*c*) *Hist.* a town at which post-horses were kept; **post-village** a village where there is a post office; **postwoman** a woman who delivers or collects mail (to be) sent through the post.

post /pəʊst/ *noun*³. *obsolete* exc. *Hist.* E16.

[App. from Italian *posta* stake laid down, repr. Latin *posita*: see POST *noun*².]

CARDS. Now only more fully ***post and pair***. A gambling game involving hands of three cards.

post /pəʊst/ *noun*⁴. M16.

[French *poste* from Italian *posto* from Proto-Romance contr. of popular Latin *positum* neut. pa. pple of *ponere* to place. Cf. POST *noun*².]

1 An office or situation to which a person is appointed; a position of paid employment, a job. M16.

2 The place where a soldier etc. is stationed; a soldier's or sentry's patrol; *gen.* a person's chosen or appointed station, one's place of duty. E17.

3 A (strategic) position taken up by a body of soldiers etc.; the force occupying such a position. L17. ▸**b** A place where an armed force is permanently quartered; a fort; *US* the occupants of such a place, a garrison (now *esp.* in names of veterans' groups). E18. ▸**c** In full ***trading-post***. A place occupied for purposes of trade, esp. in a remote or unsettled region. L18.

4 NAUTICAL (now *Hist.*). The status or rank of full-grade captain in the Royal Navy. Chiefly in phrs. & comb. (see below). E18.

📖 **1** A. BULLOCK He would not make political appointments to the top posts in the Foreign Service. W. RAEPER MacDonald applied for the post of librarian. **2** P. F. BOLLER Adams still at his post, diligently firing away at the enemy. R. INGALLS He took up his post at the window again. **3** WELLINGTON Posts will sometimes be surprised and the troops . . roughly handled. P. L. FERMOR The frontier post was at the end of the bridge. **b** LD MACAULAY The troops . . would not have been sufficient to garrison the posts.

Phrases: ***Cossack post***: see COSSACK *adjective.* ***first-aid post***: see FIRST *aid.* **make post** NAUTICAL (now *Hist.*) (usu. in *pass.*) appoint as post captain, place on the list of captains in the Royal Navy. ***OBSERVATION post***. **take post** *verb phr*². (*a*) (of soldiers etc.) occupy a (strategic) position; (*b*) NAUTICAL (now *Hist.*) receive the rank of post captain in the Royal Navy.

Comb.: **post captain** NAUTICAL (now *Hist.*) a Royal Navy officer holding the full rank of captain, as opp. to a commander receiving the courtesy title of captain; **post exchange** *US* a shop at a military post where goods and services are available to military personnel and authorized civilians; **postholder** (*a*) *Hist.* a civil official in charge of a trading settlement in a Dutch colony; (*b*) a person who fills a post; a jobholder; **post rank** NAUTICAL (now *Hist.*) the rank of post captain in the Royal Navy; **post ship** NAUTICAL (now *Hist.*) a Royal Navy ship of not less than 20 guns, the commission to command which gave post rank to a captain.

post /pəʊst/ *noun*^{5}. **M18.**
[App. from German *Posten* parcel, lot, batch of ore from Italian *posto*: see POST *noun*^{4}.]
PAPER-MAKING. A pile of sheets of handmade paper laid with alternate sheets of felt or other material ready for pressing.

post /pəʊst/ *noun*^{6}. **L19.**
[App. from POST *noun*^{4}.]
Any of a number of military bugle-calls giving notice of the hour of retiring for the night.
first post the earliest such call to be sounded. **last post** the final such call, customarily also blown at military funerals.

post /pəʊst/ *noun*^{7}. *colloq.* (chiefly *US*). **M20.**
[Abbreviation.]
A post-mortem, an autopsy.

post /pəʊst/ *verb*^{1} *trans.* **E16.**
[from POST *noun*^{1}. Cf. earlier POSTING *noun*^{1}.]
1 a Give a square or rectangular cross-section to (timber); make into posts. *obsolete* exc. *dial.* **E16.** ▸**b** Provide or set with posts. *rare.* **E18.**
2 Fix (a notice etc.) to a post, board, etc.; stick up in a prominent or public place. Freq. foll. by *up*. **M17.** ▸**b** Put up notices etc. on or in; cover *with* posters etc. **M19.**
3 Make known, advertise, bring before the public (as) by means of a placard or notice; *spec.* (now *rare*) make known as a defaulter etc., expose to ignominy or ridicule, in this way. **M17.** ▸**b** Publish the name of (a ship, soldier, etc.) *as* overdue or missing. **L19.** ▸**c** Achieve, score. *N. Amer.* **M20.** ▸**d** Announce, publish. *N. Amer.* **M20.**

> 📖 **2** M. FORSTER Handbills offering a reward were . . posted everywhere. **3** R. SOUTH Infallible Cures, which we daily see posted up in every Corner. THACKERAY I'll post you for a swindler. J. O'HARA To be posted at the Gibbsville Club . . could mean . . you had not paid your bill. **c** *New Yorker* He won nineteen games . . and lost . . eight, posting an earned-run average of 2.48. **d** *Times* Companies that posted big price increases . . will be audited.

Comb.: **Post-it**, **Post-it note** (proprietary name for) a small piece of coloured paper with an adhesive strip on one side, used for written notes which can be attached prominently to an object or surface and easily removed.

post /pəʊst/ *verb*^{2}. **M16.**
[from POST *noun*^{2} or French †*poster*.]
▶**I** *verb intrans.* **1** Travel with relays of horses (orig. as a messenger or carrier of letters). *obsolete* exc. *Hist.* **M16.**
2 Ride, run, or travel with speed or haste; make haste, hurry. *arch.* **M16.**
3 HORSEMANSHIP. Rise and fall in the saddle (like a post-boy) when riding at trot. **L19.**

> 📖 **2** *fig.*: POPE He wastes away Old age untimely posting ere his day.

▶**II** *verb trans.* †**4** Foll. by *over*, *off*: hand over or transfer (a duty, responsibility, etc.) to another; shift, delegate; pass off; also, put off, postpone, defer, delay. **M16–M17.**
†**5** Cause to travel speedily; dispatch in haste; hurry (a person). **L16–E19.**
†**6** Carry in the manner of an express messenger; convey swiftly. Only in **17.**
7 †**a** Send by special messenger. **E17–E18.** ▸**b** Send through the post office; put into a post office or postbox for transmission by the post. **M19.**
8 BOOKKEEPING. Transfer (an entry) from an auxiliary book to a more formal one (esp. from a daybook to a journal or to a ledger) or from one account to another; enter (an item) in proper form in a book. **E17.** ▸**b** Complete (a ledger etc.) by entering all appropriate items; keep (a record) up to date thus. Usu. foll. by *up*. **E18.**
9 *fig.* (from sense 8b). Supply with full information or the latest news on a subject; inform. Freq. in ***keep a person posted***, ***keep oneself posted***. Orig. usu. foll. by *up*. *colloq.* (orig. *US*). **M19.**
10 COMPUTING. Send or link (an item of data) to a particular location in a memory etc. (usu. foll. by *to*). Also, record the occurrence of a specified event. **M20.**

> 📖 **5** G. FARQUHAR My father . . posts me away to travel. **6** SHAKES. *Cymb.* The swiftest harts have posted you by land. **7b** J. RHYS I will post the short stories to you tomorrow. V. BROME He wrote a letter but did not post it. **9** J. D. CARR Keep me posted . . Let me know everything. C. CHAPLIN He wrote . . regularly, and kept me posted about Mother. T. ALLBEURY We want you to . . post us on troop movements.

post /pəʊst/ *verb*^{3} *trans.* **L17.**
[from POST *noun*^{4}.]
Orig. MILITARY. **1** Place or station (a sentry, guard, etc.) on duty. **L17.**
2 Appoint to a post, command, or situation, esp. in a different location; *spec.* (NAUTICAL, now *Hist.*) appoint to command a post ship, commission as captain. Freq. in *pass.* **E19.**

> 📖 **1** P. ROSE Guardsmen were posted at Kennington Common. P. AUSTER He posted himself in front of gate twenty-four. **2** S. BRILL The California authorities . . posted someone to follow Fitzsimmons. A. C. GRAYLING He was posted to a mountain artillery regiment. *Guardian* A young Indian civil servant is posted to . . a small provincial town miles away from the . . metropolis.

post /pəʊst/ *verb*^{4} *trans. slang.* **L18.**
[App. from POST *noun*^{3} or perh. from Italian *posta* a stake.]
Lay down, as a stake or payment; deposit (esp. bail money).

post /pəʊst/ *adverb.* Now *arch.* or *Hist.* **M16.**
[from POST *noun*^{2}.]
With post-horses; express; with speed or haste.

post- /pəʊst/ *prefix.*
[Repr. Latin *post* (adverb & preposition) after, behind.]
Used in words adopted from Latin and in English words modelled on these, and as a freely productive prefix.
1 Prefixed adverbially to verbs, verbal derivs., and adjectives, and adjectivally to (chiefly verbal) nouns, with the senses 'later, after, behind (in time, order, or position), occurring, placed, etc., later', 'afterwards, subsequently', as ***postdate***, ***postpone***, ***postpose***, ***postcure***, etc.
2 Prefixed prepositionally to nouns and noun-stems with the sense 'occurring after, situated behind, later than, posterior to, following', as ***postgraduate***, ***postnatal***, ***post-postscriptum***, ***postwar***, etc.; freq. with (words derived from) proper names, as ***post-Cambrian***, ***post-Darwinian***, ***post-Newtonian***, ***post-Renaissance***, ***post-Vedic***, ***post-Victorian***, etc.
■ **post-a'bortal** *adjective* (MEDICINE) occurring or performed after an abortion **E20.** **post-a'bortum** *adjective & adverb* (MEDICINE) (occurring or performed) after an abortion **E20.** **postace'tabular** *adjective* (ANATOMY) situated behind the acetabulum or socket of the hip-bone **M19.** **post-al'veolar** *adjective* (PHONETICS) (of a consonant) articulated with the tongue against the back part of the ridge of the upper teeth **M20.** **post-apo'stolic** *adjective* subsequent to the apostles, later than the apostolic age **E19.** **post-au'ricular** *adjective* situated behind the ear(s) **E20.** **post-'axial** *adjective* (ANATOMY) situated behind an axis **L19.** **post-'axially** *adverb* (ANATOMY) in a post-axial direction **L19.** **postbase** *noun* (LINGUISTICS) a derivational suffix **M20.** **post-Bloom'fieldian** *adjective* (LINGUISTICS) subsequent to Leonard Bloomfield (see BLOOMFIELDIAN) and his work; *spec.* designating or pertaining to American structural linguistics in the 1950s: **M20.** **post-'boarding** *noun* the shaping of a garment by heating on a form after dyeing (rather than before) **M20.** **post'cenal** *adjective* (*joc.*) [Latin *cena* dinner] after-dinner **M19.** **post'central** *adjective* situated behind the centre; *spec.* (ANATOMY) designating a convolution of the brain: **L19.** **post-'climax** *noun* (ECOLOGY) a point in a plant succession at which development has continued beyond the balanced state of climax **E20.** **post'clitic** *noun* (LINGUISTICS) an unemphatic word stressed as part of the preceding word **M20.** **post-'clypeus** *noun*, pl. **-ei**, (in certain insects) the upper section of a divided clypeus **L19.** **post-co'lonial** *adjective* occurring or existing after the end of colonial rule **M20.** **post-'common** *noun* (*obsolete* exc. *Hist.*) = POST-COMMUNION **LME.** **post-Co'mmunion** *noun* the portion of the Eucharist which follows the receiving of the sacrament **L15.** **post-'conquest** *adjective* occurring or existing after a conquest, *spec.* (*post-Conquest*) after the Norman Conquest of England **E20.** **post-conso'nantal** *adjective* occurring in a word after a consonant **M20.** **post'costal** *adjective* situated behind a rib or (ENTOMOLOGY) a costal vein of a wing **E19.** **post'cranial** *adjective* (ANATOMY) situated posterior to the cranium **E20.** **post'cyclic** *adjective* occurring or operating after the end of a cycle or cycles **M20.** **post'dental** *adjective* behind the teeth; PHONETICS (of a consonant) pronounced by placing the tongue against the gum or palate just behind the teeth: **L19.** **post-diluvial** *adjective* (*a*) GEOLOGY subsequent to the diluvial or drift period; (*b*) = POST-DILUVIAN *adjective*: **E19.** **post-di'luvian** *adjective & noun* (*a*) *adjective* existing or occurring after the Flood described in Genesis; (*b*) *noun* a person who lived, or lives, after the Flood: **L17.** **post-di'sseisin** *noun* (LAW, now *Hist.*) a second or subsequent disseisin **M16.** **post-'echo** *noun* a faint repetition of a loud sound occurring in a recording soon after the original sound **M20.** **post-e'mergence** *adjective* occurring, performed, or applied after the emergence of seedlings from the soil **M20.** **postface** *noun* [after *preface*] a brief explanatory comment or note at the end of a book etc. **L18.** **post-fine** *noun* (LAW, now *Hist.*) = ***king's silver*** s.v. KING *noun*. **post'form** *verb trans.* give a shape to (thermosetting laminated plastic) on reheating before setting is complete **M20.** **postgangli'onic** *adjective* (ANATOMY) (of an autonomic nerve) running from a ganglion to an organ **L19.** **post-'genitive** *noun* (GRAMMAR) a possessive noun following the noun it qualifies **E20.** **post-hi'storic** *adjective* pertaining to or designating a period after recorded history or in the future **E20.** **post-hyp'notic** *adjective* (of a suggestion) made during hypnosis and intended to cause the subject to act in a certain way when conscious **E20.** **post-'ictal** *adjective* (MEDICINE) after a stroke or (esp. epileptic) fit **M20.** **postin'dustrial** *adjective* designating, relating to, or characteristic of a society in which heavy industry has been superseded as the basis of the economy, esp. by service industries **M20.** **post-in'fectious** *adjective* (MEDICINE) caused by an infection but arising after it has ceased **E20.** **post-'larval** *adjective* (ZOOLOGY) of, pertaining to, or designating stages in development after the larval stage, esp. those in which some larval characteristics are retained, before the animal attains fully adult form **L19.** **post'medial** *adjective* occurring or situated in front of the medial line or a medial position **L17.** **post-mei'otic** *adjective* (CYTOLOGY) occurring after meiosis; that has undergone meiosis: **E20.** **post-me'narchal**, **postme'narcheal** *adjectives* (MEDICINE) occurring or existing after the menarche; (of a young female) who has begun to menstruate: **M20.** **postmeno'pausal** *adjective* occurring after the menopause **E20.** **post-'mineral** *adjective* (GEOLOGY) occurring after the formation of a mineral deposit **E20.** **postmi'totic** *adjective* (CYTOLOGY) after mitosis; (of a cell) having ceased (reversibly or irreversibly) to undergo division: **M20.** **postmultipli'cation** *noun* (MATH.) non-commutative multiplication by a following factor **M19.** **post'multiply** *verb trans.* (MATH.) multiply non-commutatively by a following factor **M19.** **post'nasal** *adjective* (chiefly MEDICINE) situated or occurring at the back of or behind the nose or nasal cavity; ***postnasal drip***, secretion of mucus into the nasopharynx: **L19.** **postneo'natal** *adjective* (MEDICINE) pertaining to or designating the period from four weeks after a child's birth to the end of the first year **M20.** **post'nominal** *adjective* (GRAMMAR) following a substantive or a proper name **M20.** **post-note** *noun* (*US*, *obsolete* exc. *Hist.*) a note issued by a bank or banking association, payable to order at a future specified date, and designed as part of the bank's circulating medium **L18.** **post-o'bituary** *adjective* occurring, existing, etc., after someone's death; post-obit, post-mortem: **E19.** **post-'ocular** *adjective* (ANATOMY & ZOOLOGY) situated behind the eye **L19.** **post-'oral** *adjective* (ANATOMY & ZOOLOGY) situated behind the mouth; *esp.* designating segments of the head in arthropods: **L19.** **post-'ovulative** *adjective* (MEDICINE) = POST-OVULATORY **M20.** **post-ovu'latory** *adjective* (MEDICINE) occurring after ovulation **E20.** **post'palatal** *adjective* (*a*) ANATOMY situated behind the palate or palatal bones; (*b*) PHONETICS (of a consonant) articulated with the tip or middle of the tongue against the hard palate: **L19.** **post-pre'cipitate** *verb trans. & intrans.* (CHEMISTRY) deposit or be deposited by post-precipitation **M20.** **post-precipi'tation** *noun* (CHEMISTRY) precipitation of a compound spontaneously following that of another from the same solution **M20.** **post-'primary** *adjective* (of education etc.) subsequent to that which is primary; (of a pupil) receiving such education: **E20.** **postre'duction** *noun* (GENETICS) separation of homologous chromatids, or (earlier) reduction of chromosome number, at the second meiosis rather than the first **E20.** **post-repro'ductive** *adjective* occurring after the period of life when an individual is capable of reproduction **E20.** **postscu'tellum** *noun*, pl. **-lla**, ENTOMOLOGY the fourth (hindmost) of the sclerites making up each segment of an insect's thorax **E19.** **post-'season** *adjective* (chiefly *N. Amer.*) (of a baseball match, football game, or other sporting fixture) taking place after the end of the regular season **E20.** **postsy'naptic** *adjective* (*a*) CYTOLOGY existing or occurring after meiotic synapsis; (*b*) PHYSIOLOGY of, pertaining to, or designating a neurone that receives a nerve impulse at a synapse: **E20.** **post-'sync**, **-synch** *noun & verb* (*colloq.*) (*a*) *noun* = POST-SYNCHRONIZATION; (*b*) *verb trans.* = POST-SYNCHRONIZE: **M20.** **post-synchroni'zation** *noun* the action of post-synchronizing a sound recording **M20.** **post-'synchronize** *verb trans.* add (a sound recording) to the corresponding images of a film or video recording **M20.** **post-'tax** *adjective* (of earnings, profits, etc.) remaining after the deduction of tax **L20.** **post-tec'tonic** *adjective* (GEOLOGY) occurring or existing after tectonic activity **M20.** **post-'tension** *verb trans.* strengthen (reinforced concrete) by applying tension to the reinforcing rods after the concrete has set (freq. as ***post-tensioned*** *ppl adjective*) **M20.** **post-'tonic** *adjective* (LINGUISTICS) following the stressed syllable **L19.** **post-trau'matic** *adjective* (MEDICINE) occurring after injury or psychological shock **L19.** **post-'treatment** *noun & adjective* (*a*) *noun* treatment carried out after some other process or treatment is completed; (*b*) *adjective* arising or occurring after treatment is completed: **M20.** **post'velar** *adjective* behind or at the back of the velum or soft palate; PHONETICS (of a consonant) articulated with the tongue against the rear half of the soft palate: **M20.** **post'verbal** *adjective* (GRAMMAR) occurring following a verb **M20.** **post'viral** *adjective* (MEDICINE) following a viral infection; ***postviral fatigue syndrome***, ***postviral syndrome***, myalgic encephalomyelitis: **M20.**

postabdomen /pəʊst'abdəmən/ *noun.* **M19.**
[from POST- 1 + ABDOMEN.]
The posterior part of the abdomen, esp. in insects, crustaceans, etc.
■ **postab'dominal** *adjective* **L19.**

postage /'pəʊstɪdʒ/ *noun.* **L16.**
[from POST *noun*^{2} + -AGE.]
†**1 a** The carriage or conveyance of letters etc. by postal messenger. **L16–L17.** ▸**b** The postal service; a postal service between particular points. **M17–L18.**
†**2** Travel by means of post-horses; rapid travel. Also, the charge for hire of a post-horse. **E17–E19.**
3 The amount (orig. paid to a postal messenger) charged for carrying a letter or postal packet. Now *esp.*, the charge made by the post office for the conveyance of a letter etc., usu. prepaid by means of a stamp or stamps. **M17.**
Comb.: **postage currency** (*obsolete* exc. *Hist.*) = POSTAL ***currency***; **postage due** *noun & adjective* (*a*) *noun* the balance of postage not prepaid; (*b*) *adjective* designating a special postage stamp indicating postage still to be paid on a letter etc.; **postage meter** *N. Amer.* a franking machine; **postage stamp** an official stamp embossed or impressed on an envelope etc., or (now usu.) having the form of a small adhesive label of specified face value and bearing a distinctive design, to be affixed to any letter or packet sent by post as a means of prepayment of postage and as evidence of such payment; **postage-stamp** *attrib. adjective* very small, very cramped.

postal /'pəʊst(ə)l/ *adjective & noun.* **M19.**
[French *postal(e)*, from *poste* POST *noun*^{2}: see -AL^1.]
▶**A** *adjective.* Of or pertaining to the post; conveyed by or using the post. **M19.**
go postal *US colloq.* [with ref. to cases in which postal employees have run amok and shot colleagues] become irrational and violent, esp. from stress. **postal ballot** = ***postal vote*** below.

postal card *US* a postcard. **postal code** = POSTCODE. **postal currency** *US* (*obsolete* exc. *Hist.*) a paper currency bearing designs similar to those of postage stamps of the appropriate values and issued during the American Civil War to replace the actual postage stamps then being used instead of lower denomination silver coin. **postal note** (chiefly *US, Austral., & NZ*) a postal order. **postal order** an order issued by a post office for the payment of a specified sum to a named payee at a post office. **Postal Union** a union of the governments of various countries for the regulation of international postage. **postal vote** a vote in an election, on a resolution, etc., submitted by post on a special form.
▶**B** *ellipt.* as *noun*. **1** A postcard; a postal order. *US colloq.* L19.
2 A mail train or carriage. *US colloq.* L19.
■ **postali'zation** *noun* the act or process of postalizing a public service M20. **postalize** *verb trans.* make (a public service) like the postal system in respect of fixed prices for delivery regardless of distance L19. **postally** *adverb* for postal purposes; in the post; as far as postal matters are concerned: L19.

post-bellum /pəʊs(t)ˈbɛləm/ *adjective*. L19.
[from Latin *post* after + *bellum* war.]
Existing, occurring, etc., after a (particular) war, esp. (*US*) the American Civil War.

postcard /ˈpəʊs(t)kɑːd/ *noun, verb, & adjective*. L19.
[from POST *noun*² + CARD *noun*².]
▶**A** *noun*. A card designed to be conveyed by post without an envelope, *spec.* (***a***) with space for a message on one side and the address on the reverse; (***b***) = ***picture postcard*** s.v. PICTURE *noun* L19.
📖 M. FLANAGAN A coloured postcard of the Blue Mosque.
▶**B** *verb trans.* Communicate with, inform, or announce by postcard. L19.
▶**C** *attrib.* or as *adjective*. Such as is depicted on a postcard; picturesque, ideally pretty. M20.
📖 *Spectator* A postcard land of blossom and bridges.

postcaval /pəʊs(t)ˈkeɪv(ə)l/ *adjective*. M19.
[from POST- 1 + CAVA + -AL¹.]
ANATOMY. ***postcaval vein***, the inferior vena cava.

post-chaise /ˈpəʊs(t)ʃeɪz/ *noun*. Pl. pronounced same. L17.
[from POST *noun*² + CHAISE.]
Hist. A horse-drawn usu. four-wheeled carriage (in Britain usu. with a closed body, the driver riding on one of the horses) used for carrying mail and passengers, esp. in the 18th and early 19th cents.

post-Christian /pəʊs(t)ˈkrɪstʃ(ə)n, -tɪən/ *adjective & noun*. M19.
[from POST- 2 + CHRISTIAN *adjective*.]
▶**A** *adjective*. **1** Occurring in or dating from a time after the lifetime of Jesus or the rise of Christianity. M19.
2 Occurring in or dating from a time after the decline of Christianity in a region. E20.
▶**B** *noun*. A person in a nominally Christian society who has no professed religion. M20.

postclassic /pəʊs(t)ˈklasɪk/ *adjective*. In ARCHAEOLOGY usu. **P-**. L19.
[from POST- 2 + CLASSIC.]
Post-classical; *spec.* in ARCHAEOLOGY, of, pertaining to, or designating the period of Meso-American civilization that succeeded the Classic, from *c* 900 to 1520.

post-classical /pəʊs(t)ˈklasɪk(ə)l/ *adjective*. M19.
[from POST- 2 + CLASSICAL.]
Occurring in or characteristic of a period after one regarded as classical, esp. the classical age of Greek and Roman literature; MUSIC belonging to the Romantic period.

postcode /ˈpəʊs(t)kəʊd/ *noun & verb*. M20.
[from POST *noun*² + CODE *noun*.]
▶**A** *noun*. A series of letters and numbers included in a postal address to facilitate the sorting and speedy delivery of mail. M20.
▶**B** *verb trans.* Give a postcode to; write a postcode on. M20.

post-coital /pəʊs(t)ˈkəʊɪt(ə)l/ *adjective*. E20.
[from POST- 2 + COITAL.]
Occurring, existing, etc., after sexual intercourse. (Cf. next).
■ **post-coitally** *adverb* M20.

post coitum /pəʊs(t) ˈkəʊɪtəm/ *adjectival & adverbial phr.* E20.
[from Latin *post* after + *coitum* accus. of COITUS.]
After sexual intercourse; post-coital(ly).
¶ Freq. with allusion to the Latin proverb *post coitum omne animal triste est* after intercourse every animal is sad.

postcure /*as verb* pəʊs(t)ˈkjʊə, *as noun* ˈpəʊs(t)kjʊə/ *verb & noun*. M20.
[from POST- 1 + CURE *noun*¹, *verb*.]
▶**A** *verb trans.* Cure (plastic) after fabrication in order to complete the cure. M20.
▶**B** *noun*. The process or an instance of postcuring plastic. M20.

post-dam /ˈpəʊs(t)dam/ *verb & noun*. E20.
[from POSTERIOR + DAM *noun*¹.]
DENTISTRY. ▶**A** *verb trans. & intrans.* Infl. **-mm-**. Construct a ridge along the upper posterior border of (a palatal denture) so as to form a seal with the soft palate. E20.
▶**B** *noun*. A ridge constructed by post-damming. M20.

postdate /pəʊs(t)ˈdeɪt/ *verb trans.* E17.
[from POST- 1 + DATE *verb*.]
1 Affix or assign a date to (an event) later than the actual or currently accepted one. E17.
2 Follow in date, belong to a later date than. E20.
📖 **1** *Financial Times* It is perfectly lawful to post-date a cheque. **2** *New York Times* The lid is painted with . . scenes that post-date the 1658 instrument.
■ **postdating** *noun* the action of the verb; an instance of this; *esp.* a later occurrence of something: M20.

post-date /ˈpəʊs(t)deɪt/ *noun*. *rare*. E17.
[from POST- 2 + DATE *noun*².]
A date affixed to a document etc., or assigned to an event, which is later than the actual or currently accepted date.

postdiction /ˈpəʊs(t)dɪkʃ(ə)n/ *noun*. M20.
[from POST- 2 after *prediction*.]
The making of an assertion or deduction about a past event; an instance of this. Cf. RETRODICTION.
■ **postdict** *verb trans.* [back-form.] make a postdiction about M20.

postdoc /pəʊs(t)ˈdɒk/ *noun & adjective*. *colloq.* L20.
[Abbreviation.]
▶**A** *noun*. A post-doctoral fellow or appointment. L20.
▶**B** *adjective*. = POST-DOCTORAL *adjective*. *rare*. L20.

post-doctoral /pəʊs(t)ˈdɒktər(ə)l/ *adjective & noun*. M20.
[from POST- 2 + DOCTORAL.]
▶**A** *adjective*. Designating advanced research work carried out by a person already holding a doctor's degree; of, relating to, or engaged in work of this kind. M20.
▶**B** *noun*. A post-doctoral fellow or appointment. *rare*. L20.

postea /ˈpəʊstɪə/ *noun*. E17.
[Latin = afterwards (being the first word of the usual beginning of the record).]
LAW (now *Hist.*). The part of the record of a civil process which sets out the proceedings at the trial and the verdict given.

posted /ˈpəʊstɪd/ *adjective*. L16.
[from POST *noun*¹, *verb*¹: see -ED², -ED¹.]
Provided with or having posts (of a specified number or kind).

post-edit /pəʊstˈɛdɪt/ *verb trans.* M20.
[from POST- 1 + EDIT *verb*.]
Edit after production or processing by a machine.
■ **post-editor** *noun* a person who performs post-editing M20.

posteen *noun* see POSHTEEN.

post-entry /*as noun* ˈpəʊstɛntri, *as adjective* pəʊˈstɛntri/ *noun & adjective*. M17.
[from POST- 1, 2 + ENTRY.]
▶**A** *noun*. A late or subsequent entry, esp. in a race or a ship's manifest. M17.
▶**B** *adjective*. Designating a closed shop in which new employees are required to join a trade union after appointment. M20.

poster /ˈpəʊstə/ *noun*¹. E17.
[from POST *verb*² + -ER¹.]
1 A person who travels post; a prompt or swift traveller. Also, a post-horse. Now *rare* or *obsolete*. E17.
2 A person who posts a letter etc. L19.

poster /ˈpəʊstə/ *noun*². M19.
[from POST *verb*¹ + -ER¹.]
1 A person who puts up notices, a billposter. M19.
2 A printed or written notice posted or displayed in a public place as an announcement or advertisement. Now also, a large printed picture (which may or may not be an advertisement) suitable for decorative display on a wall. M19. ▸**b** (A presentation at) a poster session (see below). L20.
3 COMPUTING. A person who sends a message to a newsgroup. L20.
📖 **2** E. LONGFORD Posters . . announcing . . a public meeting. M. GARDINER A vintage year for London Underground posters.
Comb.: **poster boy** *N. Amer.* (***a***) a male poster child; (***b***) a male model who appears in a print advertisement; **poster child** *N. Amer.* a child who appears on a poster in an advertisement for a charitable organization; *transf.* a person who epitomizes or represents a specified quality, cause, etc.; **poster colour** an opaque paint with a water-soluble binder, such as is used on posters; **poster girl** *N. Amer.* (***a***) a female poster child; (***b***) a female model who appears in a print advertisement; **poster paint** = ***poster colour*** above; **poster paper**: of a kind used for posters; **poster session** a meeting of scientists etc. at which their work is displayed pictorially.
■ **posterish** *adjective* (esp. of a painting) characteristic or suggestive of a poster or posters M20. **posterist** *noun* a designer of posters E20. **posteri'zation** *noun* (PHOTOGRAPHY) the process of posterizing a photograph M20. **posterize** *verb trans.* (PHOTOGRAPHY) print (a photograph) using only a small number of different tones M20.

poster /ˈpəʊstə/ *noun*³. *rare*. M19.
[from POST *noun*¹ + -ER¹.]
RUGBY FOOTBALL. A ball that passes directly over the top of a goalpost.
¶ See also ***FOUR-poster (bed)***.

poste restante /pəʊst ˈrɛst(ə)nt, rɛˈstant; *foreign* pɔst rɛstɑ̃ːt/ *adverb & noun phr.* M18.
[French = letter(s) remaining.]
1 *adverb & noun phr.* (A direction written on a letter indicating that it is) to remain at the post office specified until called for by the addressee. M18.
2 *noun*. The department in a post office where such letters are kept. M19.

posterial /pɒˈstɪərɪəl/ *adjective*. *rare*. LME.
[Irreg. from Latin *posterus*: see POSTERIOR, -IAL.]
1 Pertaining to the posterior or buttocks. LME.
2 Turned towards the hinder side. M19.

posterior /pɒˈstɪərɪə/ *noun & adjective*. E16.
[Latin, compar. of *posterus* following, future, from *post* after: see -IOR.]
▶**A** *noun*. **1** In *pl.* Those who come after; descendants, posterity. Now *rare* or *obsolete*. E16.
†**2** The later part. *joc. rare*. L16–E17.
3 *sing.* & (now *rare*) in *pl.* The buttocks. E17.
📖 **1** SIR W. SCOTT Neither he, nor his posteriors from generation to generation, shall sit upon it ony mair. **3** S. BECKETT The sensation of a chair coming together with his drooping posteriors at last was so delicious. T. CALLENDER Jerome felt the whip . . stinging into his posterior.
▶**B** *adjective*. **1** Later, coming after in time, series, or order; subsequent (*to*). Opp. ***prior***. M16.
2 Chiefly ANATOMY. Situated at the back; hinder; situated behind or further back than something else. Opp. ***anterior***. L16.
📖 **1** C. LYELL Proofs of the posterior origin of the lava. R. G. COLLINGWOOD The sensum is here not prior but posterior to the emotion. **posterior probability** STATISTICS the probability that a hypothesis is true calculated in the light of relevant observations.
■ **posteriorly** *adverb* (***a***) (chiefly ANATOMY) in a posterior position; behind; †(***b***) at a later time, subsequently: L16. **posteriormost** *adjective* (chiefly BIOLOGY) in the furthest back position, nearest to the posterior E20.

posteriority /pɒˌstɪərɪˈɒrɪti/ *noun*. LME.
[medieval Latin *posterioritas*, from Latin POSTERIOR: see -ITY.]
1 The state or quality of being later or subsequent in time. LME.
2 Inferiority in order, rank, or dignity. Now *rare*. M16.

posterity /pɒˈstɛrɪti/ *noun*. LME.
[Old & mod. French *postérité* from Latin *posteritas*, from *posterus*: see POSTERIOR, -ITY.]
1 The descendants collectively of a person. LME.
2 All succeeding generations collectively; *transf.* future fame or recognition. LME. ▸†**b** In *pl.* Later generations. M16–M17.
📖 **1** COVERDALE *Job* 5:25 Thy posterite shalbe as the grasse vpon the earth. **2** E. LONGFORD Posterity must be grateful to the Duke for his eighteen years' service to Oxford. S. QUINN A formal banquet . . recorded for posterity in an official photograph.

postern /ˈpɒst(ə)n, ˈpəʊst-/ *noun & adjective*. ME.
[Old French *posterne* (mod. *poterne*) alt. of *posterle* from late Latin *posterula* dim. of *posterus*: see POSTERIOR.]
▶**A** *noun*. **1** A back door; a door or gate distinct from the main entrance; a side way or entrance. ME. ▸**b** *fig.* A way of escape. Also, a back-door or underhand means of entry. Now *rare*. L16.
†**2** The latter or hinder part; the buttocks. *rare*. E17–E18.
📖 **1** J. R. GREEN She escaped in white robes by a postern. **b** SIR T. BROWNE So closely shut up . . as not to find some escape by a postern of resipiscency.
▶**B** *attrib.* or as *adjective*. Of a gate, door, etc.: placed at the back or side, secondary, lesser. LME.

postero- /ˈpɒstərəʊ/ *combining form*.
[from POSTER(IOR: see -O-.]
Chiefly ANATOMY. Forming adjectives and corresp. adverbs with the sense 'posterior and —'.
■ **postero'lateral** *adjective* both posterior and lateral M19. **postero'laterally** *adverb* in a posterolateral position M20. **postero'ventral** *adjective* placed on the hinder part of the ventral aspect E20. **postero'ventrally** *adverb* in a posteroventral position E20.

post eventum /pəʊst ɪˈvɛntəm/ *adverbial phr.* M19.
[Latin = after the event.]
= POST FACTUM.

For other words beginning with *post-* see the entry for **post-**

post-exilian /pəʊstɪɡˈzɪlɪən, -ɪkˈsɪ-, -ɛɡ-, -ɛk-/ *adjective*. L19.
[from POST- 2 + EXILIAN.]
Existing or occurring in the period of Jewish history following the Babylonian exile.
■ Also **post-exilic** *adjective* L19.

post-exist /pəʊstɪɡˈzɪst, -ɛɡ-/ *verb intrans. rare*. L17.
[from POST- 1 + EXIST.]
Exist at a later period, esp. after the present life; live subsequently.
■ **post-existence** *noun* L17. **post-existent** *adjective* L17.

post factum /pəʊs(t) ˈfaktəm/ *adverbial phr.* L17.
[Latin = after the fact.]
After the event; with hindsight.

post festum /pəʊs(t) ˈfɛstəm/ *adverbial phr.* L19.
[Latin = after the festival.]
= prec.

postfix /ˈpəʊs(t)fɪks/ *noun*. E19.
[from POST- 1 after *prefix*.]
An element (e.g. *-ly*) appended to the end of a word; a suffix.

postfix /pəʊs(t)ˈfɪks/ *verb trans.* E19.
[from POST- 1 + FIX *verb*.]
1 Append as a postfix. E19.
2 ANATOMY. As ***postfixed*** *ppl adjective*: (of a nerve) connected to the spinal cord relatively caudally. L19.
3 BIOLOGY. Fix a second time; treat with a second fixative. M20.
■ **postfiˈxation** *noun* (*a*) ANATOMY the condition of a nerve of being postfixed; (*b*) BIOLOGY fixation of tissue that has already been treated with a fixative: M20.

post-Fordism /pəʊs(t)ˈfɔːdɪz(ə)m/ *noun*. L20.
[from POST- + FORDISM.]
ECONOMICS. The theory that modern industrial production should change from the large-scale mass-production methods pioneered by Henry Ford towards the use of small flexible manufacturing units.
■ **post-Fordist** *noun & adjective* L20.

post-Freudian /pəʊs(t)ˈfrɔɪdɪən/ *noun & adjective*. M20.
[from POST- 2 + FREUDIAN.]
► **A** *noun*. A psychoanalyst whose views and practice have developed and diverged from, or have been influenced by, those of Freud; a person influenced by Freudian ideas. M20.
► **B** *adjective*. Influenced by Freud's work in psychoanalysis; occurring after the impact and influence of Freud's ideas. M20.

postfrontal /pəʊs(t)ˈfrʌnt(ə)l/ *adjective & noun*. M19.
[from POST- 2 + FRONTAL *adjective, noun*.]
ANATOMY & ZOOLOGY. ►**A** *adjective*. **1** Situated behind the forehead, or at the back of the frontal bone. M19.
2 Situated in the posterior part of the frontal lobe of the brain. L19.
► **B** *ellipt.* as *noun*. A bone behind the orbit of the eye in some vertebrates. M19.

postglacial /pəʊs(t)ˈɡleɪʃ(ə)l, -sɪəl/ *adjective & noun*. M19.
[from POST- 2 + GLACIAL.]
GEOLOGY. ►**A** *adjective*. Existing, occurring, or formed subsequent to the glacial period or ice age. M19.
► **B** *ellipt.* as *noun*. A postglacial deposit; the postglacial period. E20.
■ **postglacially** *adverb* M20.

postgrad /pəʊs(t)ˈɡrad/ *noun & adjective*. *colloq.* M20.
[Abbreviation.]
= next.

postgraduate /pəʊs(t)ˈɡradjʊət/ *adjective & noun*. M19.
[from POST- 2 + GRADUATE *noun & ppl adjective*.]
► **A** *adjective*. Of a course of study: carried on after graduation, *spec.* after taking a first degree. Also, of or relating to a student or students following such a course of study. M19.
► **B** *noun*. A student who takes a postgraduate course or who goes on to further study after graduation. L19.

posthabit /pəʊstˈhabɪt/ *verb trans. rare*. M17.
[Latin *posthabere* place after, from *post* POST- 1 + *habere*, *habit-* hold, have.]
Make secondary or subordinate *to*.

post-haste /pəʊstˈheɪst, ˈpəʊstheɪst/ *noun & adverb*. M16.
[From the former direction on letters 'haste, post, haste', later taken as a comb. of POST *noun*[2] and HASTE *noun*.]
► **A** *noun*. Haste or speed like that of a person travelling post; promptness or swiftness of travel. *arch.* M16.

T. HEARNE You did not use to write in Post-Hast.

► **B** *adverb*. With the speed of a person travelling post; as rapidly as possible; hurriedly, swiftly; promptly. L16.

T. HARDY Sending post-haste for somebody or other to play to them. J. MAY Soldiers came galloping posthaste out of the barbican and rushed off.

posthitis /pɒsˈθʌɪtɪs/ *noun*. M19.
[from Greek *posthē* prepuce + -ITIS.]
MEDICINE. Inflammation of the prepuce.

post hoc /pəʊst ˈhɒk/ *adverbial & adjectival phr.* M19.
[Latin.]
After this; after the event; consequent(ly).
¶ Chiefly with ref. to the fallacy *post hoc, ergo propter hoc* after this, therefore because of this.

post-house /ˈpəʊsthaʊs/ *noun*. E17.
[from POST *noun*[2] + HOUSE *noun*[1].]
1 An inn etc. where post-horses were kept for the use of travellers. Now only *Hist.* and in names of inns, hotels, etc. E17.
2 A post office. Long *obsolete* exc. *dial.* M17.

posthuma /ˈpɒstjʊmə/ *noun pl. rare*. M17.
[Latin, neut. pl. of *post(h)umus*: see next, -A[3].]
Posthumous writings.

posthumous /ˈpɒstjʊməs/ *adjective & noun*. E17.
[from Latin *postumus* last, superl. from *post* after; in late Latin referred to *humus* earth or *humare* bury: see -OUS.]
► **A** *adjective*. Occurring, existing, appearing, etc., after a person's death; *esp.* (of a child) born after the father's death; (of a book etc.) published after the author's death; (of a medal) awarded to a person who has died. E17.

L. WOOLF His friend A. F. Wedgwood . . had recently died leaving a posthumous novel. P. LARKIN Hardy's reputation has not taken the accustomed posthumous dip. D. A. THOMAS He was awarded a posthumous V.C.

►†**B** *noun*. A posthumous child. *rare*. M17–E18.
■ †**posthume** *adjective & noun* [French] (*a*) *adjective* = POSTHUMOUS *adjective*; (*b*) *noun* a posthumous child; a posthumous work: L16–L17. **posthumously** *adverb* L18. †**posthumus** *adjective & noun* (pl. **-humi**) [late Latin] = POSTHUMOUS LME–L17.

postica *noun* pl. of POSTICUM.

postical /ˈpɒstɪk(ə)l/ *adjective*. M17.
[from Latin *posticus* hinder, from *post* behind: see -IC, -AL[1].]
Hinder, posterior. Now only BOTANY, designating the back or ventral portion of a stem or leaf.
■ Also **posticous** /pɒˈstʌɪkəs/ *adjective* M19.

postiche /pɒˈstiːʃ/ *adjective & noun*. As adjective also (earlier) †**-ique**. E18.
[French from Italian *posticcio* counterfeit, feigned.]
► **A** *adjective*. Artificial; (of a decoration in architecture etc.) added to a finished work, esp. inappropriately or superfluously. *rare*. E18.
► **B** *noun*. **1** An imitation substituted for the real thing; *esp.* a piece of false hair worn as an adornment. L19.
2 Imitation, pretence. *rare*. L19.

posticum /pɒˈstʌɪkəm/ *noun*. Pl. **-ca** /-kə/. E18.
[Latin, use as noun of neut. of *posticus*: see POSTICAL.]
ARCHITECTURE. A back door or gate; *spec.* a portico or apartment at the back of an ancient Roman temple, equivalent to the Greek opisthodomos.

postie /ˈpəʊsti/ *noun*. *colloq.* Also **posty**. L19.
[from POST *noun*[2] + -IE.]
(A familiar name for) a postman or postwoman.

postil /ˈpɒstɪl/ *noun*. *obsolete* exc. *Hist.* LME.
[Old French *postille* from medieval Latin *postilla*, perh. from Latin *post illa (verba)* after those (words), used as a direction to a scribe.]
1 A marginal note or comment on a text, esp. of Scripture. LME.
2 A series of such comments, a commentary; *spec.* an expository discourse or homily on a Gospel or Epistle, to be read in a church service. Also, a book of such homilies. L15.

postil /ˈpɒstɪl/ *verb trans.* Long *obsolete* exc. *Hist.* Infl. **-ll-**. LME.
[French †*postil(l)er* from medieval Latin *postillare*, from *postilla*: see prec.]
Annotate; inscribe with marginal notes.

postilion /pɒˈstɪlɪən/ *noun*. Also **-ll-**. M16.
[French *postillon* from Italian *postiglione* post-boy, from *posta* POST *noun*[2].]
†**1** A person who rides a post-horse; a courier or swift messenger. Also, a guide or forerunner (for such a person). M16–E18.
2 A person who rides the (leading) nearside horse drawing a coach etc.; *esp.* one who rides the near horse when one pair only is used and there is no coachman. E17.

postillate /ˈpɒstɪleɪt/ *verb trans. rare* (*obsolete* exc. *Hist.*). LME.
[medieval Latin *postillat-* ppl stem of *postillare* POSTIL *verb*: see -ATE[3].]
= POSTIL *verb*
■ **postiˈllation** *noun* M19.

postillion *noun* var. of POSTILION.

post-impressionism /pəʊstɪmˈprɛʃ(ə)nɪz(ə)m/ *noun*. E20.
[from POST- 2 + IMPRESSIONISM.]
A school or style of painting developed from, or as a reaction against, impressionism in the late 19th and early 20th cents., which rejected concern with momentary effects and naturalistic representation, and sought to express the artist's individual conception of the subject.
■ **post-impressionist** *noun & adjective* (*a*) *noun* a practitioner or adherent of post-impressionism; (*b*) *adjective* of or pertaining to post-impressionists or post-impressionism: E20. **post-impressioˈnistic** *adjective* E20.

posting /ˈpəʊstɪŋ/ *noun*[1]. ME.
[from POST *noun*[1], *verb*[1] + -ING[1].]
1 The action of providing something with posts; posts collectively. Long *rare*. ME.
2 The action of sticking up a notice etc., or of making something public by this or similar means; public advertisement by posters. M17.

posting /ˈpəʊstɪŋ/ *noun*[2]. L16.
[from POST *verb*[2] + -ING[1].]
1 The action of POST *verb*[2]. Also (*obsolete* exc. *Hist.*), the business or occupation of keeping post-horses, post-vehicles, etc. L16.
2 An amount of mail posted during a given period. E20.

posting /ˈpəʊstɪŋ/ *noun*[3]. M19.
[from POST *verb*[3] + -ING[1].]
Orig. MILITARY. The action of POST *verb*[3]; an instance of this; a command, situation, etc., to which someone is appointed. Also, the location of such a post or appointment.

C. TOMALIN Marion's parents were moved to another posting, and Katherine lost her friend.

†**postique** *adjective* see POSTICHE.

postlapsarian /pəʊs(t)lapˈsɛːrɪən/ *adjective*. M18.
[from POST- 2 after *sublapsarian*.]
THEOLOGY. Occurring or existing after the Fall of Man. Formerly also = INFRALAPSARIAN *adjective*.

postliminary /pəʊs(t)ˈlɪmɪn(ə)ri/ *adjective*. E18.
[Sense 1 from next; sense 2 from Latin POST- 2 + *limin-*, *limen* threshold: see -ARY[1].]
1 LAW. Pertaining to or involving the right of postliminy. E18.
2 Subsequent. Opp. ***preliminary***. *rare*. E19.
■ **postliminious** /-lɪˈmɪnɪəs/, **postliminous** /-ˈlɪmɪnəs/ *adjectives* †(*a*) = POSTLIMINARY 1; (*b*) = POSTLIMINARY 2: M17.

postliminy /pəʊs(t)ˈlɪmɪni/ *noun*. Also in Latin form **postliminium** /pəʊs(t)lɪˈmɪnɪʌm/. M17.
[Latin *postliminium*, from POST- 2 + *limin-*, *limen* threshold: see -Y[3].]
LAW. In Roman Law, the right of a banished person or captive to resume civic privileges on return from exile. In International Law, the restoration to their former status of people and things taken in war.

postlude /ˈpəʊs(t)luːd/ *noun*. M19.
[from POST- 1 after *prelude*, *interlude*.]
1 MUSIC. A concluding movement played at the end of an oratorio or other work; a concluding voluntary. M19.
2 A written or spoken epilogue; an afterword or conclusion. E20.

postman /ˈpəʊs(t)mən/ *noun*[1]. Pl. **-men**. E16.
[from POST *noun*[2] + MAN *noun*.]
1 A courier who rides post. *obsolete* exc. *Hist.* E16.
2 A man who delivers or collects mail (to be) sent through the post. M18.
2 postman's knock (*a*) a sharp knock on a door, said to be typical of a postman; (*b*) a parlour game in which the players in turn act as postman and deliver letters which are paid for by kisses.

postman /ˈpəʊs(t)mən/ *noun*[2]. *obsolete* exc. *Hist.* Pl. **-men**. M18.
[from POST *noun*[1] + MAN *noun*: so called from the post used as a measure of length in excise cases, beside which the postman stood. Cf. TUBMAN.]
A barrister in the former Court of Exchequer who had precedence in motions except in Crown business.

postmaster /ˈpəʊs(t)mɑːstə/ *noun*[1]. E16.
[from POST *noun*[2] + MASTER *noun*[1].]
1 a An officer in charge of the system of postal messengers. *obsolete* exc. *Hist.* E16. ►**b** ***Postmaster General***, the administrative head of the postal service of a country or State (usu. a government minister). (The post was abolished in the UK in 1969.) E17.
2 The master of a posting station, who provides post-horses; a person who keeps a posting establishment. *obsolete* exc. *Hist.* L16.
3 Orig., a post-office servant at a stage of a post-road whose primary duty was to carry the mail to the next stage and receive and deliver or send out letters for his own town or district (cf. POST *noun*[2] 1). Now, a person in charge of a post office (cf. POSTMISTRESS). E17.
■ **postmastership** *noun* E17.

postmaster /ˈpəʊs(t)mɑːstə/ *noun*[2]. M16.
[Origin unkn.]
At Merton College, Oxford: a portionist.

For other words beginning with *post-* see the entry for **post-**

postmaster /ˈpəʊs(t)mɑːstə/ *noun*³. *Canad.* M19.
[from POST *noun*⁴ + MASTER *noun*¹.]
The master of a fur-trading post.

postmature /pəʊs(t)məˈtjʊə/ *adjective.* L19.
[from POST- 2 + MATURE *adjective.*]
1 MEDICINE. Of an infant: born after a pregnancy lasting significantly longer than normal. L19.
2 Pertaining to or designating a person who is over the age of maturity. L19.
▪ **postmaturely** *adverb* M20. **postmaturity** *noun* E20.

postmen *noun* pl. of POSTMAN *noun*¹, *noun*².

postmenstrual /pəʊs(t)ˈmɛnstrʊəl/ *adjective.* L19.
[from POST- 2 + MENSTRUAL.]
MEDICINE. Occurring after menstruation.
▪ **postmenstruum** *noun,* pl. **-strua, -struums,** the stage of the menstrual cycle which follows menstruation E20.

post meridiem /pəʊs(t) məˈrɪdɪəm/ *adjectival & adverbial phr.* M17.
[Latin: see MERIDIAN *adjective.*]
After midday; between noon and midnight. Abbreviation ***p.m.***
▪ ***postmeˈridian*** *adjective* occurring after midday; of or pertaining to the afternoon: E17.

post-millennial /pəʊs(t)mɪˈlɛnɪəl/ *adjective.* M19.
[from POST- 2 + MILLENNIAL.]
Of or belonging to the period following the millennium.
▪ **post-millennialism** *noun* the doctrine that a second Advent will follow the millennium L19. **post-millennialist** *noun* a believer in post-millennialism M19.

postmistress /ˈpəʊs(t)mɪstrɪs/ *noun.* L17.
[from POST *noun*² + MISTRESS *noun.*]
A woman in charge of a post office (cf. POSTMASTER *noun*¹ 3).

post-modern /pəʊs(t)ˈmɒdən/ *adjective.* M20.
[from POST- 2 + MODERN *adjective.*]
Later than what is 'modern' in literature, architecture, etc.; *spec.* of, pertaining to, or designating a movement reacting against modernism esp. by self-consciously drawing attention to earlier styles and conventions.
▪ **post-modernism** *noun* a movement in literature, architecture, etc., constituting a reaction against modernism, esp. by self-conscious use of earlier styles and conventions L20. **post-modernist** *noun & adjective* (**a**) *noun* a practitioner or adherent of post-modernism; (**b**) *adjective* of or pertaining to post-modernists or post-modernism: M20.

postmodification /ˌpəʊs(t)mɒdɪfɪˈkeɪʃ(ə)n/ *noun.* M20.
[from POST- 1 + MODIFICATION.]
LINGUISTICS. The modification of a word or phrase by another coming after.
▪ **postˈmodifier** *noun* a word or phrase that modifies one coming before it M20. **postˈmodify** *verb trans.* modify the sense of (a word or phrase) by being placed after it M20.

post-mortem /pəʊs(t)ˈmɔːtəm/ *adverb, adjective, noun, & verb.* Also (esp. as adjective) **post mortem.** M18.
[Latin.]
▶ **A** *adverb.* After death. M18.
▶ **B** *adjective.* Taking place, formed, or done after death or (*colloq.*) after the conclusion of a matter (cf. sense C.2 below). M18.

📖 R. RENDELL Doreen Bett's denial had . . been . . a post-mortem whitewashing of her mother's character. A. CLARE The only consistent change . . in the postmortem schizophrenic brain is an increase . . of dopamine receptors.

▶ **C** *noun.* **1** An examination of a body performed after death esp. in order to determine the cause of death; an autopsy. M19.
2 An analysis or discussion conducted after the conclusion of a game, examination, or other event. Cf. INQUEST *noun* 3c. *colloq.* E20.

📖 **1** A. CROSS No question that it was cyanide: the post-mortem had established that. **2** R. MARKUS The post-mortem centred the blame on East for not ducking the jack of diamonds at trick two. TOECKEY JONES I mooched about . . holding endless postmortems on our conversations.

▶ **D** *verb trans.* Conduct a post-mortem examination of. L19.

📖 N. FREELING Who looks twice at a couple post-morteming a traffic scrape.

postnatal /pəʊs(t)ˈneɪt(ə)l/ *adjective.* M19.
[from POST- 2 + NATAL *adjective*¹.]
Occurring after birth; characteristic of or pertaining to the period after a birth.
postnatal depression depression in a mother in the period after a birth.
▪ **postnatally** *adverb* E20.

†**postnate** *adjective.* M17–L18.
[formed as next.]
Born, made, occurring, etc., after something else; of later date, subsequent *to.*

postnatus /pəʊs(t)ˈneɪtəs/ *noun. obsolete* exc. *Hist.* Pl. **-ti** /-tʌɪ/. E17.
[medieval Latin = born after: see PUISNE.]
1 A person born after a particular event; *spec.* a person born in Scotland after the uniting of the Scottish and English crowns (1603) or in the US after the Declaration of Independence (1776). E17.
†**2** A second son. Only in Dicts. E18–M19.

post-nuclear /pəʊs(t)ˈnjuːklɪə/ *adjective.* M20.
[from POST- 2 + NUCLEAR *adjective.*]
1 PHONETICS. Occurring after a nucleus. M20.
2 Following the development or use of nuclear weapons. M20.

post-nuptial /pəʊs(t)ˈnʌpʃ(ə)l/ *adjective.* E19.
[from POST- 2 + NUPTIAL.]
Existing, occurring, or performed after marriage. Also, subsequent to mating (of animals).
▪ **postnuptially** *adverb* L19.

post-obit /pəʊstˈəʊbɪt, -ˈɒbɪt/ *noun & adjective.* M18.
[Latin *post obitum* after decease.]
▶ **A** *noun.* A bond given by a borrower, securing to the lender a sum of money to be paid on the death of a specified person from whom the borrower expects to inherit. M18.
▶ **B** *adjective.* **1** Taking effect after someone's death. L18.
2 Taking place, existing, etc., after death; post-mortem. *rare.* E19.
1 ***post-obit bond*** = sense A. above.

post office /ˈpəʊst ɒfɪs/ *noun phr.* Also **post-office.** M17.
[from POST *noun*² + OFFICE *noun.*]
1 (**P- O-.**) The public department, agency, or organization responsible primarily for the collection, transmission, and distribution of mail and (in some countries) also for telecommunications and some other services. M17.
2 A local branch of this department; a building or room where postal business is carried on. L17.
3 = ***postman's knock*** s.v. POSTMAN *noun*¹. *US.* M19.
4 A person who receives information for further transmission or collection, esp. in espionage. *slang.* L19.
Comb.: **post-office box** (**a**) a private box or pigeon-hole at a post office, in which mail for an individual or firm is put and kept until called for; (**b**) = ***post-office bridge*** below; **post-office bridge** ELECTRICITY a portable self-contained Wheatstone bridge containing a large number of resistors which are selected using plugs; **post-office red** (of) a bright-red colour formerly used for British public postboxes and telephone kiosks; **post-office savings bank** *Hist.* a bank in the UK having branches at local post offices where sums within fixed limits were received on government security at a fixed rate of interest.

post-op /pəʊstˈɒp/ *adjective & noun. colloq.* L20.
[Abbreviation.]
= next.

postoperative /pəʊstˈɒp(ə)rətɪv/ *adjective & noun.* L19.
[from POST- 2 + OPERATIVE.]
MEDICINE. ▶**A** *adjective.* Occurring in or pertaining to the period following a surgical operation; having recently undergone an operation. L19.
▶ **B** *noun.* A person who has recently had an operation. M20.
▪ **postoperatively** *adverb* E20.

postorbital /pəʊstˈɔːbɪt(ə)l/ *adjective & noun.* M19.
[from POST- 2 + ORBITAL.]
ANATOMY & ZOOLOGY. ▶**A** *adjective.* Situated behind or on the hinder part of the orbit or eye socket; *spec.* designating a process of the frontal bone, forming a separate bone in some reptiles. M19.
▶ **B** *noun.* The postorbital bone or process. M19.

post-partum /pəʊs(t)ˈpɑːtəm/ *adjective & adverb.* M19.
[Latin *post partum* after childbirth.]
MEDICINE. (Occurring, existing, etc.) after childbirth; postnatal(ly).

postpone /pəʊs(t)ˈpəʊn, pəˈspəʊn/ *verb.* L15.
[Latin *postponere,* from *post* after + *ponere* to place.]
1 *verb trans.* Put off to a future time; arrange (an event etc.) to take place at a later time; defer. L15. ▶†**b** Keep (a person) waiting for something promised or expected. L16–E18.
2 *verb trans.* Place later in serial order; put at or nearer to the end. E16.
3 *verb trans.* Place lower in order of rank, importance, etc.; subordinate *to.* Now *rare.* M17.
4 *verb intrans.* MEDICINE. Of a disease: be later in coming on or recurring. Now *rare.* M19.

📖 **1** M. FRAYN Vote to postpone a decision until the next meeting. A. LURIE It would not prevent scandal . . merely postpone it. E. FEINSTEIN I postponed telling my father of my engagement. **2** G. HICKES He hath Postponed the most scandalous part of his Speech . . and put it towards the end. **3** T. JEFFERSON Postponing motives of delicacy to those of duty.

¶ Orig. *Scot.*: otherwise rare before 1700.
▪ **postponable** *adjective* L19. **postponement** *noun* the action or fact of postponing (an event etc.); an instance of this: E19.

postponence *noun* (*rare*) postponement M18. **postponer** *noun* M16.

postpose /pəʊs(t)ˈpəʊz/ *verb trans.* L16.
[French *postposer,* from POST- 1 + *poser* POSE *verb*¹.]
Place after or later than in (temporal or serial) order. Now chiefly GRAMMAR, place (a modifying particle or word) after the word modified.

📖 O. JESPERSEN Postposed adjectives are not in general accord with colloquial English.

¶ Not recorded L17–L19.

postposit /pəʊs(t)ˈpɒzɪt/ *verb trans. rare.* M17.
[Latin *postposit-* pa. ppl stem of *postponere* POSTPONE.]
= POSTPONE 2, 3.

postposition /pəʊs(t)pəˈzɪʃ(ə)n/ *noun.* M16.
[Late Latin *postpositio(n-),* formed as prec.: see -ITION.]
†**1** The action of postponing; postponement; delay. *Scot. rare.* Only in M16.
2 Chiefly GRAMMAR. The action of placing something after another, esp. a modifying particle or word after the word modified; the condition or fact of being postposed. M17.
3 GRAMMAR. A particle or relational word placed after another word; *esp.* a particle or word having the function of a preposition but following its object, as English ***-ward(s)*** in ***homeward(s)*** etc. M19.
▪ **postpositional** *adjective* of, pertaining to, or of the nature of a postposition; postpositive: M19.

postpositive /pəʊs(t)ˈpɒzɪtɪv/ *adjective & noun.* L18.
[Late Latin *postpositivus,* formed as POSTPOSIT: see -IVE.]
GRAMMAR. ▶**A** *adjective.* (Of a word, particle, etc.) that should be placed after a word or letter; of or pertaining to postposition. L18.
postpositive preposition: see PREPOSITION 1.
▶ **B** *noun.* A postpositive particle or word. M19.
▪ **postpositively** *adverb* M20.

postprandial /pəʊs(t)ˈprandɪəl/ *adjective.* Chiefly *joc.* exc. MEDICINE. E19.
[from POST- 2 + PRANDIAL.]
Done, made, taken, happening, etc., after dinner or (MEDICINE) any large meal; after-dinner.

📖 D. MORTMAN As a postprandial surprise, Zoltán and Andras invited everyone into the music room.

▪ **postprandially** *adverb* M19.

post-pubertal /pəʊs(t)pjʊˈbəːt(ə)l/ *adjective.* L19.
[from POST- 2 + PUBERTAL.]
Occurring after the attainment of puberty; that has attained puberty.
▪ Also **post-ˈpuberal** *adjective* M20.

post rem /pəʊst ˈrɛm/ *adjectival & adverbial phr.* E20.
[medieval Latin = after the thing.]
PHILOSOPHY. Subsequent to the existence of something else; (of a universal) existing only as a mental concept or as an abstract word after the fact of being experienced from particulars. Cf. ANTE REM, IN RE.

postscript /ˈpəʊs(t)skrɪpt/ *noun & verb.* M16.
[from next.]
▶ **A** *noun.* **1** A paragraph or remark at the end of a letter after the signature, containing an afterthought or additional matter. M16.
2 An additional passage at the end of any text. M17.
3 A thing appended; an additional or conclusory action; an afterthought, a sequel. L19.
4 (**PostScript.**) COMPUTING. (Proprietary name for) a language used as a standard for describing pages of text. Freq. *attrib.* L20.

📖 **1** S. WEINTRAUB The Duke's equerry, the letter added in a postscript, would be sent . . to handle all details. **2** C. WILSON He wrote a postscript to his article . . admitting that his earlier views were inadequate. **3** G. W. THORNBURY Brentford always a mere ecclesiastical postscript to Hanwell or Ealing. *Listener* Would he have expanded . . , or remained as much a postscript from the nineties as Max?

▶ **B** *verb trans.* Put a postscript to. Also, provide as a postscript. *rare.* M19.
▪ **postˈscriptal** *adjective* of the nature of or relating to a postscript L19.

postscriptum /pəʊs(t)ˈskrɪptəm/ *noun.* Pl. **-ta** /-tə/. E16.
[Latin, use as noun of neut. pa. pple of *postscribere* write after, from *post* after + *scribere* write.]
= POSTSCRIPT *noun* 1, 2.

post-structuralism /pəʊs(t)ˈstrʌktʃ(ə)r(ə)lɪz(ə)m/ *noun.* L20.
[from POST- 2 + STRUCTURALISM.]
An extension and critique of structuralism, esp. as used in critical textual analysis, in which the concepts of representation are questioned, and which is therefore characterized by an emphasis on plurality and deferral of meaning.
▪ **post-structural** *adjective* L20. **post-structuralist** *noun & adjective* (**a**) *noun* a practitioner or adherent of post-structuralism; (**b**) *adjective* of or pertaining to post-structuralists or post-structuralism: L20.

For other words beginning with *post-* see the entry for **post-**

post-term /pəʊs(t)ˈtəːm/ *adjective*. **M20.**
[from POST- 2 + TERM *noun*.]
MEDICINE. = POSTMATURE 1.

Post Toastie /pəʊs(t) ˈtəʊsti/ *noun phr.* Chiefly *US*. **E20.**
[from Charles William *Post* (1854–1914), US manufacturer + TOASTIE.]
In *pl.* (Proprietary name for) a breakfast cereal made from toasted maize. Also (*sing.*), a piece of this breakfast cereal.

postulant /ˈpɒstjʊl(ə)nt/ *noun*. **M18.**
[French, or Latin *postulant-* pres. ppl stem of *postulare* POSTULATE *verb*: see -ANT[1].]
A candidate for appointment to some honour, office, or position; *esp.* a candidate for admission into a religious order.

📖 A. WEST She followed up on her conversion by becoming a postulant in a Dominican Convent.

▪ **postulancy** *noun* the condition of being a postulant; the period during which this lasts: **L19.**

postulata *noun* pl. of POSTULATUM.

postulate /ˈpɒstjʊlət/ *noun*[1]. **L15.**
[Latin *postulatus* pa. pple of *postulare* POSTULATE *verb*: see -ATE[1].]
SCOTTISH HISTORY. A person nominated by the monarch to a bishopric or other high ecclesiastical office.

postulate /ˈpɒstjʊlət/ *noun*[2]. **L16.**
[Latin *postulatum* use as noun of neut. pa. pple of *postulare*: see next, -ATE[1].]
1 A demand, a request; a stipulation. Now *rare*. **L16.**
2 A postulated proposition; *esp.* a thing assumed as a basis of reasoning, discussion, or belief; a fundamental condition or principle; an unproved or necessary assumption, a hypothesis. **M17.** ▸**b** MATH. A simple (esp. geometric) operation whose possibility is taken for granted, e.g. the drawing of a straight line between two points. **M17.**

📖 **2** N. FRYE The first postulate of this hypothesis is . . the assumption of total coherence. J. MASSON Therapy depends . . on the postulate that the truth of a person's life can be uncovered in therapy. ***Koch postulates***, ***Koch's postulates***: see KOCH. **b** ***Peano postulates***, ***Peano's postulates***: see PEANO.

postulate /ˈpɒstjʊleɪt/ *verb trans.* Pa. t. & pple **-ated**, (earlier) †**-ate**. **LME.**
[Latin *postulat-* pa. ppl stem of *postulare* ask, demand, request: see -ATE[3].]
1 ECCLESIASTICAL LAW. Nominate or elect to an ecclesiastical office or dignity subject to the sanction of a higher authority. **LME.**
2 Demand; require; claim. Now *rare*. **L16.**
3 Claim (explicitly or tacitly) the existence, fact, or truth of; take for granted; assume, esp. as a basis of reasoning, discussion, or belief. **M17.** ▸**b** MATH. Assume the possibility of (some geometric construction or operation). Cf. POSTULATE *noun*[2] 2b. **E19.**

📖 **1** W. STUBBS The chapter was then allowed to postulate the bishop of Bath. **2** J. S. MILL *Logic* . . postulates to express in words what is already in the thoughts. **3** *Scientific American* The postulated corpuscles are invisible. W. GOLDING It is . . scientifically respectable to postulate that . . the laws of nature no longer apply. A. STORR Freud postulated an agency within the mind which devoted itself to self-observation.

▪ **postulator** *noun* a person who postulates someone or something; *spec.* (ROMAN CATHOLIC CHURCH) a pleader for a candidate for beatification or canonization: **M19. postulatory** *adjective* (now *rare*) [Latin *postulatorius*] (*a*) supplicatory; (*b*) of the nature of an assumption; hypothetical: **M17.**

postulation /pɒstjʊˈleɪʃ(ə)n/ *noun*. **LME.**
[Old French *postulacion* (mod. *-ation*) from Latin *postulatio(n-)*, formed as prec.: see -ATION.]
1 ECCLESIASTICAL LAW. The nomination of a person for an ecclesiastical office, the appointment being subject to the sanction of a higher authority. **LME.**
2 The action of requesting or demanding something; a request, demand, or claim. Now *rare*. **LME.**
3 The action of assuming the truth or existence of something, esp. as a basis of reasoning, belief, etc.; an assumption. **M17.**
▪ **postulational** *adjective* of or pertaining to postulation; based on or involving deduction from a set of postulates: **E20. postulationally** *adverb* **M20.**

postulatum /pɒstjʊˈleɪtəm/ *noun*. Now *rare* or *obsolete*. Pl. **-ta** /-tə/. **E17.**
[Latin: see POSTULATE *noun*[2].]
1 = POSTULATE *noun*[2] 2. **E17.**
†**2** = POSTULATE *noun*[2] 1. **M17–M18.**
†**3** A problem; a desideratum. **M17–E19.**

Postum /ˈpəʊstəm/ *noun*. Orig. *US*. **L19.**
[Pseudo-Latin, from C. W. *Post* (see POST TOASTIE + *-um*).]
(Proprietary name for) a coffee substitute.

postural /ˈpɒstʃ(ə)r(ə)l/ *adjective*. **M19.**
[from next + -AL[1].]
1 Of or pertaining to posture or position. **M19.**
2 MEDICINE. Of hypotension etc.: brought on by an upright posture. **L19.**

posture /ˈpɒstʃə/ *noun*. **L16.**
[French from Italian *postura* from Latin *positura* position, situation, formed as POSIT: see -URE.]
1 The relative disposition of the various parts of something; *esp.* the position and carriage of the limbs and the body as a whole; attitude, pose. **L16.** ▸**b** A particular pose adopted by an animal or bird, interpreted as a signal of a specific pattern of behaviour. **M20.**
2 Position (relative to that of another), situation. Now *rare* or *obsolete*. **E17.**
3 A state of being; a condition or state of affairs; *spec.* a military or political position (in relation to an issue etc.), a condition of armed readiness. **E17.**
4 A mental or spiritual attitude or condition. **M17.**

📖 **1** V. WOOLF He jerked himself up into a sitting posture. D. LEAVITT As he stands, his posture is hunched and awkward. **b** N. TINBERGEN Powerful wings raised aloft and their necks still in the rigid threat posture. **2** J. WOODWARD An imaginary . . Earth, whose Posture to the sun he supposes to have been much different. **3** T. H. WHITE Lancelot must be stopped . . until the castle had been put in posture of defence. *Times* Urging the party to adopt a unilateralist non-nuclear defence posture. *Defense Update International* Improving our conventional posture . . would give . . a more convincing basis for deterrence. **4** S. PEPYS Therewith we broke up, all in a sad posture.

Comb.: **posture-maker**, **posture-master** *arch.* (*a*) an expert in assuming postures; *esp.* a contortionist or acrobat; (*b*) an instructor in callisthenics.
▪ **posturist** *noun* = POSTURER **L19. posturize** *verb* (*a*) *verb trans.* (*rare*) compose into a particular posture; (*b*) *verb intrans.* assume a physical posture or mental attitude, esp. for effect; pose: **E18.**

posture /ˈpɒstʃə/ *verb*. **E17.**
[from the noun.]
1 *verb trans.* Place in a particular attitude; dispose the body or limbs of (a person) in a particular way. Now *rare*. **E17.**
†**2** *verb trans.* Place in position; set. **M–L17.**
3 *verb intrans.* Assume a particular posture; *esp.* adopt an artificial pose. **M19.**
4 *verb intrans. fig.* Act in an affected manner; pose for effect; adopt an artificial mental attitude. **L19.**

📖 **3** C. KINGSLEY Laughing . . as they postured and anticked on the mole-hills. P. L. FERMOR Statues posture in their scalloped recesses. **4** F. G. LEE Jewell . . sometimes became witty, and occasionally postured as a buffoon. H. JAMES Their tone had truth . . ; they weren't posturing for each other.

▪ **posturer** *noun* a person who assumes postures; a poser: **M19. posturing** *noun* (*a*) the action of the verb; an instance of this; (*b*) the adoption of particular poses by birds etc. as signals of specific behaviour patterns: **E17.**

Posturepedic /pɒstʃəˈpiːdɪk/ *noun* & *adjective*. Orig. *US*. **M20.**
[from POSTURE *noun* + ORTHO)PEDIC.]
(Proprietary name designating) a kind of mattress designed to give support to the relaxed body.

postvocalic /pəʊstvə(ʊ)ˈkalɪk/ *adjective*. **L19.**
[from POST- 2 + VOCALIC.]
Situated or occurring after a vowel; of or pertaining to the position after a vowel.
▪ **postvocalically** *adverb* **M20.**

postwar /pəʊs(t)ˈwɔː, ˈpəʊs(t)-/ *adjective* & *noun*. **E20.**
[from POST- 2 + WAR *noun*[1].]
▶ **A** *adjective*. Of, pertaining to, or characteristic of the period after a war, now esp. that of 1939–45. **E20.**
postwar credit (a payment or promissory note associated with) a system of additional taxation introduced in Britain in 1941 to supplement wartime expenditure, intended to be repaid after the war.
▶ **B** *noun*. The period following a war. *US*. **M20.**

posty *noun* var. of POSTIE.

posy /ˈpəʊzi/ *noun*. **LME.**
[Syncopated from POESY.]
1 A short motto, usu. a line of verse, inscribed within a ring, on a knife, etc. *arch.* **LME.**
2 A small bunch of flowers. **L15.**
3 An anthology of verse etc. *arch.* **M16.**
†**4** A poetical composition (= POESY 2). **L16–M17.**
Comb.: **posy-ring** a finger-ring with a motto inside.

posy *adjective* var. of POSEY.

pot /pɒt/ *noun*[1] & *adjective*. In sense A.7 usu. **pott**.
[Old English *pott* corresp. to Old Frisian, Middle & mod. Low German, Middle & mod. Dutch *pot*, from popular Latin (whence Old French, Provençal *pot*); cf. late Latin *potus* drinking-cup, Anglo-Latin *pottus*, *-um*. Prob. reinforced in Middle English from Old & mod. French *pot*. Ult. origin unkn.]
▶ **A** *noun*. **1** A deep rounded or cylindrical vessel, usu. made of earthenware, metal, glass, or plastic, and used for holding liquid or solid substances or for various other purposes. **OE.**
2 *spec.* **a** A pot (now usu. of metal) used in cooking, esp. boiling. **ME.** ▸**b** A pot for holding drink and for drinking from or (now chiefly) for pouring a (usu. hot) drink into smaller vessels. Now chiefly with specifying word. **LME.** ▸**c** A chamber-pot. Also, a lavatory pan. **L16.** ▸**d** A flower-pot. **E17.** ▸**e** A chimney-pot. **M19.** ▸**f** A prize in a sports contest, *esp.* a silver cup. *slang*. **L19.** ▸**g** A protuberant stomach; = POT-BELLY 1. **E20.** ▸**h** A cylinder or carburettor in an engine. *slang*. **E20.**
3 A pot with its contents; a potful; *spec.* (*a*) a pot of some (hot) drink; (*b*) a glass of liquor, esp. beer. **ME.** ▸**b** A pot as a conventional measure of various commodities; *spec.* (*Austral.*) a measure of beer of approx. half a pint. **LME.**
4 Earthenware, baked clay. Also (chiefly *dial.*), a fragment of this used in hopscotch and other games; (a part of) the game of hopscotch itself. **ME.**
5 a Either of a pair of baskets or tubs for carrying manure, sand, etc. (usu. in *pl.*). Also *spec.*, a dung-pot. *dial.* **LME.** ▸**b** A wicker basket used as a trap for fish or crustaceans. Chiefly with specifying word. **M17.**
6 A sausage. Now *dial.* **LME.**
7 In full ***pot-paper***. A size of paper, usu. 15½ × 12½ inches (394 × 318 mm), orig. watermarked with a pot. *obsolete* exc. *Hist.* **L16.**
8 A steel helmet worn by a soldier. **M17.**
9 a A large sum staked or betted, esp. in horse-racing. Also, a horse on which a large sum is staked. *slang*. **E19.** ▸**b** A large sum of or *of* money. *colloq.* **M19.** ▸**c** The betting pool in poker etc. Cf. JACKPOT. **M19.** ▸**d** An important person. Chiefly in ***big pot*** s.v. BIG *adjective*. **L19.**
10 BILLIARDS & SNOOKER etc. A shot which results in a ball being potted. **E20.**

📖 **1** ***glue-pot***, ***jam-pot***, ***mustard-pot***, etc. **2a** E. COXHEAD Poached game is never sold, it goes into the pot. J. IRVING There was a pot of water already boiling on the stove. **b** ***coffee-pot***, ***pint-pot***, ***teapot***, etc. **d** M. GIROUARD A sunflower and a lily, each in a pot to either side of the door. **3** E. FERRARS The tea had got cold, so Christine made a fresh pot. J. RATHBONE Will you share a pot of coffee with me, Reverend Mother? C. S. FORESTER He was sitting in . . the Lamb Inn . . with a pot of beer . . at his elbow. **b** *Canberra Times* In my youth I used to drink up to 30 pots a day. **5b** ***crab-pot***, ***lobster-pot***, etc. **9b** F. TROLLOPE He went to India . . and came back . . with a pot of money.

Phrases: **boil the pot** = ***keep the pot boiling*** below. **for the pot** for food, for cooking. **go to pot**, †**go to the pot** *colloq.* be ruined or destroyed; deteriorate, go to pieces. **in one's pots** in a state of intoxication (cf. CUP *noun* 4). ***in the melting-pot***: see MELTING *noun*. **keep the pot boiling** earn a living. **pot of gold** an imaginary reward; a jackpot; an ideal. †**pot of the head** the skull. **put a person's pot on** *Austral.* & *NZ slang* inform against a person. ***shit or get off the pot***: see SHIT *verb*.
Comb.: **pot-ale** the completely fermented wash in distillation; **pot-arch**: an arch in a glass-making furnace, in which pots are annealed; **pot-ball** (*obsolete* exc. *dial.*) a dumpling; **pot-bank** *dial.* a pottery; **pot-board** a board upon which pots are placed; *spec.* the shelf nearest the floor underneath a dresser; **pot-boil** *verb intrans.* & *trans.* produce (a literary, artistic, or other work) simply to earn a living; **pot-boiler** (*a*) *colloq.* a literary, artistic, or other work produced simply to earn a living; a writer or artist who produces such a work; (*b*) ARCHAEOLOGY any of a number of small stones heated in a fire and then placed in a container of liquid in order to boil it; **pot-bound** *adjective* (of a plant in a pot) having roots which fill the pot, leaving no room to expand; **pot-boy** *arch.* a publican's young male assistant, a bartender; **pot-bunker** GOLF an artificially constructed small deep bunker; **pot-cheese** *US* cottage cheese; **pot clay** (*a*) clay free from iron and so suitable for making earthenware; (*b*) a bed of this clay; **pot-companion** *arch.* a companion in drinking; **pot courage** *arch.* = ***Dutch courage*** s.v. COURAGE *noun* 4; **pot cupboard** a bedside cupboard designed to hold a chamber-pot; **pot-earth** potter's clay, *spec.* brick-earth; **pot-furnace**: containing pots for glassmaking, or in which crucibles are heated; **pot-garden** a kitchen garden; †**pot-gun** (*a*) a short piece of ordnance with a large bore; (*b*) a pop-gun; **pot-gut(s)** *colloq.* = POT-BELLY 1, 2; **pot-gutted** *adjective* (*colloq.*) = POT-BELLIED; **pot hat** *colloq.* a bowler hat; **pothead** *colloq.* (*a*) a stupid person; (*b*) *Canad.* (in full ***pothead whale***) the pilot whale, *Globicephala melaena*; (*c*) ELECTRICITY an insulated connector used to make a sealed joint between conductors, esp. between insulated and uninsulated lines; **pot-herb** a herb grown or suitable for growing in a kitchen garden; **pot holder** *N. Amer.* a piece of quilted or thick fabric for handling hot dishes etc.; **pot-hook** (*a*) a (usu. S-shaped) hook, orig. suspended over a fireplace, for hanging a pot etc. on, or (formerly) for lifting a hot pan or lid; (*b*) a curved or hooked stroke in handwriting, esp. made when learning to write; **pot-house** (*a*) a small tavern or public-house; (*b*) a place where pottery is made; **pot-hunter** (*a*) a person who hunts, esp. by shooting, for food or profit only and disregards the rules of the sport; (*b*) a person who takes part in a contest merely for the sake of winning a prize; (*c*) a person who finds or obtains archaeological objects, esp. by unorthodox or illicit methods, for the purpose of private collection or profit; **pot-hunting** *noun* & *adjective* (*a*) *noun* the action or activities of a pot-hunter; (*b*) *adjective* that engages in pot-hunting; **pot-kiln** a small lime-kiln; **pot-lace**: having the figure of a pot or vase (often containing flowers) in the pattern; **pot-layering** a method of plant propagation in which a ball of soil is attached to a cut on a branch until enough roots have grown for the branch to be planted independently; **potleg** *arch.* broken scraps of cast iron, used as shot; **pot-licker** *N. Amer.* a mongrel dog; **pot-lid** (*a*) the lid of a pot; (*b*) CURLING a stone played so as to rest on the tee; **pot life** the length of time that a glue, resin, etc., remains usable after preparation; **pot-likker** (chiefly *US*) = ***pot-liquor*** below; **pot-line**

a line of retorts used for the electrolytic production of aluminium; **pot-liquor** liquor in which meat, vegetables, etc., have been boiled, stock; **potman** (*a*) a publican's assistant, a bartender; (*b*) a man who attends to the filling, emptying, firing, etc., of pots at a foundry etc.; ***pot marigold***: see MARIGOLD *noun* 1; ***pot*** MARJORAM; **pot-mess** *Nautical slang* (*a*) a stew made from various scraps; (*b*) *fig.* a state of confusion or disorder; **pot-oven** (*a*) a round covered cooking-pot for placing in a fire; (*b*) a kiln in which pottery is fired; *pot-paper*: see sense 7 above; **pot-pie** (chiefly *N. Amer.*) (*a*) a usu. savoury mixture enclosed in a pastry crust and steamed or baked; (*b*) a usu. savoury pie with a top crust only; **pot plant** a plant grown or suitable for growing in a flowerpot, esp. indoors; **pot roast** a piece of meat, esp. beef, cooked slowly in a closed container with a small amount of liquid; **pot-roast** *verb trans.* cook (meat) as a pot roast; **pot stand** a stand designed to hold pots or potted plants; **pot still** a still to which heat is applied directly (as to a pot) and not by means of a steam-jacket; **pot-train** *verb trans.* = ***potty-train*** s.v. POTTY *noun*; **pot-valiant** *adjective* courageous through the influence of drink; **pot-valour** courage induced by drink; **pot-washings** food removed from pots by washing; **pot-water** (*obsolete exc. dial.*) water for cooking purposes; **pot-woman** (*a*) a woman who sells pots; (*b*) (*obsolete* exc. *Hist.*) a barmaid; **pot-work** a place where pottery is made; **pot-wrestler** *US slang* a person who washes dishes.

▶ **B** *attrib.* or as *adjective*. Made of pot or baked clay, earthenware. M19.

pot /pɒt/ *noun*². ME.

[Perh. same word as prec., or of Scandinavian origin: cf. Swedish dial. *putt*, *pott* water-hole, abyss. Cf. also POTHOLE.]

1 A deep hole, a pit; *spec.* (*a*) a hole out of which peat has been dug; (*b*) a deep hole in a river-bed. *Scot. & dial.* ME.

2 A natural deep hole or pit esp. in limestone. L18.

📖 **2** *Caves & Caving* Grabbing hard at the line to prevent himself falling down into this pot.

pot /pɒt/ *noun*³. L19.

[Abbreviation of POT-SHOT.]

1 A pot-shot. L19.

2 RUGBY FOOTBALL. A dropped goal. *Austral. & NZ.* M20.

pot /pɒt/ *noun*⁴. *slang*. M20.

[Prob. from Mexican Spanish *potiguaya* marijuana leaves.]

= MARIJUANA 1.

Comb.: **pot-head** a person who smokes marijuana.

pot /pɒt/ *noun*⁵. *colloq.* M20.

[Abbreviation.]

= POTENTIOMETER.

pot /pɒt/ *verb*¹. Infl. **-tt-**. M16.

[from POT *noun*¹.]

▶ **I 1** *verb trans.* Outwit, deceive. *arch. slang.* M16.

2 *verb trans.* Inform against (a person). *Austral. slang.* E20.

▶ **II 3** *verb intrans. & trans.* (with *it*). Drink beer etc. out of a pot; indulge in drinking. Now *rare* or *obsolete*. L16.

▶ **III 4** *verb trans.* **a** Preserve (meat etc.) in a sealed pot, jar, etc. Chiefly as POTTED *adjective*. E17. ▶**b** In sugar-making, put (crude sugar) into a perforated pot to allow the molasses to drain off. M18. ▶**c** *fig.* Summarize, condense; epitomize. Chiefly as POTTED *adjective*. M19. ▶**d** Encapsulate (an electrical component or circuit) in a liquid insulating material, usu. a synthetic resin, which sets solid. M20.

5 *verb trans.* Set (a plant) in a flowerpot filled with earth for cultivation; plant in or transplant into a pot. Formerly also, put (earth) into a flowerpot. E17.

6 a *verb intrans.* Take a pot-shot, shoot (*at*). *colloq.* M19. ▶**b** *verb trans.* Shoot at, hit, or kill (game), esp. with a pot-shot. *colloq.* M19.

7 *verb trans.* Pocket (a ball) in billiards, snooker, etc. M19.

8 *verb trans.* Seize, win, secure. M19.

📖 **5** *Independent* Between five and eight cuttings are taken from each plant and potted. **pot off** transplant (a seedling) into an individual pot. **pot on** transplant from a smaller pot to a larger one. **pot up** transplant (esp. a seedling) into a pot. **6** *Shooting Times* He used to creep about his father's woods potting pigeon off the trees. **7** *Pot Black* The order of play after all the reds have been potted.

▶ **IV 9** *verb intrans. & trans.* Make (articles) from earthenware or baked clay, make (pottery). M18.

▶ **V 10** *verb trans.* Sit (a young child) on a chamber-pot. *colloq.* M20.

pot /pɒt/ *verb*² *trans. Austral. & NZ.* Infl. **-tt-**. M20.

[from POT *noun*³.]

RUGBY FOOTBALL. Score (a dropped goal) from a kick.

potable /ˈpəʊtəb(ə)l/ *adjective & noun*. LME.

[Old & mod. French, or late Latin *potabilis*, from *potare* to drink: see -ABLE.]

▶ **A** *adjective*. Drinkable. LME.

†**potable gold** a liquid preparation containing dissolved gold or gold salts, formerly used as a medicine.

▶ **B** *noun*. In *pl.* Drinkable substances; liquor. E17.

■ **pota'bility** *noun* L17. **potableness** *noun* E18.

potage /pɔtaːʒ (*pl. same*), pɒˈtaːʒ/ *noun*. ME.

[Orig. from Old & mod. French, lit. 'what is put in a pot', from *pot* POT *noun*¹ (see -AGE); later reintroduced from French See also POTTAGE.]

(A) soup, *esp.* (a) thick (vegetable) soup.

📖 P. VAN RJNDT Giering's potage was served along with black bread and butter.

¶ Formerly Anglicized with stress on 1st syll. (whence POTTAGE).

†**potager** *noun*¹. ME–E18.

[Old & mod. French, formed as prec.: see -ER².]

A maker of pottage or soup.

potager /ˈpɒtədʒə, *foreign* pɔtaʒe (*pl. same*)/ *noun*². Also (earlier) †**potagere**. M17.

[French (also *-gère*) in (*jardin*) *potager* (garden) for the kitchen.]

A kitchen garden.

potagerie /pəʊˈtadʒ(ə)ri, *foreign* pɔtaʒri (*pl. same*)/ *noun*. Also (earlier) Anglicized as †**-ery**. L17.

[French.]

Herbs and vegetables collectively. Also, a kitchen garden.

potamic /pəˈtamɪk/ *adjective*. L19.

[from Greek *potamos* river + -IC.]

Of or pertaining to rivers; fluviatile.

potamogale /pɒtəˈmɒgəliː/ *noun*. L19.

[mod. Latin *Potamogale* genus name, from Greek *potamos* river + *galē* weasel.]

ZOOLOGY. An otter shrew. Chiefly as mod. Latin genus name.

potamogeton /pɒtəmə(ʊ)ˈgiːtɒn/ *noun*. M16.

[mod. Latin (see below), use as genus name of Latin *potamogeton* from Greek *potamogeitōn* pondweed, from *potamos* river + *geitōn* neighbour.]

Any of various aquatic plants of the genus *Potamogeton* (family Potamogetonaceae); a pondweed.

potamology /pɒtəˈmɒlədʒi/ *noun*. E19.

[from Greek *potamos* river + -LOGY.]

The branch of science that deals with rivers.

■ **potamo'logical** *adjective* L19. **potamologist** *noun* M19.

potamoplankton /pɒtəməʊˈplaŋktɒn/ *noun*. E20.

[formed as prec. + PLANKTON.]

Plankton found in rivers or streams.

potash /ˈpɒtaʃ/ *noun*. Also †**pot-ash**. Pl. (sense 1 only) **-ashes**. E17.

[Du †*potasschen* (mod. *potasch*): cf. POT *noun*¹, ASH *noun*².]

1 In *pl.* An alkaline substance consisting largely of impure potassium carbonate and originally obtained by leaching the ashes of burnt plant material and evaporating the solution in large iron pots. *obsolete* exc. *Hist.* E17. ▶**b** Purified potassium carbonate. M18.

2 An oxide or hydroxide base containing potassium; *spec.* (more fully ***caustic potash***), potassium hydroxide, KOH, a white caustic deliquescent solid which gives a strongly alkaline solution in water. In names of compounds, minerals, etc.: = POTASSIUM (*arch.* in CHEMISTRY use). L18. ▶**b** Chiefly AGRICULTURE & HORTICULTURE. (Soluble) salts of potassium. M19.

3 Carbonated water containing potassium bicarbonate. Also more fully ***potash-water***. Now *rare* or *obsolete*. E19.

📖 **1b** *attrib.*: *Endeavour* Potash glasses give a purer blue than the corresponding sodium glasses. **2** ***carbonate of potash***, ***sulphate of potash***, etc. **b** *attrib.*: *Garden News* Use a high potash feed . . at weekly intervals to sustain good growth. **3** J. K. JEROME White wine with a little soda-water; perhaps occasionally a glass of . . potash But beer, never.

Comb.: **potash alum** a hydrated double sulphate of potassium and aluminium; **potash feldspar** = POTASSIUM ***feldspar***.

■ **potashery** *noun sing.* & in *pl.* a factory where potash is made L18.

†**potass** *noun*. L18–E20.

[French *potasse* POTASH.]

Potash, potassa. Later also, potash-water.

potassa /pəˈtasə/ *noun*. Now *rare* or *obsolete*. E19.

[mod. Latin form of POTASH after *soda*, *magnesia*, etc.]

CHEMISTRY. Potassium monoxide, K_2O. Also, potassium hydroxide, KOH.

potassic /pəˈtasɪk/ *adjective*. M19.

[from POTASSIUM + -IC.]

1 CHEMISTRY. Of, pertaining to, or containing potassium or potash. Now *rare*. M19.

2 GEOLOGY. Of a mineral or rock: containing an appreciable or a greater than average quantity of potassium, often as compared with sodium. Also, designating a metamorphic process in which such minerals are formed. E20.

potassium /pəˈtasɪəm/ *noun*. E19.

[from POTASH or POTASS + -IUM.]

A soft light pinkish-white, highly reactive chemical element, atomic no. 19, belonging to the alkali metal group, which is present in numerous minerals, and whose salts are essential to biological processes. (Symbol K.)

Comb.: **potassium-argon** *attrib. adjective* designating or pertaining to a method of isotopic dating based on measuring the proportions in rock of potassium-40 and its decay product, argon-40; **potassium feldspar** MINERALOGY any of a group of potassium-rich feldspars including orthoclase and microcline.

potation /pə(ʊ)ˈteɪʃ(ə)n/ *noun*. LME.

[Old French, or Latin *potatio(n-)*, from *potat-* pa. ppl stem of *potare* to drink: see -ATION.]

1 The action or an act of drinking; *spec.* the action or an act of drinking alcohol; a bout of drinking. LME. ▶†**b** A drinking party. Only in 16.

2 A drink, a beverage. LME.

potato /pəˈteɪtəʊ/ *noun & verb*. M16.

[Spanish *patata* var. of BATATA.]

▶ **A** *noun*. Pl. **-oes**.

1 More fully ***sweet potato***. A plant of the bindweed family, *Ipomoea batatas*, cultivated in tropical and subtropical regions for its sweetish edible tubers; the root of this plant, usu. eaten boiled and mashed. M16.

2 A plant of the nightshade family of S. American origin, *Solanum tuberosum*, widely cultivated for its starchy tubers (also ***potato-plant***); the root of this plant, eaten as a vegetable. Also (now *US*) ***Irish potato***, (*US*) ***white potato***. L16.

3 With specifying word: any of various plants having tubers or tuberous roots, mostly edible. E17.

4 a A large or conspicuous hole in (esp. the heel of) a sock etc. *colloq.* L19. ▶**b** In *pl.* Money; *spec.* dollars. *US slang*. M20. ▶**c** [ellipt. for ***potato peeler*** (b) below.] A girl, a woman. *Austral. slang*. M20.

2 ***kidney potato***, ***pink-eye potato***, etc. ***baked potato***, ***boiled potatoes***, ***mashed potatoes***, ***sautéed potatoes***, etc. **3** ***air potato***, ***Indian potato***, ***native potato***, ***Telinga potato***, etc.

Other phrases: **hot potato** *colloq.* a controversial or awkward matter or situation. ***meat and potatoes***: see MEAT *noun*. **small potatoes** *colloq.* (a person who or thing which is) insignificant or unimportant. **the clean potato**, **the potato** *colloq.* the correct or socially acceptable thing; a socially acceptable or honourable person.

Comb.: **potato-apple** the (poisonous) berry of the potato-plant, *Solanum tuberosum*; **potato-balls** mashed potatoes formed into balls and fried; **potato-bean** a N. American leguminous plant, *Apios americana*, which bears edible tubers on its root; **potato-beetle** a beetle which infests potato-plants; *spec.* = COLORADO BEETLE; **potato blight** a very destructive disease of potatoes caused by a parasitic fungus, *Phytophthora infestans*; **potato-bogle** *Scot.* a scarecrow; **potato bread**: made partly from potato flour; **potato-bug** (chiefly *N. Amer.*) a beetle, esp. an American blister-beetle, which infests potato-plants; **potato-cake** a small patty made of potatoes and flour; **potato chip** (*a*) a thin strip of potato fried or for frying (cf. CHIP *noun* 3); (*b*) *N. Amer.* = ***potato crisp*** s.v. CRISP *noun* 6; **potato creeper** = ***potato-vine*** below; ***potato crisp***: see CRISP *noun* 6; **potato disease** = ***potato blight*** above; **potato dumpling**: made with sieved cooked potatoes; **potato-eater** *slang* (*offensive*) an Irish person; **potato-eye** a bud on a potato tuber; **Potato Famine** *the* famine in Ireland in 1846–7 caused by the failure of the potato crop; **potato fern** either of two Australasian ferns, *Dryopteris cordifolia* and *Marattia salicina*, with an edible rootstock; **potato flour**: made from ground potatoes; **potato-fly** = ***potato-bug*** above; **potato hook** a tool with bent tines for digging up potatoes; **potato masher** (*a*) an implement for mashing potatoes, consisting of a perforated flat plate (formerly, a solid wooden cylinder) attached to a handle; (*b*) (in full ***potato masher grenade***) a type of hand-grenade resembling a potato masher; **potato mould**, **potato murrain** = ***potato blight*** above; **potato onion** a variety of onion which produces small lateral bulbs from the base of the main bulb, within an outer set of scales; **potato pancake**: made with sieved cooked potatoes; **potato patch** a plot of ground on which potatoes are grown; **potato peeler** (*a*) an implement with a blade used for peeling potatoes; (*b*) *Austral. rhyming slang* [= SHEILA] a girl, a woman; **potato pie** (*a*) a pie made with potatoes; (*b*) = ***potato pit*** below; **potato pit** a shallow pit, usu. covered with a mound of straw and earth, for storing potatoes in winter; ***potato-plant***: see sense 2 above; **potato-ring** *Hist.* an 18th-cent. Irish (usu. silver) ring used as a stand for a bowl etc.; **potato rot** = ***potato blight*** above; **potato-salad** cold cooked potato chopped and mixed with mayonnaise etc.; **potato scone**: made with sieved cooked potatoes; ***potato set***: see SET *noun*¹ 8b; **potato straw** a very thin strip of potato, fried until crisp; **potato-trap** *arch. slang* the mouth; **potato-vine** any of several S. and Central American climbing plants of the genus *Solanum*, esp. *S. jasminoides*, bearing blue or white flowers.

▶ **B** *verb trans.* Plant with potatoes. *rare*. M19.

potator /pəˈteɪtə/ *noun*. *rare*. M17.

[Latin, from *potat-*: see POTATION, -OR.]

A drinker, a tippler.

potatory /ˈpəʊtət(ə)ri/ *adjective*. E19.

[from POTATION, after pairs in *-ation*, *-atory*: see -ORY².]

1 Drinkable. *rare*. E19.

2 Of, pertaining to, or given to drinking. M19.

pot-au-feu /pɔtofø/ *noun*. Pl. (*rare*) ***pots-au-feu*** (pronounced same). L18.

[French, lit. 'pot on the fire'.]

A large cooking pot of a kind common in France; the (traditional) soup cooked in this.

Potawatomi /pɒtəˈwɒtəmi/ *noun & adjective*. L17.

[Ojibwa *po:te:wa:tami:*.]

▶ **A** *noun*. Pl. same, **-s**.

1 A member of an Algonquian people inhabiting the Great Lakes region, principally in Michigan and Wisconsin. L17.

2 The language of this people. E20.

▶ **B** *adjective*. Of or pertaining to the Potawatomi or their language. L18.

pot-belly /ˈpɒtbɛli, pɒtˈbɛli/ *noun*. **E18**.
[from POT *noun*[1] + BELLY *noun*.]
1 A protuberant stomach. **E18**.
2 A person with such a stomach. **L19**.
3 A small bulbous stove. Also ***pot-belly stove***. **L20**.
■ **pot-bellied** *adjective* having a pot-belly **M17**.

potch /pɒtʃ/ *noun*. **L19**.
[Origin unkn.]
Opal of inferior quality, being dull and having no play of colour.

potch /pɒtʃ/ *verb*[1] *trans. slang*. **L19**.
[Yiddish *patshn* from German *patschen*.]
Slap, smack.

potch *verb*[2] see POACH *verb*[2].

potcher *noun* see POACHER *noun*[1].

pot de chambre /po də ʃɑ̃br/ *noun phr*. Pl. ***pots de chambre*** (pronounced same). **L18**.
[French.]
A chamber-pot.

pote /pəʊt/ *noun. obsolete* exc. *dial*. **E18**.
[Rel. to POTE *verb*.]
1 A stick or rod for poking, thrusting, or stirring. **E18**.
2 A prod, a shove, a kick. **E18**.

pote /pəʊt/ *verb. obsolete* exc. *dial*. **OE**.
[Origin unkn.: cf. PUT *verb*[1].]
1 *verb trans. & intrans*. Push, thrust; *esp*. push with the foot, kick. **OE**.
†**2** *verb trans*. Crimp (linen). Only in **17**.
3 *verb trans. & intrans*. Poke (esp. a fire) with a stick. **E18**.

poteen /pɒˈtiːn/ *noun. Anglo-Irish*. Also **potheen** /pɒˈθiːn/, **potsheen** /pɒˈtʃiːn/. **E19**.
[Irish (*fuisce*) *poitín* little pot (whiskey): see -EEN[2].]
Alcohol made from potatoes on an illicit still.

Potemkin village /pəˈtɛmkɪn ˈvɪlɪdʒ/ *noun phr*. **M20**.
[Grigorii Aleksandrovich *Potëmkin* (1739–91), favourite of Empress Catherine II of Russia.]
Any of a number of sham villages reputedly built on Potemkin's orders for Catherine II's tour of the Crimea in 1787; *transf*. any sham or unreal thing.

> 🕮 A. HUTSCHNECKER Their promises were delusions and their beautiful homes Potemkin villages.

potence /ˈpəʊt(ə)ns/ *noun*[1]. **LME**.
[Old French = power from Latin *potentia*, from *potent-*: see POTENT *adjective*[2], -ENCE.]
1 = POTENCY 1. **LME**. ▸**b** = POTENCY 1d. **L19**.
2 = POTENCY 4. **E19**.

potence /ˈpəʊt(ə)ns/ *noun*[2]. **LME**.
[Old & mod. French = †crutch, (mod.) gallows from Latin *potentia*: see prec., cf. POTENT *noun*[1] & *adjective*[1].]
†**1** A crutch. Also, a heraldic device shaped like the crosspiece of a crutch. Cf. POTENT *noun*[1] 3. **LME–L15**.
†**2** A cross; a gibbet. **L15–M19**.
3 *HOROLOGY*. A piece fastened to a plate of a clock or watch to form the lower pivot of the spindle. **L17**.
4 *Hist*. A military formation in which a line is thrown out at right angles to the main body. **M18**.
5 *Hist*. A revolving post with a ladder, used for collecting eggs in a dovecote. **L19**.

potencé /ˈpəʊt(ə)nseɪ/ *adjective*. Also **potence** /ˈpəʊt(ə)ns/. **L16**.
[French, formed as prec.]
HERALDRY. = POTENT *adjective*[1].

potency /ˈpəʊt(ə)nsi/ *noun*. **LME**.
[Latin *potentia*: see POTENCE *noun*[1], -ENCY.]
1 (Great) power, authority, or influence. **LME**. ▸**b** Power to cause a physical effect; *spec*. power to intoxicate. **M17**. ▸**c** *HOMOEOPATHY*. The degree of dilution of a drug, taken as a measure of its efficacy. **M19**. ▸**d** Ability to achieve erection of the penis; (esp. of a male) ability to have sexual intercourse or to reach orgasm or (*popularly*) to procreate. **E20**. ▸**e** *GENETICS*. The extent of the contribution of an allele towards the production of a phenotypic character. **E20**. ▸**f** *PHARMACOLOGY*. The strength of a drug, as measured by the amount needed to produce a certain response. **M20**.
2 *transf*. A person or thing wielding or possessing power or influence. Now *rare*. **E17**.
3 a Potentiality, inherent capability or possibility. **M17**. ▸**b** *EMBRYOLOGY*. A capacity in embryonic tissue for developing into a particular specialized tissue or organ. **E20**.
4 Degree of power. **L17**.
5 *MATH*. = POWER *noun* 12b. **E20**.

> 🕮 **1a** V. PACKARD The potency of television in conditioning youngsters to be loyal enthusiasts of a product. B. BETTELHEIM The child's steps towards independence are experienced as a threat to the parent's potency. **b** *Highlife* Intoxicated by the sun . . and the potency of rum punches.

potent /ˈpəʊt(ə)nt/ *noun*[1] & *adjective*[1]. **LME**.
[Alt. of (Old French) POTENCE *noun*[2]: see -ENT.]
▸**A** *noun*. †**1** A crutch; a staff with a crosspiece to lean on. **LME–L15**.
2 *fig*. A support, a stay. Long *arch*. **LME**.
3 *HERALDRY*. A T-shaped form or figure; a fur potent. **E17**.
▸**B** *adjective*. *HERALDRY*. (Of a cross) having the limbs terminating in potents; (of a fur) consisting of interlocking T-shaped areas of alternating tinctures and orientations; (of a line) formed into an open T-shape at regular intervals. Usu. *postpositive*. **L16**.
■ **potented** *adjective* having or formed into a potent or potents **E19**.

potent /ˈpəʊt(ə)nt/ *adjective*[2] & *noun*[2]. **LME**.
[Latin *potent-* pres. ppl stem of *posse* be powerful or able, for *potis esse*: see -ENT.]
▸**A** *adjective*. **1** Powerful; having great power, authority, or influence. **LME**. ▸**b** Of a principle, motive, idea, etc.: cogent, convincing. **L16**.
2 Having power to cause a physical effect; *spec*. having the power to intoxicate easily. **E17**.
3 Able to achieve erection of the penis; (esp. of a male) able to have sexual intercourse or to reach orgasm or (*popularly*) to procreate. **L19**.

> 🕮 **1** S. BIKO The most potent weapon . . of the oppressor is the mind of the oppressed. B. PYM Sloth and sex are less potent temptations for a writer in her sixties. **b** C. LAMBERT Their most potent arguments were drawn from the era . . we all imagined to be closed. **2** TOLKIEN It must be potent wine to make a wood-elf drowsy. W. S. BURROUGHS They know an aphrodisiac so potent that it shatters the body to quivering pieces.

▸†**B** *noun*. **1** Power; a power. **E16–M17**.
2 A potent person, a potentate; ***the potent***, potent people. **M16–M17**.
3 A military warrant or order. **E17–E18**.
■ **potently** *adverb* **M16**. **potentness** *noun* (*rare*) **L16**.

potentate /ˈpəʊt(ə)nteɪt/ *noun & adjective*. **LME**.
[Old & mod. French *potentat* or Latin *potentatus* power, dominion, (in late Latin) potentate, formed as prec.: see -ATE[1].]
▸**A** *noun*. **1** A person endowed with independent power; a monarch, a ruler. **LME**.
2 A powerful city, State, or body. **E17**.

> 🕮 **1** J. KLAUBER He was a potentate administering imaginary empires. S. WEINTRAUB The Eastern potentates whose jewels and orders gleamed. **2** LD MACAULAY Nothing indicated that the East India Company would ever become a great Asiatic potentate.

▸†**B** *adjective*. Powerful, ruling. **M16–M17**.
■ †**potentacy** *noun* the state or rule of a potentate **L16–E18**.

potential /pə(ʊ)ˈtɛnʃ(ə)l/ *adjective & noun*. **LME**.
[Old French *potenciel* (mod. *-tiel*) or late Latin *potentialis*, from *potentia*: see POTENCE *noun*[1], -AL[1].]
▸**A** *adjective*. **1** Possible as opp. to actual; capable of coming into being or action; latent. **LME**. ▸**b** *GRAMMAR*. Designating or pertaining to the subjunctive mood when used to express possibility. **M16**.
2 Possessing (great) power; potent, powerful. Now *rare*. **L15**.
3 *PHYSICS*. Of a property etc.: that would be manifested under certain different, esp. standard, conditions. **L19**.

> 🕮 **1** A. STORR Those with potential gifts . . whose talents have remained unrealized for lack of recognition. J. KLEIN How mysterious a baby is, its personality still largely potential. ***potential cautery***: see CAUTERY 1. **2** J. S. MILL Without any potential voice in their own destiny. **3 potential energy** energy which a body possesses by virtue of its state or position not its motion (cf. *KINETIC energy*). **potential temperature** the temperature that a given body of gas or liquid would have if it were brought adiabatically to a standard pressure of 1 bar or 1 atmosphere.

▸**B** *noun*. †**1** = ***potential cautery*** s.v. CAUTERY 1. *rare*. Only in **LME**.
†**2** A thing which gives power. *rare*. Only in **M17**.
3 That which is possible as opp. to actual; a possibility; *spec*. capacity for use or development, resources able to be used or developed. **E19**.
4 *PHYSICS*. A mathematical function or quantity by the differentiation of which can be expressed the (gravitational, electromagnetic, etc.) force at any point in space arising from a system of bodies, electrical charge, etc. (also ***potential function***; the quantity of energy or work denoted by this, considered as a quality or condition of the matter, electricity, etc., and equivalent to that required to move a body, charge, etc., from the given point to a reference point of zero potential (e.g. the earth, infinity); *gen*. any function from which a vector field can be derived by differentiation (also ***potential function***). **E19**. ▸**b** Any of a group of thermodynamic functions mathematically analogous to electric and gravitational potentials, including free energy, enthalpy, internal energy, and chemical potential. **L19**.
5 *GRAMMAR*. The potential mood. **L19**.

> 🕮 **3** J. BRONOWSKI Every cell in the body carries the complete potential to make the whole animal. G. PALEY A soft job in advertising, using a fraction of his potential. S. BRETT The young man read the play, recognized its potential. **4 *action potential***, ***chemical potential***, ***ionization potential***, ***Madelung potential***, ***resting potential***, etc.

Comb.: **potential barrier** a region in a field of force in which the potential is significantly higher than at points either side of it, so that a particle requires energy to pass through it; *spec*. that surrounding the potential well of an atomic nucleus; **potential difference** the difference of electric potential between two points; **potential flow** flow which is irrotational and for which there therefore exists a velocity potential; ***potential function***: see sense B.4 above; **potential gradient** (the rate of) change of (electrical) potential with distance; **potential scattering** *NUCLEAR PHYSICS* elastic scattering of a particle by an atomic nucleus in which the scattering cross-section varies smoothly with the energy of the incident particle; **potential wall** a region in a field of force in which the potential increases sharply; **potential well** a region in a field of force in which the potential is significantly lower than at points immediately outside it, so that a particle in it is likely to remain there unless it gains a relatively large amount of energy; *spec*. that in which an atomic nucleus is situated.
■ **potentialize** *verb trans*. make potential, give potentiality to; *spec*. convert (energy) into a potential condition: **M19**. **potentially** *adverb* **LME**. **potentialness** *noun* **M17**.

potentiality /pə(ʊ)ˌtɛnʃɪˈalɪti/ *noun*. **E17**.
[medieval Latin *potentialitas*, from late Latin *potentialis*: see prec., -ITY.]
1 The quality of being powerful or potent. Now *rare*. **E17**.
2 The state or quality of possessing latent power or capacity capable of coming into being or action; an instance of this, a thing in which this is embodied. **E17**.
3 *ELECTRICITY*. = POTENTIAL *noun* 4. *rare*. **L19**.

> 🕮 **2** J. D. DANA Characteristics before only foreshadowed, or existing only in potentiality. *Scientific American* We feel that the potentialities of the human brain are inexhaustible.

potentiate /pə(ʊ)ˈtɛnʃɪeɪt/ *verb trans*. **E19**.
[from POTENCE *noun*[1] or POTENCY + -ATE[3], after *substance*, *substantiate*. Cf. German *potenzieren*.]
1 Endow with power. **E19**.
2 Make possible. **M19**.
3 Chiefly *PHYSIOLOGY*. Increase the effect of (a drug or its action); act synergistically with; promote or enhance the physiological or biochemical effect of. **E20**.

> 🕮 **3** DOUGLAS CLARK Though the phenobarbitone had caused death, it had been potentiated by the alcohol.

■ **potentiˈation** *noun* (*a*) the action of endowing someone or something with power; (*b*) synergistic activity between two drugs or other agents: **E19**. **potentiator** *noun* (*PHARMACOLOGY*) an agent that increases the effect of a drug **M20**.

potentilla /pəʊt(ə)nˈtɪlə/ *noun*. **M16**.
[medieval Latin from Latin *potent-* (see POTENT *adjective*[2]) + dim. *-illa*.]
Any of various chiefly yellow-flowered plants of the genus *Potentilla*, of the rose family, *esp*. any of those grown for ornament.

potentiometer /pə(ʊ)ˌtɛnʃɪˈɒmɪtə/ *noun*. **L19**.
[from POTENTIAL + -OMETER.]
1 A device for measuring potential difference or an electromotive force by balancing it against a variable potential difference of known value produced by passing a known (usu. fixed) current through a known (usu. variable) resistance. **L19**.
2 A voltage divider which is regulated by varying a resistance. Also *loosely*, a rheostat. **E20**.
■ **potentioˈmetric** *adjective* of, pertaining to, or by means of a potentiometer or potentiometry **E20**. **potentioˈmetrically** *adverb* **E20**. **potentiometry** *noun* the use of potentiometers, esp. in chemical analysis **M20**.

potentiostat /pə(ʊ)ˈtɛnʃɪəʊstat/ *noun*. **M20**.
[from POTENTIAL + -O- + -STAT.]
A device used to regulate automatically the potential difference between electrodes in electrolysis.
■ **potentioˈstatic** *adjective* of, pertaining to, or involving a potentiostat; with the potential difference between electrodes held constant: **M20**. **potentioˈstatically** *adverb* **M20**.

potentize /ˈpəʊt(ə)ntʌɪz/ *verb trans*. Also **-ise**. **M19**.
[from POTENT *adjective*[2] + -IZE.]
Make potent; *spec*. in *Homoeopathy*, make (a medicine) more powerful or effective by dilution and succussion.
■ **potentiˈzation** *noun* (a) dilution of a (homoeopathic) medicine in order to increase its power or efficacy **M19**.

poter /ˈpəʊtə/ *noun*. *rare*. **M17**.
[App. from Latin *potare* to drink or *potus* drink + -ER[1].]
A drinker, a tippler.

potestas /pə(ʊ)ˈtɛstas/ *noun*. Pl. ***-states*** /-ˈsteɪtiːz/. **M17**.
[Latin = power.]
†**1** *MATH*. A power, an exponent. **M–L17**.
2 *ROMAN LAW*. The power or authority of the male head of a family over those legally subject to him; *esp*. parental authority. **L19**.
3 *PHILOLOGY*. The phonetic or phonemic value of a letter in an alphabet. **M20**.

potestative /pə(ʊ)ˈtɛstətɪv/ *adjective*. **M17**.
[French *potestatif*, *-ive* or late Latin *potestativus*, from *potestat-*, POTESTAS: see -IVE.]
Having power or authority.
potestative condition: within the power or control of one of the parties concerned.

pot-et-fleur /pɒtəflœ:r (pl. *same*), pɒteɪˈflə:/ *noun*. **M20.**
[French, lit. 'pot and flower'.]
A style of floral decoration using pot plants together with cut flowers.

potful /ˈpɒtfʊl, -f(ə)l/ *noun*. **LME.**
[from POT *noun*[1] + -FUL.]
As much as a pot will hold.

📖 P. CAREY They drank tea by the potful.

pothecary /ˈpɒθɪk(ə)ri/ *noun*. Now *dial.* **LME.**
[Aphet.]
= APOTHECARY 1.
■ Also †**pothecar** *noun* (*Scot.* & *north.*) **L15–M19.**

potheen *noun* var. of POTEEN.

pother /ˈpɒðə/ *noun* & *verb*. Also (*arch.*) **pudder** /ˈpʌdə/. **L16.**
[Origin uncertain: perh. rel. to BOTHER.]
▶ **A** *noun*. **1** Disturbance, commotion, turmoil; an uproar, a din; a fuss; mental disturbance or turmoil. **L16.**
2 A choking atmosphere of dust. Now *dial.* **E17.**

📖 **1** F. T. BULLEN Smiting the sea with his mighty tail, making an almost deafening noise and pother. V. WOOLF All this pother about a brooch really didn't do at all. P. ZIEGLER The Home Fleet was in a pother about Mountbatten's activities.

▶ **B** *verb*. **1** *verb trans.* Disturb, fluster, worry, trouble. **L17.**
2 *verb intrans.* Make a fuss; fuss, worry. **E18.**
3 *verb intrans.* Of smoke or dust: move or gather in a cloud. *dial.* **M19.**
■ **pothery** *adjective* choking, stifling; close, sultry: **L17.**

pothole /ˈpɒthəʊl/ *noun* & *verb*. **E19.**
[from POT *noun*[2] + HOLE *noun*[1].]
▶ **A** *noun*. **1** A deep (esp. cylindrical) hole, esp. formed by the wearing away of rock by the rotation of a stone or stones in an eddy of running water etc.; a system of holes, caves, and underground river-beds formed in this way. **E19.**
2 A deep hole in the ground or in a river-bed. **L19.**
3 *spec.* **a** A shallow excavation made in prospecting for gold or opal. *Austral.* **L19.** ▶**b** A pond formed by a natural hollow in the ground in which water has collected. *N. Amer.* **E20.** ▶**c** A depression or hollow in a road surface caused by wear or subsidence. **E20.**
▶ **B** *verb*. **1** *verb intrans.* Explore underground potholes or caves, esp. as a pastime. Chiefly as ***potholing*** *verbal noun*. **L19.**
2 *verb trans.* Produce potholes in; *spec.* (*Austral.*) search (an area) for gold or opal by digging potholes. **L19.**
■ **potholed** *adjective* having potholes **M20.** **potholer** *noun* a person who goes potholing, esp. as a pastime **E20.** **potholey** *adjective* having many potholes **E20.**

pothos /ˈpəʊθɒs/ *noun*. **M19.**
[mod. Latin (see below), from Sinhalese *pōtha*, *pōtæ*.]
Any of various climbing aroid shrubs of the genus *Pothos*, of tropical Asia, Australia, etc., some of which are cultivated as foliage plants.

potiche /pɒtiʃ/ *noun*. Pl. pronounced same. **L19.**
[French.]
A large (esp. Chinese) porcelain jar or vase with a rounded bulging shape and a wide mouth, freq. having a lid.

potichomania /pɒˌtiːʃəˈmeɪnɪə/ *noun*. *arch.* **M19.**
[French *potichomanie*, formed as prec. + *-manie* -MANIA.]
The process of covering the inner surface of a glass vase etc. with designs on paper or sheet gelatin in order to imitate porcelain; the fashion for doing this.

potin /pɒtɛ̃/ *noun*. Pl. pronounced same. **E17.**
[French, from *pot* POT *noun*[1] + *-in*: cf. -INE[4].]
Hist. **1** = POT-METAL 1a, b. Now *rare*. **E17.**
2 An alloy of tin, copper, lead, and zinc, used by the ancient Gauls to make coins. **M19.**

potion /ˈpəʊʃ(ə)n/ *noun* & *verb*. **ME.**
[Old French from Latin *potio(n-)* drink, poisonous draught, from *pot-* pa. ppl stem of *potare* to drink: see -ION.]
▶ **A** *noun*. **1** A (dose of) liquid medicine or poison. **ME.**
†**2** A drink; a kind of drink. *rare*. **LME–M17.**
▶ **B** *verb trans.* Treat or dose with a potion; drug. **E17.**

potlatch /ˈpɒtlatʃ/ *noun* & *verb*. Chiefly *N. Amer.* Also **-lache**. **M19.**
[Chinook Jargon from Nootka *p'ačitl* make a gift at a potlatch.]
▶ **A** *noun*. Among some N. American Indians of the Pacific coast, an extravagant and competitive ceremonial feast at which a person, esp. a chief, gives presents and gives away or destroys possessions in order to enhance his or her status; *transf.* (*N. Amer. colloq.*) a wild party. **M19.**
▶ **B** *verb*. **1** *verb intrans.* Hold a potlatch. **L19.**
2 *verb trans.* Give. **E20.**

potluck /ˈpɒtlʌk, pɒtˈlʌk/ *noun*. *colloq.* Also **pot luck**. **L16.**
[from POT *noun*[1] + LUCK *noun*.]
1 Whatever food may have been prepared or is available; *gen.* whatever is available. Chiefly in ***take potluck***. **L16.**
2 In full ***potluck dinner***, ***potluck supper***. A meal to which the guests bring food to be shared. **L19.**

pot-metal /ˈpɒtmɛt(ə)l/ *noun*. **L17.**
[from POT *noun*[1] + METAL *noun*.]
1 a *Hist.* An alloy of lead and copper of which pots were formerly made. **L17.** ▶**b** A kind of cast iron suitable for making pots. **M19.**
2 Stained glass coloured in a melting-pot. **M19.**

potoo /pəˈtuː/ *noun*. **M19.**
[Jamaican creole from Twi *patú* of imit. origin.]
Any of several American nocturnal insectivorous birds of the genus *Nyctibius*, related to the nightjars.

potoroo /pɒtəˈruː/ *noun*. **L18.**
[Aboriginal.]
Any of several Australian rat-kangaroos. Now usu. *spec.*, any member of the nocturnal genus *Potorous*, found in dense scrub and grassland.
long-footed potoroo a rare potoroo, *Potorous longipes*, of eastern Victoria. **long-nosed potoroo** a potoroo, *Potorous tridactylus*, widespread in southern and eastern Australia.

pot-pourri /pəʊˈpʊəri, -ˈriː, pɒtˈpʊəri/ *noun*. Also **potpourri**. **E17.**
[French, lit. 'rotten pot', from *pot* POT *noun*[1] + *pourri* pa. pple of *pourrir* rot: translating Spanish OLLA PODRIDA.]
†**1** A stew made of different kinds of meat. **E17–E18.**
2 Dried flower petals, leaves, etc., mixed with spices and kept in a jar or bowl to scent the air. Also, a container for holding this. **M18.**
3 *fig.* A medley, *esp.* a musical or literary one. **M19.**

potrero /pɒˈtrɛːrəʊ/ *noun*. Pl. **-os**. **M19.**
[Spanish, formed as next.]
1 In S. America and the south-western US, a paddock or pasture for horses or cattle. **M19.**
2 In the south-western US, a narrow steep-sided plateau. **L19.**

potro /ˈpɒtrəʊ/ *noun*. *US*. Pl. **-os**. **L19.**
[Spanish.]
A colt, a pony.

pots-au-feu *noun pl.* see POT-AU-FEU.

pots de chambre *noun phr.* pl. of POT DE CHAMBRE.

potsheen *noun* var. of POTEEN.

potsherd /ˈpɒt-ʃəːd/ *noun*. *arch.* exc. ARCHAEOLOGY. **ME.**
[from POT *noun*[1] + SHERD.]
A fragment of broken pottery, esp. of a broken earthenware pot.

pot-shoot /ˈpɒt-ʃuːt/ *verb trans.* & *intrans.* *US*. Pa. t. & pple **-shot** /-ʃɒt/. **E20.**
[from POT *noun*[1] + SHOOT *verb*, after next.]
Take a pot-shot at (a person or thing).
■ **pot-shooter** *noun* **E20.**

pot-shot /ˈpɒt-ʃɒt/ *noun* & *verb*[1]. **M19.**
[from POT *noun*[1] + SHOT *noun*[1].]
▶ **A** *noun*. **1** A shot taken at an animal purely to kill it for food, without regard to skill or the rules of the sport. **M19.**
2 A shot aimed, esp. unexpectedly or without giving any chance for self-defence, at a person or animal within easy reach; a random shot. **M19.**
3 *fig.* A piece of esp. random or opportunistic criticism. Also, a random attempt to do something. **E20.**

📖 **2** B. W. ALDISS Someone was . . taking pot-shots through the boarded windows with a revolver. F. SMYTH Rawlings took a pot-shot at the fleeing poacher. **3** *Newsweek* The tobacco industry is leaving no radioisotope unturned to counter medical potshots at its product.

▶ **B** *verb trans.* & *intrans.* Infl. **-tt-**. Take a pot-shot at or *at* (a person or thing). **E20.**
■ **pot-shotter** *noun* **E20.**

pot-shot *verb*[2] *pa. t.* & *pple* of POT-SHOOT.

potsie *noun* var. of POTSY.

potstick /ˈpɒtstɪk/ *noun*. Now *dial.* **LME.**
[from POT *noun*[1] + STICK *noun*[1].]
A stick for stirring food or for moving washing about in a pot.

potstone /ˈpɒtstəʊn/ *noun*. **L18.**
[from POT *noun*[1] + STONE *noun*.]
A granular variety of soapstone (steatite).

potsy /ˈpɒtsi/ *noun*. *US*. Also **potsie**. **E20.**
[Perh. from POT *noun*[1] (in sense 4) + -SY.]
1 (The object thrown in) a children's game similar to hopscotch. **E20.**
2 A badge of office worn by a police officer or fire officer. **M20.**

Pott /pɒt/ *noun*[1]. **M19.**
[Sir Percivall Pott (1713–88), English surgeon.]
MEDICINE. **1** ***Pott's disease***, tuberculosis of the spine, transmitted in infected cow's milk and leading to deformity if untreated. **M19.**
2 ***Pott's fracture***, a fracture of the fibula and tibia at the level of the malleoli, close to the ankle, due to forced eversion of the foot. **M19.**

pott *noun*[2] see POT *noun*[1].

pottage /ˈpɒtɪdʒ/ *noun*. **M16.**
[Anglicized form of POTAGE. Cf. PORRIDGE.]
1 = POTAGE. Also, a thin stew. **M16.**
2 Oatmeal porridge. *obsolete* exc. *Scot. dial.* **L17.**

pottah /ˈpɒtɑː/ *noun*. **L18.**
[Hindi *paṭṭā* from Sanskrit *paṭṭa* document.]
In the Indian subcontinent: a lease, a deed of tenure.

potted /ˈpɒtɪd/ *adjective*. **M17.**
[from POT *verb*[1] + -ED[1].]
1 Of meat etc.: preserved in a sealed pot or jar. **M17.**
2 Of a plant: planted or grown in a flowerpot, esp. indoors. **M19.**
3 *fig.* Of a literary work, descriptive account, etc.: put into a short and easily assimilable form; condensed, summarized. **L19.** ▶**b** = CANNED 2. *arch.* **E20.**
4 Of pottery: (*well*, *badly*, etc.) fashioned or made. **E20.**
5 Intoxicated by alcohol or drugs, esp. marijuana. *N. Amer. slang*. **E20.**
6 Of an electrical component or circuit: encapsulated in insulating material. **M20.**

📖 **2** M. DORRIS I sat . . in the solarium, surrounded by abandoned potted plants. **3** *Holiday Which?* A multi-lingual audio-visual show . . gives a potted history of the city's development. **5** D. W. GOODWIN I was drinking at noontime . . going home potted.

potter /ˈpɒtə/ *noun*[1]. **LOE.**
[from POT *noun*[1] + -ER[1].]
1 A maker of earthenware pots or vessels. **LOE.** ▶†**b** A maker of metal pots or vessels. *rare*. **LME–M16.**
2 A vendor or hawker of earthenware. Also, a vagrant; a Gypsy. *north.* **L15.**
Comb.: **potter's clay**, **potter's earth** clay free from iron and so suitable for making earthenware; **potter's field** [after *Matthew* 27:7] a burial place for paupers, strangers, etc.; ***potter's lathe***: see LATHE *noun*[3] 2; **potter's lead**, **potter's ore** lead ore used for glazing pottery, galena; **potter's rot**, **potters' rot** silicosis or other lung disease caused by the continued inhalation of dust in a pottery; **potter wasp** a wasp which builds a cell or cells of clay, as several of the genus *Eumenes*; **potter's wheel** a horizontal revolving disc mounted on a potter's lathe, on which prepared clay is moulded into shape.

potter /ˈpɒtə/ *noun*[2]. **E19.**
[from the verb.]
(A) desultory but agreeable action; *esp.* a gentle or idle stroll.

📖 E. BOWEN A potter through the boundary woods.

potter /ˈpɒtə/ *verb*. **M16.**
[Frequentative of POTE *verb*: see -ER[5].]
1 *verb intrans.* Make a succession of small thrusts; poke repeatedly. Now *dial.* **M16.** ▶**b** *verb trans.* Poke. Now *dial.* **M18.**
2 *verb intrans.* Meddle, interfere; tamper (*with*). Now *dial.* **M17.**
3 *verb trans.* Trouble, disturb, worry. Cf. POTHER *verb* 1. *dial.* **M18.**
4 *verb intrans.* Occupy oneself in a desultory but agreeable manner; move or go *about* whilst occupied in such a way; go or walk slowly, idly, or in a desultory manner; dabble *in* a subject. **M18.** ▶**b** *verb trans.* Spend, while *away*, (time) in such a manner. **L19.**

📖 **4** J. GALSWORTHY He . . pottered in and out of his dressing-room. E. M. FORSTER The walk sounded rather far: he could only potter about these days. S. BARSTOW Nothing left but pottering in the garden till the end. C. TOMALIN They all pottered about, fishing, sailing and flying kites.

■ **potterer** *noun* **M19.** **potteringly** *adverb* in a pottering manner **L19.**

pottery /ˈpɒt(ə)ri/ *noun* & *adjective*. **L15.**
[Old & mod. French *poterie*, from *potier* a potter (see POTTER *noun*[1]); later from POT *noun*[1]: see -ERY.]
▶ **A** *noun*. **1** A potter's workshop; a factory where earthenware or baked clay vessels etc. are made. **L15.**
2 The potter's art; the making of earthenware or baked clay vessels etc. **E18.**
3 Vessels or other objects made of earthenware or baked clay. **L18.**

📖 **1** P. GZOWSKI Because I was firing my kiln this morning, I wasn't able to leave the pottery. **the Potteries** a district in North Staffordshire, the seat of the English pottery industry. **2** *South African Panorama* Raku pottery is another of her favourite pastimes. **3** V. BROME Scattered bones and broken pottery from a very primitive culture. E. LEONARD He . . wondered if this piece of pottery was more authentic than the ten-buck . . stuff. ***Newcastle pottery***.

Comb.: **pottery-bark tree** = ***pottery tree*** below; **pottery clay** = ***potter's clay*** s.v. POTTER *noun*[1]; **pottery mould** a brick of soft stone mixed with pipeclay, used for whitening hearths etc.; **pottery tree** a S. American tree, *Licania octandra* (family Chrysobalanaceae), the bark of which is mixed with clay to make it heat-resistant.

▸ **B** *attrib.* or as *adjective.* Made of baked clay, earthenware. **M19.**

📖 M. MAHY Laura put the pottery mugs down on the table.

potting /ˈpɒtɪŋ/ *verbal noun.* **L16.**
[from POT *verb*[1] + -ING[1].]
The action of POT *verb*[1].
Comb.: **potting compost** a mixture of loam, peat, sand, and nutrients, used as a growing medium for plants in containers; **potting shed**: in which plants are potted and tools etc. are stored.

†**pottingar** *noun. Scot.* **L15–E19.**
[Alt. of POTHECAR.]
= APOTHECARY 1.

pottinger /ˈpɒtɪndʒə/ *noun.* Now *dial.* **LME.**
[Old & mod. French *potager*, from POTAGE: see -ER[2] (for intrusive *n* cf. *harbinger*). Cf. PODDINGER, PORRINGER.]
= PORRINGER 1.

pottle /ˈpɒt(ə)l/ *noun.* **ME.**
[Old French *potel* dim. of *pot* POT *noun*[1]: see -EL[2].]
1 A former unit of capacity for corn, fruit, liquids, etc., equal to two quarts or half a gallon (approx. 2.3l). *arch.* **ME.** ▸**b** A pot or vessel of (about) this capacity. *arch.* **L17.**
2 A small esp. conical punnet for strawberries etc.; *NZ* an open cardboard or plastic container in which chips etc. are sold. **L18.**
3 (The object thrown in) a children's game similar to hopscotch. **E19.**
Comb.: **pottle-pot** *arch.* a two-quart pot or tankard.

potto /ˈpɒtəʊ/ *noun.* Pl. **-os**. **E18.**
[App. W. African.]
1 A slow-climbing folivorous primate of equatorial African forests, *Perodicticus potto*, of the loris family. **E18.**
2 A kinkajou. Now *rare* or *obsolete.* **L18.**
1 golden potto = ANGWANTIBO.

potty /ˈpɒti/ *noun. colloq.* **M20.**
[from POT *noun*[1] + -Y[6].]
A chamber-pot, *esp.* a small easily portable one for use by a young child. Also, a lavatory pan.
Comb.: **potty-chair** a child's commode; **potty-train** *verb trans.* train (a young child) to use a chamber-pot instead of nappies.

potty /ˈpɒti/ *adjective. slang.* **M19.**
[Origin unkn.]
1 Insignificant, trivial. Chiefly foll. by *little.* **M19.** ▸**b** Easy to manage or deal with; simple. *arch.* **L19.**
2 Mad, crazy. **E20.** ▸**b** Madly in love; extremely enthusiastic. Foll. by *about, on.* **E20.**

📖 **1** J. GRENFELL She could . . vault over the potty little low box hedge. **2** B. PYM He has a grandfather . . who is a bit potty—and spits on the floor. **b** *Best* I'm potty about my two sons . . . I've always loved children.

▪ **pottily** *adverb* **L20.** **pottiness** *noun* **M20.**

†**potulent** *adjective.* **M17.**
[Latin *potulentus*, from *potus* drink, from *pot-*: see POTION, -ENT.]
1 Drinkable. **M17–L18.**
2 Given to drink; drunken. **M17–M19.**

POTUS /ˈpəʊtəs/ *noun. US slang.* Also **Potus**. **E20.**
[Acronym.]
(The) President of the US; the office of the President of the US.

potwaller /ˈpɒtwɒlə/ *noun.* **E18.**
[from POT *noun*[1] + WALL *verb*[1] + -ER[1].]
Hist. A male householder or lodger with his own separate fireplace on which to cook, which qualified him as a voter in some English boroughs before 1832.

pot-walling /ˈpɒtwɒlɪŋ/ *noun. rare* (now *Hist.*). **LME.**
[from POT *noun*[1] + WALL *verb*[1] + -ING[1].]
The possession of a fireplace on which to cook, qualifying a person as an official resident and later as a voter.

potwalloper /ˈpɒtwɒləpə/ *noun.* **E18.**
[Alt. of POTWALLER after WALLOP *verb.*]
1 *Hist.* = POTWALLER. **E18.**
2 A scullion; a cook. *arch. slang.* **M19.**
▪ **potwalloping** *adjective* (*Hist.*) designating a borough in which the voters were predominantly potwallers, designating such a voter **L18.**

potzer *noun* var. of PATZER.

pou *noun* var. of POUW.

pouch /paʊtʃ/ *noun.* **ME.**
[Old Northern French *pouche* var. of Old & mod. French *poche* bag, pouch, (now) pocket: cf. POKE *noun*[1].]
1 A (usu. small) bag, sack, or other receptacle, used for various purposes. Later also, a (detachable) outside pocket worn on the front of a garment; (chiefly *Scot.*) a pocket in a garment. **ME.**
2 *spec.* **a** A small bag for carrying money; *arch.* a purse. **LME.** ▸**b** *MILITARY.* A leather bag or case for carrying ammunition. **E17.** ▸**c** A lockable bag for carrying mail; *esp.* a diplomatic bag. **L19.**
3 a *ANATOMY, MEDICINE, & ZOOLOGY.* An enclosed cavity or hollow structure resembling a bag or pocket; *spec.* †(*a*) the stomach of a fish; (*b*) a distensible sac for food storage, as beneath the bill of some birds (e.g. pelicans), in the cheeks of some mammals (esp. rodents and certain monkeys), etc.; (*c*) a cavity enclosed by a fold of tissue in which certain animals, esp. marsupial mammals, carry their young; a marsupium; (*d*) *BOTANY* a short or rounded seed-vessel of a cruciferous plant; a silicle. **LME.** ▸**b** A baggy fold of loose skin, esp. under the eye. Usu. in *pl.* **E20.**
4 *NAUTICAL.* Any of several divisions made by bulkheads in a ship's hold, for stowing cargo which might shift. *obsolete* exc. *Hist.* **E17.**

📖 **1** J. FOWLES Those little pouches Victorian gentlemen . . put their watches in. **2a** P. S. BUCK He took from his girdle a small greasy pouch . . and counted the money in it. **3a** *cheek-pouch*: see CHEEK *noun*. *Douglas's pouch*: see DOUGLAS *noun*[2]. *gill pouch*: see GILL *noun*[1]. **b** J. HELLER The pouches under the sad man's eyes were tinged with blue.

Comb.: **pouch-mouth**, **pouch-mouthed** *adjectives* (long *rare*) having thick or protruding lips.
▪ **pouchless** *adjective* (*rare*) **E19.** **pouchlike** *adjective* resembling a pouch **M19.** **pouchy** *adjective* having pouches; resembling a pouch; baggy: **E19.**

pouch /paʊtʃ/ *verb.* In sense 3 also **pooch** /puːtʃ/. **M16.**
[from the noun.]
1 *verb trans.* **a** Put or enclose in a pouch; put into one's pocket, pocket. **M16.** ▸**b** *CRICKET.* Catch (the ball) in the hand, dismiss (a batsman) with a catch. **E20.** ▸**c** Send by diplomatic bag. **M20.**
2 *verb trans.* Chiefly of a bird or fish: take into the mouth or stomach, swallow; take into a pouch in the mouth or gullet. **M17.**
3 a *verb trans.* Purse (the lips); push *out* (the mouth), pout. Now *dial.* & *US.* **M17.** ▸**b** *verb intrans.* Make a pouting face; swell or bulge *out. dial.* & *US.* **M18.**
4 *verb intrans.* Form a pouch or pouchlike cavity. Chiefly as ***pouching*** *verbal noun.* **L17.**
5 *verb trans.* Give money to (a person), give as a present of money. *slang.* **E19.**
6 *verb trans.* Cause (part of a garment) to hang loosely like a pouch. **L19.**

📖 **1** F. TROLLOPE A pretty sum you must have pouched last night. **3a** *New York Review of Books* Beaming idiotically, he pooched out his lips and attempted to kiss her.

pouched /paʊtʃt/ *adjective.* **E19.**
[from POUCH *noun, verb*: see -ED[2], -ED[1].]
Having or provided with a pouch or pouches.
pouched mouse a marsupial mouse.

pouchong /puːˈ(t)ʃɒŋ/ *noun.* **M19.**
[Chinese *bāozhǒng* (Wade–Giles *paochung*), lit. 'wrapped sort', with ref. to the method of packing the leaves when picked.]
A kind of China tea made by fermenting the withered leaves only briefly, and typically scented with rose-petals.

poudre /ˈpuːdrə/ *noun. Canad.* **L18.**
[French: see POWDER *noun*[1].]
Light powdery snow.

poudré /pudre, puːˈdreɪ/ *adjective.* Fem. ***-ée***. **E19.**
[French, pa. ppl adjective of *poudrer* to powder, formed as prec.]
Of the hair, a wig, etc.: powdered.

poudrette /puːˈdrɛt/ *noun.* **M19.**
[French, dim. of *poudre* POWDER *noun*[1]: see -ETTE.]
A manure made from excrement dried and mixed with charcoal, gypsum, etc.

poudreuse /pudrøːz/ *noun.* Pl. pronounced same. **E20.**
[French, formed as POUDRE.]
A lady's dressing-table of a kind made in France in the time of Louis XV.

†**pouer** *adjective & noun* see POOR *adjective & noun.*

pouf /puːf/ *noun*[1]. In sense 3 usu. **pouffe**. **E19.**
[French, ult. imit.]
1 An elaborate female head-dress fashionable in the late 18th cent. (*Hist.*); a high roll or pad of hair worn by women. **E19.**
2 *DRESSMAKING.* A part of a dress gathered up to form a soft projecting mass of material. **M19.**
3 A large firm cushion with a stable base, used as a low seat or footstool. Also, a soft stuffed ottoman or couch. **L19.**

pouf *noun*[2] var. of POOF *noun*[1].

pouf *interjection & noun*[3] var. of POOF *interjection & noun*[2].

pouffe *noun* see POUF *noun*[1].

†**pough** *noun.* **OE–L17.**
[Old English *pohha* from Germanic.]
A bag.
¶ Perh. rel. to POGUE.

†**pough** *interjection* var. of POH.

poui /ˈpuːi/ *noun.* **M19.**
[Local name in Trinidad.]
Any of several trees of the W. Indies and Central and S. America, of the genus *Tabebuia* (family Bignoniaceae), esp. *T. rosea* and *T. serratifolia*, which bear terminal clusters of trumpet-shaped flowers, pink and yellow respectively. Also, the wood of these trees.

Poujadism /ˈpuːʒɑːdɪz(ə)m/ *noun.* **M20.**
[French *Poujadisme*, from *Poujade* (see below) + *-isme* -ISM.]
The conservative political philosophy and methods advocated by the French publisher and bookseller Pierre Poujade (b. 1920), who in 1954 founded a movement for the protection of artisans and small shopkeepers, protesting chiefly against the French tax system then in force. Also, any organized protection of the interests of small business.
▪ **Poujadist** *noun & adjective* (*a*) *noun* an advocate or supporter of Poujadism; (*b*) *adjective* of or pertaining to Poujadists or Poujadism: **M20.**

poulaine /puːˈleɪn/ *noun.* **M16.**
[Old French, lit. 'Poland', in *souliers à la Polaine* shoes in a Polish style, crakows.]
Hist. The long pointed toe of a shoe of a style worn in the 14th and 15th cents.

poulard /puːˈlɑːd/ *noun.* **M18.**
[French *poularde*, from *poule* hen + *-arde* -ARD.]
A spayed domestic hen (usu. fattened for the table). Cf. CAPON.
Comb.: **poulard wheat** [French *blé poulard*] rivet-wheat, *Triticum turgidum*.

pouldron *noun* var. of PAULDRON.

poule /pul/ *noun. slang.* Pl. pronounced same. **E20.**
[French, lit. 'hen'.]
A young woman, *esp.* a promiscuous one.
poule de luxe /pul də lyks/ [= of luxury] a prostitute.

poule au pot /pul o po/ *noun phr.* Pl. ***poules au pot*** (pronounced same). **L19.**
[French.]
A boiled chicken.

poulet /pulɛ (*pl. same*), ˈpuːleɪ/ *noun.* **M19.**
[French: see PULLET.]
1 A chicken; a chicken dish, esp. in French cooking (usu. with qualifying adjective). **M19.**
2 A (neatly-folded) billet-doux. **M19.**

poulette /ˈpuːlɛt/ *noun.* **E19.**
[French: see PULLET.]
More fully ***poulette sauce***. In French cooking, a sauce made with butter, cream, and egg-yolks.

poulp /puːlp/ *noun.* Now *rare* or *obsolete.* Also **poulpe**. **E17.**
[French, ult. from Latin POLYPUS.]
An octopus, cuttlefish, or other cephalopod.

Poulsen arc /ˈpəʊls(ə)n ɑːk/ *noun phr. obsolete* exc. *Hist.* **E20.**
[from Valdemar *Poulsen* (1869–1942), Danish electrical engineer.]
An arc discharge between a carbon electrode and a water-cooled copper electrode in a hydrogen or hydrocarbon vapour atmosphere and a strong magnetic field, formerly used in the generation of short-wave radio waves.

poult /pəʊlt/ *noun*[1]. Also (*dial.*) **pout** /paʊt/. **LME.**
[Contr. of PULLET.]
1 A young domestic fowl, a chicken. Also, a young turkey, pheasant, pigeon, guinea-fowl, etc. **LME.**
2 A child; a youth. *colloq.* & *dial.* **M18.**

poult /puːlt, pʊlt/ *noun*[2]. **M20.**
[Abbreviation.]
Poult-de-soie. Also, a similar synthetic fabric.

poult-de-soie /puːdəˈswɑː/ *noun & adjective.* **M19.**
[French, alt. of *pou-de-soie* (see PADUASOY) of unkn. origin.]
(Made of) a fine corded silk or taffeta, usu. coloured.

poulter /ˈpəʊltə/ *noun. arch.* **ME.**
[Old French *pouletier*, from *poulet* PULLET: see -ER[2].]
1 = POULTERER. **ME.**
2 An officer of a noble household, a monastery, etc., in charge of the purchase of poultry and other provisions. *obsolete* exc. *Hist.* **LME.**
1 poulter's measure *PROSODY* (now *rare*) a metre consisting of lines of 12 and 14 syllables alternately.

poulterer /ˈpəʊlt(ə)rə/ *noun.* **L16.**
[Extended from prec., perh. infl. by POULTRY.]
A dealer in poultry and usu. game.
poulterer's measure *PROSODY* (now *rare*) = POULTER*'s measure*.

poultice /ˈpəʊltɪs/ *noun & verb.* **LME.**
[Latin *pultes* (pl.), from *pult-*, *puls* thick pottage, pap: see PULSE *noun*[2].]
▸ **A** *noun.* **1** A soft, moist, usu. heated mass of material applied to the skin to alleviate pain, inflammation, or irritation, to act as an emollient, or to stimulate the circulation locally; a fomentation, a cataplasm. **LME.**
2 *fig.* A (large) sum of money; a mortgage. Formerly also, a large wager. *Austral. slang.* **E20.**
▸ **B** *verb trans.* Apply a poultice to; treat with a poultice. **M18.**
▪ **poultice-wise** *adverb* in the manner of a poultice **E17.**

poultry /ˈpəʊltri/ *noun*. ME.
[Old French *pouletrie* formed as POULTER: see -RY.]
1 *pl.* (usu. *collect.*, treated as *sing.* or *pl.*) Domestic fowl; birds commonly reared for meat, eggs, or feathers in a yard, barn, or other enclosure, as chickens, ducks, geese, turkeys, or guinea-fowl (usu. excluding game-birds, as pigeons, pheasants, etc.). Also, such birds as a source of food. ME.
†**2** A place where fowl are reared or sold for food. ME–L16.
†**3** The office or position of a poulter in a noble household. Cf. POULTER 2. LME–E17.

📖 **1** *Daily Telegraph* More than two million poultry have now been lost in the . . fowl pest epidemic. *Which?* To eat more white meat (especially poultry) and fish in place of red meat.

■ **poultryless** *adjective* L19.

pounamu /pəʊˈnɑːmuː/ *noun*. *NZ*. M19.
[Maori.]
Nephrite, jade; an object made of this.

pounce /paʊns/ *noun*[1]. LME.
[Perh. shortening of PUNCHEON *noun*[1] or directly from Old French *poinson*, *po(i)nchon*: cf. PUNCH *noun*[1].]
†**1** A stamp or punch for impressing marks on metal etc. LME–M16.
†**2** A dagger. *rare*. L15–M16.
3 A claw, a talon, esp. of a hawk or other bird of prey. L15.
4 A forcible poke, esp. with the foot; a push, a nudge. *obsolete* exc. *dial.* M18.

📖 **3** G. W. THORNBURY Had hawk ever a fuller eye, or larger pounces? *fig.*: J. ELPHINSTON Whether gives thy wonder more to rove, The power of Caesar, or the pounce of Jove?

pounce /paʊns/ *noun*[2]. E18.
[Old French *ponce*, from popular Latin form of Latin *pumic-*, *pumex* PUMICE.]
1 *Hist.* A fine powder formerly used to prevent ink from spreading (esp. in writing on unsized paper) or to prepare parchment to receive writing. E18.
2 A fine powder, esp. powdered charcoal, for dusting over a perforated pattern sheet to transfer the design to a surface beneath. E18.

pounce /paʊns/ *noun*[3]. M19.
[from POUNCE *verb*[3].]
An act of pouncing; a sudden swoop or spring.
on the pounce ready to pounce, watching for an opportunity to pounce.

pounce /paʊns/ *verb*[1] *trans*. LME.
[Var. of PUNCH *verb*, prob. from Old French: cf. POUNCE *noun*[1].]
1 Emboss (plate or other metalwork) by raising the surface with blows struck on the underside. *obsolete* exc. *Hist.* LME.
2 Ornament (cloth etc.) by cutting or punching eyelets, figures, etc.; pink. *obsolete* exc. *Hist.* LME. ▸**b** Cut the edges of (cloth or a garment) into points and scallops; jag. Usu. in *pass.* *obsolete* exc. *Hist.* M16. ▸†**c** In *pass.* Of leaves etc.: be marked with jags, points, and indentations on the edges. L16–E18.
†**3** Prick, puncture, pierce, stab. LME–M17.
4 Poke or thrust forcibly, esp. with the foot or a stick. Now chiefly *Scot.* LME.
†**5** Bruise, comminute, or pulverize by blows. E16–M17.
6 Beat, thump, thrash, (a person). E19.
■ **pouncer** *noun*[1] a person or thing which pounces something M16.

pounce /paʊns/ *verb*[2] *trans*. L16.
[Old French *poncer*, formed as POUNCE *noun*[2].]
1 Smooth down by rubbing with pumice or pounce; *spec.* smooth or finish (the surface of a hat) with pumice, sandpaper, etc. L16.
2 Transfer (a design) to a surface by dusting a perforated pattern with pounce; dust (a pattern's perforations) with pounce. Also, transfer a design to (a surface) using pounce. L16.
†**3** Sprinkle with powder; *spec.* powder (the face) with a cosmetic. L16–L17.
■ **pouncer** *noun*[2] a device for applying pounce L19.

pounce /paʊns/ *verb*[3]. L17.
[from POUNCE *noun*[1].]
1 *verb trans.* Seize (prey) with claws or talons; swoop down on and grab. L17.
2 *verb intrans.* **a** Swoop down like a bird of prey; spring suddenly by way of attack. (Foll. by *on*, *upon*.) M18. ▸**b** *transf.* & *fig.* Seize on suddenly or eagerly. Usu. foll. by *on*, *upon*. E19.
3 *verb intrans. gen.* Spring or jump unexpectedly. Now *rare*. M19.

📖 **2a** D. HIGHSMITH The Bogeyman was standing in the gloom, waiting to pounce. *New Scientist* Trapdoor spiders pounce on their prey from below. **b** M. DIBDIN If a woman makes the slightest mistake it's pounced on. P. GROSSKURTH Ernest Jones pounced on any talk of archaic inheritance as suspiciously Jungian.

Comb.: **pounce commerce** a card-game resembling snap.

pounced /paʊnst/ *adjective*. Long *rare* or *obsolete*. L17.
[from POUNCE *noun*[1] + -ED[2].]
Having talons like a hawk. Usu. in *comb.*

pouncet /ˈpaʊnsɪt/ *noun*. M19.
[App. deduced from next.]
= next.

pouncet-box /ˈpaʊnsɪtbɒks/ *noun*. *arch.* L16.
[Perh. orig. misprint for *pounced* (=perforated) *box*: see POUNCE *verb*[1], BOX *noun*[2].]
A small box with a perforated lid, for holding perfumes etc.
¶ A Shakespearian term revived by Sir Walter Scott.

pound /paʊnd/ *noun*[1]. Pl. **-s**, (in senses 1 and 2, also *colloq.*) same.
[Old English *pund* = Old Frisian, Old Saxon *pund* (Middle Dutch *pont*, Dutch *pond*), Old High German *pfunt* (German *Pfund*), Old Norse, Gothic *pund*, from Germanic, from Latin (*libra*) *pondo* a pound (by) weight.]
▸**I 1** A unit of weight originally derived from the ancient Roman libra, varying at different periods, in different countries, and for different commodities. Now chiefly, a standardized unit of weight and mass equal to 16 ounces avoirdupois (0.4536 kg). Also, a unit of weight equal to 12 troy ounces (0.3732 kg). Abbreviation ***lb***. OE. ▸**b** *fig.* A large quantity, a lot. E16. ▸†**c** A weight, *esp.* one equal to a pound. Only in 17.

📖 **1** G. BERKELEY Excellent balsam may be purchased for a penny a pound. P. MAILLOUX His weight had dropped to 108 pounds. **b** T. BROWN An hundred Pound of Sorrow pays not an Ounce of our Debts.

▸**II 2** Orig., an English money of account (orig. a pound weight of silver) equal to 20 shillings or 240 pence. Later, the basic British monetary unit (also ***pound sterling***), since decimalization equal to 100 pence (formerly equal to 240 pence) used also in various British dependencies (also more fully ***Falkland Island pound***, ***Gibraltar pound***, ***St Helena pound***, etc.) and formerly in Ireland (cf. ***Irish pound*** below). Also, a coin or note of the value of one pound. OE. ▸**b** *fig.* A large sum of money. ME.
3 More fully ***pound Scots***. A former Scottish monetary unit, orig. of the same value as the pound sterling, but debased to one twelfth of that by the time of the Union of the Crown in 1603. *obsolete* exc. *Hist.* LME.
4 The basic monetary unit in Cyprus, Egypt, Lebanon, Sudan, Syria, and various other countries, equal to 100 cents in Cyprus, and 100 piastres in Egypt, Lebanon, Sudan, and Syria; a note or coin of this value. L19.
5 Five dollars; a five-dollar note. *US slang*. M20.

📖 **2** DICKENS 'It's twenty-four pound, sixteen and sevenpence ha'penny', observed the stranger. H. E. BATES There was always money in the hat, twenty or thirty pounds. *Observer* The current weakness of the dollar against the pound.

Phrases: ***in for a penny, in for a pound***: see PENNY *noun*. **in the pound** for each pound. **Irish pound** = PUNT *noun*[5]. ***penny wise and pound foolish***: see PENNY *adjective*. **pound and pint** *Nautical slang* (*obsolete* exc. *Hist.*) a sailor's ration **pound for pound** one pound for another, at the same rate. **pound of flesh** [with allus. to Shakes. *Merch. V.*] a payment, penalty, etc., which is strictly due but which it is ruthless or inhuman to demand. ***pound Scots***: see sense 3 above. **pounds, shillings, and pence** *colloq.* (**a**) British money; (**b**) *arch.* monetary, viewing things in monetary terms.
Comb.: **pound brush** a large paintbrush; **pound cake** a rich cake containing a pound (or equal weights) of each main ingredient; **pound coin** a coin worth one pound sterling; **pound-force**, pl. **pounds-force**, a unit of force equal to the weight of a mass of one pound avoirdupois, esp. under standard gravity; **pound-meal** *adverb* (long *obsolete* exc. *dial.*) pound by pound, by the pound; **pound note** a banknote worth one pound; **pound-noteish** *adjective* (*slang*) affected, pompous; **pound sign** the symbol £, placed before a number to denote that many pounds of money; **poundstone** a natural stone or pebble weighing a pound, formerly used as a weight; **pound-weight** a weight of one pound.

pound /paʊnd/ *noun*[2]. LOE.
[Origin uncertain: cf. PIND *verb*, POND *noun*.]
▸**I 1 a** An enclosure for detaining stray or trespassing cattle etc., or for keeping distrained cattle or goods until redeemed. Earliest in *comb.* LOE. ▸**b** An enclosure for sheltering or accommodating sheep or cattle; an enclosure in which wild animals are trapped. L18. ▸**c** An enclosure in which vehicles impounded by the police are kept. L20.
2 *transf.* & *fig.* A place of confinement; a trap; a prison. LME.

📖 **1a pound close**, **pound covert**: to which the owner of impounded animals has no right of access. **pound open**, **pound overt**: that is unroofed and may be entered by the owner of impounded animals to feed them. **b** G. CARTWRIGHT A pound for taking deer alive. **c** *Daily Telegraph* The Vauxhall . . had been towed to a pound because it was found parked on an urban clearway.

▸**II 3** A body of still water, a pond; *spec.* (**a**) a millpond; (**b**) the reach of a canal above a lock. ME.
4 A place where fish are caught or kept; *spec.* (**a**) a compartment for stowing fish on board a fishing vessel; (**b**) the second compartment of a pound-net. L18.

📖 **3** B. MARSH The water levels in canal pounds are maintained by means of weirs.

Comb.: **pound-boat** *US* a flat-bottomed boat used for carrying fish from a pound-net; **pound-breach** (**a**) the breaking open of a pound; (**b**) the illegal removal by an owner of goods lawfully impounded; **pound-fee**: paid for the release of cattle or goods from a pound; **pound-keeper** a person in charge of a public pound; **pound lock** a lock on a river with two gates to confine water, and often a side reservoir to maintain the water-level; **poundmaster** = ***pound-keeper*** above; **pound-net** an enclosure of nets in the sea near the shore, consisting of a long straight wall of net leading the fish into a first enclosure, and a second enclosure from which they cannot escape.

pound /paʊnd/ *noun*[3]. M16.
[from next.]
†**1** In *pl.* The products of pounding. *rare*. Only in M16.
2 An apparatus for pounding or crushing apples for cider. M19.
3 (The sound made by) a heavy beating blow; a thump. L19.

📖 **3** S. NAIPAUL There was the heavy pound of rhythm and blues.

pound /paʊnd/ *verb*[1].
[Old English *pūnian* rel. to Dutch *puin*, Low German *pün*.]
▸**I** *verb trans.* **1** Break down and crush by beating, as with a pestle; reduce to pulp; pulverize. OE.
†**2** Land (heavy blows) *on* a person. *rare* (Spenser). Only in L16.
3 Strike severely with the fists or a heavy instrument; strike or beat with repeated heavy blows; thump, pummel. E18. ▸**b** Knock or hammer (a thing) *in*, *out*, etc., by repeated blows. L19. ▸**c** Foll. by *out*: type (a letter, article, etc.) with heavy keystrokes. E20. ▸**d** Walk (the streets etc.), cover on foot, esp. in search of work, business, etc.; *spec.* (of a police officer) patrol (a beat). *colloq.* (orig. *US*). E20.

📖 **1** V. S. REID The cassava will be dried and pounded . . to make the . . flour. J. HERRIOT We . . pounded the tablets until we had five initial doses. *fig.*: P. CUTTING Chatila was being pounded to rubble. **3** J. S. LE FANU I danced every day, and pounded a piano. G. STEIN He pounded his pillow with his fist. A. J. CRONIN Women, kneeling on the stony river bank, were pounding linen. **b** R. KIPLING The big drum pounded out the tune. L. STEPHEN Not simply state a reason, but pound it into a thick head by repetition. **d** S. MARCUS He personally pounded the pavements calling on . . businessmen.

▸**II** *verb intrans.* **4** Beat or knock heavily; make a heavy beating sound; deliver heavy blows; fire heavy shot. (Foll. by *at*, *on*.) E19. ▸**b** Of a ship or boat: beat the water, rise and fall heavily. E20.
5 Move with heavy steps that beat the ground; run or ride hard and heavily. (Foll. by *over*, *up*, etc.) E19.

📖 **4** W. H. RUSSELL Our guns pounding at the Martinière. B. MOORE Suddenly . . someone pounded on the kitchen door. R. GUY Standing in the hall sweating, heart pounding. N. HINTON The music pounded so loudly that the bass notes rattled the window. **b** *Ships Monthly* Because of her . . shallow draft she tends to pound in a heavy sea. **5** M. WEBB Oxen and cows . . went pounding away into the woods. P. PEARCE James pounded up the doorsteps and into the house.

Phrases: **pound away** continue pounding, deliver repeated blows, (*at*). **pounded meat** *N. Amer.* the flesh of buffalo or other game cut up, dried, and pulverized to form the basic ingredient of pemmican. **pound one's ear** *slang* (orig. *US*) sleep.
Comb.: **pound-house** a building in which material is pounded, pulverized, or crushed.
■ **pounding** *noun* (**a**) the action of the verb; (**b**) (a quantity of) pounded material; (**c**) a heavy crushing or beating; a resounding defeat; an onslaught resulting in heavy losses; freq. in ***take a pounding***: L16.

pound /paʊnd/ *verb*[2] *trans*. LME.
[from POUND *noun*[2].]
1 Enclose in a pound, impound. LME. ▸**b** HUNTING. In *pass.* Of a rider: become confined in an enclosed place so as to be unable to follow the chase. E19.
2 Dam (water); dam *up*. Now chiefly *dial.* M17.

pound /paʊnd/ *verb*[3]. L16.
[from POUND *noun*[1].]
▸**I** †**1** *verb trans.* Weigh. *rare*. Only in L16.
2 *verb intrans.* Test the weight of coins (or of blanks to be minted) by weighing the number which ought to make a pound weight or a certain number of pounds. L19.
▸**II 3** *verb trans.* with *it*. Bet a pound or an extravagant amount; state as a certainty or strong conviction. *slang*. Now *rare* or *obsolete*. E19.

poundage /ˈpaʊndɪdʒ/ *noun*[1]. LME.
[from POUND *noun*[1] + -AGE.]
1 A duty or tax of so much per pound sterling, payable on merchandise; *spec.* a subsidy granted by Parliament to

the Crown on all imports and exports except bullion and commodities paying tonnage. *obsolete* exc. *Hist.* LME.

2 A payment or charge of so much per pound weight. L15.

3 a A payment of so much per pound sterling on the sum involved in a transaction; *spec.* a charge made on a postal order etc. L16. ▸**b** A percentage of the total earnings of a business, paid as wages. L19.

4 *BETTING.* Extravagant odds. *slang.* Now *rare* or *obsolete.* E19.

5 a (A) weight stated in pounds. E20. ▸**b** A person's weight, *esp.* that which is regarded as excess. M20.

> 📖 **3a** *Independent* The poundage, at 34.8p in the pound, will be slightly lower than the expected 36p. **5a** *Sport* Anything can happen at the featherweight poundage. *Health & Strength* How does one become strong? By exercising with weights of varying poundages. **b** *Fortune* People with a predisposition toward poundage must . . eat sensibly.

poundage /ˈpaʊndɪdʒ/ *noun*². M16.
[from POUND *noun*², *verb*² + -AGE.]
1 The action or right of impounding stray or trespassing cattle; the charge levied on the owner of impounded cattle etc. Now *rare* or *obsolete.* M16.
2 The keeping of cattle in a pound; a pound for cattle. M19.

poundal /ˈpaʊnd(ə)l/ *noun.* L19.
[from POUND *noun*¹, perh. after *quintal.*]
A unit of force equal to that which when applied to a pound mass for a period of one second gives it a velocity of one foot per second (equivalent to 0.1382 newtons). Also ***foot-poundal.***

pounder /ˈpaʊndə/ *noun*¹. LOE.
[from POUND *verb*¹ + -ER¹.]
1 A thing for pounding; *spec.* a pestle. LOE.
2 A person who pounds something. E17. ▸**b** A police officer, *esp.* one who patrols a beat. *US slang.* M20.

pounder /ˈpaʊndə/ *noun*². Now *rare.* L15.
[from POUND *verb*² + -ER¹.]
A person whose job it is to impound cattle, a pound-keeper.

pounder /ˈpaʊndə/ *noun*³. L17.
[from POUND *noun*¹ + -ER¹.]
▸**I** Usu. with prefixed qualifying numeral.
1 A thing which or person who weighs a specified number of pounds. Also, a gun carrying a shell of a specified number of pounds. L17.
2 A person possessing or earning, or a thing worth, a specified number of pounds. E18.
1 *hundred-pounder, quarter-pounder, six-pounder,* etc.
▸**II 3** A thing which weighs one pound. M19.

Poundian /ˈpaʊndɪən/ *adjective.* M20.
[from *Pound* (see below) + -IAN.]
Of, pertaining to, or characteristic of the American writer and poet Ezra Pound (1885–1972) or his work.

Poupart's ligament /ˈpuːpɑːz ˌlɪɡəm(ə)nt/ *noun phr.* M18.
[François *Poupart* (1661–1708), French surgeon.]
ANATOMY. The inguinal ligament which runs from the anterior superior spine of the ilium to the pubic tubercle.

poupée /pupe/ *noun.* Pl. pronounced same. L18.
[French = doll, puppet, wax figure.]
A figure used in making and displaying dresses, wigs, and other items of dress.

†**poupiets** *noun pl.* see PAUPIETTE.

pour /pɔː/ *noun.* M18.
[from the verb.]
1 A pouring stream (*lit. & fig.*). M18.
2 A heavy fall of rain, a downpour. E19.
3 *FOUNDING.* An act or the process of pouring melted metal etc.; the amount of melted metal etc. poured at one time. L19.

pour /pɔː/ *verb.* Also †**poor**, †**powre**, & other vars. ME.
[Origin unkn.]
▸**I** *verb trans.* **1** Emit in a stream; cause or allow (a liquid or granular substance) to flow, esp. from a container or other source. Usu. foll. by *down, out, over,* etc. ME. ▸**b** *refl.* Of a river etc.: flow stongly, flow *into* the sea. M17.
2 *transf. & fig.* Send out as in a stream; emit or discharge freely or copiously; *spec.* (**a**) discharge (missiles etc.) simultaneously or in rapid succession; (**b**) bestow or spend (money etc.) lavishly or profusely; (**c**) utter or express (words, feelings, etc.) freely and fully. (Foll. by *forth, out,* etc.) L16. ▸**b** Put or fit (a person) *into* a tight-fitting garment. *colloq.* M20.
†**3** Send (a thing) down a stream. *rare* (Spenser). Only in L16.
4 *FOUNDING.* Form by running molten metal into a mould; cast, found. *rare.* L19.

> 📖 **1** W. IRVING The sun had poured his last ray through the lofty window. J. JOHNSTON Her hand shook . . as she poured the coffee. S. BELLOW I was pouring sweat. ***pour cold water on***: see COLD *adjective.* **pour oil on the waters, pour oil on troubled waters** calm a disagreement or disturbance, esp. with conciliatory words. **2** LYNDON B. JOHNSON The Indians had been pouring most of their energy . . into a strenuous campaign. R. P. JHABVALA I managed . . to pour my tale of woe into his . . ear. ***pour down the throat***: see THROAT *noun.*

▸**II** *verb intrans.* **5** Dispense a liquid, esp. tea, from a container. M16.
6 Of a liquid etc.: gush out or flow in a stream; flow strongly; (of rain) fall heavily. Freq. foll. by *down, out,* etc. M16. ▸**b** *impers.* in ***it pours, it is pouring,*** etc., it rains, is raining, etc., heavily or copiously. E18.
7 *transf. & fig.* Come or go in great numbers, continuously, or in rapid succession; rush in a stream, swarm. Freq. foll. by *in, out,* etc. L16.

> 📖 **5** R. FULLER 'Shall I pour?' she asked. **6** DRYDEN When impetuous Rain Swells hasty Brooks, and pours upon the Plain. WILLIAM COLLINS The sweat poured off my face like water. **b** *Proverb:* It never rains but it pours. **7** J. STEINBECK Waves of excitement poured over the flat. A. SILLITOE Arthur joined the thousands that poured out through the factory gates. F. TOMLIN Books on Eliot continue to pour from the press.

■ **pourable** *adjective* able to be poured; capable of flowing easily: M20. **pourer** *noun* L16.

pourboire /purbwaːr/ *noun.* Pl. pronounced same. E19.
[French, lit. 'for drinking'.]
A gratuity, a tip.

†**pourcuttle** *noun.* L16–M18.
[Origin of 1st elem. unkn.; 2nd prob. CUTTLE *noun*¹.]
An octopus.

pour encourager les autres /pur ɑ̃kuraʒe lez oːtr/ *adverbial phr.* E19.
[French, lit. 'to encourage the others'.]
As an example to others; to encourage others.

pouring /ˈpɔːrɪŋ/ *noun.* LME.
[from POUR *verb* + -ING¹.]
The action of POUR *verb*; an instance of this; a quantity poured at one time.
Comb.: **pouring cream** (**a**) cream that flows readily; (**b**) single cream.

pouring /ˈpɔːrɪŋ/ *adjective & adverb.* E17.
[from POUR *verb* + -ING².]
▸**A** *adjective.* That pours; *spec.* (of rain) heavy. E17.
▸**B** *adverb.* Of rain falling: heavily. M19.

pour le sport /pur lə spɔːr/ *adverbial phr.* E20.
[French.]
For fun, amusement, or sport.

pourparler /purparle/ *noun.* Pl. pronounced same. E18.
[French, use as noun of Old French *po(u)rparler* discuss, from *po(u)r-* PRO-¹ + *parler* speak.]
An informal discussion or conference preliminary to actual negotiation.

pour passer le temps /pur pɑse lə tɑ̃/ *adverbial phr.* L17.
[French.]
To pass the time; to amuse oneself.

pourpoint /ˈpʊəpɔɪnt/ *noun & verb. obsolete* exc. *Hist.* ME.
[Old French *po(u)rpoint* orig. pa. pple of *pourpoindre* perforate, quilt, from *po(u)r-* PRO-¹ + *poindre* to prick, ult. from Latin *per* through + *pungere* to prick.]
▸**A** *noun.* **1** A close-fitting padded doublet worn by men in the 14th and 15th cents. ME.
†**2** A quilt, as a bed-covering. LME–M16.
▸**B** *verb trans.* Make in the style of a pourpoint; quilt. M19.

pour-point /ˈpɔːpɔɪnt/ *noun.* E20.
[from POUR *verb* + POINT *noun*¹.]
The temperature below which an oil is too viscous to be poured.

†**pourprise** *noun.* ME–E18.
[Old French, from *pour* for, before + *prendre* take.]
A precinct, an enclosure, a circuit.

pour rire /pur riːr/ *adjectival & adverbial phr.* L19.
[French, lit. 'in order to laugh'.]
(In a manner) that causes amusement or suggests jocular pretence; not serious(ly).

> 📖 *Punch* A flight of facetious fancy, a suggestion *pour rire.*

pourriture /purityːr/ *noun.* L17.
[French = rot, (a) rotting.]
1 Rotten or decomposed material. *rare.* L17.
2 In full ***pourriture noble*** /nɔbl/. A common grey mould, *Botrytis cinerea,* as deliberately cultivated on grapes to perfect certain French and German wines and Tokay; the condition of being affected by this mould; noble rot. E20.

pour-soi /purswa/ *noun.* M20.
[French, lit. 'for itself, for oneself'.]
PHILOSOPHY. In the philosophical thinking of J. P. Sartre, the spontaneous free being of consciousness; being for itself.

pousada /pəʊˈsɑːdə/ *noun.* M20.
[Portuguese, lit. 'resting-place', from *pausar* to rest.]
An inn or hotel in Portugal, *esp.* one of a chain of hotels administered by the State.

pousse-café /puskafe/ *noun.* Pl. pronounced same. L19.
[French, lit. 'push coffee'.]
A glass of various liqueurs or cordials poured in successive layers, taken immediately after coffee.

poussette /puːˈsɛt/ *noun & verb.* E19.
[French, dim. of *pousse* a push: see -ETTE.]
▸**A** *noun.* An act of poussetting. E19.
▸**B** *verb intrans.* Dance round one another with hands joined, as a couple in a country dance. E19.

poussin /ˈpuːsã, *foreign* pusɛ̃ (*pl. same*)/ *noun.* M20.
[French.]
A young chicken for eating. Earlier in ***petit poussin*** s.v. PETIT *adjective*².

Poussinesque /puːsaˈnɛsk/ *adjective.* M19.
[from *Poussin* (see below) + -ESQUE.]
Pertaining to or characteristic of the French painter Nicolas Poussin (1594–1665) or his work, esp. his landscapes.

poustie /ˈpaʊsti/ *noun.* Now only *Scot. arch.* ME.
[Old French *pousté* from Latin POTESTAS.]
Power; strength, might; authority.

pou sto /paʊ ˈstəʊ, puː ˈstɔː/ *noun.* M19.
[Greek (*dos moi*) *pou stō* (*kai kinō tēn gēn*) (give me (a place)) where I may stand (and I will move the earth), a saying attributed to Archimedes.]
A place to stand on, a standing-place; *fig.* a basis of operation.

pout /paʊt/ *noun*¹. OE.
[App. formed as POUT *verb*: earliest in *eel-pout*]
Any of various fishes esp. of the gadid genus *Trisopterus* or related genera; *esp.* (more fully ***whiting-pout***) the bib or pouting, *T. luscus.* Also = ***eelpout*** s.v. EEL *noun.*
HORNED ***pout.*** **ocean pout** a bottom-dwelling eelpout, *Macrozoarces americanus,* of the western N. Atlantic. *SILVERY* ***pout.***

pout *noun*² see POULT *noun*¹.

pout /paʊt/ *verb & noun*³. ME.
[Perh. from base of Swedish dial. *puta* be inflated, Danish *pude* cushion. Cf. POUT *noun*¹.]
▸**A** *verb.* **1** *verb intrans.* Push the lips forward, usu. as an expression of displeasure, sullenness, or flirtatiousness; show displeasure, sulk. ME. ▸**b** Of the lips: protrude, be pushed forward. Also (*transf.*), swell out like lips. L16.
2 *verb trans.* Push *out,* protrude, (the lips). L18.
3 *verb trans.* Utter sulkily or with a pout. L19.

> 📖 **1** *Patches* 'It's not fair,' said our Judey, stamping her size 6's . . and pouting. **b** M. M. HEATON The full childish lips pout out as if waiting to be kissed. **3** J. HELLER 'Do you like my wool?' 'Of course,' he replied. 'You never say so,' she pouted.

▸**B** *noun.* A protrusion of the lips; a pouting expression or mood. L16.

> 📖 J. BRAINE I saw Susan's mouth assume the pout which was always . . the precursor of a quarrel. **in the pouts** in a pouting mood, sulky.

poutassou /puˈtasuː/ *noun.* M19.
[Provençal.]
= ***blue whiting*** s.v. BLUE *adjective.*

pouter /ˈpaʊtə/ *noun.* E18.
[from POUT *verb* + -ER¹.]
1 (A bird of) a breed of domestic pigeon characterized by a greatly inflatable crop. Also ***pouter pigeon.*** E18.
2 A person who pouts. E19.

pouting /ˈpaʊtɪŋ/ *noun.* L16.
[from POUT *noun*¹ + -ING³.]
= BIB *noun* 2.

pouty /ˈpaʊti/ *adjective.* Chiefly *N. Amer.* M19.
[from POUT *noun*³ or *verb* + -Y¹.]
Of a person, the lips, etc.: inclined to pout. Also, sullen, petulant.

pouw /pəʊ/ *noun. S. Afr.* Also **pou.** L18.
[Afrikaans *pauw* from Dutch *paauw* peacock.]
A bustard.

POV *abbreviation.*
Point of view.

†**povere** *adjective & noun* see POOR *adjective & noun.*

poverish /ˈpɒv(ə)rɪʃ/ *verb trans. obsolete* exc. *dial.* LME.
[Old French *po(u)veriss-* lengthened stem of *po(u)verir,* from *povre* POOR *adjective*: see -ISH². Cf. IMPOVERISH.]
Make poor, impoverish.

poverty /ˈpɒvəti/ *noun*. **ME.**
[Old French *poverte*, *poverté* from Latin *paupertas*, *-tatis* from *pauper* poor: see **-TY**[1].]
▶ **I 1** The condition of having little or no wealth; indigence, destitution, want; relative lack of money or material possessions. Also *spec.* (ECCLESIASTICAL), renunciation of the right to individual ownership of property. **ME.** ▸**b** In *pl.* Material deprivations, hardships. Now *rare* or *obsolete*. **M16.**
†**2** *transf.* The poor collectively. **LME–L16.**

📖 **1** S. BELLOW Father blamed himself bitterly for the poverty that forced him to bring us up in a slum. A. STORR Freud was . . neat in dress . . even when early poverty made this difficult. ***primary poverty***, ***secondary poverty***. **b** M. TWAIN The household poverties . . had been made to blossom like the rose.

▶ **II 3** Deficiency in or lack of an appropriate or a particular property, quality, or ingredient; inferiority, paltriness, meanness; unproductiveness. **ME.** ▸**b** Poor physical condition, feebleness. **E16.**
4 Scantiness, dearth, scarcity; smallness of amount. **LME.**

📖 **3** SHAKES. *Sonn.* Alack, what poverty my Muse brings forth. I. WATTS The poverty of your understanding. S. HAUGHTON The extraordinary poverty of . . north-eastern Africa in river-producing power.

Comb.: **poverty-grass** (*a*) any of several N. American grasses that grow on poor soil, esp. *Aristida dichotoma*; (*b*) = ***poverty-plant*** below; **poverty level**, **poverty line** the estimated minimum income sufficient for maintaining the necessities of life; **poverty-plant** a small shrubby N. American heathlike plant, *Hudsonia ericoides*, of the rockrose family; **poverty programme** *US* a programme or policy designed to alleviate poverty; **poverty-stricken** *adjective* reduced to or suffering from poverty, extremely poor; **poverty-struck** *adjective* (now *rare* or *obsolete*) poverty-stricken; **poverty trap** a situation in which an increase of income is offset by a consequent loss of State benefits, making real improvement impossible.

povidone /ˈpɒvɪdəʊn/ *noun*. **M20.**
[Contr. of polyvinyl pyrrolidone.]
PHARMACOLOGY & MEDICINE. = **POLYVINYL** ***pyrrolidone***. Freq. *attrib.*, esp. in ***povidone iodine***, a complex of povidone and iodine in the form of a brown powder, used as a topical antiseptic.

Povindah *noun & adjective* var. of **POWINDAH.**

POW *abbreviation.*
1 Prince of Wales.
2 Prisoner of war.

pow /paʊ/ *interjection*. Orig. *US*. **L19.**
[Imit.]
Repr. the sound of a punch, blow, explosion, etc.

powan /ˈpəʊwən, ˈpaʊən/ *noun*. **M17.**
[Scot. form of **POLLAN**.]
A form of the freshwater houting, *Coregonus lavaretus*, occurring in Loch Lomond and Loch Eck, Scotland. Cf. **GWYNIAD**, **SKELLY** *noun* 1.

powder /ˈpaʊdə/ *noun*[1]. **ME.**
[Old & mod. French *poudre*, earlier *pol(d)re* from Latin *pulver-*, *pulvis* dust.]
1 Solid matter in the form of dry particles; a mass of dry impalpable particles produced by the grinding, crushing, or disintegration of a solid substance; dust. **ME.** ▸†**b** = **DUST** *noun* 2. **ME–M16.** ▸**c** Pollen; spores. **L17.** ▸**d** In full ***powder snow***. Loose dry (esp. newly fallen) snow. **E20.**
2 A preparation in the form of fine dry particles, esp. for a particular purpose; *spec.* (*a*) a medicament for external application; a (dose of) powdered medicine to be taken internally, usu. dissolved or suspended in a liquid (freq. in *pl.*); (*b*) a cosmetic to be applied to the face or skin or (formerly) to be sprinkled on the hair or a wig. Freq. with specifying word. **ME.**
3 = **GUNPOWDER 1. LME.**

📖 **1** *Essentials* Crush praline to a powder, with a rolling pin or in a food processor. **2** THACKERAY Two superior officers . . in livery with their hair in powder. D. CUSACK Mrs Mac brings Sheila a powder and a drink of water. *Practical Hairstyling & Beauty* Loose powder is important if you want your make-up to stick. ***baby powder***, ***baking-powder***, ***curry powder***, ***custard powder***, ***dusting powder***, ***emery powder***, ***face-powder***, ***milk powder***, ***rice powder***, ***scouring powder***, ***Seidlitz powder***, ***soap powder***, ***talcum powder***, etc. **3** J. CLAVELL His pistols were in his belt but he had no . . powder and no more shot.

Phrases: ***be* FOOD *for powder***. ***black powder***: see **BLACK** *adjective*. **keep one's powder dry** act providently or cautiously, be on the alert. ***lycopodium powder***: see **LYCOPODIUM** 2. **powder and shot** (*a*) the *matériel* expended in warfare; (*b*) *fig.* effort expended for some result. ***powder of projection***: see **PROJECTION** 1. ***priming powder***: see **PRIMING** *noun*[1] 2(a). **take a powder**, **take a run-out powder** depart, run away, abscond.
Comb.: **powder-bag**: for carrying or holding powder; **powder base** foundation cream; **powder-box**: for carrying or holding powder; **powder-burn** a burn made by the hot gases emitted by a firearm; **powder-chest** *Hist.* a chest for holding gunpowder; *spec.* a kind of petard charged with gunpowder, scrap iron, old nails, etc., for discharging from a ship's deck at a boarding enemy; **powder closet** (*obsolete* exc. *Hist.*) a small room used for powdering hair or wigs; **powder-coat** *verb trans.* cover (an object) with a polyester or epoxy powder, which is then heated to fuse into a protective layer; **powder colour** an opaque watercolour in powder form; ***powder compact***: see **COMPACT** *noun*[2] 2; **powder-down** a down feather which disintegrates into a powder when broken (more fully ***powder-down feather***); such feathers collectively; **powder-flask** *Hist.* a case for carrying gunpowder, usu. with a special device for measuring out a charge; **powder-horn** *Hist.* a powder-flask made of the horn of an ox, cow, etc., with a wooden or metal bottom at the larger end; **powder hound** *colloq.* a person who enjoys skiing on powder snow; **powder-house** *Hist.* a building for storing gunpowder; **powder keg** (*a*) a small barrel or container for gunpowder or blasting powder; (*b*) *fig.* a volatile or dangerous situation; **powder magazine** *Hist.* a place for the storage of gunpowder in a fort etc. or on board ship; **powder-man** a person who attends to the gunpowder used in blasting operations etc.; **powder metallurgy** the production of metals and carbides as fine powders and their pressing and sintering into compact forms; **powder-mill** a mill for making gunpowder; **powder paint** = ***powder colour*** above; **powder pattern** (*a*) an X-ray diffraction pattern produced from powdered crystals; (*b*) a pattern showing the domain structure of a magnetized solid, formed by a colloidal magnetic powder allowed to settle on it; **powder-plot** (now *rare*) = ***Gunpowder Plot*** s.v. **GUNPOWDER**; **powder-post beetle** any small brown beetle of the family Lyctidae, the boring larva of which reduces wood to powder; **powder-puff** (*a*) a soft pad for applying powder to the skin, esp. the face; (*b*) *Hist.* an instrument like a small bellows, for powdering the hair; **powder rag** a piece of cloth for applying face-powder; **powder slope**: covered in powder snow; ***powder snow***: see sense 1d above.
■ **powderize** *verb trans.* pulverize **L18.** **powderless** *adjective* without powder; (of a method of etching) not employing powder: **L19.** **powder-like** *adjective* resembling (that of) a powder **E19.**

powder /ˈpaʊdə/ *noun*[2]. Long *obsolete* exc. *dial.* Also **pooder** /ˈpuːdə/. **L16.**
[Origin unkn.]
A rush. Chiefly in ***with a powder***, ***at a powder***, ***in a powder***, impetuously, violently.

powder /ˈpaʊdə/ *verb*[1]. **ME.**
[Old & mod. French *poudrer*, from *poudre* **POWDER** *noun*[1]. In some senses from **POWDER** *noun*[1].]
1 *verb trans.* †**a** Sprinkle (food) with a powdery condiment; season (*with*) (*lit.* & *fig.*). **ME–L18.** ▸**b** *spec.* Sprinkle (meat) with salt or powdered spice, esp. for preserving; cure. *obsolete* exc. *dial.* **LME.**
2 *verb trans.* **a** Decorate or ornament with a multitude of small objects, figures, spots, or heraldic devices; sprinkle or spangle (a surface etc.) *with*. Usu. in *pass.* **ME.** ▸**b** Sprinkle or scatter (objects, figures, etc.) on a surface etc. Now *rare*. **LME.**
3 a *verb trans.* Sprinkle powder on; cover (as) with some powdery substance. (Foll. by *with*.) **LME.** ▸**b** *verb trans.* & *intrans.* Apply cosmetic powder (to). **L16.**
4 *verb trans.* Reduce to powder, pulverize; *spec.* reduce (a foodstuff) to powder by dehydration. Now chiefly as ***powdered*** *ppl adjective*. **LME.**
5 *verb intrans.* Turn to powder, become like powder. **M19.**

📖 **2a** J. ENTICK Gold shoes powdered with pearls. *London Gazette* The cape furred with miniver . . , and powdered with bars or rows of ermine. **3a** J. A. SYMONDS Ridges powdered with light snow. **b** V. SACKVILLE-WEST Sylvia Roehampton powders her face. **powder one's nose** *euphem.* (of a woman) go to the lavatory. **4** *Sunday Times* I have orange juice . . then . . a cup of powdered coffee. *Antique Collector* Made of powdered glass blown on to a sticky background.

■ **powderable** *adjective* (*rare*) **M17.**

powder /ˈpaʊdə/ *verb*[2] *intrans. colloq.* & *dial.* **M17.**
[from **POWDER** *noun*[2].]
Rush; hurry impetuously.

powder blue /paʊdə ˈbluː/ *noun & adjectival phr.* **M17.**
[from **POWDER** *noun*[1] + **BLUE** *noun*, *adjective*.]
▶ **A** *noun phr.* **1** Powdered smalt, esp. for use in laundry. **M17.**
2 Orig., the deep blue colour of smalt. Now chiefly, a soft pale shade of blue. **L19.**
▶ **B** *adjectival phr.* Of the colour of powder blue. **M19.**

powdering /ˈpaʊd(ə)rɪŋ/ *noun*. **LME.**
[from **POWDER** *verb*[1] + **-ING**[1].]
1 The action of **POWDER** *verb*[1]; an instance of this. **LME.**
2 (Decoration consisting of) a multitude of spots or small figures on a surface. **LME.**
3 A powdery deposit, esp. of snow; a thin sprinkling. **M19.**
Comb.: **powdering-closet** = ***powdering-room*** below; **powdering-gown** *Hist.* an overgarment worn to protect ordinary clothes while the hair was being powdered; **powdering-room** *Hist.* a room used for powdering hair or wigs; **powdering-tub** *Hist.* (*a*) a tub in which meat was salted and pickled; (*b*) *joc.* a sweating-tub used for treating venereal disease.

powder-monkey /ˈpaʊdəmʌŋki/ *noun*. **L17.**
[from **POWDER** *noun*[1] + **MONKEY** *noun*.]
1 a *Hist.* A boy employed on board ship to carry powder to the guns. **L17.** ▸**b** A member of a blasting crew; a powder-man. *US*. **E20.**
2 A compressed mass of damp gunpowder. **L19.**

powder-room /ˈpaʊdəruːm/ *noun*. **E17.**
[from **POWDER** *noun*[1] + **ROOM** *noun*[1].]
1 *Hist.* A room on board ship for the storage of gunpowder; a powder magazine. **E17.**
2 = ***powder closet*** s.v. **POWDER** *noun*[1]. **E20.**
3 A ladies' cloakroom or lavatory, esp. in a hotel or shop. **M20.**

powdery /ˈpaʊd(ə)ri/ *adjective*. **LME.**
[from **POWDER** *noun*[1] + **-Y**[1].]
1 Of the nature or consistency of powder; consisting of fine loose particles. **LME.**
2 Covered with or full of powder; having a deposit of powder; dusty. **E18.**
Special collocations: **powdery mildew** a plant disease caused by a parasitic fungus of the family Erysiphaceae and characterized by a white floury covering of conidia; the fungus itself.
■ **powderiness** *noun* **E19.**

Powellise *verb* var. of **POWELLIZE.**

Powellism /ˈpaʊ(ə)lɪz(ə)m/ *noun*. **M20.**
[from *Powell* (see below) + **-ISM**.]
The political and economic policies advocated by the British politician J. Enoch Powell (1912–98); *spec.* the restriction or termination of the right of immigration from Commonwealth countries into the United Kingdom.

powellite /ˈpaʊ(ə)lʌɪt/ *noun*[1]. **L19.**
[from J. W. *Powell* (1834–1902), US geologist + **-ITE**[1].]
MINERALOGY. Calcium molybdate, a rare fluorescent yellow mineral crystallizing in the tetragonal system and freq. also containing tungsten.

Powellite /ˈpaʊ(ə)lʌɪt/ *noun*[2] & *adjective*. **M20.**
[formed as **POWELLISM** + **-ITE**[1].]
▶ **A** *noun*. An advocate or supporter of Powellism. **M20.**
▶ **B** *adjective*. Of or pertaining to Powellites or Powellism. **M20.**

Powellize /ˈpaʊ(ə)lʌɪz/ *verb trans.* Now *rare*. Also **-ise**. **E20.**
[from William *Powell* of London, inventor of the process + **-IZE**.]
Preserve (timber) by boiling in a sugar solution to reduce shrinkage. Chiefly as ***Powellized*** *ppl adjective*, ***Powellizing*** *verbal noun*.

power /ˈpaʊə/ *noun*. **ME.**
[Anglo-Norman *poer*, *po(u)air*, Old French *poeir* (mod. *pouvoir*) from Proto-Romance alt. of Latin *posse* be able.]
▶ **I 1** Ability (*to do*), capacity (*of doing*, *to do*); an active property or principle. **ME.** ▸**b** A particular mental or physical faculty, capacity, or ability. Usu. in *pl.* **L15.**
2 (Possession of) control or authority over others; dominance; government, command; personal, social, or political influence or ascendancy. **ME.** ▸**b** (With specifying word.) A movement to enhance the status or influence of a specified group, lifestyle, etc. **M20.**
3 Ability to act or affect something strongly; strength, might; vigour, energy; effectiveness. **ME.**
4 Legal authority to act for another, esp. in a particular capacity; delegated authority; authorization; an instance of this. **ME.**

📖 **1** G. BERKELEY Is it not in your power to open your eyes? J. TYNDALL The red rays of the spectrum possess a very high heating power. R. HOGGART Mistrust of science has been strengthened by the latest revelations of its power to harm. J. BARZUN Material success had extinguished . . the power of speculative thought. **b** DAY LEWIS Aged voters . . through failing . . powers of concentration confused C. S. with C. D. Lewis on their voting papers. **2** H. HALLAM The council of ten had . . power over the senate. J. GALSWORTHY The revolution which had restored his Party to power. D. ROWE When we were small children we were . . fully in the power of other people. V. J. SCATTERGOOD A . . power struggle between the leading members of a politically irresponsible nobility. **b** *Howard Journal* The growth of 'pupil power' and the increase in truancy. ***Black Power*** etc. **3** V. BROME The power of his presence gave the illusion of height to his personality. W. RAEPER Dickens acknowledged the power of fairy-tales for moral good. **4** J. A. FROUDE The bishops . . had power to arrest laymen on suspicion of heresy. W. CRUISE Powers . . by which one person enabled another to do an act for him. E. L. DOCTOROW The enormous power of the immigration officials.

▶ **II 5** A military force; an army. *arch.* **ME.**
6 a A powerful or influential person, body, or thing; *spec.* (*arch.*) a person in authority, a ruler. **LME.** ▸**b** A State or nation with regard to its international authority or influence. **E18.**
7 A celestial being; *spec.* (*a*) in Christian theology, a member of the sixth order of the ninefold celestial hierarchy, ranking directly below the virtues and above the principalities (usu. in *pl.*); (*b*) a pagan god. **LME.**

8 Orig. (now *dial.*), a large number *of*. Later (now *colloq.*), an abundance *of*, a great deal *of*. LME.

9 A document, or clause in a document, giving a person legal authority to act for another, esp. in a particular capacity. Freq. in ***power of attorney*** s.v. ATTORNEY *noun* 4. L15.

†**10** In biblical translations and allusions [translation of Greek *exousia* (*1 Corinthians* 11:10)]: a woman's head-covering. E16–E17.

> 📖 **6a** T. S. ELIOT I want to be a power in the City. **b** V. CRONIN Catherine had recognised Prussia to be the strongest European power. **8** J. DISKI It'll do you a power of good.

▶ **III 11** The sound indicated by a character or symbol; the meaning in context of a word or phrase. M16.

12 *MATH.* A value obtained by multiplying a quantity by itself a (specified) number of times (the number of equal factors of the resulting product being the exponent). Also, an exponent. Freq. with preceding ordinal, as ***first power*** (the quantity itself), ***second power*** (the square of a quantity), ***third power*** (the cube of a quantity), or following cardinal, as ***(to) the power ten***, ***(to) the power of ten***. (Earliest in narrower *GEOMETRY* sense.) L16. ▸**b** That property of a set that is the same for any two sets whose elements can be placed in a one-to-one correspondence (in the case of a finite set, equal to the number of elements it contains); = POTENCY 5. E20.

13 *MECHANICS.* In full ***mechanical power***. = ***simple machine*** s.v. MACHINE *noun*. *obsolete* exc. *Hist.* L17.

14 a A form or source of energy or force available for application to work, or applied to produce motion, heat, or pressure; (***a***) mechanical or electrical energy as distinct from hand-labour; (***b***) a (public) supply of energy, esp. electricity (often viewed as a commodity); occas. *spec.*, an electricity supply other than that for lighting. E18. ▸**b** Capacity for exerting mechanical force, doing work, or producing some physical effect; *spec.* in *PHYSICS*, the rate of energy output, the rate at which work is done. E19. ▸**c** An engine; engines or machines collectively. *slang*. M20.

15 *OPTICS.* **a** The magnifying capacity of a lens or combination of lenses; also, the lens itself. E18. ▸**b** [from *refractive power*.] The reciprocal of the focal length of a lens. E19.

> 📖 **14a** G. GREENE What's the good of a vacuum cleaner if the power's cut off? ***hydroelectric power***, ***nuclear power***, ***solar power***, etc.

Phrases: ***balance of power***: see BALANCE *noun*. ***Black Power***: see BLACK *adjective*. ***Central Powers***: see CENTRAL *adjective*. ***corridors of power***: see CORRIDOR 4. ***Great Power***: see GREAT *adjective*. ***have the power of record***: see RECORD *noun*. **more power to you** etc., **more power to your arm**, **more power to your elbow**, etc. *colloq.*: expr. encouragement for a person or approval of a person's actions. **power behind the throne** a person without constitutional status who covertly exercises power by personal influence over a ruler or leader. ***power of attorney***: see ATTORNEY *noun* 4. **powers-that-be** [*Romans* 13:1] the authorities concerned, the people exercising political or social control. ***resolving power***: see RESOLVE *verb* 2d. ***residuary powers***: see RESIDUARY 2. ***separation of powers***: see SEPARATION 1. ***specific rotary power***: see SPECIFIC *adjective*. ***to the best of one's power***: see BEST *adjective* etc.. ***vital power***: see VITAL *adjective*.

Attrib. & comb.: In the senses 'operated, driven, or done by mechanical power', as ***power-crane***, ***power drill***, ***power-hammer***, ***power-lathe***, ***power mower***, etc.; 'designating a sportsman or sportswoman or a style of play in which great muscular power is used', as ***power hitter***, ***power tennis***, etc; 'pertaining to the generation and use of (esp. commercial electrical) power', as ***power industry***, ***power loss***, ***power supply***, etc; 'designating fuel of a grade suitable for producing mechanical power', as ***power alcohol***, ***power kerosine***, etc. Special combs., as **power-assistance** (the equipment for) the application of power to assist manual operation; **power-assisted** *adjective* (esp. of brakes and steering in motor vehicles) employing an inanimate source of power to assist manual operation; **power base** a source of authority or support; **power block** *POLITICS* a group of allied States, a great power with its allies and dependencies; **power board** (***a***) a board or panel containing switches or meters for an electricity supply; (***b***) (chiefly *NZ*) a controlling authority for the supply of electricity in an area; **powerboat** a motorboat, *esp.* one with a powerful engine; **power brake** a power-assisted brake (in a motor vehicle); **power breakfast** (orig. *US*) a working breakfast at which powerful politicians, business executives, etc., hold high-level discussions; **power broker** (chiefly *N. Amer.*) a person who exerts influence or affects the distribution of political power by intrigue; **power cable**: transmitting electrical power; **power car** (chiefly *US*) a railway carriage incorporating an engine; **power centre** a locus of political authority, *esp.* a powerful person or institution; **power-centred** *adjective* concerned with the study, acquisition, or exercise of political authority; **power cut** a temporary withdrawal or failure of an electricity supply; **power density** *NUCLEAR PHYSICS* the power produced per unit volume of a reactor core; **power dive** a steep dive of an aircraft with its engine or engines providing thrust; **power-dive** *verb intrans.* perform a power dive; **power dressing**: in a style intended to show that one holds a powerful position in business etc.; **power-drive** (***a***) (equipment for) the driving of machinery by mechanical or electrical power; (***b***) the impulse to exercise power; **power-egg** an ovate housing for an engine, esp. on an airship; **power élite** a social or political group that exercises power; **power factor** *ELECTRICITY* the ratio of the actual power delivery by (part of) an a.c. circuit to the product of the root mean square values of current and voltage; **power failure** a failure of a power supply, esp. of electricity; **power forward** *BASKETBALL* a large forward who typically plays close to the basket and has good shot-blocking and rebounding skills; **power frequency** *ELECTRICITY*: in the range used for alternating currents supplying power (commonly 50 or 60 Hz); **power game** a contest for authority or influence, esp. in politics; **power law** a relationship between two quantities such that one is proportional to a fixed power of the other; **power level** the amount of power being transmitted, produced, etc. (often relative to a reference level); **powerlifter** a person who takes part in powerlifting; **powerlifting** a form of competitive weightlifting in which contestants attempt three types of lift in a set sequence; **power line** a conductor supplying electrical power, a mains transmission line, esp. supported by poles or pylons; **power-load** *ELECTRICITY* the amount of current delivered for use in driving machinery, as distinct from that used for lighting; **power-loader** a machine for loading coal on to a conveyor belt at the coalface; **power loading** (***a***) *MINING* the loading of coal on to a conveyor belt at the coalface by means of a machine; (***b***) see LOADING *noun* 6; **power-loom** a weaver's loom worked by machine rather than by hand; **power lunch** (orig. *US*) a working lunch, esp. one at which people of authority or influence can hold discussions in a relatively informal or neutral setting; the food served at such a lunch; **power-net** a knitted stretch fabric used in women's underwear; **power-operated** *adjective* operated by power from an inanimate source; **power outage** *N. Amer.* = ***power cut*** above; **power pack** a unit for supplying power; *spec.* one for converting an alternating current (from the mains) to a direct current at a different (usu. lower) voltage; **power package** a self-contained source of power; **powerplant** (an) apparatus or an installation which provides power for industry, a machine, etc.; **power play** (***a***) *SPORT* (tactics involving) a concentration of players at a particular point; (***b***) *TENNIS* (tactics requiring) the hitting of every ball with maximum speed and strength; (***c***) *ICE HOCKEY* (play involving) a formation of players adopted when the opponents are one or more players down; (***d***) a political or business strategy involving a concentration of effort, resources, etc.; **power point** a socket in a wall etc. by which an electrical appliance or device can be connected to the electricity supply; **power pole** a pole supporting an overhead power line; **power-political** *adjective* pertaining to or characterized by power politics; **power-politician** a person who practises power politics; **power politics** political action based on or backed by power or threats to use force; **power-rating** the electrical power which an appliance is designed to receive or operate at; **power series** *MATH.* an infinite series of the form $\Sigma a_n x^n$ (where n is a positive integer); a generalization of this for more than one variable; **power set** *MATH. & LOGIC* the set of all the subsets of a given set; **power-sharing** (***a***) the sharing among rival political interests of governmental responsibilities; (***b***) a policy for such sharing agreed between parties or within a coalition; **power shovel** a mechanical excavator; **power shower** a shower bath using an electric pump to produce a high-pressure spray; **power slide** *noun & verb* (***a***) *noun* a deliberate controlled skid in a vehicle, usu. done in order to turn corners at high speed; (***b***) *verb trans.* (***power-slide***) turn (a car) in this way; **power spectrum** the distribution of the energy of a waveform among its different components; **power station** a building or works where electricity is generated for distribution; **power steering** power-assisted steering (in a motor vehicle); **power stroke** the stroke of an internal-combustion engine in which the piston is moved downward by the expansion of gases in the cylinder; **power supply** the supply of power, esp. electricity; **power take-off** (equipment for) the transmission of mechanical power from an engine, esp. that of a tractor or similar vehicle, to another piece of equipment; **power tool** an electrically powered tool; **power train** *MECHANICS* the mechanism that transmits the drive from the engine of a vehicle to its axle; this together with the engine and axle; **power transformer** *ELECTRONICS* a transformer designed to accept a relatively large power, esp. from a mains supply or an amplifier, for transmission at a usu. lower voltage to a circuit or device; **power transistor** *ELECTRONICS* a transistor designed to deliver a relatively high power; **power unit** a device supplying, or controlling the supply of, power; a power plant; **power-up** (***a***) the action of switching on an electrical device, esp. a computer; (***b***) (in a computer game) a bonus which a player can collect and which gives his or her character an advantage such as more strength or firepower; **power user** *COMPUTING* a user who needs products having the most features and the fastest performance.

power /ˈpaʊə/ *verb*. M16.
[from the noun.]

†**1** *verb trans.* Make powerful, strengthen. *rare*. M16–E18.

2 *verb trans.* Supply with power, esp. for propulsion; propel. L19.

3 *verb intrans.* Travel using an engine, esp. as an alternative or supplement to sail. L20.

4 *verb intrans.* Move or travel with great speed or force; surge. L20.

> 📖 **2** A. YORK The police launch . . was powered by two big Perkins engines. *Nordic Skiing* Cold air . . sweeps . . across the country, powered by the prevailing westerly winds. **4** *Daily Telegraph* The majestic locomotives that powered along the track in the first half of the century. *Gridiron* New Orleans . . powered to a 17–0 lead.

†**powerable** *adjective*. L16.
[from POWER *noun* + -ABLE.]

1 Powerful. L16–M17.

2 Able to be done; possible. *rare*. Only in M19.

■ †**powerableness** *noun* L16–M17. †**powerably** *adverb* powerfully L16–E17.

powered /ˈpaʊəd/ *adjective*. M17.
[from POWER *noun* + -ED².]

†**1** *MATH.* Squared. *rare*. Only in M17.

2 Having or using power of a specified kind or degree (freq. as 2nd elem. of comb.); using a fuel-burning source of power, esp. for propulsion. L19.

> 📖 **2** C. G. BURGE The introduction of powered flight in 1903. ***high-powered***, ***low-powered***, ***nuclear-powered***, ***rocket-powered***, etc.

Powerforming /ˈpaʊəfɔːmɪŋ/ *noun*. M20.
[from POWER *noun* + *re*)*forming* (see REFORM *verb*¹ 8).]

A process for reforming petroleum using a platinum catalyst.

■ **Powerformer** *noun* an installation for Powerforming M20.

powerful /ˈpaʊəfʊl, -f(ə)l/ *adjective & adverb*. LME.
[from POWER *noun* + -FUL.]

▶ **A** *adjective*. **1** Having great power, mighty; politically or socially influential. LME.

2 (Capable of) exerting great force or producing great effect; (of an argument etc.) impressive, convincing, telling. L16.

3 Great in quantity or number. *dial. & colloq.* E19.

▶ **B** *adverb*. Very, extremely. *dial. & colloq.* E19.

■ **powerfully** *adverb* E17. **powerfulness** *noun* L16.

powerhouse /ˈpaʊəhaʊs/ *noun & adjective*. L19.
[from POWER *noun* + HOUSE *noun*¹.]

▶ **A** *noun*. **1** A building where power is produced on a large scale for driving machinery or generating electricity for distribution. L19.

2 *fig.* A source of energy or inspiration; a very strong or energetic person or animal; a powerful group of people. E20. ▸**b** A very strong hand at cards. M20.

▶ **B** *attrib.* or as *adjective*. Of, pertaining to, or characteristic of a powerhouse; *spec.* (*MUSIC*) performed or performing with a powerful driving rhythm. M20.

powerless /ˈpaʊəlɪs/ *adjective*. LME.
[from POWER *noun* + -LESS.]

Lacking power or strength; helpless; wholly unable *to do*.

■ **powerlessly** *adverb* E19. **powerlessness** *noun* M19.

Powhatan /ˈpaʊətan/ *noun & adjective*. E17.
[Virginia Algonquian.]

▶ **A** *noun*. **1** A member of an Algonquian people of eastern Virginia. E17.

2 The language (now extinct) of this people, Virginia Algonquian. E20.

▶ **B** *adjective*. Of or pertaining to this people or their language. L18.

Powindah /ˈpaʊwɪndə/ *noun & adjective*. Also **Pov-**. M19.
[Pashto from Persian *parvanda* bundle, merchandise.]

▶ **A** *noun*. A member of a nomadic trading people of Afghanistan. M19.

▶ **B** *attrib.* or as *adjective*. Of or pertaining to the Powindahs. L19.

powldoody /paʊlˈduːdi/ *noun*. E19.
[from *Pouldoody*, the inner part of a creek near Corcomroe Abbey in Co. Clare, Ireland.]

A celebrated variety of Irish oyster.

†**powre** *verb* var. of POUR *verb*.

powwow /ˈpaʊwaʊ/ *noun & verb*. Also **pow-wow**. E17.
[Narragansett *powah*, *powwaw* shaman.]

▶ **A** *noun*. **1** A N. American Indian priest, sorcerer, or medicine man, a shaman. E17. ▸**b** The art of a powwow, esp. as used in healing. M19.

2 A N. American Indian ceremony, *esp.* one involving magic, feasting, and dancing. Also, a council or conference of or with Indians. E17.

3 *transf.* Any meeting for discussion; a conference, congress, or consultation, esp. among friends or colleagues. Also, noisy bustle or activity. Orig. *US*. E19.

> 📖 **2** J. A. MICHENER The defeated Comanche and Apache chiefs sought pow-wow with the Cheyenne. **3** *Spectator* Congresses and pow-wows . . are certainly a feature of the age. *Sunday Express* A family pow-wow . . decided that the afternoon . . be spent on a secluded beach. N. MAILER Allen Dulles and . . John. F. Kennedy had a powwow.

▶ **B** *verb*. **1** *verb intrans.* Of N. American Indians: practise powwow; hold a powwow. M17.

2 *verb trans.* Treat with powwow. E18.

3 *verb intrans. transf.* Confer, discuss, deliberate. Chiefly *N. Amer.* L18.

■ **powwower** *noun* (now *rare* or *obsolete*) a person who powwows M17.

Powysian /pəʊˈɪsɪən, paʊ-/ *adjective & noun*. M19.
[from *Powys* (see below) + -IAN.]

Chiefly *Hist.* ▶ **A** *adjective*. Of or pertaining to the former Welsh principality or (less commonly) the modern Welsh county of Powys. M19.

▶ **B** *noun*. A native or inhabitant of Powys. L19.

pox /pɒks/ *noun & verb.* Also (earlier) †**pocks**. LME.
[from POCK *noun* + -S[1], with later alt. of consonants.]
▶ **A** *noun.* **I 1** Usu. ***the pox.*** (Any of several diseases characterized by) a rash of pocks or eruptive pustules on the skin; *esp.* (now *colloq.*) a venereal disease, syphilis; formerly also *spec.*, smallpox. LME.
2 In imprecations expr. irritation or impatience. *arch. slang.* E16.

> 📖 **1** ***chickenpox, cowpox, smallpox,*** etc. ***French pox***: see FRENCH *adjective.* ***great pox***: see GREAT *adjective.* **2** CLARENDON Some said, 'a Pox take the House of Commons.' V. WOOLF Hand me the mirror, girl . . . A pox on the girl—she's dreaming!

▶†**II** Pl. of POCK *noun*
Comb.: **pox-doctor** *slang* a doctor specializing in the treatment of venereal diseases; **poxvirus** any of a group of large DNA viruses that cause smallpox and similar infectious diseases in vertebrates.
▶ **B** *verb trans.* Infect with the pox (usu., with syphilis); ruin, botch (a piece of work). Freq. as ***poxed*** *ppl adjective. colloq.* L17.

poxy /ˈpɒksi/ *adjective. colloq.* E20.
[from POX *noun* + -Y[1].]
Infected with pox; spotty; *fig.* trashy, worthless.

poya /ˈpəʊjə/ *noun.* M19.
[Sinhalese *pōya*, from Sanskrit *upavasatha* fast-day.]
BUDDHISM. More fully **poya day**. Each of the days on which the moon enters one of its four phases, observed as a day of special religious observance in Sri Lanka.

poy-bird *noun* var. of POË-BIRD.

Poynings' Law /ˈpɔɪnɪŋz lɔː/ *noun phr.* E17.
[Sir Edward *Poynings* (1459–1521), Lord Deputy in Ireland, 1494–6.]
Hist. A series of statutes, passed at Drogheda in 1494–5 and repealed in 1782, by which the Irish parliament was subordinated to the English Crown.

Poynting /ˈpɔɪntɪŋ/ *noun.* L19.
[J. H. *Poynting* (1852–1914), English physicist.]
PHYSICS. Used *attrib.* and in *possess.* to designate concepts in electromagnetism.
Poynting's theorem: that the rate of flow of electromagnetic energy through a closed surface is equal to the integral over the surface of the Poynting vector. **Poynting's vector**, **Poynting vector** the vector product of the electric and magnetic field strengths at any point, often interpretable as the rate of flow of electromagnetic energy.

pozole *noun* var. of POSOLE.

pozzolana /pɒtsəˈlɑːnə/ *noun.* E18.
[Italian *pozz(u)olana* (sc. *terra*) '(earth) belonging to Pozzuoli', a town near Naples (from Latin *Puteoli* little springs).]
A volcanic ash, containing silica, alumina, lime, etc., used in the preparation of hydraulic cement. Also, an artificial preparation resembling this. Freq. *attrib.*, esp. in ***pozzolana cement.***
■ **pozzolanic** *adjective* of the nature of or containing pozzolana E19. **pozzolaˈnicity** *noun* the property of combining with lime in the presence of water to form a cement M20.

pozzy /ˈpɒzi/ *noun*[1]. *Military slang.* E20.
[Origin unkn.]
Jam, marmalade.

pozzy *noun*[2] var. of POSSIE.

PP *abbreviation*[1].
Parish priest.

pp *abbreviation*[2].
1 Latin *per procurationem* by proxy, on behalf of.
2 MUSIC. Pianissimo, very softly.

pp. *abbreviation.*
Pages.

ppb *abbreviation.*
Parts per billion.

PPC *abbreviation.*
French *Pour prendre congé* in order to take leave (written on cards etc.).

PPE *abbreviation.*
Politics, Philosophy, and Economics (a course of study at Oxford University).

PPI *abbreviation*[1].
Plan position indicator (in radar).

ppi *abbreviation*[2].
COMPUTING. Pixels per inch.

PPLO *abbreviation.*
Pleuropneumonia-like organism(s).

ppm *abbreviation.*
Parts per million.

PPN *abbreviation.*
Public packet network.

PPP *abbreviation*[1].
1 Pakistan People's Party.
2 COMPUTING. Point to point protocol, which allows data conforming to the Internet protocol IP to be handled on a serial line.
3 ECONOMICS. Purchasing power parity (a way of measuring what an amount of money will buy in different countries).

ppp *abbreviation*[2].
MUSIC. Pianissimo, very softly.

PPS *abbreviation.*
1 Parliamentary Private Secretary.
2 Latin *post-postscriptum* additional postscript.

PPV *abbreviation.*
Pay-per-view.

PQ *abbreviation. Canad.*
1 French *Parti Québécois* Quebec Party.
2 Province of Quebec.

PR *abbreviation.*
1 Proportional representation.
2 Public relations.
3 Puerto Rico, Puerto Rican. *US.*

Pr *symbol.*
CHEMISTRY. Praseodymium.

pr. *abbreviation.*
Pair.

PRA *abbreviation.*
President of the Royal Academy of Arts.

praam *noun* var. of PRAM *noun*[1].

prabble /ˈprab(ə)l/ *noun. obsolete* exc. *dial. rare.* L16.
[Alt. of BRABBLE. Cf. PRIBBLE.]
A quarrel, a squabble.

practic /ˈpraktɪk/ *noun.* Also (now only in sense 2b) **-ick**. LME.
[Old French *practique* (mod. *pratique*) from medieval Latin *practica* from Greek *praktikē* use as noun of fem. of *praktikos*: see next, -IC.]
1 The action of doing something; practical work; practice as opp. to theory. *arch.* LME. ▸**b** An action, a deed; in *pl.*, works, practices; practical things or matters. *arch.* M17.
2 †**a** Custom, habit, usage. LME–E19. ▸**b** Chiefly SCOTS LAW (now *Hist.*). Legal usage; case-law. M16.
3 Artful dealing, cunning. Also, an art, a practical skill; an artful stratagem, a deception. *obsolete* exc. *Scot. dial.* LME.
†**4** Practical acquaintance; familiarity; experience. L16–M18.
¶ Earlier English and esp. Scot. equivalent of PRACTICE *noun.*

practic /ˈpraktɪk/ *adjective. arch.* LME.
[French †*practique* var. of *pratique* or late Latin *practicus*, from Greek *praktikos*, from *prattein* do: see -IC.]
1 = PRACTICAL *adjective* 2a. LME.
†**2** Experienced, practised, skilled. L16–M17.
†**3** Artful, crafty, cunning. Only in L16.
†**4** = PRACTICAL *adjective* 3, 5. E–M17.

practicable /ˈpraktɪkəb(ə)l/ *adjective.* M17.
[French, from *pratiquer* put into practice, use, from *pratique*: see PRACTIC *noun*, -ABLE.]
1 Able to be put into practice; able to be effected, accomplished, or done; feasible. M17.
2 Of a road, passage, etc.: able to be used or traversed. E18. ▸**b** THEATRICAL & CINEMATOGRAPHY. = PRACTICAL *adjective* 2C. M19.
■ **practicaˈbility** *noun* M18. **practicableness** *noun* M17. **practicably** *adverb* M17.

practical /ˈpraktɪk(ə)l/ *adjective & noun.* M16.
[from PRACTIC *adjective* + -AL[1] (see -ICAL).]
▶ **A** *adjective.* †**1** Practising art or craft; crafty, scheming. Only in M16.
2 a Of or pertaining to practice; consisting or shown in practice or action, as opp. to theory or speculation. L16. ▸**b** Available or useful in practice; able to be used. Also, useful but dull. M17. ▸**c** Of a prop in a theatre or film set: able to be used as in real life; working, operable. M20.
3 Engaged in practising an occupation; practising, working. E17.
4 Inclined or suited to action as opp. to speculation etc.; capable of action. Also, skilled at manual tasks. E17.
5 That is such in practice or effect, though not theoretically or nominally; virtual. M17.

> 📖 **2a** U. LE GUIN It has no practical application—no relevance to real life. **b** T. HARDY A practical skill in the various processes of farming. I. MURDOCH A flying leap from the High Table . . was not a very practical idea. P. V. WHITE The house had been stained a practical brown. **4** J. M. BARRIE Being a practical man he busies himself gathering firewood. R. C. HUTCHINSON Steve'll fix it up . . . He's quite practical when he's got to be. **5** E. A. FREEMAN The great advantage of our practical republic over your avowed republic. F. O'CONNOR I have finished my novel for all practical purposes, but am still tinkering with it.

Special collocations: **practical attitude** an attitude concerned with material facts and actual events. **practical criticism** an analytical form of literary criticism. ***practical joke***: see JOKE *noun.* ***practical joker***: see JOKER *noun.* **practical nurse** (chiefly *N. Amer.*) a nurse who has completed a training course but is not registered. **practical politics** the reality of political life, sometimes implying lack of moral principle.
▶ **B** *noun.* †**1** In *pl.* Practical matters; points of practice. M17–M18.
2 An examination, course, or lesson devoted to practice in a subject. M20.
■ **practicalism** *noun* devotion to practical affairs or methods; *spec.* (in Communism) overemphasis on practical matters leading to disregard of theory: M19. **practiˈcality** *noun* (*a*) the quality of being practical; (*b*) a practical matter or affair: E19. **practicalize** *verb trans.* (*rare*) (*a*) make practical; (*b*) subject to practical jokes: E19. **practicalness** *noun* E18.

practically /ˈpraktɪk(ə)li/ *adverb.* E17.
[from PRACTICAL + -LY[2].]
1 In a practical manner; as a matter of fact, actually, in reality. E17.
2 For practical purposes; to all intents and purposes; virtually, almost. M18.

> 📖 **1** E. H. HUTTEN Such extremes of temperature are practically difficult to produce. JOAN SMITH 'Why don't we make a list of things that have to be done?' she suggested practically. **2** W. S. MAUGHAM Miss Ley pursed her lips till they practically disappeared. E. WAUGH Practically no one ever sets out to write such trash.

practicant /ˈpraktɪk(ə)nt/ *noun.* M17.
[medieval Latin *practicant-* pres. ppl stem of *practicare*, *-ari* practise medicine: see -ANT[1].]
Orig., a medical practitioner. Now *gen.*, a practitioner.

practice /ˈpraktɪs/ *noun.* Also (earlier) †**-ise**. LME.
[from PRACTISE, after such pairs as *advice, advise, device, devise.* Superseded PRACTIC *noun.*]
1 a The habitual doing or carrying out *of* something; usual or customary action or performance; action as opp. to profession, theory, knowledge, etc. LME. ▸**b** A custom; a habit; a habitual action. M16. ▸**c** LAW. An established method of legal procedure. E17.
2 *spec.* The carrying out or exercise of a profession or occupation; the business to which a lawyer, doctor, etc., belongs for this purpose. LME.
3 a The action of scheming or planning, esp. in an underhand or evil way; treachery; trickery, artifice, deception. *arch.* L15. ▸**b** Dealings, negotiation; *esp.* underhand dealings, intrigue. *arch.* M16. ▸**c** A scheme, a conspiracy; an artifice, a trick. *arch.* M16.
4 Repeated exercise in or performance of an activity so as to acquire or maintain proficiency in it; activity undertaken to this end. Formerly also, proficiency so acquired. E16.
5 a The action *of* doing something; performance, operation; method of action or working. *obsolete* exc. as passing into sense 1a. M16. ▸**b** An action, a deed; in *pl.*, doings, proceedings. *obsolete* exc. as passing into sense 1b. M16. ▸**c** PHILOSOPHY. The practical aspect or application of something as opp. to the theoretical aspect. L19. ▸**d** In Marxism, the social activity which should result from and complement the theory of Communism. Cf. PRAXIS 1C. L19.
†**6** An exercise; a practical treatise. M16–E18.
7 An arithmetical method of finding the price of a given number of articles or the quantity of a commodity at a given price, where quantity or price or both are expressed in several denominations. Now *rare* or *obsolete.* L16.

> 📖 **1a** J. BARZUN It being accepted practice to start conversation by asking people what they do. D. ACHESON Not all the arts of diplomacy are learned solely in its practice. **b** H. JAMES I can put her off her guard only by ingratiating diplomatic practices. *Dissent* Exchanging goods by barter, a practice that the Russians call *blat.* **2** C. A. LINDBERGH He began his law practice in Little Falls where he served as County Attorney. W. C. WILLIAMS My first job was to resume my practice of medicine. **3** E. A. FREEMAN He . . died a martyr's death, through the practice of the Lady Ælfthryth. **4** G. S. HAIGHT Though she knew German thoroughly, Marian had had little practice in speaking it. N. HINTON He found that his own guitar playing improved rapidly with the constant practice. *Guardian* He was allowed to use the Luger for target practice.

Phrases: ***choir practice***: see CHOIR *noun.* ***corrupt practice***: see CORRUPT *adjective.* ***general practice***: see GENERAL *adjective.* ***group practice***: see GROUP *noun.* **in practice** (*a*) in reality, as a fact, when actually applied; (*b*) skilled at something through recent exercise in it or performance of it. **make a practice of** do regularly, make a habit of. ***old Spanish practice***: see SPANISH *adjective.* **out of practice** no longer skilled at something through lack of recent exercise in it or performance of it. ***private practice***: see PRIVATE *adjective.* **put into practice** apply, use, actually carry out. ***restrictive practice***: see RESTRICTIVE *adjective* 3. ***sharp practice***: see SHARP *adjective.* ***transfer of practice***: see TRANSFER *noun* 2C.
Attrib. & comb.: In the senses 'for repeated exercise; so as to maintain or acquire proficiency', as ***practice game, practice-ground, practice-room, practice run,*** etc. Special combs., as **practice bar** = BARRE 2; **practice-curve** a curve or graph showing the relation of progress to practice.

practice *verb*, **practicer** *noun* see PRACTISE *verb*, PRACTISER.

practician /prakˈtɪʃ(ə)n/ *noun*. Now *rare*. L15.
[Old French †*practicien* (mod. *praticien*), from *practique* (mod. *pratique*): see PRACTIC *noun*, -IAN.]
A person who practises an art, profession, or occupation; a practitioner; a practical person.

practico- /ˈpraktɪkəʊ/ *combining form*. M20.
[from PRACTICAL *adjective* or PRAXIS: see -O-.]
Forming adjectives with the sense 'practically; practical and', as ***practico-empirical***, ***practico-social***.

practicum /ˈpraktɪkəm/ *noun*. *N. Amer.* E20.
[Late Latin, neut. of *practicus*: see PRACTIC *adjective*.]
A practical exercise; a course of practical training.

†**practisant** *noun*. *rare* (Shakes.). Only in L16.
[French †*pra(c)tisant* pres. pple of Old & mod. French †*pra(c)tiser* PRACTISE *verb*: see -ANT[1].]
A plotter, a conspirator.

practise *noun* see PRACTICE *noun*.

practise /ˈpraktɪs/ *verb*. Also ***practice**. LME.
[Old & mod. French †*pra(c)tiser* or medieval Latin *practizare* (Anglo-Latin *practizans* medical practitioner) alt. of *practicare*, from *practica* PRACTIC *noun*.]
1 *verb trans.* Perform, do, carry out. *obsolete* exc. as passing into sense 2. LME. ▸**b** *verb intrans.* Go on with an activity; act, operate. (Foll. by *upon*.) Now *rare*. M16.
2 *verb trans.* Carry out or perform habitually or constantly; make a practice of; carry out in action (as opp. to believing, professing, etc.). LME.
3 *verb trans. & intrans.* Work at, exercise, or pursue (a profession, occupation, etc., as law or medicine). Also, observe or pursue actively the teaching and duties of (a religion). LME. ▸†**b** *verb intrans.* Perform music. LME–L18.
†**4** *verb trans.* Put into practice, actually carry out (a law, command, etc.). LME–L18.
5 *verb trans. & intrans.* Perform (an action) repeatedly or continuously in order to acquire or maintain proficiency; exercise oneself in (a skill, art, etc.) for this purpose; (foll. by *on* a person) do this before another person as critic, audience, etc. LME. ▸**b** Exercise (someone) *in* an activity in order to make him or her proficient; train, drill. L16.
†**6** *verb trans.* Put to practical use; make use of, employ. LME–M18. ▸**b** Frequent, haunt. M17–E18.
†**7** *verb trans.* Bring about, effect, accomplish. LME–M18. ▸**b** Attempt (a thing); try (*to do*). LME–L17. ▸**c** Devise means to bring about, plan; plot (an evil or unlawful act). M16–E18.
8 *verb intrans.* Scheme, plot, esp. for an evil purpose. (Foll. by *with* or *against* a person, *to do* a thing.) *arch.* M16.
9 *verb intrans.* Have dealings; negotiate or deal *with* a person, esp. in order to influence or win over. Now *rare*. M16. ▸†**b** *verb trans.* Persuade or influence (a person etc.) into some course of action, esp. an evil one; win over, corrupt. L16–E18.
10 *verb intrans.* Foll. by *on*, *upon*: perform a trick on, delude; persuade, esp. by artifice, to do or believe something; impose on. L16.
†**11** *verb trans.* Try out, use experimentally. M17–E19.
†**12** *verb trans.* Construct. *rare*. M18–E19.

> 📖 **2** H. ELLIS 75 per cent of the inmates of the Parisian venereal hospitals have practised homosexuality. L. MUMFORD Instead of practicing poverty, chastity, and obedience. W. PLOMER Not everybody practised what he preaches. **3** T. HARDY He had practised gardening in his own plot for . . many years. G. STEIN He was a doctor who had just begun to practise. T. BENN There are unemployed teachers and nurses who cannot practise their professions. D. MADDEN Robert doesn't practise his religion any more. **5** V. BRITTAIN We were practising tennis strokes against a brick wall. N. SEDAKA I spent so much time practising, Mom had to bring my meals to the piano. *Clothes Show Magazine* We went north to practise our . . floral wizardry on a few of those bright young Mancunians. **10** H. JAMES I had not been practised upon by the servants, nor made the object of any 'game'.

▪ **practised** *ppl adjective* that has had practice; experienced, skilled, proficient: M16. **practising** *ppl adjective* that practises; *spec.* (of a person) actively involved in or pursuing a profession, occupation, or religion: E17.

practiser /ˈpraktɪsə/ *noun*. Also ***-cer**. LME.
[Prob. from Anglo-Norman = Old French *practiser* PRACTISE *verb*: see -ER[2].]
1 A person who practises a profession or occupation; a practitioner. LME. ▸**b** A person who carries out or makes a practice of an activity, way of life, etc. M16.
†**2** A schemer, a conspirator. M16–M17.

practitional /prakˈtɪʃ(ə)n(ə)l/ *adjective*. *rare*. E17.
[formed as next + -AL[1].]
†**1** Given to scheming or plotting. Only in E17.
2 Relating to practice, practical. E19.

practitioner /prakˈtɪʃ(ə)nə/ *noun*. M16.
[Extension with -ER[1] of obsolete var. of PRACTICIAN.]
1 A person involved in the practice of an art, profession, or occupation, esp. medicine or law; a practical or professional worker. M16.
2 A person who does anything habitually; a person who carries out a practice or action. M16.
†**3** A person who uses artifice or trickery; a schemer, a conspirator. M16–E17.
†**4** A person who repeatedly performs an activity in order to acquire or maintain proficiency in it; a learner, a probationer. L16–E19.

> 📖 **1** J. P. STERN Nietzsche was not much of a practitioner of 'the will to power'; he only described it. R. CHRISTIANSEN He . . trained for the Law, of which he was always a diligent and methodical practitioner. ***general practitioner***: see GENERAL *adjective*. ***medical practitioner***: see MEDICAL *adjective*.

prad /prad/ *noun*. *slang* (now chiefly *Austral.*). L18.
[from (with metathesis) Dutch *paard* from late Latin *paraveredus*: see PALFREY. Cf. PROD *noun*[3].]
A horse.

pradakshina /prəˈdʌkʃɪnə/ *noun*. E19.
[Sanskrit *pradakṣiṇa*, from *pra* in front + *dakṣiṇa* right.]
HINDUISM & BUDDHISM. Circumambulation of an object in a clockwise direction as a form of worship.

Prader–Willi syndrome /prɑːdəˈvɪli ˌsɪndrəʊm/ *noun phr.* M20.
[Andrea *Prader* (b. 1919) and Heinrich *Willi* (1900–71), Swiss paediatricians.]
MEDICINE. A congenital disorder characterized by sexual infantilism, mental handicap, obsessive eating, and obesity.

prae- *prefix* see PRE-.

praecipe /ˈpriːsɪpiː/ *noun*. LME.
[Latin, imper. of *praecipere*: see PRECEPT *noun*.]
LAW. **1** *Hist.* A writ demanding action, or an explanation of non-action. Also ***praecipe quod reddat*** [lit. 'enjoin (him) that he render']. LME.
2 A note containing particulars of a writ or other legal document to be issued or prepared. M19.

praecocial *adjective* see PRECOCIAL.

praecognitum /priːˈkɒɡnɪtəm/ *noun*. Pl. ***-ta*** /-tə/. E17.
[Latin, neut. pa. pple of *praecognoscere* know beforehand, from *prae* PRE- + *cognoscere* know.]
A thing known beforehand; *esp.* a thing needed or assumed to be known in order to infer or ascertain something else. Usu. in *pl.*

praecordia /priːˈkɔːdɪə/ *noun*. Also ***pre-**. L17.
[Latin pl. = diaphragm, entrails, from *prae* PRE- + *cord-*, *cor* heart.]
ANATOMY. = PRECORDIUM.

†**praecordial** *adjective* var. of PRECORDIAL *adjective*.

Praedesque /preɪˈdɛsk/ *adjective*. *rare*. M19.
[from W. M. *Praed* (see below) + -ESQUE.]
In the manner or style of the English poet and essayist Winthrop Mackworth Praed (1802–39), writer of society verse.

praedial *adjective & noun* var. of PREDIAL.

praefect *noun* see PREFECT.

praefervid /priːˈfəːvɪd/ *adjective*. L17.
[Latin *praefervidus*, formed as PRE- + FERVID. Cf. PERFERVID.]
Very fervid.

praelector *noun* var. of PRELECTOR.

praeludium *noun* var. of PRELUDIUM.

praemunientes /ˌpriːmjuːnɪˈɛntiːz/ *noun*. E18.
[medieval Latin alt. of Latin *praemonentes* pl. pres. pple of *praemonere*: see PREMONITION.]
LAW (now *Hist.*). A clause (opening with the word *praemunientes*, 'warning') in the writ of Edward I by which bishops and abbots summoned to Parliament were required to summon representatives of the lesser clergy to attend with them (also ***praemunientes clause***); the writ itself (also ***praemunientes writ***).

praemunire /*as noun* priːmjuːˈnʌɪri; *as verb* -ˈnʌɪə, -ˈnɪə/ *noun & verb*. LME.
[Latin = fortify or protect in front, (in medieval Latin, by assoc. with *praemonere*: see PREMONITION) forewarn, admonish: see PREMUNITION. So called from the words *praemunire facias* ('that you warn') occurring in the writ.]
Hist. ▸**A** *noun*. **1** LAW (now *Hist.*). A writ charging a sheriff to summon a person accused of asserting or maintaining papal jurisdiction in England (orig., one accused of prosecuting abroad a suit cognizable by English law), so denying the ecclesiastical supremacy of the monarch. Also, the statute of Richard II on which this writ was based, later applied to various actions seen as questioning or diminishing the royal jurisdiction. LME.
2 *transf.* †**a** An offence against the statute of praemunire; any offence incurring the same penalties. M16–L17. ▸**b** The penalties, usu. forfeiture of goods or property, incurred by such an offence. *obsolete* exc. *Hist.* L16.
†**3** A situation or condition resembling that of someone who has incurred a praemunire; *joc.* a difficulty, a scrape, a predicament. L16–E19.
▸**B** *verb trans.* Issue a writ of praemunire against; convict of offending against the statute of praemunire. Now *rare*. L17.

Praenestine /prʌɪˈnɛstiːn, priː-/ *adjective & noun*. L19.
[Latin *Praenestinus*, from *Praeneste*: see below, -INE[1].]
▸**A** *adjective*. Of or pertaining to Praeneste, an ancient city in Latium (the modern Palestrina, near Rome) from which come the earliest known examples of Latin. L19.
▸**B** *noun*. A native or inhabitant of Praeneste. E20.

praenomen /priːˈnəʊmɛn/ *noun*. E17.
[Latin = forename, from *prae* PRE- + *nomen* name.]
An ancient Roman's first or personal name preceding the nomen and cognomen (as *Marcus* Tullius Cicero); *gen.* a first name, a forename.

praepositi *noun* pl. of PRAEPOSITUS.

praepositor *noun* var. of PREPOSITOR *noun*[1].

praepositus /priːˈpɒzɪtəs/ *noun*. Pl. **-ti** /-tʌɪ/. E17.
[Latin = head, chief, (in medieval Latin) provost, use as noun of pa. pple of *praeponere* place or set over, from *prae* PRE- + *ponere* to place. Cf. PREVOST, PROVOST *noun*.]
(A title of) the head of various clerical or civil institutions.

praepostor /prɪˈpɒstə/ *noun*. Also **pre-**. M18.
[Syncopated from *praepositor* PREPOSITOR *noun*[1].]
A prefect or monitor at various English public schools. Cf. PREPOSITOR *noun*[1].

praeputium /priːˈpjuːʃɪəm/ *noun*. Now *rare* or *obsolete*. LME.
[Latin.]
ANATOMY. = PREPUCE 1.

Praesepe /prɪˈsiːpi/ *noun*. M17.
[Latin *praesaepe* enclosure, manger, hive, from *prae* PRE- + *saepire* to fence.]
ASTRONOMY. = BEEHIVE 2.

praeses /ˈpriːsiːz/ *noun*. Chiefly *Scot.* Also **preses**. Pl. **-sides** /-sɪdiːz/. M17.
[Latin = president, chief, guardian, from *praesidere* PRESIDE.]
1 The president or chairman of a meeting. M17.
2 A university moderator. M19.

Praesidium *noun* var. of PRESIDIUM.

praeter- *prefix*, **praetergress** *verb*, **praeterhuman** *adjective*, etc. vars. of PRETER- etc.

praetexta /priːˈtɛkstə/ *noun & adjective*. E17.
[Latin, use as noun (sc. *toga*) of fem. pa. pple of *praetextere*: see PRETEXT *noun*.]
ROMAN HISTORY. ▸**A** *noun*. A toga with a purple border, worn by curule magistrates and boys up to the age of manhood. E17.
▸**B** *adjective*. ***toga praetexta*** = sense A. above. E20.

praetor /ˈpriːtə, -tɔː/ *noun*. Also **pre-**. LME.
[French *prêteur* or Latin *praetor*, perh. from *prae* PRE- + *it-* pa. ppl stem of *ire* go: see -OR.]
1 ROMAN HISTORY. Any of several annually elected magistrates (of which there were usually two) who were subordinate to the consuls. Also, a consul as leader of the army, at a time before the development of this magistracy. LME.
2 *transf.* A person holding high civic office, as a mayor or chief magistrate. Now *rare*. L15.
1 ***peregrine praetor***: see PEREGRINE *adjective*.
▪ **praetorship** *noun* the position or office of praetor; the term of this office: M16.

praetoria *noun* pl. of PRAETORIUM.

praetorial /priːˈtɔːrɪəl/ *adjective*. Also **pre-**. L16.
[from Latin *praetorius*, from *praetor*: see PRAETOR, -AL[1].]
Of or pertaining to a Roman praetor; praetorian.

praetorian /priːˈtɔːrɪən/ *adjective & noun*. Also **pre-**. LME.
[Latin *praetorianus*, from *praetor*: see PRAETOR, -IAN.]
ROMAN HISTORY. ▸**A** *adjective*. **1** Designating or belonging to (a soldier of) the bodyguard of a Roman military commander or the Roman Emperor. Freq. in ***praetorian guard***. LME.
2 Of or pertaining to a Roman praetor or his position. L16. ▸**b** *transf.* Of or pertaining to a judge, court, etc., analogous to that of the praetor of ancient Rome. Now *rare* or *obsolete*. E17.

> 📖 **2** E. POSTE Another guardian . . called a praetorian guardian, because he was appointed by the praetor of the city.

▸**B** *noun*. **1** A soldier of the praetorian guard. E17. ▸**b** *fig.* A member of a group or class that seeks to defend an established system. M17.
2 A person of praetorian rank. M18.

> 📖 **1** A. DUGGAN Only legionaries of good character were chosen for the Praetorians.

▪ **praetorianism** *noun* a system like that of the Roman praetorian organization; military despotism: L19.

praetorium /priːˈtɔːrɪəm/ *noun*. Also **pre-**. Pl. **-ia** /-ɪə/. E17.
[Latin, use as noun of *praetorius* adjective, belonging to a praetor.]
ROMAN HISTORY. **1** The tent of the commanding general in a Roman camp; the space where this was placed. E17.

2 The court or palace of the governor of a Roman province; *transf.* an official building, *esp.* the court or palace of an ancient king. **E17.**
3 The quarters of the praetorian guard in Rome. **L17.**

pragmatic /prag'matɪk/ *noun & adjective.* **L16.**
[Late Latin *pragmaticus* (in *pragmatica sanctio* pragmatic sanction, earlier 'skilled in affairs') from Greek *pragmatikos*, from *pragmat-*, *pragma* act, deed, affair, from *prak-* stem of *prattein* do.]
▶ **A** *noun.* **1** = ***pragmatic sanction*** below. **L16.**
†**2** A person skilled in business, *esp.* one appointed to represent someone else in business; an agent. **L16–E17.**
3 An officious or meddlesome person; a conceited person. **M17.**
4 In *pl.* (treated as *sing.*). LINGUISTICS. The branch of linguistics that deals with the use of sentences in actual situations. **M20.**
5 In *pl.* Practical considerations as opp. to theoretical or idealistic ones. **L20.**

> 📖 **5** *Broadcasting* The pragmatics of managing broadcasters: getting the most from your employees.

▶ **B** *adjective.* **1** Busy, active; *esp.* officiously busy, meddlesome. Now *rare.* **E17.**
2 Conceited, self-important, opinionated; dictatorial, dogmatic. **E17.**
3 Pertaining to the affairs of a State or community. Chiefly in ***pragmatic sanction*** below. **M17.**
4 Treating the facts of history systematically and with reference to their practical causes and results. Cf. PRAGMATISM 2. *rare.* **M19.**
5 Matter-of-fact; dealing with matters with regard to their practical requirements or consequences. **M19.**
6 Pertaining to philosophical or political pragmatism. **E20.**
7 LINGUISTICS. Of or pertaining to pragmatics. **M20.**

> 📖 **3 pragmatic sanction** (now chiefly *Hist.*) a decree or ordinance issued by a head of State that refers to the affairs of that State; an imperial or royal ordinance with the force of law. **5** D. MACDONALD Its emphasis on the facts suits our pragmatic temper. **6** S. QUINN America's pragmatic bias, placing greater emphasis on what is observed and less on theory to explain it.

pragmatica /prag'matɪkə/ *noun.* **M17.**
[Spanish, from late Latin *pragmatica sanctio*: see prec.]
Hist. A pragmatic sanction, *esp.* a Spanish one.

pragmatical /prag'matɪk(ə)l/ *adjective.* **M16.**
[formed as PRAGMATIC + -AL¹.]
1 = PRAGMATIC *adjective* 3. Now *rare.* **M16.**
2 = PRAGMATIC *adjective* 5. **L16.**
3 †**a** Involved in action; active; energetic. Cf. PRAGMATIC *adjective* 1. **E–M17.** ▸**b** Experienced, expert; skilled, shrewd. Now *rare.* **M17.**
4 a Officiously busy, meddlesome. Cf. PRAGMATIC *adjective* 1. Now *rare.* **E17.** ▸**b** = PRAGMATIC *adjective* 2. **E18.**
5 = PRAGMATIC *adjective* 6. **E20.**
6 LINGUISTICS. = PRAGMATIC *adjective* 7. **M20.**

> 📖 **2** E. CRANKSHAW The sort of pragmatical and level-headed guide whom the generations . . to come so sorely lacked.

■ **pragmati'cality** *noun* **M19.** **pragmaticalness** *noun* = PRAGMATICISM 1 **M17.**

pragmatically /prag'matɪk(ə)li/ *adverb.* **E17.**
[from PRAGMATIC *adjective* or PRAGMATICAL: see -ICALLY.]
In a pragmatic manner; from the point of view of pragmatism or pragmatics.

pragmaticism /prag'matɪsɪz(ə)m/ *noun.* **M19.**
[from PRAGMATIC + -ISM.]
1 The quality of being pragmatic. **M19.**
2 PHILOSOPHY. The doctrine that concepts are to be understood in terms of their practical implications. **E20.**

pragmatise *verb* var. of PRAGMATIZE.

pragmatism /'pragmətɪz(ə)m/ *noun.* **M19.**
[from Greek *pragmat-*, *pragma* deed, act + -ISM.]
1 Officiousness; pedantry; an instance of this. **M19.**
2 A method of treating history in which events are considered with reference to their causes and results. Now *rare.* **M19.**
3 PHILOSOPHY. = PRAGMATICISM 2. Also, the view that the truth of any assertion is to be evaluated from its practical consequences and its bearing on human interests. **L19.**
4 The theory that advocates dealing with social and political problems by practical methods adapted to the circumstances rather than by methods that conform to an ideology; *gen.* attention to the feasibility and practical consequences of actions, rather than any principles that may underlie them. **M20.**

pragmatist /'pragmətɪst/ *noun & adjective.* **M17.**
[formed as prec. + -IST.]
▶ **A** *noun.* **1** A meddlesome person, a busybody. **M17.**
2 An adherent or practitioner of pragmatism; a person concerned with practical rather than theoretical or ideological matters. **L19.**

> 📖 **2** *Mind* The Pragmatist holds that what works is true.

▶ **B** *adjective.* Pertaining to pragmatism or pragmatists. **E20.**

> 📖 A. J. AYER Pragmatist and idealist theories of truth.

■ **pragma'tistic** *adjective* pertaining to or characteristic of pragmatism **E20.** **pragma'tistically** *adverb* **E20.**

pragmatize /'pragmətʌɪz/ *verb.* Also **-ise.** **M19.**
[formed as prec. + -IZE.]
1 *verb trans.* Represent as real or actual (what is imaginary or subjective). **M19.**
2 *verb intrans.* Express or behave in a pragmatic way. **E20.**
■ **pragmati'zation** *noun* **M20.** **pragmatizer** *noun* **M19.**

Prägnanz /prɛg'nants/ *noun.* **E20.**
[German = conciseness, definiteness.]
In gestalt psychology, the tendency of every perceptual or mental form to be integrated into a whole and become coherent and simple. Cf. PREGNANCE 2.

Prague /prɑːg/ *noun.* **M20.**
[The capital of the Czech Republic.]
Used *attrib.* to designate things originating from or associated with Prague.
Prague circle: see ***Prague linguistic circle*** below. **Prague ham** a type of salted smoked ham. **Prague linguistic circle**, **Prague circle** a group of linguists founded in 1926, who developed a linguistic theory relating primarily to phonology. **Prague school** the views and methods of the Prague linguistic circle. **Prague Spring** a brief period of liberalization in Czechoslovakia, ending in August 1968, during which a programme of political, economic, and cultural reform was initiated.
■ **Praguean** *adjective & noun* (**a**) *adjective* of or pertaining to the Prague school; (**b**) *noun* an adherent or advocate of the Prague school: **L20.** **Praguian** *adjective* = PRAGUEAN *adjective* **M20.**

prahu *noun* var. of PROA.

praia /prʌɪə/ *noun.* Also **praya.** **M19.**
[Portuguese.]
In Portugal and Portuguese-speaking countries: a seashore; a river-bank; a waterfront.

praire /prɛːr/ *noun.* Pl. pronounced same. **E20.**
[French.]
The European clam or the N. American hard-shell clam esp. as an item of food.

Prairial /'prɛːrɪəl, *foreign* prɛrjal/ *noun.* **E19.**
[French, from *prairie* meadow.]
Hist. The ninth month of the French Republican calendar (introduced 1793), extending from 20 May to 18 June.

prairie /'prɛːri/ *noun.* **L18.**
[French from Old French *praerie* from Proto-Romance, from Latin *pratum* meadow: see -RY.]
1 An extensive tract of treeless grassland, esp. in N. America; a savannah, a steppe. Also (*US dial.*), a marsh, a swampy pond or lake. **L18.**
2 (**P-**.) A steam locomotive with a 2-6-2 wheel arrangement. **E20.**

> 📖 G. MILLAR We found ourselves on a wide and noble prairie rolling north to . . the river Doubs. DAY LEWIS I race down the meadow, which seems as big as a prairie.

Attrib. & comb.: In the sense 'pertaining to or characterized by prairies', as ***prairie country***, ***prairie farm***, ***prairie fire***, ***prairie land***, ***prairie region***, etc. Special combs., as **prairie bottom** a low-lying expanse of prairie land; **prairie-breaker** a plough for cutting and overturning a wide shallow furrow; **prairie-breaking** the action of using a prairie-breaker; **prairie-buster** = *prairie-breaker* above; **prairie chicken** either of two grouse native to the N. American plains, *Tympanuchus cupido* (more fully ***greater prairie chicken***) and *T. pallidicinctus* (more fully ***lesser prairie chicken***); **prairie clover** any of various N. American leguminous plants of the genus *Dalea*, with pinnate leaves and dense heads of pink or white flowers; **prairie coal** *N. Amer.* dried cattle or horse dung used as fuel; cf. ***buffalo chips*** s.v. BUFFALO *noun*; **prairie cock** = *prairie chicken* above; **prairie crocus** the pasque-flower of N. America, *Pulsatilla nuttalliana*; **prairie dock** a rosinweed, *Silphium terebinthinaceum*, with very large leaves shaped like those of burdock; **prairie dog** any rodent of the N. American genus *Cynomys*, the members of which resemble marmots, live gregariously in burrows in grassland, and have a cry like a dog's bark; **prairie falcon** a falcon, *Falco mexicanus*, with pale brown upperparts, native to western N. American plains and Mexico; **prairie fox** *N. Amer.* a kit-fox, *Vulpes velox*; **prairie hawk** *N. Amer.* the American kestrel, *Falco sparverius*; **prairie hen** = *prairie chicken* above; **prairie marmot** = ***prairie dog*** above; **prairie oyster** (**a**) a seasoned raw egg, often served in spirits and swallowed in one as a cure for a hangover; (**b**) in *pl.*, calves' testicles cooked and eaten as a delicacy; **Prairie Province** (**a**) *Hist.* the Canadian province of Manitoba; (**b**) in *pl.*, the Canadian provinces of Manitoba, Saskatchewan, and Alberta; **prairie rattler**, **prairie rattlesnake** any of various rattlesnakes of the N. American prairies, esp. *Crotalus viridis*; **prairie rose** the American climbing rose, *Rosa setigera*; ***prairie schooner***: see SCHOONER *noun*¹ 2; **prairie smoke** = *prairie crocus* above; **prairie soil** soil of the kind characteristic of the N. American prairies; *spec.* (SOIL SCIENCE) a soil having a deep dark-coloured surface horizon with a high organic content, occurring under long grass in subhumid temperate regions; **Prairie State** *US* the State of Illinois; in *pl.*, the States of Illinois, Wisconsin, Iowa, Minnesota, and others to the south; **prairie turnip** = *bread-root* s.v. BREAD *noun*¹; **prairie wagon** = *prairie schooner* above; **prairie warbler** a yellow-breasted olive-backed warbler, *Dendroica discolor*, of open country in eastern N. America; **prairie-wolf** *N. Amer.* = COYOTE; **prairie wool** *Canad.* the natural grassy plant cover of prairie land.
■ **prairied** *adjective* containing or characterized by prairies **M19.**

praise /preɪz/ *noun.* **ME.**
[from next. Superseding LOSE *noun*¹, PRICE *noun*.]
1 a The action or an act of praising; (an) expression in speech of approval, admiration, or honour; eulogy. **ME.** ▸**b** The fact or condition of being praised. Now *rare.* **M16.** ▸**c** = ***praise poem*** below. **M19.**
2 The expression of admiration and the ascription of glory as an act of worship, esp. in song. **ME.**
3 a Praiseworthiness, merit, virtue. *arch.* **E16.** ▸**b** Formerly, an object of praise. Now only (*Scot. colloq.*) God as an object of praise. **M16.**

> 📖 **1a** P. F. BOLLER Johnson loved praise and was upset by even the gentlest criticism. W. M. CLARKE Carlyle . . gave high praise both to the play and to Dickens's performance. *Independent* Mr Sarney may be basking in the bland praises of Mr Santos. **2** J. H. NEWMAN Praise to the holiest in the height, And in the depth be praise.

Phrases: **heap praises on** praise enthusiastically. **praise be** *arch.* thank goodness. ***prick and praise***: see PRICK *noun*. ***sacrifice of praise (and thanksgiving)***: see SACRIFICE *noun*. **sing the praises of** praise enthusiastically.
Comb.: **praise-house** *US* a small meeting-house for religious services; **praise name** in Africa, a ceremonial name or title, a name given to the subject of a praise poem; **praise poem**, **praise song** a laudatory poem or song, *esp.* one belonging to the oral tradition of certain African peoples; **praise poet**, **praise-reciter**, **praise-singer** a composer, reciter, or singer of praise poems or praise songs; ***praise song***: see ***praise poem*** above.
■ **praiseless** *adjective* without praise; not deserving praise: **M16.**

praise /preɪz/ *verb.* **ME.**
[Old French *preisier* price, value, prize, praise, from late Latin *pretiare*, from Latin *pretium* price: cf. PRICE *verb*, PRIZE *verb*¹.]
▶ **I 1** *verb trans.* Set a price on; value, appraise. Now *obsolete* or *dial.* **ME.**
†**2** *verb trans.* Attach value to; esteem, prize. **ME–M16.**
▶ **II 3 a** *verb trans.* Express or commend the excellence or merits of; express warm approval or admiration of; laud, extol. **ME.** ▸**b** *verb intrans.* Give praise, express warm approval. **LME.**
4 *verb trans.* Extol the glorious attributes of (God or a deity), esp. in song; glorify, magnify. **LME.**

> 📖 **3a** M. AMIS She had been good at art as a schoolgirl, often praised by her art master. *New Yorker* His administration and the city in general were praised to the skies for their handling of the event. **be to praise** (now *rare* or *obsolete*) deserve praise; be commended or extolled. **4** T. KEN Praise God from whom all blessings flow. *Times* Praise the Lord for a television interviewer who does not ram his personality down our throats.

■ **praisable** *adjective* (now *rare*) deserving of praise; praiseworthy: **LME.** **praisably** *adverb* (*rare*) **M16.** **praiser** *noun* a person who praises; *spec.* = ***praise poet*** s.v. PRAISE *noun*: **LME.** **praisingly** *adverb* in a praising or laudatory manner; with praise: **M19.**

praiseach /prə'ʃax/ *noun. Anglo-Irish.* Also **praisseagh** & other vars. **L17.**
[Irish from Latin *brassica* cabbage.]
1 An oatmeal porridge; *fig.* a mess, a confusion. **L17.**
2 Any wild cruciferous plant resembling the cabbage; *spec.* charlock, *Sinapis arvensis.* **E18.**

praiseful /'preɪzfʊl, -f(ə)l/ *adjective.* **LME.**
[from PRAISE *noun* or *verb* + -FUL.]
1 Worthy of praise or honour; praiseworthy, laudable. *rare.* **LME.**
2 Full of praise; eulogistic, laudatory. **E17.**
■ **praisefully** *adverb* **M18.** **praisefulness** *noun* **M19.**

praiseworthy /'preɪzwəːði/ *adjective.* **LME.**
[from PRAISE *noun* + -WORTHY.]
Worthy of or deserving praise; laudable, commendable.
■ **praiseworthily** *adverb* **L16.** **praiseworthiness** *noun* **L16.**

praisseagh *noun* var. of PRAISEACH.

prajna /'praʒna/ *noun.* **E19.**
[Sanskrit *prajñā*.]
BUDDHISM. Direct insight into the truth taught by the Buddha, as a faculty required to attain enlightenment.
■ ***prajnaparamita*** /ˌpraʒnaparamɪ'tɑː/ *noun* [Sanskrit *pāramitā* perfection] (any of) a group of ancient Mahayana Buddhist texts **E19.**

Prakrit /'prɑːkrɪt/ *noun & adjective.* **M18.**
[Sanskrit *prākṛta* natural, unrefined, vernacular: cf. SANSKRIT.]
▶ **A** *noun.* (Any of) the group of (esp. ancient) vernacular Indic languages and dialects of northern and central India which existed alongside or developed from Sanskrit. **M18.**
▶ **B** *attrib.* or as *adjective.* Of or pertaining to a Prakrit or Prakrits. **L18.**

prakriti /ˈprʌkrɪti, ˈprak-/ *noun*. L18.
[Sanskrit *prakṛti* nature.]
HINDUISM. Matter as opp. to spirit; primordial matter; nature; *spec.* in Sankhya philosophy, the passive principle (personified as female) which with the active (male) principle produces the universe. Cf. PURUSHA.

pralaya /ˈprʌləjə/ *noun*. E20.
[Sanskrit.]
INDIAN MYTHOLOGY. Destruction, esp. of the whole world.

pralidoxime /pralɪˈdɒksiːm/ *noun*. M20.
[from ALDOXIME with insertion of *p*, *r*, and *i* from PYRIDINE.]
PHARMACOLOGY. A quaternary ammonium derivative of pyridine which is used to treat poisoning by cholinesterase inhibitors such as malathion.

praline /ˈprɑːliːn/ *noun*. E18.
[French, from Marshal de Plessis-*Praslin* (1598–1675), French soldier, whose cook invented praline.]
A confection made by heating together a mixture of almonds or nuts and sugar until it turns to a brown liquid and letting it cool, used esp. as a filling for chocolates.

pralltriller /ˈpraltrɪlər/ *noun*. Pl. same, **-s**. M19.
[German, from *prallen* to bounce + *Triller* trill.]
MUSIC. An ornament consisting of rapid alternation of the note written with the one immediately above it. Cf. MORDENT.

pram /prɑːm, pram/ *noun*[1]. Also **praam**. LME.
[Middle Dutch *prame*, *praem* (Dutch *praam*), Middle Low German *prâme* (whence also German *Prahm*) = Old Frisian *prām*, perh. from Czech *prám*.]
1 A flat-bottomed cargo boat or lighter as used in the Baltic and the Netherlands. LME.
2 A large flat-bottomed gunboat used as a floating battery. E18.
3 A ship's dinghy. M19.
4 A small lightweight sailing boat. *US*. M20.

pram /pram/ *noun*[2]. L19.
[Abbreviation of PERAMBULATOR.]
1 A four-wheeled horizontal carriage for a baby, pushed by a person on foot; a baby carriage. L19.
2 A milkman's hand-cart for delivering milk. Now *rare* or *obsolete*. L19.

> 📖 **1** H. E. BATES She pushed an old hoodless pram, with a baby in it, up the hillside.

Comb.: **pram-park** an area where prams may be left; **pram-pusher** a person who pushes a pram; *spec.* a young mother.

Pramnian /ˈpramnɪən/ *adjective*. E17.
[from Latin *Pramnium* Greek *Pramnios* + -AN.]
CLASSICAL HISTORY. ***Pramnian wine***, a wine from the neighbourhood of Smyrna in Asia Minor.

prana /ˈprɑːnə/ *noun*. M19.
[Sanskrit *prāṇa*.]
HINDUISM. A life-giving force, the breath of life; the breath, breathing.

> 📖 C. DE SILVA My own *prana* seemed to have ebbed away from my body.

pranayama /prɑːnɑːˈjɑːmɑ, prɑːnəˈjɑːmə/ *noun*. M20.
[Sanskrit, from prec. + *āyāma* restraint, from *yam* sustain, hold up.]
Exercises in the regulation of the breath in yoga; breath control.

> 📖 J. HEWITT For Pranayama and meditation the yogis use certain seated postures.

prance /prɑːns/ *verb & noun*. LME.
[Origin unkn.]
▶**A** *verb*. **1** *verb intrans*. Of a horse: rise by springing from the hind legs, either of its own accord or at the rider's will; move (*about*) by a succession of such springs. LME. ▸**b** *verb trans*. Cause (a horse) to prance. M16.
2 *verb intrans*. Of a person: ride with the horse prancing; ride gaily or proudly. LME.
3 *verb intrans*. **a** Walk or behave in a proud or arrogant manner suggestive of a prancing horse; swagger (*about*, *around*). LME. ▸**b** Dance (*about*); gambol, caper. *colloq*. LME.

> 📖 **1** J. WOODFORDE The Postilon's Horse was rather restive and pranced about a little. **3a** T. O'BRIEN You prance around with this holier than thou outlook.

▶**B** *noun*. An act of prancing; a prancing movement or walk. M18.
■ **prancy** *adjective* resembling or suggestive of a prance M20.

prancer /ˈprɑːnsə/ *noun*. M16.
[from PRANCE *verb* + -ER[1].]
1 a A horse. *Criminals' slang*. M16. ▸**b** A lively or prancing horse; a steed. L16.
†**2** Orig., a mounted robber; a highwayman. Later, a horse thief. *slang*. L16–E18.
3 a A rider on a prancing horse; *slang* a cavalry officer. M19. ▸**b** A person who capers or dances. M19.

prandial /ˈprandɪəl/ *adjective*. *formal* or *joc*. E19.
[from Latin *prandium* late breakfast + -AL[1].]
Pertaining to a meal, esp. lunch or dinner.

> 📖 W. GADDIS He interrupted the silent prandial industry beside him to ask for something else.

■ **prandially** *adverb* in connection with a meal, esp. lunch or dinner M19.

Prandtl number /ˈprant(ə)l nʌmbə/ *noun phr*. M20.
[Ludwig *Prandtl* (1875–1953), German physicist.]
PHYSICS. A dimensionless parameter used in calculations of heat transfer between a moving fluid and a solid body, equal to $c_p v/k$, where c_p is the heat capacity of unit volume of the fluid, *v* its kinematic viscosity, and *k* its thermal conductivity.

prang /praŋ/ *verb & noun*. *slang* (orig. *RAF slang*). M20.
[Origin unkn.]
▶**A** *verb*. **1 a** *verb trans. & intrans*. Crash or damage (an aircraft), esp. in a crash-landing. M20. ▸**b** *verb trans*. Bomb (a target) successfully from the air. M20. ▸**c** *verb trans*. Involve (a vehicle) in an accident, crash. Also, collide with. M20.
2 *verb trans*. Hit, strike heavily (*against*); injure. M20.

> 📖 **1b** F. DONALDSON Some RAF pilots had attempted to 'prang' the Wodehouse villa at Le Touquet. **c** *Guardian* If your bike is . . pranged in an accident in Portugal, who's going to foot the bill? **2** *Slipstream* Don't prang yourselves against the table. *Beano* I . . pranged the baddie with a sucker arrow!

▶**B** *noun*. **1 a** An accident in which an aircraft is damaged; a crash-landing. M20. ▸**b** A bombing raid. M20.
2 A collision involving a road vehicle; a crash. M20.

> 📖 **1b** *fig.*: *Spectator* The Prime Minister was questioned about the RAF's wizard prang on the Government's defence policy. **2** *Truckin' Life* I was . . 15 km north of Moree and there was a head on prang right in front of me.

prank /praŋk/ *noun*. E16.
[Origin unkn.]
†**1** A trick of a malicious nature; a wicked deed. E16–M18.
†**2** A conjuring trick, performed formerly to deceive but in later times to amuse or surprise. M16–M19.
3 An act of a frolicsome or mischievous nature; a practical joke. L16.
4 A capricious or frolicsome action on the part of an animal. L17.

> 📖 **3** K. M. E. MURRAY Still a boy at heart in his sense of fun and enjoyment of family pranks.

■ **prankful** *adjective* full of pranks; mischievous, frolicsome: E19. **prankish** *adjective* of the nature of a prank; inclined to pranks, mischievous: E19. **prankishness** *noun* L19. **pranksome** *adjective* prankish E19. **pranky** *adjective* (*rare*) prankish M16.

prank /praŋk/ *verb*[1]. Pa. t. & pple **pranked**, (*arch*.) **prankt**. LME.
[Rel. to Middle Low German *prank* pomp, display, Dutch *pronk* show, finery, German *Prunk* pomp, ostentation: cf. Dutch *pronken*, German *prunken* show off, display.]
1 *verb intrans. & trans*. (with *it*). Show off; act ostentatiously; swagger. LME.
2 *verb trans*. **a** Dress or adorn in a bright or showy manner; decorate colourfully; brighten. Also foll. by *out*. M16. ▸**b** *refl*. Deck oneself *out*, dress oneself *up*. L16.

> 📖 **2a** E. BLUNDEN Amid great trees . . pranked with blue and russet wings. *fig.*: *Times* Laurie Lee's book . . is pranked out with countless small pleasures of light and colour.

†**prank** *verb*[2] *trans*. LME–L17.
[Origin unkn.]
Fold, plait, arrange in pleats; *fig*. put in order.

prank /praŋk/ *verb*[3] *intrans*. M16.
[App. from PRANK *noun*.]
Play pranks or tricks, formerly from wickedness, now usu. in fun; play (*around*).

> 📖 *Virginia Quarterly Review* He may . . prank with the young 'uns while the crops go to naught. H. HORNSBY He laughed, just to let everybody know he was pranking.

pranker /ˈpraŋkə/ *noun*. L16.
[from PRANK *verb*[1] + -ER[1].]
†**1** *Criminals' slang*. = PRANCER 1a. Only in L16.
2 = PRANCER 3b. *rare*. E17.

prankle /ˈpraŋk(ə)l/ *verb intrans*. Now *dial*. E18.
[Frequentative of PRANK *verb*[1]: see -LE[3].]
Prance lightly, move in a capering way.

prankster /ˈpraŋkstə/ *noun* orig. *US*. E20.
[from PRANK *noun* + -STER.]
A person who plays pranks; a hoaxer, a practical joker.

> 📖 J. BARNES Some pranksters at an end-of-term dance released into the hall a piglet.

■ **pranksterism** *noun* L20.

prankt *verb pa. t. & pple*: see PRANK *verb*[1].

p'raps /praps/ *adverb*. M19.
[Repr. colloq. pronunc.]
Perhaps.

prasad /prəˈsɑːd/ *noun*. Also **prasada**. E19.
[Sanskrit *prasāda* clearness, kindness, grace.]
HINDUISM. **1** A propitiatory offering of food made to a god or an image, often afterwards shared among devotees. E19.
2 Divine grace or favour. L19.

prase /preɪz/ *noun*. L18.
[French, from Latin *prasius*, from Greek *prasios* adjective leek-green, from *prason* leek.]
MINERALOGY. A leek-green variety of translucent quartz. Cf. earlier PRASIUS.

praseodymium /preɪzɪəˈdɪmɪəm/ *noun*. L19.
[from German *Praseodym*, from Greek *prasios* leek-green (the typical colour of praseodymium salts) + German *Didym* DIDYMIUM: see prec., -IUM.]
A metallic chemical element of the lanthanide series, atomic no. 59, which occurs in association with neodymium. (Symbol Pr.)

prasine /ˈpreɪzɪn/ *adjective*. *rare*. LME.
[Latin *prasinus* from Greek *prasinos*, from *prasos* leek.]
Leek-green.

†**prasius** *noun*. LME–M18.
[Latin: see PRASE.]
= PRASE.

praskeen /prəˈskiːn/ *noun*. *Anglo-Irish*. M19.
[Irish *práiscín*.]
An apron, esp. a large coarse one.

prat /prat/ *noun*[1]. Now only *Scot*.
[Late Old English *prætt*: cf. Middle Dutch *parte*, Dutch *part* crafty trick, prank; also Middle Dutch, Flemish *perte*, Dutch, East Frisian, Low German *pret*, Old Norse *prettr*, Norwegian *pretta* roguish trick. Ult. origin unkn. Cf. PRETTY *adjective*.]
A piece of trickery or fraudulence; a prank, a frolic.

prat /prat/ *noun*[2]. Also **-tt**. M16.
[Origin unkn.]
1 a Formerly, a buttock (usu. in *pl*.). Now, the buttocks, the backside. *slang* (orig. *Criminals'*). M16. ▸**b** A hip-pocket. *US Criminals' slang*. E20.
2 An insignificant person; a fool, a blockhead. *slang*. M20.

> 📖 **1a** S. BELLOW He wore diplomatist's pants . . that accommodated his wide prat. **2** *Listener* He was a gormless prat of the first order. K. WATERHOUSE I've already told you once, you pink-faced pratt.

Comb.: **prat digger** *US slang* a pickpocket; **prat-digging** *US slang* pickpocketing; **pratfall** *noun & verb* (**a**) *noun* (THEATRICAL) a fall on the buttocks as performed on stage etc.; (**b**) *verb intrans*. fall on the buttocks (deliberately or accidentally); **prat-kick** *US slang* a hip-pocket.

prat /prat/ *verb intrans*. Infl. **-tt-**. L16.
[App. from PRAT *noun*[1].]
1 Practise tricks. *Scot. rare*. L16.
2 Act in a silly or annoying manner; lark about, fool around. Also foll. by *about*. Now *slang*. E18.

pratal /ˈpreɪt(ə)l/ *adjective*. *rare*. M19.
[from Latin *pratum* meadow + -AL[1].]
BOTANY. Growing in meadows.

pratchant /ˈpratʃ(ə)nt/ *adjective*. *obsolete* exc. *dial*. L16.
[Origin unkn.]
Conceited, forward; swaggering.

prate /preɪt/ *verb & noun*. LME.
[Middle & mod. Low German, Middle & mod. Dutch *praten*, prob. of imit. origin. Cf. PRATTLE *verb*.]
▶**A** *verb*. **1** *verb intrans*. Talk, chatter, esp. idly or for too long. Formerly also, speak insolently, boastfully, or officiously; tell tales, blab. LME.
2 *verb trans*. Say or tell in a prating or chattering manner; relate or repeat to little purpose. L15.

> 📖 **1** A. S. NEILL Those who prate about marriage as an emancipation for a woman. STEVIE SMITH Prate not to me of suicide. **2** N. GOULD Prating mere polite nothings to a young lady.

▶**B** *noun*. The action of prating; talk. Now *esp*. idle or irrelevant chatter; prattle. L16.
Comb.: **prate-apace** *arch*. a person given to prating; a chatterbox; †**prate-rost** *slang* = *prate-apace* above.
■ **pratement** *noun* (*rare*) prating, talking M17. **prater** *noun* a person who prates, *esp*. an idle talker, a chatterer L16.

pratie /ˈpreɪti/ *noun*. Chiefly *Anglo-Irish*. L18.
[Irish *prátaí* pl. of *práta*.]
A potato.

pratincole /ˈpratɪŋkəʊl/ *noun*. L18.
[mod. Latin *pratincola*, from Latin *pratum* meadow + -COLE.]
ORNITHOLOGY. Any of several birds of the Old World genus *Glareola* (family Glareolidae), closely related to the coursers, which resemble swallows in flight and live near rivers and marshes. Also, (more fully ***Australian pratincole***), a long-legged bird, *Stiltia isabella*, of

semidesert and open grassland in Australia and Indonesia, which provides a link between the other pratincoles and the coursers.

pratiquant /pratikɑ̃/ *adjective*. E20.
[French.]
Observant of religious duties or practices.

pratique /ˈpratiːk, *foreign* pratik/ *noun*. E17.
[Old & mod. French = practice, intercourse, corresp. to or from Italian *pratica* from medieval Latin *practica* use as noun (sc. *ars* art) of *practicus* PRACTIC *adjective*.]
Permission granted to a ship to use a port after quarantine or on showing a clean bill of health.

pratt *noun* var. of PRAT *noun*².

Pratt /prat/ *adjective*. E20.
[See below.]
Designating a coloured earthenware manufactured by members of the Pratt family of Staffordshire, England, in the late 18th and early 19th cents.

prattle /ˈprat(ə)l/ *verb & noun*. M16.
[Middle Low German *pratelen*, from *praten* PRATE *verb*: see -LE³. Cf. TATTLE.]
▶ **A** *verb*. **1** *verb intrans*. Chatter or talk at length in a childish or inconsequential manner. Also foll. by *on*. M16.
2 *verb trans*. Say in the course of prattling. M16. ▸**b** Bring or force *into* by prattling. *rare*. E17.

> **1** *Times* Those who prattle on about 'Victorian Values'. M. WESLEY She felt like an adult listening to prattling children and gave them only half her attention. *fig.*: B. TAYLOR A fountain prattles to the night. **2b** SHAKES. *All's Well* If you prattle me into these perils.

▶ **B** *noun*. The action of prattling; *esp.* inconsequential talk, childish chatter. M16.

> R. GRAVES How the prattle of young children Vexed more than if they whined.

Comb.: †**prattle-box** *slang & joc.* a chatterbox.
▪ **prattlement** *noun* (*rare*) idle talk, prattle, prattling L16. **prattler** *noun* a person who prattles, a chatterbox M16.

pratyahara /prətjɑːˈhɑːrə/ *noun*. L19.
[Sanskrit *pratyāhāra* withdrawal.]
YOGA. Withdrawal of the senses; restraint of response to external stimuli.

prau *noun* var. of PROA.

Prausnitz–Küstner /ˌpraʊznɪtsˈkuːstnə, -ˈkɪst-/ *noun*. E20.
[C. W. *Prausnitz* (1876–1963), German bacteriologist, and Heinz *Küstner* (1897–1963), German gynaecologist.]
MEDICINE. Used *attrib.* with ref. to a test for allergic sensitivity in which an individual is injected with serum from someone with the allergy, and after a day or two with the allergen, which produces a weal if a reagin is present. Abbreviation *PK*.

pravity /ˈpravɪti/ *noun*. L15.
[Latin *pravitas*, from *pravus* crooked, perverse: see -ITY. Superseded by DEPRAVITY.]
1 Moral corruption; wickedness, depravity. Now *rare*. L15.
2 *gen.* Corrupt or defective quality; badness. E17.
1 natural pravity, **original pravity** THEOLOGY the innate corruption of human nature due to original sin; depravity.

prawn /prɔːn/ *noun & verb*. LME.
[Origin unkn.]
▶ **A** *noun*. **1** Any of various marine decapod crustaceans resembling shrimps but usu. larger and with two pairs of pincers; *loosely* a large shrimp. LME.
2 A (usu. cheeky or impertinent) person. *joc. & colloq.* M19.
Phrases: **come the raw prawn on**, **come the raw prawn over**, **come the raw prawn with** *Austral. slang* attempt to deceive.
Comb.: **prawn cracker** a light crisp made from rice or tapioca flour and prawn flavouring which puffs up when deep-fried, eaten esp. with Chinese food (usu. in *pl.*).
▶ **B** *verb intrans*. Chiefly as ***prawning*** *verbal noun*.
1 Fish for prawns. L19.
2 Fish for salmon using a prawn as bait. E20.
▪ **prawner** *noun* (*a*) a person who fishes for prawns; (*b*) a fishing boat for catching prawns: L19.

Praxean /ˈpraksɪən/ *noun & adjective*. E18.
[from *Praxeas* (see below) + -AN. Cf. -EAN.]
ECCLESIASTICAL HISTORY. ▶**A** *noun*. A follower of Praxeas, a 3rd-cent. Monarchian. E18.
▶ **B** *adjective*. = MONARCHIAN *adjective*. L19.

praxeology /praksɪˈɒlədʒi/ *noun*. Also **-iology**. E20.
[French *praxéologie*, or directly from Greek *praxis*: see PRAXIS, -OLOGY.]
The branch of knowledge that deals with practical activity and human conduct; the science of efficient action.
▪ **praxeoˈlogical** *adjective* M20. **praxeologist** *noun* a person who studies practical activity M20.

praxinoscope /ˈpraksɪnəskəʊp/ *noun*. L19.
[French, irreg. from Greek PRAXIS + -O- + -SCOPE.]
A device resembling a zoetrope but having in the middle a series of mirrors in which reflections of the moving pictures are viewed.

praxiology *noun* var. of PRAXEOLOGY.

praxis /ˈpraksɪs/ *noun*. L16.
[medieval Latin from Greek, from *prattein* do.]
1 a Action, practice; *spec.* the practice of a technical subject or art, as opp. to or arising out of the theory of it. L16. ▸**b** Habitual action, accepted practice, custom. L19. ▸**c** In Marxism, the willed action by which a theory or philosophy becomes a practical social activity. Cf. PRACTICE *noun* 5d. M20.
2 An example or collection of examples used for practice in a subject, esp. in grammar; a practical specimen. E17.

> **1** COLERIDGE In theory false, and pernicious in praxis. *Church Times* Our faith determines our praxis.

Praxitelean /prakˌsɪtɪˈliːən/ *adjective*. E19.
[from Greek *Praxiteleios*, from *Praxitelēs*: see -EAN.]
Of or pertaining to Praxiteles, a Greek sculptor of the 4th cent. BC.

pray /preɪ/ *noun*. *rare*. ME.
[from the verb.]
An act of praying; a prayer.

pray /preɪ/ *verb*. ME.
[Old French *preier* (mod. *prier*) from late Latin *precare* alt. of classical Latin *precari* entreat.]
▶ **I** *verb trans*. **1** Ask earnestly or humbly; beseech; ask (a person) for something as a favour; *esp.* make devout and humble supplication to (God or an object of worship). (Foll. by *to do*, *for*, *that*, etc.) Now *literary*. ME. ▸**b** In *imper.* Please. (Adding deference or politeness to a question etc.) Now *arch. & formal*. ME.
†**2** Ask (a person) to come for a meal etc.; invite. ME–E17.
3 Ask for earnestly or in prayer; ask earnestly or of God *that* or *to be*; beg (a thing). Also, say (a prayer) to ask for something. ME.
4 Get or bring about by praying. (Foll. by *down*, *out*.) M17.

> **1** SHAKES. *Merch. V.* I pray you, which is the way to master Jew's? E. BOWEN He . . prayed them to keep still that he might count them. **b** G. B. SHAW What business is it of yours, pray? W. GOLDING Ladies and gentlemen, pray let us be seated. **3** SHAKES. *Meas. for M.* I'll pray a thousand prayers for thy death. J. RUSKIN He prayed permission to introduce his mother and sisters to us. **4** POPE I would not pray them out of purgatory.

▶ **II 5** *verb intrans*. Make earnest request or entreaty, esp. to God or an object of worship in the form of prayer. More widely, address oneself to God in prayer. ME.

> **5** K. LINES To this temple came long-robed Ionians to worship and to pray for protection. B. EMECHETA She knelt and prayed to God to forgive her. ***pray extempore***: see EXTEMPORE *adverb* 1. **pray for** (*a*) ask for in prayer; (*b*) pray on behalf of. **pray in aid** beg the assistance (*of*).

Comb.: **pray-TV** *N. Amer. colloq.* religious broadcasting, *esp.* television evangelism.
▪ **prayable** *adjective* (*a*) that may be prayed to or entreated; (*b*) (of a prayer) that may be made: LME.

praya *noun* var. of PRAIA.

prayer /prɛː/ *noun*¹. ME.
[Old French *preiere* (mod. *prière*) from Proto-Gallo-Romance use as noun of fem. of Latin *precarius* obtained by entreaty.]
1 a A solemn request to God or an object of worship; a supplication, thanksgiving, or other verbal or mental act addressed to God. ME. ▸**b** The action or practice of praying, esp. to God. ME. ▸**c** A formula or form of words used in praying. ME. ▸**d** In *pl.* Requests to God for his blessing on someone; earnest good wishes. Now *rare*. L16.
2 Religious worship, esp. of a public nature (chiefly in ***common prayer***, ***evening prayer***, etc., below). In *pl.*, an occasion of (esp. private) worship, a service of prayer. ME.
3 An entreaty made to a person; an earnest request or appeal. ME.
4 The subject matter of a petition or formal request; the thing requested or entreated; *spec.* the part of a petition to a monarch or a public body that specifies the thing desired. LME.

> **1a** P. CUTTING Hannes was a devout Christian, always offering a silent prayer before he ate. G. SAYER Because his prayers were not answered, he soon lost his faith. **b** R. WARNER We heard the clergyman's voice raised in prayer. K. AMIS Prayer and meditation are sure to guide me. **c** B. MOORE Do you actually say prayers, things like the Hail Mary, the Our Father, and so on? **d** SHAKES. *Per.* Madam, my thanks and prayers. **2** P. TOYNBEE At school prayers would have already begun. E. LONGFORD Early next day there were family prayers in the private chapel. **4** *Times* Since the hearing in the Inner House, the prayer of the petition had been amended.

Phrases: ***answer to a maiden's prayer***: see MAIDEN *noun*. ***a wing and a prayer***: see WING *noun*. ***bidding-prayer***: see BIDDING *noun*. ***common prayer***: see COMMON *adjective*. ***evening prayer***: see EVENING. ***House of prayer***: see HOUSE *noun*¹. ***lead in prayer***, ***lead the prayers***: see LEAD *verb*¹. ***MORNING prayer***. **not have a prayer** (chiefly *N. Amer. colloq.*) have no chance. ***the Lord's Prayer***: see LORD *noun*.
Attrib. & comb.: In the sense 'pertaining to or for the purpose of prayer', as ***prayer-group***, ***prayer-house***, ***prayer-room***, ***prayer-time***, etc. Special combs., as **prayer-bead** (*a*) any of the beads of a string used in prayer, *spec.* a bead of a rosary; (*b*) a seed of the jequirity, *Abrus precatorius*, used for making rosaries; **prayer-bell** a bell rung to call people to prayer in a school, monastery, etc.; **prayer bones** *US* the knees; **prayer-book** a book of forms of prayer, *spec.* (***the Prayer-Book***) the Book of Common Prayer; **prayer card** a card used by a Member of Parliament for reserving a seat at prayers; **prayer-carpet** = ***prayer rug*** below; **prayer-desk** a desk from which prayers are read in a church; **prayer-flag** in Tibet and Nepal, a flag on which prayers are inscribed; **prayer-mat** = ***prayer rug*** below; **prayer-meeting** a religious meeting for prayer; **prayer-mill** = ***prayer-wheel*** below; ***prayer niche***: see NICHE *noun* 1c; **prayer-nut** in a chaplet of beads, a nut-shaped bead which opens to form a diptych with reliefs; **prayer plant** a house-plant, *Maranta leuconeura*, (family Marantaceae), native to Brazil, with variegated leaves which are erect at night but prostrate during the day; **prayer rug** a small rug, carpet, or mat used (esp. by a Muslim) when praying; **prayer-shawl** = TALLITH; **prayer-stick** a stick decorated with feathers, used by the Zuñi of New Mexico in their religious ceremonies; **prayer-wall** a wall on which prayers are inscribed, *spec.* = MANI *noun*²; **prayer-wheel** a revolving cylindrical box inscribed with or containing prayers, used esp. by Tibetan Buddhists.
▪ **prayerwise** *adverb* (*rare*) after the manner of a prayer L16.

prayer /ˈpreɪə/ *noun*². Also **pray-er**. LME.
[from PRAY *verb* + -ER¹.]
A person who prays.

prayerful /ˈprɛːfʊl, -f(ə)l/ *adjective*. E17.
[from PRAYER *noun*¹ + -FUL.]
1 Of a person: given to praying; devout. E17.
2 Of speech, action, etc.: characterized by or expressive of prayers. M17.
▪ **prayerfully** *adverb* E19. **prayerfulness** *noun* M19.

prayerless /ˈprɛːlɪs/ *adjective*. M17.
[from PRAYER *noun*¹ + -LESS.]
Without prayer; not in the habit of praying.
▪ **prayerlessly** *adverb* M19. **prayerlessness** *noun* E17.

praying /ˈpreɪɪŋ/ *verbal noun*. ME.
[from PRAY *verb* + -ING¹.]
The action of PRAY *verb*; prayer, earnest request.
Comb.: **praying-desk** = ***prayer-desk*** s.v. PRAYER *noun*¹; **praying machine** = ***prayer-wheel*** s.v. PRAYER *noun*¹; **praying mat**, **praying rug** = ***prayer rug*** s.v. PRAYER *noun*¹; **praying-shawl** = ***prayer-shawl*** s.v. PRAYER *noun*¹.

praying /ˈpreɪɪŋ/ *ppl adjective*. LME.
[from PRAY *verb* + -ING².]
That prays.
praying band a group of people who habitually pray together. ***praying MANTIS***.

prazosin /ˈpreɪzəsɪn/ *noun*. L20.
[Arbitrary formation from components (PIPERAZINE, AZO-) of the chemical structure.]
PHARMACOLOGY. A vasodilator drug used to treat hypertension, with a molecular structure incorporating quinazoline, piperazine, and furyl rings.

PRB *abbreviation*.
Pre-Raphaelite Brother(hood).

pre /priː/ *preposition*. *US*. M20.
[Developed from PRE- 2.]
Earlier than, before.

pre- /priː, *unstressed* prɪ/ *prefix*. Also (now only in words regarded as Latin or relating to Roman antiquity) **prae-**.
[Repr. Latin *prae* (adverb & preposition) before, in front, in advance.]
Used in words adopted from Latin and in English words modelled on these, and as a freely productive prefix.
1 Prefixed adverbially to verbs, verbal derivs., and adjectives, and adjectivally to (chiefly verbal) nouns, with the senses 'earlier, prior (in time or order)', 'beforehand, previously', 'in front, anterior(ly)', and (not productive) 'before in importance, more than, beyond', 'exceedingly', as ***prearrange***, ***precaution***, ***precede***, ***precordial***, ***predominant***, etc.
2 Prefixed prepositionally to nouns and noun-stems with the sense 'situated or occurring before or in front of, earlier than, anterior to, preceding' as ***Precambrian***, ***prenatal***, ***prewar***, etc.
▪ **pre-ˈact** *verb intrans. & trans.* act or carry out beforehand M17. **pre-ˈaction** *noun* previous action M17. **pre-ˈadjunct** *noun* (GRAMMAR) an adjunct that precedes the word it modifies L19. **preadˈmission** *noun* admission beforehand: *spec.* the admission of a certain amount of steam into the cylinder of a steam engine before the end of the back stroke: L19. **preadoˈlescence** *noun* the preadolescent period M20. **preadoˈlescent** *adjective & noun* (*a*) *adjective* nearly adolescent; belonging to the two or three years before adolescence; (*b*) *noun* a preadolescent child: E20. **pre-adult** /priːˈadʌlt, priːəˈdʌlt/ *adjective* that has not yet reached adulthood, that occurs prior to adulthood E20. **preadˈvise** *verb trans.* advise or warn beforehand L17. **pre-ˈagonal** *adjective* occur-

ring immediately before the moment of death L19. **pre-agri'cultural** *adjective* (ANTHROPOLOGY) that has not yet developed agriculture as a means of subsistence E20. **pre-'Aids** *adjective* (*a*) before the onset of full-blown Aids but after infection with HIV; (*b*) before the recognition of Aids as a disease: L20. **pre'albumin** *noun* (BIOCHEMISTRY) a plasma protein with an electrophoretic mobility slightly greater than that of albumin; *spec.* one in human blood which binds thyroxine and the retinol-binding protein M20. **pre-'animism** *noun* (ANTHROPOLOGY) a stage of religious development held to have preceded animism, in which material objects were invested with spiritual energy E20. **pre-ani'mistic** *adjective* (ANTHROPOLOGY) characterized by or pertaining to pre-animism E20. **pre-a'nnounce** *verb trans.* announce beforehand M19. **pre-a'nnouncement** *noun* the action of pre-announcing something; an announcement made beforehand: L19. **prean'ticipate** *verb trans.* (*rare*) anticipate beforehand M17. **pre-a'ppoint** *verb trans.* appoint beforehand E17. **pre-a'ppointment** *noun* previous appointment, prearrangement M17. **pre'aspirate** *verb trans.* (PHONETICS) aspirate (a sound) in advance of another sound M20. **pre-aspi'ration** *noun* (PHONETICS) aspiration in advance of another sound M20. **pre-a'ssign** *verb trans.* assign beforehand M20. **pre-a'tomic** *adjective* existing or occurring before the utilization of atomic energy or atomic weapons; characteristic of such a time: E20. **prea'ttune** *verb trans.* attune beforehand L18. **pre'audience** *noun* (LAW) the right to be heard before another, relative rank M18. **pre-au'ricular** *adjective* (ANATOMY) (*a*) designating a groove situated immediately anterior to the inferior margin of the auricular surface of the ilium, and better developed in the female than in the male; (*b*) situated in front of the ear(s): L19. **pre-'axial** *adjective* (ANATOMY) situated in front of an axis L19. **pre-bacterio'logical** *adjective* before the discovery of the relationship of bacteria to disease L19. **pre-'baiting** *noun* the practice of accustoming vermin to harmless bait so that they will take poisoned bait more readily M20. **pre'cancer** *noun* (MEDICINE) a condition which is expected to lead to the development of cancer M20. **pre'cancerous** *adjective* (MEDICINE) occurring as a precursor of cancer, tending to be followed by cancer L19. **pre'carcinogen** *noun* (MEDICINE) a precursor of a carcinogen M20. **pre,carcino'genic** *adjective* (MEDICINE) of or pertaining to a precarcinogen; capable of causing a preneoplastic condition: M20. **pre'cellular** *adjective* (BIOLOGY) existing or occurring before the origin of cellular life M20. **pre'central** *adjective* (ANATOMY) designating parts of the cerebrum anterior to the central sulcus L19. **pre'civilized** *adjective* existing or occurring before the development of civilization M20. **pre'climax** *noun* (ECOLOGY) a point in a plant succession at which development has ceased before the state of climax is reached E20. **pre'clinical** *adjective* (MEDICINE) (*a*) pertaining to or designating the first stage of medical education, consisting chiefly of scientific studies; (*b*) preceding the onset of recognizable symptoms that make a diagnosis possible; (*c*) preceding clinical testing of a drug: M20. **pre-Co'lumbian** *adjective* occurring or existing before the arrival in America of Columbus L19. **precommi'ssural** *adjective* (ANATOMY) anterior to a commissure of the brain L19. **pre-'Communist** *adjective* existing or occurring before the time of Communist government; characteristic of such a time: L20. **precom'pose** *verb trans.* compose beforehand M17. **precom'press** *verb trans.* (BUILDING) compress prior to some other treatment M20. **pre-com'pression** *noun* (BUILDING) the compressive force exerted in prestressed concrete by the reinforcing rods M20. **precon'demn** *verb trans.* condemn beforehand M17. **precon'figure** *verb trans.* configure in advance; adapt beforehand: E19. **pre'conquest** *adjective* occurring or existing before a conquest, *spec.* (*pre-Conquest*) before the Norman Conquest of England in 1066 L19. **precon'sider** *verb trans.* consider beforehand M17. **preconside'ration** *noun* prior consideration; a preliminary consideration: L16. **preconso'nantal** *adjective* occurring in a word before a consonant M20. **pre'contour** *noun* (PHONETICS) an unstressed syllable which precedes the peak of a contour M20. **pre'cook** *verb trans.* cook in advance, cook before the warming given at the time of eating M20. **pre'cool** *verb trans.* cool prior to use or some further treatment, esp. further cooling to a very low temperature E20. **pre'cooler** *noun* a device for precooling something E20. **pre'coracoid** *adjective & noun* (ANATOMY) (a bone or cartilage) situated anterior to the coracoid L19. **pre'costal** *adjective* situated in front of a rib or (ENTOMOLOGY) a costal vein of a wing M19. **pre-'critical** *adjective* occurring prior to the critical treatment of a subject L19. **pre'cut** *verb trans.* cut prior to some other operation M20. **pre'cystic** *adjective* (ZOOLOGY) (of a protozoan) that is preparing to encyst E20. **pre-'decimal** *adjective* existing at or dating from a time before the introduction of decimal currency in the UK (in 1971) L20. **prede'clare** *verb trans.* (*rare*) declare or announce beforehand M17. **pre-de'linquency** *noun* behaviour which is likely to lead to (juvenile) delinquency M20. **pre-de'linquent** *adjective & noun* (*a*) *adjective* of, pertaining to, or characterized by pre-delinquency; (*b*) *noun* a person engaged in pre-delinquency: M20. **prede'sign** *verb trans.* design, contrive, or intend beforehand L17. **predi'luvian** *noun & adjective* (*a*) *noun* a person who lived before the Flood described in Genesis; (*b*) *adjective* = ANTEDILUVIAN *adjective* 1: E19. **predis'cover** *verb trans.* discover beforehand M17. **predis'covery** *noun & adjective* (*a*) *noun* previous discovery; (*b*) *adjective* occurring or performed before the discovery of something: M17. **predissoci'ation** *noun* (PHYSICS) the passage of a molecule between a quantized vibrational and rotational excited state and an unquantized dissociated state of the same energy, resulting in certain bands in the spectrum of the molecule being diffuse and lacking rotational fine structure E20. **pre'doom** *verb trans.* (*a*) condemn beforehand; (*b*) foreordain, predestine, (*to*): E17. **predy'nastic** *adjective* (*Hist.*) existing or occurring before the recognized Egyptian dynasties L19. **pre-'echo** *noun* (*a*) a faint copy of a loud sound occurring in a recording shortly before the original sound; (*b*) *fig.* a foreshadowing, an anticipation: M20. **pre-e'lectric** *adjective* belonging to the time before the use of electricity, esp. in the making of gramophone records M20. **pre-e'mergence**, **pre-e'mergent** *adjectives* occurring, performed, or applied before the emergence of seedlings from the soil M20. **pre-'emphasis** *noun* a systematic distortion of an audio signal prior to transmission or recording in anticipation of a corresponding decrease (de-emphasis) made during reception or playback (a technique aimed at improving the signal-to-noise ratio) M20. **pre-'emphasize** *verb trans.* subject to pre-emphasis M20. **pre-'entry** *adjective* prior to entry; *spec.* designating a closed shop in which trade-union membership is a prerequisite of appointment to a post: M20. **pre-es'tablish** *verb trans.* establish beforehand M17. **pre-expo'nential** *adjective* (MATH.) occurring as a non-exponential multiplier of an exponential quantity M20. **pre-fade** *noun* (BROADCASTING) (an instance of) monitoring of programme material prior to fading up M20. **pre'fashion** *verb trans.* fashion or shape beforehand E17. **pre-'feudal** *adjective* of the time before a country's adoption of a feudal system M20. **pre-fine** *noun* (LAW, now *Hist.*) a fee due on the issue of a writ before the fine was passed M17. **pre'finished** *adjective* (of metal) coated or treated before leaving the mill so as to make further finishing unnecessary M20. **pre'fire** *verb trans.* fire (pottery, clay, etc.) beforehand, esp. before glazing M20. **prega'lactic** *adjective* (ASTRONOMY) existing or occurring before the galaxies were formed L20. **pregangli'onic** *adjective* (ANATOMY) (of an autonomic nerve) running from the central nervous system to a ganglion L19. **pregeo'logical** *adjective* pertaining to or designating the period of the earth's history before the formation of the oldest known rocks L19. **pre-'graduate** *adjective* = UNDERGRADUATE *adjective* E20. **pre'harvest** *adjective* occurring before a crop is ready to be gathered M20. **pre-'ictal** *adjective* (MEDICINE) preceding a stroke or (esp. epileptic) fit M20. **pre-implan'tation** *adjective* (BIOLOGY) occurring or existing between the fertilization of an ovum and its implantation in the wall of the uterus M20. **pre-'Inca** *adjective* existing or occurring in S. America before the time of the Incas E20. **pre-in'cline** *verb trans.* incline or dispose beforehand L17. **pre-'indicate** *verb trans.* indicate or point out beforehand E19. **pre-in'dustrial** *adjective* of or pertaining to the time before industrialization L19. **pre-in'form** *verb trans.* inform beforehand L18. **pre-in'stall** *verb trans.* (COMPUTING) load (software) on to a computer before use L20. **pre-in'terpret** *verb trans.* interpret beforehand M17. **pre-'intimate** *verb trans.* intimate beforehand E19. **,pre-inti'mation** *noun* (a) previous intimation E19. **pre-in'vasive** *adjective* (MEDICINE) (of a tumour) that has not yet become invasive M20. **pre-Is'lamic** *adjective* before the time of Islam L19. **pre-'Latin** *adjective* pertaining to or designating any of the Italic languages older than Latin M20. **preload** *noun* a load applied beforehand M20. **pre'load** *verb trans.* load beforehand; *esp.* give (a bearing etc.) an internal load independent of any working load (e.g. to reduce noise in operation): M20. **pre,lumirho'dopsin** *noun* (BIOCHEMISTRY) an isomer of rhodopsin, stable at low temperatures, which is formed by the action of light on rhodopsin and changes spontaneously to lumirhodopsin M20. **pre-'makeready** *noun* (PRINTING) the preparations made before a letterpress block or forme goes to press M20. **pre'medial** *adjective & noun* (a thing) occurring or situated in front of the medial line or a medial position M19. **pre-mei'otic** *adjective* (CYTOLOGY) occurring before meiosis; that has not yet undergone meiosis: E20. **preme'narchal**, **preme'narcheal**, **preme'narchial** *adjectives* (MEDICINE) occurring or existing before the menarche; (of a female) who has not yet menstruated: M20. **premeno'pausal** *adjective* (MEDICINE) preceding the menopause; of or pertaining to the premenopause: M20. **pre'menopause** *noun* the stage of a woman's life immediately preceding the menopause M20. **pre-'mention** *verb trans.* (*rare*) mention previously or beforehand M16. **pre'merit** *verb trans.* (*rare*) merit or deserve beforehand E17. **pre-'milking** *noun* the removal of milk from a cow's udder before the birth of her calf M20. **pre-'moral** *adjective* pertaining to or designating a stage of development prior to the acquisition of moral responsibility M19. **pre'morbid** *adjective* (MEDICINE) preceding the occurrence of symptoms of disease M20. **pre'motor** *adjective* (ANATOMY) designating the anterior part of the precentral area of the frontal lobe of the brain, concerned with coordinating activities in the adjacent motor area M20. **pre'moult** *adjective & noun* (ZOOLOGY) (*a*) *adjective* preceding the moult in birds, insects, etc.; (*b*) *noun* a premoult stage or period: M20. **premultipli'cation** *noun* (MATH.) non-commutative multiplication by a preceding factor M19. **pre'multiply** *verb trans.* (MATH.) multiply non-commutatively by a preceding factor M19. **pre'myelocyte** *noun* (MEDICINE) = PROMYELOCYTE E20. **prename** *noun* a forename L19. **prenegoti'ation** *noun & adjective* (*a*) *noun* a preliminary negotiation; (*b*) *adjective* occurring before a negotiation: M20. **preneo'plastic** *adjective* (MEDICINE) occurring prior to the development of a neoplasm, tending to be followed by neoplasia M20. **pre'neural** *adjective* (ZOOLOGY) designating a skeletal element in chelonians that lies between the nuchal bone and the neural bones E20. **pre-'notice** *noun* (*rare*) previous notice or intimation L17. **prenotifi'cation** *noun* (*rare*) previous notification M18. **prenoun** *noun* (GRAMMAR) a word which usu. precedes and is closely related to a noun M19. **pre'nova** *noun* (ASTRONOMY) a star prior to its becoming a nova M20. **pre'ocular** *adjective* (ZOOLOGY) situated in front of the eye E19. **pre-'Oedipal** *adjective* (PSYCHOLOGY) existing or occurring before the onset of the Oedipal phase of development M20. **pre-'option** *noun* an option before anyone else; right of first choice: M17. **pre-'oral** *adjective* (ZOOLOGY) situated in front of the mouth L19. **pre-'orbital** *adjective* (ANATOMY & ZOOLOGY) situated in front of the orbit or eye socket M19. **pre-'order** *verb trans.* (*rare*) order, arrange, or appoint beforehand M17. †**pre-ordinance** *noun* previously established ordinance or rule LME–E17. **pre-ovu'latory** *adjective* (MEDICINE) occurring before ovulation M20. **pre'palatal** *adjective* (*a*) ANATOMY situated in front of the palate or palatal bones; (*b*) PHONETICS (of a consonant) articulated with obstruction of the air-stream in front of the palate: M19. **prepa'tellar** *adjective* (ANATOMY & MEDICINE) situated above or in front of the patella; ***prepatellar bursitis***, inflammation of the prepatellar bursa, housemaid's knee: L19. **pre'patent** *adjective* (MEDICINE) designating the period between parasitic infection of a host and the time when the parasite can first be detected E20. **preper'ception** *noun* previous perception; a condition preceding perception: L19. **pre'plan** *verb trans.* plan in advance M20. **pre'planetary** *adjective* (ASTRONOMY) existing before the formation of planets; *spec.* (of matter) from which the planets were formed: M20. **pre-'preference** *adjective* (of shares, claims, etc.) ranking before preference shares etc. M19. **pre'primate** *noun* (ZOOLOGY) an evolutionary ancestor of the primates; a related animal showing characteristics more highly developed in the primates: M20. **pre-pro'fessional** *adjective & noun* (*a*) *adjective* preliminary to professional training; (*b*) *noun* a person who is training for a profession: M20. **pre'program** *verb trans.* program (a computer or calculator) beforehand M20. **pre'prohormone** *noun* (BIOCHEMISTRY) a natural precursor of a prohormone L20. **prepsy'chotic** *adjective* (MEDICINE) occurring prior to the onset of psychosis; (displaying symptoms) indicative of the imminent onset of psychosis: E20. **prepubli'cation** *adjective & noun* (*a*) *adjective* issued or occurring in advance of publication; (*b*) *noun* publication in advance: E20. **prepulse** *noun* a preliminary pulse of electricity M20. **pre'punched** *ppl adjective* (of a card) having holes already punched in it; (of information) already represented as a pattern of holes: M20. **prepy'ramidal** *adjective* (ANATOMY) situated in front of the pyramids of the medulla oblongata in the brain M19. **pre'qualify** *verb intrans. & trans.* qualify in advance, esp. in advance of a sporting event L20. **prequark** *noun* (PARTICLE PHYSICS) = PREON L20. **pre-'rational** *adjective* based on mental processes more primitive than reason; intuitive: E20. **pre-'reader** *noun* (a book designed for) a person who is about to learn to read M20. **prere'duction** *noun* (GENETICS) separation of homologous chromatids, or (earlier) reduction of chromosome number, at the first meiosis rather than the second E20. **pre-re'flective** *adjective* prior to reflection or reasoning thought M20. **pre-re'flexive** *adjective* = PRE-REFLECTIVE L20. **pre-repro'ductive** *adjective* occurring before the time when an individual becomes capable of reproduction E20. **pre-revo'lutionary** *adjective* (*a*) existing before a (particular) revolution; (*b*) verging on revolution: M19. **pre-rinse** *noun* a preliminary rinse given to something before washing, esp. in an automatic washing machine M20. **pre-'Roman** *adjective* of or pertaining to the time before the rise of Rome, esp. before the founding of the republic in 509 BC M19; **pre-Ro'mantic** *adjective & noun* (a composer or writer) of the period before the Romantic Movement M20. **pre'scapular** *adjective* anterior to the spine or long axis of the shoulder-blade L19. **prescien'tific** *adjective* of or pertaining to the times before the development of modern science or the application of scientific method M19. **pre-'scoring** *noun* (CINEMATOGRAPHY) the recording of a sound track in advance of the shooting of the film it is to accompany M20. **pre'screen** *verb trans.* screen beforehand M20. **pre'senile** *adjective* (MEDICINE) occurring in or characteristic of the period of life preceding old age, esp. the period of middle age L19. **prese'nility** *noun* (MEDICINE) premature senility E20. **presensiti'zation** *noun* sensitization beforehand L20. **pre-'sensitize** *verb trans.* sensitize beforehand M20. **pre-'service** *adjective* of or pertaining to a period before a person or thing is ready for service or use E20. **pre'sexual** *adjective* preceding or not yet influenced by sexual activity or sexual awareness; prepubertal: E20. **pre'sign** *verb trans.* (*arch.*) signify or indicate beforehand L16. **pre-soak** *noun* a soaking given prior to some subsequent treatment E20. **pre-So'cratic** *adjective & noun* (PHILOSOPHY) (*a*) *adjective* of or pertaining to the period before Socrates; (*b*) *noun* any of the Greek philosophers of the 6th and 5th cents. BC who preceded Socrates: L19. **pre'solar** *adjective* (ASTRONOMY) = PRESTELLAR L20. **pre'sphenoid** *noun & adjective* (ANATOMY) (designating) the most anterior bone of the floor of the cranium (in humans the front part of the sphenoid bone) M19. **pre'stellar** *adjective* (ASTRONOMY) not (yet) having formed a star or stars M20. **pre'store** *verb trans.* (esp. COMPUTING) store beforehand M20. **pre-'stretch** *verb trans.* (BUILDING) = PRE-TENSION *verb* M20. **presy'naptic** *adjective* (*a*) CYTOLOGY existing or occurring prior to meiotic synapsis; (*b*) PHYSIOLOGY of, pertaining to, or designating a neurone that transmits a nerve impulse across a synapse: E20. **pre'systole** *noun* (PHYSIOLOGY) the period immediately preceding systole L19. **presys'tolic** *adjective* (PHYSIOLOGY) preceding systole; of or pertaining to presystole: M19. **pre'tape** *verb trans.* pre-record on tape M20. **'pre-tax** *adjective* (of earnings, profits, etc.) considered before the deduction of tax M20. **pre'tectal** *adjective* (ANATOMY) situated in front of the tectum; of or pertaining to the pretectum: E20. **pre'tectum** *noun* (ANATOMY) the pretectal region of the brain M20. **pre-'teen** *adjective & noun* (orig. *US*) (*a*) *adjective* in or suited to the years (immediately) prior to one's teens; (*b*) *noun* a pre-teenager: M20. **pre-'teenager** *noun* a child (just) under the age of thirteen M20. **pre'terminal** *adjective* preceding that which is terminal M20. **pre'tibial** *adjective* (MEDICINE) situated or occurring in front of, or on the front part of, the tibia M19. **pre'train** *verb trans.* (PSYCHOLOGY) train in advance of an experiment or test M20. **pre'treat** *verb trans.* treat beforehand M20. **pre'treatment** *noun & adjective* (*a*) *noun* treatment given beforehand; (*b*) *adjective* existing before treatment: E20. **pre'typify** *verb trans.* typify beforehand, prefigure, foreshadow M17. **pre'vernal** *adjective* (chiefly ECOLOGY) pertaining to or designating a period before or very early in spring E20. **pre'viable** *adjective* (MEDICINE) before the stage when a foetus has developed sufficiently to survive outside the womb E20. **prevo'cational** *adjective* given or performed as preparation for vocational training E20. **pre'warn** *verb trans.* (*rare*) (*a*) give advance warning of (an event); (*b*) warn (a person) beforehand; forewarn: E17. **pre-wash** *noun* a preliminary wash, esp. as performed in an automatic washing machine M20. **pre'wash** *verb trans.* give a preliminary wash to; wash before putting on sale: L20. **pre'wire** *verb trans.* wire beforehand; *spec.* put in (a building or vehicle) during construction wiring for services such as alarms or communications that are normally installed afterwards: M20. **prezy'gotic** *adjective* (BIOLOGY) occurring before or independently of fertilization M20.

preach /priːtʃ/ *noun*[1]. *colloq.* L15.
[from PREACH *verb.*]
An act of preaching; a solemn discourse, a lecture.

preach /priːtʃ/ *noun*[2]. *US colloq.* M20.
[Abbreviation Cf. TEACH *noun.*]
A preacher.

preach /priːtʃ/ *verb.* ME.
[Old French *prechier* (mod. *prêcher*), earlier *preëchier*, from Latin *praedicare* proclaim, (in ecclesiastical Latin) preach: see PREDICATE *noun.*]
1 *verb intrans.* Deliver a sermon or religious address. ME.
▸**b** Utter an earnest exhortation. Now usu., give moral

or religious advice in an obtrusive or tiresome way (foll. by *at*). LME.
2 *verb trans.* Publicly proclaim or expound (God, a religious message, etc.); advocate or teach with earnest exhortation. ME.
†**3** *verb trans.* Address, esp. on a religious subject; preach to. ME–E18.
4 *verb trans.* Formerly, utter publicly. Now only, deliver (a sermon or a religious address). LME.
5 *verb trans.* Bring into or out of some specified state by preaching. E17.

> 🕮 **1** E. WILSON The great Calvinist evangelist . . who preached every Sunday . . and reduced his congregation to weeping. *Grimsby Evening Telegraph* A baptist minister who preaches against gambling. **b** G. B. SHAW When you have preached at and punished a boy until he is a mad cripple. **2** B. BUNTING I am not preaching the simple life to those who enjoy being rich. S. BIKO The bible must . . preach that it is a sin. S. TERKEL I heard the gospel preached in its fullness. **4** G. GREENE Mr Powell is made to preach a sermon to the assembled family on social reform. **5** JONSON We had a Preacher that would preach folke asleepe still.

Phrases: **preach down** decry or oppose by preaching; silence by preaching. **preaching friar** a Dominican friar. **preach to the converted** commend an opinion to those who already assent to it. **preach up** extol by preaching; speak in praise of.
■ **preachable** *adjective* LME.

preacher /ˈpriːtʃə/ *noun.* ME.
[Anglo-Norman *prech(o)ur*, Old French *prech(e)or* from ecclesiastical Latin *praedicator*, formed as PREDICATE *verb*: see -ER[2].]
1 A person who preaches, *esp.* one whose function it is to preach the gospel, a minister of religion; *spec.* a person licensed to preach. ME.
2 In full ***friar preacher***. A Dominican friar. Cf. ***preaching friar*** s.v. PREACH *verb*. *obsolete* exc. *Hist.* ME.
3 ***the Preacher***, Solomon as supposed speaker in the Book of Ecclesiastes. Also, that book of the Bible. M16.

> 🕮 **1** S. PEPYS To church, and there being a lazy preacher I slept out the sermon. ***lay preacher***: see LAY *adjective*. ***local preacher***: see LOCAL *adjective*.

Comb.: **preacher-man** *US dial.* a male preacher.
■ **preacheress** *noun* a female preacher M17. **preacherly** *adjective* of or pertaining to a preacher or preachers E20. **preachership** *noun* the position or office of preacher M17.

preachify /ˈpriːtʃɪfʌɪ/ *verb intrans.* *colloq.* L18.
[from PREACH *verb* + -I- + -FY: cf. *speechify*.]
Preach, esp. in a tedious way.
■ **preachifiˈcation** *noun* M19.

preaching /ˈpriːtʃɪŋ/ *noun.* ME.
[from PREACH *verb* + -ING[1].]
1 The action of PREACH *verb*; an instance of this; the practice or art of preaching. ME.
2 A message or doctrine preached; a sermon. LME.
3 A public religious service, *esp.* one at which a sermon is preached. Chiefly *Scot.* & *US.* M16.
Comb.: **preaching-cross** a cross by the roadside or in an open place, at which monks etc. held evangelistic services; **preaching-house** a building devoted to preaching; *spec.* (the early name for) a Methodist place of worship; **preaching-station** a place to which a preacher comes from time to time to hold a religious service.

preachment /ˈpriːtʃm(ə)nt/ *noun.* Now usu. *derog.* ME.
[Old French *prechement* from late Latin *praedicamentum* that which is predicated, (in medieval Latin) preaching, sermon: see PREDICAMENT.]
A (tedious or obtrusive) sermon or exhortation; delivery of such a discourse, sermonizing.

> 🕮 D. ACHESON The moralistic . . preachments of the State Department.

preachy /ˈpriːtʃi/ *adjective.* *colloq.* E19.
[from PREACH *verb* + -Y[1].]
Inclined to preach; *esp.* tediously moralistic.

> 🕮 ALDOUS HUXLEY If I seem to be smug and preachy, forgive me.

■ **preachily** *adverb* M20. **preachiness** *noun* M19.

pre-acquaint /priːəˈkweɪnt/ *verb trans.* E17.
[from PRE- 1 + ACQUAINT *verb*.]
Acquaint beforehand, inform previously. (Foll. by *with*.)
■ **pre-acquaintance** *noun* previous acquaintance M17.

pre-adamic /priːəˈdamɪk/ *adjective.* M19.
[from PRE- 2 + ADAMIC.]
= PRE-ADAMITE *adjective*.

pre-adamite /priːˈadəmʌɪt/ *noun & adjective.* M17.
[from PRE- 2 + ADAM *noun* + -ITE[1].]
▶ **A** *noun.* **1** A person of a race formerly believed to have existed before the time of Adam. M17.
2 A believer in the existence of men before Adam. *obsolete* exc. *Hist.* E18.
▶ **B** *adjective.* Belonging to a race or to the time previous to Adam; prehuman. L17.
■ **pre-adaˈmitic** *adjective* = PRE-ADAMITE *adjective* E18. **pre-adamitism** *noun* the doctrine of the existence of pre-adamite man L18.

preadapt /priːəˈdapt/ *verb trans.* M19.
[from PRE- 1 + ADAPT.]
Adapt beforehand; *spec.* (BIOLOGY) adapt (an organism) for life in future conditions different from those currently obtaining. Freq. in *pass.*

> 🕮 T. H. EATON Some thecodonts were 'preadapted' in certain ways for the life of birds.

■ **preadaptive** *adjective* causing or characterized by preadaptation E20. **preadapˈtation** *noun* the fact or condition of being preadapted; a feature which is an instance of this: L19.

preadmonish /priːədˈmɒnɪʃ/ *verb trans.* M17.
[from PRE- 1 + ADMONISH.]
1 Admonish beforehand, forewarn. M17.
†**2** Give prior warning of. M17–E18.
■ **preadmoˈnition** *noun* a forewarning M17.

preallable /prɪˈaləb(ə)l/ *adjective.* *rare.* E17.
[Obsolete French (now *préalable*), from Old French *preal(l)er* precede, formed as PRE- + *aller* go.]
Preceding, preliminary.
■ **preallably** *adverb* previously M17.

preamble /priːˈamb(ə)l, ˈpriːamb(ə)l/ *noun.* LME.
[Old & mod. French *préambule* from medieval Latin *praeambulum* use as noun of neut. of late Latin *praeambulus* going before, (in medieval Latin) preliminary, from *praeambulare*: see next.]
1 A preliminary statement in speech or writing; an introductory paragraph, section, or clause. LME. ▶**b** *spec.* An introductory paragraph in a statute, deed, or other formal document, setting forth its grounds and intention. L16. ▶**c** A musical prelude. *poet.* E17.
2 *gen.* A preceding fact or circumstance; *esp.* a presage, a prognostic. M16.

> 🕮 **1** R. PARK Ma had launched into conversation without preamble. *Early Music* The editorial preamble is excellent on the overall background to the two works. **b** E. WHARTON The lawyer . . began to rattle through the preamble of the will. **2** K. TYNAN A convivial meeting of the summit is always the preamble to war.

preamble /priːˈamb(ə)l/ *verb.* LME.
[In sense 1 from Latin *praeambulare*, from *prae-* PRE- + AMBLE *verb*. In later senses from PREAMBLE *noun*.]
†**1** *verb intrans.* Walk in front. *rare.* Only in LME.
2 a *verb trans.* Utter by way of preamble. Long *rare* or *obsolete*. E17. ▶**b** *verb intrans.* Make an introductory statement. M17.
3 *verb trans.* Make a preamble to; preface. E17.

> 🕮 **3** *fig.*: W. SANSOM She might think this was a trick of Harry's . . to preamble the marriage-bed.

preambular /priːˈambjʊlə/ *adjective.* Now *rare.* M17.
[from medieval Latin *praeambulum* PREAMBLE *noun*: see -AR[1].]
Of the nature of a preamble; introductory.
■ Also **preambulary** *adjective* M17.

preambulate /priːˈambjʊleɪt/ *verb intrans.* *rare.* L16.
[In sense 1 late Latin *praeambulat-* pa. ppl stem of *praeambulare*: see PREAMBLE *verb*; in sense 2 from medieval Latin *praeambulum* PREAMBLE *noun*: see -ATE[3].]
†**1** Walk in front. L16–M17.
2 = PREAMBLE *verb* 2b. E17.
■ **preambuˈlation** *noun* LME. **preambulatory** *adjective* prefatory, preliminary E17.

pre-amp /ˈpriːamp/ *noun.* M20.
[Abbreviation.]
= PREAMPLIFIER.

preamplify /priːˈamplɪfʌɪ/ *verb trans.* M20.
[from PRE- 1 + AMPLIFY.]
Subject to a preliminary amplification; amplify in a preamplifier.
■ **preamplifiˈcation** *noun* M20. **preamplifier** *noun* an amplifier designed to amplify a very weak signal (as from a microphone, pickup, etc.) and deliver it to another amplifier for further amplification M20.

pre-anaesthetic /ˌpriːanɪsˈθɛtɪk/ *adjective & noun.* Also ***-anes-**. L19.
[from PRE- 2 + ANAESTHETIC.]
MEDICINE. ▶**A** *adjective.* **1** Occurring before the introduction of anaesthetics into surgical practice. L19.
2 Used or carried out as a preliminary to the induction of anaesthesia. M20.
▶ **B** *noun.* A drug used before the induction of anaesthesia. M20.
■ **pre-anaesthetically** *adverb* M20.

preapprehension /ˌpriːaprɪˈhɛnʃ(ə)n/ *noun.* E17.
[from PRE- 1 + APPREHENSION.]
1 Fearful anticipation; a foreboding. E17.
2 A preconceived notion. M17.

prearrange /priːəˈreɪndʒ/ *verb trans.* E19.
[from PRE- 1 + ARRANGE.]
Arrange beforehand.

> 🕮 N. PICKARD People who are happy they've prearranged their funerals.

■ **prearrangement** *noun* arrangement beforehand; a prior arrangement: L18.

For other words beginning with *pre-* see the entry for **pre-**

pre-assemble /priːəˈsɛmb(ə)l/ *verb trans.* M20.
[from PRE- 1 + ASSEMBLE.]
Assemble beforehand, esp. before being delivered or transported.
■ **pre-assembly** *noun* preliminary assembly M20.

preassume /priːəˈsjuːm/ *verb trans.* E17.
[from PRE- 1 + ASSUME.]
†**1** Take beforehand. E–M17.
2 Assume or take for granted beforehand. L18.

preassure /priːəˈʃʊə/ *verb trans.* L17.
[from PRE- 1 + ASSURE.]
Assure or make certain beforehand.
■ **preassurance** *noun* (**a**) a previous guarantee; (**b**) a previous feeling of certainty: M17.

Preb. *abbreviation.*
Prebendary.

prebend /ˈprɛb(ə)nd/ *noun.* LME.
[Old & mod. French *prébende* from late Latin *praebenda* lit. 'things to be supplied', neut. pl. of gerundive of *praebere* to supply, from *prae-* PRE- + *habere* have, hold: see -END.]
1 *Hist.* The portion of the revenues of a cathedral or collegiate church formerly granted to a canon or member of the chapter as his stipend. LME.
2 *Hist.* The property from which such a stipend was derived; the tenure of this as a benefice. LME.
3 = PREBENDARY *noun* 1. LME.
■ **prebendal** *adjective* of or pertaining to a prebend or a prebendary; ***prebendal stall***, the cathedral stall or benefice of a prebendary: LME. **prebender** *noun* (long *arch.*) a prebendary LME. †**prebendship** *noun* a prebendaryship L16.

prebendary /ˈprɛb(ə)nd(ə)ri/ *noun & adjective.* LME.
[medieval Latin *praebendarius*, from late Latin *praebenda*: see PREBEND, -ARY[1].]
▶ **A** *noun.* **1** Formerly, a canon of a cathedral or collegiate church whose income orig. came from a prebend. Now, an honorary canon of an English cathedral of the Old Foundation. LME.
†**2** = PREBENDARYSHIP. L15–E18.
▶ **B** *attrib.* or as *adjective.* Prebendal. M17.
■ **prebendaryship** *noun* the position or office of prebendary; the benefice of a prebendary: M17.

prebiological /ˌpriːbʌɪəˈlɒdʒɪk(ə)l/ *adjective.* M20.
[from PRE- 2 + BIOLOGICAL.]
Existing or occurring before the appearance of life; pertaining to the origin of life.
■ **prebiˈologist** *noun* a specialist in prebiology M20. **prebiˈology** *noun* the branch of science that deals with the origin of life and with conditions preceding it M20.

prebiotic /priːbʌɪˈɒtɪk/ *adjective.* M20.
[from PRE- 2 + BIOTIC.]
= PREBIOLOGICAL.

preboard /priːˈbɔːd/ *verb.* M20.
[from PRE- 1 + BOARD *verb*.]
1 *verb trans.* Shape by heating on a form before dyeing rather than after. M20.
2 *verb trans. & intrans.* Admit to, or go on board, an aircraft in advance of others. L20.

Preboreal /priːˈbɔːrɪəl/ *adjective & noun.* Also **Pre-Boreal**. E20.
[from PRE- 2 + BOREAL.]
▶ **A** *adjective.* Designating or pertaining to the climatic period in northern Europe following the last glaciation and preceding the Boreal period, marked by the spread of birch and pine forests. E20.
▶ **B** *noun.* The Preboreal period. M20.

prebuttal /priːˈbʌt(ə)l/ *noun.* L20.
[from PRE- + RE)BUTTAL.]
In politics: a response formed in anticipation of a criticism.

precalculate /priːˈkalkjʊleɪt/ *verb trans.* M19.
[from PRE- 1 + CALCULATE.]
Calculate or reckon beforehand; forecast.
■ **precalculable** *adjective* able to be precalculated M19. ˌ**precalcuˈlation** *noun* M19.

Precambrian /priːˈkambrɪən/ *adjective & noun.* Also **pre-C-**. M19.
[from PRE- 2 + CAMBRIAN.]
GEOLOGY. ▶**A** *adjective.* Designating, or pertaining to the period of geological time preceding the Cambrian period and Palaeozoic era, covering the period before the widespread occurrence of living organisms on earth. M19.
▶ **B** *noun.* The Precambrian period; the rocks collectively dating from this time. E20.

precancel /priːˈkans(ə)l/ *verb & noun.* Chiefly *US.* Infl. **-ll-**, ***-l-**. E20.
[from PRE- 1 + CANCEL *verb*, *noun*.]
▶ **A** *verb trans.* Cancel (a postage stamp) in advance of use to facilitate bulk mailing. E20.
▶ **B** *noun.* A precancelled stamp. M20.
■ ˌ**precanceˈllation** *noun* M20.

precantation /priːkanˈteɪʃ(ə)n/ *noun*. E17.
[Late Latin *praecantatio(n-)*, from Latin *praecantare* foretell, from *prae-* PRE- + *cantare* sing, CHANT *verb*: see -ATION.]
†1 A singing before. *rare* (only in Dicts.). Only in E17.
2 A prophesying, a foretelling. M19.

precaria *noun* pl. of PRECARIUM.

precarious /prɪˈkɛːrɪəs/ *adjective*. M17.
[from Latin *precarius*, from *prec-*, *prex* prayer, entreaty: see -ARIOUS. Cf. Old & mod. French *précaire*.]
1 **a** Held at the pleasure of another; uncertain. M17. ▸**b** Dependent on chance; insecure, unstable. L17.
2 Assumed gratuitously; unfounded, doubtful. M17.
†3 Suppliant, supplicating; importunate. M–L17.
4 Exposed to danger, risky. E18.

> 1a HOR. WALPOLE Though the tenure is precarious, I cannot help liking the situation for you. ANNE STEVENSON She would lose her husband, the chief prop of her precarious happiness. **b** A. S. DALE Gilbert . . earned a precarious living for years. V. BROME At this stage he did not wish to undermine his precarious authority. **2** J. MARTINEAU His mode of proof is precarious and unsatisfactory. **4** A. KENNY The German night raids . . made life in Liverpool . . a precarious affair.

■ **precariously** *adverb* in a precarious manner; *esp.* insecurely, unstably: M17. **precariousness** *noun* L17.

precarium /prɪˈkɛːrɪəm/ *noun*. Pl. **-ia** /-ɪə/. L17.
[Latin, use as noun of neut. of *precarius*: see PRECARIOUS.]
ROMAN & SCOTS LAW. A loan granted on request but revocable whenever the owner may please.

precary /ˈprɛk(ə)ri/ *noun*. *obsolete* exc. *Hist.* LME.
[In sense 1 formed as prec. In sense 2, from medieval Latin *precaria*.]
†1 A grant made on request but revocable whenever the grantor may please. LME–L16.
2 *FEUDAL LAW*. An additional service which the lord of a manor had a right to require. E20.

precast /priːˈkɑːst/ *adjective & verb*. E20.
[from PRE- 1 + CAST *ppl adjective, verb*.]
▸**A** *adjective*. Formed by casting before being placed in position; composed of units so made; involving such a process. E20.
▸**B** *verb trans*. Pa. t. & pple **-cast**. Cast before placing in position. M20.

precative /ˈprɛkətɪv/ *adjective*. M17.
[Late Latin *precativus*, from Latin *precat-* pa. ppl stem of *precari* PRAY *verb*: see -ATIVE.]
Of a word, form, etc.: expressing a wish or request.

> O. SHIPLEY The indicative or the precative form of absolution.

■ **precatively** *adverb* M19.

precatory /ˈprɛkət(ə)ri/ *adjective*. M17.
[from late Latin *precatorius*, from *precat-*: see prec., -ORY[2].]
Of, pertaining to, or expressing a wish or request.
precatory words *LAW* words in a will expressing a wish that a thing should be done.

precaution /prɪˈkɔːʃ(ə)n/ *noun*. L16.
[French *précaution* from late Latin *praecautio(n-)*, from *praecaut-* pa. ppl stem of *praecavere*, from *prae-* PRE- + *cavere* take heed.]
1 Caution exercised beforehand; prudent foresight. L16.
2 A measure taken beforehand to avoid a danger or ensure a good result. E17. ▸**b** *spec.* A precaution against conception in sexual intercourse. Usu. in *pl. colloq.* M20.

> 1 F. CLISSOLD The danger in this place defies precaution. **2** I. FLEMING As a precaution, the storm shutters were battened down over the portholes. J. HERRIOT Jeff never took any hygenic precautions such as washing his hands. **b** G. PALEY He got onto me right where we were, and . . we were so happy we forgot the precautions.

■ **precautional** *adjective* (*rare*) precautionary M17. **precautionary** *adjective* (**a**) advising caution; (**b**) of the nature of a precaution: M18.

precaution /priːˈkɔːʃ(ə)n/ *verb trans*. Now *rare* or *obsolete*. M17.
[French *précautionner*, formed as prec.]
†1 Caution or warn beforehand. M17–M18.
†2 Mention beforehand as a caution. M–L17.
3 Put (a person) on guard *against*; *refl.* take precautions *against*. E18.

precautious /prɪˈkɔːʃəs/ *adjective*. E18.
[from PRECAUTION *noun* after *caution*, *cautious*.]
Displaying forethought or anticipatory caution.
■ **precautiously** *adverb* E18.

precaval /priːˈkeɪv(ə)l/ *adjective*. Now *rare*. M19.
[from PRE- 1 + CAVA + -AL[1].]
ANATOMY. **precaval vein**, the superior vena cava.

†**precedaneous** *adjective*. M17–L18.
[App. from PRECEDE *verb* + *-aneous* (cf. *succedaneous*), perh. by assoc. with Latin *praecidaneus* slaughtered first, (in medieval Latin also) preliminary.]
Happening or existing before something else; preceding.

precede /prɪˈsiːd/ *verb*. LME.
[Old & mod. French *précéder* from Latin *praecedere*, from *prae-* PRE- + *cedere* CEDE.]
▸**I** *verb trans*. †1 Surpass in quality or degree; exceed. LME–M18.
2 Come before in time; occur earlier than. LME.
3 Go before in rank or importance; take precedence over. L15.
4 Go or come before in order or arrangement; occupy a position in front of. L15.
5 Travel in front of or ahead of; *ASTRONOMY* (of a celestial object) rise earlier than (another) in the apparent diurnal rotation of the heavens, be situated to the west of celestially. M16.
6 Cause to be preceded (*by*); preface, introduce, (*with*, *by*). E18.

> 2 B. CHATWIN The stillness that precedes a storm. **4** A. BAIN When the adjective ends in y *preceded by* a consonant, the y is changed into i. **5** J. STEINBECK Carlson stepped back to let Slim precede him. J. HELLER News of his arrival preceded him into the city. **6** A. M. BENNETT The old man . . never . . addressed her, without preceding Winifrid with Mrs. or Miss.

▸**II** *verb intrans*. **7** Go or come before or first in rank, order, place, or time. LME.

> 7 OED A statement different from anything that precedes or follows.

precedence /ˈprɛsɪd(ə)ns, ˈpriː-, prɪˈsiːd(ə)ns/ *noun*. L15.
[from PRECEDENT *adjective*: see -ENCE.]
†1 = PRECEDENT *noun* 2, 3. L15–M16.
†2 A thing said or done before; an antecedent. L16–E17.
3 **a** The right of preceding others in ceremonies and social formalities; *gen.* the order to be ceremonially observed by people of different rank, according to an acknowledged or legally determined system. L16. ▸**b** *gen.* Priority in importance, rank, order, or time. Freq. in ***take precedence*** (foll. by *over*, (arch.) *of*). E17.

> 3a S. WEINTRAUB She complained . . about proper precedence being ignored in her seating. **b** G. M. TREVELYAN The wagon . . had precedence, and all other traffic must draw aside to let it pass. A. STORR For the deeply religious . . attachment to God takes precedence over attachment to persons.

■ Also **precedency** *noun* = PRECEDENCE *noun* (now only senses 3a, b) L16.

precedent /ˈprɛsɪd(ə)nt/ *noun*. LME.
[Old & mod. French *précédent*, use as noun of the adjective: see PRECEDENT *adjective*.]
†1 **a** A thing just mentioned. Usu. in *pl.*, the preceding facts, statements, etc. LME–E17. ▸**b** A sign, an indication. Only in 16. ▸**c** An original of which a copy is made. *rare* (Shakes.). Only in L16. ▸**d** A prior event; an antecedent. L17–L18.
2 A previous instance taken as an example or rule for subsequent cases, or used to support a similar act or circumstance; *spec.* (*LAW*) a judicial decision which constitutes a source of law for subsequent cases of a similar kind. LME.
†3 A record of past proceedings, serving as a guide for subsequent cases. LME–M17.
4 **a** An example to be copied; a pattern, an exemplar. *obsolete* exc. *LAW*. M16. ▸†**b** An instance, an illustration. M16–L17.

> 2 C. HILL The execution of Mary Queen of Scots . . set a precedent for sitting in judgment on the Lord's Anointed. P. GAY He had no precedent for this work . . but had to invent the rules for it. **without precedent** unprecedented.

precedent /prɪˈsiːd(ə)nt/ *adjective*. Now *rare*. LME.
[Old & mod. French *précédent* pres. pple of *précéder*, repr. Latin *praecedent-* pres. ppl stem of *praecedere*: see PRECEDE, -ENT.]
1 Preceding in time; former, antecedent. LME.
2 Preceding in order; foregoing, aforesaid. LME.
3 Having or taking precedence. E17.
■ **precedently** *adverb* E17.

precedent /ˈprɛsɪd(ə)nt/ *verb trans*. *obsolete* exc. as PRECEDENTED. E17.
[from PRECEDENT *noun*.]
Provide with or justify by a precedent. Also, quote as a precedent.

precedented /ˈprɛsɪdɛntɪd/ *adjective*. M17.
[from PRECEDENT *verb*, *noun*: see -ED[1], -ED[2].]
Having or supported by a precedent. Usu. *pred.* Opp. earlier UNPRECEDENTED.

precedential /prɛsɪˈdɛnʃ(ə)l/ *adjective*. Now *rare*. M17.
[from PRECEDENT *noun* or PRECEDENCE, after *consequential* etc.]
1 Constituting a precedent. M17.
2 Introductory, preliminary; having or pertaining to precedence. M17.

preceding /prɪˈsiːdɪŋ/ *ppl adjective*. L15.
[from PRECEDE + -ING[2].]
1 That precedes in order or time; *esp.* occurring or mentioned immediately before. L15.
2 *ASTRONOMY*. Of a star etc.: situated further west, or to the west of another, and therefore rising earlier in the apparent diurnal rotation of the heavens. E18.

> 1 C. MATHEWSON Mr. George had helped with the team the preceding spring. J. RAZ The rejection of neutrality in the preceding chapter. *New Yorker* Designers . . borrow from the styles of preceding generations.

†**precel** *verb intrans. & trans.* Infl. **-ll-**. LME–M18.
[Latin *praecellere*, from *prae-* PRE- + base of *celsus* towering: cf. EXCEL.]
Be conspicuously superior (to). Freq. as ***precelling*** *ppl adjective*.

precellence /priːˈsɛl(ə)ns/ *noun*. Now *rare*. LME.
[Late Latin *praecellentia*, formed as prec.: see -ENCE.]
The fact or quality of excelling; pre-eminence.

precent /prɪˈsɛnt/ *verb*. M17.
[Back-form. from next.]
1 *verb intrans*. Officiate as precentor; lead the singing of a choir or congregation. M17.
2 *verb trans*. Lead the singing of (a psalm etc.). L19.

precentor /prɪˈsɛntə/ *noun*. E17.
[French *précenteur* or Latin *praecentor*, from *praecent-* pa. ppl stem of *praecinere*, from *prae-* PRE- + *canere* sing: see -OR.]
A person who leads or directs the singing of a choir or congregation; *spec.* (**a**) a cathedral cleric responsible for choral services (in a cathedral of the Old Foundation, a member of the chapter, ranking next below the dean; in one of the New Foundation, a minor canon or chaplain); (**b**) in a church or chapel in which there is no choir or instrumental accompaniment, a person appointed to lead congregational singing; (**c**) in a synagogue, a person who leads the prayers of the congregation.
■ **precentorship** *noun* the position or office of precentor E19. **precentrix** *noun* a female precentor E18.

precept /ˈpriːsɛpt/ *noun*. LME.
[Latin *praeceptum* use as noun of pa. pple of *praecipere* take beforehand, warn, instruct, from *prae-* PRE- + *capere* take. Cf. French *précepte*.]
†1 An order to do a particular act; a command. LME–E16.
2 A general instruction or rule for action, a maxim; *esp.* an injunction (freq. a divine command) regarding moral conduct. LME. ▸**b** Any of the rules of an art; a direction for the performance of a technical operation. M16.
3 *spec.* **a** A written order to attend a parliament or court, to serve on a jury, to hold an assize, to produce an offender or record, etc.; a written order, usu. from a sheriff to a returning officer, to make arrangements for an election; a writ, a warrant. LME. ▸**b** An instrument granting possession or conferring a privilege. *SCOTS LAW*. E16. ▸**c** An order issued by one local authority to another specifying the rate of tax to be charged on its behalf; the rate or tax itself. L19.
†4 A written authorization. E16–M18.

> 2 ALDOUS HUXLEY He knew . . how much he had learnt from her example and precept. V. BROME Jones did not subscribe to the precept that people should know their place in society. **b** S. QUINN True to Freudian precepts, she interpreted these fantasies as wishes. **3c** *Times* Essex county council have increased their rate precept by 10.8 per cent.

precept /ˈpriːsɛpt/ *verb*. Pa. pple **precepted**, †**precept**. LME.
[Earliest as pa. pple *precept* from Latin *praeceptus* pa. pple of *praecipere*: see prec. In sense 3 from PRECEPT *noun*.]
†1 *verb trans*. **a** Lay down as a precept or rule. LME–M17. ▸**b** Instruct (a person) by precepts. E–M17.
2 **a** *verb intrans*. Of a local authority: issue a precept; make a demand *on* a rating authority for funds. E20. ▸**b** *verb trans*. Take (rates) by means of a precept. M20.

preceptee /priːsɛpˈtiː/ *noun*. *US*. L20.
[from PRECEPT(OR + -EE[1].]
A medical student under training by a preceptor (PRECEPTOR 1b).

preceptial /prɪˈsɛpʃ(ə)l/ *adjective*. *rare*. L16.
[Irreg. from PRECEPT *noun* + -IAL.]
= PRECEPTUAL.

preception /prɪˈsɛpʃ(ə)n/ *noun*. E17.
[Latin *praeceptio(n-)*, from *praecept-* pa. ppl stem of *praecipere*: see PRECEPT *noun*, -ION.]
†1 A presumption, a preconception. *rare*. E–M17.
2 *ROMAN LAW*. The right of an heir to receive a legacy before partition of the inheritance. L19.

preceptive /prɪˈsɛptɪv/ *adjective*. LME.
[Latin *praeceptivus*, from *praecept-*: see prec., -IVE.]
1 Conveying a command, mandatory. LME.
2 Conveying an instruction or maxim, didactic. L17.

preceptor /prɪˈsɛptə/ *noun*. LME.
[Latin *praeceptor*, from *praecept-*: see PRECEPTION.]
1 A person who gives instruction; a teacher, a tutor. LME. ▸**b** *spec.* A physician or specialist who gives a medical student practical clinical training. *US*. E19.

For other words beginning with *pre-* see the entry for **pre-**

2 The head of a preceptory of Knights Templars. E18.

▪ **preceptoral** *adjective* = PRECEPTORIAL M19. **preceptorate** *noun* = PRECEPTORSHIP L19. **precep'torial** *adjective* (*a*) of or pertaining to a preceptor; (*b*) didactic: M19. **preceptorship** *noun* (*a*) the position or office of preceptor; (*b*) *US* the position of a medical student under training by a preceptor: E19. **preceptress** *noun* a female preceptor L18.

preceptory /prɪˈsɛpt(ə)ri/ *noun*. M16.
[medieval Latin *praeceptoria* use as noun of fem. of *praeceptorius*: see next, -ORY¹.]
Hist. A subordinate community of the Knights Templars; the buildings of such a community; an estate or manor supporting such a community.

preceptory /prɪˈsɛpt(ə)ri/ *adjective*. *rare*. L16.
[medieval Latin *praeceptorius*, formed as PRECEPTOR: see -ORY².]
Commanding, enjoining.

preceptual /prɪˈsɛptjʊəl/ *adjective*. *rare*. Also **preceptial** /-ˈsɛpʃ(ə)l/. E17.
[Irreg. from PRECEPT *noun* after *concept*, *conceptual*.]
Pertaining to or conveying a precept.

preces /ˈpriːsiːz/ *noun pl.* LME.
[Latin = prayers.]
ECCLESIASTICAL. Orig., liturgical prayers. Now *spec.* short petitions said as verse and response by minister and congregation alternately.

precess /prɪˈsɛs/ *verb*. E16.
[Latin *praecess-* pa. ppl stem of *praecedere* PRECEDE.]
†**1** *verb trans.* Precede, take precedence over. *rare*. Only in E16.
2 *verb intrans.* Undergo precession (*about* an axis). L19.

precession /prɪˈsɛʃ(ə)n/ *noun*. ME.
[Late Latin *praecessio(n-)*, from Latin *praecess-* pa. ppl stem of *praecedere* PRECEDE: see -ION.]
†**1** [By confusion.] A procession. ME–E16.
2 a ASTRONOMY. In full ***precession of the equinoxes***: the earlier occurrence of the equinoxes in each successive sidereal year (due to precession of the earth's axis); the slow change of direction of the earth's axis, which moves so that the pole of the equator rotates around the pole of the ecliptic once in about 25,800 years. Also, any motion (e.g. of the equinoctial points or the celestial pole or equator) associated with the precession of the equinoxes. L16. ▸**b** PHYSICS. A motion analogous to that of the earth's axis in the precession of the equinoxes; a rotation of the axis of a spinning body about another axis due to a torque acting to change the direction of the first axis; *spec.* the rotation of the spin axis of a nucleus, electron, etc., about the direction of a magnetic or an electric field. L19.
3 The action or fact of preceding in time, order, or rank. E17.
4 PHONETICS. Advance in oral position. M19.
2a ***LARMOR precession***. **lunisolar precession** the part of the precession of the equinoxes caused by the gravitational attraction of the moon and sun on the earth. **planetary precession** the part of the precession of the equinoxes caused by the gravitational attraction of the other planets.
▪ **precessional** *adjective* (ASTRONOMY & PHYSICS) E19.

pre-Christian /priːˈkrɪstʃ(ə)n, -tɪən/ *adjective*. E19.
[from PRE- 2 + CHRISTIAN *noun*, *adjective*.]
1 Occurring in or dating from a time before the birth of Jesus or the Christian era. E19.
2 Occurring in or dating from a time before the introduction of Christianity in a region. M19.

précieux /presjø/ *noun & adjective*. Also (fem.) ***-euse*** /-øːz/. E18.
[French = PRECIOUS.]
▸ **A** *noun*. Pl. ***-eux*** /-øːz/, (fem.) ***-euses*** /-øːz/. A person affecting an overrefined delicacy of language and taste. E18.
▸ **B** *adjective*. Overrefined, affectedly fastidious in taste etc.; = PRECIOUS *adjective* 3. L18.

precinct /ˈpriːsɪŋ(k)t/ *noun*. LME.
[medieval Latin *praecinctum* use as noun of neut. pa. pple of Latin *praecingere* gird about, encircle, from *prae* PRE- 2 + *cingere* gird.]
1 An administrative district, a district over which a person or body has jurisdiction; a division of a city, town, parish, etc. Now chiefly *US*, a subdivision of a county or ward for election purposes, or of a city for the purpose of police control. LME. ▸**b** *ellipt.* A police precinct house. *US colloq.* L19.
2 *sing.* & (usu.) in *pl.* The area within the boundaries (real or imaginary) of a building or place; the grounds; the interior; *esp.* an enclosed or clearly defined area around a cathedral, college, etc. Also, the surroundings or environs *of* a place. L15.
3 An enclosing line or surface; a boundary, a limit. Freq. in *pl.* M16.
4 A specially designated part of a town, *esp.* one from which motor vehicles are excluded. M20.

🕮 **1** *Listener* The 18th Precinct . . took in . . Times Square and . . Hell's Kitchen. **b** W. S. BURROUGHS They drove back to the precinct and I was locked in. **2** K. J. FRANKLIN He was offered an official residence in the precincts of Bart's. A. POWELL The Close remained . . a precinct of immense beauty. **3** H. E. MANNING Girdled the world about with the precinct of His own holiness. **4** K. ISHIGURO Three side streets intersected to form a paved precinct. ***pedestrian precinct***, ***shopping precinct***.

Comb.: **precinct captain** *US* a leader of a political party in a precinct; **precinct house** *US* (*a*) the headquarters of an election precinct; (*b*) a police station; **precinct station** *US* = *precinct house* (b) above.

precinct /prɪˈsɪŋ(k)t/ *pa. pple & ppl adjective*. *rare*. M17.
[Latin *praecinctus* pa. pple of *praecingere*: sec. prec.]
Girt about; girdled, encompassed.

precinctual /prɪˈsɪŋ(k)tjʊəl/ *adjective*. M20.
[from PRECINCT *noun*, perh. after *instinct*, *instinctual*.]
Of, pertaining to, or characteristic of a precinct.

preciosity /prɛʃɪˈɒsɪti/ *noun*. LME.
[Old & mod. French *préciosité* from Latin *pretiositas*, from *pretiosus*: see next, -ITY.]
†**1** The quality of being precious or costly; preciousness, great value or worth. LME–L17.
2 A very costly thing, an article of value. Now *rare* or *obsolete*. L15.
3 Affectation of refinement or distinction, esp. in the choice of words; fastidious refinement in literary or artistic style. M19.

precious /ˈprɛʃəs/ *adjective, adverb, & noun*. ME.
[Old French *precios* (mod. *précieux*) from Latin *pretiosus*, from *pretium* PRICE *noun*: see -OUS.]
▸ **A** *adjective*. **1** Of great value; having a high price, costly. ME.
2 Of great moral, spiritual, or non-material worth; beloved, much prized. Occas. *derog.*, expr. the speaker's contempt of something valued by another. ME.
3 Affectedly refined in conduct, manners, language, etc., (over-)fastidious. LME.
4 As an intensive or *iron.*: worthless; consummate; considerable. *colloq.* LME.

🕮 **1** D. M. THOMAS Water was precious: one . . had to go every day . . to fetch it. F. WELDON Jack took my hand and held it . . as if I were a precious possession. **2** TOLKIEN We have already lost precious hours. A. DJOLETO Safety of the boys was more precious to me than my own welfare. *California* Must universities give up their precious overhead projectors? **3** D. MACDONALD English pre-Raphaelites, a decadent and precious group. **4** KEATS I would have made precious havoc of her house. C. DARWIN I find I am writing most precious nonsense. CLIVE JAMES I shall look a precious fool if all other sources of income . . dry up.

Special collocations: **precious blood** THEOLOGY the blood of Jesus, as shed for the redemption of humankind. **precious coral** a coral of the order Antipatharia, members of which form branching plantlike growths. **precious metal** an expensive and rare metal suitable for use in ornaments, high-value coinage, etc.; *spec.* gold, silver, platinum. **precious opal**: showing colourful iridescence. **precious stone** a (piece of) mineral which on account of its beauty, hardness, and rarity is prized for use in ornamentation and jewellery and has a high commercial value; a gemstone.

▸ **B** *adverb*. **1** With intensive force: extremely, very, indeed (chiefly foll. by *few*, *little*, etc.) *colloq.* LME.
2 *lit.* Preciously; expensively, valuably. Long *rare* or *obsolete*. L15.

🕮 **1** THACKERAY I . . took precious good care to have it. F. WARNER There's precious few like him around.

▸ **C** *noun*. Used as a form of address: precious one, (*my* etc.) darling. L16.
▪ **preciously** *adverb* †(*a*) in a costly manner, expensively; †(*b*) valuably, as a precious thing; (*c*) fastidiously, with affected refinement of language etc.; (*d*) *colloq.* very greatly; exceedingly, extremely: LME. **preciousness** *noun* LME.

precip /prɪˈsɪp, ˈpriːsɪp/ *noun*. *N. Amer. colloq.* L20.
[Abbreviation.]
Atmospheric precipitation, such as rain or snow.

†**precipe** *noun*. Pl. **-pes**, **-pies**. E17–M18.
[Latin *praecipes* var. of *praeceps*: see next.]
A steep descent; a precipice.

precipice /ˈprɛsɪpɪs/ *noun*. L16.
[French *précipice* or Latin *praecipitium*, from *praeceps*, *praecip(it)-* headlong, steep, or *praecipitare* PRECIPITATE *verb*.]
†**1** A precipitate fall or descent. Freq. *fig.* L16–M17.
2 A high cliff, crag, or steep mountainside from which one might fall; a vertical or very steep rock face. E17.
3 *fig.* A dangerous or hazardous situation. M17.

🕮 **1** P. MASSINGER His precipice from goodness. **2** W. M. CLARKE They were teetering on the edge of precipices. *fig.*: *Independent* The country was sliding down the precipice of crisis.

†**precipies** *noun pl.* see PRECIPE.

precipit /prɪˈsɪpɪt/ *adjective*. *rare*. M17.
[Latin *praecipit-*: see PRECIPICE.]
Steep, precipitous.

precipitable /prɪˈsɪpɪtəb(ə)l/ *adjective*. L17.
[from PRECIPITATE *verb* + -ABLE.]
Able to be precipitated from solution in a liquid, or from a state of vapour.
▪ **precipita'bility** *noun* L18.

precipitancy /prɪˈsɪpɪt(ə)nsi/ *noun*. E17.
[from next + -ANCY.]
1 a Excessive or unwise haste in action; hastiness, rashness. E17. ▸**b** An instance of this; a hasty or rash act. *rare*. M17.
2 Rapid headlong or onward movement; violent hurry, suddenness of action. M17.
▪ **precipitance** *noun* (*a*) = PRECIPITANCY 1a; (*b*) *rare* = PRECIPITANCY 2: M17.

precipitant /prɪˈsɪpɪt(ə)nt/ *adjective & noun*. E17.
[French *précipitant* (now only as noun) pres. pple of *précipiter* PRECIPITATE *verb*: see -ANT¹.]
▸ **A** *adjective*. = PRECIPITATE *adjective*. E17.
▸ **B** *noun*. **1** CHEMISTRY. A substance that causes precipitation (*of* a particular substance) when added to a solution. L17.
2 A cause or stimulus which precipitates a particular action or (esp. psychological) condition. (Foll. by *of*, *for*.) E20.
▪ **precipitantly** *adverb* M17.

precipitate /prɪˈsɪpɪteɪt/ *noun*. M16.
[mod. Latin *praecipitatum* use as noun of neut. pa. pple of Latin *praecipitare* PRECIPITATE *verb*.]
1 CHEMISTRY. Any of various mercury compounds formed by precipitation. Later only with defining word. *obsolete* exc. *Hist.* and in phrs. below. M16.
2 *gen.* A substance precipitated from a solution; a solid, often powdery or flocculent, deposited from a solution by chemical action, cooling, etc. L16.
3 PHYSICS & METEOROLOGY. Atmospheric moisture condensed from water vapour by cooling and deposited as rain, dew, etc. M19.
1 red precipitate mercury(II) oxide, HgO. **white precipitate** either of two complexes formed by the action of ammonia on mercury(II) chloride, the ammine $Hg(NH_3)_2Cl_2$ (***fusible white precipitate***), and the amide $HgNH_2Cl$ (***infusible white precipitate***).

precipitate /prɪˈsɪpɪtət/ *adjective*. E17.
[Latin *praecipitatus* pa. pple of *praecipitare*: see next, -ATE².]
1 Headlong; falling or descending steeply or vertically. E17. ▸**b** Very steep, precipitous. *rare*. E17.
2 Actuated by violent or sudden impulse; overhasty, hurried; rash, headstrong. E17.
3 Rushing or driven along headlong; moving or moved with excessive haste or speed. M17.
4 Performed or occurring very rapidly; very sudden or abrupt. M17.

🕮 **1** J. S. BLACKIE And Dadaces . . spear-struck fell Precipitate from his ship. **2** J. SMEATON I was determined not to be precipitate in purchasing. W. GERHARDIE Conscious of the danger of precipitate action. K. MOORE Rather precipitate marriages did run in the family. **3** GIBBON The general escaped by a precipitate flight. P. V. WHITE They were all a little out of breath from precipitate arrival. **4** W. S. CHURCHILL Gladstone's precipitate conversion to Home Rule.

▪ **precipitately** *adverb* M17. **precipitateness** *noun* M17.

precipitate /prɪˈsɪpɪteɪt/ *verb*. E16.
[Latin *praecipitat-* pa. ppl stem of *praecipitare* throw or drive headlong, from *praecipit-*, *praeceps* headlong, from *prae* PRE- + *caput* head: see -ATE³.]
▸ **I** *verb trans.* **1** Throw down headlong; hurl or fling down; *fig.* send violently or suddenly into a state or condition. E16.
2 a Cause to move, pass, act, etc., very rapidly; hasten, hurry, urge on. Now *rare*. M16. ▸**b** Bring about quickly, suddenly, or unexpectedly; hasten the occurrence of. E17.
3 a Cause (a substance) to be deposited in solid form from solution in a liquid or (METALLURGY) a solid; cause (dust or other particulate matter) to be deposited on a surface from suspension in a gas. Formerly also, deposit as a sediment from suspension in a liquid. M17. ▸**b** Cause precipitation in (a liquid, gas, etc.). E19. ▸**c** PHYSICS & METEOROLOGY. Condense (moisture) into drops from vapour; cause (moisture) to fall as rain, dew, etc. M19.

🕮 **1** T. PENNANT No alternative but to perish by the . . sword, or to precipitate themselves into the ocean. T. HARDY He became aware . . that there was suddenly nothing to tread on, and found himself precipitated downwards. R. LYND Is it into this world of jangling suspicion . . that the clergy of the future are to be precipitated? **2a** J. BUTLER Men are impatient, and for precipitating things. **b** E. J. HOWARD She attracted those people most likely to precipitate her doom. V. BROME He had the ability to precipitate quarrels. **3a** F. HOYLE Oxygen changes the dissolved ferrous iron to insoluble ferric, which is then precipitated. **c** D. BAGLEY The hurricane will also precipitate a lot of water.

▸ **II** *verb intrans.* †**4** Fall headlong; fall, plunge; descend steeply; *fig.* fall *into* a state or condition, come suddenly to ruin. L16–L18.

For other words beginning with *pre-* see the entry for **pre-**

†**5** Rush headlong; hasten, hurry; move, act, or proceed very quickly. Also, act rashly, be precipitate in action. E17–M18.

6 a Be deposited as a solid from solution, or from suspension in a gas; settle as a precipitate. Also foll. by *out*. E17. ▸**b** Fall or be deposited as condensed vapour. E19.

> **6a** *Engineering* To accelerate charged particles . . towards a negatively charged wire on which they tend to precipitate. **b** *Scientific American* The atmosphere would have cooled and the water vapor . . would have condensed and precipitated.

■ **precipitated** *ppl adjective* (*a*) (now *rare*) hastened, hurried; precipitate; (*b*) deposited from solution, from a state of vapour, or from a state of suspension in a gas: M17. **precipitator** *noun* a person who or thing which precipitates; an apparatus for precipitation; *esp.* an electrostatic device for removing particulate matter from gases: M17.

precipitation /prɪˌsɪpɪˈteɪʃ(ə)n/ *noun*. LME.
[French *précipitation* or Latin *praecipitatio(n-)*, formed as prec.: see -ATION.]
▸**I 1** The action or an act of throwing down or falling from a height; headlong fall or descent. LME. ▸**b** Steepness of descent; precipitousness. *rare*. E17.
2 Sudden and hurried action; sudden or inconsiderate haste; rashness. E16.
3 Headlong rush, violent onward motion. Now *rare*. E17.
4 The bringing about of something rapidly, suddenly, or unexpectedly. E17.

> **1** SHAKES. *Coriol.* We . . banish him our city, In peril of precipitation From off the rock Tarpeian. **2** DICKENS The lady having seized it, with great precipitation, they retired. DISRAELI We must not act with precipitation. **4** F. W. FARRAR He attributes to his death the precipitation of the ruin of Jerusalem.

▸**II 5** Separation and deposition of a substance as a precipitate; condensation and deposition of moisture from vapour; the process of precipitating a substance. L15.
6 A precipitated substance, a precipitate; METEOROLOGY water that falls to or condenses on the ground, as rain, snow, dew, etc.; the amount of this. E17.

> **6** *Scientific American* Precipitation coalesces from cloud water.

Comb.: **precipitation hardening** METALLURGY hardening of an alloy by heat treatment that causes crystals of a solute phase to separate from solid solution.

precipitato /preˌtʃipiˈtaːto, prɪˌtʃɪpɪˈtɑːtəʊ/ *adjective & adverb*. L19.
[Italian.]
MUSIC. A direction: in a hurried or headlong manner; (to be) played in this manner.

precipitin /prɪˈsɪpɪtɪn/ *noun*. E20.
[from PRECIPIT(ATE *verb* + -IN[1].]
IMMUNOLOGY. An antibody that on reacting with its antigen produces a visible precipitate.
■ **precipiˈtinogen** *noun* an antigen which induces the production of a precipitin E20.

†**precipitious** *adjective*. E17.
[from Latin *praecipitium* PRECIPICE + -OUS.]
1 Precipitous, steep. E17–E18.
2 Sudden, rash, precipitate. Only in 17.

precipitous /prɪˈsɪpɪtəs/ *adjective*. M17.
[French †*précipiteux* from Latin *praecipit-*: see PRECIPITATE *verb*, -OUS.]
1 = PRECIPITATE *adjective* 2, 3, 4. Now *rare*. M17.
2 Of the nature of a precipice; dangerously high and steep; consisting of or characterized by precipices. E19.
3 Of a decline or fall: large and sudden. L19.

> **1** TENNYSON The sweep Of some precipitous rivulet to the wave. A. CROSS Anxiety . . in murder cases . . led to precipitous conclusions. **2** J. BERGER The precipitous edge of an infinitely deep fissure. P. THEROUX The land was too precipitous for crops. **3** L. STARKE A precipitous drop in ivory prices.

■ **precipitously** *adverb* E17. **precipitousness** *noun* M19.

précis /ˈpreɪsiː/ *noun & verb*. M18.
[French, use as noun of *précis*: see next.]
▸**A** *noun*. Pl. same /-siːz/.
1 A summary or abstract, esp. of a text or speech. M18.
2 The action or practice of précis-writing. L19.
▸**B** *verb trans*. Make a précis of; summarize. M19.

precise /prɪˈsʌɪs/ *adjective & adverb*. LME.
[French *précis*, *-ise* from Latin *praecisus* pa. pple of *praecidere* cut short, abridge, from *prae-* PRE- + *caedere* cut.]
▸**A** *adjective*. **1** Marked by definiteness or exactness of expression; strictly defined; (of a person) definite and exact in statement. LME. ▸**b** Of an instrument: exact, accurate. M16. ▸**c** Of the voice, language, etc.: distinct in utterance or enunciation. M19.
2 Distinguished with precision from any other; identified with exactness; *the* particular, *the* identical, *the* exact. LME.
3 Strict in observing rules etc.; formal, correct; punctilious, scrupulous; (of a practice) strictly observed; *occas.* overnice, fastidious. M16. ▸**b** *esp.* Strict in religious observance. Formerly *spec.* puritanical. M16.
4 That is exactly what it is stated to be; perfect, complete; neither more nor less than. L16.

> **1** DAY LEWIS My own passionate sense of justice—or rather, to be precise, of injustice. *Nature* Most geophysical theories tend to be more precise than accurate. S. NAIPAUL The government, unafraid of precise commitment, . . said that it would 'feed, clothe and house' all the people. **c** DICKENS The low precise tone of one who endeavours to awaken a sleeper. **2** V. BROME The precise directon which his . . career should follow. TOECKEY JONES What Dave was doing at that precise moment. W. M. CLARKE Its precise shape is difficult to describe. **3** W. COWPER Learned without pride, exact, yet not precise. F. MARRYAT He . . was very precise about doing his duty. **b** E. B. PUSEY Men are now called 'precise', who will not connive at sin. **4** L. STEPHEN The precise adaptation of the key to every ward of the lock.

▸**B** *adverb*. = PRECISELY. Long *obsolete* exc. *Scot.* LME.
■ **preciseness** *noun* M16.

precise /prɪˈsʌɪs/ *verb trans*. M19.
[French *préciser*, formed as prec.]
Define precisely or exactly; particularize.

precisely /prɪˈsʌɪsli/ *adverb*. LME.
[from PRECISE *adjective* + -LY[2].]
†**1** Definitely; expressly. LME–M17.
2 Strictly; punctiliously; with propriety. E16.
†**3** Specifically, in particular. M16–L17.
4 With exact correspondence; with precise identification or definite knowledge; exactly, just; *colloq.* (as a comment or reply) just so, quite so. M16.

precisian /prɪˈsɪʒ(ə)n/ *noun*. L16.
[from PRECISE *adjective* + -IAN.]
A person who is rigidly precise or punctilious in the observance of rules or forms, esp. religious ones; orig. (*obsolete* exc. *Hist.*) a Puritan.
■ **precisianism** *noun* the practice or conduct of a precisian (cf. PRECISIONISM) L16. **precisianist** *noun* E19.

precision /prɪˈsɪʒ(ə)n/ *noun & adjective*. L16.
[French *précision* or Latin *praecisio(n-)*, from *praecis-* pa. ppl stem of *praecidere*: see PRECISE *adjective*, -ION. In sense 1 used as a noun corresp. to PRESCIND.]
▸**A** *noun*. †**1** The cutting off of one thing from another; *esp.* the mental separation of a fact or idea. Also (*rare*), a precise definition. L16.
2 The fact, condition, or quality of being precise; exactness, definiteness; distinctness, accuracy. M18. ▸**b** STATISTICS. (A quantity expressing) the reproducibility of a measurement or numerical result. L19. ▸**c** The degree of refinement in measurement or specification, esp. as represented by the number of digits given. Cf. ACCURACY 2. M20. ▸**d** The accuracy of an act of information retrieval, expressed as the proportion of the retrieved items that are relevant or desired. M20.

> **2** T. H. HUXLEY The precision of statement which . . distinguishes science from common information. M. KEANE With careful and delicate precision I poured the ginger ale. **c** *Journal of Navigation* To chart the crystal field with high precision requires observations at intervals of 1km or less. ***double precision***: see DOUBLE *adjective & adverb*.

▸**B** *attrib.* or as *adjective*. Marked by or adapted for precision. L19.

> *Technology* The repair of indicator gauges and other precision instruments. *Farmers Weekly* Precision drilling of sugar beet. **precision approach radar** a ground-based radar system used to follow accurately the approach of an aircraft and to enable landing to be supervised from the ground.

■ **precisional** *adjective* of or pertaining to precision L19. **precisionism** *noun* the practice or beliefs of precisionists (cf. PRECISIANISM) M19. **precisionist** *noun & adjective* (*a*) *noun* a person who makes a practice of precision or exactness in expression etc.; a purist; *spec.* (**P-**) any of a group of US painters of the 1920s who employed a smooth, precise technique; (*b*) *adjective* employing or exhibiting precision as an artistic technique: M19.

precisive /prɪˈsʌɪsɪv/ *adjective*. *rare*. L17.
[from PRECISION *noun* after *incision*, *incisive*: see -IVE.]
†**1** That cuts off, separates, or distinguishes one thing from another. L17–E18.
2 Characterized by precision or exactitude. E19.

Preclassic /priːˈklasɪk/ *adjective*. M20.
[from PRE- 2 + CLASSIC.]
ARCHAEOLOGY. Of, pertaining to, or designating a period of Meso-American civilization that existed between about 1500 BC and AD 300. Also called ***Formative***.

pre-classical /priːˈklasɪk(ə)l/ *adjective*. L19.
[from PRE- 2 + CLASSICAL.]
Occurring in or characteristic of a period before one regarded as classical, esp. the classical age of Greek and Roman literature, or the period between baroque and classical music.

preclose /prɪˈkləʊz/ *verb trans*. *rare*. M16.
[from PRE- 1 + CLOSE *verb*.]
= FORECLOSE 6.

preclude /prɪˈkluːd/ *verb trans*. L15.
[Latin *praecludere*, from *prae* PRE- + *claudere* to shut.]
†**1** Close or bar (a passage, route, etc.) against any attempt to pass. L15–L18.
2 Shut out, exclude; prevent, frustrate; make impossible. E17.
3 Esp. of a situation or condition: prevent (a person) *from* an action or (*from*) *doing* something. M18.

> **2** G. GREENE Immature—an adjective which does not preclude a university professor here or there. P. NORMAN Dad said, 'No, Louis' in a clipped voice that precluded all further enquiries. A. S. BYATT The ward . . was so constituted that it precluded rest or sleep. **3** C. C. TRENCH Her intellectual limitations . . precluded her from lengthy discussions. *Air Force Magazine* The weather precluded us from seeing where they . . launch the Scuds.

■ **preclusion** *noun* (now *rare*) the action of precluding something; prevention by anticipatory measures: E17. **preclusive** *adjective* that tends to preclude or has the effect of precluding something; preventive (*of*): L17. **preclusively** *adverb* L17.

precoce /prɪˈkəʊs/ *adjective*. *rare*. M17.
[French *précoce* from Latin *praecoc-*, *praecox*: see PRECOCIOUS.]
†**1** Of plants: early flowering. M17–E18.
2 = PRECOCIOUS 2. L17.

precocene /prɪˈkəʊsiːn/ *noun*. L20.
[from PRECOC(IOUS + -ENE.]
BIOCHEMISTRY. Either of two plant hormones able to induce the premature metamorphosis of some insect larvae into (freq. sterile) adults.

precocial /prɪˈkəʊʃ(ə)l/ *adjective*. Also (earlier) **prae-**. L19.
[from mod. Latin *Praecoces*, a former division of birds, pl. of Latin *praecox*: see PRECOCIOUS, -IAL.]
ZOOLOGY. (Having young which are) able to move about and feed independently soon after hatching or birth; nidifugous. Cf. ALTRICIAL.

precocious /prɪˈkəʊʃəs/ *adjective*. M17.
[from Latin *praecoc-*, *praecox*, from *praecoquere* boil beforehand, ripen fully, from *prae* PRE- + *coquere* to cook: see -IOUS.]
1 BOTANY. Flowering or fruiting early; *spec.* bearing blossom before the leaves. M17.
2 a Of a person, esp. a child: prematurely developed in some faculty or proclivity. Often mildly *derog.* L17. ▸**b** Of, pertaining to, or indicative of premature development; (of a thing) of early development. L17.
3 ZOOLOGY. = PRECOCIAL. L19.

> **2a** R. CHURCH I was a precocious reader. J. I. M. STEWART My brother Ninian had been sexually precocious. **b** LD MACAULAY Untimely decrepitude was the penalty of precocious maturity. L. GRANT-ADAMSON His precocious talent as an artist.

■ **precociously** *adverb* M19. **precociousness** *noun* L17.

precocity /prɪˈkɒsɪti/ *noun*. M17.
[French *précocité*, from *précoce* PRECOCE: see -ITY.]
The quality of being precocious; early maturity, premature development; BOTANY early flowering or fruiting.

precog /ˈpriːkɒg/ *noun*. *colloq.* M20.
[Abbreviation.]
Precognition; a person having this.

precogitation /ˌpriːkɒdʒɪˈteɪʃ(ə)n/ *noun*. Long *rare*. L16.
[Late Latin *praecogitatio(n-)*, from *praecogitat-* ppl stem of *praecogitare*, from *prae* PRE- + *cogitare* COGITATE: see -ATION.]
Previous consideration or meditation.

precognise *verb* var. of PRECOGNIZE.

precognition /priːkɒgˈnɪʃ(ə)n/ *noun*. LME.
[Late Latin *praecognitio(n-)*, formed as PRE- + COGNITION.]
1 Antecedent cognition or knowledge; (supposed) foreknowledge, esp. as a form of extrasensory perception. LME.
2 SCOTS LAW. The preliminary examination of witnesses or other people concerned with a case in order to obtain a general picture of the available evidence; *esp.* such an examination carried out by a Procurator-fiscal in order to know whether there is ground for trial. Also, a statement so obtained from a witness before a trial. M17.

> **1** W. MARCH He must have had some precognition of his own end. V. BROME Jung was . . very preoccupied with precognition and the occult.

■ **preˈcognitive** *adjective* of the nature of, or giving, precognition E20.

precognize /ˈpriːkɒgnʌɪz/ *verb trans*. Also **-ise**. E17.
[from PRE- 1 + COGNIZE.]
Have foreknowledge of.

precognosce /priːkɒgˈnɒs/ *verb trans*. M17.
[from PRE- 1 + COGNOSCE.]
SCOTS LAW. Make a preliminary examination of (a witness etc.) as part of the process of precognition.

precoital /priːˈkəʊɪt(ə)l/ *adjective*. M20.
[from PRE- 2 + COITAL.]
Occurring or performed as a preliminary to sexual intercourse.
■ **precoitally** *adverb* L20.

preconceive /priːkənˈsiːv/ *verb trans.* **M16.**
[from PRE- 1 + CONCEIVE.]
Conceive or imagine beforehand; form (an idea about something) in anticipation of one's actual knowledge or experience. Freq. as ***preconceived*** *ppl adjective.*

N. HAWTHORNE The Coliseum was very much what I had preconceived it. R. G. COLLINGWOOD The result . . is preconceived or thought out before being arrived at. P. LARKIN We came to our work without any preconceived ideas.

preconception /priːkənˈsɛpʃ(ə)n/ *noun.* **E17.**
[from PRE- 1 + CONCEPTION.]
The action or result of preconceiving something; *esp.* a conception or opinion formed prior to actual knowledge or experience; a prepossession, a prejudice.

M. DIBDIN An outsider, someone free of any preconceptions. *What Mortgage* A million preconceptions of the perfect dream house.

preconceptional /priːkənˈsɛpʃ(ə)n(ə)l/ *adjective.* **E20.**
[from PRE- 2 + CONCEPTION + -AL¹.]
Occurring or existing before conception.

preconcert /priːkənˈsəːt/ *verb trans.* **M18.**
[from PRE- 1 + CONCERT *verb.*]
Concert or arrange beforehand. Freq. as ***preconcerted*** *ppl adjective.*

precondition /priːkənˈdɪʃ(ə)n/ *noun.* **E19.**
[from PRE- 1 + CONDITION *noun.*]
A prior condition; a condition required to be fulfilled beforehand; a preliminary stipulation, a pre-requisite.

H. KISSINGER An end of American military aid . . was an absolute precondition of settlement. J. BARNES Three preconditions for happiness—stupidity, selfishness and good health.

precondition /priːkənˈdɪʃ(ə)n/ *verb trans.* **E20.**
[from PRE- 1 + CONDITION *verb.*]
Bring into a desired or necessary condition beforehand.

preconize /ˈpriːkənʌɪz/ *verb trans.* Also **-ise. LME.**
[medieval Latin *praeconizare*, from Latin *praeco(n-)* public crier, herald: see -IZE.]
1 Proclaim or announce publicly; sing the praises of, extol. **LME.** ▸**b** Call on publicly, summon by name. **M19.**
2 ROMAN CATHOLIC CHURCH. Of the Pope: publicly approve the appointment of (a bishop). **L17.**
■ **preconiˈzation** *noun* **M17.**

preconscious /priːˈkɒnʃəs/ *adjective & noun.* **M19.**
[from PRE- 2 + CONSCIOUS.]
PSYCHOLOGY. ▶**A** *adjective.* Antecedent to consciousness or conscious action; *spec.* = FORECONSCIOUS *adjective.* **M19.**
▶**B** *noun.* = FORECONSCIOUS *noun.* **M20.**
■ **preconsciousness** *noun* the condition of being preconscious; the preconscious part of the mind: **M20.**

pre-contract /priːˈkɒntrakt/ *noun.* **LME.**
[from PRE- 1 + CONTRACT *noun*¹.]
A contract or agreement previously entered into, *esp.* one whose existence precludes the making of another similar contract.

W. STUBBS Edward being already bound by a pre-contract of marriage.

pre-contract /priːkənˈtrakt/ *verb.* Pa. pple **-contracted**, (*rare, poet.*) **-contract. M16.**
[from PRE- 1 + CONTRACT *verb.*]
1 *verb trans.* Engage in a previous contract, esp. of marriage; affiance or betroth beforehand (*to*). **M16.**
2 *verb trans. & intrans.* Enter into (an agreement) in advance. *rare.* **M17.**

precordia *noun* see PRAECORDIA.

precordial /priːˈkɔːdɪəl/ *adjective.* Also †**prae-. LME.**
[medieval Latin *praecordialis*, from *prae* PRE- + *cordialis* CORDIAL.]
1 MEDICINE. Situated in front of or about the heart; of or pertaining to the precordium. **LME.**
†**2** Exceedingly cordial; very hearty, warm, or sincere. **M16–M18.**

precordium /prɪˈkɔːdɪəm/ *noun.* **L19.**
[Sing. of PRAECORDIA.]
ANATOMY. The forepart of the thoracic region; the part of the body immediately over the heart.
¶ Superseding earlier pl. PRAECORDIA.

precure /*as verb* priːˈkjʊə, *as noun* ˈpriːkjʊə/ *verb & noun.* **M20.**
[from PRE- 1 + CURE *noun*¹, *verb.*]
▶**A** *verb intrans.* Of a synthetic resin: undergo premature curing, so as to impede subsequent mechanical processing. **M20.**
▶**B** *noun.* Premature curing. **M20.**

precurrent /prɪˈkʌr(ə)nt/ *adjective. rare.* **E17.**
[Latin *praecurrent-* pres. ppl stem of *praecurrere*: see PRECURSOR, -ENT.]
Occurring beforehand; precursory.

†**precurse** *noun. rare* (Shakes.). Only in **E17.**
[Latin *praecursus*, formed as next.]
Forerunning, heralding.

precurse /prɪˈkəːs/ *verb trans. rare.* **M19.**
[Latin *praecurs-* ppl stem of *praecurrere*: see PRECURSOR.]
Precede, occur before; herald, portend.

precursive /prɪˈkəːsɪv/ *adjective.* **E19.**
[from next + -IVE.]
= PRECURSORY *adjective.*

precursor /prɪˈkəːsə/ *noun & adjective.* **LME.**
[Latin *praecursor*, from *praecurs-* pa. ppl stem of *praecurrere* run before, precede, from *prae* PRE- + *currere* run: see -OR.]
▶**A** *noun.* **1** A person who or thing which precedes another as a forerunner or presage; a person who or thing which heralds the approach of someone or something else, a harbinger. **LME.**
2 A predecessor. **L18.**
3 a A substance, esp. a naturally occurring one, from which another is formed by metabolism, decay, or other (esp. chemical) process. **L19.** ▸**b** BIOLOGY. A cell which precedes another in a process of differentiation. **E20.**

1 E. H. ERIKSON Infantile fears . . are the precursors of many . . anxieties entertained by adults A. N. WILSON There is no evidence that Jesus, or his precursor John, taught pacifism as such. **2** M. ARNOLD Cowper . . by his genuine love of nature was a precursor of Wordsworth A. C. CLARKE A score of ships . . each with more advanced technology than its precursor. **3a** *Scientific American* Ozone and its precursor, atomic oxygen, are destroyed by catalytic reactions.

▶**B** *attrib.* or as *adjective.* That is a precursor. **M19.**
■ **precursorship** *noun* (*a*) the status or function of a precursor; (*b*) antecedence, prior occurrence: **M19.**

precursory /prɪˈkəːs(ə)ri/ *adjective & noun.* **L16.**
[Latin *praecursorius*, from *praecurs-*: see prec., -ORY².]
▶**A** *adjective.* Having the character of a precursor; preceding, esp. as the harbinger or presage of something to follow; preliminary, introductory. (Foll. by *of.*) **L16.**

Nature The precursory behaviour of a volcano as it builds towards an eruption.

▶**B** *noun.* A precursory fact or condition; an antecedent. *rare.* **M17.**

predacious /prɪˈdeɪʃəs/ *adjective.* Also **-eous. E18.**
[from Latin *praeda* booty, plunder + -ACIOUS.]
1 Of an animal: that naturally preys on other animals, that subsists by the capture of living prey; predatory, raptorial. Also, (of a fungal etc. parasite) that actually kills its host. **E18.**
2 Of or pertaining to predatory animals. **E19.**
■ **predaciousness** *noun* **E20. predacity** /-ˈdas-/ *noun* **M19.**

predamn /priːˈdam/ *verb trans.* Now *rare.* **E17.**
[from PRE- 1 + DAMN *verb.*]
Damn or condemn beforehand.
■ **predamˈnation** *noun* **E17.**

predate /priːˈdeɪt/ *verb*¹ *trans.* **M19.**
[from PRE- 1 + DATE *verb.*]
1 Affix or assign a date to (an event etc.) earlier than the actual or currently accepted one; = ANTEDATE *verb* 1, 4. **M19.**
2 Precede in date, belong to an earlier date than; = ANTEDATE *verb* 6. **L19.**

predate /prɪˈdeɪt/ *verb*² *intrans. & trans.* **L20.**
[Back-form. from PREDATOR, PREDATION.]
Act as a predator (of); catch and eat (prey).

predation /prɪˈdeɪʃ(ə)n/ *noun.* **L15.**
[Latin *praedatio(n-)*, from *praedat-*: see PREDATORY, -ATION.]
1 The action of plundering or pillaging; depredation; rapacious or exploitative behaviour. **L15.**
2 The natural preying of one animal on others; the behaviour of a predator. **M20.**

2 *Science* Predation of sea urchins by sea otters can initiate a change in kelp bed communities.

predator /ˈprɛdətə/ *noun.* **E20.**
[Latin *praedator* plunderer, from *praedat-*: see PREDATORY, -OR.]
1 An animal that naturally preys on others; an animal that habitually catches and eats prey. **E20.**
2 A person whose behaviour is rapacious or exploitative. **M20.**
3 COMMERCE. A company, director, etc., that seeks to take over another company or is expected to do so. **M20.**

1 A. STORR Isolated animals are more likely to be attacked by predators. **3** *Financial Weekly* O' Reilly . . is no longer interested in buying the ailing company and . . few other predators are likely to emerge.

predatory /ˈprɛdət(ə)ri/ *adjective.* **L16.**
[Latin *praedatorius*, from *praedator* plunderer, from *praedat-*, *praedari* seize as plunder, pillage, from *praeda* booty, plunder: see -ORY².]
1 Of, pertaining to, or involving predation (PREDATION 1). **L16.**
†**2** Destructive, wasteful, deleterious. **E17–E18.**
3 Of an animal: that preys on other animals, predacious. Also, of or concerned with predation. (PREDATION 2). **M17.**
4 Given to or living by plunder or marauding. Now usu. (often coloured by sense 3), ruthlessly acquisitive at the expense of others, rapacious, exploitative; unfairly competitive or aggressive in business etc. **L18.**

1 GIBBON Revenge might justify his praedatory excursions by sea and land. G. F. MACLEAR Predatory instincts. N. COWARD She . . went into the bedroom with a predatory look in her eye. **predatory pricing** the setting of uneconomically low prices in order to put smaller competitors out of business. **4** A. FRASER Care was taken to present the invaders as alien and predatory. ROSEMARY MANNING She could be predatory She expected people to . . advance her.

■ **predatorily** *adverb* **M19. predatoriness** *noun* **L19.**

predecease /priːdɪˈsiːs/ *verb & noun.* **L16.**
[from PRE- 1 + DECEASE *verb, noun.*]
▶**A** *verb.* **1** *verb trans.* Die earlier than (another person); *occas.* die before (an event). **L16.**
2 *verb intrans.* Die first or before another person. *rare.* **L18.**
▶**B** *noun.* The death of one person before another (specified or implied). **L18.**

predecessor /ˈpriːdɪsɛsə/ *noun.* **LME.**
[Old & mod. French *prédécesseur* from late Latin *praedecessor*, from Latin *prae* PRE- + *decessor* retiring officer, from *decedere* depart: see -OR.]
1 A former holder of a position or office with respect to a later holder. **LME.** ▸**b** A thing to which another has succeeded. **M18.**
2 An ancestor; a forefather. Now *rare.* **LME.**
†**3** A person who goes before as a leader or guide. **LME–M17.**

1 G. L. CRAIK Eadmer's immediate predecessor in the see of St. Andrews was Turgot. A. N. WILSON Nicholas II . . travelled more than any of his predecessors. **b** D. A. THOMAS The ship is . . given a list of predecessors which have borne the same name.

■ **predeˈcession** *noun* (*rare*) the action or fact of being a predecessor **M17.**

predefine /priːdɪˈfʌɪn/ *verb trans.* **M16.**
[from PRE- 1 + DEFINE.]
Define, limit, or settle previously; predetermine. Freq. as ***predefined*** *ppl adjective.*

predella /prɪˈdɛlə/ *noun.* **M19.**
[Italian = stool.]
1 A step or platform on which an altar is placed, an altar-step; a painting or sculpture on the vertical face of this. **M19.**
2 A raised shelf at the back of an altar (= GRADINE 2); a painting or sculpture on the front of this, forming an appendage to an altarpiece above; any painting that is subsidiary to another painting. **M19.**

predesignate /priːˈdɛzɪgneɪt/ *verb trans. rare.* **E19.**
[from PRE- 1 + DESIGNATE *verb.*]
1 Designate or specify beforehand. **E19.**
2 LOGIC. Prefix a sign of quantity to. **M19.**
■ **predesigˈnation** *noun* (*a*) previous designation or specification; (*b*) LOGIC a prefixed sign of quantity: **M17.**

predestinarian /prɪˌdɛstɪˈnɛːrɪən/ *noun & adjective.* **M17.**
[from PREDESTINATION or PREDESTINY + -ARIAN.]
▶**A** *noun.* A person who believes in the doctrine of predestination; a fatalist. **M17.**
▶**B** *adjective.* Of or pertaining to predestination; holding or maintaining the doctrine of predestination. **M17.**
■ **predestinarianism** *noun* **E18.**

predestinate /priːˈdɛstɪnət/ *adjective & noun.* **LME.**
[ecclesiastical Latin *praedestinatus* pa. pple of *praedestinare*: see next, -ATE².]
▶**A** *adjective.* **1** THEOLOGY. Foreordained by divine purpose or decree (*to* a specified fate, *to do*); *spec.* predestined for salvation or eternal life. **LME.**
2 *gen.* Predestined, fated. **E16.**
▶**B** *noun.* THEOLOGY. A person predestined for eternal life; one of God's elect. **E16.**
■ **predestinately** *adverb* by predestination **L16.**

predestinate /priːˈdɛstɪneɪt/ *verb trans.* Pa. pple **-ated**, †**-ate. LME.**
[ecclesiastical Latin *praedestinat-* pa. ppl stem of *praedestinare*, from *prae* PRE- + *destinare* make fast or firm, establish: see DESTINE, -ATE³.]
1 THEOLOGY. Of God: preordain by divine decree or purpose (*to* a particular fate, *to do*); *spec.* predestine for salvation or eternal life. **LME.**
2 *gen.* Predestine. **L16.**
■ **predestinator** *noun* a predestinarian **L16.**

predestination /priːˌdɛstɪˈneɪʃ(ə)n/ *noun.* **ME.**
[ecclesiastical Latin *praedestinatio(n-)*, from *praedestinat-*: see prec., -ATION.]
1 THEOLOGY. (Belief in, a doctrine teaching) the action by which God is held to have immutably determined all (or

some particular) events by an eternal decree or purpose, *spec.* the preordained salvation of God's elect. ME.
2 *gen.* Predetermination; fate, destiny. E16.

📖 **1** W. H. FREMANTLE He reduces predestination to God's foreknowledge of human determination. J. HELLER Major's father had a Calvinist's faith in predestination and could perceive how everyone's misfortunes . . were expressions of God's will.

■ **predestinationism** *noun* belief in predestination; the doctrine of predestination: E20.

predestine /priːˈdɛstɪn/ *verb trans.* LME.
[Old & mod. French *prédestiner* or ecclesiastical Latin *praedestinare*: see PREDESTINATE *verb*.]
Usu. in *pass.* **1** THEOLOGY. = PREDESTINATE *verb* 1. LME.
2 Determine or settle beforehand; ordain as if by fate or destiny; fate, doom. M17.

📖 **1** E. LONGFORD Calvinists believing in predestined salvation by faith. *absol.*: F. W. FARRAR God predestines; man is free. How this is we cannot say. **2** C. DARWIN The white man who seems predestined to inherit the country. T. T. LYNCH The bird of paradise Predestined for the sunniest skies.

predestiny /priːˈdɛstɪni/ *noun. rare.* LME.
[from PRE- 1 + DESTINY *noun*.]
Preappointed destiny or fate; predestination.

predeterminate /priːdɪˈtəːmɪnət/ *adjective.* M17.
[Late Latin *praedeterminatus* pa. pple of *praedeterminare* PREDETERMINE: see -ATE².]
Predetermined.

predetermination /ˌpriːdɪtəːmɪˈneɪʃ(ə)n/ *noun.* M17.
[medieval Latin *praedeterminatio(n-)*, from late Latin *praedeterminat-* pa. ppl stem of *praedeterminare*: see next, -ATION.]
1 The action of settling or ordaining beforehand what is to take place; the fact of being so settled; predestination, fate. M17.
2 A prior decision; a decision given beforehand or in advance. M17.
3 A previous mental determination or intention. L18.

📖 **3** CARLYLE In spite of her rigorous predeterminations, some kindness for him is already gliding in.

■ **predeterminative** *adjective (rare)* (**a**) having the quality of predetermining; (**b**) GRAMMAR having the quality of a predeterminer: L17.

predetermine /priːdɪˈtəːmɪn/ *verb.* E17.
[Late Latin *praedeterminare*, from *prae* PRE- + Latin *determinare* DETERMINE.]
1 *verb trans.* Settle, decide, ordain, or decree beforehand; predestine. Usu. in *pass.* E17.
2 *verb trans.* Give an antecedent direction or tendency to; impel beforehand (*to*). Now *rare.* M17.
3 *verb intrans.* & *trans.* (in *pass.*). Determine or resolve beforehand or previously (*to do*). M18.

📖 **1** F. MYERS The Gospel . . came to pass as God had predetermined. W. LIPPMANN The doctrine that all human rights and virtues are biologically predetermined. *Independent* ABC hopes . . to be able to predetermine the sex of embryos. **2** H. T. BUCKLE Predetermining the nation to habits of loyalty. **3** L. STERNE I was predetermined not to give him a single sous. LYTTON He had almost predetermined to assent to his brother's prayer.

■ **predeterminable** *adjective* able to be predetermined M19.

predeterminer /priːdɪˈtəːmɪnə/ *noun.* L17.
[In sense 1 from prec. + -ER¹; in sense 2 from PRE- 1 + DETERMINER *noun*².]
†**1** A believer in predetermination. *rare.* Only in L17.
2 GRAMMAR. Any of a class of limiting expressions that precede the determiner (as *all, both, half*, etc.). M20.

prediabetic /ˌpriːdʌɪəˈbɛtɪk/ *adjective & noun.* E20.
[from PRE- 2 + DIABETIC.]
MEDICINE. ▶**A** *adjective.* Of, pertaining to, or designating a person who appears likely to develop diabetes mellitus but does not exhibit its full symptoms. E20.
▶**B** *noun.* A prediabetic person. L20.
■ **prediabetes** /-ˈbiːtiːz/ *noun* the prediabetic state M20.

predial /ˈpriːdɪəl/ *adjective & noun.* Also **praedial**. LME.
[medieval Latin *praedialis*, from Latin *praedium* farm, estate: see -AL¹.]
▶**A** *adjective.* **1** Consisting of, pertaining to, or derived from farmland or its occupation; rural, agrarian. LME.
2 Of (the labour etc. of) a serf or tenant: attached to a farm or to the land. L17.

📖 **1** *Blackwood's Magazine* To repress the predial or rural disorders of Ireland. *Caribbean Quarterly* 'Bitter Bessie' . . is sometimes planted round the edges of cultivations to . . discourage praedial thieves. **predial tithe**: derived from the produce of the soil. **2 predial servitude** SCOTS LAW a servitude constituted over one piece of land in favour of the owner of another, e.g. a right of way through another's property.

▶**B** *noun.* Orig., a predial tithe. Later, a predial serf or bondman. M16.
■ **prediˈality** *noun* the state of being predial L19.

predicable /ˈprɛdɪkəb(ə)l/ *noun & adjective.* M16.
[medieval Latin *praedicabilis* predicable (in classical Latin = praiseworthy), from Latin *praedicare*: see PREDICATE *verb*, -ABLE.]
▶**A** *noun.* That which may be predicated; *spec.* in Aristotelian logic, each of the five (orig. four) classes of predicate (genus, species, difference, property, accident) to which every predicated thing may be referred. M16.
▶**B** *adjective.* Able to be predicated or affirmed. L16.

📖 CARLYLE A people of whom great good is predicable.

■ **predicaˈbility** *noun* L18.

predicament /prɪˈdɪkəm(ə)nt/ *noun.* LME.
[Late Latin *praedicamentum* (translation of Greek *katēgoria* CATEGORY), from Latin *praedicare*: see PREDICATE *verb*, -MENT.]
1 A thing which is predicated or asserted; *spec.* in LOGIC, each of the ten categories of Aristotle (see CATEGORY 1). LME.
2 A class, a category. M16.
3 A state of being, a condition, a situation. Now *spec.* an unpleasant, difficult, or embarrassing situation. L16.

📖 **2** HENRY FIELDING Irish ladies of strict virtue, and many Northern lasses of the same predicament. **3** A. HOPKINS An author who rescues his hero from one predicament, only to pitch him into another.

■ **predicaˈmental** *adjective* E17. **predicaˈmentally** *adverb* E17.

predicant /ˈprɛdɪk(ə)nt/ *noun & adjective.* L16.
[Latin *praedicant-* pres. ppl stem of *praedicare*, in ecclesiastical Latin = preach: see PREDICATE *verb*, -ANT¹.]
▶**A** *noun.* **1** *Hist.* A preacher; *spec.* a member of a predicant religious order. L16.
2 See PREDIKANT.
▶**B** *adjective. Hist.* Given to or characterized by preaching; *spec.* (of a religious order, esp. the Dominicans or Black Friars) engaged in preaching. E17.

predicate /ˈprɛdɪkət/ *noun.* Formerly also in Latin form †**-atum**. LME.
[Late Latin *praedicatum* (translation of Greek *katēgoreuomenon*) neut. of *praedicatus* pa. pple of *praedicare*: see next, -ATE¹.]
1 LOGIC. What is affirmed or denied of the subject of a proposition by means of the copula (e.g. *my father* in *this man is my father*). LME. ▸**b** A quality, an attribute. *rare.* L15.
2 GRAMMAR. The part of a sentence or clause containing what is said about a subject, including the logical copula (e.g. *went home* in *John went home yesterday*), but sometimes excluding any adjunct (*yesterday* in this example). M17.
▸**b** MATH. & LOGIC. An assertion or relation in the absence of any specified term or terms (e.g. *is greater than*); a propositional function. M20.
3 A personal appellation or title that asserts something. L19.
4 [German *Prädikat*.] In a German or other foreign university: the judgement pronounced upon a candidate's work in an examination; the class obtained by a candidate. L19.

📖 **2** W. V. QUINE 'Is true' and 'is false' . . are predicates by means of which we speak *about* statements.

Comb.: **predicate calculus** the branch of symbolic logic that deals with propositions containing arguments and quantifiers; also called ***functional calculus***.

predicate /ˈprɛdɪkeɪt/ *verb.* M16.
[Latin *praedicat-* pa. ppl stem of *praedicare* declare, (in medieval Latin) predicate, from *prae* PRE- + *dicare* make known, rel. to *dicere* say: see -ATE³.]
▶**I 1 a** *verb trans.* Declare or affirm as true or existent; postulate, assume. Also (now *rare* or *obsolete*) preach; extol, commend. M16. ▸**b** *verb intrans.* Make an assertion. E19.
2 *verb trans.* **a** LOGIC. Assert (something) about the subject of a proposition; make (a term) the predicate in a proposition. L16. ▸**b** Affirm as a quality or attribute *of* something. E17.
3 *verb trans.* Foll. by *on*: affirm or postulate on the basis of; base or found on. Usu. in *pass.* Orig. *US.* M18.

📖 **1** *Blackwood's Magazine* Composing discourses, which . . might not have been unprofitably predicated from the pulpit. *Nature* The Pleistocene colonisation of Tasmania has long been predicated. F. WELDON Who is there to punish us? Unless . . we predicate some natural law of male dominance. **b** G. A. SALA It is perilous to predicate dogmatically as to the locality. **2a** F. BOWEN Whatever is predicated . . universally of any Class . . may also be predicated of any part of that Class. **b** E. WAUGH Humour and compassion are the qualities . . predicated of him. **3** L. APPIGNANESI A set of values which were predicated on a rejection of all previous assumptions. C. BRAYFIELD The other great families . . did not choose lives predicated totally on loyalty to the ruling house.

▶**II 4** *verb trans.* [By confusion.] Predict. E17.

📖 **4** W. H. DIXON That shrewd Venetian envoy heard enough to predicate the rising of domestic storms.

predication /prɛdɪˈkeɪʃ(ə)n/ *noun.* ME.
[Old & mod. French *prédication* or Latin *praedicatio(n-)*, formed as prec.: see -ATION.]
1 Preaching; a sermon, an oration. Now *rare.* ME.
2 The action or an act of predicating something; an assertion; GRAMMAR & LOGIC the assertion of something about a subject, the constructing of a predicate. L15.
†**3** The action of extolling or commending something. E16–M17.
2 verb of incomplete predication GRAMMAR a verb introducing a word, phrase, or clause identifying, defining, or describing the subject (as English *be, seem*), a copular verb.
■ **predicational** *adjective* L19.

predicative /prɪˈdɪkətɪv/ *adjective & noun.* M19.
[Latin *praedicativus*, formed as PREDICATE *verb*: see -IVE.]
▶**A** *adjective.* **1** Having the quality of predicating something; GRAMMAR (of an adjective or noun) forming a predicate, contained in the predicate (opp. ***attributive***). M19.
2 LOGIC. Of a function: of order one greater than that of its argument of greatest order. E20.

📖 **1** *English Studies* Intransitive verbs combined with a predicative 'apposition' (e.g. *he died young, he died an admiral*).

▶**B** *noun.* GRAMMAR. A word used predicatively. E20.
■ **predicatival** /prɛˌdɪkəˈtʌɪv(ə)l/ *adjective* of or forming a predicate L19. **predicatively** *adverb* as a predicate L19. **predicaˈtivity** *noun* the quality of being predicative M20.

predicator /ˈprɛdɪkeɪtə/ *noun.* ME.
[Old French *predicatour* (mod. *prédicateur*) or Latin *praedicator*, formed as PREDICATE *verb*: see -OR.]
1 A preacher; *spec.* a preaching friar. Now *rare.* ME.
2 GRAMMAR. The part of a clause or sentence (usu. a verb) that introduces a predicate. L19.
■ **predicatory** /ˈprɛdɪkət(ə)ri, -keɪt(ə)ri/ *adjective* of or pertaining to a preacher or preaching E17.

†**predicatum** *noun* see PREDICATE *noun*.

†**predict** *noun. rare* (Shakes.). Only in L16.
[Latin *praedictum*: cf. French *prédit* (obsolete form *predict*.]
A prediction.

predict /prɪˈdɪkt/ *verb.* M16.
[Latin *praedict-* pa. ppl stem of *praedicere*, from *prae* PRE- + *dicere* say.]
†**1** *verb trans.* Mention previously in speech or writing. Only as ***predicted*** *ppl adjective rare.* M–L16.
2 *verb trans.* Announce as an event that will happen in the future; say *that* (a thing) will happen; foretell. E17. ▸**b** Of a theory, observation, etc.: have as a deducible consequence; imply. M20.
3 *verb intrans.* Utter prediction; prophesy. M17.
4 *verb trans.* MILITARY. Direct fire at (a person etc) with the aid of a predictor. M20.

📖 **2** W. MARCH She had predicted the direst consequences if her son persisted in 'this mad folly'. A. BROOKNER His tutors predicted that he would be lucky to get a third. **b** *Nature* Sensitivity to the taste of PTC predicts sensitivity to caffeine. **3** J. CARLYLE No one can predict as to the length of her life.

predictable /prɪˈdɪktəb(ə)l/ *adjective.* M19.
[from PREDICT *verb* + -ABLE.]
Able to be predicted. Also (of a person), acting in a way that is easy to predict.

📖 C. FREEMAN The weather was no more predictable than the events of a person's life. C. PRIEST Nothing I could do would ever surprise her, because . . I was completely predictable.

■ **predictaˈbility** *noun* M19. **predictably** *adverb* E20.

prediction /prɪˈdɪkʃ(ə)n/ *noun.* M16.
[Latin *praedictio(n-)*, formed as prec.: see -ION. Cf. French *prédiction*.]
1 The action of predicting future events; an instance of this, a forecast, a prophecy. M16.
†**2** A portent. *rare* (Shakes.). Only in E17.

📖 **1** M. SEYMOUR Garland's prediction was borne out when the novel was hailed with glowing reviews.

■ **predictionism** *noun* belief in prediction or prophecy E20.

predictive /prɪˈdɪktɪv/ *adjective.* M17.
[Late Latin *praedictivus*, from *praedicere*: see PREDICT *verb*, -IVE.]
Having the character or quality of predicting the future; indicative. (Foll. by *of*.)

📖 *British Medical Journal* He had all the features predictive of a poor clinical outcome.

■ **predictively** *adverb* M19. **predictiveness** *noun* E20. **predicˈtivity** *noun* predictive power, predictiveness M20.

predictor /prɪˈdɪktə/ *noun.* M17.
[medieval Latin, formed as PREDICT *verb*: see -OR.]
1 A person who or thing which predicts. M17. ▸**b** STATISTICS. A variable whose value can be used in estimation. Also ***predictor variable***. M20.
2 MILITARY. An apparatus for automatically providing tracking information for an anti-aircraft gun from telescopic or radar observations. M20.
■ **predictory** *adjective* of or pertaining to a predictor; predictive: M17.

predigest /priːdɪˈdʒɛst, -dʌɪ-/ *verb trans.* M17.
[from PRE- 1 + DIGEST *verb*.]
1 Digest beforehand; *spec.* treat (food) by a process similar to digestion, in order to make more digestible when subsequently eaten. M17.
2 *fig.* Make (an author, reading matter) easier to read or understand. E20.

For other words beginning with *pre-* see the entry for **pre-**

■ **predigestion** *noun* †(*a*) overhasty digestion; (*b*) artificial treatment of food to make it more digestible: **E17.**

predikant /prɛdɪˈkant/ *noun.* Also **-cant. E19.**
[Dutch, formed as PREDICANT.]
A minister of the Dutch Reformed Church or one of its sister churches, esp. in South Africa.

predilect /priːdɪˈlɛkt/ *adjective. rare.* **LME.**
[medieval Latin *praedilectus* pa. pple of *praediligere*: see next.]
Chosen or favoured in preference to others.
■ Also **predilected** *adjective* (*rare*) **L18.**

predilection /priːdɪˈlɛkʃ(ə)n/ *noun.* **M18.**
[French *prédilection*, repr. noun of action from medieval Latin *praedilect-* pa. ppl stem of *praediligere* choose or love before others, from *prae* PRE- + *diligere*: see DILIGENT, -ION.]
A mental preference or partiality; a favourable predisposition. Usu. foll. by *for.*

J. R. ACKERLEY I had not concealed from her my homosexual predilections. M. HUNTER His predilection for the bottle that was eventually to make him an alcoholic.

predisponent /priːdɪˈspəʊnənt/ *adjective & noun.* **M17.**
[from PRE- 1 + DISPONENT.]
▶ **A** *adjective.* Predisposing. Now *rare.* **M17.**
▶ **B** *noun.* A predisposing influence or cause. **L18.**

predispose /priːdɪˈspəʊz/ *verb.* **M17.**
[from PRE- 1 + DISPOSE *verb.*]
1 a *verb trans.* Make (a person etc.) liable or susceptible (*to*) beforehand; make inclined (*to do*) beforehand. **M17.** ▸**b** *verb intrans.* Make a person susceptible *to.* **E19.**
2 Dispose of or give away beforehand. **M17.**

1a J. S. BLACKIE The majority of his judges . . came predisposed to condemn him. A. STORR Early bereavement . . acts as a trigger for depression in those who are already genetically predisposed. **b** *Lancet* This alteration . . would predispose to gallstones.

■ **predispoˈsition** *noun* (*a*) the condition of being predisposed (*to* a thing, *to do*); also, a tendency in a person to react in a certain way; (*b*) *spec.* a physical condition which makes a person susceptible to a disease: **E17.**

Predmost /ˈprɛdməʊst/ *noun.* Also **Předmost-** /ˈpʒɛd-/. **E20.**
[See below.]
ARCHAEOLOGY. Used **attrib.** to designate (remains of) a race of upper palaeolithic man known from discoveries at Predmost (Předmostí), Moravia, and from other sites in central Europe and round the eastern Mediterranean.

prednisolone /prɛdˈnɪsələʊn/ *noun.* **M20.**
[from next with inserted -OL.]
PHARMACOLOGY. A synthetic steroid having similar properties and uses to prednisone, of which it is a reduced derivative.

prednisone /ˈprɛdnɪsəʊn/ *noun.* **M20.**
[Prob. arbitrarily from PRE(GNANE + D(IE)N(E + CORT)ISONE.]
PHARMACOLOGY. A synthetic steroid, resembling cortisone but possessing greater glucocorticoid activity, which is used as an anti-inflammatory agent and to depress immune responses, esp. in the treatment of autoimmune diseases.

predoctoral /priːˈdɒkt(ə)r(ə)l/ *adjective.* **L20.**
[from PRE- + DOCTORAL.]
Pertaining to work or a course that leads to the award of a doctorate; (of a person) engaged in such work.

predominant /prɪˈdɒmɪnənt/ *adjective & noun.* **M16.**
[Old & mod. French *prédominant* or medieval Latin *predominant-* pres. ppl stem of *predominari*: see PREDOMINATE *verb.*]
▶ **A** *adjective.* **1** Orig. ASTROLOGY & PHYSIOLOGY. Having supremacy or ascendancy over others; predominating. **M16.**
2 Constituting the main or strongest element; prevailing. **E17.**
3 Rising high *over.* **L18.**

1 JAS. MILL After the power of the English became predominant. **2** R. NIEBUHR The maxim that egoism is . . the predominant inclination of human nature. E. BOWEN Generations of odours . . had been absorbed into the limewashed walls, leaving . . lamp oil freshly predominant. **3** T. HOLCROFT The Cupola rises predominant over every object.

▶ **B** *noun.* **1** A predominating person, influence, or power; a predominating quality or feature. **M16.**
†**2** A besetting sin. **M–L17.**
■ **predominance** *noun* **L16.** **predominancy** *noun* (now *rare*) **L16.** **predominantly** *adverb* in a predominant manner or degree; preponderatingly, chiefly: **L17.**

predominate /prɪˈdɒmɪnət/ *adjective.* Now *rare.* **L16.**
[App. a mistaken form for PREDOMINANT, prob. after such adjectives as *moderate, temperate.*]
Predominant, preponderating.
■ **predominately** *adverb* **L16.**

predominate /prɪˈdɒmɪneɪt/ *verb.* **L16.**
[medieval Latin *predominat-* pa.ppl stem of *predominari*, formed as PRE- + DOMINATE.]
1 *verb intrans.* Orig. ASTROLOGY. Have or exert controlling power (*over*); be superior. **L16.**
2 *verb intrans.* Be the stronger or leading element; preponderate. (Foll. by *over.*) **L16.**
3 *verb trans.* Dominate, prevail over, control. Now *rare.* **E17.**
4 *verb intrans.* Rise high or tower *over.* **E19.**

1 H. H. MILMAN The Frenchman soon began to predominate over the Pontiff. **2** E. BOWEN Pasture predominates; there are lesser proportions of plough, moor and wood land. C. ISHERWOOD The dark heads far predominating over the blond. **3** CONAN DOYLE In his eyes she eclipses and predominates the whole of her sex. **4** GEO. ELIOT The tall gables and elms of the rectory predominate over the tiny white-washed church.

■ **predominating** *ppl adjective* that predominates; *esp.* preponderating, predominant: **L16.** **predominatingly** *adverb* **L19.**

†**predomination** *noun.* **L16–L18.**
[from PREDOMINATE *verb* + -ATION.]
Chiefly ASTROLOGY & PHYSIOLOGY. Predominance, ascendancy.

predy /ˈprɛdi/ *adjective & verb.* Long *arch.* **E17.**
[Origin uncertain: perh. rel. to READY *adjective.*]
NAUTICAL. ▶**A** *adjective.* Prepared for action, ready. **E17.**
▶†**B** *verb trans.* Make (a ship etc.) ready. **E17–E18.**

pree /priː/ *verb trans. Scot. & north.* Pa. t. & pple **preed. L17.**
[Abbreviation of *preve* obsolete var. of PROVE *verb.*]
Try what (a thing) is like, esp. by tasting.

pre-eclampsia /priːɪˈklam(p)sɪə/ *noun.* **E20.**
[from PRE- 2 + ECLAMPSIA.]
MEDICINE. A disorder of pregnancy characterized by high blood pressure, albuminuria, and oedema. Cf. TOXAEMIA 2.
■ **pre-eclamptic** *adjective* **L19.**

pre-edit /priːˈɛdɪt/ *verb trans.* **M20.**
[from PRE- 1 + EDIT *verb.*]
Edit or sort as a preliminary to later editing; prepare for computer processing by the addition or alteration of material.
■ **pre-editor** *noun* a person, apparatus, or program that performs pre-editing **M20.**

pre-elect /priːɪˈlɛkt/ *adjective.* Now *rare.* **L15.**
[medieval Latin *praeelectus* pa. pple of *praeeligere* choose beforehand, or from PRE- 1 + ELECT *adjective.*]
Chosen beforehand or before others; chosen in preference to others.

pre-elect /priːɪˈlɛkt/ *verb trans.* **L16.**
[from PRE- 1 + ELECT *verb.*]
Elect or choose beforehand; *spec.* (at Oxford and Cambridge Universities) elect as head of a college or as fellow by anticipation.

pre-election /priːɪˈlɛkʃ(ə)n/ *noun & adjective.* **L16.**
[from PRE- 1, 2 + ELECTION.]
▶ **A** *noun.* †**1** Choice of one person or thing in preference to others. **L16–E17.**
2 Previous choice; an anticipatory election. **E17.**
▶ **B** *adjective.* Occurring or given before a parliamentary etc. election. **L19.**

Guardian The final pre-election opinion poll.

pre-embryo /priːˈɛmbrɪəʊ/ *noun.* Pl. **-os. L19.**
[from PRE- 2 + EMBRYO.]
BIOLOGY & MEDICINE. A body which develops into an embryo. Now *spec.* a fertilized human egg up to fourteen days after fertilization.
■ ˌ**pre-embryˈonic** *adjective* **L19.**

preemie /ˈpriːmi/ *noun. N. Amer. slang.* **E20.**
[from PREM(ATURE *adjective & noun* + -IE.]
A baby born prematurely.

pre-eminent /priːˈɛmɪnənt/ *adjective.* **LME.**
[Latin *praeeminent-* pres. ppl stem of *praeeminere* tower above the rest, excel, from *prae* PRE- + *eminere*: see EMINENT.]
Excelling others in a quality or in rank, authority, etc.; outstandingly superior.

J. LUBBOCK As an object of worship . . the serpent is pre-eminent among animals.

■ **pre-eminence** *noun* (*a*) outstanding excellence; superiority; †(*b*) a quality present in a pre-eminent degree; a distinguishing privilege: **ME.** **pre-eminency** *noun* (now *rare*) = PRE-EMINENCE **M16.** **pre-eminently** *adverb* in the highest degree, supremely: **M18.**

pre-empt /priːˈɛm(p)t/ *noun.* **L19.**
[formed as next.]
1 A pre-emptive right. *Austral. colloq.* **L19.**
2 BRIDGE. A pre-emptive bid. **M20.**

pre-empt /priːˈɛm(p)t/ *verb.* Orig. *US.* **M19.**
[Back-form. from next.]
1 *verb trans.* Obtain by pre-emption; *US* occupy (public land) so as to establish a pre-emptive title. **M19.** ▸**b** Acquire or appropriate in advance of another. **M19.**
2 BRIDGE. **a** *verb intrans.* Make a pre-emptive bid. **E20.** ▸**b** *verb trans.* Thwart (a player) by making a pre-emptive bid. **M20.**
3 *verb trans.* Prevent (an occurrence) or stop (a person) by anticipatory action; forestall, preclude. Also, override. **M20.**

1b BETTY SMITH They pre-empted a whole front pew by laying Laurie full length on the seat. J. K. GALBRAITH A large proportion of the federal revenues are pre-empted by defence. **3** A. HALL He would kill me . . unless I could pre-empt him. B. TRAPIDO She got pregnant immediately to pre-empt any attempt . . to tear her away.

■ **pre-emptible** *adjective* able to be pre-empted **L19.**

pre-emption /priːˈɛm(p)ʃ(ə)n/ *noun.* **E17.**
[medieval Latin *praeemptio(n-)*, from *praeempt-* pa. ppl stem of *praeemere*, from *prae* PRE- + *emere* buy: see -ION.]
1 The purchase by one person or party before an opportunity is offered to others; the right to make such purchase; *Hist.* the prerogative of the monarch to buy household provisions in preference to other people and at special rates. **E17.** ▸**b** N. AMER. & AUSTRALIAN HISTORY. The preferential purchase, or right of purchase, of public land by an occupant, on condition of his or her improving it; a piece of land so obtained **M18.** ▸**c** INTERNATIONAL LAW. The right of a belligerent to seize goods of neutrals which are considered doubtfully or conditionally contraband. **M19.**
2 BRIDGE. The action of making a pre-emptive bid. **M20.**
3 The action or an act of setting aside or overriding something. **L20.**
4 MILITARY. The action or strategy of making a pre-emptive attack. **L20.**

1 N. HAWTHORNE The papal government . . has the right of pre-emption whenever any relics of ancient art are discovered.

■ **pre-emptioner** *noun* a person with a prior right to buy certain public land **M19.**

pre-emptive /priːˈɛm(p)tɪv/ *adjective.* **L18.**
[formed as PRE-EMPTION + -IVE.]
1 Pertaining to or of the nature of pre-emption. **L18.**
2 BRIDGE. Of a bid: intended to be high enough to prevent opponents from bidding normally and so obtaining adequate information. **E20.**
3 MILITARY. Of an attack: intended to forestall an enemy who is thought to be about to attack. Freq. in ***pre-emptive strike.*** **M20.**
■ **pre-emptively** *adverb* **E20.**

pre-emptor /priːˈɛm(p)tə/ *noun.* **M19.**
[formed as PRE-EMPTION + -OR.]
1 N. AMER. HISTORY. A person who acquires land by pre-emption. **M19.**
2 BRIDGE. A person who makes a pre-emptive bid. **L20.**

preen /priːn/ *noun & verb*[1]. Now *Scot. & north.* Also **prin** /prɪn/ (verb infl. **-nn-**).
[Old English *prēon*, corresp. to Middle Low German *prēme*, Middle & mod. Dutch *priem(e* bodkin, dagger, Middle High German *pfrieme* (German *Pfriem*) awl, Old Norse *prjónn* pin, peg.]
▶ **A** *noun.* A pin; a brooch. Freq. typifying a thing of small value. **OE.**

C. GIBBON You got to like books, and he didna care a prin for them.

▶ **B** *verb trans.* †**1** Sew; stitch up. **ME–E16.**
2 Fasten with a pin. **M16.**

preen /priːn/ *verb*[2]. **LME.**
[Perh. alt. of PRUNE *verb*[1] by assim. to PREEN *noun & verb*[1], with ref. to the pricking action of a bird's beak.]
1 *verb trans. & intrans.* Of a bird: tidy and clean (its feathers) with the beak. **LME.** ▸**b** *verb trans.* Of a bird: preen the feathers of. Usu. *refl.* **LME.**
2 *verb refl. & intrans.* **a** Smarten up one's appearance. **LME.** ▸**b** *fig.* Congratulate oneself, show self-satisfaction. Usu. foll. by *on.* **L19.**

1 G. WHITE The feathers of these birds must be well preened to resist so much wet. P. ANGADI A duck oiled its feathers by preening. **b** R. DAWKINS An individual bird can pull off its own ticks when preening itself. **2a** K. MANSFIELD The gentlemen . . preened themselves in front of the admiring ladies. S. FUGARD He preened before a mirror. **b** E. JONES He preened himself on a purely spontaneous discovery of his own.

Comb.: **preen-gland** ZOOLOGY = ***oil-gland*** s.v. OIL *noun.*
■ **preener** *noun* **M20.** **preening** *ppl adjective* that preens; smugly self-confident: **E20.**

pre-engage /ˌpriːɪnˈɡeɪdʒ, -ɛn-/ *verb.* Also †**-ing-. M17.**
[from PRE- 1 + ENGAGE *verb.*]
1 *verb trans.* Bind (a person) in advance by a pledge or promise; *spec.* betroth beforehand (usu. *refl.* or in *pass.*). **M17.** ▸**b** *verb intrans.* Pledge oneself, guarantee beforehand, (*that, to do*). **M17.**
2 *verb trans.* Win over beforehand; secure for oneself beforehand, bespeak. **M17.**
3 *verb trans.* Occupy beforehand, preoccupy. **M17.**

1 G. A. BELLAMY She pressed me to stay dinner, but . . I informed her that I was pre-engaged. **2** JOHN BOYLE They had pre-engaged all readers in his favour.

■ **pre-engagement** *noun* **M17.**

For other words beginning with *pre-* see the entry for **pre-**

pre-English /priːˈɪŋglɪʃ/ *adjective & noun.* **E20.**
[from PRE- 2 + ENGLISH *adjective & noun.*]
▶ **A** *adjective.* **1** Designating or pertaining to the period before the settlement of speakers of English in the British Isles. **E20.**
2 Designating or pertaining to the period before the emergence of English, or the West Germanic or Anglo-Frisian dialect from which English developed. **E20.**
▶ **B** *noun.* The pre-English dialect. **E20.**

pre-excellent /priːˈɛks(ə)l(ə)nt/ *adjective. rare.* **L15.**
[medieval Latin *preexcellent-*, *-ens*, formed as PRE- + EXCELLENT.]
Of outstanding excellence.

pre-exilian /priːɪgˈzɪlɪən, -ɪkˈsɪ-, -ɛg-, -ɛk-/ *adjective.* **L19.**
[from PRE- 2 + Latin *exilium* EXILE *noun*[1] + -IAN.]
Existing or occurring in the period of Jewish history before the Babylonian exile.
■ Also **pre-exilic** *adjective* **L19.**

pre-exist /priːɪgˈzɪst, -ɛg-/ *verb.* **L16.**
[from PRE- 1 + EXIST.]
1 *verb intrans.* Exist at an earlier period, esp. before the present life. **M17.** ▸**b** Exist ideally or in the mind, before material embodiment. **L18.**
2 *verb trans.* Exist earlier than. **L18.**
■ **pre-existence** *noun* (a) previous existence, esp. of the soul before its union with the body **M17. pre-existent** *adjective* = PRE-EXISTING *ppl adjective* **E17. pre-existing** *ppl adjective* existing beforehand, or before some person, thing, event, etc., referred to **L16.**

pre-exposure /priːɪkˈspəʊʒə, -ɛk-/ *noun.* **M20.**
[from PRE- 1 + EXPOSURE *noun.*]
A preliminary or premature exposure; *spec.* in PHOTOGRAPHY, one given uniformly to a film in order to increase its sensitivity prior to use.
■ **pre-expose** *verb trans.* expose beforehand or in advance; PHOTOGRAPHY give a pre-exposure to: **E19.**

pref. *abbreviation.*
1 Preface.
2 Preference.
3 Preferred.
4 Prefix.

prefab /ˈpriːfab/ *adjective & noun. colloq.* **M20.**
[Abbreviation.]
▶ **A** *adjective.* Prefabricated. **M20.**
▶ **B** *noun.* A prefabricated house or building; *spec.* a light, often single-storey house of the kind built in Britain in large numbers during and after the war of 1939–45. **M20.**

prefab /ˈpriːfab/ *verb trans. colloq.* Infl. **-bb-.** **M20.**
[Abbreviation.]
= PREFABRICATE *verb.*

prefabricate /priːˈfabrɪkeɪt/ *verb trans.* **M20.**
[from PRE- 1 + FABRICATE.]
Manufacture (sections of a building etc.) in a factory or yard prior to their assembly on a site; build (a house etc.) from sections manufactured thus. Freq. as ***prefabricated*** *ppl adjective.*

> F. L. WRIGHT We have eliminated the need for skilled labor by prefabricating all plumbing, heating and wiring. *fig.*: S. NAIPAUL He shivered with prefabricated distaste.

■ ˌ**prefabriˈcation** *noun* **M20. prefabricator** *noun* **M20.**

preface /ˈprɛfəs/ *noun.* **LME.**
[Old & mod. French *préface* from medieval Latin *praefatia* alt. of classical Latin *praefatio*, from *praefat-*, *-fari* say beforehand, from *prae* PRE- + *fari* speak.]
▶ **I 1** ECCLESIASTICAL. The introduction to the central part of the Eucharist, consisting of an exhortation to thanksgiving and an offering of praise to God, and ending with the Sanctus. **LME.**
▶ **II 2** The introduction to a literary work, stating its subject, purpose, plan, etc. **LME.**
3 The introductory part of a speech; a preliminary explanation. **E16.**
4 *fig.* A preliminary or introductory event etc. **L16.**

> **1 proper preface** any of various special formulas interpolated in the ordinary preface on major feast-days. **2** P. GAY *The Interpretation of Dreams*, he confessed in the preface to the second edition, was 'hard to read'. **3** POPE With artful preface to his host he spoke. **4** J. REED Yesterday's horrors are but a preface to what you are preparing.

preface /ˈprɛfəs/ *verb.* **E17.**
[from the noun.]
1 *verb intrans.* Make introductory or prefatory remarks; write, speak, etc., a preface. **E17.** ▸**b** *Hist.* Give a commentary on the verses of the psalms about to be sung in a church service. *Scot.* **E18.**
2 *verb trans.* Write or say (something) as a preface; state beforehand. Now *rare* or *obsolete.* **E17.**
3 *verb trans.* **a** Introduce, precede, herald. Now *esp.* (*a*) (of an event or action) lead up to (another); (*b*) introduce (a remark or action) (foll. by *with*, *by doing*). **E17.** ▸**b** Provide (a book etc.) with a preface. **L17.**
4 *verb trans.* Provide with something placed in front; occupy a position in front of. Usu. foll. by *with.* **M17.**

> **1** I. WALTON I will preface no longer, but proceed. **2** J. STRYPE The author thought fit to preface a very apt quotation. **3a** M. DRABBLE His dangerous encouragement of this scheme . . prefaced her final disillusion with him. A. PRYCE-JONES She prefaced each trivial remark by saying . . '*Ecoutez, Paul.*' **4** W. TREVOR It was a white building . . pillars and steps prefacing its entrance doors.

■ **prefacer** *noun* a person who writes a preface **M17.**

prefatorial /prɛfəˈtɔːrɪəl/ *adjective.* **L18.**
[formed as next + -AL[1].]
Of or pertaining to a preface; prefatory.
■ **prefatorially** *adverb* **E20.**

prefatory /ˈprɛfət(ə)ri/ *adjective.* **L17.**
[from Latin *praefat-* past ppl stem of *praefari* (see PREFACE *noun*) + -ORY[2].]
Of the nature of a preface; introductory, preliminary.

> J. TYNDALL The Prefatory Note which precedes the volume.

■ **prefatorily** *adverb* **M18.**

prefect /ˈpriːfɛkt/ *noun.* In sense 1 also **praefect.** **LME.**
[Old French *prefect* (mod. *préfet*) from Latin *praefectus* use as noun of pa. pple of *praeficere* put in charge, from *prae* PRE- + *facere* make, constitute.]
1 A chief officer, magistrate, or governor; *esp.* (*a*) ROMAN HISTORY any of various civil and military officers, e.g. the civil governor of a province or city; (*b*) the chief administrative officer of a department in France; = PRÉFET; (*c*) ROMAN CATHOLIC CHURCH a cardinal presiding over a congregation of the Curia. **LME.**
2 In a British secondary (esp. public) school: a senior pupil given authority over and disciplinary responsibility for his or her juniors. **E19.**
1 Prefect of Police the head of police administration in Paris.
■ **prefectship** *noun* the position or office of prefect; the period of office of a prefect: **E17.**

prefectoral /prɪˈfɛkt(ə)r(ə)l/ *adjective.* **L19.**
[French *préfectoral*, irreg. from Latin *praefectus*: see next, -AL[1].]
= PREFECTORIAL.

prefectorial /priːfɛkˈtɔːrɪəl/ *adjective.* **M19.**
[from late Latin *praefectorius*, from Latin *praefectus*: see PREFECT, -ORY[2], -AL[1].]
1 Of or pertaining to a prefect or prefects, esp. in a school. **M19.**
2 Of or pertaining to a prefecture or *préfet's* residence. **M20.**
■ **prefectorially** *adverb* **L19.**

prefecture /ˈpriːfɛktjʊə/ *noun.* **LME.**
[Old & mod. French *préfecture* or Latin *praefectura*, from *praefectus*: see PREFECT, -URE.]
1 The position or office of prefect; the period during which this is held. **LME.**
2 A district under the administration of a prefect; *spec.* an administrative division of a Japanese or Chinese province. **L16.**
3 The official residence of a French *préfet.* **M19.**
■ **preˈfectural** *adjective* **E19. preˈfecturate** *noun* = PREFECTURE **M18.**

prefer /prɪˈfəː/ *verb trans.* Infl. **-rr-.** **LME.**
[Old & mod. French *préférer* from Latin *praeferre*, from *prae* PRE- + *ferre* to bear.]
▶ **I 1** Advance in status, rank, etc; promote. Now chiefly, appoint *to* a more senior position. **LME.** ▸†**b** *refl.* Further one's interests or career. **LME–M17.** ▸†**c** Advance to a position in life; *esp.* settle in marriage. **M16–E17.**
†**2** Help forward or promote (a result). **L16–E17.**

> **1** T. FULLER He was preferred Chief Baron of the Exchequer. W. H. PRESCOTT Ferdinand promised . . to prefer no foreigners to municipal offices.

▶ **II 3** Favour (one person or thing) in preference to or *to* another (also foll. by *over*); like better. Also, choose rather (*to do, that*). **LME.** ▸**b** LAW. Give preference to as a creditor. Cf. PREFERENCE 5. **LME.**
†**4** Surpass, excel. *rare.* **LME–L16.**

> **3** D. CECIL Bath had ceased to be as fashionable as it had been . . : the smart set of London had begun to prefer Regency Brighton. A. KENNY He preferred to deal with annulments in the mornings, and canonizations in the afternoon. *Sunday Express* She still prefers lace to silk.

▶ **III** †**5** Put in front or before. **M–L16.**
6 Submit formally (a statement, charge, claim, etc.) to an authority for consideration or approval. **M16.**
7 Present for acceptance, proffer; introduce, recommend. Now *rare* or *obsolete.* **M16.**
†**8** Refer, ascribe. **L16–M17.**

> **6** M. PUZO Do you want to prefer charges against whoever did this to you? *Times* Wimbledon magistrates dismissed an information preferred against him. **7** POPE Each am'rous nymph prefers her gifts in vain.

preferable /ˈprɛf(ə)rəb(ə)l/ *adjective & adverb.* **M17.**
[French *préférable*, from *préférer*: see PREFER, -ABLE. Cf. PREFERRABLE.]
▶ **A** *adjective.* **1** Worthy to be preferred; to be chosen rather than another; more desirable. **M17.**
†**2** Displaying preference; preferential. **M18–E19.**

> **1** L. APPIGNANESI Their sensuality made them far preferable as companions to men.

▶†**B** *adverb.* Preferably, in preference. **L17–M18.**
■ **preferaˈbility** *noun* **E19. preferableness** *noun* **M17. preferably** *adverb* in a preferable manner; *esp.* as a thing to be preferred: **E18.**

preferee /prɛfəˈriː/ *noun. rare.* **L17.**
[from PREFER *verb* + -EE[1].]
A person who receives preferment.

preference /ˈprɛf(ə)r(ə)ns/ *noun.* **LME.**
[Old & mod. French *préférence* from medieval Latin *preferentia*, from Latin *praeferent-* pres. ppl stem of *praeferre*: see PREFER, -ENCE.]
1 Preferment; promotion. Now *rare.* **LME.**
†**2** The quality of being preferable; precedence, superiority. **E17–L18.**
3 The action or an act of preferring or being preferred; liking for one thing rather than another, predilection. (Foll. by *for.*) **M17.** ▸**b** That which one prefers; one's prior choice. **M19.** ▸**c** *spec.* In preferential voting: the numbering of candidates in the order desired by a voter; the position in that order assigned to a candidate by a voter. **E20.**
4 A prior claim to something; *spec.* priority of payment given to a certain debt or class of debts. **M17.** ▸**b** = ***preference share***, ***preference stock*** below. **M19.**
5 CARDS. **a** A game for three people resembling whist in which the trump is determined by bidding. **M19.** ▸**b** BRIDGE. In full ***preference bid.*** A bid indicating in which of two or more suits bid by one's partner one wishes to play. **E20.**
6 ECONOMICS. The favouring of, or an advantage given to, one customer over others in business relations; *esp.* the favouring of a country by admitting its products free or at a lower import duty than those of other countries. **L19.**

> **3** J. KOSINSKI He was somewhat surprised by my preference for some prayers and indifference to others. **for preference** if one follows one's inclination. **in preference to** rather than, more than. **b** *Muscle Mag International* I really like any type of music, but my preference is rock. **4 fraudulent preference** such priority fraudulently given by a bankrupt in order to prevent the equal distribution of his or her assets. **6 *imperial preference***: see IMPERIAL *adjective.*

Comb.: ***preference bid***: see sense 5b above; **preference share**, **preference stock** a share, stock, whose entitlement to interest takes priority over that of ordinary shares.

preferent /ˈprɛf(ə)r(ə)nt/ *adjective. rare.* **L19.**
[from PREFERENCE, after *difference*, *different*: see prec., -ENT.]
Having a right to priority of payment or consideration.

preferential /prɛfəˈrɛnʃ(ə)l/ *adjective.* **M19.**
[from PREFERENCE + -IAL, after *difference*, *differential*.]
1 Of or pertaining to preference; involving or exhibiting a preference. **M19.** ▸**b** Of voting or an election: in which a voter puts candidates in order of preference. **L19.** ▸**c** ECONOMICS. Of the nature of or characterized by import duties favouring particular countries, esp. (*Hist.*) trade between Britain and its colonies. **E20.** ▸**d** ANTHROPOLOGY. Designating a type of marriage in which the parties are expected to have a particular relationship to each other within a tribe or kinship group. **E20.**
2 = PREFERRED *ppl adjective* 4. **E20.**

> **1** J. VIORST Although parents are supposed to love their children . . equally, sometimes . . one child will receive preferential treatment.

■ **preferentially** *adverb* (*a*) by preference; (*b*) to a greater extent or degree: **L19.**

preferment /prɪˈfəːm(ə)nt/ *noun.* **LME.**
[from PREFER + -MENT.]
▶ **I** †**1** Furtherance or encouragement of an action or undertaking. **LME–M16.**
2 Advancement to an office or position, promotion. Formerly also, advancement of a child by marriage or pecuniary settlement. **L15.**
3 An appointment, esp. in the Church of England, which gives social or pecuniary advancement. **M16.**

> **2** P. LEVI He still half hoped for preferment at court. R. HARRIES A bishop . . came to the vicarage door to offer the incumbent preferment. **3** E. A. FREEMAN Spiritual preferments being turned into means of maintenance for . . bastards of the royal house.

▶ **II 4** Prior right or claim, esp. to receive payment or to make an offer for a thing on sale. *arch.* **LME.** ▸†**b** *gen.* Preference, advantage. **E16–M18.**

†**preferrable** *adjective.* **E17–E18.**
[from PREFER + -ABLE: cf. PREFERABLE.]
= PREFERABLE 1.
■ Also †**preferrible** *adjective* **M–L17.**

preferred /prɪˈfəːd/ *ppl adjective.* **LME.**
[from PREFER + -ED[1].]
1 That has obtained preferment; advanced to high office; distinguished. (*rare* before **18.**) **LME.**

For other words beginning with *pre-* see the entry for **pre-**

2 Having a prior claim to payment. M19.
3 Most favoured; desired by preference; *spec.* forming one of an officially approved series of sizes, values, etc. L19.
4 SCIENCE. Of a property, attribute, or value of a system: exhibited more often than other possible ones. E20.

2 preferred share *US* = PREFERENCE *share*. **preferred stock** *US* = PREFERENCE *stock*. **3** M. McCARTHY Bourbon (Gus's preferred tipple). **4** *Nature* The wind has a strongly preferred direction up and down the . . Loch. D. M. ADAMS The relative sizes of the ions in a crystal could be related to preferred coordination arrangements.

■ **preferredness** *noun* M19.

préfet /prefe/ *noun.* E19.
[French = PREFECT.]
= PREFECT 1(b).

prefetch /*as noun* 'pri:fɛtʃ, *as verb* pri:'fɛtʃ/ *noun & verb.* M20.
[from PRE- 1 + FETCH *verb.*]
COMPUTING. ▶**A** *noun.* The action or an act of transferring an instruction from main memory to a register or cache memory in readiness for later execution. M20.
▶**B** *verb trans.* Transfer in this way. L20.

prefetto /pre'fɛtto/ *noun. rare.* Pl. **-tti** /-tti/. M18.
[Italian from Latin *praefectus*: see PREFECT.]
An Italian prefect.

prefigurate /pri:'fɪgjʊreɪt/ *verb trans.* Now *rare.* Pa. t. & ppl adjective **-ated**, (*arch.*) **-ate** /-ət/. M16.
[ecclesiastical Latin *praefigurat-*: see next, -ATE³.]
= PREFIGURE.

prefiguration /pri:ˌfɪgə'reɪʃ(ə)n, -gjʊ-/ *noun.* LME.
[ecclesiastical Latin *praefiguratio(n-)*, from *praefigurat-* pa. ppl stem of *praefigurare* PREFIGURE: see -ATION.]
1 The action of prefiguring something; representation beforehand by a figure or type. LME.
2 That in which something is prefigured; a prototype. L16.

prefigurative /pri:'fɪgərətɪv, -gjʊ-/ *adjective.* E16.
[medieval Latin *praefigurativus*, from ecclesiastical Latin *praefigurat-*: see prec., -IVE.]
That prefigures something.
■ **prefiguratively** *adverb* L16.

prefigure /pri:'fɪgə/ *verb trans.* LME.
[ecclesiastical Latin *praefigurare*, from Latin *prae* PRE- + *figurare* FIGURE *verb.*]
1 Represent or indicate beforehand, foreshadow; *spec.* be an earlier figure or type of. LME.
2 Imagine beforehand. E17.

1 F. KERMODE The Old Testament made sense only insofar as it prefigured Christianity. P. ACKROYD Is it the secret of dreams that they prefigure reality? F. SPALDING The interior monologue technique which Stevie [Smith] pursues is prefigured in Pater.

■ **prefigurement** *noun* the action or fact of prefiguring something; an instance of this: M19.

prefix /'pri:fɪks/ *noun.* M17.
[mod. Latin *praefixum* use as noun of neut. of Latin *praefixus* pa. pple of *praefigere* fix in front, from *prae* PRE- + *figere* FIX *verb.*]
1 GRAMMAR. An element (e.g. *re-, dis-*) placed at the beginning of a word or stem to adjust or qualify its meaning or (in some languages) as an inflection. M17.
2 The action or an act of prefixing something. *rare.* L18.
3 a A title used before a person's name, e.g. *Mr, Sir, Dame.* M19. ▸**b** A word placed at the beginning of the registered name of a pedigree animal, esp. a dog, to indicate where it was bred. L19.
4 A sequence of symbols placed at the beginning of a coded message, data item, product code, etc., often to categorize what follows. L19.
■ **prefixable** *adjective* L19. **pre'fixal** *adjective* pertaining to or of the nature of a prefix M19. **pre'fixally** *adverb* E20.

prefix /pri:'fɪks, *in branch II also* 'pri:fɪks/ *verb trans.* LME.
[Old & mod. French *préfixer*, from Latin *prefixus*: see prec.]
▶**I 1** Fix, appoint, or determine beforehand. LME.
2 BIOLOGY. Fix with the first of two consecutively used fixatives. M20.

1 *Daily Telegraph* Suspending the 'pre-fixing' of export subsidies on butter sales to Moscow.

▶**II 3** Place before or at the beginning of a book or other text, esp. as an introduction or title. M16.
4 *gen.* Fix, fasten, or put in front. *rare.* E17.
5 Place (a word or element) before a word, esp. in combination with it; use as a prefix. (Foll. by *to*.) E17.
6 ANATOMY. As ***prefixed*** *ppl adjective*: (of a nerve) connected to the spinal cord relatively cranially. L19.

3 B. WILLEY M. Julien Benda prefixes his *Trahison des Clercs* with a quotation from Renouvier. **5** J. IMISON The same syllables are prefixed to chlorides and iodides. W. H. RUSSELL All the people who addressed me by name prefixed 'Major' or 'Colonel'.

prefixation /pri:fɪk'seɪʃ(ə)n/ *noun.* L19.
[from prec. + -ATION.]
1 The use of prefixes in grammar. L19.
2 ANATOMY. The condition of a nerve of being prefixed. M20.
3 BIOLOGY. The initial fixation of tissue that is to be treated with a second fixative. M20.

1 *Canadian Journal of Linguistics* Forming a passive by prefixation occurs in Hebrew and Arabic.

prefixion /pri:'fɪkʃ(ə)n/ *noun.* Now *rare* or *obsolete.* E16.
[Old & mod. French *préfixion* or medieval Latin *praefixio(n-)* preappointment, from Latin *praefix-* pa. ppl stem of *praefigere*: see PREFIX *noun*, -ION.]
†**1** The action of fixing or appointing beforehand. E16–M18.
2 GRAMMAR. = PREFIXATION 1. E19.

prefixoid /'pri:fɪksɔɪd/ *noun.* M20.
[from PREFIX *noun* + -OID, after Italian *prefissoido*.]
LINGUISTICS. A combining form, esp. one with no prior currency as an independent word.

prefixture /pri:'fɪkstʃə/ *noun.* Now *rare.* E19.
[from PREFIX *verb* after FIXTURE.]
1 GRAMMAR. The action of prefixing something. E19.
2 A prefixed word, esp. as a title. E19.

preflight /pri:'flʌɪt/ *adjective & verb.* E20.
[from PRE- 2 + FLIGHT *noun*¹.]
▶**A** *adjective.* **1** Of or pertaining to the time before powered flight. *rare.* E20.
2 Of or pertaining to the preparations for a flight, or for flying in general. M20.
▶**B** *verb trans.* Prepare (an aircraft) for a flight. L20.

prefloration /pri:flə'reɪʃ(ə)n/ *noun.* M19.
[from PRE- 2 + Latin *flor-*, *flos* flower + -ATION, after French *préfloraison*.]
BOTANY. = AESTIVATION 2.

prefocus /pri:'fəʊkəs/ *adjective & verb.* M20.
[from PRE- 1 + FOCUS *noun, verb.*]
▶**A** *adjective.* Designating or pertaining to a bulb so constructed that a lamp (esp. a vehicle headlamp) is automatically focused when fitted with it. M20.
▶**B** *verb trans.* Infl. **-s-**, **-ss-**. Focus beforehand; *spec.* make or adjust (a lamp, bulb, etc.) to ensure automatic focusing of the lamp when the bulb is fitted. M20.

prefoliation /ˌpri:fəʊlɪ'eɪʃ(ə)n/ *noun.* M19.
[French *préfoliation*.]
BOTANY. = VERNATION 1.

preform /'pri:fɔ:m/ *noun.* M20.
[from next.]
1 A moulded object which requires further processing to give it its final shape. M20.
2 PHILOLOGY. A linguistic form reconstructed from later evidence. M20.

preform /pri:'fɔ:m/ *verb trans.* E17.
[from PRE- 1 + FORM *verb*¹. Cf. French *préformer*.]
1 Form or shape beforehand. E17.
2 *spec.* Give a shape to (plastic or other moulding material) before further processing. E20.
■ **preformer** *noun* a press or similar device for preforming plastic M20.

preformation /pri:fɔ:'meɪʃ(ə)n/ *noun.* M18.
[from PRE- 1 + FORMATION. Cf. French *préformation*.]
The action or process of forming or shaping beforehand; previous formation.
theory of preformation BIOLOGY (now *Hist.*) = **theory of** EVOLUTION (a).

preformationist /pri:fɔ:'meɪʃ(ə)nɪst/ *noun & adjective.* L19.
[from prec. + -IST.]
BIOLOGY (now *Hist.*).
▶**A** *noun.* An advocate of the theory of preformation. L19.
▶**B** *adjective.* Of or pertaining to preformationism or preformationists. M20.
■ **preformationism** *noun* (belief in) the theory of preformation L19.

preformative /pri:'fɔ:mətɪv/ *noun & adjective.* E19.
[from PRE- 1 + FORMATIVE.]
▶**A** *noun.* Chiefly SEMITIC GRAMMAR. A particle prefixed as a formative element. Cf. AFFORMATIVE. E19.
▶**B** *adjective.* **1** Chiefly SEMITIC GRAMMAR. Of a particle: prefixed as a formative element. E19.
2 Having the quality or capacity of forming beforehand. M19.

preformist /prɪ'fɔ:mɪst/ *noun & adjective.* L19.
[from PREFORM *verb* + -IST.]
BIOLOGY (now *Hist.*). = PREFORMATIONIST.
■ **preformism** *noun* L19.

pre-Freudian /pri:'frɔɪdɪən/ *adjective.* M20.
[from PRE- 2 + FREUDIAN.]
Designating or characterized by attitudes that were accepted before Freud's work in psychoanalysis; occurring before the impact and influence of Freudian ideas.

For other words beginning with *pre-* see the entry for **pre-**

prefrontal /pri:'frʌnt(ə)l/ *adjective & noun.* M19.
[from PRE- 2 + FRONTAL *adjective, noun.*]
ANATOMY & ZOOLOGY. ▶**A** *adjective.* **1** Situated in front of the frontal bone of the skull. M19.
2 Situated in or pertaining to the forepart of the frontal lobe of the brain. L19.
▶**B** *ellipt.* as *noun.* A portion of the ethmoid, which forms a distinct bone in some reptiles, anurans, and fishes. M19.

preg /prɛg/ *adjective. colloq.* M20.
[Abbreviation.]
= PREGNANT *adjective*¹ 1.

pregenital /pri:'dʒɛnɪt(ə)l/ *adjective.* L19.
[from PRE- 2 + GENITAL.]
1 Situated in front of the genital region. L19.
2 Occurring before the development of genital sexuality; characteristic of the period of this. M20.
■ **pregeni'tality** *noun* the state or condition of being in the pregenital period M20.

pregermination /ˌpri:dʒə:mɪ'neɪʃ(ə)n/ *noun.* M20.
[from PRE- 1 + GERMINATION.]
The treatment of seed to start the process of germination before planting.
■ **pregerminated** *adjective* subjected to pregermination L20.

preggers /'prɛgəz/ *adjective. slang.* M20.
[from PREG(NANT *adjective*¹: see -ER⁶.]
= PREGNANT *adjective*¹ 1.

preggo /'prɛgəʊ/ *adjective. Austral. slang.* Also **prego**. M20.
[from PREG(NANT *adjective*¹ + -O.]
= PREGNANT *adjective*¹ 1.

preggy /'prɛgi/ *adjective. slang.* M20.
[from PREG(NANT *adjective*¹ + -Y¹.]
= PREGNANT *adjective*¹ 1.

preglacial /pri:'gleɪʃ(ə)l, -sɪəl/ *adjective.* M19.
[from PRE- 2 + GLACIAL.]
GEOLOGY. Existing, occurring, or formed before the glacial period or ice age.
■ **preglacially** *adverb* L19.

preglottalized /pri:'glɒt(ə)lʌɪzd/ *adjective.* Also **-ised**. M20.
[from PRE- 1 + GLOTTALIZE + -ED¹.]
PHONETICS. Preceded by a glottalized sound.
■ **preglottali'zation** *noun* M20.

pregnable /'prɛgnəb(ə)l/ *adjective.* LME.
[Old & mod. French *prenable* takable (Old French also *pregnable*), from *pren-* stem of *prendre* take from Latin *prehendere*: see -ABLE.]
1 Of a fortress etc.: able to be taken by force, not impregnable. LME.
2 *fig.* Open to attack; assailable, vulnerable. M19.

1 *Times* An Englishman's home is a structure pregnable by all sorts of officials. **2** *Daily Chronicle* He attacks Arnold's very pregnable idea that Christianity is only stoicism 'touched with emotion'.

■ **pregna'bility** *noun* M19.

pregnance /'prɛgnəns/ *noun.* M16.
[from PREGNANT *adjective*¹: see -ANCE.]
1 = PREGNANCY *noun* 1, 3, 4; a pregnant quality. M16.
2 = PRÄGNANZ. M20.

pregnancy /'prɛgnənsi/ *noun.* L15.
[from PREGNANT *adjective*¹: see -ANCY.]
1 Fertility of the mind, inventiveness, imaginative power; quickness or readiness *of* wit. L15.
2 The condition or an instance of being pregnant. E16.
3 Fertility of soil, plants, etc.; fruitfulness; abundance. E17.
4 a Latent capacity to produce results; potentiality. E19. ▸**b** Latent significance of words, speech, etc.; suggestiveness. M19.

1 CLARENDON He was chosen to . . deceive a whole Nation . . : which he did with notable pregnancy and dexterity. P. HEYLIN A pregnancy of judgment above his years. **2** J. H. BURN Women require much larger amounts of iron during pregnancy to supply the foetus. A. MASSIE She worked through the first months of her pregnancy. *Newsweek* There were a million teenage pregnancies last year. ***multiple pregnancy***: see MULTIPLE *adjective*. ***PHANTOM pregnancy***. ***toxaemia of pregnancy***: see TOXAEMIA 2. ***tubal pregnancy***: see TUBAL 2. **4a** G. SARTON Revolutionary efforts comparable in their pregnancy to those of Eudoxos.

Comb.: **pregnancy test**: to establish whether a woman (or female animal) is pregnant.

pregnane /'prɛgneɪn/ *noun.* M20.
[German *Pregnan*, from Latin *praegnans*: see PREGNANT *adjective*¹, -ANE.]
CHEMISTRY. A synthetic saturated tetracyclic hydrocarbon, $C_{21}H_{36}$, whose molecule is the framework of those of progesterone, pregnanediol, and related steroids.
■ **pregnanediol** /-'dʌɪɒl/ *noun* (BIOCHEMISTRY) a steroid, $C_{21}H_{36}O_2$, which is a product of progesterone metabolism and occurs in the urine during pregnancy M20.

pregnant /'prɛgnənt/ *adjective*¹. LME.
[French *prégnant* or Latin *praegnant-*, *-ans*, alt. (by assim. to *-ant-* -ANT¹) of *praegnat-*, prob. from *prae* PRE- + base of *(g)nasci* be born.]

▶ **I 1** Of a woman or female mammal: having a child or offspring developing in the uterus; manifesting this condition to a specified degree; having been in this condition for a specified time since conception. (Foll. by *with* the offspring, *by* the male parent.) **LME.** ▸**b** *fig.* Large and swollen. **M17.**
†**2** Of soil etc.: fertile, prolific; teeming *with*. Of a plant or seed: fertilized, capable of germinating; fruitful. **E17–L18.**

> 🕮 **1** D. MARECHERA She got pregnant, was cast out of school. *Observer* At the moment she is very pregnant with her third child. U. BENTLEY I was picturing the reaction . . were I to come home pregnant by a married man. *Health & Fitness* The women performed exercise bike tests when they were six months pregnant. **b** DONNE A pregnant banke swel'd up. V. NABOKOV A huge pregnant envelope.

▶ **II 3 a** Of a person or the mind: full of ideas; imaginative, inventive. (Foll. by *in*, *with*, etc.) *arch.* **LME.** ▸†**b** Esp. of a young person: quick to understand, perceptive, quick-witted; full of promise. **M16–E18.** ▸†**c** Easily influenced; receptive; inclined, ready. *rare* (chiefly Shakes.). **E–M17.**
4 Of words, an action, etc.: full of meaning, highly significant; suggestive, implying more than is obvious; (foll. by *with*). Formerly also, full *of*. **LME.**
5 Fruitful in results; momentous; fraught. (Foll. by *with*.) **L16.**

> 🕮 **3a** M. ARNOLD That Oxford scholar poor Of pregnant parts and quick inventive brain. **4** W. S. MAUGHAM Resuming the significance of an episode in a single pregnant phrase. E. HEATH With . . voice still pregnant with emotion, she urged support for her party. **5** G. MORRIS A critical business, . . pregnant with dangerous consequences. W. S. CHURCHILL The accession of Henry II began one of the most pregnant and decisive reigns in English history.

Special collocations & phrases: **negative pregnant** *LAW* a negative implying or involving an affirmative. **pregnant construction** a construction in which more is implied than the words express (e.g. *not have a chance*, implying *of success* etc.).

pregnant /ˈprɛɡnənt/ *adjective*[2]. *arch.* **LME.**
[French *preignant* pres. pple of *preindre* (earlier *priembre*) from Latin *premere* **PRESS** *verb*[1]: see **-ANT**[1].]
Of evidence, an argument, proof, etc.: compelling, cogent, convincing; clear, obvious.

†**pregnantly** *adverb*[1]. **LME–M17.**
[from **PREGNANT** *adjective*[2] + **-LY**[2].]
Cogently, forcibly, clearly.

pregnantly /ˈprɛɡnəntli/ *adverb*[2]. **M18.**
[from **PREGNANT** *adjective*[1] + **-LY**[2].]
In a pregnant manner or state; *spec.* in a manner implying more than is expressed; significantly; suggestively.

prego *adjective* var. of **PREGGO**.

prehallux /priːˈhaləks/ *noun*. Pl. **-lluces** /-ljʊsiːz/. **L19.**
[from **PRE-** 2 + **HALLUX**.]
ZOOLOGY. A rudimentary digit found on the inner side of the tarsus of some mammals, reptiles, and anurans.

pre-head /*as noun* ˈpriːhɛd, *as adjective* priːˈhɛd/ *noun & adjective*. **M20.**
[from **PRE-** 2 + **HEAD** *noun*.]
▶ **A** *noun*. *PHONETICS.* A syllable or sequence of syllables occurring before the head in a tone-group. **M20.**
▶ **B** *adjective*. *LINGUISTICS.* Preceding the head in a phrase. **L20.**

preheat /priːˈhiːt/ *verb trans.* **L19.**
[from **PRE-** 1 + **HEAT** *verb*.]
Heat before use or other treatment.

> 🕮 J. GRIGSON Preheat the oven to gas 6, 200°C.

▪ **preheater** *noun* a device for preheating something **E20.**

prehend /prɪˈhɛnd/ *verb trans.* **M16.**
[Latin *prehendere* grasp, seize, catch, for earlier *praehendere*, from *prae* **PRE-** + Latinized form of Greek *khandanein* take in, hold. Occas. perh. aphet. from **APPREHEND**.]
†**1** Seize, catch, grasp. *rare*. **M16–M19.**
2 *PHILOSOPHY.* Perceive and respond to, interact with, (an object or event). **E20.**

> 🕮 **2** R. G. COLLINGWOOD A plant prehends the sunlight. J. B. COBB The new occasion prehends all the entities in its past.

prehensible /prɪˈhɛnsɪb(ə)l/ *adjective*. *rare*. **M19.**
[from Latin *prehens-*: see next, **-IBLE**.]
Able to be grasped or perceived.

prehensile /prɪˈhɛnsʌɪl/ *adjective*. **L18.**
[French *préhensile*, from Latin *prehens-* pres. ppl stem of *prehendere*: see **PREHEND**, **-ILE**.]
Capable of prehension; *spec.* (of a tail or limb) capable of grasping or holding.
▪ **prehensility** /priːhɛnˈsɪlɪti/ *noun* the quality of being prehensile **M19.**

prehension /prɪˈhɛnʃ(ə)n/ *noun*. **M16.**
[Latin *prehensio(n-)* seizing, from Latin *prehens-*: see prec., **-ION**.]
†**1** Seizure or arrest in the name of the law; physical apprehension. **M16–E19.**
2 Chiefly *ZOOLOGY.* The action of physically grasping or holding something. **E19.**
3 The action of grasping with the mind; mental apprehension. **M19.** ▸**b** *PHILOSOPHY.* Perception of and response to an object or event, irrespective of cognition. **E20.**

> 🕮 **2** *Nature* Long fore-limbs with short digits adapted for running and not prehension. **3** *Blackwood's Magazine* Mr. Churchill's instinctive prehension of her claims to fashionable distinction.

prehensive /prɪˈhɛnsɪv/ *adjective*. **M19.**
[from Latin *prehens-* (see **PREHENSILE**) + **-IVE**.]
Prehensile; pertaining to or involving prehension.
▪ **prehensiveness** *noun* **L19.**

prehistorian /priːhɪˈstɔːrɪən/ *noun*. **L19.**
[formed as next, after **HISTORIAN**.]
An expert in or student of prehistory.

prehistoric /priːhɪˈstɒrɪk/ *adjective*. **M19.**
[from **PRE-** 2 + **HISTORIC**.]
1 Of, pertaining to, or dating from the time before written historical accounts. **M19.**
2 Extremely old or out of date. Chiefly *joc.* **M19.**

> 🕮 **1** P. AUSTER An archaeologist inspecting a shard at some prehistoric ruin. P. FARMER Prehistoric cave paintings. **prehistoric archaeology** the archaeology of the prehistoric period. **2** J. BUCHAN I obediently sampled an old hock, an older port, and a most pre-historic brandy.

▪ **prehistorical** *adjective* **M19.** **prehistorically** *adverb* **L19.**

prehistory /priːˈhɪst(ə)ri/ *noun*. **L19.**
[from **PRE-** + **HISTORY** *noun*, after **PREHISTORIC**.]
1 (The branch of knowledge that deals with) events or conditions before written or recorded history; the time when such events occurred; prehistoric matters. **L19.**
2 *transf.* Events or conditions leading up to a particular occurrence, period, etc. (Foll. by *of*.) **M20.**

> 🕮 **1** *Guardian* A lecturer in European prehistory at the University of Leeds. **2** *Encycl. Brit.* The latter third of the 19th century was a crucial point in the prehistory of jazz.

prehnite /ˈpreɪnʌɪt/ *noun*. **L18.**
[from Col. van *Prehn*, late-18th-cent. Dutch governor of the Cape + **-ITE**[1].]
MINERALOGY. An orthorhombic basic silicate of aluminium and calcium, usu. occurring in pale green vitreous masses.

prehominid /priːˈhɒmɪnɪd/ *noun & adjective*. **M20.**
[from **PRE-** 2 + **HOMINID**.]
▶ **A** *noun*. An anthropoid primate that is considered to be an evolutionary ancestor of the hominids. **M20.**
▶ **B** *adjective*. Of or pertaining to prehominids; of the nature of a prehominid. **M20.**

prehuman /priːˈhjuːmən/ *adjective*. **M19.**
[from **PRE-** 2 + **HUMAN**.]
Occurring before, or belonging to the time before, the appearance of humankind on the earth.

pre-ignition /priːɪɡˈnɪʃ(ə)n/ *noun*. **L19.**
[from **PRE-** 1 + **IGNITION**.]
Ignition of the fuel and air mixture in an internal-combustion engine before the passage of the spark.

pre-imagine /priːɪˈmadʒɪn/ *verb trans.* *rare*. **M17.**
[from **PRE-** 1 + **IMAGINE**: cf. medieval Latin *praeimaginare*.]
Imagine beforehand, preconceive.
▪ **pre-imagiˈnation** *noun* imagination of something before the actual existence or experience of it **M19.**

pre-impregnate /priːˈɪmprɛɡneɪt/ *verb trans.* **M20.**
[from **PRE-** 1 + **IMPREGNATE** *verb*.]
Impregnate with a substance prior to mechanical processing.
▪ ˌ**pre-impregˈnation** *noun* **M20.**

pre-impregnated /priːˈɪmprɛɡneɪtɪd/ *ppl adjective*. **M20.**
[from prec. + **-ED**[1].]
1 (Of paper insulation) impregnated with oil and resin before use in electric cables; (of a cable) containing such insulation. **M20.**
2 Of reinforcing material for plastics: impregnated with synthetic resin before fabrication. **M20.**

pre-incarnate /priːɪnˈkɑːneɪt, -ət/ *adjective*. **M19.**
[from **PRE-** 2 + **INCARNATE** *adjective*.]
Existing before the Incarnation.

pre-incarnation /ˌpriːɪnkɑːˈneɪʃ(ə)n/ *noun*. **E20.**
[from **PRE-** 1 + **INCARNATION**.]
A previous incarnation or embodiment.

pre-intone /priːɪnˈtəʊn/ *verb trans.* **M19.**
[from **PRE-** 1 + **INTONE** *verb*.]
ECCLESIASTICAL. Intone quietly the opening of (a melody) for the officiant, who then intones it aloud.

preiotation /ˌpriːʌɪəˈteɪʃ(ə)n/ *noun*. **L19.**
[from **PRE-** 1 + **IOTA** + **-ATION**.]
PHILOLOGY. In Slavonic languages, the development of a palatal glide before a vowel.
▪ ˌ**preiotiˈzation** *noun* preiotation **L19.**

For other words beginning with *pre-* see the entry for **pre-**

prejacent /priːˈdʒeɪs(ə)nt/ *adjective*. Now *rare*. **L15.**
[Old French *préjacent* placed in front, pre-existent, or medieval Latin *praejacent-*, *-ens* pre-existent, prior to modification (in classical Latin, lying in front), from *prae* **PRE-** + *jacere* lie: see **-ENT**.]
†**1** Previously existing; pre-existent. **L15–E18.**
2 Lying or situated in front. **M18.**
3 *LOGIC.* Laid down previously; constituting the original proposition from which another is inferred. **M19.**

prejudge /priːˈdʒʌdʒ/ *verb trans.* **M16.**
[from **PRE-** 1 + **JUDGE** *verb*, after French *préjuger* or Latin *praejudicare*.]
†**1** Affect adversely or unjustly; prejudice, harm, injure. *Scot.* **M16–M18.**
2 Pass judgement or pronounce sentence on before trial or without proper inquiry; form a judgement on (a person, opinion, action, etc.) prematurely and without due consideration. **L16.**
†**3** Anticipate (another) in judging. **L16–E18.**

> 🕮 **2** GIBBON The emperor had prejudged his guilt. Bosw. SMITH She knew that the case was prejudged against her.

▪ **prejudger** *noun* (*rare*) a person who prejudges someone or something **M19.**

prejudgement /priːˈdʒʌdʒm(ə)nt/ *noun*. Also **-dgm-**. **M16.**
[French †*prejugement*, from *pre-* **PRE-** + *jugement* **JUDGEMENT**.]
The action or fact of prejudging someone or something; a conclusion formed before examination of the facts; prejudice.

†**prejudical** *adjective*. *rare*. **L16–L18.**
[App. from Latin *praejudicare* (see **PREJUDICATE** *verb*) + **-AL**[1], or perh. erron. for **PREJUDICIAL**.]
= **PREJUDICIAL** *adjective* 1.

prejudicate /priːˈdʒuːdɪkeɪt/ *verb*. Now *rare* or *obsolete*. Pa. t. & pple **-ated**, **-ate** /-ət/. **M16.**
[Latin *praejudicat-* pa. ppl stem of *praejudicare* judge before, prejudice, etc., from *prae* **PRE-** + *judicare* judge: see **-ATE**[3].]
†**1** *verb trans.* = **PREJUDICE** *verb* 1. **M16–E19.**
2 †**a** *verb trans.* = **PREJUDGE** 1. **L16–M18.** ▸**b** *verb intrans.* & *trans.* Form a judgement prematurely or without due consideration. **E17.**
†**3** *verb trans.* = **PREJUDICE** *verb* 3. **L16–E18.**
▪ †**prejudicately** *adverb* in a prejudiced manner; with prejudice: **L16–E18.** **prejudiˈcation** *noun* (a) prejudgement **E17.** †**prejudicative** *adjective* characterized by prejudgement **M17–E19.**

prejudice /ˈprɛdʒʊdɪs/ *noun*. **ME.**
[Old & mod. French *préjudice* from Latin *praejudicium*, from *prae* **PRE-** + *judicium* judgement. Cf. **PRE-JUDICIAL**.]
▶ **I 1** Harm or injury to a person or thing that may result from a judgement or action, esp. one in which his or her rights are disregarded. **ME.** ▸†**b** *gen.* Injury, damage, harm. **M16–L18.**

> 🕮 **1** *Independent* A finding . . which caused substantial prejudice to the applicant. **terminate with extreme prejudice** *US slang* kill, assassinate. **to the prejudice of** with resulting harm to. **without prejudice** without detriment to any existing right or claim; *spec.* in *LAW*, without damage to one's own rights or claims.

▶ **II** †**2 a** A prior judgement; *esp.* a judgement formed hastily or before due consideration. **LME–M19.** ▸**b** The action of judging an event beforehand; prognostication. *rare*. Only in **L16.**
3 Preconceived opinion not based on actual experience; bias, partiality. Also, an instance of this; an unreasoning preference or objection; a bias. Usu. *derog.* **LME.**
†**4** A preliminary or anticipatory judgement; a preconceived idea of what will happen; an anticipation. **M–L18.**

> 🕮 **3** *Guardian* I have to accept that there are still prejudices against women. V. BROME Freud returned with a bad impression of the United States . . . based more on prejudice than fact. M. MOORCOCK For years they suffered the prejudice of their white neighbours.

prejudice /ˈprɛdʒʊdɪs/ *verb trans.* **LME.**
[Old & mod. French *préjudicier* to prejudice, from *préjudice*: see prec.]
▶ **I 1** Affect adversely or unfavourably; injure or impair the validity of (a right, claim, etc.). **LME.** ▸**b** Injure materially; damage. Now *rare*. **L15.**

> 🕮 **1** A. F. DOUGLAS-HOME A temporary concession did not prejudice their ultimate goal.

▶ **II** †**2** Judge beforehand; *esp.* prejudge unfavourably. *rare*. **L16–M17.**
3 Affect or fill with a prejudice; give a bias to, influence the mind or judgement of beforehand and often unfairly. (Foll. by *against*, *in favour of*.) (Earlier as **PREJUDICED**.) **E17.**

> 🕮 **3** C. KINGSLEY I wished . . to prejudice my readers' minds in their favour rather than against them.

prejudiced /ˈprɛdʒʊdɪst/ *ppl adjective*. **L16.**
[from prec. + **-ED**[1].]
Affected or influenced by prejudice; biased beforehand. (Foll. by *against*, *in favour of*.)

📖 R. TRAVERS The defence counsel was determined to show up Roche as a prejudiced witness.

prejudicial /prɛdʒʊˈdɪʃ(ə)l/ *adjective.* LME.
[Old & mod. French *préjudiciel* †causing prejudice (now = next).]
1 Causing prejudice; of a harmful tendency; detrimental or damaging to rights, interests, etc. LME.
†**2** Of the nature of prejudice; prejudiced, unfavourably prepossessed. M16–M17.

📖 **1** R. C. A. WHITE Judges have a discretion to exclude evidence the prejudicial effect of which . . outweighs its probative value.

■ **prejudicially** *adverb* in a prejudicial manner; harmfully, detrimentally: LME. **prejudicialness** *noun* (*rare*) M17.

pre-judicial /priːdʒuːˈdɪʃ(ə)l/ *adjective.* M17.
[Late Latin *praejudicialis*, from Latin *praejudicium* a judicial examination previous to trial: see PREJUDICE *noun*, -AL[1].]
ROMAN LAW. Designating an action to determine preliminary questions, e.g. as to status, which may affect the outcome of a suit.

prejudicious /prɛdʒʊˈdɪʃəs/ *adjective.* Long *rare.* L16.
[from Latin *praejudicium* PREJUDICE *noun* + -OUS.]
1 Harmful, detrimental; = PREJUDICIAL 1. L16.
†**2** Full of prejudice; = PREJUDICED. L16–E17.
■ **prejudiciously** *adverb* L19.

†**preke** *noun.* E17–M18.
[Origin unkn.]
An octopus, a cuttlefish.

prelacy /ˈprɛləsi/ *noun.* ME.
[Anglo-Norman *prelacie* from medieval Latin *prelatia*, from *praelatus* PRELATE: see -ACY.]
1 The position, or office, or rank of prelate. ME.
†**2** The authority of a prelate; ecclesiastical power; the authority of any superior. ME–L16.
3 Ecclesiastical dignitaries collectively. LME.
4 The system of church government by prelates or bishops. Freq. *derog.* LME.

prelanguage /ˈpriːlaŋgwɪdʒ/ *noun.* M20.
[from PRE- 2 + LANGUAGE *noun*[1].]
A form of communication preceding the emergence or acquisition of language.

prelapsarian /priːlapˈsɛːrɪən/ *adjective.* L19.
[from PRE- 2 after *sublapsarian*.]
Pertaining to the condition of innocence before the Fall of Man (*THEOLOGY*); innocent and carefree.

📖 P. AUSTER Some saw the Indians as living in prelapsarian innocence.

prelate /ˈprɛlət/ *noun.* ME.
[Old & mod. French *prélat* from medieval Latin *praelatus* use as noun of pa. pple corresp. to Latin *praeferre* PREFER: see -ATE[1].]
1 An ecclesiastical dignitary of high rank and authority, as a bishop, archbishop, or (now *Hist.*) an abbot or prior. ME. ▸†**b** A chief priest of a religion other than Christianity, esp. the Jewish religion. LME–E17.
†**2** *gen.* A person with superiority or authority; a chief, a superior. LME–L18.
■ **prelatist** *noun* a supporter or adherent of prelacy or episcopacy M17. **prelatry** *noun* prelacy M17.

prelateship /ˈprɛlətʃɪp/ *noun.* L16.
[from prec. + -SHIP.]
The rank or position of prelate; the tenure of office of a prelate. Also (with possess. adjective, as ***your prelateship*** etc.): a title of respect given to a prelate.

prelatess /ˈprɛlətɪs/ *noun.* M17.
[formed as prec. + -ESS[1].]
A female prelate; an abbess, a prioress. Also (*joc.*), the wife of a prelate.

prelatial /prɪˈleɪʃ(ə)l/ *adjective.* L19.
[from medieval Latin *praelatia* PRELACY + -AL[1].]
Of or pertaining to prelacy or a prelate.

prelatic /prɪˈlatɪk/ *adjective.* M17.
[from PRELATE + -IC.]
1 That is a prelate; pertaining to or of the nature of a prelate. M17.
2 Governed by or adhering to prelates or prelacy; episcopal. M17.

📖 **1** H. H. MILMAN Prelatic magnificence. **2** SIR W. SCOTT The prelatic clergy.

■ Also **prelatical** *adjective* M17.

prelation /prɪˈleɪʃ(ə)n/ *noun.* Now *rare.* LME.
[Old French *prelacion* (mod. *prélation*) from Latin *praelatio(n-)*, from *praelat-* pa. ppl stem corresp. to *praeferre* PREFER: see -ATION.]
†**1** Utterance, pronunciation. *rare.* LME–M17.
2 The action of preferring; the condition of being preferred; preference, promotion; pre-eminence, superiority. LME.

prelatize /ˈprɛlətʌɪz/ *verb.* Also **-ise.** M17.
[from PRELATE + -IZE.]
†**1** *verb intrans.* Be or become prelatical. *rare.* Only in M17.
2 *verb trans.* Make prelatical; bring under prelatic or episcopal government. M19.

prelature /ˈprɛlətjʊə/ *noun.* E17.
[Old & mod. French *prélature* from medieval Latin *praelatura*, from *praelatus*: see PRELATE, -URE.]
1 = PRELACY 1. E17.
2 = PRELACY 3. M19.

pre-law /priːˈlɔː/ *adjective & noun. N. Amer.* M20.
[from PRE- 2 + LAW *noun*[1].]
(Of or pertaining to) subjects studied in preparation for a course in law.

prelect /prɪˈlɛkt/ *verb.* E17.
[Latin *praelect-* pa. ppl stem of *praelegere* read to others, lecture on, from *prae* PRE- + *legere* choose, read.]
†**1** *verb trans.* Choose in preference to others. E–M17.
2 *verb intrans.* Lecture (*to* an audience, *on* a subject); deliver a lecture. L18.

prelection /prɪˈlɛkʃ(ə)n/ *noun.* L16.
[Latin *praelectio(n-)*, formed as prec.: see -ION.]
1 A public lecture or talk; *esp.* a college or university lecture given to students. L16.
2 A prior reading. M17.

prelector /prɪˈlɛktə/ *noun.* Also **prae-**. L16.
[Latin *praelector*, from *praelegere*: see PRELECT, -OR.]
A public reader or lecturer, esp. in a college or university.
■ **prelectorship** *noun* the position or office of prelector L19.

prelibation /priːlʌɪˈbeɪʃ(ə)n/ *noun.* E16.
[Late Latin *praelibatio(n-)*, from *praelibat-* pa. ppl stem of *praelibare* taste beforehand, formed as PRE- + *libare*: see LIBATE, -ATION.]
1 A foretaste. Chiefly *fig.* E16.
2 An offering of the first fruits or the first taste of something. Now *rare.* M17.

📖 **1** *Blackwood's Magazine* That mysterious ante-dawn—that prelibation of the full daylight.

prelim /ˈpriːlɪm, prɪˈlɪm/ *noun. colloq.* L19.
[Abbreviation of PRELIMINARY.]
1 A preliminary practice, examination, contest, etc. L19.
2 The preliminary matter of a book. Usu. in *pl.* Cf. PRELIMINARY *noun* 2. E20.

📖 **1** D. MORAES I had passed Prelims, which meant that I was sure of three clear years at Oxford. *Sports Illustrated* The prelims of the 400-meter free relay. **2** *Indexer* The index . . should be provided by the publisher much as he provides prelims and jacket copy.

preliminary /prɪˈlɪmɪnəri/ *noun, adjective, & adverb.* M17.
[French *préliminaire* or mod. Latin *praeliminaris*, from *prae* PRE- + Latin *limin-*, *limen* threshold: see -ARY[2].]
▸ **A** *noun.* **1** An action, measure, statement, etc., that precedes another to which it is introductory or preparatory. Usu. in *pl.*, preparatory measures or arrangements. M17. ▸**b** A preliminary examination. L19. ▸**c** *SPORT.* A contest used to select competitors for a more important event; a boxing-match put on before the main match. L19.
2 The preliminary matter of a book, preceding the main text (including title-page, contents, preface, etc.). Usu. in *pl.* Cf. PRELIM 2. L19.

📖 **1** B. MAGEE We can never get to the discussion at all, because we can never complete the necessary preliminaries.

▸ **B** *adjective.* Preceding and leading up to the main subject or business; introductory; preparatory. M17.

📖 J. ROSENBERG A preliminary study for a larger life-sized portrait. P. GARDINER During his first year he covered preliminary courses in a wide range of subjects.

▸ **C** *adverb.* Preliminarily. (Foll. by *to*.) M18.

📖 E. J. NICHOLS A pitcher's straightening of his arms above his head preliminary to delivering the ball.

■ **prelimiˈnarily** *adverb* in a preliminary manner; as an introduction: M18.

prelimit /priːˈlɪmɪt/ *verb trans.* M17.
[from PRE- 1 + LIMIT *verb*.]
Limit or set bounds to beforehand; confine within previously fixed limits.
■ Also **prelimitate** *verb trans.* (*rare*) [Latin *limitare* LIMIT *verb*] M17.

prelingual /priːˈlɪŋgw(ə)l/ *adjective.* L19.
[from PRE- 2 + LINGUAL.]
1 Existing or occurring before the development of language or the acquisition of speech. L19.
2 Located in front of the tongue. M20.
■ **prelingually** *adverb* from a time before the acquisition of speech L20.

prelinguistic /priːlɪŋˈgwɪstɪk/ *adjective & noun.* E20.
[from PRE- 2 + LINGUISTIC.]
▸ **A** *adjective.* = PRELINGUAL 1. E20.
▸ **B** *noun.* In *pl.* (treated as *sing.*). The branch of science that deals with the biological and physiological aspects of speech. M20.

preliterate /priːˈlɪt(ə)rət/ *adjective & noun.* E20.
[from PRE- 2 + LITERATE.]
▸ **A** *adjective.* **1** Of an individual, social group, or culture: having no written language. E20.
2 (Of a child) at a stage of development before the acquisition of literacy; pertaining to this stage. M20.
▸ **B** *noun.* A preliterate person. Cf. NON-LITERATE. E20.
■ **preliteracy** *noun* the state of being preliterate M20.

prelogical /priːˈlɒdʒɪk(ə)l/ *adjective.* L19.
[from PRE- 2 + LOGICAL *adjective*.]
Preceding logic or logical reasoning; *spec.* (*ANTHROPOLOGY*) designating thinking based on myth, magic, etc.

prelude /ˈprɛljuːd/ *noun.* M16.
[French *prélude* or medieval Latin *praeludium*, from *praeludere*: see next.]
1 A preliminary performance, action, or condition, preceding and introducing one that is more important; an introduction or preface to a literary work. (Foll. by *to*.) M16.
2 *MUSIC.* A piece forming the introduction to a work, usually establishing its pitch or mood; *esp.* a movement preceding a fugue or forming the first piece of a suite. Also, a short independent piece for the piano. M17.

📖 **1** V. BROME This period of uneasy compromise was merely the prelude to far worse frictions.

prelude /ˈprɛljuːd/ *verb.* M17.
[Latin *praeludere* play beforehand, preface, from *prae* PRE- + *ludere* to play, from *ludus* play.]
1 *verb trans.* **a** Precede as a prelude or preliminary action; prepare the way for, introduce; foreshadow. M17. ▸**b** Of a person: introduce with a prelude or preliminary action. L17.
2 *verb intrans.* **a** Give a prelude or introductory performance *to* a subsequent action. M17. ▸**b** Form or act as a prelude, be introductory (*to*). E18.
3 *MUSIC.* **a** *verb intrans.* Play a prelude before the main work. L17. ▸**b** *verb trans.* Play as a prelude. Also, introduce with a prelude. L18.

📖 **1a** DRYDEN When the gray Of morn preludes the splendour of the day. **b** A. S. BYATT She gave a peremptory little tug on Stephanie's arm, preluding a confidence. **2b** T. ARNOLD The skirmishing of the light-armed troops preluded as usual to the battle.

¶ Formerly pronounced with stress on 2nd syll.
■ **preluder** *noun* (*rare*) a person who plays or performs a prelude L18.

preludia *noun pl.* see PRELUDIUM.

preludial /prɪˈljuːdɪəl/ *adjective.* M17.
[from medieval Latin *praeludium* PRELUDE *noun* + -AL[1].]
Pertaining to or of the nature of a prelude; serving to introduce something.

Preludin /prɪˈl(j)uːdɪn/ *noun.* M20.
[Origin unkn.]
PHARMACOLOGY. (Proprietary name for) the drug phenmetrazine.

preludio /prɪˈluːdɪəʊ/ *noun. rare.* Pl. **-os.** E18.
[Italian from medieval Latin *praeludium* PRELUDE *noun*.]
MUSIC. = PRELUDE *noun* 2.

preludious /prɪˈljuːdɪəs/ *adjective.* Now *rare.* M17.
[formed as PRELUDIAL + -OUS.]
= PRELUDIAL.

preludise *verb* var. of PRELUDIZE.

preludium /priːˈljuːdɪəm/ *noun.* Now *rare.* Also **prae-**. Pl. **-diums**, **-dia** /-dɪə/. M16.
[medieval Latin *praeludium* PRELUDE *noun*.]
A prelude, an introduction; a preliminary.

preludize /ˈprɛljuːdʌɪz/ *verb intrans.* Also **-ise.** M19.
[from PRELUDE *noun* + -IZE.]
Play or write a prelude.

prelusion /prɪˈl(j)uːʒ(ə)n/ *noun.* Now *rare.* L16.
[Latin *praelusio(n-)*, from *praelus-* pa. ppl stem of *praeludere*: see PRELUDE *verb*, -ION.]
The performance of a prelude; a prelude, an introduction.

prelusive /prɪˈl(j)uːsɪv/ *adjective.* E17.
[formed as prec. + -IVE.]
Of the nature of a prelude; preliminary, introductory.
■ **prelusively** *adverb* (*rare*) in a prelusive manner, by way of a prelude M19.

prelusory /prɪˈl(j)uːs(ə)ri/ *adjective.* Now *rare.* M17.
[Late Latin *praelusorius*, formed as prec.: see -ORY[2].]
= prec.

prem /prɛm/ *noun & adjective.* M20.
[Abbreviation of PREMATURE *adjective & noun*.]
▸ **A** *noun.* A premature baby. M20.
▸ **B** *adjective.* Premature; of or pertaining to premature babies. M20.

📖 D. HALLIDAY The incubator lights had cut out in a prem ward.

For other words beginning with *pre-* see the entry for **pre-**

pre-man /as noun 'priːman; *as adjective* priː'man/ *noun & adjective.* E20.
[from PRE- 2 + MAN noun.]
▶ **A** *noun.* Pl. **-men** /-mɛn/. A hominid or manlike creature that lived before the appearance of *Homo erectus* and *H. sapiens.* E20.
▶ **B** *adjective.* = PREHUMAN. M20.

premarital /priː'marɪt(ə)l/ *adjective.* L19.
[from PRE- 2 + MARITAL.]
Occurring before marriage.

📖 *Drum* Your girl is one of those . . who do not like to indulge in premarital sex.

■ **premaritally** *adverb* L20.

prematuration /prɛmətjʊ'reɪʃ(ə)n, ˌpriːmatjʊ'reɪʃ(ə)n/ *noun. rare.* E20.
[from PREMATURE *adjective & noun* + -ATION, or PRE- 1 + MATURATION.]
Early maturing or maturation. Also, prematureness.

prematuration /priːmatjʊ'reɪʃ(ə)n/ *adjective.* E20.
[from PRE- 2 + MATURATION.]
Occurring before maturation.

premature /'prɛmətjʊə, 'priː-/ *adjective & noun.* LME.
[Latin *praematurus* very early, from *prae* PRE- + *maturus* MATURE *adjective.*]
▶ **A** *adjective.* †**1** Ripe, mature. Only in LME.
2 Occurring, existing, or done before the usual or proper time; too early; overhasty. E16.
3 Born or occurring before the end of the full term of pregnancy (but usu. after the stage when the foetus normally becomes viable); *spec.* (of an infant) weighing less than 2.5 kg at birth. M18.

📖 **2** J. CHEEVER The white in her hair is premature. P. GAY Freud was regretful about his friend's premature death. ***premature ejaculation***: see EJACULATION 1. ***premature* PUBARCHE. 3** L. LAWRENCE Gwenlian Harris' baby was born six weeks premature. S. WEINTRAUB The Duke was willing to risk a premature and possibly fatal birth.

▶ **B** *noun.* MEDICINE. A premature infant. E20.
■ **prematurely** *adverb* (*a*) in a premature manner; too soon, too hastily; (*b*) before the end of the full term of pregnancy; as a premature infant: M17. **prematureness** *noun* E18.

premature /'prɛmətjʊə/ *verb intrans.* E20.
[from the adjective.]
MILITARY. (Of a shell or other projectile) explode before the proper time; (of a gun) fire such a projectile.

prematurity /prɛmə'tjʊərɪti, priː-/ *noun.* E17.
[from PRE- 1 + MATURITY, after French *prématurité.*]
†**1** Early ripening or flowering in a plant. E17–E18.
2 Undue earliness or haste; hastiness, precipitancy. E18.
3 Early development, esp. of mental or physical faculties; precociousness. L18.
4 MEDICINE. The fact or condition of giving birth to a premature infant. L19.

📖 **2** J. S. BRISTOWE Their early sickliness and prematurity of death.

premaxilla /priːmak'sɪlə/ *noun.* Pl. **-llae** /-liː/. M19.
[from PRE- 2 + MAXILLA.]
ANATOMY & ZOOLOGY. A premaxillary bone.

premaxillary /priːmak'sɪləri/ *adjective & noun.* M19.
[from PRE- 2 + MAXILLARY.]
ANATOMY & ZOOLOGY. ▶**A** *adjective.* Situated in front of the upper jaw; *esp.* designating either of a pair of bones of the upper jaw situated in front of and between (and in humans fused with) the maxillae. M19.
▶ **B** *noun.* A premaxillary bone. M19.

premed /priː'mɛd, 'priːmɛd/ *noun*[1]. *colloq.* M20.
[Abbreviation.]
Premedication.

premed /priː'mɛd/ *adjective & noun*[2]. *colloq.* (chiefly *N. Amer.*). M20.
[Abbreviation.]
▶ **A** *adjective.* Premedical. M20.
▶ **B** *noun.* A premedical student. Also, premedical studies, a premedical course. M20.

premedical /priː'mɛdɪk(ə)l/ *adjective.* Chiefly *N. Amer.* E20.
[from PRE- 2 + MEDICAL.]
Studied in preparation for a medical course; of or pertaining to studies of this kind.

premedicant /priː'mɛdɪk(ə)nt/ *noun & adjective.* M20.
[formed as next + -ANT[1].]
(A drug) given as premedication.

premedicate /priː'mɛdɪkeɪt/ *verb trans.* M19.
[from PRE- 1 + MEDICATE.]
Give preparatory medication to, esp. (now) before anaesthesia.
■ **premedi'cation** *noun* medication given prior to or in preparation for the main treatment; *spec.* (the giving of) a preanaesthetic: E20.

†**premeditate** *adjective.* M16.
[Latin *praemeditatus* pa. pple of *praemeditari*: see next, -ATE[2].]
1 = PREMEDITATED. M16–M18.
2 Using premeditation; considerate, deliberate. Only in L16.
■ †**premeditately** *adverb* M17–E19.

premeditate /priː'mɛdɪteɪt/ *verb.* Pa. t. & pple **-ated**, †**-ate**. M16.
[Latin *praemeditat-* pa. ppl stem of *praemeditari*, from *prae* PRE- + *meditari* MEDITATE.]
1 *verb trans.* Think about with a view to subsequent action; think out beforehand; plan in advance. M16.
2 *verb intrans.* Deliberate beforehand or in advance. L16.

📖 **1** R. COBB He had persisted in maintaining that he had premeditated his mother's murder.

■ **premeditatingly** *adverb* (*rare*) with or by premeditation M19. **premeditative** *adjective* (*rare*) given to or characterized by premeditation M19.

premeditated /priː'mɛdɪteɪtɪd/ *ppl adjective.* L16.
[from prec. + -ED[1].]
Thought about or planned beforehand.

📖 CONAN DOYLE A woman who, in a cold, premeditated fashion, is about to get rid of a rival. J. AGEE An irreverence which had not been premeditated but spontaneous.

■ **premeditatedly** *adverb* E18. **premeditatedness** *noun* M17.

premeditation /ˌpriːmɛdɪ'teɪʃ(ə)n/ *noun.* LME.
[Old & mod. French *préméditation* or Latin *praemeditatio(n-)*, formed as PREMEDITATE *verb*: see -ATION.]
The action of premeditating something; previous planning or deliberation.

📖 J. G. COZZENS Without premeditation their mouths fell open, chanting the spontaneous antiphon.

pre-men *noun pl.* of PRE-MAN.

premenstrua *noun pl.* see PREMENSTRUUM.

premenstrual /priː'mɛnstrʊəl/ *adjective.* L19.
[from PRE- 2 + MENSTRUAL.]
Occurring or experienced before menstruation.
premenstrual syndrome a syndrome affecting women in the latter part of the menstrual cycle which may include nervous tension, depression, and physical symptoms; abbreviation ***PMS***. **premenstrual tension** nervous tension felt prior to menstruation; abbreviation ***PMT***.
■ **premenstrually** *adverb* M20.

premenstruum /priː'mɛnstrʊəm/ *noun.* Pl. **-strua** /-strʊə/, **-struums**. E20.
[from PRE- 2 + MENSTRUUM.]
MEDICINE. The stage of the menstrual cycle which precedes menstruation.

premiate /'priːmɪeɪt/ *verb trans. rare.* M16.
[Latin *premiat-* pa. ppl stem of *praemiari* stipulate for a reward, from *praemium* PREMIUM: see -ATE[3].]
Reward; award a prize to.
■ **premi'ation** *noun* (*rare*) reward; an act of rewarding, a prize-giving: L15.

premie /'priːmi/ *noun.* L20.
[Sanskrit *premī* lover, from *preman* to love.]
A follower of the guru Maharaj Ji (b. 1957) or the religious organization Divine Light that he founded.

premier /'prɛmɪə, 'priː-/ *adjective & noun.* LME.
[Old & mod. French from Latin *primarius* PRIMARY *adjective.*]
▶ **A** *adjective.* **1** First in order or importance; leading, foremost. LME.
2 First in time; earliest. LME.

📖 **1** *National Observer (US)* Television is now the premier instrument for political campaigning. †**minister premier**, †**premier minister** = sense B.1 below. **2** *Belfast Telegraph* Lady De Ros . . holds the premier barony in the UK—created in 1264.

▶ **B** *noun.* **1** (Also **P-**.) (Used as a title preceding the name of) the first or chief minister in a government, *spec.* (*a*) the Prime Minister of the United Kingdom; (*b*) *Austral. & Canad.* the chief minister of the government of a State or Province. E18.
2 = PREMIÈRE *noun.* M20.
■ **premiership** *noun* (*a*) the position or office of premier; the period of office of a premier; (*b*) the state of being first in order, as in a competition; a competition to be first in order, esp. in the top division of the English soccer league: E19.

premier /'prɛmɪə, 'priː-/ *verb trans. & intrans.* M20.
[from prec. after PREMIÈRE *verb.*]
= PREMIÈRE *verb.*

premier cru /prəmje kry, prɛmɪə 'kruː/ *noun phr.* Pl. ***-s -s*** (pronounced same). M19.
[French, lit. 'first growth'.]
A wine of the best quality.

premier danseur /prəmje dɑ̃sœːr/ *noun phr.* Pl. ***-s -s*** (pronounced same). E19.
[French, lit. 'first dancer'.]
A leading male dancer in a ballet company. Cf. PREMIÈRE DANSEUSE.

For other words beginning with *pre-* see the entry for **pre-**

première /'prɛmɪɛː, *foreign* prəmjɛːr (*pl. same*)/ *noun & adjective.* Also **premiere**. L19.
[French, fem. of *premier* (see PREMIER *adjective & noun*). As noun short for *première représentation* first representation.]
▶ **A** *noun.* A first performance or showing of a play, film, etc.; a first night. L19.
▶ **B** *adjective.* = PREMIER *adjective* 1. L19.
PREMIÈRE DANSEUSE.

première /'prɛmɪɛː/ *verb.* Also **premiere**. M20.
[from prec.]
1 *verb trans.* Present or perform (a play, film, etc.) for the first time; reveal (a new product). M20.
2 *verb intrans.* Of a play, film, etc.: be premièred. M20.

première danseuse /prəmjɛːr dɑ̃søːz/ *noun phr.* Pl. ***-s -s*** (pronounced same). E19.
[French, fem. of PREMIER DANSEUR.]
A leading female dancer in a ballet company; a ballerina.

premiers crus, premiers danseurs *noun phrs.* pls. of PREMIER CRU, PREMIER DANSEUR.

premillenarian /ˌpriːmɪlɪ'nɛːrɪən/ *noun & adjective.* M19.
[from PRE- 2 + MILLENARIAN.]
▶ **A** *noun.* A person who believes that the second coming of Christ will precede the millennium; a premillennialist. M19.
▶ **B** *adjective.* Of or pertaining to this belief or its holders. M19.

premillennial /priːmɪ'lɛnɪəl/ *adjective.* M19.
[from PRE- 2 + MILLENNIAL.]
Of an event, esp. the second coming of Christ: occurring before the millennium. Also, pertaining to the world before the millennium.
■ **premillennialism** *noun* the doctrine or belief that the second coming of Christ will precede the millennium M19. **premillennialist** *noun* a person who holds this doctrine or belief M19.

premio /'priːmɪəʊ/ *noun.* Now *rare.* Pl. **-os**. E17.
[Italian, from Latin *praemium* PREMIUM.]
= PREMIUM 1, 2.

premisal /prɪ'mʌɪz(ə)l/ *noun.* Now *rare.* M17.
[from PREMISE *verb* + -AL[1].]
The action or an act of premising something.

premise /'prɛmɪs/ *noun.* Also (the usual form in sense 1) **premiss**. LME.
[Old & mod. French *prémisse* from medieval Latin *praemissa* use as noun (sc. *propositio*) of fem. sing. and neut. pl. pa. pple of Latin *praemittere* send or set before, from *prae* PRE- + *mittere* put, send.]
▶ **I** LOGIC. **1** A previous statement or proposition from which another is inferred or follows as a conclusion; *spec.* in *pl.*, the two propositions in a syllogism. LME.

📖 **1** A. J. AYER Descartes attempted to derive all human knowledge from premises whose truth was intuitively certain. ISAIAH BERLIN The Soviet pattern is . . deduced from 'scientifically demonstrated' premisses. ***INSTANTIAL premiss***.

▶ **II** Now only in *pl.*
2 Chiefly LAW. Things already stated or mentioned; the aforesaid, the foregoing. Now *rare.* LME.
3 LAW. The opening part of a deed or conveyance, which gives the names of the grantor, the grantee, and details about the grant. LME.
4 LAW. The houses, lands, or tenements previously specified in a deed or conveyance. LME.
5 A house or building with its grounds etc. Also, (a part of) a building housing a business etc. E17.
†**6** Previous circumstances or events; things happening before. E17–M18.

📖 **5** J. GALSWORTHY Bosinney rose to go, and Soames rose too, to see him off the premises. F. WYNDHAM The Slade School . . had also moved . . to premises in Oxford. A. LURIE It still kept its premises above an expensive antique shop.

premise /prɪ'mʌɪz/ *verb trans.* Also (esp. in sense 1) **premiss** /'prɛmɪs/. LME.
[from prec.]
1 State or mention before something else; say or write by way of introduction to a main subject. Foll. by obj. clause or simple obj. LME. ▸†**b** Put (words etc.) before as an introduction, explanation, etc. Foll. by *to.* E17–E19. ▸**c** LOGIC. State in the premisses. L17.
2 Make, do, or use beforehand; *esp.* (MEDICINE), perform (an operation) or administer (a remedy) as the beginning of a course of treatment. *arch.* M16.
†**3** Send in advance or before the expected time. *rare.* M16–E17.
4 Preface or introduce (something) *with* or *by* something else. *rare.* E19.

📖 **1** SYD. SMITH Having premised these observations, I proceed to consider. J. R. LOWELL I will premise generally that I hate this business of lecturing.

premiss *noun, verb* see PREMISE *noun, verb.*

†**premit** *verb trans.* Infl. **-tt-**. E16–L18.
[Latin *praemittere*: see PREMISE *noun.*]
= PREMISE *verb* 1, 1C.

premium /ˈpriːmɪəm/ *noun & adjective.* E17.
[Latin *praemium* booty, profit, reward, from *prae* PRE- 1 + *emere* buy, (orig.) take.]
► **A** *noun.* **1** A reward, a prize. E17.
2 The amount payable for a contract of insurance. M17.
3 A sum added to interest, wages, etc.; a bonus; a sum paid in addition to the rent on a leased property. L17.
4 a A charge made for changing one currency into another of greater value; the excess value of one currency over another. E18. ▸**b** The excess of the prospective price of a currency or commodity over the present price; *STOCK EXCHANGE* the amount by which the price of a stock exceeds its issue price or the value of the assets it represents; *gen.* the excess of an actual over a nominal price. M19.
5 A fee paid for instruction in a profession or trade. M18.
6 An item given away or sold cheaply to persuade people to buy, sample, or subscribe to something. E20.

📖 **1** H. ALLEN It was a rich Eastern cargo and premiums might follow. **2** *Which?* Many . . policies . . offer an 'all risks' extension: you pay an extra premium. **4b** *Financial Times* Shares . . jumped to a 70 per cent premium on the first day.

Phrases: **at a premium** at more than the nominal value or price; *fig.* in high esteem: opp. ***at a discount***. **Premium Savings Bond** = ***premium bond*** (b) below. **put a premium on** put a high value on; provide or act as an incentive to.
Comb.: **premium apprentice** *Hist.*: who has paid a premium for his or her instruction; **premium bond** (*a*) a bond earning no interest but eligible for lotteries; (*b*) *spec.* (also with cap. initials) since 1956, a British Government bond without interest but with regular chances of cash prizes.
► **B** *attrib.* or as *adjective.* (Of a commodity etc.) superior in quality and therefore more expensive; (of a price) suited to an item of superior quality, higher than usual. E20.

📖 *Marketing Week* Newcastle Brown is competing against . . premium lagers like Lowenbräu.

■ **premiumed** *adjective* that has won a premium or prize; that has paid a premium: L18.

premix /ˈpriːmɪks/ *noun & adjective.* M20.
[from PRE- 1 + MIX *noun*.]
► **A** *noun.* **1** A mixture prepared beforehand of various, esp. granular or resinous, materials. M20.
2 A preliminary dub or mix of a musical or film soundtrack. M20.
► **B** *adjective.* Mixed beforehand, premixed. Also, that mixes beforehand. M20.

premix /priːˈmɪks/ *verb trans.* M20.
[from PRE- 1 + MIX *verb*.]
Mix beforehand.

premixture /priːˈmɪkstʃə/ *noun.* M20.
[from PRE- 1 + MIXTURE.]
A mixture prepared beforehand.

premodify /priːˈmɒdɪfʌɪ/ *verb trans.* M20.
[from PRE- 1 + MODIFY.]
LINGUISTICS. Modify (a word or phrase) by an immediately preceding word or phrase.
■ **premodifiˈcation** *noun* M20. **premodifier** *noun* a word or phrase which modifies one coming after it M20.

premolar /priːˈməʊlə/ *noun & adjective.* M19.
[from PRE- 2 + MOLAR *adjective*[1].]
► **A** *noun.* A premolar tooth (see below). M19.
► **B** *adjective.* Designating each of a set of teeth (eight in a complete human dentition) situated in pairs between the canine and molar teeth. L19.

premonish /priːˈmɒnɪʃ/ *verb.* Now *rare.* M16.
[from Latin *praemonere* forewarn, after ADMONISH, MONISH.]
1 *verb trans.* = FOREWARN *verb*[1] 1. M16.
2 *verb intrans.* Give warning beforehand. M16.
■ †**premonishment** *noun* M16–L18.

premonition /prɛməˈnɪʃ(ə)n, priː-/ *noun.* M16.
[French *prémonition* or late Latin *praemonitio(n-)*, from Latin *praemonit-* pa. ppl stem of *praemonere*: see prec., -ITION. Cf. PREMUNITION.]
The action of warning in advance; an advance notification or warning. Now usu., a presentiment, esp. of something bad.

📖 D. CECIL A chilling premonition of death began to steal into his heart. H. ROBBINS She had a sudden premonition that something was wrong.

premonitor /prɪˈmɒnɪtə/ *noun.* E17.
[Latin *praemonitor*, from *praemonit-*: see prec., -OR.]
A person who or thing which gives a forewarning; a premonitory sign or token.

premonitory /prɪˈmɒnɪt(ə)ri/ *adjective & noun.* M17.
[Late Latin *praemonitorius*, formed as prec.: see -ORY[2].]
► **A** *adjective.* Conveying premonition; that warns or notifies in advance. M17.

📖 A. BROOKNER Premonitory rumours that something was afoot had reached me.

► **B** *noun.* In *pl.* Premonitory symptoms. *rare.* M19.

■ **premonitorily** *adverb* M19.

Premonstrant /priːˈmɒnstr(ə)nt/ *noun & adjective. rare.* E18.
[Old French, pres. pple of *premonstrer* show beforehand, used to repr. medieval Latin *Praemonstratensis* PREMONSTRATENSIS: see -ANT[1].]
ECCLESIASTICAL. ►**A** *noun.* = PREMONSTRATENSIAN *noun.* E18.
► **B** *adjective.* = PREMONSTRATENSIAN *adjective.* L19.

premonstrate /priːˈmɒnstreɪt/ *verb trans. rare.* L16.
[Latin *praemonstrat-* ppl. stem of *praemonstrare* show beforehand, from *prae* PRE- + *monstrare* to show.]
Point out or make known beforehand; foreshadow, portend.

Premonstratenses *noun pl.* see PREMONSTRATENSIS.

Premonstratensian /ˌpriːmɒnstrəˈtɛnsɪən/ *noun & adjective.* L15.
[from medieval Latin *Praemonstratensis* (see next) + -AN.]
ECCLESIASTICAL. ►**A** *noun.* A member of a Roman Catholic order of regular canons founded by St Norbert at Prémontré in France, in 1120. Also, a member of a corresponding order of nuns. L15.
► **B** *adjective.* Of or belonging to this order. L17.

Premonstratensis /ˌpriːmɒnstrəˈtɛnsɪs/ *adjective & noun.* Pl. of noun **-tenses** /-ˈtɛnsiːz/. LME.
[medieval Latin = belonging to Prémontré, (*locus*) *Praemonstratus* lit. '(the place) shown beforehand', so called because prophetically pointed out by St Norbert.]
ECCLESIASTICAL. = PREMONSTRATENSIAN.

premonstration /priːmɒnˈstreɪʃ(ə)n/ *noun. rare.* LME.
[Late (eccl.) Latin *praemonstratio(n-)*, formed as PREMONSTRATE: see -ATION.]
The action of showing beforehand; a making known or manifesting in advance.

premorse /priːˈmɔːs/ *adjective.* M18.
[Latin *praemorsus* pa. pple of *praemordere* bite off, from *prae* PRE- + *mordere* to bite.]
BOTANY & ZOOLOGY. Having the end abruptly truncated, as if bitten or broken off.

premortal /priːˈmɔːt(ə)l/ *adjective.* M19.
[from PRE- 2 + MORTAL.]
†**1** Existing or occurring before the creation of mortal creatures. Only in M19.
2 *MEDICINE.* Existing or occurring shortly before death. E20.

pre-mortem /priːˈmɔːtəm/ *adjective & noun.* L19.
[Latin *prae mortem* before death.]
► **A** *adjective.* Taking place or performed before death (opp. ***post-mortem***). L19.
► **B** *noun.* A discussion or analysis of a presumed future death. Chiefly *fig.* L20.

premotion /priːˈməʊʃ(ə)n/ *noun.* M17.
[medieval Latin *praemotio(n-)*, from late Latin *praemovere* move (something) beforehand, from Latin *prae* PRE- + *movere* MOVE *verb* (cf. *motio(n-)* MOTION *noun*).]
Motion or impulse given beforehand; *esp.* divine action as determining will.

premove /priːˈmuːv/ *verb trans. rare.* L16.
[Late Latin *praemovere*: see prec.]
Move or influence beforehand; impel or incite to action.

premunise *verb* var. of PREMUNIZE.

premunition /priːmjuːˈnɪʃ(ə)n/ *noun.* LME.
[Latin *praemunitio(n-)* (in rhet. 'preparation'), from *praemunire* fortify or protect in front, from *prae-* PRE- + *munire* fortify, defend. Cf. PRAEMUNIRE.]
1 [By confusion.] = PREMONITION. Now *rare* or *obsolete.* LME.
2 The action of fortifying or guarding beforehand; a forearming. Now *rare.* E17.
3 *MEDICINE.* (The production of) resistance to disease due to the presence of the causative agent in the host in a harmless or tolerated state. M20.

premunitory /priːˈmjuːnɪt(ə)ri/ *adjective. rare.* E18.
[from Latin *praemunit-* ppl stem of *praemunire* (see prec.) + -ORY[2].]
= PREMONITORY *adjective.*

premunize /ˈpriːmjʊnʌɪz/ *verb trans.* Also **-ise**. E20.
[from PREMUNITION + -IZE.]
MEDICINE. Introduce pathogens into (a host) so as to produce premunition; immunize.
■ **premuniˈzation** *noun* M20.

prenasal /priːˈneɪz(ə)l/ *adjective & noun.* L19.
[from PRE- 2, 1 + NASAL *adjective, noun*.]
► **A** *adjective.* **1** *ANATOMY & ZOOLOGY.* Situated in front of the nose or nasal region. L19.
2 *LINGUISTICS.* Occurring before a nasal consonant. *rare.* L20.
► **B** *noun. LINGUISTICS.* A prenasalized consonant. M20.
■ ˌ**prenasaliˈzation** *noun* pronunciation as a prenasalized consonant M20. **prenasalized** *adjective* (of a consonant) pronounced with initial nasalization M20.

prenatal /priːˈneɪt(ə)l/ *adjective.* E19.
[from PRE- 2 + NATAL *adjective*[1].]
= ANTENATAL.
■ **prenatally** *adverb* L19.

prender /ˈprɛndə/ *noun.* Now *rare.* L16.
[Use as noun of Anglo-Norman *prender* = Old & mod. French *prendre* take: see -ER[4].]
LAW. The power or right of taking a thing without its being offered.

prenex /ˈpriːnɛks/ *adjective.* M20.
[Late Latin *praenexus* tied or bound up in front, from Latin *prae* PRE- + NEXUS.]
MATH. & LOGIC. Pertaining to or designating a quantifier at the beginning of a formula which affects the whole formula.

prenominal /priːˈnɒmɪn(ə)l/ *adjective.* M17.
[from Latin *praenomin-* stem of PRAENOMEN + -AL[1].]
1 Pertaining to a Roman praenomen. Also (*rare*), pertaining to the first word in a binominal plant-name. M17.
2 Of a word, part of speech, etc.: that precedes a noun. M20.

†**prenominate** *adjective.* E16–E17.
[Late Latin *praenominatus* pa. pple of *praenominare*: see next, -ATE[2].]
Before-named, above-named.

†**prenominate** *verb trans.* M16–L17.
[from late Latin *praenominare* name in the first place, from Latin *prae* PRE- + *nominare* NOMINATE *verb*.]
Name beforehand, mention previously.

prenotion /priːˈnəʊʃ(ə)n/ *noun.* Now *rare.* L16.
[Latin *praenotio(n-)* (translation of Greek *prolēpsis*: see PROLEPSIS), from *prae* PRE- + *notio(n-)* NOTION.]
1 A mental perception of something before it exists or happens. Also, foreknowledge, prescience. L16.
2 A notion of something prior to actual knowledge of it; a preconceived idea. E17.

prentice /ˈprɛntɪs/ *noun, adjective, & verb.* Now chiefly *dial.* & *N. Amer.* ME.
[Aphet. from APPRENTICE.]
► **A** *noun.* **1** = APPRENTICE *noun* 1. ME.
†**2** = APPRENTICE *noun* 2. LME–M16.
†**3** = APPRENTICE *noun* 3. L15–L16.
► **B** *attrib.* or as *adjective.* Characteristic of or pertaining to an apprentice or beginner; apprenticed; inexperienced, gauche. L16.

📖 *Times Lit. Suppl.* It is unfair to print such academic prentice-work . . with the work of experienced professionals.

► **C** *verb trans.* = APPRENTICE *verb.* L16.
■ **prenticeship** *noun* = APPRENTICESHIP M16.

pre-nuclear /priːˈnjuːklɪə/ *adjective.* M20.
[from PRE- 2 + NUCLEAR *adjective*.]
1 *PHONETICS.* Occurring before a nucleus. M20.
2 Preceding the development of nuclear weapons. M20.

†**prenunciate** *verb trans.* Also **-tiate**. E–M17.
[Latin *praenuntiat-* pa. ppl stem of *praenuntiare* foretell, from *prae* PRE- + *nuntiare* announce: see -ATE[3].]
Announce beforehand; foretell, predict.
■ †**prenunciation** *noun* E–M17. †**prenunciative** *adjective* (*rare*) M16–M19.

prenup /ˈpriːnʌp/ *noun. N. Amer.* L20.
[Abbreviation.]
A prenuptial agreement.

prenuptial /priːˈnʌpʃ(ə)l/ *adjective.* M19.
[from PRE- 2 + NUPTIAL.]
Existing, occurring, or performed before marriage; premarital.

📖 *Daily Telegraph* Prenuptial conceptions and illegitimate births. **prenuptial agreement**: made by a couple before they marry concerning their respective assets subsequent to the marriage.

preoccupancy /priːˈɒkjʊp(ə)nsi/ *noun.* M18.
[from PRE- 1 + OCCUPANCY.]
1 = PREOCCUPATION 3. M18.
2 = PREOCCUPATION 4. M19.

preoccupant /priːˈɒkjʊp(ə)nt/ *adjective & noun. rare.* M17.
[from PRE- 1 + OCCUPANT.]
► **A** *adjective.* Preoccupying, mentally engrossing. M17.
► **B** *noun.* A person who occupies a place beforehand or before another person. E19.

†**preoccupate** *verb trans.* L16.
[Latin *praeoccupat-*: see next, -ATE[3].]
1 Take possession of or seize beforehand or before another person; usurp. L16–E18.
2 Take unawares, surprise. L16–M17.
3 Prepossess; influence, prejudice. L16–L17.
4 Anticipate; forestall. L16–L17.

preoccupation /ˌpriːɒkjʊˈpeɪʃ(ə)n/ *noun.* L16.
[French *préoccupation* or Latin *praeoccupatio(n-)*, from *praeoccupat-* pa. ppl stem of *praeoccupare* beforehand, from *prae* PRE- + *occupare* OCCUPY: see -ATION.]

For other words beginning with *pre-* see the entry for **pre-**

†**1** The meeting of objections beforehand; *spec.* in RHETORIC, a figure of speech in which objections are anticipated and prevented, prolepsis. L16–L17.
2 Mental prepossession leading to a particular disposition; bias, prejudice. E17.
3 Occupation of a place beforehand. M17.
4 The state or condition of being preoccupied; mental absorption. M19.
5 A thing that dominates a person's thoughts. L19.

> **2** J. LOCKE 'Tis your preoccupation in favour of me, that makes you say what you do. **4** GEO. ELIOT Gravity and intellectual preoccupation in his face. **5** J. RATHBONE His main preoccupation was Astronomy. P. FITZGERALD Gradually the class returned to their preoccupations.

preoccupied /priːˈɒkjʊpʌɪd/ *ppl adjective.* L16.
[from next + -ED[1].]
†**1** Prejudiced, prepossessed. L16–E17.
2 Engrossed in thought; mentally abstracted; expressive of such a state. Also foll. by *with.* M19.
3 TAXONOMY. Of a name: already in use for another organism or taxon. M19.

> **2** J. BARTH I did a lot of staring at nothing, as though preoccupied with my thoughts. I. MURDOCH He gazed at her with remote brooding preoccupied eyes. TOECKEY JONES His mind was preoccupied and he had little time to devote to family matters.

■ **preoccupiedly** *adverb* in a preoccupied manner; with preoccupation of thought: L19.

preoccupy /priːˈɒkjʊpʌɪ/ *verb trans.* M16.
[from PRE- 1 + OCCUPY, after Latin *praeoccupare* (see PREOCCUPATION).]
1 Dominate or engross mentally to the exclusion of other things. Formerly also, prepossess, prejudice. M16.
2 Occupy or appropriate for use beforehand or before another person. E17.
†**3** Anticipate; possess by anticipation. E17–L18.

> **1** *Bella* A distant issue may preoccupy your mind. **2** B. POTTER The ground was pre-occupied by a belligerent assembly.

preon /ˈpriːɒn/ *noun.* L20.
[from PRE- 1 + -ON.]
PARTICLE PHYSICS. A hypothetical particle proposed as a constituent of quarks and leptons.

pre-op /ˈpriːɒp/ *adjective. colloq.* M20.
[Abbreviation.]
= PREOPERATIVE, PRE-OPERATION *adjective.*

pre-operation /ˌpriːɒpəˈreɪʃ(ə)n/ *noun & adjective. rare.* E17.
[from PRE- 1, 2 + OPERATION.]
► **A** *noun.* **1** Action beforehand. E17.
2 A preoperational activity. L20.
► **B** *adjective.* Preoperative. L20.

preoperational /ˌpriːɒpəˈreɪʃ(ə)n(ə)l/ *adjective.* M20.
[from PRE- 2 + OPERATIONAL.]
PSYCHOLOGY. Pertaining to or designating a stage of a child's development (between about two and seven years) in which it is regarded as able to understand or foresee the effects of its actions only in an unsystematic and sometimes contradictory way.

preoperative /priːˈɒp(ə)rətɪv/ *adjective.* E20.
[from PRE- 2 + OPERATIVE.]
MEDICINE. Given or occurring before a surgical operation.
■ **preoperatively** *adverb* M20.

pre-operculum /priːəˈpəːkjʊləm/ *noun.* Pl. **-la** /-lə/. E19.
[from PRE- 1 + OPERCULUM.]
ICHTHYOLOGY. The foremost of the four bones forming the operculum in fishes.
■ **pre-opercular** *adjective* M19.

preordain /priːɔːˈdeɪn/ *verb trans.* M16.
[from PRE- 1 + ORDAIN *verb*, repr. late Latin *praeordinare* predestine, French †*préordiner* (mod. *préordonner*).]
Ordain or appoint beforehand; foreordain.
■ **preordainment** *noun* M19.

pre-ordinate /priːˈɔːdɪnət/ *ppl adjective. arch.* LME.
[Late Latin *praeordinatus* pa. pple of *praeordinare*: see prec., -ATE[2].]
Foreordained, predestined.

pre-ordination /ˌpriːɔːdɪˈneɪʃ(ə)n/ *noun.* Now *rare.* M16.
[from PRE- + ORDINATION.]
The action of preordaining or settling beforehand; the condition of being preordained; predestination.

pre-owned /priːˈəʊnd/ *adjective.* M20.
[from PRE- 1 + *owned* pa. pple of OWN *verb*.]
Second-hand.

prep /prɛp/ *noun*[1]. *colloq.* M19.
[Abbreviation of PREPARATION.]
1 = PREPARATION 1d. M19. ►**b** *gen.* (A) preparation. E20.
2 *US.* A horse-race that is a preparation for a more important event. M20.

> **1** A. DJOLETO Some eating toffee and others doing their prep. *attrib.*: E. S. TURNER At prep time they were not allowed to use ink. **2** *New Yorker* Quiet Little Table . . won the prep. *Dirt Rider* During his race prep of the bike, Wageman discovered a broken silencer mount.

Comb.: **prep chef**, **prep cook**: who undertakes the initial preparation of food in a kitchen.

prep /prɛp/ *adjective & noun*[2]. *colloq.* L19.
[Abbreviation of PREPARATORY *adjective*.]
► **A** *adjective.* **1** ***prep school***, a preparatory school. L19.
2 A pupil at such a school; a student who is preparing for college. *US.* L19.
► **B** *noun.* = ***prep school*** in sense A.1. L19.

prep /prɛp/ *verb*[1] *intrans. US colloq.* Infl. **-pp-**. E20.
[from PREP *noun*[2].]
Attend or be a pupil at a preparatory school.

prep /prɛp/ *verb*[2]. *colloq.* Infl. **-pp-**. E20.
[from PREP *noun*[1] or abbreviation of PREPARE *verb*.]
1 *verb trans.* Prepare, train, make ready or suitable; *spec.* (***a***) train (an animal) for racing; (***b***) prepare (a patient) for surgery. E20.
2 *verb intrans.* Prepare oneself for an event; practise, train, esp. in sport. *US.* M20.

> **1** *New Yorker* She had been prepped and given an epidural anesthesia.

prep. *abbreviation.*
Preposition.

prepack /*as verb* priːˈpak; *as noun* ˈpriːpak/ *verb & noun.* E20.
[from PRE- 1 + PACK *noun*, *verb*[1].]
► **A** *verb trans.* Pack or wrap (an article, esp. of food) at the place of production or before sale. E20.

> *Times Educ. Suppl.* The coffee is weak, and the lunches are pre-packed. *fig.*: E. ANTHONY The average pre-packed American beauty.

► **B** *noun.* A container or wrapper in which an article is prepacked. M20.

pre-package /priːˈpakɪdʒ/ *verb trans.* M20.
[from PRE- 1 + PACKAGE *verb*.]
= PREPACK *verb*. Chiefly as ***pre-packaged*** *ppl adjective*, ***pre-packaging*** *verbal noun*.

> *Times* The growing popularity of pre-packaged foods. *fig.*: *National Times* A pre-packaged night-time TV documentary-type speech.

prepaid *verb pa. t. & pple* of PREPAY.

preparable /ˈprɛp(ə)rəb(ə)l/ *adjective. rare.* M17.
[French *préparable*, formed as PREPARE *verb*: see -ABLE.]
Able to be prepared.

preparate /ˈprɛp(ə)rət/ *adjective. rare.* LME.
[Latin *preparatus* pa. pple of *preparare* PREPARE *verb*: see -ATE[2].]
Prepared.

preparation /prɛpəˈreɪʃ(ə)n/ *noun.* LME.
[Old & mod. French *préparation* from Latin *praeparatio(n-)*, from *praeparat-* pa. ppl stem of *praeparare*: see PREPARE *verb*, -ATION.]
1 The action or process, or an act, of preparing; the condition of being prepared; making or getting ready. LME. ►**b** The acts or observances preliminary to the celebration of the Jewish Sabbath or other festival. Also, the day before such a festival. M16. ►**c** ECCLESIASTICAL. The action of preparing for the Eucharist; a set of prayers used before its celebration. Also, the first part of the Eucharistic rite. E17. ►**d** School work done outside teaching periods by a pupil preparing for subsequent lessons, esp. in a public school or preparatory school; (a) time in a school routine set aside for this. Cf. PREP *noun*[1] 1. M19.
2 A preparatory act or procedure; usu. in *pl.*, things done to make ready (*for* something). M16.
†**3** A personal accomplishment. *rare* (Shakes.). Only in L16.
†**4** A thing which is prepared for any action, esp. warfare; a piece of equipment; a force or fleet fitted out for attack or defence. L16–L18.
5 **a** A specially prepared or made up substance, as a medicine, foodstuff, etc. M17. ►**b** A specimen of a natural object specially prepared or treated for dissection, display, or other purpose. M18.
6 MUSIC. The sounding of the dissonant note in a discord as a consonant note in the previous chord, so lessening the effect of the discord. E18.

> **1a** *Bookman* A new edition is in active preparation. *Studio News* Each stage in the preparation of a piece of music is important. **2** *Times* The final preparations are made for the . . ballot of miners next week. J. DISKI Mo had finished her preparations and made her arrangements. **5a** F. O'CONNOR White skin that glistened with a greasy preparation. C. PRIEST The profusion of bottles, pills and other preparations—herbal remedies, powders, salts.

preparative /prɪˈparətɪv/ *noun, adjective, & adverb.* LME.
[Old & mod. French *préparatif, -ive* or medieval Latin *preparativus*, from Latin *praeparat-*: see prec., -IVE.]
► **A** *noun.* **1** A preparatory act or procedure; a thing that prepares; a preparation. LME. ►†**b** MEDICINE. A preparation administered before medication or other treatment, to prepare the body for it. L15–L18.
†**2** A precedent. *Scot.* M16–E18.
3 MILITARY & NAUTICAL. A signal sounded as an order to make ready. M17.

> **1** G. BURNET The first Step, without any Preamble or Preparative, is downright Beastliness.

► **B** *adjective.* **1** That prepares; preliminary, preparatory. L15.
2 Used in or for preparing. *rare.* M18.
1 preparative meeting a local meeting of the Society of Friends, preparatory and subordinate to a monthly meeting.
► **C** *adverb.* By way of preparation; preparatory. *rare.* M17.
■ **preparatively** *adverb* E17.

preparator /ˈprɛpəreɪtə/ *noun.* LME.
[Late Latin *praeparator*, from Latin *praeparat-*: see PREPARATION, -OR.]
Orig., a thing which prepares or promotes. Later, a person who makes a preparation; a preparer of medicine, specimens, etc.

preparatory /prɪˈparət(ə)ri/ *adjective, noun, & adverb.* LME.
[Late Latin *praeparatorius*, from Latin *praeparat-*: see PREPARATION, -ORY[1], -ORY[2].]
► **A** *adjective.* That prepares or serves to prepare for something following; preliminary, introductory. LME.
preparatory school in Britain, a junior school in which pupils are prepared for public school; in the US, a usu. private school in which pupils are prepared for college entrance.
► **B** *noun.* †**1** In *pl.* A (military) vanguard. Only in LME.
†**2** = PREPARATIVE *noun* 1. L15–E19.
3 A preparatory school. E20.
► **C** *adverb.* In or by way of preparation; as a preliminary. Foll. by *to.* M17.

> D. HAMMETT Cutting up the body preparatory to eating it. B. MONTGOMERY As we were circling the airfield preparatory to landing the engine cut out.

■ **preparatorily** *adverb* M17.

prepare /prɪˈpɛː/ *noun.* M16.
[from the verb.]
1 The act of preparing; preparation. Long *obsolete* exc. *dial.* M16.
2 A substance used to prepare something for dyeing. L19.

prepare /prɪˈpɛː/ *verb.* LME.
[French *préparer* or Latin *praeparare*, from *prae* PRE- + *parare* make ready.]
1 **a** *verb trans.* Put beforehand into a suitable condition for some action; bring into a proper state for use; get or make ready; fit out, equip. LME. ►**b** *verb trans.* Bring into a state of mental or spiritual readiness; incline or dispose beforehand. E16. ►**c** *verb trans. & intrans.* Make ready (a speech, sermon, lesson, etc.) by previous study. L17. ►**d** *verb trans.* Compose and write out; draw up (a text or document). L18. ►**e** *verb trans.* Fit or make ready (a person) by preliminary instruction or training. (Foll. by *for.*) L19.
2 *verb trans.* Make ready (food, a meal) for eating; cook or assemble in eatable form and serve. L15.
3 *verb intrans. & refl.* Put oneself, or things, in readiness; make preparation. (Foll. by *for, to do.*) E16.
†**4** *verb intrans. & refl.* Make ready for a journey; get ready to go. Also, go, set off. E16–L18.
5 *verb trans.* Produce or form (esp. a chemical or medicinal product) by a regular process; manufacture, make. M16.
6 *verb trans.* MUSIC. Lead up to (a discord) by preparation (see PREPARATION *noun* 6). E18.

> **1a** R. GRAVES Tiberius had a fleet standing by prepared. *Guardian* The union prepares national industrial action against overcrowding . . in the jails. **b** E. LYALL I am trying to prepare you . . He is dead. **c** J. WAIN He . . launched into what seemed like a . . prepared speech. **d** A. CARNEGIE I prepared a prospectus which I had printed. **e** M. BARING Mr Owen . . was a specialist in preparing boys for Oxford and Cambridge. **2** S. BELLOW On a summer evening . . she'd probably prepare vichyssoise. P. ABRAHAMS She prepared the day's main meal. **3** D. H. LAWRENCE He was probably preparing to go out somewhere. O. MANNING He spoke like a man preparing for a difficult time ahead. W. M. CLARKE London was already preparing itself for . . winter. **5** H. WATTS Hydrogen prepared by dissolving zinc or iron in sulphuric acid.

Phrases: **be prepared** be ready (*for, to do*); be mentally inclined or willing. **prepare the way** make preparations; prepare a receptive environment or setting; ***prepare the way for***, contribute to, lead to, encourage or facilitate the occurrence of.
■ **preparedly** *adverb* in a prepared manner or condition; in a state of readiness: E17. **preparedness** /prɪˈpɛːrɪdnɪs, -ˈpɛːdnɪs/ *noun* the state or condition of being prepared, esp. (MILITARY) against attack; readiness: L16. **preparer** *noun* a person who or thing which prepares L15.

For other words beginning with *pre-* see the entry for **pre-**

prepartum /priːˈpɑːtəm/ *adjective.* M19.
[Latin *prae partum* before birth.]
MEDICINE. = ANTEPARTUM.

prepay /priːˈpeɪ/ *verb trans.* Pa. t. & pple **-paid** /-ˈpeɪd/. M19.
[from PRE- 1 + PAY *verb*[1].]
1 Pay postage on (a letter, parcel, etc.) before posting. M19.
2 Pay (a charge) in advance. E20.
■ **prepayable** *adjective* that may or must be prepaid L19. **prepayment** *noun* the action of prepaying something, (a) payment in advance M19.

prepend /prɪˈpɛnd/ *verb trans. rare.* M16.
[from PRE- 1 + Latin *pendere* weigh.]
Weigh mentally, ponder; premeditate.

prepense /priːˈpɛns/ *adjective.* E18.
[Alt. of earlier *prepensed* pa. pple of PREPENSE *verb*, after Latin pa. pples in *-ensus*.]
1 Considered and planned beforehand; premeditated, deliberate. Chiefly in ***malice prepense*** (LAW), malice aforethought. Cf. PROPENSE 3. E18.
2 Of a person: acting with intention, deliberate. *rare.* L19.

> 📖 **1** *joc.*: L. STEPHEN He . . plunges into slang, not irreverently . . but of malice prepense. **2** G. MACDONALD He was an orator wilful and prepense.

■ **prepensely** *adverb* M19.

†**prepense** *verb trans.* E16–E18.
[Alt. of earlier PURPENSE, with substitution of prefix PRE- to emphasize the notion of 'beforehand'.]
Plan, devise, or consider beforehand. Chiefly as ***prepensed*** *ppl adjective.*
malice prepensed LAW = *malice prepense* S.V. PREPENSE *adjective* 1.

prepollent /prɪˈpɒl(ə)nt/ *adjective.* Now *rare.* M17.
[Latin *praepollent-* pres. ppl stem of *praepollere* exceed in power, from *prae* PRE- + *pollere* be strong: see -ENT.]
Having superior power, weight, or influence; predominating, prevailing.
■ **prepollency** *noun* L17.

prepolymer /priːˈpɒlɪmə/ *noun.* M20.
[from PRE- 2 + POLYMER.]
CHEMISTRY. An intermediate in polymerization which is convenient for manipulation and is fully polymerized at a later stage in the process.
■ **prepolymeriˈzation** *noun* the formation of a prepolymer M20. **prepolymerize** *verb trans.* convert (a monomer) into a prepolymer M20.

preponder /prɪˈpɒndə/ *verb.* Now *rare.* E16.
[French *prépondérer* or Latin *praeponderare*: see PREPONDERATE *verb*[1].]
†**1** *verb trans.* Attach greater importance to. *rare.* Only in E16.
2 *verb trans.* Outweigh in importance, preponderate over. E17.
3 *verb intrans.* Have greater weight, influence, etc. L17.

preponderance /prɪˈpɒnd(ə)r(ə)ns/ *noun.* L17.
[from next: see -ANCE.]
1 Superiority in physical weight. L17. ▸**b** MILITARY. The excess weight of the part of a gun behind the trunnions over that in front of them. M19.
2 Superiority in moral weight, influence, or importance. L18.
3 Superiority in number or amount. M19.

> 📖 **2** J. BENTHAM The good would have an incontestible preponderance over the evil. **3** *Railway Magazine* The narrow-gauge preponderance in industry is such that only 14 . . sites are standard gauge. *Independent* The pub now attracts a preponderance of families with children and young couples.

■ Also **preponderancy** *noun* (now *rare*) M17.

preponderant /prɪˈpɒnd(ə)r(ə)nt/ *adjective.* LME.
[Latin *praeponderant-* pres. ppl stem of *praeponderare*: see next, -ANT[1].]
Having greater influence, power, or importance; predominant.

> 📖 W. LIPPMANN The dominion which Great Britain exercised . . and the preponderant influence . . were not felt to be intolerable.

■ **preponderantly** *adverb* E19.

preponderate /prɪˈpɒnd(ə)rət/ *adjective. rare.* E19.
[Latin *praeponderatus* pa. pple of *praeponderare*: see next, -ATE[2].]
Preponderating, predominant.
■ **preponderately** *adverb* E19.

preponderate /prɪˈpɒndəreɪt/ *verb*[1]. E17.
[Latin *praeponderat-* pa. ppl stem of *praeponderare*, from *prae* PRE- + *ponderare*: see PONDER *verb*, -ATE[3].]
1 *verb intrans.* **a** Weigh more, be heavier; *fig.* have greater moral or intellectual weight. E17. ▸**b** Be superior in power, amount, number, etc.; predominate. L18.
†**2** *verb trans.* Exceed in weight; *fig.* exceed in importance, value, or influence. E17–M18.
†**3** *verb trans.* Cause (one scale of a balance etc.) to descend on account of greater weight; *fig.* cause to incline more strongly. M17–L18.
4 *verb intrans.* Of the scale of a balance: incline downwards on account of greater weight. L17. ▸**b** Gravitate, incline more strongly. *rare.* L17.

> 📖 **1a** W. R. D. FAIRBAIRN Although one of these attitudes may come to preponderate, there is . . a constant oscillation between them. **b** D. LODGE Caribbean faces now preponderate on the pavement.

■ **preponderatingly** *adverb* in a preponderating degree, predominantly M19. **preponderˈration** *noun* (now *rare*) (*a*) preponderance, predominance; (*b*) greater inclination or bias: M17.

†**preponderate** *verb*[2] *trans. & intrans.* L16–M19.
[from PRE- 1 + PONDERATE *verb*.]
Weigh in the mind or ponder beforehand.

preponderous /priːˈpɒnd(ə)rəs/ *adjective. rare.* E18.
[from PRE- 1 + PONDEROUS, after PREPONDERATE *adjective* etc.]
Greater in weight, amount, or number; having the preponderance.

prepone /priːˈpəʊn/ *verb trans.* L20.
[from PRE- after *postpone*.]
Bring forward to an earlier date or time.

prepose /priːˈpəʊz/ *verb trans.* L15.
[French *préposer*, after Latin *praeponere* put before. Cf. PRAEPOSITUS.]
†**1** Place in authority. L15–M17.
†**2** Propose, purpose, intend. E16–M17.
3 Now chiefly LINGUISTICS. Place in front; preface, prefix. M16.

preposition /prɛpəˈzɪʃ(ə)n, *in sense 3* priːpə-/ *noun.* In sense 3 now usu. **pre-position**. LME.
[Latin *praepositio(n-)* putting in front, (translation of Greek *prothesis*) preposition, from *praeponere*: see PRE-, POSITION *noun*.]
1 GRAMMAR. One of the traditional parts of speech, an indeclinable word governing (and usu. preceding) a noun, pronoun, etc., and expressing a relation between it and another word, e.g. Stratford *on* Avon, good *for* food, come *after* dinner, what did you do it *for*? Also, such a word when combined as prefix with a verb or other word. LME. ▸†**b** Any word or particle prefixed to another word; a prefix. M16–M17.
†**2** [By confusion of *pre-* and *pro-*.] A proposition; an exposition. L15–M16.
3 Chiefly LINGUISTICS. The action of placing in front; the fact of being so placed, position in front. L16. ▸†**b** A thing placed in front. M17–E19.
1 postpositive preposition a preposition which follows its noun, e.g. he goes home*wards*.
■ **prepositional** *adjective* of, pertaining to, or expressed by a preposition; formed with or functioning as a preposition; GRAMMAR designating or pertaining to a case (in Russian etc.) of nouns and pronouns (and words in agreement with them) used after certain prepositions: M19. **prepositionally** *adverb* M19. **prepositionless** *adjective* M20.

pre-position /priːpəˈzɪʃ(ə)n/ *verb trans.* M20.
[from PRE- 1 + POSITION *verb*.]
Position (esp. military equipment) in advance.

prepositive /prɪˈpɒzɪtɪv/ *adjective & noun.* L16.
[Late Latin *praepositivus*, from Latin *prae* PRE- + POSITIVE.]
▸ **A** *adjective.* Of a word, particle, etc.: that should be placed in front of a word or letter. L16.
▸ **B** *noun.* A prepositive word or particle. L17.
■ **prepositively** *adverb* by placing in front L19.

prepositor /prɪˈpɒzɪtə/ *noun*[1]. Now *rare.* Also **prae-**. E16.
[Alt. of Latin PRAEPOSITUS: cf. PRAEPOSTOR.]
1 = PRAEPOSTOR. E16.
†**2** The manager of an establishment; the head of a monastic house. L17–L19.
■ **preposiˈtorial** *adjective* M19.

†**prepositor** *noun*[2]. L17–M19.
[Latin *praepositor*, from *praeposit-* pa. ppl stem of *praeponere* put in charge: see -OR.]
SCOTS LAW. The principal who deputes the management of a business or commercial undertaking to a factor, consignee, or institor.

†**preposíture** *noun.* LME–M18.
[Late Latin *praepositura* office of overseer (in medieval Latin in English sense), from Latin PRAEPOSITUS: see -URE.]
The office of praepositus or provost in a collegiate church or priory.

prepossess /priːpəˈzɛs/ *verb trans.* E17.
[from PRE- 1 + POSSESS, prob. after medieval Latin *prepossessus* seized beforehand.]
†**1** Take or have prior possession of; *refl.* possess oneself *of* beforehand; in *pass.*, have possession *of* beforehand. E17–M18.
2 Cause (a person) to be imbued *with* or strongly affected beforehand *by* a feeling or idea. Formerly also, cause to think *that*. M17.
3 Influence (a person) in advance in favour of or against a person or thing. Now chiefly, impress favourably beforehand. M17.

> 📖 **1** R. L'ESTRANGE Without more ado they prepossess'd themselves of the Temple. R. SOUTH Hope is that which . . prepossesses a future good. **2** J. AUSTEN Strongly prepossessed that neither she nor her daughters were such kind of women. J. KEBLE The Creed . . had prepossessed them with these truths, before ever they thought of proving them. **3** E. A. POE An attempt was made . . to prepossess the public against his 'Classical Dictionary'.

prepossessing /priːpəˈzɛsɪŋ/ *ppl adjective.* M17.
[from prec. + -ING[2].]
1 Causing prejudice. Now *rare* or *obsolete.* M17.
2 Creating a favourable first impression, attractive. E19.

> 📖 **2** C. P. SNOW He was pallid and not prepossessing, with . . a flattish Slav nose.

■ **prepossessingly** *adverb* E19. **prepossessingness** *noun* L19.

prepossession /priːpəˈzɛʃ(ə)n/ *noun.* M17.
[from PREPOSSESS *verb* after POSSESSION.]
1 Prior possession or occupancy. Now *rare* or *obsolete.* M17.
2 A preconceived opinion which tends to bias the mind; unfavourable or (now chiefly) favourable predisposition. M17.

> 📖 **2** R. FRY According to his prepossessions he is likely to be shocked or pleased.

preposterous /prɪˈpɒst(ə)rəs/ *adjective.* M16.
[from Latin *praeposterus* reversed, from *prae* PRE- + *posterus* coming after: see -OUS.]
1 Having last what should be first; inverted. Now *rare.* M16.
2 Contrary to nature, reason, or common sense; monstrous, perverse; utterly absurd, outrageous. M16.

> 📖 **2** W. BUCHAN Nothing can be more preposterous than a mother who thinks it below her to take care of her . . child. R. K. NARAYAN He expressed his gay mood by tying a preposterous turban round his head. F. TOMLIN Accusations that he was a 'fascist' . . are little short of preposterous.

■ **preposterously** *adverb* M16. **preposterousness** *noun* E17.

prepostor *noun* var. of PRAEPOSTOR.

prepotency /priːˈpəʊt(ə)nsi/ *noun.* M17.
[Latin *praepotentia*, formed as next: see -ENCY.]
The quality of being prepotent.
■ Also **prepotence** *noun* E19.

prepotent /priːˈpəʊt(ə)nt/ *adjective.* LME.
[Latin *praepotent-*, *-ens*, from *prae* PRE- + POTENT *adjective*[2].]
1 Having great power or influence; more powerful than others. LME.
2 BIOLOGY. Having a greater power of fertilization or of transmitting hereditary characters. M19.
3 PSYCHOLOGY. Designating the stimulus which determines the response when stimuli with conflicting responses occur together. E20.

> 📖 **1** F. B. YOUNG His grandmother, that prepotent, regal figure of his early years. **2** J. A. MICHENER This prepotent gentleman had sired seven sons in a row.

■ **prepotently** *adverb* L19.

prepper /ˈprɛpə/ *noun. slang.* M20.
[from PREP *noun*[2] + -ER[1], -ER[6].]
1 (A member of) a preparatory school sports team. *US.* M20.
2 A preparatory school. M20.

preppy /ˈprɛpi/ *adjective & noun.* Chiefly *N. Amer. colloq.* (freq. *derog.*). Also **preppie**. E20.
[from PREP *noun*[2] + -Y[1], -Y[6], -IE.]
▸ **A** *adjective.* Orig., silly, immature. Now usu., traditional in outlook, style, etc.; (of clothes) tastefully neat and stylish, in a way suggestive of a person who has been to an expensive school. E20.

> 📖 *Times* He looks prosperously preppy with curly hair cut neat . . subtle grey Armani trousers.

▸ **B** *noun.* **1** A pupil or former pupil of a preparatory school, esp. an expensive one. E20.
2 A person with 'preppy' characteristics; a wearer of 'preppy' fashions. L20.
¶ Rare before L20.
■ **preppiness** *noun* L20.

preprandial /priːˈprandɪəl/ *adjective.* E19.
[from PRE- 2 + Latin *prandium* lunch + -AL[1].]
Done, taken, etc., before dinner.

> 📖 A. WILSON Chicken sandwiches are all right with the preprandial sherry, but they're not a meal.

prepreg /ˈpriːprɛg/ *noun.* M20.
[from PRE-(IM)PREG(NATED).]
A fibrous material pre-impregnated with synthetic resin for use in making reinforced plastics.

preprint /ˈpriːprɪnt/ *noun.* L19.
[from PRE- 1 + PRINT *noun*.]
A thing printed in advance; a portion of a work printed and issued before the publication of the whole.

For other words beginning with *pre-* see the entry for **pre-**

preprint /priːˈprɪnt/ *verb trans.* E20.
[from PRE- 1 + PRINT *verb*.]
Print in advance; *spec.* print and issue (part of a work) before publication of the whole.

preprocess /priːˈprəʊsɛs/ *verb trans.* M20.
[from PRE- 1 + PROCESS *verb*[1].]
Subject to a preliminary processing.
■ **ˈpreprocessor** *noun* a machine for preprocessing something; a computer program that modifies data to conform with the input requirements of a standard program: M20.

preproduction /priːprəˈdʌkʃ(ə)n/ *noun & adjective.* M20.
[from PRE- 1, 2 + PRODUCTION.]
▶ **A** *noun.* **1** (A) preliminary or trial production. M20.
2 Work prior to production, esp. of a film; preparation for production. L20.
▶ **B** *adjective.* Prior to or preliminary to (a) production. M20.

prepubertal /priːpjuːˈbəːt(ə)l/ *adjective.* M19.
[from PRE- 2 + PUBERTAL.]
Occurring prior to the attainment of puberty; that has not yet attained puberty.
■ Also **preˈpuberal** *adjective* M20.

prepuberty /priːˈpjuːbəti/ *noun.* E20.
[from PRE- 2 + PUBERTY.]
The period of life preceding puberty, esp. the two or three years immediately before.

prepubes *noun* pl. of PREPUBIS.

prepubescent /priːpjʊˈbɛs(ə)nt/ *adjective & noun.* E20.
[from PRE- 2 + PUBESCENT.]
▶ **A** *adjective.* = PREPUBERTAL. E20.
▶ **B** *noun.* A prepubescent boy or girl. M20.
■ **prepubescence** *noun* = PREPUBERTY E20.

prepubis /priːˈpjuːbɪs/ *noun.* Pl. **-pubes** /-ˈpjuːbiːz/. L19.
[from PRE- 1, 2 + PUBIS.]
ANATOMY & ZOOLOGY. **1** The portion of the pubis in front of the acetabulum, esp. in dinosaurs. L19.
2 = EPIPUBIS. M20.
■ **prepubic** *adjective* (*a*) of or pertaining to the prepubis; (*b*) situated in front of the pubis: L19.

prepuce /ˈpriːpjuːs/ *noun.* LME.
[French *prépuce* from Latin PRAEPUTIUM.]
1 The foreskin. Also, the fold of skin surrounding the clitoris. LME.
†**2** *fig.* The state of uncircumcision. LME–L16.

prepunctual /priːˈpʌŋktjʊəl/ *adjective. rare.* L19.
[from PRE- 1 + PUNCTUAL.]
Arriving or occurring earlier than the appointed time.
■ ˌ**prepunctuˈality** *noun* L19.

prepupa /priːˈpjuːpə/ *noun.* Pl. **-pae** /-piː/. E20.
[from PRE- 2 + PUPA.]
ENTOMOLOGY. An insect larva during a relatively quiescent phase just before the transformation into a pupa; a distinct instar preceding the pupa stage of certain beetles.
■ **prepupal** *adjective* E20.

preputial /priːˈpjuːʃ(ə)l/ *adjective.* E17.
[from Latin *praeputium* PREPUCE + -AL[1].]
Of or pertaining to the prepuce.

prequel /ˈpriːkw(ə)l/ *noun.* L20.
[from PRE- 1 + SE)QUEL.]
A book, film, etc., portraying events which precede those of an existing work.

Pre-Raphael /priːˈrafeɪɛl/ *adjective.* Now *rare.* M19.
[from PRE- 2 + *Raphael* (see next).]
Of a painter (or painting): dating from before the time of Raphael. Also = PRE-RAPHAELITE *adjective* 1.
■ **Pre-Raphaelism** *noun* (*a*) the art of the painters who preceded Raphael; (*b*) Pre-Raphaelitism: M19.

Pre-Raphaelite /priːˈrafəlʌɪt/ *noun & adjective.* M19.
[from PRE- 2 + *Raphael*, Italian *Raffaello*, *-aele* (see below) + -ITE[1].]
▶ **A** *noun.* Any of a group of 19th-cent. English painters (including Holman Hunt, Millais, and D. G. Rossetti) who called themselves 'the Pre-Raphaelite Brotherhood' and sought to return to a style and spirit prevalent before the time of the Italian artist Raphael (1483–1520); *gen.* any artist working in such a style. M19.
▶ **B** *attrib.* or as *adjective.* **1** Of, belonging to, or characteristic of the Pre-Raphaelites or their principles or style. M19. ▸**b** Resembling the female models favoured by the Pre-Raphaelites in slenderness, long wavy hair, etc. L20.
2 Existing before Raphael. M19.

> **1b** N. BAWDEN She was a lovely girl in a rather droopy, Pre-Raphaelite way.

■ **Pre-Raphaelitic** /-ˈlɪtɪk/ *adjective* L19. **Pre-Raphaelitically** /-ˈlɪt-/ *adverb* L19. **Pre-Raphaelitism** *noun* the principles, or the style of painting, of the Pre-Raphaelite Brotherhood and their followers; a similar tendency in poetry and other arts: M19.

pre-record /priːrɪˈkɔːd/ *verb trans.* M20.
[from PRE- 1 + RECORD *verb*.]
Record (esp. material for broadcasting) in advance.

> S. BRETT *The Alexander Harvey Show* was prerecorded some four hours before its . . transmission. **pre-recorded tape** (a) magnetic tape offered for sale with a recording on it.

pre-register /priːˈrɛdʒɪstə/ *verb.* M20.
[from PRE- 1 + REGISTER *verb*.]
1 *verb trans.* Bring into alignment or coincidence beforehand. M20.
2 *verb intrans.* Register in advance (*for* an event etc.). L20.

> **2** *Independent* Three million people have pre-registered for water privatisation.

preregistration /ˌpriːrɛdʒɪˈstreɪʃ(ə)n/ *adjective & noun.* E20.
[from PRE- 1, 2 + REGISTRATION.]
▶ **A** *adjective.* Of or pertaining to the period of a doctor's training between qualification and registration. E20.
▶ **B** *noun.* Registration in advance; the action of pre-registering. M20.

pre-release /priːrɪˈliːs/ *adjective, noun & verb.* E20.
[from PRE- 1, 2 + RELEASE *noun*, *verb*.]
▶ **A** *adjective.* Of or pertaining to the period before the release of a film, record, etc., or of a suspect or prisoner. E20.
▶ **B** *noun.* A film or record given restricted availability before being generally released. E20.
▶ **C** *verb trans.* Release in advance; release to a limited extent in advance of a general release. M20.

prerequire /priːrɪˈkwʌɪə/ *verb trans.* Now *rare.* E17.
[from PRE- 1 + REQUIRE *verb*.]
Require as a prior condition; have as a prerequisite.

> *Christian* There are two levels of psychotherapy, the second prerequiring the first.

prerequisite /priːˈrɛkwɪzɪt/ *adjective & noun.* M17.
[from PRE- 1 + REQUISITE.]
▶ **A** *adjective.* Required as a prior condition. M17.

> COLERIDGE For the human soul to prosper in rustic life, a certain vantage-ground is prerequisite.

▶ **B** *noun.* A thing required as a prior condition. (Foll. by *for*, *to*.) M17.

> H. KISSINGER The indispensable prerequisite of a Secretary of State is the complete confidence of the President. M. EDWARDES Changes at the top were a pre-requisite to the company's survival.

prerogative /prɪˈrɒgətɪv/ *noun.* LME.
[Old & mod. French *prérogative* from Latin *praerogativa*, orig. '(the verdict of) the century which voted first in the Roman comitia', use as noun of fem. of *praerogativus*: see next.]
1 Chiefly *Hist.* The special right or privilege exercised by a monarch or head of State over all other people, which overrides the law and is in theory subject to no restriction. LME. ▸**b** *gen.* A special right or privilege possessed by a person, class, or body. LME.
2 *fig.* A faculty or property by which a person, animal, or (formerly) thing, is specially and advantageously distinguished. LME. ▸†**b** Precedence, pre-eminence. LME–L17.
3 Chiefly ROMAN HISTORY. The right of voting first and thus serving as a guide to the votes that follow. E17.

> **1 prerogative of mercy** the royal prerogative exercised to commute a death sentence or (formerly) to change the mode of execution or to pardon an offender. **royal prerogative** the prerogative of the British monarch under common law. **b** J. BRAINE 'Mistresses mustn't nag,' she said. 'That's a wife's prerogative'. V. BROME Psychopathology was exclusively the prerogative of organic neurologists. **2** H. T. BUCKLE It is the peculiar prerogative of certain minds to be able to interpret as well as . . originate.

Comb.: **prerogative court** (*a*) *Hist.* the court of an archbishop for the probate of wills in which effects to the value of five pounds had been left in each of two or more dioceses in his province; (*b*) *US* (in New Jersey) a probate court; **prerogative writ**: issued in the exercise of the royal prerogative.
■ **prerogatived** *adjective* possessed of a prerogative E17.

prerogative /prɪˈrɒgətɪv/ *adjective.* LME.
[Latin *praerogativus*, from *praerogat-* pa. ppl stem of *praerogare* ask first, from *prae* PRE- + *rogare* ask: see -IVE.]
1 Pertaining to, arising from, or enjoyed by prerogative or special privilege. LME.
2 ROMAN HISTORY. Having the right to vote first. Of a vote: given first and serving as a precedent for those that follow. E17.
3 Having precedence; pre-eminent. *rare.* M17.

> **1** R. C. A. WHITE The Privy Council is the body . . through which the sovereign exercises . . prerogative powers.

prerupt /prɪˈrʌpt/ *adjective. rare.* E17.
[Latin *praeruptus* pa. pple of *praerumpere* break off short, from *prae* PRE- + *rumpere* break.]
1 Abrupt, precipitous. E17.
2 Sudden, unexpected. M19.

pres *noun* var. of PREZ *noun*[2].

For other words beginning with *pre-* see the entry for **pre-**

presa /ˈpreːza/ *noun.* E18.
[Italian = a taking, use as noun of fem. of *preso* pa. pple of *prendere* take.]
MUSIC. A symbol used in a canon etc. to mark the entry of a voice or instrument.

presage /ˈprɛsɪdʒ/ *noun.* LME.
[French *présage* or Latin *praesagium*, from *praesagire* forebode.]
1 An indication, esp. a supernatural one, of what is about to happen; an omen, a portent. LME.
2 An utterance foretelling something in the future; a prediction. Now *rare.* L16.
3 A presentiment, a foreboding. L16.

> **1** N. SHERRY This last night was to be a grim presage of the future. **of evil presage** etc., auguring evil etc. things to come. **2** CLARENDON He might reasonably have expected as ill a presage for himself from these Fortune tellers. **3** J. HODGSON He had a strong presage . . that he had only a very short time to live.

■ **preˈsageful** *adjective* (*a*) full of significance about the future; portentous; (*b*) full of foreboding: L16. **preˈsagefully** *adverb* M19.

presage /ˈprɛsɪdʒ, prɪˈseɪdʒ/ *verb.* M16.
[French *présager* or Latin *praesagire* forebode, from *prae* PRE- + *sagire* perceive keenly.]
1 *verb trans.* Constitute a supernatural or natural indication of (a future event); portend, foreshadow. M16.
2 *verb trans.* Of a person: predict, forecast. L16. ▸†**b** *verb trans.* Point out, make known. *rare* (Spenser). Only in L16. ▸**c** *verb intrans.* Make or utter a prediction. L16.
3 *verb trans.* & †*intrans.* Have a presentiment of (some misfortune). L16.

> **1** JOYCE Have not eclipses been esteemed as omens presaging some direful calamity? P. L. FERMOR The sky presaged snow. M. RICHLER A newly constructed hotel . . opened on the bay outside . . San Antonio, presaging a tourist boom. **2** V. BROME He wrote a letter to Freud which presaged coming events. **3** A. M. BENNETT God forgive me if I don't presage some mischief to poor Miss Rosy.

■ **presager** *noun* a person who or thing which presages or portends something L16. **presagingly** *adverb* in a presaging manner E17.

†**presagious** *adjective.* L15–E18.
[from Latin *praesagium* PRESAGE *noun* + -OUS: cf. French †*presagieux*.]
Of the nature of a presage; portentous. Also, having a presentiment.

pré-salé /presale/ *noun.* Pl. pronounced same. M19.
[French.]
In France: a salt meadow, *esp.* one on which sheep are reared; the flesh of sheep reared on such a meadow.

presanctify /priːˈsaŋktɪfʌɪ/ *verb trans.* M18.
[from PRE- 1 + SANCTIFY.]
Sanctify beforehand. Chiefly in ***Liturgy of the Presanctified, Mass of the Presanctified*** [translation of medieval Latin *missa praesanctificatorum*], a form of the Eucharist at which elements consecrated at a previous celebration are consumed, used in the Roman Catholic and Anglican Churches on Good Friday and in the Orthodox Church during Lent.

presbycusis /prɛzbɪˈkuːsɪs/ *noun.* Also **presbyacusis** /prɛzbɪəˈkuːsɪs/, **-(a)cusia** /-(ə)kuːsɪə/, **-cous-**. L19.
[formed as next + Greek *akousis* hearing, from *akouein* hear: see -IA[1].]
MEDICINE. Loss of acuteness of hearing due to age.

presbyopia /prɛzbɪˈəʊpɪə/ *noun.* L18.
[from Greek *presbus* old man + -OPIA.]
Inability of the eye to adjust its focus to near objects, occurring esp. in old age, owing to loss of elasticity in the lens.
■ **ˈpresbyope** *noun* a person with presbyopia M19. **presbyopic** *adjective & noun* (*a*) *adjective* pertaining to or affected with presbyopia; (*b*) *noun* = PRESBYOPE: E19.

presbyter /ˈprɛzbɪtə/ *noun.* L16.
[ecclesiastical Latin from Greek *presbuteros*, in New Testament = elder of the Sanhedrin or apostolic church, use as noun of compar. of *presbus* old (man): cf. PRIEST.]
1 a In the early Christian church: one of a number of people having oversight of the affairs of a local church or congregation. Cf. BISHOP *noun* 1b. L16. ▸**b** In an Episcopal Church: a minister of the second degree of holy orders, between bishop and deacon; a priest. L16. ▸**c** In a Presbyterian Church: an elder; *esp.* a member of a presbytery. L16.
†**2** A Presbyterian. M17–E19.

> **1c** H. T. BUCKLE The main object was, to raise up presbyters, and to destroy bishops.

■ **presˈbyteral** *adjective* (*a*) of or pertaining to a presbyter or priest; consisting of presbyters; (*b*) = PRESBYTERIAN *adjective* 1: E17. **presbytership** *noun* L16.

presbyterate /prɛzˈbɪt(ə)rət/ *noun.* M17.
[ecclesiastical Latin *presbyteratus*, formed as PRESBYTER: see -ATE[1].]
1 The position or office of presbyter. M17.
2 A body or order of presbyters. M17.

presbyterate /prɛzˈbɪt(ə)reɪt/ *verb trans.* E18.
[from PRESBYTER + -ATE[3].]
Constitute or organize on Presbyterian lines. Chiefly as ***presbyterated*** *ppl adjective.*

presbytère /prɛzbitɛːr/ *noun.* Pl. pronounced same. M19.
[French from late Latin PRESBYTERIUM.]
In France, the house of a Roman Catholic priest.

presbyteress /ˈprɛzbɪt(ə)rɪs/ *noun.* M16.
[medieval Latin *presbyterissa*, formed as PRESBYTERATE *noun* + *-issa* -ESS[1].]
†**1** The wife of a presbyter. M16–L17.
2 *Hist.* A member of an order of women in the early Church, having some of the functions of presbyters. M17.

presbyterial /prɛzbɪˈtɪərɪəl/ *adjective.* L16.
[medieval Latin *presbyterialis*, from ecclesiastical Latin PRESBYTERIUM: see -IAL.]
1 Of or pertaining to a body of elders. L16.
2 (Usu. **P-**.) Presbyterian. Now *rare.* L16.
▪ **presbyterially** *adverb* M17.

presbyterian /prɛzbɪˈtɪərɪən/ *adjective & noun.* Now usu. **P-**. M17.
[from ecclesiastical Latin PRESBYTERIUM + -AN.]
► **A** *adjective.* **1** Pertaining to church government by presbyters or presbyteries; belonging to or maintaining a Church or system of this kind. M17.
2 Characteristic of (a member of) a Presbyterian Church. *rare.* L17.
1 Free Presbyterian Church a Scottish Church formed by secession from the Free Church of Scotland in 1892. **Presbyterian Church** any of various Christian denominations (e.g. the Church of Scotland) in which the Church is governed by elders through a hierarchy of courts. **Reformed Presbyterian Church** a Scottish Church formed by Presbyterians who refused to accept the settlement of 1690 which established the Church of Scotland. **United Presbyterian Church** *Hist.* the Church formed in Scotland in 1847 by the union of the United Secession and Relief Churches.
► **B** *noun.* (**P-**.) An adherent of the Presbyterian system; a member of a Presbyterian Church. M17.
▪ **Presbyterianism** *noun* the Presbyterian doctrines or system of church government M17. **Presbyterianize** *verb trans.* make Presbyterian; organize on Presbyterian lines: M19. **Presbyterianly** *adverb* in a Presbyterian manner or direction M17.

presbyterion *noun* var. of PRESBYTERIUM.

presbyterism /ˈprɛzbɪt(ə)rɪz(ə)m/ *noun. rare.* M17.
[from PRESBYTER + -ISM.]
†**1** (**P-**.) = PRESBYTERIANISM. Only in M17.
2 The position or office of presbyter. E19.

presbyterium /prɛzbɪˈtɪərɪəm/ *noun.* Also **-ion** /-ɪɒn/. M16.
[ecclesiastical Latin *presbyterium* from ecclesiastical Greek *presbuterion*, from *presbuteros* PRESBYTER.]
= PRESBYTERY 1, 5.

presbytery /ˈprɛzbɪt(ə)ri/ *noun.* LME.
[Old French *presbiterie* from ecclesiastical Latin PRESBYTERIUM: see -Y[4].]
1 A part of a cathedral or church reserved for the clergy; the eastern part of the chancel of a cathedral, beyond the choir. LME.
2 In the Presbyterian system: an ecclesiastical court above the kirk-session and below the synod, consisting of all the ministers and one ruling elder (or sometimes two) from each parish or congregation within a given area; the area represented by this court. L16.
3 The Presbyterian system of Church government; Presbyterianism. Now *rare.* L16.
†**4** The position or office of presbyter. L16–E18.
5 A body of presbyters or elders in the early Church. E17.
6 The residence of a priest, esp. one of the Roman Catholic Church. Also ***presbytery-house***. E19.

presbytia /prɛzˈbɪtɪə/ *noun.* Now *rare* or *obsolete.* E18.
[mod. Latin, from Greek *presbutēs* old man: see -IA[1].]
= PRESBYOPIA.

prescaler /priːˈskeɪlə/ *noun.* M20.
[from PRE- 1 + SCALER *noun*[1].]
ELECTRONICS. A scaling circuit used to scale down the input to a counting circuit so that it can deal with high counting rates.

preschool /*as adjective* priːˈskuːl, ˈpriː-; *as noun* ˈpriː-/ *adjective & noun.* E20.
[from PRE- 2 + SCHOOL *noun*[1].]
► **A** *adjective.* Of or pertaining to the time or age before a child is old enough for school, or a child of this age. E20.
📖 *Sun* Educational tapes . . aimed at pre-school children. *Times Educ. Suppl.* The first pre-school playgroup specifically for homeless children.
► **B** *noun.* A kindergarten or nursery school for children of preschool age. M20.
▪ **preˈschooler** *noun* a child who is too young to attend school or who attends preschool M20.

prescience /ˈprɛsɪəns/ *noun.* LME.
[Old French from ecclesiastical Latin *praescientia*, formed as next: see -ENCE.]
1 Knowledge of events before they happen; foreknowledge; *spec.* divine foreknowledge. LME.
2 An instance of this. *rare.* M18.
📖 **1** D. H. LAWRENCE She had a strange prescience, an intimation of something yet to come. **2** S. DONALDSON Kevin was . . gifted or blighted with presciences.

prescient /ˈprɛsɪənt/ *adjective.* E17.
[Latin *praescient-* pres. ppl stem of *praescire* know before, from *prae* PRE- + *scire* know: see -ENT.]
Having foreknowledge or foresight; foreseeing.
📖 P. MAILLOUX Kafka . . an amazingly prescient political writer who had foreseen . . totalitarianism.
▪ **presciently** *adverb* E19.

prescind /prɪˈsɪnd/ *verb.* M17.
[Latin *praescindere* cut off in front, from *prae* PRE- + *scindere* to cut.]
1 *verb trans.* Cut off beforehand, prematurely, or abruptly. M17.
2 *verb trans.* Cut off or separate *from*; abstract *from*. M17.
3 *verb intrans.* Foll. by *from*: leave out of consideration. M17.
📖 **2** J. F. FERRIER Nor have universal things prescinded from the particular any absolute existence. **3** W. S. LILLY In what I am about to write I prescind entirely from all theological theories.

prescribe /prɪˈskraɪb/ *verb.* LME.
[Latin *praescribere* write before, direct in writing, etc., from *prae* PRE- + *scribere* write.]
► **I** *LAW.* †**1** *verb trans.* Hold or claim by prescription. *rare.* LME–E17.
2 *verb intrans.* Make a claim on the basis of prescription; assert a prescriptive right or claim (*to, for, that*). M16.
†**3** *verb intrans.* Of a person: plead prescription of time *against* an action etc.; cease to be liable through lapse of time. L16–L17.
4 *verb intrans. SCOTS LAW.* (Of an action) suffer prescription; lapse through passage of time; (of a claim, debt, etc.) cease to be capable of prosecution. E17.
📖 **2** J. WILLIAMS A man might . . prescribe that he and his ancestors had . . exercised a certain right. **4** *Times* In the law of Scotland . . heritable rights . . did not prescribe unless there had been adverse possession.
► **II 5** *verb trans.* Limit, restrict; confine within bounds. LME.
6 a *verb trans.* Write or lay down as a rule or direction; impose authoritatively; appoint, dictate, direct. L15. ▸**b** *verb intrans.* Lay down rules. M16.
†**7** *verb trans.* Write first or beforehand; write with foreknowledge. M16–M17.
8 *verb trans.* & (now *rare*) *intrans.* Advise or order the use of (a medicine, remedy, etc.), esp. by an authorized prescription; *fig.* recommend as something beneficial. Also foll. by double obj.: advise or order (a person) to take (a medicine etc.). L16.
📖 **6a** W. S. CHURCHILL He made no attempt to prescribe the succession. P. ROTH The gate . . other than the one prescribed for tourists. **b** *American Speech* A modern dictionary that describes but does not prescribe. **8** J. HERRIOT I prescribed a kaolin antacid mixture. M. ROBERTS Dr Felton prescribed me a different tonic.
▪ **prescribable** *adjective* M20. **prescriber** *noun* a person who prescribes M16.

prescript /ˈpriːskrɪpt/ *noun.* M16.
[Latin *praescriptum* use as noun of neut. of *praescriptus*: see next.]
1 A thing that is prescribed or laid down; an ordinance, a law, a command; a direction, an instruction. M16.
2 Medicine prescribed; a medical prescription. Now *rare* or *obsolete.* E17.

prescript /prɪˈskrɪpt/ *adjective.* Now *rare.* LME.
[Latin *praescriptus* pa. pple of *praescribere*: see PRESCRIBE.]
Prescribed as a rule; ordained, appointed, settled.

prescriptible /prɪˈskrɪptɪb(ə)l/ *adjective. rare.* M16.
[from Latin *praescript-*: see next, -IBLE.]
Liable or subject to prescription; based on prescription.
▪ **prescriptiˈbility** *noun* M18.

prescription /prɪˈskrɪpʃ(ə)n/ *noun.* LME.
[Old & mod. French from Latin *praescriptio(n-)*, from *praescript-* pres. ppl stem of *praescribere*: see PRESCRIBE, -ION.]
► **I** *LAW.* **1 a** Uninterrupted use or possession from time immemorial, or for a period fixed by law as giving a title or right; a title or right acquired by such use or possession. Also ***positive prescription***. LME. ▸**b** Limitation of the time within which an action or claim can be raised; the extinction of a title or right by failure to claim it or exercise it over a long period. Also ***negative prescription***. L15.
†**2** The action of claiming on the basis of prescription. M16–E19.
3 Ancient custom, esp. when regarded as authoritative. Also, claim based upon long use. L16.
1a ***short prescription***: see SHORT *adjective.*
► **II 4** The action or an act of prescribing by rule; a thing which is so prescribed. M16.
5 A doctor's instruction, usu. in writing, for the composition and use of a medicine; the action of prescribing a medicine; a medicine prescribed. Also, any treatment ordered by a doctor. L16.
†**6** Restriction, limitation. L16–E18.
📖 **5** P. CAREY His dark glasses . . made to prescription in Dallas, Texas. *Independent* Prescription of drugs by GPs is being closely monitored. *Which?* Antibiotics can be bought . . without . . a prescription. *fig.*: F. RAPHAEL Watered gin, his prescription for poetic fertility.
Comb.: **prescription charge** a usu. fixed charge for a medicine etc. obtained on prescription; **prescription drug**: obtainable only with a doctor's prescription.
▪ **prescriptionist** *noun* †(***a***) a person who writes prescriptions; (***b***) a person who makes up medical prescriptions; (***c***) a prescriptivist: E18.

prescriptive /prɪˈskrɪptɪv/ *adjective.* M18.
[Late Latin *praescriptivus* pertaining to a legal exception or demurrer, from Latin *praescript-*: see prec., -IVE.]
1 That prescribes or directs; giving definite precise directions or instructions. M18. ▸**b** *LINGUISTICS.* Laying down rules of usage. M20. ▸**c** *PHILOSOPHY.* Having or implying an imperative force. M20.
2 *LAW.* Of a right, title, etc.: derived from or based on prescription or lapse of time. M18.
3 Prescribed by long-standing custom or usage. M18.
4 *ANTHROPOLOGY.* Pertaining to or designating marriage traditionally considered obligatory between certain people in a tribe or kinship group. M20.
📖 **3** R. C. HUTCHINSON For her own mother . . she had felt no more than a prescriptive affection. N. ALGREN The prescriptive rights of master over men.
▪ **prescriptively** *adverb* L18. **prescriptiveness** *noun* E19. **prescriptivism** *noun* (***a***) *LINGUISTICS* the practice or advocacy of prescriptive grammar; (***b***) *PHILOSOPHY* the theory that evaluative judgements have prescriptive force like to that of imperatives: M20. **prescriptivist** *noun & adjective* (***a***) *noun* an adherent of prescriptivism; (***b***) *adjective* pertaining to or characteristic of prescriptivism: M20. **prescripˈtivity** *noun* prescriptiveness M20.

preselect /priːsɪˈlɛkt/ *verb trans.* M19.
[from PRE- 1 + SELECT *verb*.]
Select in advance.
▪ **preselective** *adjective* involving or permitting preselection E20.

preselection /priːsɪˈlɛkʃ(ə)n/ *noun & adjective.* E20.
[from PRE- 1, 2 + SELECTION.]
► **A** *noun.* Selection in advance; *spec.* the operation or use of a preselector. E20.
► **B** *adjective.* Occurring before selection. L20.

preselector /priːsɪˈlɛktə/ *noun.* E20.
[from PRE- 1 + SELECTOR.]
1 *TELEPHONY.* A switch in a telephone exchange which, when a receiver is lifted, automatically connects the calling line to a free trunk. E20.
2 *TELECOMMUNICATIONS.* A tuned circuit preceding the first mixer in a superheterodyne receiver; an analogous filter in a microwave receiver. M20.
3 A gearbox that enables a driver to select a gear before the change is actually made. M20.

pre-sell /priːˈsɛl/ *verb trans.* Pa. t. & pple **-sold** /-ˈsəʊld/. M20.
[from PRE- 1 + SELL *verb*.]
COMMERCE. Promote (a product) before it is available to the consumer; persuade (a consumer) in advance to buy a product.

presence /ˈprɛz(ə)ns/ *noun.* ME.
[Old & mod. French *présence* from Latin *praesentia*, from *praesent-*: see PRESENT *adjective & adverb*, -ENCE.]
1 The fact or condition of being present; the state of being with or in the same place as a person or thing; attendance, association. ME. ▸**b** = ***presence of mind*** below. L20.
2 The place or space around or in front of a person; the company or society of someone; *spec.* that of a monarch or other distinguished person. ME. ▸†**b** = ***presence chamber*** below. M16–M18.
†**3** A number of people assembled together; an assembly, a company. LME–L18.
4 a With *possess.*: a person's self or embodied personality. Chiefly *poet.* LME. ▸**b** A person (or thing) that is physically present, *esp.* a person of impressive appearance or bearing; a person of good appearance or aspect. E19.
5 Demeanour, carriage, esp. when stately or impressive; nobleness or handsomeness of bearing or appearance. L15.
6 A spiritual or incorporeal being or influence felt or conceived as present. M17.

For other words beginning with *pre-* see the entry for **pre-**

7 *POLITICS.* The maintenance by a nation of political interests and influence in another country or region; the representation of a nation's interests at an event. **M20.** ▸**b** *spec.* The maintenance of personnel, esp. armed forces, in an allied or friendly State. Also, armed forces stationed in this way. **M20.** ▸**c** *COMMERCE.* A representation *in* a place or market by virtue of business activity of a specified kind. **L20.**

8 A quality in reproduced sound which gives the impression that the recorded activity is occurring in the listener's presence. **M20.**

📖 **1** M. MEAD We are a gregarious people, needing the presence of others. R. WHELAN The presence of U-boats was detected. ***real presence***: see **REAL** *adjective*[2]. **b** *Undercurrents* Somehow I had the presence to see . . a nurse shark sheltered in the ripped hull. **2** M. PATTISON Being admitted to his presence they saluted him. **4a** POPE Her ample presence fills up all the place. S. WOODS Saving your presence, Vicar. **b** WORDSWORTH That Presence fair and bright . . Victoria the Queen. **5** BARONESS ORCZY Tall, above the average, with magnificent presence and regal figure. **6** A. UTTLEY A feeling of a presence came upon her. A. LURIE They feel you as a rather hostile presence. **7** *Time* A formula that would allow some Palestinian presence at Geneva. **b** *Punch* The Americans have a presence of 380,000 men in Vietnam. **c** *Creative Review* Saatchi & Saatchi is stepping up its design presence in Britain.

Phrases: †**chamber of presence** = ***presence chamber*** below. **in a person's presence** before or with a person; in a person's company. **in presence** (now *rare*) present; in the room, company, vicinity, etc. **in the presence of** in the company of, observed by. ***make one's presence felt***: see **FEEL** *verb*. **presence of mind** calmness and self-command in sudden difficulty, an emergency, etc. ***real presence***: see **REAL** *adjective*[2].

Comb.: **presence chamber**, **presence-room** a reception room in a palace etc. where a monarch or other distinguished person receives people.

presenium /priːˈsiːnɪəm/ *noun*. **E20.**
[from **PRE-** 2 + Latin *senium* feebleness of age.]
MEDICINE. The period of life preceding old age.

presensation /priːsɛnˈseɪʃ(ə)n/ *noun*. **M17.**
[from **PRE-** 1 + **SENSATION**.]
Feeling or perception of something before it exists, occurs, or manifests itself; foreknowledge; presentiment.

presension /priːˈsɛnʃ(ə)n/ *noun*. Now *rare* or *obsolete*. **L16.**
[Latin *praesensio(n-)*, from *praesens-* pres. ppl stem of *praesentire*, from *prae* **PRE-** + *sentire* feel: see **-ION**.]
= prec.

present /ˈprɛz(ə)nt/ *noun*[1]. **ME.**
[Ellipt. or absol. use of **PRESENT** *adjective*.]
1 = **PRESENCE** 1, 2. Long *rare* or *obsolete*. **ME.**
†**2** A thing or person that is before one or here; an affair in hand; a present occasion. **ME–M18.**
3 *The* present time; the time now passing or that now is. **ME.** ▸†**b** The current month. Cf. **INSTANT** *noun* 2. **E16–M17.** ▸**c** *GRAMMAR.* (A form of) present tense. **M16.**

📖 **3** U. LE GUIN There is no past and future, only a sort of eternal present. E. LEONARD The next part brought the story to the present. **c** B. UNSWORTH I speak of her . . still in the present I do not always remember . . she is dead.

Phrases: **at present** at the present time, now. †**at that present** at that time, then. †**at this present** = ***at present*** above. **for the present** so far as this time is concerned, just now. †**in present** (*a*) now; (*b*) immediately; (*c*) then. †**on the present** *rare* at present, now. ***prophetic present***: see **PROPHETIC** 1. **these presents** *LAW* this document or writing; these words or statements. **until the present**, **up to the present** until now, up till now.

present /ˈprɛz(ə)nt/ *noun*[2]. **ME.**
[Old French (mod. *présent*), orig. in *mettre un chose en present à quelqu'un* put a thing before (in the presence of) someone, in which *en present* effectively = *en don* as a gift.]
1 A thing that is offered, presented, or given; = **GIFT** *noun* 3. **ME.**
2 The action or an act of presenting or giving something; (a) presentation; = **GIFT** *noun* 1. **ME.**
3 An offering to God or a god; = **GIFT** *noun* 4. Now *rare* or *obsolete*. **M16.**

📖 **1** R. INGALLS Maybe he'd be saying he loved her, bringing her flowers, buying her presents. **2** **make a present of** give or present as a gift.

present /prɪˈzɛnt/ *noun*[3]. **M19.**
[from **PRESENT** *verb* 9a.]
MILITARY. The action of presenting or aiming a firearm or other weapon; the position of the weapon when presented or fired.

present /ˈprɛz(ə)nt/ *adjective & adverb*. **ME.**
[Old & mod. French *présent* from Latin *praesent-*, *praesens* pres. pple of *praeesse* be before, be at hand, from *prae* **PRE-** + *esse* be.]
▸ **A** *adjective*. **I** Senses relating to place.
1 a Being beside, with, or in the same place as the person or thing which is the point of reference; being in the place in question. Chiefly *pred.* **ME.** ▸**b** Existing in the thing, case, etc., under consideration; not wanting or lacking. **E19.**
2 That is currently being discussed, considered, etc.; (of a writer or speaker) actually writing or speaking. **LME.**
3 Having the mind or thought intent on what one is about; attentive, alert; self-possessed (also ***present to oneself***). Now *rare* or *obsolete*. **LME.**
4 Being in the mind or consciousness; directly thought of, remembered, or imagined. Usu. foll. by *to*. Now *rare*. **LME.**
5 Esp. of help or assistance: ready at hand, immediately accessible or available. *arch.* **M16.**

📖 **1a** A. DAVIS Jon was present at the next meeting. C. MCWILLIAM I had not wanted him to be present when I introduced Hal and Cora. **present company excepted** excluding those who are here or being addressed now. **b** *Which?* A manufacturing fault, present but not active. *BioFactors* Two other substances were present in the extract. **2** *Times* The present survey aims to update and develop that document.

▸ **II** Senses relating to time.
6 Existing or occurring now; that is or is so at this time; current, contemporary; modern. **ME.**
7 *GRAMMAR.* Of a participle or tense: expressing an action now going on or habitually performed, or a condition now existing. **LME.**
8 Existing in or belonging to a particular time; that is or was so at that time. Now *rare*. **LME.**
†**9** Immediate, instant. **M16–L18.**

📖 **6** I. MURDOCH A life in Australia which would be . . the reverse of her present life. A. S. BYATT Pieces of furniture which had no present function. I. WATSON The present moment, the moment you're living through. ***at that present speaking***, ***at the present speaking***, ***at this present speaking***: see **SPEAKING** *noun*. ***sacrament of the present moment***: see **SACRAMENT** *noun*. **7** *Saturday Review* Writing in the present tense and autobiographically. **8** J. HUMPHREYS My troubles would soon be over. The present discombobulation was temporary.

Comb. & special collocations: **present-day** *adjective* of this time; current, modern; **present value**, **present worth** the sum of money which, together with the compound interest on it, amounts to a specified sum at a specified future date.

▸†**B** *adverb*. **1** Immediately, instantly; now; = **PRESENTLY** *adverb* 2, 3. **LME–M17.**
2 In or into the presence of someone; there; here. **LME–M16.**

present /prɪˈzɛnt/ *verb*. **ME.**
[Old & mod. French *présenter* from Latin *praesentare* place before etc., (in medieval Latin) present as a gift, from *praesent-*: see prec.]
▸ **I** Make present, bring into the presence of.
1 *verb trans.* **a** Bring (a person) before or into the presence or notice of another; introduce, esp. formally or ceremonially; *spec.* introduce at court or before a monarch or other distinguished person. **ME.** ▸**b** Bring before or into the presence of God; dedicate by so bringing. **ME.** ▸**c** Put forward (oneself, a candidate) for examination or to receive a degree. **M17.** ▸†**d** Offer greetings from (a person) by proxy; remember (one person) *to* another. **M17–L18.**
2 *verb trans. & intrans. ECCLESIASTICAL.* Recommend (a member of the clergy) to a bishop for institution *to* a benefice (cf. sense 15 below). Also, recommend (a candidate) to a presbytery for licence as a preacher. **ME.**
3 *verb refl.* & (now *rare*) *intrans.* Come forward into the presence of another or into a particular place; appear, attend. **LME.**
4 *verb trans.* **a** Symbolize, represent; stand for, denote. *arch.* **LME.** ▸**b** Represent (a character) on the stage. *arch.* **L16.** ▸†**c** Perform (a play, a scene). **E–M17.**
5 *verb trans. LAW.* Bring or lay before a court, magistrate, etc., for consideration or trial; *spec.* (*a*) bring formally under notice, submit, (a complaint, offence, etc.); (*b*) bring a formal charge or accusation against. **LME.**
6 *verb trans.* **a** Put before the eyes of someone; offer to sight or view; show, exhibit, display. Also, exhibit (a quality or attribute). **LME.** ▸**b** (Of a company, producer, etc.) put or bring (a form of entertainment) before the public; (of a person) introduce or announce the various items of (a radio or television programme) as a participant; (of a performer) perform (an item). **M20.**
7 *verb trans.* Make clear to the mind or thought; convey or present to the mental perception; set forth, describe. **LME.**
8 *verb refl.* & (now *rare*) *intrans.* Of a thing: offer itself to view or thought; come before one's sight or notice; show or suggest itself. **L16.**
9 a *verb trans. & intrans.* Hold out or aim (a weapon) at something, so as to be ready to fire. **L16.** ▸†**b** *verb trans. & intrans.* Point or turn to face something, or in a specified direction. (Foll. by *to*.) **L18.**
10 *MEDICINE.* **a** *verb trans.* Of a foetus: direct (a particular part) towards the cervix during labour. Now *rare*. **L16.** ▸**b** *verb intrans.* Of a part of a foetus: be directed towards the cervix during labour. **E18.**
11 *verb trans.* Bring or put (a substance) into close contact with another. (Foll. by *to*.) Now *rare*. **M18.**
12 *verb intrans. & refl. MEDICINE.* (Of a condition or lesion) show itself, be manifest, appear, occur (in a certain manner etc.); (of a patient) come forward for or undergo an examination (*with* a symptom etc.). **L19.**

📖 **1a** P. MORTIMER An aunt in London . . was going to present her at court. L. GORDON After completing high school, Emily was presented to Boston society. **3** *Law Times* He presented himself at the museum. **5** H. PRIDEAUX The Church-wardens are also to present all such as come not to Church. **6a** CONAN DOYLE The matter must be presented in such a way as may interest the reader. E. M. FORSTER Except for the Marabar Caves . . the city of Chandrapore presents nothing extraordinary. **present arms** hold a rifle etc. vertically in front of the body as a salute. **b** *New York Times* Ellie Mao . . presented a program of folksongs. **7** *Manchester Examiner* The arguments . . were presented with clearness and precision. **8** J. TYNDALL The terrible possibility of his losing his hands presented itself to me. W. S. MAUGHAM The opportunity presented itself sooner than . . foreseen. **12** *Nature* These complications may present as hypersensitivity reactions. *British Medical Journal* A woman . . presented with hirsutism, deepening voice, and amenorrhea.

▸ **II** Make a present of; offer, deliver, give.
13 *verb trans.* **a** Bring or place (a thing) before or into the hands of a person for acceptance; offer, hand over, or give (*to* a person), esp. formally or ceremonially; *spec.* (*a*) offer as an act of worship, a sacrifice, etc.; (*b*) offer or make accessible (a literary work) to readers. **ME.** ▸**b** Deliver, convey, give (something non-material, as a message, greeting, etc.); offer (compliments, regards, etc.). Formerly also, offer (service or assistance). **LME.** ▸**c** Deliver up (a person) as a prisoner. **LME.** ▸**d** Formally hand over (a petition, cheque, bill, etc.) for payment, acceptance, or other action. **E16.** ▸**e** Of a thing: afford, offer, supply. **E17.**
14 *verb trans.* Make a presentation or gift to; make available to; cause to have. Now only foll. by *with* the thing given etc. **ME.**
†**15** *verb trans. ECCLESIASTICAL.* Give (a benefice) to a member of the clergy. Cf. sense 2 above. **LME–L18.**

📖 **13a** J. CONRAD He went to present a letter of introduction to Mr. Tesman. *Harpers & Queen* She attended the final afternoon's racing . . and presented some of the prizes. **e** *Outrage* The blackout often presented the opportunity for a good grope. **14** A. PATON He . . had presented his parents with a pair of fine grandchildren. H. MACMILLAN I was presented with a two-volume history of Moscow University.

presentable /prɪˈzɛntəb(ə)l/ *adjective*. **LME.**
[Orig. from medieval Latin *praesentabilis*; later from prec. + **-ABLE**.]
1 *LAW.* That may or should be formally brought up or charged, as an offence etc.; liable to presentment. **LME.**
2 *ECCLESIASTICAL.* = **PRESENTATIVE** 2. **LME.**
3 That can or may be presented; capable of or suitable for presentation to a person, to the mind, as a gift, etc. **E17.**
4 Fit to be presented or introduced into society or company; of good or respectable appearance, fit to be seen. **E19.**

📖 **4** G. GISSING Then go into my bedroom and make yourself presentable. P. L. FERMOR I was lent something more presentable than my canvas trousers.

■ **presentableness** *noun* (*rare*) **E20.** **presenta'bility** *noun* **M19.** **presentably** *adverb* **L19.**

presentation /prɛz(ə)nˈteɪʃ(ə)n/ *noun*. **LME.**
[Old & mod. French *présentation* from late Latin *praesentatio(n-)*, from Latin *praesentat-* pa. ppl stem of *praesentare*: see **PRESENT** *verb*, **-ATION**.]
▸ **I** The action of presenting or introducing.
1 The action or an act of presenting a person. **LME.**
2 a The action of presenting a thing for acceptance. **LME.** ▸**b** A thing offered for acceptance; a present, a gift, a donation. Now *rare* or *obsolete*. **E17.**

📖 **1** *Book of Common Prayer* The Presentation of Christ in the Temple, commonly called, the Purification of Saint Mary the Virgin. M. HOWITT I was promised an early presentation to Her Majesty.

▸ **II 3 a** An image, a likeness; a symbol. *rare*. **L15.** ▸**b** The action of presenting something to sight or view; theatrical, pictorial, or symbolic representation; a display, an exhibition. Also, a show or demonstration of materials, information, etc.; a lecture. **E17.** ▸**c** The action of supervising the broadcast of a radio or television programme. **M20.**
4 The action of presenting something to the mind or mental perception; a description, a statement. **L16.** ▸**b** The style or manner in which something is presented, described, or explained. **M20.**
5 *MEDICINE.* The directing of a particular part of the foetus towards the cervix during labour; the position and orientation of the foetus in relation to the cervix. **M18.**
6 *METAPHYSICS & PSYCHOLOGY.* [translation of German *Vorstellung*.] All the modification of consciousness required to know

or be aware of an object in a single moment of thought; *spec.* perceptual cognition as opp. to ideational cognition. Now *rare*. M19.

> **3b** *Marketing Week* The airline is . . looking at presentations from three London agencies. L. GORDON She directed . . Comus . . to mark the three-hundredth anniversary of its presentation at Ludlow Castle. **4** H. KISSINGER In an extraordinarily effective presentation Rogers argued that the risks were excessive. **b** *Daily Telegraph* These are small points, matters of presentation.

Comb.: **presentation copy** a copy of a book etc. presented as a gift, esp. for promotional reasons.

presentational /prɛz(ə)nˈteɪʃ(ə)n(ə)l/ *adjective*. L19.
[from prec. + -AL[1].]
Of or pertaining to presentation.

> *Listener* This new . . series on photography sees a shift in presentational style.

■ **presentationalism** *noun* L19. **presentationally** *adverb* M20.

presentationism /prɛz(ə)nˈteɪʃ(ə)nɪz(ə)m/ *noun*. Now *rare*. M19.
[from prec. + -ISM.]
PHILOSOPHY. The doctrine that in perception the mind has immediate cognition of the object.
■ **presentationist** *noun* a person who holds this doctrine M19.

presentative /prɪˈzɛntətɪv/ *adjective*. LME.
[Prob. orig. from medieval Latin, from Latin *praesentat-*: see PRESENTATION, -IVE.]
†**1** Representative; that symbolizes or stands in place *of*. LME–M17.
2 ECCLESIASTICAL. Of a benefice: to which a patron has the right of presentation. Opp. DONATIVE. M16.
3 That presents or is capable of presenting an idea or notion to the mind. M19.
4 METAPHYSICS & PSYCHOLOGY. Of, pertaining to, or of the nature of presentation (PRESENTATION 6). Now *rare*. M19.

presentee /prɛz(ə)nˈtiː/ *noun*[1]. L15.
[Anglo-Norman, from French *présenté* pa. pple of *présenter*: see PRESENT *verb*, -EE[1].]
1 a ECCLESIASTICAL. A member of the clergy presented for institution to a benefice. L15. ▸**b** A person presented at court. E19.
2 A person to whom something is presented; the recipient of a present or gift. M19.

presentee /prɛz(ə)nˈtiː/ *noun*[2]. *joc.* L19.
[from PRESENT *adjective & adverb*, after ABSENTEE: see -EE[1].]
A person who is present.
■ **presenteeism** *noun* M20.

pre-sentence /priːˈsɛnt(ə)ns/ *noun & adjective*. M20.
[from PRE- 2 + SENTENCE *noun*.]
▶ **A** *noun*. LINGUISTICS. A construct that precedes or underlies the formation of a sentence. M20.
▶ **B** *adjective*. **1** That occurs before a judicial sentence. M20.
2 LINGUISTICS. That occurs before a spoken or written sentence. M20.

presenter /prɪˈzɛntə/ *noun*. LME.
[from PRESENT *verb* + -ER[1]. Cf. PRESENTOR.]
A person who presents; *spec.* (*a*) a person who presents someone to a benefice, for a degree, etc.; (*b*) a person who formally introduces someone, esp. at court; (*c*) LAW (now *rare*) a person who makes a presentment; (*d*) a person who presents a petition, bill, etc.; (*e*) a person who takes part in a radio or television programme and introduces its various items.

> *Sunday Times* Sue MacGregor . . has been presenter of BBC Radio Four's *Woman's Hour* since 1972. *Philadelphia Record* The rules of the bank required that the presenter of a check should be identified.

presential /prɪˈzɛnʃ(ə)l/ *adjective*. Now *rare*. L15.
[medieval Latin *praesentialis* present, from Latin *praesentia* PRESENCE: see -AL[1].]
1 Of or pertaining to presence; having or implying actual presence with a person or in a place; present. L15.
2 Mentally present; having presence of mind; attentive, alert. M17.
■ **presentiˈality** *noun* (now *rare*) E17. †**presentially** *adverb* LME–L17. †**presentialness** *noun* L17–E18.

presentiate /prɪˈzɛnʃɪeɪt/ *verb trans.* Now *rare*. M17.
[Perh. from PRESENT *adjective & adverb* + -ATE[3], after *different*, *differentiate*.]
Make present in space or time; cause to be perceived or realized as present.

presentient /priːˈsɛnʃ(ə)nt, -ˈzɛn-/ *adjective*. E19.
[Latin *praesentient-* pres. ppl stem of *praesentire* feel or perceive beforehand, from *prae* PRE- + *sentire* feel: see -ENT.]
Feeling or perceiving beforehand; having a presentiment.

presentiment /prɪˈzɛntɪm(ə)nt, -ˈsɛn-/ *noun*. E18.
[French †*présentiment* (mod. *press-*), from *pré-* PRE- + SENTIMENT.]
1 A mental impression or feeling about a future event; a vague expectation; a foreboding, esp. of misfortune. E18.
2 A preconceived sentiment or opinion. *rare*. M18.

> **1** M. BARING Both . . felt a presentiment that they would never see him again. J. BRIGGS A curious, and apparently unconscious, presentiment of death.

■ **presentiˈmental** *adjective* E19.

presentist /ˈprɛz(ə)ntɪst/ *adjective & noun*. L19.
[from PRESENT *adjective & adverb* + -IST.]
▶ **A** *adjective*. Of or pertaining to presentism or presentists. L19.
▶ **B** *noun*. An advocate of the present; a person who is influenced by present-day attitudes; THEOLOGY a person who believes that the prophecies of the Apocalypse etc. are in the course of fulfilment. E20.
■ **presentism** *noun* the doctrines or beliefs of a presentist L19.

presently /ˈprɛz(ə)ntli/ *adverb*. LME.
[from PRESENT *adjective & adverb* + -LY[2].]
†**1** So as to be present; on the spot; in person, personally. LME–L16.
2 a At the present time; now. Now chiefly *Scot.* & *N. Amer.* LME. ▸†**b** At the time referred to; just then. E16–M18.
3 Without delay; immediately, instantly; quickly, promptly. Now *arch.* *rare*. LME.
4 In a little while, after a short time; soon, shortly. LME.
†**5** Immediately (in space or relation); so as to be adjacent or contiguous; directly, closely. E–M17.
6 As a direct result or conclusion. Now *rare*. M17.

> **2a** N. MANDELA Two thousand Africans are presently languishing in jail. **3** HENRY FIELDING The poor woman . . no sooner looked at the serjeant, than she presently recollected him. **4** E. M. FORSTER Presently the waitress entered. G. VIDAL I'm sure he'll be along presently.

presentment /prɪˈzɛntm(ə)nt/ *noun*. ME.
[Old French *presentement*, formed as PRESENT *verb*: see -MENT.]
1 = PRESENTATION 1, 2. ME.
2 LAW. The action or an act of laying before a court, magistrate, etc., a formal statement of a matter requiring legal action; *spec.* (*a*) a statement on oath by a jury of a fact known to them; †(*b*) a similar statement by a magistrate, justice of the peace, or constable; (*c*) ECCLESIASTICAL a formal complaint or report made by a churchwarden etc. to a bishop or archdeacon. LME.
3 = PRESENTATION 3, 4, 6. E17.

> **3** G. BANCROFT The presentment of a burlesque masque. F. R. LEAVIS This poem . . is particularly dramatic in presentment.

presentness /ˈprɛz(ə)ntnɪs/ *noun*. M16.
[from PRESENT *adjective & adverb* + -NESS.]
The quality or condition of being present in space, time, or thought.

presentoir /prɛz(ə)nˈtwɑː; *foreign* prezɑ̃twaːr/ *noun*. Also **pré-** /preɪ-, *foreign* pre-/. Pl. pronounced same. M19.
[French *présentoire*.]
Hist. An item of decorative tableware used in the 16th and 17th cents., *esp.* a serving knife.

presentor /prɪˈzɛntə/ *noun*. LME.
[Anglo-Norman *presentour*, from *presenter*, formed as PRESENT *verb*: see -OR. Cf. PRESENTER.]
†**1** LAW. A person who makes a presentment. LME–E17.
2 ECCLESIASTICAL. A person who presents someone to a benefice. *rare*. M19.

presepio /preˈsɛpjo/ *noun*. Pl. **-pii** /-pji/. M18.
[Italian from Latin *praesaepe* enclosure, stall.]
A crib; a model of the manger in which Jesus was laid.

preserval /prɪˈzəːv(ə)l/ *noun*. *rare*. M17.
[from PRESERVE *verb* + -AL[1].]
= next.

preservation /prɛzəˈveɪʃ(ə)n/ *noun*. LME.
[Old & mod. French *préservation* from medieval Latin *praeservatio(n-)*, from late Latin *praeservat-* pa. ppl stem of *praeservare*: see PRESERVE *verb*, -ATION.]
1 The action or an act of preserving or protecting something; the fact of being preserved. LME.
†**2** A means of preservation; a preservative. L16–E17.
3 The condition of being well or badly preserved; state of keeping. M18.

> **1** *Discovery* A point was raised as to the preservation of some untouched heathland. *Antiquity* The preservation of bone . . may be due to a reduced soil acidity. **3** G. L. HARDING The remarkable state of preservation of buildings which are now . . 1,400 years old.

Comb.: **preservation order** a legal obligation laid on an owner to preserve a building of historic interest or value.
■ **preservationism** *noun* the practice or advocacy of preservation M20. **preservationist** *noun* a person who advocates preservation, esp. of historic buildings or antiquities E20.

preservative /prɪˈzəːvətɪv/ *adjective & noun*. LME.
[Old & mod. French *préservatif* from medieval Latin *praeservativus*, *-um*, from late Latin *praeservat-*: see prec., -IVE.]
▶ **A** *adjective*. Having the quality of preserving; protective. LME.
▶ **B** *noun*. **1** A medicine that gives protection from disease or infection; a prophylactic. Now *rare* or *obsolete*. LME. ▸**b** *gen.* A safeguard *against* danger; a thing that prevents injury. Now *rare*. E16
2 A thing which preserves something from damage or loss. LME. ▸**b** *spec.* A substance (now esp. a synthetic one) used to preserve perishable foodstuffs, wood, etc. LME.

> **2b** V. BRAMWELL Additives like preservatives and colouring in processed foods . . can have adverse effects on some people.

preservatory /prɪˈzəːvət(ə)ri/ *adjective & noun*. *rare*. M17.
[from PRESERVAT(IVE + -ORY[1], -ORY[2].]
▶ **A** *adjective*. = PRESERVATIVE *adjective*. M17.
▶ **B** *noun*. **1** = PRESERVATIVE *noun* 2. M17.
2 = PRESERVE *noun* 3. E19.

preserve /prɪˈzəːv/ *noun*. M16.
[from next.]
1 †**a** A preservative. M16–M19. ▸**b** In *pl.* Weak spectacles. *Scot.* *rare*. M17. ▸**c** In *pl.* Goggles used to protect the eyes from dust, bright light, etc. L19.
2 A confectionary preparation of fruit etc. preserved with sugar; jam. L16.
3 a A stretch of land or water set apart for the protection and rearing of game, fish, etc.; a vivarium. E19. ▸**b** A place or sphere of activity regarded as belonging to a particular person, group, etc. E19.

> **3b** *Accountancy* Golf is still predominantly a male preserve. ***trespass on a person's preserve***: see TRESPASS *verb* 4.

Comb.: **preserve jar** = PRESERVING *jar*.

preserve /prɪˈzəːv/ *verb*. LME.
[Old & mod. French *préserver* from late Latin *praeservare*, from *prae* PRE- + *servare* keep, protect.]
1 *verb trans.* Keep safe from harm, injury; take care of, protect. (Foll. by *from*.) LME.
2 *verb trans.* Keep (a person) alive, save (*arch.*); keep in existence, keep free from decay; maintain (a state of things). LME. ▸**b** Continue to possess (a quality etc.). E17.
3 a *verb trans.* Prepare (fruit, meat, etc.) by boiling with sugar, salting, or pickling to prevent decomposition or fermentation; treat (esp. food) to prevent these processes. L16. ▸**b** *verb intrans.* Remain without physical or chemical change; remain wholesome or intact. Now *rare*. L16.
4 *verb trans.* & *intrans.* Keep (game, an area where game is found) undisturbed for private use. E17.

> **1** SHAKES. *2 Hen. IV* The Lord preserve thy Grace! D. ROWE No amount of goodness and obedience can preserve you from danger. **2** R. HAYMAN The army was in attendance to preserve order. *Natural World* Vast sums are spent preserving the nation's architectural heritage. *Choice* He is working to preserve breeds like the . . North Ronaldsay sheep. **b** W. S. CHURCHILL Buckingham . . for the moment preserved his new Parliamentary prestige. G. GREENE It isn't that I'm without money, but I like to preserve it for essentials. **3a** G. VIDAL Their diet appears to consist entirely of onions and preserved fish. **b** C. M. YONGE How well Lady Martindale preserves! **4** A. TROLLOPE A man who preserves is always respected by the poachers.

■ **preservaˈbility** *noun* ability to be preserved L19. **preservable** *adjective* able to be preserved M17.

preserver /prɪˈzəːvə/ *noun*. L15.
[from prec. + -ER[1].]
1 A thing that preserves something or someone. L15. ▸**b** = ***life-preserver*** (b) s.v. LIFE *noun*. E20.
2 A person who preserves something or someone; *spec.* a saviour. M16. ▸**b** A person who preserves game, fish, etc., for sport. M19.

> **2** *Book of Common Prayer* O God the creator and preserver of all mankind.

■ **preserveress** *noun* (chiefly *poet.*) a female preserver L16.

preserving /prɪˈzəːvɪŋ/ *verbal noun*. LME.
[from PRESERVE *verb* + -ING[1].]
The action of PRESERVE *verb*; an instance of this.
Comb.: **preserving jar** a jar with a lid that screws on, for putting jam in after it has been made.

preses *noun* var. of PRAESES.

pre-set /*as adjective* priːˈsɛt; *as noun* ˈpriːsɛt/ *adjective & noun*. M20.
[from PRE- 1 + SET *adjective*.]
▶ **A** *adjective*. Determined in advance; (of apparatus etc.) set or adjusted in advance of its operation or use. M20.
▶ **B** *noun*. A control on electronic, esp. audio, equipment that is set or adjusted beforehand to facilitate its use. M20.

> *Smash Hits* Digital tuning and twenty-four presets make finding the right wavelength a breeze.

pre-set /priːˈsɛt/ *verb trans.* Infl. **-tt-**. Pa. t. & pple **-set**. M20.
[from PRE- 1 + SET *verb*[1].]
Set or adjust (a device) in advance of its operation.
■ **presettable** *adjective* L20.

preshrink /priːˈʃrɪŋk/ *verb trans.* Pa. t. **-shrank** /-ˈʃraŋk/; pa. pple **-shrunk** /-ˈʃrʌŋk/. M20.
[from PRE- 1 + SHRINK *verb*.]
Shrink (fabric, a garment) during manufacture, to prevent further shrinkage after washing.
■ **preshrinkage** *noun* the process of preshrinking something M20.

preside /prɪˈzʌɪd/ *verb*. E17.
[French *présider* from Latin *praesidere*, from *prae* PRE- + *sedere* sit.]
1 *verb intrans.* Occupy the seat of authority in an assembly or meeting; act as chairman or president; ECCLESIASTICAL act as the celebrant (*at* a Eucharist). (Foll. by *at*, *over*.) E17.
2 *verb intrans.* Exercise authority or control; be in charge. (Foll. by *over*.) M17.
3 *verb trans.* Direct, control; chair. M17.
4 *verb intrans.* Orig., conduct or lead an orchestra while playing the piano, harpsichord, etc. Now (*colloq.*), play the organ, piano, etc., at any kind of gathering. L18.

1 B. WEBB The assembly, presided over by Clifford Allen, was good-tempered and orderly. *Daily Telegraph* Judge Abdela, presiding at the Old Bailey trial. **2** M. BARING The nursery . . was presided over by a brisk and rather sharp-tongued Nanny. J. N. ISBISTER Franz Joseph . . had presided over this Empire for twelve years. **3** *English World-Wide* The court presided by X . . . found them guilty after a four-month trial.

■ **presider** *noun* a person who presides L17.

presidence /ˈprɛzɪd(ə)ns/ *noun*. L15.
[Old & mod. French *présidence* from medieval Latin *praesidentia*: see next, -ENCE.]
1 The action or fact of presiding; control, authority. L15.
2 The function or office of president. Now *rare*. E17.

presidency /ˈprɛzɪd(ə)nsi/ *noun*. L16.
[Spanish, Portuguese *presidencia*, Italian *presidenza*, from medieval Latin *praesidentia*, from Latin *praesident-*: see next, -ENCY.]
1 The function or office of president; the term during which a president holds office. L16.
†**2** Superior or leading position. E17–E19.
3 A district under the administration of a president; *spec.* (*Hist.*) each of the three divisions of the East India Company's territory in India. L18.

1 S. QUINN The gracious manner that was to become the trademark of his presidency.

president /ˈprɛzɪd(ə)nt/ *noun*. LME.
[Old & mod. French *président* from Latin *praesident-*, *-ens* use as noun of pres. pple of *praesidere*: see PRESIDE, -ENT.]
1 The appointed governor or lieutenant of a province, colony, city, etc. Now chiefly *Hist.* LME. ▸**b** *fig.* A presiding or tutelary god, a guardian. *poet.* Long *rare* or *obsolete*. E16.
2 The appointed or elected head of an academy, society, etc., who presides over its meetings and proceedings. LME. ▸**b** The chairman of a company. *N. Amer.* L18. ▸**c** ECCLESIASTICAL. The celebrant at the Eucharist. M20. ▸**d** In some sports, a referee, an official in charge. M20.
†**3** The head of a religious house or a hospital. LME–E17.
4 The head of certain colleges; *N. Amer.* the head of a university. LME.
5 a The head of certain advisory councils, administrative boards, and judicial bodies. LME. ▸**b** *Hist.* The chief magistrate in some of the British N. American colonies and in the States to which they gave rise (a title superseded by that of governor). E17.
6 The elected head of a republican State, having some of the functions of a constitutional monarch in addition to the role of head of the government. L18.
7 A heavy cotton and woollen fabric. L19.

2 L. HUXLEY He became President of the Geological Society in 1872. **4** A. N. WILSON The President of Magdalen . . had been tutor to the Prince of Wales. **5** *Times* The President of the Board of Trade would take powers to control inertia selling campaigns. **Lord President of the Council** the cabinet minister with the responsibility of presiding at meetings of the Privy Council. **6** *Guardian* The Somali President . . has fired two ministers.

Comb.: **president-elect**, pl. **presidents-elect**, a person elected to be president who has not yet taken up office; **president-general**, pl. **presidents-general**, a president with authority over all the subordinate presidents of a system.
■ **presidentship** *noun* = PRESIDENCY 1 E16.

president /ˈprɛzɪd(ə)nt/ *adjective*. Now *rare*. LME.
[Latin *praesident-*: see prec.]
That occupies the chief place; presiding, in charge.

presidentess /ˈprɛzɪd(ə)ntɛs/ *noun*. L18.
[from PRESIDENT *noun* + -ESS[1].]
A female president; the wife of a president.

presidential /prɛzɪˈdɛnʃ(ə)l/ *adjective*. E17.
[medieval Latin *praesidentialis*, from *praesidentia* PRESIDENCY: see -AL[1].]
1 Of or pertaining to a president or presidency. E17.
2 Of the nature of a president; presiding. M17.
3 *Hist.* Of or belonging to one of the presidencies of the East India Company. M19.

1 S. BELLOW Politicians with presidential ambitions. *Japan Times* The presidential term is six years.

■ **presidentialism** *noun* the system or practice of presidential government M20. **presidentialist** *noun* a supporter or advocate of presidentialism M20. **presidentially** *adverb* L19.

Presidia *noun pl.* see PRESIDIUM.

presidial /prɪˈsɪdɪəl/ *adjective*[1]. L16.
[from Latin *praesidium*: see PRESIDIARY, -AL[1].]
†**1** = PRESIDIARY *adjective*. L16–M17.
2 Of or pertaining to a presidio. L19.

presidial /prɪˈsɪdɪəl/ *adjective*[2] & *noun*. E17.
[French *présidial* noun & adjective, from late Latin *praesidialis*, formed as PRAESES: see -AL[1].]
▶ **A** *adjective*. **1** FRENCH HISTORY. Of or pertaining to a province, provincial; *spec.* designating a court of justice having limited jurisdiction, formerly established in certain French towns. E17.
†**2** Of a Roman province: under a governor (Latin *praeses*). M17–L18.
3 Of or pertaining to a president or the action of presiding. *rare*. M17.
▶ **B** *noun*. FRENCH HISTORY. A presidial court of justice. L17.

presidiary /prɪˈsɪdɪəri/ *adjective* & *noun*. L16.
[Latin *praesidiarius* that serves for defence, from *praesidium* garrison, fort, from *praesidere* PRESIDE: see -ARY[1].]
▶ **A** *adjective*. Pertaining to or serving as a garrison; having a garrison; fortified. L16.
▶ **B** *noun*. A guard, a protection. *rare*. E17.

presiding /prɪˈzʌɪdɪŋ/ *ppl adjective*. M17.
[from PRESIDE + -ING[2].]
That presides.
presiding elder *US* an elder in charge of a district in the Methodist Church. **presiding officer** an official in charge of a polling station at an election.

presidio /prɪˈsɪdɪəʊ, *foreign* preˈsiðjo/ *noun*. Pl. **-os** /-əʊz, *foreign* -ɔs/. M18.
[Spanish from Latin *praesidium*: see PRESIDIARY.]
In Spain and Spanish America: a fort, a fortified settlement, a garrison town. Also, a Spanish penal settlement in a foreign country.

Presidium /prɪˈsɪdɪʌm, -ˈzɪ-/ *noun*. Also **Prae-**. Pl. **-ia** /-ɪə/, **-iums**. E20.
[Russian *prezidium* from Latin *praesidium*: see PRESIDIARY.]
The presiding body or standing committee in a Communist organization, *esp.* (*Hist.*) that in the Supreme Soviet.

presignify /priːˈsɪɡnɪfʌɪ/ *verb trans*. L16.
[French †*présignifier* or Latin *praesignificare*, from *prae-* PRE- + *significare* SIGNIFY.]
Signify or intimate beforehand.
■ ˌ**presignifiˈcation** *noun* (now *rare*) the action of presignifying something; an indication or sign of what is coming: E17.

pre-sold *verb pa. t.* & *pple* of PRE-SELL.

press /prɛs/ *noun*[1]. ME.
[Old & mod. French *presse*, from *presser* PRESS *verb*[1].]
▶ **I 1** The action or fact of pressing together in a crowd; a thronging together; the condition of being crowded; a crowd, a multitude, (*of* people etc.). ME. ▸**b** *spec.* A melée in battle; the thick of the fight. *arch.* ME.
2 The condition of being hard-pressed; a position of difficulty, a critical situation; distress, tribulation. *arch.* ME.
3 Pressure of affairs; the compelling influence *of* a circumstance etc.; urgency, haste. LME.
4 PSYCHOLOGY. An influence in a person's environment which tends to affect his or her behaviour. M20.

1 D. H. LAWRENCE In the cattle-market she shrank from the press of men. M. M. KAYE So crowded that . . two had fallen because of the press and been killed. K. WARREN The press of vehicles in Central London caused considerable confusion on the streets. **b** LD MACAULAY He . . fought, sword in hand, in the thickest press. **3** B. ENGLAND The press of heat within the jungle fiercely oppressive. *Underground Grammarian* How we speak, in the press of the moment, is usually the result of habit.

▶ **II 5** The action or an act of pressing something; pressure. LME. ▸**b** In GYMNASTICS, a raising of the body by continuous muscular effort. In WEIGHTLIFTING, a raising of a weight up to shoulder-height followed by its gradual extension above the head. E20. ▸**c** The action or an act of pressing clothes. M20. ▸**d** BASKETBALL. Any of various forms of close guarding by the defending team. M20.
6 A mark made by pressing; a crease; *fig.* an impression. E17.
7 The action of pressing *forward* etc. L19.

5 L. SPALDING With the press of his fingers still on my back I tried to sound businesslike. *Amiga User International* A press of the freeze button resets the machine. **c** J. OSBORNE I'll give them a press while I've got the iron on.

▶ **III 8** A device for compressing, flattening, or shaping a substance by pressure. LME. ▸**b** *Hist.* The apparatus for inflicting the torture of *peine forte et dure*. M18.
9 An apparatus for extracting juice, oil, etc., out of fruit, seed, or other produce by pressure. LME.
10 a A machine for leaving the impression of type on paper etc.; a machine for printing. Also ***printing-press***. M16. ▸**b** A place of business of which the printing-press is the centre; a printing-house; (esp. in titles) a publishing business; the personnel of such an establishment. L16. ▸**c** The work or function of the printing-press; the art or practice of printing. L16.
11 a *The* newspapers, journals, and periodical literature generally; *the* newspapers etc. of a country, district, party, subject, etc. Also in titles of newspapers. L18. ▸**b** Usu. with *the*: journalists, reporters (from newspapers or other media) collectively. E20. ▸**c** Usu. with *bad*, *good*, etc.: publicity or opinion regarding a particular person or thing, esp. as presented in print; journalistic reaction or opinion. E20.

8 ***cheese press***, ***cotton press***, ***garlic press***, ***hydraulic press***, etc. ***hot-press***: see HOT *adjective*. **9** ***CIDER-press***. **10a** C. V. WEDGWOOD They contrived to . . print their sheets on small movable presses that could be easily concealed. ***CYLINDER press***. ***job press***: see JOB *noun*[1]. **b** LD MACAULAY The Athenian Comedies . . have been reprinted at the Pitt Press and the Clarendon Press. E. HUXLEY There are several Polish presses in London. **c** *Guardian* The first Royal Commission on the Press in 1949. **11a** *Times* For years we have heard Labour politicians screaming about the Tory press. V. BROME Freud's teachings had . . caused a considerable stir in the Swiss and German press. **b** P. N. WALKER As the police were . . trying to clear the streets the . . press were trying to drive in. M. BUTTERWORTH Arrange for the exhumation forthwith. Seal off Highgate Cemetery . . No Press No television. **c** P. M. M. KEMP In Britain General Franco had not enjoyed a good Press. *Observer* The Phoenicians had a largely hostile press from the Bible. *New Yorker* He's getting an enormous amount of press out of it.

▶ **IV 12** A large, usu. shelved, cupboard for holding clothes, books, etc.; *esp.* one placed in a wall recess. LME.

12 R. BURNS Coffins stood round like open presses, That shaw'd the dead in their last dresses. K. AMIS A battered press of unvarnished wood.

Phrases: **at press**, **at the press** in the process of printing, being printed. ***corrector of the press***: see CORRECTOR 1. **freedom of the press** the right to print and publish anything without official approval. ***gentlemen of the press***: see GENTLEMAN. **go to press** go to be printed. **in press**, **in the press** = *at press* above. **liberty of the press** = *freedom of the press* above. **off the press** finally printed, issued. **press of sail** NAUTICAL as much sail as it is possible to carry in the prevailing conditions. **see through the press** oversee the printing of. **send to press** send to be printed. ***stop the press***: see STOP *verb*.
Attrib. & comb.: In the sense 'connected with journalism, newspapers, etc.' as ***press coverage***, ***press cutting***, ***press notice***, ***press photograph***, etc. Special combs., as **press agency** = ***news agency*** (b) s.v. NEWS *noun*; **press-agent** a person employed by an organization etc. to attend to advertising and press publicity; **press agent** *verb trans.* advertise in the manner of or by means of press agents; **press attaché** a diplomat responsible for the dealings of an embassy with the press; **press baron** = ***press lord*** below; **press bed** a bed constructed to fold up into a cupboard when not in use; a bed in an alcove with folding doors; **press book** (*a*) a volume of press cuttings; (*b*) a book printed at a private press, a type of fine book; **press-box** an enclosure for newspaper reporters, esp. at a sports ground; **press card** an official authorization carried by a reporter, esp. one that gains him or her admission; **press cloth** a piece of cloth placed between the fabric and the iron while ironing; **press conference** an interview given to journalists by a person or persons in order to make an announcement or answer questions; **press corps** a group of reporters (in a specified place); **press correction** (*a*) the action or process of correcting errors in a text during preparation for publication; (*b*) an error marked for correction; ***press corrector***: see CORRECTOR 1; **Press Council** a body established in the UK in 1953 to raise and maintain professional standards among journalists; **press day** (*a*) a day on which journalists are invited to an exhibition, performance, etc.; (*b*) the day on which a journal goes to press; **press-forged** *adjective* forged by pressure; **press gallery** a gallery or other area set apart for reporters, as in the House of Commons or other legislative chamber; **press-house** a house or building containing a press; a place where pressing is done; **press lord** a newspaper magnate, *esp.* one who is a member of the peerage; **press-mark** *noun* & *verb* (chiefly *Hist.*) (*a*) *noun* a mark or number written or stamped on a book or manuscript and also listed in a library catalogue, specifying the location of the book etc.; (*b*) *verb trans.* give a press-mark to; **press mark**: left on fabric by the impress of an iron; **press number** a number at the foot of the page of an early printed book showing on which press or by which printer the page was printed; **press office** an office within an organization or government department responsible for dealings with the press; **press officer** an official appointed by an individual or institution to handle publicity and public relations; **press proof** the last proof examined before printed matter goes to press; **press release** an official statement offered to newspapers for information and possible publication; **press revise** = ***press proof*** above; **press roll** (*a*) PAPER-MAKING a heavy roll used to press out moisture from the web; (*b*) JAZZ a drum roll in which the sticks are pressed against the drumhead; **press-room** (*a*) a room containing a press; *esp.* the room in a printing-office containing the presses; (*b*) a room reserved for the use of reporters; **press secretary** a secretary who deals with publicity and public relations; **press show** a performance given for the press, *esp.* a showing of a film to journalists before general release; **press view** a viewing of an exhibition by journalists before it is open to the general public;

presswork (*a*) the business of a printing-press; work turned out from a press, esp. from the point of view of its quality; (*b*) the pressing or drawing of metal into a shaped hollow die; a piece of metal shaped by such means; **press-yard** *Hist.* a yard at the former Newgate Prison, London, where the torture of *peine forte et dure* is believed to have been carried out, and from which, at a later period, condemned prisoners started for the place of execution.

press /prɛs/ *noun*[2]. L16.
[Alt. of PREST *noun*[1], prob. by assoc. with PRESS *noun*[1].]
Hist. **1** The impressing of men for service in the army or navy; compulsory enlistment; impressment into service of any kind; a requisition. L16.
†**2** = *press-warrant* below. L16–M17.

📖 **1** D. HUME An English army . . was levied by a general press throughout the kingdom.

Comb.: **press-money**: paid to a sailor or soldier on enlistment, acceptance of which was held to constitute legal proof of engagement in the service; **press-warrant** giving legal authority to impress men for navy or army service. See also PRESS-GANG.

press /prɛs/ *verb*[1]. Pa. t. & pple **pressed**, (*arch.*) **prest**. ME.
[Old & mod. French *presser* from Latin *pressare* frequentative of *press-* pa. ppl stem of *premere*.]
▶ **I 1** *verb trans.* Cause to move in some direction or into some position by pressure; push, drive, thrust. ME. ▸**b** *verb intrans.* In golf and other games: misdirect the ball through trying to hit too hard. E20.
2 *verb trans.* Act on (an object) with a continuous force directed towards the object by means of physical contact with it; exert a steady force on (a thing in contact); subject to pressure. LME. ▸**b** *verb trans.* Execute the punishment of *peine forte et dure* on (a person). Usu. in ***press to death***. *obsolete* exc. *Hist.* M16. ▸**c** *verb trans.* Caress or embrace by squeezing; hold affectionately *against* etc. E18. ▸**d** *verb intrans.* Exert pressure; bear (*down*) with weight or force (*up*)*on*, *against*. E19.
3 *verb trans.* Subject to pressure so as to alter the shape, consistency, bulk, etc., or to extract juice etc. from; compress, squeeze; *spec.* smooth (fabric or clothes) with an iron or a clothes press. LME. ▸**b** Dry and flatten (a leaf, flower, etc.) in order to preserve it. L18. ▸**c** Make a gramophone record or compact disc of (music); *colloq.* record (a song etc.). E20.
4 *verb trans.* Extract by pressure, express; squeeze (juice etc.) *out of* or *from*. LME.
5 *verb trans.* Print. Now *rare*. L16.

📖 **1** W. DAMPIER The Wind being on our broad side, prest her down very much. H. ROTH He pressed his brow against the cold window pane. M. FLANAGAN He pressed into her hand a packet of birth-control pills. **2** SHELLEY Her step seemed to pity the grass it prest. G. LORD He pressed one of the triggers of his gun. **c** SIR W. SCOTT The Minstrel's hand he kindly pressed. E. M. FORSTER He put his arm round her waist and pressed her against him. **d** D. NOBBS He pressed too hard . . and it broke in his hands. JEREMY COOPER They pressed tightly together in the dark. *fig.*: C. RAYNER Amy felt the weight of years of this family's history pressing down on her. **3** E. TEMPLETON The dress is on the bed, I've just pressed it. J. S. FOSTER Cold-formed steel sections are pressed or rolled to shape. *Scientific American* The small seeds of sesame are chiefly pressed for their oil. **4** *Cook's Magazine* Extra virgin is the highest quality, pressed from hand-picked fine olives.

▶ **II 6** *verb intrans.* & †*trans.* Come up or gather closely round (a person or place); crowd, throng. ME.
7 *verb intrans.* Push or strain forward, as through a crowd or against obstacles; push one's way, advance forcefully; hasten onward. Freq. foll. by *on*. ME.
8 *verb intrans.* Thrust oneself or advance presumptuously or insistently; push oneself forward, intrude. *arch.* LME.
†**9** *verb intrans.* Try hard, attempt *to do* something, usu. with eagerness or haste; aim at, strive after something. LME–E19.
10 *verb intrans.* Strive, contend. Long *rare*. LME.

📖 **6** T. PYNCHON Trees press close: overhead you can see barely enough sky for the rocket's ascent. J. M. COETZEE The crowd . . presses in so tight around them that I can hardly see. **7** R. WEST She . . pressed on with the delicate task. A. TYLER She pressed forward in her seat. J. BRIGGS The family pressed on to Rouen, their first port of call. **8** SWIFT You ne'er consider whom you shove, But rudely press before a duke.

▶ **III 11** *verb trans.* **a** Of an attacking force etc.: bear heavily on, assail with much force; beset, harass. LME. ▸†**b** Of a tyrant, misfortune, etc.: oppress, crush, distress, afflict. LME–L18. ▸**c** Weigh down, oppress, (the feelings, mind, spirits, etc.). *arch.* E17. ▸**d** Put in difficulty, esp. by a lack. Now only in ***be pressed for***, have barely enough of, be short of. L17.
12 a *verb trans.* Constrain, compel, force. LME. ▸**b** *verb intrans.* Of time, danger, etc.: compel haste, be urgent, necessitate immediate action. LME. ▸**c** *verb trans.* Impel to rapid movement, drive quickly. *rare*. E17. ▸**d** *verb trans.* Hasten (a movement etc.), execute quickly. M18.
13 *verb intrans.* & *trans.* Ask earnestly, beg, implore; try hard to persuade, importune, urge. (Foll. by *for*, *to do*.) LME.
14 *verb trans.* Insist on the doing of; solicit, request earnestly. (Foll. by (*up*)*on* a person.) LME.
15 *verb trans.* Insist on the belief, admission, or mental acceptance of; impress on the mind, emphasize, present earnestly; plead (a claim etc.) insistently. (Foll. by (*up*)*on*.) LME.
16 *verb intrans.* Produce a strong mental or moral impression, bear heavily, have an influence. Foll. by (*up*)*on*. M16.
17 *verb trans.* Push forward or develop (an argument, view, consideration, etc.). L17.
18 *verb trans.* Insist that a person receive or accept; thrust *on* a person. L18.

📖 **11a** W. ROBERTSON The castle of Milan was pressed more closely than ever. A. DUGGAN Our opponents, also well trained, still pressed us. **d** G. A. LAWRENCE You can have money sooner, if you are much pressed for it. **12a** SHAKES. *Mids. N. D.* Why should he stay whom love doth press to go? **b** SIR W. SCOTT Time presses: I must go. **13** H. JAMES The ponderous probity that kept him from pressing her for a reply. F. RAPHAEL He sent Scrope and Hobhouse back and forth to press for details. *Which?* We are continuing to urge the Government to press the EEC to reform its policy. **14** J. JORTIN Such a person might easily press the observance of a duty. *Daily Telegraph* The Brooklyn district attorney decided not to press charges against three adult children who had turned off their father's respirator. **15** C. P. SNOW The scientists . . were pressing the case against using the bomb. R. L. FOX The Delphic oracle had long pressed Philip's cause. **16** M. EDGEWORTH The reflection that he had wasted his time . . pressed upon his mind. DAY LEWIS The adult world pressed only lightly upon me. **17** G. GREENE One must not press the comparison with Browning or Wilde too far. **18** S. RAVEN You shouldn't press details on people who don't ask for them.

Phrases: ***press flesh***: see ***press the flesh*** below. **press home** (*a*) MECHANICS press (a part) to achieve the maximum penetration or the desired fit in something; (*b*) continue with (a course of action) as far as possible; (*c*) make sure a person understands or appreciated (a matter). ***press one's luck***: see LUCK *noun*. ***press the button***: see BUTTON *noun*. **press the flesh**, **press flesh** *colloq.* (chiefly *US*) shake hands. ***press the panic button***: see PANIC *adjective* & *noun*[2]. **press the point** insist on making a point, make sure a matter is understood or appreciated. ***press to death***: see sense 2b above.

Comb.: **press-board** a small ironing-board for use on the lap while sewing; **pressboard** a material made of compressed paper laminations, used as a separator or insulator in electrical equipment; **press-button** *noun* & *adjective* = PUSH-BUTTON; **press-fastener** = ***press-stud*** below; **press fit** MECHANICS an interference fit between two parts in which one is forced under pressure into a slightly smaller hole in the other; **press-on** *adjective* (of a material) that can be pressed or ironed on to something; **press-stud** a fastener used for joining parts of a garment etc., consisting of two components, one with a short shank which is pressed into a corresponding hollow in the other; **press-up** an exercise in which the body is raised from a prone position by straightening the arms while keeping the hands and feet on the ground and the legs and trunk straight.

■ **pressable** *adjective*[1] (*rare*) M17. **presser** *noun* a person who or thing which presses; (a worker who operates) a press; ***presser-foot***, the footplate of a sewing-machine which holds the material down over the feed: E16.

press /prɛs/ *verb*[2] *trans.* L16.
[Alt. of PREST *verb* by assoc. with prec.]
1 *Hist.* Force (a man) to serve in the army or navy; subject to impressment. L16. ▸**b** Seize authoritatively for royal or public use; requisition. M17.
2 *gen.* Force into service or use of any kind; bring into use as a makeshift. Also ***press into service***. L16.

📖 **1** J. WESLEY The Constables and Churchwardens came to press you for a soldier. F. MARRYAT He had been pressed out of an American ship. **2** U. LE GUIN Everything the federation had on wings or wheels was pressed into service. C. LASCH The secularization of sport . . began as soon as athletes were pressed into the cause of patriotism.

■ **pressable** *adjective*[2] (*rare*) M19.

pressel /ˈprɛs(ə)l/ *noun*. L19.
[from PRESS *verb*[1] + *-el* (arbitrary ending).]
A press-button switch, orig. one attached to a flexible pendent conductor. Also ***pressel-switch***.

press-gang /ˈprɛsgaŋ/ *noun* & *verb*. L17.
[from PRESS *noun*[2] or (sense A.2, punningly) PRESS *noun*[1] + GANG *noun*.]
▶ **A** *noun*. **1** *Hist.* A body of men employed, under the command of an officer, to press men for service in the army or navy. L17. ▸**b** *gen.* A group engaged in compelling people to do something. *colloq.* L18.
2 A group of journalists; the press. *joc.* M19.
▶ **B** *verb trans.* Force to serve by means of or in the manner of a press-gang; coerce. (Foll. by *into*.) M19.

📖 *Listener* The men on the *Mary Rose* . . were not press-ganged, and pay . . was good. V. SETH She and her sister . . were press-ganged into lessons.

pressie *noun* var. of PREZZIE.

pressing /ˈprɛsɪŋ/ *noun*. ME.
[from PRESS *verb*[1] + -ING[1].]
1 The action of PRESS *verb*[1]; an instance of this. ME.
2 a *sing.* & (usu.) in *pl.* Juice, wine, etc., produced by pressing. Also, solid matter left after expressing juice. E17. ▸**b** An article formed or shaped in a press; *esp.* a gramophone record, a compact disc; a series of discs made at one time. E20.
Comb.: **pressing board** (*a*) either of a pair of boards used in bookbinding to compress the sheets or volumes; (*b*) an ironing-board.

pressing /ˈprɛsɪŋ/ *ppl adjective*. L16.
[from PRESS *verb*[1] + -ING[2].]
1 That weighs heavily on a person; burdensome. L16.
2 That presses physically; exerting or causing pressure. E17.
3 Calling for immediate attention; urgent. E17. ▸**b** Of a request, invitation, etc.: strongly expressed. Of a person: persistent in solicitation, importunate. E18.

📖 **3** B. MONTGOMERY The most pressing task . . in Greece was to assist in the training of the Greek Army. *Oxford Today* To meet its pressing financial needs the University was aiming to raise £220 million. **b** R. FORD They are very pressing in their invitations.

■ **pressingly** *adverb* E17. **pressingness** *noun* L17.

pression /ˈprɛʃ(ə)n/ *noun*. Now *rare*. M16.
[French from Latin *pressio(n-)*, from *press-*: see PRESS *verb*[1], -ION.]
The action or an act of pressing; pressure.

pressive /ˈprɛsɪv/ *adjective*. *rare*. E17.
[French †*pressif*, *-ive*, from *presser*: see PRESS *verb*[1], -IVE.]
†**1** Pressing, urgent; oppressive; impressive. Only in E17.
2 Characterized by or pertaining to pressure. E19.

pressman /ˈprɛsmən/ *noun*[1]. Pl. **-men**. L16.
[from PRESS *noun*[1] + MAN *noun*.]
1 A man who operates or manages a press; *esp.* a hand-press printer. L16.
2 A man who writes or reports for the press; a male reporter or journalist. M19.

pressman /ˈprɛsmən/ *noun*[2]. Pl. **-men**. M17.
[from PRESS *noun*[2] + MAN *noun*.]
Chiefly *Hist.* **1** A man pressed into (military or naval) service; an impressed man. M17.
2 A member of a press-gang. Only in Dicts. M18.

pressor /ˈprɛsə/ *adjective*. L19.
[Attrib. use of agent-noun in Latin form from *press-*: see PRESS *verb*[1], -OR.]
PHYSIOLOGY. That increases blood pressure or vasoconstriction.

pressoreceptor /ˈprɛsərɪˌsɛptə/ *noun*. M20.
[from PRESS(URE *noun* + -O- + RECEPTOR.]
PHYSIOLOGY. A specialized receptor which responds to changes in blood pressure.

pressure /ˈprɛʃə/ *noun*. LME.
[Latin *pressura*, from *press-*: see PRESS *verb*[1], -URE.]
▶ **I 1** The action or fact of pressing; the fact or condition of being pressed; the exertion of continuous force on or against an object by something in contact with it. LME. ▸†**b** *fig.* A form produced by pressing; impression, image, stamp. E17–E19.
2 Force exerted on an object by something in contact with it, regarded as a measurable quantity and usu. expressed as weight per unit area. M17.

📖 **1** R. GUY The door opened to the pressure of his hand. **2** L. DEIGHTON He reset the barometer . . when the pressure started to rise. *Scientific American* A downward pressure of about two pounds is exerted . . to squeeze out the excess concrete.

▶ **II 3** The action of bearing painfully on the sensations, feelings, etc.; the state or condition of being oppressed by circumstances, problems, hardship, etc.; affliction, trouble, stress, strain; (freq. in *pl.*) a problem that is hard to cope with, a difficulty. LME. ▸**b** Urgency; the demand of affairs on one's time or energies. E19.
4 The action of moral or mental force; influence exerted by collective opinion; constraining influence. E17.

📖 **3** A. RADCLIFFE Emily struggled against the pressure of grief. L. DUNCAN Anything, to leave this room and the pressure of the confrontation. *Observer* Even a day's house arrest would be quite a new pressure. P. CUTTING The psychological pressure of weeks of bombardment was beginning to tell. *Independent* Lecturers' morale had been eroded by economic pressures. **b** D. H. LAWRENCE In spite of his pressure of business he had become a County Councillor. T. K. WOLFE You aren't on the fiftieth floor . . because you cave in under pressure. *Oxford Mail* There is still a tremendous pressure on hospital beds. **4** M. MEAD When fecundity threatens vigour, social pressures against child-bearing may become apparent. G. SWIFT I resisted all pressure to become an engineer.

Phrases: ***atmospheric pressure***: see ATMOSPHERIC *adjective* 1. ***blood pressure***: see BLOOD *noun*. **bring pressure (to bear)** exert influence to a specific end. **bring pressure on** = ***put pressure on*** below. ***centre of pressure***: see CENTRE *noun*. ***CRITICAL pressure***.

For other words beginning with *pre-* see the entry for **pre-**

dynamic pressure: see **DYNAMIC** *adjective*. *high pressure*: see **HIGH** *adjective*. *internal pressure*: see **INTERNAL** *adjective*. *low pressure*: see **LOW** *adjective*. *moral pressure*: see **MORAL** *adjective*. *osmotic pressure*. *partial pressure*: see **PARTIAL** *adjective*. **put pressure on** urge or press (someone) strongly in order to persuade.

Comb.: **pressure cabin** an airtight cabin in an aircraft in which the air is maintained at a pressure safe and comfortable for the occupants; **pressure casting** die-casting in which metal is forced into a mould under pressure; a casting so made; **pressure chamber**: for holding material under pressure; **pressure-cook** *verb trans.* cook in a pressure cooker; **pressure cooker** (*a*) an airtight pan in which food can be cooked in steam under pressure, so that a higher water temperature is reached and the food is cooked more quickly; (*b*) *fig.* (freq. *pressure-cooker* attrib.) an environment or situation of great pressure or stress; **pressure drag** AERONAUTICS = *form drag* s.v. **FORM** *noun*; **pressure-feed** *verb & noun* (*a*) *verb trans.* supply (fuel etc.) by means of applied pressure; (*b*) *noun* (the supplying of fuel etc. by) a system in which flow is maintained by applied pressure; **pressure flaking** ARCHAEOLOGY the removal of flakes, in the shaping of stone tools, by applying pressure with a hard point rather than by striking; **pressure gauge** an instrument for showing the pressure of a fluid, esp. steam or gas; **pressure group** a group or association representing some special interest and seeking to bring concerted pressure to bear on a matter of public policy; **pressure head** (*a*) the pressure exerted by a fluid expressed as the height of a column of fluid which would produce that pressure by virtue of its weight (cf. **HEAD** *noun* 19); (*b*) a pitot-static tube; **pressure hold** MOUNTAINEERING a hold maintained by the exertion of sideways or downward pressure; **pressure hull** the hull (or part of the hull) of a submarine which is designed to withstand the pressure of the sea when the vessel is submerged; **pressure-jet** *attrib.* designating a type of oil burner in which the fuel is burned at a fine nozzle through which it is passed under pressure; **pressure lamp** a portable lamp in which the fuel is forced up into the mantle or burner by the pressure of air drawn in by pumping with a plunger; **pressure mine** an explosive mine designed to be activated by the temporary reduction in hydrostatic pressure caused by a passing ship; **pressure pad**: designed to transmit or absorb pressure; **pressure plate** a plate for detecting, receiving, or applying pressure; **pressure point** (*a*) a small area on the skin especially sensitive to pressure; (*b*) a point where an artery can be pressed against a bone to inhibit bleeding; (*c*) a person or thing which can be used as a means of exerting (esp. political) pressure on another; **pressure ridge** a ridge caused by pressure; *esp.* a ridge of ice in the polar seas forced up by lateral pressure; **pressure sore** MEDICINE a sore produced by continued pressure on a part of the body; **pressure suit** a garment that can be made airtight and inflated to protect the wearer against low ambient pressure (as in high-altitude flight); **pressure tank**: in which a fluid, esp. fuel, is held under pressure; **pressure-test** *noun & verb* (*a*) *noun* a test of pressure, or of ability to withstand or sustain pressure; (*b*) *verb trans.* subject to a test of this nature; **pressure-treat** *verb trans.* subject to pressure treatment; **pressure treatment** (*a*) impregnation of timber with a preservative fluid under applied pressure; (*b*) BIOLOGY subjection of cells, organisms, etc., to increased pressure; **pressure tube** (*a*) a tube open at one or more points to a surrounding fluid whose velocity or pressure it is used to measure; (*b*) a tube in which pressurized coolant or moderator is passed through a nuclear reactor core; **pressure vessel** a vessel designed to contain material at high pressures; *esp.* a vessel containing a nuclear reactor core immersed in pressurized coolant.

pressure /ˈprɛʃə/ *verb*. M20.
[from the noun.]
1 *verb trans.* Exert pressure on. Chiefly *fig.*, coerce; urge, impel; drive or force by applying mental or moral pressure. (Foll. by *to*, *into*, *out of*, *to do*, etc.). M20. ▸**b** *verb intrans.* Exert pressure, press (*for*). L20.
2 *verb trans.* = **PRESSURIZE** *verb* 1. M20.

> 🕮 **1** H. CHEETHAM The trouble about an Oxford education . . is that no-one . . pressures you into working. R. JAFFE Richard began to pressure Daphne to get rid of Elizabeth. P. ROSE She felt pressured to be cheerful . . when doing so cost her great pain. **b** E. JONG Cicely pressured constantly for more nights off. **2** *Daily Telegraph* The engine . . would have continued to pressure the No 3 . . system under normal circumstances.

■ **pressured** *ppl adjective* subjected to pressure, pressurized; urgent, pressing: L20.

pressurize /ˈprɛʃərʌɪz/ *verb trans.* Also **-ise**. M20.
[from **PRESSURE** *noun* + **-IZE**.]
1 Produce or maintain pressure artificially in; apply pressure to; *spec.* maintain normal atmospheric pressure in (an aircraft cabin etc.) at high altitudes. Freq. as ***pressurized*** *ppl adjective*. M20.
2 Subject to moral, mental, or other non-physical pressure; urge, coerce, influence. (Foll. by *to do*, *into*, *to*, *out of*.) M20.

> 🕮 **1** *Nature* The camera and payload section were sealed and pressurized to two atmospheres. **pressurized-water reactor** a nuclear reactor in which the coolant is water at high pressure. **2** *Listener* White is now able to gain space and pressurize the black squares on the king's side. W. M. CLARKE Dickens . . pressurised the Duke of Devonshire to provide Devonshire House for the occasion.

■ **pressuriˈzation** *noun* M20.

prest /prɛst/ *noun*[1]. *obsolete* exc. *Hist.* LME.
[Old French (mod. *prêt*), from *prester* lend.]
†**1** A loan of money, esp. to a monarch in an emergency. LME–M17.
2 A payment of wages in advance. LME.
†**3** *spec.* A sum of money paid to a sailor or soldier on enlistment; an enlistment of a person by such payment. L15–E17.
†**4** A tax, an impost. L15–M16.
2 in prest as an advance.
¶ Cf. **IMPREST** *noun*.

†**prest** *noun*[2]. LME–E18.
[Origin unkn.]
A sheet of parchment.

prest *verb pa. pple*: see **PRESS** *verb*[1].

prestable /ˈprɛstəb(ə)l/ *adjective*. *Scot.* Now *rare*. E17.
[Obsolete French (now *prêtable*), from Old French *prester* (mod. *prêter*) lend: see **-ABLE**.]
Able to be paid or performed in discharge of an obligation.

prestance /ˈprɛst(ə)ns/ *noun*. *rare*. L19.
[Latin *praestantia*, from *praestare* excel: see next, **-ANCE**.]
Superiority, pre-eminence.

prestation /prɛˈsteɪʃ(ə)n/ *noun*. L15.
[Old French = action of lending, tendering, etc. (also mod. French in other senses), or from late Latin *praestatio(n-)* payment etc., in classical Latin = warranty, from *praestare* stand before, excel, vouch for, (in late Latin) lend, from *prae* **PRE-** + *stare* stand: see **-ATION**.]
1 The action of paying, in money or service, what is due; a payment or the performance of a service so imposed. L15.
2 ANTHROPOLOGY. A gift, payment, or service that forms part of some traditional function in a society. L19.

> 🕮 **2** *American Ethnologist* The prestations and festivities associated with marriage.

Prestel /ˈprɛstɛl/ *noun*. L20.
[from **PRESS** *noun*[1] + **TEL(ECOMMUNICATION)**.]
(Proprietary name for) a British viewdata system.

prester /ˈprɛstə/ *noun*. LME.
[Latin from Greek *prēstēr*.]
1 A mythical serpent, the bite of which caused death by swelling. LME.
†**2** A scorching whirlwind. E17–L18.

Prester John /prɛstə ˈdʒɒn/ *noun*. ME.
[Old French *prestre Jehan* (mod. *prêtre-Jean*), medieval Latin *presbyter Johannes* 'priest John'.]
A legendary Christian priest and king, believed in the Middle Ages to reign in the extreme east and later generally identified with the King of Ethiopia.

prestidigitator /prɛstɪˈdɪdʒɪteɪtə/ *noun*. Also in French form ***prestidigitateur*** /prɛstidiʒitatœːr/. E18.
[from French *preste* nimble or Italian **PRESTO** + Latin *digitus* finger + **-ATOR**, prob. pseudo-etymological alt. of earlier **PRESTIGIATOR**.]
A person who practises sleight of hand; a conjuror, a juggler.
■ ˌ**prestidigiˈtation** *noun* sleight of hand M19. ˌ**prestidigiˈtatory** *adjective* M19.

prestige /prɛˈstiːʒ, -ˈstiːdʒ/ *noun & adjective*. M17.
[French from late Latin *praestigium* illusion, in classical Latin as pl. *praestigiae* juggler's tricks.]
▸**A** *noun*. †**1** An illusion; a conjuring trick; a deception, an imposture. Usu. in *pl.* M17–M19.
2 Influence, reputation, or popular esteem derived from character, achievements, associations, etc. E19.

> 🕮 **2** ISAIAH BERLIN Thinkers whose views enjoyed prestige among the serious public. V. PACKARD They set out to give their beer prestige by showing . . the best people drank it.

▸**B** *attrib.* or as *adjective*. Having or conferring prestige. M20.

> 🕮 L. P. HARTLEY If only they could . . change into their old clothes! But no; this was a prestige occasion.

Comb.: **prestige advertising** advertising with the principal aim of furthering the prestige of the advertiser (rather than increasing sales etc.).
■ **prestigeful** *adjective* having or conferring prestige M20. **prestigey** *adjective* (*colloq.*) = **PRESTIGEFUL** M20.

prestigiation /ˌprɛstɪdʒɪˈeɪʃ(ə)n/ *noun*. Now *rare*. M16.
[from late Latin *praestigiat-* pa. ppl stem of *praestigiare*, *-ari* deceive, from *praestigium*, classical Latin *praestigiae*: see **PRESTIGE**, **-ATION**.]
The practice of conjuring or juggling; sorcery; deception by such means.
■ **preˈstigiator** *noun* L16.

prestigious /prɛˈstɪdʒəs/ *adjective*. M16.
[Latin *praestigiosus*, formed as prec.: see **PRESTIGE**, **-OUS**.]
1 Practising legerdemain, deluding, deceptive; *fig.* dazzlingly skilful or impressive. Now *rare*. M16.
2 Enjoying or conferring prestige. E20.

> 🕮 **1** *English Language Teaching* Prestigious virtuosity in paraphrase. **2** N. SYMINGTON The post was not paid, but it was very prestigious.

■ **prestigiously** *adverb* L16. **prestigiousness** *noun* M17.

prestissimo /prɛˈstɪsɪməʊ/ *adverb, adjective, & noun*. E18.
[Italian, superl. of **PRESTO** *adverb & adjective*.]
MUSIC. ▸**A** *adverb & adjective*. A direction: very rapid(ly). E18.
▸**B** *noun*. Pl. **-mos**, **-mi** /-mi/. A very rapid movement or passage. E20.

presto /ˈprɛstəʊ/ *adverb, interjection, noun, & adjective*. L16.
[Italian = quick, quickly, from late Latin *praestus* ready, for Latin *praesto* at hand.]
▸**A** *adverb & interjection*. **1** In various commands used by conjurors: quickly, at once. Also as *interjection*, announcing the climax of a trick or a surprising dénouement. Freq. in ***hey presto***. L16.
2 MUSIC. A direction: rapidly. L17.

> 🕮 **1** *Saturday Evening Post* Hey, presto! I'm off by the first train. R. MACAULAY To clap one's hands, twice, thrice, and presto! an elegant meal.

▸**B** *noun*. Pl. **-os**.
1 An exclamation of 'presto!' E17.
2 MUSIC. A rapid movement or passage. M19.

> 🕮 **2** A. HOPKINS The same cascade of notes . . sweeps us back into a final tumultuous Presto.

▸**C** *attrib.* or as *adjective*. **1** Orig., in readiness. Now, rapid, instantaneous; of the nature of a magical transformation. M17.
2 MUSIC. In a rapid tempo. M20.

prestress /ˈpriːstrɛs/ *noun*. M20.
[from **PRE-** 1 + **STRESS** *noun*.]
BUILDING. Tension applied prior to some other treatment, usu. in order to counteract applied compressive loads.

prestress /priːˈstrɛs/ *verb trans.* M20.
[from **PRE-** 1 + **STRESS** *verb*[1].]
BUILDING. Apply stress to prior to some other treatment; *spec.* reinforce (concrete) by steel rods or wires which have been tensioned while the concrete is setting. Freq. as ***prestressed*** *ppl adjective*.

presumable /prɪˈzjuːməb(ə)l/ *adjective*. L17.
[from **PRESUME** *verb* + **-ABLE**: cf. French *présumable*.]
That may reasonably be assumed; likely; to be expected.

> 🕮 *American Speech* A presumable influence here is the form for a Catholic priest.

■ **presumably** *adverb* †(*a*) *rare* so as to take things for granted; (*b*) (qualifying a statement) as may reasonably be assumed: M17.

presume /prɪˈzjuːm/ *verb*. LME.
[Old & mod. French *présumer* from Latin *praesumere*, from *prae* **PRE-** + *sumere* take.]
1 *verb trans.* **a** Undertake without adequate authority or permission; venture on. Now *rare*. LME. ▸**b** Take the liberty or be audacious enough *to do*. LME.
2 *verb trans.* Assume to be true or (LAW) proved in the absence of evidence to the contrary, presuppose (*that*); assume (a person or thing) *to be*. LME.
3 *verb intrans.* Act with an assumption of authority; take liberties. Foll. by *(up)on*: act presumptuously on the strength of, take (unscrupulous) advantage of; also (now *rare*), count confidently on. LME.
†**4** *verb intrans.* Make one's way overconfidently into an unwarranted position; presume to go. LME–L17.
†**5** *verb trans.* Make pretension, profess, *to do*. L15–M17.

> 🕮 **1a** P. P. READ He looked surprised . . as if a servant had presumed too great a familiarity. **b** H. KISSINGER He is a reckless ambassador who would presume to preempt his chiefs. **2** *Law Reports* Death is presumed from the person not being heard of for seven years. BETTY SMITH You have a sweetheart or a brother, I presume? L. DURRELL Those who . . presume that if he spent his time with me I must also . . be rich. A. MACLEAN In law every man is presumed innocent until proved otherwise. **3** R. SHAW Forgive me if I have presumed. F. RAPHAEL Shelley . . presumed . . on Byron's goodwill. **4** MILTON Into the Heaven of Heavens I have presumed, An earthly guest.

■ **presumedly** *adverb* as is presumed, supposedly M19. **presumer** *noun* E16. **presuming** *ppl adjective* presumptuous, arrogant E17. **presumingly** *adverb* E17.

presumption /prɪˈzʌm(p)ʃ(ə)n/ *noun*. ME.
[Old French *presumpcion*, *presompcion* (mod. *présomption*) from Latin *praesumptio(n-)*, from *praesumpt-* pa. ppl stem of *praesumere*: see prec., **-ION**.]
1 The taking upon oneself of more than one's position etc. warrants; overconfident opinion or conduct, arrogance. ME.
2 The action of taking something for granted; a belief based on reasonable evidence; an assumption, a supposition. ME.
†**3** Seizure and occupation without right; usurpation *of* a position or office. *rare*. LME–E19.
4 Ground for presuming; presumptive evidence. L16.

For other words beginning with *pre-* see the entry for **pre-**

📖 **1** W. BELSHAM It would be great presumption in me to attempt a reply. **2** G. GROTE The presumptions are all against it. G. GORER If the children say prayers . . it is a strong presumption that the parents . . are actively religious. **presumption of fact** *LAW* the inference from known facts of a fact not certainly known. **presumption of law** (*a*) the assumption of the truth of anything until the contrary is proved; (*b*) an inference established by the law as universally applicable to certain circumstances. **4** H. HALLAM There seems strong internal presumption against the authenticity of these epistles.

presumptious /prɪˈzʌm(p)ʃəs/ *adjective.* Now *rare.* LME.
[Old French *presoncieux* from late Latin *praesumptiosus*, from *praesumptio(n-)* PRESUMPTION: see -IOUS.]
Presumptuous, impertinent.

presumptive /prɪˈzʌm(p)tɪv/ *adjective.* LME.
[French *présomptif*, *-ive* from late Latin *praesumptivus*, formed as PRESUMPTION: see -IVE.]
1 Based on presumption or inference; presumed, inferred. LME. ▸**b** *EMBRYOLOGY.* Of tissue: that is not yet differentiated but will develop into a specified part. M20.
2 Of evidence: giving reasonable grounds for inferences. M16.
3 = PRESUMPTUOUS. Now *rare* or *obsolete.* E17.

📖 **1** W. KENNEDY He avoided the Phelan headstones on the presumptive grounds that they belonged to another family. **heir presumptive** a person whose right of inheritance can be superseded by the birth of another (cf. ***heir apparent*** s.v. APPARENT *adjective* 2).

■ **presumptively** *adverb* L17.

presumptuous /prɪˈzʌm(p)tʃʊəs/ *adjective.* ME.
[Old French *presumptueux* (mod. *présomptueux*) from late Latin *praesumptuosus* var. of *praesumptiosus*: see PRESUMPTIOUS.]
Characterized by presumption or undue confidence; forward, impertinent.

📖 A. BRINK Isn't it presumptuous to pretend we can speak for someone else?

■ **presumptuously** *adverb* LME. **presumptuousness** *noun* LME.

presuppose /priːsəˈpəʊz/ *verb trans.* LME.
[Old & mod. French *présupposer* (after medieval Latin *praesupponere*), from *pré-* PRE- + SUPPOSE *verb*.]
1 Of a person: assume or postulate beforehand; take for granted, presume. LME.
2 Suppose or believe in advance of actual knowledge or experience. E16.
3 Of a thing: require as a necessary preceding condition; imply. E16.

📖 **1** J. MOXON All the Authors I have met with seem to presuppose their Reader to understand Geometry. **2** BACON Corrupted minds presuppose that honesty groweth out of simplicity of manners. **3** B. RUSSELL Logical principles . . cannot be themselves proved by experience, since all proof presupposes them. C. S. LEWIS Alexandrian poetry was difficult because it presupposed a learned reader.

■ **presupposal** *noun* (now *rare*) a presupposition L16.

presupposition /ˌpriːsʌpəˈzɪʃ(ə)n/ *noun.* M16.
[medieval Latin *praesuppositio(n-)*, from *praesupponere*, from Latin *prae* PRE- + *supponere*: see SUPPOSITION.]
1 The action or an act of presupposing something. M16.
2 A thing which is presupposed; an idea assumed as a basis of argument, action, etc. L16.

📖 **2** A. S. DALE Both men shared certain ethical presuppositions about the universe.

■ **presuppositional** *adjective* E20. **presuppositionless** *adjective* L19.

prêt-à-porter /prɛtəˈpɔːteɪ, *foreign* prɛtapɔrte/ *adjective & noun.* M20.
[French.]
▸ **A** *adjective.* Of clothes: sold ready to wear. M20.
▸ **B** *noun.* Ready-to-wear clothes. M20.

pretaxation /priːtakˈseɪʃ(ə)n/ *noun.* M18.
[from medieval Latin *praetaxare* estimate beforehand: see -ATION.]
Hist. The action of voting first for a prospective ruler and then submitting him to others for approval.

pretence /prɪˈtɛns/ *noun.* Also ***pretense**. LME.
[Anglo-Norman *pretense* from use as noun of fem. sing. or neut. pl. of medieval Latin *pretensus* pretended, alleged, for classical Latin *praetentus* pa. pple of *praetendere* PRETEND *verb*.]
1 An assertion of a right; a claim. Now *rare.* LME.
2 Pretension (esp. false or ambitious) to or to merit or personal worth. Also, ostentatious display, affectation. LME.
3 An alleged (now usu. trivial or fallacious) ground for an action; a pretext, an excuse. LME.
4 The action or an act of pretending; (an instance of) make-believe, (a) fiction. LME.
†**5** A professed aim; an object, a purpose. L15–L18.
6 A false show or profession. L15.

📖 **1** LD MACAULAY Marlborough . . politely showed that the pretence was unreasonable. **escutcheon of pretence** *HERALDRY* an inescutcheon bearing a shield or device in pretence. **in pretence** *HERALDRY* borne to indicate a claim, e.g. that of a husband to represent his wife when she is herself an heiress or coheir of her father. **2** H. READ His characteristic sayings reflect his modesty and his lack of pretence. **3** *Scribner's Magazine* And ring for the servants on the smallest pretense. **4** R. WEST A pretence . . existed . . that children do not belong to the same species as adults. **5** W. CONGREVE To please, this time, has been his sole pretence. **6** E. O'NEILL That's the hardest job we have . . keeping up the pretense of work. M. MITCHELL She must go on making a pretence of enthusiasm. W. TREVOR She agreed she had been having them on, trying on a pretence.

■ **pretenceless** *adjective* without pretext or excuse M17.

pretenced /prɪˈtɛnst/ *ppl adjective.* Also (earlier) **pretensed**. LME.
[from medieval Latin *pretensus* (see prec.) + -ED¹.]
1 Alleged or claimed, esp. falsely; feigned, counterfeit, pretended. *arch.* LME.
†**2** Intended, designed. Freq. in ***pretenced malice*** = ***malice prepense*** s.v. PREPENSE *adjective.* L15–L16.
■ **pretencedly** *adverb* (*rare*) M16.

pretend /prɪˈtɛnd/ *noun & adjective.* E17.
[from the verb.]
▸ **A** *noun.* †**1** The action of pretending; a pretension, an assertion. *rare.* Only in E17.
2 In (imitation of) children's use: the action or an act of pretending in imagination or play. L19.

📖 **2** P. SCOTT Occasionally I play a game of pretend in this hut . . imagining it to be the palace in Jundapur.

▸ **B** *attrib.* or as *adjective.* In (imitation of) children's use: make-believe, imaginary. E20.

📖 W. REES-MOGG Gold is real money and paper is pretend money.

pretend /prɪˈtɛnd/ *verb.* LME.
[French *prétendre* or Latin *praetendere* stretch forth, put forward, allege, claim, from *prae* PRE- + *tendere* stretch, TEND *verb*².]
▸ **I** *verb trans.* †**1** Present for consideration or acceptance; bring (a charge, an action at law). LME–L17.
†**2** *refl.* Profess to be or *to be.* LME–L17.
3 a Profess to have (a quality etc.); profess *to do.* LME. ▸†**b** Lay claim to (a thing, esp. a right, title, etc.). Also, claim the right *to do.* LME–L18.
4 Make oneself appear *to be, to do,* or make it appear *that* something is the case, in order to deceive others or in play; (now *rare*) make a false profession or outward show of (a quality, feeling, etc.). LME.
†**5** Put forward as a reason or excuse. LME–L18.
6 a Assert, claim, *that.* LME. ▸**b** Allege the existence or presence of. L16.
†**7** Intend, plan. LME–E18.
†**8** Portend, foreshow. LME–M17.
9 Aspire or presume *to do.* L15.
†**10** Signify, mean. E16–M17.
†**11** Extend in front of or over a person or thing, esp. as a covering or defence. L16–L17.

📖 **2** T. FULLER Poor, petty, pitiful persons who pretended themselves princes. **3a** H. JAMES I don't pretend to have contributed anything to the amusement of my contemporaries. **4** L. CARROLL Nurse! do let's pretend that I'm a hungry hyaena, and you're a bone! J. BUCHAN I pretended to retreat over the skyline, but instead went back the way I had come. W. S. MAUGHAM Her heart sank, but she pretended that she was as excited as he. O. MANNING It was a mild December night, pretending spring. F. POHL He no longer had to pretend to be cheerful, he was so in fact. **5** T. GATAKER I pretended mine unfitness for such a place and imployment. **6a** HUGH WALPOLE It is pretended that to satisfy their natural impatience, he formed a hasty manner. **b** H. ROGERS In any 'type' it is only analogical resemblance that is pretended. **9** A. BAIN How many ultimate nerve fibres are contained in each nerve unit, we cannot pretend to guess.

▸ **II** *verb intrans.* †**12** Move forward, direct one's course. (Foll. by *to, for.*) LME–M17. ▸**b** *fig.* Tend to an end in action, speech, etc. LME–M17.
13 Foll. by *to*: (*a*) *arch.* pay court to (a prospective wife); formerly, aspire to (a position etc.); (*b*) lay claim to; profess to have (a quality etc.). L15.
14 Make pretence, esp. in imagination or play; make believe. E16.

📖 **13** E. WAUGH Barbara herself pretended to no illusions about Basil. **14** R. INGALLS I thought actors were supposed to like pretending. ***let's pretend***: see LET *verb*¹.

pretendant /prɪˈtɛnd(ə)nt/ *noun.* Also **-ent**. L16.
[French *prétendant* pres. pple of *prétendre*: see prec., -ANT¹.]
†**1** A person who intends something. *rare.* Only in L16.
2 A claimant; *esp.* a fraudulent claimant to a throne or office. Now *rare.* E17.
3 A suitor, a wooer. Also, a plaintiff in a lawsuit. M17.

pretended /prɪˈtɛndɪd/ *ppl adjective.* LME.
[from PRETEND *verb* + -ED¹.]
▸ **I 1** Falsely claimed to be such, so-called; spurious, counterfeit. LME.
2 Falsely asserted to exist or to be the case; alleged, reputed. E16.
3 Professed falsely or insincerely. M17.

📖 **1** STEELE One Isaac Bickerstaff, a Pretended Esquire. **2** P. LUCKOMBE Dr Barnes was prior, who was burnt for pretended heresy. **3** H. ROGERS They . . made the pretended service of God a reason for evading the most sacred obligations.

▸ **II** †**4** Intended, proposed. L16–E18.
■ **pretendedly** *adverb* ostensibly, professedly, not really E17.

pretendent *noun* var. of PRETENDANT.

pretender /prɪˈtɛndə/ *noun.* L16.
[from PRETEND *verb* + -ER¹.]
†**1** A person who intends. *rare.* Only in L16.
2 A person who puts forward a claim to a title or office, esp. to a throne. E17. ▸†**b** A suitor, a wooer. E17–L18.
3 A person who has pretensions to a quality or who makes a profession or assertion, esp. falsely or without adequate grounds. (Foll. by *to.*) M17.

📖 **2** *Times Lit. Suppl.* A . . laughable pretender, whose periodical attempts to win the throne of France always ended . . in ridicule. **the Old Pretender, the Young Pretender** *Hist.* the designation respectively of James Stuart (1688–1766), the son of James II of England, and Charles Stuart (1720–80), son of James, who successively asserted their claim to the British throne against the house of Hanover. **3** F. WELDON Here was no pretender to the mad state: this was the real thing.

■ **Pretenderism** *noun* (*Hist.*) adherence to the cause of the Old or Young Pretender E18. **pretendership** *noun* E18.

pretending /prɪˈtɛndɪŋ/ *ppl adjective.* LME.
[from PRETEND *verb* + -ING².]
That pretends; *esp.* (*a*) pretentious; (*b*) (of a thing or action) imitative, imaginary; (of a game etc.) that involves pretence.

📖 J. WILSON Remembered when more pretending edifices are forgotten. C. M. YONGE They called all 'pretending games' falsehood.

■ **pretendingly** *adverb* M17.

prétendu /pretɑ̃dy/ *noun.* Now *rare* or *obsolete.* Also (fem.) ***-ue***. Pl. pronounced same. M19.
[French.]
An intended husband or wife; a fiancé(e).

pretense *noun* see PRETENCE.

pretensed *ppl adjective* see PRETENCED.

pretension /prɪˈtɛnʃ(ə)n/ *noun.* Also †**-tion**. LME.
[medieval Latin *praetensio(n-)*, *-tio(n-)*, from *praetens-* pa. ppl stem of *praetendere*: see PRETEND *verb*, -ION.]
1 An (unfounded) assertion, *esp.* one put forward to deceive or serve as an excuse; a pretext, an excuse. LME.
†**2** An intention; an aspiration. LME–L18.
3 An assertion of a claim as of right; a claim made, a demand. E17. ▸**b** A rightful claim, a title. E18.
4 The claim that one is or has something; a profession. (Foll. by *to, to be.*) M17. ▸**b** (An instance of) the unwarranted assumption of merit or dignity; (a piece of) pretentiousness. E18.

📖 **1** S. JOHNSON The only things of which we . . could find any pretensions to complain. R. L. STEVENSON Miss Bird . . declares all the viands of Japan to be uneatable—a staggering pretension. **3** CHESTERFIELD The pretensions also of France . . upon Naples. **b** JOHN BROOKE The Hanoverians had no pretensions to the throne except by parliamentary right. **4** E. A. FREEMAN A house . . of no great pretensions. K. M. E. MURRAY A good-natured . . man, making no pretensions to be better-spoken . . than those amongst whom he moved. **b** A. N. WILSON She had abandoned . . the pretensions which had kept her mother's eyes . . on the goals of gentility. A. KENNY A kindly . . man, devoid of pomp or pretension.

■ **pretensionless** *adjective* E19.

pre-tension /priːˈtɛnʃ(ə)n/ *noun & verb.* M20.
[from PRE- 1 + TENSION *noun, verb.*]
▸ **A** *noun.* Tension in an object applied previously or at an early stage of a process, *esp.* that applied to the steel reinforcements in prestressed concrete. M20.
▸ **B** *verb trans.* Apply tension to (something) before some other treatment. Freq. as ***pre-tensioned*** *ppl adjective.* M20.

pretensive /prɪˈtɛnsɪv/ *adjective. rare.* M17.
[from late Latin *praetens-* pa. ppl stem of Latin *praetendere* PRETEND *verb* + -IVE.]
1 Characterized by pretence; professed, feigned. M17.
2 Pretentious, ostentatious. L19.
■ **pretensively** *adverb* E17. **pretensiveness** *noun* †(*a*) a claim, a pretension; (*b*) pretentiousness: L19.

†**pretention** *noun* var. of PRETENSION.

pretentious /prɪˈtɛnʃəs/ *adjective.* M19.
[French *prétentieux*, from *prétention*, formed as PRETENSION: see -IOUS.]
Making excessive or unwarranted claim to merit or importance; making an exaggerated outward show, ostentatious.

DYLAN THOMAS The pretentious palming off of *doggerel* . . as 'arty' poetry is too much. J. STEINBECK An immaculate . . house, grand enough, but not pretentious.

■ **pretentiously** *adverb* M19. **pretentiousness** *noun* M19.

pretenture /priːˈtɛntjʊə/ *noun*. Now *rare* or *obsolete*. M17.
[Late Latin *praetentura*, from *praetendere*: see PRETEND *verb*, -URE.]
ROMAN ANTIQUITIES. A Roman frontier wall, *esp*. either of the two defending Roman Britain from the unsubdued tribes in the north; a Roman garrison guarding a frontier.

†**preter** *adjective & noun*. L15.
[Latin *praeter* contr. of *praeteritum* preterite.]
▶ **A** *adjective*. **1** *GRAMMAR*. = PRETERITE *adjective* 2. Chiefly in ***preter tense*** (orig. one word). L15–L18.
2 Past, gone by in time. L15–E17.
▶ **B** *noun*. **1** *GRAMMAR*. The preterite tense. Only in E17.
2 Past time, the past. Only in 17.

preter- /ˈpriːtə/ *prefix*. Also **praeter-**.
[Latin *praeter* (adverb & preposition) past, beyond, besides, compar. of *prae* before.]
Forming words, esp. adjectives, with the senses 'past', 'beyond', 'more than', as ***preterhuman***, ***preternatural***, etc.

pretergress /priːtəˈgrɛs/ *verb trans*. *rare*. Also **prae-**. L16.
[Latin *praetergress-* pa. ppl stem of *praetergredi* walk past, go by, surpass, formed as PRETER- + *gredi* to step.]
Go beyond; surpass.
■ **pretergression** *noun* the action of going beyond bounds; failure to conform to a law etc.: E17.

preterhuman /priːtəˈhjuːmən/ *adjective*. Also **prae-**. E19.
[from PRETER- + HUMAN *adjective*.]
Beyond or outside of what is human; superhuman.

preterimperfect /priːt(ə)rɪmˈpəːfɪkt/ *adjective & noun*. Long *rare*. M16.
[Latin *praeteritum imperfectum* uncompleted past, from *praeteritum* use as noun of neut. sing. of *praeteritus* (see PRETERITE) + *imperfectus* IMPERFECT *adjective*.]
GRAMMAR. ▶**A** *adjective*. = IMPERFECT *adjective* 5. M16.
▶ **B** *noun*. = IMPERFECT *noun* 1. L16.

preterist /ˈprɛt(ə)rɪst/ *noun & adjective*. M19.
[from PRETER- + -IST.]
THEOLOGY. (Of or pertaining to) a person who holds that the prophecies of the Apocalypse have been already fulfilled.

preterite /ˈprɛt(ə)rɪt/ *adjective & noun*. Also ***-it**. ME.
[Old & mod. French *prétérite* or Latin *praeteritus* pa. pple of *praeterire* go by, pass, formed as PRETER- + *ire* go: see -ITE².]
▶ **A** *adjective*. **1** Of or pertaining to past time; that occurred or existed earlier; past, former. *arch*. ME.
2 *GRAMMAR*. Of a tense or participle: expressing a past action or state. Cf. PAST *adjective* 3. LME.
▶ **B** *noun*. †**1** Past time, the past. *rare*. Only in LME.
2 *GRAMMAR*. A preterite tense or form. M16.
■ **preteriteness** *noun* M17.

preterite-present /prɛt(ə)rɪtˈprɛz(ə)nt/ *adjective & noun*. L19.
[mod. Latin *praeterito-praesens*, formed as PRETERITE + PRESENT *adjective*.]
GRAMMAR. (Designating) a verb of which the tense now used as the present was originally a preterite (e.g. *can*, *dare*); (designating) a tense now present but formerly preterite.

preterition /priːtəˈrɪʃ(ə)n/ *noun*. L16.
[Late Latin *praeteritio(n-)*, from Latin *praeterit-* pa. ppl stem of *praeterire*: see PRETERITE, -ION.]
1 *RHETORIC*. Summary mention made of a thing by professing to omit it. Now *rare*. L16.
2 The action of passing over a matter; the fact of being passed over without notice; omission, disregard. Also, an instance of this. L17.
3 *THEOLOGY*. The passing over of the non-elect; non-election to salvation. Now *rare*. L17.
4 *ROMAN LAW*. Omission to mention in a will one of the testator's children or natural heirs. Now *rare*. E18.

preteritive /prɪˈtɛrɪtɪv/ *adjective*. *rare*. M19.
[from Latin *praeterit-*: see prec., -IVE.]
1 *THEOLOGY*. Of or pertaining to preterition or non-election. M19.
2 Gram. ***preteritive present***, = PRETERITE-PRESENT. L19.

preterlabent /priːtəˈleɪbənt/ *adjective*. *rare*. Also **prae-**. L17.
[Latin *praeterlabent-* pres. ppl stem of *praeterlabi* glide or flow by, formed as PRETER- + *labi* glide: see -ENT.]
Gliding or flowing past.

preterlegal /priːtəˈliːg(ə)l/ *adjective*. *rare*. Also **prae-**. M17.
[from PRETER- + LEGAL *adjective*.]
Beyond or outside of what is legal; not according to law.

preterm /priːˈtəːm/ *adjective*. E20.
[from PRE- 2 + TERM *noun*.]
MEDICINE. Born or occurring after a pregnancy significantly shorter than normal, *spec*. after no more than 37 weeks of pregnancy.

pretermission /priːtəˈmɪʃ(ə)n/ *noun*. Now *rare*. Also **prae-**. L16.
[Latin *praetermissio(n-)*, from *praetermiss-* pa. ppl stem of *praetermittere*: see next, -ION.]
1 The overlooking or disregarding of something; omission, neglect. L16.
2 Ceasing of an action or practice; disuse. L17.
3 *RHETORIC*. = PRETERITION 1. E18.
4 *ROMAN LAW*. = PRETERITION 4. L18.

pretermit /priːtəˈmɪt/ *verb trans*. Infl. **-tt-**. L15.
[Latin *praetermittere*, formed as PRETER- + *mittere* let go, send.]
1 Fail to do or deal with; leave undone, neglect. L15.
2 Leave out of a narrative; leave unmentioned; omit. E16. ▶**b** *ROMAN LAW*. Omit mention of (a descendant or natural heir) in a will. Cf. PRETERITION 4. L19.
3 Allow to pass without notice or regard; overlook intentionally. M16.
4 Fail to take advantage of; allow (time or an opportunity) to pass unused; miss, lose. Now *rare*. M16.
5 Leave off for a time; interrupt, suspend. M16.

1 HUGH WALPOLE Was the necessary defence of her colonies to be pretermitted? **2** GLADSTONE Some points of conduct relating to the present war . . we advisedly pretermit. **5** B. HARTE The monotonous strokes of an axe were suddenly pretermitted.

preternatural /priːtəˈnatʃ(ə)r(ə)l/ *adjective*. Also **prae-**. L16.
[medieval Latin *praeternaturalis*, from Latin phr. *praeter naturam*: see PRETER-.]
1 Outside the ordinary course of nature; differing from or surpassing what is natural; non-natural. Formerly also, exceptional, unusual; unnatural. L16.
2 Supernatural. L18.

1 A. N. WILSON The clue to what makes him special resides in this preternatural ability to be aware.

■ **preternaturally** *adverb* in a preternatural manner; extraordinarily, unusually: E17. **preternaturalness** *noun* E18.

preternaturalism /priːtəˈnatʃ(ə)r(ə)lɪz(ə)m/ *noun*. M19.
[from prec. + -ISM.]
1 The quality or condition of being preternatural. Also, a preternatural occurrence. M19.
2 Recognition of what is preternatural; a system or doctrine of preternatural things. M19.
■ **preternaturalist** *noun* (*rare*) a believer in preternatural things M19.

†**preterperfect** *adjective*. Also **prae-**. M16–L18.
[Late Latin *praeteritum perfectum* complete past, from Latin *praeteritum*: see PRETERIMPERFECT, PERFECT *adjective*, *adverb*, & *noun*.]
GRAMMAR. Of a tense: indicating a past or completed state or action; past perfect.

preterpluperfect /ˌpriːtəpluːˈpəːfɪkt/ *adjective*. M16.
[Late Latin *praeteritum plusquamperfectum*, from Latin *praeteritum*: see PRETERIMPERFECT, PLUPERFECT.]
†**1** *GRAMMAR*. = PLUPERFECT *adjective* 1. M16–M19.
2 Absolutely perfect. Chiefly *joc*. L16.

pretest /ˈpriːtɛst/ *noun*. M20.
[from PRE- 1 + TEST *noun*¹.]
A preliminary or qualifying test; *spec*. in *PSYCHOLOGY*, a test to assess methods or questions intended for use in a projected test.

pretest /priːˈtɛst/ *verb trans*. M20.
[from PRE- 1 + TEST *verb*².]
Test beforehand; *spec*. in *PSYCHOLOGY*, test (methods or questions) in advance of use in a projected test.

pretext /ˈpriːtɛkst/ *noun*. E16.
[Latin *praetextus* outward display, from *praetext-* pa. ppl stem of *praetexere* weave in front, border, disguise, from *prae* PRE- + *texere* weave. Cf. French *prétexte*.]
A reason put forward to conceal the real purpose or object; an ostensible motive of action; an excuse, a pretence.

W. TREVOR She had written the letter herself as a pretext to gain admittance. S. SONTAG The Romantics invented invalidism as a pretext for leisure. **on the pretext of**, **under the pretext of** claiming as one's object or motive.

¶ Formerly stressed on 2nd syll.

pretext /prɪˈtɛkst/ *verb trans*. E17.
[French *prétexter*, from *prétexte* PRETEXT *noun*.]
Use as a pretext; allege as an excuse; pretend.

W. S. MAUGHAM Pretexting an appointment . . he left.

pretone /ˈpriːtəʊn/ *noun*. L19.
[from PRE- 2 + TONE *noun*.]
PHONOLOGY. The syllable or vowel preceding a stressed syllable.

■ **preˈtonic** *adjective & noun* (**a**) *adjective* occurring immediately before a stressed syllable; (**b**) *noun* = PRETONE: M19. **preˈtonically** *adverb* as regards a pretone M20.

pretor *noun*, **pretorial** *adjective & noun*, **pretorian** *adjective & noun*, etc., vars. of PRAETOR etc.

pretrial /*as noun* ˈpriːtrʌɪəl; *as adjective* priːˈtrʌɪəl/ *noun & adjective*. M20.
[from PRE- 1, 2 + TRIAL *noun*.]
▶ **A** *noun*. A preliminary hearing before a trial. *US*. M20.
▶ **B** *adjective*. Of or pertaining to the period before a trial. M20.

prettify /ˈprɪtɪfʌɪ/ *verb trans*. M19.
[from PRETTY *adjective* + -FY.]
Make pretty; represent prettily in a painting or in writing; *spec*. make pretty in an affected or superficial way.

M. AMIS The good champagne, the prettified canapés. *Independent* Rundown areas of Camden . . have been prettified into small parks.

■ **prettifiˈcation** *noun* E20. **prettifier** *noun* M20.

prettily /ˈprɪtɪli/ *adverb*. LME.
[from PRETTY *adjective* + -LY².]
†**1** In a cunning or clever manner; ingeniously, skilfully. LME–E18. ▶†**b** To the point; aptly, neatly. L16–L18.
2 In a way that is pleasing to the eye, the ear, or the aesthetic sense; attractively; charmingly. LME. ▶**b** Gently, softly, quietly. Now *dial*. L15.
†**3** = PRETTY *adverb* 1. M16–M19.

2 E. FEINSTEIN It was a modest apartment, but prettily painted.

prettiness /ˈprɪtɪnɪs/ *noun*. M16.
[from next + -NESS.]
1 Beauty of a delicate, dainty, or diminutive kind, without stateliness. M16.
†**2** Pleasantness, agreeableness. E–M17.
3 A thing which is pretty; a pretty act, feature, ornament, etc. M17.
4 Affected or trivial beauty of expression or style in literature, art, etc. Also, an instance of this, a prettyism. M17.

1 ALDOUS HUXLEY The prettiness, the cosy sublimities of the Lake District. **4** G. B. SHAW I was in no humour to be consoled by elaborate prettinesses from harp and English horn.

pretty /ˈprɪti/ *adjective & noun*.
[Old English *prættig* corresp. to Middle Low German *prattich* capricious, overbearing, Middle Dutch (*ghe*)*pertich* brisk, clever, roguish, Dutch †*prettig* sportive, humorous, from West Germanic base meaning 'trick': ult. origin unkn.]
▶ **A** *adjective*. **1** Orig., cunning, crafty. Later, (of a person) clever, skilful; (of a thing) cleverly made or done; ingenious, artful. *arch*. OE.
2 a Of a person: excellent or admirable in appearance, manners, or other qualities; *spec*. (chiefly *Scot*.) (of a soldier) brave, gallant, warlike. *arch*. LME. ▶**b** Of a thing: fine, pleasing, nice; agreeable, proper. M16.
3 a Of a person, esp. a woman or child: attractive and pleasing in appearance; beautiful in a delicate, dainty, or diminutive way without stateliness. LME. ▶**b** Of a thing: pleasing to the eye, the ear, or the aesthetic sense. LME.
4 Of a quantity or amount: considerable, great. Now *rare* exc. in ***pretty packet***, ***penny*** below. L15.

2b A. F. DOUGLAS-HOME A master of English . . with as pretty and sharp a wit as any politician. *iron*.: W. BLACK Well, young lady . . and a pretty mess you have got us into! **3a** SHAKES. *Wint. T.* My prettiest Perdita. V. BRITTAIN A pretty young Scotswoman, pink-cheeked . . and dewy-eyed. **b** G. CATLIN A pretty little town. E. BOWEN A black dress with pretty touches of white.

Phrases: ***a pretty kettle of fish***: see KETTLE 1. **(as) pretty as a picture** extremely pretty. ***as pretty as paint***: see PAINT *noun*. ***come to a pretty pass***: see PASS *noun*². **not just a pretty face** *colloq*. intelligent as well as attractive.
Special collocations & comb.: **pretty-boy** *slang* a foppish or effeminate man; a male homosexual; *iron*. a thug. **pretty-by-night** *US* = ***marvel of Peru*** s.v. MARVEL *noun*¹. **pretty-face (wallaby)** = ***whiptail wallaby*** s.v. WHIPTAIL *adjective*. **pretty fellow** *arch*. a fine fellow, a fop. **pretty packet**, **pretty penny** a considerable sum, a good deal of money. **pretty please**: a wheedling form of request.
▶ **B** *noun*. **1** A pretty thing, an ornament. M18.
2 A pretty man, woman, or child; a pretty one. Chiefly (also ***my pretty***) as a form of address. L18.
3 = ***pretty penny*** above. *US*. M19.
4 The fluted or ornamented part of a glass or tumbler. M19.
5 The fairway of a golf course. E20.

1 J. D. MACDONALD 'Here is a pretty I got for you . . .' She . . gasped at the lovely ring. **2** GOLDSMITH If you would but comprehend me, my pretty. **3** G. STRATTON-PORTER I'd give a pretty to know that secret.

■ **prettyish** *adjective* somewhat pretty M18. **prettyism** *noun* studied prettiness of style or manner; an instance of this: L18.

pretty /ˈprɪti/ *verb.* **E19.**
[from the adjective.]
1 *verb refl. & intrans.* Make oneself pretty; make or dress oneself *up* to look attractive. **E19.**
2 *verb trans.* Make (a thing or person) attractive; *iron.* spoil, damage. Freq. foll. by *up.* **M20.**

📖 **1** M. M. ATWATER Prettying up for company. **2** *Sunday Express* They've prettied it up now with hanging baskets and window boxes.

pretty /ˈprɪti/ *adverb. colloq.* **M16.**
[from the adjective.]
1 To a considerable extent, considerably; fairly, moderately, tolerably. **M16.**
†**2** Ingeniously. Only in **M17.**
3 = PRETTILY 2. **L18.**

📖 **1** H. SECOMBE He was pretty strong for his size. E. LEONARD He'll be home pretty soon. **3** M. EDGEWORTH How pretty behaved he is.

Phrases: **pretty much**, **pretty near**, **pretty well** almost, very nearly; approximately. **sitting pretty** *colloq.* in a comfortable or advantageous position.

pretty-pretty /ˈprɪtɪˌprɪti/ *adjective, adverb, & noun.* **L19.**
[Redupl. of PRETTY *adjective & noun.*]
► **A** *adjective.* Excessively or affectedly pretty; in which the aim at prettiness is overdone. **L19.**

📖 I. MURDOCH He sometimes did pretty-pretty representations of flowers or animals, of which he felt .. mildly ashamed.

► **B** *adverb.* In a pretty-pretty manner. **L19.**
► **C** *noun.* **1** In *pl.* Pretty things; ornaments, knick-knacks. **L19.**
2 *the pretty-pretty*, that which is pretty-pretty. **E20.**
■ **pretty-ˈprettiness** *noun* **E20.**

prettyprint /ˈprɪtɪprɪnt/ *verb trans.* **L20.**
[from PRETTY *adjective & noun* + PRINT *verb.*]
COMPUTING. Print in a way that displays the structure of a program by the use of spacing and indentation.
■ **prettyprinter** *noun* a printer or program for producing prettyprinted text **L20.**

pretzel /ˈprɛts(ə)l/ *noun.* Also (now *rare* or *obsolete*) **bretzel** /ˈbrɛts(ə)l/. **M19.**
[German.]
A hard salted biscuit usu. in the form of a knot, eaten orig. in Germany.

preux /prø/ *adjective.* **L18.**
[French: see PROUD.]
Brave, valiant. Chiefly in ***preux chevalier***, gallant knight.

prevail /prɪˈveɪl/ *verb.* **LME.**
[Latin *praevalere* have greater power, from *prae* PRE- + *valere* (see VAIL *verb*[1]), with assim. to AVAIL *verb.*]
†**1** *verb intrans.* Become very strong; gain vigour or force, increase in strength. *rare.* **LME–M18.**
2 *verb intrans.* Be superior in strength or influence; have or gain the advantage; be victorious. (Foll. by *against, over.*) **LME.**
3 *verb intrans.* Be effectual or efficacious; succeed. **LME.** ►†**b** *verb trans.* = ***prevail on*** below. **L15–M19.**
†**4** *verb trans. & intrans.* Be of advantage or use (to); = AVAIL *verb* 1. **LME–E17.** ►**b** *verb intrans. & refl.* Make use *of*; obtain the benefit *of*; = AVAIL *verb* 2. Only in **17.**
5 *verb intrans.* **a** Be or become the more widespread or more usual; predominate. **E17.** ►**b** Be in general use or practice; be prevalent or current; exist. **L18.**

📖 **2** W. SALMON It .. prevails against all cold Diseases of the Head, Brain, Nerves and Womb. A. G. GARDINER In the end the moral law prevails over the law of the jungle. D. LESSING On you go, jolly and optimistic that right will prevail. **5a** *International Affairs* The tensions and conflict that have long prevailed in the Gulf. **b** P. G. WODEHOUSE In the drawing-room a tense silence prevailed. A. FRASER Those who had decided to sit out the times until better ones prevailed.

With prepositions in specialized senses: **prevail on**, **prevail upon** succeed in persuading, inducing, or influencing.
■ **prevailer** *noun* (now *rare*) a person who prevails **E17.** †**prevailment** *noun* (*rare*) the action or fact of prevailing **L16–M17.**

prevailing /prɪˈveɪlɪŋ/ *ppl adjective.* **L16.**
[from prec. + -ING[2].]
That prevails; *spec.* (*a*) superior, victorious, effective; (*b*) predominant in extent or amount; generally current or accepted.

📖 *Japan Times* At prevailing prices the mines are incurring substantial losses. **prevailing wind** the wind that most frequently occurs at a place (as regards direction).

■ **prevailingly** *adverb* **L18.** **prevailingness** *noun* (*rare*) **L19.**

prevalence /ˈprɛv(ə)l(ə)ns/ *noun.* **L16.**
[French †*prévalence* from late Latin *praevalentia* superior force, predominance, from Latin *praevalere*: see PREVAIL *verb*, -ENCE.]
1 The fact or action of prevailing; mastery. Now *rare.* **L16.**
2 Effective force or power; influence; efficacy. Now *rare.* **M17.**
3 The condition of being prevalent; general occurrence or existence; common practice; *MEDICINE* the number or proportion of cases at any one time. **E18.**

📖 **1** T. CHALMERS The final prevalence of the good over the evil. **3** M. SCHORER The prevalence of American slang in British speech. *Lancet* Populations with a high prevalence of the virus.

■ Also **prevalency** *noun* (now *rare*) **E17.**

prevalent /ˈprɛv(ə)l(ə)nt/ *adjective.* **L16.**
[Latin *praevalent-* pres. ppl stem of *praevalere*: see PREVAIL *verb*, -ENT.]
1 Having great power or force; effective, powerful; influential (*with* a person). Now *rare.* **L16.** ►†**b** Of a medicine etc.: efficacious. **E17–E18.**
2 Having the advantage; predominant, victorious. Now *rare.* **E17.**
3 Generally occurring or existing; in general use; usual. **M17.**

📖 **3** M. STOTT Diseases currently more prevalent among men.

■ **prevalently** *adverb* **M17.**

prevaricate /prɪˈvarɪkeɪt/ *verb.* **M16.**
[Latin *praevaricat-* pa. ppl stem of *praevaricari* go crookedly, deviate from the right path, transgress, (of an advocate) practise collusion, from *prae* PRE- + *varicare* spread the legs apart, straddle, from *varus* bow-legged: see -ATE[3].]
► **I** *verb intrans.* †**1** Go aside from the right course, method, etc.; deviate, go astray, transgress. **M16–L17.**
2 Deviate from straightforwardness; act or speak evasively; quibble, equivocate. **M17.**
†**3** *LAW.* Betray the cause of a client by collusion with an opponent; undertake a matter deceitfully in order to defeat the professed object. **M17–E18.**

📖 **2** J. H. INGRAHAM It is impossible .. for me either to conceal or to prevaricate. M. WESLEY He had rung off before she could prevaricate or protest.

►†**II** *verb trans.* **4** Deviate from, transgress, (a law etc.). **L16–E17.**
5 Turn from the straight course, application, or meaning; pervert. **M17–E18.**

prevarication /prɪˌvarɪˈkeɪʃ(ə)n/ *noun.* **LME.**
[Latin *praevaricatio(n-)*, formed as prec.: see -ATION.]
†**1** Divergence from the right course, method, etc.; deviation from truth or rectitude; violation of moral law; departure from a principle or normal state. Also foll. by *from, of.* **LME–E18.**
†**2** Deviation from duty; violation of trust; corrupt action. **M16–E18.** ►**b** *LAW.* Betrayal of a client's cause by collusion with an opponent. **M16–E18.**
3 Avoidance of plain dealing or straightforward statement of the truth; evasion, quibbling, equivocation, deception. Also, an instance of this. **M17.**

📖 **3** R. CHRISTIANSEN Timothy Shelley was not deceived by prevarications. M. FORSTER What he wanted was an end to all this prevarication.

prevaricator /prɪˈvarɪkeɪtə/ *noun.* **LME.**
[Latin *praevaricator* a person who violates his duty, (in ecclesiastical Latin) transgressor, formed as prec.: see -OR.]
†**1** A person who goes astray or deviates from the right course; a transgressor. **LME–M18.** ►**b** A person who betrays a cause or violates a trust; a renegade; a traitor. **L15–M17.**
2 At Cambridge University, an orator who made a jocose or satirical speech at commencement. Cf. TERRAE FILIUS 2. *obsolete* exc. *Hist.* **E17.**
3 A person who acts or speaks evasively; a quibbler, an equivocator. **M17.**
†**4** *LAW.* A person who betrayed a client's cause by collusion with an opponent. **M17–L18.**
5 A person who diverts something from its proper use; a perverter. Long *rare* or *obsolete.* **L17.**

prevaricatory /prɪˈvarɪkət(ə)ri/ *adjective. rare.* **M17.**
[formed as PREVARICATE *verb* + -ORY[2].]
Characterized by prevarication; prevaricating, evasive.

†**preve** *noun* see PROOF *noun.*

†**preve** *verb* var. of PROVE *verb.*

prevenance /ˈprɛvɪnəns/ *noun.* Also ***prévenance*** /prɛvnɑ̃s, pre-/ **E19.**
[French *prévenance*, from *prévenir* anticipate, prepossess, formed as next: see -ANCE.]
Courteous anticipation of the desires or needs of others; complaisance; an obliging manner.

prevene /prɪˈviːn/ *verb trans.* Chiefly *Scot.* Now *rare* or *obsolete.* **LME.**
[Latin *praevenire*: see next.]
†**1** Take action before or in anticipation of; frustrate, evade; forestall. **LME–M18.**
†**2** Take in advance. Only in **16.**
3 Come or go before; precede. *rare.* **M16.**

prevenient /prɪˈviːnɪənt/ *adjective.* **E17.**
[Latin *praevenient-* pres. ppl stem of *praevenire* come before, anticipate, from *prae* PRE- + *venire* come: see -ENT.]
1 Coming before, preceding, previous; antecedent, esp. to human action. **E17.**
2 Anticipatory, expectant. (Foll. by *of.*) **E19.**
1 prevenient grace *THEOLOGY* the grace of God which precedes repentance and conversion, and predisposes the heart to seek God prior to any initiative on the part of the recipient.
■ **preveniently** *adverb* antecedently, previously **M17.**

prevent /prɪˈvɛnt/ *verb.* **LME.**
[Latin *praevent-* pa. ppl stem of *praevenire* precede, anticipate, hinder: see PREVENE.]
► **I** Act or do in advance.
†**1 a** *verb trans.* Act before, in anticipation of, or in preparation for (a future event, a point in time). **LME–E19.** ►**b** *verb trans.* Meet beforehand or anticipate (an objection, question, desire, etc.). **M16–M19.** ►**c** *verb intrans.* Come, appear, or act before the time or in anticipation. **M16–E17.**
†**2** *verb trans.* Act before or more quickly than (another); anticipate in action. **LME–E19.**
†**3** *verb trans.* Come, arrive, or appear before; precede; outrun, outstrip. **L15–M18.** ►**b** Come in front of, meet in front. **M16–E17.** ►**c** *fig.* Outdo, excel. **M16–M17.**
†**4** *verb trans.* Hasten or bring about prematurely; anticipate. **M16–L17.**
†**5** *verb trans.* Occupy or use beforehand. Also, preoccupy or prejudice (the mind). **M16–M18.**
6 *verb trans.* Of God or his grace: go before with spiritual guidance and help, in anticipation of human action or need. *arch.* **M16.**

📖 **2** GIBBON The fortunate soil assisted, and even prevented, the hand of cultivation. **6** *Book of Common Prayer* By thy special grace preventing us, thou dost put into our minds good desires.

► **II** Stop, hinder, avoid.
7 *verb trans.* Forestall or thwart by previous or precautionary measures. *obsolete* exc. as passing into sense 12. **LME.**
8 *verb trans.* Preclude *from* or deprive *of* a purpose, expectation, etc. Now *rare* exc. as passing into sense 12. **M16.**
9 *verb trans.* Provide beforehand against the occurrence of (something); make impracticable or impossible by anticipatory action; stop from happening. **M16.** ►†**b** *verb intrans.* Use preventive measures. *rare* (Shakes.). Only in **E17.**
†**10** *verb trans.* Frustrate, defeat, make void (an expectation, plan, etc.). **M16–E18.**
†**11** *verb trans.* Stop (something) from happening to oneself; escape or evade by timely action. **L16–E18.**
12 *verb trans.* Cause to be unable to do or be something, stop (foll. by *from doing, from being*). Also (with ellipsis of *from*), stop from *doing* or *being.* **M17.**

📖 **9** F. MARRYAT I shall not prevent your going. I. MURDOCH She put her hands to her eyes as if to prevent tears. **12** J. CONRAD A vague nervous anxiety .. prevented him from getting up. G. GREENE I want to abandon .. everybody but you: only fear and habit prevent me. N. MOSLEY We had nailed the trap door .. to prevent the children falling through it.

■ **preventable** *adjective* (earlier in UNPREVENTABLE) **M17.** **preventaˈbility** *adjective* **M19.** **preventiˈbility** *noun* (*rare*) **M19.** **preventible** *adjective* **M19.**

preventative /prɪˈvɛntətɪv/ *adjective & noun.* **M17.**
[from PREVENT + -ATIVE.]
= PREVENTIVE *adjective & noun.*
■ **preventatively** *adverb* **L20.**

preventer /prɪˈvɛntə/ *noun.* **L16.**
[formed as prec. + -ER[1].]
1 A person who or thing which hinders, restrains, or stops something from happening or being done. **L16.**
2 *NAUTICAL.* A rope, chain, etc., used to provide temporary additional support to rigging in high winds or storms. Also more fully ***preventer-rope.*** **E17.**
3 In full ***blow-out preventer.*** A heavy valve or assembly of valves fitted above an oil or gas well during drilling and closed in the event of a blow-out. **E20.**

prevention /prɪˈvɛnʃ(ə)n/ *noun.* **LME.**
[Old & mod. French *prévention* or late Latin *praeventio(n-)*, from Latin *praevent-*: see PREVENT, -ION.]
1 The action of stopping something from happening or making impossible an anticipated or intended act. **LME.** ►†**b** A means of preventing; a safeguard; an obstruction. **L16–E19.**
2 *ECCLESIASTICAL.* The privilege possessed or claimed by an ecclesiastical superior of taking precedence over or forestalling an inferior. Now *rare* or *obsolete.* **E16.**
†**3** The arrival, occurrence, or action of one person or thing before another, or before the due time; action or occurrence before or in anticipation of the expected or usual time. **M16–E18.**

†**4 a** The action of forestalling or thwarting a person by previous action. L16–M17. ▸**b** Action intended to provide against an anticipated danger; (a) precaution. E17–L18. †**5** A mental anticipation; a presentiment. E17–E19. †**6** Bias, prejudice. L17–E19.

> 📖 **1** *Gentleman's Magazine* Lord Erskine's Bill for the Prevention of Cruelty towards Animals. J. WYNDHAM Prevention being better than cure, the sensible course was to see that the situation should never develop.

■ **preventional** *adjective* (*rare*) M17. **preventionism** *noun* (*rare*) a policy of prevention E20. **preventionist** *noun* (*rare*) a person who favours preventionism E20.

preventive /prɪˈvɛntɪv/ *adjective & noun*. M17.
[from PREVENT + -IVE. Cf. PREVENTATIVE.]
▶**A** *adjective*. †**1** That comes or goes before something else; antecedent, anticipatory. M–L17.
2 That anticipates in order to preclude; that stops something from happening; that acts as a hindrance or obstacle; (of a drug etc.) prophylactic. M17. ▸**b** Of or belonging to the customs department which is concerned with the prevention of smuggling. E19.

> 📖 **2** B. V. BOWDEN The technique of preventive maintenance . . has considerably reduced the number of valve failures. *Which?* Many headaches may be tackled by simple preventive measures. **b** *Hongkong Standard* Officers of both Immigration and the Preventive Services.

Special collocations: **preventive detention** imprisonment with the aim of preventing the person concerned from committing further offences. **preventive medicine** the branch of medicine that deals with the prevention of disease.
▶**B** *noun*. **1** A preventive agent or measure; a means of prevention; a hindrance, an obstacle. M17.
2 a MEDICINE. A drug or other agent for preventing disease; a prophylactic. L17. ▸**b** A contraceptive. E19.

> 📖 **1** J. R. ACKERLEY She was looking around for . . some lemon as a preventive of sea-sickness.

■ **preventively** *adverb* M17.

preventorium /priːvɛnˈtɔːrɪəm/ *noun*. Chiefly *US*. Pl. **-ria** /-rɪə/, **-riums**. E20.
[from PREVENT *verb* after SANATORIUM.]
An establishment where preventive care is given to people at risk from tuberculosis or other diseases.

preverb /*as noun* ˈpriːvəːb; *as adjective* priːˈvəːb/ *noun & adjective*. M20.
[from PRE- 2 + VERB.]
GRAMMAR. ▶**A** *noun*. A particle or prefix preceding the stem of a verb. M20.
▶**B** *adjective*. = PREVERBAL 2. L20.

preverbal /priːˈvəːb(ə)l/ *adjective*. M20.
[from PRE- 2 + VERBAL.]
1 Existing or occurring before speech or the development of speech. M20.
2 GRAMMAR. Occurring before a verb. M20.

preview /ˈpriːvjuː/ *noun*. In sense 2b also ***prevue**. M19.
[from PRE- 1 + VIEW *noun*.]
1 Foresight, prevision. *rare*. M19.
2 A previous view or inspection. Also, a foretaste, a preliminary glimpse. L19. ▸**b** *spec*. A showing or presentation of a film, play, exhibition, etc., before it is available to the public or before an official opening. Also (chiefly *N. Amer.*), a trailer for a film. E20.

> 📖 **2** *Sun (Baltimore)* His preview of the budget probabilities for the fiscal year now current. **b** *Independent* Their own latest musical production . . is playing in preview at London's Victoria Palace.

preview /*in sense* 1 priːˈvjuː; *in sense* 2 ˈpriːvjuː/ *verb*. E17.
[from PRE- 1 + VIEW *verb*.]
1 *verb trans*. View or look at beforehand; foresee. *rare*. E17.
2 a *verb trans*. Show or present (a film etc.) before its public presentation or official opening; give a preview or foretaste of. E20. ▸**b** *verb intrans*. Of a production, performance, etc.: be previewed. L20.

> 📖 **1** R. CONNOR Every act of importance had to be previewed from all possible points. **2a** *Listener* The first edition previewed the Commonwealth Conference.

■ ˈ**previewer** *noun* L20.

previous /ˈpriːvɪəs/ *adjective, adverb, & noun*. E17.
[Latin *praevius* going before, leading the way, from *prae* PRE- + *via* way: see -OUS.]
▶**A** *adjective*. **1** Coming or going before in time or order; foregoing, preceding, antecedent. (Foll. by *to*.) E17.
†**2** Going before or in front; leading the way. M–L17.
3 Occurring, acting, etc., before the proper time; hasty, premature. *colloq*. L19.

> 📖 **1** E. HEMINGWAY Commanders who had sprung to arms . . without any previous military training. J. F. LEHMANN We had made friends on his previous visit. **3** E. COXHEAD I think it's a bit previous. Why not put the chappie off.

Special collocations: **Previous Examination** *Hist*. the first examination for the degree of BA at Cambridge University. **previous question** in parliamentary procedure, the question whether a vote shall be taken on the main question or issue, moved before the main question is put.
▶**B** *adverb*. = PREVIOUSLY. E18.

> 📖 A. N. WILSON Maudie could only have received his letter some three hours previous.

▶**C** *noun*. A thing which is previous; *spec*. (**a**) *Hist*. = ***Previous Examination*** above; (**b**) *slang* previous convictions. E20.

> 📖 L. GRIFFITHS Never been in bother, no previous, never known to mix with bad company.

■ **previousness** *noun* L17.

previously /ˈpriːvɪəsli/ *adverb*. E18.
[from prec. + -LY[2].]
At a previous or preceding time; before, beforehand. (Foll. by *to*.)

> 📖 T. HARDY The fiddlers were doing the up bow-stroke previously to . . the opening chord. L. APPIGNANESI A despair greater than any she had previously felt.

previse /prɪˈvʌɪz/ *verb trans*. LME.
[Latin *praevis-* pa. ppl stem of *praevidere* foresee, anticipate, from *prae-* PRE- + *videre* see.]
†**1** Provide, supply, furnish. *rare*. Only in LME.
2 Foresee; forecast. L16.

prevision /prɪˈvɪʒ(ə)n/ *noun*. LME.
[Late Latin *praevisio(n-)* foresight, formed as prec.: see -ION.]
The action or faculty of foreseeing; foresight, foreknowledge. Also, an instance of this.
■ **previsional** *adjective* M19. **previsionary** *adjective* E19.

prevocalic /priːvə(ʊ)ˈkalɪk/ *adjective*. E20.
[from PRE- 2 + VOCALIC.]
Situated or occurring before a vowel; of or pertaining to the position before a vowel.
■ **prevocalically** *adverb* M20.

prevost /ˈprɛvɒst/ *noun*. Also (esp. in sense 2) ***prévôt*** /prevo (*pl. same*)/. L15.
[Old French (mod. *prévôt*) from Latin PRAEPOSITUS. Cf. PROVOST.]
†**1** The provost or president of a chapter or collegiate church. Cf. PROVOST. L15–M19.
2 a Orig., an officer or deputy of the French king who collected imposts and administered justice. Later, the judge of a French prevotal court. M17. ▸**b** In Guernsey, an officer of justice equivalent to a High Sheriff in England. Also, in Jersey and Guernsey, a bailiff of an estate or fief. L17.
■ **prevotal** /ˈprɛvət(ə)l/ *adjective* of or pertaining to a French *prévôt*; ***prevotal court***, a French temporary criminal tribunal, from which there is no appeal: E19.

prevoyance /prɪˈvɔɪəns/ *noun*. *rare*. E19.
[French *prévoyance*, from *prévoir* from Latin *praevidere*, from *prae* PRE- + *videre* see.]
Foresight.

prevue *noun* see PREVIEW *noun*.

pre-war /priːˈwɔː/ *adjective & adverb*. E20.
[from PRE- 2 + WAR *noun*[1].]
▶**A** *adjective*. Pertaining to or characteristic of the period before a war, esp. the wars of 1914–18 or 1939–45. E20.
▶**B** *adverb*. Before a war, esp. the wars of 1914–18 or 1939–45. E20.

Prex /prɛks/ *noun*. *US College slang*. E19.
[Alt. of abbreviation of PRESIDENT *noun*.]
A president, *esp*. the president of a college.

Prexy /ˈprɛksi/ *noun*. *US slang*. L19.
[from prec. + -Y[6].]
= PREX.

prey /preɪ/ *noun*. ME.
[Old French *preie* (mod. *proie*) from Latin *praeda* booty.]
1 That which is taken in war, or by pillage or violence; booty, spoil, plunder. *arch*. ME. ▸**b** *fig*. In biblical use, that which one takes away or saves from a contest etc. LME.
2 An animal that is hunted or killed, esp. (and now only) by another animal for food. ME. ▸†**b** That which is procured or serves for food. LME–L17.
3 A person who or thing which is influenced by or vulnerable to someone or something injurious. ME.
4 The action of preying; seizing by force or violence, or in order to devour; pillage, capture, seizure. Now *rare*. E16.

> 📖 **2** A. HARDY Sea-anemones capture larger prey. D. MORRIS Hyaenas start tearing at the legs of any prey in reach. **3** S. T. WARNER At night I become prey to the gloomiest suspicions. S. WEINTRAUB She was easy prey to someone influential.

Phrases: ***beast of prey***: see BEAST *noun*. ***bird of prey***: see BIRD *noun*.
■ †**preyful** *adjective* (*rare*) killing much prey, prone to prey L16–E17.

prey /preɪ/ *verb*. ME.
[Old French *preier*, *preer* from late Latin *praedare* alt. of earlier *praedari*, from *praeda* PREY *noun*.]
†**1** *verb trans*. **a** Plunder, pillage, spoil; rob, ravage. ME–M17. ▸**b** Make prey or spoil of; take as booty. *rare*. L16–E17.
2 *verb intrans*. Pillage, plunder. (Foll. by *(up)on*.) Now *rare*. ME.
3 *verb intrans*. Take or look for prey. Usu. foll. by *(up)on*, seize and kill as prey; *fig*. make a victim of, make harmful use of for one's own purposes. ME.
4 *verb intrans*. Exert a baneful, wasting, or destructive influence *(up)on*. E18.

> 📖 **3** A. C. CLARKE Alert for the mountain lions that would prey upon his father's sheep. G. GREENE You are obviously preying on her good nature. R. CHRISTIANSEN Oswald is a hard-hearted cynic who preys on the weakness of others. **4** H. KELLER Anger and bitterness had preyed upon me continually for weeks. B. CHATWIN The thought of it preyed on their minds and made them ill.

■ **preyer** *noun* L16.

prez /prɛz/ *noun*[1]. *colloq*. L19.
[Abbreviation.]
= PRESIDENT *noun*.

prez /prɛz/ *noun*[2]. *colloq*. Also **pres**. E20.
[Abbreviation.]
= PRESENT *noun*[2].

prezzie /ˈprɛzi/ *noun*. *colloq*. Also **pressie**. M20.
[from PREZ *noun*[2] + -IE.]
A present, a gift.

prial /ˈprʌɪəl/ *noun*. E19.
[Alt.]
= ***pair royal*** s.v. PAIR *noun*[1].

Priamel /prɪˈɑːm(ə)l/ *noun*. Also **p-**. Pl. **-meln** /-məln/. M20.
[German from Latin *praeambulum* PREAMBLE *noun*.]
Hist. An epigrammatic verse form popular in Germany in the 15th and 16th cents. Also, a similar verse form in ancient Greek poetry.

prian *noun* var. of PRYAN.

Priapi *noun pl*. see PRIAPUS.

priapic /prʌɪˈapɪk/ *adjective*. Also **P-**. L18.
[from PRIAPUS + -IC.]
Of, pertaining to, or characteristic of the god Priapus. Also, phallic.
■ Also **priapean** /prʌɪəˈpiːən/ *adjective* L17.

priapism /ˈprʌɪəpɪz(ə)m/ *noun*. Earlier in Latin form †**priapismus**. LME.
[Late Latin *priapismus* from Greek *priapismos*, from *priapizein* act Priapus, be lewd, formed as PRIAPUS: see -ISM. Cf. French *priapisme*.]
1 MEDICINE. Persistent erection of the penis, commonly due to a blood clot in the erectile tissue. LME.
2 = PRIAPUS 2. *rare*. M17.
3 Lewdness, licentiousness. M18.
■ **Priapist** *noun* (*rare*) a worshipper of Priapus; a lecher: M16.

priapulid /prʌɪˈapjʊlɪd/ *noun & adjective*. E20.
[mod. Latin *Priapulida* (see below), from *Priapulus* genus name, dim. of PRIAPUS: see -ID[3].]
ZOOLOGY. ▶**A** *noun*. Any of various wormlike marine animals of the minor phylum Priapulida, which burrow in sand or mud and possess an eversible proboscis or pharynx. E20.
▶**B** *adjective*. Of, pertaining to, or designating this phylum. E20.

Priapus /prʌɪˈeɪpəs/ *noun*. Also **p-**. Pl. **-pi** /-pʌɪ, -piː/, **-puses**. LME.
[Latin from Greek *Priapos*, the Greek and Roman god of procreation whose symbol was the phallus, later adopted as a god of gardens.]
1 A statue or image of the god Priapus, esp. characterized by having large genitals. LME.
2 *transf*. (A representation of) the penis, esp. when erect. L16.

pribble /ˈprɪb(ə)l/ *noun*. L16.
[Alt. of PRABBLE *noun*.]
Petty disputation, vain chatter. Chiefly in ***pribble-prabble***.

pribumi /ˈprɪbuːmi/ *noun & adjective*. Also **P-**. L20.
[Indonesian or Javanese Cf. Sanskrit *bhūmi* earth.]
▶**A** *noun*. Pl. same, **-s**. In Indonesia and Malaysia, a member of the indigenous population. L20.
▶**B** *attrib*. or as *adjective*. Of or pertaining to the pribumi. L20.

price /prʌɪs/ *noun & adjective*. Also †**prise**, (as noun, now *dial*.) **prize** /prʌɪz/. See also PRIZE *noun*[1]. ME.
[Old French *pris* (mod. *prix*) from Latin *pretium* price, value, wages, reward. Cf. PRAISE *noun*.]
▶**A** *noun*. **I 1** The (esp. stated) sum in money or goods for which a thing is or may be bought or sold, or a thing or person ransomed or redeemed; *spec*. in *pl*., the current level of prices charged by a shop, hotel, etc., for goods or services. Formerly also, a rate for labour, wages. ME. ▸**b** Payment in purchase of something. *obsolete* exc. in ***without price*** (a) below. LME. ▸**c** Reckoning or statement of the value of something, estimation of value. Only in ***above price***, ***beyond price***, ***without price*** (b), below. L16.

▸**d** ECONOMICS. The actual cost of acquiring, producing, etc., something calculated according to some specific measure. **L17.**

2 *fig.* The cost of a thing in expenditure of effort, endurance, suffering, etc.; what is borne, sacrificed, surrendered, etc., to obtain some advantage. **LME.**

3 A sum of money offered as a reward for the capture or killing of a person. Chiefly in ***put a price on a person's head, set a price on a person's head*** below. **M18.**

4 The amount of money etc. needed to procure a person's interest or support. **M18.**

5 The odds in betting. **L19.**

📖 **1** A. KENNY Cigarettes at duty-free prices. E. LEONARD All they get .. are tourists .. the way their prices are. *Which?* An average price for each item. **2** B. NEIL Was madness the price for a few hours' living? P. DE VRIES The stops .. were small price to pay for the stimulations .. of that journey. **4** J. BENTHAM It is a well-known adage, .. that every man has his price.

▸**II 6** Value, worth; *esp.* high value. Formerly also, honourableness, virtue. *arch.* **ME.**

†**7** Esteem, regard; *esp.* high esteem. **ME–M17.** ▸**b** Valuation, assessment. *rare* (Shakes.). Only in **E17.**

📖 **6** AV *Matt.* 13:46 One pearle of great price.

▸†**III 8** = PRAISE *noun* 1a. **ME–M16.**

9 = PRAISE *noun* 1b. **ME–E17.**

▸†**IV** See PRIZE *noun*¹.

Phrases: **above price** = ***beyond price*** below. **a price on one's head** a reward on offer for one's capture or death. *ASKING* **price**. **at any price** whatever it may cost, whatever loss, sacrifice, etc., is or may be entailed. **at a price** at a high cost, entailing considerable loss, sacrifice, etc. **beyond price** so valuable that no price can be stated. ***long price***: see LONG *adjective*¹. *MARKED* **price**. ***maximum price***: see MAXIMUM *adjective*. ***middle price***: see MIDDLE *adjective*. †**of price** (*a*) (of a thing) precious, valuable; (*b*) (of a person) worthy, honourable. **put a price on a person's head, set a price on a person's head** offer a reward for a person's capture or death. ***reserve price***: see RESERVE *noun* 5b. ***retail price index, retail price maintenance***: see RETAIL *noun, adjective*. ***set a price on a person's head***: see ***put a price on a person's head*** above. ***short price***: see SHORT *adjective*. ***unit price***: see UNIT *noun*¹ & *adjective*. ***upset price***: see UPSET *adjective*. **what price —?** what is the value or use of —?; what is the likelihood of —? **without price** (*a*) *arch.* without payment, free; (*b*) = ***beyond price*** above.

Comb.: **price buster** (*colloq.*, orig. *US*) (*a*) a person who or thing which inflates or reduces the price of an item or commodity; (*b*) an item or commodity selling at a reduced price; **price control** governmental establishment and maintenance of a maximum price to be charged for specified goods and services; **price-current** a price-list for a particular range of goods etc.; **price-cut** *verb & noun* (*a*) *verb trans. & intrans.* practise price-cutting (on); (*b*) *noun* a reduction made by price-cutting; **price-cutting** the action of reducing the price of goods for sale, esp. in order to compete with other traders; **price discrimination** the action of charging different prices to different customers for the same goods or services; **price–earnings multiple, price–earnings ratio** ECONOMICS the ratio between the current market price of a company's stock and its annual per-share income; **price elasticity** the extent to which demand for goods etc. is affected by a change in price; **price-fixed** *adjective* (of goods for sale etc.) maintained at a certain price level by price fixing; **price-fixing** the action of maintaining prices at a certain level by agreement between traders; **price index**: showing the variation in the prices of a set of goods etc. since a chosen base period; **price leader** a dominant firm that determines the prices within an industry; **price-list**: giving current prices of goods for sale etc.; **price-mark** *noun & verb* (*a*) *noun* a mark on an item for sale indicating its price; (*b*) *verb trans.* (*US*) put a price-mark on (an item for sale); **price movement** a fluctuation in price; **price point** (chiefly *US*) a point on a scale of possible prices at which something might be marketed; **price ring** an association of traders formed to control certain prices; **price shading** the action of changing prices by small gradations; **price stop** a ban on price increases; **price support** assistance in maintaining the levels of prices regardless of supply or demand; **price system** an economic system in which prices are determined by market forces; **price tab** *US* a bill; **price tag, price ticket** (*a*) a label on an item indicating its price; (*b*) ECONOMICS the estimated value of a company, esp. as the sum required for a takeover etc.; **price war** intense competition among traders by price-cutting.

▸†**B** *adjective.* Precious, valuable; (of a person) worthy, honourable. **ME–E17.**

price /prʌɪs/ *verb trans.* Also (earlier) †**prise**. **LME.**
[Var. of PRIZE *verb*¹, assim. to prec. Cf. PRAISE *verb*.]

1 Set or state the price of (a thing for sale); *esp.* attach a price-tag or ticket to. **LME.** ▸**b** *fig.* Value relatively, estimate. **L19.**

†**2** = PRIZE *verb*¹ 2. **LME–M17.**

†**3** Pay for by some sacrifice etc. Only in **16.**

4 Inquire the price of. **M19.**

📖 **1** *HomeFlair* Finished in tough melamine .. it is priced at £279. **price out** charge a prohibitive price to (a potential customer); ***price out of the market***, eliminate (oneself or another) from commercial competition through charging prohibitive prices, charge a prohibitive price for (goods etc.) or to (a potential customer). **price up** increase the price of. **b** GEO. ELIOT The girls' doings are .. priced low. **4** R. KIPLING Colonel Creighton, pricing Tibetan ghost-daggers at Lurgan's shop.

▪ **priceable** *adjective* (*US*) able to be priced, having a calculable value **M20.** **pricer** *noun* a person who prices goods etc. **LME.** **pricing** *noun* the action or process of establishing a price or prices; the overall level of prices so fixed; ***predatory pricing***: see PREDATORY *adjective*: **M19.**

priced /prʌɪst/ *adjective.* **LME.**
[from PRICE *noun, verb*: see -ED², -ED¹.]

†**1** Prized, highly valued. *Scot.* **LME–L15.**

2 Having the price set or stated; containing a statement of prices; having a price-tag or ticket attached. Freq. with specifying word, as ***high-priced, low-priced***, etc. **E16.**

priceless /ˈprʌɪslɪs/ *adjective.* **L16.**
[from PRICE *noun* + -LESS.]

1 Beyond price; invaluable, inestimable. **L16.**

2 Valueless, worthless. *rare.* **L18.**

3 Very amusing or absurd. *colloq.* **E20.**

📖 **1** E. M. FORSTER Italy was offering her the most priceless of all possessions—her own soul. *Great Hospitality* Illuminated .. vitrines for displaying priceless porcelain. **3** S. NAIPAUL Can you imagine how they must have .. rolled their eyes? Absolutely priceless. B. BAINBRIDGE 'You're priceless,' his wife told him, giving little whoops of resurrected joy.

▪ **pricelessly** *adverb* **M19.** **pricelessness** *noun* **L19.**

pricey /ˈprʌɪsi/ *adjective. colloq.* Also **pricy**. **M20.**
[from PRICE *noun* + -Y¹.]
Expensive.

📖 *Truck & Driver* Chain restaurants .. tend to be .. pricey. *Listener* The priciest areas of New York.

▪ **priciness** *noun* **L20.** **pricily** *adverb* **L20.**

prick /prɪk/ *noun & adjective.*
[Old English *prica, pricca, price* = Middle Low German *pricke* (Low German, Dutch *prik*), of unkn. origin. Cf. PRICKLE *noun*¹, PRITCH *noun*.]

▸**A** *noun.* **I** The result of pricking.

1 A small hole in a surface made by pricking or piercing; a puncture, a perforation. **OE.** ▸**b** A hare's footprint. **L16.** ▸**c** A wound in the sole of a horse's foot. **E17.**

2 A minute indentation or mark on a surface made with a pointed instrument, formerly esp. the point of a pen or pencil; a dot. Now *rare* or *obsolete*. **OE.** ▸†**b** Any of the marks dividing a clock dial. *rare* (Shakes.). Only in **L16.**

3 A punctuation or metrical mark; a diacritical mark. *obsolete* exc. *Hist.* **OE.** ▸†**b** A point or dot in musical notation. **L16–M18.**

▸**II** †**4** A minute part or amount (*of* something); a jot, a fraction. **OE–M17.** ▸**b** An instant, a moment. **ME–L16.**

▸**III 5** The action or an act of pricking; the fact of being pricked; *fig.* a feeling of mental pain or torment. **ME.**

📖 **5** M. WEST Bear the pricks and the poison with .. dignity.

▸**IV** A thing that pricks.

6 A projecting spike on a plant or animal; a thorn, a spine. Now *rare* or *obsolete*. **ME.**

7 A goad for oxen; a spur (*lit.* & *fig.*). Now *arch.* exc. in ***kick against the pricks*** s.v. KICK *verb*¹. **ME**

8 A slender tapering piece of wood or metal, esp. used as a fastening; a skewer, a pin. Now *Hist.* **LME.**

9 The point of a spear etc., a pointed weapon or implement. Now *rare*. **LME.**

†**10** An upright spike in ironwork etc.; a spire, a pinnacle. Chiefly *Scot.* **L15–E20.**

11 *coarse slang.* †**a** As a term of endearment: a young man, a lover. **M16–L17.** ▸**b** The penis. **L16.** ▸**c** As a term of abuse: an objectionable man. **E20.**

12 A small roll of tobacco. **M17.**

📖 **11c** M. GEE Harold is just a stupid prick.

▸**V** A point in space or time.

13 A stage in a process or scale, a degree; spec. *the* height or highest point of something, *the* apex. Long *arch.* **LME.**

†**14** A specified point in time; *esp.* the critical moment. **LME–L16.**

15 ARCHERY. (A mark in the centre of) a target. **LME.** ▸†**b** *fig.* An aim, an object. **LME–L16.**

†**16** *gen.* A point in space; a geometrical point. **M16–E17.**

Phrases: ***kick against the pricks***: see KICK *verb*¹. **prick and praise** success and its acknowledgement. **prick of conscience** (orig. a thing causing) compunction, remorse.

Comb.: **prick-hedge** a thorn hedge; **prick-mark** †(*a*) ARCHERY a mark aimed at, the bull's-eye; (*b*) a mark on a surface made by pricking; **prick-post** ARCHITECTURE = ***queen-post*** s.v. QUEEN *noun*; **prick punch**: used to impress a small round mark on metal etc.; **prick-seam** a type of stabbing-stitch used esp. in glove-making; **prick-shooting** ARCHERY (now *rare* or *obsolete*) the action of shooting at a prick or target; **prick-spur** *Hist.* a spur having a single point, as opp. to a rowel; **prick-stitch** *noun & verb* = ***stab-stitch*** s.v. STAB *noun*¹; **prick-sucker** *coarse slang* a fellator; **prick-teaser** *coarse slang* (*derog.*) a woman regarded as provocatively refusing sexual intercourse; **prickwood** either of two trees, the spindle tree, *Euonymus europaeus*, and dogwood, *Cornus sanguinea*, whose wood was used to make skewers.

▸**B** *adjective.* Of the ears: pricked up, erect. Cf. PRICK-EARED. *rare.* Chiefly *Scot.* **LME.**

▪ **pricky** *adjective* (now *dial.*) = PRICKLY 1a **M16.**

prick /prɪk/ *verb.*
[Old English *prician* = Middle & mod. Low German, Middle & mod. Dutch *prikken*, of unkn. origin. Cf. PRITCH *verb*.]

▸**I 1** *verb trans.* Pierce slightly, puncture, perforate, esp. with a fine or sharp point. **OE.** ▸†**b** Of an insect etc.: sting, bite. **ME–L17.** ▸**c** Pierce the foot of (a horse), causing lameness. **L16.**

2 *verb trans. fig.* Cause mental pain or torment to; vex. **OE.**

3 *verb intrans.* (Have the capacity to) make a slight puncture or perforation; be prickly or sharp. **OE.**

4 *verb intrans.* Thrust or stab *at* something as if to pierce it. **LME.** ▸†**b** ARCHERY. Shoot or aim *at* a target. **M16–E17.**

5 *verb intrans.* Of a hare: make a track in running. **LME.** ▸**b** *verb trans. & intrans.* Track (a hare) by its footprints. **LME.**

6 *verb intrans.* Of liquor: turn sour. **L16.**

7 *verb intrans.* = PRICKLE *verb* 3a. **M19.**

📖 **1** W. TREVOR The elderly maid pricked sausages. P. FARMER The princess pricked her finger on the spindle. *fig.*: ALDOUS HUXLEY That half century pricked .. many .. pleasant bubbles. **2** S. NAIPAUL He had been pricked by a desire to see Aubrey. R. THOMAS Jealousy still pricked her. **4** *fig.*: J. MARK A forgotten remark .. pricked at Viner.

▸**II 8 a** *verb trans.* Drive or goad (esp. a horse); *fig.* incite, provoke. *arch.* **ME.** ▸**b** *verb intrans.* Spur a horse on; ride fast. *arch.* **ME.**

▸**III 9** *verb trans. & intrans.* Dress (*up*) elaborately, esp. using pins as fastenings. *obsolete* exc. *dial.* **ME.**

†**10** *verb trans.* Impale *on* or *upon* a point. **LME–L17.**

†**11** *verb trans.* Fasten with a pin, skewer, etc. **LME–E19.**

†**12** *verb trans.* Pluck or remove, esp. with a sharp point. **L16–L17.**

13 Plant (seedlings etc.) in small holes made in the ground at regular intervals. Foll. by *in, off, out*. **E17.**

14 *verb trans.* Score the surface of (plaster) in preparation for an additional coating. Foll. by *up*. **L18.**

📖 **13** ELLIS PETERS To .. prick out early lettuces.

▸**IV 15** *verb trans.* Record (music) by means of pricks or marks. Formerly also, record music in (a book etc.) by this method. Now chiefly *Hist.* **LME.**

16 *verb trans.* Place a mark against (an item in a list); mark off, pick out; *esp.* select (a person) to be sheriff from a list of candidates. *arch.* **M16.**

17 *verb trans.* Mark out (a surface) with pricks or dots; mark out (a pattern, a ship's course, etc.) on a surface in pricks or dots. Foll. by *off, out*. **L16.**

▸**V** †**18** *verb trans.* Stick (a pointed instrument) *in, into*, or *on* something. **LME–M17.**

†**19** *verb trans.* Stud, mark, or dot, esp. *with* pointed objects. **M16–M19.**

▸**VI 20** *verb trans. & intrans.* Make or become erect, raise or rise. Usu. foll. by *up*. **L16.**

Phrases: ***prick in the garter, prick the garter***: see GARTER *noun* 4b. **prick one's ears, prick up one's ears, prick up the ears** (*a*) (of a dog etc.) make the ears erect when alert; (*b*) *fig.* (of a person) become suddenly attentive.

Comb.: **pricklouse** (now *Scot. & north., derog.*) a tailor; **prick-me-dainty** *noun & adjective* (now *arch. & Scot.*) (a person who is) excessively or affectedly precise, esp. about personal appearance or dress.

prick-eared /prɪkˈɪəd/ *adjective.* **LME.**
[from PRICK *noun & adjective* + EARED *adjective*¹.]

1 Of an animal, esp. a dog: having erect pointed ears. **LME.** ▸**b** *fig.* Of a person or animal: listening attentively, alert. **M16.**

2 Of a person: having ears made conspicuous by the hair being cut short and close to the head, in a style favoured by Puritan supporters of Parliament in the English Civil War; *derog.* puritanical, priggish. Cf. ***crop-eared*** (b) s.v. CROP *noun*. *arch.* **M17.**

▪ **prick-ear** *noun* (usu. in *pl.*) (*a*) an animal's, esp. a dog's, erect pointed ears; (*b*) *arch.* a person's ear made conspicuous by the hair being cut short and close to the head: **M17.**

pricked /prɪkt/ *adjective.* **LME.**
[from PRICK *verb, noun* + -ED¹, -ED².]

1 That has been pricked; provided with a prick or pricks; *spec.* (of pottery etc.) ornamented with designs traced in pricks or dots. **LME.**

†**2** Pointed, tapering; prickly. **LME–L16.**

3 Of an animal's, esp. a dog's, ears: erect and pointed, cocked *up*. **L16.**

4 Of liquor: turned or turning sour. **L17.**

5 Of a game-bird: wounded by shooting. **M20.**

1 †**pricked song** = PRICK-SONG.

pricker /ˈprɪkə/ *noun.* **ME.**
[from PRICK *verb* + -ER¹.]

1 A rider; *spec.* (*a*) a light horseman employed as a skirmisher or scout; (*b*) (more fully ***yeoman pricker***) a mounted attendant at a hunt. Now *arch.* or *Hist.* **ME.**

2 A person who drives or goads an animal etc.; *fig.* a person who incites or provokes another. **LME.**

3 A sharply pointed instrument for pricking or piercing; an awl, a prong. **LME.**

4 The basking shark, *Cetorhinus maximus*, so called from its habit of swimming with its dorsal fin projecting out of the water. Also, the spur-dog, *Squalus acanthias*. *obsolete* exc. *dial.* E18.

5 A thorn or spine on a plant. *dial. & US colloq.* L19.

Phrases: **get the pricker**, **have the pricker** *Austral. & NZ slang* become or be angry.

pricket /ˈprɪkɪt/ *noun.* LME.
[from PRICK *noun* + -ET¹: earlier (Middle English) in Anglo-Latin *prikettus*, *-um*.]
†**1** A candle, a taper. LME–M17.
2 A male deer, esp. a fallow deer, in its second year, having straight unbranched horns. LME. ▸†**b** *transf.* A boy. *rare*. L16–L18.
3 A spike for holding a candle. LME.
4 = PRICK *noun* 10. *Scot.* Now *rare* or *obsolete*. M16.

pricking /ˈprɪkɪŋ/ *noun.* OE.
[from PRICK *verb* + -ING¹.]
1 The action of PRICK *verb*; an instance of this. OE.
2 A series of pricks or marks used for ornamentation or as a pattern or guide; *spec.* (**a**) LACE-MAKING a pattern transferred by means of pricks on to a template, a template used in this; (**b**) PALAEOGRAPHY a series of holes on a leaf as a guide for ruling lines. E16.
1 pricking of one's thumbs, **pricking in one's thumbs** an intuitive feeling, a premonition, a foreboding (with allus. to Shakes. *Macb.*).
Comb.: **pricking-iron** SADDLERY an implement used to make regular points for stitching; **pricking-up** BASKET-MAKING the action of turning up (esp. willow) stakes after insertion in the base of a basket.

prickle /ˈprɪk(ə)l/ *noun*¹.
[Old English *pricel* corresp. to Middle Low German, Middle Dutch *prickel*, *prēkel* (Dutch *prikkel*), from Germanic base of PRICK *noun*: see -LE¹.]
1 An instrument used for pricking; *esp.* a spur, a goad. Now *Scot.* OE.
2 Orig., the sensation of being pricked or goaded with a sharp instrument. Later, a tingling feeling (*lit. & fig.*). OE.
3 A short slender sharp-pointed outgrowth (a modified trichome) on the bark or epidermis of a plant. Cf. SPINE 1, THORN *noun* 1. LME.
4 A hard-pointed spine or outgrowth of the epidermis of an animal (e.g. the hedgehog). M16.
5 *fig.* **a** Something that pricks the mind or feelings. Usu. in *pl.* Chiefly *poet.* M17. ▸**b** In *pl.* Defensive or esp. aggressive reactions or disposition. L20.

> 🕮 **2** J. WINTERSON I felt a prickle at the back of my neck. *Decanter* A nice prickle on the tongue. **3** W. O. JAMES A blackberry . . has hard prickles which can tear the flesh. **5** L. GILLEN 'You've got the McCourt prickles anyway,' he told her tactlessly.

Comb.: **prickle-back** †(**a**) the three-spined stickleback; (**b**) any of various elongated perciform fishes of the family Stichaeidae, found chiefly in the N. Pacific and having a spinous dorsal fin; **prickle-cell** ANATOMY a flattened cell forming a middle layer in the mammalian epidermis, having a surface with complex folds and numerous desmosomes; **prickle-layer** ANATOMY a middle layer in the epidermis, made up of prickle-cells; †**prickle-pear** = PRICKLY *pear*.
■ †**prickled** *adjective* = PRICKLY *adjective* 1a L16–E18. **pricklet** *noun* a small prickle, esp. (BOTANY) of a bramble L19.

prickle /ˈprɪk(ə)l/ *noun*². E17.
[Origin unkn.]
Hist. A type of open wicker basket formerly used esp. as a measure for fruit, nuts, etc.

prickle /ˈprɪk(ə)l/ *verb.* ME.
[Partly from PRICKLE *noun*¹, partly dim. of PRICK *verb*: see -LE³.]
1 *verb intrans.* Protrude sharply, point, rise or stand *up* like prickles. Chiefly *Scot.* ME.
2 *verb trans.* Prick or goad, esp. with a sharp instrument. Now *rare*. E16.
3 a *verb intrans.* Be affected with a pricking sensation; tingle, smart. M17. ▸**b** *verb trans.* Cause to prickle. M19.
4 *verb intrans.* React defensively or esp. aggressively to a situation etc.; bristle *with* anger etc. L20.

> 🕮 **3a** W. BRERETON His finger burned and prickled. T. MORRISON Jadine's neck prickled at the description. **b** G. VIDAL The heat prickled me unpleasantly. J. E. GORDON The horsehair stuffing prickled . . her legs. **4** S. COOPER The field was still, prickling with tension. *Los Angeles Times* Lawyers will prickle at the . . approach he takes.

■ **prickling** *noun* (**a**) the action of the verb; (**b**) a pricking or tingling sensation, esp. on the skin: M17.

prickly /ˈprɪkli/ *adjective.* L16.
[from PRICKLE *noun*¹ + -Y¹.]
1 a Having prickles, covered with prickles; causing a prickling sensation. L16. ▸**b** *fig.* (Of a topic, argument, etc.) full of contentious or irritating points; (of a person) quick to react angrily, touchy. M19.
2 Having a prickling sensation, tingling. M19.

> 🕮 **1a** G. LORD Prickly grasses and stunted brush tore at bare legs. JAYNE PHILLIPS I sat and sweated on the prickly car seats. **b** B. MASON He was . . prickly . . sensing insults and quickly avenging them. **2** J. BUCHAN The skin grows hot and prickly.

Special collocations: **prickly ash** any of several spiny N. American shrubs or trees whose bark is used medicinally; esp. *Zanthoxylum americanum* and *Z. clava-herculis*, of the rue family, and the angelica tree *Aralia spinosa* (family Araliaceae). ***prickly glasswort***: see GLASS *noun*. **prickly heat** an itchy rash of small raised red spots caused by inflammation of the sweat glands, most common in hot moist weather; also called ***heat rash***, ***miliaria***. ***prickly Moses***: see MOSES 3. **prickly pear** any of various usu. very spiny cacti constituting the genus *Opuntia*, with jointed stems freq. having flattened segments; the fleshy, freq. edible fruit of such a plant. **prickly poppy** = *MEXICAN poppy*. **prickly rat** = TUCO-TUCO. **prickly rhubarb** a S. American plant, *Gunnera manicata* (see GUNNERA), with prickly hairs on the petioles of its huge leaves. ***prickly saltwort***: see SALTWORT 1. **prickly withe** a climbing cactus of the W. Indies, *Hylocereus triangularis*.
■ **prickliness** *noun* M17.

prick-madam /ˈprɪkmadəm/ *noun. obsolete* exc. *Hist.* M16.
[Alt. of French *trique-madame* TRICK-MADAM. Cf. TRIP-MADAM.]
Any of several stonecrops, esp. *Sedum acre*.

prick-song /ˈprɪksɒŋ/ *noun.* E16.
[Alt. of ***pricked song*** s.v. PRICKED 1.]
EARLY MUSIC. **1** Music sung from written notes, as opp. to from memory or by ear. E16.
2 A descant or accompaniment to a simple melody or theme, esp. a written one. E16.
¶ *pricked song* recorded from LME.

pricy *adjective* var. of PRICEY.

pride /prʌɪd/ *noun*¹ & *verb*.
[Late Old English *pryde* var. of *prȳte*, *prȳtu*, from PROUD.]
▶ **A** *noun.* **I 1** The quality of having a high, esp. an excessively high, opinion of one's own worth or importance; inordinate self-esteem. Also (*rare*), an instance of this. LOE.
2 Arrogant or overbearing conduct, demeanour, etc., arrogance, haughtiness. ME.
3 A consciousness of what befits, is due to, or is worthy of oneself or one's position; self-respect. ME.
4 A person who or thing which causes a feeling of pride (freq. in ***pride and joy*** below); the foremost, the best, *of* a group, country, etc. ME.
5 Pleasure or satisfaction derived from some action, possession, etc., that does one credit. Chiefly in ***have pride in***, ***take pride in***, etc., below. L16.

> 🕮 **1** MILTON High conceits ingendring pride. J. IRVING The greatest sin was moral pride. **2** SHAKES. *Twel. N.* I love thee . . maugre all thy pride. **3** C. P. SNOW Having swallowed his pride. M. GEE Clothilde had her pride, she would rather die . . than complain. **4** *Daily Colonist* A three-legged chicken is the pride of a brood. R. E. KNOWLES You're the pride of Hamilton. **5** C. CARSWELL Great pride in her unmanageable flock.

▶ **II 6** Magnificence; pomp, display; *esp.* magnificent or ostentatious adornment. *poet.* ME. ▸†**b** Love of display or ostentation. LME–L17.
†**7 a** Honour, glory. *rare*. ME–L16. ▸**b** Exalted rank or status. LME–E18.
8 Vitality in an animal, *spec.* mettle or spirit in a horse. ME. ▸†**b** Sexual desire, esp. in a female animal. L15–E17.
9 The best state or condition; the prime *of*. Chiefly *literary*. LME.
10 A group of animals, esp. lions, forming a social unit. LME.

> 🕮 **8** T. H. WHITE In the pride of youth.

Phrases etc.: BARBADOS ***pride***. **have pride in**, **have a pride in** be proud of or conscientious about; maintain in good condition or appearance. **in his pride** (HERALDRY) (of a peacock) represented looking towards the spectator with expanded tail and drooping wings. ***in pride of grease***: see GREASE *noun* 1b. LONDON ***pride***. **pride and joy** a cherished person or thing. **pride-of-California** a wild pea of California, *Lathyrus splendens*, with very large pink or crimson flowers. **pride of China** = ***pride of India*** (a) below. **pride of India** either of two trees of southern Asia widely grown in the tropics for their showy flowers, (**a**) the azedarac, *Melia azedarach*; (**b**) the jarool, *Lagerstroemia speciosa*. **pride of life** *arch.* worldly pride or ostentation. ***pride of place***: see PLACE *noun*¹ 7a. **pride of the morning** a mist or shower at sunrise, supposedly indicating a fine day to come. **pride of the world** *arch.* = ***pride of life*** above. **take pride in**, **take a pride in** = ***have pride in*** above.
▶ **B** *verb.* †**1** *verb trans.* Adorn magnificently. ME–M17.
†**2** *verb intrans. & trans.* (with *it*). Possess, show, or develop pride. ME–E19.
3 *verb trans.* Cause to have or feel pride. Usu. in *pass.* Now *rare*. ME.
4 *verb refl.* & (now *rare*) *intrans.* Take pride in or credit to oneself for something. Foll. by *on*, *upon*, *that*, etc. ME.

> 🕮 **4** JAN MORRIS The women's colleges pride themselves on their . . proportion of first-class degrees. P. ACKROYD She prided herself upon being 'good in a crisis'.

■ **prideful** *adjective* (chiefly *Scot. & N. Amer.*) (**a**) proud, arrogant; (**b**) pleased or satisfied at some action, achievement, etc.: L15. **pridefully** *adverb* M17. **prideless** *adjective* LME. **pridy** *adjective* (now *dial.*) characterized by pride, proud LME.

pride /prʌɪd/ *noun*². *obsolete* exc. *dial.* L15.
[Perh. alt. of medieval Latin *lampreda*, *lamprida* LAMPREY.]
A freshwater lamprey, esp. the lampern, *Lampetra fluviatilis*.

Pride's Purge /prʌɪdz ˈpəːdʒ/ *noun phr.* E18.
[from Thomas *Pride* (see below) + -'S¹ + PURGE *noun*.]
Hist. The exclusion or arrest in 1648 of about 140 Members of Parliament thought likely to vote against the trial of Charles I, by soldiers under the command of Colonel Thomas Pride (d. 1658).

pridian /ˈprɪdɪən/ *adjective. rare.* M17.
[Latin *pridianus*, from *pridie* on the day before: see -AN, -IAN.]
Of or pertaining to the previous day.

pried *verb*¹, *verb*² *pa. t. & pple* of PRY *verb*¹, PRY *verb*².

prie-dieu /priːˈdjəː, *foreign* pridjø/ *noun.* Pl. **prie-dieux** (pronounced same), same. M18.
[French, lit. 'pray God'.]
A desk for prayer consisting of a kneeling surface and a narrow upright front surmounted by a ledge for books etc. Also, (more fully ***prie-dieu chair***) a chair with a low seat and a tall sloping back, used esp. as a prayer seat or stool and fashionable in the mid 19th cent.

prier /ˈprʌɪə/ *noun.* M16.
[from PRY *verb*¹ + -ER¹.]
A person who pries.

priest /priːst/ *noun & verb*.
[Old English *prēost* corresp. to Old High German *priast*, *prēst*, Old Norse *prestr*, from base of Old Frisian *prēstere*, Old Saxon, Old High German *prēster* (Middle & mod. Dutch, Middle High German, German *Priester*), ult. from ecclesiastical Latin PRESBYTER (whence Old French *prestre*: see PRESTER JOHN).]
▶ **A** *noun.* **I 1** CHRISTIAN CHURCH. **a** In the episcopal Churches, a member of the second order of the ministry, ranking above deacons and below bishops and having authority to perform certain rites and administer certain sacraments; *spec.* a celebrant of the Eucharist or other sacerdotal office. OE. ▸†**b** In the early Church, a presbyter. *rare*. LME–M16.
2 *gen.* A clergyman, a minister of religion. OE.
3 An official minister of a religion other than Christianity, *esp.* one performing public religious (*spec.* sacrificial) functions. OE. ▸†**b** = PRIESTESS. *rare*. L16–E17.
4 *fig.* Christ regarded as a mediator and offerer of sacrifice on behalf of humankind. ME. ▸**b** (A member of) the Christian Church regarded as the body of Christ, sharing the mediating and sacrificial character of Christ. LME.
5 A person whose function is likened to that of a priest; a devotee or minister *of* a practice or thing. L17.

> 🕮 **1a** J. H. BLUNT The chief sacerdotal function of the Christian priest is to offer up . . the Eucharistic Sacrifice. **3** TENNYSON The Priest in horror about his altar To Thor and Odin lifted a hand. **5** WORDSWORTH The Youth . . still is Nature's Priest.

▶ **II 6** ANGLING. A mallet etc. for killing caught fish. M19.
Phrases: *transf.* **be a person's priest** (long *rare* or *obsolete*) preside over or cause a person's death (with allus. to a priest's function in performing the last rites. ***poor priests***: see POOR *adjective*. SEM ***priest***. ***seminary priest***: see SEMINARY *noun*¹ 4b. SPOILED ***priest***.
Comb.: **priest-cap** (**a**) a cap worn by a priest; (**b**) FORTIFICATION an outwork with three salient and two re-entrant angles; **priestcraft** (**a**) the training, knowledge, and work of a priest; (**b**) *derog.* the self-interested policies, practice, and influence attributed to some priests; **priest-ridden** *adjective* (*derog.*) managed or controlled by a priest or priests; **priest's hole** *Hist.* a concealed room or other hiding place for a Roman Catholic priest in times of religious persecution; **priest's pintle** (now *dial.*) (**a**) cuckoo-pint, *Arum maculatum*; (**b**) the early purple orchid, *Orchis mascula*; **priest-shire** *Hist.* (*rare*) a district to which a priest ministered, a parish.
▶ **B** *verb.* †**1** *verb intrans. & trans.* (with *it*). Exercise the ministry or functions of a priest. LME–M17.
2 *verb trans.* Make (a person) a priest; ordain to the priesthood. E16.
3 *verb trans.* Bless or serve as a priest. *rare*. E17.

> 🕮 **2** E. SAINTSBURY Ordained deacon in the Church of England but . . never priested.

■ **priestdom** *noun* (*rare*) †(**a**) the office of priest, priesthood; (**b**) rule or government by priests: E16. **priesti'anity** *noun* (*derog.*, *rare*) a priestly system or doctrine E18. **priestless** *adjective* ME. **priestlike** *adjective & adverb* (**a**) *adjective* of, pertaining to, resembling, characteristic of, or befitting a priest; †(**b**) *adverb* (*rare*) in a priestly manner: LME. **priestling** *noun* (*derog.*) (**a**) a young, small, or insignificant priest; (**b**) a weak or servile follower of a priesthood: E17. **priestship** *noun* (now *rare*) the office of priest, the function of a priest E17.

priestess /ˈpriːstɪs/ *noun.* L17.
[from PRIEST *noun* + -ESS¹.]
A female priest of a religion other than Christianity.

priesthood /ˈpriːsthʊd/ *noun.* OE.
[from PRIEST *noun* + -HOOD.]
1 The office of priest, the function of a priest; the condition of being a priest. OE. ▸†**b** With possess. adjective (***your priesthood*** etc.): a mock title of respect given to a priest. *rare* (Shakes.). Only in L16.
2 A priestly system; priests collectively, *transf.* a group having specialized (freq. arcane) knowledge or power and (usu.) high social status. LME.

🕮 **1** *Tablet* A few students . . training for the priesthood. *Times* The ordained priest's special priesthood will seem . . just a superior case of the unordained's general priesthood. **2** J. GILMOUR Sacred books used by the priesthood and laity of Mongolia.

priestly /ˈpriːstli/ *adjective.* OE.
[from PRIEST *noun* + -LY[1].]
1 Of or pertaining to a priest or priests; sacerdotal. Formerly also, canonical. OE.
2 Having the character or aspect of a priest; like a priest; befitting or characteristic of a priest. LME.

🕮 **1** *Christadelphian* The sacrifice of praise was a priestly duty. **2** CARLYLE The priestliest man I . . under any ecclesiastical guise was privileged to look upon. A. F. LOEWENSTEIN Dave raised his arm in a forgiving, priestly gesture. B. VINE He had an ascetic, even priestly, look.

Phrases: **priestly code** the Levitical elements of the Pentateuch.
■ **priestliness** *noun* priestly quality or character L17.

priestly /ˈpriːstli/ *adverb. rare.* LME.
[from PRIEST *noun* + -LY[2].]
In the character of, or in a manner befitting, a priest.

prig /prɪg/ *noun*[1]. Now *dial.* E16.
[Origin unkn. Cf. PIG *noun*[2].]
A small brass or tin pan.

prig /prɪg/ *noun*[2] *& adjective.* M16.
[Origin unkn.]
▶ **A** *noun.* **1** Orig. (*rare*), a tinker. Later, a (petty) thief. *arch. slang.* M16.
2 An unpleasant or unsympathetic person. Long *obsolete* exc. as passing into sense 3 below. *slang.* L17.
3 An affectedly or self-consciously precise person; *spec.* †(*a*) *slang* a dandy, a fop; †(*b*) *slang* a precisian in religion, *esp.* a Nonconformist minister; (*c*) a self-righteously correct or moralistic person. L17.

🕮 **3** P. H. GIBBS He was no prig, but liked a laugh. *Guardian* Isabel is such a prig that she values her chastity more than her brother. C. FORBES Perhaps I'm a prig . . , but it'd be too much like taking a salary and not doing any work.

▶ **B** *attrib.* or as *adjective.* Priggish. *rare.* E18.
■ **priggery** *noun* the behaviour of a prig E19. **priggism** *noun* †(*a*) *rare* professional crime, esp. theft; (*b*) priggishness: M18.

prig /prɪg/ *verb.* Infl. **-gg-**. E16.
[Origin unkn.: rel. to prec.]
1 *verb intrans.* Negotiate or haggle over price, terms, etc. Chiefly *Scot. & north.* E16. ▸**b** *verb trans.* Decrease (a price) by haggling; negotiate better terms from (a person). Foll. by *down.* M19.
2 *verb trans.* Steal. *slang.* M16.
3 *verb intrans.* Entreat, beg, importune. Chiefly *Scot.* E18.
■ **priggable** *adjective* that may be stolen E19. **prigger** *noun* (*slang*) a thief M16. †**prigster** *noun* (*slang, rare*) (*a*) a prig; (*b*) a thief: L17–E19.

priggish /ˈprɪgɪʃ/ *adjective.* L17.
[from PRIG *noun*[2] *& adjective* + -ISH[1].]
Of the nature of or characteristic of a prig; self-righteously correct, moralistic.

🕮 R. WEST To these unhappy creatures Augustine addressed priggish rebukes. E. FEINSTEIN 'Alternative medicine doesn't interest me,' said Halina. She knew she sounded priggish.

■ **priggishly** *adverb* M19. **priggishness** *noun* M19.

prikaz /prjiˈkaz/ *noun.* Pl. **-y** /-i/. E18.
[Russian.]
In Russia: an office or department of (esp. central government) administration (now *Hist.*); an order, a command.

prill /prɪl/ *noun*[1]. Now *dial.* E17.
[Metath. alt. of PURL *noun*[2].]
A small stream of running water; a rill.

prill /prɪl/ *noun*[2]. L18.
[Origin unkn.]
1 In copper-mining, (a piece of) rich copper ore remaining after separation and removal of low-grade material. L18.
2 A granule or globule, orig. *spec.* of metal obtained by assaying a specimen of ore in the cupel. *US.* M19.
■ **prilled** *adjective* made into granules by solidifying molten droplets M20.

prim /prɪm/ *noun.* Now *dial.* L16.
[App. abbreviation of PRIMPRINT. Cf. PRIMP *noun*[1].]
Privet, *Ligustrum vulgare.*

prim /prɪm/ *adjective.* Compar. & superl. **-mm-**. E18.
[Origin uncertain: perh. ult. from Old French *prin*, fem. *prime* = Provençal *prim* excellent, fine, delicate, from Latin *primus* PRIME *adjective.*]
1 Of a person, manner, etc.: (affectedly) strict or precise; formal; demure, prudish. E18.
2 Of a thing: ordered, regular, formal. L18.

🕮 **1** E. GLASGOW The nurse sat prim and straight. *Guardian* One very prim and proper lady. **2** A. TROLLOPE A square prim garden, arranged in parallelograms.

prim /prɪm/ *verb.* Infl. **-mm-**. L17.
[Origin uncertain: rel. to prec. Cf. PRIMP *verb.*]
1 *verb intrans. & trans.* (with *it*). Assume a formal, precise, or demure attitude or appearance. L17.
2 *verb trans.* Form (the face, mouth, lips, etc.) into a prim expression; make prim in appearance, manner, etc. Freq. foll. by *up.* E18.

🕮 **2** K. O'HARA Aunt May primmed her seamed little mouth.

prima /ˈpriːmə/ *noun.* M18.
[from Italian, fem. of *primo* first.]
A prima donna, a prima ballerina.

prima ballerina /ˌpriːmə baləˈriːnə/ *noun phr.* L19.
[Italian, formed as prec. + BALLERINA.]
The principal female dancer in a ballet or ballet company; a ballerina of the highest accomplishment or rank.
prima ballerina assoluta /asəˈluːtə/ [= complete] a prima ballerina of outstanding excellence.

Primacord /ˈprʌɪməkɔːd/ *noun. N. Amer.* M20.
[from PRIMER *noun*[2] + CORD *noun*[1].]
MILITARY. (Proprietary name for) a type of detonating fuse consisting of a core of high explosive in a textile and plastic sheath.

primacy /ˈprʌɪməsi/ *noun.* LME.
[Old & mod. French *primatie* or medieval Latin *primatia* (for earlier *primatus*) from Latin *primat-*: see PRIMATE, -ACY.]
1 The state or position of being first in order, importance, or authority; the first or chief place; pre-eminence, precedence, superiority. LME. ▸**b** PSYCHOLOGY. The predominance of earlier impressions over subsequent or derived ones, esp. as it affects ease of recall. Esp. in ***primacy effect***. Cf. RECENCY 2. L19.
2 ECCLESIASTICAL. Leadership in spiritual matters; the office, rank, or authority of a primate; the chief office in an ecclesiastical province. Cf. PRIMATE *noun* 1. LME. ▸**b** The ecclesiastical province of a primate. *rare.* M16.

🕮 **1** G. STEINER Trotsky acknowledged Lenin's primacy. G. VIDAL His masculine primacy. *British Journal of Aesthetics* The primacy of questioning over answering. **2** H. A. L. FISHER Christ had given . . Peter the primacy over the Apostles. G. PRIESTLAND The Church had expected great things under Archbishop Runcie's primacy.

prima donna /ˌpriːmə ˈdɒnə/ *noun phr.* L18.
[Italian, formed as PRIMA + DONNA.]
1 The principal female singer in an opera or opera company; a female opera singer of the highest accomplishment or rank. L18.
2 *transf.* Orig., a person of high standing in a particular field of activity. Now chiefly, a temperamentally self-important person. M19.

🕮 **1 prima donna assoluta** /asəˈluːtə/ [= complete] a prima donna of outstanding excellence. **2** *attrib.*: D. CECIL The most trivial points . . were enough to produce a violent explosion of prima donna temperament.

■ **prima donna-ish** *adjective* M20.

primaeval *adjective* var. of PRIMEVAL.

prima facie /prʌɪmə ˈfeɪʃiː/ *adverbial & adjectival phr.* L15.
[Latin = at first sight, from fem. abl. of *primus* PRIME *adjective* and of *facies* FACE *noun.*]
▶ **A** *adverb.* At first sight; from a first impression. L15.

🕮 *Modern Law Review* The recommendation was prima facie unlawful.

▶ **B** *adjective.* Arising at first sight; based on a first impression. E19.

🕮 *Times Lit. Suppl.* Prima facie evidence of a Germanic . . source.

primage /ˈprʌɪmɪdʒ/ *noun.* L15.
[Anglo-Latin *primagium*, from Latin *primus* PRIME *adjective*: see -AGE. Cf. PRIME *noun*[1], *verb*[1].]
1 A small sum for the loading and care of cargo, payable by the owner or consignee of goods to the master of the ship carrying them. Also called ***hat-money***. L15.
2 A small duty on cargo paid to a local society of harbour-pilots. *obsolete* exc. *Hist.* E17.

prima inter pares *adjectival & noun phr.* see PRIMUS INTER PARES.

primal /ˈprʌɪm(ə)l/ *adjective, noun, & verb.* M16.
[medieval Latin *primalis*, from Latin *primus* PRIME *adjective*: see -AL[1].]
▶ **A** *adjective.* †**1** = PRIMATIAL. *rare.* Only in M16.
2 Belonging to the first age or earliest stage; original; primitive, primeval. E17. ▸**b** PSYCHOLOGY. Of, pertaining to, or designating the needs, fears, behaviour, etc., that are postulated (esp. in Freudian theory) to form the origins of emotional life. E20.
3 Of first rank, standing, or importance; chief; fundamental, essential. E19.

🕮 **2** E. F. BENSON Imitation . . the most primal instinct. **3** P. TOYNBEE The primal message of the . . NT.

Special collocations: **primal father** the dominant male of a primal horde. **primal horde** a postulated early form or unit of human social organization. **primal scene** PSYCHOLOGY: during which, in Freudian theory, a child becomes aware of his or her parents' sexual intercourse. **primal scream** PSYCHOLOGY: releasing emotion uncovered in primal therapy. **primal therapy** PSYCHOLOGY: in which a person attempts to recover his or her earliest (esp. emotional) experiences.
▶ **B** *ellipt.* as *noun.* PSYCHOLOGY. (An experience of) a primal emotion. L20.

🕮 *Listener* A true, deep primal, . . a reliving of . . childhood experience.

▶ **C** *verb.* Infl. **-ll-**, ***-l-**. PSYCHOLOGY.
1 *verb intrans.* Participate in primal therapy; release emotion, tension, etc., in a primal scream. L20.
2 *verb trans.* Subject to primal therapy. L20.
■ **priˈmality** *noun* (*a*) *rare* the quality or condition of being primal; an instance of this; (*b*) MATH. the property of being a prime number: L16. **primally** *adverb* L19.

prima materia /ˌprʌɪmə məˈtɪərɪə/ *noun phr.* E20.
[Latin, lit. 'first matter'.]
= ***first matter*** s.v. MATTER *noun.*

primaquine /ˈprʌɪməkwiːn, ˈpriːm-/ *noun.* M20.
[App. from Latin *prima* fem. of *primus* first + QUIN(OLIN)E.]
PHARMACOLOGY. A synthetic quinoline derivative, $C_{15}H_{21}N_3O$, used to treat malaria.

primary /ˈprʌɪm(ə)ri/ *adjective & noun.* LME.
[Latin *primarius* chief, from *primus* PRIME *adjective*: see -ARY[1].]
▶ **A** *adjective.* **I** *gen.* **1** Original, not derivative; not derived from, caused by, based on, or dependent on anything else. LME.
2 Of or pertaining to a first period of time or a first stage; primitive. L15.
3 Principal, chief, of major importance. M16.

🕮 **1** R. A. KNOX St. Thomas . . distinguished God as the primary cause. C. POTOK Primary source material, research papers based on direct experimental data. **2** D. ATTENBOROUGH The proportion of the secondary element to the primary one in rock. **3** G. SANTAYANA The primary use of conversation. *Nursing* Overall responsibility rests with the primary nurse.

▶ **II** *spec.* **4** GEOLOGY. Of the first or earliest formation; *spec.* (**P-**) = PALAEOZOIC *adjective* 1. E19.
5 BIOLOGY. Belonging to or directly derived from the first stage of development or growth, and often forming the foundation of the subsequent structure. Cf. PRIMITIVE *adjective* 8. M19.
6 CHEMISTRY. (Of an organic compound) having the characteristic functional group located on a saturated carbon atom which is itself bonded to not more than one other carbon atom; designating, involving, or characterized by such an atom. Also, (of an amide, amine, or ammonium compound) derived from ammonia by replacement of one hydrogen atom by an organic radical. M19.
7 ELECTRICITY. **a** (Of current) supplied directly from a source, not induced; of, pertaining to, or carrying the input electrical power in a transformer etc. M19. ▸**b** Of a cell or battery: generating electricity by an irreversible chemical reaction and therefore unable to store applied electrical energy. M19.
8 BIOLOGY. Designating sexual characteristics (esp. the ovaries and testes) that are essential to reproduction. L19.
9 GEOLOGY. Of a mineral or rock: that has crystallized from magma and undergone no alteration. L19.
10 ECOLOGY. Forming part of the lowest trophic level in a community, either as a producer or as a consumer that feeds on a producer; of or pertaining to producers. M20.
Special collocations: **primary cause** a cause which is the ultimate cause, a first cause. **primary colour** †(*a*) each of the seven colours of the rainbow; (*b*) any of the colours from a mixture of which all other colours can be produced, i.e. red, green, and violet, or for paints etc., red, blue, and yellow. ***primary* COSMIC *radiation***. ***primary* COSMIC *rays***. **primary education** the first stage of formal education, providing instruction at an elementary level in basic subjects for young children of school age. **primary election** a first or preliminary election, *spec.* in the US, a preliminary election to appoint delegates to a party conference or to select the candidates for a principal (esp. presidential) election. **primary evidence** LAW evidence, such as the original of a document, that by its nature does not suggest that better evidence is available. **primary feather** any of the large flight-feathers of a bird's wing, growing from the manus. **primary group** SOCIOLOGY a group held together by relationships formed by family and environmental associations, regarded as basic to social life and culture. **primary industry** industry (such as mining, fishing, agriculture, forestry, etc.) that provides raw materials for conversion into commodities and products for the consumer. **primary oocyte**: that gives rise in the first division of meiosis to a secondary oocyte and a polar body. ***primary planet***: see PLANET *noun*[1]. **primary poverty** effective poverty due to insufficiency of means rather than waste, inefficiency or some other drain on resources. **primary production** the production of raw materials for primary industry. **primary quality** PHILOSOPHY (*a*) *Hist.* each of the four original qualities of matter (hot, cold, wet, and dry) recognized by Aristotle, from which other

qualities were held to derive; (*b*) a property or quality (as size, motion, shape, number, etc.) belonging to physical matter independently of an observer. ***primary radar***: see RADAR 1. **primary school** a school providing primary education. **primary sector** *ECONOMICS* the sector of the economy concerned with or relating to primary industry. **primary structure** (*a*) *AERONAUTICS* the parts of an aircraft whose failure would seriously endanger safety; (*b*) *BIOCHEMISTRY* the sequence of amino acids forming a protein or polypeptide chain. **primary succession** *ECOLOGY* = PRISERE. ***primary SYPHILIS***. **primary teacher** a teacher in a primary school. **primary treatment** the first major (or only) treatment for sewage effluent, including sedimentation and removal of most suspended matter. **primary wave** *SEISMOLOGY* an earthquake P wave.

▸ **B** *ellipt.* as *noun*. **1** *ASTRONOMY*. A primary planet; the body orbited by a satellite etc. **E18.**

2 A primary person or thing, a person who or thing which is first in order, rank, or importance, or from which another thing may derive. Usu. in *pl.* **M18.** ▸**b** *GRAMMAR*. A word or group of words, usu. a noun or noun-phrase, of primary importance in a phrase or sentence. **E20.** ▸**c** A primary school. *colloq.* **E20.**

3 *ORNITHOLOGY*. A primary feather. Usu. in *pl.* **L18.**

4 A primary colour. **M19.**

5 *ELECTRICITY*. A primary circuit, coil, etc. **M19.**

6 A primary election. *US.* **M19.**

7 *PHYSICS & ASTRONOMY*. A primary ray or particle, *esp.* a primary cosmic ray. **E20.**

> 📖 **6** *Guardian* Yuppies . . supported Senator . . Hart in the primaries.

▪ **primarily** /ˈprʌɪm(ə)rɪli, prʌɪˈmɛr-/ *adverb* **E17.** **primariness** *noun* **L17.** **primarize** *verb trans.* (*rare*) **M19.**

primase /ˈprʌɪmeɪz/ *noun.* **L20.**
[from PRIM(ER *noun*[2] + -ASE.]
BIOCHEMISTRY. An enzyme which catalyses the synthesis of primers, esp. of primer DNA or RNA.

primate /ˈprʌɪmeɪt/ *noun.* **ME.**
[Old & mod. French *primat* from medieval Latin use as noun of Latin *primat-* of the first rank, from *primus* PRIME *adjective*: see -ATE[1].]

1 *ECCLESIASTICAL*. An archbishop; the chief or highest-ranking bishop of a province. Also, a patriarch or exarch of the Orthodox Church. **ME.**

2 *gen.* A person of the first rank or importance; a chief, a superior, a leader. Now *rare.* **LME.**

3 *ZOOLOGY*. A member of the mammalian order Primates, which includes man, apes, monkeys, and prosimians. **L19.**

1 Primate of All England the Archbishop of Canterbury. **Primate of All Ireland** a title of both the Catholic and Anglican Archbishops of Armagh. **Primate of England** the Archbishop of York.

▪ **primateship** *noun* the office or position of (a) primate **M17.**

primatial /prʌɪˈmeɪʃ(ə)l/ *adjective.* **E17.**
[French from medieval Latin *primatialis*, from *primatia*: see PRIMACY, -AL[1].]
Of, pertaining to, or having ecclesiastical primacy; of or pertaining to a primate.

primatic /prʌɪˈmatɪk/ *adjective.* Now *rare* or *obsolete.* **L17.**
[medieval Latin *primaticus*, from Latin *primat-*: see PRIMATE, -IC.]
Of or pertaining to ecclesiastical primacy, primatial.
▪ **primatical** *adjective* **L17.**

primatology /prʌɪməˈtɒlədʒi/ *noun.* **M20.**
[from PRIMATE + -OLOGY.]
The branch of zoology that deals with primates.
▪ **primatoˈlogical** *adjective* **M20.** **primatologist** *noun* **M20.**

primavera /priːməˈvɛrə/ *noun.* **L19.**
[Spanish (see next), in ref. to its early flowering.]
A tall Central American tree, *Cybistax donnell-smithii* (family Bignoniaceae); the wood of this tree, much used for furniture-making in the US.

primaveral /priːməˈvɛr(ə)l/ *adjective. rare.* **E19.**
[from Italian, Spanish, Portuguese, Provençal *primavera* spring-time (from use as fem. sing. of Latin *prima vera* pl. *primum ver* first or earliest spring) + -AL[1].]
Of, pertaining to, or suggesting the earliest spring-time.

prima vista /ˌprima ˈvista/ *adverbial phr.* **M19.**
[Italian, lit. 'first sight'.]
MUSIC. At first sight.

prime /prʌɪm/ *noun*[1]. **OE.**
[from Latin *prima* (sc. *hora*) first (hour), reinforced in Middle English by Old & mod. French *prime*, from Latin *primus* PRIME *adjective*. In later senses partly from the adjective.]

▸ **I 1** *ECCLESIASTICAL*. The second of the daytime canonical hours of prayer, appointed for the first hour of the day (about 6 a.m.); the office appointed for this hour. **OE.**

2 *gen.* The first hour of the day, the early morning. *literary.* **ME.**

3 The general meeting of a guild; the hour or time of this. Long *obsolete* exc. *Hist.* **LME.**

> 📖 **1** S. HEANEY Ringing the bell for prime. **2** SIR W. SCOTT Early and late, at evening and at prime.

▸ **II 4** = ***golden number*** s.v. GOLDEN *adjective. arch.* **ME.**

5 The beginning or first age of something; *spec.* †(*a*) the first appearance of the new moon; (*b*) *literary* the first season of the year; spring; (*c*) (now *rare*) the beginning or early period of adulthood; (*d*) *arch.* the first or primeval age of the world. **LME.**

6 The best, most flourishing, or most perfect, stage or state of a thing; *spec.* the stage or state of greatest perfection or vigour in human life. **M16.**

7 The principal, best, or chief among a group of people or things. Chiefly *poet.* **L16.** ▸**b** The best or most desirable part of a thing. **M17.**

8 a *MATH.* A prime number. **L16.** ▸**b** *LINGUISTICS*. A simple indivisible linguistic unit, *spec.* a phoneme. **M20.**

9 a A subdivision of any standard measure of dimension, which is itself subdivided in the same ratio, e.g. one-sixtieth of a degree, a minute (one-sixtieth of which is a *second*), etc. *obsolete* exc. *Hist.* **E17.** ▸†**b** The first decimal place; a tenth. **E17–E19.** ▸**c** *TYPOGRAPHY*. A symbol (′) written above and to the right of a letter etc. as a distinguishing mark, or after a figure to denote minutes or feet. **L19.**

10 *FENCING*. The first of eight recognized parrying positions, used to protect the upper inside of the body, with the sword-hand at head-height in pronation and the tip of the blade pointing downwards; a parry in this position. **E18.**

11 *MUSIC.* = ***prime tone*** s.v. PRIME *adjective.* Also, the interval of a unison; the original ordering of a tone-row. **L18.**

12 *CYCLING*. A special section in a cycle race, attracting a special prize. **M20.**

13 = ***prime rate*** s.v. PRIME *adjective.* **L20.**

> 📖 **5** POPE The fields are florid with unfading prime. TENNYSON Dragons of the prime. **6** K. M. E. MURRAY Years when most men would have passed their prime. H. CARPENTER Past his intellectual prime. ***in prime of grease***: see GREASE *noun* 1b. **7** POPE: Prime of the flock, and choicest of the stall.

▸† **III 14** *CARDS*. A hand in primero consisting of one card in each suit. Also, a card-game, *spec.* primero. **L16–E19.**

▪ **primed** *adjective* having a prime (the symbol ′) as a superscript **E20.**

†**prime** *noun*[2]. **M17.**
[from PRIME *verb*[2].]
1 (The pan for) the priming of a gun. **M17–E19.**
2 A first coat of paint; priming. **M17–M18.**

prime /prʌɪm/ *adjective & adverb.* **LME.**
[Old & mod. French from Latin PRIMUS *adjective*.]

▸ **A** *adjective.* **1** First in order of time or occurrence; early, young; primitive. **LME.** ▸**b** First in order of development; fundamental, basic; from which another thing may derive or proceed. **M17.**

2 Of the best or highest quality or value; excellent, wonderful. **LME.**

3 *MATH.* Of a number: having no integral factors except itself and unity. Also, (of two or more numbers in relation to each other) having no common integral factor except unity (foll. by *to*). **L16.**

4 Most important, principal, chief; (of a person) first in rank, authority, influence, etc. **E17.**

†**5** Sexually excited. *rare* (Shakes.). Only in **E17.**

> 📖 **1** W. LAUD If the speech be of the prime Christian Church. **b** J. S. BLACKIE According to the prime postulate . . of the philosophy of Socrates. **2** *Listener* Sirloin steaks, fillet mignon, prime ribs, . . and so on. *Observer* Sponsors' products receive prime exposure on screen. **3** ***twin prime***: see TWIN *adjective & noun*. **4** J. GALSWORTHY The prime motive of his existence. A. STORR The prime biological necessity of reproducing ourselves.

Special collocations & comb.: **prime cost** the direct cost of a commodity in terms of materials, labour, etc. **prime lens** a lens of fixed focal length (cf. ***zoom lens***). **prime meridian** the meridian from which longitude is reckoned (orig. variable, being that on which magnetic variation of compass was zero in a certain latitude; since 1794, fixed at Greenwich, England); longitude 0°. **prime rate** the lowest rate of interest at which money can be borrowed commercially. **prime-sign** *verb trans.* (*obsolete* exc. *Hist.*) [Old Norse *prim-signa* from ecclesiastical Latin *prima signatio* lit. 'the first signing'] mark (a person) with the sign of the cross before baptism; make (a person) a catechumen. **prime time** †(*a*) springtime; (*b*) *BROADCASTING* the time at which a radio or television audience is expected to be at its largest; a peak listening or viewing period. **prime tone** *MUSIC* the fundamental note or generator of a compound tone. **prime vertical** *ASTRONOMY* a great circle of the celestial sphere which passes through the east and west points of the horizon and through the zenith where it cuts the meridian at right angles.

▸ **B** *adverb.* In prime order; excellently. *colloq.* **M17.**

▪ **primely** *adverb* †(*a*) firstly, primarily, originally; (*b*) *colloq.* exceedingly well, excellently: **E17.** **primeness** *noun* **E17.**

prime /prʌɪm/ *verb*[1] *intrans.* **LME.**
[from PRIME *adjective* or *noun*[1].]
†**1** Of the moon: begin the first phase; become new. **LME–M17.**
2 Of a tide: come at progressively shorter intervals. Chiefly as ***priming*** *verbal noun.* **M19.**

prime /prʌɪm/ *verb*[2]. **E16.**
[Origin uncertain: perh. rel. to PRIMAGE.]

1 *verb trans.* Fill, charge, load. Now chiefly *dial.* **E16.**

2 *verb trans.* Supply with gunpowder for communicating fire to a charge; prepare (a gun) for firing; prepare (a charge) for detonation. **L16.**

3 *verb trans.* Cover (wood, canvas, metal, etc.) with a preparatory coat of paint etc., esp. to prevent the absorption of subsequent layers of paint or the development of rust. **E17.** ▸†**b** Put or wear cosmetics on (the face etc.). **E17–L18.**

4 *verb trans. transf. & fig.* Prepare or equip, esp. *with* information, *for* a particular purpose, or *to* perform a specific task. **L18.** ▸**b** Fill or ply with food or drink. **E19.**

5 *verb trans.* Pour or spray liquid into (a pump) to facilitate operation. **E19.** ▸**b** Inject fuel into (a cylinder, carburettor, or internal-combustion engine) to facilitate starting. **E20.**

6 *verb intrans. ENGINEERING*. Of an engine boiler: spray water with the steam into the cylinder. **M19.**

7 *verb trans. BIOLOGY & MEDICINE*. Treat (an animal or tissue) so as to induce a desired susceptibility or proclivity. **M20.**

> 📖 **2** J. G. FARRELL Fleury . . primed the vent. **3** C. HAYES They are primed with a suitable ground. **4** A. MASSIE Primed with musical terms. S. HILL Horses . . primed for the . . race. **b** E. WAUGH Primed with champagne. **5b** J. C. OATES He primed the engine.

Phrases: **prime the pump** *fig.* stimulate, promote, or support an implied action or process.

prime /prʌɪm/ *verb*[3] *trans.* Now *dial.* **M16.**
[Origin unkn.]
Prune or trim (a plant, esp. a tree); thin out (a wood, crop, etc.).

prime /prʌɪm/ *verb*[4] *intrans.* **L18.**
[Origin unkn.]
Of a fish: leap or rise out of the water.

prime minister /prʌɪm ˈmɪnɪstə/ *noun phr.* Also (as a title) **P- M-.** **M17.**
[from PRIME *adjective* + MINISTER *noun*.]

†**1** *gen.* A principal or chief minister, servant, or agent. Freq. in *pl.* **M17–E20.**

2 The first or principal minister or servant of a monarch or State (or formerly, of any person of rank or position); the first minister or leader of an elected government; *spec.* (*a*) the head of the executive branch of government of Great Britain and Northern Ireland; (*b*) *Austral. & Canad.* the chief minister of the federal government. **M17.**

▪ **prime-minister** *verb intrans. & trans.* act as prime minister of (a State etc.) **M18.** **prime-ministerial** /-mɪnɪˈstɪərɪəl/ *adjective* of or pertaining to a prime minister **L19.** **prime-ministership** *noun* = PRIME MINISTRY **M19.** **prime ministry** *noun* the office or position of (a) prime minister **M18.**

prime mover /prʌɪm ˈmuːvə/ *noun phr.* **L17.**
[from PRIME *adjective* + MOVER. Cf. PRIMUM MOBILE.]

1 A person who or thing which originates or promotes an action, event, etc.; an initiator. **L17.**

2 An initial source of activity, esp. movement; *spec.* a mechanism which translates energy into motion. **E19.**

3 *PHYSIOLOGY*. = AGONIST 3. **E20.**

4 A towing vehicle; *spec.* one for towing heavy artillery. **M20.**

> 📖 **1** C. MACKENZIE The prime mover in that boot business. D. MACDONALD Love . . is . . a prime mover.

primer /ˈprʌɪmə, *in senses 2d, 3* ˈprɪm-/ *noun*[1]. **LME.**
[Anglo-Norman from medieval Latin *primarius* (sc. *liber* book), *primarium* (sc. *manuale* manual), uses as nouns of masc. and neut. of Latin *primarius* PRIMARY *adjective*: see -ER[2].]

1 A prayer-book or devotional manual for the laity. Now *Hist.* **LME.**

2 An elementary textbook (orig. a small prayer-book) used in teaching children to read. **LME.** ▸**b** A small introductory book on any subject; *fig.* something introducing or providing initial instruction in a particular subject, practice, etc. **E17.** ▸**c** (A child in) an elementary class in a primary school. *NZ.* **E20.**

3 *Hist.* A size of type. Chiefly & now only in ***great primer***, ***long primer*** below. **L16.**

> 📖 **2** G. CRABBE Students gilded primers read. W. STYRON Using my Bible as a primer. **b** G. S. FRASER A primer of English poetry. P. GAY The *Outline of Psychoanalysis* looks like a primer. **3** ***great primer*** a former size of type (equal to about 18 points) between paragon and English. ***long primer*** a former size of type (equal to about 10 points) between small pica and bourgeois.

primer /ˈprʌɪmə/ *noun*[2]. **L15.**
[from PRIME *verb*[2] + -ER[1].]

1 a = ***priming-wire*** s.v. PRIMING *noun*[1]. Now *rare.* **L15.** ▸**b** A cap, cylinder, etc., containing a compound which responds to friction, electrical impulse, etc., and ignites the charge in a cartridge etc. **E19.**

2 A substance used as a preparatory coat on previously unpainted wood, metal, canvas, etc., esp. to prevent the absorption of subsequent layers of paint or the development of rust. L17.

3 A person who primes something. L19.

4 *AERONAUTICS.* A small pump in an aircraft for pumping fuel to prime the engine. Also called ***priming pump***. E20.

5 a *BIOCHEMISTRY.* A molecule that serves as a starting material for a polymerization. M20. ▸**b** *ZOOLOGY & PHYSIOLOGY.* A pheromone that acts initially on the endocrine system, and is thus more general in effect than a releaser. M20.

> 🕮 **1b** *Sporting Gun* Primers . . give . . ignition to the powder. **2** C. HAYES Oil-based primers . . to prime raw canvas. **5a** attrib.: *primer DNA*, *primer RNA*, etc.

primer /ˈprɪmə, ˈprʌɪmə/ *adjective.* LME.
[Anglo-Norman = Old French *primer* var. of Old & mod. French *premier* from Latin *primarius* PRIMARY *adjective*.]
1 First in order of time or occurrence; early; primitive. Long *obsolete* exc. in phrs. below. LME.
2 First in rank or importance; principal, chief. L15–M18.
1 primer fine (*LAW*, now *Hist.*) a sum, usu. about one-tenth of the annual income of the land in question, to be paid to the Crown by a plaintiff suing for the recovery of land by writ of covenant. **primer seisin** (*LAW*, now *Hist.*) a feudal right of the English Crown to receive, from the heir of a tenant of the Crown who died in possession of a knight's fee, the profits of the inherited estate for the first year.
¶ Recorded earlier in ME as a surname.

primero /prɪˈmɛːrəʊ/ *noun.* M16.
[Alt. of Spanish *primera* fem. of *primero* first, from Latin *primarius* PRIMARY.]
Hist. A gambling card-game, fashionable in the 16th and 17th cents., in which each player was dealt four cards.

primeur /primœːr/ *noun.* Pl. pronounced same. L19.
[French = newness, something quite new, formed as PRIME *adjective* + *-eur* -OR.]
A new or early thing; *spec.* (*a*) in *pl.*, fruit or vegetables grown to be available very early in the season; (*b*) new wine.

primeval /prʌɪˈmiːv(ə)l/ *adjective.* Also **-aeval**. M17.
[from Latin *primaevus*, from PRIMUS *adjective* + *aevum* age: see -AL¹.]
Of or pertaining to the first age of the world; ancient; primitive.

> 🕮 D. H. LAWRENCE He belongs to the primeval world. L. T. C. ROLT The primeval . . landscape of Western Cornwall. ***primeval soup***: see SOUP *noun*.

■ **primevally** *adverb* in the first age of the world; in a primeval manner: M19. **primevalness** *noun* E18. †**primevous** *adjective* primeval, primitive M17–L19.

primi *adjective & noun* see PRIMO.

primidone /ˈprɪmɪdəʊn/ *noun.* M20.
[from P(Y)RIMID(INE + -DI)ONE.]
PHARMACOLOGY. A pyrimidine derivative, $C_{12}H_{14}N_2O_2$, used as an anticonvulsant in the treatment of epilepsy.
¶ A proprietary name for this drug is MYSOLINE.

primigene /ˈprʌɪmɪdʒiːn/ *adjective. rare.* E17.
[Latin *primigenus*, *primigenius*: see next.]
= next.

primigenial /prɪmɪˈdʒiːnɪəl/ *adjective.* Now *rare.* Also **primo-** /prʌɪməʊ-/. E17.
[from Latin *primigenius* first of its kind (from *primi-* combining form of PRIMUS *adjective* + *genus* kind, or *gen-* stem of *gignere* beget) + -AL¹. Var. *primo-* app. arose by confusion with PRIMOGENITAL.]
First generated or produced; belonging to the earliest stage of existence of anything; original, primitive, primary.
■ †**primigenious** *adjective* E17–L18.

primigravida /priːmɪˈgravɪdə, prʌɪ-/ *noun.* Pl. **-dae** /-diː/, **-das**. L19.
[mod. Latin, fem. adjective, from PRIMUS *adjective* + *gravidus* pregnant, after PRIMIPARA.]
MEDICINE & ZOOLOGY. A female pregnant for the first time. Cf. MULTIGRAVIDA, SECUNDIGRAVIDA.
■ **primigravid** *adjective & noun* (*a*) *adjective* pregnant for the first time; (*b*) *noun* = PRIMIGRAVIDA: M20.

primine /ˈprʌɪmɪn/ *noun.* M19.
[French, from Latin PRIMUS *adjective* + -INE¹.]
BOTANY. One of the two integuments of an ovule where two are present, orig., the outer one, now, the inner one (which is formed first). Cf. SECUNDINE 3.

priming /ˈprʌɪmɪŋ/ *noun*¹. LME.
[from PRIME *verb*² + -ING¹.]
1 The action of PRIME *verb*²; *spec.* (*a*) the placing of gunpowder in the pan of a firearm; the preparation of a gun for firing; (*b*) the coating of wood, canvas, metal, etc. with primer; (*c*) *fig.* hasty preparation for examinations etc.; cramming. LME.
2 A thing which primes something; primer; *spec.* (*a*) gunpowder placed in the pan of a firearm to ignite a charge (also ***priming powder***); a train of powder connecting a fuse with a charge in blasting etc.; (*b*) a substance used to prime wood, canvas, metal, etc., before painting (= PRIMER *noun*² 2); a coat or layer of this. E17.
3 A preparation of sugar added to beer. L19.
Comb.: **priming-hole** a vent through which a charge of a firearm etc. is ignited; **priming-iron** = ***priming wire*** below; ***priming powder***: see sense 2 above; **priming pump** = PRIMER *noun*² 4; **priming-wire** a sharp pointed wire used to ascertain whether the priming-hole of a firearm, charge, etc., is unobstructed, and to pierce the cartridge.

priming /ˈprʌɪmɪŋ/ *noun*². M19.
[from PRIME *verb*¹ + -ING¹.]
A shortening of the interval between corresponding states of the tide, taking place from the neap to the spring tides (cf. ***lag of the tide*** s.v. LAG *noun*²). Chiefly in ***priming of the tides***.

priming /ˈprʌɪmɪŋ/ *noun*³. *US.* L19.
[from PRIME *verb*³ + -ING¹.]
The action or process of pruning or trimming a plant, esp. a tree, or of thinning out a wood, crop, etc.; an instance of this; the leaves, branches, plants, etc., removed in this process.

primipara /prʌɪˈmɪp(ə)rə/ *noun.* Pl. **-rae** /-riː/, **-ras**. M19.
[mod. Latin, fem. adjective, from *primus* PRIME *adjective* + *-parus* (from *parere* bring forth).]
MEDICINE & ZOOLOGY. A female giving birth for the first time; a female who has had one pregnancy that resulted in viable offspring. Cf. MULTIPARA.
■ **primiˈparity** *noun* the condition of being primiparous M19. **priˈmiparous** *adjective* giving birth for the first time M19.

primipilar /prʌɪmɪˈpʌɪlə/ *adjective.* E17.
[Latin *primipilaris*, formed as next: see -AR¹.]
ROMAN HISTORY. Of or belonging to a primipilus, that is a primipilus.

primipilus /ˈprʌɪmɪpʌɪləs/ *noun.* Pl. **-li** /-liː/. Also Anglicized as **-pile** /-pʌɪl/. LME.
[Latin, from PRIMUS *adjective* + *pilus* a body of pikemen (from *pilum* javelin).]
ROMAN HISTORY. The chief centurion of the first maniple of the third rank in a legion.

primitial /prʌɪˈmɪʃ(ə)l/ *adjective.* Now *rare* or *obsolete.* M17.
[medieval Latin *primitialis*, from *primitiae*, the first things of their kind, first-fruits, from Latin PRIMUS *adjective*: see -AL¹.]
1 Of, pertaining to, or of the nature of, first-fruits. M17.
2 First, primitive, original. M18.

primitive /ˈprɪmɪtɪv/ *adjective & noun.* LME.
[Old & mod. French *primitif*, *-ive* or Latin *primitivus* first or earliest of its kind, from *primitus* in the first place, from PRIMUS *adjective*: see -IVE.]
▶ **A** *adjective.* **I 1** Original, not derivative; not developed or derived from any other thing; from which another thing develops or is derived. LME.
2 Of or pertaining to the first age, period, or stage; early, ancient. LME.
3 Having a quality or style associated with an early or ancient period or stage; old-fashioned; simple, unsophisticated; undeveloped, crude. L17.

> 🕮 **1** G. GROTE The primitive ancestor of the Trojan line of kings is Dardanus. **2** R. H. TAWNEY The aim of religious leaders was to reconstruct . . the forgotten purity of primitive Christianity. **3** P. DICKINSON The heavy . . gear felt primitive and inefficient.

▶ **II** *spec.* **4** Of a word, base, or root, or of a language: radical; not derived; from which another word, base, or root, or language develops or is derived. M16.
5 *MATH.* **a** Of an algebraic or geometric expression: from which another is derived, or which is not itself derived from another. L17. ▸**b** Of a root of an integer *n*: such that the least power to which the root can be raised to yield unity modulo *n* is the totient of *n*. M19. ▸**c** Of a substitution group: having letters which cannot be partitioned into disjoint proper subsets in a way that is preserved by every element of the group. L19. ▸**d** Of an *n*th root of unity: having the *n*th power, but no lower power, equal to unity. E20.
6 *GEOLOGY.* Of a rock or formation: believed to belong to the earliest geological period. Cf. PRIMARY *adjective* 4. L18.
7 *CRYSTALLOGRAPHY.* Of, pertaining to, or designating a fundamental crystalline form from which all other forms may be derived by geometrical processes; of the form obtained by cleavage. E19.
8 *BIOLOGY.* **a** Of a part or structure: in the first or early stage of formation or growth; rudimentary, primordial. M19. ▸**b** Of, pertaining to, or designating the minute or ultimate elements of a structure. M19. ▸**c** Of an anatomical structure: from which secondary structures arise by branching, as in a blood-vessel. M19.
9 Pertaining to or designating pre-Renaissance western European art. Also, (of art etc.) simple or straightforward in style, eschewing subtlety or conventional technique; suggesting the artist's lack or rejection of formal training (cf. NAÏF *adjective* 1b, NAIVE *adjective* 1b). M19.
10 *ANTHROPOLOGY.* Belonging or pertaining to a culture characterized by isolation, low technology, and simple social and economic organization. E20.
11 Of behaviour, thought, emotion, etc.: originating in unconscious needs or desires, and unaffected by objective reasoning. E20.
12 *LOGIC.* (Of a concept) not defined in terms of any other concept; (of a proposition) not based on inference from any other proposition. E20.

> 🕮 **11** D. BAGLEY He could not control the primitive reaction of his body.

Special collocations: **primitive accumulation** *ECONOMICS* in Marxist theory, the posited original accumulation of capital by expropriation of small producers, from which capitalist production was able to start; ***primitive socialist accumulation***, the accumulation of capital by expropriation of small producers thought to be needed to start socialist production. **Primitive Baptist** *US* a member of an association of conservative Baptists, formed by secession from the Baptist Church. **primitive cell** *CRYSTALLOGRAPHY* the smallest unit cell of a lattice, having lattice points at each of its eight vertices only. **Primitive Church** the Christian Church in its earliest and (supposedly) purest era. **primitive circle** *MATH. & CRYSTALLOGRAPHY* the circle on which a projection is made. **primitive colour** = ***primary colour*** s.v. COLOUR *noun*. ***primitive Germanic***. **primitive groove** *EMBRYOLOGY* (*a*) = ***primitive streak*** below; (*b*) a groove or furrow which appears in the upper surface of the primitive streak, marking the beginning of the vertebral column. **primitive lattice** *CRYSTALLOGRAPHY* a lattice generated by the repeated translation of a primitive cell. **Primitive Methodist** *Hist.* a member or adherent of a society of Methodists founded in 1810 by Hugh Bourne by secession from the main body, reunited with the Methodist Church in 1932. **primitive plane** *MATH. & CRYSTALLOGRAPHY* the plane on which a projection is made. **primitive streak**, **primitive trace** *EMBRYOLOGY* the faint streak which is the earliest trace of the embryo in the fertilized ovum of a higher vertebrate.

▶ **B** *noun.* **I** †**1** An original ancestor or progenitor. Also (*rare*), a first-born child. LME–L17.
2 †**a** An early Christian; a member of the primitive Church. M16–L17. ▸**b** An original inhabitant, an aboriginal; a person of primitive (esp. prehistoric) times; *transf.* an uncivilized, uncultured person. L18.
3 = ***Primitive Methodist*** above. M19.
4 *ART.* **a** A pre-Renaissance painter; a modern painter who imitates pre-Renaissance style. Also, an artist employing a primitive or naive style. L19. ▸**b** A work of art, esp. a painting, by a primitive artist. L19.
▶ **II 5 a** A word, base, or root from which another develops or is derived; a root-word. Opp. ***derivative***. LME. ▸**b** = PHONETIC *noun* 1. E19.
6 *MATH.* An algebraic or geometric expression from which another is derived; a function which satisfies a differential equation; a curve of which another is the polar, reciprocal, etc. L19.
7 *LOGIC.* A primitive concept or proposition. M20.
8 *COMPUTING.* A simple operation or procedure, esp. one of a limited set from which complex operations or procedures may be constructed; *spec.* a simple geometric shape which may be generated in computer graphics by such an operation or procedure. Cf. sense A.5a above. M20.
■ **primitively** *adverb* L16. **primitiveness** *noun* M17. **primitivism** *noun* (*a*) primitive belief, thought, or behaviour; (*b*) preference for, or idealization or practice of, what is simple, unsophisticated, or primitive (in society, art, etc.): M19. **primitivist** *noun & adjective* (*a*) *noun* a person who advocates or practises primitivism; a person who uses obsolete methods or techniques; (*b*) *adjective* of or pertaining to primitivists, primitivism, or what is primitive: E20. **primitiˈvistic** *adjective* = PRIMITIVIST *adjective* M20. **primiˈtivity** *noun* primitiveness M18. **primitiviˈzation** *noun* the action or process of primitivizing M20. **primitivize** *verb trans. & intrans.* make primitive; simplify; return to an earlier stage: M20.

primly /ˈprɪmli/ *adverb.* M19.
[from PRIM *adjective* + -LY².]
In a prim or precise manner; with primness.

primness /ˈprɪmnɪs/ *noun.* E18.
[from PRIM *adjective* + -NESS.]
The quality of being prim; formal or affected preciseness.

primo /ˈpriːməʊ/ *adjective & noun.* Pl. (in senses A.1, B.) **-mi** /-mi/, (in sense B.) **-mos**. M18.
[Italian = first. Cf. PRIMA *noun*.]
▶ **A** *adjective.* **1** *MUSIC.* Of a musician, performer, role, etc.: principal, chief; of highest quality or importance. M18.
2 First-class, first-rate; of top quality. *slang* (chiefly *US*). L20.
1 primo buffo /ˈbʊfəʊ/, pl. **primi buffi** /-fi/, **primo buffos**, [BUFFO] the principal male comic singer or actor in an opera or opera company. **primo tenore** /tɛˈnɔːri/, pl. **primi tenori** /-ri/, [TENORE] the principal tenor in an opera or opera company; a tenor of the highest accomplishment or rank; ***primo tenore assoluto*** /asəˈluːtəʊ/ [= complete], a primo tenore of outstanding excellence. **primo uomo** /ʊˈəʊməʊ/, pl. **primi uomi** /-mi/, **primo uomos**, [= man] the principal male singer in an opera or opera company.
▶ **B** *noun. MUSIC.* (The pianist who plays) the upper part in a piano duet. L18.

primogenial *adjective* var. of PRIMIGENIAL.

primogenital /prʌɪmə(ʊ)ˈdʒɛnɪt(ə)l/ *adjective*. L17.
[Late Latin *primogenitalis*, use as noun of Latin *primogenitus*, from *primo* at first + *genitus* pa. pple of *gignere* beget, + -AL¹.]
Of or pertaining to a first-born or primogeniture.

primogenitary /prʌɪmə(ʊ)ˈdʒɛnɪt(ə)ri/ *adjective*. E19.
[from Latin *primogenitus* (see prec.) + -ARY¹.]
= PRIMOGENITAL.

primogenitive /prʌɪmə(ʊ)ˈdʒɛnɪtɪv/ *noun & adjective*. *rare*. E17.
[from Latin *primogenitus* (see PRIMOGENITAL) + -IVE.]
▸†**A** *noun*. = PRIMOGENITURE 2. *rare* (Shakes.). Only in E17.
▸ **B** *adjective*. = PRIMOGENITAL. M19.

primogenitor /prʌɪmə(ʊ)ˈdʒɛnɪtə/ *noun*. M17.
[Var. of PROGENITOR after *primogeniture*.]
An ancestor, *esp*. the earliest ancestor of a people, a forefather, a progenitor.

primogeniture /prʌɪmə(ʊ)ˈdʒɛnɪtʃə/ *noun*. E17.
[medieval Latin *primogenitura*, from Latin *primo* at first + *genitura* GENITURE.]
1 The fact or condition of being a first-born child. Freq. in ***right of primogeniture***. E17.
2 The right of the first-born child of a family, esp. a son, to succeed or to inherit property or title to the exclusion of other claimants; *spec*. the feudal rule by which the whole real estate of an intestate passes to the eldest son. M17.

> 📖 **2** E. A. FREEMAN Primogeniture . . supplanted the . . custom of equal partition of lands.

■ **primogenitureship** *noun* (now *rare*) = PRIMOGENITURE *noun* 2 E17.

primordia *noun* pl. of PRIMORDIUM.

primordial /prʌɪˈmɔːdɪəl/ *adjective & noun*. LME.
[Late Latin *primordialis* that is first of all, formed as next: see -AL¹.]
▸ **A** *adjective*. **1** Of, pertaining to, or existing at or from the beginning; first in time, original, primeval. Also, from which another thing develops or is derived; on which another thing depends; fundamental, radical. LME.
2 BIOLOGY. Designating (temporary) parts, structures or tissues in their earliest, simplest, or rudimentary stage. L18.
3 BOTANY. Of a cell, organ, etc.: in the earliest stage of development. Of a leaf etc.: that is formed first. L18.
†**4** GEOLOGY. = PRIMITIVE *adjective* 6. Also = CAMBRIAN *adjective* 2. L18–L19.

> 📖 **1** D. ATTENBOROUGH Compounds that had taken . . millions of years to accumulate in the primordial seas. *Times Lit. Suppl.* Primordial scenes . . associated with the Surrealists. P. GROSSKURTH Linking sex to some . . primordial fear. ***primordial soup***: see SOUP *noun* 1b.

▸ **B** *noun*. A primordial, original, or fundamental thing; a beginning, an origin; a first principle, an element. *rare*. E16.
■ **primordialism** *noun* primordial nature or condition L19. **primordiˈality** *noun* the quality of being primordial; a primordial thing: L19. **primordially** *adverb* (*a*) at or from the beginning; originally; (*b*) in relation to the beginning or starting-point; radically, fundamentally: M19. **primordian** *noun* (long *rare* or *obsolete*) a small pale early variety of plum (also more fully ***primordian plum***) E17.

primordium /prʌɪˈmɔːdɪəm/ *noun*. Pl. **-ia** /-ɪə/. L16.
[Latin, use as noun of neut. of *primordius* original, from PRIMUS *adjective* + *ordiri* begin: see -IUM.]
1 The very beginning, the earliest stage; an introduction; a source, an origin. L16.
2 BOTANY & EMBRYOLOGY. An organ, structure, etc., in its earliest stage of development; = ANLAGE. L19.

primp /prɪmp/ *noun*¹. Now *dial*. E17.
[App. abbreviation of PRIMPRINT. Cf. PRIM *noun*.]
Privet, *Ligustrum vulgare*.

primp /prɪmp/ *verb, adjective, & noun*². L16.
[Rel. to PRIM *verb*.]
▸ **A** *verb*. **1** *verb trans. & intrans*. Make (the hair, one's clothes, etc.) neat and tidy, make (oneself) smart, esp. in a fussy or affected manner. Also foll. by *up*. L16.
2 *verb intrans*. Behave or talk in a prim or affected manner. *Scot*. E19.
3 *verb intrans*. Walk affectedly or mincingly. M20.

> 📖 **1** T. SHARPE She looked . . in the mirror and primped her hair. *Village Voice* 'You putting me in . . ?' he asked, primping for the camera.

▸ **B** *adjective*. Orig., (of the mouth etc.) pursed, set. Later, (of a person or thing) prim, tidy; affected. L16.
▸ **C** *noun*. A person who behaves primly or affectedly. *Scot*. M19.
¶ As adjective not recorded between L16 and M19.

†**primprint** *noun*. M16–M18.
[Origin unkn. Cf. PRIM *noun*, PRIMP *noun*¹.]
Privet, *Ligustrum vulgare*.

primrose /ˈprɪmrəʊz/ *noun & adjective*. LME.
[Corresp. to Old French *primerose* medieval Latin *prima rosa* first or earliest rose.]
▸ **A** *noun*. **1** An early flowering primula, *Primula vulgaris*, of woods, banks, etc., with solitary pale yellowish flowers, which is cultivated in many varieties as a garden plant; a flower or flowering stem of this plant. Also (with specifying word), (a flower or flowering stem of) any of various plants related to or resembling this. LME.
†**2** *fig*. The finest or best; a fine example (*of*). LME–M17.
3 HERALDRY. A charge representing a primrose. M16.
4 The colour of the primrose, a pale greenish-yellow. L19.
1 ***bird's eye primrose***, ***Cape primrose***, ***evening primrose***, etc. **primrose peerless** an old-fashioned form of poetaz narcissus, *Narcissus* × *medioluteus*.
Comb.: **Primrose Day** the anniversary of the death of Disraeli (19 Apr. 1881); **Primrose League** a political association to promote and sustain conservative principles in Britain, formed in 1883 in memory of Benjamin Disraeli (1804–81), whose favourite flower was reputedly the primrose; **Primrose Leaguer** a member of the Primrose League; **primrose path**, **primrose way** the pursuit of pleasure, esp. with disastrous consequences (with allus. to Shakes. *Haml*.).
▸ **B** *adjective*. Of the colour of the primrose, of a pale greenish yellow. L18.
■ **primrosed** *adjective* (*poet*.) covered with or having many primroses M17. **primrosing** *noun* looking for or gathering primroses M19. **primrosy** *adjective* having many primroses; resembling a primrose, esp. in colour: E19.

primstaff /ˈprɪmstɑːf/ *noun*. Pl. **-staves** /-steɪvz/. M17.
[Swedish *primstaf* (= Norwegian, Danish *primstav*), from *prim* prime + *stafr* stave, letter.]
Hist. A Scandinavian (esp. Norwegian) runic calendar or almanack.

primula /ˈprɪmjʊlə/ *noun*. M18.
[mod. Latin (see below) from medieval Latin, fem. of Latin *primulus* (orig. in name *primula veris* applied to several flowers of early spring) dim. of PRIMUS *adjective*.]
Any of numerous usu. low perennial plants constituting the genus *Primula* (family Primulaceae), which have dimorphic (pin-eyed and thrum-eyed), chiefly umbellate, esp. yellow, pink, or purple, flowers on leafless stems, and include the primrose and cowslip and many ornamental garden flowers; a flower or flowering stem of such a plant.
■ **primuˈlaceous** *adjective* of or pertaining to the family Primulaceae, of which *Primula* is the type genus M19.

primuline /ˈprɪmjʊliːn/ *noun*. L19.
[from prec. + -INE⁵.]
CHEMISTRY. A synthetic yellow dyestuff which is a sulphonate of primuline base (see below).
Comb.: **primuline base** a yellow thiazole derivative, $C_{21}H_{15}N_3S_2$, obtained when *p*-toluidine is heated with sulphur; *loosely* any of the related compounds also formed by this process; **primuline red** a red dyestuff obtained from primuline base by diazotization followed by coupling with β-naphthol.

primum mobile /ˌpriːməm ˈməʊbɪli, ˌprʌɪməm ˈməʊbɪliː/ *noun phr*. Pl. ***primum mobiles***. L15.
[medieval Latin, lit. 'first moving thing', from Latin neut. of PRIMUS *adjective* + *mobilis* MOBILE *adjective*.]
1 In the medieval version of the Ptolemaic system, an outermost sphere supposed to revolve round the earth in twenty-four hours, carrying with it the inner spheres. Cf. MOBILE *noun*¹ 1, MOVABLE *noun* 1. L15.
2 *transf*. = PRIME MOVER 1, 2. E17.

primus /ˈprʌɪməs/ *noun*. Also **P-**. L16.
[from (the same root as) next.]
1 In an episcopal Church, *spec*. the Episcopal Church of Scotland, the bishop chosen by colleagues to preside over episcopal meetings but having no metropolitan authority. L16.
2 (Proprietary name for) a type of portable usu. paraffin-burning stove used for cooking etc. E20.

primus /ˈpriːməs, ˈprʌɪməs/ *adjective*. L16.
[Latin = first. Cf. PRIME *adjective*.]
1 First, original, principal. Orig. & chiefly in Latin phrs. L16.
2 = MAJOR *adjective* 1b. Cf. SECUNDUS, TERTIUS. L18.
1 primus motor (long *rare*) = PRIME MOVER 1, 2.
¶ See also PRIMUS INTER PARES.

primus inter pares /ˌpriːməs ɪntə ˈpɑːriːz, ˌprʌɪməs/ *adjectival & noun phr*. Fem. also ***prima inter pares*** /ˌpriːmə, ˌprʌɪmə/. E19.
[Latin.]
(The) first among equals, (the) senior in a group.

> 📖 *Sun (Baltimore)* The Army, in terms of the personnel strength of units . . , remains primus inter pares.

prince /prɪns/ *noun & verb*. ME.
[Old & mod. French from Latin *princeps*, *princip-* chief man, leading citizen, PRINCEPS, use as noun of adjective 'first, chief, sovereign', from PRIMUS *adjective* + *cip-* combining form of *capere* take.]
▸ **A** *noun*. Also (esp. in titles) **P-**.
▸ **I** *gen*. **1** A monarch; *esp*. a king. Formerly also, a person whose authority is paramount, a ruler, a chief; a leader, a commander. *arch*. ME.
2 A person who or thing which is pre-eminent in a specified class or sphere. Usu. foll. by *of*. ME. ▸**b** A powerful or influential person; *esp*. a magnate in a specified industry etc. Orig. & chiefly *US*. M19. ▸**c** An admirable or generous man. *colloq*. Chiefly *N. Amer*. E20.

> 📖 **1** GOLDSMITH These animals are often sent as presents to the princes of the East. **2** DELIA SMITH A prince of fish, in my opinion, a true delicacy when freshly caught. **b** *Times* The . . retailing prince who founded the stores. **c** J. D. SALINGER He's crazy about *you*. He thinks you're a goddam prince.

▸ **II** *spec*. **3** The ruler of a State actually, nominally, or originally, subject to a king or emperor. ME.
4 A male member of a royal family other than a reigning king; *esp*. a son or grandson of a monarch (also ***prince of the blood***). ME.
5 In France, Germany, and other (esp. Continental European) countries, a nobleman (usu. ranking next below a duke). Also, as a courtesy title, a duke, a marquess, an earl. E18.

> 📖 **3** J. MASSON He was the prince of a small kingdom that was now part of Pakistan. **4** *Daily Chronicle* Prince George of Denmark was elected to the throne of Greece.

Phrases & comb.: **Prince Albert** (*a*) *Hist*. a man's double-breasted frock-coat orig. made fashionable by Prince Albert Edward, later Edward VII; (*b*) *Austral. slang* in *pl*., rags worn inside boots by tramps, sailors, etc.; **prince-bishop** (*a*) a man holding the ranks of both bishop and prince (sense 3); (*b*) a man having the temporal possessions and authority of a bishopric, with princely rank. **Prince Charming** an idealized young hero or lover, esp. in fairy tales. **Prince Consort** the husband of a reigning female monarch who is himself a prince. **prince-elector** *Hist*. = ELECTOR 2. ***Prince of Darkness***: see DARKNESS 2. **Prince of Peace** Jesus Christ. ***prince of the blood***: see sense 5 above. **Prince of the Church**, **Prince of the Holy Roman Church** ROMAN CATHOLIC CHURCH (the title of) a Cardinal. **Prince of this world** = ***Prince of Darkness*** s.v. DARKNESS 2. **Prince of Wales** (the title of) the ruler of the Principality of Wales; *spec*. (*a*) *Hist*. (the title adopted by) any of several medieval Welsh rulers; (*b*) (the title, conferred by the monarch, of) the heir apparent to the British throne. **Prince of Wales' feathers** (*a*) the plume of three ostrich feathers, first adopted as a crest by the eldest son of Edward III (Edward Plantagenet, the Black Prince, 1330–76); (*b*) *NZ* the crape-fern, *Leptopteris superba*. **Prince of Wales check** (a fabric in) a large check pattern. **Prince Regent** a prince who acts as regent of a country during the minority, incapacity, or absence of the monarch; *spec*. (*Hist*.) George Prince of Wales (later George IV), Regent of Great Britain and Ireland (1811–20). **Prince Royal** the eldest son of a reigning monarch. ***Prince Rupert's drop***: see DROP *noun* 5. **prince's feather** either of two ornamental amaranths, *Amaranthus hybridus* var. *erythrostachys* and *A. cruentus*, bearing feathery spikes of small red or purple flowers. **Prince's metal** [Prince Rupert of the Rhine (1619–82), nephew of Charles I, Royalist general, and scientist] (*obsolete* exc. *Hist*.) an alloy, resembling brass, of about three parts copper and one zinc, used esp. for cheap jewellery. **prince's pine** the pipsissewa, *Chimaphila umbellata*. **prince-wood** (the dark-coloured, light-veined wood of) a W. Indian tree, *Cordia gerascanthus*, of the borage family; also called ***Spanish elm***. ***Red Prince***: see RED *adjective*. ***restraint of princes***: see RESTRAINT 3b.
▸ **B** *verb trans*. with *it*. Behave or conduct oneself as a prince. Now *rare* or *obsolete*. L16.
■ **princedom** *noun* (*a*) a State or country ruled by a prince; (*b*) the position or rank of a prince; *rare* (with possess. adjective, as ***your princedom*** etc.) a title of respect given to a prince; (*c*) = PRINCIPALITY 5: M16. **princehood** *noun* (now *rare*) the condition of being a prince LME. **princekin** *noun* (*joc. & derog*.) = PRINCELING (a) M19. **princelet** *noun* = PRINCELING (b) L17. **princelike** *adjective & adverb* (*a*) *adjective* like or resembling a prince; characteristic of or befitting a prince; princely; (*b*) *adverb* (now *rare* or *obsolete*) in a princely manner: M16. **princeling** *noun* (*a*) a young or small prince; (*b*) a petty prince, the ruler of a small principality: E17. **princeship** *noun* (*a*) the rank or position of a prince; *rare* the personality of a prince; with possess. adjective, as ***your princeship*** etc.) a title of respect given to a prince); (*b*) the period of a prince's rule: L16.

princely /ˈprɪnsli/ *adjective & adverb*. L15.
[from PRINCE *noun* + -LY¹.]
▸ **A** *adjective*. **1** Of or pertaining to a prince or princes; held or exercised by a prince; royal, kingly. L15.
2 Having the character, appearance, or qualities of a prince; dignified, noble. E16.
3 Having the rank of a prince. M16.
4 Befitting a prince; sumptuous, magnificent. Now freq. *iron*. M16.

> 📖 **1 princely State** *Hist*. in the Indian subcontinent, any of those States that were ruled by an Indian prince before the Indian Independence Act of 1947. **4** J. R. ACKERLEY A princely allowance of £2,000.

▸ **B** *adverb*. Now *rare*. In a princely manner; royally. M16.
■ **princeliness** *noun* L16.

princeps /ˈprɪnkɛps, -sɛps/ *noun*. Also (as a title) **P-**. Pl. **-cipes** /-sɪpiːz/. E17.
[Latin: see PRINCE.]
ROMAN HISTORY. Head of the State (a title adopted by Augustus Caesar, emphasizing the non-military nature of his rule), emperor. Cf. IMPERATOR 1.

princess /prɪnˈsɛs, ˈprɪnsɛs/ *noun & adjective*. LME.
[Old & mod. French *princesse*, formed as PRINCE *noun*: see -ESS¹.]
▸ **A** *noun*. Also (esp. in titles) **P-**.
▸ **I 1** A female sovereign; a queen. *arch*. LME.

2 A female member of a royal family other than a queen; *esp.* a daughter or granddaughter of a monarch (also ***princess of the blood***). Also, the wife of a prince. LME.

> 1 SWIFT So excellent a princess, as the present queen. 2 *Daily Telegraph* The Queen, Princess Margaret and other members of the royal family.

▶ **II 3** A woman who or thing which is pre-eminent in a specified class or sphere. Usu. foll. by *of*. LME. ▸**b** A woman, a girl. Chiefly as a form of address. *colloq.* M20.
4 A large (size of) roofing-slate. L19.

> 3 G. BOATE The Liffie is the princess of the Irish Rivers. *Ski* Twenties' skating princess, Sonja Henie. **b** A. LASKI Ah come on, princess, you're being morbid. N. MAILER Stephanie . . was one beautiful princess.

Phrases & comb.: **Princess Regent** (*a*) a princess who acts as regent of a country during the minority, incapacity, or absence of the monarch; (*b*) the wife of a Prince Regent. **Princess Royal** (the title of) the eldest daughter of a reigning monarch, *spec.* (the title, conferred by the monarch) of the eldest daughter of the British monarch. **Princess telephone** (US proprietary name for) a style of telephone incorporating the dial in the handset. ***sleeping princess***: see SLEEPING *ppl adjective*.
▶ **B** *adjective.* Designating (a garment in) a style of woman's clothing characterized by a close fitted bodice and flared skirt with seamless waist. M19.
■ **princessdom** *noun* (*rare*) (*a*) a State or country ruled by a princess; (*b*) the position or rank of a princess: L19. ˈ**princessly** *adjective* having the rank of princess; of, pertaining to, or befitting a princess: M18. ˈ**princess-ship** *noun* (*rare*) (*a*) the position or rank of a princess; (*b*) (with possess. adjective, as ***your princess-ship*** etc.) a title of respect given to a princess: M18.

princesse lointaine /prɛ̃sɛs lwɛ̃tɛn/ *noun phr.* Pl. **-s -s** (pronounced same). E20.
[French, lit. 'distant princess', title of a play by E. Rostand (1868–1918), based on a theme in troubadour poetry.]
An idealized unattainable woman.

Princetonian /prɪnˈstəʊnɪən/ *noun & adjective.* L19.
[from *Princeton* University + -IAN.]
▶ **A** *noun.* A student or graduate of Princeton University, New Jersey, USA. L19.
▶ **B** *adjective.* Of or pertaining to Princeton University. L19.

principal /ˈprɪnsɪp(ə)l/ *adjective, noun, & adverb.* ME.
[Old & mod. French from Latin *principalis* first, chief, original, from *princip-*: see PRINCE, -AL[1].]
▶ **A** *adjective.* **I 1** First or highest in rank; most important, foremost; greatest. Also *postpositive* in titles, denoting senior status. ME.
2 Belonging to the highest group or first rank; prominent, leading. Formerly freq. in superl. & (occas.) compar. ME.
†**3** Princely, royal. LME–L16.
4 Relatively or especially great or important; special, eminent. Now *rare* or *obsolete*. LME.
5 Of especially fine quality; excellent, choice. *obsolete* exc. *Scot.* LME.

> 1 J. THURBER His principal and most successful business venture. N. GORDIMER The principal source of information. ***Official Principal***: see OFFICIAL *noun* 2. ***sheriff principal***: see SHERIFF 1. **2** H. JAMES The master's principal productions. *Times* The survey . . is . . to contain five principal features.

▶ **II** *spec.* **6** Of money: constituting an original sum invested or lent; capital. ME.
†**7** *LAW.* (Of a person) being the actual perpetrator of or directly responsible for a crime. ME–M16.
8 Of a document: original, not a copy. *obsolete* exc. *Scot.* LME.
9 *GRAMMAR.* (Of a sentence or clause) superordinate to a dependent sentence or clause; (of a verb) superordinate to an auxiliary verb. L16.
10 Of a post, rafter, etc.: supporting the chief strain of a framework or building. L16.
Special collocations: **principal axis** *MATH.* (*a*) the axis of a conic which passes through the foci, the transverse axis (opp. ***conjugate axis***); (*b*) each of three chief lines of reference in a body or system. **principal boy** (an actress taking) the leading male role in a pantomime. **principal challenge** an objection, such as would lead to disqualification if proved, made against a jury or juror. **principal-component(s)** *attrib. adjective* (*STATISTICS*) designating a method of analysis which involves finding the linear combination of a set of variables that has maximum variance and removing its effect, repeating this successively. **principal focus** the focus of rays that impinge on a lens or spherical mirror parallel to its axis. **principal girl** (an actress taking) the leading female role in a pantomime. **principal meridian** *Canad.* a geographical meridian established by an authority as a meridian of reference for land surveying purposes; *spec.* the north-south line, 97° 27′ west, from which land in the prairies is surveyed. **principal parts** the parts of a (Latin or Greek) verb from which all the other parts can be deduced. **principal point** in perspective, the point where the principal ray meets the plane of delineation; in a lens or lens system, the point where the optic axis intersects the image plane. **principal quantum number** *PHYSICS* the quantum number symbolized by *n* (see N, N 6b). **principal ray** in perspective, the straight line from the point of sight perpendicular to the plane of delineation. **principal section** *CRYSTALLOGRAPHY* any section passing through the optic axis. **principal stress** *ENGINEERING* each of the three purely tensile or compressive stresses acting in mutually perpendicular directions into which any combination of stresses acting at a point can be resolved.
▶ **B** *noun.* **I 1** A person having the highest authority in an organization or institution; a chief, a head, a ruler; *esp.* the head of a school, college, or university. ME. ▸†**b** In *pl.* Leading or prominent people in a community etc.; notables. LME–E17. ▸**c** A fully qualified practitioner in some profession. LME. ▸**d** In Britain, a civil servant of the grade below Secretary. L19.
2 *LAW.* **a** A person directly responsible for a crime. ME. ▸**b** A person who is the chief actor in or perpetrator of some action; *spec.* a person for whom another acts as agent or deputy. LME. ▸**c** A person for whom another is surety for a debt etc. LME.
3 Either of the combatants in a duel. E18.
4 Any of the solo or leading performers in a play, opera, concert, etc. Also, the leading player in each section of an orchestra. L19.

> 1 B. HEAD He resigned as principal of Swaneng Hill School. **c** *British Medical Journal* A random sample of 1824 principals in general practice was selected. **2a** ***principal in the first degree***: see FIRST *adjective* etc. ***principal in the second degree***: see SECOND *adjective*. **4** P. G. WODEHOUSE Principals and chorus rehearsed together.

▶ **II 5** A principal or main part, thing, etc. Now *rare* or *obsolete* exc. in phr. below. ME.
6 The best chattel belonging to an estate, bequeathed, or inherited by custom. *obsolete* exc. *Hist.* LME.
7 A main rafter supporting purlins; a main girder. LME.
8 A capital sum of money as distinguished from interest or income. LME.
9 a An original document, drawing, painting, etc., as opp. to a copy. *obsolete* exc. *Scot.* L15. ▸†**b** An origin, a source. M16–E17.
†**10** An upright attachment used for holding candles on a hearse. M16–M19.
11 *FALCONRY.* Either of the two outermost primary feathers in each wing. Now *rare*. L16.
12 *MUSIC.* An organ-stop sounding an octave above the diapason. E17.
5 in principal *arch.* in the main, principally.
▶ **III 13** = PRINCIPLE. Now considered *erron.* M16.
■ **principalness** *noun* (*rare*) M16. **principalship** *noun* the function or office of a principal, *esp.* the headship of a school, college, or university L16.

principality /prɪnsɪˈpalɪti/ *noun.* ME.
[Old & mod. French *principalité* var. of Old French *principalté* (mod. *principauté*) from late Latin *principalitas*, from Latin *principalis*: see prec., -ITY.]
1 The position or rank of a prince; sovereignty; supreme authority; the rule or government of a prince. ME.
2 The territory held or governed by a prince. LME.
3 The quality, condition, or fact of being principal; pre-eminence. Now *rare*. LME. ▸†**b** A principal or chief part etc. *rare*. M16–E17.
4 In Christian theology, a member of the seventh order of the ninefold celestial hierarchy, ranking directly below the powers and above the archangels (usu. in *pl.*). Formerly called ***might***. E17.
5 = PRINCIPALSHIP. Now *rare*. E17.
2 the Principality Wales.

principally /ˈprɪnsɪp(ə)li/ *adverb.* ME.
[from PRINCIPAL *adjective* + -LY[2].]
1 In the chief place; above all; pre-eminently. ME. ▸†**b** In the first instance; originally. LME–M16.
†**2** In a special or marked degree; especially. LME–M17.
3 For the most part; in most cases. M19.

principate /ˈprɪnsɪpət/ *noun.* ME.
[Old & mod. French *principat* or Latin *principatus* first place, from *princip-*: see PRINCE, -ATE[1].]
1 = PRINCIPALITY 1. Now *rare*. ME. ▸**b** *ROMAN HISTORY.* (The period of) the rule of the *princeps* or emperor. M19.
†**2** = PRINCIPALITY 4. ME–M17.
†**3** A person having the chief position or pre-eminence; a chief, a prince. LME–M17.
4 = PRINCIPALITY 2. LME.

principe /ˈprintʃipe/ *noun.* Pl. **-pi** /-pi/. M20.
[Italian from Latin *princip-*: see PRINCE.]
In Italy, a prince.

principes *noun* pl. of PRINCEPS.

principessa /printʃiˈpessa/ *noun.* Pl. **-se** /-se/. E19.
[Italian (fem. of PRINCIPE) from medieval Latin *principissa*, from Latin *princip-* (see PRINCE) + *-issa* -ESS[1].]
In Italy, a princess.

principi *noun* pl. of PRINCIPE.

principium /prɪnˈkɪpɪəm, -ˈsɪp-/ *noun.* Pl. **-ia** /-ɪə/. L16.
[Latin, from *princip-*: see PRINCE.]
1 *ROMAN HISTORY.* In *pl.* The general's quarters in an army camp. L16.
2 = PRINCIPLE *noun* 1, 2, 3. E17.
2 *principium individuationis* /ɪndɪˌvɪdjʊɑːtɪˈəʊnɪs, ɪndʌɪˌvɪdjʊeɪt-/ [INDIVIDUATION] *PHILOSOPHY* the criterion for distinguishing one individual from another.

principle /ˈprɪnsɪp(ə)l/ *noun & verb.* LME.
[Anglo-Norman var. of Old & mod. French *principe* formed as prec.]
▶ **A** *noun.* **I** †**1** Beginning, commencement; the original state of something. LME–L17.
2 The origin or source of something. *obsolete* exc. as in sense 3 below. LME.
3 A fundamental cause or basis of something; a primary element, force, or law determining a particular result. LME.
4 An original or native tendency; a natural disposition, esp. as the source of some action. LME.

> 3 R. L. FOX Weaponry, the main principle of his military success. **4** W. JAMES The deepest principle of Human Nature.

▶ **II 5** A fundamental truth or proposition on which others depend; a general statement or tenet forming the basis of a system of belief etc.; a primary assumption forming the basis of a chain of reasoning. LME. ▸**b** *PHYSICS* etc. A general or inclusive theorem or law, having numerous special applications across a wide field. Cf. LAW *noun*[1] 15. E18.
6 a A general law or rule adopted or professed as a guide to action; a fundamental motive or reason for action. M16. ▸**b** A personal code of right action; rectitude, honourable character. Usu. in *pl.* M17.
7 A fundamental quality or attribute determining the nature of something; (an) essence. M17.
†**8** A motive force, esp. in a machine. M17–M19.
9 A natural law forming the basis of the construction or operation of a machine etc. E19.

> 5 D. CUSACK His two sacred principles . . the significance . . and the progressive deterioration of all literature. ***anthropic principle***, ***Archimedes' principle***, ***exclusion principle***, ***Mach's principle***, etc. **6a** A. S. DALE Destroy himself and his party for a principle. S. NAIPAUL Cherished principles of racial and economic equality. **b** M. DICKENS You've got no principles. R. P. JHABVALA Some principles, some sense of right and wrong. **7** *Times* The principle of active energetic evil. D. LODGE The combination of male and female principles.

▶ **III 10** In *pl.* The elementary aspects *of* a field of study; rudiments. *obsolete* exc. as passing into sense 5. M16.
11 A component part, a constituent, an element. *obsolete* exc. as below. E17. ▸**b** *CHEMISTRY* (now *Hist.*). Each of five simple substances or elements of which all bodies were once believed to be composed, usu. comprising spirit, oil, salt, water, and earth. M17. ▸**c** *CHEMISTRY.* A constituent of a substance obtained by simple analysis, esp. (as ***active principle***, ***bitter principle***, etc.) one giving rise to a characteristic property. *arch.* M17.

> 11c H. DAVY The narcotic principle is found . . in opium.

Phrases: ***concupiscible principle***: see CONCUPISCIBLE *adjective* 1. **first principle** a primary proposition upon which further reasoning is based (freq. in *pl.*). **in principle** theoretically. **on general principles** in general, for no specified reason. **on principle** (*a*) on the basis of a moral code or principle; (*b*) according to a fixed rule. ***principle of Archimedes***: see ARCHIMEDES 2. ***principle of bivalence***: see BIVALENCE *noun* 2. **principle of duality** *MATH.* the principle that all theorems relating to points and lines have reciprocal theorems by substituting line for point and point for line. ***principle of equivalence***: see EQUIVALENCE 1. ***principle of excluded middle***, ***principle of excluded third***: see EXCLUDE *verb* 5. ***principle of*** INDETERMINACY. ***principle of*** LEAST ***action***. ***principle of*** LEAST ***constraint***. ***principle of least squares***: see SQUARE *noun*.
▶†**B** *verb trans.* **1** Ground (a person) in the principles or elements of a subject; instruct, train. E17–M18.
2 Give rise to; originate. M–L17.

principled /ˈprɪnsɪp(ə)ld/ *adjective.* M17.
[from prec. + -ED[2].]
1 (Of a person) instructed in, holding, or motivated by particular principles. M17.
2 Having praiseworthy principles of behaviour etc.; morally upright, honourable. L17.
3 Of an action, belief, etc.: founded on or involving a principle. L18.
4 Based on or guided by technical principles or rules; not arbitrary. M20.

> 2 *Guardian* The principled man is . . worthy of . . respect. **3** *Times* They had 'no principled objections' to the . . demands. **4** *American Speech* Expansion of . . grammar . . must include a principled base.

■ **principledness** *noun* the quality of being principled in behaviour etc., uprightness M20.

princock /ˈprɪŋkɒk/ *noun.* Long *arch.* & *dial.* Also (earlier) †**-cocks**, †**-cox**. M16.
[Origin unkn.]
A pert or conceited boy or youth; a coxcomb.

pringle /ˈprɪŋg(ə)l/ *verb intrans.* L19.
[Alt. of PRICKLE *verb*, app. after *tingle*.]
Cause or experience a tingling sensation; prickle.

prink /prɪŋk/ *verb*[1] *trans. & intrans.* Now *dial.* ME.
[Origin unkn.]
Wink.

prink /prɪŋk/ *verb*[2]. L16.
[Rel. to PRANK *verb*[1].]
†**1** *verb trans. & intrans.* Show off ostentatiously. Usu. foll. by *up*. L16–E17.
2 *verb trans.* Make spruce or smart; deck *out*; dress *up*. *colloq.* L16. ▸**b** *verb intrans.* Dress up; make oneself look smart. *colloq.* L17.
3 *verb trans. & intrans.* Of a bird: preen (the feathers). L16.
4 *verb intrans.* Be pert or forward. *dial.* E19.

📖 **2** A. HOLLINGHURST A wonderful black pidgin, prinked out with more exotic turns of speech.

■ **prinky** *adjective* (*colloq.*) prinked or dressed up, smart E19.

prinkum-prankum /prɪŋkəmˈpraŋkəm/ *noun.* Long *arch. rare.* L16.
[In sense 1 rel. to PRANK *noun*; in sense 3 rel. to PRANK *verb*[1].]
†**1** A prank, a trick. Only in L16.
†**2** = ***cushion-dance*** s.v. CUSHION *noun.* M–L17.
3 Fine clothing, adornment, etc. E18.

print /prɪnt/ *noun.* ME.
[Old French *priente, preinte*, use as noun of fem. pa. pple of *preindre* press from Latin *premere*. Cf. PRUNT.]
▶**I 1** An impressed mark or image, an impression; *esp.* (*a*) the impress made by a stamp or seal; (*b*) a design impressed on a coin; (*c*) *fig.* (now *rare*) an image, idea, or character impressed on the mind or soul. ME.
2 An indentation or mark formed and left on a surface by the pressure of a body; *spec.* (*a*) a footprint; (*b*) a fingerprint. ME. ▸†**b** A vestige, a trace. M16–E18.
3 An instrument or device for producing a mark by pressing; a stamp, a die; a mould. LME. ▸**b** FOUNDING. A support for the core of a casting. M19.
4 A printed (usu. cotton) fabric or piece of cloth; a pattern printed on fabric or cloth. Now also, a garment or other article made of printed fabric. M18.
5 A pat of butter moulded to a shape. M18.

📖 **2** E. WAUGH The prints of ass and pig . . mingled indifferently with those of barefoot children. J. GARDNER The prints of his hands left . . in the dust. L. DUNCAN Wipe your prints off the steering wheel. **4** V. S. REID Bright prints to make dresses. G. NAYLOR The curtains . . had . . fern prints. P. BAILEY Nurse Barrow took the orange print from its hanger.

▶**II 6 a** The state of being printed; printed form. L15. ▸**b** Language in printed form; printed lettering or writing; typography, esp. with ref. to size, form, or style. E17.
†**7** A printing-press; the process of printing. E16–L17.
8 An impression of a work printed at one time; an edition. M16.
9 a A printed publication; *esp.* a newspaper. Now chiefly *US.* L16. ▸**b** A printed copy of a document. E19.
10 A picture or design printed from a block or plate; an impression from an engraved or otherwise prepared plate. M17.
11 PHOTOGRAPHY. A picture produced from a negative; *spec.* (*a*) a photograph produced on paper (as opp. to a transparency); (*b*) a positive copy of a motion picture on a transparent medium. M19.
12 An accidental signal on magnetic tape produced by print-through. M20.

📖 **6a** E. V. LUCAS I have no recollection that the article ever reached print. H. G. WELLS This success whetted my appetite for print. **b** M. MAHY Tiny print under the picture. *Library* No owner of a . . library expected to see only print coming on to his shelves. **8** *Listener* A new novel . . has a print of 20,000. **9a** *Daily Express* Published in the popular prints. **b** *Daily Mail* Prints of the Memorandum . . can be inspected. **10** HOR. WALPOLE There is a print of him . . engraved by Vosterman. **11** *Amateur Photographer* Keeping the dust away from prints is a major problem.

Phrases: **appear in print** have one's work published. ***fine print***: see FINE *adjective*. **in print** (*a*) in printed form; (*b*) (of a book etc.) available from the publisher; (*c*) (*obsolete* exc. *dial.*) in a precise manner, with exactness. **in the print** in the printing trade. ***large print***: see LARGE *adjective* etc. ***married print***: see MARRIED *adjective*. ***original print***: see ORIGINAL *adjective*. ***silver print***: see SILVER *noun* & *adjective*. ***small print***: see SMALL *adjective*. See also OUT OF PRINT.
Comb.: **print chain** COMPUTING an endless chain of printing types in some printers; **print hand** handwriting imitating or resembling print; **printhead** COMPUTING the part of a printer in which characters are held or assembled immediately before printing, and from which their images are transferred to the printing medium; **print journalism** reporting or writing for newspapers (as opp. to television); **print journalist**: reporting or writing for newspapers (as opp. to television); **print media** newspapers (as opp. to broadcasting); **print order** an order for a certain number (of copies of a book, paper, etc.) to be printed; **print-room** a room, esp. in a museum, containing a collection of prints; **print run** the number of copies of a book etc. printed at one time; **print-script** a style of handwriting that imitates typography; **print-seller** a person who sells prints or engravings; **print-shop** (*a*) a print-seller's shop; (*b*) *N. Amer.* a printing-office; **print spooler** COMPUTING a program which controls print spooling; **print spooling** COMPUTING a technique of storing and automatically outputting files to a printer; **print train** COMPUTING = ***print chain*** above; **print union** a trade union for printers; **print wheel** a disc with printing types round the rim that are brought into position by rotating the disc; **printworks** a factory where fabrics are printed.

print /prɪnt/ *adjective.* L15.
[Partly from the noun, partly as if pa. pple of the verb.]
1 Orig., printed. Now chiefly *spec.*, made from a printed fabric or pattern. L15.
2 Of moonlight etc.: clear, bright. *dial.* M18.

📖 **1** A. MILLER She wore a flowered blue cotton print dress.

print /prɪnt/ *verb.* LME.
[from the noun.]
▶**I 1** *verb trans.* **a** Impress or stamp (a soft surface) with a seal, die, etc.; mark (a surface) with any impressed or coloured figure or pattern; brand. LME. ▸†**b** Coin (money). LME–M16.
2 *verb trans.* **a** Impress or stamp (a figure, mark, etc.) on a soft substance; set or trace (a figure, mark, etc.) on a surface by carving, writing, etc. LME. ▸**b** *fig.* Impress *on* or fix *in* the mind, memory, etc. LME.
3 a *verb trans.* Press (something hard) into a substance or on a surface, so as to leave an imprint. Freq. foll. by *in*. LME. ▸**b** *verb intrans.* SHOOTING. (Of a bullet) strike the target; (of a gun) cause bullets to strike the target (too high, too low, etc.). Now *rare.* M20.
†**4** *verb trans.* Express in writing; inscribe. LME–L16.

📖 **3a** SHAKES. *Hen. V* Horses . . Printing their proud hoofs i' th' receiving earth.

▶**II 5** *verb trans.* Produce or reproduce (text, a picture, etc.) by mechanically transferring characters or designs to paper, vellum, etc., esp. from inked types, blocks, or plates. E16.
6 *verb trans.* **a** Of an author or editor: cause (text etc.) to be printed; send (text etc.) to press. M16. ▸**b** Express or publish (ideas etc.) in print. M17.
7 *verb intrans.* **a** Work as a printer; produce or reproduce text etc. in print. L17. ▸**b** Of text etc.: appear in print; be printed. L18. ▸**c** Of a manuscript etc.: run *up* or amount in type (to a certain quantity). *rare.* M19. ▸**d** Of type, a block, a plate: produce an impression on paper etc. L19.
8 *verb trans.* Use (a forme of type, a plate, block, etc.) in printing. E18.
9 *verb trans. & intrans.* Write (letters) separately in the style of printed characters. M19.
10 *verb trans. & intrans.* Transfer (a signal on magnetic tape) as a result of print-through. M20.

📖 **5** *London Gazette* His Majesty's Picture, printed in natural Colours. *Athenaeum* Titles of books are printed in italics. **6a** BUNYAN Some said, John, print it J. W. CLARK To print the Latin text alone. **b** *New Scientist* A campaign . . which would force tampon manufacturers to print a warning on the box. **7a** S. JOHNSON Maps were printing in one of the rooms. M. RUSSELL The first editions were still printing. **9** E. KRAFT The Graffitist leaves messages . . printed in small, precise capital letters.

▶**III 11** *verb trans.* Stamp or mark (a textile fabric) with a coloured pattern or decorative design. L16.
12 *verb trans.* Transfer (a decorative design) from paper etc. to the unglazed or glazed surface of ceramic ware. L18.
13 PHOTOGRAPHY. **a** *verb trans.* Produce (a positive picture) by the transmission of light via a negative on to the sensitized surface; produce (a copy) of a motion picture film, or (a photograph) from a positive transparency. Also foll. by *off, out.* M19. ▸**b** *verb intrans.* Of a negative: produce a photograph (*well, badly*, etc.). M19. ▸**c** *verb trans.* Produce a print from (a negative or transparency). E20.
14 *verb trans.* Test (an object) for fingerprints; record the fingerprints of (a person). M20.
15 *verb trans.* Make (a printed circuit or component). M20.

📖 **14** D. SHANNON The lab men had printed the patent leather tote bag.

With adverbs in specialized senses: **print down** transfer a photographic image from (a negative) to a printing plate. **print in** transfer (an image on a negative) to another negative that has already been exposed once. **print out** (*a*) COMPUTING produce in or as a printout; (*b*) PHOTOGRAPHY produce an image (or, of an image, appear) without chemical development.
Comb.: **printfield** (*obsolete* exc. *Scot.*) a cotton-printing factory; **print-out** *adjective* (PHOTOGRAPHY) of, pertaining to, or resulting from printing out; **printout** COMPUTING (an instance of) output in printed form; **print-through** (*a*) the accidental transfer of recorded signals to adjacent layers in a reel of magnetic tape; (*b*) (the degree of) visibility of print through the reverse side of a printed sheet.
■ **printaˈbility** *noun* (*a*) ability of paper etc. to take print; (*b*) suitability or fitness of language, a statement, etc., to be printed: M20. **printable** *adjective* able or fit to be printed M19.

printanier /prɛ̃tanje/ *adjective & noun.* Fem. **-ière** /-jɛːr/. M19.
[French, lit. 'of springtime', from *printemps* spring, from Latin PRIMUS *adjective* + *tempus* time.]
(A soup) made from or garnished with spring vegetables.

printed /ˈprɪntɪd/ *adjective.* LME.
[from PRINT *verb* + -ED[1].]
1 That has been printed; *esp.* produced, reproduced, or decorated by a process of printing. LME.
2 Produced on magnetic tape by print-through. M20.

📖 **1** *Guardian* A . . printed cotton satin. *Times Educ. Suppl.* An enlarged printed version of *Peter Rabbit*. **printed circuit** ELECTRICITY a circuit with thin strips of conductor on a flat insulating sheet, usu. made by a process that resembles printing. **printed circuitry** ELECTRICITY printed circuits collectively; the components of a printed circuit.

printer /ˈprɪntə/ *noun.* LME.
[from PRINT *verb* + -ER[1].]
1 A person who prints; *esp.* one who prints books, magazines, advertising matter, etc. Also, the owner or manager of a printing business. LME.
2 A device that prints; *spec.* (*a*) a teleprinter; (*b*) PHOTOGRAPHY & CINEMATOGRAPHY an apparatus for producing positive prints from negatives; (*c*) COMPUTING an output device which produces a printed record of data, text, etc. Freq. with specifying word. M19.
3 A cotton cloth made to be printed on. M19.
2 ***drum printer, line printer, matrix printer, thermal printer***, etc.
Comb.: **printer buffer** COMPUTING = ***print spooler*** s.v. PRINT *noun*; **printer plotter** COMPUTING a printer which can produce line drawings and halftone pictures as well as text; **Printers' Bible** an impression of the Bible reading *printers* instead of *princes* in *Psalms* 119:161; ***printer's devil***: see DEVIL *noun* 7(a); **printer-slotter** a machine used for printing on cardboard or other packaging materials; **printer's mark** a device used as a printer's trade mark; **printer's pie** = PIE *noun*[4] 1; ***printer's ream***: see REAM *noun*[2] 1.
■ **printergram** *noun* a telegram transmitted by telex M20.

printery /ˈprɪnt(ə)ri/ *noun.* Chiefly *US.* M17.
[from prec.: see -ERY.]
1 A printer's office or works. M17.
2 A cotton-printing factory. M19.

printing /ˈprɪntɪŋ/ *noun.* LME.
[from PRINT *verb* + -ING[1].]
1 The action of PRINT *verb*; an instance of this. LME.
2 The total number of copies of a book etc. printed at one time; an impression. M16.
3 PHOTOGRAPHY. The production of a print from a negative or a transparency. M19.
4 = ***print-through*** (a) s.v. PRINT *verb.* M20.
1 ***rotary printing***: see ROTARY *adjective*. **3 printing out** PHOTOGRAPHY the production of an image without chemical development.
Comb.: **printing-frame** a holder in which sensitized paper is placed beneath a negative and exposed to light to make a print; **printing-house** an establishment in which books, newspapers, etc., are printed; **printing-office** a printing-house; ***printing-press***: see PRESS *noun*[1] 10a; **printing-sheet** a large usu. rectangular sheet of paper for printing, to be printed without cutting or folding or to be cut or folded into any of various standard sizes of book or paper, as folio, octavo, etc.; **printing union** = ***print union*** s.v. PRINT *noun*.

printless /ˈprɪntlɪs/ *adjective & adverb.* E17.
[from PRINT *noun* + -LESS.]
▶**A** *adjective.* **1** Making or leaving no print or trace. E17.
2 That has received or that retains no print. L18.
▶**B** *adverb.* Without leaving or receiving a print. L18.

prion /ˈprʌɪən/ *noun*[1]. M19.
[mod. Latin *Prion* former genus name from Greek *priōn* a saw.]
Any of various small saw-billed petrels of the genus *Pachyptila* (family Procellariidae), found in southern seas.

prion /ˈpriːɒn/ *noun*[2]. L20.
[from rearrangement of 'proteinaceous infectious particle'. Cf. VIRION.]
MICROBIOLOGY. A hypothetical infectious particle consisting only of protein, thought to be the cause of diseases such as scrapie and kuru.

prior /ˈprʌɪə/ *noun.* LOE.
[medieval Latin use as noun of Latin *prior* former, elder, superior, compar. of *prae*: see PRE-.]
1 A superior of a house or group of houses of any of various religious orders; *spec.* (*a*) the deputy of an abbot; (*b*) *Hist.* the superior of a house of canons regular; (*c*) the superior of a house of friars. LOE.
2 a In some western European countries, the elected head of a guild of merchants or craftsmen. E17. ▸**b** *Hist.* A chief magistrate in any of various former Italian republics. E17.
3 COMMERCE. The head of a firm. Now *rare* or *obsolete.* M19.
4 *ellipt.* A prior criminal conviction. *US slang.* L20.
■ **priorship** *noun* the office or dignity of a prior M16.

prior /ˈprʌɪə/ *adjective*. E18.
[Latin: see prec.]
1 Preceding in time, order, or importance; earlier, former, previous, antecedent. Freq. foll. by *to*. E18.
2 STATISTICS. Of the result of a calculation: made before or in ignorance of an observation or observations. E20.

> 📖 **1** D. LODGE Gary . . pleaded a prior commitment to homework. P. VAN SOMMERS Jealous about his wife's prior sexual experience.

Special collocations & phrases: **prior charge** FINANCE stock, capital, etc., on which claims for payment take precedence over the claims of ordinary stock etc. **prior probability** STATISTICS a probability as assessed before making reference to certain relevant observations. **prior to** before.
■ **priorly** *adverb* L18.

priorate /ˈprʌɪərət/ *noun*. LME.
[Late Latin *prioratus*, from *prior*: see PRIOR *noun*, -ATE¹.]
1 The office, dignity, or term of office of a prior or prioress. LME.
2 A priory; the community living in a priory. M18.

prioress /ˈprʌɪərɪs, -rɛs/ *noun*. ME.
[Old French *prioresse* = medieval Latin *priorissa*; formed as PRIOR *noun*: see -ESS¹.]
A female superior of a house of any of various orders of nuns; the deputy of an abbess.

prioritize /prʌɪˈɒrɪtʌɪz/ *verb*. Also **-ise**. L20.
[from next + -IZE.]
1 *verb trans.* Designate as requiring prior attention, give priority to. L20.
2 *verb trans. & intrans.* Determine the order for dealing with (items), establish priorities for (a set of items). L20.

> 📖 **1** *Precision Marketing* Segmenting your effort prioritises what is most important. **2** *Which Computer?* The program allows you . . to prioritize the tasks. *Methodist Recorder* We are having to prioritize . . in terms of areas of work.

■ **prioritiˈzation** *noun* L20.

priority /prʌɪˈɒrɪti/ *noun & adjective*. LME.
[Old & mod. French *priorité* from medieval Latin *prioritas*, from Latin *prior*: see PRIOR *noun*, -ITY.]
▶ **A** *noun*. **1** The fact or condition of being earlier in time or of preceding something else. LME. ▸**b** TAXONOMY. The claim of the earliest validly published Latin name to be taken as the correct one for any given organism. M19.
2 Precedence in order, rank, or dignity; the right to receive attention, supplies, etc., before others. Now also *transf.*, an interest with prior claim to consideration; an important consideration. LME.
3 LAW. A precedence among claims; a preference in order of payment. E16.

> 📖 **2** M. MOORCOCK Giving the community priority over individuals. S. HASTINGS A clear idea of her order of priorities. *Which?* Priority is now . . given to traffic already on the roundabout.

▶ **B** *attrib.* or as *adjective*. Of or pertaining to priority or priorities; having priority. M19.

> 📖 *Guardian* To increase the ratio of teachers to children in educational priority areas. *Broadcast* A shorter working week . . is a priority objective. R. DAHL The list of priority candidates.

priory /ˈprʌɪəri/ *noun*. ME.
[Anglo-Norman *priorie*, medieval Latin *prioria*, from Latin *prior*: see PRIOR *noun*, -Y³.]
1 A monastery or convent governed by a prior or prioress. Also (*Hist.*), a house of canons regular. ME.
2 = PRIORATE 1. LME.
1 *Alien Priory*: see ALIEN *adjective* 1b.

prisage /ˈprʌɪzɪdʒ/ *noun*. E16.
[Anglo-Norman, from *prise* PRISE *noun*¹: see -AGE.]
Hist. An ancient duty levied on imported wine until 1809.
■ **prisable** *adjective* liable to prisage L19.

priscan /ˈprɪsk(ə)n/ *adjective*. *rare*. L19.
[from Latin *priscus* old + -AN.]
Ancient, primitive, of early times.

Priscian /ˈprɪʃ(ə)n/ *noun*. E16.
[A famous 6th-cent. Roman grammarian.]
A grammarian (esp. as a type). Chiefly in ***break Priscian's head***, ***knock Priscian's head***, violate the rules of grammar.

Priscillianist /prɪˈsɪlɪənɪst/ *noun & adjective*. LME.
[French *Priscillianiste* or late Latin *Priscillianista*, from Latin *Priscillianus* Priscillian (see below): see -IST.]
ECCLESIASTICAL HISTORY. ▶**A** *noun*. A follower of Priscillian, a 4th-cent. Bishop of Avila in Spain, or of the Gnostic or Manichaean doctrines he is alleged to have taught. LME.
▶ **B** *adjective*. Of or pertaining to the Priscillianists or their doctrines. L19.
■ **Priscillian** *noun* = PRISCILLIANIST *noun* L17. **Priscillianism** *noun* the doctrines of Priscillian or his followers E17. **Priscillianite** *noun* = PRISCILLIANIST *noun* L16.

Priscoan /prɪˈskəʊən, ˈprɪ-/ *adjective & noun*. L20.
[Irreg. from Latin *priscus* ancient + -AN.]
GEOLOGY. ▶**A** *adjective*. Of, relating to, or denoting the aeon that (in some schemes) constitutes the earliest part of the Precambrian, extending from the origin of the earth to the beginning of the Archaean aeon about 4,000 million years ago, and which has left no identifiable rocks. L20.
▶ **B** *noun*. The Priscoan aeon. L20.

Priscol /ˈprɪskɒl/ *noun*. M20.
[Invented word.]
PHARMACOLOGY. (Proprietary name for) tolazoline.
■ Also **Priscoline** *noun* (US proprietary name) M20.

prise /prʌɪz, priːz/ *noun*¹. See also PRIZE *noun*². ME.
[Old & mod. French, use as noun of fem. pa. pple of *prendre* take, seize. Cf. Anglo-Latin *prisa*.]
Hist. **1** The seizing of anything by a lord for his own use from his feudal tenants or dependants; a requisition; a thing requisitioned for the use of the monarch or the garrisons in his or her castles. ME.
†**2** A portion taken from or a duty levied on imported goods by the monarch. Usu. in *pl.* LME–E17.

prise /prʌɪz/ *noun*². Also **prize**. LME.
[formed as prec. Cf. PRY *noun*⁴.]
1 An instrument used for prising or levering something off; a lever. Now *dial.* LME.
2 The action of prising something; leverage. M19.

†**prise** *noun*³, *noun*⁴ & *adjective*, *noun*⁵ see PRICE *noun*, PRIZE *noun*¹ & *adjective*, PRIZE *noun*².

prise /prʌɪz/ *verb*¹ *trans.* Also **prize**. L17.
[from PRISE *noun*². Cf. PRY *verb*².]
1 Raise, move, or open by force of leverage. Usu. foll. by adverb or compl. L17.
2 Compress (cured tobacco) in a hogshead or box. *US*. E18.

> 📖 **1** S. BRETT Two were . . fighting, while the rest . . struggled to prise them apart. G. LORD She prised the cover off. R. THOMAS Chunks of debris were prised loose.

†**prise** *verb*², *verb*³, *verb*⁴ see PRIZE *verb*¹, *verb*², PRICE *verb*.

priser *noun*¹, *noun*² vars. of PRIZER *noun*¹, *noun*².

prisere /ˈprʌɪsɪə/ *noun*. E20.
[from PRI(MARY *adjective* + SERE *noun*².]
ECOLOGY. A sere that began on an area not previously colonized; a primary succession. Cf. SUBSERE.

prisiadka /prjiˈsjatkə/ *noun*. M20.
[Russian *prisyadka*.]
A dance step in which a squatting male dancer kicks out each leg alternately to the front; the dance which uses this step. Cf. KAZACHOC.

prism /ˈprɪz(ə)m/ *noun*. L16.
[Late Latin *prisma* from Greek, lit. 'thing sawn', from *prizein* to saw.]
1 GEOMETRY. A solid figure of which the two ends are similar, equal, and parallel rectilineal figures, and the sides parallelograms. L16.
2 OPTICS. A transparent body of this form, *esp.* a triangular geometrical prism of which the refracting surfaces are at an acute angle with each other. E17. ▸**b** A spectrum produced by refraction through a prism; in *pl.*, prismatic colours. M19.
3 Any body or object of the shape of a geometric or optical prism. M17.
4 CRYSTALLOGRAPHY. An open form consisting of three or more planes that meet in edges parallel to the vertical axis. L19.
2 ***Nicol prism***, ***roof prism***, ***Wollaston prism***, etc.
Phrases: ***prunes and prism(s)***: see PRUNE *noun*.
■ **prismal** /ˈprɪzm(ə)l/ *adjective* of, pertaining to, or produced by a prism M19. **prismed** *adjective* produced by refraction in a prism; having prismatic colours: E19. **prismy** /ˈprɪzmi/ *adjective* (now *rare* or *obsolete*) produced (as) by a prism, refracted, refracting L18.

prismane /ˈprɪzmeɪn/ *noun*. M20.
[from prec. + -ANE.]
CHEMISTRY. Any saturated hydrocarbon whose molecule contains six carbon atoms linked together in the shape of a triangular prism; *spec.* the form of the benzene molecule which has this structure.

prismatic /prɪzˈmatɪk/ *adjective*. E18.
[French *prismatique*, from Greek *prismat-*, *prisma*: see PRISM, -IC.]
1 Of or pertaining to a prism; having the form of a prism or prisms. E18.
2 Of or pertaining to the optical prism; formed, separated, or distributed (as) by a transparent prism; of varied colours, brightly coloured, brilliant. E18.
3 Of an optical or measuring instrument: incorporating or making use of a prism or prisms. M19.
4 CRYSTALLOGRAPHY. = ORTHORHOMBIC. M19.
Special collocations: **prismatic astrolabe** an astrolabe designed specifically for the determination of latitude and longitude. **prismatic compass** a magnetic compass using a prism to enable an object and its bearing to be viewed simultaneously. **prismatic layer** ZOOLOGY the middle layer of a molluscan shell, consisting of crystalline calcite or aragonite.
■ **prismatical** *adjective* (now *rare*) = PRISMATIC 1 M17. **prismatically** *adverb* L17.

prismatoid /ˈprɪzmətɔɪd/ *adjective & noun*. M19.
[from Greek *prismat-*, *prisma* PRISM + -OID.]
▶ **A** *adjective*. CRYSTALLOGRAPHY. Of a plane: parallel to one of the three coordinate axes and intersecting the other two. Cf. PINACOID. M19.
▶ **B** *noun*. GEOMETRY. A solid figure having parallel polygonal ends connected by triangular faces. L19.

prismoid /ˈprɪzmɔɪd/ *noun & adjective*. E18.
[from PRISM + -OID, app. after *rhomboid*.]
▶ **A** *noun*. A body resembling a prism in form, with similar but unequal parallel polygonal bases. E18.
▶ **B** *adjective*. Prismoidal. *rare*. M19.
■ **prisˈmoidal** *adjective* of, pertaining to, or of the form of a prismoid E19.

prison /ˈprɪz(ə)n/ *noun & verb*. LOE.
[Old French *prisun*, (also mod.) *prison* from Latin *prensio(n-)* var. of *prehensio(n-)*, from *prehendere* seize.]
▶ **A** *noun*. **1** The condition of being kept in custody, captivity, or confinement; imprisonment. Also, a place in which a person is confined or held captive; *spec.* a building to which people are legally committed for custody while awaiting trial or for punishment; a jail. LOE. ▸**b** ROULETTE etc. A position on the board where bets are held in abeyance until the next round of play. M19.
†**2** A prisoner. ME–L15.

> 📖 **1** *Daily News* Prison for lads should be the last . . resort. D. EDEN The key turned in the lock. He and Sarah were in prison. *Guardian* The new maximum security prison. *fig.*: SHAKES. *Haml.* Denmark's a prison.

Comb.: **prison bars** (*a*) the bars of a prison; (*b*) = BAR *noun*¹ 11; **prison-bird** = *jailbird* s.v. JAIL *noun*; **prison-breaking** escape from prison; **prison camp** a camp for detaining prisoners of war or of the State; **prison-crop** = *prison haircut* below; **prison editor** a newspaper editor who takes legal responsibility for what is published and serves any resulting term of imprisonment; **prison-fever** = *jail fever* s.v. JAIL *noun*; **prison haircut** a style in which the hair is worn very short; **prison-house** a house or other structure that serves as a prison; **prison sentence**: committing an offender to prison or served in prison; **prison-van** a secure van for transporting prisoners; **prison-without-bars** *colloq.* an open prison.
▶ **B** *verb trans.* Put in prison, take or keep prisoner, imprison; confine, restrain, restrict the movement of. Now *north. & poet.* ME.

> 📖 SHAKES. *Lucr.* His true respect will prison false desire. C. BRONTË I arrested his wandering hand, and prisoned it in both mine.

■ **prisonful** *noun* as much or as many as a prison will hold E20. **prisoniˈzation** *noun* the fact or process of becoming prisonized M20. **prisonize** *verb trans.* cause (a prisoner) to adopt the characteristic psychological attitudes and social behaviour of prison life (usu. in *pass.*) M20. **prisonment** *noun* (now *rare*) = IMPRISONMENT LME.

prisoner /ˈprɪz(ə)nə/ *noun*. LME.
[Anglo-Norman = Old French *prisonier* (mod. -*nn*-), from *prison*: see prec., -ER².]
1 A person who is being kept in prison; *spec.* one who is in custody as the result of a legal process. LME.
2 A person who has surrendered to or been captured by an enemy or opponent; a prisoner of war. LME. ▸**b** A captive in the game of prisoners' base. E19.
3 *transf. & fig.* A person or thing confined or restricted by illness, circumstances, etc. LME.

> 📖 **1** *Chambers's Journal* The twenty years, which all life-sentenced prisoners must serve. **2** D. FRASER More than 230,000 of the enemy became prisoners. **3** SHAKES. *Hen. VIII* An untimely ague Stay'd me a prisoner in my chamber. I. MURDOCH I was a prisoner of the situation.

Phrases: **prisoner at the bar** a person on trial in a court of justice on a criminal charge. ***prisoner of* CONSCIENCE**. **prisoner of State** a person imprisoned for political reasons. **prisoner of war** a person captured in war. **prisoners' bars** = *prisoners' base* s.v. BASE *noun*². ***prisoners' base***: see BASE *noun*². **prisoner's dilemma** GAME THEORY a situation in which two players each have two options whose outcome depends crucially on the simultaneous choice made by the other (often formulated in terms of two prisoners separately deciding whether to confess to a crime). **prisoner's friend** MILITARY an officer representing a defendant at a court martial. **State prisoner** = *prisoner of State* above. **take prisoner** seize and hold as a prisoner.

priss /prɪs/ *noun*. *US colloq.* E20.
[Back-form. from next.]
A prissy person.

prissy /ˈprɪsi/ *adjective*. *colloq.* (orig. *US*). L19.
[Perh. blend of PRIM *adjective* and SISSY.]
Fussy, overparticular; excessively or affectedly prim, prudish.

> 📖 J. GASH The police woman was . . speculating whether this prissy missie was a secret raver and who with. S. KING A prissy attention to detail that takes all the fun out of writing.

■ **prissily** *adverb* M20. **prissiness** *noun* M20.

pristaf /ˈprɪstaf/ *noun.* M17.
[Russian *pristav*, from *pri-* before + *stavit'* set up, place, post.]
RUSSIAN HISTORY. A commissioner, a police officer, an overseer.

pristane /ˈprɪsteɪn/ *noun.* E20.
[from Latin, Greek *pristis* sawfish, shark + -ANE.]
CHEMISTRY. A saturated hydrocarbon which is a colourless oil occurring in the liver oils of some sharks; 2,6,10,14-tetramethylpentadecane, $C_{19}H_{40}$.

pristine /ˈprɪstiːn, -stʌɪn/ *adjective.* M16.
[Latin *pristinus* former: see -INE[1].]
1 Of or pertaining to the earliest period; original, former; primitive, ancient. M16.
2 Of a thing: having its original condition; unmarred, uncorrupted, unspoilt; *spec.* (of a manufactured product) spotless, fresh as if new; brand-new. Orig. *US.* E20.

🕮 **1** H. ACTON She retained her pristine naïvety. *Theatre Research International* Country communities embody a pristine innocence. **2** P. USTINOV A pristine kingdom, unaffected by . . Tartar invasions. R. FRAME I took a clean, pristine sheet of paper.

■ **pristinely** *adverb* L19.

pritch /prɪtʃ/ *noun. obsolete* exc. *dial.* ME.
[App. by-form of PRICK *noun.*]
1 †**a** A prick, a goad, a spur. Only in ME. ▸**b** Any of various sharp-pointed tools or implements. E19.
†**2** Offence taken (*against* a person). L16–M17.
3 Small or poor beer. L17.

pritch /prɪtʃ/ *verb trans. obsolete* exc. *dial.* ME.
[App. by-form of PRICK *verb.*]
1 Prick; affect with a pricking sensation. ME.
2 Prick or punch holes in. M18.

prithee /ˈprɪðiː/ *interjection. arch.* L16.
[Abbreviation of (*I*) *pray thee.*]
Please, pray.

prittle-prattle /ˈprɪt(ə)lprat(ə)l/ *noun & verb.* Now *rare.* M16.
[Redupl. of PRATTLE Cf. TITTLE-TATTLE.]
▶ **A** *noun.* Trivial, worthless, or idle talk; childish prattle. M16.
▶†**B** *verb intrans.* Chatter, talk idly. M16–E17.

prius /ˈprʌɪəs/ *noun.* L19.
[Latin, neut. of *prior*: see PRIOR *noun.*]
That which is prior; *esp.* that which is a necessary prior condition.

privacy /ˈprɪvəsi, ˈprʌɪ-/ *noun.* LME.
[from PRIVATE *adjective* + -CY.]
1 The state or condition of being withdrawn from the society of others or from public attention; freedom from disturbance or intrusion; seclusion. LME. ▸**b** In *pl.* Private or retired places; places of retreat. Now *rare.* L17.
2 Absence or avoidance of publicity or display; secrecy. L16.
3 A private or personal matter; a secret. Now *rare.* L16.
4 The state of being privy to something, privity. *rare.* E18.

🕮 **1** A. LURIE She values . . privacy and dislikes official social life. R. P. GRAVES He was a shy man, who relished his privacy. P. CUTTING There was an atmosphere of friendly coexistence but the lack of privacy was sometimes a strain. **b** C. THUBRON The palaces . . succeeded each other in ever more intense barriers and deeper privacies. **2** JOHN SAUNDERS A marriage . . was solemnised with strict privacy in the chapel of Leigh Court. **3** M. ANGELOU Listening winds overhear my privacies spoken aloud.

†**privado** *noun.* Pl. **-os.** L16–E19.
[Spanish = private, particular, a favourite.]
An intimate friend, a confidant.

Privatdozent /priˈvaːtdoˌtsɛnt/ *noun.* Also **-docent.** M19.
[German = private teacher or lecturer.]
In German and some other universities: a private teacher or lecturer not on the salaried staff but usu. accorded official recognition, access to university resources, etc.; also in extended use.

private /ˈprʌɪvət/ *adjective, adverb, & noun.* LME.
[Latin *privatus* withdrawn from public life, peculiar to oneself, a man in private life, use of pa. pple of *privare* bereave, deprive, from *privus* single, individual, private: see -ATE[2].]
▶ **A** *adjective.* **1** Of a person: not holding public office or an official position. LME.
2 Of or pertaining to a person in a non-official capacity. LME.
3 Not open to the public; restricted or intended only for the use of a particular person or persons. LME. ▸**b** That belongs to or is the property of a particular person; one's own; of, pertaining to, or affecting a particular person or group of people, individual, personal. LME. ▸†**c** Peculiar to a particular person or persons; particular. E16–M17. ▸**d** Of a service, business, etc.: provided or owned by an individual rather than the State or a public body; *spec.* (of a system of education or medical treatment) conducted outside the State system and charging fees to the individual concerned; of or pertaining to such a system. M18.
4 Kept or removed from public view or knowledge; not generally known; secret; confidential, not to be disclosed to others. Also, without the presence of another person or persons, alone (*with*). L15. ▸†**b** Privy; enjoying another's confidence, intimate. Foll. by *to, with.* L16–M18.
5 Of a place: secluded, unfrequented, affording privacy. L15.
6 Of a person: retiring; reserved; unsociable. Formerly also, secretive. L16.

🕮 **1** G. B. SHAW We cannot do this as private persons. It must be done by the Government. N. FREELING I'm just a private individual. *Journal of Navigation* Like the private sailor, the private aviator relies . . on magnetic heading systems. **2** J. F. KENNEDY We believe that groups will co-ordinate their private interests with national interests. J. STEINBECK He never mixed his professional life with his private pleasures. W. S. CHURCHILL His private letters reveal his bitterness. **3** C. MACINNES I was up very early . . as if with a private alarm clock in my brain. DAY LEWIS I sang once, at a private party. A. ALVAREZ They had private jokes and rituals from which everyone was excluded. J. AIKEN A stone tunnel . . defended by a PRIVATE sign. **b** A. MILLER Conscience was no longer a private matter but one of state administration. S. BELLOW A Texas builder . . flew up . . in his private jet. *Asian Art* Qing emperors . . confiscated important private art collections. L. DUNCAN They sat and talked . . sharing . . private thoughts and longings. **d** P. WILLMOTT Private beds amount to little over one per cent of the total . . in use. P. D. JAMES 'I'm on the list of the orthopaedic hospital.' 'Forgive me, but why not go private?' J. WILSON He'd always been against private education. **4** T. HARDY Though this conversation had been private, . . its import reached . . those around. J. LINGARD Black wanted to be private, you could tell that at a glance. M. M. R. KHAN He was not . . sure how much to tell me and how much to keep private. **6** A. S. DALE Frances was such an intensely private person . . that her reactions were not left for posterity.

Special collocations & phrases: **private army** an army not recruited by the State; a mercenary force. ***private attorney***: see ATTORNEY *noun* 1. ***private bank***: see BANK *noun*[3] 3. **private bar** = ***lounge bar*** s.v. LOUNGE *noun*[1]. **private bill** a parliamentary bill affecting an individual or corporation only. **private branch exchange** TELEPHONY an exchange by which private lines may be connected to the public network; abbreviation ***PBX***. **private car** (*a*) a motor car owned and used privately, as distinct from a commercial vehicle; (*b*) *US* a railway carriage owned and used privately. **private company** a company with restricted membership and no issue of shares. **private detective** a person who undertakes special enquiries for private employers. **private enterprise** (*a*) a business etc. that is privately owned and not under State control; (*b*) individual initiative esp. in business. **private enterpriser** an advocate of or participant in private enterprise. **private eye** *colloq.* = ***private detective*** above. **private hotel** (*a*) a hotel not obliged to take all comers; (*b*) *Austral.* a hotel without a licence to serve alcohol. **private house** the dwelling-house of a private person, as distinct from a shop, office, or public building. **private income** an unearned income, derived from investments, property, etc. **private inquiry**: undertaken by a private detective. **private investigator** = ***private detective*** above. ***private JUDGEMENT***. **private key** a cryptographic key, unique to a particular recipient, used to decipher messages encrypted using a public key (see ***PUBLIC key***). **private language** a language which can be understood by the user or users only. **private law**: relating to dealings between individuals or institutions, rather than the State. **private life**: as a private individual rather than as an official, public performer, etc. **private line** TELEPHONY (*a*) a line for the exclusive use of a subscriber, or not connected to the public network; (*b*) = ***private wire*** (a) below. **private means** = ***private income*** above. **private member** a member of a legislative body not holding a government office (***private member's bill***, a bill introduced by a private member, not part of government legislation). **private number** TELEPHONY (*a*) an ex-directory number; (*b*) a number at a private address. **private parts** the genitals. **private patient** (in Britain) a patient treated by a doctor other than under the National Health Service. **private practice** (in Britain) medical practice that is not part of the National Health Service. **private press** a usu. privately operated printing establishment which prints a limited number of books to a very high standard, esp. for collectors. **private residence** = ***private house*** above. **private room**: in a club, hotel, etc., that may be hired for private use. **private school** (*a*) an independent school supported wholly by the payment of fees and esp. owned by an individual; (*b*) *US* a school not supported mainly by the State. ***private secretary*** see SECRETARY *noun* (***parliamentary private secretary***: see PARLIAMENTARY *adjective*). **private sector** the part of an economy, industry, etc., which is free from direct State control. ***private sentinel***: see SENTINEL *noun* 4. **private service** domestic service in a private house. **private soldier** an ordinary soldier as opp. to an officer or (*US*) an officer or a recruit. **private treaty** an agreement for the sale of a property at a price negotiated directly between the vendor and purchaser or their agents. **private view** the viewing of an exhibition (esp. of paintings) before it is open to the public. **private war** (*a*) a feud between a restricted number of people from personal motives; (*b*) hostilities against members of another State without the sanction of one's own government. **private wire** TELEPHONY (*a*) a wire in an exchange used to test whether a line is in use without intrusion on a call in progress; (*b*) = ***private line*** (a) above. **private wrong** an offence against an individual but not against society as a whole.
▶ **B** *adverb.* Privately. LME.
▶ **C** *noun.* **I** †**1** A private person; a person not holding a public office or position. L15–L17.
†**2** An intimate, a favourite. *rare* (Shakes.). Only in E17.
3 A private soldier. L18.

🕮 **3** A. HUTSCHNECKER They wanted to make me an officer . . I wanted to remain a private.

▶ **II** †**4** A private or personal matter; private business. M16–M17.
†**5** A private or confidential communication. *rare* (Shakes.). Only in L16.
†**6** Privacy, seclusion. E–M17.
7 In *pl.* The genitals. *colloq.* E17.
8 A private school. *slang.* E20.

🕮 **7** S. TOWNSEND Bert doesn't get on with his district nurse. He says he doesn't like having his privates mauled about by a woman.

Phrases: **in private** privately, not publicly. **private first class** *US* a soldier ranking above an ordinary private but below officers.
¶ In sense C.7 rare (Shakes.) before M20.
■ **privately** *adverb* (*a*) in a private capacity, unofficially; (*b*) without publicity, quietly, secretly; (*c*) individually, personally: LME. **privateness** *noun* L16.

privateer /prʌɪvəˈtɪə/ *noun & verb.* M17.
[from PRIVATE *adjective* + -EER, after *volunteer.*]
▶ **A** *noun.* **1** An armed vessel owned and crewed by private individuals and holding a government commission authorizing its use in war, esp. in the capture of merchant shipping; the commander or a member of the crew of such a vessel. Now chiefly *Hist.* M17.
2 An advocate or exponent of private enterprise. M20.
3 MOTOR RACING. A competitor who races as a private individual rather than as a member of a works team. L20.
Comb.: **privateersman** US HISTORY an officer or a member of the crew of a privateer.
▶ **B** *verb intrans.* Engage in the activities of a privateer; (of a vessel) be used as a privateer. Chiefly as ***privateering*** *verbal noun.* M17.

privation /prʌɪˈveɪʃ(ə)n/ *noun.* ME.
[Latin *privatio(n-)*, from *privat-* pa. ppl stem of *privare*: see PRIVATE, -ATION.]
1 The action of depriving a person or thing of or taking something away; the fact of being deprived; *spec.* the action of depriving someone of office or position; deprivation. Now *rare.* ME.
2 In LOGIC, the condition of being deprived of or being without some attribute formerly or properly possessed; *gen.* the loss or absence of a quality. LME.
3 (A) lack of the usual comforts or necessities of life. L18.

🕮 **3** J. H. NEWMAN Prepared by penury . . for the privations of a military life. R. WEST We foresaw distress . . and privation . . no holidays, no new clothes, no concerts. M. SCAMMELL Besides the physical privations, there was the mental anguish.

privatise *verb* var. of PRIVATIZE.

privatism /ˈprʌɪvətɪz(ə)m/ *noun.* M20.
[from PRIVATE *adjective* + -ISM.]
A tendency to be concerned with ideas, matters, etc., only as affecting one as an individual.
■ **privaˈtistic** *adjective* L20.

privative /ˈprɪvətɪv/ *adjective & noun.* L16.
[French *privatif, -ive* or Latin *privativus* denoting privation, from *privat-*: see PRIVATION, -IVE.]
▶ **A** *adjective.* **1** Having the quality of depriving a person or thing. L16.
2 Consisting in or characterized by the removal of or lack of some attribute normally or properly present; *gen.* characterized by the absence of a quality. L16. ▸**b** Of a term: denoting privation or absence of a quality or attribute. M17.
3 GRAMMAR. Of a particle or affix: expressing privation or negation. L16.
▶ **B** *noun.* A privative attribute, quality, proposition, or particle. L16.
■ **privatively** *adverb* †(*a*) to the deprivation or exclusion of others; (*b*) by the removal or absence of something; negatively: LME. **privativeness** *noun* (*rare*) M17.

privatize /ˈprʌɪvətʌɪz/ *verb trans.* Also **-ise.** M20.
[from PRIVATE *adjective* + -IZE.]
1 Make private as opp. to public; *esp.* (of the State) assign (a business, service, etc.) to private as distinct from State control or ownership; denationalize. M20.
2 View (a concept, discipline, activity, etc.) in terms of its relation to or significance for the individual only as opp. to (a part of) society. M20.
■ **privatiˈzation** *noun* M20. **privatizer** *noun* L20.

privet /ˈprɪvɪt/ *noun.* M16.
[Obscurely rel. to PRIMPRINT, PRIM *noun*, PRIMP *noun*[1].]
1 Any of several stiff semi-evergreen shrubs constituting the genus *Ligustrum*, of the olive family, with white flowers and black berries, much used for garden hedges; *esp.* (more fully ***common privet***) *L. vulgare*, native to chalk scrub etc., and (more fully ***garden privet, Japanese privet***) *L. ovalifolium*, which has largely superseded it in cultivation. M16.

2 In full ***swamp privet***. A small evergreen tree of the southern US, *Forestiera acuminata*, related to and resembling common privet. **L19.**

Phrases: ***common privet***, ***garden privet***: see sense 1 above. **Japanese privet** (*a*) an evergreen privet, *Ligustrum japonicum*, of Japan and Korea; (*b*) see sense 1 above. ***mock privet***: see MOCK *adjective*. ***swamp privet***: see sense 2 above.

Comb.: **privet hawk**, **privet hawkmoth** a large hawkmoth, *Sphinx ligustri*, whose larvae feed on privet.

■ **privet-like** *adjective* resembling (that of) privet **M19.**

privilege /ˈprɪvɪlɪdʒ/ *noun*. **ME.**

[from Anglo-Norman word = Old & mod. French *privilège* from Latin *privilegium* legal provision affecting an individual, prerogative, from *privus* (see PRIVATE) + *lex*, *leg-* law.]

1 A right, advantage, or immunity granted to or enjoyed by a person or a class of people, beyond the usual rights or advantages of others. **ME.** ▸**b** *gen.* A special right, an honour. **ME.** ▸†**c** An advantage yielded. *rare* (Shakes.). Only in **L16.**

2 Such a right or immunity attaching to some office, rank, or station; *spec.* freedom of speech during a meeting and immunity from arrest in a civil case granted to the members of a legislative assembly. **ME.**

3 A privileged position; the possession of special advantages or rights. **LME.**

4 A grant to an individual, corporation, etc., of special rights or immunities, sometimes to the prejudice of the general right; a franchise, a monopoly. **LME.** ▸**b** *ROMAN HISTORY.* A special ordinance having reference to an individual. **L15.**

†**5** The right of asylum or sanctuary. **LME–L17.**

6 *US STOCK EXCHANGE.* = OPTION *noun* 5. **M19.**

> 🕮 **1** R. NIEBUHR The . . victory of universal suffrage was not final, because women were excluded from the privilege. T. CAPOTE The privileges granted ordinary prisoners were denied . . no radios or card games. A. CROSS Kate had had . . the privilege of wealth. F. TUOHY Long holidays which are the privilege of schoolteachers. **b** D. L. SAYERS A woman whom it is a privilege to call one's friend. A. C. BOULT I had the privilege of conducting at Petersfield for twenty years. A. HARDING Philip offers me his arm; but Charles, more swift . . to claim the privilege, has seized my hand. **2** H. HALLAM The commons voted Skinner into custody for a breach of privilege. V. BROME They were accorded diplomatic privilege, and avoided the delays . . of passing through Customs. **3** G. GORER This concept of privilege and conditional enjoyment would appear to have . . ramifications. R. CHRISTIANSEN There were many closed avenues in a France rotten with privilege and exclusiveness.

Phrases: **bill of privilege** a petition of a peer demanding to be tried by his peers. ***Pauline privilege***: see PAULINE *adjective* 1. **writ of privilege** a writ to deliver a privileged person from custody when arrested in a civil suit.

privilege /ˈprɪvɪlɪdʒ/ *verb trans.* **ME.**

[Old & mod. French *privilégier* from medieval Latin *privilegiare*, from *privilegium*: see prec.]

1 Invest with a privilege or privileges; grant a particular right or immunity to; allow as a privilege *to do*. **ME.**

2 Give (a person) special freedom or immunity *from* some liability etc.; exempt. **M16.**

3 *transf.* Authorize contrary to the usual rule or practice; justify, excuse. **L16.**

> 🕮 **1** BUNYAN To privilege the worst of sinners with the first offer of mercy. **2** S. DANIEL Kings cannot privilege what God forbade.

privileged /ˈprɪvɪlɪdʒd/ *adjective*. **LME.**

[from PRIVILEGE *noun*, *verb*: see -ED[2], -ED[1].]

Invested with or enjoying a certain privilege or privileges; allowed as a privilege, honoured, (*to do*).

> 🕮 V. WOOLF He mixes the salad with his own hands for some privileged guest. N. MANDELA Congress declined and became an organisation of the privileged few. G. ADAIR He had been offered privileged access to a secret world. *Guardian* I feel privileged to have known Collins. **privileged communication** *LAW* (*a*) a communication which a witness cannot be legally compelled to divulge; (*b*) a communication made between such people and in such circumstances that it is not actionable. **privileged debt**: having a prior claim to satisfaction. **privileged deed** *SCOTS LAW*: valid without witnesses' signatures.

priviligentsia /ˌprɪvɪlɪˈdʒɛn(t)sɪə/ *noun*. Also **-leg-**. **M20.**

[Blend of PRIVILEGE *noun* and INTELLIGENTSIA.]

Esp. in a Communist State: the section of society (regarded as) enjoying certain social and economic privileges over ordinary citizens.

privity /ˈprɪvɪti/ *noun*. **ME.**

[Old French *priveté*, *-ité* from medieval Latin *privitas*, from Latin *privus*: see PRIVATE, -ITY.]

†**1 a** A divine or heavenly mystery. **ME–L15.** ▸**b** A secret; a person's own private business or affairs. **ME–E17.**

†**2** Privacy, seclusion; secrecy. Chiefly in ***in privity***, in private. **ME–M17.**

†**3** Intimacy, familiarity. **ME–L15.**

4 In *pl.* & †*sing.* The genitals. *arch.* **LME.**

5 *LAW.* A relation between two parties that is recognized by law, e.g. that of blood, service, a contract, etc.; a mutual interest. **E16.**

6 The fact of being privy to or *to* something. **M16.** ▸**b** *MARITIME LAW.* Knowledge of (and failure to rectify) a circumstance which subsequently contributes to damage or loss. **M19.**

5 privity of contract the relation between the parties in a contract which entitles them to sue each other but prevents a third party from doing so. **privity of estate** the relation between landlord and tenant which allows them to sue each other even though no privity of contract exists between them.

privy /ˈprɪvi/ *adjective & noun*. **ME.**

[Old & mod. French *privé* (as noun in Old French, familiar friend, private place) from Latin *privatus* PRIVATE: see -Y[5].]

▶ **A** *adjective*. **I** †**1** That is of one's own private circle; intimate, familiar. **ME–M17.**

2 Of or pertaining exclusively to a particular person or persons, private, personal. *obsolete* exc. in special collocations (see below). **ME.** ▸†**b** Peculiar to or characteristic of an individual; (of a word) idiomatic. *rare.* **LME–M17.**

†**3** = PRIVATE *adjective* 2. **LME–M16.**

4 Sharing in the knowledge of something secret or private. Foll. by *to*, †*of*. **LME.**

> 🕮 **4** R. C. HUTCHINSON He must be privy to all kinds of cryptic intelligence. W. STYRON Proud to be privy to portentous tidings. D. LEAVITT Suzanne isn't privy to the secrets of Linda and Sam's lives.

▶ **II 5** Secret, concealed; clandestine, surreptitious. *arch.* **ME.**

†**6** Not visible; hidden. **M16–M17.**

Special collocations: **privy chamber** *Hist.* (*a*) a room reserved for the private use of a particular person or persons; (*b*) *spec.* a private apartment in a royal residence. **privy council** (*a*) (with cap. initials) a body of advisers appointed by the British monarch, usu. as a personal honour but automatically in the case of Cabinet Ministers, and including those who hold or have held high political, legal, or ecclesiastical office in Britain or the Commonwealth (***Judicial Committee of the Privy Council***: see JUDICIAL *adjective*); (*b*) any similar select body of advisers, *spec.* (chiefly *Hist.*) that of a (foreign) monarch, governor-general, etc. **privy councillor** = ***privy counsellor*** below. **privy counsellor** (*a*) (with cap. initials) a member of the Privy Council; (*b*) *gen.* a private or confidential adviser. ***privy member(s)***: see MEMBER *noun*. **privy parts** *arch.* the genitals. **privy purse** (*a*) an allowance from the public revenue for private expenses of the monarch; (*b*) (with cap. initials) an officer of the royal household in charge of this. **privy seal** (*a*) a seal affixed to documents that are afterwards to pass the Great Seal or that do not require it; in Scotland, a seal authenticating a royal grant of personal or assignable rights; (*b*) (with cap. initials) the keeper of this (now called ***Lord Privy Seal*** and having chiefly nominal official duties) (see also ***Keeper of the Privy Seal*** s.v. KEEPER *noun*); (*c*) *Hist.* a document to which the privy seal was affixed.

▶ **B** *noun*. **I** †**1** An intimate or trusted friend or counsellor; a confidant. Only in **ME.**

2 *LAW.* A person who has a part or interest in any action, matter, or thing. Opp. ***stranger***. **L15.** ▸†**b** A person privy to a secret matter. **M16–M17.** ▸†**c** A native or inhabitant of a place, as opp. to a stranger. **M16–M17.**

▶ **II 3** A lavatory, *esp.* an outside one or one without plumbing. **ME.**

†**4** Secrecy. Only in ***in privy***. **LME–M16.**

■ **privily** *adverb* (*arch.*) secretly **ME.**

Prix de Rome /pri də rɔm/ *noun phr.* Pl. ***Prix de Rome*** (pronounced same). **L19.**

[French = prize of Rome.]

(A winner of) any of a group of prizes awarded annually by the French Government in a competition for artists, sculptors, architects, and musicians.

prix fixe /pri fiks/ *noun phr.* **L19.**

[French, lit. 'fixed price'.]

A meal consisting of several courses served at a total fixed price. Cf. À LA CARTE.

> 🕮 *attrib.*: S. CHITTY At a *prix fixe* restaurant a franc or two bought a three course meal.

prizable *adjective* var. of PRIZEABLE.

prize /prʌɪz/ *noun*[1] & *adjective*. As noun also (earlier) †**price**, †**prise**. See also PRICE *noun*. **ME.**

[Var. of PRICE *noun*.]

▶ **A** *noun*. **I 1** A reward as a symbol of victory or superiority in a contest or competition. Also, a reward given in recognition of some non-competitive achievement. **ME.**

2 Something (as a sum of money or a valuable object) that can be won in a lottery or other game of chance. **M16.**

3 *fig.* **a** An advantage, a privilege; something highly valued. Long *rare*. **L16.** ▸**b** Anything striven for or worth striving for. **E17.**

> 🕮 **1** *Glasgow Herald* He won first prize in . . a model-making competition. E. BLISHEN In a grammar school, prizes are plotted for, swotted for, expected. *Journal of Navigation* The Daily Mail had offered a prize of £10,000 for the first successful transatlantic crossing. ***booby prize***, ***consolation prize***, etc. ***Nobel prize***, ***Pulitzer prize***, etc. **2** H. ALLEN An official lottery with several very large prizes. **3b** A. BEVAN Material success . . is the prize awarded by society to the individual who has served it best.

▶ **II** See PRICE *noun*.

▶ **B** *attrib.* or as *adjective*. **1** To or for which a prize is awarded; *fig.* supreme, outstanding, unrivalled. **L18.**

2 That is given as a prize. **M19.**

> 🕮 **1** J. H. B. PEEL The owners of prize bulls will not accept responsibility if the brass band suddenly lets-go. M. TRIPP I've been made a fool, a prize bloody fool.

Comb.: **prize-giving** an award of prizes, *esp.* a formal one at a school etc.; **prize-list** *noun*[1] a list of people winning prizes; **prizeman** a winner of a prize, esp. a specified academic one; **prize-money** *noun*[1] money constituting a prize or prizes.

■ **prizeless** *adjective* not having won a prize **L19.** **prizeworthy** *adjective* **M17.**

prize /prʌɪz/ *noun*[2]. Also (earlier) †**prise**. **LME.**

[Specialized use of PRISE *noun*[1], later identified with PRIZE *noun*[1].]

1 Something seized or captured by force, esp. in war; booty, plunder. Now only *spec.*, a ship or other item of property captured in naval warfare. **LME.** ▸**b** Property seized (as) in war. Chiefly in ***make prize***. **L16.** ▸**c** *fig.* A find, a windfall. **L16.**

†**2** The action of taking or stealing something; capture, seizure. **L15–E18.**

Comb.: **prize agent**: appointed for the sale of prizes taken in maritime war; **prize court** a department of an admiralty court responsible for adjudication concerning prizes; **prize-list** *noun*[2] a list of people entitled to receive prize-money on the capture of a ship; **prize-master** an officer appointed to command a prize ship; **prize-money** *noun*[2]: realized by the sale of a prize and distributed among the captors.

prize /prʌɪz/ *noun*[3]. *obsolete* exc. in PRIZEFIGHTER & derivs. **M16.**

[Perh. transf. use of PRIZE *noun*[1]: cf. Greek *athlon* prize, contest.]

A contest, a match. Later *spec.*, a prizefight.

†**play a prize** engage in a contest or match. †**play one's prize** play one's part.

prize *noun*[4] var. of PRISE *noun*[2].

prize /prʌɪz/ *verb*[1] *trans.* Also (earlier) †**prise**. **LME.**

[Old French *pris-* tonic stem of *preisier*: see PRAISE *verb*. Cf. PRICE *verb*.]

▶ **I 1** Estimate the (relative or monetary) value of; value; appraise; reckon. Now *arch.* & *dial.* **LME.**

2 Value or esteem highly, think much of. **LME.** ▸†**b** With neg.: think nothing of, care nothing for. *rare* (Shakes.). **L16–E17.**

> 🕮 **2** F. FITZGERALD Peasants who prized their bullocks and . . ancestral tombs above all things. V. BROME Wit was not something he prized.

▶†**II 3** = PRAISE *verb* 3a. *north.* **LME–M16.**

prize /prʌɪz/ *verb*[2] *trans.* Now *rare* or *obsolete*. Also (earlier) †**prise**. **LME.**

[from PRIZE *noun*[2].]

Seize, capture. Long *spec.*, seize (a ship or a ship's cargo) as a prize in naval warfare.

prize *verb*[3] var. of PRISE *verb*[1].

prizeable /ˈprʌɪzəb(ə)l/ *adjective*. Now chiefly *dial.* Also **prizable**. **E17.**

[from PRIZE *verb*[1] + -ABLE.]

Able or worthy to be prized, valuable.

prizefight /ˈprʌɪzfʌɪt/ *noun*. **E19.**

[Back-form. from next.]

A public contest between prizefighters; a boxing-match, esp. an unlicensed one, for money.

prizefighter /ˈprʌɪzfʌɪtə/ *noun*. **E18.**

[Orig. from PRIZE *noun*[3] + FIGHTER, from phr. *fight a prize*; now assoc. with PRIZE *noun*[1].]

Orig., a person who engaged in a public boxing-match. Now, a professional boxer, *esp.* an unlicensed one.

■ **prizefighting** *noun* **E18.**

prizer /ˈprʌɪzə/ *noun*[1]. Now *rare*. Also †**priser**. **LME.**

[from PRIZE *verb*[1] + -ER[1].]

†**1** An estimator of the value of something; an appraiser, a valuer. **LME–M17.**

2 A person who values or esteems something highly. (Foll. by *of*.) **E17.**

prizer /ˈprʌɪzə/ *noun*[2]. *arch.* Also †**priser**. **L16.**

[from PRIZE *noun*[3] + -ER[1].]

A prizefighter.

prize-ring /ˈprʌɪzrɪŋ/ *noun*. **E19.**

[from *prize* in PRIZEFIGHTER + RING *noun*[1].]

A boxing ring; *transf.* boxing.

PRO *abbreviation*.

1 Public Record Office.

2 Public relations officer.

pro /prəʊ/ *noun*[1] & *adjective*[1]. *colloq.* Also **pro.** (point). **M19.**

[Abbreviation.]

▶ **A** *noun*. Pl. **pros**.

1 At Oxford University, a pro-proctor. Now *rare* or *obsolete*. **M19.**

2 A professional (in sport or art). **M20.**

3 A prostitute. **M20.**

Comb.: **pro-am** *adjective & noun* (a game) involving professionals and amateurs; **pro shop**, **pro's shop** a workshop run by the resident professional at a golf club.

▶ **B** *adjective*. Professional. **M20.**

pro /prəʊ/ *preposition, adverb, noun*², & *adjective*². LME.
[Latin = before, in front of, for, on behalf of, instead of, in return for, on account of.]
▸ **A** *preposition*. **1** For: in Latin phrs. LME.
2 For, in favour of. M19.

📖 **1 pro aris et focis** /ˌɑːrɪs ɛt ˈfəʊkiːs, ˌɛːrɪs ɛt ˈfəʊsɪs/ [lit. 'for altars and hearths'] on behalf of religion and domestic life. **pro-bono** *adjective* (US) designating legal work undertaken without charge as for someone on a low income, and lawyers undertaking such work. **pro bono publico** /ˌbɒnəʊ ˈpʊblɪkəʊ, ˌbəʊnəʊ ˈpʌblɪkəʊ/ for the public good. **pro hac vice** /hɑːk ˈvʌɪsɪ, ˈviːkeɪ/ for this occasion only. **pro re nata** /reɪ ˈnɑːtə, riː ˈneɪtə/ [lit. 'for the affair born'] for an occasion as it arises. **pro tanto** /ˈtantəʊ/ [lit. 'for so much'] to such an extent, to that extent. **2** R. HARRIS It's nice of you to be so pro the idea.

▸ **B** *adverb*. In favour (of a proposition etc.). Chiefly in ***pro and con***, ***pro and contra*** below. LME.
▸ **C** *noun*. Pl. **-os**. A reason, argument, or arguer in favour of something. Now chiefly in ***pros and cons*** below. LME.
▸ **D** *adjective*. Favourable, supportive; that is in favour. E18.

pro-attitude PHILOSOPHY a positive attitude such as approval, pleasure, or satisfaction.

Other phrases: **con and pro** = ***pro and con*** (a) below. **pro and con** (*a*) *adverbial phr.* for and against a proposition etc.; (*b*) *verb phr. intrans. & trans.* weigh arguments for and against; debate both sides of (a matter). **pro and contra** (*a*) for and against a proposition etc., pro and con; (*b*) argument for and against something. **pro or con** for or against a proposition etc. **pros and cons**, **pros and contras** reasons or considerations for and against something, arguments on both sides, advantages and disadvantages.

pro- /prəʊ/ *prefix*¹.
[Latin, formed as PRO *preposition, adverb, noun*², & *adjective*². Sense 7 (rare before L19) app. from PRO *noun*¹. Cf. PUR-.]
▸ **I** In words derived or adopted from Latin.
1 Forward, to or toward the front, as ***produce***, ***project***, ***protrude***; forward and down, as ***procumbent***, ***prolapse***, ***prostrate***; into a public position, as ***proclaim***.
2 From its place, away, as ***prodigal***.
3 Onward (in space or time), as ***proceed***, ***progress***, ***propel***.
4 Out, outward, as ***propagate***, ***protract***.
5 Before (in space or time), in front of, in provision for, as ***prohibit***, ***protect***.
▸ **II** As a living prefix.
6 Prefixed to nouns to form nouns (and derived adjectives) with the sense 'deputizing for, standing in place of', as ***pro-cathedral***, ***proconsul***.
7 Prefixed to nouns and adjectives to form nouns and adjectives with the sense '(a person) favouring or supporting', as ***pro-abortion***, ***pro-abortionist***, ***pro-Israeli***.

▪ **probiˈotic** *adjective*¹ & *noun* [after ANTIBIOTIC] (pertaining to or designating) a substance which stimulates the growth of micro-organisms, esp. those with beneficial or desirable properties (such as those of the intestinal flora) M20. **pro-caˈthedral** *noun* & *adjective* (designating) a church used instead of or as a substitute for a cathedral M19. **pro-ˈchoice** *noun* & *adjective* (a policy of) advocating a legal right for women to choose whether to have an abortion L20. **pro-ˈchoicer** *noun* a person in favour of pro-choice L20. **proˈcurved** *adjective* curved in a forward direction L19. **proˈcyclical** *adjective* tending to enhance the trade cycle L20. **pro-Euroˈpean** *noun* & *adjective* (a person) favouring or supporting Europe; *spec.* (a person) supporting (British membership of) the European Community: M20. **pro-ˈfamily** *adjective* (US) promoting family life; *spec.* opposed to abortion on demand: L20. **proˈfluvium** *noun*, pl. **-ia** /-ɪə/, (esp. MEDICINE) a copious flow or discharge E17. **pro-form** *noun* (LINGUISTICS) a form, as a pronoun, whose reference or meaning is determined by the context. M20. **pro-ˈknock** *adjective* & *noun* (a substance) tending to cause knocking when present in the fuel burnt in an internal-combustion engine E20. **pro-ˈlife** *adjective* in favour of the maintenance of life; *spec.* against inducing abortion: M20. **pro-ˈlifer** *noun* a person with pro-life views L20. †**pronotary** *noun* = PROTONOTARY M16–E18. **proˈsiphonate** *adjective* (PALAEONTOLOGY) (of a (fossil) cephalopod shell) having the siphonal funnel directed forward M20. **pro-ˈtutor** *noun* (SCOTS LAW) a person acting as tutor or guardian to one in the state of pupillarity, though not legally appointed as such M17.

pro- /prəʊ/ *prefix*².
[Greek, from *pro* preposition, before.]
1 Before in time: forming (***a***) nouns (and derived adjectives) denoting a thing that is earlier or more primitive; (***b***) adjectives denoting earlier occurrence.
2 Before in space: forming (***a***) nouns (and derived adjectives) denoting an anterior part or an anterior thing; (***b***) adjectives denoting an anterior position.

▪ **proˈactivator** *noun* (BIOCHEMISTRY) a precursor of the activator of a compound M20. **pro-aˈnaphoral** *adjective* (CHRISTIAN CHURCH) designating the part of the Eucharist which precedes the anaphora, esp. in the Orthodox Church M19. **probaˈsidium** *noun*, pl. **-dia**, BOTANY in some basidiomycetes, a part or early stage of a basidium in which nuclear fusion takes place E20. **probiˈotic** *adjective*² = PREBIOTIC M20. **proˈcarcinogen** *noun* (MEDICINE) a substance that is not directly carcinogenic itself but is converted in the body into one that is M20. **proˌcarcinoˈgenic** *adjective* (MEDICINE) having the activity of a procarcinogen M20. **proˈchiral** *adjective* (CHEMISTRY) designating or containing a carbon atom attached to two identical and two distinct groups, and so readily forming chiral products from certain reactions M20. **prochiˈrality** *noun* (CHEMISTRY) the state of being prochiral M20. **procoˈagulant** *noun* & *adjective* (BIOCHEMISTRY) (of or pertaining to) any substance that promotes the conversion of the inactive prothrombin to the clotting enzyme thrombin M20. **proˈcoelous** *adjective* (ANATOMY & ZOOLOGY) (of vertebral centra) concave in front L19. **proˈcuticle** *noun* the inner, thicker layer of the cuticle of an arthropod, below the epicuticle M20. **proˈdelta** *adjective* & *noun* (GEOLOGY) (*a*) *adjective* lying underneath and beyond the sloping front of a delta; (*b*) *noun* the prodelta part of a delta: M20. **prodelˈtaic** *adjective* (GEOLOGY) = PRODELTA *adjective* M20. **pro-ˈethnic** *adjective* (PHILOLOGY) prior to the division of the Indo-Europeans into separate peoples or tribes M19. **profibrinoˈlysin** *noun* (BIOCHEMISTRY) = PLASMINOGEN M20. **proˈfilmic** *adjective* occurring or situated in front of a camera L20. **progenote** /-ˈdʒiːn-/ *noun* [from GENE after *prokaryote*] BIOLOGY a putative ancestor of all prokaryotes L20. **proˈglacial** *adjective* situated or occurring just beyond the edge of an ice sheet or glacier M20. **proˈhormone** *noun* a natural precursor of a hormone M20. **proˈinsulin** *noun* (BIOCHEMISTRY) the natural precursor of insulin E20. **proˈmeristem** *noun* (BOTANY) in an apical meristem, the initial cells together with their most recent derivatives L19. **proˈmyelocyte** *noun* (PHYSIOLOGY & MEDICINE) a cell intermediate in development between a myeloblast and a myelocyte E20. **proˈnotal** *adjective* of or pertaining to the pronotum L19. **proˈnotum** *noun*, pl. **-ta**, ENTOMOLOGY the dorsal part of the prothorax of an insect, completely covering the thorax in coleopterans, orthopterans, etc.: M19. **pro-ode** *noun* (*rare*) (*a*) an introductory ode in a Greek chorus; (*b*) a short verse preceding a longer one: M19. **proˈpeptide** *noun* (BIOCHEMISTRY) a peptide which is eliminated from a protein in the course of the protein's synthesis L20. **propneustic** /-ˈnjuːstɪk/ *adjective* [Greek *-pneustos* breathing] ENTOMOLOGY having only a prothoracic pair of functional spiracles E20. **proˈpodium** *noun*, pl. **-ia** /-ɪə/, ZOOLOGY in some gastropod molluscs, the anterior lobe of the foot M19. **proˈsternal** *adjective* (ENTOMOLOGY) of or pertaining to a prosternum M19. **proˈsternum** *noun*, pl. **-na**, **-nums**, ENTOMOLOGY the median ventral piece of the prothorax of an insect E19. **proˈstomial** *adjective* (ZOOLOGY) of or pertaining to a prostomium L19. **proˈstomium** *noun* (ZOOLOGY) in various invertebrates, a part of the body situated in front of the mouth L19. **proˈtheca** *noun* (ZOOLOGY) the primary wall of a foraminifer M20. **prothoˈracic** *adjective* of or pertaining to an insect's prothorax E19. **proˈthorax** *noun* the first, anterior segment of an insect's thorax E19.

proa /ˈprəʊə/ *noun*. Also ***pra(h)u*** /ˈprɑːuː/. L16.
[Malay *p(ā)rā(h)ū* boat.]
A Malay boat capable of sailing with either end first; *spec.* an undecked one with a large triangular sail and a canoe-like outrigger.

proactive /prəʊˈaktɪv/ *adjective*. M20.
[from PRO-² + ACTIVE *adjective*.]
1 PSYCHOLOGY. That affects the remembering of what is subsequently learned. Esp. in ***proactive inhibition***, the impairment of memory of some learned material or task by a condition present prior to the learning of it. M20.
2 Of a person, policy, etc.: creating or controlling a situation by taking the initiative or anticipating events; ready to take initiative, tending to make things happen. L20.

📖 **2** *NATFHE Journal* Members should take a proactive role with regard to the marketing of their college.

▪ **proactively** *adverb* L20. **proacˈtivity** *noun* proactive behaviour or practice L20.

proavis /prəʊˈeɪvɪs/ *noun*. Pl. **-aves** /-ˈeɪviːz/. E20.
[from PRO-² + Latin *avis* bird.]
PALAEONTOLOGY. A hypothetical animal forming an evolutionary link between fossil reptiles and fossil birds.
▪ **proavian** *adjective* & *noun* E20.

prob /prɒb/ *noun*. Chiefly *colloq.* Also **prob.** (point). M20.
[Abbreviation.]
A problem, a difficulty.

prob. /prɒb/ *adverb*. M18.
[Abbreviation.]
Probably. Chiefly in written English

probabilify /prɒbəˈbɪlɪfʌɪ/ *verb trans.* M20.
[from PROBABILI(TY + -FY.]
PHILOSOPHY. Give probability to; give (a proposition) reasonable grounds for being true.
▪ ˌ**probabilifiˈcation** *noun* M20.

probabiliorism /prɒbəˈbɪlɪərɪz(ə)m/ *noun*. M19.
[from Latin *probabilior* more probable, from *probabilis*: see PROBABLE, -ISM.]
PHILOSOPHY. The doctrine that the side on which the evidence preponderates is more probably right and therefore ought to be followed.
▪ **probabiliorist** *noun* an adherent of the doctrine of probabiliorism E18.

probabilism /ˈprɒbəbɪlɪz(ə)m/ *noun*. M19.
[from Latin *probabilis*: see PROBABLE, -ISM.]
1 ROMAN CATHOLIC CHURCH. The doctrine that in matters of conscience on which there is disagreement among authorities, it is lawful to follow any course in support of which the authority of a recognized doctor of the Church can be cited. M19.
2 PHILOSOPHY. The theory that there is no absolutely certain knowledge, but that there may be grounds of belief sufficient for practical life. E20.
3 PHILOSOPHY. The theory that the laws of nature are not deterministic but merely give probabilities or tendencies. M20.

probabilist /ˈprɒbəbɪlɪst/ *noun* & *adjective*. M17.
[formed as prec. + -IST.]
▸ **A** *noun*. An adherent or advocate of probabilism. M17.
▸ **B** *adjective*. Probabilistic. M20.

probabilistic /prɒbəbəˈlɪstɪk/ *adjective*. M19.
[from prec. + -IC.]
1 Pertaining to probabilists or probabilism. M19.
2 Pertaining to or expressing probability; subject to or involving chance variations or uncertainties. M20.
▪ **probabilistically** *adverb* in a probabilistic manner; in terms of probabilities: M20.

probability /prɒbəˈbɪlɪti/ *noun*. LME.
[(Old & mod. French *probabilité* from) Latin *probabilitas*, from *probabilis*: see PROBABLE, -ITY.]
1 The quality or fact of being probable; degree of likelihood; the appearance of truth, or likelihood of being realized, which a statement or event bears in the light of present evidence. LME.
2 An instance of this; a probable event, circumstance, belief, etc.; a thing judged likely to be true, to exist, or to happen. Usu. in *pl.* LME. ▸**b** *The* most probable thing. M19.
3 MATH. As a measurable quantity: the extent to which a particular event is likely to occur, or a particular situation be the case, expressed by a number between 0 and 1 and commonly estimated by the ratio of the number of favourable cases to the total number of all possible cases. E18.

📖 **1** A. STORR Protracted imprisonment actually increases the probability that subsequent offences will be committed. **in all probability** probably; considering what is probable. **2** J. A. FROUDE Wolsey's return to power was discussed openly as a probability. **b** *Financial Review (Melbourne)* The probability is that the commission will deliver another of its weasel judgements. **3** F. KEAY In throwing a . . six-sided dice, the probability of throwing a four is ⅙. ***posterior probability***: see POSTERIOR *adjective* 1. ***prior probability***: see PRIOR *adjective*.

Comb.: **probability curve** MATH. a graph of a probability distribution; **probability density** MATH. a probability distribution that is a continuous function; **probability distribution** MATH. a function whose integral over any interval is the probability that the variate specified by it will lie within that interval; **probability theory** a branch of mathematics that deals with quantities having random distributions.

probable /ˈprɒbəb(ə)l/ *adjective* & *noun*. LME.
[(Old & mod. French from) Latin *probabilis* provable, credible, from *probare* PROVE *verb*: see -ABLE.]
▸ **A** *adjective*. †**1** Worthy of acceptance or belief; (of a person) worthy of approval or trust. Also, plausible, specious. LME–L19.
2 Able to be proved; demonstrable, provable. Now *rare* or *obsolete*. LME.
3 Having an appearance of truth or fact; that may reasonably be expected to happen or be the case; likely. Also with *impers. it*, foll. by *that*. LME.

📖 **3** F. SMYTH The problem of fixing the probable time of death. J. G. BALLARD It seems probable that the kidnappers intended to shoot . . us.

Special collocations: **probable cause** (now US LAW) reasonable cause or grounds (for making a search, preferring a charge, etc.). **probable error** STATISTICS the difference between the mean of a distribution and the first or third quartiles, i.e. an error of such a magnitude that larger and smaller errors are equally likely (now largely superseded by the standard error).

▸ **B** *noun*. †**1** A probable event or circumstance. M–L17.
2 A person who will probably, though not certainly, be successful; a likely candidate, competitor, etc.; *spec.* a member of the supposedly stronger team in a trial match. E20.
3 MILITARY. An aircraft recorded as probably shot down; a submarine probably destroyed. M20.
▪ **probableness** *noun* LME.

probably /ˈprɒbəbli/ *adverb*. LME.
[from prec. + -LY².]
1 In a way that commends itself to one's reason for acceptance or belief; with likelihood. Now *rare*. LME.
2 Qualifying a clause or sentence: as is likely; so far as the evidence goes; most likely; (introducing a sentence) it is likely that; (as a sentence) that is likely. E17.

📖 **1** GOLDSMITH Thirty men only, as Nepos says; but, as Xenophon more probably says . . near seventy. **2** D. H. LAWRENCE Probably she suffered more than he did. V. WOOLF A steamer, probably bound for Cardiff, now crosses the horizon. DAY LEWIS 'Has he got it here?' 'Probably'. J. MITCHELL This was probably a covered way between the main house and the outbuildings.

†**probal** *adjective*. *rare* (Shakes.). Only in E17.
[Origin uncertain: perh. alt. of PROBABLE.]
Worthy of acceptance or belief.

proband /ˈprəʊband/ *noun.* E20.
[Latin *probandus* gerundive of *probare* PROVE *verb*: see -AND.]
MEDICINE & GENETICS. An individual chosen as a propositus because of the presence of some trait whose inheritance is to be studied.

probang /ˈprəʊbaŋ/ *noun.* Now *rare.* Orig. †**prov-**. M17.
[Origin unkn.: prob. altered after *probe*.]
MEDICINE. A long slender strip of flexible material with a sponge or the like at the end, used to remove a foreign body from the throat or apply a medication to it.

probate /ˈprəʊbeɪt, -bət/ *noun.* LME.
[Latin *probatum* thing proved, use as noun of neut. pa. pple of *probare* PROVE *verb*: see -ATE¹.]
1 LAW. The official proving of a will. Also, the officially verified copy of the will together with the certificate of its having been proved, as delivered to the executors. LME.
†**2** The action of proving something; the fact of being proved; proof; evidence. LME–M19.
Comb.: **probate court**: having jurisdiction of probate, administration, and other testamentary matters.

probate /ˈprəʊbeɪt/ *verb trans.* Pa. pple **-ated**, †**-ate**. L15.
[Latin *probat-* pa. ppl stem of *probare*: see prec., -ATE³. In sense 3 back-form. from next.]
†**1** Prove, demonstrate. *rare.* L15–E17.
2 Obtain probate of, prove, (a will). Now *N. Amer.* L18.
3 Place (a person) on probation; reduce (a sentence) by placing the convicted person on probation. *US.* M20.

probation /prəˈbeɪʃ(ə)n/ *noun.* LME.
[(Old & mod. French from) Latin *probatio(n-)*, formed as prec.: see -ATION.]
► **I 1** The testing of the character, conduct, or abilities of a person, esp. one who has provisionally joined a religious body or a company; a period allocated for this; CHRISTIAN THEOLOGY moral trial or discipline, esp. as taking place in this life preparatory to a future life. LME. ►†**b** *gen.* The action or process of putting something to the test; trial, experiment; investigation, examination. LME–M19. ►†**c** (A) surgical examination with a probe. LME–L17. ►**d** The examining of students for proficiency; a school or college examination. Now *US.* E18.
2 LAW. A system of suspending the sentence on an offender subject to a period of good behaviour under the supervision of a person appointed for the purpose. L19.

🕮 **1** D. CECIL Clerks were only paid a proper salary after . . three years of probation.

► **II 3** †**a** Evidence, proof. Chiefly *Scot.* LME–M18. ►**b** The action or an act of showing something to be true; (a) proof, (a) demonstration. *obsolete* exc. *Scot.* L15. ►†**c** The proving of a will, probate. Only in 16.
Comb. & phrases: **on probation** undergoing probation, *spec.* as an offender; **probation officer** an official who supervises an offender on probation; **probation order** a court order committing an offender to a period of probation; **probation service** a service responsible for the supervision of offenders on probation and the care of accused people and discharged prisoners.
■ **probational** *adjective* = PROBATIONARY *adjective* 1 M17. **probationship** *noun* (*rare*) the state or condition of probation; a term or period of probation: E17.

probationary /prəˈbeɪʃ(ə)n(ə)ri/ *adjective & noun.* M17.
[from prec. + -ARY¹.]
► **A** *adjective.* **1** Of, pertaining to, or of the nature of probation. M17.
2 Undergoing probation; consisting of probationers. E19.

🕮 **1** P. DICKINSON We might both regard the arrangement as probationary. **2** M. BANTON A number of new recruits (probationary constables).

► **B** *noun.* A probationer. *rare.* M18.

probationer /prəˈbeɪʃ(ə)nə/ *noun.* M16.
[formed as prec. + -ER¹.]
1 A person placed on probation to test his or her suitability for something, esp. a job or the ministry of some non-episcopal Churches; a recently appointed person yet to be confirmed or fully trained, esp. in the teaching and nursing professions. M16.
2 An offender placed on probation. E20.
■ **probationership** *noun* the position or condition of a probationer M17.

probative /ˈprəʊbətɪv/ *adjective.* LME.
[Latin *probativus*, formed as PROBATE *verb*: see -IVE.]
1 Having the quality or function of testing. Now *rare.* LME.
2 Having the quality or function of proving or demonstrating something; affording proof; evidential. L17.

🕮 **2** R. C. A. WHITE Judges have a discretion to exclude evidence the prejudicial effect of which . . outweighs its probative value.

■ **probatively** *adverb* in a probative manner; by way of proof: M19. **probativeness** *noun* E20.

probatory /ˈprəʊbət(ə)ri/ *adjective.* Now *rare.* L16.
[medieval Latin *probatorius*, formed as prec.: see -ORY².]
= PROBATIVE.

†**probatum** *noun.* L16.
[Latin: see PROBATE *noun*.]
1 A thing proved or demonstrated; *esp.* a means or remedy found to be effective. L16–M17.
2 A seal of approval, a recommendation. M17–M18.

probe /prəʊb/ *noun.* LME.
[Late Latin *proba* proof, (in medieval Latin) examination, from Latin *probare* PROVE *verb*.]
► **I 1** A slender blunt-ended surgical instrument, usu. of metal, for exploring wounds, sinuses, and other body cavities. LME.
2 An electrode or other small device placed in or on something to obtain and relay information or measurements about it, or excite radiation in it. E20. ►**b** NUCLEAR PHYSICS. A subatomic particle which can be used to penetrate nuclei, atoms, etc., to provide information about their internal structure. M20.
3 AERONAUTICS & ASTRONAUTICS. A tube on an aircraft's nose or wing which is fitted into the drogue of a tanker aircraft in order to take on fuel from it in aerial refuelling; a projecting device on a spacecraft designed to engage with the drogue of another craft during docking. M20.
4 More fully ***space probe***. An unmanned spacecraft (other than an earth satellite) for transmitting information about its environment; a rocket or an instrument capsule for obtaining measurements in the upper atmosphere. M20.
► **II** [from the verb.]
5 An act of probing; *Scot.* a prod, a jab. LME.
6 A penetrating investigation or inquiry. E20.

🕮 **5** *Icarus* A radar probe of the Martian surface. **6** *Oxford Journal* Amateur sleuths . . launched a top-level probe into an Oxford business.

probe /prəʊb/ *verb.* M17.
[from the noun; occas. infl. by Latin *probare* PROVE *verb*.]
1 *verb trans.* Examine or look into closely, esp. in order to discover something; investigate; interrogate closely. M17.
2 *verb trans.* Explore (a wound etc.) with a probe; examine (a person) with a probe. L17.
3 *verb trans.* Pierce or penetrate with something sharp, esp. in order to test or explore. L18.
4 *verb intrans.* Perform the action of piercing with or as with a probe; ask searching questions; look closely *into.* M19.

🕮 **1** T. ROETHKE Let others probe the mystery if they can. D. ARKELL A period of intense letter-writing, during which they endlessly probed one another's characters. **4** A. J. CRONIN Christine probed amongst the dust and cobwebs. R. MACAULAY The police probed into their past lives. D. LEAVITT She wanted to probe more deeply, to learn more about Nathan.

■ **probeable** *adjective* able to be probed M20. **prober** *noun* L19. **probing** *ppl adjective* that probes; piercing, penetrating: L18. **probingly** *adverb* L19. **probingness** *noun* E19.

probenecid /prəʊˈbɛnɪsɪd/ *noun.* M20.
[from PRO(PYL + BEN(ZOIC + *-e-* + A)CID *noun*.]
PHARMACOLOGY. A uricosuric agent used esp. to treat gout.

probie *noun* var. of PROBY.

probit /ˈprəʊbɪt/ *noun.* M20.
[from PROB(ABILITY + UNIT *noun*¹.]
STATISTICS. The unit which forms the scale into which percentages may be transformed so that data evenly distributed between 0 and 100 per cent become normally distributed with a standard deviation of one. Chiefly in ***probit analysis***, the technique of using probits in statistical analysis.

probity /ˈprəʊbɪti, ˈprɒb-/ *noun.* LME.
[(French *probité* from) Latin *probitas*, from *probus* good, honest: see -ITY.]
Integrity, uprightness of character; conscientiousness, honesty, sincerity.

problem /ˈprɒbləm/ *noun.* LME.
[(Old & mod. French *problème* from) Latin *problema* from Greek *problēma*, from *proballein* put forth, formed as PRO-² + *ballein* throw.]
1 A puzzle, a riddle. Long *obsolete* exc. as below. LME.
2 A question proposed for academic discussion or scholastic disputation. Long *obsolete* exc. *Hist.* LME. ►**b** LOGIC. The question (usu. only implied) involved in a syllogism, of which the conclusion is the solution. M17.
3 A doubtful or difficult matter; a matter that exercises the mind. LME. ►**b** Usu. with preceding noun or adjective: a seemingly insoluble quandary affecting a specified group of people or a nation; a long-standing personal difficulty. E20.
4 A contrived or imagined situation in which the task is to produce or prove some specified result by the exercise of thought, esp. in mathematics or chess. L16.
5 SCIENCE. An inquiry starting from given conditions to investigate or demonstrate some fact, result, or law. L16.

🕮 **3** T. S. ELIOT The problem with Lucasta Is how to keep her fed between meals. LYNDON B. JOHNSON One of the most pressing problems was a stagnant economy. D. ROWE Listening to his friends . . telling him about their problems. M. HUGHES The problem lay in explaining her presence on Floor One. **b** *Time* What Nazis call 'the biggest library in the world dealing exclusively with the Jewish problem'. *Guardian* One of the reasons for Britain's housing problem. R. INGALLS Gina . . was worried about her daughter's weight problem. **5** ***Delian problem***, ***four-colour problem***, ***Kepler's problem***, ***three-body problem***, etc.

Phrases: ***Indian problem***: see INDIAN *adjective*. **no problem** *colloq.* (that is) simple or easy. **that's your problem**, **that's his problem**, etc.: said to disclaim responsibility or connection. ***travelling salesman problem***: see TRAVELLING *ppl adjective*.
Attrib. & comb.: In the sense 'in which a problem is treated or discussed', as **problem column**, **problem page**, **problem story**; in the sense 'in which problems of a personal or social character are manifested', as **problem child**, **problem family**. Special combs., as **problem-oriented** *adjective* (COMPUTING) (of a programming language) devised in the light of the requirements of a certain class of problem.
■ **problematist** *noun* a problemist M17. **problematiˈzation** *noun* the action of problematizing something L20. **problematize** *verb* †(*a*) *verb intrans.* (*rare*) propound problems; (*b*) *verb trans.* make a problem of, view as a problem requiring solution: M17. **problemist** *noun* a person who devotes himself or herself to problems; *esp.* a composer of chess problems: E17. **problemless** *adjective* unaffected by problems, presenting no problems E20.

problematic /prɒbləˈmatɪk/ *adjective & noun.* E17.
[(French *problématique* from) late Latin *problematicus* from Greek *problēmatikos*, from *problēma*: see prec., -ATIC.]
► **A** *adjective.* **1** Of the nature of a problem; constituting or presenting a problem; difficult of solution or decision; uncertain, questionable. E17.
2 LOGIC. Of a proposition: asserting that something is possible as opp. to actual or necessary. E17.
3 Of or pertaining to chess problems. L19.

🕮 **1** I. MURDOCH The concept of a personal God began to seem to her more and more problematic. R. SCRUTON If form and content always change together, it seems problematic to claim . . they are distinct. *Times* The company is . . considering the disposal of its problematic United States operations.

► **B** *noun.* A thing that constitutes a problem or an area of difficulty in a particular field of study. Freq. in *pl.* M20.
■ **problematical** *adjective* †(*a*) of the nature of a scholastic problem; (*b*) = PROBLEMATIC *adjective* 1, 2: L16. **problematically** *adverb* in a problematic manner; in the form of a problem; doubtfully: L16. **problematicalness** *noun* M20.

problematique /prɒbləməˈtiːk, *foreign* prɔblematik/ *noun.* Also ***problématique*** /prɔblematik/. L20.
[French: see PROBLEMATIC.]
The problematic area of a subject etc.; *spec.* environmental and other global problems collectively.

probosces *noun pl.* see PROBOSCIS.

proboscidal /prəʊˈbɒsɪd(ə)l/ *adjective. rare.* M19.
[from Latin *proboscid-*, PROBOSCIS + -AL¹.]
Having the nature or appearance of a proboscis.

†**proboscide** *noun.* E17–E18.
[French, formed as prec.]
A heraldic charge representing an elephant's trunk.

proboscidean /prɒbəˈsɪdɪən/ *adjective & noun.* Also **-ian**. M19.
[from mod. Latin *Proboscidea* neut. pl., name of order, formed as PROBOSCIDAL: see -EAN, -IAN.]
► **A** *adjective.* **1** Of or belonging to the mammalian order Proboscidea, which includes elephants and related extinct animals. M19.
2 Having a proboscis. M19.
3 Of, pertaining to, or resembling a proboscis. L19.
► **B** *noun.* A mammal of the order Proboscidea. M19.

proboscides *noun pl.* see PROBOSCIS.

proboscidiferous /prə(ʊ)ˌbɒsɪˈdɪf(ə)rəs/ *adjective.* E19.
[formed as PROBOSCIDAL + -I- + -FEROUS.]
Having a proboscis.

proboscidiform /prɒbəˈsɪdɪfɔːm/ *adjective.* M19.
[formed as prec. + -I- + -FORM.]
Having the form or shape of a proboscis.

proboscis /prə(ʊ)ˈbɒsɪs/ *noun.* Pl. **-sces** /-siːz/, **-scides** /-sɪdiːz/, **-scises**. E17.
[Latin from Greek *proboskis* lit. 'means of providing food', formed as PRO-² + *boskein* (cause to) feed.]
1 An elephant's trunk; the long flexible snout of some other mammals, e.g. the tapir and the proboscis monkey. E17.
2 A person's nose. *joc.* M17.
3 An elongated, often tubular and flexible, mouth part of many insects; an extensible tubular sucking organ in some worms. M17.
Comb.: **proboscis monkey** a large leaf-monkey, *Nasalis larvatus*, of Borneo, the male of which has a long pendulous nose.

probouleutic /prəʊbuːˈl(j)uːtɪk/ *adjective.* M19.
[from PRO-[2] + Greek *bouleutikos* deliberative, from *boulē* council: see -IC. Cf. Greek *probouleuein* pass a preliminary decree.]
That deliberates preliminarily; *spec.* (GREEK HISTORY) designating the Athenian council which discussed measures before they were submitted to the general Assembly.

proby /ˈprəʊbi/ *noun. colloq.* Also **-ie**. L19.
[from PROB(ATIONER + -Y[6], -IE.]
A probationer; *spec.* (US) a fire-fighter undergoing probation.

†**procaccio** *noun.* Pl. **-os**. M17–M19.
[Italian, lit. 'purveying, procuring'.]
In Italy = CARRIER 2; a carrier's vehicle.

procacious /prəˈkeɪʃəs/ *adjective.* Now *rare.* M17.
[from Latin *procac-*, *procax* bold + -OUS.]
Forward, insolent, pert.

procacity /prəˈkasɪti/ *noun.* Now *rare.* E17.
[(French †*procacité* from) Latin *procacitas*, formed as prec.: see -ITY.]
Forwardness, insolence, pertness.

procaine /ˈprəʊkeɪn/ *noun.* Also **-cain**. E20.
[from PRO-[1] + -CAINE.]
PHARMACOLOGY. A synthetic derivative of benzoic acid, used as a local anaesthetic; 2-diethylaminoethyl *p*-aminobenzoate, $NH_2C_6H_4{\cdot}COO{\cdot}C_2H_4N(C_2H_5)_2$.
Comb.: **procaine penicillin** an insoluble salt of procaine and benzylpenicillin which releases penicillin slowly after intramuscular injection.
¶ A proprietary name for this drug is NOVOCAIN.
■ **proˈcainamide** *noun* an amide used in cardiac therapy, esp. to control arrhythmia M20.

procambium /prəʊˈkambɪəm/ *noun.* L19.
[mod. Latin, formed as PRO-[2] + CAMBIUM.]
BOTANY. The young tissue of an apical meristem, usu. composed of elongated cells, which differentiates into the primary vascular tissue.
■ **procambial** *adjective* L19.

procarbazine /prəʊˈkɑːbəziːn/ *noun.* M20.
[from PRO(PYL + CARB(AMIC + HYDR)AZINE.]
PHARMACOLOGY. A hydrazine derivative used to treat some neoplastic diseases, esp. Hodgkin's disease.

procarp /ˈprəʊkɑːp/ *noun.* L19.
[mod. Latin *procarpium*, formed as PRO-[2] + Greek *karpos* fruit.]
BOTANY. In a red alga, a carpogonium when associated with auxiliary cells as part of a common branch system.

procaryotic *adjective* var. of PROKARYOTIC.

†**procatarctic** *adjective.* E17.
[mod. Latin *procatarcticus* from Greek *prokatarktikos* antecedent, from *prokatarkhein* begin first, from *arkhein* begin: see PRO-[2], CATA-, -IC.]
1 Designating an immediate or exciting cause, esp. of a disease. E17–E19.
2 Designating a primary cause. M17–E18.

procédé /prɔsede/ *noun.* Pl. pronounced same. L19.
[French.]
Manner of proceeding; a method, a procedure, a process.

procedendo /prəʊsɪˈdɛndəʊ/ *noun.* Pl. **-os**. LME.
[Latin (*de*) *procedendo* (*ad judicium*) of proceeding (to judgement), abl. gerund of *procedere* PROCEED *verb*.]
LAW (now *Hist.*). A writ commanding a subordinate court to proceed to judgement, either when judgement had been wrongfully delayed or when the action had been removed to a superior court on insufficient grounds. Also ***procedendo ad judicium*** /ad juːˈdɪkɪəm/.

procedural /prəˈsiːdʒ(ə)r(ə)l/ *adjective.* L19.
[from next + -AL[1].]
1 Of or pertaining to procedure. L19.
2 COMPUTING. Designating programming languages in which the procedure to be followed is specified, rather than the desired result. L20.
■ **procedurally** *adverb* M20.

procedure /prəˈsiːdʒə/ *noun.* L16.
[Old & mod. French *procédure*, from *procéder* PROCEED *verb*: see -URE.]
► **I 1** The fact or manner of proceeding; a system of proceeding; conduct, behaviour; *spec.* (**a**) LAW the formal steps to be taken in a legal action; the mode of conducting judicial proceedings; (**b**) POLITICS the mode of conducting business in Parliament. L16.
2 A particular mode or course of action, a proceeding. M19. ▸**b** COMPUTING. A set of instructions for performing a specific task which may be invoked in the course of a program; a subroutine. M20.

> 🕮 **1** *Times* The collective dispute procedure had been agreed nationally. B. CHATWIN The procedure was to go to your usual physician. **2** P. QUILLIN Most surgical procedures and drugs . . carry with them . . hazards and side-effects. D. LEAVITT Late in the pregnancy, the procedure was painful and complicated.

► **II** †**3** Proceeds, produce. Only in E17.
4 The fact of proceeding *from* a source; origination. *rare.* M17.
†**5** Continuance or progress *of* something. M17–E18.

proceed /ˈprəʊsiːd/ *noun.* LME.
[from the verb.]
†**1** The action or manner of proceeding; a proceeding, a procedure. LME–L17.
2 In *pl.* & †*sing.* Money produced or gained by a transaction or undertaking, profit; an outcome, a result. E17.

> 🕮 **2** V. S. PRITCHETT The estate should be sold and the proceeds invested in securities.

proceed /prəˈsiːd/ *verb.* LME.
[Old & mod. French *procéder* from Latin *procedere*, formed as PRO-[1] + *cedere* go.]
1 *verb intrans.* Go or travel forward, esp. after stopping or after reaching a certain point; resume one's movement or travel. LME.
2 *verb intrans.* Carry on, continue, or resume an activity or action, esp. in a specified manner (foll. by *with* the activity); *spec.* (without *with*) continue or resume speaking; adopt a course of action. LME. ▸**b** Go on *to do*; advance *to* another action, subject, etc.; pass on from one point to another in a series. LME. ▸†**c** Argue, debate. *rare.* LME–E18. ▸**d** Deal *with*; act in some way, esp. judicially, with regard to. Now chiefly, institute legal action, take legal proceedings, (*against*). LME. ▸**e** Carry on an action to a particular point; make some progress. Now *rare* exc. as passing into sense 2. M16. ▸†**f** Get on; prosper, fare. L16–L18.
3 a *verb intrans.* Of an action, process, etc.: be carried on, take place; continue. LME. ▸†**b** *verb trans.* Cause to proceed; carry on, carry forward. LME–L18.
4 *verb intrans.* Go or come *from* or *out of*; arise, originate, result, be derived, (*from*). Formerly also, happen *that* or *to*. LME. ▸**b** *spec.* Be the descendant *of*; be descended *from*. Long *rare* or *obsolete*. L15.
5 *verb intrans.* (foll. by *to* or with compl.). Advance in a university course from a first degree to a second or higher one; (now *rare* or *obsolete*) in the Inns of Court, advance or be admitted to the status of a barrister. LME. ▸†**b** *verb trans.* Advance to the status of, develop into. L16–E18.

> 🕮 **1** G. GREENE After a short . . conversation they proceeded . . to a quiet and secluded restaurant. **2** SHAKES. *L.L.L.* The conqueror is dismay'd. Proceed, good Alexander. L. STEFFENS The man proceeded with his work quickly . . without fear or pity. W. GOLDING I decided I must proceed on the principle of the use of *least force*. **b** D. BREWSTER From the globular clusters of stars our author proceeds to the binary systems. *Scotsman* Banks are lending too much money to their customers who proceed to spend it. **d** *Observer* The authorities empowered to proceed against litterers. **3a** G. B. SHAW The further municipalization of the gas industry is proceeding with great rapidity. R. GRAVES As the history proceeds the reader will be . . ready to believe . . I am hiding nothing. **4** J. G. COOPER Despair . . proceeds From loosen'd thoughts, and impious deeds. A. JESSOPP The most sumptuous work that has ever proceeded from the Cambridge Press.

■ **proceeder** *noun* a person who proceeds LME.

proceeding /prəˈsiːdɪŋ/ *noun.* LME.
[from prec. + -ING[1].]
1 The action of PROCEED *verb*; onward movement; conduct, behaviour. LME.
†**2** A company of people marching along in regular order; (a) procession. LME–E18.
3 In *pl.* & †*sing.* The fact or manner of taking legal action; a legal action; an act done by authority of a court of law; a step taken by a party in a case. LME.
4 A particular action or course of action; a piece of conduct or behaviour. In *pl.*, doings, actions; the business transacted by a court, assembly, or society; *esp.* a published record of papers delivered at a meeting of a learned society or a conference. M16.

> 🕮 **1** S. PEPYS The manner of my friend's proceeding with me. **3** A. J. AYER To marry her as soon as the divorce proceedings . . were completed. **4** B. WEBB The meeting turned out to be a useless and painful proceeding. F. L. WRIGHT Only . . one proceeding which can rid the city of its congestion. R. CHRISTIANSEN The proceedings of the Revolutionary Tribunal.

proceleusmatic /ˌprɒsɪljuːsˈmatɪk/ *noun & adjective.* M18.
[Late Latin *proceleusmaticus* from Greek *prokeleusmatikos*, from *prokeleusmat-*, *-ma* incitement, from *prokeleuein* incite: see -IC.]
► **A** *noun.* PROSODY. A proceleusmatic foot. M18.
► **B** *adjective.* †**1** Arousing enthusiasm, animating. Only in L18.
2 PROSODY. Designating, pertaining to, or containing a metrical foot of four short syllables. E19.

procello *noun* see PUCELLAS.

†**procellous** *adjective.* M17–M19.
[from French †*procelleux* from Latin *procellosus*, from *procella* storm: see -OUS.]
Stormy.

procerity /prəʊˈsɛrɪti/ *noun.* Now *rare.* M16.
[(French †*procérité* from) Latin *proceritas*, from *procerus* tall, high: see -ITY.]
Tallness, loftiness, height; length.

process /ˈprəʊsɛs/ *noun.* ME.
[Old & mod. French *procès* from Latin *processus*, from *process-* pa. ppl stem of *procedere* PROCEED *verb*.]
1 The action or fact of going on or being carried on; progress, course; PHILOSOPHY the course of becoming as opp. to being. Now chiefly in ***in process***, ***in process of***, ***in the process of*** below. ME.
2 Passage or lapse *of* time, seasons, etc. Chiefly in ***by process of time***, ***in process of time*** below. ME.
†**3 a** A narration, a story, a play; a discourse, a treatise; an argument, a discussion. Also, a passage of a discourse. ME–L18. ▸**b** The course of a narrative, treatise, argument, etc.; drift, tenor, gist. ME–M17.
4 A thing that goes on or is carried on; a continuous series of actions, events, or changes; a course of action, a procedure; *esp.* a continuous and regular action or succession of actions occurring or performed in a definite manner; a systematic series of actions or operations directed to some end, as in manufacturing, printing, photography, etc. ME. ▸**b** A method of straightening and styling the hair by chemical means; hair so treated; the chemicals used. *US Black English.* M20.
5 a LAW. (The proceedings in) an action at law; *spec.* a mandate, summons, or writ by which a person or thing is brought to court for litigation. ME. ▸†**b** A formal command or edict issued by a person in authority. *rare* (Shakes.). Only in E17.
6 †**a** Onward movement in space. LME–L19. ▸**b** Progress to a better or more advanced state. Now *rare.* M17. ▸†**c** Degree of progress. *rare.* M17–L18.
7 The action of proceeding from a source, emanation. Cf. PROCESSION *noun* 3a. *rare.* M16.
8 Chiefly ANATOMY, ZOOLOGY, & BOTANY. A projection from the main body of something; an outgrowth, a protuberance, esp. of a bone. L16.

> 🕮 **1** *Guardian* The process of government in Northern Ireland. S. HASTINGS In the process of writing a novel, she discussed every stage with him. **4** J. TYNDALL Explained to me the process of making cheese. B. STEWART Ice is not instantly converted into water but the process is gradual. W. TREVOR He felt himself dying, a process which began below and overcame his body. J. BRIGGS Edith wrote . . ghost stories, and sometimes frightened herself in the process. ***batch process***, ***Bessemer process***, ***Markov process***, ***three-colour process***, etc. **8** ***coronoid process***, ***odontoid process***, ***transverse process***, etc.

Phrases: †**by process of time** = *in process of time* below. **due process (of law)**: see DUE *adjective* 2. **final process**: see FINAL *adjective*. ILLICIT **process**. **in process** going on, being done. **in process of** = *in the course of* s.v. COURSE *noun*[1]. **in process of time** as time goes on, in the course of time. **in the process of** = *in the course of* s.v. COURSE *noun*[1]. **mesne process**: see MESNE *adjective* 1. **process of** EXCLUSION(S).
Attrib. & comb.: With ref. to printing other than by hand engraving, as **process lens**, **process reproduction**, **process work**; with ref. to colour printing in which a wide continuous range of colours is produced by superimposing halftones in each of three or four different colours, as **process ink**, **process printing**, etc.; with ref. to industrial processes, esp. continuous ones (as opp. to batch processes), as **process engineering**, **process operation**, **process work**, etc. Special combs., as **process annealing** METALLURGY heat treatment applied to an alloy after cold working to prepare it for further cold working; **process black** a black printing ink suitable for use in process work; **process camera**: designed for taking photographs for use in process work; **process chart**: showing the sequence and sometimes the time and place of the different stages in an industrial or commercial process, or the different activities performed by an employee; **process cheese** = *processed cheese* s.v. PROCESS *verb*[1] 2; **process control** the regulation and control of the physical aspects of an industrial process, esp. automatically by instruments; **process heat**: supplied or required for an industrial process; **process projection** CINEMATOGRAPHY projection on to the back of a translucent screen, the front of which is used as a background for ordinary filming; **process-paid** *adjective* (of film) sold with the cost of developing and printing included in the price; **process schizophrenia** endogenous schizophrenia that does not seem connected with environmental causes; **process server** a sheriff's officer who serves processes or summonses; a bailiff; **process shot** CINEMATOGRAPHY: taken using process projection; **process steam**: supplied or required for an industrial process other than power generation; **process water**: used in an industrial process.
■ **proˈcessal** *adjective* (*rare*) pertaining to a legal process M17.

process /ˈprəʊsɛs/ *verb*[1]. M16.
[Sense 1 from Old French *processer*, formed as prec.; sense 2 from prec.]
1 *verb trans.* Institute a legal action against, sue, prosecute; obtain a summons against; serve a process on. Chiefly *Scot.* Now *rare.* M16.
2 *verb trans.* Subject to or treat by a process or in a processor; *spec.* (**a**) reproduce (a drawing etc.) by a mechanical or photographic process; (**b**) preserve (food) by some process; (**c**) operate on (data) using a computer; (**d**) purée or liquidize (food) in a food processor. L19. ▸**b** Subject (a

person) to a process, e.g. of registration, examination, or analysis. Orig. *US*. M20.

> 2 B. PYM Fresh vegetables .. would be better than processed peas. *Photographer* I can process a batch of E6 film almost immediately after shooting. *Which?* 11 or 12 weeks for a passport application to be processed. **processed cheese**: made by melting, blending, and freq. emulsifying other cheeses.

■ **processable** *adjective* able to be processed M20. **processa'bility** *noun* the capacity to be processed M20.

process /prə'sɛs/ *verb*². E19.
[Back-form. from next.]
1 *verb intrans.* Go, walk, or march in procession. E19.
2 *verb trans.* Lead or carry in procession; go along or through in procession. M20.

procession /prə'sɛʃ(ə)n/ *noun & verb*. LOE.
[Old & mod. French from Latin *processio(n-)*, from *process-*: see PROCESS *noun*, -ION.]
▶**A** *noun*. **1** The action of a number of people going along in orderly succession in a formal or ceremonial way, esp. at a ceremony, demonstration, or festivity; a similar movement by boats or vehicles. Chiefly in ***in procession***. LOE. ▶**b** *CRICKET*. A rapid succession of batsmen; a batting collapse. L19.
2 A number of people, vehicles, etc., going in procession; *transf.* & *fig.* a regular succession of things. ME.
3 a Chiefly *CHRISTIAN THEOLOGY*. The action of proceeding from a source, emanation, esp. of the Holy Spirit. Cf. PROCESS *noun* 7. LME. ▶**b** The action of proceeding or advancing; onward movement, progression, advance. Now *rare* or *obsolete* exc. as passing into sense 1. L16.
4 *ECCLESIASTICAL HISTORY*. A litany, prayer, or office, said or sung in a religious procession. M16.

> 2 W. S. CHURCHILL A procession of wars which had lasted for thirty years. S. WEINTRAUB The procession, from Buckingham Palace .. to Westminster Abbey.

▶**B** *verb*. **1** *verb trans*. Celebrate (a saint etc.) by a procession; carry (an image etc.) in procession. M16.
2 *verb intrans*. Make a procession, go in procession; *spec*. perambulate boundaries. L16.
3 *verb trans*. Go round in procession; *spec*. (*US HISTORY*) perambulate (a piece of land, a boundary). Also, walk along (a street etc.) in procession. E18.
■ **processioner** *noun* (*a*) orig., a person going in procession; now *spec*. (*US HISTORY*) an official responsible for perambulating boundaries; †(*b*) *ECCLESIASTICAL* = PROCESSIONAL *noun* 1: LME. **processionist** *noun* a person who goes in a procession E19. **processionize** *verb intrans*. go in procession L18.

processional /prə'sɛʃ(ə)n(ə)l/ *noun & adjective*. LME.
[As noun from medieval Latin *processionale* use as noun of neut. of *processionalis*. As adjective from medieval Latin *processionalis*, from Latin *processio(n-)*: see prec., -AL¹.]
▶**A** *noun*. **1** *ECCLESIASTICAL*. A book containing litanies, hymns, etc., for use in religious processions. LME.
2 A processional hymn. L19.
3 A procession. L19.
▶**B** *adjective*. **1** Used, carried, or sung in processions; (of a road, route, etc.) traversed by a procession or processions. M16.
2 Of, pertaining to, or of the nature of a procession; characterized by processions. E17.
3 Walking or going in procession, forming a procession; *joc.* forming a long line. M19.
■ **processionally** *adverb* in a processional manner; in procession: LME.

processionary /prə'sɛʃ(ə)n(ə)ri/ *adjective*. L16.
[medieval Latin *processionarius*, from Latin *processio(n-)*: see PROCESSION, -ARY¹.]
1 = PROCESSIONAL *adjective*. *obsolete* exc. as in sense 2. L16.
2 Designating caterpillars which move *en masse*; designating a moth which has such caterpillars, esp. one of the family Thaumetopoeidae. M18.

processive /prə'sɛsɪv/ *adjective*. *rare*. E17.
[from PROCEED *verb*, PROCESSION, after *recede*, *recession*, *recessive*, perh. infl. by *progressive*: see -IVE.]
†**1** Of the nature of a legal process; serving to initiate legal proceedings. Only in E17.
2 Having the quality of proceeding; progressive. E19.

processor /'prəʊsɛsə/ *noun*. E20.
[from PROCESS *noun*, *verb*¹ + -OR.]
A machine, organization, or person that performs a process or processes things; *spec*. (*a*) a central processing unit; (*b*) a food processor.
data processor, ***food processor***, ***list processor***, ***text processor***, ***word processor***, etc.

processual /prə'sɛsjʊəl/ *adjective*. L19.
[from Latin *processus* PROCESS *noun* + -AL¹.]
1 *ROMAN LAW*. Pertaining to a legal process, procedural. Now *rare*. L19.
2 Pertaining to a social or linguistic process. M20.

procès-verbal /prɒsɛvɛrbal, prɒseɪvə:'bɑ:l/ *noun*. Pl. ***-baux*** /-bo, -bəʊ/. M17.
[French.]
A detailed written report of proceedings; minutes; an authenticated written statement of facts in support of a charge.

prochain /'prɒʃeɪn/ *adjective*. Also **-ein**. L15.
[French, from *proche* near from Latin *propius*: see APPROACH *verb*.]
Neighbouring, nearest, next. Long *obsolete* exc. as below.
prochain ami /a'mi:/ *LAW* = ***next friend*** s.v. NEXT *adjective*.

prochloraz /prəʊ'klɔ:raz/ *noun*. L20.
[from PRO-¹ + CHLOR-¹ + IMID)AZ(OLE.]
An imidazole derivative used as a systemic fungicide.

prochlorophyte /prəʊ'klɔ:rəfʌɪt/ *noun*. L20.
[from PRO-² + mod. Latin *Prochlorophyta* (see below), formed as PRO-² + CHLORO-¹ + -PHYTE.]
BIOLOGY. Any prokaryote of the division Prochlorophyta, characterized by the presence of two types of chlorophyll and the absence of phycobilins (and so resembling the chloroplasts of higher plants).

prochlorperazine /prəʊklɔ:'pɛrəzi:n/ *noun*. M20.
[from PRO(PYL + CHLOR-¹ + PI)PERAZINE.]
PHARMACOLOGY. A phenothiazine derivative used as a tranquillizer.

prochronism /'prəʊkrənɪz(ə)m/ *noun*. M17.
[from PRO-² + Greek *khronos* time + -ISM. Cf. ANACHRONISM.]
An error in chronology consisting in placing an event earlier than its real date (opp. METACHRONISM 1). Cf. PARACHRONISM.

procidentia /prəʊsɪ'dɛnʃɪə/ *noun*. Also Anglicized as **procidence** /'prəʊsɪd(ə)ns, 'prɒs-/ E17.
[mod. Latin from (French *procidence* from) Latin *procidentia*, from *procidere* fall forward, formed as PRO-¹ + *cadere* fall: see -ENCE.]
MEDICINE. Prolapse, *esp*. severe prolapse of the uterus.

†**procinct** *noun*¹. LME–E19.
[medieval Latin *procinctus* for *praecinctum* PRECINCT *noun*.]
= PRECINCT *noun* 1, 2, 3.

†**procinct** *noun*² & *adjective*. M16–M19.
[Latin *procinctus* verbal noun & ppl adjective of *procingere* gird up, equip, formed as PRO-¹ + *cingere* gird.]
▶**A** *noun*. Readiness for action. Only in ***in procinct***, in readiness, ready, prepared, (foll. by *of*). M16–M19.
▶**B** *adjective*. Ready, prepared. E17–L18.

Procion /'prəʊsɪən/ *noun*. M20.
[Origin unkn.]
(Proprietary name for) any of a large class of reactive dyestuffs based on 1,3,5-triazine and covering a wide range of colours. Chiefly in ***Procion dye***.

†**proclaim** *noun*. *rare*. LME–E19.
[from the verb.]
(A) proclamation.

proclaim /prə'kleɪm/ *verb*. LME.
[Latin *proclamare* cry out, formed as PRO-¹ + *clamare* to shout.]
1 *verb trans*. Make official announcement of (something, *that*), esp. by word of mouth in a public place; cause this to be done by officers or agents; cause to become widely and publicly known; declare publicly (*that*). LME. ▶†**b** *LAW*. Read (a fine) in open court in order to make it less liable to be levied by fraud. L15–M18. ▶**c** Publish (banns of marriage); *Scot.* publish the banns of (a couple). L16.
2 *verb trans*. With double obj. & compl.: officially or publicly declare (a person or thing) to be. LME. ▶**b** Without compl.: declare to be a rebel or outlaw; denounce. E16. ▶**c** Proclaim the accession of (a monarch). E18. ▶**d** Place (a district etc.) under legal restrictions by proclamation. Also, forbid by official decree. E19.
†**3** *verb intrans*. Make a public announcement. L15–E17.
4 *verb trans*. Of a thing: be an indication of, make manifest, demonstrate; reveal *as*; show or prove *to be*. L16.

> 1 P. BROOK Every now and then an actor .. proclaims that directors are unnecessary. P. MAILLOUX Martial law had to be proclaimed. **proclaim war** = ***DECLARE war***. 2 C. HILL Oliver Cromwell was proclaimed Lord Protector. N. SEDAKA I .. sang at the famed San Remo festival, where .. I was proclaimed a star. **d** *Southern Star (Eire)* The play was proclaimed by the British authorities. 4 E. WAUGH Their clothes and demeanour proclaimed them as belonging to the middle rank. M. HOLROYD His drawings proclaimed an amazing genius. J. ARCHER The cut of the collar .. proclaimed him as West German. A. MASSIE His birth, character and history all proclaimed him to be a masterful man.

■ **proclaimer** *noun* M16.

proclamation /prɒklə'meɪʃ(ə)n/ *noun*. LME.
[Old & mod. French from Latin *proclamatio(n-)*, formed as prec.: see -ATION.]
1 The action of proclaiming something; *spec*. the public and formal announcement of the accession of a monarch, the fact of being proclaimed monarch. (Foll. by *of*.) LME.
2 A thing proclaimed; a formal order issued by a monarch or other legal authority and made public; *Hist.* a royal decree of the kind issued in the 16th and 17th cents., by which it was sought to legislate without the assent of Parliament. LME.
†**3** *transf.* Open declaration; manifestation; favourable or unfavourable notice. L16–E17.

> 1 *New York Times* After the proclamation of the new State of Israel. 2 P. NORMAN A proclamation on the book's frontispiece announced that it belonged to Gaye Nevinson, Parkfield Lodge.

Comb.: **proclamation money** *US HISTORY* coin valued according to a royal proclamation of 1704, according to which the Spanish dollar of 17½ pennyweight was to be rated at six shillings in all the colonies.

†**proclamator** *noun*. M17–E18.
[Latin, formed as PROCLAIM *verb*: see -OR.]
A person who made proclamations; *spec*. an officer of the Court of Common Pleas.

proclamatory /prə'klamət(ə)ri/ *adjective*. M17.
[formed as prec.: see -ORY².]
1 That proclaims something. M17.
2 Of, pertaining to, resembling, or of the nature of a proclamation. M19.

Proclian /'prɒklɪən/ *adjective*. E20.
[from *Proclus* (see below) + -IAN.]
Of or pertaining to Proclus, a Neoplatonist philosopher of the 5th-cent. AD, or his views or works.
■ Also **Procline** *adjective* M20.

procline /prəʊ'klʌɪn/ *verb intrans*. *rare*. L19.
[Latin *proclinare*, formed as PRO-¹ + *clinare* to bend.]
Lean or slope forward.

proclisis /'prəʊklɪsɪs/ *noun*. L19.
[from PRO-² + Greek *klisis* inclination, from *klinein* to lean, slope.]
GRAMMAR. Pronunciation as a proclitic; the transference of accentuation to a following word.

proclitic /prəʊ'klɪtɪk/ *adjective & noun*. M19.
[mod. Latin *procliticus*, from Greek *proklinein* lean forward, after late Latin *encliticus* ENCLITIC.]
GRAMMAR. ▶**A** *adjective*. Designating a word so unemphatic as to be pronounced as if part of the following word, as *an* in *an ounce*, *at* in *at home*. M19.
▶**B** *noun*. A proclitic word. M19.
■ **proclitically** *adverb* E20.

proclive /prəʊ'klʌɪv/ *adjective*. *arch*. E16.
[(Obsolete French from) Latin *proclivis*, *-us*: see next.]
†**1** Sloping steeply forwards and downwards. E16–E17.
†**2** (Of a person) having a proclivity or inclination to an action; (of a thing) conducive *to* something (usually something bad). M16–E18.
3 Headlong, hasty, rash. E17.

proclivity /prə'klɪvɪti/ *noun*. L16.
[Latin *proclivitas*, from *proclivis*, *-us* sloping, formed as PRO-¹ + *clivus* slope: see -ITY.]
A predisposition, tendency, or propensity on the part of a person. (Foll. by *for* or *to* an action, habit, or thing; *to do*.)

> ROSEMARY MANNING At last my sexual proclivities .. were out in the open. P. MAILLOUX His proclivity for making friends.

Procne *noun* var. of PROGNE.

proconsul /prəʊ'kɒns(ə)l/ *noun*. LME.
[Latin, from earlier *pro consule* (person acting) for the consul, formed as PRO *preposition*, *adverb*, etc. + CONSUL.]
1 *Hist.* In the Roman Republic, an officer, usu. an ex-consul, who acted as governor or military commander of a province and had most of the authority of a consul; in the Roman Empire, the governor of a senatorial province. LME.
2 A governor of a modern dependency, colony, or province. L17.
3 (**P-**.) *PALAEONTOLOGY* [Named as being the ancestor of a London Zoo chimpanzee named *Consul*.] A fossil hominoid primate of the genus *Proconsul*, found in Lower Miocene deposits in East Africa, one of the last common ancestors of both humans and the great apes. M20.
■ **proconsular** *adjective* (*a*) of or pertaining to a proconsul; (*b*) (of a province) under the administration of a Roman proconsul: L17. †**proconsulary** *adjective* (*rare*) proconsular L16–E18. **proconsulate** *noun* (*a*) the district under the government of a proconsul; (*b*) a proconsulship: L18. **proconsulship** *noun* the position or office of a proconsul L16.

procrastinate /prə(ʊ)'krastɪneɪt/ *verb*. L16.
[Latin *procrastinat-* pa. ppl stem of *procrastinare*, formed as PRO-¹ + *crastinus* belonging to tomorrow, from *cras* tomorrow: see -ATE³.]
1 *verb trans*. Postpone, put off, defer; prolong. Now *rare*. L16.
2 *verb intrans*. Defer action, delay; be dilatory. L16.
■ **procrasti'nation** *noun* [Latin *procrastinatio(n-)*] the action or habit of procrastinating, dilatoriness; an instance of this; the deferring *of* something: M16. **procrastinative** *adjective* that tends to procrastinate E19. **procrastinator** *noun* a person who procrastinates E17. **procrastinatory** *adjective* given to or implying procrastination; dilatory: M19.

procreant /ˈprəʊkrɪənt/ *adjective & noun.* L16.
[(Old & mod. French *procréant* from) Latin *procreant-* pres. ppl stem of *procreare*: see next, -ANT[1].]
▸ **A** *adjective.* **1** That procreates; producing young; productive. L16.
2 Of or pertaining to procreation. E17.
▸†**B** *noun.* A person who or thing which procreates. E–M17.

procreate /ˈprəʊkrɪeɪt/ *verb.* Pa. pple & ppl adjective **-ated**, †**-ate**. LME.
[Orig. pa. pple, from Latin *procreatus* pa. pple of *procreare*, formed as PRO-[1] + CREATE *verb*: see -ATE[3].]
1 *verb trans. & intrans.* Bring (offspring) into existence by the natural process of reproduction; beget. LME.
2 *verb trans.* Produce, give rise to, occasion. Now *rare* or *obsolete.* M16.
■ **procreative** *adjective* pertaining to procreation; having the power or function of producing offspring: M17. **procreator** *noun* a person who or thing which procreates; a parent: M16.

procreation /prəʊkrɪˈeɪʃ(ə)n/ *noun.* LME.
[(Old French *procreacion* (also mod.), *-tion* from) Latin *procreatio(n-)*, from *procreatus*: see prec., -ATION.]
1 The action of procreating; reproduction; the fact of being begotten; *transf. & fig.* origination, production. LME.
†**2** Offspring, progeny. LME–M17.

Procrustean /prə(ʊ)ˈkrʌstɪən/ *adjective.* M19.
[from *Procrustes* from Greek *Prokroustēs* lit. 'stretcher', from *prokrouein* beat or hammer out: see below, -AN.]
Of or pertaining to Procrustes, a robber who in Greek legend stretched or mutilated his victims in order to make them fit the length of his bed; seeking or tending to produce uniformity by forceful or arbitrary methods.

> B. JOWETT Neither must we . . confine the Platonic dialogue on the Procrustean bed of a single idea. C. LAMBERT Vaughan Williams . . rarely submits his themes to a Procrustean development.

■ **Procrusteanism** *noun* Procrustean nature or character; an instance of this: M19.

procryptic /prəʊˈkrɪptɪk/ *adjective.* L19.
[from PRO-[1] + Greek *kruptikos* CRYPTIC, app. after *protective.*]
ZOOLOGY. Designating colouring of insects and some other animals that gives protection by helping to conceal them from predators.
■ **procrypsis** *noun* protective colouring E20. **procryptically** *adverb* E20.

procto- /ˈprɒktəʊ/ *combining form.* Before a vowel **proct-**.
[from Greek *prōktos* anus: see -O-.]
Chiefly MEDICINE. The rectum; the anus; the rectum and anus.
■ **procˈtalgia** *noun* pain in the anus E19. **procˈtitis** *noun* inflammation of the rectum and anus E19. **proctoˈdaeal**, **-ˈdeal** *adjective* (ZOOLOGY & EMBRYOLOGY) of, pertaining to, or taking place through the proctodaeum L19. **proctoˈdaeum**, **-deum** *noun* [Greek *hodaios* that is on or by the road] ZOOLOGY the posterior portion of the alimentary canal, esp. in an insect or an embryo (cf. STOMODAEUM) L19. **proctoscope** *noun* an instrument for the visual examination of the rectum L19. **procˈtoscopy** *noun* use of, or examination with, a proctoscope L19. **proctoˈscopic** *adjective* of or pertaining to proctoscopy L19.

proctology /prɒkˈtɒlədʒi/ *noun.* L19.
[from prec. + -OLOGY.]
The branch of medicine that deals with the anus and rectum, or with the anus and the whole colon.
■ **proctoˈlogic**, **proctoˈlogical** *adjectives* L19. **proctologist** *noun* L19.

proctor /ˈprɒktə/ *noun & verb.* ME.
[Syncopated form of PROCURATOR.]
▸ **A** *noun.* **I 1** A person employed to manage the affairs of someone else; an agent, a manager; a steward; *spec.* an agent for the collection of tithes and other church dues (also ***tithe-proctor***). Long *obsolete* exc. *Hist.* and as below. ME.
†**2** An advocate, a supporter, a guardian. ME–M17.
3 LAW. A person whose profession is to represent others in a court of canon or (formerly) civil law; *spec.* (***a***) in the Church of England, a representative of the clergy of a diocese in convocation; (***b***) (in full ***King's Proctor***, ***Queen's Proctor***) an official with the right to intervene on behalf of the Crown in divorce, nullity, and probate cases when collusion or suppression of the facts is alleged. LME.
4 Each of two or more officers periodically elected by the members of certain ancient universities, with administrative, disciplinary, and (formerly) legal duties. LME. ▸**b** An invigilator at a university or college examination. *US.* M20.
†**5** A person who collected alms on behalf of people who were debarred from begging for themselves, esp. the occupants of an almshouse etc. E16–E17.
▸ **II** †**6** *Hist.* A Roman procurator. LME–L15.
▸ **B** *verb.* **1** *verb intrans.* Officiate as a university proctor. L17.
2 *verb intrans.* Swagger, bully. *dial.* E18.
3 *verb trans.* Invigilate (an examination). *US.* M20.
■ **procˈtorial** *adjective* M19. **procˈtorially** *adverb* in a proctorial capacity; in the manner of a proctor: L19. **proctorize** *verb trans.* (of a university proctor) exercise proctorial authority on (an undergraduate etc.); arrest and punish (an offender): M19. **proctoriˈzation** *noun* the act of proctorizing someone; the fact of being proctorized: L19. **proctorship** *noun* the position, office, or function of a proctor M16.

proctotrupid /prɒktəˈtruːpɪd/ *adjective & noun.* M19.
[mod. Latin *Proctotrupidae* (see below), from *Proctotrupes* genus name, from PROCTO- + Greek *trupan* to bore: see -ID[3].]
ENTOMOLOGY. (Of, pertaining to, or designating) a wasp of the family Proctotrupidae or the superfamily Proctotrupoidea, which include parasitoids of insects and spiders.

procumbent /prəʊˈkʌmb(ə)nt/ *adjective.* M17.
[Latin *procumbent-* pres. ppl stem of *procumbere* fall forwards, formed as PRO-[1] + *-cumbere*: see CUMBENT.]
1 BOTANY. Of a plant or stem: lying flat on the ground without throwing out roots; growing along the ground. M17.
2 Lying on the face, prone; prostrate. E18.
3 ZOOLOGY. Of a tooth: lying along the jaw. L19.

procurable /prəˈkjʊərəb(ə)l/ *adjective.* LME.
[from PROCURE + -ABLE.]
Able to be procured, obtainable.

procuracy /prəˈkjʊərəsi/ *noun.* ME.
[medieval Latin *procuratia* from Latin *procuratio* PROCURATION: see -ACY. Cf. PROXY.]
†**1** ECCLESIASTICAL. = PROCURATION 3. Only in ME.
2 The position or office of a procurator; management or action for another. LME.
†**3** A document empowering a person to act as the representative of another; a proxy, a letter of attorney. LME–E17.

procural /prəˈkjʊər(ə)l/ *noun.* M19.
[from PROCURE + -AL[1].]
The action or process of procuring something.

procurance /prəˈkjʊər(ə)ns/ *noun.* M16.
[from PROCURE + -ANCE.]
The action of procuring something; the action by which something is attained; agency.

procuration /prɒkjʊˈreɪʃ(ə)n/ *noun.* LME.
[(Old French *procuracion*, (also mod.) *-tion* from) Latin *procuratio(n-)*, from *procurat-* pa. ppl stem of *procurare*: see PROCURE, -ATION.]
†**1** Management, superintendence; attention, care; stewardship. LME–L17.
2 The action of appointing a person with legal authority to act on one's behalf; the authority so delegated; the function or action of one's agent. LME. ▸**b** A formal document conveying such authority; a letter or power of attorney. Now *rare.* LME.
3 ECCLESIASTICAL HISTORY. The provision of necessary entertainment for a bishop or other visitor by a parish or religious house visited; a payment of money in lieu. LME.
4 The action of procuring something, procurement; *spec.* the negotiation of a loan for a client; the fee for this. L15. ▸**b** The action of a procurer or procuress; pimping. L17.

procurator /ˈprɒkjʊreɪtə/ *noun.* ME.
[(Old French *procuratour* from) Latin *procurator* manager, agent, deputy, tax-collector in a province, from *procurat-*: see prec., -ATOR. Cf. PROCTOR.]
1 *Hist.* A Roman officer who collected the taxes, paid the troops, and attended to the interests of the treasury in an imperial province, sometimes with other administrative duties. ME.
2 A person employed to manage the affairs of someone else; a person appointed with legal authority to act on behalf of another; a manager, a steward; an agent, an attorney. Long *obsolete* exc. *Hist.* ME.
3 LAW. A proctor representing others in a court of law, esp. in countries retaining Roman civil law and in English ecclesiastical courts; *spec.* in Scotland, a lawyer practising before the lower courts. LME.
†**4** An advocate, a supporter, a guardian. LME–E17.
†**5** A person who or thing which brings or helps to bring something about; a producer *of.* L15–M17.
6 = PROCTOR *noun* 4. (The official name at certain Scottish universities.) E16.
7 In some Italian cities, a public administrator or magistrate. E17.
3 procurator fiscal in Scotland, the public prosecutor of a district, appointed by the Lord Advocate.
■ **procuratorship** *noun* the position, function, or period of office of a procurator L16.

pro-curator /prəʊˈkjʊərətə/ *noun.* L17.
[from PRO-[1] + CURATOR.]
SCOTS LAW. A person who performs the duties of a curator towards a minor etc. though not legally appointed as such.

procuratory /ˈprɒkjʊrət(ə)ri/ *noun & adjective.* ME.
[Late Latin *procuratorius*, from Latin PROCURATOR: see -ORY[2].]
▸ **A** *noun.* LAW. Authorization of one person to act for another; an instrument or a clause in an instrument giving such power. ME.
▸†**B** *adjective.* Of or pertaining to a procurator or procuration. LME–L16.
■ **procuraˈtorial** *adjective* of or pertaining to a procurator or proctor M17.

procuratrix /prɒkjʊˈreɪtrɪks/ *noun.* M16.
[Latin, fem. of PROCURATOR: see -TRIX.]
The occupant of a nunnery responsible for its temporal concerns.

procure /prəˈkjʊə/ *verb.* ME.
[Old & mod. French *procurer* from Latin *procurare* take care of, attend to, manage, formed as PRO-[1] + *curare* look after.]
▸ **I** †**1** *verb intrans.* Endeavour, labour, use means, (*to do*). Also foll. by *for* or *to* a thing. ME–E17.
†**2** *verb trans.* Contrive (an action or proceeding); try to bring about (esp. something bad). ME–L17.
3 *verb trans.* Bring about, esp. by care or with effort; cause *to be done*; arrange *that.* Now *rare.* ME. ▸†**b** Manage (*to do*). M16–L17.
4 *verb trans.* Obtain, esp. by care or with effort; gain, acquire, get. ME. ▸**b** *verb intrans. & trans.* Act as a procurer; obtain (women) for prostitution. E17.
5 *verb trans.* Prevail on or persuade (a person) *to do.* Now *Scot.* exc. LAW. ME. ▸†**b** Bribe, suborn. LME–E17. ▸†**c** Prevail on (a person) to come; bring, lead. L16–E17.
†**6** *verb trans.* Try to induce; urge. M–L16.

> **3** SMOLLETT This second sneer procured another laugh against him. W. D. HOWELLS An ingenious lover procured his . . rival to be arrested for lunacy. R. BRIDGES Could you procure that I should speak with her? **4** A. JOHN We . . procured the services of a . . lad to convey our baggage by train. A. J. AYER They procured his election to the secret society. **5c** SHAKES. *Rom. & Jul.* What unaccustom'd cause procures her hither?

▸ **II** †**7** *verb intrans.* Act as a procurator or legal agent; *fig.* plead, make supplication. LME–M17.
▸ **III** †**8** *verb intrans.* Proceed, advance. *rare.* L15–L16.
■ **procurative** *adjective* tending to produce something; productive *of*: M17. **procurement** *noun* (***a***) the action or an act of causing or arranging something; instigation; (***b***) acquisition; an instance of this; *spec.* the action or occupation of procuring military equipment and supplies: ME. **procurer** *noun* [Anglo-Norman *procurour*, Old French *procureur* from Latin PROCURATOR] †(***a***) a procurator; (***b***) (now *rare*) a promoter, an instigator, (*of*); (***c***) a person who obtains something; *spec.* one who obtains women for prostitution, a pimp: LME. **procuress** *noun* a female procurer, *spec.* a bawd LME.

procureur /prɔkyrœːr/ *noun.* Pl. pronounced same. L16.
[French, from *procurer* PROCURE + *-eur* -OR.]
1 In France, a procurator, *esp.* a legal one. L16.
2 A procurer, a pimp. E20.
■ ***procureuse*** /prɔkyrøːz (pl. *same*)/ *noun* a procuress M20.

procurrent /prəʊˈkʌr(ə)nt/ *adjective.* E20.
[Latin *procurrent-* pres. ppl stem of *procurrere* run forward, formed as PRO-[1] + *currere* run: see -ENT.]
Of a fish's fin: having rays that are almost parallel.

procyclidine /prəʊˈsʌɪklɪdiːn/ *noun.* M20.
[from PRO(PANOL + CYCLO- + -IDINE.]
PHARMACOLOGY. A tricyclic anticholinergic drug, $C_{19}H_{29}NO$, used to treat Parkinsonism.

procyonid /prəʊsɪˈɒnɪd, -sʌɪ-/ *adjective & noun.* E20.
[mod. Latin *Procyonidae* (see below), from *Procyon* genus name from Latin from Greek *Prokuōn*, brightest star of Canis Minor, formed as PRO-[2] + *kuōn* dog: see -ID[3].]
(Of, pertaining to, or designating) a mammal of the family Procyonidae, which includes racoons, coatis, and kinkajous.

prod /prɒd/ *noun*[1]. M18.
[from the verb.]
1 Any of various pointed instruments, as a goad, skewer, etc. M18. ▸**b** FOUNDING. Any of a number of pointed projections for holding the loam when preparing a loam mould. L19.
2 An act of prodding; a poke with a pointed instrument etc.; *fig.* a stimulus to action. E19.

> **1** R. INGALLS Kelsoe . . used the electric prod to tease. **2** J. CARY Set a donkey running . . by a skilful prod. JULIAN GLOAG Gave the coals a prod with . . his shoe. **on the prod** *N. Amer. colloq.* on the attack, on the offensive.

prod /prɒd/ *noun*[2]. Also (earlier, now *Hist.*) **prodd**. L18.
[Alt. of ROD *noun.*]
A lightweight crossbow designed to shoot stones or bullets (*Hist.*); the bow or bow assembly of a modern crossbow.

prod /prɒd/ *noun*[3]. *slang.* L19.
[App. var. of PRAD.]
A horse, *esp.* an old one.

Prod /prɒd/ *noun*[4] *& adjective. slang* (chiefly *Anglo-Irish*). *offensive.* **M20.**
[Abbreviation after pronunc.]
= PROTESTANT *noun* 2, *adjective* 1. Cf. PROT.

prod /prɒd/ *verb.* Infl. **-dd-**. **M16.**
[Perh. symbolic, or a blend of POKE *verb*[1] and BROD *verb*.]
1 *verb trans.* Poke with a pointed instrument, finger, etc. **M16.** ▸**b** Make (a hole etc.) by prodding. **M19.**
2 *verb intrans.* Thrust, poke. Foll. by *at*, †*in*. **L17.**
3 *verb trans. fig.* Stimulate or goad into action. **L19.**

> **1** R. C. HUTCHINSON He prodded the body with his toe. D. BAGLEY If they don't move, prod them with bayonets. **2** R. THOMAS Gwyn had taken a pot . . and was prodding at the contents. **3** E. WAUGH The Duke . . has been prodded into . . a remonstrance. P. MAILLOUX Prodded by his parents, Kafka . . reluctantly acknowledged . . he had to go. *absol.*: K. CHERNIN She likes to prod and challenge.

Comb.: **prodnose** *noun & verb* (*colloq.*) (*a*) *noun* an inquisitive person; *spec.* a detective; (*b*) *verb intrans.* pry.
■ **prodder** *noun* **M17.**

prodd *noun* see PROD *noun*[2].

Proddy /ˈprɒdi/ *noun & adjective. slang* (chiefly *Anglo-Irish*). *offensive.* **M20.**
[from PROD *noun*[4] *& adjective* + -Y[6].]
= PROTESTANT *noun* 2, *adjective* 1.

prodelision /prəʊdɪˈlɪʒ(ə)n/ *noun.* **E20.**
[from Latin *prod* earlier form of *pro* PRO-[1] + ELISION.]
PROSODY. Elision of an initial vowel.

prodigal /ˈprɒdɪg(ə)l/ *adjective, noun, & adverb.* **LME.**
[Late Latin *prodigalis* (implied in but recorded later than *prodigalitas*, *-aliter*) from Latin *prodigus* lavish: see -AL[1].]
▸ **A** *adjective.* **1** Recklessly wasteful of one's property or means; extravagant. (Foll. by *of*, *with*.) **LME.**
2 (Wastefully) lavish. (Foll. by *of*, *with*.) **E16.**
3 Proud, conceited. *dial.* **M18.**

> **1** P. BOWLES Ahmed refused to be prodigal with the wood. J. M. COETZEE He . . knew it was bad to be prodigal. **2** T. C. WOLFE Cherries hung . . in prodigal clusters. R. V. JONES We were . . prodigal with the information. R. RENDELL People are . . prodigal of effort.

Special collocations: **prodigal son** = sense B.2 below.
▸ **B** *noun.* **1** A person who spends money extravagantly and wastefully; a spendthrift. **L16.**
2 *spec.* [with ref. to *Luke* 15:11–32] Such a person who subsequently regrets such behaviour. Now *esp.* a returned wanderer. Cf. ***prodigal son*** above. **L16.**

> **2** DEFOE Like a true Prodigal, go home to . . Father. A. WILSON Well! . . so the prodigal's returned.

▸†**C** *adverb.* Prodigally, lavishly. *rare* (Shakes.). Only in **E17.**
■ **prodiˈgality** *noun* [Old & mod. French *prodigalité*] the quality of being prodigal; a prodigal act: **ME. prodigalize** *verb trans.* (*arch.*) spend extravagantly **E17. prodigally** *adverb* **M16.**

prodigiosin /prədɪdʒɪˈəʊsɪn/ *noun.* **E20.**
[from mod. Latin (*Bacillus*) *prodigiosus* (Latin = marvellous), former name of *Serratia marcescens* (see below): see -IN[1].]
BIOCHEMISTRY. A dark red pigment with antibiotic properties produced by the bacterium *Serratia marcescens* and having a molecule containing three pyrrole rings linked to a central carbon atom.

prodigious /prəˈdɪdʒəs/ *adjective & adverb.* **L15.**
[Latin *prodigiosus*, from *prodigium*: see next, -OUS.]
▸ **A** *adjective.* †**1** Of the nature of a prodigy or omen; ominous. **L15–E18.**
2 Marvellous, amazing; appalling, monstrous. Also (*arch.*) as *interjection.* **L15.**
3 Unnatural, abnormal. *arch.* **L16.**
4 Of great size, extent, amount, etc.; enormous. Freq. *hyperbol.* **E17.**

> **2** M. SEYMOUR Henry, whose memory was prodigious, had forgotten . . nothing. **4** H. CARPENTER He . . had a prodigious appetite; one evening he ate six eggs at a sitting. S. QUINN The early steam engine required prodigious amounts of coal. P. VAN SOMMERS All four were prodigious letter-writers.

▸ **B** *adverb.* Prodigiously, amazingly. *arch. colloq.* **L17.**
■ **prodigiˈosity** *noun* (*rare*) (*a*) an enormous person or thing; (*b*) something marvellous: **L19. prodigiously** *adverb* **L16. prodigiousness** *noun* **M17.**

prodigy /ˈprɒdɪdʒi/ *noun.* **L15.**
[Latin *prodigium*, from *prod-* (see PRODELISION) + elem. perh. from *aio* I say or *agere* to act: see -Y[4].]
1 Something extraordinary regarded as an omen. Now *rare.* **L15.**
2 An amazing, marvellous, or unusual thing. Also, something abnormal or monstrous. **L16.** ▸**b** A wonderful example *of* some quality. **M17.**
3 *spec.* A person endowed with some exceptional (freq. specified) quality or ability; *esp.* a very precocious child. **M17.**

> **2b** J. AGATE Preserving his balance with prodigies of skill. **3** D. LEAVITT Charles is a computer prodigy. F. SPALDING Jacobson had been a child prodigy and . . could play . . Bach's preludes.

prodition /prəˈdɪʃ(ə)n/ *noun.* Now *rare.* **LME.**
[Old French *prodicion* from Latin *proditio(n-)*, from *prodit-* pa. ppl stem of *prodere* betray: see -ITION.]
Betrayal, treachery.

†**proditor** *noun.* **LME–L17.**
[Anglo-Norman *proditour* = Old French *proditeur* from Latin *proditor*, from *prodit-*: see prec., -OR.]
A betrayer; a traitor.
■ †**proditorious** *adjective* traitorous **LME–E19.** †**proditoriously** *adverb* **LME–E17.**

prodroma /prɒˈdrəʊmə/ *noun.* Now *rare* or *obsolete.* Pl. **-mas**, **-mata** /-mətə/. **M19.**
[mod. Latin from Greek, neut. pl. of *prodromos* adjective: see next.]
MEDICINE. = PRODROME 2.

prodrome /ˈprəʊdrəʊm, ˈprɒdrəʊm/ *noun.* Also (now *rare*) in Latin form **-dromus** /-drəʊməs/, pl. **-mi** /-mʌɪ/. **E17.**
[French from mod. Latin *prodromus* from Greek *prodromos* precursor, formed as PRO-[2] + -DROME.]
1 A precursor, a forerunner, a premonitory event. Long *rare.* **E17.**
2 *MEDICINE.* A premonitory symptom. **L17.**
3 A preliminary treatise or book. **L17.**
■ **proˈdromal** *adjective* (*a*) introductory, preliminary; (*b*) (of a symptom) premonitory: **E18. prodroˈmatic** *adjective* = PRODROMAL **E18. proˈdromic** *adjective* = PRODROMAL **M19.**

prodrug /ˈprəʊdrʌg/ *noun.* **M20.**
[from PRO-[2] + DRUG *noun*[1].]
BIOCHEMISTRY. A compound (usu. a biologically inactive one) which can be metabolized in the body to produce a drug; a compound from which a given drug is produced by metabolic action.

produce /ˈprɒdjuːs/ *noun.* **M16.**
[from the verb.]
1 The fact of producing; production. *rare.* **M16.**
2 That which is produced, either by natural growth or as the result of some action; *spec.* agricultural and natural products collectively, as opp. to manufactured goods. **L17.** ▸**b** *gen.* Result, consequence. **M18.** ▸**c** Offspring, *esp.* that of a horse (*spec.* a mare). Cf. GET *noun*[1] 1a. **M19.**
3 The amount produced; the return, the yield. Now chiefly *techn.* **E18.**

> **2** A. DJOLETO Saw him . . loaded with farm produce. J. DISKI The supermarket filled with the produce of the world.

produce /prəˈdjuːs/ *verb.* **LME.**
[Latin *producere*, formed as PRO-[1] + *ducere* to lead.]
1 *verb trans.* Bring forward or out, esp. for inspection or consideration, present to view or notice. **LME.** ▸**b** Introduce (a person or thing) *to*. Now *spec.* bring (a performer or performance) before the public (cf. sense 3e below). **L16.** ▸†**c** Bring *into* a specified condition. **E17–M18.**
2 *verb trans.* Extend in length; *esp.* (*GEOMETRY*) extend or continue (a line). **LME.** ▸†**b** Extend in duration; prolong. **E–M17.**
3 *verb trans. & intrans.* **a** Bring (a thing) into existence; bring about, effect, cause, (an action, result, etc.). **L15.** ▸**b** Give birth to (offspring); (of a plant) bear (seed, fruit, etc.). **L15.** ▸**c** Of a country, region, process, etc.: yield or supply (a commodity etc.). **L16.** ▸**d** Compose, make, or bring into existence by mental or physical labour (a material object). **M17.** ▸**e** Administer and supervise the making of (a play, film, broadcast, etc.); supervise the making of (a record), esp. by determining the overall sound. **L19.**

> **1** E. WAUGH He produced from under his coat a gardenia. C. P. SNOW Milly produced these views with . . satisfaction. A. MACLEAN From her . . handbag she produced a set of . . keys. **b** S. JOHNSON Hilarius . . produced me to all his friends. P. CAMPBELL He'd written a play . . . It was produced at the Abbey Theatre. **3a** H. JAMES The effect she produced upon people. I. MURDOCH A thundersheet . . when shaken produces a . . rumbling noise. *Gridiron* Dorsey failed to produce so . . Dawson was brought in. **c** N. F. DIXON This planet is quite capable of producing enough food. *Investors Chronicle* £1,000 invested . . would have produced only £3,483. **d** H. CARPENTER He . . produced some of his best and most moving work.

produceable /prəˈdjuːsɪb(ə)l/ *adjective.* **M17.**
[from prec. + -ABLE. Cf. PRODUCIBLE.]
= PRODUCIBLE.

producent /prəˈdjuːs(ə)nt/ *adjective & noun.* Now *rare.* **M16.**
[Latin *producent-* pres. ppl stem of *producere*: see PRODUCE *verb*, -ENT.]
▸ **A** *adjective.* That produces something or someone; *ECCLESIASTICAL LAW* that brings forward a witness or document. **M16.**
▸ **B** *noun.* A person who or thing which produces something or someone; *ECCLESIASTICAL LAW* the party producing a witness or document. **E17.**

producer /prəˈdjuːsə/ *noun.* **L15.**
[from PRODUCE *verb* + -ER[1].]
1 *gen.* A person who or thing which produces something or someone. **L15.**
2 A person who produces a commodity. Opp. to ***consumer***. **L17.**
3 *esp.* A person who produces a play, film, broadcast, etc., or a record. **L19.**
4 In full ***gas producer***. A furnace for producing fuel gas by passing air and steam through hot solid fuel. **L19.**
5 *ECOLOGY.* (A part of) an organism that produces organic compounds from simple substances such as water, carbon dioxide, or nitrogen. Freq. *attrib.* **M20.**
Comb.: **producer gas** a low-grade fuel gas formed in a gas producer, consisting mainly of nitrogen and carbon monoxide.
■ **producership** *noun* the position or function of a producer **E20.**

producible /prəˈdjuːsɪb(ə)l/ *adjective.* **M17.**
[Late Latin *producibilis*, formed as PRODUCE *verb*: see -IBLE. Cf. PRODUCEABLE.]
Able or fit to be produced.
■ **produciˈbility** *noun* **M17.**

product /ˈprɒdʌkt/ *noun.* **LME.**
[Latin *productum* use as noun of neut. pa. pple of *producere*: see PRODUCE *verb*.]
1 *MATH.* The quantity obtained by multiplying two or more quantities together. Also, any of various other entities obtained by defined processes of combination. **LME.**
2 A thing produced by an action, operation, or natural process; a result, a consequence; *spec.* that which is produced commercially for sale. Also, (agricultural) produce. **L16.** ▸†**b** A quantity; a supply, a stock. *rare.* **M17–M18.** ▸**c** The value of goods produced. **L19.**
3 *CHEMISTRY.* A substance produced in a chemical or nuclear reaction. Cf. BY-PRODUCT. **E19.**

> **2** R. NIEBUHR Universal education was a product of the democratic movement. D. LODGE How many different products this firm made. *collect.*: *Sounds* Not a . . wonderful year for albums; too many disappointments, too much product.

Phrases: ***gross domestic product***, ***gross national product***: see GROSS *adjective*. ***logical product***: see LOGICAL *adjective*. ***national product***: see NATIONAL *adjective*. ***net national product***: see NET *adjective*[2] *& adverb*. ***partial product***: see PARTIAL *adjective*. **product of inertia** (with ref. to a body or system of bodies with respect to two given planes at right angles to each other or to the two axes perpendicular to such planes) the sum of the elements of mass each multiplied by the product of its distances from the two given planes.
Comb.: **product differentiation** *ECONOMICS* the marketing of generally similar products with minor variations that are used by consumers when making a choice; **product liability** the legal liability a manufacturer or trader incurs for producing or selling a faulty product; **product moment** *STATISTICS* in a set of pairs of data, the sum of the products of the elements of each pair; **product-moment** *attrib. adjective* (*STATISTICS*) designating a correlation coefficient calculated from the product moment and equal to the covariance divided by the geometric mean of the variances; **product placement** a practice in which manufacturers of goods or providers of a service gain exposure for their products by paying for them to be featured in films and television programmes.

product /prəˈdʌkt/ *verb trans.* Now *rare.* Pa. pple & ppl adjective **producted**, (earlier) †**product**. **LME.**
[Orig. pa. pple, from Latin *productus* pa. pple of *producere*: see PRODUCE *verb*. Orig. pa. pple *product*.]
1 = PRODUCE *verb* 3a, b, c, d. **LME.**
†**2** = PRODUCE *verb* 1. Only in **M16.**
3 = PRODUCE *verb* 2. **M17.**
■ **productiˈbility** *noun* ability to be produced **M19. productor** *noun* **E17. productress** *noun* **M18.**

production /prəˈdʌkʃ(ə)n/ *noun.* **LME.**
[Old & mod. French from Latin *productio(n-)*, from *product-* pa. ppl stem of *producere*: see PRODUCE *verb*, -ION.]
1 Something which is produced by an action, process, etc.; a product. Formerly also, a result, a consequence. **LME.** ▸**b** *spec.* A literary or artistic work; a play, a film, a broadcast, etc. Also, a heavy undertaking; a fuss, a commotion. **M17.** ▸**c** The total yield or output produced. **L19.**
2 The action or an act of producing, making, or causing something; the fact or condition of being produced. **LME.** ▸**b** *spec.* The process of being manufactured commercially, esp. in large quantities; the rate of this. **L18.**
3 The action of bringing forward or exhibiting something or someone; *spec.* (*LAW*) the exhibiting of a document in court. **L15.** ▸**b** *SCOTS LAW.* A document or piece of evidence produced in an action. **M19.**
4 Extension in space or (formerly) time. **M16.**
†**5** *ANATOMY.* = PROCESS *noun* 8. **L16–M19.**
Phrases: ***flow-line production***, ***flow production***: see FLOW *noun*[1]. ***mass production***: see MASS *noun*[2] *& adjective*. ***primary production***: see PRIMARY *adjective*.
Comb.: **production line** a systemized sequence of mechanical or manual operations involved in the manufacture of a commodity; an assembly line; **production number** a spectacular

song or dance in a musical show etc.; **production platform** a platform which houses equipment necessary to keep an oil or gas field in production, with facilities for temporarily storing the output of several wells; **production reactor** a nuclear reactor designed to produce fissile material; **production rule** ARTIFICIAL INTELLIGENCE any rule which associates a particular condition with an action to be taken when the condition is satisfied.
■ **productional** *adjective* M20. **productionize** *verb trans.* produce for general use M20.

productive /prəˈdʌktɪv/ *adjective.* E17.
[French (also *productif*), or late Latin *productivus*, from Latin *product-*: see prec., -IVE.]
1 Having the quality of producing something, esp. in large quantities. (Foll. by *of*.) E17. ▸**b** Of a cough: that raises mucus. E20. ▸**c** GRAMMAR. Of an affix: frequently or actively used in word formation. E20.
2 That causes or results in. Foll. by *of*. M17.
3 ECONOMICS. That produces or increases wealth or value; of or engaged in the production of commodities of exchangeable value. L18.
■ **productively** *adverb* E17. **productiveness** *noun* E18.

productivity /prɒdʌkˈtɪvɪti/ *noun.* E19.
[from late Latin *productivus* PRODUCTIVE + -ITY.]
1 The quality or fact of being productive; capacity to produce. E19.
2 ECONOMICS. The rate of output per unit of input, used esp. in assessing the effective use of labour, materials, etc. L19.
3 ECOLOGY. The rate of production of new biomass by an individual, population, or community; the fertility or capacity of a given habitat or area. E20.
Comb.: **productivity coefficient** ECOLOGY the ratio of gross community production to respiration.

†**proegumenal** *adjective.* M17–M19.
[from Greek *proēgoumen-* pres. ppl stem of *proēgeisthai* lead, precede: see -AL¹.]
LOGIC. Of a cause: preceding, predisposing.

proem /ˈprəʊɪm/ *noun.* Also (earlier) †**proheme**. LME.
[Old French *pro(h)eme* (mod. *proème*) or Latin *prooemium* (medieval Latin *prohemium*) from Greek *prooimion* prelude, formed as PRO-² + *oimē* song. Cf. PROOEMIUM.]
1 A preface or preamble to a book or speech. LME.
2 *fig.* A beginning, a prelude. M17.
■ **proˈemial** *adjective* LME.

proembryo /prəʊˈɛmbrɪəʊ/ *noun.* M19.
[German, formed as PRO-² + AS EMBRYO.]
BOTANY. The group of cells formed by the early divisions of the zygote after fertilization, before the embryo proper and the suspensor become differentiated. Also, the protonema of a moss.
■ **proembryˈonic** *adjective* L19.

proenzyme /prəʊˈɛnzʌɪm/ *noun.* E20.
[from PRO-² + ENZYME.]
BIOCHEMISTRY. A biologically inactive precursor of an enzyme.

proestrus *noun* var. of PROOESTRUS.

proette /prəʊˈɛt/ *noun. colloq.* M20.
[from PRO *noun*¹ + -ETTE.]
A female professional golfer.

prof /prɒf/ *noun. colloq.* M19.
[Abbreviation.]
= PROFESSOR 1, 2.

†**proface** *interjection.* E16–M17.
[French †*prou fasse!* (in full *bon prou vous fasse!* may it do you good), from *prou* profit, advantage + *fasse* 3rd person sing. pres. subjunct. of *faire* do.]
Expr. welcome or good wishes at a meal.

profanation /prɒfəˈneɪʃ(ə)n/ *noun.* M16.
[French, or late Latin *profanatio(n-)*, from *profanat-* pa. ppl stem of *profanare*: see PROFANE *verb*, -ATION.]
The action or an act of profaning; (a) desecration, (a) defilement.

profane /prəˈfeɪn/ *adjective & noun.* Also (earlier) †**proph-**. LME.
[Old French *prophane* (mod. *profane*) or Latin *profanus* (medieval Latin *prophanus*) not sacred, uninitiated, impious, lit. 'before or outside the temple', formed as PRO-¹ + *fanum* temple.]
▸ **A** *adjective.* **1** Ritually unclean; *esp.* heathen, pagan. LME.
2 Not pertaining or devoted to what is sacred or biblical; secular; civil. L15. ▸**b** Of a person: not initiated into a religious rite; *transf.* not admitted to some esoteric knowledge. E17.
3 Characterized by disregard or contempt of sacred things; *esp.* irreverent, blasphemous. L15.

> 🕮 **1** G. F. MACLEAR Rewarded by seeing many won from their profane rites. **2** K. CLARK Images of a pleasant earthly life were a . . motive of profane decoration. **3** J. C. OATES By the sacrament of death . . their profane love redeemed. R. WHELAN Famous for his wildly profane language.

▸ **B** *absol.* as *noun.* A profane person; *esp.* (*collect.*) that which is or those who are profane. E16.
■ **profanely** *adverb* M16. **profaneness** *noun* L16.

profane /prəˈfeɪn/ *verb.* Also (earlier) †**proph-**. LME.
[Latin *profanare* (medieval Latin *proph-*), from *profanus*: see prec.]
1 *verb trans.* Treat (what is sacred) with irreverence or contempt; desecrate. LME.
2 *verb trans.* Abuse or defile (a thing) where reverence or respect is due. M16.
3 *verb intrans.* Speak profanely; swear. *rare.* L17.

> 🕮 **2** P. F. BOLLER The place where men had . . died . . should not be profaned by gaiety.

■ **profaner** *noun* M16.

profanity /prəˈfanɪti/ *noun.* M16.
[Late Latin *profanitas*, formed as prec.: see -ITY.]
The quality or condition of being profane; profane conduct or speech; a profane word or act.

> 🕮 M. MEYER 'Damnation!'—the only profanity he permitted himself. A. N. WILSON He could . . attack the profanity and violence of the extreme left.

profecticious *adjective* var. of PROFECTITIOUS.

profection /prəʊˈfɛkʃ(ə)n/ *noun.* *obsolete* exc. ASTROLOGY. M16.
[Partly from French †*profection* progression (Astrol.), from Latin *profect-* pa. ppl stem of *proficere* go forward; partly from Latin *profectio(n-)* setting out, departure, from *proficisci* set out: see -ION.]
1 The action or fact of going forward; progression, advance. M16. ▸†**b** Proficiency. E–M17.
†**2** An advancement or promotion in rank. M16–M17.
†**3** Setting out, (a) departure. L16–M17.

profectitious /prɒfɛkˈtɪʃəs/ *adjective.* Also **-icious**. M17.
[from late Latin *profecticius*, *-itius* that proceeds from someone (from Latin *profect-*: see prec.) + -OUS.]
ROMAN LAW. Of property: coming from a parent or ancestor. Opp. ***adventitious***.

profer /ˈprɒfə/ *verb trans.* Long *arch.* Infl. **-rr-**. ME.
[App. from Old & mod. French *proférer* utter from Latin *proferre* bring forth, offer, utter.]
1 Utter (words). ME.
†**2** Put forth, extend. LME–L16.
†**3** Produce; yield. LME–E17.
†**4** Bring or put near. E16–L17.

proferens /prəˈfɛrɛnz/ *noun.* Pl. ***proferentes*** /prɒfəˈrɛntiːz/. M20.
[Latin, pres. pple of *proferre*: see prec.]
LAW. The party which proposes or adduces a contract or a condition in a contract.
¶ Cf. earlier CONTRA PROFERENTEM.

profert /ˈprəʊfət/ *noun. obsolete* exc. *Hist.* E18.
[from Latin *profest (in curia)* he produces (in court), from *proferre*: see PROFER.]
LAW. The production of a deed in court.

profesh /prəˈfɛʃ/ *noun. slang.* E20.
[Abbreviation.]
= PROFESSION 3.

profess /prəˈfɛs/ *verb.* Pa. pple & ppl adjective **professed**, †**profess**. ME.
[Orig. pa. pple & ppl adjective, from Old & mod. French *profes* from Latin *professus*. Later from Latin *profess-* pa. ppl stem of *profiteri* declare aloud or publicly, formed as PRO-¹ + *fateri* declare, avow.]
1 *verb trans.* Orig. in *pass.*, have taken the vows of a religious order. Later, receive or admit into a religious order. ME. ▸**b** *verb refl. & intrans.* Take the vows of a religious order. LME.
2 *verb trans.* Declare openly, affirm, avow (something, *that*, *to be*, *to do*). Also *refl.* with compl. Passing into sense 3. E16.
3 *verb trans.* Lay claim to (a quality, feeling, etc.), esp. falsely or insincerely; pretend (*to be* or *to do*). M16. ▸**b** *verb refl. & intrans.* Profess friendship. Long *rare.* L16.
4 *verb trans.* Affirm or declare one's faith in or allegiance to (a religion, principle, action, etc.). M16.
5 *verb trans. & intrans.* Teach (a subject) as a professor. M16.
6 *verb trans.* Declare oneself expert or proficient in; make (a thing) one's profession or business. L16.

> 🕮 **2** F. A. KEMBLE She professed herself much relieved. M. H. ABRAMS Theorists . . quick to profess that much . . that has been said . . is wavering, chaotic. A. N. WILSON Abolitionists, such as Belloc professed himself to be. P. GAY To profess nothing less than his 'unconditional devotion'. **3** I. MURDOCH I've seen her looking at French newspapers, though she professes not to know French. A. BROOKNER She professed ignorance of the whole affair. G. ADAIR She professed to be as mystified as her grandchildren when the losses were discovered. **4** C. G. SELIGMAN The Danakil profess Islam.

professed /prəˈfɛst/ *ppl adjective.* LME.
[from prec. + -ED¹.]
1 Of a person: that has taken the vows of a religious order; of or pertaining to people who have taken such vows. LME.
2 Self-acknowledged; alleged, ostensible. M16.
3 That professes to be duly qualified; professional. L17.
■ **professedly** *adverb* L16.

profession /prəˈfɛʃ(ə)n/ *noun.* ME.
[Old & mod. French from Latin *professio(n-)* public declaration, from *profess-*: see PROFESS, -ION.]
1 The declaration or vow made by a person entering a religious order; the action of entering a religious order; the ceremony or fact of being professed in a religious order. ME. ▸**b** Any solemn declaration or vow. LME.
†**2** A religious order. Only in LME.
3 A vocation, a calling, *esp.* one requiring advanced knowledge or training in some branch of learning or science, *spec.* law, theology, or medicine; *gen.* any occupation as a means of earning a living. LME. ▸**b** The body of people engaged in a profession; (THEATRICAL) *the* body of actors collectively, *the* theatre. E17.
4 The declaration of belief in and obedience to a religion; the faith or religion which a person professes. Also, a religious system. L15.
5 The action or an act of declaring, affirming, or avowing an opinion, belief, custom, etc., esp. as opp. to putting it into practice. E16.
†**6** The function or office of a professor in a university or college. L16–E18.

> 🕮 **3** B. MONTGOMERY Many of them were not soldiers by profession. DAY LEWIS Beard and profession combined to . . identify him with St Peter. *Bella* The way female-dominated professions are portrayed. ***profession of letters***: see LETTER *noun*¹. **the oldest profession** *joc.* prostitution. **5** M. L. KING Men seldom bridge the gulf between practice and profession. ISAIAH BERLIN Repeated professions of his . . devotion.

■ †**professionary** *adjective* = PROFESSIONAL *adjective* 2, 4 M18–E19. †**professionist** *noun* (*a*) a person of a particular profession; (*b*) *rare* a person who professes something, esp. insincerely: only in 19. **professionless** *adjective* L18.

professional /prəˈfɛʃ(ə)n(ə)l/ *adjective & noun.* LME.
[from prec. + -AL¹.]
▸ **A** *adjective.* †**1** Marking entrance into a religious order. *rare.* Only in LME.
2 Of, pertaining to, or proper to a profession. M18.
3 Engaged in a profession, esp. one requiring advanced knowledge or training. L18.
4 Engaged in a specified occupation or activity for money or as a means of earning a living, rather than as a pastime. L18. ▸**b** Of a sports match etc.: undertaken or engaged in for money. M19. ▸**c** Engaged in a specified activity regarded with disfavour; habitual. *derog.* L19. ▸**d** Having or showing the skill of a professional person, competent; worthy of a professional person. E20. ▸**e** Of, done by, or of a type or standard used by a person in a (particular) profession. M20.
†**5** Professorial. *rare.* L18–M19.

> 🕮 **2** S. BIKO Professional possibilities for blacks. R. WHELAN Both his professional and his family life. *Journal of Theological Studies* An element of professional envy . . between humanists and theologians. **3** J. DISKI Functional but elegant, an ideal place for a professional couple. **4** J. SIMMS A professional musician. M. CHABON He was a professional golfer. J. B. MORTON Professional hecklers (1s. per hour) sent by his opponents. **d** D. FRANCIS A professional job: no amateur could have produced that. *Daily Mail* Those . . guiding university students . . were highly professional. **e** *Wireless World* Professional audio amplifiers. K. VONNEGUT The wisdom to seek professional help.

Special collocations: **professional class(es)** = ***professional middle class*** below. **professional foul** a deliberate foul in football and other games, to prevent an opponent or opposing team from scoring. **professional middle class(es)** people engaged in (skilled) professions regarded collectively.
▸ **B** *noun.* **1** A person who makes a profession of an occupation or activity usually engaged in as a pastime. Opp. ***amateur***. E19. ▸**b** *spec.* A prostitute. M19.
2 A person engaged in a profession, esp. one requiring advanced knowledge or training. M19.
3 A person highly skilled or competent in some activity or field. M20.

> 🕮 **1** G. B. SHAW Johnson . . boxes with professionals. **2** J. BARTH Only a hardened professional could sleep . . during a battle. *Highlife* Docklands . . for the new urban professionals to live in. **3** *Business Week* Real professionals and sophisticated investors. A. MASSIE A professional in literature.

■ **professioˈnality** *noun* = PROFESSIONALISM 1 M19. **professionaliˈzation** *noun* the action of professionalizing an occupation etc. E20. **professionalize** *verb trans.* make (an occupation etc.) professional M19. **professionally** *adverb* in a professional manner, as a professional, (***professionally speaking***: see SPEAK *verb*) L18.

professionalism /prəˈfɛʃ(ə)n(ə)lɪz(ə)m/ *noun.* M19.
[from prec. + -ISM.]
1 The body of qualities or features, as competence, skill, etc., characteristic of a profession or professional. M19.
2 Engagement in an occupation, esp. a sport, for money rather than as a pastime. L19.
■ **professionalist** *noun* (now *rare*) a professional E19.

professor /prəˈfɛsə/ *noun*. **LME.**
[Old & mod. French *professeur* or Latin *professor*, from *profess-*: see **PROFESS**, **-OR**.]
▶ **I 1** A university academic of the highest rank, esp. in a specified faculty or branch of learning; *spec.* the holder of a university chair; a person of similar status in other institutions. Also used as a title preceding a name and as a form of address. **LME.** ▸**b** A teacher at a university, college, or secondary school. *US.* **E20.**
2 A professional person. *arch.* **M16.** ▸**b** (A title for) a teacher or exponent of a non-academic subject etc. *joc.* **L18.**
1 ***associate professor***, ***full professor***, ***Regius professor***, ***visiting professor***, etc.
▶ **II** †**3** A professed member of a religious order. *rare.* **L15–M18.**
4 A person who professes something, esp. insincerely. **M16.** ▸**b** *spec.* A person who professes a religion. Now chiefly *Scot.* & *US.* **L16.**
■ **professorate** *noun* (*a*) the office or function of professor; (*b*) a body of professors: **E19.** **professordom** *noun* the realm of professors; professors collectively: **L19.** **professoress** *noun* (now *rare* or *obsolete*) a female professor **M18.** **profeˈssorial** *adjective* of, pertaining to, or characteristic of a professor or body of professors **E18.** **profeˈssorialism** *noun* the professorial system, professorial practice **M19.** **profeˈssorially** *adverb* **L19.** **profeˈssoriat** *noun* = **PROFESSORIATE M19.** **profeˈssoriate** *noun* (*a*) the professorial staff of a university; (*b*) the office or function of professor: **M19.** **professorship** *noun* the office or function of a professor **M17.**

proffer /ˈprɒfə/ *verb & noun*. **ME.**
[Anglo-Norman *proffrer*, -*ir*, Old French *proffrir*, earlier *poroffrir*, *pur-*, from *por* (from Latin **PRO-**[1]) + *offrir* **OFFER** *verb*.]
▶ **A** *verb*. **1** *verb trans.* Bring or put before a person for acceptance; offer, present. Now *literary*. **ME.** ▸†**b** *verb trans.* Attempt to engage in or inflict (battle, injury, etc.). **ME–L16.** ▸†**c** *verb intrans.* & *trans.* Make an offer. **LME–L16.**
2 *verb trans.* Offer or propose *to do*. *arch.* **ME.**
†**3** *verb trans.* Attempt or venture *to do*. **ME–M17.** ▸†**b** *verb intrans.* Esp. of a stag: make a movement as if to do something; begin to move and then stop. **LME–M17.**
📖 **1** G. SANTAYANA The Captain . . proffered a broad and muscular hand. J. WAINWRIGHT Barker . . took one of the proffered cigarettes.
▶ **B** *noun*. **1** An act of proffering; an offer. Now *literary*. **LME.**
2 *LAW* (now *Hist.*). A provisional payment of estimated dues into the Exchequer by a sheriff or other officer at certain appointed times. **LME.**
†**3** An indication, a sign, a trace. **M16–M18.**
■ **profferer** *noun* **E16**

proficiency /prəˈfɪʃ(ə)nsi/ *noun*. **M16.**
[from next: see **-ENCY**.]
†**1** Improvement in skill or knowledge, progress. **M16–M19.**
2 The quality or fact of being proficient; expertness, skill. **M17.** ▸**b** A skill. *rare.* **M17.**
Comb.: **proficiency badge**: worn by Scouts, Guides, etc., to mark achievement in a test of skill or endurance; **proficiency pay** *MILITARY* increased pay given in respect of proficiency.
■ Also †**proficience** *noun* **E17–L18.**

proficient /prəˈfɪʃ(ə)nt/ *adjective & noun*. **L16.**
[Latin *proficient-* pres. ppl stem of *proficere* advance, formed as **PRO-**[1] + *facere* do, make: see **-ENT**.]
▶ **A** *adjective*. **1** Possessed of or advanced in acquiring a skill; expert, skilled, adept. (Foll. by *in*, *at*.) **L16.**
†**2** Making progress, improving. *rare.* **E–M17.**
▶ **B** *noun*. †**1** A learner making progress in a skill etc. **L16–M18.**
2 A person who has made good progress in a skill etc.; an expert, an adept. Now *rare.* **L16.**
■ **proficiently** *adverb* **M19.**

†**proficuous** *adjective*. **E17–E18.**
[from late Latin *proficuus*, from Latin *proficere*: see prec., **-OUS**.]
Profitable, advantageous, useful.

profile /ˈprəʊfʌɪl/ *noun*. **M17.**
[Italian †*profilo*, now *proffilo* (whence also French *profil*, whence perh. some of the English senses), from †*profilare*: see next.]
1 A drawing or other representation of the outline of something, esp. the face or head, as seen from the side. **M17.**
2 The actual outline of something, *spec.* a person's face (freq. in ***in profile*** below); *PHYSICAL GEOGRAPHY* the outline of part of the earth's surface, e.g. a river, as seen in a vertical section. **M17.** ▸**b** The shape of a wave. **E20.**
3 A sectional drawing of a building etc.; *FORTIFICATION* a transverse vertical section of a fort; the relative thickness of an earthwork etc.; an earthwork of strong or weak thickness. **M17.**
†**4** A ground plan. **L17–E18.**
5 a A short biographical sketch or character study, esp. of a public figure. **M18.** ▸**b** The manner or attitude of a person, government, etc.; the extent to which a person, organization, etc., attracts public notice or comment. **M20.**
6 A plate in which is cut one half of the outline of an object to be made (esp. from clay) by turning or moulding. **M18.**
7 *THEATRICAL*. A flat piece of scenery or stage property cut out in outline. **E19.**
8 a *SOIL SCIENCE*. The set of horizons of which a soil is composed, as displayed in a vertical cross-section down to the parent material. Also ***soil profile***. **E20.** ▸**b** *GEOLOGY*. A representation of the form of the interface between strata obtained from measurements made at points lying on a straight line; the line itself. **E20.** ▸**c** The outline formed on a chart by joining the scores that a person has obtained in personality tests; a similar type of diagrammatic representation of measured individual attributes for purposes of comparison. **M20.** ▸**d** *ASTRONOMY*. (A diagram of) the way the intensity of radiation varies with wavelength from one side of a line in a stellar spectrum to the other. **M20.** ▸**e** (A diagram of) the way a quantity varies along a line, esp. a vertical line through the earth or the atmosphere; any graph of empirical results in the form of a line. **M20.** ▸**f** *ASTRONAUTICS*. A particular sequence of accelerations undergone by a rocket in flight; the plan of a space flight as regards the nature and duration of successive trajectories. **M20.**
📖 **2** C. P. SNOW His profile confronted hers. V. J. CHAPMAN The beach profile . . allows the waves to break close in-shore. **5a** *Listener* A film profile of Julian Bream. **b** *Guardian* The British profile during the present crisis in Vietnam has been . . low. **8c** *Physics Bulletin* Abstracts . . sent selectively to subscribers . . according to their interest 'profiles'.
Phrases etc.: ***high profile***, ***high-profile***: see **HIGH** *adjective*, *adverb*, & *noun*. **in profile** as seen from one side. ***low profile***, ***low-profile***: see **LOW** *adjective*. **profile of equilibrium** a the profile of a graded river or stream; the profile of a beach such that the amount of sediment deposited is balanced by the amount removed. **shoot a profile** *GEOLOGY* make measurements of a profile (sense 8b), e.g. in geophysical surveying.
Comb.: **profile component** *EDUCATION* a target for attainment in a particular subject, forming part of a general assessment of a pupil; **profile cut** a method of cutting a diamond in which it is sliced into thin plates that are polished on one side, finely grooved on the other, and bevelled on the edge; **profile cutter** a cutting tool in wood- or metalworking machines which corresponds in shape to the profile to be produced; **profile drag** the part of the drag on an aerofoil or aircraft which is not attributable to lift; **profile grinding** *ENGINEERING*: in which the grinding wheel is given a profile which, when viewed at right angles to the axis of rotation, is the negative of the one to be produced on the work; **profile machine** *ENGINEERING*: for shaping the profile of small parts of machinery, in which the cutting tool is guided by a pattern; **profile shot** a photograph or view of the face in profile.
■ **profilist** /-fɪl-/ *noun* a person who produces profile portraits or silhouettes **L18.**

profile /ˈprəʊfʌɪl/ *verb*. **E18.**
[Italian †*profilare* draw in outline, formed as **PRO-**[1] + *filare* spin, (formerly) draw a line from Latin, from *filum* thread. Cf. **PURFLE** *verb*.]
1 *verb trans.* **a** Represent in profile; draw in cross-section; outline. **E18.** ▸**b** Compose or present a biographical profile of (a person); present a summary of information about. **M20.**
2 *verb trans.* Provide (an object) with a profile of a specified nature; *ENGINEERING* shape, esp. by means of a tool guided by a template. **E19.**
3 *verb trans.* Chiefly *GEOLOGY*. Measure or investigate the profile of, esp. by means of measurements made at collinear points. **E20.**
4 *verb intrans.* Present one's profile to view; *BULLFIGHTING* stand in profile in preparation for a charge. **M20.**
📖 **1b** *Listener* H. O. Nazareth profiles the work of Farrukh Dhondy. **2** DYLAN THOMAS Fasten your affections on some immaculately profiled young man. *Practical Woodworking* The same cutter is used to profile an ovolo mould.
■ **profiler** *noun* (*a*) *ENGINEERING* a profile machine; (*b*) an instrument for measuring profiles, esp. of strata of rock or the seabed: **E20.** **profiling** *noun* the action of the verb; *spec.* the recording and analysis of a person's psychological and behavioural characteristics, so as to assess or predict their capabilities in a certain sphere or to assist in identifying a particular subgroup of people: **L19.**

profilin /prəʊˈfɪlɪn/ *noun*. **L20.**
[from **PRO-**[1] + **FIL**(**AMENTOUS** + **ACT**)**IN**.]
BIOCHEMISTRY. One of the proteins which inhibits the polymerization of actin in eukaryotic cells.

profilograph /prəʊˈfʌɪləgrɑːf/ *noun*. **L19.**
[French *profilographe*, from *profil* **PROFILE** *noun*: see **-O-**, **-GRAPH**.]
= **PROFILOMETER** 2.

profilometer /prəʊfʌɪˈlɒmɪtə/ *noun*. **L19.**
[French *profilomètre*, from *profil* **PROFILE** *noun*: see **-OMETER**.]
1 An instrument for measuring a person's profile. **L19.**
2 (**P-**.) (Proprietary name for) an instrument for measuring or recording the roughness of a surface; *spec.* (*a*) one in which a fine stylus is drawn over a metal surface; (*b*) one consisting of a wheeled frame for travelling along a road. Cf. **ROUGHOMETER**. **M20.**
■ **profilometry** *noun* **L20.** **profiloˈmetric** *adjective* **L20.**

profil perdu /prɔfil pɛrdy/ *noun phr*. Pl. **-s -s** (pronounced same). **M20.**
[French, lit. 'lost profile'.]
A profile in which the head is more than half turned away from the onlooker.

profit /ˈprɒfɪt/ *noun*. **ME.**
[Old & mod. French from Latin *profectus* progress, profit, from *profect-* pa. ppl stem of *proficere*: see **PROFICIENT**.]
1 Advantage or benefit to a person or group; (one's) good. Also, advantage or benefit residing in a thing, use. **ME.** ▸†**b** That which is to the advantage or benefit of someone or something. *rare* (Shakes.). Only in **E17.**
2 a Income from an estate, position, etc; revenue, proceeds. Usu. in *pl.* **ME.** ▸**b** The financial gain in a transaction or enterprise; the excess of returns over outlay; the surplus of a company or business after deducting wages, cost of raw materials, interest, and other expenses. Also, the state of being profitable. **L15.** ▸†**c** *sing.* & in *pl.* Interest on capital. *Scot.* **M16–M17.**
†**3** Respect, honour; reputation. Only in **LME.**
†**4** = **PROFICIENCY** 1. **LME–E17.**
📖 **1** ADDISON Posts of Honour, Dignity, and Profit. G. B. SHAW Before the Peace Conference can be discussed with any profit. **2a** JOHN BROOKE The colonelcy of a regiment was a place of considerable profit. **b** *Daily Telegraph* Pergamon Press . . is back in profit. *Times* The corporation would make a profit of about £12m.
Phrases: **at a profit** with financial gain. ***mesne profits***: see **MESNE** *adjective* 1. **profit and loss** the gain and loss made in a commercial transaction or series of transactions; (***profit and loss account***, an account to which all gains are credited and losses debited, so as to ascertain the overall profit or loss; a financial statement showing a company's net profit after offsetting all other ordinary expenses against the gross profit from trading). **profit à prendre** /ɑː ˈprɑːndrə/ [French, lit. 'profit to take'] *LAW* a right to go on another's land and take produce from it, as by logging, mining, drilling, grazing animals, etc. ***retained profit***: see **RETAIN** 3c. ***small profits and quick returns***: see **SMALL** *adjective*. ***turn a profit***: see **TURN** *verb*. ***violent profits***: see **VIOLENT** *adjective*. ***with-profit(s)***: see **WITH** *preposition*.
Comb.: **profit centre** a part of an organization with assignable revenues and costs and hence ascertainable profitability; a profitable part of an organization; **profit margin** the amount by which revenue from sales exceeds cost of sales, usu. considered as a percentage of the latter; **profit motive** the incentive that the possibility of making profits gives to individual or free enterprise; **profit-sharing** the sharing of profits, esp. between a company and its employees; **profit-taking** *STOCK EXCHANGE* the action of selling shares etc. that have risen in price in order to realize the profit.
■ **profitless** *adjective* unprofitable, useless **L16.** **profitlessly** *adverb* **M19.** **profitlessness** *noun* **E19.**

profit /ˈprɒfɪt/ *verb*. **ME.**
[Old & mod. French *profiter*, formed as prec.]
▶ **I 1** *verb trans.* & *intrans.* Be of advantage or benefit (to). **ME.** ▸†**b** Of a person: bring profit or benefit to or *to* someone. **LME–M17.**
2 *verb intrans.* Derive a benefit. Usu. foll. by *by*, *from*, *of*. **LME.**
📖 **1** J. H. NEWMAN What will it ultimately profit a man to profess without understanding? **2** E. BLISHEN We could watch teachers at work, and profit from doing so.
▶†**II 3** *verb intrans.* Make progress, improve, prosper. **ME–L17.**
▶†**III 4** Bring forward, present. *rare.* **LME–E17.**

profitable /ˈprɒfɪtəb(ə)l/ *adjective & noun*. **ME.**
[Old & mod. French, formed as **PROFIT** *noun*: see **-ABLE**.]
▶ **A** *adjective*. **1** Beneficial, useful, fruitful, valuable. **ME.**
2 Yielding a financial profit; gainful, remunerative. **LME.**
📖 **1** O. MANNING He moved away to find more profitable companionship.
▶†**B** *noun*. Benefit, gain; a useful or profitable thing. **LME–L17.**
■ **profitaˈbility** *noun* the quality or state of being profitable; (a) capacity to make a profit: **ME.** **profitableness** *noun* **LME.** **profitably** *adverb* **LME.**

profiteer /prɒfɪˈtɪə/ *verb & noun*. **E19.**
[from **PROFIT** *noun* + **-EER**.]
▶ **A** *verb intrans.* & *trans.* Make or seek to make an excessive profit (from). **E19.**
▶ **B** *noun*. A person who profiteers. **E20.**
¶ Rare before **E20.**

profiter /ˈprɒfɪtə/ *noun*. **LME.**
[from **PROFIT** *verb* + **-ER**[1].]
†**1** A person who makes progress. **LME–E16.**
†**2** A benefactor. Only in **LME.**
3 A person who makes a profit or gains by something. **E19.**

profiterole /prəˈfɪtərəʊl/ *noun*. **E16.**
[French, dim. of *profit* **PROFIT** *noun*: see **-OLE**[1].]
†**1** Some kind of cooked food. **E16–E18.**
2 A small hollow case of choux pastry usu. filled with cream and covered with chocolate sauce. **L19.**

proflavine /prəʊˈfleɪviːn/ *noun.* E20.
[from PRO-^{2} + FLAVINE.]
PHARMACOLOGY. An acridine derivative, $C_{13}H_{11}N_3$, which is used as an antiseptic.

profligate /ˈprɒflɪgət/ *adjective & noun.* M16.
[Latin *profligatus* ruined, dissolute, pa. pple of *profligare* overthrow, ruin, formed as PRO-^{1} + *fligere* to strike: see -ATE^{2}.]
▶ **A** *adjective.* **I** †**1** Overthrown, overwhelmed, routed. M16–M17.
▶ **II 2** Abandoned to vice or indulgence; recklessly licentious, dissolute. E17.
3 Recklessly extravagant. L18.

> **3** L. DEIGHTON The energy he . . wasted with profligate disregard.

▶ **B** *noun.* A profligate person. E18.
■ **profligacy** *noun* the quality, state, or condition of being profligate M18. **profligately** *adverb* L17. **profligateness** *noun* (now *rare*) M17.

profligate /ˈprɒflɪgeɪt/ *verb trans.* Now *rare* or *obsolete.* M16.
[Latin *profligat-* pa. ppl stem of *profligare*: see prec., -ATE^{3}.]
Overcome, overthrow, defeat; dispel, disperse; ruin, destroy.
■ †**profligated** *adjective* (*a*) overthrown, dissipated; (*b*) profligate: L16–E18. **profliˈgation** *noun* [Late Latin *profligatio(n-)*] LME.

profluent /ˈprəʊflʊənt/ *adjective.* LME.
[Latin *profluent-* pres. ppl stem of *profluere*, formed as PRO-^{1} + *fluere* to flow: see -ENT.]
Flowing onward or out; flowing in a full stream.
■ **profluence** *noun* (*arch.*) [Latin *profluentia*] †(*a*) a flowing onward or out; a current, a flow; †(*b*) fluency (of speech); (*c*) abundance, profusion: M16.

pro forma /prəʊ ˈfɔːmə/ *adverbial, adjectival, & noun phr.* E16.
[Latin.]
▶ **A** *adverbial phr.* As a matter of form. E16.
▶ **B** *adjectival phr.* Done or produced as a matter of form; designating a model or standard document or form; *spec.* (of an invoice) sent in advance of goods supplied or with goods sent on approval. M19.

> S. QUINN All that remained . . was a dissertation, almost a *pro forma* exercise.

▶ **C** *noun phr.* Pl. **pro formas**. A pro forma invoice or form. E20.

> M. GILBERT Inside of every . . file cover . . is a pro forma into which you fill the essential details.

profound /prəˈfaʊnd/ *adjective & noun.* ME.
[Anglo-Norman, Old French *profund*, (also mod.) *profond* from Latin *profundus*, formed as PRO-^{1} + *fundus* bottom.]
▶ **A** *adjective.* **1** Of a person, personal attribute or action, statement, etc.: that penetrates deeply into a subject; having or showing great insight; very learned. Formerly also, crafty, cunning. ME.
2 a Of a subject or thought: demanding much study or thought; abstruse, recondite; difficult to understand. LME. ▸**b** Of an emotion, condition, quality, etc.: intense, thorough, unqualified; deep-seated, far-reaching; (of silence, sleep, etc.) completely unbroken, difficult to break. E16.
3 a Having considerable downward or inward measurement, very deep; situated or extending far beneath the surface, deep-seated. LME. ▸**b** Originating in or coming from a depth; (of a sigh) deeply drawn; (of a bow etc.) carried far down or very low. M16.

> **1** J. BUCHAN A profound knowledge of Scottish songs, both words and tunes. G. VIDAL My profound analysis of the military situation. **2a** H. CARPENTER A slow learner of more profound things. **b** T. HARDY A profound distaste for the situation. H. A. L. FISHER While the differences of custom . . were superficial the resemblances were profound. P. LOMAS A profound effect on the victim's attitude to life. **3a** SHAKES. *Meas. for M.* Which of your hips has the most profound sciatica? W. OWEN I escaped Down some profound dull tunnel.

▶ **B** *noun.* †**1** The or an inner part. Only in LME.
2 (Usu. with *the*.) A profound or very deep thing; a vast depth; an abyss; *spec.* the depths of the sea. Chiefly *poet.* E17.
■ **profoundly** *adverb* deeply, intensely; with great insight or understanding; to or at a great depth, so as to come from or sink to a great depth: LME. **profoundness** *noun* †(*a*) an abyss; the or an inner or deep part; (*b*) the quality of being profound, profundity: LME.

profugate /ˈprɒfjʊgeɪt/ *verb trans. rare.* Pa. pple **-ated**, (*poet.*) **-ate** /-ət/. E17.
[from PRO-^{1} + Latin *fugare* put to flight + -ATE^{3}.]
Drive or chase away.

profulgent /prəʊˈfʌldʒ(ə)nt/ *adjective. rare.* L15.
[from PRO-^{1} + Latin *fulgent-* FULGENT.]
Shining forth, effulgent, radiant.

profunda /prəʊˈfʌndə/ *adjective & noun.* Pl. of noun **-dae** /-diː/. LME.
[Latin, fem. of *profundus* deep (sc. *vena*, *arteria*): see PROFOUND.]
ANATOMY. (Designating) any of various deep-seated arteries and veins.

profundal /prəʊˈfʌnd(ə)l/ *adjective & noun.* M20.
[from German *profund* profound + -AL^{1}.]
ECOLOGY. (Designating or pertaining to) the region of the bed of a lake lying below the limit of light penetration.

profundi *noun* pl. of PROFUNDUS *noun.*

profundity /prəˈfʌndɪti/ *noun.* LME.
[Old French *profundité* (mod. *-fond-*) or late Latin *profunditas*, from Latin *profundus*: see PROFOUND, -ITY.]
1 The quality of being profound, depth (*lit.* & *fig.*); abstruseness; intensity of feeling, understanding, etc. LME.
2 A very deep place; the deepest part *of* something; an abyss. LME. ▸†**b** = DEPTH 1. L15–L17. ▸**c** In *pl.* Depths of thought or meaning; deep matters. L16.

profundus /prəʊˈfʌndəs/ *noun & adjective.* Pl. of noun **-di** /-dʌɪ/. E18.
[Latin = deep (sc. *musculus*): see PROFOUND.]
ANATOMY. (Designating) any of various deep-seated muscles.

profuse /prəˈfjuːs/ *adjective.* LME.
[Latin *profusus* use as adjective of pa. pple of *profundere* pour out, formed as PRO-^{1} + *fundere* pour.]
1 Of a person or agent: giving or producing abundantly; lavish, extravagant. (Foll. by *in*, *of*.) LME.
2 Of an action, condition, or thing: very abundant, copious; excessive. E17.

> **2** E. YOUNG-BRUEHL A startling episode of profuse bleeding from Freud's mouth.

■ **profusely** *adverb* E17. **profuseness** *noun* L16.

†**profuse** *verb trans.* E17–L18.
[Latin *profus-* pa. ppl stem of *profundere*: see prec.]
Give or produce profusely or lavishly; squander, waste.

profusion /prəˈfjuːʒ(ə)n/ *noun.* M16.
[(French from) Latin *profusio(n-)*, formed as prec.: see -ION.]
1 a Lavish or wasteful expenditure; squandering, waste. M16. ▸**b** The fact, condition, or quality of being profuse; lavishness, extravagance; (a) great abundance. L17.
2 The action of pouring out, esp. wastefully; an outpouring, a shedding. Now *rare.* E17.

> **1a** CHESTERFIELD This idle profusion of time. **b** S. J. PERELMAN The reckless profusion of orchids on everyone's dinner table. *Daily Telegraph* Explanations of the left-handed brain are beginning to appear in profusion.

■ **profusive** *adjective* characterized by or tending to profusion M17.

prog /prɒg/ *noun*^{1}. *obsolete* exc. *Scot. dial.* E17.
[Origin unkn.: cf. BROG.]
1 A piercing instrument or weapon. E17.
2 A stab, a thrust, a prod. E19.

prog /prɒg/ *noun*^{2}. M17.
[Perh. from PROG *verb*^{1}.]
1 Food; *esp.* provisions for a journey. *slang* & *Canad. dial.* M17.
2 A hoard of money. *dial.* M19.

prog /prɒg/ *noun*^{3}. *Univ. slang.* Now *rare.* E20.
[Alt. of PROCTOR *noun.*]
A proctor at Oxford or Cambridge University.
■ Also **proggins** *noun* L19.

prog /prɒg/ *noun*^{4}. *slang.* L20.
[Abbreviation.]
A television or radio programme.

> J. HAWES We were watching some prog on the telly about the Evils of Drink.

prog /prɒg/ *adjective & noun*^{5}. *slang.* M20.
[Abbreviation.]
▶ **A** *adjective.* Progressive. M20.
▶ **B** *noun.* A progressive. M20.

prog /prɒg/ *verb*^{1}. *obsolete* exc. *dial.* Infl. **-gg-**. E17.
[Rel. to PROG *noun*^{2}.]
1 *verb intrans.* Search about, hunt about, esp. for food; go about begging. E17.
†**2** *verb trans.* Search out. Only in M17.
†**3** *verb trans.* Hoard. Only in E18.
■ **progger** *noun*^{1} L17.

prog /prɒg/ *verb*^{2} *trans. & intrans. dial.* Infl. **-gg-**. E19.
[from PROG *noun*^{1}.]
Poke, prod, prick.
■ **progger** *noun*^{2} (*a*) a butcher's stabbing instrument; (*b*) *US* a person who searches for clams: E19.

prog /prɒg/ *verb*^{3} *trans. Univ. slang.* Now *rare.* Infl. **-gg-**. E20.
[from PROG *noun*^{3}.]
= PROCTORIZE.

progenerate /prə(ʊ)ˈdʒɛnəreɪt/ *verb trans. rare.* E17.
[Latin *progenerat-* pa. ppl stem of *progenerare*, formed as PRO-^{1} + *generare*: see GENERATE *verb.*]
Beget, procreate.
■ †**progeneration** *noun* (*rare*) [Latin *progeneratio(n-)*] M16–M18.

progenitive /prə(ʊ)ˈdʒɛnɪtɪv/ *adjective.* M19.
[from Latin *progenit-*: see next, -IVE.]
Having reproductive power or properties.
■ **progenitiveness** *noun* M19.

progenitor /prə(ʊ)ˈdʒɛnɪtə/ *noun.* LME.
[Old French *progeniteur* from Latin *progenitor* ancestor, from *progenit-* pa. ppl stem of *progignere* beget, formed as PRO-^{1} + *gignere* create: see -OR.]
1 A person from whom another person, a family, or a race is descended; an ancestor; a parent; BIOLOGY an ancestral species. LME.
2 A spiritual, political, or intellectual predecessor. L16.
3 The original of which a thing is a copy. L19.
■ **progeniˈtorial** *adjective* of, pertaining to, or of the nature of a progenitor E19. **progenitorship** *noun* the position or fact of being a progenitor E19.

progenitress /prə(ʊ)ˈdʒɛnɪtrɪs/ *noun.* Now *rare.* E17.
[from prec. + -ESS^{1}.]
A female progenitor.

progenitrix /prə(ʊ)ˈdʒɛnɪtrɪks/ *noun.* Now *rare.* Also †**-trice**. Pl. **-trices** /-ˌtrɪsiːz/. L15.
[Late Latin, from Latin PROGENITOR: see -TRIX.]
= PROGENITRESS.

progeniture /prə(ʊ)ˈdʒɛnɪtʃə/ *noun.* L15.
[from Latin *progenit-*: see PROGENITOR, -URE.]
1 Begetting of offspring. L15.
2 Offspring, progeny. L15.

progeny /ˈprɒdʒ(ə)ni/ *noun.* ME.
[Old French *progenie* from Latin *progenies* descent, family, formed as PRO-^{1} + *gen-* base of *gignere* create, beget: see -Y^{3}.]
1 The offspring of a parent or couple; children, descendants; BIOLOGY & AGRICULTURE the offspring of an animal or plant; *fig.* successors, followers, disciples. ME.
†**2** = GENERATION 2. *rare.* ME–L15.
†**3** A race, stock, or line descended from a common ancestor. LME–L17.
†**4** Lineage, parentage, ancestry. LME–L18.
5 A product, an outcome, a result. LME.

> **1** B. GUEST The only one of their progeny not to graduate from college.

Comb.: **progeny test** AGRICULTURE an assessment of the genetic value of an animal or plant made by examining its progeny.

progeria /prə(ʊ)ˈdʒɪərɪə/ *noun.* E20.
[from Greek *progērōs* prematurely old, formed as PRO-^{2} + *gērōs* old age: see -IA^{1}.]
A syndrome of children characterized by physical symptoms suggestive of premature senility.
■ **progeric** *adjective* M20.

progestagen *noun* var. of PROGESTOGEN.

progestational /prəʊdʒɛˈsteɪʃ(ə)n(ə)l/ *adjective.* E20.
[from PRO-^{2} + GESTATION + -AL^{1}.]
PHYSIOLOGY. Pertaining to, promoting, or forming part of the physiological preparations for pregnancy; (of a substance) resembling progesterone in its effects.
■ **progestationally** *adverb* as regards progestational activity or state M20.

progesterone /prə(ʊ)ˈdʒɛstərəʊn/ *noun.* M20.
[German, blend of PROGESTIN and its German synonym *Luteosteron*, from *luteo-* repr. CORPUS **luteum**: see -STERONE.]
PHYSIOLOGY. A female steroid sex hormone secreted by the corpus luteum which is responsible for the cyclical changes in the uterus in the latter part of the menstrual cycle and is necessary for the maintenance of pregnancy.

progestin /prə(ʊ)ˈdʒɛstɪn/ *noun.* M20.
[from PRO-^{1} + GEST(ATION + -IN^{1}.]
PHYSIOLOGY. = PROGESTOGEN; *spec.* progesterone, esp. as an unpurified preparation.

progestogen /prə(ʊ)ˈdʒɛstədʒ(ə)n/ *noun.* Also **-gesta-**. M20.
[from prec. + -O- + -GEN.]
PHYSIOLOGY. Any of various steroid hormones, including progesterone, having progestational effects. Also called ***gestagen***.

> S. KITZINGER Not as reliable a contraceptive as the combined oestrogen and progestogen pill.

■ **progestoˈgenic** *adjective* M20.

proglottid /prəʊˈglɒtɪd/ *noun.* L19.
[from Greek *proglōssid-*, *-glōssis* point of the tongue, after Greek *glōtta*, *glōssa* tongue: see PRO-^{2}, GLOTTO-.]
A sexually mature segment or joint of a tapeworm, with a complete reproductive system.
■ Also **proglottis** *noun*, pl. **-ides** /-ɪdiːz/, M19.

prognathous /prɒgˈneɪθəs, ˈprɒgnəθəs/ *adjective.* M19.
[from PRO-^{2} + Greek *gnathos* jaw + -OUS.]
Having a projecting jaw; (of jaws) prominent, protruding. Cf. OPISTHOGNATHOUS, ORTHOGNATHOUS.
■ **prognathic** /prɒgˈnaθɪk/ *adjective* = PROGNATHOUS M19. **prognathism** /ˈprɒgnəθɪz(ə)m, prɒgˈnaθ-/ *noun* the condition or state of being prognathous M19. **prognathously** *adverb* in a prognathous manner; with the jaw prominent or protruding: L20. **prognathy** /ˈprɒgnəθi/ *noun* prognathism L19.

Progne /ˈprɒgni/ *noun. poet.* Also **Procne** /ˈprɒkni/. LME.
[Latin, alt. of *Procne*, Greek *Proknē*, Philomela's sister in mythol., who was transformed into a swallow (or in some accounts, a nightingale). Cf. PHILOMEL.]
The swallow (esp. wrongly regarded as a songbird).

prognose /prɒgˈnəʊz/ *verb trans. & intrans.* E20.
[Back-form. from next, after DIAGNOSE.]
Make a prognosis (of).

prognosis /prɒgˈnəʊsɪs/ *noun.* Pl. **-noses** /-ˈnəʊsiːz/. M17.
[Late Latin from Greek *prognōsis*, from *progignōskein* know beforehand, formed as PRO-[2] + *gignōskein* KNOW *verb*.]
1 *MEDICINE.* (A prediction of) the likely outcome of a disease (in general or in a particular case). M17.
2 *gen.* (A) prognostication. E18.

📖 **1** *Lancet* The prognosis of Pick's disease without surgical treatment is unfavourable for health. A. HUTSCHNECKER The cancer had invaded connective tissues, which gave the case a rather poor prognosis.

prognostic /prɒgˈnɒstɪk/ *noun.* Also (earlier) †**pron-**. LME.
[Old French *pronostique* (mod. *-ic*) from Latin *prognosticum*, *-con* from Greek *prognōstikon* use as noun of neut. of *prognōstikos*: see next, -IC.]
1 A thing which gives warning of something to come or about to happen; an omen, a portent. LME.
2 *MEDICINE.* A symptom or sign on which a prognosis is based. Formerly also, a prognosis. LME.
3 A prediction of the future, a forecast. M17.

prognostic /prɒgˈnɒstɪk/ *adjective.* LME.
[medieval Latin *prognosticus* from Greek *prognōstikos*, from *progignōskein*: see PROGNOSIS, -IC.]
1 Foretelling, predictive, (*of*). LME.
2 *MEDICINE.* Of or pertaining to prognosis. M17.
▪ **prognostical** *adjective* (*rare*) prognostic LME. **prognostically** *adverb* in a prognostic manner; by or with prognostication: E17.

prognosticate /prɒgˈnɒstɪkeɪt/ *verb.* LME.
[medieval Latin *prognosticat-* pa. ppl stem of *prognosticare*, from Latin *prognosticum*: see PROGNOSTIC *noun*, -ATE[3].]
†**1** *verb intrans.* Make or utter a prognostication or prediction (*of*). LME–M17.
2 *verb trans.* Know or tell of (an event etc.) beforehand; foresee, foretell, predict. L15.
3 *verb trans.* Of a thing: betoken, presage. L15.
▪ **prognosticable** *adjective* †(*a*) *rare* capable of prognosticating; (*b*) able to be prognosticated: M16. **prognosticative** *adjective* [French †*prognosticatif*, *-ive*] = PROGNOSTIC *adjective* 1 L16. **prognosticator** *noun* (*a*) a person who or thing which prognosticates something; a person who claims to know the future; (*b*) a maker or publisher of almanacs containing predictions of weather and events of an ensuing year; an almanac containing these: M16. **prognosticatory** *adjective* of the nature of a prognostication; serving to prognosticate something: L17.

prognostication /prɒgˌnɒstɪˈkeɪʃ(ə)n/ *noun.* LME.
[Old French *prognosticacion*, *-tion* from medieval Latin *prognosticatio(n-)*, formed as prec.: see -ATION.]
1 The action or fact, or an act, of prognosticating something; (a) prediction, (a) prophecy; foreboding. LME.
2 = PROGNOSTIC *noun* 1. Now *rare*. LME.
†**3** *MEDICINE.* = PROGNOSIS 1. LME–M18.
4 Orig., a prediction of the weather and events of a coming year, published in an almanac. Later (now *Hist.*), an almanac containing such a prediction. E16.

progradation /prəʊgrəˈdeɪʃ(ə)n/ *noun.* E20.
[from PROGRADE *verb* + -ATION.]
PHYSICAL GEOGRAPHY. The seaward advance of a beach or coastline as a result of the accumulation of river-borne sediment or beach material.

prograde /ˈprəʊgreɪd/ *adjective.* M20.
[from PRO-[1] + RETRO)GRADE *adjective*.]
1 *PETROGRAPHY.* Of a metamorphic change: resulting from an increase in temperature or pressure. Opp. RETROGRADE *adjective* 3c. M20.
2 *ASTRONOMY.* = DIRECT *adjective* 2a. M20.

prograde /prə(ʊ)ˈgreɪd/ *verb intrans. & trans.* E20.
[from PRO-[1] + RETRO)GRADE *verb*.]
PHYSICAL GEOGRAPHY. (Cause to) undergo progradation.

program *noun, verb* see PROGRAMME *noun, verb*.

†**programma** *noun.* Pl. **-grammata**. M17.
[Late Latin: see PROGRAMME *noun*.]
1 A written notice or proclamation displayed in a public place; *spec.* one giving information about a forthcoming event. M17–E19.
2 A written preface or introduction; in *pl.*, prolegomena. E18–L19.

programme /ˈprəʊgram/ *noun.* Also (earlier, now *US & COMPUTING*) **program**. E17.
[Orig. from late Latin *programma* from Greek, from *prographein* write publicly, formed as PRO-[2] + *graphein* write. Later reintroduced from French *programme*.]
▶ **I** †**1** = PROGRAMMA 1. *Scot.* E17–E19.
2 A written preface or introduction; an essay. Cf. PROGRAMMA 2. Now *rare*. M19.
▶ **II 3** A descriptive notice, issued beforehand, of any formal series of proceedings, e.g. an entertainment or a course of study; *esp.* a list of the events, pieces of music, or performers at a concert or show, in the order of their occurrence or appearance; such events etc., such a performance. E19. ▸**b** *gen.* A plan or outline of (esp. intended) activities; *transf.* a planned series of activities or events. M19. ▸**c** *MUSIC.* A sequence of objects, scenes, or events intended to be suggested by a musical composition or used to determine its structure. M19. ▸**d** = ***dance-card*** s.v. DANCE *noun.* Also ***dance programme***. L19.
4 *BROADCASTING.* **a** A broadcast presentation treated as a single item for scheduling purposes, being broadcast between stated times and without interruption except perhaps for news bulletins or advertisements. E20. ▸**b** A radio service or station providing a regular succession of programmes on a particular frequency. E20.
5 *ELECTRONICS.* A signal corresponding to music, speech, or other activity. Also ***programme signal***. M20.
6 a A sequence of operations that a machine can be set to perform automatically. M20. ▸**b** A series of coded instructions to control the operation of a computer or other machine. M20.

📖 **3** G. GREENE They sat two programmes round at the cinema. H. ROSENTHAL I have kept my programme and ticket stubs. **b** *Economist* Huge military and space programmes. E. HEATH A tour of . . vineyards completed our programme. **4a** B. MOORE American television is planning . . a special one-hour programme. ***magazine programme***, ***request programme***, ***schools programme***, etc. **b** *Times* Radio 3 . . the most civilised and broad-ranging programme. **6a** *Which?* There was a pre-rinse and . . two washing programmes. **b** *Which Micro?* Our . . home computer with four . . built-in programs.

Comb.: **programme-building** the selection of items for a concert or for a period of broadcasting; **programme chairman** *US* the person who arranges the programme of events or the agenda for a particular event for a society etc.; **programme company**: authorized to make programmes and advertisements for broadcasting on British commercial television; **programme movie** = *programme picture* below; **programme music**: intended to convey the impression of a definite series of objects, scenes, or events; **programme note** a note about the contents of a programme (at a concert, or broadcast); **programme picture** a cinema film for showing as part of a programme that includes another film as the main feature; **programme trading** *STOCK EXCHANGE* the purchase and sale of many different stocks at a time with the use of a computer program to exploit price differences in different markets; *esp.* the simultaneous purchase of stocks and sale of futures contracts on them, or vice versa.
▪ **progra'mmatic** *adjective* pertaining to or of the nature of a programme or programme music: L19. **progra'mmatically** *adverb* in the manner of a programme or programme music; in accordance with a programme; with regard to a programme: M20. **pro'grammatist** *noun* a person who composes or draws up a programme L19.

programme /ˈprəʊgram/ *verb.* Also (earlier, now *US & COMPUTING*) **program**, infl. **-mm-**, ***-m-**. L19.
[from the noun.]
1 *verb trans.* Arrange according to a programme; draw up a programme of; plan definitely. L19.
2 *verb trans. & intrans.* Broadcast. *US.* M20.
3 *verb trans. & intrans.* Express (a task or operation) in terms appropriate to its performance by a computer etc.; cause (an activity or property) to be automatically regulated in a prescribed way; incorporate (a property) *into* a computer etc. by programming. M20.
4 *verb trans. & intrans.* Cause (a computer etc.) automatically to do a prescribed task or perform in a prescribed way; supply with a program; *fig.* train to behave in a predetermined way. M20.
5 *verb intrans.* *ASTRONAUTICS.* Of a spacecraft: perform a scheduled and automatically controlled manoeuvre. M20.

📖 **1** *Listener* Americans . . are now being taught by . . programmed texts. *Daily Telegraph* He tried to programme her day into housework and study. *Church Times* The General was programmed to leave the gathering. **programmed cell death** (*MEDICINE & BIOLOGY*) = APOPTOSIS 2. **3** *Scientific American* The algorithm is easy to program and can be executed quickly with a computer. **4** M. FRAYN Another job . . a computer could . . be programmed to do.

▪ **programma'bility** *noun* the property of being programmable M20. **programmable** *adjective & noun* (*a*) *adjective* able to be programmed; (*b*) *noun* a programmable calculator: M20.

programmer /ˈprəʊgramə/ *noun.* Also ***programer**. L19.
[from PROGRAMME *noun*, *verb* + -ER[1].]
1 A person who arranges programmes or programmes things; *spec.* one who writes computer programs. L19.
2 = ***programme picture*** s.v. PROGRAMME *noun.* M20.
3 A device that automatically controls the operation of something in accordance with a prescribed programme. M20.

programming /ˈprəʊgramɪŋ/ *noun.* Also ***programing**. L19.
[formed as prec. + -ING[1].]
†**1** The writing of (musical) programme notes. *rare.* Only in L19.
2 The choice, arrangement, or broadcasting of radio or television programmes. M20.
3 The action of programming; planning for management or administrative purposes; the writing of computer programs. M20.

📖 **2** M. MCLUHAN TV caused drastic changes in radio programming.

progress /ˈprəʊgrɛs/ *noun.* LME.
[Latin *progressus*, from *progress-* pa. ppl stem of *progredi* go forward, formed as PRO-[1] + *gradi* proceed, walk, from *gradus* step.]
1 a The action or an act of journeying or moving onward; *spec.* (*a*) an official, esp. royal, visit or tour; (*b*) a state procession. *arch.* LME. ▸**b** Forward movement in space, as opp. to regress or rest; advance. E16. ▸**c** The physical path or course of water, a celestial object, etc. Chiefly *poet.* L16.
2 *fig.* **a** The course or process of a series of actions or events, a narrative, etc. LME. ▸**b** Advancement, esp. to a better state or condition; growth, development. LME.
3 *SCOTS LAW.* More fully ***progress of titles***. A series of title-deeds, extending over several years, constituting a person's title to land etc. M16.

📖 **1a** H. JAMES Her cool June progress through the charming land. **b** DAY LEWIS Lilies interfered with my progress. J. RATHBONE Once off we made good progress. **c** SHAKES. *Jul. Caes.* I cannot by the progress of the stars Give guess how near to day. **2a** G. W. KNIGHT Second-hand or vague knowledge reported during the play's progress. **in progress** in the course of developing, taking place. ***rake's progress***: see RAKE *noun*[4]. **b** G. M. TREVELYAN The constant progress of medical knowledge. JULIETTE HUXLEY They loved the children and followed their progress.

Comb.: **progress chaser** an employee responsible for ensuring that work is done efficiently and to schedule; **progress report** an interim report on progress made to date.

progress /prəˈgrɛs/ *verb.* L16.
[from the noun.]
1 *verb intrans.* Make a journey, travel; *spec.* (*arch.*) make a State progress, travel ceremoniously. Now chiefly as passing into sense 2. L16. ▸†**b** *verb trans.* Travel through; traverse. *poet.* L16–M17.
2 *verb intrans.* Of a person, action, etc.: go or move forward or onward; proceed. L16. ▸**b** *MUSIC.* Of melody or harmony: proceed from one note or chord to another. L19.
3 *verb intrans. fig.* Proceed to a further (esp. better) state or condition; advance, develop, grow. E17. ▸**b** Proceed by stages; form an advancing series. M19.
4 *verb trans.* Cause (a situation, condition, etc.) to move forward or improve; cause (work etc.) to proceed towards completion; *spec.* (*US*) secure the passage of (a bill) through a legislative body. E19.

📖 **2** J. BUCHAN As my studies progressed. *USA Today* As the day progressed. **3** M. SPARK Master Laurence is progressing. R. SHAW To progress, to add to the knowledge he had already obtained. B. EMECHETA Intensity of the knocks progressed . . to a final thunderous one. **4** *Marxism Today* To progress the possibility of women being represented. *Landscape* Every endeavour will be made to progress your interest.

progression /prəˈgrɛʃ(ə)n/ *noun.* LME.
[French, or Latin *progressio(n-)*, from *progress-*: see PROGRESS *noun*, -ION.]
1 The action or an act of progressing or moving forward (*lit.* & *fig.*); (an) advance. LME. ▸**b** The action or an act of progressing through a series; (a) succession. M16.
2 *MATH.* (The succession of) a series of quantities, between every two successive terms of which there is a constant relationship. LME.
3 *ASTROLOGY.* Movement of a planet, from west to east, in the order of the zodiacal signs. Opp. RETROGRADATION 1. M16.
4 *MUSIC.* The action of passing from one note or chord to another; a succession of notes or chords. Also = SEQUENCE *noun* 4b. E17.
5 *PHYSICS.* A series of regularly spaced lines or bands in a spectrum which arise from a series of energy levels of consecutive quantum numbers. E20.

📖 **1** D. ROWE The structure . . is that of linear progression. P. MONETTE A grim progression towards this . . catastrophe. **2** ***arithmetical progression***, ***geometrical progression***, ***harmonic progression***, etc.

▪ **progressional** *adjective* of, pertaining to, or involving progression L16. **progressionism** *noun* the theory or principles of progressionists M19. **progressionist** *noun* an advocate of or believer in progress, a progressive; *spec.* an advocate of or believer in the theory of gradual evolution towards higher forms of life or society M19.

progressist /ˈprəʊgrɛsɪst, prəˈgrɛsɪst/ *noun.* Now chiefly *Hist.* Also **P-**. M19.
[French *progressiste*, formed as PROGRESS *noun*: see -IST.]
= PROGRESSIVE *noun* 1.

progressive /prəˈɡrɛsɪv/ *adjective & noun.* E17.
[Old & mod. French *progressif, -ive* or medieval Latin *progressivus*, from Latin *progress-*: see PROGRESS *noun*, -IVE.]
▶ **A** *adjective.* **1** Proceeding by stages in a series; successive. E17. ▸**b** Of a card-game or dance: involving successive changes of partners. L19.
2 Characterized by progress or advance, esp. to a better state or condition; growing, developing. E17. ▸**b** MEDICINE. Of a disease: continuously increasing in severity or extent. M18. ▸**c** Of taxation: at a rate increasing with the sum taxed. L18. ▸**d** GRAMMAR = CONTINUOUS *adjective* 2. E20.
3 Moving forward or onward. Also (now *rare*), characterized by or designating motion involving forward movement. M17.
4 Of a person, group, etc.: advocating or supporting esp. political or social progress or reform. Of an educational method, school, etc.: stressing individual needs, informal and without strict discipline. M19. ▸**b** Favouring or promoting change or innovation; advanced, avant-garde. E20. ▸**c** Of music: modern, experimental, avant-garde, esp. in a specified area, as ***progressive jazz***, ***progressive rock***, etc. M20.

📖 **1** N. HAWTHORNE Pictures arranged . . in a progressive series. **b** R. MACAULAY Whist? . . We have . . progressive drives on Wednesday nights. **2** J. S. MILL A people . . may be progressive for a certain . . time. **4** R. CHRISTIANSEN The virtues of . . the progressive and . . conservative positions. **b** E. H. GOMBRICH The most 'progressive' . . innovator . . was Antonio Allegri. JAN MORRIS Progressive of appearance, having long sideburns and a droopy moustache.

Special collocations: **progressive assimilation** PHILOLOGY the process whereby a sound is modified by one closely preceding it. **Progressive Judaism** Liberal or Reform Judaism. **progressive kiln** a long kiln through which timber is passed to dry. **progressive metamorphism** PETROGRAPHY prograde metamorphism (see PROGRADE *adjective* 1). **progressive proofs** in colour printing, a test series of proofs made with cumulative layers of colour.

▶ **B** *noun.* **1** An advocate or supporter of esp. political or social progress; a member of a progressive political group or party. M19.
2 In *pl.* = ***progressive proofs*** above. E20.
3 An advocate or practitioner of a progressive method of education. M20.
4 GRAMMAR. The progressive aspect or tense; a form of a verb in this. M20.
■ **progressively** *adverb* E17. **progressiveness** *noun* E18. **progressivism** *noun* the principles or practice of a progressive; advocacy or support of progress or reform: L19. **progressivist** *noun* = PROGRESSIVE *noun* 1 L19. **progreˈssivity** *noun* the condition or degree of being progressive, esp. with ref. to taxation L19. **progressor** *noun* a person who progresses or makes progress E17.

proguanil /prəʊˈɡwɑːnɪl/ *noun.* M20.
[from PRO(PYL + BI)GUAN(IDE + -IL.]
PHARMACOLOGY. A bitter-tasting synthetic biguanide derivative, 1-*p*-chlorophenyl-5-isopropylbiguanide, $C_{11}H_{16}ClN_5$, used in the prevention and treatment of malaria.
¶ A proprietary name for this drug is PALUDRINE.

Progymnasium /ˈproːɡʏmˌnaːzɪʊm/ *noun.* Pl. ***-sien*** /-zɪən/. M19.
[German from mod. Latin, formed as PRO-¹ + GYMNASIUM.]
In Germany, a secondary school preparatory to a gymnasium.

†**proheme** *noun* see PROEM.

prohibit /prə(ʊ)ˈhɪbɪt/ *verb trans.* Pa. pple **prohibited**, †**prohibit**. LME.
[Latin *prohibit-* pa. ppl stem of *prohibere*, formed as PRO-¹ + *habere* hold.]
1 Forbid (a thing) as by a command; forbid (a person) *from* doing, (arch.) *to do*. Also with double obj. LME.
2 Prevent or hinder by physical means; debar; make impossible. M16. ▸†**b** With neg. in following clause: command *not to do* a thing, command or cause *that . . not*. M16–E18.

📖 **1** A. RANKEN Parents were prohibited from selling, gifting, or pledging their children. P. FUSSELL Purchase of tires was prohibited. **2** MILTON Gates . . Barr'd over us prohibit all egress. P. TOYNBEE Degrees of pain and discomfort which almost prohibit wise thoughts.

■ **prohibiter**, **prohibitor** *nouns* E17.

prohibited /prə(ʊ)ˈhɪbɪtɪd/ *ppl adjective.* M16.
[from prec. + -ED¹.]
That has been prohibited; forbidden, debarred.
prohibited area a region which only authorized people may enter. ***prohibited degrees***: see DEGREE *noun*.

prohibition /prəʊhɪˈbɪʃ(ə)n, prəʊɪ-/ *noun.* LME.
[Old & mod. French, or Latin *prohibitio(n-)*, formed as PROHIBIT: see -ITION.]
1 *gen.* The action or an act of forbidding a thing or person (as) by a command; a decree or order prohibiting something, an interdict. LME.
2 LAW. **a** An order or (formerly) writ from a superior court, now *spec.* the High Court, forbidding an inferior court from proceeding in a suit deemed to be beyond its cognizance. LME. ▸**b** Each of three clauses in a deed of entail prohibiting the heir from selling, incurring debt on, or altering the succession to an estate. *Scot.* M19.
3 The legal ban on the trade or importation of a specified commodity. L17. ▸**b** *spec.* The legal proscription of the manufacture and sale of alcohol for consumption; *esp.* (*Hist.*, freq. **P-**) (the period of) such a proscription in the US from 1920 to 1933. M19.

📖 **1** DAY LEWIS Few prohibitions about what I might read. E. FEINSTEIN Forbidden fruit, all the sweeter for being under prohibition. **3** A. HUTSCHNECKER The prohibition of the drug traffic is . . ineffective. **b** A. LOOS There is prohibition and nobody can get anything to drink. *Economist* Bright . . supported temperance, but opposed prohibition.

Comb.: **Prohibition party** a political party in the US, formed in 1869 to nominate or support advocates of the prohibition of alcohol.
■ **prohibitionary** *adjective* of or pertaining to prohibition, esp. of the manufacture and sale of alcohol L19. **prohibitionism** *noun* the principles or practice of prohibition, esp. of the manufacture and sale of alcohol L19. **prohibitionist** *noun* an advocate or supporter of prohibition, esp. of the manufacture and sale of alcohol M19.

prohibitive /prə(ʊ)ˈhɪbɪtɪv/ *adjective.* LME.
[Orig. from French *prohibitif, -ive* or medieval Latin *prohibitivus*, formed as PROHIBIT; later from PROHIBIT + -IVE.]
1 Having the quality or effect of prohibiting something; forbidding, debarring. (Foll. by *of*.) LME.
2 Of a tax, price, etc.: set so high as to prevent the purchase, use, or abuse of something. L19.
3 GRAMMAR. Expressing prohibition; negative in an imperative use. L19.

📖 **1** A. BROOKNER His smile, vague, pleasant, prohibitive of deeper enquiries. **2** *Guardian* Insurance rates against banditry, mutiny and storm were getting prohibitive.

■ **prohibitively** *adverb* M19. **prohibitiveness** *noun* L19.

prohibitory /prə(ʊ)ˈhɪbɪt(ə)ri/ *adjective.* L16.
[Latin *prohibitorius* restraining, formed as PROHIBIT: see -ORY².]
1 = PROHIBITIVE 1; *esp.* of or pertaining to the prohibition of alcohol, supporting or advocating prohibition. L16.
2 = PROHIBITIVE 2. M19.

project /ˈprɒdʒɛkt, ˈprəʊ-/ *noun.* LME.
[Latin *projectum*, formed as next.]
†**1** An (esp. written or drawn) outline or draft; a tabulated statement; a preliminary design or pattern. LME–E17.
†**2** (A) mental conception, (a) speculation. L16–E18.
3 = PROJECTION 5. *rare*. E17.
4 A planned or proposed undertaking; a scheme. E17.
†**5** A projectile. E17–E18.
6 *spec.* **a** A usu. long-term exercise or study of a set topic undertaken by a pupil or group of pupils. E20. ▸**b** An individual or collaborative enterprise undertaken usu. for industrial or scientific research, or having a social purpose. M20. ▸**c** A government-subsidized estate or block of houses or apartments with relatively low rents. Also more fully ***housing project***. *N. Amer.* M20.

📖 **4** J. MASEFIELD He had no project outlined. DAY LEWIS The project—I mean the burning—was fortunately abandoned. **6a** R. CARSON One of the local schools made the collection of insecticide-poisoned birds a science project. *Beano* Our project this week is helping old folk. **b** J. DISKI Back in the forest working on my project, checking over the information I had gathered. *Guardian* A wave power research project at Queen's University, Belfast.

project /prəˈdʒɛkt/ *verb.* Pa. pple & ppl adjective **-ed**, (earlier) †**project**. LME.
[Latin *project-* pa. ppl stem of *pro(j)icere* throw out, expel, formed as PRO-¹ + *jacere* throw.]
▶ **I** †**1** *verb trans.* Throw away or out (*lit.* & *fig.*); reject, abandon. LME–E17.
2 a *verb trans.* Place in a protruding position; cause to jut or stand out. Now *rare*. LME. ▸**b** *verb intrans.* Jut or stand out; protrude. L17.
3 *verb trans.* Chiefly ALCHEMY. Throw or cast (a substance) *in, into, on*, or *upon* something. Cf. PROJECTION 1. Now *rare*. L15.
4 *verb trans.* Throw or cause to move forward or outward; propel. L16. ▸**b** *verb intrans.* Wander (*around*), stroll; trifle *with*. *US dial.* E19.
5 *verb trans.* Cause (light, an image, shadow, etc.) to fall on a surface or extend into space. Now *esp.* cause (a cinematic, photographic, etc., image) to be visible on a screen. Foll. by *against, on, upon*. M17. ▸**b** PSYCHOANALYSIS. Transfer (an emotion, state of mind, etc.) to an external person or thing, esp. unconsciously. Cf. PROJECTION 5b. E20.
6 *verb trans.* CARTOGRAPHY. Make a geometric or other projection or representation on a plane surface of (the earth, sky, etc., or any portion of them); GEOMETRY draw a projection of (a figure etc.). Cf. PROJECTION 4a. M17.
7 *verb trans.* **a** Imagine (oneself, an image, situation, etc.) removed in space or time, esp. into the future. M19. ▸**b** Chiefly ECONOMICS. Calculate or forecast on the basis of present trends. M20.
8 *verb trans.* & *intrans.* **a** Express (oneself, an idea, etc.) to others forcefully or effectively. M20. ▸**b** (Cause to) be audible at a distance. M20.

📖 **2b** M. GIROUARD A . . bay window projects from the drawing-room. **5** A. GRAY Blackness on which Lanark's dazzled eyes projected stars. G. ADAIR On the . . screen was projected the logo of Paramount pictures. **7a** G. CLARK Careful not to project into the remote past the elaborate social arrangements of the recent Indians. **b** *Times* Inflation is projected to remain . . subdued. **8a** V. PACKARD The problem is to project yourself as a person. **b** M. ATWOOD You have to project to three sides.

▶ **II 9** *verb trans.* Plan or design (a course of action, scheme, etc., or (now *rare*) *to do*). LME. ▸†**b** *verb intrans.* Form a plan; scheme. Only in 17.
†**10** *verb trans.* Display; exhibit. Only in 17.

📖 **9** H. JAMES Another visit . . was projected.

▶ **III 11** *verb trans.* (in *pass.*) & *intrans.* ANATOMY. Be connected with a specified part of the nervous system by nerve fibres. Foll. by *on, to, upon*. E20.
■ **projectable** *adjective* able to be projected E20.

projectile /prə(ʊ)ˈdʒɛktʌɪl, -tɪl/ *noun & adjective.* M17.
[mod. Latin, formed as prec.: see -ILE.]
▶ **A** *noun.* An object projected or propelled through space, the air, etc.; *esp.* a missile designed to be fired from a gun or rocket. M17.
▶ **B** *adjective.* **1** Caused by propulsion or projection; propelled. Now *rare* or *obsolete*. L17.
2 Projecting or driving forward, propelling. E18.
3 Able to be projected by force; *esp.* able to be fired from a gun etc. as a missile. M19.
4 LITERARY CRITICISM. Of an adjective: expressing the author's view of a thing rather than being objectively descriptive. E20.
3 projectile anchor a collapsible anchor designed to be shot out of a tube, used esp. in life-saving.

projection /prəˈdʒɛkʃ(ə)n/ *noun.* L15.
[Latin *projectio(n-)*, formed as PROJECT *verb*: see -ION.]
▶ **I 1** ALCHEMY. The throwing of an ingredient into a crucible; *esp.* the casting of the powder of philosopher's stone on a molten metal to effect its transmutation into gold or silver; the transmutation of metals. Now *Hist.* L15. ▸**b** *fig.* Transmutation, change. Now *rare*. M17.
2 The action of throwing something forward; propulsion. L16.
▶ **II 3** The action of drawing a map or plan of a surface or three-dimensional object; *esp.* the representation on a plane surface of (part of) a spherical surface, esp. that of the earth or of the celestial sphere; any of the geometrical or cartographic methods by which this may be done. Also, a drawing, plan, or map so made. M16.
4 a GEOMETRY. The drawing of straight lines or rays through every point of a given figure, usu. so as to fall on a surface or line and produce on it a new figure each point of which corresponds to a point of the original figure; such a ray; a point of the resulting figure; the whole resulting figure. M17. ▸**b** MATH. Any homomorphism from a vector space etc. into a part of itself such that each element of the part is mapped on to itself. Also, a homomorphism from a group into a quotient group. M20. ▸**c** Chiefly ECONOMICS. A forecast or estimate based on present trends. M20.
5 An external (esp. visual) manifestation of a mental image, idea, etc. E18. ▸**b** PSYCHOANALYSIS. The process or fact of (usu. unconsciously) transferring one's own feelings, desires, fantasies, etc., to another person, thing, or situation, to avoid recognizing them as one's own and thereby to justify one's behaviour. Cf. PROJECT *verb* 5b. E20. ▸**c** The action of conveying a positive self-image to others. M20.
6 The action of projecting an image on to a surface, esp. a cinema screen; the fact of being so projected. L19. ▸**b** MUSIC. The projective quality of sound; acoustic penetration. L20.
7 PHYSIOLOGY & PSYCHOLOGY. More fully ***eccentric projection***. The process whereby a stimulus is perceived as being located at a point other than where the sensation or perception occurs. L19.
8 ANATOMY. The spatial distribution in the cerebral cortex etc. of the points to which nerves or nerve impulses go from any given area or organ. Cf. PROJECT *verb* 11. L19.

📖 **1 powder of projection** powder of the philosopher's stone. *New Statesman* Sales were way above projections. **3 *clinographic projection, conical projection, homolographic projection, Mercator's projection, orthogonal projection, spherical projection, stereographic projection***, etc. **5** R. W. EMERSON A . . projection of God in the unconscious. E. WILSON Myths . . are projections of . . human imagination. **6** *Times* Amplified sound . . slide projection . . all the tools of the professional. **b** *Oxford Times* The increased projection of the viola was remarkable.

▶ **III 9** The action of forming a mental project or plan; scheming. Now *rare*. L16.
†**10** = PROJECT *noun* 4. M17–E19.

▶ **IV 11 a** The action of placing a thing or part in a projecting or protruding position; the fact or condition of being so placed; *esp.* the representation of relief in a painting. L16. ▸**b** A protruding thing or part. M18.

Comb.: **projection booth**, **projection box** = *projection room* below; **projection fibre** a nerve fibre connecting the cerebral cortex with another part of the central nervous system, esp. with the brainstem or spinal cord; **projection lens** the objective lens in a film or slide projector, which projects an enlarged image; **projection printer** PHOTOGRAPHY an apparatus for projection printing; an enlarger; **projection printing** PHOTOGRAPHY printing in which a lens system is placed between the negative and the printing paper, so that variable enlargement or reduction of the projected image is possible; **projection room** a room in a cinema or film studio containing the projector and projectionist; **projection rule** GRAMMAR a rule for predicting the semantic structure of a sentence, from its syntactic structure; **projection television** a large television receiver in which the image is projected optically on to a large viewing screen; **projection test** = *PROJECTIVE test*; **projection welder**, **projection welding** (an apparatus for) resistance welding in which welding is carried out at one or more projecting points of contact previously formed in the components by pressing.

■ **projectional** *adjective* L19. **projectionist** *noun* a person who operates a film projector E20.

projective /prəˈdʒɛktɪv/ *adjective.* M17.
[from PROJECT *verb* + -IVE.]
1 That projects or can project; of, pertaining to, or marked by projection. M17.
2 *spec.* In GEOMETRY etc., of, pertaining to, or produced by the projection of lines or figures on a surface. In PSYCHOLOGY, mentally projecting or projected. L17.

Special collocations: **projective geometry** the branch of geometry that deals with projective properties. **projective plane** MATH. a two-dimensional manifold which is a spherical shell with all pairs of antipodal points identified. **projective property** a property (of a figure) which remains unchanged after projection. **projective space** MATH. a space obtained by taking a vector space of the next higher dimension, identifying all vectors which are multiples of one another, and omitting the origin. **projective test** PSYCHOLOGY a test designed to reveal unconscious elements of personality by asking a person to respond freely to words, pictures, etc., placed before him or her. **projective verse** a type of free verse seeking to replace traditional ideals of poetic form with open or natural structures.

■ **projectively** *adverb* L19. **projecˈtivity** *noun* (*rare*) E20.

projector /prəˈdʒɛktə/ *noun.* L16.
[from PROJECT *verb* + -OR.]
1 A person who forms a project or plan; the originator of an enterprise. L16. ▸**b** A schemer, *esp.* a promoter of speculative companies; a cheat. *arch.* E17.
2 A person who or thing which projects or throws something forward. L17.
3 A person who forecasts or makes projections. M19.
4 a An apparatus for projecting a powerful light; a searchlight. L19. ▸**b** An apparatus comprising a light source and lens system for projecting an enlargement of a slide, film, or opaque surface on to a screen. L19.

■ **projectress** *noun* (now *rare* or *obsolete*) a female projector E17.

projecture /prəˈdʒɛktjʊə/ *noun.* Now *rare.* M16.
[French from Latin *projectura*, formed as PROJECT *verb*: see -URE.]
The fact or state of projecting or protruding; *spec.* (ARCHITECTURE) a projecting moulding on a column etc.

projet /prɔʒɛ/ *noun.* Pl. pronounced same. E19.
[French, formed as PROJECT *noun.*]
A proposal or a draft, esp. of a treaty.

projicient /prəˈdʒɪʃ(ə)nt/ *adjective.* E20.
[from Latin *projicient-* pres. ppl stem of *pro(j)icere* PROJECT *verb*: see -ENT.]
Concerned with or pertaining to an individual's perception of his or her surroundings at a distance, as with the senses of vision, hearing, and smell.

■ **projicience** *noun* projicient activity or ability E20.

prokaryotic /ˌprəʊkarɪˈɒtɪk/ *adjective.* Also **-cary-**. M20.
[from PRO-² + Greek *karuon* nut, kernel + *-ōtēs* -OT²: see -IC.]
BIOLOGY. (Of a cell) having no nuclear membrane; (of an organism) composed of such a cell, belonging to the group which comprises bacteria and blue-green algae; of or pertaining to a prokaryotic cell or organism. Opp. EUKARYOTIC.

■ **proˈkaryote** *noun* a prokaryotic organism (opp. EUKARYOTE) M20.

proke /prəʊk/ *verb.* Now *Scot.* & *dial.* ME.
[Origin uncertain: perh. rel. to PRICK *verb*, POKE *verb*¹, PROG *verb*². Cf. Low German *proken* prod, poke, scratch, scrawl.]
1 *verb trans.* = POKE *verb*¹ 1, 2. ME.
2 *verb intrans.* = POKE *verb*¹ 10. E17.

prokinesis /prəʊkɪˈniːsɪs, -kʌɪ-/ *noun.* M20.
[from PRO-² + (AS) KINESIS.]
ZOOLOGY. A form of upper jaw mobility, found in many birds, in which the flexing occurs at the junction of the upper jaw and neurocranium. Cf. RHYNCHOKINESIS.

■ **prokinetic** /-ˈnɛtɪk/ *adjective* M20.

prolabium /prəʊˈleɪbɪəm/ *noun.* Pl. **-bia** /-bɪə/. L17.
[medieval Latin, formed as PRO-¹ + LABIUM.]
ANATOMY. The prominent or outer part of a lip.

prolactin /prəʊˈlaktɪn/ *noun.* M20.
[from PRO-¹ + LACT(ATION + -IN¹.]
PHYSIOLOGY. A gonadotrophic polypeptide hormone which promotes lactation, secreted by the anterior pituitary. Cf. LACTOGEN.

prolamine /ˈprəʊləmiːn/ *noun.* Also (now *rare*) **-in** /-ɪn/. E20.
[from PROLINE with inserted *-am* (from AMIDE).]
BIOCHEMISTRY. Any of certain proteins which occur in the seeds of cereals and are insoluble in water.

prolan /ˈprəʊlan/ *noun.* M20.
[from Latin *proles* progeny + -AN.]
A mixture of female sex hormones, comprising follicle-stimulating hormone and luteinizing hormone.

prolapse /ˈprəʊlaps, prəˈlaps/ *noun.* L16.
[Anglicized from PROLAPSUS.]
†**1** The lapse or passage *of* time. Only in L16.
2 MEDICINE & VETERINARY MEDICINE. A slipping forward or down of a part or organ from its normal position, freq. into a cavity; the eversion of an organ etc., *spec.* the uterus or rectum, through an opening. Also, the prolapsed part or organ. E19.

prolapse /prəʊˈlaps/ *verb intrans.* M18.
[Latin *prolaps-* pa. ppl stem of *prolabi* slip forward or down: see PRO-¹, LAPSE *verb*.]
MEDICINE & VETERINARY MEDICINE. Of an organ etc.: slip forward or downward out of place. Freq. as ***prolapsed*** *ppl adjective.*

†**prolapsion** *noun.* L16.
[Latin *prolapsio(n-)*, formed as prec.: see -ION.]
1 MEDICINE. = PROLAPSUS. L16–E19.
2 The action or an act of falling into sin or error. E–M17.

prolapsus /prəʊˈlapsəs/ *noun.* L18.
[mod. Latin from late Latin = fall, formed as PROLAPSE *verb.*]
MEDICINE. = PROLAPSE *noun* 2.

prolate /ˈprəʊleɪt/ *adjective.* L17.
[Latin *prolatus* pa. pple of *proferre* carry forward, extend, prolong, formed as PRO-¹ + *ferre* carry: see -ATE².]
1 GEOMETRY. Of a spheroid: lengthened in the direction of the polar diameter, (as) by the revolution of an ellipse about its longer axis. Opp. ***oblate***. L17.
2 Extended or extending in width; *fig.* widely spread. Also (GRAMMAR) = PROLATIVE 2. M19.

📖 **2** H. G. WELLS There shone brightly a prolate moon.

■ **prolately** *adverb* M19. **prolateness** *noun* M18.

prolate /prəʊˈleɪt/ *verb trans.* Now *rare* or *obsolete.* E17.
[Latin *prolat-* pa. ppl stem of *proferre*: see prec., -ATE³.]
Extend, increase, lengthen; *esp.* lengthen (a word etc.) in articulation.

prolation /prə(ʊ)ˈleɪʃ(ə)n/ *noun.* LME.
[Latin *prolatio(n-)*, formed as prec.: see -ATION.]
†**1** (A) production, *esp.* (an) utterance of words. LME–M18. ▸**b** CHRISTIAN THEOLOGY. The generation or procession of the Logos. L17–E18.
2 MEDIEVAL MUSIC. The relative duration of minim to semibreve in a particular rhythm. Formerly also *gen.*, melody, measure. LME.

prolative /prə(ʊ)ˈleɪtɪv/ *adjective.* L17.
[from PROLATE *adjective* + -IVE.]
†**1** Spoken, declaratory. *rare.* Only in L17.
2 GRAMMAR. Esp. of an infinitive: serving to continue or complete a predication. M19.

prole /prəʊl/ *noun & adjective. colloq. derog.* L19.
[Abbreviation.]
▶ **A** *noun.* = PROLETARIAN *noun.* L19.
▶ **B** *adjective.* = PROLETARIAN *adjective.* M20.

proleg /ˈprəʊlɛg/ *noun.* E19.
[from PRO-¹ + LEG *noun.*]
ENTOMOLOGY. Any of the fleshy appendages or tubercles of some insect larvae, e.g. caterpillars, serving as legs but distinct from the true legs. Also called ***prop-leg***.

prolegomenon /prəʊlɪˈgɒmɪnən/ *noun.* Pl. **-mena** /-mɪnə/. M17.
[Latin from Greek, use as noun of neut. pres. pple of *prolegein* say beforehand, formed as PRO-² + *legein* say.]
An esp. critical or discursive introduction prefaced to a literary work; *transf.* a preliminary remark; *fig.* an event, action, etc., serving as an introduction *to* something. Freq. in *pl.* (treated as *sing.* or *pl.*).

■ **prolegomenal** *adjective* prefatory, introductory L19. **prolegomenous** *adjective* (*a*) = PROLEGOMENAL; (*b*) (of a person) long-winded, prolix: M18.

prolepsis /prəʊˈlɛpsɪs, -ˈliːpsɪs/ *noun.* Pl. **-lepses** /-ˈlɛpsiːz, -ˈliː-/. LME.
[Late Latin from Greek *prolēpsis*, from *prolambanein* anticipate, formed as PRO-² + *lambanein* take.]
1 RHETORIC. Orig., a brief introductory summary to an argument. Later, a preface to an argument intended to anticipate and preclude objection. LME. ▸**b** The anticipatory use of an adjective. M19.
2 The representation of a future act, state, etc., as already done or existing; anticipation; an instance of this. L16.
†**3** A presupposed or a priori principle or idea. M–L17.

proleptic /prəʊˈlɛptɪk, -ˈliːptɪk/ *adjective.* M17.
[Greek *prolēptikos*, from *prolambanein*: see prec., -IC.]
1 Of, pertaining to, or characterized by prolepsis; anticipatory. M17.
†**2** Of a principle, idea, etc.: presupposed, a priori. M–L17.
3 MEDICINE. Of a periodical disease: of which the paroxysm recurs before the expected time. Now *rare* or *obsolete.* L17.

■ **proleptical** *adjective* (*rare*) (*a*) = PROLEPTIC; (*b*) (of a date) assigned by astronomical etc. calculations, rather than by observation: E17. **proleptically** *adverb* E17. **proleptics** *noun* the branch of medicine that deals with prediction or prognosis M19.

proletaire /prəʊlɪˈtɛː, prɒl-/ *noun.* Now *rare.* E19.
[French *prolétaire*, formed as next.]
= PROLETARIAN *noun.*

■ **proletairism** *noun* = PROLETARIANISM M19. **proletariˈzation** *noun* = PROLETARIANIZATION E20.

proletarian /prəʊlɪˈtɛːrɪən/ *noun & adjective.* M17.
[from Latin *proletarius* a Roman citizen of the lowest class (regarded as serving the State only with their offspring), from *proles* offspring: see -AN.]
▶ **A** *noun.* A member of the proletariat. M17.
▶ **B** *adjective.* †**1** Low, vulgar. M17–M18.
2 Of, pertaining to, or characteristic of the proletariat. M19.

2 proletarian revolution in Marxist theory, the predicted stage of political development when the proletarians overthrow capitalism.

■ **proletarianism** *noun* (*a*) the condition of being a proletarian or having a proletarian class; (*b*) the political principles and practice of the proletariat: M19. **proletarianiˈzation** *noun* the fact or process of making or becoming proletarian in character E20. **proletarianize** *verb trans. & intrans.* make or become proletarian in character L17.

proletariat /prəʊlɪˈtɛːrɪət/ *noun.* Also **-ate**. M19.
[French *prolétariat*, formed as prec.: see -AT¹.]
1 a ROMAN HISTORY. The lowest class of citizens. M19. ▸**b** *transf.* The lowest class of any community, esp. when regarded as uncultured. Usu. *derog.* M19.
2 Wage earners collectively, *esp.* those without capital and dependent on daily labour for subsistence; the working classes. M19.

2 dictatorship of the proletariat in Marxist theory, the ideal of proletarian supremacy following the overthrow of capitalism and preceding the classless state.

proletary /ˈprəʊlɪt(ə)ri/ *adjective & noun.* Now *rare.* L16.
[formed as PROLETARIAN: see -ARY¹.]
= PROLETARIAN.
¶ Fell into disuse after M17; reintroduced M19.

proletkult /prəʊˈlɛtkʊlt/ *noun.* Also **-cult**. E20.
[Russian, contr. of *proletarskaya kul'tura* proletarian culture.]
Esp. in the former USSR, (the advocacy of) cultural activities designed to reflect or encourage a purely proletarian ethos.

prolidase /ˈprəʊlɪdeɪz/ *noun.* M20.
[from PROL(INE + IM)ID(O- + -ASE.]
BIOCHEMISTRY. A proteolytic enzyme which hydrolyses peptide bonds formed with the nitrogen atom of proline.

proliferate /prəˈlɪfəreɪt/ *verb.* L19.
[Back-form. from next.]
▶ **I** *verb intrans.* **1** BIOLOGY. Reproduce or increase in extent by cellular division or budding. Also in BOTANY, develop flowers, vegetative shoots, etc., from a flower, spikelet, or other normally terminal part. L19.
2 ZOOLOGY. Produce new individuals, esp. sexual zooids in hydrozoans; *gen.* give rise to an increasing number of offspring, reproduce prolifically. L19.
3 Increase greatly, multiply; become rife. M20.

📖 **3** E. ROOSEVELT My interests seem to proliferate rather than narrow. A. MASSIE With its . . two million independent shopkeepers, its proliferating restaurants.

▶ **II** *verb trans.* **4** BIOLOGY. Produce or form (cells, tissue, structures, offspring, etc.) by proliferation. L19.
5 Produce (esp. nuclear weapons) in large or increasing quantities. L20.

📖 **5** *Scientific American* Thousands of cheap missiles proliferated in a theater of warfare will put . . tanks out of business.

■ **proliferative** *adjective* (chiefly MEDICINE) characterized by or tending to proliferation (esp. of cells or tissue) L19. **proliferator** *noun* L20.

proliferation /prəlɪfəˈreɪʃ(ə)n/ *noun.* M19.
[French *prolifération*, from *prolifère* PROLIFEROUS: see -ATION.]
▶ **I 1** BIOLOGY & MEDICINE. Increase in the extent of tissues by cellular division or budding. M19.
2 ZOOLOGY. The production of sexual zooids by some hydrozoans. L19.
3 (A) multiplication, (an) increase in number, now esp. of nuclear weapons. E20.

📖 **3** *National Observer (US)* So dominant in the nuclear field that we could stop proliferation. Jo GRIMOND The proliferation of cars takes the pleasure out of motoring. ***vertical proliferation***: see VERTICAL *adjective*.

▸ **II 4** *BOTANY*. The condition or fact of being proliferous. **M19.**

proliferous /prəˈlɪf(ə)rəs/ *adjective*. **M17.**
[from Latin *proles* offspring + -FEROUS.]
1 = PROLIFIC 1. Long *rare* or *obsolete*. **M17.**
2 Producing many flowers. *rare*. **L17.**
3 *BOTANY*. Producing flowers, vegetative shoots, etc., from a flower, spikelet, or other normally terminal part. Also, reproducing by offsets rather than by seed. **E18.**
4 *ZOOLOGY*. Reproducing or multiplying by budding; *spec.* (of a hydrozoan) producing sexual zooids. **M19.**
5 *MEDICINE*. Proliferative. **L19.**
▪ **proliferously** *adverb* **M19.**

prolific /prəˈlɪfɪk/ *adjective*. **M17.**
[medieval Latin *prolificus*, from Latin *proles* offspring: see -FIC.]
1 Generating or producing offspring; reproductive. **M17.** ▸**b** Causing fertility; fertilizing. Now chiefly *poet.* **M17.**
2 Producing many offspring or fruit; fruitful; (of a season, climate, etc.) characterized by abundant produce. **M17.** ▸**b** Having or producing an abundance of something. Foll. by *of*, *in*. **M17.** ▸**c** *spec.* Of a person, esp. a creative artist: producing much work. **M20.**

📖 **2** R. MACAULAY By nature prolific, she . . presented me with several half-brothers. *transf.*: M. SEYMOUR To live by her prolific pen. **c** H. READ Delacroix was one of the most prolific of painters.

▪ **prolificacy** *noun* the quality or condition of being prolific **L18.** †**prolifical** *adjective* = PROLIFIC: only in 17. **prolifically** *adverb* **M18.** **prolificate** *verb trans.* (*rare*) make prolific or fruitful, fertilize **M17.** **prolifiˈcation** *noun* (*a*) the generation or production of offspring; reproductive power, fertility; (*b*) *BOTANY* (now *rare*) = PROLIFERATION 1: **LME.** **proliˈficity** *noun* = PROLIFICACY **E18.** **prolificness** *noun* **L17.**

proligerous /prəˈlɪdʒ(ə)rəs/ *adjective*. Now *rare* or *obsolete*. **M19.**
[from Latin *proles* offspring + -GEROUS.]
Bearing offspring; generative; germinative.

proline /ˈprəʊliːn/ *noun*. **E20.**
[Contr. of PYRROLIDINE.]
BIOCHEMISTRY. A heterocyclic imino acid, pyrrolidine-2-carboxylic acid, $C_5H_9NO_2$, which occurs in proteins and is an important constituent of collagen.

prolix /ˈprəʊlɪks, prəˈlɪks/ *adjective*. **LME.**
[Old & mod. French *prolixe* or Latin *prolixus* extensive, extended, lit. 'poured forth', formed as PRO-¹ + pa. ppl formation on *liquere* be liquid.]
1 Of long duration, lengthy, protracted; *esp.* (of speech, writing, a speaker, etc.) verbose, long-winded. **LME.**
2 Extended, physically long. Now *rare*. **LME.**

📖 **1** E. POUND *Vers libre* has become . . prolix and . . verbose.

▪ †**prolixious** *adjective* = PROLIX **E16–E17.** **proˈlixity** *noun* the quantity, state, or degree of being prolix **LME.** **prolixly** *adverb* **M16.** **prolixness** *noun* (now *rare*) **M17.**

Prolixin /prəʊˈlɪksɪn/ *noun*. **M20.**
[Invented word.]
PHARMACOLOGY. (US proprietary name for) fluphenazine hydrochloride, $C_{22}H_{26}F_3N_3OSHCl$, a phenothiazine derivative used as a tranquillizer.

†**proll** *verb* & *noun* see PROWL.

prolly /ˈprɒli/ *adverb*. *non-standard*. **M20.**
[Repr. a pronunc.]
Probably.

proloculus /prəʊˈlɒkjʊləs/ *noun*. Pl. **-li** /-lʌɪ, -liː/. **E20.**
[from PRO-² + LOCULUS.]
ZOOLOGY. The first chamber formed by the zygote of a foraminiferan.

prolocution /prəʊləˈkjuːʃ(ə)n, ˈprɒl-/ *noun*. Now *rare*. **LME.**
[Partly from late Latin *prolocutio(n-)*, from *prolocut-* pa. ppl stem of *proloqui* speak out; partly from PRO-¹ + LOCUTION.]
1 The action or an act of speaking on behalf of another or others. **LME.**
2 A preliminary remark, an introduction. **L16.**

prolocutor /ˈprəʊləkjuːtə, ˈprɒl-, prə(ʊ)ˈlɒkjʊtə/ *noun*. **LME.**
[Latin, from *prolocut-*: see prec., -OR.]
1 A person who speaks on behalf of another or others; a spokesperson. Now *rare*. **LME.**
2 *spec.* †**a** = ADVOCATE *noun* 1. *Scot.* **M16–L18.** ▸**b** The chair of the lower house of convocation of either province of the Church of England. **M16.** ▸**c** The presiding officer or speaker of any assembly. **M16.**
▪ **prolocutorship** *noun* the office or function of prolocutor **E18.**

PROLOG /ˈprəʊlɒg/ *noun*¹. Also **Prolog**. **L20.**
[from PRO(GRAMMING + LOG(IC.]
COMPUTING. A high-level programming language comparable to Lisp and devised for use in artificial intelligence.

prolog *noun*² & *verb* see PROLOGUE.

prologue /ˈprəʊlɒg/ *noun* & *verb*. Also ***-log**. **ME.**
[Old & mod. French from Latin *prologus* from Greek *prologos*, formed as PRO-² + *logos* saying, speech: see -LOGUE. Cf. EPILOGUE.]
▸ **A** *noun*. **1** The preface or introduction to a literary or musical work; *spec.* an introductory speech or short poem addressed to the audience by one of the actors in a play. **ME.** ▸**b** *transf.* A preliminary act, event, etc.; *spec.* (*CYCLING*) a short preliminary time trial held before a race to obtain a leader. **M17.**
2 The actor who delivers the prologue in a play. **L16.**

📖 **1** *Listener* The opera opens with a Prologue of the spirits. *fig.*: SHAKES. *2 Hen. VI* My death . . is made the prologue to their play.

▸ **B** *verb trans.* Introduce or provide (a play etc.) with a prologue; *poet.* introduce, precede. Usu. foll. by *by*, *with*. Usu. in *pass.* **E17.**
▪ **prologist** *noun* (*rare*) = PROLOGUIZER **E18.** **prologize** *verb intrans.* = PROLOGUIZE **E17.** **prologizer** *noun* = PROLOGUIZER **M19.** **prologuer** *noun* (*rare*) = PROLOGUE *noun* 2 **L16.** **prologuize** *verb intrans.* compose or deliver a prologue to a play etc. **E19.** **prologuizer** *noun* a person who composes or delivers a prologue to a play etc. **M18.**

prolong /prəˈlɒŋ/ *verb* & *noun*. **LME.**
[Old & mod. French *prolonger*; later from late Latin *prolongare*, formed as PRO-¹ + *longus* LONG *adjective*¹.]
▸ **A** *verb*. **1** *verb trans.* Extend in duration; cause to last longer. **LME.** ▸**b** Lengthen the pronunciation of (a syllable etc.). **M16.**
†**2** *verb trans.* & *intrans.* Delay, postpone; keep (a person) waiting. **LME–L18.** ▸**b** *verb trans.* Extend (time) so as to cause delay; protract. **LME–L16.**
†**3** *verb trans.* = PURLOIN. *rare*. **LME–L16.**
4 *verb trans.* Extend in spatial length; lengthen out. **L16.**

📖 **1** DAY LEWIS Lack of brothers . . prolonged my childishness. R. THOMAS I don't think there's much point in prolonging this.

▸†**B** *noun*. (A) delay, (a) prolongation. *Scot.* **LME–E17**
▪ **prolongable** *adjective* able to be prolonged **M19.** **prolonged** *ppl adjective* extended in space or (esp.) time; (tediously) lengthy **L18.** **prolongedly** *adverb* **M20.** **prolonger** *noun* **M16.** **prolongment** *noun* (*rare*) **L16.**

prolongate /ˈprəʊlɒŋgeɪt/ *verb trans.* *rare*. **L16.**
[Late Latin *prolongat-* pa. ppl stem of *prolongare* PROLONG *verb*: see -ATE³.]
Prolong in time or space.

prolongation /prəʊlɒŋˈgeɪʃ(ə)n/ *noun*. **LME.**
[Old & mod. French, or late Latin *prolongatio(n-)*, formed as prec.: see -ATION.]
1 The action or an act of prolonging; the state of being prolonged. **LME.**
2 (An) extension in scope or range. **M19.**

prolonge /prɔlɔ̃ːʒ/ *noun*. Pl. pronounced same. **M19.**
[French, from *prolonger* PROLONG *verb*.]
MILITARY. A jointed length of rope forming part of the equipment of a gun-carriage.

prolusion /prəˈl(j)uːʒ(ə)n/ *noun*. **E17.**
[Latin *prolusio(n-)*, from *prolus-* pa. ppl stem of *proludere*, formed as PRO-¹ + *ludere* play: see -ION.]
1 A preliminary event before a contest, performance, etc.; a prelude. **E17.**
2 A literary essay or article intended as a precursor of a fuller treatment of a subject. **E17.**
▪ **prolusory** *adjective* preliminary, introductory **M19.**

proly /ˈprəʊli/ *noun* & *adjective*. *colloq.* *derog.* **M20.**
[Abbreviation: see -Y⁶.]
= PROLETARIAN.

PROM *abbreviation*.
COMPUTING. Programmable read-only memory.

prom /prɒm/ *noun*. *colloq.* **L19.**
[Abbreviation of PROMENADE *noun*.]
1 A dance at a school or college. *US*. **L19.**
2 (Usu. **P-**.) A promenade concert; *esp.* any of the BBC Promenade Concerts. Also ***Prom concert***. **E20.**
3 = PROMENADE *noun* 2a. **E20.**

📖 **2** *Listener* Henry Wood decreed that the nine symphonies of Beethoven should be the backbone of the Proms.

▪ **prommer** *noun* (*colloq.*) a person who attends a promenade concert **M20.**

promastigote /prəʊˈmastɪgəʊt/ *noun* & *adjective*. **L20.**
[from PRO-² + Greek *mastig-*, *mastix* whip + *-ote* (cf. -OT²).]
ZOOLOGY & MEDICINE. (Designating) a parasitic protozoan of the genus *Leishmania* in the flagellated or leptomonad form. Opp. AMASTIGOTE.

promazine /ˈprəʊməziːn/ *noun*. **M20.**
[from PRO(PYL + M(ETHYL + AZINE.]
PHARMACOLOGY. A bitter-tasting phenothiazine derivative, $C_{17}H_{20}N_2S$, related to promethazine, used as a tranquillizer.
¶ A proprietary name for this drug is SPARINE.

promenade /prɒməˈnɑːd, -ˈneɪd, ˈprɒm-/ *noun* & *verb*. **M16.**
[French, from *se promener* walk, refl. of *promener* cause to walk: see -ADE. Cf. PROM.]
▸ **A** *noun*. **1** A leisurely walk (occas. a ride or drive), *esp.* one taken in a public place for display or amusement. **M16.**
2 a A place for promenading; a paved public walk, *esp.* one along the sea-front at a resort. **M17.** ▸**b** A gallery at a music hall. Now *Hist.* **M19.**
3 = ***promenade deck*** below. **M19.**
4 a = PROM 1. *US*. **L19.** ▸**b** *DANCING*. In ballet, a slow turn made on one leg; in country dancing, a movement resembling a march made by couples in formation. **M20.**
5 = ***promenade concert*** below. *rare*. **E20.**
Comb.: **promenade concert** a concert at which (part of) the audience may stand, sit on the floor, or move about; *spec.* (usu. with cap. initials) any in an annual series instituted by the English conductor Sir Henry Wood (1869–1944) and supported by the BBC; **promenade deck** an upper deck on a passenger ship where passengers may promenade.
▸ **B** *verb*. **1** *verb intrans.* Take a leisurely walk (occas. a ride or drive), esp. in a public place for display or amusement. **L16.**
2 *verb trans.* Promenade through (a place). **E19.**
3 *verb trans.* Lead (a person or animal) about a place, esp. for display. **M19.**
▪ **promenader** *noun* (*a*) a person who promenades; (*b*) a person who attends a promenade concert: **M19.**

prometaphase /prə(ʊ)ˈmɛtəfeɪz/ *noun*. **M20.**
[from PRO-² + METAPHASE.]
CYTOLOGY. The stage in mitosis or meiosis, following prophase and preceding metaphase, during which the spindle is formed and the chromosomes become oriented towards it; a dividing nucleus at this stage.

promethazine /prə(ʊ)ˈmɛθəziːn/ *noun*. **M20.**
[from PRO(PYL + METH(YL + AZINE.]
PHARMACOLOGY. A bitter-tasting phenothiazine derivative, $C_{17}H_{20}N_2S$, related to promazine, used as an antihistamine, anti-emetic, and sedative.
¶ A proprietary name for this drug is PHENERGAN.

promethea /prəˈmiːθɪə/ *noun*. **L19.**
[mod. Latin (see below) from Latin *Promethea* fem. of *Prometheus* adjective, formed as next.]
In full ***promethea moth***. A large N. American saturniid silk moth, *Callosamia promethea*.

Promethean /prəˈmiːθɪən/ *adjective* & *noun*. **L16.**
[from *Prometheus* (see below): see -AN.]
▸ **A** *adjective*. **1** Of, pertaining to, or resembling (esp. in skill or daring) Prometheus, in Greek mythology a demigod worshipped by craftsmen, who stole fire from the gods and gave it to the human race, and was punished for this by Zeus by being chained to a rock where an eagle fed each day on his liver. **L16.**
†**2** Designating a kind of match (see sense B.1 below). Only in **M19.**
▸ **B** *noun*. †**1** A match made from a flammable mixture of sugar and potassium chlorate wrapped in a paper roll around a small glass bulb of sulphuric acid, and igniting when fractured (superseded by the friction match). **M–L19.**
2 A Promethean person. **M19.**
▪ **Prometheanism** *noun* conduct or policy resembling that of Prometheus **M20.**

promethium /prəˈmiːθɪəm/ *noun*. **M20.**
[formed as prec. + -IUM.]
A soft silvery metallic chemical element, atomic no. 61, a rare radioactive member of the lanthanide series which is produced artificially. (Symbol Pm.) Cf. ILLINIUM.

prometryne /ˈprəʊmɪtrʌɪn/ *noun*. Also **-tryn** /-trɪn/. **M20.**
[from PRO(PYL + ME(THYL + *tryne* (from TRI(AZI)NE).]
A triazine herbicide, $C_{10}H_{19}N_5S$, used to control annual grasses and broad-leaved weeds.

prominence /ˈprɒmɪnəns/ *noun*. **L16.**
[French from Latin *prominentia* jutting out, from *prominent-*: see next, -ENCE.]
1 A prominent thing, *esp.* a jutting outcrop, mountain, etc. **L16.**
2 The fact, quality, or condition of being prominent (*lit.* & *fig.*). **E17.** ▸**b** *LINGUISTICS*. The degree to which a sound or syllable stands out from its phonetic environment. **E20.**
3 A salient point or matter. **E19.**
4 *ASTRONOMY*. A major eruption of incandescent gas projecting above the sun's chromosphere. Also ***solar prominence***. **L19.**

📖 **2** *Lancet* Endothelial prominence typical of secondary syphilis. *Village Voice* Through a syndicated column . . Rowan gained a national prominence.

▪ **prominency** *noun* (*a*) (now *rare*) a projection; (*b*) prominence: **M17.**

prominent /ˈprɒmɪnənt/ *adjective* & *noun*. **LME.**
[Latin *prominent-* pres. ppl stem of *prominere* jut out: see -ENT.]
▸ **A** *adjective*. **1** Jutting out or protruding from a surface; projecting, protuberant. **LME.**

2 Standing out so as to catch the attention; conspicuous; distinguished above others of the same kind, well known, famous. M18.

1 R. P. WARREN The chin bony and prominent. J. THURBER Prominent eyes which . . seemed to bulge unnaturally. 2 E. CLODD Ancestor-worship . . was the prominent feature of the old Aryan religion. P. LARKIN A list of prominent literary people.

▶ **B** *noun.* **1** A prominent person. Now *N. Amer.* E17.

2 A moth belonging to any of several genera of the family Notodontidae, bearing a tuft projecting from the inner margin of the forewings, and one or more humps on the back of the larva. E19.

■ **prominently** *adverb* M17.

prominenti /promiˈnɛnti/ *noun pl.* M20.
[Italian, pl. of noun from *prominente* adjective, formed as prec.]
Prominent or eminent people; leading personages.

promiscuous /prəˈmɪskjʊəs/ *adjective & adverb.* E17.
[from Latin *promiscuus*, formed as PRO-¹ + *miscere* mix: see -OUS.]
▶ **A** *adjective.* **1** Consisting of parts or elements of various kinds grouped or massed together without order; of mixed and disorderly composition or character. E17.
2 Indiscriminate; making no distinctions, undiscriminating. Now *esp.*, characterized by casual or indiscriminate changes of sexual partner. E17.
3 Of common gender; epicene. *rare.* M17.
†**4** That forms part of an indiscriminately mixed or undiscriminating company. Chiefly *derog.* M18–L19.
5 Casual, carelessly irregular. *colloq.* M19.

1 C. LYELL The strata . . settled down from this promiscuous mass. 2 S. JOHNSON Made cheap by promiscuous publication. *Times Lit. Suppl.* She was promiscuous in her favours. *Daily Telegraph* Abuse suffered from promiscuous . . male employers.

▶ **B** *adverb.* Promiscuously. Now *colloq.* L17.
■ **promiscous** *adjective* (long *obsolete* exc. *dial.*) = PROMISCUOUS *adjective* M17. **promiscuity** /prɒmɪˈskjuːɪti/ *noun* (*a*) the condition of being promiscuous, an instance of this; (*b*) promiscuous sexual behaviour: M19. **promiscuously** *adverb* E17. **promiscuousness** *noun* E18.

promise /ˈprɒmɪs/ *noun.* LME.
[Old & mod. French *promesse* or directly from Latin *promissum* use as noun of neut. pa. pple of *promittere* send or put forth, promise, formed as PRO-¹ + *mittere* send.]
1 A declaration or assurance by which a person undertakes a commitment to do or refrain from doing a specified act or gives a guarantee that a specified thing will or will not happen, be done, etc. LME. ▸**b** *spec.* A divine assurance of future benefit or blessing. LME.
2 A thing promised. LME.
3 *fig.* Indication of a future event or condition; *esp.* something giving strong or reasonable grounds for the expectation of future achievements or good results. Also (*poet.*, *rare*), a precursor, a harbinger. LME.

1 J. A. FROUDE Becket had broken his promise to submit to the Constitutions. A. S. DALE Gladstone was able to redeem his campaign promise. A. COHEN He could make no promises. 2 SHAKES. *Rich. III* Claim thou of me The earldom of Hereford . . . I'll claim that promise. 3 OED This scholarship is given for promise. T. CALLENDER He had promise . . and he would succeed.

Phrases: ***a lick and a promise***: see LICK *noun* 1. **bow of promise** *poet.* a rainbow (in allus. to *Genesis* 9:12–17). ***breach of promise***: see BREACH *noun* 2. **land of promise** = ***promised land*** s.v. PROMISE *verb*.
■ **promiseful** *adjective* †(*a*) *rare* full of promises; (*b*) full of promise, promising: L16.

promise /ˈprɒmɪs/ *verb.* LME.
[from the noun.]
1 *verb trans.* Make a promise to (a person), esp. to do, give, or procure a specified thing (freq. foll. by *that*, *to do*); make a promise to give (a specified thing) to a person; (with indirect obj.) make a promise to give a specified thing to (a person). LME. ▸**b** Engage to give in marriage to another; betroth. *arch.* M16. ▸†**c** In *pass.* Have an engagement. *rare* (Shakes.). Only in E17.
2 *verb intrans.* Make a promise. LME.
3 *fig.* **a** *verb trans.* Indicate the future occurrence or condition of; *esp.* give strong or reasonable grounds for expecting (future achievements or good results). L16. ▸**b** *verb intrans.* Appear likely to turn out in a specified way; encourage expectation. E17.

1 E. A. FREEMAN The princes promised free constitutions to their people. S. J. PERELMAN Not if they promised me a bucket of free quahogs. *Economist* He promised that if elected he would serve out his term. **I promise you** *colloq.* I assure you, I tell you plainly. **promised land** (*a*) THEOLOGY the land of Canaan, as promised to Abraham and his descendants (in *Genesis* 12:7 etc.); (*b*) *fig.* a place of expected happiness, *esp.* heaven. **promise oneself** look confidently foward to providing oneself with (something welcome). *John o' London's* Her lover had promised to marry her. **b** SHAKES. *Tam. Shr.* Her father . . will not promise her to any man. **2** TENNYSON Dora promised, being meek. **3a** K. AMIS The sky promised hours of sunshine. **b** B. MASON Better-looking than he had promised as a boy.

■ **promiˈsee** *noun* (esp. LAW) a person to whom a promise is made M18. **promiser** *noun* LME. **promisor** *noun* (esp. LAW) a person who makes a promise M19.

promising /ˈprɒmɪsɪŋ/ *adjective.* L16.
[formed as prec. + -ING².]
1 Likely to turn out well; full of promise; hopeful. L16.
2 That makes a promise or promises. *rare.* L16.

1 *Garden News* Quite a few seedlings look promising. *New York Times* Cardiologists involved in the study of a promising new heart drug.

■ **promisingly** *adverb* L17.

promissor /prə(ʊ)ˈmɪsə/ *noun.* E17.
[Latin, from *promiss-* pa. ppl stem of *promittere*: see PROMISE *noun*, -OR.]
†**1** ASTROLOGY. = PROMITTOR. Only in 17.
2 ROMAN LAW. A promisor. E17.

promissory /ˈprɒmɪs(ə)ri/ *adjective.* LME.
[medieval Latin *promissorius*, formed as prec.: see -ORY².]
1 Conveying or implying a promise; of, pertaining to, or of the nature of a promise. LME.
2 *fig.* Indicative of something to come; full of promise, promising. M19.
1 promissory note a signed document containing a written promise to pay a stated sum to a particular person or the bearer at a specified date or on demand. **promissory oath**: which guarantees a future action.
■ **promissive** /prəˈmɪsɪv/ *adjective* (now *rare*) = PROMISSORY 1 E17.

†**promit** *verb trans. & intrans.* Infl. **-tt-**. LME–M18.
[Latin *promittere*: see PROMISE *noun*.]
Promise.

promittor /prəˈmɪtə/ *noun.* M17.
[from (the same root as) prec. + -OR. Cf. PROMISSOR.]
ASTROLOGY. A planet, fixed star, or point in the heavens which, when a significator is brought into some particular aspect with it, prognosticates the occurrence of some event.

promo /ˈprəʊməʊ/ *noun & adjective. colloq.* M20.
[Abbreviation of PROMOTION, PROMOTIONAL.]
▶ **A** *noun.* Pl. **-os**. Publicity, advertising. Also, a vehicle for this, *spec.* (*a*) a trailer for a television programme; (*b*) a promotional video for a pop record etc. M20.
▶ **B** *adjective.* = PROMOTIONAL *adjective.* L20.

promontory /ˈprɒm(ə)nt(ə)ri/ *noun.* M16.
[medieval Latin *promontorium* alt. (after Latin *mont-*, *mons* MOUNT *noun*¹) of Latin *promunturium*, perh. formed as PRO-¹ + *mont-*: see -ORY¹.]
1 A point of high land jutting out into the sea; a headland. M16.
2 ANATOMY. A projecting part on a bone etc. M19.
■ **promontorial** /prɒm(ə)nˈtɔːrɪəl/ *adjective* (*rare*) of, pertaining to, or resembling a promontory M19. **promontoried** *adjective* formed into or provided with a promontory M17. **promontorium** /prɒm(ə)nˈtɔːrɪəm/ *noun* (*rare*) a promontory M17.

promorphology /prəʊmɔːˈfɒlədʒi/ *noun.* Now *rare.* L19.
[from PRO-² + MORPHOLOGY.]
BIOLOGY. The morphology of fundamental forms; the branch of morphology that deals with organic forms from a mathematical standpoint; stereometric morphology.
■ **promorphoˈlogical** *adjective* L19. **promorphoˈlogically** *adverb* L19. **promorphologist** *noun* L19.

promote /prəˈməʊt/ *verb.* LME.
[Latin *promot-* pa. ppl stem of *promovere* move forward, formed as PRO-¹ + *movere* move.]
▶ **I 1** *verb trans.* Advance or raise (a person) to a higher rank or position etc.; transfer (a team) to a higher division of a league. LME. ▸**b** CHESS. Raise (a pawn reaching the opponent's end of the board) to the rank of a higher piece, esp. a queen. E19. ▸**c** BRIDGE. Enable (a relatively low card) to win a trick; secure (a trick) by this means. M20.
2 *verb trans.* Further the development, progress, or establishment of (a thing); encourage, help forward, or support actively (a cause, process, etc.). LME. ▸**b** Actively support the passing of (a law); *spec.* take the necessary steps to ensure the passing of (a local or private bill). E18. ▸**c** CHEMISTRY. Act as a promoter of (a catalyst) or in (a catalytic reaction); *loosely* catalyse, initiate. E20. ▸**d** Publicize (a product); advertise the merits of (a commodity). M20.
†**3** *verb trans.* Publish, promulgate; advance (a claim). L15–L17.
4 *verb trans.* Cause to move forward in space or time; extend. *obsolete* exc. *dial.* M17.

1 *Times* Bristol City, . . promoted a year ago, return to a lower division. M. MAHY She had been promoted to shop manager. A. MASSIE She was promoted to the rank of Officier de la Légion d'Honneur. 2 B. BETTELHEIM Enough to promote the necessary personality changes. P. MAILLOUX Able to judge the talent of others and willing to promote it. **b** *Daily Telegraph* A private Bill, promoted by the L.C.C. **d** *Melody Maker* With the group over here to promote their latest recording . . they could well make the chart.

▶ **II** †**5** *verb trans. & intrans.* Inform against (a person), lay information about (a crime etc.). LME–L16.
6 *verb trans.* ECCLESIASTICAL LAW. Set in motion (the office of the ordinary or judge) in a criminal suit; institute (a suit) by permission of the ordinary. L17.
7 *verb trans.* Borrow, obtain illicitly. *slang* (orig. *US*). M20.
■ **promotaˈbility** *noun* suitability for promotion M20. **promotable** *adjective* able or deserving to be promoted E18. **promoˈtee** *noun* a person who is or has been promoted M20. **promoting** *adjective* (*a*) that promotes; (*b*) MEDICINE that causes tumour promotion: L16. **promotive** *adjective* having the quality of promoting; tending to promotion (*of*): E16. **promotiveness** *noun* M19.

promoter /prəˈməʊtə/ *noun.* LME.
[Anglo-Norman *promotour* (= French *promoteur*) from medieval Latin *promotor*, formed as PROMOTE: see -ER¹.]
1 *gen.* A person who or thing which promotes someone or something. LME. ▸**b** A person who promotes or is party to the formation of a corporation or joint-stock company. Also more fully ***company promoter***. L19. ▸**c** CHEMISTRY. An additive which increases the activity of or otherwise improves the performance of a catalyst. Also, a substance used to initiate a catalytic polymerization reaction. E20. ▸**d** A person who organizes or finances a sporting event, theatrical production, etc., esp. for profit. M20. ▸**e** MEDICINE. An agent that promotes tumour formation following initiation by a carcinogen. M20. ▸**f** GENETICS. A part of an operon, situated between the operator and the structural gene(s), at which transcription starts. M20.
2 a A person whose business was to prosecute or denounce offenders against the law; a professional informer. *obsolete* exc. *Hist.* L15. ▸**b** ECCLESIASTICAL LAW. The prosecutor of a suit in an ecclesiastical court. M18.
3 = PROMOTOR 1. L17.

1 E. A. FREEMAN Harold . . appears as a special promoter of German churchmen. *Country Life* The promoters of turkey-meat sales.

■ **promotress** *noun* (*arch.*) a female promoter E17.

promotion /prəˈməʊʃ(ə)n/ *noun.* LME.
[Old & mod. French from Latin *promotio(n-)*, formed as PROMOTE: see -ION.]
▶ **I 1** *gen.* The action of promoting someone or something; the fact of being promoted; an instance of this. LME.
2 The publicization of a product; the advertisement of the merits of a commodity etc.; an instance of this. E20.
3 An entertainment or sporting event (esp. a boxing-match) staged for profit. M20.

1 G. CRABBE Promotion's ladder, who goes up or down. *Nature* The promotion of high standards in scientific and technical information work. T. ALLBEURY The official notification of his promotion to major. *Pulse* Increasing the number of health promotion clinics. ***Irishman's promotion***: see IRISHMAN 1. 2 *Bookseller* Applicants should have several years' experience in books promotion.

▶ **II 4 a** CHEMISTRY. The action of promoting a catalyst or a catalytic reaction. E20. ▸**b** MEDICINE. The furtherance of neoplastic growth following its initiation by a carcinogen; the conversion of latent tumour cells into active malignant ones. M20.
5 a PHONETICS. (An instance of) the intensification of normal stress levels in verse. M20. ▸**b** LINGUISTICS. In transformational grammar, the translation of material from an embedded to a main sentence. Now *rare.* M20.
■ **promotional** *adjective* E20.

promotor /prəˈməʊtə/ *noun.* E18.
[medieval Latin: see PROMOTER.]
1 In some Scottish universities, the official who presents students for degrees. E18.
2 CHEMISTRY. = PROMOTER 1C. M20.

†**promove** *verb.* LME.
[(Old French *promovoir* (mod. *promouvoir*) from) Latin *promovere* PROMOTE.]
1 *verb trans.* = PROMOTE 1. LME–L17.
2 *verb trans.* = PROMOTE 2. LME–M18.
3 *verb trans.* Provoke, instigate, incite. L15–E18.
4 *verb intrans.* Advance, make progress. L16–M17.
■ †**promovent** *adjective* (*rare*) that promotes; causing progress: E17–E19.

prompt /prɒm(p)t/ *noun.* LME.
[In branch I from Latin *promptus* (see PROMPT *adjective*); in branch II from PROMPT *verb*; in branch III from PROMPT *adjective*.]
▶ **I** †**1** Readiness. *rare.* Only in LME.
▶ **II 2** An act of prompting. Also, something said or suggested to prompt someone, *spec.* a forgotten word, sentence, etc., supplied to an actor or reciter. L16. ▸**b** THEATRICAL. A prompter. M20.
3 COMPUTING. A message or sign on a VDU screen to indicate that the system is waiting for input. L20.
▶ **III 4** COMMERCE. A time-limit for payment of an account for goods purchased; a date when payment becomes due. M18.
Comb.: **prompt-book** a copy of a play annotated with directions for the prompter's use; **prompt-box**: in front of the footlights beneath the stage where the prompter sits; **prompt-copy** = ***prompt-book*** above; **prompt-note**: given to a customer as a

reminder of payment due; **prompt side** the side of the stage where the prompter sits, usu. on the actor's left; **prompt-script** = ***prompt-book*** above; **prompt table** the table on which the prompter rests his book.

prompt /prɒm(p)t/ *adjective & adverb*. LME.
[Old & mod. French, or directly from Latin *promptus* pa. pple of *promere* bring forth, formed as PRO-¹ + *emere* take.]
▶ **A** *adjective*. **1** Quick to act; acting with alacrity; ready and willing. LME. ▶†**b** Inclined, disposed. *rare* (Shakes.). Only in E17.
2 Of action, speech, etc.: ready, quick; done, performed, etc., without delay. E16.
3 COMMERCE. (Of goods) for immediate delivery and payment; (of a payment) due at once or at the date fixed, made forthwith. L19.
4 NUCLEAR PHYSICS. Of a neutron or gamma ray: emitted within a small fraction of a second as the direct result of a fission, as distinct from radiation due to the decay of fission products. M20.

📖 **2** *Lancet* Prompt return of nausea precluded further digitalisation. *National Trust Magazine* Disease caused by fungal attacks is kept at bay by the prompt removal of both infected and damaged material.

▶ **B** *adverb*. Promptly, punctually. E20.

📖 A. PILLING Breakfast was at 5.30 prompt.

Comb.: **prompt-critical** *adjective* (NUCLEAR PHYSICS) critical even when the effect of delayed neutrons is neglected and prompt neutrons alone are considered.
■ **promptly** *adverb* in a prompt manner, without delay L15. **promptness** *noun* E16.

prompt /prɒm(p)t/ *verb trans*. ME.
[from assumed medieval Latin verb from Latin *promptus*: see PROMPT *adjective*.]
1 Incite to action; urge or induce (a person etc.) *to*, *to do*. ME.
2 Assist (a hesitating speaker) by suggesting a word etc.; supply a forgotten word, sentence, etc., to (an actor, reciter, etc.). LME. ▶†**b** Remind. *rare* (Shakes.). Only in L16.
3 Urge, suggest, or dictate (a thing); inspire or give rise to (a feeling, thought, action, etc.). E17.

📖 **1** N. GORDIMER The small child is prompted by the mother to wave. G. SWIFT Prompted by some look in his father's eyes. **2** F. C. BURNAND It was like being prompted in an examination, and being unable to catch the word. **3** R. NIEBUHR The motives which prompt human action. *Music & Letters* His lordly ways . . prompted vicious satires.

■ **prompting** *noun* (*a*) the action of the verb; (*b*) an instance of this, a prompt: LME. **promptive** *adjective* (*rare*) tending or calculated to prompt someone or something L19. **prompture** *noun* (*rare*) prompting, suggestion, instigation; an instance of this: E17.

prompter /ˈprɒm(p)tə/ *noun*. LME.
[from PROMPT *verb* + -ER¹.]
1 A person who urges or incites another to action. LME.
2 A person who prompts a hesitating speaker; *spec.* a person in a theatre stationed at one side of the stage out of sight of the audience to prompt the actors. L16.

promptitude /ˈprɒm(p)tɪtjuːd/ *noun*. LME.
[French, or late Latin *promptitudo*, from Latin *promptus* PROMPT *adjective*: see -TUDE.]
Quickness or readiness of action, promptness. Formerly also, (a) willingness or inclination (*to*).

promptuary /ˈprɒm(p)tjʊəri/ *noun*. Now *rare*. LME.
[Latin *promptuarium*, from *promptuarius*, from *promptus*: see PROMPT *adjective*, -ARY¹.]
1 A storehouse, a repository. LME.
2 A handbook or notebook containing a summary or digest of information etc. L16.

promulgate /ˈprɒm(ə)lgeɪt/ *verb trans*. M16.
[Latin *promulgat-* pa. ppl stem of *promulgare* expose to public view, formed as PRO-¹ + base of *mulgere* to milk, (hence) cause to issue forth, bring to light: see -ATE³.]
Make known to the public, publish; *spec.* (*a*) disseminate (a creed or belief); (*b*) put (a law, decree, etc.) into effect by official proclamation.

promulgation /prɒm(ə)lˈgeɪʃ(ə)n/ *noun*. L15.
[Old & mod. French, or Latin *promulgatio(n-)*, formed as prec.: see -ATION.]
The action or an act of promulgating something; the fact of being promulgated.
■ **promulgator** *noun* M17.

promulge /prəˈmʌldʒ/ *verb trans*. *arch*. L15.
[Latin *promulgare* PROMULGATE. Cf. Old & mod. French *promulguer*.]
Promulgate.
■ **promulger** *noun* M17.

†**promuscis** *noun*. Pl. **-sces**. E17.
[Late Latin, alt. of Latin PROBOSCIS.]
1 ZOOLOGY. The trunk of an elephant. E17–E18.
2 ENTOMOLOGY. The proboscis of certain insects, esp. hemipterans and hymenopterans. M17–M19.

■ †**promuscidate** *adjective* formed as or furnished with a proboscis E–M19.

promycelium /prəʊmʌɪˈsiːlɪəm/ *noun*. Pl. **-lia** /-lɪə/. M19.
[from PRO-¹ + MYCELIUM.]
BOTANY. The basidium of a rust or smut fungus.
■ **promycelial** *adjective* L19.

pronaos /prəʊˈneɪɒs/ *noun*. Pl. **-naoi** /-ˈneɪɔɪ/. E17.
[Latin from Greek, formed as PRO-² + NAOS.]
CLASSICAL ANTIQUITIES. The space in front of the body of a temple, enclosed by a portico and projecting side-walls. Also, a narthex.

Pronase /ˈprəʊneɪz/ *noun*. Also **p-**. M20.
[from PRO(TEI)NASE.]
BIOCHEMISTRY. (US proprietary name for) a purified preparation of proteinase from cultures of the bacterium *Streptomyces griseus*.

pronatalist /prəʊˈneɪt(ə)lɪst/ *adjective & noun*. M20.
[from PRO-¹ + NATAL *adjective*¹ + -IST.]
▶ **A** *adjective*. Of or pertaining to the encouragement of the practice of having a large family, esp. by the State; advocating large families. M20.
▶ **B** *noun*. A pronatalist person. M20.
■ **pronatalism** *noun* M20.

pronate /ˈprəʊneɪt/ *adjective*. *rare*. M19.
[formed as next.]
Bent into a prone position.

pronate /ˈprəʊneɪt/ *verb*. M19.
[Back-form. from next.]
1 *verb trans*. Make prone; put (a hand, a forelimb) into the prone position; turn (the palm) downwards. Opp. SUPINATE 1. M19.
2 *verb intrans*. Of a limb, esp. (in running) the foot: undergo pronation. Of a person: turn the foot outward (while running etc.) to take the weight on the inner edge. Opp. SUPINATE 2. M19.

pronation /prəʊˈneɪʃ(ə)n/ *noun*. M17.
[from PRONE *adjective* (or Latin *pronus*) + -ATION.]
The action of pronating; the position or condition of being pronated. Opp. SUPINATION.

pronator /prəʊˈneɪtə/ *noun*. E18.
[mod. Latin, from *pronus* PRONE *adjective* + -ATOR, after SUPINATOR.]
ANATOMY. A muscle that effects or assists in pronation; *spec.* either of two muscles of the forelimb. Opp. SUPINATOR.
***pronator* QUADRATUS**. ***pronator* TERES**.

prone /prəʊn/ *noun*. M17.
[French *prône* the grating or railing separating the chancel of a church from the nave, where notices were given and addresses delivered.]
ECCLESIASTICAL HISTORY. An exhortation or homily delivered in church. Also, prayers, exhortations, etc., attached to a sermon.

prone /prəʊn/ *adjective & adverb*. LME.
[Latin *pronus*, from *pro* forwards.]
▶ **I** *adjective*. **1** Disposed, inclined, or liable to some (bad or regrettable) action, condition, etc. (freq. foll. by *to*, *to do*); more than usually susceptible *to* (illness). Now also as 2nd elem. of comb. LME.
2 Willing, eager. *arch*. LME.
†**3** Easy to adopt or pursue; suiting a person's natural inclination. L15–M17.

📖 **1** M. L. KING We are prone to judge success by the index of our salaries. *Guardian* Many of these children are chesty, prone to colds. *Publishers Weekly* A wayward bus line founded by the author's failure-prone father. M. SEYMOUR Suiting his sentiments to his audience was a fault to which James was . . prone. ***accident prone*** etc. **2** J. GUILLIM The Horse . . of all beestes there is none . . more prone in battell. **3** R. SANDERSON There is not a proner way to hell.

▶ **II** *adjective & adverb*. **4** Directed or sloping downwards. Also *loosely*, descending steeply or vertically, headlong. *arch*. LME.
5 Facing downwards; bending forward and downward; lying face downwards or on the belly; *spec.* (of the hand or forelimb) with the palm downwards or backwards and the radius and ulna crossed. Later also *loosely*, lying flat. L16.

📖 **4** POPE From high Olympus prone her flight she bends. SHELLEY Down the prone vale. **5** N. P. WILLIS The broken column, vast and prone. I. MURDOCH He . . turned over to lie prone upon the bed.

■ **pronely** *adverb* in a prone manner or position M16. **proneness** *noun* M16. †**pronity** *noun* (a) propensity, proneness LME–E18.

pronephros /prəʊˈnɛfrɒs/ *noun*. Pl. **-nephroi** /-ˈnɛfrɔɪ/. Also (now *rare*) **-phron** /-frɒn/, pl. **-phra** /-frə/. L19.
[from PRO-² + Greek *nephros* kidney.]
ZOOLOGY & ANATOMY. The first of the three segments of the embryonic kidney in vertebrates, which is functional only in the larvae of lower vertebrates. Cf. MESONEPHROS, METANEPHROS.
■ **pronephric** *adjective* L19.

prôneur /prɔnœːr, prəʊˈnəː/ *noun*. *literary*. Pl. pronounced same. E19.
[French, from *prôner* address a congregation, eulogize, formed as PRONE *noun* + *-eur* -OR.]
A person who praises another; a flatterer.

prong /prɒŋ/ *noun & verb*. L15.
[Perh. rel. to Middle Low German *prange* pinching instrument, Dutch *prang* pinching, Low German, Dutch *prangen* press. Cf. PANG *noun*¹, SPRONG.]
▶ **A** *noun*. **1** Any of various piercing instruments or implements with two, three, or more piercing points or tines; a forked instrument, a fork. Now chiefly *dial*. L15.
2 A thin projecting thing, a part ending in a point; *esp.* each of the tines of a fork. M17. ▶**b** The penis. *coarse slang*. M20.
Comb.: **prongbuck** (now *rare*) a pronghorn, esp. a male; **prong-hoe** an agricultural implement with two curving prongs, used like a hoe; **pronghorn**, **prong-horned antelope** a N. American ruminant, *Antilocapra americana*, the sole member of the family Antilocapridae, resembling an antelope but having deciduous hooked horns in the male.
▶ **B** *verb trans*. Pierce or stab with a prong; turn up (soil) with a fork. M19.

pronged /prɒŋd/ *adjective*. M18.
[from PRONG *noun* + -ED².]
Having prongs or tines; *esp.* having a specified number of prongs or (*fig.*) lines of attack or advance, as ***many-pronged***, ***three-pronged***, etc.

pronk /prɒŋk/ *noun*. *slang*. M20.
[Origin uncertain: cf. Dutch *pronker* fop.]
A weak or effeminate person; a crank, a fool.

pronk /prɒŋk/ *verb intrans*. *S. Afr.* L19.
[Afrikaans = show off, strut, prance, from Dutch *pronken* strut.]
Of a springbok: leap in the air with a stiff-legged gait and raised mane, esp. as a form of display.

pronograde /ˈprəʊnəgreɪd/ *adjective*. E20.
[from Latin *pronus* PRONE *adjective* + -O- + *-gradus* walking.]
Moving on all fours.

pronominal /prəʊˈnɒmɪn(ə)l/ *adjective & noun*. M17.
[Late Latin *pronominalis* belonging to a pronoun, from Latin *pronomin-*, *pronomen* PRONOUN: see -AL¹.]
▶ **A** *adjective*. Of, pertaining to, or of the nature of a pronoun; characterized by the presence of a pronoun. M17.
▶ **B** *noun*. A pronominal word. L19.
■ **pronominaliˈzation** *noun* the replacement of a noun or noun phrase by a pronoun M20. **pronominalize** *verb trans*. make pronominal L19. **pronominally** *adverb* as, with the force of, or by means of a pronoun M17.

prononcé /prɔnɔ̃se/ *adjective*. M19.
[French, pa. pple of *prononcer* PRONOUNCE.]
Pronounced; strongly marked; conspicuous.

†**pronostic** *noun* see PROGNOSTIC *noun*.

pronoun /ˈprəʊnaʊn/ *noun*. LME.
[from PRO-¹ + NOUN, after French *pronom*, Latin *pronomen*.]
A word used instead of a noun to designate an object which is identifiable from context or usage, or which has already been mentioned or indicated (e.g. *we*, *theirs*, *this*, *ourselves*, *who*). (One of the parts of speech.)
demonstrative pronoun, ***interrogative pronoun***, ***personal pronoun***, ***possessive pronoun***, ***relative pronoun***, etc.
■ **proˈnounal** *adjective* (*rare*) = PRONOMINAL L19.

pronounce /prəˈnaʊns/ *verb*. ME.
[Old French *pronuncier* (mod. *prononcer*) from Latin *pronuntiare* proclaim, narrate, formed as PRO-¹ + *nuntiare* ANNOUNCE.]
▶ **I 1** *verb trans*. Formally or solemnly utter or deliver (esp. a judgement or sentence); proclaim or declare officially. Also, state authoritatively or definitely; declare as one's opinion or view; assert (a person, oneself) *to be*. ME.
2 *verb intrans*. Make an authoritative statement or assertion; pass judgement, give an opinion or decision. LME.

📖 **1** GOLDSMITH A Courier . . pronounced the dreadful tidings. A. CHRISTIE 'That difficulty will not exist long,' pronounced Poirot quietly. V. BRITTAIN He tested my heart and pronounced me constitutionally fit. A. DJOLETO A judge pronounces sentence. A. KENNY My grandmother . . pronounced the baptismal formula. **2** LD MACAULAY The majority . . pronounced in favour of William's undertaking. OED The Pope has pronounced against the validity of Anglican orders. M. DIBDIN It is too soon to pronounce on these matters with any certainty.

▶ **II 3** *verb trans*. Utter or articulate (a word, sound, etc.), esp. in a certain way. LME.
4 *verb trans*. Declaim or recite in a specified manner. Long *rare* or *obsolete*. M16.

📖 **4** H. JAMES She pronounced every syllable. E. TAYLOR He never could pronounce his r's properly. *Times* Female staff . . may . . use the Ms title (usu. pronounced Miz) as an alternative to the Miss or Mrs. **5** SHAKES. *Haml.* Speak the speech . . as I pronounc'd it to you.

■ **pronounceaˈbility** *noun* ability to be pronounced M20. **pronounceable** *adjective* able to be pronounced L16. **pronouncement** *noun* (*a*) the action of pronouncing; (*b*) a formal or authoritative statement, an opinion or decision given; a declaration, an assertion: L16. **pronouncer** *noun* LME.

pronounced /prəˈnaʊnst/ *adjective*. L16.
[from prec. + -ED¹.]
1 Of a word, sound, etc.: uttered, articulated. L16.
2 Strongly marked; evident, conspicuous; decided. E18.
■ **pronouncedly** /-sɪdli/ *adverb* M19.

pronto /ˈprɒntəʊ/ *adverb*¹ & *adjective*. M18.
[Italian, from Latin *promptus* PROMPT *adjective*. Cf. next.]
MUSIC. A direction: quick(ly), prompt(ly).

pronto /ˈprɒntəʊ/ *adverb*². *colloq.* (orig. US). E20.
[Spanish, from Latin *promptus* PROMPT *adjective*. Cf. prec.]
Quickly; promptly, at once.

Prontosil /ˈprɒntəsɪl/ *noun*. M20.
[Invented word.]
PHARMACOLOGY. (Proprietary name for) a reddish-brown crystalline pigment, $C_{12}H_{13}N_5O_2S$, formerly used as a bacteriostatic to treat a range of infections.

pronuba /ˈprəʊnjʊbə/ *noun*. Pl. **-bae** /-biː, -ʌɪ/. E16.
[Latin = a woman who attended a bride, formed as PRO-¹ + stem of *nubere* marry.]
1 ROMAN HISTORY. A woman presiding over or assisting in the ceremonies and arrangements of marriage. E16.
2 [Former genus name.] In full ***pronuba moth***. Any of various small white N. American moths of the genus *Tegeticula* and family Incurvariidae, *esp.* the yucca moth. L19.

pronucleus /prəʊˈnjuːklɪəs/ *noun*. Pl. **-ei** /-ɪʌɪ/. L19.
[from PRO-² + NUCLEUS.]
CYTOLOGY. Either of a pair of gametic nuclei, in the stage following meiosis but before their fusion leads to the formation of the nucleus of the zygote.

pronunciamento /prəˌnʌnsɪəˈmɛntəʊ/ *noun*. Pl. **-os**. M19.
[Spanish *pronunciamiento*, from *pronunciar* (from Latin *pronuntiare* PRONOUNCE) + *-miento* -MENT.]
Esp. in Spain and Spanish-speaking countries: a pronouncement, proclamation, or manifesto, *esp.* a political one.

pronunciation /prənʌnsɪˈeɪʃ(ə)n/ *noun*. LME.
[Old & mod. French *prononciation* or Latin *pronuntiatio(n-)*, from *pronuntiat-* pa. ppl stem of *pronuntiare* PRONOUNCE: see -ATION.]
1 The action or an act of pronouncing a word or words; the way in which a word is pronounced, esp. with ref. to a recognized standard. LME.
†**2** Elocution; *spec.* elegant or eloquent delivery. LME–M18.
3 The action of proclaiming; promulgation; a pronouncement. Long *rare*. LME.
Comb.: **pronunciation key** a list of symbols used to indicate pronunciation; **pronunciation-spelling** the spelling of words in accordance with their usual pronunciation; an instance of this.
■ **pronunciaˈbility** *noun* = PRONOUNCEABILITY E19. **proˈnunciable** *adjective* (long *rare*) = PRONOUNCEABLE M17. **proˈnunciator** *noun* (*rare*) a person who pronounces M19.

pro-nuncio /prəʊˈnʌnsɪəʊ, -ʃɪəʊ/ *noun*. Pl. **-os**. M20.
[Italian *pro-nunzio*, from *pro-* PRO-¹ + *nunzio* NUNCIO.]
ROMAN CATHOLIC CHURCH. A papal ambassador to a country which does not accord the Pope's ambassador automatic precedence over other ambassadors.

prooemium /prəʊˈiːmɪəm/ *noun*. LME.
[Latin from Greek *prooimion* PROEM.]
= PROEM.

proestrus /prəʊˈiːstrəs/ *noun*. Also **-um**, **proest-**. E20.
[from PRO-² + OESTRUS.]
BIOLOGY. The period immediately preceding oestrus in many mammals.
■ **prooestrous** *adjective* E20.

proof /pruːf/ *noun*. Also †**preve**, †**prove**. ME.
[Old French *preve*, *proeve*, *prueve* (mod. *preuve*) from late Latin *proba*, from Latin *probare* PROVE *verb*. Substitution of *o* for *e* by assim. to *prove*, of *f* for *v* from loss of final *e*.]
▶ **I 1** (A piece of) evidence or (an) argument establishing a fact or the truth or validity of a statement; *spec.* in MATH. & LOGIC, a sequence of steps by which a theorem is derived from given premises. ME. ▶**b** LAW. Orig., a person who gives evidence; a witness. Later, (a piece of) evidence determining the judgement of a tribunal; *spec.* (*a*) a document so attested as to form legal evidence; (*b*) the evidence given and officially recorded in a particular case. LME.
2 The action, process, or fact of establishing the truth or validity of a statement; demonstration. Freq. in ***burden of proof*** s.v. BURDEN *noun* 1. ME.
3 SCOTS LAW. In civil cases, evidence given before (a representative of) a judge in determining what is at issue in a trial or establishing the disputed facts in a case; the taking of such evidence. Now also, trial of a civil case before a judge without a jury. E18.

> 📖 **1** R. NIEBUHR Failure to achieve such a competence was in itself proof of a lack of virtue. A. KENNY The proofs we were offered for the existence of God all seemed to contain serious flaws. **b** G. BURNET The proof did not carry it beyond manslaughter. **2** J. TYNDALL All capable of experimental proof.

▶ **II** †**4** The action or fact of having experience of something; knowledge derived from this. ME–E17.
5 Orig., the issue, result, effect, or fulfilment of something. Later (now *dial.*), the fact or condition of turning out well or producing good results; good condition or quality. ME.
6 The action or an act of testing something; a test, a trial, an experiment. LME. ▶**b** *spec.* An operation to check the correctness of an arithmetical calculation. LME.
7 a Tried or tested strength, esp. of armour or arms; *transf.* & *fig.* resistance, impenetrability, invulnerability. *arch.* LME. ▶**b** Armour of established strength. Long *obsolete* exc. *Hist.* L16.
†**8** An attempt, an endeavour. L16–E17.
9 a The testing of cannon or small firearms by firing a heavy charge or by hydraulic pressure. M17. ▶**b** A place for testing firearms or explosives. M18.
10 a A standard of strength of distilled alcoholic liquors, equivalent in Britain to 57.1 per cent of alcohol by volume (at 51°F, 10.6°C), and in the US to 50 per cent of alcohol by volume (at 60°F, 15.6°C); the relative strength (usu. measured in degrees) of any alcoholic liquor compared to this standard as 100°. E18. ▶**b** The aeration of dough by a raising agent before baking. E20.

> 📖 **5** G. B. SHAW Put to the proof.. you behaved very sensibly.

▶ **III 11** An instrument, vessel, etc., used in testing or examining something; *spec.* †(*a*) a surgeon's probe; (*b*) a test-tube. Now *rare*. M16.
12 PRINTING. A trial impression of text, an illustration, etc., taken from type or film to be checked for errors and marked for correction before subsequent revision or final printing. Freq. with specifying word. E17.
13 Orig., a coin or medal struck as a test of the die. Later, any of various preliminary impressions of coins struck as specimens. M18.
14 ENGRAVING. Orig., an impression taken from an engraved plate, block, etc., to examine the state of a work in progress. Now, each of a limited number of impressions from a finished block, plate, etc., before the printing of the ordinary issue and usu. (in full ***proof before letters***) before the addition of an inscription or signature. L18.
15 A photographic print, *esp.* a trial print taken from a plate. M19.
16 BOOKBINDING. The rough uncut edges of the shorter or narrower leaves of a book, left in trimming it to show that it has not been cut down. L19.

> 📖 **12** T. H. HUXLEY I have carefully revised the proofs of every chapter. J. UGLOW The translation was finished, the proofs read. ***galley proof***, ***page proof***, etc.

Phrases: ***artist's proof***: see ARTIST 3. ***burden of proof***: see BURDEN *noun* 1. ***conjunct proof***: see CONJUNCT *adjective*. ***final proof***: see FINAL *adjective*. ***foul proof***: see FOUL *adjective*. **in proof** at the stage in the production of a book etc. when proofs have been printed and are undergoing correction. **over proof** (of an alcoholic liquor) above standard strength, esp. by a specified number of degrees. ***progressive proofs***: see PROGRESSIVE *adjective*. ***proof before letters***: see sense 14 above. TOUCHED ***proof***. **under proof** (of an alcoholic liquor) below standard strength, esp. by a specified number of degrees.
Comb.: **proof-glass** a deep cylindrical glass for holding liquids while under test; **proof load** MECHANICS a load which a structure must be able to bear without exceeding specified limits of permanent deformation; *loosely* proof stress; **proof-plane** a small flat conductor on an insulating handle for measuring the electrification of a body; **proof positive** absolutely certain proof; **proofread** *verb trans.* & *intrans.* read (text etc.) in proof in order to find and mark errors for correction; **proofreader** a person who proofreads; **proof-sheet**, **proof-slip** a sheet printed from a forme of type for examination and correction before final printing; **proof strain** MECHANICS the strain produced by the proof stress; *loosely* proof stress; **proof strength** = sense 10a above; **proof stress** MECHANICS the stress required to produce a specified permanent deformation of a material or structure; **proof-text** a passage of the Bible to which appeal is made in support of an argument or position in theology; **proof-theoretic** *adjective* of or pertaining to proof theory; **proof theory** the branch of mathematics that deals with the syntactic (as opp. to semantic) properties of formulae and proofs in formal systems.
■ **proofless** *adjective* (now *rare*) unsupported by proof or evidence, unfounded E17.

proof /pruːf/ *adjective*. L16.
[from the noun, app. by ellipsis of *of*.]
1 Orig., (of armour) of tried strength or quality. Now chiefly (*transf.* & *fig.*), resistant, impenetrable, impervious, invulnerable (freq. foll. by *against* or as 2nd elem. of comb.). L16.
2 Of a distilled alcoholic liquor: of standard strength. E18.

> 📖 **1** C. BOUTELL These cuirasses.. were not proof against a well-delivered thrust. A. SILLITOE It would do him no harm because he was proof against poison of all kinds. ***bulletproof***, ***childproof***, ***fireproof***, ***ovenproof***, ***soundproof***, ***waterproof***, etc.

proof /pruːf/ *verb trans.* E18.
[from PROOF *noun* or *adjective*.]
▶ **I 1** Try out, esp. by tasting; assess the quality or value of. *Scot.* E18.
2 Aerate (dough) by the action of yeast before baking. L19.
3 Make a proof of (a printed work, an engraving, etc.). Also, proofread. L19.
▶ **II 4** Make (a thing) proof against or impervious to something; *esp.* make (a fabric etc.) waterproof. L19.

proot /pruːt/ *interjection*. L19.
[Origin unkn.]
A word of command used to a donkey etc.: go on, go faster.

prop /prɒp/ *noun*¹. LME.
[Prob. from Middle Dutch *proppe* vine-prop, support.]
1 A rigid support, as a pole, beam, etc., *esp.* one not an integral part of the thing supported. LME. ▶**b** *fig.* A person or thing providing support, help, comfort, etc. L16. ▶**c** MINING. A piece of timber etc. placed upright to support a roof. M18. ▶**d** Orig. (*dial.*), the leg. Also (*slang*), the arm extended in boxing; a straight hit, a blow. Usu. in *pl.* L18. ▶**e** RUGBY FOOTBALL. Either of two outside front-row forwards who support the hooker in a scrum. Also ***prop forward***. M20.
2 A post, a cairn, esp. as a boundary-marker. *Scot.* LME.
3 A sudden stop made by a horse etc. when going at speed. Chiefly *Austral.* L19.

> 📖 **1b** SHAKES. *Merch. V.* The boy was the.. staff of my age, my very prop. P. PARISH We use alcohol as a social prop.

Comb.: ***prop forward***: see sense 1e above; **prop-leg** ENTOMOLOGY = PROLEG; **prop-root** an adventitious root springing from the base of a plant above ground level, providing extra support; **prop-word** LINGUISTICS a word of indefinite meaning, as English *one*, that refers to a previously mentioned noun or group of words and can take the modification of an adjective.

prop /prɒp/ *noun*². E16.
[Middle Dutch *proppe*, Dutch *prop* broach, skewer, plug.]
1 A plug; a wedge. *Scot. rare*. E16.
2 A scarf-pin. Also, a valuable piece of jewellery; a diamond. *slang*. M19.

prop /prɒp/ *noun*³. *colloq.* E19.
[Abbreviation.]
= PROPOSITION *noun* 5.

prop /prɒp/ *noun*⁴. *US*. M19.
[Origin unkn.]
Chiefly *Hist.* A cowrie shell modified for use in a gambling game resembling dice; this game.

prop /prɒp/ *noun*⁵. M19.
[Abbreviation of PROPERTY.]
1 A portable object other than furniture or costumes used on the set of a play or film; *transf.* an accessory, an appurtenance. Freq. in *pl.* M19.
2 In *pl.* The department of a theatre etc. responsible for stage props; (treated as *sing.*) a person in charge of stage props in a theatre etc. *colloq.* M19.

> 📖 **1** M. FONTEYN A tremendous variety of props.. garlands, scarfs.. baskets of flowers.

Comb.: **prop man**, **prop mistress**, **props man**, **props mistress**, etc.: in charge of stage props in a theatre etc.

prop /prɒp/ *noun*⁶. L19.
[Abbreviation.]
= PROPRIETOR.

prop /prɒp/ *noun*⁷. *colloq.* E20.
[Abbreviation.]
A propeller, esp. on an aircraft.

> 📖 *attrib.*: *Daily Telegraph* They make jet trainers and prop trainers.

Comb.: **prop-fan** (an aircraft engine incorporating) an airscrew having broad blades swept back from a direction perpendicular to the rotation axis; **prop-jet** = TURBOPROP; **propshaft** a propeller shaft, esp. of a motor vehicle; **prop wash** a surge or wash of air created by the action of a propeller.

prop /prɒp/ *verb*. Infl. **-pp-**. LME.
[from PROP *noun*¹.]
1 *verb trans.* Mark out (a boundary etc.) with posts or cairns. *Scot.* LME.
2 *verb trans.* Support or keep from falling (as) with a prop, hold *up*; lean (a thing or person) *against* something; keep in position with a prop. L15. ▶**b** *verb trans. fig.* Provide support, help, comfort, etc., to. Freq. foll. by *up*. M16.
3 *verb trans.* Hit or knock down (a person). *slang*. M19.
4 *verb intrans.* Of a horse etc.: come to a dead stop with the forelegs rigid. Orig. *Austral.* M19.

📖 **2** J. LONDON He propped the book before him, and propped his eyelids with his fingers. J. C. POWYS He propped up the oars . . against the house. P. ROTH Content . . to lie on the ground propped up on one elbow. **prop up the bar** *joc.* drink, esp. alone, at the bar of a public house. **b** *Times* The Government are prepared to prop up . . the . . backward sheikhs. *Private Investor* People should not be propped up . . and . . should be perfectly capable of looking after themselves.

■ **propper** *noun* M16.

prop- /prəʊp/ *combining form* of PROPANE, PROPYL, as ***propamide***, ***propidium***.

propachlor /ˈprəʊpəklɔː/ *noun*. M20.
[from PROPANE + CHLORO-¹.]
A selective herbicide used to control grass and other weeds among crops.

propadiene /prəʊpəˈdʌɪiːn/ *noun*. E20.
[from PROPANE + DI-² + -ENE.]
CHEMISTRY. A gaseous unsaturated hydrocarbon, $CH_2{=}C{=}CH_2$. Also called ***allene***.

propaedeutic /prəʊpiːˈdjuːtɪk/ *noun & adjective*. L18.
[from PRO-² + PAEDEUTICS, after Greek *propaideuein* teach beforehand: see -IC.]
► **A** *noun*. **1** A subject or course of study forming an introduction to an art or science or to more advanced study. L18.
2 In *pl.* (treated as *sing.*). The body of principles or rules introductory to any subject of special study, preliminary learning. M19.
► **B** *adjective*. Of study or a subject: introductory, preliminary. M19.
■ **propaedeutical** *adjective* = PROPAEDEUTIC *adjective* M19.

propafenone /prəʊˈpafənəʊn/ *noun*. L20.
[German *Propafenon*, from PROP(YL + A(MINO- + *fen*- PHEN- + *keton* KETONE.]
PHARMACOLOGY. A bicyclic compound, $C_{21}H_{27}NO_3$, used to control cardiac arrhythmia.

propagable /ˈprɒpəgəb(ə)l/ *adjective*. M17.
[from PROPAGATE + -ABLE.]
Able to be propagated.
■ **propagaˈbility** *noun* L19. **propagableness** *noun* L17.

propagand /prɒpəˈgand/ *noun*. Also **-ande**. L18.
[French *propagande*.]
= PROPAGANDA 2, 3.

propagand /prɒpəˈgand/ *verb trans. & intrans.* E20.
[Back-form. from next.]
= PROPAGANDIZE.

propaganda /prɒpəˈgandə/ *noun & verb*. E18.
[Italian, from mod. Latin *congregatio de propaganda fide* congregation for propagating the faith.]
► **A** *noun*. **1** *ROMAN CATHOLIC CHURCH.* (Also **P-**.) A committee of cardinals responsible for foreign missions, founded in 1622 by Pope Gregory XV. Also more fully ***Congregation of the Propaganda***, ***College of the Propaganda***. E18.
2 An organization or concerted movement for the propagation of a particular doctrine, practice, etc. Now *rare*. L18.
3 The systematic dissemination of doctrine, rumour, or selected information to propagate or promote a particular doctrine, view, practice, etc.; ideas, information, etc., disseminated thus (freq. *derog.*). E20.

📖 **3** B. CHATWIN He undertook not to spread malicious propaganda against the People's Republic. *attrib.*: J. CALLAGHAN They said that the USC had been the victim of a propaganda campaign. A. WAUGH Propaganda leaflets . . scattered behind the German lines.

► **B** *verb trans. & intrans.* = PROPAGANDIZE. E20.
■ **propagandic** *adjective* (*rare*) of, pertaining to, or of the nature of propaganda L19.

propagandise *verb* var. of PROPAGANDIZE.

propagandism /prɒpəˈgandɪz(ə)m/ *noun*. E19.
[from prec. + -ISM.]
The spreading of propaganda, propagandizing.

propagandist /prɒpəˈgandɪst/ *noun & adjective*. L18.
[formed as prec. + -IST.]
► **A** *noun*. **1** A member or agent of a propaganda organization, a person who disseminates propaganda, esp. on behalf of a particular organization or cause; an advocate of the systematic use of propaganda. L18.
2 *ROMAN CATHOLIC CHURCH.* (Also **P-**.) A missionary or convert of the Congregation of the Propaganda. E19.

📖 **1** *Daily Telegraph* Dr Goebbels, the Nazi propagandist, could not have invented a more vilifying tag. V. S. PRITCHETT An active propagandist for the conservation of the forests.

► **B** *adjective*. Given or inclined to propagandizing; of the nature of propaganda. E19.
■ **propaganˈdistic** *adjective* L19. **propaganˈdistically** *adverb* L19.

propagandize /prɒpəˈgandʌɪz/ *verb*. Also **-ise**. M19.
[formed as prec. + -IZE.]
1 *verb trans.* Disseminate (ideas, information, etc.) as propaganda; advocate (a cause). Also, subject (a person) to propaganda; attempt to influence (a person) with propaganda. M19.
2 *verb intrans.* Carry on a campaign of propaganda, disseminate propaganda. L19.

📖 **1** J. RABAN 'Mixed housing' has been heavily propagandised. **2** *New Yorker* He propagandized for wilderness preservation.

propagate /ˈprɒpəgeɪt/ *verb*. Pa. pple **-ate**, **-ated**. LME.
[Latin *propagat-* pa. ppl stem of *propagare* multiply (plants) from shoots or layers, rel. to *propago* young shoot, formed as PRO-¹ + base of verb meaning 'fix': see -ATE³. Cf. PROVINE.]
1 *verb trans.* Cause (a plant, animal, etc.) to multiply by reproduction from the parent stock; breed, reproduce. LME. ▸**b** *verb intrans.* Breed, produce offspring; reproduce. E17. ▸**c** *verb trans. transf.* Hand down (a quality etc.) from one generation to another, pass on to one's descendants. E17.
2 *verb trans.* Cause to grow in numbers or amount; extend the bounds of; spread (esp. an idea, practice, etc.) from place to place. L16. ▸**b** *verb intrans.* Grow more widespread or numerous, increase, spread. M17.
3 *verb trans.* Extend the action or operation of; transmit (motion, light, sound, etc.) in some direction or through some medium. M17. ▸**b** *verb intrans.* Be transmitted, travel. M20.

📖 **1** *Observer* Fuchsias are easy to . . propagate from cuttings. **b** R. DAWKINS Many plants propagate . . by sending out suckers. **2** P. GAY He kept on propagating Charcot's ideas. **3** T. H. HUXLEY Waves or tremors may be propagated in all directions though the . . ground. **b** *Nature* When a laser beam propagates through a mixture of gases.

¶ In isolated use as pa. pple in *-ate* before 16.
■ **propagative** *adjective* having the quality of propagating, characterized by propagation, tending to propagate M17.

propagation /prɒpəˈgeɪʃ(ə)n/ *noun*. LME.
[Old & mod. French, or Latin *propagatio(n-)*, formed as prec.: see -ATION.]
1 The action of breeding or multiplying by natural processes; procreation, generation, reproduction. LME.
2 The action of spreading an idea, practice, etc., from place to place. L16.
†**3** Increase in amount or extent; enlargement; extension in space or time. E17–M18.
4 The transmission of an action, signal, or form of energy, as motion, light, sound, etc. M17.
5 *CHEMISTRY.* The self-perpetuating step or series of steps in a chain reaction in which product molecules are formed or polymer chains lengthened by a process which generates more reagents or radicals for a repetition of the reaction. Freq. *attrib.* E20.

📖 **2** D. HALBERSTAM The propagation of ideas and values.

Comb.: **propagation constant** *PHYSICS* a measure of the loss of magnitude or retardation of a propagating wave per unit distance travelled; **propagation function** *PHYSICS* = PROPAGATOR 4.
■ **propagational** *adjective* (*rare*) L19.

propagator /ˈprɒpəgeɪtə/ *noun*. L16.
[Latin, formed as PROPAGATE: see -ATOR.]
1 A person who begets or produces offspring; a planter, a rearer of plants. L16. ▸**b** The penis. *arch.* L17.
2 A person who spreads an idea, practice, etc., from place to place. E17.
3 A forcing-frame for plants. Also, a small box with a transparent lid and a base that can be heated, for germinating seeds or raising seedlings. L19.
4 *PHYSICS.* An algebraic function representing the propagation of a particle on the subatomic scale, esp. between its space–time points of creation and annihilation. M20.
■ **propagatress** *noun* (*rare*) = PROPAGATRIX M17. **propaˈgatrix** *noun*, pl. **-trices** /-trɪsiːz/, **-trixes**, a female propagator M17.

propagule /ˈprɒpəgjuːl/ *noun*. M19.
[mod. Latin *propagulum* dim. of Latin *propago* shoot, runner: see PROPAGATE, -ULE.]
BOTANY. **1** Each of the granules of the soredium of a lichen. M19.
2 *gen.* Any structure capable of giving rise to a new plant by asexual or sexual reproduction, as a bulbil, a leafbud, etc. E20.
■ **proˈpagular** *adjective* of or pertaining to a propagule E20.

propale /prəʊˈpeɪl/ *verb trans.* Chiefly *Scot.* Long *arch.* E16.
[Late Latin *propalare*, from Latin *propalam*, formed as PRO-¹ + *palam* openly.]
Publish, divulge, disclose.
■ Also †**propalate** *verb trans.* L16–E18.

propamidine /prəʊˈpamɪdiːn/ *noun*. M20.
[from PROP- + AMIDINE *noun*².]
PHARMACOLOGY. A diamidine with bactericidal and fungicidal properties used in dressing minor wounds and burns; 1,3-di(4-amidinephenoxy)propane, $C_{17}H_{20}N_4O_2$.

propane /ˈprəʊpeɪn/ *noun*. M19.
[from PROP(IONIC + -ANE.]
CHEMISTRY. A colourless odourless flammable gaseous alkane, $CH_3CH_2CH_3$, occurring in petroleum and used esp. in liquefied form as a fuel.

■ **propanal** /-pənal/ *noun* = PROPIONALDEHYDE M20. **propaˈnoic** *adjective* = PROPIONIC E20.

propanidid /prəʊˈpanɪdɪd/ *noun*. M20.
[from PROP- + *-an*, *-idid* arbitrary elems.]
PHARMACOLOGY. An oily liquid, $C_{18}H_{27}NO_5$, which is given intravenously in solution as a short-acting anaesthetic.

propanol /ˈprəʊpənɒl/ *noun*. L19.
[from PROPANE + -OL.]
CHEMISTRY. Either of two isomeric alcohols, C_3H_7OH, widely used as solvents; propyl alcohol; *spec.* (also ***propan-1-ol***) the primary isomer, $CH_3CH_2CH_2OH$.

propanone /ˈprəʊpənəʊn/ *noun*. M20.
[from PROPANE + -ONE.]
CHEMISTRY. = ACETONE.

propantheline /prəʊˈpanθəliːn/ *noun*. M20.
[from PROP- + X)ANTH(ENE + E(THY)L + -INE⁵.]
PHARMACOLOGY. A white solid quaternary ammonium bromide derived from xanthene, $C_{23}H_{30}NO_3Br$, which is a parasympatholytic agent used esp. to relieve the symptoms of peptic ulcers. Also ***propantheline bromide***.

propargyl /prəʊˈpɑːdʒʌɪl/ *noun*. L19.
[from PROP(IONIC + Latin *arg(entum* silver (with ref. to its readily-formed silver salt) + -YL.]
CHEMISTRY. A hydrocarbon radical, $CH{\cdot}C{\cdot}CH_2{\cdot}$.
Comb.: **propargyl alcohol** a colourless fragrant liquid, $HC{\cdot}C{\cdot}CH_2OH$ (2-propyn-1-ol).
■ **propargylic** *adjective* of, containing, or derived from propargyl; ***propargylic acid***, the carboxylic acid $HC{\cdot}C{-}COOH$: M19.

proparoxytone /prəʊpəˈrɒksɪtəʊn/ *adjective & noun*. M18.
[Greek *proparoxutonos*, formed as PRO-² + PAROXYTONE.]
GRAMMAR. ► **A** *adjective*. Designating or pertaining to a word in ancient Greek having an acute accent on the antepenultimate syllable; *transf.* designating or pertaining to a word in Latin and other languages having a stress on the antepenultimate syllable. M18.
► **B** *noun*. An proparoxytone word. L19.
■ **proparoxyˈtonic** *adjective* having or characterized by proparoxytone accent or stress L19. †**proparoxytonous** *adjective* (*rare*) = PROPAROXYTONIC: only in M18.

†**propassion** *noun*. L16–L19.
[medieval Latin *propassio(n-)*, formed as PRO-¹ + PASSION *noun*.]
A feeling that precedes or anticipates passion, *esp.* an emotion experienced by Jesus before the Passion.

propatagium /prəʊpəˈteɪdʒɪəm/ *noun*. Pl. **-gia** /-dʒɪə/. L19.
[from PRO-² + PATAGIUM.]
ORNITHOLOGY. The anterior part of the patagium of a bird's wing.
■ **propatagial** *adjective* L19.

propel /prəˈpɛl/ *verb trans.* Infl. **-ll-**. LME.
[Latin *propellere* drive before one, formed as PRO-¹ + *pellere* drive.]
†**1** Drive out or away, expel. LME–M17.
2 Drive or push (a person or thing) forward, cause to move onwards. L16.
3 *fig.* Urge (a person) on, encourage; impel. M18.

📖 **2** LD MACAULAY Each galley was propelled by . . huge oars. B. BAINBRIDGE He propelled her . . up the . . ramp. **propelling pencil** a pencil of metal, plastic, etc., with a thin replaceable lead projected or retracted by twisting part of the casing. **3** S. QUINN A rejection . . propelled her toward study.

■ **propellable** *adjective* (*rare*) M19.

propellant /prəˈpɛl(ə)nt/ *adjective & noun*. Also (as adjective now usu.) **-ent**. M17.
[Orig. from Latin *propellent-* pres. ppl stem of *propellere* PROPEL *verb*; later from PROPEL *verb* + -ENT, -ANT¹.]
► **A** *adjective*. Capable of driving or pushing something forward, propelling. M17.
► **B** *noun*. **1** Something that propels, a propelling agent, *spec.* (***a***) an explosive that fires bullets etc. from a firearm; (***b***) *fig.* an incentive, a stimulus. E19.
2 A substance that is used (alone, or reacting with another) as a source of the hot gases that provide the thrust in a rocket engine. E20.
3 The inert compressed fluid in which the active contents in an aerosol container etc. are dispersed. M20.
¶ In isolated use before 19.

propeller /prəˈpɛlə/ *noun*. L18.
[from PROPEL + -ER¹.]
1 *gen.* A person who or thing which propels something. L18.
2 *spec.* A mechanical device for propelling something; *esp.* = SCREW *noun*¹ 8. E19. ▸**b** *transf.* A ship powered by a propeller or propellers. M19.
Comb.: **propeller-head** [prob. with ref. to a beanie hat with a propeller on top, popularized by science-fiction enthusiasts] *colloq.* a person who has an obsessive interest in computers or technology; **propeller shaft** a shaft transmitting power from an engine to a propeller or to the driven wheels of a motor vehicle; **propeller turbine** *noun & adjective* = TURBOPROP.
■ **propellerless** *adjective* M20. **propellor** *noun* = PROPELLER M19.

propend /prəˈpɛnd/ *verb intrans. arch.* M16.
[Latin *propendere* hang forward or down, formed as PRO-[1] + *pendere* hang.]
†1 Hang or lean forward or downwards, incline. M16–L17.
2 Have an inclination or propensity, tend, be disposed, (*to, to do*). E17.

propendent /prəˈpɛnd(ə)nt/ *adjective.* Now *rare* or *obsolete.* L16.
[Latin *propendent-* pres. ppl stem of *propendere*: see prec., -ENT.]
Hanging or leaning forwards or downward.

propene /ˈprəʊpiːn/ *noun.* M19.
[from PROP- + -ENE.]
CHEMISTRY. = PROPYLENE.
Comb.: **propenenitrile** = ACRYLONITRILE.
■ **propenal** /-pɪnal/ *noun* = ACROLEIN M20. **propeˈnoic** *adjective* = ACRYLIC *adjective* 1 M20. **propenyl** *noun* either of the radicals $CH_2{=}CHCH_2{\cdot}$ and $CH_3{=}CH{\cdot}$ derived from propylene M19.

propense /prəˈpɛns/ *adjective.* Now *rare.* E16.
[Latin *propensus* pa. pple of *propendere* PROPEND.]
1 Having an inclination or propensity, inclined, disposed; ready, willing. Foll. by *to, to do.* E16.
†2 Well-disposed, favourable, partial, (*to*). M16–L18.
†3 = PREPENSE *adjective* 1. M17–M18.
■ **propensely** *adverb* L17. **propenseness** *noun* M16.

propension /prəˈpɛnʃ(ə)n/ *noun.* Now *rare.* E17.
[Latin *propensio(n-)*, from *propens-* ppl stem of *propendere* PROPEND: see -ION.]
= next.

propensity /prəˈpɛnsɪti/ *noun.* L16.
[from PROPENSE + -ITY.]
(An) inclination, (a) tendency, (a) leaning; bent, disposition. (Foll. by *to, towards, for, to do*). Also, (a) favourable inclination, bias, partiality, (*to*).

🕮 SYD. SMITH That dreadful propensity . . for writing verses. E. FROMM Selfishness and laziness are . . propensities inherent in human beings. D. CECIL His propensity to . . morbid moods.

proper /ˈprɒpə/ *adjective, noun, & adverb.* ME.
[Old & mod. French *propre* from Latin *proprius* one's own, special, peculiar (to).]
▶ **A** *adjective.* **I 1** Belonging to as a possession or quality, owned, own; intrinsic, inherent. Usually preceded by a *possess.* Now chiefly SCIENCE. ME.
2 Belonging or relating to distinctively or exclusively; particular, peculiar; special, individual. (Foll. by *to.*) ME. ▸**b** Of a name or noun: applicable to a particular individual person, animal, place, country, title, etc. (and usu. spelt with a capital letter). Opp. ***common***. ME. ▸**c** PHYSICS. Measured as though stationary with respect to the observer. E20.
3 HERALDRY. Represented in the natural colours rather than conventional tinctures. Usu. *postpositive.* L16.
4 MATH. & PHYSICS. [translating German *eigen* own, characteristic: see EIGEN-.] ▸**a** Of an oscillation: = NORMAL *adjective* 5a. L19. ▸**b** Of a function, value, etc.; that is an eigenfunction, eigenvalue, etc. M20.

🕮 **2** P. SIPMA A certain number of peculiarities in their system of vowels and consonants: these must have been proper to the original Anglo-Frisian language.

▶ **II 5** Strictly or accurately so called; genuine, true, real; regular, normal. Now freq. *postpositive.* ME. ▸**b** MATH. Designating a subset, subgroup, etc., that does not constitute the entire set; group, etc.; *spec.* designating such a subgroup that has more than one element. E20.
6 Strictly belonging or applicable; strict, accurate, correct. LME. ▸†**b** Very, identical. *rare.* E16–M19.
7 **a** Of good quality or character; excellent, admirable, fine. *arch.* LME. ▸**b** Good-looking, handsome, attractive; elegant. *dial.* LME.
8 Answering fully to the description; thorough, complete, veritable. Now *colloq.* LME.

🕮 **5** P. LARKIN Too much trouble to make a proper meal. B. PYM A kind of ante-room leading to the restaurant proper. A. THWAITE He had never had a proper microscope. **6** COLERIDGE Felicity, in its proper sense, is . . happiness. **8** M. BINCHY She was a proper little madam.

▶ **III 9** Of requisite standard or type; fit, suitable, appropriate; fitting, right. ME.
10 Conforming to recognized social standards or etiquette; seemly, decent, decorous; (of a person) respectable, correct, esp. excessively so. M18.

🕮 **9** J. BUCHAN A tailed coat . . a garb . . he thought proper for a country laird. R. THOMAS Present your . . accusations through the proper channels. **10** E. J. WORBOISE I abominate your goody-goody, circumspect, infallibly-proper young lady. G. SANTAYANA You can't talk to an elderly man about your love affairs; it wouldn't be proper.

Special collocations & phrases: **Proper Bostonian** = BRAHMIN 2. **proper fraction** MATH. a fraction whose value is less than one, with the numerator less than the denominator. **proper lesson** ECCLESIASTICAL: appointed for a particular day, occasion, or season. **proper motion** ASTRONOMY the part of the apparent motion of a celestial object relative to the solar system due to its actual movement in space (i.e. allowing for the rotation of the earth parallax, and aberration). ***proper preface***: see PREFACE *noun* 1. **proper psalm** ECCLESIASTICAL: appointed for a particular day, occasion, or season. ***with all proper reserve***: see RESERVE *noun.*
▶ **B** *noun.* †**1** That which is one's own; a possession, one's property. LME–M16.
2 ECCLESIASTICAL. An office or part of an office, as a psalm, lesson, etc., appointed for a particular occasion or season. Opp. COMMON *noun* 4. L15.
1 in proper in individual possession, as private property, as one's own, (opp. ***in common***).
▶ **C** *adverb.* Properly; *spec.* extremely, very, thoroughly, completely; (of speech) in received pronunciation, correctly. Now *dial.* & *colloq.* LME.

🕮 K. S. PRICHARD They got proper wet out there. M. ALLINGHAM Teachin' me to speak proper. E. WAUGH We couldn't bury him proper. M. GEE He will sort her out good and proper.

properdin /prəʊˌpəːdɪn/ *noun.* M20.
[from PRO-[1] + Latin *perdere* destroy + -IN[1].]
PHYSIOLOGY. Any of a group of proteins found in the blood and involved in the body's response to certain kinds of infection.

properispomenon /prə(ʊ)ˌpɛrɪˈspəʊmɪnən/ *adjective & noun.* Pl. **-mena** /-mɪnə/. Also Anglicized as **properispome** /prəʊˈpɛrɪspəʊm/. E19.
[Greek *properispōmenon*, formed as PRO-[2] + PERISPOMENON.]
GREEK GRAMMAR. (A word) having a circumflex accent on the penultimate syllable.

properly /ˈprɒp(ə)li/ *adverb.* ME.
[from PROPER *adjective* + -LY[2].]
1 **a** Particularly, distinctively, specially. ME. ▸**b** In itself, intrinsically, essentially; as private property, privately. Now *rare* or *obsolete.* LME.
2 In the strict sense, strictly speaking; accurately, exactly. ME.
3 Fittingly, suitably, appropriately; rightly, duly; respectably, with propriety or decency. ME.
4 Excellently, finely, well. *arch.* LME.
5 Thoroughly, completely, utterly; exceedingly, very. Now *colloq.* LME.
6 MATH. So as to form a proper subset or subgroup. M20.

🕮 **2** W. CATHER The French Church, properly the Church of Sainte-Agnes, stood upon a hill. **3** H. JAMES I had not been properly introduced. E. BOWEN The doors shut properly. A. CARTER She had a chance to see him properly. **5** K. AMIS She's properly fed up.

properness /ˈprɒpənɪs/ *noun.* Now *rare.* LME.
[from PROPER *adjective* + -NESS.]
1 Excellence, goodness, esp. of appearance; handsomeness, elegance. LME.
2 Fitness, suitability; propriety, respectability. M16.
3 The fact of belonging specially to a thing or person; special quality or character. M17.

Propertian /prəˈpəːʃ(ə)n/ *adjective.* L19.
[from *Propertius* (see below) + -AN.]
Of, pertaining to, or characteristic of Sextus Aurelius Propertius, a Latin elegiac poet of the first cent. BC, or his poetry.

propertied /ˈprɒpətɪd/ *adjective.* E17.
[from next + -ED[2].]
1 Having a specified property, quality, or nature. Long *rare.* E17.
2 Owning or holding property, esp. land or real estate. M18.
3 Provided with stage props. E20.

🕮 **2** D. PIPER The . . landed and propertied classes.

property /ˈprɒpəti/ *noun & verb.* ME.
[Repr. Anglo-Norman var. of Old & mod. French *propriété*: see PROPRIETY.]
▶ **A** *noun.* **1** That which one owns; a thing or things belonging to a person or persons; possessions collectively; *spec.* real estate, housing. ME. ▸**b** A house or piece of land owned. E18. ▸**c** In *pl.* Shares or investments in property. M20. ▸**d** An artist, performer, or work regarded as a commercial asset, a success, a sensation. Freq. in ***hot property***. *colloq.* M20.
2 An attribute, quality, or characteristic, *esp.* an essential one; an inherent power or capacity, a virtue. ME. ▸†**b** The characteristic quality of a person or thing; character, nature. ME–E18. ▸**c** LOGIC. A non-essential characteristic common to all, and only, the members of a class. M16.
3 The condition or fact of owning or being owned; the (exclusive) right to the possession, use, or disposal of a thing, ownership. LME.
4 THEATRICAL. = PROP *noun*[5]. LME.
†**5** The quality of being proper or appropriate; suitability. LME–M18.
†**6** *fig.* A means to an end; a person or thing to be made use of. L16–M19.

🕮 **1** D. CARNEGIE A real-estate operator who had bought and sold property on Long Island. C. PRIEST The houses were . . council property. P. VAN SOMMERS We treat those we love as our property. **b** J. BARNES A . . white, eighteenth-century property. **2** B. RUSSELL Some property of *all* triangles. R. FRY Art had the property of conveying . . aesthetic emotion. F. HOYLE This simple property of transparency to sunlight. L. MCMURTRY The culinary properties of rattlesnake. **3** T. DRUMMOND Property has its duties. *Observer* Attacks on the rights of property.

Phrases: ***common property***: see COMMON *adjective.* ***intellectual property***: see INTELLECTUAL *adjective* 1. ***internal property***: see INTERNAL *adjective.* ***literary property***: see LITERARY *adjective.* ***lost property***: see LOST *adjective.* ***personal property***: see PERSONAL *adjective.* PROJECTIVE ***property***. TOPOLOGICAL ***property***.
Comb.: **property man**, **property mistress**, etc.: in charge of stage props in a theatre etc.; **property qualification** a qualification for office, or for the exercise of a right, based on the possession of a certain amount of property; **property tax** a tax levied directly on property.
▶†**B** *verb trans.* **1** Use (a person or thing) for one's own ends, exploit. L16–M18
2 Make one's own property, appropriate, take or hold possession of. E17–M19.
■ **propertyless** *adjective* E19. **propertylessness** *noun* M20.

prophage /ˈprəʊfeɪdʒ/ *noun.* M20.
[from PRO-[2] + PHAGE.]
BIOLOGY. The genetic material of a bacteriophage, incorporated into the genome of a lysogenic bacterium and able to produce phages if specifically activated.

propham /ˈprəʊfam/ *noun.* M20.
[from elems. of the semi-systematic name isopropyl *N*-phenylcarbamate.]
A white crystalline biodegradable substance used as a selective agricultural herbicide.

†**prophane** *adjective & noun, verb* see PROFANE *adjective & noun, verb.*

prophase /ˈprəʊfeɪz/ *noun.* L19.
[from PRO-[2] + PHASE *noun.*]
CYTOLOGY. The first stage in a mitotic or meiotic nuclear division, before metaphase, during which the chromosomes become visible and shorten and the nuclear envelope disappears.
■ **proˈphasic** *adjective* E20.

prophecy /ˈprɒfɪsi/ *noun.* ME.
[Old French *profecie*, *prophecie* (mod. *prophétie*) from late Latin *prophetia* from Greek *prophēteia*, from *prophētēs* PROPHET: see -CY.]
1 The action, practice, or faculty of prophesying; divinely inspired utterance or writing, esp. in the Bible or the Koran; an instance of this. Also, the foretelling or prediction of future events, orig. as a divinely inspired action; an instance of this. ME. ▸**b** *fig.* A foreshadowing of something to come. M18.
2 The interpretation and expounding by a preacher of Scripture or of divine mysteries; an instance of this. Now *rare.* LME.
3 CHRISTIAN CHURCH. An Old Testament lesson or reading, esp. in the Eucharist. *rare.* LME.

🕮 **1** DONNE Any of the prophecies of the Revelation concerning Antichrist. C. ISHERWOOD Among other prophecies, the astrologer has told her . . she will win some money. *Times* Panic buying . . caused largely by forecasts of . . shortage—a self-fulfilling prophecy. ***Great Pyramid prophecy***: see PYRAMID *noun* 2. **b** E. YOUNG The world's a prophecy of worlds to come.

prophesy /ˈprɒfɪsʌɪ/ *verb.* Also (earlier) †**-cy**. ME.
[Old French *prophecier*, formed as prec.: see -Y[2].]
1 *verb intrans.* Speak or write by divine inspiration, act as a prophet. Also, foretell or predict future events, orig. *spec.* by divine inspiration. ME.
2 *verb trans.* Announce, utter, or write (a thing, *that*) by divine inspiration; foretell or predict (future events), orig. *spec.* by divine inspiration. ME. ▸**b** *fig.* Foreshadow, prefigure. E17.
3 *verb intrans.* Interpret or expound Scripture or divine mysteries. Now *rare.* ME.

🕮 **1** AV *Jer.* 19:14 Then came Ieremiah from Tophet, whither the Lord had sent him to prophecie. E. WAUGH To prophesy rashly . . there will be no air attack on London. **2** G. HARRIS Marliann . . prophesied that their parents would admire them. R. DEACON They . . prophesied the Algiers coup.

■ **prophesier** *noun* L15. **prophesying** *noun* (*a*) the action of the verb; (*b*) an instance of this, a prediction: E16.

prophet /ˈprɒfɪt/ *noun.* ME.
[Old & mod. French *prophète* from Latin *propheta*, *-tes* from Greek *prophētēs* interpreter, spokesman esp. of the will of a god, formed as PRO-[2] + *phētēs* speaker, from *phēnai*, *pha-* speak.]
1 A person who speaks for God or a god; a divinely inspired teacher or interpreter of the will of God or a god. Also, a person who predicts or foretells future events, orig. *spec.* by divine inspiration. ME.
2 A minister in the Catholic Apostolic Church; *gen.* a preacher. Now *rare.* M16.
3 An omen, a portent. L16.

4 An innovative proclaimer or advocate of a cause, principle, etc.; a visionary leader or representative. M19. **5** A person who predicts the result of a race etc., a tipster. *slang*. M19.

> **1** AV *Matt.* 13:57 Iesus said vnto them, a Prophet is not without honour, saue in his owne countrey. HOBBES Prophets .. at Delphi .. of whose loose words a sense might be made to fit any event. **4** J. T. MICKLETHWAITE Durandus .. the prophet of symbolism. *New Scientist* The leading prophet of sea-farming.

Phrases: **Former Prophets** *JUDAISM* the books of Joshua, Judges, 1 & 2 Samuel, and 1 & 2 Kings, which with the Latter Prophets make up one of the three canonical divisions of the Hebrew Scriptures. **Latter Prophets** *JUDAISM* the books of Isaiah, Ezekiel, Jeremiah, and the twelve shorter prophetic books from Hosea to Malachi, which with the Former Prophets make up one of the three canonical divisions of the Hebrew Scriptures. **Major Prophet** *CHRISTIAN CHURCH* (*a*) each of the prophets, Isaiah, Jeremiah, and Ezekiel, for whom the three longer prophetic books of the Old Testament are named and whose prophecies they record (usu. in *pl.*); (*b*) in *pl.*, these books collectively. **Minor Prophet** *CHRISTIAN CHURCH* (*a*) any of the prophets, from Hosea to Malachi, for whom the twelve shorter prophetic books of the Old Testament are named and whose prophecies they record (usu. in *pl.*); (*b*) in *pl.*, these books collectively. **Prophet's flower** a plant of the borage family, *Arnebia pulchra*, native to the regions west of the Upper Indus, which has a yellow corolla bearing evanescent purple spots, believed to be the marks of Muhammad's fingers. **the Prophet** *spec.* (*a*) = MUHAMMAD; (*b*) among Mormons, Joseph Smith (1805–44), founder and first leader of the Mormon faith; any of his successors. **the Prophets** (*a*) *CHRISTIAN CHURCH* the prophetic books of the Old Testament, Isaiah, Jeremiah, Ezekiel, Daniel, and the Minor Prophets; (*b*) *JUDAISM* one of the three canonical divisions of the Hebrew Scriptures, comprising the Former and Latter Prophets, the other two divisions being the Law and the Hagiographa or Writings.

■ **prophetess** *noun* a female prophet ME. **prophethood** *noun* the position of a prophet, the state or condition of being a prophet M19. **prophetism** *noun* the action or practice of a prophet or prophets; the system or principles of the Hebrew prophets: E18. †**prophetize** *verb trans. & intrans.* prophesy ME–E18. **prophetless** *adjective* E20. **prophetship** *noun* = PROPHETHOOD M17.

prophetic /prəˈfɛtɪk/ *adjective*. L15.
[French *prophétique* or late Latin *propheticus* from Greek *prophētikos*, from *prophētēs*: see prec., -IC.]
1 Characterized by or of the nature of containing a prediction; predicting or presaging something. Freq. foll. by *of*. L15.
2 Of, pertaining to, or befitting a prophet or prophecy; having the character or function of a prophet. E17.
3 Spoken of in prophecy, predicted. Now *rare*. M17.

> **1** J. WILSON Lurid stars Prophetic of throne-shattering wars. J. R. LOWELL Verses .. prophetic of the maturer man. J. M. MURRY That sonnet was prophetic .. far in advance of .. his work at the moment. **prophetic present, prophetic perfect** *GRAMMAR* the present or perfect tense used to express a certain future.

■ **prophetical** *adjective* (*a*) = PROPHETIC 2; (*b*) = PROPHETIC 1: LME. **propheti'cality** *noun* (*rare*) M19. **propheticalness** *noun* (*rare*) E18. **prophetically** *adverb* L15. **propheticism** /-sɪz(ə)m/ *noun* a prophetic statement etc., an expression characteristic of a prophet; prophetic condition or state: L17. †**propheticly** *adverb* (*rare*) M17–E18.

propho /ˈprɒfəʊ/ *noun*. *slang* (orig. *US*). E20.
[from PROPH(YLAXIS + -O.]
Prophylaxis of venereal disease.

prophylactic /prɒfɪˈlaktɪk/ *adjective & noun*. L16.
[French *prophylactique* from Greek *prophulaktikos*, formed as PRO-² + *phulak-*: see PHYLACTERY, -IC.]
▶**A** *adjective*. Protecting against or tending to prevent disease; *transf.* protective, precautionary. L16.
▶**B** *noun*. **1** A medicine or course of action taken to prevent or as a precaution against disease etc; a preventive measure, a protection. M17.
2 A condom (esp. as used more for protection against disease than for contraceptive purposes). Chiefly *N. Amer.* M20.

> **1** J. FOWLES Camphor as a prophylactic against cholera. G. BLACK Troops were here as a prophylactic against rioting.

■ **prophylactically** *adverb* M19.

prophylaxis /prɒfɪˈlaksɪs/ *noun*. M19.
[mod. Latin, formed as PRO-² + Greek *phulaxis* an act of guarding, on the analogy of prec.]
Treatment intended to prevent disease; *transf.* precautionary action.

> A. S. NEILL My territory was prophylaxis—not curing.

■ **prophylaxy** *noun* (*rare*) L19.

prophyll /ˈprəʊfɪl/ *noun*. Orig. in Greek form **prophyllon** /-lɒn/, pl. **-lla** /-lə/. L19.
[from PRO-² + Greek *phullon* leaf.]
BOTANY. The first leaf, or either of the first two leaves, on a lateral shoot (freq. smaller than the other leaves).

propidium /prə(ʊ)ˈpɪdɪəm/ *noun*. M20.
[from PROP- + -IDE + -IUM.]
BIOCHEMISTRY. (The cation of) propidium iodide.
Comb.: **propidium iodide** an iodinated derivative of a compound analogous to ethidium bromide, and with similar uses.

propine /prəʊˈpʌɪn/ *noun*¹ *& verb*. Chiefly *Scot. arch.* LME.
[Latin *propinare* to pledge from Greek *propinein* drink before or to, formed as PRO-² + *pinein* drink.]
▶**A** *noun*. **1** A thing presented as a gift; a present. LME.
2 The power to give; disposal. *rare*. L18.
▶**B** *verb trans*. **1** Offer or give (a beverage) to drink; propose (a toast), wish a person (health etc.) in drinking. LME.
2 Offer (a thing) for acceptance or as a present, present; present (a person) *with* something, endow, reward. LME.

†**propine** *noun*². M–L19.
[from PROP- + -INE⁵.]
CHEMISTRY. = PROPYNE.

propinquant /prəˈpɪŋkwənt/ *adjective*. *rare*. M17.
[Latin *propinquant-* pres. ppl stem of *propinquare* bring near, approach, from *propinquus*: see PROPINQUITY, -ANT¹.]
Near, neighbouring, adjacent.

propinquate /prəˈpɪŋkweɪt/ *verb intrans*. *rare*. E17.
[Latin *propinquat-* pa. ppl stem of *propinquare*: see prec., -ATE³.]
Approach, draw near.

propinque /prəˈpɪŋk/ *adjective*. *rare*. L15.
[from Latin *propinquus*: see next.]
= PROPINQUANT.

propinquity /prəˈpɪŋkwɪti/ *noun*. LME.
[Old French *propinquité* or Latin *propinquitas*, from *propinquus* neighbouring, from *prope* near: see -ITY.]
Nearness or closeness in space or time, proximity; near or close kinship; similarity, affinity.

> Q. BELL In .. cosy propinquity .. diseases were shared by all.

■ **propinquitous** *adjective* nearby, adjacent, close at hand L19. **propinquous** *adjective* (*rare*) = PROPINQUITOUS M19.

propionibacterium /prəʊpɪˌɒnɪbakˈtɪərɪəm/ *noun*. Pl. **-ria** /-rɪə/. M20.
[mod. Latin (see below), from PROPIONIC + BACTERIUM.]
A bacterium of the genus *Propionibacterium*, comprising rod-shaped Gram-positive forms which metabolize carbohydrate, and some of which are involved in the fermentation of dairy products and the aetiology of acne.

propionic /prəʊpɪˈɒnɪk/ *adjective*. M19.
[French *propionique*, formed as PRO-² + Greek *piōn* fat (as the first in the carboxylic acid series to form fatty compounds): see -IC.]
CHEMISTRY. ***propionic acid***, a colourless sharp-smelling liquid carboxylic acid, CH_3CH_2COOH, used esp. to inhibit the growth of mould in bread etc. Also called ***propanoic acid***.

■ **propio'lactone** *noun* a pungent colourless liquid β-lactone, $C_3H_4O_2$, used as a disinfectant E20. **propio'naldehyde** *noun* the aldehyde, CH_3CH_2CHO, of propionic acid, a flammable colourless liquid that forms an explosive mixture with air (also called ***propanal***, ***propyl aldehyde***) E20. **'propionate** *noun* a salt or ester of propionic acid L19. **'propionyl** *noun* the radical CH_3CH_2CO- M19.

propiska /prəˈpɪskə/ *noun*. L20.
[Russian = registration, residence permit, from *propiskat'* to register.]
In the Soviet Union and post-Soviet Russia: a permit entitling a person to reside (and therefore work) in a particular city or town.

propitiate /prəˈpɪʃɪeɪt/ *verb trans*. L16.
[Latin *propitiat-* pa. ppl stem of *propitiare*, from *propitius* favourable, gracious: see -ATE³.]
Make propitious or favourably inclined; appease, conciliate, placate.

> C. FRANCIS Human sacrifices to propitiate the .. sea. P. D. JAMES His attempt to propitiate her, to get her on his side.

■ **propitiable** *adjective* L15. **propitiatingly** *adverb* in a propitiating manner, so as to propitiate M19. **propitiative** *adjective* (*rare*) tending to propitiate, propitiatory, conciliatory E20. **propitiator** *noun* L16.

propitiation /prəpɪʃɪˈeɪʃ(ə)n/ *noun*. LME.
[Late (eccl.) Latin *propitiatio(n-)*, formed as prec.: see -ATION. Cf. Old & mod. French *propitiation*.]
1 The action or an act of propitiating; appeasement, conciliation; atonement, expiation. LME.
2 A propitiatory gift, offering, or sacrifice. *arch.* M16.

> **1** *Harper's Magazine* They threw the salt over their shoulders .. in propitiation of evil powers.

propitiatory /prəˈpɪʃɪət(ə)ri/ *noun & adjective*. ME.
[As noun from ecclesiastical Latin *propitiatorium* use as noun of neut. sing. of *propitiatorius*, as adjective from *propitiatorius*, from *propitiator*, formed as PROPITIATE, rendering Greek *hilastērion*: see -ORY².]
▶**A** *noun*. **1** = ***mercy-seat*** s.v. MERCY *noun*. ME.
2 A propitiation, an offering of atonement; formerly *spec.* in *CHRISTIAN THEOLOGY*, the sacrificed Christ. Now *rare*. M16.
▶**B** *adjective*. Serving, tending, or intended to propitiate someone; appeasing, conciliating, ingratiating; atoning, expiatory. M16.
■ **propitiatorily** *adverb* M16.

propitious /prəˈpɪʃəs/ *adjective*. LME.
[Old French *propicieus* or Latin *propitius* favourable, gracious: see -IOUS.]
Well-disposed, favourably inclined; (of an omen etc.) good, boding well; (of weather, an occasion, etc.) favourable, timely, opportune. Freq. foll. by *for*, *to*.

> W. HAMILTON God is propitious to me .. my sins are forgiven. H. MACMILLAN For such an adventure that time was not .. propitious. A. FRASER A propitious storm saved them.

■ **propitiously** *adverb* L17. **propitiousness** *noun* L16.

proplasm /prəʊˈplaz(ə)m/ *noun*. *rare*. L17.
[Latin *proplasma*, formed as PRO-¹ + PLASM.]
A mould, a matrix.

propless /ˈprɒplɪs/ *adjective*. L16.
[from PROP *noun*¹ + -LESS.]
Without prop or support, unsupported.

propodeum /prəʊˈpəʊdɪəm/ *noun*. Pl. **-ea** /-ɪə/. Also (earlier) in Greek form **-podeon** /-ˈpɒdɪən/. M19.
[from PRO-² + Greek *podeōn* narrow end, neck of a wineskin, alt. to *-um* by false analogy with Latin form of Greek neuter nouns in *-on*.]
ENTOMOLOGY. The segment anterior to and partly surrounding the petiole (in origin, the first abdominal segment) of some insects, esp. hymenopterans.

propofol /ˈprəʊpəfɒl/ *noun*. L20.
[from PROP(YL + -O- + *-fol* alt. of PH(EN)OL.]
PHARMACOLOGY. A phenol derivative used as an anaesthetic and sedative; 2,6-diisopropylphenol, $C_{12}H_{18}O$.

propolis /ˈprɒp(ə)lɪs/ *noun*. E17.
[Latin from Greek, formed as PRO-² + *polis* city.]
A red resinous substance collected by bees from the bark and buds of various trees and used to fill crevices and fix and varnish the combs; bee-glue.

propone /prəˈpəʊn/ *verb trans*. Long *obsolete* exc. *Scot.* LME.
[Latin *proponere* put or set forth, formed as PRO-¹ + *ponere* to place.]
1 Put forward for consideration, propose; propound (a theory, proposal, etc). LME.
2 *LAW*. Put or state before a tribunal. LME.

proponent /prəˈpəʊnənt/ *noun & adjective*. L16.
[Latin *proponent-* pres. ppl stem of *proponere*: see prec., -ENT.]
▶**A** *noun*. A person bringing forward or advocating a theory, proposal, etc; a proposer, an advocate. (Foll. by *of*). L16.

> F. KAPLAN Proponents of industrial .. laissez-faire.

▶**B** *adjective*. That brings forward or proposes; proposing or advocating a theory etc. L17.

Propontic /prəʊˈpɒntɪk/ *adjective & noun*. E17.
[from Latin *Propontis* from Greek, the ancient name of the Sea of Marmara, formed as PRO-² + *pontos* sea, spec. the Black Sea: see -IC.]
(Designating or pertaining to) the Sea of Marmara.

proportion /prəˈpɔːʃ(ə)n/ *noun*. LME.
[Old & mod. French, or Latin *proportio(n-)*, from *pro portione* proportionally, formed as PRO-¹ + *portio(n-)*: see PORTION *noun*.]
1 A portion, a part, a share, esp. in relation to a whole; a relative amount or number. LME.
2 (A) comparative relation or ratio between things in size, quantity, number, etc. LME.
3 Relation between things in nature etc.; comparison, analogy. Now *rare*. LME.
4 Due or pleasing relation between things or parts of a thing; balance, symmetry, harmony. LME.
5 In *pl.* & (now *rare*) *sing.* Dimensions, extent, esp. in relation to something; relative measurements or size. LME.
6 *MATH*. A relationship of equivalence between two pairs of quantities, such that the first bears the same relation to the second as the third does to the fourth. Now *spec.* = ***GEOMETRICAL proportion***. Also, a set of quantities in such a relation. LME.
†**7** The action of proportioning or making proportionate; proportionate estimate or adjustment. LME–E17.
8 Form, shape; a figure or image of something. *obsolete* exc. *poet.* LME.

> **1** T. H. HUXLEY So large a proportion of the earth's surface. A. C. BOULT A small proportion of Old Boys who revisit their old school. **2** SIR T. BROWNE The proportion of the Diameter unto the Circumference. SAKI The proportions .. make such a difference .. how much liver to how much chestnut. **4** K. OKAKURA The stone Buddhas are beautiful, with a .. harmony of proportion. **5** J. TYNDALL The ice-crags .. seemed of gigantic proportions. M. FONTEYN His ideal proportions: his slender build, long legs, shoulders neither too narrow nor too wide.

Phrases: ***direct proportion***: see DIRECT *adjective*. ***divine proportion***: see DIVINE *adjective*. ***GEOMETRICAL proportion***. **in proportion** (*a*) without exaggerating the importance etc. of something, with correct emphasis; (*b*) well or appropriately proportioned; proportional, proportionally, (foll. by *to*, *with*); (*c*) (foll. by *to*, *as*) to the extent in which, by the same factor as; (*d*) (foll. by *to*) in comparison with. ***inverse proportion***: see INVERSE *adjective*. ***multiple proportion***: see MULTIPLE *adjective*. **out of proportion** (*a*) badly proportioned; (*b*) exaggerated, overemphasized; (*c*) disproportionate (foll. by *to, with*). **rule of proportion** MATH. = *rule of three* s.v. RULE *noun*.

■ **proportionless** *adjective* M17.

proportion /prəˈpɔːʃ(ə)n/ *verb trans.* LME.
[Old French *proporcioner* (mod. *proportionner*) or medieval Latin *proportionare*, from Latin *proportio(n-)*: see prec.]
1 Adjust or regulate in proportion to something, make (a thing) proportionate. Foll. by *to, with*. LME.
2 Fashion, form or shape (a thing). *obsolete* exc. as PROPORTIONED 2. LME.
†**3** Divide into proportionate parts, measure out; allot or assign (a thing) to a person, apportion. L15–L18.
†**4** Be in proportion to; correspond to, equal. L16–M17.
†**5** Compare (a thing or person) with another; estimate the relative proportions of. L16–E18.

📖 **1** H. MARTINEAU Proportion your supply exactly to the demand. J. S. MILL The punishment should be proportioned to the offence.

■ **proportioner** *noun* L16. **proportionment** *noun* (now *rare*) the action or fact of proportioning something, proportional distribution or arrangement L17.

proportionable /prəˈpɔːʃ(ə)nəb(ə)l/ *adjective*. LME.
[Old & mod. French, or late Latin *proportionabilis*, from *proportionare*: see prec., -ABLE.]
1 That is in due proportion; corresponding, commensurate, proportional. LME. ▸†**b** Suitable, appropriate; analogous. E16–M18.
2 Well-proportioned; symmetrical. Now *rare* or *obsolete*. E17.
†**3** Relative, comparative. M17–L18.
■ **proportionableness** *noun* M17. **proportionably** *adverb* LME.

proportional /prəˈpɔːʃ(ə)n(ə)l/ *noun & adjective*. LME.
[Late Latin *proportionalis*, from *proportio(n-)*: see PROPORTION *noun*, -AL[1].]
▶**A** *noun*. †**1** A proportionate part; a relative quantity. *rare*. LME–M19.
2 MATH. Each of the terms of a proportion. Now *rare*. L16.
†**3** CHEMISTRY. = EQUIVALENT *noun* 3 E–M19.
2 CONTINUED *proportionals*.
▶**B** *adjective*. **1** That is in (due) proportion; related in terms of proportion *to* something; corresponding in degree, size, amount, etc; comparable. LME.
2 Of or pertaining to proportion; relative; used in determining proportions. M16.
3 MATH. & SCIENCE. That is in proportion; having the same or a constant ratio (esp. over a range of values) *to* another quantity. L16.

📖 **1** W. ROBERTSON A zeal in defence of their religion proportional to the fierceness with which it had been attacked. **proportional representation** a system of parliamentary representation based on numerical rather than regional division of the electorate, *spec.* one by which each party gains seats in proportion to the number of votes it receives; abbreviation *PR*. **2 proportional counter** an ionization chamber in which the operating voltage is large enough to produce gas amplification but not so large that the output pulse ceases to be proportional to the initial ionization. **proportional limit** MECHANICS the point at which the strain in a stressed material or object ceases to be proportional to the stress. **3** J. B. S. HALDANE The amount of substrate transformed is proportional . . both to the enzyme concentration and the time.

■ **proportionalism** *noun* †(*a*) CHEMISTRY the combination of elements in definite proportions; (*b*) the theory or practice of proportional representation: M19. **proportionalist** *noun* (*a*) a planner of the proportions of anything, a designer; (*b*) an advocate of proportional representation: M19. **proportionally** *adverb* (*a*) in a proportional manner, in (due) proportion: †(*b*) in a well-proportioned manner: LME.

proportionality /prəpɔːʃəˈnalɪti/ *noun*. LME.
[French *proportionnalité* or medieval Latin *proportionalitas*, from *proportionalis*: see prec., -ITY.]
†**1** = PROPORTION *noun* 6. Only in LME.
2 The quality, character, or fact of being proportional. M16.
3 MATH. A formula expressing the proportional relationship of two or more quantities. M20.
Phrases: **constant of proportionality**, **factor of proportionality** MATH. & SCIENCE a value representing the ratio of one variable to a second to which it is constantly proportional. **limit of proportionality** = *proportional limit* s.v. PROPORTIONAL *adjective*.
Comb.: **proportionality constant**, **proportionality factor** = *constant of proportionality* above.

proportionate /prəˈpɔːʃ(ə)nət/ *adjective*. LME.
[Late Latin *proportionatus*, from Latin *proportio(n-)*: see PROPORTION *noun*, -ATE[2].]
That is in (due) proportion (*to*); appropriate, proportional, corresponding.

📖 F. LIEBER The toll . . on the canal is proportionate to weight.

■ **proportionately** *adverb* L15. **proportionateness** *noun* M17.

proportionate /prəˈpɔːʃ(ə)neɪt/ *verb trans.* M16.
[from prec. or medieval Latin *proportionat-* pa. ppl stem of *proportionare*: see PROPORTION *verb*, -ATE[3].]
= PROPORTION *verb*.

proportioned /prəˈpɔːʃ(ə)nd/ *adjective*. ME.
[from PROPORTION *noun, verb*: see -ED[2], -ED[1].]
1 That is in due proportion, *to* something; proportionate, proportional. ME.
2 Having proportions or dimensions of a specified kind; formed, shaped, or composed in a specified way. LME.

📖 **1** LD MACAULAY Great as were the offences . . his punishment was fully proportioned to them. **2** A. RADCLIFFE Another apartment, proportioned like the first. E. WAUGH She was . . admirably proportioned. M. SEYMOUR The . . gracefully proportioned oak staircase.

proposal /prəˈpəʊz(ə)l/ *noun*. M17.
[from PROPOSE *verb* + -AL[1].]
†**1** The action or an act of stating or propounding something. M–L17.
2 An act of proposing something; a course of action etc. proposed; a scheme, a plan, a motion; a suggestion, an idea. M17. ▸**b** A tender for a contract etc. Now *US*. M18.
3 An offer. Now only *spec.*, an offer of marriage. L17.

📖 **2** J. R. GREEN The Lords debated . . proposals of peace. *Times* The Government's . . proposals to help first-time buyers. A. BISHOP Proposals for films based on his novels. **3** W. H. AUDEN He made his proposal, She laughed, said: 'I'll never wed'.

proposant /prəˈpəʊz(ə)nt/ *noun*. *rare*. E19.
[French, pres. pple of *proposer*: see PROPOSE *verb*, -ANT[1].]
A person proposing or offering himself or herself as a candidate.

†**propose** *noun*. ME.
[Old & mod. French *propos*, formed as next. Cf. PURPOSE *noun*.]
1 Something proposed for discussion, a subject; a proposition. ME–L16.
2 Purpose, intention. L15–L16.
3 A proposal; something proposed to be done. E17–E18.

propose /prəˈpəʊz/ *verb*. ME.
[Old & mod. French *proposer* based on Latin *proponere* (see PROPONE) with substitution of Old & mod. French *poser* for *ponere*: see POSE *verb*[1].]
1 *verb trans.* Put forward as a scheme or plan, suggest (a thing), (foll. by *to do, that, doing*). Also, intend, resolve (on), purpose, (*to do, doing*). ME.
2 *verb trans.* Put forward or present for consideration, discussion, etc.; advance, propound, posit, (an argument, motion, etc.). LME. ▸†**b** Anticipate; face, confront. L16–M18. ▸†**c** Imagine, fancy, (a thing). *rare* (Shakes.). Only in L16. ▸**d** Decide on or put forward (a thing) as an aim or object. E17.
†**3** *verb trans.* Exhibit or display to view or perception. *lit. & fig.* M16–M18.
4 a *verb trans.* Present or offer for acceptance or assent; *spec.* (*a*) nominate (a person) for an office or position, esp. as a member of a society etc.; (*b*) offer (a person, a person's health, etc.) as a subject for a toast. L16. ▸**b** *verb intrans.* Make an offer of marriage, ask a person to marry one. (Foll. by *to*, (arch.) *for*.) M18.
†**5** *verb intrans.* Carry on a discussion; converse. *rare* (Shakes.). L16–E17.

📖 **1** H. JAMES She . . proposed that I should come with her. W. S. MAUGHAM Two small flats, . . one which he proposed to let. M. INNES I proposed a walkabout. We were to stroll through Auld Reekie's dusk together. **2** B. F. WESTCOTT An answer to the riddles which she proposes. *Archives of Neurology* We propose the terms light sleep, deep sleep, and sleep depth. B. EARNSHAW I proposed Classical Music against . . Pop. **4a** G. VIDAL The . . papers are going to propose you for President. C. P. SNOW The best man proposed the health of the bride. **propose marriage** make an offer of marriage (*to*). **b** V. SACKVILLE-WEST He would propose to her. J. BAYLEY Lockeley proposes, is accepted; the pair have a quiet wedding.

■ **proposable** *adjective* able or fit to be proposed E19. **proposed** *ppl adjective* that has been proposed; put forward for consideration or action; given or stated in an argument etc.: LME. **proposer** *noun* a person who proposes something; *spec.* a person propounding an argument etc., formally advancing a motion, or nominating someone for a position: E17.

proposita /prə(ʊ)ˈpɒzɪtə/ *noun*. Pl. **-tae** /-tiː/. L20.
[Latin, fem. of PROPOSITUS.]
A female propositus.

propositi *noun* pl. of PROPOSITUS.

proposition /prɒpəˈzɪʃ(ə)n/ *noun*. ME.
[Old & mod. French, or Latin *propositio(n-)*, from *proposit-* pa. ppl stem of *proponere*: see PROPONE, -ITION.]
1 The action or an act of propounding or proposing something for consideration; something proposed for consideration, *spec.* an introductory part of a speech, literary work, etc. Now *rare* or *obsolete*. ME. ▸†**b** A question proposed for solution, a problem, a riddle. LME–E17.
2 The action or an act of representing or displaying something; (a) presentation, (an) exhibition. Now *rare*. LME.
3 a A statement, an assertion; the making of a statement about something; *spec.* in LOGIC, a statement expressed in a form requiring consideration of its truth rather than its validity. LME. ▸**b** LOGIC. Either of the premisses of a syllogism, *esp.* the major premiss. Now *rare* or *obsolete*. M16.
4 A scheme or plan of action put forward, a proposal; *US* a constitutional proposal, a bill. LME.
5 MATH. A formal statement of a truth to be demonstrated (a theorem) or of an operation to be performed (a problem) (freq. including also the demonstration). LME.
†**6** The action or an act of putting something forward for acceptance; an offer. E–M17.
7 An enterprise, an undertaking, esp. with regard to the likelihood of its commercial etc. success; *colloq.* a (difficult) problem or project, a prospect with regard to its likely difficulty; a (formidable) person etc. to be dealt with. Orig. *US*. L19.
8 A sexual proposal or advance. *colloq.* (orig. *US*). M20.

📖 **3a** L. DURRELL The Cartesian proposition: 'I think, therefore I am'. G. K. WOLFE The proposition that humans enjoyed a destiny to conquer the universe. **4** A. JOHN I began to receive propositions for an autobiography from . . publishers. **7** C. E. MULFORD Knife fighters are bad propositions. *Daily Express* Every industry . . must be a business proposition. L. BLUE What a tough proposition a human life is. L. APPIGNANESI To create a *brief* portrait is something of a proposition. **not a proposition** unlikely to succeed in business etc.

proposition /prɒpəˈzɪʃ(ə)n/ *verb trans.* *colloq.* (orig. *US*). E20.
[from the noun.]
Make or present a proposition to (a person); solicit, importune; *spec.* make a sexual proposal or propose sexual activity to (a person).

📖 *Listener* The GI . . propositioned every woman in sight.

propositional /prɒpəˈzɪʃ(ə)n(ə)l/ *adjective*. E18.
[from PROPOSITION *noun* + -AL[1].]
Pertaining to or of the nature of a logical proposition; consisting of or based on propositions; *spec.* (of speech or language) in which statements and assertions occur.
propositional attitude PHILOSOPHY the relation that a person has with a proposition, such as having an opinion concerning it or responding emotionally to it. **propositional calculus** the branch of symbolic logic that deals with unanalysed propositions and the relations between them.
■ **propositionalist** *noun* a person concerned with the logic of propositions M20. **propositionally** *adverb* L19. **propositionalness** *noun* the quality of laying down propositions M19.

propositionize /prɒpəˈzɪʃ(ə)nʌɪz/ *verb intrans.* Also **-ise**. M19.
[from PROPOSITION *noun* + -IZE.]
Make or utter propositions.

propositum /prəʊˈpɒzɪtəm/ *noun*. M19.
[Latin, use as noun of neut. of *propositus*: see next.]
LOGIC. The first premiss of a syllogism; an argument, principal theme, or subject propounded.

propositus /prə(ʊ)ˈpɒzɪtəs/ *noun*. Pl. **-ti** /-tʌɪ/. M18.
[Latin, pa. pple of *proponere*: see PROPONE.]
An individual to whom the family relationships of others are reckoned; *spec.* (*a*) MEDICINE the first member of a family to be investigated by a researcher; (*b*) LAW a testator when making a will.

propound /prəˈpaʊnd/ *verb trans.* M16.
[Alt. of PROPONE: for the parasitic *d* cf. *compound, expound*.]
1 Put forward for consideration or as a question; devise, form, conceive, (a theory, plan, etc.). M16.
2 Nominate (a person) for an office or position, esp. as a member of a society etc. Now *US*. L16.
†**3** Hold up or put forward as an example, reward, aim, etc. L16–E18.
†**4** = PROPOSE *verb* 1. L16–E18.
5 LAW. Produce before the proper authority so as to establish the legality of (a will etc.). M18.

📖 **1** T. HARDY He propounded a plan for raising money. J. HELLER The ideal of the philosopher king propounded in the *Republic*.

■ **propounder** *noun* M16. **propoundment** *noun* (*rare*) the action or fact of propounding something M19. **propoundress** *noun* (*rare*) a female propounder M19.

propoxur /prəʊˈpɒksʊə/ *noun*. M20.
[from PROP- + OX(Y- = UR(ETHANE.]
A carbamate, $C_{11}H_{15}NO_3$, used as a long-lasting insecticide.

propoxyphene /prəʊˈpɒksɪfiːn/ *noun*. M20.
[from PROP- + OXY- + PH(EN- + -ENE.]
PHARMACOLOGY. A mild synthetic narcotic analgesic, chemically related to methadone.

proppy /ˈprɒpi/ *adjective*. *Austral. colloq.* M19.
[from PROP *verb* + -Y[1].]
Of a horse etc.: tending to prop or stop suddenly, restive.

For other words beginning with *pro-* see the entries for **pro-**[1], **pro-**[2]

■ **proppily** *adverb* M20.

propraetor /prəʊˈpriːtə/ *noun.* L16.
[Latin, orig. *pro praetore* (one acting) for the praetor.]
ROMAN HISTORY. A magistrate of the Roman republic who after holding the office of praetor was given the administration of a province not under military control, with the authority of a praetor. Also, a person acting in place of a praetor.
■ **propraeˈtorial** *adjective* = PROPRAETORIAN L19. **propraeˈtorian** *adjective* of, pertaining to, or under the rule of a propraetor M19. **propraetorship** *noun* the office of a propraetor E17.

propranolol /prəʊˈpranəlɒl/ *noun.* M20.
[from PRO(PYL + PR(OP)ANOL with redupl. of *-ol*.]
PHARMACOLOGY. A β-adrenergic blocking agent, $C_{16}H_{21}NO_2$ used mainly in the treatment of cardiac arrhythmia.

propria *noun* pl. of PROPRIUM.

propriate /ˈprəʊprɪət/ *adjective.* Now *rare* or *obsolete.* M16.
[Latin *propriat-* pa. ppl stem of *propriare* make one's own, from *proprius* PROPER: see -ATE².]
= APPROPRIATE *adjective.*

propriation /prəʊprɪˈeɪʃ(ə)n/ *noun. rare.* E17.
[Latin *propriatio(n-)*, formed as prec.: see -ATION.]
= APPROPRIATION 1, 2.

proprietage /prəˈprʌɪətɪdʒ/ *noun. rare.* M19.
[from PROPRIET(OR or PROPRIET(Y + -AGE.]
Private property collectively; proprietors collectively.

proprietary /prəˈprʌɪət(ə)ri/ *noun & adjective.* LME.
[Late Latin *proprietarius* (in medieval Latin as noun) a proprietor, from *proprietas* PROPRIETY: see -ARY¹.]
▶**A** *noun.* †**1** A member of a religious or monastic order holding private property in violation of a vow of poverty; *fig.* a self-seeking or selfish person. LME–M16.
†**2** *ECCLESIASTICAL.* The holder of an appropriated benefice. LME–M17.
3 A person owning something, esp. land, as property; an owner, a proprietor. Now only *spec.* (*Hist.*), a grantee or owner of a colony in N. America etc. granted with rights of government to an individual or group (also ***lord proprietary***). L15.
4 The holding of something as property; ownership. E17.
5 Something held as property, a possession; *esp.* a landed property or estate. Now *rare* or *obsolete.* E17.
6 A body of proprietors, proprietors collectively. E19.
7 A proprietary drug or medicine. M20.
▶**B** *adjective.* **1** Orig. *spec.*, (of a member of a religious or monastic order) holding private property in violation of a vow of poverty. Later, holding property; of the nature of a proprietor or proprietors. LME.
2 Owned or held as property, held in private ownership; *spec.* (of a product, esp. a drug or medicine) marketed under and protected by a registered trade name (cf. GENERIC *adjective* 2). L16.
3 *Hist.* Designating a colony in N. America etc. granted with rights of government to a group or individual; of or pertaining to these colonies or their government. E18.
4 = PROPRIETORIAL 1. M19.

> 🕮 **1** H. P. BROUGHAM The classes . . without any property . . would overpower the proprietary classes. **2** *Which?* If you have a wasp's nest, you could buy a proprietary killer. **proprietary company** *Austral.* = ***private company*** s.v. PRIVATE *adjective.* **proprietary name**, **proprietary term** a name of a product etc. registered by the name's owner as a trade mark, and not usable by another without permission. **4** H. H. WILSON Proprietary rights to lands. R. COBB He had . . a proprietary attitude towards her.

¶ As adjective rare before L16.
■ Also **proprietory** *noun & adjective* M17.

proprietor /prəˈprʌɪətə/ *noun.* L15.
[from prec. by substitution of suffix -OR.]
1 A person holding something as property; an owner, esp. of a business, as a shop, restaurant, etc., or of land. L15.
2 *Hist.* An owner or grantee of a proprietary colony. Also ***lord proprietor***. M17.

> 🕮 **1** V. BRITTAIN The proprietor of the small hotel. P. HOWARD The ambition of newspaper proprietors. **peasant proprietor** a peasant who owns the land he or she cultivates.

■ **proprietorship** *noun* (*a*) the position or condition of a proprietor, ownership; (*b*) a piece of land owned by a proprietor: M17.

proprietorial /prəprʌɪəˈtɔːrɪəl/ *adjective.* M19.
[from prec. + -AL¹.]
1 Of or pertaining to a proprietor; characteristic of or resembling a proprietor or owner, possessive. M19.
2 = PROPRIETARY *adjective* 1. M19.

> 🕮 **1** *Daily Telegraph* Strong proprietorial feelings about the untouchableness of Shakespeare. E. FEINSTEIN She continued to feel proprietorial long after their parting.

■ **proprietorially** *adverb* M19.

proprietous /prəˈprʌɪətəs/ *adjective.* E19.
[from PROPRIETY + -OUS.]
Characterized by (extreme) propriety, (excessively) correct or conventional in outlook.
■ **proprietously** *adverb* E20.

proprietress /prəˈprʌɪətrɪs/ *noun.* L17.
[from PROPRIETOR + -ESS¹.]
A female proprietor.
■ Also **proprietrix** *noun* M19.

propriety /prəˈprʌɪəti/ *noun.* LME.
[Old & mod. French *propriété* from Latin *proprietas* peculiarity, ownership, from *proprius* PROPER *adjective*: see -ITY. Cf. PROPERTY.]
▶**I 1** Particular or individual character, nature, or disposition; individuality. Now *rare.* LME.
†**2** An essential quality or attribute; = PROPERTY *noun* 2. LME–M19.
†**3** The special character or a special characteristic of a language; an idiom. M16–M18.
4 Fitness, appropriateness, suitability; rightness, correctness, accuracy. E17.
5 Conformity to conventional standards of behaviour or morals, correctness, decency; convention; in *pl.*, *the* things that are considered proper, *the* details or rules of conventionally correct conduct. L18.

> 🕮 **4** LD MACAULAY A committee to consider the propriety of impeaching Arlington. **5** A. LIVINGSTONE Lou and Rée defied propriety by sharing their home without being married. **play propriety** ensure correct behaviour by acting as a chaperon.

▶**II 6** The fact of owning or being owned; right of possession or use; ownership. Now *rare.* LME.
7 Something owned, one's property; a possession. Now only *spec.* (*N. AMER. HISTORY*), a piece of land owned by or granted to someone, an estate. L16.

proprioceptor /ˈprəʊprɪə(ʊ)septə/ *noun.* E20.
[from Latin *proprius* own + -O- + RE)CEPTOR.]
PHYSIOLOGY. A sensory receptor which receives stimuli from within the body (usu. other than the gut); *spec.* one that responds to position and movement. Cf. INTEROCEPTOR.
■ **proprioception** *noun* the reception of information by proprioceptors and its interpretation E20. **proprioceptive** *adjective* E20. **proprioceptively** *adverb* M20.

proprio-spinal /ˌprəʊprɪəʊˈspʌɪn(ə)l/ *adjective.* E20.
[formed as prec. + SPINAL *adjective.*]
ANATOMY. Situated wholly within the spinal cord.

proprium /ˈprəʊprɪəm/ *noun.* Pl. **-ia** /-ɪə/. M16.
[Latin, use as noun of neut. sing. of *proprius* PROPER.]
1 *LOGIC.* = PROPERTY *noun* 2C. M16.
2 Chiefly *THEOLOGY.* An essential attribute of something, a distinctive characteristic; essential nature, selfhood. L18.

pro-proctor /prəʊˈprɒktə/ *noun.* M17.
[from PRO-¹ + PROCTOR.]
Orig., a person acting for and under the control of university proctors. Now, an assistant or deputy university proctor.

proptosis /prɒpˈtəʊsɪs/ *noun.* Pl. **-toses** /-ˈtəʊsiːz/. L17.
[Late Latin from Greek *proptōsis*, from *propiptein* fall forwards.]
MEDICINE. Abnormal protrusion of the eyeball, esp. asymmetrically. Cf. EXOPHTHALMOS.
■ **proptosed** *adjective* (of the eye) protruding forward L19.

†**propugn** *verb trans.* L15–L17.
[Latin *propugnare* go out to fight, defend, fight for, formed as PRO-¹ + *pugnare* fight.]
Fight for, defend; champion, vindicate.
■ †**propugnation** *noun* defence, protection, vindication L16–M17.

propugnaculum /prəʊpʌgˈnakjʊləm/ *noun.* Pl. **-la** /-lə/. L18.
[Latin, formed as prec.]
A bulwark, a rampart; *fig.* a defence, a protection.
■ Also †**propugnacle** *noun* LME–M17.

propugnator /ˈprəʊpəgneɪtə/ *noun.* Now *rare.* LME.
[Latin, from *propugnat-* pa. ppl stem of *propugnare* PROPUGN + -OR.]
A defender, a champion. Freq. foll. by *of.*

propugner /prəʊˈpjuːnə/ *noun.* Now *rare* or *obsolete.* L16.
[from PROPUGN + -ER¹.]
= prec.

†**propulse** *verb trans.* M16–M17.
[from Latin *propulsare* frequentative of *propellere* PROPEL.]
Drive away, repel.

propulsion /prəˈpʌlʃ(ə)n/ *noun.* E17.
[from prec. + -ION.]
†**1** The action or an act of driving out or away; (an) expulsion. E17–M18.
2 The action or an act of driving or pushing something forward; the condition of being propelled; propulsive force. L18. ▸**b** *fig.* Impelling influence; an impulse. E19.

> 🕮 **2** J. HERSEY All he could find for propulsion was a thick bamboo pole.

Comb.: **propulsion gun** an astronaut's hand-held device expelling a jet of compressed gas to provide propulsion in space.

propulsive /prəˈpʌlsɪv/ *adjective.* M17.
[formed as prec. + -IVE.]
†**1** Able or tending to drive away or expel something. *rare.* Only in M17.
2 Having the quality or the tendency of propelling; that drives or pushes something forward. M18.

propulsor /prəˈpʌlsə/ *noun.* L20.
[from Latin *propuls-* pa. ppl stem of *propellere* PROPEL + -OR.]
A propeller mounted in a short duct or cylinder on an airship etc. that can be swivelled to vary the direction of thrust.

propulsory /prəˈpʌls(ə)ri/ *adjective. rare.* M17.
[formed as PROPULSIVE: see -ORY².]
= PROPULSIVE.

propyl /ˈprəʊpʌɪl, -pɪl/ *noun.* M19.
[from PROPIONIC + -YL.]
CHEMISTRY. Either of two isomeric radicals, C_3H_7·, derived from propane; *spec.* (more fully ***1-propyl***, ***normal propyl***) the unbranched form, $CH_3CH_2CH_2$·. Usu. in *comb.*
Comb.: **propyl alcohol** = PROPANOL; **propyl aldehyde** = PROPIONALDEHYDE; **propylthiouracil** a propyl derivative of a thiouracil; *spec.* 6-*n*-propyl-2-thiouracil, an antithyroid substance used to combat thyrotoxicosis.
■ **propylic** /prəʊˈpɪlɪk/ *adjective* (now *rare*) of or containing propyl M19.

propyla *noun* pl. of PROPYLON.

propylaeum /prɒpɪˈliːəm/ *noun.* Pl. **-laea** /-ˈliːə/. E18.
[Latin from Greek *propulaion* use as noun of neut. of adjective *propulaios* before the gate, formed as PRO-² + *pulē* gate. Cf. PROPYLON.]
The entrance to a temple or other sacred enclosure; *spec.* (**P-**) *the* entrance to the Acropolis at Athens; *gen.* a gateway, a porch.

propylene /ˈprəʊpɪliːn/ *noun.* M19.
[formed as PROPYL + -ENE.]
CHEMISTRY. A colourless gaseous alkene, $CH_2{=}CHCH_3$, used esp. in organic synthesis. Also called ***propene***.
Comb.: **propylene glycol** either of two isomeric liquid alcohols, $CH_3(OH)CH(OH)CH_3$ and $CH_2(OH)CH_2CH_2OH$; *spec.* the former, which is used esp. as a solvent, in antifreeze, and in the food, plastic, and perfume industries; **propylene imine** = PROPYLENIMINE.

propylenimine /prəʊpɪˈlɛnɪmiːn, ˌprəʊpɪliːˈnɪmiːn/ *noun.* E20.
[from prec. + IMINE.]
CHEMISTRY. A synthetic flammable liquid whose molecule is a saturated ring of formula C_3H_7N, used esp. as a binding agent with dyes and adhesives, and in the manufacture of plastics, paper, etc.

propylidene /prəʊˈpʌɪlɪdiːn, -ˈpɪl-/ *noun.* L19.
[from PROPYL + -IDENE.]
CHEMISTRY. The divalent radical $CH_3CH_2CH{=}$. Usu. in *comb.*

propylite /ˈprɒpɪlʌɪt/ *noun.* M19.
[formed as PROPYLON (with ref. to the opening of the Tertiary volcanic period) + -ITE¹.]
GEOLOGY. A greenish rock formed by hydrothermal alteration of an igneous rock, esp. andesite.
■ **propylitic** /-ˈlɪtɪk/ *adjective* of or pertaining to propylite L19. **propylitiˈzation** *noun* the hydrothermal alteration of an igneous rock to propylite, esp. around a body of ore E20.

propylon /ˈprɒpɪlɒn/ *noun.* Pl. **-lons**, **-la** /-lə/. M19.
[Latin from Greek *propulon*, formed as PRO-² + *pulē* gate.]
= PROPYLAEUM.

propyne /ˈprəʊpʌɪn/ *noun.* M20.
[from PROP- + -YNE.]
CHEMISTRY. A gaseous alkyne, $CH_3C{\equiv}CH$; methyl acetylene. Also called ***allylene***.

proquaestor /prəʊˈkwiːstə/ *noun.* E17.
[Late Latin for earlier *pro quaestore* (one acting) on behalf of a quaestor.]
ROMAN HISTORY. A person acting on behalf of a quaestor; an officer aiding a proconsul in the administration of a province after having fulfilled the quaestorship at Rome.

pro rata /prəʊ ˈrɑːtə, ˈreɪtə/ *adverbial & adjectival phr.* L16.
[Latin = according to the rate: see RATE *noun*¹.]
▶**A** *adverb.* In proportion, proportionally. L16.
▶**B** *adjective.* Proportional. M19.

pro-rate /prəʊˈreɪt/ *verb.* Chiefly *N. Amer.* M19.
[from PRO RATA.]
1 *verb trans.* Allocate, distribute, or assess (something) proportionally. M19.
2 *verb intrans.* Make an arrangement or reach agreement on a basis of proportional distribution. M19.
■ **pro-ratable** *adjective* able to be pro-rated L19. **pro-rating** *verbal noun* the action of the verb; an instance of this: E20.

proration /prəʊˈreɪʃ(ə)n/ *noun.* E20.
[from prec. + -ATION.]
The action or an instance of pro-rating; *spec.* allocation of the permitted production of oil or gas between competing operators, fields, etc.

prore /prɔː/ *noun.* Now *poet. rare.* L15.
[French †*prore* or Latin *prora* PROW *noun.*]
The prow of a ship; a ship.

pro-rector /prəʊˈrɛktə/ *noun.* E17.
[from PRO-¹ + RECTOR.]
The deputy of a rector in a university, college, etc., esp. in Scotland and Germany; a vice-rector.

prorogate /ˈprəʊrə(ʊ)geɪt/ *verb trans.* Chiefly *Scot.* LME.
[Latin *prorogat-* pa. ppl stem of *prorogare* PROROGUE: see -ATE³.]
1 Orig., = PROROGUE 1. Now chiefly (*SCOTS LAW*), extend the period of (a lease). LME.
2 = PROROGUE 2, 3. M16.
3 *SCOTS LAW.* Extend (the jurisdiction of a judge or court) by consent of the parties to a cause which would otherwise be outside the judge's or the court's jurisdiction. Cf. PROROGATION 4b. E17.

prorogation /prəʊrə(ʊ)ˈgeɪʃ(ə)n/ *noun.* LME.
[Old & mod. French, or Latin *prorogatio(n-)*, formed as prec.: see -ATION.]
1 The action of lengthening something in duration; extension of time; protraction, esp. of judicial proceedings. Now *rare* or *obsolete* exc. *SCOTS LAW.* LME.
2 The action of proroguing a legislative or other assembly, esp. Parliament; an instance of this. L15. ▸**b** *transf.* The time during which a legislative or other assembly, esp. Parliament, stands prorogued; the interval between successive sessions of such an assembly. M16.
†**3** The action of deferring to a later time; postponement. *rare.* L15–E18.
4 †**a** *gen.* Extension. *rare.* Only in E17. ▸**b** *SCOTS LAW.* The extension of the jurisdiction of a judge or court by consent of the parties to a cause which would otherwise be outside the judge's or court's jurisdiction. M19.

prorogue /prə(ʊ)ˈrəʊg/ *verb.* LME.
[Old & mod. French *proroger*, †-*guer* from Latin *prorogare* prolong, extend, formed as PRO-¹ + *rogare* ask.]
1 *verb trans.* Lengthen or extend (something) in time or duration; protract. Now *rare* or *obsolete.* LME.
2 *verb trans.* Defer, postpone. Now *rare.* LME.
3 *verb trans.* Discontinue a session of (a legislative or other assembly, esp. Parliament) without dissolution. LME. ▸**b** *verb intrans.* Be prorogued; become discontinued until the next session. M17.

proruption /prəʊˈrʌpʃ(ə)n/ *noun.* Long *rare.* M17.
[Late Latin *proruptio(n-)*, from *prorupt-* pa. ppl stem of *prorumpere* burst out, formed as PRO-¹ + *rumpere* burst: see -ION.]
The action or an act of bursting suddenly or violently.

pros *noun* var. of PROSS.

pros- /prɒs/ *prefix.*
[Repr. Greek *pros* preposition.]
Used in words adopted from Greek with senses 'to, towards', 'in addition', as ***proselyte***, ***prosody***.

prosa /ˈprəʊzə/ *noun.* Pl. **prosae** /ˈprəʊziː/. E19.
[Latin.]
ECCLESIASTICAL. = SEQUENCE *noun* 1. Cf. PROSE *noun* 2.

prosaic /prə(ʊ)ˈzeɪɪk/ *noun & adjective.* L16.
[French *prosaïque* or late Latin *prosaicus*, from Latin *prosa* PROSE *noun*: see -IC.]
▶ **A** *noun. rare.*
1 = PROSAIST 1. L16.
2 In *pl.* Prosaic things or subjects. L19.

> **1** *Times Lit. Suppl.* A . . press catering for . . poetasters and prosaics.

▶ **B** *adjective.* **1** Of or pertaining to prose; written in prose; (of an author) writing in prose. Now *rare* or *obsolete.* M17.
2 Having the character, style, or diction of prose as opp. to poetry; lacking poetic beauty or imagination; plain. M18. ▸**b** Unromantic; commonplace, dull, mundane. E19.

> **1** W. TAYLOR He published many works, chiefly prosaic. **2** I. D'ISRAELI The verse being prosaic, preserves its colloquial ease. **b** E. BLISHEN He knew I thought him prosaic and scandalously unexcitable. M. ATWOOD They . . spend prosaic evenings together, him reading the paper.

■ **prosaical** *adjective* (now *rare* or *obsolete*) = PROSAIC *adjective* M17. **prosaically** *adverb* M19. **prosaicalness** *noun* (*rare*) M19. **prosaicism** /-sɪz(ə)m/ *noun* = PROSAISM E19. **prosaicness** *noun* L19.

prosaism /ˈprəʊzeɪɪz(ə)m/ *noun.* L18.
[French *prosaïsme*, from Latin *prosa* PROSE *noun*: see -ISM.]
1 Prosaic character or style. L18.
2 A prosaic phrase or expression. Usu. in *pl.* E19.

prosaist /ˈprəʊzeɪɪst/ *noun.* E19.
[French *prosaïste*, formed as prec.: see -IST.]
1 A person who writes in prose. E19.
2 A prosaic or dull person. M19.

prosateur /ˈprəʊzətəː/ *noun.* L19.
[French from Italian *prosatore*: cf. medieval Latin *prosator*.]
A person who writes in prose; a prosaist.

prosauropod /prəʊˈsɔːrəpɒd/ *noun & adjective.* M20.
[from PRO-² + SAUROPOD.]
PALAEONTOLOGY. ▶**A** *noun.* Any of a group of herbivorous, often bipedal saurischian dinosaurs of the late Triassic and early Jurassic, widespread as fossils. M20.
▶ **B** *adjective.* Of or pertaining to an animal of this kind. M20.

proscenium /prəˈsiːnɪəm, prə(ʊ)-/ *noun.* Pl. **-iums**, **-ia** /-ɪə/. E17.
[Latin from Greek *proskēnion*, from *pro-* PRO-² + *skēnē* SCENE.]
1 a *CLASSICAL ANTIQUITIES.* The performance area between the background and the orchestra of a theatre; the stage. E17. ▸**b** The part of the stage of a modern theatre between the curtain or drop-scene and the auditorium, often including the curtain itself and the enclosing arch. Freq. *attrib.* E19.
2 *transf.* & *fig.* **a** The front, the foreground. M17. ▸**b** The theatre as a profession; dramatic art. *rare.* E19.
1b ***proscenium arch***, ***proscenium box***, ***proscenium opening***, etc.

prosciutto /prə(ʊ)ˈʃuːtəʊ/ *noun.* M20.
[Italian = ham.]
Italian cured ham, usu. served raw and thinly sliced as an hors d'oeuvre.

> S. CONRAN Paper-thin slices of dark red prosciutto.

proscribe /prə(ʊ)ˈskraɪb/ *verb trans.* LME.
[Latin *proscribere* publish in writing, formed as PRO-¹ + *scribere* write.]
†**1** Write (something) in front of another piece of writing. *rare.* Only in LME.
2 Chiefly *Hist.* Publish or post up (a person's name) as condemned to death and confiscation of property; put outside the protection of the law, outlaw; banish, exile. LME.
3 Reject, condemn, denounce (esp. a practice) as unwanted or dangerous; prohibit. E17.

> **2** J. COLVILLE She has been proscribed by the Germans and has had to leave her family in France. **3** A. STORR Aggressive threat and display are encouraged, whilst actual slaughter is proscribed.

■ **proscribable** *adjective* L19. **proscriber** *noun* (*rare*) L17.

proscript /ˈprəʊskrɪpt/ *noun.* L16.
[Latin *proscriptus* pa. pple of *proscribere*: see prec.]
An outlaw.

proscription /prə(ʊ)ˈskrɪpʃ(ə)n/ *noun.* LME.
[Latin *proscriptio(n-)*, from *proscript-* pa. ppl stem of *proscribere*: see PROSCRIBE, -ION.]
1 The action of proscribing; an instance of this; the condition or fact of being outlawed or exiled; a decree of condemnation to death or banishment. LME.
2 Denunciation; an authoritative prohibition; exclusion (by public order). M17.

> **1** J. R. GREEN No bloodshed or proscription should follow the revolution. **2** N. SHERRY Accepting its proscription of suicide—a mortal sin.

proscriptive /prə(ʊ)ˈskrɪptɪv/ *adjective.* M18.
[from prec. after *description*, *descriptive* etc.]
Characterized by proscribing; tending to prohibit or proscribe something; of the nature of proscription.
■ **proscriptively** *adverb* L19. **proscriptiveness** *noun* L19.

prose /prəʊz/ *noun.* ME.
[Old & mod. French from Latin *prosa* (sc. *oratio*) straightforward (discourse) use as noun of fem. of *prosus* from earlier *prorsus* straightforward, direct.]
1 The ordinary form of written or spoken language, without metrical structure, esp. as a literary form as distinct from poetry or verse. ME. ▸†**b** A (prose) story, a narrative. Only in LME. ▸**c** A passage of or composition in prose, *esp.* one for translation into a foreign language. L16.
2 *ECCLESIASTICAL.* = SEQUENCE *noun* 1. LME.
3 *fig.* Plain matter-of-fact expression; dull or commonplace expression, quality, etc. M16.
4 a A dull or tedious discourse or written passage; a dull or tedious person. *colloq.* L17. ▸**b** (A) chat, (a) gossip. *colloq.* Now *rare.* E19.

> **1** WORDSWORTH The only strict antithesis to Prose is Metre. *Classical Review* His . . eloquent and fine-cut prose. **c** *Punch* My tutor . . supposes I am writing Latin proses. **3** J. R. LOWELL In the frank prose of undissembling noon.

Attrib. & *comb.*: In the senses 'consisting of or written in prose', 'composing or writing prose', as ***prose account***, ***prose author***, ***prose epic***, ***prose style***, etc. Special combs., as ***Prose EDDA***; **prose fiction** the genre of fictional narratives written in prose; **prose idyll** a short description in prose of a picturesque, esp. rustic, incident, character, etc.; **proseman** a writer of prose; **prose-poem** a piece of prose poetry; **prose-poetry** prose writing characterized by poetic features such as imagery, assonance, etc.; **prose sense** the meaning of a poem as paraphrasable in prose.

■ **proseology** /-ˈɒlə-/ *noun* (*rare*) tediously lengthy or turgid prose E20. **prosist** *noun* (*rare*) a writer of prose E19.

prose /prəʊz/ *verb.* LME.
[from the noun.]
1 *verb trans.* Compose or write (a passage etc.) in prose; turn (a poem) into prose; *rare* translate (a passage etc.) into a foreign language. LME. ▸**b** *verb intrans.* Write prose. E19.
2 *verb intrans.* Talk or write in a dull or tedious manner (usu. foll. by *away*, *on*, etc.); *colloq.* (now *rare*) chat, gossip. L18. ▸**b** *verb trans.* Bring into a specified condition by talking or writing in a tedious manner. Foll. by *to*, *into*. E19.

> **1** J. JACOBS I have . . no sample in prosing a ballad. **b** *Tait's Edinburgh Magazine* I've rhymed, I've prosed . . done everything. **2** C. CONNOLLY The relief . . is more than words can say—but I prose. I. MURDOCH There will be time . . enough to prose on about my life. **b** F. M. PEARD In spite of my having prosed you to death.

■ **proser** *noun* E17. **prosing** *verbal noun* the action of the verb; an instance of this: M17.

prosector /prəʊˈsɛktə/ *noun.* M19.
[Late Latin = anatomist (formed as PRO-¹, SECTOR), perh. through French *prosecteur*.]
Chiefly *Hist.* A person appointed to dissect dead bodies (esp. of animals) in preparation for autopsy or anatomical research or demonstration.
■ **prosec'torium** *noun*, pl. **-ria**, a room or building for the dissection of dead bodies (esp. of animals) E20.

prosecute /ˈprɒsɪkjuːt/ *verb.* LME.
[Latin *prosecut-* pa. ppl stem of *prosequi* pursue, accompany, formed as PRO-¹ + *sequi* follow.]
1 *verb trans.* Follow up or pursue (an inquiry, studies, etc.); persist in or continue with (a course of action or an undertaking) with a view to its completion. LME.
2 *verb trans.* Examine, investigate; consider or deal with (a subject) systematically or in detail. M16.
†**3** *verb trans.* Pursue (a fugitive); chase (a person) with hostile intent. M16–E17.
†**4** *verb trans.* Treat (a person etc.) *with* regard, disrespect, etc. M16–M18.
5 *verb trans.* Engage in, practise, or carry on (a trade, pursuit, etc.). L16.
†**6** *verb trans.* Follow up (an advantage); take advantage of (an opportunity). L16–M18.
7 *LAW.* **a** *verb trans.* Institute or conduct legal proceedings against (a person); call (a person) before a court to answer a criminal charge. L16. ▸**b** *verb trans.* Institute or conduct legal proceedings in respect of (a crime, action, etc.). Freq. in ***prosecute an action***, ***prosecute a claim***. L16. ▸**c** *verb intrans.* Institute or conduct legal proceedings, esp. in a criminal court. E17.
†**8** *verb trans.* Seek to gain or achieve (a desired result); strive for. L16–E18.
†**9** *verb trans.* Persecute; harass. L16–E18.

> **1** J. COLVILLE Obliged to prosecute the war with greater vigour. **2** M. HANMER Which Josephus hath prosecuted at large in his histories. **4** JER. TAYLOR Prosecuting . . Jesus Christ with a singular honour. **5** J. I. M. STEWART Waiting for permission to prosecute my craft. **7a** *Daily Mirror* We doubt whether Mr. Poulson would even have been prosecuted. **c** *Listener* Even when the police prosecute, committal for trial cannot be left entirely to their discretion. ***prosecuting attorney***, ***prosecuting counsel***, etc.

■ **prosecutable** *adjective* E19.

prosecution /prɒsɪˈkjuːʃ(ə)n/ *noun.* M16.
[Old French, or late Latin *prosecutio(n-)*, formed as prec.: see -ION.]
1 The following up, continuation, or pursuit *of* a course of action etc. with a view to its completion. M16.
†**2** The pursuit of a person, esp. with hostile intent; a chase; hunting. M16–M17. ▸†**b** The action of seeking to gain possession *of* property etc. M16–E17.
3 The carrying on or practice *of* a trade, pursuit, etc. L16.
†**4** The consideration *of* a subject systematically or in detail; investigation. E17–E18.
5 *LAW.* The institution and conducting of legal proceedings in respect of a criminal charge in a court; the institution and conducting of legal proceedings against a person or in pursuit of a claim; an instance of this. Also, the prosecuting party in a case. M17.
†**6** Persecution; harassment. M17–M18.

> **1** *Manchester Examiner* The further prosecution of the war. **3** A. TATE The prosecution of special scientific interests. **5** *Headlight* Enough villainy to bring 4,000 prosecutions a year. V. BROME The prosecution's case collapsed. *attrib.*: *Hamilton (Ontario) Spectator* A long piece of prosecution evidence. **Crown Prosecution Service** an organization established in 1985 to conduct the majority of criminal prosecutions, including those proceedings instituted by the police. **Director of Public Prosecutions** an English law officer appointed as head of the Crown Prosecution Service and whose duty it is to institute and conduct criminal proceedings in the public interest.

prosecutive /ˈprɒsɪkjuːtɪv/ *adjective. rare.* **E17.**
[formed as PROSECUTE + -IVE.]
Of the nature of a prosecution; having the function of prosecuting.

prosecutor /ˈprɒsɪkjuːtə/ *noun.* **L16.**
[Partly from Latin, from *prosecut-* (see PROSECUTE), partly directly from PROSECUTE: see -OR.]
1 A person who follows up, continues, or pursues a course of action etc. Now *rare.* **L16.**
†**2** A pursuer, a hunter. **L16–M18.**
3 A person who institutes or conducts legal proceedings, esp. in a criminal court. **L17.**
†**4** A persecutor. Only in **E18.**

🕮 **1** H. SPELMAN The principal mover, and prosecutor thereof. **3** A. PATON The prosecutor . . tells the court the whole story. **public prosecutor** a law officer responsible for conducting criminal prosecutions on behalf of the Crown or State or in the public interest; *spec.* (**a**) in Scotland, a procurator fiscal; (**b**) = ***Director of Public Prosecutions*** s.v. PROSECUTION 5.

■ **prosecuˈtorial** *adjective* of or pertaining to a prosecutor, *esp.* of or pertaining to (the duties of) a prosecuting lawyer or officer **L20.**

prosecutrix /ˈprɒsɪkjuːtrɪks, -ˈkjuː-/ *noun.* Pl. **-cutrices** /-ˈkjuːtrɪsiːz/. **M18.**
[mod. Latin, fem. of Latin PROSECUTOR: see -TRIX.]
A female prosecutor.

proselyte /ˈprɒsɪlʌɪt/ *noun & verb.* **LME.**
[Late Latin *proselytus* from Greek *prosēluthos* stranger, (New Testament) convert to Judaism, from *prosēluth-* aorist stem of *proserkhesthai* come to, approach, formed as PROS- + *erkhesthai* come.]
► **A** *noun.* **1** A person who has converted, esp. recently, from one opinion, faith, political party, etc., to another. **LME.**
2 *spec.* A Gentile who has fully converted to Judaism. **LME.**

🕮 **2** *attrib.*: J. GILCHRIST Proselyte Baptism existed among the Jews.

► **B** *verb.* **1** *verb trans.* = PROSELYTIZE 2. Now chiefly *US.* **E17.**
†**2** *verb intrans.* Become a proselyte. **L17–E18.**
3 *verb intrans.* = PROSELYTIZE 1. **L18.**
■ **proselytism** *noun* (**a**) the fact of becoming or state of being a proselyte; (**b**) the practice of proselytizing: **M17.** **proselytist** *noun* a proselytizer **M19.**

proselytess /ˈprɒsɪlʌɪtɪs/ *noun.* **E17.**
[from PROSELYTE *noun* + -ESS¹.]
A female proselyte.

proselytize /ˈprɒsɪlɪtʌɪz/ *verb.* Freq. *derog.* Also **-ise.** **L17.**
[from PROSELYTE *noun* + -IZE.]
1 *verb intrans.* Convert a person or people, esp. from one religious faith to another. **L17.**
2 *verb trans.* Convert (a person or people), esp. from one religious faith to another. **L18.**

🕮 **1** J. N. ISBISTER An ardent follower of Freud proselytizing for him. **2** J. BAYLEY To proselytize the reader and inculcate in him his own . . beliefs.

■ **proselytiˈzation** *noun* the action or practice of proselytizing **L19.** **proselytizer** *noun* a person who proselytizes **M19.**

proseminary /prə(ʊ)ˈsɛmɪn(ə)ri/ *noun.* **L18.**
[from PRO-¹ + SEMINARY *noun*¹.]
A preparatory seminary or school.

prosencephalon /prɒsɛnˈkɛfəlɒn, -ˈsɛf-/ *noun.* **M19.**
[mod. Latin, from Greek *prosō* forwards + *egkephalos* brain.]
ANATOMY. The forebrain.
■ **prosenceˈphalic** *adjective* **M19.**

prosenchyma /prɒˈsɛŋkɪmə/ *noun.* **M19.**
[mod. Latin, formed as PROS- + *egkhuma* infusion, after *parenchyma*.]
BOTANY. Tissue, esp. of the wood or bast, consisting of elongated cells with tapering ends, often with the terminal partitions obliterated so as to form ducts or vessels. Cf. PARENCHYMA.
■ **prosenˈchymatous** *adjective* **M19.**

proseucha /prɒˈsjuːkə/ *noun. obsolete* exc. *Hist.* Pl. **-chae** /-kiː/. **M17.**
[Late Latin from Greek *proseukhē* (place of) prayer, from *proseukhesthai* pray to, offer prayers, formed as PROS- + *eukhestai* pray.]
A place of prayer; *spec.* a place set apart for Jewish worship.

prosify /ˈprəʊzɪfʌɪ/ *verb.* Chiefly *joc.* **L18.**
[Partly from Latin *prosa* or directly from PROSE *noun*; partly after *versify*: see -I-, -FY.]
1 *verb trans.* Convert (poetry etc.) into prose; make (a subject etc.) commonplace or tedious. **L18.**
2 *verb intrans.* Write prose. **E19.**
■ **prosifiˈcation** *noun* **M19.**

prosiliency /prəʊˈsɪlɪənsi/ *noun. rare.* **M17.**
[from Latin *prosilient-* pres. ppl stem of *prosilire* leap out: see -ENCY.]
Orig., the fact of leaping out. Now only *fig.*, great prominence.
■ **prosilient** *adjective* prominent **E20.**

prosimian /prəʊˈsɪmɪən/ *noun & adjective.* **L19.**
[from PRO-² + SIMIAN.]
ZOOLOGY. ► **A** *noun.* A mammal of the suborder Prosimii of primitive, mostly arboreal primates including lemurs, lorises, galagos, and tarsiers. **L19.**
► **B** *adjective.* Of, pertaining to, or designating a prosimian or prosimians. **L19.**
■ **prosimious** *adjective* (*rare*) = PROSIMIAN *adjective* **M19.**

prosiopesis /prɒsɪəˈpiːsɪs/ *noun.* **E20.**
[from PRO-² + Greek *siōpēsis* taciturnity, from *siōpan* be silent.]
GRAMMAR. Ellipsis of the beginning of a grammatical construction in a sentence, clause, etc.

prosit /ˈproːzɪt/ *interjection & noun.* Also ***prost*** /proːst/, (as noun) *P-*. **M19.**
[German from Latin = may it benefit.]
(An utterance of the exclamation) wishing a person good health, success, etc., esp. in drinking a toast.

proslambanomenos /ˌprɒslambəˈnɒmɪnəs/ *noun.* **L17.**
[Latin from Greek = the note taken in addition, i.e. added below the *hupatē*, use as noun of pres. pple of *proslambanein* take in addition, formed as PROS- + *lambanein* take.]
The lowest note, added a whole tone below the lowest tetrachord, in the later scales or systems of ancient Greek music.

prosobranch /ˈprɒsəbraŋk/ *adjective & noun.* **M19.**
[from mod. Latin *Prosobranchia(ta)* (see next), from Greek *prosō* forwards + *bragkhia* gills.]
ZOOLOGY. = next.

prosobranchiate /prɒsəˈbraŋkɪət/ *adjective & noun.* **L19.**
[formed as prec. + -ATE².]
ZOOLOGY. ► **A** *adjective.* Of, pertaining to, or characteristic of the subclass Prosobranchia of gastropod molluscs having the gills anterior to the heart. Cf. OPISTHOBRANCHIATE, PULMONATE. **L19.**
► **B** *noun.* A prosobranchiate gastropod. **L19.**

prosocial /prəʊˈsəʊʃ(ə)l/ *adjective.* **M20.**
[from PRO-¹ + SOCIAL *adjective*.]
PSYCHOLOGY. Of or pertaining to a type of behaviour that is automatically or rigidly loyal to the moral standards accepted by the established group. Opp. ***antisocial***, ***asocial***.

prosodeme /ˈprɒsədiːm/ *noun.* **M20.**
[from PROSOD(IC + -EME.]
LINGUISTICS. A linguistically contrastive prosodic feature (as pitch, stress, etc.); a suprasegmental phoneme.

prosodia *noun* pl. of PROSODION.

prosodiac /prəˈsɒdɪak/ *adjective & noun. rare.* **M19.**
[Late Latin *prosodiacus*, in senses A.1, B. from Greek *prosodiakos*, from PROSODION, in sense A.3 from Greek *prosōidiakos*, from *prosōidia* PROSODY: see -IC.]
► **A** *adjective.* **1** GREEK HISTORY. **a** Pertaining to or used as a prosodion; processional. **M19.** ►**b** Of or pertaining to a type of verse used in processional songs. **M19.**
2 = PROSODIC 1. **L19.**
► **B** *noun.* GREEK HISTORY. A verse consisting of three anapaests, for the first of which a spondee or iambus may be substituted. **E20.**

prosodiacal /prɒsəˈdʌɪək(ə)l/ *adjective.* **L18.**
[Late Latin *prosodiacus* from Greek *prosōidiakos*, from *prosōidia* PROSODY: see -ICAL.]
= PROSODIC 1.

prosodic /prəˈsɒdɪk/ *adjective.* **L18.**
[from Latin *prosodia* PROSODY + -IC.]
1 Of or pertaining to prosody. **L18.**
2 LINGUISTICS. Of or pertaining to suprasegmental phonological features such as intonation, stress, etc. **M20.**
2 prosodic analysis analysis employing the phonematic unit and the prosody as fundamental concepts.
■ **prosodical** *adjective* = PROSODIC 1 **L17.** **prosodically** *adverb* **E19.**

prosodion /prəˈsɒdɪən/ *noun.* Pl. **-ia** /-ɪə/. **M19.**
[Greek.]
GREEK HISTORY. A hymn sung in procession at a religious festival.

prosody /ˈprɒsədi/ *noun.* **L15.**
[Latin *prosodia* accent of a syllable from Greek *prosōidia* song sung to music, (mark indicating the) tone of a syllable, formed as PROS- + *ōidē* song, ODE: see -Y³.]
1 The theory and practice of versification; the branch of knowledge that deals with the forms of metrical composition and formerly also with the pronunciation of words, esp. in relation to versification. Also, a treatise on this. **L15.**
2 Correct pronunciation of words; observance of the rules of pronunciation. *rare.* **L16.**
3 LINGUISTICS. A suprasegmental phonological feature such as intonation, stress, etc. **M20.**
■ **proˈsodial** *adjective* (*rare*) = PROSODIC 1 **L18.** **proˈsodian** *noun & adjective* (*rare*) (**a**) *noun* = PROSODIST; (**b**) *adjective* = PROSODIC 1: **E17.**
prosodist *noun* a person who is skilled or knowledgeable in prosody **L18.**

prosoma /prə(ʊ)ˈsəʊmə/ *noun.* **L19.**
[from PRO-² + Greek *sōma* body.]
ZOOLOGY. The anterior or cephalic region of the body in various invertebrates; *esp.* the cephalothorax of an arachnid.

prosopagnosia /ˌprɒsə(ʊ)pagˈnəʊsɪə, -zɪə/ *noun.* **M20.**
[mod. Latin, from Greek *prosōpon* face + *agnōsia* ignorance.]
MEDICINE. Inability to recognize familiar faces, esp. as a result of brain damage.

prosopalgia /prɒsə(ʊ)ˈpaldʒə/ *noun.* Now *rare* or *obsolete.* **M19.**
[formed as prec. + -ALGIA.]
MEDICINE. Facial neuralgia.

prosopography /prɒsə(ʊ)ˈpɒgrəfi/ *noun.* **M16.**
[mod. Latin *prosopographia*, from Greek *prosōpon* face, person: see -GRAPHY.]
†**1** RHETORIC. = PROSOPOPOEIA 1. *rare.* Only in **M16.**
2 A description of (esp. the outward appearance of) a person. *obsolete* exc. as in sense 3 below. **L16.**
3 A description of a person's appearance, personality, social and familial connections, career, etc.; a collection of such descriptions; the study of these, esp. in Roman history. **E20.**
■ **prosopographer** *noun* **M20.** **prosopoˈgraphic**, **prosopoˈgraphical** *adjectives* of or pertaining to the method of historical study or research which makes use of prosopography **M20.** **prosopoˈgraphically** *adverb* **L20.**

prosopolepsy /prəˈsɒp(ə)lɛpsi/ *noun.* Now *rare* or *obsolete.* **M17.**
[Greek *prosōpolēpsia* (a Hebraism) acceptance of the face of a person, from *prosōpolēptēs*, from *prosōpon* face, person + *lambanein* take, accept.]
Respect for a person; (unduly) favourable reception of personal advances; favouritism.

prosopon /ˈprɒsəpɒn/ *noun.* **E20.**
[Greek *prosōpon* face, person.]
CHRISTIAN THEOLOGY. = PERSON *noun* 6a.

prosopopoeia /prɒsəpəˈpiːə/ *noun.* **M16.**
[Latin from Greek *prosōpopoiia* representation in human form, formed as prec. + *poiein* make.]
1 RHETORIC. **a** A figure of speech in which an imaginary or absent person is represented as speaking or acting; the introduction of a pretended speaker. **M16.** ►**b** A figure of speech in which an inanimate or abstract thing is personified or given human characteristics. **L16.**
2 *transf.* A person or thing as *the* embodiment *of* a quality. **E19.**
■ **prosopopoeic** *adjective* **L19.**

prosopyle /ˈprɒsəpʌɪl/ *noun.* **L19.**
[from Greek *prosō* forward + *pulē* gate.]
ZOOLOGY. A small aperture in a sponge leading from the exterior to a flagellated chamber, an incurrent opening.
■ **proˈsopylar** *adjective* **L19.**

prospect /ˈprɒspɛkt/ *noun.* **LME.**
[Latin *prospectus* view, from *prospicere* look forward, formed as PRO-¹ + *specere* look.]
► **I 1 a** The action or fact of looking out or towards a distant object etc.; the condition of facing in a specified direction; outlook, aspect (of a building etc.). *obsolete* exc. as passing into sense 2. **LME.** ►**b** A place providing an extensive view; a lookout. Now *rare* or *obsolete.* **L16.**
2 An extensive or commanding view of landscape etc. **M16.** ►**b** A person's range or scope of vision. Chiefly in ***in prospect*** below. *arch.* **M16.**
†**3** The appearance presented by something. *rare.* **E17–E18.**
4 That which is visible or seen from a place or point of view; a scene, a landscape. **M17.**
†**5** A pictorial representation of a scene, landscape, etc.; a picture, a sketch. **M17–M18.**

🕮 **1a** P. HOLLAND A prospect to the Caspian sea. **2** *Holiday Which?* A long sweeping prospect across hill spattered desert. **4** R. GRAVES The windows frame a prospect of cold skies.

► **II** †**6** A mental survey; an inspection, an examination; an investigative account. **M16–M18.**
7 Forethought; consideration or knowledge of some future event or course of action. **E17.**
8 A mental picture, esp. of a future or anticipated event. **M17.** ►**b** A future event, something to look forward to or anticipate; an expectation, esp. of wealth, success in a career, etc. (freq. in *pl.*). **M17.** ►**c** A potential or probable purchaser, customer, etc.; *slang* a selected victim of a thief etc. **E20.**

🕮 **7** S. JOHNSON His prospect of the advancement which it shall receive from the Royal Society. **8** J. HILTON A few . . would probably . . stand him drinks; it was a pleasant prospect. G. SAYER The prospect of a civilization dominated by scientists . . filled him with horror. **b** P. GALLICO Stony broke and no prospects. I. MURDOCH The prospect of food . . restored him. **c** *Accountancy* Far from being put off by a keen approach, prospects welcome it.

▶**III 9** *ellipt.* = ***prospect-glass*** below. *obsolete* exc. *Scot.* **M17.**
▶**IV 10 a** A place likely to yield a mineral deposit. **M19.** ▸**b** A test of the mineral richness of a place or of the material from which the ore etc. is extracted. **M19.** ▸**c** A sample of ore for testing; the resulting yield of ore. **L19.**
Phrases: **in prospect** (*a*) *arch.* within the range or scope of vision; in sight; within view; (*b*) (esp. of something personally advantageous) within the range of expectation; (to be) expected.
Comb.: **prospect-glass** a prospective glass, a telescope.
■ **prospectless** *adjective* (*a*) having no view or outlook; (*b*) without future expectations of success etc.: **M17.**

prospect /prəˈspɛkt, ˈprɒspɛkt/ *verb.* **M16.**
[In branch I from Latin *prospectare* frequentative of *prospicere* (see prec.); in branch II from **PROSPECT** *noun* 10.]
▶†**I 1** *verb intrans.* Look out or towards a certain direction; face; provide an outlook in a specified direction. **M16–E17.**
2 *verb trans.* (Of a person) look out upon or towards; look at, view; (of a building etc.) face; be situated towards; command a view of. **M16–L17.**
3 *verb trans.* Foresee, expect; anticipate. *rare.* **M–L17.**
📖 **1** S. PURCHAS Houses are low . . and prospect into the streets. **2** J. FRYER The College . . is on an high Mount, prospecting the whole City.
▶**II 4** *verb intrans.* Explore a region for gold, minerals, etc.; *fig.* search around, look out for something. Freq. foll. by *for.* **M19.**
5 *verb trans.* Explore (a locality) for gold, minerals, etc.; work (a mine) experimentally so as to test for richness; *fig.* survey or consider with regard to prospects. **M19.**
6 a *verb intrans.* Of a mine: promise *well, ill,* etc., in respect of yield. **M19.** ▸**b** *verb trans.* Of a mine: promise to yield (a specified amount). **L19.**
📖 **4** E. WAUGH Midwinter is no season to prospect for a house. M. DE LA ROCHE Experienced hard luck prospecting in the North. **prospecting claim** the first claim, marked out by the discoverer of the mineral deposit. ***SEISMIC prospecting.*** **5** *Daily News* Prospecting the new year, he saw grounds for caution. J. BUCHAN I got to . . the dovecot and prospected a way of ascent.
■ **prospection** *noun* (now *rare*) (*a*) the action of prospecting; (*b*) anticipation; foresight; an instance of this: **M17. prospector** *noun* a person who prospects, esp. for gold, minerals, etc. **M19.**

prospective /prəˈspɛktɪv/ *adjective & noun.* **L16.**
[As adjective from French †*prospectif, -ive* or late Latin *prospectivus* formed as **PROSPECTUS**: see **-IVE**. As noun partly from French †*prospective* view, prospect, partly from the adjective.]
▶**A** *adjective.* **1** Characterized by looking forward into the future. Formerly also, having foresight or care for the future. Now *rare.* **L16.**
†**2** Suitably situated so as to provide a fine or extensive view; *fig.* elevated, lofty. **L16–E19.**
†**3** Used or suitable for looking forward or viewing a distant object (*lit.* & *fig.*). **E–M17.**
4 Concerned with or applying to the future; operative at a future date. **E19.** ▸**b** *GRAMMAR.* Designating or pertaining to a tense of a verb which is present in form but implies a future action or state. **M20.**
5 Anticipated; hoped for; future. **E19.**
📖 **4** J. M. KEYNES Depends on the *prospective* yield of capital, and not merely on its current yield. **5** P. MAILLOUX A prospective husband had . . been chosen.
Special collocations & comb.: †**prospective glass** (*a*) a magic glass or crystal, used to foretell the future; (*b*) a field glass, a telescope; in *pl.*, spectacles, binoculars.
▶**B** *noun.* †**1 a** = ***prospective glass*** (a) above. **L16–E17.** ▸**b** = ***prospective glass*** (b) above. **E17–E18.**
2 The action of looking out or forward. Chiefly in ***in prospective***, in view, in anticipation. Now *rare.* **L16.**
†**3** A scene, a view. **L16–M18.**
†**4** The practice or skill of drawing in perspective; a perspective view. Only in **17.**
†**5** A pictorial view; *fig.* a description. *rare.* Only in **M17.**
■ **prospectively** *adverb* **M16. prospectiveness** *noun* **E19.**

prospectus /prəˈspɛktəs/ *noun.* **M18.**
[Latin = view, prospect, use as noun of pa. pple of *prospicere*: see **PROSPECT** *noun*.]
A printed document giving advance notification of the chief features of a forthcoming publication, issue of shares for a commercial enterprise, etc. Also, a brochure or pamphlet detailing the courses, facilities, etc., of an educational institution.
■ **prospectusless** *adjective* not having a prospectus; *spec.* (of a company or its shares) for which no prospectus has been issued: **L19.**

prospekt /prɒsˈpɛkt/ *noun.* **M19.**
[Russian.]
In Russia: a long wide street; a grand avenue, a boulevard.

prosper /ˈprɒspə/ *verb.* **LME.**
[Old & mod. French *prospérer* or Latin *prosperare*, from *prosper(us)* doing well or successfully.]
1 *verb intrans.* Flourish, thrive, succeed; be or become prosperous. **LME.**
2 *verb trans.* Cause to flourish; promote the prosperity or success of; be favourable to. **L15.**
📖 **1** E. NORTH Nothing in nature prospered without control. ROSEMARY MANNING The practice prospered. There were servants, a new Ford car, rounds of dinner parties. **2** *Listener* They used their . . initiative to prosper others.
■ **prospeˈration** *noun* (*obsolete* exc. *dial.*) prosperity **LME.**

prosperity /prɒˈspɛrɪti/ *noun.* **ME.**
[Old & mod. French *prospérité* from Latin *prosperitas*, from *prosper(us)*: see prec., **-ITY.**]
1 The state of being prosperous, successful, or thriving; good fortune, success, well-being. **ME.**
2 In *pl.* Instances of prosperity, prosperous circumstances. Now *poet.* **ME.**
📖 **1** P. THEROUX Costa Rica is enjoying a boom; the prosperity is obvious in San José.

prosperous /ˈprɒsp(ə)rəs/ *adjective.* **LME.**
[Old French *prospereus*, (mod. *prospère*) from Latin *prosper(us)*: see **PROSPER, -OUS.**]
1 Promoting or conducive to success; bringing prosperity; favourable, auspicious. **LME.**
2 Enjoying continued success or good fortune; wealthy; flourishing, thriving. **L15.**
📖 **1** A. UTTLEY It had been a prosperous year, and there was food for every one. **2** P. FITZGERALD The prosperous owner of a chain of dress-shops.
■ **prosperously** *adverb* **LME. prosperousness** *noun* **M17.**

prosphora /ˈprɒsfɒrə/ *noun.* **L19.**
[Greek = offering, from *prospherein* present, offer, from **PROS-** + *pherein* carry.]
In the Orthodox Church, a small loaf of bread used in the Eucharist.

prospicience /prəˈspɪʃ(ə)ns/ *noun. rare.* **L15.**
[Latin *prospicientia*, from *prospicient-* pres. ppl stem of *prospicere* look forward: see **PROSPECT** *noun*, **-ENCE.**]
The action or quality of looking forward; foresight.
■ †**prospicient** *adjective* having foresight **M17–E19.**

pross /prɒs/ *noun. slang.* Also **pros. E20.**
[Abbreviation.]
= **PROSTITUTE** *noun* 1.

prossie /ˈprɒsi, -zi/ *noun. slang.* Also **prossy. M20.**
[from prec. + **-IE, -Y**[6].]
= **PROSTITUTE** *noun* 1.

prostacyclin /prɒstəˈsʌɪklɪn/ *noun.* **L20.**
[from next + **CYCLIC** + **-IN**[1].]
BIOCHEMISTRY. A prostaglandin derivative produced in arterial walls, with properties as an anticoagulant and vasodilator.

prostaglandin /prɒstəˈglandɪn/ *noun.* **M20.**
[from **PROSTATE** + **GLAND** *noun*[2] + **-IN**[1].]
BIOCHEMISTRY. Any of a group of cyclic fatty acids related to prostanoic acid which occur in many mammalian tissues (esp. semen) and have effects resembling those of hormones.

prostanoic /prɒstəˈnəʊɪk/ *adjective.* **M20.**
[from prec. + *-anoic*, after the systematic name 7-(2-octylcyclopentyl)hept*anoic* acid.]
BIOCHEMISTRY. ***prostanoic acid***, a derivative of arachidonic acid containing a saturated five-membered ring from which the prostaglandins are formally derived.

prostate /ˈprɒsteɪt/ *noun & adjective.* **M17.**
[French, or from mod. Latin *prostata* from Greek *prostatēs* guardian, formed as **PRO-**[2] + *statos* placed, standing.]
ANATOMY. (Designating) a large gland in male mammals (including humans) or any of a number of small glands in some other animals, which surrounds the neck of the bladder and secretes a component of seminal fluid into the urethra.
Comb.: **prostate-specific antigen** *MEDICINE* an antigenic enzyme released in the prostate and found in abnormally high concentrations in the blood of men with prostate cancer.
■ **prostaˈtectomy** *noun* (an instance of) surgical removal of (part of) the prostate **L19. proˈstatic** *adjective* of or pertaining to the prostate **M19. prostatism** *noun* any condition due to disease of the prostate gland, esp. difficulty in urination **E20. prostaˈtitis** *noun* inflammation of the prostate **M19. prostatoˈrrhoea** *noun* abnormal discharge of fluid from the prostate **M19.**

†**prosternation** *noun.* **L15–E19.**
[Old & mod. French, from *prosterner* or Latin *prosternare* by-form of *prosternere*: see **PROSTRATE** *verb*, **-ATION.**]
The action or an act of prostrating someone or something; the state of being prostrated; prostration.

prosthaphaeresis /prɒsθəˈfɪərɪsɪs/ *noun.* Also ***-pher-.** Pl. **-eses** /-ɪsiːz/. **M17.**
[mod. Latin from Greek *prosthaphairesis*, from *prosthen* before + *aphairesis* subtraction, **APHAERESIS.**]
ASTRONOMY, ASTROLOGY, & NAVIGATION. The correction necessary to find the actual apparent position of a planet etc. from the mean position.

prosthesis /ˈprɒsθɪsɪs, *in sense 2 usu.* prɒsˈθiːsɪs/ *noun.* Pl. **-theses** /-θiːsiːz, *in sense 2 usu.* -ˈθiːsiːz/. **M16.**
[Late Latin from Greek, from *prostithenai* add, from **PROS-** + *tithenai* place.]
1 *GRAMMAR.* The addition of a letter or syllable at the beginning of a word. **M16.**
2 a = **PROSTHETICS.** Now *rare.* **E18.** ▸**b** An artificial replacement for a part of the body. **E20.**

prosthetic /prɒsˈθɛtɪk/ *adjective.* **M19.**
[from prec. after *synthesis, synthetic*, etc.]
1 *GRAMMAR.* (Of a letter or syllable) added to the beginning of a word; of or pertaining to prosthesis. **M19.**
2 *BIOCHEMISTRY.* Designating a non-protein group forming part of or combined with a protein. **L19.**
3 *MEDICINE.* Of or pertaining to prosthetics; pertaining to or of the nature of a prosthesis. **E20.**
■ **prosthetically** *adverb* **L19.**

prosthetics /prɒsˈθɛtɪks/ *noun.* **L19.**
[from prec.: see **-ICS.**]
The branch of surgery (including dental surgery) that deals with the replacement of defective or absent parts of the body by artificial substitutes.

prosthetist /ˈprɒsθɪtɪst/ *noun.* **E20.**
[from **PROSTHET(IC** + **-IST.**]
MEDICINE. A person who designs and fits prostheses.

prosthion /ˈprɒsθɪɒn/ *noun.* **E20.**
[Greek, neut. of *prosthios* foremost from *prosthen* before, in front.]
ANATOMY. The lowest or the most forward point of the maxilla between the two central incisors.

prosthodontia /prɒsθəˈdɒntɪə/ *noun.* **E20.**
[formed as next + **-IA**[1].]
DENTISTRY. Prosthodontics.

prosthodontics /prɒsθəˈdɒntɪks/ *noun.* **M20.**
[from **PROSTHESIS** after *orthodontics.*]
The branch of dentistry that deals with the design, manufacture, and fitting of artificial replacements for teeth and other parts of the mouth; prosthetic dentistry.
■ **prosthodontist** *noun* a person who practises prosthodontics **E20.**

prostie *noun* var. of **PROSTY.**

Prostigmin /prəʊˈstɪgmɪn/ *noun.* **M20.**
[from **PRO-**[1] + **PHYSO)STIGMIN(E.]**
PHARMACOLOGY. (Proprietary name for) neostigmine.

prostitute /ˈprɒstɪtjuːt/ *noun.* **E17.**
[Latin *prostituta* use as noun of fem. of *prostitutus* pa. pple of *prostituere* expose publicly, offer for sale, prostitute, formed as **PRO-**[1] + *statuere* set up, place.]
1 A woman who engages in sexual activity promiscuously or (now only) in return for payment. **E17.** ▸†**b** A catamite. *rare.* Only in **M17.** ▸**c** A man who engages in sexual activity, esp. with homosexual men, in return for payment. Chiefly in ***male prostitute.*** **L19.**
2 †**a** A person entirely or abjectly devoted to another. **E17–E18.** ▸**b** A person devoted to shameful or corrupt practices; *esp.* a person who misuses his or her talents, skills, etc., or who sacrifices his or her self-respect, for the sake of personal or financial gain. **M17.**
📖 **1** JAN MORRIS Prostitutes signal their services from the doorways. *attrib.*: *Globe & Mail (Toronto)* The use or possession of condoms to prosecute prostitute women undermines women's efforts to protect their health. **2b** C. FITZGIBBON Turning scientists into military prostitutes.

prostitute /ˈprɒstɪtjuːt/ *adjective.* **M16.**
[Latin *prostitutus*: see prec.]
1 Debased; debasing; devoted to corrupt profit; corrupt. Now *rare* or *obsolete.* **M16.**
2 (Of a woman) engaging in sexual activity promiscuously or (now only) in return for payment, that is a prostitute; licentious. (Foll. by *to.*) Now *rare* or *obsolete* exc. as passing into attrib. use of the noun **L16.**
†**3 a** Given over, exposed, subjected, *to.* **E17–E18.** ▸**b** Debased through being made common or cheap; hackneyed. **M17–M18.**
†**4** Prostrate. **E–M17.**
📖 **1** D. HUME No courtier, even the most prostitute, could go farther. **2** ROBERT BURTON Noblemens daughters . . were prostitute to every common souldier.

prostitute /ˈprɒstɪtjuːt/ *verb.* **M16.**
[Latin *prostitut-* pa. ppl stem of *prostituere*: see **PROSTITUTE** *noun.*]
1 *verb trans.* Offer (esp. a woman) for sexual activity in return for payment; *esp.* (*refl.*) (usu. of a woman) engage in sexual activity promiscuously or (now chiefly) in return for payment. **M16.** ▸†**b** *verb intrans.* Act as a prostitute. *rare.* **M17–M18.** ▸**c** *verb trans.* Seduce (a woman). *rare.* **M17.**
†**2** *verb trans.* **a** Offer with complete devotion or self-denial. **M16–L17.** ▸**b** Expose or subject to a destructive agency. Only in **17.** ▸**c** Exhibit shamefully or degradingly to public view. Only in **17.**

3 *verb trans. fig.* Put (one's talents, skills, etc.) to an unworthy or corrupt use or purpose, sacrifice (self-respect, honour, etc.), for the sake of personal or financial gain. L16.
†**4** *verb trans.* Prostrate. E–M17.

📖 **3** *Royal Air Force Journal* Technical skill prostituted in the name of death . . and destruction.

■ **prostitutor** *noun* E17.

prostitution /prɒstɪˈtjuːʃ(ə)n/ *noun.* M16.
[Old & mod. French, or late Latin *prostitutio(n-)*, formed as prec.: see -ION.]
1 The action of prostituting a person or oneself; *esp.* the practice of a prostitute or prostitutes; the condition of being prostituted. M16.
2 *fig.* Devotion to an unworthy or corrupt cause or purpose; corruption. M17.

prostrate /ˈprɒstreɪt/ *adjective & noun.* ME.
[Latin *prostratus* pa. pple of *prosternere*: see next, -ATE².]
▶ **A** *adjective.* **1** Lying face downwards, as a sign of submission or humility, or in reverence or supplication; *gen.* lying at full length or with the body extended flat. Freq. *pred.* ME. ▸**b** Of a thing usually upright: levelled with the ground, thrown down. *rare.* L17.
2 *fig.* Laid low emotionally; submissive; powerless; overcome with grief etc.; physically exhausted; unable to rise through exhaustion etc. LME.
3 BOTANY. Growing closely along the ground. L18.

📖 **1** A. B. EDWARDS Some lay prostrate . . foreheads touching the ground. D. H. LAWRENCE Kicking the prostrate body of his rival. **2** W. DE LA MARE Prostrate with thirst and weariness. P. THEROUX Passengers, prostrate in the heat, lay collapsed on the seats.

▶ **B** *noun.* **1** = PROSTRATOR 2. *rare.* L16.
2 A person who lies or falls prostrate. Now *rare* or *obsolete.* M17.

prostrate /prɒˈstreɪt/ *verb.* LME.
[Latin *prostrat-* pa. ppl stem of *prosternere* throw in front of, cast down, formed as PRO-¹ + *sternere* lay low: see -ATE³.]
1 *verb refl.* & (now) *rare intrans.* Fall or lay oneself flat, become prostrate, esp. in reverence or submission. LME.
2 *verb trans.* Lay (a person etc.) flat on the ground; throw down, esp. from an upright position, level (something) with the ground. L15.
3 *verb trans. fig.* Lay low; make submissive, helpless, or powerless. M16. ▸**b** Of illness, fatigue, etc.: reduce to extreme physical weakness or emotional exhaustion. E19.
†**4** *verb trans.* Submit, present, or offer submissively or reverently. M16–L17.

📖 **1** R. K. NARAYAN Everybody . . prostrated before the image. P. KAVANAGH The straw was so lovely it could almost make him want to prostrate himself upon it. **2** BROWNING Pebble from sling Prostrates a giant. **3** C. THIRLWALL Any treaty which would not . . prostrate Athens under its rule. **b** B. BAINBRIDGE So utterly prostrated by depression as to be unable to perform his usual duties.

■ **ˈprostrative** *adjective* (*rare*) (*a*) tending to weaken or prostrate a person or thing; (*b*) characterized by a submissive or prostrate attitude: E19.

prostration /prɒˈstreɪʃ(ə)n/ *noun.* LME.
[Partly from Old & mod. French; partly from prec. + -ATION.]
1 The action or an act of prostrating oneself or one's body, esp. as a sign of reverence or submission; the condition of being prostrated, or lying prostrate. LME.
2 *fig.* Veneration; submission, humiliation. Now *rare.* M17.
3 Extreme physical weakness; emotional exhaustion; depression. M17.
4 The reduction of a country etc. to a helpless or powerless condition. M19.

prostrator /ˈprɒstreɪtə, prɒˈstreɪtə/ *noun. rare.* M17.
[Late Latin, formed as PROSTRATE *verb*: see -ATOR.]
1 A person who prostrates something. M17.
2 ECCLESIASTICAL HISTORY. A penitent of the third order in the early Church. Usu. in *pl.* E18.

prosty /ˈprɒsti/ *noun. US slang.* Also **-ie**. M20.
[Abbreviation.]
= PROSTITUTE *noun* 1.

prostyle /ˈprəʊstʌɪl/ *noun & adjective.* L17.
[Latin *prostylos* having pillars in front, formed as PRO-²: see STYLE *noun.*]
ARCHITECTURE. ▶**A** *noun.* A free-standing portico, esp. of a classical temple. L17.
▶ **B** *adjective.* Of a building: having a prostyle. L17.

prosula /ˈprəʊsʊlə/ *noun.* Pl. **-lae** /-liː/. E20.
[mod. Latin, dim. of PROSA: see -ULE.]
ECCLESIASTICAL. An insertion of new words (as an embellishment or amplification) into a pre-existing text of certain liturgical chants at a point where there is a melisma.

prosy /ˈprəʊzi/ *adjective.* E19.
[from PROSE *noun* + -Y¹.]
1 Resembling or characteristic of prose; commonplace, matter-of-fact; tedious, dull, mundane. E19.
2 Apt to speak or write in a commonplace, dull, or tedious way. M19.

📖 **1** G. B. SHAW You don't loathe the scenery for being prosy.

■ **prosily** *adverb* M19. **prosiness** *noun* prosaic quality; (an instance of) dullness or tediousness in speech or writing: E19.

prosyllogism /prəʊˈsɪlədʒɪz(ə)m/ *noun.* L16.
[Late Latin *prosyllogismus* from Greek *prosullogismos*, formed as PRO-²: see SYLLOGISM.]
LOGIC. A syllogism the conclusion of which forms the major or minor premiss of another syllogism.

Prot /prɒt/ *noun & adjective. slang. derog.* E18.
[Abbreviation Cf. PROD *noun*⁴ & *adjective.*]
▶ **A** *noun.* = PROTESTANT *noun* 2. E18.
▶ **B** *adjective.* = PROTESTANT *adjective* 1. M18.

prot- *combining form* see PROTO-.

protactinium /prəʊtakˈtɪnɪəm/ *noun.* Also **protoactinium** /ˌprəʊtəʊakˈtɪnɪəm/. E20.
[from PROTO- + ACTINIUM (because the commonest isotope decays to give actinium).]
A radioactive metallic chemical element, atomic no. 91, which is a member of the actinide series and occurs as a decay product in uranium ores. (Symbol Pa.)

protagonist /prəˈtag(ə)nɪst/ *noun.* L17.
[Greek *prōtagōnistēs*, formed as PROTO- + AGONISTES.]
1 The chief person in a drama; the principal character or (usu. in *pl.*) any of the leading characters in a play, novel, narrative poem, etc. L17.
2 The leading person in a contest; a prominent supporter or champion of a cause; in *pl.*, the most prominent or most important individuals in a situation or course of events. M19.
3 [Prob. from confusion of 1st syllable with PRO-¹.] A proponent or advocate of a method, idea, or course of action. M20.

📖 **1** A. TOFFLER This book . . had change as its protagonist. **2** L. STRACHEY New protagonists—Mr. Gladstone and Mr. Disraeli—struggled together in the limelight. **3** S. BIKO Protagonists of the bantustan theory. F. WELDON A great protagonist of open decision making.

■ **protagonism** *noun* (*rare*) the defence or advocacy of a cause, idea, etc. E20.

Protagorean /prə(ʊ)ˌtagəˈriːən/ *adjective & noun.* L17.
[from *Protagoras* (see below) + -EAN.]
▶ **A** *adjective.* Of or pertaining to the Greek philosopher Protagoras (fl. 5th cent. BC) or his philosophy of extreme subjectivism. L17.
▶ **B** *noun.* An adherent or student of the philosophy of Protagoras. L19.
■ **Protagoreanism** *noun* Protagorean philosophy M20.

protalus /prəʊˈteɪləs/ *noun.* M20.
[from PRO-² + TALUS *noun*².]
PHYSICAL GEOGRAPHY. More fully ***protalus rampart***, ***protalus ridge***. A ridge marking the lower edge of an existing or melted snow-bank, composed of boulders and coarse debris that have slid or rolled from a talus or scree higher up.

protamine /ˈprəʊtəmiːn/ *noun.* L19.
[from PROTO- + AMINE.]
BIOCHEMISTRY & MEDICINE. Any of a class of simple basic proteins which occur combined with nucleic acids (esp. in fish sperm) and may be combined with insulin to slow its absorption.
Comb.: **protamine sulphate** a salt of a protamine and sulphuric acid, given as an aqueous solution to neutralize the anticoagulant effect of heparin.

protandrous /prəʊˈtandrəs/ *adjective.* L19.
[from PROTO- + -ANDROUS. Cf. PROTERANDROUS.]
BOTANY & ZOOLOGY. Of a hermaphrodite flower or animal: in which the male reproductive organs come to maturity before the female. Opp. PROTOGYNOUS.
■ **protandric** *adjective* = PROTANDROUS L19. **protandry** *noun* the condition of being protandrous L19.

protanomaly /prəʊtəˈnɒm(ə)li/ *noun.* M20.
[from PROTO- (red being regarded as the 1st component of colour vision) + ANOMALY.]
OPHTHALMOLOGY. Anomalous trichromatism involving reduced sensitivity to red; partial protanopia. Cf. DEUTERANOMALY.
■ **protanomalous** *adjective* of, pertaining to, or exhibiting protanomaly E20.

protanopia /prəʊtəˈnəʊpɪə/ *noun.* E20.
[formed as prec. + AN-⁵ + -OPIA.]
OPHTHALMOLOGY. Colour-blindness (esp. dichromatism) involving insensitivity to red, resulting in confusion of reds, yellows, greens, and some other colours; red-blindness, daltonism. Cf. DEUTERANOPIA.

■ **ˈprotanope** *noun* a protanopic individual E20. **protanopic** *adjective* of, pertaining to, or exhibiting protanopia E20.

protargol /prəʊˈtɑːgɒl/ *noun.* L19.
[from PROT(EIN + Latin *argentum* silver + -OL.]
BIOLOGY & MEDICINE. A substance made from protein and various compounds of silver, used as a stain and mild antiseptic.

protarsus /prəʊˈtɑːsəs/ *noun.* Pl. **-si** /-sʌɪ, -siː/. L19.
[from PRO-² + TARSUS.]
ENTOMOLOGY. The tarsus of the foreleg of an insect.
■ **protarsal** *adjective* E20.

protasis /ˈprɒtəsɪs/ *noun.* Pl. **-ases** /-əsiːz/. M16.
[Latin from Greek, from *proteinein* put forward, tender, formed as PRO-² + *teinein* stretch.]
1 The first part of a play, in which the characters and the subject are introduced, preceding the epitasis and the catastrophe. M16.
2 GRAMMAR & RHETORIC. The first or introductory clause in a sentence; *spec.* the clause expressing the condition in a conditional sentence. Opp. APODOSIS. L16.
3 Something which is put forward; a proposition, a maxim. *rare.* M17.
■ **proˈtatic** *adjective* of or pertaining to the protasis; *spec.* designating a character appearing only in the protasis of a play: M17. **proˈtatically** *adverb* (*rare*) in the protasis M19.

protea /ˈprəʊtɪə/ *noun.* M18.
[mod. Latin (see below), from PROTEUS, with allus. to the variety of form in the genus.]
Any of numerous shrubs or small trees constituting the genus *Protea* (family Proteaceae), of tropical and southern Africa, bearing showy conelike heads of apetalous flowers surrounded by coloured bracts.
■ **proteˈaceous** *adjective* of or pertaining to the Proteaceae, the mainly southern African and Australian family to which the genus *Protea* belongs M19.

protean /ˈprəʊtɪən, prəʊˈtiːən/ *adjective & noun.* Also **P-**. L16.
[from PROTEUS + -AN.]
▶ **A** *adjective.* **1** Of, pertaining to, or characteristic of the sea-god Proteus of classical mythology; taking or existing in many forms; changing, varying. L16.
2 (Of a theatrical performer) capable of taking several parts in the same piece; *gen.* versatile. Orig. *US.* L19.
3 BIOLOGY. Of animal behaviour: unpredictable, following no obvious pattern. M20.

📖 **1** E. H. GOMBRICH The dignity of man . . lies precisely in his Protean capacity for change. A. S. BYATT I never know what name you're working under, women these days . . are so protean.

▶ **B** *noun.* †**1** An inconstant or equivocal person. *rare.* Only in L16.
2 A theatrical performer who takes several parts in the same piece. Orig. *US.* L19.
■ **proteanism** *noun* capacity for change; changeableness, variability: M20. **proteanly** *adverb* (*rare*) L17.

protease /ˈprəʊtɪeɪz/ *noun.* E20.
[from PROTE(IN + -ASE.]
BIOCHEMISTRY. An enzyme which hydrolyses proteins and peptides.

protect /prəˈtɛkt/ *verb trans.* Pa. t. & pple **-tected**, †**-tect**. LME.
[Latin *protect-* pa. ppl stem of *protegere* to cover in front, formed as PRO-¹ + *tegere* to cover.]
1 Defend or guard against injury or danger; shield from attack or assault; support, assist, give esp. legal immunity or exemption to; keep safe, take care of; extend patronage to. Freq. foll. by *against*, *from*. LME. ▸†**b** Act as official or legal protector or guardian of. *rare* (Shakes.). Only in L16. ▸**c** Aim to preserve (a threatened plant or animal species) by legislating against collecting, hunting, etc.; restrict by law access to or development of (land) in order to preserve its wildlife or its undisturbed state; prevent by law demolition of or unauthorized changes to (a historic building etc.). Freq. as ***protected*** *ppl adjective.* L19.
2 ECONOMICS. Help or shield (a domestic industry) against outside competition by imposing duties or quotas on foreign goods. L18.
3 **a** Provide with a protective covering. *rare.* M19. ▸**b** Provide (an electrical device, machine, etc.) with safeguards against too high a current or voltage. L19. ▸**c** Provide (machinery etc.) with appliances to prevent injury to the user. E20.
4 COMMERCE. Provide funds to meet (a commercial draft or bill of exchange). L19.
5 CHEMISTRY. **a** Prevent the alteration or removal of (a group or molecule) in a reaction, by temporary conversion to an unreactive derivative. L19. ▸**b** Make (a hydrophobic sol) resistant to precipitation in the presence of an electrolyte. E20.

1 R. HAYMAN Her husband . . had to be protected from shock. M. HUGHES Hands in front . . to protect her face. **b** SHAKES. *2 Hen. VI* To be protected like a child. **c** J. S. HUXLEY To see that protected birds are not shot. S. BELLOW It's a protected landmark, and can't be demolished. **2** J. E. T. ROGERS If every producer . . were protected, foreign trade might cease.

■ **protec'tee** *noun* a person under protection; *spec.* (*Hist.*) in the 16th and 17th cents., an Irishman or Irishwoman who had accepted the protection of the English Government: E17. **protectingly** *adverb* in a protecting manner E19. **protectingness** *noun* (*rare*) the state of being protecting; an instance of this: M19.

protectable *adjective* var. of PROTECTIBLE.

protectant /prəˈtɛkt(ə)nt/ *adjective & noun.* L17.
[Irreg. from prec. + -ANT[1].]
▶**A** *adjective.* Protective; providing protection against disease or infestation, esp. to a plant or plant product. L17.
▶**B** *noun.* A protective agent, *esp.* one providing protection against disease or infestation, esp. to a plant or plant product. M20.

protectible /prəˈtɛktɪb(ə)l/ *adjective.* Also **-able** /-əb(ə)l/. M19.
[from PROTECT: see -ABLE, -IBLE.]
Able to be protected, esp. by legislation.

protection /prəˈtɛkʃ(ə)n/ *noun.* ME.
[Old & mod. French, or late Latin *protectio(n-)*, formed as PROTECT: see -ION.]
1 The action of protecting someone or something; the fact or condition of being protected. ME.
2 A person who or thing which protects someone or something. LME.
3 A document guaranteeing protection, exemption, or immunity to the person specified in it; a safe-conduct, a pass. Formerly *spec.* (more fully ***letter of protection***), a document issued by a British monarch granting immunity from arrest or lawsuit to one engaged in his or her service or going abroad with his or her cognizance. LME.
4 The keeping of a mistress in a separate establishment. Freq. in ***under a person's protection***. *arch.* L17.
5 *ECONOMICS.* The theory or practice of protecting domestic industries from the competition of foreign goods. L18.
6 Immunity from molestation obtained by paying money, esp. on a regular basis, to a person who threatens violence or retribution if payment is not made; (more fully ***protection money***) the money paid to secure such immunity. *colloq.* M19.
7 *BRIDGE.* The action of reopening with a bid or a double when the bidding of one's opponents has stopped at a low level. M20.
8 *MOUNTAINEERING.* The number and quality of running belays or other equipment employed to safeguard a pitch. M20.

1 *Scotsman* The citizen is under the protection of the law. C. HILL The King fled northwards to seek the protection of the Scottish army. J. UGLOW An innocent who craves protection. *CATHODIC protection*. *SANITARY protection*. **2** AV *Deut.* 32:38 Where *are* their gods? . . Let them . . be your protection. F. CLISSOLD Veils, as a protection from the heat. **3** J. L. DE LOLME Having been detected in selling protections. R. KIPLING Chinn never broke a protection spoken or written. **4** J. HATTON Living under his lordship's protection. **6** S. BELLOW Throwing acid on clothes in dry-cleaning shops that wouldn't buy protection. E. FAIRWEATHER The Provos were getting protection money.

Comb.: **protection forest** a forest planted to provide a dense cover of vegetation which helps to inhibit erosion and conserve water; ***protection money***: see sense 6 above; **protection racket** *colloq.* an illegal scheme for the levying of protection money.

■ **protectional** *adjective* of or pertaining to protection L19. **protectionism** *noun* (*ECONOMICS*) = PROTECTION 5 M19. **protectionist** *noun & adjective* (*a*) *noun* an advocate of protectionism; (*b*) *adjective* of or pertaining to protectionists or protectionism: M19.

protective /prəˈtɛktɪv/ *adjective & noun.* M17.
[from PROTECT + -IVE.]
▶**A** *adjective.* **1** Having the quality or character of protecting; tending to protect; defensive; preservative. M17. ▸**b** *ELECTRICITY.* Providing protection against too high a current or voltage. L19. ▸**c** Of food: providing protection against deficiency diseases. M20.
2 *ECONOMICS.* Of or pertaining to the theory or practice of the protection of domestic industries from the competition of foreign goods. E19.
3 *CHEMISTRY.* **a** Having the quality or property of protecting a sol. Chiefly in ***protective colloid*** below. E20. ▸**b** Preventing a group or molecule from alteration or removal. M20.

1 DAY LEWIS He was . . protective, taking my side against the . . world. R. THOMAS Keeping to the protective shadows, Mari followed him. V. BRAMWELL On sunbeds . . wear protective goggles.

Special collocations: **protective arrest** the detention of a person for his or her own protection. **protective clothing** clothing worn to shield the body from dangerous substances or a hostile environment. **protective colloid** a lyophilic colloid whose presence in small quantities protects a lyophobic sol. **protective coloration**, **protective colouring** *ZOOLOGY* cryptic or mimetic colouring that enables an animal to conceal or disguise itself. **protective custody** = *protective arrest* above.
▶**B** *noun.* A thing which protects someone or something; *spec.* a condom. L19.
■ **protectively** *adverb* M19. **protectiveness** *noun* M19.

protector /prəˈtɛktə/ *noun.* In sense 2b also **P-**. LME.
[Old French *protecteur* from late Latin *protector*, formed as PROTECT: see -OR.]
1 A person who protects a person or thing from injury or danger; a defender; a guardian, a patron. LME. ▸**b** *ROMAN HISTORY.* A member of one of four companies into which the imperial guard was divided. *rare.* L18. ▸**c** A man who keeps a mistress in a separate establishment (*arch.*). Also, a man who looks after a prostitute in return for a share of the earnings; a pimp. E20. ▸**d** A person from whom immunity from molestation is obtained by the payment of money. *colloq.* M20.
2 *Hist.* **a** A person in charge of a kingdom or State during the minority, absence, or incapacity of the monarch; a regent. LME. ▸**b** In full ***Lord Protector (of the Commonwealth)***. (The title of) the head of State in England during the later period of the Commonwealth between 1653 and 1659, first Oliver Cromwell (1653–8), then his son Richard (1658–9). M17.
3 *LAW.* ***protector of the settlement***, the first person entitled, under a strict settlement of land, to a life interest preceding the entailed interest or (if there is no prior life interest) the settlor. M19.
4 A thing which protects a person or thing from injury or danger; *esp.* a device for protecting a specified part of the body from injury etc. (chiefly as 2nd elem. of comb.). M19.

1 Protector of the Poor *Anglo-Indian* master, sir, (chiefly as a term of respectful address). **4** ***chest-protector***, ***eye-protector***, etc.
■ **protectoral** *adjective* (chiefly *Hist.*) of or pertaining to a protector M17. **protec'torial** *adjective* of or pertaining to a protector or a protecting State E19. **protectorless** *adjective* (*rare*) M19.

protectorate /prəˈtɛkt(ə)rət/ *noun.* Also **P-**. L17.
[from prec. + -ATE[1].]
1 *Hist.* The office, position, or government of the protector of a kingdom or State; the period of administration of a protector, *esp.* that in England under the Cromwells between 1653 and 1659. L17.
2 The relation of a State to a State or territory which it controls or protects; the relation of a suzerain to a vassal State; suzerainty. M19.
3 A State or territory controlled or protected by another State; the relation of a State or territory to the State which controls or protects it. M19.

3 F. RAPHAEL Part of the British protectorate of the Ionian Islands.

protectorship /prəˈtɛktəʃɪp/ *noun.* Also **P-**. LME.
[formed as prec. + -SHIP.]
1 *Hist.* = PROTECTORATE 1; *rare* (with possess. adjective, as ***your protectorship*** etc.) a title of respect given to a protector. LME.
2 The position, character, or function of a protector; guardianship, patronage. L16.

protectory /prəˈtɛkt(ə)ri/ *adjective & noun.* M17.
[As adjective from late Latin *protectorius*, from Latin PROTECTOR; as noun from PROTECT: see -ORY[2], -ORY[1].]
▶**A** *adjective.* Having the quality of protecting; protective. Long *rare* or *obsolete.* M17.
▶**B** *noun.* An institution for the care and education of homeless or delinquent children. M19.

protectress /prəˈtɛktrɪs/ *noun.* Also (*rare*) **-tectoress** /-ˈtɛkt(ə)rɪs/. L16.
[from PROTECTOR + -ESS[1].]
1 A female protector. L16.
2 *spec.* (*Hist.*) A female regent of a kingdom or State; the wife of a regent. L16.

protectrice /prətɛkˈtriːs/ *noun.* Now *rare.* LME.
[French, formed as next: see -TRICE.]
A protectress.

protectrix /prəˈtɛktrɪks/ *noun.* Pl. **-trixes**, **-trices** /-trɪsiːz/. L15.
[medieval Latin, fem. of Latin PROTECTOR: see -TRIX.]
A protectress.

protégé /ˈprɒtɪʒeɪ, -tɛʒeɪ, ˈprəʊ-/ *noun.* Also (fem.) **-ée**. L18.
[French, pa. ppl adjective of *protéger* from Latin *protegere* PROTECT.]
A person under the protection, care, or patronage of another, esp. of a person of superior position or influence.

P. V. WHITE To enjoy the power of patron over protégé. E. LONGFORD A young protégé of Lady Astor.

protegulum /prəʊˈtɛgjʊləm/ *noun.* L19.
[from PRO-[2] + Latin *tegulum* covering.]
ZOOLOGY. The embryonic form of a brachiopod shell.

proteid /ˈprəʊtiːɪd/ *noun.* Now *rare* or *obsolete.* L19.
[from PROTEIN + -ID[5].]
CHEMISTRY. = PROTEIN.

proteiform /ˈprəʊtiːɪfɔːm/ *adjective.* L18.
[from PROTEUS + -I- + -FORM.]
Changeable in form, assuming many forms; protean, multiform, extremely variable or various.

protein /ˈprəʊtiːn/ *noun.* M19.
[French *protéine*, German *Protein*, from Greek *prōteios* primary, from *prōtos* first: see PROTO-, -IN[1].]
Any of a large group of organic polymeric compounds which form an essential part of all living organisms as both structural and functional constituents, and are composed of amino acids linked in specific sequences by peptide bonds and coiled and folded into complex globular or fibrous structures; such substances collectively, esp. as a component of the diet.
fibrous protein, ***flavoprotein***, ***glycoprotein***, ***plasma protein***, ***textured vegetable protein***, etc.
Comb.: **protein plastic** a plastic in which protein is the chief component; *esp.* a casein plastic; **protein shock** *MEDICINE* (*a*) a disturbed state produced by the parenteral introduction into the body of a foreign protein; (*b*) protein therapy; **protein therapy** *MEDICINE* the controlled production of protein shock for therapeutic purposes.
¶ Orig. thought to be a single fundamental substance.
■ **proteinaceous** /prəʊtɪˈneɪʃəs/ *adjective* of the nature of or consisting of protein M19. **proteinic** /prəʊˈtiːnɪk/ *adjective* = PROTEINACEOUS L19 **proteinous** /prəʊˈtiːnəs/ *adjective* = PROTEINACEOUS M19.

proteinase /ˈprəʊtiːneɪz/ *noun.* E20.
[from prec. + -ASE.]
BIOCHEMISTRY. A protease which hydrolyses proteins.

proteinoid /ˈprəʊtiːnɔɪd/ *noun & adjective.* M20.
[from PROTEIN + -OID.]
BIOCHEMISTRY. ▶**A** *noun.* A polypeptide or mixture of polypeptides obtained by heating a mixture of amino acids. M20.
▶**B** *attrib.* or as *adjective.* Of, pertaining to, or of the nature of a proteinoid or proteinoids. M20.

proteinosis /prəʊtiːˈnəʊsɪs/ *noun.* Pl. **-noses** /-ˈnəʊsiːz/. M20.
[from PROTEIN + -OSIS.]
MEDICINE. The abnormal accumulation or deposition of protein in tissue.

proteinuria /prəʊtiːˈnjʊərɪə/ *noun.* E20.
[from PROTEIN + -URIA.]
MEDICINE. The presence of abnormal quantities of protein in the urine.
■ **proteinuric** *adjective* of, pertaining to, or suffering from proteinuria M20.

pro tem /prəʊ ˈtɛm/ *adverbial & adjectival phr. colloq.* E19.
[Abbreviation.]
= next.

pro tempore /prəʊ ˈtɛmpəri/ *adverbial & adjectival phr.* LME.
[Latin = for the time.]
▶**A** *adverbial phr.* For the time being, temporarily. LME.
▶**B** *adjectival phr.* Temporary. M18.

protend /prəʊˈtɛnd/ *verb.* Now *rare.* LME.
[Latin *protendere* stretch forth, extend, formed as PRO-[1] + *tendere* stretch.]
▶**I 1** *verb trans.* Stretch or hold out. LME. ▸**b** *verb intrans.* Stretch forward; stick out, protrude. E18.
2 *verb trans.* Extend (something) in length or in one dimension of space; in *pass.*, reach *from* one point *to* another. LME. ▸**b** Extend in magnitude or amount. M17.
3 *verb trans.* Extend in duration; protract, prolong. LME.
▶**II** †**4** *verb intrans. & trans.* Portend or foretoken (something). L16–E17.

†**protense** *noun. rare* (Spenser). Only in L16.
[from Latin *protens-*: see next.]
Extension in time, duration.

protension /prəʊˈtɛnʃ(ə)n/ *noun.* In sense 3b also **-tention**. L17.
[Late Latin *protensio(n-)*, from Latin *protens-* pa. ppl stem of *protendere* PROTEND: see -ION. In sense 3b after German *Protention*.]
1 The action or fact of stretching or holding something out; a stretching or reaching forward. L17.
2 Extension in length; linear extent; length. E18.
3 a Extension in time; duration. M19. ▸**b** In phenomenology, extension of the consciousness of a present act or event into the future; an instance of this. M20.

protensity /prəʊˈtɛnsɪti/ *noun.* E20.
[from Latin *protens-* (see prec.) + -ITY.]
The quality of having (a certain) protension, esp. of time.

protensive /prəʊˈtɛnsɪv/ *adjective. rare.* L17.
[from Latin *protens-* (see PROTENSION) + -IVE, after *intensive, extensive.*]
1 Extending in time; continuing, lasting, enduring. Earlier in PROTENSIVELY 2. L17.
2 Extending lengthwise; relating to or expressing linear extension or magnitude of one dimension. Earlier in PROTENSIVELY 1. M19.

protensively /prəʊˈtɛnsɪvli/ *adverb. rare.* L15.
[from prec. + -LY².]
1 In respect of lengthwise extension, so as to relate to or express linear extension or magnitude of one dimension. L15.
2 In respect of duration or extension in time. M17.

protention *noun* see PROTENSION.

proteo- /ˈprəʊtɪəʊ/ *combining form* of PROTEIN: see -O-.
■ **proteoˈclastic** *adjective* (*rare*) = PROTEOLYTIC *adjective* E20. **proteoglycan** /-ˈglʌɪkan/ *noun* a protein that is covalently bonded to one or more glycosaminoglycan chains, a mucoprotein M20. **proteoˈlipid**, **-ide** *noun* a complex that contains protein and lipid components, insoluble in aqueous media and occurring esp. in cell membranes M20.

proteolysis /prəʊtɪˈɒlɪsɪs/ *noun.* L19.
[from PROTEO- + -LYSIS.]
BIOCHEMISTRY. The splitting of protein or peptide molecules by the action of enzymes, esp. during the process of digestion.
■ **proteolyse** /ˈprəʊtɪəlʌɪz/ *verb trans.* (*rare*) decompose or split up (a protein) E20. **proteoˈlytic** *adjective* of, pertaining to, or capable of proteolysis L19. **proteoˈlytically** *adverb* as regards or by means of proteolysis E20.

proteome /ˈprəʊtɪəʊm/ *noun.* L20.
[Blend of PROTEIN and GENOME.]
GENETICS. The entire complement of proteins that is (or can be) expressed by a cell, tissue, or organism.

proteomics /prəʊtɪˈɒmɪks/ *noun pl.* (treated as *sing.*). L20.
[from prec. + -ICS.]
The branch of molecular biology concerned with the behaviour and interaction of proteins within cells.

proteose /ˈprəʊtɪəʊz, -s/ *noun.* Now *rare.* L19.
[from PROTEIN + -OSE².]
A polypeptide produced by partial proteolysis.

proter- *combining form* see PROTERO-.

proterandrous /prɒtəˈrandrəs/ *adjective.* L19.
[from PROTERO- + -ANDROUS.]
BOTANY & ZOOLOGY. = PROTANDROUS.
■ **proterandry** *noun* = PROTANDRY L19.

protero- /ˈprɒt(ə)rəʊ/ *combining form.* Before a vowel also **proter-**.
[from Greek *proteros*: see -O-.]
Former, anterior; first in place, time, order, rank, etc.
■ **proteroˈgenesis** *noun* (*BIOLOGY*, now chiefly *Hist.*) the appearance in the early stages of an organism's life of features characteristic of adult forms of its evolutionary descendants. M20. **proteroglyph** *noun* (*ZOOLOGY*) a venomous snake having grooved fangs fixed upright in the front of the mouth L19. **proteroˈglyphous** *adjective* (*ZOOLOGY*) pertaining to or of the nature of a proteroglyph L19.

proterogynous /prɒtəˈrɒdʒɪnəs/ *adjective.* L19.
[from PROTERO- + -GYNOUS.]
BOTANY & ZOOLOGY. = PROTOGYNOUS.
■ **proterogyny** *noun* = PROTOGYNY L19.

Proterozoic /prəʊt(ə)rəˈzəʊɪk/ *adjective & noun.* E20.
[from PROTERO- + Greek *zōē* life + -IC.]
GEOLOGY. (Designating or pertaining to) the later part of the Precambrian era, characterized by the oldest forms of life.

protervity /prəˈtəːvɪti/ *noun.* Now *rare.* L15.
[French †*protervité* or Latin *protervitas*, from *protervus* forward, pert, impudent: see -ITY.]
Waywardness; stubbornness; pertness, impudence, insolence; petulance; an instance of this.

protest /ˈprəʊtɛst/ *noun.* LME.
[Old French (mod. *protêt*), from *protester* PROTEST *verb.*]
1 A solemn affirmation of a fact etc.; = PROTESTATION 1. LME.
2 *LAW.* A written declaration, usu. by a notary public, that a bill has been presented and payment or acceptance refused. Also, the action taken to fix the liability for the payment of a dishonoured bill. L15.
3 a A written statement of dissent from a motion carried in the House of Lords, recorded and signed by any peer of the minority. Cf. earlier PROTESTATION 3a. E18. ▸**b** A statement, declaration, or other expression of disapproval of or dissent from, or of conditional consent to, an action or proceeding; (a) remonstrance; (an) objection. Cf. earlier PROTESTATION 3b. M18. ▸**c** *spec.* The expressing of social, political, or cultural dissent; a usu. public demonstration of objection to a policy or course of action (freq. *attrib.*). M20.
4 A written declaration made by the master of a ship, attested by a justice of the peace or a consul, stating the circumstances under which injury has happened to the ship or cargo, or under which officers or crew have incurred any liability. M18.

> 🕮 **3a** LD MACAULAY The most remarkable protests which appear in the journals of the peers. **b** *Times* Meetings of protest began to be held. G. GREENE She made no protest. M. HUGHES A laughing chorus of protests. A. DESAI He pushed out his lower lip in ready protest. **under protest** unwillingly. **c** A. POWELL A programme . . dealing with protest, counterculture, alternative societies. *attrib.*: J. RULE A few protest cartoons, directed at Nevada testing grounds. B. GELDOF I'd become involved . . with protest politics.

Comb.: **protest flag** a flag flown by a racing yacht to indicate its intention of lodging a protest against another competitor's infringement of the rules; ***protest march***: see MARCH *noun*³ 3c; **protest marcher** = MARCHER *noun*² 2; **protest vote** a vote for a party or candidate representing a protest against the actions or policies of another party or candidate; **protest voting** the action or practice of making a protest vote.

protest /prəˈtɛst/ *verb.* LME.
[Old & mod. French *protester* from Latin *protestari* declare formally, formed as PRO-¹ + *testari* be a witness, assert.]
1 *verb trans.* Declare or state formally or solemnly, esp. in relation to a stated or implied doubt; affirm or assert (one's innocence etc., *that*) formally or solemnly, esp. in response to a charge or accusation. LME. ▸**b** *verb intrans.* Make a solemn or formal affirmation about something, esp. in response to a charge or accusation. M16. ▸**c** *verb trans.* Utter or express as a protest, object. E20.
2 *verb trans.* Make a request in legal form; demand as a right; stipulate. Freq. foll. by *that. Scot.* LME.
†**3** *verb trans.* Vow; promise or undertake solemnly. LME–M17.
4 *verb trans. LAW.* Write or obtain a protest (PROTEST *noun* 2) with regard to (a bill). L15.
†**5** *verb trans.* Assert publicly; proclaim, publish; expound. M16–M17.
†**6** *verb trans.* Call to witness; appeal to. M16–L17.
7 *verb intrans.* Give (esp. formal) expression to objection, dissent, or disapproval; make a protest *against* an action, proposal, policy, etc.; remonstrate. Also foll. by *at.* L16.
8 *verb trans.* Protest against (an action or event); make (a policy or course of action) the subject of a protest; object to (a decision). Chiefly *N. Amer.* E20.

> 🕮 **1** T. KEIGHTLEY She then . . solemnly protested her innocence. F. TUOHY They'll protest any amount of pro-Western feeling. **b** SHAKES. *Haml.* The lady doth protest too much. **c** P. G. WODEHOUSE 'Please . . !' protested Jill, 'Not while I'm eating buttered toast!' **3** SHAKES. *Mids. N. D.* On Diana's altar to protest For aye austerity and single life. **5** F. QUARLES Protest His praises to the world. **6** HOBBES Protest the gods against their injuries. **7** G. VIDAL He had not protested when his half-brother Constantine became emperor. M. SHADBOLT A demonstration to protest against a wage cut. A. HARDING Protesting at the discomforts of their route. **8** *Scientific American* The Soviet has also protested some actions . . by the U.S.

■ **protestingly** *adverb* in a protesting manner; by way of protest: L19. **protestive** *adjective* protesting or constituting a protest M20.

†**Protestancy** *noun.* E17–E19.
[from next: see -ANCY.]
The condition of being a Protestant; the Protestant religion, system, or principles; Protestantism.

Protestant /ˈprɒtɪst(ə)nt/, in senses A.3, B.2 *freq.* prəˈtɛst(ə)nt/ *noun & adjective.* In senses A.4, B.2 also **p-**. M16.
[mod. Latin *protestant-*, *-ans* use as noun of pres. pple of Latin *protestari* PROTEST *verb*: see -ANT¹.]
▸ **A** *noun.* **I** *CHRISTIAN CHURCH.* **1** *Hist.* In *pl.* The German princes and free cities dissenting from the decision of the Diet of Spires (1529), which reaffirmed the edict of the Diet of Worms against the Reformation; *gen.* adherents of Reformed doctrines and worship in Germany; *esp.* Lutherans. M16.
2 A member or follower of any of the Christian Churches or sects repudiating the Roman obedience at the Reformation or of any of the Churches or sects standing in historic continuity with them; a member or follower of any of the western Christian Churches that are separate from the Roman Catholic Church in accordance with the principles of the Reformation. (Freq. opp. ***Roman Catholic.***) M16.
3 *spec.* **a** Orig., a member of the Anglican Church as opp. to a Nonconformist. Later, a member of the Anglican Church holding Low Church views (opp. ***Anglo-Catholic***). E17. ▸**b** A member of a Nonconformist or non-episcopal Church. M20.
▸ **II** *gen.* **4** A person who protests; *spec.* (***a***) *rare* a person making a protestation or affirmation, esp. of devotion or affection; a suitor; (***b***) a person protesting against error; (***c***) a person making a protest *against* an action etc.; a protester. M17.

> 🕮 **4** R. CAMPBELL First of earth's protestants, his single voice . . Was lifted in complaint. E. B. WHITE The manager has promised to fire the protestants.

▸ **B** *adjective.* **1** *CHRISTIAN CHURCH.* Of, pertaining to, or characteristic of Protestants or Protestantism; *esp.* designating or pertaining to any of the Christian Churches or sects repudiating obedience to or separate from the Roman Catholic Church (see sense A.2 above) (freq. opp. ***Roman Catholic***); *spec.* Nonconformist, non-episcopal. M16.
2 *gen.* Protesting; making a protest. M19.
Special collocations & comb.: **Protestant ascendancy** = ASCENDANCY 2. **Protestant Episcopal** *adjective* of, belonging to, or designating the Protestant Church of the Anglican Communion in the US. **Protestant Episcopalianism** (adherence to) the system, faith, and practice of the Protestant Episcopal Church. **Protestant ethic**, **Protestant work ethic** success through hard work seen as a person's duty and responsibility, attributed by Max Weber in his thesis on the origins of capitalism to the teachings of Calvin (cf. ***work ethic*** s.v. WORK *noun*).
■ **Protestantdom** *noun* Protestants collectively, the Protestant Church L17. **Protestantish** *adjective* (*rare*) Protestant; tending towards Protestantism: L17. **Protestantism** *noun* (***a***) (adherence to) the system, faith, and practice of a Protestant Church; (***b***) Protestants or the Protestant Churches collectively; (***c***) *rare* (also **p-**) the condition of protesting; an attitude of protest or objection: M17. **Protestantiˈzation** *noun* the action or fact of making a person Protestant; conversion to Protestantism: L19. **Protestantize** *verb* (***a***) *verb trans.* make Protestant; convert to Protestantism; (***b***) *verb intrans.* be or become Protestant: M19.

protestation /prɒtɪˈsteɪʃ(ə)n/ *noun.* ME.
[Old & mod. French, or late Latin *protestatio(n-)*, from *protestat-* pa. ppl stem of *protestari* PROTEST *verb*: see -ATION.]
1 The action or fact of protesting; that which is protested; a solemn affirmation of a fact, opinion, or resolution; a formal public assertion or asseveration. ME.
2 †**a** *LAW.* An affirmation or denial by a pleader of the truth of an allegation which cannot be directly affirmed or denied without duplication of his or her plea, and which cannot be passed over in case it should be held to have been tacitly waived or admitted. LME–L18. ▸**b** *SCOTS LAW.* Orig., a stipulation or assertion made to a court by or on behalf of a party to a lawsuit in order to safeguard that party's interests. Later, a note served by a defendant whereby an action that has been raised but not pursued must be proceeded with or fail. LME.
3 †**a** = PROTEST *noun* 3a. E17–E18. ▸**b** = PROTEST *noun* 3b. M17.

> 🕮 **1** D. ATHILL Protestations of absolute fidelity. **make protestation** protest in a solemn or formal manner. **3b** T. JEFFERSON A protestation against our ratification of the treaty.

protestator /ˈprɒtɪsteɪtə/ *noun.* Chiefly *Scot.* Long *rare.* LME.
[from Latin *protestat-*: see prec., -ATOR.]
A person who enters a protestation; a protester.

protestatory /prəˈtɛstət(ə)ri/ *adjective. rare.* E17.
[from Latin *protestat-*: see PROTESTATION, -ORY².]
Pertaining to or of the nature of a protest.

protester /prəˈtɛstə/ *noun.* E17.
[from PROTEST *verb* + -ER¹.]
1 A person who makes a protestation; a person who protests, esp. publicly against a policy or course of action. E17.
2 *SCOTTISH HISTORY.* (Usu. **P-**.) In *pl.* Those Presbyterians who in 1650 protested against the union with the Royalists. Also, those who on various later occasions formally protested against acts or decisions of the Church courts. M17.

> 🕮 **1** LEIGH HUNT Protesters against improper expenses. *USA Today* Police . . sealed entrances . . after groups of protesters tried to make their way inside.

protestor /prəˈtɛstə/ *noun.* M16.
[formed as prec. + -OR.]
A protester.

Proteus /ˈprəʊtɪəs, -tjuːs/ *noun.* L16.
[Latin from Greek *Prōteus*, in Greek & Roman mythol. a sea-god, the son of Oceanus and Tethys, capable of taking various forms at will.]
1 A person who or thing which takes various forms or characters; a changing, varying, or inconstant person or thing. L16.
2 a *BIOLOGY.* A micro-organism of variable shape; *esp.* an amoeba. Now usu. *spec.*, a Gram-negative intestinal or saprophytic bacterium of the genus *Proteus.* E19. ▸**b** *ZOOLOGY.* = OLM. Now only as mod. Latin genus name. E19.

Protevangel /prəʊtɪˈvandʒ(ə)l/ *noun.* M19.
[from (the same root as) next.]
= next.

Protevangelium /prəʊtˌiːvanˈdʒɛlɪəm/ *noun.* E18.
[from PROTO- + EVANGELIUM.]
CHRISTIAN CHURCH. A primitive or original gospel; *spec.* (***a***) (the title of) an apocryphal gospel, attributed to St James the Less; (***b***) the earliest utterance of the gospel (as in *Genesis* 3:15).

protext /ˈprəʊtɛkst/ *noun. rare.* **M17.**
[from PRO-¹ or PRO-² + TEXT *noun*.]
The preceding context of a passage.

prothalamium /prəʊθəˈleɪmɪəm/ *noun.* Also (earlier) **-ion** /-ɪən/. Pl. **-ia** /-ɪə/. **L16.**
[from *Prothalmion*, title of a poem by Spenser (1597), after *epithalamion* var. of EPITHALAMIUM: see PRO-².]
A song or poem in celebration of a forthcoming wedding.

prothallus /prəʊˈθaləs/ *noun.* Pl. **-lli** /-lʌɪ, -liː/. **M19.**
[mod. Latin, formed as PRO-² + Greek *thallos*: see THALLUS.]
BOTANY. The free-living gametophyte of a fern or other vascular cryptogam, a minute cellular disc or thallus produced by the germination of a spore and bearing antheridia, archegonia, or both. Also, the female gametophyte of a gymnosperm.
■ **prothallial** *adjective* pertaining to or of the nature of a prothallus; ***prothallial cell***, a small vegetative cell formed by division of the microspore in gymnosperms and in certain pteridophytes: **L19.** **prothallium** *noun*, pl. **-ia**, = PROTHALLUS **M19.** **prothalloid** *adjective* resembling or having the form of a prothallus **L19.**

prothesis /ˈprɒθɪsɪs/ *noun.* Pl. **-theses** /-θɪsiːz/. **L16.**
[Greek = a placing before or in public, formed as PRO-² + *thesis* placing.]
1 = PROSTHESIS 1. **L16.**
2 CHRISTIAN CHURCH. The placing of the Eucharistic elements in readiness for use. Also (esp. in the Orthodox Church), the table on which these are placed, a credence table; the part of a church where this stands. **L17.**
3 Something which precedes, an antecedent. *rare.* **E19.**

prothetely /prəʊˈθɛtəli/ *noun.* **M20.**
[from Greek *prothein* run before + *telos* end: see -Y³.]
ENTOMOLOGY. In certain insect larvae, the development of one part of the body, esp. the wings, at a faster rate than that of the rest.
■ **prothetelic** /-ˈtɛlɪk/ *adjective* **M20.**

prothetic /prəˈθɛtɪk/ *adjective.* **M19.**
[Greek *prothetikos*, formed as PROTHESIS: see -ETIC.]
Of, pertaining to, or involving prothesis.
■ **prothetical** *adjective* (*rare*) **M19.** **prothetically** *adverb* (*rare*) **M19.**

prothonotary *noun* var. of PROTONOTARY.

prothrombin /prəʊˈθrɒmbɪn/ *noun.* **L19.**
[from PRO-² + THROMBIN.]
BIOCHEMISTRY. A protein present in blood plasma which is converted into active thrombin during coagulation.

prothyl(e) *nouns* vars. of PROTYLE.

prothyrum /ˈprɒθɪrəm/ *noun. rare.* Pl. **-ra** /-rə/, **-rums.** **E18.**
[Latin from Greek *prothuron*, formed as PRO-² + *thura* door.]
CLASSICAL ANTIQUITIES. The porch or vestibule of a house in ancient Greece or Rome.

protic /ˈprəʊtɪk/ *adjective.* **M20.**
[from PROT(ON + -IC, prob. after APROTIC.]
CHEMISTRY. Of a liquid, esp. a solvent: able to provide a hydrogen atom for protonation, protogenic.

protide /ˈprəʊtʌɪd/ *noun. rare.* **M20.**
[French, formed as PROTEIN + -IDE.]
BIOCHEMISTRY. A protein, peptide, or amino acid.
■ **proˈtidic** *adjective* **M20.**

protist /ˈprəʊtɪst/ *noun.* **L19.**
[from mod. Latin *Protista* pl. (see below) from German *Protisten* pl., from Greek *prōtista* neut. pl. of *prōtistos* very first (superl. of *prōtos* first).]
BIOLOGY. A member of the kingdom Protista of simple organisms regarded as intermediate between or distinct from animals and plants, including protozoans, algae, and (now less commonly) bacteria and fungi; *esp.* a unicellular eukaryote, a protozoan or single-celled alga.
■ **proˈtistan** *noun* = PROTIST **E20.** **proˈtistic** *adjective* of or pertaining to the kingdom Protista **M19.** **protiˈstologist** *noun* an expert in or student of protistology **E20.** **protiˈstology** *noun* the branch of biology that deals with protists **E20.**

protium /ˈprəʊtɪəm/ *noun.* **M20.**
[from Greek *prōtos* first + -IUM.]
CHEMISTRY. The ordinary isotope of hydrogen, having only a proton in the nucleus and forming at least 99.98 per cent by volume of naturally occurring hydrogen. Symbols ^{1}H, H^1.

proto- /ˈprəʊtəʊ/ *combining form.* Before a vowel or *h* also **prot-.**
[Greek *prōto-* combining form of *prōtos* first: see -O-.]
1 First in time, earliest, original; at an early or preceding stage of development, primitive; *spec.* (LINGUISTICS) designating or pertaining to the earliest attested or hypothetically-reconstructed form of a language or language family.
2 First in rank or importance.
3 Chiefly SCIENCE. First in position, anterior. ▸**b** CHEMISTRY. Forming names of: †(***a***) (esp. binary) compounds in which an element combines in the smallest proportion with another element; (***b***) precursors or parent compounds, structures, etc.
■ **protobiont** /-ˈbʌɪɒnt/ *noun* [-BIONT] BIOLOGY a membrane-bound fluid droplet containing complex organic molecules, hypothesized as ancestral to living cells **M20.** **protocaˈnonical** *adjective* of, pertaining to, or constituting a first or primary canon (of sacred books) **E17.** **protoˈcercal** *adjective* [Greek *kerkos* tail] ICHTHYOLOGY designating or possessing a tail of primitive form, symmetrical and continuous with the dorsal and ventral fins **L19.** **protoˈchlorophyll** *noun* (BIOCHEMISTRY) a naturally occurring photoactive precursor of chlorophyll **L19.** **protoˈchordate** *adjective & noun* (ZOOLOGY) (of, pertaining to, or designating) an animal belonging or related to the chordates but lacking a skull and vertebrae (i.e. other than a vertebrate), i.e. a cephalochordate, a urochordate, or a hemichordate: **L19.** **protoconch** /-kɒŋk/ *noun* the embryonic shell in molluscs, freq. retained at the tip of the adult shell **L19.** **protocone** *noun* (ZOOLOGY) a cusp on the anterior lingual corner of the tribosphenic upper molar tooth **L19.** **protoˈconid** *noun* (ZOOLOGY) a cusp on the anterior buccal corner of the tribosphenic lower molar tooth **L19.** **protocontinent** *noun* (GEOLOGY) = SUPERCONTINENT **M20.** **protocorm** *noun* (BOTANY) a structure resembling a tuber, produced by the seedlings of certain orchids and pteridophytes which grow in association with mycorrhiza **L19.** **protoˈcultural** *adjective* pertaining to hypothetical or surmised origins of human cultural development **M20.** **protoˈdeacon** *noun* a senior deacon in the Greek Orthodox Church **L17.** **protoderm** *noun* (BOTANY) the outermost layer of the apical meristem, from which the epidermis and some of the tissue beneath it are formed **M20.** **proto-ˈdiasystem** *noun* (LINGUISTICS) a hypothetical reconstruction of the system of linguistic relationships in a proto-language **M20.** **protodyˈnastic** *adjective* (*Hist.*) designating or pertaining to the earliest (Egyptian) dynasties **E20.** **protofibril** *noun* (BIOLOGY) a protein filament that is a component structural element of a fibril or *spec.* of a microfibril **M20.** **protofilament** *noun* (BIOLOGY) a filament of protein molecules, a group of which form a microtubule **L20.** **proto-form** *noun* (LINGUISTICS) a hypothetical form of a word or part of a word from which attested words have been derived **M20.** **protogaˈlactic** *adjective* (ASTRONOMY) of, pertaining to, or of the nature of a protogalaxy **M20.** **protogalaxy** *noun* (ASTRONOMY) a vast mass of gas from which a galaxy is thought to develop **M20.** **Protogeoˈmetric** *adjective* (ARCHAEOLOGY) designating or pertaining to a period of ancient Greek culture (*c* 1100–*c* 900 BC) immediately preceding the Geometric period **E20.** **Proto-Gerˈmanic** *adjective & noun* (of, pertaining to, or designating) the unrecorded Germanic parent language from which all Germanic languages are derived **M20.** **protogram** *noun* (now *rare* or *obsolete*) an acronym **E20.** **protograph** *noun* a first or original writing **M19.** **protohaem**, **-heme** *noun* (BIOCHEMISTRY) a haem complex containing ferrous iron **M20.** **proto-hiˈstorian** *noun* (***a***) the earliest or original historian; (***b***) an expert in or student of proto-history: **M17.** **proto-hiˈstoric** *adjective* of or pertaining to proto-history **L19.** **proto-hiˈstorical** *adjective* = PROTO-HISTORIC **E20.** **proto-history** *noun* the branch of knowledge that deals with the history of the earliest times or the beginnings of historical records **E20.** **Proto-ˈHittite** *noun* the language of the Hatti, unrelated to Hittite **M20.** **protoˈhuman** *noun & adjective* (ANTHROPOLOGY) (pertaining to or designating) any of various fossil or hypothetical primates resembling and thought to be ancestral to humans **E20.** **Proto-Indo-Euroˈpean** *adjective & noun* (pertaining to or designating) the unattested and partly reconstructed language from which all Indo-European languages are believed to derive **M20.** **proto-language** *noun* (LINGUISTICS) a hypothetical parent language from which actual languages or dialects are derived (cf. URSPRACHE) **M20.** **proto-literate** *adjective* characterized by the most primitive kind of writing **M20.** **protolith** *noun* (GEOLOGY) the unmetamorphosed parent rock from which a given metamorphic rock has developed **L20.** **proˈtomerite** *noun* (ZOOLOGY) the anterior division of the body in gregarine protozoans **L19.** **protoˈmorphic** *adjective* having a primitive or the simplest form or structure **M19.** **protoneˈphridial** *adjective* (ZOOLOGY) of or pertaining to a protonephridium **L19.** **protoneˈphridium** *noun*, pl. **-dia**, ZOOLOGY a branched blind-ended nephridium containing flame cells, as in flatworms, or solenocytes, as in some annelids **L19.** **protoˈpectin** *noun* (BIOCHEMISTRY) = PECTOSE **E20.** **protopeˈtroleum** *noun* an intermediate product in the formation of petroleum from organic debris **E20.** **protophyll** *noun* (BOTANY) in clubmosses, a leaflike structure produced on the upper surface of a protocorm **L19.** **protophyte** *noun* (BOTANY) any of the primitive unicellular plantlike organisms constituting the subkingdom Protophyta, now usu. classed with protozoa among the Protista (cf. PROTIST) **M19.** **protoplanet** *noun* (ASTRONOMY) a large diffuse body of matter in a solar or stellar orbit, postulated as a preliminary stage in the evolution of a planet **M20.** **protoˈplanetary** *adjective* of, pertaining to, or of the nature of a protoplanet **M20.** **protopod** *adjective* (ENTOMOLOGY) designating or pertaining to an embryonic or larval insect lacking abdominal segmentation and limbs **E20.** **protoˈpodite** *noun* (ZOOLOGY) the basal joint of a crustacean limb **L19.** **protoˈporcelain** *noun* a form of early pottery resembling porcelain but lacking its translucent qualities, *esp.* a porcellaneous ceramic ware produced in ancient China under the Han dynasty **M20.** **protoporˈphyria** *noun* (MEDICINE) a condition characterized by the accumulation of protoporphyrin in the red blood cells **M20.** **protoˈporphyrin** *noun* (CHEMISTRY) a porphyrin of formula $C_{34}H_{34}N_4O_4$ (of which there are fifteen isomers) in which the porphin nucleus has four methyl, two vinyl, and two propanoic acid substituents, *esp.* (more fully ***protoporphyrin IX***) the isomer which occurs widely in living organisms, mainly as haem **E20.** **protoˈpresbyter** *noun* = PROTOPOPE **L19.** **Proto-Roˈmance** *adjective & noun* (pertaining to or designating) the partly reconstructed language developed from Vulgar Latin from which the Romance languages derive; (pertaining to) Vulgar Latin: **M20.** **proto-scienˈtific** *adjective* of or pertaining to primitive science, or an early stage in scientific development **M20.** **protoˈscolex** *noun*, pl. **-lices** /-lɪsiːz/, MEDICINE & ZOOLOGY a vesicle formed from a hydatid cyst and capable of developing into a tapeworm scolex **L20.** **protostele** *noun* (BOTANY) a simple type of stele, found esp. in the roots of seed plants, in which a central core of xylem is surrounded by a cylinder of phloem **E20.** **protostelic** /-ˈstiːlɪk/ *adjective* pertaining to or of the nature of a protostele **E20.** **protostar** *noun* (ASTRONOMY) a contracting mass of gas representing a star in an early stage of formation, before nucleosynthesis has begun **M20.** **protoˈstellar** *adjective* (ASTRONOMY) of, pertaining to, or of the nature of a protostar or protostars **L20.** **protostome** *noun* (ZOOLOGY) a metazoan organism whose mouth develops from the primary embryonic opening or blastopore, as an annelid, a mollusc, an arthropod **M20.** **prototroch** *noun* [Greek *trokhos* wheel] ZOOLOGY a ciliated ridge encircling the body of a trochosphere larva in front of the mouth **L19.** **prototyˈpographer** *noun* (***a***) the earliest printer; (***b***) a chief printer: **M17.** **protovirus** *noun* (BIOLOGY) a body of genetic material, esp. RNA, which cannot reproduce but from which a virus or infective particle may arise under certain circumstances **L20.** **protoˈxylem** *noun* (BOTANY) the part of the primary xylem which is formed first, found in plant tissue which is still elongating **L19.**

protoactinium *noun* var. of PROTACTINIUM.

protoceratops /prəʊtə(ʊ)ˈsɛrətɒps/ *noun.* **E20.**
[mod. Latin genus name, formed as PROTO- + TRI)CERATOPS.]
A small quadrupedal dinosaur of of the late Cretaceous period, having a bony frill above the neck and probably ancestral to triceratops.

protocol /ˈprəʊtəkɒl/ *noun & verb.* **LME.**
[Old French *prothocole* (mod. *protocole*) from medieval Latin *protocollum* from Greek *prōtokollon* first leaf of a volume, flyleaf, formed as PROTO- + *kolla* glue.]
▸ **A** *noun.* **1** The original note or minute of a transaction, agreement, etc., drawn up by a recognized public official and duly attested, forming the legal authority for any subsequent deed, agreement, etc., based on it. Also, more fully ***protocol book*** (chiefly *Scot.*, *obsolete* exc. *Hist.*), a book or register recording such a note or minute. **LME.**
2 *spec.* The original draft of a diplomatic document, esp. of the terms of a treaty agreed to in conference and signed by the parties concerned. **L17.** ▸**b** *Hist.* The first sheet of a roll of papyrus, bearing the manufacturer's official mark; such a mark. **L19.** ▸**c** PHILOSOPHY. A statement forming an essential part of a person's description of something experienced or perceived; a basic statement. Freq. *attrib.* **M20.**
3 A formal or official statement of a transaction or proceeding; *spec.* a record of (esp. scientific) experimental observations. **L19.**
4 a In France and some other countries, the formulary of the etiquette to be observed by the head of State in official ceremonies and relations with representatives of other States; a department concerned with such etiquette. **L19.** ▸**b** Official, esp. diplomatic, procedure and etiquette in affairs of State and diplomatic relations; the observance of this. **M20.** ▸**c** *gen.* The accepted or established code of procedure, rules, formalities, etc., of any group, organization, etc. **M20.**
5 Each of the official formulae used at the beginning and end of a charter, papal bull, or other similar instrument. **E20.**
6 COMPUTING & TELECOMMUNICATIONS. A (usu. standardized) set of rules governing the exchange of data between given devices, or its transmission via a given communications channel. **M20.**
▸ **B** *verb.* Infl. **-ll-**, ***-l-**.
1 *verb trans.* Set down as a protocol; record in a protocol. **LME.**
2 *verb intrans.* Draw up a protocol or protocols. **M19.**
■ **protocolar** *adjective* (*rare*) of, pertaining to, or characterized by (a) protocol or protocols; formal, ceremonial: **E20.** **protoˈcolic** *adjective* (*rare*) of or pertaining to (a) protocol or protocols **M19.** **protocolist** *noun* a person who draws up a protocol or protocols **E19.** **protocolize** *verb* (***a***) *verb intrans.* = PROTOCOL *verb* 2; (***b***) *verb trans.* = PROTOCOL *verb* 1: **M19.**

protocolaire /prɔtɔkɔlɛːr/ *adjective.* **M20.**
[French, from *protocole* PROTOCOL *noun* + *-aire*.]
Characterized by a strict regard for protocol; formal, ceremonial.

protoctist /prəʊˈtɒktɪst/ *noun.* **M20.**
[from mod. Latin *Protoctista* pl. (see below), from Greek *prōtista* (see PROTIST).]
BIOLOGY. A member of the kingdom or large grouping Protoctista, being either synonymous with the protists or equivalent to the protists together with their multicellular descendants.

protogenic /prəʊtəˈdʒɛnɪk/ *adjective*¹. **M19.**
[from PROTO- + -GENIC: cf. Greek *prōtogenēs* first-born, primeval.]
Formed first or earliest, original, primary, primeval.

protogenic /prəʊtəˈdʒɛnɪk/ *adjective*². **M20.**
[from PROTON + -GENIC.]
CHEMISTRY. Of a substance, molecular species, etc.: able to provide a hydrogen atom for protonation; protic, proton-donating. Opp. PROTOPHILIC.

protogynous /prəʊˈtɒdʒɪnəs/ *adjective.* **L19.**
[from PROTO- + -GYNOUS: cf. *proterogynous*.]
BOTANY & ZOOLOGY. Of a hermaphrodite flower or animal: in which the female organs come to maturity before the male. Opp. PROTANDROUS.
■ **protogyny** *noun* the condition of being protogynous **L19.**

protolithic /prəʊtəˈlɪθɪk/ *adjective.* L19.
[from PROTO- + -LITHIC after *neolithic* etc.]
ARCHAEOLOGY. **1** Designating a type of primitive stone implement having minimal shaping, formerly in use amongst the Seri Indians in Mexico. L19.
2 Designating or pertaining to an early stage of stone implements. M20.

protologue /ˈprəʊtəlɒg/ *noun.* Also **-log**. E20.
[from PROTO- + -LOGUE.]
TAXONOMY. The description and other details accompanying the first publication of the taxonomic name of a plant or animal.

protology /prəʊˈtɒlədʒi/ *noun.* E17.
[from PROTO- + -LOGY.]
†**1** A preface. *rare.* E–M17.
2 The study of or enquiry into origins. E20.
■ **protoˈlogical** *adjective* M20.

protolytic /prəʊtəˈlɪtɪk/ *adjective.* M20.
[from PROTON + -LYTIC.]
CHEMISTRY. Designating a reaction or process in solution involving the transfer of a proton from one molecule to another, one usu. being of the solvent; (of a solvent) in which such reactions occur.
■ **proˈtolysis** *noun*, pl. **-lyses**, a protolytic reaction, proton transfer in solution M20.

protoma /ˈprɒtəmə/ *noun.* Pl. **-mae** /-miː/, **-mas**. M20.
[mod. Latin, formed as PROTOME.]
= PROTOME.

protomartyr /prəʊtəʊˈmɑːtə/ *noun.* LME.
[from PROTO- + MARTYR *noun.*]
The first martyr in a cause; *spec.* (***a***) the first Christian martyr, St Stephen; (***b***) the first Christian martyr of a particular country.

protome /ˈprɒtəmi/ *noun.* M18.
[Greek *protomē* the foremost or upper part of a thing, from *protoenein* cut off in front.]
Chiefly CLASSICAL ANTIQUITIES. A bust; a piece of sculpture representing the forepart of an animal.

protomer /ˈprəʊtəmə/ *noun.* E20.
[from PROTO- + -MER: in sense 1 extracted from PROTOTROPIC; in sense 2 perh. infl. by *protein*.]
1 CHEMISTRY. A prototropic tautomer. E20.
2 BIOCHEMISTRY. Each of the protein subunits of which an oligomeric protein is built up. M20.
■ **protoˈmeric** *adjective* E20.

proton /ˈprəʊtɒn/ *noun.* L19.
[from Greek *prōton* neut. sing. of *prōtos* first: see -ON.]
1 BIOLOGY. = ANLAGE. Now *rare* or *obsolete.* L19.
2 PHYSICS & CHEMISTRY. A stable subatomic particle, occurring in all atomic nuclei, which is a baryon with a positive charge equal and opposite to that of the electron and a mass 1836 times the electron's mass (symbol p); in chemical reactions etc., a hydrogen ion (H^+). E20.
Comb.: **proton accelerator** a particle accelerator designed to accelerate protons; **proton-accepting** *adjective* = PROTOPHILIC; **proton acceptor** CHEMISTRY a protophilic species; **proton-donating** *adjective* = PROTOGENIC *adjective*[2]; **proton donator**, **proton donor** a protogenic species; **proton gradiometer** a vertical rod with a proton magnetometer at each end, used to measure local variations in the strength of the earth's magnetic field due to features just below the ground; **proton magnetometer**, **proton-precession magnetometer** a magnetometer in which magnetic field strength is determined from the Larmor frequency of protons in a sample of water; **proton synchrotron** a synchrotron designed to accelerate protons.

protonate /ˈprəʊt(ə)neɪt/ *verb.* M20.
[from prec. + -ATE[3].]
CHEMISTRY. **1** *verb trans.* Transfer a proton to (a molecule, group, atom, etc.), so that a coordinate bond is formed. M20.
2 *verb intrans.* Receive or accept a proton. M20.
■ **protoˈnation** *noun* the process of transferring or adding a proton M20.

protonema /prəʊtəˈniːmə/ *noun.* Pl. **-mata** /-mətə/. M19.
[from PROTO- + Greek *nēma* thread.]
BOTANY. A primitive structure in bryophytes which arises from the germination of a spore and from which the mature plant develops, in mosses usu. consisting of branched green filaments.
■ **protonemal** *adjective* L19. **protonematal** *adjective* E20.

protonic /prəʊˈtɒnɪk/ *adjective.* E20.
[from PROTON + -IC.]
1 Of, pertaining to, or characteristic of a proton or protons. E20.
2 CHEMISTRY. (Of an acid, solvent, etc.) protogenic, protic; (of a hydrogen atom in a molecule) able to take part in protonation. E20.

protonmotive /prəʊtɒnˈməʊtɪv/ *adjective.* M20.
[from PROTON + MOTIVE *adjective*, after *electromotive*.]
PHYSICS & BIOCHEMISTRY. Of, pertaining to, or characterized by the movement of protons in response to an electric potential gradient. Chiefly in ***protonmotive force*** below.
protonmotive force a force, analogous to the electromotive force, acting on the proton gradient across cell membranes and equal to the sum of the electric potential difference and the pH gradient.

protonosphere /prəʊˈtɒnəsfɪə/ *noun.* M20.
[from PROTON + -O- + -SPHERE.]
= GEOCORONA.
■ **protonospheric** /-ˈsferɪk/ *adjective* L20.

protonotary /prəʊtəˈnəʊt(ə)ri, prəˈtɒnət(ə)ri/ *noun.* Also **prothonotary** /prəʊθəˈnəʊt(ə)ri, prəˈθɒnət(ə)ri/. LME.
[medieval Latin *protonotarius*, *protho-* from Greek *prōtonotarios*, formed as PROTO- + *notarios* NOTARY.]
1 A principal notary or chief clerk of a court of law; *spec.* (***a***) *Hist.* the holder of that office in the Byzantine court; †(***b***) in England, the chief clerk or registrar in the Courts of Chancery, of Common Pleas, and of the King's or Queen's Bench; (***c***) in some Australian States, a chief administrative officer of a court. LME.
2 ROMAN CATHOLIC CHURCH. More fully ***Protonotary Apostolical***. A member of the college of twelve (formerly seven) prelates who register papal acts and keep records of beatifications and canonizations. Formerly also, (a title of) a papal envoy. L15.
3 Chiefly *Hist.* A chief secretary at the court of any of various countries. E16.
Comb.: **prothonotary warbler** an American wood warbler, *Protonotarius citrea*, with a deep yellow head and breast, green back, and blue-grey wings.
■ **protonotaryship** *noun* the office or position of a protonotary M16.

protopapas /prəʊtəˈpapəs/ *noun.* L17.
[ecclesiastical Greek *prōtopapas* chief priest, formed as PROTO- + *papas* priest.]
= PROTOPOPE.

protopathic /prəʊtəˈpaθɪk/ *adjective.* M19.
[from PROTO- + Greek *pathos* suffering, feeling, disease + -IC.]
1 MEDICINE. Of a disease: primary. M19.
2 PHYSIOLOGY. Involving the discrimination of relatively coarse sensory (esp. cutaneous) stimuli, chiefly heat, cold, and pain. E20.

protophilic /prəʊtəˈfɪlɪk/ *adjective.* M20.
[from PROTON + -PHILIC.]
CHEMISTRY. Of a substance, molecular species, etc.: able to receive a hydrogen atom in protonation, tending to remove protons, proton-accepting. Opp. PROTOGENIC *adjective*[2].

protoplasm /ˈprəʊtə(ʊ)plaz(ə)m/ *noun.* M19.
[German *Protoplasma*, formed as PROTO- + Greek *plasma* PLASM.]
BIOLOGY. The complex translucent colourless colloidal material comprising the living part of a cell, including the membrane-bound cytoplasm, nucleus, and other organelles (but excluding food particles, secretions, large vacuoles, etc.).
■ **protoˈplasmal** *adjective* (*rare*) L19. **protoplasˈmatic** *adjective* M19. **protoˈplasmic** *adjective* M19.

protoplast /ˈprəʊtəplast, -plɑːst/ *noun.* M16.
[French *protoplaste* or late Latin *protoplastus* first created being (Adam) from Greek *prōtoplastos*, formed as PROTO- + *plastos* formed, moulded, from *plassein* to form, to mould. In branch II *-plast* app. taken as repr. Greek *plastēs* former, moulder.]
▶**I 1** The first formed, fashioned, or created thing or being of its kind; the original, the archetype; *spec.* (***a***) THEOLOGY the first created member of the human race; (***b***) the first example, the original, the model; †(***c***) the first person of a line or series. M16.
2 BIOLOGY. The protoplasm of a single cell; *esp.* a living plant or bacterial cell whose cell wall has been removed. L19.
▶**II 3** The first fashioner or creator of a thing. E17.
■ **protoˈplastic** *adjective* (***a***) of the nature of a protoplast; first formed; original, archetypal; (***b***) BIOLOGY = PROTOPLASMIC: M17.

protopope /ˈprəʊtə(ʊ)pəʊp/ *noun.* M17.
[Russian *protopop*, formed as PROTOPAPAS.]
In the Orthodox Church, a chief priest.

protopterus /prəʊˈtɒpt(ə)rəs/ *noun.* M19.
[mod. Latin *Protopterus* (see below), from PROTO- + Greek *pteron* wing, fin.]
Either of two African lungfish, *Protopterus annectens* and *P. aethiopicus*. Now chiefly as mod. Latin genus name.

protospathaire /prəʊtəspəˈθɛː/ *noun.* Also **-taire** /-ˈtɛː/, (in Latin form) **-tharius** /-ˈθɛːrɪəs/, pl. **-rii** /-rɪʌɪ, -riːː/. L18.
[French from medieval Latin *protospatharius* from Byzantine Greek *prōtospatharios*, formed as PROTO- + *spatharios* swordsman.]
Hist. The captain of the imperial guards in ancient Byzantium.

prototherian /prəʊtə(ʊ)ˈθɪərɪən/ *adjective & noun.* L19.
[from mod. Latin *Prototheria* (see below), formed as PROTO- + Greek *thērion* wild animal: see -AN.]
ZOOLOGY. (Pertaining to or designating) an animal of the infraclass Prototheria of mammals, which comprises the order Monotremata and related fossil forms.

protothetic /prəʊtə(ʊ)ˈθetɪk/ *noun.* M20.
[German *Protothetik*, from PROTO- + Greek *thetikos* fit for placing, positive, from *thet-* pa. ppl stem of *tithenai* set, place: see -IC.]
PHILOSOPHY. A type of propositional calculus forming the basis of a system of logic involving functional variables and quantifiers.
■ Also **protothetics** *noun* (*rare*) M20.

prototroph /ˈprəʊtətrəʊf/ *noun.* M20.
[from next: cf. AUXOTROPH.]
BIOLOGY. A bacterium or fungus which can grow without artificial supplementary nutrients, *esp.* one of a mutant strain which has reverted to the wild-type condition.
■ **prototrophy** *noun* the state of being a prototroph M20.

prototrophic /prəʊtə(ʊ)ˈtrəʊfɪk, -ˈtrɒf-/ *adjective.* E20.
[from PROTO- + -TROPHIC.]
BIOLOGY. **1** = AUTOTROPHIC. E20.
2 That is a prototroph. M20.
■ **prototrophically** *adverb* L20.

prototropy /prəʊˈtɒtrəpi, ˈprəʊtətrəʊpi/ *noun.* E20.
[from PROTO(N + -TROPY.]
CHEMISTRY. Tautomerism in which the forms differ only in the position of a proton; migration of a proton from one part of a molecule to another.
■ **prototropic** /-ˈtrəʊpɪk, -ˈtrɒpɪk/ *adjective* of, pertaining to, or exhibiting prototropy E20.

prototype /ˈprəʊtətʌɪp/ *noun.* Also (earlier) in Greek form †**-typon**. L16.
[French, or late Latin *prototypus* from Greek *prōtotupos*, (neut. *-on*): see PROTO-, -TYPE.]
1 The first or primary type of something; the original of which a copy, imitation, representation, derivative, or improved form exists or is made; a pattern, a model, an archetype. L16. ▶**b** *spec.* That of which a model is a copy on a reduced scale. E20.
2 ELECTRONICS. A basic filter network with specified cut-off frequencies, from which other networks may be derived to obtain sharper cut-offs, constancy of characteristic impedance with frequency, etc. Freq. ***attrib.*** E20.
3 A trial model or preliminary version of a vehicle, machine, etc. M20.

> 🕮 **1** K. CLARK They look at flowers and trees not only as delightful objects, but as prototypes of the divine.
> **3** L. T. C. ROLT The derivation of these later . . locomotives from this little prototype.

■ **prototypal** *adjective* of the nature of or constituting a prototype; of or pertaining to a prototype; archetypal: L17. **prototypic** /-ˈtɪpɪk/ *adjective* prototypal L19. **protoˈtypical** *adjective* prototypal M17. **protoˈtypically** *adverb* L19. **prototyping** *noun* the design, construction, or use of a prototype M20.

protoxide /prəʊˈtɒksʌɪd/ *noun.* Now *rare* or *obsolete.* E19.
[from PROTO- + OXIDE.]
CHEMISTRY. The oxide of an element which contains the smallest proportion of oxygen.

protozoa *noun* pl. of PROTOZOON.

protozoan /prəʊtəˈzəʊən/ *noun & adjective.* M19.
[formed as PROTOZOON + -AN.]
▶**A** *noun.* Orig., an animal organism having a simple or primitive form of organization. Now *spec.* any usu. unicellular and microscopic eukaryote of the subkingdom Protozoa, including amoebas, ciliates, foraminiferans, etc. M19.
▶**B** *adjective.* Of, pertaining to, or characteristic of a protozoan. L19.
¶ Freq. regarded as constituting an animal phylum (and formerly including sponges, coelenterates, etc.) but including forms also classified as plants.
■ **protozoal** *adjective* of or pertaining to protozoans; (of a disease) caused by a parasitic protozoan: L19.

protozoic /prəʊtəˈzəʊɪk/ *adjective.* In sense 1 also **P-**. M19.
[In sense 1 from PROTO- + Greek *zōē* life + -IC; in sense 2 formed as prec. + -IC.]
†**1** GEOLOGY. **a** = PROTEROZOIC. Only in M19. ▶**b** = PALAEOZOIC. Only in M19.
2 ZOOLOGY & MEDICINE. = PROTOZOAL *adjective.* M19.

protozoology /prəʊtəʊzəʊˈɒlədʒi, -zuː-/ *noun.* E20.
[from PROTOZOA + -OLOGY.]
The branch of zoology that deals with protozoa.
■ ˌ**protozooˈlogical** *adjective* E20. **protozoologist** *noun* E20.

protozoon /prəʊtəˈzəʊɒn/ *noun.* Pl. **-zoa** /-ˈzəʊə/. M19.
[from PROTO- + Greek *zōion* animal.]
ZOOLOGY. = PROTOZOAN *noun*. Usu. in *pl.*

protract /prəˈtrakt/ *noun.* M16.
[Latin *protractus* a prolongation, from *protract-*: see next. In sense 3 from the verb.]
†**1** Extension or prolongation of time; delay, procrastination. M16–M17.
†**2** A delineation, a drawing. *rare.* Only in L16.
3 A protracted religious meeting. *US colloq.* E20.

protract /prəˈtrakt/ *verb.* M16.
[Latin *protract-* pa. ppl stem of *protrahere* prolong, defer, (in medieval Latin) draw, portray, formed as PRO-[1] + *trahere* draw. Cf. PORTRAY *verb*.]
▶**I** †**1** *verb trans.* Extend or prolong (time) so as to cause delay; waste (time). M16–M18.

2 *verb trans.* Extend (an action etc.) in time; cause to continue or last longer; prolong. M16.
†**3** *verb trans.* Put off, defer, or postpone (an action). M16–E19.
4 *verb intrans. & trans.* Delay. Long *rare* or *obsolete.* E17.
5 *verb trans.* Extend (a thing) in space or position. M17.

1 W. ROBERTSON This they did merely to protract time. **2** ALDOUS HUXLEY Long notes, a chord repeated, protracted . . effortlessly soaring on and on. H. A. L. FISHER If you wish to protract your life. A. J. CRONIN He could protract his investigation no longer. **3** GIBBON To prevent, or at least to protract, his ruin. **5** SMOLLETT To save his country, and protract his blaze Of glory, farther still!

► **II 6** Draw, represent by a drawing; *spec.* draw (a ground-plan) to scale; plot out. Cf. PROTRACTION 1. M16.

6 E. HULL We protract to a true scale the outlines of . . the British Isles.

■ **protracted** *adjective* that is protracted; *esp.* of excessive length or duration: L17. **protractedly** *adverb* M19. **protractedness** *noun* L19. †**protractive** *adjective* characterized by or tending to protraction L16–E19.

protractile /prəˈtraktʌɪl, -tɪl/ *adjective.* E19.
[from prec. + -ILE: cf. CONTRACTILE.]
ZOOLOGY. Able to be lengthened out or extended.

protraction /prəˈtrakʃ(ə)n/ *noun.* LME.
[Old & mod. French, or late Latin *protractio(n-)*, formed as PROTRACT *verb*: see -ION.]
► **I 1** †**a** The drawing or writing of figures, letters, etc. Only in LME. ►**b** The action of drawing a ground-plan, esp. of a piece of land, to scale. E17. ►**c** A chart or plan drawn to scale; a survey. M17.
► **II 2** The action or an act of extending something, esp. in time; the state of being extended, esp. in time. M16.
3 The action or process of drawing forth or out. *rare.* L17.

protractor /prəˈtraktə/ *noun.* E17.
[from PROTRACT *verb* + -OR.]
1 A person who protracts something, esp. in time. Now *rare* or *obsolete.* E17.
2 An instrument, usu. in the form of a graduated semicircle, for measuring angles. M17.
3 ANATOMY. A muscle whose contraction protracts or extends a limb or organ; an extensor. Also ***protractor muscle.*** Now *rare.* M19.

protreptic /prəˈtrɛptɪk/ *adjective & noun.* M17.
[As adjective from Greek *protreptikos* instructive; as noun from Latin *protrepticon, -um* from Greek *protreptikon* use as noun of neut. of *protreptikos.*]
► **A** *adjective.* Directive, instructive, didactic. M17.
► **B** *noun.* A book, writing, or speech intended to exhort or instruct; an exhortation, an instruction. M17.
■ **protreptical** *adjective* = PROTREPTIC *adjective* M17.

protriptyline /prəʊˈtrɪptɪliːn/ *noun.* M20.
[from PRO(PYL + TRI- + HE)PTYL + -INE⁵.]
PHARMACOLOGY. A tricyclic antidepressant, $C_{19}H_{21}N$.

protruberance /prəˈtruːb(ə)r(ə)ns/ *noun.* E19.
[Alt., prob. infl. by next.]
A protuberance.

protrude /prəˈtruːd/ *verb.* E17.
[Latin *protrudere*, formed as PRO-¹ + *trudere* to thrust.]
†**1** *verb trans.* Thrust forward (a detached body); push or drive (a thing) onward. E17–E19.
2 *verb intrans.* Extend beyond or above a surface; stick out; project. Also foll. by *from.* E17.
3 *verb trans.* Thrust out (an organ or part) into a projecting position; cause to stick out or project. M17. ►**b** *fig.* Obtrude. M19.

1 E. BANCROFT The arrow is . . protruded through the cavity of the reed. **2** P. G. WODEHOUSE His eyes . . protrude slightly. J. G. BALLARD A pair of water-skis protruded from a cupboard. A. BROOKNER The tip of his tongue protruding from his mouth. **3** T. R. JONES From each tube a polyp is protruded. C. H. SISSON Where the Habsburgs had protruded their lips You had pinched your nostrils. **b** THACKERAY Critics . . who protrude their nonsense upon the town.

protrusible /prəˈtruːsɪb(ə)l/ *adjective. rare.* M19.
[formed as PROTRUSIVE + -IBLE.]
Able to be protruded.

protrusile /prəˈtruːsʌɪl/ *adjective.* M19.
[formed as PROTRUSIVE + -ILE.]
Esp. of an organ or part: adapted or able to be protruded.

protrusion /prəˈtruːʒ(ə)n/ *noun.* M17.
[medieval Latin *protrusio(n-)*, from Latin *protrus-* pa. ppl stem of *protrudere* PROTRUDE: see -ION.]
1 The action or fact of protruding; the fact or condition of being protruded. M17.
2 That which protrudes; a thing that is protruded. E18.

protrusive /prəˈtruːsɪv/ *adjective.* L17.
[from Latin *protrus-* (see prec.) + -IVE, after *extrude, extrusive,* etc.]
Tending to protrude; able to be protruded; protruding.
■ **protrusively** *adverb* M19. **protrusiveness** *noun* L19.

protuberance /prəˈtjuːb(ə)r(ə)ns/ *noun.* M17.
[from next: see -ANCE.]
1 That which is protuberant; a rounded projection or swelling. M17.
2 The quality or condition of being protuberant. L17.
1 solar protuberance = PROMINENCE 4.
■ Also **protuberancy** *noun* M17.

protuberant /prəˈtjuːb(ə)r(ə)nt/ *adjective.* M17.
[Late Latin *protuberant-* pres. ppl stem of *protuberare*, formed as PRO-¹ + *tuber* a swelling: see -ANT¹.]
1 Bulging or swelling out beyond the surrounding surface; prominent. M17.
†**2** Moulded or formed in the round or in relief. Only in L17.

1 JOHN PHILLIPS The protuberant northern base of the dome of Vesuvius. N. SHERRY A stranger . . with protuberant eyes.

■ **protuberantly** *adverb* M19.

protuberate /prəˈtjuːb(ə)reɪt/ *verb. rare.* L16.
[Late Latin *protuberat-* pa. ppl stem of *protuberare*: see PROTUBERANT, -ATE³.]
1 *verb intrans.* Be or become protuberant. L16.
2 *verb trans.* Make protuberant. Chiefly as ***protuberated*** *ppl adjective.* L17.
■ †**protuberation** *noun* a protuberance E17–E18.

protyle /ˈprəʊtʌɪl/ *noun. obsolete* exc. *Hist.* Also **prothyl(e)** /ˈprəʊθʌɪl/. L19.
[Irreg. formed as PROTO- + Greek *hulē* matter, HYLE.]
SCIENCE. A hypothetical original undifferentiated matter from which the chemical elements were supposed to derive.

protypon /ˈprɒtɪpɒn/ *noun. rare.* Pl. **-pa** /-pə/. E17.
[Greek *protupon*, formed as PRO-² + *tupos* TYPE *noun.*]
A sculpture, moulding, etc., in bas-relief.

proud /praʊd/ *adjective & adverb.*
[Late Old English *prūd* (also *prūt*) = Old Norse *pruðr* from Old French *prud, prod,* nom. *pruz, proz, prouz* (mod. *preux*) valiant, gallant from Proto-Romance from Latin *prodesse* be of value, be good, from *prod* var. of *pro* (see PRO-¹) + *esse* be.]
► **A** *adjective.* **I 1** Having a high, esp. an excessively high, opinion of one's own worth or importance; having inordinate self-esteem. Also, having a sense of what befits, is due to, or is worthy of oneself or one's position; characterized by self-respect. (Foll. by *of.*) LOE.
2 Feeling greatly honoured, pleased or satisfied by something which or someone who does one credit, taking pride in something; (now *dial.*) gratified, glad. (Foll. by *of, to do.*) ME.
3 Arising from or showing pride; expressive of pride. ME.
4 That is a ground or cause of pride; of which one is or may be proud. ME.
5 Of a person, a person's name, etc.: of exalted status or rank, noble. *poet.* ME.
6 Of a thing: stately, magnificent, imposing, splendid. ME.
7 Valiant, brave. Now *spec.* (of an animal) spirited, fearlessly vigorous, moving with force and dignity. Chiefly *poet.* ME.

1 D. H. LAWRENCE The majority . . were much too proud to ask. DAY LEWIS Proud and poor, the Anglo-Irish exalted their snobbery into a tribal mystique. ***house-proud*** etc. **2** T. HARDY I'm proud to say . . that he's stole nothing. M. K. RAWLINGS I'd be proud to eat breakfast before I go. D. ACHESON We were proud of her. M. FORSTER She was proud of being able to comfort him when no one else could. ***proud as Punch***: see PUNCH *noun*⁴ 3. **3** ALDOUS HUXLEY A proud, defiant lifting of the chin. T. HEGGEN Her forehead was high and proud. **4** W. S. CHURCHILL One of the proudest titles that history can bestow.

► **II 8** Of (esp. injured) tissue: swollen, overgrown. Chiefly in ***proud flesh*** below. LME.
9 Of the sea, a stream, etc.: high, strong, in flood. M16.
10 Of a plant, crop, etc.: luxuriant in growth, esp. out of season. Of sap: rising vigorously. L16.
11 Sexually excited; lascivious. Now only (*obsolete* exc. *Canad. dial.*), in oestrus. L16.
12 Projecting; *spec.* slightly raised or projecting from a surface (foll. by *of*). E19.
8 proud flesh excess granulation tissue formed around a healing wound.
Comb.: **proud-heart** *adjective* (*poet.*) proud-hearted; **proud-hearted** *adjective* having a proud heart or spirit, proud, haughty.
► **B** *adverb.* Proudly, in a proud manner. ME.
do a person proud, do oneself proud: see DO *verb.*
■ **proudful** *adjective* (now *dial.*) full of pride, proud ME. **proudish** *adjective* somewhat proud, rather proud M17. **proudly** *adverb* LOE. **proudness** *noun* LME.

Proustian /ˈpruːstɪən/ *noun & adjective.* E20.
[from *Proust* (see below) + -IAN.]
► **A** *noun.* An admirer or imitator of the French novelist, essayist, and critic Marcel Proust (1871–1922). E20.
► **B** *adjective.* Of, pertaining to, or characteristic of Proust, his writings, or his style. E20.

proustite /ˈpruːstʌɪt/ *noun.* M19.
[from J. L. *Proust* (1754–1826), French chemist + -ITE¹.]
MINERALOGY. Silver arsenic sulphide, a scarlet hemimorphic mineral crystallizing in the hexagonal system. Also called ***ruby silver, light red silver ore.***

Prov. *abbreviation.*
1 Provençal.
2 Proverbs (in the Bible).
3 Province.

provable /ˈpruːvəb(ə)l/ *adjective.* Also **proveable.** LME.
[Old French *pro(u)vable* from Latin *probabilis*: see PROBABLE. Later partly from PROVE *verb* + -ABLE.]
1 Able to be proved; of which the truth or validity can be established; demonstrable. LME.
†**2** Deserving acceptance or belief; plausible. LME–L16.
†**3** Deserving approval; commendable. M16.
■ **provaˈbility** *noun* E20. **provableness** *noun* (*rare*) L19. **provably** *adverb* LME.

provand /ˈprɒv(ə)nd/ *noun.* Now *arch. rare.* ME.
[Partly var. of PROVEND *noun*, partly from Middle Low German, Middle Dutch *provande* formed as PROVEND. Cf. PROVANT, PROVIANT.]
Provisions, provender, esp. for an army.

†**provang** *noun* see PROBANG.

provant /ˈprɒv(ə)nt/ *noun & adjective.* Now *arch. rare.* LME.
[App. from Middle Low German *provant* later form of *provande*: see PROVAND.]
► **A** *noun.* Provisions, provender. LME.
► **B** *attrib.* or as *adjective.* **1** Pertaining to or characteristic of an army's provisions; of inferior quality. L16.
†**2** Mercenary. E–M17.

†**prove** *noun* var. of PROOF *noun.*

prove /pruːv/ *verb.* Also †**preve.** Pa. t. **proved**; pa. pple **proved,** (orig. *Scot.*) **proven** /ˈpruːv(ə)n, ˈprəʊv-/. See also PROVED *adjective*, PROVEN *adjective.* ME.
[Old French *prover* (mod. *prouver*) from Latin *probare* test, approve, demonstrate, from *probus* good.]
1 *verb trans. & †intrans.* with *of.* Test the genuineness or qualities of, subject to a testing process, (chiefly *techn.*); *Scot.* taste. ME. ►**b** *verb trans.* MINING. Ascertain the position and extent of a deposit of coal, ore, a well, etc. Also foll. by *up.* M19. ►**c** *verb trans.* HOMOEOPATHY. Give (a drug) to healthy people to ascertain the symptoms it produces. M19.
2 *verb trans.* Find out by experience; experience, suffer. *arch.* ME.
†**3** *verb trans. & intrans.* Endeavour, strive, (*to do*). ME–M17.
4 *verb trans.* Establish or demonstrate the truth or existence of by evidence or argument. Foll. by simple obj., subord. clause, or obj. and compl. ME.
5 *verb intrans.* Turn out well; thrive; succeed. ME–L17.
6 *verb intrans.* With complement. Be shown or found by experience or trial to be (so and so); turn out *to be*; emerge incontrovertibly as; *arch.* become, grow. LME.
7 *verb trans.* Establish the genuineness and validity of; *spec.* obtain probate of (a will); *refl.* evince proof of one's abilities or prowess. LME.
†**8** *verb trans.* Approve of. LME–M16.
9 *verb trans.* TYPOGRAPHY. Take a proof impression of. L18.
10 *verb trans.* Test the correctness of (a calculation). E19. ►**b** *verb intrans.* Of a calculation: pass a test of correctness. *rare.* M19.
11 *verb intrans.* Of dough: become aerated by the fermentation of yeast prior to baking; rise. Of yeast: cause such aeration. M19.

1 *Proverb*: The exception proves the rule. **4** G. K. CHESTERTON Buck . . had proved himself a man of the strongest type. O. MANNING She will get a rise as soon as she proves she's worth it. T. CAPOTE To prove that they had not supplied their clients with the minimum protection. **6** M. MCCARTHY Dogwood, which proved, on closer examination, to have paper flowers. *New Scientist* It may prove of interest in . . banking and finance. J. GASKELL Cook, or her daughter, will prove mines of information. P. ACKROYD In this . . he was to prove mistaken. F. WELDON Those benefits . . prove to be no use to me at all. **7** *Observer* These new experimental drinks have still to prove themselves.

Phrases: ***fend and prove***: see FEND *verb* 1. **not proven** SCOTS LAW: a verdict that there is insufficient evidence to establish guilt (having the effect of a verdict of not guilty). **prove too much** pursue an argument too far; establish a proposition so inclusive as to be unhelpful.
With adverbs in specialized senses: **prove out** (*a*) *verb phr. trans.* establish as correct or workable; test exhaustively; (*b*) *verb phr. intrans.* prove to be correct or workable. **prove up** *verb phr. intrans. & trans.* (*N. Amer.*) show that one has fulfilled the legal conditions for taking up (a grant of government land), so that a patent may be issued; (see also sense 1b above).

proveable *adjective* var. of PROVABLE.

provect /prəˈvɛkt/ *verb trans.* LME.
[Latin *provect-* pa. ppl stem of *provehere*, formed as PRO-¹ + *vehere* carry.]
†**1** Carry forward or onward (*lit. & fig.*). LME–L18.
2 PHILOLOGY. Change or mutate (a consonant) according to Grimm's Law; *esp.* in Celtic languages, change (a

voiced consonant) into the corresponding voiceless consonant. Usu. in *pass.* Now *rare.* M19.

provection /prəˈvɛkʃ(ə)n/ *noun.* M17.
[Late Latin *provectio(n-)*, formed as prec.: see -ION.]
†**1** Proficiency; advancement. Only in M17.
2 PHILOLOGY. **a** The changing or mutating of consonants according to Grimm's Law; the mutation of voiced consonants in Celtic languages to corresponding voiceless consonants. M19. ▸**b** The transposition of the final letter of a word to a succeeding one (as in English *newt, nickname*). M19.

proved /pruːvd/ *adjective.* ME.
[from PROVE *verb* + -ED¹. Cf. PROVEN *adjective.*]
That has been proved; *esp.* (*a*) tried, tested; approved, trustworthy; (*b*) shown to be true, or to be as stated; demonstrated.
■ **provedly** /ˈpruːvɪdli/ *adverb* E17.

proved *verb pa. t. & pple* of PROVE *verb.*

proveditor /prəˈvɛdɪtə/ *noun.* Also **proveditore** /prəvɛdɪˈtɔːri/. M16.
[Italian †*proveditore* (now -*vv*-) provider, purveyor, from †*provedere* (now -*vv*-) from Latin *providere* PROVIDE.]
1 *Hist.* Any of various officers of the Venetian republic, as an adviser to the commander of a military force, the governor of a dependency. M16.
2 A purveyor, a caterer, a steward. Now *rare.* L16.

provedore /prɒvɪˈdɔː/ *noun.* Now *rare.* L16.
[Venetian Italian *providore* & other Romance agent-nouns, all from verbs repr. Latin *providere* PROVIDE.]
1 A commander, an overseer; *spec.* = PROVEDITOR 1. L16.
2 = PROVEDITOR 2. E17.

proven /ˈpruːv(ə)n, ˈprəʊv-/ *adjective.* Orig. *Scot.* M16.
[from PROVE *verb* + -EN⁶. Cf. PROVED *adjective.*]
That has been proved; shown to be successful.

> *Globe & Mail (Toronto)* Opportunity exists for a proven manager. M. PUZO A proven man . . he can make the operation go. D. CECIL Proven, everyday, homely pleasures.

■ **provenly** *adverb* L19.

proven *verb pa. pple*: see PROVE *verb.*

provenance /ˈprɒv(ə)nəns/ *noun.* L18.
[French, from *provenant* pres. pple of *provenir* come out from Latin *provenire*, formed as PRO-¹ + *venir* come: see -ANCE.]
1 The place of origin, derivation, or earliest known history, esp. of a work of art, manuscript, etc. L18.
2 A record of the ultimate derivation and passage of an item through its various owners. M20.
3 FORESTRY. The location in which tree seed is collected. Also, seed from a specific location. M20.
■ **provenanced** *adjective* provided with a record of provenance; established as to origin: M20.

Provençal /prɒvɑ̃ːˈsɑːl, -vɒn-, -ˈsal/ *adjective & noun.* L16.
[French from Latin *provincialis* PROVINCIAL: see PROVENCE.]
▸ **A** *adjective.* Of or pertaining to Provence, its inhabitants, or its language; characteristic of or associated with Provence. L16.
▸ **B** *noun.* **1** A native or inhabitant of Provence. E17.
2 The Romance language of Provence, closely related to French, Italian, and Catalan; the French dialect of Provence. M17.
■ **Provençalism** *noun* an idiom or form of expression typical of Provençal M20. **Provençalist** *noun* a student of or expert in Provençal language and literature M20.

provençale /prɒvɑ̃ːˈsɑːl, -vɒn-/ *adjective.* M20.
[French, fem. of prec.]
COOKERY. Denoting a dish cooked in a sauce made with tomatoes, garlic, and olive oil.

Provence /prɒˈvɑ̃ːs, *foreign* prəvɑ̃ːs/ *noun.* E18.
[French = a region and former province in SE France east of the Rhône, from Latin *provincia* PROVINCE, colloq. name for southern Gaul under Roman rule.]
Used *attrib.* to designate things originating in or obtained from Provence.
Provence rose the cabbage rose, *Rosa centifolia*, or a variety of it, esp. one bearing fragrant red flowers, (often confused with the Provins rose).

provend /ˈprɒv(ə)nd/ *noun & verb. arch.* ME.
[Old & mod. French *provende* from Proto-Romance alt. of Latin *praebenda* PREBEND. Cf. PROVAND, PROVANT, PROVIANT.]
▸ **A** *noun.* **1** = PREBEND 1. Also, the portion or allowance of food supplied to each inmate of a monastery. ME.
2 Provisions; provender, esp. for horses etc. ME.
▸†**B** *verb trans.* Supply with provender. L16–M18.
■ †**provendry** *noun* (*rare*) (*a*) = PREBEND *noun* 1, 2; (*b*) a prebendary: LME–E18.

provender /ˈprɒvɪndə/ *noun & verb.* ME.
[Old French *provendre* var. of *provende* PROVEND.]
▸ **A** *noun.* **1** Food, provisions; *esp.* dry food, as corn or hay, for horses etc.; animal fodder; (now *joc.*) food for human beings. ME.
†**2** A prebend. Only in LME.
▸ **B** *verb.* †**1** *verb trans.* Provide with a prebend or benefice. Only in LME.
2 *verb trans.* Provide (a horse etc.) with provender; fodder. L16.
3 *verb intrans.* Eat provender; feed *on. rare.* E19.

†**provene** *verb intrans. rare.* E16–M18.
[French *provenir* or Latin *provenire*: see PROVENANCE.]
Come as proceeds or produce, arise, (*from*).

provenience /prəˈviːnɪəns/ *noun.* Chiefly *US.* L19.
[from Latin *provenient-* pres. ppl stem of *provenire*: see PROVENANCE, -ENCE.]
= PROVENANCE.

proventriculus /prəʊvɛnˈtrɪkjʊləs/ *noun.* Pl. **-li** /-lʌɪ, -liː/. M19.
[from PRO-¹ + VENTRICULUS.]
ZOOLOGY. **1** The narrow glandular first region of a bird's stomach between the crop and the gizzard. M19.
2 A glandular bulge in the lower oesophagus of some mammals. *rare.* L19.
3 A thick-walled expansion of the oesophagus above the stomach of an insect, modified as a valve or as a muscular gizzard; in other invertebrates, a gizzard or gastric mill. L19.
■ **proventricular** *adjective* of or pertaining to a proventriculus M19.

†**provenue** *noun.* L15–M18.
[Old & mod. French *provenu* use as noun of pa. pple of *provenir*: see PROVENANCE.]
Produce, profit, revenue; a product.

prover /ˈpruːvə/ *noun.* LME.
[In branch I from PROVE *verb* + -ER¹; in branch II from Anglo-Norman *provour, pruvour* (= Anglo-Latin *probator*).]
▸ **I 1** A person who proves something. LME.
2 An instrument or apparatus for testing. M18.
3 HOMOEOPATHY. A healthy person on whom the effect of a drug is tested. M19.
▸ **II** †**4** = APPROVER *noun*² 1. LME–M18.

proverb /ˈprɒvəːb/ *noun & verb.* ME.
[Old & mod. French *proverbe* or Latin *proverbium*, formed as PRO-¹ + *verbum* word + *-ium* collect. suffix.]
▸ **A** *noun.* **1** A short pithy saying in common and recognized use; a concise sentence, often metaphorical or alliterative in form, held to express some general truth. In *pl.* (treated as *sing.*) (**P-**), the Book of Proverbs, a didactic poetic book of the Old Testament and Hebrew Scriptures, consisting of maxims ascribed to Solomon and others. ME.
2 A common word or phrase of contempt or reproach; a person to whom or thing to which such a phrase is applied; a byword; a thing that is proverbial or a matter of common talk. LME.
†**3** An oracular or enigmatic saying; an allegory, a parable. LME–M19.
4 A play, esp. a French play, of which a proverb is taken as the foundation of the plot. M18.
5 In *pl.* Any of various round games played with proverbs or popular sayings, *esp.* one in which a proverb is to be guessed by asking questions of a circle of players, whose answers must introduce in order each word of it. M19.
1 to a proverb *arch.* to an extent that has become proverbial; proverbially.
▸ **B** *verb trans.* **1** Utter in the form of a proverb; speak of proverbially; make a byword of. LME.
2 Provide with a proverb. *rare.* L16.

proverbial /prəˈvəːbɪəl/ *adjective & noun.* LME.
[Latin *proverbialis*, from *proverbium*: see prec., -AL¹.]
▸ **A** *adjective.* **1** Resembling, characteristic of, or of the nature of a proverb; expressed in a proverb or proverbs. LME.
2 Used or current as a proverb; well known, notorious. Also, familiar as (part of) a proverb or catch-phrase or as a stock character. L16.
†**3** Much given to using proverbs. *rare.* Only in M17.

> **1** SIR T. BROWNE Proverbs bee popular principles, yet is not all true that is proverbiall. P. GAY It is almost proverbial that every historian is something of a biographer.
> **2** R. FRAME They had to be handled with proverbial kid gloves. L. APPIGNANESI Her . . lust for experience was proverbial amongst her friends. S. BEDFORD A foreigner, a divorcée and of course the proverbial woman old enough to be his mother.

▸†**B** *noun.* **1** A person much given to using proverbs. Only in L16.
2 A proverbial saying, a proverb. L17–L18.
■ **proverbialism** *noun* a proverbial saying M19. **proverbialist** *noun* an originator, user, or recorder of proverbial sayings E18. **proverbiˈality** *noun* the quality of being proverbial M19. **proverbialize** *verb intrans.* make or use proverbs L17. **proverbially** *adverb* in a proverbial manner; to a proverbial degree: LME.

proviant /ˈprɒvɪənt/ *noun & adjective.* Now *arch. rare.* E17.
[German from Italian *provianda* app. alt. of *provenda* PROVEND. Cf. PROVAND, PROVANT.]
▸ **A** *noun.* Provisions, provender, esp. for an army. E17.
▸ **B** *attrib.* or as *adjective.* = PROVANT *adjective* 1. M17.

pro-vice-chancellor /prəʊvʌɪsˈtʃɑːns(ə)lə/ *noun.* M17.
[from PRO-¹ + VICE-CHANCELLOR.]
An assistant or deputy vice-chancellor of a university.

provide /prəˈvʌɪd/ *verb.* LME.
[Latin *providere*, formed as PRO-¹ + *videre* see.]
†**1** *verb trans.* Foresee. LME–M17.
2 *verb intrans.* Take appropriate measures in view of a possible event; make adequate preparation. Foll. by *for, against.* LME. ▸†**b** Prepare, get ready, (*to do*). LME–E18.
3 *verb trans.* Stipulate in a will, statute, etc., *that.* Formerly also *gen.*, take measures beforehand to ensure *that.* LME.
4 *verb trans.* Prepare, get ready, or arrange (something) beforehand. Now *rare.* LME.
5 *verb trans.* Equip or fit out with what is necessary for a certain purpose; furnish or supply with something. (Foll. by *with*, †*of*, double obj.). LME. ▸**b** ECCLESIASTICAL HISTORY. Appoint (an incumbent) *to* a vacant benefice; (of the Pope) appoint (a person as successor) *to* a benefice not yet vacant. LME.
6 *verb trans.* Supply or furnish for use; make available; yield, afford. LME.
7 *verb intrans.* Make provision for the maintenance of a person etc.; supply necessary resources. Foll. by *for.* L15.

> **2** *Times* Nature . . has not provided against assaults upon the hearing. G. F. KENNAN The document provided . . for the resumption of full diplomatic relations. **4** DRYDEN The wise Ant her wintry Store provides. **5** I. FLEMING The bed was provided with an electric blanket. S. CHITTY Augustus had provided them . . with . . some cakes. H. KOHUT The analyst provides the patient with the opportunity to become more objective about himself. **6** L. DEIGHTON He threw the towel into the basket provided. M. SARTON For most people their job . . provides a saving routine in time of stress. **7** T. S. ELIOT Mrs. Guzzard brought him up, And I provided for his education. B. BETTELHEIM Feeding and otherwise providing for the child. J. FENTON Reduced in circumstances, but well enough provided for.

■ **providable** *adjective* (*rare*) able to be provided L19.

provided /prəˈvʌɪdɪd/ *conjunction.* LME.
[pa. pple of PROVIDE: see -ED¹. Cf. PROVIDING *conjunction.*]
On the condition, supposition, or understanding that, or *that*; it being stipulated or arranged that or *that.*

> R. C. HUTCHINSON Allowed to talk . . provided that they did not raise their voices. M. KEANE Jane did not mind expense provided she got what she wanted.

providence /ˈprɒvɪd(ə)ns/ *noun.* LME.
[Old & mod. French, or Latin *providentia*, formed as next: see -ENCE.]
1 The action of providing; provision, preparation, arrangement. Chiefly in ***make providence***. *obsolete* exc. *dial.* LME.
2 Foresight; anticipation of and preparation for the future; prudent management; *spec.* thrift, frugality. LME.
3 The foreknowing and protective care and government of a spiritual power; *spec.* (*a*) that of God (more fully ***providence of God, divine providence***, etc.); (*b*) that of nature. Also (usu. **P-**) such a power, *spec.* God or nature, as providing this. LME.
4 An instance or act of divine intervention. Now chiefly in ***special providence***, a particular act of direct divine intervention. M16. ▸†**b** A disastrous accident or fatality, regarded as an act of God. M18–M19.

> **3** M. L. KING The Israelites, through the providence of God, crossed the Red Sea. A. HIGGINS Just then by a merciful stroke of providence, the doorbell rang. ***tempt Providence***: see TEMPT *verb.*

provident /ˈprɒvɪd(ə)nt/ *adjective.* LME.
[Latin *provident-* pres. ppl stem of *providere* PROVIDE: see -ENT.]
1 Foreseeing; exercising or characterized by foresight; making provision for the future. LME.
2 Economical; frugal, thrifty. L16.
1 Provident Club, **Provident Society** = ***Friendly Society*** s.v. FRIENDLY *adjective.*
■ **providently** *adverb* L15. **providentness** *noun* (*rare*) E18.

providential /prɒvɪˈdɛnʃ(ə)l/ *adjective.* M17.
[from PROVIDENCE, PROVIDENT + -IAL, after *evidence, evident, evidential*, etc.]
†**1** Of the nature of or characterized by foresight; provident, prudent. M17–M19.
2 Of, pertaining to, or ordained by divine providence; *esp.* (thought to be) brought about by special interposition of Providence, opportune, lucky. E18.

> **2** W. S. CHURCHILL At a critical moment . . providential succour arrived from an English fleet.

■ **providentialism** *noun* the belief that events are predestined (whether by God or by fate) E20. **providentially** *adverb* in a providential manner; by the ordination of divine providence, by special intervention of Providence, opportunely, luckily: E17. **providentialness** *noun* (*rare*) E18.

provider /prə'vʌɪdə/ *noun.* LME.
[from PROVIDE + -ER[1].]
A person who or thing which provides something; *spec.* the breadwinner of a family etc.
the lion's provider: see LION *noun.*

providing /prə'vʌɪdɪŋ/ *noun.* E17.
[from PROVIDE + -ING[1].]
1 The action of PROVIDE. E17.
2 That which is provided, a stock; *spec.* (*Scot.*) a stock of linen and household equipment assembled for a future independent home as by a bride. E19.

providing /prə'vʌɪdɪŋ/ *conjunction.* LME.
[pres. pple of PROVIDE: see -ING[2]. Cf. PROVIDED.]
Provided (*that*).

> *She* Agree to take her this year providing she will stay at home the next. *Nature* We intend to carry out further spectroscopy on the object, providing that it does not fade too quickly.

Provie /'prəʊvi, 'prɒvi/ *noun & adjective. colloq.* L20.
[Abbreviation of PROVISIONAL: see -IE. Cf. PROVO *noun*[2].]
A member of, of or pertaining to, the Provisional IRA.

province /'prɒvɪns/ *noun.* ME.
[Old & mod. French from Latin *provincia* charge, official duty, administration or region of a conquered territory, of unkn. origin.]
▶ **I 1** *gen.* A country, a territory, a district, a region; a part of the world or of a continent. Now *rare.* ME.
2 ROMAN HISTORY. A country or territory outside Italy, under Roman dominion, and administered by a governor from Rome. LME.
3 A principal administrative division of certain countries or States; a principal division of a kingdom or empire, *esp.* one historically or linguistically distinct; *spec.* †(*a*) an English shire; (*b*) *Hist.* any of the British colonies in N. America; (*c*) ***the Province***, Northern Ireland. LME.
4 ECCLESIASTICAL. **a** A district within the jurisdiction of an archbishop or a metropolitan, usu. consisting of adjacent dioceses. Formerly also, a district within the jurisdiction of a synod of a Presbyterian Church. LME. ▸**b** A territorial division of a religious order. E18.
5 In *pl. The* parts of a country outside the capital or chief seat of government, esp. regarded as unsophisticated or uncultured. L18.
6 a BIOLOGY. An area, zone, or region containing a distinct group of animal or plant communities; a division of a biogeographical region. Also, a group of countries treated together with regard to species distribution etc. M19. ▸**b** In full ***petrographical province***, ***petrographic province***. (An area containing) a group of similar igneous rocks apparently formed during the same period of activity. L19. ▸**c** More fully ***physiographic province***. An extensive region all parts of which have a broadly similar geology and topography, differing significantly from adjacent regions. L19. ▸**d** = ***oil province*** s.v. OIL *noun.* E20.
3 *United Provinces*: see UNITED *adjective.* **6a *oceanic province***, ***neritic province***, etc.
▶ **II 7** A sphere of action, concern, responsibility, or knowledge; a department or branch of learning or of any subject. E17.

> **7** G. BERKELEY The two distinct provinces of sight and touch. H. A. L. FISHER Bede . . took all knowledge for his province. B. PYM It was not . . a man's province to fetch or carry jumble. S. QUINN Psychic life . . the province . . of philosophy as of medicine.

Comb.: †**province rose** (*a*) = PROVINS ROSE; (*b*) = PROVENCE *rose*; **province-wide** *adjective* extending throughout or pertaining to a whole province.

provincial /prə'vɪnʃ(ə)l/ *noun & adjective.* ME.
[Old & mod. French from Latin *provincialis*, from *provincia*: see prec., -AL[1].]
▶ **A** *noun.* †**1** In *pl.* The people of Provence. Only in ME.
2 A native or inhabitant of a province. LME. ▸**b** *Hist.* A native or inhabitant of any of the British colonies in N. America, *esp.* one engaged in military service. M18. ▸**c** In Canada: a member of a provincial police force. M20.
3 ECCLESIASTICAL. The ecclesiastical head of a province; the chief of a religious order in a district or province. LME.
†**4** ECCLESIASTICAL. **a** An ordinance of a provincial synod. Also, a rescript addressed to an ecclesiastical province. E16–M17. ▸**b** A provincial synod. Chiefly *Scot.* L16–M17.
5 A person who lives in or comes from the provinces, as opp. to a native or inhabitant of the capital or chief seat of government of a country; an unsophisticated or uncultured person. E18.
6 *ellipt.* A provincial newspaper. L19.
▶ **B** *adjective.* **1** Of or pertaining to an ecclesiastical province. LME.
†**2 a** Provençal. Only in LME. ▸**b** Designating the Provins rose; consisting of such roses. E–M17.
3 Of or pertaining to a province of a country, State, or empire, now esp. a province of Canada. LME. ▸**b** *Hist.* Of or pertaining to European, esp. British, colonies in N. America. L17.
†**4** Having the relation of a province to a sovereign State. L16–E18.
5 Of or pertaining to a province or provinces as opp. to the whole nation or State; of or pertaining to the provinces as opp. to the capital or chief seat of government; having the manners, speech, or character, esp. the narrowness of view or interest, associated with or attributed to inhabitants of a province or the provinces; unsophisticated, uncultured. M17. ▸**b** *transf.* Of or pertaining to places outside that or those regarded as the national centre(s) for some activity. M19.

> **5** G. GREENE The Lancashire farces he constructs . . are genuinely provincial. A. MASSIE The even tenor of . . provincial life. A. N. WILSON The Muscovites . . seemed to them provincial and conservative. **b** C. M. BOWRA Oxford and Cambridge on . . one side and 'provincial' universities on the other.

■ **provincialate** *noun* (ECCLESIASTICAL) the position of provincial, the period of office of a provincial E20. **provinciali'zation** *noun* the action of provincializing a place etc. E20. **provincialize** *verb trans.* make provincial; make into a province, give the status of a province to: E19. **provincially** *adverb* in a provincial manner or capacity; in a province or local area, in the provinces: E17. **provincialship** *noun* = PROVINCIALATE E17.

provincialism /prə'vɪnʃ(ə)lɪz(ə)m/ *noun.* L18.
[from prec. + -ISM.]
1 A manner of speech, or a word, phrase, or pronunciation, characteristic of a particular province or local area, or of the provinces; a provincial characteristic or variety. L18.
2 Attachment to one's own province or local area rather than the whole nation or State; desire for provincial autonomy rather than national unity. E19.
3 Provincial character, speech, manners, fashion, mode of thought, etc., esp. regarded as narrow, restricted, unsophisticated, or uncultured. M19.
4 ECOLOGY & PALAEONTOLOGY. The presence or development of biogeographical provinces. M20.

provincialist /prə'vɪnʃ(ə)lɪst/ *noun.* M17.
[formed as prec. + -IST.]
1 A native or inhabitant of a province or the provinces, a provincial person. M17.
2 A supporter or advocate of provincialism. E18.

provinciality /prəvɪnʃɪ'alɪti/ *noun.* L18.
[from PROVINCIAL + -ITY.]
1 = PROVINCIALISM 3. L18.
2 ECOLOGY & PALAEONTOLOGY. The degree to which plant or animal communities are restricted to particular provinces; degree of endemism. M20.

provinciate /prə'vɪnʃɪeɪt/ *verb trans.* E17.
[from Latin *provincia* (see PROVINCE) + -ATE[3].]
Reduce to the condition of a province; make provincial.

provine /prə'vʌɪn/ *verb trans.* LME.
[Old French *provaignier*, *-veign-* (mod. *proviner*), from *provain* (mod. *provin*) from Latin *propagin-*, *propago* young shoot, layer: cf. PROPAGATE.]
Propagate (a vine etc.) by layering.

Provins rose /'prɒvɛ̃ rəʊz/ *noun phr.* M19.
[*Provins*, a town east of Melun in northern France where it used to be grown.]
An old garden rose, a double-flowered variety of *Rosa gallica*.
¶ Often confused with the Provence rose (see PROVENCE), both formerly being also called ***province rose***.

provirus /prəʊ'vʌɪrəs/ *noun.* M20.
[from PRO-[2] + VIRUS.]
BIOLOGY. The genetic material of a DNA or RNA virus as incorporated into, and able to replicate with, the genome of a host cell.
■ **proviral** *adjective* M20.

provision /prə'vɪʒ(ə)n/ *noun & verb.* LME.
[Old & mod. French from Latin *provisio(n-)*, from *provis-* pa. ppl stem of *providere* PROVIDE: see -ION.]
▶ **A** *noun.* †**1** Foresight, prevision. LME–M16.
2 The action or an act of providing something; the fact or condition of being provided. Freq. in ***make provision***, make prior arrangement or preparation (*for*), supply necessary resources (*for*). LME. ▸**b** ECCLESIASTICAL HISTORY. Appointment to a benefice not yet vacant, esp. by the Pope; an instance of this. LME.
3 A supply of necessaries or materials provided, esp. of food and drink; food etc. provided. Now usu. in *pl.*, supplies of food, drink, etc., esp. for an expedition. LME.
4 (A clause or division of) a legal or formal statement providing for some particular matter or making a stipulation or condition; a proviso. LME.
5 Something provided or arranged in advance; a measure or measures taken beforehand; a precaution. L15.

> **2** T. H. HUXLEY Provision for education . . is a . . duty of the state. E. CALDWELL Wayne had made ample provision for all of Annette's financial needs. *Which?* Strong support for the provision of tea and coffee in pubs. **3** J. REED The two years' provision of grain had fallen to less than enough to feed the city for one month. D. HAMMETT Sufficient provisions for the long . . journey. **4** C. HILL Scotland and Ireland were included within the provisions of the Navigation Act. **5** I. FLEMING An electric hoist and provision for launching . . underwater craft. R. SCRUTON In every legal system . . there must be provision against sedition.

▶ **B** *verb.* **1** *verb trans.* Supply with provisions or stores, esp. with a stock of food. E19.
2 *verb intrans.* Supply oneself with provisions; lay in provisions. Also foll. by *up.* M19.
■ **provisioner** *noun* M19. **provisionless** *adjective* L18. **provisionment** *noun* the supplying or supply of provisions E19.

provisional /prə'vɪʒ(ə)n(ə)l/ *adjective & noun.* E17.
[from prec. + -AL[1], after French †*provisionnal* (now *-el*), medieval Latin *provisionalis*.]
▶ **A** *adjective.* **1** Of the nature of a temporary provision or arrangement; provided or adopted for present needs or temporarily; supplying the place of something regular, permanent, final, or better; tentative. E17. ▸**b** PHILATELY. Of a postage stamp: (overprinted and) put into circulation temporarily; not definitive. L19.
†**2** Characterized by or exhibiting foresight; provident. *rare.* E17–M18.
†**3** Done with a proviso; conditional. M17–E19.

> **1** A. HUTSCHNECKER He confirmed the provisional diagnosis. C. HARMAN All plans were provisional. **Provisional IRA** the unofficial wing of the Irish Republican Army instituted in 1970, advocating terrorism.

▶ **B** *noun.* †**1** A person for whom provision is made. *rare.* Only in E18.
2 A person whose tenure of office is temporary; a provisional governor. M19.
3 A provisional thing, *esp.* a provisional postage stamp. L19.
4 (P-.) A member of the Provisional IRA. L20.
■ **provisio'nality** *noun* E19. **provisionally** *adverb* in a provisional manner; as a temporary measure: L16. **provisionalness** *noun* L19.

provisionary /prə'vɪʒ(ə)n(ə)ri/ *adjective.* Now *rare.* E17.
[from PROVISION + -ARY[1].]
1 = PROVISIONAL *adjective* 1. E17.
†**2** Of or pertaining to provisions or food-supply. *rare.* E17–E19.
†**3** Characterized by or exhibiting foresight; provident. M17–L18.
4 ECCLESIASTICAL HISTORY. Of or pertaining to papal provisions. M18.

proviso /prə'vʌɪzəʊ/ *noun.* Pl. **-o(e)s.** LME.
[Latin, neut. abl. sing. of pa. pple of *providere* PROVIDE, as in medieval Latin *proviso quod* (or *ut*) it being provided that.]
A clause in a legal or formal document, making some condition, stipulation, exception, or limitation, or on the observance of which the operation or validity of the instrument depends; *gen.* a condition, a qualification, a stipulation, a provision.

> H. E. THOMAS Permits . . issued with the proviso that water . . be returned to the same aquifer. R. V. JONES To be accurate you must put in . . provisos and qualifications.

provisor /prə'vʌɪzə/ *noun.* LME.
[Anglo-Norman *provisour* (French *proviseur*) from Latin *provisor*, from *provis-*: see PROVISION, -OR.]
1 ECCLESIASTICAL HISTORY. The holder of a grant (esp. from the Pope) giving him the right to be appointed to the next vacant benefice. LME.
†**2** A person who provides or cares for another. LME–M18.
†**3** A person who is in charge; an agent. LME–M16.
4 A person in charge of getting provisions; a purveyor; a steward. *obsolete* exc. *Hist.* L15.
5 ROMAN CATHOLIC CHURCH. An ecclesiastic assisting and deputizing for an archbishop or bishop; a vicar-general; *Hist.* a deputy inquisitor. M16.

provisory /prə'vʌɪz(ə)ri/ *adjective.* E17.
[French *provisoire* or medieval Latin *provisorius*, from *provis-*: see PROVISION, -ORY[2].]
1 Subject to a provision or proviso; conditional. E17.
2 = PROVISIONAL *adjective* 1. L18.
■ **provisorily** *adverb* E19.

provitamin /'prəʊvɪtəmɪn/ *noun.* E20.
[from PRO-[2] + VITAMIN.]
BIOLOGY. A substance which is converted into a vitamin within an organism. Freq. with following cap. letter specifying the vitamin.

provo /prə'vəʊ/ *noun*[1]. *arch.* Pl. **-oes.** L17.
[Repr. a pronunc. after French *prévôt*.]
= PROVOST.

provo /ˈprəʊvəʊ/ *noun*² & *adjective*¹. Pl. of noun **-os**. M20.
[Dutch, abbreviation of French PROVOCATEUR.]
A member of, of or pertaining to, a group of young Dutch anarchist agitators.

Provo /ˈprəʊvəʊ, ˈprɒvəʊ/ *noun*³ & *adjective*². *colloq.* Pl. of noun **-os**. L20.
[Abbreviation of PROVISIONAL: see -O. Cf. PROVIE.]
A member of, of or pertaining to, the Provisional IRA.

provocable /ˈprɒvəkəb(ə)l/ *adjective*. *rare*. E17.
[Late Latin *provocabilis*, from Latin *provocare* PROVOKE: see -ABLE.]
= PROVOKABLE.

provocate /ˈprɒvəkeɪt/ *verb trans. rare*. LME.
[Latin *provocat-*: see PROVOCATION, -ATE³.]
Provoke, incite.

provocateur /prɔvɔkatœːr/ *noun*. Pl. pronounced same. E20.
[French = provoker. Cf. PROVOCATOR.]
A person who provokes a disturbance; an agitator; an *agent provocateur*.

provocation /prɒvəˈkeɪʃ(ə)n/ *noun*. LME.
[Old & mod. French, or Latin *provocatio(n-)*, from *provocat-* pa. ppl stem of *provocare* PROVOKE: see -ATION.]
▶ **I** †**1** The action or an act of appealing against a judgement, esp. to a higher ecclesiastical court. LME–E18.
†**2** A challenge to fight. L15–E17.
3 The action or an act of inviting or summoning someone. *obsolete* exc. as passing into sense 4. M16.
▶ **II 4** The action or an act of provoking someone; an incitement, a stimulus, *spec.* to anger, resentment, or irritation; a cause of anger, resentment, or irritation; *LAW* an action, insult, etc., held to be likely to provoke physical retaliation. LME.
Comb.: **provocation test** *MEDICINE* a test to elicit a particular response, reflex, reaction, signs of life, etc.

provocative /prəˈvɒkətɪv/ *adjective* & *noun*. LME.
[Old French *provocatif*, *-ive* from late Latin *provocativus*, from *provocat-*: see prec., -IVE.]
▶ **A** *adjective*. Having the quality of provoking or giving rise to something (foll. by *of*); *spec.* (*a*) tending to excite sexual desire; (*b*) tending to provoke anger, resentment, or irritation, intentionally annoying. LME.

> C. BEATON She could look . . provocative in a dress that covered her. A. BURGESS Such provocative questions as: 'What is religion?' A. DJOLETO Grinning in the most provocative manner. **provocative test** *MEDICINE* = *PROVOCATION* **test**.

▶ **B** *noun*. A provocative thing; an incentive; an aphrodisiac. LME.
■ **provocatively** *adverb* M17. **provocativeness** *noun* L17.

provocator /ˈprɒvəkeɪtə/ *noun*. L19.
[French PROVOCATEUR, after Latin *provocator* (from *provocat-*: see PROVOCATION): see -OR.]
= PROVOCATEUR.

provocatory /prəˈvɒkət(ə)ri/ *adjective*. *rare*. LME.
[Late Latin *provocatorius*, from Latin PROVOCATOR: see -ORY².]
= PROVOCATIVE *adjective*.

provodnik /prəvʌdˈnik/ *noun*. L19.
[Russian.]
1 A Russian guide. *rare*. L19.
2 An attendant or guard on a train in a Russian-speaking country. E20.

provoke /prəˈvəʊk/ *verb*. LME.
[Old & mod. French *provoquer* or Latin *provocare*, formed as PRO-¹ + *vocare* to call.]
▶†**I 1** *verb trans.* Invoke; summon, invite. LME–E18.
2 *verb intrans.* Appeal against a judgement (esp. *from* a lower *to* a higher ecclesiastical tribunal). LME–L17.
3 *verb trans.* Challenge to a fight. L15–L17.
▶ **II 4** *verb trans.* Incite or urge (a person or animal) *to* or *into* some act, *to do* something; stimulate to action; *spec.* incite to anger, enrage, vex, irritate, exasperate. LME. ▶**b** *verb intrans.* Incite or urge another or others *to* (now *rare*); cause anger, resentment, or irritation; be provocative. E16.
5 *verb trans.* Give rise to, bring about, induce, elicit. LME.

> **4** J. WAIN Whatever he said wouldn't provoke me. E. LONGFORD To . . provoke him to a duel. R. HAYMAN His father shouted . . provoking others to shout back. L. NKOSI Trying to provoke me into losing my temper. **5** W. CATHER Nothing pleased one more than to provoke her laughter. S. QUINN Karen managed to provoke a fight. *Times Lit. Suppl.* The lecture . . provoked a storm.

■ **provokable** *adjective* L17. **provoked** *adjective* having received provocation; irritated, angry, annoyed: M16. **provokement** *noun* (long *arch. rare*) a provocation M16. **provoker** *noun* LME.

provoking /prəˈvəʊkɪŋ/ *adjective*. LME.
[from PROVOKE + -ING².]
That provokes; provocative; exasperating, irritating.
■ **provokingly** *adverb* in a provoking manner; to a provoking degree: E17. **provokingness** *noun* M19.

provolone /prɒvəˈləʊni/ *noun*. M20.
[Italian, from *provola* buffalo's milk cheese.]
An Italian smoked cheese, often made in a variety of shapes. Also ***provolone cheese***.

provost /ˈprɒvəst, *in sense 8 usu.* prəˈvəʊ/ *noun*.
[Late Old English *profost* corresp. to Middle Low German, Middle Dutch *provest*, Middle Dutch *proofst* (Dutch *proost*), Old High German *probost* (German *Probst*, *Propst*), Old Norwegian *prófastr*; reinforced in Middle English from Anglo-Norman, Old French *provost*, *prevost* (mod. *prévôt*) from medieval Latin *propositus* used alongside Latin PRAEPOSITUS: see PRO-¹. Cf. PREVOST, PROVO *noun*¹. In sense 1b translating German *Propst*, Danish *provst*, etc.]
▶ **I 1** *ECCLESIASTICAL*. The head or president of a chapter, or of a community of religious people, a prior, (now chiefly *Hist.*); the chief dignitary or minister of some cathedrals or collegiate churches. LOE. ▶**b** A Protestant member of the clergy in charge of the principal church of a town or district in Germany, the Low Countries, Scandinavia, etc. M16.
2 The head of certain universities and colleges. LME.
▶ **II 3** A person appointed to preside, a superintendent; a representative of a ruling power; an appointed leader. Long *obsolete* in *gen.* sense. LOE.
4 *Hist.* An officer in charge of some establishment, undertaking, or body; a manager or steward of a royal or feudal establishment; an overseer or bailiff of a manor. ME.
5 *Hist.* The chief magistrate of a French, Flemish, or other Continental town; an officer in France etc. charged with the apprehension, custody, and punishment of offenders. ME.
6 The head of a Scottish municipal corporation or burgh. Now only as a courtesy title. LME.
†**7** An assistant fencing-master. Cf. USHER *noun* 3b. M16–E17.
8 *MILITARY*. A military police officer. (Earliest in ***provost marshal*** below.) M16.
6 Lord Provost the provost of one of the more important Scottish corporations, as of Edinburgh or Glasgow (now only as a courtesy title).
Comb.: **provost guard** *US* a body of soldiers acting as military police under a provost marshal; **provost marshal** any of various military or naval officers whose duties and powers have varied at different times and in different places; now *spec.* (*a*) the head of military police in camp or on active service; (*b*) the master-at-arms of a ship in which a court martial is to be held.
■ **provostal** *adjective* (*rare*) E17. **provostry** *noun* (*Hist.*) (*a*) = PROVOSTSHIP; (*b*) the benefice of an ecclesiastical provost; the revenue derived from such a benefice: LME. **provostship** *noun* the office or position of provost; the area of jurisdiction of a provost: E16. **provosty** *noun* (*Hist.*) = PROVOSTSHIP LME.

prow /praʊ/ *noun*. M16.
[Old & mod. French *proue* from Provençal *proa* or Italian dial. (Genoese, Sicilian) *prua* from Latin *prora* from Greek *prōra*, from base repr. by Latin *pro* before, in front.]
1 The forepart or bow of a boat or ship, adjoining the stem. M16. ▶†**b** *spec.* The fore gun-deck of a warship. E17–E18.
2 A point or pointed part projecting in front. M17.
3 A ship. *literary*. M18.
■ **prowed** *adjective* having a prow, freq. of a specified kind M19.

prow /praʊ/ *adjective*. Long *arch. literary*. ME.
[Old French *prou*, earlier *prud*, *prod*: see PROUD.]
Good, worthy, valiant, brave, gallant. Freq. in ***prowest knight*** (after Spenser).

prowess /ˈpraʊɪs/ *noun*. ME.
[Old French *proesce* (mod. *prouesse*), formed as prec.: see -ESS².]
1 Valour, bravery, martial daring; manly courage. Also, an act of bravery, a valiant deed, (usu. in *pl.*). Now chiefly *literary*. ME.
2 Exceptional ability or talent; skill, expertise; (in full ***sexual prowess***) sexual vigour or potency, virility. E20.

> **1** CARLYLE His excellencies and prowesses. H. CARPENTER The job of fighting demands . . daring and individual prowess in arms. **2** W. FAULKNER His proved prowess with a pistol. P. OLIVER The man who is proud of his sexual prowess, real or imaginary.

■ **prowessful** *adjective* (now *arch. rare*) full of prowess, valorous, valiant L16.

prowl /praʊl/ *verb* & *noun*. Also (earlier) †**proll**. LME.
[Origin unkn.]
▶ **A** *verb*. **1** *verb intrans.* Orig., go or move about, esp. in search of something. Later *spec.*, roam or wander about in search of plunder or prey; move about stealthily as or like a hunter. Freq. foll. by *about*, *around*. LME. ▶†**b** Search *for*; seek for or *for* gain or advantage in a mean or underhand way. LME–L17.
†**2 a** *verb trans.* Obtain by stealth, cheating, or petty theft. M16–L17. ▶**b** *verb intrans.* Plunder, steal, pilfer. L16–M17. ▶**c** *verb trans.* Steal from (a person). Only in 17.
3 *verb trans.* Roam over or around (a place or region), esp. in search of plunder or prey; traverse stealthily. L16. ▶**b** Examine, esp. in preparation for a robbery; = CASE *verb* 3. *US slang*. E20.

> **1** D. H. LAWRENCE A boy was prowling with a sling, prowling like a cat. E. BLYTON Any wild animal that might be prowling around. G. VIDAL Paul prowled restlessly about the . . room. **3** P. AUSTER They prowl the streets . . scavenging for morsels.

▶ **B** *noun*. The action or an act of prowling. Esp. in ***on upon the prowl***, ***upon the prowl***, prowling about, now esp. in search of a sexual partner. LME.
Comb.: **prowl car** *colloq.* (chiefly *US*) a police patrol car.
■ **prowler** *noun* a person who prowls, now esp. with a view to committing a crime E16.

prox. /prɒks/ *adjective*. L19.
[Abbreviation.]
Chiefly *COMMERCE*. = PROXIMO.

proxemic /prɒkˈsiːmɪk/ *adjective*. M20.
[formed as next.]
Of or pertaining to proxemics.

proxemics /prɒkˈsiːmɪks/ *noun*. M20.
[from PROXIMITY after *phonemics* etc.: see -ICS.]
The branch of knowledge that deals with the amount of space that people feel it necessary to set between themselves and others.

†**proxenete** *noun*. M17–E19.
[French *proxénète* or Latin *proxeneta* from Greek *proxenētēs* negotiator, agent, from *proxenein*, from *proxenos*: see next.]
A negotiator, a go-between, a match-maker.

proxenus /ˈprɒksɪnəs/ *noun*. Pl. **-ni** /-nʌɪ/. M19.
[mod. Latin from Greek *proxenos*, formed as PRO-² + *xenos* guest, stranger.]
GREEK HISTORY. A resident citizen of a State appointed by another State to represent and protect its interests there.
■ **proxeny** /ˈprɒksɪni/ *noun* [Greek *proxenia*] the office or function of *proxenus* M19.

proximad /ˈprɒksɪmad/ *adverb*. E19.
[formed as PROXIMAL + -AD³.]
ANATOMY. In the direction of the proximal part of a limb etc.

proximal /ˈprɒksɪm(ə)l/ *adjective*. E18.
[from Latin *proximus* nearest + -AL¹.]
1 Very near or close *to*. *rare*. E18.
2 Proximate, immediate. *rare*. E19.
3 Chiefly *ANATOMY* & *ZOOLOGY*. Situated towards the centre of a body, or the point of origin or attachment of a limb, bone, etc. Opp. DISTAL. E19.
4 *DENTISTRY*. Designating or pertaining to a surface of a tooth which faces or touches the adjacent tooth. E20.
5 *PSYCHOLOGY*. Of a stimulus: immediately responsible for the stimulation of a sense receptor, giving rise to a perception or sensation. M20.
6 *GEOLOGY*. Designating or characteristic of an area close or closest to an area of activity, as a sedimentation zone, a volcanic vent, etc. M20.
■ **proximally** *adverb* in a proximal position; towards or near the proximal part or end: L19.

proximate /ˈprɒksɪmət/ *adjective*. L16.
[Latin *proximatus* pa. pple of *proximare*, from *proximus* nearest: see -ATE².]
1 Next before or after, nearest, (in space, serial order, a chain of causation, a train of thought, quality, time, etc.); immediately adjacent, immediate. L16.
2 Nearly accurate or correct; approximate. L18.
3 *CHEMISTRY*. Designating or involving those components of a substance identifiable or separable by an initial or relatively crude procedure. Freq. in ***proximate analysis***. E19.
■ **proximately** *adverb* L16. **proximateness** *noun* L19. **proxiˈmation** *noun* approximation M20. †**proxime** *adjective* = PROXIMATE *adjective* 1 M17–M19.

proxime accessit /ˌprɒksɪmi akˈsɛsɪt/ *noun phr.* L19.
[Latin, lit. '(he or she) came very near.']
Second place in merit to the actual winner of a prize, scholarship, etc.; a person gaining this.

proximity /prɒkˈsɪmɪti/ *noun*. L15.
[Old & mod. French *proximité* or Latin *proximitas*, from *proximus* nearest: see -ITY.]
The fact, condition, or position of being near or close, nearness, (of relation, in space or time, etc.).

> E. SAINTSBURY The town's . . proximity to the River Bogie. W. M. CLARKE Collins . . and Constable continued to live in close proximity. **proximity of blood** kinship.

Comb.: **proximity fuse** an electronic detonator in a projectile that operates automatically within a predetermined distance of a target; **proximity talks** diplomatic discussions or negotiations in which opposing parties do not meet but are in close proximity to each other and talk through intermediaries.

proximo /ˈprɒksɪməʊ/ *adjective*. M19.
[Latin = in the next (sc. *mense* month). See also PROX.]
Chiefly *COMMERCE*. Of next month. Following the ordinal numeral denoting the day.

> *Times* About the 1st proximo.

proxy /ˈprɒksi/ *noun & verb.* LME.
[Contr. of PROCURACY.]
▶ **A** *noun.* **I 1** The agency of a person who acts by appointment instead of another; the action of a substitute or deputy. Chiefly in ***by proxy***, by the agency of another, by or through a substitute, not in person. LME.
2 A document empowering a person to represent and act for another; a letter of attorney. Now only *spec.*, a document authorizing a person to vote on behalf of another; a vote cast by proxy. LME.
3 A person appointed or authorized to represent and act for another; an attorney, a substitute, a representative. E17.
▶†**II 4** ECCLESIASTICAL. = PROCURATION 3. LME–M19.
▶ **III 5** PETROGRAPHY & MINERALOGY. A mineral or element that replaces another. M20.
Comb.: **proxy sitting** SPIRITUALISM a sitting arranged with a medium and attended by one person at the request of another, usu. unknown, person who hopes for news of someone recently dead; **proxy vote** a vote cast by proxy; **proxy war** US a war instigated by a major power which does not itself become involved.
▶ **B** *verb.* **1** *verb intrans.* Act or vote by proxy (*for*). M19.
2 *verb trans. & intrans.* with *for.* PETROGRAPHY & MINERALOGY. Occur in place of, in a rock or crystal lattice. E20.

Prozac /ˈprəʊzak/ *noun.* L20.
[Origin unkn.]
PHARMACOLOGY. (Proprietary name for) the antidepressant drug fluoxetine; a tablet of this.

prozoic /prəʊˈzəʊɪk/ *adjective.* M19.
[from PRO-² + Greek *zōē* life + -IC.]
GEOLOGY. = AZOIC *adjective*¹.

prozone /ˈprəʊzəʊn/ *noun.* E20.
[from PRO-¹ + (*agglutination*) ZONE *noun.*]
IMMUNOLOGY. The range of relative quantities of precipitin (or agglutinin) and antigen within which an expected precipitation (or agglutination) is inhibited, apparently by excess of one component. Freq. *attrib.*

Prozymite /ˈprɒzɪmʌɪt/ *noun.* M19.
[Late Greek *prozumitēs*, from *prozumion* leaven, formed as PRO-² + *zumē* leaven: see -ITE¹.]
ECCLESIASTICAL HISTORY. (A contemptuous name used by Western Churches for) a member of any of the Eastern Christian Churches which administer the Eucharist with leavened bread. Cf. AZYMITE.

PRR *abbreviation.*
ELECTRONICS. Pulse repetition rate.

PRS *abbreviation.*
1 Performing Rights Society.
2 President of the Royal Society.

prude /pruːd/ *adjective & noun.* Freq. *derog.* E18.
[French adjective & noun, back-form. from *prudefemme* fem. corresp. to *prud'homme* PRUDHOMME taken as adjective & noun.]
▶ **A** *adjective.* Behaving like a prude; prudish. Now *rare.* E18.

> 🕮 H. G. GRAHAM The prudest might . . enjoy Vanbrugh's *Provoked Husband.*

▶ **B** *noun.* A person, esp. a woman, having or affecting an attitude of extreme propriety or modesty, esp. in sexual matters; an excessively prim person, a prudish person. E18.

> 🕮 P. H. GIBBS I'm not a prude . . but I don't want to meet your friend's mistress. P. P. READ We can't keep our conversation clean just for a prude.

■ **prudelike** *adjective* (*rare*) resembling (that of) a prude E18.

prude /pruːd/ *verb intrans.* M18.
[from prec.]
Behave like a prude; act prudishly. Chiefly as ***pruding*** *verbal noun.*

prudence /ˈpruːd(ə)ns/ *noun.* ME.
[Old & mod. French from Latin *prudentia* contr. of *providentia* PROVIDENCE.]
1 The quality of being prudent. ME. ▸**b** An instance of this; a prudent act. *rare.* M17.
†**2** Wisdom; knowledge of or skill in a matter. Cf. JURISPRUDENCE. ME–M19.
†**3** Foresight, providence. L15–M18.
■ Also **prudency** *noun* (long *rare*) LME.

prudent /ˈpruːd(ə)nt/ *adjective.* LME.
[Old & mod. French, or Latin *prudent-* contr. of *provident-* PROVIDENT.]
1 Characterized by or proceeding from care in following the most politic and profitable course; having or showing sound judgement in practical affairs; circumspect, sensible. LME.
2 Wise, discerning, sapient. *obsolete* exc. as passing into sense 1. LME.

> 🕮 **1** A. F. DOUGLAS-HOME A diplomatic act . . was prudent and timely. M. SEYMOUR A prudent woman would have decided to stay at the . . manageable house.

■ **prudently** *adverb* LME. **prudentness** *noun* (long *rare* or *obsolete*) E18.

prudential /prʊˈdɛnʃ(ə)l/ *adverb, adjective, & noun.* LME.
[from prec. + -IAL, after *evidential* etc.]
▶†**A** *adverb.* Prudentially. *rare.* Only in LME.
▶ **B** *adjective.* **1** Of, involving, or characterized by prudence; exercising prudence, esp. in business affairs. M17.
2 US HISTORY. Designating (any of several men appointed to conduct) the business and administrative affairs of a colonial town, society, etc., in New England. M17.
▶ **C** *noun.* **1** In *pl.* Prudential matters or considerations; US minor administrative or financial matters, esp. as relating to local government. M17.
†**2** A prudential maxim or precept. E–M18.
3 A person who urges prudence. *rare.* M19.
■ **prudentialism** *noun* prudential principles and practices; an instance of these: M19. **prudentialist** *noun* a person who is guided by or acts from prudential motives; an adherent of prudentialism: M19. **prudentiality** /prʊˌdɛnʃɪˈalɪti/ *noun* (*rare*) the quality of being prudential; prudential nature or character: M17. **prudentially** *adverb* in a prudential manner; in accordance with prudence; on prudential grounds: M17.

prudery /ˈpruːd(ə)ri/ *noun.* E18.
[French *pruderie*, formed as PRUDE *adjective & noun*: see -ERY.]
The characteristic quality of a prude; prudish behaviour; an instance of this.

> 🕮 SIR W. SCOTT Her pruderies and her scruples. C. RYCROFT Victorian morality, with its prudery . . about sexual matters.

†**prudhomme** *noun.* E18–L19.
[French *prud'homme* good man and true, earlier *prodome*, from *prod* (see PROUD *adjective*) + *ome* (mod. *homme*) man. Cf. PRUDE *adjective & noun.*]
A man of valour and discretion; a knight or freeholder summoned to sit on the jury or serve in the king's council. Also (*rare*), a member of a French tribunal appointed to decide labour disputes.

prudish /ˈpruːdɪʃ/ *adjective.* E18.
[from PRUDE *noun* + -ISH¹.]
Having the character of a prude; having or affecting an attitude of extreme propriety or modesty, esp. in sexual matters; excessively demure, prim, or formal.

> 🕮 M. M. R. KHAN Her prudish bashfulness. R. OWEN Pornographic by prudish Soviet standards.

■ **prudishly** *adverb* M18. **prudishness** *noun* M19.

Prufrockian /pruːˈfrɒkɪən/ *adjective.* L20.
[from the central character of T. S. Eliot's poem *The Love Song of J. Alfred Prufrock* (1917) + -IAN.]
Resembling or characteristic of the timid, passive Prufrock and his world of middle-class conformity and unfulfilled aspirations.

pruinose /ˈpruːɪnəʊs/ *adjective.* E19.
[Latin *pruinosus*, from *pruina* hoar-frost: see -OSE¹.]
BOTANY & ZOOLOGY. Covered with a fine whitish or bluish-white powder or waxy bloom.

prunasin /ˈpruːnəsɪn/ *noun.* E20.
[from PRUNUS + -IN¹.]
CHEMISTRY. A cyanogenic glycoside related to amygdalin, found in the bird cherry and other trees.
■ **prunase** *noun* an enzyme present in bitter almonds and yeast, and in the fruit of several species of *Prunus*, which hydrolyses prunasin and some other glycosides E20.

prune /pruːn/ *noun & adjective.* ME.
[Old & mod. French, ult. from Latin *prunum* from Greek *prounon*, earlier *proumnon.*]
▶ **A** *noun.* **1** †**a** The fruit of the tree *Prunus domestica*; a plum. Also, a plum tree. ME–L17. ▸**b** A variety of plum suitable for drying. Chiefly *N. Amer.* E20.
2 Orig. more fully ***dry prune***. The wrinkled purplish-black dried fruit of several varieties of plum. ME.
3 A dull dark reddish-purple colour suggesting the juice of prunes. L19.
4 A disagreeable or disliked person. Also (esp. *RAF slang*), a stupid or incompetent person. *slang.* L19.

> 🕮 **4** *Women Speaking* If a man doesn't like a girl's looks . . she's a . . prune.

Phrases: **prunes and prism(s)** [offered by Mrs General in Dicken's *Little Dorrit* as a phrase giving 'a pretty form to the lips'] (marked by) prim, mincing affectation of speech.
Comb.: **prune tree** †(*a*) a plum tree; (*b*) a tree producing plums suitable for drying.
▶ **B** *adjective.* Of the colour prune. L19.
■ **pruniferous** /pruːˈnɪf(ə)rəs/ *adjective* (*rare*) producing or bearing plums or stone-fruits M17.

prune /pruːn/ *verb*¹. Now *rare* or *obsolete.* LME.
[Old French *poroign-* pres. stem of *poroindre*, from *por-* (mod. *pour-*), formed as PRO-¹ + *oindre* from Latin *ungere* anoint. Cf. PREEN *verb*².]
1 *verb trans. & intrans.* Of a bird: preen (itself, the feathers). LME.
2 *verb trans. & intrans.* Of a person: smarten (oneself, one's clothes, etc.); adorn (oneself), dress (oneself) smartly. LME.
†**3** *verb trans.* Set in order. *rare.* Only in L16.
†**4** *verb refl.* Pride oneself. (Foll. by *in.*) M–L17.

prune /pruːn/ *verb*² *trans.* LME.
[Old French *proignier*, earlier *prooignier* from Proto-Romance, formed as PRO-¹ + Latin *rotundus* round, ROTUND *adjective.*]
1 Cut down, shorten or abbreviate by cutting, esp. by removing superfluous or unwanted matter. Also, remove as superfluous or unwanted. LME.
2 Trim (a tree, shrub, or plant) by cutting or lopping dead or overgrown branches, twigs, or shoots, esp. to increase fruitfulness and regular growth. Freq. foll. by *down.* M16.
3 Cut or lop (dead or overgrown branches, twigs, or shoots) from a tree or shrub, esp. to increase fruitfulness and regular growth. Freq. foll. by *off, away.* L16.

> 🕮 **1** *Times Lit. Suppl.* Marston's text—judiciously pruned . . without Webster's additions. **2** *Observer* Prune the plants . . down to the last active growth.

■ **prunable** *adjective* (*rare*) able to be pruned M18. **pruner** *noun* L16.

†**prunel** *noun.* L16–E18.
[French *prunelle* or mod. Latin PRUNELLA *noun*¹.]
The plant self-heal, *Prunella vulgaris*; formerly also, the bugle *Ajuga reptans.*

prunella /prʊˈnɛlə/ *noun*¹. L16.
[mod. Latin (see below), app. used because self-heal was a reputed cure for the disease PRUNELLA *noun*³.]
Any of several small labiate plants constituting the genus *Prunella*; *esp.* self-heal, *P. vulgaris.*

prunella /prʊˈnɛlə/ *noun*² *& adjective.* M17.
[Origin uncertain: perh. from French *prunelle*, of unkn. origin.]
▶ **A** *noun.* A strong silk or worsted fabric formerly used for the gowns of graduates, members of the clergy, and barristers, and later for the uppers of women's shoes. M17.
leather and prunella *arch.* a matter of complete indifference.
▶ **B** *attrib.* or as *adjective.* Made or consisting of prunella. E18.

†**prunella** *noun*³. M17–L19.
[mod. Latin, in medieval Latin *brunella* an infectious disease with brown coating of the tongue, dim. of *brunus* brown: see -ELLA.]
MEDICINE. Orig., typhus, esp. as prevalent among the imperial troops in Germany in 1547 and 1566. Later, any of various conditions esp. of the throat, as quinsy.
Comb.: **prunella salt** [mod. Latin *lapis* or *sal prunellae*] PHARMACOLOGY a preparation of saltpetre.
¶ Long only in Dicts.

prunelle /prynɛl/ *noun.* E20.
[French, lit. 'sloe', formed as PRUNE *noun* + *-elle* -EL². Cf. PRUNELLO.]
A French brandy-based liqueur flavoured with sloes.

prunello /prʊˈnɛləʊ/ *noun.* Pl. **-o(e)s.** E17.
[Alt. of Italian †*prunella* dim. of *pruna* (now *prugna*) plum, prune.]
Orig., a variety of plum or prune. Now, a fine kind of prune, *esp.* one made from a greengage.

pruning /ˈpruːnɪŋ/ *noun.* M16.
[from PRUNE *verb*² + -ING¹.]
1 The action of PRUNE *verb*². M16.
2 In *pl.* Pieces cut off in pruning. M19.
Comb.: **pruning-hook** a long-handled curved cutting tool used for pruning; **pruning-knife** a knife used for pruning.

prunt /prʌnt/ *noun.* L19.
[Origin uncertain: perh. alt. of PRINT *noun.*]
A piece of moulded or impressed glass attached as an ornament to a glass vessel; a tool for moulding or impressing such a piece of glass.
■ **prunted** *adjective* decorated with prunts E20.

prunus /ˈpruːnəs/ *noun.* E18.
[Latin = plum tree, from Greek *prounos*, earlier *proumnē.*]
1 Any of the numerous trees and shrubs with drupaceous fruits constituting the genus *Prunus*, of the rose family, which includes the sloe, plum, peach, apricot, cherry, and other fruit trees; *esp.* any of the varieties of cherry cultivated for their ornamental pink or white flowers. E18.
2 CERAMICS. A representation of a Chinese and Japanese plum tree, *Prunus mume*, on porcelain etc. L19.

prurience /ˈprʊərɪəns/ *noun.* L17.
[formed as PRURIENT: see -ENCE.]
1 †**a** The physical fact or sensation of itching. Only in L17. ▸**b** *fig.* Mental itching; craving. Now *rare.* E19.
2 = PRURIENCY 2. L18.

pruriency /ˈprʊərɪənsi/ *noun.* M17.
[formed as next: see -ENCY.]
1 a The quality or state of itching. *rare.* M17. ▸**b** *fig.* The quality or condition of mental itching. E18.
2 Liking for lascivious thoughts, tendency towards an unhealthy concern with sexual matters; an instance of this. L18.

prurient /ˈprʊərɪənt/ *adjective.* L16.
[from Latin *prurient-* pres. ppl stem of *prurire* itch, be wanton: see -ENT.]
1 a Having a mental itching or an uneasy or morbid craving. *rare.* L16. ▸**b** That itches physically, itching. *rare.* M17.
2 Having or characterized by an unhealthy concern with sexual matters; encouraging such a concern. M18.
3 Unduly forward or excessive in growth. Now *rare.* E19.

📖 **1a** C. KINGSLEY Prurient longing after . . personal gossip. **2** J. GLASSCO A . . prurient curiosity about . . physical details. O. MANNING She was an object of prurient excitement among the boys. **3** R. SIMPSON The prurient branches of some promising fir.

■ **pruriently** *adverb* M19.

pruriginous /prʊəˈrɪdʒɪnəs/ *adjective.* LME.
[from late Latin *pruriginosus*, from *prurigin-*, *-go*: see next, -OUS.]
1 Affected by or liable to prurigo or itching; of or pertaining to prurigo. Formerly also, mangy, scabby. LME.
2 Characterized by mental itching, curiosity, or uneasiness; irritable, fretful. Long *rare* or *obsolete.* E17.

prurigo /prʊəˈrʌɪɡəʊ/ *noun.* M17.
[Latin = itching, from *prurire* to itch.]
Itching, pruritus. Now usu. *spec.*, a chronic skin condition characterized by itching and the presence of small pale pimples, sometimes associated with an allergic disorder.

pruritus /prʊəˈrʌɪtəs/ *noun.* M17.
[Latin, from *prurire* to itch.]
Itching of the skin, with or (esp.) without visible eruption. Freq. with mod. Latin specifying word.
■ **pruritic** /-ˈrɪtɪk/ *adjective* L19.

prushun /ˈprʌʃ(ə)n/ *noun. US slang.* L19.
[Origin unkn.]
A youth who travels with and begs for a tramp. Cf. JOCKER 1.

prusik /ˈprʌsɪk/ *adjective & verb.* M20.
[from Karl *Prusik*, Austrian mountaineer who devised the method.]
MOUNTAINEERING. ▸**A** *adjective.* Designating a method of ascending or descending a climbing rope by means of two loops, each attached to it by a special knot tightening when weight is applied and slackening when it is removed, enabling the loop to be moved up the rope. Also, designating a knot or loop used in this method. M20.
▸**B** *verb intrans.* Climb using the prusik method. Freq. as ***prusiking*** *verbal noun.* M20.

Prussian /ˈprʌʃ(ə)n/ *adjective & noun.* M16.
[from *Prussia* (see below), ult. from *Prussi* (or *Borussi*) a people belonging to the western Slavonic group: see -AN.]
▸**A** *adjective.* Of or pertaining to Prussia, a former Polish and later German duchy and kingdom, orig. centred in NE Europe along the south coast of the Baltic and now divided among Germany, Poland, and Russia; originating in or associated with Prussia. M16.
Old Prussian: see OLD *adjective.* †**Prussian acid** hydrocyanic acid. †**Prussian alkali** potassium ferrocyanide. **Prussian binding** a kind of binding with a silk face and cotton back used for coats, dressing-gowns, etc. **Prussian blue** (*a*) a deep blue pigment, ferric ferrocyanide, used in painting and dyeing; the colour of such a pigment; (*b*) a variety of pea with large bluish seeds. **Prussian carp** (*a*) a goldfish of an east European subspecies; †(*b*) a crucian carp. **Prussian collar** a kind of high turned-down collar.
▸**B** *noun.* **1** A native or inhabitant of Prussia. M16.
2 More fully ***Old Prussian***. The West Baltic language of the Old Prussians, spoken until the 17th cent. M19.
1 *Old Prussian*: see OLD *adjective.*
■ **Prussianism** *noun* Prussian ideas or attitudes, esp. as regards militarism and discipline; attachment to these: M19. **Prussianist** *adjective* of, pertaining to, or characteristic of Prussia or Prussianism E20. **Prussianiˈzation** *noun* the action or process of Prussianizing L19. **Prussianize** *verb* (*a*) *verb trans.* make Prussian in manners, customs, etc.; (*b*) *verb intrans.* adopt Prussian manners, customs, etc.: M18. **Prussianizer** *noun* E20. **Prussianly** *adverb* in a characteristically Prussian manner E20.

prussiate /ˈprʌsɪət, ˈprʌʃ-/ *noun.* Now *rare* or *obsolete.* L18.
[from PRUSSIC + -ATE[1].]
CHEMISTRY. A salt of prussic acid, a cyanide; a ferrocyanide, a ferricyanide.

prussic /ˈprʌsɪk/ *adjective.* L18.
[from PRUSSIAN + -IC.]
CHEMISTRY. Of, pertaining to, or derived from Prussian blue. Chiefly in ***prussic acid***, = HYDROCYANIC ***acid***.

prut /prʌt/ *interjection & noun.* ME.
[Imit.]
1 (An exclamation repr.) a slight explosive sound expr. contempt. ME.
2 (Repr.) the sound of a rifle shot. L19.

Prutenic /pruːˈtɛnɪk/ *noun & adjective.* E17.
[medieval Latin *Prutenicus*, from *Prut(h)eni* Prussians: see -IC.]
▸†**A** *noun.* In *pl.* = ***Prutenic tables*** below. Only in E17.
▸**B** *adjective.* Prussian. Only in ***Prutenic tables***, the Copernican planetary tables published in 1551 by Erasmus Reinhold, named in honour of Albert, Duke of Prussia. M17.
■ †**Prutenical** *adjective* = PRUTENIC *adjective* L16–M17.

†**pry** *noun*[1]. Chiefly *dial.* L16–E18.
[Origin unkn.]
The small-leaved lime, *Tilia parvifolia*. Also ***pry-tree***.

pry /prʌɪ/ *noun*[2]. Now *Scot. & north.* E17.
[Origin unkn.]
Any of various wiry sedges of damp hill pasture, esp. *Carex panicea* and *C. flacca*. Also ***pry-grass***.

pry /prʌɪ/ *noun*[3]. M18.
[from PRY *verb*[1].]
1 The action or an act of prying; a peeping or inquisitive glance. M18.
2 An inquisitive person. M19.
2 *PAUL Pry.*

pry /prʌɪ/ *noun*[4]. Now *dial. & US.* E19.
[from PRY *verb*[2].]
Now more fully ***pry-bar***. An instrument for prying or prising; a lever, a crowbar.

pry /prʌɪ/ *verb*[1]. Pa. t. & pple **pried** /prʌɪd/. ME.
[Origin unkn.]
1 *verb intrans.* Look, esp. closely or curiously; peep; peer inquisitively or impertinently; spy. Freq. foll. by *into.* ME.
†**2** *verb trans.* Look for, through, or at closely; observe narrowly. M16–M17. ▸**b** Search or find *out* by close examination. M16–M18.
3 *verb intrans.* Inquire *into* closely; *esp.* inquire impertinently into or *into* another's private affairs; make private investigations into. L16.

📖 **1** J. DORAN Prying about into the corners of the hall. **2** J. PORY Prying the King . . in the face. **3** H. BELLOC Prying into the most important military secrets. P. AUSTER I don't mean to pry But how . . did that lead to marriage?

■ **pryingly** *adverb* in a prying manner E17.

pry /prʌɪ/ *verb*[2] *trans.* Now *dial. & N. Amer.* Pa. t. & pple **pried** /prʌɪd/. E19.
[from PRISE *verb*[1] taken as 3rd person sing. pres.]
= PRISE *verb*[1] 1.

📖 E. L. DOCTOROW They pried open his jaws.

pryan /ˈprʌɪən/ *noun.* Chiefly *local.* Also **prian**. M16.
[Cornish = clayey ground, from *pry* clay.]
MINING. A vein of soft white gravelly clay; the material forming this.

pryce *noun* var. of PRYSE.

pryddest /ˈprʌðɛst/ *noun.* L19.
[Welsh.]
In Welsh poetry: a long poem in unrestricted metre.

pryse /prʌɪs/ *noun. arch.* Also **pryce**. ME.
[Old French, Anglo-Norman *pris* taken or Old French *prise* taking, capture.]
HUNTING. A blast on a hunting horn signalling that a stag is taken. Chiefly in ***blow the pryse***, ***sound the pryse***.

†**prytan** *noun* see PRYTANIS.

prytaneum /prɪtəˈniːəm/ *noun.* Pl. **-nea** /-ˈniːə/. E17.
[Latin from Greek *prutaneion*, formed as next.]
1 GREEK HISTORY. The public hall of a Greek State or city, in which a sacred fire was kept burning; *esp.* in Athens, the hall in which distinguished citizens, foreign ambassadors, and successive presidents of the senate were entertained at the public charge. E17.
2 *transf.* A public hall or house. L17.

prytanis /ˈprɪtənɪs/ *noun.* Pl. **-nes** /-niːz/. Also (earlier) Anglicized as †**prytan**, pl. **-s**. M17.
[Greek *prutanis* = prince, ruler.]
1 GREEK HISTORY. A member of the presiding division of the Athenian Council of Five Hundred. M17.
2 GREEK HISTORY. The chief magistrate of a Greek State, as of Rhodes, Lycia, or Miletus. L17.
3 *transf.* A president, a chief. M19.

prytany /ˈprɪtəni/ *noun.* E19.
[Greek *prutaneia*, formed as prec.]
GREEK HISTORY. **1** Each of the ten divisions of the Athenian Council of Five Hundred; the period of five weeks during which a division presided. E19.
2 The presidency of the Athenian senate; the office or dignity of a prytanis. L19.

Przewalski /pəːʒəˈvalski, pʃɛ-/ *noun.* L19.
[Polish spelling of N. M. *Przheval'skiĭ* (1839–88), Russian explorer.]
In full ***Przewalski's horse***, ***Przewalski horse***. A rare wild horse, *Equus przewalskii*, of Mongolia, having a stocky body, brownish coat, and erect mane.

PS *abbreviation.*
1 Police Sergeant.
2 Latin *postscriptum* postscript.
3 Private secretary.
4 Prompt side (in a theatre).

Ps. *abbreviation.*
Psalm(s) (in the Bible).

PSA *abbreviation.*
Prostate-specific antigen.

psalm /sɑːm/ *noun.*
[Old English (*p*)*s*(*e*)*alm* (reinforced in Middle English from Old French) corresp. to Old High German (*p*)*salmo*, Old Norse *psalmr* from late Latin *psalmus* from Greek *psalmos* song sung to a harp, from *psallein* pluck, twang.]
1 A sacred song that is or may be sung in religious worship; a hymn. Also, any song or ode of a sacred or serious character. OE.
2 *spec.* Any of the sacred songs traditionally held to have been composed by King David, contained in the Book of Psalms, a book of the Old Testament and Hebrew Scriptures, used in both Jewish and Christian worship; a version or paraphrase of any of these, esp. as set for metrical chanting. In *pl.* (treated as *sing.*) (**P-**), the Book of Psalms. OE.
Comb.: **psalm-book** †(*a*) the Book of Psalms; (*b*) a book or volume containing the psalms, esp. as set for metrical chanting; **psalm-singer** (freq. *derog.*) a person who sings psalms; a person who supports the singing of (biblical) psalms rather than hymns in public worship.
■ **psalmic** *adjective* of, pertaining to or characteristic of a psalm or psalms M19.

psalm /sɑːm/ *verb.* Now *rare.* OE.
[from the noun.]
1 a *verb intrans.* Sing a psalm or psalms. OE. ▸†**b** *verb trans.* Sing or celebrate in a psalm or psalms. LME–E17.
2 *verb trans.* Say or sing a psalm or psalms to or over. E19.

psalmist /ˈsɑːmɪst/ *noun.* L15.
[Late Latin *psalmista*, from *psalmus*: see PSALM *noun*, -IST.]
1 The author or composer of a psalm or psalms. L15. ▸**b** *fig.* A person who extols or sings the praises of someone or something. *rare.* L19.
2 ECCLESIASTICAL HISTORY. A member of one of the minor clerical orders discharging the functions of a chorister or precentor. M16.
1 the Psalmist the author or composer of (part of) the Book of Psalms; *spec.* (in traditional belief) David (d. *c* 970 BC), king of Judah and later of all Israel.

psalmodist /ˈsɑːmədɪst, ˈsalm-/ *noun.* M17.
[from PSALMODY + -IST.]
1 A person who practises or is skilled in psalmody; a singer of psalms. M17.
†**2** = PSALMIST 1. M17–L19.

psalmody /ˈsɑːmədi, ˈsalm-/ *noun & verb.* ME.
[Late Latin *psalmodia* from Greek *psalmōidia* from *psalmōidos* psalmist, from *psalmos* (see PSALM *noun*) + *ōidē* song: see -Y[3]. Cf. HYMNODY.]
▸**A** *noun.* **1** The art, practice, or action of singing psalms, hymns, etc., esp. in public worship. ME.
2 The arrangement of psalms for singing; psalms and hymns so arranged collectively. M16.
▸**B** *verb.* **1** *verb intrans.* = PSALMODIZE. *rare.* LME.
2 *verb trans.* Celebrate (as) in psalmody. *rare.* M19.
■ **psalmodic** /salˈmɒdɪk/ *adjective* of or pertaining to psalmody; having the style or character of psalmody; *loosely* = PSALMIC: M18. **psalmodize** *verb intrans.* use psalmody; sing a psalm or psalms: E16.

psalter /ˈsɔːltə, ˈsɒl-/ *noun.* Also **P-**.
[Old English (*p*)*saltere* corresp. to Old High German (*p*)*salteri*, Old Norse (*p*)*saltari*, reinforced in Middle English from Anglo-Norman *sauter*, Old French *sautier* (mod. *psautier*), from Latin *psalterium*, from Greek *psaltērion* stringed instrument, in Christian Latin & Greek the Book of Psalms, from *psallein* pluck, twang.]
▸**I 1** The Book of Psalms. OE. ▸**b** A translation or particular version (prose or metrical) of the Book of Psalms. Freq. with specifying word. OE. ▸**c** A copy of, or a volume containing, the Psalms, esp. as arranged for liturgical or devotional use. OE.
†**2** A selection from, or portion of, the Psalms, said or sung at a particular service or for a particular purpose. OE–E16.
3 Any of various old Irish chronicles in verse. L17.
1b ***English Psalter***, ***Prayer-Book Psalter***, ***Scotch Psalter***, etc. **3** ***Psalter of Cashel***, ***Psalter of Tara***, etc.
▸**II 4** = PSALTERY 1. *arch.* OE.
Phrases: **Jesus psalter** a form of devotion consisting of 15 petitions, each beginning with a tenfold repetition of the name Jesus (which is thus said as many times as there are psalms in the Psalter). **Our Lady's psalter** the rosary (so called on account of its containing as many Aves as there are psalms in the Psalter); a book containing this.
■ **psaltress** *noun* (now *poet. rare*) a female player on the psaltery M16.

psalterial /sɒlˈtɪərɪəl/ *adjective.* M19.
[from PSALTERIUM + -AL[1].]
Chiefly ZOOLOGY. Of or pertaining to the psalterium.

psalterian /sɒlˈtɪərɪən/ *adjective*. E19.
[from Latin *psalterium* (see PSALTER) + -AN.]
1 Of, like, or having a sound like that of, a psaltery. E19.
2 Pertaining to, or having the style of, the Psalter. E19.

psalterion /sɒlˈtɪərɪən/ *noun*. ME.
[Old French *salterion* from Latin *psalterium*: see PSALTER.]
1 = PSALTERY *noun* 1. Now *poet.* ME.
2 ROMAN CATHOLIC CHURCH. = PSALTER *noun* 1, 2. *rare.* L19.

psalterium /sɒlˈtɪərɪəm/ *noun*. E19.
[Latin: see PSALTER.]
▶ **I 1** ANATOMY. = LYRA 4. *rare.* E19.
2 ZOOLOGY. The omasum or third stomach of a ruminant. M19.
▶ **II 3** = PSALTERY 1. L19.

psaltery /ˈsɔːlt(ə)ri, ˈsɒl-/ *noun & verb*. ME.
[Old French *sautere*, *-erie*, from Latin *psalterium*: see PSALTER.]
▶ **A** *noun*. **1** An ancient and medieval stringed musical instrument, resembling a dulcimer but played by plucking the strings with the fingers or a plectrum. Also, a modern reproduction of this. ME.
†**2** = PSALTER 1, 2. *rare.* E17–L19.
▶ **B** *verb intrans.* Play on the psaltery. *rare.* LME.

psammic /ˈ(p)samɪk/ *adjective*. *rare.* M20.
[from Greek *psammos* sand + -IC.]
ECOLOGY. Living among or attached to grains of sand or gravel.

psammite /ˈsamʌɪt/ *noun*. M19.
[formed as prec. + -ITE[1].]
GEOLOGY. An arenaceous sediment or rock; sandstone. Also, a metamorphic derivative of a sandstone.
■ **psammitic** /-ˈmɪtɪk/ *adjective* of, pertaining to, or of the nature of a psammite; derived by metamorphism from a sandstone: M19.

psammo- /ˈsaməʊ/ *combining form* of Greek *psammos* sand: see -O-.
■ **psammophile** *noun & adjective* (BOTANY) (a plant) thriving best in sandy soil L19. **psammoˈphilic** *adjective* = PSAMMOPHILOUS L20. **psaˈmmophilous** *adjective* (BOTANY & ZOOLOGY) living in sand, growing in sandy soil M19. **psammophyte** *noun* a plant characteristic of sandy habitats E20. **psammosere** *noun* (ECOLOGY) a plant succession originating on sand E20.

psammoma /saˈməʊmə/ *noun*. Pl. **-mas**, **-mata** /-mətə/. L19.
[from PSAMMO- + -OMA.]
MEDICINE. A tumour containing calcareous particles like grains of sand, typical esp. of meningiomas and ovarian cancers.
■ **psammomatous** *adjective* of, pertaining to, or characteristic of a psammoma E20.

PSBR *abbreviation*.
Public sector borrowing requirement.

psc *abbreviation*.
MILITARY. Passed staff college.

pschent /pəˈskɛnt/ *noun*. Also **p-skhent**. E19.
[Greek *pskhent* = Egyptian (demotic) *p-skhent*, from *p* (def. article) the + *skhent* from (hieroglyphic) *sekhen(t)*, *sekhet*, *sekhte* the double crown of ancient Egypt.]
EGYPTOLOGY. The double crown of ancient Egypt, combining the white crown of Upper Egypt with the red crown of Lower Egypt, used after the union of the two kingdoms under Menes (*c* 3000 BC).

psellism /ˈsɛlɪz(ə)m/ *noun*. M19.
[Greek *psellismos* stammering, from *psellizein* stammer: see -ISM.]
A defect of enunciation or articulation, as stammering.

psephism /ˈsiːfɪz(ə)m/ *noun*. M17.
[Greek *psēphisma*, from *psēphizein* to vote (orig. with pebbles), from *psēphos* pebble: see -ISM.]
GREEK HISTORY. A decree enacted by a vote of a public assembly, esp. of the Athenians.

psephite /ˈsiːfʌɪt/ *noun*. L19.
[from Greek *psēphos* pebble + -ITE[1].]
GEOLOGY. Rudite; *spec.* the metamorphic derivative of rudite.
■ **psephitic** /-ˈfɪtɪk/ *adjective* L19.

psephocracy /sɪˈfɒkrəsi/ *noun*. *rare.* M20.
[from Greek *psēphos* pebble (for voting) + -O- + -CRACY.]
The form of government resulting from election by ballot; representative government.
■ **psephocrat** /ˈsiːfəkrat/ *noun* an adherent or advocate of government resulting from psephocracy M20.

psephology /sɛˈfɒlədʒi, sɪ-/ *noun*. M20.
[formed as prec. + -OLOGY.]
The study and statistical analysis of elections and trends in voting; *loosely* the prediction of electoral results.
■ **psephoˈlogical** *adjective* of or pertaining to psephology or psephologists M20. **psephoˈlogically** *adverb* M20. **psephologist** *noun* an expert in or student of psephology; an electoral analyst or commentator: M20.

pseud /sjuːd/ *adjective & noun*. *colloq.* M20.
[Abbreviation of PSEUDO.]
▶ **A** *adjective*. = PSEUDO *adjective* 2. M20.

> *Listener* To offer weighty statements without being pseud.

▶ **B** *noun*. = PSEUDO *noun* 2. M20.

> *Listener* The pseud's trap of labelling any film the distinct work of an *auteur*.

■ **pseudery** *noun* an intellectually or socially pretentious manner of expression; an instance of this: L20.

pseud- *combining form* see PSEUDO-.

†**pseudapostle** *noun*. LME–E18.
[from PSEUDO- + APOSTLE.]
A false or pretended apostle.

pseudepigrapha /sjuːdɪˈpɪɡrəfə/ *noun pl.* L17.
[Greek, use as noun of neut. pl. of *pseudepigraphos* with false title, from PSEUDO- + *epigraphein*: see EPIGRAPH.]
Books or writings collectively wrongly titled or attributed; spurious writings; *spec.* Jewish writings ascribed to various biblical patriarchs and prophets but composed *c* 200 BC–AD 200.
■ **pseudepigraphal** *adjective* of, pertaining to, or having the character of pseudepigrapha; wrongly titled or attributed; spurious: M17. **pseudepigraphous** *adjective* = PSEUDEPIGRAPHAL L17.

pseudish /ˈsjuːdɪʃ/ *adjective*. *colloq.* M20.
[from (the same root as) PSEUD + -ISH[1].]
Somewhat intellectually or socially pretentious; (of architecture) imitative and exaggerated.
■ **pseudishness** *noun* L20.

pseudisodomon /psjuːdʌɪˈsɒdə(ʊ)mɒn/ *noun*. Long *rare*. E17.
[Greek, use as noun of neut. of *pseudisodomos*, from PSEUDO- + *isodomos*, from ISO- + *domos* layer or course in a building.]
GREEK ARCHITECTURE. A method of building in which the courses were of unequal height, length, or thickness, but the blocks alike in each course.
■ **pseudisodomous** *adjective* of the nature of or pertaining to pseudisodomon M19.

pseudo /ˈsjuːdəʊ/ *adjective & noun*. LME.
[Independent use of (Greek) PSEUDO-.]
▶ **A** *adjective*. **1** False, counterfeit, pretended, spurious. LME.
2 Intellectually or socially pretentious; insincere, affected; meaningless. M20.

> **1** A. L. KENNEDY They had a nice wind-up gramophone, . . some pseudo Thirties junk and several clocks. **2** H. MACINNES Its patrons were a mixture of the restless rich and the pseudo avant-garde.

▶ **B** *noun*. Pl. **-o(e)s**.
†**1** A false person, a pretender. LME–M19.
2 An intellectually or socially pretentious person; an insincere person. M20.
■ **pseudoism** *noun* (*rare*) a tendency to falseness L19.

pseudo- /ˈsjuːdəʊ/ *combining form*. Before a vowel also **pseud-**.
[Greek, from *pseudēs* false, from *pseudos* falsehood: see -O-.]
Used in words adopted from Greek and in English words modelled on these, and as a freely productive prefix, with the senses (*a*) 'supposed or purporting to be but not really so, false, not genuine', as ***pseudo-intellectual***, ***pseudology***; (*b*) 'resembling, imitating' (freq. in technical applications), as ***pseudo-acid***, ***pseudo-language***, ***pseudo-paralysis***.
■ **pseudaesˈthesia** *noun* (MEDICINE) sensation in skin or muscles without an external stimulus, such as phantom pain in an amputated limb M19. **pseuˈdandry** *noun* [Greek *andr-*, *anēr* man] the use by a woman of a male pseudonym E20. **pseudaposeˈmatic** *adjective* (ZOOLOGY) of or pertaining to mimicry by a harmless organism of (esp. the warning coloration of) a harmful one L19. **pseudarˈthrosis** *noun*, pl. **-oses**, MEDICINE (the formation of) a false joint, formed around the end of a displaced or fractured bone M19. **pseuˈdergate** *noun* [Greek *ergatēs* worker] ENTOMOLOGY a wingless nymph of some termites which functions in the colony as a worker M20. **pseudoˈallele** *noun* (GENETICS) each of two or more mutations that affect different loci within a single cistron M20. **pseudoaˈllelic** *adjective* behaving as or consisting of pseudoalleles M20. **pseudo-arˈchaic** *adjective* appearing or purporting to be ancient, but not really so; artificially archaic in style, language, etc.: L19. **pseudobedding** *noun & adjective* (GEOLOGY) (a structure) resembling the bedding of sediments, esp. as produced in an igneous rock by parallel fractures M19. **pseudoˈbreccia** *noun* (GEOLOGY) a limestone in which partial and irregular dolomitization has produced a texture similar to that of a breccia E20. **pseudobulb** *noun* (BOTANY) a bulblike enlargement of the stem in many (esp. tropical and epiphytic) orchids M19. **pseudoˈbulbous** *adjective* (BOTANY) of the nature of or having a pseudobulb M19. **pseudocarp** *noun* (BOTANY) a type of fruit, e.g. in the apple and the strawberry, which is formed by the ripened ovary combining with other parts of the flower etc., esp. the modified and enlarged receptacle M19. **pseudo-ˈcatholic** *adjective & noun* (*a*) *adjective* falsely or erroneously called or claiming to be catholic; (*b*) *noun* a pseudo-catholic person: E17. **pseudocholiˈnesterase** *noun* (BIOCHEMISTRY) a cholinesterase present in the blood and certain organs which acts more slowly and has a broader effect than acetylcholinesterase M20. **pseudo-Christ** *noun* a false Christ; a person pretending to be the Christ or Messiah: LME. **pseudo-ˈChristian** *noun & adjective* (*a*) *noun* a person falsely or erroneously called or claiming to be a Christian; (*b*) *adjective* of or pertaining to pseudo-Christians or pseudo-Christianity: L16. **pseudo-Christiˈanity** *noun* false or spurious Christianity; the practice or beliefs of pseudo-Christians: L17. **pseudo-ˈclassical** *adjective* of, pertaining to, or characteristic of pseudo-classicism L19. **pseudo-ˈclassicism** *noun* false or spurious classical style, sham classicism L19. **pseudo-cleft** *adjective & noun* (GRAMMAR) (*a*) *adjective* resembling a cleft sentence conveying emphasis through the use of a relative clause (as *what we want is* — from *we want* —); (*b*) *noun* a pseudo-cleft sentence: M20. **pseudocode** *noun* (COMPUTING) a notation resembling a simplified programming language, used in program design M20. **pseudocoel** /-siːl/, **pseudoˈcoelom** *nouns* (ZOOLOGY) a body cavity which is not part of the true coelom; *esp.* in certain invertebrates (as nematodes), one derived from the blastocoel of the embryo L19. **pseudoˈcoelomate** *adjective & noun* (an animal) having a pseudocoel M20. **pseudo-concept** *noun* (PHILOSOPHY) a notion treated as a concept though it cannot be properly conceptualized or grasped by the mind M19. **pseudocopuˈlation** *noun* (BIOLOGY) an act resembling copulation; *esp.* attempted copulation by a male insect with a flower resembling the female, so pollinating it M20. **pseudocrisis** *noun* (MEDICINE, now *rare*) a temporary lowering of temperature during a fever L19. **pseudocroup** *noun* (MEDICINE) spasmodic contraction of the larynx without coughing or inflammation M19. **pseudoˈcubic**, **pseudoˈcubical** *adjectives* (CRYSTALLOGRAPHY) of, pertaining to, or designating a composite crystal of lower symmetry simulating a simple one of the cubic system L19. **pseudoˈcumene** *noun* (CHEMISTRY) an isomer of cumene, $C_6H_3(CH_3)_3$, 1,2,5-trimethylbenzene, present in coal tar L19. **pseudocyesis** /-sʌɪˈiːsɪs/ *noun* [Greek *kuēsis* conception] MEDICINE & ZOOLOGY = PSEUDOPREGNANCY M19. **pseudocyst** *noun* (MEDICINE & BIOLOGY) (*a*) a fluid-filled cystlike cavity lacking a wall or lining; (*b*) a layer of host tissue round certain tapeworm cysts; (*c*) a cluster formed in a host cell by certain protozoan pathogens, esp. those of toxoplasmosis and Chagas' disease: L19. **pseudoˈdiploid** *adjective* (GENETICS) designating or having a chromosome complement differing from the normal diploid complement in constitution but not in number E20. **pseudoˈdipteral** *adjective* (ARCHITECTURE) having a single peristyle arranged like the outer row in a double peristyle E19. **pseudodox** *noun* [Greek *doxa* opinion] a false or erroneous opinion E17. **pseudodoxy** *noun* the holding of false or erroneous opinions; an instance of this: M17. **pseudo-entity** *noun* (PHILOSOPHY) something falsely called or regarded as an entity L19. **pseudo-event** *noun* (orig. *US*) an event arranged or brought about merely for the sake of the publicity generated M20. **pseudoexˈtinction** *noun* (PALAEONTOLOGY) extinction of a group with survival of modified descendant forms L20. **pseudofaeces** *noun pl.* (ZOOLOGY) a mixture of mucus and particles from the water that collects in the mantle cavity of a mollusc and is expelled without passing through the gut M20. **pseudoˈfovea** *noun* (OPHTHALMOLOGY) a point of increased sensitivity on the retina other than the fovea, as in a squinting eye M20. **pseudofracture** *noun* (MEDICINE) a bone defect that radiographically resembles a narrow fracture M20. **pseuˈdogamous** *adjective* of, pertaining to, or exhibiting pseudogamy M20. **pseuˈdogamy** *noun* (BOTANY) in an apomictic plant, development of an embryo stimulated by pollination but without fertilization E20. **pseudogene** *noun* (GENETICS) a section of a chromosome that is an imperfect copy of a functional gene L20. **pseudogley** *noun* (SOIL SCIENCE) a gley resulting from temporary or seasonal surface waterlogging, rather than a permanently high water-table M20. **pseudo-ˈGothic** *noun & adjective* (*a*) *noun* a style of architecture, literature, etc., purporting or mistakenly held to be Gothic; (*b*) *adjective* of, pertaining to, or characteristic of the pseudo-Gothic: L19. **pseudogout** *noun* (MEDICINE) a disorder resembling gout but produced by deposition of calcium pyrophosphate crystals in a joint, esp. the knee M20. **pseudoˈhalide** *noun* (CHEMISTRY) a compound, ion, or radical formed by a pseudohalogen E20. **pseudo-halluciˈnation** *noun* (PSYCHOLOGY) a vivid sensory experience resembling an auditory or visual hallucination but recognized as subjective by the person concerned L19. **pseudoˈhalogen** *noun* (CHEMISTRY) any of a class of simple compounds of electronegative elements, resembling the halogens E20. **pseudoheˈxagonal** *adjective* (CRYSTALLOGRAPHY) of, pertaining to, or designating a composite crystal of lower than hexagonal symmetry simulating a simple one of the hexagonal system L19. **pseudohypertrophic** /-ˈtrəʊfɪk, -ˈtrɒfɪk/ *adjective* (MEDICINE) involving pseudohypertrophy; *esp.* designating a form of muscular dystrophy (Duchenne's): L19. **pseudohyˈpertrophy** *noun* (MEDICINE) enlargement of an atrophying organ by replacement of its tissue with excess fat or connective tissue L19. **pseudohypoparaˈthyroidism** *noun* (MEDICINE) a familial developmental disorder resembling hypoparathyroidism, caused by insensitivity to rather than deficiency of parathyroid hormone M20. **pseudo-instruction** *noun* (COMPUTING) an instruction that controls a compiler or assembler rather than generating a machine instruction M20. **pseudokarst** *noun* (PHYSICAL GEOGRAPHY) topography like karst but in ground other than limestone M20. **pseudoˈleucite** *noun* (MINERALOGY) a mixture of orthoclase and nepheline formed by alteration of leucite L19. **pseudoˈmalachite** *noun* (MINERALOGY) a monoclinic hydrated basic copper phosphate occurring in green amorphous masses resembling malachite M19. **pseudomembrane** *noun* (MEDICINE) a layer of exudate, esp. on the mucosa or conjunctiva, resembling a membrane M19. **pseudoˈmembranous** *adjective* (MEDICINE) characterized by a pseudomembrane L19. **pseudoneuˈrotic** *adjective* (PSYCHIATRY) of or designating types of psychosis, esp. schizophrenia, involving symptoms of neurosis M20. **pseudo-operation** *noun* (COMPUTING) = PSEUDO-INSTRUCTION M20. **pseudopatient** *noun* a person, esp. a researcher, who pretends to have the signs, symptoms, and history of a medical case in order to gain admission to a hospital as a patient L20. **pseudoˈplastic** *adjective & noun* (a liquid) that is non-Newtonian, esp. in having a viscosity that decreases with increasing shearing stress E20. **pseudoplasˈticity** *noun* the phenomenon or condition of being pseudoplastic M20. **pseudopoˈtential** *noun* (PHYSICS) a potential distribution assumed for the purposes of calculation as an approximation to the actual potential M20. **pseudoprime** *noun* (MATH.) an integer *p* such that $a^p - a$ is a multiple of *p* for a given positive integer *a* or (in full ***absolute pseudoprime***) for all positive integers L20. **pseudo-problem** *noun* a problem which is unreal either because it has no possible solution or because there exists a confusion in the formulation of it E20. **pseudoˈprophet** *noun* a false prophet; a person who falsely pre-

tends to be a prophet, or who prophesies falsely: LME. **pseudo-proposition** *noun* (PHILOSOPHY) an apparent proposition which is unreal because it does not have intelligible meaning L19. **pseudopseudo hypopara'thyroidism** *noun* (MEDICINE) a disorder in which the developmental abnormalities of pseudohypoparathyroidism are present without the biochemical abnormalities M20. **pseudorabies** *noun* (VETERINARY MEDICINE) an infectious herpesvirus disease of the central nervous system in domestic animals that causes intense itching, convulsions, and usu. death L19. **pseudo'racemate** *noun* (CHEMISTRY) a pseudoracemic substance E20. **pseudora'cemic** *adjective* (CHEMISTRY) consisting of intergrown crystals of different optical isomers L19. **pseudo'random** *adjective* (MATH.) satisfying one or more statistical tests for randomness but produced by a definite mathematical procedure M20. **pseudo'randomly** *adverb* in a pseudorandom manner M20. **pseudo-'rational** *adjective* assumed to be, or treated as, rational although beyond experience or proof E20. **pseudo-'rationalism** *noun* a theory or system based on pseudo-rational arguments or assumptions M20. **pseudo-'rationalist** *noun* an adherent of pseudo-rationalism M20. **pseudo-science** *noun* a pretended or spurious science; a collection of beliefs about the world mistakenly regarded as being based on scientific method or as having the status of scientific truths: M19. **pseudo-scien'tific** *adjective* of, pertaining to, or characteristic of pseudo-science L19. **pseudo-scientist** *noun* an adherent or practitioner of pseudo-science; a person who falsely or mistakenly claims to be or is regarded as a scientist: M20. **pseudoscorpion** *noun* (ZOOLOGY) any of various small arachnids of the order Pseudoscorpiones, resembling a scorpion but tailless, and found in soil, leaf litter, bark, etc. M19. **pseudoseizure** *noun* (MEDICINE) an attack resembling an epileptic fit but either feigned or due to emotional disturbance L20. **pseudose'matic** *adjective* (ZOOLOGY) = MIMETIC 4a L19. **pseudosex** *noun* (*a*) pseudosexual activity; (*b*) perverted sexual activity: M20. **pseudo'sexual** *adjective* (*a*) ZOOLOGY designating or pertaining to the parthenogenetic production by certain crustaceans of eggs resembling those of the sexual phase; (*b*) ZOOLOGY & PSYCHOLOGY designating sexual behaviour motivated by fear of aggression, desire for dominance, etc., (freq. in overcrowded conditions) rather than by genuinely sexual aims: E20. **pseudosolari'zation** *noun* solarization involving the Sabatier effect L19. **pseudosoph** *noun* (*rare*) [Greek *sophos* wise] a person who falsely affects, or supposes himself or herself, to be wise; a pretender to wisdom: M19. **pseudo-statement** *noun* (PHILOSOPHY) an expression that does not refer or correspond to an objective fact, but is used for its subjective effect on the hearer or reader E20. **pseudostem** *noun* the apparent trunk of a banana plant or related plant, which consists of leaf bases closely packed around a stem L19. **pseudostome** *noun* a false mouth; *spec.* in ZOOLOGY, a false osculum arising from folding in a complex sponge: L19. **pseudostratifi'cation** *noun* (GEOLOGY) = PSEUDOBEDDING L19. **pseudo'stratified** *adjective* (*a*) GEOLOGY of or exhibiting pseudostratification; (*b*) BIOLOGY designating epithelium composed of a single layer of columnar cells with nuclei at varying distances from the basal lamina, giving the appearance of several layers: L19. **pseudo'symmetry** *noun* (MINERALOGY) apparent symmetry produced by the combination (e.g. twinning) of crystals with different symmetries L19. **pseudotubercu'losis** *noun* (VETERINARY MEDICINE) any of several bacterial diseases resembling tuberculosis that occur chiefly in birds, rodents, and other mammals, esp. sheep, and are caused by pasteurellae or corynebacteria L19. **pseudo'uracil** *noun* (BIOCHEMISTRY) the uracil residue in pseudouridine M20. **pseudo'uridine** *noun* (BIOCHEMISTRY) a nucleoside, 5-ribosyluracil, found in transfer RNA and differing from uridine in having the sugar residue attached at a carbon, not a nitrogen, atom M20.

pseudocide /ˈsjuːdəsʌɪd/ *noun.* M20.
[from PSEUDO- + -CIDE, after *suicide*.]
1 An apparent attempt at suicide, undertaken with the intention of failure. M20.
2 A person making such an attempt. L20.
■ **pseudo'cidal** *adjective* of, pertaining to, or characteristic of (a) pseudocide L20.

pseudograph /ˈsjuːdə(ʊ)grɑːf/ *noun.* E17.
[Late Latin *pseudographus* from Greek *pseudographos*, from PSEUDO- + *-graphos* -GRAPH.]
1 A counterfeit writer. *rare* (only in Dicts.). E17.
2 A spurious writing; a literary work purporting to be by a person other than the real author. E19.

pseudography /sjuːˈdɒgrəfi/ *noun.* L16.
[Late Latin *pseudographia* from Greek = false drawing, writing, or description, from *pseudographos*: see prec., -GRAPHY.]
1 The writing of words falsely, esp. in respect of sound or usage; false, incorrect, or bad spelling; an instance of this. L16.
2 False argument. *rare.* E17.

pseudohermaphroditism
/ˌsjuːdəʊhəːˈmafrədʌɪtɪz(ə)m/ *noun.* L19.
[from PSEUDO- + HERMAPHRODITISM.]
MEDICINE. The condition of having the gonads and chromosomes of one sex and some anatomical characteristics of the other sex.
■ **pseudohermaphrodite** *noun* a person exhibiting pseudohermaphroditism L19.

pseudologia /sjuːdə(ʊ)ˈləʊdʒɪə/ *noun.* E20.
[mod. Latin from Greek = falsehood.]
PSYCHOLOGY. In full ***pseudologia fantastica, pseudologia phantastica*** /fanˈtastɪkə/ [medieval Latin fem. of *fantasticus* imaginary, FANTASTIC]. The telling of elaborate and fantastic stories, esp. about oneself, as if believing them true (though readily changing them if challenged), esp. as a feature of mental illness or personality disorder.

pseudology /sjuːˈdɒlədʒi/ *noun.* M17.
[Greek *pseudologia*, from *pseudologos*, from PSEUDO- + *logos* saying, speech: see -OLOGY.]
1 The (systematic) making of false statements (freq. *joc.*); the art of lying. M17.
2 The study or subject of false statements; a false or pretended branch of knowledge. M19.
■ **pseudologer** *noun* (*rare*) a maker of false statements, a (systematic) liar M17. **pseudo'logical** *adjective* of, pertaining to or characteristic of pseudology L19. **pseudologist** *noun* (*a*) = PSEUDOLOGER; (*b*) an expert in or student of pseudology: E19.

pseudomonas /sjuːdə(ʊ)ˈməʊnəs, sjuːˈdɒmənəs/ *noun.* E20.
[mod. Latin *Pseudomonas* (see below), from PSEUDO- + Greek *monas* MONAD.]
BIOLOGY. A member of the genus *Pseudomonas* of aerobic generally rod-shaped Gram-negative bacteria occurring chiefly in soil and detritus, including the pathogens of melioidosis and many plant diseases.
■ **pseudomonad** *noun* a bacterium of the genus *Pseudomonas*, the family Pseudomonadaceae, or the order Pseudomonadales E20.

pseudomorph /ˈsjuːdə(ʊ)mɔːf/ *noun & verb.* M19.
[from PSEUDO- + -MORPH.]
MINERALOGY, PALAEONTOLOGY, & ARCHAEOLOGY. ▶**A** *noun.* A lump or mass of mineral substance having the crystal form of another mineral, or the shape of an organism or artefact, having been formed by substitution or by chemical or physical alteration. M19.
▶**B** *verb trans.* Replace (another substance) to form a pseudomorph. Chiefly as ***pseudomorphed*** *ppl adjective.* E20.
■ **pseudo'morphic** *adjective* pertaining to, or of the nature of, a pseudomorph L19. **pseudo'morphically** *adverb* M20. **pseudo'morphism** *noun* the formation or occurrence of pseudomorphs; the state of being a pseudomorph: M19. **pseudo'morphous** *adjective* = PSEUDOMORPHIC E19. **pseudo'morphously** *adverb* M20.

pseudonym /ˈsjuːdənɪm/ *noun.* M19.
[French *pseudonyme* from Greek *pseudōnumon* neut. of *pseudōnumos*, formed as PSEUDO- + *onuma* name: see -NYM.]
1 A false or fictitious name, *esp.* one assumed by an author. M19.
2 TAXONOMY. A name of a species other than its taxonomic name; a common name. *rare.* L19.
■ **pseudo'nymic** *adjective* = PSEUDONYMOUS M19.

pseudonymous /sjuːˈdɒnɪməs/ *adjective.* E18.
[from Greek *pseudōnumos*: see prec., -OUS.]
1 Bearing or taking a false name; *esp.* writing under a pseudonym; of, pertaining to, or characterizing a person who writes under a pseudonym. E18.
2 Written under a pseudonym; bearing the name of a person other than the real author. E18.
■ **pseudo'nymity** *noun* the character or condition of being pseudonymous; the use of a pseudonym: L19. **pseudonymously** *adverb* M19.

pseudoperipteros /ˌsjuːdəʊpəˈrɪpt(ə)rɒs/ *noun.* Also (earlier) †**-peripter.** L17.
[Late Greek, formed as PSEUDO- + *peripteros* PERIPTER.]
ARCHITECTURE. A form of temple or other building with free columns forming a portico in front (and sometimes in the rear) as in a peripteral building, but with the rest of the columns engaged in the walls instead of standing free.
■ **pseudoperipteral** *adjective* having the structure of a pseudoperipteros M19.

pseudopod /ˈsjuːdə(ʊ)pɒd/ *noun.* L19.
[from next.]
ZOOLOGY. **1** = PSEUDOPODIUM. L19.
2 A projection serving as a foot in the larvae of certain insects. E20.

pseudopodium /sjuːdə(ʊ)ˈpəʊdɪəm/ *noun.* Pl. **-ia** /-ɪə/. M19.
[from PSEUDO- + PODIUM.]
BIOLOGY. **1** A protrusion of part of the protoplasm of an amoeboid cell, for movement, ingestion of food, etc. M19.
2 BOTANY. A leafless prolongation of the stem in certain mosses, *esp.* that supporting the capsule in sphagnum mosses. M19.
■ **pseudopodial** *adjective* of, pertaining to, or connected with a pseudopodium M19.

pseudopregnancy /sjuːdə(ʊ)ˈprɛgnənsi/ *noun.* M19.
[from PSEUDO- + PREGNANCY.]
1 MEDICINE. An abnormal condition in which signs of pregnancy such as amenorrhoea, nausea, and abdominal swelling are present in a woman who is not pregnant. M19.
2 ZOOLOGY. A state marked by changes in the reproductive organs and mammary glands similar to those of early pregnancy, occurring in many female mammals after ovulation when fertilization has not occurred. E20.
■ **pseudo'pregnant** *adjective* of, in, or characteristic of the state of pseudopregnancy E20.

pseudoscalar /sjuːdə(ʊ)ˈskeɪlə/ *noun & adjective.* M20.
[from PSEUDO- + SCALAR *noun & adjective.*]
MATH. & PHYSICS. ▶**A** *noun.* A variable quantity that transforms as a scalar under rotation but changes sign under reflection. Also, a subatomic particle whose wave function is such a quantity, having zero spin and odd parity. M20.
▶**B** *adjective.* Pertaining to, of the nature of, or described by a pseudoscalar. M20.

pseudoscopic /sjuːdə(ʊ)ˈskɒpɪk/ *adjective.* M19.
[from PSEUDO- + -SCOPE + -IC.]
Pertaining to or characteristic of a pseudoscope; involving apparent reversal of relief (convexity and concavity), esp. due to transposition of images between the left and right eyes.
■ **'pseudoscope** *noun* a binocular optical instrument which produces an apparent reversal of relief, a reversed stereoscope M19. **pseudoscopically** *adverb* L19. **pseu'doscopy** *noun* pseudoscopic optical illusion M20.

pseudosuchian /sjuːdə(ʊ)ˈsuːkɪən/ *noun & adjective.* E20.
[from PSEUDO- + Greek *soukhos* crocodile + -IAN.]
PALAEONTOLOGY. ▶**A** *noun.* A small fossil thecodont reptile of the suborder Pseudosuchia of primitive, often bipedal, carnivores of the Triassic period. E20.
▶**B** *adjective.* Of, pertaining to, or designating an animal of this kind. E20.

pseudovector /sjuːdə(ʊ)ˈvɛktə/ *noun & adjective.* E20.
[from PSEUDO- + VECTOR *noun.*]
MATH. & PHYSICS. ▶**A** *noun.* A vector whose direction is reversed when the sign of an odd number of coordinates is changed. E20.
▶**B** *adjective.* Pertaining to, of the nature of, or described by a pseudovector. M20.

pshaw /pʃɔː, ʃɔː/ *interjection, noun, & verb. arch.* L17.
[Natural exclam. Cf. PISH *verb, interjection, & noun.*]
▶**A** *interjection.* Expr. contempt, impatience, or disgust. L17.
▶**B** *noun.* An utterance of 'pshaw'. E18.
▶**C** *verb.* **1** *verb intrans.* Say 'pshaw!' (*at*). M18.
2 *verb trans.* Say 'pshaw!' at. M19.

psi *abbreviation.*
Pounds per square inch.

psi /psʌɪ, sʌɪ/ *noun.* LME.
[Greek *psei.*]
1 The twenty-third letter (Ψ, ψ) of the Greek alphabet. LME.
2 Paranormal phenomena or faculties collectively; the psychic force supposed to be manifested by these. Freq. *attrib.*, as ***psi powers*** etc. Cf. PSIONIC. M20.
3 NUCLEAR PHYSICS. A neutral, relatively long-lived strongly interacting particle with a mass of 3.1 MeV, a spin of +1, zero hypercharge and isospin, and negative parity, produced by high-energy collisions. Also (***psi prime*** or ψ′), a similar particle of mass 3.7 MeV that decays into a psi and two pions. L20.

psia *abbreviation.*
Pounds per square inch absolute.

psilanthropism /sʌɪˈlanθrəpɪz(ə)m/ *noun.* E19.
[from ecclesiastical Greek *psilanthrōpos*, from *psilos* bare, mere + *anthrōpos* man: see -ISM.]
The doctrine or belief that Jesus was human but not divine.
■ **psilanthropist** *noun* an adherent of or believer in psilanthropism E19.

psilocybin /sʌɪləˈsʌɪbɪn/ *noun.* M20.
[from mod. Latin *Psilocybe* (see below), from Greek *psilos* bare, smooth + *kubē* head: see -IN[1].]
CHEMISTRY. An alkaloid which is the phosphate ester of psilocin and is present in several toadstools (esp. of the genus *Psilocybe*), producing hallucinogenic effects similar to those of LSD but milder and more short-lived.
■ **'psilocin** *noun* the alkaloid which is the active hallucinogenic metabolite of psilocybin M20.

psilomelane /sʌɪˈlɒməleɪn/ *noun.* M19.
[from Greek *psilos* smooth + *melan* neut. of *melas* black.]
MINERALOGY. A mixture of hydrated manganese oxides occurring as smooth black amorphous, botryoidal, or stalactitic masses.

psilosis /sʌɪˈləʊsɪs/ *noun.* Pl. **-loses** /-ˈləʊsiːz/. M19.
[Greek *psilōsis*, from *psiloun* strip bare: see -OSIS.]
1 MEDICINE. = SPRUE *noun*[1] 2. M19.
2 PHILOLOGY. Esp. in Greek, the substitution of plosive for aspirated or fricative consonants (as *p* for *ph*) or of smooth for rough breathings. E20.
■ **psilotic** /-ˈlɒtɪk/ *adjective* M20.

psionic /sʌɪˈɒnɪk/ *adjective.* M20.
[from PSI + *-onic* after *electronic.*]
Pertaining to or involving psychic or paranormal phenomena or (esp.) powers; using methods related to dowsing in medical diagnosis.

■ **psionically** *adverb* L20. **psionics** *noun* (the branch of knowledge that deals with) the paranormal M20.

psittacine /ˈsɪtəkʌɪn, ˈsɪtəsʌɪn/ *adjective & noun.* L19.
[Latin *psittacinus*, from *psittacus*, Greek *psittakos* parrot: see -INE[1].]
► **A** *adjective.* Of or belonging to a parrot or the parrot family; *fig.* parrot-like, characterized by thoughtless repetition. L19.
► **B** *noun.* A bird of the parrot family. L19.

psittacism /ˈsɪtəsɪz(ə)m/ *noun.* L19.
[from Greek *psittakos* parrot + -ISM.]
The mechanical repetition of previously received ideas or images, reflecting neither true reasoning nor feeling; repetition of words or phrases parrot-fashion; an instance of this.

psittacosaurus /sɪtakəˈsɔːrəs/ *noun.* E20.
[mod. Latin genus name, formed as prec. + *sauros* -SAUR.]
A partly bipedal herbivorous dinosaur of the mid Cretaceous period, which had a parrot-like beak and was probably ancestral to other ceratopsians.

psittacosis /sɪtəˈkəʊsɪs/ *noun.* Pl. **-coses** /-ˈkəʊsiːz/. L19.
[mod. Latin, from Latin *psittacus* parrot + -OSIS.]
MEDICINE. A contagious disease of birds caused by a virus-like bacterium, *Chlamydia psittaci*, and transmissible (esp. from parrots and budgerigars) to humans, causing a form of pneumonia. Cf. ORNITHOSIS.
■ **psittacotic** /-ˈkɒtɪk/ *adjective* M20.

p-skhent *noun* var. of PSCHENT.

psoas /ˈsəʊəs/ *noun.* L17.
[Pl. (taken as *sing.*) of mod. Latin *psoa*, Greek *psoa*, usu. in pl. *psoai*, accus. *psoas*, the muscles of the loins.]
ANATOMY. A large muscle in the groin region which, with the iliacus, flexes the hip (more fully ***psoas major***). Also (in full ***psoas minor***), a smaller muscle present in mammals and some humans, having a similar action. Also ***psoas muscle***.

psocid /ˈsəʊkɪd, -sɪd/ *noun.* L19.
[mod. Latin *Psocidae* family name, from *Psocus* genus name, from Greek *psōkhein* grind: see -ID[3].]
ENTOMOLOGY. Any small insect with long antennae, of the order Psocoptera, which feeds on fragments of vegetable or animal matter in bark, straw, soil, among books and papers, etc.

psophometer /sɒˈfɒmɪtə/ *noun.* M20.
[from Greek *psophos* noise + -METER.]
ELECTRICITY. An instrument for giving a reading approximately proportional to the subjective aural effect of the noise in a communication circuit.
■ **psophoˈmetric** *adjective* M20. **psophoˈmetrically** *adverb* L20.

psora /ˈsɔːrə/ *noun. obsolete* exc. *Hist.* L17.
[Latin from Greek *psōra* itch, mange.]
MEDICINE. Any (esp. a contagious) itching skin disease; scabies.

psoralen /ˈsɔːrəlɛn/ *noun.* M20.
[from mod. Latin *Psoralea* (from Greek *psōraleos* itchy, mangy, from *psōra*: see prec.), former genus name of the clover *Trifolium unifolium*, + *-en* (cf. -ENE).]
CHEMISTRY & PHARMACOLOGY. A crystalline tricyclic lactone, $C_{11}H_6O_3$, occurring in certain plants and used in perfumery and to treat certain skin disorders; any derivative of this.

psoriasis /sɒˈrʌɪəsɪs/ *noun.* Pl. **-ases** /-əsiːz/. L17.
[mod. Latin from Greek *psōriasis*, from *psōrian* have the itch, from *psōra* PSORA.]
A chronic skin disease of unknown cause characterized by dry reddish itching scaly or flaky patches.
■ **psoriatic** /sɔːrɪˈatɪk/ *adjective & noun* (*a*) *adjective* of the nature of or affected with psoriasis; (*b*) *noun* a person affected with psoriasis: L19.

psoroptic /sɔːˈrɒptɪk/ *adjective.* E20.
[from mod. Latin *Psoroptes* genus name of a mite (formed as PSORA, after *Sarcoptes*): see -IC.]
VETERINARY MEDICINE. Of mange: caused by mites living on the skin.

PSS *abbreviation.*
COMPUTING & TELECOMMUNICATIONS. Packet-switching service; packet switch stream.

Pss. *abbreviation.*
Psalms (in the Bible).

psst /p(ə)st/ *interjection & noun.* Also **pst.** E20.
[Imit.]
► **A** *interjection.* Attracting attention or conveying a warning, esp. surreptitiously. E20.
► **B** *noun.* An utterance of 'psst!'. M20.

PST *abbreviation. N. Amer.*
Pacific Standard Time.

PSTN *abbreviation.*
Public switched telephone network.

PSV *abbreviation.*
Public service vehicle.

psych /sʌɪk/ *noun & verb. colloq.* Also (exc. in sense A.1) **psyche.** L19.
[Abbreviation of PSYCHIATRY, PSYCHOLOGY, PSYCHIC, PSYCHOANALYSE, etc.]
► **A** *noun.* **I 1** Psychology, psychiatry. L19.
2 A psychologist, a psychiatrist, a psychoanalyst. M20.
► **II 3 a** In *pl.* Psychical research. *rare.* E20. ►**b** A psychic person. L20.
4 *BRIDGE.* (Usu. **psyche.**) A psychic bid. M20.
► **B** *verb.* Pres. pple & verbal noun **-(e)ing.**
► **I 1** *verb trans.* Subject to psychoanalysis or psychological testing. E20.
2 *verb trans.* Prepare (oneself or another) mentally for an ordeal etc. (usu. foll. by *up*, also *into* a mental state, situation, etc.); gain a psychological advantage over, intimidate, demoralize (usu. foll. by *out*). Freq. in *pass.* M20.
3 *verb trans.* Foll. by *out*: analyse in psychological terms; work out. M20.
4 *verb intrans.* Foll. by *out*: break down mentally; become confused, deranged, or intimidated. L20.

> 📖 **2** P. A. WHITNEY He was absolutely without fear. Nothing ever psyched him out before a race. N. SEDAKA I'd psyched myself into thinking Festival Hall was an intimate room. R. CARVER She'd just have to tell herself she could do it, get herself psyched up for it. **3** S. BRILL Hoffa's ability . . to psyche out the opposition's thinking.

► **II 5** *verb intrans. BRIDGE.* Make a psychic bid. M20. ►**b** *verb trans.* Make as a psychic bid; deceive (one's opponents) with a psychic bid. M20.

> 📖 **5b** *Bridge Magazine* Both Souths psyched a one spade response.

psychagogic /sʌɪkəˈɡɒdʒɪk/ *adjective.* M19.
[Greek *psukhagōgikos* persuasive, from *psukhagōgia* persuasion, formed as next: see -IC.]
1 Influencing the mind; persuasive, attractive. M19.
2 Calling up the spirits of the dead. *rare.* L19.
■ **psychagogical** *adjective* = PSYCHAGOGIC E19. **psychagogically** *adverb* M19.

psychagogue /ˈsʌɪkəɡɒɡ/ *noun.* M19.
[from Greek *psukhē* PSYCHE *noun*[1] + *agōgos* leading: cf. PEDAGOGUE.]
1 A person who instructs the mind. *rare.* M19.
2 A person who calls up the spirits of the dead; a necromancer. M19.

psychal /ˈsʌɪk(ə)l/ *adjective. rare.* M19.
[from PSYCHE *noun*[1] + -AL[1].]
Of the psyche; spiritual; psychological, psychical.

psychanalysis *noun* see PSYCHOANALYSIS.

psychasthenia /sʌɪkəsˈθiːnɪə/ *noun.* E20.
[from PSYCHO- + ASTHENIA.]
PSYCHOLOGY (now *Hist.*). Neurosis in which there is fear or anxiety.
■ **psychasthenic** /-ˈθɛnɪk/ *adjective* pertaining to or affected by such neurosis E20.

psyche /ˈsʌɪki/ *noun*[1]. M17.
[Latin from Greek *psukhē* breath, life, soul, mind (also butterfly, moth), rel. to *psukhein* breathe; in some uses with allus. to *Psukhē* Psyche, in Greek mythol. the beloved of Eros (Cupid), the god of love.]
► **I 1** The soul, the spirit. Formerly also (*rare*), the animating principle of the universe. Now chiefly *Hist.* M17.
2 The mind, esp. in its spiritual, emotional, and motivational aspects; the collective mental or psychological characteristics of a nation, people, etc. E20.
► **II 3** [After Greek.] A butterfly, a moth. *rare.* E19.
► **III 4** [Said to be after Raphael's painting of Psyche.] A cheval-glass. Also ***psyche-glass***. *arch.* M19.
Comb.: ***psyche-glass***: see sense 4 above; **Psyche knot** = *GRECIAN knot.*

psyche *noun*[2] *& verb* see PSYCH *noun & verb.*

psychedelia /sʌɪkɪˈdiːlɪə/ *noun.* M20.
[Back-form. from next: see -IA[2].]
Psychedelic articles or phenomena collectively, esp. music, posters, paintings, etc.; the subculture associated with psychedelic drugs.

psychedelic /sʌɪkɪˈdɛlɪk, -ˈdiːlɪk/ *adjective & noun.* M20.
[Irreg. from PSYCHE *noun*[1] + Greek *dēloun* make manifest, reveal, from *dēlos* manifest, clear: see -IC.]
► **A** *adjective.* **1 a** Of a drug: producing a change in, esp. an apparent expansion of, consciousness through greater awareness of sensations, emotions, and unconscious motivations (freq. through symbolic hallucinations). M20. ►**b** Of, pertaining to, or produced by such a drug; concerned with or characterized by the use of such drugs. M20.
2 Imitating or inspired by an effect produced by a psychedelic drug; *spec.* having vivid colours. M20.

> 📖 **1a** C. WILSON Aldous Huxley . . advocated the use of psychedelic drugs to 'expand consciousness'. **b** V. BROME A renaissance of the irrational had turned thousands of young people toward psychedelic experience. **2** *Observer* The very latest psychedelic colours, electric purples and greens. **psychedelic rock** = *acid rock* s.v. ACID *noun.*

► **B** *noun.* **1** A psychedelic drug. M20.
2 A person who takes a psychedelic drug or has a psychedelic lifestyle. Now *rare.* M20.
■ **psychedelically** *adverb* M20. **psychedelicize** /-sʌɪz/ *verb trans.* (*colloq.*) make psychedelic or bizarrely colourful M20.

psychiater /sʌɪˈkʌɪətə/ *noun.* Now *rare* or *obsolete.* M19.
[from Greek *psukhē* PSYCHE *noun*[1] + *iatēr* healer.]
= PSYCHIATRIST.

psychiatric /sʌɪkɪˈatrɪk/ *adjective.* M19.
[formed as PSYCHIATRY + -IC.]
Of or pertaining to psychiatry; connected with or affected by mental illness or emotional disturbance.
psychiatric social work social work designed to support and supplement psychiatric treatment. **psychiatric social worker** a social worker engaged or qualified in psychiatric social work.
■ **psychiatrical** *adjective* (*rare*) L19. **psychiatrically** *adverb* M19. **psychiatrics** *noun* (now *rare*) the theory or practice of psychiatry M19.

psychiatrise *verb* var. of PSYCHIATRIZE.

psychiatrist /sʌɪˈkʌɪətrɪst/ *noun.* L19.
[from PSYCHIATRY + -IST.]
A qualified practitioner of psychiatry; a person who treats mental illness, emotional disturbance, etc.

psychiatrize /sʌɪˈkʌɪətrʌɪz/ *verb trans.* Also **-ise.** E20.
[from next + -IZE.]
Treat or analyse psychiatrically.
■ **psychiatriˈzation** *noun* L20.

psychiatry /sʌɪˈkʌɪətri/ *noun.* M19.
[from Greek *psukhē* PSYCHE *noun*[1] + *iatreia* healing, from *iatros* healer.]
The medical treatment of mental illness, emotional disturbance, and abnormal behaviour.
social psychiatry: see SOCIAL *adjective.*

psychic /ˈsʌɪkɪk/ *noun & adjective.* E19.
[Greek *psukhikos* of the mind or soul, from *psukhē* PSYCHE *noun*[1]: see -IC.]
► **A** *noun.* **1 a** In *pl.* (treated as *sing.*). Formerly, psychology. Now, psychical research. E19. ►**b** A person who is regarded as particularly susceptible to supernatural or paranormal influence; a medium, a clairvoyant. L19. ►**c** The realm or sphere of psychical phenomena. E20.
2 *BRIDGE.* A psychic bid. M20.
► **B** *adjective.* **1** = PSYCHICAL *adjective* 3. M19. ►**b** Involving or (esp. of a person) regarded as susceptible to supernatural or paranormal influence; having paranormal powers, clairvoyant. E20.
2 *CHRISTIAN THEOLOGY.* Pertaining to the natural or animal soul, as distinct from the spirit. M19.
3 Of or pertaining to the human mind or psyche; spiritual, psychological, mental. Also in *MEDICINE* (now *rare*), psychogenic. L19.
4 *BRIDGE.* Of a bid, bidder, or bidding: deliberately misrepresenting the player's hand so as to deceive the opponents. M20.

> 📖 **1b** N. COWARD I've got second sight over certain things. I'm almost psychic. **3** D. CUPITT God is the Self, the . . unified personality towards which our psychic life tends. **psychic energizer** *MEDICINE* an antidepressant drug, esp. one effective against psychotic states. **psychic income** *ECONOMICS* the non-monetary or non-material satisfactions that accompany an occupation or economic activity.

■ **psychicist** /ˈsʌɪkɪsɪst/ *noun* a psychical researcher L19.

psychical /ˈsʌɪkɪk(ə)l/ *adjective.* M17.
[formed as prec.: see -ICAL.]
1 = PSYCHIC *adjective* 3. M17.
2 *CHRISTIAN THEOLOGY.* = PSYCHIC *adjective* 2. E18.
3 Of, pertaining to, or concerned with phenomena or faculties which appear to transcend the laws of physics and are attributed by some to spiritual or hyperphysical agency; involving paranormal phenomena of the mind, parapsychological. L19.

psychically /ˈsʌɪkɪk(ə)li/ *adverb.* E19.
[from PSYCHIC *adjective* or PSYCHICAL: see -ICALLY.]
In a psychic or psychical manner; with reference to the soul or mind; mentally.

psychism /ˈsʌɪkɪz(ə)m/ *noun.* M19.
[formed as PSYCHE *noun*[1] + -ISM.]
1 a = VITALISM. Now *rare* or *obsolete.* M19. ►**b** = ANIMISM 2. Now *rare* or *obsolete.* L19.
2 The doctrine proposing the existence of psychic phenomena; psychic phenomena. Also, psychical research. L19.
3 Psychic or mental activity. L19.
■ **psychist** *noun* †(*a*) a psychologist; (*b*) a person who believes in or investigates psychic phenomena; (*c*) a bridge player who practises psychic bidding: L19.

psycho /ˈsʌɪkəʊ/ *noun, adjective, & verb. colloq.* E20.
[Abbreviation.]
► **A** *noun.* Pl. **-os.**
1 Psychoanalysis; psychology. E20.
2 A psychologist. E20.
3 A psychopath. M20.
► **B** *adjective.* **1** Psychological; psychoanalytic. E20.

2 Psychopathic. M20.
▶ **C** *verb trans.* Psychoanalyse; = PSYCH *verb* 1. Chiefly as ***psychoed*** *ppl adjective.* E20.

psycho- /ˈsʌɪkəʊ/ *combining form.* Before a vowel also **psych-.**
[Greek *psukho-*, formed as PSYCHE *noun*¹: see -O-.]
Of or pertaining to the mind or psyche; of or pertaining to psychology or psychical phenomena.
■ **psychoˈactive** *adjective* = PSYCHOTROPIC *adjective* M20. **psychoacˈtivity** *noun* psychotropic action L20. **psycho-aesˈthetic** *adjective* of or pertaining to psycho-aesthetics E20. **psycho-aesˈthetics** *noun* (the branch of knowledge that deals with) aesthetic perception in its psychological aspects E20. **psychobabble** *noun* (*colloq.*, *derog.*) lay jargon, esp. concerning personality and relationships, derived from the technical language of psychology L20. **psychobabbler** *noun* (*colloq.*, *derog.*) a user of psychobabble L20. **psychoˈcentric** *adjective* (PSYCHOLOGY) treating the mind rather than the body as the important factor in human behaviour M20. **psychoˈchemical** *adjective & noun* (*a*) *adjective* pertaining to the relationship between chemicals and the mind, esp. the way the former can be used to modify the latter; (of a drug) psychotropic; (*b*) *noun* a psychotropic drug: M20. **psychoˈcultural** *adjective* relating to the interaction between the culture in which individuals live and their psychological characteristics M20. **psychodiagˈnosis** *noun* = PSYCHODIAGNOSTICS M20. **psychodiagˈnostic** *adjective* (PSYCHOLOGY) of or pertaining to psychodiagnostics M20. **psychodiagˈnostics** *noun* (PSYCHOLOGY) the investigation of a subject's personality, *spec.* by means of the Rorschach and other projective tests M20. **psychodysˈleptic** *noun* [after *psycholeptic* with inserted DYS-] PHARMACOLOGY = PSYCHOTOMIMETIC *noun* M20. **psychoˈendocrine** *adjective* relating to or involving the endocrine glands and also mood and behaviour M20. **psychoˌendocriˈnology** *noun* the branch of science that deals with the relationship between endocrine hormones and mental states, esp. mood and behaviour M20. **psychogalˈvanic** *adjective* of, designating, or involving the galvanic skin response E20. **psychogalvaˈnometer** *noun* a galvanometer used to measure the psychogalvanic response M20. **psychogeoˈgraphic, psychogeoˈgraphical** *adjectives* of or pertaining to psychogeography M20. **psychogeˈography** *noun* (the investigation of) the effect of the geographical environment on the mind M20. **psychoˈleptic** *adjective* [Greek *lēpsis* seizing] (*a*) characterized by a sudden change to a less excited or less tense mood; (*b*) (of a drug) affecting the psyche, esp. as a sedative or antidepressant: M20. **psycholytic** /-ˈlɪtɪk/ *adjective* (of a drug) disrupting established responses and emotional reactions; ***psycholytic therapy***, therapy that combines controlled use of drugs such as LSD with psychotherapeutic instruction and discussion: M20. **psychomotor** *adjective* (MEDICINE & PHYSIOLOGY) (*a*) pertaining to or involving the origination of movement by conscious (voluntary) mental action; (*b*) designating (an attack of) a type of epilepsy freq. associated with disease of the temporal lobe and involving a state of altered consciousness sometimes characterized by automatisms, hallucinations, and disordered memory: L19. **psychoˈneural** *adjective* of or pertaining to the relationship between the mind and the nervous system E20. **psychoneuroimmuˈnology** MEDICINE the study of the effect of a person's mental state on his or her immune system and hence susceptibility to disease L20. **psychopharmaˈceutical** *noun & adjective* (a drug that is) psychotropic M20. **psychoplasm** *noun* (now *rare* or *obsolete*) [after *protoplasm*] the basis of sensibility or consciousness conceived as a substance L19. **psychopoˈlitical** *adjective* both psychological and political; relating to psychopolitics: E20. **psychoˈpolitics** *noun* (the branch of knowledge that deals with) the interaction of politics and human behaviour M20. **psychoˈsocial** *adjective* of or pertaining to the interrelation of social factors and individual thought and behaviour; pertaining to the interrelation of mind and society in human development: L19. **psychosocioˈlogical** *adjective* of or pertaining to psychosociology E20. **psychosociˈology** *noun* sociology as connected with or applying the findings of psychology E20. **psychosphere** *noun* the sphere or realm of consciousness E20. **psychoˈstimulant** *noun & adjective* (a drug) increasing one's activity and alertness M20. **psychoˈsynthesis** *noun* the integration of separated elements of the psyche or personality through psychoanalysis E20.

psychoacoustic /ˌsʌɪkəʊəˈkuːstɪk/ *adjective.* L19.
[from PSYCHO- + ACOUSTIC.]
Of or pertaining to the perception of sound, including speech, or the branch of science that deals with this.
■ **psychoacoustical** *adjective* = PSYCHOACOUSTIC M20. **psychoacoustically** *adverb* M20. **psychoacoustician** /-ˈstɪʃ(ə)n/ *noun* an expert in or student of psychoacoustics M20. **psychoacoustics** *noun* the science of the perception of sound M20.

psychoanalysis /ˌsʌɪkəʊəˈnalɪsɪs/ *noun.* Also (*rare*) **psychanalysis.** E20.
[from PSYCHO- + ANALYSIS.]
Analysis of the unconscious forces believed to affect the mind; *spec.* (*a*) a therapeutic method originated by Sigmund Freud for treating mental illnesses by bringing into consciousness a patient's unconscious fears, conflicts, and fantasies (attributed chiefly to the development of the sexual instinct) through free association of ideas, interpretation of dreams, etc., and dealing with them through transference; (*b*) a theory of personality, motivation, and neurosis derived from Freudian analysis, based on the interaction of conscious, preconscious, and unconscious levels of the mind, the ego, id, and superego, and the repression of the sexual instinct. Also, the psychology of the unconscious.
■ **psychoˈanalyse** *verb* (*a*) *verb trans.* subject to or treat by psychoanalysis; (*b*) *verb intrans.* perform psychoanalysis: E20. **psychoˈanalyst** *noun* a person who practises or has training in psychoanalysis E20. **psychoanaˈlytic** *adjective* of, pertaining to, or employing psychoanalysis E20. **psychoanaˈlytical** *adjective* (*a*) relating to the analysis of mental processes; (*b*) = PSYCHOANALYTIC: E19. **psychoanaˈlytically** *adverb* by means of or as regards psychoanalysis E20.

psychobiography /ˌsʌɪkəʊbʌɪˈɒgrəfi/ *noun.* M20.
[from PSYCHO- + BIOGRAPHY.]
(A) biography dealing esp. with the psychology of the subject.
■ **psychobiographer** *noun* a writer of psychobiography L20. **psychobioˈgraphic, psychobioˈgraphical** *adjectives* L20. **psychobioˈgraphically** *adverb* L20.

psychobiology /ˌsʌɪkəʊbʌɪˈɒlədʒi/ *noun.* E20.
[from PSYCHO- + BIOLOGY.]
The branch of science that deals with the biological basis of behaviour or mental phenomena.
■ **ˌpsychobioˈlogic** *adjective* = PSYCHOBIOLOGICAL M20. **ˌpsychobioˈlogical** *adjective* of or pertaining to psychobiology; both psychological and biological: E20. **ˌpsychobioˈlogically** *adverb* in a psychobiological manner; in relation to psychobiology: M20. **psychobiologist** *noun* an expert in or student of psychobiology M20.

psychodrama /ˈsʌɪkəʊdrɑːmə/ *noun.* M20.
[from PSYCHO- + DRAMA.]
1 An extempore psychotherapeutic play in which a patient acts out his or her feelings and problems with or in front of fellow patients and therapists; psychotherapy involving such a use of drama. M20.
2 A play, film, novel, etc., in which psychological elements are the main interest. M20.

psychodramatic /ˌsʌɪkəʊdrəˈmatɪk/ *adjective.* M20.
[from prec. after *dramatic*.]
1 Of, pertaining to, or employing therapeutic psychodrama. M20.
2 Pertaining to or of the nature of a psychodrama (sense 2). M20.
■ **psychodramatics** *noun* (*a*) the use of psychodrama as therapy; (*b*) psychological dramatics: M20. **psychodramatist** *noun* (*a*) a person who directs or takes part in therapeutic psychodrama; (*b*) a person who writes psychodramas: M20.

psychodynamic /ˌsʌɪkəʊdʌɪˈnamɪk/ *adjective.* L19.
[from PSYCHO- + DYNAMIC *adjective.*]
Of or pertaining to psychodynamics.
■ **psychodynamically** *adverb* M20.

psychodynamics /ˌsʌɪkəʊdʌɪˈnamɪks/ *noun.* L19.
[from PSYCHO- + DYNAMICS.]
The science of mental action; (the branch of science that deals with) the interrelation of the mental (esp. unconscious) forces that determine personality and motivation.

psychogenesis /sʌɪkə(ʊ)ˈdʒɛnɪsɪs/ *noun.* M19.
[from PSYCHO- + -GENESIS.]
1 (The branch of science that deals with) the origin and development of the mind. M19.
2 Origin or evolution supposedly due to the activity of the soul or mind. Now *rare* or *obsolete.* L19.
3 The psychological cause to which mental illness or behavioural disturbance may be attributed. E20.
■ **psychogeˈnetic** *adjective* of or pertaining to psychogenesis L19. **psychogeˈnetically** *adverb* in relation to, or in respect of, psychogenesis L19. **psyˈchogeny** *noun* (*rare*) = PSYCHOGENESIS 1 L19.

psychogenetics /ˌsʌɪkəʊdʒɪˈnɛtɪks/ *noun.* M20.
[from PSYCHO- + GENETICS.]
The branch of psychology that deals with the effects of genetic inheritance on behaviour.

psychogenic /sʌɪkə(ʊ)ˈdʒɛnɪk/ *adjective.* E20.
[from PSYCHO- + -GENIC.]
Having a psychological origin or cause rather than a physical one.
■ **psychogenically** *adverb* M20.

psychogeriatric /ˌsʌɪkəʊdʒɛrɪˈatrɪk/ *adjective & noun.* M20.
[from PSYCHO- + GERIATRIC.]
▶ **A** *adjective.* Of or pertaining to mental illness or disturbance in old people; (of a person) old and mentally ill or disturbed. M20.
▶ **B** *noun.* **1** In *pl.* (treated as *sing.*). The branch of medicine that deals with mental illness and disturbance in old people. M20.
2 An old person who is mentally ill or disturbed. L20.
■ **psychogeriatrician** /-ˈtrɪʃ(ə)n/ *noun* a doctor who specializes in psychogeriatrics M20.

psychogram /ˈsʌɪkə(ʊ)gram/ *noun.* L19.
[from PSYCHO- + -GRAM.]
1 A writing or message supposed to be produced by a spiritual or psychical agency. L19.
2 PSYCHOLOGY. A diagrammatic representation of someone's personality, *esp.* one based on responses to tests. E20.

psychograph /ˈsʌɪkə(ʊ)grɑːf/ *noun.* L19.
[from PSYCHO- + -GRAPH.]
1 A photographic image attributed to a supernatural or spiritualistic cause. L19.
2 = PSYCHOGRAM 2. E20.
3 A psychobiography. M20.

psychographer /sʌɪˈkɒgrəfə/ *noun.* M19.
[formed as prec. + -ER¹.]
1 An instrument which produces psychographic images; a medium who practises psychography. M19.
2 = PSYCHOBIOGRAPHER. E20.

psychographic /sʌɪkə(ʊ)ˈgrafɪk/ *adjective.* L19.
[from PSYCHO- + -GRAPHIC.]
1 Of or pertaining to psychography. L19.
2 Of or pertaining to psychographics. L20.

psychographics /sʌɪkə(ʊ)ˈgrafɪks/ *noun.* M20.
[formed as prec.: see -ICS.]
The study and classification of people according to their attitudes, aspirations, etc., esp. in market research.

psychography /sʌɪˈkɒgrəfi/ *noun.* L19.
[from PSYCHO- + -GRAPHY.]
1 Descriptive psychology. Also = PSYCHOBIOGRAPHY. L19. ▶**b** PSYCHOLOGY. The making of a psychogram; the systematic examination of an individual's personality. E20.
2 Writing, drawing, etc., supposed to be produced by a spiritual or psychical agency, esp. through the hand of a medium; automatic writing. L19.

psychohistory /sʌɪkəʊˈhɪst(ə)ri/ *noun.* M20.
[from PSYCHO- + HISTORY *noun.*]
1 The interpretation of historical events with the aid of psychological theory. Also (chiefly SCIENCE FICTION), a hypothetical predictive science based on this. M20.
2 (A) psychobiography; the psychological history of an individual. L20.
■ **psychohiˈstorian** *noun* an expert in or writer of psychohistory M20. **psychohiˈstoric** *adjective* = PSYCHOHISTORICAL M20. **psychohiˈstorical** *adjective* (*a*) *rare* of or pertaining to the history of the mind or soul; (*b*) of or pertaining to psychohistory: M19. **psychohiˈstorically** *adverb* M20.

psychoid /ˈsʌɪkɔɪd/ *noun & adjective.* Now *rare.* E20.
[from PSYCHE *noun*¹ + -OID.]
▶ **A** *noun.* The unconscious mind, regarded as directing bodily functions and instinctive or reflex actions (sometimes held to include the body itself). E20.
▶ **B** *adjective.* Of or pertaining to unconscious mental events and processes. M20.

psychokinesis /ˌsʌɪkəʊkɪˈniːsɪs, -kʌɪ-/ *noun.* E20.
[from PSYCHO- + KINESIS.]
The supposed ability to affect or move physical objects by mental effort alone.
■ **psychokiˈnetic** *adjective* E20.

psycholinguistics /ˌsʌɪkəʊlɪŋˈgwɪstɪks/ *noun.* M20.
[from PSYCHO- + LINGUISTICS.]
The branch of science that deals with psychological processes in the acquisition and use of language.
■ **psychoˈlinguist** *noun* a specialist in psycholinguistics M20. **psycholinguistic** *adjective* M20. **psycholinguistically** *adverb* M20.

psychologese /sʌɪˌkɒləˈdʒiːz/ *noun. colloq.* M20.
[from PSYCHOLOGY + -ESE.]
Language in which technical terms in psychology are used merely for effect; psychobabble.

psychologic /sʌɪkəˈlɒdʒɪk/ *adjective & noun.* L18.
[from PSYCHOLOGY: see -IC, -ICS. In sense B.2 from PSYCHOLOGY + LOGIC.]
▶ **A** *adjective.* = PSYCHOLOGICAL. Now chiefly *poet.* L18.
▶ **B** *noun.* **1** In *pl.* (treated as *sing.* or *pl.*). Psychological matters; psychology. *rare.* E19.
2 Logical reasoning based on psychological observations and judgements rather than on abstract propositions. E20.

psychological /sʌɪkəˈlɒdʒɪk(ə)l/ *adjective & noun.* L17.
[formed as PSYCHOLOGY + -ICAL.]
▶ **A** *adjective.* **1** Of, pertaining to, or of the nature of psychology; dealing with or relating to psychology. L17.
2 Of or pertaining to the functioning of the mind, mental; affecting or pertaining to the mental and emotional state of a person; *colloq.* (of an ailment) having a mental not a physical cause. L18.
3 = MENTAL *adjective*¹ 5b. *colloq.* M20.
Special collocations: **psychological** ATOMISM. **psychological block**: see BLOCK *noun* 10c. **psychological hedonism** the theory that people in fact desire only pleasure or satisfaction, or other things solely for the sake of these. **psychological moment** [French *moment psychologique*, mistranslation of German *das psychologische Moment* psychological momentum] (*a*) the moment at which something will or would have the greatest psychological effect; the psychologically appropriate moment; *loosely* the critical moment; (*b*) the short period of time within which successive stimuli are integrated and perceived as a whole. **psychological novel**: in which the mental or emotional states of characters are the main interest. **psychological operations** MILITARY (*a*) actions and operations designed primarily to influence favourably the morale or attitudes of one's own forces, or of allied and neutral forces, States, etc.; (*b*) psychological warfare. **psychological warfare** MILITARY actions and operations designed primarily to confuse, intimidate, demoralize, or discredit an enemy.
▶ **B** *noun.* A psychologist. *rare.* M19.

■ **psychologically** *adverb* in a psychological manner; in relation to psychology; mentally, emotionally: M19.

psychologise *verb* var. of PSYCHOLOGIZE.

psychologism /sʌɪˈkɒlədʒɪz(ə)m/ *noun.* M19.
[from PSYCHOLOGY + -ISM.]
1 *PHILOSOPHY.* = IDEALISM 1. M19.
2 The tendency to explain in psychological terms matters which are considered to be more properly explained in other ways. E20.

psychologist /sʌɪˈkɒlədʒɪst/ *noun.* E18.
[formed as prec. + -IST.]
1 An expert in or student of psychology. E18.
2 A person who has, or claims to have, insight into the motivation of human behaviour. *colloq.* L19.

1 psychologist's fallacy the attribution of features derived from a psychologist's own mind to that of a subject under investigation. **2** P. LAFITTE He has done something ingenious or subtle and so thinks of himself as a bit of a psychologist.

psychologistic /ˌsʌɪkɒləˈdʒɪstɪk/ *adjective.* E20.
[from PSYCHOLOGISM + -ISTIC.]
Of, pertaining to, or characterized by psychologism.
■ **psychologistically** *adverb* M20.

psychologize /sʌɪˈkɒlədʒʌɪz/ *verb.* Also **-ise**. E19.
[from next + -IZE.]
1 *verb intrans.* Theorize, speculate, or reason concerning psychology. E19.
2 *verb trans.* Analyse or describe (a person) psychologically. M19.
3 *verb trans.* Subject to psychical or psychological influence. L19.
4 *verb trans.* Analyse or regard (a subject) in psychological terms. M20.
■ **psychologiˈzation** *noun* E19. **psychologizer** *noun* L19.

psychology /sʌɪˈkɒlədʒi/ *noun.* L17.
[mod. Latin *psychologia*, formed as PSYCHO- + -OLOGY.]
1 The science of the nature, functioning, and development of the human mind (formerly, of the soul), including the faculties of reason, emotion, perception, communication, etc.; the branch of science that deals with the (human or animal) mind as an entity and in its relationship to the body and to the environmental or social context, based on observation of the behaviour of individuals or groups of individuals in particular (ordinary or experimentally controlled) circumstances. L17. ▸**b** A treatise on, or system of, psychology. L18.
2 a The mental characteristics or outlook of an individual or a group. L19. ▸**b** (The branch of science that deals with) the psychological aspects *of* an event, activity, or phenomenon. L19.

1 ***abnormal psychology, child psychology, depth psychology, ego-psychology, faculty psychology, folk psychology, gestalt psychology, introspective psychology, moral psychology, new psychology, social psychology, structural psychology***, etc. **experimental psychology** the branch of psychology that deals with experimental investigation of the responses of individuals to stimuli or controlled situations. **2a** P. G. WODEHOUSE The psychology of the Master Criminal is a thing I have never been able to understand. **b** M. ARGYLE Many . . have combined an interest in the psychology of religion with a desire to support, or . . attack, religion.

psychomachia /sʌɪkə(ʊ)ˈmeɪkɪə/ *noun.* Also (occas.) Anglicized as **psychomachy** /sʌɪˈkɒməki/. E17.
[Late Latin (title of a poem by Prudentius *c* 400), from Greek *psukhē* PSYCHE *noun*[1] + *makhē* fight: see -IA[1].]
Conflict of the soul; the battle between spirit and flesh, or virtue and vice.
¶ Obsolete after M17; revived M20 by historians of literature.

psychomancy /ˈsʌɪkə(ʊ)mansi/ *noun.* Now *rare.* E17.
[from PSYCHO- + -MANCY.]
Orig., conjuration of or communication with spirits, esp. of the dead; necromancy. Later also, occult communication between souls.

psychometer /sʌɪˈkɒmɪtə/ *noun.* Now *rare.* M19.
[from PSYCHO- + -METER.]
1 A person who makes use of psychometry (sense 1). M19.
2 A (supposed) gauge or instrument for measuring the state or power of a soul or mind. M19.

psychometric /sʌɪkəˈmetrɪk/ *adjective.* M19.
[from PSYCHOMETRY + -IC.]
Of, pertaining to, or of the nature of psychometry or psychometrics.
■ **psychometrical** *adjective* = PSYCHOMETRIC M19. **psychometrically** *adverb* by psychometry M19.

psychometrics /sʌɪkə(ʊ)ˈmɛtrɪks/ *noun.* M20.
[formed as prec.: see -ICS.]
The scientific measurement of mental capacities and processes and of personality.
■ **psychometrician** /ˌsʌɪkəʊmɪˈtrɪʃ(ə)n/ *noun* an expert in or student of psychometrics M20.

psychometrist /sʌɪˈkɒmɪtrɪst/ *noun.* M19.
[from next + -IST.]
1 = PSYCHOMETER 1. M19.
2 = PSYCHOMETRICIAN. M20.

psychometry /sʌɪˈkɒmɪtri/ *noun.* M19.
[from PSYCHO- + -METRY.]
1 The (alleged) faculty of divining, from physical contact or proximity only, the qualities or properties of an object, or of persons or things that have been in contact with it. M19.
2 Psychometrics; *esp.* the measurement of the duration and intensity of mental states or processes. L19.
■ **psychometrize** *verb trans.* practise psychometry on M19.

psychon /ˈsʌɪkɒn/ *noun.* E20.
[from PSYCHO- + -ON.]
A hypothetical unit of nervous energy or mental activity.
■ **psyˈchonic** *adjective* M20.

psychoneurosis /ˌsʌɪkəʊnjʊəˈrəʊsɪs/ *noun.* Pl. **-roses** /-ˈrəʊsiːz/. L19.
[from PSYCHO- + NEUROSIS.]
PSYCHOLOGY. (A) neurosis attributed in psychoanalytic theory to repression of unconscious conflict or fantasy rather than present sexual frustration.
■ **psychoneurotic** *noun & adjective* (*a*) *noun* a person with a psychoneurosis; (*b*) *adjective* of, pertaining to, or characterized by psychoneurosis: E20.

psychopannychy /psʌɪkə(ʊ)ˈpanɪki/ *noun. obsolete* exc. *Hist.* M17.
[mod. Latin *psychopannychia* (Calvin), from Greek *psukho-* PSYCHO- + *pannukhios* lasting all night, from *pan-* PAN- + *nukt-*, *nux* night: see -Y[3].]
THEOLOGY. The doctrine that the soul sleeps between death and the Day of Judgement.

psychopath /ˈsʌɪkəpaθ/ *noun.* L19.
[from PSYCHO- + Greek *-pathēs*, from *pathos* suffering.]
A person with chronic psychopathy, esp. leading to abnormally irresponsible and antisocial behaviour; *loosely* a mentally or emotionally unstable and aggressive person.

psychopathic /sʌɪkəˈpaθɪk/ *adjective & noun.* M19.
[formed as PSYCHOPATHY + -IC.]
▸ **A** *adjective.* Of, pertaining to, or concerned with mental illness. Now usu. *spec.*, of, pertaining to, or affected with psychopathy. M19.
▸ **B** *noun.* = PSYCHOPATH. L19.
■ **psychopathically** *adverb* E20.

psychopathology /ˌsʌɪkəʊpəˈθɒlədʒi/ *noun.* M19.
[from PSYCHO- + PATHOLOGY.]
1 The pathology of the mind; the science of the origin and treatment of mental illnesses and abnormalities. M19.
2 A mentally or behaviourally disordered state. M20.
■ **ˌpsychopathoˈlogic** *adjective* (*rare*) L19. **ˌpsychopathoˈlogical** *adjective* L19. **ˌpsychopathoˈlogically** *adverb* from the point of view of psychopathology E20. **psychopathologist** *noun* an expert in or student of psychopathology M19.

psychopathy /sʌɪˈkɒpəθi/ *noun.* M19.
[from PSYCHO- + -PATHY.]
1 Orig., mental illness. Now usu., a state characterized by persistent egocentric, irresponsible, and antisocial or aggressive behaviour, and an inability to form normal relationships with others; the state of having such a disorder. M19.
2 The treatment of disease by psychic influence, as by hypnotism. Now *rare* or *obsolete.* L19.
■ **psychopathist** *noun* (now *rare* or *obsolete*) = PSYCHIATRIST M19.

psychopharmacology /ˌsʌɪkəʊfɑːməˈkɒlədʒi/ *noun.* E20.
[from PSYCHO- + PHARMACOLOGY.]
The branch of science that deals with the effects of drugs on the mind and behaviour.
■ **psychopharmacoˈlogic** *adjective* (chiefly *US*) = PSYCHOPHARMACOLOGICAL M20. **psychopharmacoˈlogical** *adjective* of or pertaining to psychopharmacology; (of a drug) psychotropic: M20. **psychopharmacoˈlogically** *adverb* L20. **psychopharmacologist** *noun* an expert in or student of psychopharmacology M20.

psychophonetics /ˌsʌɪkəʊfəˈnɛtɪks/ *noun.* M20.
[from PSYCHO- + *phonetics*: see PHONETIC *noun* 2.]
LINGUISTICS. The branch of phonetics that deals with mental aspects of speech sound production.
■ **psychophonetic** *adjective* M20. **psychophonetically** *adverb* M20.

psychophysic /sʌɪkə(ʊ)ˈfɪzɪk/ *adjective.* L19.
[formed as next.]
= next.

psychophysical /sʌɪkə(ʊ)ˈfɪzɪk(ə)l/ *adjective.* M19.
[from PSYCHO- + PHYSICAL *adjective.*]
Of or pertaining to psychophysics; of or involving (the relation between) the mental and the physical.
■ **psychophysically** *adverb* by psychophysical means; as regards psychophysics: M19.

For other words beginning with *psycho-* see the entry for **pre-**

psychophysics /sʌɪkə(ʊ)ˈfɪzɪks/ *noun.* L19.
[from PSYCHO- + PHYSICS.]
The branch of science that deals with the relations between mental states and physical events and processes.
■ **psychophysicist** /-sɪst/ *noun* an expert in or student of psychophysics L19.

psychophysiology /ˌsʌɪkəʊfɪzɪˈɒlədʒi/ *noun.* M19.
[from PSYCHO- + PHYSIOLOGY.]
The branch of science that deals with the interaction of physiological and mental phenomena.
■ **psychophysioˈlogic** *adjective* (chiefly *US*) psychophysiological E20. **psychophysioˈlogical** *adjective* of or pertaining to psychophysiology M19. **psychophysioˈlogically** *adverb* L19. **psychophysiologist** *noun* an expert in or student of psychophysiology E20.

psychopomp /ˈsʌɪkə(ʊ)pɒmp/ *noun.* Also in Greek form **psychopompos** /-ˈpɒmpɒs/. M19.
[Greek *psukhopompos*, from *psukhē* PSYCHE *noun*[1] + *pompos* conductor.]
A mythical conductor of souls to the place of the dead. Also, the spiritual guide of a (living) person's soul.

psychoprophylaxis /ˌsʌɪkəʊprɒfɪˈlaksɪs/ *noun.* M20.
[from PSYCHO- + PROPHYLAXIS.]
MEDICINE. A method intended to reduce pain by instruction in relaxation and understanding, esp. as applied to alleviate labour pains by encouraging mental and physical cooperation with the process of birth.
■ **psychoprophylactic** *adjective* M20. **psychoprophylactically** *adverb* M20.

psychoses *noun* pl. of PSYCHOSIS.

psychosexual /sʌɪkə(ʊ)ˈsɛksjʊəl, -ʃʊəl/ *adjective.* L19.
[from PSYCHO- + SEXUAL.]
Involving or pertaining to the mental and emotional aspects of the sexual impulse.
■ **ˌpsychosexuˈality** *noun* the mental and emotional aspects of sexuality E20. **psychosexually** *adverb* M20.

psychosis /sʌɪˈkəʊsɪs/ *noun.* Pl. **-choses** /-ˈkəʊsiːz/. M19.
[from PSYCHE *noun*[1] + -OSIS, prob. after *neurosis.*]
PSYCHOLOGY. Orig., any kind of disordered mental state. Now *spec.* (a) severe mental illness, derangement, or disorder involving a loss of contact with reality, freq. with hallucinations, delusions, or altered thought processes, with or without a known organic origin. Cf. NEUROSIS.

psychosomatic /ˌsʌɪkə(ʊ)səˈmatɪk/ *adjective.* M19.
[from PSYCHO- + SOMATIC.]
1 Involving or concerned with the interdependence of mind and body. M19.
2 *MEDICINE.* Designating, pertaining or relating to illnesses having both physical and mental components, usu. involving a physical condition caused or aggravated by mental or emotional disorder. M20.
■ **psychosomatically** *adverb* in a psychosomatic manner; *esp.* through the (unconscious) effect of the mind on the body: M20. **psychosomaticist** /-sɪst/ *noun* a specialist in psychosomatic medicine M20. **psychosomatics** *noun* the branch of knowledge that deals with the relationship between mind and body M20. **psychoˈsomatist** *noun* = PSYCHOSOMATICIST M19.

†**psychosomimetic** *adjective & noun* var. of PSYCHOTOMIMETIC.

psychostasy /sʌɪˈkɒstəsi/ *noun.* M19.
[Greek *psukhostasia*, from *psukhē* PSYCHE *noun*[1] + *stasis* weighing.]
GREEK MYTHOLOGY. The judgement of souls by weighing.

psychostatics /sʌɪkə(ʊ)ˈstatɪks/ *noun. rare.* E18.
[from PSYCHO- + Greek *statikos* weighing, or STATICS.]
†**1** = PSYCHOSTASY. *rare.* Only in E18.
2 The branch of science that deals with states and conditions (as distinct from the development) of the mind. L19.
■ **psychostatical** *adjective* (*rare*) E18.

psychosurgery /sʌɪkə(ʊ)ˈsəːdʒ(ə)ri/ *noun.* M20.
[from PSYCHO- + SURGERY.]
MEDICINE. Brain surgery intended to alter the behaviour of patients with certain kinds of severe mental illness.
■ **ˈpsychosurgeon** *noun* a surgeon specializing in psychosurgery M20. **psychosurgical** *adjective* M20.

psychotechnic /sʌɪkə(ʊ)ˈtɛknɪk/ *noun & adjective.* E20.
[from PSYCHO- + TECHNIC *adjective & noun.*]
▸ **A** *noun sing.* & (usu.) in *pl.* (treated as *sing.*). = PSYCHOTECHNOLOGY. E20.
▸ **B** *adjective.* = PSYCHOTECHNICAL *adjective.* M20.

psychotechnical /sʌɪkə(ʊ)ˈtɛknɪk(ə)l/ *adjective.* E20.
[from PSYCHO- + TECHNICAL *adjective.*]
Pertaining to or concerned with the application of psychological knowledge to practical problems in industry, employment, education, etc.

psychotechnology /ˌsʌɪkəʊtɛkˈnɒlədʒi/ *noun.* E20.
[from PSYCHO- + TECHNOLOGY.]
The branch of knowledge that deals with the practical application of scientific knowledge about the human mind.
■ **psychotechnologist** *noun* an expert in or student of psychotechnology E20.

psychotherapeutic /ˌsʌɪkə(ʊ)θɛrəˈpjuːtɪk/ *adjective.* M19.
[from PSYCHO- + THERAPEUTIC.]
Of, pertaining to, or characterized by psychotherapy.
■ **psychotheraˈpeutically** *adverb* by means of psychotherapy E20. **psychotheraˈpeutics** *noun* the methods or practice of psychotherapy L19. **ˌpsychotheraˈpeutist** *noun* = PSYCHOTHERAPIST E20.

psychotherapy /sʌɪkə(ʊ)ˈθɛrəpi/ *noun.* M19.
[from PSYCHO- + THERAPY.]
The treatment of disorders of emotion or personality by psychological methods. Formerly, the treatment of disease by psychic or hypnotic influence.
■ **psychotherapist** *noun* a specialist in or practitioner of psychotherapy E20.

psychotic /sʌɪˈkɒtɪk/ *adjective & noun.* L19.
[from PSYCHOSIS + -OTIC.]
MEDICINE & PSYCHOLOGY. ▶**A** *adjective.* Of, pertaining to, or suffering from psychosis. L19.
▶**B** *noun.* A person with a psychosis. E20.
■ **psychotically** *adverb* M20. **psychoticism** /-sɪz(ə)m/ *noun* the condition or state of being psychotic; a tendency towards psychosis, esp. as a factor in certain types of personality assessment: M20.

psychotogenic /sʌɪˌkɒtəˈdʒɛnɪk/ *adjective.* M20.
[formed as next + -GENIC.]
= PSYCHOTOMIMETIC *adjective*
■ **psyˈchotogen** *noun* a psychotomimetic substance M20. **psychotogenesis** *noun* the production of a psychosis or a state resembling psychosis M20.

psychotomimetic /sʌɪˌkɒtə(ʊ)mɪˈmɛtɪk/ *adjective & noun.* Also (earlier) †**psychoso-**. M20.
[from PSYCHOSIS + -O- + MIMETIC, alt. after *psychotic*.]
▶**A** *adjective.* Having an effect on the mind originally likened to that of a psychotic state; of or pertaining to a drug with this effect (cf. PSYCHEDELIC *adjective* 1). M20.
▶**B** *noun.* A psychotomimetic drug. M20.
■ **psychotomimetically** *adverb* M20.

psychotronic /sʌɪkə(ʊ)ˈtrɒnɪk/ *adjective.* L20.
[formed as next.]
1 Of or relating to psychotronics. L20.
2 Denoting or relating to a genre of films typically with a science fiction, horror, or fantasy theme and made on a low budget or poorly received by critics. L20.

psychotronics /sʌɪkə(ʊ)ˈtrɒnɪks/ *noun.* L20.
[from PSYCHO-, on the pattern of *electronics*.]
A branch of parapsychology which supposes an energy or force to emanate from living organisms and affect matter.

psychotropic /sʌɪkə(ʊ)ˈtrəʊpɪk, -ˈtrɒp-/ *adjective & noun.* M20.
[from PSYCHO- + -TROPIC.]
▶**A** *adjective.* Affecting a person's mental state; *spec.* = PSYCHOTOMIMETIC *adjective.* M20.
▶**B** *noun.* A psychotropic drug. L20.
■ **psychotrophic** *adjective* = PSYCHOTROPIC L20. **psychotropically** *adverb* M20.

psychro- /ˈsʌɪkrəʊ/ *combining form.*
[from Greek *psukhros* cold, rel. to *psukhein* breathe, blow, cool: see -O-.]
Of or pertaining to cold.
■ **psychrophile** *noun & adjective* (an organism that is) psychrophilic M20. **psychroˈphilic** *adjective* (BIOLOGY) (of an organism, esp. a bacterium) capable of growing at temperatures close to freezing; having a low optimum temperature: M20. **psychrosphere** *noun* the colder, deeper part of the oceans M20. **psychroˈspheric** *adjective* of or inhabiting the psychrosphere L20. **psychroˈtolerant** *adjective* (of an organism) capable of growing at temperatures close to freezing (even if having a higher optimum temperature) M20. **psychrotroph** /-trəʊf/ *noun* a psychrotrophic organism M20. **psychrotrophic** /-trəʊfɪk, -ˈtrɒfɪk/ *adjective* (BIOLOGY) = PSYCHROTOLERANT M20.

psychrometer /sʌɪˈkrɒmɪtə/ *noun.* E18.
[from PSYCHRO- + -METER.]
METEOROLOGY. A hygrometer consisting of two thermometers, one of which is enclosed in material from which water is caused to evaporate, the degree of cooling indicating the relative humidity of the air. Formerly also, a thermometer.
■ **psychroˈmetric** *adjective* of or pertaining to the psychrometer or psychrometry; hygrometric: L19. **psychrometry** *noun* measurement of humidity by means of a psychrometer M19.

psykter /ˈsɪktə/ *noun.* Also **psycter**. M19.
[Greek *psuktēr*, from *psukhein* breathe, blow, cool.]
CLASSICAL ANTIQUITIES. A jar for cooling wine.

psylla /ˈsɪlə/ *noun.* M19.
[mod. Latin *Psylla* (see below) from Greek *psulla* flea.]
A jumping plant-louse of the genus *Psylla* or the family Psyllidae. Cf. next.

psyllid /ˈsɪlɪd/ *noun & adjective.* L19.
[mod. Latin *Psyllidae* (see below), formed as prec. + -ID³.]
▶**A** *noun.* A jumping plant-louse of the family Psyllidae, which includes several species that cause galls or spread virus diseases in plants. L19.
▶**B** *adjective.* Of, pertaining to, or designating this family. L19.

psyllium /ˈsɪlɪəm/ *noun.* M16.
[Latin from Greek *psullion*, from *psulla* flea.]
A leafy-stemmed Mediterranean plantain, *Plantago psafra*; the seeds (which resemble fleas) of this or several related plantains, used as a laxative.

psy-ops /ˈsʌɪɒps/ *noun pl.* Orig. *US.* Also **psy-opps**, (*attrib.*) **psy-op**. M20.
[Abbreviation.]
MILITARY. = ***psychological operations*** s.v. PSYCHOLOGICAL *adjective.* Freq. *attrib.*

psy-war /ˈsʌɪwɔː/ *noun.* Orig. *US.* M20.
[Abbreviation.]
MILITARY. = ***psychological warfare*** s.v. PSYCHOLOGICAL *adjective.*

PT *abbreviation*¹.
1 Physical training.
2 *Hist.* Purchase tax.

pt *abbreviation*².
1 Part.
2 Pint.
3 Point.
4 Portuguese.

Pt *symbol.*
CHEMISTRY. Platinum.

PTA *abbreviation.*
1 Parent–Teacher Association.
2 Passenger Transport Authority.

ptarmic /ˈtɑːmɪk/ *noun. rare.* L17.
[mod. Latin *ptarmicus* from Greek *ptarmikos*, from *ptarmos* a sneeze: see -IC.]
A substance that excites sneezing.
■ **ptarmical** *adjective* causing sneezing M17.

ptarmigan /ˈtɑːmɪg(ə)n/ *noun.* Pl. same. L16.
[Gaelic *tarmachan*, from *tarm-*, *torm-*, grumble, croak; initial *pt-* introduced L17 by false analogy with Greek words and universal from E19.]
A game-bird, *Lagopus mutus*, of the grouse family, which lives on barren moors and heaths in Arctic and subarctic areas, and at high altitudes in the Scottish Highlands, the Alps, and the Pyrenees, and has grey and black plumage which changes to white in winter. Also called ***white grouse***, ***rock grouse***.
willow ptarmigan.

PT boat *abbreviation. US.*
Patrol torpedo-boat.

PTC *abbreviation.*
Phenylthiocarbamide.

PTE *abbreviation.*
Passenger Transport Executive.

Pte. *abbreviation.*
MILITARY. Private (soldier).

pter- *combining form* see PTERO-.

pteranodon /tɛˈranədɒn/ *noun & adjective.* Also (earlier) **-dont** /-dɒnt/. L19.
[mod. Latin *Pteranodon* (see below), from Greek *pteron* wing + AN-⁵ + -ODON.]
PALAEONTOLOGY. A toothless pterosaur with a bony crest, of the pterodactyloid genus *Pteranodon*.

pteridine /ˈtɛrɪdiːn/ *noun.* M20.
[from PTERIN + -IDINE.]
CHEMISTRY. A synthetic yellow crystalline solid, $C_6H_4N_4$, which has a bicyclic structure formed from fused pyrazine and pyrimidine rings; any of the derivatives of this, many of which occur naturally as insect pigments and B group vitamins.

pterido- /ˈtɛrɪdəʊ/ *combining form* of Greek *pterid-*, *pteris* fern: see -O-.
■ **pteridoˈlogical** *adjective* of or pertaining to pteridology M19. **pteriˈdologist** *noun* an expert in or student of ferns M19. **pteriˈdology** *noun* the branch of botany that deals with ferns M19. **pteridoˈmania** *noun* an excessive enthusiasm for ferns M19. **pteridophyte** *noun* a member of the Pteridophyta, a division of plants including the ferns and their allies (horsetails, clubmosses, etc.); a vascular cryptogam: L19. **pteridophytic** /-ˈfɪtɪk/ *adjective* of or pertaining to pteridophytes L19. **pteridosperm** *noun* a fossil plant of the class Pteridospermeae, comprising plants intermediate between ferns and seed-bearing plants E20.

pterin /ˈtɛrɪn/ *noun.* M20.
[from Greek *pteron* wing + -IN¹.]
CHEMISTRY. A pteridine; *esp.* any of a class of naturally occurring pteridines found esp. as insect pigments.

pterion /ˈtɛrɪən/ *noun.* L19.
[mod. Latin, from Greek *pteron* wing (with ref. to the wings of the sphenoid) + *-ion* after *gnathion*, *inion*, etc.]
ANATOMY. An H-shaped suture at the side of the skull where the sphenoid and parietal bones meet between the frontal and temporal bones.

ptero- /ˈtɛrəʊ/ *combining form.* Before a vowel **pter-**.
[from Greek *pteron* wing, feather: see -O-.]
Of, pertaining to, or shaped like a wing or feather, winged, feathered, as ***pterobranch***, ***pterosaur***, etc.

pterobranch /ˈtɛrə(ʊ)braŋk/ *noun.* M20.
[from mod. Latin *Pterobranchia*, formed as PTERO- + Greek *bragkhia* gills.]
ZOOLOGY. Any small marine usu. colonial tube-dwelling hemichordate of the class Pterobranchia. Freq. *attrib.*

pterodactyl /tɛrəˈdaktɪl, -ʌɪl/ *noun.* Also (earlier) †**-yle**. E19.
[mod. Latin *Pterodactylus* (see below), from Greek *pteron* wing + *daktulos* finger.]
PALAEONTOLOGY. An extinct winged reptile, a pterosaur; *spec.* one of the genus *Pterodactylus*.
■ **pterodactyloid** *adjective & noun* (**a**) *adjective* having the form or character of a pterodactyl; *spec.* belonging to the extinct suborder Pterodactyloidea of long-necked, short-tailed pterosaurs; (**b**) *noun* a pterodactyloid pterosaur: L19.

pteroic /ˈtɛrəʊɪk/ *adjective.* M20.
[from PTER(IDINE + -OIC.]
BIOCHEMISTRY. ***pteroic acid***, a synthetic crystalline derivative of pteridine, $C_{14}H_{12}N_6O_3$, of which the pteroylglutamic acids are formally amides.

pteroma /təˈrəʊmə/ *noun.* Pl. **-mata** /-mətə/. M19.
[Latin from Greek *pterōma*.]
ARCHITECTURE. The space between the cella of a Greek temple and the surrounding colonnade (peristyle).

pteromorph /ˈtɛrəmɔːf/ *noun.* Also (earlier) **-morpha** /-mɔːfə/, pl. **-phae** /-fiː/. E20.
[from PTERO- + -MORPH.]
ZOOLOGY. A winglike hinged appendage on each side of the body of certain mites.

pteropine /ˈtɛrəpʌɪn, tɛˈrəʊpʌɪn/ *adjective.* M19.
[from mod. Latin *Pteropus* (see below), from Greek *pteropous* wing-footed: see PTERO-, -POD, -INE¹.]
ZOOLOGY. Designating flying foxes, esp. of the genus *Pteropus*.

pteropod /ˈtɛrəpɒd/ *noun.* M19.
[from mod. Latin *Pteropoda*, formed as PTERO-: see -POD.]
ZOOLOGY. A pelagic marine gastropod of the class Pteropoda, having a modified foot bearing lobes which act as fins. Also called ***sea butterfly***.
Comb.: **pteropod ooze** a calcareous marine sediment rich in the shells of pteropods.
■ **pteˈropodous** *adjective* pertaining to, characteristic of, or belonging to the class Pteropoda M19.

pterosaur /ˈtɛrəsɔː/ *noun.* M19.
[mod. Latin *Pterosauria* (see below), formed as PTERO-: see -SAUR.]
Any of numerous extinct reptiles of the Mesozoic order Pterosauria, having the fourth digit of each forelimb enormously prolonged to support a membrane for flight.
■ **pteroˈsaurian** *adjective & noun* (**a**) *adjective* of, pertaining to, or characteristic of a pterosaur; (**b**) *noun* a pterosaur: L19.

pterotic /təˈrəʊtɪk/ *adjective & noun.* L19.
[from PTERO- + -OTIC.]
ANATOMY & ZOOLOGY. (Designating or pertaining to) a winglike expansion of the petrosal bone or periotic capsule, occurring in some vertebrates.

pteroylglutamic /ˌtɛrəʊʌɪlgluˈtamɪk, -rəʊɪl-/ *adjective.* M20.
[from PTERO(IC + -YL + GLUTAMIC.]
BIOCHEMISTRY. ***pteroylglutamic acid***, any of a series of derivatives of pteroic acid which contain one or more glutamic acid residues and include certain B group vitamins and other animal growth factors; *spec.* = ***FOLIC acid***. Also with inserted prefix indicating the number of glutamic acid residues present, as ***pteroylmonoglutamic acid***, ***pteroylpolyglutamic acid***, etc.
■ **ˌpteroylˈglutamate** *noun* (a compound or the anion of) a pteroylglutamic acid M20.

pterygium /təˈrɪdʒɪəm/ *noun.* Pl. **-ia** /-ɪə/. M17.
[mod. Latin, from Greek *pterugion* dim. of *pterux* wing.]
BIOLOGY & ANATOMY. A small winglike structure; *spec.* in MEDICINE, a triangular overgrowth on the conjunctiva in the corner of the eye.

pterygo- /ˈtɛrɪgəʊ/ *combining form.*
[from Greek *pterug-*, *pterux* wing, fin: see -O-.]
1 Pertaining to or resembling a wing or wings.
2 ANATOMY. Connected with or relating to the pterygoid processes.
■ **pterygo-maˈxillary** *adjective* belonging to or connected with the pterygoid processes and the maxillary bones M19.

pterygoid /ˈtɛrɪgɔɪd/ *adjective & noun.* E18.
[mod. Latin *pterygoides* noun pl., formed as prec.; see -OID.]
ANATOMY. ▶**A** *adjective.* Winglike, wing-shaped; *spec.* designating, pertaining to, attached to, or forming part of a bony plate (***pterygoid process***) which descends from the junction of the body and greater wing of each sphenoid bone to form part of the back of the mouth (represented in some vertebrates by one or more distinct bones). E18.
pterygoid bone, ***pterygoid ridge***, etc. **pterygoid muscle** any of several muscles attached to the pterygoid processes and acting to move the jaw backwards, forwards, or sideways. ***pterygoid process***: see above.
▶**B** *noun.* **1** A pterygoid bone or process. M19.
2 A pterygoid muscle. M19.

For other words beginning with *psycho-* see the entry for **pre-**

pterygote /ˈtɛrɪɡəʊt/ *adjective*. L19.
[from mod. Latin *Pterygota* (see below), from Greek *pterugōtos* winged, from *pterug-*, *pterux* wing.]
ENTOMOLOGY. Designating or belonging to the subclass Pterygota of insects, characterized by the possession of wings (in at least some stage of life) or descended from winged forms.

pteryla /ˈtɛrɪlə/ *noun*. Pl. **-lae** /-liː/. M19.
[mod. Latin, from Greek *pteron* feather + *hulē* wood, forest.]
ORNITHOLOGY. Any of several defined areas of a bird's skin in which feathers grow.

pterylosis /tɛrɪˈləʊsɪs/ *noun*. Pl. **-loses** /-ˈləʊsiːz/. L19.
[from prec. + -OSIS.]
ORNITHOLOGY. The arrangement or disposition of the pterylae, or of the feathers, of a bird.
■ **pteryˈlography** *noun* the scientific description of pterylosis; a treatise on this: M19.

PTFE *abbreviation*.
Polytetrafluoroethylene.

PTI *abbreviation*.
Physical training instructor.

ptilinum /tɪˈlʌɪnəm/ *noun*. Pl. **-na** /-nə/. M19.
[mod. Latin, from French *ptiline*, perh. dim. of Greek *ptilon* downy feather, plume on a helmet.]
ENTOMOLOGY. An inflatable structure on the head of cyclorrhaphous dipterans which is used to rupture the puparium and then atrophies, leaving a suture.
■ **ptilinal** *adjective* of or pertaining to a ptilinum E20.

ptilo- /ˈtɪləʊ, ˈtʌɪləʊ/ *combining form* of Greek *ptilon* downy feather: see -O-.
■ **ptilopaedic** /-ˈpiːdɪk/ *adjective* [Greek *paid-*, *pais* child] ORNITHOLOGY (of a bird) hatched with a complete covering of down L19.

ptilosis /tɪˈləʊsɪs/ *noun*. *rare*. Pl. **-loses** /-ˈləʊsiːz/. M19.
[from prec. + -OSIS.]
ORNITHOLOGY. Plumage; the arrangement of (esp. down) feathers, pterylosis.

ptisan, **ptisane** *nouns* see TISANE.

PTO *abbreviation*.
1 Please turn over (the page).
2 Power take-off.

ptochocracy /təʊˈkɒkrəsi/ *noun*. L18.
[from Greek *ptōkhos* beggar + -CRACY.]
Government by beggars, or by the poor; *loosely* the poor as a class.

Ptolemaean /tɒləˈmiːən/ *adjective & noun*. M17.
[from Latin *Ptolemaeus* Ptolemy (see next) + -AN.]
▶ **A** *noun*. = PTOLEMAIST. *rare*. M17.
▶ **B** *adjective*. **1** = PTOLEMAIC *adjective* 2. *rare*. M18.
2 = PTOLEMAIC *adjective* 1. E19.

Ptolemaic /tɒləˈmeɪɪk/ *adjective & noun*. L17.
[from Greek *Ptolemaios* Ptolemy (see below) + -IC.]
▶ **A** *adjective*. **1** Of or pertaining to the Alexandrian astronomer Ptolemy (*c* 90–168); designating or pertaining to his theory that the planets, including the sun, revolve around the earth. L17.
2 Of or pertaining to the Ptolemies, the Macedonian rulers of Egypt from the death of Alexander the Great until the annexation by Rome (4th to 1st cents. BC). L18.
▶ **B** *noun*. = PTOLEMAIST. *rare*. M18.
■ **Ptolemaism** *noun* (belief in) the Ptolemaic theory L19. **Ptolemaist** *noun* an advocate of the Ptolemaic theory L19.

ptomaine /ˈtəʊmeɪn/ *noun*. L19.
[French *ptomaïne* from Italian *ptomaina*, irreg. from Greek *ptōma* corpse: see -INE[5].]
CHEMISTRY. Any of various alkaloids of unpleasant taste and odour found in putrefying animal and vegetable matter, formerly thought to cause food poisoning.

ptooey *interjection* var. of PTUI.

P2P *abbreviation*.
COMPUTING. Peer-to-peer (network).

ptosis /ˈtəʊsɪs/ *noun*. Pl. **ptoses** /ˈtəʊsiːz/. M18.
[Greek *ptōsis* falling, fall.]
MEDICINE. Prolapse of an organ; *spec.* drooping of the upper eyelid, usu. from a disorder of the levator muscle or its nerve supply.
■ **ptotic** /ˈtəʊtɪk/ *adjective* pertaining to or affected with ptosis L19.

PTSD *abbreviation*.
Post-traumatic stress disorder.

ptui /ˈptuːi/ *interjection*. Also **ptooey**. L20.
[Imit.]
Repr. the noise of spitting, esp. in disgust.

Pty *abbreviation*. *Austral., NZ, & S. Afr.*
Proprietary (in the name of a company).

ptyalin /ˈtʌɪəlɪn/ *noun*. M19.
[from Greek *ptualon* spittle + -IN[1].]
BIOCHEMISTRY. Salivary amylase.

ptyalism /ˈtʌɪəlɪz(ə)m/ *noun*. L17.
[Greek *ptualismos*, from *ptualizein* spit, expectorate, from *ptualon* spittle: see -ISM.]
Excessive production of saliva.

ptygma /ˈtɪɡmə/ *noun*. M20.
[Back-form. from next.]
GEOLOGY. A ptygmatic fold.

ptygmatic /tɪɡˈmatɪk/ *adjective*. E20.
[from Greek *ptugmat-*, *ptugma* folded matter + -IC.]
GEOLOGY. Designating or exhibiting highly sinuous and often discordant folding that occurs in veins in some gneisses and migmatites.
■ **ptygmatically** *adverb* E20.

p-type /ˈpiːtʌɪp/ *adjective*. M20.
[from P(OSITIVE *adjective* + TYPE *noun*.]
PHYSICS. Designating (a region in) a semiconductor in which electrical conduction is due chiefly to the movement of holes. Opp. N-TYPE.

ptyxis /ˈtɪksɪs/ *noun*. L19.
[Greek *ptuxis* folding.]
BOTANY. The way in which an individual leaf is folded in a bud. Cf. VERNATION 1.

Pu *abbreviation*.
CHEMISTRY. Plutonium.

pub /pʌb/ *noun*[1] & *verb*[1]. *colloq.* M19.
[Abbreviation of PUBLIC HOUSE.]
▶ **A** *noun*. A public house, an inn; *Austral.* a hotel. M19.

attrib.: M. AMIS I ate a lot of pub grub. ***local pub***: see LOCAL *adjective*.

Comb.: ***pub-crawl***: see CRAWL *noun*[2] 1b, *verb* 3; **pub lunch** a lunch served and eaten in a pub; **pub rock** rock music of a type played in public houses; **pub theatre** a public house at which theatrical performances take place; a theatrical performance in a public house; **pub-time** (*a*) the hour at which a public house opens or closes; (*b*) the time shown by a clock in a public house, often slightly advanced so as to bring forward closing-time.

▶ **B** *verb*. Infl. **-bb-**.
1 *verb intrans. & trans.* (with *it*). Frequent public houses. L19.
2 *verb intrans.* Own or manage a public house. *rare*. M20.
■ **pubbish**, **pubby**, **pubsy** *adjectives* of the nature or character of a public house M20.

pub /pʌb/ *noun*[2]. Also **pub.** (point). E20.
[Abbreviation Cf. PUB *verb*[2].]
PUBLISHING. = PUBLICATION *noun* 2a, b. Freq. in ***pub date***.

pub /pʌb/ *verb*[2] *trans.* Also **pub.** (point). Infl. **-bb-**. Pa. pple **pub**, **pubbed**. L19.
[Orig. pa. pple, abbreviation of (*published* pa. pple of) PUBLISH. Cf. PUB *noun*[2].]
PUBLISHING. = PUBLISH 5a.

pubarche /pjuːˈbɑːkiː/ *noun*. M20.
[from Latin PUBES *noun*[1] + Greek *arkhē* beginning.]
MEDICINE. The first appearance of pubic hair; chiefly in ***premature pubarche***, the premature occurrence of this without other sexual characteristics.

pubble /ˈpʌb(ə)l/ *adjective*. *obsolete* exc. *dial.* M16.
[Origin uncertain: perh. rel. to East Frisian *pumpel*, Low German *pümpel* a fat, burly person.]
Fat, well filled, plump.

puberal /ˈpjuːb(ə)r(ə)l/ *adjective*. Now *rare*. M19.
[medieval Latin *puberalis*, from *puber*: see PUBERTY, -AL[1].]
= next.

pubertal /ˈpjuːbət(ə)l/ *adjective*. L19.
[Irreg. from next + -AL[1].]
Of or pertaining to puberty.

puberty /ˈpjuːbəti/ *noun*. LME.
[Latin *pubertas* (or the derived French *puberté*), from *puber-*, *pubes* (an) adult, *pubes* PUBES *noun*[1]: see -TY[1].]
The period during which adolescents reach sexual maturity and become capable of reproduction, distinguished by the appearance of secondary sexual characteristics.

attrib.: *New York* Puberty rites of Sierra Leone. **age of puberty** the age at which puberty begins.

puberulent /pjuːˈbɛːjʊl(ə)nt/ *adjective*. M19.
[from Latin *puber-*, *pubes* (see prec.) + -ULENT.]
BOTANY. Minutely pubescent.
■ Also **puberulous** *adjective* L19.

pubes /ˈpjuːbiːz, ˈpjuːbz/ *noun*[1]. Pl. same. L16.
[Latin = the pubic hair, the groin, the genitals.]
1 The pubic hair. Now *colloq.* L16.
2 The lower part of the abdomen at the front of the pelvis, which becomes covered with hair from the time of puberty. L17.

pubes *noun*[2] pl. of PUBIS.

pubescence /pjʊˈbɛs(ə)ns/ *noun*. LME.
[French, or medieval Latin *pubescentia*, formed as next: see -ENCE.]
1 The fact or condition of arriving or having arrived at puberty. LME.
2 BOTANY & ZOOLOGY. The soft down which grows on the leaves, stems, etc., of many plants and on certain animals; the character or condition of being covered with this. M18.

pubescent /pjʊˈbɛs(ə)nt/ *adjective & noun*. M17.
[French, or Latin *pubescent-* pres. ppl stem of *pubescere* reach the age of puberty, from PUBES *noun*[1]: see -ESCENT.]
▶ **A** *adjective*. **1** Arriving or having arrived at the age of puberty. M17.
2 BOTANY & ZOOLOGY. Covered with short soft hair; downy. Cf. PILOSE. M18.
▶ **B** *noun*. A person at the age of puberty. L19.

pubic /ˈpjuːbɪk/ *adjective*. M19.
[from PUBES *noun*[1] + -IC.]
Of or pertaining to the pubes or pubis. Freq. in ***pubic hair***.

pubiotomy /pjuːbɪˈɒtəmi/ *noun*. L19.
[from Latin *pubi-*, PUBES *noun*[1] + -O- + -TOMY.]
MEDICINE. Surgical division of the pubic bone near the symphysis, performed during childbirth if the pelvis is too small; an instance of this.

pubis /ˈpjuːbɪs/ *noun*. Pl. **pubes** /ˈpjuːbiːz/. L16.
[In sense 1 short for Latin *os pubis*, from *os* bone + *pubis* genit. sing. of PUBES *noun*[1]; in sense 2 var. of PUBES *noun*[1].]
1 Either of two bones which form the lower and anterior part of the pelvis. L16.
†**2** = PUBES *noun*[1] 2. L17–E19.

public /ˈpʌblɪk/ *adjective & noun*. LME.
[Old & mod. French *public*, *-ique* or Latin *publicus* from *pubes* adult infl. by *poplicus*, from *populus* PEOPLE *noun*: see -IC.]
▶ **A** *adjective*. **1** Of or pertaining to the people as a whole; belonging to, affecting, or concerning the community or nation. LME.
2 Carried out or made by or on behalf of the community as a whole; authorized by or representing the community. LME. ▸**b** Orig., belonging to, authorized by, or acting for a university as a corporate body (as opp. to a college or other individual member). Now also (passing into senses 3a, 4), open to all members of a particular university. M16.
3 a Open or available to, used or shared by, all members of a community; not restricted to private use. Also (of a service, fund, amenity, etc.) provided by local or central government for the community and supported by rates or taxes. LME. ▸**b** At the service of the public in a professional capacity; working in local or central government. E19.
4 Open to general observation, sight, or knowledge; existing or done openly; accountable to the general public. Formerly also, (of a book etc.) accessible to all, published, (chiefly in ***made public***). LME.
5 Of or pertaining to a person in the capacity in which he or she comes in contact with the community, as opp. to his or her private capacity etc. M16.
6 a Of or pertaining to the international community; international. Now *rare* exc. in ***public law*** below. M16. ▸**b** Of or common to the whole human race. *rare*. M17.
7 Of or engaged in the affairs of the community; *esp.* (of a person) occupying an official position, holding a position of influence or authority. M16.
8 Devoted or directed to the promotion of the general welfare; patriotic. Now chiefly in ***public spirit***, ***public-spirited***, etc., below. E17.

1 T. HARDY A day of public rejoicing. P. WORSTHORNE The expenditure of public money. **2** *Malvern Gazette* Our public housing stock. **b** ***public examination***, ***public lecture***, ***public professor***, etc. **3a** ***public baths***, ***public library***, ***public park***, ***public rooms***, ***public telephone***, ***public toilet***, etc. **4** M. FRAYN The public glare of open committees. N. F. DIXON Whereas patriotic fervour is public, . . grief and sorrow are private. **5** C. STORR Although she was still . . difficult . . in her private relationships, she acquired a much easier public face. **7** *Daily Mirror* Corruption in public life. **8** C. P. SNOW A public benefactor.

▶ **B** *noun*. **1** ***in public***, in a place or state open to public view or access; openly. Formerly also, in a published form, in print. L15.
†**2** Organized society, *the* body politic; a nation, a State; the interest or welfare of the community. E17–M18.
3 People collectively; *the* members of the community. Treated as *sing.* or *pl.* M17.
4 a A section of the community having a particular interest in or special connection with the person or thing specified. (Freq. with possess. adjective.) E18. ▸**b** SOCIOLOGY. A collective group regarded as sharing a common cultural, social, or political interest but who as individuals do not necessarily come into contact with one another. E20.
5 *ellipt.* **a** = PUBLIC HOUSE. *colloq.* E18. ▸**b** = ***public bar*** below. *colloq.* M20.

1 B. EMECHETA He kissed her in public, with everybody looking. *Observer* Those . . most confident in public . . could be the most self-depreciatory in private.

2 SHAFTESBURY A civil State or Publick. 3 *Times* Mr Cheeseman's allegations should be brought to the attention of the public. S. JOHNSON Members of the public. **4a** R. G. COLLINGWOOD Every artist . . knows . . his public. *Gramophone* A large concert-going and record-buying public.

Special collocations, phrases, & comb.: ***certified public accountant***: see CERTIFY. ***Director of Public Prosecutions***: see PROSECUTION 5. **general public** = sense B.3 above. **go public** (*a*) (of a privately-owned company) seek a quotation on a stock exchange; (*b*) make one's intentions plain, come out into the open. ***Great British Public***: see GREAT *adjective*. **in the public domain** belonging to the public as a whole, *esp.* not subject to copyright. ***in the public eye***: see EYE *noun*. ***Joe Public***: see JOE *noun*[2]. ***John Q. Public***. ***notary public***: see NOTARY 2. ***of public resort***: see RESORT *noun*. **public access television** (orig. *US*) a form of television in which members of the public can produce their own programmes. **public act** a parliamentary act which affects the community as a whole. **public address system** a system comprising an amplifier and one or more microphones and loudspeakers, used to project speech or music to an audience. **public bar** the most basically furnished and sometimes least expensive bar in a public house. **public bill** a parliamentary bill which affects the community as a whole. †**public commoner** (*rare*, Shakes.) = ***public woman*** below. **public company** a company whose shares are traded freely on a stock exchange. **public defender** *US* a lawyer employed by the State to represent a defendant (in a criminal action) unable to afford legal assistance. **public education** (*a*) education at a public as opp. to a private school; †(*b*) education at school rather than from a private tutor. **public enemy (number one)** (*a*) (orig. *US*) a notorious wanted criminal; (*b*) the greatest threat to a community, nation, etc. **public figure** a person active in public life and known to many. **public good** the common or national good or well-being. **public health** (*a*) the health of the public in general; (*b*) the provision of adequate drainage, sanitation, etc., by the State. **public holiday** a usu. annual holiday marking a State, religious, etc., occasion and awarded to most employees. ***public inquiry***: see INQUIRY 2. **public interest** the common welfare. **public interest immunity** a principle by which the government can request that sensitive documents are not used as evidence in a trial, on the grounds that to do so would be against the public or national interest (see also ***gagging order*** s.v. GAG *verb*[1] 2). **public key** a cryptographic key that can be obtained and used by anyone to encrypt messages intended for a particular recipient, such that the encrypted messages can be deciphered only by using a second key known only to the recipient (the ***private key***). **public law** (*a*) that part of the law pertaining to the relationship between the State and a person subject to it; (*b*) a law having validity in a number of States or nations. **Public Lending Right** the entitlement of authors to a fee for books borrowed from public libraries. **public libel** a published libel. **public life**: as an official, performer, etc., rather than as a private individual. **public menace** a person who or thing which is harmful or annoying to the community. ***public notary***: see NOTARY 2. **public nuisance** (*a*) an illegal act causing harm to a community in general rather than to individual members of it; (*b*) = ***public menace*** above. **public office** (*a*) a building or set of buildings used for various departments of civic business, including the judicial, police, and coroner's courts, the meeting-place of a local authority, etc.; (*b*) a position or function involving responsibility to the public, *esp.* one in a government. **public opinion** the prevalent view or views held by the majority of the community. ***public orator***: see ORATOR 5. **public ownership** State ownership of the means of production, distribution, and exchange. ***public prosecutor***: see PROSECUTOR 3. **Public Record Office** an institution holding official archives, esp. birth, marriage, and death certificates, which are available for public inspection. **public relations** (treated as *sing.* or *pl.*) the creation or maintenance of goodwill and a favourable public image by an organization, company, famous person, etc.; the methods or profession of creating or maintaining such an image etc.; a department or organization responsible for public relations. **public school** (*a*) *Hist.* any of a class of grammar-schools founded or endowed for public use and subject to public management or control; (*b*) any of a class of private fee-paying secondary schools developing from former endowed grammar-schools and traditionally held to be characterized by a certain type of discipline and to impart a distinctive spirit; †(*c*) a lecture-room or class of the professor of any faculty in a university or similar institution; (*d*) in Scotland, the Commonwealth, and N. America, any school managed by public authority for the use of the community of a defined district, as part of a free local education system. **public sector** that part of an economy, industry, etc., controlled by the State. **public servant** a government official or employee. **public service** (*a*) government employment; (*b*) a service provided for the community, esp. under the direction of local or central government or other official agency; (*c*) *spec.* (*Austral. & NZ*) the Civil Service. **public spirit** a willingness to act in the best interests of a community, State, etc. **public-spirited** *adjective* having the best interests of a community etc. in mind; animated or actuated by a desire to promote the public good. **public-spiritedly** *adverb* in a public-spirited manner. **public-spiritedness** the quality of being public-spirited. **public transport** a system of buses, trains, etc., charging set fares and running on fixed routes. ***public utility***: see UTILITY *noun* 3c. **public weal** = ***public good*** above. **public woman** *arch.* a prostitute. **public works** construction or engineering projects carried out by or for the State on behalf of the community. **public wrong** an offence against society as a whole. ***the public purse***: see PURSE *noun*. ***wash one's dirty linen in public***: see LINEN *noun* 1. See also PUBLIC HOUSE.

■ **publically** *adverb* = PUBLICLY E20. **publicly** *adverb* (*a*) in a public or open manner; in public; (*b*) by or for the public or community collectively; by or with public action or consent: M16. **publicness** *noun* (now *rare*) E17.

publican /ˈpʌblɪk(ə)n/ *noun*[1]. ME.
[Old & mod. French *publicain* from Latin *publicanus* from *publicum* public revenue, use as noun of neut. of *publicus* PUBLIC *adjective*: see -AN.]

1 ROMAN HISTORY. A person who farmed the public taxes; a tax-gatherer. Chiefly in biblical allusions. ME. ▸**b** *transf.* A collector of toll, tribute, customs, etc. M17.
†**2** *transf.* A person regarded as a heathen; a person cut off from the Church or excommunicated. (W. ref. to *Matthew* 18:17.) ME–M17.
3 A person who keeps a public house or tavern; a licensed victualler. E18.
■ **publicanism** *noun* (*rare*) the state or profession of being a publican (PUBLICAN *noun*[1] 1) M17.

Publican /ˈpʌblɪk(ə)n/ *noun*[2]. LME.
[Old French *popelican*, *publican* from medieval Latin *Pop(e)licanus*, *Publicanus* alt. of medieval Greek *Paulikianos* PAULICIAN with allus. to Latin *publicanus* PUBLICAN *noun*[1].]
ECCLESIASTICAL HISTORY. A member of the Paulician sect living in the South of France in the 12th cent.

†**publicate** *verb trans.* M16–E19.
[from Latin *publicat-*: see next, -ATE[3].]
Publish, make (something) publicly known.

publication /pʌblɪˈkeɪʃ(ə)n/ *noun*. LME.
[Old & mod. French from Latin *publicatio(n-)*, from *publicat-* pa. ppl stem of *publicare*: see PUBLISH, -ATION.]
1 The action of making something generally known; public declaration or announcement. LME. ▸**b** LAW. Notification or communication to a third party or to a limited number of people regarded as representing the public; *spec.* (*a*) execution of a will before witnesses; (*b*) communication of defamatory words to a person or persons other than the person or organization defamed. L16.
2 a The process of producing and issuing for public sale a book, newspaper, report, piece of music, or other printed or reproduced matter. L16. ▸**b** A work published; a book etc. produced and issued for public sale. L16.

1 J. FOWLES The publication of what had hitherto been private. **2a** H. CARPENTER *The Boy's Own Paper* . . was an instant success when it began publication. *attrib.*: H. CRANE Its publication date. **b** *Times* Magazines or other publications.

publicatory /ˈpʌblɪkeɪt(ə)ri, -ət(ə)ri/ *adjective*. *rare*. E18.
[from late Latin *publicator*, from Latin *publicat-*: see prec., -ORY[2].]
Of or pertaining to publication; intended for publication.

public house /pʌblɪk ˈhaʊs/ *noun phr.* L16.
[from PUBLIC *adjective* + HOUSE *noun*[1].]
1 A building belonging or available to the community at large; a building provided for public use, public functions, etc. *obsolete* exc. as passing into sense 2. L16.
2 a An inn or hostelry usu. licensed for the supply of alcohol and providing food and lodging for travellers or members of the general public. Now passing into sense 2b. M17. ▸**b** A building with one or more bars, whose principal business is the sale of alcoholic liquors to be consumed on the premises, often now offering a range of meals; a tavern. E18.

publicise *verb* var. of PUBLICIZE.

publicist /ˈpʌblɪsɪst/ *noun*. L18.
[French *publiciste* (after *canoniste* CANONIST), from Latin (*jus*) *publicum* public (law), from neut. of *publicus* PUBLIC *adjective*: see -IST.]
1 An expert in or writer on public or international law. *arch.* L18.
2 A writer on contemporary public issues; a journalist writing chiefly on current affairs. M19.
3 A press or publicity agent; a person who promotes or publicizes something. M20.
■ **publiˈcistic** *adjective* E19.

publicitor /pʌbˈlɪsɪtə/ *noun*. *US*. M20.
[from PUBLICIT(Y + -OR.]
= PUBLICIST 3.

publicity /pʌbˈlɪsɪti/ *noun*. L18.
[French *publicité*, from *public* PUBLIC: see -ICITY.]
The quality of being public; the condition or fact of being open to public observation or knowledge; *spec.* the action or fact of publicizing someone or something or of being publicized; the technique or process of promoting or advertising a product, person, company, etc.; material or information issued for this purpose; public exposure, fame, notoriety.

F. RAPHAEL Once notoriety had been achieved, he lived always in the glare of publicity.

Comb.: **publicity agent** a person employed to gain and maintain public exposure for a person, company, etc., a publicist.

publicize /ˈpʌblɪsʌɪz/ *verb trans.* Also **-ise**. E20.
[from PUBLIC *adjective* + -IZE.]
Draw to public attention; make generally known; advertise, promote.

Weekly Dispatch Nowadays the potential star has to be managed and publicised.

■ **publiciˈzation** *noun* M20.

publish /ˈpʌblɪʃ/ *verb*. ME.
[from stem of Old French *puplier*, (also mod.) *publier* from Latin *publicare* make public, from *publicus* PUBLIC *adjective*: see -ISH[2].]
1 *verb trans.* Make generally known; declare or report openly; announce; disseminate (a creed or system). ME.
†**2** *verb trans.* Populate (a country etc.). ME–L16.
3 *verb trans.* **a** Announce (an edict etc.) in a formal or official manner; pronounce (a judicial sentence). LME. ▸**b** Proclaim (the banns) in church before a marriage. Also (*obsolete* exc. *US*), announce or list the names of (people) as intending marriage. L15.
4 *verb trans.* †**a** Proclaim (a person) publicly to be a traitor etc.; denounce. LME–M18. ▸†**b** Bring (a thing) to public notice. E16–E18.
5 a *verb trans.* Of an author, publisher, etc.: prepare and issue (a book, newspaper, report, piece of music, etc.) for sale to the public. Also, prepare and issue the work of (an author, composer, etc.). E16. ▸**b** *verb trans.* Make (a work, information, etc.) generally accessible or available; place before the public; *spec.* make (news, data, research findings, etc.) generally available through the medium of a newspaper, book, journal, etc. M17. ▸**c** *verb intrans.* Come into public circulation; be issued. E20.

1 L. STRACHEY Publish it to the world. **publish a will** LAW execute a will before witnesses. **publish a libel** LAW communicate a libel to a person or persons other than the one defamed. **5a** *Economist* A published poet. A. N. WILSON In 1947, he published a book called *Miracles*. *absol.*: C. S. LEWIS John Galsworthy (who publishes with them) had seen my MS. ***desktop publishing***: see DESKTOP *adjective*. **b** *Asian Art* This bronze was published in the Freer Gallery bronze catalog. **publish or perish** an attitude or practice existing within academic institutions, whereby researchers are under pressure to publish results in order to retain their positions or to be deemed successful.

■ **publishable** *adjective* able or fit to be published E19. **publishment** *noun* (now *rare*) (*a*) the action of publishing; publication, announcement; (*b*) *US* publication of marriage banns: L15.

publisher /ˈpʌblɪʃə/ *noun*. LME.
[from prec. + -ER[1].]
1 A person who makes something generally known; a person who declares or announces something publicly. Now *rare*. LME.
2 †**a** An author or editor of a published book or literary work. M17–L18. ▸**b** A person who or (esp.) a company which prepares and issues books, newspapers, music, etc., for sale to the public. Also (chiefly *N. Amer.*), a newspaper proprietor. M18.
2b publisher's binding, **publishers' binding** a uniform binding provided for an edition of a book before it is offered for sale. **publisher's cloth**, **publishers' cloth** a publisher's binding in which cloth is used as the covering material.

Puccinian /pʊˈtʃiːnɪən/ *adjective*. M20.
[from *Puccini* (see below) + -AN.]
Of, pertaining to, or characteristic of the Italian operatic composer Giacomo Puccini (1858–1924) or his work.
■ **Pucciniˈesque** *adjective* characteristic of or resembling Puccini's work E20.

puccoon /pʌˈkuːn/ *noun*. E17.
[Algonquian *poughkone*.]
Any of several N. American plants from which pigments are obtained; *esp.* (more fully ***red puccoon***) the bloodroot, *Sanguinaria canadensis*, and (more fully ***hoary puccoon***) *Lithospermum canescens*, which both yield a red dye, and (more fully ***yellow puccoon***) golden seal, *Hydrastis canadensis*, which yields a yellow dye.

puce /pjuːs/ *adjective & noun*. L18.
[Old & mod. French = flea (*couleur puce* flea colour) from Latin *pulex*, *-ic-* flea.]
▶ **A** *adjective*. Dark red or purple-brown in colour. L18.
▶ **B** *noun*. Puce colour; a shade of this. L19.

†**pucelage** *noun*. Also **-ll-**. M16–L18.
[Old & mod. French *pucel(l)age*, formed as PUCELLE + -AGE.]
The state or condition of being a girl; maidenhood, virginity.

pucellas /pjuːˈsɛləs/ *noun pl.* (treated as *sing.* or *pl.*). Also (now *rare* or *obsolete*) **procello** /prəʊˈsɛləʊ/, pl. **-os**. L18.
[(Pl. of alt. of) Italian *procello*.]
GLASS-MAKING. A tool for shaping a glass vessel or object being rotated on the end of a punty.

pucelle /pʊˈsɛl/ *noun*. *arch.* ME.
[Old & mod. French from late Latin *pulicella* from popular Latin dim. of Latin *puella* girl, *pullus* young animal, foal.]
1 A girl, a maiden; *spec.* (***the Pucelle***), Joan of Arc. ME.
†**2** A prostitute, a courtesan; a mistress. L16–L17.

puchero /pʊˈtʃɛrəʊ/ *noun*. Pl. **-os**. M19.
[Spanish = pot from Latin *pultarius* cooking- or drinking-vessel, from *pult-*, *puls* a kind of thick porridge + *-arius*.]
1 A glazed earthenware cooking-pot. *rare*. M19.
2 A Latin American stew of beef, sausage, bacon, and various vegetables. M19.

puck /pʌk/ *noun*¹. Also **pook** /pʊk/.
[Old English *pūca* = Old Norse *púki* mischievous demon. Cf. Welsh *pwca*, *pwci*, Irish *púca* POOKA.]
1 An evil or mischievous sprite, *spec.* (**P-**) Robin Goodfellow. Formerly also, the Devil. OE.
2 *transf.* Orig., a wicked man. Now, a person fond of playing mischievous tricks, *esp.* a mischievous child. LME.
Comb.: **puckfist** (now chiefly *dial.*) (*a*) an empty boaster; (*b*) a puffball fungus; **puck-needle** any of several weeds with long-beaked fruits; *esp.* shepherd's needle, *Scandix pecten-veneris*.

puck /pʌk/ *noun*². L19.
[Origin unkn.]
A flat rubber disc used as a ball in ice hockey or bandy.
Comb.: **puck carrier** the player in possession of the puck during play; **puck-chaser** *N. Amer. colloq.* an ice-hockey player.
■ **puckster** *noun* (*N. Amer. colloq.*) an ice-hockey player M20.

puck /pʌk/ *verb & noun*³. Now chiefly *dial.* M19.
[Perh. from base of POKE *verb*¹.]
▸ **A** *verb trans.* Hit, strike; butt. M19.
▸ **B** *noun.* A blow; in the game of hurling, a stroke at the ball. E20.

pucka *adjective* var. of PUKKA.

puckauly /pʌˈkɔːli/ *noun.* L18.
[Hindi *pakhālī* a water-carrier, from *pakhāl* a large water-skin.]
In the Indian subcontinent: a person employed as a water-carrier; a skin for carrying water.

puckaun /ˈpʌkɔːn/ *noun. Anglo-Irish.* M18.
[Irish *pocán* a small male goat.]
A billy-goat.

pucker /ˈpʌkə/ *noun.* M18.
[from next.]
1 A wrinkle, a small fold, a crease; a gathering in a piece of cloth. M18.
2 *fig.* A state of agitation or excitement. Chiefly in ***in a pucker***. *colloq.* M18.
🕮 **1** M. DE LA ROCHE The troubled pucker on his forehead.
■ **puckery** *adjective* (*a*) liable to puckering; marked with a pucker or puckers; (*b*) causing the mouth to form a pucker; bitter: M19.

pucker /ˈpʌkə/ *verb.* L16.
[Prob. frequentative from base also of POKE *noun*¹, POCKET *noun*: see -ER⁵.]
1 *verb intrans.* Become gathered or contracted into wrinkles, small folds, or creases. Freq. foll. by *up*. L16.
2 *verb trans.* Contract (the skin etc.) into wrinkles or creases; gather (a piece of cloth) into small folds. Freq. foll. by *up*. E17.
🕮 **1** ALBERT SMITH His waistcoat . . had a propensity to pucker up. **2** E. F. BENSON Lucia puckered up her eyebrows.

puckeroo /pʌkəˈruː/ *verb & adjective. NZ slang.* L19.
[Maori *pakaru* broken.]
▸ **A** *verb trans.* Ruin. Chiefly as ***puckerooed*** *ppl adjective.* L19.
▸ **B** *adjective.* Useless, broken. E20.

puckerow /ˈpʌkərəʊ/ *verb trans. Military slang.* M19.
[Hindi *pakṛo* imper. of *pakarnā* seize.]
Seize, lay hold of.

puckish /ˈpʌkɪʃ/ *adjective.* L19.
[from PUCK *noun*¹ + -ISH¹.]
Of the nature of or characteristic of a puck or Puck; impish, mischievous.
■ **puckishly** *adverb* L20. **puckishness** *noun* E20. **pucklike** *adjective* resembling (that of) a puck M19.

puckle /pʌk(ə)l/ *noun*¹. OE.
[from PUCK *noun*¹ + -LE¹.]
A sort of bogey or bugbear.

puckle /ˈpʌk(ə)l/ *noun*². *Scot.* L19.
[Origin unkn.]
An indefinite amount, a few.

pud /pʌd/ *noun*¹. *nursery & colloq.* M17.
[Origin uncertain; perh. a var. of PAD *noun*³.]
A (child's) hand; an animal's forefoot.

pud /pʊd/ *noun*². E18.
[Abbreviation.]
▸ **I 1** = PUDDING *noun* 1, 2. Now chiefly *Scot. & dial.* E18.
2 = PUDDING *noun* 5. *coarse slang.* M20.
3 *fig.* = PUDDING *noun* 9b; *spec.* an easy college course. *US slang.* M20.
2 ***pull one's pud***: see PULL *verb*.
▸ **II 4** = PUDDING *noun* 7. *colloq.* M20.

pudden *noun, verb* see PUDDING *noun, verb.*

puddening /ˈpʊd(ə)nɪŋ/ *noun.* M18.
[from *pudden* var. of PUDDING *verb* + -ING¹.]
NAUTICAL. = PUDDING *noun* 4.

pudder *noun & verb*¹ see POTHER.

pudder /ˈpʌdə/ *verb*² *intrans.* Now *rare* or *obsolete.* L16.
[Origin unkn.]
1 Poke or stir about with the hand or a stick; (of an animal) root, grub, poke at something with bill or snout. L16.
2 Potter about; meddle or dabble *in*. E17.

pudding /ˈpʊdɪŋ/ *noun.* Also (*colloq. & dial.*) **pudden** /ˈpʊd(ə)n/. ME.
[Old & mod. French *boudin* black pudding from Proto-Gallo-Romance from Latin *botellus* pudding, sausage, small intestine: see BOWEL. Cf. BOUDIN.]
▸ **I 1** The stomach or intestine of a pig, sheep, etc., stuffed with minced meat, suet, oatmeal, seasoning, etc., and boiled. Now chiefly *Scot. & dial.* or with specifying word. ME. ▸†**b** A stuffing mixture of similar ingredients, roasted within the body of an animal. L16–L18.
2 In *pl.* The bowels, the entrails, the guts. Now chiefly *Scot. & dial.* LME.
†**3** A kind of artificial light or firework; a kind of fuse for exploding a mine. E16–L17.
4 *NAUTICAL.* A plaited rope placed round the mast and yards of a ship as a support; a fender; a pad or binding to prevent cables or hawsers from chafing. E17.
5 The penis. *coarse slang.* E18.
6 A fat or dumpy person. *colloq.* L18.
1 ***black pudding***, ***white pudding***, etc.
▸ **II 7** A cooked dish consisting of various sweet or savoury ingredients, esp. as enclosed within a flour-based crust or mixed with flour, eggs, etc., and boiled or steamed; a baked batter mixture. Now also, the sweet course of a meal. M16. ▸**b** Food consisting of such a dish. L17.
8 *transf.* Anything of the consistency of or resembling a pudding. E17.
9 *fig.* **a** Material reward or advantage, esp. as opp. to ***praise***. *arch.* M17. ▸**b** Something easy to accomplish. *US slang.* L19.
10 Poisoned or drugged meat used to incapacitate a guard dog. *slang.* L19.
🕮 **7** ***bread pudding***, ***Christmas pudding***, ***milk pudding***, ***roly-poly pudding***, ***steak and kidney pudding***, ***Yorkshire pudding*** etc. **b** G. MEREDITH Our English pudding, a fortuitous concourse of all the sweets. **8** *Times* A pudding of a pitch.
Phrases: ***in the pudding club***: see CLUB *noun*. OVEREGG ***the pudding***. ***pudding in the oven***: see OVEN *noun* 2d. ***pull one's pudding***: see PULL *verb*. ***queen of puddings***: see QUEEN *noun*.
Attrib. & comb.: In the senses 'of a pudding or puddings', 'used in the making or eating of a pudding', as ***pudding course***, ***pudding bowl***, ***pudding plate***, etc. Special combs., as **pudding-bag** a bag in which a pudding is boiled; something resembling such a bag; **pudding basin** a basin in which puddings are made; *transf.* a round hat, a severe round hairstyle of uniform length; **pudding-face** *colloq.* a large fat face; **pudding-faced** *adjective* (*colloq.*) having a large fat face; **pudding-grass** (*obsolete* exc. *Hist.*) pennyroyal, *Mentha pulegium*, formerly used as a flavouring; **pudding-head** *colloq.* a stupid person; **pudding-headed** *adjective* (*colloq.*) stupid; **pudding-pie** any of various types of pastry; *esp.* a baked dough pudding containing meat or a small tart containing custard; **pudding-pipe tree** an Indian leguminous tree, *Cassia fistula*, with a very long pod; **pudding-sleeve** a large full sleeve drawn in at the wrist or above; **pudding-stone** a conglomerate in which dark-coloured round pebbles contrast with a paler fine-grained matrix; **pudding-time** (now *rare* or *obsolete*) the time when pudding or puddings are available or being served; *fig.* a favourable or useful time; **pudding-wife** †(*a*) a woman selling puddings; (*b*) (now *dial.*) a professional or expert maker of puddings; (*c*) a bluish and bronze wrasse, *Halichoeres radiatus*, found off the Atlantic coasts of tropical America.
■ **puddingy** *adjective* having the appearance, shape, or consistency of a pudding E18.

pudding /ˈpʊdɪŋ/ *verb trans.* Also (*colloq. & dial.*) **pudden** /ˈpʊd(ə)n/. M17.
[from prec.]
1 Supply or treat (as) with pudding. M17.
2 *NAUTICAL.* Bind (a cable or hawser) to prevent chafing. E18.

puddle /ˈpʌd(ə)l/ *noun.* ME.
[Dim. of Old English *pudd* ditch, furrow: see -LE¹. Cf. German dial. *P(f)udel* pool.]
1 A small pool of muddy water, *esp.* one formed on a road or path after rain. Formerly also, a larger body of water, such as a pond or swamp. ME. ▸**b** *transf.* A small pool of any liquid; *colloq.* a pool of urine (freq. in ***make a puddle*** below). E18. ▸**c** *fig.* The sea, *esp.* the Atlantic Ocean. Freq. in ***this side of the puddle*** etc. *joc.* L19. ▸**d** *ROWING.* A circular patch of disturbed water made by the blade of an oar at each stroke. M20. ▸**e** A small pool of molten metal, esp. one formed in welding; a piece of metal solidified from such a pool. M20.
2 *fig.* **a** A confused collection or heap; a state of confusion; a muddle. Now chiefly *dial.* E16. ▸**b** A sink of corruption, a source of moral defilement or false doctrine. Now *rare.* M16.
3 Foul or muddy water as found in puddles. Now *dial.* M16.
4 A preparation of clay and sometimes sand mixed with water and used as a watertight covering for embankments etc. Cf. PUDDLING *noun.* L18.
5 A muddler, a bungler. *Scot. & dial.* L18.
🕮 **1b** L. BLUE Puddles of sweet cider. **make a puddle** *colloq.* (of a child or pet animal) urinate on the floor. **2b** R. G. PRESTON In what a Puddle of Filth Impiety doth wallow.
Comb.: **puddle-duck** the domestic duck; **puddle-jumper** *N. Amer. slang* a fast highly manoeuvrable means of transport, *esp.* a small light aeroplane.
■ **puddly** *adjective* M16.

puddle /ˈpʌd(ə)l/ *verb.* LME.
[from prec. Cf. Dutch *poedelen*, Low German *pud(d)eln* dabble or splash in water.]
1 a *verb intrans.* Dabble, poke about, or wallow in mud or shallow water; *fig.* busy oneself in a disorganized way, muddle or mess *about*. LME. ▸**b** *verb refl.* Bring or get oneself into a specified condition by or as by puddling. *rare.* M18.
2 *verb trans.* Bog down in mud; wet with mud or dirty water. M16.
3 *verb trans.* Make (water) muddy; *fig.* muddle, confuse, sully. L16.
4 *verb trans.* **a** Reduce (wet ground, clay, etc.) to mud; *spec.* knead (wet clay and sand) so as to form puddle or plastic watertight material. M18. ▸**b** Cover or line with puddle; *spec.* dip (the roots of a plant) into puddle to conserve moisture. E19.
5 *verb trans. METALLURGY.* Heat (molten iron) in a reverberatory furnace with iron oxide, so as to oxidize and remove the carbon and other impurities and produce wrought iron. L18.
6 *verb trans. MINING.* Work (clayey wash-dirt) with water so as to separate gold or opals from the ore. M19.
🕮 **1a** E. M. FORSTER We puddled about in the car. **2** G. BOYCOTT The covers . . were puddled with . . water. **3** J. HOWKER I'd not puddle me mind with it.
■ **puddler** *noun* L16. **puddling** *noun* (*a*) the action or an act of the verb; (*b*) = PUDDLE *noun* 4: L16. **puddling** *ppl adjective* that puddles, *esp.* muddling M17.

puddled /ˈpʌd(ə)ld/ *adjective.* M16.
[from PUDDLE *noun, verb*: see -ED², -ED¹.]
1 Made muddy by being stirred, as water in a puddle; dirty, foul. Formerly also, muddled, confused. M16.
2 Reduced to puddle (PUDDLE *noun* 4); covered or lined with puddle so as to be watertight. L18.
3 Turned into or covered with puddles of water. M19.
4 *METALLURGY.* Of iron: purified from carbon etc. by puddling. M19.

puddock *noun* see PADDOCK *noun*¹.

puddy /ˈpʌdi/ *adjective.* Chiefly *dial.* M18.
[Origin unkn.: see -Y¹. Cf. PUD *noun*¹, SPUDDY.]
Esp. of the hands or fingers: plump; stumpy; pudgy. Also, thickset.

pudency /ˈpjuːd(ə)nsi/ *noun. literary.* E17.
[Late Latin *pudentia*, from *pudent-* pres. ppl stem of *pudere* be ashamed: see -ENCY.]
Susceptibility to the feeling of shame; modesty, bashfulness.

pudenda *noun* pl. of PUDENDUM.

†**pudendous** *adjective.* L17–E19.
[from Latin *pudendus*: see next, -OUS.]
Shameful.

pudendum /pjʊˈdɛndəm/ *noun.* Pl. **-da** /-də/. M17.
[Latin *pudenda* use as noun of neut. pl. of *pudendus* gerundive of *pudere* be ashamed.]
In *pl.* & (occas.) *sing.* The genitals, *esp.* the female external genitals.
■ **pudendal** *adjective* L18.

pudeur /pydœːr/ *noun.* M20.
[French, formed as PUDOR.]
A sense of shame or embarrassment, esp. with regard to matters of a sexual or personal nature; modesty.
🕮 A. S. BYATT She could not, out of a kind of *pudeur*, mention enemas to Daniel.

pudge /pʌdʒ/ *noun*¹. Chiefly *dial.* L17.
[Origin uncertain: perh. ult. rel. to PUDDLE *noun.*]
A ditch, a puddle.

pudge /pʌdʒ/ *noun*². Now *dial. & colloq.* E19.
[Parallel to PODGE *noun*. Cf. earlier PADGE.]
1 A short thickset or fat person; a short squat thing. E19.
2 A barn owl. Also ***pudge-owl***. L19.

pudge /pʌdʒ/ *verb intrans.* Now *dial.* Also (earlier) **podge** /pɒdʒ/. M17.
[Origin unkn.: cf. PODGE *noun*, PUDGE *noun*².]
Walk slowly and heavily.

pudgy /ˈpʌdʒi/ *adjective.* M19.
[from PUDGE *noun*² + -Y¹. Cf. PODGY.]
Short and thickset; plump, fat.
■ **pudgily** *adverb* E20. **pudginess** *noun* L20.

pudibund /ˈpjuːdɪbʌnd/ *adjective. rare.* M16.
[Latin *pudibundus* easily ashamed, bashful, shameful, from *pudere*: see PUDENDUM.]
Modest, bashful, prudish. Formerly also, shameful.
■ **pudiˈbundery** *noun* bashfulness, prudery E20.

pudic /ˈpjuːdɪk/ *adjective.* L15.
[Old & mod. French *pudique* or Latin *pudicus* chaste, from *pudere*: see PUDENDUM, -IC.]
1 Having a keen sense of shame; modest, chaste. *literary.* L15.
2 ANATOMY. = PUDENDAL. Now *rare.* L18.
■ †**pudical** *adjective* E16–L18.

pudicity /pjuːˈdɪsɪti/ *noun. literary.* M16.
[French *pudicité* from Latin *pudicitia*, from *pudicus*: see prec., -ICITY.]
Modesty, chastity.

pudor /ˈpjuːdɔː/ *noun. literary.* E17.
[Latin = shame, modesty, from *pudere*: see PUDENDUM, -OR.]
Due sense of shame; bashfulness, modesty.

pudsy /ˈpʌdzi/ *adjective. nursery & colloq.* Also **-ey**. M18.
[Perh. from PUD *noun*[2] after FUBSY: see -SY.]
Plump.

pudu /ˈpuːduː/ *noun.* L19.
[Araucanian.]
Either of two very small rare deer of the genus *Pudu*, found in the lower Andes.

pueblo /ˈpwɛbləʊ/ *noun & adjective.* Pl. **-os**. E19.
[Spanish from Latin *populus* PEOPLE *noun.*]
▸ **A** *noun.* **1** A town or village in Latin America or the south-western US; *esp.* an Indian settlement. E19.
2 (**P-**.) A member of the Pueblo Indians. M19.
▸ **B** *attrib.* or as *adjective.* Of or pertaining to a pueblo; (usu. **P-**) designating or pertaining to a group of N. American Indians living in pueblos chiefly in New Mexico and Arizona. M19.
■ **puebloan** *adjective* of or pertaining to Pueblo Indians or their culture L19.

puer *verb* see PURE *verb.*

puericulture /ˈpjʊərɪkʌltʃə/ *noun.* E20.
[French *puériculture*, from Latin *puer* boy, child + *cultura* CULTURE *noun.*]
The rearing of children as a skill or a branch of sociology.

puerile /ˈpjʊərʌɪl/ *adjective.* L16.
[French *puéril* or Latin *puerilis*, from *puer* boy, child: see -ILE.]
1 Of or like a boy or child. Freq. *derog.*, trivial, childish, immature. L16.
2 MEDICINE. Of respiration: characterized by a louder pulmonary murmur as found in children, which in adults is usu. a sign of disease. Now *rare* or *obsolete.* E19.
📖 **1** M. DICKENS She would boast, or use puerile slang expressions from school.
■ **puerilely** *adverb* M18. **puerileness** *noun* puerility E18. **puerilism** *noun* (PSYCHIATRY & PSYCHOLOGY) the state or condition of behaving like a child, childish behaviour; *spec.* (**a**) (in an adult) a reversion to infantile behaviour, usu. as a symptom of mental illness; (**b**) (in a child) that stage of normal development which follows infantilism and precedes puberty: M20.

puerility /pjʊəˈrɪlɪti/ *noun.* LME.
[French *puérilité* or Latin *puerilitas*, from *puerilis*: see prec., -ITY.]
1 a An instance of childishness or immaturity in behaviour or expression; a thing embodying or displaying childishness. Usu. in *pl.* LME. ▸**b** The quality of being puerile; childishness, immaturity, triviality. L16.
2 The condition of being a child; childhood. E16.
📖 **1a** DENNIS POTTER In the accepted parliamentary manner . . he has to get through the obligatory puerilities first. **b** LD MACAULAY That a shrewd statesman . . should, at nearly sixty . . descend to such puerility is utterly inconceivable.

puerperal /pjuːˈəːp(ə)r(ə)l/ *adjective.* M18.
[from Latin *puerperus* parturient, from *puer* child + *-parus* bringing forth: see -AL[1].]
MEDICINE. Of, pertaining to, accompanying, or following childbirth.
puerperal fever, **puerperal sepsis** septicaemia shortly after childbirth resulting from infection of the lining of the uterus or vagina.

puerperium /pjuːəˈpɛrɪəm, -ˈpiːrɪəm/ *noun.* Also (earlier, now *rare*) Anglicized as **puerpery** /pjuːˈəːp(ə)ri/. E17.
[Latin, from *puerperus*: see prec., -IUM.]
MEDICINE. The puerperal state or period; *spec.* the few weeks following delivery during which the mother's tissues return to their non-pregnant state.

Puerto Rican /pwɑːtə(ʊ) ˈriːk(ə)n/ *noun & adjective.* M19.
[from *Puerto Rico* (see below) + -AN.]
▸ **A** *noun.* A native or inhabitant of Puerto Rico, an island in the Greater Antilles group of the W. Indies; a person of Puerto Rican descent. M19.
▸ **B** *adjective.* Of or pertaining to Puerto Rico or the Puerto Ricans. L19.

puff /pʌf/ *noun.* ME.
[Imit., perh. repr. Old English *pyf(f)* corresp. to Dutch *pof*, Low German *pof*, *puf*. Cf. next.]
1 a A short quick blast of breath or wind; a light abrupt emission of air, vapour, smoke, etc.; an inhalation or exhalation from a cigarette, pipe, etc. Also as *interjection.* ME. ▸**b** An act of puffing; an utterance of 'puff' as an expression of contempt. Also as *interjection*, expr. contempt. L15. ▸**c** Breath, wind. *colloq.* E19. ▸**d** A small quantity of air, vapour, smoke, etc., emitted in one light abrupt blast; the sound of an abrupt or explosive emission. M19. ▸**e** Dynamite or other explosives used for safe-blowing. *slang* (orig. *US*). E20. ▸**f** Life. Chiefly in ***in one's puff***, ***in all one's puff***, in (all) one's life. *colloq.* E20.
2 †**a** A small container for sprinkling scent. Only in LME. ▸**b** Orig., an instrument like a small bellows, used for blowing powder on the hair (*obsolete* exc. *Hist.*). Now, a powder-puff. M17.
3 Any of various kinds of light pastry, cake, etc.; now *esp.* a small light pastry containing jam, cream, etc., usu. made of puff pastry. LME.
4 a A swelling; a blister, a protuberance. M16. ▸**b** A rounded soft mass of material gathered at the edges and full in the middle; *ellipt.* = ***puff sleeve*** below. Also, a decorative rounded mass of ribbons or feathers on a bonnet; a hairstyle formed by rolling the hair around a pad and securing it on the head. E17. ▸**c** A lightweight quilt or duvet. Chiefly *N. Amer.* E20. ▸**d** CYTOLOGY. A short swollen region of a polytene chromosome, active in RNA synthesis. M20.
5 = PUFFBALL 1. Now *dial.* M16.
6 *fig.* **a** An inflated speech, an empty boast; pride; showy adornment, inflation of style; bluff. M16. ▸†**b** Anything empty, vain, or insubstantial. L16–E17.
7 a A boaster; a person swollen with pride or vanity. *arch.* L16. ▸†**b** = PUFFER 2a. M–L18. ▸†**c** A decoy in a gambling-house; a dummy bidder at an auction. *slang.* M–L18. ▸**d** An effeminate man; a male homosexual. Cf. POOF *noun*[1]. E20.
8 Undue or extravagant praise; an excessively or falsely enthusiastic advertisement or review. M18.
📖 **1a** H. WOUK Pamela asked for a cigarette and took several puffs. J. LINGARD The leaves were going, a few more puffs of wind . . and they would all be gone. **c** *Observer* The top of a mountain is . . where climbers run out of puff. **d** J. M. COETZEE Warm breath forming puffs in the air. **3** R. GODDEN Apricot puffs and cheese. **6a** T. ARNOLD Puff, or verbal ornament. **8** H. EVANS He . . printed candid reviews instead of puffs.
Comb.: **puff box** a box to hold powder and a powder-puff; **puff-leg** any of various S. American hummingbirds of the genera *Eriocnemis* and *Haplophaedia*, having tufts of down on the legs; **puff piece** (chiefly *US*) a newspaper article, item on a television show, etc., intended to praise or promote a celebrity, book, etc.; **puff pipe** (**a**) a short ventilation pipe in a drainage system; (**b**) a pipe out of which compressed air is blown in order to control the attitude of a vertical take-off aircraft; **puff port** a vent out of which compressed air is blown in order to control the attitude of a hovercraft; **puff sleeve** a short sleeve gathered at the top and cuff and full in the middle.

puff /pʌf/ *verb.* ME.
[Imit., perh. repr. Old English *pyffan*, corresp. to Middle & mod. Dutch *puffen*, Dutch *poffen*. Cf. prec.]
1 a *verb intrans.* Blow with a short quick blast or blasts; emit a puff of air or breath. ME. ▸**b** *verb intrans.* Breathe hard, pant; run pantingly. Freq. in ***puff and blow.*** LME. ▸**c** *verb trans.* Utter breathlessly or whilst panting. Freq. foll. by *out.* L16. ▸**d** *verb intrans.* Send out or move with puffs of vapour, smoke, etc. (freq. foll. by *away, in, out*); (of a person smoking) take puffs *at* a cigarette, pipe, etc. L18. ▸**e** *verb trans.* Cause to puff, put out of breath; tire (a person) *out*. Chiefly as ***puffed*** *ppl adjective.* E19. ▸**f** *verb intrans.* Of a puffball or similar fungus: discharge a cloud of spores suddenly. L19.
2 *verb trans.* **a** Blow or carry (dust, a cloud, etc.) *away, out, up*, etc., with a short quick blast; emit (smoke, steam, etc.) in puffs. ME. ▸**b** Extinguish with a puff. Usu. foll. by *out.* M16. ▸†**c** Blow (a fire) with the mouth or bellows to make it burn well. E17–M18. ▸**d** Smoke (a cigarette, pipe, etc.) in intermittent puffs. E19. ▸**e** Apply (powder) with a powder-puff. M19.
3 a *verb trans.* Praise or commend extravagantly or unduly; *esp.* advertise or review (a product, book, etc.), with excessive or false enthusiasm. LME. ▸**b** *verb intrans.* Make exaggerated claims, boast. *rare.* M18. ▸**c** *verb intrans.* Make dummy bids at an auction to inflate or raise the price of a lot and incite others to buy. M19.
†**4** *verb intrans.* Express contempt or scorn; speak or behave scornfully or insolently, swagger. L15–L17.
5 a *verb trans. & intrans.* Become or cause to become swollen or inflated, swell; distend or become distended (as) by inflation, padding, or gathering in a bunch. Usu. foll. by *up, out.* L15. ▸**b** *verb intrans.* CYTOLOGY. Of a polytene chromosome: form a puff (PUFF *noun* 4d). Chiefly as ***puffed*** *ppl adjective*, ***puffing*** *verbal noun.* M20.
6 *verb trans. fig.* ▸**a** Cause to swell with vanity, pride, etc.; make vain, proud, or arrogant; elate; *rare* cause to swell with anger. Usu. foll. by *up*. Chiefly as ***puffed*** *ppl adjective.* E16. ▸†**b** Foll. by *up*: raise unduly in position or authority. M16–M17.
📖 **1a** SHAKES. *A.Y.L.* Foggy South, puffing with wind and rain. **b** R. INGALLS She was puffing by the time they reached the . . arena. **d** *Railway Magazine* The 7:30 a.m. from Amman . . puffs heavily round a hillside. A. MACLEAN He puffed deeply on an ancient brier. **2a** M. FRAYN A train . . puffing . . snowballs of smoke. **3a** P. ZWEIG The dubious ethics of anonymously puffing one's own work. **4** AV *Ps.* 10:5 As for . . his enemies, he puffeth at them. **5a** C. EASTON Puffed up from . . cortisone injections. P. LIVELY She was a small round woman, puffed out with frilly blouses. ***puffed rice***, ***puffed wheat***, etc. **6a** *Daedalus* Puffed-up hypocrites.
Comb.: **puff adder** (**a**) a large, very venomous African viper, *Bitis arietans*, which hisses loudly when alarmed; (**b**) (*US*) = ***hognose snake*** s.v. HOG *noun*; **puffbird** any of various American birds of the family Bucconidae, closely related to the jacamars, and having lax plumage which gives them a stout appearance.
■ **puffing** *noun* (**a**) the action of the verb; an instance of this; (**b**) a puffed frill or trimming of frills: LME.

Puffa /ˈpʌfə/ *noun.* L20.
[Origin uncertain: perh. respelling of PUFFER.]
In full ***Puffa jacket***. (Proprietary name for) a type of thick padded jacket.

puffball /ˈpʌfbɔːl/ *noun.* M17.
[from PUFF *noun* or *verb* + BALL *noun*[1].]
1 Any of the gasteromycetous fungi constituting the genera *Lycoperdon*, *Calvatia*, *Bovista*, etc., which have a ball-shaped fruiting body and at maturity burst open to discharge a cloud of powdery spores; *esp.* (in full ***giant puffball***) *Calvatia gigantea*. M17.
2 A powder-puff; an object resembling this. E19.
3 A short full skirt gathered in around the hemline to produce a soft puffy shape. M20.
📖 **3** *attrib.*: *Sunday Mail (Brisbane)* Skintight leathers and puff-ball minis.

puffer /ˈpʌfə/ *noun.* E17.
[from PUFF *verb* + -ER[1].]
1 A person who or thing which blows in short abrupt blasts, or emits puffs of smoke, steam, etc.; a steam engine, a steamboat; *spec.* (chiefly *Scot.*) a small steamboat used for carrying cargo in coastal waters. E17. ▸**b** In full ***puffer fish***. Any of various marine globe-fishes of the Tetraodontidae and related families, which inflate themselves with water when alarmed. E19. ▸**c** A porpoise. *US.* L19. ▸**d** A wheel-lock pistol. L20. ▸**e** A soft plastic container designed to blow powder out when squeezed. L20.
2 a A person who praises something excessively or unduly; a writer of puffs. M18. ▸**b** A person employed by a vendor to make dummy bids at an auction for the purpose of inflating the price of a lot and inciting others to buy. M18.
■ **puffery** *noun* (**a**) the practice of praising or commending something extravagantly or unduly; extravagant praise; (**b**) *rare* puffs collectively, a puffed frill or trimming of frills: L18.

puffick /ˈpʌfɪk/ *adjective. colloq.* M20.
[Repr. a pronunc.]
Perfect.
■ **pufficKly** *adverb* L19.

puffin /ˈpʌfɪn/ *noun.* ME.
[App. from PUFF *verb* + -ING[3], with ref. to the fat nestlings of the Manx shearwater: earlier as Anglo-Latin *puffo(nus)*, *poffo*, *paphinus*. The modern sense arose by confusion.]
1 Orig., the Manx shearwater, *Puffinus puffinus*. Now, any of various auks of the genera *Fratercula* and *Lunda*, noted for their very deep and brightly coloured bills, esp. *F. arctica*, the Atlantic puffin. ME.
2 [from *p(edestrian) u(ser) f(riendly) in(telligent)*, alt. by analogy with *pelican crossing*.] More fully ***puffin crossing***. In Britain, a pedestrian crossing with traffic lights which go green again only when no more pedestrians are detected on the crossing by infrared detectors and mats. L20.
■ **puffinry** *noun* (a place occupied by) a breeding colony of puffins M20.

puffinosis /pʌfɪˈnəʊsɪs/ *noun.* Pl. **-noses** /-ˈnəʊsiːz/. M20.
[from mod. Latin *Puffinus* (see below) + -OSIS.]
An epizootic viral disease of sea birds, originally observed in the Manx shearwater, *Puffinus puffinus*.

puff-paste /ˈpʌfpeɪst/ *noun.* L16.
[from PUFF *noun*, *verb* + PASTE *noun.*]
1 A dough rolled and folded several times, with butter incorporated at each rolling. Also (*N. Amer.*) = PUFF PASTRY. Now chiefly *arch.* & *N. Amer.* L16.
2 *fig.* A person or thing of a light, flimsy, or insubstantial nature. Now *rare.* E17.

puff pastry /pʌf ˈpeɪstri/ *noun phr.* M19.
[from PUFF *noun*, *verb* + PASTRY.]
A pastry made from dough which has been rolled and folded several times, with butter incorporated at each

rolling, and forming a rich light flaky texture when baked. Cf. PUFF-PASTE.
rough puff pastry: see ROUGH *adjective*.

puff-puff /ˈpʌfpʌf/ *noun. colloq.* or *nursery*. L19.
[Redupl. of PUFF *noun, verb*.]
A locomotive, a railway train.

puffy /ˈpʌfi/ *adjective*. L16.
[from PUFF *noun, verb* + -Y[1].]
1 Vain, pompous, inflated. Now *rare*. L16.
2 (Of wind) gusty; (of a person or animal) easily caused to puff and pant, short-winded. E17.
3 Swollen or inclined to swell; puffed out; fat; flabby. M17.

> 🕮 **1** DRYDEN He distinguished not the blown puffy style from true sublimity. **2** *Times* A strong puffy off-shore wind. **3** B. BREYTENBACH He has red puffy bags under the eyes.

■ **puffily** *adverb* M19. **puffiness** *noun* puffed-up or swollen condition; an instance of this: M17.

†**puft** *noun*. LME–L18.
[By-form of PUFF *noun*.]
A puff of wind.

puftaloon /pʌftəluːn/ *noun. Austral.* L19.
[Origin uncertain. Cf. PUFF *noun* 3.]
A small fried cake, spread with jam, sugar, or honey, and usu. eaten hot.

pug /pʌɡ/ *noun*[1]. Now *dial.* LME.
[Origin unkn.]
The chaff of wheat, oats, small seeds, etc.; the refuse corn separated in winnowing.

pug /pʌɡ/ *noun*[2]. M16.
[Perh. of Low Dutch origin: cf. Western Flemish *Pugge* substituted for male forename.]
► **I** †**1** A term of endearment: dear one. M16–E17.
†**2 a** A bargeman; *spec.* (more fully ***Western pug***) one navigating barges down the River Thames to London. L16–E17. ►**b** A ship's boy. *rare*. L16–L17.
†**3** A courtesan, a prostitute; a mistress. E17–E18.
4 An upper servant in a large establishment. CF. TAG *noun*[1] 12. *arch. colloq.* M19.
► **II 5** A monkey, an ape. Also (*rare*), a child. *obsolete exc. dial.* L16.
†**6** A small demon or imp; a sprite. Only in 17.
7 In full ***pug-dog***. (An animal of) a dwarf breed of dog resembling a bulldog, with a broad flat nose and deeply wrinkled face. M18.
8 (A name for) a fox. Chiefly *dial.* E19.
9 Any of various small geometrid moths of the genus *Eupithecia* and related genera. E19.
10 A short or stumpy person or thing; *esp.* a dwarf. *Scot. & dial.* M19.
11 In full ***pug-engine***. A small locomotive used chiefly for shunting purposes. L19.
12 A net or snood for keeping a bun or knot of hair in place. E20.
Comb.: ***pug-dog***: see sense 7 above; ***pug-engine***: see sense 11 above; ***pug-nose*** a short squat or snub nose; ***pug-nosed*** *adjective* having a pug-nose.
■ **puggish** *adjective* characteristic of or resembling a pug L17. **puggy** *adjective*[1] resembling the face or nose of a monkey or pug-dog; having such a face or nose: E18.

pug /pʌɡ/ *noun*[3]. E19.
[Origin uncertain: cf. PUG *verb*[2].]
Loam or clay mixed, kneaded, and prepared for brick-making, pottery, etc. (Earliest in ***pug-mill*** below.)
Comb.: **pug-mill** a machine for mixing and working clay etc. into pug.
■ **puggy** *adjective*[2] muddy, sticky M20.

pug /pʌɡ/ *noun*[4]. M19.
[Hindi *pag* footprint.]
More fully ***pug-mark***. The footprint of an animal.

pug /pʌɡ/ *noun*[5]. *slang*. M19.
[Abbreviation.]
= PUGILIST.

pug /pʌɡ/ *verb*[1] *trans.* Now *Scot. & dial.* Infl. **-gg-**. L16.
[Perh. symbolic cf. *lug*, *tug*.]
1 Pull, tug. L16.
2 Dirty by excessive handling. L19.

pug /pʌɡ/ *verb*[2] *trans.* Infl. **-gg-**. E19.
[Origin uncertain: cf. PUG *noun*[3], Western Flemish *pug(ge* prod, kick, knock.]
1 Poke, punch, strike. *dial. rare.* E19.
2 Pack or fill up (a space) with pug or other materials; *esp.* pack (the space) between floor joists with earth, sawdust, etc., to provide sound insulation. E19.
3 Thrust, poke, or pack into a space. *dial.* M19.
4 Prepare (clay) for brick-making or pottery, by kneading and working into a soft and plastic condition. M19. ►**b** Trample (ground) into a muddy and sticky mass. L19.
■ **pugging** *noun* composite material used to pack the space between floor joists to provide sound insulation E19.

pug /pʌɡ/ *verb*[3] *trans.* Infl. **-gg-**. M19.
[from PUG *noun*[4].]
Track (an animal etc.) by footprints.

puggaree /ˈpʌɡ(ə)riː/ *noun*. Also **pagri** /ˈpaɡri/; **puggree** /ˈpʌɡriː/. M17.
[Hindi *pagrī* turban.]
1 A turban, as worn in the Indian subcontinent. M17.
2 A thin muslin scarf wound round the crown of a sun-helmet or hat so that the ends of the scarf form a shade for the neck. M19.

puggle /ˈpʌɡ(ə)l/ *noun & adjective*. Also **poggle** /ˈpɒɡ(ə)l/. E19.
[Hindi *pāgal*, *paglā*.]
► **A** *noun*. A crazy or foolish person, an idiot. *Anglo-Indian*. Now *rare* or *obsolete*. E19.
► **B** *adjective*. Mentally unbalanced, crazy. *Military slang*. E20.

puggle /ˈpʌɡ(ə)l/ *verb trans.* Chiefly *dial.* M19.
[Frequentative of PUG *verb*[2]: see -LE[3].]
Unblock (a hole etc.) by poking with a stick or wire.

puggled /ˈpʌɡ(ə)ld/ *adjective. slang* (orig. MILITARY) & *Scot.* Also **poggled** /ˈpɒɡ(ə)ld/. E20.
[from (the same root as) PUGGLE *noun & adjective* + -ED[2].]
Exhausted, in a state of collapse; completely drunk.

puggree *noun* var. of PUGGAREE.

puggy /ˈpʌɡi/ *noun*[1]. E17.
[from PUG *noun*[2] + -Y[6].]
†**1** A term of endearment. E17–E18.
2 A monkey. *Scot.* M17.
3 = PUG *noun*[2] 8. *dial.* E19.

puggy /ˈpʌɡi/ *noun*[2]. *rare*. L19.
[Hindi *pagī*, formed as PUG *noun*[4].]
A tracker.

pugil /ˈpjuːdʒɪl/ *noun*[1]. *arch.* L16.
[Latin *pugillus* a handful, from *pug-* base of *pugnus* fist.]
Orig., a handful. Later, as much or as many as can be held between the thumb and the next two fingers; a large pinch.

pugil /ˈpjuːdʒɪl/ *noun*[2]. *US*. M20.
[Prob. from PUGIL(ISM.]
In full ***pugil stick***. A short pole with padded ends used in military training as a substitute for a rifle with fixed bayonet.

pugilant /ˈpjuːdʒɪl(ə)nt/ *adjective. rare*. L19.
[Late Latin *pugilant-* pres. ppl stem of *pugilari* to box, formed as next: see -ANT[1].]
Pugnacious, fighting.

pugilism /ˈpjuːdʒɪlɪz(ə)m/ *noun*. L18.
[from Latin *pugil* boxer + -ISM.]
The art, practice, or profession of fighting with fists; boxing.

pugilist /ˈpjuːdʒɪlɪst/ *noun*. M18.
[formed as prec. + -IST.]
A boxer, *esp.* a professional one; a fighter.
■ **pugiˈlistic** *adjective* L18. **pugiˈlistically** *adverb* L18.

pugillary /pjuːˈdʒɪləri/ *noun*. Pl. **-ries**, in Latin form **-ria** /-rɪə/. *rare*. M18.
[from Latin *pugillar* writing-tablet, from *pugillaris* that can be held in the hand, from *pug-*: see PUGIL *noun*[1], -ARY[2].]
Hist. A writing-tablet. Usu. in *pl.*

Puginesque /pjuːdʒɪˈnɛsk/ *adjective*. M19.
[from *Pugin* (see below) + -ESQUE.]
Of, pertaining to, or characteristic of the English architect Augustus Welby Northmore Pugin (1812–52) or his style of Gothic revival architecture.
■ Also **Puˈginian** *adjective* L20.

pugnacious /pʌɡˈneɪʃəs/ *adjective*. M17.
[from Latin *pugnac-*, *-ax*, from *pugnare* to fight, from *pugnus* fist: see -ACIOUS.]
Disposed to fight, quarrelsome, contentious.

> 🕮 D. WELCH Such pugnacious determination, such violence of feeling.

■ **pugnaciously** *adverb* M19. **pugnaciousness** *noun* L17.

pugnacity /pʌɡˈnasɪti/ *noun*. E17.
[Latin *pugnacitas*, formed as prec.: see -ACITY.]
The condition or character of being pugnacious; inclination to fight, quarrelsomeness.

Pugwash /ˈpʌɡwɒʃ/ *adjective & noun*. M20.
[A village in Nova Scotia (see below).]
► **A** *adjective*. Designating or pertaining to one or several of the series of international conferences first held in Pugwash in 1957 by scientists to promote the peaceful application of scientific discoveries; pertaining to or characteristic of the movement which these meetings generated. M20.
► **B** *noun*. The Pugwash movement; a Pugwash conference. M20.

puha /ˈpuːhɑː/ *noun. NZ*. M19.
[Maori.]
A sowthistle, esp. *Sonchus oleraceus*; the leaves of this plant used as a vegetable. Cf. RAURIKI.

puirt-a-beul *noun* see PORT-A-BEUL.

puisne /ˈpjuːni/ *noun & adjective*. L16.
[Old French (mod. *puîné*), from *puis* (from Latin *postea* afterwards) + *né* (from Latin *natus* born). Cf. PUNY.]
► **A** *noun*. †**1** A junior; an inferior; a novice. L16–M17.
2 A puisne judge (see sense B.1 below). E19.
► **B** *adjective*. **1** Younger, junior. Now *rare* or *obsolete* exc. in *LAW*, designating an ordinary judge of the High Court. E17.
†**2** Small, insignificant, petty. E17–L18.
3 Later, more recent, of subsequent date. Now chiefly in ***puisne mortgage*** below. M17.
3 puisne mortgage a legal mortgage of unregistered land in which the title-deeds are retained by a first mortgagee; subsequent mortgages will thus be puisne.

puissance /ˈpjuːɪs(ə)ns, ˈpwiː-, ˈpwɪ-, (*esp. in sense 1b*) ˈpwiːsɒ̃s/ *noun*. LME.
[Old & mod. French, formed as next: see -ANCE.]
1 a Power, strength, force, might; influence. Chiefly *arch. & poet.* LME. ►**b** A showjumping competition testing a horse's ability to jump large obstacles. M20.
†**2** An armed force. Also, a number or crowd of people. LME–L16.

> 🕮 **1a** P. D. JAMES The windmill . . looked a melancholy wreck of its former puissance. **b** *attrib.*: P. SMYTHE Daydreams about jumping paddocks and over Puissance courses.

puissant /ˈpjuːɪs(ə)nt, ˈpwiː-, ˈpwɪ-/ *adjective. arch. & poet.* LME.
[Old & mod. French, from Proto-Gallo-Romance (from Latin *posse* be able), for Latin *potent-*: see POTENT *adjective*[2], -ANT[1].]
Having great authority or influence; mighty, strong, powerful.
■ **puissantness** *noun* M16. **puissantly** *adverb* LME.

puja /ˈpuːdʒə/ *noun*. Also **pooja**, **-jah**. L17.
[Sanskrit *pūjā* worship.]
A Hindu religious ceremony or rite.

pujari /pʊˈdʒɑːri/ *noun*. E19.
[Hindi *pujārī*, formed as prec.]
A Hindu priest or worshipper.

puka /ˈpʊkə/ *noun*. L19.
[Maori.]
1 A New Zealand shrub or small tree, *Griselinia lucida*, of the dogwood family, freq. epiphytic, and having glossy leathery leaves and tiny flowers. L19.
2 A small evergreen tree, *Meryta sinclairii* (family Araliaceae), of Australasia and the Pacific islands, with very large thick leaves. L19.

pukatea /puːkəˈtiːə/ *noun*. M19.
[Maori.]
A tall New Zealand forest tree, *Laurelia novae-zelandiae* (family Monimiaceae), having buttresses at the base of the trunk, leathery leaves, and tiny flowers; the wood of this tree.

†**puke** *noun*[1] & *adjective*. LME.
[Middle Dutch *puuc*, *puyck* the best type of woollen cloth: ult. origin unkn.]
► **A** *noun*. **1** A fine woollen cloth. LME–E17.
2 A dye used for woollen cloth, app. a bluish-black or inky colour. M16–E18.
► **B** *attrib.* or as *adjective*. (Made) of puke. M16–E17.

puke /pjuːk/ *verb & noun*[2]. Now *colloq.* L16.
[Prob. imit. Cf. Low German (whence German) *spucken* spit, Flemish *spukken* spew, spit.]
► **A** *verb*. **1** *verb intrans.* Vomit. L16.
2 *verb trans.* Eject by vomiting; vomit (food etc.) *up*. E17.
3 *verb trans.* Cause (a person) to vomit, treat with an emetic. M18.

> 🕮 **1** L. MICHAELS She ate candy until she puked in her lap. **2** A. CARTER She puked her guts into St. George's Channel, poor thing.

► **B** *noun*. **1 a** An act of vomiting. M18. ►**b** Vomit. M20.
2 An emetic. M18.
3 A disgusting or repulsive person. Also (*US*), a native of Missouri. M19.

> 🕮 **1b** N. MAILER Shreddings of puke came up.

■ **puker** *noun* †(*a*) an emetic; (*b*) a person who pukes: E18. **pukey**, **-ky** *adjective* (*a*) sickly; about or likely to vomit; (*b*) revolting, repulsive, disgusting: M19.

pukeko /ˈpuːkɛkəʊ/ *noun. NZ*. Pl. **-os**. M19.
[Maori.]
= ***purple gallinule*** s.v. PURPLE *adjective*.

pukka /ˈpʌkə/ *adjective & noun*. Orig. *Anglo-Indian*. Also **pukkah**, **pucka**. L17.
[Hindi *pakkā* cooked, ripe, substantial.]
► **A** *adjective*. **1** Of full weight, full; genuine. L17.
†**2** Of a fever: severe; malignant. M–L18.
3 Certain, reliable; authentic, true; proper, socially acceptable. Freq. in ***pukka sahib***, a socially acceptable man, a true gentleman. L18.
4 Permanent; (of a building) solidly built. L18.
5 Excellent, of the very best; fashionable. *colloq.* L20.

📖 **3** C. MULLARD Pukka members of the white Establishment.

▶**B** *noun.* **1** A composite permanent building material. Now *rare* or *obsolete.* **E18.**

2 A copper coin. Now *rare* or *obsolete.* **E19.**

puku /ˈpuːkuː/ *noun*[1]. **L19.**
[Bantu.]
An antelope of central southern Africa, *Kobus vardonii*, related to the water-buck and distinguished by its shaggy golden-yellow coat.

puku /ˈpʊkʊ/ *noun*[2]. *NZ colloq.* **M20.**
[Maori.]
The stomach, the belly.

pul /puːl/ *noun.* Pl. **puls, puli** /ˈpuːli/. **M19.**
[Pashto from Persian *pūl* copper coin.]
Orig. (*Hist.*), any of various small copper coins of Asia. Now, a monetary unit of Afghanistan, equal to one-hundredth of an afghani.

pula /ˈpʊlə/ *noun.* **E19.**
[Setswana = rain.]
1 Rain. Chiefly as *interjection*, expr. salutation or blessing. **E19.**
2 The basic monetary unit of Botswana, equal to 100 thebe. **L20.**

pulao *noun* var. of PILAU.

pulaski /pʊˈlaski/ *noun. US.* **E20.**
[Edward C. *Pulaski* (1866–1931), Amer. forest ranger who designed it.]
A hatchet having a head forming an axe blade on one side and an adze on the other.

pulchritude /ˈpʌlkrɪtjuːd/ *noun. literary.* **LME.**
[Latin *pulchritudo*, from *pulcher* beautiful: see -TUDE.]
Beauty.
■ **pulchriˈtudinous** *adjective* beautiful **E20.**

pule /pjuːl/ *verb & noun.* Now *Scot. & literary.* Also (*Scot.*) **pewl. LME.**
[Prob. imit.: cf. French *piauler*, dial. *pioler* chirp, whine, & MEWL.]
▶**A** *verb.* **1** *verb intrans.* Of a chick, nestling etc.: pipe plaintively. Now *rare.* **LME.**
2 *verb intrans.* Esp. of an infant: cry in a thin or weak voice, whine, cry querulously. **M16.**
3 *verb trans.* Utter in a whining or querulous tone. **M16.**
4 *verb intrans.* Pine or waste away, have no appetite. Freq. as ***puling*** *ppl adjective.* **M16.**
▶**B** *noun.* **1** A small amount of food, a bite, a nibble. Also, a wisp of smoke etc. *Scot.* **E19.**
2 The action of puling; a whine, a complaint. **L19.**
■ **puler** *noun* **L16. pulingly** *adverb* in a puling manner, querulously, complainingly **E17. puly** *adjective* given to puling, whining, querulous **L17.**

Pulfrich /ˈpʊlfrɪx/ *noun.* **E20.**
[Carl *Pulfrich* (1858–1927), German physicist.]
Used *attrib.* and in *possess.* with ref. to an optical illusion in which a pendulum swinging in a plane perpendicular to the line of sight appears to describe ellipses when one eye is covered with a dark filter and the other is uncovered.

puli /ˈpuːli/ *noun*[1]. Pl. **pulik** /ˈpuːlɪk/. **M20.**
[Hungarian.]
(An animal of) a breed of black, grey, or white sheepdog characterized by a long thick coat with a corded appearance.

puli *noun*[2] *pl.* see PUL.

pulicose /ˈpjuːlɪkəʊs/ *adjective. rare.* **M18.**
[Latin *pulicosus*, from *pulic-*, *pulex* flea: see -OSE[1].]
Flea-infested, flea-bitten; caused by or resembling a flea-bite.
■ **puˈlicious** *adjective* [irreg.] = PULICOSE **M19. puliˈcosity** *noun* the condition of being flea-infested **M17. pulicous** *adjective* = PULICOSE **M17.**

pulik *noun* pl. of PULI *noun*[1].

Pulitzer /ˈpʊlɪtsə, ˈpjuːl-/ *noun.* **E20.**
[J. *Pulitzer* (1847–1911), Amer. newspaper-publisher.]
In full ***Pulitzer prize***. Each of 13 annual awards for achievements in journalism, literature, and music produced or published in the US.

pulk /pʌlk/ *noun.* Also **polk** /pɒlk/. **L18.**
[French from Polish *polk*, Russian *polk* regiment, army.]
Hist. A regiment of Cossacks.

pulka /ˈpʌlkə/ *noun.* Also **pulkha. L18.**
[Finnish *pulkka*, Lappish *pulkke*.]
A Lapp one-person travelling-sledge shaped like the front half of a boat.

pull /pʊl/ *noun.* **ME.**
[from the verb.]
▶**I 1** The action or an act of pulling; *spec.* †(*a*) a turn or bout at pulling each other in wrestling etc.; a trial of strength; (*b*) PRINTING a pull of the bar of a hand-press; (*c*) a pull at a bridle in order to check a horse; (*d*) a pull at an oar; a spell at rowing; a journey in a rowing boat; (*e*) CRICKET & GOLF a hit which pulls the ball round, a hit which causes the ball to swerve; (*f*) a pull on the handle of a beer-pump. **ME.** ▸**b** A long or deep draught of liquor; an act of taking a drink. Also, an act of drawing on a cigarette etc. **LME.**
2 The power or capacity to pull instead of being pulled; advantage; *spec.* personal or private influence employable to one's advantage. *colloq.* **L16.**
3 The force exerted in pulling; pulling power; the force of attraction or gravitation; the exertion of making an ascent; an act requiring such force or exertion; *spec.* the force required to pull the trigger of a firearm, the action of a trigger in respect of the force required to pull it. **L18.**
4 The action or an act of attempting to pick up a partner for sexual purposes; a partner picked up for sexual purposes. *slang.* **M20.**

📖 **1** J. GILMOUR With a .. strong pull, round goes the wheel. **b** J. BARTH I .. took a good pull of bourbon. A. S. BYATT Simmonds took a long pull on his milk shake. **2** R. LARDNER You've either got to have a name or a pull to get your things published. J. KRANTZ His future .. was assured .. through family pull. **3** R. CAMPBELL Leaping against the pull of the rope one got up a tremendous .. momentum. P. WARNER To draw a longbow required a pull of 70 lbs. R. GITTINGS He finds the pull of his other occupations too strong. C. SAGAN The pull on Phobos is only about one-thousandth of that on Earth. **4** M. AMIS Lady Demeter certainly looked like a brother's dream pull: blonde, rich, stacked. DAVID MITCHELL He was on the pull and got talking to a couple of girls from Scotland.

▶**II** †**5** A kind of drag-net. *rare.* Only in **ME.**
6 A part of a road etc. requiring extra exertion; *esp.* a steep ascent. **L18.**
7 A part of a mechanism by which something is pulled; a handle etc.; an instrument or device for pulling. **E19.**
8 A printer's proof. **M19.**
9 A pulled muscle or tendon. *colloq.* **M20.**
7 bell-pull, ring-pull, etc.
Phrases etc.: **have a pull, have the pull** *arch.* have an advantage (foll. by *of, over*). ***leg-pull***: see LEG *noun.* ***long pull***: see LONG *adjective*[1]. **take a pull, take a pull at oneself, take a pull on oneself** *colloq.* (chiefly *Austral.*) pull oneself together.

pull /pʊl/ *verb.*
[Old English (ā)*pullian* prob. rel. to Low German *pūlen* shell, strip, pluck, Middle Dutch *polen*, and Middle & mod. Low German *pūle*, Dutch *peul* husk, shell.]
1 *verb trans.* Remove or extract by force from a previously fixed or permanent place; *spec.* (*a*) draw up (a plant, esp. a food plant) by the root; (*b*) (now chiefly *Scot.*) gather or pick (fruit, flowers, or leaves) from a tree or plant; (*c*) extract (a tooth) from the gum; (*d*) withdraw (casing etc.) from an oil-well; (*e*) draw (beer) from a keg etc. by means of a pump or tap; (*f*) withdraw (a cork) from the neck of a bottle. **OE.** ▸**b** *verb trans.* Steal, snatch, filch. Now *slang.* **L16.** ▸**c** *verb trans. & intrans.* Draw and point or fire (a gun). Foll. by *on* a person. Chiefly *N. Amer.* **M19.** ▸**d** *verb trans.* N. AMER. SPORT. Withdraw (a player) from the game; retire, replace, substitute. **M20.**
2 *verb trans.* Strip (a bird) of feathers by plucking. Formerly also, shear (a sheep etc.). Now *rare.* **OE.** ▸†**b** Strip (a person) of property or money; fleece; rob, cheat. **LME–M17.**
3 *verb trans.* Exert force on (a thing) so as to tend to snatch, draw, or drag it towards the source of the force; drag or tug at. Also with adverb or adverbial phr. expr. direction. **OE.** ▸**b** *verb trans.* Take away forcibly or with difficulty; tear off, wrench away. **LME–E17.** ▸**c** *verb trans. & intrans.* PRINTING. Print (a sheet), orig. by drawing the bar of a hand-press towards one, so as to press down the platen; print off (an impression, proof, or copy). **M17.** ▸**d** *verb trans.* Hold in, check; *spec.* (*a*) rein in (a horse) so as to lose in a race or slow down; (*b*) ***pull one's punches***: see below. **L18.** ▸**e** *verb trans.* Pull (an oar or sculls) in rowing; propel (a boat) by rowing, row; transport or convey in a boat by rowing. **E19.** ▸**f** *verb trans.* Strike (a ball) widely in the direction in which one follows through, as from the off to the leg side in cricket or to the left of a right-handed player in golf. **M19.** ▸**g** *verb trans.* Stretch and draw (sugar candy etc.) until it is ready to set. Orig. *US.* **M19.** ▸**h** *verb trans.* Strain (a muscle or tendon) by abnormal exertion. **M20.** ▸**i** *verb trans. & intrans.* Repossess (property); recall or rescind (a document, publication, etc.); cancel or revoke (a business deal, esp. a share issue). **M20.** ▸**j** *verb trans.* COMPUTING. Retrieve (a piece of data etc.) from the top of a stack. **L20.**
4 *verb intrans.* Exert force tending to draw or drag something towards the source of the force. Freq. foll. by *at.* **ME.** ▸**b** Pull an oar so as to move a boat; row a boat. **L17.** ▸**c** Of a horse: strain against the bit, esp. habitually and persistently. **L18.** ▸**d** Snatch or tear *at*; *spec.* (of a hawk) tear or pluck at food. **E19.** ▸**e** Draw or suck *at* or *on* (a cigarette, pipe, etc.). **M19.** ▸**f** Move or proceed by pulling or by some exertion of force; drive or be driven in a specified direction. **L19.** ▸**g** Of a vehicle's engine, a motor vehicle: deliver power, afford (adequate) propulsive force. **E20.** ▸**h** Foll. by *for*: exert influence on behalf of, sympathize with, favour. Chiefly *N. Amer.* **E20.** ▸**i** AMER. FOOTBALL. Of a lineman: withdraw from and cross behind the line of scrimmage to block opposing players and clear the way for a runner. **M20.**
5 *fig.* **a** *verb trans.* Draw or move by a non-physical force or influence; bring forcibly into or out of some state or condition. Now *rare.* **LME.** ▸†**b** *verb trans.* Bring or draw (evil, calamity) *upon.* **M16–L17.** ▸**c** *verb trans.* Arrest (a person) or raid (a gambling-house etc.) in the name of justice. *slang.* **E19.** ▸**d** *verb trans.* Draw or be assigned (a task or position); carry out (a duty); perform (an action), commit (a crime). *slang* (chiefly *N. Amer.*). **L19.** ▸**e** *verb trans. & intrans.* Attract (custom etc.); secure (patronage, support). **E20.** ▸**f** *verb trans.* Earn (a sum of money) as a wage or salary. *colloq.* **M20.** ▸**g** Pick up or attract a partner for sexual purposes. *slang.* **M20.**
6 *verb trans.* Take a draught or drink of (liquor); draw or suck (a draught of liquor) into the mouth; drink from (a vessel). **LME.**
7 *verb trans.* (Uses implying an adverb) ▸†**a** Pull down. **E–M17.** ▸**b** Pull on or at (a bell, a rope, etc.). **E19.**
8 (With pass. sense.) ▸**a** *verb intrans.* Admit of being plucked or picked. Now *rare.* **M17.** ▸**b** *verb intrans.* Be pulled; (of a boat) be rowed. **E19.** ▸**c** *verb trans.* Of a boat: be fitted for or rowed with (a specified number of oars). **E19**

📖 **3** D. H. LAWRENCE He .. was pulling on his stockings. J. STEINBECK He pulled his hat down a little more over his eyes. DAY LEWIS I can remember .. pulling a wooden engine along the sands. G. VIDAL He was so large that it took two slaves to pull him out. P. MORTIMER He grabbed my wrist and pulled me round to face him. R. HILL He was roused from .. bed by Ellie pulling his hair. E. WELTY Eugene gently pulled the Spaniard's arm, and pointed to the cliffs. **4** A. BARON Sailors pulled at cords and the wet .. nets thumped over the sides. *fig.*: ADDISON Ambition pulls one Way, Interest another. **b** LD MACAULAY He ordered his men to pull for the beach. **f** *Times* The .. van pulled into the outside lane. **g** E. J. HOWARD The car did not pull well up the hill. **5d** ***pull a fast one, pull a job, pull a robbery, pull a stunt, pull a trick***, etc. **e** *Sunday Times* The Channel pulled an audience of 13.85 m. for the final episode. A. BLOND Good strong reviews .. will pull sales. **f** M. INNES I'm .. pulling twelve pounds a week. **g** L. GRIFFITHS Jack the Lad might pull one of the hostesses. **8b** F. MARRYAT The boats pulled in shore.

Phrases: (A selection of cross-refs. only is included: see esp. other nouns.) ***a crow to pull***: see CROW *noun*[1] 1. **pull a —** *colloq.* imitate or behave in the manner of (a specified person). **pull a boner** *US slang* make a stupid mistake. **pull a face** distort one's features, grimace; ***pull a — face***, assume an expression of the specified kind. **pull a person's coat** *US Black slang* give information to a person, tip a person off. ***pull a person's leg***: see LEG *noun.* ***pull a stroke***: see STROKE *noun*[1]. **pull a train** *coarse slang* copulate successively with more than one partner. **pull caps** *arch.* scuffle, quarrel. **pulled wool** wool obtained from a sheepskin (not from a living animal). **pull foot** *arch.* run away, take to one's heels. **pull leather** *US slang* grasp the saddle horn in order to avoid being thrown from a bucking horse. **pull one's freight** *US slang* depart quickly, leave promptly. **pull one's pud, pull one's pudding** *coarse slang* (of a male) masturbate. **pull one's punches** put less than one's full force into delivering blows; *fig.* use less force than one is capable of exerting, be gentle or lenient, esp. in criticism or punishment. **pull one's rank** = ***pull rank*** below. ***pull one's socks up***: see SOCK *noun*[1]. **pull one's weight** row with effect in proportion to one's weight; *fig.* perform one's share of work, take one's share of responsibility. **pull one's wire** *coarse slang* (of a male) masturbate. **pull rank** employ one's superior status in exacting obedience, cooperation, or privilege, take unfair advantage of one's seniority. ***pull strings***: see STRING *noun.* ***pull the* LABOURING *oar. pull the longbow***: see LONG *adjective*[1]. **pull the other one (it's got bells on it)** *colloq.*: expr. disbelief (with ref. to pulling a person's leg). ***pull the pin***: see PIN *noun*[1]. ***pull the plug***: see PLUG *noun.* **pull the rug from under, pull the rug out from under** *colloq.* unexpectedly withdraw support from, destroy the basis of, betray. ***pull the strings***: see STRING *noun.* ***pull the wires***: see WIRE *noun.* ***pull the wool over a person's eyes***: see WOOL *noun.* ***pull to pieces***: see PIECE *noun.* ***pull wire(s)***: see WIRE *noun.*

With adverbs in specialized senses: **pull about** *verb phr. trans.* pull from side to side; *colloq.* treat roughly, unceremoniously, or arbitrarily. **pull apart** *verb phr. trans.* separate by pulling; *fig.* criticize unmercifully, analyse thoroughly. **pull back** (*a*) *verb phr. trans. & intrans.* (cause to) retreat or withdraw; (*b*) *verb phr. trans.* (SPORT) score (a goal) restoring, or serving towards restoring, level terms between two teams. **pull down** *verb phr. trans.* (*a*) demolish (a building etc.); (*b*) *arch.* depress in health or spirits; (*c*) lower in size, strength, or value; (*d*) humble, humiliate; (*e*) depose or dethrone (a monarch) violently; overthrow (a government) by force; (*f*) *colloq.* earn (a sum of money), esp. as a wage or salary. **pull in** (*a*) *verb phr. trans.* get into one's possession, acquire, earn; (*b*) *verb phr. trans.* rein in, hold in, check; (*c*) *verb phr. intrans.* check or bring oneself to a stop in any course; (*d*) *verb phr. trans.* (*colloq.*) arrest (a person); (*e*) *verb phr. intrans.* (of a train, bus, etc.) enter a station, arrive to take passengers; (*f*) *verb phr. intrans.* drive or (of a vehicle) be driven to the side of or off a road. **pull off** (*a*) *verb phr. trans.* remove by pulling; (*b*) *verb phr. trans.* win (a prize or contest); succeed in gaining, achieving, or effecting; (*c*) *verb phr. trans.* (*coarse slang*) cause (a person, esp. oneself) to ejaculate by masturbation; (*d*) *verb phr. intrans.* (SURFING) = ***pull out*** (f) below. **pull out** (*a*) *verb phr. trans.* remove or extract by pulling; (*b*) *verb phr. intrans.* (of a train, bus, etc.) move out of a station, leave with its passengers; (of a person) go away, take one's departure; (*c*) *verb phr. intrans.* (of a vehicle) drive or be driven outwards into another lane of traffic, for overtaking etc.; move out from the side of a road; (*d*) *verb phr. intrans.* withdraw from an undertaking; (*e*) *verb phr. intrans.* (of a drawer etc.) admit of being pulled open; (*f*) *verb phr. intrans.* (SURFING) end a ride by bringing one's surfboard out of a wave. **pull over** (*a*) *verb phr. intrans.* = **pull in** (f) above; (*b*) *verb phr. trans.* cause a driver or vehicle to pull over. **pull round** (*a*) *verb phr. intrans.* recover from an illness or a faint; come round; (*b*) *verb phr. trans.* restore to health after an illness etc.; put into a healthier or better condition. **pull through** (*a*) *verb phr. trans.* get (a person) through a difficult, dangerous, or critical condition or situation; bring (a thing) to a successful issue; (*b*) *verb phr. intrans.* get through an illness, a difficult time, or a dangerous undertaking with effort or difficulty; succeed in accomplishing or enduring something difficult or severe. **pull to** *verb phr. trans.* shut (a door etc.) by pulling it towards oneself. **pull together** (*a*) *verb phr. trans.* assemble or collect in one place, esp. from diverse or difficult sources; (*b*) *verb phr. trans.* = COLLECT *verb* 8; (*c*) ***pull oneself together***, recover control of oneself; gather with an effort one's faculties or energies; (*d*) *verb phr. intrans.* act in unison; work in harmony; cooperate. **pull up** (*a*) *verb phr. trans.* drag out of the ground or from a settled place, root out; demolish; (*b*) *verb phr. trans.* cause to stop; arrest, apprehend, formerly *esp.* apprehend and take before a magistrate; (*c*) *verb phr. trans.* reprimand, reprove, rebuke; (*d*) *verb phr. intrans.* bring a horse or vehicle to a stop; stop, come to a standstill; (*e*) *verb phr. intrans.* advance one's position in a race or other contest; improve.

■ **pullable** *adjective* L19. **puller** *noun* ME. **pullery** *noun* (TANNING) a place in which wool, hair, and bristles are removed from hides E20.

pull- /pʊl/ *combining form.*

[Repr. PULL *verb, noun.*]

In combs. in various relations and with various senses, as 'that is pulled', 'that pulls', 'involving pulling'.

■ **pull-apart** *noun* the action or result of being pulled in opposite directions so as to be ruptured or separated M20. **pull-bell** *noun* a bell rung by a cord, as distinct from a handbell M16. **pullbone** *noun* (*US*) the wishbone of a cooked bird E20. **pull-cord** *noun* a cord which operates a mechanism when pulled M20. **pull-date** *noun* (*N. Amer.*) a date stamped on a container of perishable goods indicating when it becomes unsuitable for sale L20. **pull-drive** *noun* (CRICKET) a drive which pulls the ball from the off to the leg side E20. **pull-hitter** *noun* (BASEBALL) a hitter who (habitually) strikes the ball in the direction in which he or she follows through M20. **pull-in** *noun* (*a*) the action or an act of pulling something in; (*b*) a roadside café or refreshment stand; (*c*) an area where a motor vehicle may pull in, a lay-by: E20. **pull-on** *noun & adjective* (designating) a garment without fasteners that is pulled on E20. **pull-quote** *noun* (*US*) a brief, attention-catching quotation, usu. in a distinctive typeface, taken from the main text of an article and used as a subheading or graphic feature L20. **pull-stroke** *noun* a stroke effected by pulling; *CRICKET* a stroke which pulls the ball from the off to the leg side: L19. **pull-switch** *noun* a switch operated by means of a pull-cord L19. **pull-tab** *noun* a device, usu. comprising a ring and short tongue of metal, by means of which a can may be opened M20.

pull-back /ˈpʊlbak/ *noun.* L16.

[from PULL *verb* + BACK *adverb.*]

1 A thing which pulls back or opposes progress or action; a retarding influence. Now *dial.* L16.

2 The action or an act of pulling something back; *spec.* an orderly withdrawal of military troops. M17. ▸**b** *CINEMATOGRAPHY.* A shot in which the scene is observed to recede. M20. ▸**c** A tap-dancing step involving striking the floor with the front part of the foot while moving backwards. M20.

3 A contrivance or attachment for pulling something back. E18.

pull-down /ˈpʊldaʊn/ *noun & adjective.* In sense A.1b usu. **pulldown.** L16.

[from PULL *verb* + DOWN *adverb.*]

▸ **A** *noun.* **1** The action or an act of pulling something down; the fact of being pulled down. L16. ▸**b** An exercise in which a bar or handle is pulled down to raise a counterweight. M20.

2 A thing which is pulled down or which pulls something down; *esp.* (*a*) *CINEMATOGRAPHY* a mechanism which moves a film past the aperture of a camera, projector, etc.; (*b*) a wire in a pipe-organ which pulls down a pallet or valve when a key is depressed, to let air into a pipe. M19.

▸ **B** *attrib.* or as *adjective.* That may be pulled down; designed to be pulled down. Also, operated by or functioning as a pull-down. L19.

pull-down menu *COMPUTING* a menu which may be briefly displayed onscreen when required.

pullen /ˈpʊlɪn/ *noun.* Long *obsolete* exc. *dial.* ME.

[App. from Old & mod. French *poulain* foal from late Latin *pullanus* from Latin *pullus* young animal, foal, chicken, identified with *poulaille* poultry.]

Poultry; domestic fowls; the flesh of these as food.

pullet /ˈpʊlɪt/ *noun.* LME.

[Old & mod. French *poulet*, *-ette* dim. of *poule* hen from Proto-Romance use of fem. of Latin *pullus* young animal, foal, chicken: see -ET[1].]

1 A young hen between the ages of chicken and mature fowl, *spec.* from point-of-lay until first moult. LME.

2 More fully ***pullet carpet-shell***. (The shell of) a marine bivalve mollusc, *Venerupis pullastra*. Cf. PALOURDE. E19.

Comb.: **pullet disease** *VETERINARY MEDICINE* a rare disease of domestic poultry, of unknown cause, involving nephritis, disordered urate metabolism, and monocytosis, and sometimes fatal.

pulley /ˈpʊli/ *noun & verb.* ME.

[Old French *polie* (mod. *poulie*) from Proto-Romance, prob. ult. from medieval Greek dim. of *polos* pivot, axis, windlass, capstan (POLE *noun*[2]).]

▸ **A** *noun.* **1** A simple mechanical device consisting of a grooved wheel or set of wheels over which a cord etc. may pass, mounted in a block, and used esp. for raising weights by pulling downward on the cord. ME.

2 A wheel or drum fixed on a shaft and turned by a belt etc. for the application or transmission of power, or to guide such a belt. E17.

Comb.: **pulley-block** a block or casing in which a pulley is mounted; **pulley-wheel** a grooved wheel of a pulley.

▸ **B** *verb trans.* **1** Raise or hoist with a pulley. L16.

2 Provide with a pulley; work by means of a pulley. M18.

pulli *noun* pl. of PULLUS.

pullicate /ˈpʌlɪkət/ *noun.* L18.

[from *Pulicat*, a town in Tamil Nadu (formerly, in the Madras presidency) in southern India.]

Hist. (More fully ***pullicate handkerchief***), a checked coloured handkerchief of a type originally made at Pulicat; a material woven from dyed yarn, from which handkerchiefs were made.

Pullman /ˈpʊlmən/ *noun.* In branch II usu. **p-.** M19.

[George M. *Pullman* (1831–97), Amer. designer.]

I 1 Used *attrib.* to designate any of various types of railway carriage built by the American Pullman Company or of a similar type, esp. as affording special comfort or sleeping arrangements, as ***Pullman car***, ***Pullman saloon***. M19.

2 A sleeping-car; a railway carriage or (later) motor coach affording special comfort. L19.

3 In full ***Pullman train***. A train made up of Pullman cars. L19.

4 In full ***Pullman case***. A large suitcase designed to fit under the seat in a Pullman carriage. E20.

▸ **II 5** In full ***Pullman kitchen***. A compact prefabricated unit of kitchen or bathroom fixtures. Chiefly *US.* M20.

pull-off /ˈpʊlɒf/ *noun & adjective.* M19.

[from PULL *verb* + OFF *adverb.*]

▸ **A** *noun.* **1** The action or an act of pulling something off; the fact of being pulled off. M19.

2 A roadside parking area, a lay-by. M20.

▸ **B** *attrib.* or as *adjective.* That may be pulled off; designed to be pulled off. E20.

pullorum disease /pʊˈlɔːrəm dɪˌziːz/ *noun phr.* E20.

[from mod. Latin (*Bacterium*) *pullorum* (Latin = of chickens), former name of *Salmonella gallinarum* (see below).]

VETERINARY MEDICINE. An acute, infectious, often fatal disease of young chicks, caused by the bacterium *Salmonella gallinarum*. Also called ***bacillary white diarrhoea***.

pull-out /ˈpʊlaʊt/ *noun & adjective.* E19.

[from PULL *verb* + OUT *adverb.*]

▸ **A** *noun.* **1** The action or an act of pulling out; withdrawal from an undertaking or affair, esp. from military involvement or occupation. E19. ▸**b** *AERONAUTICS.* The transition from a dive or spin to normal flight. E20.

2 A thing that may be pulled out, a thing designed to be pulled out; *spec.* a self-contained detachable section of a magazine etc. M20.

▸ **B** *attrib.* or as *adjective.* That may be pulled out; designed to be pulled out. L19.

pullover /ˈpʊləʊvə/ *noun & adjective.* L19.

[from PULL *verb* + OVER *adverb.*]

▸ **A** *noun.* **1** A gap in sand-hills or a rough road where vehicles can be pulled over to a beach. *local.* L19.

2 *HAT-MAKING.* A silk or felt cover or nap drawn over a hat body; a hat made with such a cover. L19.

3 The action or an act of pulling something over or from side to side, *spec.* as a body-building exercise. E20.

4 A knitted or woven garment for the upper part of the body, designed to be put on over the head. E20.

▸ **B** *attrib.* or as *adjective.* **1** Having the function of pulling something over. *rare.* L19.

2 (Of an article of clothing) designed to be put on over the head. E20.

■ **pullovered** *adjective* wearing a pullover E20.

pullulant /ˈpʌljʊl(ə)nt/ *adjective.* M16.

[Latin *pullulant-* pres. ppl stem of *pullulare*: see next, -ANT[1]; later from French *pullulant.*]

Budding, sprouting, (*lit.* & *fig.*).

pullulate /ˈpʌljʊleɪt/ *verb intrans.* E17.

[Latin *pullulat-* pa. ppl stem of *pullulare* sprout, grow, from *pullulus* dim. of *pullus* young animal, foal, chicken: see -ATE[3].]

1 Sprout, bud; germinate; propagate by budding. Also, swarm, multiply, breed prolifically. E17.

2 *transf.* & *fig.* **a** Develop, spring up, come to life. M17. ▸**b** Teem, swarm, abound, (*with*). M19.

pullulation /pʌljʊˈleɪʃ(ə)n/ *noun.* M17.

[from prec.: see -ATION. Cf. French *pullulation.*]

The action or an act of pullulating; sprouting, budding, germination; generation, production. Also, a product of this; offspring, progeny; an outgrowth.

pull-up /ˈpʊlʌp/ *noun & adjective.* M19.

[from PULL *verb* + UP *adverb*[1].]

▸ **A** *noun.* **1** The act of pulling up a horse or vehicle; a sudden stop. M19.

2 A place for pulling up; a stopping-place for riders or drivers. L19.

3 An act of encouragement; a helping hand to attain greater happiness or success. L19.

4 The fact or action of pulling something upwards; *spec.* in physical exercise, an act of pulling up the body by means of a bar or beam held by the hands. E20.

▸ **B** *attrib.* or as *adjective.* That pulls up; designed to be pulled up. E20.

pullus /ˈpʊləs/ *noun.* Pl. **pulli** /ˈpʊlʌɪ/. L18.

[Latin = young chick.]

A young bird or nestling prior to fledging (esp. with ref. to ringed birds and museum specimens).

pully-hauly /ˈpʊlɪˌhɔːli/ *noun & adjective. colloq.* & *dial.* L18.

[from extended forms of PULL *verb* + HAUL *verb.*]

▸ **A** *noun.* The action or work of pulling and hauling; pulling with all one's strength. L18.

▸ **B** *adjective.* Involving or characterized by pulling and hauling; requiring all one's strength of arm. E19.

■ **pully-haul** *verb intrans.* & *trans.* pull or haul with all one's strength L19.

pulmo- /ˈpʌlməʊ/ *combining form* of Latin *pulmo* lung: see -O-.

■ **pulmobranchiae** /-ˈbraŋkiiː/ *noun pl.* (now *rare*) (*a*) the book-lungs of some arachnids; (*b*) the respiratory cavity of pulmonate molluscs: L19. **pulmoˈbranchial** *adjective* of, pertaining to, or of the nature of pulmobranchiae L19. **pulˈmometer** *noun* (MEDICINE) = SPIROMETER E19.

pulmonaria /pʌlməˈnɛːrɪə/ *noun.* L16.

[medieval Latin *pulmonaria* (sc. *herba*) use as noun of fem. sing. of Latin *pulmonarius* PULMONARY, from its assumed efficacy in curing lung diseases.]

Any of various spring-flowering plants of the borage family constituting the genus *Pulmonaria*, with tubular flowers changing from pink to blue; esp. *P. officinalis*, with white-spotted leaves, often grown for ornament. Also called ***lungwort***.

pulmonary /ˈpʌlmən(ə)ri/ *noun & adjective.* M17.

[Latin *pulmonarius*, from *pulmon-*, *pulmo* lung + *-arius* -ARY[1].]

▸ **†A** *noun.* **1** = PULMONARIA. Only in M17.

2 *ZOOLOGY.* A pulmonate arachnid. *rare.* Only in M19.

▸ **B** *adjective.* **1** Chiefly *ANATOMY.* Of, pertaining to, situated in, or connected with the lungs. E18. ▸**b** Of respiration: carried on by means of lungs. E19. ▸**c** *ZOOLOGY.* Of the nature of or resembling a lung. M19.

2 *MEDICINE.* Of a disease: occurring in or affecting the lungs. E18. ▸**b** Affected with or subject to lung disease, esp. tuberculosis. M19.

1 pulmonary artery the artery conveying oxygen-poor blood from the heart to the lungs. ***pulmonary pleura***: see PLEURA *noun*[1] 1. **pulmonary vein** the vein carrying oxygenated blood from the lungs to the heart. **2** ***pulmonary*** TUBERCULOSIS.

pulmonate /ˈpʌlmənət/ *noun & adjective.* M19.

[mod. Latin *pulmonatus*, from Latin *pulmon-*, *pulmo* lung: see -ATE[2].]

ZOOLOGY. ▸ **A** *noun.* Any of various gastropod molluscs of the subclass Pulmonata, which contains the terrestrial and many freshwater species, having the mantle cavity modified for breathing air. M19.

▸ **B** *adjective.* Having lungs, as the higher vertebrates, or similar respiratory organs, as gastropod molluscs of the subclass Pulmonata and certain arachnids (as spiders and scorpions). M19.

pulmonic /pʌlˈmɒnɪk/ *adjective & noun.* M17.

[French *pulmonique* or mod. Latin *pulmonicus*, from Latin *pulmon-*, *pulmo* lung: see -IC.]

▸ **A** *adjective.* **1** = PULMONARY *adjective* 1, 2. *rare.* M17.

2 *PHONETICS.* Of a sound: produced with an air-stream exhaled by the lungs. M20.

▸ **B** *noun.* **†1** A remedy for disease of the lungs; a medicine good for the lungs. L17–E18.

2 A person subject to or affected with disease of the lungs, esp. tuberculosis. Now *rare.* M18.

pulmotor /ˈpʌlməʊtə/ *noun.* E20.

[from PULMO- + Latin MOTOR *noun.*]

MEDICINE. An emergency apparatus for forcing air or oxygen into the lungs under pressure.

pulp /pʌlp/ *noun & adjective.* LME.

[Latin *pulpa.*]

▸ **A** *noun.* **1** The fleshy or succulent part of a fruit. LME.

2 Soft muscle or flesh, as the pads of the fingertips; the soft internal parts of organs etc.; the mass of connective tissue etc. in the cavity at the centre of a tooth. LME.

3 Any soft formless wet substance or mass, as of disintegrated organic matter. **L17.**
4 Soft fibrous material derived from rags, wood, etc., used to manufacture paper; a mass of this. Also ***paper pulp***. **M18.**
5 Pulverized ore mixed with water. **M19.**
6 A magazine or book printed on cheap paper, *esp.* one regarded as of poor quality or popular or sensational; ephemeral, esp. sensational, literature. **M20.**

> 📖 **3** L. CHAMBERLAIN Soak the onion . . then grate it, reserving both pulp and juice. R. FRAME The windfall lay in the grass, softening to pulp in the heat. **6** F. DONALDSON I really made a living writing for the pulps.

Phrases: **be a pulp** = ***be pulp*** below. **beat to a pulp** *hyperbol.* beat or thrash (a person) severely. **be pulp** *fig.* (of a person) have no strength of character or firmness of purpose. ***mechanical pulp***: see MECHANICAL *adjective*.
Comb.: **pulp-canal** DENTISTRY the pulp cavity of a canine tooth; **pulp-capping** DENTISTRY the covering of the exposed pulp cavity of a tooth with an artificial cap; **pulp cavity** DENTISTRY the space in the interior of a tooth which contains the pulp; **pulp-stone** a stone used like a grindstone for reducing wood to pulp; **pulpwood** wood suitable for making paper pulp.
▶**B** *attrib.* or as *adjective*. Made from paper pulp; (of paper) of a rough texture or poor quality, cheap, recycled; printed on pulp paper; designating, pertaining to, or devoted to popular or sensational literature. **E20.**

> 📖 A. KOESTLER We churned out a couple of detective stories for pulp magazines. R. ALTER Bad literature, like pulp fiction and greeting-card verse.

■ **pulpal** *adjective* (DENTISTRY) of or pertaining to the pulp of a tooth **E20.** **pulpless** *adjective* **L18.**

pulp /pʌlp/ *verb*. **M17.**
[from the noun.]
1 *verb trans.* Reduce to pulp or to a pulpy mass; *spec.* reduce (a copy of a book etc.) to paper pulp, withdraw from publication or sale, esp. recycling the paper; *fig.* destroy, scrap. **M17.**
2 *verb trans.* Remove pulp from. **L18.**
3 *verb intrans.* Become pulpy, swell with juice. Chiefly *poet.* **E19.**

> 📖 **1** C. MCCULLOUGH The mud had not completely dried, and . . eager feet . . had already pulped it to a mire. R. CHRISTIANSEN The censors . . pulped the entire first edition.

■ **pulper** *noun* a machine for pulping something **M19.**

pulpectomy /pʌlˈpɛktəmi/ *noun*. **E20.**
[from PULP *noun* + -ECTOMY.]
DENTISTRY. Surgical removal of the pulp of a tooth; an instance of this.

pulperia /pʊlpəˈriːə, *foreign* pulpeˈria/ *noun*. **E19.**
[Amer. Spanish.]
In Spanish-speaking America: a grocery; a tavern.

pulpify /ˈpʌlpɪfʌɪ/ *verb trans.* **L19.**
[from PULP *noun* + -I- + -FY.]
Reduce to a pulp, make pulpy.

pulpiness /ˈpʌlpɪnɪs/ *noun*. **M19.**
[from PULPY + -NESS.]
The quality or state of being pulpy; softness, flabbiness.

pulpit /ˈpʊlpɪt/ *noun & verb*. **ME.**
[Latin *pulpitum* scaffold, platform, stage, (in late Latin) pulpit.]
▶**A** *noun*. **1** A raised structure consisting of an enclosed platform, usu. in a church or chapel, from which a preacher delivers a sermon and in some denominations an officiating minister conducts a service; *fig.* a place from which something of the nature of a sermon, as a moral lecture, is delivered. **ME.** ▸**b** *The* Christian ministers as a body, the Christian ministry, or (formerly) a Christian minister, as occupied with preaching. **L16.**
†**2** A stage or platform for public speeches in ancient times. **LME–L17.**
3 An elevated structure giving the occupant a conspicuous or controlling position; *spec.* †(***a***) an elevated pew or seat in a church; (***b***) a standing-place on the bowsprit of a whaler or fishing vessel; a railed-in area at the bow (or stern) of a yacht etc.; (***c***) an auctioneer's desk or platform (long *dial.*); (***d***) a small raised platform or room from which machinery can be observed and controlled. **LME.**
1 ***thump the pulpit***: see THUMP *verb* 1a. ***tub-pulpit***: see TUB *noun*[1] 8. ***wayside pulpit***: see WAYSIDE *adjective*.
▶**B** *verb*. **1** *verb trans.* Provide with a pulpit; place in a pulpit. **E16.**
2 *verb intrans.* Speak from or officiate in a pulpit, preach. **M16.**
■ **pulpiˈtarian** *noun* (now *rare*) a preacher, a pulpiteer **M17.** **pulpiˈteer** *noun & verb* (usu. *derog.*) (***a***) *noun* a preacher; (***b***) *verb intrans.* preach (chiefly as **pulpiteering** *verbal noun*): **M17.** **pulpiter** *noun* (usu. *derog.*) a preacher, a pulpiteer **L17.** **pulˈpitical** *adjective* (*rare*) connected with, appropriate to, or characteristic of the pulpit as the place of preaching **L18.** **pulˈpitically** *adverb* (*rare*) **M18.** **pulpitry** *noun* (now *rare*) preaching, sermonizing **E17.**

pulpitis /pʌlˈpʌɪtɪs/ *noun*. **L19.**
[from PULP *noun* + -ITIS.]
DENTISTRY. Inflammation of the dental pulp.

pulpitum /ˈpʊlpɪtəm/ *noun*. **M19.**
[Latin: see PULPIT.]
A stone screen in a church separating the choir from the nave, freq. surmounted by an organ-loft.

pulpotomy /pʌlˈpɒtəmi/ *noun*. **E20.**
[from PULP *noun* + -O- + -TOMY.]
DENTISTRY. Surgical removal of part of the pulp of a tooth; an instance of this.

pulpous /ˈpʌlpəs/ *adjective*. **E17.**
[from Latin *pulposus*, formed as PULP *noun*: see -OUS.]
Of the nature of pulp, consisting of pulp, resembling pulp, pulpy.
■ **pulpousness** *noun* (*rare*) **E18.**

pulpy /ˈpʌlpi/ *adjective*. **L16.**
[from PULP *noun* + -Y[1].]
1 Of the nature of pulp, consisting of pulp, resembling pulp; soft, fleshy, succulent; *fig.* flabby. **L16.**
2 Pertaining to or characteristic of pulp magazines or pulp literature, sensational. **M20.**
1 pulpy kidney (disease) VETERINARY MEDICINE a clostridial enterotoxaemia of sheep often marked by rapid post-mortem degeneration of the kidneys.

pulque /ˈpʊlkeɪ, ˈpʊlki/ *noun*. **L17.**
[Amer. Spanish, from Nahuatl *puliúhki* decomposed.]
A Mexican and Central American fermented drink made from the sap of any of several agaves.
Comb.: **pulque brandy** a strong intoxicating spirit distilled from pulque.
■ **pulqueria** /pʊlkəˈriːə/ *noun* a shop or tavern selling pulque **E19.**

pulsant /ˈpʌls(ə)nt/ *adjective*. *rare*. **E18.**
[Latin *pulsant-* pres. ppl stem of *pulsare*: see PULSATE, -ANT[1].]
Pulsating.

pulsar /ˈpʌlsɑː/ *noun*. **M20.**
[from *pulsating star* after QUASAR.]
ASTRONOMY. A cosmic source of regular and rapid pulses of radiation usu. at radio frequencies, believed to be a rapidly rotating neutron star.

pulsatance /pʌlˈseɪt(ə)ns/ *noun*. **E20.**
[from next + -ANCE.]
PHYSICS. The angular frequency of a periodic motion, i.e. 2π times its actual frequency.

pulsate /pʌlˈseɪt, ˈpʌlseɪt/ *verb intrans.* **L18.**
[Latin *pulsat-* pa. ppl stem of *pulsare* frequentative of *pellere*, *puls-* drive, beat: see -ATE[3].]
1 Expand and contract rhythmically; exhibit a pulse; throb. **L18.**
2 Make a rhythmical succession of strokes; move with a regular alternating motion; vibrate, quiver, thrill. **M19.**
3 Of an electric current or voltage: flow or act in one direction but with a periodically varying strength. Chiefly as ***pulsating*** *ppl adjective*. **E20.**

pulsatile /ˈpʌlsətʌɪl/ *adjective*. **LME.**
[medieval Latin *pulsatilis* (spec. in *vena pulsatilis* artery), formed as prec.: see -ILE.]
1 (Esp. of the heart, an artery, a vesicle, etc.) having the capacity or property of pulsating; exhibiting or characterized by pulsation. **LME.**
2 Of a musical instrument: played by striking or percussion; percussive. **M18.**
■ **pulsaˈtility** *noun* **M19.**

pulsatilla /pʌlsəˈtɪlə/ *noun*. **L16.**
[mod. Latin (see below), dim. of Latin *pulsatus* beaten about, i.e. 'the flower beaten by the wind'.]
Any of various spring-flowering plants constituting the genus *Pulsatilla*, closely allied to the anemones but with the perianth segments downy outside; *esp.* pasque-flower, *P. vulgaris*. Also, a medicinal extract or tincture of this plant.

pulsation /pʌlˈseɪʃ(ə)n/ *noun*. **LME.**
[Latin *pulsatio(n-)*, formed as PULSATE: see -ATION.]
1 Rhythmical expansion and contraction, esp. of the heart, blood-vessels, etc.; beating, throbbing, vibration. **LME.**
2 A beat, a throb, a pulse. **M17.**
3 The action of striking or knocking; a knock, a blow. Now *rare*. **M17.**
■ **pulsational** *adjective* **L19.**

pulsative /ˈpʌlsətɪv/ *adjective*. Now *rare*. **LME.**
[medieval Latin *pulsativus* (spec. in *vena pulsativa* artery), formed as PULSATE: see -IVE.]
= PULSATILE.

pulsator /pʌlˈseɪtə/ *noun*. **M17.**
[from (the same root as) PULSATE + -OR.]
1 A person who or thing which knocks or strikes. *rare*. **M17.**
2 A machine which works with a vibratory or pulsating motion; *spec.* a device on a milking machine which releases the suction on the teat intermittently so as to simulate the sucking action of a calf. **L19.**

pulsatory /ˈpʌlsət(ə)ri/ *adjective*. **E17.**
[from PULSATE + -ORY[2].]
1 Having the quality of pulsating; characterized by or of the nature of pulsation; acting or moving in intermittent pulses. **E17.**
2 = PULSATILE 1. **E19.**

pulse /pʌls/ *noun*[1]. **ME.**
[Old French *pous*, later (Latinized) *pouls* from Latin *pulsus* beating (spec. *venarum* of the veins), from *puls-* pa. ppl stem of *pellere* drive, beat.]
1 The beating, throbbing, or rhythmical dilatation of the arteries as the blood is propelled along them by the heart, esp. as felt in the wrists, temples, etc. (Usu. with ref. to its rate and character as indicating the person's state of health.) **ME.** ▸**b** Each successive beat or throb of the arteries, or of the heart. Usu. in *pl.* **LME.** ▸†**c** The place where the pulse occurs or is felt, esp. in the wrist. Also, an artery. **LME–E17.**
2 The life-force *of* something; vitality, energy; a throb or thrill of life, emotion, etc. **LME.**
†**3** A stroke, a blow, an impact; an attack. **L16–L17.**
4 a The rhythmical recurrence of strokes, vibrations, or undulations; beating, vibration. **M17.** ▸**b** Each of a rhythmical succession of strokes or undulations; a single vibration or wave; a beat; a very short train of radio or sound waves, etc., a short burst of radiated energy; a sudden momentary change in amplitude etc. **L17.** ▸**c** PROSODY & MUSIC. A beat or stress in the rhythm of a verse or piece of music. **L19.** ▸**d** GEOLOGY. A temporary upward movement of magma through the earth's crust. **M20.**
5 BIOCHEMISTRY. A brief period during which a culture of cells is supplied with an isotopically labelled substrate. **M20.**
Phrases: ***feel the pulse of***: see FEEL *verb*. **have one's finger on the pulse of** be fully conversant with, be in contact with and understand. **on one's pulse(s)**, **on the pulse(s)** through one's own experience. ***SOFTNESS of the pulse***. ***strobe pulse***: see STROBE *adjective*.
Comb.: **pulse code** ELECTRONICS a code form in which groups of pulses are used to convey specific values; **pulse code modulation** TELECOMMUNICATIONS a pulse modulation technique of representing a signal by a sequence of binary codes; abbreviation *PCM*; **pulse dialling** TELEPHONY: in which each digit is transmitted as a corresponding number of electronic pulses (opp. ***tone dialling***); **pulse jet** AERONAUTICS a type of jet engine in which combustion is intermittent, the ignition and expulsion of each charge of mixture causing the intake of a fresh charge; **pulse-label** *verb trans.* (BIOCHEMISTRY) = PULSE *verb* 3; **pulse modulation** TELECOMMUNICATIONS modulation in which a series of pulses is varied in some respect so as to represent the amplitude of the signal after successive short intervals of time; **pulse pressure** MEDICINE the difference between the maximum (systolic) and the minimum (diastolic) pressure of arterial blood; **pulse radar**: that transmits pulses rather than a continuous beam of radio energy; **pulse repeater** ELECTRONICS a device for receiving pulses from one circuit and transmitting corresponding pulses into another circuit; **pulse-wave** MEDICINE a component element of the waveform recorded from a person's pulse.
■ **pulseless** *adjective* **M18.** **pulselessness** *noun* **M19.**

pulse /pʌls/ *noun*[2]. **ME.**
[Old French *pols* (mod. dial. *poul(s)*, *pou*) from Latin *puls*, *pult-* thick pottage of meal or pulse (cf. Greek *poltos* porridge), rel. to POLLEN.]
1 a *collect. sing.* (sometimes treated as *pl.*). The edible seeds of leguminous plants cultivated for food (peas, beans, lentils, etc.) **ME.** ▸**b** A particular kind of edible leguminous seed. **M16.**
2 *collect. sing.* (sometimes treated as *pl.*) Leguminous plants yielding edible seeds. **LME.**

pulse /pʌls/ *verb*. **LME.**
[Latin *pulsare* frequentative of *puls-*, *pellere* drive, beat.]
1 *verb intrans.* Pulsate, beat, throb. **LME.**
2 *verb trans.* Orig., drive, impel. Now *spec.* send out or transmit in or by pulses or rhythmic beats. **M16.**
3 *verb trans.* BIOCHEMISTRY. Subject (cells in culture) to a pulse of isotopically labelled substrate. **M20.**
4 *verb trans.* Apply a pulsed signal to. **M20.**
5 *verb trans.* Modulate (a wave, beam, etc.) so that it becomes a series of pulses. **M20.**
■ **pulsed** *ppl adjective* producing or involving pulses; consisting of pulses; in the form of pulses; ***pulsed column*** (CHEMISTRY), a solvent extraction tower in which a small-amplitude vibration is mechanically superimposed on the countercurrent flow in order to promote extraction: **M20.**

pulser /ˈpʌlsə/ *noun*. **M20.**
[from PULSE *noun*[1] or *verb* + -ER[1].]
A device that generates (esp. electrical) pulses.

pulsific /pʌlˈsɪfɪk/ *adjective*. Now *rare*. **E17.**
[from Latin *pulsus* PULSE *noun*[1] + -I- + -FIC.]
Causing the pulse or pulsation of the arteries. Also, characterized by pulsation, throbbing.

pulsimeter /pʌlˈsɪmɪtə/ *noun*. **M19.**
[from PULSE *noun*[1] + -I- + -METER.]
MEDICINE. An instrument for measuring the rate or force of a pulse.

pulsion /ˈpʌlʃ(ə)n/ *noun*. **M17.**
[Late Latin *pulsio(n-)*, from Latin *puls-* pa. ppl stem of *pellere* drive, beat: see **-ION.**]
The action or an act of driving or pushing something, propulsion.

pulsive /ˈpʌlsɪv/ *adjective*. **E17.**
[from Latin *puls-* (see prec.) + **-IVE.**]
1 Having the quality of driving or impelling something, propulsive. Now *rare*. **E17.**
2 Making a beating or throbbing sound. **M20.**

pultaceous /pʌlˈteɪʃəs/ *adjective*. **M17.**
[from Latin *pult-*, *puls* (see **PULSE** *noun*²) + **-ACEOUS.**]
Chiefly *MEDICINE*. Semifluid, pulpy.

pultan, **pulton** *nouns* vars. of **PULTUN.**

pultrude /pʊlˈtruːd, pʌl-/ *verb trans*. **M20.**
[from *pul(ling* + **EX)TRUDE.**]
Make (a reinforced plastic article) by drawing resin-coated glass fibres through a heated die.
■ **pultrusion** *noun* **M20.**

pultun /ˈpʌltʌn/ *noun*. Also **-an**, **-on**. **E19.**
[Hindi *palṭan* from Tamil *paṭṭālam* from **BATTALION** *noun*.]
Hist. A regiment of infantry in India.

pulu /ˈpuːluː/ *noun*. **M19.**
[Hawaiian.]
A fine vegetable wool obtained from the base of the leaf-stalks of the Hawaiian tree-fern *Cibotium glaucum*, formerly used for stuffing mattresses and pillows.

†**pulver** *verb trans*. **LME–L18.**
[Latin *pulverare*, from *pulver-*, *pulvis* dust.]
Reduce to powder, pulverize.

pulverable /ˈpʌlv(ə)rəb(ə)l/ *adjective*. Now *rare*. **E17.**
[from (the same root as) prec. + **-ABLE.**]
Able to be reduced to powder; pulverizable.

pulveration /pʌlvəˈreɪʃ(ə)n/ *noun*. Now *rare*. **E17.**
[from **PULVER** or from Latin *pulveratio(n-)*, formed as **PULVER**: see **-ATION.**]
Reduction to powder; pulverization.

pulverize /ˈpʌlvərʌɪz/ *verb*. Also **-ise**. **LME.**
[Late Latin *pulverizare*, from Latin *pulver-*, *pulvis* dust: see **-IZE.**]
1 *verb trans*. Reduce to powder or dust. **LME.** ▸**b** Divide into minute particles of liquid, turn into spray. **E19.**
2 *verb trans*. *fig.* Demolish, destroy, break down utterly. **M17.**
3 *verb intrans*. Crumble or fall to dust; become disintegrated; *fig.* be demolished, destroyed, or utterly broken down. **E19.**
■ **pulverizable** *adjective* **M17.** **pulveriˈzation** *noun* **M17.** **pulverizator** *noun* (*a*) an instrument for reducing something to powder; (*b*) an apparatus for scattering powder or ejecting liquid in the form of spray: **L19.** **pulverizer** *noun* **M19.**

pulverous /ˈpʌlv(ə)rəs/ *adjective*. Now *rare*. **LME.**
[from medieval Latin *pulverosus* or from Latin *pulver-*, *pulvis* dust: see **-OUS.**]
Reduced to powder, powdery; dusty.

pulverulent /pʌlˈvɛrʊl(ə)nt/ *adjective*. **M17.**
[Latin *pulverulentus*, from *pulver-*, *pulvis* dust: see **-ULENT.**]
1 Consisting of or having the form of powder or dust; powdery. **M17.**
2 Covered (as) with powder or dust; *spec.* in *ENTOMOLOGY*, covered with minute scales. **M18.**
3 Friable, crumbly; crumbling to dust. **L18.**
■ **pulverulence** *noun* (*rare*) dustiness, powder **E18.**

pulvilio /pʊlˈvɪlɪəʊ/ *noun*. *obsolete* exc. *Hist.* Also **-ill-**, & Anglicized as **pulvil** /ˈpʌlvɪl/. **L17.**
[Italian *polviglio* fine powder, from *polve*, *polvere* powder.]
Cosmetic or perfumed powder for powdering a wig or perfuming the person.

pulvillus /pʌlˈvɪləs/ *noun*. Pl. **-lli** /-lʌɪ/. **E18.**
[Latin, contr. of *pulvinulus* dim. of *pulvinus* cushion.]
1 A little cushion; *SURGERY* a small mass of lint for plugging wounds. Now *rare* or *obsolete*. **E18.**
2 *ENTOMOLOGY*. A pad or lobe beneath the pretarsal claws of certain insects, esp. dipterans, which assists in adhering to surfaces. **E19.**

pulvinar /pʌlˈvʌɪnə/ *noun*. **L16.**
[Latin = couch, formed as **PULVINUS**: see **-AR**¹.]
1 *SURGERY*. A small (medicated) pad or cushion. Now *rare* or *obsolete*. **L16.**
2 *ROMAN ANTIQUITIES*. A couch, a cushioned seat. **E17.**
3 *ANATOMY*. A cushion-like prominence formed by the posterior end of the thalamus. **L19.**

pulvinar /pʌlˈvʌɪnə/ *adjective*. **L19.**
[Latin *pulvinaris*, formed as **PULVINUS**: see **-AR**¹.]
BOTANY. Of or pertaining to a pulvinus.

pulvinate /ˈpʌlvɪnət/ *adjective*. **E19.**
[Latin *pulvinatus*, formed as **PULVINUS**: see **-ATE**².]
BOTANY & ENTOMOLOGY. Cushion-like; moderately convex. Also, having a pulvinus.

pulvinated /ˈpʌlvɪneɪtɪd/ *adjective*. **L17.**
[formed as prec. + **-ED**¹.]
Swelling, bulging; *spec.* (*a*) *ARCHITECTURE* (of a frieze) having a convex face; (*b*) *BOTANY* having a pulvinus.

pulvini *nouns* pls. of **PULVINO, PULVINUS.**

pulvino /pʌlˈviːnəʊ/ *noun*. Pl. **-ni** /-ni/, **-nos**. **E20.**
[Italian from Latin **PULVINUS.**]
ARCHITECTURE. A dosseret resembling a cushion pressed down by a weight.

pulvinus /pʌlˈvʌɪnəs/ *noun*. Pl. **-ni** /-nʌɪ/. **M19.**
[Latin = cushion, pillow.]
BOTANY. Any cushion-like swelling; *esp.* a special enlargement at the base of a petiole or petiolule in some plants, which is subject to changes of turgor leading to nastic movements of the leaf or leaflet.

pulwar /ˈpʌlwɑː, pəlˈwɑː/ *noun*. **M18.**
[Hindi *palvār*.]
A light keelless riverboat used in the north-east of the Indian subcontinent.

pulza /ˈpʊlzə/ *noun*. **M19.**
[Origin unkn.]
In full ***pulza-oil***. An oil from the seeds of the physic-nut, *Jatropha curcas*, used as a purgative and in candle-making.

puma /ˈpjuːmə/ *noun*. **L18.**
[Spanish from Quechua *púma*.]
A moderately large carnivorous mammal of the cat family, *Felis concolor*, with a tawny or greyish coat, found in parts of N. and S. America. Also called ***cougar***, ***mountain lion***, ***panther***.

†**pumex** *noun*. **L16–L18.**
[Latin.]
Pumice.

pumice /ˈpʌmɪs/ *noun & verb*. **LME.**
[Old French *pomis* from Latin dial. *pomic-* var. of *pumic-*, *pumex*; in 16 assim. to Latin form. Cf. **POUNCE** *noun*².]
▶ **A** *noun*. A light spongy form of volcanic glass, usu. of pyroclastic origin and with a high silica content, often used as an abrasive in cleaning, polishing, removing stains or dead skin, etc., or as an absorbent for moisture; a piece of this. **LME.**
▶ **B** *verb trans*. Rub with pumice; smooth, polish, or clean by rubbing with pumice. **LME.**

> 🕮 *Sunday Express* Pumice away rough . . skin.

Comb.: **pumice stone** *noun & verb* (*a*) *noun* = sense A. above; (*b*) *verb trans*. (*rare*) = sense B. above.
■ **pumiced** *adjective* (*a*) rubbed smooth with pumice; (*b*) (of a horse's hoof) spongy on account of disease: **M16.** **pumiceous** *adjective* consisting of pumice; of the nature or texture of pumice: **L17.**

pumicite /ˈpʌmɪsʌɪt/ *noun*. **E20.**
[from **PUMICE** *noun* + **-ITE**¹.]
GEOLOGY. Unconsolidated volcanic ash.

pummel *noun* var. of **POMMEL** *noun*.

pummel /ˈpʌm(ə)l/ *verb trans. & intrans*. Infl. **-ll-**, ***-l-**. **M16.**
[from *pummel* var. of **POMMEL** *noun*.]
Beat or strike repeatedly, esp. with the fists; pound, thump.

> 🕮 R. FRAME She picked up a cushion, to pummel it . . into shape. *Weekend Australian* Typhoon Agnes pummelled the country.

pummelo *noun* var. of **POMELO.**

pump /pʌmp/ *noun*¹. **LME.**
[Orig. naut.; corresp. to late Middle Dutch *pompe* wood or metal pipe, stone conduit, Dutch *pomp* ship's pump, Low German *pump(e)*, whence early mod. German *Pumpe*, Swedish *pump*, Danish, French *pompe*: perh. ult. imit.]
1 A mechanical device, usu. consisting of a cylinder in which a piston or plunger is moved up and down, used to raise water etc. by lifting, suction, or pressure; *gen.* any of various devices for the raising or moving of liquids, compression or evacuation of gases, etc. **LME.** ▸**b** *transf.* Any bodily organ having a pumping action; *colloq.* the heart. **L18.** ▸**c** *PHYSIOLOGY*. A mechanism in living cells by which energy is used to cause specific ions to pass through the cell membrane against a concentration gradient. **M20.** ▸**d** *ellipt.* A pump-action shotgun. *US*. **M20.**
2 The bilge or well of a ship. Now *rare* or *obsolete*. **M16.**
3 An act of pumping; a stroke of a pump. **L17.**
4 An attempt at extracting information from a person by exhaustive or persistent questioning. Also, a person skilled in this. **M18.**

> 🕮 **1** H. WILLIAMSON Large rotary pumps for forcing filtered water through pipes. *Which?* Garages weren't reflecting the full price at their pumps. ***bicycle-pump***, ***hand-pump***, ***petrol pump***, ***stomach-pump***, ***suction pump***, etc. ***prime the pump***: see **PRIME** *verb*². **b** E. O'NEILL I guess my old pump's busted.

Comb.: **pump-action** *adjective* (orig. *US*) designating a repeating firearm activated by a horizontally-operating slide action; **pump attendant** a person who serves petrol at a garage; **pump-brake** the handle of a pump, esp. with a transverse bar for several people to work at; **pump-handle** *noun & verb* (*a*) *noun* a handle by which a pump is worked; (*b*) *verb trans*. (*colloq.*) shake (a person's hand) vigorously; **pump island** the part of a petrol station on which the pumps stand; **pump-log** *US* a hollowed log used in the construction of a pump or as a water pipe; **pumpman** a man who works a pump; *spec.* a person in charge of the pumps in a mine; **pump-primer** a financial grant etc. aimed to stimulate economic enterprise; **pump-priming** *verbal noun & ppl adjective* (*a*) introducing fluid etc. into a pump to prepare it for working; (*b*) *fig.* stimulating commerce etc. by investment; **pump-rod** a rod connecting the piston or plunger of a pump with the motive power; **pump room** a room or building where a pump is worked; *spec.* a place at a spa where medicinal water is dispensed; **pumpset** a complete pumping installation, comprising a pump, a source of power, and all necessary fitments; **pump-tree** a length of tree-trunk used as the stock of a pump, or as a water pipe; **pump-turbine** *ENGINEERING* a machine designed to operate as a pump running in one direction or a turbine running in the other; **pump-water**: obtained from below the surface of the soil by means of a pump; **pump-well** (*a*) a compartment in a ship in which the pumps work; (*b*) a well with a pump combined.
■ **pumpless** *adjective* (*rare*) without a pump **L19.**

pump /pʌmp/ *noun*². **M16.**
[Origin unkn.]
A light low-heeled shoe, usu. without a fastening, (as) worn for dancing, gymnastics, etc.; a plimsoll. Also (*N. Amer.*), a court shoe.

pump /pʌmp/ *verb*. **E16.**
[from **PUMP** *noun*¹.]
▶ **I 1** *verb intrans*. Work a pump; raise or move water or other fluid by means of a pump. **E16.**
2 *verb trans*. Raise or remove (water etc.) by means of a pump. Freq. foll. by *out*, *up*. **M16.**
3 *verb trans*. Free from water, air, etc., by means of a pump or pumps. Also foll. by *down*. **M17.**
4 *verb trans*. Put (a person) under a stream of water from a pump, either as a punishment or as medical treatment. Now *rare*. **M17.**
5 *verb trans*. Inflate (a tyre etc.) with air by means of a pump. Freq. foll. by *up*. **L19.**

> 🕮 **2** JULIETTE HUXLEY The gardener had to . . pump up the water. *Offshore Engineer* The cuttings and solvent may be formed into a slurry . . and then pumped to a . . centrifuge. **3** F. CHICHESTER I stopped . . to pump the bilges dry with my . . bilge pump. N. SEDAKA They pumped her stomach.

▶ **II** *transf. & fig.* **6** *verb trans*. Force up or out esp. rapidly and in great quantity, as if by means of a pump; move around, pour forth or eject in this way. **E17.**
7 *verb trans*. Subject to a persistent process with the object of extracting something; *spec.* question (a person) persistently to obtain information. Also, drain, exhaust. **E17.**
8 *verb trans*. Extract, raise, or create by means of persistent effort; *spec.* elicit (information) *out of* a person by such means. **M17.**
9 *verb intrans*. Make a persistent effort, exert oneself in order to gain something; strive to obtain information etc. Freq. foll. by *for*. **M17.**
10 *verb intrans. & trans*. Copulate (with). *coarse slang*. **M18.**
11 *verb trans*. Arouse, excite; work *up*. **L18.**
12 *verb intrans. & trans*. Work or move with action like that of the handle or piston of a pump. **E19.** ▸**b** *verb intrans*. Of mercury in a barometer: fluctuate rapidly as a result of sudden local variations of pressure or of mechanical disturbance. **L19.** ▸**c** *verb trans*. Shake (a person's hand) vigorously. **E20.**
13 *verb intrans*. = **HUNT** *verb* 8. *rare*. **E20.**
14 *PHYSICS*. Raise (an atom or electron) into a higher energy state by (esp. optical) irradiation, esp. so as to produce a population inversion for laser action; excite (a substance or device) in this way. Freq. as ***pumping*** *verbal noun*. **M20.**

> 🕮 **6** B. ENGLAND The mortar was pumping star shell into the sky. *Observer* These groups pump out . . magazines and news-sheets. J. BRONOWSKI When he sprints . . the heart is pumping five times as much blood as normal. *Scientific American* Data are pumped rhythmically . . through the . . network. *Investors Chronicle* The company has pumped some £30m . . into land purchases. **7** *Muscle Power* Boys . . pumped me for my 'secrets' of training. **8** R. S. SURTEES He might pump something out of the servant about the family. **9** THACKERAY To account for his admiration, the critic pumps for words in vain. *Field & Stream* Drake mallards sprung up out of the willows, pumping for altitude. **11** M. EDGEWORTH I could not pump up any enthusiasm. *New Yorker* Everyone expected him to pump up the Party workers with enthusiasm. **12** J. HELLER His brain was pumping with fragments of ideas. R. THOMAS Martin ran faster, his legs pumping up and down. **c** H. ROBBINS She watched her father jump up and . . excitedly pump his hand.

Phrases: **pump iron** *colloq.* (orig. *US*) exercise with weights as a body-building technique. **pump ship** *colloq.* urinate.
Comb.: **pump-down** the action of reducing the pressure of air or other gas inside an enclosed volume by pumping; **pump drill** a primitive drill in which the shaft is rotated by sliding up and down a crosspiece to which is attached a cord that winds and unwinds about the shaft; **pump gun** (orig. *N. Amer.*) a rifle with a tubular magazine and a sliding forearm.

■ **pumpaˈbility** *noun* the quality of being pumpable L19. **pumpable** *adjective* able to be pumped M20. **pumpage** *noun* work done at pumping; the quantity pumped: L19.

pumped /pʌm(p)t/ *adjective*[1]. *rare.* E17.
[from PUMP *noun*[2] + -ED[2].]
Wearing pumps.

pumped /pʌm(p)t/ *adjective*[2]. L18.
[from PUMP *verb* + -ED[1].]
1 Obtained by pumping; raised by persistent effort; (artificially) worked *up*. L18.
2 Exhausted, out of breath with exertion. Also foll. by *out*. *colloq.* M19.

> 📖 **1** M. WOLLSTONECRAFT Lover-like phrases of pumped up passion. D. A. DYE Chris was still pumped up from Lerner's rescue. **pumped storage** in electricity generation, the pumping of water to a high-level reservoir when demand for electricity is low, for use in generating electricity when demand is high.

pumper /ˈpʌmpə/ *noun.* M17.
[from PUMP *verb* + -ER[1].]
1 A person who or thing which pumps or works a pump. M17. ▸**b** A race, exercise, etc., which makes one out of breath. *colloq.* L19.
2 An oil-well from which the oil has to be pumped. *N. Amer.* L19.
3 A fire engine that carries a hose and pumps water. *N. Amer.* E20.

pumpernickel /ˈpʊmpənɪk(ə)l, ˈpʌm-/ *noun.* M18.
[German, transf. use of earlier sense 'lout', 'stinker': ult. origin unkn.]
Dark German bread made from coarsely ground wholemeal rye.

pumpion *noun* var. of POMPION.

pumpkin /ˈpʌm(p)kɪn/ *noun.* Also (esp. in sense 2b) **punkin** /ˈpʌŋkɪn/. L17.
[Alt. of *pumpion* var. of POMPION, assim. to -KIN.]
1 The large yellow egg-shaped or globose fruit of several plants of the gourd family, esp. varieties of the vegetable marrow, *Cucurbita pepo*, and winter squash, *C. maxima*, which is eaten cooked as a vegetable or in a pie; any of the plants producing such a fruit. L17.
2 a A stupid person, a fool. *colloq.* M18. ▸**b** A person or matter of importance. Esp. in ***some pumpkins***. *US slang.* M19. ▸**c** Used as a term of endearment for a person. *N. Amer. colloq.* M20.
Comb.: **pumpkin-head** *US colloq.* (*a*) a head with hair cut short all round; a large head resembling a pumpkin; (*b*) a person having a pumpkin-head; a stupid person, a fool; **pumpkin-headed** *adjective* (*US colloq.*) having a pumpkin-head; stupid; **pumpkin pie**: made with pumpkin and traditionally eaten on Thanksgiving day in the US and Canada; **pumpkin pine** (the light soft wood of) a variety of the white pine, *Pinus strobus*; **pumpkinseed** a N. American freshwater fish, *Lepomis gibbosus*, of the sunfish family Centrarchidae.
■ **pumpkinifiˈcation** *noun* [translating Latin *apocolocyntosis*, title of satire by Seneca] *joc.*, *rare* transformation into a pumpkin; extravagant or absurdly uncritical glorification: M19.

pun /pʌn/ *noun.* M17.
[Origin uncertain: perh. short for PUNDIGRION.]
The humorous use of a word in such a way as to suggest two or more meanings, or of words of similar sound with different meanings; an instance of this; a play on words.

> 📖 D. BOGARDE Will of his own, Mr. Wills . . no pun intended. P. AUSTER 'Mr Farr is not far,' Isaac said, unable to resist the pun.

pun /pʌn/ *verb*[1] *trans.* Infl. **-nn-**. M16.
[Dial. var. of POUND *verb*[1].]
1 = POUND *verb*[1] 1, 3. M16.
2 *spec.* Make (earth, rubble, etc.) firm by pounding or ramming down. M19.

pun /pʌn/ *verb*[2]. Infl. **-nn-**. L17.
[from PUN *noun*.]
1 *verb intrans.* Make a pun or puns; play on words. (Foll. by *on*.) L17.
2 *verb trans.* Bring (a person) into a specified state by punning. (Foll. by *into*, *to*.) E18.
■ **punningly** *adverb* in a punning manner; with a pun or play on words: L18.

puna /ˈpuːnə/ *noun.* E17.
[Amer. Spanish, from Quechua.]
1 A high bleak plateau in the Peruvian Andes. E17.
2 Difficulty of breathing, nausea, etc., caused by climbing to high altitudes; mountain sickness. M19.

†**punaise** *noun.* E16–E19.
[French, use as noun of fem. of *punais* stinking, fetid.]
A bed-bug.

punalua /puːnəˈluːə/ *noun.* M19.
[Hawaiian.]
ANTHROPOLOGY. A form of group marriage in which one's wife's sister is also regarded as one's wife, and one's husband's brother is also regarded as one's husband.
■ **punaluan** *adjective* of or relating to punalua L19.

Punan /puːˈnɑːn/ *noun & adjective.* M19.
[Dyak.]
▶ **A** *noun.* Pl. same, **-s**.
1 A member of any of various groups of Dyak peoples inhabiting parts of Borneo. M19.
2 Any of the related languages of these peoples. L20.
▶ **B** *attrib.* or as *adjective.* Of or pertaining to the Punan or their languages. M20.

punch /pʌn(t)ʃ/ *noun*[1]. LME.
[Abbreviation of PUNCHEON *noun*[1], or from PUNCH *verb*: cf. POUNCE *noun*[1].]
†**1** A dagger; = PUNCHEON *noun*[1] 3. *rare.* LME–L15.
2 A post or beam supporting a roof. *rare.* LME.
3 a A tool or machine for making or enlarging holes, cutting out pieces, driving in nails, etc. E16. ▸†**b** DENTISTRY. An instrument for extracting the stumps of teeth. M18–M19. ▸**c** MEDICINE. An instrument for removing small pieces of skin tissue. L19.
4 A tool or machine for impressing a design or stamping a die on plate or other material. E17.
3a *bell punch*, *nail-punch*, *ticket-punch*, etc.
Comb.: **punch biopsy** MEDICINE a biopsy in which a punch is used to remove tissue; ***punch card***: see CARD *noun*[2] 3c; **punch forceps** SURGERY a punch consisting of two hinged parts like a pair of forceps; **punch graft** MEDICINE a graft of tissue removed by means of a surgical punch; **punch-mark**: punched on metal, a coin, etc.; **punch-marked** *adjective* (of a coin etc.) bearing a punch-mark; **punch-press**: designed to drive a punch for shaping metal; **punch tape** tape punched with holes in a certain pattern to represent specific information, esp. as used formerly in computing.

punch /pʌn(t)ʃ/ *noun*[2]. L16.
[from PUNCH *verb*.]
1 An act of punching; a thrusting blow, now *esp.* one delivered with the fist. Formerly also, a kick. L16.
2 *transf.* & *fig.* Forceful or effective quality in something said or done; vigour, weight, effectiveness. Orig. *US.* E20.

> 📖 **1** P. CAREY Grief came on her. It was like a punch in the stomach. ***beat to the punch***: see BEAT *verb*[1] 5. ***pull one's punches***: see PULL *verb*. ***roll with the punches***: see ROLL *verb*. *SUNDAY punch*. ***throw a punch***: see THROW *verb*. **2** *Swing* The rowdy backing . . gives plenty of punch to a good old barroom song. *Boards* A moderate camber produces the punch of acceleration.

Comb.: **punch-bag** a stuffed bag suspended at a height for boxers to practise punching; **punchball** (*a*) a stuffed or inflated ball suspended or mounted on a stand for boxers to practise punching; (*b*) *US* a ball game in which a rubber ball is punched with the fist or head; **punch board** *N. Amer.* (*a*) a board with holes containing slips of paper which are punched out as a form of gambling, with the object of locating a winning slip; (*b*) *slang*, *derog.* a promiscuous woman; **punch-drunk** *adjective & noun* (orig. *US*) (*a*) *adjective* (esp. of a boxer) dazed or stupefied (as though) from severe or continual punching of the head; *spec.* exhibiting reduced muscular coordination and slowness of speech and thought; (*b*) *noun* a person who is punch-drunk; **punch-drunkenness** the condition of being punch-drunk; **punch-line** (orig. *US*) a phrase or sentence expressing the point of a joke, story, etc.; **punch-pull** *verb intrans.* refrain from striking as hard as one can, or from expressing oneself forcefully.
■ **punchless** *adjective*[1] (*rare*) (esp. of a boxer) lacking a powerful punch M20.

punch /pʌn(t)ʃ/ *noun*[3]. M17.
[App. from Sanskrit *pañc(a)* five, five kinds of (as the drink properly had five ingredients).]
1 A drink usu. made from wine or spirits mixed with water, fruit, spices, etc., and often served hot. M17.
2 A party at which punch is drunk. L19.

> 📖 **1** DICKENS A bowl of punch was carried up . . and a grand carouse held. ***brandy punch***, ***fruit punch***, ***gin punch***, ***rum punch***, etc.

Comb.: **punch bowl** (*a*) a large bowl from which punch is served; (*b*) *fig.* a round deep hollow in a hilly region; **punch-house** a public house where punch is served.
■ **punchery** *noun* a place where punch is prepared E19. **punchless** *adjective*[2] (*rare*) without punch, having no punch to drink E19.

punch /pʌn(t)ʃ/ *noun*[4] & *adjective.* M17.
[Abbreviation of PUNCHINELLO.]
▶ **A** *noun.* **I 1** A short fat person. Now chiefly *dial.* M17.
2 In full ***Suffolk Punch***. (An animal of) a breed of heavy draught horse with a thickset body and short legs. E19.
▶ **II 3** (**P-**.) The grotesque hook-nosed humpbacked principal character of *Punch and Judy* (see below). L17.
3 pleased as Punch, **proud as Punch** showing or feeling great pleasure or pride. **Punch-and-Judy show** a traditional puppet-show in which Punch is shown nagging, beating, and finally killing a succession of characters, including his wife Judy.
▶ **B** *adjective.* Esp. of a horse: short and stout. Now *dial.* L17.

punch /pʌn(t)ʃ/ *noun*[5]. M19.
[Abbreviation.]
= PANCHAYAT.

punch /pʌn(t)ʃ/ *verb.* LME.
[Var. of POUNCE *verb*[1].]
▶ **I** *verb trans.* †**1** Stab, prick, or puncture (as) with a pointed instrument. LME–M17.
2 Poke or prod, esp. with a stick. Now *esp.* (*N. Amer.*), drive (cattle) by prodding. LME.
3 a Deliver a sharp blow or forward thrust at, esp. with the fist; beat, thump. M16. ▸**b** Strike with the foot, kick. *north.* M16. ▸**c** Press (a push-button, key, etc.); switch *on*, tune *in* (a device) by doing this. Also, (foll. by *out*) dial or type (a number, message, etc.) by pressing buttons or keys. M20.
4 a Make a hole or holes in (something); perforate, pierce, cut. L16. ▸**b** Make (a hole, a perforation) by cutting or piercing. L17. ▸**c** Take *out* (a piece) by punching. E19. ▸**d** = KEYPUNCH *verb.* M19.

> 📖 **3a** E. LONGFORD To punch his opponents as hard . . as possible. **c** *New Yorker* I pick up the phone and punch out Jean's number. E. LEONARD At the cash register punching keys. M. DIBDIN The barman punched a button on the television. **4a** A. S. NEILL A . . ticket . . the collector forgot to punch. **b** R. DAHL Machines that could punch holes . . in little cards.

▶ **II** *verb intrans.* **5** Penetrate, pierce, cut. (Foll. by *into*, *through*.) L17.
Phrases & comb.: **punch above one's weight** *colloq.* engage in an activity or contest perceived as being beyond one's capacity or abilities. **punch the clock** clock in or out. **punch-up** *colloq.* a fight, a brawl; *fig.* a noisy argument.
With adverbs in specialized senses: **punch in** clock in. **punch out** (*a*) *verb phr. intrans.* (*slang*) eject from an aircraft; (*b*) *verb phr. trans.* (*N. Amer.*) knock out, beat up. **punch up** (*a*) CINEMATOGRAPHY emphasize, increase (action, brightness, sound, etc.); (*b*) assault, beat up.
■ **punchable** *adjective* (*rare*) able to be punched L17. **puncher** *noun* (*a*) a person who or thing which punches; an instrument for punching; (*b*) *N. Amer.* = ***cowpuncher*** s.v. COW *noun*[1]: L17.

punchayat *noun* var. of PANCHAYAT.

punched /pʌn(t)ʃt/ *ppl adjective.* LME.
[from PUNCH *verb* + -ED[1].]
1 Of metalwork: beaten, hammered, wrought. *obsolete* exc. *Hist.* LME.
2 Perforated or pierced with a punch. L19.
3 MEDICINE. ***punched out***, (of a wound, ulcer, etc.) having a well-defined edge. L19.
2 *punched card*: see CARD *noun*[2] 3c. **punched tape** = ***punch tape*** s.v. PUNCH *noun*[1].

puncheon /ˈpʌn(t)ʃ(ə)n/ *noun*[1]. ME.
[Old French *poinson*, *po(i)nchon* (mod. *poinçon*), from Proto-Romance: cf. POUNCE *noun*[1], PUNCH *noun*[1]. See also next.]
▶ **I** A piece of timber.
1 BUILDING. A short upright piece of timber used to stiffen longer timbers or to support a load; a strut; a post supporting a roof in a coalmine. Formerly also, a doorpost. ME.
2 a A heavy piece of rough timber or a split trunk, used for flooring and rough building. *US.* E18. ▸**b** A piece of timber used in building a railway track or a corduroy road. *N. Amer.* M19.
▶ **II** A pointed or piercing instrument.
†**3** A dagger. LME–L17.
4 A pointed tool for piercing, chiselling, engraving, etc. LME.
5 A tool or machine for impressing a design or stamping a die on plate or other material; = PUNCH *noun*[1] 4. Now *rare* or *obsolete.* LME.

puncheon /ˈpʌn(t)ʃ(ə)n/ *noun*[2]. LME.
[Old French *poinson*, *po(i)nchon* (mod. *poinçon*), perh. identical with prec.]
A large cask for liquids, fish, etc.; *spec.* a cask of a definite capacity, used as a liquid measure.

> 📖 *Caribbean Quarterly* Puncheons of rum.

Punchinello /pʌn(t)ʃɪˈnɛləʊ/ *noun.* Pl. **-o(e)s**, **-lli** /-liː/. M17.
[Alt. of Italian (Neapolitan) *Polecenella*, (literary) *Pulcinella*, perh. from dim. of *pollecena* young of the turkey-cock (the hooked beak of which bears some resemblance to the character's nose) from *pulcino* chicken from Proto-Romance, from Latin *pullus* (see PULLET).]
1 Orig., one of the stock characters of the Italian *commedia dell'arte*, distinguished by his hooked nose, humped back, and short stout figure; an entertainment in which the character appeared. Later = PUNCH *noun*[4] 3; a Punch-and-Judy show. M17.
2 *transf.* A person, animal, or thing resembling Punchinello, esp. in being short and stout. M17.

punching /ˈpʌn(t)ʃɪŋ/ *noun.* LME.
[from PUNCH *verb* + -ING[1].]
The action of PUNCH *verb*; a mark produced by punching; a piece of sheet metal cut out by a punch.
Comb.: **punching bag** = ***punch-bag*** s.v. PUNCH *noun*[2]; **punching-ball** = ***punchball*** s.v. PUNCH *noun*[2]; **punching press** = ***punch-press*** s.v. PUNCH *noun*[1].

punchy /ˈpʌn(t)ʃi/ *adjective*[1]. L18.
[from PUNCH *noun*[4] + -Y[1].]
Short and stout, squat.
■ **punchiness** *noun*[1] (*rare*) M19.

punchy /ˈpʌn(t)ʃi/ *adjective*[2]. *rare.* M19.
[from PUNCH *noun*[3] + -Y[1].]
Of the nature of punch; smelling or tasting of punch.

punchy /ˈpʌn(t)ʃi/ *adjective*[3]. **E20.**
[from PUNCH *noun*[2] + -Y[1].]
1 Full of punch or vigour; forceful. **E20.**
2 Punch-drunk; *transf.* in a state of nervous tension or extreme fatigue. *slang* (chiefly *N. Amer.*). **M20.**

> **1** *Listener* Grappling with election issues in fine punchy form. *Caravan Life* Performance is punchy in all .. the gears.

■ **punchily** *adverb* **L20.** **punchiness** *noun*[2] **L20.**

puncta *noun* pl. of PUNCTUM.

punctal /ˈpʌŋ(k)t(ə)l/ *adjective. rare.* **LME.**
[medieval Latin *punctalis*, from *punctum* point: see -AL[1].]
Of the nature of, occupying, or relating to a point.

punctate /ˈpʌŋ(k)teɪt/ *adjective.* **M18.**
[from Latin *punctum* point + -ATE[2].]
1 Chiefly BOTANY, ZOOLOGY, & MEDICINE. Marked or studded with points, dots, spots, etc., or with small depressions resembling punctures; of the nature of or characterized by such markings. **M18.**
2 Having or coming to a point; pointed. *rare.* **E19.**
■ Also **puncˈtated** *adjective* **E18.**

punctation /pʌŋ(k)ˈteɪʃ(ə)n/ *noun.* **E17.**
[medieval Latin *punctatio(n-)*, formed as PUNCTUATE *verb* punctuate, or directly from prec.: see -ATION.]
†**1** Punctuation; *esp.* the pointing of Hebrew etc. **E17–M18.**
2 Chiefly ZOOLOGY & BOTANY. The condition of being punctate; (each of) the points etc. displayed by a punctate object. **M19.**
3 [Repr. German *Punktation*.] A treaty or agreement setting out a number of specific points. **M19.**

puncti *noun* pl. of PUNCTUS.

punctiform /ˈpʌŋ(k)tɪfɔːm/ *adjective.* **E19.**
[from Latin *punctum* point + -I- + -FORM.]
1 Having the form of a point, puncture, or dot. **E19.**
2 Formed of or having the appearance of a number of points or dots. **M19.**

punctiliar /pʌŋ(k)ˈtɪlɪə/ *adjective.* **E20.**
[from next + -AR[1].]
GRAMMAR. = PUNCTUAL *adjective* 8c.

punctilio /pʌŋ(k)ˈtɪlɪəʊ/ *noun.* Pl. **-os.** Also (earlier) †**punt-.** **L16.**
[Italian *puntiglio*, Spanish *puntillo*, dim. of *punto* POINT *noun*[1], later assim. to Latin *punctum*.]
†**1 a** A fine point or mark, as on a dial. *rare.* Only in **L16.** ▸**b** A high point; the acme, the apex. *rare.* **L16–M17.** ▸**c** A point in time, a moment, an instant. Only in **17.**
2 A minute detail of action or conduct; a delicate point of ceremony or honour. **L16.** ▸†**b** *gen.* A minute point or particular; a particle, a whit, a jot; a thing of no importance, a trifle. **M17–E19.**
3 Insistence on minutiae of action or conduct; petty formality; punctiliousness. **L16.**

> **3** S. RICHARDSON People of birth stood a little too much on punctilio. J. UPDIKE She was all precision and copyediting punctilio.

punctilious /pʌŋ(k)ˈtɪlɪəs/ *adjective.* **M17.**
[from French *pointilleux*, from *pointille* formed as prec.: see -IOUS.]
Attentive to minor details of action or behaviour; strictly observant of formality or etiquette.

> H. T. BUCKLE The punctilious honour of a Spanish gentleman. D. M. DAVIN A punctilious and generous observer of birthdays. F. KAPLAN The stylish dresser, punctilious about his clothes.

■ **punctiliously** *adverb* **L18.** **punctiliousness** *noun* **L17.**

†**punction** *noun.* **LME–E18.**
[Latin *punctio(n-)*, from *punct-* pa. ppl stem of *pungere* prick: see -ION.]
The action or an act of pricking or puncturing; a prick, a puncture. Also, a pricking sensation.

punctual /ˈpʌŋ(k)tʃʊəl, -tjʊəl/ *adjective.* **LME.**
[medieval Latin *punctualis*, from Latin *punctum* POINT *noun*[1]: see -UAL.]
▸ **I** †**1** SURGERY. Of the nature of a sharp point or puncture; sharp-pointed. **LME.**
2 Of, pertaining to, or of the nature of punctuation. **E17.**
†**3** Of the nature of or resembling a point or speck; tiny, trifling. **E–M17.**
4 Of or relating to a point in space. *rare.* **E19.**
▸ **II 5** Punctilious. Now *arch. rare.* **L16.**
6 (Now the predominant sense.) Exactly observant of an appointed time; marked by observance of appointed times; on time, neither early nor late. **L17.**

> **6** W. CONGREVE I will be punctual to the minute. T. S. ELIOT Ah, there you are, Eggerson! Punctual as always. N. MONSARRAT It was just after half past one: lunch had been punctual.

▸ **III 7** †**a** Bearing directly on the point; apposite, apt. **E–M17.** ▸**b** Express, explicit. *arch.* **E17.**
8 a Exact in every point; precise, accurate. Now *arch. rare.* **E17.** ▸**b** Precisely or aptly timed, timely. Now *arch. rare.* **E17.** ▸**c** GRAMMAR. (Of action) occurring at a point in time; (of aspect or tense) relating to something that occurs at a point in time. **E20.**
†**9** Minute, detailed, circumstantial. **E17–L18.**
■ **punctually** *adverb* **L16.** **punctualness** *noun* (now *rare*) **E17.**

punctuality /pʌŋ(k)tʃʊˈalɪti, -tjʊ-/ *noun.* **E17.**
[from prec. + -ITY.]
1 Exactness, precision; attention to detail. Now *arch. rare.* **E17.** ▸†**b** An instance of this; a nicety, a detail. **M17–M18.** ▸**c** GRAMMAR. The quality or character of occurring at a point in time; the punctual aspect of a verb. **M20.**
2 Punctiliousness of style or conduct; petty formality; precise observance of etiquette or duty. Now *arch. rare.* **E17.** ▸†**b** An instance of this; a punctilio. **E17–M19.**
3 Exact observance of an appointed time; the fact or habit of being neither early nor late. **L18.**

punctuate /ˈpʌŋ(k)tʃʊeɪt, -tjʊ-/ *adjective.* **L19.**
[from Latin *punctum* POINT *noun*[1] + -ATE[2].]
Chiefly ZOOLOGY. = PUNCTATE 1.

punctuate /ˈpʌŋ(k)tʃʊeɪt, -tjʊ-/ *verb.* **M17.**
[medieval Latin *punctuat-* pa. ppl stem of *punctuare*, from Latin *punctum* POINT *noun*[1]: see -ATE[3].]
†**1** *verb trans.* Point out. *rare.* Only in **M17.**
2 *verb trans.* Mark with points or dots, esp. with small depressions resembling punctures. Chiefly as ***punctuated** ppl adjective* (= PUNCTATE 1). *rare.* **E19.**
3 *verb trans.* Insert punctuation marks in (a sentence etc.); mark or divide with points or stops. **E19.** ▸**b** *verb intrans.* Insert or employ punctuation marks. **M19.**
4 *verb trans. fig.* Interrupt at intervals; intersperse *with*. Also, interrupt so as to bring to a close. **M19.**
5 *verb trans.* Give point to; emphasize, accentuate. *rare.* **L19.**

> **3** D. ARKELL Apollinaire does not punctuate his poems. **b** T. L. DE VINNE A knowledge of grammar is of .. value in enabling a compositor to punctuate properly. **4** D. WELCH Benches stood against the walls, punctuated by powder-blue spittoons. C. CAUSLEY The bell punctuates Visiting time. P. BARKER Conversations with Kelly were punctuated by frequent swigs from a bottle. P. GAY Freud punctuated his private correspondence with .. declarations of ignorance. **punctuated equilibrium** BIOLOGY (a theory of) evolutionary development marked by isolated episodes of rapid speciation between long periods of little or no change.

■ **punctuator** *noun* a person who punctuates something **M17.**

punctuation /pʌŋ(k)tʃʊˈeɪʃ(ə)n, -tjʊ-/ *noun.* **M16.**
[medieval Latin *punctuatio(n-)*, formed as prec.: see -ATION.]
†**1** The pointing of the psalms. *rare.* **M16–L18.**
2 The insertion of points indicating vowels etc. in Hebrew and other Semitic writing; the system of such points. **M17.**
3 The practice, method, or skill of inserting points or marks in writing or printing, in order to aid the sense; division of text into sentences, clauses, etc., by means of such marks; the system used for this; such marks collectively. Also, observance of appropriate pauses in reading or speaking. **M17.** ▸**b** *fig.* Repeated occurrence or distribution at regular intervals; something that makes repeated interruptions or divisions. **E20.** ▸**c** BIOLOGY. An episode of rapid speciation; the occurrence of such episodes, as described by the theory of punctuated equilibrium. **L20.**
4 Chiefly ZOOLOGY. = PUNCTATION 2. **M19.**

> **3** DYLAN THOMAS The punctuation in both stories is abominable, and makes nonsense of .. the sentences. L. DUNCAN You have a grasp of grammar and punctuation. **b** H. BRAUN Vertical punctuation is .. achieved by the pilasters. *Times* Stages in a continuous process rather than punctuations in an otherwise stable history.

Comb.: **punctuation mark** any of the marks (e.g. full stop, comma, semicolon) used in writing and printing to separate sentences, phrases, etc., and to clarify meaning.

punctuational /pʌŋ(k)tʃʊˈeɪʃ(ə)n(ə)l, -tjʊ-/ *adjective.* **E20.**
[from prec. + -AL[1].]
1 Of, pertaining to, or of the nature of punctuation. **E20.**
2 BIOLOGY. Of, pertaining to, or marked by punctuationalism or punctuated equilibrium. **L20.**
■ **punctuationalism** *noun* advocacy of the theory of punctuated equilibrium **L20.** **punctuationalist** *noun & adjective* (*a*) *noun* an advocate of the theory of punctuated equilibrium; (*b*) *adjective* of or pertaining to punctuationalism or punctuationalists: **L20.**

punctuationist /pʌŋ(k)tʃʊˈeɪʃ(ə)nɪst, -tjʊ-/ *noun & adjective.* **L19.**
[formed as prec. + -IST.]
▸ **A** *noun.* **1** A person who uses or is concerned with punctuation. *rare.* **L19.**
2 BIOLOGY. = PUNCTUATIONALIST *noun.* **L20.**
▸ **B** *adjective.* BIOLOGY. = PUNCTUATIONALIST *adjective.* **L20.**

punctuative /ˈpʌŋ(k)tʃʊətɪv, -tjʊ-/ *adjective.* **M19.**
[from PUNCTUATE *verb* + -ATIVE.]
Of, pertaining to, or serving for punctuation.

†**punctula** *noun pl.* see PUNCTULE.

punctulate /ˈpʌŋ(k)tʃʊlət, -tjʊ-/ *adjective.* **M19.**
[from next + -ATE[2].]
Chiefly ZOOLOGY & BOTANY. Marked or studded with small dots or puncta; minutely punctate.
■ **punctuˈlated** *adjective* †(*a*) consisting of small points or dots, dotted; (*b*) = PUNCTULATE: **L17.** **punctuˈlation** *noun* punctulate condition; a number or mass of small dots or puncta: **E19.**

punctule /ˈpʌŋ(k)tjuːl/ *noun. rare.* Also (earlier) in Latin form †**-ulum**, pl. **-la.** **M17.**
[Latin *punctulum* dim. of *punctum* POINT *noun*[1]: see -ULE.]
Chiefly ZOOLOGY & BOTANY. A small point; a small punctum.

punctum /ˈpʌŋ(k)təm/ *noun.* Pl. **puncta** /ˈpʌŋ(k)tə/. **L16.**
[Latin, orig. neut. of *punctus* pa. pple of *pungere* prick.]
1 A point. *obsolete* exc. as below. **L16.**
2 ZOOLOGY, BOTANY, & MEDICINE etc. A minute rounded speck, dot, or spot of colour; a small elevation or depression on a surface. **M17.**
3 ANATOMY. = ***punctum lachrymale*** below. **L18.**
4 PALAEOGRAPHY. A punctuation mark consisting of a point in a medieval manuscript. **M20.**
Phrases: ***punctum indifferens*** /ɪnˈdɪfərɛnz/ [= not differing] a neutral point. ***punctum lachrymale*** /lakrɪˈmeɪli/, pl. ***-lia*** /-lɪə/, [= lachrymal] ANATOMY the orifice of either of the two lacrimal canals at the corner of the eye. ***punctum saliens*** /ˈsalɪɛnz/ [= leaping] the first trace of the heart in an embryo, appearing as a pulsating point; *fig.* a starting-point or centre of activity.

puncturation /pʌŋ(k)tʃʊˈreɪʃ(ə)n, -tjʊ-/ *noun.* **M18.**
[from PUNCTURE *verb* + -ATION.]
1 The action or operation of puncturing something. Formerly also, a pricking sensation. **M18.**
2 Chiefly ZOOLOGY & BOTANY. The condition of being pitted or dotted; = PUNCTATION 2. **L19.**

puncture /ˈpʌŋ(k)tʃə/ *noun.* **LME.**
[Latin *punctura*, from *punct-* pa. ppl stem of *pungere* prick: see -URE.]
1 An act or the action of pricking; a prick; perforation with a sharp point; *spec.* (*a*) an accidental perforation of a pneumatic tyre; (*b*) MEDICINE insertion of a hollow needle into the body for removal of tissue or fluid, esp. cerebrospinal fluid. **LME.**
2 A hole, wound, or mark made by pricking. **LME.**
†**3** A sharp point or prickle. *rare.* **L16–L18.**

> **1** M. UNDERWOOD I had a puncture I had hell's own time changing the wheel. *fig.*: E. COXHEAD His power complex is about due for a puncture. ***lumbar puncture***. ***slow puncture***: see SLOW *adjective & adverb.* **2** J. H. BURN He made a puncture through the skin of the back.

■ **punctureless** *adjective* free from punctures; that cannot be punctured: **L19.**

puncture /pʌŋ(k)tʃə/ *verb.* **L17.**
[from the noun.]
1 *verb trans.* Make a puncture in; pierce with a sharp point; prick, perforate. **L17.** ▸**b** *spec.* Mark (the skin) with punctures, tattoo. Now *rare.* **L18.** ▸**c** BOTANY & ZOOLOGY etc. Mark with spots or dots resembling punctures. Usu. in *pass.* **M19.** ▸**d** *fig.* Cause to collapse as if by pricking; deflate; debunk. **L19.** ▸**e** Make repeated interruptions or divisions in, intersperse. **L19.**
2 *verb trans.* Make (a hole etc.) by pricking. **E19.**
3 *verb intrans.* Sustain a puncture (in a tyre). **L19.**

> **1** J. LE CARRÉ Grey shoes, punctured for ventilation. P. MONETTE The doctor had managed to puncture Leo's lung. **d** J. SYMONS Fisher had .. punctured many enthusiasms with kindly ridicule. *Business* The oil price collapse of 1981–2 punctured Houston's real estate boom. **e** *Blueprint* A full-height elliptical lobby punctured by a black marble balcony. **2** J. HERRIOT The jaws of the instrument clicked together, puncturing a small round hole in the hard tissue. **3** *Rally Sport* Blomqvist punctured and dropped out of contention.

punctus /ˈpʌŋktəs/ *noun.* Pl. ***-ti*** /-tʌɪ, -tiː/. **M20.**
[Latin: see PUNCTUM.]
PALAEOGRAPHY. A punctuation mark in a medieval manuscript. Chiefly in phrs. below.
punctus elevatus /ɛlɪˈvɑːtəs/, pl. ***-ti*** /-tiː/, [Latin = raised] a punctuation mark resembling an inverted semi-colon. ***punctus interrogativus*** /ɪntəˌrɒgəˈtʌɪvəs, -ˈtiːvəs/, pl. ***-vi*** /-vʌɪ, -viː/, [Latin = interrogative] a point of interrogation. ***punctus versus*** /ˈvəːsəs/, pl. ***-si*** /-sʌɪ, -siː/, [Latin = turned] a punctuation mark resembling a semi-colon.

†**pundigrion** *noun. rare.* **L17–E19.**
[Perh. fanciful alt. of PUNCTILIO. Cf. PUN *noun.*]
A pun, a quibble.

pundit /ˈpʌndɪt/ *noun & verb.* In sense A.1 also (now usu.) **pandit** /ˈpandɪt, ˈpʌn-/. **L17.**
[Sanskrit *paṇḍita* learned, conversant with.]
▸ **A** *noun.* **1** A Hindu learned in Sanskrit and in Indian philosophy, religion, and laws. **L17.**

2 A learned expert or teacher; a person who makes knowledgeable and authoritative pronouncements on current affairs. Freq. *iron.* E19.

📖 **2** M. SARTON Nixon's nonconversation with four TV pundits. C. P. SNOW He was the literary pundit of his time.

▸ **B** *verb intrans.* Make pronouncements like an expert. *rare.* M20.

■ **punditry** *noun* the characteristics or behaviour of a pundit; expert pronouncements befitting a pundit: E20.

pundonor /pundo'nɔr/ *noun.* Pl. †**-es.** M17.
[Spanish, contr. of *punto de honor* point of honour.]
In Spain: (orig., with *pl.*) a point of honour; (now) one's sense of honour, dignity, self-respect, pride.

pung /pʌŋ/ *noun*¹. *N. Amer.* E19.
[Shortened from TOM PUNG.]
A sleigh with a boxlike body drawn esp. by a single horse, used in New England. Also, a toboggan.

pung /pʌŋ/ *noun*² & *verb.* E20.
[Chinese *pèng.*]
▸ **A** *noun.* A set of three identical tiles in the game of mah-jong; the action of completing such a set in one's hand. Also as *interjection*, announcing this. E20.
▸ **B** *verb intrans.* & *trans.* Take (a discarded tile) in order to complete a pung in mah-jong. E20.

punga *noun* var. of PONGA *noun*¹.

pungency /'pʌn(d)ʒ(ə)nsi/ *noun.* M17.
[from next + -ENCY.]
1 The property of pricking; the fact of having a sharp point or points. *rare.* M17.
2 *fig.* Sharpness or intensity of feeling; intense painfulness, poignancy; incisiveness or severity of comment; an instance of this. M17.
3 The quality of having a pungent smell or taste; pungent smell or taste; a stinging, irritant, or caustic property. L17.

📖 **2** *Guardian* He . . commented with unnerving pungency.

■ **pungence** *noun* (*rare*) a pungent smell E19.

pungent /'pʌn(d)ʒ(ə)nt/ *adjective.* L16.
[from Latin *pungent-* pres. ppl stem of *pungere* prick: see -ENT.]
1 a Keenly painful or distressing; (of pain or grief) acute, poignant. Formerly also, (of appetite or desire) keen, eager. Now *arch. rare.* L16. ▸**b** *lit.* Pricking, piercing, sharp-pointed. Now only in BOTANY & ZOOLOGY (of a leaf, spine, etc.) having one or more sharp points or prickles. E17.
2 Affecting the organs of smell or taste with a pricking sensation; sharp-smelling or -tasting; penetrating and irritant. M17. ▸**b** MEDICINE. Of the skin: hot to the touch, fevered. Now *rare.* E19.
3 †**a** Of argument: telling, convincing. M17–E18. ▸**b** Of remarks etc.: trenchant, severe, penetrating, caustic, incisive, sarcastic. Later also, exciting keen interest; mentally stimulating; piquant. M17

📖 **1a** J. P. PHILIPS With pungent Colic Pangs distress'd he'll roar. **2** W. SHENSTONE Pungent radish, biting infant's tongue. J. TYNDALL Chlorine and sodium are elements, the former a pungent gas. E. FIGES The pungent odour of moth-balls. **3b** L. STEPHEN A few pungent epigrams. A. F. DOUGLAS-HOME He was pungent in all his comments. E. LONGFORD Pungent accounts of wartime life in London.

■ **pungently** *adverb* M19.

punger /'pʌŋgə/ *noun.* *obsolete* exc. *dial.* L16.
[Origin unkn.]
The edible crab, *Cancer pagurus.*

†**pungitive** *adjective.* LME–E18.
[medieval Latin *pungitivus*, irreg. from Latin *pungere* (see PUNGENT) after *fugitivus* fugitive, etc.: see -IVE.]
Having a pricking quality; sharp, keen, pungent.

pungle /'pʌŋg(ə)l/ *verb trans.* & *intrans.* *US colloq.* M19.
[Spanish *pongale*, from *poner* put, give.]
Contribute, hand over, or pay (money), pay up. Usu. foll. by *down, up.*

pungy /'pʌŋ(g)i/ *noun.* *US local.* Also (earlier) **pungo** /'pʌŋgəʊ/, pl. **-os.** M19.
[Origin unkn.]
A kind of sailing boat used in harvesting oysters.

Punic /'pju:nɪk/ *noun* & *adjective.* LME.
[Latin *Punicus* earlier *Poenicus* adjective, from *Poenus* from Greek *Phoinix* Phoenician, Carthaginian: see -IC.]
▸ **A** *noun.* †**1** = ***Punic apple*** below. *rare.* Only in LME.
†**2** A native or inhabitant of ancient Carthage in N. Africa, a Carthaginian. Only in 17.
3 The Semitic language of ancient Carthage, related to Phoenician. L17.
▸ **B** *adjective.* †**1** = PUNICEOUS. E16–E17.
2 Of or pertaining to Carthage or its language; Carthaginian. M16. ▸**b** Having the character attributed by the Romans to the Carthaginians; treacherous, perfidious. E17.

Special collocations: †**Punic apple** a pomegranate. **Punic faith** treachery. **Punic War** any of a series of three wars between the Romans and Carthaginians, 264–146 BC.

puniceous /pjʊ'nɪʃəs/ *adjective.* *rare.* LME.
[from Latin *puniceus* Punic, red, purple-coloured, formed as prec.: see -EOUS.]
Of a bright red or reddish-purple colour.

punily /'pju:nɪli/ *adverb.* L18.
[from PUNY + -LY².]
In a puny manner; weakly.

puniness /'pju:nɪnɪs/ *noun.* E18.
[from PUNY + -NESS.]
The state or quality of being puny.

punish /'pʌnɪʃ/ *verb trans.* ME.
[Old & mod. French *puniss-* lengthened stem of *punir* from Latin *punire*, earlier *poenire*, from *poena* PAIN *noun*¹: see -ISH².]
1 Cause (an offender) to suffer for an offence; inflict a penalty on as retribution or as a caution against further misconduct. ME. ▸**b** Inflict a penalty on an offender for (an offence). ME. ▸†**c** *spec.* Fine (a person). L16–E18.
2 *transf.* Subject to severe treatment, damage, injury, or loss, *esp.* inflict severe blows on (an opponent); abuse, treat improperly. Freq. *joc.* & *colloq.* LME.

📖 **1** HOBBES 'Tis against the Law of Nature, To punish the Innocent. S. BIKO We do not believe that God can create people only to punish them eternally. **b** LD MACAULAY No misdemeanour should be punished more severely than the most atrocious felonies. **2** W. G. GRACE It was a treat to watch him punish the bowling. J. B. PRIESTLEY The bottle of brandy they'd punished was prominent on the little table.

■ **punisher** *noun* a person who or (occas.) thing which punishes someone or something E19. **punishing** *adjective* (**a**) that punishes; punitive; (**b**) *colloq.* hard-hitting; (**c**) very demanding, severe and exhausting: ME. **punishingly** *adverb* to a punishing extent, in a punishing manner M20.

punishable /'pʌnɪʃəb(ə)l/ *adjective.* LME.
[Old French *punissable*, formed as prec.: see -ABLE.]
Liable to punishment, able to be punished; *esp.* (of an offence) entailing punishment.

■ **punisha'bility** *noun* M19. **punishableness** *noun* E18. **punishably** *adverb* M18.

punishment /'pʌnɪʃm(ə)nt/ *noun.* LME.
[Anglo-Norman, Old French *punissement*, formed as PUNISH *verb*: see -MENT.]
1 The action or an instance of punishing; the fact of being punished; the infliction of a penalty in retribution for an offence. Also, a loss or suffering inflicted as a penalty, a penalty imposed to ensure the application and enforcement of a law. LME. ▸**b** PSYCHOLOGY. An unpleasant consequence experienced by an organism responding incorrectly under specific conditions so that, through avoidance, a desired behaviour becomes established; the process by which this occurs. Cf. REWARD *noun* 3e. E20.
2 Rough treatment, as that inflicted by a boxer on an opponent; pain, damage, or loss inflicted; excessive use or rough handling of machinery etc. *colloq.* E19.

📖 **1** G. SWIFT They look so in need of punishment and penance. J. HELLER For a first offence . . the punishment was five years in prison. ***capital punishment, corporal punishment***, etc. **2** J. TEY He looked stupid, like a boxer who is taking too much punishment. *Times* Only the finest . . oils can withstand the punishment a tractor engine receives. V. GLENDINNING These houses . . took a lot of punishment from German bombs.

Phrases: ***a glutton for punishment***: see GLUTTON *noun* & *adjective.*

punition /pju:'nɪʃ(ə)n/ *noun.* Now *rare.* LME.
[Old & mod. French from Latin *punitio(n-)*, from *punit-*: see next, -ITION.]
The action of punishing; punishment.

punitive /'pju:nɪtɪv/ *adjective.* E17.
[French *punitif, -ive* from medieval Latin *punitivus*, from Latin *punit-* pa. ppl stem of *punire* PUNISH: see -IVE.]
Inflicting or intended to inflict punishment; retributive, LAW (of damages etc.) exceeding simple compensation and awarded to punish the defendant, exemplary; (of taxation etc.) very severe.

📖 R. SUTCLIFF Destroying the local garrison will . . mean a punitive expedition and their homes and . . crops burned. I. FLEMING Seeking alleviation from the punitive burden of the Revenue. A. STORR Punitive imprisonment for criminals.

■ **punitively** *adverb* M19. **punitiveness** *noun* E18.

punitory /'pju:nɪt(ə)ri/ *adjective.* E18.
[medieval Latin *punitorius*, from Latin *punit-*: see prec., -ORY².]
= prec.

Punjabi /pʌn'dʒɑ:bi/ *noun* & *adjective.* Also (see senses A.1, B. below) **Pan-** /pʌn-, pan-/. E19.
[Urdu *panjābī*, from *Panjāb* Punjab (see below), from Persian *panj* five + *āb* water (so called from the five main rivers of the region).]
▸ **A** *noun.* **1** (Usu. **Pan-.**) The Indo-Aryan language spoken in the Punjab, a region in the north-west of the Indian subcontinent now divided between India and Pakistan. E19.
2 A native or inhabitant of the Punjab. M19.
3 (**p-.**) A kind of loose shirt or tunic worn by Hindus; a kurta. M20.
▸ **B** *adjective.* Of or pertaining to the Punjab, Punjabis, or (usu. **Pan-**) the language Panjabi. E19.

punji /'pʌndʒi/ *noun.* Also (earlier) **panji** /'pandʒi/. L19.
[Prob. of Tibeto-Burman origin.]
Esp. in SE Asia: a sharpened (freq. poisoned) bamboo stake set in a camouflaged hole in the ground as a defence against attackers. Also ***punji stake, punji stick.***

punk /pʌŋk/ *noun*¹. *arch.* L16.
[Origin unkn. Cf. next.]
A prostitute.

punk /pʌŋk/ *noun*² & *adjective.* L17.
[Origin uncertain: perh. rel. to FUNK *noun*¹, SPUNK *noun.* Perh. also rel. to prec. in some senses.]
▸ **A** *noun.* **I 1** Soft dry crumbly wood, rotted by fungal attack, esp. used for tinder; any of several bracket fungi also so used. Cf. TOUCHWOOD 1, 2. Orig. *US.* L17. ▸**b** = AMADOU. *US.* M19.
2 Something worthless; foolish talk; nonsense, rubbish. Chiefly *US colloq.* M19.
3 Bread. *US slang.* L19.
4 Chinese incense; joss-sticks. *US.* L19.
5 a A passive male homosexual, a catamite. *US slang.* E20. ▸**b** A person of no account, a worthless fellow; a young hooligan or petty criminal. Chiefly *N. Amer. colloq.* E20. ▸**c** Esp. in show business: a youth, a novice; a young circus animal. *US slang.* E20.

📖 **5b** E. HEMINGWAY This fellow was just a punk . . a nobody. V. S. NAIPAUL The telephone rang. 'Hallo, punk'.

▸ **II 6** Punk rock; the subculture or style associated with this. Also, a punk rocker; a person who adopts or typifies a punk style. L20.

📖 **6** S. TOWNSEND Nigel brought his records round. He is into punk. R. ALTER Shakespeare has been presented in every conceivable mode from neoclassical stateliness to raucous punk. *Hair* Punks, with their super-glued spikes and day-glo colours.

▸ **B** *adjective.* **1** Worthless, bad, poor in quality, disappointing; nonsensical. Chiefly *US colloq.* L19.
2 Of timber: decayed, rotten. *US.* E20.
3 Designating or pertaining to a loud fast-moving form of rock music with crude and aggressive effects; characteristic of the subculture or style associated with this, esp. as distinguished by the wearing of leather ornamented with zips and chains and brightly dyed hair dressed in spikes. L20.

📖 **1** E. LEONARD I don't know what is the matter with me. I feel kind of punk. **3** L. R. BANKS He never liked me in my punk gear.

Comb. & special collocations: **punk chic** a fashionable style of design reflecting unconventional aspects of punk rock; **punk rocker** a player or admirer of punk rock.

■ **punker** *noun* (*colloq.*) a punk rocker L20. **punkette** *noun* (*colloq.*) a young female punk rocker L20. **punkish** *adjective* characteristic of or like a punk rocker, somewhat punk L20.

punk /pʌŋk/ *verb intrans.* *US slang.* E20.
[from PUNK *noun*² & *adjective.*]
Foll. by *out*: back out, withdraw one's support, quit.

punkah /'pʌŋkə, -kɑ:/ *noun.* Also **-ka.** E17.
[Hindi *paṅkhā* fan from Sanskrit *paksaka*, from *pakṣa* wing.]
†**1** = ***punkah-wallah*** below. Only in E17.
2 In the Indian subcontinent, a large fan to cool a room etc.; *spec.* (**a**) a large portable fan made esp. from a palmyra leaf; (**b**) a large swinging cloth fan on a frame worked manually by a cord or by electricity. L17.

Comb.: **punkah-wallah** a servant who works a punkah.

punkie /'pʌŋki/ *noun.* *US local.* M18.
[from alt. of Delaware *pońkwas*, from *pónkw* ashes: see -IE.]
A biting fly or midge common in parts of the north-eastern US.

punkin *noun* see PUMPKIN.

punky /'pʌŋki/ *adjective.* L19.
[from PUNK *noun*² & *adjective* + -Y¹.]
1 Containing or of the nature of punk or touchwood; (of fire) smouldering. *US.* L19.
2 = PUNK *adjective* 2. Chiefly *US.* L19.
3 Of, pertaining to, or resembling punk rock or the subculture or style associated with this; adopting or typifying a punk style; punkish. L20

punnable /'pʌnəb(ə)l/ *adjective.* M19.
[from PUN *verb*² + -ABLE.]
Of a word: able to be punned on or used in a pun.

punner /'pʌnə/ *noun*¹. E17.
[from PUN *verb*¹ + -ER¹.]
A person who or thing which puns earth, rubble, etc.; *spec.* a tool for ramming earth about a post etc.

punner /'pʌnə/ *noun*². L17.
[from PUN *verb*² + -ER¹.]
A person who makes puns; a punster.

punnet /ˈpʌnɪt/ *noun*. E19.
[Perh. dim. of dial. var. of POUND *noun*[1]: see -ET[1].]
A small light basket or container used esp. for strawberries, raspberries, mushrooms, and similar produce.

punny /ˈpʌni/ *adjective*. M20.
[from PUN *noun* + -Y[1].]
Consisting of or characterized by a pun or puns.

punster /ˈpʌnstə/ *noun*. E18.
[from PUN *noun* + -STER.]
A person who makes puns, esp. habitually or skilfully.

punt /pʌnt/ *noun*[1]. OE.
[Latin *ponto(n-)* PONTOON *noun*[1]; readopted in E16 from Middle Low German *punte*, *punto* (Low German *pünte*, *pünto*), Middle Dutch *ponte* (Dutch *pont*), from Latin: cf. PONT *noun*.]
A flat-bottomed shallow boat, broad and square at both ends; *spec*. a long narrow boat of this kind propelled by means of a long pole thrust against the bed of a waterway, and used on inland waterways now mainly for pleasure.
Comb.: **punt-gun** a gun used for shooting waterfowl from a punt; **punt-pole** a long pole used in propelling a punt.

punt /pʌnt/ *noun*[2]. E18.
[French *ponte* or Spanish *ponto* point; in later use from PUNT *verb*[1].]
1 A person who plays against the bank in baccarat, faro, etc. E18.
2 A point in the game of faro. M19.
3 A bet, a gamble. *colloq*. M20.
3 take a punt *Austral.* take a chance or risk.

punt /pʌnt/ *noun*[3]. M19.
[from PUNT *verb*[3].]
FOOTBALL. A kick given to the ball dropped from the hands, before it reaches the ground.
Comb.: **punt-about** a casual session of kicking a ball about for practice in rugby.

punt /pʌnt/ *noun*[4]. M19.
[from (the same root as) PUNTY.]
†**1** = PUNTY *noun* Only in M19.
2 An indentation at the bottom of a glass bottle; = KICK *noun*[2]. M19.

punt /pʊnt/ *noun*[5]. L20.
[Irish *púnt* pound.]
The basic monetary unit of the Republic of Ireland until the introduction of the euro in 2002, equal to 100 Irish pence.

punt /pʌnt/ *verb*[1] *intrans*. E18.
[French *ponter* rel. to *ponte* PUNT *noun*[2].]
1 In baccarat, faro, etc.: lay a stake against the bank. E18.
2 Bet on a horse etc.; gamble, speculate. *colloq*. L19.

punt /pʌnt/ *verb*[2]. E19.
[from PUNT *noun*[1].]
1 *verb trans*. Propel (a punt or other boat) by thrusting a pole against the bed of a waterway. E19.
2 *verb intrans*. Propel a punt etc. by punting; travel in a punt. M19.
3 *verb trans*. Convey in a punt. M19.

📖 **1** E. LONGFORD To me his cleverest trick was to punt a canoe. **2** J. K. JEROME Punting is not as easy as it looks. P. LEVI In summer we punted up rivers, streams, canals.

punt /pʌnt/ *verb*[3]. M19.
[Prob. ult. dial. var. of BUNT *verb*[2].]
1 *verb trans. & intrans.* FOOTBALL. Kick (a ball) after dropping it from the hands and before it reaches the ground. M19.
2 *verb trans*. Strike, hit, knock. *colloq. rare*. L19.

puntal /ˈpʊntɑːl/ *noun*. L16.
[Spanish, from *punto* point.]
A blockhouse or other fortification defending a harbour, orig. & long only *spec*. that of Cadiz in Spain. Usu. in *pl*.

Punt e Mes /pʊnt eɪ ˈmɛs/ *noun phr*. M20.
[Italian (Piedmontese), lit. 'point and a half'.]
(Proprietary name for) a bitter-sweet Italian vermouth, made in Piedmont; a drink of this.

punter /ˈpʌntə/ *noun*[1]. E18.
[from PUNT *verb*[1] + -ER[1].]
1 A player who plays against the bank at baccarat, faro, etc. E18.
2 A person who bets or gambles, esp. on horses or on football pools; a speculator. *colloq*. M19.
3 An accomplice of a criminal or swindler. *slang*. L19.
4 The victim of a swindler or confidence trickster. *slang*. M20.
5 A customer or client, *spec*. of a prostitute. Also, a member of an audience, a spectator, a paying guest; a participant in any activity. *colloq*. M20.

📖 **1** J. ARCHER Seven punters at the blackjack table. **2** J. HONE A punter who has just seen his money romp home on a rank outsider. **5** CLIVE JAMES The kind of modern building that will pack the punters in more efficiently. *Photography* Watching hopeful Stonehenge punters, was the Public Order Surveillance vehicle. *Time Out*: *The Shostakovich Quartet* . . inspiring superlatives from critics and punters alike.

punter /ˈpʌntə/ *noun*[2]. E19.
[from PUNT *noun*[1], *verb*[2] + -ER[1].]
A person who propels a punt; orig. *esp*. a person who goes fishing or shooting in a punt.

punter /ˈpʌntə/ *noun*[3]. L19.
[from PUNT *verb*[3] + -ER[1].]
FOOTBALL. A person who punts the ball.

†**puntilio** *noun* see PUNCTILIO.

puntilla /pʊnˈtiʎa, pʌnˈtɪljə/ *noun*. Pl. **-as** /-as, -əz/. M19.
[Spanish, dim. of *punto* point.]
A dagger used to administer the *coup de grâce* in a bullfight.
■ **puntillero** /puntiˈʎero, pʌntɪˈljɛːrəʊ/ *noun*, pl. **-os** /-ɔs, -əʊz/, a bullfighter's assistant who uses the *puntilla* in a bullfight E20.

punto /ˈpʌntəʊ, *foreign* ˈpunto/ *noun*. In sense 3 also **ponto** /ˈpɒntəʊ/. Pl. **-os** /-əʊz, *foreign* -ɔs/. L16.
[Italian or Spanish = Latin *punctum* POINT *noun*[1].]
†**1** A small point or detail; a particle, a jot. Also, a moment, an instant. L16–E18. ▸**b** A small point of behaviour, (a) punctilio. L16–M18.
†**2** FENCING. A stroke or thrust with the point of the sword or foil. L16–E17.
3 CARDS. In quadrille, the ace of trumps when trumps are either diamonds or hearts. L17.
4 LACE-MAKING. Lace, embroidery. Only in phrs. M19.
4 punto a rilievo /ə rɪˈliːvəʊ, *foreign* a riˈljeːvo/ [Italian = in relief] a type of lace worked in bold relief. **punto in aria** /ɪn ˈɑːrɪə, *foreign* in ˈaːria/ [Italian = in the air] an early form of needlepoint lace orig. made in Venice.

punto banco /ˌpʌntəʊ ˈbaŋkəʊ/ *noun phr*. L20.
[Prob. formed as prec. + BANCO.]
A form of baccarat.

punty /ˈpʌnti/ *noun*. Also **ponty** /ˈpɒnti/. M17.
[French PONTIL.]
GLASS-MAKING. = PONTIL.

puny /ˈpjuːni/ *noun & adjective*. M16.
[Phonetic spelling of PUISNE.]
▸**A** *noun*. †**1** A person younger or more junior than another or others. M16–E17.
†**2** A junior pupil or student, a freshman. M16–L17.
†**3** A novice, a tyro. L16–L17.
4 An inferior, a subordinate; a nobody. Long *arch. rare*. L16.
▸**B** *adjective*. **1** Junior; inferior in rank, subordinate; = PUISNE *adjective* 1. Long *rare*. L16.
†**2** Raw, inexperienced, novice. L16–E18.
3 Of small size, force, or importance; weak, feeble; diminutive, tiny; (of a person or animal) undersized and weakly. E17. ▸**b** In bad health; ailing. *US dial*. M19.
†**4** Later, more recent; = PUISNE *adjective* 2. E–M17.

📖 **3** B. TARKINGTON He was so puny that nobody thought he would live. I. MURDOCH Our love was puny, not powerful enough to live on. K. AMIS So he's not the puny little worm you'd taken him for.

PUO *abbreviation*.
Pyrexia of unknown origin.

pup /pʌp/ *noun*. L16.
[Back-form. from PUPPY *noun*, as if a dim. in -Y[6].]
1 a A stupid, arrogant, or unpleasant young man. L16. ▸**b** A youthful or inexperienced person, a beginner. *colloq*. (chiefly *N. Amer.*). L19.
2 A young dog, a whelp, a young puppy. L18.
3 A young animal of certain other animals, as the wolf, seal, rat, etc. E19.
4 A little creek; a stream which flows into a creek. L19.
5 A small fast aeroplane used in the war of 1914–18. *Military slang*. E20.
6 A four-wheeled trailer drawn by a lorry or other vehicle. *US slang*. M20.

📖 **2** *Dogworld* Whelping and rearing 10 pups involved the usual trauma, triumphs, and . . energy. **3** *Orcadian* 10,000-plus . . pups had been culled.

Phrases: **be a pup**, **be only a pup** *Austral. colloq.* (of the day or night) have scarcely begun, be not far advanced. **buy a pup** be swindled. **in pup** (of a bitch) pregnant. ***mucky pup***: see MUCKY *adjective* 1. **sell a person a pup** swindle a person, esp. by selling something on its supposed prospective value. **with pup** = *in pup* above.
Comb.: **pupfish** any of various small cyprinodont fishes of the genus *Cyprinodon* found in fresh or brackish water in the deserts of the south-western US and northern Mexico, several species of which are confined to single pools; **pup joint** OIL INDUSTRY a piece of drill pipe of less than the standard length; **pup-tent** (orig. *US* MILITARY) a small tent or bivouac, a dog-tent.

pup /pʌp/ *verb trans. & intrans.* Infl. **-pp-**. E18.
[from (the same root as) prec.]
Give birth to (a pup or pups); litter.

pupa /ˈpjuːpə/ *noun*. Pl. **pupae** /ˈpjuːpiː/. L18.
[mod. Latin from Latin, = girl, doll.]
ENTOMOLOGY. **1** An insect in the distinct, usually quiescent, instar which in complete metamorphosis is transitional between the larva and adult; a chrysalis; (now *rare*) any pre-adult resting form of an insect. L18.
2 A stage in the development of some other invertebrates, as copepod and cirripede crustaceans, and holothurians. L19.
Comb.: **pupa-case** the horny cuticle of a pupa.
■ **pupal** *adjective* M19.

puparium /pjuːˈpɛːrɪəm/ *noun*. Pl. **-ria** /-rɪə/. E19.
[mod. Latin, formed as PUPA + -ARIUM, after *herbarium* etc.]
ENTOMOLOGY. The hardened last larval skin which encloses a later stage in some insects, *esp*. that enclosing the pupa in higher Diptera; a pupa so enclosed.
■ **puparial** *adjective* E20. **pupariate** *verb intrans*. form a puparium L20. **pupari'ation** *noun* the formation of a puparium L20.

pupate /pjuːˈpeɪt/ *verb intrans*. L19.
[from PUPA + -ATE[3].]
Become a pupa or chrysalis.
■ **pupation** *noun* the formation of a pupa L19.

pupiform /ˈpjuːpɪfɔːm/ *adjective*. *rare*. M19.
[from PUPA + -I- + -FORM.]
Having the form or appearance of a pupa.

pupil /ˈpjuːpɪl, -p(ə)l/ *noun*[1]. LME.
[Old & mod. French *pupille* masc. & fem. or its source Latin *pupillus*, *-illa* orphan, ward, dim. (on *pupulus*, *-ula*) of *pupus* boy, *pupa* girl.]
1 An orphan who is a minor and consequently a ward (now *rare*); SCOTS LAW a person below the age of puberty (a boy under 14 or girl under 12). LME.
2 A person being taught by another; *esp*. a schoolchild or student in relation to a teacher. M16. ▸**b** LAW. A trainee barrister undergoing his or her pupillage. M19.

📖 **2** JULIETTE HUXLEY My mother was a born teacher, her pupils adored her. S. QUINN He became a favourite pupil of the Zen master.

Comb.: **pupil age** the age or period during which one is a pupil; **pupil barrister** = sense 2b above; **pupil-master** (*a*) *arch. rare* a schoolmaster; (*b*) LAW a barrister to whom a trainee barrister is apprenticed in pupillage; **pupil-room** at Eton College, the room in which a tutor teaches; the work done there by a pupil; **pupil teacher** *Hist.* a boy or girl preparing to be a teacher, whose time was divided between teaching younger pupils and being taught by the head-teacher or at a separate establishment; **pupil-teacher** *adjective* designating the relation between pupils and teachers (***pupil–teacher ratio***, the number of pupils to each teacher); **pupil-teachership** *Hist.* the post or office of a pupil teacher.
■ **pupildom** *noun* (*rare*) the condition of a pupil M19. **pupilless** /-l-l-/ *adjective*[1] (*rare*) without pupils M19. **pupilship** *noun* the condition or position of being a pupil L16.

pupil /ˈpjuːpɪl, -p(ə)l/ *noun*[2]. Also (earlier) †**pupilla**. LME.
[Old & mod. French *pupille* or Latin *pupilla*, dim. of *pupa* girl, doll, pupil of the eye (so called from the tiny images visible in the eye).]
The opening in the centre of the iris of the eye, through which light passes to reach the retina.

📖 J. D. MACDONALD Her eyes were narrow, the pupils small.

■ **pupilled** *adjective* having a central spot in the ocellus (of a butterfly's wing or bird's feather) E19. **pupilless** /-l-l-/ *adjective*[2] (of the eye) having no pupil M19.

pupilage *noun*, **pupilar** *adjective*, etc., vars. of PUPILLAGE, PUPILLAR[1], etc.

†**pupilla** *noun* see PUPIL *noun*[2].

pupillage /ˈpjuːpɪlɪdʒ/ *noun*. Also **pupilage**. L16.
[from PUPIL *noun*[1] + -AGE.]
1 The condition of being a minor or ward; the period of minority or wardship. L16.
2 The condition or position of being a pupil or scholar; pupilship. M17. ▸**b** LAW. Apprenticeship to a member of the Bar, qualifying a barrister to practise independently. M19.

pupillar /ˈpjuːpɪlə/ *adjective*. Also **pupilar**. M16.
[Latin *pupillaris*: see PUPILLARY *adjective*[1], -AR[1].]
= PUPILLARY *adjective*[1].

pupillarity /pjuːpɪˈlarɪti/ *noun*. Also **pupilarity**. M16.
[Old & mod. French *pupillarité* from medieval Latin, from Latin *pupillaris*: see next, -ITY.]
SCOTS LAW. The state of being below the age of puberty; the period during which a person remains in this state.

pupillary /ˈpjuːpɪləri/ *adjective*[1]. Also **pupilary**. E17.
[French *pupillaire* or Latin *pupillaris*, from *pupillus*, *-illa*: see PUPIL *noun*[1], -ARY[2].]
1 SCOTS LAW. Of or pertaining to a person in pupillarity. E17.
2 Belonging to a pupil or scholar. M19.

pupillary /ˈpjuːpɪləri/ *adjective*[2]. Also **pupilary**. L18.
[from Latin *pupilla* PUPIL *noun*[2] + -ARY[2].]
Of or pertaining to the pupil of the eye.

pupillize /ˈpjuːpɪlʌɪz/ *verb intrans. & trans.* Now *rare.* Also **pupilize**, **-ise**. E19.
[from PUPIL *noun*¹ + -IZE.]
Teach a pupil or pupils; tutor pupils.

pupillography /pjuːpɪˈlɒgrəfi/ *noun.* M20.
[from PUPIL *noun*² + -O- + -GRAPHY.]
MEDICINE. The recording and analysis of the size and reactions of the pupils of the eyes, esp. in order to determine neurological disorders.
■ ˈ**pupillogram** *noun* a record obtained in pupillography M20. ˈ**pupillograph** *noun* an apparatus used for pupillography M20. ˌ**pupilloˈgraphic** *adjective* M20. ˌ**pupilloˈgraphically** *adverb* M20.

pupillometer /pjuːpɪˈlɒmɪtə/ *noun.* Also (*rare*) **-ilo-**. L19.
[from PUPIL *noun*² + -OMETER.]
An instrument for measuring the size of the pupil of the eye.
■ **pupilloˈmetric** *adjective* M20. **pupilloˈmetrics** *noun* the branch of science that deals with psychological influences on the size of the pupil M20. **pupillometry** *noun* the measurement of the pupil of the eye L19.

pupiparous /pjuːˈpɪp(ə)rəs/ *adjective.* E19.
[from PUPA + -I- + -PAROUS.]
ENTOMOLOGY. Reproducing by the production of young ready to pupate, as certain dipterans.

puppet /ˈpʌpɪt/ *noun.* M16.
[Later form of POPPET *noun.*]
1 a A usu. small figure representing a human being; a child's doll; = POPPET *noun* 1b. Now *rare* or *obsolete.* M16. ▸†**b** An idolatrous image; an idol; = POPPET *noun* 1c. M16–E19.
2 a A (usu. small) figure of a human, animal, etc., made to move for entertainment by any of various means of manual control or (formerly) clockwork etc.; *spec.* (**a**) a figure with jointed limbs, moved from above by strings or wires, a marionette; (**b**) a figure supported and moved from below by rods; (**c**) a figure made to be fitted over and moved by a hand, finger, etc. Also (*transf.*), any of the characters in a puppet-show. M16. ▸**b** *fig.* A person, usu. one in a prominent position, whose actions appear to be his or her own, but are actually controlled by another. Also, a country or State nominally independent but actually under the control of another power. L16. ▸†**c** An actor, esp. in a pantomime. L16–M17.
3 A dressed-up empty-headed person, esp. a woman. L16.
†**4** A little dog; a puppy. Only in 17.
5 A lathe-head. Cf. POPPET *noun* 4. L17.

📖 **2a** R. P. JHABVALA He hops along twitching and jigging like a puppet. B. BAINBRIDGE She collapsed . . like a puppet whose strings have been cut. ***finger-puppet***, ***glove puppet***, ***rod puppet***, ***shadow puppet***, etc. **b** BROWNING God's puppets, best and worst, Are we.

Attrib. & comb.: In the senses 'that is a puppet, that is controlled by another', as ***puppet administration***, ***puppet leader***, ***puppet State***, etc., 'of a puppet or puppets', as ***puppet-maker***, ***puppet-theatre***, etc. Special combs., as †**puppet-clack** = *POPPET-valve*; **puppet-master** the manager or operator of a puppet-show, a puppeteer; *fig.* a person who is in control esp. of another or others; **puppet-play** (**a**) a play or dramatic performance acted with puppets; (**b**) the playing or acting of puppets; **puppet-player** a person who manages or puts on a puppet-play; **puppet-show** a show or exhibition of puppets; *esp.* a dramatic performance with or of puppets; a puppet-play; **puppet-showman** a man who exhibits or manages a puppet-show; **puppet-valve** (now *rare*) = *POPPET-valve*.
■ **puppeˈteer** *noun* a person who operates a puppet or puppets; *spec.* a person who creates, manages, or puts on puppet-shows: M20. **puppetish** *adjective* (*rare*) pertaining to or of the nature of a puppet M16.

puppetry /ˈpʌpɪtri/ *noun.* E16.
[from PUPPET *noun* + -RY.]
1 Mimicry or representation like that of puppets; masquerade, make-believe; artificial or unreal action; *spec.* idolatrous or superstitious observances. E16.
2 Puppet-play; inferior dramatic action. Also, the art or process of making puppets, putting on puppet-shows, etc. E17.
3 Something resembling a puppet or set of puppets, *esp.* an unreal or artificial character or set of characters in literary fiction. E17.

Puppis /ˈpʌpɪs/ *noun.* M19.
[Latin *puppis* POOP *noun*¹.]
(The name of) a constellation of the southern hemisphere, lying partly in the Milky Way south of Canis Major and orig. part of Argo; the Poop.

puppy /ˈpʌpi/ *noun.* L15.
[Old French *popée*, (also mod.) *poupée* doll, lay figure, (contextually) toy, plaything, from Proto-Romance, ult. from Latin *pup(p)a*: see POPPET *noun.* Cf. PUP *noun.*]
†**1** A small dog used as a lady's pet or plaything; a toy dog. L15–M17.
2 a A young dog, a whelp. L16. ▸**b** A young seal Also (more fully ***puppy shark***), a young shark. L19.
3 a A conceited, arrogant, or empty-headed young man. L16. ▸†**b** A sexually promiscuous or arrogant woman. L16–L17.
4 = PUPPET 2a. Long *obsolete* exc. *Scot. & dial.* M17.

📖 **2a** P. L. FERMOR Two sheepdogs and their puppies . . bounded forward in greeting. **3a** *Echoes* The impudent puppy . . can't resist pointing out that . . England has been less receptive.

Comb.: **puppy-dog** *nursery* = PUPPY *noun* 1, 2; **puppy-fat** plumpness in a child or adolescent which is usu. outgrown; **puppy foot** *US slang* a card of the club suit, *esp.* the ace of clubs; †**puppy-headed** *adjective* (*rare*, Shakes.) stupid; **puppy-love** = *calf-love* s.v. CALF *noun*¹; **puppy-tooth** a small dog-tooth or houndstooth check; **puppy walker** a person who walks and begins the training of young hounds and guide dogs.
■ †**pupplily** *adjective* characteristic of a puppy; resembling a puppy: L17–L18. **puppydom** *noun* (**a**) = PUPPYHOOD; (**b**) puppies collectively: M19. **puppyhood** *noun* the state of being a puppy or young dog; the early period of a dog's life: M18. **puppyish** *adjective* of the nature or character of a puppy, like a puppy L18. **puppyishly** *adverb* (*rare*) E19. **puppyishness** *noun* M20. **puppyism** *noun* the character, style, or manners of a puppy; *esp.* impertinent conceit, affectation: L18.

puppy /ˈpʌpi/ *verb intrans. & trans.* L16.
[from prec.]
Give birth to (a puppy or puppies); litter, pup.

pupton /ˈpʌptən/ *noun.* E18.
[French †*poulpeton*, †*poupeton*, perh. ult. from Latin *pulpa* PULP *noun.* Cf. PAUPIETTE.]
COOKERY. A dish made with fruit or meat and other ingredients, baked in a slow oven.

pupunha /pʊˈpʊnjə/ *noun.* M19.
[Portuguese from Tupi *púpuña.*]
More fully ***pupunha palm***. A S. American palm tree, *Bactris gasipaes*, with large red and yellow fruit which is edible when cooked. Also called ***peach-palm***.

pur- /pəː/ *prefix* (no longer productive).
[Anglo-Norman form of Old French *por-*, *pur-*, (also mod.) *pour-*, from Latin *por-*, *pro-*: see PRO-¹.]
= PRO-¹, in words adopted from Anglo-Norman, as ***purchase***, ***purloin***, ***purpose***, ***pursue***, etc.

†**puralé** *noun.* Also **-lee**. ME.
[Anglo-Norman *purale(e*: see PURLIEU.]
LAW. **1** A perambulation made to determine the boundaries of a county, district, etc.; *esp.* one made to ascertain the boundaries of a royal forest and to disafforest encroaching lands. ME–M17.
2 The piece of land between the wider bounds of a forest and the restricted bounds as fixed by perambulation. Also = PURLIEU 1. ME–E18.

Purana /pʊˈrɑːnə/ *noun.* L17.
[Sanskrit *purāṇa* belonging to former times, from *purā* formerly.]
Any of a class of sacred works in Sanskrit, chiefly in verse, containing the mythology and traditional lore of the Hindus.
■ ***Puranic*** *adjective & noun* (**a**) *adjective* of or pertaining to the Puranas; (**b**) *noun* a Puranic work or author; a believer in the Puranas: E19.

purau /ˈpuːraʊ/ *noun.* Also **purao**. L18.
[Tahitian.]
A small tree, *Hibiscus tiliaceus*, of the mallow family, native to tropical coasts; the light wood or fibrous bast of this tree. Also called ***mahoe***.

Purbeck /ˈpəːbɛk/ *adjective & noun.* M18.
[A peninsula on the Dorset coast.]
▸**A** *adjective.* Designating stone quarried at Purbeck, something made of this stone, or the geological formation there typically developed. M18.
Purbeck beds GEOLOGY = PURBECKIAN *noun.* **Purbeck marble** any of the finer kinds of Purbeck stone, used in ornamental architecture. **Purbeck stone** a hard limestone obtained from Purbeck, used in building and paving.
▸**B** *noun.* **1** = ***Purbeck stone*** above. Also, a paving-stone made of this. M18.
2 Any of the Purbeck strata. L19.
■ **Purˈbeckian** *adjective & noun* (**a**) *adjective* of or pertaining to Purbeck, or the Purbeck beds; (**b**) *noun* a series of strata or a stage in the British Upper Jurassic and Lower Cretaceous, above the Portlandian and below the Wealden: L19.

purblind /ˈpəːblʌɪnd/ *adjective.* Orig. two words. ME.
[from PURE *adverb* (with assim. to PUR-) + BLIND *adjective.*]
1 Orig. (*rare*), completely blind. Now, having impaired or defective vision; dim-sighted; partially-sighted. ME. ▸**b** *fig.* Of a thing: dimly lit. E18.
2 *fig.* Having imperfect perception or discernment; obtuse, dull, dim-witted. M16.

📖 **1** M. E. BRADDON Old Nanon the cook, purblind, stone-deaf. **2** *New Yorker* A Victorian despot, purblind to the feelings of his wife and children.

■ **purblindly** *adverb* (*rare*) M19. **purblindness** *noun* M16.

purblind /pəːˈblʌɪnd/ *verb trans.* L16.
[from prec.]
Make purblind; impair the sight or perception of.

Purcellian /pəːˈsɛlɪən/ *adjective & noun.* L19.
[from *Purcell* (see below) + -IAN.]
▸**A** *adjective.* Of, pertaining to, or characteristic of the first English opera composer Henry Purcell (*c* 1659–95), or his style of composition, esp. distinguished by a sensitive and effective setting of words to music and a wide emotional range. L19.
▸**B** *noun.* A person who admires or imitates the style of Purcell. M20.

purchasable /ˈpəːtʃɪsəb(ə)l/ *adjective & noun.* Also **-aseable**. E17.
[from PURCHASE *verb* + -ABLE.]
▸**A** *adjective.* Able to be purchased. E17.
▸**B** *noun.* A purchasable item. L20.
■ **purchasaˈbility** *noun* E20.

purchase /ˈpəːtʃɪs/ *noun.* ME.
[Anglo-Norman *purchas*, Old French *por-*, formed as next. Later also directly from the verb.]
▸**I** The action or an act of purchasing.
†**1** The action of hunting; the chasing and catching of prey. Also, pillage, plunder, capture. ME–E18.
†**2** An attempt to obtain or effect something; endeavour; machination; contrivance. ME–M16.
†**3** The action or process of obtaining or acquiring something for oneself in any way; acquisition, gain. ME–L16.
4 a The action of making one's living or gaining one's sustenance, esp. in an irregular way. *obsolete* exc. *Scot.* LME. ▸†**b** A means of livelihood; an occupation. L16–M17.
5 LAW. The acquisition of property, esp. land, by personal action and not by inheritance or descent. LME.
6 *spec.* **a** Acquisition by payment of money or some other valuable equivalent; the action or an act of buying. L16. ▸**b** *Hist.* The action or system of buying commissions in the army; payment made for an appointment in the commissioned ranks. L18.
7 *fig.* Acquisition by the expenditure of effort, suffering, etc. M17.

📖 **6a** F. KAPLAN The purchase of an additional . . piece of land.

▸**II** The product of purchasing; something purchased.
†**8 a** That which is obtained or acquired; gains, winnings; *esp.* spoil, booty, plunder; *spec.* a prize or booty taken by a privateer. ME–E18. ▸**b** An advantage gained or possessed. LME–L17.
9 The annual return or rent from land. L16.
10 a A thing purchased or bought. L16. ▸**b** A bargain of a specified kind. Now *rare* or *obsolete.* E17.

📖 **10a** P. H. JOHNSON They unpacked their parcels and studied each purchase.

▸**III** Senses from PURCHASE *verb* 7.
11 A hold or position on something for advantageously applying power; the advantage gained by such application. E18.
12 A device by means of which power may be usefully applied or increased; *esp.* (NAUTICAL) a rope, a pulley, a windlass. E18.
13 *fig.* A position of advantage for accomplishing something; a means by which one's power or influence is increased. L18.

📖 **11** B. ENGLAND Their boots found no purchase in the scrub. *Oxford Journal* Cutting gear to get a purchase on the . . tangled metal. **13** H. P. LIDDON The will has a . . strong purchase over the understanding in matters of belief.

Phrases: **at five years' purchase**, **at seven years' purchase**, etc., at a cost of five, seven, etc., years' rent. **compulsory purchase** the legally enforced purchase, usu. by a local authority, of privately owned land or property. **not worth an hour's purchase**, **not worth a day's purchase**, etc., not likely to last an hour, day, etc. ***offshore purchase***: see OFFSHORE *adjective*.
Comb.: **purchase-money** the sum for which anything is or may be purchased; **purchase price** the price at which something is put on sale; **purchase tax** *Hist.* a tax levied at wholesale, between 1940 and 1973, on saleable goods at a higher rate on luxuries than on essentials.

purchase /ˈpəːtʃɪs/ *verb.* ME.
[Anglo-Norman *purchacer*, Old French *pourchacier* seek to obtain, procure, formed as PUR- + *chacier* (mod. *chasser*) CHASE *verb*¹.]
†**1** *verb trans.* Try to obtain or bring about; contrive or plan (esp. something unpleasant or wicked). (Foll. by *to*, *do*, *to*, *for*, a person.) ME–M16.
†**2** *verb refl. & intrans.* Exert oneself for the attainment of something; endeavour; strive. ME–L17.
†**3 a** *verb trans.* Bring about, effect; procure. (Foll. by *to*, *for*, a person.) ME–L17. ▸**b** *verb intrans.* Arrange, provide. (Foll. by *for.*) LME–E16.
4 *verb trans.* †**a** Obtain for oneself, acquire; gain. ME–E18. ▸**b** Obtain as permission from a recognized authority (a brief, licence, etc.). *obsolete* exc. *Hist.* ME.
5 *spec.* **a** *verb trans.* LAW. Acquire (property, esp. land) other than by inheritance or descent; (now *arch. rare*) gain by conquest in war. ME. ▸†**b** *verb intrans.* Acquire possessions; become rich. ME–E17.
6 a *verb trans.* Acquire by payment; be an equivalent price for; = BUY *verb* 1, 1b. LME. ▸**b** *verb trans. fig.* Obtain in exchange for something else or by the expenditure of effort, suffering, etc.; = BUY *verb* 2. LME. ▸**c** *verb intrans.* Make a purchase or purchases; = BUY *verb* 7. *rare.* M19.

7 NAUTICAL. Haul in (a rope or cable); *spec.* haul up (an anchor etc.) by means of a pulley, lever, etc. Cf. PURCHASE *noun* III. **M16.**

> **4b purchase a writ** LAW obtain and issue a writ; commence an action. **6a** G. B. SHAW Such pleasures as money can purchase. R. DAHL I purchased a motor car. **b** F. BURNEY Dearly . . do I purchase experience! E. A. FREEMAN The victory was purchased by the death of Rhiwallon. **7** F. MARRYAT Purchase the anchor I could not; I therefore slipped the cable.

purchaseable *adjective & noun* var. of PURCHASABLE.

purchaser /ˈpəːtʃɪsə/ *noun.* **ME.**
[Anglo-Norman *purchasour*, Old French *porchaceor, pourchaseur*, from *pourchacier*: see prec., -OUR, -ER².]
†**1** A person who acquires or aims to acquire possessions **ME–L16.** ▸**b** = CAVER *noun* 1. **M16–M18.**
2 LAW. A person who acquires property, esp. land, other than by inheritance or descent. **ME.**
3 A person who purchases something for money; a buyer. **E17.**

> **3** *Consumer Reports* Many prospective purchasers want an easy-to-operate device.

purchasing /ˈpəːtʃɪsɪŋ/ *verbal noun.* **ME.**
[from PURCHASE *verb* + -ING¹.]
The action of PURCHASE *verb.*
Comb.: **purchasing power** the (potential) amount which a sum of money, investment, etc., can purchase; the financial ability of an individual to make purchases; ***purchasing power parity***, the quotient between the purchasing power of money in two different countries.

purdah /ˈpəːdə/ *noun.* **E19.**
[Persian & Urdu *parda* veil, curtain.]
1 In the Indian subcontinent and SE Asia, a curtain, a veil; *esp.* one used to screen women from men or strangers. **E19.**
2 A system in certain Muslim and Hindu societies, esp. in the Indian subcontinent, of screening women from men or strangers by means of a veil or curtain. **M19.** ▸**b** *transf.* Seclusion; (medical) isolation or quarantine; secrecy. Chiefly in ***in purdah, into purdah, out of purdah.*** **E20.**
Comb.: **purdah glass** opaque glass; **purdah party** a party held for purdah women; **purdah woman** a woman wearing a purdah or conforming to the system of purdah.
▪ **purdahed** /ˈpəːdəd/ *adjective* screened by (a) purdah; *transf.* secluded, secret: **M19.**

Purdey /ˈpəːdi/ *noun.* **M19.**
[James *Purdey* (1816–68), founder of the firm of manufacturers.]
(Proprietary name for) a type of firearm.

pure /pjʊə/ *adjective, adverb, & noun.* In sense C.3 also **puer. ME.**
[Old & mod. French *pur*, fem. *pure* from Latin *purus*.]
▸ **A** *adjective.* **I** Of something physical.
1 a Not mixed with anything else, not adulterated. (Cf. sense B.1 below.) **ME.** ▸**b** Of a sound: not discordant, perfectly in tune. **L19.** ▸**c** Of a group of plants, esp. trees: consisting of only one species. **L19.**

> **1a** J. TYNDALL The snow was of the purest white. *Maclean's Magazine* A . . pantdress in pure wool. C. THOMAS Wheat wine, almost pure alcohol. B. CORNWELL Gorgets of pure gold.

▸ **II** Of something non-physical (and extended senses).
2 a Free from anything not properly pertaining to it, without foreign or extraneous matter, homogeneous. **ME.** ▸**b** LAW. Without any condition attached, absolute, unconditional. Now *rare* or *obsolete.* **LME.** ▸**c** Of unmixed origin or descent. **L15.** ▸**d** Restricted to the essential matter of one particular subject of study, not concerned with related subjects or topics; *esp.* dealing with the theory of a subject as distinct from its practical application (freq. opp. ***applied***). Also, of or pertaining to a form of art considered as absolute, essential, or objective, as distinct from representational, didactic, or commercial. **M17.** ▸**e** LOGIC. Designating or pertaining to a proposition in which the predicate is affirmed or denied of the subject without a qualification (opp. ***modal***); (of a syllogism) containing a pure proposition as its premiss. Now *rare* or *obsolete.* **M17.** ▸**f** GRAMMAR. (Of a vowel) not joined with another in a diphthong; (of a consonant) not accompanied by another. **M17.**
3 a Taken by itself, mere, simple (with intensive force), nothing short of, absolute, sheer. Freq. in ***pure and simple*** below. **ME.** ▸**b** Real, genuine. Long *obsolete* exc. *Canad. dial.* & in ***the pure quill*** below. **ME.**
4 a Not debased or corrupt; conforming absolutely to a standard of quality or style; faultless, correct. **ME.** ▸**b** Morally undefiled, innocent, sincere. **ME.** ▸**c** Sexually undefiled, chaste. **ME.** ▸†**d** Puritan, puritanical. *derog.* **L16–L18.** ▸**e** Ritually clean. Long *rare* or *obsolete.* **E17.**
5 Fine, excellent, nice. *slang* (now *rare* or *obsolete*). **M17.**

> **2a** J. EDWARDS Castellio hath turned the whole Bible into pure, terse, elegant Latin. G. J. ADLER The transition from . . poetry in monkish Latin to . . poetry in the pure Romansh. **c** C. ISHERWOOD One drop of pure Russian blood in my . . veins. *Watsonia* On account of introgressive hybridisation there is no genetically pure *R. reptans* . . in the British Isles. **d** OED He is a pure physicist, he does not know chemistry. ***pure mathematics, pure science***, etc. **3a** M. PATTISON His delay . . was due to pure procrastination. J. BUCHAN A lot of pure nonsense. J. F. LEHMANN It was pure luck that Chamson's piece had come into my hands. **4a** LD MACAULAY They had been oppressed, and oppression had kept them a pure body. C. PEBODY His taste, if severe, was pure. **b** MILTON Nature her self, though pure of sinful thought. I. WATTS How should the sons of Adam's race Be pure before their God? **c** SHAKES. *1 Hen. VI* And yet, forsooth, she is a virgin pure.

Phrases: ***in one's pure naturals***: see NATURAL *noun* 2b. ***of the purest water***: see WATER *noun* 10b. ***pure and pute***: see PUTE. **pure and simple** (following a noun) taken absolutely by itself, nothing short of. ***pure pute***: see PUTE. **the pure quill** *N. Amer. colloq.* the genuine article, the real thing.

▸ **B** *adverb.* **1** With no admixture, esp. of any other colour. (Not always clearly distinguishable from the adjective) **ME.**
2 Absolutely, entirely, thoroughly; just; really. *obsolete* exc. *US dial.* **ME.**
3 Simply; rightly, chastely. *poet. rare.* **LME.**

> **1** J. SYLVESTER The Lily (first) pure-whitest Flow'r of any.

▸ **C** *noun.* **1** That which is pure, purity. *poet.* **LME.**
2 A pure person. *slang. rare.* **E19.**
3 TANNING (now *Hist.*). Canine or other faeces used for lye in which to steep hides; lye made with such faeces. **M19.**

> **1** TENNYSON The mask of pure worn by this court.

Special collocations & comb. (of adjective & adverb): **pure-blood** a pure-bred animal. **pure-blooded** *adjective* (of an animal) of unmixed ancestry, pure-bred. **pure-bred** *noun & adjective* (an animal) bred from parents of the same breed or variety; (an animal) of unmixed ancestry. **pure-breeding** *adjective* producing genetically similar progeny. **pure culture** MICROBIOLOGY a culture in which only one strain or clone is present. **pure line** GENETICS (an individual belonging to) an inbred line of descent. ***pure merino***: see MERINO 1b. ***pure milk***: see MILK *noun.* ***pure tone***: see TONE *noun* 2b.

pure /pjʊə/ *verb trans.* In sense 2 also **puer. ME.**
[Old French *purer* from medieval Latin *purare* refine (ore, metal), from Latin *purus* PURE *adjective.*]
†**1** Make pure; cleanse, purify (*lit.* & *fig.*). **ME–M17.**
2 TANNING (now *Hist.*). Steep (hide) in lye made with canine or other faeces. **M19.**

purée /ˈpjʊəreɪ, *as noun also foreign* pyre (*pl. same*)/ *noun & verb.* **E18.**
[Old & mod. French, in form fem. pa. pple of *purer*: see prec. Cf. PORRAY.]
▸ **A** *noun.* A pulp of vegetables, fruit, etc., reduced to the consistency of cream. **E18.**
▸ **B** *verb trans.* Reduce (food) to a purée. **M20.**

> A. TULL Foods . . should be puréed so that the baby can swallow them without choking.

purely /ˈpjʊəli/ *adverb & adjective.* **ME.**
[from PURE *adjective* + -LY².]
▸ **A** *adverb.* **I** In non-physical senses.
1 Simply, exclusively, solely. Also (now chiefly *US dial.*) thoroughly, completely. **ME.** ▸†**b** Really, genuinely. Only in **ME.** ▸**c** LAW. Absolutely, unconditionally. Now *rare* or *obsolete.* **LME.**
2 Faultlessly; innocently, chastely. *arch.* **LME.**
3 Finely, excellently. *slang* (now *rare* or *obsolete*). **L17.**
▸ **II** In physical senses.
4 Without admixture of anything else, without adulteration. **E16.** ▸†**b** So as to cleanse. **L16–L17.**
▸ **B** *pred. adjective.* In good health, well. Chiefly *dial.* **L18.**

pureness /ˈpjʊənɪs/ *noun.* **LME.**
[from PURE *adjective* + -NESS.]
The quality of being pure; purity.

pur et simple /pyr e sɛ̃ːpl/ *adjectival phr.* **M19.**
[French.]
= ***pure and simple*** s.v. PURE *adjective.*

purfle /ˈpəːf(ə)l/ *noun.* **LME.**
[Old French *porfil*, from *porfiler*: see next.]
1 An embroidered border or fur trimming of a garment. *arch.* **LME.** ▸**b** An inlaid ornamental border on the back or belly of a violin etc. **E18.**
†**2** A drawing of something in outline; a profile. Only in **17.**

purfle /ˈpəːf(ə)l/ *verb trans.* **ME.**
[Old French *porfiler* from Proto-Romance, formed as PRO-¹ + Latin *filum* thread (cf. PROFILE *verb*), perh. partly also from the noun.]
Usu. in *pass.* **1** Decorate with a purfle (*arch.*); *esp.* decorate (a garment) with an embroidered border or fur trimming. **ME.** ▸**b** Ornament, beautify. **LME.** ▸†**c** Provide with an edge or border of a distinctive colour or kind. **M16–M17.**
2 ARCHITECTURE. Ornament (the edge or ridge of a structure). Chiefly foll. by *with*. Cf. earlier PURFLED *adjective* 3. **M19.**
▪ **purfling** *noun* (*a*) the action or result of purfling; (*b*) an example of this, a purfle: **LME.**

purfled /ˈpəːf(ə)ld/ *adjective.* **LME.**
[from PURFLE *noun, verb*: see -ED², -ED¹.]
1 Provided with a purfle, that has been purfled. **LME.** ▸**b** Of a person: wearing purfled clothes. **LME.**
2 HERALDRY. Garnished. Also, purflewe. **M16.**
3 ARCHITECTURE. Of the edge or ridge of a structure: ornamented. **E19.**

purflewe /ˈpəːfljuː/ *adjective.* Now *rare* or *obsolete.* **M16.**
[Prob. ult. from PURFLE *verb* or *noun.*]
HERALDRY. Having a bordure of a fur.

purga /pʊəˈgɑː, ˈpʊəgə/ *noun.* **L19.**
[Russian.]
In the eastern Asiatic tundra, a violent blizzard of fine snow. Cf. BURAN.

purgation /pəːˈgeɪʃ(ə)n/ *noun.* **LME.**
[Old & mod. French, or Latin *purgatio(n-)*, from *purgat-* pa. ppl stem of *purgare* PURGE *verb*: see -ATION.]
1 The action of making physically clean by the removal of dirt or waste matter. **LME.**
2 Moral or spiritual purification; *spec.* in the Roman Catholic Church, the purification of a soul in purgatory. **LME.**
3 a The expulsion of ingested material from the body. Now only, the evacuation of the bowels, esp. as a result of taking a laxative. **LME.** ▸†**b** A laxative. Also, an emetic. **LME–L17.** ▸†**c** Menstruation; in *pl.* the menstrual discharge. Also, the lochia. **M16–M18.**
4 Ceremonial cleansing from defilement. Now *rare.* **LME.**
5 LAW (now *Hist.*). The action of clearing oneself from accusation or suspicion by an oath or ordeal. **LME.**

purgative /ˈpəːgətɪv/ *adjective & noun.* **LME.**
[Old & mod. French *purgatif, -ive* or late Latin *purgativus*, from Latin *purgat-*: see prec., -IVE.]
▸ **A** *adjective.* **1** MEDICINE. That causes expulsion of ingested material from the body. Now only, strongly laxative. **LME.**
2 †**a** Of or pertaining to purgatory. Only in **E17.** ▸**b** Serving to purify, esp. morally or spiritually. **L17.**
▸ **B** *noun.* **1** A purgative medicine. Now only, a powerful laxative. **LME.**
2 A thing that serves to purify. **E18.**

purgator /pəːˈgeɪtə/ *noun. rare.* **E18.**
[Late Latin, from Latin *purgat-*: see PURGATION, -OR.]
A purifier.

purgatorial /pəːgəˈtɔːrɪəl/ *adjective.* **L15.**
[from late Latin *purgatorius* or directly from PURGATORY *noun*: see -AL¹.]
Of a spiritually cleansing or purifying quality; of, pertaining to, or of the nature of purgatory.

purgatorian /pəːgəˈtɔːrɪən/ *noun & adjective. rare.* **M16.**
[from next + -AN.]
▸ **A** *noun.* A believer in purgatory. **M16.**
▸ **B** *adjective.* Relating to purgatory; purgatorial. **E17.**

purgatory /ˈpəːgət(ə)ri/ *noun.* **ME.**
[Anglo-Norman *purgatorie*, Old & mod. French *purgatoire* from medieval Latin *purgatorium*, use as noun of neut. of late Latin *purgatorius* purifying, from Latin *purgat-*: see PURGATION, -ORY¹.]
1 A condition or supposed place of spiritual cleansing, *spec.* in the Roman Catholic Church, in which the souls of those who have died in the grace of God suffer for a time to expiate venial sins or to atone for mortal sins for which they have received absolution; the duration of this condition. **ME.** ▸†**b** Expiation; an instance or means of this. **ME–M17.**
2 *fig.* A place or state of temporary suffering or expiation; the duration of this state. **LME.**
3 A cavern; (a flowing through) a narrow steep-sided gorge. Chiefly in place-names. *US local.* **M18.**
4 A space beneath a fireplace, covered with a grating, as a receptacle for ashes; a grating covering such a space. *dial.* **M19.**

> **1** D. LODGE Purgatory was a kind of penitential transit camp on the way to the gates of Heaven. **2** *Intercity Magazine* I . . sought any way possible to avoid the personal purgatory of staying in the city. *Guardian* The phoney grandeur . . that characterises the three and a half hour purgatory.

purgatory /ˈpəːgət(ə)ri/ *adjective.* **ME.**
[Late Latin *purgatorius*: see prec.]
Having the quality of cleansing or purifying; purgative.

purge /pəːdʒ/ *noun.* **M16.**
[from next or Old & mod. French, formed as next.]
1 A thing that purges; *spec.* a purgative. **M16.**
2 The action or an act of purging someone or something; *esp.* the removal from an organization, party, etc., of people regarded as undesirable. **M16.** ▸**b** Removal of one liquid by flushing with another; an instance of this. **M20.**

📖 **2** H. ARENDT Almost all higher officials owe their positions to purges that removed their predecessors. **PRIDE'S PURGE.**

purge /pəːdʒ/ *verb.* ME.
[Old French *purgier*, (also mod.) *purger* from Latin *purgare* purify, from *purus* PURE *adjective*.]
1 *verb trans.* Make physically pure or clean by the removal of dirt or waste matter. (Foll. by *of*, *from*.) ME. ▸**†b** Prune (a tree); snuff (a candle). E16–E17. ▸**c** Empty (a container etc.) of one gas or liquid by flushing with another. M20.
2 *verb trans.* Make spiritually or morally pure or clean. (Foll. by *of*, *from*.) ME. ▸**†b** Make ritually clean. LME–E17. ▸**c** Rid (an organization, party, etc.) of people regarded as undesirable. (Foll. by *of*.) L19.
3 *verb trans.* Remove or clear *away*, *out*, etc., by cleansing or purifying (*lit.* & *fig.*). ME. ▸**b** Remove (a person regarded as undesirable) from an organization, party, etc. L19.
4 *verb trans.* LAW (now *Hist.*). Clear from accusation or suspicion by an oath or ordeal. ME. ▸**b** SCOTS LAW (now *Hist.*). = ***purge of partial counsel*** below. Usu. in *pass.* E19.
5 a *verb trans.* Expel or cause expulsion of ingested material from (the body, now only the bowels) by evacuation; administer a laxative or (formerly) emetic to. LME. ▸**b** *verb refl.* Evacuate one's bowels, chiefly & now only as a result of taking a laxative. Formerly also, vomit, esp. as a result of taking an emetic. LME. ▸**c** *verb intrans.* Evacuate one's bowels. Formerly also, vomit. L16. ▸**d** *verb intrans.* Act as a laxative or (formerly) emetic. E17.
6 *verb trans.* LAW. Atone for or expunge (an offence, esp. contempt of court). Freq. in ***purge one's contempt***. M16.
7 *verb refl.* & *intrans.* Of a liquid: become clear, lose its turbidity. Now *rare* or *obsolete*. L17.

📖 **1** W. WHISTON They purge the barley from the bran. **2** E. WAUGH Suffering had purged Mr Harkness of all hypocrisy. **c** *Daily Express* Tito's officials are still purging towns and villages of Italian Fascists. **3** W. COWPER From thine eye the darkness purge. **b** *Evening News* More than twenty members .. have been purged by the East German Communist Party. **4** W. STUBBS Archbishop Arundel had to purge himself from a like suspicion. **purge of partial counsel** (SCOTS LAW, now *Hist.*) request (a witness) to take an oath as to the disinterested and impartial nature of his or her evidence (usu. in *pass.*). **5b** S. PURCHAS They purged themselves first .. and by vomit emptied their bodies. **d** H. C. WOOD Medicines which purge actively. **6** W. BLACKSTONE Bankruptcy once committed cannot be purged .. by any subsequent conduct. **7** C. LYELL Every current charged with sediment must purge itself in the first deep cavity .. it traverses.

■ **purgeable** *adjective* M17. **pur'gee** *noun* a person who is purged M20. **purger** *noun* a person who or thing which purges someone or something L15.

purging /ˈpəːdʒɪŋ/ *verbal noun.* LME.
[from PURGE *verb* + -ING¹.]
The action or an act or purging; *esp.* evacuation of the bowels, freq. as the result of taking a laxative.

📖 A. BLAISDELL There had been .. violent vomiting and purging, blood being present in both evacuations.

purging /ˈpəːdʒɪŋ/ *adjective.* M16.
[from PURGE *verb* + -ING².]
That purges; *esp.* purgative, strongly laxative.
purging* BUCKTHORN *purging flax: see FLAX *noun*. **purging nut** (*a*) (the seed of) the physic-nut, *Jatropha curcas*, the source of pulza-oil; (*b*) (the seed of) the tree *Croton tiglium*, the source of croton oil.

puri /ˈpuːri/ *noun*¹. M20.
[Indonesian.]
In Bali and other parts of Indonesia: a palace.

puri /ˈpuːri/ *noun*². M20.
[Hindi *pūrī* from Sanskrit *pūrikā*.]
In Indian cookery, a small round cake of unleavened wheat flour deep-fried in ghee or oil.

purification /ˌpjʊərɪfɪˈkeɪʃ(ə)n/ *noun.* ME.
[Old & mod. French, or Latin *purificatio(n-)*, from *purificat-* pa. ppl stem of *purificare* PURIFY: see -ATION.]
1 The action or process of making ceremonially or ritually clean, *esp.* the ritual cleansing of a woman after childbirth through the observances enjoined by Jewish law; an instance of this. ME.
2 The action or process of making physically pure or clean; the removal of dirt, blemishes, impurities, etc.; an instance of this. L16.
3 The action or process of making morally or spiritually pure; the elimination of faults, errors, or other undesirable elements; an instance of this. M17.

📖 **1 the Purification (of the Virgin Mary)** (*a*) the purification of the Virgin Mary after the birth of Jesus, culminating in her presentation of Jesus in the temple; (*b*) the feast (2 February, also called *Candlemas*) commemorating this. **2** *Which?* The purification process of some tap-water. *Nature* The research will involve .. the .. purification of samples from normal and lesional human skin. **3** A. G. MORTIMER Where the holy souls are waiting until their purification is accomplished.

purificator /ˈpjʊərɪfɪkeɪtə/ *noun.* M19.
[from (the same root as) next: see -OR.]
1 ECCLESIASTICAL. A cloth used at the Eucharist for wiping the chalice and paten, and the fingers and lips of the celebrant. M19.
2 A purifier. *rare*. M19.

purificatory /ˌpjʊərɪfɪˈkeɪt(ə)ri/ *noun.* L17.
[medieval Latin *purificatorium* use as noun of neut. of *purificatorius*: see next, -ORY¹.]
= PURIFICATOR 1.

purificatory /ˌpjʊərɪfɪˈkeɪt(ə)ri/ *adjective.* E17.
[Late Latin *purificatorius*, from Latin *purificat-*: see PURIFICATION, -ORY².]
Having the quality of purifying.

purifier /ˈpjʊərɪfʌɪə/ *noun.* L15.
[from PURIFY + -ER¹.]
A person who or thing which purifies or refines.

puriform /ˈpjʊərɪfɔːm/ *adjective. rare.* M17.
[from Latin *pur-* PUS + -I- + -FORM.]
MEDICINE. Having the character of or resembling pus; purulent.

purify /ˈpjʊərɪfʌɪ/ *verb.* ME.
[Old & mod. French *purifier* from Latin *purificare*, from *purus* PURE *adjective*: see -FY.]
▸**I** *verb trans.* Freq. foll. by *of*, *from*.
1 Make morally or spiritually clean; free from guilt or sin; remove faults, errors, or other undesirable elements from. ME.
2 Make ceremonially or ritually clean, formerly *spec.*, after childbirth. Usu. in *pass.* ME.
3 Make physically pure or clean, remove dirt, blemishes, impurities, etc. from. LME. ▸**b** ECCLESIASTICAL. Of a celebrant: cleanse (the chalice, paten, etc.) after the Eucharist. M19.
4 Remove by cleansing or purifying. *rare*. LME.
5 Fulfil (a condition) so as to make a legal obligation unconditional or absolute. Long only SCOTS LAW. L16.

📖 **1** J. FOWLES Each time she read it .. she felt elevated and purified, a better young woman. R. SILVERBERG I've been purified of all the shady bad things I used to do—forgiven. **2** J. H. NEWMAN Priests washed and purified the altars. **3** G. NAYLOR His stomach and intestines were purified by .. quantities of spring water and camomile tea.

▸**II** *verb intrans.* **6** Become pure. M17.

Purim /ˈpʊərɪm, pʊˈriːm/ *noun.* LME.
[Hebrew, pl. of *pūr*, a foreign word, explained in *Esther* 3:7, 9:24 as = LOT *noun* (from the casting of lots by Haman).]
A Jewish spring festival commemorating the defeat of Haman's plot to massacre the Jews.

purine /ˈpjʊəriːn/ *noun.* L19.
[Intended as blend of Latin *purum* pure and mod. Latin *uricum* URIC + -INE⁵.]
CHEMISTRY. A white crystalline basic substance $C_5H_4N_4$, having a bicyclic structure consisting of fused imidazole and pyrimidine rings; any of various substituted derivatives of this, *esp.* (also ***purine base***) either of the nucleotide-forming bases adenine and guanine.
■ **puri'nergic** *adjective* (PHYSIOLOGY) releasing or involving a purine derivative as a neurotransmitter L20.

puriri /ˈpuːrɪri/ *noun.* M19.
[Maori.]
A New Zealand tree, *Vitex lucens*, of the verbena family, with compound leaves and axillary clusters of red flowers; the hard durable timber of this tree.

purism /ˈpjʊərɪz(ə)m/ *noun.* M17.
[French *purisme*, from *pur* PURE *adjective*: see -ISM.]
1 Scrupulous or exaggerated observance of, or insistence on, purity or correctness, esp. in language or style; an instance of this. M17.
2 (Usu. **P-**.) An early 20th-cent. movement in painting marked by a return to basic geometric forms, arising from a rejection of excessive ornateness in cubism. M20.

📖 **1** *Dictionaries* Germans have alternated between periods of profligate borrowing and staunch purism.

puris naturalibus /ˌpjʊərɪs natjʊˈrɑːlɪbəs, -ˈreɪl-/ *adverbial phr.* E20.
[Latin: cf. earlier IN PURIS NATURALIBUS.]
In one's natural state; stark naked.

purist /ˈpjʊərɪst/ *noun* & *adjective.* E18.
[French *puriste*, from *pur* PURE *adjective*: see -IST.]
▸**A** *noun.* **1** A stickler for purity or excessive correctness, esp. in language or style. E18.
2 (Usu. **P-**.) A practitioner or adherent of Purism. M20.

📖 **1** B. FUSSELL Purists will omit tomatoes entirely as a decadent incursion from Texas.

▸**B** *adjective.* Of, pertaining to, or characteristic of purism or purists. M20.
■ **pu'ristic**, **pu'ristical** *adjectives* somewhat purist, characterized by purism L19.

puritan /ˈpjʊərɪt(ə)n/ *noun* & *adjective.* L16.
[from Latin *puritas* PURITY + -AN. Cf. French *puritain*.]
▸**A** *noun.* **1** *Hist.* (Usu. **P-**.) A member of a group of English Protestants of the late 16th and 17th cents, who regarded the Elizabethan settlement as incomplete and sought a further purification of the Church from supposedly unscriptural forms and ceremonies. Later also, any person separating from the Established Church on a point of ritual, doctrine, etc., regarded as unscriptural. L16. ▸**b** A member of any religious sect aspiring to special purity of doctrine or practice. L16.
2 A person practising or affecting extreme strictness and austerity in religion, morals, etc. L16.
3 A purist member of a party, advocating or practising strict adherence to party principles. L19.

📖 **1** H. F. OSBORN The Biblical literalism of the time of Cromwell, Milton, and the Puritans. **2** S. RAVEN I am no puritan: I should be capable of enjoying sex.

▸**B** *adjective.* Of, pertaining to, or characteristic of puritans, *spec.* (*Hist.*) the Puritans of the late 16th and 17th cents; practising or affecting extreme strictness in religion, morals, etc. L16.

📖 LONGFELLOW Singing the hundredth Psalm, the grand old Puritan anthem. *Listener* The Puritan ethic .. an ethic of discipline, work, responsibility. **Puritan spoon** *Hist.* a type of silver spoon with a flat plain stem and an oval bowl, made in the 17th cent.

puritanical /pjʊərɪˈtanɪk(ə)l/ *adjective.* Chiefly *derog.* Also **P-**. E17.
[from prec. + -ICAL.]
Characteristic of or befitting a puritan, *spec.* (*Hist.*) a Puritan; of the late 16th and 17th cents; *esp.* practising or affecting strict religious or moral behaviour.

📖 J. WAINWRIGHT The severe puritanical bulk of the chapel. *Oxford Art Journal* Greenberger's .. almost puritanical disregard for pleasure.

■ **puritanic** *adjective* (now *rare*) = PURITANICAL E17. **puritanically** *adverb* E17.

puritanise *verb* var. of PURITANIZE.

puritanism /ˈpjʊərɪt(ə)nɪz(ə)m/ *noun.* Also **P-**. L16.
[formed as prec. + -ISM.]
Puritan doctrines and principles; puritanical behaviour.

puritanize /ˈpjʊərɪt(ə)nʌɪz/ *verb trans.* Also **P-**, **-ise**. E17.
[formed as prec. + -IZE.]
†1 With *it*: behave in the manner of a puritan. Only in E17.
2 Make puritan. M17.

purity /ˈpjʊərɪti/ *noun.* ME.
[Old & mod. French *pureté*, with later assim. to late Latin *puritas*, from Latin *purus* PURE *adjective*: see -ITY.]
1 The state of being morally or spiritually pure; freedom from moral or ritual pollution; chastity; an instance of this. ME.
2 The state of being physically pure; freedom from admixture or adulteration; cleanness; an instance of this. LME.
3 *fig.* Freedom from foreign or extraneous elements; (a) faultlessness or correctness of speech, style, etc. M16.

📖 **1** MILTON No savage fierce .. Will dare to soyl her Virgin purity. **2** J. TYNDALL Snow of perfect purity. **3** J. K. JEROME The purity of my pronunciation was considered .. quite remarkable. *Scotsman* Any baby born whose racial purity is in doubt will be killed.

Purkinje /pəːˈkɪndʒi/ *noun.* M19.
[J. E. *Purkinje* (1787–1869), Bohemian physiologist.]
ANATOMY & PHYSIOLOGY. Used *attrib.* and in *possess.* with ref. to various phenomena and anatomical structures described by Purkinje.
Purkinje cell a large branching cell in the cortex of the cerebellum. **Purkinje fibre** any of the constituent fibres of an atrioventricular bundle. **Purkinje phenomenon**, **Purkinje shift**, **Purkinje's phenomenon**, **Purkinje's shift** a decrease in the apparent brightness of light of long wavelength (e.g. red) compared with light of short wavelength (e.g. blue) when the degree of illumination falls. **Purkinje's vesicle** = *PURKINJEAN vesicle*
■ **Purkinjean** *adjective* pertaining to or named after Purkinje; *Purkinjean vesicle*, the nucleus of the ovum: M19.

purl /pəːl/ *noun*¹. In senses 2, 4 also **pearl**. LME.
[Perh. symbolic: cf. PIRL *verb*. In sense 4 perh. a different word.]
▸**I 1** Thread or cord of twisted gold or silver wire, used esp. for edging; edging etc. made from this. LME.
2 (Any of) a series of minute loops or twists worked in lace, braid, etc., esp. as an ornamental edging; lace, braid, etc., made with such loops or twists. L16.
†3 A pleat or fold of a ruff or band; a frill. L16–M17.
▸**II 4** A knitting stitch made by putting a needle through the front of the corresponding stitch of the previous row and behind the needle on which this row is held and passing the yarn from the front round the back of the first needle (also ***purl stitch***); knitting using this stitch (also ***purl knitting***). M17.

purl /pəːl/ *noun*². E16.
[Rel. to or from PURL *verb*². Cf. PRILL *noun*¹.]
†**1** A small stream flowing with a swirling motion. E16–M17.
2 The action or sound of a small stream flowing with a swirling motion. M17.
3 An act of whirling, hurling, or pitching head over heels or head first; a heavy fall; an overturn, an upset. *colloq.* E19.

purl /pəːl/ *noun*³. *obsolete exc. Hist.* M17.
[Origin unkn.]
Orig., an infusion of wormwood or other bitter herbs in ale or beer. Later, hot beer mixed with gin and sometimes also with ginger and sugar.

purl /pəːl/ *verb*¹. In senses 1, 3 also †**pearl**. E16.
[from PURL *noun*¹.]
▶**I** †**1** *verb trans.* Embroider or edge with gold or silver thread. E16–L17.
2 Make (lace, braid, etc.) with a series of minute loops or twists, esp. as an ornamental edging. Chiefly as ***purled*** *ppl adjective.* E16.
†**3** *verb trans.* Pleat or frill like a ruff; frill the edge of. Chiefly as ***purled*** *ppl adjective.* L16–M17.
▶**II 4** *verb trans. & intrans.* Knit with a purl stitch. E19.

purl /pəːl/ *verb*² *intrans.* L16.
[Prob. imit.: cf. Norwegian *purla* bubble up, gush out, Swedish dial. *porla* ripple, gurgle, PIRL *verb.*]
1 *verb intrans.* Of water, a stream, etc.: flow with a swirling motion and a murmuring sound. L16.
2 *verb intrans.* Revolve or whirl round rapidly; spin round. L18.
3 *verb trans. & intrans.* Turn upside down, overturn, capsize; turn head over heels. *dial. & colloq.* M19.

> **1** N. ROWE Neverceasing Waters . . That purl and gurgle o'er their Sands.

purler /ˈpəːlə/ *noun. colloq.* In sense 2 also **pearler**. M19.
[from prec. + -ER¹.]
1 A throw or blow that hurls a person or animal head first; a heavy fall; *fig.* a sudden misfortune, failure, etc. M19.
2 Something of excellence; a thing of outstanding quality. Orig. & chiefly *Austral. & NZ.* M20.

> **1 come a purler, go a purler** fall heavily head first; *fig.* suffer sudden misfortune, failure, etc. **2** *Listener* I hope the next goal . . is an absolute purler.

purlieu /ˈpəːljuː/ *noun.* Also (earlier) †**-lew**. L15.
[Prob. alt. (by assim. to *leu* LIEU) of Anglo-Norman *purale(e*, Old French *pourallee* a going round to settle the boundaries, from *po(u)raler* traverse, from *po(u)r-* PUR- + *aller* go. Cf. PURALÉ.]
1 *Hist.* A tract of land on the border of a forest, *esp.* one formerly included within the forest boundaries and still partly subject to the forest laws. L15.
2 An outlying district of a city or town, a suburb. Also, a squalid or disreputable street or quarter. E17.
3 In *pl.* The outskirts or surroundings of a place (*lit. & fig.*). M17.
4 *transf. & fig.* A place where a person has the right to range at large; a person's usual haunts; bounds, limits. M17.

> **2** *New Yorker* Some godforsaken street in the . . endlessly sprawling purlieus of Memphis. **3** G. ETHEREGE I walk within the purlieus of the law. H. MANTEL Fierce cats spit and howl . . in the purlieus of the buildings. **4** SWIFT Wit has . . its purlieus, out of which it may not stray.

Comb.: **purlieu-man** *Hist.* the owner of freehold land within the purlieu of a forest.

purlin /ˈpəːlɪn/ *noun.* Also **-ine**. LME.
[Anglo-Latin *perlio(n-)*, perh. from Latin *per* through + stem of *ligare* bind: cf. French *lien* tie in carpentry.]
A horizontal beam along the length of a roof, resting on principals and supporting the common rafters or boards of the roof.

purloin /pəːˈlɔɪn/ *verb trans.* ME.
[Anglo-Norman *purloigner*, Old French *porloigner*, from PUR- + *loign* (mod. *loin*) far.]
†**1** Put far away; remove. ME–M17.
2 Make away with, take by deception; steal, filch. LME.

> **2** D. LESSING A nice neat skirt . . purloined from her mother.

■ **purloiner** *noun* L16.

puro /ˈpuro/ *noun.* Pl. **-os** /-ɔs/. M19.
[Spanish, lit. 'pure'.]
In Spain and Spanish-speaking countries, a cigar.

puromycin /pjʊərə(ʊ)ˈmʌɪsɪn/ *noun.* M20.
[from PUR(INE + -O- + -MYCIN.]
PHARMACOLOGY. An antibiotic produced by the bacterium *Streptomyces alboniger*, used esp. to treat sleeping sickness and amoebic dysentery.

purparty /pəːˈpɑːti/ *noun.* ME.
[Anglo-Norman *purpartie* (Anglo-Latin *purpartia*), from PUR- + *partie* PARTY *noun.*]
LAW (now *Hist.*). A proportion or share, esp. of an inheritance.
■ Also †**purpart** *noun* L15–E19.

†**purpense** *verb trans.* LME–M16.
[Old French *purpenser*, from PUR- + *penser* think. Superseded in 16 by PREPENSE *verb.*]
Think of, meditate on; determine beforehand.

purpie /ˈpəːpi/ *noun. Scot.* LME.
[Old French *porpié*, later *pourpié*, *pourpied*, alt. of *polpié*, *poulpied* from medieval Latin *pullipedem* accus. of *pulli pes* lit. 'foot of a colt'.]
A salad plant, orig. purslane, *Portulaca oleracea*, now (in full ***water purpie***) brooklime, *Veronica beccabunga*.

purple /ˈpəːp(ə)l/ *adjective & noun.* OE.
[Reduced and dissimilated late Northumbrian form of *purpuran* oblique case of PURPURE from Latin *purpura* (whence also Old High German *purpura* (German *Purpur*), Old Norse *purpuri*, Gothic *paurpaura*), from Greek *porphura* (molluscs that yielded) a crimson dye, cloth dyed with this. For the change of *r* to *l* cf. MARBLE *noun*, TURTLE *noun*¹.]
▶**A** *adjective.* **1** Of or pertaining to the costly fabric traditionally worn by a person of imperial, royal, etc., rank, esp. an emperor or senior magistrate of ancient Rome (with ref. to the distinguishing colour of the fabric from the dye originally used: see sense B.1 below). OE. ▶**b** Of a person: wearing or entitled to wear such fabric; of imperial or royal rank. *poet. rare.* M17.
2 a Of the colour purple, *esp.* of a deep rich shade between crimson and violet. LME. ▶**b** Of the colour of blood; bloodstained. *poet.* L16.
3 *fig.* Brilliant, striking; splendid, rich; *esp.* (of literary composition) elaborate, ornate; overwritten. L16.

> **2a** S. BELLOW The purple mulberries have a better flavour. P. CAREY The Bishop's face became as purple as his vest. **b** T. GRAY Where he points his purple spear, Hasty, hasty Rout is there. **3** M. MEYER Couched in hideous purple prose.

Special collocations: **purple airway** *colloq.* a route reserved for an aircraft on which a member of royalty is flying. ***purple amaranth***: see AMARANTH 1. **purple bacterium** any of various bacteria of the suborder Rhodospirillineae, and of similar groups, which contain a purple photoactive pigment. **purple copper (ore)** *MINERALOGY* = BORNITE. **purple emperor** a large Eurasian nymphalid butterfly, *Apatura iris*, the male of which has mainly black wings with purple iridescence. †**purple fever** = any of various fevers characterized by purplish cutaneous eruptions, esp. purpura. **purple finch** a common N. American finch, *Carpodacus purpureus*, the male of which is mainly rose red. †**purple-fish** = sense B.4 above. **purple gallinule** (*a*) a large Old World rail, *Porphyrio porphyrio*, having mainly blue plumage and red bill and legs; (*b*) a similar but smaller American bird, *Porphyrula martinica*, with more iridescent plumage and yellow legs. **purple gland** the gland in some gastropods which yields a purple dye. **purple grackle** the common grackle, *Quiscalus quiscula*. **purple haze** *slang* the drug LSD. **purpleheart** any of several large leguminous tropical American trees of the genus *Peltogyne*, esp. *P. paniculata*; the dark purplish-brown timber of such a tree, used for furniture. **purple heart** (*a*) *US* (with cap. initials) a decoration awarded to a member of the armed services wounded in action; (*b*) *colloq.* (usu. in *pl.*) a tablet of the stimulant drug Drinamyl, so named because of its shape and colour. **purple heron** a slender Old World heron, *Ardea purpurea*, having a chestnut-coloured neck and breast. **purple lake** a purple pigment. ***purple laver***: see LAVER *noun*¹ 2. ***purple loosestrife***. **purple martin** a large American martin, *Progne subis*, having mainly purplish-blue plumage. **purple membrane** a membrane containing photoactive pigments found within the cell membrane of the bacterium *Halobacterium salinarium*. ***purple moor-grass***: see MOOR *noun*¹. **purple osier** a Eurasian willow, *Salix purpurea*, used in basketry, with glaucous leaves and often purple twigs. **purple passage** = ***purple patch*** (a) below. **purple patch** (*a*) an elaborate, ornate, or overwritten passage in a literary composition; (*b*) *Austral. slang* a run of good luck or success. **purple sandpiper** a small northern and subarctic wader, *Calidris maritima*, with very dark upperparts in winter. **purple sea urchin, purple urchin** a small echinoid, *Psammechinus miliaris*, found on rocky shores of the N. Atlantic. **purple-shell** (*a*) = sense B.4 above; (*b*) = ***violet snail*** s.v. VIOLET *adjective.* **purple swamphen** = ***purple gallinule*** above. ***purple urchin***: see ***purple sea urchin*** above. †**purple waterhen** = ***purple gallinule*** above. **purple wreath** a liana of the W. Indies and tropical America, *Petrea volubilis*, of the vervain family, with long sprays of purple or blue flowers. **purple zone** = ***purple airway*** above.

▶**B** *noun.* **1** Orig. (now *Hist.*), a shade of crimson (more fully ***Tyrian purple***), the colour of a dye obtained from various gastropod molluscs (see sense 1b below) and traditionally used for fabric worn by people of imperial, royal, etc., rank (see sense A.1 above); formerly also more widely, any of various shades of red. Now, a colour intermediate between red and blue, *esp.* a deep rich shade between crimson and violet. LME. ▶**b** The dye obtained from the secretion of the hypobranchial gland of various gastropod molluscs esp. of the genera *Murex*, *Nucella*, and *Thais*; *gen.* any purple pigment. M17.
2 a Purple cloth or clothing, a purple robe or garment, *spec.* as worn by a person of imperial, royal, etc., rank. Also, *the* position or authority of a person of imperial, royal, etc., rank or office. LME. ▶**b** *The* scarlet official dress of a cardinal; *the* rank or office of a cardinal. L17.
3 In *pl.* (treated as *sing.*). ▶**a** Any of various diseases characterized by an eruption of purplish pustules; *esp.* = PURPURA 1. Now *rare* or *obsolete.* LME. ▶**b** A form of cockle in wheat. E19. ▶**c** *VETERINARY MEDICINE.* Swine fever. L19.
4 Any of the molluscs which yielded Tyrian purple (see sense B.1b above), or their allies. Now *esp.* the dog-whelk *Nucella (Thais) lapillus.* L16.
5 A purple flower. Earliest in ***long purples*** s.v. LONG *adjective*¹. *poet.* E17.
6 = ***purple heart*** (b) above. Also, the drug LSD. *slang.* M20.
7 Obscene or indecent writing (*rare*); elaborate or ornate written material, overwriting. *colloq.* M20.

Phrases: **born in the purple** born into an imperial or royal reigning family; belonging to the highest or most privileged rank of an organization. ***LONDON purple***. ***long purples***: see LONG *adjective*¹. ***mineral purple***: see MINERAL *adjective.* ***Perkin's purple***: see PERKIN 1. ***purple of CASSIUS***. ***Tyrian purple***: see sense B.1 above. ***visual purple***: see VISUAL *adjective.* ***wear the purple***: see WEAR *verb*¹.
■ **purpleness** *noun* E20. **purplish** *adjective* somewhat purple M16. **purply** *adjective* of a purple colour or tint; purplish: E18.

purple /ˈpəːp(ə)l/ *verb.* LME.
[from PURPLE *adjective.*]
1 *verb trans.* Make purple; colour, dye, or tinge with purple. LME.
2 *verb intrans.* Become purple. M17.

purpled /ˈpəːp(ə)ld/ *adjective.* LME.
[from PURPLE *noun, verb*: see -ED², -ED¹.]
Coloured, dyed, or tinged with purple; clothed in purple; that has been made purple.

purport /ˈpəːpɔːt/ *noun.* LME.
[Anglo-Norman, Old French *purport*, *por-* produce, contents, formed as next.]
1 That which is expressed or stated, esp. by a formal document or speech; import, effect; meaning, substance; an instance of this. LME. ▶†**b** Outward bearing. *rare* (Spenser). Only in L16.
2 That which is intended to be done or effected by something; (an) object, (a) purpose, (an) intention. E17.

> **1** G. WASHINGTON The purport of your private letter. J. CONRAD Words . . too indistinct for him to understand their purport. **2** M. HOWITT The purport of our steamer's visit . . is to promote . . commerce.

■ **purportless** *adjective* (*rare*) having no purport; meaningless, pointless: E19.

purport /pəˈpɔːt/ *verb trans.* LME.
[Anglo-Norman, Old French *purporter* (formed as PUR- + *porter*) from medieval Latin *proportare*, from Latin PRO-¹ + *portare* carry, bear.]
1 a Esp. of a document or speech: express, state; mean, signify, imply. LME. ▶**b** Profess *to be* or *do*; be intended to seem, appear ostensibly to be. L18.
2 Intend. *rare.* E19.

> **1b** D. L. SAYERS What purported to be the draft of a will. A. ROBERTSON His paintings purport to show the domestic scenes . . of the ancients. *Sun* Those who purport to act in their name. **2** F. W. ROBINSON What Matthew purports doing, I don't know.

■ **purportedly** *adverb* allegedly, ostensibly M20.

purpose /ˈpəːpəs/ *noun.* ME.
[Old French *purpos*, *porpos*: (mod. *propos*: see PROPOSE *noun*), formed as next.]
1 A thing to be done; an object to be attained, an intention, an aim. ME.
2 The action or fact of intending to do something; resolution, determination. ME.
†**3** A proposition, a question, an argument; a riddle. ME–E17.
4 The subject of a discourse; the matter in hand, the point at issue. Now only in ***to the purpose*** below. ME.
5 The reason for which something is done or made, or for which it exists; the result or effect intended; an instance of this. LME.
6 Import, effect, meaning, esp. of words. Chiefly in ***to this purpose, to that purpose***, etc. Now *rare.* LME.

> **1** SHAKES. *Mids. N. D.* Fair Helen told me . . Of this their purpose hither to this wood. E. WILSON Studied . . with the purpose of profiting by their experience. *Blackwood's Magazine* A meeting at the Summit may well have served its purpose. *USA Today* Our purpose was to avoid casualties. **2** P. BENSON We . . walked . . with an air of purpose. M. COREN Gilbert was drifting without purpose. **3** SPENSER Oft purposes, oft riddles, he devysed. **5** G. ORWELL Winston wanted the room for the purpose of a love affair. A. TOFFLER The purpose of temporary classrooms is to . . cope with rapidly shifting population densities. B. BETTELHEIM The reclamation of land for agricultural purposes. **6** D. GARNETT I had heard him say a great deal to the same purpose.

Phrases: †**be in purpose to** intend to. ***for all intents and purposes***: see INTENT *noun* 6. **of purpose, of a set purpose** (now *rare*) purposely, intentionally. **on purpose** by design; purposely, intentionally; in order *that*, *to do*. ***serve the purpose***: see SERVE *verb*¹. ***to all intents and purposes***: see INTENT *noun* 6. **to good**

purpose, **to no purpose**, **to some purpose**, etc., with good, no, some, etc., effect or result. **to the purpose** pertinent, apposite, to the point.
Comb.: **purpose-built**, **purpose-designed**, **purpose-made** *adjectives* built, designed, or made for a specific purpose.
■ **purpose-like** *adjective* (*a*) *Scot.* appearing efficient or suitable for a purpose; (*b*) having a definite purpose: LME.

purpose /ˈpəːpəs/ *verb*. LME.
[Old French *purposer*, *por-* (mod. *pourposer*, from *pur-*, *por-* PUR- + *poser*) var of Old & mod. French *proposer* PROPOSE *verb*.]
†**1 a** *verb trans.* = PROPOSE *verb* 2. LME–M17. ▸**b** *verb intrans.* & *trans.* (with *it*). Converse, talk. Cf. PROPOSE *verb* 5. Only in L16.
2 *verb trans.* Have or set oneself as one's purpose; plan or intend (*that*, *to do*). LME.
†**3** *verb intrans.* & *refl.* Intend to go *to*; be bound *for*. LME–M17.
†**4** *verb intrans.* Have a purpose, plan, or design. Also, have good, bad, etc., intentions toward a person. LME–M17.
5 *verb trans.* In *pass.* Intended *to do* something; designed *for* some purpose. Now *rare*. LME.

> 📖 **2** H. BELLOC Does he also purpose great things? W. S. CHURCHILL They purposed to strike from Niagara. **3** SHAKES. *Ant. & Cl.* He purposeth to Athens.

■ **purposed** *adjective* (*a*) (of an action etc.) intentional; (*b*) (of a person) resolved, determined: LME. †**purposedly** *adverb* = PURPOSELY M16–L18. **purposer** *noun* a person who purposes something; *esp.* a person who has a particular object or intention: LME.

purposeful /ˈpəːpəsfʊl, -f(ə)l/ *adjective*. M19.
[from PURPOSE *noun* + -FUL.]
1 Having a purpose or meaning; indicating purpose; designed, intentional. M19.
2 Having a definite purpose in mind; resolute. M19.
■ **purposefully** *adverb* M19. **purposefulness** *noun* L19.

purposeless /ˈpəːpəslɪs/ *adjective*. M16.
[from PURPOSE *noun* + -LESS.]
1 Done or made without purpose or design. M16.
2 Having no purpose, plan, or aim. M19.
■ **purposelessly** *adverb* in a purposeless manner; aimlessly: M19. **purposelessness** *noun* lack of purpose, object, or use; aimlessness: M19.

purposely /ˈpəːpəsli/ *adverb*. L15.
[from PURPOSE *noun* + -LY².]
On purpose, by design; intentionally, deliberately; expressly (*for*, *to do*).

> 📖 D. CECIL Comic character parts put in purposely to make the reader laugh. J. KOSINSKI They purposely spoke in another language.

purposive /ˈpəːpəsɪv/ *adjective*. M19.
[from PURPOSE *noun* or *verb* + -IVE.]
1 Adapted to some purpose or end; serving some particular purpose. M19.
2 Acting or performed with conscious purpose or intention. M19.
3 Of or pertaining to purpose; characterized by purpose and resolution; GRAMMAR (of a conjunction or clause) expressing purpose. L19.

> 📖 **1** L. MANN This seemingly casual gathering . . at once became purposive. **2** *Times* The appellant . . told a whole string of purposive lies. **3** E. NORTH Ushers looking upright, military and purposive.

■ **purposively** *adverb* in a purposive manner; purposely: E20. **purposiveness** *noun* L19. **purposivism** *noun* the theory that all human or animal activity is purposive M20. **purposivist** *noun* & *adjective* (*a*) *noun* an advocate of purposivism; (*b*) *adjective* of or pertaining to purposivism: M20.

purpresture /pəːˈprɛstʃə/ *noun*. ME.
[Old French *purpresture*, *por-* alt. of *porpresure*, from *porprendre* occupy, usurp, enclose, from *pur-*, *por-* PUR- + *prendre* take, seize from Latin *praehendere*.]
LAW. **1** An illegal enclosure of or encroachment on the land or property of another or (now only) of the public. ME.
2 *Hist.* A payment or rent due to a feudal superior for permission to enclose or build on land. LME.

†**purpur** *noun & adjective* var. of PURPURE.

purpura /ˈpəːpjʊrə/ *noun*. M18.
[Latin: see PURPLE *adjective* & *noun*.]
1 MEDICINE. A skin rash of purple spots resulting from the rupture of small blood capillaries. Also (usu. with specifying word), any of various diseases characterized by this. M18.
2 ZOOLOGY. Any of various gastropod molluscs now or formerly of the genus *Purpura*, *esp.* any from which a purple dye was formerly obtained (cf. PURPLE *noun* 1b). Now only as mod. Latin genus name. M18.

purpurate /ˈpəːpjʊreɪt/ *noun*. E19.
[from PURPURIC + -ATE¹.]
CHEMISTRY. Any of a series of purple or red salts of an ion ($C_8H_4N_5O_6^-$) containing two heteroaromatic rings.

†**purpurate** *verb trans*. M17–E19.
[Latin *purpurat-* pa. ppl stem of *purpurare* make purple, clothe in purple, from *purpura*: see PURPLE *adjective* & *noun*, -ATE³.]
Make purple.

purpure /ˈpəːpjʊə/ *noun* & *adjective*. *obsolete* exc. HERALDRY. Also †**purpur**. OE.
[Latin *purpura*, reinforced by Old French *purpre* (mod. *pourpre*): see PURPLE *adjective* & *noun*.]
▸ **A** *noun*. †**1** Orig., a purple robe or garment, *spec.* as worn by a person of imperial, royal, etc., rank. Later also, purple cloth or clothing. Cf. PURPLE *noun* 2. OE–E17.
2 †**a** A deep crimson or scarlet colour. Cf. PURPLE *noun* 1. LME–L15. ▸**b** HERALDRY. The tincture purple. LME.
▸ **B** *adjective*. †**1** Of a purple colour, *spec.* of the distinctive colour of imperial and royal dress. ME–E17.
2 HERALDRY. Of the tincture purpure. M16.

purpureal /pəːˈpjʊərɪəl/ *adjective*. Chiefly *poet.* E18.
[from Latin *purpureus* from Greek *porphureos* (from *porphura*: see PURPLE *adjective* & *noun*): see -AL¹.]
Of a purple colour.

> 📖 JOCELYN BROOKE Coloured . . by the rich, purpureal glow of heather.

purpurean /pəːˈpjʊərɪən/ *adjective*. *rare*. ME.
[formed as prec. + -AN.]
= prec.

purpuric /pəːˈpjʊərɪk/ *adjective*. E19.
[from Latin *purpura* (see PURPLE *adjective* & *noun*) + -IC.]
1 CHEMISTRY. ***purpuric acid***, the hypothetical parent acid of purpurates. E19.
2 MEDICINE. Of, pertaining to, or of the nature of purpura; (of a disease) marked by a purple rash. M19.

purpurin /ˈpəːpjʊrɪn/ *noun*. M19.
[from Latin *purpura* (see PURPLE *adjective* & *noun*) + -IN¹.]
CHEMISTRY. A red dye orig. extracted from madder and also prepared artificially by the oxidation of alizarin; 1,2,4-trihydroxyanthraquinone, $C_{14}H_8O_5$.

†**purpurine** *adjective*. OE–L19.
[from (the same root as) PURPURE, reinforced by Old French *porprin*, *purprin* (mod. *purpurin*): see -INE¹.]
Of a purple colour.

purpurissum /pəːpjʊəˈrɪs(ə)m/ *noun*. *obsolete* exc. *Hist.* (*rare*). Also †***-isse***. E16.
[Latin, from *purpura*: see PURPLE *adjective* & *noun*.]
A red or purple colouring matter used by the ancients.

purpurite /ˈpəːpjʊraɪt/ *noun*. E20.
[from Latin *purpura* (see PURPLE *adjective* & *noun*) + -ITE¹.]
MINERALOGY. An orthorhombic phosphate of trivalent manganese and trivalent iron, occurring as red or purple crystals and containing more manganese than heterosite.

purpurogallin /ˌpəːpjʊrəʊˈgalɪn/ *noun*. L19.
[from PURPUR(IN + PYR)OGALL(IC + -IN¹.]
CHEMISTRY. An orange-red crystalline phenol, $C_{11}H_8O_5$, consisting of fused tropolone and trihydroxybenzene rings.

purr /pəː/ *noun*. E17.
[Imit. Cf. PURR *verb*¹.]
An act of purring; the low vibrating sound made by a cat when pleased or contented; a sound resembling this.

> 📖 E. BIRNEY The purr of a waterfall rose and sank with the wind. M. BINCHY Joy gave a little purr of satisfaction.

purr /pəː/ *verb*¹. E17.
[Imit. Cf. PURR *noun*.]
1 *verb intrans.* **a** Of a cat or (occas.) other feline animal: make a low continuous vibratory sound expressive of contentment or pleasure. E17. ▸**b** Of a non-feline animal: make a sound resembling this. M19.
2 *verb intrans. transf.* ▸**a** Of a person: express pleasure by low murmuring sounds, or in one's behaviour or attitude. Also, talk or behave in a quiet self-satisfied way. M17. ▸**b** Of a thing: make a sound resembling a cat's purr, as that caused by rapid vibrations, boiling or bubbling liquid, the working of a piece of machinery, etc. M17.
3 *verb trans.* Utter or express by purring. M18.

> 📖 **1a** P. FARMER A cat lay, purring loudly, on my lap. **2a** DRYDEN We love to get our mistresses, and purr over them. **3** *Westminster Gazette* 'I was at Poona in '76—' 'My dear Colonel,' purred Reginald, 'fancy admitting such a thing!'

■ **purrer** *noun* E19. **purringly** *adverb* in a purring manner E20.

purr *verb*² var. of PORR *verb*.

†**purre** *noun*. E17–L18.
[Origin unkn.]
Water cider, ciderkin, perkin.

purree /ˈpʌriː, ˈpjʊəriː/ *noun*. Also **piuri**. M19.
[Hindi *piyūrī*, *peorī*, from Sanskrit *pīta* yellow + *mṛdā* earth.]
The pigment Indian yellow in an unpurified state.

purry /ˈpʌri/ *noun*. Long *Scot.* Also †**porray** & other vars. ME.
[Old French *porée* from late Latin *porrata*, from *porrum* leek + *-ata* -ADE; in sense 2 prob. assoc. with French PURÉE.]
†**1** A soup or broth of boiled and sieved vegetables or fish, added to stock or milk. ME–L16.
2 A dish of brose with chopped kale. L18.

pur sang /pyr sɑ̃/ *adjectival & adverbial phr.* M19.
[French *pur-sang* thoroughbred animal, from *pur* PURE *adjective* + *sang* blood.]
Without admixture, genuine(ly).

purse /pəːs/ *noun*. LOE.
[Alt. (with *p* prob. after *pung* purse, *pusa* wallet) of late Latin *bursa* var. of *byrsa* from Greek *bursa* leather. Cf. BURSA, BURSE.]
▸ **I** Conn. with money.
1 A small pouch or bag of leather or other flexible material, orig. to be closed at the mouth by drawing tight two threaded strings or drawstrings, for carrying money on the person. LOE.
2 Such a pouch or bag with its contents; the contents of a purse, money, funds. ME.
3 A sum of money collected as a present or donated as a prize in a contest. Also, winnings. E17.
4 *Hist.* In the Ottoman Empire, a specific sum of money, 500 or 600 piastres. L17.
5 A fragment of live coal exploding from a fire with a report (regarded as a good omen). Chiefly *dial.* M18.

> 📖 **1** M. FLANAGAN She opened her purse There was not enough money to pay the driver. **2** F. RAPHAEL Their presence was a call on his purse and his patience. **3** *Golf World* A loss in prize money . . for the women professionals—almost a fifth of their total purse.

▸ **II** *gen.* & *transf.* **6** †**a** A bag carried for any purpose; a wallet, a pouch, a sack. ME–M19. ▸**b** *spec.* One of the official insignia of the Lord Chancellor. Cf. BURSE 1. Long *rare* or *obsolete*. L17.
7 †**a** The scrotum. ME–E18. ▸**b** BIOLOGY. A natural receptacle resembling a bag or pocket. E16.
8 A small leather bag formerly used with a pull-down to prevent the escape of wind from an organ-pipe. M19.
9 A bag-shaped net or part of a net, used in fishing or rabbit-catching. Cf. ***purse-net*** below. L19.
10 A handbag. *N. Amer.* M20.

> 📖 **10** N. MAILER She . . went to reach into her purse for a cigarette.

Phrases: †**be out of purse** be the loser, be out of pocket. ***line one's purse***: see LINE *verb*¹ 2. ***long purse***: see LONG *adjective*¹. ***privy purse***: see PRIVY *adjective*. **purse and person** one's money and oneself. **the public purse** the national treasury.
Comb.: **purse-bag** *rare* a handbag, *esp.* one with a purse incorporated; **purse-bearer** (*a*) the bearer or carrier of a purse; a person in charge of money; a treasurer; (*b*) *rare* an official who carries the burse in front of the Lord Chancellor in procession; (*c*) *rare* a marsupial; **purse-belt** = ***money-belt*** s.v. MONEY *noun*; **purse boat** a large boat used for fishing with a purse-seine; **purse-cutter** (now *rare*) a thief who cuts purses and removes their contents; a cutpurse; **purse-net** a bag-shaped net, the mouth of which may be drawn together with cords, used in fishing and rabbit-catching (cf. sense 9 above); **purse-pick**, †**purse-picker** *rare* a thief who steals purses; a pickpocket; **purse-pride** the pride or arrogance of the wealthy; **purse-proud** *adjective* proud or arrogant on account of one's wealth; **purse seine** a fishing net or seine which may be pursed or drawn into the shape of a bag, used for catching shoal fish; **purse-seiner** a vessel used in purse-seine fishing; **purse-web** a tubular spider's web supposed to resemble a kind of purse; ***purse-web spider***, any of various mygalomorph spiders of the genus *Atypus*, which spin an enclosed tube-shaped web.
■ **purseful** *noun* as much or as many as a purse will hold ME. **purseless** *adjective* without a purse L17.

purse /pəːs/ *verb*. ME.
[from prec.]
1 *verb trans.* Put into one's purse; pocket. (Foll. by *up*.) Now *rare*. ME.
†**2** *verb trans. fig.* Keep secret; contain, confine; keep back, withdraw. (Foll. by *up*.) ME–L17.
†**3** *verb trans.* In *pass.* Be (well or badly) provided with money. M16–M17.
4 a *verb trans.* Contract or draw together (the lips, brow, etc.) in wrinkles or puckers (as if by tightening the strings of a purse). (Foll. by *up*.) E17. ▸**b** *verb intrans.* Become wrinkled or puckered. E18.
5 *verb trans.* Close the mouth of (a purse-seine) by drawing the edges together. L19.

> 📖 **4a** DICKENS Mr. Brownlow looked apprehensively at Mr. Bumble's pursed-up countenance. G. GREENE She frowned . . and pursed her lips to indicate I was not to speak. **b** A. BROOKNER Under stress . . his lips would very slightly purse.

purser /ˈpəːsə/ *noun*. ME.
[from PURSE *noun* + -ER¹.]
†**1** A maker of purses. ME–M17.
2 a An officer in charge of money and accounts; a purse-bearer, a treasurer. Now *rare* or *obsolete*. LME. ▸**b** An officer on board ship who keeps the accounts and sometimes has charge of the provisions. Now (*spec.*) the head

steward in a passenger vessel; an officer with a similar function on a passenger aircraft. LME.
3 A ship fishing with purse-nets. M20.

2b G. GREENE The purser took the last landing-card. **3** *attrib.*: *Shetland Times* The whole purser fleet is fishing for mackerel.

■ **pursership** *noun* the office or position of purser E17.

purserette /pəːsəˈrɛt/ *noun*. M20.
[from prec. + -ETTE.]
A female purser on a ship or aircraft.

purse-string /ˈpəːstrɪŋ/ *noun*. LME.
[from PURSE *noun* + STRING *noun*.]
Either of two threaded strings or drawstrings drawn to close the mouth of a purse (usu. in *pl.*). Now chiefly in phrs. below.
hold the purse-strings have control of expenditure. **loosen the purse-strings** become more generous in spending money. **tighten the purse-strings** become more sparing in spending money.

pursive /ˈpəːsɪv/ *adjective*. *arch*. LME.
[Anglo-Norman *porsif* alt. of Old French *polsif* (mod. *poussif*), from *polser* breathe with difficulty, pant, from Latin *pulsare* drive or agitate violently (see PUSH *verb*). Cf. PURSY *adjective*¹.]
Esp. of a horse: short-winded, broken-winded, asthmatic.
■ **pursiveness** *noun* LME.

purslane /ˈpəːslən/ *noun*. LME.
[Old French *porcelaine*, prob. assim. of Latin *porcil(l)aca* (var. of *portulaca*), to French *porcelaine* PORCELAIN. Cf. PUSSLEY.]
1 A low succulent plant, *Portulaca oleracea* (family Portulacaceae), widely grown, chiefly in warmer countries, as a salad or pot-herb. Also (with specifying word), any of various other plants of this genus. LME.
2 Any of various plants related to purslane or resembling it. L16.
2 *pink purslane*, *sea purslane*, *water purslane*, etc.

pursuance /pəˈsjuːəns/ *noun*. L16.
[formed as next: see -ANCE.]
†**1** That which follows or is consequent upon a thing, a consequence. *rare*. Only in L16.
2 The action of continuing something; (a) continuance *of*. Now *rare*. E17.
†**3** The action of pursuing in order to catch or harm; = PURSUIT 2a. M–L17.
4 The action of trying to attain or accomplish something; = PURSUIT 6. M17.
5 The action of proceeding in accordance with something (foll. by *of*, †*to*); the carrying out or observance *of*. M17.

5 H. JAMES In pursuance of our arrangement, we met in the hall.

pursuant /pəˈsjuːənt/ *noun*. LME.
[Old French, use as noun of *poursuiant* pres. pple: see next. In later uses from next. Cf. PURSUIVANT.]
†**1** A person who prosecutes an action in court; a prosecutor. LME–M17.
2 A person who pursues or chases after; a pursuer. *rare*. E20.

pursuant /pəˈsjuːənt/ *adjective & adverb*. M16.
[Old French *poursuiant* pres. pple of *poursuir*: see PURSUE, -ANT¹.]
▶ **A** *adjective*. †**1** That prosecutes an action in court; prosecuting. Only in M16.
2 With *to*: consequent and conforming to; in accordance with. Now *rare* or *obsolete*. M17.
3 Going in pursuit; pursuing. L17.

2 ADDISON They determined, pursuant, to the Resolution they had taken . . , to retire.

▶ **B** *adverb*. With *to*: in consequence of, in accordance with. L17.

C. G. ADDISON If the act has been performed pursuant to the . . request of the party making the promise.

■ **pursuantly** *adverb* in consequence, accordantly M16.

pursue /pəˈsjuː/ *verb*. ME.
[Anglo-Norman *pursuer*, *-siwer* = Old French *poursuir*, *por-* var. of *poursivre* (mod. *-suivre*) from Proto-Romance alt. of Latin *prosequi* PROSECUTE.]
▶ **I** *verb trans*. **1** Follow with enmity; seek to injure (a person); harass, worry, torment. Now *rare* or *obsolete* exc. *Scot*. ME. ▶†**b** Avenge, follow with punishment. L16–L17.
2 Follow with intent to overtake and capture or harm; hunt, chase; *fig*. (of misfortune etc.) persistently assail. ME.
3 Prosecute in a court of law, sue (a person). Chiefly *Scot*. LME.
4 a Come after in time or order. Also, follow as an attendant. Now *rare* or *obsolete*. LME. ▶**b** Keep track of mentally or visually; trace. *poet*. L17.
5 Try to obtain or accomplish, aim at. LME. ▶†**b** Make one's aim; try (*to do* something). LME–E16. ▶†**c** Try to attain to. L15–L17.
6 Follow (a path, way, or course); proceed along. LME.
7 Proceed in compliance or accordance with (a plan, system, etc.). Cf. FOLLOW *verb* 7. LME.
8 Follow up, carry on further, continue (a course of action etc.). Also, continue to discuss (a topic etc.), utter in continuation. LME. ▶**b** LAW. Continue (an action); lay (information); present (a libel). Chiefly *Scot*. L15.
9 Follow as an occupation or profession; engage in, practise; make a pursuit of. E16.

2 D. H. LAWRENCE Suddenly he would be . . pursuing his adversary with a stone. M. MAHY Disturbing ideas pursued her. F. KAPLAN He looked over his shoulder to see who was pursuing him. **5** G. SANTAYANA Reformers blindly pursued something . . which . . would probably be worthless. **6** E. M. FORSTER The carriage was still pursuing the windings of the road. *fig*.: STEELE To consider what Course of Life he ought to pursue. **7** JAS. MILL The . . scheme was invented and pursued. **8** W. WHEWELL 'Something of this', he pursues, 'may be seen in language'. E. FORSTER The brothers then pursued their journey. B. MONTGOMERY It was useless for me to pursue the matter further. **9** W. TREVOR He was a solicitor . . by night and pursued some different trade by day. A. HIGGINS He pursued his studies in the summer house.

▶ **II** *verb intrans*. **10** Go in pursuit, chase. (Foll. by *after*.) ME.
†**11** Proceed with hostile intent; (with *on*, *to*, *upon*) attack, assail a person or thing. LME–E16.
†**12** Make one's suit; entreat. LME–M16. ▶**b** *spec*. Make suit as plaintiff or pursuer; sue. Later chiefly *Scot*. LME–M18.
†**13** Follow or come after in order. L15–L17.
†**14** Proceed continuously. Also, come forth. E16–M17.
15 Continue something. (Foll. by *on*.) Now *rare*. E16.

10 H. BROOKE To take every horse he had . . and to pursue after the fugitives. O. HENRY The rangers mounted and pursued but . . Manning gave the word to abandon the chase.

■ **pursuable** *adjective* E17. **pursual** *noun* (*rare*) the action or fact of pursuing; pursuance: E19.

pursuer /pəˈsjuːə/ *noun*. LME.
[from prec. + -ER¹.]
A person who pursues; *spec*. (*a*) *Civil & SCOTS LAW* a plaintiff, a petitioner; a prosecutor; (*b*) a person who follows after or chases with intent to capture; (*c*) a person who pursues some object or aim.

K. AMIS With his pursuer close behind . . Hubert . . ran for the doorway. *Times* A pursuer might in petitory action conclude for . . a grossly extravagant sum.

pursuit /pəˈsjuːt/ *noun*. LME.
[Anglo-Norman *purseute* = Old & mod. French *poursuite*, from *poursuir*: see PURSUE.]
†**1** Persecution, annoyance, ill treatment. LME–E17.
2 a The action of pursuing, with intent to overtake and catch or harm; an instance of this; a chase. LME. ▶**b** *spec*. In track cycling, any of various kinds of competitive race, in which competitors pursue one another round a track. Also ***pursuit race***. M20.
†**3** The action of entreating; a suit, a petition. LME–E18.
4 LAW. A legal action; a suit; a prosecution. Later chiefly *Scot*. LME.
†**5** Attack, assault, siege. *Scot*. LME–M17.
6 a The action of trying to obtain, attain, or accomplish something. Formerly also, an endeavour. LME. ▶**b** *transf*. The object aimed at. Now *rare* or *obsolete*. L16.
7 The action of following or engaging in something, as a profession, business, recreation, etc.; an instance of this; that in which one is engaged. LME.
†**8** The pursuing or following out *of* a plan, design, etc.; the action of continuing with something already begun. L15–E18.

2a H. READ The Green Child followed them leisurely, so as not to give the impression of pursuit. S. COOPER He stared in horror . . his fear of pursuit awakened. **6a** M. GIROUARD In the pursuit of beauty they toured art galleries. **7** M. MEYER She loved open-air pursuits, especially riding. A. C. GRAYLING Philosophy . . has become a pursuit for specialists.

Phrases: **hot pursuit**: see HOT *adjective*. **in pursuit (of)** pursuing, chasing, following. ***Trivial Pursuit***: see TRIVIAL *adjective* 4.
Comb.: **pursuit aeroplane**, **pursuit plane** = FIGHTER 2; ***pursuit race***: see sense 2b above.

pursuivant /ˈpəːsɪv(ə)nt/ *noun & verb*. LME.
[Old French *pursivant* use as noun of pres. pple of *pursivre*: see PURSUE, -ANT¹. Cf. PURSUANT *noun*.]
▶ **A** *noun*. **1** Formerly, a junior heraldic officer attendant on a herald or attached to a particular nobleman. Now, an officer of the College of Arms, ranking below a herald. Also ***pursuivant of arms***, †***pursuivant at arms***. LME.
2 A royal or State messenger with power to execute warrants; a warrant-officer. *obsolete* exc. *Hist*. E16.
3 A follower; an attendant. *arch*. E16.

1 O. NEUBECKER At their head . . a king-at-arms followed by heralds . . and then pursuivants. **2** A. KENNY The hair's-breadth escapes of recusants hunted by pursuivants.

▶†**B** *verb trans*. Pursue, summon, or arrest by a pursuivant. M17–E18.

pursy /ˈpəːsi/ *adjective*¹. LME.
[Later form of PURSIVE, perh. assoc. with PURSE *noun*. Cf. PUSSEL.]
1 = PURSIVE. LME.
2 Fat, corpulent. L16.
■ **pursiness** *noun* L15.

pursy /ˈpəːsi/ *adjective*². M16.
[from PURSE *noun* + -Y¹.]
1 Of cloth, skin, etc.: having puckers or wrinkles (as if resulting from tightening the drawstrings of a purse). M16.
2 Having a full purse; rich, wealthy; purse-proud. E17.

1 N. P. WILLIS His heavy oily black eyes twinkled in their pursy recesses.

purt *adjective & adverb* see PURTY.

purtenance /ˈpəːt(ə)nəns, -tɪn-/ *noun*. *arch*. LME.
[Anglo-Norman alt. of Old French *partinance*, *pert-*, from *partenant* pres. pple of *partenir*: see PERTAIN, -ANCE. Later perh. taken as aphet. from APPURTENANCE.]
That which appertains or forms an appendage to something; an accessory, an appurtenance; *spec*. †(*a*) LAW an appendage or appurtenance to a possession or estate; (*b*) the entrails of an animal.

purty /ˈpəːti/ *adjective & adverb*. *non-standard*. *Anglo-Irish* & *N. Amer*. Also (*N. Amer*. before a nasal consonant) **purt** /pəːt/. E19.
[Repr. a local pronunc.]
= PRETTY *adjective*, *adverb*.

purulent /ˈpjʊərʊl(ə)nt/ *adjective*. LME.
[French, or Latin *purulentus*, from *pur-*, *pus* PUS: see -ULENT.]
1 Of the nature of or resembling pus. Also (*rare*), corrupt, putrid. LME.
2 Containing, forming, or discharging pus; suppurating, festering; characterized or accompanied by the formation of pus. E17.
■ **purulence** *noun* (now *rare*) (*a*) the fact of being purulent; the formation of pus; (*b*) purulent matter, pus: L16. **purulency** *noun* (now *rare*) the quality or state of being purulent L16. **purulently** *adverb* M19.

Purum /ˈpʊrʊm/ *noun & adjective*. E20.
[Prob. from a Sino-Tibetan lang.]
▶ **A** *noun*. Pl. same, **-s**. A member of a people living near the border of India and Myanmar (Burma). E20.
▶ **B** *attrib*. or as *adjective*. Of or pertaining to this people. M20.

¶ The Purum's kinship system, characterized by matrilateral cross-cousin marriage, has attracted the attention of western anthropologists.

purusha /ˈpʊrʊʃə/ *noun*. L18.
[Sanskrit *puruṣa* lit. 'man', pl. 'mankind'; in Hindu mythol., a being sacrificed by the gods in order to create the universe.]
HINDUISM. The universal spirit or soul; spirit or consciousness as opp. to matter; *spec*. in Sankya philosophy, the active or animating principle (personified as male) which with the passive (female) principle produces the universe. Cf. PRAKRITI.

purvey /ˈpəːveɪ/ *noun*. M16.
[from next.]
†**1** = PURVIEW 1. Only in M16.
2 An act of providing something or supplying something provided. Long *rare*. E17.
3 *spec*. A sum provided to meet current expenses. *local*. M18.

purvey /pəˈveɪ/ *verb*. ME.
[Anglo-Norman *purveier*, *por-*, Old French *porveeir* (mod. *pourvoir*) from Latin *providere* PROVIDE.]
†**1** *verb trans*. Foresee. Only in ME.
†**2** *verb trans*. Attend to (something) in advance; arrange beforehand (a thing, *to do*, *that*); foreordain. ME–E17.
3 *verb trans*. Provide or supply (something) for someone. Now *esp*., provide (items of food) as one's business. ME.
4 *verb trans*. Provide or supply (a person etc.) *with* something. *arch*. ME. ▶†**b** Equip (a person etc.). ME–M16.
†**5** *verb refl*. Prepare or equip oneself; get ready (*for*, *to do*). ME–L15.
†**6** *verb intrans*. Make provision for some event or action, or for the supply of something needed. (Foll. by *for*, *of*.) LME–M17.
7 *verb intrans*. Provide material necessities, esp. food; act as a supplier or purveyor. Also, make provision *for* a person, material needs, etc. LME.

3 E. EDWARDS Provisions . . had been excellently purveyed under Ralegh's contract. *British Journal of Aesthetics* The image purveys . . information . . not tied by necessity to a textual function. **7** G. B. GOODE Ten or twelve Connecticut smacks, which purvey for the New York market.

purveyance /pəˈveɪəns/ *noun*. ME.
[Old French *parvea(u)nce*, *pur-* from Latin *providentia* PROVIDENCE, or (later) from *porveeir*: see PURVEY *verb*, -ANCE.]
▶ **I** †**1** Foresight; = PROVIDENCE 2. ME–L16.

†**2** Preparation, prearrangement; direction; = PROVIDENCE 1. ME–E17.

†**3** In full ***purveyance of God, divine purveyance***. = PROVIDENCE 3. LME–M16.

▶**II** †**4** Something which is ordained; (a clause in) an ordinance or statute. ME–M17.

†**5** Something which is purveyed; a supply, a provision, esp. of food, arms, or other necessities. ME–L16.

6 The requisition and collection of provisions etc. as a right or prerogative; *spec.* and long only (now *Hist.*) the right of a monarch to buy necessities for the royal household, by means of and at a price fixed by a purveyor, and to exact the use of horses and vehicles for the royal journeys. ME.

7 The provision of some necessity, esp. food. LME.

> **6** W. BLACKSTONE The powers of purveyance have declined, in foreign countries as well as our own. **7** J. H. BURTON There was busy baking of biscuits and purveyance of provender.

purveyor /pəˈveɪə/ *noun*. ME.
[Anglo-Norman *purveür*, *-eour*, Old French *porveour*, *-eur*, formed as PURVEY *verb*: see -OR.]
†**1** A person who prepares or prearranges something. Only in ME.
2 A person who supplies something, esp. a necessity; *spec.* a person whose business is the provision of food and other material necessities, esp. large-scale meals. ME. ▸**b** An official responsible for the provision of necessities to a garrison, army, city, etc. L15.
3 *Hist.* A domestic officer responsible for the provision of purveyance and costing of necessities, as food, lodging, transport, etc., for a monarch or other important person. ME.

> **2** R. FRAME The Misses Vetch, purveyors of dairy products, will shut the shop. *transf.*: K. CLARK A stylish romanticism, which later purveyors of the genre .. never surpassed.

purview /ˈpəːvjuː/ *noun*. LME.
[Anglo-Norman *purveu*, Old French *porveu* (mod. *pourvu*) pa. pple of *porveir*: see PURVEY *verb*. Orig. *purveu est* it is provided, *purveu que* provided that.]
1 LAW. The body of a statute, following the preamble, and beginning 'be it enacted'; the enacting clauses. LME.
2 The scope or range of a document, scheme, subject, etc. L17.
3 A range of physical or mental vision; an outlook; a range of experience or thought. M19.

> **3** *Early Music* Considerations that modern historians have been inclined to exclude from their purview. S. WEYMAN In a twinkling she was hidden .. from the purview of the castle.

purwanah *noun* var. of PARWANAH.

PUS *abbreviation*.
Permanent Under-Secretary.

pus /pʌs/ *noun*. LME.
[Latin.]
MEDICINE. A yellowish-white or greenish opaque viscid liquid, produced in infected tissue and containing a suspension of dead white cells etc.

puschkinia /pʊʃˈkɪnɪə/ *noun*. E19.
[mod. Latin (see below), from Count Apollos Musin-*Pushkin* (1760–1805), Russian scientist + -IA¹.]
A small spring-flowering plant of the lily family, *Puschkinia scilloides* of western Asia, bearing pale blue bell-shaped flowers with a darker stripe on the perianth segments. Also called ***striped squill***.

Puseyism /ˈpjuːzɪɪz(ə)m/ *noun*. Chiefly *derog.* M19.
[from Dr E. B. *Pusey* (1800–82), professor of Hebrew and Canon of Christ Church at Oxford + -ISM.]
Hist. The principles of Dr Pusey and his associates in the Oxford Movement who advocated the revival of Catholic doctrine and observance in the Church of England.
■ **Puseyist** *noun* (*rare*) a Puseyite L19. **Puseyˈistical** *adjective* of or pertaining to the Puseyites or Puseyism M19. **Puseyite** *noun & adjective* (*a*) *noun* a follower of Pusey; a supporter of the Oxford Movement; (*b*) *adjective* of or pertaining to Puseyites or Puseyism: M19. **Puseyˈitical** *adjective* (*rare*) = PUSEYISTICAL M19.

push /pʊʃ/ *noun*¹. M16.
[from the verb.]
▶**I** †**1** An attack, a vigorous onset. M16–E19.
2 a An act of pushing; an application of force or pressure to move someone or something away; a shove, a thrust. Formerly also, a blow, a stroke, a knock. L16. ▸**b** *fig.* An exertion of influence or pressure, esp. to promote a person's advancement. M17. ▸**c** More fully ***push-shot***, ***push-stroke***, etc. In cricket, golf, hockey, etc., a stroke in which the ball is pushed instead of being hit; *spec.* in billiards, a stroke in which the ball is pushed with the cue, or in which the cue, the cue-ball, and the object ball are all in contact at the time the stroke is made. L19.
3 An effort, an attempt; now *esp.* a vigorous effort, a determined (esp. military) advance. Freq. in ***make a push***. L16. ▸**b** The action or an act of selling drugs illegally. *colloq. rare.* L20.
4 A thrust of a weapon, or of an animal's horn. L16.
5 *fig.* Pressure of circumstances; a case of stress or emergency, a critical moment; a showdown. L16.
6 Physical pressure; *esp.* in BUILDING, the thrust of an arch etc. E18.
7 Determined and persistent effort to achieve success; drive, initiative, enterprise, esp. as characterized by a lack of consideration for others. M19.

> **2a** D. LESSING He gave the door a sharp push .. and went into a large .. hall. **b** V. S. PRITCHETT Chekhov was 'a famous man' and the acquaintance would give a push to her career. **3** P. CAREY The U.K. office .. planned a big push on the Australian market. R. WHELAN Patton's eastward push along the coast to Messina. *Waterski International* Moore made a determined push to catch the leader. **5** T. GRAY When it came to the push .. I had forgot all I intended to say. **7** J. GALSWORTHY They seemed unable to make money .. they had no push and no tenacity. C. BONINGTON His .. modesty and lack of push has stopped him achieving the reputation of some of his peers.

▶**II 8** A crowd of people; a throng; *spec.* (*slang*) a band of thieves; a gang of convicts; *Austral. slang* a gang; a particular group of people, a clique. E18.
9 A button, switch, etc., which is pressed in order to operate a mechanism; a push-button. L19.

> **8** D. MALOUF He was a member of Brisbane's toughest rugby push.

Phrases: **at a push** at a critical moment, in a showdown; *colloq.* with difficulty, if pushed. **get the push** *colloq.* be thrown out, be dismissed. **give a person the push** *colloq.* throw out or dismiss a person.
■ **pushful** *adjective* full of drive and energy, self-assertive, aggressively enterprising L19. **pushfully** *adverb* E20. **pushfulness** *noun* L19.

push /pʊʃ/ *noun*². *obsolete* exc. *dial.* LME.
[Origin unkn.]
A pustule, a pimple, a boil.

push /pʊʃ/ *verb*. ME.
[Old & mod. French *pousser*, †*pou(l)ser* from Latin *pulsare* frequentative of *puls-* pa. ppl stem of *pellere* drive, thrust.]
▶**I 1 a** *verb trans.* Exert force on (a person or thing) so as to move away; move by force; shove, thrust, drive. Formerly also, hit, strike. Freq. foll. by adverbs, as *away*, *down*, *off*, etc. ME. ▸**b** *verb trans.* Drive or repulse by force of arms; drive (game) in a hunt. M17. ▸**c** *verb intrans.* Move *off* in a boat; move *away* from a bank or shore, move *out* into open water. Also (*colloq.*), leave, go away (freq. foll. by *along*, *off*). E18. ▸**d** *verb trans.* Move or advance (a force) against opposition or difficulty. M18. ▸**e** *verb trans.* In billiards, cricket, etc., move (the ball) by pushing instead of hitting. L19. ▸**f** *verb trans.* COMPUTING. Prepare (a stack) to receive a piece of data etc. on the top (usu. foll. by *down*); transfer (data etc.) to the top of a stack. M20.
2 *verb intrans.* Exert force or pressure on a person or thing; move by force, shove, jostle. Freq. foll. by *against*, *at*, *into*, etc. ME. ▸**b** Exert muscular pressure internally, esp. during the second stage of labour. L20.
3 a *verb intrans.* Thrust *at* with a pointed weapon, stick, etc.; tilt, fence; use a spear, short sword, etc. Now *arch. rare.* LME. ▸†**b** *verb trans.* Stab with a weapon. L17–E18.
4 *verb intrans. & trans.* Of an ox etc.: thrust or butt with the horns. Now *dial.* M16.
5 *verb trans. & intrans.* Thrust (a weapon); stick out, poke out, project; (of a plant) send out (a shoot, root, etc.) as a growth. Freq. foll. by *out*, *up*. E17.
6 *verb intrans.* Make one's way with force or persistence; advance with effort. Chiefly with *along*, *on*, etc. E18.

> **1a** M. SINCLAIR Her father pushed back his chair. D. H. LAWRENCE The waves pushed the boat slowly round. M. FORSTER I pushed him off with such force that he crashed back. *fig.*: H. L. MENCKEN As dangerous to push wages too high as it is to over-expand capital. G. LORD Can any of you just forget it, push it out of your mind? **c** K. MOORE It's rather late .. I'd better be pushing off. **d** J. IRVING The Wehrmacht pushed into Yugoslavia with thirty-three divisions. **2** J. CONRAD Men pushed against one another. C. PRIEST I put my weight against the door and pushed. G. LORD I could feel the weave of the sea-grass matting pushing into my flesh. **4** AV *Exod.* 21:32 If the oxe shall push a man seruant, or a mayd seruant. **5** J. M. COETZEE New grass-shoots are beginning to push out here and there. **6** R. GITTINGS In spite of the .. rain they pushed on. R. INGALLS He pushed forward ahead of her. R. THOMAS He .. pushed through the stream of people.

▶**II 7 a** *verb intrans.* Make a strenuous effort; make an urgent request; aim *at* with endeavour; press *for*; strive *to do*. L16. ▸**b** *verb trans.* Approach (a certain number), esp. in years of age. *colloq.* M20.
8 *verb trans.* Urge, press, incite (a person) *to do*, *to* a course of action; egg *on*. L16.
9 *verb trans.* **a** Pursue (an action or operation) with vigour and insistence; urge, press (a claim etc.). (Foll. by †*on*.) E17. ▸**b** Extend or increase (an action or operation); develop further afield. M19.
10 a *verb trans.* Impel (a horse etc.) to greater speed; urge *on*; *transf.* accelerate (a vehicle) vigorously and esp. excessively. E18. ▸**b** *verb trans.* Force (a thing) into more intense action. Now *rare.* M18. ▸**c** *verb trans. & intrans.* BRIDGE. Try to force (an opponent) into a higher and more doubtful contract by overcalling. E20. ▸**d** *verb trans.* PHOTOGRAPHY. = ***push-process*** s.v. PUSH-. L20.
11 *verb trans.* Carry out (a matter, action, principle, etc.) to a further point, or to the furthest limit; press *through* to a conclusion. E18.
12 *verb trans.* **a** Advance, promote; urge the use, practice, sale, etc., of (a thing); work for the advancement of (a person). E18. ▸**b** Force or thrust (something) *on* or *upon* a person for attention or acceptance. E18. ▸**c** Sell (drugs) illegally. *colloq.* M20.
13 *verb trans.* Put pressure or strain on (a person); (in *pass.*) be hard-pressed through lack of time, means, etc. M18.

> **7a** A. S. DALE Gardiner pushed for political measures, using the paper to produce a spirit of social reform. *International Business Week* Venezuela is pushing to double aluminium output. **b** S. BELLOW Mrs Renling was pushing fifty-five .. only a little grey. J. RABAN The temperature was pushing ninety degrees. **8** G. GREENE He was pushed steadily by his father towards art. **9a** M. MOORCOCK I had learned tact .. so I did not push the point. **b** YEATS They pushed their trade to still more distant parts. **10a** H. CALVIN Dai was pushing the Land Rover all out. **11** *Scotsman* The wisdom of not pushing .. political power to extremes. *Spotlight Contacts* Walker pushed massive construction and delicate detail to new levels. **12a** A. BLOND As a publisher I am .. alert for opportunities to push my wares. ALAN BENNETT They take advantage of you. That's your trouble .. you won't push yourself. *West Highland Free Press* This is an issue we've been pushing for quite some time. **c** *Punisher* Lining his pockets by pushing the lethal cocaine derivative, Crack. **13** E. SIMPSON Once pushed beyond endurance by something his mother had done, Delmore said he hated her. *Radio Times* If pushed Jimmy will admit to being .. on the wrong side of 70. *Boardroom* He was so pushed for cash .. he didn't even have a phone.

Phrases, & with adverbs in specialized senses: **push about**, **push around** move (a person) roughly from place to place, manhandle; *fig.* (orig. *US*) browbeat, bully, domineer over. ***pushing up the daisies***: see DAISY *noun* 1. **push it** *colloq.* cause an action to be rushed; cut something fine. **push one's fortune** try to make one's fortune. ***push one's luck***: see LUCK *noun*. **push one's way** make one's way by thrusting obstacles or opponents aside. ***push the boat out***: see BOAT *noun* 1. **push things** *colloq.* = ***push it*** above. **when push comes to shove** *colloq.* when action must be taken, when a decision, commitment, etc., must be made.
■ **pushaˈbility** *noun* the quality or condition of being pushable L20. **pushable** *adjective* able to be pushed L20. **pushing** *adjective* (*a*) that pushes; (*b*) enterprising; pushy; (*c*) *colloq.* approaching (a specified age): L17. **pushingly** *adverb* (*rare*) M19. **pushingness** *noun* (*rare*) L19.

†**push** *interjection & noun*³. L16.
[Natural exclam.]
▶**A** *interjection.* Expr. contempt, impatience, or disgust. L16–E17.
▶**B** *noun.* An expression of contempt or disdain. Only in ***make a push at***, treat with disdain. *rare* (Shakes.). Only in L16.

push- /pʊʃ/ *combining form*. L16.
[Repr. PUSH *noun*¹, *verb*.]
Forming combs. in various relations and senses, as 'moved by pushing' (***push-bar***, ***push-boat***); 'used for pushing' (***push-pedal***, ***push-piece***, ***pushrod***); 'that pushes or is pushed' (***push-along***, ***push-down***). Many can be written with or without a hyphen.
push-and-go *noun & adjective* (*a*) *noun* ability to develop and carry out a scheme energetically; enterprise, initiative, ambition; (*b*) *adjective* (of a motorized toy etc.) having a mechanism that stores and releases the momentum generated by a preliminary push. **push-and-pull** *adjective & noun* (*a*) *adjective* involving (esp. alternate) pushes and pulls; *spec.* designating (the operation of) a train which can travel in either direction without having the engine turned around; (*b*) *noun* (*US* MILITARY) sighting and aiming drill. **push-ball** a game for two teams in which either side tries to push a very large ball towards the opponents' goal. **push-bicycle** a bicycle operated by pedals as opp. to a motor. **push-bike** *noun & verb* (*colloq.*) (*a*) *noun* a push-bicycle; (*b*) *verb intrans.* ride a push-bicycle. **push-car** *US* a railway car, *esp.* one connecting an engine with a train which is on a ferryboat. **pushcart** (*a*) a handcart; (*b*) a pram. **push-chain** LINGUISTICS a sound shift in which one phoneme approaches a second and this in turn shifts so that their differentiation is maintained. **pushchair** a folding chair on wheels, in which a child can be pushed along. **push-cycle** = ***push-bicycle*** above. **push-cyclist** a rider of a push-bicycle. **push-down** *noun & adjective* (*a*) *noun* (AERONAUTICS) a manoeuvre in which an aircraft in level flight loses altitude and resumes level flight; (*b*) *adjective* (COMPUTING) designating or pertaining to a linear store or list that receives and loses items at one end only, the first to be removed being the last to have been added (cf. PUSH *verb* 1f). **push fit**: enabling a part to be pushed into a hole by hand but not allowing free rotation. **push hold** MOUNTAINEERING = ***pressure hold*** s.v. PRESSURE *noun*. **push-in** (*a*) HOCKEY the act of pushing the ball into play from the sideline; (*b*) *US & Austral. slang* mugging carried out after forced entry into a house when the victim opens the door. **pushmobile** *US* a children's cart pushed by hand. **push money** *US slang* = SPIFF *noun*. **push moraine** PHYSICAL GEOGRAPHY a morainic ridge pushed up by

the snout of an advancing glacier, made up of unconsolidated rock debris. **push-off** *noun & adjective* (*a*) *noun* an act of pushing off; *spec.* an action of pushing down with the foot so as to give impetus to a leap; (*b*) *adjective* that pushes something off. **push-out** *slang* a person who is made to leave somewhere, esp. school. **push pass** SPORT a pass effected by pushing rather than hitting or kicking the ball. **push-pin** (*a*) a children's game in which each player pushes or fillips a pin with the object of crossing that of another player; *fig.* a trivial or insignificant occupation; (*b*) (chiefly *N. Amer.*) a tack or drawing-pin, usu. with a glass or plastic head. **push-pit** [joc. formation after PULPIT noun] NAUTICAL a raised safety rail in the stern of a boat. **push plate**: attached to a door by which it may be pushed open. **push poll** an ostensible opinion poll in which the true objective is to sway voters using loaded questions. **push-process** (PHOTOGRAPHY) develop (a film) so as to compensate for (deliberate) underexposure, thus increasing the effective film speed. ***push-shot***: see PUSH *noun*[1] 2C. **push-start** *verb & noun* (*a*) *verb trans.* start (a motor vehicle) by pushing to turn the engine; (*b*) *noun* the action of push-starting a vehicle. ***push-stroke***: see PUSH *noun*[1] 2C. **push technology** COMPUTING a service in which the user downloads software from a provider which then continually supplies information from the Internet in categories selected by the user. **push-through** *noun & adjective* (*a*) *noun* an instrument for cleaning the bore of a rifle; (*b*) *adjective* designating a thing in which one part is pushed through another. **push-tow** a line of connected unpowered barges with a powered one at each end to propel them. **push-towing** propulsion of a push-tow.

push-button /ˈpʊʃbʌt(ə)n/ *noun & adjective.* L19.
[from PUSH- + BUTTON *noun.*]
▶ **A** *noun.* A button that is pressed to effect some operation, usu. by closing or opening an electric circuit. L19.
▶ **B** *adjective.* **1** Operated or effected by pressing a push-button. E20.
2 Characterized by the use of push-buttons, *spec.* as a sign or result of technological advancement; fully automated or mechanized. M20.
3 Easily obtainable, as at the press of a button; instant. M20.

📖 **2** *Times* The . . woman of the future will live in an increasingly push-button home. **push-button war**, **push-button warfare** warfare conducted by means of (nuclear) missiles launched by the press of a button. **3** *Listener* The price we are paying for the alleged boon of push-button entertainment can already be discerned.

pusher /ˈpʊʃə/ *noun.* L16.
[from PUSH *verb* + -ER[1].]
1 a *gen.* A person who or thing which pushes. L16. ▸**b** A girl, a young woman; *spec.* a prostitute. *slang.* E20. ▸**c** A person who sells drugs illegally. *slang.* M20.
2 a A part of a machine with a thrusting action; a machine with such parts. M19. ▸**b** NAUTICAL. The seventh mast of a seven-masted schooner. E20. ▸**c** AERONAUTICS. An aircraft with an airscrew behind the main wings. Cf. TRACTOR 2C. E20.
3 A utensil used by infants to push food on to a spoon or fork. Also, a piece of bread used for this purpose. E20.
4 A pushchair. *Austral. colloq.* M20.

📖 **1a** O. S. NOCK Steam-operated coal pushers were first introduced on the . . 'Pacific' engines. T. TANNER Elton is indeed a pusher, or social climber. **c** *Cincinnati Enquirer* The drug ring's security man and pusher. **2c** *attrib.*: *Flying* Pusher propellers . . contribute to both directional and longitudinal stability.

Comb.: **pusher set** an infant's spoon and pusher; **pusher-tug**: used to push a group of connected barges.

pushily /ˈpʊʃɪli/ *adverb.* M20.
[from PUSHY *adjective* + -LY[2].]
In a pushy manner.

pushiness /ˈpʊʃɪnɪs/ *noun.* E20.
[from PUSHY *adjective* + -NESS.]
1 PHILOSOPHY. The property inherent in a material object which enables it to be apprehended and identified by touch. Now *rare.* E20.
2 The quality of being pushy. M20.

pushmi-pullyu /pʊʃmiːˈpʊljuː/ *noun & adjective.* Also **pushme-pullyou**. E20.
[from phrs. *push me* and *pull you*; invented by Hugh Lofting (1886–1947) in *Doctor Dolittle.*]
▶ **A** *noun.* An imaginary creature resembling a llama or an antelope, but with a head at both ends. E20.
▶ **B** *attrib.* or as *adjective.* Of an attitude or policy: incoherent, ambivalent. M20.

pushover /ˈpʊʃəʊvə/ *noun.* L19.
[from PUSH *verb* + OVER *adverb.*]
1 Something easily accomplished or overcome; an easy task or victory. *slang.* L19.
2 A person who is easily pushed over or overcome; *spec.* (*a*) a boxer, player of a game, etc., who is easily knocked out or beaten; (*b*) a woman who makes little resistance to demands for sexual intercourse; (*c*) an easy victim; (*d*) a person who is easily influenced or attracted by something; (foll. by *for*). *slang.* E20.
3 RUGBY FOOTBALL. In full ***pushover try***. A try in which one side in a scrum pushes the ball over the opponents' goal-line. M20.

📖 **2** *Rugby World & Post* We may not win all our matches, but we will not be a pushover. G. CHARLES I'm a push-over for all Eastern music.

push-pull /pʊʃˈpʊl/ *adjective, noun, & adverb.* E20.
[from PUSH- + PULL *verb, noun.*]
▶ **A** *adjective.* **1** Able to be pushed or pulled; responding to or exerting both pushes and pulls. E20.
2 ELECTRONICS. Having or involving two matched valves or transistors that operate 180 degrees out of phase, conducting alternately for increased output. E20.
3 CINEMATOGRAPHY. Of an optical soundtrack: divided into equal parts exposed to light modulated in opposite phase. M20.
▶ **B** *noun.* Chiefly ELECTRONICS. A push-pull arrangement or state. E20.
▶ **C** *adverb.* ELECTRONICS. In a push-pull manner. M20.

push-up /ˈpʊʃʌp/ *noun & adjective.* E20.
[from PUSH *verb* + UP *adverb*[1].]
▶ **A** *noun.* **1** = ***press-up*** s.v. PRESS *verb*[1]. Also, an exercise on parallel bars in which the body is supported by the bent arms and raised by straightening them. Chiefly *N. Amer.* E20.
2 An act of picking a pocket in which the victim's arm is pushed away from his or her pocket by the pickpocket's accomplice. *Austral. slang.* E20.
3 A muskrat's resting-place, formed by pushing up vegetation through a hole in the ice. *N. Amer.* M20.
▶ **B** *adjective.* **1** That pushes up or may be pushed up. M20. ▸**b** Designating a brassière or similar garment which is underwired or padded to provide uplift for the breasts. M20.
2 COMPUTING. = ***push-down*** (b) s.v. PUSH-. M20.

pushy /ˈpʊʃi/ *adjective. colloq.* M20.
[from PUSH *noun*[1], *verb* + -Y[1].]
Excessively or unpleasantly forward or self-assertive; aggressive.

📖 *Melody Maker* A gaggle of pushy European journalists thrust microphones under his nose. M. FORSTER I gave John every encouragement I could, without being indecently pushy.

pusill /ˈpjuːsɪl/ *adjective & noun. rare.* E17.
[Latin *pusillus* very small.]
▶†**A** *adjective.* Small, insignificant, petty. E–M17.
▶ **B** *noun.* †**1** A variety of pear. Only in E17.
2 A small or weak child; a weakling. L19.

pusillanimity /ˌpjuːsɪləˈnɪmɪti/ *noun.* LME.
[Old & mod. French *pusillanimité* or late (eccl.) Latin *pusillanimitas*, from *pusillanimis* (translating Greek *olugopsukhos*), from *pusillus* very small, weak + *animus* mind: see -ITY.]
The quality or character of being pusillanimous; lack of courage; timidity; meanness of spirit.

pusillanimous /pjuːsɪˈlanɪməs/ *adjective.* LME.
[Late (eccl.) Latin *pusillanimis*: see prec., -OUS.]
1 Of a person: lacking in courage; timid, cowardly; mean-spirited. LME.
2 Of a quality, action, etc.: resulting from or displaying meanness of spirit or a lack of courage. E17.
■ **pusillanimously** *adverb* M17. **pusillanimousness** *noun* = PUSILLANIMITY E18.

puss /pʊs/ *noun*[1]. E16.
[Prob. from Middle Low German *pūs* (also *pūskatte*), Dutch *poes*: cf. Lithuanian *puž*, *puiž*, Gaelic *puis*, *puiseag*, Irish *puisín* of unkn. origin.]
1 (A pet name for) a cat. Also ***puss-cat***. *colloq.* E16.
2 (Orig. a term of contempt, now one of endearment for) a girl or woman. E17.
3 (A name for) a hare. M17.
4 = PUSSY *noun* 4. *coarse slang.* M17.

📖 **1** R. L'ESTRANGE For Puss even when she's a Madam, will be a Mouser still. **puss in the corner** a children's game in which one player in the centre tries to capture one of the other players' bases as they change places. **2** M. M. KAYE Major Harlowe pinched his daughter's chin . . his pretty little puss. **3** *Hounds* Puss ran . . and . . hounds caught their hare next to the . . bales.

Comb.: **puss boot** *Jamaican* a plimsoll, a tennis shoe; ***puss-cat***: see sense 1 above; **puss-moth** a large European moth, *Cerura vinula*, of the family Notodontidae, having a very fluffy body and whitish wings with darker markings.

puss /pʊs/ *noun*[2]. *dial. & slang* (chiefly *Anglo-Irish & N. Amer.*). L19.
[Irish *pus* lip, mouth.]
A (pouting) mouth; a (sour or ugly) face. Also, the mouth or face considered as the object of a blow.

📖 W. C. WILLIAMS Once mother . . laid the old gal out with a smack across the puss.

pussel /ˈpʌs(ə)l/ *adjective.* Chiefly *US dial.* Also **pussy** /ˈpʌsi/. M19.
[Alt.]
= PURSY *adjective*[1] 2.

pusser /ˈpʌsə/ *noun. Nautical slang.* E20.
[Repr. a pronunc.]
A naval purser.

pussley /ˈpʌsli/ *noun. US colloq.* Also **-ly**. E19.
[Alt. of PURSLANE.]
Purslane, *Portulaca oleracea.*

pussums /ˈpʊsəmz/ *noun. colloq.* E20.
[from PUSS *noun*[1] + *-ums*, after *diddums*.]
(A term of endearment for) a cat or (*transf.*) a sweetheart.

pussy /ˈpʊsi/ *noun & adjective*[1]. L16.
[from PUSS *noun*[1] + -Y[6].]
▶ **A** *noun.* **1** (A term of endearment for) a girl or a woman. Also *slang*, a finicky or effeminate man; a homosexual. L16.
2 (A pet name for) a cat. *colloq.* E18.
3 (A name for) a hare. Also (*Austral.*), a rabbit. E18.
4 The female external genitals. Also (*transf.*), sexual intercourse; women considered sexually. *coarse slang.* L18.
5 a Something soft and furry, as a fur necklet, a willow catkin, etc. M19. ▸**b** A fur garment. *Criminals' slang.* M20.

📖 **2** E. PEACOCK A saucer of milk . . on the rug for pussy. **4 eat pussy** *coarse slang* perform cunnilingus.

Comb.: **pussy hair** *coarse slang* a woman's pubic hair; **pussy palm** a branch of pussy-willow; **pussy posse** *US slang* the vice squad; **pussy-toes** *US* any of various small woolly plants of the genus *Antennaria*, of the composite family, esp. *A. plantaginifolia*; **pussy-wants-a-corner** *US* = ***puss in the corner*** s.v. PUSS *noun*[1] 1; **pussy-whip** *verb trans.* (*slang*) henpeck (usu. in *pass.*); **pussy-willow** *colloq.* (orig. *US*) any willow with soft fluffy catkins appearing before the leaves, *esp.* (in the US) the glaucous willow, *Salix discolor*, and (in Britain) the goat willow, *S. caprea*, and grey willow, *S. cinerea*; the catkins of such a willow.
▶ **B** *adjective.* Soft or furry like a cat. Also, finicky, effeminate. M19.

📖 C. KINGSLEY She was the most . . soft . . pussy cuddly delicious creature who ever nursed a baby.

pussy /ˈpʌsi/ *adjective*[2]. *rare.* L19.
[from PUS *noun* + -Y[1].]
Full of pus.

pussy *adjective*[3] var. of PUSSEL.

pussy /ˈpʊsi/ *verb intrans.* E20.
[from PUSSY *noun & adjective*[1].]
Behave or move like a cat; move stealthily; play *around*.

pussy-cat /ˈpʊsɪkat/ *noun.* E19.
[from PUSSY *noun* + CAT *noun*[1].]
1 A cat. *nursery & colloq.* E19.
2 A willow or hazel catkin. M19.
3 A person compared to a cat; now *esp.* one who is attractive, amiable, or submissive. M19.

📖 **3** *News of the World* He's a tough businessman but he's a pussycat in private.

Comb.: **pussy-cat bow** a soft floppy bow worn at the neck of a blouse etc.

pussyfoot /ˈpʊsɪfʊt/ *noun, adjective, & verb.* E20.
[from PUSSY *noun* + FOOT *noun, verb.*]
▶ **A** *noun.* **1** A person who moves stealthily or acts cautiously. E20.
2 [Nickname of W. E. Johnson (1862–1945), US supporter of prohibition known for his stealthy methods as a magistrate.] An advocate or supporter of prohibition; a teetotaller. E20.
▶ **B** *attrib.* or as *adjective.* Teetotal; non-alcoholic. E20.

📖 D. H. LAWRENCE Even the word Marsala will smack of preciosity Soon in the pussyfoot West.

▶ **C** *verb intrans.* Tread softly or lightly to avoid being noticed; act cautiously or non-committally. Also foll. by *around*. E20.

📖 J. O'FAOLAIN Larry's pussyfooting. Maybe he doesn't trust me? *Creative Review* There's been a lot of pussyfooting around about Aids.

■ **pussy-footed** *adjective* having a light step; cautious; non-committal: L19. **pussy-footedness** *noun* (*rare*) M20. **pussyfooter** *noun* (*a*) a person who pussyfoots; (*b*) an advocate or supporter of prohibition: E20. **pussyfootism** *noun* teetotalism, advocacy or enforcement of prohibition E20.

pustulan /ˈpʌstjʊlan/ *noun.* M20.
[from mod. Latin *pustulata*, specific epithet of a lichen, fem. of late Latin *pustulatus*: see next, -AN.]
BIOCHEMISTRY. A glucan present in various lichens.

pustulate /ˈpʌstjʊlət/ *adjective.* LME.
[Late Latin *pustulatus* pa. pple, formed as next: see -ATE[2].]
MEDICINE & ZOOLOGY. Having or covered with pustules; pustulous, pustular.

pustulate /ˈpʌstjʊleɪt/ *verb trans. & intrans.* M18.
[Late Latin *pustulat-* pa. ppl stem of *pustulare* blister, from Latin *pustula* PUSTULE: see -ATE[3].]
Form (into) pustules.
■ **pustu'lation** *noun* the action of pustulating; formation of pustules: L19.

pustule /ˈpʌstjuːl/ *noun.* LME.
[Old & mod. French, or Latin *pustula*: see -ULE.]
1 MEDICINE. A small blister on the skin containing pus; a pimple. LME.
2 ZOOLOGY & BOTANY. A small raised spot or rounded swelling. L18.

3 An eruptive swelling of the ground. *rare.* M19.
1 malignant pustule the characteristic lesion of cutaneous anthrax.
■ **pustular** *adjective* of or pertaining to pustules, affected or characterized by pustules M18. **pustulous** *adjective* = PUSTULAR M16.

puszta /ˈpʊstə/ *noun.* M19.
[Hungarian = plain, steppe, waste.]
In Hungary, flat treeless countryside; a plain in Hungary.

put /pʊt/ *noun*[1]. Also (*obsolete* exc. *Scot.*) **-tt**. See also PUTT *noun*[2]. ME.
[from PUT *verb*[1].]
1 A throw of a stone, shot, or other heavy weight. ME.
2 An act of thrusting or pushing; a shove; a butt by an animal. Now *rare.* LME.
3 *Hist.* A card-game for two, three, or four players, in which three cards are dealt to each player, the game being won either by winning two or more tricks or by bluffing the other player or players into conceding. L17.
4 *STOCK EXCHANGE.* The option of selling a specified amount of stock at a certain price within a specified time. E18.
Comb.: **put-and-call** *STOCK EXCHANGE* the option of buying or selling stock at a certain price by a certain date.

put /pʌt/ *noun*[2]. *arch. colloq.* Also **-tt**. L17.
[Origin unkn.]
A stupid man, a blockhead.
country put a lout, a bumpkin.

put /pʊt/ *verb*[1]. Infl. **-tt-**. Pa. t. & pple **put** /pʊt/, (*obsolete* exc. *Scot.*) **putted**. Also (*obsolete* exc. *Scot.*) **-tt**. See also PUTT *verb*
[Old English (in verbal noun *putung*), with parallel forms *potian* POTE *verb*, *pȳtan*: ult. origin unkn.]
▶ **I 1** *verb trans. & intrans.* Thrust, push, shove; give a push or knock (to); *fig.* urge. Now only *Scot. & north.*, butt with the head or horns. OE.
2 *verb trans.* & †*intrans.* (with *at, with*). Propel (a stone or weight) mainly by the swing of the body from the hand raised and placed close to the shoulder and neck, esp. as an athletic exercise. Chiefly in ***putting the shot***, ***putting the stone***, ***putting the weight***, etc. ME.
3 *verb trans.* Thrust or plunge (a weapon), fire or send (a missile, bullet, etc.), *into, through*, etc. ME.
4 *verb trans.* †**a** Drive; impel by force or command; *esp.* (of the wind) drive (a ship) in a specified direction. LME–L18. ▸**b** *MINING.* Propel (a barrow of coal etc.), orig. by pushing behind, later also by hauling. E18.
5 *verb trans.* & †*refl.* Foll. by adverb: launch or embark on a sea voyage. LME.
6 *verb intrans.* **a** Set out, start; pass, make one's way. Now only *US colloq.*, leave, quit. LME. ▸**b** *NAUTICAL.* Foll. by adverb: (of a ship etc.) set out, proceed, follow a course in a specified direction. L16. ▸**c** Of a stream etc.: flow *into*, *out of*. *US.* E17.
7 *verb intrans.* Of a plant: send out shoots, sprout, bud. Cf. ***put forth*** (b) below. Now *dial.* E17.

> 📖 **3** SHAKES. *Oth.* Wear thy good rapier bare, and put it home. **5** C. M. YONGE He put a fleet to sea. **6b** C. THIRLWALL Clearchus . . having put into Delos for shelter, returned to Greece.

▶ **II 8** *verb trans.* Move physically into or out of some position; cause to get into or be in some place or position expressed or implied; place, lay, set. ME. ▸**b** Foll. by adverb: remove, expel, send away; divert, cause to give up. *arch.* ME. ▸**c** Place (a garment, an ornament, etc.) *on, upon* the body. LME. ▸**d** Foll. by *to, against*: write (a signature or name) fix (a seal etc.) on a document etc. LME. ▸**e** Couple (an animal) *to* another of the opposite sex for breeding. E16. ▸**f** Foll. by *to, in*: harness (a draught animal) to a vehicle. M16. ▸†**g** Commit (a person) *to* another for education or training. M17–L18. ▸**h** Convey, transport, *across, over*, etc. M17. ▸**i** *STOCK EXCHANGE.* Deliver (stock) at a specified price within a specified time. E19.

> 📖 **8** LD MACAULAY A sealed packet was put into his hands. J. RUSKIN You have put a railroad bridge over the fall of Schaffhausen. E. WAUGH Basil put his hand to the iron bell. A. WILSON She put a record onto an old gramophone. W. BRONK A man putting pole-bean seeds in the ground. **b** F. MANN She could not put from her some feeling of pride. **d** J. H. NEWMAN To this number . . I also put my initials. OED Put a tick against the names you know. **e** *Horse & Hound* The foals which the Oldenburg mares produced when put to . . Cleveland Bay stallions.

▶ **III 9** *verb trans.* Place *in* or bring *into* a specified condition, relation, or state; cause to be or go, habitually or temporarily. ME. ▸**b** Place with or in by way of addition; add. Foll. by *to, in*. LME.
10 *verb trans.* Subject *to* death, suffering, expense, trouble, etc. ME.
11 *verb trans.* Apply or devote to a use or purpose; *spec.* use (ground) for the raising of a particular crop. Usu. foll. by *to*. ME.
12 *verb trans.* Propose to or place before a person for consideration or attention; propound. ME. ▸**b** *spec.* Submit (a motion etc.) formally to the vote of an assembly. L17.
13 *verb trans.* Foll. by *in, into*: express or translate in words, another language, form of expression, etc. Also, express, state, or write in a particular way. ME.
14 *verb trans.* Force or drive (a person) reluctantly into performing some action, e.g. making a choice, etc. ME. ▸**b** Oblige, compel, call on, (*to do*). *arch.* E17.
15 *verb trans.* Place in a scale of magnitude, rank, kind, etc.; estimate or price at (a specified amount etc.). LME.
16 *verb trans.* **a** Assign or set (a quality, meaning, value, etc.) *on, upon, to*, †*in*. LME. ▸**b** Regard as based on or arising from; base, found, *(up)on*. E18.
17 *verb trans.* Impose or enforce the existence of, bring to bear, (a state, condition, relation, etc.) *on* or *to* an existing thing, action, or state. LME. ▸**b** Place, repose (trust, confidence, etc.) *in*, †*to*. L15.
18 *verb trans.* Impose (something) *on, upon*, (†*to*, †*unto*) a person etc. as a burden, an obligation, an indignity, blame, etc.; encumber a person with (something unwelcome or unpleasant). LME. ▸**b** Play (a trick) or practise (a deception) *on* or *upon*. *arch.* E17.
19 *verb trans.* Lay the blame of (something) *on* or *upon*. LME.
20 *verb trans.* Set to do something, or on a course of action; *refl.* (*arch. & dial.*) set about, apply oneself. Foll. by *to, to do, on, upon*. LME. ▸**b** Set to learn, study, or practise. LME. ▸**c** Direct or urge (a horse etc.) towards an obstacle etc.; cause to perform a particular movement. L16. ▸**d** Set (cattle etc.) to feed on something; restrict (a person) to a specified diet or regimen. E17.
21 *verb trans.* Set conceptually *in the place of* something else; substitute *for* another thing; imagine (oneself) in a specified situation. L15.
22 *verb trans.* Place, insert, or enter (a name, an item) in a list, table, etc. Now usu. foll. by *down*. E16.
23 *verb trans.* Commit *to* a risk or hazard; stake *on, upon*, bet (money) *on* a horse etc.; invest (money) *in* or *into*. E17.

> 📖 **9** DEFOE This put my mother into a great passion. R. J. GRAVES A very fine . . man put himself under my care. F. MARRYAT You have put me under an obligation which I never can repay. H. R. MILL The least mistake . . would put the calculation all wrong. J. RHYS Now to put you wise about the book. J. GATHORNE-HARDY Every night . . Mary would cry when she was put to bed. E. SAINTSBURY A homeopath . . who put Dodgson in touch with a . . stammer-curer. **10** HENRY FIELDING She had put herself to the expense of a long hood. SOUTHEY Foy . . put the defenders to the bayonet. G. DURRELL Tremendous dark eyes, eyes that would have put any self-respecting owl to shame. J. UGLOW She wanted to put to the test her theories about . . the social novel. **11** MILTON O glorious strength Put to the labour of a Beast. **12** HENRY MORE The Queen . . put hard and weighty questions to him. *Daily Telegraph* The militant wing . . was putting its case to the meeting. **b** GIBBON On the question being put, it was carried without a division. **13** F. MARRYAT This new feature of the case, so aptly put by the old lawyer. A. WILSON Let's see if I can succeed . . in putting my thoughts into words. L. P. HARTLEY He was so ashamed . . of the word 'love' that he . . had to put it in inverted commas. JULIAN GLOAG 'You think it's naïve to be religious?' 'That's —one way of putting it.' **14** MILTON Thank him who puts me loath to this revenge. J. P. STERN The . . subterfuges Marxist . . interpreters are put to when attempting to isolate the major motive force of politics. **b** SIR W. SCOTT Put me not . . to dishonour myself by striking thee. **15** J. RUSKIN Whether you think I am putting the motives of popular action too low. G. F. NEWMAN He put her age around twenty-two. **16a** ADDISON That was the Interpretation which the Neighbourhood put on it. **b** J. BUTLER A plain rule of life . . has . . put the principle of virtue upon the love of our neighbour. **17** LD MACAULAY To solicit the Lords to put some check on . . the Commons. K. LINES He made up his mind to put an end to the friendship. M. WESLEY Rose had . . let the telephone ring . . to put a stop to conversation. **b** F. MARRYAT Of course I put implicit confidence in you. **18** W. CONGREVE Sir Joseph has found out your trick, and does not care to be put upon. DEFOE We were very sensible of the obligation he had put upon us. SWIFT There wants nothing to be put upon the publick, but a false . . Cause. C. BURNEY The contempt which lyric poets put upon instrumental music. **20** SHAKES. *Lear* 'Tis they have put him on the old man's death. J. CONRAD Stevie was put to help wash the dishes. **b** JOHN CLARKE They are . . put upon Versifying. **c** F. MARRYAT Edward put the pony to a trot. DICKENS Mr Pumblechook then put me through my pence-table. **d** LD MACAULAY To put the garrison on rations of horse flesh. **21** C. READE Put yourself in his place. **22** SHAKES. *Wint. T.* Let me be unroll'd and my name put in the book of virtue! **23** SHAKES. *Cymb.* Would I had put my estate . . on th'approbation of what I have spoke. F. HOYLE Forced to admit that he put his money on Kingsley's prediction being wrong.

▶ **IV** [Latin *ponere*.]
†**24** *verb trans.* Posit, suppose, assume; state, affirm; ordain. LME–L17.
†**25** Lay down (one's life) *for, on behalf of*. Only in LME.
Phrases, & with adverbs & prepositions in specialized senses: (A selection of cross-refs. only is included: see esp. other nouns.) ***be hard put to***: see HARD *adjective, adverb, & noun*. ***be put through the hoop(s)***: see HOOP *noun*[1] 10. **not know where to put oneself** feel extremely embarrassed. ***not put a foot wrong***: see FOOT *noun*. **put about** (*a*) *NAUTICAL* place or turn on to the opposite tack; *gen.* cause to turn round; (*b*) spread, circulate, publish (information, a rumour, etc.); (*c*) (chiefly *Scot. & north.*) trouble, inconvenience, distress. **put across** make (an idea) acceptable or effective, convey the significance of, express in an understandable way (see also ***put it across, put one across*** below). ***put a girdle about***: see GIRDLE *noun*[1] 2. ***put a person's back up***: see BACK *noun*[1]. ***put a pistol to one's head, put a pistol to someone's head***: see HEAD *noun*. ***put a slur on***: see SLUR *noun*[3] 1. **put at** *Scot.* proceed against, attack, prosecute. **put away** (*a*) replace where normally kept, put into a receptacle etc. for safe-keeping; (*b*) lay (money etc.) aside for future use; (*c*) *arch.* get rid of, reject, divorce; dispel, abolish, put an end to; (*d*) *colloq.* consume as food or drink, esp. in large quantities; (*e*) *colloq.* imprison; commit to a home or mental institution; (*f*) *slang* pawn; (*g*) *colloq.* bury; kill, put down (an old or sick animal); (*h*) *colloq.* (esp. in sport) dispatch, deal with. **put back** †(*a*) repulse, reject; (*b*) reduce to a lower position or condition, check the advance of; (*c*) move the hands or display of (a clock etc.) back to an earlier time; (*d*) put off, defer; (*e*) replace; restore to a proper or former place or position; (*f*) *NAUTICAL* reverse one's course, return to the port which one has left; (*g*) *colloq.* cost (a person) a specified sum of money. **put by** (*a*) *arch.* thrust or turn aside, reject, ward off, evade, put off with an excuse etc.; (*b*) lay aside, save (esp. money), for future use. **put down** (*a*) suppress by force or authority, crush; (*b*) *arch.* depose, dethrone, degrade; (*c*) lower the pride or self-esteem of, snub, humiliate, disparage; †(*d*) excel, surpass; (*e*) kill, put to death (now esp. an old or sick animal); (*f*) set down in writing, enter in a list etc.; enter the name of, esp. as a member or subscriber; (*g*) attribute *to*; estimate *as, at*, take *for*; (*h*) sink (a shaft, pit, etc.); (*i*) *CRICKET* hit (a wicket), dislodging a bail; (*j*) *CRICKET* drop (a catch); (*k*) (orig. *US*) preserve or store (food) for future use; (*l*) land (an aircraft etc.); (*m*) *US slang* reject, abandon; (*n*) put (a young child) to bed; (*o*) pay (a specified sum) as a deposit; (*p*) *slang* record (music). †**put for** try for, strive to do or attain. **put forth** (*a*) *arch. & formal* stretch out, extend (the hand etc.); display, exhibit; propound, assert; bring into operation, exert (one's strength etc.); publish, put in circulation; (*b*) (of a plant) send out (buds or leaves); (*c*) *arch.* set out, esp. to sea. **put forward** (*a*) advance the hands or display of (a clock etc.); (*b*) (freq. *refl.*) put into a prominent position, draw attention to; (*c*) advance for consideration or acceptance, propose, suggest, nominate; †(*d*) come forward, hasten on. ***put ideas into a person's head***: see IDEA. **put in** (*a*) place within a receptacle or containing space; insert, introduce; plant (seeds, a crop); (*b*) install in or appoint to an office or position; (*c*) *CRICKET* send in to bat; *esp.* make (the opposing team) take first innings; (*d*) enter, submit (a claim etc.); (*e*) submit a claim etc. *for*, apply, enter, bid, *for*; (*f*) (of a ship) enter or call at a port, harbour, etc., esp. as a deviation from a regular course; (*g*) interpose (a blow, shot, remark, etc.); (*h*) intervene, esp. in conversation or discussion; (*i*) provide in addition; (*j*) contribute as one's share; perform (a spell of work etc.) as part of a larger effort; (*k*) *colloq.* pass, spend (a portion or period of time) in some specified or understood activity; (*l*) *slang* inform against, secure the conviction of. ***put in an APPEARANCE***. ***put in mind***: see MIND *noun*[1]. **put it across, put one across** *colloq.* get the better of, get even with; deceive, convince by deceit. **put it there** *colloq.* (in *imper.*) shake hands with the speaker as a sign of agreement, congratulations, etc. **put it to** present or submit a question, statement, etc., to (a person) for consideration or by way of appeal; challenge (a person) to deny *that*. **put off** (*a*) set down from a boat, train, etc.; (*b*) postpone to a later time, defer; postpone an engagement with; (*c*) *arch.* remove, take off (a garment etc.), divest oneself of; †(*d*) dismiss, dispense with, put out of one's mind; (*e*) evade by an excuse etc.; placate with minimal compliance; (*f*) hinder, dissuade, esp. by diverting the attention of; (*g*) (*obsolete* exc. *dial.*) pass (time); (*h*) *arch.* dispose of, sell; dispose of fraudulently; palm off *on*; (*i*) *NAUTICAL* leave the shore or bank, set out or start on a voyage; (*j*) *colloq.* offend, disconcert; cause to lose interest in, discourage. **put on** (*a*) place on or attach to something; *esp.* place (a garment etc.) on oneself or another, clothe with; (*b*) impose as a burden or charge; (*c*) adopt, assume (a character or quality), *esp.* assume deceptively or falsely, affect, pretend; (*d*) *colloq.* impose on, take advantage of, deceive intentionally; (*e*) add, make an addition of; add to a price, score, etc.; develop additional (bodily weight, fat); (*f*) stake, bet (money); †(*g*) encourage, impel, promote; †(*h*) go faster, hasten onward; (*i*) advance (the hands or display of a clock, etc.); (*j*) bring into action or operation, cause to act or function; apply, exert; switch or turn on; (*k*) set or appoint to do something; *CRICKET* send (a person) on to bowl; (*l*) stage (a play, show, etc.); broadcast (a programme); cause (a train, bus, aircraft, etc.) to be available as transport; (*m*) *colloq.* draw the attention of or introduce (a person) *to* a particular person or thing. ***put one across***: see ***put it across*** above. ***put one's back into***: see BACK *noun*[1]. ***put one's feet up***: see FOOT *noun*. ***put one's finger on***: see FINGER *noun*. ***put one's foot down, put one's foot in it***: see FOOT *noun*. ***put one's hands on, put one's hands to***: see HAND *noun*. ***put one's heart into***: see HEART *noun*. ***put one's house in order***: see HOUSE *noun*[1]. ***put on flesh***: see FLESH *noun*. **put out** (*a*) expel, eject; blind (an eye); (*b*) put out of joint, dislocate; †(*c*) remove from office, possession, etc., depose, dismiss; (*d*) eliminate from a contest, knock out; *CRICKET* dismiss (a batsman); *BASEBALL* cause to be out; (*e*) put an end to, destroy; (now only *slang*) kill; †(*f*) expunge, erase, efface; (*g*) extinguish (fire, a light, etc.); (*h*) disconcert, upset, annoy; inconvenience (freq. *refl.*); (*i*) exert; (*j*) publish, issue, put in circulation, broadcast; (*k*) *NAUTICAL* set out on a voyage, leave port; (*l*) stretch out, extend, (a hand etc.); cause to stick out or project; display, show; send out (buds, shoots, etc.); (*m*) place (a person) away from home for some purpose; turn out (an animal) to feed, *esp.* send or allow out (a pet) for exercise etc; (*n*) lend (money) at interest, invest; (*o*) allocate (work) to be done off the premises; (*p*) *slang* (chiefly *N. Amer.*) (of a woman) offer oneself for sexual intercourse (foll. by *for* a man). **put out of** (*a*) *arch.* remove or expel from (a place, position, one's thoughts, memory, etc.); †(*b*) dismiss from the possession or occupation of property, an office or position, etc.; (*c*) remove, liberate, or extricate from a condition of; cause no longer to be in a specified condition. ***put out of one's MISERY***. ***put out of one's mind***: see MIND *noun*[1]. ***put out to grass***: see GRASS *noun* 2. **put over** (*a*) *US* defer, postpone; (*b*) (now *dial.*) get over, get through (time); (*c*) make acceptable or effective; convey or communicate; present convincingly; (*d*) impose (something false or deceptive) *on* a person;

achieve by deceit; (*e*) **put it over (on)**, **put one over (on)**, get the better of, outsmart, defeat, upstage, trick. ***put paid to***: see PAY *verb*[1]. ***put the boot in***: see BOOT *noun*[2]. ***put the finger on***: see FINGER *noun*. ***put the hard word on (a person)***: see HARD *adjective, adverb, & noun*. ***put the hooks in***: see HOOK *noun*. **put them up** *colloq.* (usu. in *imper.*) (*a*) raise the fists for a fight; (*b*) raise the hands above the head in surrender. **put through** (*a*) cause to pass through a process; carry (successfully) through; carry out, bring to a finish; (*b*) connect (a person) by telephone to another through one or more exchanges. **put through it** *colloq.* impose a severe test on, subject to an ordeal or trying experience. **put to** (*a*) *arch.* exert, apply, set to work; (*b*) *arch.* attach (a horse etc.) to a vehicle; (*c*) *dial.* shut (a door etc.); (*d*) NAUTICAL put in to shore, take shelter; (*e*) in *pass.* (freq. with *it*) be hard-pressed. **put to a vote**, **put to the vote** (*a*) = sense 12b above; (*b*) *colloq.* decide on a matter by voting. ***put to*** DEATH. ***put to expense***: see EXPENSE 3b. ***put to flight***: see FLIGHT *noun*[2]. **put together** (*a*) join, combine, unite (parts) into a whole; (*b*) form (a whole) by combination of parts; construct, compile, compose; (*c*) combine mentally; add or consider together. ***put to grass***: see GRASS *noun* 2. ***put to great expense***: see EXPENSE 3b. ***put to the horn***: see HORN *noun*. ***put to the vote***: see ***put to a vote*** above. **put under** (*a*) *colloq.* kill, bury; (*b*) make unconscious by means of an anaesthetic, hypnosis, etc. **put up** (*a*) put into a higher position, raise, lift; fix up for public view, display; CRICKET score (runs); (*b*) set up or mount (esp. a jockey) on horseback; employ as a jockey, give (a jockey) a particular ride; (*c*) HUNTING cause (game) to rise from cover; start; (*d*) raise in amount; (*e*) engage in (a fight, struggle, etc.) as a form of resistance; (*f*) offer (thanks, a prayer, etc.); (*g*) bring before a magistrate, bring into court, accuse formally; (*h*) propose for election or adoption, or for an award etc.; bring forward as a speaker etc.; (*i*) offer oneself for election, set oneself up *for* something; (*j*) send in (esp. banns) to be published in church; publish (banns); (*k*) offer for sale by auction, or for competition; (*l*) submit (a question etc.) *to* a person; (*m*) place in a receptacle for future use or safe-keeping; put into a bag, pocket, etc.; pack up, make up into a parcel; *arch.* put by, store; (*n*) *arch.* replace (a sword) in a sheath; (*o*) deposit, stake (money); provide (money) as backing for an enterprise; (*p*) provide (temporary) accommodation for, esp. in one's own home; (*q*) accept (temporary) accommodation, lodge; †(*r*) = ***put up with*** below; (*s*) annoy, vex; (*t*) erect, set up (a building, tent, etc.), construct, build; make up or compose by putting together; *colloq.* concoct, prearrange. **put upon** *colloq.* make unfair or excessive demands on, take advantage of (a person). ***put up one's hair***: see HAIR *noun*. **put up or shut up** *colloq.* (in *imper.*) defend or justify yourself or remain silent. **put up to** *colloq.* make aware of, inform of, instruct in; (now usu.) incite or persuade (a person or persons) to (an action, *doing*). **put up with** endure, tolerate, submit to. ***put words into a person's mouth***: see MOUTH *noun*. ***put to it*** MILDLY.

Comb.: **put-and-take** (*a*) a gambling game played with a six-sided spinning-top; a spinning-top used in this game; (*b*) the stocking of waters with fish for anglers to catch (freq. *attrib.*); **put-away** (TENNIS etc.) = KILL *noun*[1] 3; **put-down** *colloq.* a snub, a humiliating remark or criticism; **put-in** (*a*) *US colloq.* one's turn to speak, one's affair; (*b*) the act of putting the ball into a scrum in rugby; **put-off** an evasive or procrastinating reply, a pretext for inaction or delay; a postponement, a delay; **put-on** *colloq.* (chiefly *N. Amer.*) a deception, a ruse, a hoax; **put-through** (*a*) = THROUGHPUT 2; (*b*) STOCK EXCHANGE a financial transaction in which a broker arranges the sale and the purchase of shares simultaneously; **putting-off** *adjective* = OFF-PUTTING; **put-up** *adjective* (*colloq.*) prearranged, esp. in an underhand manner (freq. in ***put-up job***); **put-you-up**, (proprietary) **Put-u-up** a sofa or settee which can be converted into a bed.

put *verb*[2] var. of PUTT *verb*.

puta /ˈputa/ *noun*. *slang*. M20.
[Spanish.]
A prostitute; a slut.

putamen /pjʊˈteɪmɛn/ *noun*. M19.
[Latin, from *putare* prune.]
1 BOTANY. The hardened endocarp (stone) of a fleshy fruit. M19.
2 ANATOMY. The outer part of the lentiform nucleus of the brain. L19.

putanism /ˈpjuːt(ə)nɪz(ə)m/ *noun*. *rare*. L17.
[from Old & mod. French *putain* prostitute, ult. from Latin *putida* stinking, disgusting: see -ISM. Cf. French *putanisme*.]
The occupation of a prostitute; prostitution.

putative /ˈpjuːtətɪv/ *adjective*. LME.
[Old & mod. French *putatif*, *-ive* or late Latin *putativus*, from Latin *putat-* pa. ppl stem of *putare* think, suppose: see -ATIVE.]
That is believed to be such; reputed, supposed.

> C. MCWILLIAM Tease her by inventing absurd putative events and making her select clothes to wear to . . them. **putative father** LAW a man deemed to be the father of an illegitimate child. **putative marriage** LAW a marriage which though legally invalid was contracted in good faith by at least one of the parties.

■ **putatively** *adverb* E18.

putcher /ˈpʌtʃə/ *noun*. *local*. Also (earlier) **putcheon** /ˈpʌtʃ(ə)n/. M19.
[Origin unkn.: cf. PUTT *noun*[1].]
A funnel-shaped wickerwork fish-trap, used esp. on the R. Severn in England to catch salmon, eels, etc. Cf. PUTT *noun*[1].

putchock /ˈpʊtʃək, ˈpʌ-/ *noun*. Also **putchuk**. E17.
[Malay *pūcok*.]
In the Indian subcontinent, = COSTUS.

pute /pjuːt/ *adjective*. Now *arch. rare*. E17.
[Latin *putus* clean, pure.]
Pure, clean, simple, absolute. Only in ***pure and pute***, ***pure pute***.

puteal /ˈpjuːtɪəl/ *noun*. M19.
[Latin, orig. neut. of *putealis*, from *puteus* well: see -AL[1].]
ROMAN ANTIQUITIES. A stone curb surrounding the mouth of a well.

putid /ˈpjuːtɪd/ *adjective*. Now *rare* or *obsolete*. L16.
[Latin *putidus*, from *putere* stink: see -ID[1].]
Stinking, rotten. Chiefly *fig.*, foul, base, despicable, worthless.
■ **putidly** *adverb* L19. **putidness** *noun* M17.

putlog /ˈpʌtlɒg/ *noun*. Also (earlier) **-lock** /-lɒk/. M17.
[Perh. from *put* pa. pple of PUT *verb*[1] + LOG *noun*[1].]
A short horizontal timber projecting from a wall to serve as a support for scaffold-boards.
Comb.: **putlog-hole** a hole left in a wall to receive a putlog.

putonghua /puːˈtʊŋhwɑː/ *noun*. M20.
[Chinese *pǔtōnghuà*, from *pǔtōng* common + *huà* spoken language. Cf. PAI-HUA.]
The standard spoken form of modern Chinese, based on the northern dialects, esp. that of Beijing.

put-put /ˈpʌtpʌt/ *noun & verb*. Also **putt-putt**. E20.
[Imit.]
▸**A** *noun*. A rapid intermittent sound characteristic of a small internal-combustion engine; a vehicle, boat, etc., fitted with such an engine. E20.
▸**B** *verb intrans*. Infl. **-tt-**. Make such a sound; move under the power of such an engine. E20.

> J. BARNES I hired a Solex . . and put-putted off to . . Vincennes.

†**putredinous** *adjective*. M17–E18.
[French *putrédineux*, from late Latin *putredo* rottenness, from Latin *putrere* rot: see PUTRID, -OUS.]
Characterized or formed by putrefaction; *fig.* filthy, abominable.

putrefacient /pjuːtrɪˈfeɪʃ(ə)nt/ *adjective*. L19.
[Latin *putrefacient-* ppl stem of *putrefacere*: see PUTREFY, -FACIENT.]
= PUTREFACTIVE.

putrefaction /pjuːtrɪˈfakʃ(ə)n/ *noun*. LME.
[Old & mod. French *putréfaction* or late Latin *putrefactio(n-)*, from Latin *putrefact-* pa. ppl stem of *putrefacere* PUTREFY: see -FACTION.]
1 The action or process of putrefying; the bacterial decomposition of animal or vegetable matter, accompanied by the formation of foul-smelling substances; rotting, corruption; suppuration, festering. LME. ▸†**b** ALCHEMY. Chemical disintegration, decomposition, oxidation, corrosion. L15–L17.
2 Decomposed or putrid matter. LME.
3 *fig.* Moral corruption and decay. M17.

putrefactive /pjuːtrɪˈfaktɪv/ *adjective*. LME.
[Old & mod. French *putréfactif*, *-ive* or medieval Latin *putrefactivus*, from Latin *putrefact-*: see prec., -IVE.]
1 Causing or inducing putrefaction; putrefying. Formerly also, subject to putrefaction, corruptible. LME.
2 Of, pertaining to, produced by, characterized by, or indicative of putrefaction. M17.

putrefy /ˈpjuːtrɪfʌɪ/ *verb*. LME.
[Latin *putrefacere*, from *putr-*, *puter* rotten + *facere* make: see -FY.]
1 *verb trans*. Make putrid; cause to decompose with a foul smell. Now *rare*. LME. ▸†**b** ALCHEMY. Decompose, corrode, oxidize. L15–M17. ▸†**c** *fig.* Corrupt morally. M16–L17.
2 *verb intrans*. Become putrid; decompose with a foul smell; rot, go bad; become gangrenous, fester, suppurate; *fig.* become corrupt, decay morally. LME.

> **2** C. DARWIN The ground is concealed by a mass of slowly putrefying vegetable matter. A. N. WILSON All the hams . . sent to Moscow arrived in a putrefied state.

■ **putrefiable** *adjective* L19. **putrefier** *noun* a putrefying agent M17.

putrescence /pjuːˈtrɛs(ə)ns/ *noun*. M17.
[formed as next + -ENCE.]
1 The action or process of rotting or becoming putrid; incipient or advancing putrefaction. M17.
2 Putrescent or rotting matter. M19.

> **1** *fig.*: CARLYLE Am I to sink ever lower into falsehood, stagnant putrescence?

■ **putrescency** *noun* = PUTRESCENCE 1 M18.

putrescent /pjuːˈtrɛs(ə)nt/ *adjective*. M18.
[Latin *putrescent-* pres. ppl stem of *putrescere* inceptive of *putrere* rot: see PUTRID, -ESCENT.]
1 Becoming putrid; in the process of putrefaction. M18.
2 Of, pertaining to, or accompanying putrescence. L18.

putrescible /pjuːˈtrɛsɪb(ə)l/ *adjective*. L18.
[formed as prec. + -IBLE.]
Liable to rot or become putrid; subject to putrefaction.
■ **putresciˈbility** *noun* E19.

putrescine /pjuːˈtrɛsiːn/ *noun*. L19.
[formed as prec. + -INE[5].]
CHEMISTRY. A crystalline amine, 1,4-diaminobutane, $H_2N(CH_2)_4NH_2$, formed by putrefaction of proteins.

putrid /ˈpjuːtrɪd/ *adjective*. LME.
[Latin *putridus* or (sense 4) *putris*, from *putrere* rot, from *putr-*, *puter* rotten: see -ID[1].]
1 In a state of decomposition; putrefied, rotten. LME.
2 Pertaining to, causing, resulting from, or infected with putrefaction; foul. LME.
3 *fig.* Morally corrupt; aesthetically abominable; suggestive of putrefaction; noxious, corrupting; *colloq.* appalling, very unpleasant, contemptible. E17.
†**4** Of soil: loose, crumbling, friable. M17–L18.

> **1** J. S. HUXLEY The putrid remains of a whale carcass. **2** SHELLEY Their bones Bleaching unburied in the putrid blast. B. ENGLAND They fell through the green scum . . releasing a great gout of putrid gases. †**putrid fever** typhus. **3** MILTON Teaching to his Son all those putrid and pernicious documents, both of State and Religion. D. L. SAYERS Some putrid fool sliced a ball . . and got me slap-bang in the eye. M. ATWOOD I hate those neo-expressionist dirty greens and putrid oranges.

■ **puˈtridity** *noun* (*a*) putrid condition, corruption, rottenness, decay (*lit.* & *fig.*); (*b*) putrid matter: M17. **putridly** *adverb* L19. **putridness** *noun* putrid condition, rottenness L17.

putriform /ˈpjuːtrɪfɔːm/ *adjective*. *rare*. L19.
[from Latin *putr-*, *puter* rotten + -I- + -FORM.]
Of putrid form or appearance.

putrilage /ˈpjuːtrɪlɪdʒ/ *noun*. M17.
[Late Latin *putrilago*, from Latin *putr-*, *puter* rotten: see -AGE.]
Putrid matter.
■ **putrilaginous** /pjuːtrɪˈladʒɪnəs/ *adjective* L16.

putsch /pʊtʃ/ *noun*. E20.
[Swiss German = thrust, blow.]
1 An attempt at political revolution; a violent uprising. E20.
2 A sudden vigorous effort or campaign. *colloq.* M20.
■ **putschism** *noun* advocacy of a putsch or of the use of violence in a political revolution L19. **putschist** *noun & adjective* (*a*) *noun* an advocate of or participant in a putsch; (*b*) *adjective* of or pertaining to putschism or putschists: L19.

putt /pʌt/ *noun*[1]. *local*. E17.
[Var. of BUTT *noun*[7].]
A basket for catching fish. Cf. PUTCHER.

putt /pʌt/ *noun*[2]. Orig. *Scot*. Also **put**. See also PUT *noun*[1]. M17.
[Var. of PUT *noun*[1].]
GOLF. An act of putting; a gentle stroke given to the ball to make it roll across the green and into a hole.
make one's putt good *Scot.* succeed in one's attempt.

putt *noun*[3] var. of PUT *noun*[2].

putt /pʌt/ *verb trans. & intrans*. Orig. *Scot*. Also **put**. Pa. t. & pple **putted** /ˈpʌtɪd/. See also PUT *verb*[1]. M18.
[Var. of PUT *verb*[1].]
GOLF. Strike (the ball) gently and carefully so that it rolls across the green and into a hole.

puttanesca /pʊtəˈnɛskə/ *noun & adjective*. L20.
[Italian, from *puttana* prostitute (the sauce is said to have been devised by prostitutes as one which could be cooked quickly between clients' visits).]
(Denoting) a dish of pasta in a sauce of tomatoes, garlic, olives, anchovies, etc.

puttee /ˈpʌti/ *noun*. L19.
[Hindi *paṭṭī* band, bandage from Sanskrit *paṭṭikā*. Cf. PATTAWALLA.]
A long strip of cloth wound spirally round the leg from the ankle to the knee, worn for protection and support, esp. by soldiers in the war of 1914–18. Also (*US*), a leather legging.
■ **putteed** *adjective* wearing a puttee or puttees E20.

putter /ˈpʊtə/ *noun*[1]. LME.
[from PUT *verb*[1] + -ER[1].]
1 a An animal that pushes or butts with the head or horns. *obsolete* exc. *Scot. & north*. LME. ▸**b** MINING. A person employed to propel barrows of coal from the workings; a haulier, a trammer. Cf. PUT *verb*[1] 4b. Now *rare* or *obsolete*. E18.
2 *gen*. A person who or thing which puts. Freq. with adverb, as ***putter-down***, ***putter-off***, ***putter-on***, ***putter-out***, ***putter-up***, etc. LME.
3 A person who puts the shot or other weight. E19.

> **2** C. LAMB The putter of the said question. *Country Life* As a putter-up of game one cannot imagine the clumber outdoing the springer [spaniel]. *New York Review of Books* The Medawars are indeed great putters down of . . pretensions.

putter /ˈpʌtə/ *noun*[2]. M18.
[from PUTT *verb* + -ER[1].]
GOLF. **1** A club used in putting. M18.
2 A player who putts; a golfer considered in terms of ability at putting. M19.

putter /ˈpʌtə/ *noun*³ & *verb*¹ *intrans.* M20.
[Imit.]
= PUT-PUT.

putter /ˈpʌtə/ *verb*² *intrans.* & *trans.* Orig. *US.* L19.
[Alt.]
= POTTER *verb* 4, 4b.
▪ **putterer** *noun* L19. **putteringly** *adverb* L19.

putting /ˈpʌtɪŋ/ *noun.* E19.
[from PUTT *verb* + -ING¹.]
GOLF. The action of PUTT *verb.* Also, a game of miniature golf involving only putting strokes and played on a special course.
Comb.: **putting-green** (*a*) the smooth area of grass round a hole; (*b*) a miniature golf course.

putto /ˈpʊtəʊ, *foreign* ˈputto/ *noun.* Pl. **putti** /ˈpʊti, *foreign* ˈputti/. M17.
[Italian from Latin *putus* boy.]
A representation of a (boy) child, naked or in swaddling clothes, in (esp. Renaissance and baroque) art, a cherub, a cupid.

puttock /ˈpʌtək/ *noun*¹. *obsolete* exc. *dial.* ME.
[Origin unkn.]
1 A kite; a buzzard. ME.
†**2** *fig.* An ignoble or greedy person; *spec.* a catchpole. E17–M19.

†**puttock** *noun*². ME–M19.
[Origin unkn.: cf. FUTTOCK.]
NAUTICAL. = FUTTOCK ***shroud***. Also ***puttock shroud***.

puttony /ˈputoɲ/ *noun.* Pl. **-s**, **-os** /-oz/. M20.
[Hungarian; *puttonyos* is an attrib. form meaning 'holding as much as goes into a (specified) number of *puttonys*'.]
In Hungary, a basket for grapes; *esp.* (a measure equal to the contents of) a container of dried overripe grapes added to the fermentation cask in making Tokay, the number of baskets determining the richness of the wine.

puttoo /ˈpʌtuː/ *noun* & *adjective.* M19.
[Hindi *paṭṭū* from Sanskrit *paṭṭa* cloth.]
▶**A** *noun.* A fabric made of the coarse refuse hair of the Kashmir goat. M19.
▶**B** *adjective.* Made of this fabric. M19.

putt-putt *noun* & *verb* var. of PUT-PUT.

putty /ˈpʌti/ *noun* & *verb.* M17.
[Old & mod. French *potée*, orig. = potful, from *pot* POT *noun*¹: see -Y⁵.]
▶**A** *noun.* **1** A powder of tin or lead oxides, or of tin and lead oxides, used for polishing glass or metal. Also ***jewellers' putty***, ***putty powder***. M17.
2 A fine mortar made of lime and water without sand, used in pointing brickwork etc. Also ***plasterers' putty***. M17.
3 A cement of powdered whiting made into a stiff paste with raw linseed oil, used esp. in fixing panes of glass, filling holes in woodwork, etc. Also ***glaziers' putty***. E18.
4 a Any of various materials resembling (esp. glaziers') putty; *esp.* (*slang*) sticky mud at the bottom of a body of water. L19. ▸**b** A light shade of yellowish grey. L19.
3 like putty in a person's hands, **putty in a person's hands** totally under the influence of someone, malleable. ***Silly putty***: see SILLY *adjective.* **up to putty** *Austral. colloq.* worthless, useless.
Comb.: **putty-colour** a light yellowish grey; **putty-coloured** *adjective* of putty-colour, of a light yellowish grey; **putty-knife**: with a blunt flexible spatulate blade for spreading (glaziers') putty; **putty medal** *colloq.* a worthless reward for insignificant service or achievement; ***putty powder***: see sense 1 above; **putty-root** a N. American orchid, *Aplectrum hyemale*, the corm of which contains a glutinous substance.
▶**B** *verb trans.* Cover, smear, fix, mend, join, or fill with putty. M18.
▪ **putty-like** *adjective* resembling (esp. glaziers') putty in consistency; malleable, plastic: M19.

puture /ˈpjuːtʃə/ *noun. obsolete* exc. *Hist.* L15.
[Anglo-Norman = Old Northern French *pulture*, Old French *pouture* etc. (mod. dial. *pouture*, *peuture* food for animals) from medieval Latin *pu(l)tura*.]
LAW. Food and drink claimed by foresters for themselves, their attendants, and their animals, from others living within the bounds of the forest; the custom of giving or the right of demanding this.

putwary *noun* var. of PATWARI.

putz /pʊts, pʌts/ *noun.* E20.
[German = decoration, finery. In sense 2 from Yiddish.]
1 In areas of Moravian influence in the US: a representation of the Nativity scene traditionally placed under a Christmas tree. *US.* E20.
2 a The penis. *US slang.* M20. ▸**b** A fool; a stupid or objectionable person. *N. Amer. slang.* M20.

puy /pwiː/ *noun.* Pl. pronounced same, /-z/. M19.
[French = hill, from Latin PODIUM.]
A small extinct volcanic cone; orig. & *spec.* any of those in the Auvergne, France.

puya /ˈpuːjə/ *noun.* E19.
[mod. Latin (see below) from Amer. Spanish from Spanish = goad.]
Any of numerous freq. giant bromeliads constituting the genus *Puya*, of dry regions of the Andes, having rosettes of spiny leaves and blue or yellow flowers.

puzzle /ˈpʌz(ə)l/ *noun.* E17.
[from the verb.]
1 The state of being puzzled or bewildered; confusion, perplexity; an instance of this. E17.
2 A puzzling or perplexing question; a difficult problem, an enigma; something mysterious or baffling. M17.
3 Something devised or made for the purpose of testing ingenuity, knowledge, etc.; a toy or problem of this kind. E19.

🕮 **1** M. ARNOLD The result would be . . utter puzzle and bewilderment. **2** E. K. KANE It is a puzzle . . where they have retreated to. A. STORR Freud continued to find women a puzzle throughout his life. **3** ***Chinese puzzle***: see CHINESE *adjective.* CROSSWORD ***puzzle***. ***jigsaw puzzle***: see JIGSAW *noun* 2. ***monkey-puzzle (tree)***: see MONKEY *noun.*

Comb.: **puzzle-box** *PSYCHOLOGY* a box with no obvious connection between its door and the opening device, designed to test the learning abilities of an animal in trying to release itself; **puzzlehead** a puzzle-headed person; **puzzle-headed** *adjective* having confused ideas; **puzzle-pate** a puzzle-headed person; **puzzle-pated** *adjective* puzzle-headed; **puzzle-peg** a pointed piece of wood (to be) fastened to a dog's lower jaw to keep the animal's nose away from the ground.
▪ **puzzledom** *noun* the realm of puzzles; the state of being puzzled, perplexity, bewilderment: M18. **puzzlist** *noun* (*US*) a person who devises puzzles M20.

puzzle /ˈpʌz(ə)l/ *verb.* L16.
[Origin unkn.]
1 *verb trans.* Orig., beset with difficulties, cause to be at a loss, baffle, confound. Now, disconcert mentally, perplex, bewilder, (as) by a difficult problem or question. Freq. as ***puzzled*** *ppl adjective.* L16.
2 a *verb intrans.* & *refl.* Be perplexed or bewildered; exercise oneself with the solution of a problem. Freq. foll. by *about*, *over*, *upon*, refl. *with*. L16. ▸**b** *verb intrans.* Search in a confused way; fumble, grope *for*, get *through*, with some perplexity. E19.
3 *verb trans.* Make puzzling or confused; complicate; mix up. Now *rare.* M17.
4 *verb trans.* Foll. by *out*: make out by using ingenuity and patience, solve or understand by hard thought. L18.

🕮 **1** SHAKES. *Twel. N.* Thou art more puzzled than the Egyptians in their fog. E. PEACOCK The question has always puzzled me. **2a** B. JOWETT When he was young he had puzzled himself with physics. *Guardian* He puzzled over migration. Do at least some swallows hibernate here? **4** N. HAWTHORNE Inscriptions . . not sufficiently legible to induce us to puzzle them out. L. MCMURTRY Dish tried to puzzle out the real motive.

▪ **puzzledly** *adverb* in a puzzled manner L19. **puzzlement** *noun* (*a*) the fact or condition of being puzzled; perplexity, bewilderment, confusion; (*b*) a puzzle, a problem: E19. **puzzler** *noun* (*a*) a puzzling thing, a puzzle; (*b*) a person who puzzles; a person who is fond of solving puzzles: M17. **puzzlingly** *adverb* in a puzzling manner L19. **puzzlingness** *noun* (*rare*) puzzling quality E18.

PVA *abbreviation.*
1 Polyvinyl acetate.
2 Polyvinyl alcohol.

PVC *abbreviation.*
Polyvinyl chloride.

PVS *abbreviation.*
1 Persistent vegetative state.
2 Postviral (fatigue) syndrome.

Pvt. *abbreviation.*
Private; (*US*) private soldier.

PW *abbreviation.*
Policewoman.

p.w. *abbreviation.*
Per week.

PWA *abbreviation.*
Person with Aids.

PWD *abbreviation.*
Public Works Department.

pwe /pwe/ *noun.* Also ***pooay***. M19.
[Burmese.]
A Myanmar (Burmese) festival of drama, dancing, sports, or other entertainments.

PWR *abbreviation.*
Pressurized-water reactor.

PX *abbreviation.*
US MILITARY. Post Exchange.

py- *combining form* see PYO-.

pya /ˈpjɑː/ *noun.* M20.
[Burmese.]
A monetary unit of Myanmar (Burma), equal to one-hundredth of a kyat.

pyaemia /pʌɪˈiːmɪə/ *noun.* Also ***pyemia**. M19.
[from PYO- + -AEMIA.]
MEDICINE. Blood-poisoning and fever caused by pus-forming bacteria released from an abscess, which may be followed by the widespread formation of abscesses; septicaemia.
▪ **pyaemic** *adjective* of, pertaining to, or of the nature of pyaemia; affected with pyaemia: M19.

Pybuthrin /pʌɪˈbuːθrɪn/ *noun.* Also **p-**. M20.
[Blend of PYRETHRIN and BUTOXIDE.]
(Proprietary name for) an insecticide compounded of pyrethrins and piperonyl butoxide.

pycn- *combining form* see PYCNO-.

pycnic *adjective* & *noun* var. of PYKNIC.

pycnidium /pɪkˈnɪdɪəm/ *noun.* Pl. **-ia** /-ɪə/. M19.
[mod. Latin, formed as next + -IDIUM.]
BOTANY. A flask-shaped fruiting body found in certain imperfect fungi and in the fungal component of certain lichens.
▪ **pycnidial** *adjective* L19. **pycnidiospore** *noun* a spore formed in a pycnidium L19.

pycnium /ˈpɪknɪəm/ *noun.* Pl. **-ia** /-ɪə/. E20.
[mod. Latin, from Greek *puknos* thick, dense.]
BOTANY. A flask-shaped structure found in rust fungi, analogous to the spermogonium of ascomycetes.
▪ **pycnial** *adjective* M20. **pycniospore** *noun* a spore formed in a pycnium M20.

pycno- /ˈpɪknəʊ/ *combining form* of Greek *puknos* thick, dense: see -O-. Also **pykno-**; before a vowel **pycn-**.
▪ **pycnoˈchlorite** *noun* (*MINERALOGY*) a chlorite having the same silicon content as clinochlore but more iron E20. **pycnocline** *noun* a layer in which water density increases rapidly with depth, esp. in oceans M20. **pycnocoˈnidium** *noun* (*BOTANY*) = PYCNIDIOSPORE L19. **pycnogon** *noun* = PYCNOGONID *noun* E20. **pycnohyˈdrometer** *noun* a combination of a pycnometer and a hydrometer L19. **pycˈnometer** *noun* a vessel used for measuring the relative density of a liquid, using a calibrated capillary M19. **pycnoˈmetric** *adjective* involving or employing a pycnometer E20. **pycnospore** *noun* (*BOTANY*) (*a*) = PYCNIDIOSPORE; (*b*) = PYCNIOSPORE: L19.

pycnogonid /pɪknəˈgɒnɪd/ *noun* & *adjective.* L19.
[mod. Latin *Pycnogonida* (see below), from *Pycnogonum* genus name, formed as PYCNO- + Greek *gonu* knee: see -ID³.]
ZOOLOGY. ▶**A** *noun.* Any of various marine chelicerate arthropods of the class Pycnogonida, having very small bodies and long legs which contain extensions of the gut and gonads; a sea-spider, a pantopod. L19.
▶**B** *adjective.* Of, pertaining to, or designating this class of arthropods. M20.

pycnosis *noun* var. of PYKNOSIS.

pycnostyle /ˈpɪknə(ʊ)stʌɪl/ *adjective* & *noun.* L17.
[Latin *pycnostylos* from Greek, formed as PYCNO- + *stulos* column.]
ARCHITECTURE. (A building) having close intercolumniation such that the space between the columns equals one diameter and a half of a column.

pye *noun*¹ see PIE *noun*³.

†**pye** *noun*² var. of PIE *noun*⁴.

pye-dog /ˈpʌɪdɒg/ *noun.* Orig. *Anglo-Indian.* Also **pi-dog**, **pie-dog**. M19.
[Prob. contr. of *PARIAH-dog*.]
A half-wild stray dog, esp. in the Indian subcontinent.

pyel- *combining form* see PYELO-.

pyelitis /pʌɪəˈlʌɪtɪs/ *noun.* M19.
[formed as PYELO- + -ITIS.]
MEDICINE. Inflammation of the pelvis of the kidney, usu. as a result of bacterial infection.
▪ **pyelitic** /-ˈlɪtɪk/ *adjective* M19.

pyelo- /ˈpʌɪələʊ/ *combining form.* Before a vowel also **pyel-**.
[from Greek *puelos* trough: see -O-.]
Used in *MEDICINE* with the sense 'of the pelvis of the kidney'.
▪ **pyelocyˈstitis** *noun* pyelitis accompanied by cystitis L19. **pyelogram** *noun* an X-ray photograph showing the pelvis of the kidney E20. **pyeˈlography** *noun* X-ray examination of the kidneys, esp. using radio-opaque contrast material E20. **pyeloliˈthotomy** *noun* (an instance of) surgical removal of a renal calculus through an incision made into the pelvis of the kidney L19. **pyeloneˈphritic** *adjective* affected by pyelonephritis L19. **pyeloneˈphritis** *noun* inflammation of the substance of the kidney as a result of bacterial infection M19. **pyeloplasty** *noun* a surgical operation to relieve obstruction at the junction of the pelvis of the kidney and the ureter E20.

pyemia *noun* see PYAEMIA.

pyet *noun* & *adjective* var. of PIET.

pygal /ˈpʌɪɡ(ə)l/ *adjective.* M19.
[from Greek *pugē* rump + -AL¹.]
ZOOLOGY. Of or pertaining to the rump or posterior part of an animal.

pygarg /ˈpʌɪɡɑːɡ/ *noun.* Long *rare* or *obsolete.* LME.
[Latin *pygargus* from Greek *pugargos* white-rump (applied to various creatures), formed as prec. + *argos* white. Usu. translating Hebrew *dīšōn*.]
Chiefly in biblical translations: a kind of antelope, perh. an ibex.

pygidium /pʌɪˈdʒɪdɪəm, -ɡ-/ *noun.* Pl. **-ia** /-ɪə/. M19.
[mod. Latin, formed as PYGAL: see -IDIUM.]
ZOOLOGY. The caudal part of the body posterior to the last segment in certain invertebrates, esp. insects, crustaceans, and worms.
■ **pygidial** *adjective* L19.

pygmaean /pɪɡˈmiːən/ *noun & adjective.* Also **-mean.** LME.
[from Latin *pygmaeus* (see PYGMY) + -AN.]
▶†**A** *noun.* = PYGMY *noun* 1. LME–E17.
▶ **B** *adjective.* Of or pertaining to pygmies; of the nature or size of a pygmy; diminutive, dwarfish. M17.

Pygmalion /pɪɡˈmeɪlɪən/ *adverb. joc. euphem.* M20.
[A play by G. B. Shaw (1856–1950) which caused a sensation when first produced in 1914 because it contained the phr. 'not bloody likely'.]
= BLOODY *adverb.* Only in ***not Pygmalion likely.***

Pygmalionism /pɪɡˈmeɪlɪənɪz(ə)m/ *noun.* E20.
[from *Pygmalion*, Greek *Pugmaliōn* a legendary king of Cyprus who fell in love with a statue of a woman which was then brought to life by Aphrodite: see -ISM.]
PSYCHOLOGY. The condition of loving a statue, image, or inanimate object, esp. one of one's own making.

pygmean *noun & adjective* var. of PYGMAEAN.

pygmoid /ˈpɪɡmɔɪd/ *adjective & noun.* M20.
[from next + -OID.]
(A person) resembling or having characteristics of a pygmy.

pygmy /ˈpɪɡmi/ *noun, adjective, & verb.* Also **pig-.** LME.
[In earliest use in pl., from Latin *pygmaei* pl. of *pygmaeus* from Greek *pugmaios* dwarf(ish) from *pugmē* measure of length from elbow to knuckles, fist.]
▶ **A** *noun.* **1** A member of any of several peoples of very short stature inhabiting equatorial Africa and parts of SE Asia. Formerly also, a member of a (mythological) race of very small people traditionally inhabiting parts of Ethiopia or India. LME.
2 a *gen.* A person of very small stature; a dwarf. E16. ▸**b** *fig.* A person of very little significance, or having some quality to a very small degree. L16. ▸**c** *transf.* A thing that is much smaller than the average of its kind. M19.
3 An elf, a pixie. E17.

> **2b** *Sunday Times* Maxwell and Lord Stevens are scarcely financial pygmies. A. N. WILSON The . . volume established Lewis . . as a giant among the pygmies of the Oxford English Faculty.

▶ **B** *adjective.* **1** (Of a person or animal) of very small size or stature; *gen.* very small, diminutive, tiny; *esp.* designating animal species much smaller than related forms. Also (*fig.*), of very little significance. L16.
2 Of or pertaining to pygmies. M17.

> **1** *Courier-Mail (Brisbane)* My pygmy effort is just a gesture. *BBC Wildlife* The world's smallest monkeys, the pygmy marmosets.

Special collocations & comb.: **pygmy chimpanzee** a small chimpanzee, *Pan paniscus*, found in the Democratic Republic of Congo (Zaire). **pygmy-flint** ARCHAEOLOGY any of a class of small flint artefacts (now usu. classed as microliths). **pygmy glider** = ***flying mouse*** s.v. FLYING *ppl adjective.* **pygmy goose** any of various small Old World geese of the genus *Nettapus*. **pygmy hippopotamus** a small W. African hippopotamus, *Choeropsis liberiensis*. **pygmy owl** any of various small owls of the genus *Glaucidium*, esp. *G. passerinum* of Eurasia. **pygmy possum** any of various small Australasian possums of the family Burramyidae. **pygmy shrew** a shrew, *Sorex minutus* (Eurasia) or *S. hoyi* (America), which is one of the smallest known mammals.
▶ **C** *verb trans.* Make a pygmy of, reduce to insignificance, dwarf. *rare.* M17.

pygo- /ˈpʌɪɡəʊ/ *combining form* of Greek *pugē* rump: see -O-.
■ **pyˈgomelus** *noun*, pl. **-li** /-lʌɪ/, MEDICINE either of unequal conjoined twins in which the lesser is represented by a fleshy mass or supernumerary limb behind or between the posterior limbs E20. **pyˈgopagus** *noun*, pl. **-gi** /-ɡʌɪ, -dʒʌɪ/, MEDICINE (the condition of) a pair of Siamese twins joined at the buttocks, often back to back M19. **pygostyle** *noun* (ZOOLOGY) the triangular plate, formed of the fused caudal vertebrae, which supports the tail feathers in most birds L19.

pyinkado /ˈpjɪŋkədəʊ/ *noun.* Also **pying-** /ˈpjɪŋ-/. M19.
[Burmese.]
A leguminous tree, *Xylia xylocarpa*, of southern Asia; the hard durable timber of this tree, used in heavy construction work.

pyjamas /pəˈdʒɑːməz/ *noun pl.* Also ***paj-.** In attrib. use & in comb. usu. in sing. **-ama** (otherwise *rare*). E19.
[Persian & Urdu *pāy-jāmah*, *pā-jāmah*, from *pa(y)* leg + *jāmah* garment. Cf. JAMA *noun*¹.]
Orig., loose trousers, usu. of silk or cotton, tied round the waist, worn by both sexes in Turkey, India, and other Eastern countries. Now also, nightclothes consisting of loose trousers and a jacket; a daytime outfit of a loose blouse and wide-legged trousers worn by women. Also ***pair of pyjamas.***
Attrib. & comb.: In the sense 'pertaining to a part of a pair of pyjamas' as ***pyjama bottom***, ***pyjama jacket***, etc. Special combs., as **pyjama case** a bag etc. in which pyjamas may be kept when not being worn; **pyjama party** a party at which people wear pyjamas.
■ **pyjamaed** *adjective* wearing pyjamas L19.

pyjams /ˈpʌɪdʒamz/ *noun pl. colloq.* E20.
[Contr.]
Pyjamas.

pyknic /ˈpɪknɪk/ *adjective & noun.* Also **pycnic.** E20.
[from Greek *puknos* thick, close-packed + -IC.]
▶ **A** *adjective.* Of, pertaining to, or designating a stocky physique with a rounded body and head, thickset trunk, and a tendency to fat, freq. associated with a cyclothymic temperament. E20.
▶ **B** *noun.* A person with a pyknic physique. E20.

pykno- *combining form* var. of PYCNO-.

pyknolepsy /ˈpɪknə(ʊ)lɛpsi/ *noun.* E20.
[formed as PYCNO- + EPI)LEPSY.]
MEDICINE. An epileptic condition in which attacks of petit mal occur with great frequency.
■ **pyknoˈleptic** *adjective* E20.

pyknosis /pɪkˈnəʊsɪs/ *noun.* Also **pyc-.** E20.
[formed as PYCNO- + -OSIS.]
CYTOLOGY. Condensation of the heterochromatin of a nucleus into a densely-staining mass, esp. in a dying cell.
■ **pyknotic** /pɪkˈnɒtɪk/ *adjective* of, pertaining to, or displaying pyknosis E20.

py korry /pʌɪ ˈkɒri/ *interjection. NZ slang* (now *rare*). M20.
[Repr. a Maori alt. of *by golly*.]
= ***by golly!*** s.v. GOLLY *noun*¹.

pylagore /ˈpɪləɡɔː/ *noun.* M18.
[Greek *Pulagoras*, from *Pulai* Thermopylae (the older place of assembly of the Pythian Amphictyony) + *agora* assembly.]
GREEK HISTORY. Either of the two deputies sent by each constituent State to the Amphictyonic Council.

Pylian /ˈpʌɪlɪən, ˈpiː-/ *noun & adjective.* E17.
[Greek *pulos*, Latin *Pylos* Pylos (see below): see -IAN.]
▶ **A** *noun.* A native or inhabitant of the Homeric town of Pylos in the southern Peloponnese, traditionally regarded as the birthplace of Nestor and the name of his dynasty; a native or inhabitant of the territory ruled by Nestor or his dynasty. E17.
▶ **B** *adjective.* Of or pertaining to Pylos or its inhabitants. E17.

pylon /ˈpʌɪlən, -ɒn/ *noun & adjective.* In sense A.2a also †**-one.** M19.
[Greek *pulōn* gateway, from *pulē* gate.]
▶ **A** *noun.* **1** ARCHITECTURE. A gateway; *spec.* a monumental gateway to an Egyptian temple, usu. formed by two truncated pyramidal towers connected by a lower architectural part containing the gate. M19.
2 a A structure used to mark out a course for light aircraft, cars, etc. E20. ▸**b** Orig., a post to which wires for supporting or warping an aircraft wing were attached. Now, a pillar projecting from an aircraft wing or fuselage to support an engine, weapon, etc. E20.
3 SURGERY. A temporary, unjointed, artificial leg. E20.
4 A tall structure erected as a support; *spec.* a lattice-work metal tower for overhead electricity lines. E20.
5 A small pillar or column, used to support a sign or signal. *US.* M20.

> **4** *Scotland on Sunday* Cables underground can cost . . more than overhead pylons.

▶ **B** *attrib.* or as *adjective.* [from sense A.4 above, after Spender's poem *The Pylons* (1933).] Designating or pertaining to those poets of the 1930s (chiefly W. H. Auden, C. Day Lewis, L. MacNeice, and S. Spender) who used industrial scenes and imagery as themes of their poetry. M20.

pylor *combining form* see PYLORO-.

pyloric /pʌɪˈlɒrɪk/ *adjective.* E19.
[from PYLORUS + -IC.]
ANATOMY. Of or pertaining to the pylorus.
pyloric stenosis narrowing of the pylorus, leading to repeated vomiting.

pyloro- /pʌɪˈlɔːrəʊ/ *combining form* of PYLORUS, used in MEDICINE: see -O-. Before a vowel **pylor-.**
■ **pyloˈrectomy** *noun* (an instance of) surgical removal of the pylorus L19. **pyloroplasty** *noun* (an instance of) surgical widening of the pylorus L19. **pylorospasm** *noun* closure of the pylorus due to muscle spasm L19.

pylorus /pʌɪˈlɔːrəs/ *noun.* Pl. **-ri** /-rʌɪ/. E17.
[Late Latin from Greek *pulōros*, *pulouros* gatekeeper, from *pulē* gate + *ouros* warder.]
1 ANATOMY. The opening from the stomach into the duodenum, controlled by a strong sphincter muscle. Also, the adjacent part of the stomach. E17.
2 ZOOLOGY. An analogous part in an invertebrate, e.g. the posterior opening of the stomach in an insect. E19.

PYO *abbreviation.*
Pick your own (fruit).

pyo- /ˈpʌɪəʊ/ *combining form* of Greek *puon* pus, used esp. in MEDICINE: see -O-. Before a vowel **py-.**
■ **pyarˈthrosis** *noun*, pl. **-throses** /-ˈθrəʊsiːz/, an infected joint filled with pus; suppurative arthritis: M19. **pyoˈcoccal** *adjective* of or pertaining to a pyococcus L19. **pyoˈcoccus** *noun*, pl. **-cci** /-k(s)ʌɪ, -k(s)iː/, any of various cocci causing suppuration, esp. *Streptococcus pyogenes* L19. **pyoˈcyanase** *noun* a preparation, formerly used as an antibiotic, obtained from the bacterium *Pseudomonas aeruginosa* E20. **pyoˈcyanine**, **-in** *noun* a toxic blue pigment, $C_{13}H_{10}N_2O$, produced by the bacterium *Pseudomonas aeruginosa* and responsible for colouring pus blue or green M19. **pyoˈderma** *noun* any pyogenic infection of the skin M20. **pyoˈdermia** *noun* = PYODERMA L19. **pyoˈdermic** *adjective* of or pertaining to pyoderma L19. **pyoˈgenesis** *noun* the formation of pus, suppuration M19. **pyogeˈnetic**, **pyoˈgenic** *adjectives* of or pertaining to pyogenesis; producing pus: M19. **pyoneˈphrosis** *noun* the presence of pus in the kidney following obstruction and infection L19. **pyopneumoˈthorax** *noun* the presence of pus and air in the pleural cavity L19. **pyoˈrrhoea**, ***-rrhea** *noun* orig., discharge of pus; now (in full ***pyorrhoea alveolaris***), periodontitis: E19.

pyoid /ˈpʌɪɔɪd/ *adjective.* M19.
[Greek *puoeidēs* like pus, from *puon* pus: see -OID.]
MEDICINE. Of the nature of or resembling pus.

pyosis /pʌɪˈəʊsɪs/ *noun.* Now *rare.* L17.
[mod. Latin from Greek *puōsis*.]
MEDICINE. Formation and discharge of pus.

pyot *noun & adjective* var. of PIET.

pyr- *combining form* see PYRO-.

pyracantha /ˈpʌɪrəkanθə/ *noun.* Also (now *rare*) Anglicized as **-canth** /-kanθ/. E17.
[mod. Latin (see below), use as genus name of Greek *purakantha* an unidentified plant, from *pur* fire + *akantha* thorn.]
An evergreen thorny shrub of the rose family, *Pyracantha coccinea*, of southern Europe, with clusters of white flowers and persistent scarlet or yellow berries, in Britain often trained against walls as an ornamental shrub.

pyralid /pʌɪˈralɪd, -ˈreɪl-/ *noun & adjective.* L19.
[from mod. Latin *Pyralidae*, from *Pyralis* (see below), use as genus name of Greek *puralis* a mythical fly said to live in fire, from *pur* fire: see -ID³.]
ENTOMOLOGY. ▶**A** *noun.* Any of various small moths of the family Pyralidae or the genus *Pyralis*. L19.
▶ **B** *adjective.* Of or pertaining to the family Pyralidae. L19.

pyramid /ˈpɪrəmɪd/ *noun & adjective.* As noun also (earlier) in Latin form †**pyramis**, pl. **-mides.** LME.
[Latin *pyramis*, *-id-* from Greek *puramis*, pl. *puramides*: ult. origin unkn.]
▶ **A** *noun.* **1** A polyhedron of which one face is a polygon of any number of sides, and the other faces are triangles with a common vertex. LME.
2 A monumental structure, often serving as a tomb, built of stone etc., with a usu. square base and sloping sides meeting centrally at an apex; *esp.* (also **P-**) any of the ancient structures of this kind built in Egypt as royal tombs. L15.
3 ARCHITECTURE. A structure of the form of a pyramid, as a spire, obelisk, etc. *obsolete* exc. as in sense 2. M16.
4 a An object of the form of a pyramid; a number of things arranged or piled up in this form. L16. ▸**b** A tree, esp. a fruit tree, trained in the form of a pyramid. E18.
5 a A plane figure suggesting the profile of a pyramid; a triangular formation, as a wedge-shaped body of people; a poem the successive lines of which increase or decrease in length. L16. ▸**b** *sing.* & (usu.) in *pl.* (treated as *sing.*). A game played on a billiard-table with fifteen red balls arranged in a triangle and one cue-ball. M19.
6 CRYSTALLOGRAPHY. A set of triangular faces meeting in a point. Also, two such sets of faces on opposite sides of a common base. M18.
7 ANATOMY & ZOOLOGY. Any of various parts or structures of more or less pyramidal form; *spec.* (***a***) (more fully ***renal pyramid***) each of the conical masses that constitute the medulla of the kidney, projecting into the pelvis of the kidney; (***b***) either of two rounded prominences on the anterior surface of the medulla oblongata; (***c***) a subdivision of the vermis of the cerebellum; (***d***) (in full ***pyramid of the vestibule***) a protrusion of the crest of the vestibule in the inner ear; (***e***) any of the five main radial elements of the chewing apparatus of sea urchins, each consisting of two joined calcareous plates enclosing a tooth. E19.
8 a FINANCE. A system of financial growth achieved by a small initial investment, usu. in stock or in a company.

Orig. *US.* E20. ▸**b** A lottery in which each participant recruits two or more further participants. *US.* M20.

📖 **2** E. H. GOMBRICH For the mummy of the king . . the pyramid had been piled up. G. GREENE A man in his forties was to me as old as the pyramids. **Great Pyramid** the pyramid of the fourth-dynasty Pharaoh Cheops at Giza which has supposed mystical powers; ***Great Pyramid prophecy***, the prediction of events of worldwide importance, based on a belief in the occult significance of the internal measurements of the Great Pyramid, pyramidology. **4a** A. BROOKNER Her hair, a heavily lacquered pyramid. M. DIBDIN A tray on which a pyramid of empty cups and glasses was balanced. *fig.*: DISRAELI The apex of the pyramid of his ambition was at length visible. **b** *attrib.*: *Garden* Lines of pyramid Apples and Pears. **5a** *Gymnast* A squad of 28 men . . showed different pyramids . . some of the 'corner stones' gave way occasionally. **7** ***MALPIGHIAN pyramid***.

Comb.: **pyramid-rest** BILLIARDS & SNOOKER etc. = ***spider-rest*** s.v. SPIDER *noun*; **pyramid selling** a system of selling goods in which agency rights are sold to an increasing number of distributors at successively lower levels; **pyramid shell** (the shell of) any of various small gastropod molluscs of the family Pyramidellidae, which are elongated and conical in shape; **pyramid-spot** the spot on a billiard-table midway between the centre spot and the face of the top cushion, which in snooker is where the pink ball is placed at the start of a frame etc., and in pyramids where the apex ball is positioned at the beginning of a game; **pyramid-text** an ancient Egyptian text found in the Pyramids.

▸**B** *attrib.* or as *adjective*. Designating a system of profit involving extensive subcontracting of work, or a system of selling in which each buyer secures the participation of further buyers. M20.

📖 *Observer* Pyramid distributors . . may make more money by recruiting other people to sell products.

■ **pyra'midic** *adjective* (*rare*) of or like a pyramid; heaped up; lofty, massive: M18. **pyra'midical** *adjective* = PYRAMIDAL *adjective* 1 E17. **pyra'midically** *adverb* (*rare*) = PYRAMIDALLY L17. **pyramidist** /'pɪrəmɪdɪst, pɪ'ram-/ *noun* (*rare*) a person who investigates or is an expert on the structure and history of the Egyptian pyramids L19. **pyramidize** *verb intrans.* (*rare*) form a pyramid; converge towards a summit or apex: M19. **pyramid-like** *adjective* resembling a pyramid M19. **pyramido'logical** *adjective* of or pertaining to pyramidology M20. **pyrami'dologist** *noun* a student of or an expert in pyramidology L20. **pyrami'dology** *noun* the branch of knowledge that deals with the mathematical or occult significance of the measurements of the Great Pyramid E20. **pyramidwise** *adverb* in the manner or form of a pyramid E17.

pyramid /'pɪrəmɪd/ *verb.* M19.
[from the noun.]
1 *verb intrans.* Of a group in a painting: be arranged in a form suggesting a pyramid, symmetrically about a central figure in an elevated position. *rare.* M19.
2 *verb trans.* FINANCE. ▸**a** Accumulate (assets); *spec.* (STOCK EXCHANGE) build up (stock) from the proceeds of a series of advantageous sales. E20. ▸**b** Set up (a company) as part of a pyramid aiming at financial growth from a small initial investment. M20.
3 *verb trans.* Distribute (assets or costs), *esp.* pass on (costs) by means of a pyramid of subcontracted work. M20.
4 *verb trans.* Arrange in the form of a pyramid; *gen.* pile up. M20.
5 *verb intrans.* (Of a person) become rich; (of a thing) increase greatly in value or amount. Also foll. by *up.* M20.

📖 **4** J. STEINBECK Canned goods are piled in mountains, the champagne and wine . . are pyramided. **5** *Time* Winter stress can be aggravated by the thought of pyramiding fuel bills.

pyramidal /pɪ'ramɪd(ə)l/ *adjective.* LME.
[medieval Latin *pyramidalis*: see PYRAMID *noun & adjective*, -AL[1].]
1 Of the nature or shape of a pyramid; resembling a pyramid. Also (*rare*), sloping, as an edge or face of a pyramid. LME. ▸**b** Huge, colossal. *rare. colloq.* E20.
2 a ANATOMY. Of, pertaining to, or designating certain structures of more or less pyramid-like form. Also, pertaining to any of the structures called pyramids (see PYRAMID *noun* 7). E18. ▸**b** CRYSTALLOGRAPHY. = TETRAGONAL *adjective* 2. L18. ▸**c** BOTANY. Designating any of various plants having a pyramid-like inflorescence, esp. a species of orchid (see below). L18.

📖 **1** V. S. NAIPAUL The building had a pyramidal roof. ***inversely pyramidal***: see INVERSELY *adverb* 2.

Special collocations: **pyramidal muscle** ANATOMY any of various pyramid-shaped muscles in the abdomen, nose, and heart. **pyramidal numbers** MATH. any of a series of numbers obtained by continued summation of terms in a series of polygonal numbers. **pyramidal orchid** an orchid of calcareous grassland, *Anacamptis pyramidalis*, with dense conical spikes of rosy-purple flowers. **pyramidal system**, **pyramidal tract** ANATOMY a tract of motor nerve fibres within the pyramid of the medulla oblongata.

■ **pyramidally** *adverb* in a pyramidal manner; in the form of a pyramid: M16.

pyramidate /pɪ'ramɪdət/ *adjective. rare.* L16.
[Late Latin *pyramidatus*, from *pyramidem*, from Latin *pyramid-*: see PYRAMID *noun*, -ATE[2].]
Resembling a pyramid, pyramidal.

■ **pyramidated** *adjective* formed with pyramids, or into a pyramid E19.

†**pyramides** *noun pl.* see PYRAMID *noun.*

pyramidion /pɪrə'mɪdɪɒn/ *noun.* Pl. **-ia** /-ɪə/, **-ions**. M19.
[from Greek *puramis*, *-id-* PYRAMID *noun* + *-ion* dim. suffix.]
A small pyramid; *spec.* in ARCHITECTURE, the pointed pyramidal portion forming the apex of an obelisk.

pyramidon /pɪ'ramɪdɒn/ *noun*[1]. L19.
[from PYRAMID *noun* after *accordion*, *harmonicon*, etc.]
MUSIC (now *Hist.*). A pedal organ-stop having wooden pipes in the form of an inverted pyramid, and producing very low notes.

Pyramidon /pɪ'ramɪdɒn/ *noun*[2]. Also **p-**. L19.
[from PYR(AZOL)ONE with inserted *amid-*: see AMIDO-.]
PHARMACOLOGY. (US proprietary name for) a pyrazoline derivative, $C_{13}H_{17}N_3O$, used as an antipyretic and analgesic.

†**pyramis** *noun & adjective* see PYRAMID *noun & adjective.*

pyran /'pʌɪran/ *noun.* Also **-ane** /-eɪn/. E20.
[from PYR(ONE + -AN, -ANE.]
CHEMISTRY. A colourless liquid heterocyclic compound, C_5H_6O, having a doubly unsaturated six-membered ring in its molecule. Also, any compound containing a ring of five carbon atoms and one oxygen atom.

■ **pyranose** *noun* a sugar with a molecular structure containing the six-membered (C_5O) ring present in pyran (freq. *attrib.*) E20. **py'ranoside** *noun* a glycoside of a sugar in the pyranose form M20.

pyranometer /pʌɪrə'nɒmɪtə/ *noun.* E20.
[from Greek *pur* fire + *ana* up + -OMETER.]
An instrument for measuring the amount of radiation incident from the entire sky on a horizontal surface.

pyrargyrite /pʌɪ'rɑːdʒɪrʌɪt/ *noun.* M19.
[from PYR(O- + Greek *arguros* silver + -ITE[1].]
MINERALOGY. Silver antimony sulphide, a dark red or grey rhombohedral ore of silver. Also called ***ruby silver***, ***dark red silver ore***.

pyrazine /'pʌɪrəziːn, 'pɪr-/ *noun.* L19.
[from PYR(ID)INE with inserted *az-* (from AZO-).]
CHEMISTRY. A weakly basic crystalline heteroaromatic compound, $C_4H_4N_2$, which is a diazine with the nitrogen atoms at opposite positions in the ring; any substituted derivative of this.

■ **pyra'zinamide** *noun* (PHARMACOLOGY) a pyrazine derivative used to treat tuberculosis, pyrazine-2-carboxamide, $C_4H_3N_2{\cdot}CONH_2$: M20.

pyrazole /'pʌɪrəzəʊl, 'pɪr-/ *noun.* L19.
[from PYR(R)OLE with inserted *az-* (from AZO-).]
CHEMISTRY. A weakly basic white crystalline compound, $C_3H_4N_2$, whose molecule is an unsaturated five-membered ring containing adjacent nitrogen atoms; any derivative of this containing such a ring.

■ **pyrazoline** /-'razəliːn/ *noun* a dihydro derivative of pyrazole, of formula $C_3H_6N_2$, of which three isomers exist; a substituted derivative of such a compound: L19. **pyrazolone** /-'razələʊn/ *noun* a keto derivative of a pyrazoline, of formula $C_3H_4N_2O$; any of the substituted derivatives of such a compound: L19.

pyre /pʌɪə/ *noun.* M17.
[Latin *pyra* from Greek *pura*, from *pur* fire.]
A heap of combustible material, esp. wood; *spec.* a funeral pile for burning a dead body.

■ **pyral** *adjective* (*rare*) of or pertaining to a pyre M17.

pyrene /'pʌɪriːn/ *noun*[1]. M19.
[mod. Latin *pyrena*, from Greek *purēn*.]
BOTANY. A stone in a fruit; *esp.* a single one in a small drupe.

pyrene /'pʌɪriːn/ *noun*[2]. M19.
[from Greek *pur* fire + -ENE.]
CHEMISTRY. A tetracyclic aromatic hydrocarbon, $C_{16}H_{10}$, present in coal tar and isolated as colourless crystals.

Pyrenean /pɪrə'niːən/ *adjective & noun.* M16.
[from Latin *Pyrenaeus*, from *Pyrene* from Greek *Purēnē* daughter of Bebryx, beloved of Hercules, said to be buried in the Pyrenees: see -AN, -EAN.]
▸**A** *adjective.* Of or belonging to the Pyrenees, a range of mountains along the border between France and Spain. M16.
Pyrenean mountain dog, **Pyrenean dog** (an animal of) a breed of large heavily built white dog, often with grey or brown markings on the head, distinguished by a thick shaggy double coat. **Pyrenean sheepdog** (an animal of) a breed of small fawn or grey long-coated sheepdog, often with white markings; also = ***Pyrenean mountain dog*** above. **Pyrenean wolfhound** = ***Pyrenean mountain dog*** above.
▸**B** *noun.* †**1** In *pl.* The Pyrenees. *rare.* M–L18.
2 A Pyrenean mountain dog or sheepdog. E20.

pyrenocarp /pʌɪ'riːnə(ʊ)kɑːp/ *noun.* L19.
[formed as PYRENE *noun*[1] + Greek *karpos* fruit.]
BOTANY. The perithecium of a pyrenomycete.

■ **pyreno'carpous** *adjective* L19.

pyrenoid /pʌɪ'riːnɔɪd/ *adjective & noun.* M19.
[from PYRENE *noun*[1] + -OID.]
▸**A** *adjective.* ANATOMY. Resembling the stone of a fruit in form. *rare.* M19.
▸**B** *noun.* BOTANY. A small colourless protein body found in the chloroplasts of certain algae and associated with the storage of starch. L19.

pyrenomycete /pʌɪ,riːnə(ʊ)'mʌɪsiːt/ *noun.* Orig. only in pl. **-mycetes** /-'mʌɪsiːts, -mʌɪ'siːtiːz/. L19.
[Anglicized sing. of mod. Latin *Pyrenomycetes* (see below), formed as prec. + Greek *mukētes* pl. of *mukēs* fungus.]
MYCOLOGY. An ascomycete of the class Pyrenomycetes, typically producing a flask-shaped ascocarp (perithecium).

■ **pyrenomy'cetous** *adjective* L19.

pyret- *combining form* see PYRETO-.

pyrethrin /pʌɪ'riːθrɪn/ *noun.* E20.
[from PYRETHRUM + -IN[1].]
CHEMISTRY. Any of a class of insecticidal terpenoid esters obtained from the flower-heads of *Tanacetum cinerariifolium* and related plants, or prepared synthetically.

■ **pyrethroid** *noun* any substance possessing the terpenoid structure and insecticidal properties characteristic of the pyrethrins M20.

pyrethrum /pʌɪ'riːθrəm, -'rɛθrəm/ *noun.* ME.
[Latin from Greek *purethron* feverfew, perh. from *puretos* fever.]
1 Chiefly *Hist.* = PELLITORY 1. ME.
2 Any of several plants of the composite family belonging to the former genus *Pyrethrum* and now included in the genus *Tanacetum*; esp. *T. coccineum*, much grown in various colours as a garden flower, and feverfew, *T. parthenium*. L19. ▸**b** In full ***pyrethrum powder***. An insecticide (containing pyrethrins) obtained from the flower-heads of *Tanacetum cinerariifolium* and related plants. L19.

pyretic /pʌɪ'rɛtɪk, pɪ-/ *noun & adjective.* E18.
[mod. Latin *pyreticus*, from Greek *puretos* fever: see -IC.]
▸**A** *noun.* A remedy for fever; an antipyretic. *rare* (only in Dicts.). E18–M19.
▸**B** *adjective.* **1** Of, pertaining to, or characterized by fever; tending to produce fever. M19.
†**2** Antipyretic. Only in M19.

📖 **1** *fig.*: *Times* The purge of the Justice Department has raised political tempers . . to a pyretic level.

pyreto- /'pʌɪrɪtəʊ, 'pɪ-/ *combining form* of Greek *puretos* fever, used in MEDICINE: see -O-. Before a vowel **pyret-**.

■ **pyre'tology** *noun* (now *rare*) the branch of medicine that deals with fevers L18.

†**pyrewinks** *noun* see PILLIWINKS.

Pyrex /'pʌɪrɛks/ *noun.* E20.
[Invented word.]
(Proprietary name for) a hard heat-resistant borosilicate glass often used for cookware. Freq. *attrib.*

pyrexia /pʌɪ'rɛksɪə, pɪ-/ *noun.* M18.
[mod. Latin from Greek *purexis*, from *puressein* be feverish, from *pur* fire: see -IA[1].]
MEDICINE. Raised body temperature, fever.

■ **pyrexial** *adjective* pyretic M19. **pyrexic** *adjective* L19. **pyrexical** *adjective* M19.

pyrheliometer /pəː,hiːlɪ'ɒmɪtə/ *noun.* *obsolete* exc. *Hist.* M19.
[from Greek *pur* fire + *hēlios* sun + -METER.]
An instrument for measuring solar radiation by allowing the rays to fall on water or mercury in a blackened vessel and observing the rise of temperature in the liquid.

Pyribenzamine /pɪrɪ'bɛnzəmiːn/ *noun.* M20.
[from PYRI(DINE + BENZ(O- + AMINE.]
PHARMACOLOGY. (US proprietary name for) the antihistamine tripelennamine hydrochloride.

pyridazine /pɪ'rɪdəziːn/ *noun.* L19.
[from PYRO- + -ID(E + AZINE.]
CHEMISTRY. A weakly basic heteroaromatic liquid, $C_4H_4N_2$, which is a diazine with the nitrogen atoms adjacent in the ring; a substituted derivative of this.

pyridine /'pɪrɪdiːn/ *noun.* M19.
[from Greek *pur* fire + -IDINE.]
CHEMISTRY. A colourless volatile liquid with a pungent odour present in coal tar, whose molecule is an unsaturated heterocycle of formula C_5H_5N.
Comb.: **pyridine nucleotide** BIOCHEMISTRY either of the two oxidizing coenzymes NAD and NADP (nicotinamide adenine dinucleotide and its phosphate).

■ **pyridyl** *noun* the radical $C_5H_4N{\cdot}$ E20.

pyridostigmine /,pɪrɪdəʊ'stɪgmiːn/ *noun.* M20.
[from PYRID(INE + NE)OSTIGMINE.]
PHARMACOLOGY. A compound containing the quaternary ion $(CH_3)_2N{\cdot}CO{\cdot}O{\cdot}C_5H_4N^{+}CH_3$, similar in action to neostigmine but weaker and longer-acting.

pyridoxine /pɪrɪˈdɒksɪn, -iːn/ *noun*. M20.
[from PYRIDINE with inserted *ox*-.]
BIOCHEMISTRY. One of the three common forms of vitamin B_6, a colourless weakly basic solid present esp. in cereals, liver oils, and yeast, and also prepared synthetically, which is important in the metabolism of unsaturated fatty acids; 3-hydroxy-4,5-di(hydroxymethyl)-2-methylpyridine, $C_8H_{11}NO_3$.
■ **pyridoxal** *noun* an oxidized derivative of vitamin B_6 which is a coenzyme in transamination and other processes M20. **pyridoxamine** *noun* a derivative of vitamin B_6 which is a co-enzyme in protein metabolism M20. **pyridoxic** *adjective*: ***pyridoxic acid***, an inactive oxidized derivative of pyridoxine which is the form in which excess vitamin B_6 is usu. excreted M20. **pyridoxol** *noun* = PYRIDOXINE M20.

pyriform /ˈpɪrɪfɔːm/ *adjective*. Also **piri-**. M18.
[mod. Latin *pyriformis*, from *pyrum* misspelling of *pirum* pear: see -FORM.]
Chiefly *ANATOMY*. Pear-shaped.
pyriform fossa either of two depressions on each side of the opening to the larynx. **pyriform muscle** a hip muscle which rotates the extended thigh laterally and abducts the flexed thigh.

pyrimethamine /pɪrɪˈmɛθəmiːn/ *noun*. M20.
[from PYRIM(IDINE + ETH(YL + AMINE.]
PHARMACOLOGY. A pyrimidine derivative used to treat malaria; 2,4-diamino-5-*p*-chlorophenyl-6-ethylpyrimidine, $C_{12}H_{13}N_4Cl$.

pyrimidine /pɪˈrɪmɪdiːn/ *noun*. L19.
[formed as PYRIDINE with inserted *-im* (from IMIDE).]
CHEMISTRY. A basic colourless solid, $C_4H_4N_2$, which is a diazine with the nitrogen atoms separated by one carbon atom; any compound containing this ring structure, *esp.* (also ***pyrimidine base***) any of the nucleotide-forming bases cytosine, thymine, and uracil.

†**pyritae** *noun pl.* see PYRITES.

pyrite /ˈpʌɪrʌɪt/ *noun*. L15.
[Old & mod. French, or Latin PYRITES: see -ITE[1].]
†**1** Orig. (also ***pyrite stone***), = PYRITES 1. Later, = PYRITES 2. L15–L18.
2 *MINERALOGY*. Native iron disulphide, FeS_2, crystallizing in the cubic system as a brassy-yellow mineral with a metallic lustre. Cf. next. M19.

pyrites /pʌɪˈrʌɪtiːz/ *noun*. Pl. (*rare*) †**-tae**. LME.
[Latin from Greek *puritēs* use as noun (sc. *lithos* stone) of adjective from *pur* fire: see -ITE[1].]
†**1** A mineral that can be used for striking fire. LME–L18.
2 *MINERALOGY*. Either of the two common forms of iron disulphide, pyrite and marcasite (also ***iron pyrites***). Also (with specifying word), any of various other metal sulphides and arsenides. LME.
2 copper pyrites = CHALCOPYRITE. **white iron pyrites** = MARCASITE.
■ **pyritic** /pʌɪˈrɪtɪk/ *adjective* of or pertaining to pyrites, containing or resembling pyrites; (of copper smelting) utilizing heat produced by the oxidation of sulphide ores: E19. **py'ritical** *adjective* (now *rare*) = PYRITIC M18. **pyritiferous** /pʌɪrɪˈtɪf(ə)rəs/ *adjective* yielding pyrites E19.

pyritify /pʌɪˈrɪtɪfʌɪ/ *verb trans*. Now *rare*. M19.
[from PYRITES after *petrify*.]
= PYRITIZE.
■ **pyritifi'cation** *noun* M18.

pyritize /ˈpʌɪrɪtʌɪz/ *verb trans*. Also **-ise**. E19.
[from PYRITES + -IZE.]
GEOLOGY. Impregnate with pyrites; *esp*. replace the original material of (wood, a fossil, etc.) with iron pyrites. Chiefly as ***pyritized*** *ppl adjective*.
■ **pyriti'zation** *noun* L19.

pyritohedron /ˌpʌɪrɪtəˈhiːdrən, -ˈhɛd-, ˌpɪ-/ *noun*. Pl. **-dra** /-drə/, **-drons**. M19.
[from PYRITE + -O- + -HEDRON.]
CRYSTALLOGRAPHY. A form of pentagonal dodecahedron common esp. in crystals of pyrite.
■ **pyritohedral** *adjective* M19.

pyritous /ˈpʌɪrɪtəs/ *adjective*. M18.
[from PYRITES + -OUS.]
GEOLOGY. Of or pertaining to pyrites; of the nature of or containing pyrites.
■ Also **pyritose** *adjective* (now *rare*) M18.

pyro /ˈpʌɪrəʊ/ *noun*[1]. *colloq*. L19.
[Abbreviation.]
Pyrogallic acid used as a photographic developer.

pyro /ˈpʌɪrəʊ/ *noun*[2]. *colloq*. Pl. **-os**. L20.
[Abbreviation.]
A pyromaniac.

pyro- /ˈpʌɪrəʊ/ *combining form*. Before a vowel or *h* also **pyr-**.
[Greek *puro-*, from *pur* fire: see -O-.]
Of, pertaining to, done with, or produced by fire; *spec*. denoting substances formed by the action of heat or fire, or behaving distinctively when heated; of a fiery red or yellow colour.
■ **pyro'bitumen** *noun* any of a class of bitumens that are infusible and relatively insoluble in organic solvents E20. **pyrobi'tuminous** *adjective* of or pertaining to pyrobitumens; of the nature of a pyrobitumen: E20. **pyro'cellulose** *noun* a form of nitrocellulose of relatively low nitrogen content, used in explosives E20. **pyrochlore** *noun* (*MINERALOGY*) any of a group of cubic minerals of the general formula $A_2B_2O_6(O,OH,F)$, where A is sodium, potassium, calcium, etc., and B is niobium, tantalum, titanium, etc.; *spec*. an ore of niobium found in pegmatites derived from alkaline igneous rocks: M19. **pyromag'netic** *adjective* pertaining to or exhibiting pyromagnetism; *spec*. (of a dynamo) operating by the diminution of the magnetization of iron with increase of temperature: L19. **pyro'magnetism** *noun* magnetism that is dependent on the temperature of the material E20. **pyrometa'llurgical** *adjective* of or pertaining to pyrometallurgy E20. **pyrome'tallurgist** *noun* a person who studies pyrometallurgy M20. **pyrome'tallurgy** *noun* metallurgy in which high temperatures are employed for the extraction of metals E20. **pyrometa'morphic** *adjective* (*GEOLOGY*) of, pertaining to, or characterized by pyrometamorphism L19. **pyrometa'morphism** *noun* (*GEOLOGY*) metamorphism resulting from the action of heat alone L19. **pyro'morphite** *noun* (*MINERALOGY*) a hexagonal chloride and phosphate of lead, occurring as green, yellow, or brown crystals in the oxidized zones of lead deposits E19. **py'rophanite** *noun* [Greek *phanos* bright] *MINERALOGY* a deep-red trigonal manganese titanate, also containing ferrous iron and forming a series with ilmenite E20. **pyro'phyllite** *noun* (*MINERALOGY*) a hydrous silicate of aluminium, occurring as foliated masses which exfoliate when heated M19. **pyrosphere** *noun* (*GEOLOGY*) = BARYSPHERE E20. **pyro'sulphate** *noun* (*CHEMISTRY*) a salt of pyrosulphuric acid L19. **pyrosul'phuric** *adjective* (*CHEMISTRY*): ***pyrosulphuric acid***, a powerful oxyacid of sulphur, $H_2S_2O_7$: L19. **pyro'synthesis** *noun* synthesis by the action of heat M20. **pyrosyn'thetic** *adjective* of, pertaining to, or produced by pyrosynthesis M20. **pyro'toxin** *noun* (*a*) *MEDICINE* (now *rare*) = PYROGEN 3; (*b*) a toxic substance produced by fire, *esp*. an environmental pollutant produced by combustion: L19.

Pyroceram /ˈpʌɪrəʊsɛˌram/ *noun*. M20.
[from PYRO- + CERAM(IC.]
(US proprietary name for) a strong, heat-resistant, partially devitrified glass.

pyroclastic /pʌɪrə(ʊ)ˈklastɪk/ *adjective* & *noun*. L19.
[from PYRO- + CLASTIC.]
GEOLOGY. ▶**A** *adjective*. Pertaining to or designating fragmental rocks of volcanic origin. L19.
▶**B** *noun*. A pyroclastic rock or rock fragment. E20.
■ **'pyroclast** *noun* a pyroclastic rock fragment E20.

pyroelectric /ˌpʌɪrəʊɪˈlɛktrɪk/ *adjective*. M19.
[from PYRO- + ELECTRIC.]
Of a crystal or crystalline substance: that becomes electrically polar when heated. Also, of, pertaining to, or utilizing this effect.
■ **pyroelec'tricity** *noun* (the property of displaying) electric polarization induced by heating M19.

pyrogallic /pʌɪrə(ʊ)ˈgalɪk/ *adjective*. M19.
[from PYRO- + GALLIC *adjective*[2].]
CHEMISTRY. **1** ***pyrogallic acid***, 1,3,5-trihydroxybenzene, $C_6H_3(OH)_3$, a weakly acid crystalline substance used esp. in photographic developers. M19.
2 Containing or using this acid. M19.
■ **pyrogallate** *noun* a salt or ester of pyrogallic acid M19.

pyrogallol /pʌɪrə(ʊ)ˈgalɒl/ *noun*. L19.
[from prec. + -OL.]
CHEMISTRY. = PYROGALLIC ***acid***.

pyrogen /ˈpʌɪrədʒ(ə)n/ *noun*. M19.
[from PYRO- + -GEN.]
†**1** Electricity considered as a material substance. *rare*. Only in M19.
†**2** A substance produced by the action of heat on organic compounds. *rare*. Only in M19.
3 *MEDICINE*. A substance which when introduced into the blood produces fever; a pyrogenic agent. L19.

pyrogenetic /ˌpʌɪrə(ʊ)dʒɪˈnɛtɪk/ *adjective*. M19.
[from PYRO- + -GENETIC.]
1 Having the property of producing heat, esp. in the body; thermogenic; pyrogenic. Now *rare* or *obsolete*. M19.
2 *GEOLOGY*. Of a mineral: crystallizing from a magma at high temperature. E20.

pyrogenic /pʌɪrə(ʊ)ˈdʒɛnɪk/ *adjective*. M19.
[from PYROGEN + -IC.]
†**1** *GEOLOGY*. = PYROGENOUS 1. *rare*. M19–E20.
2 *MEDICINE*. Having the property of producing heat in the body; *spec*. inducing fever. L19.
3 *CHEMISTRY*. Of a reaction etc.: caused by the application of heat. L19.
■ **pyrogenicity** /-ˈnɪsɪti/ *noun* M20.

pyrogenous /pʌɪˈrɒdʒɪnəs/ *adjective*. M19.
[from PYROGEN + -OUS.]
1 Of a substance: produced by fire or heat; *GEOLOGY* (now *rare*) igneous. M19.
2 *MEDICINE*. = PYROGENIC 2. L19.

pyrography /pʌɪˈrɒgrəfi/ *noun*. L17.
[from PYRO- + -GRAPHY.]
†**1** A description of firearms. Only in L17.
2 The art of decorating wood etc. by burning a design on the surface with a heated metallic point; poker-work. L19.
■ **'pyrograph** *verb trans*. burn a design on by pyrography L19. **pyro'graphic** *adjective* of or pertaining to pyrography E19.

pyrogravure /ˌpʌɪrəʊgrəˈvjʊə/ *noun*. L19.
[French, from PYRO- + *gravure* engraving.]
= PYROGRAPHY 2.

pyrola /ˈpɪrələ/ *noun*. M16.
[medieval & mod. Latin, dim. of PYRUS, from the resemblance of the leaves to those of the pear tree.]
A wintergreen of the genus *Pyrola*. Cf. WINTERGREEN 1(a).

pyrolatry /pʌɪˈrɒlətri/ *noun*. M17.
[from PYRO- + -LATRY.]
Worship of fire.

pyroligneous /pʌɪrə(ʊ)ˈlɪgnɪəs/ *adjective*. L18.
[from PYRO- + LIGNEOUS.]
CHEMISTRY. Produced by the action of fire or heat on wood; now only in ***pyroligneous acid***, = ***wood vinegar*** s.v. WOOD *noun*[1].

pyrology /pʌɪˈrɒlədʒi/ *noun*. *rare*. M18.
[mod. Latin *pyrologia*, formed as PYRO-: see -LOGY.]
The science of fire or heat; the branch of chemistry that deals with the application of fire to chemical analysis etc.
■ **pyro'logical** *adjective* L19. **pyrologist** *noun* L18.

pyrolusite /pʌɪrə(ʊ)ˈluːsʌɪt/ *noun*. E19.
[from PYRO- + Greek *lousis* washing (from the mineral's use in decolourizing glass) + -ITE[1].]
MINERALOGY. Native manganese dioxide, MnO_2, a black or dark-grey tetragonal mineral with a metallic lustre.

pyrolyse /ˈpʌɪrəlʌɪz/ *verb trans*. & *intrans*. Also ***-lyze**. E20.
[from next after *analyse*.]
CHEMISTRY. (Cause to) undergo pyrolysis.

pyrolysis /pʌɪˈrɒlɪsɪs/ *noun*. L19.
[from PYRO- + -LYSIS.]
CHEMISTRY. Decomposition of a substance by the action of heat; *loosely* any chemical change produced by heating.

pyrolytic /pʌɪrəˈlɪtɪk/ *adjective*. E20.
[from prec. + -LYTIC.]
CHEMISTRY. Of, involving, or produced by pyrolysis.
pyrolytic carbon, pyrolytic graphite a strong heat-resistant form of graphite deposited from vaporized products of hydrocarbon pyrolysis.
■ **pyro'lytically** *adverb* by pyrolysis M20.

pyrolyze *verb* see PYROLYSE.

pyromancy /ˈpʌɪrə(ʊ)mansi/ *noun*. Now *rare*. LME.
[Old French *piromance*, *pyromancie* from late Latin *pyromantia* from Greek *puromanteia*: see PYRO-, -MANCY.]
Divination by signs derived from fire.

pyromania /pʌɪrə(ʊ)ˈmeɪnɪə/ *noun*. M19.
[from PYRO- + -MANIA.]
A mania for setting things on fire.
■ **pyromaniac** *noun* & *adjective* (designating or pertaining to) a person with pyromania L19. **pyroma'niacal** *adjective* pertaining to or suffering from pyromania L19. **pyromanic** *adjective* = PYROMANIACAL E20.

pyrometer /pʌɪˈrɒmɪtə/ *noun*. M18.
[from PYRO- + -METER.]
Orig., an instrument for measuring the expansion of solid bodies under the influence of heat. Now, any instrument for measuring high temperatures, usu. those higher than can be measured by a mercury thermometer.
optical pyrometer: see OPTICAL *adjective*.
■ **pyrometry** *noun* the measurement of very high temperatures (using a pyrometer) L18.

pyrometric /pʌɪrə(ʊ)ˈmɛtrɪk/ *adjective*. E19.
[from PYRO- + -METRIC.]
Of or pertaining to a pyrometer or pyrometry; of the nature of, or measurable by, a pyrometer.
pyrometric cone a small clay cone which melts at a certain temperature, used to determine the temperature of a kiln.
■ **pyrometrically** *adverb* E20.

pyromucic /pʌɪrə(ʊ)ˈmjuːsɪk/ *adjective*. L18.
[from PYRO- + MUCIC.]
CHEMISTRY. ***pyromucic acid***, furan-2-carboxylic acid, $C_5H_4O_3$, a crystalline acid produced by the dry distillation of mucic acid.
■ **pyromucate** /-keɪt/ *noun* a salt or ester of pyromucic acid E19.

pyrone /ˈpʌɪrəʊn/ *noun*. L19.
[from PYRO- + -ONE.]
CHEMISTRY. A keto derivative of a pyran.

pyronin /ˈpʌɪrənɪn/ *noun*. Also **-ine** /-iːn/. L19.
[German, prob. formed as PYRO- + *-n-* + -IN[1], -INE[5].]
BIOLOGY & CHEMISTRY. Any of a class of synthetic red xanthene dyes employed chiefly as microscopic stains.

pyrope /ˈpʌɪrəʊp/ *noun*. ME.
[Old French *pirope*, from Latin *pyropus* from Greek *purōpos* gold-bronze, lit. 'fiery-eyed', from *pur* fire + *ōps* eye, face.]
1 A red or fiery gem, as a ruby or carbuncle. *poet*. Long *rare*. ME.
2 *MINERALOGY*. More fully ***pyrope garnet***. A deep red variety of garnet. E19.

pyrophori *noun* pl. of PYROPHORUS.

pyrophoric /pʌɪrə(ʊ)ˈfɒrɪk/ *adjective.* M19.
[from next + -IC.]
CHEMISTRY. Liable to ignite spontaneously on exposure to air; (of an alloy) emitting sparks when scratched or struck.
▪ Also **pyrophorous** /pʌɪˈrɒf(ə)rəs/ *adjective* E19.

pyrophorus /pʌɪˈrɒf(ə)rəs/ *noun.* Now *rare* or *obsolete.* Pl. **-ri** /-rʌɪ/. L18.
[mod. Latin, from Greek *purophoros* fire-bearing, from *pur* fire + *-phoros* -bearing.]
CHEMISTRY. Any substance capable of igniting spontaneously on exposure to air.

pyrophosphoric /ˌpʌɪrəʊfɒsˈfɒrɪk/ *adjective.* M19.
[from PYRO- + PHOSPHORIC.]
CHEMISTRY. ***pyrophosphoric acid***, a tetrabasic acid, $H_4P_2O_7$, obtained as a glassy solid by heating orthophosphoric acid.
▪ **pyroˈphosphatase** *noun* (*BIOCHEMISTRY*) an enzyme which hydrolyses pyrophosphates or pyrophosphoric acid E20. **pyroˈphosphate** *noun* a salt or ester of pyrophosphoric acid M19.

pyrosis /pʌɪˈrəʊsɪs/ *noun.* Chiefly *US.* L18.
[mod. Latin from Greek *purōsis*, from *puroun* set on fire, from *pur* fire: see -OSIS.]
MEDICINE. Heartburn.

pyrosoma /pʌɪrəˈsəʊmə/ *noun.* Also **†-ome.** E19.
[mod. Latin (see below), formed as PYRO- + Greek *sōma* body.]
ZOOLOGY. A colonial thaliacean of the genus *Pyrosoma*, consisting of brilliantly phosphorescent individuals united into a hollow cylinder closed at one end. Now only as mod. Latin genus name.

pyrotartaric /ˌpʌɪrəʊtɑːˈtarɪk/ *adjective.* L18.
[from PYRO- + TARTARIC *adjective*¹.]
CHEMISTRY. ***pyrotartaric acid***, a colourless crystalline compound, $C_5H_8O_4$, obtained by the dry distillation of tartaric acid; methylsuccinic acid.
▪ **pyroˈtartrate** *noun* a salt or ester of pyrotartaric acid M19.

pyrotechnic /pʌɪrə(ʊ)ˈtɛknɪk/ *adjective & noun.* E18.
[from next: see -IC.]
▶**A** *adjective.* †**1** Of or pertaining to the use of fire in chemistry, metallurgy, or gunnery. E–M18.
2 a Pertaining to fireworks or to their manufacture and handling; of the nature of a firework. Also, able to be ignited for technical or military purposes. E19. ▸**b** *fig.* Of wit, rhetoric, etc.: resembling or suggesting fireworks; brilliant, sensational. M19.

> **2a** N. F. DIXON Stellar explosions and other pyrotechnic marvels.

▶**B** *noun.* **1 a** In *pl.* (treated as *sing.*). Orig. = PYROTECHNY 1. Now, the art of manufacturing or using fireworks; the art of putting on firework displays. E18. ▸**b** In *pl.* A display of fireworks. Also (*transf.*), lightning. M19. ▸**c** In *pl. fig.* Any brilliant or sensational display. E20.
2 A pyrotechnist. *rare.* E19.
3 A device or material which can be ignited to produce light, smoke, or noise. E20.

> **1c** H. ROSENTHAL Joan . . stunned us all with a display of vocal pyrotechnics.

▪ **pyrotechnical** *adjective* = PYROTECHNIC *adjective* E17. **pyrotechnically** *adverb* M19. **pyrotechnician** /-ˈnɪʃ(ə)n/ *noun* a person skilled in pyrotechnics; a maker of gunpowder etc., or of fireworks: E18.

pyrotechny /ˈpʌɪrə(ʊ)tɛkni/ *noun.* L16.
[French *pyrotechnie* from mod. Latin *pyrotechnia*, from PYRO- + Greek *tekhnē* art: see -Y³.]
†**1** The manufacture and use of gunpowder, bombs, firearms, etc. Also, the use of fire in chemistry or metallurgy. L16–E18.
2 Pyrotechnics; the art of making or displaying fireworks. M17. ▸**b** *fig.* Brilliant or sensational wit, style, etc. M19.
▪ **pyroˈtechnist** *noun* a person employed or skilled in pyrotechnics; *fig.* a person of brilliant or sensational wit, etc.: L18.

pyrothere /ˈpʌɪrəθɪə/ *noun.* E20.
[from mod. Latin *Pyrotheria* (see below), formed as PYRO- + Greek *thēria* pl. of *thēr*, *thērion* wild animal.]
PALAEONTOLOGY. A member of the extinct order Pyrotheria of large ungulate mammals resembling elephants, of the S. American Oligocene.

†**pyrotic** *adjective & noun.* M17–M19.
[mod. Latin *pyroticus* from Greek *purōtikos* burning, from *puroun* burn, from *pur* fire: see -IC.]
MEDICINE. = CAUSTIC *adjective* 1, *noun* 1.

pyroxene /pʌɪˈrɒksiːn/ *noun.* E19.
[from PYRO- + Greek *xenos* stranger, because the mineral group was thought alien to igneous rocks.]
MINERALOGY. Orig., any of a large group of silicate minerals containing calcium and one or more other bases, usu. magnesium and iron. Now, any of a group of silicate minerals characterized by a structure of chains of SiO_4 tetrahedra and prismatic cleavage at nearly 90 degrees.
▪ **pyroxenic** /pʌɪrɒkˈsɛnɪk/ *adjective* of, pertaining to, of the nature of, or containing pyroxene E19. **pyroxenite** *noun* (*GEOLOGY*) an igneous rock consisting chiefly of pyroxenes and olivine M19. **pyroxeˈnitic** *adjective* of, pertaining to, or of the nature of pyroxenite M20. **pyroxenoid** /pʌɪˈrɒks(ə)nɔɪd/ *noun* any of a small group of triclinic silicates resembling pyroxenes in chemical constitution M20.

pyroxferroite /pʌɪrɒksˈfɛrəʊʌɪt/ *noun.* L20.
[formed as next + FERRO-: see -ITE¹.]
MINERALOGY. A yellow iron-rich analogue of pyroxmangite occurring in lunar rocks.

pyroxmangite /pʌɪrɒksˈmaŋgʌɪt/ *noun.* E20.
[from PYROX(ENE + MANG(ANESE + -ITE¹.]
MINERALOGY. A manganese- and iron-containing pyroxenoid occurring in metamorphic and metasomatic rocks.

†**pyroxylic** *adjective.* L18–L19.
[formed as next + -IC.]
CHEMISTRY. Obtained from wood by heating.
†**pyroxylic spirit** = ***wood alcohol*** s.v. WOOD *noun*¹.

pyroxylin /pʌɪˈrɒksɪlɪn/ *noun.* M19.
[from PYRO- + Greek *xulon* wood + -IN¹.]
CHEMISTRY. Nitrocellulose; an explosive consisting of this, as gun-cotton.
▪ Also **pyroxyle** *noun* (now *rare*) M19.

pyrrhic /ˈpɪrɪk/ *noun*¹ *& adjective*¹. L16.
[Latin *pyrrhicha* or Greek *purrhikhē* a dance in armour, said to have been so named after its inventor *Purrhikhos*; use as noun of adjective (sc. *orkhēsis* dancing): see -IC.]
GREEK HISTORY. ▶**A** *noun.* A war dance of the ancient Greeks, incorporating the movements of actual warfare performed in armour to a musical accompaniment. L16.
▶**B** *adjective.* Of or pertaining to this dance. E17.

pyrrhic /ˈpɪrɪk/ *noun*² *& adjective*². As noun also in Latin form **pyrrhichius** /pɪˈrɪkɪəs/, pl. **-chii** /-kɪʌɪ/. E17.
[Latin *pyrrhichius* from Greek *purrhikhios* of or pertaining to the pyrrhic (dance), formed as prec. As noun *sc.* Latin *pes*, Greek *pous* foot (a metrical foot used in the war-song accompanying the pyrrhic dance): see -IC.]
CLASSICAL PROSODY. (A metrical foot) consisting of two short syllables.

Pyrrhic /ˈpɪrɪk/ *adjective*³. L19.
[Greek *purrhikos*, from *Purrhos*, Latin *Pyrrhus*, king of Epirus: see -IC.]
Of a victory: gained at too great a cost, like that of Pyrrhus over the Romans at Asculum in 279 BC.

pyrrhichii, **pyrrhichius** *nouns* see PYRRHIC *noun*².

Pyrrhonian /pɪˈrəʊnɪən/ *noun & adjective.* Also **-nean.** L16.
[French *pyrrhonien* from Latin *pyrrhonius*, *-eus*, from *Pyrrho*, Greek *Purrhōn*: see next, -AN.]
▶**A** *noun.* A Pyrrhonist. L16.
▶**B** *adjective.* Pyrrhonic. M17.

Pyrrhonism /ˈpɪrənɪz(ə)m/ *noun.* L17.
[from Greek *Purrhōn* Pyrrho (see below) + -ISM.]
A system of sceptic philosophy taught by Pyrrho of Elis (*c* 300 BC), founder of the first school of Greek sceptic philosophy; the doctrine of the impossibility of attaining certainty of knowledge; absolute or universal scepticism. Also (*gen.*), scepticism, incredulity.

> *Philosophical Quarterly* Pyrrhonism comes from failing to distinguish between a demonstration, a proof and a probability.

▪ **Pyˈrrhonic** *noun & adjective* (*a*) *noun* = PYRRHONIST; (*b*) *adjective* of or pertaining to Pyrrho or his doctrines; purely sceptical: L16. **Pyrrhonist** *noun* a follower or adherent of Pyrrho; an advocate of Pyrrhonism; a sceptic: L16. **Pyrrhoˈnistic** *adjective* of the nature of a Pyrrhonist or of Pyrrhonism L19. **pyrrhonize** *verb* (*rare*) (*a*) *verb intrans.* practise Pyrrhonism; be sceptical; (*b*) *verb trans.* treat sceptically: E17.

pyrrhotite /ˈpɪrətʌɪt/ *noun.* M19.
[from Greek *purrhotēs* redness + -ITE¹.]
MINERALOGY. A bronze-yellow or reddish-brown magnetic ferrous sulphide crystallizing in the hexagonal system and usu. forming massive or granular deposits.
▪ Also **pyrrhotine** /ˈpɪrətiːn/ *noun* [-INE⁵] M19.

pyrrole /ˈpɪrəʊl/ *noun.* Also (now *rare*) **-ol** /-ɒl/. M19.
[from Greek *purrhos* reddish + Latin *oleum* oil: see -OL.]
CHEMISTRY. A weakly basic sweet-smelling liquid heteroaromatic compound, C_4H_4NH, present in bone-oil and coal tar; any substituted derivative of this.
Comb.: **pyrrole ring** an aromatic ring of four carbon atoms and one nitrogen atom.
▪ **pyrrolic** /pɪˈrɒlɪk/ *adjective* E20.

pyrrolidine /pɪˈrɒlɪdiːn/ *noun.* L19.
[from prec. + -IDINE.]
CHEMISTRY. A weakly basic pungent liquid, C_4H_8NH, which is a saturated heterocyclic compound obtained by catalytic reduction of pyrrole; any substituted derivative of this.

pyrrolidone /pɪˈrɒlɪdəʊn/ *noun.* E20.
[from prec. + -ONE.]
CHEMISTRY. A keto derivative of pyrrolidine; *esp.* (more fully ***2-pyrrolidone***) a colourless weakly basic solid, C_4H_7NO, in which the keto group is adjacent to the nitrogen atom in the ring.

pyrroline /ˈpɪrəliːn/ *noun.* L19.
[from PYRROLE + -INE⁵.]
CHEMISTRY. A partially reduced derivative of pyrrole of formula C_4H_7N, of which three isomers exist; a substituted derivative of such a compound.

pyrrolizidine /pɪrəˈlɪzɪdiːn/ *noun.* M20.
[from PYRROLIDINE with inserted *-iz-* (rel. to AZO-).]
CHEMISTRY. A colourless basic liquid, $C_7H_{13}N$, which has a structure consisting of two fused pyrrolidine rings sharing a carbon and a nitrogen atom; any derivative of this.
Comb.: **pyrrolizidine alkaloid** any of a large class of toxic alkaloids based on this structure which occur widely in plants.

pyrus /ˈpʌɪrəs/ *noun.* M19.
[medieval Latin var. of Latin *pirus*.]
Any of various small trees constituting the genus *Pyrus*, of the rose family; *esp.* the cultivated pear tree, *P. communis*. Also, any of various other trees and shrubs formerly included in this genus, esp. japonicas (genus *Chaenomeles*), and whitebeams and mountain ashes (genus *Sorbus*).

pyruvic /pʌɪˈruːvɪk/ *adjective.* M19.
[from PYRO- + Latin *uva* grape + -IC.]
BIOCHEMISTRY. ***pyruvic acid***, a yellowish odoriferous weakly acidic liquid, $CH_3COCOOH$, which is an important intermediate in many metabolic processes, esp. glycolysis.
▪ **pyruvate** *noun* a salt or ester of pyruvic acid M19.

Pythagoras /pʌɪˈθag(ə)rəs/ *noun.* L19.
[See next.]
GEOMETRY. ***Pythagoras' theorem***, ***Pythagoras's theorem***, ***theorem of Pythagoras***, the theorem, attributed to Pythagoras, that the square on the hypotenuse of a right-angled triangle is equal to the sum of the squares on the other two sides.

Pythagorean /pʌɪˌθagəˈriːən/ *noun & adjective.* Also (earlier) **Pythagorian** /pʌɪθaˈgɔːrɪən/. M16.
[from Latin *Pythagoreus*, *-ius* from Greek *Puthagoreios*, from personal name *Puthagoras* Pythagoras: see below, -AN, -EAN.]
▶**A** *noun.* A follower of the Greek philosopher and mathematician Pythagoras (fl. 6th cent. BC); *transf.* a person whose doctrine or practice agrees with that attributed to Pythagoras, esp. regarding belief in the transmigration of souls. M16.
▶**B** *adjective.* **1** Of or pertaining to Pythagoras or his philosophical system or school. L16.
2 *MUSIC.* Designating a diatonic scale of eight notes, or interval of this scale, attributed to Pythagoras, and based on fifths. L17.
▪ **Pythagoreanism** *noun* the Pythagorean philosophy E18.

Pythagoric /pʌɪθəˈgɒrɪk/ *adjective & noun.* Now *rare.* M17.
[Latin *Pythagoricus* from Greek *Puthagorikos*, from *Puthagoras*: see prec., -IC.]
▶**A** *adjective.* = PYTHAGOREAN *adjective.* M17.
▶†**B** *noun.* = PYTHAGOREAN *noun.* M–L17.
▪ **Pythagorician** /-ˈrɪʃ(ə)n/ *noun* = PYTHAGOREAN *noun* M18.

pythagorise *verb* var. of PYTHAGORIZE.

†**Pythagorist** *noun.* L16–L18.
[Greek *Puthagoristēs*, from *puthagorizein*: see next.]
= PYTHAGOREAN *noun.*

pythagorize /pʌɪˈθagərʌɪz/ *verb.* Long *rare.* Also **-ise.** E17.
[Greek *puthagorizein* be a disciple of Pythagoras, from *Puthagoras* Pythagoras: see -IZE.]
1 *verb intrans.* Follow Pythagoras; speculate after the manner of Pythagoras. E17.
†**2** *verb trans.* Change (a person or thing) into another as by transmigration of souls. M17–E18.

Pythiad /ˈpɪθɪad/ *noun. rare.* M19.
[Greek *Puthiad-*, *-as*, from *Puthia* pl. (sc. *hiera*) the Pythian games: see -AD¹.]
The four-year period between two celebrations of the Pythian games.

pythiambic /pɪθʌɪˈambɪk/ *adjective & noun.* M19.
[mod. Latin *pythiambicus*, from *Pythius* Pythian + *iambicus* IAMBIC.]
CLASSICAL PROSODY. (Designating) a metre consisting of a dactylic hexameter followed by an iambic colon.

Pythian /ˈpɪθɪən/ *noun & adjective.* L16.
[Latin *Pythius* from Greek *Puthios*, from *Puthō* Delphi (see DELPHIC) + -IAN.]
▶**A** *noun.* A native or inhabitant of Delphi; *spec.* in ancient Greece, the Delphic priestess of Apollo who delivered the oracles. Also (*transf.*), a person who is ecstatic or frenzied like this priestess. L16.
▶**B** *adjective.* Of or pertaining to Delphi or the oracle and priestess of Apollo there. E17.
Pythian games one of the four national festivals of ancient Greece, and celebrated near Delphi in the third year of each Olympiad.

For other words beginning with *pyro-* see the entry for **pre-**

Pythic /ˈpɪθɪk/ *adjective*. **E17.**
[Latin *Pythicus*, Greek *Puthikos*, formed as prec.: see **-IC**.]
1 = **PYTHIAN** *adjective*. **E17.**
2 Of the nature of the Pythian priestess; ecstatic, frenzied. **M19.**

pythogenic /pʌɪθə(ʊ)ˈdʒɛnɪk/ *adjective*. Now *rare*. **M19.**
[from Greek *puthein* rot + **-GENIC**.]
Chiefly MEDICINE. Generated by decay or decomposition.

python /ˈpʌɪθ(ə)n/ *noun*¹. **LME.**
[Latin from Greek *Puthōn*.]
1 In GREEK MYTHOLOGY (**P-**), the huge serpent or monster killed by Apollo near Delphi; *transf.* (*poet.*) any monster or plague. **LME.**
2 Any of various large non-venomous snakes of the family Pythonidae occurring mainly in the Old World tropics, which kill their prey by constriction, and have vestigial hind limbs; *loosely* any large snake which crushes its prey. **M19.**

python /ˈpʌɪθ(ə)n/ *noun*². **L16.**
[Late Latin (Vulgate) *pytho(n-)* or late Greek (New Testament) *puthōn* familiar spirit.]
ANCIENT HISTORY. A familiar or possessing spirit. Also, a person possessed by and uttering the words of such a spirit.

python /ˈpʌɪθ(ə)n/ *noun*³. **M20.**
[A code-name.]
MILITARY HISTORY. Leave granted at the end of the war of 1939–45 to members of the British forces who had served a long period overseas.

Pythonesque /pʌɪθəˈnɛsk/ *adjective*. **L20.**
[from Monty *Python*'s Flying Circus (see below) + **-ESQUE**.]
Pertaining to or characteristic of *Monty Python's Flying Circus*, a popular British television comedy series of the 1970s, noted esp. for its absurdist or surrealist humour.

pythoness /ˈpʌɪθənɛs/ *noun*. Also (now *rare*) in Latin form **pythonissa** /pʌɪθəˈnɪsə/. **LME.**
[Old French *phitonise* (mod. *pythonisse*) from medieval Latin *phitonissa* alt. of late Latin *pythonissa* fem. of *pytho(n-)* from late Greek *puthōn* **PYTHON** *noun*²: see **-ESS**¹.]
ANCIENT HISTORY. A woman said to be possessed by and utter the words of a familiar spirit; a woman with powers of divination; a witch. Also, the Pythian priestess.

pythonic /pʌɪˈθɒnɪk/ *adjective*¹. **M17.**
[Latin *pythonicus* from Greek *puthōnikos* prophetic, from *puthōn* **PYTHON** *noun*²: see **-IC**.]
Of or pertaining to divination; prophetic, oracular.
■ Also **pythonical** *adjective* (now *rare*) **L16.**

pythonic /pʌɪˈθɒnɪk/ *adjective*². **E19.**
[from **PYTHON** *noun*¹ + **-IC**.]
Of, pertaining to, or resembling a python (the snake); monstrous, huge.

pythonissa *noun* see **PYTHONESS**.

pythonomorph /pʌɪˈθɒnəmɔːf/ *noun*. Now *rare*. **L19.**
[from mod. Latin *Pythonomorpha*, former taxonomic division, formed as **PYTHON** *noun*¹ + Greek *morphē* form: see **-MORPH**.]
PALAEONTOLOGY. A mosasaur.

pyuria /pʌɪˈjʊərɪə/ *noun*. **E19.**
[from **PYO-** + **-URIA**.]
MEDICINE. The presence of pus in the urine.

pyx /pɪks/ *noun & verb*. Also **pix**. **LME.**
[Latin *pyxis* from late Greek *puxis* **BOX** *noun*².]
▶ **A** *noun*. **1** ECCLESIASTICAL. The vessel in which the consecrated bread of the Eucharist is kept. **LME.**
2 At the Royal Mint, the chest in which specimen gold and silver coins are deposited to be tested annually. Esp. in ***trial of the pyx***, the annual test of such specimen coins. **L16.**
3 A box; a vase. *rare*. **E17.**
†**4** A mariner's compass; = **PYXIS** *noun* 3. *rare*. **L17–E18.**
Comb.: **pyx-box**, **pyx-chest** = sense 2 above; **pyx-cloth**: used to veil the Eucharistic pyx.
▶ **B** *verb trans*. **1** ECCLESIASTICAL. Keep or put (the consecrated bread of the Eucharist) in a pyx. Long *rare*. **M16.**
2 Deposit (specimen coins) in the pyx of the Royal Mint; test (coins) by weight. **M16.**

pyxides *noun* pl. of **PYXIS**.

pyxidium /pɪkˈsɪdɪəm/ *noun*. Pl. **-ia** /-ɪə/. **M19.**
[mod. Latin from Greek *puxidion* dim. of *puxis* a box: see **PYX** *noun*.]
BOTANY. A seed-capsule opening by transverse dehiscence, so that the top comes off like the lid of a box.

pyxie /ˈpɪksi/ *noun*. *US*. **L19.**
[Abbreviation of mod. Latin *Pyxidanthera* (see below), from Greek *puxidion* (see prec.) + fem. of *anthēros* flowery.]
In full ***pyxie moss***. A small prostrate evergreen shrub, *Pyxidanthera barbulata* (family Diapensiaceae), of the pine-barrens of the eastern US, with needle-like leaves and tiny white flowers. Also called ***pine-barren beauty***.

pyxis /ˈpɪksɪs/ *noun*. Pl. **pyxides** /ˈpɪksɪdiːz/. **LME.**
[Latin: see **PYX** *noun*.]
†**1** ANATOMY. The acetabulum. **LME–M19.**
2 A small box or vase; a casket. **M16.**
3 More fully ***Pyxis Nautica*** /ˈnɔːtɪkə/ [Latin, fem. of *nauticus* **NAUTICAL**]. (The name of) an inconspicuous constellation of the southern hemisphere, lying in the Milky Way between Vela and Puppis and orig. part of Argo; the Mariner's Compass. **L17.**
4 BOTANY. = **PYXIDIUM**. **M19.**

pzazz *noun* var. of **PIZZAZZ**.

Qq

Q, q /kjuː/.
The seventeenth letter of the modern English alphabet and the sixteenth of the ancient Roman one, in the latter an adoption of the ϙ (*koppa*) of some of the early Greek alphabets, in turn derived from the Phoenician letter used to represent voiced uvular. In Latin, Q was regularly used with *v* to represent the double sound /kw/; subsequently in Romance languages, esp. French, it also represented simple /k/. In Old English the ordinary representation of the sound was *cw-* (earlier also *cu-*). After the Norman Conquest *qu-* was introduced, and by the end of the 13th cent. *cw-* was entirely discontinued, with *qu-* (or its variants *qv-*, *qw-*) being the established spelling for all cases of the sound /kw/, whether of English, French, or Latin origin. In ordinary modern English Q is normally only used in *qu*, whether initially as in ***quake***, ***quality***, medially as in ***equal***, ***sequence***, or finally with the sound /k/ as in ***cheque***, ***grotesque***. Q used alone varies with *k* and *kh* in transliterations of Semitic languages, as ***qat***, ***Qur'an*** for ***khat***, ***Koran***. Q in transliterations of Chinese is normally pronounced /tʃ/. Pl. **Q's**, **Qs**.
► **I 1** The letter and its sound.
2 The shape of the letter.
1 ***mind one's P's and Q's***: see P, P. Q-CELTIC.
► **II** Symbolical uses.
3 Used to denote the serial order; applied e.g. to the seventeenth (or often the sixteenth, either I or J being omitted) group or section, sheet of a book, etc.
4 a ***Q-boat***, ***Q-ship***, an armed and camouflaged merchant ship used as a decoy or to destroy submarines. ▸**b** ***Q car***, a disguised police car. ▸**c** ***Q fever*** [abbreviation of *query*], a febrile disease resembling influenza, caused by a rickettsia.
5 PHYSICS. [Initial letter of *quantity*.] Representing electric charge.
6 THEOLOGY. [Prob. abbreviation of German *Quelle* source.] (Cap. Q.) Used to denote the hypothetical source of the passages shared by the gospels of Matthew and Luke, but not found in Mark.
7 (Cap. Q.) The ratio of the reactance of an inductor or capacitor to its resistance; a parameter of an oscillatory system or device (as a laser) representing the degree to which it is undamped and hence expressing the relationship between stored energy and energy dissipation. Also ***Q factor***.
8 PSYCHOLOGY. More fully ***Q-sort***, ***Q-technique***. A personality testing method in which each subject has to rate in order those personality traits that seem most applicable to himself or herself.
9 (Cap. Q.) A unit of energy equal to 10^{18} British thermal units (approx. 10^{21} joule).
10 ***Q-Tip***, (proprietary name for) a cotton swab on a small stick.
7 Q meter ELECTRICITY an instrument for measuring the Q of a component. **Q-spoiling** ELECTRONICS Q-switching. **Q-switch** *noun* & *verb* (PHYSICS) (***a***) *noun* A means of suddenly increasing or decreasing the Q of a laser by unblocking the optical path to one of the mirrors; (***b***) *verb trans.* Use a Q-switch on (a laser), esp. to increase the Q and produce a single pulse of very high power (chiefly as ***Q-switched*** *ppl adjective*, ***Q-switching*** *verbal noun*).
► **III 11** Abbrevs.: **Q** = quartermaster, quartermaster-general, -sergeant; quarto; Queen; query, question.

QA *abbreviation.*
Quality assurance.

qabalah *noun* var. of CABBALA.

qadi *noun* var. of CADI.

qaimaqam *noun* var. of KAIMAKAM.

Qajar /ˈkɑːdʒɑː/ *adjective & noun.* Also **K-**. L19.
[Persian *ḳājār*.]
► **A** *adjective.* Of or pertaining to a northern Iranian people of Turcoman origin, who formed the ruling dynasty of Persia from 1794 to 1925. L19.
► **B** *noun.* Pl. same, **-s**. A member of this people. E20.

qanat /kəˈnɑːt/ *noun.* Also **k-**. M19.
[Persian from Arab. *ḳanāt* reed, lance, pipe, channel.]
A gently sloping underground channel or tunnel, *esp.* one constructed to lead water from the interior of a hill to a village below.

Q and A *abbreviation.*
Question and answer.

QANTAS /ˈkwɒntəs/ *abbreviation.*
Queensland and Northern Territory Aerial Services, Australia's national airline.

QARANC *abbreviation.*
Queen Alexandra's Royal Army Nursing Corps.

Qashgai *noun & adjective* var. of KASHGAI.

qasida /kaˈsiːdə/ *noun.* E19.
[Arab. *ḳaṣīda*.]
A classical Arabic or Persian monorhyme poem in uniform metre, consisting of ten or more distichs and usu. a tripartite structure, freq. having a panegyric or elegiac theme.

qat *noun* var. of KHAT.

Qatabanian /katəˈbeɪnɪən/ *adjective & noun.* E20.
[from *Qataban* (see below) + -IAN.]
Hist. ►**A** *adjective.* Of or pertaining to the ancient kingdom of Qataban in southern Arabia, or its Semitic language. E20.
►**B** *noun.* A native or inhabitant of Qataban; the Qatabanian language. M20.

Qatari /ˈkataːri, kəˈtɑːri, g-/ *noun & adjective.* M20.
[from *Qatar* (see below) + -I².]
► **A** *noun.* A native or inhabitant of Qatar, a State situated on a peninsula on the west coast of the Persian Gulf. M20.
► **B** *adjective.* Of or pertaining to Qatar or its people. M20.

qawwal /kaˈwɑːl/ *noun.* E20.
[Urdu, Persian *qawwāl* from Arab. = reciter, chanter (esp. of religious verse), lit. 'a person who speaks well', from *qāla* speak.]
A performer of qawwali.

qawwali /kaˈwɑːli/ *noun.* M20.
[Urdu, Persian *qawwālī* from Arab., lit. 'singing of a qawwal'.]
A style of Muslim devotional music, associated particularly with Sufis in Pakistan, characterized by a fervent, often improvisatory vocal delivery and with an accompanying rhythm articulated on drums and harmonium; a song in this style.

QB *abbreviation.*
Queen's Bench.

QBI *abbreviation. RAF slang.*
Quite bloody impossible (of flying conditions).

QC *abbreviation.*
1 Quality control.
2 LAW. Queen's Counsel.

QCD *abbreviation.*
PARTICLE PHYSICS. Quantum chromodynamics.

qds *abbreviation.*
MEDICINE. Latin *Quater in die sumendus* to be taken four times a day.

QED *abbreviation.*
1 PARTICLE PHYSICS. Quantum electrodynamics.
2 Latin *Quod erat demonstrandum* which was to be demonstrated, (*loosely*) as has been demonstrated.

QEF *abbreviation.*
Chiefly MATH. Latin *Quod erat faciendum* which was to be done.

qere /kəˈreː/ *noun.* Also **Q-**; ***keri***, **K-**. M17.
[Aramaic from *qrā* read.]
A word in the margin of a Hebrew text of the Old Testament to be substituted in reading for a traditional reading or *kethib* in the text.

QF *abbreviation.*
MILITARY quick-firing.

QI *abbreviation.*
Quartz-iodine.

qi /tʃi/ *noun.* M19.
[Chinese *qì* air, breath.]
The physical life-force postulated by certain Chinese philosophers; the material principle.
qi gong [Chinese *kung* work] a system of techniques to focus and strengthen qi, including breathing exercises, meditation, and hand and arm movements, used in alternative medicine and as a basis for training in martial arts.

Qiana /kɪˈɑːnə/ *noun & adjective.* Chiefly *US.* Also **q-**. M20.
[Invented word.]
Nylon.
¶ Proprietary name in the US.

qibla(h) *nouns* vars. of KIBLAH.

qibli *noun* var. of GHIBLI.

qid *abbreviation.*
MEDICINE. Latin *Quater in die* four times a day.

Qin /tʃɪn/ *noun & adjective.* Also **Chin**, **Tsin**. L18.
[Chinese *Qín*.]
(Designating or pertaining to) a dynasty ruling in China for a short period in the 3rd cent. BC.

qindar(ka) *nouns* vars. of QINTAR.

Qing /tʃɪŋ/ *noun & adjective.* Also **Ching**, **Tsing**. L18.
[Chinese *Qīng* (Wade–Giles *Ch'ing*).]
(Designating or pertaining to) the Manchu dynasty ruling China from the 17th to the 20th cent.

qinghaosu /ˌtʃɪŋaʊˈsuː/ *noun.* L20.
[Chinese *qīnghāosù*, from *qīnghāo* a medicinal plant of the genus *Artemisia*.]
PHARMACOLOGY. A sesquiterpenoid extracted from a Chinese wormwood, *Artemisia annua*, used to treat malaria.

qintar /ˈkɪntɑː/ *noun.* Also **-dar** /-dɑː/, **-darka** /-dɑːkə/. Pl. **-s**, same. E20.
[Albanian *qindar*, *qindarke*, from *qind* a hundred.]
A monetary unit of Albania, now equal to one-hundredth of a lek.

qirsh *noun* var. of QURSH.

qiviut /ˈkɪvɪət/ *noun.* M20.
[Inupiaq, pl. of *qiviuq*.]
The underwool of the musk ox; fibre made from this.

Qld. *abbreviation.*
Queensland.

QM *abbreviation.*
Quartermaster.

QMG *abbreviation.*
Quartermaster-General.

QMS *abbreviation.*
Quartermaster-Sergeant.

QPM *abbreviation.*
Queen's Police Medal.

qr. *abbreviation.*
1 Quarter(s).
2 Quire(s).

QSO *abbreviation.*
ASTRONOMY. Quasi-stellar object (= QUASAR).

QSS *abbreviation.*
ASTRONOMY. Quasi-stellar radio source.

qt. *abbreviation.*
1 Quantity.
2 Quart(s).

q.t. *abbreviation. colloq.*
Quiet, esp. in ***on the q.t.***

qu *abbreviation.*
Query, question.

qua /kweɪ, kwɑː/ *adverb.* M17.
[Latin, abl. sing. fem. of *qui* who.]
In so far as; in the capacity of.

> 📖 *Word* Qua phonetician, de Saussure has no interest in making precise the notion of species. S. BRETT Wayland Ogilvie's dissatisfaction with the pictures *qua* pictures.

Quaalude /ˈkweɪl(j)uːd, ˈkwaː-/ *noun.* Chiefly *US.* M20.
[Invented word.]
Orig. PHARMACOLOGY. (Proprietary name for) the drug methaqualone; a tablet of this.

quab /ˈkwɒb/ *noun¹.* Long *obsolete* exc. *dial.* ME.
[Prob. already in Old English: cf. Anglo-Latin *quabba*, Middle Low German *quabbe*.]
A marshy spot, a bog.

†**quab** *noun².* *rare.* E17.
[Middle Dutch, Middle Low German *quabbe* (Dutch *kweb(be)*, (Low) German *quabbe*): cf. prec., SQUAB *noun*.]
1 a A sea-cucumber. Only in E17. ▸**b** A burbot. E17–L18.
2 *fig.* A shapeless thing. Only in E17.

qua-bird /ˈkwɑːbəːd/ *noun. US.* Now *rare*. L18.
[from 1st elem. imit. of the call + BIRD *noun*.]
The black-crowned night heron, *Nycticorax nycticorax*.

quack /kwak/ *noun¹ & adjective.* M17.
[Abbreviation of QUACKSALVER.]
► **A** *noun.* **1** A person who pretends to have medical skill or knowledge. M17.

2 *gen.* Any person who professes a knowledge or skill which he or she does not have; a charlatan. **M17.** **3** A doctor; a physician, a surgeon. *slang.* **E20.**

📖 **1** K. TYNAN Hatred of quacks may lead us to despise the true healers. **3** J. IGGULDEN I'll get the quack at the Bush Hospital to have a look at it.

▶ **B** *attrib.* or as *adjective.* That is a quack or charlatan; pertaining to or characteristic of a quack. **M17.**

📖 V. S. NAIPAUL In those days people went by preference to . . the quack dentist. W. TREVOR Potatoes on string, badger's oil, rhubarb—there's not a quack cure I haven't heard of.

■ **quackery** *noun* the characteristic practices or methods of a quack; charlatanry: **L17.** **quackish** *adjective* of the nature of a quack or quackery **M18.** **quackism** *noun* quackery **E18.**

quack /kwak/ *noun*[2]. *N. Amer.* **E19.**
[Var. of QUICK *noun*[2].]
Couch grass, *Elytrigia repens*. Also ***quack-grass***.

quack /kwak/ *noun*[3] *& interjection.* **M19.**
[Imit.: cf. Dutch *kwak*, German *Quack*, Icelandic *kvak* twittering of birds. Cf. next.]
(Repr.) the harsh cry characteristic of a duck or a sound resembling or imitating this.

quack /kwak/ *verb*[1] *intrans.* **M16.**
[Imit.: cf. Du *kwakken*, German *quaken* croak, quack (from prec.).]
1 a Of a duck: utter its characteristic abrupt harsh sound. **M16.** ▶**b** Of a raven or frog: croak. *rare.* **E18.** **2** *transf.* Make a harsh sound like that of a duck; (of a person) talk loudly or foolishly. **E17.**

■ **quacker** *noun* (*colloq.*) (*a*) a duck; (*b*) a person who talks loudly or foolishly: **M19.**

quack /kwak/ *verb*[2]. **E17.**
[from QUACK *noun*[1].]
1 *verb intrans.* Pretend to have medical skill or knowledge; dabble ignorantly in medicine. Also, talk pretentiously and ignorantly, like a quack. **E17.** **2** *verb trans.* Advertise or promote (esp. a medicine) with fraudulent or exaggerated claims. **M17.** **3** *verb trans.* Treat in the manner of a quack; administer quack medicines to; seek to remedy by ignorant treatment. **M18.**

quackle /ˈkwak(ə)l/ *verb*[1] *trans. & intrans. obsolete* exc. *dial.* **E17.**
[Imit.]
Choke.

quackle /ˈkwak(ə)l/ *verb*[2] *intrans.* **M16.**
[from QUACK *verb*[1] + -LE[3]. Cf. Middle Low German *quackelen*, German *quackeln* prattle.]
Of a duck: quack.

quack-quack /ˈkwakkwak/ *verb, interjection, & noun.* **E19.**
[Redupl. of QUACK *verb*[1], *noun*[3].]
▶ **A** *verb intrans.* = QUACK *verb*[1] 1a. *rare.* **E19.**
▶ **B** *interjection.* Repr. a (duck's) quack. **M19.**
▶ **C** *noun.* A duck's quack. Also (*joc. & nursery*), a duck. **M19.**

quacksalver /ˈkwaksalvə/ *noun.* Now *rare.* **L16.**
[Early mod.Dutch (now *kwakzalver*, whence German *Quacksalber*): 1st elem. prob. stem of †*quacken*, *kwakken* prattle, 2nd elem. from *salf*, *zalf* SALVE *noun*[1].]
1 = QUACK *noun*[1] 1. **L16.** **2** = QUACK *noun*[1] 2. **E17.**

quad /kwɒd/ *noun*[1]. *colloq.* **E19.**
[Abbreviation.]
= QUADRANGLE *noun* 2.

quad /kwɒd/ *noun*[2]. **L19.**
[Abbreviation.]
TYPOGRAPHY. A small metal block in various sizes, lower than type height, used by letterpress printers for filling up short lines etc.; = QUADRAT *noun* 2.
EM quad. ***mutton quad***: see MUTTON 5.

quad /kwɒd/ *noun*[3]. *colloq.* **L19.**
[Abbreviation.]
= QUADRUPLET.

quad /kwɒd/ *noun*[4]. *colloq.* Also **Q-.** **E20.**
[Abbreviation of QUADRUPLE *noun*.]
A vehicle with four-wheel drive.
Comb.: **quad bike** an off-road, four-wheeled motorcycle used for sport and recreation.

quad /kwɒd/ *noun*[5]. **E20.**
[Abbreviation of QUADRUPLEX *adjective*.]
TELEPHONY. A group of four insulated conductors twisted together, usu. forming two circuits.

quad /kwɒd/ *noun*[6]. **M20.**
[Abbreviation of QUADRILATERAL *adjective & noun*.]
1 *NAUTICAL.* A four-sided jib used on racing yachts. **M20.** **2** *RADIO.* An aerial in the form of a square or rectangle broken in the middle of one side. **M20.**

quad /kwɒd/ *noun*[7]. *slang.* **M20.**
[Abbreviation.]
= QUADRICEPS. Usu. in *pl.*

quad /kwɒd/ *noun*[8]. **L20.**
[Abbreviation.]
= QUADRAPHONY.

quad /kwɒd/ *noun*[9]. **L20.**
[Abbreviation of QUADRILLION.]
A unit of energy equal to 10^{15} British thermal units (approx. 10^{18} joule).

quad /kwɒd/ *noun*[10]. *N. Amer. colloq.* **L20.**
[Abbreviation.]
= QUADPLEX, QUADROMINIUM.

quad *noun*[11] var. of QUOD *noun*.

quad /kwɒd/ *adjective*[1]. *slang* exc. *PRINTING.* **L19.**
[Abbreviation.]
= QUADRUPLE *adjective*

📖 *Times* Posters ranging from quad-crown to crown-folio.

quad /kwɒd/ *adjective*[2]. **L20.**
[Abbreviation.]
= QUADRAPHONIC *adjective.*

quad /kwɒd/ *verb*[1] *trans.* Infl. **-dd-.** **L19.**
[Abbreviation.]
= QUADRUPLEX *verb.*

quad *verb*[2] var. of QUOD *verb.*

Quadi /ˈkwaːdiː, ˈkweɪ-/ *noun pl.* **E17.**
[Latin.]
An ancient Germanic people of the Suevian group who migrated to Moravia in about 8 BC.

quadplex /ˈkwɒdplɛks/ *noun.* *N. Amer.* Also **quadra-**, **quadri-**, **quadru-**, /ˈkwɒdrə-/. **L20.**
[from QUAD(RI-, QUADR(U-, + -PLEX[1], after DUPLEX *noun* 1.]
A building divided into four self-contained residences.

quadra /ˈkwɒdrə/ *noun.* **M17.**
[Latin = a square.]
ARCHITECTURE. The plinth of a podium. Also, a platband, a fillet, *esp.* one above or below the scotia in an Ionic base.

quadrable /ˈkwɒdrəb(ə)l/ *adjective.* Now *rare* or *obsolete.* **L17.**
[medieval Latin *quadrabilis*, from Latin *quadrare*: see QUADRATE *verb*, -ABLE.]
MATH. Able to be represented by an equivalent square.

quadragenarian /kwɒdrədʒɪˈnɛːrɪən/ *adjective & noun.* **M19.**
[Late Latin *quadragenarius*, from Latin *quadrageni* distrib. of *quadraginta* forty: see -ARIAN.]
(A person who is) forty years old or between forty and fifty.
■ **quadragenarious** *adjective* **M17.**

Quadragesima /kwɒdrəˈdʒɛsɪmə/ *noun.* **LME.**
[Late (eccl.) Latin, use as noun (sc. *dies* day) of fem. of Latin *quadragesimus* fortieth, ordinal of *quadraginta* forty.]
ECCLESIASTICAL. †**1** (The forty days of) Lent. **LME–M17.** **2** The first Sunday in Lent. Also more fully ***Quadragesima Sunday***. **E17.**

quadragesimal /kwɒdrəˈdʒɛsɪm(ə)l/ *adjective.* **E17.**
[Late Latin *quadragesimalis*, formed as prec.: see -AL[1].]
1 Pertaining or appropriate to the period of Lent; Lenten. **E17.** **2** Of a fast, esp. that of Lent: lasting for forty days. **M17.**

quadraminium *noun* var. of QUADROMINIUM.

quadrangle /ˈkwɒdraŋg(ə)l/ *noun.* **LME.**
[Old & mod. French, or late Latin *quadrangulum* use as noun of *quadrangulus* adjective, formed as QUADRI- + Latin *angulus* ANGLE *noun*[3].]
1 *GEOMETRY.* A figure having four angles and therefore four sides. Cf. QUADRILATERAL. **LME.** ▶**b** *PALMISTRY.* An area of the human palm bounded by four lines. **LME.** **2** A square or rectangular space or courtyard entirely or mainly surrounded by buildings, as in some colleges. Cf. QUAD *noun*[1], QUADRANT *noun*[2] 2. **L16.** **3** A rectangular building or block of buildings; a building containing a square or rectangular courtyard. **E17.**

📖 **2** JAN MORRIS The college is probably divided into two or three quadrangles, lawns in their centres.

■ **quadrangled** *adjective* (*a*) (now *rare* or *obsolete*) quadrangular; (*b*) having a quadrangle: **M16.**

quadrangular /kwɒˈdraŋgjʊlə/ *adjective.* **LME.**
[Late Latin *quadrangularis*, from *quadrangulum*: see prec., -AR[1].]
Shaped like a quadrangle; having four angles or sides.
■ **quadrangularly** *adverb* **E18.**

quadrant /ˈkwɒdr(ə)nt/ *noun*[1]. **LME.**
[Latin *quadrant-*, *-ans* quarter (orig. of an as), from *quadr-* QUADRI-. Cf. OCTANT, SEXTANT.]
†**1** A quarter of a day; six hours. **LME–M17.** **2** An instrument for taking angular measurements of altitude (formerly esp. in astronomy and navigation), usu. consisting of a graduated quarter-circle and a sight-ing mechanism. **LME.** †**3 a** A farthing. **LME–E17.** ▶**b** A Roman coin equal to a quarter of an as. **M16–M17.** **4 a** A plane figure bounded by two radii of a circle at right angles and the arc cut off by them. **L16.** ▶**b** A quarter of a circle's circumference. **M17.** ▶**c** A quarter of a sphere or spherical body. **L19.** **5** *gen.* Something having the form of a quarter-circle. **M17.** ▶**b** (Freq. **Q-.**) A street or part of a street curved in a quarter-circle. **E19.** ▶**c** *NAUTICAL.* A metal frame shaped like a quadrant, fixed to a rudder head and to which steering ropes or chains are attached. **L19.** ▶**d** A slotted segmental guide through which an adjusting lever is operated. **L19.** **6** Each of four parts into which something may be divided. **L19.**

📖 **5** M. HUGHES The circles were broken by four main aisles that divided the seating into four quadrants. **quadrant of altitude** a graduated strip on an artificial globe round which it revolves, extending from the meridian round one quarter of the circumference. **6** *Nature* A child . . with swelling in all four quadrants of the jaw.

Comb.: **quadrant electrometer** an electrometer in which the index moves within a metal cylinder that is divided into four insulated parts; **quadrant method** *ARCHAEOLOGY* a method of excavating circular features by removing diagonally opposite quadrants.

†**quadrant** *noun*[2]. **LME–M17.**
[App. alt. of QUADRAT or QUADRATE *noun* after prec.]
1 A square; a square thing. **LME–M17.** **2** = QUADRANGLE 2. **LME–M17.**

quadrant /ˈkwɒdr(ə)nt/ *adjective.* Long *rare* or *obsolete.* **E16.**
[Latin *quadrant-* pres. ppl stem of *quadrare* to square: see QUADRATE *noun*, -ANT[1].]
1 Square; of a square form. **E16.** †**2** Agreeing, conformable (*to* or *with*). **M16–E18.**

quadrantal /kwɒˈdrant(ə)l/ *adjective.* **L17.**
[Latin *quadrantalis*, formed as QUADRANT *noun*[1]: see -AL[1].]
Having the shape of, consisting of, or pertaining to a quadrant or quarter-circle.

📖 B. STEWART A quadrantal arc of a meridian on the earth's surface.

quadrantanopia /ˌkwɒdrantəˈnəʊpɪə/ *noun.* Also (earlier) **-nopsia** /-ˈnɒpsɪə/. **E20.**
[from QUADRANT *noun*[1] + AN-[5] + -OPIA.]
OPHTHALMOLOGY. A quadrantic loss of vision in an eye.

quadrantic /kwɒˈdrantɪk/ *adjective.* **E20.**
[from QUADRANT *noun*[1] + -IC.]
OPHTHALMOLOGY. Involving one quarter of the visual field.

Quadrantid /kwɒˈdrantɪd/ *noun & adjective.* **L19.**
[from Latin *Quadrant-* stem of *Quadrans* (see below) + -ID[3].]
ASTRONOMY. (Designating) any of a shower of meteors seeming to radiate from the former constellation of Quadrans Muralis (now in Boötes) in early January.

quadraphonic /kwɒdrəˈfɒnɪk/ *adjective.* Also **quadro-.** **M20.**
[from QUADRI- after *stereophonic* etc.]
AUDIO. Produced by, pertaining to, or designating a system of sound recording and reproduction that uses four signal sources and four loudspeakers, enabling both front-to-back and side-to-side sound distribution to be reproduced.
■ **quadraphonically** *adverb* **L20.** **quadraphonics** *noun pl.* (usu. treated as *sing.*) = QUADRAPHONY **L20.** **quadraphony** /kwɒˈdrɒf(ə)ni/ *noun* quadraphonic reproduction; the use of quadraphonic techniques: **M20.**

quadraplegia *noun* var. of QUADRIPLEGIA.

quadraplex *noun* var. of QUADPLEX.

quadrat /ˈkwɒdrət/ *noun.* Also †**quadrate.** **LME.**
[Var. of QUADRATE *noun*.]
▶ **I** †**1 a** A geometrical instrument formerly used to measure altitude or distance. **LME–E17.** ▶**b** A square with two graduated sides, marked on the right-angled corner of a quadrant to facilitate its use. **LME–E18.**
2 *TYPOGRAPHY.* A small metal block in various sizes, lower than type height, used by letterpress printers for filling up short lines etc.; = QUAD *noun*[2]. **L17.**
3 *ECOLOGY.* A small area, freq. of one square metre, marked out for studying the local distribution of plants and animals. Also, a portable square frame or grid used to mark out such an area. **E20.**

📖 **2** *EM* ***quadrat***. ***mutton quadrat***: see MUTTON 5. ***n quadrat***: see N, N 3. **3** J. DISKI She measured the growth of everything within the designated quadrats.

▶ **II** See QUADRATE *noun*.

quadrate /ˈkwɒdrət/ *noun.* Also †**quadrat**. See also QUADRAT. **LME.**
[Latin *quadratum* use as noun of *quadratus* pa. pple of *quadrare* to square, from *quadr-* QUADRI-: see -ATE[1].]
▶†**I 1** See QUADRAT. **LME.**
▶ **II** †**2** A square; a square area or space. Also, a rectangle; a rectangular space. **L15–L17.** ▶**b** A square number, the square *of* a number. **L16–M17.** **3** A square or rectangular object. **M17.** †**4** *ASTRONOMY.* Quadrate aspect; quadrature. **M–L17.** **5 a** *ZOOLOGY.* The quadrate bone. **L19.** ▶**b** *ANATOMY.* A quadrate muscle. **L19.**

quadrate /ˈkwɒdrət/ *adjective*. LME.
[Latin *quadratus* pa. pple of *quadrare*: see prec., -ATE².]
1 Of a square or rectangular form. LME. ▸†**b** *MATH*. Of a number or root: square. LME–M17.
†**2** *ASTRONOMY & ASTROLOGY*. = QUARTILE *adjective*. M16–L17.
†**3** *fig*. Complete, perfect. Only in 17.
†**4** Agreeing, conformable (*to* or *with*). M17–E18.
5 *HERALDRY*. Designating a cross which expands into a square at the junction of the limbs. Usu. *postpositive*. L18.
Special collocations: **quadrate-bone** a bone in the skull of reptiles and birds with which the lower jaw articulates. **quadrate muscle** = QUADRATUS.

quadrate /ˈkwɒdreɪt/ *verb*. M16.
[Latin *quadrat-* pa. ppl stem of *quadrare*: see QUADRATE *noun*, -ATE³.]
1 *verb trans*. Make square. M16. ▸†**b** *MATH*. Square (a circle etc.). M17–M19.
2 *verb intrans*. Square, agree, correspond, conform, (*with*). E17. ▸**b** *verb trans*. Make conformable (*to*). *rare*. M17.
3 *verb trans*. *ARTILLERY*. Place correctly or adjust (a gun) on its carriage. E18.

quadrathlon /kwɒˈdraθlɒn, -lən/ *noun*. L20.
[from QUADR(I- + Greek *athlon* contest, after *triathlon* etc.]
An athletic or sporting contest in which competitors engage in four different events.

quadratic /kwɒˈdratɪk/ *adjective & noun*. M17.
[French *quadratique* or mod. Latin *quadraticus*, from *quadratus*: see QUADRATE *adjective*, -IC.]
▶ **A** *adjective*. **1** Square. M17.
2 *MATH*. Of the second degree; involving a second power but no higher one. M17.
2 *quadratic* RESIDUE.
▶ **B** *noun*. *MATH*. A quadratic equation. L17.
■ **quadratical** *adjective* (now *rare*) L17. **quadratically** *adverb* L19.

quadrato- /kwɒˈdreɪtəʊ/ *combining form* of Latin *quadratus* QUADRATE *adjective*, or of QUADRATE *noun*: see -O-.
■ †**quadratoˈcubic** *adjective* (*MATH*.) of the fifth power or degree M17–L18. **quadratoˈjugal** *adjective & noun* (*ZOOLOGY*) (of, pertaining to, or designating) a bone connecting the quadrate and jugal bones of the skull in birds and some reptiles L19.

quadratrix /kwɒˈdreɪtrɪks/ *noun*. Now *rare*. Pl. **-trices** /-trɪsiːz/. M17.
[mod. Latin, from Latin *quadrat-*: see QUADRATE *verb*, -TRIX.]
MATH. A curve used in the process of squaring other curves.

quadrature /ˈkwɒdrətʃə/ *noun*. LME.
[Old & mod. French, or Latin *quadratura* a square, act of squaring: see QUADRATE *verb*, -URE.]
†**1** Square shape, squareness. Also, a square formation. LME–M17.
2 *MATH*. Calculation of the area bounded by or lying under a curve; the process of constructing a square equal in area to that of a given surface, esp. a circle. M16.
3 *ASTRONOMY*. The aspect of a celestial object in the solar system (esp. the moon) when situated 90 degrees from the sun as seen from earth; the point (in space or time) at which this occurs. Also (*ASTROLOGY*), a similar aspect between any two planets, a square aspect. L16.
4 *ELECTRICITY*. A phase difference of 90 degrees. Usu. *attrib*. or in ***in quadrature (with)***. L19.

quadratus /kwɒˈdreɪtəs/ *noun*. M18.
[Latin: see QUADRATE *adjective*.]
ANATOMY. Any of various square-shaped muscles. Also called ***quadrate muscle***, ***quadrate***.
pronator quadratus a pronating muscle of the forearm, extending across the radius and ulna.

quadrennia *noun pl.* see QUADRENNIUM.

quadrennial /kwɒˈdrɛnɪəl/ *adjective & noun*. M17.
[from next + -AL¹.]
▶ **A** *adjective*. **1** Lasting for four years. M17.
2 Occurring every four years. *rare*. E18.
▶ **B** *noun*. †**1** A period of four years. Only in M17.
2 An event occurring every four years. *rare*. M19.
■ **quadrennially** *adverb* every fourth year L18.

quadrennium /kwɒˈdrɛnɪəm/ *noun*. Also (earlier) **quadriennium** /kwɒdrɪˈɛnɪəm/. Pl. **-iums**, **-ia** /-ɪə/. E19.
[Latin *quadriennium*, formed as QUADRI- + *annus* year.]
A period of four years.

quadri- /ˈkwɒdri/ *combining form*.
[Latin, combining form of *quattuor* four: see -I-.]
Having four, fourfold.
■ **quadricenˈtennial** *adjective & noun* (**a**) *adjective* consisting of or pertaining to a period of four centuries; (**b**) *noun* a four-hundredth anniversary: L19. **quadricycle** *noun* a four-wheeled cycle L19. **quadriˈdentate** *adjective* (**a**) *BOTANY & ZOOLOGY* having four toothlike projections or notches; (**b**) *CHEMISTRY* (of a ligand) forming four separate bonds; (of a complex) formed by such a ligand: M18. **quadrifid** *adjective* (*BOTANY & ZOOLOGY*) divided into four parts by deep clefts or notches M17. **quadriˈfoliate** *adjective* (*BOTANY*) consisting of four leaves M19. **quadriform** *adjective* having four forms or aspects M17. **quaˈdrigamist** *noun* (*rare*) a person who has four spouses at once M17. **quadriˈlingual** *adjective* using or able to use four languages; in four languages: L19. **quadriˈlocular** *adjective* (*BOTANY*) having four loculi or compartments L18. **quaˈdrilogy** *noun* a tetralogy M19. **quadriˈnomial** *adjective* (*rare*) consisting of four (algebraic) terms E18. **quadriˈpinnate** *adjective* (*BOTANY*) having four pinnae L19. **quadrisyllable** *adjective & noun* (a word) consisting of four syllables M17. **quadrituˈberculate** *adjective* (of a tooth) having four cusps M19. **quadriˈvoltine** *adjective* (of a moth) producing four broods in a year L19.

quadric /ˈkwɒdrɪk/ *adjective & noun*. M19.
[from Latin *quadra* square + -IC.]
MATH. ▶ **A** *adjective*. Of a curve or surface: having a cartesian equation which is algebraic and of the second degree. M19.
▶ **B** *noun*. An expression of the second degree. M19.

quadriceps /ˈkwɒdrɪsɛps/ *noun*. Pl. same. M16.
[Latin, formed as QUADRI- + *-ceps*, *caput* head.]
ANATOMY. A large muscle forming the front of the thigh, the chief extensor of the knee. Also ***quadriceps muscle***.

quadriennium *noun* see QUADRENNIUM.

quadriga /kwɒˈdriːɡə, -ˈtrʌɪɡə/ *noun*. Pl. **-gae** /-ɡiː/. E17.
[Latin, sing. form of pl. *quadrigae* contr. of *quadrijugae*, formed as QUADRI- + *jugum* yoke.]
ROMAN ANTIQUITIES. A chariot drawn by four horses harnessed abreast; *esp*. a representation of this in sculpture or on a coin.

quadrilateral /kwɒdrɪˈlat(ə)r(ə)l/ *adjective & noun*. M17.
[from late Latin *quadrilaterus* + -AL¹.]
▶ **A** *adjective*. Four-sided; having four sides. M17.
▶ **B** *noun*. **1** A four-sided figure; a space or area having four sides. M17.
2 The space lying between and defended by four fortresses; *spec*. (*Hist*.) that in northern Italy formed by the fortresses of Mantua, Verona, Peschiera, and Legnano. M19.
3 *ECCLESIASTICAL*. The essence of Anglicanism comprising four essential principles, orig. enunciated in 1870 and approved by the Lambeth Conference of 1888 as a basis for the reunion of the Christian Church. Also ***Lambeth Quadrilateral***. L19.
■ **quadrilateralness** *noun* (*rare*) E18.

quadriliteral /kwɒdrɪˈlɪt(ə)r(ə)l/ *adjective & noun*. L18.
[from QUADRI- + LITERAL.]
▶ **A** *adjective*. Consisting of four letters; *spec*. (of a Semitic root) having four consonants instead of the usual three. L18.
▶ **B** *noun*. A word of four letters; a (Semitic) root containing four consonants. L18.

quadrille /kwəˈdrɪl/ *noun*¹. E18.
[French, perh. from Spanish *cuartillo* (from *cuarto* fourth) with assim. to French QUADRILLE *noun*².]
A card-game, fashionable in the 18th cent., played by four people with forty cards, the eights, nines, and tens of the ordinary pack being discarded.

quadrille /kwəˈdrɪl/ *noun*² & *verb*. M18.
[French from Spanish *cuadrilla*, Italian *quadriglia* troop, company, from *cuadro*, *quadro* square.]
▶ **A** *noun*. **1** Each of four groups of riders taking part in a tournament or carousel, each being distinguished by a special costume or colours; *gen*. a riding display. M18.
2 A square dance usu. performed by four couples and containing five figures, each of which is a complete dance in itself; a piece of music for such a dance. L18.
▶ **B** *verb intrans*. Dance a quadrille or quadrilles. E19.

quadrille /kwəˈdrɪl/ *adjective & noun*³. Also **-llé** /-leɪ/. L19.
[French *quadrillé*, from *quadrille* small square from Spanish *cuadrillo* square block.]
(Something, esp. paper) marked with small squares.

quadrilled /kwəˈdrɪld/ *adjective*. M19.
[formed as prec. + -ED².]
Marked with small squares.

quadrillion /kwɒˈdrɪljən/ *noun*. L17.
[French, formed as QUADRI- after *million*, *billion*, etc.]
Orig. (esp. in the UK), the fourth power of a million (10^{24}). Now usu. (orig. *US*), the fifth power of a thousand (10^{15}).
■ **quadrillionth** *adjective & noun* L19.

quadripartite /kwɒdrɪˈpɑːtʌɪt/ *adjective*. Also **quadru-** /kwɒdrʊ-/. LME.
[Latin *quadripartitus*, formed as QUADRI-, PARTITE.]
1 Divided into or consisting of four parts. LME. ▸**b** *spec*. Of a contract, indenture, etc.: drawn up in four identical versions. LME.
2 Divided among, shared by, or involving four parties. L16.
1 quadripartite division division into four parts, classes, etc.; *spec*. (*ECCLESIASTICAL HISTORY*) a fourfold division of tithes.

quadripartition /ˌkwɒdrɪpɑːˈtɪʃ(ə)n/ *noun*. M17.
[Latin *quadripartitio(n-)*, formed as QUADRI-, PARTITION *noun*.]
Division into or by four.

quadriplegia /kwɒdrɪˈpliːdʒə/ *noun*. Also **quadra-** /kwɒdrə-/, **quadru-** /kwɒdrʊ-/. E20.
[from QUADRI- + PARA)PLEGIA.]
MEDICINE. Paralysis of all four limbs.
■ **quadriplegic** *adjective & noun* (a person) suffering from quadriplegia E20.

quadripole /ˈkwɒdrɪpəʊl/ *noun*. E20.
[from QUADRI- + POLE *noun*².]
ELECTRICITY. A network, esp. a balanced filter network, having two input terminals and two output terminals.

quadrireme /ˈkwɒdrɪriːm/ *adjective & noun*. E17.
[Latin *quadriremis*, from QUADRI- + *remus* oar.]
CLASSICAL ANTIQUITIES. (A galley) having four rowers on each bank of oars.

quadrivalent /*esp*. *CHEMISTRY* kwɒdrɪˈveɪl(ə)nt, *esp*. *CYTOLOGY* kwɒˈdrɪv(ə)l(ə)nt/ *adjective & noun*. M19.
[from QUADRI- + -VALENT.]
▶ **A** *adjective*. **1** *CHEMISTRY*. = TETRAVALENT. M19.
2 *CYTOLOGY*. That is (part of) a quadrivalent. L19.
▶ **B** *noun*. †**1** *CHEMISTRY*. A quadrivalent element. *rare*. Only in L19.
2 *CYTOLOGY*. A multivalent consisting of four chromosomes. E20.
■ **quadrivalence** *noun* E20. **quadrivalency** *noun* M20.

quadrivial /kwɒˈdrɪvɪəl/ *adjective & noun*. LME.
[medieval Latin *quadrivialis*, formed as next + -AL¹.]
▶ **A** *adjective*. **1** Belonging to the quadrivium. LME.
2 Having four roads or ways meeting in a point; (of a road) leading in four directions. L15.
▶ **B** *noun*. †**1** A group of four. *rare*. Only in LME.
2 In *pl*. The four sciences constituting the quadrivium. *obsolete* exc. *Hist*. E16.

quadrivium /kwɒˈdrɪvɪəm/ *noun*. E19.
[Latin = place where four ways meet, formed as QUADRI- + *via* way: see -IUM.]
In the Middle Ages, the higher division of a course of study of seven sciences, comprising arithmetic, geometry, astronomy, and music. Cf. ART *noun*¹ 4, TRIVIUM.

quadro /ˈkwɒdrəʊ/ *noun*. *colloq*. L20.
[Abbreviation Cf. QUAD *noun*⁸.]
= QUADRAPHONY.

quadrominium /kwɒdrəˈmɪnɪəm/ *noun*. *N. Amer*. Also **quadra-**. L20.
[from QUADR(I- + COND)OMINIUM.]
A condominium consisting of four apartments.

quadroon /kwɒˈdruːn/ *noun*. Orig. †**quarteron**. E18.
[Spanish *cuarterón* (through French *quarteron*) quarter. Later assim. to words in *quadr-*: see -OON.]
1 A person having one quarter black blood. Also (*rare*), a person fourth in descent from a black person, one in each generation being white. E18.
2 *transf*. The offspring resulting from any similar admixture of blood, or from crossing certain animals. E19.

📖 **1** E. MITTELHOLZER Katrina is fair and has lovely wavy brown hair. She must be a quadroon.

quadrophonic *adjective & noun* var. of QUADRAPHONIC.

quadru- /ˈkwɒdruː/ *combining form*.
[Latin, var. of QUADRI-.]
Having four, fourfold.

quadrumanous /kwɒˈdruːmənəs, kwɒdrʊˈmɑːnəs/ *adjective*. L17.
[from mod. Latin *Quadrumana* (see below), formed as prec. + *manus* hand: see -OUS.]
ZOOLOGY. Of, pertaining to, or designating the former order of Quadrumana, comprising primates other than humans; four-handed.
■ **quadrumanal** *adjective* = QUADRUMANOUS L19. ˈ**quadrumane** *noun & adjective* (**a**) *noun* a non-human primate; (**b**) *adjective* = QUADRUMANOUS: E19.

quadrumvirate /kwɒˈdrʌmvɪrət/ *noun*. M18.
[from QUADRU- + TRIU)MVIRATE.]
A union of four men.
■ **quadrumvir** *noun* (*rare*) a member of a quadrumvirate L18.

quadrupartite *adjective* var. of QUADRIPARTITE.

quadruped /ˈkwɒdrʊpɛd/ *noun & adjective*. Also (earlier) †**-pede**. M17.
[French *quadrupède* or Latin *quadruped-*, *-pes*, formed as QUADRU- + *ped-*, *pes* foot.]
▶ **A** *noun*. **1** An animal which has four feet, *esp*. an ungulate mammal. M17.
†**2** *spec*. A horse. M17–M19.
▶ **B** *adjective*. Of or pertaining to quadrupeds; quadrupedal. M18.
■ **quadrupedal** /kwɒdrʊˈpiːd(ə)l/ *adjective* four-footed; using all four feet for walking or running; of, pertaining to, or designating a quadruped: E17. **quadruˈpedalism** *noun* = QUADRUPEDISM M20. **quadruˈpedally** *adverb* M19. †**quadrupeded** *adjective* quadrupedal M16–E18. **quadrupedism** *noun* the condition of being quadrupedal M19.

quadruplane /ˈkwɒdrʊpleɪn/ *noun.* E20.
[from QUADRU- + PLANE *noun*⁴.]
An aeroplane having four sets of wings, one above another.

quadruple /ˈkwɒdrʊp(ə)l, kwɒˈdruːp(ə)l/ *noun & adjective.* LME.
[Old & mod. French, from Latin *quadruplus*, formed as QUADRU- + *-plus* as in *duplus* DUPLE.]
▶ **A** *noun.* A fourfold number or amount. LME.
▶ **B** *adjective.* Consisting of four parts or things; having four participants; four times as many or as much, fourfold. M16.

LD MACAULAY The value of silver was more than quadruple of what it now is. **quadruple counterpoint** four-part counterpoint in which the parts may be interchanged. **quadruple time** MUSIC a rhythm or time having four beats in a bar. **quadruple alliance** *Hist.* an alliance of four powers, *esp.* that of Britain, France, Germany, and the Netherlands in 1718, and of Britain, France, Spain, and Portugal in 1834.

quadruple /ˈkwɒdrʊp(ə)l, kwɒˈdruːp(ə)l/ *verb.* LME.
[Old & mod. French *quadrupler* or late Latin *quadruplare*, from Latin *quadruplus*: see prec.]
1 *verb trans.* Make four times as great or as many; multiply by four. Also, outnumber four to one. LME.
2 *verb intrans.* Increase fourfold. L18.

1 E. BOWEN The mirrors opposite one another, which quadrupled the figure of each lady. **2** *New Scientist* These objects are quadrupling in number every 10 years.

■ **quaˈdrupler** *noun* a device that makes something four times as great M20.

quadruplegia *noun* var. of QUADRIPLEGIA.

quadruplet /ˈkwɒdrʊplɪt, kwɒˈdruːplɪt/ *noun.* L18.
[from QUADRUPLE *noun & adjective* + -ET¹, after *triplet*.]
1 Each of four children born at one birth. L18.
2 a A set of four things or parts working together. M19.
▶**b** MUSIC. A group of four notes to be played in the time of three. L19.
3 A bicycle for four riders. *rare.* L19.

quadruplex *noun* var. of QUADPLEX.

quadruplex /ˈkwɒdrʊplɛks/ *adjective & verb.* L19.
[Latin = fourfold, formed as QUADRU- + -PLEX¹.]
TELEPHONY. ▶**A** *adjective.* Of a system etc.: such that four messages can be sent over one wire at the same time. L19.
▶ **B** *verb trans.* Make (a circuit etc.) quadruplex. L19.

quadruplicate /kwɒˈdruːplɪkət/ *adjective & noun.* M17.
[Latin *quadruplicatus* pa. pple of *quadruplicare*, formed as prec.: see -ATE², -ATE¹.]
▶ **A** *adjective.* **1** Fourfold. M17.
2 Forming four identical copies. E19.
1 quadruplicate proportion, **quadruplicate ratio** the proportion or ratio of fourth powers in relation to that of the radical quantities.
▶ **B** *noun.* **1** *in quadruplicate*, in four identical copies. L18.
2 In *pl.* Four things exactly alike; *esp.* four identical copies. L19.

1 *Daily Times (Lagos)* Applications should be forwarded in quadruplicate naming two referees.

quadruplicate /kwɒˈdruːplɪkeɪt/ *verb trans.* M17.
[Latin *quadruplicat-* pa. ppl stem of *quadruplicare*: see prec., -ATE³.]
1 Multiply by four; quadruple. M17.
2 Make or provide in quadruplicate. L19.

quadruplication /kwɒˌdruːplɪˈkeɪʃ(ə)n/ *noun.* L16.
[Latin *quadruplicatio(n-)*, formed as prec.: see -ATION.]
1 The action or process of multiplying by four; the result of this. L16.
2 LAW (now *Hist.*). A pleading on the part of a defendant, in reply to a triplication. Cf. QUADRUPLY *noun.* M17.

quadruplicity /kwɒdrʊˈplɪsɪti/ *noun.* L16.
[from Latin QUADRUPLEX *adjective* after *duplicity*, *triplicity*: see -ITY.]
The condition of being fourfold or of forming a set of four.

quadruply /ˈkwɒdrʊpli/ *noun.* E17.
[French †*quadruplique*. Cf. DUPLY.]
SCOTS LAW (now *Hist.*). = QUADRUPLICATION 2.

quadruply /ˈkwɒdrʊpli/ *adverb.* L16.
[from QUADRUPLE *noun & adjective* + -LY².]
Four times; in a fourfold degree or manner.

quadrupole /ˈkwɒdrʊpəʊl/ *noun & adjective.* E20.
[from QUADRU- + POLE *noun*².]
PHYSICS. ▶**A** *noun.* **1** A multipole of order 2; *esp.* a system of four magnetic or electric monopoles with no net pole strength or charge. E20.
2 An arrangement of four magnetic (or electric) poles, of alternate polarity, directed at one point to focus beams of subatomic particles. M20.
▶ **B** *attrib.* or as *adjective.* That is a quadrupole; of or pertaining to a quadrupole or quadrupoles. E20.
quadrupole moment the (electric, magnetic) moment associated with a quadrupole, a function of the magnitudes of the charges etc. and the distance between them, and dependent on the configuration of the quadrupole.
■ **quadruˈpolar** *adjective* M20.

quaere /ˈkwɪəri/ *verb & noun.* Also (earlier) †**quere**. M16.
[Latin, imper. sing. of *quaerere*: see QUAESTOR. See also QUERY.]
1 *verb trans.* (in *imper.* now also interpreted as *noun*). Ask, inquire, query. Chiefly & now only in *imper.* introducing a question. M16.
2 *noun.* A question, a query. L16.

1 *Modern Law Review*: *Quaere* whether such refusal is . . justified.

quaesitum /kwiːˈsʌɪtəm/ *noun.* Pl. **-ta** /-tə/. M18.
[Latin, neut. sing. of *quaesitus* pa. pple of *quaerere*: see next.]
That which is sought; the answer to a problem.

quaestor /ˈkwiːstə/ *noun.* LME.
[Latin, from old form of *quaesit-* pa. ppl stem of *quaerere* ask, inquire, seek.]
1 ROMAN HISTORY. Any of a number of Roman officials who had charge of public revenue and expenditure, acting as treasurers of State, paymasters of the troops, etc. Also, a public prosecutor in certain criminal cases. LME.
2 The chief financial officer of St Andrews University and, formerly, of other (esp. Scottish) universities. L17.
■ **quaeˈstorial** *adjective* of or pertaining to (the position of) a quaestor M18. **quaeˈstorian** *adjective* = QUAESTORIAL M17. **quaestorship** *noun* the office or position of quaestor M16.

quaestuary /ˈkwiːstjʊəri/ *adjective & noun.* L16.
[Latin *quaestuarius*, from *quaestus* gain: see -ARY¹.]
▶ **A** *adjective.* Pertaining to or concerned with gain; moneymaking. L16.
▶†**B** *noun.* A person who seeks for gain; *spec.* = QUESTOR 1. E–M17.

quaff /kwɒf, kwɑːf/ *verb & noun.* E16.
[Perh. from Middle Low German *quassen* eat or drink immoderately.]
▶ **A** *verb.* **1** *verb intrans. & trans.* Drink (liquor etc.) deeply or in a long draught. Also, drink copiously or repeatedly of (liquor etc.) in this manner. E16.
2 *verb trans.* Drain (a cup etc.) in one draught or in long draughts. Also foll. by *off*, *up*. E16.
3 *verb trans.* Drive *away* by drinking; bring *down to* or *into* (a specified state) by copious drinking. *rare.* E18.

1 GODFREY SMITH The company quaff their wine. **2** P. CAREY He lifted his tankard, tried to quaff it in one gulp. **3** J. WILSON He quaffs, guzzles and smokes himself into stupidity.

▶ **B** *noun.* An act of quaffing; liquor quaffed; a deep draught. L16.
■ **quaffable** *adjective* (of a wine) that can be drunk copiously L20. **quaffer** *noun* E16.

quag /kwag, kwɒg/ *noun.* L16.
[Rel. to next.]
A marshy or boggy spot, *esp.* one covered with turf which gives way underfoot.

quag /kwag/ *verb intrans. obsolete* exc. *dial.* Infl. **-gg-**. L16.
[Symbolic: cf. prec., WAG *verb*, SWAG *verb*.]
Shake in the manner of something soft or flabby.

quagga /ˈkwagə/ *noun.* L18.
[Dutch from Nama *qua-ha'*, perh. imit. of the animal's call or rel. to Nguni *iqwara* striped thing.]
A southern African zebra, *Equus quagga*, which was yellowish brown with stripes only on the head, neck, and foreparts, and has been extinct since 1883.

quaggy /ˈkwagi, ˈkwɒgi/ *adjective.* E17.
[from QUAG *noun*, *verb* + -Y¹.]
1 (Of ground) boggy, soft; (of a stream) flowing through boggy soil. E17.
2 (Of flesh etc.) soft, yielding, flabby; (of a person) fat, flabby. E17.

1 G. SWIFT Weeks of autumn rain . . turning the ground quaggy. **2** S. RICHARDSON Spreading the whole . . bed with her huge quaggy carcase.

■ **quagginess** *noun* M17.

quagma /ˈkwagmə/ *noun.* L20.
[from QUA(RK² + G(LUON + PLAS)MA (partly after *magma*).]
PARTICLE PHYSICS. A hypothetical state of matter consisting of free quarks and gluons; a body of matter in this state.

quagmire /ˈkwagmʌɪə, ˈkwɒg-/ *noun & verb.* L16.
[from QUAG *noun*, *verb* + MIRE *noun*¹.]
▶ **A** *noun.* **1** A wet boggy area of land that gives way underfoot; a fen, a marsh. L16.
2 *transf. & fig.* **a** Anything soft, flabby, or yielding. M17.
▶**b** An awkward, complex, or hazardous situation. L18.

1 D. GARNETT Smith stepped into a quagmire in which he sank up to his middle. **2** T. BROWN The rich . . drown'd in foggy quagmires of fat and dropsy. **b** A. FRANCE Trust them . . to guide us through the quagmire of our own conflicts.

▶ **B** *verb trans.* In *pass.* Be sunk or stuck in a quagmire. *rare.* E18.
■ **quagmiry** *adjective* (*rare*) of the nature of a quagmire; boggy: M17.

quahog /ˈkwɔːhɒg, ˈkwɑː-, kwəˈhɔːg/ *noun & verb.* *N. Amer.* Also **-haug**, (now *rare*) **cohog** /ˈkəʊhɒg, kəˈhɔːg/. M18.
[Narragansett *poquaûhock*.]
▶ **A** *noun.* The common edible round clam, *Venus mercenaria*, of eastern N. America. M18.
▶ **B** *verb intrans.* Infl. **-hogg-**, **-haug-**. Dig or collect quahogs. Chiefly as ***quahogging*** *verbal noun*. E20.

quai /keɪ, *foreign* kɛ (*pl. same*)/ *noun.* L19.
[French: see QUAY *noun*.]
1 A public street or path along the embankment of a stretch of navigable water, usu. having buildings on the land side; *spec.* such a street on either bank of the Seine in Paris. L19.
2 In full ***Quai d'Orsay*** /ˈdɔːseɪ, *foreign* dɔrsɛ/ [the quai on the south bank of the Seine where the French Foreign Office is situated]. The French Foreign Office. E20.

quaich /kweɪk, -x/ *noun.* *Scot.* Also **quaigh**. M16.
[Gaelic *cuach* cup, perh. from *cua* hollow. Cf. Latin *caucus* (Greek *kauka*), Welsh *caurg* bowl.]
A shallow cup, usu. made of wooden staves hooped together and having two handles, but sometimes made of silver or fitted with a silver rim.

quail /kweɪl/ *noun.* Pl. same, **-s**. ME.
[Old French *quaille* (mod. *caille*) from medieval Latin *coacula*, prob. of imit. origin as, or from, synon. Middle Low German, Middle Dutch *quackele* (Dutch *kwakkel*), Old High German *wahtala*, *qua(h)tala* (German *Wachtel*). Cf. Anglo-Latin *quaila*.]
1 Any of various small Old World gallinaceous birds of the genus *Coturnix* and family Phasianidae, *esp.* (more fully ***common quail***) the migratory *C. coturnix*, which is reared for its edible flesh and eggs. Also (with specifying word), any of various similar birds of other genera occurring in America, Asia and Australasia. ME.
2 *fig.* [With allus. to the supposed amorousness of the bird.] A courtesan, a prostitute. *obsolete* exc. *Hist.* E17.
3 A girl, a young woman. *US slang.* M19.
1 ***button-quail***, ***painted quail***, ***Virginian quail***, etc.
Comb.: **quail-call** = *quail-pipe* below; **quail-dove** any of several Central and S. American doves of the genera *Geotrygon* and *Starnoenas*; **quailfinch** any of several African waxbills of the genus *Ortygospiza*; **quail hawk** the New Zealand falcon, *Falco novaezeelandiae*; **quail-pipe** a pipe or whistle on which the call of the quail is imitated, formerly used to attract and capture the birds; **quail-thrush** any of various Australasian babblers of the genus *Cinclosoma*.
■ **quailery** *noun* (*rare*) a place where quails are kept, esp. to be fattened for food L19.

quail /kweɪl/ *verb*¹. LME.
[Origin unkn. Cf. QUAY *verb*¹.]
▶ **I** *verb intrans.* **1** Of a person, plant, etc.: decline from a natural or flourishing condition; waste away; fade; wither. *obsolete* exc. *dial.* LME.
2 a Of an action, state etc.: orig., fail, come to nothing; now, yield *to* or *before* something. LME. ▶**b** Of courage etc.: fail, give way, become faint. Now *rare.* M16.
3 Of a person, the spirits, etc.: lose courage or heart, flinch; give way through fear *to* or *before* someone or something. M16.

3 R. L. STEVENSON His eye . . quails before so vast an outlook. E. TEMPLETON His keen and unpleasant glance travelled over them and made them quail beneath it. E. EAGER A weaker spirit might have quailed, or hid its head in the sand.

▶ **II** *verb trans.* **4 a** Frighten (a person) into submission, cause to quail; daunt, intimidate. E16. ▶**b** Depress (the heart, courage) with fear or dejection; dispirit. M16.
†**5** Spoil, impair; overpower, destroy, put an end to. M16–M17.

4a J. WILSON As thunder quails Th' inferior creatures of the air.

¶ Rare after M17 until revived in E19 app. by Sir Walter Scott.

quail /kweɪl/ *verb*² *intrans. obsolete* exc. *dial.* LME.
[Old French *quailler* (mod. *cailler*) from Latin *coagulare* COAGULATE *verb*.]
Curdle, coagulate.

quaint /kweɪnt/ *adjective, adverb, & noun.* ME.
[Old French *cointe*, *queinte* from Latin *cognitus* pa. pple of *cognoscere* ascertain, formed as CO- + *gnoscere* know.]
▶ **A** *adjective.* **I** †**1** Of a person: wise, clever, ingenious. Later *spec.*, skilled in the use of fine language. ME–E18.
▶**b** Crafty, given to scheming. ME–L17.
2 Of an action, scheme, device, etc.: marked by ingenuity, cleverness, or cunning. *arch.* ME.
3 Of a thing: skilfully made, ingeniously designed; elaborate. Also, beautiful, fine, elegant. Long *rare.* ME.
†**4** Of a person: beautiful or handsome in appearance; finely dressed, elegant. ME–L18.
†**5** Of speech, language, words, etc.: elegant, refined; clever, smart; affected. ME–M19.

6 Strange or odd in character or appearance; curious, mysterious. *obsolete* exc. as passing into sense 7. ME.
7 Attractively unusual or unfamiliar in character or appearance, esp. in an old-fashioned way. L18. ▸**b** Of furniture: designed in the style of art nouveau. L19.

> 📖 **7** J. K. JEROME The quaint back streets of Kingston. D. CECIL Personalities as . . quaint and idiosyncratic as characters in a novel by Dickens. *Classical Quarterly* However quaint this may sound today, it is a notion which has persisted well into our century.

▸†**II 8** Proud, haughty. *rare.* Only in ME.
9 Dainty, fastidious; prim. L15–L17.
▸†**B** *adverb.* Skilfully, cunningly. *rare.* ME–M16.
▸**C** *noun.* An unusual or strange person. *rare.* M20.
■ **quaintish** *adjective* L16. **quaintly** *adverb* ME. **quaintness** *noun* ME.

quaiss /kwʌɪs/ *adjective. Military slang.* Also **quies** & other vars. L19.
[Colloq. Arab. *kuwáyyis* nice, fine.]
Good, fine, satisfactory.
quaiss kitir /kɪˈtɪə/ (also **quaiss kateer** & other vars.) [colloq. Arab. *kitīr* very from classical Arab. *kaṭīr* much] very good, very well, excellent.

quaite /kweɪt/ *adverb.* Chiefly *joc. & derog.* E20.
[Repr. an affected pronunc.]
= QUITE *adverb.*

quake /kweɪk/ *noun* (In sense 2) also **'quake**. ME.
[from the noun In sense 2 now interpreted as abbreviation of *earthquake.*]
1 An act of quaking or trembling. ME.
2 *spec.* An earthquake. *colloq.* L19.

quake /kweɪk/ *verb.*
[Old English *cwacian* rel. to *cweċċan* QUETCH: cf. Old Saxon *quekilīk* waving to and fro.]
1 *verb intrans.* Of a thing, esp. the earth: shake, tremble, move or rock to and fro. OE.
2 *verb intrans.* Of a person, animal, limb, etc.: shake from fear, cold, etc.; tremble, shudder; *fig.*, take fright, be afraid. OE.
3 *verb trans.* Cause to quake. Long *obsolete* exc. *dial.* LME.

> 📖 **1** S. COOPER He saw . . the ground begin to quake and heave. **2** J. HERRIOT The enemy would have quaked at that chilling sound. P. KURTH The Danish ambassador quaking in his boots.

■ **quaky** *adjective* inclined to quake; trembling: M19.

quaker /ˈkweɪkə/ *noun.* Also (esp. in sense 2) **Q-**. L16.
[from prec. + -ER¹.]
1 In *pl.* Quaking-grass, *Briza media. dial.* L16.
2 [Orig. derog., perh. with allus. to George Fox's direction to his opponents to 'tremble at the word of the Lord', or to the fits supposedly suffered when moved by the Spirit.] A member of the Society of Friends, a Christian movement founded by George Fox *c* 1650, noted for its belief in the Inner Light and in pacifist principles, and for its rejection of sacraments, ordained ministry, and set forms of worship; formerly also distinguished by plainness of dress and speech. M17.
3 Any of various drab-coloured European noctuid moths of the genera *Orthosia* and *Agrochola*, esp. *O. stabilis*. L18.
4 In full ***quaker gun***. A dummy gun in a ship or fort, usu. made of wood. *US.* E19.
Attrib. & comb.: In the sense 'of, pertaining to, or characteristic of that formerly worn by Quakers', as ***Quaker brown***, ***Quaker cap***, ***Quaker dress***, ***Quaker grey***, etc. Special combs., as **Quaker City** *US* Philadelphia, USA; **Quaker collar** a broad flat collar; ***quaker gun***: see sense 4 above; **quaker-ladies** *US* (the small pale blue flowers of) the plant bluets, *Hedyotis caerulea*; **Quaker meeting** a religious meeting of members of the Society of Friends, characterized by periods of silence until members feel moved by the Spirit to speak; **Quaker Oats** (proprietary name for) oats used esp. for making porridge; **Quaker State** *US* the State of Pennsylvania.
■ **Quakerdom** *noun* (*a*) Quakers collectively; (*b*) Quakerism: E19. **Quakeress** *noun* (*arch.*) a female Quaker E18. **Quakerish** *adjective* resembling or characteristic of a Quaker or Quakers M18. **Quakerishly** *adverb* (*rare*) L19. **Quakerism** *noun* the principles or practice of the Quakers M17. **Quakerly** *adjective* & *adverb* (*a*) *adjective* of or befitting a Quaker; (*b*) *adverb* in a Quakerly manner: L17.

quaking /ˈkweɪkɪŋ/ *ppl adjective.* OE.
[from QUAKE *verb* + -ING².]
1 That quakes. OE.
†**2** That is or is like a member of the Society of Friends. M17–M18.
Special collocations: **quaking aspen** a N. American aspen, *Populus tremuloides*. **quaking bog** bog-land formed over water or soft mud, which shakes underfoot. **quaking-grass** any of several grasses of the genus *Briza*, esp. *B. media*, with broad laterally compressed spikelets dangling on slender pedicels. **quaking pudding** a pudding made from breadcrumbs, cream, eggs, and spices.
■ **quakingly** *adverb* M16.

quale /ˈkweɪli/ *noun.* Pl. **-lia** /-lɪə/. L17.
[Latin, neut. sing. of *qualis* of what kind.]
A property, a quality; a thing having certain qualities.

qualification /ˌkwɒlɪfɪˈkeɪʃ(ə)n/ *noun.* M16.
[French, or medieval Latin *qualificatio(n-)*, from *qualificat-* pa. ppl stem of *qualificare*: see QUALIFY, -FICATION.]
1 Modification, limitation; a modifying element, an added restriction; a thing detracting from completeness or absoluteness. M16. ▸**b** *ACCOUNTANCY.* A statement in an auditor's report indicating items excluded from examination owing to some doubt or disagreement; the action of recording such a statement. E20.
2 The action of qualifying or the condition of being qualified for a position etc. M16.
†**3** The distinctive quality of a person or thing; condition, character, nature. E17–M18.
4 A quality, an attribute, a property; an accomplishment. Now *rare* or *obsolete* in *gen.* sense. M17.
5 A quality, skill, or desire of knowledge or expertise which qualifies or fits a person for a certain office or function or which is formally or officially recognized. M17.
6 a A condition which must be fulfilled or complied with before a certain right can be exercised, office held, etc.; a requirement. E18. ▸**b** A document attesting that such a condition has been fulfilled or complied with. *rare.* M18.
7 The action of determining the quality, nature, or merit of a thing; the attribution of a quality to a thing. E19.

> 📖 **1** K. M. E. MURRAY Every comment . . was so wrapped about with qualifications as to be rendered meaningless. A. BURGESS She loved him too, though with qualifications there was no time to elucidate. **2** *Flight International* To equip . . prototype engines for . . testing before qualification of the powerplant. **5** *Newsweek* His main qualifications for office were an unswerving loyalty to Peron. J. RABAN A degree in Arabic . . must be an unusual qualification in the building trade.

Comb.: **qualification shares**: which a person must hold in order to be qualified for a directorship of a company.

qualificative /ˈkwɒlɪfɪkətɪv/ *noun & adjective. rare.* M17.
[from prec., after *predication*, *predicative*, etc.]
(A word or phrase) denoting a quality.

qualificator /ˈkwɒlɪfɪkeɪtə/ *noun.* L17.
[medieval Latin, from *qualificat-*: see QUALIFICATION, -OR.]
Hist. A member of a board of theologians attached to the Inquisition, who judged and reported on whether propositions submitted to them were heretical.

qualificatory /ˈkwɒlɪfɪkeɪt(ə)ri/ *adjective.* E19.
[from QUALIFICATION: see -ORY².]
Having the character of qualifying, modifying, or limiting.

qualified /ˈkwɒlɪfʌɪd/ *adjective & noun.* E16.
[from QUALIFY *verb* + -ED¹.]
▸**A** *adjective.* **I 1** Possessing qualities or qualifications fitting or necessary for a certain office, function, or purpose. (Foll. by *for*, *to do.*) E16.
2 Capable of doing or being something, esp. by law or custom. E16.
†**3** Possessing certain qualities; *spec.* possessing good qualities, accomplished. L16–L17.
4 Belonging to the upper classes of society. *obsolete* exc. *dial.* E17.

> 📖 **1** A. URE He was . . little qualified to cope with the hardships of a new manufacturing enterprise. *Hindu* Candidates should be qualified electrical engineering graduates. **2** *London Gazette* The next winning Horse that is duly qualified to run for this Plate.

▸**II 5 a** Limited, modified, or restricted in some respect. L16. ▸**b** *euphem.* Bloody, damn. *colloq.* L19.

> 📖 **5a** J. S. MILL Unfit for more than a limited and qualified freedom. J. SIMMS 'Teaching' becomes a qualified term when the pupil is . . self-taught. **b** E. C. R. LORAC I . . knocked my head on those qualified rocks.

▸**B** *absol.* as *noun.* A person eligible for a position, office, etc.; a person possessing an officially recognized qualification for a particular profession. E20.

> 📖 *Accountancy* Increasing demand for newly qualifieds.

■ **qualifiedly** *adverb* M19. **qualifiedness** *noun* (*rare*) L17.

qualifier /ˈkwɒlɪfʌɪə/ *noun.* M16.
[from QUALIFY *verb* + -ER¹.]
1 A person who or thing which qualifies; *spec.* a person eligible for (the final rounds of) a competition etc.; *transf.* a preliminary round of a competition etc. M16.
2 *GRAMMAR.* A word or phrase, as an adjective or adverb, used with another word to qualify it. Also, a subordinate clause. L16.
3 = QUALIFICATOR. M19.

> 📖 **1** *Daily Express* England put nine goals past Luxemburg . . in the away leg of a World Cup qualifier.

qualify /ˈkwɒlɪfʌɪ/ *verb.* LME.
[Old & mod. French *qualifier* from medieval Latin *qualificare*, from Latin *qualis* of what kind, from base of *qui*, *quis* WHO + *-alis* -AL¹: see -FY.]
▸**I 1** *verb trans.* Describe or designate in a particular way; characterize, name. (Foll. by *as*, †*with.*) LME.
†**2** *verb trans.* Impart a certain quality to (a thing). L15–L17.
3 *verb trans. SCOTS LAW.* Establish by evidence. Now *rare.* M16.
4 *verb trans.* **a** Invest (a person) with the qualities or accomplishments essential for being something. (Foll. by *for*). Now *rare.* L16. ▸**b** Endow with legal power or capacity, as by administering an oath; give a recognized status to (a person). L16. ▸**c** Provide with qualities or qualifications fitting or necessary for a certain office, function, or purpose. (Foll. by *as*, *for*, *to do.*) M17.
5 *verb intrans.* Be or become eligible for a certain office, benefit, competition, etc., by fulfilling some necessary condition; possess qualities or qualifications fitting or necessary for a certain office or function; become eligible to proceed to a further round of a competition etc.; acquire an officially recognized qualification for a particular profession. (Foll. by *for.*) L16.

> 📖 **1a** J. REED I qualify such acts . . as acts of treason. **4c** M. BARING He would . . learn some foreign language sufficiently well to qualify him for employment. G. G. COULTON She had just qualified herself as a typist. **5** *Milton Keynes Express* In the first qualifying round of the FA Cup, City face an away match with Marlow. A. N. WILSON He had qualified as a barrister, but had been unable to practise . . because of ill health. G. PRIESTLAND We did not qualify for a petrol ration.

▸**II 6** *verb trans.* Modify (a statement, opinion, etc.) by the addition of some limitation or reservation; make (an assertion etc.) less strong or positive. M16. ▸**b** *GRAMMAR.* Limit the sense of (a word, phrase, etc.); *spec.* (of an adjective) express some quality which describes or limits the reference of (a noun). M19. ▸**c** *ACCOUNTANCY.* Enter a statement in (an auditor's report) indicating items excluded from examination. E20.
7 *verb trans.* Moderate, mitigate, reduce to a more satisfactory or normal condition; *esp.* make less severe or unpleasant. M16.
†**8** *verb trans.* Appease, calm. M16–L17.
†**9** *verb trans.* Bring or keep under control; regulate, modulate. L16–L17.
10 *verb trans.* Alter the strength or flavour of (a liquid). (Foll. by *with.*) L16.
11 *verb trans.* Orig., harm, damage. Now, diminish; make less perfect or complete. L16.

> 📖 **6** R. MACAULAY 'Be good . . as good as you can manage,' she added, lightly qualifying an impossible admonition. **7** SIR W. SCOTT A voice in which the authority of the mother was qualified by her tenderness. **10** SMOLLETT Tea, which he drank . . qualified with brandy. **11** R. SCRUTON Freedom should be qualified only by the possibility that someone might suffer through its exercise.

qualitated /ˈkwɒlɪteɪtɪd/ *adjective. rare.* M17.
[from mod. Latin *qualitatus*, from Latin *qualitas*: see QUALITY *noun & adjective*, -ATE², -ED¹.]
= QUALITIED.

qualitative /ˈkwɒlɪtətɪv/ *adjective.* LME.
[Late Latin *qualitativus*, from Latin *qualitas*: see QUALITY *noun & adjective*, -IVE.]
Relating to or concerned with quality or qualities. (Freq. opp. ***quantitative***.)

> 📖 R. BERTHOUD Moore's work took a qualitative leap forward with a *Reclining Figure*. **qualitative analysis** *CHEMISTRY* identification of the constituents present in a substance; cf. ***quantitative analysis*** s.v. QUANTITATIVE *adjective* 3.

■ **qualitatively** *adverb* L17.

qualitied /ˈkwɒlɪtɪd/ *adjective.* E17.
[from QUALITY *noun*, *verb*: see -ED², -ED¹.]
Possessing some (esp. good) quality or qualities.
■ **qualitiedness** *noun* M19.

quality /ˈkwɒlɪti/ *noun & adjective.* ME.
[Old & mod. French *qualité* from Latin *qualitas* (translating Greek *poiotēs*), from *qualis*: see QUALIFY, -ITY.]
▸**A** *noun.* **I** Of people.
1 a Character, disposition, nature. Now *rare.* ME. ▸**b** Excellence of character; good nature, virtue. E17. ▸**c** Ability, skill, talent. Cf. sense 7c. M19.
2 Title, description, character, capacity. Chiefly in ***in quality of***, ***in the quality of***. Now *rare.* ME.
3 a Rank, social position. Now *rare.* LME. ▸**b** High rank, high social position; *collect.* people of high social position. *arch.* L16.
†**4 a** A profession, an occupation, *esp.* that of an actor; *collect.* a body of people of the same profession, esp. acting. E16–M17. ▸**b** One's party, a side. *rare* (Shakes.). Only in L16.

5 a A personal attribute, a trait, a feature of a person's character. **M16.** ▸**b** An accomplishment, an attainment; a skill. **L16.**

📖 **3b** F. MARRYAT They will make very nice tire-women to some lady of quality. A. T. ELLIS There were servants to perform the morning tasks while the quality lounged around in negligé. **5a** N. COWARD Possessiveness, petty jealousy. All those qualities come out in us. C. ODETS Moody's explosiveness covers a soft, boyish quality. ***the defects of a person's qualities***: see DEFECT *noun* 2. **b** M. BINCHY His strongest quality was an ability to compartmentalize his life.

▶ **II** Of things.

6 An attribute, a property, a special feature or characteristic. **ME.** ▸†**b** A manner, a style. *rare.* **L16–M17.** ▸†**c** A substance of a certain nature. *rare.* **E18–E19.**

7 a Orig., the nature or kind of something. Now, the relative nature or standard of something; the degree of excellence etc. possessed by a thing; a particular class or grade of something as determined by this. **LME.** ▸†**b** Origin, cause. *rare* (Shakes.). Only in **E17.** ▸**c** Excellence; superiority. Cf. sense 1C. **L19.** ▸**d** = ***quality newspaper*** below. **L20.**

8 That aspect by which a thing is considered in thinking or speaking of its nature, condition, or properties. **M16.**

9 *spec.* **a** LOGIC. The condition of a proposition of being affirmative or negative. Also, comparative distinctness of a concept. **M16.** ▸**b** GRAMMAR. Manner of action as denoted by an adverb. **M16.** ▸**c** LAW. The manner in which an estate is to be held. **E19.** ▸**d** The tone or timbre of a sound. **M19.** ▸**e** ENGINEERING. The proportion by weight of a given vapour that is actually in the gas phase (as opp. to liquid droplets). **L19.** ▸**f** RADIOLOGY. The penetrating power of a beam of X-rays. **E20.** ▸**g** The degree to which reproduced sound resembles the original; fidelity. **E20.**

📖 **6** J. LAWRENCE The distinguishing qualities of Hereford oxen. J. CONRAD The even, mysterious quality of her voice. **b** SHAKES. *Merch. V.* Hate councels not in such a quality. **7a** M. GIROUARD Houses of good architectural quality. F. TOMLIN Conversation of a high quality was not easy to come by. A. TAYLOR In a hospice the concept of care shifts from quantity to quality of life. *New Musical Express* The albums . . are illegal and poor quality. **c** A. ROBERTSON The picture's quality comes from Grimshaw's care over his handling of paint. ***primary quality***: see PRIMARY *adjective*. ***secondary quality***: see SECONDARY *adjective*. **9b adverb of quality** = ***adverb of manner*** s.v. MANNER *noun*[1].

▶†**III 10** A qualification, a proviso. *Scot. rare.* **E17–L18.**

▶ **B** *attrib.* or as *adjective*. Designating a thing or person of high quality. **E18.**

📖 *Times* We are buying a quality business. V. BRAMWELL Hours of quality sleep are more important than overall time.

Comb. & special collocations: **quality assurance** the maintenance of the desired quality in a service or product, esp. by means of attention to every stage of the process of delivery or production; **quality circle** a group of employees who meet to consider ways of resolving problems and improving production in their organization; **quality control** the maintenance of the desired quality in a manufactured product, esp. by comparison of a sample of the output with the specification; **quality controller** a person responsible for quality control; **quality factor** = Q, Q 7; **quality mark**: designating the grade or class of a product; **quality newspaper**, **quality paper** a newspaper considered to be of a high cultural standard; **quality time**: spent productively or profitably.

■ **qualityless** *adjective* **M19.**

quality /ˈkwɒlɪti/ *verb trans. rare.* **L16.**
[from the noun.]
Orig., endow with a quality or qualities. Now, rate at a certain quality or value.

qualm /kwɑːm, kwɔːm/ *noun.* **E16.**
[Origin uncertain: cf. Old English *cw(e)alm* pestilence, pain (rel. to QUELL *verb*[1]), Middle Low German *quallem*, German *Qualm* (Dutch *kwalm*) thick vapour or smoke.]

1 A sudden feeling of sickness, faintness, or nausea. **E16.**

2 *transf.* **a** A sudden feeling of fear, misgiving, or depression. **M16.** ▸**b** A sudden intense feeling of some quality, principle, etc.; *esp.* a scruple of conscience, a doubt, a pang of guilt. **E17.**

📖 **1** F. C. BURNAND No qualms to interfere with appetite. **2a** S. BELLOW A nervous qualm went through him. **b** A. BROOKNER Frederick has no qualms in asking for some of the profits.

■ **qualmless** *adjective* **E20.** **qualmlessness** *noun* (*rare*) **M19.**

qualm /kwɑːm, kwɔːm/ *verb. rare.* **M16.**
[from the noun.]
†**1** *verb intrans.* Have a qualm or qualms. **M16–E17.**
2 *verb trans.* Make sick; affect with qualms. **E17.**

qualmish /ˈkwɑːmɪʃ, ˈkwɔːmɪʃ/ *adjective.* **M16.**
[from QUALM *noun* + -ISH[1]. Cf. SQUALMISH.]
1 Of a person: affected with a qualm or qualms; *esp.* nauseous. **M16.**
2 Of a feeling etc.: of the nature of a qualm. **L18.**
3 Liable to induce qualms. *rare.* **E19.**

■ **qualmishly** *adverb* (*rare*) **M19.** **qualmishness** *noun* **M17.**

qualmy /ˈkwɑːmi, ˈkwɔːmi/ *adjective.* **M16.**
[from QUALM *noun* + -Y[1].]
= prec.
■ **qualminess** *noun* the condition of being qualmy; nausea: **L18.**

qualup bell /ˈkwɒləp ˈbɛl/ *noun phr.* **E20.**
[*Qualup*, an estate in Western Australia.]
A western Australian shrub, *Pimelea physodes* (family Thymelaeaceae), with reddish-yellow bracts forming bells round the flowers.

quamash /kwəˈmaʃ, ˈkwɒmaʃ/ *noun.* Also **camas(s)**, **kam-**, /ˈkaməs, kəˈmas/. **E19.**
[Chinook Jargon *kamass*, perh. from Nootka.]
A N. American plant of the lily family, *Camassia quamash*, the bulbs of which are used as food by N. American Indians; any of various other plants of this genus, and of the related genus *Zigadenus*, having starry blue or purple flowers.

quamoclit /ˈkwaməklɪt/ *noun.* **M18.**
[Nahuatl *qua'mochitl*, from *qua-* combining form of *quaiutl* tree + unkn. 2nd elem.]
Any of various morning glories constituting the former genus *Quamoclit* (now included in *Ipomoea*), which are tropical American climbing plants with brilliant scarlet or crimson flowers; *esp.* the cypress-vine, *Ipomoea quamoclit*.

quandary /ˈkwɒnd(ə)ri/ *noun & verb.* **L16.**
[Origin uncertain: perh. from Latin *quando* when + *-are* inf. ending (cf. BACKARE).]
▶ **A** *noun.* A state of perplexity or uncertainty; a practical dilemma, a difficult problem. Freq. in ***in a quandary*** **L16.**

📖 K. M. E. MURRAY He could not see his map and was in a quandary which way to turn. E. PAWEL Kafka resolved such quandaries on a case-by-case basis.

▶†**B** *verb intrans. & trans.* Be or put in a quandary. *rare.* **E17–L18.**

quand même /kɑ̃ mɛm/ *adverbial phr.* **E19.**
[French.]
All the same, even so, nevertheless.

quandong /ˈkwɒndɒŋ, ˈkwan-/ *noun.* **M19.**
[Aboriginal.]
1 a A small shrubby Australian tree, *Eucarya acuminata*, of the sandalwood family; the round red fruit of this, which has an edible pulp and kernel. Also called ***native peach***. **M19.** ▸**b** More fully ***silver quandong***, ***blue quandong***. A forest tree of NE Australia, *Elaeocarpus grandis* (family Elaeocarpaceae), bearing insipid blue berries. **M19.**
2 A person living by his or her wits. *Austral. slang.* **M20.**

quango /ˈkwaŋgəʊ/ *noun.* Pl. **-os.** **L20.**
[Acronym, from *quasi non-government(al) organization*; later often glossed as *quasi-autonomous non-government(al) organization*.]
A semi-public administrative body outside the Civil Service but with financial support from and senior members appointed by the Government.

📖 *Economist* A quango covers just about everything from the Price Commission to the Police Complaints Board.

■ **quangocrat** *noun* (*colloq.*) a member of a quango, esp. regarded as exercising unelected authority **L20.**

quant /kwɒnt, kwant/ *noun*[1] *& verb.* **LME.**
[Perh. from Latin *contus* (Greek *kontos*) boat-pole. Cf. KENT *noun*[1] & *verb*[1].]
▶ **A** *noun.* **1** A pole for propelling a Norfolk wherry or other barge, *esp.* one with a prong at one end to prevent it from sticking in mud. Also ***quant-pole***. **LME.**
2 A vertical spindle used to drive millstones in a windmill. **E20.**
▶ **B** *verb trans. & intrans.* Propel (a boat) with a quant. **M19.**

quant /kwɒnt/ *noun*[2]. *colloq.* **L20.**
[Abbreviation.]
A quantity analyst.

quanta *noun pl.* see QUANTUM.

quantal /ˈkwɒnt(ə)l/ *adjective.* **L17.**
[Sense 1 from Latin *quantus* how great; sense 2 from QUANTUM: see -AL[1].]
†**1** Of a part: that is contained in the whole but does not divide it evenly. Cf. ALIQUOT *adjective. rare.* Only in **L17.**
2 a Composed of discrete units; varying in steps rather than continuously; PHYSIOLOGY designating an all-or-none response. **E20.** ▸**b** PHYSICS. Of the nature of a quantum or quanta; of or pertaining to the quantum theory. **M20.**
■ **quantally** *adverb* **M20.**

quantic /ˈkwɒntɪk/ *noun.* **M19.**
[from Latin *quantus* how great + -IC.]
MATH. A rational integral homogeneous function of two or more variables.

quantification /ˌkwɒntɪfɪˈkeɪʃ(ə)n/ *noun.* **M19.**
[formed as next + -FICATION.]
The action or an instance of quantifying something; the indication of quantity or scope, the use of quantifiers; *spec.* in LOGIC, the process of giving formal expression to the scope of variables in general propositions.
■ **quantificational** *adjective* **M20.**

quantifier /ˈkwɒntɪfʌɪə/ *noun.* **L19.**
[from next + -ER[1].]
1 *gen.* A person who or thing which quantifies something. **L19.**
2 In LOGIC, an expression (e.g. *all*, *some*) that indicates the scope of a term to which it is attached. In GRAMMAR, a word or phrase having the same function; a determiner indicative of quantity. **L19.**

quantify /ˈkwɒntɪfʌɪ/ *verb.* **M16.**
[medieval Latin *quantificare*, from *quantus* how great: see QUANTITY, -FY.]
1 *verb trans.* Endow with quantity (now *rare*); treat or express as a quantity; determine the quantity of, measure. **M16.**
2 *verb trans.* LOGIC. Make explicit the scope of a term in (a proposition), by prefixing a quantifier. **M19.**
3 *verb intrans.* LOGIC & GRAMMAR. Act as a quantifier. Chiefly as ***quantifying ppl adjective***. **M19.**
■ **quantifiaˈbility** *noun* ability to be quantified **L20.** **quantifiable** *adjective* able to be quantified **L19.**

quantile /ˈkwɒntʌɪl/ *noun.* **M20.**
[from Latin *quantus* how great + -ILE.]
STATISTICS. Each of any set of values of a variate which divide a frequency distribution into equal groups, each containing the same fraction of the total population; any of the groups so produced, e.g. a quartile, percentile, etc.

quantise *verb* var. of QUANTIZE.

quantitate /ˈkwɒntɪteɪt/ *verb trans.* **M20.**
[from QUANTITY + -ATE[3].]
BIOLOGY & MEDICINE. Ascertain the quantity or extent of, measure.
■ **quantiˈtation** *noun* **M20.**

quantitative /ˈkwɒntɪtətɪv, -teɪtɪv/ *adjective.* **L16.**
[medieval Latin *quantitativus*, from Latin *quantitas*, *-at-*, from *quantus*: see QUANTITY, -ATIVE.]
1 Possessing quantity, magnitude, or spatial extent. Now *rare.* **L16.**
2 That is or may be considered with respect to the quantity or quantities involved; estimable by quantity, measurable. **M17.**
3 Pertaining to or concerned with quantity or its measurement; ascertaining or expressing quantity. **M17.**
4 Of, pertaining to, or based on vowel-quantity. **L18.**
5 CHEMISTRY. Of a reaction etc.: acting on the whole quantity of a particular substance or species; having or designating an efficiency or a yield of 100 per cent. **E20.**

📖 **2** J. MARTINEAU Not as its quantitative equal . . but as a moral equivalent. **3** M. KLINE The quantitative knowledge that science and technology needed. **quantitative analysis** CHEMISTRY measurement of the amounts of constituents present in a substance (cf. ***QUALITATIVE analysis***). **5** N. G. CLARK On careful combustion there remains a quantitative residue of metallic silver.

■ **quantitatively** *adverb* (*a*) in a quantitative manner; in respect of quantity; (*b*) CHEMISTRY with a yield of 100 per cent: **L16.** **quantitativeness** *noun* **M19.** **quantiˈtativist** *noun & adjective* (*a*) *noun* a person for whom quantity is a criterion of value; (*b*) *adjective* of or pertaining to quantitativists, resulting from an evaluation of quantity: **M20.**

quantité négligeable /kɑ̃tite neglіʒabl/ *noun phr.* Pl. **-s -s** (pronounced same). **L19.**
[French = negligible quantity.]
A factor of no account, something insignificant.

quantitive /ˈkwɒntɪtɪv/ *adjective.* **M17.**
[from QUANTITY + -IVE.]
= QUANTITATIVE.
■ **quantitively** *adverb* **E19.**

quantity /ˈkwɒntɪti/ *noun.* **ME.**
[Old & mod. French *quantité* from Latin *quantitas* (translating Greek *posotēs*), from *quantus* how great, how much, from base of *qui*, *quis* who: see -ITY.]
1 A (specified) portion or amount *of* an article, commodity, quality, etc., or a (specified) number *of* things; *the* portion, amount, or number (*of* something) present in a particular instance. **ME.** ▸**b** An indefinite (usu. fair or considerable) portion, amount, or number (*of*). **ME.** ▸**c** A certain space or surface; an area (*of*). Now *rare.* **LME.** ▸**d** A great or considerable amount or bulk. Freq. in *pl.* **M18.**
2 Size, extent, dimensions. *obsolete* exc. as passing into sense 5. **LME.**
3 The amount or sum of a material or immaterial thing not usually estimated by spatial measurement; weight; magnitude, number. **LME.** ▸†**b** Monetary amount. **LME–L18.**

4 a Length in time, duration. *obsolete* in *gen.* sense. LME. ▸**b** Length or shortness of vowel sounds or syllables. M16. ▸**c** *MUSIC.* Length or duration of notes. L16.
5 a *PHILOSOPHY & MATH.* That property of things that is (in principle) measurable. M16. ▸**b** *MATH.* A thing having this property; a value, component, etc., that can be expressed in numbers; a figure or symbol standing for such a thing. L16.
†**6** Relative size or amount, proportion. *rare.* M16–E17.
7 *LOGIC.* The degree of extension which a proposition gives to the term forming its subject. M16.

📖 **1** S. JOHNSON A certain quantity or measure of renown. A. DJOLETO At lunchtime he takes large quantities of illicit gin. R. BRAUTIGAN A pound of anchovies, and the same quantity of bay-salt. *Studio News* The quantity of data processing involved made it impossible to run the system. **b** D. L. SAYERS She wore a quantity of little bangles on her . . wrists. P. FITZGERALD Light . . entered at an angle through a quantity of dust. **d** W. HOGARTH Windsor castle is a noble instance of the effect of quantity. R. POSTGATE A pleasant, not very distinctive drink . . served in quantities in railway trains. **3** J. BENTHAM Any punishment is subservient to reformation in proportion to its quantity. **4b** J. RUSKIN A . . scholar who knew his grammar and his quantities. **5a** F. BOWEN Mathematics is the science of pure quantity. **b** D. BREWSTER He considered quantities not as composed of indivisibles, but as generated by motion.

Phrases: ***bill of quantities***: see BILL *noun*^{3}. ***false quantity***: see FALSE *adjective*. **quantity of estate** *LAW* the length of time during which the right of enjoyment of an estate is to continue. ***unknown quantity***: see UNKNOWN *adjective*.
Comb.: **quantity mark** a mark put over a vowel or syllable etc. to indicate its length; ***quantity surveyor***: see SURVEYOR 2; **quantity theory** (more fully ***quantity theory of money***) the hypothesis that prices correspond to changes in the monetary supply.

quantize /ˈkwɒntʌɪz/ *verb trans.* Also **-ise**. E20.
[from QUANTUM + -IZE.]
1 Orig. & chiefly *PHYSICS.* Apply quantum theory to, form into quanta; *esp.* restrict the number of possible values of (a quantity) or states of (a system) so that certain variables can assume only certain discrete magnitudes. Freq. as ***quantized*** *ppl adjective.* E20.
2 *ELECTRONICS.* Approximate (a continuously varying signal) by one whose amplitude is restricted to a prescribed set of values. M20.

📖 **1** F. SMYTH The position was then quantized, that is, expressed as a whole number of unit distances.

■ **quantiˈzation** *noun* E20. **quantizer** *noun* (*ELECTRONICS*) a device that quantizes a signal applied to it M20.

quantophrenia /kwɒntəˈfriːnɪə/ *noun.* M20.
[from QUANT(ITATIVE + -O- + *-phrenia* as in HEBEPHRENIA etc.]
Undue reliance on or use of mathematical methods or statistics, esp. in social sciences research.

quant. suff. /kwɒnt ˈsʌf/ *adverb & noun phr.* M19.
[Abbreviation.]
= QUANTUM SUFFICIT.

quantum /ˈkwɒntəm/ *noun & adjective.* M16.
[Latin, neut. of *quantus* how much.]
▶ **A** *noun.* Pl. **-ta** /-tə/, †**-tums**.
1 Quantity; a quantity. Now *esp.* in *LAW*, an amount of or *of* money payable in damages etc. Cf. sense 3b below. M16.
2 One's (required or allowed) share or portion. M17.
3 *PHYSICS.* A discrete quantity of electromagnetic energy proportional in magnitude to the frequency of the radiation it represents; an analogous discrete amount of any other physical quantity (as momentum, electric charge). E20. ▸**b** *transf. & fig.* A small discrete amount of anything. M20.
4 *PHYSIOLOGY.* The unit quantity of acetylcholine which is released at a neuromuscular junction by each single synaptic vesicle, corresponding to a certain small voltage, integral multiples of which go to make up the measured end-plate potential at the junction. M20.

📖 **1** *Times* The Court of Appeal dismissed an appeal on quantum of damages. R. C. A. WHITE The victim receives legal advice as to the amount of damages (quantum) appropriate. **2** SWIFT He will double his present quantum by stealth. J. LE CARRÉ Each man has only a quantum of compassion . . and mine is used up. **3** *Scientific American* Waves of elastic crystal vibrations generate quanta of sound called phonons. J. BRONOWSKI The energy difference between the two is emitted as a light quantum. **b** L. MUMFORD Every new quantum of accurate knowledge was precious.

▶ **B** *attrib.* or as *adjective. PHYSICS* etc. Involving quanta or quantum theory; quantized. E20.

📖 P. DAVIES The concept of a continuous space and time . . seems threatened when quantum effects are taken into account. S. HAWKING The methods . . were not able to answer questions such as whether singularities would occur in quantum gravity. *New Scientist* The possibilities for implementing computation that is intrinsically quantum.

Comb. & special collocations: **quantum chemistry** the branch of physical chemistry that deals with the quantum-mechanical explanation of chemical phenomena; ***quantum chromodynamics***: see CHROMODYNAMICS; **quantum computer** a (hypothetical) computer which makes use of the quantum states of physical systems (such as spinning subatomic particles) to store and manipulate information; **quantum efficiency** the proportion of incident photons that are effective in causing photodecomposition, photo-emission, or similar photo-effect; **quantum-electrodynamic**, **quantum-electrodynamical** *adjectives* of or pertaining to quantum electrodynamics; **quantum electrodynamics** the branch of quantum field theory that deals with the electromagnetic field and its interaction with electrically charged particles; **quantum electronics** the branch of physics that deals with the practical consequences of the interaction of quantized energy states with electromagnetic radiation; **quantum field theory** a field theory that incorporates quantum mechanics and the principles of the theory of relativity; **quantum gravity** a theory that attempts to explain gravitational physics in terms of quantum mechanics; **quantum increase** a sudden large increase; **quantum jump**, **quantum leap** (*a*) *PHYSICS* an abrupt transition between one stationary state of a quantized system and another, with the absorption or emission of a quantum; (*b*) *transf. & fig.* a sudden large increase or advance; **quantum-mechanical** *adjective* of or pertaining to quantum mechanics; **quantum-mechanically** *adverb* by means of or as regards quantum mechanics; **quantum mechanics** (the branch of physics that deals with) the mathematical description of the motion and interaction of (subatomic) particles that incorporates the concepts of quantization of energy, wave-particle duality, the uncertainty principle, and the correspondence principle; **quantum number** a number which occurs in the theoretical expression for the value of some quantized property of a particle, atom, molecule, etc., and can only have certain integral or half-integral values; ***principal quantum number***: see PRINCIPAL *adjective*; **quantum state** a state of a physical system (such as an atom or molecule) which is described by a particular set of quantum numbers; **quantum-theoretical** *adjective* of or pertaining to quantum theory; **quantum-theoretically** *adverb* by means of or as regards quantum theory; **quantum theory** *PHYSICS* a theory of matter and energy based on the concept of quanta; *esp.* = ***quantum mechanics*** above; ***old quantum theory***, the early theory of quanta (due to Planck and Einstein) based on classical mechanics, prior to the development of wave mechanics etc.; **quantum yield** = ***quantum efficiency*** above.

quantum meruit /kwɒntəm ˈmɛrʊɪt/ *noun phr.* M17.
[Latin = as much as he has deserved.]
LAW. A reasonable sum of money to be paid for services rendered or work done, when the amount due is not stipulated in a legally enforceable contract.

quantum sufficit /kwɒntəm ˈsʌfɪsɪt/ *adverbial & noun phr.* L17.
[Latin.]
As much as suffices; (in) a sufficient quantity; (to) a sufficient extent.

†**quap** *verb* var. of QUOP.

Quapaw /ˈkwɔːpɔː/ *noun & adjective.* L18.
[Quapaw *okáxpa* (orig. a village name).]
▶ **A** *noun.* Pl. same, **-s**.
1 A member of a N. American Indian people inhabiting the Arkansas River region, now mainly in north-eastern Oklahoma. L18.
2 The Siouan language of this people. M19.
▶ **B** *attrib.* or as *adjective.* Of or pertaining to the Quapaw or their language. L18.
¶ Also called ***Arkansas***.

quaquaversal /kweɪkwəˈvəːs(ə)l/ *adjective.* E18.
[from late Latin *quaqua versus*, *-sum*, from Latin *quaqua* wheresoever + *versus* turned: see -AL^{1}.]
Chiefly *GEOLOGY.* Turned or pointing in every direction.
■ **quaquaversally** *adverb* L19.

quar /kwɔː/ *noun. obsolete* exc. *dial.* ME.
[Abbreviation of QUARRY *noun*^{2}.]
A stone-quarry.

quar /kwɔː/ *verb trans. & intrans. obsolete* exc. *Canad. dial.* M16.
[Origin unkn.]
Block or become blocked up.

†**quarantain** *noun.* M17.
[French *quarantaine* QUARANTINE.]
1 A period of forty days or nights. M17–E19.
2 = QUARANTINE *noun* 2. M17–M18.
1 King's quarantain [French *quarantaine du roi*] a compulsory forty days' truce between quarrelling parties in France, in force esp. during the reign of Louis IX in the 13th cent.

quarantine /ˈkwɒr(ə)ntiːn/ *noun & verb.* In senses A.1, 3 also †**quaren-**. E16.
[medieval Latin *quarantena*, *quadrantena* ult. from Latin *quadraginta* forty, or (sense 2) from Italian *quarantina*, from *quaranta* forty.]
▶ **A** *noun.* **1** *LAW* (now *Hist.*). A period of forty days in which a widow, entitled to a dower, had the right to remain in her deceased husband's chief dwelling; such a right. E16.
2 A period of isolation, orig. of forty days, imposed on a person, animal, or thing that might otherwise spread a contagious disease, esp. on one that has just arrived from overseas etc. or has been exposed to infection; the fact or practice of isolating someone or something or of being isolated in this way. Freq. in ***in quarantine***. M17. ▸**b** *fig.* Any comparable period, instance, or state of isolation or detention; *esp.* a blockade, boycott, or severance of diplomatic relations intended to isolate a nation. L17. ▸**c** A place where quarantine is kept or enforced. M19.
3 *gen.* A period of forty days. *rare.* M17.

📖 **2** P. PEARCE He was in quarantine for measles. A. KOESTLER Plague broke out, and the strict quarantine made communications between Rome and Florence difficult. *Scientific American* The lunar samples were placed in quarantine for seven weeks. *attrib.*: T. HEALD All dogs coming into Britain had to spend six weeks in quarantine kennels. **b** *New York Herald Tribune* President Roosevelt . . advocated instead a collective 'quarantine' of aggressor nations. W. GARNER Putting him in emotional quarantine. **c** R. L. STEVENSON Somnolent Inverkeithing, once the quarantine of Leith.

Comb.: **quarantine flag** a yellow flag used in signalling the presence of disease on a ship.
▶ **B** *verb trans.* Put in quarantine; isolate by the imposition of quarantine. E19.

📖 J. WYNDHAM Coker quarantined them at the first symptoms. *fig.*: J. VIORST We quarantine our anger, afraid our hateful feelings will wipe out those we cherish.

■ **quarantinable** *adjective* subject or liable to quarantine M19.

Quarant' Ore /kwarant ˈoːre/ *noun phr.* E17.
[Italian, contr. of *quaranta ore*.]
= ***forty hours*** s.v. FORTY *adjective*.

quaranty /ˈkwɒr(ə)nti/ *noun.* Long *obsolete* exc. *Hist.* M17.
[Italian *quarantia*, from *quaranta* forty.]
A Venetian court of judicature having forty members.

quare /kwɛː/ *adjective. Anglo-Irish.* E19.
[Repr. a pronunc.]
Queer, strange, eccentric.
quare and — very, extremely.
■ **quarely** *adverb* E19.

quare impedit /kwɛːrɪ ˈɪmpɪdɪt/ *noun phr.* L15.
[Latin = why he impedes.]
LAW (now *Hist.*). A writ issued in cases of disputed presentation to a benefice, requiring the defendant to state the reason(s) for hindering the plaintiff from making the presentation.

quarentene /ˈkwɒr(ə)ntiːn/ *noun. rare.* Also **-ten** /-t(ə)n/. L15.
[medieval Latin *quarentena* QUARANTINE *noun*.]
Hist. A linear or square measure containing forty poles; a furlong (201.17m); a rood (1012.5 m^{2}.)

†**quarentine** *noun* see QUARANTINE.

quark /kwɑːk, kvɑːk/ *noun*^{1}. M20.
[German = curd(s), cottage or curd cheese.]
A low-fat soft cheese of German origin.

quark /kwɑːk/ *noun*^{2}. M20.
[Invented word, assoc. with the line 'Three quarks for Muster Mark' in Joyce's *Finnegans Wake*.]
PARTICLE PHYSICS. Any of a group of (orig. three) subatomic particles postulated to have fractional electric charge, to combine in different ways to form the hadrons, and not to occur in the free state.
■ **quarkonium** /kwɑːˈkəʊnɪəm/ *noun*, pl **-ia**, a meson consisting of a quark and corresponding antiquark bound together; matter in the form of such mesons: L20.

quark /kwɔːk/ *verb intrans.* M19.
[Imit. Cf. SQUARK *noun*^{1} & *verb*.]
Of a frog or bird: croak.

quarl /kwɔːl/ *noun*^{1}. *rare.* E19.
[Perh. from German *Qualle*, Dutch *kwal*.]
A jellyfish.

quarl /kwɔːl/ *noun*^{2}. Also **-le**. L19.
[Alt. of QUARREL *noun*^{1}.]
A large brick or tile; *esp.* a cylindrically curved firebrick.

quarrel /ˈkwɒr(ə)l/ *noun*^{1}. ME.
[Old French *quar(r)el* (mod. *carreau*) from Proto-Romance dim. of late Latin *quadrus* a square. Cf. QUARRY *noun*^{3}.]
1 Chiefly *Hist.* A short heavy square-headed arrow or bolt used with a crossbow or arbalest. ME.
2 A square or (usu.) diamond-shaped pane of glass used in lattice-windows. Now *rare.* LME.
3 A square tile. Cf. QUARL *noun*^{2}. *obsolete* exc. *dial. rare.* E17.
■ **quarrelled** *adjective* (of a window) made of quarrels; (of glass) formed into quarrels: M19.

quarrel /ˈkwɒr(ə)l/ *noun*^{2}. Long *obsolete* exc. *north.* ME.
[from medieval Latin *quarrera* etc., from Latin *quadrare* to square (stones), perh. alt. after QUARREL *noun*^{1}. Cf. QUARRY *noun*^{2}.]
A stone-quarry.

quarrel /ˈkwɒr(ə)l/ *noun*^{3}. ME.
[Old French *querele* (mod. *-elle*) from Latin *querella* var. of *querela* complaint, from *queri* complain.]
1 A complaint against or disagreement with a person or his or her action or opinion; a ground or occasion for this, a cause of unfriendly feeling. (Foll. by *with*, *against*, †*to*.) ME. ▸**b** One's cause or side in a dispute; a cause considered in terms of its justice etc. Now *rare.* LME. ▸†**c** *transf.* A ground or reason for anything. (Foll. by *to*.) LME–M17.
†**2** *spec.* A complaint in law against a person; an accusation; a suit. LME–M17.

†**3** An objection, an aversion. Foll. by *to*, *with*. L16–E18.
4 A violent contention or altercation, an argument, a dispute, a breaking off of friendly relations. (Foll. by *between* people etc., *with* another person etc.) L16. ▸†**b** Quarrelling; quarrelsomeness. *rare*. Only in E17.

> **1** C. LAMB I have no quarrel with you. **b** SHAKES. 2 *Hen. VI* Thrice is he arm'd, that hath his Quarrel just. POPE Perhaps their swords some nobler quarrel draws. **4** C. THIRLWALL The quarrels between the Phocians and their Locrian neighbours. V. S. PRITCHETT She had run away . . after a violent quarrel with her stepfather. A. LIVINGSTONE Between the quarrels they got on extremely well. ***lovers' quarrel***, ***lover's quarrel***: see LOVER.

quarrel /ˈkwɒr(ə)l/ *verb*. Infl. **-ll-**, ***-l-**. LME.
[Orig. from Old French *quereler*, from *querele*; later directly from the noun: see prec.]
1 *verb intrans*. Foll. by *with*, †*at*: make a complaint, protest, or objection against; find fault with, take exception to. LME.
2 *verb intrans*. Contend violently, have a dispute, fall out, break off friendly relations, argue. Foll. by *with* a person, *over*, *for*, or *about* a thing. M16.
3 *verb trans*. Find fault with (a person); reprove angrily; dispute, call into question, object to, (an act, word, etc.). *obsolete* exc. *Scot*. L16.
†**4** *verb trans*. With compl.: force or bring by quarrelling. Only in 17.

> **1** MILTON I must not quarrel with the will Of highest dispensation. *Observer* I would not quarrel with Mr. Buchan's analysis. **quarrel with one's bread and butter**: give up a means of livelihood for insufficient reasons. **2** L. STEFFENS His followers began to quarrel among themselves. I. MURDOCH She never quarrelled with her husband. **3** JAS. HOGG They might kill a good many without being quarrelled for it. **4** JONSON You must quarrel him out o' the house.

■ **quarreller** *noun* a person who quarrels LME.

†**quarrellous** *adjective*. LME–M17.
[Old French *querelous* (mod. *querelleux*), formed as QUARREL *noun*³ + -OUS.]
Quarrelsome; contentious; querulous; fault-finding.

quarrelsome /ˈkwɒr(ə)ls(ə)m/ *adjective*. L16.
[from QUARREL *noun*³ + -SOME¹.]
Inclined to quarrel; given to or characterized by quarrelling.

> E. LONGFORD A witty talker, he was also said to be hot-tempered and quarrelsome.

■ **quarrelsomely** *adverb* M18. **quarrelsomeness** *noun* E17.

quarrenden /ˈkwɒr(ə)nd(ə)n/ *noun*. Also **-don**, **-der** /-də/, & other vars. LME.
[Origin uncertain: perh. a place-name.]
A variety of red-skinned eating apple particularly associated with Somerset and Devon.

quarrian *noun* var. of QUARRION.

quarrier /ˈkwɒrɪə/ *noun*. ME.
[Old French *quarreour*, *-ieur* (mod. *carrier*), from *quarrer* from Latin *quadrare* to square (stones): see -ER².]
A person who quarries stone.

quarrion /ˈkwɒrɪən/ *noun*. *Austral*. Also **-ian**. E20.
[Prob. from Aboriginal.]
= COCKATIEL.

quarrons /ˈkwɒr(ə)nz/ *noun*. *slang*. Long *arch*. Also †**-oms**. M16.
[Origin unkn.]
The body.

quarry /ˈkwɒri/ *noun*¹. ME.
[Anglo-Norman var. of Old French *cuiree* (mod. *curée*) alt. after *cuir* leather, *curer* disembowel, (lit.) cleanse (from Latin *curare* CURE *verb*), of *couree* from Proto-Romance, from Latin *cor* heart: see -EE¹, -Y⁵.]
1 *collect*. Parts of a deer's body placed on the hide and given to the hounds as a reward. Long *obsolete* exc. *Hist*. ME.
†**2** A heap made of the deer killed in hunting; *transf*. a pile of dead bodies. LME–M17.
3 The object(s) of pursuit or attack by a bird of prey, hound, hunter, predator, etc.; *gen*. that which is hunted, pursued, or sought, an intended prey or victim. L15.
4 The swoop of a hawk on its prey; an act of seizing or tearing prey. Cf. SOUSE *noun*² 2b. E17.

> **3** SPENSER When Joue's . . bird from hye Stoupes at a flying heron . . The stone dead quarrey falls. W. BRONK In the white winter, rabbits are your quarry. *Bird Watching* The Hawfinch is shy and elusive, so . . a far more challenging quarry than most rarities.

quarry /ˈkwɒri/ *noun*². ME.
[medieval Latin *quarreia* alt. of *quareria* from Old French *quarriere* (mod. *carrière*), ult. from Latin *quadrum* a square.]
1 An open-air excavation from which stone for building etc. is or has been obtained by cutting, blasting, etc. ME. ▸**b** Any place from which stone may be extracted. M19.
†**2** A large mass of stone suitable for quarrying. E17–M18.

> **1** *fig*.: *Classical Review* The treatment of ancient philosophy as . . a quarry for ideas to be developed in the light of modern theories.

Comb.: **quarryman** a worker in a quarry.

quarry /ˈkwɒri/ *noun*³. M16.
[Alt. of QUARREL *noun*¹, prob. after QUARRY *adjective*.]
1 A square stone, tile, or brick; *esp*. (in full ***quarry tile***) an unglazed square floor-tile. M16.
†**2** = QUARREL *noun*¹ 1. Only in 17.
3 A small usu. diamond-shaped pane of glass; = QUARREL *noun*¹ 2. E17.
■ **quarried** *adjective* (of flooring) paved with quarries; (of a window) decorated with quarries: M19.

†**quarry** *adjective*. ME–E17.
[Old French *quarré* (mod. *carré*) from Latin *quadratus* QUADRATE *adjective*.]
Square; squarely built, stout.

quarry /ˈkwɒri/ *verb*¹. L16.
[from QUARRY *noun*¹.]
†**1** *verb trans*. Teach (a hawk) to seize its quarry; supply with a quarry. L16–E17.
†**2** *verb intrans*. Of a hawk etc.: pounce *on*, prey *on*. E17–E18.
3 *verb trans*. Hunt down or kill (game). *rare*. E19.

quarry /ˈkwɒri/ *verb*². L18.
[from QUARRY *noun*².]
1 *verb trans*. Extract (stone etc.) from a quarry. Also, form (a cavity) by or as if by such extraction. Also foll. by *out*. L18. ▸**b** *fig*. Obtain or extract by laborious methods. M19. ▸**c** GEOLOGY. = PLUCK *verb* 1C. L19.
2 *verb trans*. Form a quarry or quarries in, cut into (rock, ground, etc.). M19.
3 *verb intrans*. Cut or dig (as) in a quarry. M19.

> **1** GOLDSMITH In the mountains . . they quarry out a white stone. MOLLIE HARRIS Roofed with grey stone slates quarried at Stonesfield. *Antiquaries Journal* An approximately square or rectangular chamber quarried in the soft bedrock. **b** L. DURRELL Were these words . . quarried from his own experience? **3** J. MASEFIELD A hundred years ago they quarried for the stone here.

■ **quarriable** *adjective* M19.

quart /kwɔːt/ *noun*¹. ME.
[Old & mod. French *quarte* from Latin *quarta* use as noun of fem. (sc. *pars* part) of *quartus* fourth, ordinal of *quattuor* four.]
1 a A unit of liquid capacity equal to a quarter of a gallon or two pints: in Britain equivalent to approx. 1.13 litres, in the US equal to approx. 0.94 litre. Also (*US*), a unit of dry capacity equal to approx. 1.10 litres. ME. ▸**b** A vessel holding or able to hold a quart. ME.
†**2** A quarter or fourth part of something. LME–L16.
†**3** A quarter or region. *rare* (Spenser). Only in L16.
4 MUSIC. An interval of a fourth. *rare*. L19.

> **1** *attrib*.: W. SANSOM From that polished oak cupboard take very carefully . . four fat quart bottles of black stout. ***reputed quart***: see REPUTED 2. ***Winchester quart***: see WINCHESTER 1.

Comb.: **quart-pot** = sense 1b above; *Austral*. a billycan holding a quart, for boiling tea etc.

quart /kɑːt/ *noun*². In sense 1 also **quarte**, **carte**. M17.
[French *quarte*: see prec.]
1 FENCING. The fourth of eight recognized parrying positions, used to protect the upper inside of the left of the body, with the sword-hand at chest-height and the tip of the blade pointing at the opponent's eyes; a parry in this position. M17.
2 A sequence of four cards, in piquet and other card-games. M17.
1 quart and tierce practice between fencers who thrust and parry in quart and tierce alternately. **2 quart major** the sequence of ace, king, queen, jack.

quart /kɑːt/ *verb*. L17.
[French *quarter*, formed as QUART *noun*².]
FENCING. **1** *verb trans*. & *intrans*. Draw back (the head and shoulders) when in the quart position. L17.
2 *verb intrans*. Use the quart position. L19.

quartal /ˈkwɔːt(ə)l/ *adjective*. M20.
[from Latin *quartus* fourth (see QUART *noun*¹) + -AL¹.]
MUSIC. Of a harmony: based on the interval of a fourth.

quartan /ˈkwɔːt(ə)n/ *adjective* & *noun*. ME.
[Old & mod. French *quartaine* (sc. *fièvre* fever) from Latin *quartana* (sc. *febris*) fem. of *quartanus*, from *quartus*: see QUART *noun*¹, -AN.]
MEDICINE. ▸**A** *adjective*. Designating a fever recurring every third (by inclusive reckoning every fourth) day. ME.
quartan malaria, (*arch*.) **quartan ague** a relatively mild form of malaria due to infection by *Plasmodium malariae*.
▸**B** *noun*. A quartan fever. LME.

quartation /kwɔːˈteɪʃ(ə)n/ *noun*. Now *rare* or *obsolete*. E17.
[from Latin *quartus* (see QUART *noun*¹) + -ATION.]
= INQUARTATION.

quarte *noun* see QUART *noun*².

quarter /ˈkwɔːtə/ *noun*. ME.
[Anglo-Norman, Old & mod. French *quartier* from Latin *quartarius* fourth part of a measure, gill, from *quartus* fourth: see QUART *noun*¹, -ER².]
▸**I 1** Each of four equal or corresponding parts into which a thing is or may be divided. ME.
2 a Each of the four parts, each including a limb, into which the carcass of an animal or bird may be divided. ME. ▸**b** *Hist*. In *pl*. The four parts of a human body similarly divided, as was commonly done to a traitor after execution. ME. ▸**c** Each of the four similar parts of a live person or animal, esp. of a horse (usu. in *pl*.); *spec*.. *sing*. & in *pl*. the hindquarters, the haunches. LME.
3 HERALDRY. **a** Each of the four or more parts into which a shield is divided by quartering (see QUARTER *verb* 3). LME. ▸**b** A charge occupying one-fourth of a shield, placed in chief. L16. ▸**c** = QUARTERING *noun* 1b. E18.

> **1** H. GLASSE Garnish with a Seville orange cut in quarters. M. BINCHY He has a good quarter of it drunk . . by this stage. **2a** P. V. WHITE The sheep had been dressed and cut up into convenient quarters. **c** E. BAIRD The horse's quarters are a guide to a square stance.

▸**II** The fourth part of a measure or standard.
4 A measure of capacity for grain etc.; *spec*. (*a*) in Britain (more fully ***imperial quarter***) a grain measure equal to eight bushels; (*b*) (now *rare*) one-fourth of a chaldron. ME. ▸**b** A bottle one-fourth of the size of a standard bottle of wine, spirits, etc.; the quantity held by this. L20.
5 a One-fourth of a pound weight. LME. ▸**b** A fourth of a hundredweight: in Britain 28 lb (approx. 12.7 kg), in the US 25 lb (approx. 11.3 kg). LME.
6 A measure of length or area, *spec*. (*a*) one-fourth of a yard, nine inches (22.86 cm); (*b*) NAUTICAL one-fourth of a fathom; (*c*) *N. Amer*. one-fourth of a mile or square mile. LME.
7 a One-fourth of a year, esp. as divided by the quarter days. Later also, each of four terms into which a school or (*US*) university year may be divided. LME. ▸**b** One-fourth of a lunar period. Also, the moon's position when halfway between new and full moon (***first quarter***) or between full and new moon (***last quarter***); quadrature. LME. ▸**c** One-fourth of an hour, the space of fifteen minutes. Also, the moment at which one quarter of an hour ends and the next begins, *esp*. the moment fifteen minutes before (foll. by *to*, (N. Amer.) *of*) or after (foll. by *past*, (N. Amer.) *after*) any hour (specified or understood). L15. ▸**d** SPORT (chiefly AMER. FOOTBALL). Each of four equal periods of play in a match. Also (*gen*.), one-fourth of the time taken to play a match. E20.
8 a A farthing. *obsolete* exc. *Hist*. LME. ▸**b** (A coin worth) one-fourth of a US or Canadian dollar. *N. Amer*. M19.
9 A quarterly payment. *rare*. L17.
10 One-fourth of a point on a compass. Also ***quarter-point***. E18.

> **4** R. H. TAWNEY The pawnbroker who took a hundred quarters of wheat when he had lent ninety. **b** *Time* Daily quarters of whisky could not erase the awful memories. **7a** T. S. ELIOT Claude gave her . . a regular allowance . . . It was always spent before the end of the quarter. **c** J. S. CLOUSTON It was then quarter-past eleven. V. WOOLF The clock struck the quarter. M. LASKI If I'm not there by quarter to, you'll know I couldn't make it. C. LARSON He got here at a quarter after nine. **8b** D. BARTHELME The . . waiter took six quarters from another pocket.

▸**III** (A) locality.
11 a A region, a place, a locality. ME. ▸**b** *transf*. A certain part or member of a community etc., without reference to locality and esp. as regarded as a source of something. M18.
12 The region lying about or under each of the four principal points of the compass or divisions of the horizon; each such point or division. Later also, any direction or point of the compass. LME. ▸†**b** The boundary or limit of a place towards one of the cardinal points. M16–E17.
13 †**a** A particular place or point in a building etc. LME–E16. ▸**b** A particular division or district of a town or city, *esp*. that occupied by a certain class or group. E16. ▸†**c** A part of a gathering, army, camp, etc. Only in L16.
14 Assigned or appropriate position. Now *rare*. M16.
15 A place of residence; lodgings; *spec*. (MILITARY) the living accommodation of troops etc. Usu. in *pl*. L16. ▸†**b** The compulsory provision by civilians of lodging for troops. M17–L18. ▸**c** US HISTORY. The cabins in which the Blacks on a plantation lived. E18.
16 †**a** Relations with or conduct towards a person. L16–L17. ▸**b** Good, fair, etc., treatment or terms. *arch*. M17.
17 Reprieve from death, granted to a defeated opponent by a victor in a battle or fight; mercy offered or granted to an enemy in battle etc. on condition of surrender. E17.

📖 **11a** W. H. Prescott The marquis . . had left the place on a visit to a distant quarter. **b** J. F. Kennedy Opposition to the White Paper came from another quarter. R. D. Laing In some quarters there is a point of view that science is neutral. **12** John Ross Venus was also seen in the southern quarter. L. Strachey There flowed . . from every quarter of the globe, a constant stream of gifts. R. Shaw The wind changed quarter, blew from astern. *Prediction* Burn it . . scattering the ashes to the four quarters. **13b** R. L. Stevenson There are rough quarters where it is dangerous o'nights. J. Rosenberg He lived at the edge of the Jewish quarter in Amsterdam. E. Heath The only attractive part of the town was the old Arab quarter. **15a** P. Gallico Williams will show you to your quarters. D. Attenborough Mole-rats live in families and excavate elaborate underground quarters. ***summer quarters, winter quarters***, etc. **17** Defoe The tradesman can expect no quarter from his creditors. *Boxing Scene* He was determined, gave no quarter, asked for no quarter, and had the will to win.

▶ **IV** *techn.* **18** CARPENTRY. A piece of wood; *spec.* a small piece of wood used as an upright beam or scantling in framing. Also more fully †***quarter-board***. Usu. in *pl.* **LME.**

19 a FARRIERY. A part of a horse's hoof, *esp.* either half of the coffin, running from heel to toe. Also, the corresponding part of a horseshoe. **E16.** ▸**b** The upper part of a shoe or boot extending from the back round either side of the foot; the piece of material forming this part. **M18.**

†**20** The skirt of a coat or other garment. Also, (in *pl.*) pieces of leather or other material which are attached to and hang from a saddle. **E16–M18.**

†**21** A bed or plot in a garden. **M16–M18.**

22 NAUTICAL. **a** The upper part of a ship's side abaft the beam. **L16.** ▸**b** Of a yard: the section between the slings and the yard-arm; a part of this section. **M18.**

23 Each of the four parts into which an unsurfaced road or track may be divided by the horse-track and the wheel-ruts. *obsolete* exc. *dial.* **M18.**

24 Each of the four teats of a cow's udder with the part it drains. **M18.**

25 a RUGBY FOOTBALL. (The position of) a half-back. *rare.* **M19.** ▸**b** AMER. FOOTBALL. (The position of) a quarter-back. **L19.**

26 MILITARY. A quartermaster. Also, a quartermaster-sergeant. **E20.**

27 In *pl.* In full ***quarter-finals***. (The four matches constituting) the round before the semi-finals in a tournament. **E20.**

📖 **22** L. T. C. Rolt She lay with her stern and port quarter fully exposed. **27** *Times* I had never won . . at Wimbledon and here I am in the quarters.

Phrases: **a bad quarter of an hour, an unpleasant quarter of an hour** a short but very unpleasant period of time. ***at close quarters***: see CLOSE *adjective & adverb*. ***beat to quarters***: see BEAT *verb*¹ 17. ***close quarters***: see CLOSE *adjective & adverb*. ***collision quarters***. ***false quarter***: see FALSE *noun & adjective*. ***first quarter***: see sense 7b above. ***imperial quarter***: see sense 4 above. †**keep a heavy quarter**, †**keep a quarter** maintain a disturbing or riotous state of affairs, behave riotously. †**keep fair quarters with**, †**keep fair quarter with** keep on good terms with. †**keep good quarter** (*a*) keep good watch; preserve good order; (*b*) ***keep good quarter with, keep good quarters with*** = ***keep fair quarters with*** above. ***last quarter***: see sense 7b above. ***Latin Quarter***: see LATIN *adjective*. **quarter of an hour** one-fourth of an hour, the space of fifteen minutes. ***straiten a person's quarters***: see STRAITEN *verb*¹. ***Westminster quarters***: see WESTMINSTER 2.

Attrib. & comb.: Esp. in the sense (with or without hyphen) 'that is one-fourth in size, amount, extent, etc.', as ***quarter century, quarter hour, quarter litre, quarter mile, quarter pint***, etc. Special combs., as **quarter-bell** a bell in a clock which sounds the quarters; **quarter-binding** a style of bookbinding in which the spine is bound in one material, usu. leather, and the rest of the cover in another; **quarter-block** NAUTICAL a block fitted under the quarter of a yard; **quarter-bloke** *Military slang* a quartermaster; a quartermaster-sergeant; **quarter-blood** *US* a person who is only one-fourth descended from a particular racial group, esp. from the N. American Indians; ***quarter-board***: see sense 18 above; **quarter-boat** *US* a boat containing living quarters for river workers; **quarter-boot** a boot designed to protect the heels of a horse's forefoot from being injured by a hind foot; **quarter-bound** *adjective* (of a book) bound using quarter-binding; **quarter-boy** a quarter-jack in the form of a boy; **quarter-bred** *noun & adjective* (an animal, esp. (*Austral. & NZ*) a sheep) of mixed breed; **quarter-breed** *noun & adjective* (*US*) (a person) born of a half-breed and a white; **quarter-caste** *noun & adjective* (*Austral. & NZ*) (a person) of mixed descent, being one-quarter Aboriginal or Maori and three-quarters white; **quarter-cleft** (now *arch. & dial.*) (*a*) wood that has been quarter-sawn; each of the pieces produced by quarter-sawing a log; (*b*) an eccentric person; **quarter-clock** a clock that strikes the quarters; **quarter-elliptic, quarter-elliptical** *adjectives* (of a leaf spring) having the profile of a quarter of an ellipse; **quarter-evil** = BLACKLEG *noun* 1a; **quarter-final** each of the four matches constituting the quarter-finals in a tournament; ***quarter-finals***: see sense 27 above; **quarter-gallery** NAUTICAL a kind of balcony with windows, projecting from the quarter of a large vessel; **quarter girth measure** a Hoppus measure; **quarter-grain** the grain of wood shown when a log is quarter-sawn; **quarter-guard** MILITARY a small guard mounted a short distance in front of each battalion in a camp; **quarter-gunner** *Hist.* an officer subordinate and assistant to a gunner in the navy; **quarter-horse** *US* (an animal of) a small stocky breed of horse noted for agility and speed over short distances; **quarter-hour** a period of fifteen minutes; the moment fifteen minutes before or after any hour; **quarter-ill** = BLACKLEG *noun* 1a; **quarter-jack** a jack of the clock which strikes the quarters (see JACK *noun*¹ 2); **quarterland** (*obsolete* exc. *Hist.*) a certain division of land in Scotland and the Isle of Man; **quarter leather** quarter-binding in leather; **quarter-light** a window in the side of a motor vehicle, closed carriage, etc., other than the main door window; **quarter-line** RUGBY FOOTBALL (chiefly *Austral.*) the 22-metre line; the space enclosed by this and the goal-line; **quarterman** a foreman of shipwrights; **quarter-miler** an expert at or specialist in running a quarter-mile race; **quarter-moon** a crescent moon; **quarter note** MUSIC (chiefly *N. Amer.*) a crotchet; **quarter-partition** CARPENTRY a partition whose framework is made of quarters; **quarter peal** CAMPANOLOGY a peal comprising one quarter of the number of changes in a full peal; **quarter-piece** NAUTICAL any of several pieces which together form the quarters and stern of a ship; **quarter-pierced** *adjective* (HERALDRY) (of a cross) having a square opening in the centre; **quarter-plate** a photographic plate measuring 3¼ × 4¼ inches (approx. 8.3 × 10.8 cm); a photograph reproduced from such a plate; ***quarter-point***: see sense 10 above; **quarter pole** *US* a pole marking the quarter-mile on a racecourse; **quarter-pounder** something, esp. a hamburger, that weighs a quarter of a pound; **quarter-race** *US* a horse-race over a quarter of a mile; **quarter-racing** *US* the holding of quarter-races; **quarter-repeater** a repeater-watch which strikes the quarters; **quarter-repeating** *adjective* (of a repeater-watch or clock) striking the quarters; **quarter-round** ARCHITECTURE a convex moulding with an outline of a quarter-circle, an ovolo, an echinus; **quarter-saw** *verb trans.* saw (a log) radially into quarters and then into boards; produce (a board) by quarter-sawing; **quarter-section** *N. Amer.* a quarter of a square mile of land, 160 acres (approx. 64.7 hectares); **quarter sessions** LAW (now *Hist.*) (*a*) in England, Wales, and Ireland (latterly Northern Ireland), a court of limited criminal and civil jurisdiction, and of appeal, usu. held quarterly in counties or boroughs, and largely replaced by the crown court; (*b*) in Scotland, a court of review and appeal held quarterly on days appointed by statute; **quarterstaff** (*a*) *Hist.* a stout pole, six to eight feet long and freq. iron-tipped, formerly used as a weapon esp. by the English peasantry; (*b*) fighting or exercise with a quarterstaff; **quarter stretch** *US* (a part of) a racecourse that is a quarter of a mile long; **quarter-tonal** *adjective* (MUSIC) based on quarter tones; **quarter-tonality** MUSIC quarter-tonal quality; **quarter-tone** MUSIC one half of a semitone; **quarter-watch** NAUTICAL a ship's watch composed of a quarter of the crew; **quarter-wave** *adjective* (PHYSICS) having a thickness or a length equal to a quarter of a wavelength; ***quarter-wave plate***, a plate of a birefringent substance cut parallel to the optic axis and of such a thickness that it introduces a phase difference of ninety degrees between ordinary and extraordinary rays passing normally through it; **quarter-wind** NAUTICAL a wind blowing on a vessel's quarter.

quarter /ˈkwɔːtə/ *verb.* **LME.**
[from the noun.]

1 *verb trans.* Cut into quarters; divide into four equal or corresponding parts; *spec.* (*Hist.*) divide (a human body) into four parts after execution. **LME.**

2 *verb trans.* Divide into parts fewer or more than four. **LME.**

3 *verb trans.* HERALDRY. Place or bear (a coat of arms) quarterly on a shield; add (another's coat) to one's hereditary arms; place in alternate quarters *with*; divide (a shield) into four or more parts by vertical and horizontal lines. **L15.**

4 *verb trans.* **a** Put (troops etc.) into quarters; station or lodge in a particular place. **L16.** ▸**b** Impose (troops etc.) on a householder, town, etc., to be lodged and fed. Foll. by *on, upon.* **M17.**

5 *verb intrans.* Take up quarters; stay, reside, lodge. **L16.**

6 *verb trans.* BUILDING. Construct (a wall or partition) with quarters of wood. **L16.**

7 *verb intrans.* NAUTICAL. Sail with the wind on the quarter or between beam and stern. **E17.**

8 *verb trans.* NAUTICAL. Assign (crew members) to a particular quarter on board ship; station for action. **L17.**

9 a *verb trans.* Esp. of a hunting dog or bird of prey: range over or traverse (ground etc.) in every direction. **E18.** ▸**b** *verb intrans.* Range to and fro; shift from point to point. **M19.** ▸**c** *verb intrans.* Move in a slanting direction. **L19.**

10 *verb intrans.* Of the moon: pass from one quarter to another. Also foll. by *in.* **L18.**

11 *verb intrans.* **a** Drive a cart or carriage so that the right and left wheels are on the quarters of an unsurfaced road, with a rut between. Also, (of a horse) walk with the feet so placed. Now *arch. & dial.* **E19.** ▸**b** Drive a cart or carriage to the side to allow another vehicle to pass. *arch.* **M19.**

📖 **1** K. O'Hara I think there's *enough* . . If we just quarter the tomatoes. **3 be quartered by** be a quartering of. **be quartered with** be marshalled with (in a quartered shield). **4a** B. Malamud A detachment of Ural Cossacks quartered in Kiev. P. Scott Smith's Hotel where we were quartered throughout the war. **b** E. Waugh Micky bit the wife of the roadman on whom he was quartered. **5** Defoe The man in whose house I quartered was exceedingly civil. **9a** J. Buchan My pursuers were patiently quartering the hill-side and moving upwards. J. Wainwright A police helicopter was quartering the area. *Bird Watching* Several . . owls have appeared and quarter the rough ground in search of rodents.

■ **quarterer** *noun* a person who quarters, *esp.* a person who takes up quarters or lodgings: **M17.**

quarterage /ˈkwɔːt(ə)rɪdʒ/ *noun.* **LME.**
[from QUARTER *noun* + -AGE, or from Old French.]

1 A contribution, subscription, tax, or other payment made quarterly. **LME.**

2 A sum paid or received quarterly. **LME.**

3 Place of abode, quarters; (the expense of) quartering of troops. *rare.* **L16.**

quarterback /ˈkwɔːtəbak/ *noun & verb.* **L19.**
[from QUARTER *noun* + BACK *noun*¹.]

▶ **A** *noun.* **1** AMER. FOOTBALL. (The position of) a player stationed behind the centre, who directs a team's attacking play. **L19.**

2 *transf.* A supporter or critic of an American football team. **M20.**

3 *fig.* A person who directs or coordinates an operation; a leader. *N. Amer.* **M20.**

2 Monday morning quarterback a person who analyses and criticizes a game retrospectively; *fig.* a person who is wise after the event.

Comb.: **quarterback club** an association of supporters actively interested in promoting their team's success; **quarterback sack** an attack on a quarterback before he or she can make a pass; **quarterback sneak** play in which a quarterback carries the ball instead of passing it to another back.

▶ **B** *verb trans.* **1** AMER. FOOTBALL. Play quarterback for (a team); direct as quarterback. **M20.**

2 *fig.* Direct or coordinate (an operation). **M20.**

■ **quarterbacking** *verbal noun* the action of the verb; ***Monday morning quarterbacking***, criticizing after the event: **M20.**

quarter day /ˈkwɔːtə deɪ/ *noun phr.* **L15.**
[from QUARTER *noun* + DAY *noun.*]

Each of four days fixed by custom as marking off the quarters of the year, on which some tenancies begin and end, and quarterly payments of rent and other charges fall due.

¶ In England, Wales, and Ireland the quarter days are Lady Day (25 March), Midsummer Day (24 June), Michaelmas (29 September), and Christmas (25 December). In Scotland they are Candlemas (2 February), Whitsunday (28 May, formerly 15 or 26 May), Lammas (1 August), and Martinmas (11 November).

quarterdeck /ˈkwɔːtədɛk/ *noun & verb.* **E17.**
[from QUARTER *noun* + DECK *noun*¹.]

NAUTICAL. ▶**A** *noun.* Orig., a smaller deck situated above the half-deck, covering about a quarter of a vessel. Now, that part of a ship's upper deck near the stern, usu. reserved for officers or more privileged passengers; *transf.* the officers of a ship or the navy. **E17.**

▶ **B** *verb intrans.* Walk up and down as on a quarterdeck. **E20.**

quartered /ˈkwɔːtəd/ *ppl adjective.* **L15.**
[from QUARTER *verb* + -ED¹.]

1 a HERALDRY. (Of a shield or arms) divided into four or more parts by vertical and horizontal lines; quarterly; (of a cross) quarterly-pierced. **L15.** ▸**b** Cut into quarters; divided in four; *spec.* (of timber) sawn radially into quarters and then into planks. **E16.**

2 MILITARY. Lodged in or belonging to quarters. **E17.**

†**3** Pertaining to a quarter or part of the horizon. *rare* (Milton). Only in **L17.**

quartering /ˈkwɔːt(ə)rɪŋ/ *noun.* **LME.**
[from QUARTER *verb* + -ING¹.]

1 HERALDRY. The dividing of a shield into quarters; the marshalling or bringing together of various coats on one shield, to denote family alliances. **LME.** ▸**b** Each of the four or more divisions of a quartered shield. Also, a further division of a quarter on a quartered shield. Usu. in *pl.* **E18.**

2 Division into four equal parts. Also, division in general. **M16.**

3 The assigning or taking up of quarters; *spec.* the provision of quarters for troops. Formerly also, a place suitable as quarters. **E17.**

4 BUILDING. The use of quarters in construction; *sing.* & in *pl.*, quarters collectively. **E18.**

5 The moon's passage from one quarter to another. Also = QUARTER *noun* 7b. **M19.**

📖 **1b** Geo. Eliot Families with many quarterings.

quartering /ˈkwɔːt(ə)rɪŋ/ *ppl adjective.* **L16.**
[from QUARTER *verb* + -ING².]

That quarters; *spec.* (NAUTICAL) (*a*) (of a wind) that blows on the quarter of a ship; (*b*) (of the sea) flowing or surging under the effect of a quartering wind.

quarterly /ˈkwɔːtəli/ *adverb, adjective, & noun.* **LME.**
[from QUARTER *noun* + -LY², -LY¹. In sense A.2 after Anglo-Norman *esquartelé*, Old French *quartilé*.]

▶ **A** *adverb.* **1** Every quarter of a year; once a quarter. **LME.**

2 HERALDRY. In or into the quarters of a shield; in two diagonally opposite quarters. **E17.**

📖 **1** W. S. Jevons Managers, officers, secretaries, and others, are paid quarterly. **2** Hor. Walpole A banner with the arms of Vicenza and Otranto quarterly.

▶ **B** *adjective.* **1** That occurs, is done, etc., every quarter of a year; relating to or covering a quarter of a year. **M16.**

2 Pertaining or relating to a quarter; *spec.* (*a*) (of a wind) blowing on the quarter of a ship; (*b*) HERALDRY (of a shield) divided into four or more parts by vertical and horizontal lines; quartered. **M18.**

📖 **1** M. EDGEWORTH Quarterly and half-yearly payments.

▶**C** *noun.* A quarterly publication, as a review, magazine, etc. **M19.**

Comb.: **quarterly meeting** *spec.* (*a*) a general meeting of the Society of Friends; (*b*) an administrative meeting of officials within a circuit of the Methodist Church; **quarterly-pierced** *adjective* (HERALDRY) (of a cross) having a square opening in its centre large enough for the limbs of the cross to be no longer joined; **quarterly-quartered** *adjective* (HERALDRY) having one or more quarters divided into four.

quartermaster /ˈkwɔːtəmɑːstə/ *noun & verb.* **LME.**
[from QUARTER *noun* + MASTER *noun*[1].]
▶**A** *noun.* **1** NAUTICAL. **a** A naval petty officer in charge of steering, signals, stowing of the hold, etc. **LME.** ▸**b** *transf.* Steering equipment. **L19.**
†**2** A person having a quarter of a responsibility which is shared with another or others. **M16–L17.**
3 MILITARY. A regimental officer, ranking as lieutenant, responsible for providing quarters, laying out the camp, and looking after supplies. **E17.**
Comb.: **quartermaster captain** a captain in the US army with duties similar to those of a quartermaster; **Quartermaster-General** the head of the army department responsible for quartering, encamping, marching, and equipment of troops; **quartermaster-sergeant** a sergeant who assists an army quartermaster.
▶**B** *verb intrans.* Perform the duties of a quartermaster. *rare.* **M19.**

quartern /ˈkwɔːt(ə)n/ *noun.* **ME.**
[Anglo-Norman *quartrun*, Old French *quart(e)ron*, from *quart(e* fourth (see QUART *noun*[1]) or *quartier* QUARTER *noun.*]
1 A quarter of something. (Foll. by *of*.) *obsolete exc. dial.* **ME.**
2 *spec.* A quarter of any of various weights and measures, now only of a pint. *arch.* **LME.** ▸**b** In full ***quartern loaf***. A four-pound loaf. *arch.* **M18.**
†**3** A quarter of a hundred, twenty-five. **L15–M17.**

†**quarteron** *noun* see QUADROON.

quartet /kwɔːˈtɛt/ *noun.* Also **-ette.** **E17.**
[French *quartette* from Italian *quartetto*: see next, -ET[1], -ETTE.]
1 A set of four things, as lines in a sonnet, runs at cricket, etc. **E17.**
2 MUSIC. A composition for four voices or instruments, *esp.* one for four stringed instruments. **L18.**
3 A group of four persons or things; *esp.* (MUSIC) a group of four singers or instrumentalists. **E19.**
Comb.: **quartette table** (*obsolete exc. Hist.*) = *QUARTETTO table.*

quartetto /kwɔːˈtɛtəʊ/ *noun.* Now *rare* or *obsolete.* Pl. **-os.** **L18.**
[Italian, from *quarto* fourth.]
1 MUSIC. = QUARTET 2. **L18.**
2 = QUARTET 1, 3. **L18.**
Comb.: **quartetto table** (*obsolete exc. Hist.*) each of a nest of four small tables.

quartic /ˈkwɔːtɪk/ *noun & adjective.* **M19.**
[from Latin *quartus* fourth + -IC.]
▶**A** *noun.* MATH. A quantic or function of the fourth degree; a curve or surface of the fourth order. **M19.**
▶**B** *adjective.* **1** MATH. Of the fourth degree or order. **L19.**
2 Of a steering wheel: shaped like a rectangle with rounded corners. **L20.**

quartier /kartje/ *noun.* Pl. pronounced same. **E19.**
[French: cf. QUARTER *noun* 13b.]
In France: a district or area, esp. of a city; *ellipt.* = ***Quartier Latin*** below.
Quartier Latin /latɛ̃/ = ***Latin Quarter*** s.v. LATIN *adjective & noun.*

quartiere /kwarˈtjɛːre/ *noun.* Pl. ***-ri*** /-ri/. **L19.**
[Italian: cf. prec.]
In Italy: a district or area, esp. of a city. Cf. SESTIERE.

quartile /ˈkwɔːtʌɪl/ *adjective & noun.* **LME.**
[Old French *quartil*, from Latin *quartus* fourth: see -ILE.]
▶**A** *adjective.* ASTROLOGY. Designating the aspect of two planets which are a quarter of a circle (90 degrees) apart in the sky; square. **LME.**
▶**B** *noun.* **1** ASTROLOGY. A quartile aspect. *obsolete exc. Hist.* **E16.**
2 STATISTICS. The first or third (or occas. the second) of three values of a variate which divide a frequency distribution into four groups each containing a quarter of the total population; each of the four groups so produced. **L19.**

quarto /ˈkwɔːtəʊ/ *noun & adjective.* **LME.**
[Latin (*in*) *quarto* (in) a fourth (*sc.* of a sheet), from *quartus* fourth.]
▶**A** *noun.* Pl. **-os.**
1 ***in quarto***, in four parts. **LME.**
2 A size of book or paper in which each sheet is a quarter of a standard printing-sheet. **L16.**
3 A book or page of this size. **M17.**
2 ***royal quarto***: see ROYAL *adjective.*
▶**B** *adjective.* (Of paper) folded twice so as to produce four leaves out of one sheet; (of a book) formed of such sheets. **M17.**

Quartodeciman /kwɔːtəʊˈdɛsɪmən/ *noun & adjective.* **E17.**
[medieval Latin *quartodecimanus*, *quarta-*, from *quartus decimus* fourteenth.]
ECCLESIASTICAL HISTORY. ▶**A** *noun.* Any of a group of early Christians who celebrated Easter on the day of the Jewish Passover, whether or not it was a Sunday. **E17.**
▶**B** *adjective.* Of or pertaining to the Quartodecimans or their method of observing Easter. **E18.**

quartz /kwɔːts/ *noun.* **M18.**
[German *Quarz* from Polish dial. *kwardy* = Polish *twardy*, Czech *tvrdý* hard.]
MINERALOGY. A trigonal rock-forming mineral consisting of silica, massive or crystallizing in colourless or white hexagonal prisms, often coloured by impurities (as amethyst, citrine, cairngorm), and found widely in igneous and metamorphic rocks.
rose quartz, ***sapphire quartz***, ***smoky quartz***, etc.
Comb.: **quartz clock**: in which accuracy is achieved by using a vibrating quartz crystal to regulate the current; **quartz glass** glass consisting almost entirely of silica, silica glass; **quartz-halogen**, **quartz-iodine** *adjectives* (of an electric lamp) having a quartz envelope containing the vapour of a halogen (iodine); **quartz lamp**: in which the envelope is of quartz, enabling ultraviolet light to pass through it; **quartz-locked** *adjective* maintained at a constant speed of rotation by means of a vibrating quartz crystal, as in a quartz clock; **quartz watch**: in which a quartz crystal is employed as in a quartz clock.
■ **quartˈziferous** *adjective* bearing or containing quartz **M19.** **quartzose** *adjective* mainly or entirely composed of quartz; of the nature of quartz: **M18.** **quartzy** *adjective* (now *rare*) of the nature of quartz; resembling quartz: **L18.**

quartzite /ˈkwɔːtsʌɪt/ *noun.* **M19.**
[from prec. + -ITE[1].]
GEOLOGY. An extremely compact, hard, granular rock consisting essentially of quartz.
■ **quartˈzitic** *adjective* **L19.**

quasar /ˈkweɪzɑː, -sɑː/ *noun.* **M20.**
[from QUAS(I-STELL)AR.]
ASTRONOMY. A celestial object that resembles a star optically but is inferred to be an extremely remote and immensely powerful source of light and other radiation.

quash /kwɒʃ/ *noun. rare.* **L17.**
[Alt.]
= SQUASH *noun*[2].

quash /kwɒʃ/ *verb.* **ME.**
[Old French *quasser*, (also mod.) *casser* annul from late Latin *cassare* (medieval Latin also *quassare*), from Latin *cassus* null, void. Cf. SQUASH *verb.*]
▶**I 1** *verb trans.* Annul, make null or void; reject as invalid, esp. by legal procedure; put an end to (legal proceedings). **ME.**
2 *verb trans.* Destroy, ruin, overcome; suppress or stifle (a feeling, idea, undertaking, etc.). **ME.**
3 *verb trans.* Quell or crush, completely subdue (a person). Now *rare.* **M17.**

📖 **1** *Times* On appeal, the convictions of the driver and Kennedy were quashed. **2** E. BOWEN Many functions were quashed by the rain. M. DORRIS I had to quash an impulse to shake her conscious.

▶**II** †**4** *verb trans.* Break in pieces, smash. Also, squeeze, squash. **LME–M18.** ▸**b** Dash or smash *on* or *against* something. **M16–M17.**
†**5** *verb intrans.* Shake; splash, make a splashing noise. **LME–M18.**

Quashee /ˈkwɒʃi/ *noun. slang* (chiefly *W. Indies*). Also **Quashie.** **L18.**
[Akan *Kwasi* name given to a boy born on Sunday.]
A black person.

quasi /ˈkweɪzʌɪ, -sʌɪ, *esp. in sense 3* ˈkwɑːzi/ *adverb & conjunction.* **L15.**
[Latin = as if, almost.]
1 Almost, virtually. *rare.* **L15.**
2 As it were; so to speak. **L16.**
3 [Italian.] MUSIC. As if, almost, like. **E20.**

📖 **3** V. C. CLINTON-BADDELEY A fine girl . . singing, *quasi parlando*, in a fruity baritone.

quasi- /ˈkweɪzʌɪ, -sʌɪ, ˈkwɑːzi/ *combining form.*
[from prec.]
Forming words with the senses 'seemingly, apparently but not really', 'being partly or almost', as ***quasi-crystalline***, ***quasi-equilibrium***, ***quasi-ethical***, ***quasi-existence***, ***quasi-independent***, ***quasi-religion***, ***quasi-scientific***.
■ **quasi-contract** *noun* (LAW) an obligation of one party to another imposed by law independently of an agreement between the parties **E18.** **quasi-conˈtractual** *adjective* (LAW) pertaining to or constituting a quasi-contract **L19.** **quasicrystal** *noun* (PHYSICS) a locally regular aggregation of molecules resembling a crystal in certain properties (as that of diffraction of radiation) but not having a consistent spatial periodicity **L20.** **quasiparticle** *noun* (PHYSICS) an excitation of a many-body system, esp. a crystal lattice, that has some of the properties of a free particle, such as momentum and position **M20.** **quasi-ˈstellar** *adjective* (ASTRONOMY) (of a celestial object) resembling a star; esp. in ***quasi-stellar object***, = QUASAR: **M20.**

quasi in rem /ˌkweɪzʌɪ ɪn ˈrɛm, ˌkweɪs-/ *adjectival phr.* **L19.**
[Latin, lit. 'as if against a thing'.]
US LAW. Brought against a person in respect of his or her interest in a property within the jurisdiction of the court. Freq. *postpositive.*

Quasimodo /kwɑːzɪˈməʊdəʊ/ *noun.* Pl. **-os.** **E18.**
[In sense 1 from Latin *quasi modo*, the first words of the introit for this day. In sense 2 from the name of the hunchback in Victor Hugo's novel *Notre-Dame de Paris.*]
1 In full ***Quasimodo Sunday***. The Sunday after Easter, Low Sunday. *obsolete exc. Hist.* **E18.**
2 SURFING. An act of riding on a wave in a crouched position with one arm forward and one arm back. **M20.**

quasquicentennial /ˌkwaskwɪsɛnˈtɛnɪəl/ *noun & adjective. US.* **M20.**
[Irreg. from Latin *quadrans* quarter, after SESQUICENTENNIAL.]
(Of or pertaining to) a one-hundred-and-twenty-fifth anniversary.

quass *noun* var. of KVASS.

quassia /ˈkwasɪə, ˈkwaʃ-, ˈkwɒʃ-/ *noun.* **M18.**
[mod. Latin (see below), from Surinamese slave Graman *Quassi* (= QUASHEE), who first discovered the medicinal properties of *Quassia amara.*]
A medicinal wood or bark, orig. (more fully ***Suriname quassia***) that of the simarouba, *Quassia amara* (family Simaroubaceae), now chiefly that of several related trees, esp. the bitter ash, *Picrasmia excelsa*, of the W. Indies; the bitter drug obtained from the wood etc. of any of these trees, formerly much used as a tonic and as an insecticide. Also, any of the trees yielding quassia.

quat /kwɒt/ *noun. obsolete exc. dial.* **L16.**
[Origin unkn.]
1 A pimple, a pustule, a small boil; a stye. **L16.**
†**2** A (young) person. *contempt.* Only in **E17.**

quat /kwɒt/ *adjective. obsolete exc. dial.* **LME.**
[Rel. to next: cf. SQUAT *adjective.*]
Crouching down, lying close to the ground, as in hiding.

quat /kwɒt/ *verb. obsolete exc. dial.* Infl. **-tt-.** **LME.**
[Old French *quaitir*, *quatir* beat or press down, force in, hide (mod. *catir* press), from Provençal *quait*, Italian *quatto* squatting, cowering from Latin *coactus* pressed together (see COACT).]
1 *verb trans.* Beat or press down; squash, flatten; extinguish. **LME.**
2 *verb intrans.* Crouch down, lie close, as in hiding; squat. **LME.**

quatercentenary /kwatəsɛnˈtiːn(ə)ri, -ˈtɛn-, -ˈsɛntɪn-, kweɪtə-/ *noun.* **L19.**
[from Latin *quater* four times + CENTENARY.]
(A celebration of) a four-hundredth anniversary.

quatercentennial /kwatəsɛnˈtɛnɪəl, kweɪtə-/ *adjective.* **M20.**
[from Latin *quater* four times + CENTENNIAL.]
Of or pertaining to a four-hundredth anniversary.

quatern /kwɒˈtəːn/ *noun. rare.* **L16.**
[French *quaterne* set of four numbers from Latin *quaterni*: see next.]
†**1** A quire of paper. *Scot.* Only in **L16.**
2 A set of four numbers in a lottery. **M19.**

quaternary /kwəˈtəːn(ə)ri/ *noun & adjective.* **LME.**
[from Latin *quaternarius* (adjective), from *quaterni* four at once, set of four, from *quater* four times, from *quattuor* four: see -ARY[1].]
▶**A** *noun.* **1** A set of four things; (*obsolete exc. Hist.*) the number four. **LME.**
2 GEOLOGY (**Q-**). The Quaternary period or sub-era; the system of rocks dating from this time. **E20.**
3 CHEMISTRY. A quaternary ammonium compound. **M20.**
1 †**quaternary of numbers** the tetractys of Pythagoreanism; ten (= 1 + 2 + 3 + 4).
▶**B** *adjective.* **1** Composed of four parts; characterized by the number four; of or belonging to the fourth order or rank, fourth in a series. **E17.**
2 GEOLOGY (**Q-**). Designating or pertaining to the most recent period or sub-era, following the Tertiary and comprising the Pleistocene and Holocene epochs. **M19.**
3 CHEMISTRY. Designating or containing a principal atom which forms four bonds to organic radicals. Of a carbon atom: bonded to four other carbon atoms. **L19.**
Special collocations: †**quaternary number** (*a*) four; (*b*) ten (see ***quaternary of numbers*** above). **quaternary structure** BIOCHEMISTRY the relative configuration of polypeptide subunits in a protein molecule.
■ **quaterˈnarian** *adjective* (*rare*) = QUATERNARY *adjective* 1 **M17.**

quaternate /kwəˈtəːnət/ *adjective.* **M18.**
[from Latin *quaterni* (see prec.) + -ATE[2].]
Arranged in a set or sets of four; composed of four parts.

quaternion /kwəˈtəːnɪən/ *noun.* Also (*rare*) **-io** /-ɪəʊ/, pl. **-os. LME.**
[Late Latin *quaternio(n-)*, from Latin *quaterni*: see QUATERNARY.]
1 A group of four persons or things; *spec.* a set of four poems. **LME.**
2 A quire of four sheets of paper folded in two. **E17.**
†**3** The number four; the number ten. Cf. ***quaternary number*** s.v. QUATERNARY *adjective.* **M17–M18.**
4 *MATH.* A complex number of the form *w* + *xi* + *yj* + *zk*, where *w*, *x*, *y*, *z* are real numbers and *i*, *j*, *k* are imaginary units that satisfy certain conditions. **M19.**
Comb.: **quaternion group** *MATH.* the group which is generated by multiplication of the unit quaternions, *i*, *j*, and *k*.
▪ **quaterniˈonic** *adjective* of or pertaining to quaternions **L19.** **quaternionist** *noun* a student of quaternions **L19.**

quaternise *verb* var. of QUATERNIZE.

Quaternitarian /kwətəːnɪˈtɛːrɪən/ *noun. rare.* **E19.**
[from next after *Trinitarian*, *Unitarian*.]
CHRISTIAN THEOLOGY. A person who believes that there are four persons in the Godhead.

quaternity /kwəˈtəːnɪti/ *noun.* **E16.**
[Late Latin *quaternitas*, formed as QUATERNION: see -ITY.]
1 A set of four persons or things; *spec.* (**Q-**) in *CHRISTIAN THEOLOGY*, a set of four persons in the Godhead. **E16.**
2 The fact or condition of being four in number. *rare.* **M19.**

quaternize /ˈkwɒtənʌɪz/ *verb trans. & intrans.* Also **-ise. M20.**
[from QUATERN(ARY *adjective* + -IZE.]
CHEMISTRY. Convert or be converted into a quaternary compound.
▪ **quaterniˈzation** *noun* **M20.**

quatorzain /ˈkatəzeɪn/ *noun.* **L16.**
[French *quatorzaine* a set of fourteen, from *quatorze*: see next.]
A poem of fourteen lines. Orig. *spec.*, a sonnet.

quatorze /kəˈtɔːz/ *noun.* **E18.**
[French, from Latin *quattuordecim* fourteen.]
1 In piquet, a set of four aces, kings, queens, or jacks held by one player, scoring fourteen. **E18.**
2 In full ***Quatorze Juillet*** /ˈʒwiːjeɪ/ [French = 14 July]. Bastille Day. **M20.**

quatrain /ˈkwɒtreɪn/ *noun.* **L16.**
[French *quatrain*, †*quadrain*, from *quatre* four + *-ain* -AN.]
1 A stanza of four lines, usu. with alternate rhymes. **L16.**
2 A quarter of a sheet of paper. *rare.* **E19.**

quatre /ˈkɑːtə, ˈkatrə/ *noun.* **M16.**
[French = four.]
The four on a die or in a pack of cards; a throw of four at dice; = CATER *noun*[2] 1.

quatre-couleur /katrəkuːˈləː/ *adjective.* Also **-leurs** /-ˈləː/. **M20.**
[French *quatre-couleurs*, from *quatre* four + *couleurs* colours.]
Of an *objet d'art*: made of or decorated with carved gold of several (esp. four) different colours.

quatrefoil /ˈkatrəfɔɪl, ˈkwɒtrə-/ *noun.* **LME.**
[Anglo-Norman, from Old & mod. French *quatre* four + *foil* leaf, FOIL *noun*[1].]
†**1** A set of four leaves. *rare.* Only in **LME.**
2 A leaf or flower consisting of four (usu. rounded) leaflets or petals radiating from a common centre; a representation or imitation of this, esp. as a charge in heraldry; *ARCHITECTURE* an opening or ornament having an outline divided by cusps so as to give the appearance of such a leaf or flower, esp. a clover leaf. **L15.**
▪ **quatrefoiled** *adjective* (*ARCHITECTURE*) having the form of a quatrefoil, divided into four parts by cusps **M19.**

quatrin /ˈkwɒtrɪn/ *noun. obsolete* exc. *Hist.* **LME.**
[Old French *quatrin*, *quadrin* or Italian *quattrino*, from *quattro* four.]
A small piece of money; a farthing.

quatro /ˈkwatrəʊ/ *noun. W. Indies.* Also **cua-**. Pl. **-os. M20.**
[Spanish *cuatro* lit. 'four'.]
A small four-stringed guitar, originating in Latin America.

quatsch /kvatʃ/ *noun.* **E20.**
[German.]
Nonsense, rubbish. Freq. as *interjection*

quattie /ˈkwɒti/ *noun. W. Indies.* **M19.**
[Alt. of QUARTER *noun*.]
A coin worth a quarter of six old pence; the amount represented by this.

quattrocento /kwatrə(ʊ)ˈtʃɛntəʊ/ *noun & adjective.* **L19.**
[Italian = four hundred.]
▶ **A** *noun.* The fifteenth century in Italy; the Italian style of art, architecture, etc., of this period. **L19.**
▶ **B** *attrib.* or as *adjective.* Of or pertaining to the quattrocento. **E20.**
▪ **quattrocentist** *noun* a fifteenth-century Italian artist or writer **M19.**

quave /kweɪv/ *verb intrans.* Long *obsolete* exc. *dial.* **ME.**
[Prob. repr. Old English form parallel to *cwacian* QUAKE *verb*.]
Quake, tremble; palpitate.

quaver /ˈkweɪvə/ *noun.* **M16.**
[from the verb.]
1 *MUSIC.* A symbol for a note with the time value of half a crotchet or an eighth of a semibreve, having a solid head and a straight stem with a hook on the end; a note of this length. **M16.**
2 *MUSIC.* A trill in singing or (*rare*) instrumental music. **E17.**
3 A shake or tremble in the voice. **M18.**
4 A quivering or tremulous movement. **M18.**

quaver /ˈkweɪvə/ *verb.* **LME.**
[Frequentative of QUAVE: see -ER[5].]
1 *verb intrans.* **a** Vibrate, tremble, quiver; proceed with a quivering or tremulous movement. **LME.** ▸**b** Of the voice: shake, tremble. **M18.**
2 a *verb intrans. & trans.* Sing (a note, song, etc.) with trills or quavers. **M16.** ▸**b** *verb trans.* Utter in a quavering tone. **L19.**

> 🕮 **1b** P. D. JAMES Her voice . . quavered like the voice of an old, impotent woman. **2b** C. S. FORESTER 'My name is Hornblower,' he quavered at length.

▪ **quaverer** *noun* (*rare*) **E17.** **quaveringly** *adverb* in a quavering manner **L16.** **quaverous** *adjective* (*rare*) tremulous, quavering **E20.** **quavery** *adjective* apt to quaver; quavering: **E16.**

†**quaviver** *noun.* **L16–L18.**
[from unkn. 1st elem. + VIVER *noun*[2].]
= DRAGONET 2.

quawk /kwɔːk/ *noun. US.* **M19.**
[Imit.]
The black-crowned night-heron, *Nycticorax nycticorax*. Cf. QUA-BIRD.

quay /kiː/ *noun.* Also (earlier) †**key. LME.**
[Old French *kay*, *kai*, *cay* (see CAY). Later spelling *quay* (from 18) after French *quai*.]
A stationary artificial bank or landing-stage, built esp. of stone and lying alongside or projecting into water for loading and unloading ships.
Comb.: **quay crane** = ***wharf crane*** s.v. WHARF *noun*; **quay-punt** a small fore-and-aft rigged two-masted sailing boat, orig. used for transporting stores between ship and shore; **quayside** the land along the edge of a quay.
▪ **quayage** *noun* (**a**) dues levied on goods landed or shipped at a quay, or on ships using a quay; (**b**) the area of a quay: **LME.** **quayful** *noun* (*rare*) as much or as many as will fill a quay **M19.**

†**quay** *verb*[1] *trans. rare.* **L16–L17.**
[Perh. alt. of QUAIL *verb*[1].]
Depress, subdue, daunt.

> 🕮 SPENSER His sturdie corage soon was quayd.

quay /kiː/ *verb*[2] *trans.* **L18.**
[from the noun.]
Provide with a quay. Chiefly as ***quayed*** *ppl adjective.*

Que. *abbreviation.*
Quebec.

queach /kwiːtʃ/ *noun. obsolete* exc. *dial.* **ME.**
[Origin unkn.]
A dense growth of bushes; a thicket.
¶ Earliest in place-names.

queachy /ˈkwiːtʃi/ *adjective.* **L15.**
[from prec. + -Y[1].]
1 Of ground: swampy, boggy. *obsolete* exc. *dial.* **L15.**
†**2** Forming a dense growth or thicket. *rare.* **M–L16.**
3 Feeble, weak, small. *dial.* **M19.**

quean /kwiːn/ *noun.*
[Old English *cwene* = Old Saxon *cwena* (Dutch *kween* barren cow), Old High German *quena*, *quina*, Old Norse *kvenna*, *kvinna* (genit. pl. *kona*), Gothic *qino* woman from Germanic, from Indo-European base repr. by Greek *gunē* woman. Cf. QUEEN *noun*.]
1 Orig. *gen.*, a woman, a female. Later, a bold or impudent woman, a hussy; *spec.* a prostitute. *arch.* exc. *Scot.* **OE.**
2 A young woman, a girl, esp. of a healthy and robust appearance. *Scot.* **LME.**
3 A male homosexual of effeminate appearance. Cf. QUEEN *noun* 9. *slang.* **M20.**

queasy /ˈkwiːzi/ *adjective.* **LME.**
[Origin uncertain: perh. rel. to unrecorded Anglo-Norman or Old French adjectives rel. to Old French *coisier* hurt, wound.]
1 Of a time, matter, or state of affairs: unsettled, troubled, uncertain, hazardous. Now *rare* or *obsolete.* **LME.**
2 a Of food: unsettling to the stomach; causing sickness. Now *rare* or *obsolete.* **LME.** ▸**b** Of the stomach: easily upset; inclined to sickness. **M16.** ▸**c** Of a person: having an unsettled stomach; affected with nausea. **L16.**
3 Of the mind, conscience, etc.: delicate, tender, scrupulous. **M16.**
4 Of a feeling, pain, etc.: uneasy, uncomfortable. **L16.**
▪ **queasily** *adverb* **M19.** **queasiness** *noun* **L16.**

Quebec /kwɪˈbɛk, kə-/ *noun.* **L18.**
[A city and province in eastern Canada.]
Used *attrib.* to designate things found in or associated with Quebec.
Quebec heater a solid-fuel, domestic heating stove with a tall cylindrical firebox.

Quebecker /kwɪˈbɛkə, kə-/ *noun.* Also **-becer. M19.**
[from prec.: see -ER[1].]
= QUÉBECOIS *noun.*

Québecois /kwɪˈbɛkwɑː, *foreign* kebɛkwa/ *noun & adjective.* **L19.**
[French, from QUEBEC.]
▶ **A** *noun.* Pl. same.
1 A native or inhabitant of Quebec, *esp.* a French-Canadian one. **L19.**
2 The French spoken in Quebec. **M20.**
▶ **B** *adjective.* Of or pertaining to Quebec or its inhabitants. **M20.**

quebracho /kɪˈbrɑːtʃəʊ/ *noun.* Pl. **-os. L19.**
[Spanish, from *quebrar* break + *hacha* axe.]
Any of several S. American trees whose timber and bark are a rich source of tannin, esp. (in full ***white quebracho***) of the genus *Aspidosperma* (family Apocynaceae) and (in full ***red quebracho***) of the genus *Schinopsis* (family Anacardiaceae). Also, the bark or hard timber of any of these trees.

quebrada /keˈbraða, kɪˈbrɑːdə/ *noun.* Pl. ***-as*** /-as, -əz/. **M19.**
[Spanish, fem. of *quebrado* pa. pple of *quebrar* break.]
A mountain stream or ravine in S. America.

Quechua /ˈkɛtʃwə/ *noun & adjective.* Also **Quichua** /ˈkɪtʃwə/. **M19.**
[Spanish, from Quechua *qʰeswa*, *ghechwa* temperate valleys.]
▶ **A** *noun.* Pl. same, **-s.**
1 A member of a S. American Indian people of Peru and neighbouring parts of Bolivia, Chile, Colombia, and Ecuador. **M19.**
2 The language of this people. **M19.**
▶ **B** *attrib.* or as *adjective.* Of or pertaining to the Quechua or their language. **M19.**
▪ Also **Quechuan** *noun & adjective* **M19.**

Queckenstedt test /ˈkwɛk(ə)nstɛt ˌtɛst/ *noun phr.* Also **Queckenstedt's test. E20.**
[Hans Heinrich Georg *Queckenstedt* (1876–1918), German physician.]
MEDICINE. Compression of a patient's jugular veins while observing the pressure of the cerebrospinal fluid in a lumbar puncture, a marked increase indicating normal flow of the fluid.

queen /kwiːn/ *noun.* Also (esp. in titles) **Q-.**
[Old English *cwēn* = Old Saxon *quān*, Old Norse *kvæn* (also *kván*), Gothic *qēns* (wife), from Germanic, from Indo-European base of QUEAN.]
1 A female sovereign (esp. hereditary) ruler of an independent State, a female monarch; the wife or consort of a king. **OE.** ▸**b** *ellipt.* (Usu. **Q-**.) The British national anthem in the reign of a female monarch, 'God save the Queen'. **L19.**
2 a The Virgin Mary. Freq. in ***Queen of glory***, ***Queen of grace***, ***Queen of heaven***, etc. **OE.** ▸**b** Any of the goddesses of ancient religions or mythologies. **LME.** ▸**c** (A term of endearment for) a fine and honourable woman. **L16.** ▸**d** A woman pre-eminent in a given sphere or class; a mock sovereign on some occasion. **L16.** ▸**e** An attractive woman; a girlfriend, a female partner. *slang.* **E20.**
3 A thing (e.g. a plant, country, or city) regarded as supreme or outstandingly beautiful or excellent of its kind; that which in a particular sphere has pre-eminence comparable to that of a queen. **OE.**
4 a *CHESS.* The piece which has greatest freedom of movement, and hence is most effective for defending the king, next to which it is placed at the beginning of the game. Also (*rare*), the position on the board attained by a pawn when it is queened. **LME.** ▸**b** *CARDS.* One card in each suit, bearing the representation of a queen, ranking next below the king and above the jack or knave. **L16.**
5 A reproductive female in a colony of social insects (freq. the only one in a colony). Also ***queen ant***, ***queen bee***, ***queen termite***, ***queen wasp***, etc. **E17.**
6 A litter-bearing female cat. Also more fully ***queen cat.*** **L17.**
7 = ***queen scallop*** below. Cf. QUIN *noun*[1]. **E19.**
8 a In *pl.* One of the classes into which fullers' teasels are sorted. **E19.** ▸**b** A roofing-slate measuring three feet by two (approx. 0.91 by 0.61 m). **E19.** ▸**c** = REINETTE *noun.* **M19.**
9 A male homosexual, *esp.* one of effeminate behaviour or appearance. *slang.* **L19.**

📖 **1** SHAKES. *Wint. T.* Hermione, Queen to the worthy Leontes, King of Sicilia. DRYDEN Spenser . . flourished in the reign of Queen Elizabeth. **2b** MILTON Mooned Ashtaroth, Heav'n's Queen and mother both. **c** SHAKES. *L.L.L.* O queen of queens! how far dost thou excel. **d** H. ACTON Madame de Pompadour . . already a queen of fashion. *Face* Molly's . . stable home-life . . contrasts sharply with that of seventies teen queens. **e** S. CLARKE He . . took his blood-stained shirt back . . for his queen, Joice to wash. **3** SHAKES. *Wint. T.* Each your doing . . Crowns what you are doing . . That all your acts are queens. J. SHEFFIELD Paris, the queen of cities.

Phrases & comb.: ***beauty queen***: see BEAUTY *noun*. ***closet queen***: see CLOSET *adjective*. ***drag queen***: see DRAG *noun*. ***Nine Days' Queen***: see NINE *adjective*. ***Pearly Queen***: see PEARLY *adjective*. **Queen and country** the objects of allegiance for a patriot whose head of State is a queen. ***queen ant***: see sense 5 above. **Queen At, Queen AT** *Military slang* a Chief Commander of the ATS. **queen bee** (*a*) see sense 5 above; (*b*) the chief or dominant woman in an organization or social group; (*c*) MILITARY a remote-controlled aeroplane used as a target in firing practice. **queen-cake** a small usu. heart-shaped currant-cake. ***queen cat***: see sense 6 above. **queen-cell** an oval wax structure built by bees, in which a new queen is reared. **Queen City** *N. Amer.* the chief or pre-eminent city of a region. **queen closer** a brick split in half lengthways. **queen conch** (the shell of) a large marine gastropod, *Strombus gigas*, found in the Caribbean. **queen consort** the wife of a reigning king. **queen dowager** the widow of a king. **queen excluder** a screen in a beehive with holes large enough for the workers to pass through but not for the queen. **queenfish** (*a*) a small edible drum-fish, *Seriphus politus*, found along the Pacific coast of America; (*b*) a large carangid game-fish, *Scomberoides sanctipetri*, found in the tropical seas of Australia. ***queen hornet***: see sense 5 above. **queen lily** a Peruvian ornamental plant of the lily family, *Phaedranassa carmiolii*. **Queen Mary** (now *rare*) a long low-loading road trailer. **Queen Mary hat, Queen Mary toque** a variety of toque popularized by Queen Mary (1867–1953), wife of King George V, who favoured the hat because it enabled the public to see her face clearly. **queen mother** (*a*) a queen dowager who is the mother of the reigning monarch; (*b*) a queen who is a mother. **Queen Mum** *colloq.* Queen Elizabeth, the queen mother (1900–2002). ***Queen of glory, Queen of grace, Queen of heaven***: see sense 2a above. **queen of night** the moon. **queen of puddings** a pudding made of breadcrumbs, milk, etc., with a topping of jam and meringue. **Queen of Spain fritillary** an orange nymphalid butterfly with black markings, *Issoria lathonia*, widely distributed in Europe, N. Africa, and parts of Asia. ***Queen of the May***: see MAY *noun*². **queen-of-the-meadow** meadowsweet, *Filipendula ulmaria*. **queen-of-the-night** a W. Indian night-blooming cereus, *Selenicereus grandiflorus*, cultivated in the tropics. **queen-of-the-prairie** a N. American plant, *Filipendula rubra*, allied to meadowsweet, with clusters of small pink flowers. **Queen of the West** Cincinnati, Ohio. **queen of tides** the moon. **queen olive** any very large pickling olive, *esp.* one from Seville. **queen-pin** *colloq.* a woman who controls the organization of an institution or event (cf. KINGPIN). **queen-post** CARPENTRY either of two upright posts in a roof-truss, extending from the principal rafters down to the tie-beam on either side of the king-post. **queen pudding** = ***queen's pudding*** below. **queenright** *adjective* (of a colony of bees etc.) that has a properly functioning queen. ***Queen's Attorney***: see ATTORNEY *noun* 2. **Queen's Award** any of a number of annual awards given to firms in the UK for achievements in exporting goods or services or in advancing technology. ***Queen's Bench***: see BENCH *noun* 3b. **queen's bishop, queen's knight, queen's rook** CHESS the bishop etc. on the queen's side of the board at the start of a game. ***Queen's bounty***: see BOUNTY 4. **queen scallop** (the shell of) a small scallop, *Chlamys opercularis*, found off northern and Mediterranean coasts. **queen's conch** = ***queen conch*** above. ***Queen's counsel***: see COUNSEL *noun*. **queen's cushion** the mossy saxifrage, *Saxifraga hypnoides*. **queen's flower** the jarool, *Lagerstroemia speciosa*. **queen's gambit** CHESS: in which a sacrifice of the queen's bishop's pawn is offered. **Queen's Guide** a holder of the highest award in Guiding during the reign of a queen. **queen's head** (now *rare*) a postage stamp. ***Queen's highway***: see HIGHWAY 1. **queen-side** *adjective & noun* (CHESS) (of or pertaining to) the half of the board on which both queens stand at the start of the game. **queen-size, queen-sized** *adjectives* of an extra large size, though usu. smaller than king-size. ***queen's knight***: see ***queen's bishop*** above. **queen's lace** *US* wild carrot or Queen Anne's lace, *Daucus carota*. ***Queen's messenger***: see MESSENGER *noun*. **queen's pattern** an ornamental pattern used on porcelain. **queen's pawn** CHESS the pawn immediately in front of the queen at the start of a game; ***queen's pawn opening***: in which White begins by advancing the queen's pawn two squares. **queen's pigeon** = ***Victoria crowned pigeon*** s.v. VICTORIA *noun* 6. ***Queen's Proctor***: see PROCTOR *noun* 3. **queen's pudding** (*a*) a steamed suet pudding; (*b*) = ***queen of puddings*** above. ***Queen's Remembrancer***: see REMEMBRANCER 1a. ***queen's rook***: see ***queen's bishop*** above. ***Queen's Scout***: see SCOUT *noun*³. ***Queen's SHILLING***. **queen staysail** a triangular maintopmast staysail in a schooner yacht. **queen-stitch** a fancy stitch in embroidery. **queen substance** a pheromonal substance produced by the queen in a colony of social insects to inhibit the production of more queens. **queen's ware** (*a*) cream-coloured Wedgwood earthenware; (*b*) a type of stoneware; **queen's weather** (now *rare*) fine weather. ***queen termite***: see sense 5 above. **queen trigger fish** a deep-bodied, blue and yellow trigger fish, *Balistes vetula*, found in the Indian and Atlantic Oceans. ***queen wasp***: see sense 5 above. **the Queens** *Hist.* the Cunard passenger liners, 'Queen Mary' and 'Queen Elizabeth'. ***The Queen's Bays***: see BAY *noun*⁶ 2. ***the Queen's colour***: see COLOUR *noun* 7. ***the Queen's English***: see ENGLISH *adjective & noun*. ***the Queen's peace***: see PEACE *noun*. ***the Queen's speech***: see SPEECH *noun*. ***turn Queen's evidence***: see EVIDENCE *noun*. ***virgin queen***: see VIRGIN *noun & adjective*.

■ **queendom** *noun* (*a*) the territory or country ruled over by a queen; (*b*) the rank or position of a queen, queenhood: E17. **queenhood** *noun* the rank, authority, or office of a queen; queenly spirit or character: M19. **Queenite** *noun* (*Hist.*) a partisan or supporter of a queen, esp. in the 19th cent. of Queen Caroline against George IV, or of Queen Isabella of Spain against Don Carlos E19. **queenless** *adjective* M19. **queenlet** *noun* a minor queen; a queen ruling over a small territory: M19. **queenlike** *adjective* resembling, characteristic of, or befitting a queen; queenly; majestic, haughty: L16. **queenship** *noun* (*a*) the rank or office of queen; (*b*) (with possess. adjective, as ***her queenship, your queenship***, etc.) majesty: M16.

queen /kwiːn/ *verb*. E17.
[from the noun.]
1 *verb intrans. & trans.* (with *it*). Act or rule as queen; *transf.* behave as if a queen, be ostentatious or overbearing. Also foll. by *over*. E17.
2 CHESS. **a** *verb trans.* Convert (a pawn) into a queen when it reaches the opponent's end of the board. L18. ▸**b** *verb intrans.* Of a pawn: reach the position of conversion into a queen. M19.
3 *verb trans.* Make (a woman) a queen. M19.
4 *verb trans.* Rule over as a queen. *rare*. M19.

📖 **1** J. GATHORNE-HARDY Nan . . still queened it over the rest of the staff. V. S. PRITCHETT The bride was in full folly, queening it before the groom. **2a queening square** the square on a chessboard on which a particular pawn may be queened.

Queen Anne /kwiːn 'an/ *noun phr.* E19.
[Queen of Great Britain and Ireland who reigned from 1702 to 1714.]
Used *attrib.* and in *possess.* to designate things associated with Queen Anne or her reign; *spec.* (*attrib.*) designating furniture, architecture, etc., characteristic of the early 18th cent.

Queen Anne's bounty: see BOUNTY 4. **Queen Anne's daffodil, Queen Anne's double daffodil** a creamy-yellow double form of daffodil, with perianth segments in six whorls. **Queen Anne's jonquil** a double-flowered variety of the jonquil, *Narcissus jonquilla*. **Queen Anne's lace** any of several umbelliferous plants bearing lacy clusters of small white flowers, *esp.* cow parsley and (*N. Amer.*) wild carrot, *Daucus carota*.

■ **Queen Anneish, Queen Annish** *adjective* (of furniture or architecture) suggestive of or designed in a Queen Anne style E20.

queenie /'kwiːni/ *noun, adjective, & adverb*. *colloq.* Also **queeny**. M20.
[from QUEEN *noun* + -IE.]
▸**A** *noun*. An effeminate male; a homosexual. M20.
▸**B** *adjective*. Effeminate. M20.
▸**C** *adverb*. In an effeminate manner. M20.

queening /'kwiːnɪŋ/ *noun*. LME.
[Perh. from QUEEN *noun* + -ING³.]
Any of several red-flushed varieties of apple, *esp.* (more fully ***winter queening***) one that keeps well in winter.

queenly /'kwiːnli/ *adjective & adverb*. LME.
[from QUEEN *noun* + -LY¹.]
▸**A** *adjective*. **1** Resembling, characteristic of, or befitting a queen; queenlike. LME.
2 Characteristic of a male homosexual. *slang*. M20.
▸**B** *adverb*. Like, or in a manner befitting, a queen. M19.
■ **queenliness** *noun* M19.

Queensberry rules /kwiːnzb(ə)ri 'ruːlz/ *noun phr. pl.* L19.
[Sir John Sholto Douglas (1844–1900), eighth Marquis of *Queensberry*, who supervised the preparation of the rules.]
A code of rules drawn up in 1867 to govern the sport of boxing in Great Britain; the standard rules of modern boxing. Also *transf.*, standard rules of polite or acceptable behaviour.

Queensland /'kwiːnzlənd/ *noun*. L19.
[A State in NE Australia.]
Used *attrib.* in the names of things, esp. trees, occurring in or associated with Queensland.

Queensland blue = ***blue heeler*** s.v. BLUE *adjective*. **Queensland hemp** Paddy's lucerne, *Sida rhombifolia*. **Queensland lungfish** a freshwater dipnoan, *Neoceratodus forsteri*, found in Queensland. **Queensland maple** (the high-grade wood of) either of two evergreen trees, *Flindersia brayleyana* and *F. pimenteliana*, of the rue family. **Queensland nut** (the fruit of) either of two species of macadamia, *Macadamia integrifolia* and *M. tetraphylla*, which yield edible nuts. **Queensland sore** a sore which does not heal readily because of scurvy. **Queensland walnut** an evergreen tree, *Endiandra palmerstonii*, of the laurel family; its variegated wood, used for panelling.
■ **Queenslander** *noun* a native or inhabitant of Queensland M19.

queeny *adjective & adverb* var. of QUEENIE.

queer /kwɪə/ *adjective & noun*. E16.
[Perh. from German *quer* cross, oblique, squint, perverse (Middle High German *twer*: see THWART *adjective, adverb, & preposition*).]
▸**A** *adjective*. **1** Strange, odd, eccentric; of questionable character, suspicious. E16.
2 a Bad; worthless. M16. ▸**b** Of a coin or banknote: counterfeit, forged. *Criminals' slang*. M18.
3 Out of sorts; giddy, faint, ill. Freq. in ***feel queer***. L18.
4 Esp. of a man: homosexual. *slang. derog.* L19.

📖 **1** R. H. HORNE The queer-looking little houses. A. DJOLETO People think I'm queer because I train my children differently.

▸**B** *noun*. **1** Counterfeit coin. Also (*US*), forged paper currency or bonds. *Criminals' slang*. E19.
2 A (usu. male) homosexual. *slang. derog.* E20.

Phrases: **on the queer** *Criminals' slang* living dishonestly; *spec.* engaged in the forging of currency. **queer for** *US colloq.* fond of, keen on; in love with. ***shove the queer***: see SHOVE *verb*.

Special collocations & comb.: **queer-basher** *slang* a person who attacks homosexuals. **queer-bashing** *slang* physical or verbal attack on homosexuals. **queercore** [-*core* after *hardcore* etc.] a cultural movement amongst young homosexuals which deliberately rebels against and dissociates itself from the established gay scene, having as its primary form of expression an aggressive type of punk-style music. **queer fish, queer fellow** an odd or eccentric person. ***queer screen***: see SCREEN *noun*². **Queer Street** *slang* a difficult situation; trouble, debt, difficulty.

■ **queerdom** *noun* (*slang, derog.*) the state of being a homosexual M20. **queerie** *noun* (*slang, derog.*) a person who is queer; *esp.* an effeminate or homosexual person: M20. **queerish** *adjective* somewhat queer M18. **queerishness** *noun* (*rare*) E19. **queerity** *noun* (now *rare*) queerness; (an) oddity: E18. **queerly** *adverb* strangely, oddly E18. **queerness** *noun* (*a*) strangeness; (*b*) *slang, derog.* homosexuality: L17.

queer /kwɪə/ *verb trans. slang*. L18.
[from the adjective.]
1 Ridicule; puzzle; swindle, cheat. Now *rare*. L18.
2 Spoil, put out of order; spoil the reputation or chances of (a person). E19.
3 Upset, disconcert; make (a person) feel queer. *rare*. M19.

2 queer a person's pitch interfere with or spoil someone's chances, business, etc.

■ **queerer** *noun* (*rare*) a person who queers someone or something E19.

queest /kwiːst/ *noun*. *obsolete* exc. *dial.* LME.
[Alt. of CUSHAT.]
The woodpigeon. Cf. ***woodquest*** s.v. WOOD *noun*¹.

†**queise** *verb trans. rare*. LME–E17.
[Origin unkn. See also SQUEEZE *verb*.]
Squeeze.

quel /kɛl/ *adjective*. Pl. **quels**. Fem. **quelle**, pl. **quelles**. L19.
[French.]
With following noun: what — Only in French phrs. and in English phrs. imitating them.

📖 K. A. PORTER Oh, what sophistication, what aplomb, quel savoir faire. M. KRAMER *Quelle horreur*, it is not a classic tulip. C. BRAYFIELD *Quel* shit, Louise thought to herself.

quelch /kwɛltʃ/ *verb intrans. & trans. rare*. M17.
[Rel. to SQUELCH *verb* as *quash* to *squash* etc.]
Squelch.

quelea /'kwiːlɪə/ *noun*. M20.
[mod. Latin (see below), perh. from medieval Latin *qualea* QUAIL *noun*.]
Any of various African weaver-birds of the genus *Quelea*, esp. (more fully ***red-billed quelea***) *Q. quelea*, which is an important pest of grain crops. Also called ***dioch***.

quell /kwɛl/ *noun*¹. Long *rare*. LME.
[from QUELL *verb*¹.]
Killing, slaughter.

📖 SHAKES. *Macb.* His spongy officers . . shall bear the guilt Of our great quell.

quell /kwɛl/ *noun*². *rare*. L19.
[German *Quelle*: cf. QUELL *verb*².]
A spring, a fountain.

quell /kwɛl/ *verb*¹.
[Old English *cwellan* = Old Saxon *quellian* (Dutch *kwellen*), Old High German *quellen* (German *quälen*), Old Norse *kvelja*, from Germanic base repr. also by Old English *cwalu* death.]
1 *verb trans.* Kill, put to death. Now *rare* or *obsolete*. OE.
2 *verb trans.* Put an end to, suppress, extinguish (a thing, state, feeling, etc.). ME.
3 *verb trans.* Subdue, oppress, reduce to submission. E16.
†**4** *verb intrans.* Quail, break down, fail. L16–E17.

📖 **2** J. CONRAD He quelled mutinies on the high seas. A. BRINK The old man was shockingly frail . . but nothing could quell his exuberant spirit. **3** C. V. WEDGWOOD The . . skill with which he quelled the Royalist insurgents. J. G. FARRELL His anger impressed the twins sufficiently to quell them. **4** SPENSER Old January, wrapped well . . Yet did he quake and quiver, like to quell.

■ **queller** *noun* a person who quells someone or something (freq. as 2nd elem. of comb., as ***manqueller***) OE.

quell /kwɛl/ *verb*² *intrans. rare*. ME.
[Orig. app. repr. Old English form corresp. to Old Saxon, Old High German *quellan*; later from German *quellen*.]
Well out, flow.

quelle *adjective* see QUEL.

Quellenforschung /'kvɛlənfɔrʃʊŋ/ *noun*. M20.
[German, from *Quelle* source + *Forschung* research.]
The investigation of the sources of, or influences on, a literary work.

quelles, quels *adjectives* see QUEL.

quemadero /kemaˈðero/ *noun.* Pl. **-os** /-ɔs/. **M19.**
[Spanish, from *quemar* to burn.]
Hist. In Spain and former Spanish territories during the Inquisition, a place where convicted heretics were executed by burning.

queme /kwiːm/ *adjective & adverb.* Long *obsolete* exc. *Scot. & north.* Also **weme** /wiːm/.
[Old English *ġecwēme*: cf. Old Norse *kvæmr*, Old High German *fiquāmi* (German *bequem*), Middle Dutch *bequame* (Dutch *bekwaam*): ult. rel. to COME *verb*.]
▶ **A** *adjective.* **1** †**a** Pleasing, agreeable, acceptable. **OE–ME.** ▸**b** Of pleasing appearance; neat; (of words) specious. **ME.** ▸†**c** Protected from the wind, snug; smooth, still. **L17–E19.**
2 Fit, fitting; convenient, handy. **OE.**
†**3 a** Friendly (*to*); intimate (*with*). **ME–M18.** ▸**b** Skilled, clever. *rare.* **LME–E17.**
▶ **B** *adverb.* = QUEMELY. **LME.**
■ **quemely** *adverb* (**a**) agreeably; (**b**) smoothly: **ME.**

†**queme** *verb trans.* **OE.**
[formed as prec.]
1 Please, be agreeable to, gratify. **OE–E17.**
2 Satisfy; appease. *rare.* Only in **ME.**
3 Join or fit closely. *Scot. rare.* **E16–L19.**

quench /kwɛn(t)ʃ/ *verb & noun.*
[Old English *-cwenċan* (in *ācwenċan*), from Germanic: rel. to Old Frisian *quinka*.]
▶ **A** *verb.* **I** *verb trans.* **1** Extinguish (a fire, light, etc.) (*lit.* & *fig.*). **OE.** ▸**b** Blind (an eye). *rare.* **LME.**
2 *transf.* **a** Put an end to, stifle, suppress, (a feeling, (occas.) an action, etc.). **ME.** ▸**b** Satisfy (thirst or desire). Formerly also, satisfy (hunger). **ME.** ▸†**c** Stifle or satisfy the feelings of (a person). *rare.* Only in **E17.**
3 a Oppress or kill (a person). Now *poet. rare.* **ME.** ▸**b** *transf.* Put down in a dispute etc., reduce (a person) to silence. **M19.**
4 a Extinguish (heat) by cooling. **LME.** ▸**b** Chiefly METALLURGY. Cool (a heated object, esp. a metal one) rapidly in cold water, air, oil, etc. **LME.** ▸†**c** Slake (lime). *rare.* **LME–M17.**
5 a RADIO. Extinguish by cooling etc. (the spark in a spark transmitter). Now *rare.* **E20.** ▸**b** PHYSICS & CHEMISTRY. Suppress (a property or effect, esp. luminescence or electronic angular momentum); de-excite (an atom). **E20.** ▸**c** Damp (successive discharges in a radiation counter); damp the discharges in (a counter). **M20.**

> 🕮 **1** S. BECKETT His efforts to rekindle the light that Nelly had quenched. N. GORDIMER The embers of the cooking-fires had been quenched by the rain. ***quench a person's light***: see LIGHT *noun.* **2a** T. CAPOTE She did not quench the old woman's curiosity. M. SEYMOUR A couple of months . . had been enough to quench her enthusiasm for country life. **b** H. ARENDT The thirst for power could be quenched only through destruction. B. TRAPIDO We quenched our thirst on tumblers of frozen black coffee. **3b** L. M. MONTGOMERY She . . quenched Anne by a curt command to hold her tongue. W. GOLDING A . . roar from the quarterdeck quenched him like a bucket of cold water.

▶ **II** *verb intrans.* †**6** Of a fire, light, etc.: be extinguished; *fig.* come to an end, disappear. **ME–M17.** ▸**b** Of a person: cool down. *rare* (Shakes.). Only in **E17.**
7 PHYSICS. Change from a superconducting to a non-superconducting state. **M20.**
▶ **B** *noun.* **1** The action or an act of quenching; the state or fact of being quenched. **E16.**
2 ELECTRONICS. The process of stopping an oscillation, esp. in a superregenerative receiver; a signal used for this. Freq. *attrib.* **M20.**
Comb.: **quench ageing** METALLURGY improvements in the properties of steel, esp. hardening, which occur after the metal has been rapidly quenched from a high temperature; **quench-cracking** METALLURGY fracture of a metal caused by thermal stresses during rapid cooling; **quench hardening** METALLURGY hardening of steel by holding it at high temperature for some time and then quenching rapidly.
■ **quenchable** *adjective* (earlier in UNQUENCHABLE) **E17.** **quencher** *noun* a person or thing which quenches something; *colloq.* a drink: **LME.** **quenchless** *adjective* that cannot be quenched **M16.**

quenelle /kəˈnɛl/ *noun.* **M19.**
[French, of unkn. origin.]
A seasoned ball or roll of meat or fish ground to a paste.

quercetin /ˈkwəːsɪtɪn/ *noun.* **M19.**
[Prob. from Latin *quercetum* oak grove (from *quercus* oak: see -ETUM) + -IN[1].]
CHEMISTRY. A yellow crystalline pigment, 3, 3′, 4′, 5, 7-pentahydroxyflavone, $C_{15}H_{10}O_7$, found in plants and used as a food supplement to reduce allergic responses or boost immunity.

quercine /ˈkwəːsʌɪn/ *adjective.* **M17.**
[Latin *quercinus*, from *quercus* oak: see -INE[1].]
Of, pertaining to, or made of oak.

quercitron /ˈkwəːsɪtr(ə)n/ *noun.* **L18.**
[Blend of Latin *quercus* oak + CITRON.]
The black oak of the southern US, *Quercus velutina* (also ***quercitron oak***); (more fully ***quercitron bark***) the inner bark of this, used as a source of the dye quercitrin and in tanning.
Comb.: **quercitron lake**, **quercitron yellow** = QUERCITRIN.
■ **quercitrin** *noun* the pale yellow crystalline pigment of quercitron bark, quercetin 3-rhamnoside, $C_{21}H_{20}O_{11}$, which yields quercetin and rhamnose on hydrolysis **M19.**

quere /ˈkwɪə/ *verb*[1] *trans. & intrans.* Long *arch. rare.* **ME.**
[Old French *querre* (mod. *querir*) from Latin *quaerere* ask.]
Ask; inquire.

†**quere** *verb*[2] *& noun* see QUAERE.

querencia /keˈrenθja/ *noun.* **M20.**
[Spanish = lair, haunt, home ground, from *querer*: see QUERIDA.]
1 BULLFIGHTING. The part of the arena where the bull takes its stand. **M20.**
2 *fig.* A person's home ground, a refuge. **M20.**

querent /ˈkwɪər(ə)nt/ *noun.* **L16.**
[Latin *quaerent-* pres. ppl stem of *quaerere* inquire: see -ENT.]
A person who inquires; *spec.* a person who consults an astrologer.

querida /keˈriða/ *noun.* Masc. **-do** /-ðo/, pl. **-os** /-ɔs/. **M19.**
[Spanish from *querido* pa. pple of *querer* desire, love from Latin *quaerere* seek, inquire.]
In Spain and Spanish-speaking countries: a sweetheart; a darling. Freq. as a form of address.

querimonious /kwɛrɪˈməʊnɪəs/ *adjective. arch.* **E17.**
[from medieval Latin *querimoniosus*, from Latin *querimonia*: see next, -OUS.]
Full of complaints; given to complaining.

querimony /ˈkwɛrɪməni/ *noun. arch.* **LME.**
[Latin *quaerimonia*, from *queri* complain: see -Y[3].]
(A) complaint, complaining.

querist /ˈkwɪərɪst/ *noun.* **M17.**
[from Latin *quaerere* inquire + -IST.]
A person who inquires; a questioner.

querken /ˈkwəːk(ə)n/ *verb trans. obsolete* exc. *dial.* **LME.**
[Prob. from Old Norse *kvirkja*, *kyrkja* (from *kverk* throat) or Old Frisian *querka*: see -EN[5].]
Choke; suffocate.

querl /kwəːl/ *verb & noun. US.* Also **quirl**. **L18.**
[Prob. var. of CURL *verb* or from German *Querl*, *Quirl* from Middle High German *twirl*.]
▶ **A** *verb intrans. & trans.* Twist, coil. **L18.**
▶ **B** *noun.* A curl, a twist. **M19.**

quern /kwəːn/ *noun.*
[Old English *cweorn(e)* = Old Frisian, Old Saxon *quern* (Dutch *kweern*), Old High German *quirn(a)*, Old Norse *kvern*, Gothic *-qairnus*, from Germanic.]
A hand-mill for grinding corn, *esp.* one consisting of two circular stones. Also, a small hand-mill for grinding pepper etc.
rotary quern: see ROTARY *adjective.*
Comb.: **quern-stone** a millstone.

†**querry** *noun* var. of EQUERRY.

querulous /ˈkwɛrʊləs, -jʊləs/ *adjective.* **L15.**
[from late Latin *querulosus* or Latin *querulus*, from Latin *queri* complain: see -ULOUS.]
1 Given to complaining; full of complaints; peevish. **L15.** ▸**b** Of an animal etc.: producing sounds suggestive of complaint. **M17.**
2 Expressing complaint; characterized by complaining. **M16.**

> 🕮 **1** D. ROWE Sick people can be querulous and difficult. P. TOYNBEE If I am ill and in pain I shall die in querulous misery. **2** C. BLACKWOOD Grumbling relentlessly in their high-pitched querulous tones. B. BAINBRIDGE The baby . . , bored and fretful, was uttering querulous little cries.

■ **querulist** *noun* (*rare*) a person who complains **L18.** **queˈrulity** *noun* (*rare*) the habit of complaining **M19.** **querulously** *adverb* **M17.** **querulousness** *noun* **M17.**

query /ˈkwɪəri/ *noun & verb.* **M17.**
[Anglicized from *quere* obsolete var. of QUAERE.]
▶ **A** *noun.* A question, esp. one expressing some doubt or objection; (chiefly TYPOGRAPHY) a question mark (?). Also used to introduce a question or to question the accuracy or validity of any following word or statement (partly repr. the verb in *imper.*, partly a spoken substitute for the symbol ?). **M17.**

> 🕮 R. LEHMANN 'You reminded me of someone I once knew . . .' (Query her sister?) N. YOUNG He punctured the . . rhetoric of the conference with simple incisive queries. H. KISSINGER His queries had been answered several times.

Comb.: **query language** COMPUTING a language for the specification of procedures for the retrieval (and sometimes also modification) of information from a database.
▶ **B** *verb.* **1** *verb trans.* Put as a question. Long *rare* or *obsolete.* **M17.**
2 *verb trans.* Ask, inquire, (*whether*, *if*, *what*, etc., in *imper.* now also interpreted as *noun*). Also with direct speech as obj. **M17.** ▸**b** *verb intrans.* Ask a question or questions. **L17.**
3 Ask a question of (a person). Now chiefly *US.* **M17.**
4 Question the accuracy of; mark as doubtful. **L18.**

> 🕮 **2** HOR. WALPOLE Should not one query whether he had . . those proofs . . antecedent to the cabinet? L. M. MONTGOMERY 'Did you hear what I said, Anne?' queried Mr. Phillips. **3** *Daily Times (Lagos)* When these officers were queried, they felt unhappy. **4** C. HAMPTON The Company's final decision And it wasn't for him to query it. M. FORSTER Mrs Jameson's mind was sharp and . . she queried all received ideas.

■ **querier** *noun* (*rare*) **L17.** **querying** *noun* the action of the verb; an instance of this, a query: **L19.** **queryingly** *adverb* in a querying manner **L19.**

quesadilla /kesaˈðiʎa, keɪsəˈdiːljə/ *noun.* Pl. **-as** /-as, -əz/. **M20.**
[Spanish.]
A tortilla stuffed with cheese (or occas. other filling) and heated.

quesited /kwɪˈsʌɪtɪd/ *adjective & noun. rare.* **M17.**
[from medieval Latin *quesitum* (from Latin *quaesitum* neut. pa. pple of *quaerere* seek, inquire) + -ED[1].]
ASTROLOGY. ▶†**A** *adjective.* Inquired about. **M–L17.**
▶ **B** *noun.* The thing or person inquired about. **M17.**

quest /kwɛst/ *noun.* **ME.**
[Old French *queste* (mod. *quête*), from Proto-Romance var. of Latin *quaesita* use as noun of fem. pa. pple of *quaerere* seek, inquire.]
▶ **I 1** = INQUEST *noun* 1. *obsolete* exc. *dial.* **ME.**
2 = INQUEST *noun* 2. Now *rare.* **ME.**
3 Any inquiry or investigation; the object of this. **L16.**
▶ **II 4** A search; the action of searching. **ME.** ▸†**b** A person or group engaged in searching. *rare* (Shakes.). Only in **E17.**
5 The search for game made by hounds; the baying of hounds in pursuit or sight of game. *obsolete* exc. *dial.* **ME.**
6 In medieval romance: an expedition or adventure made by a knight or group of knights to obtain some thing or achieve some exploit. **LME.**
7 ROMAN CATHOLIC CHURCH. The collection of donations. **E16.**

> 🕮 **4** J. BUCHAN They were looking for me and I wished them joy of their quest. M. L. KING Oppressed people in their quest for freedom. E. BLISHEN We might . . go in quest of leaf-mould, in our local woods. **6** C. KINGSLEY By the laws of chivalry . . you must fulfil my quest. *transf.*: A. BROOKNER This search, for him, has become a mythic quest.

Comb.: **questman** †(**a**) a person appointed to undertake or participate in an official inquiry; (**b**) ECCLESIASTICAL (*obsolete* exc. *Hist.*) a churchwarden's assistant.

quest /kwɛst/ *verb.* **ME.**
[Old French *quester* (mod. *quêter*), from *queste*: see prec.]
1 *verb intrans.* Of a hound: search (*about*) for game (*obsolete* exc. *dial.*); bay at the sight of game. **ME.**
2 *verb intrans.* Go (*about*) in search of something; search. Also foll. by *after*, *for.* **E17.** ▸**b** ROMAN CATHOLIC CHURCH. Ask for donations. **M18.**
3 *verb trans.* Search for, pursue. *poet.* **M18.**

> 🕮 **2** I. FLEMING Beneath his conscious thoughts his senses were questing for enemies. E. BOWEN A car could be heard going slowly by, turning and coming past again, still questing. **3** *American Poetry Review* They deliberately quest wisdom.

■ †**questant** *noun* (*rare*, Shakes.) = QUESTER: only in **E17.** **questingly** *adverb* in a questing manner **E20.**

quester /ˈkwɛstə/ *noun.* **M16.**
[from prec. + -ER[1].]
A person who quests.

question /ˈkwɛstʃ(ə)n/ *noun.* **ME.**
[Anglo-Norman *questiun*, Old & mod. French *question* from Latin *quaestio(n-)*, from *quaest-* pa. ppl stem of *quaerere* seek, inquire: see -ION.]
▶ **I** What is inquired (about).
1 A sentence worded or expressed in a form such as to elicit information from a person; inquiry. **ME.** ▸**b** In *pl.* The catechism. *Scot.* **L18.**
2 The interrogative statement of a point to be investigated; a problem, a difficulty; a doubt; *gen.* a matter forming or capable of forming the basis of a problem. Also (foll. by *of*), a matter or concern depending on or involving a specified condition or thing. **ME.** ▸**b** *spec.* A subject or proposal to be debated, decided, or voted on, in a meeting or deliberative assembly, esp. Parliament. **M16.**
3 A dispute (*between* parties). Now *rare.* **LME.**

> 🕮 **1** GOLDSMITH Ask me no questions and I'll tell you no fibs. C. ISHERWOOD Excused from having to ask those ghastly sickroom questions. **2** R. MACAULAY It was now only a question of time; she would recover. *Scotsman* A number of important questions which he is likely to raise. G. F. KENNAN The Russian question was not on the agenda . . but the senior statesmen could scarcely fail to talk about it. A. PRICE Devious and ruthless men, no question about that. A. CROSS The question is . . whether to believe him at all. *Tennis World* The game today is more a question of service and return. **3** W. CRUISE A question arose between the heir at law and the younger children.

▶ **II** The action of inquiring.

4 The stating or investigation of a problem; inquiry into a matter; the expression of some doubt; discussion of a doubtful point. LME.
5 The action of questioning a person; the fact of being questioned; judicial examination; interrogation. Formerly also, talk, discourse. *arch.* LME. ▸**b** *Hist.* ***the question***, torture as part of interrogation. L16.

📖 **4** F. SPALDING She throws into question accepted literary values. A. STORR Various details of the Oedipus theory are open to question. **5** TENNYSON Fixing full eyes of question on her face.

Phrases: ***a good question***: see GOOD *adjective*. ***beg the question***: see BEG *verb* 4. **beyond question**, **beyond all question** undoubtedly. ***call in question***, ***call into question***: see CALL *verb*. ***categorical question***: see CATEGORICAL *adjective*. **come into question** be discussed, be a practical proposition. ***direct question***: see DIRECT *adjective*. ***Homeric question***. ***indirect question***. **in question** (*a*) that is being discussed or referred to; (*b*) in dispute (now chiefly in ***call in question***). ***leading question***: see LEADING *adjective*. **no question of** no possibility of. **no questions asked** with no need to account for one's conduct etc. ***open question***: see OPEN *adjective*. **out of the question** too impracticable to be considered or discussed, impossible. ***pop the question***: see POP *verb* 2b. ***previous question***: see PREVIOUS *adjective*. **put the question** require members of a deliberative assembly or meeting to vote on a proposal. ***rhetorical question***: see RHETORICAL 1. ***unstarred question***. **without question** undoubtedly. ***x-question***: see X, x 5e.
Comb.: **question mark** (*a*) a punctuation mark (?) indicating a question; (*b*) *fig.* a doubtful point or matter, an unresolved problem; a person about whom there is some mystery or doubt; **question-master** a person who presides over a quiz game etc.; **question time** a period during parliamentary proceedings when MPs may question ministers; **question word** an interrogative pronoun etc., used to introduce a question.

question /ˈkwɛstʃ(ə)n/ *verb*. LME.
[Old & mod. French *questionner*, from *question*: see prec.]
1 *verb trans.* & †*intrans.* (with *with*). Ask a question or questions of; *fig.* seek information from the study of (phenomena, facts). LME. ▸**b** *verb trans.* Examine judicially, interrogate; accuse (*of*). Now *rare*. E17.
2 *verb trans.* Raise the question (*if, whether*); doubt. M16.
3 *verb intrans.* Ask questions. L16.
4 *verb trans.* Ask (*how, what*, etc.). Now only with direct speech as obj. L16.
†**5** *verb trans.* Ask or inquire about. *rare*. L16–M17.
6 *verb trans.* Call in question, dispute. M17. ▸**b** Bring into question, make doubtful. *rare*. M17.

📖 **1** J. STEINBECK The friends . . questioned one another with their eyes. E. LONGFORD I questioned John half a century later about that suit. JOAN SMITH An unidentified man was still being questioned in connection with Puddephat's murder. **b** LD MACAULAY Questioned before any tribunal. **2** LYNDON B. JOHNSON *The New York Times* questioned whether the moon program was justified. **3** POPE I scarce uplift my eyes, Nor dare to question. **4** E. BLAIR 'Who's Harry Pollitt?' she questioned. **6** J. A. FROUDE Any one who openly questioned the truth of Christianity was treated as a public offender. A. S. NEILL Don't question anything—just obey.

■ **questio'nee** *noun* a person who is questioned M19. **questioner** *noun* LME. **questioningly** *adverb* in a questioning manner M19.

questionable /ˈkwɛstʃ(ə)nəb(ə)l/ *adjective*. LME.
[from prec. + -ABLE.]
1 a That may be called in question; open to dispute; doubtful as regards truth or quality. LME. ▸**b** Of obscure meaning. *rare*. M18. ▸**c** Of doubtful nature, character, or quality; not clearly in accordance with honesty, honour, respectability, wisdom, etc. E19.
†**2** Of a person: of whom questions may be asked. *rare* (Shakes.). Only in E17.
†**3** Liable to be called to account or examined with judicially. M–L17.

📖 **1a** J. BERMAN He uses questionable logic that he passes off as profound psychological truth. L. KENNEDY To say that she did not love me is questionable. **c** A. THWAITE She cast a cold eye on Edmund, as one of Louis' questionable English friends. *Natural History* Alleging that their money was made by dealing in illicit products or using questionable methods.

■ **questiona'bility** *noun* M19. **questionableness** *noun* M17. **questionably** *adverb* M19.

†**questionary** *noun*¹. *rare*. LME.
[medieval Latin *questionarius*, from Latin *quaestio(n-)* QUESTION *noun*: see -ARY¹.]
1 = QUESTIONIST. LME–L18.
2 = QUESTOR 1. *rare*. Only in E19.

questionary /ˈkwɛstʃ(ə)n(ə)ri/ *noun*². Now *rare* exc. MEDICINE. M16.
[medieval Latin *questionarium*; reintroduced in L19 from French *questionnaire*: see -ARY¹.]
Orig. (*rare*), a catechism. Now = QUESTIONNAIRE.

questionary /ˈkwɛstʃ(ə)n(ə)ri/ *adjective*. M17.
[App. from QUESTION *noun* + -ARY¹.]
Having the form of a question; conducted by means of questioning.

questionist /ˈkwɛstʃ(ə)nɪst/ *noun*. E16.
[medieval Latin *questionista*, from Latin *quaestio(n-)* QUESTION *noun* + -IST.]
1 A habitual questioner, *spec.* in theological matters. E16.
2 *Hist.* At Cambridge and Harvard universities: an undergraduate in the last term before final examinations. L16.

questionless /ˈkwɛstʃ(ə)nlɪs/ *adverb & adjective*. LME.
[from QUESTION *noun* + -LESS.]
▸ **A** *adverb*. Without question; undoubtedly. Now *rare*. LME.
▸ **B** *adjective*. **1** Not admitting of question; indubitable. M16.
2 That asks no questions, unquestioning. L19.
■ **questionlessly** *adverb* (*a*) undoubtedly; (*b*) without asking questions: M17.

questionnaire /kwɛstʃəˈnɛː, kɛstjə-/ *noun*. L19.
[French, from *questionner* QUESTION *verb* + *-aire* -ARY¹.]
A formulated series of questions by which information is sought from a selected group, usu. for statistical analysis; a document containing these.

questor /ˈkwɛstə/ *noun*. LME.
[medieval Latin, or Latin QUAESTOR.]
1 ROMAN CATHOLIC CHURCH. An official appointed to grant indulgences on the gift of alms to the Church. LME.
2 In France: any of the treasurers of the National Assembly. M19. ▸**b** = QUESTORE. *rare*. M19.
3 A person who quests or searches for something. L19.

questore /kwesˈtoːre/ *noun*. Pl. ***-ri*** /-ri/. M20.
[Italian, formed as prec.]
In Italy: a chief of police.

†**questrist** *noun*. *rare* (Shakes.). Only in E17.
[from QUESTER + -IST.]
A person who goes in quest of another.

questura /kwesˈtuːra/ *noun*. Pl. ***-re*** /-re/. E20.
[Italian from Latin *quaestura*, formed as QUAESTOR.]
In Italy: a police station; the police.

quetch /kwɛtʃ/ *verb*. *obsolete* exc. *dial.*
[Old English *cweċċan* causative from QUAKE *verb*. Cf. SQUITCH *verb*.]
†**1** *verb trans.* Shake, brandish. OE–ME. ▸**b** *verb intrans.* Of a thing: shake, tremble. Only in ME.
†**2** *verb intrans.* Go, travel. Only in ME.
3 *verb intrans.* Twitch; move (a part of) the body. Later *esp.*, shrink; wince. Usu. in neg. contexts. ME. ▸**b** Utter a sound. Usu. in neg. contexts. M16.

quête /kɛt/ *noun*. E20.
[French = quest.]
The traditional act of begging for food or alms to the accompaniment of folk-song.

†**quethe** *verb*. Pa. t. QUOTH.
[Old English *cweþan* = Old Frisian *qwetha*, Old Saxon *queþan*, Old High German *quedan*, Old Norse *kveða*, Gothic *qiþan*, from Germanic.]
1 *verb trans.* & (*rare*) *intrans.* Say, tell, declare, (something). OE–M16.
2 *verb trans.* Bequeath. ME–M16.

quetsch /kvɛtʃ, kwɛtʃ/ *noun*. M19.
[German *Quetsche* dial. form of *Zwetsche* plum.]
An oval dark-skinned variety of plum; the tree bearing this fruit. Also, a liqueur made from these plums.

quetzal /ˈkɛts(ə)l/ *noun*. Pl. **-zals**, in sense 2 **quetzales** /kɛtˈsɑːlɪz/. E19.
[Spanish (also (earlier) *quetzale*), from Aztec *quetzalli* brightly coloured tail feather.]
1 Any of various Central and S. American trogons of the genus *Pharomachrus*, the males of which are noted for their iridescent green plumage with red to yellow underparts, *esp.* (more fully ***resplendent quetzal***) *P. mocinno*, which has extremely long tail coverts. E19.
2 The basic monetary unit of Guatemala, equal to 100 centavos. E20.

queue /kjuː/ *noun*. See also CUE *noun*³. L16.
[French, ult. from Latin *cauda* tail; branch II perh. a different word.]
▸ **I 1** HERALDRY. The tail of an animal. L16.
2 A plait of hair worn at the back; a pigtail. M18.
3 A line of people, vehicles, etc., awaiting their turn to proceed, be attended to, etc. M19. ▸**b** COMPUTING. A list of data items, commands, etc., stored in such a way that they are only retrievable in a definite order (either the order of storage or its reverse). M20.
4 *Hist.* A support for the butt of a lance. M19.

📖 **1 queue fourché(e)** having a forked or double tail. **3** E. FIGES The queue of office employees at the bus stop. *transf.*: *Listener* The railways had to take their place in the queue after housing. ***jump the queue***: see JUMP *verb*.

▸ **II 5** Chiefly *Hist.* A barrel holding approx. one and a half hogsheads of wine; this quantity of wine. L18.
Comb.: **queue-jump** *verb intrans.* go ahead of one's position in a queue (chiefly as ***queue-jumping*** *verbal noun*); **queue-jumper** a person who queue-jumps.

■ **queued** *adjective* (HERALDRY) (of an animal) having a tail, *spec.* of a different colour from that of the body L17.

queue /kjuː/ *verb*. Pres. pple & verbal noun **queuing**, **queueing**. L18.
[from the noun.]
1 *verb trans.* Put up (the hair) in a queue or pigtail. L18.
2 *verb intrans.* **a** Move along in line. Foll. by *in*. *rare*. L19. ▸**b** Stand or take one's place in a queue; form a queue. Also foll. by *up*. E20. ▸**c** *verb trans.* Arrange in line (as) in a queue or queues. E20.

📖 **2b** A. BROOKNER She liked queuing for the bus. G. SWIFT People queued up for hours.

Comb.: **queue theory** the statistical investigation of the structure and behaviour of queues.
■ **queuer** *noun* a person who queues M20.

quey /kweɪ/ *noun*. *Scot.* & *north*. LME.
[Old Norse *kviga*, app. from *ku* cow.]
A young cow before it has had a calf.

quia timet /kwiːə ˈtɪmɛt/ *adverbial & adjectival phr.* E17.
[Latin, lit. 'because he or she fears'.]
LAW. ▸ **A** *adverbial phr.* So as to prevent a possible future injury. E17.
▸ **B** *adjectival phr.* Of an injunction: brought for this purpose. L17.

†**quib** *noun*. M16.
[Prob. from Latin *quibus* dat. and abl. pl. of *qui, quae, quod* who, what, which, as a word frequently occurring in legal documents and so associated with verbal niceties or subtle distinctions.]
1 = QUIBBLE *noun* 2. M16–E17.
2 A gibe, a taunt. *rare*. M17–E19.

quibble /ˈkwɪb(ə)l/ *noun*. E17.
[Dim. of prec.: see -LE¹.]
1 A play on words, a pun. *arch*. E17.
2 An evasion of the point at issue; an insubstantial argument depending on an ambiguity etc.; a petty objection, a trivial point of criticism. L17. ▸**b** The use of quibbles. E18.

📖 **2** *Business Traveller* My only complaints are quibbles . . there is no telephone in the bathroom.

quibble /ˈkwɪb(ə)l/ *verb*¹ *intrans.* E17.
[from the noun.]
†**1** Play on words, pun. E17–M18.
2 Raise a petty objection; argue about a triviality; evade the point at issue by a quibble. M17.

📖 **2** E. H. GOMBRICH Quibbling with very subtle and unreal distinctions. L. GRANT-ADAMSON Her work took too long . . But he was not going to quibble about it.

■ **quibbler** *noun* L17. **quibbling** *noun* the action of the verb; an instance of this, a quibble: E17. **quibblingly** *adverb* in a quibbling manner M17.

quibble /ˈkwɪb(ə)l/ *verb*² *intrans.* *obsolete* exc. *dial.* E18.
[Perh. imit.]
Quiver; shake.

†**quiblet** *noun*. M17–L19.
[from QUIB or QUIBBLE *noun*: see -LET.]
= QUIBBLE *noun*.

quiche /kiːʃ/ *noun*. M20.
[French from Alsatian dial. *Küchen* (German *Kuchen* cake).]
An open flan consisting of a pastry case filled with a savoury mixture of milk, eggs, and other ingredients, and baked until firm.
quiche Lorraine /lɒˈreɪn/ a quiche made with bacon and cheese.

Quiché /kiːˈtʃeɪ/ *noun & adjective*. E19.
[Quiché.]
▸ **A** *noun*. Pl. **-s**, same. A member of a people inhabiting the western highlands of Guatemala; the Mayan language of this people. E19.
▸ **B** *adjective*. Of or pertaining to this people or their language. E19.
■ **Quichean** *adjective & noun* (designating) the subgroup of the Mayan language family to which Quiché belongs M20.

Quichua *noun & adjective* var. of QUECHUA.

quick /kwɪk/ *noun*¹. OE.
[Absol. use of the adjective.]
1 *collect.* Those or all who are living. Chiefly with *the*. OE. ▸†**b** That which is alive. OE–ME.
2 A living thing. *rare* (now *dial.*). OE.
3 *collect.* Hedging consisting of living plants (as opp. to dead wood), *spec.* hawthorn; any of the plants forming such hedging. ME.
4 *The* tender or sensitive flesh in a part of the body, *esp.* that under the nails, or surrounding a sore or wound; *the* sensitive part of a horse's foot, above the hoof. L15. ▸**b** *fig.* *The* central, vital, or most sensitive part; the seat of feeling or emotion. E16.
5 *The* life; living semblance. Chiefly in **to the quick**. M16.
6 CRICKET. A fast bowler. M20.

📖 **1** W. Trevor The wishes of the departed take precedence over those of the quick. **4** N. Lowndes Her nails were bitten down to the quick. **b** V. Woolf The scene . . does . . come so close to the quick of the mind. A. Maupin The tableau cut Brian to the quick, underscoring everything that was missing from his life.

quick /kwɪk/ *noun*[2]. **LME.**
[North. form of QUITCH: cf. QUICKEN *noun*[2].]
collect. sing. & in *pl.* Weedy grasses with creeping rhizomes; *esp.* couch grass.
Comb.: **quick-grass** (*a*) = QUICK *noun*[2]; (*b*) *S. Afr.* = KWEEK.

quick /kwɪk/ *adjective & adverb.*
[Old English *cwic(u)* = Old Frisian, Old Saxon *quik* (Dutch *kwik*), Old High German *quek* (German *keck*, dial. *kweck* lively, sprightly), Old Norse *kvikr*, Gothic *qius*, from Germanic from Indo-European base repr. also by Latin *vivus*.]
▶ **A** *adjective.* **I** Characterized by the presence of life.
1 Living, animate. Now *arch.* & *dial.* **OE.** ▸†**b** Of property: consisting of animals; live. **OE–M18.**
2 In a live state, alive. Now *arch.* & *dial.* **OE.**
3 Of (a part of) a plant: alive, growing. Of a hedge: consisting of living plants, esp. hawthorn (cf. QUICKSET). **OE.**
4 a Orig., pregnant with a live foetus. Later *spec.*, at a stage of pregnancy when movements of the foetus have been felt. Chiefly & now only in ***quick with child***. *arch.* **LME.** ▸**b** *fig.* Alive *with* some feeling or quality. Passing into sense 12 below. **M19.**

📖 **4b** W. H. Dixon In Barcelona everyone was quick with rage.

▶ **II** Having a quality characteristic or suggestive of a living thing.
5 Of a spring, stream, etc.: running, flowing. Now *rare* exc. in ***quick water*** below. **OE.** ▸**b** *MINING.* Of a vein etc: containing ore, productive. **L17.** ▸**c** Of stock, capital, etc.: productive of interest, profitable. **E18.**
6 Of a coal: live, burning. Now only (*arch.*), of a fire: burning strongly. **OE.** ▸†**b** Of sulphur: readily flammable, fiery. **ME–M17.**
7 Of soil etc.: mobile, shifting, readily yielding to pressure. Cf. QUICKSAND. **ME.**
†**8** (Of speech, writing, etc.) lively, full of wit or acute reasoning; (of a place or time) full of activity, busy. **ME–M18.**
9 †**a** (Of colour) bright; (of the complexion) ruddy, fresh. **ME–L17.** ▸**b** Of a feeling: keen, strongly felt. Formerly also, of a thing seen: lifelike, vivid. *arch.* **ME.**
10 †**a** (Of a taste or smell) sharp, pungent; (of a thing) having a sharp taste or smell. **L16–L18.** ▸†**b** Of speech or writing: sharp, caustic. **L16–M18.** ▸**c** Of air or light: sharp, piercing. *poet. rare.* **E17.**
▶ **III** Distinguished by or capable of prompt or rapid action or movement.
11 Mentally active or agile; prompt to understand, learn, think, etc.; acute, intelligent, alert. **OE.** ▸**b** Of the eye, ear, etc.: keenly perceptive; capable of ready perception. **LME.**
12 Full of vigour or energy (now *rare*); prompt to do something; able to do something with speed. Passing into sense 13. **ME.**
13 Moving or able to move with speed; rapid, swift. **ME.**
14 Of an action, occurrence, etc.: that is done or happens rapidly or with speed, or with a short interval; *esp.* that is over or completed within a short space of time. **M16.**
15 a Hasty, impatient, hot-tempered. *obsolete* exc. *dial.* **M16.** ▸**b** Of a temper: easily roused. **M19.**
16 Of a bend, turn, etc.: sharp. **E18.**

📖 **11** H. James An alertness of action that matched her quick intelligence. R. Hoggart A smart young son with a quick brain. G. Charles 'I take it she was your Personal Assistant.' . . 'How very quick of you.' **b** *Cornhill Magazine* The quick ear of Midwinter detected something wrong in the tone of Brock's voice. **12** Tennyson The quick lark's closest-caroll'd strains. E. Jolley She was not very quick at arithmetic and it took a little time to do the addition. M. Forster Miss Mitford . . was . . quick to spot new talent. **13** Shelley The young stars glance Between the quick bats in their twilight dance. A. Christie He turned sharply . . . But he was not quick enough. **14** R. Graves A plunge in the swimming pool and a quick lunch. *Scientific American* The needle is held . . to the skin and 15 quick punctures are made. J. Harvey Forbes smiled again the quick tired smile.

▶ **B** *adverb.* = QUICKLY. Now *non-standard* exc. in *imper.* use (also interpretable as the adjective with *be* understood), in certain idioms, and in comb. **ME.**

📖 J. Buchan Get us some food, . . for we're starving. Quick, man. *Listener* I've never known a journey go so quick. *Times* The brash and selfish values of a 'get rich quick' society.

Comb., special collocations, & phrases: ***a quick buck***: see BUCK *noun*[8]; ***be quick off the mark***: see MARK *noun*[1]; **quick-and-dirty** *adjective* (*colloq.*, chiefly *N. Amer.*) makeshift, done etc. hastily; **quick bread** bread or cake made with a leavening agent that permits immediate baking; **quick-break** *adjective* (of a switch or its action) designed to break an electric circuit quickly regardless of the speed at which it is operated; **quick-change** *adjective* (of an actor etc.) changing costume etc. quickly during a performance in order to play a different part; **quick-clay** clay that may spontaneously liquefy and flow down a gentle slope under certain conditions; **quick death** *US* (*a*) an unexpected or sudden death; (*b*) = ***sudden death*** s.v. SUDDEN *adjective*; **quick-eyed** *adjective* keen-sighted; **quick-fire** *adjective* (*a*) (of a gun) that can fire shots in rapid succession; (*b*) (of repartee etc.) rapid, in rapid succession; **quick-firer** a quick-fire gun; **quick-firing** *adjective* = ***quick-fire*** (*a*) above; **quick fix** *colloq.* a speedy solution to a problem, likely to prove inadequate in the long term; **quick-freeze** *verb & noun* (*a*) *verb trans.* freeze (food etc.) rapidly for storage; deep-freeze; (*b*) *noun* the process of quick-freezing food etc.; **quickgold** (chiefly *literary*) liquid gold; **quick kill** a sudden or quick victory; **quick-knit** *adjective* (*a*) (of wool) consisting of several strands giving a thick yarn with which a garment can be knitted quickly; (*b*) (of a garment) made with such wool; **quick-loader** a device to enable a gun to be loaded quickly; **quick-look** *adjective* involving the rapid provision of information, esp. from a satellite or spacecraft; **quick march** *MILITARY* a march in quick time; the order to march at this pace; **quick-match** a quick-burning fuse used for firing cannon, igniting fireworks, etc.; **quick one** *colloq.* a drink, esp. an alcoholic one, intended to be taken rapidly; ***quick on the trigger***: see TRIGGER *noun*[1] 1; **quick-reference** *adjective* giving quick and easy access to information; **quick-release** *adjective* (of a device) designed for rapid release; **quick-return** *adjective* (of a mechanism etc.) in which the speed in one direction is greater than the speed in the other; **quick-sighted** *adjective* keen-sighted; **quick-sticks** *slang* quickly, without delay (also ***in quick-sticks***); **quick succession** *LAW* a change in ownership of property twice within a limited period; **quickthorn** thorny bushes used for hedging; *spec.* hawthorn; **quick time** *MILITARY* a brisk marching pace consisting of about 120 steps per minute; *adverb* at this pace; **quick trick** *BRIDGE* (a card or combination of cards which should provide) a trick in the first or second round of the suit; **quick water** the part of a river etc. with a strong current.
■ **quickish** *adjective* **E20.** **quicklike** *adverb* (chiefly *US*) quickly **E20.**

quick /kwɪk/ *verb*[1]. Now *arch. rare.* **OE.**
[from QUICK *adjective & adverb.*]
†**1** *verb intrans.* = QUICKEN *verb* 1b. **OE–E16.**
†**2** *verb trans.* = QUICKEN *verb* 1a. **OE–LME.**
3 = QUICKEN *verb* 2b. **ME.**

quick /kwɪk/ *verb*[2] *trans.* **LME.**
[from QUICK *noun*[1], *adjective.*]
1 Provide with a quickset hedge. *rare.* Chiefly as ***quicking*** *verbal noun.* **LME.**
2 Coat with mercury by immersion. Chiefly as ***quicked*** *pa. pple*, ***quicking*** *verbal noun.* **M19.**

quickbeam /ˈkwɪkbiːm/ *noun. obsolete* exc. *dial.* **OE.**
[App. from QUICK *adjective* + BEAM *noun*. Cf. next.]
= next.

quicken /ˈkwɪk(ə)n/ *noun*[1]. Chiefly *north.* Also **whicken** /ˈwɪkən/. **ME.**
[App. from QUICK *adjective*, with unexpl. ending.]
The mountain ash, *Sorbus aucuparia*. Formerly also, the juniper, *Juniperus communis*. Also more fully ***quicken tree***.

quicken /ˈkwɪk(ə)n/ *noun*[2]. *Scot. & north.* **LME.**
[from QUICK *noun*[2] + -EN[2].]
Couch grass; in *pl.*, the creeping rhizomes of this and other grasses.

quicken /ˈkwɪk(ə)n/ *verb.* **ME.**
[from QUICK *adjective* + -EN[5].]
1 a *verb trans.* Give or restore life to; revive; animate. **ME.** ▸**b** *verb intrans.* Come to life, become living. Formerly also, revive. **ME.**
2 *fig.* **a** *verb intrans.* Come into a state of existence or activity comparable to life. **ME.** ▸**b** *verb trans.* Give or restore vigour to; stimulate, rouse. **LME.**
3 *verb trans.* Kindle (a fire); cause to burn strongly. *arch.* **ME.** ▸**b** *verb intrans.* Grow bright. *poet.* **E18.**
4 *verb intrans.* (Of a woman) reach the stage of pregnancy when movements of the foetus can be felt; (of a foetus) begin to move. **M16.**
5 *verb trans.* Make (a liquor or medicine) sharper or more stimulant. Now *rare* or *obsolete.* **L16.**
6 *verb trans. & intrans.* Make or become quicker, accelerate. **E17.** ▸**b** *verb trans.* Make (a curve) sharper; make (a slope) steeper. **E18.**

📖 **1a** Shelley Ill things Shall, with a spirit of unnatural life, Stir and be quickened. **b** Sir W. Scott The seed which is sown shall one day sprout and quicken. **2a** E. Waugh Her perennial optimism quickened within her and swelled to a great . . confidence. V. S. Naipaul Her tired face quickened with scorn. **b** P. G. Wodehouse Peril quickens the wit, and she had thought of a plan of action. J. Gathorne-Hardy The memory of childhood suffering quickened his sympathy in relation to the sufferings of . . children. **6** S. Middleton They . . began to quicken their pace, until . . they ran together.

■ **quickener** *noun* **LME.** **quickening** *noun* (*a*) the action of the verb; (*b*) *dial.* (a quantity of) yeast: **LME.**

quickhatch /ˈkwɪkhatʃ/ *noun.* **M18.**
[from Cree *kwi:hkoha:če:w*. Cf. CARCAJOU, KINKAJOU.]
The wolverine.

quickie /ˈkwɪki/ *noun & adjective. colloq.* **E20.**
[from QUICK *adjective* + -IE.]
▶ **A** *noun.* **1** Something made or done quickly; *spec.* (*a*) a drink, esp. an alcoholic one, taken quickly; (*b*) a brief or hurried act of sexual intercourse. **E20.**
2 *CRICKET.* A fast bowler. **M20.**
▶ **B** *attrib.* or as *adjective.* (Able to be) made or done quickly. **E20.**

quicklime /ˈkwɪklʌɪm/ *noun.* **LME.**
[from QUICK *adjective* + LIME *noun*[1], after Latin *calx viva*.]
= LIME *noun*[1] 3.

quickly /ˈkwɪkli/ *adverb.* **OE.**
[from QUICK *adjective* + -LY[2].]
†**1** In a lively manner; with animation or vigour. **OE–E19.** ▸**b** With quickness of perception. **OE–L16.** ▸**c** In a lifelike manner. **L15–E17.**
2 Rapidly; at a fast rate; within a short space of time; without delay, very soon. **ME.**

📖 **2** T. Hardy She moved about quickly as if anxious to save time. G. Greene He would rather die quickly than slowly suffocate. B. Pym 'I don't suppose I shall be in very much,' said Mrs. Napier quickly. A. Carter She stepped back quickly into the bushes.

quickness /ˈkwɪknɪs/ *noun.* **ME.**
[from QUICK *adjective* + -NESS.]
The quality of being quick; rapidity; an instance of this.

quicksand /ˈkwɪksand/ *noun.* **ME.**
[from QUICK *adjective* + SAND *noun*.]
1 (A bed of) loose wet sand, easily yielding to pressure and sucking in any object resting on it or falling into it. **ME.**
2 *fig.* A treacherous thing or (*rare*) person. **L16.**

📖 **2** P. Arrowsmith By confiding in her . . he had trodden unwarily into the quicksand of emotional dependence on her.

■ **quicksandy** *adjective* (*rare*) of the nature of (a) quicksand **E17.**

quickset /ˈkwɪksɛt/ *noun, adjective, & verb.* **L15.**
[from QUICK *adjective* + SET *noun*[1], *adjective*.]
▶ **A** *noun.* **1** *collect.* Live slips or cuttings of plants, esp. hawthorn, set in the ground to grow into a hedge. **L15.**
2 Such a slip or cutting; a hedge formed of such slips or cuttings. **E16.**
▶ **B** *adjective.* **1** Of a hedge etc.: formed of living plants. **M16.**
2 *fig.* Rough, bushy. **L16.**
▶†**C** *verb trans.* Infl. **-tt-**. Provide or plant with quickset. **E16–M18.**

quick-set /ˈkwɪksɛt/ *adjective.* **M20.**
[from QUICK *adverb* + SET *verb*[1].]
1 Designating a type of surveyor's level with a ball-and-socket joint in the levelling head to facilitate quick setting. **M20.**
2 That hardens or dries quickly. **M20.**

quicksilver /ˈkwɪksɪlvə/ *noun, adjective, & verb.* **OE.**
[from QUICK *adjective* + SILVER *noun*.]
▶ **A** *noun.* The liquid metal mercury. **OE.**

📖 *fig.*: Sir W. Scott Thou hast quicksilver in the veins of thee to a certainty.

▶ **B** *attrib.* or as *adjective.* **1** Of, pertaining to, or containing quicksilver. **M16.**
2 Resembling quicksilver in motion etc.; rapid, unpredictable. **M17.**

📖 **2** K. Douglas Kew Tinker's quicksilver dash and brilliance in action.

▶ **C** *verb.* Treat, imbue, or mix (as) with quicksilver, *esp.* coat (a mirror-glass) with an amalgam of tin. Earliest as ***quicksilvered*** *ppl adjective.* **L16.**
■ **quicksilvery** *adjective* resembling quicksilver **E17.**

quickstep /ˈkwɪkstɛp/ *noun & verb.* **E19.**
[from QUICK *adjective* + STEP *noun*[1].]
▶ **A** *noun.* **1** *MILITARY.* The step used in marching in quick time. **E19.**
2 *MUSIC.* A march in military quick time. **E19.**
3 A fast foxtrot in 4/4 time. **L19.**
▶ **B** *verb intrans.* Infl. **-pp-**.
1 March in quick time. **E20.**
2 Dance the quickstep. **M20.**

quick-witted /kwɪkˈwɪtɪd/ *adjective.* **M16.**
[from QUICK *adjective* + WITTED.]
Having a quick wit; quick to grasp, or react to, a situation; sharp; witty.
■ **quick-wittedness** *noun* **M19.**

Quicunque /kwiːˈkʊŋkweɪ/ *noun.* **L19.**
[formed as next or abbreviation of next.]
= next.

Quicunque vult /kwiːˈkʊŋkweɪ vʊlt/ *noun phr.* **LME.**
[Latin *quicunque* (also *quicumque*) *vult* (*salvus esse*) lit. 'whosoever will (be saved)', the opening words.]
The Athanasian Creed. Also ***Quicunque***.

quid /kwɪd/ *noun*¹. L16.
[Latin = what, anything, something, neut. sing. of *quis* who, anyone, etc.; in sense 3 abbreviation of TERTIUM QUID.]
†**1** = QUIDDITY 2. *rare*. Only in L16.
2 The nature of something; that which a thing is. E17.
3 *US HISTORY*. A section formed within the Republican Party, 1805–11. E19.

quid /kwɪd/ *noun*². *slang*. Pl. same, (*rare* exc. in **quids in**) -**s**. L17.
[Origin unkn.]
Orig., a sovereign; a guinea. Now, one pound sterling.
A. BURGESS I had fifty quid in fivers. **make a quid** *Austral. slang* earn money. **not the full quid** *Austral. & NZ slang* of low intelligence, not very bright. **quids in** *slang* in luck or profit.
■ **quidlet** *noun* (*slang*, now *rare*) = QUID *noun*² E20. **quidsworth** *noun* (*slang*) as much or as many as might be bought for one pound sterling M20.

quid /kwɪd/ *noun*³ & *verb*. E18.
[Var. of CUD *noun*.]
▶**A** *noun*. **1** A small piece of tobacco, gum, etc., for chewing. E18.
2 A cast or pellet regurgitated by a bird of prey. M19.
▶**B** *verb*. Infl. -**dd**-.
1 *verb intrans*. Chew tobacco; (of an animal) chew the cud. L18.
2 *verb trans. & intrans*. Of a horse: drop (partly-chewed food) from the mouth, esp. as a symptom of tooth decay. M19.

quiddany /ˈkwɪdəni/ *noun*. Long *obsolete* exc. *Hist*. E17.
[French †*codignat*, †*condoignac* (now *cotignac*), medieval Latin *condoniatum* var. of *cydoniatum*, from Latin *cydonia*: see QUINCE.]
A thick syrup or jelly made from fruit, esp. quinces.

quiddity /ˈkwɪdɪti/ *noun*. In sense 1 also in Latin form **quidditas** /ˈkwɪdɪtɑːs, -tas/; in sense 2 also (*arch*.) **quiddit**. LME.
[medieval Latin *quidditas*, formed as QUID *noun*¹ + -ITY. Cf. HAECCEITY, SEITY.]
1 Chiefly *PHILOSOPHY*. The inherent nature or essence of a person or thing; that which constitutes a person or thing. LME.
2 A nicety in argument; a quibble. Cf. QUODDITY. M16. ▸**b** Ability or tendency to use quiddities in argument. E17.
1 H. GARDNER The critic needs a sense of the work's quiddity or essence, its individuality. *Daily Telegraph* As people, the three characters have no personal quiddity, no individual tincture.
■ **quiddative** *adjective* (*rare*) of or pertaining to the quiddity or essence of a person or thing M17.

quiddle /ˈkwɪd(ə)l/ *verb & noun*. Now chiefly *dial. & US*. M16.
[Prob. from prec., after *fiddle* etc.]
▶**A** *verb intrans*. **1** Speak in a trifling way. M16.
2 Trifle or waste time *with*. M19.
▶**B** *noun*. A fastidious person. E19.

quidnunc /ˈkwɪdnʌŋk/ *noun*. *arch*. E18.
[Latin *quid nunc?* what now?]
An inquisitive person; a gossip; a newsmonger.

quid pro quo /kwɪd prəʊ ˈkwəʊ/ *noun phr*. M16.
[Latin = something for something.]
1 A thing (orig. a medicine) given or used in place of another; a substitute. M16. ▸**b** The action or fact of substituting one thing for another. Also, a mistake or blunder arising from such substitution. L17.
2 An action performed or thing given in return or exchange for another. L16.
2 *British Medical Journal* The quid pro quo by which . . academic staff treat patients and . . doctors teach students. *attrib*.: *Scientific American* Companies and unions have . . explored a quid-pro-quo arrangement.

quies *adjective* var. of QUAISS.

quiesce /kwɪˈɛs, kwʌɪ-/ *verb intrans*. E19.
[Latin *quiescere* be still, from *quies* quiet: see QUIET *noun*, -ESCE.]
Become quiescent; *spec*. (*SEMITIC GRAMMAR*) (of a consonant) become silent when following a vowel.

quiescence /kwɪˈɛs(ə)ns, kwʌɪ-/ *noun*. M17.
[Late Latin *quiescentia*, formed as QUIESCENT: see -ENCE.]
1 The state or condition of being quiescent; inertia, dormancy; an instance of this. M17.
2 *SEMITIC GRAMMAR*. The process of a consonant's becoming quiescent or silent. E19.
1 R. LINDNER A period of quiescence and recovery necessarily follows each high point in therapy. J. C. OATES Hiram's sleepwalking . . flared up again . . after some months of quiescence.
■ **quiescency** *noun* = QUIESCENCE *noun* 1 M17.

quiescent /kwɪˈɛs(ə)nt, kwʌɪ-/ *adjective & noun*. E17.
[Latin *quiescent*- pres. ppl stem of *quiescere* QUIESCE: see -ENT.]
▶**A** *adjective*. **1** *SEMITIC GRAMMAR*. Of a consonant: silent. Opp. ***movable***. E17.
2 Motionless, inert; dormant. M17.
3 *ELECTRONICS*. Corresponding to or characterized by the absence of input to a device ready to receive it. E20.
1 ***quiescent sheva***: see SHEVA 1. **2** I. MURDOCH In telling her the story he . . released . . the desire for her which had been quiescent before. M. FLANAGAN The ulcers had been quiescent for the past two weeks.
▶**B** *noun*. *SEMITIC GRAMMAR*. A quiescent consonant. E18.
■ **quiescently** *adverb* E19.

quiet /ˈkwʌɪət/ *noun*. ME.
[Old French *quieté*, Anglo-Norman *quiete*, from Latin *quiet*-, *quies* rest, repose, quiet.]
1 Absence of disturbance in social or political life; peace as opp. to war or strife. ME.
2 Freedom from personal disturbance or interruption, esp. by others; rest, repose. ME.
3 Absence of excessive noise or motion in the surrounding environment; silence; stillness, tranquillity. LME.
4 Freedom from mental agitation or excitement; peace of mind. *arch*. L15.
5 The condition of remaining quiet or refraining from excessive noise, exertion, etc. M16.
1 BURKE Why is not the nation's quiet secured? **2** A. PRICE Desperate to get back to the loving quiet of his home. P. AUSTER He wants to be left alone . . all he wants is peace and quiet. **3** H. ALLEN The profound quiet which precedes the first stir of dawn. K. ISHIGURO My country house and the quiet that surrounds it. **5** F. NORRIS Turbulent in trifling matters, when actual . . danger threatened he was of an abnormal quiet. A. LURIE She warned him to observe quiet in the hallways.
Phrases: **at quiet**, †**at a good quiet** (now *Scot*.) in a state of calm or repose; at rest. **on the quiet** *colloq*. privately, in secret; unobtrusively.

quiet /ˈkwʌɪət/ *adjective & adverb*. LME.
[Old French *quiet*(*e* from Latin *quietus* pa. pple of *quiescere* QUIESCE.]
▶**A** *adjective*. **I 1** Of a person or thing: making little or no sound or movement; causing no trouble or disturbance; at rest, inactive. LME. ▸**b** *ASTRONOMY*. Of the sun: marked by an absence of transient and localized radio emissions such as accompany sunspots. M20.
2 Tranquil by nature, gentle; reserved, not outspoken. LME.
3 (Of a person) acting discreetly or (esp.) secretly; (of an action, thought, etc.) undivulged, hidden, private. E16.
4 Free from excess; moderate; (of colour, clothing, etc.) unobtrusive; understated, muted; (of a social occasion) simple, informal. M16.
1 F. WELDON The little girls fall quiet: terror silences them. U. BENTLEY Had the class been quieter and more orderly it might have been easier. ***quiet as a mouse***: see MOUSE *noun*. **2** P. S. BUCK A small, quiet man, ever unwilling to speak. **3** A. J. P. TAYLOR There was a good deal of quiet anti-semitism in England. **4** G. DALY Most Victorian weddings were quiet affairs, but wealthier families . . threw big parties. O. NASH Two new suits! The first is a tasteful quiet gray.
▶**II 5 a** Of an action, state, etc. (formerly also of a person): undisturbed, uninterrupted; not interfered with. LME. ▸**b** Partaken of or enjoyed in quiet. M19.
6 (Of a place, a period of time, etc.) characterized by the absence of noisy activity or commotion; peaceful, not busy; (of a place) secluded. E16. ▸**b** Of a period of time: spent in seclusion for the purpose of prayer or meditation. L19.
7 Of a person, the mind, etc.: untroubled; free from (mental) agitation or excitement. M16.
5a AV *Job* 3:26 I was not in safetie, neither had I rest, neither was I quiet. ***anything for a quiet life***: see LIFE *noun*. **b** J. WAINWRIGHT Enjoying a quiet pint at the time. **6** M. MOORCOCK The streets were unusually quiet, virtually deserted. A. BISHOP Life in Oxford was very quiet . . partly because of . . financial difficulties. *Investors Chronicle* Invest the proceeds while the market remains quiet.
▶**B** *adverb*. = QUIETLY. *rare*. M16.
Special collocations: **quiet American** (freq. *iron*.) [with allus. to Graham Greene's *The Quiet American* (1955)] a person suspected of being an undercover agent or spy. **quiet number** *Nautical slang* an easy job. **quiet-room** (*a*) a room set aside for quiet activities; (*b*) a soundproof room, esp. in a hospital. **quiet time** a daily session of private Bible study or prayer.
■ **quietish** *adjective* somewhat quiet E20. **quietlike** *adjective & adverb* (orig. *Scot*.) (*a*) *adjective* apparently quiet; (*b*) *adverb* quietly: L15. **quietness** *noun* LME. **quietsome** *adjective* (*obsolete* exc. *dial*.) quiet, calm L16.

quiet /ˈkwʌɪət/ *verb*. LME.
[from prec., partly after late Latin *quietare*, from Latin *quietus* QUIET *adjective*.]
†**1** *verb trans*. Free (oneself or another) from obligation; acquit. LME–L15.
2 *verb trans*. Make quiet; quieten; soothe, pacify. E16. ▸**b** *ELECTRONICS*. = SQUELCH *verb* 5. M20.
3 *verb intrans*. Become quiet; quieten. Freq. foll. by *down*. Now chiefly *N. Amer*. M16.
4 *verb trans*. *LAW*. Settle or establish the fact of ownership of (a title etc.). L16.
2 G. SANTAYANA Medicinal sherry to quiet his nerves. **3** C. POTOK The noise quieted a little. A. MILLER The audience was quieting down.
■ **quieter** *noun* a person who or thing which makes someone or something (esp. the mind) quiet M16.

quieta non movere /kwiːˌeɪtə nəʊn məʊˈveːriː/ *verb phr*. (*inf. & imper*.). L18.
[Latin, lit. 'not move settled things'.]
= ***let sleeping dogs lie*** s.v. DOG *noun*.

†**quietation** *noun*. E16–E18.
[medieval Latin *quietatio*(*n*-), from late Latin *quietat*- pa. ppl stem of *quietare* QUIET *verb*: see -ATION.]
The action or an act of quieting someone or something; the state of being quieted or quiet.

quieten /ˈkwʌɪət(ə)n/ *verb*. E19.
[from QUIET *adjective* + -EN⁵. Cf. earlier QUIET *verb*.]
1 *verb trans*. Make quiet; soothe, pacify. Also foll. by *down*. E19.
2 *verb intrans*. Become quiet. Freq. foll. by *down*. L19.
1 M. BINCHY Sister Nessa had quietened the baby. C. BRAYFIELD Richard breathed deeply as if he could quieten his thoughts with the air. **2** P. BENSON The storm had quietened. E. O'BRIEN Even dogs that barked and marauded . . had quietened down.
■ **quietener** *noun* = QUIETER M19.

Quietism /ˈkwʌɪɪtɪz(ə)m/ *noun*. L17.
[Italian *quietismo*: see -ISM.]
1 Religious mysticism based on the teaching of the Spanish priest Miguel de Molinos (*c* 1640–97), rejecting outward forms of devotion in favour of passive contemplation and extinction of the will; *gen*. (usu. **q**-) any (esp. spiritual) system or philosophy emphasizing human passivity and non-resistance. L17.
2 (**q**-.) A state of calmness and passivity of mind or body; repose. L18.
■ **Quietist** *noun & adjective* (*a*) *noun* an adherent or practitioner of Quietism; a person who follows the principles of Quietism in political or social philosophy; (*b*) *adjective* of or pertaining to the Quietists or Quietism: L17. **quieˈtistic** *adjective* of, pertaining to, or characteristic of Quietism or its adherents M19.

quietly /ˈkwʌɪətli/ *adverb*. L15.
[from QUIET *adjective* + -LY².]
In a quiet manner.
just quietly *Austral. & NZ colloq*. confidentially, between ourselves.

quietude /ˈkwʌɪətjuːd/ *noun*. L16.
[French *quiétude* or medieval Latin *quietudo*, from Latin *quietus* QUIET *adjective*: see -TUDE. Cf. earlier INQUIETUDE.]
The state or condition of being quiet or calm; tranquillity; repose.
B. VINE She could draw and paint, but she preferred to sit for hours in quietude.

quietus /kwʌɪˈiːtəs/ *noun*. LME.
[Abbreviation of medieval Latin *quietus est* lit. 'he is quit.']
1 a Orig. more fully †***quietus est***. An acquittance granted on payment of a debt; a receipt. LME. ▸†**b** A discharge or release from office or duty. L16–L18.
2 *fig*. Death regarded as a release from life; something which causes death. M16. ▸**b** A final settlement, an ending. E19.
3 [By assoc. with *quiet*.] A sedative, a salve; a state of quiet or repose, a lull. M18.
2 R. CAMPBELL Giving the quietus to half-drowned snakes. **b** E. JONES Any remaining military interest . . received a final quietus from the . . experience of spending a year in the army. **3** *Washington Post* A . . quietus on the creative front, a non-development dance has shared with other media.

quiff /kwɪf/ *noun*¹. *US & dial*. M19.
[Var. of WHIFF *noun*¹.]
A whiff, a puff, esp. of tobacco smoke.

quiff /kwɪf/ *noun*². *dial. & slang*. L19.
[Origin unkn.]
A clever trick or stratagem; a dodge.

quiff /kwɪf/ *noun*³ & *verb*¹. L19.
[Origin unkn.]
▶**A** *noun*. A curl or lock of hair plastered down on the forehead, worn esp. by soldiers. Now *esp*. a tuft of hair brushed upwards over the forehead. L19.
Face An Australian ted who'd had his quiff flattened.
▶**B** *verb trans*. Arrange (hair) into a quiff. Also foll. by *up*. M20.

quiff /kwɪf/ *noun*⁴. *dial. & coarse slang*. E20.
[Origin unkn. Cf. next.]
A young woman; *spec*. a prostitute.

†**quiff** *verb*² *intrans*. *coarse slang*. Only in 18.
[Origin unkn. Cf. prec.]
Copulate.

qui hi *noun* var. of KOI HAI.

quile /kʌɪl/ *noun. obsolete* exc. *Scot.* Also †**quill**. L16.
[Perh. from Old French (mod. *cuielle* gathering, harvest), from var. of *coillir* (mod. *cueillir*) gather: see COIL *verb*.]
Orig., a coil, a spiral. Now *Scot.*, a small haystack.
†**in a quile**, †**in the quile** together, in a body.

quill /kwɪl/ *noun*¹ *& verb.* LME.
[Prob. from Middle & mod. Low German *quiele* rel. to synon. Middle High German *kil* (German *Kiel*).]
▶ **A** *noun.* **1** †**a** *gen.* A hollow stem or stalk, esp. of a reed. LME–L17. ▶**b** A hollow stem on which yarn is wound; a bobbin, a spool. LME. ▶**c** A musical pipe made from a hollow stem; in *pl.* (*US colloq.*) pan-pipes. M16. ▶**d** A curled piece of dried cinnamon or cinchona bark. L18. ▶**e** The whistle of a steam engine. *US.* M20. ▶**f** A thin tube or straw used to inhale or smoke narcotics. *US colloq.* M20.
2 a A small pipe or tube; now *esp.* one used for applying slip to pottery. LME. ▶**b** A hollow rotating sleeve of metal etc., *esp.* one used to transmit the drive from a motor to a concentrically mounted axle. L19.
3 The shaft of a feather, esp. the calamus; *loosely* a quill-feather. LME. ▶**b** A pen formed from a main wing or tail feather of a large bird (esp. a goose) by pointing and slitting the end of the shaft. M16. ▶**c** A plectrum formed from the quill of a feather, used for plucking a musical instrument; *spec.* in instruments of the harpsichord type, a piece of quill attached to a jack causing the string to be plucked when the key is pressed down. M16.
4 Any of the hollow sharp spines of a porcupine, hedgehog, etc. E17.
Phrases: ***pure quill***: see PURE *adjective*.
Comb.: **quillback** a N. American sucker (fish), *Carpiodes cyprinus*, which has one ray of the dorsal fin greatly elongated; **quill-coverts** the feathers covering the base of the quill-feathers; **quill drive** (the apparatus for) the transmission of power from a motor by means of a quill (sense 2b); **quill-driver** *joc. & derog.* a clerk, an author; **quill-feather** any of the main wing and tail feathers (remiges and retrices) of a bird; **quill pen** = sense 3b above; **quillwork** a type of applied decoration for clothing, bags, etc., characteristic of certain N. American Indian peoples, using softened and freq. dyed porcupine quills in usu. elaborate designs; **quillwort** any of various plants constituting the genus *Isoetes* (family Isoetaceae), allied to the ferns, with dense rosettes of tubular leaves having sporangia embedded in their bases; esp. *I. lacustris* and *I. echinospora*, submerged aquatic plants.
▶ **B** *verb.* **1** *verb intrans.* Wind yarn on a quill or spool. M17.
2 *verb trans.* Form (a lace edge etc.) into small cylindrical folds; goffer. E18.
3 *verb trans.* Cover (as) with quills; *spec.* fit (a harpsichord) with quills to pluck the strings. L18.
4 *verb trans.* Write (orig. with a quill), pen. L19.
■ **quilling** *noun* (*a*) the action of the verb; (*b*) a piece of quilled lace edging etc.; (*c*) *US* the art or practice of producing various sounds on a steam engine whistle; (*d*) *US* the craft of making ornamental filigree from tightly rolled columns of paper: M17. **quilly** *adjective* (*a*) of, pertaining to, or resembling a quill or quills; (*b*) consisting of or covered by quills: M16.

†**quill** *noun*² var. of QUILE.

quillaja /kwɪˈleɪdʒə/ *noun.* Also **quillaia**. M19.
[mod. Latin (see below) from Spanish from Araucanian *quillai*, *quillay* soapbark tree, from *quillcan* to wash.]
Any tree of the S. American genus *Quillaja*, of the rose family; *esp.* the soapbark tree, *Q. saponaria*.

quilled /kwɪld/ *adjective.* L16.
[from QUILL *noun*¹ *& verb*: see -ED², -ED¹.]
1 Having or fitted with a quill or quills. L16.
2 Having the form of a quill or quills; *spec.* (of a lace edge etc.) formed into quills, goffered. E18. ▶**b** BOTANY. (Of the florets of a composite flower) abnormally tubular instead of ligulate, as in certain horticultural varieties; (of a flower-head) having florets of this form. E19.

quillet /ˈkwɪlɪt/ *noun*¹. Now *dial. & Hist.* M16.
[Origin unkn.]
A small plot or narrow strip of land.

quillet /ˈkwɪlɪt/ *noun*². *arch.* L16.
[Perh. rel. to QUIDDITY.]
A verbal nicety; a quibble.

quillet /ˈkwɪlɪt/ *noun*³. L19.
[from QUILL *noun*¹ + -ET¹.]
(A thing resembling) a small quill.

quillon /kijɔ̃/ *noun.* Pl. pronounced same. L19.
[French.]
Either of the two limbs of the cross-guard of a sword.

quilombo /kiˈlombo/ *noun.* Pl. **-os** /-ɔs/. M19.
[Brazilian Portuguese.]
Hist. In 18th- and 19th-cent. Brazil, an organized community of escaped slaves.

quilt /kwɪlt/ *noun & verb*¹. ME.
[Old French *coilte*, *cuilte*, var. *coute*, (mod. *couette*) from Latin *culcita* mattress, cushion.]
▶ **A** *noun.* **1** An article consisting of two pieces of fabric, either whole or formed from patchwork or applique, stuffed with a layer of wool, cotton batting, etc., and joined together with stitches or lines of stitching freq. in a decorative design, used esp. as a bedspread or blanket. ME. ▶**b** *transf.* A layer of padding; a thick covering; *spec.* such a covering used to insulate a beehive. L17.
2 A piece of padded material worn as a substitute or lining for armour. LME.
†**3** A pad impregnated with a medicinal substance for applying to the skin. Only in 17.
1 continental quilt = DUVET.
▶ **B** *verb.* **1** *verb trans. & intrans.* Join together (layers of fabric and stuffing) with lines of esp. decorative stitching to form a quilt etc.; cover (fabric etc.) *with* a particular stitched design. M16.
2 *verb trans.* Line or cover with some soft material as padding. M16. ▶**b** Cover or line (esp. a ball) with interlaced cord. E17.
3 *verb trans.* Secure (an object) between two layers of fabric etc. by stitching; sew *in* or *into*. M16.
4 *verb trans. fig.* Compile (esp. a literary work) by assembling various parts; patch together. Chiefly as ***quilted*** *ppl adjective.* E17.

📖 **1** A. COLBY Jackets . . quilted with . . diamond pattern. *Embroidery* Some women quilted in their . . homes. A. PRYCE-JONES The walls were . . hung with Lyons silks . . sometimes quilted. **3** J. BYROM He had three guineas quilted in the flap of his waistcoat.

■ **quilter** *noun* (*a*) a person who quilts, esp. as a hobby or profession; (*b*) a foot attached to a sewing machine for quilting: ME.

quilt /kwɪlt/ *verb*² *trans.* M19.
[Perh. transf. use of prec.]
1 Beat, thrash. *dial. & slang* (chiefly *US & Austral.*). M19.
2 CRICKET. Hit (the ball) about the field with force, esp. repeatedly. M19.

quilting /ˈkwɪltɪŋ/ *noun*¹. E17.
[from QUILT *verb*¹ + -ING¹.]
1 The action of QUILT *verb*¹. E17.
2 Work made or in the process of being made by quilting; the pattern of stitching used for quilting. E17.
3 = ***quilting-party*** below. *dial. & N. Amer.* M18.

📖 **1** *Workbox* Patchwork was a . . drawing room occupation . . quilting was the poor relation. *attrib.*: *Quilting Today* The quilting design . . is . . to further the artwork. ***Italian quilting***: see ITALIAN *adjective.* ***Marseilles quilting***: see MARSEILLES 1.

Comb.: **quilting bee** = ***quilting party*** below; **quilting frame** a free-standing or hand-held frame on which fabric is kept taut while quilting; **quilting hoop** a hand-held circular quilting frame; **quilting party** a social gathering for the purpose of making a quilt or quilts.

quilting /ˈkwɪltɪŋ/ *noun*². *dial. & slang* (chiefly *US & Austral.*). E19.
[from QUILT *verb*² + -ING¹.]
A beating, a thrashing.

quim /kwɪm/ *noun. coarse slang.* M18.
[Origin unkn.]
1 The vulva; the vagina. M18.
2 A woman; women collectively. Chiefly *N. Amer.* M20.

quin /kwɪn/ *noun*¹. M19.
[Origin unkn.]
= ***queen scallop*** s.v. QUEEN *noun*.

quin /kwɪn/ *noun*². *colloq.* M20.
[Abbreviation.]
= QUINTUPLET 2.

quina /ˈkiːnə, ˈkwʌɪnə/ *noun.* Now *rare.* M19.
[Spanish from Quechua *kina* bark. Cf. earlier QUINQUINA.]
Cinchona bark; quinine.

quinacridone /kwɪˈnakrɪdəʊn/ *noun.* E20.
[from QUIN(OLINE + ACRID(INE + -ONE.]
CHEMISTRY. Each of four synthetic isomeric compounds, $C_{20}H_{12}N_2O_2$, or their substituted derivatives, which have molecules containing three benzene and two pyridine rings arranged alternately, and include a number of red to violet pigments.

quinacrine /ˈkwɪnəkriːn/ *noun.* M20.
[from QUIN(INE + ACR(ID)INE.]
PHARMACOLOGY. = MEPACRINE.
Comb.: **quinacrine mustard** a nitrogen mustard derived from quinacrine and used as a fluorescent stain for chromosomes.

quinalbarbitone /kwɪnalˈbɑːbɪtəʊn/ *noun.* M20.
[from Latin *quin(que* five + AL(LYL + BARBITONE.]
PHARMACOLOGY. A sedative and hypnotic derivative of barbituric acid, $C_{12}H_{17}N_2O_3Na$, used esp. for pre-operative sedation.
¶ A proprietary name for this drug is SECONAL.

†**quinaquina** *noun* var. of QUINQUINA.

quinarius /kwɪˈnɑːrɪəs/ *noun.* Pl. **-rii** /-rɪiː/. E17.
[Latin, from *quini* distrib. of *quinque* five. Cf. DENARIUS.]
Hist. An ancient Roman silver coin equivalent to half a denarius.

quinary /ˈkwʌɪnəri/ *adjective & noun.* E17.
[formed as prec.: see -ARY¹.]
▶ **A** *adjective.* **1** Of, pertaining to, characterized by, or compounded of, five. E17.
2 ZOOLOGY. Pertaining to or designating a former system of classification in which the animal kingdom is divided into five subkingdoms, and each subkingdom into five classes. *obsolete* exc. *Hist.* E19.
3 Of the fifth order or rank; fifth in a series. E20.
▶ **B** *noun.* A set or compound of five things. Now *rare.* M17.
■ **quiˈnarian** *adjective & noun* (ZOOLOGY) (*a*) *adjective* pertaining to or characterized by a quinary division; (*b*) *noun* an advocate of the quinary system of classification: M19.

quinate /ˈkwʌɪneɪt/ *adjective.* E19.
[mod. Latin *quinatus*, formed as prec.: see -ATE².]
BOTANY. Of a compound leaf: composed of five leaflets.

quinazoline /kwɪˈnazəliːn/ *noun.* L19.
[from QUINOLINE with inserted *-az-* (see AZO-).]
CHEMISTRY. A yellow basic crystalline solid, $C_8H_6N_2$, which has a bicyclic structure of fused benzene and pyrimidine rings; any substituted derivative of this.

quincaillerie /kɛ̃kajri/ *noun.* Pl. pronounced same. L19.
[French.]
1 Metalwork; metal artefacts. *rare.* L19.
2 In France, a hardware or ironmonger's shop. M20.

quince /kwɪns/ *noun.* ME.
[Old French *cooin* (mod. *coing*) from late Latin (*malum*) *cotoneum* var. of (*malum*) *Cydonium* lit. 'apple of Cydonia' (now Canea, in Crete), translating Greek *mēlon kudōnion*: cf. MELOCOTON.]
1 The tart yellowish pear-shaped fruit of a small tree of the rose family, *Cydonia oblonga*, used to make preserves, to flavour fruit tarts, etc.; the tree bearing this fruit. ME.
2 With specifying word: (the fruit of) any of several other trees related to or resembling the quince. M19.
2 BENGAL *quince.* **Japan quince**, **Japanese quince** (the fruit of) the japonica, *Chaenomeles speciosa*. **native quince** *Austral.* a quinine-tree, *Petalostigma quadriloculare*.
Phrases: **get on a person's quince** *Austral. slang* irritate or exasperate a person.
¶ Orig. a pl. used *collect.*

quincentenary /kwɪnsɛnˈtiːn(ə)ri, -ˈtɛn-, kwɪnˈsɛntɪn-/ *adjective & noun.* L19.
[from Latin *quin(que* five + CENTENARY.]
(The celebration of) a five-hundredth anniversary.
■ **quincenˈtennial** *noun & adjective* L19.

quinch /kwɪn(t)ʃ/ *verb intrans.* Long *rare* exc. *dial.* M16.
[Perh. var. of QUETCH.]
Start, stir; flinch.

†**quincunce** *noun* var. of QUINCUNX.

quincuncial /kwɪnˈkʌnʃ(ə)l/ *adjective.* E17.
[Latin *quincuncialis*, formed as next + -AL¹.]
1 (Esp. of a tree plantation) arranged in the form of a quincunx or quincunxes; involving or characterized by this arrangement. E17.
2 BOTANY. Of aestivation: having five perianth segments imbricated in such a way that two are exterior and two interior, while the fifth is partly exterior and partly interior. M19.
■ **quincuncially** *adverb* M17.

quincunx /ˈkwɪnkʌŋks/ *noun.* M17.
[Latin = five-twelfths, from *quinque* five + *uncia* twelfth. Cf. OUNCE *noun*¹.]
1 ASTROLOGY. The aspect of two planets which are five signs (150 degrees) apart in the sky. M17.
2 An arrangement of five objects in a square or rectangle in which four occupy the corners, and one the centre, esp. used in planting trees; a set of five objects (esp. trees) so arranged. M17.

Quincy /ˈkɛ̃si, ˈkwɪnsi/ *noun.* M20.
[A region in the upper Loire valley, France.]
Any of several dry white wines produced in the Quincy region.

quindecagon /kwɪnˈdɛkəg(ə)n/ *noun.* L16.
[Irreg. from Latin *quindecim* fifteen + -GON, after *decagon*.]
GEOMETRY. A plane figure with fifteen straight sides and fifteen angles.

quindecemvir /kwɪndɪˈsɛmvə/ *noun.* E17.
[Latin, from *quindecim* fifteen + *vir* man.]
ROMAN HISTORY. A member of a group of fifteen; *esp.* any of the priests in charge of the Sibylline books.

quindecim /ˈkwɪndɪsɪm/ *noun.* Also †**-disme**. LME.
[Alt. of Anglo-Norman *quinzisme* QUINZIÈME, after Latin *quindecim* fifteen and *disme* DIME.]
1 A fifteenth part, as a tax or duty. *obsolete* exc. *Hist.* LME.
2 = next. L15.

quindene /ˈkwɪndiːn/ *noun.* L15.
[medieval Latin *quindena*, from Latin *quindeni* distrib. of *quindecim* fifteen.]
ECCLESIASTICAL HISTORY. The fifteenth (mod. fourteenth) day after a church festival.

†**quindisme** *noun* var. of QUINDECIM.

Quinean /ˈkwʌɪnɪən/ *adjective.* M20.
[from *Quine* (see below) + -AN.]
Of, pertaining to, or characteristic of the US logician and philosopher Willard Van Orman Quine (1908–2000) or his theories, esp. on empiricism.

quinella /kwɪˈnɛlə/ *noun.* Orig. *US.* Also (earlier) **-iela** /-ɪˈɛlə/. E20.
[Amer. Spanish *quiniela.*]
A form of betting in which the better must select the first two place-winners in a race etc., not necessarily in the correct order.

quinestrol /kwɪˈniːstrɒl/ *noun.* M20.
[from QUIN(IC + OESTR(OGEN + -OL.]
PHARMACOLOGY. A synthetic oestrogen, $C_{25}H_{32}O_2$, included in some oral contraceptives.

quingenary /kwɪnˈdʒiːn(ə)ri/ *noun & adjective.* E20.
[from Latin *quingenarius*, from *quingeni* distrib. of *quingenti*: see next, -ARY¹.]
▶ **A** *noun.* A quincentenary. *rare.* E20.
▶ **B** *adjective. ROMAN HISTORY.* Of a military unit: consisting of five hundred men. M20.

quingentenary /kwɪndʒ(ə)nˈtiːn(ə)ri, -ˈdʒɛntɪn(ə)ri/ *adjective & noun. rare.* L19.
[from Latin *quingenti* five hundred, after *centenary* etc.]
= QUINCENTENARY.

quinhydrone /kwɪnˈhʌɪdrəʊn/ *noun.* M19.
[formed as QUINA + HYDRO- + -ONE.]
CHEMISTRY. A dark green crystalline substance which is a complex formed by benzoquinone and hydroquinone molecules. Also, any similar complex formed by a quinone and another aromatic compound.

quinia /ˈkwɪnɪə/ *noun.* Now *rare* or *obsolete.* E19.
[formed as QUINA: see -IA¹.]
CHEMISTRY. = QUININE.

quinic /ˈkwɪnɪk/ *adjective.* Also †**kinic**. E19.
[formed as QUINA + -IC.]
CHEMISTRY. ***quinic acid***, a cyclic carboxylic acid, $C_6H_7(OH)_4COOH$, found in cinchona bark and in various fruits and leaves.
■ **quinate** *noun* a salt or ester of quinic acid M19.

quinidine /ˈkwɪnɪdiːn/ *noun.* M19.
[formed as QUINA + -IDINE.]
PHARMACOLOGY. A cinchona alkaloid, $C_{20}H_{24}N_2O_2$, which is an optically active isomer of quinine and is used to treat cardiac arrhythmia.

quiniela *noun* see QUINELLA.

quinine /ˈkwɪniːn, kwɪˈniːn/ *noun.* E19.
[formed as QUINA + -INE⁵.]
An alkaloid, $C_{20}H_{24}N_2O_2$, found in cinchona barks; a bitter drug containing this, formerly used as an antipyretic, tonic, and abortifacient, and now chiefly (with chloroquine etc.) as a specific remedy for malaria, and as an additive to tonic water.
Comb.: **quinine-tree** any of several Australian trees with a bitter bark, esp. *Petalostigma quadriloculare*, of the spurge family, and *Alstonia constricta* (family Apocynaceae).

quinion /ˈkwɪnɪən/ *noun.* L19.
[Abbreviation of QUINTERNION.]
BIBLIOGRAPHY. A gathering of five sheets of paper.

quinnat /ˈkwɪnət/ *noun.* E19.
[Lower Chinook *ikʷanat.*]
The Chinook salmon, *Oncorhynchus tshawytscha.* Also ***quinnat salmon***.

quinoa /ˈkiːnəʊə, kwɪˈnəʊə/ *noun.* Also **-ua**. E17.
[Spanish spelling of Quechua *kinua, kinoa.*]
Any of several annual goosefoots, esp. *Chenopodium quinoa* and *C. pallidicaule*, grown by the Indians of the Andes for their edible starchy seeds; these seeds, used as food.

quinoid /ˈkwɪnɔɪd/ *adjective & noun.* E20.
[from QUIN(ONE + -OID.]
CHEMISTRY. = QUINONOID.
■ **quiˈnoidal** *adjective* E20.

quinol /ˈkwɪnɒl/ *noun.* L19.
[from QUINA + -OL.]
CHEMISTRY. = HYDROQUINONE.

quinoline /ˈkwɪnəliːn/ *noun.* Also †**chin-**. M19.
[formed as prec. + -INE⁵.]
CHEMISTRY. A pungent colourless liquid, C_9H_7N, whose molecule contains fused benzene and pyridine rings.

quinology /kwɪˈnɒlədʒi/ *noun.* M19.
[from QUINA + -OLOGY.]
The scientific investigation of quinine.
■ **quinologist** *noun* M19.

quinone /ˈkwɪnəʊn, kwɪˈnəʊn/ *noun.* Also †**ki-**. M19.
[from QUINA + -ONE.]
CHEMISTRY. Any of a series of aromatic compounds derived from benzene and its homologues by the replacement of two atoms of hydrogen by two of oxygen; *spec.* = BENZOQUINONE.
■ **ˈquinonoid** *adjective & noun* (**a**) *adjective* resembling or characteristic of a quinone; having a molecular structure like that of quinone; (**b**) *noun* a quinonoid compound: L19.

quinovic /kwɪˈnəʊvɪk/ *adjective.* Also **quinovaic** /kwɪnə(ʊ)ˈveɪɪk/, †**kinovic**. M19.
[from mod. Latin *quina nova*, formed as QUINA + Latin *nova* new: see -IC.]
CHEMISTRY. ***quinovic acid***, a polycyclic carboxylic acid found in the bark of the plant *Cinchona nova.*

quinoxaline /kwɪˈnɒksəliːn/ *noun.* L19.
[from QUIN(OLINE + GLY)OXAL + -INE⁵.]
CHEMISTRY. A weakly basic solid, $C_8H_6N_2$, with a bicyclic structure of fused benzene and pyrazine rings; any substituted derivative of this.

quinquagenarian /ˌkwɪŋkwədʒɪˈnɛːrɪən/ *noun & adjective.* M16.
[Latin *quinquagenarius*, from *quinquageni* distrib. of *quinquaginta* fifty + -ARIAN.]
▶ **A** *noun.* †**1** A military commander of fifty men. *rare.* M16–E17.
2 A person from 50 to 59 years old. M19.
▶ **B** *adjective.* †**1** (Of a military commander) in charge of fifty men. *rare.* Only in E17.
2 From 50 to 59 years old; of or pertaining to a quinquagenarian or quinquagenarians. E19.

quinquagenary /kwɪnˈkwadʒɪn(ə)ri/ *noun & adjective. rare.* LME.
[formed as prec.: see -ARY¹.]
▶ **A** *noun.* †**1** = QUINQUAGENARIAN *noun* 1. LME–L15.
2 A fiftieth year or anniversary. L16.
▶ **B** *adjective.* = QUINQUAGENARIAN *adjective* 2. E18.

Quinquagesima /kwɪŋkwəˈdʒɛsɪmə/ *noun.* LME.
[medieval Latin, use as noun (sc. *dies* day) of fem. of Latin *quinquagesimus* fiftieth, from *quinquaginta* fifty, after QUADRAGESIMA.]
ECCLESIASTICAL. The Sunday before the beginning of Lent (also more fully ***Quinquagesima Sunday***). Formerly also, the period beginning with this day and ending on Easter Sunday.
■ **quinquagesimal** *adjective* constituting or belonging to a set of fifty days M19.

†**quinquangle** *noun. rare.* M17–L18.
[Late Latin *quinquangulum*, from Latin *quinque* five + *angulus* ANGLE *noun*³.]
GEOMETRY. A pentagon.

quinquangular /kwɪŋˈkwaŋgjʊlə/ *adjective.* M17.
[formed as prec. + -AR¹.]
= PENTAGONAL *adjective* 1.

quinquarticular /kwɪŋkwɑːˈtɪkjʊlə/ *adjective.* M17.
[mod. Latin *quinquarticularis*, from *quinque* five + *articulus* ARTICLE.]
ECCLESIASTICAL HISTORY. Of or pertaining to the five articles of Arminian doctrine condemned at the Synod of Dort in 1618.

quinque- /ˈkwɪŋkwi/ *combining form.* Also **quinqui-**.
[from Latin *quinque* five. Cf. QUINTI-.]
Having five, fivefold.
■ **quinqueˈdentate** *adjective* (**a**) *BOTANY & ZOOLOGY* having five teeth or toothlike projections; (**b**) *CHEMISTRY* (of a ligand) forming five separate bonds; (of a complex) formed by such a ligand: M18. **quinquefid** *adjective* (*BOTANY*) divided into five parts by deep clefts or notches E18. **quinqueˈfoliate** *adjective* (*BOTANY*) having five leaflets L17. **quinqueˈlobate** *adjective* having five lobes E19. **quinqueˈlocular** *adjective* (*BOTANY*) having five loculi M18. **quinqueˈvalent** *adjective* (*CHEMISTRY*) = PENTAVALENT L19.

quinquennia *noun pl.* see QUINQUENNIUM.

quinquenniad /kwɪŋˈkwɛnɪəd/ *noun.* M19.
[formed as next + -AD¹, after *decad.*]
= QUINQUENNIUM 2.

quinquennial /kwɪŋˈkwɛnɪəl/ *adjective.* L15.
[from Latin *quinquennis*, from *quinque* five + *annus* year + -AL¹. Cf. ANNUAL.]
1 Lasting, esp. holding office, for five years. L15.
▶**b** Consisting of five years. M19.
2 Occurring every five years. E17.
■ **quinquennially** *adverb* every five years E19.

quinquennium /kwɪŋˈkwɛnɪəm/ *noun.* Pl. **-nniums**, **-nnia** /-nɪə/. E17.
[Latin, from *quinque* five + *annus* year.]
1 A fifth anniversary. E17.
2 A period of five years. M17.

quinquepartite /kwɪŋkwɪˈpɑːtʌɪt/ *adjective.* L16.
[Latin *quinquepartitus*, from QUINQUE- + *partitus* pa. pple of *partiri* divide.]
Divided into or consisting of five (equal) parts.

quinquereme /ˈkwɪŋkwɪriːm/ *noun & adjective.* M16.
[Latin *quinqueremis*, from QUINQUE- + *remus* oar.]
Hist. ▶**A** *noun.* A galley prob. having five rowers to each bank of oars. M16.
▶ **B** *attrib.* or as *adjective.* That is a quinquereme. M17.

quinquesect /ˈkwɪŋkwɪsɛkt/ *verb trans.* L17.
[from QUINQUE- + Latin *sect-* ppl stem of *secare* cut, after *bisect* etc.]
Cut or divide into five (equal) parts.
■ **quinqueˈsection** *noun* division into five (equal) parts L17.

quinquevirate /kwɪŋˈkwɛvɪrət/ *noun.* Now *rare.* E18.
[Latin *quinqueviratus*, from *quinqueviri* five men.]
An official body consisting of five people.

quinqui- *combining form* var. of QUINQUE-.

quinquina /kwɪŋˈkwʌɪnə, kɪnˈkiːnə/ *noun.* Also †**quinaquina**. M17.
[Spanish from Quechua *kin(a)-kina*, redupl. of *kina* QUINA.]
1 Cinchona bark, the source of quinine etc.; any of the trees producing this bark. M17.
2 Any of several fortified French wines containing quinine. E20.

quinsy /ˈkwɪnzi/ *noun.* ME.
[Old French *quinencie* from medieval Latin *quinancia* from Greek *kunagkhē* CYNANCHE. Cf. SQUINANCY, SQUINSY.]
MEDICINE. (A case of) a pus-filled swelling in the soft palate around the tonsils, usu. as a complication of tonsillitis.
Comb.: **quinsy-wort** squinancy-wort, *Asperula cynanchica.*
■ **quinsied** *adjective* M19.

quint /kwɪnt/ *noun*¹. In sense 2 also **-te**. LME.
[Old & mod. French (also *quinte*) from Latin *quintus* fifth.]
1 *Hist.* A tax of one-fifth. LME.
2 *MUSIC.* An interval of a fifth. M19.

quint /kɪnt, kwɪnt/ *noun*². L17.
[French: see prec.]
In piquet, a sequence of five cards of the same suit counting as fifteen. Cf. TIERCE *noun*¹ 4.
quint major the ace, king, queen, jack, and ten of a suit. **quint minor** the five cards from the jack to the seven.

quint /kwɪnt/ *noun*³. *N. Amer. colloq.* M20.
[Abbreviation.]
= QUINTUPLET 2.

quint- *combining form* see QUINTI-.

quinta /ˈkɪnta, ˈkwɪntə/ *noun.* M18.
[Spanish & Portuguese, from *quinta parte* fifth part, orig. the amount of a farm's produce paid as rent.]
In Spain, Portugal, and Latin America: a large house or villa in the country or on the outskirts of a town; a country estate; *spec.* a wine-growing estate in Portugal.

quintain /ˈkwɪntɪn/ *noun.* LME.
[Old French *quintaine, -eine*, medieval Latin *quintana, -ena*, usu. taken as identical with Latin *quintana* market of a camp, from *quintus*: see QUINTAN.]
Hist. (An object mounted on) a post or plank as a target for tilting at with a lance etc., used esp. as an exercise of skill for a horseman. Also, the exercise of tilting at such a target.

quintal /ˈkwɪnt(ə)l/ *noun.* Also †**kintal**, †**kentle**. LME.
[Old French from medieval Latin *quintale* from Arab. *ḳinṭār*, ult. from Latin *centenarius*. Cf. KANTAR, KENTLEDGE.]
1 Orig., a weight of one hundred pounds. Later, a hundredweight. LME.
2 A weight of 100 kilograms. L20.

quintan /ˈkwɪnt(ə)n/ *adjective & noun.* Now *rare* or *obsolete.* M17.
[medieval Latin *quintana* (sc. *febris* fever) use as noun of fem. of *quintanus*, from *quintus* fifth: see -AN. Cf. QUARTAN, SEXTAN.]
MEDICINE. (Designating) a fever recurring every fourth day (by inclusive reckoning every fifth day).

quinte /kwɪnt/ *noun.* E18.
[French: see QUINT *noun*¹.]
FENCING. The fifth of eight recognized parrying positions, used to protect the head (in sabre fencing) or the lower inside of the body (in foil and épée fencing), with the sword-hand across the body at waist-height in pronation and lower than the point of the blade; a parry in this position.

quinternion /kwɪnˈtəːnɪən/ *noun.* M17.
[from Latin *quinque* five, or *quintus* fifth, after *quaternion*: see -ION.]
= QUINION.

quintessence /kwɪnˈtɛs(ə)ns/ *noun & verb.* LME.
[French (also †*quinte essence*), from medieval Latin *quinta essentia* fifth essence.]
▶ **A** *noun.* **1** In classical and medieval philosophy, a fifth substance in addition to the four elements, thought to compose the celestial bodies and to be latent in all things. LME.
2 The most essential part of a substance; a refined essence or extract; *CHEMISTRY* (long *obsolete* exc. *Hist.*) an alcoholic tincture obtained by infusion at a gentle heat. M16.
3 The purest, most typical, or most perfect form, manifestation, or embodiment *of* some quality or class. L16.

📖 **2** *fig.*: *Writer (US)* The poet has to pare down her material to its quintessence. **3** D. MURPHY To me running barefoot symbolised the very quintessence of liberty. M. DORRIS He had been deprived of.. transcendent imagination, a.. grace that was the quintessence of being human.

▶ **B** *verb trans.* Extract the quintessence of. Now *rare* or *obsolete*. **L16.**

▪ **quinte'ssentiate** *verb trans.* (*rare*) = QUINTESSENCE *verb* **E17.**

quintessential /kwɪntɪˈsɛnʃ(ə)l/ *adjective & noun.* **E17.**
[formed as prec. + -IAL.]
▶ **A** *adjective.* Of, pertaining to, or of the nature of (a) quintessence; *esp.* purest, most typical, or most refined of its kind. **E17.**

📖 *Bon Appetit* That quintessential, most sublime of gastronomic gifts—French foie gras. R. FRAME A calendar.. with photographs of quintessential English scenes.

▶ **B** *noun.* = QUINTESSENCE 2, 3. *rare.* **L19.**

▪ **quintessenti'ality** *noun* (*rare*) **M19.** **quintessentialize** *verb trans.* (*rare*) make quintessential; *esp.* refine or purify to the highest degree **E19.** **quintessentially** *adverb* **L19.**

quintet /kwɪnˈtɛt/ *noun.* Also **-ette**, (earlier) †**-etto**. **L18.**
[Italian *quintetto* or French *quintette*, from Italian *quinto* fifth: see -ET^{1}.]
1 MUSIC. A composition for five voices or instruments. **L18.**
2 A group of five persons or things; *esp.* (MUSIC) a group of five singers or instrumentalists. **L19.**

quinti *noun* pl. of QUINTUS.

quinti- /ˈkwɪnti/ *combining form. rare.* Before a vowel also **quint-**.
[from Latin *quintus* fifth. Cf. QUINQUE-.]
Having five, fivefold.
▪ †**quintipartite** *adjective* divided into five parts **L17.** **quint'angular** *adjective* having five angles **L18.**

quintic /ˈkwɪntɪk/ *adjective & noun.* **M19.**
[from Latin *quintus* fifth + -IC.]
MATH. ▶ **A** *adjective.* Of the fifth order or degree. **M19.**
▶ **B** *noun.* A quantic or surface of the fifth degree. **M19.**

quintile /ˈkwɪntɪl, -ʌɪl/ *adjective & noun.* **E17.**
[from Latin *quintilis* (sc. *mensis*) fifth month, July, from *quintus* fifth: see -ILE. Cf. *quartile*, *sextile*.]
▶ **A** *adjective.* ASTROLOGY. Designating the aspect of two planets which are one-fifth of a circle (72 degrees) apart in the sky. **E17.**
▶ **B** *noun.* **1** ASTROLOGY. A quintile aspect. **M17.**
2 STATISTICS. Each of the four values of a variate which divide a frequency distribution into five equal groups; each of the five groups so produced. **M20.**

quintillion /kwɪnˈtɪljən/ *noun.* **L17.**
[from Latin *quintus* fifth after *million*, *billion*, etc.]
Orig. (esp. in the UK), the fifth power of a million (10^{30}). Now usu. (orig. *US*), the sixth power of a thousand (10^{18}).
▪ **quintillionth** *adjective & noun* the ordinal numeral or fraction corresponding to this **M19.**

quintole /ˈkwɪntəʊl/ *noun.* **L19.**
[German *Quintole* arbitrary formation from Latin *quintus* fifth. Cf. SEPTIMOLE.]
MUSIC. A group of five notes to be played in the time of four.

quinton /kɛ̃tɔ̃/ *noun.* Pl. pronounced same. **L19.**
[French.]
Hist. A 17th-cent. treble viol. Also, an 18th-cent. five-stringed hybrid between the viol and violin families.

quintuple /ˈkwɪntjʊp(ə)l/ *adjective, verb, & noun.* **L16.**
[French from medieval Latin *quintuplus*, from Latin *quintus* fifth + *-plus* as in *duplus* double.]
▶ **A** *adjective.* Consisting of five things or parts; five times as many or as much, fivefold; MUSIC (of a rhythm or time) having five beats in a bar. **L16.**
▶ **B** *verb.* **1** *verb trans.* Multiply by five; make five times as large, numerous, etc. **M17.**
2 *verb intrans.* Increase fivefold in amount or degree. **E19.**
▶ **C** *noun.* A fivefold amount; a set of five. **L17.**
▪ **quintuply** *adverb* **L19.**

quintuplet /ˈkwɪntjʊplɪt, kwɪnˈtjuːplɪt/ *noun.* **L19.**
[from prec. + -ET^{1}, after *triplet*.]
1 A set of five things; MUSIC a group of five notes to be performed in the time of three or four. **L19.**
2 Each of five children born at one birth. **L19.**

quintuplicate /kwɪnˈtjuːplɪkət/ *adjective & noun.* **M17.**
[from QUINTUPLE after *duplicate* etc.]
▶ **A** *adjective.* Quintuple; *esp.* copied or repeated to produce a set of five. **M17.**
▶ **B** *noun.* A set of five. **M19.**
in quintuplicate in five identical copies.

quintuplicate /kwɪnˈtjuːplɪkeɪt/ *verb trans. & intrans.* **L20.**
[from prec. after *duplicate* etc.]
Multiply by five.

quintuplication /kwɪnˌtjuːplɪˈkeɪʃ(ə)n/ *noun.* **L17.**
[from QUINTUPLICATE *adjective & noun* after *duplication* etc.]
The action or an act of multiplying a thing by five or of making five identical copies.

quintus /ˈkwɪntəs/ *noun.* Pl. **-ti** /-tʌɪ, -tiː/. **L19.**
[Latin = fifth.]
MUSIC. The fifth part in a vocal quintet.

quinua *noun* var. of QUINOA.

quinzaine /ˈkwɪnzeɪn, *foreign* kɛ̃zɛn/ *noun.* **M19.**
[French, formed as next.]
ECCLESIASTICAL HISTORY. = QUINDENE.

quinze /kwɪnz, *foreign* kɛ̃ːz/ *noun.* **E18.**
[French, from Latin *quindecim* fifteen.]
A card-game resembling pontoon in which the object is to obtain or come nearest to fifteen points.

quinzième /kɛ̃zjɛm/ *noun. obsolete* exc. *Hist.* **ME.**
[Anglo-Norman *quinzisme*, *quinzième*, ordinal from prec.]
†**1 a** = QUINDENE. **ME–L15.** ▶**b** A period of fifteen days; *esp.* the day of a church festival and the two weeks following. **LME–L15.**
2 A tax or duty of a fifteenth part. **LME.**
¶ Formerly naturalized.

quip /kwɪp/ *noun & verb.* **M16.**
[Origin uncertain: perh. from Latin *quippe* indeed, forsooth.]
▶ **A** *noun.* **1** Orig., a sharp or sarcastic remark. Now usu., a clever or witty saying; an epigram. **M16.** ▶**b** A verbal equivocation; a quibble. **L16.**
2 A curious or odd action, feature, or object. *arch.* **E19.**

📖 **1** I. BANKS A.. bright fellow, always ready with a joke or a quip.

▶ **B** *verb.* Infl. **-pp-**.
1 *verb intrans.* Make a quip or quips; be wittily sarcastic. **M16.**
2 *verb trans.* **a** Make the object of a quip or quips; mock. **L16.** ▶**b** Say as a quip. **M20.**

📖 **1** *Smart Set* Audrey.. would quip and jest with roguish glee. **2a** HENRY MILLER She began to quip him about his strength of will. **b** D. LESSING 'Ask no questions.. get told no lies,' quipped Faye.

▪ **quipper** *noun* **L16.** **quippery** *noun* (*rare*) the making of quips; quips collectively: **M20.** **quippish** *adjective* given to or characterized by quips **M19.** **quipster** *noun* a person who quips **L19.**

quipu /ˈkiːpuː, ˈkwɪ-/ *noun.* Also †**-po**, pl. **-o(e)s**. **E18.**
[Quechua *khipu* knot.]
An ancient Peruvian device for recording information, events, etc., consisting of variously coloured cords arranged and knotted in different ways.

quire /kwʌɪə/ *noun^{1} & verb.* **ME.**
[Old French *qua(i)er* (mod. *cahier* quire, copybook) from Proto-Romance, from Latin *quaterni*, four at once, set of four: see QUATERNARY.]
▶ **A** *noun.* **1** A small pamphlet or book consisting of four folded sheets of parchment; a short poem, treatise, etc., which is or might be contained in such a pamphlet. Long *obsolete* exc. *Scot.* **ME.**
2 A set of four sheets of parchment or paper folded to form eight leaves, as in many medieval manuscripts; *gen.* any gathering of sheets folded into leaves and set one within another in a manuscript or printed book. Also, 25 (formerly 24) sheets of writing-paper; a twentieth of a ream. **LME.**
2 in quires unbound, in sheets.
▶ **B** *verb trans.* Arrange in quires. **L17.**
▪ **quiring** *noun* (a series of signatures indicating) the order or arrangement of a series of quires, esp. in a bound manuscript **E20.**

quire *noun^{2}* see CHOIR *noun.*

Quirinal /ˈkwɪrɪn(ə)l/ *adjective & noun.* **M19.**
[Latin *Quirinalis* from *Quirinus* a name of Romulus.]
▶ **A** *adjective.* Designating or pertaining to one of the seven hills of Rome. **M19.**
▶ **B** *noun.* The presidential (formerly royal) palace on the Quirinal hill in Rome; *transf.* the Italian government (formerly the monarchy), esp. as distinct from the papacy or Vatican. **M19.**

quiritary /ˈkwɪrɪt(ə)ri/ *adjective.* **M19.**
[Late Latin *quiritarius*, from Latin *Quirites* Roman citizens: see -ARY^{1}.]
ROMAN LAW. Of or pertaining to the legal position or title of a person as a Roman citizen; (of property) held by legal right or title.
▪ Also **quiri'tarian** *adjective* **M19.**

quiritian /kwɪˈrɪʃ(ə)n/ *noun. rare.* **M19.**
[from Latin *Quirites* (see prec.) + -IAN.]
A citizen of ancient Rome.

quirk /kwəːk/ *noun.* **M16.**
[Origin unkn.]
▶ **I 1** A verbal subtlety, evasion, or trick; a quibble; use of quibbles, quibbling. Now *rare.* **M16.** ▶**b** A clever or witty saying; a quip. **L16.**
2 A sudden or unexpected twist, turn, or bend; *spec.* a stylistic variation or flourish in music, drawing, writing, etc. **L16.**
3 a A peculiarity of behaviour. **E17.** ▶**b** A sudden or peculiar feature or result (*of* an event); an anomaly, a freak. **M20.**

📖 **3a** D. ATHILL They had their charms, their interesting quirks. E. PAWEL This.. quirk of his made it.. impossible for anyone to share their meals with him. **b** A. N. WILSON An odd and cruel quirk of Fortune. T. HEALD There were too many elections under consideration for this to be some sort of statistical quirk.

▶ **II 4** An addition or removal; (a piece of) a thing inserted or cut out; *spec.* (**a**) = CLOCK *noun^{2}*; (**b**) a square or diamond-shaped insert between the fingers of a glove to allow greater movement and flexibility; (**c**) *rare* an irregular pane of glass; (**d**) ARCHITECTURE an acute hollow between convex or other mouldings. **M16.**
▪ **quirkily** *adverb* in a quirky manner **M20.** **quirkiness** *noun* the quality of being quirky **L19.** **quirkish** *adjective* (**a**) of the nature of a quirk; (**b**) idiosyncratic; erratic: **L17.** **quirky** *adjective* (**a**) subtle, tricky; (**b**) characterized by twists, turns, or flourishes; (**c**) characterized by unexpected or peculiar traits; idiosyncratic; eccentric: **E19.**

quirk /kwəːk/ *verb^{1}.* **E16.**
[Origin uncertain: cf. QUIRK *noun.*]
1 *verb intrans.* Move suddenly or jerkily. **E16.**
2 *verb trans. & intrans.* Make a quip or quips (about or against); mock. Now *rare.* **L16.**
3 *verb trans.* ARCHITECTURE. Make or provide (esp. a moulding) with a quirk; groove. Chiefly as ***quirked** ppl adjective.* **M19.**

📖 **1** *New Yorker* The body quirked back and forth.

quirk /kwəːk/ *verb^{2} intrans. dial.* **M18.**
[Imit.]
Grunt, groan, croak; *transf.* grumble.

quirked /kwəːkt/ *adjective.* **E19.**
[from QUIRK *noun*, *verb^{1}*: see -ED^{1}, -ED^{2}.]
1 ARCHITECTURE. Having a quirk. **E19.**
2 Of the mouth, eyebrow, etc.: set in an attitude by quirking. **M20.**

quirl *verb & noun* var. of QUERL.

quirley /ˈkwəːli/ *noun. US & Austral. slang.* **M20.**
[from *quirl* var. of QUERL + -Y^{6}.]
A (usu. hand-rolled) cigarette.

quirt /kwəːt/ *noun & verb.* Orig. *US.* **M19.**
[Spanish *cuerda* cord or Mexican Spanish *cuarta* whip.]
▶ **A** *noun.* A short-handled riding-whip with a braided leather lash. **M19.**
▶ **B** *verb trans.* Strike with a quirt. **L19.**

quisby /ˈkwɪzbi/ *adjective. arch. slang.* **E19.**
[Origin unkn.]
Queer, not quite right; idle; bankrupt.

quisling /ˈkwɪzlɪŋ/ *noun & adjective.* Also **Q-**. **M20.**
[Major Vidkun *Quisling* (1887–1945), Norwegian army officer and diplomat who collaborated with the German occupying force in Norway (1940–5).]
▶ **A** *noun.* A person cooperating with an occupying enemy; a collaborator (esp. with ref. to the war of 1939–45). Also, a traitor. **M20.**
▶ **B** *attrib.* or as *adjective.* Collaborating with an enemy, traitorous. **M20.**
▪ **quisle** *verb intrans.* (*joc. & colloq.*) [back-form.] betray one's country, esp. by collaborating with an occupying enemy **M20.** **quislingism** *noun* the practice or political doctrine of collaboration with an occupying enemy **M20.** **quislingist**, **quislingite** *adjectives & nouns* (*rare*) = QUISLING **M20.**

quit /kwɪt/ *noun^{1}. Jamaican.* **M19.**
[Prob. imit.]
Any of various small birds. Now chiefly in ***bananaquit***, ***orangequit***.

quit /kwɪt/ *noun^{2}.* **L19.**
[from QUIT *verb.*]
1 A point of departure. *rare.* **L19.**
2 The act or an instance of quitting; a person who quits. *US.* **E20.**
Comb.: **quit rate** *US* the proportion of people in a section of society who voluntarily leave their jobs.

quit /kwɪt/ *adjective* (chiefly *pred.*). Also †**quite**. **ME.**
[Latin *quietus* QUIET *adjective*; later from Old & mod. French *quitte* from medieval Latin *quittus* from Latin *quietus*.]
1 Free, clear, rid, (*of*, *from*). **ME.**
†**2** Destitute, deprived, *of*; parted *from*. **ME–L16.**
†**3** = QUITS 2. **LME–M18.**

📖 **1** R. L. STEVENSON If you keep on drinking rum, the world will soon be quit of a.. scoundrel.

Comb.: **quit-rent** (**a**) a (usu. small) rent paid by a freeholder or copyholder in lieu of services which might be required of him or her; (**b**) a charge on or payment from an estate for some special purpose.

quit /kwɪt/ *verb*. Infl. **-tt-**; pa. t. & pple also **quit**. Also †**quite**. ME.
[Old & mod. French *quitter*, earlier *quiter*, from Latin *quietus* QUIET *adjective*, QUIT *adjective*.]
1 *verb trans.* Set free, deliver, redeem. Foll. by *from, out, out of*. Long *rare*. ME. ▸**b** Free or rid (a person, oneself) *of*. Now *rare*. ME.
†**2** *verb trans.* Prove (a person) innocent of suspicion or accusation; absolve, acquit. Foll. by *from, of*. ME–M18.
3 *verb trans.* Repay, reward, (a person), esp. with an equivalent or for a favour, injury, etc.; repay a person for (a favour, injury, etc.); be equal to, balance, redress. *obsolete* exc. *dial.* ME.
4 *verb trans.* Pay off or clear (a debt etc.). Formerly also with double obj. Now *rare*. ME.
5 a *verb refl.* Behave, perform a task, esp. in a specified way. *arch.* LME. ▸†**b** *verb trans.* Discharge (a duty); play (one's part). *rare* (Shakes.). Only in E17.
†**6** *verb trans.* Remit (a debt etc.). *rare*. LME–L17.
7 a *verb trans.* Relinquish, renounce; cease to have, use, or be occupied with. LME. ▸**b** *verb trans.* Yield or hand over (a thing *to*). Now *rare* or *obsolete*. LME.
8 *verb trans.* Put, take, or send away (a person or thing). Also with double obj. Now *rare*. L16.
9 *verb trans.* Leave, go away from; separate from; part *with*. E17. ▸**b** *verb intrans.* (Of a tenant) leave occupied premises; *US & dial.* go away, depart. M18.
10 *verb trans. & intrans.* Cease, stop, discontinue (an action or activity, esp. a job). Now chiefly *N. Amer. colloq.* M17.

> 🕮 **5a** BROWNING I . . danced and gamed, Quitted me like a courtier. **7a** J. BUTLER Resentment has taken possession of the temper, . . and will not quit its hold. **9** T. HARDY The bench he had quitted. *Japan Times* She will quit the Liberal Democratic Party. **b** S. O'CASEY What are we . . to do with . . notices to quit? **10** W. MARCH Go on in the house and quit bothering me. G. VIDAL Diana had quit her job. **quitting-time** *colloq.* (chiefly *N. Amer.*) the time at which work is ended for the day.

Phrases: **quit claim to** = QUITCLAIM *verb* 2. **quit hold of** loose, free. *quit the* SCENE.

qui tam /kwʌɪ 'tam/ *noun phr.* M18.
[Latin, lit. 'who as well' (beginning the clause of the action).]
LAW (now *Hist.*).
1 An action brought on a penal statute by an informer on his or her own and the government's behalf. Cf. TANQUAM. M18.
2 *transf.* An informer. E19.

quitch /kwɪtʃ/ *noun*.
[Old English *cwiċe* (= Middle Low German *kweke*), perh. rel. to QUICK *adjective*. Cf. KWEEK, QUICK *noun*[2].]
Couch grass, *Elytrigia repens*. Also ***quitch-grass***.

quitclaim /'kwɪtkleɪm/ *noun*. ME.
[Anglo-Norman *quiteclame*, formed as next.]
LAW. A formal renunciation or relinquishing of a claim. Formerly also, a formal discharge or release. Now *N. Amer.*

quitclaim /'kwɪtkleɪm/ *verb trans.* ME.
[Anglo-Norman *quiteclamer* declare free, from *quite* free, clear + *clamer* proclaim; later assoc. with QUIT *verb* and CLAIM *noun*.]
†**1** Declare (a person) free; release, acquit, discharge. ME–M17.
2 LAW (now *Hist.*). Renounce or give up (a possession, claim, right, pursuit, etc.). Cf. ***quit claim to*** s.v. QUIT *verb*. ME.

quite /'kite/ *noun*. E20.
[Spanish.]
BULLFIGHTING. A series of passes made with the cape to distract the bull from a vulnerable picador, horse, etc.

†**quite** *adjective*[2], *verb* vars. of QUIT *adjective, verb*.

quite /kwʌɪt/ *adverb & adjective*[1]. ME.
[Adverbial use of †*quite* var. of QUIT *adjective*.]
▶ **A** *adverb*. **1** Completely, fully, entirely; to the utmost extent or degree; in the fullest sense. Also, exceptionally. ME. ▸**b** As a comment on a statement or a reply to a question: just so; I entirely agree. Freq. in ***quite so***. *colloq.* L19.
2 Actually, truly, absolutely; plainly, definitely. Also used as an intensive (freq. *iron.*) before a determiner and noun. L16.
3 Somewhat; moderately; fairly. M19.

> 🕮 **1** T. HARDY Ethelberta would have been disappointed quite. J. BUCHAN The place is quite bare and empty. M. DE LA ROCHE There were quite eight books in the packet. A. T. ELLIS I can quite see why Evvie comes so often. **b** P. G. WODEHOUSE 'The thing's impossible.' 'Quite,' agreed Sir Herbert. **2** W. S. MAUGHAM His red cheeks . . had . . a purple tinge that was quite alarming. G. VIDAL In thirty years one picks up quite a bit, you know. D. BOGARDE This is quite a place? Or should I say Palace? M. FORSTER Cream was quite the worst colour for her mistress to wear. **3** R. DINNAGE She was all right, I suppose—quite nice.

▶ **B** *ellipt.* as *adjective*. Socially acceptable. Usu. in neg. contexts. *colloq.* M19.

Phrases: **not quite** *colloq.* socially unacceptable. ***quite a*** FEW. **quite another**, **quite other** very different. **quite something** *colloq.* a remarkable thing; a good deal.

Quiteño /kiː'tɛnjəʊ, *foreign* ki'teɲo/ *adjective & noun*. M20.
[Amer. Spanish, from *Quito* (see below).]
▶ **A** *adjective*. Of, pertaining to, or characteristic of Quito, the capital city of Ecuador in S. America. M20.
▶ **B** *noun*. Pl. **-os** /-əʊz, *foreign* -ɔs/. A native or inhabitant of Quito. M20.

quiteron /'kwɪtərɒn/ *noun*. L20.
[from *quasiparticle injection tunnelling effect* (the phenomenon by which the device operates) + -T)RON.]
ELECTRONICS. A superconducting device with characteristics similar to those of a transistor but capable of operating at lower power levels.

quits /kwɪts/ *pred. adjective & noun*. L15.
[Prob. colloq. use of medieval Latin *quittus* QUIT *adjective*.]
▶ **A** *adjective*. †**1** Clear, discharged (*of* a liability). L15–L16.
2 Even or equal (*with*), esp. by repayment or retaliation. M17.
Phrases: **call it quits**, **cry quits** acknowledge that terms are now equal; agree to abandon a quarrel etc.; abandon a venture etc., esp. to cut one's losses. ***double or quits***: see DOUBLE *adverb*.
▶ **B** *noun*. A recompense; retaliation. *rare*. E19.

†**quittal** *noun*. L15–M17.
[from QUIT *verb* + -AL[1].]
Orig., discharge of payment, acquittance. Later, requital, retaliation.

quittance /'kwɪt(ə)ns/ *noun*. ME.
[Old French *quitance* (later *quitt-*), from *quiter* QUIT *verb*: see -ANCE.]
1 The action of freeing or clearing someone; release. Freq. foll. by *from*. *arch.* ME.
2 A release or discharge from a debt or obligation; a document certifying this; a receipt. *arch.* exc. *Scot.* ME.
3 Recompense; repayment; reprisal. Now *arch.* or *poet.* L16.

> 🕮 **2** R. BARBER The purchase of knighthood . . became a . . quittance for future taxes.

quitter /'kwɪtə/ *noun*[1]. Now *rare*. Also (esp. in sense 2) **-or**. ME.
[Perh. from Old French *quiture*, *cuiture* cooking etc. Cf. TWITTER *noun*[2].]
1 Pus; purulent discharge from a wound or sore. *obsolete* exc. *Jamaican*. ME.
2 An ulcer or suppurating sore on the coronet of a horse's hoof. Also more fully ***quitter-bone***. L16.

quitter /'kwɪtə/ *noun*[2]. E17.
[from QUIT *verb* + -ER[1].]
A person who or thing which quits something. Now only *spec.*, a person who or thing which gives up something, esp. easily; a shirker.

quitter /'kwɪtə/ *verb intrans.* Orig. *Scot.* Now *arch. rare*. E16.
[Origin unkn.]
Flicker, quiver. Also, twitter.

quittor *noun* see QUITTER *noun*[1].

quiver /'kwɪvə/ *noun*[1]. ME.
[Anglo-Norman var. of *quiveir*, Old French *quivre*, *coivre* from West Germanic word repr. by Old English *cocor*: see COCKER *noun*[1].]
1 A case for holding arrows (and occas. a bow). ME.
2 A quiverful of arrows. L16.
1 have an arrow left in one's quiver, **have a shaft left in one's quiver** not be resourceless.
■ **quiverful** *noun* (***a***) as much or as many as a quiver will hold; (***b***) *fig.* (with allus. to *Psalms* 127:5) many children of one parent: M19.

quiver /'kwɪvə/ *noun*[2]. E18.
[from QUIVER *verb*[1].]
A quivering motion or sound. Formerly also = QUAVER *noun* 1.

> 🕮 D. PARKER She began to feel . . little quivers of excitement.

quiver /'kwɪvə/ *adjective*. *obsolete* exc. *dial.* OE.
[Prob. symbolic.]
Active, nimble; quick, rapid.

quiver /'kwɪvə/ *verb*[1]. L15.
[from prec.]
1 *verb intrans.* Shake, tremble, vibrate, with a slight rapid motion. L15.
2 *verb trans.* Cause to quiver. L16.

> 🕮 **1** K. MANSFIELD Wind moving through . . so that the grass quivers. J. STEINBECK Lennie's lip quivered and tears started. T. HEGGEN He was . . quivering with rage. **2** E. WELTY The bird quivered its wings rapidly.

■ **quiveringly** *adverb* in a quivering manner; with a quiver in the voice: L16. **quivery** *adjective* tending to quiver; characterized by quivers: L19.

quiver /'kwɪvə/ *verb*[2] *trans.* M17.
[from QUIVER *noun*[1].]
Put (as) into a quiver. Usu. in *pass.*

quivered /'kwɪvəd/ *adjective*. Chiefly *poet.* M16.
[from QUIVER *noun*[1], *verb*[2]: see -ED[2], -ED[1].]
1 Equipped with a quiver. M16.
2 Placed or kept (as) in a quiver. M17.

qui vive /kiː 'viːv, *foreign* ki viv/ *noun phr.* L16.
[French, lit. '(long) live who?', a sentry's challenge, to discover to whom an approaching person is loyal.]
An alert or watchful state or condition. Chiefly in ***on the qui vive***, on the alert or lookout.

Quixote /'kwɪksət, *foreign* ki'xote/ *noun*. M17.
[from Don *Quixote* (see below) = Spanish *quixote* (now *quijote*) thigh armour.]
A person who resembles Don Quixote, the eponymous hero of a romance (1605–1615) by Cervantes, esp. in chivalry, romantic vision, and naive idealism.
■ **quixotism** *noun* quixotic principles, character, or practice; a quixotic action, statement, or idea: L17. **quixotry** *noun* = QUIXOTISM E18.

quixotic /kwɪk'sɒtɪk/ *adjective*. L18.
[from prec. + -IC.]
1 Of a person: visionary; naively idealistic; enthusiastically and actively chivalrous or romantic; impractical. L18.
2 Of an act, statement, etc.: characteristic of or appropriate to Don Quixote; showing or motivated by naive idealism, chivalry, or romanticism; impracticable. M19.

> 🕮 **1** P. FARMER Paid for the whole thing in a manner typically quixotic and extravagant. **2** CLIVE JAMES To . . maintain so many . . old edifices would seem quixotic even supposing it were technically possible.

■ **quixotically** *adverb* M19.

quiz /kwɪz/ *noun*[1]. *arch.* Pl. **quizzes**. L18.
[Origin unkn. Cf. QUIZ *verb*[1].]
1 An odd or eccentric person; a person of ridiculous appearance. L18.
2 A person who makes practical jokes, engages in banter, a hoaxer, a joker. L18.
3 A practical joke; a hoax; a piece of ridicule or banter; a witticism. E19. ▸**b** An act or the practice of quizzing or ridiculing someone. *rare*. E19.
■ **quizzy** *adjective* L18.

quiz /kwɪz/ *noun*[2]. Orig. *US*. Pl. **quizzes**. M19.
[from QUIZ *verb*[2].]
An act of questioning; a set of questions to be answered; *spec.* (***a***) a questionnaire; (***b***) an examination, esp. on a specified topic; (***c***) a test of knowledge, as a competition (esp. for entertainment) between individuals or teams.
attrib.: ***quiz game***, ***quiz paper***, ***quiz show***, etc.
Comb.: **quiz kid** *colloq.* a child, usu. a member of a team, who answers (extempore) questions in a quiz show; *transf.* a person who ostentatiously displays his or her knowledge; **quiz-master** a person who asks questions in or presides over a quiz.

quiz /kwɪz/ *verb*[1] *trans. arch.* Infl. **-zz-**. L18.
[Origin unkn. Cf. QUIZ *noun*[1].]
Make fun of, ridicule; regard with mockery. Also, look curiously at; observe the ways or eccentricities of; survey (as) through a quizzing-glass.
quizzing-glass a single eyeglass; a monocle.
■ **quizzable** *adjective* L18. **quiz'zee** *noun*[1] a person who is quizzed or ridiculed E19. **quizzer** *noun* L18. **quizzery** *noun* the practice or an instance of quizzing E19. **quizzingly** *adverb* in a quizzing manner M19.

quiz /kwɪz/ *verb*[2] *trans.* Infl. **-zz-**. M19.
[Origin unkn.]
Question, interrogate; *spec.* (*N. Amer.*) examine (a student or class) using questions requiring very short factual answers. Also, find *out* (a thing) by questioning.

> 🕮 S. MIDDLETON By quizzing Arthur . . he could . . get the fellow's name. M. SPARK I had come for a serious interview and was being frivolously quizzed. *Sunday Mirror* Two men were being quizzed by police.

■ **quiz'zee** *noun*[2] a person who is quizzed or questioned; a participant in a quiz game or show: M20.

quizzical /'kwɪzɪk(ə)l/ *adjective*. E19.
[from QUIZ *noun*[1], *verb*[1] + -ICAL.]
1 Unusual, odd; comical. Also, expressing or done with mild or amused puzzlement. E19.
2 Given to quizzing or joking; pertaining to or characterized by quizzing or mockery. *rare*. E19.

> 🕮 **1** E. LONGFORD His quizzical and original mind. He never said what one expected. *Twenty Twenty* He has never mastered the quizzical knitted brow.

■ **quizzi'cality** *noun* E19. **quizzically** *adverb* E19. **quizzicalness** *noun* E19.

quizzy /'kwɪzi/ *adjective*[1]. *rare*. L18.
[from QUIZ *noun*[1] + -Y[1].]
= QUIZZICAL 1.

quizzy /'kwɪzi/ *adjective*[2]. M20.
[from QUIZ *verb*[2] + -Y[1].]
Inquisitive.

Qum /kuːm/ *noun & adjective.* M20.
[A city in NW Iran.]
(Designating) a type of elaborately patterned rug or carpet produced in Qum.

Qumran /kʊmˈrɑːn/ *adjective.* M20.
[A region on the western shore of the Dead Sea.]
Of, pertaining to, or designating the Dead Sea Scrolls, discovered in caves at Qumran, or the religious community located in Khirbet Qumran during the beginning of the Christian era, which preserved the scrolls.
■ **Qumranite** *noun & adjective* of or pertaining to, a member of, the religious community of Qumran M20.

quoad /ˈkwəʊad/ *preposition.* E17.
[Latin = so far as, as much as, as to, from *quo* where, whither + *ad* to.]
To the extent of, as regards, with respect to.
quoad hanc /haŋk/, **quoad hunc** /hʌŋk/ [accus. fem., masc., of *haec, hic* this] LAW as far as this woman, man, is concerned (used with ref. to the nullity of a marriage or to sexual impotence). ***quoad hoc*** /hɒk/ [neut., = this] to this extent, with respect to this. ***quoad hunc***: see ***quoad hanc*** above. ***quoad sacra*** /ˈseɪkrə/ [pl. of *sacrum* sacred thing] ECCLESIASTICAL with respect to sacred matters (used esp. in Scotland with ref. to parishes constituted for purely ecclesiastical rather than civil purposes).

quod /kwɒd/ *noun & verb. slang.* Also **quad**. L17.
[Origin uncertain: perh. abbreviation of QUADRANGLE.]
▶ **A** *noun.* Prison. Freq. in ***in quod***. L17.
▶ **B** *verb trans.* Infl. **-dd-**. Put in prison. E19.

quoddity /ˈkwɒdɪti/ *noun. rare.* L17.
[from Latin *quod* (that) which + -ITY.]
A subtlety, a quibble, esp in argument. Cf. QUIDDITY 2.

quodlibet /ˈkwɒdlɪbɛt/ *noun.* LME.
[medieval Latin *quodlibet(um)* from Latin *quodlibet*, from *quod* what + *libet* it pleases.]
1 *Hist.* A question proposed as an exercise in philosophical or theological debate; a scholastic debate, thesis, or exercise. LME.
2 MUSIC. A light-hearted combination of several tunes; a medley. E19.
■ **quodlibetal** *adjective* (*rare*) = QUODLIBETICAL M19. **quodlibeˈtarian** *noun* (*Hist.*) a person who discusses quodlibets E18. **quodliˈbetic** *adjective* (*rare*) = QUODLIBETICAL M17. **quodliˈbetical** *adjective* (*Hist.*) of the nature of or concerned with a quodlibet or quodlibets L16.

quoin /kɔɪn/ *noun.* Also (earlier) **coin**. ME.
[Var. of COIN *noun*: cf. COIGN *noun*.]
1 An external angle of a wall or building; any of the stones or bricks forming this angle, a cornerstone. ME.
2 a A wedge for keeping a thing securely in position; *spec.* (*a*) PRINTING either of a pair of wooden wedges for locking up a forme of type; a metal device operated by a key performing a similar function; (*b*) NAUTICAL a wedge for preventing casks, cannons, etc. from rolling freely on a ship. L16. ▸**b** A wedge with a handle at the thick end, for adjusting the level of a gun barrel. E17. ▸**c** Any of the wedge-shaped stones of an arch, esp. the keystone. *rare.* M18.
3 An angle; a wedge-shaped object. M19.
3 *trigonal quoin*: see TRIGONAL 1b. ***trihedral quoin***: see TRIHEDRAL *adjective*.
■ **quoining** *noun* stone or brick (for) forming a quoin of a wall or building LME.

quoin /kɔɪn/ *verb trans.* Also (earlier) **coin**, **coigne**. L15.
[from prec., partly as var. of COIN *verb*².]
1 Secure or raise with a quoin or wedge. Also foll. by *up*. L15.
2 Provide with quoins or corners. E18.

quoit /kɔɪt, kwɔɪt/ *noun & verb.* LME.
[Origin unkn.]
▶ **A** *noun.* **1** A flat disc of stone or metal, thrown as an exercise of strength or skill; now *spec.* a heavy flattened sharp-edged iron ring thrown to encircle or land as near as possible to an iron peg. Also, a ring of rope, rubber, etc., used similarly. LME. ▸**b** A curling-stone. *rare.* E19.
2 In *pl.* & (rare) *sing.* Aiming and throwing quoits, as a game. LME.
3 Orig., a quoit-shaped stone or piece of metal. Now only, the flat covering stone of a dolmen; *transf.* a dolmen. L16. ▸**b** The buttocks. *Austral. slang.* M20.
2 *deck quoits*: see DECK *noun*¹.
▶ **B** *verb.* **1** *verb intrans.* Play quoits. Now *rare.* LME.
2 *verb trans.* Throw like a quoit. Also foll. by *away, down, out*, etc. L16.
■ **quoiter** *noun* a person who throws or plays quoits LME.

quokka /ˈkwɒkə/ *noun.* M19.
[Aboriginal.]
A small rare short-tailed wallaby, *Setonix brachyurus*, of coastal scrub in SW Australia.

quoll /kwɒl/ *noun.* L18.
[Aboriginal.]
The dasyure (native cat), *Dasyurus viverrinus*, of SE Australia.

quomodo /ˈkwəʊmədəʊ/ *noun.* Now *rare.* Also **quo modo** /kwəʊ ˈməʊdəʊ/. L17.
[Latin = in what way?]
The manner, *the* way, *the* means.

quondam /ˈkwɒndəm, -dam/ *adverb, noun, & adjective.* M16.
[Latin = formerly.]
▶ **A** *adverb.* At one time, formerly. *rare.* M16.
▶ **B** *noun.* The former holder of an office or position; *derog.* a person who has been deposed or ejected. M16.
▶ **C** *adjective.* That once was or existed; former. L16.

Quonset /ˈkwɒnsɪt/ *noun & adjective.* Orig. & chiefly *US*. Also **q-**. M20.
[*Quonset* Point, Rhode Island, where the buildings were first made.]
(Designating or resembling) a type of prefabricated building consisting of a semi-cylindrical corrugated metal roof on a bolted steel foundation.
¶ Proprietary name in the US.

quop /kwɒp/ *verb intrans.* Long *rare* exc. *dial.* Also †**quap**. Infl. **-pp-**. LME.
[Imit.]
Beat, throb, palpitate.

quorate /ˈkwɔːrət, -reɪt/ *adjective.* M20.
[from QUOR(UM + -ATE².]
Of a meeting: attended by a quorum, and thereby constitutional.

Quorn /kwɔːn/ *noun.* L20.
[from *Quorn* Specialities Ltd, original manufacturers, from the name of a village (now Quorndon) in Leicestershire.]
(Proprietary name for) a type of mycoprotein made from an edible fungus and used as a meat substitute in cooking.

quorum /ˈkwɔːrəm/ *noun.* LME.
[Latin, lit. 'of whom (we wish that you be one, two, etc.)' in the wording of commissions for members of bodies, committees, etc.]
1 Orig., certain (usu. eminent) justices of the peace whose presence was necessary to constitute a deciding body. Later *gen.*, all justices collectively. LME. ▸**b** *transf.* Distinguished or essential members of any body; a select company. L16.
2 A fixed minimum number of members whose presence is necessary to make the proceedings of an assembly, society, etc., valid. E17.

quota /ˈkwəʊtə/ *noun & verb.* E17.
[medieval Latin *quota* (sc. *pars*) how great (a part) fem. of *quotus*, from Latin *quot* how many.]
▶ **A** *noun.* **1** The share which an individual or group is obliged to contribute to a total; *spec.* (ECCLESIASTICAL) the proportion of the funds of a parish contributed to the finances of the diocese (chiefly in ***diocesan quota***). Now also, the minimum number or quantity of a particular product which under official regulations must be produced, exported, imported, etc. E17. ▸**b** In a system of proportional representation, the minimum number of votes required to elect a candidate. M19.
2 The share of a total or the maximum number or quantity belonging, due, given, or permitted to an individual or group. L17. ▸**b** The maximum number (of immigrants or imports) allowed to enter a country within a set period; (a) regulation imposing such a restriction on entry to a country. Also, the number of students allowed to enrol for a course, at a college, etc., at the start of or over an academic year. E20.

> 🕮 **1** W. ROBERTSON The . . troops were . . inferior in number to the quota stipulated. N. SHERRY The number of words written and the quotas fulfilled. *Washington Post* They will have to meet minimum quotas for the specific grains. **2** A. SHAW The collector disburses to each . . authority its respective quota. *Financial Times* It . . voted for a reduced quota on minke whales. **b** *Japan Times* Classed as a Japanese import and hence subject to quota.

Comb.: **quota method** the statistical method of using quota samples (usu. for opinion polls); **quota quickie** *colloq.* (now *rare*) a film made quickly and cheaply in a country outside the US to offset American films shown there; **quota sample**: from a stratified population obtained by sampling until a pre-assigned quota or number in each stratum is represented; **quota sampling** the use of the quota method; **quota system** a law, rule, or custom prescribing the maximum or minimum number or proportion of persons or goods to be admitted to a country, institution, etc.
▶ **B** *verb trans.* Impose a quota on. L18.

quotable /ˈkwəʊtəb(ə)l/ *adjective.* E19.
[from QUOTE *verb* + -ABLE.]
Able to be quoted; suitable for quoting.

> 🕮 S. BEDFORD He was a quotable judge, a witty judge, a talking judge.

■ **quotaˈbility** *noun* M19.

quotation /kwə(ʊ)ˈteɪʃ(ə)n/ *noun.* LME.
[medieval Latin *quotatio(n-)*, from *quotat-* pa. ppl stem of *quotare*: see QUOTE *verb*, -ATION.]
†**1** A numbering; a number. *rare.* Only in LME.
2 †**a** A (marginal) reference to a passage of text. Cf. QUOTE *verb* 2. M16–L17. ▸**b** TYPOGRAPHY. A large (usu. hollow) quadrat for filling blanks in letterpress printing (orig. between marginal references). *obsolete* exc. *Hist.* L17.
†**3** A note or observation; a matter noted. E–M17.
4 a A quoted passage or remark; *transf.* a short passage or tune taken from one piece of music and quoted in another; a visual image taken from one work of art and used in another. E17. ▸**b** The action or an act of quoting. M17.
5 The amount stated as the current price of a stock or commodity; a contractor's estimate for a specified job etc. E19.

> 🕮 **4a** *Guardian* Time to sprinkle his . . speech with quotations from Shakespeare and Burns. **b** *Early Music* The quotation of well-known refrains was the Trivial Pursuit of the day.

Comb.: **quotation mark** either of a set of punctuation marks (in English, single or double inverted commas) used to mark the beginning and end of a quotation, book title, etc., or words regarded as slang or jargon.
■ **quotational** *adjective* M19. **quotationist** *noun* (*rare*) a person who (habitually) makes quotations M17.

quote /kwəʊt/ *noun*¹. *rare.* LME.
[Old French *cote, quote* QUOTA.]
†**1 a** MATH. An aliquot part. Only in LME. ▸**b** A quotient. L17–M18.
2 †**a** = QUOTA 1. LME–E17. ▸**b** SCOTS LAW (now *Hist.*). The portion of a deceased person's movable estate payable to the bishop of the diocese where the deceased resided at death. E16.

quote /kwəʊt/ *verb & noun*². Orig. †**cote**. LME.
[medieval Latin *quotare* to number, from Latin *quot* how many or medieval Latin QUOTA. Cf. French *coter*.]
▶ **A** *verb.* **I** †**1** *verb trans.* Mark (esp. a book) with numbers (as of chapters etc.), (marginal) references, or lines. *rare.* LME–E17.
†**2 a** *verb trans.* Give the page, chapter, reference to (a passage of text). L16–M17. ▸**b** *verb intrans.* Set down references. *rare.* L16–M17.
3 *verb trans.* Repeat a passage from or statement by; cite or refer to (a person or text), esp. as the source of or authority for a statement. L16.
4 *verb trans.* Repeat or copy out (a passage, statement, etc.), usu. with an indication that one is borrowing another's words; *transf.* repeat (a passage or tune) from one piece of music to another. Also foll. by *from*. L17. ▸**b** *verb intrans.* Make quotations. Freq. foll. by *from*. L18. ▸**c** *verb trans.* Used parenthetically to indicate the start of a quotation. Cf. UNQUOTE *verb*. M20.

> 🕮 **3** *Observer* If the devil can quote scripture, surely a bishop can quote Lenin. *New Yorker* I wouldn't want to be quoted on this. *Guardian* 'Martyrs are nobler than us all', the president is quoted as saying on a . . plaque nearby. **4** *Guardian* He quoted some well-known lines from Goethe. **b** E. BLISHEN Someone quoting from a railway timetable. **c** K. HULME My radiophone operator said, quote, he's a wellknown . . oddity, unquote.

▶ **II** †**5** *verb trans.* Make a note or record of; notice, observe; write down. L16–M17.
6 *verb trans.* †**a** Note, or mention, *for* some quality or action. L16–E18. ▸**b** Cite or put forward *as* an instance or example of or *as* having a particular quality or doing a particular thing. E19.
7 *verb trans.* State the price of (a stock, commodity, service, etc.); state the odds in (a race, bet, etc.). Also, give (a person) a quotation for goods, services, etc. E19.

> 🕮 **6b** N. YOUNG Shifts in Labour policy . . were quoted as CND successes. **7** *Which?* Give them full details of the product . . , and they quote you the . . price. *County Cuisine* David quoted him £1,000 . . and won the order. *Wall Street Journal* The dollar was quoted at 1.8548 marks.

▶ **B** *noun.* †**1** A (marginal) reference; a note. Only in E17.
2 a A passage or remark quoted; a quotation. L19. ▸**b** A quotation mark. Usu. in *pl.* L19.
3 A price or amount quoted. M20.

> 🕮 **2a** T. S. ELIOT Not use the Conrad quote? **b** *Scottish Leader* The portion of this quotation which we have put within quotes.

■ **quotative** *adjective & noun* (*a*) *adjective* (chiefly LINGUISTICS) pertaining to, inclined to, or indicating quotation; (*b*) *noun* (LINGUISTICS) a quotative word or expression: E19. **quotativeness** *noun* (*rare*) the quality of being quotative L19. **quoˈtee** *noun* a person who is quoted E19. **quoter** *noun* L16.

quoth /kwəʊθ/ *verb trans. pa.* (*1 & 3*, chiefly *sing.*). Now *arch. & dial.* ME.
[pa. t. of QUETHE.]
Said. Chiefly with direct speech as obj.

quotha /ˈkwəʊθə/ *interjection. arch.* E16.
[Contr. of *quoth he*: see A *pronoun*.]
Expr. irony, contempt, incredulity, etc. Usu. following a repeated statement etc.

> 🕮 R. L. STEVENSON Learning quotha! After what fashion?

quotidian /kwɒˈtɪdɪən, kwəʊ-/ *adjective & noun.* ME.
[Old French *cotidien* (mod. *quotidien*), assim. to Latin *quotidianus* (earlier *cotidianus*), from *cotidie* every day: see -IAN.]
▶ **A** *adjective.* **1** Daily; of or pertaining to every day; (of a fever etc.) recurring every day; *spec.* designating malignant malaria caused by *Plasmodium falciparum*. ME.
2 Of a person: performing some act or sustaining some characteristic daily. *rare.* LME.
3 Ordinary; everyday, commonplace; trivial. LME.
🕮 **1** A. POWELL A lacerating quotidian regime of business luncheons. **3** J. BARNES Gillian's rebarbatively quotidian motor-car. Definitely not a Lagonda.
▶ **B** *noun.* **1** A quotidian fever or ague. LME.
2 A daily allowance or portion. *rare.* E19.
3 *absol.* The ordinary, commonplace, or trivial. M20.
▪ **quotidianly** *adverb* (*rare*) LME.

quotient /ˈkwəʊʃ(ə)nt/ *noun.* LME.
[Latin *quotiens* how many times (from *quot* how many), erron. taken as a ppl form in *-ens, -ent-*: -ENT.]
1 MATH. The result obtained by dividing one quantity by another; the number of times one number is contained in another as ascertained by division. LME.
†**2** = QUOTUM. *rare.* E–M17.
1 *intelligence quotient*: see INTELLIGENCE *noun.* RESPIRATORY *quotient.*
Comb.: **quotient group** = *factor group* s.v. FACTOR *noun.*

quotity /ˈkwɒtɪti/ *noun. rare.* E17.
[formed as QUOTA + -ITY, perh. after French *quotité*: cf. QUANTITY.]
1 = QUOTUM. E17.
2 A certain number (*of* individuals etc.). M19.

quotum /ˈkwəʊtəm/ *noun.* M17.
[Latin, neut. sing. of *quotus*: see QUOTA.]
A number or quantity considered in proportion to a larger number or amount of which it forms part; a quota.

quo warranto /kwəʊ wəˈrantəʊ/ *noun.* E16.
[Law Latin = by what warrant, abl. sing. of *quod* what and *warrantum* warrant.]
LAW (now *Hist.*). Orig., a King's or Queen's Bench writ obliging a person to show by what warrant an office or franchise was held, claimed, or exercised. Later, a legal action testing the legality of exercise of powers, as by a corporation.

Qur'an *noun* var. of KORAN.

Quraysh, **Qureysh** *nouns pl. & adjectives* vars. of KOREISH.

qursh /kʊəʃ, g-/ *noun.* Also †**cursh**, **girsh**, **kirsh**, **qirsh**. L18.
[Arab. *kirsh* from Slavonic *grossus*. Cf. GROSCHEN.]
Orig., a silver coin of various Middle-Eastern countries. Now, a monetary unit of Saudi Arabia equal to one-twentieth of a rial.

q.v. *abbreviation.*
Latin *Quod vide* which see.

qwerty /ˈkwəːti/ *adjective.* E20.
[The first six letters from the left on the top row of letter keys on a standard English-language typewriter.]
Pertaining to or designating a keyboard, typewriter, word processor, etc., having the standard non-alphabetical letter arrangement.
🕮 *Personal Computer World* The MZ 800 . . has . . a standard qwerty layout.

q.y. *abbreviation.*
Query.

Rr

R, r /ɑː/.
The eighteenth letter of the modern English alphabet and the seventeenth of the ancient Roman one, is derived through early Greek ρ from Phoenician, repr. the twentieth letter of the early Semitic alphabet. In general R denotes a post-alveolar voiced consonant, in the formation of which the point of the tongue approaches the palate a little way behind the teeth; in many languages this is accompanied by a vibration of the tongue, in which case the R is said to be 'trilled' or 'rolled'. This trill is almost or altogether absent in the R of mod. standard British English, which moreover retains its consonantal value only when it precedes a vowel (see ***linking r*** s.v. LINKING 1); in other positions it has been vocalized to an /ə/ sound, and even this is entirely lost after certain vowels. In Scotland R is still often strongly trilled in all positions, and other varieties of the sound are characteristic of certain districts of the UK. In other parts of the English-speaking world there are similarly varieties both with R only before vowels and with retention of its consonantal value in other historical positions. By southern British speakers R is frequently introduced between word-final and word-initial vowels (see ***intrusive r*** s.v. INTRUSIVE *adjective* 2). In all periods of English, R has exercised a marked effect on a preceding vowel, in modern English being associated with the lengthening of it. Pl. **R's, Rs.**
▶ **I 1** The letter and its sound.
1 r-colour the modification of a vowel sound caused by a following *r*, with retraction of the tongue, as in one US pronunciation of *bird*. **r month** a month in whose name an *r* appears, as being one of those (September to April) during which oysters are in season. **the three R's** reading, writing, and arithmetic (as the basis of elementary education).
▶ **II** Symbolical uses.
2 Used to denote serial order; applied e.g. to the eighteenth (or often the seventeenth, either I or J being omitted) group or section, sheet of a book, etc.
3 *CHEMISTRY.* [Abbreviation of *radical*.] (Cap. R.) In chemical formulae, an unspecified radical or group of radicals (usu. organic).
4 *PHYSICAL CHEMISTRY.* (Cap. R.) The gas constant.
5 *BIOLOGY.* (Italic *r*.) The rate of increase of a population, usually representing the factor by which its size is multiplied in each generation, or the value which this factor would have if resources were unlimited.
6 *PHYSICS.* (Cap. R.) The Rydberg constant.
7 *CHEMISTRY.* [Abbreviation of Latin *rectus* right.] (Cap. R.) Designating (compounds having) a configuration about an asymmetric carbon atom in which the substituents, placed in order according to certain rules, form a clockwise sequence when viewed from a particular direction. Opp. **S, S** 10.
8 *ASTRONOMY.* [Initial letter of *rapid*.] ***r-process***, a process believed to occur in stars in circumstances of high neutron flux (e.g. in supernova explosions), in which heavy atomic nuclei are formed from lighter ones by a combination of rapid neutron captures and slower beta decays. Opp. ***s-process***.
9 *MICROBIOLOGY.* [Initial letter of *resistance*.] (Cap. R.) Denoting certain plasmids which confer drug-resistance on bacteria and can be transferred to other bacteria by conjugation.
5 r selection the form of natural selection which acts on populations having ample resources and little or no competition.
▶ **III 10** Abbrevs.: **R** = Rabbi; radius; Railway; rand(s) (as monetary unit); Réaumur; (*MEDICINE*) Recipe; Regiment; Regina; registered (of a trade mark); (*US*) Republican; restricted (in US film classification); reverse (on the selector mechanism in a motor vehicle); Rex; right (as opp. left); River; roentgen; (*CHESS*) rook; Royal (in names of organizations). ℞ = (*MEDICINE*) Recipe; (*ECCLESIASTICAL*) Response. ® = registered (of a trade mark). **r** = radius (vector); (*NAUTICAL*) rain (in a logbook); recto; right (as opp. left); run(s) (in cricket).

RA *abbreviation.*
1 Rear Admiral.
2 *ASTRONOMY.* Right ascension.
3 Royal Academy; Royal Academician.
4 Royal Artillery.

Ra *symbol.*
CHEMISTRY. Radium.

raad /rɑːt/ *noun*[1]. M19.
[Dutch.]
In South Africa: a council, an assembly; *Hist.* (**R-**) the legislative assembly of one of the former Boer republics.

raad /rəˈɑːd, rɑːd/ *noun*[2]. M19.
[Arab. *raʿād* lit. 'thunder-striker'.]
The electric catfish, *Malapterurus electricus*, of the family Malapteruridae, found in the Nile and other rivers of central and western tropical Africa, and capable of giving a strong electric shock.

RAAF *abbreviation.*
Royal Australian Air Force.

rab /rab/ *noun*[1]. Chiefly *Cornish*. L19.
[Cornish *rabman*.]
Rough or stony subsoil; rubble, gravel.

rab *noun*[2] see RAV.

rabanna /rəˈbanə/ *noun.* L19.
[Malagasy *rabane*.]
A fabric woven from raffia and used as matting.

rabat /raˈbat/ *noun.* L16.
[French = collar.]
1 = RABATO. Long *obsolete* exc. *Hist.* L16.
2 A false shirt-front, a stock. M20.

rabat /rəˈbat/ *verb trans.* Infl. **-tt-**. L19.
[Old & mod. French *rabattre*: see REBATE *verb*[1].]
GEOMETRY. Rotate (a plane) about its line of intersection with another plane (*esp.* the horizontal plane) until the two coincide.
■ **rabatment** *noun* the process of rabatting a plane E20.

rabate /rəˈbeɪt/ *verb trans.* & †*intrans.* Long *obsolete* exc. *dial.* LME.
[formed as prec.]
= REBATE *verb*[1].

rabato /rəˈbɑːtəʊ/ *noun.* Long *obsolete* exc. *Hist.* Also **re-**. Pl. **-os.** L16.
[from French *rabat* collar etc., after Italian words in *-ato*.]
A stiff collar fashionable from the late 16th to the mid 17th cent.; such a collar, or a wire frame, used to support a ruff.

rabbet /ˈrabɪt/ *noun & verb.* LME.
[Old French *rab(b)at*, from *rabattre* beat back or down: see REBATE *verb*[1].]
▶ **A** *noun.* **1** A channel (usually rectangular in section) cut along the edge, face, or projecting angle of a piece of wood, stone, etc., usually to receive the edge or tongue of another piece. LME.
2 A side of such a channel in a projecting angle or corner. Formerly, a tongue to fit into a rabbet. L17.
3 A beam fixed so as to cause the rebounding of a large steam hammer. E19.
Comb.: **rabbet plane** a paring tool for cutting a groove along an edge.
▶ **B** *verb.* **1** *verb trans.* Join or fix by means of a rabbet or rabbets. Also foll. by *in*. M16.
2 *verb trans.* Form a rabbet in; cut *away* or *down* as in making a rabbet. L16.
3 *verb intrans.* Join *on* or lap *over* by means of a rabbet. M19.
■ **rabbeting** *noun* (*a*) the process of rabbeting boards or fitting rabbeted boards together; (*b*) the rabbeted portion of such boards: LME.

rabbi /ˈrabʌɪ/ *noun*[1]. LOE.
[ecclesiastical Latin & Greek, from Hebrew *rabbī* my master, from *rab* master.]
1 A Jewish scholar or teacher having authority on law and doctrine; now *spec.* one authorized by ordination to deal with questions of law and ritual and to perform certain functions. Also as a title of respect and form of address (usu. with following personal name). LOE.
2 *transf.* A person whose learning, authority, or status is comparable to that of a Jewish rabbi; *spec.* (*US slang*) a senior official who exerts influence or patronage on behalf of a person. M16.
1 Chief Rabbi *esp.* the religious head of the Jewish communities in Britain.
■ **rabbinate** *noun* (*a*) the position or office of a rabbi; (*b*) the period during which a person is a rabbi; (*c*) *collect.* rabbis as a body or a class: E18. **rabbiship** *noun* the position or office of rabbi M17.

rabbi /ˈrabi, ˈrabʌɪ/ *noun*[2]. E20.
[Alt. of RABAT *noun*.]
A stock, a rabat.

rabbin /ˈrabɪn/ *noun.* Now *rare.* Pl. **-s**, same. M16.
[French, or mod. Latin *rabbinus*, alt. of RABBI *noun*[1]; the *-n* may be due to a Semitic pl. form.]
†**1** = RABBI *noun*[1] 2. M16–M17.
2 = RABBI *noun*[1] 1. Usu. in *pl.* L16.
■ **rabbindom** *noun* the rule and government of rabbis L19. **rabbinship** *noun* (*rare*) a rabbinate; (with possess. adjective, as ***your rabbinship*** etc.) a title of respect given to a rabbi: L16.

rabbinic /rəˈbɪnɪk/ *adjective & noun.* E17.
[from prec. + -IC.]
▶ **A** *adjective.* = RABBINICAL. E17.
▶ **B** *noun.* **1** Rabbinical Hebrew. M19.
2 In *pl.* The branch of learning that deals with the writings or doctrines of rabbis. E20.

rabbinical /rəˈbɪnɪk(ə)l/ *adjective.* E17.
[formed as prec. + -ICAL.]
1 Pertaining to or characteristic of rabbis or their learning, writings, etc.; *spec.* designating the later form of Hebrew used by rabbis. E17.
2 Of a person: belonging to the class of rabbis; resembling a rabbi; occupied with or skilled in rabbinical literature. M17.
■ **rabbinically** *adverb* L17.

rabbinise *verb* var. of RABBINIZE.

rabbinist /ˈrabɪnɪst/ *noun.* L16.
[formed as prec. + -IST.]
A follower or adherent of rabbis; a person who accepts the teaching of the Talmud and the rabbis.
■ **rabbinism** *noun* the teaching or doctrines of the rabbis M17. **rabbiˈnistic** *adjective* L19.

rabbinize /ˈrabɪnʌɪz/ *verb. rare.* Also **-ise.** M17.
[from RABBIN + -IZE.]
†**1** *verb intrans.* Adopt or conform to rabbinism. Only in M17.
2 *verb trans.* Imbue with rabbinism. M19.

rabbit /ˈrabɪt/ *noun.* LME.
[Origin uncertain: perh. from an Old French form repr. by French dial. *rabbotte*, *rabouillet* young rabbit, *rabouillère* rabbit burrow, perh. of Low Dutch origin (cf. Flemish *robbe*, dim. *robbeke*, Dutch †*robett*, Walloon *robète*).]
1 Any of various gregarious burrowing plant-eating mammals of the family Leporidae (order Lagomorpha), with long ears (but not as long as a hare's) and a short stumpy tail; esp. *Oryctolagus cuniculus*, native to Europe and of a brown colour in the wild, and widely kept as a pet and for meat; the flesh of this as food. Formerly *spec.*, a young animal of this kind (the adult being called a cony). Also (*US*), a hare. LME. ▶**b** A thing resembling a rabbit. M19. ▶**c** Rabbit's fur. E20.
2 A person; *spec.* (*slang*) a poor performer at a sport or game, a novice. *derog.* L16.
3 A smuggled or stolen article. *Nautical & Austral. slang.* E20.
4 A conversation, a talk. Also, jargon, dialect. Also more fully ***rabbit-and-pork***. *rhyming slang.* M20.
5 = PIG *noun*[1] 8. M20.
6 A pneumatically or hydraulically propelled container used to convey material into a nuclear reactor etc. M20.
Phrases: **buy the rabbit** *slang* fare badly, come off worse. ***Welsh rabbit***: see WELSH *adjective*.
Comb.: ***rabbit-and-pork***: see sense 4 above; **rabbit ball** *US* a baseball that is springy in construction and lively in action; **rabbit-bandicoot** a small Australian marsupial of the genus *Macrotis* which lives in a burrow and has ears like a rabbit's; **rabbit berry** (the berry of) the buffalo berry, *Shepherdia argentea*; **rabbit brush, rabbit bush** a shrub of the composite family, *Chrysothamnus nauseosus*, of the western US, bearing clusters of yellow flowers like goldenrod; **rabbit-dog**: that is good for hunting rabbits; **rabbit drive** *US* a drive of jackrabbits for slaughtering; **rabbit-eared bandicoot** = ***rabbit-bandicoot*** above; **rabbit fever** *colloq.* tularaemia; **rabbit-fish** any of several fishes with points of resemblance to a rabbit, *esp.* (*a*) a chimaera, esp. *Chimaera monstrosa* of the Atlantic Ocean and the Mediterranean; (*b*) any fish of the family Siganidae, of tropical waters of the Indian and Pacific Oceans, caught as a food fish; esp. *Sigamus oranim* of the Indian Ocean; **rabbit food** *slang* lettuce, green salad; **rabbit-foot** *US* (*a*) (more fully ***rabbit-foot clover***) = ***rabbit's foot*** (b) below; (*b*) ***rabbit-foot grass***, a naturalized European grass, *Polypogon monspeliensis*, with a silky panicle; (*c*) ***work the rabbit-foot on*** = ***work the rabbit's foot on*** below; **rabbit-proof** *adjective & noun* (*a*) *adjective* proof against rabbits; *esp.* designating a fence through which rabbits cannot pass; (*b*) *noun* (*Austral.*) a rabbit-proof fence, *esp.* one marking a border between States; **rabbit punch** a sharp chopping blow with the side of the hand to the back of another person's neck; **rabbit-punch** *verb trans.* hit with a rabbit punch; **rabbit's ear** (*a*) lamb's ears, *Stachys*

byzantina; (**b**) an indoor television aerial consisting of a base supporting two stiff wires that form a V; **rabbit's foot** (*a*) the foot of a rabbit carried to bring luck (***work the rabbit's foot on*** (*US*), cheat, trick); (**b**) *US* (more fully ***rabbit's foot clover***) hare's-foot trefoil, *Trifolium arvense*; (**c**) *US* (more fully ***rabbit's foot fern***) an epiphytic fern, *Phlebodium aureum*, native to tropical America and grown for ornament, so called from its prominent brown rhizome; **rabbit test** a pregnancy test in which rabbit ovaries are used; **rabbit tobacco** *US* the sweet everlasting, *Gnaphalium obtusifolium*, bearing fragrant white flowers; its dried flowers, used as a substitute for tobacco; **rabbit tooth** *slang* = ***buck-tooth*** s.v. BUCK *noun*[1]; ***rabbit warren***: see WARREN *noun*[1] 2.

■ **rabbitish** *adjective* characteristic of or resembling a rabbit **M19**. **rabbit-like** *adjective* resembling (that of) a rabbit **M19**. **rabbitry** *noun* (*a*) a place in which rabbits are kept; a collection of rabbits; (*b*) rabbit-breeding; (*c*) *slang* in sport, poor performers; poor play or performance in any game: **M19**. **rabbity** *adjective* (*a*) containing many rabbits; (*b*) somewhat like (that of) a rabbit, suggestive of a rabbit: **E19**.

rabbit /ˈrabɪt/ *verb*[1] *trans. & intrans. slang.* **M18.**
[Prob. alt. of *rat* in *od-rat*: see DRAT *verb*.]
= DRAT.

rabbit /ˈrabɪt/ *verb*[2]. **M19.**
[from RABBIT *noun*.]
1 *verb intrans.* Hunt for or catch rabbits. Chiefly as ***rabbiting*** *verbal noun & ppl adjective.* **M19.**
2 *verb intrans.* Go; move quickly, run; run away. *colloq. & dial.* **L19.**
3 *verb trans.* Borrow, steal. *nautical & Austral. slang.* **M20.**
4 *verb intrans.* Talk volubly; gabble. Freq. foll. by *on*. *colloq.* **M20.**

📖 **2** J. STEINBECK That girl rabbits in an' tells the law she been raped. **4** *Guardian Weekly* A girl reporter . . rabbits on about the Maharishi.

■ **rabbiter** *noun* a person or dog that hunts rabbits **L19**.

rabbit-o /ˈrabɪtəʊ/ *noun. Austral. slang.* Pl. **-os**. Also **-oh**. **E20.**
[from RABBIT *noun* + -O.]
An itinerant seller of rabbits as food.

rabble /ˈrab(ə)l/ *noun*[1] *& adjective.* **LME.**
[Prob. from RABBLE *verb*[1].]
▶ **A** *noun.* **1** †**a** A long series *of* words etc. having little meaning or value. **LME–M17.** ▶†**b** A pack, string, or swarm of animals. **LME–L16.** ▶**c** A rigmarole. Long *obsolete* exc. *dial.* **L16.**
2 A disorderly crowd of people, a mob; *derog.* a category of people imagined as collected in a mob; (without article) people of the lowest class, *the* common or disorderly part of a populace or (formerly) group. **E16.**
3 A disorderly collection of things. Now only with direct ref. to sense 2. **E16.**

📖 **2** TENNYSON To mob me up with all The soft and milky rabble of womankind. C. SANDBURG As a fence, it . . will shut off the rabble and all the vagabonds. S. WEINTRAUB Viscount Melbourne . . blamed all discontent upon a rabble of agitators. **3** R. W. EMERSON We live in youth amidst the rabble of passions.

Comb.: **rabble-rouser** (*a*) a person who arouses the emotions of a crowd or of the people for social or political purposes; a demagogue; (*b*) a piece of music that excites an audience; **rabble-rousing** *adjective & noun* (*a*) *adjective* tending to arouse the emotions of a crowd, inflammatory; (*b*) *noun* the action of a rabble-rouser, demagoguery; **rabble rout** = sense 2 above.

▶ **B** *attrib.* or as *adjective*. Forming a rabble, belonging to the rabble; characteristic of the rabble. **M16.**

📖 S. JOHNSON To burn the jails . . was a good rabble trick.

rabble /ˈrab(ə)l/ *noun*[2]. **M17.**
[French *râble* (earlier *roable*) from medieval Latin *rotabulum* = Latin *rutabulum* fire-shovel, oven rake, from *rut-*, *ruere* rake up.]
1 A shovel used by charcoal-burners to remove the covering from the burned pile. Long *obsolete* exc. *dial.* **M17.**
2 *METALLURGY.* An iron bar for stirring and skimming molten metal or cleaning the hearth of a furnace. **M19.**

rabble /ˈrab(ə)l/ *verb*[1]. *obsolete* exc. *dial.* **ME.**
[Prob. from Middle Dutch *rabbelen*, Low German *rabbeln*, of imit. origin.]
1 *verb intrans. & trans.* = GABBLE *verb* 1, 3. Also foll. by *forth*, *out*, etc. **ME.**
2 *verb intrans.* Work in a hurried slovenly manner. **M19.**

rabble /ˈrab(ə)l/ *verb*[2]. **L16.**
[from RABBLE *noun*[1].]
1 *verb intrans.* Become a rabble; behave as a rabble. Long only as ***rabbling*** *ppl adjective.* **L16.**
2 *verb trans.* Attack as a rabble or along with a rabble; mob; drive *out of* a place in this way. Chiefly *Hist.*, with ref. to attacks made on Episcopalian clergy in Scotland by bands of Presbyterians in 1688–9. **M17.**

rabble /ˈrab(ə)l/ *verb*[3] *trans.* **M19.**
[from RABBLE *noun*[2].]
METALLURGY. Stir, skim, or rake with a rabble.

rabblement /ˈrab(ə)lm(ə)nt/ *noun.* **M16.**
[from RABBLE *noun*[1] + -MENT.]
1 A rabble, a mob. Now *dial.* **M16.**
†**2** = RABBLE *noun*[1] 3. **M16–M17.**
†**3 a** = RABBLE *noun*[1] 1A. **M16–E18.** ▶**b** = RABBLE *noun*[1] 1C. **M16–M19.**
4 Confusion, riotous conduct. *rare.* **L16.**

Rabelaisian /rabəˈleɪzɪən/ *adjective & noun.* **E19.**
[from *Rabelais* (see below) + -IAN.]
▶ **A** *adjective.* Pertaining to, characteristic of, or resembling the French satirist François Rabelais (*c* 1494–1553) or his writing; marked by exuberant imagination and language, coarse humour, and satire. **E19.**
▶ **B** *noun.* An admirer or student of Rabelais or his writing. **L19.**

■ **Rabelaisianism** *noun* the characteristic style or attitude of Rabelais; a Rabelaisian feature or characteristic: **L19**. **Rabelaism** /-ˈleɪz(ə)m/ *noun* Rabelaisianism **E19**.

Rabfak /ˈrabfak/ *noun.* **E20.**
[Russian, from *rabochiĭ fakul'tet* workers' school.]
A workers' school of the kind established after the Russian Revolution to prepare workers and peasants for higher education.

rabi /ˈrabiː/ *noun.* **M19.**
[Persian & Urdu from Arab. *rabī'* spring.]
In the Indian subcontinent: the grain crop sown in September and reaped in the spring.

rabid /ˈrabɪd, ˈreɪ-/ *adjective.* **E17.**
[Latin *rabidus*, from *rabere* be mad: see -ID[1].]
1 Furious, raging; madly violent in nature or behaviour. **E17.**
2 Of a person: that is something to an unreasoning extent; fanatical. **E19.**
3 Affected with rabies; pertaining to or of the nature of rabies. **E19.**

📖 **1** R. GRAVES Honest men sleeping Start awake with rabid eyes, Bone-chilled, flesh creeping. *Health Express* I . . cannot stop feeling this rabid hunger. **2** C. LAMB B. was a rabid pedant. R. CAMPBELL Those strapping girls whose love . . Would make a rabid Mormon of a priest.

■ **raˈbidity** *noun* **M19**. **rabidly** *adverb* **L19**. **rabidness** *noun* **M17**.

rabies /ˈreɪbiːz, -ɪz/ *noun.* **L16.**
[Latin, from *rabere* be mad.]
A contagious virus disease that affects the central nervous system of warm-blooded animals and is transmitted to humans in saliva, esp. by dog bites, causing throat spasm on swallowing, aversion to water, convulsions, paralysis, and death. Also called ***hydrophobia***.

■ **rabic** /ˈrab-/ *adjective* pertaining to, caused by, or affected with rabies **L19**. **rabious** *adjective* (*arch.*) [Latin *rabiosus*] rabid **E17**.

rabinet /ˈrabɪnɛt/ *noun. obsolete* exc. *Hist.* **L16.**
[Alt. of ROBINET.]
A kind of small cannon.

RAC *abbreviation.*
1 Royal Armoured Corps.
2 Royal Automobile Club.

Racah /ˈrɑːkɑː/ *noun.* **M20.**
[Giulio *Racah* (1909–65), Italian-born Israeli physicist.]
PHYSICS. ***Racah coefficient***, ***Racah parameter***, either of two coefficients representing electrostatic interactions within a system of equivalent charged particles, esp. electrons within an atom.

†**raccommode** *verb trans.* **L17–M18.**
[French *raccommoder*, from *re-* RE- + *accommoder* ACCOMMODATE *verb*.]
Set right, repair; *refl.* reconcile (oneself) *with*.

raccoon *noun* var. of RACOON.

raccourci /rakursi/ *noun.* Pl. pronounced same. **M20.**
[French, use as noun of pa. pple of *raccourcir* shorten.]
BALLET. A movement in which the toe is made to touch the bent knee of the other leg.

race /reɪs/ *noun*[1]. **LOE.**
[Old Norse *rás* = Old English *rǣs*, Middle Low German *rās* current.]
▶ **I** With ref. to motion.
1 (Esp. rapid) forward movement; *spec.* (and now only) the regular course or movement of the sun or moon through the heavens. **LOE.** ▶†**b** Rapid action, haste. **LOE–LME.** ▶†**c** An impact resulting from (esp. rapid) forward motion. *rare.* **LME–M16.** ▶**d** A strong current in the sea, river, etc. **LME.**
2 An act or instance of (esp. rapid) forward movement; a run; a rush; an attack. *obsolete* exc. *Scot.* **LOE.** ▶†**b** A journey, a voyage. **LME–M16.** ▶**c** *fig.* The course or progress of life, time, a period of time, etc. **E16.**
3 A contest of speed between runners, horses, vehicles, etc.; in *pl.* a series of these held at a fixed time on a regular course. **E16.** ▶**b** *fig.* A contest or competition between individuals, groups, etc., to (be first to) achieve some objective, esp. superiority; *spec.* (*N. Amer.*) an election. **M19.** ▶**c** *ELECTRONICS.* A condition in a switching circuit in which the operation may depend on the relative arrival time of input signals. Also more fully ***race condition***. **M20.**

📖 **1d** *Lifeboat* Eddies and races . . can become . . violent. **2c** TENNYSON Whom I shall not see Till all my widow'd race be run. **3** AV *Eccles.* 9:11 The race is not to the swift. LONGFELLOW Swimming, skating, snow-shoe races. DAY LEWIS I was as breathless . . as if I had . . run a 440-yards race. ***boat race***, ***classic races***, ***drag race***, ***flat race***, ***pancake race***, ***sack race***, ***welter race***, etc. **be in the race** have a chance (freq. in neg. contexts). **b** G. B. SHAW A race of armaments. *Australian Financial Review* After . . tight races, Republicans were expected to pick up about 14 . . seats. *City Limits* The race is on to see if Lambeth . . can carry out more Labour policies. ***arms race***: see ARM *noun*[2]. **make the race** run for public office. ***space race***: see SPACE *noun*.

▶ **II** With ref. to what is traversed.
4 a A portion of time or space; a period of time; the distance between two points. *rare.* Long *obsolete* exc. *dial.* **ME.** ▶**b** A straight level stretch of ground, suitable for running or racing on. *rare.* **E17.**
5 †**a** A course or path, esp. as taken by a person or a moving body. **LME–L16.** ▶**b** A water channel, the bed of a stream; *spec.* a channel built to lead water to or from a mill, mine, etc. Cf. MILL-RACE. **L16.** ▶**c** *MINING.* A small vein of spar or ore. *rare.* **L16.** ▶**d** A groove, channel, passage, or path directing or restricting movement; *spec.* (*a*) the channel in the batten of a loom, along which the shuttle moves; (*b*) *rare* a circular path to be followed by a horse that is driving machinery; (*c*) (chiefly *dial.*) a fenced passageway for drafting sheep etc. **M19.** ▶**e** Either of the two grooved rings of a ball-bearing or roller bearing. **E20.**

Comb.: **race card** a printed card giving information about races; a programme of races; ***race condition***: see sense 3C above; **racecourse** an area marked out as the site or route of a race; *spec.* a ground or track for horse-racing; **race game** a board game simulating a race, in which rival tokens or counters proceed, often at the throw of a dice; **race glasses** field glasses for use at races; **race meeting** an event consisting of a sequence of horse-races at one place; **race-reader** a person who broadcasts, comments on, or forecasts the performance of competitors in a race; **racetrack** (orig. *US*) = ***racecourse*** above; **race walker** a person who engages in race walking; **race walking** an act or the practice or sport of walking as a contest of speed, requiring a continuous progress of steps in which one or other of the feet is always in contact with the ground.

race /reɪs/ *noun*[2]. **LME.**
[Old French *rais*, *raiz* from Latin *radic-*, *radix* root.]
A root of ginger.

race /reɪs/ *noun*[3]. **E16.**
[French from Italian *razza*.]
▶ **I 1** A group or set, esp. of people, having a common feature or features. **E16.**
2 A particular class of wine; the characteristic flavour of this. Now *rare* or *obsolete.* **E16.** ▶**b** *fig.* A characteristic individual style or manner of speech, writing, etc., esp. liveliness, piquancy. **L17.**

📖 **1** SIR W. SCOTT The faded race of fallen leaves. JO GRIMOND Writers to the papers are . . a race on their own.

▶ **II** A group of living things connected by common descent or origin.
3 a A person's offspring; a set of children or descendants; a limited group of people descended from a common ancestor; a family, a kindred. Also (*rare*, now chiefly *dial.*) a particular generation. **M16.** ▶**b** A tribe, nation, or people, regarded as of common stock. **L16.** ▶†**c** Breeding; the production of offspring. **E–M17.**
4 †**a** A herd of horses. **M16–M17.** ▶**b** A breed or stock of animals or plants; *BIOLOGY* a genetically or morphologically distinct (subspecific) variety of an animal or plant. **L16.** ▶**c** A kind or species of animal or plant. Chiefly *poet.* **L16.**
5 (Without article.) ▶**a** The stock, class, family, etc. to which a living thing belongs; descent; kindred. **M16.** ▶**b** Natural or inherited disposition. *rare* (Shakes.). Only in **E17.** ▶**c** The fact or condition of belonging to a particular people, ethnic group, etc.; the qualities or characteristics associated with this. **L18.**
6 a (Usu. with *the*.) Humankind. **L16.** ▶**b** Any of the major divisions of living creatures. Chiefly *poet.* **L17.** ▶**c** Any of the major divisions of humankind, having in common distinct physical features or ethnic background. **L18.**

📖 **3a** TENNYSON Two daughters of one race. **4b** P. MATTHIESSEN As for the argali . . the best-known race is the Marco Polo sheep. E. T. SETON Distinctions on which the scientist founds . . species and races. ANTHONY HUXLEY New races of . . food plants. **c** SHELLEY I wish the race of cows were perished. **5a** T. GRAY Two Coursers of ethereal race. A. J. TOYNBEE In race he is pure Indian. **c** *Financial Times* Education . . regardless of race. **6a** B. WEBB The future of the race and the search for the Purpose of Human Life. **b** DRYDEN There dwells below a Race of Demi-Gods. ***human race***: see HUMAN *adjective*. **c** HENRY MILLER Not the home of the white . . or the black race but . . of *man*. ***master race***: see MASTER *noun*[1] *& adjective*.

Comb.: **race consciousness** (emotional) awareness of racial differences between people or social groups; the supposed intuitive awareness of the common heritage of a race or culture; **race man** *US colloq.* a black person, esp. a black rights advocate or activist; **race memory** (a) posited subconscious memory of events in human history (esp. that of one's race), allegedly transmitted genetically; **race music** a style of music, freq. in a twelve-bar sequence, originating among black people of the southern US; music that is liked by black audiences; **race record**: recording or playing race music; **race relations**: between racial groups within a particular area; **race riot**: caused by racial hostility; **race suicide** the decline in population, cultural vitality, influence, etc.; through low birth rate, esp. in contrast to a racial group sharing the same geographical area and having a high birth rate; the self-destruction of a race; **race theorist** an advocate of a race theory; **race theory**: asserting that each race possesses specific characteristics, abilities, qualities, etc., esp. distinguishing it as superior or inferior; **race-thinking** formulation of ideas about humankind, society, etc., based on perception of racial differences.

■ **raci'ologist** *noun* an expert in or student of raciology M20. **raci'ology** *noun* the characteristics of a race or races of humankind; the branch of knowledge that deals with these: E20.

†**race** *noun*[4]. E16–E18.
[Origin unkn. Cf. RACHE *noun*[2].]
A (white) mark down the face of a horse etc.

race /reɪs/ *noun*[5]. *obsolete* exc. *dial.* M17.
[from RACE *verb*[2].]
The heart, liver, and lungs, esp. of a calf.

race /reɪs/ *noun*[6]. E18.
[Origin unkn.]
A nodular calcareous substance in brick-clay.

race *noun*[7] see RAZE *noun*.

†**race** *verb*[1] *trans.* Also **rase**. ME–L16.
[Aphet. of ARACE.]
Pull or pluck *away, down, from, off, out, up*.

race /reɪs/ *verb*[2]. L15.
[from RACE *noun*[1].]
1 *verb intrans.* **a** Take part in a race; compete in speed with. L15. ▸**b** Move, perform, or progress swiftly or at full speed; (of an engine, wheel, etc.) run or revolve too swiftly, without resistance, or uncontrolledly; (of the heart, pulse, etc.) beat fast. M18.
2 *verb trans.* Compete with in a race; attempt to surpass in speed. E19.
3 *verb trans.* **a** Cause to take part in a race. M19. ▸**b** Cause to move, perform, or progress swiftly or at full speed; cause (an engine, wheel, etc.) to race (cf. sense 1b above). M19.

> 🕮 **1b** TOLKIEN Aragorn raced down the .. slope. M. SHADBOLT The creek raced beside them .. towards the .. sea. J. M. COETZEE An ambulance .. turned about .. and raced off. **2** E. M. FORSTER 'Race you round it then', cried Freddy. **3b** *Daily News* No attempt .. by the Government to race the Bill through. W. MCCARTHY He started the car and raced the engine noisily. **race off** *verb phr. trans.* (*Austral. slang*) (entice or hurry away in order to) seduce.

race *verb*[3] see RAZE *verb*.

raceabout /'reɪsəbaʊt/ *noun*. *US.* L19.
[from RACE *verb*[2] + ABOUT *adverb*.]
A sloop-rigged racing yacht, usu. having a small keel and large sailyards.

racehorse /'reɪshɔːs/ *noun*. E17.
[from RACE *noun*[1] + HORSE *noun*.]
1 A horse bred or kept for racing. E17. ▸**b** *transf.* & *fig.* Any speedy, sleek, or competitive thing. Freq. *attrib.* M19.
2 A steamer duck. Now *rare* or *obsolete*. L18.
3 Any of various swift-running lizards, as (in full ***racehorse lizard***) the small *Amphibolurus caudicinctus* and (in full ***racehorse goanna***) the large *Varanus tristis*. *Austral.* E20.

race-knife /'reɪsnʌɪf/ *noun*. Pl. **-knives** /-nʌɪvz/. L19.
[from *race* var. of RAZE *verb* + KNIFE *noun*.]
A knife having a bent point, used for marking timber, etc.

racemate /'rasɪmeɪt/ *noun*. M19.
[from RACEMIC + -ATE[1].]
CHEMISTRY. **1** A salt of racemic acid. Now *rare* or *obsolete*. M19.
2 A substance which is a racemic mixture. E20.

raceme /'rasiːm, rə'siːm/ *noun*. L18.
[Latin *racemus* cluster of grapes.]
BOTANY. A simple inflorescence in which the flowers are arranged on pedicels at intervals along a central axis. Cf. SPIKE *noun*[2] 2.
compound raceme: having the lower pedicels developed into secondary racemes.
■ **racemed** *adjective* arranged in racemes M19.

racemic /rə'siːmɪk, rə'sɛmɪk/ *adjective*. M19.
[formed as prec. + -IC.]
CHEMISTRY. **1** ***racemic acid***, a compound consisting of equal proportions of *l*- and *d*- isomers of tartaric acid. Now *rare*. M19.
2 *gen.* Composed of dextro- and laevorotatory isomers of a compound in equal molecular proportions, and therefore optically inactive. L19.

racemiferous /rasɪ'mɪf(ə)rəs/ *adjective*. *rare.* M17.
[from Latin *racemifer*, from *racemus* (see RACEME) + -OUS: see -FEROUS.]
Bearing racemes or clusters.

racemize /'rasɪmʌɪz/ *verb*. Also **-ise**. L19.
[from RACEMIC + -IZE.]
CHEMISTRY. **1** *verb trans.* Convert (an optically active substance) into a racemic form. L19.
2 *verb intrans.* Undergo conversion to a racemic form. M20.
■ **racemi'zation** *noun* L19.

racemose /'rasɪməʊs/ *adjective*. L17.
[Latin *racemosus*, from *racemus*: see RACEME, -OSE[1].]
1 *BOTANY.* Arranged in racemes; having the form of a raceme. L17.
2 *ANATOMY.* (Esp. of a compound gland) resembling a bunch of grapes. M19.
■ **racemous** *adjective* (*rare*) = RACEMOSE 1 M17.

racer /'reɪsə/ *noun*. M17.
[from RACE *verb*[2] + -ER[1].]
1 A person who races or takes part in a race. M17.
2 A very swift animal, *esp.* one suitable for racing; *spec.* a racehorse. L17. ▸**b** Any of several N. American snakes of the genus *Coluber* and related genera, *esp.* the common black *C. constrictor*. E19.
3 A very swift means of transport used for racing, as a bicycle, yacht, etc.; anything capable of great speed. L18.
4 A rail forming a horizontal arc, on which the carriage or traversing-platform of a heavy gun moves. M19.
5 An article of clothing designed (as) for racing, *esp.* a streamlined swimming costume. M20.

raceway /'reɪsweɪ/ *noun*. Chiefly *US*. E19.
[from RACE *noun*[1] + WAY *noun*.]
1 A water channel or the bed of a stream etc.; = RACE *noun*[1] 5b. E19. ▸**b** A man-made channel of running water for rearing fish. L19.
2 A groove or channel directing or restricting movement. Cf. RACE *noun*[1] 5d. E19. ▸**b** A pipe or tubing (for) enclosing electrical wires. L19.
3 A racecourse; *spec.* a track or circuit for running horses in harness races. M20.

rache /ratʃ/ *noun*[1]. *obsolete* exc. *arch.* & *Scot.* Also **ratch**.
[Old English *ræćć* rel. to Old Norse *rakki* dog.]
A hunting dog which pursues its prey by scent.

rache /reɪtʃ, ratʃ/ *noun*[2]. *obsolete* exc. *dial.* Also **ratch**. E16.
[Origin unkn. Cf. RACE *noun*[4], RAKE *noun*[2].]
A (white) line or streak down a horse's face.

rachel /rə'ʃɛl/ *noun*. L19.
[*Rachel*, stage name of Eliza Félix (1820–58), French actress.]
A light tan colour (orig. and chiefly of face-powder).

rachi- /'reɪki/ *combining form*. Also **rhachi-**, **r(h)achio-**.
[from RACHIS: see -I-.]
Of or pertaining to a rachis; *MEDICINE* of or pertaining to the spine.
■ **rachi'otomy** *noun* (an instance of) surgical incision into the spine; laminectomy: L19.

rachides *noun* pl. of RACHIS.

rachilla /rə'kɪlə/ *noun*. Also **rha-**. Pl. **-llae** /-liː/. M19.
[mod. Latin, dim. of RACHIS.]
BOTANY. The short slender axis on which the florets are inserted in a spikelet.

rachio- *combining form* var. of RACHI-.

rachis /'reɪkɪs/ *noun*. Also (esp. *BOTANY*) **rha-**. Pl. **-ides** /-ɪdiːz/. L18.
[mod. Latin, from Greek *rhakhis*, *rhakios* spine, ridge, etc.: pl. by false analogy with *cuspis*, *iris*, etc.]
1 *BOTANY.* The main axis of a compound leaf (esp. the frond of a fern) or of an inflorescence. L18.
2 *ANATOMY.* The vertebral column, or the primitive cord from which it develops. *rare.* M19. ▸**b** *ZOOLOGY.* The axial part of the odontophore of a mollusc. M19.
3 *ORNITHOLOGY.* The shaft of a feather, *esp.* the part bearing the vanes. L19.
■ **rachial** *adjective* (chiefly *BOTANY*) of, pertaining to, or having a rachis M19. **ra'chidial** *adjective* rachial, rachidian; *MEDICINE* spinal: E20. **ra'chidian** *adjective* (chiefly *ZOOLOGY*) of or pertaining to a rachis M19.

rachischisis /ra'kɪskɪsɪs/ *noun*. L19.
[from RACHI- + Greek *skhisis* division, cleavage.]
MEDICINE. Spina bifida.

rachitic /rə'kɪtɪk/ *adjective*. L18.
[from next + -IC.]
MEDICINE. Of or pertaining to rickets; affected with rickets, rickety.

rachitis /rə'kʌɪtɪs/ *noun*. Now *rare*. E18.
[mod. Latin, from Greek *rhakhitis* (formed as RACHIS + -ITIS), lit. 'inflammation of the spine' but adopted as learned form of *rickets*.]
MEDICINE. = RICKETS.

rachitogenic /ˌrakɪtə'dʒɛnɪk/ *adjective*. M20.
[from prec. + -O- + -GENIC.]
MEDICINE. Tending to cause rickets.

Rachmaninovian /rakˌmanɪ'nəʊvɪən, rax-/ *adjective* & *noun*. M20.
[from *Rachmaninov* (see below) + -IAN.]
► **A** *adjective*. Of or resembling the style or the music, emotional and often sombre, of the Russian pianist and composer Sergei Rachmaninov (1873–1943). M20.
► **B** *noun*. An interpreter, student, or admirer of Rachmaninov or his music. M20.

Rachmanism /'rakmənɪz(ə)m/ *noun*. M20.
[from Peter *Rachman* (1919–62), London landlord + -ISM.]
Exploitation or intimidation of a slum tenant by an unscrupulous landlord.
■ **Rachman** *noun* an unscrupulous landlord M20. **Rachmanite** *adjective* (freq. *attrib.*) of or resembling a Rachman M20.

racial /'reɪʃ(ə)l/ *adjective*. M19.
[from RACE *noun*[3] + -IAL.]
Of or pertaining to race.

> 🕮 M. L. KING The problem is not .. purely racial .. with Negroes set against whites. *Maledicta* Racial jokes are .. insulting.

■ **racialism** *noun* = RACISM *noun* E20. **racialist** *noun* & *adjective* = RACIST *noun* & *adjective* E20. **racia'listic** *adjective* M20. **raciali'zation** *noun* the process of making or becoming racist E20. **racialize** *verb trans.* make or become racist M20. **racially** *adverb* in respect of race L19.

raciation /reɪsɪ'eɪʃ(ə)n/ *noun*. *rare.* M20.
[from RACE *noun*[3] after *speciation*.]
The (supposed) evolutionary development of distinct biological races.

racily /'reɪsɪli/ *adverb*. M19.
[from RACY *adjective*[1] + -LY[2].]
In a racy manner or style; vigorously, spiritedly, uninhibitedly.

raciness /'reɪsɪnɪs/ *noun*. L17.
[from RACY *adjective*[1] + -NESS.]
The fact or condition of being racy; vigour, spirit, absence of inhibition.

racing /'reɪsɪŋ/ *noun*. L17.
[from RACE *verb*[2] + -ING[1].]
The action of RACE *verb*[2]; *spec.* the sport in which horses and their riders take part in races.
greyhound-racing, ***harness-racing***, ***horse-racing***, ***motor-racing***, etc.
Comb.: **racing car**: built for competitive racing; **racing colours**: worn by a jockey to identify the owner of a racehorse; ***racing demon***: see DEMON *noun*[1] 7; **racing flag** a private flag raised on a yacht etc. when racing, and lowered when the race is finished or has been abandoned; **racing form** a record of previous performances by a racehorse, athlete, etc.; ***racing-line***: see LINE *noun*[2] 25d; **racing pigeon** a homing pigeon competing in a race from and to specific points.

Racinian /rə'siːnɪən/ *adjective* & *noun*. E20.
[from *Racine* (see below) + -IAN.]
► **A** *adjective*. Of, pertaining to, or characteristic of the French dramatic poet Jean Racine (1639–99) or his writing. E20.
► **B** *noun*. An admirer, student, or imitator of Racine or his writing. E20.

racism /'reɪsɪz(ə)m/ *noun*. M20.
[from RACE *noun*[3] + -ISM.]
(Belief in, adherence to, or advocacy of) the theory that all members of each race possess characteristics, abilities, qualities, etc., specific to that race, esp. distinguishing it as inferior or superior to another race or races; prejudice, discrimination, or antagonism based on this.

> 🕮 *New Left Review* The incipient racism of his electorate. E. PAWEL A racism that relegated all Jews to the status of subhumans. ***White racism***: see WHITE *adjective*.

racist /'reɪsɪst/ *noun* & *adjective*. M20.
[from RACE *noun*[3] + -IST.]
► **A** *noun*. A person believing in, advocating, or practising racism. M20.

> 🕮 G. NAYLOR Lousy racists .. tried to keep black people down. ***White racist***: see WHITE *adjective*.

► **B** *adjective*. Of, pertaining to, or characterized by racism. M20.

> 🕮 *Christian Science Monitor* A .. racist strain of .. old-fashioned virulence.

■ **ra'cistic** *adjective* (*rare*) M20.

rack /rak/ *noun*[1]. In sense 2 also **wrack**. ME.
[Prob. of Scandinavian origin: cf. Norwegian & Swedish dial. *rak* (Swedish *vrak*, Danish *vrag*) wreck, wreckage, refuse, from *reka* to drive. Cf. RAKE *noun*[2].]
1 A hard blow or push; a rush, a collision, a crash; a noise as of this. Long *obsolete* exc. *Scot.* ME.
2 (A mass of) high thick fast-moving cloud; driving mist or fog. Formerly also (*rare*), a rush of wind; a gale, a storm. LME.
3 A (narrow) path or track; *esp.* a track or breach made by an animal, as a deer. LME.

> 🕮 **2** W. STYRON A white rack of cloud hovered.

rack /rak/ *noun*². ME.
[Dutch *rak*, Low German *rack*, also Middle Dutch *rek* (Dutch *rek*, *rekke*), Middle Low German *rek(ke)* horizontal bar, shelf, prob. from *recken* stretch (see RACK *verb*¹).]
1 A bar or framework on which to suspend, support, or secure, or in which to contain, a (specified) thing or set of things, as a cooking spit, luggage, dishes, pipes, etc. Formerly *spec.*, an iron bar or frame to which a prisoner was secured. ME. ▸**b** A vertically barred (portable) frame for holding animal fodder. ME. ▸**c** *NAUTICAL.* A wooden or iron frame containing or securing belaying pins, pulleys, etc. M18. ▸**d** A framework, usu. of metal and of standard size, with vertical or horizontal grooves or rails for supporting items of electrical or electronic equipment so as to be readily accessible. L19. ▸**e** *spec.* A (portable) framework, usu. consisting of a horizontal rail set at chest height (esp. on vertical supports), for transporting and displaying items of clothing for sale. M20.
2 A framework of crossing horizontal and vertical bars or slats, *spec.* as the side of a cart or wagon, a strainer or separator, etc. L16.
3 *MECHANICS.* A cogged or toothed bar for engaging a wheel, pinion, etc., or for holding or adjusting a thing's position. Freq. in ***rack and pinion***. L18.
4 A set of antlers. *N. Amer.* M20.
5 A bed, a bunk. *N. Amer.* (orig. *slang*). M20.

🕮 **1** W. BOYD Cases . . strapped to the rack at the rear of the car. P. CAREY Mrs Williams filled the toast rack. *Field & Stream* Hunters will keep their waterfowl guns in the rack.

Phrases: **at rack and manger** amid abundance or plenty; wanting for nothing. **off the rack** = ***off the peg*** s.v. PEG *noun*¹. **rack and manger** (now *dial.*) lack of proper economy or management; waste and destruction. ***rack and pinion***: see sense 3 above. **stand up to the rack** *US* face or bear consequences; take one's share of work or responsibility.
Comb.: **rack-bar** (***a***) = sense A.3 above; (***b***) *NAUTICAL* a (wooden) stick for tightening a binding rope; **rack-block** *NAUTICAL* a (wooden) frame securing several sheaves through which a ship's rigging is run; **rack chain**: by which a horse is fastened to a rack in a stall; **rack chase** (*PRINTING*, now *Hist.*): having racked sides into which fit two adjustable bars; **rack-deal** deal dried in a rack or framework by exposure to the air; **rack-jobbing** supplying goods to a retailer for display on racks on condition that unsold stock will be taken back after an agreed period; **rackman** *US* a person who distributes newspapers from a publishing office to local newspaper racks; **rack mount** a rack mounting; **rack mounting** (the use of) the standardized racks for supporting electrical or electronic equipment; **rack-rail** a cogged rail on which a cogged train wheel travels; **rack-railway**: having a rack-rail; **rack wheel** a cog-wheel.

rack /rak/ *noun*³. ME.
[Prob. spec. use of prec. Cf. RACK *verb*¹.]
1 A frame on which to stretch cloth, parchment, etc. *obsolete* exc. *dial.* ME.
2 *Hist.* An instrument of torture, usu. consisting of a frame on which the victim was stretched by turning rollers fastened to his or her wrists and ankles. ME. ▸**b** *fig.* A thing which or person who causes great difficulty, pain, suffering, etc. L16.
†**3** A windlass or winch for bending a crossbow. E16–L17.
4 = RACK-RENT *noun*. Now *rare* or *obsolete*. E16.

🕮 **2** F. KING His joints were all aching . . as from a . . sojourn on the rack.

Phrases & comb.: **on the rack** (***a***) distressed, suffering, anxious; (***b***) at full capacity, strained, stretched. **rack-master** a torturer using the rack.

rack /rak/ *noun*⁴. L16.
[Origin unkn.]
1 A joint, esp. of lamb or mutton or of pork, including the neck or forepart of the spine; a rib of mutton or lamb. L16.
†**2** A section of the backbone of a person or animal, a vertebra. Also ***rack-bone***. E17–M19.
3 ***rack of bones***, a skeleton; an emaciated person or animal (esp. a horse). E19.

rack /rak/ *noun*⁵. L16.
[Var. of WRACK *noun*¹, WRECK *noun*¹.]
1 Destruction. Chiefly in ***go to rack (and ruin)***, ***fall to rack (and ruin)***, ***run to rack (and ruin)***. Cf. WRACK *noun*¹ 2. L16.
2 Orig., a wrecked ship. Later, wreckage, flotsam. *rare.* M17.

🕮 **1** L. MACNEICE The garden is going to rack, the gardener Only comes three days. R. RENDELL A . . house . . going to rack and ruin for want of looking after.

rack /rak/ *noun*⁶. L16.
[Origin unkn.]
Either of two gaits of a horse: (***a***) a fast walk with high action; (***b***) a gait in which both hoofs on either side in turn are lifted almost simultaneously, and all four hoofs are off the ground together at certain moments.

rack /rak/ *noun*⁷. E17.
[Aphet.]
= ARRACK.
Comb.: **rack-punch**: made with arrack.

rack /rak/ *verb*¹. Also **wrack**. LME.
[Middle Low German, Middle Dutch *racken*, *recken* = Old English *reććan*, Old Saxon *rekkian*, Old High German *recchan* (German *recken*), Old Norse *rekja*, Gothic *uf)rakjan* stretch, from Germanic.]
1 *verb trans.* Torture by stretching, *spec.* with an apparatus for this purpose (see RACK *noun*³). LME. ▸**b** *transf.* Afflict (a person) with severe physical, mental, or emotional pain; torture or torment (the body, mind, soul, etc.). L16.
2 a *verb trans.* Stretch or extend, esp. severely or beyond normal capacity. *obsolete* exc. in ***rack one's brains***, ***rack one's memory***, ***rack one's wits***, etc. LME. ▸†**b** *verb intrans.* Undergo stretching, strain, or dislocation. Chiefly *Scot.* E16–L19. ▸**c** *verb trans.* Pull or tear apart; break up. *obsolete* exc. *dial.* M16. ▸**d** *verb trans.* Shake, strain, or stress severely; injure by this means. L16.
3 *verb trans.* Raise (rent) above a fair or normal amount. Cf. RACK-RENT. M16. ▸**b** Charge an excessive rent for (land). Now *rare* or *obsolete*. L16. ▸**c** Oppress, exhaust, extort money (esp. in excessive rent) from. Formerly also, extort (money etc.). L16.

🕮 **1** J. BRONOWSKI An Englishman who had been racked . . by the Spanish Inquisition. **b** A. WILSON A headache that racked her. Z. TOMIN She was racked by a . . feeling of . . loss. **2a** A. KOESTLER He racked his memory, but could not place . . this apparition. **d** S. TROTT I cried so hard that the sobs racked my body. **3c** S. C. HALL Tenants were to be racked to the utmost.

Phrases: ***rack one's brains***: see BRAIN *noun*.
Comb.: **racked-out** *adjective* (***a***) completely exhausted; (***b***) survived with difficulty.
■ **racker** *noun*¹ M16. **racking** *noun*¹ (***a***) the action of the verb; (***b***) great pain, difficulty, distress, etc.: LME.

rack /rak/ *verb*² *trans.* L15.
[Provençal *arracar*, from *raca* the stem and husks of grapes, thick dregs.]
1 Draw off (wine, cider, etc.) from the lees. Also foll. by *off*. L15. ▸**b** *fig.* Distil, refine. M17.
†**2** Empty (a cask) by racking. *rare.* L15–E18.
■ **racker** *noun*² E17.

rack /rak/ *verb*³ *intrans.* Also **wrack**. M16.
[Origin unkn. Cf. RACK *noun*⁶.]
1 *verb intrans.* Esp. of a horse: move with a rack. M16.
2 *verb trans.* Foll. by *off*: go missing; get lost. *Austral.* M20.
■ **racker** *noun*³ a racking horse E19.

rack /rak/ *verb*⁴ *intrans.* L16.
[from RACK *noun*¹.]
Of a cloud: be driven before the wind.

rack /rak/ *verb*⁵. L16.
[from RACK *noun*².]
1 *verb trans.* Provide (a stable) with racks. *rare.* L16.
2 Foll. by *up*: ▸**a** *verb trans.* & *intrans.* Fill a rack (for). M18. ▸**b** *verb trans.* Fasten (a horse) to a rack in a stable. M19. ▸**c** *verb trans. fig.* Chalk up; achieve, score. *N. Amer.* M20.
3 *verb trans.* Place (a thing) in or on a rack; *spec.* place (a length of oil-drilling pipe) in a derrick. M19.
4 *verb trans.* & *intrans.* Move or be moved by a rack and pinion. M19.

🕮 **2c** *Boxing News* Shrimpy racked up five . . wins. **3** *Woman's Day (US)* Rack up your plants on a stand. S. BELLOW Dingbat had had charge of the poolroom . . Now he . . racked up balls. **4** *Camera Weekly* Rack the lens out to bring the focus closer.

■ **racking** *noun*² (***a***) the action of the verb, providing with or placing in a rack; (***b***) functional, inexpensive (rather than decorative) shelving: M19.

rack /rak/ *verb*⁶ *intrans.* M18.
[Origin unkn.]
NAUTICAL. Bind two ropes together with a third smaller rope woven alternatively over and under each.
■ **racking** *noun*³ (***a***) the action of the verb; (***b***) a small rope used for racking: E18.

rack /rak/ *verb*⁷ *trans.* L19.
[Var. of RAKE *verb*³.]
BUILDING. Build (a brick wall) by making each successive row a little shorter than the one below, so that the end slopes (usu. temporarily until the work is completed). Also foll. by *back*.
■ **racking** *noun*⁴ (***a***) the action of the verb; (***b***) the resulting arrangement of bricks: L19.

rackan /ˈrak(ə)n/ *noun*. Long *obsolete* exc. *north*. Also **reckon** /ˈrɛk(ə)n/.
[Old English *racente* = Old Norse *rekendi*, Old High German *rahchinza*.]
†**1** A chain, a fetter. OE–LME.
2 An apparatus (orig. a chain, later a vertical bar having holes into which a pot-hook may be inserted) for hanging cooking pots over a fire. LME.
Comb.: **rackan-crook**, **rackan hook** (***a***) a rackan serving as a pot-hook; (***b***) a pot-hook used with a rackan.

rackarock /ˈrakərɒk/ *noun*. L19.
[from RACK *verb*¹ + A *adjective* + ROCK *noun*¹.]
An explosive consisting of potassium chlorate and nitrobenzene.

racket /ˈrakɪt/ *noun*¹. Also **racquet**, (esp. in sense 2) **raquette**. LME.
[French *raquette* from Italian *racchetta*, from Arab. *rāhat*, construct form of *rāḥa* palm of the hand.]
1 *sing.* (now only *attrib.* & in *pl.* (treated as *sing.*). A game in which either of two (or occas. four) players alternately strike a ball against a wall with a racket (sense 2), endeavouring to keep the ball rebounding. LME.
2 A bat with a handle ending in a round or oval frame across which a taut network of (catgut, nylon, etc.) cord is strung, used in tennis, squash, etc. E16.
3 A snowshoe resembling a racket. Chiefly *N. Amer.* E17. ▸**b** A broad wooden shoe for a person or horse, to facilitate walking over marshy ground. M19.
4 *ORNITHOLOGY.* A feather, esp. a main tail feather, broadened at the end and resembling a racket. L19.
1 ***racket-court***, ***racket-match***, ***racket-player***, etc. ***squash rackets***: see SQUASH *noun*¹ 4b.
Comb.: **racket abuse** *TENNIS* aggressive or unsportsmanlike behaviour by a player in which the racket is thrown or struck against something, incurring a penalty from the umpire; **racket-press**: for keeping a racket taut and in shape; **racket-tail** a tail (feather) shaped like a racket; any of various humming-birds, kingfishers, and motmots having such tails; **racket-tailed** *adjective* having a racket-tail.

racket /ˈrakɪt/ *noun*². M16.
[Perh. imit. of clattering noise.]
1 (A) disturbance, a loud noise, (an) uproar; *spec.* (a) noisy expression of opinion or feeling. M16.
2 a A large or noisy social gathering. M18. ▸**b** (Excessive) social excitement; gaiety. L18.
3 *slang.* A trick, an underhand scheme; now usu. a scheme for obtaining money etc. by fraudulent or violent means; a form of organized crime. E19. ▸**b** *gen.* An activity, a way of life; a line of business. L19.
4 An exciting or trying situation or experience; an ordeal. Chiefly in ***stand the racket***, withstand or cope with difficulty, stress, etc. E19.

🕮 **1** J. OSBORNE Banging . . irons and saucepans—the eternal flaming racket. P. AUSTER The racket got so loud . . that it disrupted . . sleep. B. BAINBRIDGE She made an awful racket. **2a** R. GORDON Dreadful rackets, all scientific meetings. **b** THACKERAY With all this racket and gaiety, do you understand that a gentleman feels very lonely? **3** *Sun (Baltimore)* One racket . . —that of fake securities. R. MAY The . . crook . . has to join a racket. ***numbers racket***, ***protection racket***, etc. **b** P. G. WODEHOUSE He was going to work for somebody in the publishing racket.

■ **racketiness** *noun* (fondness for) noise, excitement, gaiety, etc. M20. **rackety** *adjective* fond of or characterized by noise, excitement, gaiety, etc. L18.

racket *noun*³ var. of RACKETT.

†**racket** *verb*¹ *trans.* E17–M19.
[from RACKET *noun*¹.]
Strike (as) with a racket; toss or bandy about.

racket /ˈrakɪt/ *verb*². M18.
[from RACKET *noun*².]
1 *verb intrans.* Take part in social excitement. Also foll. by *about*. Now *rare.* M18.
2 *verb trans.* Enliven, disturb, or destroy (also foll. by *away*), by racketing. *rare.* M18.
3 *verb intrans.* Make a racket, esp. by noisy movement. Also foll. by *about*, *along*, *around*. E19.

🕮 **3** P. LEACH He and his sister have been racketing around. J. POYER A lorry racketed to life.

racket-ball /ˈrakɪtbɔːl/ *noun*. Also (the usual form in sense 2) **racquetball**. M17.
[from RACKET *noun*¹ + BALL *noun*¹.]
1 A small hard (orig. kid-covered) ball of cork and string; a game of rackets played with this. M17.
2 *spec.* A game played with a small hard ball and a short-handled racket in a four-walled handball court. Orig. & chiefly *N. Amer.* L20.

racketeer /rakɪˈtɪə/ *noun* & *verb*. Orig. *US*. E20.
[from RACKET *noun*² + -EER.]
▸ **A** *noun*. A person participating in or operating a dishonest or illegal business, freq. practising fraud, extortion, intimidation, or violence; *transf.* a person who uses illegitimate means to achieve a quick result. E20.

🕮 S. BELLOW They were average minor hoodlums and racketeers. G. PRIESTLAND The school had been founded by an Elizabethan racketeer . . to save his soul.

▸ **B** *verb trans.* & *intrans.* Practise fraud, extortion, intimidation, or violence (on), esp. as part of a dishonest or illegal business. E20.
■ **racketeering** *noun* the practices or business of a racketeer, esp. as (part of) a system of organized crime E20.

racketer /ˈrakɪtə/ *noun*¹. *rare.* L16.
[from RACKET *noun*¹ + -ER¹.]
A person who plays games with a racket.

racketer /ˈrakɪtə/ *noun*². *rare.* M17.
[from RACKET *noun*² or *verb*² + -ER¹.]
A person who rackets or makes a racket.

rackett /ˈrakɪt/ *noun*. Also **racket**, **ranket** /ˈraŋkɪt/. L19.
[German *Rackett*, *Rankett*.]
MUSIC. **1** A Renaissance wind instrument related to the oboe, consisting of about nine parallel channels joined alternately at top and bottom to form a continuous tube which emerges from the centre of the top of a containing cylinder. L19.
2 An organ-stop having an eight or sixteen foot pitch and producing a smothered tone. *obsolete* exc. *Hist.* L19.

Rackhamesque /rakəˈmɛsk/ *adjective*. M20.
[from *Rackham* (see below) + -ESQUE.]
Characteristic of or resembling the drawings of the British book illustrator Arthur Rackham (1867–1939).

rackle /ˈrak(ə)l/ *adjective*. *obsolete* exc. *Scot. & north.* Also **raukle** /ˈrɔːk(ə)l/. ME.
[Origin unkn.]
Hasty, impetuous, headstrong; rough, coarse; *Scot.* strong, vigorous.
■ **rackleness** *noun* LME.

rack-rent /ˈrakrɛnt/ *noun & verb*. L16.
[from RACK *verb*[1] + RENT *noun*[1].]
▶ **A** *noun*. A very high, excessive, or extortionate rent; a rent (nearly) equal to the annual income obtainable by the tenant from the property. L16.
▶ **B** *verb trans.* **1** Make (a person) pay excessive or extortionate rent, or rent (nearly) equal to the annual income obtainable by the tenant from the property. M17.
2 Let (a property) at a rack-rent. L19.
■ **rack-renter** *noun* a person who pays or exacts rack-rent L17.

raclette /in sense 1 raˈklɛt, in sense 2 *foreign* raklɛt (*pl. same*)/ *noun*. M20.
[French = small scraper.]
1 ARCHAEOLOGY. A stone tool of the scraper type discovered in the valley of the Vézère in SW France, dating from the early Magdalenian period. M20.
2 A dish of cheese melted before an open fire, scraped on to a plate, and served with potatoes. M20.

racloir /ˈraklwɑː/ *noun*. L19.
[French = scraper.]
ARCHAEOLOGY. = ***side scraper*** s.v. SIDE *noun*.

racon /ˈreɪkɒn/ *noun*. Orig. *US*. M20.
[from RA(DAR + BEA)CON *noun*.]
= ***RADAR beacon***.

raconteur /rakɒnˈtəː/ *noun*. E19.
[French, from *raconter* relate + -*eur* -OR.]
A (usu. skilled) teller of anecdotes.
■ **raconteuse** /-ˈtəːz/ *noun* a female raconteur M19.

racoon /rəˈkuːn, raˈkuːn/ *noun*. Also **raccoon**. E17.
[Virginia Algonquian *aroughcun*.]
1 Either of two catlike American nocturnal carnivorous mammals of the genus *Procyon* (family Procyonidae), *esp.* the common greyish-brown N. American species *P. lotor*, with a ringed bushy tail, a sharp snout, and a dark stripe across the face. E17.
2 The skin or fur of the racoon. E19.
Comb.: **racoon dog** a small wild dog, *Nyctereutes procyonoides*, of eastern Asia, resembling a racoon in markings.

Racovian /rəˈkəʊvɪən/ *adjective*. M17.
[from *Raków* (see below) + -IAN.]
Of or pertaining to Raków, a town in Poland, or the Socinians who made it their chief centre in the 17th cent.

racquet *noun* var. of RACKET *noun*[1].

racquetball *noun* see RACKET-BALL.

racy /ˈreɪsi/ *adjective*[1]. M17.
[from RACE *noun*[3] + -Y[1].]
1 a Of a wine, fruit, flavour, etc.: having a characteristic (usu. desirable) quality, esp. in a high degree. M17. ▸**b** Having a distinctive character reflecting origin or breeding. M17.
2 Vigorous, spirited, lively; *spec.* (of speech, writing, etc.) vivid, piquant, uninhibited, risqué. M17.

> **1b** C. BRONTË Yorkshire has families . . peculiar, racy. *Century Magazine* The Gordon setter . . should have a . . racy front. **racy of the soil** characteristic of a certain country or people. **2** J. HOLLINGSHEAD The power of racy narrative. *Princeton Alumni Weekly* Slang . . seeks a racy synonym for the normal.

racy /ˈreɪsi/ *adjective*[2]. M20.
[from RACE *verb*[2] or *noun*[1] + -Y[1].]
Designed or suitable for racing.

RAD *abbreviation*.
Royal Academy of Dance.

rad /rad/ *noun*[1]. E19.
[Abbreviation.]
= RADICAL *noun* 5.

rad /rad/ *noun*[2]. Pl. same. E20.
[Abbreviation.]
= RADIAN.

rad /rad/ *noun*[3]. Pl. same, **-s**. E20.
[from *radiation absorbed dose*.]
PHYSICS. A unit of absorbed dose of ionizing radiation, corresponding to the absorption of 0.01 joule of energy per kilogram of irradiated material, equivalent to 0.01 gray.

rad /rad/ *noun*[4]. M20.
[Abbreviation.]
= RADIATOR.

rad /rad/ *adjective*[1] *& adverb*. Long *obsolete* exc. *dial.*
[Old English *hrad*, *hræd* = Old High German *hrad*, *hrat*, Old Norse *hraðr* (Middle Swedish *radh*).]
▶ **A** *adjective*. Quick, hasty; active, ready; eager, elated. OE.
▶†**B** *adverb*. Quickly, readily, soon. ME–E16.

rad /rad/ *adjective*[2]. *obsolete* exc. *Scot.* ME.
[Old Norse *hræddr* (Swedish *rädd*, Danish *ræd*), from *hræða* frighten.]
Frightened, afraid, alarmed.

rad /rad/ *adjective*[3]. *slang* (orig. *N. Amer.*). L20.
[Perh. abbreviation of RADICAL *adjective*.]
Fine, excellent; admirably up to date; outstandingly enjoyable.

RADA /ˈrɑːdə/ *abbreviation*.
Royal Academy of Dramatic Art.

Rada /ˈrɑːdə/ *noun*. E20.
[App. from *Allada*, a former principality of Dahomey (now Benin).]
(The worship of) a group of deities of W. African derivation venerated in Haiti.

radappertization /raˌdapətʌɪˈzeɪʃ(ə)n/ *noun*. Also **-isation**. M20.
[from RAD(IATION + French *appertisation* method of heat treatment of food, from N.-F. *Appert* (d. 1841), French inventor: see -IZATION.]
The treatment of food with ionizing radiation so as to reduce the number of micro-organisms sufficiently to prevent spoilage in the absence of recontamination. Cf. RADICIDATION, RADURIZATION.
■ **raˈdappertize** *verb trans.* treat by radappertization (chiefly as ***radappertized*** *ppl adjective*) L20.

radar /ˈreɪdɑː/ *noun*. Orig. *US*. M20.
[from *radio detection and ranging*.]
1 A system (more fully ***primary radar***) for detecting the presence of objects at a distance and determining their position or motion by transmitting short radio waves and detecting or measuring the return of these after being reflected by the objects; a similar system (more fully ***secondary radar***) in which a return signal is automatically transmitted by the target when it receives the outgoing waves. Cf. RADIOLOCATION. M20.
2 (An) apparatus or an installation used for this system. M20.
3 *fig.* (A capacity for) intuitive perception or awareness. M20.
4 *transf.* A detection system which works on the principle of radar but uses signals other than radio waves; *esp.* lidar, sonar. M20.
Comb.: **radar beacon** a radio transmitter that automatically transmits a return signal (esp. a coded identification signal) when it receives a signal from a radar transmitter; **radar fence** a line of radar stations for giving warning of intrusions into the air space behind it; **radar gun** a hand-held device which uses Doppler radar to measure the speed of a moving object, as a vehicle or the ball in tennis, cricket, etc.; **radar map**: compiled from radar observations; **radar net** a network of radar stations, esp. a radar fence; **radar picket** a picket-boat specially equipped with radar; **radar plotter** a person who plots the direction and course of objects from radar observations; **radar scanner** a rotatable aerial for transmitting and receiving radar signals; **radar screen** the screen of a radarscope; **radar-sonde** a sonde which can be tracked by radar to obtain information on wind speed, wind direction, etc.; **radar-track** *verb trans.* track by radar; **radar trap** a speed trap in which a motorist's speed is measured using radar and the Doppler effect.
■ **radarscope** *noun* (the screen of) a cathode-ray oscilloscope on which radar echoes are represented for observation M20.

RADC *abbreviation*.
Royal Army Dental Corps.

Radcliffian /radˈklɪfɪən/ *adjective*. Also **-ean**. E19.
[from *Radcliffe* (see below) + -IAN.]
Of or characteristic of the English Gothic novelist Ann Radcliffe (1764–1823) or her works.

raddle /ˈrad(ə)l/ *noun*[1] *& verb*[1]. E16.
[Rel. to RED *adjective*: cf. RUDDLE *noun*[1].]
▶ **A** *noun*. Red ochre, ruddle. E16.
▶ **B** *verb trans.* Paint or mark with raddle; colour coarsely with red or rouge. M17.
■ **raddled** *adjective* (*a*) that has been raddled; (*b*) *fig.* (of a person, face, etc.) worn, worn out: L17.

raddle /ˈrad(ə)l/ *noun*[2] *& verb*[2]. *obsolete* exc. *dial.* M16.
[Anglo-Norman *reidele*, Old French *reddalle* (mod. *ridelle*).]
▶ **A** *noun*. **1** †**a** The rail of a cart. *rare*. Only in M16. ▸**b** A wooden bar with upright pegs for keeping the threads of the warp in place as it is wound upon the beam. M19.
2 A thin rod, wattle, or lath, fastened to or twisted between upright stakes or posts to form a fence, partition, or wall. L16. ▸**b** A hurdle, door, hedge, etc., made with intertwined rods etc. L17.
▶ **B** *verb trans.* Weave or twist together, intertwine. L17.

radeau /raˈdəʊ/ *noun*. M18.
[French, from Provençal *radel*, from Latin dim. of *ratis* raft.]
A raft; *spec.* (MILITARY) a floating battery.

radi- *combining form* see RADIO-.

radial /ˈreɪdɪəl/ *adjective & noun*. LME.
[medieval Latin *radialis*, from Latin RADIUS: see -AL[1].]
▶ **A** *adjective*. †**1** Of a cauterizing instrument: thin and sharply pointed. Only in LME.
2 Of light, beams, etc.: proceeding as rays from a common centre; of or pertaining to a ray or rays. L16.
3 Arranged like rays or the radii of a circle; having the position or direction of a radius; diverging from a common centre. M18. ▸**b** BOTANY & FORESTRY. Designating a longitudinal section or cut along a radius or diameter, or the surface so exposed. L19. ▸**c** Of a road, route, etc.: running directly from a town or city centre to an outlying district (esp. as part of a system of such roads). M20.
4 Having, involving, or characterized by lines or parts extending or proceeding from a centre; acting or moving along lines proceeding from a centre. M18. ▸**b** PHYSICAL GEOGRAPHY. Of (a pattern of) drainage: involving a number of divergent streams flowing outwards from a central elevated region. M20. ▸**c** Designating a tyre in which the layers of fabric have their cords running at right angles to the circumference of the tyre and the tread is strengthened by further layers round the circumference. M20.
5 ANATOMY & ZOOLOGY. Of, pertaining to, or associated with the radius; designating or situated on the outer (thumb) side of the forearm or foreleg, as ***radial artery***, ***radial nerve***, ***radial vein***, etc. M18.
Special collocations & comb.: **radial axle** an axle (of a railway carriage, tram, etc.) which on a curve of the track assumes the position of a radius to that curve. **radial engine** a type of internal-combustion engine (used chiefly in aircraft) having its cylinders fixed radially around a rotating crankshaft. **radial-flow** *adjective* designating or employing a turbine, pump, etc., in which fluid is forced to move at right angles to an axis of rotation. **radial keratotomy** OPHTHALMOLOGY an operation for myopia, in which a number of equally-spaced radial cuts are made through part of the thickness of the cornea in such a way as to flatten its curvature. **radial-ply** = sense 4C above. **radial symmetry**: about an axis. **radial velocity** ASTRONOMY the velocity of a star or other body along the line of sight of an observer.
▶ **B** *noun*. **1** ZOOLOGY. Each of a set of radial structures, as fin rays, echinoderm ossicles, etc. L19.
2 ANATOMY. A radial nerve, artery, etc. L19.
3 A radial tyre, road, engine, etc. E20.
4 RADIO. Each of a number of wires attached radially (and freq. horizontally) to a vertical aerial to approximate the reception and transmission characteristics of a sheet of material. M20.
5 RADAR. A straight line joining all points on the same bearing from a radar station. M20.
■ **radially** *adverb* in a radial manner, in the form of radii or rays M17.

radiale /reɪdɪˈeɪli/ *noun*. Pl. **-lia** /-lɪə/. L19.
[mod. Latin use as noun of neut. of medieval Latin *radialis* (sc. *os* bone): see prec.]
1 = RADIAL *noun* 1. *rare*. L19.
2 ANATOMY & ZOOLOGY. The carpal situated on the radial side of the wrist or carpus. L19.

radian /ˈreɪdɪən/ *noun*. L19.
[from RADIUS + -*an*.]
MATH. A unit of plane angle (now in the SI), equal to that subtended at the centre of a circle by an arc equal to the radius, 2π radians being equal to 360°.

radiance /ˈreɪdɪəns/ *noun*. M16.
[formed as next: see -ANCE.]
1 The quality of being radiant. M16.
†**2** = RADIATION 1C. *rare*. Only in 19.
3 PHYSICS. The flux of radiation emitted per unit solid angle in a given direction by a unit area of a source. E20.

radiancy /ˈreɪdɪənsi/ *noun*. M17.
[from next: see -ANCY.]
= RADIANCE 1.

radiant /ˈreɪdɪənt/ *adjective & noun*. LME.
[Latin *radiant-* pres. ppl stem of *radiare* emit rays: see -ANT[1].]
▶ **A** *adjective*. **1** Emitting rays of light; appearing in the form of rays (of light); shining, bright, splendid, dazzling. LME. ▸**b** Represented as emitting rays, esp. of light. E17. ▸**c** Of a person or a person's eyes, looks, etc.: bright or beaming with joy, hope, love, etc. E17.
2 Pertaining to or emitting electromagnetic radiation; (esp. of heat) transmitted by (electromagnetic) radiation, rather than conduction or convection. LME. ▸**b** Designed to send out radiant heat. M20.

3 Chiefly *BIOLOGY*. (Having parts) extending radially. **M19.**

> 1 M. L. KING The radiant light of the rising moon. K. LINES The immortal gods were . . radiant in . . beauty. I. MURDOCH The quiet water was a . . radiant blue. **c** A. N. WILSON Her face glowing with a radiant smile. A. FINE He had a huge smile on his face. In fact, he looked positively radiant.

Special collocations: **radiant efficiency** the ratio of the radiant flux emitted to the power consumed. **radiant energy** energy in the form of (usu. electromagnetic) radiation. **radiant flux** the rate of flow of radiant energy. **radiant heat** heat transmitted by radiation; infrared radiation. **radiant point** a central point from which rays or radii proceed; *spec.* in *ASTRONOMY*, the apparent focal point of a meteoric shower. **radiant power** = *radiant flux* above. **radiant region** *ASTRONOMY* the region of the sky from which a meteoric shower appears to originate.

▶ **B** *noun*. **1 a** *PHYSICS*. A point, small region, or object from which light or heat radiates. **E18.** ▸**b** Each of the heating units or elements in a radiant heater. **E20.**

2 *ASTRONOMY*. A radiant point or region. **M19.**

▪ **radiantly** *adverb* **M16.**

Radiata /reɪdɪˈɑːtə, -ˈeɪtə/ *noun*[1] *pl.* **E19.**
[mod. Latin (see below), neut. pl. of Latin *radiatus*: see **RADIATE** *adjective & noun*.]
ZOOLOGY (now chiefly *Hist.*). Members, collectively, of a former division of the animal kingdom comprising animals with radial structure, including most coelenterates and echinoderms.

radiata /reɪdɪˈɑːtə/ *noun*[2]. Chiefly *NZ*. **M20.**
[mod. Latin (see below), fem. of Latin *radiatus*: see next.]
In full ***radiata pine***. The Monterey pine, *Pinus radiata*, grown for timber in New Zealand.

radiate /ˈreɪdɪət/ *adjective & noun*. **M17.**
[Latin *radiatus* pa. pple of *radiare*: see next, **-ATE**[2], **-ATE**[1].]
▶ **A** *adjective*. **1** Having rays or parts proceeding from a centre; having radial symmetry; (of the capitulum in certain composite plants) having a circle of ligulate florets surrounding a central region of tubular florets. **M17.**

2 Arranged like rays, diverging from a centre. **E19.**

▶ **B** *noun*. **1** *ZOOLOGY*. A member of the Radiata. Now *rare* or *obsolete*. **M19.**

2 A classical coin with rays issuing from a central device. **M20.**

▪ **radiately** *adverb* **M19.**

radiate /ˈreɪdɪeɪt/ *verb*. **E17.**
[Latin *radiat-* pa. ppl stem of *radiare* furnish with or emit rays, from *radius* ray: see **-ATE**[3].]
▶ **I** *verb intrans*. **1** Spread from or as from a centre; diverge from a central point. **E17.** ▸**b** Converge to or towards a centre. *rare*. **M19.** ▸**c** *BIOLOGY*. Of an animal or plant group: diversify or spread into new habitats. **E20.**

2 a Emit rays of light; shine brightly. **M17.** ▸**b** Orig., emit rays of heat. Now more widely, emit energy of any kind in the form of rays or waves. **M19.**

3 Of light or heat: issue in rays. **E18.**

> 1 E. HEMINGWAY Lines . . radiated from . . each eye. A. TOFFLER Consequences of . . events radiate . . around the world.

▶ **II** *verb trans*. **4** Illuminate (*lit.* & *fig.*). *rare*. **E17.**

5 a Emit (light or heat) in rays. More widely, emit (energy of any kind) in the form of rays or waves. (Foll. by *away*.) **L18.** ▸**b** *fig.* Transmit as from a centre; exude an aura or atmosphere of (love, happiness, power, etc.). **E19.** ▸**c** Transmit (radio waves); broadcast. **E20.**

> 5a *Nature* Stars radiate their heat away. **b** D. FRASER He radiated confidence. A. LEE She radiated a fresh scent.

▪ **radiating** *adjective* (*a*) that radiates; (*b*) characterized by radiation: **E18.** **radiature** /ˈreɪdɪətʃə/ *noun* (*rare*) (an instance of) radiation **E18.**

radiated /ˈreɪdɪeɪtɪd/ *adjective*. **M17.**
[from prec. + **-ED**[1].]
1 Provided with rays; made or depicted with radiating projections. **M17.**

2 Arranged like rays; = **RADIATE** *adjective* 2. **M18.**

3 Having parts or markings arranged like rays or radii. Cf. **RADIATE** *adjective* 1. **L18.**

4 Of or characterized by a radial arrangement. **L18.**

5 Of light, energy, a signal, etc.: emitted by radiation. **E20.**

6 = **IRRADIATED** *ppl adjective* (a). *rare*. **E20.**

3 radiated mole the star-nosed mole.

radiation /reɪdɪˈeɪʃ(ə)n/ *noun*. **LME.**
[Latin *radiatio(n-)*, formed as **RADIATE** *verb*: see **-ATION**.]
1 a The action or condition of sending out rays of light. Now *rare* exc. as passing into sense 1c. **LME.** ▸**b** Orig., a ray or beam of light emitted by a radiant body (usu. in *pl.*). Now, energy transmitted in the form of (esp. electromagnetic) waves or moving subatomic particles; *spec.* (in non-*techn.* use) ionizing radiation (e.g. from a radioactive source). **L16.** ▸**c** The emission and transmission of energy (orig. *spec.*, of heat) in the form of waves (esp. electromagnetic waves) or moving subatomic particles. **E19.**

2 †**a** *ASTROLOGY*. = **ASPECT** *noun* 4. *rare*. **M16–L17.** ▸**b** Divergence from a central point; radial arrangement or structure. **M17.** ▸**c** Each of a set of radiating things or parts. **M19.** ▸**d** *BIOLOGY*. The spread of an animal or plant group into new areas. Also (more fully ***adaptive radiation***), the diversification of a group into forms that fill different ecological niches. **M20.**

1b ***cosmic radiation***, ***electromagnetic radiation***, ***gravitational radiation***, ***infrared radiation***, ***ionizing radiation***, ***thermal radiation***, ***ultraviolet radiation***, ***X-radiation***, etc. ***radiation dermatitis***, ***radiation dose***, ***radiation hazard***, ***radiation injury***, ***radiation level***, ***radiation meter***, ***radiation monitor***, etc.

Comb.: **radiation belt** *PHYSICS & ASTRONOMY* a region surrounding a planet where charged particles accumulate under the influence of the planet's magnetic field; **radiation burn** a burn caused by overexposure to ionizing radiation; **radiation chemistry** the branch of science that deals with chemical changes arising from the impact of ionizing radiation; **radiation counter** *PHYSICS* an instrument for counting or recording ionizing events; **radiation efficiency** *RADIO* the efficiency of conversion of input power to power radiated by an aerial etc.; **radiation fog**: formed when the ground loses heat by radiation and cools overlying moist air; **radiation frost**: formed when the ground loses heat by radiation; **radiation pattern** (a representation of) the directional variation in intensity of the radiation from an aerial or other source; **radiation pressure** mechanical pressure exerted by electromagnetic radiation or by sound waves; **radiation pyrometer** a pyrometer which functions by measuring radiant energy; **radiation resistance** the part of the electrical resistance of an aerial that is due to its radiation of power; an analogous property of a sound-radiator; **radiation sickness** illness caused by exposure of the body to ionizing radiation, characterized by nausea, hair loss, diarrhoea, bleeding, and damage to the bone marrow and central nervous system; **radiation therapy**, **radiation treatment** radiotherapy (esp. of cancer).

▪ **radiational** *adjective* **E20.** **radiationless** *adjective* **E20.**

radiative /ˈreɪdɪətɪv/ *adjective*. **M19.**
[from **RADIATE** *verb* + **-IVE**.]
Of or pertaining to radiation; occurring by means of radiation; involving or accompanied by the emission of radiation.

radiative capture capture of a particle by an atomic nucleus with accompanying emission of gamma radiation. **radiative equilibrium** a state of equilibrium in which the total energy flux emitted is equal to that absorbed; a state of equilibrium in which radiation is the predominant energy transport mechanism.

▪ **radiatively** *adverb* by means of (esp. electromagnetic) radiation; with emission of radiation: **M20.**

radiator /ˈreɪdɪeɪtə/ *noun*. **M19.**
[from **RADIATE** *verb* + **-OR**.]
1 A thing which radiates something (esp. light, heat, or sound waves). **M19.**

2 A small chamber, tank, or compact array of pipes usu. with a large surface area, heated by steam, hot air, or (now usu.) circulating hot water and giving off warmth into a room etc. by radiation and convection. **M19.**

3 In a liquid cooling system (as in some internal-combustion engines), a bank of thin tubes in which circulating fluid (freq. water) is cooled by the surrounding air. **E20.**

4 An aerial for transmitting (and often also receiving) radio waves. **E20.**

> 1 W. T. BRANDE Polished metals are very imperfect radiators . . of heat. **2** N. MAILER She has . . neglected to turn off the radiator.

radical /ˈradɪk(ə)l/ *adjective & noun*. **LME.**
[Late Latin *radicalis*, from Latin *radic-*, **RADIX** root: see **-AL**[1].]
▶ **A** *adjective*. **1** Forming the root, basis, or foundation; original, primary. **LME.**

2 a Of a quality etc.: inherent in the nature of a thing or person; fundamental. **LME.** ▸**b** Of action, change, an idea, etc.: going to the root or origin; pertaining to or affecting what is fundamental; far-reaching, thorough. **M17.** ▸**c** *POLITICS*. Advocating thorough or far-reaching change; representing or supporting an extreme section of a party; *spec.* (*a*) *Hist.* belonging to an extreme wing of the Liberal Party; (*b*) *US HISTORY* seeking extreme action against the South at the time of the Civil War. Now also, left-wing, revolutionary. **E19.** ▸**d** Characterized by departure from tradition; progressive; unorthodox. **E20.**

3 *MATH*. Pertaining to or forming the root of a number or quantity. **M16.**

4 *PHILOLOGY*. Of or belonging to the roots of words; connected with or based on roots. **L16.**

†**5** *ASTROLOGY*. Belonging to or forming the basis of an astrological calculation. Only in **17.**

6 *MUSIC*. Belonging to the root of a chord. **M18.**

7 *BOTANY*. Of or belonging to the root of a plant; *esp.* (of a leaf) springing directly from the rootstock or from the base of the stem (opp. ***cauline***). **M18.**

> 1 S. JOHNSON The radical idea branches out. **2a** R. H. HUTTON The radical rottenness of human nature. *Times Lit. Suppl.* None of our individualities is radical. **radical humour** = **MOISTURE** 2b. **b** *Times* Radical measures and socialist programmes. B. TARKINGTON Conservative people seldom form radical new habits. **c** W. LIPPMANN Though some . . were opposed to drastic change . . others were in favor of radical reform. *Japan Times* Radical students pelted police with rocks. **radical chic** (the people given to) the fashionable affectation of radical left-wing views or an associated style of dress, life, etc. **radical right** (the proponents of) extreme conservative or fascist views favouring group action to protect or reinstate certain social traditions. **3 radical sign** the sign √ used to indicate a root (without qualifying superscript numeral, the square root) of the number to which it is prefixed. **4 radical word**: having the form of or directly based on a root.

▶ **B** *noun*. **1** *PHILOLOGY*. **a** A root; a radical word or letter. **M17.** ▸**b** Any of the basic Chinese characters constituting usu. semantically significant elements in the composition of other characters and used as a means of classifying characters in dictionaries. Cf. **PHONETIC** *noun* 1. **E19.**

2 A basis, a fundamental thing or principle. **M17.**

3 *MATH*. **a** A quantity forming or expressed as a root of another quantity. **M18.** ▸**b** The radical sign. **L18.**

4 *CHEMISTRY*. Orig., an element, atom, or group of atoms which can form the basis of a compound and remain unaltered during ordinary chemical reactions. Now (*a*) = **GROUP** *noun* 2b; (*b*) = ***free radical*** s.v. **FREE** *adjective, adverb, & noun* **E19.**

5 A politically radical person. **E19.**

5 ***philosophical radical***: see **PHILOSOPHICAL** *adjective*.

▪ **radicalism** *noun* (*a*) politically radical attitudes, principles, or practice; (*b*) thoroughness of method: **E19.** **radiˈcality** *noun* the state, condition, or fact of being radical, radicalism **M17.** **ˌradicaliˈzation** *noun* the process of radicalizing **L19.** **radicalize** *verb trans. & intrans.* make or become politically radical **E19.** **radically** *adverb* **LME.** **radicalness** *noun* **M17.**

radicand /ˈradɪkand/ *noun*. **L19.**
[from Latin *radicandus* gerundive of *radicare*: see **RADICATE** *verb*, **-AND**.]
MATH. A number or expression of which a root is to be extracted.

radicate /ˈradɪkət/ *adjective*. **M17.**
[Latin *radicatus* pa. pple of *radicare*: see next, **-ATE**[2].]
†**1** Rooted, attached, firmly established. **M17–M18.**

2 *BOTANY*. Having a root. *rare*. **M19.**

radicate /ˈradɪkeɪt/ *verb trans.* Now *rare*. **L15.**
[Latin *radicat-* pa. ppl stem of *radicare* or *radicari* take root, from *radic-*, **RADIX** root: see **-ATE**[3].]
Cause to take root; plant or establish firmly. Chiefly *fig.* Usu. in *pass.*

▪ **radiˈcation** *noun* the process of taking root; the fact of being rooted or firmly established: **L15.**

†**radicative** *adjective*. *rare*. **E18–E19.**
[formed as **RADICATE** *verb* + **-IVE**.]
= **RADICAL** *adjective* 2b.

radicchio /raˈdiːkɪəʊ/ *noun*. Pl. **-os**. **L20.**
[Italian = chicory.]
A variety of chicory from Italy, with reddish-purple white-veined leaves.

radicel /ˈradɪsel/ *noun*. *rare*. **E19.**
[mod. Latin *radicella* dim. of Latin *radic-*, **RADIX** root: see **-EL**[2].]
BOTANY. = **RADICLE** 1a.

▪ **radiˈcellar** *adjective* of the nature of rootlets **M19.** **radicellose** *adjective* having rootlets **L19.**

radices *noun pl.* see **RADIX**.

radicidation /ˌradɪsʌɪˈdeɪʃ(ə)n/ *noun*. **M20.**
[from **RAD(IATION** + **-CIDE** + **-ATION**.]
The treatment of food with ionizing radiation to reduce the number of micro-organisms in it to an undetectable level. Cf. **RADAPPERTIZATION**, **RADURIZATION**.

radicle /ˈradɪk(ə)l/ *noun*. **L17.**
[Latin *radicula*, from *radic-*, **RADIX** root + *-ula* dim. suffix: see **-ULE**.]
1 a *BOTANY*. The embryonic root in a seedling plant. Also, one of the stout rhizoids matting the lower part of the stem in certain mosses. **L17.** ▸**b** *transf.* A minute branch of a vein, nerve, etc. **M19.**

2 *CHEMISTRY*. = **RADICAL** *noun* 4. Now *rare* or *obsolete*. **M19.**

radicular /rəˈdɪkjʊlə/ *adjective*. **M19.**
[formed as prec. + **-AR**[1].]
1 *BOTANY*. Of or belonging to a radicle. **M19.**

2 *ANATOMY*. Of or belonging to the root of an artery, nerve, etc.; *MEDICINE* affecting the root (of a tooth, nerve, etc.). **L19.**

radicule /ˈradɪkjuːl/ *noun*. **M19.**
[formed as **RADICLE**.]
BOTANY. = **RADICLE** 1a.

▪ **raˈdiculose** *adjective* (of a moss) having numerous radicles **L19.**

radiculitis /raˌdɪkjʊˈlʌɪtɪs/ *noun*. **E20.**
[formed as **RADICLE** + **-ITIS**.]
MEDICINE. Inflammation of the root in one or more spinal nerves.

radiesthesia /ˌreɪdɪɪsˈθiːzɪə/ *noun.* M20.
[French *radiesthésie*: see RADIO-, AESTHESIS, -IA[1].]
The detection of radiated energy by the human body, proposed as the basis of the use of dowsing rods, pendulums, etc., to locate buried substances, diagnose illness, etc.
▪ **radiesthesic** *adjective* = RADIESTHETIC M20. **radiesthesist** /-ˈiːsθɪ-/ *noun* = RADIESTHETIST M20. **radiesthetic** /-ˈθɛtɪk/ *adjective* of or pertaining to radiesthesia M20. **radiesthetically** *adverb* by means of radiesthesia M20. **radiesthetist** /-ˈiːsθɪ-/ *noun* a person skilled in the techniques of radiesthesia M20.

radii *noun* pl. of RADIUS *noun.*

radio /ˈreɪdɪəʊ/ *noun.* Pl. **-os.** E20.
[Independent use of RADIO- in RADIO-TELEPHONY, RADIO-TELEGRAM.]
▶ **I 1** The transmission and reception of radio-frequency electromagnetic waves, esp. as a means of communication that does not need a connecting wire; wireless telephony or telegraphy. E20.
2 Organized sound broadcasting by such means; sound broadcasting as a medium of communication or an art form. E20.
3 (**R-.**) (Forming part of the proper name of) a radio station or service. E20.
4 Radio equipment; *spec.* a receiving set. E20.
5 The radio-frequency part of the electromagnetic spectrum; radio wavelengths. M20.

📖 **1** A. L. ALBERT In radio, the feed-back coil of an oscillator is sometimes called a tickler. *Police Review* They . . sent a message by radio. **2** *Daily Telegraph* The programme itself was not an outstanding piece of radio. *Times* He welcomed the competition of commercial radio. ***local radio***: see LOCAL *adjective*. ***steam radio***: see STEAM *noun* 8b. **3** *Listener* Ask Goose Bay Radio if they have any other traffic. *Daily Telegraph* Radio Uganda, monitored in Nairobi. **Radio One, Radio Two, Radio Three, Radio Four, Radio Five** the five national radio networks of the BBC since 1967 (***Radio Five*** since 1990). **4** EDWARD VIII To speak to you all over the radio. ***transistor radio***: see TRANSISTOR 2.

▶ **II** †**6** A radio-telegram. Only in E20.
Attrib. & comb.: Esp. in the senses 'pertaining to, participating in, or transmitted as part of organized sound broadcasting', as ***radio announcer***, ***radio programme***, ***radio script***, etc.; 'controlled or operated by radio, employing radio', as ***radio cab***, ***radio compass***, etc.; 'pertaining to or characterized by the emission of radio waves, esp. by celestial objects', as ***radio buoy***, ***radio galaxy***, ***radio noise***, ***radio observatory***, etc. Special combs., as **radio amateur** a person who makes a hobby of picking up, and often also transmitting, radio messages; **radio astronomer** a person engaged in radio astronomy; **radio astronomy** the branch of astronomy that deals with the interpretation of radio waves reaching the earth from space, and with the astronomical use of radio echoes; **radio beacon** = BEACON *noun* 4b; **radio car**: equipped with a two-way radio; **radio contact** the state or an instance of being in communication by radio; **radio-controlled** *adjective* controlled from a distance by means of radio signals; **radio energy**: transmitted in the form of radio waves; ***radio fix***: see FIX *noun* 4; ***radio ham***: see HAM *noun*[1] 5; **radio horizon** the line round a radio transmitter at which direct radio waves from it are tangential to the earth's surface; **radio licence** a licence to use a radio; **radio map** ASTRONOMY a diagram showing the strength of the radio emission from different parts of the sky; **radio net** a system of intercommunicating radio sets, operated esp. by a police force or similar body; **radio network** a system of radio stations for navigation, communication, or broadcasting; a sound broadcasting organization or channel; **radio range** (*a*) = ***radio spectrum*** below; (*b*) a radio beacon transmitting directional radio signals which can be used by aircraft to determine the bearing of the transmitter; **radio shack** a small building or (esp. NAUTICAL) a room housing radio equipment; **radio silence** deliberate abstention from radio transmission; failure to communicate by radio; **radio spectrum** the radio-frequency part of the electromagnetic spectrum; the spectrum of any particular source at these frequencies; **radio star** any discrete source of radio waves outside the solar system (rarely an actual star); **radio station** an installation or establishment transmitting signals by radio; a sound broadcasting establishment or organization; ***radio telephone***: see TELEPHONE *noun* 2; **radio telescope** ASTRONOMY an apparatus or installation for detecting and recording radio waves from the sky, consisting of a large directional aerial together with a receiver and recording equipment; **radio wave** an electromagnetic wave with a frequency within the range used for telecommunication; usu. in *pl.*; **radio wavelength**: corresponding to a radio frequency.
▪ **radioless** *adjective* M20.

radio /ˈreɪdɪəʊ/ *verb.* E20.
[from the noun.]
1 *verb trans.* Transmit or send (a message or information) by radio. E20. ▸**b** Communicate with (a person, a place) by radio. Chiefly *US*. M20.
2 *verb intrans.* Send a message etc. by radio; give information or make a request by radio. E20.

📖 **2** *Daily Telegraph* The police radioed for assistance.

radio- /ˈreɪdɪəʊ/ *combining form.* Before *o* also **radi-.**
[from RADIUS, RADIO *noun*, RADIOACTIVE, RADIATION: see -O-.]
1 ANATOMY. Of or pertaining to the radius and (some other part), as ***radio-carpal***.
2 Connected with or employing radio.
3 Connected with radioactivity. ▸**b** Prefixed to the names of chemical elements and compounds to designate (*a*) a radioactive isotope (usu. one prepared artificially) of the named element, as ***radio-cobalt***, ***radio-silver***, etc.; (*b*) a compound containing a radioactive label, as ***radiothyroxine***.
4 Connected with rays or radiation, esp. ionizing radiation.
▪ **radio'assay** *noun & verb* (*a*) *noun* an assay performed by measuring radioactivity from a radioisotope present in a sample; (*b*) *verb trans.* assay in this way: M20. **radiocast** *noun & verb* (*US*) (*a*) *noun* a radio broadcast; (*b*) *verb trans.* broadcast by radio: M20. **radio-'dating** *noun* isotopic dating (e.g. radiocarbon dating) M20. **radio'density** *noun* the degree to which a material will absorb ionizing radiation; radio-opacity: M20. **radio-element** *noun* a naturally radioactive element E20. **radioenzy'matic** *adjective* (MEDICINE) designating a method of measuring concentrations of hormones etc. by the injection of radioactively labelled enzymes L20. **radio'heliograph** *noun* (ASTRONOMY) an interferometric radio telescope system designed to record instantaneous high-resolution pictures of the sun as observed at radio wavelengths M20. **radio-'iodine** *noun* a radioactive isotope of iodine; *esp.* iodine 131, an artificial isotope with a half-life for beta decay of about 8 days, widely used as a tracer and for radiotherapy of the thyroid gland: M20. **radio-label** *verb & noun* (BIOLOGY & CHEMISTRY) (*a*) *verb trans.* label with a radioactive isotope; (*b*) *noun* a radioactive label: M20. **radioland** *noun* the realm of radio; a region regarded as the place where radio listeners are: M20. **radio'ligand** *noun* (MEDICINE) a radio-labelled compound that has a strong chemical affinity for a particular receptor L20. **radiolocate** *verb trans.* locate by means of radar (or radio) M20. **radiolo'cation** *noun* the determination of the position and course of ships, aircraft, etc., by means of radar (or radio) M20. **radio'lucency** *noun* the state or property of being radiolucent M20. **radio'lucent** *adjective* transparent to X-rays E20. **radiolysis** /-ˈɒlɪsɪs/ *noun* (CHEMISTRY) decomposition of a compound by the action of ionizing radiation M20. **radio'lytic** *adjective* (CHEMISTRY) of, pertaining to, or formed by radiolysis M20. **radiometal** *noun* an alloy of nickel and iron with a high magnetic permeability M20. **radio-o'pacity** *noun* the state or property of being radio-opaque M20. **radio-o'paque** *adjective* impervious to X-rays M20. **radio'pacity** *noun* = RADIO-OPACITY E20. **radio'paque** *adjective* = RADIO-OPAQUE E20. **radiophare** *noun* a navigational radio beacon E20. **radiophoto** *noun* a photograph transmitted by means of radio M20. **radio-pro'tection** *noun* the prevention or countering by chemical means of the harmful effects produced in living tissues by ionizing radiation M20. **radio-re'sistance** *noun* the property of being radio-resistant E20. **radio-re'sistant** *adjective* (esp. of living tissue) resistant to the action of ionizing radiation E20. **radio-te'lemetry** *noun* telemetry by means of radio M20. **radio'teletype** *noun* a teleprinter which transmits and receives information by radio M20. **radio'telex** *noun* a telex transmitted by radio, esp. between ship and shore L20. **radio'toxic** *adjective* possessing radiotoxicity M20. **radioto'xicity** *noun* the property of a radioactive substance of being injurious to a living organism when present in its tissue M20. **radiovision** *noun* (*a*) *Hist.* a method of transmitting pictures by wire or radio; (*b*) the combination of a radio programme with a specially prepared film strip or series of slides, esp. as an educational aid (freq. *attrib.*): E20.

radioactivate /ˌreɪdɪəʊˈaktɪveɪt/ *verb trans.* E20.
[from next + -ATE[3].]
Make radioactive.
▪ **ˌradioacti'vation** *noun* the process of making something radioactive (***radioactivation analysis*** = ACTIVATION *analysis*) M20.

radioactive /ˌreɪdɪəʊˈaktɪv/ *adjective.* L19.
[from RADIO- 4 + ACTIVE.]
1 Of an atomic nucleus, a substance, etc.: (capable of) undergoing spontaneous nuclear decay involving emission of ionizing radiation in the form of particles or gamma rays. L19.
2 Of a process, phenomenon, etc.: of, pertaining to, involving, or produced by radioactivity. E20.

📖 **2** M. MARRIN Measure the age of the substance . . from its radioactive decay.

Special collocations: **radioactive equilibrium** a condition in which the quantities of radioactive daughter nuclides in a material remain constant because each is formed as fast as it decays. **radioactive series** a series of radioactive nuclides each member of which decays into the next, together with a non-radioactive end-product; the series of transformations relating such a set of nuclides. **radioactive waste** waste material that is radioactive, *esp.* spent nuclear fuel.
▪ **radioactively** *adverb* by radioactive decay; with radioactive material; by means of a technique dependent on radioactivity: E20.

radioactivity /ˌreɪdɪəʊakˈtɪvɪti/ *noun.* L19.
[from RADIO- + ACTIVITY.]
1 The property or condition of being radioactive; (the branch of science that deals with) the phenomena displayed by radioactive materials. Also, the radiation emitted by a radioactive material; such material itself in a dispersed form. L19.
2 ASTRONOMY. The property of emitting radio waves. M20.

radioautograph /ˌreɪdɪəʊˈɔːtə(ʊ)grɑːf/ *noun.* M20.
[from RADIO- + AUTO-[1] + -GRAPH.]
= AUTORADIOGRAPH *noun*.
▪ **ˌradioauto'graphic** *adjective* M20. **ˌradioau'tography** *noun* M20.

radiobiology /ˌreɪdɪəʊbʌɪˈɒlədʒi/ *noun.* E20.
[from RADIO- + BIOLOGY.]
The branch of biology that deals with the effects of radiation and radioactivity on living organisms, and with the biological application of radiological techniques.
▪ **ˌradiobio'logic** *adjective* (chiefly *US*) E20. **ˌradiobio'logical** *adjective* M20. **ˌradiobio'logically** *adverb* M20. **radiobiologist** *noun* M20.

radiocarbon /ˌreɪdɪəʊˈkɑːb(ə)n/ *noun.* M20.
[from RADIO- + CARBON *noun*.]
A radioactive isotope of carbon; *spec.* = ***carbon-14*** s.v. CARBON *noun*.
Comb.: **radiocarbon dating** a method of isotopic dating applicable to dead organic matter, in which the proportion of carbon-14 is measured and compared with the known natural abundance of the isotope.

radiochemical /ˌreɪdɪəʊˈkɛmɪk(ə)l/ *adjective & noun.* E20.
[from RADIO- + CHEMICAL.]
▶ **A** *adjective.* **1** Of, pertaining to, or considered in terms of radiochemistry. E20.
2 Of or pertaining to chemical changes caused by radiant energy. *rare.* E20.
▶ **B** *noun.* A radioactive chemical. E20.
▪ **radiochemically** *adverb* by a radiochemical method or process; in terms of radiochemistry: E20.

radiochemistry /ˌreɪdɪəʊˈkɛmɪstri/ *noun.* E20.
[from RADIO- + CHEMISTRY.]
The branch of chemistry that deals with radioactive substances.
▪ **radiochemist** *noun* M20.

radio-frequency /ˈreɪdɪəʊˌfriːkw(ə)nsi/ *adjective & noun.* E20.
[from RADIO *noun* + FREQUENCY.]
▶ **A** *attrib. adjective.* Pertaining to electromagnetic radiation with a frequency in the range used for telecommunication, greater than that of the highest audio frequency and less than that of the shortest infrared waves (i.e. between about 10^4 and 10^{11} or 10^{12} Hz); operating at or having such a frequency; employing alternating current with such a frequency. E20.
▶ **B** *noun.* (Usu. as two words.) A frequency in the radio-frequency range. E20.

radiogenic /ˌreɪdɪə(ʊ)ˈdʒɛnɪk, -ˈdʒiːnɪk/ *adjective.* E20.
[from RADIO- + -GENIC (in sense 1 after PHOTOGENIC).]
1 Well suited for broadcasting by radio; providing an attractive subject for a radio broadcast. E20.
2 Produced by or resulting from radioactive decay or ionizing radiation. M20.
▪ **radiogenically** *adverb* by means of radioactive decay M20.

radiogoniometer /ˌreɪdɪəʊgəʊnɪˈɒmɪtə/ *noun.* E20.
[from RADIO- + GONIOMETER.]
An apparatus for determining the direction from which radio waves are coming without using a rotating aerial.
▪ **ˌradiogonio'metric** *adjective* E20. **ˌradiogonio'metrical** *adjective* M20. **radiogoniometry** *noun* direction-finding by means of a radiogoniometer E20.

radiogram /ˈreɪdɪə(ʊ)gram/ *noun*[1]. L19.
[from RADIO- + -GRAM.]
1 = RADIOGRAPH *noun* 2. L19.
2 A radio-telegram. E20.

radiogram /ˈreɪdɪə(ʊ)gram/ *noun*[2]. E20.
[Abbreviation.]
= next.

radio-gramophone /ˌreɪdɪəʊˈgraməfəʊn/ *noun.* E20.
[from RADIO *noun* + GRAMOPHONE.]
A combined radio and record-player.

radiograph /ˈreɪdɪə(ʊ)grɑːf/ *noun & verb.* L19.
[from RADIO- + -GRAPH.]
▶ **A** *noun.* †**1** An instrument by which the duration and intensity of sunshine is measured and recorded. Only in L19.
2 An image of an object produced by means of X-rays or other ionizing radiation. L19.
†**3** = RADIO-TELEGRAPH. Only in E20.
▶ **B** *verb trans.* Make a radiograph of; study by radiography. L19.
▪ **radi'ographer** *noun* a person who practises radiography; a person qualified to operate radiographic equipment: L19. **radio'graphic** *adjective* (*a*) of, pertaining to, or carried out by means of radiography; †(*b*) = RADIO-TELEGRAPHIC: L19. **radio'graphical** *adjective* (*rare*) L19. **radio'graphically** *adverb* by means of radiography; as regards radiography: L19. **radi'ography** *noun* (*a*) the science or process of making radiographs (***mass radiography***: see MASS *noun*[2] & *adjective*); †(*b*) = RADIO-TELEGRAPHY: L19.

radioimmuno- /ˌreɪdɪəʊɪˈmjʊnəʊ, -ˈɪmjʊnəʊ/ *combining form.*
[from RADIO- + IMMUNO-.]
Forming terms pertaining to analytical techniques combining immunological and radioisotopic methods.
▪ **radioimmuno'assay** *noun* an immunological assay in which the sample is determined by allowing it to react with a prepared antiserum in competition with a known quantity of antigen labelled with a radioisotope, the extent of reaction

being measured from the radiation emitted M20. **radioimmuno'chemical** *adjective* deriving from both immunology and radiochemistry; employing radioisotopically labelled antigens and antibodies as reagents for chemical analysis M20. **radioimmunoelectropho'resis** *noun* immunoelectrophoresis carried out using radioisotopically labelled samples M20. **,radioimmuno'logic** *adjective* (chiefly *US*), **,radioimmuno'logical** *adjectives* combining radiological and immunological methods; of or pertaining to radioimmunology: M20. **,radioimmuno'logically** *adverb* by radioimmunological means L20. **,radioimmu'nology** *noun* the application of radiological techniques in immunology L20. **radioimmunoprecipi'tation** *noun* the use of radioisotopically labelled antigen or antibody in a precipitin test M20.

radioisotope /ˌreɪdɪəʊˈʌɪsətəʊp/ *noun*. M20.
[from RADIO- + ISOTOPE.]
A radioactive isotope.
■ **radioisotopic** /-ˈtɒpɪk/ *adjective* M20. **radioisotopically** /-ˈtɒpɪk-/ *adverb* L20.

radiolaria /ˌreɪdɪə(ʊ)ˈlɛːrɪə/ *noun pl.* L19.
[mod. Latin *Radiolaria* former order name, from late Latin *radiolus* faint ray, dim. of Latin RADIUS.]
Radiolarians collectively.

radiolarian /ˌreɪdɪə(ʊ)ˈlɛːrɪən/ *noun & adjective*. L19.
[from prec. + -AN.]
▶ **A** *noun*. A protozoan of any of several classes of the superclass Actinopoda, comprising marine planktonic organisms that have radiating axopodia and usu. siliceous skeletons with projecting spines. L19.
▶ **B** *adjective*. Of, pertaining to, or derived from radiolarians. L19.
radiolarian chert (a cryptocrystalline type of) radiolarite. **radiolarian earth** unconsolidated siliceous rock formed from the remains of radiolaria. **radiolarian ooze** a siliceous marine sediment rich in the remains of the tests of radiolarians.
■ **radiolarite** *noun* (GEOLOGY) (a) sedimentary rock formed mainly from skeletal remains of radiolarians E20.

radiole /ˈreɪdɪəʊl/ *noun*. E20.
[Late Latin *radiolus*: see RADIOLARIA, -OLE[1].]
A spine or prickle of a sea urchin. Also ***radiole spine***.

radiology /reɪdɪˈɒlədʒi/ *noun*. E20.
[from RADIO- + -OLOGY.]
The medical use of X-rays and other forms of radiation, esp. in diagnosis.
■ **radio'logic** (chiefly *US*), **radio'logical** *adjectives* of, pertaining to, or concerned with radiology; (of warfare, weapons, etc.) involving the deliberate release of ionizing radiation or radioactive material in harmful quantities: E20. **radio'logically** *adverb* E20. **radiologist** *noun* a person employing ionizing radiation or radioactive material in any field, *esp.* a medically qualified practitioner trained in the diagnostic use of X-rays E20.

radiometer /reɪdɪˈɒmɪtə/ *noun*. E18.
[from RADIO- + -METER.]
†**1** An instrument for measuring angles. *rare*. Only in E18.
2 An instrument for detecting or measuring the intensity of (esp. infrared) electromagnetic radiation. Also, an instrument for measuring the intensity of sound by means of its radiation pressure. L19.
3 An instrument for determining the amount of X-radiation administered to a patient. E20.
■ **radio'metric** *adjective* (*a*) of or pertaining to a radiometer or its use; (*b*) of, pertaining to, or involving the measurement of radioactivity or ionizing radiation (***radiometric dating***, isotopic dating): L19. **radio'metrically** *adverb* by a radiometric method E20. **radiometry** *noun* the use of a radiometer; *spec.* the detection and measurement of infrared radiation: L19.

radionic /reɪdɪˈɒnɪk/ *adjective*. M20.
[from RADIO- after ELECTRONIC.]
†**1** Of or pertaining to electronics, esp. as applied to radio. Only in M20.
2 Of, pertaining to, or practising radionics. M20.

radionics /reɪdɪˈɒnɪks/ *noun*. M20.
[from RADIO- after ELECTRONICS.]
†**1** Electronics, *esp.* those aspects of electronics connected with radio. *US*. Only in M20.
2 A form of fringe medicine based on the interpretation of characteristic radiation supposed to be emitted by living and other substances, and to be detectable by special electrical instruments. M20.

radiophonic /ˌreɪdɪə(ʊ)ˈfɒnɪk/ *adjective*. L19.
[from RADIO- + PHONIC.]
1 Belonging to radiophony. Now *rare* or *obsolete*. L19.
2 Pertaining to or designating synthetic sound, esp. music, produced electronically with the aid of tape recorders, usually for use in broadcasting in conjunction with conventional material. M20.
■ **'radiophone** *noun* (*a*) (now *rare* or *obsolete*) an instrument for producing sound by radiant energy; (*b*) a radio-telephone: L19. **radiophonics** *noun* (*a*) (treated as *sing.*) the production and use of radiophonic sound; (*b*) (treated as *pl.*) radiophonic sounds: M20. **radi'ophony** *noun* (now *rare* or *obsolete*) the production of sound by radiant energy L19.

radioscopy /reɪdɪˈɒskəpi/ *noun*. L19.
[from RADIO- + -SCOPY.]
The examination of objects by means of X-rays; *spec.* fluoroscopy.
■ **'radioscope** *noun* (*obsolete* exc. *Hist.*) a fluoroscope L19. **radio'scopic** *adjective* L19.

radiosensitive /ˌreɪdɪəʊˈsɛnsɪtɪv/ *adjective*. E20.
[from RADIO- + SENSITIVE *adjective*.]
Sensitive to the action of ionizing radiation.
■ **,radiosensi'tivity** *noun* E20. **,radiosensiti'zation** *noun* M20. **radiosensitize** *verb trans.* M20. **radiosensitizer** *noun* a substance used to increase the sensitivity of an organism or tissue to ionizing radiation M20.

radiosonde /ˈreɪdɪəʊsɒnd/ *noun*. M20.
[from RADIO- + AS SONDE.]
A set of meteorological instruments and a radio which transmits measurements of conditions at various heights when carried through the atmosphere, usu. by a balloon.
■ **radio'sondage** *noun* (a) sounding of the atmosphere by radiosonde M20.

radio-telegraphy /ˌreɪdɪəʊtɪˈlɛɡrəfi, -tɛ-/ *noun*. L19.
[from RADIO- 2 + TELEGRAPHY.]
Telegraphy by means of radio (rather than wires); wireless telegraphy.
■ **radio-'telegram** *noun* a telegraphic message sent by radio E20. **radio-'telegraph** *noun* an instrument for sending radiotelegrams E20. **radio-tele'graphic** *adjective* E20.

radio-telephony /ˌreɪdɪəʊtɪˈlɛfəni, -tɛ-/ *noun*. E20.
[from RADIO- + TELEPHONY.]
Telephony in which the signal is transmitted by radio over part of the route; wireless telephony.
■ **radio-tele'phonic** *adjective* E20.

radiotherapy /ˌreɪdɪə(ʊ)ˈθɛrəpi/ *noun*. E20.
[from RADIO- + THERAPY.]
The treatment of disease by means of X-rays or other forms of ionizing radiation.
■ **radiothera'peutic** *adjective* of, pertaining to, or employing radiotherapy E20. **radiothera'peutically** *adverb* M20. **radiothera'peutics** *noun* = RADIOTHERAPY L19. **radiotherapist** *noun* a person who practises radiotherapy E20.

radiothon /ˈreɪdɪə(ʊ)θɒn/ *noun*. *US*. M20.
[from RADIO- + -ATHON.]
A prolonged radio broadcast by a person or group, usu. as a fund-raising event.

†**radious** *adjective*. LME.
[from Latin *radiosus*, from RADIUS: see -OUS.]
1 Radiant, bright. LME–L17.
2 Forming rays of light. *rare*. E–M18.

radish /ˈradɪʃ/ *noun*. OE.
[from Latin *radic-*, RADIX root; *-ish* perh. by blending with French *radis*.]
The crisp pungent root, most freq. with a pinkish-red skin and white flesh, of a widely cultivated cruciferous plant, *Raphanus sativus*, eaten raw in salads; this plant. Also (with specifying word), any of several other plants of the genus *Raphanus*.
sea radish, ***wild radish***, etc. RAT-TAILED ***radish***.

radium /ˈreɪdɪəm/ *noun*. L19.
[formed as next + -IUM.]
▶ **I 1** A radioactive metallic chemical element, atomic no. 88, which is one of the alkaline earth metals and occurs in pitchblende and other uranium ores. (Symbol Ra.) L19.
2 (With following cap. letter.) Designating substances (mostly radioactive) now recognized as isotopes of other elements, which are formed successively in the radioactive series of radium. E20.
▶ **II 3** A smooth plain fabric with the sheen of silk. E20.
Comb.: **radium beam** a beam of gamma radiation from a radium source, used in radiotherapy; **radium bomb** a container holding a large quantity of radium, used in radiotherapy as a source of a gamma ray beam; **radium burn**: caused by overexposure to radiation from radium; **radium dial** a watch or clock dial with the numbers and hands marked with radium to make them luminescent; **radium needle**: containing radium which can be inserted into tissue for radiotherapy; **radium therapy** radiotherapy using radiation from radium.
■ **radiumize** *verb trans.* subject to the action of radium E20.

radius /ˈreɪdɪəs/ *noun & verb*. L16.
[Latin = staff, spoke, ray.]
▶ **A** *noun*. Pl. **-ii** /-ɪʌɪ/.
†**1** A straight object such as a staff or bar. L16–M18.
2 ANATOMY & ZOOLOGY. One of the two bones of the forearm, extending from the humerus to the thumb side of the wrist and slightly shorter than the ulna; the corresponding bone of a tetrapod's foreleg or a bird's wing. L16.
3 A straight line from the centre of a circle or sphere to the circumference; a radial line of a curve, drawn from a given point such as a focus to any point on the curve. E17.
4 Any of a set of lines, rods, spokes, etc., diverging from a point like the radii of a circle; a radiating part. E18.
5 A circular area of which the extent is measured by the length of the radius of the circle which bounds it. M19.

3 LARMOR *radius*. *radius of curvature*: see CURVATURE 1b. SCHWARZSCHILD *radius*. TURNING *radius*. **5** H. GREEN The roads are to be watched within a radius of twenty miles. *Times* The wreckage was scattered over a radius of a mile. **radius of action** the distance that an aircraft can cover so as to leave sufficient fuel for its return to base;

Comb.: **radius bar** a bar pivoted at one end so that it can move in a circle or arc of a circle; **radius rod** = ***radius bar*** above; **radius vector** a variable line drawn from a fixed point as origin; *spec.* (ASTRONOMY) one joining a satellite or other celestial object to its primary.
▶ **B** *verb trans.* Round off, give a rounded form to (a corner or end). M20.

radix /ˈradɪks, ˈreɪ-/ *noun*. Pl. **-ices** /-ɪsiːz/, **-ixes**. L16.
[Latin *radix*, *radic-* root of a plant.]
1 †**a** MATH. A root of a number. L16–E18. ▸**b** MATH. & COMPUTING. = BASE *noun*[1] 7. L18.
†**2** ASTROLOGY & ASTRONOMY. A fact used as a basis of calculation, as a nativity, a position of a planet, etc. E17–L18.
3 A thing in which something originates; a source. E17.
†**4** PHILOLOGY. An original word or form from which other words are derived. M17–L18.

radknight /ˈradnʌɪt/ *noun*. LOE.
[from *rād* ROAD *noun* + *cniht* KNIGHT.]
ENGLISH HISTORY. Under the feudal system, a tenant holding land on condition of performing service on horseback.
■ Also **radman** *noun* LOE.

radly /ˈradli/ *adverb*. Long *obsolete* exc. *Scot.* OE.
[from RAD *adjective*[1] + -LY[2].]
Quickly, promptly.

Radnor /ˈradnə/ *adjective & noun*. M19.
[Abbreviation of *Radnorshire*, a former county in Wales.]
▶ **A** *adjective*. Designating (a breed of) dark-faced sheep raised chiefly for meat. M19.
▶ **B** *noun*. A Radnor sheep; the Radnor breed. M19.

radome /ˈreɪdəʊm/ *noun*. M20.
[Blend of RADAR and DOME.]
A dome or other structure, transparent to radio waves, protecting a radar aerial.

radon /ˈreɪdɒn/ *noun*. E20.
[from RADIUM after ARGON.]
A radioactive chemical element with a short half-life, atomic no. 86, which belongs to the group of noble gases and occurs naturally in trace amounts as a result of the decay of radium and other radioactive elements. (Symbol Rn.)
Comb.: **radon seed** a short tube containing radon that is used in radiotherapy as a source of alpha radiation.

radula /ˈradjʊlə/ *noun*. Pl. **-lae** /-liː/. M18.
[Latin = scraper, from *radere* scrape: see -ULE.]
†**1** SURGERY. An instrument for scraping bones. Only in M18.
2 ZOOLOGY. The movable toothed or rasping structure in the mouth of a mollusc, used for scraping off and drawing in food particles. L19.
■ **radular** *adjective* L19.

radurization /ˌradjʊrʌɪˈzeɪʃ(ə)n/ *noun*. Also **-isation**. M20.
[from Latin *radiare* provide with rays, shine + *durare* make hard, preserve + -IZATION.]
The treatment of food with ionizing radiation so as to enhance its keeping qualities by killing many of the micro-organisms in it. Cf. RADAPPERTIZATION, RADICIDATION.

radwaste /ˈradweɪst/ *noun*. L20.
[Contr.]
= RADIOACTIVE ***waste***.

RAE *abbreviation*.
Royal Aircraft Establishment.

Raelian /rʌɪˈiːlɪən/ *noun & adjective*. L20.
[from *Rael*, assumed name of Claude Vorilhon, French singer and journalist, author of *The Message Given to me by Extraterrestrials* (1974).]
▶ **A** *noun*. A member of an atheistic cult based on the belief that humans originated from alien scientists who came to earth in UFOs. L20.
▶ **B** *adjective*. Of or relating to this cult or its members. L20.

Raetic *adjective & noun* see RHAETIC.

RAF /*colloq.* raf/ *abbreviation*.
Royal Air Force; the members of this collectively.

rafale /rafal/ *noun*. Pl. pronounced same. E20.
[French, lit. 'gust of wind'.]
A series of bursts of gunfire; a drum roll.

raff /raf/ *noun*[1]. ME.
[Last elem. of ***riff and raff*** s.v. RIFF *noun*[1] (whence RIFF-RAFF). Cf. also Swedish *rafs* rubbish. See also RAFT *noun*[2].]
†**1** A class of people or things. See also ***riff and raff*** s.v. RIFF *noun*[1]. Only in ME.
2 Alliteration; verse, esp. alliterative verse, of a low standard. Long *arch.* ME.

3 Worthless material, rubbish. *obsolete* exc. *Scot. & dial.* LME.
4a = RIFF-RAFF *noun* 1. L17. **▸b** A member of the riff-raff. L18.
5 A large number *of*. Now *rare*. L17.
4a *scaff and raff*, *scaff-raff*: see SCAFF *noun*² 2.
■ **raffy** *adjective* (*obsolete* exc. *Scot.*) of loose or coarse texture M19.

raff /raf/ *noun*². LME.
[Perh. from German *Raf*, *Raff(e)* dial. form of *Rafe* rafter, beam.]
Foreign timber, usu. in the form of planks.

raff /raf/ *verb trans. obsolete* exc. *dial.* E17.
[Origin uncertain: cf. Swedish *rafsa*.]
Sweep together.

Raffaelle ware /rafʌɪˈɛlɪ wɛː/ *noun phr.* M19.
[from *Raffaello* Sanzio (Raphael) (1483–1520), Italian painter.]
A type of 16th-cent. Italian majolica; a modern imitation of this.

raffee /raˈfiː/ *noun.* L19.
[Origin unkn.]
NAUTICAL. A small square sail above the sky-sail.

Rafferty rules /ˈrafətɪ ˌruːlz/ *noun. Austral. & NZ colloq.* Also **Rafferty's rules**. E20.
[Prob. alt. of *refractory*, assoc. with the Irish surname.]
No rules at all, esp. in boxing.

raffia /ˈrafɪə/ *noun.* In sense 1 also **raphia**, (earliest) **rofia**. E18.
[Malagasy.]
1 A palm of the African genus *Raphia*, esp. *R. farinifera* of Madagascar. E18.
2 The soft fibre from the leaves of such a palm, used as garden twine, in basketwork, etc. L19.

raffinate /ˈrafɪneɪt/ *noun.* E20.
[German or French *raffinat*, from German *raffinieren* (French *raffiner*) refine: see -ATE².]
The refined fraction which results after removal of impurities by solvent extraction, *spec.* in oil refining.

raffiné /rafine/ *adjective.* L19.
[French.]
Of manners or judgement: refined.

raffinose /ˈrafɪnəʊz, -s/ *noun.* L19.
[from French *raffiner* refine + -OSE².]
CHEMISTRY. A trisaccharide sugar containing glucose, galactose, and fructose units, found in sugar beet, cottonseed, and many cereals.

raffish /ˈrafɪʃ/ *adjective.* E19.
[from RAFF *noun*¹ + -ISH¹.]
Vulgar, tawdry; disreputable, *esp.* attractively disreputable in appearance or behaviour; rakish.

> *Spectator* A certain raffish elegance. A. T. ELLIS A horse doctor, raffish and loud. J. GATHORNE-HARDY A fairly raffish past with three husbands.

■ **raffishly** *adverb* L19. **raffishness** *noun* M19.

raffle /ˈraf(ə)l/ *noun*¹. LME.
[Old French *raffle*, (also mod.) *rafle*, medieval Latin *raffla*, of unkn. origin.]
1 A game of chance played with three dice, a win being the throwing of a triplet or the highest doublet. *obsolete* exc. *dial.* LME.
2 A usu. fund-raising lottery with prizes numbered to correspond to tickets drawn as lots. M18.

raffle /ˈraf(ə)l/ *noun*². LME.
[Perh. from Old French *raf(f)le* in *rifle ou rafle* anything at all, *ne rifle ne rafle* nothing at all. Cf. RAFF *noun*¹, RIFF-RAFF.]
1 A rabble. LME.
2 Rubbish, refuse; *spec.* (NAUTICAL) lumber, debris. M19.

raffle /ˈraf(ə)l/ *verb*¹. L17.
[from RAFFLE *noun*¹ or French *rafler*.]
1 *verb intrans.* Cast dice, draw lots, etc., *for* a thing; take part in a raffle. L17.
2 *verb trans.* Dispose of by means of a raffle. Also foll. by *off*. M19.
■ **raffler** *noun* L18.

raffle /ˈraf(ə)l/ *verb*² *trans. rare.* E18.
[Perh. var. of RUFFLE *verb*¹.]
1 Indent or serrate (a leaf). E18.
2 Crumple. E18.

raffle /ˈraf(ə)l/ *verb*³ *trans. north.* E19.
[Var. of RAVEL *verb*.]
Ravel, entangle.

Raffles /ˈraf(ə)lz/ *noun.* E20.
[A. J. *Raffles*, hero of *The Amateur Cracksman* (1899) and other books by E. W. Hornung (1866–1921).]
A man of good birth who engages in crime, esp. burglary.

rafflesia /rəˈfliːʒɪə, -ˈiːzɪə/ *noun.* E19.
[mod. Latin (see below), from Sir T. Stamford *Raffles* (1781–1826), Brit. governor of Sumatra + -IA¹.]
Any of various stemless leafless parasitic plants constituting the genus *Rafflesia* (family Rafflesiaceae), native to Java and Sumatra; esp. *R. arnoldii*, with flowers over 60 cm (two feet) across.

Rafi /raˈfiː/ *noun.* M20.
[Hebrew acronym, from *Rěšīmat Pōʿălē Yiśrāʾēl* Israel Workers List.]
A left-wing political party in the State of Israel.

rafik /raˈfik/ *noun.* M19.
[Arab. *rafīk*.]
In Arabia: a companion, an escort.

raft /rɑːft/ *noun*¹. LME.
[Old Norse *raptr* rafter, rel. to Old High German *ravo*, Old Norse *ráfr*, *ræfr*. Cf. RAFTER *noun*¹.]
1 A beam, a spar, a rafter. Now *arch. & dial.* LME.
2 A collection of logs, planks, casks, etc., fastened together for transportation by floating. L15.
3 A flat floating structure of logs or other materials for transporting people or things on water. Also *spec.*, a lifeboat or small (often inflatable) boat, esp. for use in emergencies. L16.
4 A large floating mass of fallen trees, vegetation, ice, etc. Also, a dense flock of swimming birds or animals, esp. ducks. Chiefly *US*. E18.
5 BUILDING. A layer of reinforced concrete forming the foundation of a building. E20.

> **3** B. GREENHILL The simplest rafts comprise a few logs or bundles of reeds joined together. **4** D. ATTENBOROUGH Rafts of vegetation that float . . out to sea. *Bird Watching* A raft of 20 Puffins.

Comb.: **raft-bridge**: made of a raft, or supported by rafts; **raft-dog** an iron bar bent at the ends, used to secure logs in a raft; **raft-duck** a duck which forms thick flocks on the water; *spec.* the scaup, *Aythya marila*; **raft foundation** = sense 5 above; **raftsman** a person who works on a raft; **raft spider** a large spider of the genus *Dolomedes*, which frequents pools and swamps and catches insects etc. on the surface film.

raft /rɑːft/ *noun*². M19.
[Alt. of RAFF *noun*¹, perh. by assoc. with prec.]
A large collection; a crowd, a lot, (*of*).

> J. RABAN A . . raft of American oil millionaires. *Nature* A raft of theoretical puzzles.

raft /rɑːft/ *verb*¹. L17.
[from RAFT *noun*¹.]
1 *verb trans.* Transport by water on or in the form of a raft. L17. **▸b** Float *off* (water casks) from the shore to a ship. M18.
2 *verb trans.* Form into a raft or rafts. M18.
3 *verb trans.* Cross (water) by means of a raft. M18.
4 *verb intrans.* Use a raft, esp. for crossing water; go on a raft. M18.
5 *verb intrans.* Of an ice floe: be driven on top of or underneath another floe. L19.

> **1** J. BELKNAP The lumber . . is rafted down that river. **2** J. A. MICHENER There must have been three thousand ducks rafted there. **4** A. R. AMMONS Drowning snakes / rafting down the . . river.

■ **rafting** *noun* the action of the verb; the sport or pastime of travelling down a river on a raft: L17.

raft /raft/ *verb*² *trans. English & Canad. dial.* M19.
[Origin unkn.]
Rouse; disturb, unsettle.

rafter /ˈrɑːftə/ *noun*¹ & *verb.*
[Old English *ræfter* = Old Saxon *rehter*, Middle Low German *rafter*, *rachter* rel. to RAFT *noun*¹.]
▸ A *noun.* **1** Each of the sloping beams forming the framework of a roof and bearing the outer covering of tiles, thatch, etc. OE.
†**2** Any large beam. M16–L17.
▸ B *verb.* **1** *verb trans.* Build or provide with rafters. M16.
2 *verb trans.* Form narrow ridges in ploughing (land) by leaving sections undisturbed. *obsolete* exc. *dial.* M18.
3 *verb intrans.* Of ice: = RAFT *verb*¹ 5. *N. Amer.* L18.
■ **raftered** *adjective* roofed with or composed of (esp. visible) rafters M18. **raftering** *noun* (*a*) the action of the verb; (*b*) the arrangement of rafters; wood for rafters: M16. **rafterless** *adjective* M19.

rafter /ˈrɑːftə/ *noun*². E19.
[from RAFT *noun*¹ or *verb*¹ + -ER¹.]
1 A person employed in rafting timber. E19.
2 A person who travels on a raft. L20.

rafty /ˈrɑːfti/ *adjective.* Now *dial.* M17.
[Origin unkn.]
1 Damp; muggy. M17.
2 Of bacon: rancid. E18.

> **1** A. JOBSON The weather was a bit rafty.

rag /rag/ *noun*¹. ME.
[Prob. back-form. from RAGGED or RAGGY *adjective*¹.]
1 A torn, frayed, or worn piece of woven material; in *pl.*, tattered or worn clothes. ME. **▸b** A very small scrap of cloth or article of clothing. Usu. in neg. contexts. L16. **▸c** A garment of any kind. Usu. in *pl. colloq.* (orig. *US*). M19.
2 An irregularly shaped piece of anything; a fragment, a scrap, (*lit. & fig.*). LME. **▸b** *spec.* (A small amount of) money. *arch. slang.* L16.
3 a A low-class or disreputable person. See also BOBTAIL *noun* 3b. Cf. RAGTAG *noun*, TAGRAG *noun* 1. M16. **▸b** A newspaper, *esp.* one regarded as inferior or worthless. *colloq.* M18. **▸c** A handkerchief. *colloq.* M18. **▸d** A flag. *slang.* M18. **▸e** A banknote. Usu. in *pl. arch. slang.* M19. **▸f** *The* curtain in a theatre. *slang.* M19. **▸g** A sanitary towel. Chiefly in ***be on the rag***, ***have the rags on***, be menstruating. *slang* (chiefly *N. Amer.*). M20.
4 A sharp or jagged projection. Chiefly *Scot.* M17.
5 = RAGWORM. L19.

> **1** N. STREATFEILD Nobody . . was going to curl their hair in rags every night. SIAN EVANS A dirty white rag tied round his throat in lieu of a collar. J. MCPHEE His clothes have become rags. **c** E. LANGLEY Every rag we possessed. **2** SHELLEY Rags of loose flesh. V. SCANNELL In the . . hedges pale rags of mist hung. S. MIDDLETON His private life was in rags. **3b** A. WILSON Not John's ghastly rag, of course, but the more reputable papers. B. TRAPIDO The front page of the local rag.

Phrases: ***be on the rag***: see sense 3g above. ***chew the rag***: see CHEW *verb*. **get one's rag out** *slang* = ***lose one's rag*** below. ***glad rags***: see GLAD *adjective*. ***have the rags on***: see sense 3g above. **in rags** (*a*) much torn; (*b*) in old torn clothes. **lose one's rag** *slang* become angry, lose one's temper. **rags to riches** poverty to wealth. ***tag and rag***: see TAG *noun*¹ 11. **take the rag off the bush**, **take the rag off the hedge**, **take the rag off** (chiefly *US*) surpass everything or everyone.

Comb.: **rag-and-bone-man** an itinerant dealer in old clothes, furniture, etc.; **rag-bag** (*a*) a bag in which scraps of cloth are collected or stored; (*b*) a miscellaneous collection; (*c*) *slang* a sloppily dressed woman; **rag-bolt** *noun & verb* (*a*) *noun* a bolt with barbs to keep it tight when it has been driven in; (*b*) *verb trans.* fasten by means of a rag bolt; **rag book** a children's book made of untearable cloth; **rag-chewing** protracted discussion or argument; **rag content** the proportion of rag in paper; **rag doll** a stuffed doll made of cloth; **rag frame** MINING an inclined table for partially concentrating slimes; **rag-head** *N. Amer. slang*, (*racially offensive*) a person who wears a turban or cloth around the head; **rag-lamp** *US HISTORY* a lamp with a rag as a wick; **rag-merchant** a dealer in rags; **rag-out** *slang* a sudden short unofficial strike by coalminers; **rag paper**: made from rags; **rag picker** a collector and seller of rags; **rag-roll** *verb trans.* create a marbled or mottled effect on (a surface) by painting it using a crumpled rag (chiefly as ***rag-rolling*** *verbal noun*); **rag rug**: made from small strips of fabric hooked into or pushed through a base material such as hessian; **rag-shop**, *N. Amer.* **rag-store** a shop dealing in rags and old clothes; **ragtop** *US slang* a convertible car with a soft hood; **rag trade** *colloq.* the business of designing, making, and selling clothes; **rag-wheel** a sprocket-wheel with projections catching in the links of a chain passing over it.
■ **raggie** *noun* †(*a*) *Military slang* a mess jacket; (*b*) *Nautical slang* a close friend: M19.

rag /rag/ *noun*². ME.
[Origin unkn.: later assoc. with prec.]
1 a A piece or bed of hard or rough stone. *obsolete* exc. *dial.* ME. **▸b** A large coarse roofing-slate. E19.
2 Any of various different kinds of stone of a hard coarse texture, which break up in flat pieces several inches thick. Freq. with specifying word, as ***coral rag***, ***Kentish rag***, etc. LME.

rag /rag/ *noun*³. E19.
[from RAG *verb*².]
A noisy disorderly scene or dispute; a rowdy celebration; *colloq.* a prank; *esp.* a programme of stunts, parades, and entertainment organized by students to raise money for charities.

rag /rag/ *noun*⁴. L19.
[Perh. from RAGGED. Cf. RAGTIME.]
1 A dance, a ball; *esp.* a dance performed to ragtime music. Now *rare* or *obsolete*. L19.
2 A ragtime composition or tune. L19.

rag *noun*⁵ var. of RAGA.

rag /rag/ *verb*¹. Infl. **-gg-**. LME.
[from RAG *noun*¹.]
1 *verb trans.* †**a** Tear in pieces. Only in LME. **▸b** Make ragged. E16.
2 *verb intrans.* †**a** Become ragged. *rare.* M–L17. **▸b** Foll. by *out*: dress up. *US slang.* M19.

rag /rag/ *verb*². Infl. **-gg-**. M18.
[Origin unkn.]
1 *verb trans.* Scold, reprove severely. M18.
2 *verb trans.* Tease, torment; annoy in a rough manner, play a boisterous practical joke on. E19.
3 *verb intrans.* Be noisy and riotous; engage in rough play. L19.
■ **ragger** *noun* E20.

rag /rag/ *verb*³ *trans.* Infl. **-gg-**. L19.
[Origin unkn. Cf. earlier RAGGING *noun*¹.]
Break up (ore) preparatory to sorting.

rag /rag/ *verb*⁴. Infl. **-gg-**. L19.
[from RAG *noun*⁴.]
1 *verb intrans. & trans.* (with *it*). Play, sing, or dance in ragtime. L19.

2 *verb trans.* Convert (a melody etc.) into ragtime; play ragtime music on (an instrument). **E20.**

raga /ˈrɑːɡə/ *noun.* Also **rag** /rɑːɡ/. **L18.**
[Sanskrit *rāga* colour, passion, melody.]
In Indian music: a pattern of notes used as a basis for melodies and improvisations; a piece of music based on a particular raga.
Comb.: **raga rock** rock music characterized by improvisation or melody in the style of a raga.

ragabash /ˈraɡəbaʃ/ *noun & adjective.* Long *obsolete* exc. *Scot. & north.* **E17.**
[App. from RAG *noun*¹, with fanciful ending.]
1 An idle worthless person. **E17.**
2 *collect.* The rabble, the common people. **E19.**

ragamala /ˈrɑːɡəmɑːlə, rɑːɡəˈmɑːlə/ *noun & adjective.* **L18.**
[Sanskrit *rāgamālā*, formed as RAGA + *mālā* necklace, garland.]
In Indian art: (designating) (each of) a series of miniature paintings based on situations and vernacular poems inspired by ragas.

ragamuffin /ˈraɡəmʌfɪn/ *noun & adjective.* **ME.**
[Prob. from RAG *noun*¹, with fanciful ending.]
▶ **A** *noun.* **1** A person, esp. a child, in ragged dirty clothes. **ME.**
2 (Also **-gg-**.) An exponent or follower of a style of popular music derived from reggae and incorporating elements from faster, more electronically based styles such as hip-hop; this style of music. Cf. RAGGA. **L20.**
▶ **B** *adjective.* Ragged and dirty. **E17.**
■ **ragamuffinly** *adjective* = RAGAMUFFIN *adjective* **L17.**

ragazzo /raˈɡaddzo/ *noun.* Pl. **-zzi** /-ddzi/. **M19.**
[Italian.]
In Italy, a young boy, a youth.
■ ***ragazza*** /raˈɡaddza/ *noun*, pl. **-zze** /-ddze/, (in Italy) a young girl **E20.**

rage /reɪdʒ/ *noun.* **ME.**
[Old & mod. French from Proto-Romance var. of Latin RABIES.]
1 (A fit of) madness or insanity. *obsolete* exc. *poet.* **ME.** ▸†**b** (An act of) folly or rashness. Only in **ME.**
2 (A fit of) violent anger. **ME.** ▸**b** As 2nd elem. of comb.: denoting irrationally violent or aggressive behaviour caused esp. by pent-up anger or frustration associated with a stressful environment or activity, as ***road rage***, ***air rage***, etc. **L20.**
†**3** Violent or impetuous action, ferocity, esp. in battle. **ME–L15.**
4 *transf.* **a** Violence of weather or other natural agency. **ME.** ▸**b** A flood, a high tide. Now *rare* or *obsolete.* **LME.**
5 †**a** Fun, sport; riotous behaviour; a trick, a prank. Only in **ME.** ▸**b** A party; a good time. *Austral. & NZ colloq.* **L20.**
6 Intensity or violence of or *of* a feeling; a violent feeling or passion; *spec.* (*poet.*) enthusiasm, ardour. **ME.** ▸**b** Sexual passion. Long *rare.* **LME.** ▸†**c** (A fit of) intense grief; (a) severe pain. *rare.* **LME–L16.**
7 a A violent passion or desire. (Foll. by *for, of, to do.*) **L16.** ▸**b** A widespread and usu. temporary fashion. **L18.**

> 🕮 **2** J. WAINWRIGHT His fingers trembled with controlled rage. G. DALY He flew into a rage, shouting and cursing at Gabriel. **5b** *Skyline* Have a rage at our Castaway BBQ. **7a** G. SAINTSBURY The present rage for reprints of old work. **b** *Honey* Large, military looking metal pins are definitely the rage this season. **all the rage** very popular or fashionable.

■ **rageful** *adjective* (*a*) full of rage or anger; (*b*) (of a thing) furious: **L16.** **ragefully** *adverb* **E17.** **rageless** *adjective* (*rare*) **L16.** **rageous** *adjective* (now *arch. & dial.*) furious, full of rage **LME.**

rage /reɪdʒ/ *verb.* **ME.**
[Old & mod. French *rager*, formed as prec.]
†**1** *verb intrans.* Go or be mad; act insanely. **ME–M16.**
2 *verb intrans.* Rave in madness or fury; be full of anger; act wildly; speak furiously. Freq. foll. by *against, at.* **ME.** ▸**b** *verb trans. & intrans.* (with *at, on*). Exercise one's rage on, scold. Long *obsolete* exc. *Scot.* **M16.**
3 †**a** *verb intrans.* Behave riotously; indulge in licentious pleasure. **ME–M17.** ▸**b** Revel; have a good time. *Austral. & NZ colloq.* **L20.**
4 *verb intrans.* (Of a storm, battle, disease, etc.) be violent, be at its height, continue unchecked; (of the wind etc.) move with violence. **LME.** ▸**b** Esp. of a tooth: ache severely. Now *rare.* **M16.** ▸**c** Of a feeling etc.: have or reach a high degree of intensity. **L16.**
5 *verb intrans.* Move or go in a rage. Foll. by *about, over, up*, etc. **L16.**
†**6** *verb trans.* Enrage. *rare* (Shakes.). Only in **L16.**

> 🕮 **2** J. OSBORNE I rage, and shout my head off. A. CROSS She . . raged at the world that had killed him so needlessly. **4** TENNYSON The wind is raging. E. WAUGH Discussion had raged for some days. I. MURDOCH The battle raged to and fro with particular ferocity. D. LESSING They had lit fires and let them . . rage over the mountain slopes. **c** E. MANNIN Thirst was beginning to rage. **5** J. HILTON Men . . would rage so hotly over the world that every precious thing would be in danger. T. KENEALLY Oskar raged up to him and hit him.

■ **rager** *noun* a person who or thing which rages; *esp.* (*Austral. & NZ colloq.*) a dedicated party-goer: **ME.** **raging** *adjective* (*a*) that rages; (*b*) *colloq.* highly successful, tremendous: **L15.** **ragingly** *adverb* **M16.**

ragee /ˈrɑːɡiː/ *noun.* Also **raggee**, **ragi**. **L18.**
[Sanskrit & Hindi *rāgī* from Telugu *rāgi*.]
In the Indian subcontinent: a cereal grass, finger millet, *Eleusine coracana*.

ragga /ˈraɡə/ *noun.* **L20.**
[Abbreviation.]
= RAGAMUFFIN *noun* 2.

raggamuffin *noun* var of RAGAMUFFIN *noun* 2.

ragged /ˈraɡɪd/ *adjective.* **ME.**
[Old Norse *rǫggvaðr* tufted (cf. Norwegian *ragget* shaggy). Cf. RAG *noun*¹.]
▶ **I 1** Of an animal: having a rough shaggy coat. **ME.** ▸†**b** Of a bird: having broken or irregular feathers. *rare.* **E16–E17.**
2 Having a rough, irregular, or uneven surface, edge, or outline. **ME.**
3 *transf.* Faulty, imperfect; lacking finish, smoothness, or uniformity; (of a sound) harsh, discordant. **L15.**
4 *HERALDRY.* = RAGULY. Usu. *postpositive.* **L15.**

> 🕮 **2** C. MCCULLERS A ragged line of trees. C. MACKENZIE His grey moustache usually so trim was slightly ragged. M. SHADBOLT The feeble moonlight showed the hills in ragged silhouette. **3** P. FITZGERALD When the carrier van arrived it drew . . a ragged cheer from the bystanders. R. CARVER He could hear her ragged breathing.

▶ **II 5** Of cloth, a garment, etc.: torn, frayed, worn. **ME.** ▸**b** Of a place: dilapidated. **E19.**
6 Of a person: in ragged clothes. Also *transf.*, exhausted, run-down; esp. in ***run ragged***, exhaust. **LME.**

> 🕮 **5** G. DALY Ragged work clothes. **b** SCOTT FITZGERALD The room had been redecorated . . , but already it was ragged again. **6** W. GOLDING The children were ragged and dirty.

Special collocations & phrases: **on the ragged edge** *US slang* on the extreme edge; *fig.* in a state of distress. **ragged-hipped** *adjective* (of a horse) having hips standing away from the backbone; **ragged right** *PRINTING* (with) an unjustified right-hand margin. **ragged robin** a plant of damp meadows, *Lychnis flos-cuculi*, of the pink family, with deeply four-cleft pink petals. **ragged school** *Hist.* a free school for poor children. **ragged staff**: with projecting knobs (chiefly in ref. to the crest of the Earls of Warwick). ***run ragged***: see sense 6 above.
■ **raggedly** *adverb* **M16.** **raggedness** *noun* **M16.** **raggedy** *adjective* (*colloq.*) (*a*) = RAGGED 2, 3, 5, 6; (*b*) contemptible, very poor or inferior: **L19.**

raggee *noun* var. of RAGEE.

ragging /ˈraɡɪŋ/ *noun*¹. **M19.**
[from (the same root as) RAG *verb*³ + -ING¹.]
Broken-up ore of a certain size.

ragging /ˈraɡɪŋ/ *noun*². **L20.**
[from RAG *noun*¹ + -ING¹.]
The process or technique of decorating a wall etc. by applying or smudging paint with a rag or piece of material; the effect or finish so produced.

raggle /ˈraɡ(ə)l/ *noun. Scot.* **M19.**
[Rel. to RAGGLE *verb.* Cf. earlier RAGGLING.]
A groove cut in stone, esp. on a wall to receive the end of a roof.

raggle /ˈraɡ(ə)l/ *verb trans.* **E19.**
[Rel. to RAGGLE *noun.* Cf. earlier RAGGLING.]
Cut a raggle or groove in (stone).

raggle-taggle /ˈraɡ(ə)ltaɡ(ə)l/ *adjective & noun.* Also **wr-**. **E20.**
[Fanciful extension of RAGTAG.]
▶ **A** *adjective.* (Of a person or (esp.) group of persons) ragged, disreputable; straggling, rambling; characteristic of such a group. **E20.**
▶ **B** *noun.* A wanderer; a disreputable or straggling group of people. **M20.**

raggling /ˈraɡlɪŋ/ *noun. Scot.* **E16.**
[Origin uncertain: cf. RAGGLE *noun, verb.*]
= RAGGLE *noun.*

raggy /ˈraɡi/ *adjective*¹.
[Late Old English *raggiġ* (cf. Swedish *raggig* shaggy), from Old Norse *rǫgg* tuft, strip of fur (cf. Norwegian, Swedish *ragg* rough hair), of unkn. origin. Cf. RAG *noun*¹.]
= RAGGED.

raggy /ˈraɡi/ *adjective*². **M20.**
[from RAG *noun*⁴ + -Y¹.]
Of music: pertaining to or resembling ragtime; characterized by ragtime.

ragi *noun* var. of RAGEE.

ragini /ˈrɑːɡiːniː/ *noun.* **L18.**
[Sanskrit *rāgiṇī*. Cf. RAGA.]
In Indian music: a raga represented as female, a female raga.

raglan /ˈraɡlən/ *noun & adjective.* **M19.**
[Lord Raglan (1788–1855), Brit. commander in the Crimean war.]
(Designating) a sleeve with sloping edges running up to the neck and so without a shoulder seam; (designating) a garment with such sleeves. Also, (designating) either of the sloping edges forming (the armhole of) such a sleeve.

ragman /ˈraɡmən/ *noun*¹. Pl. **-men**. **ME.**
[from RAG *noun*¹ + MAN *noun.* In sense 4 from RAG *noun*⁴.]
†**1** A ragged person. *rare.* Only in **ME.**
†**2** (A name for) a devil or the Devil. *rare.* **LME–E16.**
3 A person who collects or deals in rags, old clothes, etc. **L16.**
4 A musician who plays ragtime music. **M20.**

†**ragman** *noun*². **ME.**
[Perh. from Old Norse. Cf. next.]
▶ **I 1** A document recording (alleged) offences; any legal document, *spec.* that acknowledging Edward I as the Scottish nobles' overlord. **ME–M16.**
2 A list, a catalogue. Only in **LME.** ▸**b** *fig.* A long discourse, a rigmarole. *Scot.* Only in **16.**
▶ **II 3** A game of chance involving the selection of items, each attached to a string and hidden in a roll. Only in **ME.**

ragman roll /ˈraɡmən rəʊl/ *noun phr. obsolete* exc. *Hist.* **LME.**
[from prec. + ROLL *noun*¹. Cf. RIGMAROLE.]
▶ **I 1** †**a** = RAGMAN *noun*² 1. **LME–M17.** ▸**b** A set of rolls recording the instruments of homage made to Edward I by the Scottish King, nobles, etc., in 1296. **E18.**
†**2** A list, a catalogue. **E16–M18.**
▶†**II 3** The roll used in the game of ragman. **LME–E16.**

ragmen *noun* pl. of RAGMAN *noun*¹.

Ragnarok /ˈraɡnarɒk/ *noun.* Also **-rök**. **L18.**
[Old Norse *ragnarǫk*, *-røkkr* (Icelandic *Ragnarök*), from *ragna* genit. of *regin* the gods + *rǫk* destined end or (later) *røkr*, *røkkr* twilight.]
SCANDINAVIAN MYTHOLOGY. The destruction of the gods; *spec.* the defeat of gods and men by monsters in a final battle. Cf. GÖTTERDÄMMERUNG.

ragout /raˈɡuː/ *noun & verb.* **M17.**
[French *ragoût*, from *ragoûter* revive the taste of, formed as GOÛT.]
▶ **A** *noun.* **1** A highly seasoned dish of meat cut into small pieces and stewed with vegetables. **M17.**
†**2** A sauce, a relish. **L17–M18.**
▶ **B** *verb trans.* †**1** Appreciate, understand. Only in **L17.**
2 Make a ragout of. **E18.**

ragstone /ˈraɡstəʊn/ *noun.* **LME.**
[from RAG *noun*² + STONE *noun.*]
1 = RAG *noun*² 2. **LME.**
2 = RAG *noun*² 1a, b. **M16.**

ragtag /ˈraɡtaɡ/ *noun & adjective.* **E19.**
[from RAG *noun*¹ + TAG *noun*¹, superseding earlier TAGRAG.]
▶ **A** *noun.* A low-class or disreputable person (see also BOBTAIL *noun* 3b, & cf. RAG *noun*¹ 3a, TAGRAG *noun* 1). *rare.* **E19.**
▶ **B** *adjective.* Ragged; disreputable. **L19.**

ragtail /ˈraɡteɪl/ *adjective.* Chiefly *US.* **L20.**
[from RAG *noun*¹ + TAIL *noun*¹, perh. infl. by ***ragtag and bobtail*** s.v. BOBTAIL *noun* 3b.]
Disorganized; untidy; disreputable.

ragtime /ˈraɡtʌɪm/ *noun & adjective.* **L19.**
[Prob. from RAG *noun*⁴ + TIME *noun.*]
▶ **A** *noun.* Music characterized by a syncopated melodic line and regularly accented accompaniment, evolved among black American musicians in the 1890s and played esp. on the piano. **L19.**
▶ **B** *adjective.* Of, pertaining to, or resembling ragtime; *slang* disorderly, disreputable. **E20.**
■ **ragtimer** *noun* a person who plays ragtime **E20.** **ragtimey**, **-my** *adjective* suggestive of ragtime **E20.**

†**raguled** *adjective.* **L16–E18.**
[from (the same root as) next + -ED².]
HERALDRY. = RAGULY. Usu. *postpositive.*

raguly /ˈraɡjʊli/ *adjective.* **M17.**
[Perh. from RAGGED (cf. ***RAGGED staff***), after *nebuly* var. of NEBULÉ.]
HERALDRY. Of a cross or other charge: having short oblique projections, like a row of sawn-off branches. Usu. *postpositive.*

Ragusan /rəˈɡuːz(ə)n/ *noun & adjective.* **E20.**
[from *Ragusa* (see below) + -AN. Cf. earlier RAGUSIAN.]
Hist. ▶ **A** *noun.* **1** A native or inhabitant of Ragusa (now Dubrovnik) on the Adriatic coast. **E20.**
2 A dialect of Dalmatian formerly used by natives of Ragusa. **M20.**
▶ **B** *adjective.* Of or pertaining to Ragusa. **M20.**

†**Ragusian** *noun & adjective.* **M17.**
[formed as prec. + -IAN.]
▶ **A** *noun.* = RAGUSAN *noun* 1. Only in **M17.**
▶ **B** *adjective.* = RAGUSAN *adjective.* Only in **L18.**

†**ragusye** *noun* see ARGOSY.

ragweed /ˈragwiːd/ *noun*. M17.
[from RAG *noun*¹ + WEED *noun*¹. Cf. RAGWORT.]
1 = RAGWORT. M17.
2 Any of various greyish N. American plants of the genus *Ambrosia*, of the composite family, esp. *A. trifida* and *A. artemisiifolia*, major causes of hay fever. L18.

ragworm /ˈragwəːm/ *noun*. M19.
[from RAG *noun*¹ + WORM *noun*.]
Any polychaete worm of the family Nereidae, esp. *Nereis diversicolor*, found in sand or under stones and often used as bait.

ragwort /ˈragwəːt/ *noun*. LME.
[from RAG *noun*¹ + WORT *noun*¹, in ref. to the shape of the leaves.]
Any of various plants of the genus *Senecio*, of the composite family, with yellow-rayed flower-heads and irregularly lobed leaves; *esp.* (more fully ***common ragwort***) *Senecio jacobaea*, a weed of pastures.
Oxford ragwort: see OXFORD *adjective*.

rah /rɑː/ *noun & interjection*. *N. Amer.* L19.
[Aphet. from HURRAH.]
(A cry) expr. encouragement, approval, etc.

rahat /ˈrɑːhat/ *noun*. M19.
[Turkish *rahat (lokum)* from Arab. *rāḥat (al-ḥulḳūm)* ease (of the throat). Cf. LOKUM.]
In full ***rahat lokum*** /lɒˈkuːm/. Turkish delight.

rah-rah /ˈrɑːrɑː/ *noun, interjection, & adjective*. E20.
[Redupl. of RAH.]
► **A** *noun & interjection*. = RAH. Chiefly *N. Amer.* E20.
► **B** *adjective*. Characteristic of college students; *esp.* marked by great enthusiasm or excitement. *US slang*. E20.
rah-rah girl a cheer-leader. **rah-rah skirt** a very short flounced skirt, as worn by a cheer-leader.

Rai /rʌɪ/ *noun*¹ *& adjective*. E20.
[Rai.]
► **A** *noun*. Pl. same.
1 A member of a people of eastern Nepal. E20.
2 The Tibeto-Burman language of this people. L20.
► **B** *attrib.* or as *adjective*. Of or pertaining to the Rai or their language. E20.

rai /rʌɪ/ *noun*². L20.
[Arab.]
A style of popular music, orig. from N. Africa, combining Algerian and Arabic elements with Western styles.

raia *noun* var. of RAJA *noun*².

raid /reɪd/ *noun*. LME.
[Scot. var. of Old English *rād* ROAD *noun*.]
► **I 1** A military expedition on horseback; a hostile incursion; a rapid surprise attack by troops, aircraft, etc., in warfare; an air raid. LME.
2 A rush, a hurried movement. M19.
3 A sudden or vigorous descent or attack on a thing which it is intended to seize, suppress, or destroy; (more fully ***police raid***) a surprise attack by police to arrest suspected people or seize illicit goods. L19. ▸**b** *STOCK EXCHANGE*. A hostile attempt by a company to buy a major or controlling interest in the shares of another company. L20.

📖 **1** J. H. BURTON The Earls . . swept the country . . with more than the usual ferocity of a Border raid. D. A. THOMAS The Admiralty planned a raid on German patrols. **3** B. TARKINGTON He did not make his normal healthy raid upon the dainty tray. *Times* A gunman carrying out a raid.

► **II 4** A roadstead for ships. Long *obsolete* exc. *Scot.* LME.
Phrases: ***dawn raid***: see DAWN *noun*.
¶ Revived by Sir Walter Scott in E19 and subsequently extended in sense.

raid /reɪd/ *verb*. M19.
[from the noun.]
1 *verb intrans.* Go on or take part in a raid. M19.
2 *verb trans.* Make a raid on (a place, person, cattle, etc.); plunder, deplete the stocks of. L19.

📖 **1 raiding party** a small military group taking part in an organized foray into enemy territory, esp. to seize prisoners or supplies. **2** *Observer* Her friends bring along the drinks . . raiding their family cellars. A. E. STEVENSON Natural resources . . we have seen . . raided for private profit.

■ **raider** *noun* (**a**) a person who takes part in a raid (***corporate raider***: see CORPORATE *adjective* 1b); (**b**) an aircraft on a bombing operation: M19.

raik /reɪk/ *noun*. Now *rare* or *obsolete* exc. *Scot. dial.* ME.
[Old Norse (& Norwegian dial.) *reik* walking, strolling, rel. to *reika* RAIK *verb*.]
1 The action or an act of going or walking about; a course, a way; a walk, a journey. ME.
2 The ground over which cattle etc. usually move or graze; a piece of pasture-land. LME.
3 = RAKE *noun*² 4. L16.

raik /reɪk/ *verb*. *obsolete* exc. *Scot. dial.* ME.
[Old Norse *reika* (Norwegian dial. *reike*).]
1 *verb intrans.* Go, proceed, make one's way; walk, stroll, wander; move quickly. ME.
2 *verb trans.* Wander through or over (a place). E18.

rail /reɪl/ *noun*¹. *obsolete* exc. *dial.*
[Old English *hrægl(e)l* = Old Frisian *(h)reil*, Old High German *(h)regil*, of unkn. origin.]
†**1** A garment, a cloak. OE–ME.
†**2** A piece of cloth formerly worn about the neck by women; a neckerchief. L15–E18.
3 A woman's dress or upper garment. E17.

rail /reɪl/ *noun*². ME.
[Old French *reille* iron rod from Latin *regula* staff, rod, RULE *noun*.]
1 A bar, orig. of wood, fixed in a horizontal position to provide support or for hanging things on. Now chiefly as 2nd elem. of comb. ME. ▸**b** Such a bar forming part of the sides of a cart. M16.
2 A horizontal or sloping bar fixed on upright supports, e.g. as part of a fence, on banisters up a staircase, or round an altar; a continuous series of bars forming the horizontal part of a fence; a fence, a railing; ***the rails***, the fence forming the inside boundary of a racecourse. ME. ▸**b** The edge of a surfboard or sailboard. M20.
3 A bar or continuous line of bars (now usu. of metal) laid on or near the ground in pairs to support and guide the wheels of a vehicle. Usu. in *pl.* E17. ▸**b** A railway, a railway line, (usu. *attrib.* or in ***by rail***); *STOCK EXCHANGE* (in *pl.*) shares in railway companies. M19. ▸**c** A railwayman. *N. Amer.* M20.
4 A horizontal piece in a panelled door or other wooden framework. L17.
5 *ELECTRONICS*. A conductor which is maintained at a fixed potential and to which other parts of a circuit are connected. M20.

📖 **1 *curtain-rail*, *towel rail***, etc. **2** L. GRANT-ADAMSON A gull alighted on the rail of the boat. T. PARKS The child . . rattled the cot rails. **3b** *Daily Telegraph* 70 feared dead in rail crash. *USA Today* The eastbound rail was re-opened.

Phrases: **as thin as a rail** (of a person) very thin. ***middle rail***: see MIDDLE *adjective*. **off the rails** *fig.* out of the proper or normal condition; disorganized; deranged. **on the rails** (**a**) on the track of a racecourse nearest the rails; (**b**) in a proper or normal condition; organized; sane. **over the rails** over the side of a ship. ***post-and-rail***: see POST *noun*¹. **ride on a rail**, **ride out of town on a rail** carry or parade (a person) astride a rail as a punishment (*Hist.*); *fig.* punish or send away with ridicule. ***ride the rails***: see RIDE *verb*. **run on a rail**, **run out of town on a rail** = *ride on a rail* above. ***split rail***: see SPLIT *adjective*. ***third rail***: see THIRD *adjective & noun*.
Comb.: **rail-bird** *US* a person who watches from the rails or sidelines (*lit. & fig.*); **rail bond** an electrical connection between consecutive lengths of rail in a railway or tramway; **rail-bus** (**a**) a vehicle resembling a bus but running on a railway track; (**b**) in Denmark etc., a tramcar running on tramlines set in the road; **rail-car** (**a**) = CAR 5; (**b**) (a train including) a powered railway carriage; **railcard** a pass entitling the holder to reduced fares on a railway; **rail-fence** (**a**) a fence made of wooden posts and rails; (**b**) (in full ***rail-fence cipher***) cipher obtained by splitting the plain text between two or more lines in a zigzag pattern; **rail gun** a weapon in which a projectile is accelerated electromagnetically along a pair of rails, used esp. as an anti-missile weapon; **rail-head** (**a**) the furthest point reached by a railway; (**b**) the point on a railway from which branch-line or road transport of supplies begins; **rail-line** a railway line; **rail link** a railway service joining two established transport systems; **railman** a man employed on a railway, a railwayman; **rail-splitter** *noun & adjective* (*US colloq.*) (**a**) *noun* a Republican; ***the railsplitter*** (*Hist.*), Abraham Lincoln; (**b**) *adjective* Republican; **rail timber** (*US*): suitable for making rails; **rail yard** a railway yard.
■ **railage** *noun* conveyance by rail; the charges for this: L19. **railless** /-l-l-/ *adjective* devoid of rails; having no railway: L19.

rail /reɪl/ *noun*³. LME.
[Old French (Norman and Picard) *raille* from Proto-Romance, perh. of imit. origin.]
Any bird of the family Rallidae (order Gruiformes), which includes the coot, corncrake, and water rail; *esp.* one of the genus *Rallus*.
Virginia rail, ***weka rail***, etc.

rail /reɪl/ *noun*⁴. *rare*. E16.
[from RAIL *verb*².]
An act of railing or reviling.

rail /reɪl/ *noun*⁵. M20.
[Origin uncertain: perh. from RAIL *noun*².]
A hot-rod, a dragster.

rail /reɪl/ *verb*¹. LME.
[from RAIL *noun*².]
†**1** *verb trans.* Provide (vines etc.) with rails, train on rails. LME–L15.
2 *verb trans.* Provide or enclose with rails. LME.
3 *verb trans.* Lay with rails. M18.
4 *verb trans.* Convey by rail. M19.
5 *verb intrans.* Travel by rail. M19.
6 *verb trans. & intrans.* Sail (a sailboard) on its edge. L20.

📖 **2** D. H. LAWRENCE Mother and son went into the small railed garden. **rail in** enclose with rails. **rail off** separate or protect by rails. **3** *Scientific American* Attempts to build steam engines and to introduce railed ways.

■ **railer** *noun*¹ (**a**) a person who travels by rail; (**b**) a racehorse or greyhound that stays close to the rails: L19.

rail /reɪl/ *verb*². LME.
[French *railler*, †*ragler* from Portuguese *ralhar* jest from Proto-Romance word derived from a crossing of Latin *rugire* to bellow with Proto-Romance precursor of BRAY *verb*¹.]
1 *verb intrans.* Utter abusive language; complain persistently and abusively, rant. Freq. foll. by *against*, *at*. LME.
†**2** *verb intrans.* Jest, use banter. E16–L17.
3 *verb trans.* Bring or put *into* a certain condition, or remove *from* or *out of*, by railing. L16.

📖 **1** P. D. JAMES She railed at me like a woman possessed.

■ **railer** *noun*² E16.

†**rail** *verb*³ *intrans.* LME–E17.
[Origin unkn.]
Esp. of blood: flow, gush.

rail /reɪl/ *verb*⁴ *trans. & intrans. rare*. L18.
[Prob. imit.]
Rattle.

railing /ˈreɪlɪŋ/ *noun*¹. LME.
[from RAIL *verb*¹ + -ING¹.]
1 The action of RAIL *verb*¹. LME.
2 *sing.* & in *pl.* A fence or barrier made of uprights and a transverse rail. LME.
3 Material for railings. E19.
Comb.: **railing-line** a handline used over the rail of a boat.
■ **railinged** *adjective* enclosed by a railing M19.

railing /ˈreɪlɪŋ/ *noun*². L15.
[from RAIL *verb*² + -ING¹.]
The action of RAIL *verb*²; an instance of this; in *pl.*, abuse.

raillery /ˈreɪləri/ *noun*. M17.
[French *raillerie*, from *railler*: see RAIL *verb*², RALLY *verb*², -ERY.]
Good-humoured ridicule, banter; an instance of this.

†**railleur** *noun*. M17–M18.
[French, from *railler* (see RAIL *verb*²) + *-eur* -OR.]
A person who practises raillery.

†**railly** *verb*. M17.
[French *railler*: see RAIL *verb*².]
1 *verb intrans.* Jest, use banter. M17–M19.
2 *verb trans.* Ridicule, tease. L17–M18.
■ †**raillier** *noun* E–M18.

railroad /ˈreɪlrəʊd/ *noun*. Now *US* exc. in certain combs. M18.
[from RAIL *noun*² + ROAD *noun*.]
1 = RAILWAY *noun* 1. M18.
2 = RAILWAY *noun* 2. E19. ▸**b** In *pl.* Shares in railway companies. M19.
Phrases: ***underground railroad***: see UNDERGROUND *adjective*.
Comb.: **railroad bull** *US slang* a railway policeman; **railroad commission** *US* a committee to safeguard the public interest in relation to railways; **railroad flat** *US*: consisting of a series of long narrow rooms; **railroad guide** *US* a railway timetable; **railroad service** in real tennis, an overhead service delivered from near the wall; **railroad tie** *US* a railway sleeper; **railroad worm** the larva or the adult female of the S. American beetle *Phrixothrix tiemanni*, of the family Phengodidae, which has luminous red and green patches on its body.
¶ In Britain superseded by *railway* in M19.
■ **railroadiˈana** *noun pl.* railwayana M19.

railroad /ˈreɪlrəʊd/ *verb*. E19.
[from the noun.]
1 *verb trans.* Provide (a country etc.) with a railway or railways. *US*. E19.
2 *verb intrans.* Travel by rail. *US*. M19.
3 *verb intrans.* Work on the railway or in the railway industry. *US*. L19.
4 *verb trans.* Put *through* a process forcefully and rapidly; press (a person) hastily or forcefully *into* an action etc., hustle. Orig. *US*. L19. ▸**b** Send to prison with summary speed or by means of false evidence. Chiefly *US*. L19.

📖 **4** M. DICKENS How had he let himself be railroaded into this?

railroader /ˈreɪlrəʊdə/ *noun*. *US*. M19.
[from RAILROAD *noun*, *verb* + -ER¹.]
A person employed in the management or working of a railway.

railway /ˈreɪlweɪ/ *noun*. L17.
[from RAIL *noun*² + WAY *noun*.]
1 A way or road laid with rails (orig. of wood, later usually of metal) on which the wheels of wagons are made to run; the way composed of rails so laid; any set of rails intended to facilitate the motion of wheels. L17.
2 *spec.* A track consisting of a pair of metal rails on which carriages or wagons conveying passengers or goods are moved by a locomotive or powered carriage; a set or network of such tracks; an organization or company whose business is the conveyance of passengers or goods on such tracks. L17.

📖 **2** P. THEROUX The sleeping cars . . were . . from a railway in the States which had gone bankrupt.

Phrases: ***atmospheric railway***: see ATMOSPHERIC *adjective* 1. ***junction railway***: see JUNCTION *noun* 2. ***underground railway***: see UNDERGROUND *adjective*.

Comb.: **railway crossing** a level crossing; **railway guide** a train timetable; **railway hotel** a hotel built close to a railway station, orig. with the aim of providing accommodation for rail travellers; **Railway Institute** a social club for railway workers, esp. in India; **railway letter**: carried by train and left by the railway authorities either at a specified station or in a letter-box for subsequent collection; **railwayman** a railman; **railway novel** *Hist.* a light novel, suitable for reading on a railway journey; **railway rug** *Hist.*: used for warmth during railway journeys; **railway spine** MEDICINE (now *Hist.*) traumatic neurosis affecting the spine, orig. when resulting from a railway accident; ***railway station***: see STATION *noun* 16; **railway time** *Hist.* a standard time adopted throughout a railway system to supersede local time for railway operations (in Great Britain, London time before the adoption of Greenwich Mean Time); **railway-yard** an area where rolling-stock is kept and made up into trains.

■ **railway'ana** *noun pl.* publications or other items concerning or associated with railways L20. **railwaydom** *noun* railways considered collectively; the realm of railways: L19. **railwayless** *adjective* M19.

railway /ˈreɪlweɪ/ *verb*. M19.
[from the noun.]
1 *verb intrans.* Travel by rail. M19.
2 *verb trans.* Provide (a country etc.) with a railway or railways. L19.

raiment /ˈreɪm(ə)nt/ *noun & verb*. Now *arch.* & *poet.* LME.
[Aphet. from ARRAYMENT.]
▶ **A** *noun*. **1** Clothing. LME.
†**2** An article of clothing, a garment. L15–M17.
▶ **B** *verb trans.* Clothe. *obsolete* exc. as ***raimented*** *ppl adjective*. M17.

rain /reɪn/ *noun*[1].
[Old English *reġn*, *rēn* = Old Frisian *rein*, Old Saxon, Old High German *regan* (Dutch, German *Regen*), Old Norse *regn*, Gothic *rign*.]
1 The condensed moisture of the atmosphere, falling in drops large enough to attain a perceptible velocity; the fall of such drops. OE.
2 In *pl.* Showers of rain; *the* rainy season in tropical countries; (in the Indian subcontinent) a rainy season. OE. ▶**b** NAUTICAL. A part of the N. Atlantic Ocean in which rain is frequent. E18.
3 †**a** A shower of rain. ME–L16. ▶**b** A specified kind of rain or shower. L15.
4 A descent of liquid or solid particles or objects falling in the manner of rain; the collective particles or objects so falling; *fig.* a large or overwhelming quantity *of* something. ME.
5 A kind of firework producing a shower of bright-coloured sparks. M17.

📖 **2** T. GRAY Swoll'n with . . late descending rains. B. M. CROKER One rains he died. C. MCCULLOUGH The summer rains didn't come. **3b** *National Geographic* A steady rain slanted across . . the island. **4** *Royal Air Force Journal* The continuous rain of pamphlets . . told of the enemy's defeats. J. WAIN I watched her hands, ready to beat off any sudden rain of blows.

Phrases: *acid rain*: see ACID *adjective* 2. ***as right as rain***: see RIGHT *adjective*. **come rain or shine** = *rain or shine* below. **know enough to come in out of the rain** & vars., be sensible enough to act prudently when necessary. ***long rains***: see LONG *adjective*[1]. **rain or shine** whether it rains or not; come what may. ***red rain***: see RED *adjective*. ***yellow rain***: see YELLOW *adjective*.

Comb.: **rain band** an absorption band in the solar spectrum caused by the presence of water vapour in the atmosphere; **rainbird** a bird said to foretell rain by its cry; *spec.* the green woodpecker, *Picus viridis*; **rain bonnet** (chiefly *N. Amer.*) a plastic fold-up bonnet worn as a protection against rain; **rain-cape** a waterproof cape worn as a protection against rain; **rain-caped** *adjective* wearing a rain-cape; **rain-charm** an object, action, or incantation used by a rainmaker to summon rain; **rain check** (chiefly *N. Amer.*) (***a***) a ticket given to a spectator providing for a refund of entrance money or admission at a later date, should the event be interrupted or postponed by rain; a ticket allowing one to order an article before it is available, for later collection; (***b***) *fig.* a right to take up an offer on a subsequent occasion; esp. in ***take a rain check (on)***, reserve such a right, postpone a pre-arranged meeting, appointment, etc.; **raincoat** a waterproof or showerproof coat worn as a protection against rain; ***raincoat brigade*** (*slang*), habitual watchers of pornographic films; **raincoated** *adjective* wearing a raincoat; **rain crow** *US* either of two cuckoos of N. America and northern S. America, the yellow-billed cuckoo, *Coccyzus americanus*, and the black-billed cuckoo, *C. erythrophthalmus*; **rain dance**: performed by a tribal group in the hope of summoning rain; **rain date** *N. Amer.* an alternative date on which an event can be held if postponed because of rain; **rain-day** METEOROLOGY a day, commencing for statistical purposes at 9 a.m. GMT, on which the recorded rainfall is not less than 0.01 inch or 0.2 mm; **rain-doctor** a person who professes to bring rain by incantations; **rain-door** an outside door in Japanese houses; **raindrop** (***a***) a single drop of rain; (***b***) *rare* the dropping of rain or rainwater; **rain-fly** a horsefly, *esp.* the common cleg *Haematopota pluvialis*; **rainforest** a dense forest in an area of high rainfall with little seasonal variation; *esp.* one in the tropics, characterized by a rich variety of plant and animal life; **rain-fowl** (*obsolete* exc. *dial.*) a rainbird; **rain frog** in North and Central America, a small tree frog of the genus *Hyla*; **rain-gauge** an instrument for measuring the amount of precipitation; **rain-god**, **rain-goddess**: supposedly having control of rain; **rain-goose** the red-throated diver, *Gavia stellata*; **rain-hat**, **rain-hood**: worn as a protection against rain; **rain jungle** (a) rainforest; **rainlight** daylight as affected by falling rain; **rainmaker** a person who seeks to cause rain to fall, either by magic in some communities or by a technique such as seeding; **rain print** GEOLOGY a pit in the surface of a sedimentary stratum believed to have been caused by the impact of a raindrop when it was at the surface; **rainproof** *adjective & noun* (***a***) *adjective* impervious to rain; (***b***) *noun* a rainproof garment, esp. a coat; **rainproofer** a maker of rainproof fabrics; **rain-shadow** an area where the annual rainfall is low because it is sheltered from prevailing rain-bearing winds by a range of hills; **rain-shower** a shower of rain; **rain-slick** *adjective* (of a surface) made slippery by rain; ***rain slicker***: see SLICKER *noun* 2; **rain stick** a ceremonial instrument originating in the Andes, consisting of a hollow branch sealed at both ends and containing seeds, small pebbles, etc., which make a noise like falling rain when the branch is tilted; **rain-stone** a stone used in rain-making rituals; **rainstorm** a storm with heavy rain; **rainsuit** a jacket and leggings worn as a protection against rain; **rain-tree** (***a***) a Jamaican evergreen shrub of the nightshade family, *Brunfelsia undulata*, bearing white bell-shaped flowers; (***b***) a tropical American leguminous tree, *Albizia saman*, with flowers having prominent pink stamens, much grown as a street tree in the tropics; **rain-wash** the effect of rain in washing away earth etc.; material thus washed away; **rainwear** clothing worn as a protection against rain; **rainworm** the common earthworm.

■ **rainful** *adjective* (*rare*) rainy L15. **rainless** *adjective* M16.

rain /reɪn/ *noun*[2]. *obsolete* exc. *dial.* LME.
[Old Norse *rein* (Norwegian *rein*, Swedish & Danish *ren*) = Middle Low German *rein*, Old High German *rain*, *rein* (German *Rain*). Cf. REAN.]
1 A strip of land, a ridge, esp. as a boundary. LME.
2 A furrow between the ridges or lands in a field. LME.

rain /reɪn/ *verb*. OE.
[from RAIN *noun*[1].]
▶ **I** *verb intrans.* **1** Of the sky, clouds, etc.: send down rain. Now *rare*. OE.
2 *impers.* in ***it rains***, ***it is raining***, etc., rain falls, rain is falling, etc. Also in indirect pass., ***be rained on***, have rain fall on one. ME.
3 Of rain: fall. Now *rare*. ME.
4 Fall like rain. ME.

📖 **2** I. MURDOCH We must put the chairs on the verandah, otherwise they will be rained on. *Proverb*: It never rains but it pours. **rain on someone's parade** detract from someone's enjoyment of or success in a situation, spoil an occasion for someone. **3** SHAKES. *Twel. N.* The rain it raineth every day. **4** L. M. MONTGOMERY The tears . . rained down over my cheeks. T. HEGGEN Ticker-tape rained from Wall Street windows.

▶ **II** *verb trans.* **5** *impers.* in ***it rains*** or ***is raining*** —, etc., there is (etc.) a shower of (something) falling from above or through the air; *fig.* there is (etc.) a large or overwhelming quantity of. ME.
6 Send down like rain; send in large quantities, give lavishly; shed (tears) copiously. ME.
7 With compl.: bring into a specified condition by raining. Usu. in *pass.* ME.

📖 **5** SHAKES. *Ant. & Cl.* Bestow'd his lips . . As it rain'd kisses. C. BRONTË It rained a November drizzle. ***rain cats and dogs***: see CAT *noun*[1]. ***rain pitchforks***: see PITCHFORK *noun*[1]. **6** H. STURGIS She began . . to rain letters upon her son. *Time* Fans rained bottles . . on to the ground. **7 be rained off**, (*N. Amer.*) **be rained out** be cancelled or prematurely ended because of rain.

■ **rainer** *noun* M19.

rainbow /ˈreɪnbəʊ/ *noun & adjective*.
[Old English *reġnboga* (= Old High German *reginbogo*, Old Norse *regnbogi*), formed as RAIN *noun*[1], BOW *noun*[1].]
▶ **A** *noun*. **1** An arch of concentric coloured bands (conventionally described as red, orange, yellow, green, blue, indigo, violet) seen in the sky in a direction opposite to the sun when its light reaches an observer after having been reflected and refracted by raindrops; a similar phenomenon caused by mist, spray from a waterfall, etc., or produced by moonlight. OE.
2 †**a** The iris of the eye. *rare*. E–M17. ▶**b** A brightly coloured arch, ring, etc., resembling a rainbow. E18. ▶**c** A discoloured bruise. *Boxing slang*. E19.
3 More fully ***rainbow trout***. A large trout, *Salmo gairdneri*, native to the Pacific coast of N. America and farmed elsewhere for food. L18.
4 A very wide variety or range *of* things. M19.
5 A capsule containing the barbiturates amylobarbitone and quinalbarbitone, one end of which is red and the other blue. *slang*. M20.

📖 **4** *New Yorker* A rainbow of timbres and tones.

Phrases: ***secondary rainbow***: see SECONDARY *adjective*. **the end of the rainbow**, **the rainbow's end**: used with allusion to the proverbial belief in the existence of a crock of gold (or something else of great value) at the end of a rainbow.

Comb.: **rainbow-bird** *Austral.* a bee-eater, *Merops ornatus*, of N. Australia; **rainbow boa** a large iridescent snake, *Epicrates cenchris*, of the family Boidae, found in forests of northern S. America; **rainbow cactus** a cactus of Mexico and the south-western US, *Echinocereus pectinatus*, bearing pink flowers and spines in bands of various colours; **rainbow coalition** (orig. *US*) a political grouping of minority peoples and other disadvantaged elements, esp. for the purpose of electing a candidate; a coalition or alliance of several different political groups; **rainbow fish** any of various fishes with bright or distinctive coloration; ***rainbow runner***: see RUNNER 5c; **rainbow-serpent** in Australian Aboriginal mythology, a large snake associated with water; ***rainbow smelt***: see SMELT *noun* 3; **rainbow snake** a glossy red and black non-venomous snake, *Abastor erythrogrammus*, of the eastern US; ***rainbow trout***: see sense 3 above; **rainbow wrasse** a wrasse, *Coris julis*, of the Mediterranean and eastern N. Atlantic, the male of which has an orange stripe along its side.
▶ **B** *attrib.* or as *adjective*. Having many or bright colours. Also, curved like a rainbow. M18.

📖 R. HEBER Rainbow paths of heaven.

■ **rainbow-like** *adjective* resembling a rainbow, showing a spectrum of colours M19. **rainbowy** *adjective* of the nature of a rainbow M19.

†**Raines** *noun*. ME–E18.
[Old French place-name, now *Rennes*.]
(A piece of) fine linen or lawn made at Rennes in Brittany.

rainfall /ˈreɪnfɔːl/ *noun*. M19.
[from RAIN *noun*[1] + FALL *noun*[2].]
1 The quantity of rain that falls or has fallen at a particular place, usually expressed as so many inches or millimetres of depth. M19.
2 A fall or shower of rain; the falling of rain. M19.

rain-out /ˈreɪnaʊt/ *noun*. M20.
[from RAIN *verb* + OUT *adverb*. In sense 2 after FALLOUT.]
1 The cancellation or premature ending of an event because of rain. *N. Amer.* M20.
2 Incorporation into raindrops of radioactive debris from a nuclear explosion and its localized deposition on the earth's surface. M20.

rainwater /ˈreɪnwɔːtə/ *noun*.
[Old English *reġnwæter* (= Middle High German *regenwazzer*, Old Norse *regnvatn*), formed as RAIN *noun*[1] + WATER *noun*.]
Water that falls or has fallen from the sky as rain.
Comb.: **rainwater goods** exterior pipework, guttering, etc., designed to conduct rainwater from a building.

rainy /ˈreɪni/ *adjective*. OE.
[from RAIN *noun*[1] + -Y[1].]
1 (Of weather or climate) characterized by rain; (of a period of time) during or within which rain falls or usually falls; (of a place) in which it is raining, where rain is frequent. OE. ▶†**b** Of an action: done in the rain. *rare* (Shakes.). Only in L16.
2 Of clouds, the sky, etc.: bringing rain; laden with rain; connected with rain. LME. ▶**b** *fig.* Of the eyes: tearful. M16.
Special collocations: **rainy day** *fig.* a time of special need in the future. **rainy season** a period of a month or more each year in tropical and subtropical regions when a large quantity of rain falls.
■ **rainily** *adverb* in a rainy manner; with rain falling: M19. **raininess** *noun* E18.

rais *noun* var. of REIS.

raise /reɪz/ *noun*. L15.
[from the verb.]
†**1** A levy. *rare*. Only in L15.
2 †**a** The action of raising something; uplifting, elevation. L15–E17. ▶**b** WEIGHTLIFTING. An act of lifting or raising a part of the body while holding a weight. E20.
3 An increase in amount, price, value, etc.; *spec.* (***a***) CARDS a raised stake or bid; (***b***) (chiefly *N. Amer.*) a pay rise. E18.
4 A rising passage; *esp.* (MINING), a sloping shaft excavated from the lower end. L19.
Phrases: **make a raise** *US* secure a loan, make a profit.

raise /reɪz/ *verb*. ME.
[Old Norse *reisa*: see REAR *verb*[1].]
▶ **I** Set upright; make stand up.
1 *verb trans.* Bring into or towards a vertical position; set upright or on end; restore to an upright position. ME. ▶**b** *spec.* Cause (pastry etc.) to stand without support. L16.
2 *verb trans.* Lift or help (a person or animal) up to standing position; *refl.* rise, get up. ME.
3 *verb trans.* Restore to life; resurrect. ME.
4 *verb trans.* Wake (a person) from sleep (now *rare*); make (a person) get up; rouse (an animal), esp. from a lair or covert. ME.
5 *verb trans.* Rouse, stir up, incite, (a person or persons). (Foll. by *against*, *to*, *to do*, *upon*.) LME. ▶**b** Agitate, provoke to excitement or anger. Chiefly *Scot.* M18.
6 *verb trans.* Strengthen (the mind, spirit, etc.); animate, stimulate. LME. ▶†**b** Imbue or inspire *with* courage, confidence, etc. M16–L17.

📖 **2** E. W. LANE Take my hand and raise me. **3** J. JORTIN God was able to raise him from the dead. **5** BYRON A word's enough to raise mankind to kill. **6** DEFOE His spirits being a little raised with the dram I had given him, he was very cheerful.

▶ **II** Build up, construct, create, produce.
7 *verb trans.* Lift and put in position the parts of (a building); construct, build up. ME. ▶**b** Form (a small projection); *spec.* cause (a blister etc.) to form. M16. ▶†**c** MATH. Draw or erect (a figure or perpendicular line) *upon* a given base line. M17–E18.
8 *verb trans.* Bring into existence or action; cause to appear, produce. Also (now *rare*), beget. ME. ▶**b** Establish

contact with (a person etc.), esp. by radio or telephone. E20.

9 *verb trans.* Give rise to, institute, set going, (a report, feeling, process, condition, etc.). ME.

10 *verb trans.* **a** LAW. Draw up (a summons, letter, etc.); institute (proceedings, an action, etc.). Now *rare.* LME. ▸**b** Bring up (a question, difficulty, objection, etc.). M17.

11 *verb trans.* **a** Utter, produce, (a sound, esp. a loud cry). LME. ▸**b** (Begin to) sing. E17.

12 *verb trans.* **a** Cause or promote the growth of (plants), grow (fruit, vegetables, flowers, etc.); breed (animals). M17. ▸**b** Rear, bring up, (a person or animal). Now chiefly *N. Amer.* M18.

> 📖 **7** P. ACKROYD Ugly buildings were torn down and uglier ones raised. **8** HOR. WALPOLE Her gentleness had never raised her an enemy. W. E. NORRIS All she can do is to raise a storm in a tea-cup. *Nature* Rabbit antiserum was raised against human plasma. **b** M. HEBDEN She's . . off the air . . . We can't raise her. **9** SIR W. SCOTT A variety of sham suits, raised against him by Newgate solicitors. B. JOWETT Do not raise a quarrel . . between Thrasymachus and me. R. BROOKE The town never knew such a hullabaloo As that little dog raised. **10b** M. BERGMANN To raise the question about the purpose of life is already a sign of depression. **11a** SHAKES. *Haml.* He rais'd a sigh so piteous. **b** J. BALDWIN Elisha sat down at the piano and raised a song. **12a** H. KELLER He raised the finest watermelons and strawberries in the county. *Harpers & Queen* British oyster farms now raise clams too. **b** R. B. MARCY Horses . . raised exclusively upon grass. E. PAWEL She gave birth to six children and raised them all in that one-room shack.

▸ **III** Cause to move to a higher position.

13 *verb trans.* Lift up, elevate, (a thing); put or take into a higher position; *spec.* draw or bring up from below the ground. ME. ▸**b** Turn (the eyes, one's gaze) upwards. LME.

14 *verb trans. fig.* ▸**a** Promote to a higher rank, position, etc. ME. ▸**b** Exalt (a person's name, state, etc.). *rare.* LME. ▸**c** Extol, laud. *rare.* M17.

15 *verb trans. fig.* Give a higher or nobler character to (a person, style, thoughts, etc.); *spec.* heighten (consciousness or sensitivity). ME.

16 *verb trans.* Conjure up (a spirit, demon, etc.). LME.

17 *verb trans.* Make (the voice) heard. See also sense 27 below. LME.

18 *verb trans.* Cause to rise; send or force up. LME.

19 *verb trans.* NAUTICAL. Come in sight of (a ship, land, etc.); make (a ship etc.) appear higher in the water by approaching. M16.

20 *verb trans.* Reach the crest or summit of (a hill, ridge, etc.). *US.* E19.

21 *verb trans.* PHONETICS. Modify (a vowel) by articulating with the tongue closer to the roof of the mouth. L19.

> 📖 **13** J. CONRAD The tall student, raising his shoulders, shoved his hands deep into his pockets. J. B. MORTON He . . raised his glass of port, and held it up to the light. **14a** R. W. CLARK His theories raised him to the level of Galileo, Darwin and Einstein. *Library* Hugh Hare . . was raised to the Irish peerage by Charles I. **15** F. A. KEMBLE They are doing their best to raise and improve the degraded race. R. BUSH Eliot's intellectual clarity . . raises his work a step above the achievements of his . . contemporaries. **17** N. MANDELA They have raised their voices in condemnation of the grinding poverty of the people. **19** H. ALLEN They raised the low coast by evening.

▸ **IV** Remove, levy.

22 *verb trans.* Gather by compulsion (a tax, an army, etc.); collect (rents, funds, etc.); bring together, obtain, procure. ME.

23 *verb trans.* **a** Abandon or force an enemy to abandon (a siege or blockade). LME. ▸**b** Remove, rescind, (a prohibition, embargo, etc.). L19.

24 *verb trans.* Set in motion (an army or camp). LME.

> 📖 **22** A. S. NEILL I shall try to raise funds by giving a school concert. V. CRONIN He received permission to raise 30,000 recruits. P. DALLY Edward . . raised a further mortgage on the property.

▸ **V** Increase.

25 *verb trans.* Increase in height or bulk; cause to rise or swell up; *spec.* (*a*) make a nap on (cloth); (*b*) cause (a hide) to thicken; (*c*) cause (dough or bread) to rise. LME.

26 *verb trans.* Increase the amount or value of. E16. ▸**b** MATH. Increase (a number or quantity) to a given power. E18. ▸**c** CARDS. Bet or bid more than (another player). Orig. *US.* E19.

27 *verb trans.* Increase the degree, intensity, or force of (a thing); *spec.* (*a*) make (the voice) louder or higher (see also sense 17 above); (*b*) brighten (a colour), esp. in dyeing. M17.

> 📖 **26** J. S. MILL Free trade would relieve their distress by raising the price of wine. **27** H. ROTH He . . raised his voice to a shout. S. BELLOW Voices raised in argument.

▸ **VI** **28** *verb intrans.* Rise. Now *US.* LME.

29 *verb intrans.* Be raised. Only as ***raising*** pres. pple. M17.

30 *verb intrans.* MINING. Drive a raise. L19.

Phrases: **raise a dust** (*a*) cause turmoil; (*b*) obscure the truth. ***raise a finger***: see FINGER *noun*. **raise a laugh** cause people to laugh. **raise a person's spirits** give a person new courage or cheerfulness. ***raise Cain***: see CAIN *noun*[2] 2. ***raise hell***: see HELL *noun*. ***raise hob***: see HOB *noun*[1]. **raise its head**, **raise its ugly head** *fig.* (of a situation, problem, etc.) make an (unwelcome) appearance. ***raise one's eyebrows***: see EYEBROW *noun*. **raise one's glass to** drink the health of. **raise one's hand to** make as if to strike (a person). ***raise one's hat***: see HAT *noun*. ***raise one's sights***: see SIGHT *noun*. ***raise one's standard***: see STANDARD *noun*. ***raise sand***: see SAND *noun*. **raise the Devil** (*a*) make a disagreeable disturbance; (*b*) create trouble, uproar, or confusion. **raise the roof** (*a*) create an uproar; (*b*) make a resounding noise. **raise the wind** (*a*) cause the wind to blow; (*b*) procure money or necessary means for a purpose.

¶ In trans. senses, formerly freq. (and now occas.) foll. by *up* to strengthen the verb.

■ **raisable** *adjective* M17. **raisure** /ˈreɪʒə/ *noun* (*rare*) (an) elevation E17.

raised /reɪzd/ *adjective*. ME.

[from prec. + -ED[1].]

1 That has been raised. ME.

2 Of a cake etc.: made with baking-powder or other raising agent. *N. Amer.* L19.

Special collocations & comb.: ***raised-arm salute***: see SALUTE *noun*[1] 3b. ***raised beach***: see BEACH *noun* 2. **raised bog** a peat bog in which growth is most rapid at the centre, giving a domed shape. **raised pie** a pie with a raised crust.

■ **raisedly** *adverb* (*obsolete* exc. *Scot.*) in an elevated or excited manner L16. **raisedness** *noun* (now *rare* or *obsolete*) M17.

raiser /ˈreɪzə/ *noun*. ME.

[from RAISE *verb* + -ER[1].]

1 A person who or thing which raises something; *spec.* a person who cultivates new varieties of plants. ME.

2 A riser of a stair. L17.

3 BRIDGE. A player who increases his or her partner's bid; a card or combination of cards which justifies such an increase. E20.

raisin /ˈreɪz(ə)n/ *noun*. ME.

[Old & mod. French = grape, from Proto-Romance alt. of Latin *racemus* cluster of grapes.]

1 A grape partially dried, either in the sun or artificially. ME. ▸**b** The dark purplish-brown colour of raisins. E20.

†**2** A cluster of grapes; a grape. ME–E17.

1 ***muscatel raisin***, ***sultana raisin***, etc.

Phrases: ***raisins of Corinth***, ***raisins of Corauntz***: see CORINTH 1. **raisins of the sun** sun-dried grapes.

Comb.: **raisin tree** (more fully ***Japanese raisin tree***) a Chinese, Japanese, and Korean tree, *Hovenia dulcis*, of the buckthorn family, with sweet fleshy edible pedicels.

■ **raisiny** *adjective* like or suggestive of (the taste of) raisins M19.

raising /ˈreɪzɪŋ/ *noun*. ME.

[from RAISE *verb* + -ING[1].]

1 The action of RAISE *verb*; an instance of this. ME.

2 A thing that is raised; a raised place. L16. ▸**b** *spec.* A crop raised. M19.

raising-piece /ˈreɪzɪŋpiːs/ *noun*. M16.

[from RASEN *noun* (by assoc. with prec.) + PIECE *noun*.]

A wall-plate.

■ Also **raising-plate** *noun* L17.

raison d'état /rɛzɔ̃ deta/ *noun phr.* Pl. ***raisons d'état*** (pronounced same). M19.

[French.]

= ***reason of State*** s.v. REASON *noun*[1].

raison d'être /rɛzɔ̃ dɛtr, ˈreɪzɔ̃ dɛtrə/ *noun*. Pl. ***raisons d'être*** (pronounced same). M19.

[French = reason for being.]

A purpose or reason accounting for or justifying the existence of a thing.

raisonné /rɛzɔne/ *adjective*. L18.

[French, pa. pple of *raisonner* reason, from *raison* REASON *noun*[1].]

Reasoned out, logical, systematic. Chiefly in CATALOGUE RAISONNÉ.

raisonneur /rɛzɔnœːr/ *noun*. Pl. pronounced same. E20.

[French, lit. 'person who reasons or argues'.]

A character in a play etc. who expresses the author's message or standpoint.

raisons d'état, ***raisons d'être*** *noun phrs.* pls. of RAISON D'ÉTAT, RAISON D'ÊTRE.

rait *noun* var. of REATE.

raita /rɑːˈiːtə/ *noun*. M20.

[Hindi *rāytā*.]

An Indian dish consisting of chopped vegetables (or fruit) in curd or yoghurt.

raj /rɑː(d)ʒ/ *noun*. E19.

[Hindi *rāj* from Sanskrit *rājya*. Cf. next.]

1 Sovereignty, rule; kingdom. E19.

2 *spec. Hist.* (Usu. **R-**.) In full ***British Raj***. (The period of) British rule in the Indian subcontinent before 1947. M19.

raja /ˈrɑːdʒə/ *noun*[1]. Also **-ah**, (as a title) **R-**. M16.

[(Prob. from Portuguese from) Sanskrit *rājan* king, from *rāj* to reign or rule, rel. to Latin *rex*, *regis*, Old Irish *rí*, *ríg* king. Cf. RICH *adjective*.]

Hist. Orig., an Indian king or prince. Later also, a petty dignitary or noble in India; a Malay or Javanese ruler or chief.

White Raja: see WHITE *adjective*.

■ **rajaship** *noun* the territory, rank, or title of a raja L17.

raja /ˈreɪə/ *noun*[2]. Also **raia**. M17.

[Latin *raia*.]

A ray (the fish). Now *rare* or *obsolete* exc. as mod. Latin genus name (*Raja*).

rajah *noun* var. of RAJA *noun*[1].

Rajasthani /rɑːdʒəˈstɑːni/ *noun & adjective*. E20.

[from *Rajasthan* (see below) + -I[2].]

▸ **A** *noun*. (Any of) the group of Indo-Aryan dialects spoken in Rajasthan, a State in NW India. Also, a native or inhabitant of Rajasthan. E20.

▸ **B** *attrib.* or as *adjective*. Of or pertaining to the dialects or people of Rajasthan. M20.

raja yoga /rɑːdʒə ˈjəʊgə/ *noun phr.* L19.

[Sanskrit, from *rājan* king + *yoga* YOGA.]

A form of yoga aimed at gaining control over the mind and emotions.

rajkumar /ˈrɑːdʒkʊmɑː/ *noun*. Fem. **-ri** /-ri/. E20.

[Sanskrit *rājakumāra*, from *rājan* king + *kumāra* (fem. *kumari*) child.]

A prince or princess of the Indian subcontinent.

Rajmahali /ˈrɑːdʒməˌhɑːli/ *noun & adjective*. M19.

[from *Rajmahal*, a range of hills in northern India + -I[2].]

(Of) the Dravidian language of the Maler, also called ***Maler***, ***Malto***.

Rajpoot *noun* var. of RAJPUT.

rajpramukh /ˈrɑːdʒprəmʊk/ *noun*. M20.

[Hindi from *rāj* RAJ + Sanskrit *pramukha* chief.]

Hist. In India between 1948 and 1962, a governor of a State covering the territory of one or more former princely States.

Rajput /ˈrɑːdʒpʊt/ *noun*. Also **-poot**. L16.

[Hindi *rājpūt*, from Sanskrit *rājan* king + *putra* son: see RAJ.]

A member of a Hindu military caste claiming descent from the four or five original Kshatriyas.

Rajya Sabha /ˈrɑːdʒjə səˈbɑː/ *noun*. M20.

[Sanskrit *rājya* State + *sabhā* SABHA.]

The upper house of the Indian parliament. Cf. LOK SABHA.

Rakah /ˈrɑːkə, *foreign* ˈrakax/ *noun*. M20.

[mod. Hebrew acronym, from *Rĕšimāh Qomunisṭit Ḥădāšāh* New Communist List (of candidates).]

A Communist party in Israel, formed in 1965.

rake /reɪk/ *noun*[1].

[Old English *raca*, *racu* = Middle Low German, Middle Dutch *rāke* (Dutch *raak*) rel. to Gothic *ufrakjan* stretch out, and by ablaut to Middle Low German, Middle Dutch *rēke* (Dutch *reek*), Old High German *rehho* (German *rechen*), Old Norse *reka*, and Old High German *rehhan*, Gothic *rikan* heap up, from Germanic.]

1 An implement consisting of a toothed bar fixed across the end of a long handle, used for drawing together hay, grass, etc., or levelling and smoothing the surface of the ground. Also, a similar larger agricultural implement mounted on wheels. OE. ▸**b** Any of various implements used in a similar way; *spec.* one with a blade instead of teeth for gathering money or chips staked at a gaming-table. M16.

2 *transf.* A very lean person. E16.

3 A kind of rasp or scraper. E18.

4 An act of raking. M19.

1 as thin as a rake (of a person) very thin.

rake /reɪk/ *noun*[2]. LME.

[Old Norse *rák* stripe, streak (Norwegian dial. *raak* footpath, channel), from alt. of *rek-* to drive. Cf. RACK *noun*[1].]

▸ **I** *Scot. & north.* **1** A way, a path; *esp.* (*a*) a steep narrow path up a hillside, cliff, ravine, etc.; (*b*) a path used by grazing cattle. Also, a (right of) pasture. LME.

2 A rush; speed. *rare.* LME.

3 A leading vein of ore with a more or less perpendicular lie. Also ***rake-vein***. M17.

4 (A load carried on) a single journey conveying anything from one place to another. L18.

5 A rut, a groove. L18.

▸ **II** Orig. *Scot. & north.*

6 A row, a series; *spec.* a series of wagons or carriages on a railway or of wagons or trucks in a mine or factory. E20.

rake /reɪk/ *noun*[3]. E17.

[Rel. to RAKE *verb*[3].]

1 NAUTICAL. **a** The projection of the upper part of a ship's hull at stem and stern beyond the keel. Also, the slope of the stern or rudder. E17. ▸**b** The inclination of a mast or funnel, usu. towards the stern, from the perpendicular along the line of the keel. E19.

2 *transf.* The inclination of any object from the perpendicular or to the horizontal; the slope of a thing, as (*a*) the slope of the stage or the auditorium in a theatre; (*b*) the slope of a seat-back; (*c*) the angle of an edge or face of a cutting tool. **E17.**

rake /reɪk/ *noun*[4]. **M17.**
[Abbreviation of **RAKEHELL.**]
A fashionable or stylish person, esp. a man, of dissolute or promiscuous habits.
rake's progress [the title of a series of engravings by William Hogarth (1735)] a progressive degeneration or decline, esp. through self-indulgence.
■ **rakery** *noun* (now *rare*) the habits or conduct of a rake **E18.**

rake /reɪk/ *verb*[1] *intrans.*
[Old English *racian*, perh. = Swedish *raka* run, rush, slip.]
1 Proceed or move forward, esp. with speed; go at a rapid pace. Also, go or wander *about*, roam. *obsolete* exc. *dial.* **OE.**
2 *spec.* **a** *FALCONRY.* Of a hawk: fly along after a quarry. **L16.** ▸**b** *HUNTING.* Of a dog: run with the nose close to the ground. **E19.**

rake /reɪk/ *verb*[2]. **ME.**
[Partly from Old Norse *raka* scrape, shave, rake; partly from **RAKE** *noun*[1].]
▸ **I** *verb trans.* **1 a** Collect, gather, or draw *together* (scattered objects) (as) with a rake. **ME.** ▸**b** Draw or drag in a specified direction (as) with a rake. **LME.**
2 †**a** Cover with or bury under something brought together (as) with a rake. **LME–L18.** ▸**b** Bank *up* or cover (a fire) with ashes, coal, etc., to keep it smouldering. *obsolete* exc. *dial.* **LME.**
3 a Make level and smooth with a rake (also foll. by *over*); bring (a surface) into a specified condition with or as with a rake. **LME.** ▸**b** *transf.* Search as if with a rake. **E17.**
†**4** Draw along like a rake. *rare.* **L16–M17.**
5 a Scratch, scrape; *spec.* in *FARRIERY*, remove excrement from a constipated horse by scraping with the hand. **L16.** ▸**b** Rub sleep from (the eyes). *Scot.* **E18.**
6 a *MILITARY.* Sweep from end to end with gunfire; enfilade. **M17.** ▸**b** Of a hawk: strike (a quarry) in the air. **M18.** ▸**c** Dominate, overlook, (a position etc.). Also, sweep with the eyes. **M19.**

> 📖 **1a** W. LAMBARDE Odo raked together great masses of silver and gold. JOYCE Jack raked the cinders together with a piece of cardboard. **b** R. THOMPSON Wooden rakes . . are required for raking off grass. J. G. WHITTIER She strove to hide her bare feet by raking hay over them. M. WESLEY She raked leaves into piles. *fig.*: N. BLAKE Had tea? No? . . I'll see what Mrs Raikes can rake up. **3a** H. STEPHENS The . . field-worker rakes clean the half ridge he has cleared. J. STEINBECK He raked the gravel and watered the flowers at that station. **b** *Manchester Examiner* To rake history . . for proofs of the wickedness of Dissenters. **5a** K. KESEY The hand pulled down his cheek, raking long red marks. **6a** *Time* A French ship . . was raked . . by rocket and machine-gun fire. **c** M. SINCLAIR The window of the Vicar's study raked the orchard. M. GEE Raking the row of women with her eyes.

▸ **II** *verb intrans.* **7** Use a rake; scrape, esp. with the fingers; search (as) with a rake, make investigations. **L16.**
8 Move like a rake. **L16.**

> 📖 **7** J. A. FROUDE It has been no pleasure . . to rake among the evil memories of the past. M. O. W. OLIPHANT Students rake into the dust of old histories. *Scots Magazine* I enjoy getting filthy raking through attics.

Phrases: **raking light** *ART & PHOTOGRAPHY* bright light, usu. beamed obliquely, revealing texture, detail, technique, etc.
With adverbs in specialized senses: **rake down** *US slang* win (money) at cards etc. **rake in** *colloq.* amass (money, profits, etc.). **rake out** clear the embers of (a fire) out of a grate. **rake over** revive the memory of (past quarrels, grievances, etc.). **rake up** (*a*) = *rake over* above; (*b*) search for and adduce (evidence etc.) against a person.
Comb.: **rake-off** *colloq.* (freq. *derog.*) a share of the winnings, profits, etc., of an enterprise; a commission; **rakeshame** (now *rare* or *obsolete*) a disreputable or dissolute person, esp. a man; a rogue.

rake /reɪk/ *verb*[3]. See also **RACK** *verb*[7]. **E17.**
[Prob. rel. to German *ragen* project (whence Swedish *raka*, Danish *rage*), of unkn. origin. Cf. **RAKE** *noun*[3].]
1 *NAUTICAL. verb intrans.* ▸**a** Of a ship, its hull, timbers, etc.: have a rake at stem or stern. **E17.** ▸**b** Of a mast or funnel: incline, usu. towards the stern, from the perpendicular. **L17.**
2 *verb trans.* Cause to incline or slope back. Chiefly as ***raked*** *ppl adjective.* **M19.**
■ **raking** *adjective*[1] slanting, sloping **E18.**

rake /reɪk/ *verb*[4] *intrans.* **E18.**
[from **RAKE** *noun*[4].]
Be a rake; live a dissolute life.
■ **raking** *adjective*[2] dissolute, dissipated **E18.**

rakehell /ˈreɪkhɛl/ *noun & adjective. arch.* **M16.**
[from **RAKE** *verb*[2] + **HELL** *noun.* See also **RAKEL.**]
▸ **A** *noun.* = **RAKE** *noun*[4]. **M16.**
▸ **B** *attrib.* or as *adjective.* = **RAKEHELLY** *adjective.* **M16.**

rakehelly /ˈreɪkhɛli/ *adjective & noun. arch.* **L16.**
[from prec. + **-Y**[1].]
▸ **A** *adjective.* Of the nature of, resembling, or characteristic of a rakehell. **L16.**
▸ **B** *noun.* A rakehell. **M18.**

rakel /ˈreɪk(ə)l/ *noun.* Long *obsolete* exc. *dial.* **E17.**
[Contr.]
= **RAKEHELL** *noun.*

raker /ˈreɪkə/ *noun*[1]. **ME.**
[from **RAKE** *verb*[2] + **-ER**[1]. Sense 4 perh. from **RAKE** *verb*[3].]
1 A person who rakes; *spec.* (*arch.*) a street-cleaner. **ME.**
2 Any of various implements for raking. **M17.**
3 A large lump of coal placed on a fire to keep it smouldering. *dial.* **M19.**
4 An inclined beam or strut. **L19.**

raker /ˈreɪkə/ *noun*[2]. *colloq.* **M19.**
[from **RAKE** *verb*[1] + **-ER**[1].]
1 A heavy bet on a horse. *slang.* **M19.**
2 An extremely fast pace. **L19.**

rakhi /ˈrɑːkiː/ *noun.* Pl. **-is.** **L19.**
[Hindi *rākhī.*]
HINDUISM. An elaborate cotton bracelet given at a festival of friendship (Raksha Bandhan), by a girl to a brother or close male friend who must then treat and protect her as a sister; the festival itself, held in August.

raki /rəˈkiː, ˈraki/ *noun.* **L17.**
[Turkish *rāqī* (now *rakı* whence also mod. Greek *rhakē, rhaki*) brandy, spirits.]
Orig., an aromatic liquor made from grain-spirit or grape juice in Greece, Turkey, and the Middle East. Now also, a liquor made from various other ingredients in eastern Europe and the Middle East; a drink of this.

rakia /raˈkija, ˈrakia/ *noun.* **M19.**
[Bulgarian *rakíya*, Serbo-Croat *ràkija*: cf. prec.]
In the Balkans: brandy, liquor; raki.

raking /ˈreɪkɪŋ/ *noun.* **LME.**
[from **RAKE** *verb*[2] + **-ING**[1].]
1 The action of **RAKE** *verb*[2]; an instance of this. **LME.** ▸**b** In *pl.* Things collected with a rake, objects or matter raked up. **M17.**
2 A rebuke, a scolding. Chiefly *US.* **M19.**

rakish /ˈreɪkɪʃ/ *adjective*[1]. **E18.**
[from **RAKE** *noun*[4] + **-ISH**[1].]
Having the character, appearance, or manner of a rake; characteristic of a rake; dashing, jaunty, raffish.
■ **rakishly** *adverb* **M19.**

rakish /ˈreɪkɪʃ/ *adjective*[2]. **E19.**
[from **RAKE** *noun*[3] + **-ISH**[1].]
Of a ship: smart and fast-looking, freq. with a suggestion of suspicious or piratical character.

rakshasa /ˈrɑːkʃasa/ *noun.* Also ***-sasa.*** **M19.**
[Sanskrit *rākṣasa* demon.]
HINDU MYTHOLOGY. A malignant demon, *esp.* any of a band at war with Rama and Hanuman; a representation of such a demon.

rakshi /ˈrakʃi/ *noun.* **L19.**
[Nepali *raksi* from Tibetan *rag-śi.*]
In Nepal and Tibet, a liquor distilled from rice or grain.

raku /ˈrɑːkuː/ *noun & adjective.* **L19.**
[Japanese, lit. 'ease, relaxed state, enjoyment'.]
(Designating) a kind of usu. lead-glazed Japanese pottery, often used as tea-bowls and similar utensils.

rale /rɑːl/ *noun.* Also **râle.** **E19.**
[French *râle*, from *râler* rattle in the throat, of unkn. origin.]
MEDICINE. An abnormal coarse crackling sound heard in a stethoscope during breathing, caused by opening of air-sacs or bubbling of air through fluid in the lungs. Cf. **CREPITATION.**

rall. *abbreviation.*
MUSIC. Rallentando.

rallentando /ralənˈtandəʊ/ *adverb, adjective, & noun.* **E19.**
[Italian, pres. pple of *rallentare* slow down.]
MUSIC. ▸**A** *adverb & adjective.* A direction: with gradual decrease of speed. **E19.**
▸ **B** *noun.* Pl. **-dos, -di** /-di/. A gradual decrease of speed; a passage (to be) played with a gradual decrease of speed. **M19.**

ralli /ˈrali/ *noun.* **L19.**
[from *Ralli*, the first purchaser.]
Hist. ***ralli car, ralli cart***, a light two-wheeled horse-drawn vehicle for four people.

ralline /ˈralʌɪn/ *adjective.* **L19.**
[from mod. Latin *Rallus* **RAIL** *noun*[3] + **-INE**[1].]
ORNITHOLOGY. Of, pertaining to, or belonging to the rail family Rallidae.

rally /ˈrali/ *verb*[1] & *noun*[1]. **E17.**
[French *ral(l)ier*, from *re-* **RE-** + *allier* **ALLY** *verb.* Cf. **RELY.**]
▸ **A** *verb.* **I** *verb trans.* **1** Reassemble, bring together again, (a scattered army or company). **E17.**
2 Bring together (persons) to one's support or for concentrated action. **E17.**
3 a Concentrate or renew (courage, energy, etc.) by effort of will. **M17.** ▸**b** Revive, rouse, (a person or animal). **L18.**
4 Drive (a vehicle) in a motor rally. *colloq.* **M20.**

> 📖 **1** E. EDWARDS Ralegh was the first to rally his men under the unexpected charge. **2** J. R. GREEN Even this blow failed to rally the Country under the Queen. C. MILNE Rallying others to the cause. **3** LD MACAULAY He rallied the last energies of his failing body. P. GALLICO Sears was gathering his forces and rallying himself.

▸ **II** *verb intrans.* **5** Come together again, reassemble, esp. to renew a conflict or contest. **M17.**
6 Revive, recover; pull oneself together; acquire or assume fresh vigour or energy. Now also *fig.*, (of share prices etc.) rise rapidly after a fall. **M18.** ▸**b** *BOXING.* Return and renew the attack. **E19.** ▸**c** Begin to recover from an illness, temporarily recover strength when ill. **M19.**
7 Come (esp. in a body) to the help or support of a person, cause, etc.; unite for a common purpose; hold a rally. Freq. foll. by *round, to.* **E19.**

> 📖 **5** DEFOE The battalions rallied . . to charge a second time. **6** W. BOYD As spring approached my spirits rallied and I began to feel a little better. **7** J. K. GALBRAITH Conservatives rally to the defence of inequality. P. WILLMOTT When . . the neighbour's children married . . we all rallied round. **rally round the flag** demonstrate loyalty to a cause which is under threat or attack.

▸ **B** *noun.* **1** A rapid reassembling of forces for renewed effort or conflict. **M17.**
2 a A quick or sudden recovery from exhaustion, a renewal of strength or energy; *spec.* an initial or temporary recovery of strength during illness. **E19.** ▸**b** *fig.* A rapid rise in share prices after a fall. **M20.**
3 a *BOXING.* A sustained exchange of blows. **E19.** ▸**b** *TENNIS* etc. An extended series of strokes exchanged between the players. **L19.**
4 A mass meeting of the supporters of a cause; *esp.* a political mass meeting. Orig. *US.* **M19.** ▸**b** A crowd of people. *dial.* **M19.** ▸**c** *THEATRICAL.* A general mêlée or chase of the characters in a pantomime. **L19.**
5 A competition for motor vehicles, usu. over a long distance on public roads or rough terrain. Freq. *attrib.* **M20.**

> 📖 **1** S. JOHNSON They yielded at last . . with frequent rallies, and sullen submission. *Observer* In a belated rally . . Jones scored for Llanelly. **4** A. P. HERBERT An annual rally of the Boy Scouts. MALCOLM X At great Muslim rallies . . I have seen . . ten thousand black people applauding and cheering. ***Nuremberg rally***: see **NUREMBERG** 2.

Comb.: **rally-cross** a form of motor racing combining elements of rallying and autocross.
■ **rallied** *ppl adjective* (of an army) that has rallied to make a stand **M17.** **rallier** *noun*[1] (*rare*) **L19.** **rallying** *verbal noun* the action of the verb; the practice or sport of participating in a rally or rallies: **M19.** **rallyist** *noun* a person who competes in a motor rally or rallies **M20.**

rally /ˈrali/ *verb*[2] & *noun*[2]. **M17.**
[French *railler*: see **RAIL** *verb*[2].]
▸ **A** *verb.* **1** *verb trans.* Subject to banter or good-humoured ridicule; make fun of. **M17.**
2 *verb intrans.* Engage in banter, joke. Now *rare.* **M17.**
▸ **B** *noun.* A piece of rallying or banter. *rare.* **M19.**
■ **rallier** *noun*[2] (long *rare*) **L17.** **rallyingly** *adverb* in a rallying manner **M17.**

RAM *abbreviation.*
Royal Academy of Music.

ram /ram/ *noun*[1].
[Old English *ram(m)*, corresp. to Frisian *ram, room*, Middle & mod. Low German, Middle & mod. Dutch *ram*, Old High German, Middle High German *ram* ram (German *Ramme* rammer), perh. rel. to Old Norse *ram(m)r* strong.]
1 An uncastrated adult male sheep; in domestication, one kept for breeding purposes. **OE.**
2 (Usu. **R-**.) *The* constellation and zodiacal sign Aries. **OE.**
3 A battering ram. **OE.** ▸**b** *NAUTICAL* (now *Hist.*). A solid projection from the bows of a warship for piercing the sides of other ships; a battleship fitted with this. **M19.** ▸**c** An underwater projection from an iceberg or other body of ice. **M20.**
4 The weight or hammer of a pile-driving machine. **LME.**
5 a A machine in which a descending body of water in a pipe is brought to rest suddenly and the resulting pressure used to raise some of the water or lift something else. **E19.** ▸**b** The piston of the large cylinder of a hydrostatic press. **E19.** ▸**c** The reciprocating arm on which the tool is mounted in a shaping or slotting machine. **M19.** ▸**d** The plunger of a force-pump. **L19.**
6 A sexually aggressive man; a lecher. *colloq.* **E20.**
1 ***milk the ram***: see **MILK** *verb.* ***run-with-ram***: see **RUN** *adjective* 1.
Comb.: **ram-cat** (*obsolete* exc. *dial.*) a male cat; **ram's head** (*a*) a N. American lady's-slipper orchid, *Cypripedium arietinum*; (*b*) the tiller of a narrow boat; **ram's horn** (*a*) the horn of a ram; the material of this; (*b*) a curled motif resembling a ram's horn; (*c*) a perforated container in which fish are washed; (*d*) (in full ***ram's-horn snail, ram's-horn pond snail***) any member of the family Planorbidae, which comprises herbivorous aquatic snails with flat spiral shells.

ram /ram/ *noun*[2]. *rare*. L17.
[Origin unkn.]
Ore.

ram /ram/ *noun*[3]. E18.
[Origin unkn. Perh. rel. to earlier RAM LINE.]
The overall length of a boat. Also, the centre plank of a coble.

ram /ram/ *noun*[4]. M19.
[from RAM *verb*[1].]
1 The action or process of ramming. M19.
2 The compressive effect exerted on air which is constrained to enter a moving aperture or restricted space, esp. the intake of a jet engine. Freq. *attrib.* M20.
Comb.: **ram air** air which is constrained to enter a moving aperture.

ram /ram/ *noun*[5]. *slang* (chiefly *Austral.*). M20.
[Origin unkn.]
An accomplice in petty crime.

RAM /ram/ *noun*[6]. Also **ram**. M20.
[Acronym.]
COMPUTING. Random-access memory.

ram /ram/ *verb*[1]. Infl. **-mm-**. ME.
[from RAM *noun*[1].]
▶ **I 1** *verb intrans. & trans.* Beat (earth, the ground, etc.) with a heavy implement so as to produce hardness and firmness; make (a thing) firm in this way. ME.
2 *verb trans.* Force or drive by heavy blows; push forcefully or firmly. Foll. by *down*, *in*, *into*, *up*. E16. ▶**b** Force (a charge) into a firearm by means of a ramrod. L16.
3 *verb trans.* Block *up*. M16.
4 *verb trans.* Force in or compress the contents of (a thing) by ramming; cram *with* something. L16.
5 *verb trans.* Dash or drive (one thing) *on*, *at*, or *into* another. E18.
6 *verb trans.* Move forcefully against and collide with; strike with great force; *spec.* (*Hist.*) (of a ship) strike (another ship) with a ram. M19.
7 *verb intrans.* Move or crash forcefully *into*, *through*, or *against* something. L19.

> 🕮 **1** J. S. FOSTER Traditional rammed earth construction for walling. **2** J. CONRAD He . . rammed all his papers into his pockets. *fig.*: L. NAMIER It must have been rammed into him . . to what high station he was born. ***ram down a person's throat***: see THROAT *noun*. **ram home** stress forcefully (an argument etc.) **4** H. CAINE He took . . his pipe and rammed it with his forefinger. **6** R. BRADBURY The boat rammed the wharf hard. **7** R. K. NARAYAN She . . knocked me off my feet by ramming into me.

▶†**II 8** *verb trans.* Of a ram: copulate with (a ewe). L16–M18.
Comb.: **ram-raid** an instance of ram-raiding; **ram-raider** a person who engages in ram-raiding; **ram-raiding** the action of crashing a car into the windows of a shop in order to raid the contents.

ram /ram/ *verb*[2] *intrans. slang* (chiefly *Austral.*). Infl. **-mm-**. M20.
[from RAM *noun*[5].]
Act as an accomplice in petty crime.

r.a.m. *abbreviation.*
CHEMISTRY. Relative atomic mass.

ramada /rəˈmɑːdə/ *noun. US.* M19.
[Spanish.]
An arbour, a porch.

Ramadan /ˈramədan, raməˈdan/ *noun.* Also **-dhan**, **-zan**, /-zan/. L15.
[Arab. *ramaḍān* (whence Persian *ramażān*, Turkish *ramazàn*), from *ramiḍa* be parched or hot: reason for the name is uncertain.]
The ninth month of the year in the Islamic calendar, during which Muslims observe strict fasting between dawn and sunset.

ramage /ˈramɪdʒ/ *noun.* E17.
[French from Proto-Gallo-Romance, from Latin *ramus* branch: see -AGE.]
†**1** The song or cry of birds. Only in 17.
2 The branches of a tree or trees collectively. *arch.* M17.
3 ANTHROPOLOGY. A corporate descent group which includes members of both maternal and paternal lineages. M20.

ramage /ˈramɪdʒ/ *adjective.* ME.
[Old French (whence also Anglo-Latin *ramagius*, in sense 2) from Proto-Gallo-Romance: see prec. Cf. RAMMISH *adjective*[2].]
1 Wild, untamed, violent; furious, frenzied. Long *obsolete* exc. *Scot.* ME.
†**2** Of a hawk: having left the nest and begun to fly from branch to branch; shy, wary. LME–L18.
†**3** Of a place: full of thickets, rough. L15–E19.
†**4** Of velvet or taffeta: having a branching design. L16–E18.

ramal /ˈreɪm(ə)l/ *adjective.* M19.
[from Latin RAMUS + -AL[1].]
BOTANY. Of or pertaining to a branch; growing on or out of a branch.

Raman /ˈrɑːmən/ *noun.* E20.
[Sir Chandrasekhara Venkata *Raman* (1888–1970), Indian physicist.]
Used *attrib.* to designate concepts arising from the work of Raman.
Raman effect, **Raman scattering** the scattering of light with a change in frequency characteristic of the scattering substance, representing a change in the vibrational, rotational, or electronic energy of the substance. **Raman spectroscopy** spectroscopy in which the Raman effect is used to investigate molecular energy levels. **Raman spectrum** a spectrum of scattered light showing additional bands produced by the Raman effect.

ramanas rose /ramənəs ˈrəʊz/ *noun phr.* L19.
[from Japanese *hamanas*, from *hama* seashore + *nas* pear.]
The Japanese rose, *Rosa rugosa*.

Ramapithecus /rɑːməˈpɪθɪkəs/ *noun.* M20.
[from *Rāma*, an Indian prince + Greek *pithēkos* ape.]
A fossil anthropoid ape of the genus *Ramapithecus*, sometimes considered a hominid, and known from Miocene remains found in SW Asia and E. Africa.
■ **ramapithecine** /-ˈpɪθɪsiːn/ *noun & adjective* (designating or pertaining to) a fossil anthropoid ape of or closely related to the genus *Ramapithecus* L20.

ramarama /ˈrɑːmərɑːmə/ *noun.* M19.
[Maori.]
A New Zealand evergreen shrub or small tree of the myrtle family, *Lophomyrtus bullata*, with small white flowers and puckered red-tinged leaves.

†**ramass** *verb trans. rare.* E16–L18.
[French *ramasser*, from *ramasse* sledge of branches from Italian *ramazza*, from *ramo* branch from Latin RAMUS.]
Convey on a sledge of branches.

Ramazan *noun* var. of RAMADAN.

rambai /ˈrambʌɪ/ *noun.* E19.
[Malay.]
Either of two Malaysian evergreen trees of the spurge family, *Baccaurea motleyana* and *B. sapida*, bearing large dark green leaves and racemes of tiny yellowish-green flowers; the buff plumlike fruit of either tree, which has white flesh and pale brown seeds.

rambla /ˈrambla/ *noun.* E19.
[Spanish from Hispano-Arab. *ramla* sandy place from Arab. *raml* sand.]
1 A Spanish ravine, usu. waterless; the dry bed of an ephemeral stream. E19.
2 A broad street in an eastern Spanish city, built on a shallow watercourse; *spec.* (now usu. in *pl.*) a broad avenue in Barcelona. E19.

ramble /ˈramb(ə)l/ *noun*[1]. M17.
[from the verb.]
1 An act of rambling; a walk (formerly, any journey) without definite route or other aim than pleasure. M17.
2 Rambling, incoherence. *rare.* E18.

ramble /ˈramb(ə)l/ *noun*[2]. *rare.* M19.
[Origin uncertain: cf. Swedish *ramla* fall down.]
MINING. A thin bed of shale lying above a coal seam, which falls down as the coal is taken out.

ramble /ˈramb(ə)l/ *verb.* LME.
[Cf. Middle Dutch *rammelen* (of cats, rabbits, etc.) be on heat and wander about, frequentative of *rammen* copulate with, corresp. to Old High German *rammalōn* (German *rammeln*), ult. from Old High German *ram* RAM *noun*[1]: see -LE[3]. Cf. RAMMLE.]
1 *verb intrans.* Write or talk incoherently or inconsequentially; (of the mind or thoughts) wander. LME.
2 *verb intrans.* Travel freely and without definite aim or direction. Now usu. *spec.*, walk for pleasure, with or without a definite route but usu. in the country. E17.
3 *verb trans.* Ramble over. *rare.* E19.

> 🕮 **1** P. INCHBALD He . . let his mind ramble Thoughts, memories, pictures, came and went. P. O'DONNELL She had thought he was awake, but then realized he was rambling.

rambler /ˈramblə/ *noun.* E17.
[from prec. + -ER[1].]
1 A person who rambles or goes rambling. E17.
2 Any of various garden roses, freq. derived from *Rosa luciae*, which straggle over other vegetation. M19.
3 A single-storey suburban house; a ranch house. *US.* M20.

rambling /ˈramblɪŋ/ *noun.* E17.
[from RAMBLE *verb* + -ING[1].]
The action of RAMBLE *verb*; an instance of this; in *pl.*, incoherent talk.

> 🕮 A. WILSON In and out of her ramblings . . came clear threads of memory.

rambling /ˈramblɪŋ/ *adjective.* E17.
[formed as prec. + -ING[2].]
1 That rambles; (of life, destiny, etc.) characterized by wandering; (of a plant) straggling, spreading, or climbing freely and irregularly. E17.
2 Having an irregular straggling form or plan. E18.

> 🕮 **1** G. SWIFT I have long, rambling conversations with him. **2** F. WITTS A large rambling mansion.

■ **ramblingly** *adverb* M17. **ramblingness** *noun* M19.

rambo /ˈrambəʊ/ *noun*[1]. *US.* Pl. **-os.** E19.
[Prob. alt. of RAMBURE.]
A variety of eating or cooking apple which ripens late in autumn and has a yellowish skin streaked with red.

Rambo /ˈrambəʊ/ *noun*[2]. Pl. **-os.** L20.
[The hero of David Morrell's novel *First Blood* (1972), a Vietnam war veteran represented as bent on violent retribution, popularized in the films *First Blood* (1982) and *Rambo: First Blood Part II* (1985).]
A man given to displays of physical violence or aggression, a macho man.
■ **Ramboˈesque** *adjective* involving or characterized by a great deal of violence or aggression L20. **Ramboism** *noun* conduct or attitude resembling those of a Rambo L20.

rambootan *noun* var. of RAMBUTAN.

†**rambooze** *noun.* M17–E19.
[Origin unkn.]
A drink made with wine, eggs or milk, and sugar.

Rambouillet /ˈrambəleɪ, *foreign* rɑ̃bujɛ (*pl. same*)/ *noun.* E19.
[A town in northern France, the site of a sheep farm founded by Louis XVI.]
†**1** = RUMBULLION *noun*[2] 1. Only in E19.
2 (An animal of) a hardy breed of sheep developed from the Spanish merino but bred elsewhere for its meat and its heavy fleece of fine wool. M19.

rambunctious /ramˈbʌŋkʃəs/ *adjective. colloq.* (chiefly *N. Amer.*). M19.
[Origin unkn.: cf. earlier RUMBUSTIOUS.]
Of a person: boisterous, unruly; flamboyant. Of an animal: wild, high-spirited.
■ **rambunctiously** *adverb* M20. **rambunctiousness** *noun* E20.

†**rambure** *noun.* E17–E18.
[French *rambour*, from *Rambures*, a place near Amiens in N. France.]
A large variety of cooking apple.

rambutan /ramˈbuːt(ə)n/ *noun.* Also **-bootan.** E18.
[Malay, from *rambut* hair, in ref. to the covering of the fruit.]
A Malaysian tree, *Nephelium lappaceum* (family Sapindaceae); the fruit of this tree, resembling a lychee and covered with soft bright red spines or prickles.

RAMC *abbreviation.*
Royal Army Medical Corps.

rame /reɪm/ *noun*[1]. Long *obsolete* exc. *dial.* L15.
[Perh. = Middle Dutch *rame* (Dutch *raam*), Old High German *rama* (Middle High German *ram(e)*, German *Rahm*, *Rahmen*) frame, framework.]
A bone (of a person or animal). Usu. in *pl.*, bones, a skeleton.

rame /reɪm/ *noun*[2]. *rare.* L16.
[French from Latin RAMUS.]
A branch of a tree or shrub, or of a nerve etc.

Ramean /ˈreɪmɪən/ *adjective & noun.* M18.
[from *Ramus* (see RAMIST) + -EAN.]
= RAMIST.

ramekin /ˈramɪkɪn, ˈramkɪn/ *noun.* M17.
[French *ramequin* of Low Dutch origin (cf. Flemish †*rameken* toasted bread), perh. from Middle Dutch (cf. German *Rahm* cream, -KIN).]
1 A small quantity of cheese with breadcrumbs, eggs, etc., usually baked and served in a special mould. Usu. in *pl.* M17.
2 A small mould or dish in which ramekins or other individual portions of food are baked and served. L19.
Comb.: **ramekin case**, **ramekin dish** = sense 2 above.

ramellose /ˈraməl əʊs/ *adjective.* M19.
[from mod. Latin *ramellus* dim. of Latin RAMUS: see -OSE[1]. Cf. RAMULUS.]
ANATOMY, BOTANY, & ZOOLOGY. Bearing, or having the form of, small ramuli.

ramen /ˈrɑːmɛn/ *noun* (treated as *sing.* or *pl.*). L20.
[Japanese, from Chinese *lā* to pull + *miàn* noodles.]
Quick-cooking Chinese noodles, usu. served in a broth with meat and vegetables.

ramenas /ˈramənəs/ *noun. S. Afr.* Also **ramnas** /ˈramnəs/. E20.
[Afrikaans from Dutch *ram(m)enas* black radish.]
Wild radish, *Raphanus raphanistrum*. Formerly also, the similar weed charlock, *Sinapis arvensis*.

ramentum /rəˈmɛntəm/ *noun.* Pl. **-ta** /-tə/. M17.
[Latin, from *radere* to scrape: see -MENT.]
1 A fragment scraped off. Formerly also, a tiny particle, an atom. Usu. in *pl.* M17.
2 BOTANY. A thin membraneous scale on the surface of leaves and stalks (esp. of ferns). E19.
■ **ramenˈtaceous** *adjective* (BOTANY) covered with or resembling ramenta E19. **ramenˈtiferous** *adjective* (BOTANY) bearing ramenta L19.

Ramessid /ˈraməsɪd/ *noun & adjective.* Also **-ide** /-ʌɪd/. **M19.**
[German *Ramesside*, from Greek *Rhamessēs* Rameses + *-ide* -ID[3].]
▶ **A** *noun.* A member of the Egyptian royal family during the 19th and 20th dynasties (*c* 13th to 11th cents. BC). **M19.**
▶ **B** *adjective.* Of or pertaining to the Ramessids. **M19.**

ramet /ˈreɪmət/ *noun.* **E20.**
[from Latin RAMUS + -ET[1].]
BOTANY. An individual plant belonging to a clone.

ramfeezled /ramˈfiːz(ə)ld/ *adjective. Scot.* **L18.**
[App. an invented word.]
Worn out, exhausted.

ramgunshoch /ramˈgʌnʃʌk, -x/ *adjective. Scot.* **E18.**
[Origin unkn.]
Bad-tempered, rude.

rami *noun* pl. of RAMUS.

rami- /ˈrami/ *combining form* of Latin RAMUS: see -I-.
■ **ramicorn** *noun* [Latin *cornu* horn] a horny sheath along the edge of a bird's lower mandible **M19.** **ramiform** *adjective* branched, dendritic **M19.** **ramiˈsection** *noun* (*MEDICINE, rare*) cutting of some of the rami communicantes so as to prevent sympathetic nerve impulses from reaching a particular part of the body **E20.**

ramie /ˈrami/ *noun.* **M19.**
[Malay *rami*.]
A tropical Asian plant of the nettle family, *Boehmeria nivea*, (also called ***China grass***); its tough silky fibre, used to weave grass-cloth etc.

ramification /ˌramɪfɪˈkeɪʃ(ə)n/ *noun.* **M17.**
[French, formed as RAMIFY: see -FICATION.]
1 A subdivision of a complex structure analogous to the branches of a tree, as a network of blood-vessels or branches of a river; a branch. **M17.**
2 Each of many points of detail about a matter; a consequence, esp. when unwelcome or problematic, a complication. **M18.**
3 The action or an act of ramifying; the state of being ramified. **M18.**

📖 **2** J. D. SALINGER I couldn't quite take in this information whole, let alone consider its many possible ramifications. A. POWELL The ramifications of aristocratic life.

■ ˈ**ramificate** *verb intrans.* (*rare*) branch out **M19.**

ramify /ˈramɪfʌɪ/ *verb.* **LME.**
[Old & mod. French *ramifier* from medieval Latin *ramificare* branch out, from Latin RAMUS: see -FY.]
1 *verb intrans.* Form branches, subdivisions, or offshoots; spread out as branches or ramifications, branch. **LME.**
2 *verb trans.* Divide into or arrange in branches or ramifications. Usu. in *pass.* **LME.**

📖 **1** B. MAGEE Argument has ramified through the pages of academic journals.

■ **ramified** *adjective* branched, characterized by ramification **L17.**

ramillie /ˈramɪli/ *noun.* Also **-illies** /-ɪlɪz/. **M18.**
[*Ramillies*, a town in Belgium, the scene of a battle in 1706 won by the British.]
Hist. A wig with a long plait behind tied with a bow at the top and bottom. Also more fully ***ramillie wig***.

ramin /raˈmiːn/ *noun.* **M20.**
[Malay.]
Any of the trees of the genus *Gonystylus* (family Thymelaeaceae), natives of swamps in Malaysia, Sarawak, etc.; the light-coloured hardwood of such a tree.

Ramist /ˈreɪmɪst/ *noun & adjective.* **L16.**
[from *Ramus*: see below, -IST.]
▶ **A** *noun.* A follower of Ramus (Pierre de la Ramée (1515–72)), a French philosopher and logician who taught a controversial revised version of Aristotelian logic. **E17.**
▶ **B** *adjective.* Of, pertaining to, or characteristic of Ramists or Ramism. **M19.**
■ **Ramism** *noun* the logical system of Ramus **E18.** **Raˈmistic** *adjective* pertaining to Ramus or his system **M20.** †**Ramistical** *adjective* = RAMISTIC **L16–M17.**

ram-jam /ramˈdʒam/ *adverb. dial. & slang.* **L19.**
[from RAM *verb*[1] + JAM *verb*[1].]
ram-jam full, crammed full.

ramjet /ˈramdʒɛt/ *noun.* **M20.**
[from RAM *verb*[1] + JET *noun*[2]. See also RAM *noun*[4].]
A simple form of jet engine in which the air drawn in for combustion is compressed solely by the forward motion of the engine.

ramkie /ˈramki/ *noun. S. Afr.* **E19.**
[Afrikaans from Nama *rangi-b*, perh. from Portuguese *rabequinha* dim. of *rabeca* fiddle, REBEC.]
A stringed instrument somewhat like a guitar, played by the Nama and Bushmen of southern Africa.

ram line /ˈram lʌɪn/ *noun phr.* **M17.**
[from unkn. 1st elem. (cf. RAM *noun*[3]) + LINE *noun*[2].]
NAUTICAL. A cord used for setting a straight line, e.g. along a mast or spar.

rammel /ˈram(ə)l/ *noun.* Long *obsolete* exc. *dial.* **ME.**
[In senses 1 & 2 from Old French *ramaille* (= Anglo-Latin *ramaillum*, *ramella*) branches, loppings, from *rame* branch from Latin RAMUS. Senses 3 & 4 may repr. a different word.]
†**1** Brushwood, small trees or bushes. *Scot. & north.* **ME–L16.**
2 Small or rubbishy branches, esp. from trees which have been felled and trimmed. **ME.**
3 Rubbish of any kind. **LME.**
4 Hard infertile earth. **M19.**

rammelsbergite /ˈram(ə)lzbəːgʌɪt/ *noun.* **M19.**
[from K. F. *Rammelsberg* (1813–99), German mineralogist + -ITE[1].]
MINERALOGY. An arsenide of nickel that occurs as white granular or fibrous masses.

rammer /ˈramə/ *noun.* **LME.**
[from RAM *verb*[1] + -ER[1].]
†**1** A battering-ram. **LME–M16.**
2 An instrument for ramming or compacting material; *spec.* a block of wood fixed at the end of a staff for driving home the charge of a cannon; (formerly) a ramrod of a firearm. **L15.**
3 A pile-driver. **L17.**
4 A person engaged in ramming a material. **L19.**

rammies /ˈramɪz/ *noun pl. Austral. & S. Afr. slang.* **E20.**
[Origin uncertain: perh. from RAMIE + -S[1].]
Trousers.

rammish /ˈramɪʃ/ *adjective*[1]. **LME.**
[App. from RAM *noun*[1] + -ISH[1]. Sense 2 may belong to RAMMISH *adjective*[2].]
1 (Of a smell, taste, etc.) rank, strong, highly disagreeable; having a rank smell or taste. Now *dial.* **LME.**
2 Lascivious, lustful. Now *rare* or *obsolete.* **M16.**
■ **rammishly** *adverb* **M16.** **rammishness** *noun* **M16.**

rammish /ˈramɪʃ/ *adjective*[2]. *obsolete* exc. *dial.* **E16.**
[Alt. of RAMAGE *adjective*.]
†**1** = RAMAGE *adjective* 2. **E16–M17.**
2 = RAMAGE *adjective* 1. **E17.**

rammle /ˈram(ə)l/ *verb & noun. Scot.* **E18.**
[Var. of RAMBLE *verb*, *noun*[1].]
▶ **A** *verb intrans.* **1** Wander about without definite aim or direction, esp. when under the influence of alcohol. **E18.**
2 Ramble. **E19.**
▶ **B** *noun.* A row, an uproar; a drinking-bout, a binge. **E18.**

rammy /ˈrami/ *noun. Scot.* **M20.**
[Origin uncertain: perh. from RAMMLE *noun*.]
A brawl, a fight, esp. between gangs; a quarrel.

rammy /ˈrami/ *adjective.* Now chiefly *north.* **E17.**
[from RAM *noun*[1] + -Y[1].]
Characteristic of or resembling (that of) a ram; *esp.* = RAMMISH *adjective*[1] 1.

ramnas *noun* var. of RAMENAS.

ramon *noun* var. of RAMOON.

ramonda /rəˈmɒndə/ *noun.* **E19.**
[mod. Latin (see below), from L. F. E. von *Ramond* de Carbonnières (1753–1827), French botanist and politician.]
Any of several small European rock-plants constituting the genus *Ramonda* (family Gesneriaceae), having hairy leaves in a basal rosette and purple flowers.

ramoon /rəˈmuːn/ *noun.* Also **ramon** /rəˈməʊn, *foreign* raˈmon/. **M18.**
[Spanish *ramón*, from *ramo* branch from Latin RAMUS: see -OON.]
(In full ***ramoon-tree***) a W. Indian and Central American tree, *Brosimum alicastrum*, of the mulberry family; its leaves and tops, used as fodder.

ramose /ˈraməʊs, ˈreɪ-/ *adjective.* **L17.**
[Latin *ramosus*, formed as RAMUS: see -OSE[1].]
Branched, branching; dendritic.
■ **raˈmosely** *adverb* **L19.**

ramous /ˈreɪməs/ *adjective.* Now *rare.* **LME.**
[formed as prec.: see -OUS.]
1 = RAMOSE. **LME.**
2 Of, pertaining to, or characteristic of branches. **E19.**

ramp /ramp/ *noun*[1]. **LME.**
[from RAMP *verb*[1]. In branch III through French *rampe*, from Old & mod. French *ramper*.]
▶ **I 1** A bold lively woman or girl; a tomboy. Cf. ROMP *noun* 1. Long *arch. & dial.* **LME.**
▶ **II 2** The action or an act of ramping. **L17.**
▶ **III 3** *ARCHITECTURE.* The difference in level between the abutments of a rampant arch. **E18.**
4 A slope; an inclined plane connecting two different levels; *spec.* (***a***) a temporary bridge used when boarding or leaving a boat; (***b***) a sloping board by which an animal enters or leaves a horsebox, cattle truck, etc.; (***c***) a movable set of stairs used when boarding or leaving an aeroplane. **L18.** ▸**b** An inclined slip road leading on to or off a main highway. *N. Amer.* **M20.** ▸**c** An abrupt change in the level of a road. **M20.** ▸**d** A low platform from which competitors leave successively at timed intervals at the start of a motor rally. **M20.**
5 Part of the handrail of a stair with a concave or upward bend, as at a landing. **L18.**
6 The apron of an airfield. **M20.**
7 *ELECTRONICS.* An electrical waveform in which the voltage increases linearly with time. Freq. *attrib.* **M20.**
Comb.: **rampway** *N. Amer.* a sloping passageway formed by a ramp between different levels.

ramp /ramp/ *noun*[2]. **M16.**
[In sense 1, of unkn. origin. In sense 2, abbreviation of RAMPION. In sense 3, back-form. from RAMPS.]
†**1** Wild arum, *Arum maculatum*. **M16–E17.**
2 The garden rampion, *Campanula rapunculus*. **L16.**
3 a Wild garlic, ramsons. *dial.* **E19.** ▸**b** The N. American wild leek, *Allium tricoccum*. Cf. RAMPS 2. *US.* **E20.**

ramp /ramp/ *noun*[3]. *slang.* **E19.**
[from RAMP *verb*[2].]
1 A swindle, a fraudulent action; *spec.* the action or practice of obtaining profit by an unwarranted increase in the price of a commodity. **E19.**
2 A search made of a prisoner or prison cell. *Austral.* **E20.**

📖 **1** R. G. COLLINGWOOD The gigantic ramp by which the trade . . passes itself off as art. **bankers' ramp** a financial crisis deliberately brought about by financial institutions.

ramp /ramp/ *verb*[1]. **ME.**
[Old & mod. French *ramper* creep, crawl, climb = Italian *rampare*: ult. origin unkn.]
▶ **I 1** *verb intrans.* Of an animal, esp. a lion: rear or stand on hind legs, as if in the act of climbing; assume or be in a threatening posture; *HERALDRY* be rampant. Of a person: raise or gesticulate with the arms. **ME.**
2 *verb intrans.* Behave in a furious or threatening manner. **LME.**
†**3** *verb intrans.* Creep or crawl on the ground. *rare.* **LME–L16.**
4 *verb intrans.* Climb, scramble, (now *dial.*); (of a non-climbing plant) grow rankly or luxuriantly. **E16.**
5 *verb intrans.* †**a** Gad about licentiously, gallivant. **M16–E17.** ▸**b** = ROMP *verb* 1. Now *dial.* **M17.**
6 *verb intrans.* **a** Rush (*about*) in a wild or excited manner. **E17.** ▸**b** Sail swiftly, scud. Freq. foll. by *along*. **L19.**

📖 **6a** X. HERBERT Norman ramped about . . trying to get in.

▶ **II** [from RAMP *noun*[1].]
7 *verb trans.* Provide with a ramp, build with ramps. Chiefly as ***ramped*** *ppl adjective.* **E19.**
8 *verb intrans. ARCHITECTURE.* Of a wall: ascend or descend from one level to another. **M19.**

ramp /ramp/ *verb*[2] *trans.* **M16.**
[Origin unkn.]
1 Formerly, snatch, take violently. Now (*dial.*), sprain, tear. **M16.**
2 Rob, swindle; *spec.* force (a bookmaker) to pay a pretended bet. *slang.* **E19.** ▸**b** *COMMERCE.* Drive up the price of (a share) in order to gain a financial advantage; cause to increase sharply. Freq. foll. by *up*. **L20.**
3 Conduct a search of (a prisoner or prison cell). *Austral. slang.* **E20.**

📖 **2b** *Sunday Times* The Fed is under pressure from Wall Street to ramp up interest rates.

■ **ramper** *noun* **E19.**

rampacious /ramˈpeɪʃəs/ *adjective. rare.* **M19.**
[Alt. of RAMPAGEOUS after -ACIOUS.]
= RAMPAGEOUS.

rampage /ˈrampeɪdʒ, ramˈpeɪdʒ/ *noun.* **M19.**
[from the verb.]
The action or an act of rampaging; violent or furious behaviour. Chiefly in ***on the rampage***, rampaging.

rampage /ramˈpeɪdʒ/ *verb intrans.* Orig. *Scot.* **L17.**
[Origin uncertain: perh. based on RAMP *verb*[1] and RAGE *noun*.]
Behave violently or furiously, storm, rage; rush about in a wild, agitated, or confused manner.
■ **rampager** *noun* **L19.**

rampageous /ramˈpeɪdʒəs/ *adjective.* **E19.**
[from prec. + -OUS.]
Violent, unruly, boisterous; given to rampaging.

📖 ELIZABETH PETERS Now who is allowing a rampageous imagination to run away with him?

■ **rampageously** *adverb* **M19.** **rampageousness** *noun* **L19.**

†**rampallion** *noun.* **L16–E19.**
[Origin uncertain: perh. based on RAMP *verb*[1]. Cf. later RASCALLION.]
A ruffian, a scoundrel.

rampant /ˈrampənt/ *adjective.* **ME.**
[Old & mod. French, pres. pple of *ramper*: see RAMP *verb*[1], -ANT[1].]
1 Of an animal, esp. a lion: rearing or standing on the hind legs; *spec.* (*HERALDRY*) standing on the sinister hind leg,

with both forelegs elevated, the dexter above the sinister, and the head in profile. Freq. (esp. in HERALDRY) *postpositive*. ME.

2 Fierce, high-spirited; violent and extravagant in action, opinion, etc.; fully fledged, absolute. LME.

3 Of a thing: unchecked, unrestrained; *esp.* having full sway or unchecked course in a society or individual. LME.

†**4** Lustful; vicious. L17–E19.

5 ARCHITECTURE. Of an arch or vault; having the abutments on different levels. E18.

6 Of a plant or its growth: rank, luxurious. M18.

📖 **2** EVELYN Being . . discovered to be a rampant Socinian, he was discharged of employment. **3** H. ROBBINS Inflation was rampant in Germany. *Times Lit. Suppl.* Academicism has run rampant.

▪ **rampancy** *noun* the fact or condition of being rampant M17. **rampantly** *adverb* LME.

rampart /ˈrampɑːt/ *noun & verb*. L16.
[French *rempart*, †*rampart* alt. (after *boulevart* boulevard) of †*rempar*, from *remparer*: see RAMPIRE *verb*.]
▶ **A** *noun*. **1** A defensive mound of earth or wall with a broad top and usually a stone parapet; a walkway along the top of such a structure; *fig.* a defence, a protection. L16.
2 A steep bank of a river or gorge. Usu. in *pl. Canad.* M19.
▶ **B** *verb trans.* Fortify or surround with a rampart. L19.
▪ **ramparted** *adjective* L16.

rampick /ˈrampɪk/ *adjective. obsolete* exc. *dial.* L16.
[Origin unkn.: cf. RAMPIKE.]
Of a tree or bough: partially decayed or dead; bare of leaves or twigs.

rampier *noun, verb* vars. of RAMPIRE *noun, verb*.

rampike /ˈrampʌɪk/ *noun. dial. & N. Amer.* M19.
[Origin unkn.: cf. RAMPICK.]
A decaying or dead tree; a spiky stump or stem of a tree.
▪ **rampiked** *adjective* of the nature of a rampike L18.

rampion /ˈrampɪən/ *noun*. L16.
[from Proto-Romance var. of medieval Latin *rapuncium*, *rapontium* (Italian *raperonzo*, French *raiponce*; cf. German *Rapunzel*), app. from Latin *rapum* RAPE *noun*³.]
1 A kind of bellflower, *Campanula rapunculus*, of which the white tuberous roots are sometimes used as a salad. Also ***rampion bellflower***. L16.
2 A plant of the related genus *Phyteuma*, the members of which have heads or spikes of curved tubular blue, violet, or white flowers; *esp.* (more fully ***round-headed rampion***) *P. orbiculare*, of dry grassland, esp. chalk downs in southern England. M18.

rampire /ˈrampʌɪə/ *noun*. Also **-pier** /-pɪə/. M16.
[French †*rempar*, †*ramper*, formed as next.]
1 A rampart (*lit. & fig.*). *arch.* M16.
†**2** A dam, a barrier. L16–M18.
3 A raised road or way; the highway. *dial.* M19.

rampire /ˈrampʌɪə/ *verb trans. arch.* Also **-pier** /-pɪə/. M16.
[French *remparer* fortify, formed as RE- + *emparer* take possession of from Provençal *amparer* from Proto-Romance word, from Latin ANTE- + *parare* PREPARE *verb*. English endings unexpl.]
†**1** Strengthen (a bulwark, gate, etc.) against attack; block or close *up*, esp. by piling earth behind. M16–M17.
2 Fortify or protect (a place), esp. by a rampart. M16.
3 Shut *up* or *out* as with a rampart. *rare*. M16.
†**4** Fix or establish firmly. *rare*. M16–M17.

ramps /ram(p)s/ *noun* (treated as *sing.* or *pl.*). LME.
[Var. of RAMS.]
1 = RAMSONS. *Scot. & north.* LME.
2 = RAMP *noun*² 3b. *US*. M20.

rampsman /ˈram(p)smən/ *noun. slang.* Pl. **-men**. M19.
[from RAMP *noun*³ + -S¹ + MAN *noun*.]
A man who commits robbery with violence.

ramrod /ˈramrɒd/ *noun, adjective, adverb, & verb*. M18.
[from RAM *verb*¹ + ROD *noun*.]
▶ **A** *noun*. **1** A rod for ramming down the charge of a muzzle-loading firearm; *transf.* a thing that is very straight or rigid. Cf. RAMMER. M18.
2 A foreman, a manager. *N. Amer.* L19.
3 The erect penis. *slang*. E20.
▶ **B** *attrib.* or as *adjective*. Rigid, inflexible; solemn, formal. E20.

📖 J. A. MICHENER A man of . . ramrod rectitude.

▶ **C** *adverb*. Like a ramrod. M20.

📖 A. BROOKNER Sofka's back is ramrod straight.

▶ **D** *verb trans.* Infl. **-dd-**. Force or drive as with a ramrod; *N. Amer.* manage, direct. M20.

rams /ramz/ *noun* (treated as *sing.* or *pl.*). Long *obsolete* exc. *dial.* See also RAMPS.
[Old English *hramsa*, *-se* = Middle Low German *ramese*, German *Rams*, Danish, Swedish, & Norwegian dial. *rams*, cogn. with Old Irish *crem* (Irish & Gaelic *creamh*, Welsh *cra*), Lithuanian *kermùszė*, Russian *cheremsha* wild garlic, Greek *kromuon* onion.]
= RAMSONS.

ram-sammy /ramˈsami/ *noun. slang* (orig. *dial.*). L19.
[Origin unkn.]
A family quarrel; a noisy gathering; a fight.

Ramsauer /ˈramzaʊə/ *noun*. M20.
[from C. W. *Ramsauer* (1879–1955), German physicist.]
PHYSICS. More fully ***Ramsauer–Townsend*** [J. S. E. *Townsend* (1868–1957), Irish physicist.]
1 ***Ramsauer effect***, the sharp decrease, almost to zero, of the scattering cross-section of atoms of noble gases for electrons with energies below a critical value. M20.
2 ***Ramsauer minimum***, the minimum in the scattering cross-section for electrons exhibiting the Ramsauer effect. M20.

Ramsch /ramʃ/ *noun*. M19.
[German = junk, soiled goods.]
CARDS. A round or game of skat in which jacks are trumps and the object is to score the fewest points.

Ramsden /ˈramzd(ə)n/ *noun*. L18.
[Jesse *Ramsden* (1735–1800), English instrument-maker.]
Used *attrib.* and in *possess.* to designate an eyepiece particularly suited to the use of a graticule, consisting of two planoconvex lenses of equal focal length with their convex surfaces towards each other and a separation of two-thirds of their focal length.

ramshack /ˈramʃak/ *verb trans. US Black English*. E20.
[Alt.]
Ransack.

ramshackle /ˈramʃak(ə)l/ *adjective & noun*. E19.
[Alt. of next.]
▶ **A** *adjective*. **1** Of a person, action, etc.: unsteady, irregular, disorderly. Chiefly *dial.* E19.
2 Esp. of a building or vehicle: loose and shaky, as if ready to fall to pieces; rickety, tumbledown. M19.
▶ **B** *noun*. **1** A thoughtless or reckless person. *dial.* E19.
2 A ramshackle object. *rare*. E19.
▪ **ramshackledom** *noun* ramshackleness M20. **ramshackleness** *noun* ramshackle character or state E20. **ramshackly** *adjective* = RAMSHACKLE *adjective* M19.

ramshackled /ˈramʃak(ə)ld/ *adjective*. L17.
[Alt. of *ransackled* pa. pple of RANSACKLE.]
= RAMSHACKLE *adjective* 1.
▪ Also **ramshackling** *adjective* E19.

ramsons /ˈrams(ə)nz/ *noun pl.* (now treated as *sing.*). Also (earlier, now *dial.*) **ramson** /-s(ə)n/.
[Old English *hramsan* pl. of *hramsa*, *-se* (see RAMS), but later taken as sing., with pl. *-s*.]
A wild garlic, *Allium ursinum*, with broad flat leaves and umbels of white flowers, native to damp woods; its bulbous root, formerly eaten as a relish.

ram-stam /ˈramstam/ *adverb, adjective, & noun. Scot. & north.* M18.
[Origin unkn. Sense C.2 may be a different word.]
▶ **A** *adverb*. Impetuously, headlong. M18.
▶ **B** *adjective*. Impetuous, headstrong. L18.
▶ **C** *noun*. **1 a** Impetuous or headstrong action. L18. ▶**b** An impetuous or headstrong person. E19.
2 Beer drawn from the first mash in brewing. L18.

ramtil /ˈramtɪl/ *noun*. M19.
[Bengali *rāmtil*, from *rām* beautiful, excellent (freq. prefixed to names of plants to denote special varieties) + TIL *noun*.]
In the Indian subcontinent: the plant *Guizotia abyssinica* of the composite family, cultivated for the oil pressed from the seeds (Niger seeds).

ramulus /ˈramjʊləs/ *noun*. Pl. **-li** /-lʌɪ, -liː/. L18.
[Latin, dim. of next.]
ANATOMY & BIOLOGY. A small ramus or branch.
▪ **ramulet** *noun* (*rare*) = RAMULUS L17. **ramulose** *adjective* possessing or characterized by ramuli M18. **ramulous** *adjective* = RAMULOSE M17.

ramus /ˈreɪməs/ *noun*. Pl. **-mi** /-mʌɪ, -miː/. M17.
[Latin = branch.]
1 ANATOMY. **a** A major branch of a nerve. M17. ▶**b** An arm or branch of a bone, esp. of the ischium and pubes; either of the two arms of the jawbone. M18.
2 ZOOLOGY. **a** Any of various structures in invertebrates that have the form of a projecting arm, often one of two or more that are conjoined or adjacent. M19. ▶**b** A barb of a feather. L19.
1a ramus communicans /kəˈmjuːnɪkanz/, pl. **rami communicantes** /kəmjuːnɪˈkantiːz/ [= communicating] a branch of one nerve that joins another; *esp.* one joining a sympathetic ganglion with a spinal nerve.

ramuscule /rəˈmʌskjuːl/ *noun. rare.* Also in Latin form **-culus** /-kjʊləs/, pl. **-li** /-lʌɪ, -liː/. M19.
[Late Latin *ramusculus* dim. of Latin RAMUS: see -CULE.]
ANATOMY & BIOLOGY. A small branch or ramus.

RAN *abbreviation*.
Royal Australian Navy.

ran /ran/ *noun*. L16.
[Origin unkn.]
1 A certain width of a net. *dial.* L16.
2 A certain length of twine. Now *Canad. dial.* M18

ran *verb pa. t.* of RUN *verb*.

Rana /ˈrɑːnə/ *noun*. M20.
[Hindi & Nepali *rānā* prince, from Prakrit *rāṇa* from *rānī* RANEE.]
Chiefly *Hist.* (The title of) a member of the family which virtually ruled Nepal from 1846 to 1951.

†**ranai** *noun* var. of LANAI.

ranalian /rəˈneɪlɪən/ *adjective*. E20.
[from mod. Latin *Ranales*, from RAN(UNCULUS + Latin *-ales* pl. of *-alis* -AL¹: see -IAN.]
BOTANY. Of or pertaining to the Ranales, a subclass of dicotyledons which includes the Ranunculales, the Magnoliales, the Laurales, and several other orders.

ranarian /rəˈnɛːrɪən/ *adjective. rare*. E19.
[from Latin *rana* frog + -ARIAN.]
Resembling (that of) a frog.

rance /rɑːns/ *noun*¹. L16.
[Prob. from French.]
A kind of variegated white, red, and blue marble.

rance /rans/ *noun*² *& verb*. Chiefly *Scot. & techn.* E17.
[Prob. from Old & mod. French *ranche*, of unkn. origin.]
▶ **A** *noun*. A bar, a prop, a support. E17.
▶ **B** *verb trans.* Support with a rance, prop up, brace. E19.

rancel /ˈrans(ə)l/ *verb intrans. & trans. Scot.* Also **-sel**. Infl. **-ll-**. E17.
[Origin uncertain: cf. Old Norse *rannsaka* RANSACK *verb*, *reyna* try, investigate.]
Search for (stolen goods).
Comb.: **rancelman** a local officer formerly appointed in Orkney and Shetland to inquire into thefts and petty offences and to preserve good order.
▪ **rancellor** *noun* a rancelman E17.

ranch /rɑːn(t)ʃ/ *noun*. E19.
[Anglicized from RANCHO.]
1 a A hut or house in the country. *US*. E19. ▶**b** In full ***ranch bungalow***, ***ranch house***, etc. A single-storey or split-level house. *N. Amer.* M19.
2 A large cattle-breeding establishment, esp. in N. America; a large establishment where animals of some other kind (esp. foxes or mink) are bred, or a particular crop grown (freq. with specifying word). E19.
3 (Usu. **R-**.) More fully ***Ranch dressing***. (Proprietary name for) a type of thick white salad dressing made with sour cream and garlic. Chiefly *N. Amer.* L20.
Comb.: ***ranch bungalow***: see sense 1b above; ***Ranch dressing***: see sense 3 above; **ranch egg** *US* a fresh egg; **ranch house** *N. Amer.* (*a*) a house on a ranch; (*b*) see sense 1b above; **ranchman** = RANCHER 1; **ranch mink** a mink bred on a ranch; the fur of such a mink; a coat made of such fur; **ranchslider** *NZ* an exterior glass sliding door; **ranch wagon** *US* (*a*) a horse-drawn wagon used on a ranch; (*b*) an estate car.
▪ **ranˈchette** *noun* (*US*) a small modern ranch house M20.

ranch /rɑːn(t)ʃ/ *verb*¹. M19.
[from the noun.]
1 *verb intrans.* Run a ranch. M19.
2 *verb trans.* Put (an animal) on a ranch; breed or rear on a ranch or in large numbers. M19.
3 *verb trans.* Use (land) as a ranch. E20.

📖 **2** *Daily Telegraph* Salmon ranching . . and tourism are the immediate projects.

ranch /rɑːn(t)ʃ/ *verb*² *trans. obsolete* exc. *dial.* L15.
[Nasalized form of RACE *verb*³.]
Tear, cut, scratch.

rancher /ˈrɑːn(t)ʃə/ *noun*. Chiefly *N. Amer.* M19.
[from RANCH *noun* + -ER¹.]
1 An owner of a ranch; a person employed on a ranch. M19.
2 A modern ranch house. M20.

ranchera /rɑːnˈtʃɛːrə/ *noun*. E20.
[from Spanish *cancion ranchera* farmers' songs.]
A type of Mexican country music typically played with guitars and horns; a tune or song of this type.

rancheria /rɑːn(t)ʃəˈriːə/ *noun*. E17.
[Spanish *ranchería*, formed as RANCHO.]
In Spanish America and the western US: a collection of Indian huts; a place or house where a number of rancheros live.

ranchero /rɑːnˈtʃɛːrəʊ/ *noun*. Pl. **-os**. E19.
[Spanish, formed as RANCHO.]
A rancher or ranchman, esp. in Mexico.

ranchito /rɑːnˈtʃiːtəʊ/ *noun*. Pl. **-os**. M19.
[Spanish, dim. of *rancho* RANCHO.]
In the western US: a small ranch or farm.

rancho /ˈrɑːn(t)ʃəʊ/ *noun.* Pl. **-os**. E19.
[Spanish = a group of people who eat together.]
1 In Latin America: a hut, a hovel, a very simple building; a group of these, a small village; *esp.* one put up to accommodate travellers. Later also, a roadhouse, an inn; a meal at such a place. E19.
2 In the western US: a cattle-farm, a ranch. M19.

ranchy /ˈrɑːn(t)ʃi/ *adjective. US slang.* E20.
[Perh. alt. of RAUNCHY.]
Dirty, disgusting, indecent.

rancid /ˈransɪd/ *adjective.* E17.
[Latin *rancidus*: see -ID[1].]
Having the rank unpleasant taste or smell characteristic of oils and fats when no longer fresh; designating such a taste or smell; *fig.* nasty, disagreeable, odious.
■ **ranˈcidity** *noun* the quality or state of being rancid M17. **rancidness** *noun* M18.

rancíéite /ransɪˈeɪʌɪt/ *noun.* E20.
[from *Rancié*, a mountain in the French Pyrenees + -ITE[1].]
MINERALOGY. A hydrated oxide of calcium and manganese, occurring as soft flakes and as compact or friable masses.
■ Also †**rancierite** *noun* M19–E20.

rancio /ˈrɑːnθɪəʊ, *foreign* ˈranθio/ *adjective & noun.* M19.
[Spanish, lit. 'rancid', formed as RANCID.]
▶ **A** *adjective.* Of wine: having the distinctive bouquet, nutty flavour, or tawny colour characteristic of certain well-matured, fortified, or dessert wines. M19.
▶ **B** *noun.* Pl. **-os** /-əʊz, *foreign* -ɔs/. A rancio wine. M20.

rancour /ˈraŋkə/ *noun.* Also ***-or**. ME.
[Old French (mod. *rancœur*) from late Latin *rancor* rankness, (in Vulgate) bitter grudge, rel. to Latin *rancidus* RANCID: see -OUR.]
1 Inveterate and bitter ill feeling; malignant hatred or spitefulness. ME.
†**2** Rancid smell; rancidity; rankness. *rare.* LME–M16.

> **1** S. K. PENMAN Sarcasm was offered almost absently, without rancour.

■ **rancorous** *adjective* (*a*) of the nature of rancour; proceeding from or exhibiting rancour; †(*b*) (of a wound or sore) festering, inflamed: E16. **rancorously** *adverb* M17.

rancour /ˈraŋkə/ *verb.* Now *rare* or *obsolete*. Also **-or**. M16.
[from the noun.]
1 *verb intrans.* Have rancorous feelings; (of a feeling) rankle. M16.
2 *verb trans.* Instil rancour in; make rancorous. E17.

rand /rand/ *noun*[1]. See also ROND.
[Old English *rand*, corresp. to Old Frisian *rond*, Old Saxon (Dutch) *rand*, Old High German *rant* (German *Rand*), Old Norse *rǫnd* edge, rim of shield, from Germanic.]
1 A border or margin of esp. marshy land. *obsolete* exc. *dial.* OE. ▸**b** *gen.* A rim, a margin. Chiefly *Scot.* M18.
2 A strip or long slice of meat or fish. *obsolete* exc. *dial.* ME.
3 A strip of leather placed under the counter of a boot or shoe to make it level before the lifts of the heel are attached. L16.
†**4** A piece or mass of ice. *rare.* M17–E18.
5 In basket-making, a single rod worked alternately in front of and behind the stakes. E20.

rand /rand, rant/ *noun*[2]. *S. Afr.* Pl. **-s**, (in sense 2 also) same. M19.
[Afrikaans from Dutch *rand* edge: see prec.]
1 A rocky ridge or area of high sloping ground, esp. overlooking a river-valley; *spec.* (**the Rand**), the Witwatersrand, the chief gold-mining area of Transvaal. M19.
2 The basic monetary unit of South Africa since 1961, equal to 100 cents, and also of Namibia and (formerly) certain other countries of southern Africa. M20.

rand /rand/ *verb*[1]. ME.
[from RAND *noun*[1].]
†**1** *verb trans.* Cut into strips. ME–M17.
2 *verb trans. & intrans.* Weave with rands. E20.

†**rand** *verb*[2] *intrans. rare.* E17–E18.
[Dutch †*randen* var. of *ranten* RANT *verb*.]
Rave, rant.

randan /ranˈdan/ *noun*[1]. Now chiefly *Scot.* E18.
[Perh. alt. of French *randon* RANDOM.]
Riotous or disorderly behaviour; a spree. Freq. in **on the randan**.

randan /ranˈdan/ *adverb & noun*[2]. E19.
[Origin unkn.]
▶ **A** *adverb.* With a pair of sculls and a pair of oars (see sense B.1). E19.
▶ **B** *noun.* **1** A style of rowing in which the middle one of three rowers pulls a pair of sculls and the stroke and bow an oar each. M19.
2 A boat for rowing in this way. Also **randan boat** etc. L19.

R & B *abbreviation.*
Rhythm and blues. Cf. R'N'B.

R & D *abbreviation.*
Research and development.

randem /ˈrandəm/ *adverb & noun.* E19.
[Prob. alt. of RANDOM after TANDEM.]
▶ **A** *adverb.* With three horses harnessed in tandem. E19.
▶ **B** *noun.* A carriage or team driven in this fashion. L19.

randing /ˈrandɪŋ/ *noun.* M19.
[Perh. from RAND *noun*[1] + -ING[1].]
A kind of basketwork used in making gabions (MILITARY); the action or process of weaving with rands; randed work.

randjie /ˈraŋki/ *noun. S. Afr.* L19.
[Afrikaans from Dutch *randje* dim. of *rand* RAND *noun*[2].]
A narrow ridge of rocky ground.

randkluft /ˈrantklʊft/ *noun.* Pl. **-klufts**, ***-klüfte*** /-klyftə/. E20.
[German, lit. 'edge, crevice'.]
A crevasse between the head of a glacier and a surrounding rock wall.

Randlord /ˈrandlɔːd/ *noun. S. Afr.* E20.
[from RAND *noun*[2] + LORD *noun*, after *landlord*.]
A mining tycoon on the Rand.

random /ˈrandəm/ *noun, adverb, & adjective.* ME.
[Old French *randon* great speed, rel. to *randir* run impetuously, gallop, from Germanic base also of RAND *noun*[1]. For the dissimilation of *n . . n* to *n . . m* cf. RANSOM *noun*.]
▶ **A** *noun.* †**1** Great speed, force, or violence in riding, running, striking, etc. (chiefly in **with great random**, **in great random**). Also, an impetuous rush, a rapid headlong course (chiefly in **in a random**, **on a random**, **with a random**). ME–L19.
2 A haphazard or aimless course (now *rare*); that which is haphazard or without definite aim or purpose; randomness. M16.
†**3** The range of a piece of ordnance; *esp.* the long or full range obtained by elevating the muzzle; the degree of elevation given to a gun, *esp.* that supposed to give the greatest range. L16–M18.
4 MINING. The direction of a rake, vein, etc. M17.
5 PRINTING. A sloping board forming part of a compositor's frame, used for making up pages. L19.
Phrases: **at random** †(*a*) at great speed, with great violence; (*b*) haphazardly, without aim, purpose, or principle; †(*c*) in a neglected condition; †(*d*) at liberty, free from restraint; †(*e*) at any range other than point-blank.
▶ **B** *adverb.* At random. Chiefly & now only in comb. with pa. pples. E17.

> TENNYSON A drift of foliage random-blown.

▶ **C** *adjective.* **1** Not sent or guided in a special direction; having no definite aim or purpose; made, done, occurring, etc., without method or conscious choice. M17. ▸**b** STATISTICS. Governed by or involving equal chances for each of the actual or hypothetical members of a population; produced or obtained by a process of this kind (and therefore completely unpredictable in detail). L19.
2 Of masonry: in which the stones are of irregular sizes and shapes. E19.
3 Of a person: leading an unconventional or lawless life. *rare.* E19.

> **1** P. BARKER The suitcase into which he'd thrown an almost random selection of clothes. **b** F. C. MILLS Great care is . . needed in securing a purely random selection. *Which?* A random telephone survey of pubs.

Special collocations: **random-access** *adjective* (COMPUTING) (of a memory or file) having all parts directly accessible, so that it need not be read sequentially; *esp.* such that the access time for any item is effectively independent of both the location and the access time of the item last accessed. **random distribution** a probability distribution, *esp.* the Poisson distribution. **random error** an error in measurement caused by factors which vary unpredictably from one measurement to another. **random number** (*a*) a number selected from a given set of numbers in such a way that all the numbers in the set have the same chance of selection; (*b*) a pseudorandom number. **random sample** a sample drawn at random from a population, each member of it having an equal or other specified chance of inclusion (sometimes contrasted with a quota sample). **random shot** a shot fired at random (orig., other than point-blank). **random variable**: whose values are distributed in accordance with a probability distribution. **random walk** STATISTICS the movement of something in successive steps, the direction etc. of each step being governed by chance independently of preceding steps.
■ **randoˈmicity** *noun* randomness M20. **randomiˈzation** *noun* the action, process, or result of randomizing something E20. **randomize** *verb trans.* make unpredictable, unsystematic, or random in order or arrangement; employ random selection or sampling in (an experiment or procedure): E20. **randomizer** *noun* a device which generates random output L20. **randomly** *adverb* M19. **randomness** *noun* the quality or state of being random M19.

randori /ranˈdɔːri/ *noun.* E20.
[Japanese, from *ran* disorder + *tori* bout, participation.]
Free or informal judo practice.

R & R *abbreviation.*
1 MEDICINE. Rescue and resuscitation.
2 Rest and recreation. *colloq.* (orig. MILITARY).
3 Rock and roll. Cf. R'N'R.

randy /ˈrandi/ *noun*[1] *& verb. dial.* E19.
[Origin uncertain: perh. abbreviation of RENDEZVOUS *noun*, *verb* or from RANDY *adjective*.]
▶ **A** *noun.* A noisy merrymaking or revel, a spree. E19.
▶ **B** *verb intrans.* Make merry. M19.

randy /ˈrandi/ *adjective & noun*[2]. M17.
[Origin uncertain: perh. from RAND *verb*[2] + -Y[1].]
▶ **A** *adjective.* **1** Esp. of a beggar or (later) a woman: having a rude aggressive manner; loud and coarse-spoken. Of language: coarse. *Scot.* M17.
2 Boisterous, riotous, disorderly; unruly, unmanageable. *Scot. & dial.* E18.
3 Lustful, lewd, sexually promiscuous; eager for sexual gratification. Orig. *dial.* M19.
▶ **B** *noun.* An aggressive beggar; a scold, a virago. *Scot. & north.* E18.
■ **randily** *adverb* lustfully L20. **randiness** *noun* eagerness for sexual gratification E20.

ranee /ˈrɑːniː/ *noun.* Also **rani**, (as a title) **R-**. L17.
[Hindi *rānī* from Prakrit from Sanskrit *rājñī* fem. of *rājan* RAJA *noun*[1].]
Hist. A Hindu queen; a raja's wife or widow.

Raney nickel /ˈreɪnɪ nɪk(ə)l/ *noun phr.* M20.
[Murray *Raney* (1885–1966), US engineer.]
CHEMISTRY. (Proprietary name for) a form of nickel catalyst with a high surface area, used in organic hydrogenation reactions.

rang *verb pa. t.*: see RING *verb*[1].

rangatira /rangaˈtira/ *noun. NZ.* E19.
[Maori.]
A member of the Maori nobility.

range /reɪn(d)ʒ/ *noun*[1]. See also RINGE. ME.
[Old French, formed as RANGE *verb*[1].]
▶ **I 1** A row, line, or series of people or things. Now *rare* exc. as in sense 2 below. ME.
2 *spec.* **a** A row of buildings; a continuous stretch of building. E17. ▸**b** A series of hills or esp. mountains; *Austral.* a mountain (usu. in *pl.*). E18. ▸**c** A series of townships extending north and south parallel to the principal meridian of a survey. *N. Amer.* L18. ▸**d** MATH. A set of points on a straight line. M19.
3 A rank, a class. *rare.* E17.
4 a The position of a gun in firing. Formerly also, the direction of a shot. M17. ▸**b** *gen.* Lie, direction. L17.

> **1** N. FREELING In a range of little drawers were small objects wrapped in tissue. **2a** HUGH MILLER The range had been inhabited . . by a crew of fishermen. **b** N. CALDER The coast ranges of western North America. **4b** M. CUTLER The range of the . . valleys is . . from north to south.

▶ **II 5 a** The action or an act of ranging or moving about (now *rare*); *Scot.* a walk, a stroll. LME. ▸**b** Opportunity or scope for ranging; space. LME.
6 An area of ground intended or suitable for ranging; *esp.* (an extensive stretch of) grazing or hunting ground. Formerly also *spec.*, the lists in a tournament. LME.
7 The maximum distance attainable by something; the distance between an object and its target; *spec.* (*a*) the maximum distance to which a weapon can propel a missile; (*b*) NUCLEAR PHYSICS the maximum distance which an ionizing particle of a given energy can travel in a given medium; (*c*) the maximum distance at which a radio transmission can be effectively received; (*d*) the distance that can normally be covered by a vehicle or aircraft without refuelling; (*e*) the distance between a camera and the subject to be photographed. L16. ▸**b** An open or enclosed area having a target or targets for shooting practice. Also, an area of land or sea used as a testing-ground for military equipment etc. M19.
8 a The area or extent covered by or included in some concept etc. M17. ▸**b** A series or scale extending between certain limits and representing variation. Freq. foll. by *of*. Cf. sense 1 above. E19.
9 The area between limits of variation over which a person or thing is effective; *spec.* (*a*) the compass of a voice or musical instrument; (*b*) the scope of a person's knowledge or abilities. E19. ▸**b** STATISTICS. The difference observed in any sample between the largest and the smallest values of a given variate; the difference between the largest and smallest possible values of a random variable. E20. ▸**c** MATH. The set of values that the dependent variable of a function can take; the set comprising all the second elements of the ordered pairs constituting some given set. E20.
10 The area or period over or during which the occurrence of something is possible; *spec.* (BOTANY & ZOOLOGY) the geographical area, depth of water, or period of geological time over which a certain plant or animal is found. M19.

📖 **5b** E. YOUNG Eliminate my spirit, give it range Through provinces of thought. **6** *Poultry World* On range . . birds . . were also more at risk from disease. *attrib.*: *Times* Range animals have . . less fat than domestic livestock. **7** R. V. JONES Radar gave an indication of the range . . of the target. F. HOYLE The range of a . . stone or spear. **8a** A. BRIGGS The range of . . discussion was limited. D. M. DAVIN The range of his interests was . . wide. **b** F. SPALDING A motley range of acquaintance. *Antiquity* A range of arrow types were used with the Medieval longbow. *Truck* The . . Leyland and Daf truck ranges. **9** M. PUZO My client can do things . . that even Mr. Hoover might find out of his range. R. FRAME I drifted out of hearing range.

▶**III 11** Orig., a fireplace or simple apparatus used for cooking. Now *spec.* a large cooking stove heated by solid fuel, oil, gas, or electricity, having hotplates or burners on the top and one or more ovens, all of which are kept continually hot; *N. Amer.* any gas or electric cooker. LME. **12 a** A strip of some material, esp. leather. *rare.* E16. ▶†**b** A fence, a railing; an enclosed area. M16–L18. ▶**c** A wooden pole or shaft for attaching a rope to, esp. on a ship. Now chiefly *dial.* & *Hist.* M17.

📖 **11** M. FRAYN They cooked on a skilfully restored . . Victorian range.

Phrases: **at close range** at a short distance, very near. **at long range** at a long distance, far away. **at short range** = *at close range* above. **cooking range** = sense 11 above. ***dynamic range***: see DYNAMIC *adjective*. ***free range***: see FREE *adjective*. ***main range***: see MAIN *adjective*. ***open range***: see OPEN *adjective*. ***visual range***: see VISUAL *adjective*.

Comb.: **range beacon** a radio beacon for navigation; **range-change** *noun* & *adjective* (a gearbox) having the gears arranged progressively in series rather than in a zigzag design; **rangefinder** an instrument attached to a gun, camera, etc., for estimating the distance from the target or subject; **rangefinding** the action of estimating the distance from a target or subject; **rangeland** (an extensive area of) open country used for grazing or hunting animals (cf. sense 6 above); **range-plate** a ring-burner on top of a cooking range; **range-proof** *adjective* (*N. Amer.*) (of a cooking pot etc.) suitable for use on a hot-plate or burner; **range safety crew** a team responsible for ensuring general safety on a missile range in the event of a missile straying off course; **range safety officer** the principal member of a range safety crew; **range war** *US HISTORY* a struggle for the control of a cattle or sheep range;

■ **ran'gette** *noun* (*N. Amer. & NZ*) a small gas or electric cooker M20.

range /reɪn(d)ʒ/ *noun*[2]. Long *dial.* M16.
[Origin unkn. Cf. RANGE *verb*[2].]
A kind of sieve.

range /reɪn(d)ʒ/ *verb*[1]. LME.
[Old French *rangier*, *rengier* (mod. *ranger*), formed as RANK *noun*.]
▶**I 1** *verb trans.* Draw up (an army etc.) in ranks; set out in a row or rows; *gen.* arrange, dispose. Usu. in *pass.* or *refl.* LME. ▶**b** Lay out or set down (a line or curve); *NAUTICAL* lay out (a cable) before lowering the anchor. LME. ▶**c** Make straight or level; *esp.* (*TYPOGRAPHY*) make (type) lie flush at the ends of successive lines, align. M19. ▶**d** In *pass.* Be provided *with* a row or rows of something. M19.
2 *verb intrans.* Stretch out or stand in a row; extend. LME. ▶**b** Lie in the same line or plane *with*; *TYPOGRAPHY* (of type etc.) lie flush, be in alignment. L16.
3 *verb trans.* Place in a specified position, situation, or company. Foll. by *against*, *among*, *round*, *with*, etc. Usu. in *pass.* or *refl.* L16. ▶†**b** Cause to submit or obey. Foll. by *to*, *under*. E–M17.
4 *verb intrans.* Move into or occupy a certain position; be part of or ally oneself with a certain group. Usu. foll. by *in*, *with*. L16.
5 *verb trans.* Place *in* a certain class or category; divide *into* classes. E17.
6 *verb refl.* [French *se ranger*.] = RANGER *verb*[1]. M19.

📖 **1** J. BETJEMAN Hereditary peers Are ranged in rows. W. BOYD A large cinema screen with rows of seats ranged in front of it. P. ANGADI Everyone . . ranged themselves . . on cushions and chairs. **b ranging-pole**, **ranging-rod** *SURVEYING* a pole or rod for setting a straight line. **d** D. WELCH The bathroom shelves . . were ranged with medicine bottles. **2** T. DREISER The small stores which ranged in a row on this street. **3** H. MACMILLAN The . . powers now ranged round Russia and America. D. MAY Unhappy politicians ranged against enthusiastic businessmen. **4** THACKERAY In the . . matrimonial differences . . Beatrix ranged with her father.

▶**II 7** *verb intrans.* Move in all directions over or traverse a comparatively large area; rove, roam. Also (now *Scot.*), make a search; rummage. LME. ▶**b** *fig.* Change one's affections, be inconstant. Chiefly *poet.* L16. ▶**c** Of the eyes: glance over each of a series of objects in turn. E17.
8 *verb trans.* Traverse in all directions; roam over or through. M16. ▶**b** Sail along or about (the coast etc.). E17.
9 a *verb intrans.* With compl. (Of a projectile) cover a specified distance; (of a gun) send a projectile over a specified distance. M17. ▶**b** *verb trans.* (with *in*) & *intrans.* (with *on*). Assess the range of (a target), esp. before shooting. M20.
10 *verb intrans.* Vary within certain limits; form a varying set or series. Foll. by *between*, *from*, *within*, etc. M19. ▶**b** *BOTANY & ZOOLOGY.* Of a plant or animal: occur over a certain area or throughout a certain period of time. M19.
11 *verb trans.* Pasture (cattle) on a range. *US.* M19.

📖 **7** J. STEINBECK The paisanos ranged . . through the woods, calling Danny's name. *fig.*: J. N. ISBISTER The four essays range over a wide variety of topics. **b** BYRON I am given to range . . I've loved a great number. **c** E. L. DOCTOROW As she spoke her eyes ranged restlessly over the audience. **8** *fig.*: M. MOORCOCK Crime ranged the capital unchecked. **9b** R. V. JONES Radar-type transmissions . . appeared to be ranging on our convoys. **10** *Social History of Medicine* The papers presented ranged geographically from Finland . . to New Guinea. W. M. CLARKE Thirty pupils, ranging between the ages of nine and fifteen.

■ †**rangement** *noun* (*rare*) arrangement L17–M18.

range /reɪn(d)ʒ/ *verb*[2] *trans.* Long *dial.* M16.
[Origin unkn. Cf. RANGE *noun*[2].]
Sift (meal).

rangé /rɑ̃ʒe/ *adjective.* In sense 2 also (fem.) ***-ée***. L18.
[French, pa. ppl adjective of *ranger* RANGE *verb*[1].]
1 *HERALDRY.* Of charges: in a row, set within a band etc. Only in Dicts. L18.
2 Of a person, lifestyle, etc.: orderly, regular, settled. Cf. RANGE *verb*[1] 6. L19.

ranger /ˈreɪn(d)ʒə/ *noun.* ME.
[from RANGE *verb*[1] + -ER[1].]
1 a Orig., a forester, a gamekeeper; later, a keeper of a royal park. Now, a warden of a national or State park or forest; = ***forest ranger*** s.v. FOREST *noun.* ME. ▶**b** An officer employed to round up straying livestock etc. Orig. & chiefly *US.* M18.
2 *gen.* A person who or thing which ranges; *esp.* a rover, a wanderer; a horse or dog used to travel or hunt over a wide area. Also *spec.* (*Austral.*) = ***bush-ranger*** s.v. BUSH *noun*[1]. L16.
3 a A member of a body of armed (formerly esp. armed and mounted) troops employed in ranging over a tract of country (chiefly *US HISTORY*); *N. Amer.* a member of any of various regional police forces. L17. ▶**b** A member of an American commando unit. M20.
4 (**R-**.) More fully ***Ranger Guide***. A member of the senior branch of the Guides. E20.
2 lone ranger: see LONE *adjective* & *adverb*. **3** ***Texas Ranger***.
■ **rangership** *noun* the office or position of a forest or park ranger LME.

ranger /rɑ̃ʒe/ *verb*[1] *refl.* (*inf.*). M19.
[French *se ranger*.]
Adopt a more regular lifestyle; settle down. Cf. RANGE *verb*[1] 6.

📖 J. BUCHAN I heard . . you were goin' to be married . . What do you call it—*ranger* yourself?

ranger /ˈreɪn(d)ʒə/ *verb*[2] *intrans. US.* E20.
[from the noun.]
Act as a ranger; *esp.* round up straying livestock etc.

rangiora /raŋɪˈɔːrə/ *noun.* M19.
[Maori.]
A New Zealand evergreen shrub or small tree, *Brachyglottis repanda*, of the composite family, with woolly shoots and panicles of small greenish-white flowers.

rangle /ˈraŋg(ə)l/ *noun. rare.* L17.
[Origin unkn.]
Gravel given to a hawk to improve its digestion.

rangled /ˈraŋg(ə)ld/ *adjective.* M16.
[Origin uncertain: cf. WRANGLE *verb*.]
Wreathed; twisted.

rangoli /raŋˈgəʊli/ *noun.* M20.
[Marathi *rāgoḷī*.]
A Hindu symbolic design painted in coloured powdered stone, rice, etc.

Rangoon /raŋˈguːn/ *noun.* L19.
[The capital of Myanmar (Burma).]
Used *attrib.* to designate things found in or associated with Rangoon.
Rangoon bean the Lima bean, *Phaseolus lunatus* var. *limensis*. **Rangoon creeper** a climbing shrub of SE Asia, *Quisqualis indica* (family Combretaceae), bearing spikes of fragrant white flowers having an elongated calyx tube.

rangy /ˈreɪn(d)ʒi/ *adjective.* M19.
[from RANGE *noun*[1] or *verb*[1] + -Y[1].]
1 a Of an animal: adapted for or capable of ranging; having a long slender form. M19. ▶**b** Of a person: tall and thin. L19.
2 Mountainous. *Austral.* M19.
3 Of a place: giving scope for ranging; spacious. L19.

📖 **1a** N. LOWNDES The dog, once rangy and fit, had declined from lack of exercise. **b** P. D. JAMES His rangy graceless figure, over six feet high.

■ **rangily** *adverb* L20. **ranginess** *noun* L19.

rani *noun* var. of RANEE.

ranid /ˈreɪnɪd, ˈra-, ˈrɑː-/ *noun & adjective.* L19.
[mod. Latin *Ranidae* (see below), from Latin *rana* frog: see -ID[3].]
▶**A** *noun.* A frog of the family Ranidae, which includes the typical semi-aquatic frogs with protrusible tongues. L19.
▶**B** *adjective.* Of, pertaining to, or designating this family. E20.

raniform /ˈreɪnɪfɔːm, ˈran-, ˈrɑː-/ *adjective.* M19.
[from Latin *rana* frog + -I- + -FORM.]
Chiefly *ZOOLOGY.* Frog-shaped, having the form of a frog.

ranine /ˈreɪnʌɪn, ˈra-/ *adjective*[1]. E19.
[from RANULA + -INE[1].]
ANATOMY. Designating vessels etc. situated on the underside of the tip of the tongue (the part affected by ranula).

ranine /ˈreɪnʌɪn, ˈra-/ *adjective*[2]. *rare.* M19.
[from Latin *rana* frog + -INE[1].]
Of or pertaining to a frog or frogs; resembling (that of) a frog.

ranitidine /raˈnɪtɪdiːn, -ˈnʌɪt-/ *noun.* L20.
[from FU)RAN and NIT(RO- + -IDINE.]
PHARMACOLOGY. An antihistamine drug which is a sulphur-containing substituted furan used to treat ulcers and related conditions. Cf. ZANTAC.

ranivorous /rəˈnɪv(ə)rəs/ *adjective. rare.* E19.
[from Latin *rana* frog + -I- + -VOROUS.]
Frog-eating.

ranjau /ˈrandʒaʊ/ *noun.* Pl. same, **-s**. L18.
[Malay.]
Hist. In SE Asia: a bamboo or iron stake placed in the ground as a defence against attack.

rank /raŋk/ *noun.* See also RANK AND FILE. ME.
[Old French *ranc*, *renc*, (mod. *rang*) from Germanic base also of RING *noun*[1].]
1 A row, line, or series of things. Now chiefly *spec.* (***a***) a set of organ-pipes; (***b***) *TELEPHONY* a row of selectors; (***c***) (more fully ***taxi rank***) a row of taxis awaiting hire; the area where these wait. ME. ▶**b** A row or line of people. Now *rare* exc. as in sense 3 below. L16.
2 a High social position; professional, military, etc., distinction. LME. ▶**b** A distinct class or level within a hierarchy; a person's professional etc. position or status; *spec.* (*STATISTICS*) (a number specifying) position in a numerically ordered series. L16. ▶**c** *LINGUISTICS.* The position of a unit in a grammatical or phonological hierarchy. M20.
3 A line of soldiers drawn up abreast, esp. forming part of a formation; in *pl.*, forces, an army, *transf.* a group of people of a specified type. L16. ▶**b** *CHESS.* Each of the eight lines of squares running across the board from side to side. L16. ▶**c** In *pl.* *The* body of common soldiers; privates and corporals collectively. E19.
4 Order, array. Chiefly in phrs. below. L16.
†**5** A class, a set. L16–E18.
6 A tier. Now *rare*. L16.
7 *MATH.* The value or the order of the largest non-zero determinant of a given matrix; an analogous quantity in other kinds of group. M19.
8 The degree of metamorphic maturity, carbon content, and hardness of coal; grade. E20.

📖 **1** D. L. SAYERS The taxi-driver . . was standing on the rank. **2a** S. WEINTRAUB Her position required that someone of rank act *for* her. **b** H. BELLOC My rank . . is that of a merchant. S. BELLOW His rank was given in the paper as ensign. M. MOORCOCK Two generals . . together with a few soldiers of lesser rank. **3** J. HELLER The men . . groped their way into ranks of twelve outside the barracks. S. BIKO In the white ranks, too, the idea was heavily criticised. **c** J. REED Kerensky opened the officered schools to the ranks.

Phrases: **break rank(s)** fail to remain in line; move out of line; *fig.* end solidarity. ***close ranks***: see CLOSE *verb* 6. **keep rank** remain in line. ***other ranks***: see OTHER *adjective*. ***post rank***: see POST *noun*[4]. ***pull one's rank***, ***pull rank***: see PULL *verb*. ***reduce to the ranks***: see REDUCE 20. **rise from the ranks** (***a***) (of a private or non-commissioned officer) receive a commission; (***b***) *transf.* advance in status by one's own exertions. ***taxi rank***: see sense 1 above.

Comb.: **rank correlation** *STATISTICS* correlation between two ways of assigning ranks to the members of a set; **rank difference** *STATISTICS* the difference between two ranks assigned to the same thing; **rank order** *STATISTICS* an arrangement of the members of a set in order, with consecutive integers assigned to them; **rank-order** *verb trans.* arrange in rank order; **rankshift** *noun* & *verb trans.* (*LINGUISTICS*) (cause) a downgrading in the rank of a grammatical unit; **ranksman** *rare* (***a***) = RANKER (a); (***b***) a fishing boat accompanying another at sea.

■ **ranker** *noun* (***a***) a soldier in the ranks; (***b***) an officer who has risen from the ranks: L19.

rank /raŋk/ *adjective*, *verb*[1], & *adverb*.
[Old English *ranc* = Middle & mod. Low German *rank* long and thin, Old Norse *rakkr* erect, from Germanic.]
▶**A** *adjective.* **I** †**1** Proud, haughty; rebellious. OE–M16.
2 Stout, sturdy, strong. *obsolete* exc. *dial.* OE.
3 Having great speed or force; driving; violent. Now *rare.* ME.
▶**II** †**4** Fully grown, mature. *rare.* OE–M16.

5 Orig., vigorous or luxuriant in growth. Now, growing too luxuriantly, large and coarse; (of growth etc.) too luxuriant. ME. ▸**b** Covered (esp. excessively) with a luxuriant growth of vegetation; choked *with* weeds etc. LME. ▸**c** Esp. of land: excessively rich or fertile; liable to produce excessive vegetation. LME.

6 †**a** Abundant, copious. ME–M19. ▸**b** In close array; thick, dense. *obsolete* exc. *north.* LME. ▸**c** Numerous, frequent. *obsolete* exc. *north.* M16.

7 †**a** Excessively great or large; *esp.* fat, swollen; *fig.* too full *of* a specified quality etc. ME–M17. ▸**b** Of a sum of money: high, excessive. Now *rare* or *obsolete.* E17. ▸**c** *techn.* Projecting, standing out. L17.

> 🕮 **5** H. READ A rank growth of nettles. R. MACAULAY Dripping greenery that grew high and rank. **b** G. A. HENTY The patch . . now rank with weeds. R. ADAMS Hedgerows and verges were at their rankest and thickest. **7a** SHAKES. *Sonn.* A healthful state Which rank of goodness, would by ill be cured.

▸**III 8 a** Highly offensive or loathsome; *esp.* grossly coarse or indecent. Now *rare.* ME. ▸**b** Corrupt, foul; festering. L16.

9 Lustful, libidinous, (now *dial.*); (of a female bird or animal) in heat. LME.

10 a Having an offensive smell; rancid. E16. ▸**b** Of a smell: offensively strong. L16.

11 Esp. of a negative quality or condition: absolute, downright, thorough. E16. ▸**b** Grossly apparent. *rare.* E17.

> 🕮 **10a** E. BOWEN The hall was . . rank with cooling cigar-smoke. **b** C. MCCULLERS The rank odour of wet refuse. **11** L. MUMFORD Bacon's work brought him into rank disfavour. *Tennis World* Kramer's downfall . . was obviously rank bad luck. ***rank outsider***: see OUTSIDER.

▸**B** *verb. rare.*

†**1** *verb intrans.* Grow rank; fester, rot. ME–E17.

2 *verb trans.* In *pass.* Be projected outwards. M19.

▸**C** *adverb.* Now *dial.*

†**1** Rankly. Only in L16.

2 Completely, extremely. L16.

▪ **rankly** *adverb* OE. **rankness** *noun* LME.

rank /raŋk/ *verb*². L16.

[from the noun.]

1 a *verb trans.* Arrange (esp. soldiers) in a rank or in ranks; arrange in a row or rows, set in line. Freq. *refl.* or as ***ranked*** *ppl adjective.* L16. ▸**b** *verb intrans.* Form, or stand in, a rank or ranks. L16. ▸†**c** *verb trans.* In *pass.* Of a place: be surrounded *with* rows of something. Only in 17.

2 a *verb trans.* Assign to a certain rank in a scale or hierarchy; classify, rate; include within a specified rank or class (foll. by *among, with,* etc.). Freq. in *pass.* L16. ▸**b** *verb intrans.* Occupy a certain rank in a hierarchy; belong to a specified rank or class (foll. by *among, as, with,* etc.); be on a par *with.* L16.

†**3** *verb trans.* Divide *into* ranks or classes. M–L17.

4 LAW. **a** *verb trans.* Admit as a claimant in a bankruptcy. *Scot.* L17. ▸**b** *verb intrans.* Be admitted as a claim or claimant in a bankruptcy. Also, qualify *for.* L19.

5 *verb trans.* Outrank. Orig. & chiefly *US.* E19. ▸**b** MILITARY. Turn (a person) *out* of quarters etc. by virtue of superior rank. *US.* L19. ▸**c** Insult; put (a person) down. *US Black slang.* L20.

6 *verb intrans.* MILITARY. Move or march in rank. M19.

7 *verb trans.* Betray or expose (a person); spoil or thwart (an action). *US slang.* E20.

> 🕮 **1a** CARLYLE They all ranked themselves round me. *Harper's Magazine* The prisoners were then drawn up . . ranked six deep. **c** SHAKES. *Timon* The base o' th' mount Is ranked with . . deserts. **2a** W. H. AUDEN The sin of Gluttony Is ranked among the Deadly Seven. *Tennis* The British number 1, who was ranked 19 in the world. G. SAYER Students were ranked according to first-, second-, third-, or fourth-class honours. **b** C. CONNOLLY Proust . . so familiar as almost to rank as an English writer. T. CAPOTE Mr Clutter was entitled to rank among the . . patricians. H. MOORE Sumerian sculpture ranks with Early Greek. **5** *Delineator* The Secretary of State ranks all the other members of the Cabinet. **6** *Daily Telegraph* The King's Troop . . ranked past The Queen.

▪ **ranking** *noun & adjective* (**a**) *noun* the action of the verb; the relative position at which a person or thing is ranked; (**b**) *adjective* that ranks; *US* having a high rank or position: L16.

rank and file /raŋk (ə)nd 'fʌɪl/ *noun & adjectival phr.* Also (the usual form as adjective) **rank-and-file**. L16.

[from RANK *noun* + AND *conjunction*¹ + FILE *noun*².]

▸**A** *noun collect.* **1** The rows and columns of soldiers in military formation. Chiefly in ***in rank and file***. L16.

2 The ordinary soldiers, the ranks, (MILITARY); *transf.* the ordinary members of any group or society as opp. to the leader or principals. Treated as *pl.* or *sing.* L18.

> 🕮 **2** *Shop Assistant* We want . . the rank and file to back the Executive. *Honey* Top models . . earn good money, but what about the rank and file. C. A. MACARTNEY The rank and file . . were as a rule conscripted.

▸**B** *adjective.* Of, pertaining to, or characteristic of the rank and file; that is a member of the rank and file. L19.

> 🕮 V. G. KIERNAN The musket was a rank-and-file weapon. *Far Eastern Economic Review* A vacuum between rank-and-file workers and senior management.

▪ **rank-and-filer** *noun* a member of the rank and file E20.

ranket *noun* var. of RACKETT.

Rankine /'raŋkɪn/ *noun.* M19.

[W. J. M. *Rankine* (1820–72), Scot. physicist and engineer.]

Used *attrib.*, *postpositive*, and in *possess.* to designate concepts propounded by Rankine or arising out of his work.

degree Rankine a degree of the Rankine scale. **Rankine cycle** a thermodynamic cycle which describes the operation of an ideal composite engine worked by steam or vapour, used as a standard of efficiency. **Rankine degree** = ***degree Rankine*** above. **Rankine efficiency** the efficiency of an engine relative to that of an ideal engine following the Rankine cycle. **Rankine scale** a scale of absolute temperature (zero being identified with absolute zero) in which the degrees are equal in size to those of the Fahrenheit scale. **Rankine's formula** any of a number of formulae derived by Rankine, *spec.* a formula for the load under which a given column will collapse.

rankle /'raŋk(ə)l/ *verb & noun.* ME.

[Old French *ra(o)ncler* (cf. medieval Latin *ranclare, ranquillare*) var. of *draoncler* (mod. dial. *drancler*), from *ra(o)ncle* var. of *draoncle* ulcer, festering sore from medieval Latin *dranculus*, alt. of Latin *dracunculus* dim. of *draco* DRAGON.]

▸**A** *verb.* **1** *verb intrans.* Orig. of the body, later of a wound, sore, etc.: fester, esp. to a painful degree; suppurate. *arch.* ME.

2 †**a** *verb intrans.* Inflict a painful festering wound; cause a wound to fester. LME–L17. ▸**b** *verb trans.* Cause (a wound or flesh) to fester or become painful. *arch.* M16.

3 *verb intrans.* (Of a bad feeling) continue to be felt by a person; (of an experience, event, etc.) continue to cause bad, esp. bitter feelings. E16. ▸**b** *verb intrans.* Of a person: feel bitter; fret or chafe angrily. L16.

4 *verb trans.* Exacerbate (a bad feeling); embitter (a person); (of an experience, event, etc.) cause, or continue to cause, bad, esp. bitter, feelings in (a person). E17.

5 *verb intrans.* Change in state, pass *into*, as by festering. M18.

> 🕮 **3** E. TAYLOR The indiscretion . . remained to rankle. A. N. WILSON His nickname, as the Lady . . , rankled. **b** G. S. HAIGHT Rankling under the sense of injustice. **4** *Tennis* It rankles Mayotte . . to constantly have to defend the position. **5** *Times Lit. Suppl.* The Atomic Age into which the Machine Age has now rankled.

▸**B** *noun.* †**1** A festering sore. LME–L16.

2 A rankling thought or feeling; bitterness. L18.

rann /ran/ *noun.* M19.

[Irish.]

A piece of (Irish) verse; *spec.* (**a**) a stanza; (**b**) a quatrain.

rannel-tree /'ran(ə)ltriː/ *noun. Scot. & north.* Also (*Scot.*) **rantle-** /'rant(ə)l-/. L17.

[App. of Scandinavian origin: cf. Norwegian dial. *randa-tre*, from *rand* space above a fireplace.]

A wooden or iron bar fitted across a chimney, on which to hang pot-hooks etc.

ranny /'rani/ *noun. obsolete* exc. *dial.* M16.

[App. from Latin *araneus mus* lit. 'spider mouse' (cf. mod. Latin *Sorex araneus* common shrew).]

A shrew.

rannygazoo /ˌranɪgə'zuː/ *noun.* Chiefly *US dial. & slang.* E20.

[Origin unkn.]

A prank, a trick; horseplay.

ransack /'ransak/ *verb & noun.* ME.

[Old Norse *rannsaka*, from *rann* house + *-saka* rel. to *sækja* SEEK verb.]

▸**A** *verb.* †**1** *verb trans.* Search (a person) for a stolen or missing item. ME–L15.

2 *verb trans.* Search thoroughly in or throughout (a place, receptacle, collection of things, etc.) for or *for* something (formerly esp. for something stolen), esp. causing disorder or damage as a result. ME. ▸**b** *verb intrans.* Make a thorough search. Now *rare* or *obsolete.* ME. ▸†**c** *verb trans. & intrans.* Of a thing: penetrate (*through*). *poet.* M–L16.

3 *verb trans.* Examine thoroughly; investigate in detail. *arch.* ME.

4 a *verb trans. & intrans.* Rob (a person); plunder or pillage (a place). ME. ▸**b** *verb trans.* Carry off as plunder. Now *rare.* LME.

> 🕮 **2** E. BLISHEN Ransacked the desks, throwing open drawers, glancing at letters. *fig.*: *Listener* Ransacking the English language for . . epithets. **3** T. H. WHITE Surgeons carefully ransacking the wounds. **4a** L. GORDON Cromwell's soldiers ransacked the church.

▸**B** *noun.* The action or an act of ransacking. L16.

▪ **ransacker** *noun* ME.

ransackle /'ransak(ə)l/ *verb trans. obsolete* exc. *Scot. & north.* Also (*Scot.*) **-shackle** /-ʃak(ə)l/. E17.

[from RANSACK *verb* + -LE³.]

Search thoroughly, ransack.

ransel *verb* var. of RANCEL.

ransom /'rans(ə)m/ *noun.* ME.

[Old French *ransoun, raençon* (mod. *rançon*), from Latin *redemptio(n-)* REDEMPTION. For the dissimilation of *n . . n* to *n . . m* cf. RANDOM.]

1 A sum of money etc. paid or demanded for the release of a prisoner or the restoration of captured property. ME. ▸**b** *fig.* CHRISTIAN THEOLOGY. Christ regarded as a redeemer. ME. ▸**c** An exorbitant price or sum. *Scot.* E19.

2 The paying of a ransom; the action of procuring the release of a prisoner or recovering captured property by doing this. Now chiefly in ***hold to ransom*** s.v. HOLD *verb.* ME.

†**3** An action, payment, etc., demanded or done or made to obtain pardon; a fine. ME–M18.

> 🕮 **1** S. NAIPAUL He would not pay the ransom demanded for his kidnapped grandson. ***king's ransom***: see KING *noun.*

Comb.: **ransom-bill**, **ransom-bond** an undertaking to pay a ransom for something (formerly esp. for a captured ship); **ransom money**: demanded or given as a ransom; **ransom note** a usu. threatening letter from a kidnapper or kidnappers demanding money etc. as a ransom.

▪ **ransomer** *noun* (**a**) a person who pays a ransom; †(**b**) a person held to ransom for a ship: E18. **ransomless** *adjective* LME.

ransom /'rans(ə)m/ *verb trans.* ME.

[Old French *ransouner* (mod. *rançonner*), formed as prec.]

1 a CHRISTIAN THEOLOGY. Esp. of Christ: redeem or deliver (a person). ME. ▸**b** Atone or pay for; expiate. ME. ▸**c** Procure the release or restoration of by paying a ransom. LME.

2 Release (a prisoner) or restore (property etc.) on payment of a ransom. LME.

3 Demand or extract a ransom from or for. LME.

> 🕮 **1b** SHAKES. *Sonn.* Those tears . . are rich, and ransom all ill deeds. **c** C. THIRLWALL They were obliged to ransom not only their prisoners but their dead. **2** *International Combat Arms* Terrorists abducted and later ransomed five foreign businessmen. **3** J. BARTH Sindbad's daughter . . was ransomed and released.

▪ **ransomable** *adjective* E17.

rant /rant/ *verb & noun.* L16.

[Dutch *ranten* talk foolishly, rave.]

▸**A** *verb.* **1** *verb intrans.* & †*trans.* (with *it*). Behave in a boisterous or riotous manner; revel, romp. Also, sing loudly. Now chiefly *Scot.* L16.

2 *verb intrans.* & †*trans.* (with *it*). Use bombastic or grandiloquent language. E17. ▸**b** *verb trans.* Recite in a bombastic or declamatory style. M17.

3 *verb intrans.* †**a** Scold violently. Usu. foll. by *at.* M17–E18. ▸**b** Speak vehemently or intemperately; rave at length. (Foll. by *about, on.*) L19.

> 🕮 **1** R. BURNS Wi' quaffing and laughing, They ranted and sang. **2b** M. BARING Actors shout and rant Racine now. **3b** S. CHAPLIN People that rant on about . . religion. C. MUNGOSHI Father shouted in his sleep, ranting and raving.

▸**B** *noun.* **1** The action or an act of ranting; a piece of bombastic or declamatory speech or writing; a tirade. M17. ▸**b** Bombastic or declamatory language or sentiment. E18.

2 a A boisterous or riotous scene or occasion; a romp. *Scot. & north.* M17. ▸**b** A lively tune, song, or dance. Chiefly *Scot.* E18.

3 A state or condition characterized by ranting. E18.

> 🕮 **1** *Independent* I had little rant about the extent to which . . music fans were discriminated against. **b** E. LEWIS Excuse me laughing at this bit of newspaper rant.

▪ **rantingly** *adverb* in a ranting manner L18. **ranty** *adjective* (*Scot. & north.*) boisterous, riotous, lively L18.

ran-tan /'rantan/ *noun & verb.* M17.

[Imit.]

▸**A** *noun.* **1** A loud banging noise. M17.

2 A riot; a drinking-bout. M19.

▸**B** *verb intrans. & trans.* Infl. **-nn-**. Make a loud unruly noise outside the house of (a wife-beater). *north.* Now *rare.* M19.

ranter /'rantə/ *noun.* M17.

[from RANT *verb* + -ER¹.]

1 A person who rants or declaims noisily or bombastically. M17.

†**2** A person who leads a riotous or dissipated life; a rake. M17–E19. ▸**b** A lively singer or musician. *Scot.* E18–E19.

3 *Hist.* (**R-**.) ▸**a** A member of a 17th-cent. English antinomian sect. M17. ▸**b** A Primitive Methodist. E19.

▪ **Ranterism** *noun* (*Hist.*) the doctrine or practices of the Ranters L17.

ranter /'rantə/ *verb trans.* E17.

[French *rentrer, rentraire*: cf. RENTER *verb.*]

1 Darn, mend. *Scot. & dial.* E17.

2 = RENTER *verb.* E20.

ranterpike /ˈrantəpʌɪk/ *noun.* L19.
[Origin unkn.]
Hist. A type of three-masted schooner used esp. to transport pig-iron.

rantipole /ˈrantɪpəʊl/ *noun, adjective, & verb.* L17.
[Origin unkn. Cf. RAMP *noun*[1], RANTER *noun.*]
▶ **A** *noun.* A wild or ill-behaved person; a scolding or quarrelsome person. Now *rare* or *obsolete.* L17.
▶ **B** *adjective.* Wild, disorderly; rakish. E18.
▶ **C** *verb intrans.* Behave in a wild or noisy manner; romp about. E18.

rantle-tree *noun* see RANNEL-TREE.

†**rantum-scantum** *interjection, noun, & adjective. colloq.* E17.
[Rhyming comb., prob. from RANT.]
▶ **A** *interjection & noun.* Nonsense, rubbish. E17–L18.
▶ **B** *adjective.* Disorderly, hotchpotch. Only in 18.

ranula /ˈranjʊlə/ *noun.* M17.
[Latin, dim. of *rana* frog: see -ULE.]
MEDICINE. A cyst under the tongue, caused by the obstruction of the salivary ducts or glands; the condition characterized by this.
■ **ranular** *adjective* (*a*) of or pertaining to ranula; (*b*) *rare* = RANINE *adjective*[1]: M17.

ranunculi *noun pl.* see RANUNCULUS.

ranunculin /rəˈnʌŋkjʊlɪn/ *noun.* M20.
[from next + -IN[1].]
BIOCHEMISTRY. A glycoside produced by various buttercups, esp. *Ranunculus bulbosus*, which if eaten is liable to be metabolized to a toxic vesicant.

ranunculus /rəˈnʌŋkjʊləs/ *noun.* Pl. **-luses**, **-li** /-lʌɪ, -liː/. L16.
[Latin, lit. 'little frog', dim. of *rana* frog: see -CULE.]
A plant of the genus *Ranunculus* (family Ranunculaceae), which includes the buttercups, spearworts, water-crowfoots, and lesser celandine; *esp.* (more fully ***garden ranunculus***) the buttercup *R. asiaticus*, cultivated in various colours.
■ **ranuncuˈlaceous** *adjective* of or pertaining to the family Ranunculaceae, which includes the genus *Ranunculus* and also the anemones, hellebores, columbines, clematises, and delphiniums M19.

Ranvier /ˈrɑːnvɪeɪ, *foreign* rɑ̃vje/ *noun.* L19.
[L. A. *Ranvier* (1835–1922), French histologist.]
ANATOMY. ***node of Ranvier***, ***Ranvier's node***, each of the interruptions of the myelin which occur regularly along the sheaths of myelinated nerves between adjacent Schwann cells.

ranz-des-vaches /rɑ̃devaʃ/ *noun.* Pl. same. L18.
[Swiss French, from unkn. 1st elem. + 'of the cows'.]
A melody played esp. by Swiss cowherds, consisting of irregular phrases formed from the harmonic notes of the Alpine horn.

Rao /raʊ/ *noun.* L18.
[Hindi *rāo*, from Sanskrit *rājan* RAJA *noun*[1].]
In the Indian subcontinent: (the title of) a chief or prince.

RAOC *abbreviation.*
Royal Army Ordnance Corps.

Raoult's law /ˈraʊlz lɔː, raˈuːlz, ˈraʊlts/ *noun phr.* L19.
[François-Marie *Raoult* (1830–1901), French chemist.]
PHYSICAL CHEMISTRY. Either of two laws propounded by Raoult, (*a*) that the freezing and boiling points of an ideal solution are respectively depressed and elevated relative to that of the pure solvent by an amount proportional to the mole fraction of solute, (*b*) that the vapour pressure of an ideal solution is proportional to the mole fraction of solvent.

rap /rap/ *noun*[1]. ME.
[Rel. to RAP *verb*[1]: cf. Swedish *rapp*, Danish *rap.*]
1 a Orig., a severe blow with a weapon etc. Now, a smart light blow or stroke with a stick etc. ME. ▸**b** A sharp distinct knock (as) on a wooden surface; *esp.* a knock at a door. Also repr. the sound of such a knock. M17.
2 A moment. *Scot.* L17.
3 a A rebuke; an adverse criticism. *slang.* L18. ▸**b** A criminal accusation, a charge. Freq. with specifying word or words. *slang* (chiefly *N. Amer.*). E20. ▸**c** An identification from a group of suspects. *slang.* E20. ▸**d** A prison sentence. *slang* (chiefly *N. Amer.*). E20.
4 a Conversation, talk. *dial.* L19. ▸**b** A style of verbal display or repartee among black Americans; *gen.* (an) impromptu talk or discussion. *slang* (chiefly *US*). M20. ▸**c** A style of popular music developed by black New Yorkers in which words, usu. improvised and freq. rhyming, are recited rhythmically (rather than sung) over an instrumental backing with a pronounced beat (also ***rap music***); a song etc. in this style. L20.
5 A commendation. *Austral. colloq.* M20.

> 🕮 **1b** M. AMIS I.. rapped, with an upper-crust rap, on the knocker. **3a** *Cumberland News* Got a council room rap.. for jumping the gun over planning. *National Observer (US)* 'Mr Fixit' is coming to town and that is no rap on.. Carter. **b** *New Statesman* Hoffman was wanted on a drug peddling rap. **4b** T. LEARY He started a three-hour rap about energy. *Black Scholar* Indigenous, enduring black folk rap. **c** *Guardian* The music is up to standard, with the rap cleverly mixed with reggae and soul.

Phrases: **beat the rap** *slang* (chiefly *N. Amer.*) escape punishment, esp. a prison sentence. **bum rap**: see BUM *adjective.* **get the rap** *slang* suffer a rebuke; be blamed. **hang the rap on** *slang* charge (a suspect) with usu. circumstantial evidence. ***murder rap***: see MURDER *noun.* **pin the rap on** *slang* = ***hang the rap on*** above. **take the rap** accept responsibility and punishment (orig. for a crime). **tie the rap on** *slang* = ***hang the rap on*** above.
Comb.: **rap centre** *US slang* a meeting-place for group discussions; **rap group** (*a*) *US slang* a group that meets to discuss problems etc.; (*b*) a group which plays rap music; ***rap music***: see sense 4c above; **rap sheet** *slang* a police record.

rap /rap/ *noun*[2]. E18.
[Contr. of Irish *ropaire* robber, counterfeit coin.]
1 *Hist.* A counterfeit coin, worth about half a farthing, common in 18th-cent. Ireland. E18.
2 *transf. & fig.* **a** A worthless person. *arch. slang.* L18. ▸**b** Any small coin of low denomination (*arch.*); a very small amount, a jot. Chiefly in neg. contexts. E19.

> 🕮 **2b** H. JAMES The English don't care a rap what you say. M. MITCHELL She doesn't give a rap about him. **not a rap** *arch.* no money whatever.

rap /rap/ *noun*[3]. Now *Scot. & dial.* E18.
[Origin uncertain: cf. Norwegian *rabb* ridge of land.]
A strip of (esp. arable) land.

rap /rap/ *noun*[4]. Now *dial.* M18.
[from RAP *verb*[3].]
An exchange, esp. of horses.

rap /rap/ *verb*[1]. Infl. **-pp-**. ME.
[Prob. imit. (cf. CLAP *verb*[1], FLAP *verb*); perh. of Scandinavian origin (cf. Swedish *rappa* beat, drub).]
1 *verb trans.* Orig., deliver a severe blow to. Now, strike smartly with a stick etc. ME. ▸**b** *fig.* Criticize adversely; rebuke. E20. ▸**c** Charge; prosecute. *US slang.* E20.
2 *verb trans.* Drive, dash, knock, etc., with a rap. Foll. by *against, in, on,* †*to.* Chiefly *Scot.* LME. ▸**b** *verb intrans.* Of arrows, tears, etc.: fall in rapid succession; rain *down.* E16.
3 a *verb intrans.* Strike a hard surface with an audible sharp blow, knock, *spec.* at a door. LME. ▸**b** Strike (a hard surface) with an audible sharp blow, knock. E18. ▸**c** *SPIRITUALISM.* Foll. by *out*: express (a message or word) by a succession of raps. M19.
4 a *verb trans.* Utter sharply or suddenly. Usu. foll. by *out.* M16. ▸†**b** *verb trans. & intrans.* Swear; give (evidence) *against. slang.* E18–E19. ▸**c** *verb intrans.* Talk or chat in an easy manner, banter, (*with*); *esp.* converse on equal terms, have a rapport, *with. colloq.* (chiefly *US*). E20. ▸**d** *verb intrans.* Perform rap music; talk or sing in the style of rap. L20.

> 🕮 **1** W. VAN T. CLARK He.. rapped Gil right under the base of the skull. **rap on the knuckles**, **rap over the knuckles** *fig.* reprimand, reprove. **b** *Times* DoT raps two in enquiry. **3a** G. KENDALL He rapped twice.. paused, then knocked again. **b** A. LEE The walls.. gave a suspicious hollow sound when rapped. **4a** B. PYM 'Do you believe in the celibacy of the clergy?' rapped out Miss Clovis. **c** *Time* Buckley.. claims to rap with the Silent Majority, curries the hardhat vote.

rap /rap/ *verb*[2] *trans.* Now *rare.* Infl. **-pp-**. E16.
[In sense 1 perh. rel. to Middle Low German *rappen* seize, snatch; in sense 2 app. back-form. from RAPT *adjective.*]
†**1** Seize, snatch, steal. E16–M18.
2 Carry off; remove; *fig.* enrapture. Cf. RAPE *verb* 2. L16.

rap /rap/ *verb*[3] *trans. dial. & arch. slang.* Infl. **-pp-**. L17.
[Origin unkn.]
Exchange, barter.

rapacious /rəˈpeɪʃəs/ *adjective.* M17.
[from Latin *rapac-*, *rapax* grasping, from *rapere* RAPE *verb*: see -IOUS.]
1 Grasping; excessively or violently greedy. M17.
2 Of an animal, esp. a bird: predatory. M17.

> 🕮 **1** I. MURDOCH The machine.. like some animal through whose rapacious mouth Nina was drawing the cotton. A. STORR Sections of human society which are especially ruthless and rapacious.

■ **rapaciously** *adverb* M18. **rapaciousness** *noun* M17.

rapacity /rəˈpasɪti/ *noun.* M16.
[French *rapacité* or Latin *rapacitas*, formed as prec.: see -ACITY.]
The quality or state of being rapacious; rapacious behaviour.

rapadura /rapaˈðura/ *noun.* M19.
[Portuguese, lit. 'scraping', from *rapar* scrape.]
In Latin America, a kind of unrefined sugar formed into blocks or cakes.

rapakivi /rapəˈkiːviː, ˈrapəkiːviː/ *noun.* L18.
[Finnish = crumbly stone, from *rapa* mud + *kivi* stone.]
GEOLOGY. More fully ***rapakivi granite***. A type of granite characterized by large crystals of potash feldspar surrounded by plagioclase; orig. *spec.* that occurring in southern Finland.

RAPC *abbreviation.*
Royal Army Pay Corps.

rape /reɪp/ *noun*[1]. OE.
[Var.]
1 = ROPE *noun*[1]. *obsolete* exc. *Scot. & north.* OE.
2 *Hist.* [With ref. to the fencing-off of land with a rope.] Each of the six administrative districts into which Sussex was formerly divided, each comprising several hundreds. LOE.
1 ***thack and rape***: see THACK *noun* 2b.

rape /reɪp/ *noun*[2]. LME.
[Anglo-Norman *rap(e)*, *raap*, formed as RAPE *verb.*]
†**1** The action or an act of taking a thing by force; *esp.* violent seizure of property etc. LME–E18.
2 The action or an act of carrying away a person, esp. a woman, by force. Now *arch. & poet.* LME.
3 The action or an act of forcing a person, esp. a woman or girl, to have sexual intercourse against his or her will. Also, the action or an act of buggering a man or boy against his will. L15.
†**4** A person, esp. a woman, who has been raped. L16–L17.

> 🕮 **3** *transf.*: J. IRVING The only impediments to their rape of the forest were the black flies and mosquitoes. ***gang-rape***: see GANG *noun.* ***MARITAL rape***. ***STATUTORY rape***.

Comb.: **rape crisis centre** an agency offering advice and support to victims of sexual rape.

rape /reɪp/ *noun*[3]. LME.
[Latin *rapum*, *rapa* turnip.]
†**1** More fully ***round rape***. The turnip plant, *Brassica rapa*; the globular root of this. LME–E18.
2 A yellow-flowered plant, *Brassica napus*, allied to the turnip; *esp.* (*a*) (more fully ***long rape***) a variety of this plant, *B. napus* subsp. *rapifera*, grown as a vegetable; formerly also, the spindle-shaped root of this; (*b*) a variety of this plant, *B. napus* subsp. *oleifera*, grown as green feed for livestock and (more fully ***oil-seed rape***) for its seed which yields an edible oil. Also called ***coleseed***, ***colza***. LME.
3 ***wild rape***, charlock or wild mustard, *Sinapis arvensis.* M16.
Comb.: **rape-cake** a flat cake made of pressed rape-seeds from which the oil has been extracted, used as manure or cattle food; **rape-oil** a thick brownish-yellow oil expressed from rape-seeds, used as a lubricant and to produce foodstuffs; **rape-seed** (*a*) (now *rare*) the plant rape; (*b*) the oil-rich seed of rape.

rape /reɪp/ *noun*[4]. *obsolete* exc. *dial.* E16.
[Old French *raspe* (mod. *râpe*): see RASP *noun*[1].]
= RASP *noun*[1] 1.

rape /reɪp/ *noun*[5]. E17.
[In sense 1 prob. from French (*vin*) *râpé*, from *râpe*; in senses 2, 3 from Old & mod. French *râpe*, medieval Latin *raspa.*]
†**1** In full ***rape wine***. Wine made from the stalks or refuse of grapes with water added, or from a mixture of fresh grapes and light wine. E17–M18.
2 *sing.* & in *pl.* (treated as *sing.*). The refuse of grapes after wine-making, used in making vinegar. M17.
3 A vessel used in making vinegar. E19.

rape /reɪp/ *verb trans.* LME.
[Anglo-Norman *raper* from Latin *rapere* take by force, seize.]
1 Take (a thing) by force; seize. Now chiefly *poet.* LME. ▸**b** Rob (a person or place); plunder, strip. E18.
2 Carry off (a person, esp. a woman) by force. Now *rare* or *obsolete.* L16. ▸**b** Enrapture; transport with the strength of an emotion etc. *literary.* Now *rare.* E17.
3 Commit sexual rape on (a person, esp. a woman). L16.

> 🕮 **1** R. HUGHES It was the meal which raped José's attention. **b** *Sunday Express* Suggested.. I tour around and rape them of all their money. **3** *New Yorker* Claimed he had been.. raped by four prisoners. P. THEROUX Dragging women.. into bushes and raping them.

■ **rapable** *adjective* (of a person) regarded as a potential victim of rape L20. **raper** *noun* = RAPIST E20.

raphae *noun* pl. of RAPHE.

Raphaelesque /ˌrafeɪəˈlɛsk/ *adjective.* L18.
[from *Raphael* Anglicization of *Raffaello* (see below) + -ESQUE.]
Characteristic of or resembling the work of the Italian Renaissance painter Raffaello Sanzio (1483–1520) (widely known as Raphael).

raphanus /ˈraf(ə)nəs/ *noun.* M18.
[Latin from Greek *raphanos* radish.]
A plant of the cruciferous genus *Raphanus*, of which the common radish, *R. sativus*, is the most important species.

raphe /ˈreɪfi/ *noun.* Pl. **raphae** /ˈreɪfiː/. Also **raphé**. M18.
[mod. Latin from Greek *rhaphē* seam, suture.]
1 ANATOMY & ZOOLOGY. A groove, ridge, or seam in an organ or tissue, *esp.* one marking a line of fusion between two halves or parts; a median plane between two halves of a part of the brain, *esp.* that of the medulla oblongata and that of the tegmentum of the midbrain. M18.
2 BOTANY. **a** A longitudinal ridge in an anatropous ovule, representing the adherent funicle. M19. ▸**b** A groove in the valve of many pennate diatoms, through which cytoplasmic streaming occurs which is believed to cause their motion. L19.

raphia *noun* see RAFFIA.

raphide /ˈreɪfʌɪd/ *noun.* Also (now *rare*) **raphis** /ˈreɪfɪs/. Pl. **raphides** /-ɪdiːz/. M19.
[(French from) Greek *rhaphid-*, *rhaphis* needle.]
BOTANY. Any of the needle-like calcium oxalate crystals occurring in bundles in the vegetative parts of certain flowering plants. Usu. in *pl.*

rapid /ˈrapɪd/ *adjective, noun, & adverb.* M17.
[Latin *rapidus*, from *rapere*: see RAPE *verb*, -ID¹.]
▶ **A** *adjective.* **1** Moving or capable of moving with great speed; quick-moving, swift. M17.
2 Characterized by great speed; swift in action or execution. L17. ▸**b** PHOTOGRAPHY. = FAST *adjective* 8c. L19.
3 Progressing quickly; developed or completed within a short time. L18.
4 Of a slope: descending steeply. L19.

> 🕮 **1** J. CONRAD The scratch of rapid pens. **2** G. ORWELL His . . Adam's apple made a . . rapid up-and-down movement. A. MACLEAN For a man of his years . . he made a remarkably rapid exit. **3** E. PAWEL Rapid industrialization led to major dislocations. A. CROSS An extremely virulent cancer . . often leads to rapid death.

Special collocations & comb.: **rapid deployment** *noun & adjective* (MILITARY) (designating) a body of troops able to be quickly sent into action. **rapid eye movement** jerky binocular movement of a person's eyes, occurring in a distinctive kind of sleep (cf. REM *noun*²); an instance of this. **rapid-fire** *adjective* fired or capable of firing in quick succession; *fig.* spoken, asked, etc., at a rapid rate or in quick succession. **rapid transit** *noun & adjective* (designating) a high-speed public transport system usu. within a metropolitan area.

▶ **B** *noun.* **1** A steep descent in a river-bed causing a swift current; a current caused by such a descent. Usu. in *pl.* Orig. *US.* M18.
2 The action of firing shots in quick succession. Usu. in *pl.* E20.
▶ **C** *adverb.* With great speed; swiftly. *rare.* L18.
■ **raˈpidity** *noun* the quality of being rapid; swiftness of motion or action: M17. **rapidly** *adverb* E18. **rapidness** *noun* M17.

rapide /rapid, raˈpiːd/ *noun.* Pl. pronounced same. E20.
[French.]
In France, an express train.

rapido /ˈrapɪdəʊ, *foreign* ˈrapido/ *adverb, adjective, & noun.* L19.
[Italian.]
▶ **A** *adverb & adjective.* MUSIC. A direction: in rapid time. L19.
▶ **B** *noun.* Pl. **-di** /-di/, **-dos** /-dəʊz/. In Italy, an express train. M20.

rapier /ˈreɪpɪə/ *noun.* Also (*dial.*) **rapper** /ˈrapə/. E16.
[Prob. from Dutch, or Low German *rappir*, from French (†*espee*) *rapière*, of unkn. origin.]
Orig., a long pointed two-edged sword for cutting or esp. thrusting. Later, a light slender sharp-pointed sword for thrusting only.
Comb.: **rapier dance**, **rapier sword dance** a type of English folk-dance using swords.

rapine /ˈrapʌɪn, -pɪn/ *noun & verb. literary.* LME.
[Old & mod. French, or Latin *rapina*, from *rapere* RAPE *verb*: see -INE⁴.]
▶ **A** *noun.* The action or an act of seizing property etc. by force; plunder, pillage. Also (*rare*), the action or an act of raping someone, esp. a woman. LME.
▶† **B** *verb intrans. & trans.* Plunder, pillage. *rare.* L16–M17.

rapist /ˈreɪpɪst/ *noun.* L19.
[from RAPE *noun*² + -IST.]
A person who commits rape.

raploch /ˈraplək, -x/ *noun & adjective. Scot.* M16.
[Origin unkn.]
▶ **A** *noun.* (A garment made from) coarse undyed woollen fabric. M16.
▶ **B** *adjective.* Coarse, crude; uncouth. L16.

> 🕮 R. BURNS Muse . . ! Tho' rough an' raploch be her measure She's seldom lazy.

rapontic *adjective* var. of RHAPONTIC.

rapparee /rapəˈriː/ *noun.* L17.
[Prob. partly from Irish deriv. of *rapaire* rapier, partly from *ropaire* robber.]
Hist. A 17th-cent. Irish pikeman or irregular soldier; *transf.* an Irish bandit or robber; *gen.* any irregular soldier or bandit.

rappee /raˈpiː/ *noun.* M18.
[French (*tabac*) *râpé* rasped (tobacco), from *râper* RASP *verb*¹.]
A coarse snuff made from dark strong-smelling tobacco leaves, orig. obtained by rasping or grating a piece of tobacco.

rappel /raˈpɛl/ *noun.* M19.
[French, formed as next.]
1 A drum roll calling soldiers to arms. *rare.* M19.
2 MOUNTAINEERING. An abseil. M20.

rappel /raˈpɛl/ *verb.* Infl. **-ll-**. L16.
[French *rappeler* recall.]
†**1** *verb trans.* Recall (a hawk). *rare.* Only in L16.
2 *verb intrans.* MOUNTAINEERING. Abseil. M20.

rappen /ˈrap(ə)n/ *noun.* Pl. same. M19.
[German *Rappe(n)* from Middle High German *rappe* var. of *rabe* (also mod.) raven, orig. with ref. to the head of the bird as depicted on a medieval coin.]
A monetary unit in the German-speaking cantons of Switzerland and in Liechtenstein, equal to one-hundredth of the Swiss franc.

rapper /ˈrapə/ *noun*¹. E17.
[from RAP *verb*¹ + -ER¹.]
1 A deliberate falsehood, a lie; an oath; an imprecation. *obsolete* exc. *dial.* E17.
2 A thing used for rapping; *spec.* a door-knocker. M17.
3 A remarkably good, large, etc., person or thing. Cf. RAPPING *adjective* 2. *obsolete* exc. *dial.* M17.
4 A person who raps. M18.
5 A complainant, a plaintiff; a prosecutor. Cf. RAP *verb*¹ 1c. *US slang.* M19.
6 A travelling antiques buyer; *esp.* a person who buys valuable objects cheaply from credulous owners. Cf. KNOCKER 8. E20.

rapper *noun*² see RAPIER.

rapping /ˈrapɪŋ/ *noun.* LME.
[from RAP *verb*¹ + -ING¹.]
1 The action of RAP *verb*¹; an instance of this. LME.
2 *spec.* **a** FOUNDING. The tapping of a pattern to release it from the mould. L19. ▸**b** The action of performing rap music; rap music. L20.
Comb.: **rapping bar** FOUNDING a pointed iron bar for loosening patterns from moulds; **rapping iron** a tool for tapping the woven rows of a basket into position as it is being made; **rapping plate** FOUNDING a metal plate attached to a pattern to prevent damage to it when loosened from a mould.

rapping /ˈrapɪŋ/ *adjective.* L16.
[from RAP *verb*¹ + -ING².]
1 That raps or knocks. L16.
2 Uncommonly big or striking. Now *dial.* M17.

Rappist /ˈrapɪst/ *noun. US.* M19.
[from George *Rapp* (see below) + -IST.]
A member of a 19th-cent. communistic Christian religious sect founded by George Rapp (1757–1847) in Pennsylvania; a Harmonist.
■ Also **Rappite** *noun* M19.

rapport /raˈpɔː/ *noun.* M16.
[French, from *rapporter*, formed as RE- + *apporter* APPORT.]
†**1** Report, talk. *rare.* Only in M16.
2 Relationship; connection; communication. Now usu., harmonious accord, understanding and empathy; a relationship characterized by these. M17. ▸**b** *spec.* A posited state of deep spiritual, emotional, or mental connection between people, *esp.* one in which one person may mesmerize another; a feeling of sympathy and cooperation between therapist and patient, or tester and subject. M19.

> 🕮 **2** C. EASTON The extraordinary rapport between soloist, conductor and orchestra produced an inspired performance. *Guardian* His instinct for establishing an intimate rapport with those he photographed. EN RAPPORT. **b** A. STORR That minimum degree of rapport and co-operation without which the psychotherapist is helpless.

rapportage /rapɔrtaːʒ, rapɔːˈtɑːʒ/ *noun.* E20.
[French, lit. 'tale-telling', infl. by REPORTAGE.]
The reporting or describing of events in writing; mere description, uncreative recounting.

rapporteur /rapɔːˈtəː/ *noun.* L15.
[Old & mod. French, from *rapporter* (see prec.) + *-eur* -OR.]
†**1** A reporter, a recounter. *rare.* Only in L15.
2 A person who makes a report of the proceedings of a committee etc. for a higher body. Cf. REPORTER 1b. L18.

rapprochement /raprɔʃmɑ̃, raˈprɒʃmɒ̃/ *noun.* E19.
[French, from *rapprocher*, formed as RE- + *approcher* APPROACH *verb*: see -MENT.]
(An) establishment or resumption of harmonious relations, esp. between foreign States.

> 🕮 A. F. DOUGLAS-HOME There can be no unity in Europe without the *rapprochement* of France and Germany. G. BATTISCOMBE Christine and Lizzie were . . . very shy creatures, so that a *rapprochement* between them would have been difficult.

rapscallion /rapˈskalɪən/ *noun.* L17.
[Alt. of RASCALLION.]
A rascal, a rogue; a vagabond.
■ **rapscallionly** *adjective* L17.

rapt /rapt/ *noun.* Now *rare.* LME.
[Old & mod. French, or Latin *raptus*: see next.]
1 A trance, a rapture. LME.
†**2** Abduction; rape. Chiefly *Scot.* LME–L17.
†**3** The power *of* an emotion to inspire, transport, etc. M–L17.

rapt /rapt/ *adjective.* LME.
[Latin *raptus* pa. pple of *rapere* seize, RAPE *verb.* Cf. next.]
1 †**a** Carried away by force; (of a woman) raped. LME–M17. ▸**b** Removed from one place or situation to another. Now *poet.* M16.
2 CHRISTIAN THEOLOGY. Transported *up* or *into* heaven. *arch.* LME.
3 a Transported in spirit by religious feeling or inspiration. LME. ▸**b** *gen.* Transported with or *with* joy, intense delight, etc., enraptured; *Austral. colloq.* very pleased. M16.
4 Absorbed, enthralled, intent. Cf. ***wrapped***, ***wrapt*** pa. pple of WRAP *verb.* E16.
5 Indicating, proceeding from, or characterized by a state of rapture. L18.

> 🕮 **1b** W. IRVING The aspiring family was rapt out of sight in a whirlwind. **2** C. KINGSLEY He was rapt up on high and saw S. Peter. **3a** WORDSWORTH Rapt into still communion. S. COX St Paul when he was rapt in the spirit into Paradise. **b** R. P. JHABVALA She . . shut her eyes and seemed rapt . . with longing and desire. **4** W. GASS My . . friend, rapt in a recollection of her youth that lasted seven courses. **5** G. CLARE We listened with rapt attention. M. GARDINER The rapt look on his face, his eyes unseeing, utterly absorbed and delighted.

■ **raptly** *adverb* †(**a**) quickly; (**b**) (*rare*) rapturously; (**c**) intently, absorbedly: M17. **raptness** *noun* †(**a**) swiftness; (**b**) rapt condition: L16.

rapt /rapt/ *verb trans.* Long *poet. rare.* Pa. t. & pple †**-ed**, pa. t. also **rapt**. L16.
[from prec.]
1 Carry away by force. L16.
2 Transport in spirit; enrapture. L16.

raptor /ˈraptə/ *noun*¹. LME.
[Latin, formed as RAPT *adjective*: see -OR.]
1 ORNITHOLOGY. = ***bird of prey*** s.v. BIRD *noun.* LME.
†**2** A plunderer, a robber. LME–E18.
3 An abductor; a rapist. *rare.* E17.
■ **rapˈtorial** *adjective* predatory; pertaining to or characteristic of predatory birds or animals; adapted for seizing prey: E19. **rapˈtorious** *adjective* = RAPTORIAL E19.

raptor /ˈraptə/ *noun*². *colloq.* L20.
[Abbreviation.]
= VELOCIRAPTOR.

rapture /ˈraptʃə/ *noun & verb.* L16.
[French †*rapture* or medieval Latin *raptura*; partly infl. by RAPT *adjective*: see -URE.]
▶ **A** *noun.* **1** †**a** Seizure, capture; the carrying off of something as prey or plunder. Also, the rape of a woman. L16–E18. ▸**b** The action or an act of transporting a person from one place to another, esp. (CHRISTIAN THEOLOGY) up to heaven (*arch.*); *spec.* (**R-**) the transporting of believers to heaven at the second coming of Christ, according to some Millenarian teaching. M17.
2 Mental exaltation, *spec.* as a result of religious feeling or inspiration; *esp.* joy, intense delight; a state of intense delight or enthusiasm, the expression of this (usu. in *pl.*). E17. ▸**b** A state of excitement; a paroxysm or fit (*of* a specified emotion). *rare.* E17.
3 Force of movement. Now *rare.* E17.

> 🕮 **2** M. BARING Soaring ecstasy, the rapture of the successful creative artist. C. MACKENZIE He crossed himself in a devout rapture of humble human gratitude. W. CATHER Marie was gazing in rapture at the soft blue color of the stones. ANNE STEVENSON Sylvia had . . as great a gift for rapture as she had for misery. **be in raptures**, **go into raptures** be enthusiastic; talk enthusiastically. **rapture of the deep**, **raptures of the deep**, **rapture of the depths**, **raptures of the depths** nitrogen narcosis. **b** R. L. STEVENSON Give way to perfect raptures of moral indignation against . . abstract vices.

▶ **B** *verb.* **1 a** *verb trans.* Enrapture (*with*). Now *rare.* M17. ▸**b** *verb intrans.* Delight *in*; be excited or enthusiastic *over*. E20.
2 *verb trans.* CHRISTIAN THEOLOGY. Transport (a believer) to heaven at the second coming of Christ. Usu. in *pass.* M20.
■ **rapturous** *adjective* characterized by, feeling, or expressing rapture L17. **rapturously** *adverb* M17. **rapturousness** *noun* L19.

raptus /ˈraptəs/ *noun.* M19.
[Latin: see RAPT *adjective*.]
1 A state of rapture. M19.
2 MEDICINE. A sudden violent attack. Usu. with mod. Latin specifying word. M19.

raquette *noun* var. of RACKET *noun*¹.

rara avis /rɛːrə ˈeɪvɪs, rɑːrə ˈavɪs/ *noun phr.* Pl. ***rarae aves*** /rɛːriː ˈeɪviːz, rɑːriː, -reɪ ˈaviːz/. **E17.**
[Latin = rare bird.]
1 A kind of person rarely encountered; an unusual or exceptional person. **E17.**
2 A rarity; an unusual or exceptional occurrence or thing. **L19.**

rare /rɛː/ *adjective*[1] & *adverb*[1]. **LME.**
[Latin *rarus*.]
▶ **A** *adjective.* †**1** Orig., having the constituent parts widely spaced. Later *spec.* (of air, a gas) having low density, thin. **LME–M19.** ▸**b** Thinly attended or populated. **E17–L18.**
†**2** Widely spaced; standing far apart. **LME–M17.**
3 Of a kind seldom found, done, or occurring, uncommon, infrequent; unusual, exceptional; few and far between. **LME.**
4 Unusually good, fine, or worthy; splendid, excellent. Also (*colloq.*) as a mere intensive. **L15.**

> **3** G. B. SHAW Accidents . . , being accidents, are necessarily rare. V. S. PRITCHETT Beyond a rare cold, he was never ill in his long life. M. ROBERTS They adored the rare treat of their father cooking for them. *absol.*: SIR W. SCOTT That bower . . Hath wondrous store of rare and rich. **4** H. MARTINEAU They put me in a rare passion. M. GEE Priceless human foibles and folly, too rare to deploy in his short official reports. **rare and** — *arch. colloq.* very —.

Special collocations: **rare bird** = RARA AVIS. **rare book** a book of special value or interest on account of its age, limited issue, binding, or other historical factors. **rare earth** CHEMISTRY orig., any of various naturally occurring oxides, esp. of elements of the lanthanide series; now usu. (also ***rare-earth element***, ***rare-earth metal***), an element of a group comprising the lanthanide series and often scandium and yttrium. **rare gas** CHEMISTRY = *noble gas* s.v. NOBLE *adjective.*
▶ **B** *adverb.* Rarely. Chiefly *poet.* in comb. **E17.**

> D. H. LAWRENCE A rare-spoken, almost surly man.

■ **rareness** *noun* **LME.** **rarish** *adjective* somewhat rare **M19.**

rare /rɛː/ *adjective*[2] & *adverb*[2]. *obsolete* exc. *dial.* **L16.**
[Var. of RATHE *adjective.*]
Early. Freq. in ***rare-ripe***, (a fruit or vegetable) ripening early.

rare /rɛː/ *adjective*[3]. **M17.**
[Later form of REAR *adjective*[2].]
†**1** Of an egg: left soft in cooking. **M17–M19.**
2 Of meat, esp. beef: only lightly cooked, underdone. **L18.**

> **2** A. D. FOSTER She hungrily devoured a disgustingly rare chunk of steak.

rare /rɛː/ *verb. US, Austral., & dial.* **M19.**
[Var. Cf. RARING.]
1 *verb intrans.* = REAR *verb*[1] 15b. **M19.**
2 *verb trans.* = REAR *verb*[1] 9. **E20.**

rarebit /ˈrɛːbɪt/ *noun.* **L18.**
[Alt. of RABBIT *noun* in *Welsh rabbit* s.v. WELSH *adjective & noun.*]
(In full ***Welsh rarebit***) a dish of melted and seasoned or simply toasted cheese on toast; any dish consisting of grilled cheese and various other ingredients on toast.
buck rarebit: see BUCK *noun*[1] & *adjective.*
¶ Not recorded independently until **L19.**

raree-show /ˈrɛːriːʃəʊ/ *noun.* **L17.**
[Repr. pronunc. of *rare show* by foreign (*spec.* Savoyard) showmen.]
1 A show, a spectacle, a display. **L17.**
2 A show contained or carried about in a box, a peep-show. **E18.**

rarefaction /rɛːrɪˈfakʃ(ə)n/ *noun.* **E17.**
[medieval Latin *rarefactio(n-)*, from Latin *rarefact-* pa. ppl stem of *rarefacere*: see RAREFY, -FACTION.]
1 The action of rarefying or process of being rarefied; lessening of density. Now chiefly of the air or gases, or (MEDICINE) of (the X-ray appearance of) bones. **E17.**
2 An instance of this. **M19.**
■ **rarefactional** *adjective* characterized by rarefaction **E20.**

rarefactive /rɛːrɪˈfaktɪv/ *adjective.* **LME.**
[medieval Latin *rarefactivus*, from Latin *rarefact-*: see prec., -IVE.]
Having the quality of rarefying; characterized by rarefaction.

rarefied /ˈrɛːrɪfʌɪd/ *adjective.* **L16.**
[from next + -ED[1].]
Esp. of air, a gas, etc.: thinner or less dense than before or than usual. Freq. *fig.*, refined, subtle; elevated, exalted; select.

> W. S. MAUGHAM Philip could not live long in the rarefied air of the hill-tops. J. CAREY The art-lover as a rarefied being struck him as ridiculous. *absol.*: *Sound Choice* The pieces tend towards the spartan and rarefied.

rarefy /ˈrɛːrɪfʌɪ/ *verb.* **LME.**
[Old & mod. French *raréfier* or medieval Latin *rareficare* extension of Latin *rarefacere*, formed as RARE *adjective*[1]: see -FY.]
1 *verb trans. & (rare) intrans.* Make or become thin, esp. by expansion; make or become less dense or solid. **LME.**
2 *verb trans. fig.* Make less material; make (an idea, argument, etc.) more subtle; refine, purify. **L16.**
■ **rarefiˈcation** *noun* (*rare*) = RAREFACTION **E17.** **rarefier** *noun* (*rare*) **L16.**

rarely /ˈrɛːli/ *adverb.* **E16.**
[from RARE *adjective*[1] + -LY[2].]
†**1** Thinly, scantily. *rare.* **E16–M17.**
2 Seldom, infrequently; in few instances. **M16.**
3 Unusually well; splendidly, excellently. Now *rare.* **L16.**
4 To an unusual degree; exceptionally. **E17.**

> **2** H. BELLOC Mass is to be said but rarely, sometimes but once a year. *Radio Times* I rarely if ever play any record . . not pleasing to me. **4** J. FOTHERGILL I believed him to be rarely good and wise.

Rarey /ˈrɛːri/ *noun.* **L19.**
[John Solomon *Rarey* (1827–66), US horse-breaker.]
Used *attrib.* and in *possess.* to designate methods or equipment used by Rarey to tame horses.

rariki *noun* var. of RAURIKI.

raring /ˈrɛːrɪŋ/ *adjective. colloq.* **E20.**
[pres. pple of RARE *verb*: see -ING[2]. Cf. REARING 2.]
Eager, keen, fully ready, *to do.*

> *Church Times* We were at the starting-gate and raring to go.

rariora /rɛːrɪˈɔːrə, rarɪ-/ *noun pl.* **M19.**
[Latin, neut. pl. compar. of *rarus* RARE *adjective*[1].]
Rare books.

rarissime /rɛːˈrɪsɪmeɪ, ra-/ *adjective.* **E20.**
[Latin, lit. 'very rarely (sc. found)'.]
Extremely rare.
■ ***rarissima*** /-mə/ *noun pl.* extremely rare books **L20.**

rarity /ˈrɛːrɪti/ *noun.* **LME.**
[French *rareté*, †*-ité* or Latin *raritas*, formed as RARE *adjective*[1]: see -ITY.]
1 Thinness of composition or texture. Now usu. of air. Opp. DENSITY. **LME.**
2 Relative fewness in number; infrequency; the fact of being or occurring seldom or in few instances. **M16.**
3 An uncommon thing, *esp.* one valued for this. **L16.**
4 Unusual, exceptional, or excellent character or quality. **E17.**

> **1** H. BELLOC Height above the sea and consequent rarity of the air. **2** *Antiquaries Journal* Jade was valued for its rarity. **3** *Lancashire Life* A collection of wildlife . . included rareties now extinct. M. GIROUARD For early Victorian gentry to work in the garden had been something of a rarity. **4** J. A. SYMONDS Sappho's exquisite rarity of phrase.

Rarotongan /rarəˈtɒŋg(ə)n/ *noun & adjective.* **M19.**
[from *Rarotonga* (see below) + -AN.]
▶ **A** *noun.* **1** A native or inhabitant of Rarotonga, the largest of the Cook Islands in the S. Pacific. **M19.**
2 The Polynesian language of Rarotonga. **M19.**
▶ **B** *adjective.* Of or pertaining to Rarotonga, its people, or their language. **M19.**

ras /rɑːs/ *noun*[1]. **L17.**
[Amharic *rās* head, from Arab. *ra's* (colloq. *rās*). Cf. REIS *noun.*]
1 *Hist.* (The title of) an Ethiopian king, prince, or feudal lord. **L17.**
2 *transf.* A petty despot; *spec.* a high-ranking or influential member of the Fascist government of Italy between 1922 and 1945. **E20.**

Ras /ras/ *noun*[2] & *adjective.* Also **r-**. **M20.**
[Abbreviation.]
= RASTAFARIAN *noun & adjective.*

ras *noun*[3], *noun*[4] vars. of RASA *noun*[1], *noun*[2].

rasa /ˈrʌsə/ *noun*[1]. Also ***ras*** /rʌs/. **L18.**
[Sanskrit, lit. 'juice, essence, flavour'.]
The mood or aesthetic impression of an artistic work.

rasa /ˈrɑːsə/ *noun*[2]. Also ***ras*** /rɑːs/. **E19.**
[Sanskrit *rāsa.*]
A traditional Indian dance (commemorating that) performed by Krishna and the gopis in Hindu mythology; a festival celebrating this.

rasamala /rasəˈmɑːlə/ *noun.* **E19.**
[Malay (Javanese etc.) *ras(a)mala.*]
A tall tree of SE Asia, *Altingia excelsa*, related to the liquidambar, which yields a scented resin used in perfumes.

rasant /ˈreɪz(ə)nt/ *adjective.* Also **raz-**. **L17.**
[Old & mod. French, pres. pple of *raser* shave close: see RAZE *verb & noun*, -ANT[1].]
MILITARY. Of a line of defence: sweeping; long and curving (orig. so that the shot would graze the target).

rascal /ˈrɑːsk(ə)l/ *noun & adjective.* In sense 1 also **rascaille**. **ME.**
[Old French *rascaille* (mod. *racaille*), prob. from Old Northern French var. of Old French *rasche*, Provençal *rasca* scab, scurf, from Proto-Romance, from Latin *ras-* pa. ppl stem of *radere* scrape, scratch, shave.]
▶ **A** *noun.* **1** *collect.* The common soldiers or camp-followers of an army; those people belonging to the lowest social class, the rabble. Long *arch.* **ME.** ▸†**b** A rabble, a mob. *rare.* **ME–M16.** ▸†**c** A person of the lowest social class, a member of the rabble; *rare* a camp-follower. **ME–L17.**
2 *collect.* The young, lean, or inferior animals of a herd of esp. deer. Long *obsolete* exc. *dial.* **LME.** ▸**b** An animal, esp. a deer, of this kind. Long *obsolete* exc. *dial.* **E16.**
3 A low, unprincipled, or dishonest person; a rogue; a hooligan; a criminal. Now usu. *joc.*, a mischievous person, esp. a child, a scamp. **M16.**

> **3** WILKIE COLLINS Shifty Dick and the other rascal had been caught, and were in prison. R. P. GRAVES An engaging rascal, with an eye for the main chance. W. HORWOOD A happy day . . if you're at my side, you unkempt and grubby old rascal!

▶ **B** *adjective.* **1** Belonging to or forming the rabble or the lowest social class. Long *arch.* **LME.** ▸**b** Pertaining or appropriate to the rabble or the lowest social class. Later (now *rare*), roguish, mischievous. **E16.**
†**2** Of an animal, esp. a deer: young, lean, inferior. **L15–M17.**
†**3** Wretched, miserable, mean. **L16–M18.**
■ **rascaldom** *noun* (*a*) rascals collectively; (*b*) rascally behaviour: **M19.** **rascalism** *noun* the character or practices of a rascal **M19.** **rascality** *noun* (*a*) = RASCAL *noun* 1; (*b*) rascally character or behaviour; a rascally act or practice: **L16.** **rascalry** *noun* = RASCALITY **M19.**

rascallion /raˈskalɪən/ *noun.* **M17.**
[Prob. from prec. with fanciful ending, after RAMPALLION. Cf. RAPSCALLION.]
A wretch, a rascal.

rascally /ˈrɑːsk(ə)li/ *adjective & adverb.* **L16.**
[from RASCAL *noun* + -LY[1].]
▶ **A** *adjective.* **1** Unprincipled or dishonest in character or conduct. **L16.** ▸**b** Appropriate to a rascal. **L16.**
†**2** Belonging to the rabble or the lowest social class; (*rare*) small, inferior, of little worth. Only in **17.**
3 Wretched, miserable, mean. **E17.**
▶ **B** *adverb.* In a rascally manner. **E17.**

rascasse /rasˈkas/ *noun.* **E20.**
[French.]
A small, chiefly Mediterranean scorpion fish, *Scorpaena scrofa*, which has brick-red skin and spiny fins, used esp. as an ingredient of bouillabaisse.

rasceta /raˈsiːtə/ *noun pl.* Orig. †**-tta**. **M17.**
[Prob. from medieval Latin *racetta*, *ras(c)eta* the part of the hand where such lines are found, ult. from Arab. *rāḥa(t)* palm of the hand.]
PALMISTRY. Transverse lines running across the wrist at the base of the palm; the rascettes.

rascette /raˈsɛt/ *noun.* **M19.**
[French = the part of the hand where such lines are found, rascette: cf. prec.]
PALMISTRY. Each of the transverse lines running across the wrist at the base of the palm.

raschel /ˈraʃ(ə)l/ *noun.* Also **R-**. **M20.**
[German *Raschel(maschine*, from *Rachel*: see RACHEL.]
A type of knitting-machine noted for its versatility and capable of producing embossed patterns and netlike effects; knitting produced by this machine.

Raschig /ˈrɑːʃɪg/ *noun.* **E20.**
[Friedrich *Raschig* (1863–1928), German chemist.]
Used *attrib.* to designate various processes and devices used in industrial chemistry.
Raschig process a process in which benzene vapour is heated with hydrogen chloride and air over a catalyst to yield chlorobenzene, which is then hydrolysed to form phenol. **Raschig ring** a small cylindrical ring used in large numbers as a packing material in towers and columns for fractionation, solvent extraction, etc.

rase *verb*[1] & *noun* see RAZE *verb & noun.*

†**rase** *verb*[2] var. of RACE *verb*[1].

†**rasen** *noun.* **OE–E18.**
[Origin unkn. Cf. RAISING-PIECE, REASON *noun*[2].]
A wall-plate.

†**raser** *noun* see RAZER.

rasgado /razˈgaðo, razˈgɑːdəʊ/ *noun.* Pl. **-os** /-ɒs, -əʊz/. **M19.**
[Spanish, pa. pple of *rasgar* strum, make a flourish.]
MUSIC. (An arpeggio produced by) the act of sweeping the strings of a guitar with the fingertips.

rasgulla /rʌsˈgʊlə/ *noun.* Also **-oola**, **-ula**. **M20.**
[Hindi *rasgullā*, from *ras* juice + *gullā* ball.]
An Indian sweet consisting of a ball of soft milk cheese soaked in syrup.

rash /raʃ/ *noun*[1]. **L16.**
[French *ras* use as noun of adjective corresp. to Latin *rasus* scraped, shaven, smooth, from *radere*: see RAZE *verb.*]
Hist. A smooth textile fabric made of silk or worsted.

rash /raʃ/ *noun*². E18.
[Perh. rel. to Old French *ra(s)che* skin eruption = Italian *raschia* itch.]
1 An eruption of the skin in (esp. red) spots or patches, as in measles, scarlet fever, allergic reactions, etc. E18.
2 *transf.* & *fig.* A proliferation; a sudden widespread outbreak *of* something, esp. something unwelcome. E19.

> **1** B. SPOCK Nappie rash . . and rough patches on the cheeks. **2** B. HINES Great rashes of buttercups spread across the fields. E. P. THOMPSON A rash of rioting broke out throughout England.

rash /raʃ/ *noun*³. E20.
[Prob. from the adjective.]
MINING. = RASHING *noun*. Usu. in *pl.*

rash /raʃ/ *adjective & adverb*. LME.
[Corresp. to Middle Dutch *rasch*, Old High German *rasc* (German *rasch*), Old Norse *røskr* doughty, brave, ult. from Germanic base rel. to RATHE *adjective*. Prob. already in Old English.]
▶ **A** *adjective*. **1** Active, vigorous; nimble, quick; eager. *Scot. & north.* LME.
2 Hasty, reckless; acting without due consideration or regard for consequences; unrestrained. LME. ▸**b** Of a thing: operating quickly and strongly. *rare*. L16.
3 Of speech, action, etc.: characterized by or proceeding from undue haste or recklessness. M16. ▸†**b** Urgent, pressing. *rare* (Shakes.). Only in E17.

> **2** E. F. BENSON She had not been rash, only daring. **3** H. CARPENTER He warned McAlmon against rash remarks. G. GREENE I don't want him scared . . . He might do something rash.

▶ **B** *adverb*. Rashly. Long *obsolete* exc. *dial.* LME.
■ **rashful** *adjective* (*rare*) rash M16. **rashling** *noun* (*rare*) a rash person E17. **rashly** *adverb* LME. **rashness** *noun* E16.

rash /raʃ/ *verb*¹. Chiefly *Scot.* Now *rare* or *obsolete*. LME.
[Prob. imit.]
1 *verb intrans.* Rush hastily or violently. LME.
†**2** *verb trans.* Cast or pour *out* hurriedly or forcibly. L15–E18.
†**3** *verb trans.* Dash *against, in, through, together.* M16–M17.

†**rash** *verb*² *trans.* LME.
[Alt. of RAZE *verb*.]
1 Cut, slash. LME–L16.
2 Scrape out, erase. *rare*. LME–M17.

rasher /ˈraʃə/ *noun*¹. L16.
[Origin unkn.]
A thin slice of bacon or ham.

rasher /ˈraʃə/ *noun*². *US*. L19.
[Portuguese (local) *rasciera*.]
A red rockfish of California, *Sebastes miniatus*.

rashing /ˈraʃɪŋ/ *noun*. L19.
[Prob. from RASH *adjective* + -ING¹. Cf. RASH *noun*³.]
MINING. (A deposit of) loose brittle shale or poor coal. Usu. in *pl.*

raskol /raˈskɒl/ *noun*. L19.
[Russian = separation, schism.]
ECCLESIASTICAL HISTORY. The schism in the Russian Orthodox Church which followed the excommunication in 1667 of those who refused to accept the liturgical reforms of the patriarch Nikon (1605–81); *collect.* the dissenters under the raskol.

Raskolnik /rʌˈskɒlnɪk/ *noun*. E18.
[Russian *raskol'nik*, formed as prec. + *-nik* -NIK.]
ECCLESIASTICAL HISTORY. A member of a Russian Orthodox group which refused to accept the liturgical reforms of the patriarch Nikon (1605–81); an Old Believer.

rasolnik *noun* var. of RASSOLNIK.

rasophore /ˈrazə(ʊ)fɔː/ *noun*. L19.
[medieval Greek *rasophoros*, from *rason* cassock + -PHORE.]
(A monk of) the lowest level of the monastic hierarchy of the Greek Orthodox Church.

†**rasor** *noun & verb* see RAZOR.

rasp /rɑːsp/ *noun*¹. M16.
[Old French *raspe* (mod. *râpe*), formed as RASP *verb*¹.]
1 A type of coarse file with many projections or teeth on its surface; any similar tool for scraping, filing, or rubbing down. M16.
2 a ENTOMOLOGY. A ribbed band in some insects, used in sound production. Now *rare*. E19. ▸**b** ZOOLOGY. The radula of a mollusc; any of the teeth on this. Now *rare*. L19.
3 A rough grating sound, as of a rasp. M19.

> **1** *Which?* The Powerfile gave as good a finish as a rasp. **3** R. WEST We heard the rasp of matches on the box. B. MALAMUD He coughed with a heavy rasp.

■ **rasplike** *adjective* resembling (that of) a rasp M19.

rasp /rɑːsp/ *noun*². Now *Scot. & dial.* M16.
[Abbreviation of RASPIS *noun*².]
= RASPBERRY 1.

rasp /rɑːsp/ *verb*¹. ME.
[Old French *rasper* (mod. *râper*) from Proto-Romance (cf. medieval Latin *raspare*) from West Germanic (= Old High German) *raspōn* scrape together.]
1 *verb trans.* Scrape or grate with a rasp, file, etc. ME. ▸**b** Scrape or rub roughly. E18. ▸**c** *fig.* Irritate, grate on. E19.
2 *verb trans.* Scrape *off* or *away*. L18.
3 *verb intrans.* **a** Scrape or bow a stringed instrument. E19. ▸**b** Make a harsh grating sound. M19. ▸**c** *fig.* Foll. by *on*: irritate, grate on. L19.
4 *verb trans.* Utter with a harsh grating sound. Also foll. by *out*. M19.

> **1** W. BORLASE As if it had been rasped by a rough rounded file. **b** G. ORWELL The gritty dark-brown soap which rasped your skin like sandpaper. **c** L. P. HARTLEY What she saw and heard offended her: it rasped her tender unused sensibility. **3b** J. BETJEMAN The old lock rusty That opens rasping. T. ROETHKE The blue jay rasping from the stunted pine. **4** M. GEE 'You don't have to *know* a girl,' rasped the slow harsh voice.

■ **rasper** *noun* (*a*) a person who or thing which rasps; (*b*) HUNTING a high difficult fence; (*c*) *slang* a harsh or unpleasant person or thing; (*d*) *slang* a remarkable or extraordinary thing: E18. **rasping** *noun* (*a*) the action or an act of rubbing or scraping (as) with a rasp; (*b*) a harsh grating sound; (*c*) in *pl.*, small particles produced by rasping; *spec.* dry breadcrumbs: LME. **rasping** *adjective* (*a*) that rasps; (*b*) HUNTING difficult to jump, cross, etc.; (*c*) *slang* remarkable, extraordinary: M17. **raspingly** *adverb* L19. **raspy** *adjective* (*a*) harsh, grating; (*b*) irritable: M19.

rasp /rɑːsp/ *verb*² *intrans. & trans.* Now *dial.* E17.
[Imit.]
Belch.

raspatory /ˈrɑːspət(ə)ri/ *noun*. LME.
[medieval Latin *raspatorium*, from *raspat-* pa. ppl stem of *raspare* RASP *verb*¹: see -ORY¹.]
A type of rasp used in surgery, esp. for scraping bone.

raspberry /ˈrɑːzb(ə)ri/ *noun & adjective*. E17.
[from RASP *noun*² + BERRY *noun*¹. See also RAZZBERRY.]
▶ **A** *noun*. **1** The soft edible fruit of several shrubs of the genus *Rubus*, of the rose family (esp. the Eurasian *Rubus idaeus* and its N. American variety), which is red or sometimes yellow and composed of numerous drupelets arranged on an easily separated conical receptacle; a plant bearing this fruit. E17.
2 Raspberry wine. M18.
3 a [App. ellipt. for *raspberry tart* below.] A sound of derision or contempt made by blowing through closed lips with the tongue between. L19. ▸**b** *fig.* A refusal; a reprimand; a dismissal. E20.
4 The red colour of a raspberry, varying in shade from pink to scarlet. E20.
1 black raspberry (the fruit of) a black-berried N. American raspberry, *Rubus occidentalis*. ***flowering raspberry***: see FLOWERING *ppl adjective* 4.
Comb.: **raspberry beetle** any of various beetles of the genus *Byturus*, esp. *B. tomentosus*, the larvae of which attack raspberries etc.; **raspberry fruitworm** *US* (the larva of) either of two raspberry beetles, *Byturus bakeri* and *B. rubi*; **raspberry jam** (*a*) jam made with raspberries; (*b*) an Australian wattle, *Acacia acuminata*, so called from the smell of its wood (also ***raspberry jam tree***); this wood; **raspberry tart** (*a*) a tart filled with raspberries; (*b*) *rhyming slang* the heart; (*c*) *rhyming slang* an emission of wind from the anus, a fart; **raspberry vinegar** vinegar made from raspberries.
▶ **B** *adjective*. Of the colour of a raspberry, red, pink, scarlet. M20.

rasp-house /ˈrasphaʊs/ *noun*. Pl. **-houses** /-haʊzɪz/. M17.
[Dutch *rasphuis* (German *Raspelhaus*), from *raspen* RASP *verb*¹.]
Hist. In the Netherlands, Germany, etc., a house of correction where prisoners were employed in rasping wood.

†**raspis** *noun*¹. LME–L16.
[Origin unkn.]
Wine made from unbruised grapes or raspberries.

†**raspis** *noun*². M16–L17.
[Origin uncertain: perh. rel. to prec.]
1 A raspberry; *collect.* raspberries. M16–L17.
2 The raspberry-plant. M16–L17.

Rasputin /raˈspjuːtɪn/ *noun*. M20.
[Nickname of Grigory Yefimovich Novykh (*c* 1865–1916), mystic and influential favourite at the court of Tsar Nicholas II, from Russian *rasputnik* debauchee.]
A person exercising an insidious or corrupting influence, esp. over a ruler, governor, etc.
■ **Rasputinism** *noun* the licentious practices and insidious influence held to be characteristic of Rasputin E20.

rass /rɑːs/ *noun & verb*. *Black coarse slang*. Orig. †**rassa**. L18.
[from ARSE *noun* by metathesis and perh. partly from *your arse* by metanalysis.]
▶ **A** *noun*. The buttocks; the anus; *transf.* a contemptible person. L18.
▶ **B** *verb trans.* Bugger. E20.

rasse /ˈrasə, ras/ *noun*. E19.
[Javanese *rase*.]
The small Indian civet, *Viverricula indica*, found in India, Sri Lanka, Java, S. China, etc., kept for its musk.

rassle *noun, verb*, **rassler** *noun*, etc., see WRESTLE *noun* etc.

rassolnik /rʌsˈsɒljnjik/ *noun*. Also ***rasol-***. E20.
[Russian *rassol'nik*, from *rassol* brine + -NIK.]
A chilled Russian soup of brine, salted dill cucumbers, and pickled vegetables, meat, or fish.

rasta /rasta/ *noun*¹. Pl. pronounced same. E20.
[French, abbreviation.]
= RASTAQUOUÈRE.

Rasta /ˈrastə/ *noun*² & *adjective*. Also **r-**. M20.
[Abbreviation.]
▶ **A** *noun*. **1** = RASTAFARIAN *noun*. M20.
2 = RASTAFARIANISM. M20.
▶ **B** *adjective*. = RASTAFARIAN *adjective*. M20.
Rastaman a (male) Rastafarian.

Rastafari /rastəˈfɑːri/ *adjective & noun*. Also **Ras Tafari**. M20.
[from *Ras Tafari*, the name by which Emperor Haile Selassie of Ethiopia (1892–1975) was known between 1916 and his accession in 1930.]
▶ **A** *adjective*. Designating or pertaining to a sect originating in Jamaica, regarding black people as the chosen people and former Emperor Haile Selassie of Ethiopia as God. M20.
▶ **B** *noun*. Pl. same, **-s**. A member of this sect, a Rastafarian. M20.
■ **Rastafarism** *noun* = RASTAFARIANISM M20.

Rastafarian /rastəˈfɑːrɪən, -ˈfɛːrɪən/ *noun & adjective*. M20.
[from prec. + -AN.]
▶ **A** *noun*. A member of the Rastafari sect. M20.

> *Times* The image of the young Rastafarian with dreadlocks was based on the Masai warrior.

▶ **B** *adjective*. Of, pertaining to, or designating the Rastafari sect. M20.
■ **Rastafarianism** *noun* the beliefs and practices of Rastafarians M20.

rastaquouère /rastakwɛːr/ *noun & adjective*. Pl. pronounced same. L19.
[French from S. Amer. Spanish *rastacuero* tycoon in the hide trade, upstart.]
▶ **A** *noun*. A person (esp. from a Mediterranean or S. American country) intruding into a particular social group and having an exaggerated manner or style of dress; a dashing but untrustworthy foreigner. L19.
▶ **B** *attrib.* or as *adjective*. Of, pertaining to, or characteristic of *rastaquouères*; of the nature of a *rastaquouère*. E20.

raster /ˈrastə/ *noun*. M20.
[German = screen, frame from Latin *rastrum* rake, from *ras-* pa. ppl stem of *radere* scrape.]
1 A usu. rectangular pattern of parallel scanning lines as in the display on a cathode-ray tube etc. Also ***scanning raster***. M20.
2 CINEMATOGRAPHY & PHOTOGRAPHY. A fine grid or screen of wires, slits, or lenticular elements, placed in front of the projection screen in some stereoscopic systems. Also ***raster screen***. M20.
■ **rastered** *adjective* (of an electron beam) made to scan an area L20.

rasterize /ˈrastərʌɪz/ *verb trans.* Also **-ise**. L20.
[from prec. + -IZE.]
COMPUTING. Convert (an image stored as an outline) into pixels that can be displayed on a screen or printed.
■ **rasteriˈzation** *noun* L20. **rasterizer** *noun* a device for rasterizing images L20.

rastle *noun, verb*, **rastler** *noun*, etc. see WRESTLE *noun* etc.

Rastus /ˈrastəs/ *noun*. *US slang. derog. & racially offensive*. L19.
[Prob. aphet. from male forename *Erastus*.]
(A nickname for) a hypothetically average or typical black person.

rasure /ˈreɪʒə/ *noun*. Now *rare*. LME.
[Old & mod. French, or Latin *rasura*, from *ras-*: see RAZE *verb*, -URE.]
†**1** The action or an act of scraping or shaving; a scratch, a slit, a mark. LME–E18. ▸**b** A particle or (*collect.*) particles scraped off. LME–M17.
2 The action or an act of scraping out something written; (an) erasure. LME. ▸**b** *transf.* Obliteration, effacement; cancelling. E17.
†**3** The action or an act of shaving the head, hair, etc.; a tonsure. L15–M18.

rat /rat/ *noun*¹. OE.
[from Proto-Romance, whence other Germanic forms: ult. origin unkn. Later reinforced by Old & mod. French *rat*. Cf. RATTON.]
1 a An animal of any of various larger species of rodent, mostly of the family Muridae, usu. having a pointed snout and a long sparsely haired tail, *esp.* (more fully ***black rat***) *Rattus rattus* and (more fully ***brown rat***, ***Norway rat***) *Rattus norvegicus*, both of which are common scavengers around human settlements. OE. ▸**b** Any of various animals resembling rats, such as a muskrat, water-rat, or kangaroo-rat. L16.

2 a An unpleasant or contemptible person, esp. a man. Formerly also *spec.*, a disorderly person. *colloq.* L16. ▸**b** [From the superstition that rats desert a sinking ship.] A person who deserts a party, cause, difficult situation, etc. L18. ▸**c** A worker who refuses to join a strike or who takes a striker's place. E19. ▸**d** A person who is associated with or frequents a specified place. *colloq.* (chiefly *US*). M19. ▸**e** A new student; *esp.* a newly recruited cadet. *US slang.* M19. ▸**f** A police informer. *slang.* E20.
3 A pad with tapering ends, used in hairdressing to give shape, height, body, etc. *US.* M19.
4 In *pl.* As *interjection*: expr. annoyance, contempt, etc. L19.

📖 **1a** *cane-rat*, *jumping rat*, *mole-rat*, *pack rat*, *tree rat*, etc. *fig.*: R. BARR A little rat of a boat . . which dare not venture out in a storm. **2a** *Sun* When the rat protested that he loved Sal, she chucked a drink in his face. **d** H. ASBURY The police found him . . with a gang of notorious . . dock rats. **3** J. DOS PASSOS Her hair done in a pompadour askew so that the rat showed through. **4** *Funny Fortnightly* Aw, rats! I just *can't* win!

Phrases: **get a rat**, **get rats** *Austral. & NZ slang* be eccentric or insane. **give a person rats** *slang* berate or rebuke a person. **not give a rat's ass** *US slang* not care at all about something. **smell a rat** suspect something. **white rat** an albino form of the brown rat, widely bred as a pet and laboratory animal.
Comb.: **rat-arsed** *adjective* (*slang*) drunk; **ratbag** *slang* an unpleasant or disgusting person; ***rat-bat***: see BAT *noun*[3]; **rat-bite fever** MEDICINE an acute fever resulting from the bite of a rat, caused by either the bacterium *Spirillum minus* or the fungus *Streptobacillus moniliformis*; **rat-catcher** (*a*) a person or animal which catches rats; *spec.* a person whose occupation is to catch, kill, or drive away rats; (*b*) *colloq.* informal hunting dress; **rat cheese** *US colloq.* = MOUSETRAP *noun* 2; **ratfink** *slang* (*derog.*, chiefly *US*) an unpleasant contemptible person, *spec.* an informer; **rat-fish** (*a*) a chimaera or rabbit-fish, esp. *Chimaera monstrosa* of the Atlantic and Mediterranean, and (more fully ***spotted rat-fish***) *Hydrolagus colliei* of the N. Pacific; (*b*) = ***mouse-fish*** (b) s.v. MOUSE *noun*; **rat flea** a flea infesting rats, *esp.* any of the genera *Nosopsyllus* and *Xenopsylla*, which are vectors of typhus and bubonic plague; **rat-hare** = PIKA; **rat-house** *Austral. & NZ slang* a mental hospital; **rat kangaroo** any of various small ratlike Australian marsupials of the family Potoroidae, having hind legs adapted for jumping like those of the kangaroos (cf. POTOROO); **rat pack** *slang* a gang of disorderly young people; **rat race** a fiercely competitive struggle or contest, *spec.* working life regarded as a continuous round of this; **rat-racer** a person engaged in a rat race; **rat-racing** *noun & adjective* (*a*) *noun* competitive struggle, esp. at work; (*b*) *adjective* engaged in this; **rat-run** (*a*) (any of) a mazelike series of small passages by which rats move about their territory; (*b*) *colloq.* an alternative route on minor roads used by motorists to avoid congestion at peak periods; **rat-snake** a snake which kills rats, esp. a colubrid snake of the southern Asian genus *Ptyas*, as the dhaman.
■ **ratlike** *adjective* resembling (that of) a rat M19.

rat /rat/ *noun*[2]. Long *obsolete* exc. *north.* ME.
[Origin unkn. Cf. RATTED *adjective*[1].]
A rag, a scrap.

rat /rat/ *verb*[1]. Infl. **-tt-**. E19.
[from RAT *noun*[1].]
1 *verb intrans.* **a** Desert one's party, side, cause, etc. *colloq.* E19. ▸**b** Let a person down; behave disloyally; inform. Chiefly foll. by *on*. *colloq.* M20.
2 *verb intrans.* Hunt, catch, or kill rats. E19.
3 *verb trans.* Search (a person) for things to steal, rob; pilfer. *slang* (chiefly *Austral. & NZ*). L19.

📖 **1b** *Literary Review* Witnesses . . ratting on former colleagues. K. LETTE He's a solicitor who's ratted on a client! He could be struck off for that, you know!

rat /rat/ *verb*[2]. *arch. colloq.* Infl. **-tt-**. L17.
[Repr. affected pronunc. of ROT *verb*. Cf. DRAT.]
= DRAT.

rata /ˈrɑːtə/ *noun*. L18.
[Maori.]
Any of several New Zealand trees or woody climbers of the genus *Metrosideros*, of the myrtle family, bearing terminal clusters of red flowers with long stamens; esp. *M. robusta*, a large tree which begins its growth as an epiphyte.

ratable *adjective* var. of RATEABLE.

ratafia /ratəˈfɪə/ *noun*. L17.
[French, perh. rel. to TAFIA *noun*[1].]
1 A liqueur flavoured with almonds or kernels of peach, apricot, or cherry. L17.
2 A kind of small macaroon. M19.

ratal /ˈreɪt(ə)l/ *noun*. M19.
[from RATE *noun*[1] + -AL[1], prob. after *rental*.]
The amount on which rates are assessed.

ratamacue /ˈratəməkjuː/ *noun*. M20.
[Imit.]
A drum rhythm comprising a two-beat figure, the first beat of which is played as a triplet and preceded by two grace-notes.

ratan *noun* var. of RATTAN *noun*[1].

ratanhia /rəˈtanɪə/ *noun*. E19.
[Portuguese *ratânia*, Spanish *ratania*, prob. from Quechua *ratánya*. Cf. RHATANY.]
= RHATANY.

rataplan /ratəˈplan/ *noun & verb*. M19.
[French, of imit. origin.]
▶ **A** *noun*. A drumming or beating noise; a tattoo. M19.
▶ **B** *verb*. Infl. **-nn-**.
1 *verb trans.* Play (a tune) (as) on a drum. M19.
2 *verb intrans.* Make a rataplan. L19.

ratatat, **rat-a-tat** *noun & verb* see RAT-TAT.

ratatouille /ratəˈtuːi, -ˈtwiː/ *noun*. L19.
[French dial. (cf. French *touiller* stir up).]
†**1** A ragout. Only in L19.
2 A vegetable dish of aubergines, courgettes, tomatoes, onions, and peppers fried and stewed in oil. M20.

ratch /ratʃ/ *noun*[1]. L16.
[Perh. from German *Ratsche*, *Rätsche* ratchet-wheel. Cf. RATCHET.]
†**1** The barrel of a gun. *Scot.* L16–M17.
2 A ratchet. E18.
3 A ratchet-wheel. E18.

ratch *noun*[2], *noun*[3] vars. of RACHE *noun*[1], *noun*[2].

ratch /ratʃ/ *verb*[1]. *obsolete* exc. *dial.* ME.
[from obsolete pa. t. & pple of REACH *verb*[1], on the analogy of *caught*, *catch*.]
1 *verb intrans.* †**a** Go, proceed. *rare*. Only in ME. ▸**b** NAUTICAL Sail on a tack, reach. L19.
2 *verb trans.* Draw out, stretch; pull or tear apart. E16.

ratch /ratʃ/ *verb*[2] *trans. rare*. L18.
[from RATCH *noun*[1].]
Cut (a wheel) into teeth like those of a ratch.

ratch /ratʃ/ *verb*[3] *intrans. Scot. & north.* E19.
[from RACHE *noun*[1].]
Search about, esp. for food; forage *about*, *around*.

ratchet /ˈratʃɪt/ *noun & verb*. Also (earlier) †**rochet**. M17.
[French *rochet* (orig.) blunt lancehead, (later) bobbin, spool, ratchet (wheel), corresp. to or partly from Italian *rocchetto* spool, ratchet, dim. from Proto-Romance, rel. to base of ROCK *noun*[2]. Later assim. to synon. RATCH *noun*[1].]
▶ **A** *noun*. **1** *sing.* & (*rare*) in *pl.* A set of angled teeth on the edge of a bar or wheel in which a device (as a cog, tooth, etc.) engages to prevent reversed motion. Freq. *attrib.* M17.
2 A bar or wheel (more fully ***ratchet-wheel***) provided with such teeth. E18.
3 A click or detent engaging in the ratchet of a wheel. M19.
4 In full ***ratchet-knife***. A type of knife with a curved blade. *W. Indies*. L20.
1 ratchet effect an effect by which a process, policy, cost, etc., continues or increases without any compensatory movement in the opposite direction, so that it comes to be perceived as irreversible.
▶ **B** *verb*. **1** *verb trans.* Provide with a ratchet; make into a ratchet. L19.
2 *verb intrans. & trans.* Move (as) by means of a ratchet. L19.

📖 **2** *Daily Telegraph* The union movement has not been responsible for ratcheting up inflation.

■ **ratchety** *adjective* resembling the movement of a ratchet, jerky M19.

rate /reɪt/ *noun*[1]. LME.
[Old French from medieval Latin *rata* (from *pro rata* abbreviation of *pro rata parte* or *portione* according to the proportional share) use as noun of fem. of Latin *ratus*: see RATIFY.]
▶**I** **1** (Estimated) value or worth. *arch.* LME. ▸†**b** Estimation, consideration. E17–E18.
†**2** The total quantity, amount, or sum *of* something, esp. as a basis for calculation. L15–L16. ▸†**b** A fixed quantity. *rare*. M16–E17.
3 a The price paid or charged for a thing or class of things; *esp.* an amount paid or charged for a certain quantity of a commodity, work, etc.; a fixed or assigned price, charge, or value. L15. ▸**b** The amount of or *of* a charge or payment as a proportion of some other amount or as a basis of calculation. L15. ▸**c** A charge formerly levied by a British local authority, expressed as a proportion of the assessed value of a property owned or leased; *esp.* (in *pl.*) the amount of this payable. E18. ▸**d** In full ***rate of exchange***. The value assigned to a currency for the purpose of exchange. E18.
4 A stated numerical amount of one thing corresponding proportionally to a certain amount of some other thing (usu. expressed as unity). L15.
5 Speed of movement, change, etc.; the rapidity with which something takes place; frequency of a rhythmic action. M17. ▸**b** The amount of gain or loss made on the correct time by a clock or watch. M19. ▸**c** MECHANICS. In full ***spring rate***. A quantity relating the load applied to a spring to the compression or extension produced. M20.

📖 **1** M. HALE They mightily prize them and set a great rate upon them. **3a** W. COWPER At how dear a rate He sells protection. B. BEHAN A fourth-year apprentice . . would get a bigger rate per hour. P. D. JAMES They pay me four pounds an hour which is above the going rate. *Holiday Which?* We give rates for one person sharing a twin room. **b** *Manchester Examiner* The rate of . . income tax ought to vary. *Which?* Rates . . lower than those offered by building societies. **4** L. DEIGHTON Firing at the rate of 520 rounds per minute. H. MACMILLAN The rate of expenditure would be . . £2 million a month. *Australian Financial Review* The jobless rate fell from 8.8 per cent to 8.6. **5** W. STYRON My heart pounding at a great rate. B. CASTLE Try to reduce the rate of inflation. C. FRANCIS The rate at which the sea uses up oxygen. A. KENNY We went on at a great rate up the summit ridge.

▶ **II** †**6** A standard of conduct; a manner, a style. L15–L18.
7 A standard or measure of quality; class, rank, kind. Now chiefly with ordinal numeral, as ***first-rate*** etc. E16. ▸**b** NAUTICAL. Any of various classes into which ships, esp. (*Hist.*) warships, are divided according to their size or (*Hist.*) the number of guns carried. M17. ▸**c** NAUTICAL. = RATING *noun*[1] 2a. E18. ▸**d** *Hist.* Any of various classes into which buildings are divided according to purpose or size. L18.
Phrases: **at an easy rate** *arch.* without great expense; *fig.* without great suffering. ***at any rate***: see ANY *adjective* 1a. ***at a rate of knots***: see KNOT *noun*[1]. **at that rate** in that case, under those circumstances. **at this rate** in this case, under these circumstances. ***flat rate***: see FLAT *adjective*. ***minimum lending rate***: see MINIMUM *adjective*. ***mortgage rate***: see MORTGAGE *noun*. ***net reproduction rate***: see NET *adjective*[2] & *adverb*. ***prime rate***: see PRIME *adjective*.
Comb.: **rate-buster** *US slang* a piece-worker whose high productivity causes or threatens to cause a reduction in rates; **rate-cap** *verb trans.* subject to rate-capping; **rate-capping** the imposition by central government of an upper limit on the amount of money which a local authority could spend and so levy through the rates; **rate-card** a list of charges for advertising; **rate constant** PHYSICAL CHEMISTRY a coefficient of proportionality relating the rate of a chemical reaction at a given temperature to the concentration of reactant (in a unimolecular reaction) or to the product of the concentrations of reactants; **ratemeter** an instrument which displays or records the rate, usu. averaged over a period, of pulses in an electronic counter, esp. those resulting from incidence of ionizing radiation; **ratepayer** a person liable to local rates.

rate /reɪt/ *noun*[2]. L16.
[from RATE *verb*[2].]
HUNTING. A reproof to a hound or dog.

rate /reɪt/ *verb*[1]. LME.
[from RATE *noun*[1].]
1 *verb trans.* Estimate the worth or value of, appraise; assign a value to, esp. according to a set scale. LME. ▸**b** *spec.* Assign a fixed value to (a metal) in relation to a monetary standard. M18. ▸**c** Assign a standard, optimal, or limiting rating to (a piece of equipment, a material, etc.). Usu. foll. by *at* the value concerned. Usu. in *pass.* L19. ▸**d** COMMERCE. Estimate the value, performance, or or profitability of (securities, a company, etc.). E20.
†**2** *verb trans.* **a** Fix or assign the amount of (a payment etc.). L15–E17. ▸**b** Divide proportionally; allocate; share out. L15–M17.
3 *verb trans.* Consider, regard. M16. ▸**b** Set a high value on, think much of. *colloq.* L20.
4 *verb trans.* Calculate or estimate the amount or sum of. Now *rare*. L16.
5 *verb trans.* In *pass.* Be subjected to or (*arch.*) *to* payment of a local rate; be valued for the purpose of assessing local rates. L16.
6 a *verb trans.* Place in a certain class or rank. E18. ▸**b** *verb intrans.* Have a certain rank or position; rank or count (*as*); *spec.* rank highly, be of importance, be highly esteemed. E19. ▸**c** *verb trans.* Merit, deserve; be worthy of. E20.
7 *verb trans.* Ascertain the variation of (a clock etc.) from true time. M19.
8 *verb trans.* HORSE-RACING. Ride (a horse) at a moderate pace to conserve the animal's energy for the finish. Chiefly *US*. E20.

📖 **1** M. MITCHELL Each job was rated on a five-point scale. G. GREENE He had the modesty of a good fellow . . and he rated himself too low. ***x-rated***: see X, X 11. **c** *Practical Wireless* Variable resistors, . . rated at 25 amps. **3** N. SHUTE She could not rate it equal in importance. **b** E. DUNPHY He's a . . pro., but . . Benny doesn't rate him. J. BARNES If Heaven was gained by courage . . then Gregory didn't rate his chances. **4** T. CAMPBELL To rate What millions died—that Caesar might be great. **6a** J. AGATE Maurice Evans . . is . . rated above Gielgud. **b** D. ATHILL Warmth did not rate as a necessity. *Southern Rag* My programme . . continues to rate near the top in the commercial radio surveys. **c** F. FORSYTH Retired colonels did not rate a personal driver.

■ **rater** *noun*[1] (*a*) a person or thing which rates something; (*b*) NAUTICAL a ship of a specified rate: E17.

rate /reɪt/ *verb*[2]. LME.
[Origin unkn.]
1 *verb trans. & intrans.* (with *at*). Chide, scold, reprove angrily, (a person or dog). LME.
†**2** *verb trans.* Drive *away*, *back*, etc., by rating. L16–L19.
■ **rater** *noun*[2] M19.

raté /rate/ *adjective & noun.* Pl. pronounced same. E20.
[French.]
▶ **A** *adjective.* Ineffective; unsuccessful. E20.
▶ **B** *noun.* A person who has failed in his or her vocation. E20.

rateable /ˈreɪtəb(ə)l/ *adjective.* Also **ratable**. E16.
[from RATE *verb*[1] + -ABLE.]
1 Able to be rated or estimated, esp. in accordance with some scale. E16.
2 Liable to payment of local rates. M18.
2 rateable value the value formerly ascribed to a building for the assessment of the local rates to be levied on it.
■ **ratea'bility** *noun* M19. **rateably** *adverb* L15.

ratel /ˈreɪt(ə)l, ˈrɑː-/ *noun.* L18.
[Afrikaans, of unkn. origin.]
A badger, *Mellivora capensis*, of Africa and southern Asia, black in colour with a light grey back and head, having powerful claws on the front feet, and feeding on honey, insects, and small animals and birds. Also called ***honey-badger***.

ratelier /rɑtəlje/ *noun.* Pl. pronounced same. M17.
[French *râtelier*.]
†**1** A stand for arms. *rare.* Only in M17.
2 A set of (esp. false) teeth. M19.

rat-goose /ˈratguːs/ *noun. Scot. & north.* Now *rare* or *obsolete.* Also **road-goose** /ˈrəʊd-/, **rood goose** /ˈruːd-/, & other vars. Pl. **-geese** /-giːs/. L17.
[1st elem. perh. rel. to ROUT *verb*[1]: cf. Icelandic *hrotgæs*, Norwegian *ratgås*, Dutch *rotgans*.]
The brent-goose, *Branta bernicla*.

rath /rɑːθ/ *noun.* LME.
[Irish = Gaelic †*ráth*, Gaulish *rātin*, *-rātum* (recorded in place-names).]
IRISH ANTIQUITIES. A strong usu. circular earthen wall forming an enclosure and serving as a fort and residence for a tribal chief.

rath *adjective* var. of RATHE *adjective*.

Rathaus /ˈrɑːthaʊs/ *noun.* Pl. **-häuser** /-hɔyzər/. E17.
[German, from *Rat* council + *Haus* house.]
A town hall in a German-speaking country.

rathe /reɪð/ *noun.* Now *dial.* See also RAVE *noun*[1]. LME.
[Origin unkn.]
1 A rail of a cart; = RAVE *noun*[1] 1. LME.
2 *WEAVING.* A bar with teeth, used to separate and guide the warp-threads. M16.

rathe /reɪð/ *adjective.* Now *poet. & dial.* Also **rath** /rɑːθ/.
[Old English *hræþ*, *hræd* = Old High German *(h)rad*, Old Norse *hraðr*, from Germanic base perh. rel. to base of RASH *adjective & adverb*. Cf. RARE *adjective*[2] & *adverb*[2].]
1 Quick in action; prompt; eager. OE.
2 Early; done or occurring before the fitting, usual, or natural time; *spec.* (of a flower or fruit) blooming or ripening early in the year. ME.
3 Of or pertaining to the first part of some period of time; *esp.* early in the day, belonging to the dawn or morning. LME.
Comb.: **rathe-ripe** *adjective & noun* (*a*) *adjective* (of a fruit, vegetable, or grain) ripening early in the year; *fig.* precocious; (*b*) *noun* an early-ripening fruit etc.
■ **ratheness** *noun* (*rare*) earliness M17.

rathe /reɪð/ *adverb.* Now *poet. & dial.* Compar. RATHER *adverb*. Superl. **rathest**.
[Old English *hraþe*, *hræþe* (= Middle Low German *rade*, Old High German *(h)rado*), formed as prec.]
†**1** Quickly, rapidly; *esp.* without delay, promptly. OE–M17.
2 Early; before the fitting, usual, or natural time. Now only, early in the morning or day. ME.

rather /ˈrɑðə/ *noun. US dial.* E20.
[from the adverb.]
A choice, a preference.

rather /ˈrɑːðə, *in sense A. 4b* rɑːˈðəː/ *adverb & adjective* (in mod. use also classed as a *determiner*).
[Old English *hraþor* (= Gothic *raþizo*) compar. of *hræþe* RATHE *adverb*: see -ER[3].]
▶ **A** *adverb.* **I 1** Earlier, sooner; at an earlier time, season, etc. Formerly also foll. by *the*. Now *dial.* OE.
2 Previously, formerly. Long *obsolete* exc. *dial.* ME.

> 🕮 **1** SHAKES. *Macb.* When Duncan is asleep—Whereto the rather shall his day's hard journey Soundly invite him. C. BUTLER Dry weather may cause them come . . rather.

▶ **II 3** (All) the more; the more readily. Chiefly & long only with *the. arch.* OE.
4 In preference; more willingly; sooner (as a matter of choice). (Foll. by *than*, †*or*.) ME. ▸**b** As *interjection.* Expr. affirmation: very much so; decidedly. *colloq.* M19.
5 With better reason; more properly. Foll. by *than*. ME.
6 More correctly; more correctly speaking; on the contrary, instead. (Foll. by *than*.) LME.
7 In a certain degree; to some extent; somewhat, slightly. Also, to a somewhat excessive extent, a little too. L16.

> 🕮 **4** H. JAMES He would rather chop off his hand than offer her a cheque. L. P. HARTLEY Don't change unless you'd rather. G. GREENE He paid a fine . . rather than be an alderman. P. D. JAMES Perhaps you'd rather I went. **b** J. BUCHAN 'Have you . . heard of . . Kynæthо?' 'Rather.' **5** T. HARDY Such a remark was rather to be tolerated than admired. **6** GOLDSMITH Say rather, that he loves all the world. SCOTT FITZGERALD They talked shop . . or rather she listened while he talked shop. I. MURDOCH Feeling rather than seeing . . the iron bedsteads. *Scotsman* Designing cities for vehicles . . rather than for people. **7** D. H. LAWRENCE A rather delicate baby at first. J. B. PRIESTLEY The morning was . . rather misty. C. P. SNOW Standing rather uncertainly in some . . public-house. R. WEST A . . wreath . . set rather to the back of her head. E. BOWEN She was rather an awful child. H. SECOMBE He rather liked being bossed about.

▶ **B** *adjective.* Before an article and noun: that is the noun specified to a certain (slight or considerable) extent. L18.

> 🕮 F. E. SMEDLEY Is it my trap you're talking about? rather the thing isn't it . . ? E. BOWEN He said he had had rather a day. D. EDEN Your Aunt Annabel is rather a pet.

Phrases: **had rather** would rather. *HEAR rather.*
■ **ratherest** *adverb* (*obsolete* exc. *dial.*) most of all LME. **ratherish** *adverb* (*colloq.*) somewhat, slightly M19.

rathest *superl. adverb* see RATHE *adverb*.

Rathke /ˈrɑːtkə/ *noun.* L19.
[M. H. *Rathke* (1793–1860), German anatomist.]
EMBRYOLOGY. Used *attrib.* and in *possess.* to designate a pouch or pocket in the oral cavity of developing vertebrates which forms the anterior lobe of the pituitary gland.

rat-hole /ˈrathəʊl/ *noun & verb.* E19.
[from RAT *noun*[1] + HOLE *noun*[1].]
▶ **A** *noun.* **1** A hole lived in or used by a rat; *fig.* a cramped or squalid building etc., *esp.* one that is a refuge or hiding place. E19. ▸**b** *fig.* A seemingly bottomless hole, esp. one down which expenditure disappears. *N. Amer.* M20.
2 *OIL INDUSTRY.* A shallow hole drilled near a well to accommodate the kelly when not in use; a small hole drilled at the bottom of a larger hole. E20.

> 🕮 **1b** *Time* To build . . more airplanes would . . amount to pouring half a billion dollars down a rat-hole.

▶ **B** *verb intrans. & trans.* **1** *OIL INDUSTRY.* Drill a small hole at the bottom of (a hole of larger diameter). E20.
2 Hide or store (esp. money). *US slang.* M20.

rathskeller /ˈrɑːtskɛlə/ *noun. US.* E20.
[German †*Rathskeller* (now *Ratskeller*) cellar in a town hall where beer or wine is sold, from *Rat(haus)* town hall + *Keller* cellar.]
A beer-hall or restaurant in a basement.

†**rati** *noun* var. of RUTTEE.

raticide /ˈratɪsʌɪd/ *noun.* M19.
[from RAT *noun*[1] + -I- + -CIDE.]
A person who or thing which kills rats, *esp.* a chemical substance used as a rat poison.

ratification /ratɪfɪˈkeɪʃ(ə)n/ *noun.* LME.
[Old & mod. French, or medieval Latin *ratificatio(n-)*, from *ratificat-* pa. ppl stem of *ratificare*: see next, -ATION.]
The action or an act of ratifying something; (a) formal sanction or confirmation.

ratify /ˈratɪfʌɪ/ *verb trans.* LME.
[Old & mod. French *ratifier* from medieval Latin *ratificare*, from Latin *ratus* fixed, established, from *reri* reckon, think: see -FY.]
1 Confirm or validate (an act, agreement, etc., esp. one made in one's name) by signing or giving formal consent or sanction. LME. ▸†**b** Ensure the fulfilment of (a purpose, hope, etc.). L16–M17. ▸†**c** Confirm the possession of. *rare.* Only in E17.
2 Declare or confirm the truth of (a statement etc.). Now *rare* or *obsolete.* LME.
†**3** Consummate (a marriage); complete. *rare.* M16–E18.
■ **ratifiable** *adjective* M20. **ratifier** *noun* E17.

ratihabition /ˌratɪhəˈbɪʃ(ə)n/ *noun.* Now *rare* or *obsolete.* E16.
[Late Latin *ratihabitio(n-)*, from *ratihabit-* pa. ppl stem of *ratihabere* confirm, from *ratus* (see prec.) + *habere* have, hold: see -ION.]
LAW. (An) approval, (a) sanction.

ratine /rəˈtiːn/ *noun & adjective.* Also **-né** /-neɪ/. E20.
[from French *ratiné* pa. pple of *ratiner* frieze or put a nap on (cloth), from *ratine* RATTEEN.]
(Made of) a plain-woven (usu. cotton) fabric with a loose open weave and rough surface, used for linings, furniture covers, etc.

rating /ˈreɪtɪŋ/ *noun*[1]. M16.
[from RATE *verb*[1] + -ING[1].]
1 The action of RATE *verb*[1]. M16. ▸**b** An amount fixed as a rate. M19.
2 *NAUTICAL.* **a** The position or class held by a person on a ship's books; *transf.* any of the classes into which racing yachts are distributed by measurement. E18. ▸**b** A non-commissioned sailor. L19.
3 The value of a property or condition which is claimed to be standard, optimal, or limiting for a piece of equipment, a material, etc. L19.
4 An assessment of a person's or thing's performance, skill, status, etc.; *spec.* the estimated status of a person as regards creditworthiness; a comparative assessment of the value or performance of a commodity offered for sale. E20. ▸**b** The estimated size of the audience of a particular radio or television programme as a measure of its popularity; the relative popularity of a programme so estimated. Usu. in *pl.* M20.

> 🕮 **2b** A. HAILEY The boat was operated by two naval ratings. ***leading rating***: see LEADING *adjective*. **3** *OCTANE* ***rating***. **4** *Elle* His restaurant has received stellar ratings in both the Michelin and Gault Millau foodie bibles. *New York Times* The war in the Persian Gulf, which . . left Mr. Bush with towering approval ratings. **b** *Broadcast* A talent show gets very good ratings.

rating /ˈreɪtɪŋ/ *verbal noun*[2]. L16.
[from RATE *verb*[2] + -ING[1].]
The action of RATE *verb*[2]; an instance of this.

ratio /ˈreɪʃɪəʊ, *in sense 1 usu.* ˈrɑːtɪəʊ/ *noun.* Pl. **-os**, in sense 1 **rationes** /rɑːtɪˈəʊniːz/. M17.
[Latin *ratio(n-)* reason, reckoning from *rat-* pa. ppl stem of *reri*: see RATIFY.]
1 a Reason, rationale. Chiefly in Latin phrs. M17. ▸**b** *LAW.* In full ***ratio decidendi*** /desɪˈdɛndiː, -dʌɪ/. The principle forming the basis of a judicial decision. M19.
2 a *MATH. & SCIENCE.* The relation between two magnitudes in respect of quantity, as determined by the number of times that one contains the other (integrally or fractionally), and usu. expressed in terms of the smallest integers between which the same relation of division holds. Also (now *rare*) ***geometrical ratio***. M17. ▸**b** A proportional relationship between things not precisely measurable. E19.
†**3** = RATION *noun* 3. M18–E19.
1a ratio cognoscendi /kɒgnəˈsɛndiː, -dʌɪ/ *PHILOSOPHY* that in virtue of which knowledge of something is possible. **ratio essendi** /ɛˈsɛndiː, -dʌɪ/, (*rare*) **ratio existendi** /ɛgzɪsˈtɛndiː, -dʌɪ/ *PHILOSOPHY* that in virtue of which something exists. **2a** ***aspect ratio***, ***compression ratio***, ***inverse ratio***, ***likelihood ratio***, ***power ratio***, ***Wiedemann–Franz ratio***, etc. **arithmetical ratio** (now *rare*) the relation between two magnitudes expressed as the amount by which one exceeds the other. **b** ***mental ratio***: see MENTAL *adjective*[1].

ratio /ˈreɪʃɪəʊ/ *verb trans.* M20.
[from the noun.]
Enlarge, amplify, or reduce by a certain ratio.

ratiocinate /ratɪˈɒsɪneɪt, raʃɪ-/ *verb intrans.* Now *literary.* M17.
[Latin *ratiocinat-* pa. ppl stem of *ratiocinari* calculate, deliberate, formed as RATIO *noun*: see -ATE[3].]
Go through logical processes, reason, esp. using syllogisms.
■ **ratiocinator** *noun* E19.

ratiocination /ˌratɪɒsɪˈneɪʃ(ə)n, ˌraʃɪ-/ *noun.* Now *literary.* E16.
[Latin *ratiocinatio(n-)*, formed as prec.: see -ATION.]
1 The action or process of reasoning, esp. by using syllogisms. E16. ▸**b** An instance of this; a conclusion arrived at by reasoning. E17.
2 The power of reasoning. *rare.* M17.

ratiocinative /ratɪˈɒsɪnətɪv, raʃɪ-/ *adjective.* Now *literary.* E17.
[Latin *ratiocinativus*, formed as RATIOCINATE: see -IVE.]
Characterized by or given to ratiocination.

ration /ˈraʃ(ə)n/ *noun & verb.* M16.
[(French from Italian *razione* or Spanish *ración*) formed as RATIO *noun*: see -ION.]
▶ **A** *noun.* †**1** Reasoning. *rare.* Only in M16.
†**2** = RATIO *noun* 2. M17–E19.
3 A fixed (daily) allowance of provisions for a person, esp. in the armed forces (usu. in *pl.*); *gen.* (in *pl.*) provisions, food. Formerly also (*MILITARY*), a daily allowance of forage for an animal. E18.
4 A fixed official allowance of or *of* (a specified type of) food, clothing, fuel, etc., for each person in time of war or shortage. E18.

> 🕮 **3** R. CONQUEST We . . pull out our rations and begin to eat. P. SCOTT Provided basic rations in the shape of monthly doles of flour, tea, salt. **given out with the rations** *Military slang* (of a medal etc.) awarded automatically, without regard to merit. **4** R. MACAULAY Our meals are rather austere . . our meat ration is so tiny. E. YOUNG-BRUEHL They ate . . cautiously in order not to disturb stomachs accustomed to war rations. **off ration**, **off the ration** in addition to the allowance.

Comb.: **ration book**, **ration card**, **ration coupon**: entitling the holder to a ration; **ration sheep** *Austral.* the sheep to be killed for food for the workers on a station; **ration strength** the number of soldiers in an armed force, estimated by the rations supplied to them.
▶ **B** *verb trans.* **1** Supply with rations; limit to a fixed allowance of food etc. M19.
2 Share out (food etc.) in fixed quantities. Also foll. by *out.* L19.

1 W. GOLDING I *did* ration myself to a daily bottle. 2 G. SAYER There were . . logs . . for the fires, because coal was rationed.

rational /ˈraʃ(ə)n(ə)l/ *noun*¹. LME.
[Absol. use of adjective.]
†1 Power of reasoning. Only in LME.
2 A rational being; a human being. Usu. in *pl.* Now *rare* or *obsolete.* E17.
3 MATH. A rational number or quantity. L17.
4 That which is rational or reasonable. L17.
5 *Hist.* In *pl.* Knickerbockers for women. L19.

rational /ˈraʃ(ə)n(ə)l/ *noun*². LME.
[Late Latin (Vulgate) *rationale* use as noun of neut. of *rationalis* (see next.), translating Hebrew *ḥōšen*, after Greek (Septuagint) *logeion* oracle, oracular instrument.]
1 The breastplate worn by an Israelite high-priest; a similar ornament worn by a bishop during the celebration of mass. *obsolete* exc. *Hist.* LME.
2 = RATIONALE 2. *rare.* M17.

rational /ˈraʃ(ə)n(ə)l/ *adjective.* LME.
[Latin *rationalis*, formed as RATIO *noun*: see -AL¹.]
1 Having the faculty of reasoning; endowed with reason. LME. ▸b *Hist.* Designating (any of) an ancient class of physicians, who deduced their treatment of cases from general principles. Formerly also, (of a field of study, esp. psychology) employing or based on deduction from general principles. M16. ▸c Using the faculty of reasoning; having sound judgement; sensible, sane. M17.
2 Of, pertaining to, or based on reason or reasoning. LME. ▸†b Existing (only) in the mind, not real. Only in 17.
†3 GRAMMAR. Of a conjunction: expressing a reason for a statement. LME–L17.
4 a MATH. (Of a number, quantity, etc.) expressible as a ratio of integers; (of an expression etc.) including no radical quantities which cannot be reduced to such a ratio. L16. ▸b PHYSICS. Of electrical units and equations: rationalized (see RATIONALIZE *verb* 2b). L19.
5 In accordance with reason; not foolish, absurd, or extreme. M17.

1 J. PLAMENATZ Man as a self-conscious, rational . . being who can make choices. c P. LIVELY What had got into Helen, normally as rational as himself. 2 A. CROSS That . . is such nonsense. I refuse to pay it the compliment of rational refutation. G. SAYER Jack often experienced a conflict between his intuitive and rational sides. 5 A. S. NEILL In Australia, fear of a spider is rational, for a spider can be death-dealing.

Special collocations: **rational dress** *Hist.* a style of women's dress of the late 19th cent., characterized by the wearing of bloomers or knickerbockers. ***rational horizon***: see HORIZON *noun* 3. **rational mechanics**: as deduced logically from first principles.
■ **rationally** *adverb* E17. **rationalness** *noun* (now *rare*) M17.

rationale /raʃəˈnɑːl/ *noun.* M17.
[mod. Latin, use as noun of neut. of Latin *rationalis* RATIONAL *adjective.*]
1 A reasoned exposition of principles; an explanation or statement of reasons. M17.
2 The fundamental or underlying reason for or basis of a thing; a justification. L17.

1 *American Speech* A rationale which states how that work meets . . stated goals. 2 R. G. MYERS The main rationale for promoting rapid educational expansion was . . an economic one.

rationalise *verb* var. of RATIONALIZE.

rationalism /ˈraʃ(ə)n(ə)lɪz(ə)m/ *noun.* E18.
[from RATIONAL *adjective* + -ISM, after French *rationalisme*, German *Rationalismus.*]
1 a THEOLOGY. The practice of treating reason as the ultimate authority in religion. Also, the practice of explaining supernatural or miraculous events on a rational basis. E18. ▸b PHILOSOPHY. The doctrine or belief that reason should be the only guiding principle in life, obviating the need for reliance on or adherence to any form of religious belief. L19.
2 *Hist.* The principles of the rational physicians. E19.
3 PHILOSOPHY. The doctrine or theory that reason rather than sense-experience is the foundation of certainty in knowledge. Opp. EMPIRICISM 2. Cf. SENSATIONALISM 1. M19.
4 The principle or practice of using reasoning and calculation as a basis for analysis, a course of action, etc. E20.
5 ARCHITECTURE. A theory of architecture of the mid 19th cent., characterized by geometrical simplicity, functionalism, and sparing use of ornamentation. M20.

rationalist /ˈraʃ(ə)n(ə)lɪst/ *noun & adjective.* E17.
[from (the same root as) prec. + -IST.]
▶ A *noun.* 1 A person whose opinions are based on pure reasoning. E17.
2 An advocate or practitioner of rationalism. M17.
▶ B *adjective.* Characterized by rationalism; supporting or practising rationalism. E19.
■ **rationaˈlistic** *adjective* = RATIONALIST *adjective* M19. **rationaˈlistically** *adverb* M19.

rationality /raʃəˈnalɪti/ *noun.* L16.
[Late Latin *rationalitas*, formed as RATIONAL *adjective*: see -ITY.]
1 MATH. The quality of being rational as a number, quantity, etc. L16.
2 The quality of possessing reason. E17.
3 The fact of being based on reason; a rational or reasonable view, practice, etc. M17.
4 The tendency to regard everything from a purely rational point of view. L18.

2 E. L. DOCTOROW He was calm and courteous, the picture of rationality. 3 F. W. FABER Quite as much danger from the mysticisms of Newman as from the rationalities of Whately. 4 A. LIVINGSTONE Nietzsche was withdrawing from . . metaphysics towards a cooler rationality.

rationalize /ˈraʃ(ə)n(ə)lʌɪz/ *verb.* Also -ise. L18.
[from RATIONAL *adjective* + -IZE.]
1 *verb trans.* Explain on a rational basis; make rational and consistent; explain *away* rationally. L18. ▸b *verb trans.* & *intrans.* PSYCHOLOGY. Explain or justify (one's behaviour or attitude) with plausible but specious reasons, usu. unwittingly. E20.
2 *verb trans.* a MATH. Convert (a function, expression, etc.) to a rational form. E19. ▸b PHYSICS. Reformulate (units or equations of electromagnetism) in such a way that the factor 4π appears only when a system with spherical symmetry is involved. Chiefly as ***rationalized*** *ppl adjective.* L19.
3 *verb intrans.* Employ reason; think rationally. M19.
4 *verb trans.* Make (a business etc.) more efficient by reorganizing it according to rational principles so as to reduce or eliminate waste of labour, time, or materials. E20.
■ **rationaliˈzation** *noun* the action or an act of rationalizing M19. **rationalizer** *noun* M19.

rationate /ˈraʃ(ə)neɪt/ *verb intrans. rare.* M17.
[Late Latin *rationat-* pa. ppl stem of *rationari* to reason, formed as RATIO *noun*: see -ATE³.]
Reason, ratiocinate.
■ **rationative** *adjective* that gives a reason M17.

rationes *noun pl.* see RATIO *noun.*

ratite /ˈratʌɪt/ *adjective & noun.* L19.
[from Latin *ratis* raft + -ITE¹.]
ORNITHOLOGY. ▶ A *adjective.* Of, pertaining to, or designating (any of) a group of flightless birds having a flat breastbone with no keel, as the ostrich, emu, cassowary, etc. Opp. ***carinate***. L19.
▶ B *noun.* A ratite bird. M20.

ratline /ˈratlɪn/ *noun & verb.* Also -lin, (earlier) -ling /-lɪŋ/. LME.
[Origin unkn.]
NAUTICAL. ▶ A *noun.* Any of the small lines fastened across the shrouds of a sailing ship like ladder-rungs and used to climb the rigging (usu. in *pl.*); thin line or rope used for these (more fully ***ratline stuff***). LME.
▶†B *verb trans.* Provide with ratlines. L15–E18.

ratling /ˈratlɪŋ/ *noun*¹. L19.
[from RAT *noun*¹ + -LING¹.]
A young or small rat.

ratling *noun*² & *verb* var. of RATLINE.

ratoon /rəˈtuːn/ *noun.* M17.
[Spanish *retoño* a fresh shoot or sprout. Cf. next.]
A new shoot or sprout springing from the base of a crop plant, esp. sugar cane, after cropping.

ratoon /rəˈtuːn/ *verb.* M18.
[Spanish *retoñar* sprout again. Cf. prec.]
1 *verb intrans.* Of a plant, esp. sugar cane (formerly also, of soil): send up ratoons. M18.
2 *verb trans.* Cut down (a plant) to cause it to sprout in this way. E20.

Ratrac /ˈratrak/ *noun.* Also r-. L20.
[Origin unkn.]
(Proprietary name for) a tracked vehicle used for impacting the surface of a skiing *piste*.

rat-rhyme /ˈratrʌɪm/ *noun. Scot. & north.* E16.
[from (prob.) imit. 1st elem. (cf. RATTLE *verb*¹) + RHYME *noun.*]
A piece of doggerel verse.

ratsbane /ˈratsbeɪn/ *noun.* Now chiefly *literary.* L15.
[from RAT *noun*¹ + -'S¹ + BANE.]
Rat-poison. Formerly *spec.*, arsenic.

rat's-tail /ˈratsteɪl/ *noun.* L16.
[from RAT *noun*¹ + -'S¹ + TAIL *noun*¹.]
1 In *pl.* Scabby or suppurating cracks on a horse's pasterns, with acute soreness. Cf. SCRATCH *noun*¹ 2a. Now *rare* or *obsolete.* L16.
2 A thing resembling a rat's tail in shape; *spec.* a lank lock of hair. E19.
Comb.: **rat's-tail cactus** a pendent cactus, *Aporocactus flagelliformis*, with spiny whiplike stems bearing numerous crimson flowers; **rat's-tail fescue** an annual grass of dry rough ground, *Vulpia myuros*, with long narrow panicles; **rat's-tail plantain** the greater plantain, *Plantago major.*

rat-tail /ˈratteɪl/ *noun.* E18.
[from RAT *noun*¹ + TAIL *noun*¹.]
1 A tail resembling that of a rat; *esp.* a horse's tail with little or no hair; a horse with such a tail. E18.
2 Something resembling a rat's tail in shape; *spec.* (*a*) (in full ***rat-tail-file***) a fine rounded tapering file; (*b*) a lank lock of hair; (*c*) an extension from the handle to the back of the bowl of a spoon. M18.
3 In *pl.* = RAT'S-TAIL 1. M18.
4 Any of various deep-water marine gadoid fishes of the family Macrouridae, having a large head, short body, and long, tapering tail. L19.
Comb.: **rat-tail cactus** = *RAT'S-TAIL cactus*; ***rat-tail-file***: see sense 2(a) above; **rat-tail-grass** *Austral. & NZ* a coarse grass of pastures, *Sporobolus capensis*; **rat-tail-spoon**: with a rat-tail.

rat-tailed /ˈratteɪld/ *adjective.* L17.
[from prec. + -ED².]
Having a rat-tail.
rat-tailed maggot the aquatic larva of a drone-fly of the genus *Eristalis*, which has a long slender respiratory organ resembling a tail with which it breathes air at the surface of stagnant water. **rat-tailed radish** an Asian radish, *Raphanus caudatus*, cultivated for its long edible fruit.

rattan /rəˈtan/ *noun*¹. Also **ratan**; (earlier) **rotan** /rəʊˈtan/, **†-tang**. M17.
[Malay *rotan*, prob. from *raut* pare, trim, strip.]
1 Any of several esp. Malaysian climbing palms of the genera *Calamus*, *Daemonorops*, *Korthalsia*, etc., with long thin jointed pliable stems (also ***rattan-palm***); a stem of this used as a walking stick, an instrument of punishment, or to make cane furniture etc. M17.
2 Rattan stems collectively as a material. M18.

1 *Far Eastern Economic Review* One stroke of the rattan has been known to make tough men faint. 2 B. VINE A glass-topped table of white rattan. *attrib.*: L. SPALDING The . . rattan sofa . . looked inviting.

rattan /rəˈtan/ *noun*². L18.
[Imit.]
= RATAPLAN *noun.*

rat-tat /ratˈtat/ *noun, adverb, interjection, & verb.* Also **ratatat**, (earlier) **rat-a-tat**, /ratəˈtat/, **rat-tat-tat** /rattatˈtat/. L17.
[Imit.]
▶ A *noun.* A sharp rapping sound, esp. of a knock at a door or of reports from a gun etc. L17.
▶ B *adverb & interjection.* With a sharp rapping sound; repr. the sound of a knock etc. M19.
▶ C *verb intrans.* Infl. -tt-. Make a sharp rapping sound. E20.

ratted /ˈratɪd/ *adjective*¹. *rare.* LME.
[from RAT *noun*² + -ED².]
Ragged; torn.

ratted /ˈratɪd/ *adjective*². *slang.* L20.
[from RAT *noun*¹ + -ED². Cf. *rat-arsed adjective.* s.v. RAT *noun*¹.]
Drunk.

ratteen /rəˈtiːn/ *noun & adjective.* M17.
[French *ratine*, of unkn. origin.]
Hist. (Made of) any of various coarse twilled woollen fabrics, usu. friezed or with a curled nap and used for linings.

rattening /ˈrat(ə)nɪŋ/ *noun.* M19.
[Origin unkn.]
Hist. The practice of taking away tools, destroying machinery etc., esp. to enforce compliance with trade-union rules.

ratter /ˈratə/ *noun.* ME.
[from RAT *noun*¹, *verb*¹ + -ER¹.]
1 A rat-catcher; *esp.* a dog or cat which catches rats. ME.
2 = RAT *noun*¹ 2b, c. *slang.* M19.
3 A person who steals opal from another's mine. *Austral. slang.* M20.

rattish /ˈratɪʃ/ *adjective.* L17.
[from RAT *noun*¹ + -ISH¹.]
Somewhat resembling (that of) a rat.

rattle /ˈrat(ə)l/ *noun.* L15.
[from the verb. Cf. Low German, Dutch *rattel.*]
▶ I 1 An instrument used to make a rattling noise; *spec.* (*a*) a baby's toy consisting of a container filled with small pellets, making a noise when shaken; a musical instrument similar to this; (*b*) an instrument with a vibrating tongue fixed in a frame which slips over the teeth of a ratchet-wheel, making a loud noise when whirled round, used formerly to sound an alarm, now to express support etc. at a sports match. L15.
2 Any of several semi-parasitic meadow plants of the figwort family, having seeds which rattle in their capsules when ripe: (*a*) (in full ***yellow rattle***) *Rhinanthus minor*, with yellow flowers and round capsules containing several discoid seeds; (*b*) (in full ***red rattle***) lousewort, *Pedicularis sylvatica*, and marsh lousewort, *P. palustris*, with pink or crimson flowers. L16.

3 The set of horny loosely connected rings at the end of a rattlesnake's tail, which make a rattling noise when shaken; any of these rings. **E17.**

▶ **II 4** A rapid succession of short sharp hard sounds. **E16.** ▸**b** *transf.* A racket, an uproar; noisy gaiety. **L17.** ▸**c** A coarse bubbling sound in the throat (esp. of a dying person), caused by partial obstruction by bronchial secretions. **M18.** ▸**d** A succession of small noisy waterfalls forming rapids. *N. Amer.* **L18.** ▸**e** PAPER-MAKING. The rustling quality of a sheet of finished paper, indicative of its hardness and density. **E20.** ▸**f** HUNTING. A note sounded on the horn at the kill. **E20.**

5 a A noisy flow of words. **E17.** ▸**b** Lively talk; trivial or empty chatter. **M18.**

6 A violent blow. *Scot. & north.* **M17.** ▸†**b** A sharp reproof. **M17–M19.**

7 A person who talks incessantly in a lively or inane fashion. *arch.* **E18.**

> 🕮 **4** I. FLEMING The rattle of the . . gold chain against the coins. A. CARTER The low rattle of gunfire.

Phrases: **in the rattle** *Nautical slang* on the commander's report of defaulters; in trouble. **with a rattle** with a sudden burst of speed.

Comb.: **rattlebox** (*a*) a rattle consisting of a box with objects inside; (*b*) *colloq.* a rickety old vehicle; (*c*) *US* a leguminous plant, *Crotalaria sagittalis*, with seeds which rattle in their pod when dry; **rattle-brain** a foolish noisy person; **rattle-brained** *adjective* characterized by foolish noisy behaviour; **rattle-bush** a West Indian plant, *Crotalaria incana*, related to the American rattlebox; **rattle-head** = *rattle-brain* above; **rattle-headed** *adjective* = *rattle-brained* above; **rattle-jack** shaly coal; **rattle-mouse** (*obsolete exc. dial.*) a bat; **rattle-pate** = *rattle-brain* above; **rattle-pated** *adjective* = *rattle-brained* above; **rattle-weed** *US* any of several plants with seeds which rattle in their pods when dry: (*a*) bugbane, *Cimicifuga racemosa*; (*b*) a loco-weed, *Astragalus pomonalis*; (*c*) = *rattlebox* (c) above.

rattle /ˈrat(ə)l/ *verb*[1]. **ME.**
[Prob. from Middle & mod. Low German, Middle Dutch *ratelen*, of imit. origin. Cf. ROTTLE, RUTTLE.]

▶ **I** *verb intrans.* **1** Of a thing: give out a rapid succession of short sharp hard sounds, esp. as a result of being shaken rapidly and of striking against something. **ME.** ▸**b** Of an agent: cause such sounds by shaking or striking something. **L17.**

2 Talk rapidly in a noisy, lively, or inane manner; chatter. Usu. foll. by adverb. **ME.**

3 Make a rattling noise when breathing or speaking. Formerly also, stutter. Now *rare.* **LME.** ▸**b** Of a female goat: give a rattling cry when on heat. Now *rare* or *obsolete.* **L16.**

4 Move rapidly and with a rattling noise; *spec.* drive a vehicle in this way. Usu. foll. by adverb. **M16.** ▸**b** Hurry; work energetically. *slang.* Now *rare.* **L17.** ▸**c** *transf.* Foll. by *about, around*: occupy an undesirable or unnecessary excess of space. **M19.**

> 🕮 **1** R. L. STEVENSON Gravel was dislodged, and fell rattling and bounding. B. VINE The . . windows . . rattled in the wind. *Mandy* Sleet was rattling on the roof. **b** HOBBES Then came his father rattling at his door. **2** B. EMECHETA Everyone . . seemed to be allowing her to rattle on. R. COBB Olive would rattle away . . about Switzerland. **4** S. NAIPAUL The lorry . . roared and rattled past. D. PROFUMO They rattled over the cattle-grid. WILBUR SMITH Pebbles rattled down the embankment. **c** *New Yorker* The vicar and his wife rattle around in . . a sparsely furnished vicarage.

▶ **II** *verb trans.* **5** Say, perform, or produce in a rapid or lively manner. Usu. foll. by *off, out.* **LME.** ▸**b** CRICKET. Bowl *down* (the opposing team's wickets) rapidly; bowl *out* (a team) rapidly. **M19.**

6 Make (a thing) rattle. **M16.** ▸†**b** Assail with a rattling noise. *rare* (Shakes.). Only in **L16.** ▸**c** Drive *away* or *out* with rattling. *rare.* **E17.**

7 Scold; rail at. (Formerly foll. by *off, up*, or with compl.). Now *rare.* **M16.**

8 Stir *up*, rouse; *esp.* fluster, make nervous, agitate, alarm, frighten. *colloq.* **L18.**

9 Cause to move rapidly; bring *up*, move *along*, etc., briskly. Usu. foll. by adverb. **E19.**

> 🕮 **5** K. CHERNIN A fast talker, . . rattling off the answers she's learned by heart. C. LASSALLE She rattled off fast passages like an efficient typist. *Squash World* The top seed rattled off 20 points in succession. M. SEYMOUR Wells . . rattled his novels off with speed and verve. **6** K. WATERHOUSE Somebody rattled the loose knob of the . . door. T. MORRISON The wind tore over the hills rattling roofs. E. NORTH Richard . . rattled the ice in his otherwise empty glass. **8** A. WEST She was not going to let . . her husband . . rattle her. S. BELLOW He was badly rattled, or he wouldn't have expressed himself so strongly. **9** J. MCCARTHY A Bill . . was rattled . . through both Houses.

Phrases: *rattle one's dags*: see DAG *noun*[1]. **rattle the sabre** threaten war.

rattle /ˈrat(ə)l/ *verb*[2] *trans.* **E18.**
[Back-form. from RATLING *noun*[2].]
NAUTICAL. Provide with a ratline or ratlines. Usu. foll. by *down.*

rattler /ˈratlə/ *noun.* **ME.**
[from RATTLE *verb*[1] + -ER[1].]
1 A person who rattles; *esp.* an inane chatterer. **ME.**
2 A thing which rattles; *spec.* (*colloq.*) an old or rickety vehicle, *esp.* a train. **M17.** ▸**b** A rattlesnake. *colloq.* **E19.**
3 A violent blow. Also, a violent storm. **E19.**
4 A remarkably good specimen of something; *spec.* a fast horse. *slang.* **M19.**

rattlesnake /ˈrat(ə)lsneɪk/ *noun & verb.* **M17.**
[from RATTLE *noun, verb*[1] + SNAKE *noun.*]

▶ **A** *noun.* **1** Any of several venomous American pit vipers of the genera *Sistrurus* and *Crotalus* (family Crotalidae), having a series of loosely connected horny rings at the end of the tail which make a rattling noise when shaken. **M17.**

2 In full ***rattlesnake cocktail***. A cocktail made from whisky mixed with pernod, lemon juice, and sugar. **M19.**

Comb.: **rattlesnake fern** a N. American moonwort, *Botrychium virginianum*, with sporangia suggesting the rattles of a rattlesnake; **rattlesnake master** any of various US plants reputedly efficacious against rattlesnake bites, esp. the umbellifer *Eryngium yuccifolium*; **rattlesnake plantain** any of several N. American orchids of the genus *Goodyera*, with mottled leaves; **rattlesnake root** (the root of) any of several N. American plants reputedly curing rattlesnake bites, esp. senega root, *Polygala senega*, and white lettuce, *Prenanthes alba*; **rattlesnake's master** = *rattlesnake master* above; **rattlesnake weed** a N. American hawkweed, *Hieracium venosum*, with purple-veined leaves.

▶ **B** *verb. rare.*
1 *verb trans.* Deceive, trick. **E19.**
2 *verb intrans. & trans.* Snake *along* with a rattling sound; make (one's way) in this manner. **M20.**

rattletrap /ˈrat(ə)ltrap/ *noun & adjective. colloq.* **M18.**
[from RATTLE *noun, verb*[1] + TRAP *noun*[1].]

▶ **A** *noun.* **1** A small or worthless article, a knick-knack. **M18.**
2 A rickety old thing, esp. a vehicle. **E19.**
3 The mouth. *slang.* **E19.**

▶ **B** *adjective.* Rickety. **M19.**

rattling /ˈratlɪŋ/ *adjective & adverb.* **LME.**
[from RATTLE *verb*[1] + -ING[2].]

▶ **A** *adjective.* **1** That rattles. **LME.**
2 Characterized by a rapid flow of words or liveliness of manner. **M16.**
3 Rapid, brisk, vigorous; remarkably good. **L17.**

> 🕮 **1** K. AMIS A taxi . . with its rattling engine. **2** SHAKES. *Mids. N. D.* The rattling tongue of eloquence. **3** *Navy News* Elsegood . . started at a rattling pace. He scored 59 off 44 balls.

▶ **B** *adverb.* Remarkably, extremely. **E19.**

> 🕮 *Times* Preferred a rattling good yarn to all that highbrow twaddle.

■ **rattlingly** *adverb* **E19.**

rattly /ˈratli/ *adjective.* **L19.**
[from RATTLE *verb*[1] + -Y[1].]
Rattling; tending to rattle.

ratton /ˈrat(ə)n/ *noun.* Now *Scot. & north.* See also ROTTAN. **ME.**
[Old French *raton*, from *rat* RAT *noun*[1], with augm. suffix: see -OON.]
A rat.
■ **rattoner** *noun* (*obsolete exc. north.*) a rat-catcher **ME.**

rat-trap /ˈrattrap/ *noun.* **LME.**
[from RAT *noun*[1] + TRAP *noun*[1].]
1 A trap for catching rats. **LME.** ▸**b** *transf.* A shabby or ramshackle building. *colloq.* **M19.**
2 More fully ***rat-trap pedal***. A bicycle pedal having two parallel toothed iron plates to provide a grip. **L19.**
3 BRICKLAYING. In full ***rat-trap bond***. A form of Flemish bond in which the bricks are laid on edge and the headers span the whole thickness of wall, dividing the wall cavity into square spaces. **M20.**

ratty /ˈrati/ *adjective.* **M19.**
[from RAT *noun*[1] + -Y[1].]
1 a Infested with rats. **M19.** ▸**b** Characteristic of a rat or rats. **L19.**
2 a Shabby; wretched; nasty. *colloq.* **M19.** ▸**b** Irritable; annoyed, angry. *colloq.* **E20.** ▸**c** Mad; eccentric. *Austral. & NZ colloq.* **L19.**

> 🕮 **2a** R. JAFFE The boy was in ratty jeans. *New Yorker* He slept . . on her ratty old mattress. **b** *Nursing* She was ratty and miserable. E. O'BRIEN Admitted to having been . . ratty with her on account of her being so late.

■ **rattily** *adverb* **L20.** **rattiness** *noun* **L20.**

raucity /ˈrɔːsɪti/ *noun. rare.* **E17.**
[French *raucité* or Latin *raucitas*, from *raucus*: see next, -ITY.]
Raucousness.

raucous /ˈrɔːkəs/ *adjective.* **M18.**
[from Latin *raucus* hoarse: see -OUS.]
Of a sound, esp. a voice: hoarse, rough; loud and harsh.

> 🕮 S. K. PENMAN The Bankside would have been teeming with raucous, ribald life. R. TREMAIN The sea-birds follow: a raucous, restless choir.

■ **raucously** *adverb* **M19.** **raucousness** *noun* **M20.**

†**raught** *verb pa. t. & pple*: see REACH *verb*[1].

rauk /rɔːk, rəʊk/ *noun. Scot. & north.* **L17.**
[Alt. of RAKE *noun*[1]. Cf. ROKE *noun*[2].]
A mark, a scratch; a flaw or defect in a piece of cloth, or in stone, metal, etc.

rauli /ˈraʊli/ *noun.* **E20.**
[Amer. Spanish from Mapuche *ruili.*]
A deciduous nothofagus, *Nothofagus nervosa*, of temperate Chile and Argentina; the reddish timber of this tree.

raunch /rɔːn(t)ʃ/ *noun. colloq.* **M20.**
[Back-form. from next.]
1 Shabbiness, grubbiness, dirtiness. **M20.**
2 Coarseness, vulgarity; boisterousness, earthiness. **M20.**

raunchy /ˈrɔːn(t)ʃi/ *adjective. colloq.* (orig. *US*). **M20.**
[Origin unkn. Cf. RANCHY.]
1 Inept, slovenly; unpleasant, mean, disreputable; dirty, grubby. **M20.**
2 (Of a person, action, etc.) coarse, boisterous, earthy, lusty, sexually provocative; (of language, humour, etc.) bawdy, smutty. **M20.**

> 🕮 **2** T. KENEALLY His raunchy cattle-breeding ancestors. R. JAFFE His deep raunchy voice seemed more sensual than vulgar. *Times* His advertising is raunchy, attention-grabbing and risqué . . the key commercial for his fragrance . . was banned.

■ **raunchily** *adverb* **L20.** **raunchiness** *noun* **L20.**

raupo /ˈraʊpɔː, ˈraʊpəʊ/ *noun.* Pl. **-os.** **M19.**
[Maori.]
A New Zealand bulrush, *Typha orientalis*, used esp. as a building and thatching material.

rauque /rɔːk/ *adjective. rare.* **M19.**
[French from Latin *raucus*: see RAUCOUS.]
Of a sound: hoarse, harsh.

raurekau /raʊˈreɪkaʊ/ *noun. NZ.* **E20.**
[Maori.]
A small New Zealand evergreen tree, *Coprosma australis*, of the madder family, with small white flowers and red berries.

rauriki /ˈraʊrɪki, ˈrarɪkiː/ *noun. NZ.* Also **rariki.** **M20.**
[Maori.]
= PUHA.

rauschpfeife /ˈraʊʃ(p)fʌɪfə/ *noun.* Pl. **-fen** /-f(ə)n/. **L19.**
[German = reed-pipe. Cf. SCHREIERPFEIFE.]
MUSIC. **1** A low-pitched mixture stop in an organ. **L19.**
2 A reed-cap shawm of the Renaissance period. **M20.**

rauwolfia /raʊˈwɒlfɪə, -ˈvɒlfɪə/ *noun.* Also **-volfia.** **M18.**
[mod. Latin (see below), from Leonhard *Rauwolf* (d. 1596), German physician and botanist + -IA[1].]
1 Any of various tropical shrubs or small trees constituting the genus *Rauvolfia* (sometimes spelt *Rauwolfia*) of the family Apocynaceae, with clusters of small white flowers and red or black berries; *esp.* any of those cultivated for the medicinal drugs obtained from their roots, as *R. serpentina* and *R. vomitoria*. **M18.**
2 PHARMACOLOGY. (An extract of) the dried roots of *Rauvolfia serpentina* or related plants, containing alkaloids (esp. reserpine) and used to treat hypertension and formerly as a tranquillizer. Also ***rauwolfia serpentina*** /sɜːp(ə)nˈtiːnə, -ˈtʌɪnə/. Cf. RESERPINE. **M20.**

rav /rɒv/ *noun.* Also (in sense 1) **rab**, (in sense 2) **rov.** **E18.**
[from Hebrew and Aramaic *raḇ* master; in sense 2 partly through Yiddish. Cf. RABBI *noun*[1].]
JUDAISM. **1** *Hist.* (A title of) any of certain Babylonian rabbis of the 2nd to the 5th cents. **E18.**
2 A rabbi. Freq. as a title of respect and form of address preceding a personal name. **L19.**

ravage /ˈravɪdʒ/ *noun.* **E17.**
[Old & mod. French, alt. of *ravine* rush of water: see RAVIN *noun*[1], -AGE.]
†**1** A flood, an inundation. *rare.* Only in **E17.**
2 a The action or an instance of ravaging; devastation, extensive damage. **E17.** ▸**b** *sing.* & (now usu.) in *pl.* The destructive action or effects of disease, time, weather, etc. **E18.**

> 🕮 **2b** J. H. NEWMAN Six centuries have been unable to repair the ravages of four years. SLOAN WILSON The ravages of chicken pox on . . their faces.

ravage /ˈravɪdʒ/ *verb.* **E17.**
[French *ravager*, formed as prec.]
1 *verb trans.* Devastate, lay waste, plunder. **E17.**
2 *verb intrans.* Commit ravages; wreak havoc. **E17.**

> 🕮 **1** J. K. JEROME The Danes . . started . . to ravage all the land of Wessex. *Hindu* Floods ravaged the eastern . . parts of the country.

■ **ravaged** *adjective* devastated, laid waste **E18.** **ravager** *noun* **E17.**

ravalement /ravalmɑ̃/ *noun.* Pl. pronounced same. **M20.**
[French, from *ravaler* bring down, reduce.]
MUSIC. The action or an instance of modifying and extending the range of a keyboard instrument by rebuilding; an instrument modified in this way.

ravanastron /rɑːvəˈnɑːstrən/ *noun.* **M19.**
[Origin uncertain: perh. from Sanskrit *rāvaṇahasta*, whence Rajasthani *rāvanhattho* a kind of violin.]
An ancient Indian stringed instrument played with a bow.

rave /reɪv/ *noun*[1]. **M16.**
[Var. of **RATHE** *noun.*]
1 A rail of a cart; *esp.* (in *pl.*) permanent or removable rails or boards added to the sides of a cart to enable a greater load to be carried. **M16.**
2 A vertical side-piece in the body of a wagon or sleigh. *US.* **M19.**

rave /reɪv/ *noun*[2] *& adjective.* **L16.**
[from next.]
▶ **A** *noun.* **1** The action or an act of raving; (a) frenzy; *transf.* the roar of the wind. **L16.**
2 a A passionate (usu. transitory) infatuation with a person or thing; the object of such an infatuation. *slang.* **E20.** ▸**b** A favourable opinion; a strong recommendation; *esp.* a highly enthusiastic or laudatory review or notice of a book, play, film, etc. *colloq.* (orig. *US*). **E20.** ▸**c** More fully ***rave-up***. A lively party; a rowdy gathering. *colloq.* **M20.** ▸**d** *spec.* A large freq. illicit party or event, with dancing esp. to fast electronic popular music; music associated with such events. **L20.** ▸**e** Usu. ***rave-up***. A fast, loud, or danceable piece of popular music. *colloq.* **L20.**
▶ **B** *attrib.* or as *adjective.* Of a review, notice, etc.: highly enthusiastic or laudatory. **M20.**

rave /reɪv/ *verb*[1]. **ME.**
[Prob. from Old Northern French *raver*, rel. obscurely to Middle & mod. Low German *reven* be senseless, rave, Dutch †*travelen*, *ravotten*.]
▶ **I** *verb intrans.* **1** Orig., be mad, show signs of madness or delirium. Later, talk or declaim wildly or furiously, esp. as if mad or delirious. **ME.** ▸**b** *transf.* Of the sea, wind, etc.: rage; rush or roar furiously. **M16.**
2 Express oneself with enthusiasm or rapturous admiration. Freq. foll. by *about*, *of*, *over*. **L17.**
3 Enjoy oneself freely or with abandon. *colloq.* **M20.**
4 Attend a rave party; dance to rave music. *colloq.* **L20.**

> **1** B. BAINBRIDGE She couldn't understand why this deceived wife didn't rant and rave. L. GRANT-ADAMSON He was raving at . . people who had failed to live up to his expectations. **b** W. JONES The dark sea with angry billows raves. **2** I. BANKS You just raved about how amazing astronomy was.

▶ **II** *verb trans.* **5** Utter in a frenzied or enthusiastic manner. **E16.**
6 Bring into a specified state by raving. **E19.**

> **5** SHELLEY For he now raved enormous folly.

Phrases: **rave it up** = sense 3 above.
■ **raver** *noun* a person who raves; *esp.* (*colloq.*) (*a*) a person with a wild or uninhibitedly pleasure-seeking lifestyle; (*b*) a person attending a rave party or dancing to rave music: **LME.** **ravery** /ˈreɪv(ə)ri/ *noun* (*obsolete* exc. *dial.*) (a fit of) raging, raving, madness or delirium **LME.** **raving** *noun* the action of the verb; (an instance of) wild or delirious talk: **LME.** **raving** *adjective & adverb* (*a*) *adjective* delirious, frenzied, raging; (*b*) *adjective & adverb* used as an intensive: **L15.** **ravingly** *adverb* **L16.**

rave /reɪv/ *verb*[2] *intrans. Scot., north., & Canad. dial.* **LME.**
[Prob. of Scandinavian origin: cf. Icelandic *ráfa* in same sense. Cf. **ROVE** *verb*[1].]
Wander, rove, stray (*lit. & fig.*).

rave /reɪv/ *verb*[3]. *obsolete* exc. *dial.* **LME.**
[Origin unkn.]
1 *verb trans.* Tear, drag, pull; rake *up*. **LME.**
2 *verb intrans.* Poke or pry *into*. *rare.* **M17.**

ravel /ˈrav(ə)l/ *noun*[1]. **M17.**
[from the verb.]
1 A tangle, a knot; a complication. **M17.**
2 A broken thread, a loose end. **M19.**

ravel /ˈrav(ə)l/ *noun*[2]. **E19.**
[Origin unkn.]
WEAVING. A bar with teeth or pins for separating and guiding the threads of the warp while it is being wound on the beam.

ravel /ˈrav(ə)l/ *verb.* Infl. **-ll-**, ***-l-**. See also **RAFFLE** *verb*[3]. **LME.**
[Perh. from Dutch *ravelen* tangle, fray out, unweave, obscurely corresp. to Low German *reffeln*, *rebbeln*.]
▶ **I** *verb trans.* **1** Entangle; confuse, perplex. **LME.**
2 Unwind, unweave; draw or pull *out* by unwinding or unweaving; unravel. Also *fig.*, take to pieces; disentangle. **L16.**
3 Foll. by *out*: ▸**a** Make plain or clear. **L16.** ▸†**b** Destroy, spoil, or waste, as by pulling a fabric into threads. **E17–E18.**

> **1** P. FAIRBAIRN It ravels and complicates the meaning of the prophecies. **2** M. EDGEWORTH A fool who ravels the web of her fortune. J. A. FROUDE Ravelling out the threads of a story. **3a** SHAKES. *Haml.* Let him . . Make you to ravel all this matter out.

▶ **II** *verb intrans.* **4** Become entangled or confused. Long chiefly *dial.* **L16.**
5 a Of a fabric: fray (*out*). Also *fig.*, disintegrate. **E17.** ▸**b** Of (a) thread: unwind, come off the reel, etc. **M17.**
†**6** Examine or inquire *into* something. **E17–E18.**

> **4** MILTON By thir own perplexities involv'd, They ravel more. **5a** H. WEDGWOOD The hem of a garment . . prevents it from ravelling out.

■ **ravelling** *noun* (*a*) a thread from a woven fabric which is frayed or unravelled; (*b*) the action of the verb: **M17.** **ravelly** *adjective* (*rare*) somewhat ravelled **L19.** **ravelment** *noun* (*rare*) (an) entanglement, (a) confusion **M19.**

Ravelian /rəˈvɛlɪən/ *adjective.* **M20.**
[from *Ravel* (see below) + **-IAN.**]
Of, pertaining to, or characteristic of the French composer Maurice Ravel (1875–1937) or his music.

ravelin /ˈravlɪn/ *noun.* **L16.**
[French, from Italian †*travellina* (now *rivellino*), of unkn. origin.]
Hist. An outwork of fortifications, consisting of two faces forming a salient angle, constructed beyond the main ditch and in front of the curtain.

raven /ˈreɪv(ə)n/ *noun*[1] *& adjective*[1].
[Old English *hræfn* = Old Saxon *naht)raban* night-raven, Middle Low German, Middle Dutch *rāven* (Dutch *raaf*), Old High German *(h)raban*, Old Norse *hrafn* corresp. to Middle Dutch *rave*, Middle High German *rabo* (German *Rabe*), from Germanic.]
▶ **A** *noun.* **1** A large black bird of the crow family, *Corvus corax*, widely distributed in the northern hemisphere, feeding chiefly on carrion and having a raucous croaking call. Also, any of various other large birds of the genus *Corvus*. **OE.**
2 a *Hist.* (The image of a raven on) the flag of the Danish Vikings; *fig.* Viking military power. **LOE.** ▸**b** *HERALDRY.* A representation of a raven as an armorial bearing. **E17.**
3 (**R-**.) *The* constellation Corvus. *rare.* **LME.**

> **1** SIR T. BROWNE Ravens are ominous appearers . . presignifying unlucky events. ***night-raven***: see **NIGHT** *noun.* ***white-necked raven***: see **WHITE** *adjective.*

Comb.: **raven-duck**, **raven's duck** [German *Rabentuch*] a kind of canvas; **raven-stone** (*poet.*) *the* place of execution, *the* gallows; **raven-tree**: in which ravens build their nests.
▶ **B** *attrib.* or as *adjective.* Of the colour of a raven; glossy black; intensely dark or gloomy. **M17.**
■ **raveness** *noun* (*rare*) a female raven **E17.** **raven-like** *adjective* resembling (that of) a raven **E19.**

raven *noun*[2] *& adjective*[2] var. of **RAVIN** *noun*[1] *& adjective.*

raven /ˈrav(ə)n/ *verb.* Also †**-in**. **L15.**
[Old & mod. French *raviner* rush, ravage, (now) hollow out, furrow, ult. from Latin *rapina* **RAPINE.**]
1 *verb trans.* Take (goods) away by force; seize or divide as spoil. Long *rare* or *obsolete.* **L15.** ▸**b** *verb intrans.* Plunder; (foll. by *after*) seek spoil or booty. **E17.**
2 *verb trans.* Devour or eat *up* voraciously. **M16.**
3 *verb intrans.* **a** Eat voraciously; feed hungrily or greedily; prey *on*. **M16.** ▸**b** Have a ravenous appetite (*for*). **M17.**
4 *verb intrans.* Prowl for prey ravenously. **M16.**
■ †**ravened** *adjective* (*rare*, Shakes.) glutted; voracious: only in **E17.** **ravening** *noun* (*a*) the action of the verb; †(*b*) *rare* (a fit of) madness: **LME.** **ravening** *adjective* (*a*) that ravens, voracious, rapacious; †(*b*) mad, rabid: **LME.** **raveningly** *adverb* (long *rare*) ravenously **M16.**

ravener /ˈrav(ə)nə/ *noun.* Also †**-iner**. **ME.**
[Old French *ravineor*, *-our* from Latin *rapinator*, from *rapina* **RAPINE.**]
†**1** A ravisher, a rapist, a destroyer. *rare.* **ME–L16.**
†**2** A robber, a plunderer. **LME–L17.**
3 A ravenous person or animal; a voracious eater. Long *rare.* **LME.**

Ravenna grass /rəˈvɛnə grɑːs/ *noun phr.* **E20.**
[from *Ravenna*, a city in northern Italy + **GRASS** *noun.*]
A large grass of southern Europe, *Saccharum ravennae*, with greyish leaves and purplish-grey spikes, sometimes grown for ornament.

ravenous /ˈrav(ə)nəs/ *adjective.* **LME.**
[Old French *ravinos*, *-eus*, formed as **RAVEN** *verb*: see **-OUS.**]
1 Given to plundering; very rapacious. **LME.**
2 Of appetite, hunger, an animal, etc.: voracious, gluttonous. In pred. use also foll. by *of*. **LME.**
3 Exceedingly hungry, famished. **E18.**
■ **ravenously** *adverb* **LME.** **ravenousness** *noun* **L16.**

Ravenscroft /ˈreɪv(ə)nzkrɒft/ *noun & adjective.* **E20.**
[See below.]
(Designating) an article made of the flint glass or lead glass devised by the English glass-maker George Ravenscroft (1618–81).

ravers /ˈreɪvəz/ *pred. adjective. slang.* **M20.**
[from **RAV**(**ING** *adjective* + **-ER**[6]. Cf. **CRACKERS.**]
Raving mad; furious, angry.

ravigote /ravigɔt/ *noun.* **M19.**
[French, from *ravigoter* invigorate.]
A mixture of chopped chervil, chives, tarragon, and shallots, used to give piquancy to a sauce, as a base for a herb butter, etc.; a vinaigrette dressing containing capers and chopped hard-boiled egg flavoured with such a mixture; a velouté sauce containing such a herb butter.

ravin /ˈravɪn/ *noun*[1] *& adjective.* Now *poet. & rhet.* Also **-ven** /-v(ə)n/. **ME.**
[Old & mod. French *ravine* from Latin *rapina* **RAPINE.** See also **RAVINE** *noun.*]
▶ **A** *noun.* **1** Robbery, rapine. **ME.** ▸†**b** An act of rapine. **LME–L16.**
2 Plunder, spoil; prey. **ME.**
3 The action or practice of seizing and devouring prey or food; voracity, gluttony. **LME.**
Phrases: **beast of ravin** beast of prey.
▶†**B** *attrib.* or as *adjective.* = **RAVENOUS. LME–E17.**

†**ravin** *noun*[2]. **M18–E19.**
[French, from *raviner* hollow out.]
= **RAVINE** *noun* 2.

ravin *verb* see **RAVEN** *verb.*

ravine /rəˈviːn/ *noun.* **LME.**
[French = violent rush (now only of water), ravine, use of *ravine* **RAVIN** *noun*[1].]
†**1** Impetus, violence, force. *rare.* Only in **LME.**
2 A deep narrow gorge or cleft, *esp.* one formed by erosion by running water. **L18.**

ravine /rəˈviːn/ *verb trans. rare.* **M19.**
[from prec. or French *raviner.*]
Cut a ravine or ravines into; carve (a ravine or cleft) *out*.

ravined /rəˈviːnd/ *adjective.* **M19.**
[from **RAVINE** *noun, verb*: see **-ED**[2], **-ED**[1].]
Having or marked with ravines.

ravinement /rəˈviːnm(ə)nt/ *noun.* **E20.**
[French, formed as **RAVINE** *noun*, **-MENT.**]
PHYSICAL GEOGRAPHY. Erosion of ravines or gullies in soil or soft rock by running water. Also, an unconformity in river or shallow marine sediments caused by interruption of deposition by erosion.

†**raviner** *noun* var. of **RAVENER.**

ravioli /ravɪˈəʊli/ *noun.* **M19.**
[Italian, pl. of *raviolo.*]
Pasta in the form of small square cases filled with minced meat, vegetables, etc.; an Italian dish consisting largely of this and usu. a sauce.

ravish /ˈravɪʃ/ *verb trans.* **ME.**
[Old & mod. French *raviss-* lengthened stem of *ravir*, from Proto-Romance alt. of Latin *rapere* seize: see **RAPE** *verb*, **-ISH**[2].]
1 Forcibly seize and carry off, tear or drag away, (a person). *arch.* **ME.** ▸†**b** In *pass.* Be drawn away *from* a belief, state, etc. **LME–M18.** ▸†**c** Draw (a person) forcibly *to* or *into* some condition, action, etc. **LME–E17.**
2 a Remove from earth (esp. to heaven) or from sight; transport in spirit. Now *arch. rare.* **ME.** ▸**b** Transport with the strength of some emotion; fill with ecstasy or delight. **LME.**
†**3 a** Ravage, despoil, plunder. **ME–E17.** ▸**b** Rob or deprive (a person) *of* something. **LME–E19.**
4 a Seize and appropriate (possessions etc.) as plunder or spoil; violently seize on (a thing). *arch.* **LME.** ▸**b** Forcibly move, remove, or take away without appropriation. Now only foll. by *from*. *arch.* **LME.**
5 Rape, violate. **LME.** ▸†**b** Spoil, corrupt. *rare* (Shakes.). Only in **L16.**

> **2a** HENRY FIELDING A . . thick mist ravished her from our eyes. **b** J. BUCHAN Two landscapes . . have always ravished my fancy. **5** E. JONG He ravish'd me, then he cast me out when I was with child.

■ **ravisher** *noun* a person who ravishes someone or something; a rapist: **ME.** **ravishing** *noun* (*a*) the action of the verb; †(*b*) an ecstasy, a rapture: **ME.**

ravishing /ˈravɪʃɪŋ/ *adjective & adverb.* **ME.**
[from **RAVISH** + **-ING**[2].]
▶ **A** *adjective.* **1** Seizing on prey; ravenous. Long *rare.* **ME.**
2 Exciting ecstasy; entrancing, delightful. **LME.**
▶†**B** *adverb.* Ravishingly. *rare.* **E17–E18.**
■ **ravishingly** *adverb* in a ravishing manner, delightfully, entrancingly **L16.**

ravishment /ˈravɪʃm(ə)nt/ *noun.* **LME.**
[Old & mod. French *ravissement*, from *raviss-*: see **RAVISH**, **-MENT.**]
1 The action or an act of forcibly abducting a woman or ward; (a) rape. **LME.**
2 (A) delight, (a) rapture, (an) ecstasy. **L15.**
†**3** An act of plundering or ravaging. **L16–M17.**

ravissant /ravisɑ̃/ *adjective.* In sense 2 also (fem.) ***-ante*** /-ɑ̃ːt/. **ME.**
[French, pres. ppl adjective of *ravir*: see **RAVISH**, **-ANT**[1].]
1 †**a** Of an animal: ravening. *rare.* **ME–M16.** ▸**b** *HERALDRY.* In the half-raised posture of a wolf beginning to spring on its prey. *rare.* **E18.**

2 Ravishing, delightful. **M17.**

¶ Formerly fully naturalized.

raw /rɔː/ *adjective & noun.*

[Old English *hrēaw* = Old Saxon *hrāo* (Dutch *rauw*), Old High German *(h)rāo* (German *roh*), Old Norse *hrár*, from Germanic from Indo-European, whence Greek *kreas* raw flesh.]

► **A** *adjective.* **1** Not prepared for use as food by the action of heat, uncooked; *spec.* (of milk) unpasteurized. **OE.** ▸**b** Of clay, pottery, etc.: not hardened or fused by fire. **L17.**

2 In a natural state, unprocessed, not yet manufactured; *spec.* **(*a*)** (of silk) as reeled from cocoons; **(*b*)** (of leather or hide) untanned, undressed; **(*c*)** (of alcoholic spirit) undiluted; **(*d*)** (of grain) unmalted; **(*e*)** (of sugar) unrefined or partly refined; **(*f*)** (of sewage) untreated. **ME.** ▸**b** Of measurements, statistical data, etc.: not yet analysed or evaluated; unadjusted, uncorrected. **E20.** ▸**c** Of manufactured material: unused. **E20.**

3 Crude in form or (esp. artistic) quality; lacking finish. Also, (of cloth) without a hem or selvage. **LME.** ▸**b** Uncivilized, coarse, brutal. **L16.**

4 Unripe, immature, (*lit. & fig.*). Long *rare* or *obsolete.* **LME.** ▸**b** Inexperienced; unskilled, untrained, (*at* or *in*), naive. **L15.**

5 Stripped of skin, having the flesh exposed. **LME.** ▸**b** Painful to the touch from having the flesh exposed; *fig.* abnormally sensitive. **L16.** ▸†**c** Of bones: showing through the skin. *rare* (Spenser). Only in **L16.** ▸**d** Of a person: naked (esp. when sleeping). *colloq.* **M20.**

6 Of the weather etc.: damp and chilly; bleak. **M16.**

7 Of the taste of tea: harsh, not mellow. **L19.**

📖 **1** *Which?* The Department of Health recommends that you don't eat foods made with raw eggs. **2** *International Wildlife* Reliance . . on importing enormous quantities of raw materials for processing. *transf.:* G. DALY Losing his beloved would provide the stuff of great art, the raw material he needed. **3** L. STEPHEN The . . scenery, so provokingly raw and deficient in harmony. **4b** J. A. FROUDE With a raw and inexperienced army he engaged legions in perfect discipline. *Winning* Although Gallopin was a Tour veteran . . , Pavlov came raw to France. **5** A. FALCONBRIDGE Both flogged until their backs were raw. **6** P. S. BUCK His bones ached in the air left raw and chill when the sun withdrew.

► **B** *ellipt.* as *noun.* †**1** An unfulled portion of a cloth. Only in **LME.**

2 *The* exposed flesh; a raw place in the skin, a sore or sensitive spot. Freq. *fig.* **E19.**

3 A raw person, article, product, etc. **M19.**

Phrases: ***a raw deal***: see DEAL *noun*³ 3. ***come the raw prawn***: see PRAWN *noun.* **in the raw** (*a*) in a starkly realistic way or state; (*b*) naked. **touch on the raw** upset on a sensitive matter.

Special collocations & comb.: **raw bar** *US* a bar selling raw oysters. **raw-boned** *adjective* very lean or gaunt. **raw edge** an edge of fabric without hem or selvage. **raw feel** PSYCHOLOGY an immediate unconceptualized mental impression evoked by a stimulus. **raw head and bloody bones** (a name for) a bugbear or bogey. **rawhide** (a rope or whip of) untanned hide. **raw humus** vegetable matter not yet fully decomposed. ***raw lobster***: see LOBSTER *noun*¹. ***raw material***: see MATERIAL *noun* 1a. **raw sienna** (the colour of) a brownish-yellow ferruginous earth used as a pigment. **raw silk** (*a*) untreated silk fibres as reeled from cocoons; (*b*) a fabric made from such fibres. **raw umber** (the dark yellow colour of) umber in its natural state.

■ **rawish** *adjective* **E17.** **rawly** *adverb* (*a*) in a raw state or manner; †(*b*) (*rare*, Shakes.) at an immature age: **LME.** **rawness** *noun* †(*a*) indigestion; (*b*) the state or quality of being raw: **LME.**

raw /rɔː/ *verb.* **L15.**

[from the adjective.]

†**1** *verb intrans.* Become raw. *rare.* **L15–M18.**

2 *verb trans.* Make raw. **L16.**

Rawang /rəˈwaŋ/ *noun & adjective.* **M20.**

[Rawang.]

Of or pertaining to, a member of, a people of northern Myanmar (Burma); (of) the Tibeto-Burman language of this people.

rawin /ˈreɪwɪn/ *noun.* **M20.**

[from RA(DAR + WIN(D *noun*¹.]

METEOROLOGY. A determination of the atmospheric wind speed and direction made by tracking a balloon-borne target with radar. Also = next.

rawinsonde /ˈreɪwɪnsɒnd/ *noun.* **M20.**

[from prec. + SONDE.]

METEOROLOGY. A balloon-borne device comprising a radiosonde and a radar target which both transmits meteorological data to ground stations and permits rawin observations to be made.

rawky /ˈrɔːki/ *adjective. rare.* **E17.**

[from var. of ROKE *noun*¹ + -Y¹.]

Foggy, misty; raw.

Rawlplug /ˈrɔːlplʌg/ *noun & verb.* Also (esp. as verb) **r-.** **E20.**

[from *Rawl(ings)*, English electrical engineers who introduced the plug + PLUG *noun.*]

► **A** *noun.* (Proprietary name for) a cylindrical or conical plug which can be inserted into a hole drilled in masonry etc. to hold a screw. **E20.**

► **B** *verb trans.* Infl. **-gg-.** Attach by means of a Rawlplug; drill a hole in (a wall etc.) and insert a Rawlplug. **M20.**

†**rax** *noun.* Long only *Scot.* **L15–M19.**

[Var. of *racks* pl. of RACK *noun*².]

A set of bars to support a roasting-spit. Usu. in *pl.*

rax /raks/ *verb. Scot. & north.* **OE.**

[Origin unkn.]

► **I** *verb intrans.* **1** Stretch oneself after sleep. **OE.**

†**2** Extend one's power; rule, prevail. **LME–L16.**

3 Stretch; *rare* grow. **LME.**

4 Reach out (*for*). **L16.**

► **II** *verb trans.* **5** *refl.* Stretch, strain. **ME.**

6 Stretch by pulling. **E16.**

7 Stretch or hold *out* (the hand etc.). **M18.**

8 Hand (a thing) to (a person). **L18.**

ray /reɪ/ *noun*¹. **ME.**

[Old & mod. French *rai* from Latin *radius* RADIUS *noun.*]

► **I** **1** **a** A single line or narrow beam of light; each of the lines in which light (and heat) may seem to stream from the sun, any luminous body, a polished surface, etc., or pass through a small opening. In early scientific use, the least portion of light which can be propagated alone; now usu. the straight line in which light is propagated to a given point. **ME.** ▸**b** *fig.* An enlightening, improving, or cheering influence, esp. an initial or slight indication of one. **M17.** ▸**c** HERALDRY. A charge representing a ray of light. **E18.** ▸**d** A trace *of* anything. Usu. in neg. contexts. **L18.**

2 **a** A beam or glance of the eye. Chiefly *poet.* **M16.** ▸**b** A line of sight. **E18.**

3 Light, radiance. Chiefly *poet.* **L16.**

4 **a** A single line or wave of non-luminous physical energy, esp. electromagnetic radiation; in *pl.*, a specified form of radiation. **M17.** ▸**b** Chiefly SCIENCE FICTION. A supposed beam of (esp. destructive) energy emitted by a ray gun or similar device. **L19.**

📖 **1a** ***direct ray, extraordinary ray, ordinary ray***, etc. **ray of sunshine, little ray of sunshine** a happy or vivacious person, a person who cheers or enlivens another. **b** C. THIRLWALL Only one ray of hope broke the gloom of her prospects. **3** SHELLEY A mountain, . . whose crest . . in the ray Of the obscure stars gleamed. **4a** ***cosmic rays, gamma rays, lavender rays, Roentgen rays***, etc. ***CATHODE ray***. X-RAY.

► **II** **5** Any of a system of lines, parts, or things radially arranged. **M17.**

6 ZOOLOGY. **a** = ***fin-ray*** s.v. FIN *noun*¹. **M17.** ▸**b** Each of the radial divisions of a starfish. **M18.**

7 MATH. **a** = RADIUS *noun* 3. Now *rare* or *obsolete.* **L17.** ▸**b** Any of a set of straight lines passing through a point. **L19.**

8 BOTANY. **a** In a composite flower-head: an array of ligulate florets arranged radially round a disc of inner, tubular florets. **L18.** ▸**b** Any of the pedicels or branches of an umbel. **L18.** ▸**c** = ***MEDULLARY ray*** s.v. MEDULLARY *adjective* 1b. **L19.**

9 ASTRONOMY. Any of the long bright lines of pale material radiating from some lunar craters. **M19.**

Comb.: **ray blight** a fungus disease of chrysanthemums caused by *Ascochyta chrysanthemi*, which causes discoloration and shrivelling of the petals; **ray diagram** a diagram showing the paths of light rays through an optical system; **ray-fin** a fish belonging to the subclass Actinopterygii, to which most living bony fishes belong and which includes those having thin fins with slender dermal rays; **ray-finned** *adjective* having fins supported by rays; ***ray-finned fish***, = ***ray-fin*** above; **ray fleck** the marking caused by the exposure of a ray in sawn timber; **ray floret** a ligulate floret of the type forming the ray in certain plants of the composite family; **ray-fungus** (now *rare*) an actinomycete (bacterium); **ray gun** (esp. SCIENCE FICTION): causing injury or damage by the emission of rays; **ray therapy** the treatment of disease with radiation, radiotherapy; **ray-tracing** the calculation of the path taken by a ray of light through an optical system; **ray treatment** = ***ray therapy*** above.

■ †**rayie** *adjective* (*rare*) resembling a ray or rays **L17–L18.** **raylet** *noun* a little ray **E19.**

ray /reɪ/ *noun*². **ME.**

[Old & mod. French *raie* from Latin *raia.*]

Any of various broad flat elasmobranch fishes (e.g. skates) of the order Batiformes, with the pectoral fins greatly enlarged and winglike gill-openings on the underside, and a narrow tail. Freq. with specifying word.

electric ray, manta ray, sandy ray, stingray, thornback ray, etc.

ray /reɪ/ *noun*³. Also (earlier) **re.** **ME.**

[Latin *re(sonare)*: see UT.]

MUSIC. The second note of a scale in a movable-doh system; the note D in the fixed-doh system.

ray /reɪ/ *noun*⁴ *& adjective.* Long *obsolete* exc. *Hist.* **ME.**

[Old French *raié* from Old & mod. French *raie* stripe, streak. Cf. RAYONNÉ.]

► **A** *noun.* **1** A kind of striped cloth. **ME.**

†**2** A stripe, esp. on a piece of cloth; a streak. **ME–L16.**

► †**B** *attrib.* or as *adjective.* Striped, made of striped cloth. **LME–E17.**

ray /reɪ/ *noun*⁵. *rare.* **LME.**

[Origin unkn.]

†**1** Darnel. **LME–E17.**

2 In full ***ray-grass***. = RYEGRASS 2. **L17.**

†**ray** *noun*⁶. **LME.**

[Aphet. from ARRAY *noun.* Cf. RAY *verb*¹.]

1 = ARRAY *noun* 2. **LME–M17.** ▸**b** A line, a rank. **L15–L16.**

2 Dress, attire. **LME–M17.**

ray /reɪ/ *noun*⁷. *obsolete* exc. *dial.* **L16.**

[from RAY *verb*¹.]

Diarrhoea in sheep or cattle.

ray /reɪ/ *verb*¹ *trans. obsolete* exc. *dial.* **LME.**

[Aphet. from ARRAY *verb.* Cf. RAY *noun*⁶.]

†**1** Arrange, dispose, deal with; *spec.* draw up in battle array. **LME–E17.**

2 Put clothes on. **LME.**

†**3** Smear, bespatter, or soil *with* blood, dirt, etc.; dirty, befoul. **E16–M17.**

ray /reɪ/ *verb*². **L16.**

[from RAY *noun*¹ or French *rayer* from Old French *raier* from Latin *radiare*: see RADIATE *verb.*]

1 *verb intrans.* Of a beam or beams of light: issue or spread from a point (as if) in rays, radiate. Also foll. by *out.* **L16.**

2 *verb trans.* Send *out* or *forth*, emit, (light) in rays; *fig.* transmit as if in rays of light. **E17.**

3 *verb intrans.* Extend in the form of radii. **M17.**

4 *verb trans.* Light up, illuminate. **M19.**

5 *verb trans.* Treat or examine by means of X-rays or other radiation. **E20.**

📖 **1** J. C. OATES A boy's smile raying across his face. **2** M. C. CLARKE His presence rays life and manliness into every part of the drama.

rayah /ˈrʌɪə/ *noun. obsolete* exc. *Hist.* **E19.**

[Turkish *râya* from Arab. *raʿāyā* pl. of *raʿiyya(t)*: see RYOT.]

A non-Muslim subject of the Sultan of Turkey, liable to a poll tax.

Ray-Ban /ˈreɪban/ *noun.* **L20.**

[US company name.]

In *pl.* (Proprietary name for) a fashionable brand of sunglasses.

rayed /reɪd/ *adjective*¹. **M18.**

[from RAY *noun*¹, *verb*²: see -ED², -ED¹.]

1 **a** Having or consisting of rays, esp. of a specified number or kind. **M18.** ▸**b** ZOOLOGY. Radiate. **M19.**

2 That has been irradiated. **E20.**

rayed /reɪd/ *adjective*². *arch. & poet.* **LME.**

[from Old French *raié* (cf. RAY *noun*⁴) + -ED².]

Striped, streaked.

rayl /reɪl/ *noun.* **M20.**

[from RAYL(EIGH.]

ACOUSTICS. A unit of specific acoustic impedance equal to one dyne-second/cm³ (in the cgs system) or one newton-second/m³ (in the SI).

Rayleigh /ˈreɪli/ *noun.* In sense 2 also **r-.** **M20.**

[J. W. Strutt, 3rd Lord *Rayleigh* (1842–1919), and his son R. J. Strutt, 4th Lord *Rayleigh* (1875–1947), English physicists.]

PHYSICS. **I** *attrib.* **1** Used *attrib.* and occas. in *possess.* to designate various concepts, devices, and phenomena invented or investigated by the elder Lord Rayleigh. **M20.**

1 ***Rayleigh criterion***: see ***Rayleigh's criterion*** below. **Rayleigh instability** instability of the interface between fluids of different densities or temperatures, esp. leading to convective motion (also ***Rayleigh–Taylor instability*** [Sir Geoffrey Taylor (1886–1975), English mathematician]). **Rayleigh–Jeans law** [Sir James *Jeans* (1877–1946), English physicist] the law (valid at long wavelengths only) that the flux of radiation from a black body, at any given temperature, is proportional to its temperature divided by the fourth power of the wavelength. **Rayleigh limit** the upper limit of a quarter of a wavelength placed on the optical path difference between longest and shortest rays going to form an image if the definition is to be close to the ideal (which corresponds to no path difference). **Rayleigh number** a dimensionless parameter that is a measure of the instability of a layer of fluid due to differences of temperature and density at the top and bottom. **Rayleigh scattering** the scattering of light by particles small compared with its wavelength, the resulting intensity being inversely proportional to the fourth power of the wavelength (i.e. much greater for blue light than for red). **Rayleigh's criterion**, **Rayleigh criterion** the criterion by which adjacent lines or rings of equal intensity in a diffraction pattern are regarded as resolved when the central maximum of one coincides with the first minimum of the next. ***Rayleigh–Taylor instability***: see ***Rayleigh instability*** above. **Rayleigh wave** an undulating wave that travels over the surface of a solid (esp. of the ground in an earthquake) with a speed independent of wavelength, the motion of the particles being in ellipses.

► **II** **2** [After the younger Lord Rayleigh.] ASTRONOMY. A unit of luminous intensity equal to one million photons per square centimetre per second. **M20.**

rayless /ˈreɪlɪs/ *adjective.* **M18.**

[from RAY *noun*¹ + -LESS.]

1 Devoid of any ray of light; dark, gloomy. **M18.**

2 ZOOLOGY & BOTANY. Having no rays or ray. **M18.**

3 Emitting no rays; dull; (of the eye) expressionless. M19.

Raynaud /ˈreɪnəʊ/ *noun*. L19.
[Maurice *Raynaud* (1834–81), French physician.]
MEDICINE. ***Raynaud's disease***, ***Raynaud's phenomenon***, ***Raynaud's syndrome***, an ill-defined condition characterized by spasm of arteries in the extremities, esp. the digits (often precipitated by low temperature or continued vibration) leading to pallor, pain, numbness, and in severe cases, gangrene.

rayograph /ˈreɪə(ʊ)grɑːf/ *noun*. M20.
[from Man *Ray*, US artist and photographer (1890–1976) + -O- + -GRAPH.]
A type of photograph made without a camera by arranging objects on light-sensitive paper which is then exposed and developed.
■ Also **rayogram** *noun* M20.

rayon /ˈreɪən, *in sense 2 also foreign* rɛjɔ̃/ *noun*[1]. *rare*. L16.
[French, dim. of *rai*: see RAY *noun*[1].]
1 A ray of light. L16.
2 = RADIUS *noun* 5. L19.

rayon /ˈreɪɒn/ *noun*[2]. E20.
[Arbitrary, with suggestion of prec., RAY *noun*[1]; -*on* perh. after *cotton*. Cf. NYLON, TEFLON.]
Any of a class of fibres and filaments made of or from regenerated cellulose; fabric or cloth made from such fibres. Formerly called ***artificial silk***.

rayon /raˈjɒn/ *noun*[3]. M20.
[Russian *raĭon*.]
In the former USSR, a small territorial division for administrative purposes.

Rayonism /ˈreɪənɪz(ə)m/ *noun*. Also **-nn-**. E20.
[French *Rayonnisme*, formed as RAYON *noun*[1] + -*isme* -ISM.]
A style of abstract painting developed *c* 1911 in Russia by M. Larionov (1881–1964) and N. Goncharova (1881–1962), in which projecting rays of colour are used to give the impression that the painting floats outside time and space.
■ **Rayonist** *adjective* & *noun* (*a*) *adjective* of or pertaining to Rayonism; (*b*) *noun* an adherent or practitioner of Rayonism: M20.

rayonnant /rɛjɔnɑ̃/ *adjective*. Fem. **-ante** /-ɑ̃ːt/. E19.
[French, pres. ppl adjective of *rayonner*: see next, -ANT[1].]
Of a person: beaming, radiant.

rayonné /rɛjɔne/ *adjective*. M16.
[French, pa. pple of *rayonner*, formed as RAYON *noun*[1]. Cf. RAY *noun*[4].]
†**1** Of a kind of hood: striped, streaked. *rare*. M16–L17.
2 HERALDRY. Of a division between parts of the field: having alternate straight and wavy sided pointed projections and depressions. M19.

rayonnement /rɛjɔnmɑ̃/ *noun*. E20.
[French, formed as RAYON *noun*[1]: see -MENT.]
Radiance, splendour.

Rayonnism *noun* var. of RAYONISM.

Ray's bream /reɪz ˈbriːm/ *noun phr*. M19.
[from John *Ray* (1627–1705), English naturalist + BREAM *noun*.]
A deep-bodied, dark brown Atlantic pomfret, *Brama brama*.

Razakar /razɑːˈkɑː/ *noun*. M20.
[Urdu *razākār* volunteer, from Persian *rizā* approbation + Arab., Persian -*kār* work.]
A Muslim who voluntarily pledges to fight in defence of Islam; a member of a paramilitary faction with this end.

razant *adjective* var. of RASANT.

raze /reɪz/ *verb* & *noun*. Also (earlier) **rase**, (now only, & the only current form in, senses A.1, B.) **race** /reɪs/. ME.
[Old & mod. French *raser* shave close from Proto-Romance from Latin *ras-* pa. ppl stem of *radere* scrape, scratch.]
▶ **A** *verb*. **1** *verb trans*. Scratch, tear; cut, slash; incise (a mark or line). Now *techn*. ME. ▶**b** *verb intrans*. Make an incised mark; slash. Now *arch*. *rare*. LME. ▶**c** *verb trans*. Cut or wound slightly. Now *arch*. & *dial*. L16.
2 *verb trans*. Remove by scraping; scratch out; erase (esp. writing). Usu. foll. by adverb. Chiefly *fig*. LME.
3 *verb trans*. Scrape (a thing), esp. to remove something from a surface; *spec*. †(*a*) alter (a manuscript etc.) by erasure; (*b*) shave; (*c*) scrape down into small particles, grate. Now *rare* exc. *dial*. LME. ▶**b** Scrape, graze, or come close to (a thing) in passing. Now *rare*. M16.
4 *verb trans*. †**a** Make level. *rare*. Only in L15. ▶**b** Tear down, destroy completely, level, (a building, town, etc.). Freq. in ***raze to the ground***. M16. ▶**c** Remove completely, esp. *from* a place, situation, etc. L16.

> 📖 **4b** J. A. MICHENER This once formidable range was razed absolutely flat by erosion. P. CAREY Men raze villages and annihilate whole populations. P. ACKROYD Fire . . inflicted disaster . . razing offices and homes.

▶ **B** *noun*. **1** A scratch, a scrape; a cut, a slit. L15.
†**2** The action of scratching, scraping, or cutting; the fact of being scratched, scraped, or cut. M16–E17.
■ **razing** *noun* (*a*) the action of the verb; †(*b*) *collect*. (*rare*) shavings, scrapings: LME.

razee /rəˈziː/ *noun* & *verb*. L18.
[from French *rasé(e)* pa. ppl adjective of *raser* RAZE *verb*: see -EE[1].]
▶ **A** *noun*. *Hist*. A warship or other vessel reduced in height by the removal of the upper deck or decks. L18.
▶ **B** *verb trans*. Pa. t. & pple **-zeed**. Chiefly *Hist*. Abridge, cut down, prune; *esp*. cut down (a ship) to a lower size by reducing the number of decks. E19.

razer /ˈreɪzə/ *noun*. *obsolete* exc. *Hist*. Also (earlier) †**raser**. L15.
[Old French *rasier*, *rasiere*.]
A dry measure containing about four bushels.

razet /razɛ/ *noun*. Pl. pronounced same. M20.
[French from Provençal *raset*.]
BULLFIGHTING. In southern France, a contest in which teams compete to snatch a rosette from between the bull's horns.
■ ***razeteur*** /razətœːr/ *noun* a member of a team competing in a *razet* M20.

razoo /rəˈzuː/ *noun*[1] & *verb*. *N. Amer. slang*. L19.
[Prob. alt. of RASPBERRY with arbitrary suffix -*oo*. Cf. RAZZ, RAZZBERRY.]
▶ **A** *noun*. Ridicule; an expression or sound of contempt or derision. L19.
▶ **B** *verb trans*. Arouse, provoke, ridicule; manhandle. L19.

razoo /ˈrɑːzuː/ *noun*[2]. *Austral*. & *NZ slang*. E20.
[Origin unkn.]
An imaginary coin of trivial value; a very small sum of money. Also ***brass razoo***. Only in neg. contexts.

> 📖 R. CLAPPERTON He hasn't got two brass razoos to rub together.

razor /ˈreɪzə/ *noun* & *verb*. Also (earlier) †**rasor**. ME.
[Old French *rasor*, *ras(o)ur* (superseded by *rasoir*), from *raser* RAZE *verb*: see -OR.]
▶ **A** *noun*. **1** An instrument with a sharp edge, used for shaving or cutting hair. Now also, an electric instrument used for shaving. ME.
2 Any of various fishes or shellfish; now *spec*. a razor-shell. LME.
1 ***cutthroat razor***, ***safety razor***, ***straight razor***, etc. ***Occam's razor***: see OCCAM 1.
Comb.: **razorbill** any of various birds; *esp*. a black and white auk, *Alca torda*, of the N. Atlantic, having a narrow bill with a white stripe; **razor-billed** *adjective* having a narrow bill; ***razor-billed auk*** = *razorbill* above; ***razor-blade***: see BLADE *noun* 4c; **razor clam** *US* = *razor-shell* below; **razor-cut** *verb* & *noun* (*a*) *verb trans*. cut (hair etc.) with a razor; (*b*) *noun* a haircut effected with a razor; **razor-edge** (*a*) a keen edge; (*b*) a sharp mountain-ridge; (*c*) a critical situation; (*d*) a sharp line of division; **razor-fish** (*a*) (the mollusc which lives in) a razor-shell; (*b*) any of several fishes with a narrowly-compressed body, esp. *Centriscus scutatus* of the Indian Ocean; **razor gang** (*a*) a gang of thugs armed with razors; (*b*) *Railway slang* a team of investigators seeking ways of improving productivity; **razor-grass** any of various W. Indian sedges with sharp-edged leaves that constitute the genus *Scleria*, esp. *S. pterota*; **razor-grinder** (*a*) a person who grinds or sharpens razors; (*b*) any of various birds with a buzzing or whirring call, esp. the restless fly-catcher, or (*dial*.) a nightjar or a grasshopper warbler; **razor-man** a thug armed with a razor; **razor plug**, **razor point** a power point for plugging in an electric razor; **razor's edge** = *razor-edge* above; **razor-shell** (the shell of) any of a large group of bivalve molluscs of the superfamily Solenacea, having a long narrow shell resembling a cutthroat razor and typically burrowing in sand; **razor-slash** *verb* & *noun* (*a*) *verb trans*. slash with a razor; (*b*) *noun* (a wound made by) the action of razor-slashing; **razor strop fungus** a bracket fungus, *Piptoporus betulinus*, which grows on birch trees; **razor wire** metal wire or ribbon with sharp edges or studded with small sharp blades, used as a barrier to deter intruders.
▶ **B** *verb trans*. **1** Shave (*away*, *off*) (as) with a razor; cut *down*; cut *out* with a razor blade. ME.
2 Slash or assault with a razor. M20.

> 📖 **1** *Globe & Mail (Toronto)* Articles taken out of magazines . . I'll just say they were razored out. M. KENYON He . . had razored off the moustache.

■ †**razorable** *adjective* (*rare*, Shakes.) able to be shaved; *transf*. having attained manhood: only in E17.

razor-back /ˈreɪzəbak/ *noun* & *adjective*. E19.
[from RAZOR *noun* + BACK *noun*[1].]
▶ **A** *noun*. **1** A fin-whale, a rorqual. E19.
2 A pig having a back formed into a high narrow ridge; *esp*. a member of a half-wild breed of hogs common in the southern US. M19. ▶**b** A lean scraggy bullock or cow. *Austral*. & *NZ slang*. L20.
3 A back formed into a high ridge, esp. in cattle and horses. M19.
4 A steep-sided narrow ridge of land. Chiefly *Austral*. & *NZ*. L19.
5 A circus hand; *esp*. one who loads and unloads the wagons. *US slang*. E20.
▶ **B** *adjective*. Having a very sharp back or ridge. M19.
■ **razor-backed** *adjective* E19.

razz /raz/ *noun* & *verb*. *slang* (orig. *US*). E20.
[Abbreviation of RAZZBERRY.]
▶ **A** *noun*. = RASPBERRY 3. E20.
▶ **B** *verb trans*. Hiss, deride; tease, make fun of, (a person). E20.

razzamatazz *noun* & *adjective* var. of RAZZMATAZZ.

razzberry /ˈrazb(ə)ri/ *noun*. *N. Amer. colloq*. E20.
[Alt. to repr. pronunc.]
= RASPBERRY 3.

razzia /ˈrazɪə/ *noun*. M19.
[French from Algerian Arab. *ġāziya* raid, from Arab. *ġazā* go forth to fight, make a raid.]
A raid, a foray; *spec*. (*Hist*.) a hostile Moorish incursion for purposes of conquest, plunder, capture of slaves, etc.

razzle /ˈraz(ə)l/ *noun* & *verb*. *slang*. E20.
[Abbreviation of next.]
▶ **A** *noun*. A spree, a good time. Chiefly in ***on the razzle***. E20.
▶ **B** *verb intrans*. Enjoy oneself; have a good time. E20.

razzle-dazzle /ˈraz(ə)ldaz(ə)l/ *noun*, *adjective*, & *verb*. *slang*. L19.
[Redupl. of DAZZLE.]
▶ **A** *noun*. **1** Bustle; glamorous excitement, high living; = RAZZLE *noun*. Now also, deception, fraud; extravagant publicity. L19.
2 A kind of fairground ride. L19.
▶ **B** *attrib*. or as *adjective*. Of, pertaining to, or characterized by razzle-dazzle; (deceptively) dazzling, showy; spectacular. L19.

> 📖 P. GOODMAN Spending millions on advertising and razzle-dazzle promotional stunts. *Airgun World* A bunch of razzle-dazzle playboys.

▶ **C** *verb trans*. Dazzle, amaze. L19.

razzmatazz /razməˈtaz/ *noun* & *adjective*. *colloq*. (orig. *US*). Also **razzama-** /raz(ə)mə-/. L19.
[Perh. alt. of prec.]
(Of or pertaining to) a type of ragtime or early or sentimental jazz music; (of, pertaining to, or characterized by) showy, insincere, or extravagant publicity, display, etc.

razzo /ˈrazəʊ/ *noun*. *slang*. Pl. **-os**. L19.
[Prob. alt. of RASPBERRY.]
The nose.

Rb *symbol*.
CHEMISTRY. Rubidium.

RBC *abbreviation*.
MEDICINE. Red blood cell (count).

RBE *abbreviation*.
Relative biological effectiveness (of radiation).

RBI *abbreviation*.
BASEBALL. Run(s) batted in.

R-boat /ˈɑːbəʊt/ *noun*. Now *Hist*. M20.
[German *R-boot* abbreviation of *Räumboot* minesweeper.]
In the war of 1939–45, a German minesweeper.

RC *abbreviation*.
1 Red Cross.
2 Reinforced concrete.
3 ELECTRONICS. Resistance/capacitance; resistor/capacitor.
4 Roman Catholic.

RCA *abbreviation*.
1 Radio Corporation of America. *US*.
2 Royal College of Art.

RCAF *abbreviation*.
Royal Canadian Air Force.

RCD *abbreviation*.
ELECTRICITY. Residual current device.

RCM *abbreviation*.
Royal College of Music.

RCMP *abbreviation*.
Royal Canadian Mounted Police.

RCN *abbreviation*.
1 Royal Canadian Navy.
2 Royal College of Nursing.

RCP *abbreviation*.
Royal College of Physicians.

RCS *abbreviation*.
1 Royal College of Scientists.
2 Royal College of Surgeons.
3 Royal Corps of Signals.

RCVS *abbreviation*.
Royal College of Veterinary Surgeons.

RD *abbreviation*.
1 Refer to drawer (of a cheque).
2 Royal Naval Reserve Decoration.

Rd. *abbreviation*.
Road.

RDA *abbreviation.*
Recommended daily (or dietary) allowance, the quantity of a particular nutrient which should be consumed daily in order to maintain good health.

RDBMS *abbreviation.*
COMPUTING. Relational database management system.

RDC *abbreviation.*
Hist. Rural District Council.

RDF *abbreviation.*
Radio direction-finding, -finder; (as *verb trans.*) employ RDF against.

RDI *abbreviation.*
Recommended (or reference) daily intake (= RDA).

RDS *abbreviation.*
1 Radio data system, a radio receiving system in which a digital signal is transmitted with a normal radio signal to provide further data or control the receiver.
2 Respiratory distress syndrome.

RE *abbreviation.*
1 Religious education.
2 (Corps of) Royal Engineers.

Re *symbol.*
CHEMISTRY. Rhenium.

re *noun* see RAY *noun*[3].

†**re** *verb trans. rare* (Shakes.). Only in L16.
[from *re* var. of RAY *noun*[3].]
Sing to.

re /reɪ, riː/ *preposition.* E18.
[Latin, abl. of *res* thing.]
In the matter of, concerning, about.
S. A. BARNETT Interviewing people *re* the Garden Suburb.

re- /riː, rɪ (see note below)/ *prefix.* Before a vowel also **red-** /rɪd/ in a few words derived from Latin.
[Latin.]
1 In verbs and verbal derivs. of Latin or Romance origin, denoting (*a*) motion backwards or away, as ***recede***, ***remove***, ***revert***; (*b*) reversal, withdrawal, as ***recant***, ***redeem***, ***resign***, ***revoke***; secrecy, as ***revert***; (*c*) opposition, as ***rebel***, ***reluctant***, ***resist***; (*d*) negation, as ***reprobate***, ***reprove***; also with frequentative or intensive force, as in ***redouble***, ***redound***, ***regard***, ***research***.
2 In verbs and verbal derivs. of Latin or Romance origin, or formed in English, in which it denotes repetition, as ***reassess***, ***redecorate***, ***revise***; often with the added sense of a return to an earlier state, as in ***rebuild***, ***recross***, ***re-establish***, ***renovate***, ***revitalize***.
3 Prefixed to nouns to denote repeated or renewed supplying, treating, etc., with what is denoted by the noun, as ***regrass***, ***rewire***.
¶ In words derived from Latin or Romance *re-* usu. has the sound /rɪ/ or /rɛ/; in words formed in English, where the idea of repetition is present, the sound is a clear /riː/. The hyphen is retained in formations on English words (*a*) in cases where there is an otherwise homographic form of Latin or Romance origin, as *re-cover, recover, re-form, reform*; (*b*) where the main elem. begins with *e*, as *re-enter*; (*c*) where emphasis is laid on the idea of repetition, as *bind* and *re-bind*.

■ **reac'cept** *verb trans.* accept again E17. **reac'ceptance** *noun* the action or an act of reaccepting something M17. **re'access** *noun* return, renewed access E17. **reac'cession** *noun* a subsequent or renewed accession E19. **rea'ccommodate** *verb trans.* accommodate again E17. **rea'ccumulate** *verb intrans.* accumulate again M19. **reaccumu'lation** *noun* a repeated accumulation E19. **rea'ccustom** *verb trans.* accustom again E17. **rea'cquaint** *verb trans.* make acquainted again M17. **rea'cquaintance** *noun* renewed acquaintance M17. **rea'cquire** *verb trans.* acquire anew L17. **reacqui'sition** *noun* (*a*) the action of reacquiring something; (*b*) a thing which or a person who is reacquired: E20. **readapt** /riːə'dapt/ *verb trans. & intrans.* adapt anew M19. **readap'tation** *noun* the action or result of readapting L18. **rea'ddress** *verb trans.* (*a*) address again (a problem, a person); (*b*) put a new address on (a letter etc.): E17. †**readeption** *noun* recovery L15–M18. **rea'djust** *verb trans. & intrans.* adjust again (*to*) M18. **rea'djuster** *noun* (*a*) a person who readjusts; (*b*) US HISTORY a member of a 19th-cent. political party which advocated a legislative readjustment of the state debt: M19. **rea'djustment** *noun* the process or an act of readjusting or of being readjusted L18. **read'minister** *verb trans.* administer again L16. **rea'dopt** *verb trans.* adopt again L16. **rea'doption** *noun* (a) renewed adoption L15. **read'vise** *verb* (*a*) *verb trans.* advise again; (*b*) *verb intrans.* reconsider: L16. **reaggra'vation** *noun* (ROMAN CATHOLIC CHURCH) the second warning given to a person before excommunication E16. **re'aggregate** *verb trans. & intrans.* aggregate again M19. **reaggre'gation** *noun* (a) repeated aggregation L19. **rea'lign** *verb* (*a*) *verb intrans.* return to previously aligned positions; (*b*) *verb trans.* align again or anew: E20. **rea'lignment** *noun* a new alignment, esp. of political affiliations or alliances L19. **re'allocate** *verb trans.* allocate again or afresh M20. **reallo'cation** *noun* the action of reallocating something; a case or example of this: M20. **re-a'llot** *verb trans.* allot afresh L19. **re-a'llotment** *noun* the action of re-allotting something M19. **re'analyse** *verb trans.* analyse again M20. **reanalysis** /riːə'nal-/ *noun* a second or further analysis M20. **re-'anchor** *verb trans. & intrans.* anchor again E18. **rea'nneal** *verb* (*a*) *verb trans.* anneal again; BIOCHEMISTRY change (single-stranded nucleic acid) back into a double-stranded form; (*b*) *verb intrans.* (BIOCHEMISTRY) change from a single-stranded to a double-stranded form: M20. **rea'nnex** *verb trans.* annex again L15. **reannexation** /ˌriːanɛk'seɪʃ(ə)n/ *noun* the action of reannexing something; the fact or process of being reannexed: M19. **reappa'rition** *noun* a reappearance L16. **re-appli'cation** *noun* a fresh application L17. **re-a'pply** *verb trans. & intrans.* apply again; *spec.* submit a further application for a job: E18. **rea'ppoint** *verb trans.* appoint again to a position previously held E17. **rea'ppointment** *noun* an appointment to a position previously held L18. **rea'pportion** *verb trans.* apportion again or differently L19. **rea'pportionment** *noun* the action or an act of reapportioning something L19. **re-a'pproach** *verb trans.* (*a*) approach again; †(*b*) bring together again: M17. **re'argue** *verb trans. & intrans.* argue (esp. a law case) a second time L18. **re'argument** *noun* a fresh or repeated argument, esp. of a law case L19. **rea'rousal** *noun* a second or further arousal M20. **re-a'rouse** *verb trans.* arouse again M19. **rea'rrest** *verb & noun* (*a*) *verb trans.* arrest again; (*b*) *noun* a second or repeated arrest: M17. **re-ar'ticulate** *verb trans.* articulate again or afresh M20. **rea'scend** *verb intrans. & trans.* ascend again or to a former position LME. **rea'scension** *noun* the action or an act of reascending M17. **rea'scent** *noun* (*a*) the action of reascending; (*b*) the way by which one reascends: E18. **re-'ask** *verb trans. & intrans.* ask again E17. **re-a'spire** *verb intrans.* aspire again E17. **rea'ssail** *verb trans.* assail again L15. **rea'ssault** *noun & verb* (*a*) *noun* a renewed assault; (*b*) *verb trans.* assault again: E17. **rea'ssay** *verb* (*a*) *verb intrans.* (now *rare* or *obsolete*) make a fresh attempt; (*b*) *verb trans.* test the purity of (a metal) again: L16. **rea'ssess** *verb trans.* assess again, esp. differently E19. **rea'ssessment** *noun* the action or an act of reassessing something L18. **rea'ssimilate** *verb trans.* assimilate again E19. **reassimi'lation** *noun* the action or an act of reassimilating something L19. **rea'ssociate** *verb intrans. & refl.* (*rare*) come together again L15. **reassoci'ation** *noun* (*rare*) the action of reassociating E20. **rea'ssort** *verb trans.* assort again L19. **rea'ssortment** *noun* the action or result of reassorting something L18. **rea'ttach** *verb trans.* attach again or in a former position E17. **rea'ttachment** *noun* the action or an act of reattaching something L16. **rea'ttack** *verb trans. & intrans.* attack again E18. **rea'ttain** *verb trans.* attain again E17. **rea'ttainment** *noun* the action or an act of reattaining something M19. **rea'ttempt** *verb trans.* attempt again, esp. after failure L16. **rea'wake** *verb intrans. & trans.* awake again M19. **rea'waken** *verb intrans. & trans.* awaken again M19. **re'back** *verb trans.* replace the damaged spine of (a binding or book) E20. **re'bake** *verb trans.* bake again E18. **re'ban** *noun* an additional ban M19. **rebarbari'zation** *noun* the fact or condition of being rebarbarized M19. **re'barbarize** *verb trans.* reduce again to barbarism L18. **re'base** *verb trans.* set on a new base; *spec.* (FINANCE) establish a new base level for (a price index etc.): L20. **re-'beat** *verb trans.* beat again M17. **re-be'come** *verb intrans.* (with *compl.*) become again L16. **re-be'get** *verb trans.* beget again or a second time L16. **re-be'gin** *verb intrans.* begin again L16. **re-be'hold** *verb trans.* behold again E17. **re'bend** *verb trans.* bend again or in a new direction E17. **re'bind** *verb trans.* bind again; *esp.* give a new binding or case to (a book): E19. **re'bloom** *verb intrans.* bloom again E17. **re'blossom** *verb intrans.* blossom again E17. **re'board** *verb trans. & intrans.* board (a ship) again L16. **re'body** *verb trans.* provide (a motor vehicle) with a new body M20. **re'book** *verb trans. & intrans.* book (a seat, ticket, etc.) again or for a further stage of a journey M19. **re'boot** *verb & noun* (COMPUTING) (*a*) *verb trans.* boot (a computer etc.) again, esp. after a power failure or other breakdown; (*b*) *noun* an act or instance of rebooting a computer or an operating system: L20. **re'bottle** *verb trans.* bottle again E19. **re'brace** *verb trans.* brace again M18. **re'branch** *verb intrans.* divide into branches again L19. **re'breathe** *verb trans.* breathe (exhaled air) E17. **re'brew** *verb trans.* brew again M18. **re'bring** *verb trans.* bring back L16. **re'bud** *verb intrans.* bud again E17. **re'bunker** *verb intrans.* (of a ship) take in a further supply of coal or oil L19. **re'buoy** *verb trans.* (*rare*) (*a*) buoy up once more; (*b*) provide with a new set of buoys: E19. **re'burial** *noun* a second burial E20. **re'bury** *verb trans.* bury again L16. **re-'bush** *verb trans.* provide with a replacement bush L19. **re'button** *verb trans.* button (a garment etc.) again M19. **re'buy** *verb trans.* buy back E17. **re'calculate** *verb trans.* calculate again E17. **recalcu'lation** *noun* the action or an act of recalculating M19. **recapitali'zation** *noun* the action or an act of recapitalizing E20. **re'capitalize** *verb trans. & intrans.* capitalize (shares etc.) again E20. **re'carbonate** *verb trans.* charge (water) with carbon dioxide after softening E20. **recarburi'zation** *noun* (METALLURGY) addition of carbon to steel to produce the desired composition after refining L19. **re'carriage** *noun* the action of carrying esp. merchandise back again; the fact of being carried back: M16. **re'carry** *verb trans.* carry back or again LME. **re-'case** *verb trans.* provide with a new case; *spec.* rebind (a book) using its original case or a new one M19. **re'catch** *verb trans.* catch again E19. **recategori'zation** *noun* the action or an act of recategorizing something M20. **re'categorize** *verb trans.* categorize again or differently M20. **re-ce'ment** *verb trans.* join together again (as) with cement M17. **re-centre** *verb trans.* centre again L18. **re'charter** *noun & verb* (*a*) *noun* a new charter; (*b*) *verb trans.* give a new charter to: M19. **re'christen** *verb trans.* rename L18. **recivili'zation** *noun* the action of civilizing someone or something again E19. **re'civilize** *verb trans.* civilize again E19. **reclassifi'cation** *noun* the action or fact of reclassifying something; an instance of this: L19. **re'classify** *verb trans.* classify again; alter the classification of: L19. **re'clear** *verb trans.* make clear again; clear away again: L16. **re'climb** *verb trans.* climb again M18. **re'close** *verb trans. & intrans.* close again M16. **re'clothe** *verb trans.* clothe again or differently M17. **re'coal** *verb trans. & intrans.* supply with or take in a fresh supply of coal L19. **re'coat** *verb trans.* apply another coat of paint etc. to L19. **re'cock** *verb trans. & intrans.* cock (a gun) again L18. **re'code** *verb trans.* put into a different code; *spec.* (PSYCHOLOGY) rearrange mentally (information presented by a problem, situation, or test): M20. **re'coin** *verb trans.* coin (money) over again by repassage through a mint L17. **re'coinage** *noun* the action or process of recoining money E17. **reco'llate** *verb trans.* collate (pages or a book) again M19. **recoloni'zation** *noun* the action or an act of colonizing a place, habitat, or area again E19. **re'colonize** *verb trans.* (*a*) colonize (a place) again; (*b*) ECOLOGY (of an organism) return to (a habitat or area previously occupied): L16. **re'colour** *verb trans. & (rare, poet.) intrans.* colour again E19. **reco'mmand** *verb trans.* command again E16. **reco'mmission** *verb* (*a*) *verb trans.* commission again; (*b*) *verb intrans.* (of a ship) receive a new commission: M19. **reco'mmit** *verb trans.* commit again; *spec.* refer (a bill etc.) to a committee for further consideration: E17. **reco'mmittal** *noun* = RECOMMITMENT M19. **reco'mmitment** *noun* a renewed commitment or committal L18. **reco'mmunicate** *verb trans.* communicate again or differently E17. **recom'pact** *verb trans.* compact again E17. **recom'plete** *verb trans.* complete again M17. **re'complicate** *verb trans.* complicate again L19. **recom'pose** *verb trans. & intrans.* compose again or differently E17. **recompo'sition** *noun* (*a*) the action or an act of recomposing; (*b*) LINGUISTICS the action or an act of using a borrowed element as an affix to form a new word: L17. **recom'pound** *verb trans.* compound again L17. **recompu'tation** *noun* the action or an act of recomputing something; a new computation, a recalculation: M19. **recom'pute** *verb trans.* compute again, recalculate M18. **recon'ceive** *verb trans.* conceive again or in a new way M19. **recon'dense** *verb trans. & intrans.* condense again M17. **recon'fine** *verb trans.* confine again E17. **re'conjure** *verb trans.* conjure again; recall in the imagination: E17. **reco'nnect** *verb trans. & intrans.* connect again E19. **reco'nnection** *noun* the action or an act of reconnecting something; a second or further connection: E20. **recon'sult** *verb trans. & intrans.* consult again E17. **recon'test** *verb trans. & intrans.* contest again E17. **recontract** /riːkən'trakt, riː'kɒntrakt/ *verb trans. & intrans.* contract again or anew L16. **recon'vict** *verb trans.* convict again M19. **recon'viction** *noun* the action or an act of reconvicting someone; a second or further conviction: L19. **recon'voke** *verb trans.* convoke again M19. **re'copy** *verb trans.* copy again E18. **re'cork** *verb trans.* [CORK *verb*[1]] cork again, provide with a new cork M19. **re'couple** *verb trans.* (*rare*) join again, reunite E17. **re'cradle** *verb trans.* put (a telephone receiver) back in its cradle; = CRADLE *verb* 7: M20. **re'crystallizable** *adjective* able to be recrystallized M19. **recrystalli'zation** *noun* the process of crystallizing again; *spec.* (METALLURGY) a rearrangement of the crystalline structure of a metal at high temperatures which tends to reduce distortion of the lattice: L18. **re'crystallize** *verb trans. & intrans.* crystallize again L18. **re'cultivate** *verb trans.* cultivate anew M17. **reculti'vation** *noun* the action or an act of recultivating something M19. **re'cut** *verb trans.* cut again M17. **re'date** *verb trans.* change the date of; assign a new date to: E17. **re'decorate** *verb trans.* decorate (a room, building, etc.) again E17. **redeco'ration** *noun* the action or an act of redecorating a room, building, etc. M19. **re'dedicate** *verb trans.* dedicate afresh E17. **rededi'cation** *noun* the action or an act of rededicating L19. **rede'fect** *verb intrans.* return to a country from which one has previously defected M20. **rede'fection** *noun* the action or an act of redefecting M20. **rede'fector** *noun* a person who redefects M20. **rede'fine** *verb trans.* define again or differently L19. **redefi'nition** *noun* the action or result of redefining something; an instance of this: M19. **rede'mand** *verb trans.* demand the return of; demand or ask again: L16. **rede'posit** *verb trans.* deposit again M19. **redepo'sition** *noun* the action or fact of redepositing something or of being redeposited M19. **rede'scend** *verb intrans. & trans.* descend again L16. **rede'scribe** *verb trans.* describe again or in another way L19. **rede'scription** *noun* the action or an act of redescribing something; a new description: L19. **rede'sign** *verb & noun* (*a*) *verb trans.* design again or differently; (*b*) *noun* the action of redesigning something; a new design: L19. **redetermi'nation** *noun* the action or an act of redetermining something, a new determination M19. **rede'termine** *verb trans.* determine again or differently E17. **redi'rect** *verb trans.* direct anew, send in a new direction; *esp.* direct (a letter) to a new address: M19. **redi'rection** *noun* the action or an act of redirecting something; an instance of this: M19. **re'discount** *verb & noun* (*a*) *verb trans.* discount again; *esp.* (of a central bank) discount (a bill of exchange etc.) that has already been discounted by a commercial bank; (*b*) *noun* the action or an act of rediscounting something; an instance of this: M19. **redi'stil** *verb trans.* distil again M17. **redisti'llation** *noun* a second or renewed distillation M17. **re'district** *verb trans.* (*US*) divide or apportion into a new set of districts M19. **re'draft** *noun & verb* (*a*) *noun* a bill of re-exchange; a second or new draft; (*b*) *verb trans.* draft (a writing or document) again: L17. **re'draw** *verb* (*a*) *verb intrans.* draw a replacement bill of exchange; (*b*) *verb trans.* draw or draw up (something) again: L17. **re'drive** *verb trans.* drive back (again); drive in again: L16. **re-'edit** *verb trans.* edit again L18. **re-e'dition** *noun* the action or an act of re-editing something; a second or further edition: M17. **re-'educate** *verb trans.* educate again or in a different way, esp. with the object of changing beliefs or behaviour E19. **re-edu'cation** *noun* the action or process of re-educating someone L19. **re-e'lect** *verb trans.* elect again, esp. to a further term of office E17. **re-e'lection** *noun* the action or an act of re-electing someone; the fact of being re-elected: M18. **re-eligi'bility** *noun* eligibility for re-election to the same office L18. **re-'eligible** *adjective* eligible for re-election to the same office E19. **re-em'brace** *verb trans. & intrans.* embrace again E17. **re-em'broider** *verb trans.* ornament with additional or new embroidery E20. **re-e'mission** *noun* a second or subsequent emission; emission following absorption; *US* a reissue of banknotes etc.: M18. **re-e'mit** *verb trans.* emit again or after absorption; *US* reissue (banknotes etc.): M18. **re-en'dow** *verb trans.* endow again E17. **re-en'dowment** *noun* a new or further endowment M19. **re-'engine** *verb trans.* equip with a new engine or new engines L19. **re-engi'neer** *verb trans.* redesign and reconstruct; arrange or contrive anew: M20. **re-en'grave** *verb trans.* engrave again E18. **re-en'joy** *verb trans.* enjoy again E17. **re-en'joyment** *noun* the action or state of re-enjoying something; an instance of this: E17. **re-en'slave** *verb trans.* enslave again M17. **re-e'quip** *verb trans. & intrans.* provide or be provided with new or different equipment E19. **re-e'quipment** *noun* the process of re-equipping E19. **re-e'rect** *verb trans.* erect again, rebuild, refound L16. **re-e'rection** *noun* the action or process of re-erecting something M17. **re-ex'change** *noun* (*a*) COMMERCE charges incurred by the bearer when a bill of exchange is dishonoured in the country in which the bill was payable (cf. earlier RECHANGE *noun* 1); (*b*) a second or new exchange: L17. **re-exci'tation** *noun* the action or process of re-exciting something; an instance of this: L19. **re-ex'cite** *verb trans.* excite again L17. **re-express** /riːɛk'sprɛs/ *verb trans.* express again or differently M17. **re-expression** /riːɛk'sprɛʃ(ə)n/ *noun* the action or an act of re-expressing something; the fact of being re-expressed: M19. **re'face** *verb trans.*

(*a*) put a new face or surface on (a building, stone, etc.); (*b*) face (a person, a concept) again: M19. **re'fashion** verb trans. fashion again or anew L18. **re'fashioner** noun a person who refashions something E19. **re'fashionment** noun the action or process of refashioning something; a thing that has been refashioned: M19. **re'fasten** verb trans. fasten again L16. **re'feed** verb trans. feed again, esp. after a period of starvation L19. **refi'nance** verb & noun (*a*) verb trans. finance again; provide with further capital; (*b*) noun renewed or additional finance: E20. **re'finish** verb trans. apply a new finish to (a surface) M20. **re'fix** verb trans. fix again, establish anew: E17. **refixation** /riːfɪk'seɪʃ(ə)n/ noun the action or an act of refixing something; a renewed fixing: L19. **re'flag** verb trans. supply with a new flag; spec. register (a ship) under a different national flag: M20. **re'float** verb trans. float or set afloat again L19. **reflo'rescence** noun a blossoming again, a second florescence E18. **re'flourish** verb intrans. flourish anew ME. **re'flower** verb trans. (rare) & intrans. (cause to) flower or flourish again L16. **re'focus** verb trans. & intrans. focus again or differently M19. **re'fold** verb trans. fold (up) again L16. **re'foot** verb trans. replace the foot of (a boot, stocking, etc.) M19. **re'frame** verb trans. frame or fashion anew L16. **re'freeze** verb trans. & intrans. freeze again L18. **re'fuel** verb (*a*) verb trans. supply with more fuel; (*b*) verb intrans. take on more fuel: E19. **re'furnish** verb trans. furnish again or differently M16. **re'furnishment** noun (rare) the action or process of refurnishing something L19. **regasifi'cation** noun conversion back into gas M20. **re'gasify** verb trans. convert back into gas E20. **re'gauge** verb trans. gauge again E19. **re-'genesis** noun the state, fact, or process of reproducing or being reproduced M19. **re'germinate** verb intrans. germinate again E17. **regermi'nation** noun the action or process, or an instance, of regerminating M17. **re'gild** verb trans. gild again L16. **re'give** verb trans. give again, give back, give in return L16. **re'glaze** verb trans. glaze again E17. **re'ground** verb trans. provide with a new ground or basis for etching, painting, etc. M19. **re'hallow** verb trans. hallow again, reconsecrate E18. **re'handle** verb trans. handle again or differently; give a new form or arrangement to: L16. **re'harden** verb trans. & intrans. make or become hard again E17. **re'harmonize** verb trans. bring into harmony again; MUSIC give a different harmony to: E18. **re'hearten** verb trans. inspire with fresh courage or confidence E17. **re'heel** verb trans. fit (a shoe etc.) with a new heel M20. **re'home** verb trans. find a new home for (esp. a pet or domestic animal) L20. **re-identifi'cation** noun the action of reidentifying L19. **rei'dentify** verb (*a*) verb trans. identify again or in a new way; (*b*) verb intrans. identify oneself with something again: M20. **reig'nite** verb trans. ignite again M19. **reig'nition** noun the action or an act of reigniting something L19. **rei'llume** verb trans. (now rare) light up again, reignite L18. **rei'lluminate** verb trans. illuminate again M19. **reillumi'nation** noun the action or an act of reilluminating something; new illumination: E17. **rei'llumine** verb trans. illumine again E19. **reim'bibe** verb trans. imbibe again L16. **rei'mmerge** verb trans. & intrans. (long rare) immerge again M17. **rei'mmerse** verb trans. immerse again E18. **reimmi'gration** noun return after emigration L19. **reim'pel** verb trans. impel again M17. **reim'plant** verb trans. implant again M17. **reimplan'tation** noun the action or an act of reimplanting something; a thing that has been reimplanted: L17. **reim'pose** verb trans. impose (a burden, tax, etc.) again E17. **reimpo'sition** noun the action or an act of reimposing something; a reimposed tax: L18. **reim'pregnate** verb trans. impregnate again M17. **reim'press** verb trans. impress again or differently M17. **reim'pression** noun (*a*) the action or an act of reimpressing something; (*b*) the action or an act of reprinting; a reprint of a work; a renewed impression: E17. **reim'print** verb trans. imprint again or differently; reprint: M16. **reim'prison** verb trans. imprison again E17. **rein'augurate** verb trans. inaugurate afresh M19. **reinaugu'ration** noun the action of reinaugurating something; a fresh inauguration: M17. **rein'cite** verb trans. incite again E17. **rein'close** verb trans. (rare) enclose again E17. **rein'corporate** verb trans. incorporate again E17. **rein'crease** verb trans. & intrans. (rare) increase again M16. **rein'dict** verb trans. indict again E17. **rein'duce** verb trans. †(*a*) bring back, reintroduce; (*b*) induce again: L16. **rein'due** verb trans. (rare) put on again L19. **rein'fect** verb trans. infect anew E17. **rein'fection** noun the action or an act of reinfecting something; the condition of being reinfected: L19. **reinfe'station** noun a fresh infestation E20. **rein'flame** verb trans. inflame again E17. **rein'flate** verb trans. inflate again M19. **rein'form** verb trans. inform again; form anew: E17. **rein'fuse** verb trans. infuse again M17. **rein'gratiate** verb refl. ingratiate oneself again M17. **rein'gulf** verb trans. engulf again E17. **rein'habit** verb trans. & †intrans. inhabit (a place etc.) again M16. **rein'herit** verb trans. inherit again M17. **rei'nitiate** verb trans. initiate again M17. **re'ink** verb trans. ink again L19. **rei'noculate** verb trans. inoculate again E19. **reinocu'lation** noun the action or an act of reinoculating someone; a further inoculation: L19. **rein'scribe** verb trans. inscribe again L17. **rein'sert** verb trans. insert again E17. **rein'sertion** noun the action or an act of reinserting something E19. **rein'sist** verb intrans. insist again L18. **rein'spect** verb trans. inspect again E19. **rein'spection** noun the action or an act of reinspecting something; a further inspection: E19. **rein'spire** verb trans. inspire again E17. **rein'spirit** verb trans. inspirit afresh M17. **rein'stall** verb trans. install again L16. **rein'stalment** noun the action or process of reinstalling someone or something; (a) renewed instalment: E17. **rein'stil** verb trans. (rare) instil again E18. **re'institute** verb trans. institute again M19. **reinsti'tution** noun the action or an act of reinstituting something; the fact of being reinstituted: M19. **rein'struct** verb trans. instruct again or in turn M18. **rein'ter** verb trans. inter again E17. **rein'terment** noun the action or process of reinterring someone or something; a second interment: E19. **rein'terpret** verb trans. interpret again or differently E17. **reinterpre'tation** noun the action or an act of reinterpreting something; a fresh interpretation: L19. **rein'terrogate** verb trans. interrogate again E17. **rein'throne** verb trans. (now rare) enthrone again E17. **rein'trench** verb trans. entrench again M17. **reintro'duce** verb trans. introduce again M17. **reintro'duction** noun the action or an act of reintroducing someone or something; a renewed introduction: M17. **rein'vade** verb trans. invade again or in turn E17. **rein'vasion** noun the action or an act of reinvading; a renewed invasion: L19. **rein'vestigate** verb trans. & intrans. investigate again E19. **reinvesti'gation** noun the action or an act of reinvestigating something; a renewed investigation: M19. **rein'vestment** noun (*a*) fresh investment E17. **rein'vigorate** verb trans. give fresh vigour to M17. **reinvigo'ration** noun the action or an act of reinvigorating someone or something; fresh invigoration: E19. **rein'vite** verb trans. invite again E17. **re'joint** verb trans. joint together again; reunite or fill the joints of: L17. **re'judge** verb trans. judge again, re-examine; pronounce a fresh judgement on: M17. **re'jumble** verb †(*a*) verb intrans. of food: rise again in the stomach, repeat; (*b*) verb trans. jumble or toss about again: L17. **re'junction** noun (rare) the action or process of coming together again, reunion E17. **re'key** verb trans. (chiefly COMPUTING) re-enter (data, esp. text) by means of a keyboard L20. **re'kiss** verb trans. kiss again L16. **re'knit** verb trans. knit or knit up again E17. **re'label** verb trans. label again or differently L19. **re'lade** verb trans. & intrans. lade again E17. **re'land** verb trans. & intrans. land again E18. **re'learn** verb trans. learn again or differently E18. **re'lend** verb trans. lend again L18. **re'level** verb trans. level again E20. **remanu'facture** noun & verb (*a*) noun the action, process, or result of manufacturing something again or differently; (*b*) verb trans. manufacture again or differently: L18. **re'march** verb trans. & intrans. march back or again M17. **re'mast** verb trans. fit with a new mast or masts L18. **re'measure** verb trans. measure again L16. **re'measurement** noun the action or process of remeasuring something; a renewed measurement: L19. **re'meet** verb intrans. & trans. meet again M17. **re'melt** verb trans. & intrans. melt again E17. **remilitari'zation** noun the action or an act of remilitarizing a country or territory M20. **re'militarize** verb trans. rearm (a demilitarized country or territory) M20. **re'mint** verb trans. mint again E19. **remobili'zation** noun the action or an act of remobilizing someone or something; a further mobilization: E20. **re'mobilize** verb trans. (*a*) GEOLOGY make fluid or plastic again; (*b*) MILITARY recall to active service: M20. **remoneti'zation** noun the action or process of remonetizing a metal etc. L19. **re'monetize** verb trans. restore (a metal etc.) to its former use as legal tender L19. **remorali'zation** noun the action of remoralizing someone or something M20. **re'moralize** verb trans. make moral again; imbue with morals again: L20. **re'motivate** verb trans. motivate afresh L20. **re'name** verb trans. name again; esp. give a new name to: L16. **rene'gotiable** adjective able to be renegotiated M20. **rene'gotiate** verb trans. negotiate again or on different terms M20. **renegoti'ation** noun the action or process of renegotiating something; a further negotiation: M20. **re'nerve** verb trans. put fresh nerve into, strengthen the courage of again M17. **re'nominate** verb trans. nominate for a further term of office M19. **renomi'nation** noun the action or process of renominating someone; a further nomination: M19. **re'number** verb trans. number again or differently LME. **reob'tain** verb trans. obtain again; regain, recover: L16. **reoccu'pation** noun the action of occupying a place or position again; renewed occupation: M19. **re'occupy** verb trans. occupy (a place or position) again E19. **reo'ccur** verb intrans. occur again or habitually M19. **reo'ccurrence** noun the action or an act of recurring; a further occurrence, a recurrence: E19. **reo'ffend** verb intrans. (of a previously convicted offender) offend again; commit a subsequent offence: M20. **reo'ffender** noun one who reoffends L20. **re'offer** verb trans. offer again E17. **reor'dain** verb trans. ordain again; spec. invest (a person) again with holy orders: E17. **reordi'nation** noun the action or an act of reordaining someone or something; a second ordination: L16. **re'pack** verb trans. & intrans. pack again or differently L15. **re'package** verb trans. package again or differently; spec. redesign the packaging of (a product), present (a product) for sale in a different form: E20. **re'paganize** verb trans. & intrans. make or become pagan again L17. **re'paper** verb trans. & intrans. paper (a room etc.) again M19. **re'pave** verb trans. pave again or differently E17. **reper'form** verb trans. perform again M17. **reper'fume** verb trans. perfume again L16. **reper'suade** verb trans. (rare) persuade again M17. **re'phase** verb trans. readjust the proposed timing of M20. **re'pick** verb trans. pick again. L18. **re'picture** verb trans. picture again M19. **re'piece** verb trans. piece together again M17. **re'pin** verb trans. pin again M19. **re'plaster** verb trans. plaster again M19. **re'plight** verb trans. & intrans. (poet.) plight afresh L19. **re'plot** verb trans. plot or represent again L19. **re'plough** verb trans. plough again M18. **re'plumb** verb trans. replace the plumbing in (a building) E20. **repolari'zation** noun the action or an act of repolarizing; a renewed polarization: E20. **re'polarize** verb intrans. polarize again M20. **re'polish** verb trans. polish again (lit. & fig.) L16. **re'preach** verb trans. preach again L17. **repre'cipitate** verb trans. precipitate (a substance) again M19. **reprecipi'tation** noun the action of reprecipitating a substance; the fact of being reprecipitated: M19. **re-'pressuring** noun the pumping of fluid into an oil well so as to increase or maintain the pressure in the oil-bearing strata, allowing more oil to be extracted E20. **re'pressurize** verb trans. pressurize again; renew pressure in: M20. **re'pricing** noun the action or an act of pricing something again or differently M20. **re'process** verb trans. process again or differently M20. **repro'claim** verb trans. proclaim again L16. **repro'cure** verb trans. procure again L16. **re'profile** verb trans. give a new profile to; reface: M20. **re'promulgate** verb trans. promulgate again M19. **repromul'gation** noun the action or an act of repromulgating something; the fact of being repromulgated: M18. **re'purge** verb trans. purge or cleanse again M16. **repurifi'cation** noun the action or an act of repurifying something; the fact of being repurified: M20. **re'purify** verb trans. purify again L16. **re'qualify** verb trans. & intrans. qualify again L16. **re'quicken** verb trans. & intrans. quicken again, reanimate, revive L16. **requo'tation** noun a new or revised quotation of the price of a share etc. M20. **re'quote** verb trans. quote again; give a new or revised quotation for the price for (a share etc.): E19. **re-'radiate** verb trans. radiate again (something absorbed or received) E20. **re-radi'ation** noun the action or an act of re-radiating something; the fact of being re-radiated; a thing that has been re-radiated: L19. **re'rail** verb trans. replace (a train etc.) on a railway line L19. **re'raise** verb trans. raise again L17. **re-re'cord** verb trans. record (a piece of music etc.) again M20. **re-re'cording** noun the action or an act of re-recording a piece of music etc.; an instance of this; a thing that has been re-recorded: M20. **re-'reel** verb trans. wind again on to a reel, wind from one reel to another E20. **re-re'fine** verb trans. refine (a thing) again M17. **re-re'form** verb trans. reform (someone or something) again E18. **re-'register** verb & noun (*a*) verb trans. & intrans. register again; (*b*) noun (rare) a new or secondary register: M19. **re-regi'stration** noun the action or an act of re-registering someone or something; the fact of being re-registered: L19. **re-re'late** verb trans. relate (a story etc.) again L18. **re-re'peat** verb trans. repeat again E17. **re-represen'tation** noun a second or further representation L17. **re-re'solve** verb trans. & intrans. resolve again M18. **re-re'turn** verb intrans. & trans. return again E17. **re-re'veal** verb trans. reveal again M17. **re-re'vise** verb & noun (*a*) verb trans. & intrans. revise again; (*b*) noun a re-revision: L18. **re-re'vision** noun the action or process of re-revising; a second or further revision: E19. **re-'rise** verb intrans. rise again L18. **re'robe** verb trans. (arch.) dress or clothe (a person etc.) again M19. **re-'roll** verb trans. roll (a thing) again M19. **re-'roller** noun a person who or thing which re-rolls something, esp. iron or steel M20. **re-'romanize** verb trans. (derog.) make Roman Catholic again E17. **re-'roof** verb trans. provide (a building etc.) with a new roof M19. **re-'rubber** verb trans. provide (a tyre) with a fresh covering of rubber E20. **re'saddle** verb trans. & intrans. saddle again M19. **re'salt** verb trans. salt again M19. **resa'lute** verb trans. (now rare) salute (someone or something) in return or again L15. **re'sanctify** verb trans. sanctify again L17. **re'score** verb trans. revise the musical score of (a piece of music etc.) L19. **re'scoring** noun the action or an act of scoring a piece of music etc. again; an instance of this; a rescored version of a piece of music etc.: L19. **re'screen** verb trans. screen again M20. **rese'crete** verb trans. secrete again M19. **rese'cretion** noun the action of an act of resecreting something; the fact of being resecreted; a renewed or further secretion: M19. **re'sediment** verb trans. subject to resedimentation (chiefly as *resedimented ppl adjective*) M20. **resedimen'tation** noun (GEOLOGY) the action or process of resedimenting something; the movement of previously deposited sediment from one location to another by marine currents: M20. **re'see** verb trans. see (someone or something) again or for a second or further time E17. **re'seed** verb trans. sow (an area of land) with seed again, esp. grass-seed etc.: L19. **re'seek** verb trans. seek again E19. **re'segregate** verb trans. segregate again E20. **resegre'gation** noun the action or process of resegregating someone or something; the fact of being resegregated; further segregation: E20. **re'sensitize** verb trans. sensitize again M20. **re'sew** verb trans. sew again or differently L16. **re'shape** verb trans. shape or form again or differently E19. **re'ship** verb (*a*) verb intrans. take ship again; (*b*) verb trans. put (goods etc.) on board a ship again; transfer to another ship: M17. **re'shipment** noun the action or an act of reshipping goods etc.; a quantity of goods etc. reshipped: L18. **re'shoot** verb (*a*) verb intrans. sprout a shoot again; (*b*) verb intrans. & trans. shoot (a scene of a film etc.) again: E17. **re'shuffle** verb & noun (*a*) verb trans. shuffle (cards etc.) again; fig. redistribute posts within (a cabinet, organization, etc.); redistribute (ministerial or managerial posts); (*b*) noun an act or an instance of reshuffling something: M19. **re'signal** verb trans. resupply with railway signals (chiefly as *re-signalling verbal noun*) E20. **re-silver** verb trans. replate (a mirror etc.) with silver or quicksilver M19. **re'sing** verb trans. sing anew or again E17. **re'skill** verb trans. teach or equip with new or different skills; spec. retrain (workers) in the skills required by modern industry: L20 **re'skin** verb trans. †(*a*) rare put a fresh skin on (oneself); (*b*) replace or repair the skin of (an aircraft or motor vehicle): E19. **re'slash** verb trans. slash again E18. **re'slay** verb trans. slay again L18. **re'slush** verb trans. convert (dry or semi-dry paper stock) into slush by the addition of water M20. **re'smelt** verb trans. smelt again M19. **re'smooth** verb trans. smooth again M19. **resociali'zation** noun (PSYCHOLOGY) the action or process of (re)inducing conformity to accepted standards of social behaviour M20. **re'soften** verb trans. soften again L16. **re'soil** verb trans. †(*a*) rare dirty again; (*b*) cover again with soil: L16. **re'solder** verb trans. solder again E16. **re'sole** verb trans. provide (a boot, shoe, etc.) with a new sole M19. **resolidifi'cation** noun the action or process of resolidifying; the fact of being resolidified: L19. **reso'lidify** verb (*a*) verb intrans. become solid again; (*b*) verb trans. make solid again: M19. **re'sow** verb trans. sow (seed, corn, etc.) again; sow (land) with seed, corn, etc., again: E17. **re'speak** verb trans. (literary) reutter, re-echo, resound E17. **re'spell** verb trans. spell again, give an alternative spelling of, esp. according to a phonetic system E19. **re'spin** verb intrans. & trans. spin again, spin anew E17. **re'spirit** verb trans. (rare) inspire with fresh spirit or courage E17. **re'spread** verb trans. spread again or anew M17. **re'spring** verb intrans. spring up again E17. **re'stage** verb trans. stage again or in a new production E20. **re'stain** verb trans. stain again or anew M19. **re'stamp** verb trans. stamp again or anew E18. **re'steel** verb trans. fit or point with steel again M19. **re'stem** verb trans. (rare) (of a ship etc.) redirect (a course) E17. **re'stimulate** verb trans. stimulate again or anew L18. **restimu'lation** noun the action or an act of restimulating something; the fact of being restimulated; a fresh or renewed stimulation: E20. **re'stitch** verb trans. stitch or sew again or differently E17. **re'stow** verb trans. stow (something) again M19. **re'strengthen** verb trans. strengthen again, put new strength into L16. **re'stuff** verb trans. stuff again or anew M19. **resub'ject** verb trans. subdue again or anew M19. **resub'jection** noun the action or an act of resubjecting someone or something; the fact of being resubjected; a fresh or renewed subjection: E17. **re'subjugate** verb trans. subjugate again or anew M19. **resubli'mation** noun the action or process of sublimating something again or anew; the fact of being sublimated again or anew; an instance of this: M17. **resublime** verb trans. sublime again M17. **resub'mission** noun a renewed or further submission M17. **resub'mit** verb trans. submit again M19. **resu'ggest** verb trans. suggest again E18. **resu'pply** noun the action or an act of resupplying something L19. **resu'pply** verb (*a*) verb trans. supply again or anew; provide with a fresh supply; (*b*) verb intrans. take on or acquire a fresh supply: M17. **re'surface** verb (*a*) verb trans. provide (esp. a road) with a fresh surface; (*b*) verb intrans. come to the surface again (lit. & fig.): L19. **†resurprise** noun a fresh or new surprise E17–E18. **resu'rrender** verb trans. & intrans. (long rare or obsolete) surrender or give up again M16. **re'swallow** verb trans. swallow again E19. **re'swear** verb intrans. & trans. swear again or anew L17. **re'swell** verb intrans. swell again E17. **re'target** verb trans. target again L20. **re'taste** verb trans. taste again M17. **re'teach** verb trans. teach again L17. **re'telegraph** verb intrans. & trans. telegraph again;

retransmit by telegraph: **M19.** **reˈtemper** *verb trans.* temper again **L16.** **reˈtender** *verb trans.* (*rare*) †(*a*) offer back; (*b*) put out to tender again: **M17.** **reˈtexture** *noun & verb* (*a*) *noun* (*rare*) reweaving, retexturing; (*b*) *verb trans.* treat (material, a garment, etc.) so as to restore firmness to its texture: **M19.** **reˈthatch** *verb trans.* thatch again **M19.** **reˈthread** *verb trans.* thread again **E20.** **reˈthrone** *verb trans.* enthrone again **E19.** **reˈthunder** *verb* (*a*) *verb intrans.* sound or echo again like thunder; (*b*) *verb trans.* declaim again: **M18.** **reˈtie** *verb trans.* tie again **E18.** **reˈtimber** *verb trans.* (*a*) provide with timber or woodwork again or anew; (*b*) reforest: **L19.** **re-ˈtin** *verb trans.* cover or coat again with tin **M19.** **re-ˈtip** *verb trans.* supply with a new tip **M19.** **reˈtool** *verb* (*a*) *verb trans.* rework or reshape with a tool or tools; (*b*) *verb trans. & intrans.* equip (a factory etc.) with new tools, provide new manufacturing equipment (for): **M19.** **reˈtoss** *verb trans.* toss back or again **M16.** **reˈtrack** *verb trans. & intrans.* track or trace again **M19.** **reˈtrain** *verb trans. & intrans.* train again, *spec.* in a new or further skill **M20.** **retranˈscribe** *verb trans.* transcribe again **E19.** **reˈtransfer** *verb & noun* (*a*) *verb trans.* transfer (something) again or back; (*b*) *noun* the action or an act of retransferring something; *spec.* (PRINTING) an impression taken from a lithographic image using special ink and paper to transfer the image to another lithographic surface: **E19.** **retransˈform** *verb trans.* transform or change (someone or something) to a new or former condition **E17.** **retransforˈmation** *noun* the action or an act of retransforming something; the fact of being retransformed; a transformation to a new or former condition: **M19.** **retransˈlate** *verb trans.* translate again, esp. back into the original language of a text etc. **M19.** **retransˈlation** *noun* the action or an act of retranslating something; the fact of being retranslated; a fresh or new translation of a text etc., esp. back into the original language: **M17.** **retransˈmission** *noun* transmission back to a source or to a fresh destination **M19.** **retransˈmit** *verb trans.* transmit (esp. a radio signal or broadcast programme) back again or further on **M19.** **retransˈmute** *verb trans.* transmute to a new or former condition **E18.** **retransˈplant** *verb trans.* transplant again or back **M18.** **retransˈport** *verb trans.* transport again or back **M17.** **retransporˈtation** *noun* the action or an act of retransporting something; the fact of being retransported; transportation to a new or former place or condition: **M18.** **reˈtraverse** *verb trans.* traverse again or anew **M19.** **reˈtrial** *noun* the act of retrying a person or case; a second or new trial: **L19.** **retribaliˈzation** *noun* the process of making or becoming retribalized **M20.** **reˈtribalize** *verb trans.* restore (a person or society) to a tribal state; encourage the tribal habits of: **M20.** **reˈtrick** *verb trans.* (now *arch. rare*) (of a celestial body) cause (a beam) to shine again; ***retrick one's beams***, regain happiness, shrug off depression: **M19.** **reˈtrim** *verb trans. & intrans.* trim again or anew **M19.** **reˈtry** *verb trans.* try again **L17.** **reˈtube** *verb trans.* provide with a new tube or tubes **M19.** **reˈturf** *verb trans.* lay with new turf **M19.** **reˈtwist** *verb trans.* twist again or anew **M19.** **reˈundulate** *verb trans.* cause to undulate again **L17.** **re-ˈurge** *verb trans.* urge again **E18.** **reˈutter** *verb trans.* utter again **M19.** **reˈvalidate** *verb trans.* validate or confirm again or anew **E17.** **reˈvend** *verb trans.* vend or sell again **L18.** **reˈvent** *verb trans.* provide (a cannon etc.) with a new vent **M19.** **reverifiˈcation** *noun* the action or an act of reverifying something; the fact of being reverified: **M19.** **reˈverify** *verb trans.* verify again or anew **E17.** **reˈversify** *verb trans.* turn into verse again **E19.** **reviˈbrate** *verb intrans. & trans.* (cause to) vibrate again **M18.** **reˈvictual** *verb* (*a*) *verb trans.* supply with victuals again; (*b*) *verb intrans.* obtain or take in a fresh supply of victuals: **E16.** **reˈvindicate** *verb trans.* vindicate again or anew; reclaim, recover, restore: **E19.** **revindiˈcation** *noun* the action or an act of revindicating; the fact of being revindicated: **M17.** **reˈvisit** *noun* a repeated or second visit **E17.** **revisit** *verb* (*a*) *verb trans. & intrans.* visit again; †(*b*) *verb trans.* revise, reinspect, re-examine: **L15.** **revisiˈtation** *noun* (*a*) (*rare*) revisal, revision; (*b*) the action or an act of revisiting; the fact of being revisited: **M16.** **revitaliˈzation** *noun* the action or an act of revitalizing someone or something; the fact of being revitalized: **L19.** **reˈvitalize** *verb trans.* restore to vitality; put new life into: **M19.** **reˈvoice** *verb trans.* (*a*) voice again or in return; (*b*) provide (something) with a different voice; readjust the tone of (an organ-pipe): **E17.** **reˈvote** *noun & verb* (*a*) *noun* a second or repeated vote; a renewed grant; (*b*) *verb trans.* grant or settle (a sum of money etc.) by a new vote: **M19.** **reˈwake** *verb trans. & intrans.* wake again **L16.** **reˈwaken** *verb trans. & intrans.* waken again **M17.** **reˈwarm** *verb trans. & intrans.* warm again, reheat **E17.** **reˈwash** *verb trans.* wash again **E18.** **reˈweave** *verb trans.* (chiefly *fig.*) weave again **L19.** **reˈweigh** *verb trans.* weigh again **E19.** **re-ˈweight** *noun* (*rare*) a repeat weighing; the weight ascertained by this: **E19.** **re-ˈwet** *verb trans.* make wet again **M19.** **reˈwhisper** *verb trans.* express in a whisper again, reply in a whisper **M18.** **reˈwhiten** *verb trans.* whiten again or anew **L18.** **re-ˈwin** *verb trans.* win back or again; recover: **E17.** **reˈwrap** *verb trans.* wrap again or differently **M20.** **reˈyoke** *verb trans.* yoke (oxen etc.) again **E19.** **re-ˈzero** *verb trans. & intrans.* (cause to) return to a zero position **L20.** **reˈzone** *verb trans.* assign (land, property, or people) to a new zone **M20.** **reˈzoning** *noun* the action or an act of rezoning land, property, or people; the fact of being rezoned; an instance of this: **M20.**

're *verb* see BE *verb*.

reable /riːˈeɪb(ə)l/ *verb trans.* **E16.**
[from RE- + ABLE *verb*.]
†**1** Confirm, legitimize. *Scot.* **E16–L17.**
2 MEDICINE. Rehabilitate (a patient). *rare.* **M20.**
■ **reablement** *noun* rehabilitation **M20.**

reabsorb /riːəbˈzɔːb, -ˈsɔːb/ *verb trans.* **M18.**
[from RE- + ABSORB.]
Absorb again.
■ **reabsorption** *noun* **M18.** **reabsorptive** *adjective* having the quality of reabsorbing something or someone **M20.**

reach /riːtʃ/ *noun.* **LME.**
[from REACH *verb*[1].]
▶ **I** A thing that reaches or extends.
1 a An enclosed stretch of water; a bay. Long *obsolete* exc. *Canad. dial.* **LME.** ▸**b** A portion of a river, channel, or lake between two bends; a portion of a canal between two locks. **M16.** ▸**c** A headland. Long *obsolete* exc. *US dial.* **M16.**
2 *gen.* A continuous stretch, course, or extent in space or time. **E17.**
3 A bearing-shaft; a coupling-pole. **M19.**

> 🕮 **2** J. FOWLES Great reaches of clear sky. R. D. LAING The furthest reaches of the Empire.

▶ **II** Power of, or capacity for, reaching.
4 The distance to which a limb can be extended, esp. when seeking to touch or grasp something; distance from which some point may be reached (only in ***within reach***); CRICKET the extent to which a batsman can play forward without moving the back foot; *transf.* the distance to which an inanimate thing can extend itself. Freq. in ***beyond reach***, ***beyond the reach of***, ***out of reach***, ***within reach***, etc. **M16.**
5 Power of comprehension; extent of knowledge or of the ability to acquire it; range of mind or thought. **M16.**
6 Extent of application, effect, or influence; range, scope. **M16.**
7 Capacity to perform, achieve, or attain something. Chiefly with prepositions, as in sense 4. **L16.** ▸†**b** The compass of a person's voice. **L16–L17.**
8 The distance that a thing can carry or traverse; the range of a gun, the voice, the sight, etc. **L16.** ▸**b** The number of people who watch a television channel or listen to a radio station during a particular period. **M20.**

> 🕮 **4** T. HOOD Past the reach of foamy billows. J. WAIN Within easy reach of the drinks. **5** J. CHEEVER The retentiveness and reach of his memory. **6** W. D. WHITNEY Wide reach and abundant results. **7** W. IRVING Virtues . . within every man's reach. *Woman's Illustrated* My . . fee . . is within the reach of all. **8** D. NOBBS He had rigged up an electric light . . but beyond its reach there were pools of . . darkness.

▶ **III** An act of reaching.
9 An act of reaching with the arm, esp. to take hold of something or with something held in the hand. **L16.**
†**10** *fig.* An attempt to attain or achieve something; a scheme, a plan; scheming. **L16–L18.**
11 A single spell of movement, travel, flight, etc.; NAUTICAL a run on one tack; a course that is approximately at right angles to the wind. **M17.**

Comb.: **reach rod** a connecting rod for transmitting manual motion to another part of a mechanism; **reach truck** a fork-lift truck whose fork can be moved forward and backward as well as up and down.
■ **reachy** *adjective* (of an animal) having a long reach **L19.**

reach /riːtʃ/ *verb*[1]. Pa. t. & pple **reached**, †**raught**.
[Old English *rǣċan* = Old Frisian *rēka*, *rētsi(i)a*, Middle Low German, Middle & mod. Dutch *reiken*, Old High German, German *reichen*, from West Germanic. Cf. RATCH *verb*[1], RETCH *verb*[1].]
▶ **I** *verb trans.* **1** Extend from the body (a limb, hand, or foot). (Foll. by *out*, *forth*.) **OE.** ▸**b** Thrust (a weapon) *forth* or *up* by stretching out the arm; (of a tree) extend (its branches). *poet.* **L16.**
2 Stretch; draw or pull *out* or †*in*. *obsolete* exc. *dial.* **OE.**
3 Succeed in touching or grasping, esp. with the outstretched hand. **OE.** ▸**b** Formerly, acquire, get possession of, obtain; seize, take hold of, carry off. Now only (*arch.*), take or snatch *from*. **OE.** ▸**c** Take *down* with outstretched hand. **L15.**
4 †**a** Smite, strike. **OE–E19.** ▸**b** Deal or strike (a blow or, formerly, a wound). Foll. by *to*, *at*, or dat. obj. Now *rare* exc. *Scot.* **LME.**
5 Pass (a thing) to a person by extending a hand or arm to get it (freq. foll. by pers. indirect obj.); (now *rare*) extend a hand or arm to get (a thing) and pass it *to* a person. Also (*obsolete* exc. *poet.*), hold (a thing) *up*, *out*, etc., by extending a hand or arm. **OE.**
6 Extend so far as to touch, come into physical contact with. **ME.**
7 Get as far as, arrive at; get in contact with (a person); (of a communication) be received by (a person) or at (a place); (of a sound) be heard by. **ME.** ▸**b** Succeed in affecting or influencing; impress, convince, win over. **LME.** ▸**c** Bribe. *US slang.* **E20.**
8 Arrive at, attain, (a point in time or on a scale, a condition, etc.). **L16.**
†**9** Understand. **E17–E19.**

> 🕮 **3** A. UTTLEY The low . . tree whose branches she could reach. **c** F. MUIR I reached down a book. **5** H. BROOKE Taking . . your picture . . I reached it to her. C. KINGSLEY The beaker I reach back More rich than I took it. L. DEIGHTON Reach me . . those . . glasses. **7** W. CATHER An alarming telegram reached him. G. ORWELL A loft which could only be reached by a ladder. C. P. SNOW Gossip reached even Aunt Milly. O. MANNING The train, when they reached it, was . . full. S. TROTT He hadn't . . been able to reach me. **b** P. BROOK His seriousness . . reached the audience. **8** E. CALDWELL He had . . reached his sixteenth birthday. *Evening Post (Nottingham)* To reach agreement.

▶ **II** *verb intrans.* **10** Make a stretch with a limb, hand, or foot; extend the arm, esp. in order to touch or grasp something. Usu. foll. by adverb or preposition. **OE.** ▸**b** Grasp or clutch *at*. **M16.**
11 Extend or project a certain distance (in space or time) or in a certain direction. **OE.** ▸**b** Amount *to*. **L16.**
†**12** Proceed, move, go. **OE–LME.**
13 Suffice, be adequate. Foll. by *to*, *to do*. Now *rare* or *obsolete*. **LME.**
14 Undergo stretching. Long *obsolete* exc. *dial.* **LME.**
15 Succeed in coming *to* a specified place, person, etc. Also foll. by other prepositions & adverbs. **L16.**
16 NAUTICAL. Sail with the wind abeam or a little before or abaft the beam. **M19.**
17 Make an unwarranted inference; jump to a conclusion; guess. *US.* **M20.**
18 BASEBALL. Reach first base. **L20.**

> 🕮 **10** H. ROTH He reached into his . . pocket. HARPER LEE Two children could not reach around its trunk and touch hands. W. GOLDING Edwin reached down and slipped off his shoes. S. TROTT Joe reached over for his clarinet. *fig.*: D. M. FRAME Montaigne reaches out for a friend. **11** *Atlantic Monthly* Schemes of the Pan-Germanists . . reach to . . a vast confederation of states. M. MCLUHAN Assumptions that reach back . . two centuries. I. MURDOCH Objects . . in piles which . . reached up to the ceiling.

With prepositions in specialized senses: **reach for** make a movement with the hand or arm to touch or grasp; ***reach for one's gun*** (*fig.*), react with extreme hostility; ***reach for the sky***, raise one's arms above one's head. **reach to** (now *rare* or *obsolete*) accomplish, achieve; (see also senses 11b, 13 above).
Comb.: **reach-me-down** *adjective & noun* (*a*) *adjective* (of a garment) ready-made, second-hand; *transf.* & *fig.* derivative, inferior; (*b*) *noun* a reach-me-down thing (usu. in *pl.*); *spec.* (in *pl.*), trousers.
■ **reachaˈbility** *noun* (MATH.) the possibility of reaching one point of a graph from another **M20.** **reachable** *adjective* (earlier in UNREACHABLE) †(*a*) *rare* capable of reaching *to*; (*b*) able to be reached: **M17.** **reaching** *ppl adjective* that reaches or reaches far; *spec.* (now *rare*) (of thoughts, the mind, etc.) far-sighted, deep: **L16.** **reachless** *adjective* unable to be reached **E17.**

reach /riːtʃ/ *verb*[2]. *obsolete* exc. *dial.*
[Old English *hrǣċan* = Old Norse *hrǽkja* spit, from Germanic base repr. also by Old English *hrāca*, Old Norse *hráki* spittle; of imit. origin. Cf. RETCH *verb*[2].]
†**1** *verb intrans. & trans.* Spit; bring *up* (blood or phlegm); hawk. **OE–E17.**
2 *verb intrans.* Make efforts to vomit; retch. **L16.**

reacher /ˈriːtʃə/ *noun.* **L16.**
[from REACH *verb*[1] + -ER[1].]
1 A person who or thing which reaches. **L16.**
2 Formerly, an exaggerated statement. Now (*dial.*), an extraordinary thing. **E17.**
3 NAUTICAL. A kind of jib. **E20.**

react /rɪˈakt/ *verb.* **M17.**
[from RE- + ACT *verb*, orig. after medieval Latin *react-* pa. ppl stem of *reagere*, formed as RE- + *agere* do, act.]
1 *verb intrans.* Act in return *on* an agent or influence; produce a reciprocal or responsive effect; CHEMISTRY undergo a reaction (*with* another substance). **M17.**
2 *verb intrans.* Respond to a stimulus; undergo a change or show behaviour under some influence. (Foll. by *to*.) **M17.**
3 *verb intrans.* Act in opposition to some force. Foll. by *against*. **M19.**
4 *verb intrans.* Move or tend in a reverse direction; (of share prices) fall after rising. **L19.**
5 *verb trans.* Cause to react chemically or immunologically *with* or *together*. **M20.**

> 🕮 **1** N. CALDER Carbohydrate reacts with oxygen. **2** R. P. GRAVES Reacting badly to the inoculation. A. T. ELLIS She wondered how the gamekeeper would react. **3** J. GROSS The young reacting against . . their elders. **5** *New Scientist* Pupils are asked to react magnesium with dilute nitric acid.

re-act /riːˈakt/ *verb trans.* **E17.**
[from RE- + ACT *verb*.]
Act, do, or perform again.

reactance /rɪˈakt(ə)ns/ *noun.* **L19.**
[from REACTION + -ANCE, after *resistance*, *impedance*.]
1 ELECTRICITY. **a** The non-resistive component of impedance, arising from the effect of inductance or capacitance or both and causing the current to be out of phase with the electromotive force causing it. **L19.** ▸**b** = REACTOR 2. **E20.**
2 MECHANICS & ACOUSTICS. The imaginary component of a mechanical or acoustic impedance, producing a phase difference between a driving force and the resulting motion but no dissipation of energy. **E20.**
3 PSYCHOLOGY. A response of resistance aroused in a person who feels his or her freedom of choice is threatened or impeded. **M20.**

reactant /rɪˈakt(ə)nt/ *noun.* **E20.**
[from REACT + -ANT[1].]
CHEMISTRY. A reacting substance, molecule, etc.

reaction /rɪˈakʃ(ə)n/ *noun.* **M17.**
[from REACT, orig. after medieval Latin *reactio(n-)*, from *react-*: see REACT, -ION.]
1 Repulsion or resistance exerted in opposition to the impact or pressure of another body; a force equal and

opposite to the force giving rise to it; an influence exerted in return on the source of the influence. **M17.**
2 A chemical process in which two or more substances act mutually on each other and are changed into different substances, or one substance changes into two or more other substances; a chemical change. Also (*PHYSICS*), an analogous transformation of atomic nuclei or other particles. **M17.** ▸**b** The degree of acidity or alkalinity of a substance as exhibited in chemical processes. **M19.**
3 A movement towards the reversal of an existing tendency or state of affairs, esp. in politics; advocacy of or preference for a previous state of affairs. **L18.** ▸**b** A fall in share prices etc. following a rise. **M19.**
4 The occurrence in a person of an opposite physical or emotional condition to a preceding one. **E19.**
5 A bodily response to an external stimulus. **L19.**
6 A response to an event, statement, etc.; an action or feeling that expresses or constitutes a response; an immediate or first impression. **E20.**
7 Positive feedback in a radio. **E20.**

🕮 **1** S. VINCE The reaction of the sides of the vessel against the fluid. **2** N. V. SIDGWICK The reaction of boron trichloride with an alcohol. J. NARLIKAR The star's nuclear reactions generate energy. ***addition reaction, biuret reaction, chain reaction, Friedel–Crafts reaction***, etc. **3** HOR. SMITH Fanaticism provokes a reaction. C. CAUDWELL The revolting bourgeoisie . . beaten back . . by the forces of reaction. **4** J. HILTON Mallinson, after the strain of . . arguing, was experiencing a reaction. **6** S. WEINTRAUB Illness was . . a reaction to the . . warfare in the household. *Studio News* Initial reaction . . is sceptical.

Comb.: **reaction chamber** (*a*) a vessel in which a chemical reaction occurs, esp. in an industrial process; (*b*) the combustion chamber of a rocket; **reaction circuit** *ELECTRONICS* that part of the anode circuit of a valve which produces positive feedback in the grid circuit; **reaction coil** *ELECTRONICS* an inductance coil in the reaction circuit of a valve; **reaction formation** *PSYCHOLOGY* the tendency of a repressed wish or feeling to be expressed in a contrasting form; **reaction jet** a jet engine used to provide intermittent thrust for changing or correcting the velocity of a spacecraft etc.; **reaction pattern** a pattern of behaviour or response established in the nervous system; **reaction propulsion** a form of propulsion which utilizes the reaction exerted by escaping fluid as the source of motive power; *spec.* jet or rocket propulsion; **reaction shot** *CINEMATOGRAPHY & TELEVISION* the depiction of a person responding to an event or to a statement made by another; **reaction time** the time taken by a person (or any living organism) to respond to a stimulus; **reaction turbine**: driven by the pressure drop experienced by the working fluid in passing across or through the rotor; **reaction wood** modified wood that forms in branches and leaning trunks and tends to restore upward direction of growth.
▪ **reactionism** *noun* reactionaryism **L19.** **reactionist** *noun & adjective* (*a*) *noun* a marked or professed reactionary; a person who reacts *against* something; (*b*) *adjective* reactionary: **M19.**

reactionary /rɪˈakʃ(ə)n(ə)ri/ *adjective & noun.* **M19.**
[from prec. + -ARY[1], partly after French *réactionnaire*.]
▶ **A** *adjective.* Of, pertaining to, or characterized by, reaction; inclined or favourable to reaction, esp. to the reversal of an existing political state of affairs. **M19.**

🕮 B. JOWETT The fixed ideas of a reactionary statesman. R. LEHMANN Franco's abominable reactionary conspiracy.

▶ **B** *noun.* A reactionary person. **M19.**
▪ **reactionarily** *adverb* **M20.** **reactionariness** *noun* (*rare*) **E20.** **reactionaryism** *noun* reactionary principles or practice **E20.**

reactivate /rɪˈaktɪveɪt/ *verb trans.* **E20.**
[from RE- + ACTIVATE.]
Make active or operative again, restore to a state of activity.
▪ **reactiˈvation** *noun* the action or result of reactivating something **E20.**

reactive /rɪˈaktɪv/ *adjective & noun.* **E18.**
[from REACT + -IVE. Cf. French *réactif*.]
▶ **A** *adjective.* †**1** Repercussive, echoing. Only in **E18.**
2 Acting in return. **L18.**
3 Constituting a reaction to a previous state or a stimulus; caused by or exhibiting a reaction; *PSYCHOLOGY* (of mental illness) caused by environmental factors. **E19.**
4 Reactionary. **M19.**
5 Having a tendency to react chemically; involving chemical reaction; (of a dye etc.) designed to react chemically with the substrate, usu. in order to become fixed. **L19.**
6 *SCIENCE.* Possessing or pertaining to reactance; *spec.* (*ELECTRICITY*) designating the vector component of an alternating current (or voltage) which is 90 degrees out of phase with respect to the associated voltage (or current). **L19.**

🕮 **3 reactive inhibition** the inhibiting effect of fatigue or boredom on the response to a stimulus. **5** *Independent* Highly reactive, ozone-destroying chemicals form . . in stratospheric clouds. **6 reactive power** the product of the voltage and the reactive current, or of the current and the reactive voltage.

▶ **B** *noun.* A chemical reagent. *rare.* **L18.**
▪ **reactively** *adverb* **E19.** **reacˈtivity** *noun* the state or power of being reactive; the degree to which a thing is reactive; *spec.* the extent to which a nuclear reactor deviates from a steady state: **L19.**

reactor /rɪˈaktə/ *noun.* **L19.**
[formed as prec. + -OR.]
1 A person, animal, or organism that reacts to a stimulus, esp. under experimental conditions; *spec.* (*MEDICINE*) one showing an immune response to a specific antigen; a person who has a reaction to a drug. **L19.**
2 A coil or other piece of equipment which provides reactance in an electric circuit. **E20.**
3 A vessel or apparatus in which substances are made to react chemically, *esp.* one in an industrial plant. **M20.**
4 An apparatus or structure in which fissile material can be made to undergo a controlled, self-sustaining nuclear reaction with the consequent release of energy. Also more fully ***nuclear reactor***. **M20.**
4 ***fast breeder reactor***: see FAST *adjective*. ***light water reactor***: see LIGHT *adjective*[1]. ***pressurized-water reactor***: see PRESSURIZE. ***slow reactor***: see SLOW *adjective & adverb*. ***thermal reactor***: see THERMAL *adjective*.

read /riːd/ *noun*[1]. *obsolete* exc. *dial. & techn.* **OE.**
[Origin unkn.]
Orig., the stomach of an animal. Later *spec.*, the abomasum or fourth stomach of a ruminant.

read /riːd/ *noun*[2]. **E19.**
[from the verb.]
Orig. (*Scot.*), a loan of a book, newspaper, etc., for the purposes of perusal. Now also, a spell or act of reading, *COMPUTING* an act of reading data; *colloq.* a book, story, etc., as regards its readability and narrative power.

🕮 T. PARKER He'd . . gone to bed to lie down and have a read. J. I. M. STEWART Tamburlaine is a tolerable read . . As a stage play it is pretty hopeless.

read /rɛd/ *adjective.* **ME.**
[pa. pple of READ *verb*.]
1 Experienced, versed, or informed in or *in* a subject by reading; learned or informed through reading; acquainted with books or literature. Chiefly & now only with qualifying adverb. **ME.**
2 That is read; *esp.* that is read out, as opp. to being expressed spontaneously or repeated from memory. **L16.**

🕮 **1** HENRY FIELDING He was deeply read in the ancients. **2** *Westminster Gazette* The trouble of attending the meeting to hear a read speech.

read /riːd/ *verb.* Pa. t. & pple **read** /rɛd/. Also (earlier, now only *arch. & dial.* in senses 1, 2, & 8) **rede**, pa. t. & pple **red(d)** /rɛd/. See also REDE *verb*[1].
[Old English *rǣdan* = Old Frisian *rēda*, Old Saxon *rādan* (Dutch *raden*), Old High German *rātan* (German *raten*), Old Norse *ráða* advise, plan, contrive, read, Gothic *-rēdan*, from Germanic.]
▶ **I** †**1** *verb trans.* **a** Believe, think, suppose. **OE–M18.** ▸**b** Guess, make out, *what, who*, etc. Also foll. by direct obj. **OE–L16.**
2 *verb trans.* **a** Interpret (a dream); solve (a riddle); declare or expound (the meaning of a dream or the solution of a riddle) to someone. **OE.** ▸**b** Foresee or predict (a person's destiny). *poet. rare.* **L16.**
†**3** *verb trans.* Count, estimate. *rare.* **ME–L18.**
†**4** *verb trans.* See, discern, distinguish. **ME.**
▶ **II 5** *verb trans.* Inspect and silently interpret or say aloud (letters, words, sentences, etc.) by passing the eyes or fingers over written, printed, engraved, or embossed characters; render (written or printed matter) in speech, esp. *aloud* or *to* another person (also with pers. indirect obj.), take in the sense of (a book or magazine), or habitually peruse (an author's writings, a newspaper, etc.) by inspecting and interpreting letters, words, sentences, etc. **OE.** ▸**b** Inspect and interpret the written or printed form of (a specified language); understand (a specified language) sufficiently to do this; interpret the symbols of (musical notation), sight-read. **M16.** ▸**c** Check the correctness of (a proof), esp. against copy, and mark any emendations to be made, proofread. **M17.** ▸**d** *POLITICS.* Present (a bill or measure) before a legislative assembly (orig., in the English Parliament, by reading the bill or measure aloud). **M17.** ▸**e** Scan the text of (a book, journal, etc.) for the occurrence of words and phrases, *spec.* as usage evidence in the compilation of a dictionary. **L19.**
6 *verb intrans.* Read or be able to read letters, words, sentences, etc.; read *aloud* or *to* another person; occupy oneself in reading, esp. habitually. **OE.** ▸**b** Read and report on the merits of manuscripts etc. offered for publication to a prospective publisher; act as a publisher's reader. **M19.**
7 a *verb trans.* Find it recorded in print or writing *that*. Formerly also, find (a fact) so recorded. **OE.** ▸**b** *verb intrans.* Find mention *of* something in the course of reading. **ME.** ▸**c** *verb trans.* Discern (a fact, quality, etc.) *in* a person's expression, eyes, etc. **L16.**
8 a *verb trans.* Tell, relate. Formerly also, describe; call, name. Long *arch.* **ME.** ▸†**b** *verb intrans.* Tell *of* something. **ME–L16.**
†**9 a** *verb intrans.* Lecture or give oral instruction (*on* a subject). **ME–E18.** ▸**b** *verb trans.* Teach (a subject). (Foll. by *to*, indirect obj.) **ME–L19.**
10 *verb trans.* **a** Interpret or understand the significance of, *spec.* for purposes of divination. **L16.** ▸**b** Make out the character, nature, or intention of (a person) from observation of his or her expression, bodily movement, etc.; understand the feelings behind (a person's expression). **E17.** ▸**c** Interpret in a particular way; give a particular meaning to. **E17.** ▸**d** (Of an editor) give as the word or words probably used or intended by an author at a particular place in a text; (of a text) have at a particular place; (of a reader) accept as a correct or substituted word or passage. **M17.**
11 *verb intrans.* Be readable; *esp.* convey meaning or affect the reader in a specified way when read; sound *like* when read. **M17.**
12 *verb trans.* Bring *to* or *into* a specified condition by reading. **L17.**
13 *verb trans.* Interpret (a design) in terms of the setting needed to reproduce it on a loom. **M19.**
14 *verb trans.* Introduce, esp. wrongly, as an additional element; regard as present or implied. Foll. by *into* what is being read or considered. **L19.**
15 *verb trans. & intrans.* (with *for*). Study (an academic subject), esp. in preparation for a degree in it; study for (a degree). **L19.**
16 *verb trans.* Of a measuring instrument: show as the measurement of the quantity measured; indicate. **L19.**
17 *verb trans.* Of a passage or text: contain or consist of (specified words); say. **L19.**
18 *verb trans. & intrans.* Receive and understand the words of (a person) by radio or telephone; detect by sonar; *fig.* understand the meaning of (a speaker). **M20.**
19 *verb intrans.* Of an actor or actress: audition or rehearse *for* a part. **M20.**
20 *verb trans. COMPUTING.* Copy, extract, (data); transfer (data) *into* or *out of* an electronic device. **M20.**
21 *verb trans.* Of a device: respond in a pre-set way to (light, an optical stimulus). **M20.**

🕮 **5** A. CARNEGIE Leading editorials were read . . to the people. R. KIPLING I don't read Scott. S. BELLOW We had read the same . . books. K. AMIS She started reading him a story. **b** *Times Lit. Suppl.* Students . . who do not read Russian. **6** A. S. NEILL I'm going . . to learn to read. SCOTT FITZGERALD She read aloud to him. M. AMIS He read with concentration, his nose perhaps six inches from the page. **7a** J. W. EBSWORTH We read . . that the Spanish ships . . were of different classes. **b** J. G. FARRELL The Major sat . . reading of . . disasters. **c** L. M. MONTGOMERY She read disapproval in Mrs Rachel's expression. **10a** W. A. WALLACE A man . . that cannot read his own watch? H. WILSON Reading the electoral portents. D. PROFUMO Incapable of reading a simple map. *Daily Telegraph* She was . . reading Tarot cards. **c** T. HARDY She read his thoughts. A. PRICE Burton read the stricken expression on his face. **d** G. BATTISCOMBE The poem can be read at many levels. F. MADDEN For *Lovaine* some copies of Wace read *Alemaigne*. *Listener* The cultures of 'Indonesia' (read southeast Asia). **11** ANTHONY SMITH This incident reads like some account of the Black Death. N. RANKIN Stevenson reads well in French. **12** *Tempo Bar* The soothing voice . . lullingly reading him to sleep. **14** *Times* To read into the results of . . by-elections . . sinister or cheering evidence. **15** *Times* Students reading social science. **16** G. GREENE I looked at my watch—it read five minutes to eleven. **17** M. KENYON Arsenal Poofters OK, read the solitary graffito. **18** D. FRANCIS Port Ellen tower this is Golf Alpha Romeo . . , do you read? R. J. SERLING Do you read me? **19** E. BERCKMAN Ring your agent, and say you'll read for the part. **20** *Computer Journal* Reading a file into the system. **21** *Camera Weekly* The camera reads light from the frame.

Phrases: ***read a person a lesson***: see LESSON *noun* 6. ***read a person's mind***: see MIND *noun*[1]. ***read between the lines***: see LINE *noun*[2]. **read one's shirt** *slang* search one's clothes for lice. ***read someone like a book***: see BOOK *noun*. ***read the Riot Act***: see RIOT *noun*. **take as read** treat a statement, a subject, etc. as if it has been agreed, without having a discussion about it; take for granted. **you wouldn't read about it!** *Austral. & NZ colloq.*: expr. incredulity and disgust or ruefulness.
With adverbs in specialized senses: **read in** (*a*) *verb phr. trans.* take as intended by or deducible from a passage; (*b*) *verb phr. intrans. & refl.* (*Hist.*) take up office as an incumbent in the Church of England by publicly reading the Thirty-nine Articles and the Declaration of Assent; (*c*) *verb phr. trans.* formally admit to membership; *spec.* conscript; (*d*) *verb phr. trans.* (*COMPUTING*) transfer (data) into a computer etc. **read off** note (a measurement) from the indication of a graduated instrument. **read out** (*a*) read aloud; (*b*) (foll. by *of*) expel from (a party, church, etc.); (*c*) *COMPUTING* extract (data); transfer from internal storage. **read over** look at and read various parts of (a letter, book, etc.). **read through** read from beginning to end. **read up** study (a subject) intensively and systematically; familiarize oneself with (a subject) by reading.
Comb.: **read-around ratio** *COMPUTING* the number of times that a particular bit in an electrostatic store can be read without degrading bits stored nearby; **read-in** *COMPUTING* the input of data to a computer or storage device; **read-mostly** *adjective* (*COMPUTING*) designating a memory whose contents can be changed, though not by program instructions, but which is designed on the basis that such changes will be very infrequent; **read-only** *adjective* (*COMPUTING*) designating a memory whose contents cannot be changed by program instructions but which can usually be read at high speed; **read-through** (*a*) an act of reading through;

THEATRICAL an initial rehearsal at which actors read their parts from scripts; (*b*) *BIOCHEMISTRY* the continued transcription of genetic material by RNA polymerase that has overrun a termination sequence. **read-write** *adjective* (*COMPUTING*) capable of or allowing both the reading of the existing data and its alteration and supplementation.

readable /ˈriːdəb(ə)l/ *adjective & noun*. LME.
[from READ *verb* + -ABLE.]
▶ **A** *adjective*. **1** Able to be read, legible. LME.
2 Giving pleasure or interest when read; agreeable or attractive in style. L18.
▶ **B** *noun*. In *pl*. Readable works. M19.
■ **readaˈbility** *noun* the quality giving pleasure or interest when read; legibility: M19. **readableness** *noun* M19.

readathon /ˈriːdəθɒn/ *noun*. M20.
[from READ *verb* + -ATHON.]
A protracted session of reading aloud, esp. as a fund-raising event.

reader /ˈriːdə/ *noun*. OE.
[from READ *verb* + -ER¹.]
1 A person who reads or who is able to read, a person who occupies himself or herself in reading, esp. habitually. OE. ▸**b** *ECCLESIASTICAL*. A person in minor orders in the Roman Catholic and Orthodox Churches who is authorized to read lessons; a lector; *ANGLICAN CHURCH* (also, now *Hist.* in the Church of England, ***lay reader***) a lay person authorized to conduct certain services and perform certain liturgical and pastoral duties. M16. ▸**c** A person who reads and corrects proofs, a proofreader. E19. ▸**d** A person who reads and reports to a publisher or producer on the merits of works offered for publication or plays offered for production. E19. ▸**e** A person officially entitled to use a particular library. L19.
†**2** An interpreter of dreams etc. OE–LME.
3 Orig., a person who reads (and expounds) to pupils or students. Now, in some British universities, (the title of) a lecturer of the highest grade below professor. LME.
4 a A pocketbook. *Criminals' slang*. E18. ▸**b** A marked card. *slang*. L19.
5 A book containing passages for instruction or exercise in reading; an anthology of readings. L18.
6 A device for obtaining data stored on tape, cards, or other media (usu. converting the data into coded electrical signals). M20.
7 A machine for producing on a screen a magnified, readable image of any desired part of a microfilm etc. M20.

> 🕮 **1** H. ACTON Himself no reader, he had no objection to her browsing in the well-stocked library. *Daily Mirror* I disagree with your woman reader who thinks men score over women. M. MCCARTHY Weep with me, Reader. **e** A. BROOKNER He caught a bus to the Bibliothèque Nationale, presented his reader's ticket, and sat down at one of the desks. **6** ***optical character reader***: see OPTICAL *adjective*. ***tape reader***: see TAPE *noun*.

Comb.: **reader-aloud** a person who reads a literary text etc. aloud, esp. to an audience; **reader-printer** a reader (sense 7 above) that can also produce enlarged, readable copies.
■ **readerly** *adjective* (*a*) immediately accessible to a reader, not requiring a commentary or interpretation; (*b*) of or pertaining to a reader or readers: L20. **readership** *noun* (*a*) the office of a reader; (*b*) (with possess. adjective, as ***your readership*** etc.) a mock title of respect given to a reader; (*c*) the number of readers of a newspaper etc.; such readers considered collectively: M17.

readily /ˈrɛdɪli/ *adverb*. ME.
[from READY *adjective* + -LY².]
1 Without reluctance; with alacrity or willingness. ME.
2 Without delay; without difficulty. LME.
3 As may easily happen; probably. *Scot*. M17.

> 🕮 **1** A. J. AYER He too readily accused . . adversaries of . . wickedness. **2** GOLDSMITH Her gratitude may be more readily imagined than described.

readiness /ˈrɛdɪnɪs/ *noun*. LME.
[formed as prec. + -NESS.]
1 A state of preparation. Chiefly (now only) in ***in readiness***, †***in a readiness***. LME. ▸**b** *PSYCHOLOGY*. The stage of physiological or developmental maturity at which an organism is able to take in (a particular type of) new learning with ease. M20.
2 Prompt compliance, willingness. LME.
3 The quality of being prompt or quick in action, performance, expression, etc.; the quickness or facility with which something occurs or is done. LME.
†**4** A thing ready for use; convenience. *rare*. Only in 16.

> 🕮 **1** M. KEANE Aunt Tossie drained her glass in readiness. **2** C. HARMAN Atomic . . bombs, and a manifest readiness to use them, had given the United States world military dominance. **3** F. SPALDING Molly's fiery temperament and readiness to fly off the handle.

reading /ˈriːdɪŋ/ *noun*¹. OE.
[from READ *verb* + -ING¹.]
1 The action of READ *verb*; the practice of occupying oneself in this way. Also foll. by *up*, *off*. OE.
2 A single act or spell of reading; *spec*. a social or public entertainment at which the audience listens to someone reading aloud a literary work. Also, a portion read (esp. aloud) at one time. OE.
3 a Matter for reading; the specified quality of this. ME. ▸**b** An extract from a previously printed source; in *pl*., a selection of such extracts intended to be read at one time or as a unit. M19.
4 The form in which a given passage appears in a particular edition of a text; the word or words conjectured or given by an editor. M16.
5 The extent to which one reads or has read; literary knowledge. L16.
6 Ability to read; the art of reading. L16.
7 Orig., the formal recital of a bill or part of one before a legislative assembly. Now, each of the successive occasions on which a bill must be presented to a legislature for acceptance. L16.
8 The interpretation or meaning one attaches to something; the view one takes of a situation; the rendering given to a play, a character, a piece of music, etc., as expressing the actor's or performer's point of view. L18.
9 The figure etc. shown by a graduated instrument. M19.

> 🕮 **1** R. L. BOYER I did some reading . . at the British Museum. **2** A. DAVIS One station broadcast readings from George's book. ANNE STEVENSON A reading of his poems at Harvard. **3a** R. G. COLLINGWOOD The favourite reading of habitual criminals. *Bookseller* His investigations make . . compelling reading. ***REQUIRED reading***. **b** *Scientific American* Readings . . 10 or 12 pages in length. **4** E. A. FREEMAN The readings of the manuscripts are . . different. ***various reading***: see VARIOUS *adjective* 9b. **7** ***first reading***, ***second reading***, ***third reading***. **8** G. BOYCOTT My reading of his game. **9** P. V. WHITE Voss . . would take readings from . . instruments.

Comb.: **reading age** reading ability expressed in terms of the age at which an average child would achieve a comparable ability; **reading-book** †(*a*) *ECCLESIASTICAL* a lectionary; (*b*) a book containing passages for instruction in reading; **reading chair** a chair designed to facilitate reading; *spec*. one equipped with a book-rest on one arm; **reading copy** a (secondhand) copy of a book that is usable though in less than perfect condition; **reading-desk** a desk for supporting a book while it is being read; *spec*. a lectern; **reading-glass** (*a*) a large magnifying glass for use in reading; (*b*) in *pl*., a pair of spectacles for use when reading; **reading-machine** (*a*) a device for producing an enlarged, readable image from microform; (*b*) a device for automatically producing electrical signals corresponding to the characters of a text; **reading room** a room devoted to reading, *esp*. one in a club or library.

reading /ˈriːdɪŋ/ *ppl adjective*¹. L16.
[formed as prec. + -ING².]
Given to reading; studious.

> 🕮 J. LONDON It was wholly misunderstood by my reading public. **reading clerk** (the designation of) one of the clerks to the House of Lords.

Reading /ˈrɛdɪŋ/ *adjective*² *& noun*². E19.
[A town in Berkshire, southern England.]
▶ **A** *adjective*. **1** ***Reading beds***, a set of beds of sand, clay, and gravel of fluviatile origin underneath the London clay in the London and Hampshire basins. E19.
2 a ***Reading onion***, a variety of onion. M19 ▸**b** ***Reading sauce***, a sharp sauce flavoured with onions, spices, and herbs. M19.
3 Designating the Gypsy caravan of traditional design. M20.
▶ **B** *noun*. A Reading onion. M20.

readmit /riːədˈmɪt/ *verb trans*. Infl. **-tt-**. E17.
[from RE- + ADMIT.]
Admit again.
■ **readmission** *noun* M17. **readmittance** *noun* M17.

read-out /ˈriːdaʊt/ *noun*. M20.
[from *read out* s.v. READ *verb*.]
1 The extraction or transfer of data from a computer or other storage medium or device; the display of data by an automatic device in an understandable form. M20.
2 A device for extracting or displaying data. M20.
3 A record of output produced by a computer or scientific instrument. M20.

> 🕮 **1** *Wireless World* Direct meter read-out. **2** *Physics Bulletin* An easy to read 2½ digit LED read-out. **3** *Daily Telegraph* Yards of paper read-outs.

readvance /riːədˈvɑːns/ *verb & noun*. E17.
[from RE- + ADVANCE *verb*.]
▶ **A** *verb trans. & intrans*. Advance again. E17.
▶ **B** *noun*. Chiefly *GEOLOGY*. A renewed advance. L19.

readvertise /riːˈadvətʌɪz/ *verb trans*. M17.
[from RE- + ADVERTISE.]
Advertise again; *spec*. give further notice of (a job vacancy).
¶ Rare before M20.
■ **readˈvertisement** *noun* M20.

ready /ˈrɛdi/ *adjective, adverb, & noun*. ME.
[Extended form (with -Y¹) of Old English *rǣde* (usu. *gerǣde*) = Old Frisian *rēde*, Middle Low German *rēde* (Dutch *gereed*), Old High German *reiti*, Old Norse *greiðr* ready, Gothic *garaiþs* arranged, from Germanic base meaning 'prepare, arrange', ult. base also of REDE *verb*². Cf. PREDY.]
▶ **A** *adjective*. **I 1** In a state of preparation, so as to be capable of immediately performing (or becoming the object of) the action implied or expressed in the context; with preparations complete; in a fit state; *spec*. fully dressed (now only a contextual use of the general sense). Usu. *pred*. (Foll. by *for*, *to do*.) ME. ▸**b** With following pa. pple (now usu. hyphenated), denoting the prior completion of the action denoted by the pple. Orig. only *pred*. ME. ▸**c** *pred*. Prepared *for* an event, state, etc. L16.
2 So placed or constituted as to be immediately available when required; close at hand; convenient for use. Long only *attrib*. ME. ▸**b** *attrib*. Of a way, path, etc.: lying directly before one; straight, direct, near. Now *rare* or *obsolete*. ME. ▸**c** *attrib*. Immediately available as currency; having the form of coin or money. ME. ▸†**d** *attrib*. Of payment: made promptly, not deferred. LME–L17.
3 Willing; feeling or exhibiting no reluctance. Usu. *pred*. Foll. by *to do*. ME.
†**4** *pred*. Prepared, willing, or inclined to do, give, suffer, etc., something. Foll. by *to* the thing indicated. ME–L16.
5 Having the quality of being prepared or willing to act when necessary; prompt or quick in action or thought; (of the mind or a mental faculty) quick to understand, plan, etc. ME. ▸**b** *attrib*. Proceeding from or delivered with promptness of thought or expression; characterized by promptness. LME. ▸**c** *attrib*. Characterized by alacrity or willingness in some respect; taking place quickly or easily; easily available. M16.
6 In such a condition as to be immediately likely (*to do*); likely, liable. Usu. *pred*. LME.
7 Sufficiently angry or irritated *to do*, fit *to do*. Usu. *pred*. M16.
8 Having a tendency *to do*. Usu. *pred*. L16.
9 Esp. of music or musicians: excellent, fully competent. *US slang*. M20.
10 = ***streetwise*** (b) s.v. STREET *noun*. *US Black English*. M20.

> 🕮 **1** J. CONRAD Your supper may be ready. S. RAVEN Be ready to leave. *New Yorker* Ready when you are. **b** DICKENS Meat ready-cooked. L. DEIGHTON Ready-cooked pizzas. **c** M. KEANE The engine throbbed . . ready for the journey. **2** J. R. GREEN A . . ready source of revenue. **c** M. J. BRUCCOLI Fitzgerald wrote three stories for ready cash. **3** H. JAMES She was . . ready to postpone their visit. **5** R. GOWER He had a kind heart and a ready pen. Y. MENUHIN His humor was as ready as ever. **b** SIR W. SCOTT Returning a ready answer. **c** *What Mortgage* Ready access to London. **7** DEFOE: I was ready to snatch the breeches out of her hands. **8** B. JOWETT Too ready to speak evil.

▶ **II** As *interjection*.
11 Giving notice of a state of readiness. Formerly also, acknowledging a call or summons. L16.
12 a *MILITARY & NAUTICAL*. As a word of command. E19. ▸**b** Forming part of the formula used to start a race. Chiefly in ***ready, steady, go!*** M20.

> 🕮 **12a** A. RANSOME: 'Ready about,' said Dick.

Phrases: ***be ready to leap out of one's skin***: see LEAP *verb*. **make ready** prepare, put in order; make preparations; (foll. by *for*, *to do*).
Special collocations: **ready meal** a complete dish sold ready-made and requiring only brief heating in a microwave or conventional oven to prepare it for eating. **ready money** (*a*) actual coin or notes; (*b*) payment on the spot in cash. **ready reckoner** a book or table listing the results of standard numerical calculations, esp. those encountered in commerce. **ready room** *US MILITARY* a compartment in an aircraft carrier where pilots are briefed and await orders to fly.
Comb.: **ready-made** *adjective & noun* (*a*) *adjective* made in a finished state; (esp. of clothing) made to a standard size and specification, not to the order of a purchaser; dealing in or pertaining to ready-made articles; (*b*) *noun* a ready-made article, esp. of clothing; **ready-mix** *adjective & noun* = ***ready-mixed*** below; **ready-mixed** *adjective & noun* (*a*) *adjective* (of concrete, paint, food, etc.) having some or all of the constituents already mixed together; (*b*) *noun* ready-mixed concrete; **ready-witted** *adjective* of a ready wit; quick of apprehension.
▶ **B** *adverb*. Readily. Long only in compar. & superl. ME.
▶ **C** *noun*. **1** Ready money, cash (usu. with *the*); in *pl*., banknotes. *slang*. L17.
2 The position of a firearm when the person holding it is ready to raise it to the shoulder and aim or fire; *gen*. a state of readiness for action. Usu. with *the*, esp. in ***at the ready***. M19. ▸**b** The condition of being ready to start something. Freq. in ***get a good ready***, assume a favourable stance or position for this. *US colloq*. (now *rare*). L19.
3 A strand in a rope or cable. M19.

ready /ˈrɛdi/ *verb*. ME.
[from READY *adjective*.]
1 *verb trans*. Make ready, prepare; put in order. Now chiefly *N. Amer*. (freq. foll. by *up*). ME. ▸**b** *spec*. Make (food) ready for eating; cook. *Scot. & dial*. E18.
†**2** *verb trans*. Direct, guide; instruct. ME–E17.
3 *verb trans*. **a** Prevent (a racehorse) from winning, in order to secure a handicap in another race. *slang*. L19. ▸**b** Foll. by *up*: prepare or manipulate in an improper way. *Austral. slang*. L19.

For other words beginning with *re-* see the entry for **re-**

4 *verb intrans.* Make oneself ready. *US.* **M20.**

📖 **4** J. CLAVELL Blackthorne readied to parry the . . blow.

Comb.: **ready-up** *Austral. slang* a conspiracy, a swindle; a case of fraudulent manipulation; a fake.

ready-to- /ˈrɛdɪtʊ/ *combining form.*
[from READY *adjective* + TO *preposition.*]
Forming adjectives (and derived nouns) denoting preparedness for the action indicated by the following verb, as ***ready-to-eat***, ***ready-to-wear***, etc.

reafference /riːˈaf(ə)r(ə)ns/ *noun.* **M20.**
[from RE- + AFFERENT + -ENCE.]
PHYSIOLOGY. Sensory stimulation in which the stimulus changes as a result of the individual's movements in response to it.
■ **reafferent** *adjective* **M20.**

reaffirm /riːəˈfəːm/ *verb trans.* **E17.**
[from RE- + AFFIRM.]
†**1** Confirm again or anew. *rare.* Only in **E17.**
2 Affirm again or anew. **M19.**
■ **reaffirmance** *noun* a reaffirmation **E18.** ˌ**reaffirˈmation** *noun* (a) renewed or repeated affirmation **M19.**

reafforest /riːəˈfɒrɪst/ *verb trans.* **M17.**
[from RE- + AFFOREST.]
†**1** Restore to the legal status of a forest. Only in **M17.**
2 Replant with trees; cover again with forest. **L19.**
■ ˌ**reafforeˈstation** *noun* **L19.**

Reaganism /ˈreɪɡ(ə)nɪz(ə)m/ *noun.* **M20.**
[from *Reagan* (see below) + -ISM.]
The policies and principles advocated by Ronald Reagan, US president (1981–9) noted for his conservative Republicanism; adherence to or support of these.
■ **Reaganaut** *noun* [prob. after ARGONAUT] a Reaganite **L20.** **Reagaˈnesque** *adjective* of or resembling Reagan or his policies **L20.** **Reaganite** *noun & adjective* (*a*) *noun* an advocate or supporter of Reaganism; (*b*) *adjective* of or pertaining to Reaganites or Reaganism: **L20.** **Reagaˈnomic** *adjective* of or pertaining to Reaganomics **L20.** **Reagaˈnomics** *noun* [after ECONOMICS] the economic policies advocated by Reagan **L20.**

reagent /rɪˈeɪdʒ(ə)nt/ *noun.* **L18.**
[from RE- + AGENT, after *act*, *react*.]
CHEMISTRY. Orig., a substance used to test for the presence of another substance by means of the reaction which it produced. Now more widely, any substance used in chemical reactions.

📖 ***Grignard reagent***, ***Millon's reagent***, ***Schiff reagent***, ***Tollens' reagent***, etc. *fig.*: R. W. EMERSON Civilization is a reagent, and eats away the old traits.

Comb.: **reagent grade** a grade of commercial chemicals characterized by a high standard of purity; **reagent paper**: treated with a reagent for use in chemical tests.
■ **reagency** *noun* reactive power or operation **M19.**

reagin /rɪˈeɪdʒɪn/ *noun.* **E20.**
[German, from *reagieren* react + *-in* -INE[5].]
MEDICINE. **1** The complement-fixing substance in the blood of people with syphilis which is responsible for the positive response to the Wassermann reaction. **E20.**
2 The antibody which is involved in allergic reactions, causing the release of histamine when it combines with antigen in tissue, and capable of producing sensitivity to the antigen when introduced into the skin of a normal individual. **E20.**
■ **reaˈginic** *adjective* **M20.**

†**reak** *noun.* **L16–E19.**
[Origin uncertain: perh. rel. to FREAK *noun & adjective.*]
A prank, a capricious trick. Usu. in *pl.*, esp. in ***keep reaks***, ***play reaks***.

real /reɪˈɑːl/ *noun*[1]. **L16.**
[Spanish, use as noun of *real* ROYAL (in full *real de plata* royal coin of silver). Cf. RIAL *noun.*]
A small silver coin and monetary unit formerly used in Spain and Spanish-speaking countries.
real of eight: see EIGHT *noun* 1.

†**real** *adjective*[1]. **ME–E17.**
[Old French (mod. *royal*): see ROYAL. Cf. RIAL *adjective.*]
Royal, regal, kingly.

real /rɪəl/ *adjective*[2], *noun*[2], *& adverb.* **LME.**
[Orig. from Anglo-Norman (= Old French *réel*); later from its source, late Latin *realis*, from Latin *res* thing: see -AL[1]. Cf. RIAL *noun.*]
▶ **A** *adjective.* **I 1** *LAW.* **a** Of an action: for the recovery of a specific thing. **LME.** ▸**b** Consisting of or pertaining to immovable property such as lands and buildings. **LME.**
†**2** Attached or pertaining to scholastic realism. **E16–M17.**
3 Relating to or concerned with things. **L16.** ▸†**b** Of a written character: representing things instead of sounds; ideographic. **E17–E18.**

📖 **1b** A. ROBERTSON Statutes . . to prevent the Church . . from getting hold of real property. K. VONNEGUT Real estate and stocks.

▶ **II 4** That is actually and truly such; that is properly so called; genuine; natural, not artificial or depicted; actually present, not merely apparent. **M16.** ▸**b** Reckoned by purchasing power rather than monetary or nominal value. **L18.** ▸**c** *MUSIC.* Of a sequence or a fugal answer: transposed so as to preserve the intervals of the original melody or subject. Cf. TONAL 1b. **M19.**
5 Actually existing as a state or an object; having a foundation in fact; actually occurring or happening. **L16.** ▸**b** *PHILOSOPHY.* Having an existence in fact and not merely in appearance, thought, or language; having an absolute and necessary, not merely a contingent, existence. **E18.**
6 †**a** Sincere, straightforward, honest; loyal, true. **L16–E18.** ▸**b** Free from nonsense, affectation, or pretence; aware of or in touch with real life. **M19.**
7 Corresponding to actuality; correct, true. **L17.**
8 *MATH.* Of a quantity: having no imaginary part. **E18.**
9 *PHYSICS.* Of an image: such that the light forming it actually reaches it; not virtual. **M19.**

📖 **4** G. B. SHAW It would be a real kindness. E. ROOSEVELT I had no real knowledge. I. MURDOCH Surely you can't mix plastic bullrushes . . with real flowers? **b** *Glasgow Herald* Real earnings have fallen. **5** E. BOWEN Nothing was real that happened outside. W. H. AUDEN Where real toads may catch imaginary flies. E. CALDWELL Wondering if what was taking place was real or whether she was dreaming. A. THWAITE It was not until 1889 that Ibsen gained any real fame.
7 J. LOCKE Ideas of substance are real, when they agree with the existence of things.

Special collocations & phrases: ***chattels real***: see CHATTEL 2. **get real** *colloq.* (usu. in *imper.*) stop being foolishly unrealistic. **real account**: recording assets and liabilities as opp. to receipts and payments. **real ale** draught beer brewed and stored in what is regarded as the traditional way, with secondary fermentation in the container from which it is dispensed. **real line** *MATH.* a notional line in which every real number is conceived of as represented by a point. **real money** (*a*) current coin or notes; cash; (*b*) *colloq.* a large sum of money; (*c*) *colloq.* the coinage or currency in which one habitually reckons. **real presence** *CHRISTIAN CHURCH* the actual presence of Christ's body and blood in the Eucharistic elements. **real school** = REALSCHULE. ***real tennis***: see TENNIS *noun* 1. **real time** the actual time during which a process or event occurs, esp. one analysed by a computer as it happens. ***suit real***: see SUIT *noun* 1b. ***the real McCoy***: see MCCOY. ***the real Simon Pure***: see SIMON PURE *noun.* **the real thing** (*a*) the thing itself, as opp. to an imitation or counterfeit; *slang* = ***genuine article*** s.v. ARTICLE *noun* 10; (*b*) true love, as opp. to infatuation or flirtation. **the real world** the world as it actually exists, rather than any imagined, fictitious, or desired world. ***will the real — please stand up?***: see STAND *verb.*

▶ **B** *noun.* †**1** A philosophical realist. **E16–L17.**
2 A real thing; a thing having (or conceived as having) a real existence. **E17.**
3 ***the real***, that which actually exists, as opp. to a counterfeit or what is abstract or notional. **E19.**
4 *MATH.* A real number. **M19.**
Phrases: **for real** *colloq.* as a serious or actual concern; in earnest.
▶ **C** *adverb.* Really; very. *Scot. & N. Amer. colloq.* **L19.**

📖 G. JACKSON I felt real bad about that. D. LODGE You . . must have lunch . . real soon.

■ **realness** *noun* **M17.**

realgar /rɪˈalɡə/ *noun.* **LME.**
[medieval Latin from Spanish *rejalgar* from Arab. *rahj al-ğār* arsenic, lit. 'powder of the cave', from *rahj* powder + AL-[2] + *ğār* cave.]
A red monoclinic sulphide of arsenic that is an important source of that element, and was formerly used as a pigment and in fireworks. Also called ***red arsenic***, ***red orpiment***.

realia /reɪˈɑːlɪə, rɪˈeɪlɪə/ *noun pl.* **M20.**
[Late Latin, use as noun of neut. pl. of *realis* REAL *adjective*[2]: see -IA[2].]
1 Objects which may be used as teaching aids but were not made for the purpose. *N. Amer.* **M20.**
2 Real things, actual facts, esp. as distinct from theories about them. **M20.**

realisation *noun*, **realise** *verb* vars. of REALIZATION, -IZE.

realism /ˈrɪəlɪz(ə)m/ *noun.* **E19.**
[from REAL *adjective*[2] + -ISM.]
1 *PHILOSOPHY.* **a** The doctrine that universals have an objective or absolute existence. Opp. NOMINALISM. **E19.** ▸**b** The doctrine that matter as the object of perception has real existence and is neither reducible to universal mind or spirit nor dependent on a perceiving agent (opp. IDEALISM 1). Also, the doctrine that the world has a reality that transcends the mind's analytical capacity, and that propositions are to be assessed in terms of their truth to reality rather than their verifiability. **M19.**
2 Inclination or attachment to what is real; a tendency to regard things as they really are and deal with them accordingly. **E19.** ▸**b** The doctrine that the law is better understood by analysis of judges rather than the judgements given. **M20.** ▸**c** The view that the subject-matter of politics is political power, not matters of principle. **M20.**
3 Close resemblance to what is real; fidelity of representation, esp. in art and literature. **M19.**

📖 **3** M. FRAYN A . . novel, whose strength lies in the . . realism of its plot.

Phrases: ***magic realism***: see MAGIC *adjective.* *NAIVE* ***realism***. ***new realism***: see NEW *adjective.* *SELECTIVE* ***realism***. ***social realism***: see SOCIAL *adjective.* ***socialist realism***: see SOCIALIST *adjective.*

realist /ˈrɪəlɪst/ *noun & adjective.* **E17.**
[from REAL *adjective*[2] + -IST, after French *réaliste*.]
▶ **A** *noun.* †**1** A person whose occupation is with things rather than words. *rare.* Only in **E17.**
2 An adherent of realism, in philosophy, law, or politics; an artist or writer who practises realism. **L17.**
3 A person who tends to regard things as they really are. **M19.**
▶ **B** *adjective.* Pertaining to or characteristic of a realist or realists; advocating realism. **M19.**
Phrases: ***magic realist***: see MAGIC *adjective.* *NAIVE* ***realist***. ***new realist***: see NEW *adjective.*

realistic /rɪəˈlɪstɪk/ *adjective.* **E19.**
[from prec. + -IC.]
1 Characterized by fidelity of representation; representing things as they really are. **E19.**
2 Tending to regard things as they really are; characterized by a practical view of life. **M19.**
3 Of or pertaining to realists in philosophy; of the nature of philosophical realism. **M19.**

📖 **1** *Woman* To look realistic, wigs need to be of the highest quality. **2** J. BRAINE I had to be realistic about the situation. G. DALY His expectation that she would wait . . for him . . was hardly realistic.

■ **realistically** *adverb* **M19.**

reality /rɪˈalɪti/ *noun.* **L15.**
[(Old & mod. French *réalité* from) medieval Latin *realitas*, from late Latin *realis* REAL *adjective*[2]: see -ITY.]
1 What exists or is real; that which underlies and is the truth of appearances or phenomena. **L15.**
2 The quality of being real or having an actual existence. **M16.**
†**3** *LAW.* Realty. **E17–E18.**
†**4** Loyalty *to* a person; sincerity or honesty of character or purpose. **M17–M18.**
5 A real thing, fact, or state of affairs; the real nature *of* something. **M17.** ▸**b** That which constitutes the actual thing, as opp. to what is merely apparent or external. **M19.**
6 Resemblance to what is real or to an original. **M19.**

📖 **1** A. GRAY His energy had withdrawn into imaginary worlds and he had none to waste on reality. **in reality** in fact, really. **2** A. BROOKNER Her brothers have no reality for her. **5** A. N. WHITEHEAD The reality of the material object. I. MCEWAN The realities of the situation. **b** J. K. JEROME No caricature, but the living reality. **6** *Harper's Magazine* Her . . accessories were reproduced on the canvas with . . startling reality.

Comb.: **reality check** (orig. *US*) a reminder of the state of things in the real world, esp. to dispel mistaken perceptions or unrealistic expectations; **reality principle** *PSYCHOANALYSIS*: that the actual conditions of living modify the pleasure-seeking activity of the libido; **reality-testing** *PSYCHOANALYSIS* the objective evaluation of an emotion or thought against real life, as a faculty present in normal individuals but defective in some psychotics; **reality TV** television programmes about real people and situations, made to be entertaining rather than informative.

realization /rɪəlʌɪˈzeɪʃ(ə)n/ *noun.* Also **-isation**. **E17.**
[from next + -ATION, after French *réalisation*.]
1 The action or an act of realizing. **E17.**
2 A thing produced by or resulting from realizing; *spec.* (*a*) a realized piece of music; (*b*) *MATH.* an instance or embodiment of an abstract group as the set of symmetry operations etc. of some object or set; (*c*) *STATISTICS* a particular series which might be generated by a specified random process. **E19.**

📖 **1** M. FORSTER Troubled by the realisation of his position.

■ **realizational** *adjective* **M20.**

realize /ˈrɪəlʌɪz/ *verb.* Also **-ise**. **E17.**
[from REAL *adjective*[2] + -IZE, after French *réaliser*.]
1 *verb trans.* Make real or realistic; convert into actuality. **E17.** ▸**b** *LINGUISTICS.* Manifest (a linguistic feature) in a particular phonetic, graphic, or syntactic form. **M20.**
2 *verb trans.* Present as real; bring vividly before the mind. (Foll. by *to* oneself, the mind, a person.) **M17.**
3 a *verb trans.* Convert into cash or money. **M18.** ▸**b** *verb intrans.* Realize one's property; sell out. **L18.**
4 a *verb trans.* Acquire (money, a fortune, etc.) by one's own exertions; make (a profit). **M18.** ▸**b** Of property or capital: yield (a specified return); fetch as a price. **M19.**
5 *verb trans.* Conceive as real; apprehend with the clearness or detail of reality; (foll. by subord. clause) understand clearly, be fully aware, (*that*, *how*, etc.). **L18.**
6 *MUSIC.* Add to or complete (music left sparsely notated by the composer); enrich the texture of (a work), esp. by orchestrating music written for a single voice or instrument; *spec.* reconstruct (a part) in full from a figured bass. **E20.**

📖 **1** J. REED Practical measures to realize peace. L. P. HARTLEY She seems to have realized herself, become a person in her own right. H. MOORE A conception . . in a drawing will be . . wrong realised as stone. A. N. WILSON A . . figure who had never realised his . . potential. **realized eschatology** CHRISTIAN THEOLOGY the view that the kingdom of God preached by Jesus is already present, having been inaugurated by his person and activity. **2** T. ARNOLD That I may realize to my mind the things eternal. H. ADAMS Shakespeare realized the thirteenth-century woman . . vividly. **3a** H. NISBET Realizing what he could of his impoverished estates. **4a** E. BOWEN She realized money . . by selling . . lands. *Times* Chinese porcelain and hardstones realized £9,585 at Christie's. **b** S. UNWIN It is astonishing how little stock realises. **5** D. H. LAWRENCE She realized she must do something. W. CATHER Times have changed, but he doesn't realize it. P. BARKER She did not realise where he was taking her.

■ **realiza'bility** *noun* the property of being realizable **E20**. **realizable** *adjective* able to be realized **M19**. **realizableness** *noun* (*rare*) realizability **L19**. **realizably** *adverb* **L19**. **realizer** *noun* a person who or thing which realizes **E19**. **realizingly** *adverb* in a realizing manner **M19**.

really /'rɪəli/ *adverb*. **LME**.
[from REAL *adjective*² + -LY². Cf. REELY.]
▶ **I 1** In a real manner; in reality; actually. **LME**.
2 Used to emphasize the truth or correctness of an epithet or statement: positively, decidedly, assuredly. **E17**.

📖 **1** LD MACAULAY The government was really directed . . in London. E. NESBIT I shall not say what his name is really. J. MITCHELL Silly, really, to spend your . . holiday . . digging up a Roman villa. Q. CRISP Are they really your friends? **2** J. CONRAD No, . . I can't really. O. MANNING I really did hope you'd been thinking to better purpose. M. ROBERTS I'm really proud of you.

▶ **II** As *interjection*.
3 Expr. mild protest, dismay, or surprise. **E17**.
4 *interrog*. Expr. surprise, scepticism, or disbelief: is that so? **E19**.

📖 **3** M. LAVIN Really, there's no understanding you. M. BRAITHWAITE Being hauled . . by horses was bad enough. But oxen, really! **4** D. L. SAYERS Really? No kidding? G. GREENE Really? What kind of business?

Phrases: **really truly** *adjective* (*N. Amer. colloq.*) authentic, genuine.

†**re-ally** *verb*. **LME**.
[French †*real(l)ier* var. of *ral(l)ier* RALLY *verb*¹.]
1 *verb trans*. **a** = RALLY *verb*¹ 1. Also foll. by *up*. **LME–M17**. ▶**b** Unite (again) *to* or *with*. **E–M17**.
2 *verb intrans*. = RALLY *verb*¹ 5. **LME–M17**.
3 *verb trans*. Form (plans) again. *rare* (Spenser). Only in **L16**.

realm /rɛlm/ *noun*. Also (earlier) †**reaume**. **ME**.
[Old French *reaume*, *realme* (mod. *royaume*) from Latin *regimin-*, REGIMEN; the *l* arose through the infl. of Old French *real*, *reiel* vars. of *roial* ROYAL.]
1 A kingdom (now chiefly LAW). Also, any region or territory, esp. of a specified ruling power; the sphere, domain, or province of some quality, state, or other abstract conception. **ME**.
2 *spec*. A primary zoogeographical division of the earth's surface. **L19**.

📖 **1** R. BAKER That the Realm of England should be destroyed through the misgovernance of King Richard. DAY LEWIS A . . coin of the realm. P. AUSTER My motives are lofty, but my work now takes place in the realm of the everyday. M. BERGMANN Freud ventures outside the clinical realm to make observations on humanity as a whole. ***abjuration of the realm***: see ABJURATION 1. ***abjure the realm***: see ABJURE 3. ***Estates of the Realm***: see ESTATE *noun*. ***peer of the realm***: see PEER *noun*¹ 4.

■ **realmless** *adjective* **E19**.

Realo /'riːələʊ, *foreign* re'aːlo/ *noun*. *colloq*. Pl. **-os**. **L20**.
[German, from *Realist* REALIST + -O. Cf. next.]
A member of the pragmatic as opp. to the radical wing of the Green movement. Cf. FUNDI *noun*².

realpolitik /reˌaːlpoli'tiːk, reɪ'ɑːlpɒlɪtiːk/ *noun*. **E20**.
[German: cf. prec.]
Politics based on practical, rather than moral or ideological, considerations; practical politics.
■ **reˌalpo'litiker** *noun* a person who believes in, advocates, or practises *realpolitik* **M20**.

Realschule /re'aːlʃuːlə/ *noun*. Pl. **-len** /-lən/. **M19**.
[German.]
In Germany and Austria, a secondary school in which sciences and modern languages are taught.

realtor /'rɪəltə/ *noun*. *N. Amer*. **E20**.
[from REALTY + -OR.]
An estate agent; in the US *spec*. (**R-**) one who belongs to the National Association of Realtors.

realty /'rɪəlti/ *noun*. **LME**.
[from REAL *adjective*² + -TY¹.]
†**1** Reality. **LME–M17**.
†**2** Sincerity, honesty. *rare*. **E–M17**.
†**3** A real possession; a right. *rare*. **E–M17**.
4 LAW. Real estate; immovable property. **L17**.

ream /riːm/ *noun*¹.
[Old English *rēam* = Middle Low German *rōm(e*, Middle & mod. Dutch *room*, Middle High German (*milch*)*roum* (German *Rahm*, dial. *Raum*, *Rohm*), from West Germanic.]
1 The cream of milk. *obsolete* exc. *dial*. **OE**.
2 A scum, a froth. *obsolete* exc. *dial*. **LME**.
3 A nonhomogenous layer in flat glass. **M20**.

ream /riːm/ *noun*². **LME**.
[Old French *raime* etc. (mod. *rame*) ult. from Arab. *rizma* bundle.]
1 Twenty quires of paper, i.e. 500 sheets (formerly 480). Formerly also (in full ***printer's ream***), 21½ quires, i.e. 516 sheets, of printing paper. **LME**.
2 A large quantity of paper. Usu. in *pl*. **L16**.
3 In *pl*. *transf*. Large quantities (*of*). **E20**.

📖 **2** J. F. HENDRY Rilke sent her reams about his sufferings.

ream /riːm/ *adjective*. *slang*. **M19**.
[Origin unkn.]
Genuine.

ream /riːm/ *verb*¹. Long *obsolete* exc. *dial*. **ME**.
[Origin unkn.]
1 *verb intrans*. Stretch oneself after sleep or on rising. Formerly also, yawn. **ME**. ▶**b** Reach for something. **ME**.
2 *verb trans*. Draw out, stretch, distend. **LME**. ▶**b** Pull apart or to pieces; tear open. **L16**.

ream /riːm/ *verb*². Chiefly *Scot*. **LME**.
[from REAM *noun*¹.]
1 *verb intrans*. Froth, foam; be full of a frothy liquid. Of milk: form a cream. **LME**.
2 *verb trans*. Take the cream off; skim. **M18**.
■ **reamy** *adjective* creamy, frothy; made with cream: **M19**.

ream /riːm/ *verb*³ *trans*. In sense 1 also **reem**. **M18**.
[Origin unkn.]
1 NAUTICAL. Open (a seam) for caulking. **M18**.
2 Enlarge or widen (a hole, esp. in metal) with an instrument. Also foll. by *out*. **M18**.
3 Enlarge the bore of (a gun); widen, carve out, or clear of obstruction (a way, passage, etc.). Usu. foll. by *out*. **M19**. ▶**b** Extract juice from (a fruit) with a reamer; extract (juice) similarly. **M20**.
4 Cheat, swindle. *US slang*. **E20**.
5 Have anal intercourse with. *US coarse slang*. **M20**.
6 Reprimand. Usu. foll. by *out*. *US colloq*. **M20**.

📖 **3** F. SMYTH Cutting tools which reamed out the grooves in gun barrels.

■ **reamer** *noun* & *verb* (**a**) *noun* a tool for enlarging or finishing drilled holes; a kitchen implement with a central ridged dome on which a half fruit can be pressed down and turned to extract its juice; (**b**) *verb trans*. use a reamer on: **E19**. **reaming** *noun* (**a**) the action of the verb; (**b**) *US colloq*. a reprimand: **M18**.

rean /riːn/ *noun*. *obsolete* exc. *dial*. **L15**.
[Origin uncertain: perh. alt. of RAIN *noun*².]
1 = RAIN *noun*² 2. **L15**.
2 = RAIN *noun*² 1. **L18**.

reanimate /riː'anɪmeɪt/ *verb*. **E17**.
[from RE- + ANIMATE *verb*.]
▶ **I** *verb trans*. **1** Make alive again, restore to life or consciousness. **E17**.
2 Give fresh heart or courage to (a person); impart fresh vigour, energy, or activity to (a thing). **E18**.
▶ **II** *verb intrans*. **3** Recover life or spirit. **M17**.
■ **reani'mation** *noun* the action, fact, or process of reanimating **L18**.

reanswer /riː'ɑːnsə/ *verb*. **E16**.
[from RE- + ANSWER *verb*, in branch I prob. after *reply* etc.]
▶ **I** †**1** *verb trans*. & *intrans*. Reply (to), respond (to). Only in **16**.
†**2** *verb trans*. Be sufficient for or equivalent to. **L16–M17**.
▶ **II 3** *verb trans*. Answer again or a second time. *rare*. **E17**.

reap /riːp/ *noun*¹.
[Old English *reopa*, *rypa* rel. to *ripan* REAP *verb*¹.]
A bundle or handful of grain or any similar crop; a sheaf; a quantity sufficient to make a sheaf.

reap /riːp/ *noun*².
[Old English *rip*, *rip* rel. to *ripan* REAP *verb*¹. In branch II from REAP *verb*¹.]
▶ **I** †**1** Harvest, reaping. **OE–L17**.
2 A set of reapers. **E19**.
▶ **II 3** JUDO. An act of sweeping a leg into the opponent's leg, causing a loss of balance. **M20**.
Comb.: **reap-silver** *Hist*. the sum paid by a tenant to a superior, in commutation of his services at harvest-time.

reap /riːp/ *verb*¹. Also †**rip**.
[Old English *ripan*, *reopan*, of unkn. origin.]
1 *verb intrans*. & *trans*. Cut, gather, (a crop, esp. grain), orig. with a hook or sickle; *transf*. cut (plants, flowers, etc.) in a similar fashion. Freq. *fig*. **OE**. ▶**b** *verb trans*. Harvest the crop of (a field etc.). **LME**.
2 Get in return; obtain (esp. a benefit or advantage) for oneself; gain, acquire. **ME**.
3 *verb trans*. JUDO. Sweep a leg into (the opponent's leg), causing a loss of balance. **M20**.

📖 **1** M. W. MONTAGU We can reap the fruit of our labours. *Times* He will reap what he sows. **2** *Globe & Mail (Toronto)* The Manitoba Government has reaped . . $8-million from the Downs. M. SEYMOUR Conrad was reaping . . the benefits of his labours.

Comb.: **reap-hook** a reaping-hook.
■ **reapable** *adjective* (*rare*) able to be reaped; fit for reaping: **L16**.

reap /riːp/ *verb*² *trans*. **L16**.
[Alt. of RIP *verb*¹ after *rip* var. of prec.]
Foll. by *up*: rake up, bring up again, (a matter).

reaper /'riːpə/ *noun*. **OE**.
[from REAP *verb*¹ + -ER¹.]
1 A person who reaps. **OE**.
2 A machine for cutting grain (and now also, binding the sheaves). **M19**.
1 the Reaper, **the Great Reaper**, **the Grim Reaper**, **the Old Reaper** [from the portrayal of Death wielding a scythe] death personified.
Comb.: **reaper-and-binder**, **reaper-binder** = SELF-BINDER.

reaping /'riːpɪŋ/ *noun*. **LME**.
[from REAP *verb*¹ + -ING¹.]
The action of REAP *verb*¹; an amount reaped.
Comb.: **reaping-machine** = REAPER 2.

reappear /riːə'pɪə/ *verb intrans*. **E17**.
[from RE- + APPEAR.]
Appear again.
■ **reappearance** *noun* the action or an act of appearing again; a second or fresh appearance: **M17**.

reappraise /riːə'preɪz/ *verb trans*. **L19**.
[from RE- + APPRAISE.]
Make a fresh appraisal of, esp. in the light of new facts; reassess.
■ **reappraisal** *noun* **E20**. **reappraisement** *noun* **L19**.

rear /rɪə/ *adjective*¹, *noun*, & *adverb*. Also (*obsolete* exc. in comb.) **rere**. **ME**.
[Old French *rere*, *rier* from Latin *retro* back: see RETRO-.]
▶ **A** *adjective*. **1** Situated or placed at the back; last in position. **ME**.
†**2** Last in time; subsequent. **LME–L15**.

📖 **1** A. HALL The car . . was gathering speed . . when I . . got the rear door open. L. GRANT-ADAMSON Unless there were a rear access she could see no way in.

▶ **B** *noun*. **1** The back or hindmost part of something; *spec*. (MILITARY), the division of a force which is placed, or moves, last in order. Also, the space behind or at the back; the position at or towards the back. **ME**.
2 The buttocks. *colloq*. **L18**.
3 *sing*. & in *pl*. (treated as *sing*.). A (public or communal) lavatory. Orig. *School & Univ. slang*. **E20**.

📖 **1** T. LEDIARD The cavalry . . overtook the enemy's rear. *Boy's Magazine* An enclosed luggage boot at the rear. P. D. JAMES A door at the rear of the hall. *fig*.: SHELLEY The rear of the departing day.

▶ **C** *adverb*. At the rear; towards or from the rear. Long only in ***front and rear*** and in combs. **LME**.
rear-facing, ***rear-illuminated***, etc.
Phrases: ***action rear!***: see ACTION *noun*. **bring up the rear** come last. **hang on someone's rear** follow closely, in order to attack when opportunity offers. **in someone's rear** at someone's back, behind someone. **in the rear** in the hindmost part; at or from the back, behind; ***take in the rear*** (MILITARY), attack from behind.
Special collocations & comb.: **rear admiral** (**a**) a naval officer ranking next below a vice admiral; †(**b**) a ship carrying a rear admiral's flag. **rear echelon** US MILITARY the section of an army concerned with administrative and supply duties. **rear end** (**a**) the back part or section of something, esp. a vehicle; (**b**) *slang* the buttocks. **rear-end** *verb trans*. (*N. Amer*.) collide with the rear end of (a vehicle) or the vehicle of (a driver). **rear gunner** a member of the crew of a military aircraft who operates a gun from a compartment at the rear. **rear-lamp**, **rear-light** a (usu. red) lamp at the rear of a vehicle to serve as a warning light in the dark. **rear projection** = ***BACK-projection***. **rearsight** (**a**) a part of a camera viewfinder, situated at the back, to which the eye is applied; (**b**) the backsight of a rifle. **rear-view** *adjective* designating a mirror inside a motor vehicle in front of the driver, enabling him or her to see the traffic etc. behind.

rear /rɪə/ *adjective*². *obsolete* exc. *dial*. **OE**.
[Origin unkn. Cf. RARE *adjective*³.]
Esp. of an egg: slightly or imperfectly cooked, underdone.

rear /rɪə/ *verb*¹.
[Old English *rǣran* = Old Norse *reisa*, Gothic *-raisjan* awaken, from Germanic causative of the base of RAISE *verb*.]
▶ **I** Set upright; make to stand up.
1 *verb trans*. Bring into or towards a vertical position, set upright, (now usu. implying a considerable height in the thing when raised). **OE**. ▶**b** *spec*. = RAISE *verb* 1b. Long *obsolete* exc. *dial*. **LME**.
2 *verb trans*. = RAISE *verb* 4. *obsolete* exc. *dial*. **OE**.
†**3** *verb trans*. **a** = RAISE *verb* 3. **ME–L16**. ▶**b** Bring (a person) *to*, *out of*, or *from* a certain condition. **LME–E17**.
4 *verb trans*. = RAISE *verb* 5. *obsolete* exc. *dial*. **ME**.
†**5** *verb trans*. = RAISE *verb* 6. **E16–M17**.

6 *verb trans.* **a** Lift (a person or animal) to an erect or standing posture; *esp.* assist to rise. Now *dial.* L16. ▸**b** Raise (the body, a limb). L16.

📖 **1** A. UTTLEY Long ladders reared against . . trees.

▶ **II** Build up, construct, create, produce.
7 *verb trans.* = RAISE *verb* 7. OE.
†**8** *verb trans.* Bring into existence or action; cause to appear, produce. OE–L18.
9 *verb trans.* **a** Bring (animals) to maturity or to a certain stage of growth, as by the provision of food and care; breed and bring to maturity (cattle etc.) as an occupation. Also, raise (plants). LME. ▸**b** Care for or be responsible for (a child) to the point of maturity; in *pass.*, be brought up in a particular manner or place. L16.

📖 **9a** *Times* Butterflies reared on non-poisonous plants. **rearing-house** a building in which young chickens are kept. **b** K. WEATHERLY Old Sam, born and reared in the bush, a good mate.

▶ **III** Cause to move to a higher position.
10 *verb trans.* Lift up or upwards, elevate; have or hold in an elevated position; *refl.* rise to a great height, tower. OE.
†**11** *verb trans.* **a** Levy, raise, (fines, rents, etc.); raise (an army). LME–L16. ▸**b** Take away *from* someone. *rare* (Spenser). Only in L16.
12 *verb trans.* Turn or direct (esp. the eyes) upwards. Also foll. by *up*. LME.
13 *verb trans.* NAUTICAL. = RAISE *verb* 19. M16.
14 *verb trans.* = RAISE *verb* 17. E19.

📖 **10** J. AGEE Hobe reared up a rock. A. BURGESS A snake reared its head from the grass. R. MACAULAY Armenian churches . . would rear themselves up on rocky heights. **rear its head**, **rear its ugly head** = *raise its head*, *raise its ugly head* s.v. RAISE *verb*.

▶ **IV 15** *verb intrans.* **a** Rise up (towards a vertical position or into the air); rise high, tower. Also foll. by *up*. LME. ▸**b** Of a quadruped, esp. a horse: rise on the hind legs. LME.

📖 **15a** *Daily Telegraph* Moon-mountains rearing to 14,000 feet. **b** J. STEINBECK Joseph lifted the heavy saddle, and as the tapadero struck the horse's side, it reared.

■ **rearer** *noun* (*a*) a person who rears something; (*b*) a horse that rears: LME.

rear /rɪə/ *verb*[2] *trans. arch.* LME.
[Origin unkn.]
Carve (a fowl, esp. a goose).

rear-arch /ˈrɪərɑːtʃ/ *noun*. Also **rere-**. M19.
[from REAR *adjective*[1] + ARCH *noun*[1].]
ARCHITECTURE. The inner arch of a window- or door-opening, when differing in size or form from the external arch. Also called *scoinson arch*, *scoinson*.

rearguard /ˈrɪəɡɑːd/ *noun*. LME.
[Old French *rereguarde*, formed as REAR *adjective*[1] + GUARD *noun*. Cf. ARRIÈRE-GUARD.]
MILITARY. †**1** The rear of an army or fleet. LME–M17.
2 A body of troops detached from the main force to bring up and protect the rear, esp. in a retreat; *transf.* & *fig.* a defensive or conservative element in an organization, community, etc. M17.
Comb.: **rearguard action** a defensive stand by the rearguard of a retreating army; *fig.* a defensive stand in an argument etc., esp. when losing.

rear-horse /ˈrɪəhɔːs/ *noun*. M19.
[from REAR *verb*[1] + HORSE *noun*.]
A praying mantis.

rearing /ˈrɪərɪŋ/ *adjective*. L16.
[from REAR *verb*[1] + -ING[2].]
1 That rears. L17.
2 = RARING. E20.

†**rearly** *adverb*. *rare*. E17–E18.
[from alt. of RARE *adjective*[2] + -LY[2].]
Early.

rearm /riːˈɑːm/ *verb trans.* & *intrans.* E19.
[from RE- + ARM *verb*[1].]
Arm again, esp. with more modern weapons.
■ **rearmament** *noun* (*Moral Re-Armament*: see MORAL *adjective*) L19.

rearmost /ˈrɪəməʊst/ *adjective*. E18.
[from REAR *adjective*[1] + -MOST.]
Furthest in the rear, coming last of all.

rearmouse /ˈrɪəmaʊs/ *noun*. Now *arch.* & *dial.* Also **rere-**. Pl. **-mice** /-mʌɪs/.
[Old English *hrēremūs*, from unkn. 1st elem. + *mūs* MOUSE *noun*. Cf. FLICKERMOUSE, FLINDERMOUSE, FLITTER-MOUSE.]
= BAT *noun*[3].

rearrange /riːəˈreɪn(d)ʒ/ *verb*. E19.
[from RE- + ARRANGE.]
1 *verb trans.* Arrange again or differently; arrange in a new way. E19.
2 *verb intrans.* Become arranged in a new way; *esp.* (CHEMISTRY) (of a molecule or molecules) undergo a reaction which results chiefly or solely in a different arrangement of the component atoms. L20.

📖 **1** *Times* Rearranging my books . . after a house-move. *Acorn User* Windows can be created which can then be rearranged to provide any print format required.

■ **rearrangement** *noun* the action or an act of rearranging; the process of becoming differently arranged; a fresh arrangement; CHEMISTRY a reaction which results in a different arrangement of the component atoms in a molecule or molecules: M19.

rear-vassal /ˈrɪəvas(ə)l/ *noun*. M18.
[from REAR *adjective*[1] + VASSAL *noun*, after French *arrière-vassal*.]
Hist. A vassal who did not hold directly of the monarch.

rearward /ˈrɪəwɔːd/ *noun*. ME.
[Anglo-Norman *rerewarde* var. of *reregarde* REARGUARD.]
1 The rear part of an army or fleet. *arch.* ME.
2 The buttocks. Long *rare*. LME.
3 *gen.* The rear. Only in *in the rearward*, *at the rearward*, *in the rearward of*, *on the rearward of*, *to the rearward of*. L15.

rearward /ˈrɪəwəd/ *adjective* & *adverb*. L16.
[from REAR *adjective*[1] + -WARD.]
▶ **A** *adjective*. **1** Situated in the rear. L16.
2 Directed towards the rear; backward. M19.

📖 **2** W. BOYD Without a rearward glance he . . started to sprint away.

▶ **B** *adverb*. Towards the rear; backward. E17.

📖 *Daily Telegraph* Rearward-facing seats.

■ **rearwardly** *adverb* = REARWARD *adverb* M19. **rearwards** *adverb* = REARWARD *adverb* L19.

reason /ˈriːz(ə)n/ *noun*[1]. ME.
[Old French *reisun*, *res(o)un* (mod. *raison*) from Proto-Romance var. of Latin *ratio(n-)* reckoning, account, etc., from *rat-* pa. ppl stem of *reri* think, reckon: see -ION.]
1 The mental faculty (usually regarded as characteristic of humankind, but sometimes also attributed in a certain degree to animals) which is used in adapting thought or action to some end; the guiding principle of the human mind in the process of thinking; PHILOSOPHY a faculty transcending understanding by which first principles are grasped a priori. ME. ▸**b** The ordinary thinking faculty of the mind in a sound condition; sanity. ME. ▸†**c** The exercise of reason; reasoning. ME–M17.
2 A fact or circumstance forming a motive sufficient to lead a person to adopt or reject some course of action, belief, etc.; a fact etc. adduced or serving as this. (Foll. by *why, that; of, for; to do*.) ME. ▸**b** A cause of a fact, situation, event, or thing, *esp.* one adduced as an explanation; cause, ground. LME.
3 a A matter, act, proceeding, etc., agreeable to reason. Now *rare*. ME. ▸**b** The fact or quality of being agreeable to the reason; a view of things that the reason can approve of. LME.
4 A statement used as an argument to justify or condemn some act, or to prove or disprove some assertion or belief. Now *rare* exc. as *ellipt.* for sense 2. ME.
†**5** A statement, a narrative, a speech; a saying, an observation; talk, discourse; an account or explanation *of*, or answer *to*, something. (*rare* after M17.) ME–E19.
†**6** Monetary reckoning; income, revenue; in *pl.*, monies. Also, payment for services given. LME–M16.
†**7 a** A sentence. LME–M16. ▸**b** A motto. LME–M16.
†**8** That treatment which may with reason be expected by or required from a person; justice, satisfaction. Chiefly in *do a person reason*. LME–E19.
†**9** A reasonable quantity or degree; *spec.* the measure by which a miller took his toll. LME–L17.
†**10 a** Consideration, regard, respect. LME–M16. ▸**b** Way, manner, method. LME–M17. ▸**c** Possibility of action or occurrence. Foll. by *but*. *rare*. Only in L16.
†**11** MATH. A ratio. LME–E18.
†**12** Rationale, fundamental principle, basis. L16–L17.
13 LOGIC. A premiss of a syllogism; *esp.* the minor premiss when placed after the conclusion. E19.

📖 **1b** G. GREENE Ordinary life . . has saved many a man's reason. **2** *New Scientist* There is no reason to doubt its likelihood. M. AMIS Excellent reasons for agreeing to the transfer. **b** A. J. CRONIN There must be a reason, . . symptoms don't just happen of themselves. E. BLISHEN Another reason for Rowland's popularity. A. F. LOEWENSTEIN People are getting scared . . . And with good reason. **3a** B. H. MALKIN It is but reason that you . . distrust our purity. **b** G. BERKELEY There is reason in what you say.

Phrases: †**and reason**: placed after a statement to emphasize its reasonableness. **a woman's reason** *arch. derog.* a fact given as a reason for the same fact. **bring to reason** cause to adopt a reasonable view of a matter, or to cease vain resistance. **by reason** (*a*) (also *by reason that*) (now *rare*) for the reason that, because; (*b*) *by reason of*, †*for reason of*, on account of. **for reasons best known to oneself** for seemingly perverse reasons. †**have reason** be correct. **in reason** = *within reason* below. **it stands to reason** it is plainly evident or logical (*that*). *know the reason why*: see KNOW *verb*. **listen to reason** be persuaded to act sensibly. **reason of State** a purely political ground of action on the part of a ruler or government, esp. as involving some departure from strict justice, honesty, or open dealing; also without article, as a principle of political action. †**reason will**, †**reason would** it is or would be reasonable (that). **see reason** acknowledge a reason *to do*, *for doing*; acknowledge the force of an argument. **the age of reason** (*a*) the late 17th and 18th cents. in western Europe, during which cultural life was characterized by faith in human reason; the enlightenment; (*b*) esp. in the Roman Catholic Church, the age at which a child is held capable of discerning right from wrong. **with reason** with justification. **within reason** within the bounds of sense or moderation. **without reason** without justification. *without rhyme or reason*: see RHYME *noun*.

■ **reasonless** *adjective* (*a*) not endowed with reason; (*b*) devoid of ordinary reason; senseless; (*c*) not grounded on or supported by reason; acting or produced without the aid of reason: LME. **reasonlessly** *adverb* without reason L19. **reasonlessness** *noun* the state or quality of being without reason L19.

reason /ˈriːz(ə)n/ *noun*[2]. M16.
[Alt. of RASEN.]
A wall-plate.

reason /ˈriːz(ə)n/ *verb*. LME.
[Old French *raisoner* (mod. *-onner*), formed as REASON *noun*[1].]
†**1** *verb trans.* Question (a person), call to account; speak with. LME–L16.
2 *verb trans.* **a** Discuss, argue, (a matter). Now *rare*. LME. ▸**b** Discuss, ask oneself, *what*, *why*, etc. E16. ▸**c** Argue, conclude, *that* etc. E16.
†**3** *verb intrans.* Argue, talk. L15–L17.
4 a *verb intrans.* Think in a connected or logical manner; use one's reason in forming conclusions. (Foll. by *from*, *about*.) L16. ▸**b** *verb trans.* Arrange the thought of in a logical manner, embody reason in; express in a logical form. Also, think *out*, work *out*. Chiefly as *reasoned ppl adjective*. L17.
5 *verb trans.* Bring (a person) *into* or *out of* a state of mind etc. by reasoning. L16.
6 *verb trans.* Explain or deal with by reasoning. *rare*. E17.
7 *verb trans.* **a** Put *down* by reasoning. L17. ▸**b** Drive *away* or *off* by reasoning. M19.
8 *verb intrans.* Use reasoning or argument *with* a person in order to influence his or her conduct or opinions. M19.

📖 **2b** A. P. HERBERT She reasoned carefully with herself whether . . to go away . . or to fall flop under Ernest's nose. **c** C. CHAPLIN A small moustache . . I reasoned, would add age. **4a** H. KELLER He kept my mind alert . . and trained it to reason clearly. **b** L. STEPHEN He prefers . . instinct to reasoned action. **reasoned amendment** an amendment to a parliamentary bill that seeks to prevent a further reading by proposing reasons for its alteration or rejection. **6** SHAKES. *Coriol.* This boy . . Does reason our petition with more strength Than thou hast to deny't. **8** O. MANNING He had tried to reason with her.

■ **reasoner** *noun* †(*a*) *rare* a keeper of accounts; (*b*) a person who reasons: E16. **reasoning** *noun* the action of the verb; an instance of this; the arguments or reasons involved in arriving at a conclusion or judgement: LME. †**reasonist** *noun* (*rare*) a professed reasoner E17–M18.

reasonable /ˈriːz(ə)nəb(ə)l/ *adjective*, *adverb*, & *noun*. ME.
[Old French *raisonable* (mod. -nn-), formed as REASON *noun*[1], after Latin *rationabilis*: see -ABLE.]
▶ **A** *adjective*. **1** Endowed with the faculty of reason, rational. Now *rare*. ME.
2 In accordance with reason; not irrational or absurd. ME.
†**3** Proportionate. *rare*. ME–M18.
4 Having sound judgement; ready to listen to reason, sensible. Also, not asking for too much. LME.
5 Within the limits of reason; not greatly less or more than might be thought likely or appropriate; moderate, *spec.* in price. LME. ▸†**b** Of a fair, average, or considerable amount, size, etc. L16–E18.
†**6** Articulate. Only in LME.
†**7** Requiring the use of reason. *rare* (Shakes.). Only in E17.

📖 **4** J. GALSWORTHY Be reasonable Fleur! It's midsummer madness! **5** J. CONRAD The reasonable thought that the ship was like other ships, the men like other men. G. GREENE A reasonable rate of interest. *Which?* It seems reasonable to . . check the price before you order.

▶ **B** *adverb*. Reasonably. Now *non-standard*. LME.
▶†**C** *noun*. A reasonable being. LME–E19.
■ **reasonaˈbility** *noun* (*rare*) reasonableness L19. **reasonableness** *noun* LME. **reasonably** *adverb* (*a*) with good reason, justly; (*b*) sufficiently, suitably; †(*c*) at a reasonable rate; to a reasonable extent: LME.

reassemble /riːəˈsɛmb(ə)l/ *verb*. L15.
[from RE- + ASSEMBLE.]
1 *verb trans.* Bring together again. L15.
2 *verb intrans.* Meet or come together again. E17.
■ **reassemblage** *noun* the action or an act of reassembling M18. **reassembly** *noun* = REASSEMBLAGE E17.

reassert /riːəˈsəːt/ *verb trans.* M17.
[from RE- + ASSERT.]
1 Assert (a statement, claim, etc.) again. M17.
2 Claim (a thing) again. *rare*. E18.
■ **reassertion** *noun* M19. **reassertor** *noun* M19.

For other words beginning with *re-* see the entry for **re-**

reassign /riːəˈsʌɪn/ *verb trans.* E17.
[from RE- + ASSIGN *verb*.]
Assign again or differently.
■ **reassignment** *noun* the fact of having been reassigned; a new or different assignment: M19.

reassume /riːəˈsjuːm/ *verb.* L15.
[from RE- + ASSUME.]
1 *verb trans.* Take or take up again (a thing put down or handed over). L15. ▸**b** Take back (a grant, gift, etc.). E17. ▸†**c** Rescind (a vote). L17–E18.
2 *verb trans.* Resume (an action, one's place, †speech, etc.). L16. ▸†**b** *verb intrans. & trans.* (with direct speech as obj.). Continue speaking after a pause, resume. Only in 18.
3 *verb trans.* Take back (a person) into close relationship. E17. ▸**b** Take back as a constituent part. L17.
4 *verb trans.* Take again upon oneself (a charge, title, attribute, etc.); *refl.* return to one's natural character. E17.
■ **reassumption** *noun* the action or an act of reassuming something E17.

reassure /riːəˈʃʊə/ *verb trans.* L16.
[from RE- + ASSURE.]
1 Restore confidence to; dispel the fear or concern of. L16. ▸**b** Confirm in an opinion or impression (*of*). E19.
†**2** Re-establish; restore. E17–M18.
3 Reinsure. M18.

📖 **1** P. THEROUX A car drew up . . . I was alarmed, then reassured when I saw it was a taxi. E. LONGFORD 'It's a good sign to be nervous,' Hugh reassured me. **b** J. BRAINE The need to reassure myself of the presence of another human being.

■ **reassurance** *noun* (*a*) (a) renewed or repeated assurance; (*b*) reinsurance: E17. **reassurer** *noun* L18. **reassuringly** *adverb* in a reassuring manner L19.

reasty /ˈriːsti/ *adjective.* Chiefly *dial.* L16.
[Later form of RESTY *adjective*¹. Cf. next, REESED, RUSTY *adjective*².]
Rancid.

reasy /ˈriːsi/ *adjective. obsolete* exc. *dial.* L16.
[Rel. to prec.]
Rancid.

reata *noun* var. of RIATA.

reate /riːt/ *noun.* Now *arch. & dial.* Also **rait** /reɪt/. M17.
[Origin unkn.]
Any of several kinds of water-crowfoot, esp. *Ranunculus fluitans*.

†**reaume** *noun* see REALM.

Réaumur /ˈreɪəmjʊə, *foreign* reomyr/ *noun & adjective.* L18.
[René Antoine Ferchault de *Réaumur* (1683–1757), French naturalist and physicist.]
▶**A** *noun.* **1** The thermometric scale introduced by Réaumur in which water freezes at 0° and boils at 80° under standard conditions. Also more fully ***Réaumur's scale***. L18.
2 a ***Réaumur's porcelain***, a devitrified form of glass formerly used for chemical vessels. M19. ▸**b** ***Réaumur process***, a process for annealing iron leading to the production of white-heart malleable iron. E20.
▶**B** *adjective.* Designating or pertaining to Réaumur's scale; *postpositive* (with a specified temperature) on this scale. L18.

reave /riːv, reɪv/ *noun.* M19.
[Origin uncertain: perh. from REW *noun*.]
ARCHAEOLOGY. A long low bank or wall found on Dartmoor.

reave /riːv/ *verb*¹. *arch.* Also (esp. *Scot.*) **reive**. Pa. t. & pple **reaved**, (esp. *Scot.*) **reived**, **reft** /rɛft/.
[Old English *rēafian* = Old Frisian *rāv(i)a*, Old Saxon *rōbōn* (Dutch *rooven*), Old High German *roubōn* (German *rauben*), Gothic -*raubōn*, from Germanic base also of ROB *verb*. Cf. next.]
1 *verb intrans.* Make raids, plunder, pillage. Now chiefly *Scot.* OE.
2 *verb trans.* Deprive or rob (a person, †a place) of something by force. Long only foll. by *of*. Also (now *rare* or *obsolete*) with double obj. OE.
3 *verb trans.* Take forcible possession of (something belonging to another), steal. Also foll. by *away*, *from*. OE. ▸**b** *fig.* Take away (life, sight, etc.). ME.
4 *verb trans.* Take a person away (*from*). ME. ▸†**b** Deliver or rescue by carrying off. ME–M17. ▸†**c** Snatch *up*. *Scot.* M16–E18.

📖 **2** V. WOOLF A soul reft of body. **3** E. BOWEN The . . property of the landlords had been reft from its . . owners. **4** SHELLEY Wretched slaves, Who from their . . native land Are reft.

reave /riːv/ *verb*². *arch.* Pa. t. & pple **reft** /rɛft/. ME.
[Alt. of RIVE *verb* by confusion with prec. Cf. REFT *noun*.]
1 *verb trans.* Tear; split. ME.
†**2** *verb intrans.* Burst. ME–M16.
†**3** *verb trans.* Pull *up*. LME–M16.

📖 **1** *Pall Mall Gazette* The rock was reft asunder.

reaver /ˈriːvə/ *noun.* Also (orig. *Scot.*) **reiver**. OE.
[from prec. + -ER¹. Cf. ROVER *noun*¹.]
1 A robber; a marauder, a raider. OE.
†**2** A pirate. LME–E17.

reb /rɛb/ *noun*¹. Chiefly *US.* M19.
[Abbreviation.]
= REBEL *noun* 2C.

reb /rɛb/ *noun*². L19.
[Yiddish, formed as REBBE.]
A traditional Jewish courtesy title used preceding a man's forename or surname.

rebab /rɪˈbab/ *noun.* M18.
[Arab. *rabāb*.]
A bowed or (occas.) plucked stringed instrument of Arab origin, used esp. in N. Africa, the Middle East, and the Indian subcontinent.

rebadge /riːˈbadʒ/ *verb trans.* L20.
[from RE- + BADGE *verb*¹.]
Market a car or other product (esp. one bought from another manufacturer) under a new name or specification number.

rebaptize /riːbapˈtʌɪz/ *verb trans.* Also **-ise**. LME.
[Late Latin *rebaptizare*, formed as RE- + *baptizare* BAPTIZE.]
1 Baptize again. LME.
2 Give a new name to. L16.
■ **reˈbaptism** *noun* a second baptism L18. †**rebaptist** *noun* = REBAPTIZER M17–M18. †**rebaptization** *noun* the action or practice of rebaptizing a person L16–L18. **rebaptizer** *noun* a person who advocates or performs a second baptism, *spec.* an Anabaptist LME.

re-bar /ˈriːbɑː/ *noun.* Chiefly *US.* Also **rebar**. M20.
[from *re(inforcing* + BAR *noun*¹.]
A steel reinforcing rod in concrete.

rebarbative /rɪˈbɑːbətɪv/ *adjective.* L19.
[French *rébarbatif*, -*ive*, from *barbe* beard: see -ATIVE.]
Repellent; unattractive; objectionable.
■ **rebarbatively** *adverb* M20. **rebarbativeness** *noun* L20.

rebate /ˈriːbeɪt/ *noun*¹. M16.
[from REBATE *verb*¹. Cf. French *rabat*.]
A deduction from a sum of money to be paid; a discount. Also, a partial refund of money paid.

rebate /rɪˈbeɪt/ *noun*². L17.
[Alt. of RABBET *noun* after prec.]
A rabbet.
Comb.: **rebate plane** a rabbet plane.

rebate /ˈriːbeɪt/ *verb*¹. LME.
[Old & mod. French *rabattre*, from *re-* RE- + *abattre* ABATE *verb*¹; later alt. by substitution of RE- for 1st syll.]
1 *verb trans.* †**a** Deduct (a certain amount) from a sum; subtract; reduce or diminish (a sum or amount). LME–L17. ▸†**b** Give or allow a reduction to (a person). E16–M17. ▸**c** Pay back (a sum of money) as a rebate; give a rebate on. M20.
2 a *verb trans. &* †*intrans.* Diminish, lessen in force or intensity, abate. Now *rare*. LME. ▸**b** *verb trans. &* †*intrans.* Blunt (*lit. & fig.*). Now *rare*. LME. ▸†**c** *verb trans.* Repress or stop (a person, action, etc.). L16–L18.
†**3** *verb trans.* FALCONRY. Bring back (a hawk) to the hand. L15–L17.
4 *verb trans.* HERALDRY. Make (a charge) smaller by removal of a part; remove (a part) from a charge. M16.
†**5** *verb trans.* Repulse, drive back. L16–M17.
■ **rebatable** *adjective* L20. **rebater** *noun* E17.

rebate /ˈriːbeɪt/ *verb*² *trans.* L17.
[Alt. of RABBET *verb* after prec.]
1 Make a rabbet in. L17.
2 Join *together* with a rabbet. M19.

rebatement /ˈriːbeɪtm(ə)nt, rɪˈbeɪtm(ə)nt/ *noun.* Now *rare* or *obsolete*. M16.
[Old French, formed as REBATE *verb*¹: see -MENT.]
1 A discount. M16.
2 HERALDRY. = ABATEMENT *noun*¹ 3. M16.
3 Diminution in amount, force, etc. L16.

rebato *noun* var. of RABATO.

rebbe /ˈrɛbə/ *noun.* L19.
[Yiddish, from Hebrew *rabbī* RABBI *noun*¹.]
A rabbi; *spec.* a Hasidic religious leader.

rebbitzin /ˈrɛbɪtsɪn/ *noun.* L19.
[Yiddish, fem. of prec.]
The wife of a rabbi.

rebec /ˈriːbɛk/ *noun.* Also **-beck**. LME.
[French, alt. of Old French *rebebe*, *rubebe*: see RIBIBLE.]
Chiefly *Hist.* A medieval musical instrument with usu. three strings and played with a bow; a player on this in an orchestra etc.

Rebeccaite /rɪˈbɛkəʌɪt/ *noun.* M19.
[from *Rebecca* (see below) + -ITE¹.]
Hist. A follower of Rebecca, the leader, dressed as a woman, of a group of rioters who demolished toll-gates in South Wales in 1843–4.

rebeck *noun* var. of REBEC.

Rebekah /rɪˈbɛkə/ *noun. N. Amer.* M19.
[AV spelling of *Rebecca* female forename, with allus. to *Genesis* 24:60.]
A member of a women's society resembling that of the Oddfellows and founded in Indiana in 1851.

rebel /ˈrɛb(ə)l/ *adjective & noun.* ME.
[Old & mod. French *rebelle* from Latin *rebellis* (orig. with ref. to the defeated declaring war again), formed as RE- + *bellum* war.]
▶**A** *adjective.* (Long only *attrib.*)
1 Refusing allegiance or obedience to or fighting against the established government or ruler. ME. ▸**b** Of, consisting of, or in the command of rebels. L17.
2 Resisting or opposing authority or control; disobedient to some higher authority. (Formerly foll. by *against*, *of*.) ME.
3 Of words, an action, etc.: rebellious. LME.

📖 **1** H. FAST Readmission of the rebel states into the Union. **b** *Times* Using . . helicopter gunships against rebel strongholds. **2** *Times* Rebel Tories in Cheltenham . . suffered a setback.

▶**B** *noun.* **1** A person who or thing which resists authority or control. ME.
2 *spec.* **a** A person who refuses allegiance or obedience to or fights against the established government or ruler. LME. ▸**b** LAW (now *Hist.*). A person who refused to obey a legal command or summons. L16. ▸**c** A supporter of the Confederates during the American Civil War (1861–5); *colloq.* a person belonging to the Southern States of the US. Chiefly *US.* M19.

📖 **1** E. PAWEL Many students . . ended up as rebels rather than bureaucrats. **2a** *Armed Forces* Victories over Afghan rebels.

Comb.: **rebel yell** a shout or battle-cry used by the Confederates during the American Civil War.
■ **rebeldom** *noun* (now *rare*) (*a*) the domain of rebels, esp. of the Confederates during the American Civil War; (*b*) rebellious behaviour: M19. **rebelly** *adjective* = REBELLIOUS 1 E19.

rebel /rɪˈbɛl/ *verb.* Infl. **-ll-**. ME.
[Old & mod. French *rebeller* from Latin *rebellare*, formed as RE- + *bellare* make war, from *bellum* war.]
1 *verb intrans.* Resist, oppose, or be disobedient to a person in authority. (Foll. by *against*, (arch.) *to*.) ME.
2 *verb intrans.* Rise in opposition or armed resistance against the established government or ruler. (Foll. by *against*, (arch.) *to*.) LME. ▸**b** *fig.* Offer resistance; feel or show repugnance. LME.
3 *verb trans.* Oppose rebelliously. *rare*. LME.

📖 **1** A. STORR The parent who is too yielding gives the child . . no authority against which to rebel. **2** R. SUTCLIFF Queen Boadicea rebelled against the Romans. **b** J. F. HENDRY He rebelled against institutional life.

¶ Not recorded in sense 3 between LME and E20.
■ **rebeller** *noun* (now *rare*) LME.

rebellion /rɪˈbɛljən/ *noun.* ME.
[Old & mod. French *rébellion* from Latin *rebellio(n-)*, from *rebellis*: see REBEL *adjective & noun*, -ION.]
1 Open or determined disobedience or resistance to an authority. ME.
2 (An) organized armed resistance to the established government or ruler; (an) insurrection, (a) revolt; *spec.* (ENGLISH HISTORY) either of the Jacobite risings of 1715 and 1745. LME. ▸**b** LAW (now *Hist.*). Refusal to obey a legal command or summons; the penalty for this. LME.
Phrases: **the Great Rebellion** the period of English history from 1642 to 1651.

rebellious /rɪˈbɛljəs/ *adjective.* LME.
[from prec.: see -OUS.]
1 Insubordinate, tending to rebel; defying lawful authority; in rebellion. (Foll. by *against*, *to*.) LME. ▸†**b** *fig.* Of liquor: harmful to the health. *rare* (Shakes.). Only in E17.
2 Of an action etc.: characteristic of a rebel or rebels; marked by rebellion. L15.
3 Of a thing: unmanageable; refractory. L16.

📖 **1** M. E. BRADDON A . . rebellious girl . . expelled from a school. *Japan Times* The rebellious soldiers had . . formed an alliance. **2** LONGFELLOW The sword his grandsire bore In the rebellious days of yore.

■ **rebelliously** *adverb* M16. **rebelliousness** *noun* L16.

rebellow /riːˈbɛləʊ/ *verb.* L16.
[from RE- + BELLOW *verb*, after Latin *reboare*.]
1 *verb intrans.* Of a cow etc.: bellow in reply or in turn. L16. ▸**b** *transf.* Echo loudly (*to* or *with* a sound). L16.
2 *verb trans.* Bellow (a sound) in reply or repetition. M18.

rebid /ˈriːbɪd, *as verb also* riːˈbɪd/ *verb & noun.* E20.
[from RE- + BID *verb*, *noun*.]
BRIDGE. ▶**A** *verb trans. & intrans.* Infl. **-dd-**; pa. t. & pple **rebid**. Bid (a suit) again at a higher level. E20.
▶**B** *noun.* An act of rebidding; such a bid. E20.
■ **reˈbiddable** *adjective* M20.

rebirth /riːˈbəːθ/ *noun & verb*. M19.
[from RE- + BIRTH *noun*[1]. Cf. REBORN.]
▶ **A** *noun*. **1** A second or new birth; a reincarnation; *spec.* spiritual enlightenment. M19.
2 A revival (*of*). M19.

1 E. SIMPSON A fresh start, a magical rebirth. **2** A. E. STEVENSON We .. need .. a rebirth of ideas.

▶ **B** *verb trans.* Treat (a person) using the technique of rebirthing. L20.
■ **rebirther** *noun* L20. **rebirthing** *noun* a treatment for neurosis involving controlled breathing intended to simulate the trauma of being born L20.

reblochon /rəblɔʃɔ̃/ *noun*. E20.
[French.]
A soft French cheese made orig. and chiefly in Savoy.

reboant /ˈrɛbəʊənt/ *adjective*. Chiefly *poet.* M19.
[Latin *reboant-* pres. ppl stem of *reboare*, formed as RE- + *boare* roar, resound: see -ANT[1].]
Echoing loudly.

reboil /riːˈbɔɪl/ *verb trans.* E17.
[from RE- + BOIL *verb*.]
Boil again.

reboiler /riːˈbɔɪlə/ *noun*. M20.
[from prec. + -ER[1].]
A heater for vaporizing the liquid at the bottom of a fractionating column.

reboiler /riːˈbɔɪlə/ *verb trans.* L19.
[from RE- + BOILER.]
Fit (esp. the engine of a ship) with a new boiler.

rebore /*as verb* riːˈbɔː, *as noun* ˈriːbɔː/ *verb & noun*. E19.
[from RE- + BORE *verb*[1].]
▶ **A** *verb trans.* Make a new boring in; *esp.* widen the bore of (the cylinder in an internal-combustion engine). E19.
▶ **B** *noun*. An act of reboring; an engine which has had its cylinders rebored. M20.

reborn /riːˈbɔːn/ *adjective*. L16.
[from RE- + BORN *ppl adjective*. Cf. REBIRTH.]
1 Reincarnated; spiritually enlightened; *spec.* converted to Christianity. L16.
2 Of a thing: revived. E19.

reborrow /riːˈbɒrəʊ/ *verb trans. & intrans.* M17.
[from RE- + BORROW *verb*[1].]
Borrow back; borrow once more.
■ **reborrowing** *noun* (*a*) the action of the verb; (*b*) LINGUISTICS a word borrowed back from another language: M19.

reboso *noun* var. of REBOZO.

rebound /ˈriːbaʊnd/ *noun*. LME.
[from the verb.]
1 The action or an act, esp. by a ball, of bouncing back after striking something; (a) recoil; SPORT a ball that rebounds. LME. ▸**b** *transf.* A reaction, esp. to a strong emotion etc. M16. ▸**c** MEDICINE. The recurrence of an illness under certain conditions, as on withdrawal of medication. Usu. *attrib.* L20.
†**2** A violent blow. L15–E16.

1 *Dumfries Courier* A rebound after a shot had been blocked by the goalmouth. **c** *attrib.*: P. QUILLIN Ceasing nutrient intake could create a rebound deficiency.

Phrases: **on the rebound** (*a*) whilst rebounding; (*b*) *spec.* whilst still recovering from an emotional disturbance, esp. rejection by a lover.

rebound /rɪˈbaʊnd/ *verb*. LME.
[Old French *rebonder*, (also mod.) *rebondir*, from RE- + *bondir* BOUND *verb*[2].]
1 *verb intrans.* Spring back (as) from force of impact. LME. ▸**b** Of an action: have an adverse effect *on* or *upon* (the doer). LME. ▸**c** Redound *to* one's shame, honour, etc. LME. ▸**d** BASKETBALL. Catch a rebound. M20.
2 a *verb intrans.* Echo, reverberate. Now *rare*. LME. ▸**b** *verb trans.* Echo, return (a sound). Formerly also, exalt or celebrate with a re-echoing sound. Now *rare*. M16.
3 *verb intrans.* Bound, leap, esp. in response to some force or stimulus. Now *rare* or *obsolete*. LME. ▸†**b** Result or arise *from*. L15–M17.
4 *verb trans.* †**a** Reflect (light). LME–M17. ▸**b** Throw back, return (*lit.* & *fig.*). Now *rare*. M16.

1 E. BOWEN A leaden downpour .. rebounded from her silvery raincoat. **b** F. TOMLIN If one were to exaggerate .. the consequences would .. rebound upon one's own head. **c** *Times* If the Bar does not relax its rules .. it could 'rebound to its own detriment'. **3** MILTON With joy and fear his heart rebounds.

■ **rebounder** *noun* (*a*) *rare* a device in a gunlock for throwing back the hammer; (*b*) BASKETBALL a player skilled in catching rebounds; (*c*) (chiefly *US*) a small, round trampoline, esp. used for exercising at home: L19.

reboundant /rɪˈbaʊnd(ə)nt/ *adjective*. *obsolete* exc. *Hist.* L17.
[from prec. + -ANT[1].]
HERALDRY. = REVERBERANT 1.

rebours /rəbuːr/ *noun*. ME.
[Old French *rebors* (mod. *rebours*) rough, perverse, the wrong side, etc., from popular Latin *reburrum*, Latin *reburrum* rough-haired, bristly.]
Only in ***à rebours*** /a/, formerly naturalized (*Scot.*) †***at rebours***: in the wrong way; through perversity.

rebozo /rɪˈbəʊzəʊ, -s-/ *noun*. Also **-boso**. Pl. **-os**. E19.
[Spanish.]
A long scarf covering the head and shoulders, traditionally worn by Spanish-American women.

rebroadcast /riːˈbrɔːdkɑːst/ *verb & noun*. E20.
[from RE- + BROADCAST *verb*.]
▶ **A** *verb trans.* Pa. t. & pple **-cast**, (occas.) **-casted**. Broadcast again; *spec.* broadcast (a programme received from another station). E20.
▶ **B** *noun*. The action or an act of rebroadcasting a programme; a repeat broadcast. E20.
■ **rebroadcaster** *noun* M20.

rebuff /rɪˈbʌf/ *noun*. E17.
[French †*rebuffe* from Italian *ribuffo*: see next.]
1 A peremptory check given to a person who proffers help, shows interest, makes advances, etc.; a blunt refusal; a snub. E17. ▸**b** A check to further action or progress. L17.
2 A repelling puff or blast. *rare*. M17.

1 P. ROSE Never since the rebuff from Maria had he been able to display affection. V. ACKLAND I once more asked for help (.. it was harder, because of the rebuffs).

rebuff /rɪˈbʌf/ *verb trans.* L16.
[French †*rebuffer* from Italian *ribuffare*, *rabb-*, from *ribuffo*, *rabb-*, from RE- + *buffo* gust, puff, of imit. origin.]
1 Repel bluntly or ungraciously; snub. L16.
2 Blow or drive back. *rare*. M18.

1 E. WAUGH He attempted to interview the Resident, and was rebuffed. ANTHONY SMITH Every opinion uttered is rebuffed.

rebuffal /rɪˈbʌf(ə)l/ *noun*. M20.
[from prec. + -AL[1], perh. after REBUTTAL.]
An act of rebuffing; a rebuff.

rebuild /*as verb* riːˈbɪld, *as noun* ˈriːbɪld/ *verb & noun*. L15.
[from RE- + BUILD *verb*.]
▶ **A** *verb trans.* Pa. t. & pple **rebuilt** /riːˈbɪlt/. Build again or differently. L15.
▶ **B** *noun*. An act of rebuilding; a thing rebuilt. L19.
■ **rebuildable** *adjective* L20. **rebuilder** *noun* L17.

rebuke /rɪˈbjuːk/ *noun*. LME.
[from the verb.]
†**1** A shameful or disgraceful check. LME–L15. ▸**b** Shame, disgrace. L15–L16.
2 (A) reproof, (a) reprimand. LME.
†**3** A check, a stop. L15–E17.

2 W. S. CHURCHILL The uproar .. brought a .. rebuke from Mr Secretary Cecil. A. KENNY The Archbishop .. offering neither exhortation nor rebuke.

rebuke /rɪˈbjuːk/ *verb trans.* ME.
[Anglo-Norman, Old Northern French *rebuker* = Old French *rebuchier*, from RE- + *bu(s)chier*, *bukier* beat, strike (properly, cut down wood), from *busche* (mod. *bûche*) log.]
†**1** Force back; repulse; repress (a quality, action, etc.) ME–E17.
2 Reprove or reprimand severely. ME. ▸**b** Find fault with, censure, condemn (an action etc.). E16.
†**3** Despise. *rare*. ME–L15.

2 D. M. THOMAS Instead of comforting her, he coldly rebuked her. *fig.*: G. GREENE His discretion seemed to rebuke our .. curiosity. **b** DAY LEWIS All would rebuke my naughtiness.

■ **rebukeable** *adjective* (now *rare*) deserving of rebuke M16. **rebuker** *noun* LME. **rebukingly** *adverb* in a rebuking manner LME.

rebukeful /rɪˈbjuːkfʊl, -f(ə)l/ *adjective*. E16.
[from REBUKE *noun* + -FUL.]
1 Full of censure. E16. ▸**b** Inclined to rebuke a person or thing. M19.
†**2** Deserving of rebuke. M–L16.
■ **rebukefully** *adverb* M16. **rebukefulness** *noun* L19.

rebunk /riːˈbʌŋk/ *verb trans. colloq.* M20.
[from RE- + BUNK *noun*[3], after DEBUNK.]
Restore the reputation of or regard for.

rebus /ˈriːbəs/ *noun & verb*. E17.
[French *rébus* from Latin *rebus* abl. pl. of *res* thing, in *de rebus quae geruntur* lit. 'concerning the things that are taking place', title given in 16th-cent. Picardy to satirical pieces containing riddles in picture form.]
▶ **A** *noun*. A representation of a word or phrase by pictures, symbols, arrangement of letters, etc., which suggest the word or phrase, or the syllables of which it is made up; *spec.* a device, often of heraldic appearance, suggesting the name of its bearer. E17.

G. NORMAN IOU .. is a rebus for 'I owe you.'

▶ **B** *verb trans.* Infl. **-s(s)-**. Mark with a rebus or rebuses. *rare*. M17.

rebus sic stantibus /ˌreɪbəs sɪk ˈstantɪbəs/ *noun & adverbial phr.* E17.
[mod. Latin, lit. 'things standing thus'.]
INTERNATIONAL LAW. (According to) the principle that a treaty is subject to an implied condition that if circumstances are substantially different from those obtaining when it was concluded, then a party to the treaty is entitled to be released from it.
clausula rebus sic stantibus a clause in a document stating this principle.

rebut /rɪˈbʌt/ *verb*. Infl. **-tt-**. ME.
[Anglo-Norman *rebuter*, Old French *reboter*, *-bout-*, from RE- + *boter* BUTT *verb*[1]. Cf. next.]
1 *verb trans.* Rebuke or reproach violently. Long *obsolete* exc. *Scot.* ME.
†**2** *verb trans.* Repel or repulse (a person or an attack). LME–E19.
3 *verb intrans.* †**a** Retire, retreat. LME–E17. ▸**b** LAW. Bring forward a rebutter. Now *rare* or *obsolete*. E17. ▸**c** CURLING. Play a forceful random shot towards the end of a game. M19.
4 *verb trans.* Force or turn back; check. L15.
5 *verb trans.* Refute, disprove. E19.

4 ISAAC TAYLOR Fatalism .. has been rebutted. **5** H. JAMES I wished .. to rebut your charge that I am .. abnormal. A. FRASER To rebut accusations of treachery.

■ **rebutment** *noun* †(*a*) the act of rebutting; the fact of being rebutted; (*b*) *spec.* = REBUTTAL: L16. **rebuttable** *adjective* L19. **rebuttal** *noun* (a) refutation, (a) contradiction M19.

†**rebute** *noun*. *Scot.* LME–L19.
[Old French *rebo(u)t* (mod. *rebut*). Cf. prec.]
Repulse; a rebuke, a reproach.

rebutter /rɪˈbʌtə/ *noun*. M16.
[In sense 1 from Anglo-Norman *rebuter*, formed as REBUT; in sense 2 from REBUT + -ER[1].]
1 LAW. An answer made by a defendant to a plaintiff's surrejoinder. M16.
2 That which rebuts or refutes something; a refutation. L18.

rec /rɛk/ *noun*. *colloq.* Also **rec.** (point). E20.
[Abbreviation.]
Recreation; a recreation-ground.

recado /reˈkaðo, rɪˈkɑːdəʊ/ *noun*. Pl. **-os** /-ɔs, -əʊz/. E17.
[Spanish, Portuguese = gift, of unkn. origin.]
†**1** A present; a message of goodwill. Only in 17.
2 A S. American saddle or saddle-cloth. E19.

recalcitrant /rɪˈkalsɪtr(ə)nt/ *adjective & noun*. M19.
[French *récalcitrant* from Latin *recalcitrant-* pres. ppl stem of *recalcitrare*: see next, -ANT[1].]
▶ **A** *adjective*. Obstinately disobedient or refractory; objecting to restraint. M19.

A. J. TOYNBEE Human nature that is recalcitrant to any planner's regulations. C. THUBRON The yell of a recalcitrant child. *fig.*: M. AYRTON The hatchet .. he .. uses to subdue recalcitrant sculpture.

▶ **B** *noun*. A recalcitrant person. M19.
■ **recalcitrance** *noun* M19. **recalcitrancy** *noun* M19. **recalcitrantly** *adverb* L20.

recalcitrate /rɪˈkalsɪtreɪt/ *verb*. E17.
[Latin *recalcitrat-* pa. ppl stem of *recalcitrare* kick out, (later) be refractory, formed as RE- + CALCITRATE.]
1 *verb intrans.* Kick out, kick backwards. *rare*. E17.
2 *verb intrans. fig.* Show strong opposition or resistance; be obstinately disobedient or refractory. Foll. by *against*, *at*. M18.
3 *verb trans.* Kick back; *fig.* resist, oppose. *rare*. M19.
■ **recalciˈtration** *noun* the action or an act of recalcitrating M17.

recalescence /riːkəˈlɛs(ə)ns/ *noun*. L19.
[from RE- + Latin *calescere* grow warm + -ENCE.]
METALLURGY. The temporary generation of heat associated with a change in crystal structure when a metal is cooled.

recall /rɪˈkɔːl, ˈriːkɔːl/ *noun*. E17.
[from RE- + CALL *noun*, after the verb.]
1 The action or an act of calling someone or something back; a summons to return to or from a place; *esp.* a request for the return of a faulty product, issued by a manufacturer to all purchasers concerned. E17. ▸**b** A sound made as a signal to return, *spec.* (MILITARY) to call soldiers back to rank or camp. M19.
2 The action or an instance of remembering; the ability to remember. M17. ▸**b** A measure of the thoroughness of an information retrieval system, esp. expressed as the proportion of the number of relevant documents retrieved from a database in response to an enquiry. M20.
3 The action or possibility of revoking, undoing, or annulling something done or past. Chiefly in ***beyond recall***, ***past recall***, ***without recall***. M17. ▸**b** Removal of an elected government official from office by a system of

petition and vote; this method of terminating a period of office. *US.* E20.

1 *Which?* To reach owners . . manufacturers publicise their recalls. 2 P. CASEMENT Memory is usually . . conscious recall. C. TOMALIN Powers of recall. ***total recall***: see TOTAL *adjective*.

recall /rɪˈkɔːl; *in sense* 5 riːˈkɔːl/ *verb*. L16.
[from RE- + CALL *verb*, after Latin *revocare* or French *rappeler*.]
1 *verb trans.* Call back or summon (a person) to return from a place, a different occupation, inattention, etc. L16. ▸**b** Bring back (the attention, mind, etc.) to or *to* a subject. M17. ▸**c** *COMPUTING.* Transfer (a program, data, etc.) again to a location in memory that allows rapid processing, onscreen display, etc. M20.
2 *verb trans.* Restore or revive (a feeling etc.). L16.
3 *verb trans.* **a** Revoke, undo, or annul (an action or decision); *spec.* cancel or suspend the appointment of (an official sent overseas etc.). L16. ▸**b** Take back (a gift). E17.
4 *verb trans.* **a** Call or bring back (a circumstance etc.) *to* a person, a person's thoughts, etc. L16. ▸**b** Bring back to the mind; cause remembrance of. M17. ▸**c** Recollect, remember. L17.
5 *verb trans. & intrans.* Call again. *rare.* L18.

1 T. GRAY He . . recalls us from our wandering thoughts. R. GRAVES He recalled the actors whom the . . Emperor banished. G. BODDY Murry was recalled to England to face bankruptcy proceedings. 2 TENNYSON Autumn . . Recalls . . My old affection of the tomb. 4a B. MOORE A presence, a power . . recalled to his visitor a painting seen in Venice. **b** M. KEANE There was no single object to recall the room as it had been. **c** LD BRAIN Friends will recall his gaiety. G. SWIFT You only recall what is pleasant.

▪ **recallable** *adjective* M17. **recallment** *noun* = RECALL *noun* M17.

Récamier /reɪˈkamjeɪ, *foreign* rekamje (*pl. same*)/ *noun & adjective*. Also **r-**. E20.
[Jeanne *Récamier* (1777–1849), French hostess, portrayed reclining on a chaise longue in a painting.]
(Designating) a style of chaise longue.

recant /rɪˈkant/ *verb*. M16.
[Latin *recantare* sing in answer, recall, revoke, formed as RE- + *cantare* CHANT *verb*, after Greek *palinōidein*.]
▸ **I 1** *verb trans. & intrans.* Withdraw and renounce (a former statement, belief, etc.) as erroneous or heretical, esp. formally or publicly. M16. ▸†**b** *verb trans.* Renounce as wrong or repent (a course of life or conduct). L16–E18. ▸†**c** *verb intrans.* Refuse to fulfil a contract or agreement. *rare.* M17–M18.
2 *verb trans.* Withdraw or retract (a promise, vow, etc.). Now *rare.* L16. ▸**b** Give up (a design or purpose). *rare.* M17.
†**3** *verb refl.* Make retraction (*of*). L16–M17.
▸ **II 4** *verb trans.* Relate, tell again. Long *obsolete* exc. *Scot. dial.* E17.
▪ **recanˈtation** *noun* the action or an act of recanting M16. **recanter** *noun* L16.

recap /*as verb* riːˈkap, *as noun* ˈriːkap/ *verb*¹ & *noun*¹. M19.
[from RE- + CAP *verb*¹.]
▸ **A** *verb trans.* Infl. **-pp-**.
1 Put a cap on (a thing) again; *esp.* provide (a cartridge) with a new cap. M19.
2 Renew (a worn pneumatic tyre) by cementing, moulding, and vulcanizing a strip of camel-back on the tread. M20.
▸ **B** *noun.* A recapped tyre. M20.
▪ **recappable** *adjective* M20. **recapper** *noun* a person who or thing which recaps a cartridge, tyre, etc. L19.

recap /ˈriːkap/ *verb*² & *noun*². *colloq.* M20.
[Abbreviation.]
▸ **A** *verb trans. & intrans.* Infl. **-pp-**. = RECAPITULATE *verb* 1a. M20.
▸ **B** *noun.* = RECAPITULATION 1a. M20.

recapacitate /riːkəˈpasɪteɪt/ *verb trans.* L17.
[from RE- + CAPACITATE.]
†**1** Make legally capable again. L17–E18.
2 *PHYSIOLOGY.* Restore potency to (a decapacitated spermatozoon). M20.
▪ ˌ**recapaciˈtation** *noun* L20.

recapitulate /riːkəˈpɪtjʊleɪt/ *verb*. L16.
[Latin *recapitulat-* pa. ppl stem of *recapitulare*, formed as RE- + *capitulum*: see CAPITULATE.]
1 *verb trans. & intrans.* **a** Go briefly through again, go over the main points of (an argument, statement, etc.); sum up. L16. ▸**b** *verb trans. BIOLOGY.* Repeat (supposed evolutionary stages) in the development and growth of a young animal. L19. ▸**c** *verb trans. MUSIC.* Repeat (a musical theme) in a recapitulation. M20.
2 *verb trans.* Bring together again; unite. *rare.* E17.
▪ **recapitulative** *adjective* (*BIOLOGY*) characterized by recapitulation L19. **recapitulatory** *adjective* (*a*) of the nature of or characterized by recapitulation; (*b*) *BIOLOGY* = RECAPITULATIVE: M17.

recapitulation /ˌriːkəpɪtjʊˈleɪʃ(ə)n/ *noun*. LME.
[Old & mod. French *récapitulation* or late Latin *recapitulatio(n-)*, formed as prec. + -ATION.]
1 a The action or an act of recapitulating, (a) summing up. LME. ▸**b** *BIOLOGY.* The appearance during (esp. embryonic) development of successive forms resembling those of the organism's evolutionary predecessors. L19. ▸**c** *MUSIC.* A section of a composition or movement, esp. the final section of one in sonata form, in which themes from the exposition are repeated, usu. in a modified form. L19.
2 *CHRISTIAN THEOLOGY.* The summing up and redemption of all human experience in Jesus' life and death. M17.

recaption /riːˈkapʃ(ə)n/ *noun*. E17.
[Anglo-Latin *recaptio(n-)*, formed as RE- + CAPTION *noun*.]
LAW. **1 a** A second distress. E17. ▸**b** Distraint for a second time. Freq. in ***writ of recaption***. E17.
2 The peaceful seizure, without legal process, of property of one's own that has been wrongfully taken or withheld. M18.

recaptor /riːˈkaptə/ *noun*. M18.
[from RE- + CAPTOR.]
A person who recaptures something, esp. at sea.

recapture /riːˈkaptʃə/ *noun & verb*. M18.
[from RE- + CAPTURE *noun, verb*.]
▸ **A** *noun.* **1** The action of capturing, or being captured, again; recovery by capture. M18.
2 Something captured again. M19.
▸ **B** *verb trans.* Capture again; recover by capture; *fig.* re-experience (a past emotion etc.). L18.

V. BRITTAIN Only once . . did we recapture . . the lovely enchantment of New Year's Eve. S. BRETT Hair that had been helped to recapture its former redness.

recast /riːˈkɑːst/ *verb & noun*. E17.
[from RE- + CAST *verb, noun*¹; in sense 2 after French *refondre*.]
▸ **A** *verb trans.* Pa. t. & pple **recast**.
1 Cast or throw again. E17.
2 a Cast (metal) again. M18. ▸**b** *fig.* Refashion or remodel (a thing, esp. a literary work etc.); put into a new form. L18.
3 Recalculate. M19.
4 *THEATRICAL.* Assign (an actor) to another part; cast (a role, play, etc.) again. M20.
▸ **B** *noun.* The action or an act of recasting something; a thing produced by recasting. M19.

recce /ˈrɛki/ *noun & verb. colloq.* (orig. *Military slang*). M20.
[Abbreviation Cf. next.]
▸ **A** *noun.* A reconnaissance. M20.
▸ **B** *verb trans. & intrans.* Pres. pple & verbal noun **recceing**. Reconnoitre (a place etc.). M20.

recco /ˈrɛkəʊ/ *noun. Military slang.* Pl. **-os**. E20.
[Abbreviation Cf. prec.]
A reconnaissance.

recd. *abbreviation.*
Received.

recede /rɪˈsiːd/ *verb*¹. L15.
[Latin *recedere*, formed as RE- + *cedere* CEDE.]
1 *verb intrans.* **a** Depart *from* some usual state, standard, etc. Now *rare* or *obsolete.* L15. ▸**b** Differ or vary *from*. Now *rare.* L16.
2 *verb intrans.* †**a** Withdraw allegiance *from*. *rare.* L15–M16. ▸**b** Withdraw from or *from* a bargain, proposal, opinion, etc. M17.
3 *verb intrans.* Depart or retire (*from* or *to* a place). *rare.* L15.
4 *verb intrans.* **a** Go or move back or further off; (of hair) cease to grow at the front and sides of the head; be left at an increasing distance by an observer's motion. E17. ▸**b** Lie further back or away; slope backwards. L18. ▸**c** Of a colour: appear to be more distant than others in the same plane. M20.
†**5** *verb trans.* **a** Retract, withdraw. Only in M17. ▸**b** Move back or away. Only in E19.
6 *verb intrans.* **a** Go back or away in time. L18. ▸**b** Decline in character or value. E19.

4a J. GALSWORTHY The colour rushed into Bosinney's face, but soon receded. E. BOWEN The . . castle receded . . into its ink-like woods. I. MURDOCH Her footsteps on the gravel receded. V. BRAMWELL Gums recede with age. **b** W. GOLDING He thought, receding chin on white hand. 6a R. HUGHES A phase of their lives was receding into the past. **b** J. K. GALBRAITH A time of receding income.

▪ **recedence** *noun* = RECESSION M19. **receder** *noun* M18.

recede /riːˈsiːd/ *verb*² *trans.* L18.
[from RE- + CEDE.]
Cede again, give up to a former owner.

receipt /rɪˈsiːt/ *noun*. Also (earlier) †**receit**. LME.
[Anglo-Norman, Old Northern French *receite* = Old French *reçoite* var. of *rece(p)te* (mod. *recette*) from medieval Latin *recepta* use as noun of fem. pa. pple of Latin *recipere* RECEIVE.]
▸ **I 1** = RECIPE *noun* 1, 3. Formerly also, a drug etc. made according to a recipe. *arch.* exc. *Scot. dial.* LME. ▸**b** (The description of) a remedy or cure (*for* a disease). *arch.* L16. ▸**c** The formula of a preparation, or an account of the means, for effecting some end; the means *for* attaining an end. *arch.* E17.

1 SIR W. SCOTT Thin soft cakes, made of flour and honey according to the family receipt. **b** STEELE The most approved Receipt now extant for the Fever of the Spirits. **c** R. B. SHERIDAN Certainly this is . . the newest receipt for avoiding calumny.

▸ **II 2** An amount of something, now *spec.* money, received. Now usu. in *pl.* LME.

2 W. M. CLARKE The first night was a distinct success . . . Receipts in the first week reached £475.

▸ **III 3 a** The action of receiving something, or the fact of something being received, into one's possession or custody. LME. ▸**b** A written acknowledgement of this, esp. of the payment of money. E17.
†**4** The receiving of stolen goods. LME–L17.
†**5** Collection or storage of a thing in a place or container. LME–M17. ▸**b** The action or an act of taking food, medicine, etc.; an amount taken. LME–E17.
†**6** The admission of a person to a place, shelter, etc.; the fact of being so received; *fig.* (*rare*) acceptance of a person or thing. LME–L18. ▸**b** (A) welcome. *rare.* L16–M17. ▸**c** The habitual reception of strangers or travellers. Chiefly in ***place of receipt***. E–M17.
†**7** The fact of receiving a blow, wound, etc. M16–L17.

3a P. LOMAS Feelings of anguish do not . . subside on receipt of insight. K. M. E. MURRAY Had they been in receipt of the parish dole.

▸ **IV** †**8** A receptacle, esp. for water. LME–M17.
9 The main office for the reception of moneys on behalf of the Crown or government. *obsolete* exc. *Hist.* LME.
†**10** A place of reception or accommodation for people; a shelter. LME–E17.
†**11** *HUNTING.* A place where hunters await driven game with fresh hounds. LME–L17.
▸ **V 12** †**a** Mental capacity. LME–E17. ▸**b** Capacity, size. *obsolete* exc. *dial.* M16.

†**receipt** *verb*¹ *trans.* Also (*Scot.*) **resait**. ME.
[Old French *receiter* var. of *receter* RESET *verb*¹.]
1 Harbour (a person, esp. a criminal). ME–L18.
2 Receive (stolen goods) knowing of the theft. E16–E18.
▪ †**receipter** *noun* LME–M19.

receipt /rɪˈsiːt/ *verb*². L18.
[from the noun.]
1 *verb trans.* Acknowledge in writing the receipt of (a sum of money etc.) (chiefly *US*); *spec.* mark (a bill) as paid. L18.
2 *verb intrans.* Give a receipt *for* (a sum of money etc.). Chiefly *US.* M19.
▪ **receiptor** *noun* (*US*) a person who receipts property attached by a sheriff E19.

†**receit** *noun* see RECEIPT *noun*.

receivable /rɪˈsiːvəb(ə)l/ *adjective & noun*. LME.
[Anglo-Norman var. of Old & mod. French *recevable*; later from RECEIVE + -ABLE.]
▸ **A** *adjective.* **1** Able to be received. LME.
2 Capable of receiving. Formerly foll. by *of*. Now *rare.* E16.
▸ **B** *noun.* In *pl.* Debts owed to a business, esp. regarded as assets. Cf. PAYABLE *noun*. M19.

receival /rɪˈsiːv(ə)l/ *noun*. Now *rare* exc. *Austral.* M17.
[from RECEIVE + -AL¹.]
The action of receiving; reception.

receive /rɪˈsiːv/ *verb*. ME.
[Old French *receivre* var. of *reçoivre* or (later) *recevoir*, ult. from Latin *recipere*, formed as RE- + *capere* take.]
▸ **I 1** *verb trans. & intrans.* Take or accept into one's hands or one's possession (something offered or given); accept delivery of (a thing sent); be a recipient (of). ME. ▸**b** *verb trans.* Attend to, listen to, heed. LME. ▸†**c** *verb trans.* Accept the surrender of (a person or place). LME–L15. ▸**d** *verb trans. & intrans.* Accept or have dealings with (stolen property), knowing of the theft. L16.
2 *verb trans.* Be provided with or given; acquire, get. ME. ▸**b** Get by communication from another; learn or ascertain from another. E16.
3 *verb trans.* Allow (something) to be done to one; undergo, experience; endure, suffer; have bestowed or conferred on one. ME. ▸**b** Be marked more or less permanently by (an impression etc.). ME. ▸**c** Have (a blow, wound, etc.) inflicted on one or *in* some bodily part; get (a specified injury). LME. ▸**d** Have (a law etc.) imposed on one; be subject to. LME. ▸**e** Be exposed to (heat, light, etc.). LME. ▸**f** Of a radio or television set, aerial, recording instrument, etc.: be affected by, detect, or respond internally to a transmitted signal; detect and convert (a signal) to sound, images, etc. Of (the user of) a radio or television set: detect and interpret the signal transmitted by (a given station or distant operator). M19.

For other words beginning with *re-* see the entry for **re-**

4 *verb trans.* Serve as a receptacle or containing space for; allow to enter or penetrate; be able to hold (contents or a specified amount) conveniently. ME.

5 *verb trans. & intrans.* Eat or drink (the sacrament) as part of the Eucharistic service, take (Communion). ME. ▸**b** *verb trans.* Take in by the mouth; swallow. Now *rare* or *obsolete*. LME.

6 *verb trans.* Stand the weight, force, or effect of; encounter (a military attack etc.) with resistance. LME. ▸**b** *verb trans.* Catch (a falling person or thing). LME. ▸**c** *verb trans.* Perceive or hear (a sound). LME. ▸**d** *verb trans. & intrans.* TENNIS etc. Be the player to whom the server serves (the ball); be required to play against (a service). L19.

7 *verb trans.* Retain in one's mind; understand; learn. LME.

1 SHAKES. *Two Gent.* I.. Did in your name receive it. L. KENNEDY I could not write a letter or receive one without my mothers having to read it. **b** J. R. GREEN A priest .. received his confession. **d** J. B. HILTON Nobody's going to get done .. for receiving .. cutlery. **2** T. F. POWYS It was .. high time that he received assistance. W. TREVOR He knocked .. but received no response. *Which?* Red Riding Hood received £500 .. from .. her grandmother's estate. **b** SHAKES. *Merch. V.* From her eyes I did receive fair speechless messages. **3** SWIFT Those who receive orders .. enter .. the Church. T. L. PEACOCK Family interests compelled Mr. Glowry to receive .. visits from Mr. and Mrs. Hilary. E. A. STOPFORD The pleasure of receiving .. sympathy. S. BRETT He .. delivered the speech with greater power than it had ever received. *Woman* Dora .. was the next to receive his critical attention. **c** L. STERNE The wound .. my uncle .. received at the siege of Namur. I. MURDOCH He received a sudden blow on the shoulder. **f** L. DEIGHTON 'You are receiving me?' 'Loud and clear,' I said. *Times* A special aerial is required to receive satellite television. **4** SHAKES. *Tit. A.* The basin that receives your .. blood. E. BOWEN The room received less and less light from the windows. B. ENGLAND The gully .. received the torrent. **6** TENNYSON Make broad thy shoulders to receive my weight. T. HARDY She would start .. as if she had received a galvanic shock. **b** D. WELCH He fell. But .. soft grass .. received him.

▶**II 8** *verb trans.* Treat (a person) in a familiar or friendly manner; entertain as a guest. ME. ▸**b** *verb intrans.* Hold a formal reception; entertain visitors. M19.

9 *verb trans.* Meet (a person) with signs of welcome or salutation; greet, welcome, esp. in a specified manner. ME.

10 *verb trans.* Admit (a person); give accommodation or shelter to; harbour. ME.

11 *verb trans.* **a** Take or accept (a person) in some capacity. Now *rare* exc. in ***receive in marriage***. ME. ▸**b** Get (a person) into one's custody, control, etc. Now *rare* or *obsolete*. ME.

12 *verb trans.* Admit (a person or thing) *to* or *into* a state, privilege, occupation, etc. Now chiefly *spec.*, admit to membership of a society, organization, etc. (freq. foll. by *into*). LME.

13 *verb trans.* Take, accept, hear, etc., in a specified manner or with a specified expression of feeling. LME. ▸**b** Take *for*, regard *as*. LME.

14 *verb trans.* Give credit to; accept as authoritative or true. Chiefly as ***received*** *ppl adjective*. LME. ▸†**b** Pass (a law). M16–M17.

8 V. WOOLF Divorced ladies were not received at court. M. MEYER He received them in his study. **b** J. LE CARRÉ She was dressed to receive. **9** J. F. HENDRY Rilke .. was received by Prince Thurn. M. SEYMOUR Conrad received his .. visitor with .. courtesy. **12** E. LONGFORD Wulfstan was ready to receive him into the .. Church. **13** T. HARDY The proposal was received with .. commendation. *Times* The sale was well received by analysts. **14** *Times* The .. received wisdom held that the .. sector was poised to fall. *Poetry Review* Teachers .. remaining locked-in on received ideas about poetry.

Phrases: **on receive** (of a radio receiver) in the state of being able to receive radio signals, with the receiver switched on. **received pronunciation** the form of spoken British English based on educated speech in southern England and considered to be least regional. ***receive silk***: see SILK noun 3b. ***receive the spirit***: see SPIRIT *noun*. **the Received Standard** = ***received pronunciation*** above.

receiver /rɪˈsiːvə/ *noun*. ME.
[Anglo-Norman *receivo(u)r* = Old French *recevere*, *-our*; later from prec. + -ER¹.]

1 A person who receives something; *spec.* (**a**) AMER. FOOTBALL an attacking player eligible to catch a pass; a defender designated to receive a kick-off; (**b**) BASEBALL a catcher; (**c**) (TENNIS etc.) the player to whom the server serves the ball. ME.

2 a *Hist.* An official appointed to receive money due; a treasurer. ME. ▸**b** A person appointed by a court to administer the property of a bankrupt or insane person, or property under litigation. Also ***official receiver***. L18. ▸**c** The official of the Metropolitan Police Force responsible for police property, buildings, and finance. E19.

3 A person who receives stolen goods. Formerly also, a person who harboured offenders. ME.

4 A vessel for holding something; a receptacle. LME. ▸**b** *spec.* in CHEMISTRY. A vessel, usu. of glass, for receiving and condensing the product of distillation. Also, a vessel for receiving and containing gases or for containing a vacuum. L16. ▸**c** The part of a firearm housing the action and to which the barrel and other components are attached. L19.

5 MEDICINE. A piece of flannel in which a newborn baby is placed. Now *rare*. L17.

6 a A device or instrument which receives or reacts to an electric current, esp. a signal. Now freq. *spec.*, that part of a telephone apparatus contained in the earpiece, in which electric currents transmitted along the wire are converted to sounds; also freq. *loosely*, a complete telephone handset, or occas., a whole telephone unit. L19. ▸**b** An apparatus for receiving (signals transmitted as) electromagnetic waves; *esp.* a radio or television set; *spec.* in RADIO, a combined tuner and amplifier (without a loudspeaker). L19. ▸**c** A detector for sound or other compressional waves. E20.

Phrases & comb.: ***official receiver***: see sense 2b above. **receiver-general** (now *Hist.* & *N. Amer.*) a chief receiver, esp. of public revenues. **receiver of wreck** a port official to whom all objects recovered from the sea or from sunken ships must be delivered for adjudication of ownership. ***wide receiver***: see WIDE *adjective*.

receivership /rɪˈsiːvəʃɪp/ *noun*. L15.
[from prec. + -SHIP.]

1 The position, function, or office of a receiver, esp. of an official receiver. L15.

2 The condition of being dealt with by a receiver. L19.

2 F. ZWEIG The sinking enterprise .. ends up in receivership.

receiving /rɪˈsiːvɪŋ/ *noun*. LME.
[from RECEIVE + -ING¹.]

The action of RECEIVE; in *pl.*, what is received.

Comb.: **receiving-order**: authorizing an official receiver to act.

receiving /rɪˈsiːvɪŋ/ *adjective*. L16.
[formed as prec. + -ING².]

That receives; *spec.* intended or serving for the reception of people or things; of or pertaining to receiving.

be on the receiving end, **be at the receiving end** *colloq.* be the (unfortunate) recipient of some action, bear the brunt of something unpleasant. **receiving barn** *US* a stable in which horses are placed before a race to prevent tampering. **receiving blanket** *N. Amer.* a soft blanket in which to wrap a baby. **receiving line** a row of people greeting guests on arrival. **receiving ship** an old ship permanently moored in a naval port for the accommodation of recruits until drafted to seagoing ships.

recency /ˈriːs(ə)nsi/ *noun*. E17.
[from RECENT: see -ENCY.]

1 The state or quality of being recent. E17.

2 PSYCHOLOGY. The fact of being recent as it increases ease of recall. Esp. in ***recency effect***. Cf. PRIMACY 1b. L19.

recense /rɪˈsɛns/ *verb trans*. L16.
[Old & mod. French *recenser* or Latin *recensere*, formed as RE- + *censere* CENSE *verb*².]

Review, revise (*spec.* a text).

recension /rɪˈsɛnʃ(ə)n/ *noun*. M17.
[Latin *recensio(n-)*, from *recensere*: see prec., -ION.]

1 A survey, a review. Now *rare*. M17.

2 The (esp. critical or careful) revision of a text; a particular form or version of a text resulting from such revision. E19. ▸**b** *transf.* A revised form of anything. M19.

■ **recensionist** *noun* a person who makes a recension E20.

recent /ˈriːs(ə)nt/ *adjective & noun*. LME.
[French *récent* or Latin *recent-*, *recens*.]

▶**A** *adjective*. **1** Done, created, or begun lately; that has just happened. LME. ▸**b** Lately come or arrived *from* a place. *poet.* E18.

2 Not yet affected by the passage of time; *spec.* not decayed or decomposed; fresh. Now *rare*. LME.

3 Belonging to a past period of time comparatively near to the present. E17. ▸**b** Of a period of time: not long past. E19.

4 GEOLOGY. (**R-**.) Of, pertaining to, or designating the geological epoch which extends to the present, the later part of the Quaternary period; = HOLOCENE *adjective*. M19.

1 E. NORTH Informed on recent advances in medical science. **3** I. MURDOCH A recent photograph, which she had taken .. last summer. J. KLEIN Ideas, some .. which have been in the air for decades, and some .. more recent. **b** M. MCCARTHY The peasants .. till quite recent times, had lit big bonfires in honour of the Corn Maiden.

▶**B** *noun*. GEOLOGY. (**R-**.) The Recent epoch. M19.

Scientific American Their entire geological history belongs to the Recent.

■ **recently** *adverb* E16. **recentness** *noun* L17.

recep. /rɪˈsɛp/ *noun*. *informal*. Pl. same. E20.
[Abbreviation.]

A reception room.

receptacle /rɪˈsɛptək(ə)l/ *noun*. LME.
[Old & mod. French *réceptacle* or Latin *receptaculum*, from *receptare*, from *recept-* pa. ppl stem of *recipere* RECEIVE.]

1 Something into which another thing may be put; a containing vessel, place, or space. LME.

2 *spec.* A place for the shelter or secure keeping of people, animals, etc. Formerly also, a room, an apartment. *arch.* LME.

3 a ANATOMY, ZOOLOGY, & BOTANY. An organ or space which receives a secretion. M16. ▸**b** BOTANY. The enlarged and modified, freq. convex, area of the stem apex on which the parts of a single flower, or the florets of a composite flower-head, are inserted. M18. ▸**c** BOTANY. Any of various types of support for the sexual organs of certain cryptograms, e.g. the stalked structure in certain liverworts, an inflated branch-tip bearing the conceptacles in some brown algae, a small outgrowth from the indusium bearing the sporangia in some ferns. M19.

1 P. NORMAN A tall, thin receptacle, full of .. canes and .. walking sticks. A. COHEN Drinking tea from glasses held in .. metal receptacles. *fig.*: A. LIVINGSTONE He saw the Unconscious .. as a receptacle for repressed material.
3a receptacle of chyle [mod. Latin *receptaculum chyli*] the dilated lower portion of the thoracic (lymphatic) duct.

■ **recepˈtacular** *adjective* (**a**) BOTANY pertaining to the receptacle of a flower (***receptacular scale***: subtending one of the florets in the capitulum of a plant of the composite family); (**b**) of the nature of a receptacle: M19.

receptible /rɪˈsɛptɪb(ə)l/ *adjective*. Now *rare*. L16.
[(French †*réceptible* from) medieval Latin *receptibilis* from *recept-*: see prec., -IBLE.]

1 Able to be received. L16.

2 Capable of receiving something. Foll. by *of*. M17.

■ **receptiˈbility** *noun* †(**a**) capacity for receiving; (**b**) the quality or state of being receptible: M17.

reception /rɪˈsɛpʃ(ə)n/ *noun*. LME.
[Old & mod. French *réception* or Latin *receptio(n-)*, from *recept-*: see RECEPTACLE, -ION.]

1 The action or fact of acquiring or getting something. LME.

2 The action of taking in, containing, or accommodating a person or thing. LME. ▸†**b** A receptacle. M–L17. ▸**c** The action of learning or understanding. M19.

3 ASTROLOGY. The fact of either of two planets being received into the other's house or other dignity. LME.

4 The action of receiving esp. a person, or the fact of being received, into a place, group, etc. M17. ▸**b** A formal or ceremonious welcome. M17. ▸**c** In full ***reception room***. A room in a house available or suitable for receiving company or visitors. E19. ▸**d** A social occasion or formal party, esp. after a wedding. M19. ▸**e** A place where guests or clients report on arrival at a hotel, office, etc. Usu. without article. E20.

5 The action of receiving, or the fact of being received, in a certain manner. Usu. with specifying word. M17. ▸**b** The receiving of broadcast signals; the quality of this. E20.

6 The action of giving credit to or accepting something. M17.

†**7** Capacity for receiving. M–L17.

4 GEO. ELIOT The .. palace .. had been prepared for the reception of another tenant. **b** ADDISON His reception is .. recorded on a Medal. **d** L. ELLMANN A reception honouring the opening of our new office. **e** W. GOLDING I went in to reception but they said you weren't staying there.
5 S. WEINTRAUB Certain .. of no cordial reception by his brother. M. MEYER The audience .. cheered; never have I heard a reception equal to that. **6** *Church Times* It is not through reception by the people of God that a definition .. acquires authority.

Comb.: **reception centre** a centre for the reception of newcomers or visitors; *spec.* a hostel providing temporary accommodation for the homeless; **reception class** the lowest class in an infant school; **reception order** an order authorizing the entry and detention of a person in a mental hospital; ***reception room***: see sense 4c above.

■ **receptionism** *noun* (THEOLOGY) the doctrine that the faithful communicant receives the true body and blood of Christ along with the (unchanged) bread and wine E20. **receptionist** *noun* (**a**) THEOLOGY a believer in receptionism; (**b**) a person employed by a hotel, office, etc., to receive and register guests, clients, etc.: M19.

receptitious /riːsɛpˈtɪʃəs/ *adjective*. M17.
[Latin *receptitius*, from *recept-*: see RECEPTACLE, -ITIOUS¹.]

ROMAN LAW (now *Hist.*). Of goods, a dowry, etc.: remaining one's own; returnable.

receptive /rɪˈsɛptɪv/ *adjective*. LME.
[French *réceptif*, *-ive* or medieval Latin *receptivus*, from *recept-*: see RECEPTACLE, -IVE.]

1 Having the quality of or capacity for receiving; *esp.* able, willing, or quick to receive impressions, new ideas, etc. Also foll. by *of*. LME.

2 MEDICINE & PSYCHOLOGY. Affecting or relating to the comprehension of speech or writing, esp. as impaired by a brain disorder. E20.

For other words beginning with *re-* see the entry for **re-**

📖 **1** K. CLARK Anyone who looks at them in a receptive frame of mind must . . be touched by their exquisite poetry. *Financial Times* The Belgian Post Office was . . receptive to MCI's ideas. V. GORNICK Imprinted . . like dye on the most receptive of materials.

■ **receptively** *adverb* L19. **receptiveness** *noun* L17. **recep'tivity** *noun* E17.

receptor /rɪˈsɛptə/ *noun*. LME.
[Old French *receptour*, *-eur* or Latin *receptor*, from *recept-*: see RECEPTACLE, -OR.]
†**1** = RECEIVER 3. LME–M17.
†**2** The receiver of a telephone. Only in L19.
3 a IMMUNOLOGY. The region of an antibody molecule which shows specific recognition of an antigen. E20. ▸**b** BIOLOGY. Any organ or structure which on receiving stimuli of a certain kind from its environment generates nerve impulses that convey information about that aspect of the environment. E20. ▸**c** PHYSIOLOGY. A region in a tissue or molecule in a cell (esp. in a membrane) which specifically recognizes and responds to a neurotransmitter, hormone, or other substance. E20.

†**receptory** *noun*. LME–E18.
[Late Latin *receptorium*, from Latin *recepta*: see RECEIPT *noun*, -ORY[1].]
A receptacle.

recercelée /rɪˈsəːs(ə)leɪ/ *adjective*. Also **-lé**, **-ly** /-li/. M18.
[Old French *recercelé(e)* circular, curled, from *re-* RE- + *cercel* circle.]
HERALDRY. Of a cross: having the ends of the limbs curling into divergent spirals. Usu. *postpositive*.

recess /rɪˈsɛs, ˈriːsɛs/ *noun & verb*. E16.
[Latin *recessus*, from *recess-* pa. ppl stem of *recedere* RECEDE *verb*[1].]
▸ **A** *noun*. **1** †**a** An agreement. Only in E16. ▸**b** *Hist.* A resolution or decree of the Diet of the Holy Roman Empire or the Hanseatic League. E18.
†**2** The action of withdrawing or departing from or to a place. M16–L17. ▸**b** *fig.* A departure *from* some state or standard. Only in 17. ▸**c** The action of withdrawing from public life; privacy, seclusion; a period of retirement. M17–M18.
3 The action, esp. by water, of receding or going back or away from a certain point. *arch.* E17.
4 A period of cessation from work or business, esp. of a legislative body or (chiefly *N. Amer.*) of a court of law or during a school day. E17. ▸†**b** Delay; respite. *rare*. E17–E18. ▸†**c** Relaxation, leisure. Only in 18.
5 A remote, secluded, or secret place; in *pl.*, the remotest or innermost parts of a thing (*lit.* & *fig.*). E17.
6 a PHYSICAL GEOGRAPHY. A receding part or indentation in a mountain range, coast, etc. L17. ▸**b** A space set back in a wall; a niche, an alcove. L18. ▸**c** Any small depression or indentation. M19. ▸**d** The room for slopping out in a prison. Usu. in *pl. Criminals' slang*. M20.

📖 **4** J. B. MORTON The Commons . . reassembled after the Christmas recess. D. CUSACK There'll be a Staff Meeting at Recess. N. BARBER I will grant a ten-minute recess. **5** L. STRACHEY In the recesses of the palace her . . figure was . . omnipresent. A. STORR Traits . . have their place within the recesses of our . . psyches. **6b** P. D. JAMES A . . fireplace, the two recesses fitted with . . bookshelves.

Comb.: **recess-printed** *adjective* (of a stamp) printed by the recess printing method; **recess printing** a method of printing stamps so that the design is slightly raised from the surface.
▸ **B** *verb*. **1** *verb trans.* Place in a recess; set back. E19.
2 *verb trans.* Make a recess or recesses in. L19.
3 Chiefly *N. Amer.* ▸**a** *verb intrans.* Take a recess; adjourn. L19. ▸**b** *verb trans.* Order (a meeting etc.) into recess; adjourn. M20.

recessed /rɪˈsɛst/ *adjective*. E19.
[In sense 1 from RECESS *verb*; in sense 2 from RECESS(ION: see -ED[1].]
1 Set in a recess. E19.
2 Characterized by or suffering economic recession. M20.

recession /rɪˈsɛʃ(ə)n/ *noun*. M17.
[Latin *recessio(n-)* from *recess-*: see RECESS, -ION.]
1 a The action or an act of receding from a place or point; withdrawal; *rare* a setting or going back in time. M17. ▸**b** The action or an act of departing from some state or standard. M17. ▸**c** The departure *of* a quality or property from that in which it exists. M17. ▸**d** PHONETICS. The transference of accentuation towards or on to the first syllable of a word. L19.
2 A receding part of a surface or object. M18.
3 ECONOMICS. A temporary decline in economic activity or prosperity. E20.
■ **recessionary** *adjective* of, pertaining to, or characterized by economic recession M20.

recessional /rɪˈsɛʃ(ə)n(ə)l/ *adjective & noun*. M19.
[from prec. + -AL[1].]
▸ **A** *adjective*. **1** ECCLESIASTICAL. Pertaining to the withdrawal of the clergy and choir to the vestry at the close of a service; *spec.* designating a hymn sung during this. M19.
2 Pertaining to a recess of a legislative body etc. L19.
3 GEOLOGY. Designating a form of moraine resembling an end moraine deposited during a temporary halt or minor readvance of a receding glacier or ice sheet. E20.
▸ **B** *noun*. A recessional hymn. M19.

recessive /rɪˈsɛsɪv/ *adjective & noun*. L17.
[from RECESS *noun* + -IVE, after *exceed*, *excess*, *excessive*.]
▸ **A** *adjective*. **1** Tending to recede. L17. ▸**b** PHONETICS. Of an accent: falling near or on the first syllable of a word. L19. ▸**c** PHILOLOGY. Tending to fall into disuse. M20.
2 BIOLOGY. Of a gene, allele, or hereditary trait: perceptibly expressed only in homozygotes, being masked in heterozygotes by a dominant allele or trait. Also, (of an organism) expressing a recessive trait. (Foll. by *to* the dominant allele or trait.) E20.
▸ **B** *noun*. BIOLOGY.
1 An individual in which a particular recessive allele is expressed. E20.
2 A recessive allele or character. E20.
■ **recessively** *adverb* L19. **recessiveness** *noun* E20.

Rechabite /ˈrɛkəbʌɪt/ *noun*. LME.
[ecclesiastical Latin *Rechabita* (pl.) translating Hebrew *rēkābī*, from *rēkāb* Rechab: see -ITE[1].]
1 In biblical use, a member of an Israelite family descended from Rechab, which refused to drink wine, live in houses, or cultivate fields and vineyards (*Jer.* 35). LME.
2 A person who abstains from alcoholic drink. L17.

rechange /riːˈtʃeɪndʒ/ *noun & verb*. L15.
[from RE- + CHANGE *noun*, *verb*.]
▸ **A** *noun*. †**1** The re-exchange on a bill. L15–L17.
†**2** The action of re-exchanging money or goods. L15–E17.
3 The action of changing or altering again. M16.
▸ **B** *verb*. †**1** *verb trans.* Re-exchange (goods or money). M16–E17.
2 *verb trans.* & *intrans.* Change or alter again. L16.

recharge /*as verb* riːˈtʃɑːdʒ, *as noun* ˈriːtʃɑːdʒ/ *verb & noun*. LME.
[from RE- + CHARGE *verb*, *noun*, partly after Old & mod. French *recharger*, *recharge*.]
▸ **A** *verb*. **1** *verb trans.* †**a** Reload (a vessel). LME–E17. ▸**b** Put a fresh charge in; refill; *spec.* (HYDROLOGY) replenish the water content of (an aquifer). M19.
2 *verb trans.* †**a** Charge or accuse in return. L16–L17. ▸**b** Lay a new charge against. L19.
3 *verb intrans.* Charge in battle again or in return. L16.
4 *verb trans.* Impose again as a charge. *rare*. E17.
5 a *verb trans.* Restore an electric charge to (a battery or a piece of equipment powered by batteries). L19. ▸**b** *verb intrans.* Of a battery or piece of equipment: become recharged. L20.
5a *recharge one's batteries*: see BATTERY 8.
▸ **B** *noun*. **1** An act or the action of recharging; *spec.* (HYDROLOGY) the replenishment of an aquifer by the absorption of water into the zone of saturation (freq. induced artificially by sinking wells into the aquifer); the water so added. E17.
2 A renewed or return charge in battle. E17.
Comb.: **recharge area** an area of ground surface through which is absorbed the water that will percolate into a zone of saturation in one or more aquifers; **recharge basin** an artificially constructed basin used to collect water for artificial recharge of an aquifer; **recharge well**: used to inject water into an aquifer by artificial recharge.
■ **rechargeable** *adjective* L19. **recharger** *noun* a device for recharging batteries or battery-powered equipment M20.

rechase /riːˈtʃeɪs/ *verb trans. obsolete* exc. *dial.* LME.
[Old & mod. French *rechasser*, from *re-* RE- + *chasser* CHASE *verb*[1].]
1 †**a** HUNTING. Chase (a deer) back into a forest. LME–E18. ▸**b** Drive back (cattle or sheep) from one pasture to another. E17.
†**2** Drive back (an assailant); chase in turn. LME–E17.

réchaud /reʃo/ *noun*. Pl. pronounced same. E20.
[French, from *réchauffer*: see RÉCHAUFFÉ.]
A dish in which food is warmed or kept warm.

rechauffe /riːˈʃəʊf/ *verb trans. rare*. L15.
[French *réchauffer*: see next.]
Warm up (again); *fig.* rehash.

réchauffé /reʃofe, reɪˈʃəʊfeɪ/ *noun & adjective*. E19.
[French, pa. pple of *réchauffer* warm up again, from *re-* RE- + *échauffer* warm (up), formed as CHAFE *verb*.]
▸ **A** *noun*. A warmed-up dish; *fig.* a rehash. E19.
▸ **B** *adjective*. (Of food) reheated; *fig.* rehashed. E20.

recheat /rɪˈtʃiːt/ *noun. arch.* LME.
[Prob. from Anglo-Norman: cf. Old French *racheter*, *rachat*- reassemble, rally.]
A series of notes sounded on a horn to call together hounds to begin or continue the hunt.

recheck /*as verb* riːˈtʃɛk, *as noun* ˈriːtʃɛk/ *verb & noun*. E20.
[from RE- + CHECK *verb*[1], *noun*[1].]
▸ **A** *verb trans.* & *intrans.* Check again. E20.
▸ **B** *noun*. A second or further check or investigation. E20.

recherché /rəˈʃɛːʃeɪ/ *adjective*. L17.
[French, pa. pple of *rechercher*, from *re-* RE- + *chercher* seek.]
Carefully sought out; rare, exotic; far-fetched, obscure.

recherche du temps perdu /rəʃɛrʃ dy tɑ̃ pɛrdy/ *noun phr.* M20.
[French *à la recherche du temps perdu* lit. 'in search of the lost time', title of novel by Marcel Proust (1871–1922).]
A narration or evocation of one's early life.

Rechtsstaat /ˈrɛçtsʃtaːt/ *noun*. M20.
[German, from *Recht* right + *-s* genit. suffix + *Staat* State.]
A country in which the rule of law prevails.

recibiendo /reθiˈvjendo/ *adverb*. E20.
[Spanish, lit. 'receiving', from *recibir* receive.]
With ref. to a bullfighter: when in a stationary position so that the bull charges on to the sword.

recidivate /rɪˈsɪdɪveɪt/ *verb intrans.* Pa. pple (earlier) †**-ate**, **-ated**. E16.
[medieval Latin *recidivat-* pa. ppl stem of *recidivare*: see RECIDIVIST, -ATE[3].]
Fall back, relapse. Now *spec.* relapse into crime.
¶ Not recorded between L17 and 20.

†**recidivation** *noun*. LME.
[Old & mod. French *récidivation* or medieval Latin *recidivatio(n-)*, formed as prec.: see -ATION.]
1 The action of relapsing into sin, error, crime, etc. LME–L17.
2 A relapse in an illness or disease. E16–E18.

recidive /ˈrɛsɪdɪv/ *adjective & noun. rare*. M16.
[Latin *recidivus*: see next, -IVE.]
▸†**A** *adjective*. Falling back, relapsing. M16–M17.
▸ **B** *noun*. †**1** = RECIDIVATION 1. Only in E17.
2 = RECIDIVIST *noun*. M19.

recidivist /rɪˈsɪdɪvɪst/ *noun & adjective*. L19.
[French *récidiviste*, from *récidiver* from medieval Latin *recidivare*, from Latin *recidivus*, from *recidere* fall back, formed as RE- + *cadere* fall: see -IST.]
▸ **A** *noun*. A person who relapses; *esp.* a person who habitually relapses into crime. L19.
▸ **B** *adjective*. Of or pertaining to a recidivist; tending to relapse habitually into crime. E20.
■ **recidi'vistic** *adjective* = RECIDIVIST *adjective* E20. **recidivism** *noun* a tendency to relapse habitually into crime L19.

recidivous /rɪˈsɪdɪvəs/ *adjective. rare*. M17.
[from Latin *recidivus* (see prec.) + -OUS.]
Liable to fall back or relapse.

recipe /ˈrɛsɪpi/ *verb & noun*. LME.
[Latin, imper. sing. of *recipere* take, RECEIVE, used at the beginning of medical prescriptions.]
▸ **A** *verb trans.* (*imper.*) Take. Long *obsolete* exc. MEDICINE, used in speech (now *rare*) or abbreviated ***R***, ℞ at the beginning of a prescription or formula for a remedy. LME.
▸ **B** *noun*. **1** MEDICINE. A formula for the composition or use of a remedy, a prescription; a remedy prescribed. *arch.* L16.
2 *transf.* A means for attaining or effecting some end. M17.
3 A statement of the ingredients and procedure required for making something, esp. a dish in cookery. E18.

📖 **2** D. CARNEGIE To make people shun you . . here is the recipe: Never listen to anyone for long. **3** *attrib.*: P. LIVELY She had bought a recipe book and was attempting a . . casserole. **recipe dish** a dish of a type which would ordinarily require lengthy preparation, sold ready-made and requiring only to be heated before consumption.

¶ Noun senses B.1, 3 correspond to earlier RECEIPT *noun* 1.

recipiangle /rɪˈsɪpɪaŋɡ(ə)l/ *noun. obsolete* exc. *Hist.* E18.
[French *récipiangle*, from Latin *recipere*: see RECEIVE, ANGLE *noun*[3].]
An instrument formerly used for measuring and laying off angles.

recipiendary /rɪˈsɪpɪənd(ə)ri/ *noun. rare*. M17.
[from Latin *recipiend-* gerundial stem of *recipere* RECEIVE + -ARY[1].]
A person about to be received into a society.

recipient /rɪˈsɪpɪənt/ *noun & adjective*. M16.
[French *récipient* from Italian *recipiente* or Latin *recipient-* pres. ppl stem of *recipere* RECEIVE: see -ENT.]
▸ **A** *noun*. **1** A person who or thing which receives something. M16.
2 LINGUISTICS. The indirect object of a verb. M20.

📖 **1** H. KISSINGER Abrams had . . been the recipient of . . Presidential largesse. M. FORSTER He was a safe recipient of her affections. ***universal recipient***: see UNIVERSAL *adjective*.

▸ **B** *adjective*. That receives or is capable of receiving; receptive. E17.
■ **recipience** *noun* (*rare*) L19. **recipiency** *noun* L18.

reciprocal /rɪˈsɪprək(ə)l/ *adjective & noun*. L16.
[from Latin *reciprocus* moving backwards and forwards, ult. from *re-* back, *pro-* forward: see -AL[1].]
▸ **A** *adjective*. **1 a** Of the nature of a return made for something; given, felt, shown, etc., in return. L16. ▸**b** Existing on both sides; mutual; (of two or more things) done, made, etc., in exchange. L16. ▸**c** GRAMMAR. Of a pronoun or

verb: orig., reflexive; later, expressing mutual action or relationship. E17.

2 Inversely correspondent; correlative, complementary. L16. ▸**b** *MATH.* Based on an inverse relationship. E19. ▸**c** *PHYSICS.* Designating a unit defined as the reciprocal of a standard unit, as ***reciprocal centimetre***, ***reciprocal ohm***, ***reciprocal second***, etc. M20.

†**3** Having or of the nature of an alternate backward and forward motion; alternate. E17–M18.

†**4** = CONVERTIBLE *adjective* 1. E17–M18.

> **1a** P. NORMAN Each time . . the minute hand jerked . . he felt his heart give a tiny reciprocal jog. A. S. BYATT He had launched . . into passion and . . aroused a reciprocal passion. **b** SHAKES. *Lear* Let our reciprocal vows be rememb'red. A. STORR The partners are on equal terms, . . giving and taking are reciprocal. E. PAWEL The contempt, though . . reciprocal, was tempered by . . interdependence. **2** J. LOCKE Relative Terms that have . . a reciprocal Intimation, as . . Cause and Effect.

Special collocations: **reciprocal assimilation** *PHONETICS*: in which either of two adjacent sounds influences the other. **reciprocal course**: opposite in direction to a related one, as the one desired or the one followed immediately before. **reciprocal cross** *GENETICS* (either of) a pair of crosses in which the male parent in each is of the same kind as the female in the other. **reciprocal inhibition**, **reciprocal innervation** *PHYSIOLOGY* simultaneous stimulation of nerves supplying agonist and antagonistic muscles or groups of muscles.

▸**B** *noun.* **1** A thing corresponding in some way to another; an equivalent, a counterpart. L16.

2 *GRAMMAR.* †**a** A reflexive verb. M17–M18. ▸**b** A pronoun, verb, or other element expressing mutual action or relationship. M20.

3 *MATH.* A function or expression so related to another that their product is unity; an inverse. L18.

■ **recipro'cality** *noun* = RECIPROCITY M18. **reciprocally** *adverb* L16. †**reciprocalness** *noun* (*rare*) M17–M19.

reciprocate /rɪˈsɪprəkət/ *adjective. rare.* L16.
[Latin *reciprocatus* pa. pple, formed as next: see -ATE².]

1 = RECIPROCAL *adjective* 1b. L16.

†**2** Complementary. E–M17.

reciprocate /rɪˈsɪprəkeɪt/ *verb.* L16.
[Latin *reciprocat-* pa. ppl stem of *reciprocare*, from *reciprocus*: see RECIPROCAL, -ATE³.]

1 *verb intrans. & trans. LOGIC.* Be or make correspondent or equivalent. Also foll. by *with*. Now *rare* or *obsolete*. L16.

2 *verb trans.* **a** Give and receive in return or mutually; exchange. L16. ▸**b** Return or requite (a feeling etc.). E19.

3 *verb intrans.* **a** Make a return or exchange *with* (another or others). Now *rare* or *obsolete*. L16. ▸**b** *spec.* Make a return or exchange of good wishes; return love or liking. L18.

4 †**a** *verb intrans.* Go back. L16–M17. ▸**b** *verb trans. & intrans.* (Cause to) move backwards and forwards. *obsolete* exc. *MECHANICS*. M17.

5 *MATH.* **a** *verb trans.* Find the reciprocal of (a quantity or a curve). M19. ▸**b** *verb intrans.* Pass *into* by reciprocation. M19.

> **2a** M. COREN Both knew . . their respective emotions were reciprocated. **b** A. CROSS Two children . . for whom she had a great affection, greatly reciprocated. G. SAYER There would be . . invitations to dine . . that he was bound to reciprocate.

■ **reciprocator** *noun* (*a*) a person who or thing which reciprocates; (*b*) *spec.* a reciprocating engine: M19. **reciprocatory** *adjective* = RECIPROCATING 2 M19.

reciprocating /rɪˈsɪprəkeɪtɪŋ/ *adjective.* M17.
[from prec. + -ING².]

†**1** Back-flowing. *rare*. Only in M17.

2 Moving backwards and forwards; characterized by alternation in movement; *spec.* (of a machine) having a part, esp. a piston, characterized by such movement. L17.

3 *gen.* That reciprocates. E19.

2 reciprocating engine: using a piston or pistons moving up and down in cylinders.

reciprocation /ˌrɪsɪprəˈkeɪʃ(ə)n/ *noun.* M16.
[French *réciprocation* or Latin *reciprocatio(n-)*, formed as RECIPROCATE *verb*: see -ATION.]

†**1** *GRAMMAR.* Reflexive action; a reflexive expression. Cf. RECIPROCAL *adjective* 1c. M16–M17.

2 The action of doing something in return; *esp.* a mutual return or exchange of feelings etc. M16.

3 †**a** *LOGIC.* The conversion of terms or propositions; the harmonious relation involved by this. L16–L17. ▸**b** The state of being in a reciprocal or harmonious relation; correspondence. E17. ▸**c** *MATH.* The process of converting a proposition, quantity, or curve, to its reciprocal. M19.

4 †**a** Alternation; alternate change. E17–L18. ▸**b** Motion backwards and forwards; *rare* alternate action. *obsolete* exc. *MECHANICS*. M17.

reciprocity /rɛsɪˈprɒsɪti/ *noun.* M18.
[French *réciprocité*, from Old & mod. French *réciproque* from Latin *reciprocus*: see RECIPROCAL, -ITY.]

1 The state or condition of being reciprocal; mutual action. M18.

2 *spec.* A mutual exchange of advantages or privileges as a basis for commercial relations between two countries. L18.

Comb.: **reciprocity failure** *PHOTOGRAPHY* departure from the reciprocity law, in which greater than the predicted exposure is required at very low and very high light intensities, as with all real emulsions; **reciprocity law** *PHOTOGRAPHY* the principle that the degree of blackening of an ideal emulsion is constant for a given incident energy, i.e. for a given product of light intensity and exposure time; **reciprocity theorem** *PHYSICS*: stating that the response of a given physical system is unchanged if the locations of a constant excitation and of the measured response are interchanged, or *esp.* in *NUCLEAR PHYSICS*, that time-reversal leaves the transition rate for a nuclear reaction unchanged.

■ ˌ**reciproci'tarian** *noun* [after *Trinitarian* etc.] a person who advocates reciprocity in trade L19.

recirculate /riːˈsəːkjʊleɪt/ *verb.* E20.
[from RE- + CIRCULATE.]

1 *verb trans.* Cause to circulate again; *spec.* make available for reuse. E20.

2 *verb intrans.* Circulate again. M20.

Phrases: **recirculating ball** a ball-bearing running in a closed ball race; usu. *attrib.* with ref. to a form of automotive steering mechanism in which a half-nut containing an eccentrically mounted ball race can be made to move along a helical cam by rotation of the cam.

■ **recirculatory** /riːˈsəːkjʊlət(ə)ri, ˌriːsəːkjʊˈleɪt(ə)ri/ *adjective* recirculating M20.

recirculation /riːˌsəːkjʊˈleɪʃ(ə)n/ *noun.* E17.
[from RE- + CIRCULATION.]

A new or fresh circulation; the action or an act of recirculating.

recision /rɪˈsɪʒ(ə)n/ *noun.* Now *rare.* E17.
[Latin *recisio(n-)*, from *recis-* pa. ppl stem of *recidere* cut back: see -ION.]

The action or an act of cutting back or pruning something.

récit /resi/ *noun.* Pl. pronounced same. L19.
[French.]

1 *MUSIC.* A passage or composition for a solo voice or instrument. Also, a division of the classical French organ. L19.

2 The narrative of a book as opp. to the dialogue; a book or passage consisting largely of this. M20.

recital /rɪˈsʌɪt(ə)l/ *noun.* E16.
[from RECITE *verb* + -AL¹.]

1 *LAW.* The statement in a document of a fact or facts pertinent to the case; the part of a document containing such a statement. E16.

2 An account or detailed description of something; a relating of a series of connected facts or events; an enumeration, a catalogue. Freq. foll. by *of*. M16.

3 a The action or an act of reciting a text etc., esp. before an audience. E17. ▸**b** A performance of a piece or esp. a programme of music by a solo instrumentalist or singer, or by a small group. E19.

> **2** J. B. PRIESTLEY Encouraged by the reception of his previous recital, he . . told the story of the . . sportsman. J. O'HARA Mary's morning recital of her woes. **3a** *Saturday Review* The recital of the poems revealed . . new talent. **b** J. AGATE Rachmaninoff recital at the Queen's Hall. *Early Music News* Gillian Weir . . will give a joint harpsichord and organ recital. **opera recital** a concert performance of an opera.

■ **recitalist** *noun* a person who gives musical recitals L19.

recitation /rɛsɪˈteɪʃ(ə)n/ *noun.* L15.
[Old & mod. French *récitation* or Latin *recitatio(n-)*, from *recitat-* pa. ppl stem of *recitare* RECITE *verb*: see -ATION.]

The action or an act of reciting; *esp.* the action or an act of repeating a text from memory or of reading a text aloud before an audience.

> A. KENNY The daily recitation of the breviary. G. BODDY Kathleen also entertained the girls with songs and recitations at concerts.

recitative /rɛsɪtəˈtiːv/ *noun, adjective, & verb.* M17.
[formed as next: see -IVE.]

MUSIC. ▸**A** *noun.* **1** A style of musical declamation, between singing and ordinary speech, used esp. in the dialogue and narrative parts of an opera or oratorio. M17. ▸**b** A passage in a musical score or libretto (intended to be) delivered in this style. M18.

2 A performance in recitative. L19.

▸**B** *adjective.* Of or pertaining to recitative; delivered in recitative. M17.

▸**C** *verb trans. & intrans.* Deliver (a passage) in recitative. E19.

recitativo /retʃitaˈtiːvo, ˌrɛsɪtəˈtiːvəʊ/ *noun.* Pl. **-vi** /-vi/, **-vos** /-vəʊz/. M17.
[Italian, from Latin *recitat-* pa. ppl stem of *recitare* RECITE + -ivo -IVE.]

MUSIC. = RECITATIVE *noun* 1.

recitativo accompagnato /akkompaˈɲaːto/, pl. **-ti** /-ti/, [= accompanied] recitative accompanied by an orchestra. ***recitativo secco*** /ˈsekko/, pl. **-cchi** /-kki/, [lit. 'dry'] recitative usu. accompanied only by continuo instruments. ***recitativo stromentato*** /stromenˈtaːto/, pl. **-ti** /-ti/, [= instrumented] = *recitativo accompagnato* above.

recite /rɪˈsʌɪt/ *verb & noun.* LME.
[Old & mod. French *réciter* or Latin *recitare* read out, formed as RE- + *citare* CITE.]

▸**A** *verb.* **1** *verb trans. LAW.* State (a fact, *that*) in a document pertinent to the case. LME.

†**2** *verb trans. & intrans.* Give an account or detailed description (of); relate, recount (a story). L15–E18.

3 *verb trans. & intrans.* Repeat from memory or read aloud (a text etc.), esp. before an audience; *spec.* repeat or be examined on (a school lesson). L15.

†**4** *verb trans.* Compose; write *down*. *rare*. E16–M17.

5 *verb trans.* Mention in order; give a list or catalogue of; enumerate. M16.

†**6** *verb trans.* = CITE *verb* 3. M16–E19.

> **3** H. KELLER I . . recited passages from my favourite poets. P. MORTIMER You sound like someone reciting a kind of creed. **reciting note** *MUSIC* the note on which most of a Gregorian or Anglican chant is sung. **5** J. G. FARRELL Edward began to recite the list of things for which . . one should give thanks. T. KENEALLY Tabidgi recited all the . . places they had passed.

▸**B** *noun.* A recital, a recitation. *rare.* L17.

■ †**recitement** *noun* (a) recitation, (a) recital M17–M18. **reciter** *noun* (*a*) a person who recites; (*b*) a book containing passages for recitation: L16.

reck /rɛk/ *verb & noun.* Long *arch. & poet.* OE.
[Partly repr. Old English unrecorded inf. (pa. t. *rōhte*) = Old Saxon *rōkjan*, Old High German *ruohhen*, Old Norse *rœkja*, from Germanic; partly repr. Old English *reċċan*, of unkn. origin. Cf. RECKLESS.]

▸**A** *verb.* **1** *verb intrans.* (foll. by *by*, *for*, *of*) & *trans.* Take heed of or have regard for (a person or consequence) through desire, self-interest, caution, etc. OE. ▸**b** *verb intrans.* Know or be aware *of*. E19.

2 *verb intrans.* **a** Care or be disposed *to do*. OE. ▸**b** Be troubled, distressed, or unwilling *to do*. OE.

3 *verb intrans.* & †*refl.* Care, concern oneself. Also foll. by interrog. clause. OE.

4 *verb intrans. & trans.* Be of concern or interest (to); matter (to). Usu. *impers.* in ***(it) recks*** etc. ME.

5 *verb trans.* Reckon, consider. Now *Scot.* L16.

> **1** R. SUTCLIFF Holy war . . is . . the most deadly kind, for it recks nothing of consequences. **2a** SHAKES. *A.Y.L.* My master is . . churlish . . And little recks to find the way to heaven. **3** SIR W. SCOTT Whether false the news, or true . . I reck as light as you. **4** MILTON What recks it them? What need they? R. D. BLACKMORE Little it recked us . . that they were our founder's citizens.

▸**B** *noun.* Care, heed, regard. L15.

¶ Rare between 17 and 19. Chiefly in neg. and interrog. contexts.

Reckitt's blue /rɛkɪts ˈbluː/ *noun phr.* L19.
[from Isaac *Reckitt* and Sons, manufacturer + BLUE *noun* 1b.]

(Proprietary name for) a laundry whitener; the colour of this substance, a clear cobalt blue.

reckless /ˈrɛklɪs/ *adjective & adverb.* Also †**retch-**, (*arch.*) **wretch-** /ˈrɛtʃ-/.
[Old English *reċċelēas*, *reċe-* (earlier *reċċilēas*) corresp. to Middle Low German *rōkelōs*, Middle & mod. Dutch *roekeloos*, Old High German *ruahhalōs* (German *ruchlos*), from Germanic bases of RECK *verb*, -LESS.]

▸**A** *adjective.* **1** Of a person: heedless of the consequences of one's actions or of danger; incautious, rash. Also foll. by *of*. OE. ▸†**b** Negligent in one's duties etc., inattentive. OE–L17. ▸†**c** Inconsiderate of oneself or another. *rare*. LME–E18.

2 Of an action, behaviour, etc.: characterized by heedlessness or rashness, incautious; careless, esp. wilfully careless. ME.

> **1** G. SAYER He was reckless and . . could not look after money. M. KEANE Suddenly reckless she chose . . a vintage they could not afford. **2** DAY LEWIS I admired him . . for his . . reckless driving. A. BRINK Be careful . . Don't do anything reckless.

▸**B** *adverb.* Recklessly. *poet.* Now *rare*. LME.

¶ Form with *-ck-* orig. northern.

■ **recklessly** *adverb* (*a*) in a reckless manner; (*b*) *Scot.* through carelessness, accidentally: OE. **recklessness** *noun* (*a*) the quality of being reckless; (*b*) neglect or disregard *of* something: OE.

reckling /ˈrɛklɪŋ/ *noun.* Now *dial.* Also **wr-**. E17.
[Perh. of Scandinavian origin: cf. Old Norse *reklingr* outcast.]

The runt of a litter; the youngest or smallest child in a family.

Recklinghausen's disease /ˈrɛklɪŋhaʊz(ə)nz dɪˌziːz/ *noun phr.* L19.
[formed as VON RECKLINGHAUSEN'S DISEASE.]

MEDICINE. = VON RECKLINGHAUSEN'S DISEASE 1.

reckon *noun* var. of RACKAN.

reckon /ˈrɛk(ə)n/ *verb.*
[Old English *gerecenian* = Old Frisian *rekenia*, *reknia*, Middle & mod. Low German, Middle & mod. Dutch *rekenen*, Old High German *rehhanōn* (German *rechnen*), from West Germanic.]

†**1 a** *verb trans.* Recount, relate, tell. OE–L16. ▸**b** *verb intrans.* Answer for or give an account of or *of* items

For other words beginning with *re-* see the entry for **re-**

received, one's conduct, actions, etc.; *spec.* account for one's life to God after death. ME–L16. ▸**c** *verb trans.* Repeat aloud, recite. *rare.* LME–E17.

2 †**a** *verb trans.* & (*rare*) *intrans.* Mention (a number of things) in order; enumerate or list (items). Also foll. by *up*. ME–M16. ▸**b** *verb intrans.* Go over or settle an account (*lit.* & *fig.*). Freq. foll. by *with* a person. ME.

3 *verb trans.* & *intrans.* Count, esp. so as to ascertain the number or amount; determine (a sum etc.) by counting or (now esp.) calculation. Also foll. by *out*, *up*. ME. ▸**b** *verb trans.* Count or calculate *from* a particular point. M16.

4 *verb trans.* **a** Regard in a certain light; consider *as* or *to be*, take *for*. ME. ▸**b** Regard as doing something. Foll. by *to do*. Usu. in *pass.* E16.

5 *verb trans.* **a** Include *in* a calculation or account; *transf.* include *in* or *among* a particular group or class. ME. ▸†**b** In *pass.* Be assigned or attributed *to*. E16–E18. ▸**c** Accept or state as a total. M16.

6 *verb trans.* †**a** Decide the nature or value of. *rare.* LME–M16. ▸**b** Estimate or judge by calculation. Also foll. by *up*. M16. ▸†**c** Rate or value (*at*). M16–M17.

7 †**a** *verb trans.* Take account of, take into consideration. LME–L17. ▸**b** *verb intrans.* Foll. by *of*, *to*: think (much etc.) of, think highly of. *dial.* L16. ▸**c** *verb intrans.* Be worthy of consideration; count. L19. ▸**d** *verb trans.* Rate highly, value, esteem. *colloq.* M20.

8 a *verb trans.* Conclude after calculation, be of the considered opinion *that*; *loosely* think, suppose, believe. Foll. by clause as obj. Now *colloq.* E16. ▸**b** *verb intrans.* Calculate or plan *on*; expect *to do*. Now *colloq.* M16.

9 *verb intrans.* Count or depend *on* or *upon*. M17.

> 🕮 **3** J. MASEFIELD The merchants reckon up their gold. M. SEYMOUR A woman who reckoned every halfpenny spent. ***reckon without one's host***: see HOST *noun*² 2. **5a** R. H. MOTTRAM It . . was not reckoned among the subversive sciences. E. BOWEN With the £13,000 accepted . . for . . furnishings, 'preliminary expenses' had to be reckoned in. **6b** P. ACKROYD I did not reckon . . the cost, to him and to others. **7a to be reckoned with** of considerable importance; not to be ignored. **c** T. BARLING Nobody reckons Arch more than me. **8a** T. HARDY I may as well do that . . I reckon. E. WELTY I reckon I might as well tell you. J. WINTERSON 'Liverpool against the Rovers' . . 'What do you reckon?' **b** C. P. SNOW Something happened which none of us had reckoned on. H. CARPENTER They . . would reckon to do perhaps twenty miles a day.

■ **reckonable** *adjective* M17. **reckoner** *noun* (*a*) a person who or thing which reckons; (*b*) = ***ready reckoner*** s.v. READY *adjective*: E19.

reckoning /ˈrɛk(ə)nɪŋ/ *noun.* ME.
[from prec. + -ING¹.]
1 a The action of RECKON *verb*; an instance of this; *esp.* an enumeration, an account. ME. ▸**b** A specified manner of calculation. LME.
2 *spec.* **a** A computation or statement of a sum owed; an account of charges; a bill. LME. ▸**b** The calculated period of pregnancy. Now *rare* or *obsolete.* M17. ▸**c** NAUTICAL. The estimate of a ship's position calculated from the log etc. M17.
†**3** A mode of regarding a matter. LME–M17.
4 The action or an act of calculating a chance or contingency; (an) anticipation, (an) expectation. M16.
†**5** Estimation, consideration, distinction. L16–M17.

> 🕮 **1a** DEFOE An exact Reckoning of Days. *Daedalus* In the final reckoning, truth is restored. **b** LD MACAULAY The sixteenth of October, according to the English reckoning. **2a** E. MANNIN It was impossible to enjoy drinking . . with the reckoning . . hanging over you. **3** SHAKES. *Tam. Shr.* By this reck'ning he is more shrew than she. **4** *Belfast Telegraph* The reckoning is that North Sea oil will have worked wonders on the balance of payments.

Phrases: **day of reckoning** (*a*) CHRISTIAN THEOLOGY the Day of Judgement; (*b*) *transf.* the time when past actions must be atoned for or avenged. ***dead reckoning***: see DEAD *adjective*. ***Dutch reckoning***: see DUTCH *adjective*. **in the reckoning**, **out of the reckoning** in or out of contention for a place in a contest etc.

reclaim /rɪˈkleɪm/ *verb & noun.* ME.
[Old French *reclaim*- tonic stem of Old & mod. French *réclamer* from Latin *reclamare* cry out, exclaim.]
▶ **A** *verb.* †**1 a** *verb trans.* Call back (*spec.* a hawk), recall. ME–E18. ▸**b** *verb trans.* Restrain, check; *spec.* keep the growth of (trees) within bounds. E16–E18. ▸**c** *verb trans.* & *intrans.* Withdraw or revoke (a statement); recant. *rare.* L16–L17.
2 *verb trans.* Win (a person) away from vice, error, etc., or back to a previous or proper condition; reform. Freq. foll. by *from*, *to*. LME. ▸†**b** *verb intrans.* & *refl.* Undergo reformation. L16–M18. ▸**c** *verb trans.* Remedy or correct (a fault etc.). *rare.* E17. ▸**d** *verb trans.* Adapt (a people) to a new culture; civilize. Now *rare* or *obsolete.* M18.
3 *verb trans.* Freq. as ***reclaimed*** *ppl adjective.* ▸**a** Bring to obedience, tame, subdue (an animal, esp. a hawk). Now *rare.* LME. ▸**b** Bring (wasteland) under cultivation, esp. land formerly covered by water. M18. ▸**c** Make reusable; *spec.* recover (rubber) for reuse by removing impurities and restoring plasticity. L19.
4 *verb trans.* †**a** Make a claim against (a person); sue. *rare.* Only in LME. ▸**b** Claim the restoration of (one's property etc.); lay claim to again, retrieve; *spec.* claim back (a tax payment). M16.
5 *verb intrans.* **a** Exclaim or protest (*against*, *that*). Now *rare* or *obsolete.* LME. ▸**b** SCOTS LAW. Appeal. Now *spec.* appeal from the Outer to the Inner House of the Court of Session. L16. ▸†**c** Call out, exclaim. *rare. poet.* M–L17.

> 🕮 **2** LD MACAULAY Henrietta had reclaimed him from a life of vice. **3b** W. J. BURLEY Built on a promontory of reclaimed land. A. BRIGGS The monks . . constructed . . sea walls to reclaim the marshes. **4b** R. FRAME She was coming back to reclaim something . . she'd lost. T. K. WOLFE To revitalize Franz Sigel Park and reclaim it for the community.

▶ **B** *noun.* **1** The action of reclaiming something or someone; the state of being reclaimed; an instance of this; (a) reclamation. ME.
2 Reclaimed rubber. M20.

> 🕮 **1** *Accountancy* The payment and reclaim of tax. **baggage reclaim** (*a*) the action of reclaiming checked-in luggage at an airport etc.; (*b*) the place in an airport etc. where this is done.

■ **reclaimable** *adjective* (earlier in UNRECLAIMABLE) L17. †**reclaimant** *noun* a protester, a dissenter; SCOTS LAW an appellant: L16–E18. **reclaimer** *noun* L17.

reclamation /rɛkləˈmeɪʃ(ə)n/ *noun.* E16.
[French *réclamation* or Latin *reclamatio(n-)*, from *reclamat-* pa. ppl stem of *reclamare*: see prec., -ATION.]
The action of reclaiming something; an instance of this; now *esp.*, the process of reclaiming land for cultivation.
Comb.: **reclamation disease** a copper-deficiency disease affecting crops grown on reclaimed land.

réclame /reklam/ *noun.* Pl. pronounced same. L19.
[French, from *réclamer* RECLAIM *verb*.]
(An) advertisement; self-publicity; public acclaim or notoriety.

reclinate /ˈrɛklɪneɪt/ *adjective.* M18.
[Latin *reclinatus* pa. pple of *reclinare* RECLINE *verb*: see -ATE².]
BOTANY. Of a part of a plant: bending downwards, esp. on some other part.

reclination /rɛklɪˈneɪʃ(ə)n/ *noun.* L16.
[Old French, or late Latin *reclinatio(n-)*, from *reclinat-* pa. ppl stem of *reclinare* RECLINE *verb*: see -ATION.]
1 The action or an act of reclining; a reclining position or posture. L16.
†**2** The angle of the plane of a sundial to the vertical. L16–L18.
3 MEDICINE (now *Hist.*). A surgical operation in which the effect of a cataract is lessened by tilting the lens backwards. E19.

†**recline** *adjective. rare. poet.* M17–M19.
[Latin *reclinis*, from *reclinare* RECLINE *verb*.]
Reclining, recumbent.

recline /rɪˈklʌɪn/ *verb & noun.* LME.
[Old French *recliner* from Latin *reclinare*, formed as RE- + *clinare* bend.]
▶ **A** *verb.* **1** *verb trans.* Place in a horizontal position, esp. on the back; push or cause to lean backwards; rest (a part of the body, esp. the head) in this way. LME.
†**2** *verb intrans.* Tend towards a specified condition. Foll. by *to*. *rare.* LME–E18.
†**3** *verb intrans.* Of a sundial: incline backwards. L16–L18.
4 *verb intrans.* Assume a horizontal or leaning position, esp. in resting; lie back; repose. (Foll. by *in*, *on*, *upon*.) M17. ▸**b** Of a seat or chair: be adjustable backwards to a recumbent or semi-recumbent position. L20.

> 🕮 **1** SWIFT Their heads were all reclined . . to the right or the left. DICKENS The young gentleman . . reclined his head upon the table. *Daily Telegraph* A back-row . . seat is often fixed, i.e. the backrest cannot be reclined. **4** M. BARING Madame . . reclined on one of the divans. P. ROTH She reclines in the tub for twenty minutes each morning. **b** *Times* Both front seats recline, have sockets for . . head restraints. *Listener* Coaches . . with reclining seats.

▶ **B** *noun.* A reclining posture. M18.
■ **reclinable** *adjective* L19. **recliner** *noun* (*a*) a person who or thing which reclines; (*b*) a comfortable (usu. reclining) chair for reclining in (also ***recliner chair***): M17.

reclude /rɪˈkluːd/ *verb trans.* LME.
[Latin *recludere*: see next.]
†**1** Open (a gate etc.). LME–M17.
2 a Shut up, enclose, confine. Long *rare* or *obsolete.* L16. ▸**b** Seclude *from* society etc.; sequestrate. Long *rare.* L16.

recluse /rɪˈkluːs/ *noun & adjective.* ME.
[Old & mod. French *reclus*, fem. *recluse*, pa. pple of *reclure* from Latin *recludere* open, enclose, formed as RE- + *claudere* CLOSE *verb*.]
▶ **A** *noun.* **1** A person living in or preferring seclusion or isolation, esp. as a religious discipline; a hermit. ME.
†**2** A place of seclusion. L16–L18.

> 🕮 **1** R. W. EMERSON A notion . . that the scholar should be a recluse. B. UNSWORTH Something of a recluse, he doesn't often leave the island. P. P. READ The sociable man she had married had become a recluse.

▶ **B** *adjective.* Now *rare.*
1 Living or preferring a reclusive life; reclusive by nature. Formerly also, secluded *from* society etc. ME.
2 Of a state, condition, etc.: reclusive; solitary; retired; (of a place) secluded. Formerly also, hidden, secret, private. M17.

> 🕮 **1** M. TRIPP The . . town with shuttered windows and recluse inhabitants.

■ **reclusely** *adverb* (now *rare* or *obsolete*) L17. **recluseness** *noun* (now *rare*) M17.

†**recluse** *verb trans.* LME–E18.
[from Latin *reclus*-: see next.]
= RECLUDE 2a.

reclusion /rɪˈkluːʒ(ə)n/ *noun.* LME.
[medieval Latin *reclusio(n-)* shutting up, (monastic) seclusion, from Latin *reclus*- pa. ppl stem of *recludere*: see RECLUSE *noun & adjective*, -ION.]
1 The action of secluding (oneself) or the fact of being secluded from society etc., esp. as a religious discipline; a state of seclusion or retirement. LME.
2 Confinement as a prisoner; *esp.* solitary confinement. L19.

> 🕮 **1** *Washington Post* Withdrawal into brooding reclusion at . . his . . estate.

reclusive /rɪˈkluːsɪv/ *adjective.* L16.
[from RECLUSE *verb* + -IVE.]
Living in, preferring, or characterized by seclusion or isolation, esp. as a religious discipline.

> 🕮 E. PAWEL The reclusive scholar in his monk's cell. A. BROOKNER Naturally reclusive, she found it unsurprising that people left her. C. PETERS He . . lived . . in the country in increasingly reclusive simplicity.

■ **reclusively** *adverb* M20. **reclusiveness** *noun* L20.

recoct /rɪˈkɒkt/ *verb trans. arch.* M16.
[Latin *recoct*- pa. ppl stem of *recoquere*, formed as RE- + *coquere* cook.]
Cook a second time; *fig.* revamp, refurbish.

recogitate /rɪˈkɒdʒɪteɪt/ *verb intrans. rare.* E17.
[Latin *recogitat*- pa. ppl stem of *recogitare* (see -ATE³), or from RE- + COGITATE.]
Orig., reconsider, change one's mind. Now (*US*), think over again.

recognisance *noun* var. of RECOGNIZANCE.

recognise *verb*¹, *verb*² vars. of RECOGNIZE *verb*¹, *verb*².

recognition /rɛkəɡˈnɪʃ(ə)n/ *noun.* L15.
[Latin *recognitio(n-)*, from *recognit*- pa. ppl stem of *recognoscere* RECOGNOSCE: see -ION.]
†**1** SCOTS LAW. The repossession of land by a feudal superior, esp. on account of a crime committed by a vassal or on account of the vassal selling land without the superior's consent. L15–M18.
2 LAW (now *Hist.*). A form of inquest by jury used in early Norman England. L15.
3 The acknowledgement or admission of a service, achievement, ability, etc.; appreciation; acclaim. L15.
4 *gen.* The action or an act of recognizing a person or thing; the fact of being recognized. E16. ▸**b** The formal acknowledgement by subjects of a monarch etc., esp. in a British coronation ceremony. M16. ▸**c** In international law, the process by which a State declares that another political entity fulfils the conditions of Statehood and acknowledges its willingness to deal with it as a member of the international community. E19. ▸**d** PSYCHOLOGY. The mental process whereby things are identified as having been previously apprehended or as belonging to a known category. L19.

> 🕮 **3** *Nature* Boyle received the Flavelle Medal . . in recognition of his researches. A. J. CRONIN I've had some . . recognition . . my paintings are in the Municipal Gallery. *Woman* I have done special . . courses yet there's no recognition for this. **4** J. B. PRIESTLEY Delighted recognition lit up his face. 'Ello, I know you!' P. ACKROYD Perhaps . . stars . . came into existence in recognition of our wishes. G. DALY She wanted marriage and the recognition that came with it.

Phrases: **beyond recognition**, **beyond all recognition**, **out of recognition**, **out of all recognition** to such a degree as to be unrecognizable.
Comb.: **recognition colour**, **recognition mark** a conspicuous patch of colour on an animal or bird, believed to serve as a means of recognition to others of the same species; **recognition picketing** *US* the picketing of an employer to obtain union recognition; **recognition signal** MILITARY a prearranged signal used for mutual identification.

recognitive /rɪˈkɒɡnɪtɪv/ *adjective.* L19.
[Latin *recognativus*, from *recognit*-: see prec., -IVE.]
Of, pertaining to, or involving recognition.

recognitor /rɪˈkɒɡnɪtə/ *noun.* LME.
[Anglo-Latin, from Latin *recognit*-: see RECOGNITION, -OR.]
LAW. Orig. (*Hist.*), a member of a jury at an assize or inquest (cf. RECOGNITION 2). Now (*rare*), a person who enters into a recognizance.

recognitory /rɪˈkɒgnɪt(ə)ri/ *adjective*. Now *rare*. E19.
[App. from RECOGNITION + -ORY[2].]
= RECOGNITIVE.

recognizance /rɪˈkɒ(g)nɪz(ə)ns/ *noun*. Also **-isance**. ME.
[Old French *reconnissance*, *reconissance* (mod. *reconnaissance*), formed as RE- + COGNIZANCE.]
1 LAW. A bond undertaken before a court or magistrate to perform some act or observe some condition, esp. to pay a debt, or appear when summoned; a sum pledged as surety for this. ME.
2 a Recognition or acknowledgement of the existence or validity of a person or thing; recognition or appreciation of a service, achievement, etc. Now *rare*. LME. ▸**b** Recognition or identification of a person or thing as previously known or perceived. Now *rare*. L15.
3 †**a** = COGNIZANCE 3. LME–E18. ▸**b** LAW (now *Hist.*). = RECOGNITION 2. E17.
4 A token, an emblem. Cf. COGNIZANCE 1. *arch*. L15.

recognize /ˈrɛkəgnʌɪz/ *verb*[1]. Also **-ise**. LME.
[Old French *reconniss-*, *reconiss-* stem of *reconnaistre* (mod. *reconnaître*), formed as RECOGNOSCE.]
†**1** *verb trans*. SCOTS LAW. = RECOGNOSCE *verb* 1a. LME–E17.
†**2** *verb trans*. Testify to; confess or avow formally (*that*); *Scot.* testify to the genuineness of (a document). E16–M17.
†**3 a** *verb trans*. Look over (a document etc.) again; revise, review. M16–E18. ▸**b** *verb trans. & intrans.* Reconnoitre. *rare*. M17–E19.
4 *verb trans*. **a** Acknowledge the existence, legality, or validity of, esp. by formal approval or sanction; accord notice or attention to; treat as worthy of consideration; show appreciation of, reward. M16. ▸**b** Acknowledge or consider *as* or *to be*. M19. ▸**c** Of a person presiding at a meeting etc.: call on (a person) to speak in a debate etc. L19.
5 *verb trans*. Identify as previously known or perceived; know again, esp. by recollection of some distinctive feature. M16.
6 *verb trans. & intrans*. US LAW. Enter into or bind over by a recognizance. L17.
7 *verb trans*. Realize or discover the nature of; apprehend (a quality) *in*; realize or admit *that*. M19.

> 📖 **4a** O. MANNING She had not recognised Ellie's existence. H. L. MENCKEN The code they recognise and obey is . . severe. *Insight* The quasi-independent black homelands . . have never been recognized by foreign countries. **b** *Daily Telegraph* The Russians insisted on being recognised as leaders of the Communist movement. **5** R. C. HUTCHINSON I should recognize the place if I saw it again. P. H. JOHNSON One of those untroubled by dental caries who would not recognize a drill if he saw one. W. GOLDING The captain . . was to be recognised by his . . courtesy. **7** L. DURRELL I recognized in him . . a maturity . . I lacked. G. VIDAL He recognized in the other's . . smile that the time had come for politicking. A. C. BOULT No one could fail to recognise . . Kreisler's greatness.

■ **recogniza'bility** *noun* the quality of being recognizable L19. **recognizable** *adjective* able to be recognized L18. **recognizably** *adverb* in a recognizable manner M19. **re'cognizant** *adjective* showing recognition or acknowledgement (*of*); perceptive or conscious (*of*): M19. **recogni'zation** *noun* (*rare*) (an instance of) recognition, now esp. (*US*) of an achievement etc. M16. **recogni'zee** *noun* (now chiefly *US*) †(*a*) LAW a person to whom another is bound in a recognizance; (*b*) *gen.* a person who is recognized: L16. **recognizer** *noun* (*a*) a person who recognizes someone or something; (*b*) a machine capable of interpreting speech: E17. **recognizor** *noun* (LAW) (*obsolete* exc. *US*) a person who enters into a recognizance M16.

recognize /riːkɒgˈnʌɪz/ *verb*[2] *trans. rare*. Also **-ise**. L19.
[from RE- + COGNIZE.]
Cognize again.

†**recognosce** *verb*. LME.
[Latin *recognoscere*, formed as RE- + COGNOSCE.]
1 *verb trans*. SCOTS LAW. ▸**a** Of a feudal superior: repossess (land). Cf. RECOGNITION 1. LME–L18. ▸**b** *verb intrans. & trans.* Of land: return or be returned to a feudal superior. Only in M18.
2 *verb trans*. = RECOGNIZE *verb*[1] 2. *Scot.* M16–M17.
3 *verb trans*. = RECOGNIZE *verb*[1] 3a, 3b. *Scot.* M16–M18.
4 *verb trans*. = RECOGNIZE *verb*[1] 4a. Chiefly *Scot.* M16–L17.

recoil /rɪˈkɔɪl; *as noun also* ˈriːkɔɪl/ *verb & noun*. Also †**recule**. ME.
[Old & mod. French *reculer* from Proto-Romance, formed as RE- + Latin *culus* buttocks.]
▸ **A** *verb*. †**1** *verb trans*. Drive or force back or *back*; cause to retreat or retire. ME–E18.
2 *verb intrans*. Draw back or recede, esp. before an opposing force; retreat, retire. Also foll. by *from*. LME. ▸**b** Withdraw or retire *to* a place. Long *rare*. M16. ▸**c** Fall or stagger *back* after a blow. Long *rare*. M16.
†**3** *verb intrans*. Draw back from a course of action etc.; flinch from doing. Usu. foll. by *from*. L15–M18.
4 *verb intrans*. Start or spring back in fear, horror, or disgust. E16. ▸**b** *fig.* Shrink mentally or emotionally (*from*); feel repulsion (*at*). E17.
5 *verb intrans*. **a** (Of a gun etc.) spring back from the force of a discharge; PHYSICS (of an atom etc.) move backwards by the conservation of momentum on emission of a particle. M16. ▸**b** Rebound or spring back through force of impact or elasticity; PHYSICS (of an atom etc.) undergo a change of momentum due to a collision. L16.
6 *verb intrans*. Return to the original position or source; *fig.* (of an action etc.) have adverse consequences for the originator, rebound on. Usu. foll. by *on*, *upon*. L16.

> 📖 **2** E. M. FORSTER As he approached . . he found time to wish he could recoil. A. MOOREHEAD His natural instinct is to recoil from the sun and return to the nearest shade. **4** I. MURDOCH His . . hand touched something, recoiled . . touched again. ANNE STEVENSON They saw a bad bullfight. Sylvia recoiled in . . disgust. **b** A. KENNY I recoiled at the idea of learning more scholastic philosophy. M. MEYER Insanity is something that all of us recoil from. **6** DICKENS Any attempt . . will recoil on the head of the attempter.

▸ **B** *noun*. **1** The action or an act of recoiling, esp. in fear, horror, or disgust. Also, the fact or sensation of recoiling. ME.
2 *spec.* **a** The extent to which a gun etc. recoils when discharged. L16. ▸**b** PARTICLE PHYSICS. The result of collision or decay, in which the two resulting particles move in opposite directions. E20.

> 📖 **1** S. BELLOW A recoil of the crowd—the guards must have been pushing it back. D. CAUTE Elizabeth pretended to love the baby but Stern registered her suppressed recoil. **2a** *Sporting Gun* In a 7¼lb gun recoil was quite unobtrusive.

Comb.: **recoil escapement**: in a clock or watch, functioning by recoil; **recoil gear** MILITARY the mechanism in a field gun which absorbs the energy of recoil; **recoil particle** PHYSICS a particle which is ejected in a nuclear interaction; **recoil starter** a starter for a small internal-combustion engine in which a cord, wound round a pulley, is rewound by a spring after being pulled for the starting cycle.

■ **recoiler** *noun* M17. **recoilless** /-l-l-/ *adjective* having no or little recoil; *spec.* (of a firearm) having the recoil reduced by deflection of the combustion gas to the rear; PHYSICS (of a transition in an atomic nucleus bound in a crystal lattice) emitting a photon from the nucleus without recoil: M20. **recoilment** *noun* (now *rare* or *obsolete*) †(*a*) *rare* dismissal, removal; (*b*) the action or an act of recoiling: M17.

Recollect /ˈrɛkəlɛkt/ *noun*. M17.
[medieval Latin *recollectus*, formed as next. Cf. RECOLLET.]
ECCLESIASTICAL HISTORY. A member of a reformed branch of the Franciscan Observants, founded in France in the late 16th cent. Also, a member of a reformed branch of the Augustinian Hermits, founded in Spain in the late 16th cent.

recollect /rɛkəˈlɛkt/ *verb trans*. E16.
[Earlier form of next, now differentiated by pronunc. In sense 4 prob. after French *récolliger*.]
▸†**I 1** See next. E16.
▸ **II 2** Recall or bring back to one's mind, esp. through conscious effort; succeed in remembering. M16.
3 Recall (a thing) *to* a person. Now *rare*. L17.
†**4** *refl.* Reflect *with* (oneself); consider. L17–E18.
5 Concentrate or absorb (the mind, oneself, etc.) in religious meditation. L17.

> 📖 **2** B. BAINBRIDGE I left about 5.30, as near as I can recollect. A. V. ROBERTS Stephen paused, thinking about the . . man, recollecting his whiskery grin.

■ **recollectable** *adjective* (*rare*) L18. **recollectedness** *noun* (*a*) the state of being recollected or absorbed in religious meditation; (*b*) collectedness, composure: L17. **recollective** *adjective* (*a*) of or pertaining to recollection; (*b*) able to recollect things, having good recollection: L18. **recollectively** *adverb* E19. **recollectiveness** *noun* E19.

re-collect /riːkəˈlɛkt/ *verb*. Also (earlier) †**recollect**. E16.
[Latin *recollect-* pa. ppl stem of *recolligere*, formed as RE- + *colligere* COLLECT *verb*. Later also from RE- + COLLECT *verb*.]
†**1** *verb trans*. Collect, gather. E16–L17.
2 *verb trans. & (rare) intrans*. Collect or gather (together) again. E17.
†**3** *verb trans*. Bring back again *to* or *from* a place, condition, etc. E–M17.
4 *verb trans*. †**a** In *pass*. Be composed or calm again. E17–M18. ▸**b** *refl.* Recover composure; regain control of (oneself). M17.
5 *verb trans*. Summon up (strength, courage, etc.) again; rally. M17.

> 📖 **2** *Watsonia* This species was . . re-collected in 1961. **4b** M. EDGEWORTH His heart beat violently, and he . . stopped, to recollect himself. **5** R. L. STEVENSON Mr. Utterson's nerves . . gave a jerk . . but he re-collected his courage.

■ **re-collected** *ppl adjective* †(*a*) (*rare*, Shakes.) studied, practised; (*b*) collected or gathered together again: E17.

recollection /rɛkəˈlɛkʃ(ə)n/ *noun*. L16.
[Earlier form of next, now differentiated by pronunc.]
▸†**I 1** See next. L16.
▸ **II 2** Concentration of thought; *esp.* religious meditation. M17.
3 The action or an act of recollecting or recalling to the mind, esp. through conscious effort. L17. ▸**b** (The extent of) a person's ability to recollect things; the memory. M18.
4 A recollected thing or fact; the memory *of* something. L18.

> 📖 **2** M. GORDON Sister Josephine announced a day of recollection . . in prayer. **3** S. HAZZARD Thrale remembered this had been promised and was reassured by his . . ability to make the recollection. A. BROOKNER Fond recollection of the past was mere sentimentality. **b** P. CAREY This early childhood was . . 'quite normal' in her recollection. **4** B. T. WASHINGTON One of my earliest recollections is . . of my mother cooking a chicken. A. MACLEAN He has no recollection about what happened.

re-collection /riːkəˈlɛkʃ(ə)n/ *noun*. Also (earlier) †**recollection**. L16.
[French *récollection* or medieval Latin *recollectio(n-)*, formed as RE-COLLECT: see -ION.]
1 The action or an act of re-collecting or gathering things (together) again. L16.
†**2** Composure; self-possession. M18.

Recollet /ˈrɛkəleɪ/ *noun*. L17.
[French *récollet*, formed as RECOLLECT *noun*.]
= RECOLLECT *noun*.

récolte /rekɔlt/ *noun*. Pl. pronounced same. Also (earlier) †***recolt***. L18.
[French.]
In France: a harvest, a crop.

recombinant /rɪˈkɒmbɪnənt/ *adjective & noun*. M20.
[from RECOMBINE *verb* + -ANT[1].]
GENETICS. (Of, pertaining to, or designating) an organism, cell, or piece of genetic material formed by natural or artificial recombination.
recombinant DNA: produced artificially by joining segments of DNA from different organisms.

recombinase /rɪˈkɒmbɪneɪz/ *noun*. M20.
[from next + -ASE.]
BIOCHEMISTRY. An enzyme which promotes genetic recombination.

recombination /riːˌkɒmbɪˈneɪʃ(ə)n, ˌriːkɒmb-/ *noun*. E19.
[from RECOMBINE + -ATION.]
1 The action or an act of recombining something. E19.
2 PHYSICS. The coming together of ions and electrons to form neutral atoms. Freq. *attrib.* L19.
3 GENETICS. **a** The formation (by means of sexual reproduction) of genotypes that differ from both parental genotypes. E20. ▸**b** The formation (by crossing over) of chromosomes that differ from both the parental chromosomes. E20. ▸**c** The artificial production of new genetic material by joining segments of DNA from different organisms. L20.
■ **recombinational** *adjective* (GENETICS) of or pertaining to recombination M20. **recombinationally** *adverb* M20.

recombine /riːkəmˈbʌɪn/ *verb*. M17.
[from RE- + COMBINE *verb*[1].]
1 *verb trans*. Combine again or differently. M17.
2 *verb intrans*. Enter into a new or different combination. M19.
■ **recombinable** *adjective* M20.

recomfort /riːˈkʌmfət/ *verb trans*. Long *arch*. LME.
[Old & mod. French *réconforter*, formed as RE- + COMFORT *verb*.]
†**1** Hearten or encourage again; reinspire; *refl.* take courage or heart again. LME–M17.
2 Strengthen again physically; re-invigorate, refresh. LME.
3 Comfort or console again in grief or trouble. LME.

recommence /riːkəˈmɛns/ *verb trans. & intrans*. L15.
[Old & mod. French *recommencer*, formed as RE- + *commencer* COMMENCE.]
(Cause to) commence or begin again.
■ **recommencement** *noun* the action, process, or time of recommencing L18. **recommencer** *noun* E19.

recommend /rɛkəˈmɛnd/ *verb & noun*. LME.
[medieval Latin *recommendare*, formed as RE- + COMMEND *verb*.]
▸ **A** *verb trans*. **1** Commend or commit (a person, oneself, one's soul, etc.) to another's care or keeping, esp. to the care of God. LME. ▸†**b** Entrust or consign (a thing) *to* another's care, use, etc. L16–E17. ▸†**c** Communicate, report, (*to*). Also (*rare*, Shakes.), inform. L16–M17.
†**2** Ask for (oneself or another) to be remembered kindly *to* another; convey greetings from (a person) *to* another. LME–L18.
†**3** Praise, extol. LME–M18.
4 a Mention or present (a thing, course of action, etc.) as desirable or advisable to or *to* a person. LME. ▸**b** Counsel or advise *that*, *to do*; (now *rare*) suggest (a thing) *to* a person as being advisable *to do*. M18.
5 Procure a favourable reception for; make acceptable or desirable to or *to* a person. E17.
6 a Name or mention (a person) as suitable for or *for* a particular position or employment. M17. ▸**b** Present or mention (a person or thing) to or *to* another as worthy of favour or attention or *as* being of a particular character. L17.

📖 **1** R. L. STEVENSON I . . recommended my spirit to its Maker. K. CLARK Richard II with his patron saints . . recommending him to the Virgin. **2** S. JOHNSON Recommend me to the . . lady. **4a** D. FRASER A . . rearmament programme was recommended to the Cabinet. *Which?* The manufacturers recommend positioning the lock . . high on the window. **b** P. G. WODEHOUSE Mr Slippery . . recommended him to place his affairs in my hands. P. DALLY He recommended that she spend the winter in Pisa. **5** A. JOHN My abundant hair and . . beard . . failed to recommend me to strangers. **6a** D. L. SAYERS I know nothing about you, except that Mrs Arbuthnott recommended you. H. MACMILLAN To recommend this remarkable . . figure for a life peerage. **b** M. KEANE He poured . . a glass and drank . . . 'Not very nice; I can't say I recommend it.' J. F. HENDRY A little hotel . . recommended as cheap.

▶ **B** *noun.* (A) recommendation. Orig. *Scot.* Now *dial.* & *colloq.* **M16.**

■ **recommendable** *adjective* **L15. recommendatory** *adjective* (*a*) expressing or conveying (a) recommendation; (*b*) (of a resolution, appointment, etc.) in the form of a recommendation, without binding force: **L16. recommender** *noun* **L16.**

recommendation /rɛkəmɛnˈdeɪʃ(ə)n/ *noun.* **LME.**
[Old French (mod. *recommandation*), or medieval Latin *recommendatio(n-)*, from *recommendat-* pa. ppl stem of *recommendare*: see prec., **-ATION.**]
1 The action or an act of recommending a person or thing; a recommended course of action etc.; a proposal. **LME.**
†**2** Commendation; favour; esteem. **LME–L16.**
3 That which procures a favourable reception or acceptance. **M17.**
4 = ***letter of recommendation*** below. **M17.**

📖 **1** *Daily Telegraph* The decision to withdraw the ban was the . . recommendation by a . . scientific panel. M. MEYER Through the recommendation of a friend, Strindberg was offered extra work. *Which?* Levels are based on the recommendations of . . advisory bodies. **letter of recommendation** a letter or certificate recommending a person for employment etc.; a letter of introduction. **3** J. A. FROUDE His recommendation had been his connexion with a powerful . . family.

†**recompensation** *noun.* **LME.**
[Old French *recompensacion* from late Latin *recompensatio(n-)*, from *recompensat-* pa. ppl stem of *recompensare* **RECOMPENSE** *verb*: see **-ATION.**]
1 = **RECOMPENSE** *noun.* **LME–E18.**
2 *SCOTS LAW.* A counter-claim of compensation by a pursuer in an action for debt where the defender has pleaded compensation as a defence. **L17–M19.**

recompense /ˈrɛkəmpɛns/ *noun.* **LME.**
[Old & mod. French *récompense*, formed as next.]
1 Repayment or requital for a thing, action, or service. **LME.**
2 a Atonement or satisfaction for a misdeed, a wrong, etc. **LME.** ▶**b** Compensation for a loss, injury, defect, etc.; *spec.* (*SCOTS LAW*) a non-contractual obligation to restore a benefit resulting from another's loss. **LME.**
3 Retribution for an injury or wrong. **LME.**

📖 **1** P. ACKROYD In recompense I gave them presents. **2a** MILTON To shew what recompense . . I intend for what I have misdone. **b** S. KAUFFMANN That she had done this . . was more than recompense for the loss. **3** SHELLEY Such is the tyrant's recompense . . He who is evil can receive no good.

Phrases: **in recompense for**, †**in recompense of** in return or compensation for.

recompense /ˈrɛkəmpɛns/ *verb.* **LME.**
[Old & mod. French *récompenser* from late Latin *recompensare*, formed as **RE-** + Latin *compensare* **COMPENSATE.**]
1 *verb trans.* Make repayment or requital to (a person, *for* a thing, action, service, etc.); reward, pay. **LME.** ▶**b** Make repayment or requital for (an action, service, etc.). **LME.**
2 *verb trans.* Compensate or make amends to (a person, *for* a loss, injury, etc.). **LME.** ▶**b** Compensate for (a loss, injury, defect, etc.); atone for or redress (a wrong etc.). Now *rare.* **LME.**
3 *verb intrans.* Make repayment or amends (*for* or *to*). Now *rare* or *obsolete.* **LME.**
†**4** *verb trans.* Give in repayment or return (*to*). *rare.* **L15–E16.**

📖 **1** DEFOE The first Thing I did, was to recompense my . . Benefactor. C. DEXTER School masters . . aren't . . highly recompensed. **b** S. JOHNSON He . . saw his care amply recompensed. **2** A. LIVINGSTONE Wondering how he could recompense her . . for the harm done by Elizabeth. J. MALCOLM He offered to recompense Mme. Bonaparte by paying . . her expenses. **b** J. MORLEY A gracious, benevolent, all-powerful being, . . who would one day redress all wrongs and recompense all pain.

■ **recompensable** *adjective* (*a*) capable of providing recompense; (*b*) able to be recompensed: **LME. recompensive** *adjective* (*rare*) providing recompense **M17.**

recompress /riːkəmˈprɛs/ *verb trans.* **M20.**
[from **RE-** + **COMPRESS** *verb.*]
Compress again; *spec.* increase again the pressure of air etc. in (a vessel) or acting on (a person).

recompression /riːkəmˈprɛʃ(ə)n/ *noun.* **M20.**
[from **RE-** + **COMPRESSION.**]
The action or an act of recompressing a person etc.; the fact or state of being recompressed; *spec.* exposure to increased air pressure.
Comb.: **recompression chamber**, **recompression lock** = ***DECOMPRESSION chamber.***

recon /rɪˈkɒn/ *noun*¹. *US Military slang.* **E20.**
[Abbreviation.]
Military reconnaissance; a unit of troops assigned to this task. Freq. *attrib.* Cf. **RECCE** *noun.*

recon /ˈriːkɒn/ *noun*². **M20.**
[from **REC(OMBINATION** + **-ON.**]
BIOLOGY. The smallest element of genetic material which can be exchanged but not divided by recombination, usu. identified as a DNA base. Cf. **MUTON.**

recon /rɪˈkɒn/ *verb trans.* & *intrans. US Military slang.* Infl. **-nn-. M20.**
[Abbreviation.]
= **RECONNOITRE** *verb.*

reconcentrado /ˌriːkɒnsɛnˈtrɑːdəʊ/ *noun.* Pl. **-os. L19.**
[Spanish, pa. pple of *reconcentrar* gather together, concentrate.]
Hist. In the Cuban war of independence (1895–9), any of the rural Cubans concentrated in garrisoned towns or detention camps by the Spanish military authorities.

reconcentrate /riːˈkɒns(ə)ntreɪt/ *verb.* **E17.**
[from **RE-** + **CONCENTRATE** *verb*; partly (in sense 1) after Spanish *reconcentrar*: see prec.]
1 *verb trans.* Bring together, concentrate, now *spec.* for military reasons. **E17.**
2 *verb trans.* & *intrans.* Concentrate again. **L19.**
■ **reconcenˈtration** *noun* **L19.**

reconception /riːkənˈsɛpʃ(ə)n/ *noun.* **M18.**
[from **RE-** + **CONCEPTION.**]
A renewed or new conception; something reconceived.

reconcile /ˈrɛk(ə)nsʌɪl/ *verb.* **LME.**
[Old & mod. French *réconcilier* or Latin *reconciliare*, formed as **RE-** + *conciliare* **CONCILIATE.**]
▶ **I 1** *verb trans.* Restore (a person) to friendly relations with oneself or another after an estrangement. Also foll. by *with*, *to*. **LME.**
2 *verb trans.* Restore (estranged parties) to concord or harmony; reunite (people or things) in harmony. **LME.**
†**3** *verb trans.* Bring (a person) back *to*, *into* peace, favour, etc. **LME–L16.**
†**4** *verb trans.* Reunite with or readmit to a Church, orig. *spec.* the Roman Catholic Church. Also foll. by *to*, *with*. **LME–M19.**
5 *verb trans. ECCLESIASTICAL.* Cleanse, purify, reconsecrate, (a desecrated church, chapel, etc.). **LME.** ▶†**b** Absolve, cleanse, or purify (a person). **LME–M16.**
†**6** *verb trans.* Recover (a person's favour, respect, etc.). **LME–M17.**
7 *verb trans.* (freq. *refl.*). Bring into acquiescence with, acceptance of, or submission to a thing, condition, situation, etc. Foll. by *to*, (now *rare*) *with*. **M16.**
8 *verb intrans.* Become reconciled. **M17.**

📖 **1** SIR W. SCOTT He came in secret to . . reconcile her sire. W. H. DIXON The king's desire to reconcile his cousin with a friend. A. N. WILSON Mary was reconciled to Milton. **2** G. GREENE The three children . . sail for New York to . . reconcile their parents. A. G. GARDINER What miracle is this? England and America reconciled at last. **7** S. ROSENBERG I could never have become reconciled to the blind adulation of the leader. R. FRASER The . . existence he lived in his dream writing could not be reconciled with . . reality. T. PARKS Neither . . had ever reconciled themselves to so much that had happened. **8** E. S. PERSON The disenchanted lover may experience a desire to reconcile even after separation.

▶ **II 9** *verb trans.* Settle, cause agreement in (a controversy, quarrel, etc.). **LME.**
10 *verb trans.* Make or regard as compatible or consistent; show the compatibility of by argument or in practice; show to be in accordance. Also foll. by *with*, *to*. **M16.** ▶**b** *ACCOUNTANCY.* Make (one account) consistent *with* another, esp. by allowing for transactions begun but not yet completed (as when a cheque has been issued but not yet presented for payment). **E20.**
11 *verb trans.* Make even or smooth; fit together to present a uniform surface. **L17.**

📖 **9** N. LUTTRELL The lords . . reconciled a difference between the earls . . about the army. **10** H. JAMES I don't see how you can reconcile it to your conscience. D. CUSACK At a loss to reconcile the conflicting points of view. R. L. FOX They did not reconcile the claims . . of an outside leader with the hopes of Greek allies.

■ **reconcilaˈbility** *noun* the fact or quality of being reconcilable **M19. reconcilable** /rɛk(ə)nˈsʌɪləb(ə)l, ˈrɛk(ə)nsʌɪləb(ə)l/ *adjective* (*a*) able to be made, regarded as, or shown to be, consistent or compatible (*with*, *to*); (*b*) (now *rare*) (of a person, a person's character, etc.) easily conciliated or reconciled: **E17. reconcilableness** *noun* (now *rare*) = **RECONCILABILITY** *noun* **M17. reconcilement** *noun* (a) reconciliation **M16. reconciler** *noun* a person who or thing which reconciles someone or something; *spec.* Jesus Christ: **M16.**

reconciliate /rɛk(ə)nˈsɪlɪeɪt/ *verb trans.* Now *rare* or *obsolete.* **M16.**
[Latin *reconciliat-*: see next, **-ATE**³.]
Conciliate again; reconcile.
■ **reconˈciliative** *adjective* (*rare*) = **RECONCILIATORY L18. reconˈciliator** *noun* = **RECONCILER** *noun* **L16.**

reconciliation /ˌrɛk(ə)nsɪlɪˈeɪʃ(ə)n/ *noun.* **LME.**
[French *réconciliation* or Latin *reconciliatio(n-)*, from *reconciliat-* pa. ppl stem of *reconciliare* **RECONCILE** *verb*: see **-ATION.**]
1 a The action or an act of reconciling a person to oneself or another, or estranged parties to one another; the fact or condition of being reconciled; harmony, concord. **LME.** ▶**b** *CHRISTIAN THEOLOGY.* The action of reconciling humanity with God; the fact or condition of humanity's being reconciled with God. **LME.**
2 The cleansing, purification, or reconsecration of a desecrated church, chapel, etc. **M16.**
3 The action or an act of settling or causing agreement in a controversy, quarrel, etc.; the action or an act of making, regarding as, or showing to be consistent or compatible. **M16.** ▶**b** *ACCOUNTANCY.* The action or practice of making one account consistent with another, esp. by allowing for transactions begun but not yet completed. **L19.**
4 Reunion with or readmission to a Church. **L16.**

📖 **1a** J. R. ACKERLEY A reconciliation took place and she and my father became firm friends. E. YOUNG-BRUEHL There were peace treaties, but no fundamental reconciliation. **b** ***SACRAMENT of reconciliation.*** **3** A. STORR The reconciliation of opposites is a theme . . of Jung's work. *Observer* A reconciliation of Marxism and political democracy is possible.

Comb.: **reconciliation statement** a statement of account in which discrepancies are adjusted.

reconciliatory /rɛk(ə)nˈsɪlɪət(ə)ri/ *adjective.* **L16.**
[French †*réconciliatoire*, formed as **RECONCILIATE**: see **-ORY**².]
Esp. of actions, words: tending or intended to reconcile; showing a spirit of reconciliation.

recondite /ˈrɛk(ə)ndʌɪt, rɪˈkɒn-/ *adjective.* **M17.**
[Latin *reconditus* pa. pple of *recondere* put away, hide, formed as **RE-** + *condere* put together, compose, hide.]
1 Of a thing: removed or hidden from view; kept out of sight. Now *rare.* **M17.**
2 Little known; abstruse; obscure; profound. **M17.** ▶**b** Of study, discussion, etc.: consisting in or relating to little-known or profound knowledge. **M17.**
3 Of a writer or literary style: employing abstruse or obscure allusions or references. **L18.**

📖 **2** I. A. RICHARDS Subtle or recondite experiences are for most men . . indescribable. D. CECIL He encrusts his descriptions . . with recondite biblical and classical allusions. **b** M. MEYER People . . writing theses on the most recondite subjects.

■ **reconditely** *adverb* **M19. reconditeness** *noun* **M19.**

recondition /riːkənˈdɪʃ(ə)n/ *verb trans.* **E20.**
[from **RE-** + **CONDITION** *verb.*]
1 Restore to proper or usable condition; repair, renovate. **E20.**
2 *FORESTRY.* Reduce warping and collapse in (timber) by prolonged steaming. **M20.**
3 *PSYCHOLOGY.* Alter a habit or response of (a person) by behavioural conditioning; replace (an established behaviour) in this way. **M20.**
■ **reconditioned** *adjective* (of a vehicle engine, a piece of equipment, etc.) repaired and renovated for reuse; restored to good working order: **M20. reconditioner** *noun* a person who or a device or preparation which reconditions something; *spec.* (*FORESTRY*) a humidifier for reconditioning warped timber: **M20.**

reconduct /riːkənˈdʌkt/ *verb trans.* **E17.**
[Latin *reconduct-* pa. ppl stem of *reconducere* hire anew, lead back, formed as **RE-** + **CONDUCT** *verb.*]
Lead back.

reconfer /riːkənˈfəː/ *verb.* Infl. **-rr-. E17.**
[from **RE-** + **CONFER.**]
1 *verb intrans.* Discuss a subject again. **E17.**
2 *verb trans.* Confer (an honour, title, etc.) again. **E17.**

reconfigure /riːkənˈfɪgə/ *verb.* **M20.**
[from **RE-** + **CONFIGURE.**]
1 *verb trans.* Configure again or differently; *spec.* (*COMPUTING*) adapt (a system) to a new task by altering its configuration. **M20.**
2 *verb intrans. COMPUTING.* Of a system: become adapted to a new task by altering configuration. **L20.**
■ **reconfiguration** /ˌriːkənfɪgəˈreɪʃ(ə)n, -gjʊ-/ *noun* **M20.**

reconfirm /riːkənˈfəːm/ *verb trans.* **E17.**
[from **RE-** + **CONFIRM.**]
Confirm, ratify, or establish anew.
■ **ˌreconfirˈmation** *noun* **E17.**

reconnaissance /rɪˈkɒnɪs(ə)ns/ *noun.* E19.
[French, from *reconnaiss-* stem of *reconnaître*: see RECONNOITRE, -ANCE. Cf. earlier RECONNOISSANCE *noun*.]
1 *MILITARY.* A survey of a geographical area before advancing, in order to ascertain its strategic features and available resources or the position and strength of an enemy. E19. ▸**b** A unit of troops assigned to such a survey. E19.
2 *transf.* A preliminary investigation or inspection; *spec.* a survey of a geographical area for scientific or industrial purposes. E19.
3 Reconnoitring, surveying. L19.

📖 **1** ***reconnaissance mission, reconnaissance party, reconnaissance trip***, etc. **2** *Nature* Sediments observed . . in an earlier aerial reconnaissance. W. M. CLARKE Defoe had done his own literary reconnaissance along this coast.

†**reconnoissance** *noun.* L17.
[French (now RECONNAISSANCE), from †*reconnoiss-* stem of †*reconnoître*: see RECONNOITRE, -ANCE.]
1 = RECOGNIZANCE 1. *rare.* Only in L17.
2 = RECONNAISSANCE 1. M18–L19.
3 = RECONNAISSANCE 2. M–L19.

reconnoitre /rɛkəˈnɔɪtə/ *verb & noun.* Also ***-ter**. E18.
[French †*reconnoître* (now *-aître*) from Latin *recognoscere* look over, inspect: see RECOGNIZE *verb*¹.]
▶ **A** *verb.* **1** *verb trans. MILITARY.* Make a reconnaissance of. E18.
2 *verb intrans. MILITARY.* Make a reconnaissance. E18.
3 *verb trans. & intrans. transf.* Observe or inspect (a person); investigate or look into (a thing, situation, etc.); explore or survey (an area). M18.
†**4** *verb trans.* Recollect, remember; recognize. M18–E19.

📖 **1** M. E. HERBERT The guides advised a halt, while they reconnoitred the force . . of the enemy. **2** E. BLUNDEN To reconnoitre in Ypres . . to see the trenches we were to hold. **3** D. M. DAVIN We went back by the route I had reconnoitred. E. O'BRIEN I reconnoitre his white body while he's muttering on.

▶ **B** *noun.* An act of reconnoitring; a reconnaissance. L18.

📖 J. A. MICHENER Scouts . . , on a reconnoiter to the north, spotted the horses.

■ **reconnoitrer** *noun* M18.

reconquer /riːˈkɒŋkə/ *verb trans.* L16.
[from RE- + CONQUER *verb*.]
Conquer again; recover by conquest.

reconquest /riːˈkɒŋkwɛst/ *noun.* M16.
[from RE- + CONQUEST *noun*.]
The action or an act of conquering again; recovery by conquest.

reconsecrate /riːˈkɒnsɪkreɪt/ *verb trans.* E17.
[from RE- + CONSECRATE *verb*.]
Consecrate again or anew.
■ **reconseˈcration** *noun* M18.

reconsider /riːkənˈsɪdə/ *verb trans. & intrans.* L16.
[from RE- + CONSIDER.]
Consider (a thing, situation, idea, decision, etc.) again, esp. for a possible change of policy, practice, etc.

📖 GEO. ELIOT He had set himself . . to reconsider his worn . . clothes. P. MAILLOUX He wrote Felice begging her to reconsider her decision. G. DALY Twice he . . begged her to reconsider, but to no avail.

■ **ˌreconsideˈration** *noun* M18.

reconsign /riːkənˈsʌɪn/ *verb trans.* E17.
[from RE- + CONSIGN.]
Consign again or differently.
■ **reconsignment** *noun* the action or an act of reconsigning something; *spec.* (*COMMERCE*) a change in the route, destination, or consignee of goods being transported: M19.

reconsolidate /riːkənˈsɒlɪdeɪt/ *verb trans. & intrans.* M16.
[from RE- + CONSOLIDATE.]
Consolidate again or anew.

reconsolidation /ˌriːkənsɒlɪˈdeɪʃ(ə)n/ *noun.* M16.
[from RE- + CONSOLIDATION.]
A new or renewed consolidation.

reconstitute /riːˈkɒnstɪtjuːt/ *verb.* E19.
[from RE- + CONSTITUTE.]
1 *verb trans.* Constitute again; reconstruct. Also, reorganize. E19. ▸**b** *spec.* Restore the original constitution of (dehydrated or concentrated food, drink, etc.) by adding liquid. E20.
2 *verb intrans.* Undergo or take part in reconstitution. L20.

📖 **1** C. THUBRON His home has been tenderly reconstituted from photographs . . and memories. **b** *Which?* A few health food shop orange juices are reconstituted with spa water. **2** A. TULL The milk reconstitutes easily with water if in a fine powdered form.

reconstitution /ˌriːkɒnstɪˈtjuːʃ(ə)n/ *noun.* M19.
[from RE- + CONSTITUTION.]
1 A new or different constitution; a reconstruction, a reorganization. M19.
2 The restoration of dehydrated or concentrated food, drink, etc., to its original constitution by the addition of liquid. E20.

reconstruct /riːkənˈstrʌkt/ *verb trans.* M18.
[from RE- + CONSTRUCT *verb*.]
1 Construct, build, form, or put together again. M18.
2 Form an impression, esp. a visual one, or an actual model of (a past event, phenomenon, thing, etc.) based on assembled evidence; *spec.* (**a**) re-enact the circumstances of (a crime etc.); (**b**) *LINGUISTICS* deduce the forms and structures of (a protolanguage) from recorded cognate languages. M19.

📖 **1** K. CLARK Musical instruments, each so accurately depicted that one could reconstruct it and play it. I. MURDOCH He tore it up . . and tried in vain to reconstruct it. **2** R. G. COLLINGWOOD By excavation you could reconstruct the history of Roman sites. P. ROAZEN Out of these multiple sources it is now possible to reconstruct an intimate record. G. GREENE These details which I am trying so hard to reconstruct from my memory.

■ **reconstructable** *adjective* L20. **reconstructed** *adjective* (**a**) that has been reconstructed; ***reconstructed stone***, a building material made from crushed natural stone and cement; (**b**) (of any of various political theories, orig. Communism) altered or modified, esp. for pragmatic reasons; (of a person) holding pragmatically modified political views: M19. **reconstructible** *adjective* M20. **reconstructor** *noun* a person who reconstructs something L19.

reconstruction /riːkənˈstrʌkʃ(ə)n/ *noun.* L18.
[from RE- + CONSTRUCTION.]
1 The action or process of reconstructing, rebuilding, or re-organizing something. L18. ▸**b** *US HISTORY.* (Usu. **R-**.) The process by which the seceded Confederate States were restored to full membership of the Union after the American Civil War; the period during which this occurred. M19. ▸**c** The reorganization of a public company by closing down operations and disbanding personnel, followed by immediate reformation as a new company under similar ownership, in order to redistribute capital, resources, etc. L19. ▸**d** The rebuilding of, and restoration of economic stability to, an area devastated by war. E20.
2 An instance or example of reconstructing something; a reconstructed thing; a re-enactment of the circumstances of a crime. L18.

📖 **1** *Oxford Diocesan Magazine* Many old people become too involved in their reconstruction of past events. **2** E. PROKOSCH The form is not found in any document, but represents a reconstruction on a comparative basis. N. SHERRY The police will begin a reconstruction of Hale's kidnapping.

■ **reconstructional** *adjective* E20. **reconstructionary** *adjective* (*US*) of or pertaining to reconstruction L19. **reconstructionist** *noun & adjective* (**a**) *noun* a person involved in or favouring reconstruction; (**b**) *adjective* of or pertaining to reconstruction or reconstructionists: M19.

reconstructive /riːkənˈstrʌktɪv/ *adjective.* M19.
[from RE- + CONSTRUCTIVE.]
Of or pertaining to reconstruction.

recontinue /riːkənˈtɪnjuː/ *verb trans.* Now *rare.* LME.
[Old French *recontinuer*: see RE-, CONTINUE.]
Resume (a discontinued action, occupation, state, etc.).

reconvalescence /ˌriːkɒnvəˈlɛs(ə)ns/ *noun. rare.* L17.
[from RE- + CONVALESCENCE.]
(A period of) second or subsequent convalescence.

reconvene /riːkənˈviːn/ *verb trans. & intrans.* LME.
[from RE- + CONVENE.]
Orig. *spec.* (*SCOTS LAW*), bring before a court on a counterclaim. Now *gen.*, convene again; *esp.* (of a meeting etc.) convene again after a pause in proceedings.

reconvention /riːkənˈvɛnʃ(ə)n/ *noun.* LME.
[Old & mod. French, or medieval Latin *reconventio(n-)*: see RE-, CONVENTION.]
†**1** A reciprocal agreement. Only in LME.
2 The action or an act of reconvening; *spec.* (*LAW*) a counter-claim brought against a plaintiff by a defendant in a suit. LME.

reconversion /riːkənˈvəːʃ(ə)n/ *noun.* L16.
[from RE- + CONVERSION.]
The action or an act of reconverting a person or thing. Also, a reconverted thing.

reconvert /riːkənˈvəːt/ *verb trans.* E17.
[from RE- + CONVERT *verb*.]
Convert again, or back to a former state.

reconvey /riːkənˈveɪ/ *verb trans.* E16.
[from RE- + CONVEY.]
1 Convey back to a previous place or position; convey in a reverse direction. Now *rare.* E16.
2 *LAW.* Make over again or restore to a former owner. M17.

reconveyance /riːkənˈveɪəns/ *noun.* E18.
[from RE- + CONVEYANCE.]
The action or an act of reconveying; *spec.* (*LAW*), restoration to a former owner.

record /ˈrɛkɔːd, *in sense 5b* rɪˈkɔːd/ *noun.* ME.
[Old & mod. French = remembrance, from *recorder*: see next. In sense 5b from next.]
▶ **I 1** *LAW.* **a** The fact or condition of being or having been written down as evidence of a legal matter, *spec.* the proceedings or verdict of a court of law; evidence recorded in this way. ME. ▸**b** An authentic or official report entered on the rolls of the proceedings, including the judgement, in any case coming before a court of record. LME. ▸**c** A record of the material points, pleadings, and issue between defendant and plaintiff, constituting a case to be decided by a court of law; a case so constituted. E17. ▸**d** *SCOTS LAW.* A written statement by all parties to a lawsuit containing the pleadings which are the full and final statement of the averments and pleas on which the case rests. E19.
†**2** Attestation or testimony of a fact; witness; evidence; proof. ME–M17. ▸**b** A witness. E16–M18.
3 a The fact or condition of being preserved (esp. in writing) as knowledge or information; knowledge or information preserved in writing etc. LME. ▸**b** An account of the past; a piece of evidence about the past; *spec.* a written or otherwise permanently recorded account of a fact or event. Also, a document, monument, etc., on which such an account is recorded; *transf.* a person or thing giving evidence, reminding, or preserving the memory, of a fact or event; a memorial; in *pl.*, a collection of such accounts, documents, etc. L16. ▸**c** A performance or occurrence remarkable among or excelling others of the same kind; *spec.* the best recorded achievement in a competitive sport. L19.
4 The most important facts in the life or career of a (public) person; the sum of a person's acts or achievements. M19. ▸**b** An account of a person's behaviour in a particular sphere; *spec.* (more fully ***criminal record***) a list of a person's criminal convictions or prison sentences, a history of being convicted for crime. E20.
5 a A thin disc (formerly a cylinder), latterly of plastic, carrying recorded sound in an irregular spiral groove from which it is reproduced by rotation on a turntable with a vibrating stylus in the groove (also ***gramophone record***, (*US*) ***phonograph record***). L19. ▸**b** The action of recording on magnetic tape etc. Usu. *attrib.* M20.
6 *COMPUTING.* A number of related items of information which are handled as a unit. M20.

📖 **3a** H. KISSINGER All the principals were on record with some statement protecting themselves against all possible developments. **b** J. CONRAD I started an irregular, fragmentary record of my days. L. HELLMAN They . . had no record of her ever having been there. **c** *attrib.*: P. ABRAHAMS A small hut . . had been built in record time. **4b** D. HAMMETT He's an ex-con . . with a record as long as your arm. ANNE STEVENSON Fully preoccupied with establishing a successful academic record. **5a** P. AUSTER He put on a record—Haydn's opera . . —and listened to it. *Face* These bands don't realise they can't make records as good as the Stones.

▶ **II** †**7** Memory; recollection. ME–E17.
8 Reputation; repute. Long *obsolete* exc. *Scot.* LME.
†**9** Accord; reconcilement. *rare.* LME–M16.
†**10** = RECORDER *noun*². *rare.* L15–L16.

Phrases: **beat the record**, **break the record** surpass all previous performances of a particular action. **be on record** have stated one's opinion openly or officially, be recorded (as believing, saying, etc.). ***break the record***: see ***beat the record*** above. **court of record** a court whose proceedings are permanently recorded, and which can fine or imprison. ***criminal record***: see sense 4b above. **for the record** so that the true facts are recorded or known. **go on record**, **put oneself on record** state one's opinion openly or officially, esp. so that it is recorded. ***gramophone record***: see sense 5a above. **have a record** be known as a criminal. **have the power of record**, **have record** (*LAW*, now *Hist.*) be entitled to have one's judicial acts and decisions enrolled. **matter of record** something established as a fact by being (officially) recorded. **off the record** unofficially, confidentially; as an unattributable statement. **on record** (**a**) officially recorded; publicly known; (**b**) recorded on a gramophone record. ***phonograph record***: see sense 5a above. ***Public Record Office***: see PUBLIC *adjective & noun*. ***put oneself on record***: see ***go on record*** above. **put the record straight**, **set the record straight** achieve a correct account of the facts; correct a misapprehension. **travel out of the record** †(**a**) *LAW* consider a matter not contained in a legal record; (**b**) *transf.* (*arch.*) go off the subject.

Comb.: **record album** an album of music on record; **record changer** a device on a record-player which automatically replaces a record which has ended; **record club** a society whose members can buy selected gramophone records on special terms; **record hop** *arch. slang* a dance at which the music is provided by records; **record linkage** the process or practice of combining items of information or sets of data relating to the same subject; **record-player** an electrically operated apparatus for reproducing sound from a record, esp. through the vibrations of a stylus travelling in the irregular spiral groove of a record rotating on a turntable; **record sleeve** a stiff (esp. cardboard) envelope for covering a gramophone record, often with details of what is recorded on it; **record token** a voucher exchangeable for gramophone records costing up to a specified amount of money; **record type** a typeface including special sorts reproducing the contractions or particular letter forms found in medieval manuscripts.

For other words beginning with *re-* see the entry for **re-**

■ **recordless** *adjective* having no record or records; unrecorded: M19.

record /rɪˈkɔːd/ *verb*. ME.
[Old & mod. French *recorder* bring to remembrance from Latin *recordare*, *-ari* think over, remember, formed as RE- + *cor(d-)* heart.]
► **I** †**1** *verb trans.* Recite or repeat, aloud or in the mind, esp. in order to commit to memory. ME–M17. ▸†**b** Take seriously; give heed to (an example, warning, etc.). LME–M16.
2 *verb trans. & intrans.* Esp. of a bird: sing or practise singing (a tune, a series of notes, etc.), esp. repeatedly; go over (a tune etc.) inwardly or quietly. LME. ▸†**b** Sing (about). L16–E17.
► **II** †**3** *verb trans.* Relate, tell, or narrate orally. Also foll. by *to*. ME–M18
4 *verb trans.* Relate, tell, or narrate in writing; set down in writing or other permanent form; make a written record of. LME. ▸**b** Make an official record of (an action, decision, etc.); set down officially or permanently. L16.
†**5** *verb trans.* Attest, confirm, testify to (a fact, etc.). LME–E17.
6 *verb trans.* Convert (sound, a performance, a broadcast, etc.) into a permanent form for subsequent reproduction. L19. ▸**b** *verb trans. & intrans.* Perform (a piece of music, a play, etc.) while being or so as to be recorded. E20.

📖 **4** E. BOWEN Word for word . . their conversation had been recorded . . in the fluent writing. A. HOLLINGHURST Winchester itself had been recorded in the . . diary. **b** R. LARDNER Tommy parted with a twenty dollar bill and recorded the transaction in a . . book. S. RADLEY The Coroner recorded the . . verdict of accidental death. **recorded delivery** a Post Office service in which the dispatch and receipt of a letter or parcel are recorded. **recording angel**: that supposedly records each person's good and bad actions. **6** R. MACAULAY Hymn-singing recorded by the BBC for a Home Service programme. J. G. BALLARD The TV film . . introduced a . . sequence recorded at the Great Ormond Street Children's Hospital. **b** *Daily Telegraph* She . . recorded the Ave Maria from 'Otello' . . as if she had recorded all her life!

►†**III 7** *verb trans.* Recall; remember. ME–L18.
8 *verb trans.* Meditate, ponder (a thought, idea, etc.) *with* oneself. LME–L16.
9 a *verb intrans.* Have a memory or recollection *of*. LME–M16. ▸**b** *verb intrans. & trans.* Think or meditate (*on*). LME–E17.

■ **recordable** *adjective* (*a*) able to be recorded; worthy of being recorded, memorable; (*b*) able to be recorded on, suitable for recording on: L15. **recordal** *noun* (*rare*) the action of recording something M19. **recordist** *noun* a person who records something or makes recordings M20.

Recordak /rɪˈkɔːdak/ *noun*. Also **r-**. E20.
[Perh. from RECORD *verb* + KOD)AK.]
(Proprietary name for) a device for making photographic records of series of documents, as bank cheques etc.

recordation /rɛkəˈdeɪʃ(ə)n/ *noun*. LME.
[Old French, or Latin *recordatio(n-)*, from *recordat-* pa. ppl stem of *recordari*: see RECORD *verb*, -ATION.]
†**1** The faculty of memory. LME–M17.
†**2** Remembrance or recollection *of* something. LME–L19.
†**3** A commemorative act or account. M16–L17.
4 The action or process of recording something, esp. in writing. E19.

recordative /rɪˈkɔːdətɪv/ *adjective*. M16.
[French †*recordatif* or late Latin *recordativus*, from Latin *recordat-*: see prec., -IVE.]
Commemorative.

recorder /rɪˈkɔːdə/ *noun*[1]. LME.
[Anglo-Norman *recordour*, Old French *-eur*, formed as RECORD *verb*: see -ER[2]; later, partly from RECORD *verb* + -ER[1].]
1 Formerly, a magistrate or judge with criminal or civil jurisdiction in a city or borough. Now, in England and Wales, a barrister or solicitor of at least ten years' standing appointed as a part-time judge, esp. in certain Crown Courts. LME.
†**2** A witness. LME–E17.
3 A maker or keeper of (esp. written or official) records. M16.
4 An apparatus for recording audio or video signals, etc.; *spec.* a tape recorder. L19.

📖 **3** M. SEYMOUR Conrad . . was a far from reliable recorder of the past. **4** D. BAGLEY He switched on the recorder which would put . . data on to . . magnetic tape. ***tape recorder, video recorder***.

■ **recordership** *noun* the (term of) office of a recorder M16.

recorder /rɪˈkɔːdə/ *noun*[2]. LME.
[from RECORD *verb* + -ER[1].]
MUSIC. A reedless wind instrument of cylindrical shape, played by blowing directly into one end while covering differing combinations of holes along the cylinder; a player of this instrument. Also called ***English flute***.

recording /rɪˈkɔːdɪŋ/ *noun*. ME.
[from RECORD *verb* + -ING[1].]
†**1** Remembrance, recollection; meditation. ME–M16.
2 The practising or singing of birds. M16.
3 The action of setting something down on record. M17. ▸**b** The action or process of recording audio or video signals for subsequent reproduction. E20.
4 Recorded material; a recorded broadcast, performance, etc. M20.

📖 **4** P. MANN We could not tell whether these words were a recording or live speech.

Comb.: **recording amplifier**: which amplifies the signals supplied to the recording device or medium; **recording channel** a circuit or set of equipment used for audio or video recording; **recording engineer**: responsible for the technical aspects of making an audio or video recording; **recording head** = HEAD *noun* 25; **recording level** a measure of the average strength of a recorded signal.

Recordite /ˈrɛkɔːdʌɪt/ *adjective & noun*. *obsolete* exc. *Hist.* M19.
[from *Record* (see below) + -ITE[1].]
► **A** *adjective*. Of, pertaining to, or adhering to views represented by the evangelical Church of England newspaper, the *Record* (1828–1949). M19.
► **B** *noun*. An adherent of such views. M19.

recorte /reˈkorte/ *noun*. E20.
[Spanish, lit. 'cutting, trimming'.]
BULLFIGHTING. A pass by which the torero cuts short the bull's charge.

recount /rɪˈkaʊnt/ *noun*[1]. Long *rare*. L15.
[from RECOUNT *verb*[1]. In early use, perh. after Old French *raconte*.]
An account, a narrative; narration.
■ **recountless** *adjective* unable to be recounted E17.

recount /ˈriːkaʊnt/ *noun*[2]. L19.
[from RE- + COUNT *noun*[1].]
A subsequent or new count, esp. of votes in an election.

recount /rɪˈkaʊnt/ *verb*[1]. LME.
[Anglo-Norman, Old Northern French *reconter*, from *re-* RE- + *conter* COUNT *verb*.]
1 *verb trans.* Relate, narrate, give a detailed account of (a fact, event, etc.). LME. ▸**b** Relate (facts, events, etc.) in order; enumerate, itemize. L15.
†**2** *verb trans.* Consider or reflect on; debate (*with* or *within* oneself). E16–M17.
†**3** *verb trans.* Regard or consider (a person or thing) as possessing a certain character or quality, or as belonging to a certain category or class. Foll. by *as, among, for, in, to be*, or with compl. E16–M17.
†**4** *verb intrans. & trans.* Reckon, count *up*. M16–M17.

📖 **1** R. HOLMES The traveller . . recounting his most private thoughts. C. HEILBRUN *Testament of Youth*, which recounts Brittain's experience in the war.

■ **recountable** *adjective* (*rare*) L15. **recounter** *noun* (*rare*) a person who relates or recounts something L16. †**recountment** *noun* (*rare*, Shakes.) (a) narration, (a) recital: only in E17.

recount /riːˈkaʊnt/ *verb*[2] *trans.* M18.
[from RE- + COUNT *verb*.]
Count again.

†**recounter** *verb*. LME.
[from RE- + COUNTER *verb*, prob. after French *rencontrer*.]
1 *verb trans. & (rare) intrans.* Meet in battle or combat. LME–L16. ▸**b** Confront, withstand, or counteract (a feeling or action). L15–E18.
2 *verb trans.* Encounter or meet by chance; come upon, fall in with. LME–M17.
3 *verb trans.* SCOTS LAW. Offer or give a counter-pledge. LME–L17.

recoup /rɪˈkuːp/ *noun*. M19.
[from next.]
LAW. The action or an act of retaining or deducting an amount or portion from something due or an amount owing to another; a deduction, a discount. Now freq. *attrib.*

recoup /rɪˈkuːp/ *verb*. LME.
[Old French *recouper* retrench, cut back, from *re-* RE- + *couper* cut.]
► **I** †**1** *verb trans.* Cut short; interrupt. *rare*. Only in LME.
2 *verb trans. & intrans.* LAW. Deduct or retain (an amount or portion). E17.
► **II 3** *verb trans.* With double obj.: recompense or reimburse (a person) for; make up or make good (a loss, outlay, etc.) to. M17.
4 *verb trans.* Recover the amount of, make good (a loss, outlay, etc.). M19.
5 *verb trans.* Recompense or reimburse (a person). (Foll. by *for*.) M19.
6 *verb intrans.* Recover one's finances. E20.
7 *verb intrans. & trans.* Regain or recover (lost health, vitality, etc.). M20.

📖 **3** *Observer* Amounts returned in sale of land . . will tend to recoup the Metropolitan Board . . their outlay. **4** *Japan Times* The market recouped some early losses. **5** *Times* To recoup shipowners for . . losses suffered in last year's dock strike. **7** O. MANNING Alma spent half of each year on the continent recouping from . . English life. G. DALY He went . . to Bournemouth, . . to recoup his strength.

■ **recoupable** *adjective* L19. **recoupment** *noun* the action or an act of recouping; the fact of being recouped for loss, outlay, etc.: M19.

†**recour** *noun & verb*. ME.
[Var. of RECOVER *noun*. Cf. RECURE.]
► **A** *noun*. Recovery; support, help; resource. Only in ME.
► **B** *verb trans.* Recover. *rare* (Spenser). Only in L16.

recourse /rɪˈkɔːs/ *noun & verb*. LME.
[Old & mod. French *recours* from Latin *recursus*, formed as RE- + *cursus* COURSE *noun*[1].]
► **A** *noun*. †**1** A running or flowing back; a return, a reflux. Also, opportunity or passage to return. LME–M18. ▸**b** A periodic return or recurrence. L16–L17.
†**2** Movement or flow in some direction; a course or passage *to* or *into* something. LME–M17.
3 The action or an act of turning or resorting *to* a person or thing for help, advice, protection, etc. Freq. in ***have recourse to***. LME.
4 A person or thing turned or resorted to for help, advice, protection, etc. LME. ▸**b** LAW (chiefly *Scot.*). The right to demand financial compensation; *esp.* the holder's right of claim on the drawer and indorsers if the acceptor fails to honour a bill of exchange. M18.
†**5** Access or opportunity to resort *to* (esp. a person). LME–L16.
†**6** Usual or habitual visiting of a particular place. E16–E18. ▸**b** (A) gathering of people at a particular time. E16–M17.

📖 **3** M. STOTT Our mothers . . could have recourse to a hatpin if attacked. W. HORWOOD Fear is a numbing thing when there is no recourse to hope. **4** R. LYND Games are the last recourse to those who do not know how to idle. **b without recourse**: a formula used by the endorser of a bill etc. to disclaim liability for non-payment.

► **B** *verb intrans.* †**1** Return *to* (a place, thought, the mind, etc.). L15–M17.
2 Have recourse *to*. Now *rare* or *obsolete*. L16.

recover /rɪˈkʌvə/ *noun*. ME.
[Old French *recovre*, from *recouvrer* RECOVER *verb*[1]; later directly from the verb.]
†**1** (Means of) recovery from misfortune, trouble, illness, error, etc. ME–M17.
†**2** LAW. = RECOVERY 4. LME–E16.
†**3** Recovery of something lost, a debt or amount due, etc. L15–M16.
4 a MILITARY. A position of a firearm forming part of the manual exercise in which the lock is at shoulder height and the sling faces out. Also ***recover position***. L18. ▸**b** The action or an act of bringing something back or of coming back to a former or the correct or usual position. E19.

recover /rɪˈkʌvə/ *verb*[1]. ME.
[Anglo-Norman *recoverer*, Old French *recovrer* (mod. *recouvrer*) from Latin *recuperare* RECUPERATE.]
► **I** *verb trans.* **1** Restore to health, strength, or consciousness. In *pass.*, be well again. ME. ▸**b** Restore to a good or proper condition; set or make right again; rescue. Now only *from* or *out of* a state. LME.
2 Regain health, strength, or consciousness after; get better from. Now *rare*. ME. ▸**b** Make up for; make good (again); annul or remove the ill effect of. Now *rare*. LME. ▸†**c** Cure, heal. M16–M18.
3 Regain as a quality, condition, or attribute; regain as a functioning faculty; regain the bodily use of. ME. ▸**b** Restore to another as a quality, condition, or attribute. L15. ▸**c** Remember. *rare*. E17.
4 Get back into one's hands or possession; win back; *spec.* get back or obtain possession of or a right to by legal process. LME. ▸**b** Find or come across again. E17. ▸**c** Remove or extract for recycling or reuse. E20.
†**5** Get in place of or in return for. LME–E16.
6 *gen.* Get, obtain; get hold of; collect, gather up. LME.
7 Reach, arrive at. Now *rare*. LME. ▸†**b** Return to, get back to. LME–L17.
8 Restore to friendship, good relations, or willing obedience; reconcile. Now *rare*. L16.
9 Restore to a usual or recognized position; *spec.* (*a*) bring (a firearm) back to the recover position; (*b*) pull (a horse) back from a stumble etc. L16.

📖 **1** SWIFT Any more than a dead carcase can be recovered to life by a cordial. J. AUSTEN A young lady who faints, must be recovered. F. MARRYAT He . . recovered her from an imminent . . disease. **2b** C. JOHNSTON To try . . to recover the loss . . we had been too late to prevent. **3** A. HELPS I had . . recovered my usual health. W. CATHER Though he recovered his speech, it was . . clouded. **4** M. PATTISON To annex to them those districts . . he could recover for the empire. E. WELTY A child's ball thrown over her fence was never to be recovered. **6 recover the wind of** = ***gain the wind of*** s.v. GAIN *verb*[2].

For other words beginning with *re-* see the entry for **re-**

▶ **II** *verb intrans. & refl.* **10** †**a** *verb intrans. & refl.* Return; retreat; succeed in coming *into*, *to*, etc. ME–L17. ▸**b** *verb refl.* Withdraw or escape *from* or *out of*. Now *rare*. E17.

11 *verb intrans. & refl.* Regain health, strength, or consciousness; get well; regain composure. (Foll. by *from*, (arch.) *of*.) LME.

12 *verb refl. & intrans.* Regain one's footing or balance; return to a former, usual, or correct position or state. (Foll. by *from*.) LME. ▸**b** *verb intrans.* FENCING. Return to a position of guard after a thrust. E18. ▸**c** *verb intrans.* Rise again after bowing or curtseying. E18.

13 *verb intrans.* Obtain possession or restoration of a thing by legal process. LME.

> 🕮 **11** D. JACOBSON Days in bed, recovering from . . bruises and shock. L. HELLMAN Hannah did not recover She died . . after I left. L. ELLMANN He waited . . while I recovered myself. **12** DAY LEWIS Never recovered from the agnosticism into which I lapsed during my youth. A. MASON Recovering himself from a perilously off-balance position. D. ADAMS He landed awkwardly, stumbled, recovered.

■ **recove'ree** *noun* †(**a**) LAW a person from whom property is recovered, *spec.* the defendant in an action of common recovery; (**b**) a person recovering from a disease or illness: M16. **recoverless** *adjective* that cannot be recovered E17.

recover *verb*² var. of RE-COVER *verb*.

re-cover /riːˈkʌvə/ *verb trans.* Also **recover**. LME.
[from RE- + COVER *verb*².]
Cover again.

recoverable /rɪˈkʌv(ə)rəb(ə)l/ *adjective*. LME.
[from RECOVER *verb*¹ + -ABLE.]
1 Able to be recovered or regained; retrievable; able to be reclaimed or reused. LME. ▸**b** *spec.* Of mineral reserves: able to be extracted economically on account of location and quality. M20.
2 Able to be cured or revived; restorable to a healthy or former state or condition. L16.
†**3** Able to be retraced. *rare* (Shakes.). Only in E17.

> 🕮 **1** R. LINDNER People without a recoverable past, people who lived entirely in the present. N. CHOMSKY A deleted element is . . always recoverable. *Choice* Treating it as a civil debt recoverable in the . . county court. **2** C. TOMALIN Her condition was serious but recoverable.

■ **recovera'bility** *noun* M19. **recoverableness** *noun* E17.

recoverance /rɪˈkʌv(ə)r(ə)ns/ *noun*. *arch.* LME.
[Old French: see RECOVER *verb*¹, -ANCE.]
1 Recovery from misfortune, adversity, etc.; the remedy or help for this. LME.
†**2** The regaining or recovery *of* some thing, state, condition, etc. LME–M16.

recoverer /rɪˈkʌv(ə)rə/ *noun*. LME.
[from RECOVER *verb*¹ + -ER¹.]
1 A person who recovers something. LME.
†**2** LAW. = RECOVEROR. E16–M18.

†**recoveror** *noun*. E17.
[from RECOVER *verb*¹ + -OR.]
LAW. A plaintiff who receives a favourable judgement, esp. in an action of common recovery.

recovery /rɪˈkʌv(ə)ri/ *noun*. LME.
[Anglo-Norman *recoverie*, Old French *reco(u)vree*, from *recovrer*: see RECOVER *verb*¹, -ERY.]
▶ **I** †**1** Possibility or means of recovering or being restored to a former, usual, or correct state. LME–L17.
2 The action or an act of returning to a former, usual, or correct position. E16. ▸**b** GOLF. A stroke bringing the ball out of a bunker etc. M20.
3 Restoration or return to a former, usual, or correct state or condition, as health, prosperity, stability, etc.; an instance of this. L16. ▸†**b** The cure *of* an illness, wound, etc. E17–M18.

> 🕮 **2** W. COWPER Our recovery from our fall. **3** J. F. HENDRY Rodin had influenza and made . . a slow recovery. A. BULLOCK Creating the best possible conditions . . for economic recovery in the world. R. BERTHOUD The 1920s had been . . a time of recovery from the First World War.

▶ **II 4** LAW. The fact or process of gaining or regaining possession of or a right to property, compensation, etc.; *spec.* (now *Hist.*) (also ***common recovery***) a process, based on a legal fiction, by which an entailed estate may be transferred from one party to another. L15.
5 The process, fact, or possibility of regaining possession, use, or control of something, esp. a thing or things lost or taken away; the recovering *of* a debt, loss, former condition, etc. M16. ▸**b** A thing or (now usu.) an amount recovered, freq. contrasted with an initial loss etc. L18. ▸**c** The extraction or retrieval of a usable substance from raw material or a reusable substance from industrial waste etc. L19. ▸**d** The collection or gathering up of something, esp. a thing or things temporarily out of one's control or possession; an instance of this. E20.
†**6** The act or opportunity of reaching or arriving at somewhere or something. M16–M17.

> 🕮 **5** N. WANLEY He retired for recovery of his health. GIBBON The recovery of Italy and Africa by the arms of Justinian. **d** L. HELLMAN The dogs made such fine recoveries that we came back with fourteen ducks. *Times of India* The encounter resulted in the . . recovery of some arms.

Phrases: **common recovery**: see sense 4 above. **in the recovery**, **on the recovery** recovering, convalescent.
Comb.: **recovery position** a position used in first aid to prevent choking in unconscious patients, in which the body lies facing downwards and slightly to the side, supported by the bent limbs; **recovery room**: in a hospital etc., where a patient can recover after an operation or treatment; **recovery time** (**a**) the time required for a material or piece of equipment to return to a former or the usual condition following an action, as the passage of a current through electrical equipment; (**b**) RAILWAYS time allowed in a schedule excess to the usual necessary journey time; **recovery ward**: in a hospital, where a patient can recover after an operation.

recreance /ˈrɛkrɪəns/ *noun*¹. *arch.* L15.
[from RECRE(ATION *noun*¹ + -ANCE.]
Recreation; refreshment.

recreance /ˈrɛkrɪəns/ *noun*². *rare*. L19.
[formed as next: see -ANCE.]
= next.

recreancy /ˈrɛkrɪənsi/ *noun*. Now *literary*. E17.
[from next: see -ANCY.]
The quality of being recreant.

recreant /ˈrɛkrɪənt/ *adjective & noun*. Now *literary*. ME.
[Old French, use as adjective & noun of pres. pple of *recroire* yield, surrender from medieval Latin (*se*) *recredere* surrender (oneself), formed as RE- + *credere* entrust, believe: see -ANT¹.]
▶ **A** *adjective*. **1** Confessing oneself to be vanquished, surrendering to an opponent; faint-hearted, cowardly, craven. ME.
2 Unfaithful to one's duty; apostate; false. M17.

> 🕮 **2** D. G. MITCHELL The vain purposes which have made me recreant to the better nature.

▶ **B** *noun*. An apostate; a coward. LME.
■ **recreantly** *adverb* L15. **recreantness** *noun* (*rare*) E17.

recreate /riːkrɪˈeɪt/ *ppl adjective*. M19.
[from RECREATE *verb*² after CREATE *adjective*, *verb*: see -ATE².]
Recreated, created again.

recreate /ˈrɛkrɪeɪt/ *verb*¹. LME.
[Latin *recreat-* pa. ppl stem of *recreare*, formed as RE- + *creare* CREATE *verb*.]
1 *verb trans.* Refresh or cheer (a person) by giving comfort, consolation, or encouragement. Now *rare*. LME.
2 *verb trans.* Restore to a good or normal physical condition from a state of weakness or exhaustion; reinvigorate. Now only *refl.* L15.
†**3** *verb trans.* Refresh (a sense or sensory organ) by means of some agreeable object or impression. E16–E18.
4 *verb trans.* Refresh or enliven (the mind, the spirits, a person) by some pleasurable or interesting activity, pastime, etc., or (formerly) a physical influence. M16.
†**5** *verb trans.* Relieve (an occupation, state, etc.) by means of something of an opposite nature. M16–M17.
6 *verb intrans.* Take recreation; amuse oneself. Now chiefly *US*. L16.

> 🕮 **2** THOMAS HUGHES He stopped . . , and recreated himself with a glass of beer. **4** W. H. PRESCOTT Their sovereigns . . were wont to recreate their spirits with elegant poetry.

■ **recreator** *noun*¹ (**a**) a thing that refreshes or reinvigorates a person; (**b**) a person who takes recreation: L19.

recreate /riːkrɪˈeɪt/ *verb*² *trans*. L16.
[from RE- + CREATE *verb*.]
Create over again, in fact or in imagination.
■ **recreator** *noun*² a person who creates something over again L16.

recreation /rɛkrɪˈeɪʃ(ə)n/ *noun*¹. LME.
[Old & mod. French *récréation* from Latin *recreatio(n-)*, formed as RE- + *creatio(n-)* CREATION.]
†**1** Refreshment by taking food; a meal; nourishment. LME–E17.
†**2** Refreshment or comfort produced by something affecting the senses or body; mental or spiritual consolation; a comfort or consolation. LME–L15.
3 a An activity or pastime pursued, esp. habitually, for the pleasure or interest it gives. LME. ▸**b** The action or the fact of pursuing such an activity or pastime. LME. ▸**c** A person who or thing which provides recreation. *rare*. E17.
†**4** A place of refreshment or recreation. *rare*. LME–E17.

> 🕮 **3a** J. GALSWORTHY Forsytes, whose chief recreation . . is the discussion of each other's affairs. **b** E. WAUGH As recreation I am beginning a detective story.

Comb.: **recreation-ground** a piece of land available to the public for games and play.
■ **recreationist** *noun* (**a**) a person who pursues a recreation; (**b**) a person who is concerned with the provision of facilities for recreation: E20.

recreation /riːkrɪˈeɪʃ(ə)n/ *noun*². E16.
[from RE- + CREATION.]
The action of creating something over again; a new creation.

recreational /rɛkrɪˈeɪʃ(ə)n(ə)l/ *adjective*. M17.
[from RECREATION *noun*¹ + -AL¹.]
Of or pertaining to recreation; used for or as a form of recreation; concerned with recreation.

> 🕮 *Philadelphia Inquirer* Other recreational facilities include two . . tennis courts, a swimming pool and a jogging trail. **recreational drug**: taken on an occasional basis for pleasure, esp. when socializing. **recreational vehicle**: intended for recreational use, e.g. when camping or touring.

■ **recreationalist** *noun* a recreationist L20. **recreationally** *adverb* M20.

recreative /ˈrɛkrɪeɪtɪv/ *adjective*¹. L15.
[from RECREATE *verb*¹ + -IVE, after French *récréatif*.]
Tending to refresh in a pleasurable manner; amusing, diverting.

recreative /riːkrɪˈeɪtɪv/ *adjective*². M19.
[from RE- + CREATIVE.]
That creates over again.

recredential /rɛkrɪˈdɛnʃ(ə)l/ *noun & adjective*. M17.
[from RE- + CREDENTIAL.]
Hist. ▶ **A** *noun*. In *pl.* Letters serving as credentials for an ambassador returning from a foreign court. M17.
▶ **B** *adjective*. Of letters: serving as credentials in this manner. E18.

recrement /ˈrɛkrɪm(ə)nt/ *noun*. Now *rare*. L16.
[French *récrément* or Latin *recrementum*, formed as RE- + *cre-* pa. ppl stem of *cernere* separate: see -MENT.]
†**1** A waste product of an organism. Also, a fluid produced in the body and again absorbed into it, as saliva or bile. L16–M19.
2 The superfluous or useless portion of a substance; dross, scum. L16.
■ **recre'mental** *adjective* L16. **recremen'titious** *adjective* drossy, superfluous; of the nature of waste or scum: M17.

recriminate /rɪˈkrɪmɪneɪt/ *verb*. E17.
[medieval Latin *recriminat-* pa. ppl stem of *recriminari*, formed as RE- + Latin *criminare*: see CRIMINATE.]
1 *verb intrans.* Make mutual or counter accusations. E17.
2 *verb trans.* **a** Make a counter accusation against (a person). Now *rare*. E17. ▸†**b** Make as a counter accusation *against* or *upon* a person. E–M17.
■ **recriminative** *adjective* recriminatory E19. **recriminatory** *adjective* involving or of the nature of recrimination L18.

recrimination /rɪˌkrɪmɪˈneɪʃ(ə)n/ *noun*. E17.
[French *récrimination* or medieval Latin *recriminatio(n-)*, formed as prec.: see -ATION.]
1 The action of making an accusation, esp. against an accuser. E17.
2 An accusation, esp. against an accuser; an expression of reprimand or criticism. Usu. in *pl.* E17.

> 🕮 **1** K. ISHIGURO No one has ever considered Father's past something to view with recrimination. **2** D. LEAVITT Going back would mean having to listen to her recriminations and resentments.

recross /riːˈkrɒs/ *verb trans. & intrans.* LME.
[from RE- + CROSS *verb*.]
Cross or pass over again.

recrudency /rɪˈkruːd(ə)nsi/ *noun*. *rare*. E17.
[Perh. syncopated from RECRUDESCENCY.]
= RECRUDESCENCE 1.

recrudescence /riːkruːˈdɛs(ə)ns/ *noun*. E18.
[from Latin *recrudescere*, formed as RE- + *crudescere* become raw, from *crudus*: see CRUDE, -ESCENCE.]
1 The state or fact of breaking out afresh; a recurrence, esp. of a disease, a wound, or something unpleasant. E18.
2 A revival or rediscovery of something good or valuable. E20.
■ **recrudesce** *verb intrans.* [back-form.] break out again, recur, esp. after a dormant period L19. **recrudescency** *noun* (now *rare*) (**a**) recrudescence M17. **recrudescent** *adjective* recurrent E18.

recruit /rɪˈkruːt/ *noun*. M17.
[French dial. †*recrute* = French *recrue* use as noun of fem. pa. pple of *recroître* increase again from Latin *recrescere*, formed as RE- + *crescere* grow. Cf. CREW *noun*¹, ROOKIE.]
▶ **I 1** †**a** A fresh or supplementary body of troops. M17–E18. ▸**b** Orig., a member of a fresh or supplementary body of troops. Now, a person newly or recently enlisted in one of the armed forces and not yet fully trained; *transf.* a new employee or member of a society or organization; a beginner. M17.
2 *gen.* A fresh or additional supply or number; a replenishment or supplement. Now *rare* or *obsolete*. M17.
3 ECOLOGY. An animal which has recently reached the size that qualifies it to be counted as a member of the population to which it belongs, esp. at sexual maturity. M20.

> 🕮 **1b** *Financial Times* More graduate recruits go into manufacturing industries in Japan than . . in Britain. **2** E. HELME Austin carried a lamp with a recruit of oil. SIR W. SCOTT This recruit to my finances was not a matter of indifference to me.

▶ **II** †**4** Increase in numbers, esp. of an army. **M17–L18.**
5 Renewal, repair; renewal of strength or vigour; recovery. Now *rare* or *obsolete*. **M17.**
6 A thing that contributes to the development or sustenance of something. Now *rare* or *obsolete*. **M17.**

recruit /rɪˈkruːt/ *verb*. **M17.**
[French *recruter*, formed as prec.]
▶ **I** *verb trans*. **1** Reinforce, supplement, or keep up the number of (a class of people or things). **M17.**
2 Replenish (*with*). Now *rare*. **M17.**
3 Refresh, reinvigorate; renew; strengthen, sustain, (a quality). **M17.**
4 Enlist as a recruit in one of the armed forces; obtain as a new employee or member of an organization etc. Also, form (a regiment etc.) by enlisting recruits. **E19.** ▸**b** (Attempt to) induce (an athlete) to sign on as a student at a college or university. *US*. **E20.** ▸**c** *PHYSIOLOGY*. Bring (additional muscle fibres or muscular activity) into play by the recruitment of their neurones. **M20.**

> 📖 **3** J. AIKEN Going into the country . . to recruit her strength after so much nursing. **4** L. DEIGHTON You recruit ordinary people to become spies. G. SAYER The Oxford City Home Guard Battalion was being recruited to repel German troops. ***recruiting agent***, ***recruiting officer***, ***recruiting sergeant***, etc. **b** *Tucson (Arizona) Citizen* He was one of the state's most highly recruited athletes . . with every major college . . after him.

▶ **II** *verb intrans*. **5** Get or seek recruits. **M17.**
6 Recover one's vigour or health; follow a regime aimed at achieving this. **M17.**
†**7** Recoup outlay or expenditure. **L17–E18.**

> 📖 **6** L. STRACHEY To recruit for two months at Scarborough, 'with a course of quinine'.

■ **recruitable** *adjective* (earlier in **UNRECRUITABLE**) **L19.** **recruital** *noun* †(*a*) a new or fresh supply; (*b*) restoration to health: **M17.** **recruiter** *noun* (*a*) *Hist*. an additional Member of Parliament, appointed or elected to bring up the number; (*b*) a person who or thing which recruits, esp. soldiers or employees: **M17.**

recruitment /rɪˈkruːtm(ə)nt/ *noun*. **E19.**
[from **RECRUIT** *verb* + **-MENT**.]
1 A reinforcement. **E19.**
2 The action or process of recruiting. **M19.**
3 *PHYSIOLOGY*. **a** The involvement of successively more motor neurones in response to an unchanging stimulus. **E20.** ▸**b** The phenomenon shown by an ear which, while having a relatively high threshold for the perception of quiet sounds, perceives louder sounds with undiminished intensity (i.e. increases in actual intensity of sound result in abnormally great increases in perceived loudness). **M20.**
4 *ECOLOGY*. Increase in a natural population as progeny grow and become recruits; the extent of such increase. **M20.**
5 *ANATOMY*. The incorporation into a tissue or region of cells from elsewhere in the body. **L20.**

rect /rɛkt/ *adjective*. Long *rare* or *obsolete*. **LME.**
[Latin *rectus* straight.]
Direct; erect, straight; *fig*. upright.
■ **rectly** *adverb* directly **E20.**

recta *noun pl*. see **RECTUM**.

rectal /ˈrɛkt(ə)l/ *adjective*. **L19.**
[from **RECTUM** + **-AL**[1].]
ANATOMY & MEDICINE. Of or belonging to the rectum.
■ **rectally** *adverb* by way of the rectum **E20.**

rectangle /ˈrɛktaŋg(ə)l/ *noun*. **L16.**
[French, or medieval Latin *rectangulum* for earlier *rectiangulum* use as noun of neut. sing. of late Latin *rectiangulus* (after Greek *orthogōnios*), from Latin *rectus* straight + *angulus* **ANGLE** *noun*[3].]
1 A plane figure with four right angles and four straight sides, opposite sides being parallel and equal in length; *esp*. one in which adjacent sides are unequal; *gen*. a thing that has the shape of a rectangle. **L16.** ▸†**b** *MATH*. The product of two quantities. **L17–M18.**
†**2** A right angle. **M17–L18.**

†**rectangle** *adjective*. **L16–L18.**
[medieval Latin *rectangulus* from late Latin *rectiangulus*: see prec.]
Of a triangle: right-angled.

rectangled /ˈrɛktaŋg(ə)ld/ *adjective*. Now *rare*. **L16.**
[from **RECTANGLE** *noun* + **-ED**[2].]
Right-angled.

rectangular /rɛkˈtaŋgjʊlə/ *adjective*. **E17.**
[from **ANGULAR** after French *rectangulaire*.]
1 Shaped like a rectangle; having four straight sides and four right angles; (of a solid body) having the sides, base, or section in the form of a rectangle. **E17.**
2 Placed or lying at right angles. **M17.**
3 Having parts, lines, etc., at right angles to each other; characterized or distinguished by some arrangement of this kind. **E18.**

> 📖 **2** A. S. EDDINGTON The laws of mechanics . . are usually enunciated with respect to 'unaccelerated rectangular axes'. **3 rectangular coordinate** *MATH*. each of a set of coordinates measured along axes at right angles to one another (usu. in *pl*.). **rectangular hyperbola** *MATH*.: with its asymptotes at right angles to one another.

■ **rectanguˈlarity** *noun* the quality or state of being rectangular or having right angles; *fig*. stiffness: **E18.** **rectangularly** *adverb* in a rectangular manner or direction **M17.**

recte /ˈrɛkteɪ/ *adverb*. **M19.**
[Latin, lit. 'in a straight line, rightly'.]
Correctly: introducing a word or phrase as a correct version of that just given.
per recte et retro, ***recte et retro*** [medieval Latin = in the right way and backwards] *MUSIC* with a theme or subject running backwards as well as forwards in the same piece.
¶ Earliest in the above phr.

rectenna /rɛkˈtɛnə/ *noun*. **L20.**
[from *rect*(*ifying ant*)*enna*.]
A unit combining a receiving aerial and a device for rectifying the current it produces, *esp*. one used in the conversion of solar energy to electricity.

recti *noun* pl. of **RECTUS**.

rectifiable /ˈrɛktɪfʌɪəb(ə)l/ *adjective*. **M17.**
[from **RECTIFY** + **-ABLE**.]
Able to be rectified, esp. mathematically.

rectification /ˌrɛktɪfɪˈkeɪʃ(ə)n/ *noun*. **E17.**
[Old & mod. French, or late Latin *rectificatio*(*n*-), from *rectificat*- pa. ppl stem of medieval Latin *rectificare* **RECTIFY**: see **-ATION**.]
The action or an act of rectifying something; *spec*. the conversion of alternating current into direct current.

rectified /ˈrɛktɪfʌɪd/ *adjective*. **M16.**
[formed as next + **-ED**[1].]
1 That has been rectified; corrected, amended, refined. **M16.**
2 Purified by (esp. repeated or continuous) distillation; redistilled. Chiefly in ***rectified spirit(s)***, a mixture of ethanol (95.6 per cent) and water produced as an azeotrope by distillation. **L16.**
3 Of a tulip flower: having variegated colouring caused by a virus affecting the plant. **M17.**

rectifier /ˈrɛktɪfʌɪə/ *noun*. **E17.**
[from next + **-ER**[1].]
1 A person who or thing which rectifies something. **E17.**
2 *spec*. **a** A person who or apparatus which rectifies spirit; a distiller. **E18.** ▸**b** A device or substance which permits an electric current to flow preferentially in one direction; *esp*. a device for converting alternating current into direct current. **L19.**

rectify /ˈrɛktɪfʌɪ/ *verb trans*. **LME.**
[Old & mod. French *rectifier* from medieval Latin *rectificare*, from *rectus* right: see **-FY**.]
1 Put right, correct, amend; remove any errors in; reform (a person's nature etc.); restore to morality or to a satisfactory or normal condition. **LME.** ▸†**b** Restore (a diseased organ) to a healthy condition. **LME–L17.** ▸†**c** Set right (a person who is mistaken or in error). **L16–E18.** ▸**d** Correct errors of perspective in (an oblique aerial photograph, or a position derived from one) in order to obtain a plan view. **E20.**
2 Purify or refine by repeated distillation or a chemical process. **LME.**
3 Put right by calculation or adjustment; make an adjustment or correction to (an instrument or measurement). **M16.**
4 †**a** Make straight; bring into line. **L16–L18.** ▸**b** *MATH*. Obtain a straight line equal in length to (a given curve). **L17.**
5 Convert (alternating current) into direct current. **L19.**

> 📖 **1** ROBERT WATSON He found means . . to rectify their opinion of his conduct. GEO. ELIOT You can neither straighten their noses, nor . . rectify their dispositions. H. L. MENCKEN Now and then he falls into error, but . . the specialists quickly . . rectify it. P. ACKROYD He itemized the damage and took immediate steps to rectify it. **2 rectifying column** a columnar apparatus in which a substance being distilled is subjected to successive stages of purification by continually condensing and redistilling the vapour. **3** H. MARTINEAU She . . employed herself . . in rectifying the time-piece by her own watch.

rectilineal /rɛktɪˈlɪnɪəl/ *adjective*. **M17.**
[formed as next: see **-AL**[1].]
= **RECTILINEAR**.

rectilinear /rɛktɪˈlɪnɪə/ *adjective*. **M17.**
[from late Latin *rectilineus*, from Latin *rectus* straight + *linea* **LINE** *noun*[2]: see **-AR**[1].]
1 Of motion, course, or direction: taking or having the course of a straight line; tending always to the same point. **M17.**
2 Lying in or forming a straight line. **E18.**
3 Bounded or formed by straight lines; characterized by straight lines; *ARCHITECTURE* (**R-**) = **PERPENDICULAR** *adjective* 3. **E18.**
■ **ˌrectilineˈarity** *noun* the quality of being rectilinear **E19.** **rectilinearly** *adverb* in a straight line or straight lines **E19.**

rection /ˈrɛkʃ(ə)n/ *noun*. **M17.**
[Latin *rectio*(*n*-) government, from *rect*-: see **RECTOR**, **-ION**.]
GRAMMAR. = **GOVERNMENT** 8.
■ **rectional** *adjective* **M20.**

rectitude /ˈrɛktɪtjuːd/ *noun*. **LME.**
[Old & mod. French, or late Latin *rectitudo*, from Latin *rectus* right, straight: see **-TUDE**.]
1 †**a** Straightness. **LME–E18.** ▸**b** Straight line; direction in a straight line. Now *rare*. **L16.**
2 Moral uprightness; integrity; virtue. Also, self-righteousness. **M16.**
3 Correctness; an instance of this. **M17.**

> 📖 **2** F. KAPLAN A man of rectitude, benevolence and wisdom. W. M. CLARKE His religious outlook . . allied to a moral rectitude and a willingness to censure others. **3** H. E. MANNING A crookedness which hinders the faculty of discerning the rectitude of God's truth.

■ **rectiˈtudinous** *adjective* characterized by rectitude; self-righteous: **L19.**

rectius /ˈrɛktɪəs/ *adverb*. **M20.**
[Latin, compar. of **RECTE**.]
More correctly: introducing a word or phrase as a more correct version of that just given.

recto /ˈrɛktəʊ/ *noun*. Pl. **-os**. **E19.**
[Latin (sc. *folio*) abl. of *rectus* right.]
The right-hand page of an open book; the front of a leaf in a manuscript or printed book, as opp. to the back or verso.

recto- /ˈrɛktəʊ/ *combining form* of **RECTUM**: see **-O-**.
■ **rectocele** *noun* [Greek *kēlē* tumour, rupture] prolapse of the rectovaginal wall **M19.** **rectopexy** *noun* [**-PEXY**] (an instance of) the surgical attachment of a prolapsed rectum **L19.** **rectoscope** *noun* = **PROCTOSCOPE** **L19.** **recˈtoscopy** *noun* visual examination of the rectum **L19.** **rectoˈsigmoid** *noun & adjective* (designating or pertaining to) the region of the junction of the rectum and the sigmoid **E20.** **recto-ˈuterine** *adjective* pertaining to the rectum and the uterus; ***recto-uterine pouch***, a pouch of the peritoneum between the uterus and the rectum: **M19.** **rectovaˈginal** *adjective* pertaining to the rectum and the vagina **M19.**

rector /ˈrɛktə/ *noun*. **LME.**
[(Old French *rectour* (mod. -*eur*)) from Latin *rector*, from *rect*- pa. ppl stem of *regere* to rule: see **-OR**.]
†**1** A ruler, a governor. **LME–L17.** ▸**b** A person who or thing which has supreme control in any sphere. Now *rare*. **L15.** ▸†**c** The leader of a choir. **M16–L17.** ▸†**d** God, as the ruler of the world. **L16–M18.**
2 In England, an incumbent of a pre-Reformation or Anglican parish where the tithes were formerly retained by the incumbent (cf. **VICAR** 2); now also, in the Church of England, the leader of a team ministry; *ROMAN CATHOLIC CHURCH* a priest in charge of a church; a priest of the Scottish Episcopal Church or the Episcopal Church of the USA who has charge of a congregation. **LME.**
3 The head of certain universities, colleges, schools, and religious institutions. **LME.** ▸**b** One of the senior officers of a Scottish university, now an elected representative of students on its governing body. Also ***Lord Rector***. **LME.** ▸**c** The acting head, and president of the administrative body, in a university in Continental Europe. **M16.**
2 ***lay rector***: see **LAY** *adjective*.
■ **rectoral** *adjective* **M17.** **rectorate** *noun* the position or office of rector; the period during which the office is held: **M17.** **rectoress** *noun* †(*a*) a female ruler; = **RECTRESS**; (*b*) *colloq*. the wife of the rector of a parish: **L16.** **rectorship** *noun* (*a*) the position or office of rector; (*b*) (now *rare*) the position of ruler or governor; government, rule: **L16.**

rectorial /rɛkˈtɔːrɪəl/ *adjective & noun*. **E17.**
[from prec. + **-IAL**.]
▶ **A** *adjective*. **1** Of or pertaining to a university rector; connected with the office or election of a rector. **E17.**
2 Of or belonging to the rector of a parish held by a rector. **M18.**
3 Of or pertaining to a ruler or governor. *rare*. **M19.**
▶ **B** *noun*. At a Scottish university, a rectorial election. *Scot*. **L19.**

rectorite /ˈrɛkt(ə)rʌɪt/ *noun*. **L19.**
[from E. W. *Rector*, 19th-cent. US politician + **-ITE**[1].]
MINERALOGY. A mineral of the montmorillonite group that occurs as large soft white leaves or plates.

rectory /ˈrɛkt(ə)ri/ *noun*. **M16.**
[Anglo-Norman, Old French *rectorie* or medieval Latin *rectoria*, formed as **RECTOR**: see **-Y**[3].]
1 An educational establishment under the control of a rector. Long *obsolete* exc. *Hist*. **M16.**
2 a A benefice held by a rector. **L16.** ▸**b** The residence of a rector. **M19.**
†**3** (A) rectorship. **L16–E19.**

rectress /ˈrɛktrɪs/ *noun*. E17.
[from RECTOR + -ESS[1].]
†**1** A female ruler; = RECTORESS (a). E–M17.
2 The female head of a school or institution. M19.

rectrix /ˈrɛktrɪks/ *noun*. Pl. **-trices** /-ˈtrɪsiːz/. E17.
[Latin, fem. of RECTOR: see -TRIX.]
1 = RECTRESS 1. *rare*. E17.
2 A bird's strong tail feather, used in directing flight. Usu. in *pl*. M18.

rectum /ˈrɛktəm/ *noun*. Pl. **-tums**, **-ta** /-tə/. M16.
[Latin, neut. of *rectus* straight, short for *intestinum rectum* straight gut.]
The final section of the large intestine extending from the sigmoid flexure of the colon to the anus; the equivalent part of the gut in an animal.

rectus /ˈrɛktəs/ *noun*. Pl. **-ti** /-tʌɪ/. E18.
[Latin (sc. *musculus* muscle): see prec.]
1 ANATOMY. Any of several straight muscles, esp. of the abdomen, thigh, neck, and eye. Freq. with mod. Latin specifying word. Also ***rectus muscle***. E18.
2 MUSIC. In a fugal composition, the version of a theme performed in the original, as opp. to the reversed or inverted, order. M20.
2 rectus et inversus /ɛt ɪnˈvɛːsəs/ [= straight and inverted] = ***per* RECTE *et retro***.

rectus in curia /rɛktəs ɪn ˈkjʊərɪə/ *adjectival phr*. L16.
[Latin, lit. 'right in the court'.]
Innocent, acquitted, set right in point of law.

recueil /rəkœj/ *noun*. L15.
[Old & mod. French, from *recueillir* gather up from Latin *recolligere*, formed as RE- + *colligere* COLLECT *verb*.]
1 A literary compilation. L15.
†**2** Reception, welcome; succour. L15–L16.
¶ Formerly naturalized.

recueillement /rəkœjmɑ̃/ *noun*. M19.
[French, from *recueillir*: see prec., -MENT.]
Serious concentration of thought.

†**recule** *verb & noun* var. of RECOIL.

reculer pour mieux sauter /rəkyle pur mjø sote/ *noun phr*. E19.
[French, lit. 'draw back in order to leap better'.]
The use of a withdrawal or setback as a basis for further advance or success.

recumb /rɪˈkʌm/ *verb intrans. rare* (now *joc*.). L17.
[Latin *recumbere*: see RECUMBENT.]
Lean, recline, rest.

recumbent /rɪˈkʌmbənt/ *noun & adjective*. M17.
[Latin *recumbent-* pres. ppl stem of *recumbere* recline, formed as RE- + *-cumbere*: see CUMBENT.]
▶ **A** *noun*. †**1** A person who is dependent on another. *rare*. M–L17.
2 A recumbent bicycle. L20.
▶ **B** *adjective*. **1** Reclining, leaning; lying down. E18.
2 GEOLOGY. Designating a fold whose axial plane is nearly horizontal. E20.
3 ARCHAEOLOGY. Of a megalithic stone: placed so as to be lying on the ground rather than standing upright, and usu. flanked by two uprights. M20.
4 Designating a bicycle designed to be ridden in a recumbent position. L20.

> 🕮 **1** H. NEMEROV The giant recumbent Hills in their sullen haze. S. WEINTRAUB Statues of Prince Albert in every conceivable position, from recumbent to equestrian. **3 recumbent stone circle** a type of stone circle, found esp. in Scotland, characterized by a single recumbent stone forming the focus of a ring of uprights.

■ **recumbence** *noun* (now *rare*) recumbency L17. **recumbency** *noun* (*a*) the state of lying or reclining; a recumbent posture; (*b*) (now *rare*) dependence *on* a person or thing: M17. **recumbently** *adverb* in a recumbent posture M19.

recuperable /rɪˈkuːp(ə)rəb(ə)l/ *adjective*. L15.
[Orig. from Old & mod. French, from *récupérer* from Latin *recuperare* RECUPERATE; later re-formed from RECUPERATE + -ABLE.]
Recoverable.
¶ Not attested between 16 and 20.
■ **recuperaˈbility** *noun* ability to recuperate L19.

recuperate /rɪˈkuːpəreɪt/ *verb*. M16.
[Latin *recuperat-* pa. ppl stem of *recuperare*, formed as RE- + *capere* take, seize (cf. Latin *occupare* OCCUPY): see -ATE[3]. Cf. RECOVER *verb*[1].]
▶**I 1** *verb trans*. Recover or regain (health, something mislaid or lost, etc.). M16.
2 *verb intrans*. Recover from or *from* exhaustion, ill health, financial loss, etc. M19.

> 🕮 **2** P. THEROUX I used my time . . to recuperate from the strenuous train-ride. N. SHERRY Recuperating in hospital he read a history of smuggling.

▶**II 3** *verb trans*. Restore (a person) to health or vigour. Formerly also (*rare*), restore (a thing) to its original condition. L17.
■ **recuperative** *adjective* [Late Latin *recuperativus*] †(*a*) *rare* recoverable; (*b*) capable of restoring health or vigour; pertaining to recuperation; (*c*) designating, of, or pertaining to a recuperator or an air heater using the same principle: E17.

recuperation /rɪˌkuːpəˈreɪʃ(ə)n/ *noun*. L15.
[Latin *recuperatio(n-)*, formed as prec.: see -ATION.]
†**1** The recovery or regaining *of* a thing. L15–L17.
2 Restoration to health or vigour. M19.

recuperator /rɪˈkuːpəreɪtə/ *noun*. E18.
[Latin, formed as RECUPERATE: see -OR.]
1 ROMAN LAW. A member of a commission for trying certain cases. Now *rare*. E18.
2 A form of heat exchanger in which hot waste gases from a furnace are conducted continuously along a system of flues where they impart heat to incoming air or gaseous fuel. L19.
3 A mechanism that returns a gun to the firing position after recoil. E20.

recur /rɪˈkəː/ *verb intrans*. Infl. **-rr-**. LME.
[Latin *recurrere*, formed as RE- + *currere* run.]
1 a Return *into* or *to* a place. *rare*. LME. ▸†**b** Run or move back, recede. *rare*. E17–L18.
2 Have recourse *to* for assistance or argument. E16.
3 Go back in thought, memory, or speech. Usu. foll. by *to* a subject, time, etc. E17.
4 Of a question, difficulty, etc.: come up again for consideration. Of a thought, idea, etc.: come back to one's mind. M17.
5 Of an event, fact, state, etc.: occur or appear again, periodically, or repeatedly. L17. ▸**b** MATH. Of a figure or group of figures in a decimal fraction: come again in the same order indefinitely. E19.

> 🕮 **3** L. WOOLF I must recur to the great subject of food. **4** G. SWIFT This recurring hope . . that . . my sons will come to meet me at the station. **5** V. BRITTAIN Dreams which were to recur . . at frequent intervals for nearly ten years. **b recurring decimal** a decimal fraction in which a figure or group of figures recurs, e.g. 0.111 . . . = ⅑.

■ **recurringly** *adverb* in a recurring manner; repeatedly: E20.

†**recure** *verb*. LME.
[Latin *recurare*, formed as RE- + *curare* CURE *verb*, but also partly repr. RECOVER *verb*[1]. Cf. RECOUR.]
1 *verb trans*. Restore to health or to a normal or sound condition. LME–M17.
2 *verb trans*. Cure (a disease, sickness, etc.), heal (a wound or sore); remedy (a wrong). LME–M17.
3 *verb intrans*. Regain health or a former state; (of a wound) heal. LME–M16.
4 *verb trans*. Recover (something lost); obtain. LME–M17.

recurrence /rɪˈkʌr(ə)ns/ *noun*. M17.
[from next: see -ENCE.]
1 The fact or an instance of recurring; frequent or periodic occurrence. M17.
2 Recourse (*to* something). M17.
3 The action or an act of recurring in thought, memory, or speech. M18.
4 Return or reversion *to* a state, occupation, etc. E19.

> 🕮 **1** K. AMIS Whether or not these outbreaks were . . isolated, we must fear a recurrence.

Comb.: **recurrence formula**, **recurrence relation** MATH. an expression defining the general member of a series in terms of the preceding members; **recurrence surface** SOIL SCIENCE a horizon in a peat bog between highly decomposed and slightly decomposed peat, indicating the commencement of a period of active peat growth; **recurrence time** MATH. the time between two successive occasions when a Markov process enters any given state.
■ Also **recurrency** *noun* (now *rare*) E17.

recurrent /rɪˈkʌr(ə)nt/ *adjective & noun*. L16.
[Latin *recurrent-* pres. ppl stem of *recurrere* RECUR: see -ENT.]
▶**A** *adjective*. **1** ANATOMY. Of a nerve, blood-vessel, etc.: turned back so as to run in a direction opposite to its former one. L16.
2 Occurring frequently or periodically, recurring, esp. (MEDICINE) after apparent cure or remission. M17.
▶**B** *noun*. **1** A recurrent nerve or blood-vessel; *esp*. either of the right and left recurrent laryngeal nerves. L16.
†**2** A verse that reads the same backwards as forwards. *rare*. E17–E18.
■ **recurrently** *adverb* M19.

recursant /rɪˈkəːs(ə)nt/ *adjective*. *rare*. E19.
[Latin *recursant-* pres. ppl stem of *recursare* hasten back, return, from *recurs-*: see next, -ANT[1].]
HERALDRY. Of an eagle: having the back turned halfway towards the observer.

recursion /rɪˈkəːʃ(ə)n/ *noun*. E17.
[Late Latin *recursio(n-)*, from *recurs-* pa. ppl stem of *recurrere* RECUR: see -ION.]
1 (A) return. Now *rare* or *obsolete*. E17.
2 MATH., LOGIC, & LINGUISTICS. **a** The application or use of a recursive procedure or definition. M20 ▸**b** A recursive definition. M20.
Comb.: **recursion formula** MATH. an equation relating the value of a function for a given value of its argument (or arguments) to its values for other values of the argument(s).

recursive /rɪˈkəːsɪv/ *adjective & noun*. L18.
[from Latin *recurs-*: see prec., -IVE.]
▶**A** *adjective*. †**1** Periodically or continually recurring. Only in L18.
2 a MATH. & LOGIC. Involving or designating a repeated procedure such that the required result at each step except the last is given in terms of the result(s) of the next step, until after a finite number of steps a terminus is reached with an outright evaluation of the result. M20. ▸**b** LINGUISTICS. Designating a grammatical rule or category which applies at two or more successive stages in the derivation of a sentence. M20. ▸**c** COMPUTING. Designating a statement, subroutine, etc., some part of which makes use of the whole of itself, so that its explicit interpretation requires in general many successive executions; (of a language, compiler, etc.) that allows of such techniques. M20.
3 PHONETICS. Designating a consonant accompanied by glottal closure or implosion. M20.
▶**B** *noun*. PHONETICS. A recursive consonant. E20.
■ **recursively** *adverb* M20. **recursiveness** *noun* M20.

recurvate /rɪˈkəːvət/ *adjective*. L18.
[Latin *recurvatus* pa. pple, formed as next: see -ATE[2].]
Recurved.
■ **recurvature** *noun* (a) backward curvature E18.

recurvate /rɪˈkəːveɪt/ *verb*. Now *rare*. L16.
[Latin *recurvat-* pa. ppl stem of *recurvare* RECURVE *verb*: see -ATE[3].]
1 *verb trans*. = RECURVE *verb* 1. Usu. in *pass*. L16.
2 *verb intrans*. Bend or turn back. E19.
■ **recurˈvation** *noun* (now *rare*) the fact of being bent or curved back; a backward bend or curve: L16.

recurve /ˈriːkəːv/ *noun*. M20.
[from the verb.]
ARCHERY. A backward-curving end of the limb of a bow; a bow with this feature.

recurve /rɪˈkəːv/ *verb*. L16.
[Latin *recurvare* (trans.), formed as RE- + *curvare* CURVE *verb*.]
1 *verb trans*. Esp. BOTANY. bend back or backwards. Chiefly as ***recurved*** *ppl adjective*. L16.
2 *verb intrans*. Esp. of a wind or current: turn back in a curve to a previous direction. M19.

recurvous /rɪˈkəːvəs/ *adjective*. *rare*. E18.
[from Latin *recurvus*, formed as RE- + *curvus* bent, curved: see -OUS.]
Bent back.

recusal /rɪˈkjuːz(ə)l/ *noun*. Chiefly *US*. M20.
[from RECUSE + -AL[1].]
A judge's voluntary withdrawal from a case that he or she cannot or should not hear. Also, an objection to a judge as prejudiced.

recusant /ˈrɛkjʊz(ə)nt/ *noun & adjective*. M16.
[Latin *recusant-* pres. ppl stem of *recusare* refuse, formed as RE- + *causa* CAUSE *noun* (cf. *accuse*, *excuse*): see -ANT[1].]
▶**A** *noun*. **1** *Hist*. A person who refused to attend the services of the Church of England, *esp*. a Roman Catholic; any religious dissentient. M16.
2 *gen*. A person who refuses to submit to an authority or to comply with a command or regulation. L16.

> 🕮 **1** SIR W. SCOTT This remote county was full of Popish recusants.

▶ **B** *adjective*. That is a recusant. E17.
■ **recusance** *noun* recusancy L16. **recusancy** *noun* the action or practice characteristic of a recusant, esp. a Roman Catholic one M16.

recusation /rɛkjʊˈzeɪʃ(ə)n/ *noun*. Now chiefly *US*. E16.
[Old & mod. French *récusation* or Latin *recusatio(n-)*, from *recusat-* pa. ppl stem of *recusare*: see prec., -ATION.]
LAW. The interposition of an objection or appeal; *esp*. an appeal grounded on a judge's relationship with or possible antagonism to a party in a lawsuit. Cf. RECUSAL.

†**recusatory** *adjective*. *rare*. E16–E18.
[from Latin *recusat-* pa. ppl stem of *recusare*: see RECUSANT, -ORY[2].]
Of or pertaining to recusing; containing a recusal.

recuse /rɪˈkjuːz/ *verb*. LME.
[Latin *recusare*: see RECUSANT. (Cf. Old & mod. French *récuser*.)]
†**1** *verb trans*. Refuse (a thing offered). *rare*. Only in LME.
2 *verb trans*. Reject, renounce, (a person, authority, etc.); object to (a judge) as prejudiced. Now *rare*. LME.
†**3** *verb trans*. Refuse *to do*. LME–M16.
4 *verb intrans*. & *refl*. Of a judge: withdraw from hearing a case because of a possible conflict of interest or lack of impartiality. E19.

> 🕮 **4** T. CLANCY All of the new Justices would ordinarily have to recuse themselves because you selected them.

recycle /riːˈsʌɪk(ə)l/ *verb & noun*. E20.
[from RE- + CYCLE *verb*.]
▶ **A** *verb*. **1** *verb trans*. Return to a previous stage of a cyclic process; convert (waste) into or *into* a usable form; use again with little or no alteration. Also, reclaim (a material) from waste. E20.

2 a *verb trans.* Repeat (a process) on a computer or counting device. M20. ▸**b** *verb intrans.* Of a computer: repeat a procedure. L20.

3 *verb intrans.* Undergo recycling. L20.

> 📖 **1** ANTHONY HUXLEY Sewage can be recycled into fresh water. *Toronto Sun* Eggleton had recycled part of . . his speech from his . . fund-raising dinner. *Lifestyle* Turning the home into a green house with . . recycled loo paper and additive-free foods.

Comb.: **recycling time** PHOTOGRAPHY the time required to recharge the capacitor of a flash unit.

▸**B** *noun.* The operation or process of recycling something. Also, recycled material. E20.

■ **recycla'bility** *noun* the quality of being recyclable L20. **recyclable** *adjective* able to be recycled L20. **recycler** *noun* L20.

red /rɛd/ *noun.* ME.

[The adjective used ellipt. or absol.]

1 a Red colour; a shade of this (freq. with specifying word). ME. ▸**b** *ellipt.* Anything distinguished by red colour, as the red divisions in roulette or rouge-et-noir, the red ball in snooker and similar games, a red piece in a game or player using such a piece, a red signal, a red animal, fish, etc. M16. ▸**c** The red colour conventionally used to represent British territory on a map. Cf. PINK *noun*[4] 4b. Chiefly *Hist.* L19. ▸**d** *The* debit side of an account, conventionally made out in a red colour. Cf. BLACK *noun* 1b. E20.

2 Red fabric; red clothing or dress. ME.

3 A pigment or dye of a red colour (freq. with specifying word); (now *dial.*) ruddle. Formerly also, rouge. LME.

4 †**a** Gold. *rare.* LME–L17. ▸**b** Red wine. LME.

5 a In *pl.* N. American Indians. *offensive.* E19. ▸**b** (Usu. **R-**.) A radical, a republican, an anarchist; a Communist, a socialist. *colloq.* M19.

6 *ellipt.* **a** = *red cent* s.v. RED *adjective.* Chiefly *US.* M19. ▸**b** = *red alert* s.v. RED *adjective.* M20.

7 NAUTICAL. The port side of a ship. M20.

8 = *red-bird* (b), *red devil* s.v. RED *adjective. slang.* M20.

> 📖 **1a** N. TINBERGEN Women paint their lips . . shades of red. EDMUND WARD I stepped out into . . traffic as lights changed from red to green. M. BINCHY Helen . . felt a dull red come up her neck. **4b** K. MILLETT Nell goes off to seek another bottle of red. **5b** C. STEAD She's a *Red* . . always talking about the union.

Phrases: **Admiral of the Red** *Hist.*: of the Red squadron (one of the three divisions of the Royal Navy made in the 17th cent.). *Indian red*: see INDIAN *adjective.* **in the red** in debt, overdrawn, losing money. **out of the red** no longer in debt, making a profit. *Persian red*: see PERSIAN *adjective. Pompeian red*: see POMPEIAN *adjective*[2]. **reds under the bed** *colloq.* denoting an exaggerated fear of the presence and harmful influence of Communist sympathizers within a society etc. *RHODE ISLAND Red. ruby-red*: see RUBY *noun* 3. *sanguine red*: see SANGUINE *adjective* 1a. **see red** get very angry, lose one's temper. *Venetian red*: see VENETIAN *adjective.*

Comb.: **Red-bait** *verb intrans. & trans.* harass and persecute (a person) on account of known or suspected Communist sympathies (chiefly as *Red-baiting verbal noun*); **Red-baiter** a person who practises Red-baiting.

red /rɛd/ *adjective.* Compar. & superl. **-dd-**.

[Old English *rēad* = Old Frisian *rād*, Old Saxon *rōd* (Dutch *rood*), Old High German *rōt* (German *rot*), Old Norse *rauðr*, Gothic *rauþs* from Germanic from Indo-European. Cf. Latin *rufus*, *ruber*, Greek *eruthros*, Sanskrit *rudhira* red.]

1 Of the colour of blood, a ruby, etc., appearing at the least refracted end of the visible spectrum, and found in shades ranging from scarlet or crimson to pink or deep orange. OE. ▸**b** Of wine: made from dark grapes and coloured by their skins. ME. ▸**c** CARDS. Belonging to hearts or diamonds. E18. ▸**d** Designating or pertaining to British territory on a map, conventionally coloured red. Cf. PINK *adjective*[2] 1c. Chiefly *Hist.* E20.

2 a Traditionally designating gold. Cf. *red gold* below. Chiefly *poet. arch.* OE. ▸**b** Golden, made of gold. Now *slang.* LME.

3 Of cloth, clothing, etc.: dyed with red. OE. ▸**b** Wearing red; dressed in red. Now *rare.* ME.

4 a (Of a person) having hair of an auburn or ginger colour; (of hair) of this colour. OE. ▸**b** Of an animal: having reddish hair; tawny, chestnut, bay. Also, (of animal hair) of this colour. LME. ▸**c** Of certain peoples, esp. the N. American Indians: having or regarded as having a reddish skin. See *Red Indian* (a) below. L16.

5 Designating blood (chiefly *poet.*); *transf.* of superior quality or stock. ME.

6 a Of the cheeks, complexion, or lips: of a healthy reddish colour. ME. ▸**b** (Of the face) temporarily suffused with blood, esp. as the result of some sudden feeling or emotion; flushed or blushing *with* anger, shame, etc.; (of a person) flushed in the face. ME. ▸**c** Exceptionally high in colour. LME.

7 Stained or covered with blood. ME.

8 a Involving or characterized by bloodshed, burning, violence, or revolution. ME. ▸**b** (Also **R-**.) Communist, socialist; Russian, Soviet (orig. with ref. to the colour of a party badge). *colloq.* M19.

9 Heated to redness; red-hot, glowing. ME.

10 Of the eyes: inflamed, esp. with weeping; bloodshot. LME.

11 MEDICINE. Of a disease: marked by the evacuation of blood or by a rash. Now *rare.* LME.

12 SKIING. Designating a run suitable for intermediate skiers, being more challenging than a blue run but less so than a black one, as indicated by coloured markers on the run. M20.

> 📖 **1** H. STEPHENS When the sun rises red, rain may be expected. M. AMIS My back . . was scored with . . red welts. K. VONNEGUT We'd gotten two cans of . . red paint. ***blood-red***, ***cherry-red***, ***dark red***, ***light red***, ***orange-red***, ***ruby-red***, ***yellow-red***, etc. **2a** M. ALLINGHAM The . . chalice . . is made of English red gold. **3** W. COWPER Over all . . His long red cloak . . He manfully did throw. **4a** GOLDSMITH The children are born fair or . . red. C. KINGSLEY A boat rowed by one with a red beard. **5** SHAKES. *Merch. V.* Let us make incision . . To prove whose blood is reddest. **6a** A. LOVELL Women with . . black Eyes, and red Cheeks. **b** G. MACDONALD Tom's face was . . red with delight. **7** SIR W. SCOTT The scourge is red, the spur drops blood. **8a** BYRON Red Battle stamps his foot and nations feel the shock. **b** J. F. KENNEDY Poland and Roumania refused . . to permit Red troops to cross their frontiers. *Times* Anything is better than . . nuclear war . . better red than dead.

Phrases: ***neither fish, nor flesh, nor good red herring***: see FISH *noun*[1]. ***paint the town red***: see PAINT *verb.* **red, white, and blue** (the colours of) the Union Jack. **thin red line** *fig.* the British army.

Special collocations & comb.: **red adder** *US* (*a*) the copperhead snake; (*b*) a milk snake of the eastern race, with reddish blotches esp. when young. **red admiral** a holarctic nymphalid butterfly, *Vanessa atalanta*, having black wings with red and white markings. *red alder*: see ALDER *noun* 1. **red alert** an urgent warning of imminent danger; an instruction to prepare for an emergency, or, in a hospital, to admit only emergency cases; a state of readiness for an emergency. **red alga** an alga of the division Rhodophyta, members of which have a red pigment (esp. phycoerythrin) masking their chlorophyll and are found esp. in deep water of tropical seas. **red anchor** *adjective* designating a period of Chelsea porcelain manufacture during which high-quality porcelain with a distinguishing red anchor mark was produced; designating porcelain of this period. **Red and White Friesian** (an animal of) a breed of cattle resembling the Friesian but having a red and white coat. **red ant** any of various ants of this colour, *esp.* . . one of the Eurasian genus *Myrmica.* *red arsenic*: see ARSENIC *noun* 1. **Red Army** (*a*) *Hist.* the Russian Bolshevik army; the army of the former Soviet Union; (*b*) the army in other Communist countries. **red ash** (*a*) a N. American ash, *Fraxinus pennsylvanica*; (*b*) an Australian tree of the buckthorn family, *Alphitonia excelsa*, with poisonous leaves used by Aborigines to stupefy fish. **Red Astrachan** a red-skinned chiefly US variety of eating apple, of Russian origin. **red atrophy** MEDICINE a late stage of massive necrosis of the liver. **red-bait** *S. Afr.* a large ascidian, *Pyura stolonifera*, used as bait by anglers. **red ball** *adjective & noun* (*US slang*) (designating) a fast freight train or truck; (designating) high priority freight. **red-band** *slang* a privileged prisoner. **red bandfish** a mainly red bandfish, *Cepola rubescens*, found in the Mediterranean and the NE Atlantic. **red banner** = *red flag* (a), (c) below. **red bark** a kind of cinchona, the red inner bark of *Cinchona pubescens.* *red* BARTSIA. **red bass** a tropical snapper fish, *Lutjanus coatesi*, found off Queensland coasts. **red bat** a common American vespertilionid bat, *Lasiurus borealis.* **red bay** an evergreen tree of the laurel family, *Persea borbonia*, of the southern US. **red bean** an Australian tree, *Dysoxylum mollissimum* (family Meliaceae), with a dark red wood. **red-beard** a person with a red beard. **red beds** GEOLOGY sedimentary strata, usu. sandstones, coloured red by haematite coating the grains. **red beech** a nothofagus of New Zealand, *Nothofagus fusca.* **red-bellied** *adjective* having a red belly; ***red-bellied snake***, a N. American colubrid snake, *Storeria occipitomaculata*; ***red-bellied woodpecker***, either of two American woodpeckers of the genus *Melanerpes*, esp. *M. carolinus* of the US. **red belt** (*a*) an area under Communist control or influence; (*b*) (the holder of) a belt marking the attainment of a certain degree of proficiency in judo or karate. *red biddy*: see BIDDY *noun*[1] 3. **red birch** the river birch, *Betula nigra*, of N. America. **red-bird** (*a*) any of various small American birds with reddish plumage, *esp.* a tanager; (*b*) *slang* (a tablet of) the drug quinalbarbitone. **red bishop (bird)** an African weaver-bird, *Euplectes orix.* **red-blind** *adjective* colour-blind in respect of red. **red-blindness** the state of being red-blind; = PROTANOPIA. **red blood cell** = ERYTHROCYTE. **red-blooded** *adjective* having red blood; *transf.* virile, full of life, spirited. **red-bloodedness** the state or condition of being red-blooded. **red board** *US slang* (*a*) a stop signal on a railway; (*b*) a board on which a horse race is declared official. **red body** ZOOLOGY the rete mirabile of a fish; the gas gland that this supplies. **redbone** *US* (an animal of) an American breed of dog having a red or red and tan coat, formerly used to hunt racoons. **red book** (*a*) *Hist.* (the distinctive name of) any of various official books (usu. bound in red) of public significance; (*b*) ***Little Red Book***, (a popular name for) the book 'Quotations from Chairman Mao Zedong', published in English in 1966. **red box** a box, usu. covered with red leather, used by a Minister of State to hold official documents. **Red Branch** in Irish epic tradition, the most famous of the royal houses of Ulster. **red bream** (*a*) the red sea bream (see *sea bream* s.v. SEA *noun*); (*b*) = ***blue-mouth*** s.v. BLUE *adjective*; (*c*) *Austral.* an immature snapper fish, *Chrysophrys guttulatus.* **redbrick** *noun & adjective* (designating) a British university founded in the late 19th or early 20th cent. usu. in a large industrial city, esp. as distinct from Oxford and Cambridge. **Red Brigade(s)** a left-wing extremist terrorist group operating in Italy from the early 1970s. **red buck** = IMPALA. **red buckeye** a buckeye, *Aesculus pavia*, of the central and southern US, with flowers usu. red. **redbud** any of several early-flowering leguminous trees of the genus *Cercis* (which includes the Judas tree), esp. the N. American *C. canadensis.* **red bug** *US* (*a*) = ***cotton-stainer*** s.v. COTTON *noun*[1]; (*b*) = JIGGER *noun*[2] 2. **red cabbage** a variety of cabbage with purple-red leaves, used esp. for pickling. **red campion** a European campion, *Silene dioica*, with scentless deep-pink flowers, found esp. in woodland. **redcap** (*a*) a person who wears a red cap; *spec.* (chiefly *dial.*) a sprite, a goblin; (*b*) *dial.* the goldfinch; (*c*) *Military slang* a military police officer; (*d*) (chiefly *N. Amer.*) a railway porter. **red card** *noun & verb* (*a*) *noun* (esp. in SOCCER) a card shown by the referee to a player being sent off the field; (*b*) *verb trans.* (***red-card***) signal the dismissal of (a player) from the field by the showing of a red card. **red carpet** a carpet of this colour traditionally laid down on formal occasions to greet important visitors; *fig.* (also ***red carpet treatment***) a ceremonial welcome, a lavish reception. **red cat** *S. Afr.* = CARACAL. **red caviar** the red roe of fish other than the sturgeon. **red cedar** any of various conifers with reddish wood; *esp.* (*a*) *N. Amer.* a tree-sized juniper, *Juniperus virginiana*; (*b*) (more fully ***western red cedar***) (the reddish-brown timber of) *Thuja plicata*, an arbor vitae of western N. America; (*c*) *Austral.* a coniferous timber tree, *Toona ciliata* (also called **toon**). **red cell** = ERYTHROCYTE. **red cent** *N. Amer.* a coin (orig. of copper) worth a cent; a trivial amount (freq. in neg. contexts). ***Red Centre***: see CENTRE *noun* 6c. **red chalk** (*a*) reddle or red ochre; (*b*) GEOLOGY (a bed of) chalk of a red colour, occurring in Norfolk etc. **Red Chamber** the Senate chamber of the Canadian Parliament Building in Ottawa; the Senate itself. **red channel** at a customs area in a port, airport, etc., the channel through which travellers should pass who have goods to declare. **red-cheeked** *adjective* having red cheeks; rosy, ruddy. **red-chested** *adjective* having a red chest; ***red-chested cuckoo***, an African cuckoo, *Cuculus solitarius*, that is dark grey with a red throat and whose call is regarded as heralding the summer in South Africa. †**red children** N. American Indians considered as under the guardianship of a white person or agency. **Red China** *colloq.* Communist China; the People's Republic of China. **Red Chinese** *noun & adjective* (*colloq.*) (*a*) *noun* a native or inhabitant of the People's Republic of China; (*b*) *adjective* of or pertaining to the People's Republic of China or its inhabitants. **red clay** clay coloured red by its iron content; *spec.* a fine-grained red or reddish-brown deep-sea deposit of mainly terrestrial origin, covering large areas of ocean floor. ***red clover***: see CLOVER *noun.* **redcoat** a person who wears a red coat; *spec.* (*a*) *Hist.* a British soldier; (*b*) a steward at a Butlin's holiday camp; (*c*) an attendant at the door of the House of Lords. **red cobalt (ore)** = ERYTHRITE. **red-cooking** a form of Chinese cookery in which meat is fried quickly and then stewed in soya sauce. **red copper ore** = CUPRITE. **red coral** any of various red gorgonian corals of the genus *Corallium*, esp. *C. nobile* of the Mediterranean, used in jewellery. **red core** the chief root disease of strawberries, caused by the fungus *Phytophthora fragariae* which stains the stele of affected roots. **red corpuscle** = ERYTHROCYTE. **red country** land consisting of large tracts of red sand, esp. in Australia. **red-cowl** *Scot. rare* a sprite, a goblin. **red crab** an edible crab, *Cancer productus*, found off the Pacific coasts of N. America. **Red Crescent** the society corresponding to the Red Cross in Turkey and other Muslim countries. **red-crested** *adjective* (esp. of a bird) having a red crest. **red cross** (*a*) a cross of a red colour, used esp. as the national emblem of England, the St George's Cross, or the emblem of an ambulance service or of the organization known as the Red Cross (see next); (*b*) (with cap. initials) orig., an ambulance or hospital service organized in accordance with the Geneva Convention of 1864; now, an international organization bringing relief to victims of war or natural disaster. **red-crossed** *adjective* having a red cross. **red darnel** ryegrass, *Lolium perenne.* ***red dead-nettle***: see DEAD *adjective.* ***red deal***: see DEAL *noun*[2] 2. **red deer** (*a*) a large deer, *Cervus elaphus*, having a reddish-brown coat, widely distributed in Eurasia and NW Africa (cf. WAPITI); †(*b*) *US* the white-tailed deer. **Red Delicious** a variety of eating apple, a form of Delicious with deep red skin. **red devil** = ***red-bird*** (b) above. **red Devon** (an animal of) a large red-brown breed of cattle, usu. kept for beef. **red dog** = DHOLE. **red drum** a N. American drum-fish, *Sciaenops ocellatus*, found off Atlantic coasts and in fresh water. **red duster** *slang* = ***red ensign*** s.v. ENSIGN *noun* 4. **red dwarf** ASTRONOMY an old, relatively cool star lying on the main sequence. **red-ear** (*a*) = ***red-eared turtle*** below; (*b*) (in full ***red-ear sunfish***) a N. American freshwater fish, *Lepomis microlophus*, which has a red patch on its operculum. **red-eared** *adjective* having red ears; ***red-eared turtle***, (a turtle of) a race of the N. American pond slider, *Pseudemys scripta*, having a reddish stripe behind the eye (cf. YELLOW-BELLIED *turtle*). **red earth** †(*a*) reddle, red ochre; (*b*) laterite. **red elm** any of several N. American elms, esp. the slippery elm, *Ulmus rubra.* **red emperor** an Australian marine fish, *Lutjanus sebae*, found esp. on the Great Barrier Reef. ***red ensign***: see ENSIGN *noun* 4. **red eyebright** = *red* BARTSIA. **red-eyed** *adjective* having red eyes; (of a bird) having eyes surrounded by a red ring; having eyelids reddened by tears, lack of sleep, etc.; cf. RED-EYE. **red-faced** *adjective* (*a*) having a red face; (*b*) embarrassed, ashamed. **Red Fed** *NZ colloq.* (orig.) a member of the New Zealand Federation of Labour; *gen.* a socialist, a left-winger. **red fescue** a grass of meadows and pastures, *Festuca rubra*, of north temperate regions, having bristle-like basal leaves and panicles of short-awned, often purplish spikelets. **red figure** *adjective* (ARCHAEOLOGY) designating a type of Greek pottery devised in Athens in the late 6th cent. BC in which a red clay ground is reserved to create the figures, with details and features delineated in black, the background then being filled in with black. **red fin** *Austral.* the European perch, *Perca fluviatilis.* **red fir** a fir of western N. America, *Abies magnifica.* **red fire** a pyrotechnic effect; the mixture ignited to produce such an effect. **redfish** (*a*) a male salmon in the spawning season, when it assumes a red colour; (*b*) any of various red fishes, as the red gurnard, *Chelidonichthys kumu*, the sockeye salmon, *Oncorhynchus nerka*, the rose-fish or Norway haddock, *Sebastes marinus*, (*Austral.*) the nannygai, *Centroberyx affinis*; (*c*) (***red fish***) fish with dark flesh, such as herring, mackerel, sardine, pilchard, etc. **red flag** (*a*) a sign of defiance or battle; (*b*) a sign of danger, a warning, a signal to stop; (*c*) a symbol of revolution, socialism, or Communism; ***the Red Flag***, a socialist song with words by James Connell (fl. 1889). **red flannel** (*a*) flannel dyed red and formerly used esp. for underwear, nightwear, etc.; (*b*) *colloq.* (in *pl.*) clothing made from red flannel; (*c*) ***red flannel hash*** (*US*), a hash made with beetroot. **red fog** a reddish sea-haze due to the presence of sand or dust in the air. **red-footed** *adjective* having red feet; ***red-footed falcon***, a migratory Eurasian falcon, *Falco vespertinus*, of which the (mainly dark grey) male has rufous thighs, legs, and feet. **red fox** the common fox of Eurasia and N. America, *Vulpes vulpes*. **red giant** ASTRONOMY a relatively cool giant star. **red gland** ZOOLOGY the gas gland of a fish; the rete mirabile that supplies it. **red godwit** either of two godwits, the bar-tailed godwit, *Limosa lapponica*, or the black-tailed godwit, *L. limosa*. **red gold** an alloy of gold and copper (cf. sense 2a above). **red grass** *S. Afr.* [translating Afrikaans *rooigras*] any of several red-tinged pasture grasses, esp. *Themeda triandra*. **red–green** *adjective* pertaining to or affecting the ability to distinguish between red and green. **red groper** a red form of the blue groper, *Achoerodus gouldii*, found off southern Australia. **red grouper** a large serranid fish, *Epinephelus morio*, found off south-eastern N. America. ***red grouse***: see GROUSE *noun*¹ 1. **Red Guard** (a member of) any of various radical or socialist groups; *spec.* (*a*) (a member of) an organized detachment of workers during the Russian Bolshevik revolution of 1917; (*b*) (a member of) a militant youth movement supporting Mao Zedong during the Chinese Cultural Revolution (1966–76). **red gum** (*a*) [2nd elem. alt. of †*gound*: see BARNGUN] a facial rash in young children, esp. during teething; (*b*) [GUM *noun*²] a reddish resinous exudate from the bark of various tropical or semi-tropical trees; any of various trees exuding such gum, esp. (*Austral.*) any of several eucalypts, esp. *Eucalyptus camaldulensis*, and (*US*) the sweet gum, *Liquidambar styraciflua*. **red gurnard** (*a*) a gurnard, *Aspitrigla cuculus*, found in the NE Atlantic and Mediterranean; (*b*) an edible Australian gurnard, *Chelidonichthys kumu*. ***red hake***: see HAKE *noun*¹ 2. **red hand** *noun & adjective* (*a*) *noun* the arms or badge of Ulster, a red hand cut off squarely at the wrist (cf. ***bloody hand*** s.v. BLOODY *adjective & adverb*); (*b*) *adjective* (*red-hand*) *Scot.* = ***red-handed*** (a) below. **red-handed** *adjective* (*a*) in the very act of crime, having evidence of guilt still on the person (esp. in ***take red-handed***, ***catch red-handed***, etc.); fresh from committing murder, having the hands red with blood; that sheds or has shed blood, violent; (*b*) having red hands. **red hardness** METALLURGY the property exhibited by some steels of retaining a high degree of hardness up to a low red heat. **red hare** (*a*) a variety of the snowshoe hare; (*b*) = ***red rock rabbit*** below. **red hartebeest** the hartebeest, *Alcelaphus bucelaphus*, esp. a hartebeest of the southern African race. **red hat** a cardinal's hat; the symbol of the position of cardinal. **red-hat** (*a*) a cardinal; (*b*) *Military slang* a staff officer. **red-headed** *adjective* having red (ginger or auburn) hair; having a red head (***red-headed smew***, a female or a non-breeding male smew); cf. REDHEAD. **red-heart** (*a*) a heart-shaped variety of cherry with red flesh; the tree bearing this fruit; (*b*) any of several trees with reddish bark or wood, esp. a Californian ceanothus, *Ceanothus spinosus*. **red heat** (the degree of heat corresponding to) the condition of being red-hot. **red horse** *US* (*a*) any of various red or reddish fishes; *spec.* (usu. *redhorse*) any of various suckers of the genus *Moxostoma*, esp. *M. macrolepidotum*, found in N. American streams and rivers, the males having red-tipped fins in the breeding season; (*b*) *slang* (orig. MILITARY) corned beef. **red howler** a howler monkey, *Alouatta seniculus*, with long red-brown fur, found in the forests of S. America. **Red Indian** (*a*) (usu. considered *offensive*) a N. American Indian, so called from the reddish skin colour; (*b*) an Australian marine fish, *Pataecus fronto*, which resembles a blenny. **red ink** (*a*) *US colloq.* the debit side of an account (cf. RED *noun* 1d); (*b*) *US slang* cheap red wine or other inferior alcoholic drink; (*c*) ***red-ink plant***, the pokeweed, *Phytolacca americana*, whose berries yield a red colouring. ***red ironbark***: see ***ironbark*** s.v. IRON *noun*. **red iron (ore)**, **red ironstone** a specular form of haematite. ***red jasmine***: see JASMINE 1. **red judge** (orig. *Criminals' slang*) a high court judge. **red jungle fowl** the wild ancestor of the domestic fowl, *Gallus gallus*, occurring in SE Asia. **red kangaroo** a large kangaroo, *Macropus rufus*, occurring throughout Australia. ***red kite***: see KITE *noun* 1. **red lamp** (*a*) a lamp with red glass, formerly used as a doctor's sign; (*b*) = ***red light*** (b) below. **red land** *Scot.* ploughed or arable land; reddish sandy or clayey soil. **Redland** *noun & adjective* (*slang*) (of or pertaining to) the former Soviet Union. **red lane** *arch. colloq.* the throat. ***red lattice***: see LATTICE *noun* 1b. **red lead** (*a*) a bright red oxide of lead, Pb_3O_4, used in batteries, ceramics, protective paints, and formerly as an artists' pigment; minium; (*b*) ***red lead ore*** = CROCOITE; (*c*) *Nautical slang* tomato ketchup, tinned tomatoes. **red-lead** *verb trans.* paint (metal) with red lead. **red leg** (*a*) a bacterial disease of frogs causing haemolytic septicaemia and a red flush on the ventral surfaces of the hind legs; (*b*) (*redleg*) = ***redlegs*** (b) below. **red-legged** *adjective* (esp. of a bird) having red legs; ***red-legged partridge***, a partridge, *Alectoris rufa*, with a white throat-patch and red legs, native to SW Europe and introduced in Britain (also called ***French partridge***). **redlegs** (*a*) *colloq.* a red-legged bird; *esp.* a red-legged partridge or a redshank; (*b*) a red-stemmed knotweed, either redshank, *Persicaria maculosa*, or bistort, *P. bistorta*; (*c*) *US Military slang* an artilleryman. ***Red Leicester***: see LEICESTER *noun* 3. **red letter day** (*a*) a saint's day or church festival traditionally indicated in the calendar by red letters; (*b*) a pleasantly memorable, fortunate, or happy day. **red light** (*a*) a red warning light, esp. one instructing road traffic or a train to stop; *fig.* a sign of danger, a warning, a signal to pause or desist; (*b*) a sign of a brothel; chiefly in ***red-light district***, a district where prostitution and other commercialized sexual activities are concentrated. **red-light** *verb trans.* (*a*) *US slang* force (a tramp etc.) off a moving train; expel, get rid of; (*b*) *colloq.* signal, warn, or stop with a red light; alert, deter. **red line** a (red) mark on a gauge, dial, etc., indicating the maximum safe value of speed, rate of working, or other quantity; see also ***thin red line*** above. **red-line** *verb trans.* (*a*) circle, mark, or cross out in red; *fig.* (*colloq.*) refuse credit to, esp. arbitrarily; (*b*) *colloq.* operate (a machine, vehicle, etc.) at or beyond the maximum safe speed etc. **red loam** a red soil of the tropics, usu. friable and highly leached. ***red louro***. **red man** (*a*) (now *offensive*) a N. American Indian; (*b*) a member of the extinct Beothuk people of Newfoundland; (*c*) = ROMAN *noun*³ 2; (*d*) *colloq.* a symbol of a standing figure illuminated red on some types of pedestrian crossing to indicate a time not to cross. ***red mangrove***: see MANGROVE 1. **red maple** a maple of eastern N. America, *Acer rubrum*, with red twigs, buds, and flowers. **red mass** a votive mass, usu. one of the Holy Spirit, at which red vestments are worn by the priest. **red mavis** *US* the brown thrasher. **red meat** meat that is red when raw, as beef or lamb. **red menace** *colloq.* the political or military threat regarded as emanating from the former Soviet Union. **red mite** (*a*) a bloodsucking mite, *Dermanyssus gallinae*, which is a widespread parasite of domestic poultry; also called ***chicken mite***; (*b*) = ***red spider mite*** below. ***red moki***: see MOKI *noun*¹. ***red mombin***. **red monkey** the patas monkey. **red morocco** (*a*) morocco (leather) coloured red; (*b*) (now *rare*) the plant pheasant's eye, *Adonis annua*. **red mud** (*a*) a red marine mud of terrestrial origin, found on continental shelves and in other shallow waters; (*b*) a residue from the extraction of alumina from bauxite, coloured red by ferric impurities. **red mulga** an Australian wattle, *Acacia cyperophylla*. ***red mullet***: see MULLET *noun*¹. **red myrtle** an Australian tree of the myrtle family, *Syzygium australe*. **Red Ned** *Austral. & NZ slang* inferior red wine. **red nettle** = ***red dead-nettle*** above. **red noise** STATISTICS a temporal spectrum exhibiting more power or variance at lower frequencies. **red-nose** (*a*) a person who has a red nose, esp. a drunkard; (*b*) any of various marine molluscs that have red-tipped siphons, esp. the bivalve *Hiatella arctica*, which bores in soft rock; (*c*) VETERINARY MEDICINE infectious bovine rhinotracheitis. **red-nosed** *adjective* having a red nose. **red nucleus** ANATOMY either of a pair of nuclei in the tegmentum of the midbrain, forming part of the extrapyramidal motor system. **red oak** a N. American oak, *Quercus rubra*, whose leaves turn red in autumn. **red ochre** a variety of ochre, esp. used for colouring or dyeing; ruddle. **red-ochre** *verb trans. & intrans.* colour (something) with red ochre. ***red orpiment***. **red osier** (*a*) (more fully ***red osier dogwood***) a N. American dogwood, *Cornus sericea*; (*b*) a willow used in basketry, *Salix* × *rubra*. **red-out** a reddening of the vision resulting from congestion of blood in the eyes when the body is accelerated downwards, sometimes followed by loss of consciousness. **red out** *verb intrans.* undergo or experience a red-out. **Red Paint** *adjective* designating or pertaining to an ancient N. American Indian people whose burials involved large quantities of red ochre. **red palm oil** palm oil having a red colour, obtained by boiling the fruit in water. ***red panda***: see PANDA *noun*¹ 1. **red-pencil** *verb trans.* mark in red as erroneous or unacceptable; correct or delete (a piece of written work). ***red pepper***: see PEPPER *noun*. **red perch** an edible Australian serranid fish, *Caesioperca lepidoptera*. ***red peroba***. **red phalarope** *N. Amer.* the grey phalarope, *Phalaropus fulicarius*, in its breeding plumage. **red phosphorus** an amorphous red allotrope of phosphorus, having a high melting point and low reactivity and toxicity (cf. ***white phosphorus***). **red pine** (the timber of) any of several coniferous trees with reddish wood, esp. a N. American pine, *Pinus resinosa*, and (*NZ*) the rimu, *Dacrydium cupressinum*. **red planet** *the* planet Mars. ***red precipitate***: see PRECIPITATE *noun* 1. **Red Prince** Prince Frederick Charles of Prussia (1828–85). **red rain** rain that is reddish in colour because of suspended dust or, rarely, red algae. ***red rattle***: see RATTLE *noun* 2. **red-raw** *adjective* (of the flesh) broken and inflamed, esp. through friction or irritation. **red reflex** OPHTHALMOLOGY a red glow seen when the interior of a person's eye is illuminated, caused by the light reflected from the retina passing through the choroid. **red riband** (*obsolete* exc. *Hist.*) the crimson ribbon worn by Knights of the Order of the Bath; (membership of) this Order. **red ribbon** (*a*) = ***red riband*** above; (*b*) *US* an award given for coming second in a competition; (*c*) a small loop of red ribbon worn as an international symbol of Aids awareness. **Red Riding Hood** *adjectival phr.* designating a type of cloak with a hood, like that worn by Little Red Riding Hood in the fairy story of that name. **red-ripe** *adjective* fully ripe. **red river hog** = ***bush-pig*** (a) s.v. BUSH *noun*¹. ***red roan***: see ROAN *noun*². **red rock** (*a*) GEOLOGY a predominantly or wholly granophyric rock of bright red colour associated with some large gabbroic masses; (*b*) ***red rock-cod***, an Australian scorpion fish, *Scorpaena cardinalis*; (*c*) ***red rock fault*** (GEOLOGY), a fault in Permian red beds, forming part of the boundary of the Cheshire Basin. **red rockfish** any of various scorpaenid fishes of the genus *Sebastes*, occurring off N. American Pacific coasts. **red-root** any of several American plants whose roots are red or yield a red pigment; *esp.* (*a*) Jersey tea, *Ceanothus americanus*, or any other shrub of this genus; (*b*) a swamp plant, *Lachnanthes caroliniana* (family Haemodoraceae), also called ***paint-root***, with hairy yellowish flowers. ***red rose***: see ROSE *noun* 7. **red rot** (*a*) a fungal disease of standing trees or timber marked by red-brown rotted tissue; (*b*) a similar disease of sugar cane. **red route**: intended to facilitate the smooth flow of urban traffic by the imposition of severe penalties for stopping and parking along roads marked with a red line. **Red Rover**: a children's chasing game. **red sable** the fur of the kolinsky, used esp. in artists' brushes; a brush made from this fur. ***red sandalwood***. ***red sanders***: see SANDERS *noun*¹. ***Red Sandstone***: see SANDSTONE. **red scale** either of two scale insects, *Aonidiella aurantii* and *Chrysomphalus aonidum*, which infest orange trees (also ***California red scale***). ***red sea bream***: see ***sea bream*** s.v. SEA *noun*. ***red seraya***. **red setter** = ***Irish setter*** s.v. IRISH *adjective*. **red-shouldered** *adjective* having the shoulder or bend of the wing red; ***red-shouldered hawk***, a common N. American buzzard, *Buteo lineatus*. ***red siris***. **redskin** (*a*) (*derog.* & considered *racially offensive*) a N. American Indian; (*b*) a variety of potato. **red snapper** any of various important marine food fishes of the family Lutjanidae, esp. *Lutjanus campechinus* of eastern North and Central America. **red snow** (*a*) snow reddened by red dust or esp. by the growth of the alga *Chlamydomonas nivalis*, common in some Arctic and montane regions; (*b*) this alga. **red soil** any of various leached soils of the tropics and sub-tropics, coloured red by ferric compounds. ***red sorrel***: see SORREL *noun*¹ 2. **red spider (mite)** a small red mite, *Tetranychus urticae*, a serious horticultural pest. **red spinner** ANGLING (an artificial fly imitating) the adult female of the olive dun mayfly. **red spot** (*a*) ASTRONOMY (in full ***Great Red Spot***) a large reddish oval feature in the atmosphere of Jupiter; (*b*) a defect of cheese in which there are fine red spots throughout. **red-spotted** *adjective* marked with red spots; ***red-spotted trout***, any of various N. American chars of the genus *Salvelinus*. ***red squill***: see SQUILL *noun* 2a. **red squirrel** (*a*) a small N. American squirrel, *Tamiasciurus hudsonicus* (also called ***chickaree***); (*b*) the common Eurasian squirrel, *Sciurus vulgaris*, (now rare in southern Britain). **red star** a symbol of the former Soviet Union. **red steer** *Austral. slang* a fire, *esp.* a bushfire. ***red stompneus***. **red-stone** †(*a*) ALCHEMY = RUBY *noun* 3a; (*b*) a sandstone of a red colour; †(*c*) ruddle. ***red stopper***: see STOPPER *noun* 5. **red-streak** (*a*) a formerly esteemed cider apple with red streaks; the cider made from this; (*b*) *transf.* (*rare*) a girl with red cheeks. **red tabby** a cat, esp. a long-haired one, that has a reddish-orange coat patterned in a deeper red. **red-tailed** *adjective* having a red tail; ***red-tailed hawk***, a common N. and Central American buzzard, *Buteo jamaicensis*. ***red tangle***: see TANGLE *noun*² 3. **Red Terror** (*a*) = ***the Terror*** s.v. TERROR *noun*; (*b*) the persecution of opponents by the Bolsheviks after the Russian Revolution of 1917. **redthroat** an Australian warbler, *Pyrrholaemus brunneus*. **red-throated** *adjective* having a red throat; ***red-throated diver***, (US) ***red-throated loon***, a holarctic diver, *Gavia stellata*. **red thrush** the American robin, *Turdus migratorius*. **red tide** an occurrence of seawater discoloured by a bloom of toxic red dinoflagellates. ***red titi***: see TITI *noun*². ***red tombac***. **red-top** (*a*) *N. Amer.* (more fully ***red-top grass***) any of several grasses, esp. the black bent, *Agrostis gigantea*, much grown for hay in the US; (*b*) [from the red background on which the titles of certain British newspapers are printed] *colloq.* a tabloid newspaper. **red 'un** *slang* (*obsolete* exc. *Hist.*) a sovereign. **red underwing** a large Eurasian noctuid moth, *Catocala nupta*, which has mainly crimson hindwings. ***red valerian***: see VALERIAN 1. **red viper** (*a*) a reddish variety of the European viper; (*b*) *US* the copperhead snake. **red vision** OPHTHALMOLOGY = ERYTHROPSIA. **redware** (*a*) a coarse kind of unglazed pottery; (*b*) a type of fine, glazed pottery. **red warning** = ***red alert*** above. **red-water** (*a*) (usu. ***redwater***) any of various diseases of animals in which the urine is coloured red, esp. piroplasmosis and (more fully ***redwater fever***) babesiosis; (*b*) the poisonous red juice of the sassy-tree, *Erythrophleum suaveolens*, used in W. African trial by ordeal; ***red-water tree***, this tree; (*c*) = ***red tide*** above. **red-weed** (now *dial.*) the corn poppy, *Papaver rhoeas*. **red wheat** any of several varieties of wheat with reddish grains. **red whortleberry** the cowberry, *Vaccinium vitis-idaea*. **red willow** any of several willows with reddish twigs, esp. (*US*) *Salix laevigata*. **red wind** †(*a*) a wind which causes the leaves of trees to shrivel and turn red; (*b*) a wind charged with red sand particles which blows from the African deserts. **red wolf** (*a*) a small wolf, *Canis rufus*, native to the south-eastern US, but believed to be extinct in the wild; (*b*) a reddish variety of the grey wolf, *Canis lupus*. **red-wood** *adjective* (*Scot.*) completely mad. **red worm** (*a*) an earthworm, *Lumbricus rubellus*, used as bait in rod-fishing; (*b*) = WIREWORM; (*c*) any of various intestinal nematodes of the genus *Strongylus*, which chiefly affect horses. **red wrasse** the reddish female of the cuckoo wrasse, *Labrus mixtus*. **red zinc ore** = ZINCITE. **red zone** (*a*) (on a gauge or dial) a red sector corresponding to conditions that exceed safety limits; (*b*) a region that is dangerous or forbidden; an area in which a particular activity is prohibited; (*c*) AMER. FOOTBALL the region between the 20-yard line and goal-line, which is a major focus of the offensive team's attack strategy.

red /rɛd/ *verb*¹. Long *rare* exc. *Scot. & dial.* Infl. **-dd-**. OE.
[from RED *adjective*.]
1 *verb intrans.* Be or become red. OE.
2 *verb trans.* Make red. ME.

red *verb*², *verb*³ *pa. t. & pple*: see READ *verb*, REDE *verb*¹.

-red /rɛd/ *suffix*. Now *rare*.
[Repr. Old English *rǣden* condition, shortened in Middle English by the dropping of the final syll.]
Forming nouns with the sense 'condition of, relationship of', as ***gossipred***, ***hatred***, ***kindred***.

redact /rɪˈdakt/ *verb trans.* LME.
[Latin *redact-* pa. ppl stem of *redigere* bring back, collect, etc., formed as RE- + *agere* drive etc.]
†**1** Bring (reasoning or discourse) *into* or *to* a certain form; put *together* in writing. LME–M17.
†**2** Reduce (a person or thing) to a certain state, condition, etc. Foll. by *into*, *to*. LME–M18.
3 a Draw up (a statement, decree, etc.). M19. ▸**b** Put into appropriate literary form; arrange, edit. M19.
■ **redactor** *noun* a person who redacts something; an editor: E19. **redactoral** *adjective* (*rare*) = REDACTORIAL *adjective* L20. **redacˈtorial** *adjective* of or belonging to a redactor; editorial: M19.

rédacteur /redaktœːr/ *noun*. Pl. pronounced same. E19.
[French.]
A redactor, an editor.

redaction /rɪˈdakʃ(ə)n/ *noun*. E17.
[In sense 1 from late Latin *redactio(n-)*, from *redact-*: see REDACT, -ION. In sense 2 from French *rédaction*.]
†**1** The action of driving back; resistance, reaction. *rare*. E–M17.
2 a The action or process of preparing something for publication; revision, editing, arrangement in a certain form. L18. ▸**b** The result of such a process; a new edition; an adaptation, an abridged version. E19.
Comb.: **redaction critic** a person who engages in redaction criticism; **redaction-critical** *adjective* of the nature of redaction criticism; **redaction criticism** examination of the ways in which the gospel writers edited their material, with the aim of discovering their theological ideas.
■ **redactional** *adjective* L19.

redan /rɪˈdan/ *noun*. L17.
[French, for *redent* notching as of a saw, formed as RE- + *dent* tooth.]
FORTIFICATION. A simple fieldwork with two faces forming a salient angle.

For other words beginning with *re-* see the entry for **re-**

redargue /rɛˈdɑːgjuː/ *verb trans.* Chiefly *Scot.* LME.
[Latin *redarguere* disprove etc., formed as RE- + *arguere* ARGUE.]
†**1** Blame, reprove (a person, action, etc.). LME–L17.
2 Confute (a person) by argument. Long *rare* or *obsolete.* LME.
3 Refute, disprove (an argument, statement, etc.). Now *rare* exc. LAW. E17.

redargution /rɛdɑːˈgjuːʃ(ə)n/ *noun.* Now *rare.* L15.
[ecclesiastical Latin *redargutio(n-)* reproof, from Latin *redarguere*: see prec.]
†**1** Reproof, reprehension. L15–L17.
2 Confutation; (a) refutation, (a) disproof. E16.

red-back /ˈrɛdbak/ *noun.* E19.
[RED *adjective* + BACK *noun*[1].]
A red-backed animal (cf. next); *spec.* (in full ***red-back spider***) a venomous Australian spider of the genus *Latrodectus*, the female of which has a red stripe on the abdomen.

red-backed /ˈrɛdbakt/ *adjective.* E18.
[from RED *adjective* + BACKED *adjective.*]
Chiefly ZOOLOGY. Having a red back.
red-backed mouse = ***red-backed vole*** below. **red-backed sandpiper** *US* the dunlin. **red-backed shrike** a Eurasian and African shrike, *Lanius collurio*, now rare in Britain. **red-backed vole** any of various voles of the genus *Clethrionomys*.

redbreast /ˈrɛdbrɛst/ *noun.* LME.
[from RED *adjective* + BREAST *noun.*]
1 The European robin, *Erithacus rubecula*. Also ROBIN REDBREAST. LME.
2 An officer or soldier wearing a red jacket or waistcoat. *slang.* M19.
3 The sunfish *Lepomis auritus*. *US.* L19.

red-breasted /ˈrɛdbrɛstɪd/ *adjective.* E17.
[from RED *adjective* + BREASTED *adjective.*]
Having a red breast.
red-breasted flycatcher a Eurasian flycatcher, *Ficedula parva*. **red-breasted goose** a migratory goose, *Branta ruficollis*, which breeds in Siberia. ***red-breasted*** MERGANSER. **red-breasted thrush** the American robin, *Turdus migratorius*.

redcurrant /rɛdˈkʌr(ə)nt/ *noun.* Also **red currant**. E17.
[from RED *adjective* + CURRANT.]
Any of the small round edible translucent red berries of the shrub *Ribes rubrum*, of the gooseberry family, borne in loose hanging clusters; this shrub, much grown for its fruit.

redd /rɛd/ *noun*[1]. *Scot. & north.* L15.
[from REDD *verb*[2]. Cf. RID *noun.*]
1 An act of clearing away, setting in order, etc.; a clearance, a tidying-*up*, a removal. L15.
2 Waste which is cleared away; rubbish, refuse. E16.

redd /rɛd/ *noun*[2]. Orig. *Scot. & north.* M17.
[Origin unkn.]
1 The spawn of fish and frogs. Now *rare.* M17.
2 A spawning nest made in the bed of a river by a trout or salmon. E19.

redd /rɛd/ *ppl adjective. Scot. & north.* LME.
[from REDD *verb*[2].]
(Of a room, building, etc.) clean; in order, tidied *up*; (of land) cleared of growth, crops, etc.
void and redd SCOTS LAW (of a property) cleared and ready for a new occupant.

redd /rɛd/ *verb*[1] *trans. obsolete* exc. *Scot.* Pa. t. & pple **redd**.
[Old English *hreddan* = Old Frisian *hredda*, Middle & mod. Dutch *redden* (whence Danish *redde*, Swedish *rädda*), Old High German, German *retten* save, deliver, from Germanic. Cf. next, RID *verb*[1].]
1 Save, rescue, free (a person). Foll. by *from*, *out of*. *arch.* OE. ▸**b** Save from burning; put out (fire). LME–L19.
2 Free, clear, rid, (a person) *of* something. ME.

redd /rɛd/ *verb*[2] *trans.* Chiefly *Scot. & north.* Pa. t. & pple **redd**, **redded**. LME.
[Origin uncertain. Cf. prec., RID *verb*[1].]
1 Clear (a space, way, etc.); remove (an obstruction or blockage); clean out. LME.
2 a Settle, decide (a dispute, plea, etc.); put an end to (a quarrel or confusion). LME. ▸**b** Part, separate (combatants). L15.
3 a Arrange, put right, clear up (business, affairs, etc.). L15. ▸**b** Disentangle, unravel, sort out. E16.
4 a Put in order, tidy, clear up (a room, building, etc.); make neat or smart. Now usu. foll. by *up*. E16. ▸**b** Comb, arrange (hair). E18. ▸**c** Sort *out*, clear *out*, comb *out*. E19.
5 Remove from a place; clear *away*. M16.
Comb.: **redding-comb** a comb for the hair; **redding-stroke** a blow received by a person trying to separate combatants.
■ **redder** *noun* a person who redds someone or something, *spec.* one who tries to separate combatants or settle a quarrel LME.

redd *verb*[3], *verb*[4] *pa. t. & pple*: see READ *verb*, REDE *verb*[1].

redden /ˈrɛd(ə)n/ *verb.* E17.
[from RED *adjective* + -EN[5].]
1 *verb trans.* Make red. E17.
2 *verb intrans.* **a** Become red in the face *with* shame, anger, etc.; flush, blush. M17. ▸**b** Grow or become red, assume a red appearance. E18. ▸**c** Of a pullet: acquire a deeper shade of red in the comb and wattles as the bird matures. Foll. by *up*. E20.

> 📖 **1** B. VINE Two weeks in the sun had reddened her skin. **2a** A. WILSON Mr. Fleet . . reddened with fury. **b** J. MASEFIELD The sunset reddened in the west.

reddenda *noun* pl. of REDDENDUM.

reddendo /rəˈdɛndəʊ/ *noun.* Pl. **-o(e)s**. M17.
[Latin, abl. of next, lit. 'by giving in return'.]
SCOTS LAW. A clause in a charter specifying a duty to be paid or service due to a superior; the payment or service itself.

reddendum /rəˈdɛndəm/ *noun.* Pl. **-da** /-də/. E17.
[Latin, neut. gerundive of *reddere* give in return: see RENDER *verb.*]
LAW. A reserving clause in a deed.

redding /ˈrɛdɪŋ/ *noun.* ME.
[from RED *adjective* + -ING[3].]
1 Red ochre, ruddle. Now *dial.* ME.
2 A variety of apple. *rare.* E17.

reddish /ˈrɛdɪʃ/ *adjective.* LME.
[from RED *adjective* + -ISH[1].]
Somewhat red; red-tinted.
■ **reddishly** *adverb* (*rare*) M20. **reddishness** *noun* M17.

reddition /rɛˈdɪʃ(ə)n/ *noun.* LME.
[Latin *redditio(n-)*, from *reddit-* pa. ppl stem of *reddere* give back: see RENDER *verb*, -ITION.]
1 †**a** Return or restoration of something; surrender of a town, army, etc. LME–L18. ▸**b** LAW (now *Hist.*). A judicial admission by a person that he or she is not the owner of certain property being demanded. M16. ▸**c** Recompense. *poet. rare.* E20.
†**2** (A clause containing) the application of a comparison. L16–L18.
3 Rendition; translation. *rare.* E17.

reddle /ˈrɛd(ə)l/ *noun.* E18.
[Var. of RUDDLE *noun*[1]: cf. RADDLE *noun*[1].]
Red ochre, ruddle.

reddle /ˈrɛd(ə)l/ *verb trans. rare.* L18.
[from the noun.]
Paint or wash over with reddle.

red dog /rɛd ˈdɒg/ *noun & verb.* M19.
[from RED *adjective* + DOG *noun.*]
▸ **A** *noun.* **1** An unreliable banknote formerly in circulation in the US. M19.
2 A low grade of flour. L19.
3 A card-game in which each player bets that his or her hand contains a card of the same suit and a higher rank than the top card of the stock. M20.
4 AMER. FOOTBALL. A manoeuvre in which an opponent rushes the player passing the ball. M20.
▸ **B** *verb trans.* Infl. **-gg-**. AMER. FOOTBALL. Rush (a passer). M20.

reddy /ˈrɛdi/ *adjective.* LME.
[from RED *adjective* + -Y[1].]
†**1** Red, ruddy. LME–M17.
2 Reddish. L19.

rede /riːd/ *noun. arch.*
[Old English *rǣd* corresp. to Old Frisian *rēd*, Old Saxon *rād* (Dutch *raad*), Old High German *rāt* (German *Rat*), Old Norse *ráð*, from Germanic, whence also READ *verb.*]
1 Counsel, advice. Formerly also, help, remedy. OE.
2 Decision, resolve; a plan, a scheme, a method. OE.
3 The faculty or act of deliberation; judgement, reason. OE.
4 a A story, a narrative. LME. ▸†**b** Speech. *rare* (Spenser). Only in L16. ▸**c** Interpretation, explanation. *rare.* L19.

> 📖 **1** R. BURNS May you better reck the rede, Than ever did th' Adviser! **4a** SIR W. SCOTT Bid the gentles speed Who long have listened to my rede.

Comb.: **redesman** a counsellor, an adviser.
■ **redeless** *adjective* without counsel; *esp.* having no resource in a difficulty: OE.

rede /riːd/ *verb*[1]. Now *arch. & dial.* Pa. t. & pple **red(d)** /rɛd/. OE.
[Earlier form of READ *verb.*]
▸†**I 1** *verb trans.* Have control over; rule, govern. OE–LME.
2 *verb trans.* Of God, Christ, etc.: take care of; guide, protect. ME–L15.
▸†**II 3** *verb intrans.* Take counsel (together), deliberate. OE–L15.
4 *verb trans.* Agree on, decide after consultation or deliberation. OE–M16.
▸ **III 5** *verb trans.* Advise, counsel (a person). (Foll. by *to do*.) OE.
†**6** *verb intrans.* Give advice. OE–E17.
†**7** *verb trans.* Advise (a thing); give as advice or counsel. ME–M17.

> 📖 **5** W. MORRIS My son, I rede thee stay at home.

▸ **IV** See READ *verb*.

rede /riːd/ *verb*[2] *trans. obsolete* exc. *dial.*
[Old English *rǣdan* = Middle Dutch, Middle Low German *reden*, *reiden* (Dutch *reeden*) make ready, set in order, etc. (whence Danish *rede*, Swedish *reda*), ult. from Germanic base of READY *adjective.*]
= REDD *verb*[2].

redeem /rɪˈdiːm/ *verb trans.* LME.
[French *rédimer* or Latin *redimere*, formed as RE- + *emere* buy.]
1 Buy back (a former possession); make payment for (a thing held or claimed by another). LME. ▸**b** Regain, recover (an immaterial thing). E16. ▸**c** Regain or recover (land etc.) by force. M17.
2 a Free or recover (property, a thing put in pledge, etc.) by payment of an amount due or by fulfilment of an obligation; *spec.* (STOCK EXCHANGE) repay (a fixed-interest stock) at the maturity date. Also, make a payment to discharge (a charge or obligation); pay off. LME. ▸**b** Fulfil, carry out (a pledge, promise, etc.). M19. ▸**c** Of an agent or customer: exchange (trading stamps, coupons, etc.) for money or goods. E20.
3 Free (a person) from captivity or punishment, esp. by paying a ransom. LME.
4 a Save, rescue; *spec.* (of God or Christ) deliver (a person) from sin and damnation. Also foll. by *from*. LME. ▸**b** Reclaim (land). (Foll. by *from*.) E18.
5 Of a person: make amends for, atone for (an error, loss, etc.). Formerly also, avenge, repay (a wrong). LME.
6 Bring *into* some (esp. former) condition or state; restore, set right again. L15.
7 Free from a charge or claim. L15.
†**8** Buy, purchase. E16–M17. ▸**b** Go in exchange for. L16–E17.
9 Save (time). E16.
10 Of a quality, action, etc.: make up for, compensate for, counterbalance (a defect or fault). M16. ▸**b** Save (a person or thing) *from* some defect or fault. E17.

> 📖 **2a** M. PUZO Redeem your debt by some small service. J. HELLER Rembrandt . . redeemed articles of jewelry she had pawned. **4a** DRYDEN He thrusts aside The crowd of centaurs and redeems the bride. **5** GIBBON His father's sins had been redeemed at too high a price. **6** SIR W. SCOTT With his barb'd horse . . Stout Cromwell has redeem'd the day. **8b** SHAKES. *1 Hen. VI* Would some part of my young years Might but redeem the passage of your age! **10** J. BUCHAN The triviality of the stakes was redeemed by the brilliance . . of the player. A. N. WILSON Her only redeeming feature . . was her hair, which was . . abundant.

■ **redeemer** *noun* a person who redeems someone or something; *spec.* (**R-**) God or Christ regarded as delivering humankind from sin and damnation: LME. **redeemless** *adjective* (*rare*) unable to be redeemed, irrecoverable M17.

redeemable /rɪˈdiːməb(ə)l/ *adjective & noun.* E16.
[from prec. + -ABLE.]
▸ **A** *adjective.* Able to be redeemed; *spec.* (of property, stock, etc.) able to be repurchased. E16.
▸ **B** *noun.* In *pl.* Redeemable stocks, property, etc. Now *rare.* E18.
■ **redeemaˈbility** *noun* (*rare*) L19. **redeemableness** *noun* (*rare*) E18. **redeemably** *adverb* (*rare*) E19.

redeliver /riːdɪˈlɪvə/ *verb trans.* L15.
[from RE- + DELIVER *verb.*]
1 Give back, return, restore. L15.
2 Make or set free again. E17.
†**3** Repeat, report. *rare* (Shakes.). Only in E17.
4 Deliver (a message, letter, etc.) again or to a different address. M19.
■ **redeliverance** *noun* (*rare*) E16. **redelivery** *noun* L15.

redemption /rɪˈdɛm(p)ʃ(ə)n/ *noun.* ME.
[Old & mod. French *rédemption* from Latin *redemptio(n-)*, from *redempt-* pa. ppl stem of *redimere* REDEEM: see -ION. Cf. RANSOM *noun.*]
1 CHRISTIAN THEOLOGY. Humankind's deliverance from sin and damnation by the atonement of Christ. ME.
2 The action of freeing a prisoner, slave, etc., by payment; ransom. LME.
3 The action of freeing, delivering, restoring, or reclaiming something. LME. ▸**b** A redeeming feature or thing. M19.
4 The action or a way of redeeming oneself from punishment; atonement for an offence. LME.
5 The purchase of membership of a society, guild, etc. LME.
6 The action of discharging a recurring liability or charge by a single payment. LME.
7 The action of redeeming or buying something back from another. LME.
Phrases & comb.: **equity of redemption**: see EQUITY *noun* 4. **past redemption** beyond the possibility of recovery or restoration. **redemption yield** the yield of a stock calculated as a percentage of the redemption price and allowing for any capital gain or loss which that price represents relative to the current price.
■ **redemptional** *adjective* M19. **redemptioner** *noun* (*a*) *US* (*obsolete* exc. *Hist.*) an emigrant who received passage on condition that the passage-money and other expenses were repaid to the ship's master or owner out of wages earned on arrival; (*b*) a person who clears off a charge by redemption: L18.

redemptive /rɪˈdɛm(p)tɪv/ *adjective.* L15.
[from prec. + -IVE, orig. through French †*redemptif, -ive.*]
Tending to redeem, redeeming.

redemptor /rɪˈdɛm(p)tə/ *noun.* Now *rare.* Also **R-**. LME.
[Old French (mod. *rédempteur*) or Latin, from *redempt-*: see REDEMPTION, -OR.]
A redeemer; orig. *spec.* Jesus regarded as redeeming humankind.

Redemptorist /rɪˈdɛm(p)t(ə)rɪst/ *noun & adjective.* M19.
[French *rédemptoriste*, formed as prec.: see -IST.]
ROMAN CATHOLIC CHURCH. ▶**A** *noun.* A member of a Roman Catholic order founded at Naples in 1732 by St Alphonsus Liguori, devoted chiefly to work among the poor. M19.
▶**B** *attrib.* or as *adjective.* Of or pertaining to the Redemptorists or their order. M19.
■ **Redemptoˈristine** *noun & adjective* (**a**) *noun* a nun of a reclusive and contemplative order associated with the Redemptorists; (**b**) *adjective* of or pertaining to the Redemptoristines or their order: L19.

redemptory /rɪˈdɛm(p)t(ə)ri/ *adjective.* Now *rare.* L16.
[from REDEMPTION + -ORY².]
Of or pertaining to redemption; redemptive.

redeploy /riːdɪˈplɔɪ/ *verb trans.* M20.
[from RE- + DEPLOY.]
Move (troops, workers, materials, etc.) from one area of activity to another; reorganize for greater effectiveness; transfer to another job, task, or function.
■ **redeployment** *noun* M20.

†**redevable** *adjective.* E16–E18.
[French, from *redevoir*, formed as RE- + *devoir* owe: see -ABLE.]
Beholden, indebted.

redevelop /riːdɪˈvɛləp/ *verb.* L19.
[from RE- + DEVELOP.]
1 *verb trans. & intrans.* Develop again. L19.
2 *verb trans. spec.* Develop (an urban area) anew, with new buildings etc. M20.
■ **redeveloper** *noun* L19. **redevelopment** *noun* L19.

red-eye /ˈrɛdʌɪ/ *noun.* L17.
[from RED *adjective* + EYE *noun.*]
1 Any of various red-eyed fishes; *esp.* (**a**) the rudd, *Scardinius erythrophthalmus*; (**b**) *US* the rock bass, *Ambloplites rupestris.* L17.
2 Coarse fiery whiskey. *US slang.* E19.
3 = ***red-eyed*** VIREO. *US.* M19.
4 Tomato ketchup. *US slang.* E20.
5 A black Australian cicada, *Psaltoda moerens*, with three red ocelli. E20.
6 An airline flight on which a traveller is unable to get adequate sleep because of the time of arrival or differences in time-zones. Usu. *attrib.*, as ***red-eye flight*** etc. *colloq.* (orig. *US*). M20.
7 A drink made from beer and tomato juice. *Canad.* M20.
8 PHOTOGRAPHY. A red reflection from the blood-vessels of a person's retina, seen on a colour photograph taken with a flash. M20.
Comb.: **red-eye gravy** *US*: made by adding liquid to the fat from cooked ham etc.

redhead /ˈrɛdhɛd/ *adjective & noun.* M17.
[from RED *adjective* + HEAD *noun.*]
▶**A** *adjective.* = ***red-headed*** s.v. RED *adjective.* M17.
▶**B** *noun.* **1** A red-headed bird; *esp.* (**a**) an American diving duck, *Aythya americana*, resembling the common pochard; (**b**) an American red-headed woodpecker, *Melanerpes erythrocephalus*; (**c**) a female smew; (**d**) *Austral.* the red-browed waxbill, *Aegintha temporalis.* E18.
2 A red-headed person; *esp.* a person who has ginger or auburn hair. M19.

red herring /rɛd ˈhɛrɪŋ/ *noun phr.* LME.
[from RED *adjective* + HERRING.]
1 Herring turned red by curing with smoke. LME.
2 Something intended to divert attention from a more serious question or matter; a misleading clue, a distraction. Orig. in ***draw a red herring across the track***, etc. (from the practice of using the scent of a smoked herring to train hounds to follow a trail). L19.

> 📖 **1** ***neither fish, nor flesh, nor good red herring***: see FISH *noun*¹. **2** G. SWIFT History . . is a red herring; the past is irrelevant. *Holiday Which?* Three people sniffed out the red herrings, but only one had got the motive . . right.

redhibition /rɛdhɪˈbɪʃ(ə)n/ *noun. rare.* M17.
[French *rédhibition* or Latin *redhibitio(n-)*, from *redhibere* take or give back, formed as RE- + *habere* have: see -ITION.]
LAW. The annulment of a sale at the instigation of the buyer; a civil action to compel a vendor to take back a thing sold.
■ **redˈhibitory** *adjective* E18.

red-hot /ˈrɛdhɒt, rɛdˈhɒt/ *adjective & noun.* Also (esp. as pred. adjective) **red hot**. LME.
[from RED *adjective* + HOT *adjective.*]
▶**A** *adjective.* **1** Sufficiently hot to glow red. LME.
2 *fig.* Highly excited, fiery, violently enthusiastic, extreme; furious, exciting; intense, uninhibited, lively; enraged; sexy, passionate; very talented; (of news etc.) sensational, completely new. E17. ▸**b** Of the favourite in a race etc.: very strongly fancied. *colloq.* L19. ▸**c** Unfair, unreasonable. *Austral. slang.* L19.

> 📖 **2** T. MIDDLETON I shall expect my wife anon, red-hot with zeal. A. LOMAX A red-hot bass player . . a proud Creole. J. BRAINE Thought you were a red-hot Labour man. *Woman* The red-hot rumours that she was planning to leave her husband.

Phrases: **red-hot poker** any of various cultivated kniphofias, esp. *Kniphofia uvaria*, in which the upper flowers of the spike are fiery red, the lower yellow.
▶**B** *ellipt.* as *noun.* **1** Red-hot material. M19.
2 A frankfurter, a hot dog. *N. Amer. slang.* L19.

redia /ˈriːdɪə/ *noun.* Pl. **-iae** /-iiː/. L19.
[mod. Latin, from Francesco *Redi* (1626–98), Italian biologist: see -IA¹.]
ZOOLOGY. A digenean trematode (fluke) in the larval stage developed from a sporocyst in the main intermediate host, and in turn forming a number of cercariae.

redial /ˈriːdʌɪəl/ *noun.* L20.
[from the verb.]
A facility on a telephone by which a number just dialled may be redialled automatically.

redial /riːˈdʌɪəl/ *verb intrans. & trans.* Infl. **-ll-**, *__-l-__. M20.
[from RE- + DIAL *verb.*]
Dial again.

redid *verb pa. t.* of REDO *verb.*

rediffusion /riːdɪˈfjuːʒ(ə)n/ *noun.* E20.
[from RE- + DIFFUSION.]
BROADCASTING. The relaying or rebroadcasting of programmes; *spec.* the distribution of radio or television transmissions within a community by cable from a single receiver.

redingote /ˈrɛdɪŋgəʊt/ *noun.* L18.
[French from English *riding-coat.*]
Orig., a man's double-breasted greatcoat with long plain skirts not cut away in the front. Now usu., a woman's long coat with a cut-away front or a contrasting piece on the front.

redintegrate /rɛˈdɪntɪgreɪt/ *verb trans.* Pa. pple **-ated**, †**-ate**. LME.
[Latin *redintegrat-* pa. ppl stem of *redintegrare*, formed as RE- + *integrare* INTEGRATE *verb*: see -ATE³. Cf. REINTEGRATE.]
1 Restore to a state of wholeness, completeness or unity; renew, re-establish. Formerly also, restore to a previous condition. LME.
2 Restore (something) *to* (a person), *into* (a state); re-establish (a person) *in* a position, place, etc. Cf. REINTEGRATE *verb* 1. Now *rare* or *obsolete.* L16.
■ **redinteˈgration** *noun* [Anglo-Norman *redintegracioun* or Latin *redintegratio(n-)*] L15. **redintegrative** *adjective* tending to renew or restore M19.

rediscover /riːdɪˈskʌvə/ *verb trans.* M18.
[from RE- + DISCOVER.]
Discover again.
■ **rediscoverer** *noun* L19. **rediscovery** *noun* the act of discovering again; a renewed discovery: M19.

redissolve /riːdɪˈzɒlv/ *verb trans. & intrans.* E17.
[from RE- + DISSOLVE *verb.*]
Dissolve or become dissolved again; *esp.* dissolve (something previously precipitated or deposited).
■ **redissoluble** *adjective* = REDISSOLVABLE L18. **redissoˈlution** *noun* (a) second or renewed dissolution L18. **rediˈssolvable** *adjective* able to be redissolved L18.

redistribute /riːdɪˈstrɪbjuːt, riːˈdɪs-/ *verb trans.* E17.
[from RE- + DISTRIBUTE *verb.*]
Distribute again or differently.
■ **redisˈtributive** *adjective* of or pertaining to redistribution, esp. of wealth L19.

redistribution /ˌriːdɪstrɪˈbjuːʃ(ə)n/ *noun.* M19.
[from RE- + DISTRIBUTION.]
The action or process of redistributing something, esp. the redistributing of wealth by means of taxation; a second or different distribution.
■ **redistributionist** *noun & adjective* (**a**) *noun* a person who advocates a (more equal) redistribution of wealth; (**b**) *adjective* of or pertaining to redistributionists, advocating such redistribution: M20.

redivide /riːdɪˈvʌɪd/ *verb trans.* E17.
[from RE- + DIVIDE *verb.*]
Divide again or differently.
■ **redivision** *noun* the act or process of redividing something; a second or different division: L16.

redivivus /rɛdɪˈviːvəs/ *postpositive adjective.* Fem. **-viva** /-ˈviːvə/. Occas. (earlier) Anglicized as **redivive** /rɛdɪˈvʌɪv/. L16.
[Latin, formed as RE- + *vivus* living, alive.]
Come back to life; reborn, renewed.

> 📖 A. BRINK A tall, athletic, tanned man . . Clark Gable redivivus.

redly /ˈrɛdli/ *adverb.* E17.
[from RED *adjective* + -LY².]
With a red appearance, colour, or glow.

Redmondite /ˈrɛdməndʌɪt/ *adjective & noun.* L19.
[from *Redmond* (see below) + -ITE¹.]
▶**A** *adjective.* Of or pertaining to the Irish politician John Edward Redmond (1856–1918) or his nationalist ideas. L19.
▶**B** *noun.* A supporter of Redmond or his policies. L19.
■ **Redmondism** *noun* the ideas or policies of Redmond or his supporters E20.

redneck /ˈrɛdnɛk/ *noun.* M19.
[from RED *adjective* + NECK *noun*¹.]
1 An uneducated working-class white person in the southern US, esp. one holding reactionary political views; *gen.* anyone holding reactionary political views. *N. Amer.* Freq. *derog.* M19.
2 = ROOINEK. *S. Afr.* L19.

> 📖 **1** S. BELLOW 'He's a hillbilly. A Georgia red-neck.' *attrib.*: J. K. TOOLE This ignorant lily-white redneck fundamentalist led my other students to form a committee.

red-necked /ˈrɛdnɛkt/ *adjective.* L19.
[from RED *adjective* + NECKED.]
1 Chiefly ZOOLOGY. Having a red neck. L19.
2 Holding redneck views; characteristic of a redneck; reactionary, conservative. Orig. *US.* M20.
1 red-necked avocet an Australian avocet, *Recurvirostra novaehollandiae.* **red-necked grebe** a holarctic grebe, *Podiceps grisegena.* **red-necked nightjar** an Iberian and N. African nightjar, *Caprimulgus ruficollis.* **red-necked phalarope** a northern holarctic phalarope, *Phalaropus lobatus*, which has a chestnut patch on the neck when in breeding plumage. **red-necked wallaby** an Australian wallaby, *Macropus rufogriseus*, naturalized in parts of Britain.

redness /ˈrɛdnɪs/ *noun.* OE.
[from RED *adjective* + -NESS.]
The state or quality of being red (*lit. & fig.*); red colour.

redningskoite /ˈrɛdnɪŋzkɔɪtə/ *noun.* Also ***-shoite*** /-ʃɔɪtə/. E20.
[Norwegian, from *redning* rescue + *skyte* a type of fishing vessel.]
A kind of Norwegian lifeboat.

redo /ˈriːduː/ *noun.* M20.
[from next.]
A repetition; a repeated action, deed or activity.

redo /riːˈduː/ *verb trans.* Pa. t. **-did** /-ˈdɪd/; pa. pple **-done** /-ˈdʌn/. L16.
[from RE- + DO *verb.*]
1 Do again or afresh. L16.
2 Redecorate (a room). M19.

redolence /ˈrɛd(ə)l(ə)ns/ *noun.* LME.
[Old French, from *redolent*: see next, -ENCE.]
Sweet smell, fragrance, perfume.

redolent /ˈrɛd(ə)l(ə)nt/ *adjective.* LME.
[Old French, or Latin *redolent-* pres. ppl stem of *redolere*, formed as RE- + *olere* emit a smell: see -ENT.]
1 Having or diffusing a strong or pleasant odour; fragrant, odorous. Now *rare.* LME.
2 Of smell, odour, etc.: pleasant, sweet, fragrant. Now *rare.* LME.
3 Smelling *of* or *with*; full of the scent or smell *of.* E16. ▸**b** *fig.* Strongly suggestive or reminiscent *of*; impregnated *with.* E19.

> 📖 **3a** A. BRINK The whole room was redolent of old tobacco and cats. **b** R. W. EMERSON Oxford is redolent of age and authority.

■ **redolently** *adverb* L19.

redondilla /redonˈdiʎa, rɛdənˈdiːljə/ *noun.* Pl. ***-as*** /-as, -əz/. M19.
[Spanish, dim. of *redonda* fem. of *redondo* round.]
In Spanish poetry, a stanza of rhyming verse; *spec.* one of four trochaic lines of six or eight syllables, rhyming on lines one and four, and lines two and three.

redone *verb pa. pple* of REDO *verb.*

redouble /rɪˈdʌb(ə)l/ *verb & noun.* LME.
[French *redoubler*, formed as RE- + *doubler* DOUBLE *verb.*]
▶**A** *verb.* **1 a** *verb trans.* Double or double again; make twice as great or as much. More widely, make more intense or numerous, increase. LME. ▸**b** *verb intrans.* Be doubled or doubled again; become twice as great or as much. More widely, become more intense or numerous, increase. LME.
2 a *verb trans.* Repeat (a sound); reproduce, re-echo. Now *rare.* M16. ▸**b** *verb intrans.* Re-echo, resound. Now *rare.* E18.
3 *verb trans.* Reiterate; do, say, etc., a second time. L16.
4 *verb trans.* Duplicate by reflection. *rare.* E19.
5 *verb intrans.* BRIDGE. Double again a bid already doubled by an opponent. L19.

> 📖 **1a** P. DALLY She redoubled her prayers, and Robert's faith . . returned. J. HALPERIN He redoubled his efforts in literary self-improvement. **b** M. KEANE The curtains were drawn and the scent of freesias redoubled in the room.

▶ **B** *noun. BRIDGE.* The redoubling of a bid. **E20.**

■ **redoublement** *noun* (a) redoubling **E17.** **redoubler** *noun* (*rare*) a person who or thing which redoubles **E17.** **redoubling** *adverb* the action of the verb; an instance of this: **LME.**

redoubt /rɪˈdaʊt/ *noun.* **E17.**
[French *redoute*, †*ridotte* from Italian †*ridotta* (now *ridotto*) from medieval Latin *reductus* refuge, retreat, from pa. ppl stem of Latin *reducere* draw off, withdraw. The intrusive *b* is by analogy with next.]
1 *FORTIFICATION.* A usu. square or polygonal outwork or fieldwork, with little or no flanking defences. Formerly also, a small work made in or near a bastion or ravelin of a permanent fortification. **E17.** ▸**b** *fig.* Something serving as a refuge; an entrenched standpoint; a stronghold *of* a particular quality, condition, etc. **E17.**
2 A public assembly-hall in Germany used for gambling and entertainments; *transf.* an assembly held in such a hall, *esp.* a masked ball. Now *rare.* **L18.**
3 *FORTIFICATION.* = **REDUIT. E19.**

🕮 **1** *National Observer (US)* Remains of the French redoubt built . . to guard the original French settlement. **b** R. OWEN The Soviet Union—a last redoubt of male chauvinist piggery.

redoubt /rɪˈdaʊt/ *verb trans.* Now *rhet.* **LME.**
[Old & mod. French *redouter*, †*redoubter* fear, dread, formed as **RE-** + *douter* **DOUBT** *verb.*]
Dread, fear; stand in awe or apprehension of.
■ **redoubted** *ppl adjective* feared; formidable; respected; distinguished: **LME.**

redoubtable /rɪˈdaʊtəb(ə)l/ *adjective.* **LME.**
[Old & mod. French *redoutable*, from *redouter*: see prec., **-ABLE.**]
Formidable, to be feared. Also, (of a person) commanding respect.

🕮 M. IGNATIEFF Peggy . . turned out to be a redoubtable Edwardian adventuress.

■ **redoubtably** *adverb* **L19.**

redound /rɪˈdaʊnd/ *verb & noun.* **LME.**
[Old & mod. French *redonder* from Latin *redundare*, formed as **RE-** + *undare* surge, from *unda* wave.]
▶ **A** *verb.* **I** *verb intrans.* †**1** Of water, waves, etc.: swell or surge up, overflow. **LME–E18.** ▸**b** Of other liquids, esp. bodily fluids: overflow, superabound. **M16–L17.** ▸**c** *transf.* Be superfluous. **L16–M17.**
†**2** Be plentiful; abound (*in, with*). **LME–M17.**
†**3** Flow, come, or go back; come again. Also, recoil, spring back. **LME–E17.**
†**4** Resound, reverberate, re-echo. **LME–M17.**
5 Result in turning *to* some advantage or disadvantage. **LME.** ▸**b** Turn or make a great contribution *to* a person's honour, disgrace, etc. **L15.**
6 Of advantage, damage, etc.: attach or accrue *to*, or *unto* a person. Formerly also, (of wealth etc.) come or fall *to*. **LME.**
7 Of honour, disgrace, advantage, etc.: recoil or come back upon, come to as the final result. Foll. by *on, upon.* **M16.**
8 Proceed or arise *from* or *out of* something. Now *rare* or *obsolete.* **L16.**

🕮 **5** *Free-thinker* This Objection . . redounds only to the Damage of the Student. **b** A. BROOKNER It redounds to Frederick's credit that he openly shows his hand. **6** R. C. TRENCH Benefits which redound to us through the sacrifice of the death of Christ.

▶† **II** *verb trans.* **9** Reflect (honour, blame, etc.) *in, to, upon* a person. **L15–E18.**
▶ **B** *noun.* Reverberation, echo; a resounding cry. Also, the fact of redounding. *rare.* **M17.**

redowa /ˈrɛdəvə/ *noun.* **M19.**
[French or German, from Czech *rejdovák*, from *rejdovat* turn or whirl round.]
A Bohemian folk-dance; a ballroom dance in relatively quick triple time resembling this; a piece of music for such a dance.

redox /ˈriːdɒks, ˈrɛdɒks/ *noun.* **E20.**
[from **RED(UCTION** + **OX(IDATION.**]
CHEMISTRY. A reversible reaction in which one species is oxidized and another reduced; oxidation and reduction. Usu. ***attrib.***, designating, involving, or utilizing such a reaction.

redpoll /ˈrɛdpəʊl/ *noun*[1]. Also †**-pole. M18.**
[from **RED** *adjective* + **POLL** *noun*[1].]
Any of various holarctic finches of the genus *Acanthis* having red foreheads, *esp.* (more fully ***lesser redpoll***, ***mealy redpoll***) *A. flammea.* Formerly also (more fully ***greater redpoll***), the male linnet.

redpoll /ˈrɛdpəʊl/ *noun*[2]. **L19.**
[from **RED** *adjective* + **POLL** *noun*[3].]
(An animal of) a breed of red-haired polled cattle. Freq. ***attrib.***

red rag /rɛd ˈrag/ *noun phr.* Also (in sense 2) **red-rag. L17.**
[from **RED** *adjective* + **RAG** *noun*[1].]
1 The tongue. *arch. slang.* **L17.**
2 A variety of rust in grain. **M19.**
3 In full ***red rag to a bull***. A source of extreme provocation or annoyance. **L19.**
4 = ***red ensign*** s.v. **ENSIGN** *noun* 4. *Nautical slang.* **E20.**

Red Republic /rɛd rɪˈpʌblɪk/ *noun phr.* Also **r- r-. M19.**
[from **RED** *adjective* + **REPUBLIC.**]
A republic based on socialist principles, *spec.* the French Second Republic, proclaimed in 1848.
■ **Red Republican** *noun* a person who holds radical republican views and advocates force to realize them, *esp.* a supporter of the European revolutions of 1848 **M19. Red Republicanism** *noun* the principles and views of Red Republicans **M19.**

redress /rɪˈdrɛs/ *noun.* **LME.**
[Anglo-Norman *redresse*, *-esce*, from Old & mod. French *redresser*: see next.]
1 Reparation of or compensation for a wrong or consequent loss. **LME.**
2 Remedy for or relief from some trouble; assistance, aid, help. **LME.** ▸†**b** Correction or reformation of something wrong. **E16–M18.**
3 a A means of redress; an amendment, an improvement. Now *rare.* **L15.** ▸†**b** A person who or thing which affords redress. **E16–L17.**
4 The act of redressing; correction or amendment *of* a thing, state, etc. **M16.**

🕮 **1** *Which?* They find themselves unable to get redress following a complaint. **2** †**beyond redress**, †**past redress**, †**without redress** beyond the possibility of remedy, aid, or amendment.

redress /rɪˈdrɛs/ *verb.* **ME.**
[Old & mod. French *redresser*, †*-drecier*, formed as **RE-** + **DRESS** *verb.*]
†**1** *verb trans.* Repair (an action); atone for (a misdeed). **ME–L16.**
2 *verb trans.* Remedy or remove (trouble or distress). **ME.** ▸**b** Cure, heal (a disease, wound, etc.). **L15.**
†**3** *verb trans.* Set (a person or thing) upright again; *fig.* set up again, restore, re-establish. **LME–E18.** ▸**b** *verb refl.* Raise (oneself) again; resume an upright posture. **LME–E18.** ▸**c** *verb intrans.* Rise, become erect. **L15–L16.**
†**4** *verb trans. fig.* Bring back (a person) to the right course; set in the right direction. **LME–L17.** ▸**b** *HUNTING.* Bring back (hounds or deer) to the proper course. **LME–E18.** ▸**c** Amend (one's ways). **LME–M16.**
†**5** *verb trans. & refl.* Direct or address (a thing, oneself) *to* a destination, course, place, etc. **LME–L16.**
†**6** *verb trans.* Put in order; arrange. Also, shift *to* the proper place. **LME–L16.**
7 *verb trans.* †**a** Restore to proper order or a proper state; mend, repair. **LME–M17.** ▸**b** Put (a matter etc.) right again; reform, improve. Now *rare.* **LME.** ▸**c** Correct, emend. *rare.* **E17.**
†**8** *verb trans.* Restore (a person) to happiness or prosperity; deliver *from* misery, death, etc. **LME–L16.**
9 *verb trans.* Set (a person) right, by obtaining or giving reparation or compensation. **LME**
10 *verb trans.* Set right or rectify (injury, a wrong, a grievance, etc.); alter, correct, or do away with (an unsatisfactory state of affairs). **LME**

🕮 **2** R. W. EMERSON No calamity which right words will not begin to redress. **9** S. FOOTE I indeed have wrong'd, but will redress you. **10** P. WARNER Redressing wrongs, as well as restoring lost property and positions. *National Times* Survival of the . . Government . . depends on the extent to which it can redress this public perception.

Phrases: **redress the balance** restore equality.
■ **redressable** *adjective* (earlier in **UNREDRESSABLE**) **L17. redressal** *noun* the act of redressing something, redress **M19. redresser** *noun* a person who or thing which redresses something, esp. one who redresses a wrong **LME. redressive** *adjective* (*rare*) seeking to redress, bringing redress **M18. redressment** *noun* = **REDRESSAL M17. redressor** *noun* (*rare*) = **REDRESSER L19.**

re-dress /riːˈdrɛs/ *verb trans. & intrans.* **L15.**
[from **RE-** + **DRESS** *verb.*]
Dress again or differently.

Red River /rɛd ˈrɪvə/ *noun phr. Canad.* **M19.**
[A river flowing from North Dakota, USA, to Lake Winnipeg, Manitoba, Canada.]
Used ***attrib.*** to designate things from or associated with Red River.
Red River cart *Hist.* a stout two-wheeled wooden cart. **Red River fever** typhoid fever. **Red River jig** a fast, intricate jig.

redshank /ˈrɛdʃaŋk/ *noun.* **E16.**
[from **RED** *adjective* + **SHANK** *noun.*]
1 a Either of two red-legged Eurasian waders of the sandpiper family, *Tringa totanus* (more fully ***common redshank***) and *T. erythropus* (more fully ***spotted redshank***). **E16.** ▸†**b** A (male or female) duck. *slang.* **M16–E18.**
2 A person who has red legs, usu. through exposure to heat or cold; *spec.* (*Hist.*) a Celtic inhabitant of the Scottish Highlands or Ireland. **E16.**
3 A knotweed, *Persicaria maculosa*, with red stems and spikes of small pink flowers. Also called ***persicaria***. Cf. **SHANK** *noun* 4b. Chiefly *dial.* **L17.**

redshift /ˈrɛdʃɪft/ *noun & verb.* **E20.**
[**RED** *adjective* + **SHIFT** *noun.*]
Chiefly *ASTRONOMY.* ▶**A** *noun.* Displacement of spectral lines, resonance peaks, etc., towards longer wavelengths or the red end of the spectrum, implying (if this is a Doppler effect) that a celestial object exhibiting this is receding; the extent of this. **E20.**
▶ **B** *verb trans.* Displace (a spectrum) towards the red end. **L20.**
■ **redshifted** *adjective* exhibiting a redshift **M20.**

red shirt /ˈrɛd ʃəːt/ *noun phr.* Also **redshirt. M19.**
[from **RED** *adjective* + **SHIRT** *noun.*]
1 a A supporter of Garibaldi, esp. one of the thousand who sailed with him in 1860 to conquer Sicily. **M19.** ▸**b** *gen.* A revolutionary, an anarchist, a Communist. **L19.** ▸**c** A member of a Pathan nationalist organization formed in North-West Province in 1921 and lasting until the creation of Pakistan in 1947. Freq. ***attrib.*** **M20.**
2 A college athlete whose course is extended by a year during which he does not take part in university events, in order to develop his skills and extend his period of eligibility at this level of competition. *US.* **M20.**
■ **red-shirt** *verb trans.* (*US*) keep (an athlete) out of university competition for a year (freq. as **red-shirting** *verbal noun*) **M20.**

red-short /ˈrɛdʃɔːt/ *adjective.* **M18.**
[Swedish *rödskört*, neut. of *rödskör*, from *röd* red + *skör* brittle.]
METALLURGY. Of iron: brittle while red-hot due to an excess of sulphur in the metal.
■ **red-shortness** *noun* **M19.**

redstart /ˈrɛdstɑːt/ *noun.* **L16.**
[from **RED** *adjective* + **START** *noun*[1].]
1 Any of various Eurasian and N. African birds of the genus *Phoenicurus* (family Turdidae), characterized by their red tails, *esp.* (more fully ***common redstart***) *P. phoenicurus* and (more fully ***black redstart***) *P. ochruros.* **L16.**
2 An American fly-catching warbler, *Setophaga ruticilla* (family Parulidae), the breeding males of which have black plumage with orange-red markings (more fully ***American redstart***). Also (usu. with specifying word), any of various similar American warblers of the genus *Myioborus.* **M18.**

red-tail /ˈrɛdteɪl/ *noun.* **M16.**
[from **RED** *adjective* + **TAIL** *noun*[1].]
1 = **REDSTART** 1. Now *rare.* **M16.** ▸**b** The red-tailed hawk. *US.* **E19.**
2 †**a** The rudd. Only in **M18.** ▸**b** Any of various American fishes, esp. (in full ***red-tail chub***) *Nocomis effusus.* **L19.**

red tape /rɛd ˈteɪp/ *noun phr.* **E18.**
[from **RED** *adjective* + **TAPE** *noun.*]
Tape of a red colour such as is commonly used to secure legal and official documents; *transf.* excessive bureaucracy or adherence to formalities, esp. in public business.

🕮 A. WILSON Museum fellows . . as much bureaucrats as . . scholars—tied up by a lot of red tape.

■ **red-taped** *adjective* tied with red tape; affected or restricted by red-tapism **M19. red-tapery** *noun* red-tapism **M19. red-tapey** *adjective* red-tapish **E20. red-tapish** *adjective* characterized or affected by red-tapism **M19. red-tapism** *noun* the spirit or system of excessive adherence to bureaucratic formalities **M19. red-tapist** *noun* a person who adheres strictly or mechanically to bureaucratic formalities **M19. red-tapy** *adjective* red-tapish **L19.**

red tapeworm /rɛd ˈteɪpwəːm/ *noun phr. joc. rare.* **E20.**
[Blend of **RED TAPE** and **TAPEWORM.**]
Red-tapism or a red-tapist regarded as parasitic or as a disease of society.

reduce /rɪˈdjuːs/ *verb.* **LME.**
[Latin *reducere* bring back, restore, formed as **RE-** + *ducere* lead, bring.]
▶ **I** *verb trans.* †**1 a** Bring back, recall (a thing or person) *to* one's memory or mind. **LME–E17.** ▸**b** Bring back, recall (the mind, thoughts, etc.) to or from a subject. **LME–E18.**
†**2** Bring (a person or thing) back to or from a place, person, way of behaving, etc. Also foll. by *from, into, to.* **LME–E18.**
†**3** Take back or refer (a thing) *to* its origin, author, etc. **LME–M17.**
4 Restore (a condition, quality, etc.). Long *rare* or *obsolete.* **LME.**
5 *SURGERY.* Restore (a dislocated, fractured, etc., part) to the proper position. **LME.** ▸**b** Adjust, set (a dislocation or fracture). **M19.**
†**6** Lead (a person) away *from* or from error in action or belief, esp. in matters of morality or religion; restore to faith or truthfulness. **LME–L18.**
7 †**a** Bring (a person or thing) *to* or *into* a certain state or condition. Also, restore to a former state. **LME–M18.** ▸†**b** Influence (a person) towards some belief or opinion. **M16–E18.** ▸**c** Put (a theory etc.) to, *into* practice. Now *rare.* **E17.**

8 †**a** Adapt (a thing) *to* a purpose. LME–E17. ▸**b** *ASTRONOMY.* Adapt or correct (an observation) *to* a particular place or point. Now *rare* or *obsolete.* M17.
†**9** **a** Put *into* another language; translate. LME–L16. ▸**b** Set down in writing; record in a map. L15–E17.
10 **a** Turn *to* or convert *into* a different physical state; *esp.* break down, crush *to* powder etc. LME. ▸**b** *METALLURGY.* Convert (ore or oxide) into metal; smelt. M18. ▸**c** *CHEMISTRY.* Orig., decompose or resolve (a compound) into a simpler compound or its constituent elements. Now, cause to combine with hydrogen or to undergo reduction; add an electron to, lower the oxidation number of, (an atom). Opp. OXIDIZE. M18. ▸**d** Break up (soil) into fine particles. M18.
11 Bring together; confine, fit *into* a small space. LME.
12 Change, bring down, or simplify *to* a specified or smaller amount, or *to* a single thing; boil so as to concentrate (a liquid, sauce, etc.). Also, assign *to* a certain class; put in a certain order or arrangement. L15.
13 **a** Bring *to* order etc. by compulsion; force *into* obedience, constrain. L15. ▸**b** *LAW.* Bring (a thing or right) *into* possession. M18.
14 *SCOTS LAW.* Rescind, revoke, annul (a deed, decree, etc.) by judicial order. L15.
15 **a** Bring (a person or place) under control; subdue, conquer; *spec.* capture (a town, fortress, etc.); compel to surrender. (Foll. by †*into,* †*under.*) Long *rare.* L15. ▸†**b** Overcome, repress, moderate (a desire, temper, etc.). M17–E18.
16 **a** Change *into* or *to* a certain form or character. Now *rare.* L16. ▸**b** Put *into,* or commit *to,* writing. Now *rare.* M17.
17 **a** *MATH.* Change (a number or quantity) *into* or *to* a lower denomination or unit. L16. ▸**b** Change (a quantity, figure, etc.) *into* or *to* a different form. L16. ▸**c** Resolve by analysis. Foll. by *to.* M19.
18 *LOGIC.* Bring (a syllogism) into a different but equivalent form, esp. into one of the moods of the first figure. L16.
19 **a** Bring down *to* an unsatisfactory, undesirable, or helpless condition, a state of hardship, etc. L16. ▸**b** In *pass.* Be compelled by need or hardship *to do* something. L17. ▸**c** Weaken physically. M18. ▸**d** *PHOTOGRAPHY.* Decrease the density of (a negative or print). L19.
20 Bring down *to* a lower rank or position; demote. M17.
21 *MILITARY.* Break up, disband (an army or regiment). Long *rare* or *obsolete.* E18.
22 **a** Lower, diminish, cut down in size or amount (*to*); make lower in price, lessen the cost of. L18. ▸**b** *PHONETICS.* Articulate (a speech sound) in a way requiring less muscular effort; form (a vowel) in a more central articulatory position; weaken. L19.

> 🕮 **10a** F. KING Potatoes . . cooked so long that they have been reduced to a watery flour. **12** C. LUCAS The rules . . were . . reduced to the just order in which they now stand. E. A. ROSS We cannot reduce the whole man to a 'cell' in a 'social organism'. *Connoisseur* Reducing the broths to the bases for his sauces that evening. **13a** JOHN BOYLE His first step, was to reduce to reason . . his reverend brethren. **19a** J. BUCHAN He . . flung . . his suits before me, for my own had been pretty well reduced to rags. L. STRACHEY The ducal family were reduced to beggary. P. LIVELY The physical shock reduced her almost to tears. **b** J. GROSS He was reduced to asking . . for help finding work. **20 reduce to the ranks** demote (a non-commissioned officer) to the rank of private. **22a** M. FRAYN The smoke . . reduced her vision . . further. G. GREENE Our speed was practically reduced to walking-pace. *Broadcast* Staffing . . is to be reduced to the bare minimum.

▶**II** *verb intrans.* **23** **a** Become less or limited. Also, become more concentrated, come down *to.* E19. ▸**b** Lose weight, slim. E20.
24 *CHEMISTRY.* Undergo reduction. M20.

> 🕮 **23a** C. CONRAN Allow the gravy to boil and reduce (leaving roughly two tablespoons per person). *African Affairs* The number of . . white farmers may have reduced by . . 50 per cent.

■ †**reduceable** *adjective* = REDUCIBLE L16–L18. **reduceless** *adjective* (*rare*) incapable of reduction M19. **reducer** *noun* a person who or thing which reduces something; *spec.* (*a*) *CHEMISTRY* = ***reducing agent*** below; (*b*) *PHOTOGRAPHY* a chemical used to reduce the density of a print or negative; (*c*) *PRINTING* an additive used with ink to make it run more freely: E16. **reducing** *ppl adjective* that reduces something or undergoes reduction; ***reducing agent*** (*CHEMISTRY*), a substance that brings about reduction by undergoing oxidation and loss of electrons; ***reducing sugar*** (*CHEMISTRY*), a sugar which reduces copper(II) to copper(I) salts in Fehling's solution or similar test solutions (indicating the presence of an aldehyde group): M18.

reduced /rɪˈdjuːst/ *adjective.* E17.
[formed as prec. + -ED[1].]
1 **a** Of a person, his or her circumstances, etc.: impoverished. E17. ▸**b** *MILITARY HISTORY.* Of an officer: discharged from active service and put on half-pay. M17. ▸**c** Weakened, impaired. L17.
†**2** Brought back. L17–E18.
3 **a** Diminished in size or amount; *spec.* lowered in price. M18. ▸**b** *PHONETICS.* Of a vowel sound: articulated less distinctly than a stressed vowel; weakened and centralized. L19.
4 (Of a metal) obtained by reducing the ore or oxide; (of a compound) having undergone reduction. L18.
5 Put into another form; changed, modified. M19.

> 🕮 **3a** *Observer* 'Imperfects' offered at a . . reduced price. *Which?* Reduced-fat spread . . for most sorts of cookery.

¶ Earlier in UNREDUCED.

†**reducement** *noun.* L16.
[formed as prec. + -MENT.]
1 The act of bringing a person or thing back to a former (esp. better) state or condition. L16–L17.
2 Reduction *to* or *into* a specified quality, state, form, etc. E–M17.
3 Assignment to a particular type or class; deduction, inference. *rare.* E17–M18.
4 Conquest or subjugation of a town or country. Only in 17.
5 (A) reduction, (a) diminution; (an) abatement. E17–M18.

reducible /rɪˈdjuːsɪb(ə)l/ *adjective.* LME.
[In early use from medieval Latin *reducibilis*; later from REDUCE *verb* + -IBLE.]
That may be reduced; capable of reduction; *spec.* (*MATH.*) (of a polynomial) able to be factorized into two or more polynomials of lower degree; (of a group) expressible as the direct product of two of its subgroups.

> 🕮 R. M. HARE Everything that we are taught . . must . . be reducible to principles.

■ **reduciˈbility** *noun* the fact or quality of being reducible; ***axiom of reducibility*** (*LOGIC*), Russell's axiom that to any property above the lowest order there is a coextensive property of order o: L17. **reducibleness** *noun* M17. **reducibly** *adverb* (*rare*) (earlier in IRREDUCIBLY) L19.

reduct /rɪˈdʌkt/ *verb trans.* LME.
[Latin *reduct-* pa. ppl stem of *reducere* REDUCE.]
1 Bring *into, to,* or *from* a state or form; change, simplify. Now *rare.* LME.
†**2** Lead back, lead *into* or *to* a place. L16–M17.
3 Deduct (a sum). *obsolete* exc. *dial.* L16.

reductant /rɪˈdʌkt(ə)nt/ *noun.* E20.
[from REDUCT(ION + -ANT[1], after OXIDANT.]
CHEMISTRY. = ***REDUCING agent.***

reductase /rɪˈdʌkteɪz/ *noun.* E20.
[from REDUCT(ION + -ASE.]
BIOCHEMISTRY. An enzyme which promotes chemical reduction.

reductio ad absurdum /rɪˌdʌktɪəʊ ad əbˈsəːdəm/ *noun phr.* M18.
[Latin, lit. 'reduction to the absurd'.]
LOGIC. A method of proving the falsity of a premiss by showing that the logical consequence is absurd.

reductio ad impossibile /rɪˌdʌktɪəʊ ad ɪmpɒˈsɪbɪliː/ *noun phr.* M16.
[Latin, lit. 'reduction to the impossible'.]
LOGIC. A method of proving a proposition by drawing an absurd or impossible conclusion from its contradictory.

reduction /rɪˈdʌkʃ(ə)n/ *noun.* LME.
[Old & mod. French *réduction* or Latin *reductio(n-),* from *reduct-*: see REDUCT, -ION.]
†**1** The action of bringing a person or thing back to or from a state, condition, place, etc. LME–M18.
2 *SURGERY.* The restoration of a dislocated part to its normal position; the action of reducing a displacement, etc. LME.
3 **a** Conquest or subjugation *of* a place, esp. a town or fortress. Now *rare.* LME. ▸**b** *Hist.* [Spanish *reducción.*] A village or colony of S. American Indians converted and governed by the Jesuits. E18.
4 *SCOTS LAW.* The court action of annulling a deed, decree, etc. L15.
5 **a** *MATH.* The process of converting an amount from one denomination to a smaller one, or of bringing down a fraction to its lowest terms. M16. ▸**b** *ASTRONOMY.* The correction of observations by allowing for parallax, refraction, etc. E18. ▸**c** *GEOMETRY.* The process of reducing a curve etc. to a straight line. Now *rare* or *obsolete.* L18. ▸**d** The process of explaining behaviour, mental activity, etc., by reducing it to its component factors or to a simpler form. E20. ▸**e** *COMPUTING.* The transformation of data into a simpler form. M20.
6 *LOGIC.* The process of reducing a syllogism to another form, esp. by expressing it in one of the moods of the first figure. Also, the process of establishing the validity of a syllogism by showing that the contradictory of its conclusion is inconsistent with its premisses. M16.
7 Conversion *to* or *into* a certain state, form, etc. E17.
8 **a** The action or process of reducing a substance to another (usu. simpler) form, esp. by a chemical process; *spec.* in *CHEMISTRY* (opp. OXIDATION), the loss or removal of oxygen from, or the addition of hydrogen to, an atom or molecule; a decrease in the proportion of electronegative constituents in a molecule or compound; the lowering of the oxidation number of an atom. M17. ▸**b** The conversion of ore or oxide into metal; smelting. L18. ▸**c** In phenomenology, the process of reducing an object of consciousness or an idea to its pure essence for analysis as a logical structure by elimination of all that which is extraneous, contingent, or based on prior assumptions. E20.
9 **a** Diminution, lessening, cutting down; the amount by which something is reduced. L17. ▸**b** The action or process of making a copy on a smaller scale. Also, such a copy; *spec.* the ratio of a reduced copy or image to the original in photography, microphotography, etc. E18. ▸**c** *PHOTOGRAPHY.* Diminution of the density of a print or negative. L19. ▸**d** *MUSIC.* (An) arrangement of an orchestral score for a smaller number of instruments, esp. for piano. L19. ▸**e** *CYTOLOGY.* The halving of the number of chromosomes per cell that occurs at one of the two anaphases of meiosis. Cf. POSTREDUCTION, PREREDUCTION. L19. ▸**f** *PHONETICS.* Weakening of a vowel; substitution of a sound which requires less muscular effort to articulate. E20. ▸**g** A means of curing drug addiction by decreasing or limiting usage. E20.
10 *MILITARY.* Demotion to a lower rank. E19.

> 🕮 **5d** F. FERGUSSON Freud's reduction of the play (*Oedipus*) to the concepts of his psychology. **9a** *Manchester Examiner* A reduction of ten per cent in . . wages. N. F. DIXON Acquisition of knowledge is synonymous with reduction of ignorance. **d** B. MASON A . . piano reduction of 'The Shrovetide Fair' from *Petrouchka.*

Comb.: **reduction division** *CYTOLOGY* the meiotic cell division during which reduction occurs; **reduction gear** *ENGINEERING* a system of gear wheels in which the driven shaft rotates more slowly than the driving shaft; **reduction-improbation** *SCOTS LAW* suggestion that the deed or other document in question is not genuine; **reduction negative**, **reduction print** *PHOTOGRAPHY* a negative or print made from a larger original; **reduction sentence** *LOGIC* a sentence giving conditions for the use of a concept less strict than a definition.
■ **reductional** *adjective* characterized by reduction L17. **reductionally** *adverb* E20.

reductionism /rɪˈdʌkʃ(ə)nɪz(ə)m/ *noun.* M20.
[from prec. + -ISM.]
PHILOSOPHY. The principle of analysing complex things into simpler constituents; (freq. *derog.*) any doctrine that a complex theory, system, phenomenon, etc., can be fully understood in terms of simpler concepts or in terms of its isolated components.

> 🕮 A. CLARE Psychiatric diagnosis is often depicted as a sterile exercise in reductionism.

reductionist /rɪˈdʌkʃ(ə)nɪst/ *noun & adjective.* L19.
[formed as prec. + -IST.]
▶**A** *noun.* **1** A person who favours a reduction in the number of licensed public houses. *rare.* L19.
2 Chiefly *PHILOSOPHY.* An advocate of reductionism. M20.
▶**B** *adjective.* *PHILOSOPHY.* Of or pertaining to reductionism or reductionists. M20.

> 🕮 *British Medical Journal* The reductionist separation of the disease from the sick person.

■ **reductioˈnistic** *adjective* M20. **reductioˈnistically** *adverb* M20.

reductive /rɪˈdʌktɪv/ *adjective & noun.* M16.
[medieval Latin *reductivus,* formed as REDUCTION: see -IVE.]
▶**A** *adjective.* **1** **a** That reduces or tends to reduce something; connected with or of the nature of reduction. Also (*PHILOSOPHY*), reductionist. M16. ▸**b** *ART.* = MINIMAL *adjective* 3. M20.
2 **a** That leads or brings back. (Also foll. by *of.*) Long *rare.* M17. ▸**b** *PSYCHOLOGY.* That leads back to an earlier state; involving the tracing of psychological traits to an origin in infancy. E20.

> 🕮 **1** *City Limits* It's difficult to summarize 'The Century's Daughter' without sounding . . crassly reductive.

▶**B** *noun.* A thing which tends to cause reduction. *rare.* L17.
■ **reductively** *adverb* M17. **reductiveness** *noun* L20.

reductivism /rɪˈdʌktɪvɪz(ə)m/ *noun.* M20.
[from prec. + -ISM.]
1 *ART.* Minimalism. M20.
2 *PHILOSOPHY.* = REDUCTIONISM. L20.
■ **reductivist** *noun & adjective* (chiefly *PHILOSOPHY*) (*a*) *noun* an advocate or practitioner of reductivism; (*b*) *adjective* of or pertaining to reductivism or reductivists: M20.

reductorial /rɪdʌkˈtɔːrɪəl/ *adjective.* Long *rare.* L18.
[formed as REDUCT + -OR, -IAL.]
Reductive.

reduit /rəˈdwiː/ *noun.* E17.
[French, ult. from medieval Latin *reductus*: see REDOUBT *noun.*]
FORTIFICATION. A keep or stronghold into which a garrison may retire if the outworks are taken.

redund /riːˈdʌnd/ *verb. rare.* E20.
[Abbreviation of REDUNDANT *adjective & noun*.]
1 *verb intrans.* Be redundant. E20.
2 *verb trans.* Make redundant. M20.

redundance /rɪˈdʌnd(ə)ns/ *noun.* L16.
[formed as next: see -ANCE.]
= next.

redundancy /rɪˈdʌnd(ə)nsi/ *noun.* E17.
[Latin *redundantia*, formed as next: see -ANCY.]
1 a The state or condition of being redundant; superfluity; an instance of this. E17. **▸b** A redundant thing or part; a surplus amount. M17.
2 *spec.* **a** ENGINEERING. The presence of more structural components than are needed to confer rigidity. E20. **▸b** ENGINEERING & COMPUTING etc. The incorporation of extra components or processes to permit continued functioning in the event of a failure. M20. **▸c** The condition of being surplus to an organization's staffing requirements; loss of a job as a result of this; a case of unemployment due to reorganization, mechanization, etc. M20. **▸d** LINGUISTICS. (The degree of) predictability in a language arising from knowledge of its structure; superfluity of information in language. M20.

📖 **2b** H. MANTEL Rumours of sackings and redundancies. *attrib.*: V. GLENDINNING If my redundancy money runs out, and I go on the dole.

Comb.: **redundancy check** COMPUTING a check on the correctness of processed data that makes use of redundant data.

redundant /rɪˈdʌnd(ə)nt/ *adjective & noun.* L16.
[Latin *redundant-* pres. ppl stem of *redundare*: see REDOUND *verb*, -ANT[1].]
▸ A *adjective.* **1** Plentiful, copious, abundant; full. L16.
2 a Superfluous, excessive, unnecessary; having some additional or unneeded feature or part. E17. **▸b** ENGINEERING. Of a structural component or a force or moment on it: able to be removed without causing loss of rigidity. Of a structure: containing more than the minimum number of components necessary for rigidity. L19. **▸c** Of a person: surplus to staffing requirements; unemployed because of reorganization, mechanization, etc. E20. **▸d** (Of a language) containing material which is predictable from a knowledge of its context or structure; (of a language feature) predictable in this way. M20. **▸e** Orig. & chiefly COMPUTING. Designating information appended to a coded message which is not needed to convey the message but enables verification or correction. M20.
†3 Wavelike, swelling; overflowing. M17–L18.

📖 **1** G. M. TREVELYAN Their skirts became . . shorter and less redundant. **2a** W. GOLDING Polishing the mahogany trim—a redundant activity for it already shone. **c** D. LODGE Nobody will . . vote for a change . . that threatens to make anyone redundant.

▸ B *noun.* **1** **†a** Something redundant. L16–L18. **▸b** ENGINEERING. A redundant component of a structure (see sense A.2b above). M20.
2 A person who is made redundant by an organization. *rare.* L20.
■ **redundan'tee** *noun* (*rare*) a person who has been made redundant by an organization M20. **redundantly** *adverb* L17.

reduplicate /rɪˈdjuːplɪkət/ *adjective & noun.* M17.
[Late Latin *reduplicatus* pa. pple of *reduplicare*: see next, -ATE[2].]
▸ A *adjective.* **1** Doubled, repeated. M17. **▸b** GRAMMAR. Reduplicated; relating to or involving reduplication. M19.
2 BOTANY. Of the perianth segments in bud: valvate, with the edges reflexed. M19.
▸ B *noun.* A double, a duplicate. M17.

reduplicate /rɪˈdjuːplɪkeɪt/ *verb.* L16.
[Late Latin *reduplicat-* pa. ppl stem of *reduplicare*, formed as RE- + Latin *duplicare* DUPLICATE *verb*.]
1 *verb trans.* Make double; repeat, redouble. L16. **▸b** GRAMMAR. Repeat (a letter or syllable); form (a tense) by reduplication. M19.
2 *verb intrans.* Become double or doubled. *rare.* M19.

reduplication /rɪˌdjuːplɪˈkeɪʃ(ə)n/ *noun.* LME.
[Late Latin *reduplicatio(n-)*, formed as prec.: see -ATION.]
1 Orig., the action of turning back or folding something. Later, a fold. *rare.* LME.
2 a GRAMMAR. Repetition of a letter, syllable, word or phrase, esp. in the formation of certain tenses of Greek and Latin verbs. Later also, a word formed by repetition of a syllable. M16. **▸b** *gen.* The action of doubling or repeating; a double, a counterpart. M17.
†3 LOGIC. The repetition of a term with a limiting or defining force; the addition of some limiting term to one already used. E17–E18.

reduplicative /rɪˈdjuːplɪkətɪv/ *noun & adjective.* M16.
[medieval Latin *reduplicativus*, formed as prec.: see -ATIVE.]
▸†A *noun.* GRAMMAR. A word or particle formed by or expressing reduplication. *rare.* M16–M19.
▸ B *adjective.* **1** LOGIC. Relating to, expressing, or implying reduplication of terms. Now *rare.* E17. **▸b** Of a proposition: having a limiting repetition of the subject expressed. E18.
2 GRAMMAR. Formed by reduplication. E19.
3 BOTANY. = REDUPLICATE *adjective* 2. M19.
■ **reduplicatively** *adverb* M17.

reduplicature /rɪˈdjuːplɪkeɪtjʊə/ *noun. rare.* M19.
[formed as REDUPLICATE *verb* + -URE. Cf. DUPLICATURE.]
ANATOMY. A fold. Cf. REDUPLICATION 1.

reduviid /rɪˈdjuːvɪɪd/ *noun & adjective.* L19.
[mod. Latin *Reduviidae* (see below), from *Reduvius* genus name from Latin *reduvia* hangnail: see -ID[3].]
▸ A *noun.* Any of various predacious heteropteran bugs of the family Reduviidae, esp. the European *Reduvius personatus*; an assassin bug. L19.
▸ B *adjective.* Of, pertaining to, or designating this family. L19.

redux /ˈriːdʌks/ *adjective.* L19.
[Latin, from *reducere* bring back.]
1 MEDICINE. Of crepitation etc.: indicating the return of the lungs to a healthy state. Now *rare.* L19.
2 Brought back, revived, restored. Usu. *postpositive.* L19.

📖 **2** *Chatelaine* Bobby socks are strictly 50's redux.

redward /ˈrɛdwəd/ *adjective & adverb.* L19.
[from RED *adjective* + -WARD.]
SCIENCE. **▸A** *adjective.* Situated on the red side in a spectrum; occurring in the direction of the red end. L19.
▸ B *adverb.* Towards the red end. E20.

redwing /ˈrɛdwɪŋ/ *noun.* M17.
[from RED *adjective* + WING *noun*.]
1 a A migratory northern European thrush, *Turdus iliacus*, distinguished by red patches on the flanks and undersides of the wings. M17. **▸b** Any of various other red-winged birds, esp. the red-winged blackbird and the red-winged francolin. L18.
2 A small sailing boat with red sails. *rare.* L19.

red-winged /ˈrɛdwɪŋd/ *adjective.* E18.
[from RED *adjective* + WINGED *adjective*[1].]
Having red wings.
red-winged blackbird a very common North and Central American blackbird, *Agelaius phoeniceus*, of the family Icteridae. **red-winged francolin** a francolin, *Francolinus levaillantii*, of eastern and southern Africa. **red-winged starling** either of two African starlings, *Onychognathus morio* and *O. walleri*.

redwood /ˈrɛdwʊd/ *noun*[1]. E17.
[from RED *adjective* + WOOD *noun*[1].]
1 The reddish timber of any of various, chiefly tropical, trees; *spec.* that of *Sequoia sempervirens*. E17.
2 Any of the trees yielding such wood; esp. *Sequoia sempervirens*, a Californian conifer which is allied to the wellingtonia and is the tallest known tree. E18.
2 dawn redwood = METASEQUOIA.

Redwood /ˈrɛdwʊd/ *noun*[2]. L19.
[Sir Boverton *Redwood* (1846–1919), Brit. chemist.]
Used chiefly *attrib.* with ref. to a method of determining viscosity devised by Redwood.
Redwood second, **Redwood unit** a unit of viscosity used in conjunction with Redwood viscometers. **Redwood viscometer** a type of viscometer used esp. to measure the viscosity of petroleum and its products. **second Redwood** = ***Redwood second*** above.

ree /riː/ *noun*[1]. *obsolete* exc. *dial.* LME.
[Origin unkn.: cf. REEVE *noun*[2].]
The female of the ruff, the reeve.
¶ Attested earlier than *ruff*, and perh. orig. denoting the male also.

ree /riː/ *noun*[2]. *Scot.* L17.
[Origin unkn.]
1 A yard or enclosure where coal is stored. L17.
2 A walled enclosure for sheep. E19.

reebok *noun* var. of RHEBOK.

†reech *noun, verb* vars. of REEK *noun*[1], *verb*[1].

re-echo /riːˈɛkəʊ/ *verb & noun.* L16.
[from RE- + ECHO *verb*.]
▸ A *verb.* **1** *verb intrans.* **a** Of a sound: echo (again), be repeated as an echo. L16. **▸b** Of a place: resound *with* an echo. Also foll. by *to.* L16.
2 *verb trans.* **a** Echo back; return (a sound). L16. **▸b** Repeat (words) like an echo. M17.

📖 **1b** J. E. TENNENT The cicada . . makes the forest re-echo with . . noise. **2a** SIR W. SCOTT The sound was re-echoed . . from precipice to precipice.

▸ B *noun.* Pl. **-oes**. An echo; a repeated echo. E17.

reechy /ˈriːtʃi/ *adjective. obsolete* exc. *dial.* LME.
[from *reech* var. of REEK *noun*[1] + -Y[1].]
Smoky; squalid, dirty; rancid.

reed /riːd/ *noun*[1].
[Old English *hrēod* = Old Frisian *hriad*, Old Saxon *hriod*, Middle Dutch *ried*, *riet* (Dutch *riet*), Old High German *(h)riot* (German *Ried*), from West Germanic.]
▸ I 1 Each of the tall straight stalks or stems formed by plants of the genera *Phragmites* and *Arundo* (see sense 2). Formerly also, a cane. OE. **▸b** *collect.* A mass or bed of reeds; reeds as a material, used for thatching etc. OE. **▸c** *transf.* Wheat straw used for thatching. LME.
2 Any of various tall broad-leaved firm-stemmed grasses of the genera *Phragmites* and *Arundo* growing in water or marshy ground, freq. in large stands; *esp.* the common reed, *Phragmites australis*, found in most parts of the world. Also (with specifying word), any of various plants resembling the reed. LME.

📖 **1** J. T. STORY Beds of black-headed reeds in the . . pond. R. FRAME He used to be much more assertive . . . Now he bent to her like a reed. **broken reed** a weak or ineffectual person. ***bur-reed***, ***Norfolk reed***, ***sand-reed***, ***small reed***, etc.

▸ II 3 a In biblical use: a reed used as a measuring rod; a Hebrew unit of length equal to six cubits. ME. **▸b** A reed used as a dart or arrow; *poet.* an arrow. LME.
4 A reed or other plant with a hollow stem made into a rustic musical pipe; *fig.* this as a symbol of rustic or pastoral poetry. LME.
5 MUSIC. **a** A part of the mouthpiece of an oboe, bassoon, clarinet, or saxophone, consisting of one or two thin pieces of cane which vibrate to produce a sound when the instrument is blown into. Also, a similar device in the chanter of a bagpipe. M16. **▸b** In an organ, each of the small metal tubes fixed at the lower end of each pipe, having an opening covered by a metal tongue which vibrates when air enters the tube; such a metal tongue. Also, any similar reed, as that in a bagpipe drone. E18. **▸c** Any wind instrument with a reed; in *pl.*, *the* section of an orchestra playing such instruments. M19.
†6 A piece of reed on which yarn is wound; a bobbin, a spool. *rare.* M16–E18.
7 WEAVING. **a** An instrument for separating the threads of the warp and beating up the weft, formerly made of thin strips of reed or cane, now of metal wires, fastened on to two parallel bars of wood. L16. **▸b** A type of cloth, as distinguished by the number of threads per inch of the reed. *rare.* L19.
8 A comb used in tapestry-making for pressing down the threads of the weft to produce a close surface. E18.
9 Each of a set of small semicylindrical mouldings, resembling a number of reeds laid side by side. M18.

📖 **5a** A. E. WIER A sudden noise produced by the clarinet when the reed gets out of order. ***double reed***: see DOUBLE *adjective & adverb*. ***single reed***: see SINGLE *adjective*.

Comb.: **reed-and-tie** a style of decoration resembling reeds bound together; **reed-bed** a bed or growth of reeds; **reed-bird** *dial.* a reed warbler, sedge-warbler, or reedling; *US* the bobolink; **reed bunting** any of various Eurasian buntings of the genus *Emberiza*, which frequent reed-beds, esp. *E. schoeniclus*; **reed canary-grass** a reedlike aquatic grass, *Phalaris arundinacea*, with a long lobed inflorescence; **reed-cap** MUSIC a small wooden cap, with a slit in the top, enclosing the reed of certain double-reed instruments of the late 15th to 17th cents., keeping the reed from direct contact with the player's lips and preventing the instrument from being overblown; **reed dagger** a small pale brown and white noctuid moth, *Simyra albovenosa*; **reed-grass** any of various reedlike grasses; *esp.* = ***reed canary-grass*** above; **reed instrument** a musical (esp. wind) instrument with a reed or reeds; **reed-mace** either of two tall plants of the genus *Typha* (family Typhaceae), of ponds and river-margins, with long strap-shaped leaves and a dense velvety brown spadix, (in full ***greater reed-mace***) *T. latifolia* (also called ***cat's-tail***, ***bulrush***) and (in full ***lesser reed-mace***) *T. angustifolia*; **reed-man** (*a*) a player of a reed instrument; (*b*) a person who works with reeds; **reed-mark** a defect in the warp of a cloth caused by malfunctioning of the reed during weaving; **reed-organ** a keyboard instrument in which sound is produced by means of reeds; **reed-pipe** (*a*) a musical pipe made of reed; a wind instrument with sound produced by a reed; (*b*) an organ-pipe fitted with a reed; **reed relay** ELECTRICITY a small high-speed switching device consisting of a pair of contacts which can be brought together by an external magnetic field; **reed-sparrow** *dial.* a reed bunting; a sedge-warbler; **reed-stop** an organ-stop composed of reed-pipes; **reed switch** = ***reed relay*** above; **reed warbler** any of various Old World warblers of the genus *Acrocephalus*, which have plain plumage and frequent reed-beds, esp. the common Eurasian *A. scirpaceus*; **reed-wren** *dial.* the reed warbler.
■ **reedlike** *adjective* resembling (that of) a reed E17.

reed /riːd/ *noun*[2]. M18.
[Origin unkn.]
MINING. A cleavage plane in a coal seam parallel to the bedding.

reed /riːd/ *verb trans.* LME.
[from REED *noun*[1].]
1 Thatch with reed. Usu. in *pass.* LME.
2 Make (straw) into reed. *rare.* E19.
3 Fashion into or decorate with reeds. E19.
4 WEAVING. Pass (warp threads) through the splits of a reed. L19.

reedbuck /ˈriːdbʌk/ *noun.* M19.
[from REED *noun*[1] + BUCK *noun*[1], after RIETBOK.]
Any of various African antelopes of the genus *Redunca*, characterized by their whistling calls and high bouncing jumps, *esp.* (more fully ***southern reedbuck***) *R. arundinum*, of eastern and southern Africa.

reeded /ˈriːdɪd/ *adjective*. L18.
[from REED *noun*^{1}, *verb*: see -ED^2, -ED^1.]
1 Thatched with reed. L18.
2 Ornamented with or shaped into reeds. E19.
3 Of a musical instrument: having a reed or reeds. M19.
4 Overgrown with reeds. L19.

reeden /ˈriːd(ə)n/ *adjective*. Now *rare* or *obsolete*. ME.
[from REED *noun*^{1} + -EN^4.]
Made of reeds; reedlike.

reeder /ˈriːdə/ *noun*. LME.
[from REED *noun*^{1}, *verb* + -ER^1.]
1 A person who thatches with reeds, a thatcher. *obsolete* exc. *Hist.* LME.
2 A thatched frame used to protect clay blocks or tiles from rain. LME.

re-edification /ˌriːɛdɪfɪˈkeɪʃ(ə)n/ *noun*. Now *rare* or *obsolete*. LME.
[Old & mod. French *réédification* or late Latin *reaedificatio(n-)*, from *reaedificat-* pa. ppl stem of *reaedificare*: see RE-, EDIFICATION.]
The action of rebuilding, the state of being rebuilt.

re-edify /riːˈɛdɪfʌɪ/ *verb trans*. LME.
[Old & mod. French *réédifier* from late Latin *reaedificare*: see RE-, EDIFY.]
Rebuild (a house, wall, city, etc.); *fig.* restore, re-establish.
■ **re-edifier** *noun* (now *rare*) M16.

reeding /ˈriːdɪŋ/ *noun*. LME.
[from REED *noun*^{1}, *verb* + -ING^1.]
1 The action of REED *verb*. LME.
2 A small semicylindrical moulding; ornamentation of this form. E19.

reedling /ˈriːdlɪŋ/ *noun*. M19.
[from REED *noun*^{1} + -LING^1.]
†**1** A reed-bed. Only in M19.
2 A Eurasian passerine bird, *Panurus biarmicus*, which frequents reed-beds and is related to the parrotbills (also more fully ***bearded reedling***). Also called ***bearded tit***. M19.

reedy /ˈriːdi/ *adjective*. ME.
[from REED *noun*^{1} + -Y^1.]
1 Full of reeds; characterized by the presence of reeds. ME.
2 Made or consisting of reed or reeds. ME.
3 Resembling a reed or reeds; *spec.* (***a***) (of a person) weak, feeble; (***b***) (of a thing) having the form or texture of a reed. E17.
4 Of a voice or sound: having a tone resembling that produced by a musical reed; weak and shrill, thin. E19.
5 Of cloth: having the warp threads unevenly distributed. M20.

> 3 F. A. KEMBLE A . . bank . . covered with reedy coarse grass. 4 H. ROSENTHAL His top notes were thin and reedy.

■ **reedily** *adverb* M20. **reediness** *noun* E19.

reef /riːf/ *noun*^{1}. ME.
[Middle & mod. Dutch *reef*, *rif* from Old Norse *rif* RIB *noun*. Cf. next.]
NAUTICAL. **1** Each of the (usu. three or four) horizontal portions of a sail which may be successively rolled or folded up in order to reduce the area of canvas exposed to the wind. Freq. in ***take in a reef***, ***shake out a reef***, reduce or increase the area of sail by a reef. ME.
2 An act or method of reefing. E18.

> 1 *fig.*: M. TWAIN I . . shook the reefs out of my . . legs.

Comb.: **reef-knot** a double knot of two half-hitches made symmetrically to hold securely and cast off easily, used orig. to tie reef-points; **reef net** *N. Amer.* a type of net used for catching salmon; **reef-point** *NAUTICAL* each of a set of short ropes fixed in a line across a sail to secure the sail when reefed; **reef-tackle** *NAUTICAL* a tackle used to hoist the outer edge of a sail up to the yard in reefing.

reef /riːf/ *noun*^{2}. Orig. †**riff**. L16.
[Middle Low German, Middle Dutch *rif*, *ref* from Old Norse *rif* RIB *noun*. Cf. prec.]
1 A narrow ridge or chain of rock, shingle, coral, etc., lying at or near the surface of the sea or other water. L16.
2 A lode or vein of rock bearing gold etc.; the bedrock surrounding this. Orig. *Austral.* M19.

1 BARRIER *reef*. ***coral reef***: see CORAL *adjective*. ***fringing reef***: see FRINGE *verb* 1. **2** ***saddle reef***: see SADDLE *noun* 4b. **the Reef** *S. Afr.* the Witwatersrand (cf. RAND *noun*^{2} 1).

Comb.: **reef-builder** a marine organism which builds (coral) reefs; **reef flat** the horizontal upper surface of a reef; **reef heron** either of two grey or white herons inhabiting coastlines, *Egretta gularis*, of E. & W. African, Arabian, and western Indian coasts (more fully ***western reef heron***), and *E. sacra*, of SE Asian and Australasian coasts (more fully ***eastern reef heron***); **reef knoll** *PHYSICAL GEOGRAPHY* a (limestone) hillock formed from ancient coral.
■ **reefy** *adjective* full of reefs M19.

reef /riːf/ *verb*^{1} *trans*. M17.
[from REEF *noun*^{1}.]
1 *NAUTICAL*. Reduce the extent of (a sail) by taking in or rolling up a part and securing it. M17.
2 *NAUTICAL*. Shorten (a topmast or bowsprit) by lowering or by sliding inboard. E18.
3 *transf.* **a** Draw up or gather in after the manner of reefing a sail. Also (*Criminals' slang*), pick (a pocket), steal, obtain dishonestly; *gen.* remove, strip *off*, pull *down*. M19. ▸**b** Feel the genitals of (a person). *coarse slang*. M20.

> 1 *absol.*: *Practical Boat Owner* You reef as you would with a junk. ***double-reef***: see DOUBLE *adjective & adverb*. **reefing jacket** a thick close-fitting double-breasted jacket. ***single-reef***: see SINGLE *adjective & adverb*. 3a J. ASHBY-STERRY Dear little damsels . . Face the salt spray, reef their petticoats pluckily. L. GLASSOP Mugs deserve to have their dough reefed off them.

reef /riːf/ *verb*^{2} *intrans*. Chiefly *Austral.* & *NZ*. M19.
[from REEF *noun*^{2}.]
Work at a (mining) reef. Freq. as ***reefing*** *verbal noun*.

reefer /ˈriːfə/ *noun*^{1}. E19.
[from REEF *verb*^{1} + -ER^1.]
1 *NAUTICAL*. A person who reefs sails; *colloq.* a midshipman. E19.
2 More fully ***reefer jacket***, ***reefer coat***. A reefing jacket. Also (*N. Amer.*), an overcoat. L19.
3 [Perh. rel. to Mexican Spanish *grifo* (smoker of) marijuana.] A cigarette containing marijuana; marijuana. *slang*. M20.
4 A pickpocket; a pickpocket's accomplice. *Criminals' slang*. M20.

reefer /ˈriːfə/ *noun*^{2}. *Austral.* & *NZ*. M19.
[from REEF *noun*^{2} or *verb*^{2} + -ER^1.]
A person who works on a gold reef.

reefer /ˈriːfə/ *noun*^{3}. *colloq.* E20.
[Abbreviation.]
A refrigerator; *esp.* a refrigerated ship, lorry, or wagon. Also ***reefer ship*** etc.

reek /riːk/ *noun*^{1}. Also †**reech**.
[Old English *rēc* = Old Frisian *reek*, Old Saxon *rōk* (Dutch *rook*), Old High German *rouh* (German *Rauch*), Old Norse *reykr*, from Germanic, from base of REEK *verb*^{1}.]
1 Smoke. Now chiefly *Scot.*, *north.*, & *literary*. OE. ▸**b** *transf.* A house (as having a fire). *Scot. obsolete* exc. *Hist.* M16.
2 Vapour; steam; a mist; a visible or invisible exhalation; a fume. Now *esp.*, a strong and disagreeable smell. ME. ▸**b** Impure fetid atmosphere. L19.
3 A haze of fine dust, snow, etc. *rare*. M19.

> 2 R. BROOKE The musty reek that lingers About dead leaves. E. WAUGH The reek of petrol.

Comb.: **reek-hen** *Scot.* (*obsolete* exc. *Hist.*) an ancient tax of a hen paid annually by each householder on an estate; **reek penny** *north.* (*obsolete* exc. *Hist.*) a tax paid to the clergy by each house in a parish.

reek /riːk/ *noun*^{2}. L18.
[Alt. of RICK *noun*^{1}.]
In Ireland: a hill or mountain. Chiefly in place-names, as ***Macgillicuddy's Reeks***.

reek /riːk/ *verb*^{1}. Also †**reech**.
[Old English *rēocan* = Old Frisian *riāka*, Middle & mod. Dutch *rieken*, Old High German *riohhan* (German *riechen*), Old Norse *rjúka*, from Germanic.]
1 *verb intrans.* Give out smoke. Now *Scot.*, *north.*, & *literary*. OE.
2 *verb intrans.* Emit vapour, steam, or fumes. Now *esp.*, give out an unwholesome or unpleasant vapour, smell strongly and unpleasantly, stink, (foll. by *of*, *with*). OE. ▸**b** *fig.* Have unpleasant or suspicious associations *with*, be strongly suggestive *of* something disreputable. E18.
3 *verb trans.* Expose to smoke; dry, taint, etc., with smoke, fumigate. Now *rare*. OE.
4 *verb intrans.* †**a** Of smoke, vapour, etc.: be emitted or exhaled, rise, emanate. ME–E17. ▸**b** Of snow: whirl in fine particles like smoke. *rare*. E19.
5 *verb trans.* Emit (smoke, steam, etc.). Also, cause to smell, esp. unpleasantly. Freq. *fig.* Now *rare*. L16.

> 1 SIR W. SCOTT Not long after the civil war, the embers of which were still reeking. 2 SPENSER His browes with sweat did reek. W. H. MALLOCK She literally reeked of garlic. TENNYSON He reek'd with the blood of Piero. P. H. GIBBS It was crawling with vermin, and reeked with a dreadful stench. b *Listener* The plot . . reeks of the confessional. I. MURDOCH The place reeked of drugs and expertise and mental care. 3 *fig.*: H. BUSHNELL They are reeking themselves in all kinds of disorder.

reek /riːk/ *verb*^{2} *trans*. Long *dial.* L17.
[Alt. of RICK *verb*^{1}.]
Pile up.

reeky /ˈriːki/ *adjective*. Also (*arch.* & *Scot.*) **-kie**. LME.
[from REEK *noun*^{1} + -Y^1.]
That emits smoke or vapour; smoky, steamy; like smoke; full of or blackened with smoke.
Auld Reekie: see AULD.

reel /riːl/ *noun*.
[Late Old English *hrēol*, with no known cognates; in branch II from the verb.]
▸ **I 1** A cylindrical rotatory device on which thread, yarn, paper, etc., can be wound and from which easily wound off; any apparatus on which a length of material can be wound up and unwound as required. LOE.
2 *spec.* **a** A cylindrical device attached to a fishing-rod, used in winding the line. E18. ▸**b** A small cylinder of wood or plastic, with a rim at each end, on which thread is wound for sale and ordinary use; a quantity of thread made up in this way. L18. ▸**c** A cylindrical structure with a broad flange on which film or recording tape is wound; a length of film or tape wound on this; *loosely* a (long) portion of a motion picture. L19.
▸ **II 3** A tumult, a disturbance. Formerly also, (in *pl.*) revelry. Chiefly *Scot.* LME.
4 A lively folk-dance usu. in double time, esp. associated with Scotland, danced by two or more couples facing each other; a piece of music for such a dance. L16.
5 A whirl, a whirling movement; an act of reeling; a roll, a stagger. L16.

Phrases etc.: NOTTINGHAM *reel*. **off the reel** without stopping, in an uninterrupted course or succession; immediately, quickly. STRATHSPEY *reel*.

Comb.: **reel-fed** *adjective* (*PRINTING*) using reeled paper; **reel foot** *Scot.* a club-foot; **reel-to-reel** *adjective* designating a tape recorder in which the tape passes between two reels mounted separately, rather than within a cassette etc.

reel /riːl/ *verb*. LME.
[from REEL *noun* 1.]
▸ **I 1** *verb intrans.* Whirl round or about; go with a whirling motion. Also as *fig.* use of sense 6. LME. ▸**b** Of the mind, head, etc.: be in a whirl, be or become giddy or confused. Also, (of an image) swim before the eyes. L18.
2 *verb intrans.* Rush, dash, or prance about; behave recklessly or riotously. *obsolete* exc. *Scot.* LME.
3 *verb intrans.* Sway or stagger back from a blow or attack; (of an army etc.) waver, give way. Freq. as ***send reeling***. LME.
4 *verb intrans.* Sway unsteadily from side to side as if about to fall; totter or tremble, esp. as the result of intoxication, faintness, etc. LME. ▸**b** *verb intrans.* Walk with the body swinging or swaying, esp. while drunk; move rapidly and unsteadily. L16. ▸†**c** *verb trans.* Lurch through or along (a street). *rare* (Shakes.). Only in E17.
5 *verb trans.* Cause to roll, whirl, or stagger; impel violently. Now *rare*. LME.
6 *verb intrans.* Dance a reel. E16.

> 1 SHELLEY She saw the constellations reel and dance Like fireflies. b TENNYSON The golden Autumn woodland reels Athwart the smoke of burning weeds. W. S. MAUGHAM He repeated to himself the same thing . . till his brain reeled. 3 TENNYSON Cossack and Russian Reel'd from the sabre-stroke. *fig.*: *Wall Street Journal* The news sent Microsoft's share price reeling. 4 C. KINGSLEY He saw the huge carcass bend, reel, roll over slowly to one side, dead. R. L. STEVENSON He reeled a little, and caught himself with one hand against the wall. *fig.*: BOLINGBROKE [France] . . staggered and reeled under the burden of the war. b J. G. HOLLAND The little gig . . reeled off toward the mill at the highest speed. DYLAN THOMAS In you reeled . . as drunk as a deacon.

▸ **II 7** *verb trans.* Wind (thread, yarn, paper, line, etc.) on a reel. LME.
8 *verb trans.* Draw (thread etc.) *out*, *off*, *in*, etc., (as) with a reel; cause to move (as) by winding or unwinding a reel; *esp.* (usu. foll. by *in*) draw in (a hooked fish) by winding in the line. M16. ▸**b** *verb trans. transf.* & *fig.* Foll. by *off*: rattle off or recite (a story, song, list, etc.) without pause or effort; cover (a distance etc.) rapidly; accomplish or perform without pause or effort. M19. ▸**c** *verb intrans.* Foll. by *out*: become uncoiled from a reel. L20.
9 *verb intrans.* Make a buzzing or rapid clicking noise like that of a turning reel; *esp.* (of a grasshopper-warbler etc.) make its characteristic call. M18.

> 8 *Scientific American* To launch a kite . . release it . . and slowly reel out line. b A. KOESTLER The warder reeled off the regulations. *Trains Illustrated* The 11 miles . . were reeled off at an average of 93.8 m.p.h.

■ **reelable** *adjective* (earlier in UNREELABLE) L19. **reeling** *verbal noun* the action of the verb; an instance of this, *esp.* a stagger, a lurch: LME.

reeler /ˈriːlə/ *noun*. L16.
[from prec. + -ER^1.]
1 A person who reels or winds thread, yarn, etc. L16.
2 An instrument for reeling; *esp.* a machine which winds paper, yarn, etc., on to reels. L16.
3 In *comb.* with a numeral: a film considered in terms of the number of reels it occupies. Cf. ***one-reeler*** s.v. ONE *adjective, noun, & pronoun*. E20.
4 A person who reels or staggers. M20.

reel-rall *noun & adjective* see REE-RAW.

reely /ˈriːli/ *adverb*. *non-standard*. Also **-ll-**. L18.
[Repr. a pronunc.]
= REALLY.

reem *verb* see REAM *verb*³.

re-embark /riːɪmˈbɑːk, -ɛm-/ *verb intrans. & trans.* Also †**-im-**, †**-barque**. L16.
[from RE- + EMBARK *verb*¹.]
Go or put on board a ship, an aircraft, etc., again.
■ **re-embarˈkation** *noun* E18. **re-embarkment** *noun* (now *rare*) E18.

re-embody /riːɪmˈbɒdi, -ɛm-/ *verb*. L17.
[from RE- + EMBODY.]
†**1** *verb intrans.* Reunite to form a whole. Only in L17.
2 *verb trans.* Form again into a body; embody afresh. E19.
■ **re-embodiment** *noun* E20.

re-emerge /riːɪˈməːdʒ/ *verb intrans.* L18.
[from RE- + EMERGE *verb*.]
Emerge again; emerge from temporary concealment etc.
■ **re-emergence** *noun* M19.

re-emphasize /riːˈɛmfəsʌɪz/ *verb trans.* Also **-ise**. M19.
[from RE- + EMPHASIZE.]
Emphasize again, place renewed emphasis on.
■ **re-emphasis** *noun*, pl. **-ases** /-əsiːz/, M20.

re-employ /riːɪmˈplɔɪ, -ɛm-/ *verb trans.* E17.
[from RE- + EMPLOY *verb*.]
Employ again, take back into employment.
■ **re-employment** *noun* L19.

reen *noun* var. of RHINE *noun*³.

re-enable /riːɪnˈeɪb(ə)l, -ɛn-/ *verb trans.* E16.
[from RE- + ENABLE.]
1 Foll. by *to do*: make able once more. E16. ▸**b** COMPUTING. Make operational again. L20.
†**2** Rehabilitate, restore. L16–E17.

re-enact /riːɪˈnakt, -ɛˈnakt/ *verb trans.* L17.
[from RE- + ENACT.]
1 Enact (a law etc.) again. L17.
2 Act or perform again; reproduce. M19.
■ **re-enaction** *noun* M19. **re-enactment** *noun* E19.

re-encounter /riːɪnˈkaʊntə, -ɛn-/ *noun & verb*. E16.
[from RE- + ENCOUNTER *noun, verb*. Cf. RENCOUNTER *noun, verb*.]
▸ **A** *noun*. †**1** An encounter, esp. a hostile one. E16–L18.
2 A renewed meeting, a further encounter. E17.
▸ **B** *verb trans.* †**1** Encounter, esp. in a hostile manner. E16–E17.
2 Meet or encounter again. E17.

re-enfeoff /riːɪnˈfiːf, -ˈfɛf, -ɛn-/ *verb trans.* LME.
[from RE- + ENFEOFF.]
LAW (now *Hist.*). Enfeoff anew; enfeoff in return (the original feoffor).
■ **re-enfeoffment** *noun* M17.

re-enforce /riːɪnˈfɔːs, -ɛn-/ *verb trans.* Now chiefly *US*. LME.
[from RE- + ENFORCE *verb*.]
= REINFORCE *verb*.
■ **re-enforcement** *noun* E17. **re-enforcer** *noun* L19.

re-engage /riːɪnˈgeɪdʒ, -ɛn-/ *verb trans. & intrans.* E17.
[from RE- + ENGAGE *verb*.]
Engage again.
■ **re-engagement** *noun* M18.

re-enlist /riːɪnˈlɪst, -ɛn-/ *verb intrans. & trans.* Also †**-in-**. E19.
[from RE- + ENLIST.]
Enlist again, esp. in the armed services.
■ **re-enlistment** *noun* E19.

re-enter /rɪˈɛntə/ *verb*. LME.
[from RE- + ENTER *verb*.]
1 *verb intrans.* Go or come in again; (foll. by *into, on*) enter again into possession, membership, association, etc. LME.
2 *verb trans.* Enter (a place etc.) again. LME.
†**3** *verb trans.* Foll. by *in*: return (a person) to custody. *Scot.* M16–L17.
4 *verb trans.* Enter again in a book, register, etc. M19.
Phrases: **re-entering angle** an angle pointing inward, (in a polygon) an interior angle greater than 180 degrees.
■ **re-entrance** *noun* a renewed or repeated entrance L16.

re-entrant /rɪˈɛntr(ə)nt/ *adjective & noun*. L18.
[from RE- + ENTRANT, after French *rentrant*.]
▸ **A** *adjective*. **1** That re-enters or turns in on itself; *esp.* (of an angle) re-entering. Opp. ***salient***. L18.
2 MUSIC. Designating a form of tuning of a stringed instrument (esp. a cittern or a ukelele) in which the fourth course is tuned higher than the third. M20.
3 COMPUTING. Of, pertaining to, or designating a program or subprogram which may be called or entered many times concurrently from another program without altering the results obtained from any one execution. M20.
▸ **B** *noun*. **1** A re-entrant angle; *spec.* in PHYSICAL GEOGRAPHY, an inlet, valley, etc., forming a prominent indentation into a landform. L19.
2 A person who re-enters or returns to an activity, place, etc.; *spec.* a person who seeks to re-enter paid employment. M20.

■ **re-entrancy** *noun* E20.

re-entry /rɪˈɛntri/ *noun*. LME.
[from RE- + ENTRY.]
1 LAW. The action of re-entering on possession of land etc. previously granted or let to another. LME.
2 The action of re-entering or coming back into a place etc.; a second or new entry. L15. ▸**b** *spec.* The return of a spacecraft or missile into the earth's atmosphere. Freq. *attrib.* M20.
†**3** The act of returning a person to custody. *Scot.* M16–E18.
4 The act of re-entering something in a book, register, etc.; the fact of being so entered; the entry thus made. M19.
5 CARDS. The regaining of the lead in esp. whist or bridge; a card which will enable a player to regain the lead. L19.
6 PHILATELY. (A stamp displaying) a visible duplication of part of the design due to an inaccurate first impression. E20.
Comb.: **re-entry permit**, **re-entry visa**: giving permission to re-enter a country.

reeper /ˈriːpə/ *noun*. Also **reaper**. M18.
[Marathi *rīp*.]
In the Indian subcontinent: a lath used in making a roof.

Reeperbahn /ˈriːpəbɑːn/ *noun*. L20.
[German, a street in Hamburg, Germany, lit. 'rope-walk', from *Reeper* rope-maker + *Bahn* road, way.]
(The principal street in) the red-light district of a city etc.

ree-raw /ˈriːrɔː/ *noun & adjective*. *dial. & colloq.* Also (earlier) **reel-rall** /ˈriːlrɔːl/ L18.
[Imit.: perh. assoc. with REEL *verb*.]
▸ **A** *noun*. A drinking-bout; a noisy romp, a commotion. L18.
▸ **B** *adjective*. Rough, riotous, noisy. E19.

reesed /riːzd/ *adjective*. *obsolete* exc. *dial.* Also **reezed**. LME.
[Var. of RESTY *adjective*¹. Cf. REEST *verb*¹.]
Rancid.

reesle /ˈriːs(ə)l/ *noun & verb*. *Scot.* Also **reeshle** /ˈriːʃ(ə)l/. E17.
[Imit.: prob. ult. rel. to RUSTLE.]
▸ **A** *noun*. A clatter, a rattle. E17.
▸ **B** *verb*. **1** *verb trans.* Beat with rattling blows; make rattle. E18.
2 *verb intrans.* Make a clattering noise, rattle, rustle. M18.

reest /riːst/ *noun*. Long *obsolete* exc. *dial.*
[Old English *rēost*, of unkn. origin.]
Orig., the share-beam of a plough. Later, (a part fixed beneath) the mould-board.

reest /riːst/ *verb*¹ *intrans.* Long *obsolete* exc. *dial.* LME.
[Origin uncertain: rel. to REESED and RESTY *adjective*¹.]
Become rancid.

reest /riːst/ *verb*². *Scot. & north.* E16.
[Origin uncertain: perh. Scandinavian (cf. Danish *riste* grill, broil, from Old Norse *rist* gridiron).]
1 *verb trans.* Dry or cure (herring, bacon, etc.) by means of heat or smoke. E16.
2 *verb intrans.* Become smoke-dried. E18.

reest /riːst/ *verb*³ *intrans. Scot. & north.* L18.
[Prob. alt. of REST *verb*¹ or aphet. from ARREST *verb*.]
Of a horse: stop suddenly and refuse to proceed.
■ **reesty** *adjective* (*Scot.*) inclined to stop and refuse M18.

re-establish /riːɪˈstablɪʃ, riːɛ-/ *verb trans.* L15.
[from RE- + ESTABLISH.]
1 Establish again or anew, restore; set up again in the same or a similar place, position, condition, etc. L15. ▸**b** Put up again, rebuild. *rare*. M17.
2 Restore (health, strength) to the usual state; *gen.* set to rights. Usu. in *pass.* L17.

> 🕮 **1** R. K. NARAYAN She resolved to re-establish peace. J. BRODSKY He tried to re-establish paganism. *New Scientist* Trees have .. difficulty in re-establishing themselves. **2** STEELE His Health being so well re-established by the Baths.

■ **re-establishment** *noun* L16.

re-evaluate /riːɪˈvaljʊeɪt/ *verb trans.* M20.
[from RE- + EVALUATE.]
Evaluate again or differently.
■ **re-evaluˈation** *noun* M20.

reeve /riːv/ *noun*¹.
[Old English *rēfa* aphet. var. of *ġerēfa*, earlier *girǣfa*, *grǣfa* GRIEVE *noun*, from *ġe* Y- + base of *secġrōf* host of men, *stæfrōf* alphabet (= Old High German *ruova*, *ruoba*, Old Norse *stafróf*).]
1 *Hist.* In Anglo-Saxon England, an official having a local jurisdiction under the king; the chief magistrate of a town or district. OE.
2 An official supervising an estate; a minor local official; an overseer of a parish, a churchwarden, a bailiff, etc.; a mine overseer. Now chiefly *Hist.* ME.
3 In Canada, the president of a township or municipal district council. M19.
Phrases etc.: **BOROUGH-reeve**. **dyke-reeve**: see DYKE *noun*¹. PORTREEVE.

reeve /riːv/ *noun*². M17.
[Var. of REE *noun*¹, of unkn. origin.]
The female of the ruff (*Philomachus pugnax*).

reeve /riːv/ *noun*³. Long *obsolete* exc. *dial.* L17.
[Origin unkn.]
A long narrow strip; a string of onions.

reeve /riːv/ *verb*¹. Pa. t. **rove** /rəʊv/, **reeved**. E17.
[Perh. from Dutch *reven* reef (a sail).]
Chiefly NAUTICAL. **1** *verb trans.* Pass (a rope etc.) through a hole, ring, or block; fasten or attach (a rope etc.) in this way. Foll. by *through, to, on*, etc. E17. ▸**b** *verb intrans.* Of a rope: pass *through* a block etc. M19.
2 *verb trans.* Thread a rope etc. through (a block etc.); secure or attach by means of a rope passed through a hole. M17.

reeve /riːv/ *verb*² *intrans.* *dial.* E19.
[Origin unkn.]
Twine, twist; wind, unwind.

reevesite /ˈriːvzʌɪt/ *noun*. M20.
[from Frank *Reeves*, 20th-cent. Amer. geologist + -ITE¹.]
MINERALOGY. A trigonal hydrated basic carbonate of nickel and iron, usu. occurring as yellowish plates.

Reeves pheasant /riːvz ˈfɛz(ə)nt/ *noun phr.* Also **Reeves's pheasant** /ˌriːvzɪz/. E19.
[John *Reeves* (1774–1856), English naturalist.]
A long-tailed pheasant, *Syrmaticus reevesii*, native to northern China and occas. introduced elsewhere.

re-examine /riːɪgˈzamɪn, -ɛg-/ *verb trans.* L16.
[from RE- + EXAMINE *verb*.]
Examine again or further; *spec.* (LAW) examine (a witness) again after cross-examination.
■ **re-examiˈnation** *noun* E17.

re-exist /riːɪgˈzɪst, -ɛg-/ *verb intrans.* M19.
[from RE- + EXIST.]
Exist again.
■ **re-existence** *noun* E19. **re-existent** *adjective* M17.

re-expand /riːɪkˈspand, -ɛk-/ *verb trans. & intrans.* M17.
[from RE- + EXPAND.]
Expand again.
■ **re-expansion** *noun* L19.

re-export /riːˈɛkspɔːt/ *noun*. M18.
[from RE- + EXPORT *noun*.]
1 A commodity re-exported; (usu. in *pl.*) the amount (*of* something) re-exported. M18.
2 The process of re-exporting. M18.

re-export /riːɪkˈspɔːt, -ˈɛk-/ *verb trans.* L17.
[from RE- + EXPORT *verb*.]
Export again (imported goods), esp. after further processing or manufacture.
■ **re-exporˈtation** *noun* E18. **re-exporter** *noun* M20.

reezed *adjective* var. of REESED.

ref /rɛf/ *noun*¹ *& verb*. *colloq.* Also **ref.** (point). L19.
[Abbreviation.]
▸ **A** *noun*. = REFEREE *noun* 2b. L19.
▸ **B** *verb trans. & intrans.* Infl. **-ff-**. = REFEREE *verb*. E20.

ref /rɛf/ *noun*². *colloq.* Also **ref.** (point). E20.
[Abbreviation.]
(A) reference.

ref. *abbreviation*.
Refer to (see also prec.).

refained /rɪˈfeɪnd/ *adjective*. *joc. & affected*. E20.
[Repr. a pronunc.]
= REFINED *ppl adjective* 2.
■ **refainment** *noun* M20.

refan /ˈriːfan/ *adjective & noun*. L20.
[from next.]
AERONAUTICS. ▸**A** *adjective*. That refans a turbofan or is refanned. L20.
▸ **B** *noun*. A refanned engine. L20.

refan /riːˈfan/ *verb trans.* Infl. **-nn-**. E17.
[from RE- + FAN *verb, noun*¹.]
1 Fan again. E17.
2 AERONAUTICS. Fit (a turbofan) with a new fan. L20.

refect /rɪˈfɛkt/ *verb trans.* LME.
[Latin *refect-* pa. ppl stem of *reficere* remake, renew, formed as RE- + *facere* make; later back-form. from next.]
1 Refresh, esp. with food or drink; restore after fatigue. Now *formal* or *literary*. LME.
2 Of an animal, esp. a rabbit: eat (faecal pellets) to be digested again. M20.

refection /rɪˈfɛkʃ(ə)n/ *noun*. ME.
[Old & mod. French *réfection* from Latin *refectio(n-)*, formed as prec.: see -ION.]
1 a The action of refreshing a person or of being refreshed; refreshment with food or drink after hunger

or fatigue; comfort or revivification through spiritual or intellectual influence. Also, an instance of this. Now *formal* or *literary*. ME. ▸**b** Entertainment with food and drink; the official demanding or supplying of such entertainment. Now *Hist.* E17.

2 An occasion of partaking of food; a (light) meal; a portion of food or drink. Now *formal* or *literary*. LME.

3 Repair, restoration. *rare*. LME.

4 The eating of semi-digested faecal pellets, esp. by rabbits. M20.

> 🕮 **1a** R. BRATHWAIT God is the true food and refection of our minds. **2** J. CARLYLE A miserable refection of weak tea and tough toast.

■ **refectioner** *noun* the person in charge of the refectory and food supplies in a monastery or convent E19.

refective /rɪˈfɛktɪv/ *adjective & noun. rare.* E17.
[French †*refectif*, *-ive*, formed as REFECT: see -IVE.]
▶ **A** *adjective.* Refreshing, nourishing; pertaining to food and drink. E17.
▶ **B** *noun.* A medicine etc. that restores the strength. M17.

refectorian /rɪfɛkˈtɔːrɪən/ *noun. rare.* M17.
[formed as next + -AN.]
= REFECTIONER.

refectory /rɪˈfɛkt(ə)ri/ *noun.* LME.
[Late Latin *refectorium*, from Latin *reficere*: see REFECT, -ORY[1].]
A room used for communal meals, esp. in a college or monastery.

> 🕮 B. GELDOF I ate . . tea in the refectory with the boarders.

Comb.: **refectory table** a long narrow table.

†**refel** *verb trans.* Also **-ll**. Infl. **-ll-**. LME.
[Latin *refellere* disprove, refute, formed as RE- + *fallere* deceive.]
1 Refute or disprove (an argument, error, etc.); confute (a person). LME–M18.
2 Reject (a request, a thing offered, etc.). M16–E17.
3 Repel, force or drive back, repress. M16–M17.

refer /rɪˈfəː/ *verb.* Infl. **-rr-**. LME.
[Old & mod. French *référer* from Latin *referre* carry back, formed as RE- + *ferre* bear, carry.]
▶ **I** *verb trans.* **1** Trace or attribute (something) *to* a person or thing as the ultimate cause or source. LME.

2 Assign *to* a particular class, place, date, etc., as being properly a part of such; regard as naturally belonging, pertaining, or having relation *to*; attach or attribute *to*. LME.

3 Commit or entrust (oneself) *to* some person or thing for assistance, advice, etc., or in a spirit of submission, acquiescence, or confidence. Now *rare* or *obsolete*. LME.

4 a Commit or hand over (a question, cause, or matter) *to* some authority for consideration, decision, execution, etc. LME. ▸**b** *SCOTS LAW.* Submit (the fact at issue, as a debt etc.) *to* the oath of the defender. L16.

5 †**a** Foll. by *to*, *until*: defer, postpone, or put off until another time. LME–M18. ▸**b** Reserve (a subject etc.) for later treatment. Usu. foll. by *to*. Now *rare*. M16. ▸**c** Postpone passing (a candidate) in an examination or accepting (an application) for a degree, provision being made for later re-examination. E20.

6 Relate, report, record. Now *rare*. M16.

7 Send or direct *to* a person, book, or other source for information. Also, direct *to* a fact, event, etc., by drawing attention to it. M16. ▸**b** Send or direct (a person) to a medical consultant or institution for specialist treatment. M20.

†**8 a** Give back, restore. M16–E17. ▸**b** Hand over, give, transfer. E17–E18. ▸**c** Reproduce, represent. *rare*. Only in E18.

> 🕮 **1** M. R. MITFORD It seems impossible to refer all these well-attested stories to imposition. **4a** *Daily Telegraph* Schedule Six of the Finance Bill is expected to be referred to the . . House of Lords. **5c** *Daily Times (Lagos)* Twenty-four students . . passed the prescribed test while four . . were referred. **7** DICKENS I . . refer you to the Registrar . . for the certified cause of death. G. B. SHAW I must . . refer you back to him for further consideration. **b** R. F. HOBSON Sam was fourteen when he was referred for treatment.

▶ **II** *verb intrans.* **9 a** Have a particular relation *to* something; be directed or apply *to*. LME. ▸**b** Make reference or allusion or direct the attention *to* something. L17.

†**10** Suggest or leave *to* a person to do something. *rare*. L16–M17.

11 Have recourse or make appeal *to* something, esp. for information. L16.

> 🕮 **9a** T. HARDY My revelation refers to where my parents are. **b** *Classical Quarterly* When Pindar refers to Homer it is subject matter that interests him. **11** DICKENS 'Mother will be expecting me,' he said, referring to a . . watch in his pocket. **refer to drawer**: an instruction from a bank to return to the drawer a cheque that cannot be honoured.

■ **refera'bility** *noun* (*rare*) the fact or quality of being referable M20. **referable** /ˈrɛf(ə)rəb(ə)l, rɪˈfəː-/ *adjective* able to be referred or assigned *to*; assignable, ascribable: M17. **referred** *ppl adjective* (*a*) that has been referred; (*b*) *MEDICINE* proceeding from some other part or organ, *esp.* (of pain) felt in a different place from that where it originates L19. **referrer** *noun* L17. **referrible** *adjective* = REFERABLE L16.

referee /rɛfəˈriː/ *noun & verb.* M16.
[from prec. + -EE[1].]
▶ **A** *noun.* **1** †**a** A person appointed by Parliament to examine and report on applications for monopolies or letters patent. M16–M17. ▸**b** *Hist.* A person entrusted with the management or superintendence of something. E18. ▸**c** *Hist.* A member of certain committees and courts appointed by the House of Commons to deal with private bills. M19.

2 a A person to whom any matter or question in dispute is referred for decision; an arbiter, an umpire; *spec.* (*LAW*) a person to whom a dispute between parties is referred by mutual consent. M16. ▸**b** An umpire in various games or sports, esp. football or boxing. M19. ▸**c** A person appointed to examine and assess for publication a scientific or other academic work. L19.

3 A person willing to testify to the character of someone, esp. an applicant for employment. M19.

> 🕮 **2a** *Accountancy* The referee's main aim will be to achieve an agreed settlement through conciliation.

▶ **B** *verb trans. & intrans.* Pa. t. & pple **-reed**.
1 Preside over (a game or match) as umpire. L19.
2 Examine and assess for publication (a scientific paper, thesis, etc.). M20.

> 🕮 **2** *Nature* Congressional inquiries are not the best way of refereeing research reports.

reference /ˈrɛf(ə)r(ə)ns/ *noun & verb.* L16.
[formed as prec. + -ENCE.]
▶ **A** *noun.* **1 a** The referring or submitting of a matter, esp. a dispute or controversy, to a person or authority for consideration, decision, or settlement. L16. ▸**b** An authority or standard referred to. *rare*. L16. ▸**c** *SCOTS LAW.* The referring of a fact at issue to the oath of a defendant. Cf. REFER *verb* 4b. M18.

2 a Relation, respect, or regard *to* a thing or person. L16. ▸**b** *LOGIC & LINGUISTICS.* The action or state of referring by which a word or expression is related to an entity. L19. ▸**c** *SOCIOLOGY & PSYCHOLOGY.* The process by or extent to which an individual establishes relationships with elements in society, as a standard for comparison. Freq. *attrib.* M20.

†**3** Assignment. *rare* (Shakes.). Only in E17.

4 (An) allusion to or *to* a thing or person. E17.

5 a (A) direction to a book, passage, etc., where information may be found; (an) indication of an author, page, etc., to be looked at. Also, a book or passage so cited. E17. ▸**b** A mark or sign referring a reader to another part of a work, as from the text to a note, or indicating a part of a figure or diagram referred to. L17.

6 a The action of referring one person to another for information; a person to whom one may be referred; *spec.* = REFEREE *noun* 3. E19. ▸**b** A usu. written testimonial produced by a referee, esp. about an applicant for employment. L19.

7 ***book of reference***, ***reference book***, a book intended to be consulted for information on individual matters rather than read continuously. M19. ▸**b** A reference book. Chiefly *US*. L20.

8 An object, physical property, value, etc., used as the basis for comparative measurement or standardization. M20.

> 🕮 **1a** L. GARFIELD The gaoler would do what he'd been paid for without further reference to his employer. **2a** J. BUTLER The world is a . . system, whose parts have a mutual reference to each other. **4** *Asian Art* Reference here is to the Ningshoudian, where bronzes were kept. M. FORSTER Elizabeth took Robert up on a passing reference he had made. **5a** M. COREN Gilbert was still a careless biographer, refusing to check his references.

Phrases: ***book of reference***: see sense 7 above. **for reference** for consultation. ***frame of reference***: see FRAME *noun*. **framework of reference** = ***frame of reference*** s.v. FRAME *noun*. **in reference to** with respect or regard to; about. **point of reference** = ***reference-point*** below. ***quick reference***: see QUICK *adjective & adverb*. ***terms of reference***: see TERM *noun*. **without reference to** without regard to, without consideration of or for. **with reference to** = ***in reference to*** above.

Attrib. & comb.: In the sense 'of a thing used as a reference', as ***reference level***, ***reference signal***, ***reference solution***, etc. Special combs., as **reference book** (*a*) see sense 7 above; (*b*) a library book for consultation not loan; (*c*) *S. AFR. HISTORY* an identity document or group of documents which all non-white residents in South Africa were obliged to carry between 1952 and 1977; **reference daily intake** = RDA; **reference electrode** *ELECTRICITY* an electrode having an accurately maintained potential, used as a reference for measurement by other electrodes; **reference frame** = ***frame of reference*** s.v. FRAME *noun*; **reference group** *SOCIOLOGY & PSYCHOLOGY* a group which a person, perhaps subconsciously, refers to as a standard in forming attitudes and behaviour; **reference library**: in which the books are for consultation not loan; **reference-point** a basis or standard for evaluation, assessment, or comparison; a criterion; **reference room** a room, esp. in a library, in which reference books are available for consultation; **reference tube** *ELECTRICITY* a cold-cathode gas-filled tube which can maintain an accurately fixed voltage.

▶ **B** *verb trans.* **1** †**a** Refer or assign *to*. *rare*. Only in E17. ▸**b** Relate (a measurement) *to* a defined base or zero level. L20.

2 Provide with a reference or references; give a reference to (a passage); find by reference. L19.

> 🕮 **2** *Antiquaries Journal* The book is . . fully referenced and indexed.

referend /ˈrɛf(ə)rɛnd, rɛfəˈrɛnd/ *noun.* E20.
[Latin REFERENDUM.]
LOGIC & LINGUISTICS. That by which or to which reference is made; *spec.* that which is signified by a particular sense or use of a word, a referent.

referendary /rɛfəˈrɛnd(ə)ri/ *noun.* LME.
[Late Latin *referendarius*: see next, -ARY[1].]
1 *Hist.* (A title given to) any of various officials in the papal, imperial, and some royal courts, responsible esp. for dealing with petitions and requests. LME.
2 A person to whom a matter in dispute is referred for decision; a referee. Now *rare*. M16.
†**3** A person or thing which provides news or information; a reporter. L16–M17.

referendum /rɛfəˈrɛndəm/ *noun.* Pl. **-dums**, **-da** /-də/. M19.
[Latin, gerund or neut. gerundive of *referre* REFER.]
The process or principle of referring an important political question, e.g. a proposed constitutional change, to the entire electorate to be decided by a general vote; a vote taken by referendum. Cf. PLEBISCITE 2.

referent /ˈrɛf(ə)r(ə)nt/ *noun.* M19.
[Latin *referent-* pres. ppl stem of *referre* REFER: see -ENT.]
1 A person who is referred to or consulted. M19.
2 a *GRAMMAR.* A word which refers to another. *rare*. L19. ▸**b** *LOGIC & LINGUISTICS.* The object or entity referred to, symbolized by, or qualified by a word or expression. E20.
3 *LOGIC.* Any member of the class of all terms bearing a given relation to any term. Cf. RELATUM 1. E20.

> 🕮 **2b** A. LURIE Many . . of these apparently 'meaningless' verses . . have hidden historical and social referents.

referential /rɛfəˈrɛnʃ(ə)l/ *adjective.* M17.
[from REFERENCE after *inferential* etc.: see -IAL.]
1 Having reference (*to*); pertaining to, containing, or of the nature of a reference or references. M17.
2 *LOGIC & LINGUISTICS.* Of or pertaining to a referent; (of language or symbolism) that indicates a referent or has a referent as object; *spec.* having the external world, as opp. to text, language, etc., as a referent. L19.
■ **referenti'ality** *noun* the fact or quality of being referential or of having a referent L20. **referentially** *adverb* M19.

referral /rɪˈfəːr(ə)l/ *noun.* M20.
[from REFER + -AL[1].]
1 The act of referring; *spec.* the passing on to a third party of personal information concerning another. M20.
2 The referring of an individual to an expert or specialist for advice; *spec.* the directing of a patient, usu. by a general practitioner, to a medical consultant or institution for specialist treatment. M20.

> 🕮 **2** V. BRAMWELL Ask your GP for referral to a plastic surgeon.

reffo /ˈrɛfəʊ/ *noun. Austral. slang. derog. obsolete* exc. *Hist.* Pl. **-os**. M20.
[Abbreviation of REFUGEE *noun* + -O-.]
A European refugee; *spec.* a refugee who left Germany or German-occupied Europe before the war of 1939–45.

refigure /riːˈfɪɡə/ *verb trans.* LME.
[medieval Latin *refigurare* recall in imagination, refashion: see RE-, FIGURE *verb*.]
Figure again; represent anew.

refill /ˈriːfɪl/ *noun & adjective.* L19.
[from RE- + FILL *noun*[1].]
▶ **A** *noun.* **1** That which serves to refill anything; a new filling. L19.
2 The renewed contents of a glass; a further drink. E20.
▶ **B** *adjective.* That serves as or is designed to take a refill. E20.

refill /riːˈfɪl/ *verb trans. & intrans.* L17.
[from RE- + FILL *verb*.]
Fill again.
■ **refillable** *adjective* E20.

refine /rɪˈfʌɪn/ *verb.* L16.
[from RE- + FINE *verb*[3], partly after French *raffiner*.]
▶ **I** *verb trans.* **1** Purify (a metal) by removing oxides, gas, etc. L16.
†**2 a** Clear (the spirits, mind, etc.) from dullness; make clearer or more subtle. L16–E18. ▸**b** Purify morally, raise to a higher spiritual state. M17–E18.
3 Free from impurities; purify, cleanse; *spec.* purify (oil, sugar, etc.) by a series of special processes. E17.
4 Free from imperfections or defects; *spec.* make (a language, composition, etc.) more elegant or cultured. E17.

5 Free from rudeness or vulgarity; make more polished, elegant, or cultured. **M17.**
6 a Bring *into* or raise *to* a certain state by refining. **M17.** ▸**b** Purify or cleanse *from* something. **M17.** ▸**c** Clear *away* or *out of* by refining. **M19.**

🕮 **4** G. DALY Her poetry . . gained simplicity and directness as she refined it. **5** LYTTON He had sought less to curb, than to refine and elevate her imagination.

▸ **II** *verb intrans.* **7** Become pure; grow clear or free from impurities. **E17.**
8 Become more polished, elegant, or cultured. **E17.**
9 Use or affect a subtlety of thought or language. (Foll. by *on, upon.*) **M17.**
10 Improve *on* or *upon* something by introducing refinements. **M17.**

🕮 **9** W. GOLDING Not to refine upon it, my mind is all at sea.

■ **refinable** *adjective* **E17.** **refining** *verbal noun* the action of the verb; an instance of this: **E17.** **refiningly** *adverb* (*rare*) in a refining manner **E19.**

refined /rɪˈfʌɪnd/ *adjective.* **L16.**
[from prec. + -ED[1].]
1 Esp. of sugar, a metal, etc.: purified, freed from impurities or extraneous matter. **L16.**
2 Polished, elegant, cultured; free from rudeness or vulgarity. **L16.**
3 †**a** Having or affecting a subtlety of mind or judgement. **L16–E18.** ▸**b** Raised to a high degree of subtlety or precision. **M17.**

🕮 **1** P. PARISH Refined sugar is . . suspected of being a contributory factor in causing coronary artery disease. **2** R. PILCHER The voice was female . . and immensely refined. **3b** E. LONGFORD Birkenhead elevated the part of best man to one of refined artistry.

■ **refinedly** /rɪˈfʌɪnɪdli/ *adverb* **M17.** **refinedness** *noun* **E17.**

refinement /rɪˈfʌɪnm(ə)nt/ *noun.* **E17.**
[from REFINE + -MENT, after French *raffinement.*]
1 The act or process of refining or purifying something; the result of refining; the state of being refined. **E17.**
2 Fineness of feeling, taste, or thought; elegance of manners; culture, polish. **E18.** ▸**b** An instance of this; something indicative of refined manners, feelings, or taste. **E18.**
3 The action or practice of improving or clarifying something in thought, reasoning, etc.; an instance of this. **E18.** ▸**b** A piece of subtle reasoning; a fine distinction. **E18.**
4 An added development or improvement; a thing thus improved. **E18.**

🕮 **4** *Music & Letters* Many pages contain subtle modifications and refinements.

refiner /rɪˈfʌɪnə/ *noun.* **L16.**
[from REFINE + -ER[1].]
A person who or thing which refines; *spec.* (*a*) a person whose business is to refine metal, sugar, etc.; (*b*) PAPER-MAKING a machine which breaks down knots and lumps in the pulp.

refinery /rɪˈfʌɪn(ə)ri/ *noun.* **E18.**
[from REFINE + -ERY, after French *raffinerie.*]
A place, building, or establishment where sugar, oil, metal, etc., is refined.

refit /ˈriːfɪt, riːˈfɪt/ *noun.* **L18.**
[from next.]
An act or instance of refitting, esp. of refitting a ship; a fresh fitting-out.

refit /riːˈfɪt/ *verb.* Infl. **-tt-**. Pa. t. & pple **-fitted**, (*dial. & US*) **-fit**. **M17.**
[from RE- + FIT *verb*[1].]
1 *verb trans.* Fit out (esp. a ship, fleet, etc.) again; restore to a serviceable condition by renewals and repairs. Also, fit again. **M17.**
2 *verb intrans.* (Esp. of a ship etc.) become refitted, have renewals or repairs effected; renew supplies or equipment. **M17.**

🕮 **1** D. LODGE The kitchen . . had been extended and . . refitted.

■ **refitment** *noun* **E18.**

reflate /riːˈfleɪt/ *verb trans. & intrans.* **M20.**
[from RE- after *deflate, inflate.*]
Cause reflation of (a currency, an economy, etc.)

reflation /riːˈfleɪʃ(ə)n/ *noun.* **M20.**
[from RE- after *deflation, inflation.*]
Inflation (esp. as a deliberate policy) designed or tending to restore an economy etc. to its previous condition after deflation.
■ **reflationary** *adjective* characterized by or leading to reflation **M20.** **reflationist** *noun* an advocate of a policy of reflation **M20.**

reflect /rɪˈflɛkt/ *noun.* Long *rare* or *obsolete.* **L16.**
[from the verb.]
(A) reflection.

reflect /rɪˈflɛkt/ *verb.* **LME.**
[Old French *reflecter* or Latin *reflectere*, formed as RE- + *flectere* bend.]
▸ **I** *verb trans.* **1** Direct in a certain course; divert, turn away or aside, deflect. Now *rare* exc. as transf. use of sense 3. **LME.**
2 Chiefly ANATOMY & MEDICINE. Bend or fold back; give a backward bend or curve to, recurve. Chiefly as ***reflected*** pa. pple. **LME.** ▸†**b** Cast (the eye, mind, etc.) *on, upon.* Only in **17.**
3 Of a body or surface: send back or cause to rebound (light, heat, sound, or other form of radiation); *esp.* (of a smooth or polished surface) cause (incident light) to return in the general direction from which it came. Also, give out or emit (light) in this way. **LME.** ▸**b** PHYSIOLOGY. Give out (an impulse) along a motor nerve, in response to one received along a sensory nerve. Usu. in *pass.* **M19.**
4 Of a mirror or other smooth or polished surface: give back or show an image of (a person or thing); mirror. **L16.**
5 *fig.* Reproduce or display after the fashion of a mirror; correspond in appearance or effect to; have as a cause or source. **E17.**
6 Of an action, circumstance, etc.: cast or bring (dishonour, credit, etc.) *on, upon.* Also (*rare*), (of a person) put (blame etc.) *on, upon.* **L17.**
7 Consider, remind oneself, (*that, how*, etc.). Also, (with speech as obj.) say on reflection, utter as a spoken thought. Cf. sense 11 below. **E18.**

🕮 **2** T. PENNANT The bill is . . not quite strait, but a little reflected upwards. L. SHAINBERG A full-thickness scalp was reflected including pericranium. **3** R. BENTLEY The Light of the Moon reflected from frozen Snow. DEFOE The Walls reflected a hundred thousand Lights . . from my two Candles. *Discovery* The ionosphere—that region in the upper atmosphere where free electrons reflect wireless waves. E. MANNIN Although it was only mid-morning . . every rock . . was reflecting the heat. **reflecting telescope**: in which a mirror is used to collect and focus light. **4** G. VIDAL She could see her own face twice reflected in his eyes. **5** H. J. LASKI The State . . reflects with singular exactness the dominating ideas of its environment. H. WILSON The quality of the top appointment was reflected in those lower down. C. EASTON Jacqueline's face reflected the intense joy or anguish in the music. **6** W. PLOMER The naturalness of this proceeding reflected credit on both. D. JACOBSON My glory reflects glory upon him. **reflected glory** fame or approval achieved through association with someone else rather than through one's own efforts. **7** E. WAUGH No kipper, he reflected, is ever as good as it smells. J. HELLER 'It all sounds a bit crazy,' Yossarian reflected.

▸ **II** *verb intrans.* **8 a** Of light, a ray, etc.: undergo reflection, turn back after striking a surface; *poet.* (*rare*) appear reflected. **LME.** ▸†**b** Shine, cast a light. **L16–M17.**
†**9** *gen.* Return; come or go back; bend or be bent back; *rare* deviate, go or come in a certain direction. **M16–L18.**
†**10** Foll. by (*up*)*on*: direct a look or glance; have a bearing; *rare* direct attention or regard, set a value. **E–M17.**
11 Turn one's thoughts (back), fix the mind or attention; ponder, meditate; employ reflection. Freq. foll. by (*up*)*on.* **E17.**
12 Cast a slight or reproach *on, upon*, make disparaging remarks. **M17.**
13 Foll. by *on, upon*: (of an action, circumstance, etc.) show in a certain (esp. unfavourable) light, bring discredit on. **M17.**

🕮 **8** J. CLARE Brooks . . On whose tide the clouds reflect. *Which?* Don't use flash: it will . . reflect off the screen. **11** H. KELLER I used to have time to think, to reflect, my mind and I. E. BOWEN In the afternoons one drove . . to reflect on a Roman ruin or . . admire a village church. F. TOMLIN From an early age he had reflected . . about the oriental mind. **12** LD MACAULAY Clergy were strictly charged not to reflect on the Roman Catholic religion in their discourses. **13** HENRY FIELDING Mrs. Miller . . related everything . . suppressing only those circumstances which . . most reflected on her daughter. J. A. FROUDE His conduct, though creditable to his ingenuity, reflects less pleasantly on his character.

■ **reflectingly** *adverb* by way of reflection, thoughtfully **L17.**

reflectance /rɪˈflɛkt(ə)ns/ *noun.* **E20.**
[from prec. + -ANCE.]
PHYSICS. The proportion of the incident light which a surface (of a particular substance) reflects or scatters; *spec.* a complex number whose modulus is the proportion of the radiant flux (of specified wavelength) reflected, and whose argument indicates the change of phase undergone by the reflected light.

reflecter /rɪˈflɛktə/ *noun.* Now *rare* or *obsolete.* **L17.**
[formed as prec. + -ER[1].]
= REFLECTOR (esp. senses 1, 2).

reflection /rɪˈflɛkʃ(ə)n/ *noun.* Also **reflexion**. **LME.**
[Old & mod. French *réflexion* or late Latin *reflexio(n-)* (medieval Latin also *-flect-*), from Latin *reflex-* pa. ppl stem of *reflectere*: see REFLECT *verb*, -ION.]
1 The action of a surface etc. in reflecting light, heat, sound, or other forms of radiation incident on the surface; the fact, phenomenon, or an instance of being reflected. Cf. REFLECT *verb* 3. **LME.** ▸**b** Reflected light, heat, etc. **M16.**
2 The action of a mirror or other smooth or polished surface in reflecting an image; the fact, phenomenon, or an instance of an image being produced in this way. **LME.** ▸**b** An image thus produced; *esp.* one's own likeness in a mirror. **L16.** ▸**c** The fact of colour being reflected by one thing on another; a tinge imparted in this way. Also, an iridescence. **E17.** ▸**d** *fig.* A near-perfect image or counterpart; something corresponding closely to or arising as a consequence *of* something else. **E19.**
3 The action of bending, turning, or folding back; recurvation. **LME.** ▸†**b** The action of turning back; return, retrogression. *rare.* **E–M17.** ▸**c** The action of causing an object to rebound after impact. Now *rare.* **M17.** ▸**d** PHYSIOLOGY. The action of generating a nerve impulse in response to one received; reflex action. Cf. REFLECT *verb* 3b. **M19.**
4 The action of turning (back) or fixing the thoughts on some subject; meditation, serious consideration. **LME.** ▸†**b** Recollection or remembrance (*of*). **E17–E18.** ▸**c** PHILOSOPHY. The process or faculty by which the mind has knowledge of itself and its workings. **L17.**
5 A thought occurring to or occupying the mind; a thought expressed in words; a remark made after reflecting on a subject. **M17.**
6 Censure, reproof; a remark or statement casting some imputation on a person; an imputation; a fact etc. bringing discredit on someone or something. **M17.**
7 CRYSTALLOGRAPHY, MATH., & PHYSICS. The conceptual operation of inverting a system or event with respect to a plane, each element being transferred perpendicularly through the plane to a point the same distance the other side of it. **L19.**

🕮 **1 angle of reflection** the angle which the reflected ray makes with a perpendicular to the reflecting surface. *seismic **reflection***, *total internal **reflection***: see TOTAL *adjective.* **2** SHAKES. *Jul. Caes.* The eye sees not itself But by reflection, by some other things. **b** F. CHICHESTER A reflection of the planet Jupiter in the sea. P. MARSHALL Her . . gaze was caught and held by a reflection in one of the . . mirrors. **d** N. PODHORETZ It was a fair reflection of a widespread American sentiment. J. HALIFAX His face, a rugged reflection of the Badlands. **3b** SHAKES. *Macb.* As whence the sun gins his reflection Shipwrecking storms and direful thunders break. **4** SAKI Calmness did not in this case come with reflection. Z. GREY A hearty slap on my back disturbed my reflection. S. UNWIN A moment's reflection would tell them that an immediate answer . . was out of the question. **5** V. SACKVILLE-WEST The reflections usual to a gentleman in that . . situation . . began to course through his mind. D. M. FRAME Book III . . is full of Montaigne's reflections about man. **6** SIR W. SCOTT Robertson uttered not a word of reflection on his companion for the consequences of his obstinacy. CONAN DOYLE I withdraw any reflection I have made upon your amazing professional powers. *Nature* A second edition so soon afterwards is no reflexion on the quality of the first.

Comb.: **reflection coefficient**, **reflection factor** PHYSICS = REFLECTANCE; **reflection profiling**, **reflection shooting** GEOLOGY the use of shock waves generated at the earth's surface and reflected at the interfaces between strata to investigate underground geological structure, esp. in prospecting.
■ **reflectional** *adjective* pertaining to or due to reflection **M19.** **reflectionless** *adjective* **M19.**

reflective /rɪˈflɛktɪv/ *adjective.* **E17.**
[from REFLECT *verb* + -IVE.]
1 That reflects light etc.; that reflects an image of an object, that mirrors or reproduces. **E17.**
2 Produced by reflection of light etc; reflected. **M17.**
†**3** That makes or contains reflections *on* or *upon* a person. **M–L17.**
4 a Of, pertaining to, or concerned in mental reflection. **L17.** ▸**b** Given to thought or reflection, meditative, thoughtful. Also, proceeding from or due to reflection, considered. **E19.**
■ **reflectively** *adverb* **L18.** **reflectiveness** *noun* **M19.** **reflecˈtivity** *noun* the property of reflecting light etc.; *esp.* the degree to which light incident on a surface is reflected, or to which a surface reflects incident light: **L19.**

reflectometer /riːflɛkˈtɒmɪtə/ *noun.* **L19.**
[formed as prec. + -OMETER.]
Any of various instruments for measuring quantities associated with reflection, *spec.* (*a*) for determining the refractive index of a solid by measuring the critical angle for total reflection; (*b*) for determining reflectance by measuring the intensity of light reflected or scattered by a surface; (*c*) (***time domain reflectometer***) for locating discontinuities (e.g. faults in electrical cables) by detecting and measuring reflected pulses of energy.
■ **reflectometry** *noun* **M20.**

For other words beginning with *re-* see the entry for **re-**

reflector /rɪˈflɛktə/ *noun*. **M17**.
[formed as prec. + **-OR**. Cf. **REFLECTER**.]
1 A person who reflects or meditates. *rare*. **M17**. ▸†**b** A person who casts reflections; a critic. **L17–M18**.
2 An instrument which uses a mirror to produce an image; *esp*. a reflecting telescope. **M18**.
3 An object or surface of metal, glass, etc., designed to reflect light, heat, sound, etc., in a required direction. Also, a polished surface displaying reflected images. **L18**. ▸**b** The speculum of a reflecting telescope. **E19**. ▸**c** A piece of reflective material, *esp*. a red disc, mounted at the rear of a vehicle or by the roadside to show its presence by reflecting the light from headlights. **E20**.
4 Any body or surface which reflects light, heat, sound, etc.; something considered in terms of its reflective properties; *GEOLOGY* a stratum etc. that reflects seismic waves. **E19**.
■ **reflectorize** *verb trans*. treat or coat with a reflective substance **M20**.

reflet /rəflɛ/ *noun*. Pl. pronounced same. **M19**.
[French.]
Colour due to reflection; lustre, iridescence; *spec*. a metallic lustre on pottery.

reflex /ˈriːflɛks/ *noun & adjective*. **E16**.
[Latin *reflexus* from pa. ppl stem of *reflectere* **REFLECT** *verb*.]
► **A** *noun*. **1 a** Reflection of light, heat, etc.; reflected light; light or colour resulting from reflection. Now *literary*. **E16**. ▸**b** Reflection (as) in a mirror etc.; a reflected image. Now chiefly *literary*. **M17**.
†**2** (An act of) mental reflection. Also, a remark made after reflection. **L16–M17**.
†**3** Return, rebound; indirect action. Only in **17**.
4 An image, a reproduction; something which reproduces essential features or qualities of something else; a sign or secondary manifestation. *literary*. **L17**. ▸**b** *LINGUISTICS*. A word, sound unit, etc., corresponding to or derived from the corresponding word etc. of another language or an earlier stage of the language. **L19**.
5 A reflex action, an involuntary action. Also, (in *pl*.) a person's faculty or power of performing such actions. **M19**.
6 A reflex camera. **E20**.

> 🕮 **1a** C. BRONTË The reflex from the window . . lit his face. **b** WORDSWORTH To cut across the reflex of a star That . . gleamed Upon the glassy plain. ***red reflex***: see **RED** *adjective*. **4** W. E. H. LECKY Make legislation a reflex of the popular will. J. I. M. STEWART My own pride in my father . . was . . a reflex of his pride in Norman. **5** L. DEIGHTON He lost consciousness . . but somewhere a reflex . . ordered his hands to pull. P. DE VRIES I jumped back from the window in a reflex. ***myenteric reflex***. ***spinal reflex***: see **SPINAL** *adjective*. ***unconditioned reflex***: see **UNCONDITIONED** 2. **6** ***single-lens reflex***: see **SINGLE** *adjective & adverb*.

► **B** *adjective*. **1** Bent or turned back; recurved. **M17**.
2 (Of thinking or a thought) directed or turned back on the mind itself or its operations; introspective; derived from or consisting in such thinking. **M17**.
3 Of light etc.: reflected. **L17**.
4 Coming by way of return or reflection. **E19**.
5 (Of an action) performed independently of the will, as an automatic response to a stimulus; characterized by or pertaining to such actions; *loosely* automatic, unthinking. **M19**.
6 *GRAMMAR*. Reflexive. **L19**.
7 *ELECTRONICS*. Of, pertaining to, or designating a circuit, amplifier, etc., in which the same valves or transistors are used for amplification of both high- and low-frequency signals (usu. the radio and audio frequencies respectively). Now chiefly *Hist*. **E20**.

> 🕮 **5** C. DARWIN Coughing and sneezing are familiar instances of reflex actions. P. P. READ A reflex bureaucratic distaste for oddballs.

Special collocations & comb.: ***reflex arc***: see **ARC** *noun* 5. **reflex camera**: in which an image from the main lens is reflected on to a ground-glass screen and can be seen and adjusted up to the moment of exposure. **reflex copying** a photocopying process in which the original document is illuminated by light passing through a piece of sensitized paper placed in contact with it, a negative image being formed on the paper according to the amount of light reflected by the original. **reflex klystron**: in which the same resonant cavity serves to modulate the electron beam and to produce an amplified microwave signal.
■ **reflexly** /ˈriːflɛksli, rɪˈflɛksli/ *adverb* in a reflex manner **M19**.

reflex /rɪˈflɛks/ *verb*. **LME**.
[Latin *reflex-* pa. ppl stem of *reflectere* **REFLECT** *verb*. Sense 3 from the adjective.]
†**1** *verb trans*. Reflect (light etc.). Also, give out (light) by reflection. **LME–M17**. ▸**b** Reflect or mirror (an object). Only in **M17**.
2 *verb trans*. Chiefly *HERALDRY & BOTANY*. Bend, fold back, recurve. Only as ***reflexed*** *ppl adjective*. **L16**.
3 *verb intrans*. *ELECTRONICS*. Make use of a reflex circuit. Only as ***reflexing*** *verbal noun*. Now chiefly *Hist*. **E20**.
2 ***FLEXED and reflexed***.

reflexible /rɪˈflɛksɪb(ə)l/ *adjective*. **E18**.
[from prec. + **-IBLE**.]
Able to be reflected.
■ **reflexiˈbility** *noun* **L17**.

reflexion *noun* var. of **REFLECTION**.

reflexive /rɪˈflɛksɪv/ *adjective & noun*. **L16**.
[from **REFLEX** *verb* + **-IVE**.]
► **A** *adjective*. **1 a** Capable of turning or bending back. *rare*. **L16**. ▸**b** Capable of reflecting light. *rare*. **L17**.
†**2** (Of a mental operation) turned or directed back on the mind; characterized by reflection or serious thought. **M17–M18**.
†**3** Reciprocal, correspondent. **M–L17**.
4 *LINGUISTICS*. Of a word or form, esp. a pronoun (as *myself*): that refers back to the subject of a sentence. Of a verb: that has a reflexive pronoun as its object. **M19**.
5 Of the nature of a reflex action; involving reflexes; *loosely* automatic, unthinking. **L19**.
6 *MATH. & LOGIC*. Of a relation: that always holds between a term and itself. Cf. **IRREFLEXIVE**. **E20**.
7 *SOCIAL SCIENCES*. Of a method, theory, etc.: that takes account of itself or esp. of the effect of the personality or presence of the researcher on what is being investigated. **M20**.
► **B** *noun*. †**1** An object reflecting light. Only in **L17**.
2 A reflexive word or form, esp. a pronoun. **M19**.
■ **reflexively** *adverb* (*a*) in a reflexive or reflecting manner, by way of reflection; (*b*) *rare* in the manner of a reflex action, automatically: **L17**. **reflexiveness** *noun* **M17**. **refleˈxivity** *noun* (*a*) reflexive quality, reflexiveness; (*b*) the property in language, text, etc., of self-consciously referring to itself or its production: **M17**. **reflexiviˈzation** *noun* (*LINGUISTICS*) the action of making a verb etc. reflexive; the process or fact of being made reflexive: **M20**. **reflexivize** *verb* (*LINGUISTICS*) (*a*) *verb trans*. make (a verb etc.) reflexive; (*b*) *verb intrans*. become reflexive: **M20**.

reflexogenous /riːflɛkˈsɒdʒɪnəs/ *adjective*. **L19**.
[from **REFLEX** *noun & adjective* + **-O-** + **-GENOUS**.]
MEDICINE. Producing reflex action.
■ Also **reflexogenic** /rɪˌflɛksəˈdʒɛnɪk/ *adjective* **L19**.

reflexology /riːflɛkˈsɒlədʒi/ *noun*. **E20**.
[formed as prec. + **-LOGY**.]
1 *PSYCHOLOGY*. The theory that all behaviour consists merely of innate or conditioned responses; the branch of knowledge that deals with reflex action as it affects behaviour. **E20**.
2 A technique for relaxing nervous tension through foot massage or pressure applied to different parts of the sole. **L20**.
■ **reflexoˈlogical** *adjective* **E20**. **reflexologist** *noun* **M20**.

reflow /ˈriːfləʊ/ *noun*. **E17**.
[from **RE-** + **FLOW** *noun*[1].]
A flowing back, a reflux; the ebb of the tide.

reflow /riːˈfləʊ, ˈriːfləʊ/ *verb intrans*. **LME**.
[from **RE-** + **FLOW** *verb*.]
1 Flow back; *esp*. (of the tide) ebb. Freq. as ***flow and reflow***. **LME**.
2 Flow again. *rare*. **E19**.

refluent /ˈrɛflʊənt/ *adjective*. **LME**.
[Latin *refluent-* pres. ppl stem of *refluere* flow back, formed as **RE-** + *fluere* flow: see **-ENT**.]
Flowing back, reflowing. Also, characterized by refluence, tidal.
■ **refluence** *noun* a flowing back; reflux: **L15**.

reflux /ˈriːflʌks/ *noun & verb*. **LME**.
[from **RE-** + **FLUX** *noun*.]
► **A** *noun*. **1** A flowing back, as of the tide, an ebb, (esp. in ***flux and reflux***); a reverse flow, esp. (*MEDICINE*) of gastric fluid etc. **LME**.
2 *CHEMISTRY*. The condition, process, or action of refluxing; the condensed vapour involved in this. **L19**.

> 🕮 **1** C. LYELL Heat and cold . . are in . . universal flux and reflux. **2 at reflux, under reflux** in a vessel fitted with a reflux condenser.

► **B** *verb*. *CHEMISTRY*.
1 *verb intrans*. Of a liquid: boil in circumstances such that the vapour returns to the stock of liquid after condensing. **E20**.
2 *verb trans. & intrans*. Boil (a liquid) in this way, esp. using a reflux condenser. **E20**.
Comb.: **reflux condenser** *CHEMISTRY* a condenser which enables condensed vapour to run back into the stock of boiling liquid; **reflux oesophagitis** *MEDICINE*: caused by the reverse flow of gastric fluid into the oesophagus from the stomach; **reflux valve** = ***check-valve*** s.v. **CHECK-**.

refocillate /riːˈfəʊsɪleɪt/ *verb trans*. Now *rare*. **E17**.
[from late Latin *refocillare*, formed as **RE-** + Latin *focillare* revive, refresh, from *focus* **FOCUS** *noun*: see **-ATE**[3].]
Revive, refresh, reanimate.

> 🕮 A. BURGESS Seeing . . Sophia on the screen has refocillated many a wilting male appetite.

■ **refociˈllation** *noun* (*rare*) **L16**.

reforest /riːˈfɒrɪst/ *verb trans*. **L19**.
[from **RE-** + **FOREST**.]
= **REAFFOREST** 2.
■ **reforesˈtation** *noun* **L19**.

reforge /riːˈfɔːdʒ/ *verb trans*. **LME**.
[from **RE-** + **FORGE** *verb*[1].]
1 Forge (metal or articles of metal) over again. **LME**.
2 Remake, fashion afresh. **M16**.

reform /rɪˈfɔːm/ *noun & adjective*. **M17**.
[from next or French *réforme*.]
► **A** *noun*. **1** The removal of faults or errors, esp. of a moral, political, or social kind; amendment, change for the better; reformation of character. **M17**. ▸**b** A particular instance of this; an improvement made or suggested; a change for the better. **L18**.
2 (Also **R-**.) A religious order created from another by the adoption of stricter observances. **E18**.
3 *ellipt*. (**R-**.) *The* Reform Club in London (see below). **M19**.

> 🕮 **1** W. COWPER Remorse begets reform. SHELLEY Choose reform or civil war! R. W. EMERSON The . . necessity of the reform of the calendar. D. H. LAWRENCE Gerald rushed into the reform of the office. **b** *Law Times* The public and the Profession were . . calling for sweeping reforms.

Comb.: **Reform Act**, **Reform Bill** an act or bill to amend the system of parliamentary representation, *esp*. either of those introduced in Britain in 1832 and 1867; **Reform Club** a London club in Pall Mall founded in 1836 to promote political reform; **reform school** an institution to which young offenders are sent to be reformed.
► **B** *adjective*. (**R-**.) *JUDAISM*. Of, pertaining to, characterized by, or designating a simplified and rationalized form of Judaism initiated in the 18th cent. under the influence of the European intellectual enlightenment. **M19**.

> 🕮 A. BLAISDELL I never was very religious, we were Reform.

reform /rɪˈfɔːm/ *verb*[1]. In sense 8 also **re-form**. **ME**.
[Old & mod. French *réformer* or Latin *reformare*, formed as **RE-** + *formare* **FORM** *verb*[1].]
†**1** *verb trans*. Restore or re-establish (peace). **ME–M16**.
†**2** *verb trans*. **a** Foll. by *to*: convert, bring back, or restore to the original form or a previous condition. **ME–L16**. ▸**b** Rebuild or repair (a building). **LME–M17**.
3 *verb trans*. Convert into another and better form; make a change for the better in, improve; remove faults or errors in, amend. **LME**. ▸**b** Orig., correct, emend, revise, (a book, document, etc.). Now only *LAW* (chiefly *US*), correct (a legal document) according to the original intention. **L15**. ▸**c** Remove by or by way of reformation. **M17**.
4 *verb trans*. Cause to abandon wrongdoing; bring about a thorough improvement in (a person, his or her character, etc.). Also foll. by *from*, †*of*, †*to*. **LME**. ▸†**b** *verb trans*. Reprove or punish for some fault. **L15–L16**. ▸**c** *verb intrans*. Abandon wrongdoing; thoroughly improve one's conduct. **L15**.
5 *verb trans*. Abolish or remedy (an abuse, malpractice, etc.) by enforcing or introducing a better procedure; put right (an error). **LME**. ▸†**b** Redress (a wrong, loss, etc.), make good. Chiefly *Scot*. **LME–E17**.
†**6** *verb trans*. Cut back, trim, prune. **L16–L17**.
†**7** *verb trans*. *MILITARY*. Form into a new regiment or company; break up, partially or completely, for this purpose. **E17–M18**.
8 *verb trans*. *SCIENCE*. Change the composition of (a hydrocarbon mixture) by heating over a catalyst, esp. so as to increase the octane number. Also, convert (a hydrocarbon) to carbon monoxide and hydrogen by heating with steam over a catalyst. Freq. as ***reforming*** *verbal noun*. **E20**.

> 🕮 **3** S. AUSTIN He was bound . . to reform the administration of justice. J. H. NEWMAN He . . reformed the calendar. G. SAYER To reform the university, a succession of royal commissions was set up. **4** JOHN BAXTER Far be it from us to discourage any effort made to reform juvenile offenders. CARLYLE Buddenbrock . . is now reformed from those practices. **c** J. CONRAD You may keep it till the day I reform and enter a convent. **5** M. EDGEWORTH He could reform every abuse.

reform *verb*[2] var. of **RE-FORM** *verb*[1].

re-form /riːˈfɔːm/ *verb*[1] *trans. & intrans*. Also **reform**. **ME**.
[Orig. identical with **REFORM** *verb*[1]; later from **RE-** + **FORM** *verb*[1].]
Form a second time, form over again or differently.

> 🕮 LYTTON Order was . . restored, and the line reformed. R. INGALLS The . . writings seemed to be changing shape, running into each other and reforming.

re-form *verb*[2] see **REFORM** *verb*[1].

reformable /rɪˈfɔːməb(ə)l/ *adjective*. **LME**.
[from **REFORM** *verb*[1] + **-ABLE**.]
Able to be reformed; admitting or susceptible of reformation.
■ **reformaˈbility** *noun* **E20**.

For other words beginning with *re-* see the entry for **re-**

reformado /rɛfɔːˈmeɪdəʊ/ *noun.* Pl. **-oes**. Also Anglicized as †**-ade**. L16.
[Spanish, use as noun of pa. pple of *reformar* REFORM *verb*¹: see -ADO.]
1 *Hist.* A military officer left without a command owing to reorganization but retaining his rank and seniority, and receiving full or half pay. Cf. REFORM *verb*¹ 7. Also, a volunteer serving in the army or navy without a commission but with the rank of an officer. L16.
2 A reformed person. Also, a reformer. Now *rare* or *obsolete*. M17.

reformat /riːˈfɔːmat/ *verb trans.* Infl. **-tt-**. M20.
[from RE- + FORMAT *verb*.]
Chiefly COMPUTING. Give a new format to, revise or represent in another format.

reformate /rɪˈfɔːmeɪt/ *noun.* M20.
[from REFORM *verb*¹ + -ATE².]
The end-product of the process of reforming petroleum products (REFORM *verb*¹ 8).

reformation /rɛfəˈmeɪʃ(ə)n/ *noun*¹. LME.
[Old & mod. French *réformation* or Latin *reformatio(n-)*, formed as RE- + FORMATION.]
†**1** Restoration (of peace). LME–M16.
2 The action or process or an instance of reforming or being reformed; removal of faults or abuses; a radical change for the better, esp. in political, moral, or social matters. LME. ▸**b** (**R-**.) *The* 16th-cent. European religious movement for the reform of the doctrines and practices of the Church of Rome, ending in the establishment of the Reformed and Protestant Churches. M16.
†**3** Reparation, redress. LME–L16.
†**4** MILITARY. A disbanding of troops; removal of an officer from the active list. Cf. REFORM *verb*¹ 7. M–L17.

> **2** SHAKES. *L.L.L.* I shall find you empty of that fault, Right joyful of your reformation. ADAM SMITH The late reformation of the gold coin. J. A. FROUDE Wolsey talked of reformation, but delayed its coming.

■ **reformational** *adjective* M19. **reformationist** *noun* a person who supports or advocates reformation E20.

reformation *noun*² var. of RE-FORMATION.

re-formation /riːfɔːˈmeɪʃ(ə)n/ *noun.* Also **reformation**. LME.
[Orig. identical with prec.; later from RE- + FORMATION.]
The action of forming again; a second, new, or different formation.

reformative /rɪˈfɔːmətɪv/ *adjective.* L16.
[Old French *reformatif* or medieval Latin *reformativus*, from pa. ppl stem of Latin *reformare* REFORM *verb*¹: see -ATIVE.]
Inclined or tending to reform; reformatory.
■ **reformatively** *adverb* (*rare*) L19. **reformativeness** *noun* (*rare*) E19.

reformatory /rɪˈfɔːmət(ə)ri/ *adjective & noun.* L16.
[from REFORMATION *noun*¹ + -ORY², -ORY¹.]
▸**A** *adjective.* Having a desire or tendency to produce reform; designed for reforming. L16.
▸**B** *noun.* An institution to which young offenders are sent to be reformed. Now chiefly *N. Amer.* M19.

Reformatsky /rɛfɔːˈmatski/ *noun.* Also **-skii**. E20.
[S. N. *Reformatskii* (1860–1934), Russian chemist.]
CHEMISTRY. ***Reformatsky reaction***, ***Reformatsky's reaction***, the condensation of a carbonyl compound with an α-halogenated ester in the presence of metallic zinc to form a β-hydroxy ester.

reformed /rɪˈfɔːmd/ *ppl adjective & noun.* In sense A. 5 also **re-formed**. M16.
[from REFORM *verb*¹ + -ED¹.]
▸**A** *ppl adjective.* **1** (**R-**.) (Of a Church) that has accepted the principles of the Reformation; *spec.* Calvinist as opp. to Lutheran. Also, of or pertaining to a Reformed Church. M16.
2 *gen.* That has been reformed; improved or amended morally, politically, or socially. L16.
†**3** MILITARY. Of an officer: left without a command (see REFORM *verb*¹ 7). E17–E19.
4 JUDAISM. (**R-**.) Subscribing to or characteristic of Reform Judaism. M19.
5 Of petroleum products: subjected to or obtained by reforming (REFORM *verb*¹ 8). E20.
1 ***Reformed Presbyterian Church***: see PRESBYTERIAN *adjective*. ***United Reformed Church***: see UNITED *adjective*.
▸**B** *noun.* Pl. **-s**, same. A member of a Reformed Church. L16.

reformer /rɪˈfɔːmə/ *noun.* LME.
[from REFORM *verb*¹ + -ER¹.]
1 *gen.* A person who reforms or brings about reformation; an advocate of reform. LME.
2 (**R-**.) *Hist.* A leader or supporter of the Reformation; a member of a Reformed Church. M16.
3 (Freq. **R-**.) An advocate or supporter of political or parliamentary reform; *esp.* (*Hist.*) a member of the British reform movement of the mid 19th cent. L18.
4 (**R-**.) An advocate or adherent of Reform Judaism (see REFORM *adjective*). M19.
5 An installation or apparatus for the reforming of petroleum products (REFORM *verb*¹ 8). M20.
■ **reformeress** *noun* (*rare*) a female reformer E17.

reformism /rɪˈfɔːmɪz(ə)m/ *noun.* E20.
[from REFORM *noun* + -ISM.]
A policy of social, political, or religious reform; *esp.* advocacy of reform rather than revolution.

reformist /rɪˈfɔːmɪst/ *noun & adjective.* L16.
[from REFORM *verb*¹ + -IST.]
▸**A** *noun.* An advocate or supporter of reform. Orig. *spec.* (**R-**) = REFORMER 2; now *esp.* an advocate or supporter of reformism. L16.
▸**B** *adjective.* Of or pertaining to reformists or reformism. M19.

reformulate /riːˈfɔːmjʊleɪt/ *verb trans.* L19.
[from RE- + FORMULATE.]
Formulate again or differently.
■ **reformuˈlation** *noun* E20.

refortify /riːˈfɔːtɪfʌɪ/ *verb trans.* L16.
[from RE- + FORTIFY.]
Fortify again; rebuild the fortifications of.
■ **refortifiˈcation** *noun* L16.

refound /riːˈfaʊnd/ *verb*¹ *trans.* E16.
[from RE- + FOUND *verb*¹.]
Found something again; re-establish a thing.
■ **refounˈdation** *noun* (*a*) the action of the verb; (*b*) a new foundation: M17. **refounder** *noun* E16.

refound /riːˈfaʊnd/ *verb*² *trans.* M17.
[from RE- + FOUND *verb*².]
Cast (a metal object) again; recast.

refract /rɪˈfrakt/ *verb.* Pa. pple & ppl adjective **-acted**, (*arch.*) **-act**. E17.
[Latin *refract-* pa. ppl stem of *refringere*, formed as RE- + *frangere* break.]
1 a *verb trans.* PHYSICS. Deflect the course of (light, radio waves, etc.) by refraction. E17. ▸**b** *verb trans.* Produce by refraction. *rare.* E18. ▸**c** *verb intrans.* Undergo refraction. M20.
†**2** *verb trans.* Throw back; reflect, return. Only in 17.
†**3** *verb trans.* Break up; impair. *rare.* M–L17.
4 *verb trans. & intrans.* Measure the focusing characteristics of (an eye) or of the eyes of (a person). L19.

†**refractary** *noun & adjective.* L16.
[Latin *refractarius*, formed as prec.: see -ARY¹.]
▸**A** *noun.* = REFRACTORY *noun* 1. L16–M17.
▸**B** *adjective.* = REFRACTORY *adjective* 1. E17–M18.

refractile /rɪˈfraktʌɪl, -tɪl/ *adjective.* M19.
[from REFRACT + -ILE.]
Capable of producing refraction.
■ **refracˈtility** *noun* M19.

refracting /rɪˈfraktɪŋ/ *ppl adjective.* M17.
[from REFRACT + -ING².]
1 Causing refraction; refractive. M17.
2 Provided with a lens etc. for refracting light. M18.
Special collocations: **refracting angle** the angle between two faces of a prism or lens. **refracting telescope**: which uses a converging (objective) lens to collect the light.

refraction /rɪˈfrakʃ(ə)n/ *noun.* L16.
[French *réfraction* or late Latin *refractio(n-)*, formed as REFRACT: see -ION.]
†**1** The action of breaking open or breaking up. *rare.* L16–M17.
2 PHYSICS. The fact or phenomenon of light, radio waves, etc., being deflected in passing obliquely through the interface between one medium and another or through a medium of varying density; change in direction of propagation of any wave as a result of its travelling at different speeds at different points along the wave front; an instance of this. E17.
3 The action *of* a medium in refracting light; refractive power or effect. M17.
†**4** A reduction on a charge or bill. Only in 18.
†**5** (The process of determining) the percentage of impurities in a sample of nitre. M–L19.
6 Measurement of the focusing characteristics of an eye or eyes. E20.
Phrases: **angle of refraction** the angle made by a refracted ray with the perpendicular to the refracting surface. ***double refraction***: see DOUBLE *adjective*. **index of refraction** = ***refractive index*** S.V. REFRACTIVE 4. SEISMIC ***refraction***. ***specific refraction***: see SPECIFIC *adjective*.
Comb.: **refraction profiling** GEOLOGY profiling by means of refraction shooting; **refraction shooting** GEOLOGY seismic prospecting in which shock waves generated at the earth's surface are detected along a line some miles long, giving information about the nature and depth of underlying strata.
■ **refractionist** *noun* a person skilled in applying the laws of refraction, esp. for the correction of visual defects L19.

refractive /rɪˈfraktɪv/ *adjective.* E17.
[from REFRACT + -IVE.]
1 Stubborn, resistant. *rare.* E17.
2 That refracts light etc.; possessing or characterized by the power of refracting. L17.
3 Due to or caused by refraction. E18.
4 Of or pertaining to refraction. E18.
4 refractive index the ratio of the speed of electromagnetic radiation (esp. light) in a vacuum to its speed in a specified medium. ***specific refractive constant***: see SPECIFIC *adjective*.
■ **refractively** *adverb* M20. **refractiveness** *noun* M19. **refracˈtivity** *noun* L19.

refractometer /riːfrakˈtɒmɪtə/ *noun.* L19.
[from REFRACT + -OMETER.]
An instrument for measuring the refractive indices of substances.
■ **reˌfractoˈmetric** *adjective* made by means of refractometry: E20. **reˌfractoˈmetrically** *adverb* E20. **refractometry** *noun* the measurement of refractive indices E20.

refractor /rɪˈfraktə/ *noun.* M17.
[from REFRACT + -OR.]
†**1** A refractory person. *rare.* Only in M17.
†**2** That which breaks or repels something. *rare.* Only in L17.
3 a A refracting telescope. M18. ▸**b** A medium which refracts light; a refracting lens. M19.
4 GEOLOGY. A stratum, or an interface between strata, detected in refraction shooting. M20.

refractory /rɪˈfrakt(ə)ri/ *adjective & noun.* E17.
[Alt. of REFRACTARY by substitution of -ORY².]
▸**A** *adjective.* **1** Stubborn, obstinate; unmanageable, rebellious. E17.
†**2** Strongly opposed, refusing compliance, *to* something. E17–E18.
3 MEDICINE. **a** Of a wound, disease, etc.: resistant, not yielding *to* treatment. M17. ▸**b** Of a person etc.: resistant *to* (a) disease. Now *rare.* L19.
4 Resisting the action of heat; very difficult to melt or fuse. M18.
5 PHYSIOLOGY. Temporarily unresponsive to nervous or sexual stimuli. L19.

> **1** H. B. STOWE The slave-owner can whip his refractory slave. **3a** E. JONES Incapacitating spells of migraine, quite refractory to any treatment. **5 refractory period** a period immediately following stimulation during which a nerve, muscle, etc., is unresponsive to further stimulation.

▸**B** *noun.* †**1** A refractory person. E17–M19.
2 A piece of refractory or heat-resistant ware used in glazing pottery; *gen.* any refractory material. M19.
■ **refractorily** *adverb* M17. **refractoriness** *noun* M17.

refrain /rɪˈfreɪn/ *noun.* LME.
[Old & mod. French *refrain*, †*refrein*, prob. from Provençal *refranh* bird's song, from *refranhar* from Proto-Romance var. of Latin *refringere*: see REFRACT.]
A recurring phrase or verse, esp. at the end of each stanza of a poem or song; a chorus; the music accompanying this.

> P. MANN The song . . had a popular refrain in which everyone joined.

refrain /rɪˈfreɪn/ *verb.* ME.
[Old & mod. French *refréner* from Latin *refrenare* to bridle, formed as RE- + *frenum*, *fraenum* bridle.]
▸**I** *verb trans.* **1** Put a restraint or check on (a feeling, thought, etc.); repress, keep back. Now *rare.* ME.
2 Hold back or restrain (a person or thing) *from* an action etc. Now *rare.* LME.
†**3** Curb, check, stay, (an action, proceeding, quality, etc.). LME–L17.
†**4** Keep or desist from (an action). M16–L18.
†**5** Abstain from (a habit, indulgence, etc.); give up, avoid. M16–M18.
†**6** Avoid or shun (a person's company). M16–E18. ▸**b** Keep or go away from (a place). L16–M18.

> **1** B. JOWETT We were ashamed, and refrained our tears. **2** *Westminster Gazette* The Party . . refrained themselves and kept low.

▸**II** *verb intrans.* **7** Abstain, forbear; stop oneself from doing something. (Foll. by *from*, †*to do*.) E16.

> **7** D. ROWE I refrained from telling others of my problems. S. BEDFORD I was tempted to tell him . . but refrained.

■ **refrainment** *noun* (*rare*) refraining, abstinence E18.

†**refraination**, †**refranation** *nouns* see REFRENATION.

refrangible /rɪˈfrandʒɪb(ə)l/ *adjective.* Now *rare* or *obsolete*. L17.
[mod. Latin *refrangibilis*, from *refrangere* for classical Latin *refringere*: see REFRACT, -IBLE.]
Able to be refracted; susceptible to refraction.
■ **refrangiˈbility** *noun* the property of being refrangible; the degree to which this property is present: L17.

†**refrenation** *noun.* In sense 2 also **refra(i)nation**. LME.
[Latin *refrenatio(n-)*, from *refrenat-* pa. ppl stem of *refrenare*: see REFRAIN *verb*, -ATION.]
1 The action of refraining or restraining. LME–M17.
2 ASTROLOGY. The prevention of a conjunction by retrogression of one of the planets. L16–E18.

refresh /rɪˈfrɛʃ/ *noun.* L16.
[from next.]
†**1** The action of refreshing; renewal of supplies. L16–M17.
2 A refreshment, esp. of liquor; a refresher. *colloq.* L19.
3 COMPUTING & ELECTRONICS. The process of renewing the data stored in a memory device or displayed on a cathode-ray tube. Usu. *attrib.* M20.
Comb.: **refresh rate** the frequency with which a computer monitor's display is updated.

refresh /rɪˈfrɛʃ/ *verb.* LME.
[Old French *refreschier, refreschir* (mod. *rafraîchir*), formed as RE- + *fres*, fem. *fresche* fresh.]
1 *verb trans.* Of water, air, etc.: impart freshness to (a place or thing) by cooling or wetting. Also, plunge (cooked vegetables etc.) into cold water. LME.
2 a *verb trans.* Impart fresh strength or energy to (a person, the spirits, the eyes, etc.); reinvigorate, revive. LME. ▸**b** *verb refl.* & *intrans.* Of a person: make oneself fresher or more energetic by resting, walking, having food or drink, etc. LME. ▸†**c** *verb trans.* Relieve or clear *of*. LME–M18.
†**3** *verb trans.* Restore or renovate (a building). *rare.* LME–M16.
4 *verb trans.* **a** Maintain in or restore to a certain condition by providing a fresh supply of something. LME. ▸†**b** Provide with fresh supplies or reinforcements. (Foll. by *with*.) LME–M18.
5 *verb trans.* **a** Brighten or clean up (a thing); give a fresh or new appearance to. Long *rare*. LME. ▸**b** Make (a surface) fresh, esp. (SURGERY) remove (epithelium) from a wound to assist healing. M17.
6 *verb trans.* Renew, revive; *esp.* stimulate (the memory), remind, make clear again. E16.
7 *verb intrans.* Provide fresh supplies. Now *rare*. L17.

> **2a** E. LONGFORD After a good day's sleep I awoke refreshed. P. P. READ She would breathe in the fresh air .. to refresh her body. **b** F. L. OLMSTED Working .. for three weeks, and then refreshing for about one. R. K. NARAYAN Tables were laid and gentlemen sat around refreshing themselves. V. S. PRITCHETT Chekhov was a restless man, continually working, who refreshed himself by travel. **4a** A. TYLER Best-groomed, with my .. lipstick refreshed in the restroom hourly. **6** B. PYM Let me refresh your memory. J. UPDIKE The Museum .. was a temple where I might refresh my own sense of artistic purpose.

refreshen /riːˈfrɛʃ(ə)n, rɪ-/ *verb trans.* Now *rare*. L18.
[from RE- + FRESHEN.]
Make fresh again; refresh.
▪ **refreshener** *noun* E19.

refresher /rɪˈfrɛʃə/ *noun.* LME.
[from prec. + -ER[1].]
1 a A person who or thing which refreshes. LME. ▸**b** A refreshment; a drink. E19.
2 LAW. An extra fee paid to counsel in a prolonged case. E19.
3 a A reminder. M19. ▸**b** In full ***refresher course***. A short course for reviewing or updating previous studies or training. E20.

refreshful /rɪˈfrɛʃfʊl, -f(ə)l/ *adjective.* Now *rare*. E17.
[formed as prec. + -FUL.]
Full of refreshment; refreshing.
▪ **refreshfully** *adverb* E19.

refreshing /rɪˈfrɛʃɪŋ/ *noun.* LME.
[formed as prec. + -ING[1].]
1 The action of REFRESH *verb*; refreshment given or received. LME.
†**2** *sing.* & in *pl.* Fresh supplies of food. LME–E18.

refreshing /rɪˈfrɛʃɪŋ/ *adjective.* L16.
[formed as prec. + -ING[2].]
1 That refreshes a person or thing physically, mentally, or spiritually; pleasingly fresh or different. L16.
2 LAW. Of a fee: paid as extra to counsel in a prolonged case. E18.

> **1** H. ROBBINS The clean refreshing scent of pine. INA TAYLOR It was so refreshing to be able to talk to a woman.

▪ **refreshingly** *adverb* E19. **refreshingness** *noun* (*rare*) M17.

refreshment /rɪˈfrɛʃm(ə)nt/ *noun.* LME.
[Old French *refreschement*, from *refrescher*: see REFRESH *verb*, -MENT.]
1 The action of refreshing a person or thing physically, mentally, or spiritually; the fact of being thus refreshed. Also, something refreshing in this way; a means of restoring strength or vigour. LME. ▸**b** *spec.* A light snack or drink. Usu. in *pl.* M17.
†**2** In *pl.* Fresh supplies of people or provisions. L15–E19.

> **1** W. GOLDING Even the air .. from the sea was hot and held no refreshment. **b** G. DALY Georgie could offer few refreshments, mostly tea and cakes. ***refreshment bar***, ***refreshment stall***, ***refreshment stand***, etc.

Comb.: **Refreshment Sunday** the fourth Sunday in Lent.

refrigerant /rɪˈfrɪdʒ(ə)r(ə)nt/ *adjective & noun.* L16.
[(French *réfrigérant* from) Latin *refrigerant-* pres. ppl stem of *refrigerare*: see next, -ANT[1].]
▸ **A** *adjective.* **1** MEDICINE. Of a drug, lotion, or appliance: cooling (part of) the body; allaying heat or fever. Now *rare*. L16.
2 *gen.* Cooling, producing coolness. M18.
▸ **B** *noun.* **1 a** MEDICINE. A drug, lotion, or appliance used to reduce abnormal heat, as in inflammation or fever; a cooling medicine. Now *rare*. L17. ▸**b** *gen.* A cooling substance, esp. a drink. L18.
†**2** = REFRIGERATORY *noun*. L17–E18.
3 A substance which reduces the temperature below freezing point. Also, the fluid used to transmit heat to the evaporating coils in a refrigerator. L19.

refrigerate /rɪˈfrɪdʒəreɪt/ *verb.* Pa. pple & ppl adjective **-ated**, (earlier, *arch.*) **-ate** /-ət/. LME.
[Orig. pa. pple, from Latin *refrigeratus* pa. pple of *refrigerare*, formed as RE- + *frigus, frigor-* cold: see -ATE[3].]
1 *verb trans.* Cool, cause to become cold. LME. ▸**b** Expose (food etc.) to cold for the purpose of freezing or preserving. L19.
2 *verb intrans.* Grow cold. M16.
▪ **refrigerated** *ppl adjective* cooled, frozen; (of a container etc.) used to keep or transport food in a refrigerated condition: M17.

refrigeration /rɪˌfrɪdʒəˈreɪʃ(ə)n/ *noun.* L15.
[Latin *refrigeratio(n-)*, from *refrigerat-* pa. ppl stem of *refrigerare*: see prec., -ATION.]
1 a The action of refrigerating something; the process of being refrigerated. L15. ▸**b** GEOLOGY. The gradual cooling of the earth from natural causes. Now *rare*. L18.
2 Orig., cooling and refreshing of the blood or spirits. Now (MEDICINE), the action of lowering the temperature of (part of) the body, to reduce metabolic activity or to provide local anaesthesia; controlled hypothermia. E16.

refrigerative /rɪˈfrɪdʒ(ə)rətɪv/ *adjective & noun.* LME.
[Late Latin *refrigerativus* cooling, from Latin *refrigerat-*: see prec., -IVE.]
▸ **A** *adjective.* Cooling, refrigerant. LME.
▸ **B** *noun.* A cooling medicine. *rare*. E18.

refrigerator /rɪˈfrɪdʒəreɪtə/ *noun.* E17.
[from REFRIGERATE + -OR.]
1 A thing which refrigerates or cools something. E17.
2 *spec.* A container, room, or appliance for producing or maintaining a low temperature, *esp.* one in which food etc. is kept cold. E19.

refrigeratory /rɪˈfrɪdʒ(ə)rət(ə)ri/ *noun. obsolete* exc. *Hist.* E17.
[mod. Latin *refrigeratorium* use as noun of Latin *refrigeratorius*: see next, -ORY[1].]
Any appliance, vessel, or chamber used for cooling or freezing; *spec.* a vessel at the head of a still for condensing the distillate.

refrigeratory /rɪˈfrɪdʒ(ə)rət(ə)ri/ *adjective.* E18.
[Latin *refrigeratorius*, from *refrigerat-*: see REFRIGERATION, -ORY[2].]
Tending to make things cold; cooling.

refringent /rɪˈfrɪn(d)ʒ(ə)nt/ *adjective.* L18.
[Latin *refringent-* pres. ppl stem of *refringere*: see REFRACT, -ENT.]
= REFRACTIVE.

refry /riːˈfrʌɪ/ *verb trans.* M20.
[from RE- + FRY *verb*.]
Fry again. Chiefly in ***refried beans*** [translating Spanish *frijoles refritos*] (orig. *US*), pinto beans boiled and fried in advance and refried when required.

reft /rɛft/ *noun. rare.* E19.
[Alt. of RIFT *noun*[1] after *reft* pa. pple of REAVE *verb*[2], or on the analogy of *cleft*.]
A rift, a fissure.

reft *verb pa. t. & pple*: see REAVE *verb*[1], *verb*[2].

refuge /ˈrɛfjuːdʒ/ *noun.* LME.
[Old & mod. French from Latin *refugium*, formed as RE- + *fugere* flee.]
1 Shelter from danger or trouble; protection, aid. LME.
2 a A person who or thing which provides shelter, protection, aid, etc. Formerly also, a means of obtaining such shelter. LME. ▸**b** A pretext, an excuse. M16.
3 a A place of safety or security; a shelter, a stronghold; *spec.* an establishment offering shelter to battered wives. L15. ▸**b** A mountain hut in which climbers and walkers can shelter. E19. ▸**c** A traffic island. M19. ▸**d** BIOLOGY. A region in which a population of organisms can survive through an unfavourable period. E20. ▸**e** A bird sanctuary. *US*. M20.

> **1** E. VENABLES Catacombs became places of refuge in times of persecution. G. SWIFT I had this feeling of calm, of refuge. I was safe here. ***city of refuge***: see CITY 2. **take refuge** seek safety or shelter (*in* or *at* a place); *transf.* (foll. by *in*) turn to (something) as a means of escape, consolation, etc., take comfort in. **2a** G. DALY Books had always been a refuge in time of trouble. **b** E. F. BENSON Frankness was the refuge of the tactless. **3a** D. LEAVITT I consider my apartment my refuge, my haven.

refuge /ˈrɛfjuːdʒ/ *verb.* L16.
[from prec. or French (*se*) *réfugier*, †*refuger* take refuge.]
1 *verb trans.* Provide a refuge or retreat for (a person); shelter, protect. Now *rare*. L16.
2 *verb intrans.* & †*refl.* Take refuge, flee; seek shelter or protection in a place. *arch.* E17.

refugee /rɛfjʊˈdʒiː/ *noun & adjective.* L17.
[French *réfugié* pa. pple of (*se*) *réfugier* take refuge, from *refuge*, the ending assim. to -EE[1].]
▸ **A** *noun.* **1** A person driven from his or her home to seek refuge, esp. in a foreign country, from war, religious persecution, political troubles, natural disaster, etc.; a displaced person. Orig. (*spec.*), any of the French Huguenots who came to England after the revocation of the Edict of Nantes in 1685. L17. ▸**b** A runaway; a fugitive. *rare*. M18.
2 US HISTORY. = COWBOY *noun* 2. L18.

> **1** L. STRACHEY The swarms of refugees, who fled eastward over Germany as the French power advanced. P. MAILLOUX When the Nazis invaded .. she .. harboured refugees in her home.

▸ **B** *attrib.* or as *adjective*. Designating or pertaining to a refugee or refugees. E18.

> *Observer* I travelled in a refugee train .. taking 700 homeless wanderers .. to Courtrai. *Peace News* The British government .. refuses to give him refugee status. **refugee capital** = ***hot money*** s.v. HOT *adjective*.

▪ **refugeedom** *noun* the condition of a refugee M19. **refugeeism** *noun* (*rare*) = REFUGEEDOM L19.

refugee /rɛfjʊˈdʒiː/ *verb trans. & intrans.* Pa. t. & pple **-geed**. M18.
[from the noun.]
(Cause to) become a refugee or live as a refugee.

refugium /rɪˈfjuːdʒɪəm/ *noun.* Pl. **-ia** /-ɪə/. M20.
[Latin = place of refuge.]
BIOLOGY. A refuge (REFUGE *noun* 3d), *spec.* one in which a species survived a period of glaciation.

refulgence /rɪˈfʌldʒ(ə)ns/ *noun. literary.* M17.
[Latin *refulgentia*, formed as next: see -ENCE.]
The quality of being refulgent; brilliance, radiance.
▪ Also **refulgency** *noun* (long *rare*) E17.

refulgent /rɪˈfʌldʒ(ə)nt/ *adjective. literary.* L15.
[Latin *refulgent-* pres. ppl stem of *refulgere*, formed as RE- + *fulgere* shine: see -ENT.]
Shining with a brilliant light; radiant, gleaming.

> I. COLEGATE Scintillating with a fine refulgent light. *transf.*: DICKENS Bestowing upon the locksmith a most refulgent smile, he left them.

▪ **refulgently** *adverb* E17.

refund /ˈriːfʌnd/ *noun.* M19.
[from next.]
Repayment; a sum repaid.

> *Which?* As the radio was faulty, you can ask for a .. refund.

refund /rɪˈfʌnd/ *verb*[1]. LME.
[Old French *refonder* or Latin *refundere*, formed as RE- + *fundere* pour; later based on FUND *verb*.]
1 *verb trans.* **a** Pour back, pour in or out again. Now *rare* or *obsolete*. LME. ▸**b** Give back, restore. Now *rare*. LME. ▸**c** PHILOSOPHY. Put back *into* something antecedent. *rare*. L17.
2 a *verb trans.* Return or repay (a sum of money); hand back. M16. ▸**b** *verb intrans.* Make repayment. M17. ▸**c** *verb trans.* Reimburse or repay (a person). M18.

> **2a** *Smart Set* Warranted to cure in thirty days or money refunded. **c** J. M. LUDLOW A proposal to refund him out of the Treasury.

▪ **refundable** *adjective* able or liable to be refunded M20. **refunder** *noun*[1] L17. **refundment** *noun* (*rare*) the action of refunding something E19.

refund /riːˈfʌnd/ *verb*[2] *trans.* Also **re-fund**. M19.
[from RE- + FUND *verb*.]
Fund (a debt etc.) again.
▪ **refunder** *noun*[2] L19.

refurbish /riːˈfəːbɪʃ/ *verb trans.* E17.
[from RE- + FURBISH *verb*.]
Brighten up, clean up; renovate, restore, redecorate.

> ANNE STEVENSON They bought and refurbished a large newspaper-and-tobacco shop.

▪ **refurbishment** *noun* the action or process of refurbishing something, esp. a building L19.

refusal /rɪˈfjuːz(ə)l/ *noun.* L15.
[from REFUSE *verb* + -AL[1].]
1 The action of refusing; a denial or rejection of something demanded or offered. L15. ▸**b** An instance of a horse stopping short or running aside at a jump. M19. ▸**c** ENGINEERING. Absolute resistance of a pile to further driving. M19.
2 An opportunity to accept or reject something before it is offered to others; the privilege or right of having such an option. Freq. in ***first refusal***. (Foll. by *of*.) L16.

3 That which has been refused or rejected. *rare.* L17.

📖 **1** M. GIROUARD Refusal to join the . . party was considered bad form. **b** *Your Horse* The first fence always supplies a good crop of refusals. **2** *Times* Virginia . . wants the refusal of her next book.

refuse /rɪˈfjuːz/ *noun*[1]. ME.
[Old & mod. French *refus*, from *refuser*: see REFUSE *verb*.]
1 †**a** ***of refuse***, ***without refuse***, not worth, well worth, hunting. Only in ME. ▸**b** = REFUSAL 1. Long *obsolete* exc. *Scot.* LME.
2 = REFUSAL 2. *rare.* M18.

refuse /ˈrɛfjuːs/ *noun*[2] & *adjective*. ME.
[Perh. from Old French *refusé* pa. pple of *refuser* REFUSE *verb*.]
▶ **A** *noun*. **1** A worthless or outcast section *of* a class of people; the scum, the dregs. ME.
2 That which is thrown away or rejected as worthless; rubbish, waste. LME.
3 The remains left by something. Foll. by *of*. M17.

📖 **2** DICKENS Slipping over the stones and refuse on the shore.

▶ **B** *adjective*. Rejected as worthless or of little value; discarded, useless. Also, of or pertaining to refuse. LME.

refuse /rɪˈfjuːz/ *verb*. ME.
[Old & mod. French *refuser* from Proto-Romance, prob. alt. of Latin *recusare* refuse (see RECUSANT) after *refutare* REFUTE.]
▶ **I** **1** *verb trans.* Decline to take or accept (something offered or presented); reject, turn down; decline *to do*. ME.
2 *verb intrans.* Decline acceptance or compliance; withhold permission. LME.
†**3** *verb trans.* Avoid, keep clear of, (sin, vice, etc.). LME–L17.
4 *verb trans.* Decline to submit to (a command, rule, etc.); decline to undergo (a penalty). LME. ▸**b** *verb intrans.* & *trans.* Of a horse: stop short or run aside at (a fence etc.) instead of jumping. (Foll. by *at*.) E16.
5 *verb trans.* **a** Decline to admit (a person) to a certain position; *spec.* decline to marry (someone). LME. ▸†**b** Decline to meet (an opponent). *rare.* E16–E17.
†**6** *verb trans.* Deny (a person) permission *to do* something; prohibit *from*, forbid *that*. LME–L17.
7 *verb trans.* Decline to give or grant; deny (something) *to* a person; decline to give (a person) something requested. Also with double obj. E16.
†**8** *verb refl.* Refrain from giving oneself over *to* (something). M18–E19.
9 *verb trans.* MILITARY. Decline to oppose (troops) to the enemy; withdraw from the regular alignment. L18.

📖 **1** E. WAUGH No cheque is bad until it's refused by the bank. R. H. MORRIESON The windows all refused to open. JOAN SMITH He flatly refused to say why he was there. K. VONNEGUT I refused all promotions beyond captain. **2** SCOTT FITZGERALD Wilson refused, saying . . he'd miss a lot of business. **5a** G. BATTISCOMBE She refused . . Colonel Macgregor and married Gabriele Rossetti. **b** SHAKES. *Ant. & Cl.* No disgrace Shall fall you for refusing him at sea, Being prepar'd for land. **7** A. TROLLOPE If refused once, he might . . ask again. H. T. LANE Do not refuse him the comfort for which he asks.

▶†**II** **10** *verb trans.* Renounce, give *up* (a thing); abandon (a place); forsake. ME–L17. ▸**b** Decline to bear (a name). LME–M17.
11 *verb trans.* Renounce (God or Christ); abandon or dismiss (a person); divorce (a wife). LME–L16.
12 *verb trans.* Deny (a charge or allegation). *rare.* LME–L18.

📖 **10b** SHAKES. *Rom. & Jul.* Deny thy father and refuse thy name.

■ **refusable** *adjective* (now *rare*) that may be refused or rejected LME. **refuser** *noun* L15.

refusenik /rɪˈfjuːznɪk/ *noun*. Also **refusnik**. L20.
[Partial translation of Russian *otkaznik*, from stem of *otkazat'* to refuse: see -NIK.]
1 In the former Soviet Union, a Jew who was refused permission to emigrate, esp. to Israel; *transf.* anyone denied an official request. Now chiefly *Hist.* L20.
2 A person who refuses to follow orders, esp. as a protest. L20.

†**refusion** *noun*[1]. *rare.* M17.
[French †*réfusion* from late Latin *refusio(n-)*: see RE-, FUSION.]
1 The action of pouring something back. M17–M18.
2 The action of refunding money. Only in E18.

refusion *noun*[2] var. of RE-FUSION.

re-fusion /riːˈfjuːʒ(ə)n/ *noun*. Also **refusion**. E19.
[from RE- + FUSION.]
A renewed or repeated fusion; a recast.

refusnik *noun* var. of REFUSENIK.

refutable /ˈrɛfjʊtəb(ə)l, rɪˈfjuː-/ *adjective*. M16.
[Late Latin *refutabilis*, from Latin *refutare*: see REFUTE, -ABLE.]
Able to be refuted or disproved.
■ **refuta'bility** *noun* (*rare*) M17. **refutably** *adverb* (*rare*) E19.

refutal /rɪˈfjuːt(ə)l/ *noun*. E17.
[from REFUTE + -AL[1].]
= next.

refutation /rɛfjʊˈteɪʃ(ə)n/ *noun*. M16.
[Latin *refutatio(n-)*, from *refutat-* pa. ppl stem of *refutare*: see next, -ATION.]
The action or an act of refuting a statement, charge, person, etc.; (a) disproof, (a) confutation.

refute /rɪˈfjuːt/ *verb trans.* E16.
[Latin *refutare* repel, rebut.]
†**1** Refuse or reject (a thing or person). E16–L17.
2 Prove (a person) to be wrong: confute. M16.
3 Prove (a statement, accusation, etc.) to be false or incorrect; disprove. L16.
4 Deny, repudiate. Freq. considered *erron.* M20.

📖 **3** *Oxford Art Journal* They engaged with and refuted Trotsky's arguments. **4** P. DALLY Indignantly she refuted the accusation.

■ **refutative** *adjective* (*rare*) tending to refutation M17. **refuter** *noun* a person who refutes an argument etc. E17.

reg /rɛg/ *noun*[1]. E20.
[Colloq. Arab.]
PHYSICAL GEOGRAPHY. A desert plain covered with small rounded pebbles; a stony desert.

reg /rɛg/ *noun*[2]. *colloq.* M20.
[Abbreviation of REGULATION.]
A regulation, a rule.

reg /rɛdʒ/ *noun*[3]. *colloq.* L20.
[Abbreviation of REGISTRATION.]
A vehicle's registration mark; *spec.* the letter denoting the year of manufacture of the vehicle.

Reg. /rɛdʒ/ *noun*. L18.
[Abbreviation.]
= REGINA.

regain /rɪˈɡeɪn/ *noun*. E20.
[from the verb.]
1 An act of regaining something; recovery. Also, an amount regained. E20.
2 The amount of moisture in a textile fibre or fabric, expressed as a proportion of the weight of the dry material. E20.

regain /rɪˈɡeɪn/ *verb trans.* M16.
[Old & mod. French *regagner*: see RE-, GAIN *verb*[2].]
1 Get (something) back; recover possession of. M16.
2 Get back to, reach (a place) again; rejoin (a person). M17.

📖 **1** D. EDEN Before she regained consciousness the Doctor was there. W. S. CHURCHILL King James was . . given his chance of regaining the throne. **2** E. BOWEN She could regain the courtyard . . without retracing her steps.

■ **regainable** *adjective* (earlier in UNREGAINABLE) M19. **regainer** *noun* L18. **regainment** *noun* the action of regaining something M17.

regal /ˈriːɡ(ə)l/ *noun*[1] & *adjective*. ME.
[Old French, or Latin *regalis*, from *rex*, *reg-* king: see -AL[1].]
▶ **A** *noun*. †**1** **a** Royalty, sovereignty, royal authority. Only in ME. ▸**b** A royal right or privilege. M16–L18.
2 ***the Regal of France***, a ring set with a ruby, offered at St Thomas's shrine at Canterbury by a king of France. *obsolete* exc. *Hist.* LME.
†**3** In *pl.* = REGALIA *noun*[1] 2. L15–E17.
4 *Hist.* The chalice used for the Eucharist at the coronation of a British monarch. E17.
▶ **B** *adjective*. **1** Of or belonging to a king or queen; royal. LME.
2 Befitting or resembling a king or queen; magnificent, stately. L18.

📖 **1** DRYDEN Thus make they Kings to fill the Regal Seat. **2** F. HERBERT She walked with a . . regal stride.

Phrases: **regal lily** = REGALE *noun*[3]. **regal moth** = ***regal walnut moth*** below. **regal pelargonium** any of a group of hybrid pelargoniums, *Pelargonium* × *domesticum*, having petals with dark blotches or veins. **regal walnut moth** a large brown and yellow moth, *Citheronia regalis* (family Citheroniidae), found in the eastern US. ***suit regal***: see SUIT *noun* 1b.
■ **regally** *adverb* LME.

regal /ˈriːɡ(ə)l/ *noun*[2]. M16.
[French *régale*, of uncertain origin.]
1 EARLY MUSIC, *sing.* & (usu.) in *pl.* A small portable reed-organ popular in the 16th and 17th cents. M16.
2 Any of certain reed-stops in an organ. L18.

†**regal** *noun*[3] see RIGOL.

regale /rɪˈɡeɪli, reɪˈɡɑːl/ *noun*[1]. E17.
[French *régale* (Old French *regales*) from medieval Latin *regalia* use as noun of neut. pl. (sc. *jura* prerogatives) of Latin *regalis* REGAL *adjective*.]
1 ECCLESIASTICAL HISTORY. The right of the King of France to make use of the revenue of a vacant bishopric or abbey. E17.
†**2** A privilege or prerogative of royalty. Only in 18.

regale /rɪˈɡeɪl/ *noun*[2]. L17.
[French †*regale* (mod. *régal*) from Old French *gale*: see REGALE *verb*.]
1 A sumptuous meal, a feast, a banquet; an entertainment, a fête. L17.
2 A choice item of food or drink; a delicacy. L17.
†**3** A gift, a present. *rare.* E–M18.
4 Regalement, refreshment. M18.

📖 **1** C. BRONTË This sort of impromptu regale . . was Shirley's delight. W. IRVING This pageant . . is a regale of which we never get tired.

regale /rɪˈɡeɪli/ *noun*[3]. M20.
[Use as specific epithet of neut. of Latin *regalis* REGAL *adjective*.]
A fragant white-flowered lily of western China, *Lilium regale*, much cultivated.

regale /rɪˈɡeɪl/ *verb*. M17.
[French *régaler*, formed as RE- + Old French *gale* pleasure, rejoicing. Cf. GALLANT *adjective* & *noun*.]
1 *verb trans.* Entertain (a person) with lavish food or drink; provide with a feast. M17.
2 *verb trans.* Please or delight (a person) by some agreeable activity, gift, etc.; entertain, amuse. Also, affect with a pleasurable sensation. L17.
3 *verb intrans.* Feast, feed, (*on*, *with*, *upon*). L17.
4 *verb refl.* Entertain or treat oneself with food, drink, or amusement. E18.

📖 **1** J. H. NEWMAN The food which regaled the . . Scythians. **2** A. BROOKNER Mrs Pusey went on to regale us with anecdotes. **4** F. KAPLAN He regaled himself with a culinary treat.

■ **regalement** *noun* (**a**) the action of regaling; refreshment, entertainment; (**b**) a delicacy: E18.

regalia /rɪˈɡeɪlɪə/ *noun*[1] *pl.* & *collect. sing.* M16.
[medieval Latin = royal residence, royal rights, use as noun of neut. pl. of Latin *regalis* REGAL *adjective*: see -IA[2].]
1 Rights belonging to a king or queen; royal powers or privileges. M16.
2 The emblems or insignia of royalty; the crown, sceptre, and other ornaments used at the coronation of a king or queen. Also (*transf.*), the decorations or insignia of an order; any distinctive or elaborate clothes. E17.

📖 **2** *Japan Times* Mengistu appeared . . in full military regalia.

regalia /rɪˈɡeɪlɪə/ *noun*[2]. E19.
[Spanish = royal privilege.]
A Cuban or other large high-quality cigar.

regalian /rɪˈɡeɪlɪən/ *adjective*. E19.
[French *régalien*, formed as REGAL *adjective*: see -IAN.]
Pertaining to a monarch; regal.

regalism /ˈriːɡ(ə)lɪz(ə)m/ *noun*. M19.
[from REGAL *adjective* + -ISM.]
The doctrine of a monarch's supremacy in ecclesiastical matters.
■ **regalist** *noun* orig., a royal partisan; later, a supporter of regalism: L16.

regality /rɪˈɡalɪti/ *noun*. LME.
[Old French *regalité* or medieval Latin *regalitas*, from Latin *regalis* REGAL *adjective*: see -ITY.]
1 **a** The state or condition of being a king or queen; royalty, sovereignty, sovereign rule. LME. ▸**b** Royal dignity or demeanour. L16.
2 SCOTTISH HISTORY. **a** Territorial jurisdiction granted by the king to a powerful subject. Also, land or territory subject to such jurisdiction. Freq. in ***lord of regality***, the person to whom such jurisdiction was granted. LME. ▸**b** A particular territory or area subject to a lord of regality. LME.
3 A country or district subject to royal authority; a kingdom, a monarchical state. L15.
4 **a** A right or privilege belonging to or befitting a monarch. Usu. in *pl.* E16. ▸†**b** In *pl.* Rights and privileges granted by the monarch to the Church. *rare.* M17–M18.

regalo /rɛˈɡɑːləʊ/ *noun*. Now *rare*. Also **-galio** /-ˈɡɑːlɪəʊ/. Pl. **-os**. E17.
[Italian (also Spanish & Portuguese) = gift, rel. to *regalare* REGALE *verb*.]
A present, esp. of choice food or drink; a lavish meal or entertainment.

†**regalty** *noun*. ME–E18.
[Prob. from Anglo-Norman *regauté*, formed as REGALITY. Cf. ROYALTY.]
= REGALITY.

regard /rɪˈɡɑːd/ *noun*. ME.
[Old & mod. French, from *regarder*: see next.]
▶ **I** †**1** Repute, importance; estimation in which a person or thing is held. ME–L18.
2 Attention, care, or consideration given *to* a thing or person; concern *for*, heed *of*. ME.
3 **a** A thing or circumstance taken into account in determining action; a consideration, a motive. L16. ▸†**b** The action of looking *to* a person, God, etc., to direct one's actions. *rare.* E–M18.

4 a Esteem, admiration, kindly feeling. L16. ▸†**b** A token or sign of esteem or affection. M18–E19. ▸**c** In *pl.* An expression of goodwill in a letter etc. L18.

> 📖 **1** R. BURNS I am a bard of no regard Wi' gentlefolks. **2** C. MACKENZIE We hope that they will pay regard to our feelings. H. J. EYSENCK Others commit thefts without regard for the .. consequences. *Music & Letters* Lassus shows no regard for the Counter-Reformation principles of Trent. **4a** J. LONDON He fell an immense distance in her regard. N. SHERRY Verschoyle held him in high regard as a book reviewer. **c** M. R. MITFORD Kindest regards and best wishes from all.

▸**II 5** Orig., aspect, appearance. Later, facial expression, manner of looking. LME.
6 A look, a glance, a gaze. Formerly also, an object of sight. LME.
7 An official inspection of a forest in order to discover any trespasses committed in it. Also, the office or position of a person appointed to make such an inspection; the district within this person's jurisdiction. *obsolete* exc. *Hist.* E16.
†**8 a** Reference *to* a person or thing. Chiefly in ***have a regard to, have regard to***. M16–L17. ▸**b** Intention, design, purpose. *rare* (Shakes.). Only in L16.
9 Respect, point, particular. E17.

> 📖 **5** MILTON With stern regard thus Gabriel spake. **6** B. W. ALDISS She turned to look at him. Their regards met. **9** SHELLEY Pay .. attention to your instructions in this regard.

Phrases: ***have a regard to***: see sense 8a above. **have regard to** †(*a*) see sense 8a above; (*b*) give attention or consideration to, take care of. **in one's regard** †(*a*) *rare* (Shakes.) in one's opinion or estimation; (*b*) with respect or reference to one. †**in regard** since, inasmuch as, considering that. **in regard of** (*a*) *arch.* in comparison with; (*b*) in respect of, with reference to; (*c*) (long *rare* or *obsolete*) out of consideration for. †**in regard that** = ***in regard*** above. **in regard to**, **with regard to** in respect of, with reference to.

Comb.: **regard ring**: set with a row of stones whose initial letters spell 'regard' (ruby, emerald, garnet, amethyst, ruby, diamond).

regard /rɪˈɡɑːd/ *verb.* ME.
[Old & mod. French *regarder*, from *re-* RE- + *garder* GUARD *verb*.]
▸**I** *verb trans.* **1 a** Consider, look on, view (*as*). ME. ▸**b** Look on *with* some feeling. E17.
2 Heed, take into account; pay attention to, take notice of, show an interest in; show consideration for (a thing or person). LME.
†**3** Look after (oneself), take care of (one's own interest, health, etc.). L15–L17.
4 a Look at, observe. E16. ▸†**b** Of a place etc.: face towards. L16–M18.
5 Hold in great esteem; admire, respect, value highly. E16.
6 Concern, have relation or respect to. See also REGARDING. E17.

> 📖 **1a** J. ORR Views differ as to how the book is to be regarded. B. PYM She tended to regard most men .. as children. **b** O. MANNING She came to regard her work with admiration. **2** SHAKES. *1 Hen. IV* He talk'd very wisely, but I regarded him not. B. JOWETT The perfect citizen .. regards not only the laws but the .. legislator. **4a** BETTY SMITH Francie and Neeley sat regarding each other with steady eyes. ***regard one's navel***: see NAVEL 1. **5** R. B. SHERIDAN She does not regard you enough. *Antiquity* Literacy was not a highly regarded accomplishment. **6** CARLYLE If these things regarded only myself, I could stand it with composure. **as regards** concerning, with respect to.

▸**II 7** *verb intrans.* **a** Look, gaze. *rare.* E16. ▸**b** Pay attention, take notice, (foll. by *on*, *whether*). Orig. also, take heed or care *to do*. M16.
†**8** *verb intrans.* Consider or take into account *that*. Only in L16.
9 *verb intrans.* Seem, appear. *rare.* E19.

> 📖 **7b** T. HARDY She took no heed .. nor regarded whether her .. slippers became scratched. **8** SHAKES. *Two Gent.* Neither regarding that she is my child Nor fearing me.

■ **regardable** *adjective* (long *rare*) worthy of being regarded; noticeable: L16.

regardant /rɪˈɡɑːd(ə)nt/ *adjective & noun.* LME.
[Anglo-Norman, Old & mod. French, pres. pple of *regarder*: see prec., -ANT¹.]
▸**A** *adjective.* **1** LAW (now *Hist.*). Attached to a manor. Esp. in ***villein regardant***. LME.
2 HERALDRY. Usu. of a lion: looking backwards over the shoulder. Usu. *postpositive*. LME.
3 Observant, watchful, contemplative. L16.
▸†**B** *noun.* **1** A spectator. L16–E17.
2 A villein regardant, a serf, (see sense A.1 above). Only in L18.
■ †**regardancy** *noun* (*rare*) the fact of being regardant E17–L18.

regarder /rɪˈɡɑːdə/ *noun.* E16.
[from REGARD *verb* + -ER¹; in early use after Anglo-Norman *regardour*, Anglo-Latin *regardor*, *-ator*.]
A person who or thing which regards; *spec.* (*Hist.*) an officer responsible for the supervision and inspection of a forest.

regardful /rɪˈɡɑːdfʊl, -f(ə)l/ *adjective.* L16.
[from REGARD *noun* + -FUL.]
Attentive, observant; mindful *of*; respectful.
■ **regardfully** *adverb* E17. **regardfulness** *noun* L16.

regarding /rɪˈɡɑːdɪŋ/ *preposition.* L18.
[from REGARD *verb* + -ING². Cf. CONCERNING *preposition*.]
In reference or relation to, about, concerning. Also ***as regarding***.

> 📖 F. MACLEAN The authorities .. had received no instructions regarding my journey.

regardless /rɪˈɡɑːdlɪs/ *adjective & adverb.* L16.
[from REGARD *noun* + -LESS.]
▸**A** *adjective.* **1** Heedless, indifferent, careless; without consideration *of*. L16.
2 Unregarded, slighted; unworthy of regard. L16.

> 📖 **1** GEO. ELIOT A man .. openly regardless of religious rites. R. LEHMANN He had had a regardless way with money.

▸**B** *adverb.* Without regard to or consideration *of* something; despite the consequences, nonetheless. L19.

> 📖 H. ARENDT Jews were murdered .. regardless of what they had done. *Independent* Mrs Thatcher determined to press on regardless.

■ **regardlessly** *adverb* L16. **regardlessness** *noun* heedlessness, carelessness E17.

regather /riːˈɡaðə/ *verb.* L16.
[from RE- + GATHER *verb*.]
1 a *verb trans.* Collect or bring together again. L16. ▸**b** *verb intrans.* Meet or come together again. M19.
2 *verb trans.* Gather (a garment) again. M19.

regatta /rɪˈɡatə/ *noun.* E17.
[Venetian Italian †*regatta*, †*rigatta*, *regata* a fight, a struggle, a contest.]
1 Any of certain boat races held on the Grand Canal in Venice. E17.
2 An organized series of boat or yacht races. L18.
3 A cotton fabric, usu. made in twill; a striped garment made in this fabric. M19.

regd. *abbreviation.*
Registered.

regelate /riːdʒɪˈleɪt/ *verb intrans. & refl.* M19.
[from RE- + Latin *gelat-* pa. ppl stem of *gelare* freeze: see -ATE³.]
Freeze together again.

regelation /riːdʒɪˈleɪʃ(ə)n/ *noun.* M19.
[See prec. and GELATION *noun*¹.]
The action of freezing together again; *spec.* the fusion of two pieces of ice with moist surfaces, at a temperature above freezing point.

Régence /reʒɑ̃s/ *adjective.* E20.
[French, from *régent* REGENT *noun*: see -ENCE.]
Designating a style of costume, furniture, and interior decoration characteristic of the French Regency (see REGENCY *noun* 6).

regency /ˈriːdʒ(ə)nsi/ *noun & adjective.* LME.
[medieval Latin *regentia*, from Latin *regens*, *regent-*: see REGENT *noun*, -ENCY.]
▸**A** *noun.* **1** The position or office of ruler; exercise of rule or authority; government, control. Now *rare* or *obsolete*. LME.
2 The office and jurisdiction of a regent or vicegerent; government by a regent. LME.
3 The office or function of a university regent. L15.
4 The governing body of certain (chiefly European) towns and Muslim states; a town or State under the control of such a body. *obsolete* exc. *Hist.* M17.
5 A body of people appointed to govern during the absence, minority, or incapacity of a monarch or hereditary ruler. Also *gen.*, a group that manages or administers in the absence of a manager or leader. E18.
6 The period during which a regent governs; *spec.* (usu. **R-**.) the period in France from 1715 to 1723 when Philip, Duke of Orleans, was regent, or in Britain from 1811 to 1820 when George, Prince of Wales, was regent. E18.

> 📖 **2** GIBBON Count Henry assumed the regency of the empire. **6** W. E. H. LECKY The moral tone .. in France under the Regency.

▸**B** *attrib.* or as *adjective.* Designating a style of architecture, clothing, furniture, etc., characteristic of the Regency of 1811–20 or, more widely, of the late 18th and early 19th cents. L18.

> 📖 C. MCCULLOUGH The Louis Quinze sofa and chairs, the Regency escritoire.

regenerant /rɪˈdʒɛn(ə)r(ə)nt/ *adjective & noun. rare.* M19.
[formed as next + -ANT¹.]
▸**A** *adjective.* Regenerating. M19.
▸**B** *noun.* A regenerating agent. M20.

regenerate /rɪˈdʒɛn(ə)rət/ *ppl adjective & noun.* LME.
[Latin *regeneratus* pa. pple, formed as next: see -ATE².]
▸**A** *ppl adjective.* **1** Brought again into existence; reborn. Now *rare* or *obsolete*. LME.
2 Spiritually reborn. M16.
3 Restored to a better state or condition; reformed. M17.
4 BIOLOGY. Of tissue: formed or modified by regeneration. M20.

> 📖 **2** H. E. MANNING Born again, we are regenerate, we are sons of God.

▸**B** *noun.* †**1** A regenerate person. M16–M17.
2 BIOLOGY. A limb or other part formed by regeneration. M20.
■ **regeneracy** *noun* the state of being regenerate E17.

regenerate /rɪˈdʒɛnəreɪt/ *verb.* M16.
[Latin *regenerat-* pa. ppl stem of *regenerare*: see RE-, GENERATE *verb*.]
1 *verb trans.* **a** Cause to be spiritually reborn; invest with a new and higher spiritual nature. M16. ▸**b** Reform completely; effect a thorough moral change and improvement in (a person, state, etc.). M19.
2 *verb trans. & intrans.* Reproduce; bring or come into renewed existence; generate again. M16.
3 MEDICINE & BIOLOGY. **a** *verb intrans.* Of an organ or tissue: regrow after loss or damage. M16. ▸**b** *verb trans.* Regrow or cause to be regrown (bodily organs or tissue) in order to replace lost or damaged parts. L16.
4 *verb trans.* Reconstitute in a new and improved form; impart new and more vigorous life to (a person, institution, etc.), revive. L18.
5 CHEMISTRY & TEXTILES. Reprecipitate (a natural polymer, as cellulose, protein) following chemical processing, esp. in the form of fibres; make (fibres) in this way. E20.

> 📖 **1** T. C. FINLAYSON Perhaps .. infants dying in infancy are regenerated in the article of death. **2** C. MCCULLOUGH A .. percentage of the timber would not regenerate at all, but remain dead. **4** *Times Lit. Suppl.* Re-use of older buildings can help regenerate inner cities.

■ **regenerable** *adjective* E20.

regeneration /rɪˌdʒɛnəˈreɪʃ(ə)n/ *noun.* ME.
[Old & mod. French *régénération* or Latin *regeneratio(n-)*, formed as prec.: see -ATION.]
1 The action of regenerating; the process or fact of being regenerated; re-creation, re-formation. ME. ▸**b** *fig.* Revival, renaissance; reconstitution in an improved form. E17. ▸**c** FORESTRY. The natural regrowth of a forest which has been felled or thinned. L19.
2 The process or fact of being spiritually reborn; the state resulting from this. LME.
3 MEDICINE & BIOLOGY. The formation of new animal tissue; the natural replacement of lost parts or organs. LME.
4 ELECTRONICS. Positive feedback. E20.
5 CHEMISTRY & TEXTILES. The action or process of regenerating polymeric fibres. E20.
1c ***natural regeneration***: see NATURAL *adjective*.

regenerative /rɪˈdʒɛn(ə)rətɪv/ *adjective.* LME.
[Old & mod. French *régénératif* or medieval Latin *regenerativus*, formed as prec.: see -IVE.]
1 Tending to or characterized by regeneration. LME.
2 MECHANICS. **a** Constructed on or employing the principle of the regenerator (REGENERATOR 2). LME. ▸**b** Designating a technique of refrigeration by which the uncooled portion of the working fluid loses some heat prior to the major cooling step by exchange with the cooled portion. L19. ▸**c** ASTRONAUTICS. Designating a method of cooling the walls of a rocket engine by circulating the fuel through them. M20.
3 Designating any method of braking in which energy is extracted from the parts braked, to be stored and reused. E20.
4 ELECTRONICS. Designating, pertaining to, or employing positive feedback. E20.
■ **regeneratively** *adverb* L19.

regenerator /rɪˈdʒɛnəreɪtə/ *noun.* M16.
[from REGENERATE *verb* + -OR.]
1 A person who or thing which regenerates. M16.
2 A form of heat-exchanger in which hot waste gases from a furnace are conducted through a system of flues alternately with the incoming air or gas, to which their residual heat is imparted. M19.

regeneratory /rɪˈdʒɛn(ə)rət(ə)ri/ *adjective. rare.* E19.
[formed as REGENERATE *verb* + -ORY².]
Of the nature of regeneration; regenerative.

regent /ˈriːdʒ(ə)nt/ *noun.* LME.
[Old & mod. French *régent* or Latin *regens*, *regent-* use as noun of pres. pple of *regere* rule: see -ENT.]
1 a That which rules, governs, or has supremacy; a ruling power or principle. Now *rare*. LME. ▸**b** A person who rules or governs. Now *rare* or *obsolete*. L15.
2 a A person invested with royal authority by or on behalf of another; *esp.* a person appointed to administer a kingdom or State during the minority, absence, or incapacity of the monarch. LME. ▸†**b** A member of the municipal authorities in certain Continental cities; a native chief in Java. E18–E19.
3 a At Oxford and Cambridge universities, a master of arts ruling over disputations in the Schools, a duty held

orig. for one and later for five years after graduation. Later also, a master of arts of not more than five years standing. Now *Hist.* LME. ▸**b** In the ancient Scottish universities, an instructor in a college responsible for the tuition of a certain number of students for the duration of their course. Now *Hist.* E16. ▸**c** In France, a university instructor in arts or science, esp. in the more elementary classes. E17. ▸**d** In N. America, a member of the governing board of certain universities; at some universities, a person who oversees the students' conduct and welfare. E19.
†**4** The headmaster of a school. L16–L18.
5 A variety of potato. M19.
6 The chairwoman of a branch of the Daughters of the American Revolution. L19.

📖 **1a** JOHN FOSTER Christianity ought . . to be the supreme regent of all moral feelings. **2a** L. STRACHEY The Prince . . was appointed Regent in case of the death of the Queen.

Comb.: **regent bird** an Australian bowerbird, *Sericulus chrysocephalus*, the male of which has golden-yellow and black plumage; **regent honeyeater** a honeyeater, *Xanthomyza phrygia*, of eucalyptus forests in SE Australia, having black plumage with yellow bars and spots; **regent oriole** = ***regent bird*** above; **regent parrot** a long-tailed southern Australian parrot, *Polytelis anthopeplus*, the male of which is chiefly yellow and the female olive-green.
■ **regentess** *noun* (*rare*) a female regent E17. **regentship** *noun* the office or position of a regent L16.

regent /ˈriːdʒ(ə)nt/ *adjective*. LME.
[Old & mod. French *régent* or Latin *regens*, *regent-* pres. pple of *regere*: see prec.]
1 a Holding the position of a university regent. Freq. ***postpositive***. Now chiefly *Hist.* LME. ▸**b** Acting as or holding the position of regent of a country. Usu. ***postpositive***. M16.
2 Ruling, governing, controlling. Now *rare*. E17.

📖 **1b** J. HOWELL She was made Queen Regent . . during the Kings Minority. ***Prince Regent***: see PRINCE *noun*. ***Princess Regent***: see PRINCESS *noun*.

regent /ˈriːdʒ(ə)nt/ *verb*. Now *rare*. E17.
[from the noun.]
1 *verb trans.* Superintend or teach (a college, class, etc.) as a regent. E17.
2 *verb intrans.* Act as a university regent. M17.

reggae /ˈrɛɡeɪ/ *noun*. M20.
[W. Indian, ult. origin uncertain. Cf. Jamaican English *rege-rege* quarrel, row.]
A style of popular music of Jamaican origin, with a strongly accentuated offbeat and often a prominent bass; a dance or song set to this music. Cf. SKA.

📖 *attrib.*: F. DHONDY The beat of a reggae record thumping through the . . air.

■ **reggaefied** *adjective* (of a song or piece of music) put into the style of reggae music L20.

Regge /ˈreɪdʒeɪ, ˈrɛdʒeɪ/ *noun*. M20.
[T. E. *Regge* (b. 1931), Italian physicist.]
NUCLEAR PHYSICS. Used ***attrib.*** to designate a theory of the scattering of subatomic particles, and associated concepts.
Regge pole a pole of a complex function relating the scattered amplitude of partial waves to angular momentum. **Regge trajectory** a path traced in the complex angular momentum plane by a Regge pole as the energy varies; *esp.* a plot of spin against the square of the rest mass for a group of particles.
■ **Reggeization** /ˌrɛdʒeɪʌɪˈzeɪʃ(ə)n/ *noun* treatment or modification in accordance with Regge theory M20. **Reggeized** *adjective* treated or modified in accordance with Regge theory L20.

Reggeon /ˈrɛdʒeɪɒn/ *noun*. M20.
[from prec. + -ON.]
NUCLEAR PHYSICS. (A particle represented by) a Regge pole or trajectory, or a virtual particle regarded as exchanged in the type of scattering they represent.
■ **regge'onic** *adjective* M20.

reggo *noun* var. of REGO.

regicide /ˈrɛdʒɪsʌɪd/ *noun*. M16.
[from Latin *rex*, *reg-* king + -CIDE, prob. after French *régicide*.]
1 A person who kills a king; a person who commits the crime of regicide; *spec.* (***a***) ENGLISH HISTORY any of those involved in the trial and execution of Charles I; (***b***) FRENCH HISTORY any of those involved in the execution of Louis XVI. M16.
2 The action or an act of killing a king. L16.
■ **regi'cidal** *adjective* L18. **regicidism** *noun* the practice or principle of regicide M17.

regidor /rexiˈdɔr, rɛhiˈdɔː/ *noun*. Pl. **-dores** /-ˈdɔres/, **-dors** /-ˈdɔːz/. E17.
[Spanish, from *regir* to rule.]
In Spain and Spanish-speaking countries: a member of a *cabildo* or municipal council; a councillor; a village official.

régie /reʒi/ *noun*. Pl. pronounced same. L18.
[French, fem. pa. pple of *régir* to rule.]
In some European countries, a government department that controls an industry or service; *spec.* (*Hist.*) one with complete control of the importation, manufacture, and taxation of tobacco, salt, etc.

regifuge /ˈrɛdʒɪfjuːdʒ/ *noun*. M17.
[Latin *regifugium*, from *rex*, *reg-* king: see -FUGE.]
ROMAN HISTORY. The flight or expulsion of the kings from Rome.

regime /reɪˈʒiːm/ *noun*. Also **régime**. L15.
[French *régime* from Latin REGIMEN.]
1 = REGIMEN 2. L15.
2 A method or system of rule or government; a system or institution having widespread influence or prevalence. Now freq. (usu. *derog.*), a particular government. L18.
3 PHYSICAL GEOGRAPHY. **a** The condition of a watercourse with regard to changes in its form or bed; *esp.* an equilibrium between erosion and deposition. Cf. REGIMEN 4. M19. ▸**b** The condition of a body of water with regard to the rates at which water enters and leaves it. L19.
4 SCIENCE & ENGINEERING. The set of conditions under which a system occurs or is maintained. L19.

📖 **1** G. GREENE A patient . . accepts . . the strict regime required for a cure. **2** G. F. KENNAN The political disintegration of the old Tsarist regime. **the ancient regime**, **the old regime** [translating French] = ANCIEN RÉGIME.

regimen /ˈrɛdʒɪmən/ *noun*. LME.
[Latin, from *regere* rule.]
1 The action of governing; government, rule. Later also, a particular system of government; a regime. *arch.* LME.
2 Chiefly MEDICINE. A prescribed course of exercise, way of life, or diet, esp. for the promotion or restoration of one's health. LME.
3 GRAMMAR. The government of one word by another; the relationship between one word and another dependent word; the object of a preposition, gerund, etc. Now *rare*. M16.
4 PHYSICAL GEOGRAPHY. = REGIME 3a. E19.

📖 **2** P. ROTH From the daily regimen of swimming . . and hiking . . , we each grow more and more fit. I. HAMILTON A stern . . regimen: mass in the morning, benediction in the evening.

regiment /ˈrɛdʒɪm(ə)nt/ *noun*. LME.
[Old & mod. French *régiment* from late Latin *regimentum* rule, from *regere* rule: see -MENT.]
1 Rule or government over a person, people, or country; *esp.* royal authority. Now *rare*. LME. ▸†**b** A method or system of rule or government; a regime. L15–L17.
†**2 a** The office or function of a ruler. LME–M17. ▸**b** The period during which a ruler rules; a reign. M16–M17.
†**3 a** Restraint, self-control. LME–L17. ▸**b** Control or influence over another thing or person. LME–L17.
†**4** A place or country under a particular rule; a kingdom, a domain, a district. LME–M17.
†**5** MEDICINE. A prescribed diet or way of life; a regimen. LME–M18.
†**6** The ruling or governing *of* a person or place. Also, the management or control *of* a thing. L15–M18.
†**7** A rule, a regulation. M16–E17.
8 MILITARY. A large body of troops under the command of a superior officer, forming a permanent unit of an army or military force and usu. consisting of several companies, troops, or batteries, (now usu. *spec.*, two or more battalions). L16. ▸**b** *transf.* & *fig.* A large array or number (*of*); an organized array (*of*). E17. ▸†**c** A class, a kind. E–M17.

📖 **8** C. RYAN The remaining battalions of Tucker's 504th Regiment were moving east. ***line regiment***: see LINE *noun*[2]. ***Territorial Regiments***: see TERRITORIAL *adjective*. **b** J. RUSKIN A regiment of poplars beside a straight road. C. O. SKINNER Fill the . . wagon with provisions enough to feed a regiment.

regiment /ˈrɛdʒɪm(ə)nt/ *verb trans*. Usu. in *pass*. E17.
[from prec.]
1 MILITARY. Form into a regiment or regiments. E17.
2 Organize (people, society, etc.), esp. strictly or oppressively, into definite groups or according to an order or system. L17.
3 Assign to a regiment or group. L18.

📖 **2** N. F. DIXON People's working lives are regimented by the clock.

■ **regimen'tation** *noun* the action or process of regimenting people, society, etc. L19.

regimental /rɛdʒɪˈmɛnt(ə)l/ *adjective & noun*. M17.
[from REGIMENT *noun* + -AL[1].]
▸ **A** *adjective*. **1** Of or pertaining to a regiment. M17.
2 Maintaining or observing strict discipline. *Military slang*. E20.
1 *regimental sergeant-major*: see SERGEANT-MAJOR *noun* 2. ***the regimental colour***: see COLOUR *noun* 7.
▸ **B** *noun*. In *pl.* Military uniform, esp. of a particular regiment. M18.
■ **regi'mentally** *adverb* E18.

regimentary /rɛdʒɪˈmɛnt(ə)ri/ *noun & adjective*. *rare*. M18.
[formed as prec. + -ARY[1].]
▸†**A** *noun*. A Polish military officer. M–L18.
▸ **B** *adjective*. Regimental. M19.

regiminal /rɪˈdʒɪmɪn(ə)l/ *adjective*. Now *rare*. E19.
[from Latin *regimin-* stem of *regimen* REGIMEN: see -AL[1].]
MEDICINE. Of, pertaining to, or of the nature of (a) regimen.

Regina /rɪˈdʒʌɪnə/ *noun*. E18.
[Latin = queen.]
A queen; the prosecution, as representing a reigning queen, in criminal proceedings. Cf. REX 1.

📖 W. BOSCAWEN Upon the statute of . . Regina v. Matthews, the Court seem to have thought otherwise. ***Salve Regina***: see SALVE *noun*[2] 1.

reginal /rɪˈdʒʌɪn(ə)l/ *adjective*. M16.
[medieval Latin *reginalis*, formed as prec. + -AL[1].]
Queenly, queenlike.

region /ˈriːdʒ(ə)n/ *noun*. ME.
[Old & mod. French *région* from Latin *regio(n-)* direction, line, boundary, district, province, from *regere* rule: see -ION.]
1 A large tract of land; a country; a definable portion of the earth's surface, *esp.* one distinguished by natural features, climate, fauna or flora, etc. Formerly also, a realm, a kingdom. ME. ▸**b** An area of more or less definite extent or character; in *pl.*, *the* parts of a country outside the capital or chief seat of government. E18.
2 a A separate part of the world or universe, as the air, heaven, etc. ME. ▸**b** *fig.* A place or condition with a certain character or subject to certain influences; the sphere or realm *of* something. E16.
3 A part or division of the body round or near some organ etc. LME.
4 Any of several successive divisions of the atmosphere or the sea made according to height or depth. LME.
5 a An administrative division of a city or district. L16. ▸**b** A relatively large administrative division of a country; *spec.* each of the nine local government areas into which mainland Scotland has been divided since the abolition of counties in 1975. E20. ▸**c** An area of the world made up of neighbouring countries which are considered socially, economically, or politically interdependent. E20. ▸**d** BROADCASTING. A part of a country covered by a particular programme service or broadcasting company; *transf.* such a company. E20.
6 A space occupied by something. M17.

📖 **1b** J. BUCHAN A region of coal-pits and industrial towns. G. BATTISCOMBE One of the most backward regions of southern Italy. **2b** B. JOWETT He . . followed philosophy into the region of mythology. I. MURDOCH The human soul is a vast region. **3** D. M. THOMAS Severe pains in her left breast and pelvic region.

Phrases: **in the region of** round about, approximately. ***lower regions***: see LOWER *adjective*. ***nether regions***. ***plage region***: see PLAGE 4. ***radiant region***: see RADIANT *adjective*. ***sporadic region***: see SPORADIC *adjective*. **standard administrative region**, **standard region** each of the eight (formerly nine) areas into which England is divided for industrial planning, demographic surveying, etc. ***upper regions***: see UPPER *adjective*.
■ **regioned** *adjective* (*rare*) divided into regions; placed in a region: E19.

regional /ˈriːdʒ(ə)n(ə)l/ *adjective & noun*. LME.
[Late Latin *regionalis*, from Latin *regio(n-)*: see prec., -AL[1].]
▸ **A** *adjective*. Of, pertaining to, or characteristic of a region. LME.

📖 M. UNDERWOOD His voice still carried traces of a regional accent. *Social History of Medicine* Regional contrasts . . have proved to be very large. **regional metamorphism** GEOLOGY: affecting rocks over an extensive area as a result of the large-scale action of heat and pressure.

▸ **B** *noun*. **1** The part of a gravity anomaly or magnetic anomaly that is due to deep features and varies only gradually from place to place. M20.
2 *ellipt.* A regional newspaper, stamp, etc. M20.
■ **regio'nality** *noun* M20. **regionally** *adverb* L19.

regionalise *verb* var. of REGIONALIZE.

regionalism /ˈriːdʒ(ə)n(ə)lɪz(ə)m/ *noun*. L19.
[from prec. + -ISM.]
1 Tendency to or practice of regional systems or methods. Also, the theory or practice of regional rather than central systems of administration or economic, cultural, or political affiliation. L19.
2 A linguistic feature peculiar to a particular region and not part of the standard language of a country; regional distinctiveness in literature. M20.

📖 **1** *Listener* She glories in her regionalism and dependence on local community.

■ **regionalist** *noun* a person inclined to regionalism E20. **regiona'listic** *adjective* L19.

regionalize /ˈriːdʒ(ə)n(ə)lʌɪz/ *verb trans*. Also **-ise**. E20.
[from REGIONAL *adjective* + -IZE.]
Bring under the control of a region for administrative purposes; divide into regions; organize regionally.

For other words beginning with *re-* see the entry for **re-**

■ **regionali'zation** *noun* E20.

regionary /ˈriːdʒ(ə)n(ə)ri/ *adjective*. L17.
[Late Latin *regionarius*, from Latin *regio(n-)*: see REGION, -ARY¹.]
Of or pertaining to a region.
regionary bishop: without a particular diocese.

regiospecific /ˌriːdʒɪəʊspəˈsɪfɪk/ *adjective*. M20.
[from Latin *regio* REGION + SPECIFIC *adjective*.]
CHEMISTRY. Of a reaction or process; occurring preferentially at a particular site or sites on a molecule.
■ **regiospeci'ficity** *noun* the state of being regiospecific; the degree to which a reaction etc. is regiospecific: M20.

régisseur /reʒisœːr/ *noun*. Pl. pronounced same. E19.
[French.]
THEATRICAL & BALLET. A stage-manager, an artistic director.

register /ˈrɛdʒɪstə/ *noun*¹. LME.
[Old & mod. French *registre*, †*regestre* or medieval Latin *registrum*, *-estrum*, alt. of *regestum* sing. of late Latin *regesta* list, neut. pl. of pa. pple of Latin *regerere* enter, transcribe, record, register.]
▶ **I 1** A book or volume in which important particulars of any kind are regularly and accurately recorded; a written record or collection of entries thus formed. Also ***register book***. LME.
2 *collect.* Official records of a legal, parliamentary, or public nature, later *esp.* those relating to the transfer of heritable property. *Scot.* Now *Hist.* LME.
3 An entry in a register. E16.
4 An official record or record-book of some public or commercial importance, as (***a***) of the baptisms, marriages, and burials in a parish, or, later, of all births, marriages, and deaths, kept by a registrar; (***b***) of shipping; (***c***) of professionally qualified people; (***d***) of those entitled to vote in a constituency. Also ***register book***. M16.
5 Registration, registry. M17.

🕮 **1** ALAN JACKSON I take the register And call the fifty names. P. M. HUBBARD The hotel register . . lay open on the desk where I had signed it. M. LANE She kept a register of each individual's intellectual growth.

▶ **II 6** An index; a table of contents. *rare*. LME.
7 a A sliding device controlling a set of organ-pipes which share a tonal quality; a set of pipes so controlled. L16. ▶**b** The compass of a voice or musical instrument; a particular range of this compass. E19. ▶**c** *ART*. Any of a number of bands or sections into which a design is divided. M20. ▶**d** *LINGUISTICS*. A variety of a language or a level of usage, *spec.* one determined by degree of formality and choice of vocabulary, pronunciation, syntax, etc., according to the social context or standing of the user. M20. ▶**e** *PHONETICS*. A type of phonation, essentially controlled by the larynx, and used contrastively in some languages. M20.
8 a A device, usu. consisting of a metal plate or plates, by which an opening may be widened or narrowed, used esp. in a fire-grate to regulate the passage of air, heat, or smoke. E17. ▶**b** *ROPE-MAKING*. A disc of concentric holes through which the component yarns of a strand are passed, and which rotates to twist them together. Also ***register plate***. L18.
9 *PRINTING*. Precise positioning of printed matter; *esp.* the exact correspondence of matter on two sides of a sheet; the exact correspondence of position of superimposed images, esp. of colour-components in colour printing. L17.
10 a A registering device; an instrument for the automatic recording of data; an indicator. M19. ▶**b** A cash register. Chiefly *US*. L19. ▶**c** In a mechanical calculator, a device in which numbers representing data or results of operations are stored or displayed; in an electronic computer or calculator, a location in a store of data having a small capacity but very quick access time and used for a specific purpose. E20.

🕮 **7b** GEO. ELIOT Musical laughs in all the registers. *Early Music* Treble and middle registers were served by . . violins and . . violas. **d** *Notes & Queries* Chaucer must . . have used . . a more formal, possibly more archaic register.

Phrases: **Deputy Clerk Register** *Scot.* the official who performs the duties of the titular Lord Clerk Register. **in register** (of printed matter or superimposed images) in exact correspondence. ***LLOYD's Register (of Shipping)***. **Lord Clerk Register** *Scot.* a Scottish officer of state, formerly in charge of the national records or registers, now holding only a titular post. ***medical register***: see MEDICAL *adjective*. **out of register** (of printed matter or superimposed images) out of exact correspondence. ***social register***: see SOCIAL *adjective*. ***thick register***: see THICK *adjective*.
Comb.: **register board** a flat surface with pegs or guides such that sheets of paper or film placed on it may be brought into the same relative position; ***register book***: see senses 1, 4 above; **Register House** *Scot.* the house appointed for the keeping of the registers, now a special building (the ***General Register House***) in Princes Street, Edinburgh; **register mark** *PRINTING* a mark to control the position of the paper in colour printing; **register office** (*a*) an office at which a register of any kind is kept or where registration is made; (*b*) *spec.* a State office where civil marriages are conducted and births, marriages, and deaths are recorded with the issue of certificates (cf. ***REGISTRY office***); ***register plate***: see sense 8b above; ***register ton***: see TON *noun*¹ 2; ***register tonnage***: see TONNAGE *noun* 5.

■ **registral** *adjective* pertaining to, derived from, or authenticated by a register M17.

register /ˈrɛdʒɪstə/ *noun*². Now *rare*. LME.
[Prob. alt. of REGISTRER.]
The keeper of a register; a registrar.

register /ˈrɛdʒɪstə/ *verb*. LME.
[Old & mod. French *registrer* or medieval Latin *registrare*, from *registrum* REGISTER *noun*¹.]
1 *verb trans.* **a** Set down (a fact, name, etc.) formally or officially, esp. in writing; enter or record accurately. Also (*transf.*), make a mental note of. LME. ▶†**b** Set (a person) down *for* or as something. L16–E17.
2 *spec.* **a** *verb trans.* Formally enter or cause to be entered (a document, fact, name, etc.) in a particular register. LME. ▶**b** *verb refl.* Enter oneself in a register. E16. ▶**c** *verb trans.* & (usu.) *intrans.* Enter the name of (a guest or visitor) in the register of a hotel or guest-house; enter one's name in such a register. Orig. *US*. M19. ▶**d** *verb intrans.* Enter oneself or have one's name recorded in a list of people, as being of a specified category or having a particular eligibility or entitlement. M20.
3 a *verb trans.* Of an instrument: record by some automatic device; indicate. L18. ▶**b** *verb trans.* Of a person: indicate or convey (a feeling or emotion), esp. by facial expression. E20. ▶**c** *verb intrans.* (Of a person, esp. a film actor) portray a role with conviction; (of an idea or emotion) be successfully communicated, be convincing. Also, (of a feeling, thought, utterance, etc.) make an impression on a person's mind, produce a desired effect. Freq. foll. by *on*, *upon*, *with*. E20. ▶**d** *verb intrans.* Produce a response or appear on a recording or measuring instrument. M20.
4 *verb trans.* & *intrans.* *ROPE-MAKING*. Form (a strand) by the use of a register. L18.
5 a *verb intrans.* Coincide or correspond exactly. M19. ▶**b** *verb trans.* Adjust with precision, so as to secure an exact correspondence of parts. M19. ▶**c** *MILITARY*. Sight a gun or guns on (a target); align (artillery) with a target. M20.

🕮 **1a** *Daily Telegraph* The . . share markets registered record falls. R. F. HOBSON A message has been . . registered . . and responded to. M. SEYMOUR The temptation to register a last protest was too strong. **2a** J. HIGGINS The name on the stern was *L'Alouette*, registered Granville. J. MARSH Catherine's birth . . does not seem to have been registered. **c** *Rolling Stone* We . . registered at the Airport Inn. **d** P. D. JAMES Lady Berowne . . registered . . under the National Health Service. **3b** J. T. STORY Her face registering terrible disappointment. **c** A. T. ELLIS She had been so apprehensive . . nothing had registered. **d** *Belfast Telegraph* The appropriate light will not register.

■ **registerer** *noun* L15. **regis'tree** *noun* a person who is registered E20.

registered /ˈrɛdʒɪstəd/ *ppl adjective*. L16.
[from prec. + -ED².]
Recorded, officially set down; entered in a register; *spec.* (of a postal item) recorded at the point of dispatch and indemnified against loss or damage.
registered nurse a nurse with a State certificate of competence. ***State Registered Nurse***: see STATE *noun*.

†**registership** *noun*. L16–E18.
[from REGISTER *noun*² + -SHIP.]
The office or position of registrar.

register-ship /ˈrɛdʒɪstəʃɪp/ *noun*. *obsolete* exc. *Hist.* E18.
[from REGISTER *noun*¹ + SHIP *noun*.]
A Spanish ship with a registered licence authorizing it to trade with the Spanish possessions in America.

registrable /ˈrɛdʒɪstrəb(ə)l/ *adjective*. L17.
[from REGISTER *verb* + -ABLE.]
That may be registered.
■ **registra'bility** *noun* (*rare*) L19.

registrant /ˈrɛdʒɪstr(ə)nt/ *noun*. Orig. *US*. L19.
[from REGISTER *noun*¹ or *verb* + -ANT¹.]
A person who registers, *esp.* a person who by so doing gains a particular entitlement.

registrar /ˈrɛdʒɪstrɑː, rɛdʒɪˈstrɑː/ *noun*. L17.
[medieval Latin *registrarius*, from *registrum* REGISTER *noun*¹: see -AR².]
1 A person responsible for keeping a register; an official recorder; *spec.* (in Britain) the judicial and administrative officer of the High Court or a county court. Also, a judge in the Family Division. L17.
2 The chief administrative officer in a university. M18.
3 A local official responsible for keeping an index of births, marriages, and deaths in his or her area. M19.
4 Orig., a junior hospital doctor whose duties included keeping a register of patients. Now usu., a middle-ranking hospital doctor undergoing training as a specialist or consultant. M19.

🕮 **3** G. GISSING We have . . been married by registrar's licence.

Comb.: **Registrar General** a government official responsible for holding a population census.
■ **registrarship** *noun* the office or position of registrar M19.

registrary /ˈrɛdʒɪstrəri/ *noun*. M16.
[formed as prec.: see -ARY¹.]
A university registrar, now only at Cambridge.

registrate /ˈrɛdʒɪstreɪt/ *verb trans.* Chiefly *Scot.* Now *rare*. Pa. t. & pple **-ate**, **-ated**. LME.
[medieval Latin *registrat-* pa. ppl stem of *registrare*: see REGISTER *verb*, -ATE³.]
Register.

registration /rɛdʒɪˈstreɪʃ(ə)n/ *noun*. M16.
[French †*régistration* or medieval Latin *registratio(n-)*, formed as prec.: see -ATION.]
1 a The action of registering or recording; the process of being registered. Also, an act or instance of this. M16. ▶**b** *spec.* The action or process, open to a Commonwealth resident or a person of British descent, of acquiring full British citizenship. M20.
2 The balance of tone and its musical effect in the organ and other keyboard instruments, esp. the harpsichord. L19.
3 *PRINTING*. The state of being in or action of putting in register. L19.
4 In full ***registration mark***, ***registration number***. The series of letters and figures assigned to a motor vehicle on registration. E20.

🕮 **1a** *Nature* Registration of temperature is . . the most difficult of meteorological problems. L. DEIGHTON A car with East German registration.

Comb.: ***registration mark***, ***registration number***: see sense 4 above; **registration plate** a plate on a motor vehicle bearing a registration number; a number-plate.

registrer /ˈrɛdʒɪstrə/ *noun*. Now *rare*. LME.
[Anglo-Norman = Old French *registreur* from medieval Latin *registrator*, formed as REGISTRATE: see -ER². Cf. REGISTER *noun*².]
†**1** A person who registers; a registrar. LME–L16.
2 = REGISTER *noun*¹ 10a. M19.

registry /ˈrɛdʒɪstri/ *noun*. E16.
[from REGISTER *verb* + -RY. Cf. medieval Latin *registerium*.]
1 A register, a record-book. Also, an entry in a register. E16.
2 A place where registers are kept. Also, a court of the Family Division. M16.
3 The act of registering, registration. L16.

🕮 **1** P. AUSTER His name was entered in the . . marriage registry.

Comb.: **registry office** = ***register office*** s.v. REGISTER *noun*¹.

regium donum /ˌrɛdʒɪəm ˈdɒnəm, ˌreɡɪəm ˈdɔːnəm/ *noun phr.* L18.
[Latin, lit. 'royal gift'.]
Hist. An annual grant made from public funds to Nonconformist clergy in Britain and Ireland from the late 17th to the mid 19th cent.

Regius /ˈriːdʒɪəs/ *adjective*. E17.
[Latin = royal, from *reg-*, *rex* king.]
Designating (a professor holding) a university chair founded by a monarch or filled by Crown appointment.

reg'lar /ˈrɛɡlə/ *adjective & adverb*. *non-standard*. M19.
[Repr. a pronunc.]
Regular.

reglement /rɛɡləmɑ̃/ *noun*. Pl. pronounced same. L16.
[French *règlement*, †*reigle-*, from Old & mod. French *regler*, †*reigler* to rule from late Latin *regulare* REGULATE *verb*.]
†**1** The action of regulating or controlling something. L16–M18.
2 A regulation. M17.

reglementary /rɛɡləˈmɛnt(ə)ri/ *adjective*. *rare*. L19.
[French *règlementaire*, formed as prec.: see -ARY¹.]
Regular, according to regulations.

reglet /ˈrɛɡlɪt/ *noun*. Also †**riglet**. L16.
[Old & mod. French *réglet*, *-ette* dim. of *règle* RULE *noun*: see -ET¹. In sense 2 from Italian *regoletto* from *regola* rule.]
†**1** A narrow division of a page of a book; a column. *rare*. Only in L16.
2 *ARCHITECTURE*. A narrow strip used to separate mouldings or panels from one another. M17.
3 *TYPOGRAPHY*. A thin narrow strip of wood or metal used to separate type. L17.

regma /ˈrɛɡmə/ *noun*. Pl. **-mata** /-mətə/. M19.
[Greek *rhēgma* a break, a fracture.]
BOTANY. A dry fruit with elastically dehiscent cells, a form of schizocarp.

regnal /ˈrɛɡn(ə)l/ *adjective*. E17.
[Anglo-Latin *regnalis*, from Latin *regnum* kingdom: see -AL¹.]
Of or pertaining to a reign or monarch.
regnal year a year reckoned from the date or anniversary of a monarch's accession.

regnancy /ˈrɛɡnənsi/ *noun*. M19.
[from Latin *regnare* to reign: see -ANCY.]
The fact of ruling or reigning; predominance.

For other words beginning with *re-* see the entry for **re-**

regnant /ˈrɛɡnənt/ *adjective*. E17.
[Latin *regnant-* pres. ppl stem of *regnare* to reign: see -ANT¹. In sense 2 after French *régnant*.]
1 Reigning, ruling. Freq. *postpositive*. E17.
2 Of a thing, quality, etc.: predominant, dominating; prevalent, widespread. E17.

📖 **1** L. STRACHEY A Queen Regnant must accede to the wishes of her Prime Minister. **2** L. OLIVIER The regnant high-class English public schools.

rego /ˈrɛdʒəʊ/ *noun*. *Austral. slang*. Also **reggo**. Pl. **-os**. M20.
[from REG(ISTRATION + -O.]
= REGISTRATION 4.

regolith /ˈrɛɡəlɪθ/ *noun*. L19.
[from Greek *rhēgos* blanket + -LITH.]
GEOLOGY. The unconsolidated solid material (ash, dust, soil, rock fragments, etc.) covering the bedrock of the earth or another planet.
■ **regoˈlithic** *adjective* M20.

regorge /riːˈɡɔːdʒ/ *verb*. E17.
[Old & mod. French *regorger*, or from RE- + GORGE *verb*.]
1 *verb trans*. Disgorge or cast up again; throw or cast back. E17.
2 *verb intrans*. Gush or flow back again. M17.
3 *verb trans*. Engorge or swallow again. *rare*. E18.

regosol /ˈrɛɡəsɒl/ *noun*. M20.
[formed as REGOLITH + -SOL.]
SOIL SCIENCE. A poorly developed soil without definite horizons, overlying and formed from deep unconsolidated deposits such as sand or loess.
■ **regoˈsolic** *adjective* M20.

regrade /riːˈɡreɪd/ *verb trans*. E19.
[from RE- + GRADE *verb*.]
Grade again or differently.
■ **regrading** *noun* (**a**) the action of the verb; (**b**) a new or different grade: E20.

regrant /riːˈɡrɑːnt/ *verb & noun*. L16.
[from RE- + GRANT *verb*.]
▶ **A** *verb trans*. Grant (a privilege, estate, etc.) again. L16.
▶ **B** *noun*. The action of granting something again; the renewal of a grant. E17.

†**regrate** *noun*. *Scot*. LME.
[from REGRATE *verb*¹, or from Old French var. of *regret* REGRET *noun*.]
1 Lamentation, complaint; (an) expression of grief or distress. LME–L17.
2 Sorrow, regret. LME–E18.

†**regrate** *verb*¹ *trans*. *Scot*. LME.
[Old French *regrater* var. of *regreter* REGRET *verb*.]
1 Lament, feel or express grief or sorrow at. LME–E18.
2 Mourn for the loss or death of. LME–L17.

regrate /rɪˈɡreɪt/ *verb*² *trans*. *obsolete* exc. *Hist*. LME.
[Old French *regrater*, prob. from *re-* RE- + *grater* (mod. *gratter*) scratch, of Germanic origin.]
Buy up (market commodities) in order to sell again at a profit; resell (articles so bought), retail.

regrater /rɪˈɡreɪtə/ *noun*. Also **-or**. ME.
[Anglo-Norman *regrater*, *-tour* = Old French *regratier*, *regratteur* formed as prec.: see -ER², -OR.]
1 A person who buys commodities in order to resell at a profit; a retailer. *obsolete* exc. *Hist*. ME.
2 A person who collects commodities from producers and brings them to market; a middleman. *obsolete* exc. *Hist*. or *dial*. E19.
■ **regratress** *noun* (*rare*) a female regrater E17.

regreet /riːˈɡriːt/ *verb & noun*. Now *rare*. L16.
[from RE- + GREET *verb*¹.]
▶ **A** *verb trans*. Greet again; greet in return. Also, greet, give salutation to. L16.
▶†**B** *noun*. (A return of) a salutation or greeting; in *pl*., greetings. L16–M17.

regress /ˈriːɡrɛs/ *noun*. LME.
[Latin *regressus*, formed as next.]
1 The action or an instance of going or coming back; return; re-entry. LME.
†**2** LAW. = RECOURSE *noun* 4b. LME–M18.
3 The fact of going back from or in relation to a state or condition, regression. L16.
4 The action of working back in thought from one thing to another, *spec*. from an effect to a cause. E17.
5 Chiefly ASTRONOMY. Retrograde or reverse motion, retrogradation. M17.

📖 **3** S. CAUDWELL The progress, regress and termination of the liaison. **4** *infinite regress*: see INFINITE *adjective*.

regress /rɪˈɡrɛs/ *verb*. E16.
[Latin *regress-* pa. ppl stem of *regredi*, formed as RE- + *gradi* proceed, walk.]
1 *verb intrans*. Chiefly ASTRONOMY. Move in a backward or retrograde direction. E16.
2 *verb intrans*. Recede *from*; return *to* or *into* a state or condition. M16. ▶**b** *verb intrans. & trans*. PSYCHOLOGY. Return mentally to an earlier period or stage of development through hypnosis, psychoanalysis, mental illness, etc. E20.
3 *verb intrans*. GENETICS. Tend or evolve towards the mean value for the population; display regression to the mean. L19.
4 *verb trans*. STATISTICS. Calculate the coefficient(s) of regression of (a variable) *against* or *on* another variable. L20.

📖 **2** U. LE GUIN They would not regress to .. pre-technological tribalism. **b** J. KLEIN She was willing to let Renée .. regress to a very infantile way of being.

■ **regressor** *noun* (STATISTICS) any of the independent variables in a regression equation (also *regressor variable*) M20.

regression /rɪˈɡrɛʃ(ə)n/ *noun*. LME.
[Latin *regressio(n-)*, formed as prec.: see -ION.]
†**1** Recurrence or repetition of a word or words. *rare*. LME–L16.
†**2** Return to a subject of discussion etc. E16–E17.
3 The action or an act of returning to or towards a place or point of departure. L16.
4 Return *to* or *into* a state or condition; relapse; reversion to a less developed form. M17. ▶**b** GENETICS. The tendency of parents who are exceptional in respect of some partially inherited character to produce offspring in which this character is closer to the mean value for the general population. Freq. as *regression to the mean*. L19. ▶**c** STATISTICS. The relationship between the mean value of a random variable and the corresponding values of one or more other variables. L19. ▶**d** PSYCHOLOGY. The process of returning or a tendency to return to an earlier stage of development through hypnosis, psychoanalysis, mental illness, etc. E20.
5 = REGRESS *noun* 4. M17.
6 Chiefly ASTRONOMY. = REGRESS *noun* 5. E19.

📖 **3** *Scientific American* Marine transgressions onto the continents and regressions from them. **4** W. LIPPMANN A regression to a more primitive mode of production.

Comb.: **regression coefficient** a coefficient in the regression equation; *esp*. the first-order coefficient, which is estimated by the covariance of the two variables divided by the variance of the independent variable; **regression curve** a graph of the expected value of the dependent variable plotted against the value of the independent variable(s); **regression equation** an equation which relates the value of the dependent variable to the value(s) of the independent variable(s); **regression line** = *regression curve* above; **regression therapy** PSYCHOANALYSIS the induction of regression, esp. by hypnosis, in order to discover possible causes of a patient's disorder in his or her earlier life, or to bring repressed memories, feelings, etc., to the conscious mind.

regressive /rɪˈɡrɛsɪv/ *adjective*. M17.
[from REGRESS *verb* + -IVE.]
1 Marked by regression; retrogressive; returning, going back. Opp. *progressive*. M17. ▶**b** Acting in a backward direction, retroactive; (of a tax) that bears proportionately harder on people with lower incomes. L19. ▶**c** PSYCHOLOGY. Of, pertaining to, or marked by psychological regression. E20.
2 PHILOSOPHY. Proceeding from effect to cause, or from particular to universal. M19.
■ **regressively** *adverb* M19. **regressiveness** *noun* M19. **regreˈssivity** *noun* E20.

regret /rɪˈɡrɛt/ *noun*. L15.
[Old & mod. French, formed as the verb. Cf. earlier REGRATE *noun*.]
†**1** (An expression of) complaint, (a) lament. L15–M16.
2 A feeling of sorrow, disappointment, or pain due to some external circumstance (freq. loss or deprivation) or to reflection on something one has or has not done. (Foll. by *at*, *of*.) Freq. in *pl*. L16.
3 An expression of disappointment or sorrow at one's inability to do something, *esp*. to accept an invitation. Freq. in *pl*. M19.

📖 **2** W. COWPER Frantic with regret Of her he loves. GEO. ELIOT A face .. less bright than usual, from regret at appearing so late. J. CONRAD Don't .. think that I have the slightest regret. P. AUSTER At times my life seems nothing but a series of regrets, of wrong turnings. **3** **give one's regrets**, **send one's regrets** formally decline an invitation.

regret /rɪˈɡrɛt/ *verb trans*. Infl. **-tt-**. LME.
[Old French *regreter* bewail (the dead) (mod. *regretter*), perh. formed as RE- + Germanic base of GREET *verb*². Cf. REGRATE *verb*¹.]
1 Remember or think of (something lost) with distress or longing; feel sorrow for the loss of. LME.
2 Feel or express sorrow, disappointment, or pain on account of (some event, fact, action, etc.), be or feel sorry etc. *that*, *to do*. M16.

📖 **1** S. KEYES I regret the speaking rivers I have known. **2** V. WOOLF She .. regretted the impulse which had entangled her with .. another human being. J. B. PRIESTLEY As the lorry went .. he began to regret .. that he had ever set eyes on it. P. AUSTER He would live to regret what he was doing.

■ **regretter** *noun* M19.

regretful /rɪˈɡrɛtfʊl, -f(ə)l/ *adjective*. M17.
[from REGRET *noun* + -FUL.]
Feeling or showing regret. Also foll. by *of*.
■ **regretfully** *adverb* (**a**) in a regretful manner; (**b**) *non-standard* regrettably: L17. **regretfulness** *noun* L19.

regrettable /rɪˈɡrɛtəb(ə)l/ *adjective*. E17.
[from REGRET *verb* + -ABLE.]
Deserving of or calling for regret: *esp*. (of conduct, an event, etc.) undesirable, unwelcome, deserving censure.

📖 P. H. GIBBS There were several regrettable incidents, which Val found distressing. *Journal of Theological Studies* It is .. regrettable that the book should be .. so inaccessible. A. N. WILSON The regrettable young man enjoyed a position of eminence.

■ **regrettably** *adverb* (**a**) in a regrettable manner; (**b**) (modifying a sentence) it is regretted (that): M19. **regrettableness** *noun* E20.

regrew *verb pa. t.*: see REGROW.

regrind /ˈriːɡraɪnd/ *noun*. M20.
[from the verb.]
An act of regrinding something.

regrind /riːˈɡraɪnd/ *verb trans*. Pa. t. & pple **-ground** /-ˈɡraʊnd/. M19.
[from RE- + GRIND *verb*.]
Grind again.

regroup /riːˈɡruːp/ *verb trans. & intrans*. L19.
[from RE- + GROUP *verb*.]
Group again or differently; rearrange or regather in groups.
■ **regroupment** *noun* E20.

regrow /riːˈɡrəʊ/ *verb intrans. & trans*. Infl. as GROW *verb*; pa. t. usu. **-grew** /-ˈɡruː/, pa. pple usu. **-grown** /-ˈɡrəʊn/. L19.
[from RE- + GROW *verb*.]
Grow again.
■ **regrowth** *noun* the process or action of growing or increasing again; *esp*. the renewed growth of vegetation after harvesting, fire, etc.; the new vegetation that results: M18.

Regt. *abbreviation*.
Regiment.

†**reguerdon** *noun*. *rare*. LME–L16.
[Old French, formed as next.]
Recompense, reward.

reguerdon /rɪˈɡəːd(ə)n/ *verb trans*. *rare*. LME.
[Old French *reguerdoner*, from *re-* RE- + GUERDON *verb*.]
Reward.

regula /ˈrɛɡjʊlə/ *noun*. Pl. **-lae** /-liː/. M16.
[Latin: see RULE *noun*.]
1 ARCHITECTURE. A fillet, a reglet; *spec*. a short band, with guttae on the lower side, below the taenia in Doric architecture. M16.
†**2** A rule, a norm. *rare*. M17–L19.

regulable /ˈrɛɡjʊləb(ə)l/ *adjective*. M17.
[from REGULATE + -ABLE.]
Able to be regulated.

regulae *noun* pl. of REGULA.

regular /ˈrɛɡjʊlə/ *adjective, noun, & adverb*. LME.
[Old French *reguler* (mod. *régulier*) from Latin *regularis*, from *regula* RULE *noun*: see -AR¹.]
▶ **A** *adjective*. **1** ECCLESIASTICAL. Subject to or bound by a religious rule; belonging to a religious or monastic order. Opp. *secular*. LME.
2 Having a form, structure, or arrangement which follows some rule or principle; characterized by harmony or proper correspondence between parts or elements; symmetrical. LME. ▶**b** GEOMETRY. (Of a figure) having all sides and all angles equal; (of a solid) bounded by a number of equal figures. L16. ▶**c** BOTANY. Of a flower: radially symmetrical; actinomorphic. L18.
3 Characterized by the presence or operation of a definite principle; steady or uniform in action, procedure, or occurrence; *esp*. recurring or repeated at fixed times, recurring at short uniform intervals. E16. ▶**b** Habitually or customarily used, received, or observed; habitual, constant; (of a client or customer) of long standing. L18. ▶**c** (Of merchandise) of average, medium, or standard size, composition, or quality; designating such a size etc. E20.
4 Pursuing a definite course or observing a uniform principle of action or conduct. Now *esp*. observing fixed times for or never failing in the performance of certain actions or duties. E17. ▶**b** Orderly, well-behaved, steady. E18. ▶**c** Defecating or menstruating at predictable times or intervals. L18.
5 a GRAMMAR. Of a word, esp. a verb: following the usual or normal mode of inflection or conjugation. E17. ▶**b** Conformable to a rule or standard; made or carried out in a prescribed manner; formally correct. M17.
6 Properly constituted; having all the essential attributes, qualities, or parts; normal. M17. ▶**b** Of a person:

properly qualified or trained, full-time, professional. M18. ▸**c** Thorough, complete, absolute. *colloq.* E19.

7 *MILITARY.* (Of forces or troops) properly and permanently organized, constituting a permanent professional body; of or relating to such forces etc. E18.

📖 **2** GEO. ELIOT The conjurer . . showed his small regular teeth. S. RAVEN He was tall . . with very fair hair and pleasant, regular features. **b** ***regular octagon, regular tetrahedron***, etc. **3** W. COWPER How regular his meals, how sound he sleeps! BYRON With awful footsteps regular as rhyme. J. F. LEHMANN The drone of aircraft . . rose and fell in regular rhythm. B. CHATWIN He . . took regular exercise. **b** DICKENS It's past my regular time for going to bed. G. GORDON The regular postie was on holiday. **c** *Which?* A bun with a regular portion of chips. D. DELILLO I chew regular gum or . . sugarless gum. **4** POPE No prodigies remain, Comets are regular. T. HARDY They were regular in their visits to their parents. **b** G. STEIN His old way of regular and quiet living. **5b** *Society* Ladies making acquaintances . . without regular introductions. **6** J. BUCHAN Do you mean regular staircases—all steps, so to speak? C. A. LINDBERGH There was no regular airport in Meridian. **c** A. H. CLOUGH We had a regular flood, and it has been raining . . ever since. L. GARFIELD The mistress was a regular demon. **7** *Daily Telegraph* The withdrawal of British regular units from Oman. M. MOORCOCK Regular Don Cossack cavalry.

Phrases & special collocations: ***canon regular***: see CANON *noun*² 1. **keep regular hours** do the same thing, esp. getting up and going to bed, at the same time each day. **regular army** a or *the* permanently constituted professional standing army. ***regular canon***: see CANON *noun*² 1. **regular clergy**: belonging to a religious order. **regular fellow**, **regular guy** *colloq.* (chiefly *N. Amer.*) an agreeable, ordinary, or sociable person. **regular satellite** *ASTRONOMY*: following a nearly circular orbit in or near the equatorial plane of the primary. **regular soldier** a full-time professional soldier.

▸**B** *noun.* **1** *ECCLESIASTICAL.* A member of the regular clergy. LME.

2 a A regular soldier; a member of the regular forces. Usu. in *pl.* M18. ▸**b** A fully qualified or professional practitioner of medicine etc. Now *rare.* M18. ▸**c** A regular customer, visitor, participant, etc. M19.

3 In *pl.* A share of the profits of a crime etc. Chiefly in ***go regulars*** share profits. *Criminals' slang. arch.* E19.

4 *Hist.* In medieval computation, each of a set of fixed numbers used for ascertaining on which day of the week each month began (***solar regular***), or for finding the age of the moon on the first of each month (***lunar regular***). M19.

📖 **2c** S. GIBBONS Mr. Waite was . . a Regular at The Peal of Bells. F. KAPLAN The British Museum, where he became a regular for the next year.

▸**C** *adverb.* Regularly. *non-standard.* E18.

📖 P. DRISCOLL Quinn likes to get his rocks off pretty regular.

■ **regularly** *adverb* LME.

regularise *verb* var. of REGULARIZE.

regularity /rɛgjʊˈlarɪti/ *noun.* E17.
[from REGULAR + -ITY.]
The state or character of being regular; a regular arrangement.

📖 *Woman's Journal* Get . . back to regularity with Kellogg's . . natural laxative food. G. ORWELL The . . distinguishing mark of Newspeak grammar was its regularity. J. BRONOWSKI The regularities which nature . . imposes on . . atomic structures.

regularize /ˈrɛgjʊlərʌɪz/ *verb trans.* Also **-ise**. E17.
[from REGULAR *adjective* + -IZE.]
†**1** Govern, rule. *rare.* Only in E17.
2 Make regular. M19.
■ **regulariˈzation** *noun* M19. **regularizer** *noun* (*rare*) E20.

regulate /ˈrɛgjʊleɪt/ *verb.* LME.
[Late Latin *regulat-* pa. ppl stem of *regulare*, from Latin *regula* RULE *noun*: see -ATE³.]
1 *verb trans.* Control, govern, or direct by rule or regulations; subject to guidance or restrictions; adapt to circumstances or surroundings. LME. ▸**b** Bring or reduce (a person or group) to order. Cf. REGULATOR 2. *obsolete* exc. *Hist.* LME.

2 *verb trans.* Alter or control with reference to some standard or purpose; adjust (a clock or other machine) so that the working may be accurate. M17.

3 *verb refl. & intrans. BIOLOGY.* Exhibit regulation. E20.

📖 **1** J. GILBERT Mercy must . . be regulated by . . righteousness. P. WARNER He regulated gambling. *Proverb*: Accidents will happen in the best-regulated families. **2** A. CARTER A swivelling chair whose speed she could regulate. B. VINE He has a pacemaker to regulate his heart.

■ **regulatable** *adjective* L19.

regulation /rɛgjʊˈleɪʃ(ə)n/ *noun & adjective.* M17.
[from prec. + -ATION.]
▸**A** *noun.* **1** The action or process of regulating a thing or person; the state of being regulated. M17. ▸**b** *BIOLOGY.* The property whereby the nature and growth of the parts of an organism are interrelated so as to produce an integrated whole, and whereby the organism can adapt to injury or other changes. E20.

2 A rule prescribed for controlling some matter, or for the regulating of conduct; an authoritative direction, a standing rule. E18.

3 *ELECTRICITY.* (A measure of) the constancy of the output etc. of an apparatus under conditions of varying load. L19.

📖 **1** C. G. W. LOCK Regulation is effected by raising the pendulum bob to make the clock go faster. F. TOMLIN The regulation of his private life was a matter of genuine Catholic concern. **2** DICKENS It's against regulations for me to call at night. A. MACLEAN Army regulations state that . . helicopters must be kept in . . readiness.

▸**B** *attrib.* or as *adjective.* That is prescribed by or in accordance with regulations; of the correct type, size, etc.; ordinary, usual, regular. M19.

📖 DICKENS The regulation cap . . of female servants. V. WOOLF The regulation number of socks and drawers.

regulative /ˈrɛgjʊlətɪv/ *adjective.* L16.
[formed as prec. + -ATIVE.]
1 Chiefly *PHILOSOPHY.* Tending to regulate a thing or person. L16.
2 *BIOLOGY.* Of, pertaining to, or of the nature of regulation; displaying or characterized by regulation. E20.
■ **regulatively** *adverb* M19.

regulator /ˈrɛgjʊleɪtə/ *noun.* M17.
[formed as prec. + -OR.]
1 *gen.* A person who or thing which regulates a thing or person. M17.

2 *Hist.* **a** A member of a commission appointed in 1687 to investigate and revise the constitution of various boroughs, esp. as regards parliamentary representation. L17. ▸**b** A member of any of various vigilante bands in parts of the US. M18.

3 a A device for controlling the rate of working of machinery, or for controlling fluid flow; *spec.* one controlling the supply of steam to the cylinders of a railway locomotive. E18. ▸**b** A device for adjusting the balance of a clock or watch in order to regulate its speed. E18. ▸**c** *ECONOMICS.* (The power to operate) the mechanism of taxation etc. by which a finance minister may seek to control a nation's economy between budgets. M20.

4 A clock or watch keeping accurate time, by which other timepieces may be regulated. Also ***regulator clock***. M18.

📖 **1** LD MACAULAY The weakest Ministry has . . power as a regulator of parliamentary proceedings. *Times* Federal regulators have closed down two . . savings banks. **3a** *Railway World* I . . opened the regulator and we moved . . back over the junction.

Comb.: **regulator gene** *GENETICS* a gene which codes for a polypeptide that modifies the transcription of structural genes.

regulatory /ˈrɛgjʊlət(ə)ri/ *adjective.* E19.
[formed as prec. + -ORY².]
1 Of or pertaining to regulation(s). Also, required by or resulting from regulation. E19.
2 *BIOLOGY.* = REGULATIVE 2. E20.

reguli *noun pl.* see REGULUS.

regulo /ˈrɛgjʊləʊ/ *noun.* Also (esp. in sense 1) **R-**. Pl. **-os**. E20.
[from REGULATE + -O.]
1 (Proprietary name for) a thermostatic control for a domestic gas oven. E20.
2 *attrib.* Esp. with following numeral: a setting on a scale of numbers denoting temperatures in a gas oven. M20.

📖 **2** *Times* Preheat the oven to 420 deg. F. (Regulo 7.). *fig.*: D. HALLIDAY Stultifying in the sunshine at a low regulo setting.

regulon /ˈrɛgjʊlɒn/ *noun.* M20.
[formed as prec. + -ON.]
GENETICS. A unit comprising all the genetic material whose transcription is regulated by a single substance.

regulus /ˈrɛgjʊləs/ *noun.* Pl. **-luses**, **-li** /-lʌɪ, -liː/. L16.
[Latin, dim. of *reg-*, *rex* king.]
1 *CHEMISTRY.* A metallic form of a substance obtained by smelting or reduction. Freq. *attrib.* or with *of*; orig. in ***regulus of antimony***, metallic antimony (app. so called because it combined readily with gold). Now *arch.* or *Hist.* L16.
2 A petty king or ruler. L17.
3 A bird of the genus *Regulus*, a kinglet; orig. *spec.* the goldcrest. E18.
■ **reguline** *adjective* (*CHEMISTRY*, now *rare* or *obsolete*) of, pertaining to, or of the nature of a regulus M17.

regur /ˈrɛgə, ˈreɪgə/ *noun.* E19.
[Hindi *regar* from Telugu *rē-gaḍa*, *rē-gaḍi* clay.]
SOIL SCIENCE. Rich dark calcareous soil rich in clay, formed mainly from weathered basalt and occurring typically on the Deccan Plateau of India. Also ***regur soil***.

regurgitate /rɪˈgəːdʒɪteɪt/ *verb.* L16.
[medieval Latin *regurgitat-* pa. ppl stem of *regurgitare*, formed as RE- + late Latin *gurgitare* GURGITATE.]
1 *verb trans.* Pour or cast out again; *esp.* bring (swallowed food) up again to the mouth. L16.
2 *verb intrans.* Gush or pour back (again). Now *rare.* M17.

📖 **1** N. TINBERGEN The parent [gull] . . regurgitates . . half-digested food. *fig.*: *Accountancy* Candidates . . regurgitate lists of points, demonstrating learning by rote.

■ **regurgitant** *adjective* (*MEDICINE*) regurgitating; characterized by regurgitation M19. **regurgˈitation** *noun* [medieval Latin *regurgitatio(n-)*] E17.

rehab /ˈriːhab/ *noun & verb. colloq.* M20.
[Abbreviation.]
▸**A** *noun.* = REHABILITATION 2a, b. M20.
▸**B** *verb trans.* Infl. **-bb-**. = REHABILITATE 2a, b. M20.
■ **rehabbed** *noun* rehabilitated; (of a building) renovated or refurbished: L20.

rehabilitate /riːhəˈbɪlɪteɪt/ *verb trans.* L16.
[medieval Latin *rehabilitat-* pa. ppl stem of *rehabilitare*, formed as RE- + HABILITATE.]
1 Orig., formally restore to former privileges, rank, and possessions. Now usu., re-establish the good name, character, or reputation of; clear from unfounded accusations or misrepresentations. L16.
2 a Restore to a previous condition; set up again in proper condition. M19. ▸**b** Restore (a person) to some degree of normal life by training etc., esp. after illness, injury, or imprisonment. M20.

📖 **1** W. SEWARD Pope Calixtus the Third . . rehabilitated her memory. P. KAVANAGH He would be able to rehabilitate himself with Mary Reilly. Z. TOMIN The concept of private property had been rehabilitated. **2a** *Times* The . . latest project is to rehabilitate . . railway cottages. **b** S. NAIPAUL Their drug programme . . rehabilitated . . addicts.

■ **rehabilitative** *adjective* of or pertaining to rehabilitation; designed to rehabilitate a person or thing M20.

rehabilitation /ˌriːhəbɪlɪˈteɪʃ(ə)n/ *noun.* L15.
[medieval Latin *rehabilitatio(n-)*, formed as prec.: see -ATION.]
1 Orig., the formal restoration of a person's privileges, rank, possessions, etc.; reinstatement in a previous position. Now usu., re-establishment of a person's reputation, vindication of character. L15.
2 a The action of restoring something to a previous (proper) condition or status. M19. ▸**b** Restoration of a disabled person, a criminal, etc., to some degree of normal life by appropriate training etc. M20.

📖 **2b** *attrib.*: R. RENDELL Screaming like an addict in a rehabilitation centre.

rehalogenize /riːˈhalədʒ(ə)nʌɪz, -ˈheɪl-/ *verb trans.* Also **-ise**. M20.
[from RE- + HALOGEN + -IZE.]
PHOTOGRAPHY. Convert (metallic silver in a developed image) back to a silver halide.
■ **rehalogeniˈzation** *noun* M20.

rehang /riːˈhaŋ/ *verb trans.* Pa. t. & pple **-hung** /-ˈhʌŋ/. E19.
[from RE- + HANG *verb.*]
Hang (esp. a picture or curtain) again or differently.

rehash /ˈriːhaʃ/ *noun.* Also **re-hash**. M19.
[from the verb.]
The action or an instance of rehashing something; rehashed material, a thing rehashed under a different form or name.

📖 *Zigzag* Not a 60s rehash . . let's do something which is '76. D. LODGE Turpitz's last book . . . It's just a rehash of Iser and Jauss.

rehash /riːˈhaʃ/ *verb trans.* Also **re-hash**. E19.
[from RE- + HASH *verb.*]
1 Put into a new form without real change or improvement; restate (old ideas, opinions, etc.) in new language. E19.
2 Consider, mull over, or discuss (an idea, performance, etc.) afterwards. Chiefly *N. Amer.* M20.

📖 **1** A. BURGESS Cookery manuals that rehash other cookery manuals. **2** LADY BIRD JOHNSON Our houseguests . . were all gathered around . . rehashing the events of the evening.

rehear /riːˈhɪə/ *verb trans.* Pa. t. & pple **-heard** /-ˈhəːd/. L17.
[from RE- + HEAR.]
1 Hear again in a court of law or in a judicial manner. L17.
2 Hear (a sound) again. L18.
■ **rehearing** *noun* a second or subsequent hearing, esp. of a cause or appeal L17.

rehearsal /rɪˈhəːs(ə)l/ *noun.* LME.
[from next + -AL¹.]
1 Recounting, recital; repetition; enumeration; an instance of this. LME. ▸**b** *PSYCHOLOGY.* Oral or mental repetition of information it is intended to memorize. M20.
2 The practising of a play, piece of music, ceremony, etc., in preparation for public or actual performance; a

trial performance; a meeting of actors or performers for this purpose. L16.

> 📖 **1** J. S. KNOWLES A pretext for rehearsal of old grievances. *Nature* A rehearsal of the old controversy . . of a decade earlier. **2** J. AGATE Have seen no rehearsals, and have no idea how the play is getting on. *Times* Trip by Princess becomes rehearsal for Queen's visit. *attrib.*: H. ROSENTHAL The theatre's rehearsal rooms. **in rehearsal** in process of being rehearsed.

Comb.: **rehearsal dinner**, **rehearsal party** *N. Amer.* a dinner, party, held after a wedding rehearsal, usu. on the evening before the wedding.

rehearse /rɪˈhəːs/ *verb.* ME.
[Anglo-Norman *rehearser*, Old French *reherc(i)er*, perh. from *re-* RE- + *hercer* to harrow (formed as HEARSE *noun*[1]).]
1 *verb trans.* Recite or read aloud, say over; repeat after previously saying, hearing, reading, etc., (something). ME. ▸†**b** Utter, speak; state, declare (*how, that, what*, etc.). LME–M17. ▸**c** PSYCHOLOGY. Mentally or orally repeat so as to memorize (information). E20.
2 *verb trans.* Give an account of, recount, describe at length. Now *rare*. ME.
3 *verb trans.* Recount in order; enumerate. ME. ▸†**b** Mention; cite, quote. LME–L16.
4 *verb trans.* Go through or practise (a play, piece of music, ceremony, etc.) in preparation for public or actual performance. L16. ▸**b** Perform again or repeatedly as if practising. *rare*. E18. ▸**c** Exercise, train, or make proficient (a person, group, etc.) by rehearsal. M18.
5 *verb intrans.* Hold a rehearsal, practise. L17.

> 📖 **1** W. COWPER Words learned by rote a parrot may rehearse. R. H. TAWNEY In the matter of prices he . . rehearses traditional doctrines. **2** R. L. STEVENSON He rehearsed to me the course of a meeting. **3** W. COWPER I will rehearse the captains and their fleets. **4** SHAKES. *Mids. N. D.* Come, sit down, . . and rehearse your parts. E. M. FORSTER How often had Lucy rehearsed this bow, this interview! **b** E. K. KANE He kept on rehearsing his limited solfeggio. **5** W. S. MAUGHAM They rehearsed every morning.

■ **rehearser** *noun* M16.

reheat /ˈriːhiːt/ *noun.* E20.
[from the verb.]
1 The action or an instance of reheating something; *spec.* heating of the working fluid in a turbine between stages. E20.
2 AERONAUTICS. The burning of extra fuel in the exhaust of a jet engine in order to provide greater thrust, afterburning; a fitment for this, an afterburner. M20.

reheat /riːˈhiːt/ *verb.* E18.
[from RE- + HEAT *verb*.]
1 *verb trans.* Heat again. E18. ▸**b** *verb intrans.* Of cooked food: undergo heating again (*well, badly*). L20.
2 *verb trans.* AERONAUTICS. As **reheated** *ppl adjective*: equipped or augmented with reheat. M20.
■ **reheater** *noun* an apparatus for reheating something L19.

rehoboam /riːhəˈbəʊəm, riːə-/ *noun.* M19.
[*Rehoboam*, son of Solomon, King of Judah (*1 Kings* 12–14).]
†**1** A shovel hat. *rare*. Only in M19.
2 A large wine bottle between a jeroboam and a methuselah in size, equivalent to six ordinary bottles. L19.

Rehoboth /ˈriːəbɒθ/ *noun & adjective.* L19.
[A river, town, and district in Namibia, in origin a biblical place-name (*Genesis* 26:22).]
▸ **A** *noun.* A member of a people of mixed African and European descent living in Namibia. L19.
▸ **B** *adjective.* Of, pertaining to, or designating this people. M20.
■ **Rehobother** *noun* M20. **Rehoˈbothian** *noun* (*rare*) L19.

rehouse /riːˈhaʊz/ *verb trans.* E19.
[from RE- + HOUSE *verb*[1].]
Provide with new housing; house again.

rehung *verb pa. t. & pple* of REHANG.

rehydrate /riːhʌɪˈdreɪt/ *verb.* E20.
[from RE- + HYDRATE *verb*.]
1 *verb intrans.* Absorb water again, esp. after dehydration. E20.
2 *verb trans.* Add water to again after dehydration; *esp.* restore (dehydrated food) to a palatable state by adding water. M20.
■ **rehydration** *noun* M19.

rei /reɪs/ *noun.* M16.
[Back-form. from Portuguese *reis* pl. of *real* = Spanish *real* REAL *noun*[1].]
Hist. A former monetary unit of Portugal and Brazil of very small value, of which one thousand formed a milreis. Usu. in *pl.*

Reich /rʌɪk, -x/ *noun.* Pl. **-e** /-ə/. E20.
[German = kingdom, empire, State.]
Chiefly *Hist.* Any of several former German State or commonwealth, *esp.* the Third Reich (see below).

First Reich the Holy Roman Empire, 962–1806. **Second Reich** the German Empire, 1871–1918. **Third Reich** the Nazi regime, 1933–45.
Comb.: **Reichsmark** the basic monetary unit of the Reich, replaced in 1948 by the Deutschmark; **Reichsrat** [German *Rat* council: cf. BUNDESRAT] (*a*) the parliament of the Austrian part of the Habsburg Empire; (*b*) the council of the federated States of Germany from 1918 to 1933; **Reichstag** [German *Tag* diet: cf. BUNDESTAG] the diet or parliament of the North German Confederation (1867–71), of the German Empire (1871–1918), and of post-Imperial Germany until 1945; the building in Berlin in which this parliament met; **Reichsthaler** = RIX-DOLLAR 1.
¶ Of *First*, *Second*, and *Third Reich*, only *Third Reich* is standard historical terminology.

Reichert /ˈrʌɪkət, -x-/ *noun.* L19.
[Emil *Reichert* (1838–94), German food scientist.]
Used in *possess.* and *attrib.* with ref. to standard procedures for determining the proportion of volatile water-soluble fatty acids present in butter, fats, and oils. Freq. in *comb.* with another name, as *Meissl*, *Polenske*, *Wollny*.

Reichian /ˈrʌɪkɪən, -x-/ *noun & adjective.* M20.
[from Wilhelm *Reich* (see below) + -IAN.]
▸ **A** *noun.* A supporter of the theories or practices of the Austrian psychologist Wilhelm Reich (1897–1957), esp. those relating to vital or sexual energy derived from orgone or to the importance of sexual freedom. M20.
▸ **B** *adjective.* Of, pertaining to, or following Reich or his theories. L20.

reif /riːf/ *noun.* Chiefly *Scot. arch.*
[Old English *rēaf* = Old Frisian *rāf*, Old Saxon *rōf*, Old High German *roub*, from Germanic: see REAVE *verb*[1].]
†**1** Property etc. taken by force or robbery; plunder, booty. OE–M19.
2 The act of plundering; robbery. ME.

reification /ˌriːɪfɪˈkeɪʃ(ə)n, ˌreɪɪf-/ *noun.* M19.
[from Latin *res*, *re-* thing + -FICATION.]
The mental conversion of a person or abstract concept into a thing. Also, depersonalization, *esp.* (in Marxist theory) that due to capitalist industrialization in which the worker is considered as a commodity.
■ **reificatory** *adjective* of, pertaining to, or characterized by reification M20.

reify /ˈriːɪfʌɪ, ˈreɪɪ-/ *verb trans.* M19.
[formed as prec. + -FY.]
Convert (a concept etc.) mentally into a thing; materialize.
■ **reifier** *noun* M20.

reign /reɪn/ *noun.* ME.
[Old French *reigne*, (also mod.) *règne* kingdom from Latin *regnum* rel. to *rex*, *reg-* king.]
1 Royal power or rule, sovereignty; *transf.* power or influence comparable to that of a monarch. Now *rare*. ME.
2 †**a** A kingdom, a realm; a territory ruled over by a monarch. ME–E18. ▸**b** CHRISTIAN THEOLOGY. The kingdom of heaven or of God. ME. ▸**c** A place or sphere in which some specified person, thing, or quality is dominant or supreme. *poet.* Now *rare*. LME. ▸†**d** = KINGDOM *noun* 5. *rare*. M–L18.
3 The period of a monarch's rule. ME.

> 📖 **3** W. TREVOR An imposing building that suggested the reign of Victoria. ***reign of terror***: see TERROR *noun*.

Comb.: **reign mark**: on oriental ceramic ware indicating in whose reign it was made; **reign name**, **reign title** the symbolic name adopted by a Japanese or (formerly) Chinese ruler.

reign /reɪn/ *verb.* ME.
[Old French *reignier* (mod. *régner*) from Latin *regnare*, from *regnum*: see prec.]
1 *verb intrans.* Hold or exercise sovereign power in a State; rule as king or queen; hold royal office. (Foll. by *over*, †*upon*.) ME. ▸**b** *transf.* Of God, Christ, etc.: have supreme power on earth, in heaven, etc. ME.
2 *verb intrans.* Have power or predominance; dominate, have a commanding influence, (*over*); prevail. ME.
3 *verb trans.* †**a** Rule or govern (a person etc.). *rare*. Only in LME. ▸†**b** Live *out* (a number of years) as ruler. *rare*. Only in M17. ▸**c** Put *down* by reigning. *rare*. E19.
4 *verb intrans.* Be in a predominant position; be in the majority. E18.

> 📖 **1** T. E. MAY The king reigned, but his ministers governed. *fig.*: SHELLEY Truth . . enthroned o'er his lost empire reigns! **b** M. L. KING God may yet reign in the hearts of men. **2** E. BOWEN Chaos reigned on his desk. *Daily Telegraph* Quilting reigns supreme in . . fashion. H. S. STREAN She reigned over our house like a queen.

■ **reigner** *noun* (*rare*) a person who reigns, a ruler LME. **reigning** *ppl adjective* that reigns or rules; prevailing, predominating; (of a champion etc.) currently holding a title: M17.

reiki /ˈreɪki/ *noun.* L20.
[Japanese, lit. 'universal life energy'.]
A technique of complementary medicine based on the principle that the therapist can channel energy into the patient by means of touch, to activate natural healing processes and restore physical and emotional well-being.

Reil /rʌɪl/ *noun.* Now *rare*. M19.
[Johann Christian *Reil* (1759–1813), German anatomist.]
ANATOMY. ***island of Reil***, = INSULA 2.

Reilly *noun* var. of RILEY.

†**re-imbark** *verb* var. of RE-EMBARK.

reimburse /riːɪmˈbəːs/ *verb trans.* E17.
[from RE- + IMBURSE, after French *rembourser*.]
Repay (a sum of money spent); repay or recompense (a person). Also foll. by *for*, †*of*, or double obj.

> 📖 LD MACAULAY His friends . . proposed to reimburse him the costs of his trial. *refl.*: SIR W. SCOTT Resolving to reimburse himself for his losses.

■ **reimbursable** *adjective* that is to be reimbursed; repayable: L18. ˌ**reimbursaˈbility** *noun* (*rare*) the quality of being reimbursable L20. **reimburser** *noun* E17. **reimbursement** *noun* the action of reimbursing a sum or person; (a) repayment: E17.

reim-kennar /ˈrʌɪmkɛnə/ *noun. rare. pseudo-arch.* E19.
[App. formed by Sir Walter Scott on German *Reim* rhyme + *Kenner* knower.]
A person skilled in magic rhymes.

reimplace /riːɪmˈpleɪs/ *verb trans.* Now *rare*. M17.
[from RE- + IN-[2] + PLACE *verb*, after French *remplacer*.]
Put in place again; replace.

reimport /riːˈɪmpɔːt/ *noun.* L19.
[from RE- + IMPORT *noun*.]
The action or an instance of reimporting something, reimportation; a reimported item.

reimport /riːɪmˈpɔːt/ *verb trans.* M18.
[from RE- + IMPORT *verb*.]
Bring back; *spec.* import (goods) after processing from exported materials has taken place.
■ ˌ**reimporˈtation** *noun* M19.

rein /reɪn/ *noun*[1]. ME.
[Old French *rene*, *reigne*, earlier *resne*, Anglo-Norman *redne* (mod. *rêne*) from Proto-Romance, from Latin *retinere* RETAIN.]
1 *sing.* & in *pl.* A long narrow strap of leather on the bridle or bit of a horse or other animal, attached on either side of the head and used by the rider or driver to control and guide the animal. ME. ▸**b** In *pl.* A harness with a strap attached, used to restrain a young child while walking etc. E20.
2 *fig. sing.* & in *pl.* Any means of guiding or controlling; a curb, a restraint; guidance, control. ME.
3 In *pl.* The handles of a blacksmith's tongs. *rare*. M19.

> 📖 **1** ***bridle-rein***, ***leading-rein***, etc. **2** M. MCLUHAN Fathers are able to hand the reins directly to their sons. J. M. COETZEE I made a vow to keep a tighter rein on my tongue.

Phrases: ***break a horse to the rein***: see BREAK *verb*. ***draw rein***: see DRAW *verb*. **free rein**, **full rein** freedom, full scope. **give a horse the rein(s)** allow a horse free motion. **give rein (to)** allow full scope or freedom (to). ***loose rein***: see LOOSE *adjective*.
Comb.: **rein-arm**, **rein-hand** the arm or hand used to hold the reins in driving.
■ **reinless** *adjective* without a rein or reins; *fig.* unchecked, unrestrained: M16.

rein /reɪn/ *noun*[2]. LME.
[Swedish, Danish *ren*, †*reen* from Old Norse *hreinn* = Old English *hrān*; perh. of Finno-Ugric origin.]
A reindeer.

rein *noun*[3] see REINS.

rein /reɪn/ *verb.* ME.
[from REIN *noun*[1].]
†**1** *verb trans.* Tie (a horse etc.) *to* something by the rein; tie up, tether. ME–M17.
2 *verb trans.* Fit or provide with a rein or reins. Now *rare*. LME.
3 *verb trans.* Control, turn, or direct (a horse) by means of reins. LME. ▸**b** *fig.* Rule, guide, govern. L16.
4 *verb trans.* Check or stop by pulling at a rein; restrain. L15.
5 *verb trans.* & *intrans.* Pull (a horse) *up* or *back* by means of the reins; check and hold *in* in this way. M16.
6 *verb intrans.* Of a horse: bear or submit to the rein; move under the influence of the rein. Also foll. by *back*. M16.
7 *verb trans.* Keep enclosed or preserve (a field etc.) *from* stock. Also foll. by *up*. *US*. L18.

> 📖 **4** TENNYSON Edyrn rein'd his charger at her side. *fig.*: SHAKES. *L.L.L.* Sweet Lord . . rein thy tongue. **5** J. M. COETZEE At the bend in the road I rein in. *fig.*: *Times* Firms who failed to rein back costs. **6** *Horse & Tack* The Quarter Horse must rein with . . elegance.

reincarnate /riːɪnˈkɑːneɪt, -ət/ *adjective.* L19.
[from RE- + INCARNATE *adjective*.]
Incarnate again.

reincarnate /riːɪnˈkɑːneɪt/ *verb trans.* & *intrans.* M19.
[from RE- + INCARNATE *verb*.]
Incarnate anew; be reborn.

reincarnation /ˌriːɪnkɑːˈneɪʃ(ə)n/ *noun.* M19.
[from RE- + INCARNATION.]
1 Renewed incarnation; *esp.* (in some beliefs) the rebirth of a soul in a new body. M19.

2 A fresh embodiment *of* a person. L19.
■ **reincarnationism** *noun* a belief in or doctrine of reincarnation E20. **reincarnationist** *noun* a believer in reincarnation L19.

reindeer /ˈreɪndɪə/ *noun*. Pl. same, (*rare*) **-s**. LME.
[Old Norse *hreindýri*, from *hreinn* (see REIN *noun*²) + *dýr* DEER.]
1 An animal of the deer family, *Rangifer tarandus*, both males and females of which have large branching or palmated antlers, now confined to subarctic regions, where it is used domestically for drawing sledges and as a source of milk, meat, and hides. Also (chiefly *N. Amer.*) called ***caribou***. LME.
2 HERALDRY. A stag with double attires, one pair turned down. LME.
Comb.: **reindeer-fly** a botfly, *Hypoderma tarandi*, which attacks reindeer; **reindeer lichen**, **reindeer moss** a clump-forming Arctic lichen, *Cladonia rangiferina*, the chief winter food of reindeer.

reindustrialize /riːɪnˈdʌstrɪəlʌɪz/ *verb trans. & intrans.* Also **-ise**. L20.
[from RE- + INDUSTRIALIZE.]
Modernize or develop industrially; increase in industrial capacity.
■ **reindustriali'zation** *noun* M20.

Reinecke /ˈrʌɪnɛkə/ *noun*. L19.
[A. *Reinecke*, 19th-cent. German chemist.]
CHEMISTRY. **1** ***Reinecke's salt***, ***Reinecke salt***, a red crystalline complex ammonium salt whose anion consists of a chromium(III) atom coordinated to two ammonia molecules and four thiocyanate groups, used esp. to precipitate large organic cations. L19.
2 ***Reinecke's acid***, ***Reinecke acid***, the parent acid of Reinecke's salt, $H[Cr(NCS)_4(NH_3)_2]$, which can be isolated as red crystals. E20.
■ **reineckate** /ˈrʌɪnəkeɪt/ *noun* a salt of, or the anion present in, Reinecke's acid E20.

Reine Claude /rɛn klod/ *noun phr*. Pl. **-s -s** (pronounced same). M18.
[French, lit. 'Queen Claude', perh. in ref. to *Claude* (1499–1524), daughter of Louis XII and wife of François I.]
A (French) greengage.

reinette /reɪˈnɛt/ *noun*. LME.
[French *reinette*, *rainette*, perh. from *raine* tree frog (from Latin *rana* frog), from the spots in certain varieties. Cf. RENNET *noun*².]
Any of several eating apples of French origin, chiefly small and late-ripening, with dry skin and firm juicy flesh.

re infecta /reɪ ɪnˈfɛktə, riː/ *adverbial phr*. E16.
[Latin.]
With the matter unfinished or not accomplished.

reinforce /riːɪnˈfɔːs/ *noun*. M17.
[from next.]
†**1** MILITARY. A reinforcement of troops. *rare*. Only in M17.
2 A part of a gun next to the breech, made stronger than the rest in order to resist the explosive force of the powder. M18.
3 Any part added to an object to strengthen it. M19.
Comb.: **reinforce ring** a flat ring round a gun at the points where the reinforces meet or terminate.

reinforce /riːɪnˈfɔːs/ *verb*. LME.
[Alt., by assim. to RE- and *inforce* var. of ENFORCE *verb*, of RENFORCE, in military sense prob. from Italian *rinforzare*. Cf. RE-ENFORCE.]
1 *verb trans.* Make stronger, strengthen, (a material object, a quality, etc.); provide with additional support. LME. ▸**b** PSYCHOLOGY. Strengthen (a response), usu. by repetition of a painful or rewarding stimulus. E20.
2 *verb trans.* Orig. *spec.*, strengthen (a military or naval force) by adding fresh troops etc. Now also *gen.*, strengthen or increase (any group or thing) with fresh supplies or additions to the number. L15.
3 *verb trans.* **a** Add to the force or power of (an argument, statement, etc.); make more forcible or cogent. E17. ▸**b** Increase by giving fresh force to; intensify, make greater. M17.
4 *verb intrans.* Obtain reinforcements. *rare*. E17.
†**5** *verb trans.* Renew or repeat with fresh force. E–M17.
†**6** *verb trans.* Enforce again. M17–E18.

> 🕮 **1** H. SEGAL Narcissism can be reinforced as a defence against envy. V. BRAMWELL Glass lenses . . can be reinforced to make them less likely to smash. **2** A. ALISON Fresh troops . . came up to reinforce those . . exhausted.
> **3a** A. LIVINGSTONE Lou's final words on Rilke reinforce the judgement made in her book. **b** E. YOUNG-BRUEHL Illness reinforced his desire to have his daughter with him.

Phrases: **reinforced concrete** concrete with steel bars or wire mesh embedded in it to increase its tensile strength. **reinforced plastic** plastic strengthened by the inclusion of a layer of fibre, esp. of glass.
■ **reinforcer** *noun* a person who or thing which reinforces something; *spec.* in PSYCHOLOGY, that which serves to reinforce or strengthen a response: L19. **reinforcing** *noun* (*a*) the action of the verb; (*b*) strengthening material: E17.

reinforcement /riːɪnˈfɔːsm(ə)nt/ *noun*. E17.
[from prec. + -MENT.]
†**1** A renewal of force; a fresh assault. *rare* (Shakes.). Only in E17.
2 The action of reinforcing a military or naval force with fresh troops; a fresh supply of troops etc. (freq. in *pl.*). Now also, any additional supply or contribution (freq. in *pl.*). E17.
3 a Increase of strength or force; the action of strengthening or increasing something. M17. ▸**b** Increase in the intensity or amplitude of sound. L19. ▸**c** PSYCHOLOGY. The strengthening or establishing of a response through the repetition of a painful or rewarding stimulus or the satisfaction of a need. L19.
4 The action of enforcing something again. Now *rare*. M17.
5 That which reinforces something; *spec.* (*a*) the strengthening structure or material used in reinforced concrete or plastic; (*b*) a ring of paper or plastic stuck over a punched hole in paper to prevent the paper from tearing. E20.

> 🕮 **2** D. A. THOMAS Reinforcements arrived too late to prevent the French escaping. **3a** ANNE STEVENSON Having little confidence . . her ego . . craved reinforcement.
> ***c secondary reinforcement***: see SECONDARY *adjective*.

Reinga /reɪˈɪŋə/ *noun*. E19.
[Maori, lit. 'place of leaping'.]
In Maori tradition, the place where a dead person's spirit goes; the land of departed spirits.

reingestion /riːɪnˈdʒɛstʃ(ə)n/ *noun*. M20.
[from RE- + INGESTION.]
ZOOLOGY. The ingestion of soft faecal pellets to be digested again (as by rabbits); = REFECTION 4.

†**re-inlist** *verb* var. of RE-ENLIST.

reins /reɪnz/ *noun pl. arch.* In *attrib. & comb.* use in sing. **rein** (otherwise *rare*). OE.
[Old & mod. French from Latin *renes*.]
1 The kidneys. OE. ▸**b** The region of the kidneys; the loins. LME.
2 In biblical use, the seat of the feelings or affections; the heart. LME.
3 ARCHITECTURE. The parts of a vault between the crown and abutment. E18.
2 running of the reins: see RUNNING *noun*.

reinsman /ˈreɪnzmən/ *noun*. *US, Austral., & NZ*. Pl. **-men**. M19.
[from REIN *noun*¹ + -S¹ + MAN *noun*.]
A person skilled in handling reins; a driver of a horse-drawn vehicle.

reinstate /riːɪnˈsteɪt/ *verb trans.* L16.
[from RE- + INSTATE.]
1 Bring or put back (a person etc.) into a former position or condition; reinstall, re-establish, (*in* office etc.). L16.
2 Restore (a thing) to a proper state; replace. L18.
3 Restore to health. *rare*. E19.

> 🕮 **1** *Daily Express* Having sacked the party's . . chairman, he promptly reinstated him. *Independent on Sunday* Rolls-Royce decided to cancel then reinstate its staff's contracts.
> **2** *Independent* The path has been ploughed up and not reinstated.

■ **reinstatement** *noun* (*a*) the action of reinstating a person or thing; restoration, re-establishment, replacement; (*b*) MILITARY re-establishment of a serviceman in a previously held civilian job after demobilization: L18. **reinstation** *noun* reinstatement L17. **reinstator** *noun* (*rare*) a person who reinstates a person or thing L19.

reinsure /riːɪnˈʃʊə/ *verb trans. & intrans.* M18.
[from RE- + INSURE.]
Insure again; *esp.* (of an insurer) transfer (all or part of a risk) to another insurer to provide protection against the risk of the first insurance.
■ **reinsurance** *noun* (a) renewed or second insurance M18. **reinsurer** *noun* M18.

reintegrate /riːˈɪntɪgreɪt/ *verb trans.* L15.
[Var. of REDINTEGRATE after Old & mod. French *réintégrer* or medieval Latin *reintegrare*.]
1 Restore or re-establish to a position, state, etc. Now *esp.* integrate (a person) back into society. Cf. REDINTEGRATE *verb* 2. L15.
2 = REDINTEGRATE *verb* 1. E17.
■ **reinte'gration** *noun* [Old & mod. French *réintégration* or medieval Latin *reintegratio(n-)*, from *reintegrare*] L16. **reintegrative** *adjective* having the quality or tendency of reintegrating a person or thing M20.

reintermediation /ˌriːɪntəmiːdɪˈeɪʃ(ə)n/ *noun*. L20.
[from RE- + INTERMEDIATION.]
ECONOMICS. Transfer of investments and borrowings from an outside credit business back into the banking system.

reinvent /riːɪnˈvɛnt/ *verb trans.* L17.
[from RE- + INVENT.]
1 Invent (something) again. L17.
2 *refl.* Adopt a new image or identity, esp. in order to respond to a change in environment or react to opportunity. L20.

> 🕮 **1 reinvent the wheel** (esp. needlessly) make or do something which has already been made or done.
> **2** I. SINCLAIR Cook, between wives, . . decided to reinvent himself as a novelist.

■ **reinvention** *noun* the action or an act of reinventing something; a renewed invention: E18.

reinvest /riːɪnˈvɛst/ *verb*. E17.
[from RE- + INVEST.]
1 *verb trans.* **a** Invest or cover again *with* or as with a garment. E17. ▸**b** Re-endow *with* a possession, power, etc. M17.
2 *verb trans.* Replace, re-establish. Foll. by *in*. E17.
3 *verb trans. & intrans.* Invest (money) again. M19.

reis /reɪs/ *noun*. Also ***rais*** /rʌɪs/. L16.
[Arab. *ra'īs* chief from *ra's* head.]
1 The captain of a boat or ship. L16.
2 A chief, a governor. L17.
2 *Reis Effendi* *Hist.* an officer of State in the Ottoman Empire who acted as chancellor and minister of foreign affairs.

Reisner /ˈrʌɪsnə/ *noun*. M19.
[German artist in wood of the time of Louis XIV (1643–1715).]
In full ***Reisner-work***. A method of inlaying in wood of different colours.

Reissner /ˈrʌɪsnə/ *noun*. L19.
[Ernst *Reissner* (1824–78), German anatomist.]
ANATOMY. ***Reissner's membrane***, = VESTIBULAR ***membrane***.

reissue /riːˈɪʃuː, -ˈɪsjuː/ *verb & noun*. E17.
[from RE- + ISSUE *verb, noun*.]
▶ **A** *verb trans. & intrans.* Issue again or in a different form. E17.
▶ **B** *noun*. A second or renewed issue, esp. of a record or a previously published book. E19.
■ **reissuable** *adjective* (esp. of a note, bill, etc.) able to be reissued L18.

reitbok, **reitbuck** *nouns* vars. of RIETBOK.

reiter /ˈrʌɪtə/ *noun*¹. L16.
[German = rider, trooper, from *reiten* RIDE *verb*.]
Hist. A German cavalry soldier, *esp.* one who fought in the wars of the 16th and 17th cents.

Reiter /ˈrʌɪtə/ *noun*². E20.
[Hans *Reiter* (1881–1969), German bacteriologist.]
MEDICINE. ***Reiter's disease***, ***Reiter's syndrome***, a condition typically affecting young men, characterized by arthritis, conjunctivitis, and urethritis, and caused by an unknown pathogen, possibly the bacterium *Chlamydia trachomatis*.

reiterant /riːˈɪt(ə)r(ə)nt/ *adjective*. E17.
[from REITERATE *verb* + -ANT¹.]
Reiterating or repeating something.
■ **reiterance** *noun* (*rare*) repetition L19.

reiterate /riːˈɪtəreɪt/ *verb trans.* Pa. pple & ppl adjective **-ated**, (*arch.*) **-ate** /-ət/. LME.
[Latin *reiterat-* pa. ppl stem of *reiterare*: see RE-, ITERATE *verb*.]
1 Repeat (an action); do again or repeatedly. LME. ▸†**b** Repeat the use or application of (a thing, esp. a medicine). L16–L18.
2 Repeat, say again, (a statement, word, etc.); give renewed expression to (a feeling etc.). M16.

> 🕮 **1** SIR W. SCOTT The knocking was reiterated in every room. **2** E. MANNIN The question reiterated itself endlessly in his mind.

■ **reiteratedly** *adverb* in a reiterated manner, repeatedly L18. †**reiterately** *adverb* (*rare*) reiteratedly M17–L18.

reiteration /rɪˌɪtəˈreɪʃ(ə)n/ *noun*. LME.
[French *réitération* or medieval Latin *reiteratio(n-)*: see RE-, ITERATION.]
1 a Repetition of an action, process, etc. LME. ▸**b** Repetition of something said. L16.
2 PRINTING. The action of printing on the back of a sheet; an impression made in this way. *obsolete* exc. *Hist.* L17.

reiterative /rɪˈɪt(ə)rətɪv/ *noun & adjective*. E19.
[from REITERATE + -IVE.]
▶ **A** *noun*. A word expressing reiteration. E19.
▶ **B** *adjective*. Characterized by reiteration. M19
■ **reiteratively** *adverb* E17.

Reithian /ˈriːθɪən/ *adjective*. Also **-ean**. M20.
[from Lord *Reith* (1889–1971), first Director-General of the British Broadcasting Corporation, 1927–38: see -IAN, -EAN.]
Of, pertaining to, or characteristic of Lord Reith or his principles, esp. belief in the responsibility of broadcasting to enlighten and educate public taste.

reive *verb*, **reiver** *noun* see REAVE *verb*¹, REAVER.

reja /ˈrexa/ *noun*. M19.
[Spanish.]
In Spain, a wrought-iron screen or grille used to protect windows, chapel tombs, etc.

Rejang /reɪˈdʒʌŋ/ *noun*. Pl. **-s**, same. L18.
[Indonesian.]
A member of an Indonesian people of southern Sumatra; the language of this people.

For other words beginning with *re-* see the entry for **re-**

reject /ˈriːdʒɛkt, *in sense B.2 also* rɪˈdʒɛkt/ *noun & adjective.* LME.
[from next.]
▸ **A** *noun.* †**1** Refusal, denial. Only in LME.
2 †**a** A person who is rejected or cast out. M16–E17. ▸**b** A person who is rejected by others, esp. as unsuitable for some activity. E20.
3 A thing rejected as unsatisfactory or substandard. L19.

📖 **2b** R. M. WILSON The rejects, the drop-outs, the addicts and the tragedies. **3** D. CARNEGIE Lay out the rejects .. and .. put the good pieces in another pile.

▸ **B** *attrib.* or as *adjective.* **1** Of or pertaining to a reject or rejects. Also, that rejects or is rejected. M20.
2 *spec.* Designating a switch or device on a record player that causes the turntable to stop and usu. the arm to return to its rest. M20.

reject /rɪˈdʒɛkt/ *verb trans.* LME.
[Latin *reject-* pa. ppl stem of *reicere, rejicere* throw back, formed as RE- + *jacere* throw.]
1 Refuse to recognize, acquiesce in, or adopt (a command, practice, etc.); refuse to believe in (a statement etc.). LME.
†**2** Dismiss (a person) from some relation to oneself; cast out *from*. M16–E17.
3 Turn down for some purpose; put aside or throw away as useless or worthless. M16.
4 a Rebuff or snub (a person); refuse to accept or listen to. Also *spec.*, turn down as a lover or a spouse. M16. ▸†**b** Deny a request of (a person). Only in E17. ▸**c** Of a parent or guardian: spurn (a child) by denying him or her the normal emotional relationship between parent and offspring. Also, (of a child) spurn (a parent or guardian) in this way. M20.
†**5 a** Refer (a matter or person) *to* another for decision. M16–E17. ▸**b** Cast (a fault etc.) back *upon* or *to* a person. M16–L17.
6 Refuse to grant, entertain, or agree to (a request, proposal, etc.). E17.
7 a Throw back. Formerly also, drive back. *rare.* E17. ▸†**b** Cut off *from* a resource. E17–M18.
8 Expel from the mouth or stomach; vomit. M17.
9 Decline to receive or accept. L17.
10 MEDICINE. Show an immune response to (a transplanted organ or tissue) so that it fails to survive in the body of the recipient. M20.

📖 **1** LD BRAIN He rejected .. hypotheses for which there was no evidence. JULIETTE HUXLEY Mary attended church, but rejected belief in miracles. **3** L. P. HARTLEY Many were the cars he saw, inspected and rejected. **4a** MILTON Not to reject The penitent, but ever to forgive. **6** C. P. SNOW I had rejected George's proposition. **9** A. KENNY I offered the article to the Jesuit periodical *The Month*, but it was rejected as frivolous.

■ **rejectable** *adjective* E17. **rejected** *ppl adjective* refused, turned down, thrown back or out; *spec.* refused or denied the normal emotional relationship between parent and offspring: L16. **rejecˈtee** *noun* (US) a person who is rejected, esp. as unfit for military service: M20. **rejecter** *noun* a person who rejects a thing or person L16. **rejectingly** *adverb* in a rejecting manner M19. **rejective** *adjective* E19. **rejectment** *noun* (*rare*) †(*a*) (a) rejection; (*b*) rejected matter, in *pl.*, excrement: L17.

rejectament /rɪˈdʒɛktəm(ə)nt/ *noun. rare.* M17.
[mod. Latin *rejectamentum*, formed as prec. + -MENT after *additament*.]
Refuse; an item of rubbish; *esp.* rubbish cast up by the sea.

rejectamenta /rɪˌdʒɛktəˈmɛntə/ *noun pl.* E19.
[mod. Latin, pl. of *rejectamentum*: see prec.]
1 Things rejected as useless or worthless; refuse. E19.
2 Rubbish cast up by the sea. E19.
3 Excrement. Now *rare.* M19.

rejection /rɪˈdʒɛkʃ(ə)n/ *noun.* LME.
[French *réjection* or Latin *rejectio(n-)*, formed as REJECT *verb*: see -ION.]
1 a The action or process of rejecting a thing or person; the state of being rejected. LME. ▸**b** That which is rejected; *spec.* excrement. E17. ▸**c** The emotional inability to accept one's own child; the state of rejecting a child or parent or of being rejected in this way. M20.
2 ELECTRONICS. The process of attenuating an unwanted electrical signal. Freq. *attrib.* M20.
3 MEDICINE. The induction by a transplanted organ or tissue of an immune response in the recipient which prevents its survival. M20.

📖 **1a** D. LEAVITT Simplicity .. was a rejection of male standards of beauty. F. KAPLAN Pain and pleasure, rejection and acceptance, were closely allied in his .. life. **c** T. CAPOTE Deprivation may have involved .. an outright rejection of the child by one or both parents.

Comb.: **Rejection Front** an alliance of Arab groups, who refuse to consider a negotiated peace with Israel; **rejection slip** a formal notice sent by an editor or publisher to an author with a rejected manuscript or typescript.

■ **rejectionism** *noun* the policy of rejectionists L20. **rejectionist** *noun & adjective* (*a*) *noun* an Arab who refuses to accept a negotiated peace with Israel; (*b*) *adjective* of or pertaining to rejectionism or rejectionists: L20.

rejector /rɪˈdʒɛktə/ *noun.* M18.
[Latin, from *reicere, rejicere* REJECT *verb*: see -OR.]
1 = REJECTER. M18.
2 ELECTRONICS. In full ***rejector circuit***. A circuit consisting of a capacitor and an inductor connected in parallel providing very high impedance to signals of a particular frequency. E20.

rejig /ˈriːdʒɪɡ/ *noun.* M20.
[from RE- + JIG *noun*[1].]
(A) reorganization, (a) rearrangement.

rejig /riːˈdʒɪɡ/ *verb trans.* Infl. **-gg-**. M20.
[from RE- + JIG *verb*.]
Refit; repair; rearrange, reorganize, alter.

rejigger /riːˈdʒɪɡə/ *verb trans.* M20.
[from RE- + JIGGER *verb*.]
Alter, rearrange, rejig.

rejoice /rɪˈdʒɔɪs/ *verb.* ME.
[Old French *re(s)joir*, later *réjouir*, from *re-* RE- + *esjoir* (mod. *éjouir*), formed as ES- + *joir* JOY *verb*.]
†**1** *verb trans.* Enjoy by possessing; have full possession and use of; have for oneself. ME–L16.
2 *verb trans.* Gladden, make joyful, exhilarate, (a person, his or her spirits, etc.). LME.
†**3** *verb trans.* Feel joy on account of (an event etc.). LME–E17.
4 *verb intrans.* & (now *rare*) *refl.* Be full of joy; be glad or delighted; exult. (Foll. by *at, in, that, to do*, etc.) LME.
5 Foll. by *in*: possess as a source of pride; *gen.* have, possess. Freq. *joc.* M19.

📖 **2** L. WHISTLER He had just had news .. that rejoiced him. I had won the school prize. **4** E. WAUGH I rejoice in the Côte d'Azur. J. WAIN Charles found time to rejoice that he was not .. Hutchins. **5** JULIETTE HUXLEY A furniture-dealer .. who rejoiced in the name of Jarnim.

■ **rejoiceful** *adjective* (now *rare*) joyful, joyous M16. **rejoicement** *noun* (now *rare*) joy, exultation, rejoicing E16. **rejoicer** *noun* a person who rejoices; a person or thing which causes rejoicing: L16. **rejoicingly** *adverb* in a rejoicing manner M16.

rejoicing /rɪˈdʒɔɪsɪŋ/ *noun.* LME.
[from prec. + -ING[1].]
1 The action of REJOICE *verb*; an instance or expression of rejoicing; a festival, a celebration. LME. ▸**b** ***Rejoicing of the Law, Rejoicing over the Law*** [translating Hebrew SIMCHAT TORAH], the Jewish feast at the conclusion of the Feast of Tabernacles, celebrating the conclusion of the annual cycle of reading the Pentateuch. M19.
†**2** A cause or source of rejoicing or gladness. LME–E17.

rejoin /rɪˈdʒɔɪn/ *verb*[1]. LME.
[Old & mod. French *rejoign-* stem of *rejoindre*: see RE-, JOIN *verb*.]
1 *verb intrans.* LAW. Reply to a charge or pleading; *spec.* answer a plaintiff's replication. LME.
†**2** *verb intrans.* Answer. Orig. *spec.*, answer a reply. M16–M17.
3 *verb trans.* Say in answer, retort. M17.

📖 **3** D. BLOODWORTH 'You can ruddy well stop.' .. 'So can you,' rejoined Ivansong.

rejoin /riːˈdʒɔɪn/ *verb*[2]. M16.
[Old & mod. French *rejoign-* (see prec.), or from RE- + JOIN *verb*.]
1 *verb intrans.* Of things: come together again; reunite. M16.
2 *verb trans.* Put together again; reunite (people or things). (Foll. by *to, with.*) L16.
3 *verb trans.* Join (a person, company, etc.) again. E17.

📖 **3** A. KENNY To assist in the translation work, I rejoined the .. Library.

rejoinder /rɪˈdʒɔɪndə/ *noun.* LME.
[from Anglo-Norman inf. used as noun: see -ER[4]. Cf. REJOIN *verb*[1].]
1 LAW. A defendant's answer to a plaintiff's replication. LME.
2 An answer. Orig. *spec.*, an answer to a reply. M16.

📖 **2** M. WESLEY Rose gritted her teeth, biting back the rejoinder. **in rejoinder** in response.

†**rejoindure** *noun. rare* (Shakes.). Only in E17.
[App. from REJOIN *verb*[2] (infl. by prec.) or from RE- + JOINDER, with ending assim. to -URE. Cf. EMBRASURE *noun*[1].]
Reunion.

rejon /reˈxɔn/ *noun.* Pl. ***-es*** /-es/. M19.
[Spanish *rejón* lance, spear, from *rejo* pointed iron bar, *reja* ploughshare, from Latin *regula* straight piece of wood, from *regere* keep straight.]
BULLFIGHTING. A wooden-handled spear, usu. thrust at a bull from horseback.

rejoneador /rexoneaˈdɔr/ *noun.* Pl. ***-res*** /-res/. Also (fem.) ***-ra*** /-ra/, pl. ***-ras*** /-ras/. E20.
[Spanish, formed as prec.]
BULLFIGHTING. A mounted bullfighter who thrusts *rejones*.

rejoneo /rexoˈneo/ *noun.* M20.
[Spanish, formed as REJON.]
BULLFIGHTING. The art of bullfighting on horseback with *rejones*.

rejones *noun* pl. of REJON.

†**rejourn** *verb trans. & intrans.* LME–E19.
[from RE- + AD)JOURN.]
Adjourn.

rejuvenate /rɪˈdʒuːvɪneɪt/ *verb trans.* E19.
[Irreg. from RE- + Latin *juvenis* young + -ATE[3], after French *rajeunir*.]
1 Restore to youth; make young or as if young again. E19.
2 PHYSICAL GEOGRAPHY. Restore to a condition characteristic of a younger landscape. Chiefly as ***rejuvenated*** *ppl adjective.* E20.

📖 **1** I. MURDOCH He felt rejuvenated, renewed, filled with energy.

■ **rejuvenant** *adjective* (*rare*) that rejuvenates a person or thing L19. **rejuvenator** *noun* a thing which rejuvenates a person or thing L19. **rejuvenatory** *adjective* tending to cause rejuvenation L20.

rejuvenation /rɪˌdʒuːvɪˈneɪʃ(ə)n/ *noun.* L19.
[from prec. + -ATION.]
The action or process of rejuvenating something or of being rejuvenated; PHYSICAL GEOGRAPHY the development or restoration of features characteristic of a younger landscape, esp. by initiation of a new cycle of erosion.

rejuvenesce /rɪˌdʒuːvɪˈnɛs/ *verb.* L19.
[Late Latin *rejuvenescere*, formed as RE- + Latin *juvenis* young: see -ESCE.]
1 *verb intrans.* Become young again; *spec.* in BIOLOGY, (of cells) gain fresh vitality. L19.
2 *verb trans.* BIOLOGY. Impart fresh vitality to (cells). L19.

rejuvenescence /rɪˌdʒuːvɪˈnɛs(ə)ns/ *noun.* M17.
[formed as prec. + -ESCENCE.]
1 A physical, mental, or spiritual renewal of youth. M17.
2 BIOLOGY. The process by which a vegetative cell transforms itself into a new one. M19.
■ Also †**rejuvenescency** *noun* M17–L18.

rejuvenescent /rɪˌdʒuːvɪˈnɛs(ə)nt/ *adjective.* M18.
[formed as prec. + -ENT.]
That rejuvenesces.

rejuvenize /rɪˈdʒuːvɪnʌɪz/ *verb trans.* Also **-ise**. E19.
[App. from REJUVENATE: see -IZE.]
Rejuvenate, make young again.

rekindle /riːˈkɪnd(ə)l/ *verb.* L16.
[from RE- + KINDLE *verb*[1].]
1 *verb trans.* Kindle again, set fire to afresh; *fig.* inflame or rouse anew. L16.
2 *verb intrans.* Catch fire or be inflamed again. L16.

📖 **1** D. MADDEN She .. tried to rekindle the dying fire. *Times* This .. flurry of activity .. rekindled speculation.

-rel /rɛl/ *suffix.*
[Repr. Old French *-erel(le)* (mod. *-ereau*).]
Forming nouns with dim. or derog. sense, as ***cockerel***, ***doggerel***, ***mongrel***, ***scoundrel***.

relâche /rəlɑːʃ/ *noun.* Pl. pronounced same. M19.
[French.]
A period of rest, an interval; a break *from* something.

re-laid *verb pa. t. & pple* of RE-LAY.

relais /rəlɛ/ *noun.* Pl. same. M20.
[French.]
In France, a café, a restaurant, sometimes also providing overnight accommodation.

relance /rəlɑ̃s/ *noun.* Pl. pronounced same. L20.
[French.]
POLITICS. A relaunch, a revival, esp. of a policy.

relapse /rɪˈlaps, ˈriːlaps/ *noun & adjective.* LME.
[from the verb, after LAPSE *noun*, or from Old & mod. French *relaps* (noun & adjective) from medieval Latin use as noun of Latin *relapsus* pa. pple of *relabi* RELAPSE *verb*. In branch II directly from medieval Latin.]
▸ **A** *noun.* **I 1** The action or an act of falling back into heresy or wrongdoing; backsliding. LME.
2 A deterioration in a patient's condition after a partial or apparently complete recovery. L16.
3 An act of falling or sinking back again. L19.

📖 **2** P. CUTTING Bilar was cheerfully recovering ... Then he had a relapse.

▸ **II 4** A person who has fallen back into heresy or wrongdoing. Cf. RELAPSER. Now *rare.* M16.
▸ **B** *adjective.* Fallen back into a previous condition; relapsed. *rare.* M16.

relapse /rɪˈlaps/ *verb.* LME.
[Latin *relaps-* pa. ppl stem of *relabi*, formed as RE- + *labi* slip.]
†**1** *verb trans.* Renounce, leave off, (an evil practice). Only in LME.

For other words beginning with *re-* see the entry for **re-**

2 *verb intrans.* Fall back into wrongdoing; *spec.* fall back into heresy after recantation; backslide. (Foll. by *into*, †*to*.) L15.
3 *verb intrans.* Experience a return of an illness after partial or apparently complete recovery. M16.
4 *verb intrans.* Fall back or sink again into any state, practice, etc. (Foll. by *into*.) L16.
†**5** *verb trans.* Cause to relapse. M17–L18.

> 2 P. L. FERMOR The country was on the point of relapsing into heathen barbarism. **3** A. WILSON At the end of a week she became herself again, only relapsing when Kay's accident was mentioned. **relapsing fever** an infectious disease characterized by recurrent fever, caused by spirochaetes of the genus *Borrelia* and transmitted by lice and ticks. **4** P. FITZGERALD She seemed to have relapsed into her old sloth.

▪ **relapser** *noun* a person who relapses, esp. into wrongdoing E17.

relata *noun* pl. of RELATUM.

relate /rɪˈleɪt/ *noun.* Now *rare* or *obsolete*. E17.
[Latin *relatus* use as noun of pa. pple of *referre*: see next, -ATE[1]. Cf. medieval Latin *relata* (neut. pl.) relative terms.]
1 *LOGIC.* = RELATUM *noun* 1. E17.
†**2** = RELATION 5a. Only in M17.

relate /rɪˈleɪt/ *verb.* L15.
[Latin *relat-* pa. ppl stem of *referre* REFER *verb*: see -ATE[3].]
▶ **I** *verb trans.* †**1** In *pass.* Be supported or thrust *between*. *rare*. Only in L15.
2 Give an account of (an action, event, fact, †a person); recount, narrate, tell. M16.
†**3** Bring back, restore. *rare* (Spenser). Only in L16.
4 Bring (a thing or person) into relation with; establish a connection between. Foll. by *to*, *with*. L17.

> 2 T. HARDY He related . . all that he had heard. L. GARFIELD He went on to relate exploits . . he'd told of many times before. **4** HOR. WALPOLE The following paragraph, relating to Cromwell. W. R. GROVE Volta . . enabled us definitely to relate the forces of chemistry and electricity.

▶ **II** *verb intrans.* **5** *LAW.* Of a decision etc.: apply from a date earlier than that on which it was made, be retrospectively valid. L16.
6 Have reference *to*, concern. E17.
†**7** Discourse; give an account. E17–M18.
8 a Have some connection with, be connected *to*. M17. ▸**b** Feel emotionally or sympathetically involved or connected. (Foll. by *to*.) M20.

> 6 A. BELL Most of the surviving anecdotes relate to his later years. **8a** POPE The critic Eye . . examines bit by bit: How parts relate to parts. **b** *Guardian* Married people can still relate. *Underground Grammarian* Teach children to relate to the Eskimo experience by chewing blubber. R. D. LAING The ways we love, hate, and generally relate to each other.

▪ **relataˈbility** *noun* ability to be related M20. **relatable** *adjective* able to be related E19. **relater** *noun* a narrator; a historian: E17.

related /rɪˈleɪtɪd/ *adjective.* E17.
[from prec. + -ED[1].]
1 Narrated, recited. *rare*. E17.
2 Having relation; having mutual relation; connected. (Foll. by *to*, *with*.) Also as 2nd elem. of comb. M17.
3 Of a person: connected by blood or marriage. (Foll. by *to*.) E18.

> 2 *Petroleum Economist* Oil-related employment will increase as more companies enter the . . market. G. GORDON He had sited an airport and related paraphernalia close to the castle. **3** J. T. STORY She was distantly related to the Mussolini family.

▪ **relatedness** *noun* M19.

relation /rɪˈleɪʃ(ə)n/ *noun.* LME.
[Old & mod. French, or Latin *relatio(n-)*, formed as RELATE *verb*: see -ATION.]
1 The action of giving an account of something, narration, report; an instance of this, a narrative, an account. LME. ▸**b** *LAW.* An account of a complaint or claim made for the Attorney-General by a relator; the laying of an information (cf. INFORMATION 4b). M17.
2 The existence or effect of a connection, correspondence, or contrast between things; the particular way in which one thing stands in connection with another; any connection or association conceivable as naturally existing between things. LME. ▸**b** *LOGIC.* A constituent of a proposition or propositional function that predicates a connection of two or more terms. L19.
3 a The position which one person holds with another by means of social or other mutual connections; the connection of people by circumstances, feelings, etc. LME. ▸**b** In *pl.* The social contacts or ways of contact by which a person is brought into and kept in touch with another. L17. ▸**c** In *pl.* The various ways by which a country, State, etc., maintains political or economic contact with another. L18. ▸**d** *euphem.* In *pl.* Sexual intercourse, a sexual relationship. E20.
4 *LAW.* **a** Treatment of a decision etc. as applying to a date earlier than that on which it was made; retrospective validity. Chiefly in ***have relation back***. L15. ▸†**b** The regarding of two things, esp. times, as legally identical. L16–M18.
5 a A person related to another by blood or marriage; a relative. Freq. in *pl.* E16. ▸**b** Connection between people arising out of the ties of blood or marriage; kinship. M17.

> 2 E. J. HOWARD She seemed to bear no relation to the gawky . . schoolgirl he'd dimly remembered. R. SCRUTON The relation of wealth to social and political well-being. *Mind* The most obvious relation which events can enter into is that of one event being later . . than another. **3a** E. A. FREEMAN The relation of every man to his lord. **b** S. BUTLER No . . close relations had been maintained between the sisters for some years. I. MURDOCH My relations with women always followed a certain disastrous . . pattern. **c** H. KISSINGER US-Soviet relations were . . in for a long chilly period. **5a** L. M. MONTGOMERY I've never had an aunt or any relation at all. A. PRYCE-JONES To the distress of her relations, Aunt May became a Catholic. **b** S. HAYWARD The relation is as real as that of husband and wife.

Phrases: **be no relation** be unconnected by blood or marriage despite having the same surname. **external relation** *PHILOSOPHY* a connection between two things which is not intrinsic to the identity of the first thing. ***false relation***: see FALSE *adjective*. ***have relation back***: see sense 4a above. **have relation to** have reference or allusion to. ***HUMAN relations***. ***INDUSTRIAL relations***. **in relation to** as regards. **internal relation** *PHILOSOPHY* a connection between two things which is intrinsic to the identity of the first thing. ***labour relations***: see LABOUR *noun*. **make relation to** make reference or allusion to. ***poor relation***: see POOR *adjective*. ***public relations***: see PUBLIC *adjective & noun*. **with relation to** = ***in relation to*** above.
▪ **relationary** *adjective* relational M19. **relationless** *adjective* having no relations; without relation: E19.

relational /rɪˈleɪʃ(ə)n(ə)l/ *adjective & noun.* M17.
[from prec. + -AL[1].]
▶ **A** *adjective.* Of, pertaining to, or characterized by relation; having the function of relating one thing to another. M17.
relational database *COMPUTING* a database structured to store items of information in accordance with recognized relations between them. **relational grammar** a kind of generative grammar based on grammatical relations rather than syntactic structures. **relational word** *LINGUISTICS* a word expressing relation between other words; a preposition; a conjunction.
▶ **B** *noun. LINGUISTICS.* A relational word. M20.
▪ **relatioˈnality** *noun* M19. **relationally** *adverb* M19.

relationism /rɪˈleɪʃ(ə)nɪz(ə)m/ *noun. rare.* M19.
[formed as prec. + -ISM.]
PHILOSOPHY. The doctrine of the relativity of knowledge; relativism. Also, the doctrine that relations have a real existence.

relationist /rɪˈleɪʃ(ə)nɪst/ *noun.* M19.
[formed as prec. + -IST.]
Chiefly *PHILOSOPHY.* A person who maintains a theory based on a relation between ideas. Also, a person who holds that space and time are not entities but relations between entities.

relationship /rɪˈleɪʃ(ə)nʃɪp/ *noun.* M18.
[formed as prec. + -SHIP.]
The state or fact of being related; a connection, an association, *spec.* an emotional (esp. sexual) association between two people.

relative /ˈrɛlətɪv/ *adjective & noun.* LME.
[Old & mod. French *relatif*, *-ive* or late Latin *relativus* having reference or relation, formed as RELATE *verb*: see -IVE.]
▶ **A** *adjective.* **1** *GRAMMAR.* (Of a word, esp. a pronoun) relating or referring to an expressed or implied antecedent, and attaching a subordinate clause to it; (of a clause) attached to an antecedent by a relative word. LME.
2 Arising from or determined by relation to something else or to each other; comparative. Also, existing only by relation to something else; not absolute or independent. LME.
3 a Having mutual relationship; related to or connected with each other. L16. ▸**b** *MUSIC.* That is the major or minor key having the same key signature as a minor or major key. E19. ▸**c** Corresponding; *spec.* in *MILITARY*, (of a service rank) corresponding in grade to another in a different service. M19.
4 Related to the subject under discussion; pertinent, relevant. E17.
5 Of worship: offered indirectly by means of or through an image. M17.
6 Having or standing in a relation *to* something else; correspondent or proportionate *to*. M17.
7 Chiefly *PHILOSOPHY.* Of a term etc.: involving or implying relation; depending for meaning or significance on some relationship of things or people. L17.
8 Having application or reference *to*; relating *to*. M18.
9 *adverb.* In relation or proportion *to*. L18.

> 2 E. WAUGH Discussed the relative advantages of tulips and asparagus. G. W. KNIGHT The evil is not relative, but absolute. A. BROOKNER Age is relative . . you're as old as you feel. **3a** N. HAWTHORNE Several different, yet relative designs. **4** SOUTHEY All relative matter . . should go in the form of supplementary notes. **6** A. KOESTLER Positions of the planets relative to the sun. **7** J. S. MILL A name is relative when . . its signification cannot be explained but by mentioning another. **8** L. M. MONTGOMERY She said nothing to him, relative to the affair.

Special collocations: **relative address** *COMPUTING* an address which is defined with respect to another address. **relative atomic mass** the ratio of the average mass of an atom of an element to 1/12 the mass of an atom of carbon-12; abbreviation ***r.a.m.***; also called ***atomic weight***. **relative density** the ratio of the density of a substance to that of a standard substance (usu. water for a liquid or solid, air for a gas); also called ***specific gravity***. **relative deprivation** *SOCIOLOGY* social deprivation relative to the living standards of other members of one's class or social group. ***relative HUMIDITY***. **relative molecular mass** the ratio of the average mass of a molecule or entity of a substance to 1/12 the mass of an atom of carbon-12; also called ***molecular weight***. ***relative permeability***: see PERMEABILITY 2. ***relative PERMITTIVITY***. **relative pitch** (*a*) *MUSIC* the pitch of a note with respect to another; the ability to distinguish this; (*b*) *PHONETICS* the pitch of a speech sound with respect to another. **relative sexuality** *BIOLOGY* a phenomenon in which the individual or gamete of a simple organism may act as either male or female according to whether it is more or less male than the one it interacts with.
▶ **B** *noun.* **1** *GRAMMAR.* A relative word or clause; *esp.* a relative pronoun. LME.
2 a A thing standing in some relation to another. LME. ▸**b** Chiefly *PHILOSOPHY.* A relative term. M16. ▸**c** *MUSIC.* A relative major or minor key. E19.
3 A person who is connected with another or others by blood or marriage. Also, a species related to another by common origin. M17.
†**4** A relationship. *rare*. M–L17.
▪ **relatival** /rɛləˈtʌɪv(ə)l/ *adjective* (chiefly *GRAMMAR*) of or pertaining to a relative M19. **relatively** *adverb* (*a*) in a relative manner, in relation to something else; (*b*) with reference *to* something: LME. **relativeness** *noun* L17.

relativise *verb* var. of RELATIVIZE.

relativism /ˈrɛlətɪvɪz(ə)m/ *noun.* M19.
[from prec. + -ISM.]
Chiefly *PHILOSOPHY.* The doctrine or theory that knowledge, truth, morality, etc., are relative and not absolute.
cultural relativism the theory that there are no objective standards by which to evaluate a culture, and that a culture can only be understood in terms of its own values or customs; the practice of studying a culture from this viewpoint. **ethical relativism** the theory that there are no universal or objective ethical standards, and that each culture develops its own. **historical relativism** the theory that there can be no objective standard of historical truth, as the interpretation of data will be affected by subjective factors.

relativist /ˈrɛlətɪvɪst/ *noun & adjective.* M19.
[formed as prec. + -IST.]
▶ **A** *noun.* **1** *PHILOSOPHY.* A person who holds the doctrine of relativism. M19.
2 *PHYSICS.* A student or proponent of the theory of relativity. E20.
▶ **B** *attrib.* or as *adjective.* Of or pertaining to relativism; of or pertaining to the theory of relativity. E20.

relativistic /rɛlətɪˈvɪstɪk/ *adjective.* L19.
[from prec. + -IC.]
1 *PHILOSOPHY.* Of, pertaining to, or characterized by relativism. L19.
2 *PHYSICS.* **a** Pertaining to or based on the theory of relativity. E20. ▸**b** Characterized by or designating circumstances in which discrepancies between the predictions of the theory of relativity and of Newtonian mechanics or classical electromagnetism become significant, esp. those involving speeds approaching that of light or large gravitational potentials. M20.

> 2b *Discovery* The principles of thermodynamics as they apply in a relativistic universe.

▪ **relativistically** *adverb* M20.

relativitist /rɛləˈtɪvɪtɪst/ *noun.* M20.
[from RELATIVITY + -IST.]
PHYSICS. = RELATIVIST *noun* 2.

relativity /rɛləˈtɪvɪti/ *noun.* M19.
[from RELATIVE + -ITY.]
1 The fact or condition of being relative, relativeness. M19.
2 *PHYSICS.* The dependence of observations on the relative motion of the observer and the observed object; the branch of physics that deals with the description of space and time allowing for this. L19.
2 general theory of relativity, **general relativity** a theory extending the special theory of relativity to systems accelerating with respect to one another, covering gravitation and the curvature of space–time. **special theory of relativity**, **special relativity** a theory based on the principles that all uniform rectilinear motion is relative and that light has the same speed in a vacuum for all observers, regarding space–time as a four-

dimensional continuum, and modifying previous conceptions of geometry.

relativize /ˈrɛlətɪvʌɪz/ *verb trans.* Also **-ise**. M20.
[from RELATIVE + -IZE.]
1 *PHYSICS.* Treat according to the principles of the theory of relativity. M20.
2 Chiefly *LINGUISTICS.* Make relative; make relative to or dependent on something else. M20.
■ **relativiˈzation** *noun* E20. **relativizer** *noun* a person who or thing which relativizes something; *spec.* (*LINGUISTICS*) a relative word or form: M20.

relator /rɪˈleɪtə/ *noun.* L16.
[Latin, formed as RELATE *verb*: see -OR.]
1 = RELATER. L16.
2 *LAW.* A person who recounts a complaint or claim for an information by the Attorney-General (cf. RELATION 1b); *Hist.* a person who filed an application for a *quo warranto* or mandamus, or on whose behalf this was done. E17.
3 *GRAMMAR.* An element of a sentence, esp. a preposition, which relates one phrase to another. M20.

relatum /rɪˈlɑːtəm, -ˈleɪtəm/ *noun.* Pl. **-ta** /-tə/. L19.
[Latin, neut. pa. pple of *referre* REFER.]
1 *LOGIC.* Each of two or more objects between which a relation subsists. Cf. REFERENT *noun* 3. L19.
2 *GRAMMAR.* The object of a prepositional phrase. *rare.* M20.

relaunch /ˈriːlɔːn(t)ʃ/ *noun.* L20.
[from RE- + LAUNCH *noun*¹.]
A renewed launch, esp. of a business or new product.

relaunch /riːˈlɔːn(t)ʃ/ *verb trans. & intrans.* M18.
[from RE- + LAUNCH *verb*.]
Launch again.

relax /rɪˈlaks/ *noun.* E17.
[from the verb.]
(A) relaxation.

relax /rɪˈlaks/ *adjective. rare.* E17.
[from the verb, after LAX *adjective*.]
Lax, lacking in strictness.

relax /rɪˈlaks/ *verb.* LME.
[Latin *relaxare*, formed as RE- + *laxus* LAX *adjective*.]
▸**I** *verb trans.* **1** †**a** Make less compact or dense; loosen or open up by separation of parts. LME–L17. ▸**b** Make (a part of the body) less stiff or rigid by reducing muscle tension; make (a muscle) less tense; make loose or slack; *spec.* (chiefly *ENTOMOLOGY*) make (a specimen) flexible prior to setting. E17. ▸**c** Diminish the force or tension of; *esp.* loosen (one's grasp). L18.
2 Free or discharge (a person) from restraint, legal process, or penalty (*spec.* that of diligence or outlawry). Also, dismiss (a legal process). *Scot. obsolete* exc. *Hist.* LME. ▸**b** *Hist.* [Spanish *relaxar*.] Of the Inquisition: hand over (a heretic) for execution. M19.
3 a Make less severe, strict, or exacting; make less formal; mitigate, tone down. Also, make less tense or anxious. M17. ▸**b** Make less zealous or forceful. *rare.* M17. ▸**c** *refl.* Take recreation; rest. *rare.* M18. ▸**d** Allow (one's efforts, attention, etc.) to slacken or diminish. L18.

> **1b** J. TYNDALL The heat relaxed my muscles. **c** JOHN BROOKE In the last years . . the late King had relaxed his hold on the reins. **3a** J. CARY Even in . . intimate relations she did not relax her dignity. J. HERRIOT The iron discipline was relaxed . . to let the Yuletide spirit run free. **d** J. GALSWORTHY She never moved from his room, never relaxed her noiseless vigilance.

▸**II** *verb intrans.* **4** Become loose or slack; become less tense or rigid. Also foll. by *from, into.* LME.
5 Abate in degree or force. *rare.* E18.
6 a Become less severe, strict, or exacting. M18. ▸**b** Of a person: become less stiff or formal; assume a more open or friendly manner. Also (freq. in *imper.*), become less tense or anxious. M19.
7 Cease one's efforts; take recreation; rest. Also foll. by *from, into.* M18.
8 Chiefly *PHYSICS.* Return towards a state of equilibrium. M20.

> **4** DICKENS His features would relax into a look of fondness. H. ROTH His body relaxed, yielding to the rhythm. **5** T. COLLINS The hard swelling . . seemed to have relaxed a little. **6b** A. CHRISTIE She had been strung up . . never relaxing for a moment. *Woman* Relax, darling. Our problem is soon to be solved. **7** C. P. SNOW They relaxed into their long and restful evening. *Rage* Us tender souls at the office like nothing better than to relax . . in front of the gogglebox.

■ **relaxed** *adjective* freed from restraint; diminished in strictness, firmness, etc.; *esp.* at ease, unperturbed, free from tension: LME. **relaxedly** *adverb* E19. **relaxedness** *noun* M19. **relaxer** *noun* L17. **relaxity** *noun* (*rare*) relaxedness, the state of being relaxed L18.

relaxant /rɪˈlaks(ə)nt/ *adjective & noun.* L18.
[Latin *relaxant-* pres. ppl stem of *relaxare*: see prec., -ANT¹.]
▸**A** *adjective.* Causing or distinguished by relaxation. L18.
▸**B** *noun.* A drug or practice that reduces tension and produces relaxation, esp. of muscles. M19.

relaxation /riːlakˈseɪʃ(ə)n/ *noun.* LME.
[Latin *relaxatio(n-)*, from *relaxat-* pa. ppl stem of *relaxare*: see RELAX *verb*, -ATION.]
1 a Partial (or, formerly, complete) remission of a penalty, burden, duty, etc. Formerly also, the document granting this. LME. ▸**b** Release from a legal penalty, *spec.* that of diligence or outlawry. *Scot. obsolete* exc. *Hist.* M16. ▸**c** Release from captivity. E17. ▸**d** *Hist.* The process of handing over a heretic to the Inquisition for judgement and execution. Cf. RELAX *verb* 2b. E19.
2 a Release from mental or physical tension, esp. by recreation or rest. M16. ▸**b** *PHYSIOLOGY.* The loss of tension in a part of the body, *spec.* in a muscle when it ceases to contract; the state of a resting muscle. E17.
3 Diminution or reduction of strictness or severity. E17.
4 Abatement of force or intensity. L17.
5 Chiefly *PHYSICS.* The gradual return of a system towards equilibrium; the reduction of stress caused by gradual plastic deformation in material held at constant strain. Freq. *attrib.* M19.
6 *ENGINEERING & MATH.* A method of solving a set of simultaneous equations by guessing a solution and successively modifying it to accord with whichever equation or constraint is currently least closely satisfied. Freq. *attrib.* M20.

> **3** D. M. THOMAS I mixed a little painting with my poetry, just as relaxation. P. DALLY The beneficial effects of opium are relaxation and tranquillity. **4** F. SPALDING Some penalties . . disappeared and there was a slight relaxation of the rules. **5** C. PEBODY Stuart complains . . of his relaxation of energy.

Comb.: **relaxation oscillator** *ELECTRICITY*: in which sharp, sometimes aperiodic oscillations result from the rapid discharge of a capacitor or inductance; **relaxation time** *PHYSICS* the time taken for a system to return to a state of equilibrium; *spec.* (when the process of return is exponential) the time taken for the deviation from equilibrium to be reduced by a factor *e* (approx. 2.718).

relaxative /rɪˈlaksətɪv/ *adjective. rare.* E17.
[from RELAX *verb* after LAXATIVE.]
Tending to relax; of the nature of relaxation. *rare.*

relaxin /rɪˈlaksɪn/ *noun.* M20.
[from RELAX *verb* + -IN¹.]
PHYSIOLOGY. A hormone secreted by the placenta that causes the cervix to dilate and prepares the uterus for the action of oxytocin during labour.

relay /ˈriːleɪ/ *noun.* LME.
[Old French *relai* (mod. *relais*), from *relayer*: see next.]
1 *HUNTING.* A set of fresh hounds posted to replace a tired set in a chase for a deer; *spec.* a set released after the first hounds have come up. Cf. VAUNTLAY. Now *rare* or *obsolete.* LME.
2 a A set of fresh horses posted at various stages along a route to replace a tired set. E17. ▸**b** The place where such a set is posted. E18. ▸**c** A series of motor vehicles intended to cover a prescribed route; an operation involving this. M20. ▸**d** *BRIDGE.* In full ***relay bid***. A low bid designed to invite the bidder's partner to describe his or her hand. M20.
3 a A set of people, esp. workers, appointed to relieve others or to operate in shifts. E19. ▸**b** In full ***relay race***. A race of team-members in competing sequence; *spec.* one performed by teams of usu. four in which each member in turn covers part of the distance, and a baton is often passed from one member to the next. L19.
4 a Orig., a device used in telegraphy to enable a weak signal to initiate a stronger one, for onward transmission or to actuate a recording instrument; a repeater. Now, any electrical device, usu. incorporating an electromagnet, whereby a current or signal in one circuit can open or close another circuit. M19. ▸**b** An installation or satellite which receives, amplifies, and retransmits a transmission or broadcast. Freq. *attrib.* E20. ▸**c** A message or broadcast which has been relayed. E20.

> **2a** H. ALLEN They galloped south along the post, pausing only for relays. **3a** HANNAH MORE Relays of musicians . . to sing the whole Psalter. **b** *Times* The main hopes . . lie in the men's four by 100 and four by 400 metres relays.

Comb.: ***relay bid***: see sense 1d above; ***relay race***: see sense 3b above; **relay rack** a rack on which relays are mounted, esp. in a telephone exchange; **relay station** a radio station that serves as a relay; **relay valve** *ENGINEERING* a valve in which fluid flow is controlled by a diaphragm actuated by a weep derived from the main flow.

relay /rɪˈleɪ, ˈriːleɪ/ *verb*¹. LME.
[from the noun or from Old & mod. French *relayer*, formed as RE- + *laier*, ult. repr. Latin *laxare*: see LEASE *noun*³.]
†**1** *verb trans. & intrans. HUNTING.* Release (fresh hounds) on the track of a deer; hunt (a deer) with relays. Only in LME.
2 *verb trans.* Arrange in relays; provide with or replace by relays. LME.
3 *verb intrans.* Obtain a fresh relay (of horses). E19.
4 *verb trans.* Receive and pass on or retransmit (a broadcast, message, information, etc.). L19.

> **4** R. G. COLLINGWOOD The wireless relaying evensong from Canterbury Cathedral. I. MCEWAN They relayed Radio One through speakers. R. JAFFE She relayed all the juicy stories to Alexander.

relay *verb*² var. of RE-LAY.

re-lay /riːˈleɪ/ *verb trans.* Also **relay**. Pa. t. & pple **-laid** /-ˈleɪd/. L16.
[from RE- + LAY *verb*¹.]
Lay again or differently; *esp.* lay down again (something previously taken up).

release /rɪˈliːs/ *noun.* ME.
[Old French *reles*, from *relesser*: see next.]
1 Deliverance or liberation from trouble, pain, sorrow, etc.; liberation from emotional or physical tension. ME.
2 a Deliverance or liberation from some obligation, duty, or demand. ME. ▸†**b** Remission *of* a tax, debt, obligation, etc. LME–M17. ▸**c** A written discharge from a debt or obligation; an acquittance, a receipt. LME. ▸**d** A written authorization or permission for publication, esp. from a copyright owner or person depicted in a photograph. M20.
3 *LAW.* The action of conveying an estate or right to another or of legally disposing of it; a deed or document effecting this. ME.
4 a The action of freeing or fact of being freed from restraint or imprisonment; permission to go free. Also, a document giving formal discharge from custody. L16. ▸**b** The action of letting go something fixed or confined in a mechanism; a device, as a handle or catch, by which this is effected. L19. ▸**c** *TELEPHONY.* The action of freeing for further use apparatus or circuitry which has been engaged. L19. ▸**d** *PHONETICS.* The action or manner of ending the obstruction involved in the articulation of a stop consonant (by which the plosion is produced). E20. ▸**e** A passage of jazz music that links repetitions of a main melody. Chiefly *US.* M20.
5 a The action of making available for publication a document or piece of information; the document etc. itself. E20. ▸**b** The action of making a film, recording, etc., available to the public; the film, recording, etc., itself. E20.

> **1** G. GREENE What a sense of release you must have experienced when you set fire to Thomas Earl Parkman, junior. DAY LEWIS The release of first love long dammed up. M. HOLROYD From his innate melancholy he sought release through multifarious love-affairs. ***happy release***: see HAPPY *adjective.* **4** J. HALPERIN Upon Gissing's release from prison . . he returned to Wakefield. **b** K. ROOS He buzzed the button of the apartment; . . the click of the release sounded immediately. *Antiquity* Upon release this energy is transferred to the arrow. *attrib.*: J. AIKEN It is quite safe, unless anyone presses the release spring. **5a** S. BOOTH The release also said the tour 'will take in 13 cities'. **b** C. CHAPLIN With the release of my first film . . the debt was wiped out.

Comb.: **release agent** a substance applied to a surface in order to prevent adhesion to it; **release note** a note authorizing the release of something, *spec.* (part of) an aircraft as fit for service.
■ **releasable** *adjective* E17.

release /rɪˈliːs/ *verb trans.* ME.
[Old French *relesser*, *relaiss(i)er* from Latin *relaxare* RELAX *verb*.]
▸**I** †**1** Withdraw, recall, or revoke (a sentence, punishment, condition, etc.). ME–L17.
†**2** Relieve or remove (pain, trouble, etc.). ME–L16.
3 Chiefly *LAW.* Remit or discharge (a debt, tax, etc.). Formerly also, discharge (a vow or task). ME.
4 a Give up, relinquish, surrender (esp. a right or claim). LME. ▸**b** Chiefly *LAW.* Make over or transfer (property or money) to another. LME. ▸**c** Of an authority: make publicly available (requisitioned property etc.); return to general use. E20.
†**5** Relax, moderate, mitigate. LME–L17.
▸**II 6** Set or make free; liberate; deliver from pain, an obligation, etc.; free from physical restraint, confinement, or imprisonment; allow to move, drop, or operate, by removing a restraining part; let go (one's hold etc.). (Foll. by *from.*) ME. ▸**b** Give free rein to (an emotional or instinctual drive); ease (tension). M20.
7 Publish or make available for publication (a document, piece of information, etc.); make available to the public (a film, recording, etc.). E20.

> **6** H. REED The safety-catch . . is . . released with an easy flick of the thumb. W. GASS Fender's fork poked through the crust of his pie, releasing steam. A. KENNY I had not been released from the Church's law of celibacy. M. DAS It should not be too difficult to get Sudhir Babu released on bail. I. MURDOCH He released Patrick's hand and stood up. **b** L. NKOSI Something was released within her that . . transformed her. **7** *Blitz* Too many records get released and the distribution network gets clogged up. P. D. JAMES We shan't release any forensic information.

Comb.: **releasing factor** *PHYSIOLOGY* any of several oligopeptides released from the hypothalamus which promote the release of a specific hormone from the adenohypophysis.
■ **releaˈsee** *noun* (*a*) *LAW* (now *rare*) a person to whom an estate is released; (*b*) *US* a person released from confinement or imprison-

For other words beginning with *re-* see the entry for **re-**

ment: E18. **releasement** *noun* (now *rare*) release from prison, obligation, debt, trouble, etc. M16. **releasor** *noun* (chiefly LAW) a person who releases property, a claim, etc., in favour of another E17.

releaser /rɪˈliːsə/ *noun*. LME.
[from RELEASE *verb* + -ER¹.]
A person who or thing which releases something; *spec.* (*a*) in dairy farming, a device which removes milk from the vessel in which the output of a milking machine accumulates; (*b*) ZOOLOGY a sign stimulus, *esp.* one that acts between animals of the same species; (*c*) PHYSIOLOGY a pheromone that results in a rapid response not mediated by hormones (cf. *primer*); (*d*) PSYCHOLOGY an external stimulus which produces a specific non-reflex behavioural response.

relection /rɪˈlɛkʃ(ə)n/ *noun*. Long *rare*. E17.
[Latin *relect-* ppl stem of *relegere* read again: see -ION. Cf. LECTION.]
The action of reading something again; a correction made upon re-reading something.

relegate /ˈrɛlɪɡeɪt/ *verb trans.* LME.
[Latin *relegat-* pa. ppl stem of *relegare* send away, refer, formed as RE- + *legare* send: see LEGATE *noun*, -ATE³.]
1 Send (a person) into exile; banish *to* a particular place. Cf. RELEGATION 1a. LME.
2 a Banish or dismiss to some unimportant or obscure place; consign *to* a usu. inferior place or position. L18. ▸**b** SPORT. Demote (a team, esp. a football team) to a lower division of a league. E20.
3 a Refer (a matter) *to* another for decision or implementation. M19. ▸**b** Refer (a person) *for* something *to* some person or thing. L19.

> 1 H. B. TRISTRAM The fortress to which Herod relegated his wife. **2a** A. BURGESS He is, like Tolstoy or Hardy, too large a writer to be relegated to a slot. R. FRASER She was considered exceedingly ignorant and relegated to the lowest class. **b** *Times* Swansea . . moved into third place after beating relegated Bristol Rovers.

■ **relegable** *adjective* able to be relegated or referred L19.

relegation /rɛlɪˈɡeɪʃ(ə)n/ *noun*. LME.
[Latin *relegatio(n-)*, formed as prec: see -ATION.]
1 a Banishment; a state of temporary exile; *spec.* in ROMAN HISTORY, banishment to a certain place or distance from Rome for a limited time and without loss of civil rights. LME. ▸**b** SPORT. The demotion of a team, esp. a football team, to a lower division of a league. E20.
2 The action of referring or consigning a thing to another for some purpose. M19.

> **1b** *attrib.*: *Tennis* There's more pressure in a relegation match because you're faced with . . going down to the second tier.

relent /rɪˈlɛnt/ *noun*. *rare*. L16.
[from the verb.]
†**1** Slackening of speed. Only in L16.
2 Relenting, giving way. L16.

relent /rɪˈlɛnt/ *verb*. LME.
[Ult. from Latin *re-* RE- + *lentare* bend, (in medieval Latin) soften, from *lentus* flexible: cf. Latin *relentescere* slacken.]
†**1** *verb intrans.* Melt under the influence of heat; become liquid; dissolve. LME–L18. ▸**b** Become soft or moist. Also, (of a colour) fade. M16–E17.
†**2** *verb trans.* Dissolve; melt; make soft. LME–M17. ▸**b** Soften (one's heart, mind, etc.); cause to soften in temper. E16–L18.
3 *verb intrans.* Soften in temper; become more gentle or forgiving; abandon a harsh intention; become less severe. E16. ▸†**b** Yield; give up a previous determination or obstinacy. E16–M17.
†**4** *verb trans.* Abate; slacken. M–L16. ▸**b** Relinquish, abandon. M16–L17.
†**5** *verb trans.* Repent (an action etc.). *rare* (Spenser). Only in L16.

> **3** S. BEDFORD My mother sent him packing . . . Then relented; then sent him off again.

■ **relenting** *verbal noun* the action of the verb; an instance of this: L16. **relentingly** *adverb* in a relenting manner E17. **relentment** *noun* (now *rare*) relenting E17.

relentless /rɪˈlɛntlɪs/ *adjective*. L16.
[from prec. + -LESS.]
Incapable of relenting; pitiless; insistent and uncompromising. Also, sustained, continuous, oppressively constant.

> C. EKWENSI Mrs Nwuke hated her with a relentless hatred. A. CROSS Forgive me . . if I seem a bit relentless in my questions.

■ **relentlessly** *adverb* E19. **relentlessness** *noun* E19.

†**reles** *noun* see RELISH *noun*.

re-let /ˈriːlɛt/ *noun*. M20.
[from RE- + LET *noun*².]
A property that is re-let.

re-let /riːˈlɛt/ *verb trans.* Infl. **-tt-**. Pa. t. & pple **-let**. L18.
[from RE- + LET *verb*¹.]
Let (a property) for a further period or to a new tenant.

relevance /ˈrɛlɪv(ə)ns/ *noun*. M17.
[from RELEVANT + -ANCE.]
Relevancy. Now also *spec.*, pertinency to important current issues.

> *International Affairs* The . . proposals for improving NATO's capacity for dealing with extraregional developments have a special relevance today.

relevancy /ˈrɛlɪv(ə)nsi/ *noun*. M16.
[from RELEVANT + -ANCY.]
The quality or fact of being relevant.

relevant /ˈrɛlɪv(ə)nt/ *adjective*. E16.
[medieval Latin *relevant-*, *-ans* pres. pple of Latin *relevare* raise up, relieve, (in medieval Latin) take up, take possession of (a fief), pay a relief for: see -ANT¹.]
1 SCOTS LAW. Legally pertinent or sufficient. E16.
2 Bearing on, connected with, or pertinent to the matter in hand. (Foll. by *to*.) M16.

> **2** J. G. COZZENS Why they are no good is another matter, not relevant at this point. P. GARDINER He passed all the relevant examinations with distinction.

■ **relevantly** *adverb* M16.

†**relevate** *verb trans.* Pa. pple & ppl adjective **-ate**, **-ated**. L16.
[Latin *relevat-* pa. ppl stem of *relevare* relieve: see -ATE³.]
1 Raise the spirits of; restore to cheerfulness. L16–E18.
2 Raise, elevate. E17–M18.
■ †**relevation** *noun* LME–M17.

relevé /rələˈveɪ/ *noun*. E19.
[French = raised up.]
1 A course of a meal; a remove. *arch.* E19.
2 BALLET. A step in which the body is raised on half or full point. M20.
3 ECOLOGY. An enumeration of the species and environmental factors in a small stand of vegetation, taken as a sample of a wider area; the stand of vegetation itself. M20.

relexification /ˌriːlɛksɪfɪˈkeɪʃ(ə)n/ *noun*. M20.
[from RE- + Greek *lexis* word + -FICATION.]
LINGUISTICS. The process of replacing a word or group of words in one language with a corresponding word or group of words from another language, or of introducing into one language a word or group of words from another language, without grammatical alteration of the introduced terms.

relexify /riːˈlɛksɪfʌɪ/ *verb trans.* M20.
[formed as prec. + -FY.]
LINGUISTICS. Subject (a language) to the process of relexification.

reliable /rɪˈlʌɪəb(ə)l/ *adjective & noun*. M16.
[from RELY *verb* + -ABLE.]
▶ **A** *adjective*. **1** That may be relied on; in which reliance or confidence may be put; trustworthy, safe, sure. M16.
2 STATISTICS. Yielding concordant results when repeated. M20.

> **1** M. KEANE She had an entirely accurate and reliable memory. S. BELLOW He . . has been a reliable son, very much alive to his duties. A. C. CLARKE The fence is practically one hundred per cent reliable—there's been no major breakdown for three years.

▶ **B** *ellipt.* as *noun*. A reliable person, animal, or thing. Usu. in *pl.* L19.
■ **relia'bility** *noun* (*a*) the quality of being reliable, reliableness; (*b*) STATISTICS the extent to which a measurement made repeatedly in identical circumstances will yield concordant results; ***reliability coefficient***, a measure of this, *esp.* the coefficient of correlation between two sets of measurements of the same set of quantities: E19. **reliableness** *noun* M19. **reliably** *adverb* M19.

reliance /rɪˈlʌɪəns/ *noun*. E17.
[from RELY *verb* + -ANCE.]
1 The action or fact or (formerly) an act of relying *on*, *upon*, or *in* something or someone; the condition or character of being reliant; dependence, confidence, trust. E17.
2 A person or thing on which one relies or depends. L18.

> **1** TENNYSON Those in whom he had reliance . . Sold him unto shame. R. L. STEVENSON I give these two versions as I got them. But I place little reliance on either. **2** E. K. KANE Dogs, the indispensable reliance of the party.

reliant /rɪˈlʌɪənt/ *adjective*. M19.
[formed as prec. + -ANT¹.]
Having reliance (*on*).

relic /ˈrɛlɪk/ *noun & adjective*. Also †**relique**. ME.
[Old & mod. French *relique* (orig. pl.) from Latin RELIQUIAE.]
▶ **A** *noun*. **1** A part of the body, clothing, or belongings of a saint, martyr, or other deceased holy person which is carefully preserved as an object of veneration, esp. in the Roman Catholic and Orthodox Churches. ME. ▸**b** Something kept as a remembrance or souvenir of a person, thing, or place; a memento. E17.
2 (A part of) the body of a deceased person, a person's remains. Usu. in *pl.* ME. ▸**b** An old person. Usu. with *old* or similar adjective *colloq.* M19.
3 Something which remains or is left behind, esp. after destruction or decay; a fragment, remnant, or residue *of* something. Usu. in *pl.* ME.
4 Something surviving as a memorial *of* an event, period, people, etc; a surviving trace *of* some practice, idea, quality, etc. L15. ▸**b** BIOLOGY. A relict species. M20. ▸**c** LINGUISTICS. A relict form. M20.
5 Any object interesting because of its antiquity or associations with the past. L15.

> **1** N. MONSARRAT The relic . . was a minuscule fragment of bone from the forearm of the blessed Saint. **b** *Classical Quarterly* Before she was to be sacrificed she gave her mother locks of hair as a relic. **2** SHELLEY All round The mouldering relics of my kindred lay. **3** QUILLER-COUCH The relics of supper lay on the . . table. R. FRAME Beneath the temple may lie relics of an earlier pagan religious site. **4** C. HARE Titles and peerages are interesting relics of the past. JO GRIMOND A hundred or so dairy farms, relics of the wars when the services needed milk. **5** SHAKES. *Twel. N.* What's to do? Shall we go see the reliques of this town?

Comb.: **relic area** LINGUISTICS a region noted for the survival of relict forms; **Relic Sunday** (*obsolete* exc. *Hist.*) the third Sunday after Midsummer, on which the relics preserved in a church were specially venerated.
▶ **B** *attrib.* or as *adjective*. Chiefly BIOLOGY, GEOLOGY, & LINGUISTICS. = RELICT *adjective* 2. L19.

relicary *noun* see RELIQUARY.

relict /ˈrɛlɪkt/ *noun*. LME.
[Latin *relictus* pa. pple of *relinquere* RELINQUISH.]
1 The widow *of* a man; a widow. Now *arch.* exc. *Anglo-Irish*. LME.
†**2** A reliquary. *Scot.* E16–L17.
3 = RELIC *noun* 1, 2. Now *rare* or *obsolete*. M16.
4 = RELIC *noun* 3, 4, 5. Now *rare* exc. as below. M16.
5 a Chiefly BIOLOGY & GEOLOGY. A species, structure, etc., surviving from a previous age or in changed circumstances after the disappearance of related species, structures, etc. E20. ▸**b** LINGUISTICS. A dialect, word, etc., that is a survival of otherwise archaic or old forms. M20.

> **1** E. LONGFORD Mollie . . was now venerated as Erskine's relict. **5a** *Nature* Rare plant species are often relicts surviving in restricted ecological niches.

relict /ˈrɛlɪkt/ *adjective*. LME.
[formed as the noun; in recent use prob. attrib. use of the noun.]
†**1** Left behind, remaining; left by death, surviving; (of land) uncultivated, deserted. LME–L17.
2 Chiefly BIOLOGY, GEOLOGY, & LINGUISTICS. That is a relict; surviving from a previous age or in changed circumstances after the disappearance of related forms. L19.

> **2** H. C. DARBY Another example of relict names is found on Dunsmore Heath. *Scientific American* Relict populations of . . salmon survive in lakes . . landlocked for thousands of years.

relief /rɪˈliːf/ *noun*¹. ME.
[Anglo-Norman *relef*, Old & mod. French *relief*, from *relever* RELIEVE.]
1 LAW. A payment made to the overlord by the heir of a feudal tenant on taking up possession of the vacant estate. (*obsolete* exc. *Scot.*) ME.
2 The alleviation of or deliverance from pain, distress, anxiety, monotony, etc.; the feeling accompanying this; mental relaxation. Also, an instance of this. LME. ▸**b** A thing providing such alleviation; a feature which breaks up visual or other monotony. E18.
3 Assistance given to a person or persons in circumstances of need, danger, war, famine, or other difficulty; aid, help, succour; *spec.* financial and other assistance given to the poor from State or local community funds. LME. ▸**b** Reinforcement or military support to those besieged or threatened; *esp.* the raising of a siege *of* a besieged town etc. M16. ▸†**c** A fresh supply of some article of food or drink. L16–E18.
†**4** HUNTING. The seeking of food by a hare or deer. LME–M17.
5 LAW. Release from or remission of an obligation or imposition; *spec.* (*Scot.*) a right to reimbursement of the expenses incurred by some obligation. L15.
6 Release from some occupation or post; *spec.* the replacement of a person or persons on duty by another or others. E16. ▸**b** A person or body of people relieving another or others in this way; *esp.* a soldier or body of soldiers relieving another soldier or company on guard. E18. ▸**c** A dish succeeding another. Now *rare*. L18. ▸**d** A thing supplementing another in providing a service; *esp.* a train, bus, etc., providing an extra service at peak times. Usu. *attrib.* L19.
7 Alleviation *of* some pain, burden, etc., esp. taxation; *spec.* (a) remission of income tax due on a proportion of earned income. E16.

8 (**R-**.) A Scottish Presbyterian Church founded in 1761 in protest against the General Assembly and later amalgamated in the United Presbyterian Church. Chiefly as ***Relief Church***, ***Church of Relief*** *obsolete* exc. *Hist.* M18.

> 🕮 **2** L. M. Montgomery It would be a relief to sit down and have a good cry. R. Dahl Mrs Pratchett was alive! The relief was tremendous. J. Briggs To her great relief she . . had not been sent back to school. R. Dinnage Some just hoped for relief from misery. **b** H. Martineau A clump of beeches . . were a relief to the eye. ***comic relief***: see COMIC *adjective*. **3** Shakes. *Hen. V* To relief of lazars and weak age . . A hundred alms-houses. Goldsmith Prudence once more comes to my relief. A. Lewis He got . . the dole and then parish relief. *Sunday Telegraph* School-children are to be asked to contribute money for famine relief. ***relief agency***, ***relief organization***, ***relief work***, ***relief worker***, etc. **on relief** (chiefly *US*) receiving State assistance because of (financial) need. **b** Gibbon Stilicho . . advanced . . to the relief of the faithful city. P. Warner He built two temporary wooden forts to cut off the castle from any external relief. **6 in relief** *BASEBALL* as relief pitcher. **b** P. Matthiessen My relief on bow watch . . failed to appear. **d** D. Lodge The coach had broken down . . and a relief vehicle had taken an hour to arrive. *Railway Magazine* The 6.59 p.m . . . operated . . as a relief to the 7.10 p.m. from Hastings. **7** P. O'Donnell If it's a phony charity account . . they probably get tax relief. *Money & Family Wealth* Make full use of reliefs and allowances . . at . . current income tax rates.

Comb.: ***Relief Church***: see sense 8 above; **relief pitcher** *BASEBALL*: who relieves another pitcher, *spec.* the opening pitcher, in a match; **relief road**: designed to divert traffic from congested areas; **relief roll** *US* a list of people receiving State relief; **relief valve**: serving to relieve excess pressure in a system; **relief well**: drilled to intersect an oil or gas well so as to provide a route for water or mud to stop a fire or blow-out.

■ **reliefer** *noun* a person receiving financial relief M20. **reliefless** *adjective* E18.

relief /rɪˈliːf/ *noun*[2]. E17.

[French from Italian *rilievo*, †*rilevo*, from *rilevare* raise, ult. from Latin *relevare* RELIEVE *verb*. Cf. RELIEVO *noun*[1].]

1 A method of moulding, carving, stamping, etc., in which the design stands out from a plane surface so as to have a natural and solid appearance; the degree to which a design projects in this way. E17. ▸**b** A composition or design executed by such a method. L17.

2 The appearance of solidity or detachment given to a design or composition on a plane surface by the arrangement and disposition of the lines, colours, shades, etc.; distinctness of outline due to this; *fig.* vividness, distinctness, or prominence due to contrast or artistic presentation. L18.

3 (The extent of) variation in elevation of an area, geographical feature, etc.; difference in height from the surrounding terrain. M19.

> 🕮 **1** A. Ure The face of the block . . is carved in relief. **half-relief**: in which figures etc. project to the extent of half their true proportions. **high relief**, **low relief**: in which the projections of the design correspond more (or less) closely to those of the object depicted. **middle-relief** = ***half-relief*** above. **b** M. Bergmann In the Vatican Museum he comes across a relief of a young beauty lifting her hemline. **2** W. Irving A church with its dark spire in strong relief against the . . sky. E. Wharton The return to town threw into stronger relief the charms of the life she was leaving. **3** *Nature* These lavas form a faulted dissected plateau of considerable relief.

Comb.: **relief map**: that indicates the relief of an area, either by the analogous form of its surface or by a system of colouring, shading, etc.; **relief printing** = ***letterpress*** (b) s.v. LETTER *noun*[1].

relieve /rɪˈliːv/ *verb*. ME.

[Old & mod. French *relever* from Latin *relevare* raise again, succour, alleviate, formed as RE- + *levare* raise, from *levis* light.]

▸ **I** *verb trans.* **1** Raise out of some trouble, difficulty, or danger; bring or provide aid or assistance to; deliver *from* something troublesome or oppressive. Now chiefly *spec.* (***a***) bring military support to (a besieged town etc.), free from siege; (***b***) supply (the poor) with money or other necessities. ME. ▸†**b** Assist *with* munitions etc.; provide *with* fresh troops. LME–E17. ▸†**c** Feed; supply with nourishment. LME–E17. ▸**d** *LAW*. Free from an obligation; give legal relief to. M16.

2 Ease or free from sorrow, fear, doubt, or other source of mental discomfort. Also, give relief from physical pain or discomfort. LME. ▸**b** Ease (a device) by making slacker or wider. E19. ▸**c** *refl.* Defecate; urinate. M20.

3 Ease or mitigate (what is painful or oppressive); make less grievous or burdensome. LME. ▸**b** Make less tedious, monotonous, or disagreeable by the introduction of variety or of something striking or pleasing. L18.

4 a Set free, release. Chiefly *Scot.* Now *rare*. LME. ▸**b** Release from a duty by acting as or providing a replacement. E17. ▸**c** Set free *from*, ease *of*, any task, burden, or responsibility; *euphem.* dismiss *from* a position, deprive *of* membership etc., deprive *of* by stealing. L17. ▸**d** Replace (a dish of food) by another. *rare*. M18.

†**5** Lift or raise up (again); bring into prominence, make clear; exalt. LME–M17.

†**6** Take up or hold (an estate) from a feudal superior (cf. RELIEF *noun*[1] 1). L15–E16.

7 Bring into relief; make (something) stand out. L18.

> 🕮 **1** Pope Behold the hand . . Stretch'd to relieve the . . Poor. Sir W. Scott Neither trees nor bushes to relieve the eye from the russet . . of absolute sterility. D. Fraser The successes of convergent Allied Armies in North Africa would relieve Malta. **relieving officer** *Hist.* an official appointed by a parish or union to administer relief to the poor. **2** Shakes. *Temp.* My ending is despair Unless I be reliev'd by prayer. R. Graves One smile relieves A heart that grieves. **3** J. Raban Relieved his feelings by throwing a rock at a stray goat. D. Athill The explosion had done nothing to relieve the tension between us. V. Bramwell Painkillers . . help to relieve aches. **relieving arch** *ARCHITECTURE*: formed in a wall to distribute the weight of the structure. **relieving tackle** *NAUTICAL*: used to prevent a ship overturning when being careened, or to ease the strain on the tiller in rough weather. **b** M. Moorcock The paleness of his face was relieved by his slightly pinkish eyes. A. Kenny The hearing of confessions consists of hours of tedium occasionally relieved by embarrassment. **4b** K. Grahame Rat, whose turn it was to go on duty, went upstairs to relieve Badger. ***relieve guard***: see GUARD *noun*. **c** E. Waugh A steady stream of . . imports . . relieved the Ishmaelites of the need to practise their few clumsy crafts. E. O'Neill He relieves her of the pitcher and tumblers as she comes down the steps. **7** R. L. Stevenson He may see a group of washerwomen relieved . . against the blue sea.

▸ **II** *verb intrans.* †**8** Rise again; return; rally in battle. LME–M16.

9 Stand out in relief. E19.

10 *BASEBALL*. Act as relief pitcher. M20.

■ **relievable** *adjective* that may be relieved or assisted; able to receive (esp. legal) relief: L17. **reliever** *noun* (***a***) a person who or thing which relieves someone or something; (***b***) (*obsolete* exc. *Hist.*) a member of the Relief Church; (***c***) *BASEBALL* a relief pitcher: LME.

relieved /rɪˈliːvd/ *adjective*. E19.

[from prec. + -ED[1].]

That has been relieved; *esp.* eased or freed from anxiety or distress.

¶ Earlier (M16) in UNRELIEVED.

■ **relievedly** /-vd-, -vɪd-/ *adverb* in a relieved manner, with relief from anxiety E20.

relievo /rɪˈliːvəʊ/ *noun*[1]. Pl. **-os**. Also **rilievo** /rɪˈljeɪvəʊ/. E17.

[Italian *rilievo*: see RELIEF *noun*[2].]

= RELIEF *noun*[2] 1, 2.

alto-relievo, ***basso-relievo***, ***mezzo-relievo***, etc.

relievo /rɪˈliːvəʊ/ *noun*[2]. L19.

[Prob. from RELIEVE *verb* + -O.]

A children's seeking game in which a captured player can be released by another member of the same side calling 'relievo'.

religate /riːlɪˈɡeɪt/ *verb trans. rare*. L16.

[Latin *religat-* pa. ppl stem of *religare*, formed as RE- + LIGATE.]

†**1** *SURGERY*. Tie up (a vein etc.) to stop bleeding. Only in L16.

2 Bind together, unite; constrain. M17.

■ **religation** *noun* E17.

relight /ˈriːlʌɪt/ *noun*. M20.

[from the verb.]

AERONAUTICS. A re-ignition of a jet engine in flight.

relight /riːˈlʌɪt/ *verb*. Pa. t. & pple **-lighted**, **-lit** /-ˈlɪt/. M17.

[from RE- + LIGHT *verb*[2].]

1 *verb trans.* Light again, re-ignite; *spec.* (*AERONAUTICS*) re-ignite (a jet engine) in flight. M17.

2 *verb intrans.* Take fire again, rekindle. M19.

religieuse /rəliʒjøːz/ *noun*. Pl. pronounced same. L17.

[French, fem. of next.]

1 A woman bound by religious vows; a nun. L17.

2 A confection consisting of two round cakes of choux pastry sandwiched together with cream and decorated with icing. M20.

religieux /rəliʒjø/ *noun*. Pl. same. M17.

[French: see RELIGIOUS.]

A man bound by religious vows; a monk.

religio- /rɪˈlɪdʒɪəʊ/ *combining form*. M19.

[from RELIGION or RELIGIOUS: see -O-.]

Forming adjectives with the sense 'religious and —', as ***religio-historical***, ***religio-philosophic***, ***religio-philosophical***, ***religio-political***.

religion /rɪˈlɪdʒ(ə)n/ *noun*. ME.

[Anglo-Norman *religiun*, Old & mod. French *religion* from Latin *religio(n-)* obligation, bond, scruple, reverence, (in late Latin) religious (monastic) life, prob. from *religare*: see RELIGATE, -ION.]

1 A state of life bound by religious vows; the condition of belonging to a religious order, esp. in the Roman Catholic Church. ME.

2 A particular monastic or religious order or rule. Now *rare*. ME.

3 Belief in or sensing of some superhuman controlling power or powers, entitled to obedience, reverence, and worship, or in a system defining a code of living, esp. as a means to achieve spiritual or material improvement; acceptance of such belief (esp. as represented by an organized Church) as a standard of spiritual and practical life; the expression of this in worship etc. Also (now *rare*), action or conduct indicating such belief; in *pl.*, religious rites. ME.

4 A particular system of such belief. ME.

†**5** Devotion, fidelity; conscientiousness; pious attachment. L16–L17.

†**6** The sanction or obligation *of* an oath etc. E17–E18.

> 🕮 **1** Hor. Walpole My father . . was retired into religion. **3** Gibbon The public religion of the Catholics was uniformly simple. H. Martineau The best part of religion is to imitate the benevolence of God. Day Lewis Religion . . formed a natural part of my life. *personified*: Pope There stern Religion quench'd th' unwilling flame. **4** W. Cather What religion did the Swedes have way back? *fig.*: *Ladies Home Journal (US)* Care of the hair has become a religion. **5** Shakes. *A.Y.L.* Keep your promise . . . With no less religion than if thou wert . . my Rosalind.

Phrases: **experience religion**, **find religion** *colloq.* = ***get religion*** below. **freedom of religion** the right to follow whatever religion one chooses. **get religion** *colloq.* be converted to religious belief, become religious. †**house of religion** a religious house, a monastery or nunnery. **make a religion of** be scrupulously careful of doing, habitually make a point of. ***minister of religion***: see MINISTER *noun* 2a. ***natural religion***: see NATURAL *adjective*. ***old religion***: see OLD *adjective*. ***revealed religion***: see REVEAL *verb* 1.

■ **religioner** *noun* (***a***) a person bound by religious vows; (***b***) = RELIGIONIST: E19. **religionize** *verb* (***a***) *verb intrans.* be addicted to or affect religion; (***b***) *verb trans.* imbue with religion, make religious: E18. **religionless** *adjective* without religion; (of Christianity) dissociated from many of the doctrines and practices of conventional religion: M18.

religionary /rɪˈlɪdʒ(ə)n(ə)ri/ *noun & adjective*. Now *rare*. M17.

[from prec. + -ARY[1], or from French *religionnaire* Protestant, Calvinist.]

▸†**A** *noun*. **1** A person bound by religious vows. Only in M17.

2 A Protestant. L17–M18.

▸ **B** *adjective*. Pertaining to religion; religious. L17.

religionism /rɪˈlɪdʒ(ə)nɪz(ə)m/ *noun*. E19.

[from RELIGION + -ISM.]

Excessive inclination to religion; exaggerated or affected religious zeal.

religionist /rɪˈlɪdʒ(ə)nɪst/ *noun*. M17.

[formed as prec. + -IST.]

A person devoted to religion; *esp.* an affectedly or exaggeratedly religious person. Also, a person professionally occupied with religion.

religiose /rɪˈlɪdʒɪəʊs/ *adjective*. M19.

[Latin *religiosus* RELIGIOUS: see -OSE[1].]

Affectedly or excessively religious; unduly occupied with religion.

religiosity /rɪˌlɪdʒɪˈɒsɪti/ *noun*. LME.

[Latin *religiositas*, from *religiosus* RELIGIOUS: see -ITY.]

1 Religious feeling or belief. LME.

2 Affected or excessive religiousness. L18.

religioso /relidʒiˈoːzo, rɪˌlɪdʒɪˈəʊzəʊ/ *adverb & adjective*. M19.

[Italian = religious.]

MUSIC. A direction: with a devotional quality.

religious /rɪˈlɪdʒəs/ *adjective & noun*. ME.

[Anglo-Norman *religius*, Old French *religious* (mod. *religieux*) from Latin *religiosus*, from *religio(n-)* RELIGION: see -OUS.]

▸ **A** *adjective*. **1** Devoted to religion; exhibiting the spiritual or practical effects of religion, following the requirements of a religion; pious, godly, devout. ME.

2 Bound by vows of religion; belonging to or connected with an order bound by such vows; monastic. ME.

3 Of the nature of, pertaining to, or concerned with religion. M16. ▸**b** Regarded as sacred. Chiefly *poet.* E17.

4 Scrupulous, exact, strict, conscientious. L16.

> 🕮 **1** J. Gross He grew up in a rigidly religious atmosphere. B. Vine Her husband was . . religious in a conventional Anglican way. **2** Addison A shaved Head, and a religious Habit. **3** Day Lewis It made everything she sang sound like religious music. C. Priest There had been a renewal of religious faith. **b** Dryden Brown with the shade of a religious wood. **4** Dickens Letters I am taking religious care of.

▸ **B** *noun*. Pl. same, (now *rare*) **-es**. A person devoted to a religious or monastic life; a monk; a nun. ME.

> 🕮 M. Spark He never would have made a religious. R. Harries Three religious were arguing about . . their orders.

■ **religiously** *adverb* LME. **religiousness** *noun* LME.

reline /riːˈlʌɪn/ *verb trans.* M19.

[from RE- + LINE *verb*[1], *verb*[2].]

1 Line again, provide with a fresh lining. M19. ▸**b** Attach a new backing canvas to (a painting). E20.

2 Mark with new lines; renew the lines of. L19.

■ **reliner** *noun* (***a***) a person who relines paintings with fresh linings; (***b***) (a piece of) material providing a fresh lining: E20.

relinquish /rɪˈlɪŋkwɪʃ/ *verb trans.* LME.

[Old French *relinquiss-* lengthened stem of *relinquir* from Latin *relinquere*, formed as RE- + *linquere* leave: see -ISH[2].]

1 Give up (an idea, belief, etc.); desist from (an action or practice). LME.

2 Resign, surrender, (a possession, right, etc.). Also foll. by *to*. **L15.** ▸**b** Let go (something held). **M19.**
†**3** *gen.* Withdraw from; desert, abandon; leave behind. *rare*. **L15–L18.**

> 📖 **1** GIBBON Alarmed . . he hastily relinquished the siege. A. JOHN I relinquished my plan with sorrow. M. GARDINER The English had relinquished their customary reticence. **2** K. A. PORTER Man . . cannot relinquish . . himself to oblivion. G. BODDY An unfeeling husband who would not relinquish her. **b** F. KING The dying woman . . relinquished her grip.

■ **relinquishment** *noun* **L16.**

reliquary /ˈrɛlɪkwəri/ *noun*. Also (*rare*) **-cary**, & in French form **-quaire** /-kwɛː/. **M16.**
[Old & mod. French *reliquaire*, from *relique* RELIC: see -ARY[1].]
A small box or other receptacle in which a relic or relics are kept.

†**relique** *noun & adjective* var. of RELIC.

reliquiae /rɪˈlɪkwiː/ *noun pl.* **M17.**
[Latin, use as noun of fem. pl. of *reliquus* remaining, formed as RE- + *liq-* stem of *linquere* leave.]
Remains; *spec.* (*a*) GEOLOGY fossilized remains of animals or plants; (*b*) literary remains, unpublished or uncollected writings.

relish /ˈrɛlɪʃ/ *noun*. Also (earlier) †**reles**. **ME.**
[Ult. from Old French *relais* remainder, from *relaisser* leave behind, RELEASE *verb*. Branch III perh. repr. a different word.]
▸ **I 1** Orig., odour, scent, taste. Later, a taste, a flavour; the distinctive taste *of* something. Freq. *fig.* **ME.** ▸**b** A trace, a tinge; a sample; a small quantity. Foll. by *of*. **L16.**
†**2** An individual taste or liking. **E17–M18.**
3 a An appetizing flavour; a savoury or piquant taste. Freq. *fig.*, a pleasant or attractive quality. **M17.** ▸**b** A condiment or item of strongly flavoured food eaten with plainer food to add flavour; *spec.* a sauce made of pickled chopped vegetables. **L18.**
4 Enjoyment of the taste or flavour of something. Freq. *fig.*, pleasure obtained from something agreeable; a liking, a zest; keen or pleasurable anticipation. (Foll. by *for*, *of*.) **M17.**

> 📖 **1** D. HUME A Laplander . . has no notion of the relish of wine. **b** SHAKES. *Haml.* Some act That has no relish of salvation in't. **3a** E. EDWARDS No amount of favour has relish for the Earl, if his rival has favour too. **b** J. F. COOPER Eat their venison raw and without a relish too. Here . . we have plenty of salt. **4** J. BUCHAN I never ate a meal with greater relish, for I had had nothing all day. D. ATHILL An excellent raconteur with . . an immense relish for the absurd.

▸ **II 5** A projection, esp. in building or joinery work. *rare*. **LME.**
▸ **III** †**6** MUSIC. A grace, an ornament, an embellishment. **M16–M17.**
¶ Forms with *-sh* not recorded until **M16.**
■ †**relished** *adjective* having a (specified) taste or flavour **M16–E18.**

relish /ˈrɛlɪʃ/ *verb*. **E16.**
[from (the same root as) the noun.]
▸†**I 1** *verb trans. & intrans.* Sing, warble. **E16–E17.**

> 📖 **1** SHAKES. *Lucr.* Relish your nimble notes to pleasing ears.

▸ **II 2** *verb trans.* Give or impart a relish to; make pleasant, enjoyable, or satisfying. **L16.** ▸†**b** Provide with something tasty; please, delight. **E17–L18.**
†**3** *verb trans.* Taste, distinguish by tasting; sense. *rare*. **L16–E17.**
4 *verb trans.* Enjoy greatly, take pleasure in; look forward to, anticipate with pleasure; (in neg. contexts) find agreeable, approve of. **L16.** ▸**b** Take or receive in a particular manner. Now *rare*. **E17.** ▸†**c** Appreciate, understand. *rare*. Only in **E17.**
†**5** *verb intrans.* Be agreeable or pleasant, find acceptance or favour (*with*). **L16–M18.**
6 *verb intrans.* Have the taste *of*, have a trace *of*, savour or smack *of*. Now *rare*. **E17.** ▸†**b** Have a trace of, savour or smack of. **E17–E18.**
7 *verb intrans.* With adverbs: have a specified taste or relish; *fig.* sound, seem, feel. **E17.**

> 📖 **2** LD MACAULAY I have also a novel . . to relish my wine. **4** A. SILLITOE Arthur enjoyed the gins and relished the beer. JOAN SMITH The prospect of inquiring into a murder single-handed was not one she relished. M. SEYMOUR They were expected to relish argument. **6** JER. TAYLOR It will make everything relish of religion. **7** B. H. MALKIN That precaution relished well with his excellency.

▸ **III** †**8** *verb intrans.* Project, jut out. *rare*. Only in **E17.**
9 *verb trans.* Cut or carve projections on (wood). *rare*. **L19.**
■ **relishable** *adjective* able to be relished, enjoyable **E17.** **relisher** *noun* (*rare*) **L18.** **relishingly** *adverb* with relish; pleasantly: **L17.**

relit *verb pa. t. & pple*: see RELIGHT *verb*.

relive /riːˈlɪv/ *verb*. **M16.**
[from RE- + LIVE *verb*; in early use after REVIVE.]
†**1** *verb trans.* Restore to life, resuscitate. **M–L16.**
2 *verb intrans.* Come to life again; live anew. *literary*. **M16.**
3 *verb trans.* Live (a period of time, an experience) over again, esp. in the imagination. **E18.**

> 📖 **2** SHAKES. *Per.* Will you deliver How this dead queen re-lives? **3** H. FAST He lay awake . . reliving his experience on the . . plane.

†**reliver** *verb trans. rare*. **LME–E17.**
[Old French *relivrer*, formed as RE- + *livrer* deliver. Cf. LIVER *verb*.]
Give back, restore.

relleno /rɛˈljeɪnəʊ/ *noun*. Pl. **-os**. **E20.**
[Abbreviation.]
= CHILLI ***relleno***.

rellie /ˈrɛli/ *noun*. *colloq.* (orig. and chiefly *Austral.*). **L20.**
[from RELATIVE *noun* + -IE.]
In *pl.* Relatives.

> 📖 C. BATEMAN Someone's got their rellies in from the States.

■ Also **rello** *noun* (pl. **-os**) **L20.**

reload /ˈriːləʊd/ *noun*. **E20.**
[from the verb.]
An instance of reloading; a film, cartridge, etc., used to reload a camera, firearm, etc.

reload /riːˈləʊd/ *verb*. **L18.**
[from RE- + LOAD *verb*.]
1 *verb trans.* Make up or put in again as a load. **L18.**
2 *verb trans. & intrans.* Provide (with) a fresh load; *esp.* load (a firearm, camera, etc.) again. **L18.**
■ **reloader** *noun* **E20.**

relocate /riːlə(ʊ)ˈkeɪt/ *verb*. Orig. *US*. **M19.**
[from RE- + LOCATE.]
1 *verb trans. & intrans.* Move to a new location, esp. to live or to work; locate or be located in a new place. **M19.**
2 *verb trans.* Find the place of again. **L19.**

> 📖 **1** *New York Times* Paving the way for the Nestlé Company to relocate its White Plains headquarters. *Times* The successful applicant must be . . willing to relocate to our Midlands base.

■ **relocatable** *adjective* **L19.**

relocation /riːlə(ʊ)ˈkeɪʃ(ə)n/ *noun*. **L16.**
[Sense 1 from late Latin *relocatio(n-)*, from *relocat-* pa. ppl stem of *relocare* re-let; sense 2 from prec.: see -ATION.]
1 SCOTS LAW. ***tacit relocation***, the implied renewal of a lease on a year-to-year basis when the landlord allows a tenant to continue without a fresh agreement after the expiry of the lease. **L16.**
2 The action or fact of relocating; an instance of this. Orig. *US*. **M19.**

> 📖 **2** *attrib.*: *Navy News* Relocation expenses will be considered where appropriate.

relucent /rɪˈluːs(ə)nt, -ˈljuː-/ *adjective*. Now *rare*. **LME.**
[Old French *reluisant* from Latin *relucent-* pres. ppl stem of *relucere* shine back, formed as RE- + *lucere*: see LUCENT.]
Casting back light; shining, gleaming.
■ **relucence** *noun* (*rare*) **E18.** **relucency** *noun* (*rare*) **E17.**

reluct /rɪˈlʌkt/ *verb intrans. arch.* **E16.**
[Latin *reluctari* struggle against, formed as RE- + *luctari* to struggle.]
†**1** Strive or struggle *to do*. **E16–M17.**
2 Be reluctant; show reluctance, offer opposition, rebel, object. (Foll. by *against*, *at*, *to*.) **M16.**

reluctance /rɪˈlʌkt(ə)ns/ *noun*. **M17.**
[from RELUCTANT + -ANCE.]
1 The action of struggling *against* something; resistance, opposition. Now *rare*. **M17.**
2 Unwillingness, disinclination; an instance of this. (Foll. by *at*, †*to*, *to do*.) **M17.**
3 PHYSICS. (A measure of) the property of a magnetic circuit of opposing the passage of magnetic flux lines, equal to the ratio of the magnetomotive force to the magnetic flux. **L19.**

> 📖 **1** MILTON The Reluctance . . which is in all Kings against Presbyterian and Independent Discipline. **2** P. G. WODEHOUSE The maid . . showed a reluctance to let Bailey in. JANET MORGAN With great reluctance Agatha agreed to divorce him.

reluctancy /rɪˈlʌkt(ə)nsi/ *noun*. Now *rare*. **E17.**
[from next + -ANCY.]
†**1** An internal or mental struggle. **E–M17.**
†**2** = RELUCTANCE 1. **M–L17.**
3 = RELUCTANCE 2. **M17.**

reluctant /rɪˈlʌkt(ə)nt/ *adjective*. **M17.**
[Latin *reluctant-* pres. ppl stem of *reluctari*: see RELUCT, -ANT[1].]
1 Struggling, writhing; offering opposition (*to*). *rare*. **M17.**
2 Unwilling, averse, disinclined. (Foll. by *to do*.) **M17.**
3 Done or produced with reluctance; characterized by unwillingness or disinclination. **E18.**

> 📖 **2** J. STEINBECK What light and beauty could be forced down the throats of her reluctant pupils, she forced. DAY LEWIS I was slow to grow up—reluctant . . to leave the state of childhood. *transf.*: A. BROOKNER She turned to go, . . wrestled with the reluctant swing door. **3** E. K. KANE Fastened to the sledge, he commenced his reluctant journey. E. LANGLEY His reluctant words . . that . . I had forced from him!

■ **reluctantly** *adverb* **L17.**

reluctate /rɪˈlʌkteɪt/ *verb*. **M17.**
[Latin *reluctat-* pa. ppl stem of *reluctari*: see RELUCT, -ATE[3].]
1 *verb intrans.* Offer resistance; show reluctance; strive or struggle *against*. Now *rare*. **M17.**
2 *verb trans.* Strive against, refuse, reject. *rare*. **L17.**

reluctation /rɛlʌkˈteɪʃ(ə)n/ *noun*. Now *rare*. **L16.**
[Late Latin *reluctatio(n-)*, formed as prec.: see -ATION.]
†**1** Reluctance, unwillingness; (an) internal or mental struggle. **L16–L17.**
2 Resistance, opposition. **E17.**

reluctivity /rɛlʌkˈtɪvɪti/ *noun*. **L19.**
[from RELUCTANCE after *resistance*, *resistivity* etc.]
PHYSICS. Reluctance per unit volume, equivalent to the reciprocal of magnetic permeability.

relume /rɪˈl(j)uːm/ *verb trans. poet.* **E17.**
[from RE- + ILLUME, partly after French *rallumer*, late Latin *reluminare*.]
1 Relight, rekindle (*lit. & fig.*). **E17.**
2 Make clear or bright again. **M18.**
3 Re-illuminate; shine on anew. **L18.**
■ Also **relumine** *verb trans.* (*rare*) **M18.**

rely /rɪˈlʌɪ/ *verb*. **ME.**
[Old French *relier* bind together from Latin *religare* bind closely, formed as RE- + *ligare* bind. Cf. RALLY *verb*[1] & *noun*[1].]
†**1** *verb trans. & intrans.* Gather together; assemble, rally; betake (oneself) *to* a place etc. **ME–M17.**
†**2** *verb intrans.* Turn *to*, adhere *to*, associate *with*. *rare*. **L16–E17.**
3 *verb intrans.* Depend *on* or *upon* with full trust or confidence; be dependent *on*. **L16.** ▸**b** Put trust or confidence *in*. *rare*. **E17.**
†**4** *verb intrans.* Consist *in*. **L16–M17.**
†**5** *verb trans.* Repose (oneself, one's soul, etc.) *on*, *upon*, or *in*. **L16–M17.**

> 📖 **3** E. TAYLOR She had relied on that friendship too much and was lost without it. D. LESSING She could rely on me to do exactly as I said I would. A. PRICE Mother's massive double-volumed *Shorter Oxford English Dictionary*, ever to be relied on. A. TYLER They relied on him for money.

■ **relier** *noun* (*rare*) a person who relies (*on* a person or thing) **L16.**

rem /rɛm/ *noun*[1]. Pl. **-s**, same. **M20.**
[Acronym, from roentgen equivalent *man*.]
A unit of effective absorbed dose of ionizing radiation in human tissue, orig. (now *loosely*) equivalent to the effect of one roentgen of X-rays. Cf. REP *noun*[7].

REM /rɛm/, ɑːriːˈɛm/ *noun*[2]. **M20.**
[Acronym.]
= ***rapid eye movement*** s.v. RAPID *adjective*. Usu. *attrib.* designating a kind of sleep that occurs at intervals during the night and is characterized by rapid eye movements, more dreaming and bodily movement, and faster pulse and breathing.

remade *verb pa. t. & pple* of REMAKE *verb*.

remain /rɪˈmeɪn/ *noun*. **LME.**
[Partly from Old French, from *remaindre* (see REMAIN *verb*); partly directly from the verb.]
▸ **I 1** In *pl.* (occas. treated as *sing.*) & †*sing.* The remaining parts or part; what remains after other members or parts have gone or been removed, used, or dealt with. **LME.** ▸†**b** = REMAINDER *noun* 4. **M16–L17.**
2 A remaining or surviving thing, a relic; *esp.* (*a*) an author's (esp. unpublished) works left after death; (*b*) relics of antiquity, esp. ancient buildings; (*c*) (a part or parts of) a person's body after death. Now *rare* exc. in *pl.* (passing into sense 1). **M16.**

> 📖 **1** SHAKES. *Cymb.* I know your master's pleasure, and he mine; All the remain is, welcome. R. H. FROUDE The remains of an Ionic temple. J. N. LOCKYER Coal is the remains of an ancient vegetation. B. PYM No cake, only the remains of a . . stale loaf. **2** W. GOLDING Year by year life lays down another layer of remains. N. CALDER The oldest human remains so far discovered. *Times* One possible Punic remain, a vase . . believed till now to be Roman. L. SPALDING They went to the Museum of Indian Remains. ***removal of remains***: see REMOVAL 1c.

▸†**II 3** An instance of remaining, a stay. *rare*. **LME–E17.**

> 📖 **3** SHAKES. *Macb.* A most miraculous work . . Which often since my here-remain in England I have seen him do.

remain /rɪˈmeɪn/ *verb*. **LME.**
[Old French *remain-*, *remein-* tonic stem of *remanoir* from Latin *remanere*, formed as RE- + *manere* remain, or Old French *remaindre* from Proto-Romance from Latin *remanere*.]

For other words beginning with *re-* see the entry for **re-**

1 *verb intrans.* Be left behind or over after others or other parts have gone or been removed, used, or dealt with. Also foll. by *to* (a person etc.), *to do*. LME.
2 *verb intrans.* Be in the same place or condition during further time; continue to stay or exist (in a specified place or state); (with compl.) continue to be, stay. LME. ▸†**b** Have one's abode; dwell. LME–E17. ▸**c** Foll. by *with*: stick in the mind of. E17.
†**3** *verb intrans.* Continue to belong *to*; LAW fall *to* as a remainder. L15–E17.
†**4 a** *verb intrans.* Foll. by *on*: wait for. *Scot.* L15–M16. ▸**b** *verb trans.* Await, be left for, wait for. *rare.* L16–M17.

📖 **1** TENNYSON What I learn And what remains to tell. D. H. LAWRENCE He had so . . nearly lost his life that what remained was wonderfully precious. H. READ Half of all that remained to me. R. RENDELL When he left Olson ten minutes on the meter still remained to run. **remain to be seen** be not yet known or certain. **2** W. ROBERTSON Charles remained six days in Paris. G. GREENE While the three strangers rose he remained seated. R. WARNER I was prepared to allow it to remain a secret. S. HAZZARD He might easily have moved away . . but instead remained there. K. VONNEGUT It was and remains easy . . to go somewhere else to start anew. M. MARRIN The fact remained that two men were dead. **c** T. HARDY The tunes they . . essayed remained with him for years.

■ **remainer** *noun* (*rare*) a person who remains or stays M16.

remainder /rɪˈmeɪndə/ *noun & verb.* LME.
[Anglo-Norman = Old French *remaindre* use as noun of inf.: see prec., -ER⁴.]
▸ **A** *noun.* **1** LAW. **a** An interest in an estate that becomes effective in possession only on the ending of a prior interest, created by the same conveyance by which the estate itself was granted. Also ***remainder over***. LME. ▸**b** The right to succeed to a peerage etc., esp. where expressly assigned to a certain person or line of descent in default of male issue in the direct line. E19.
2 Those still left out of a number of people or things; that which is left when a part has been taken away, used, dealt with, etc.; the remaining ones, the rest, the residue. M16.
3 A remaining or surviving part or fragment; a remaining trace. Freq. in *pl.*, remains. Now *rare*. L16.
4 a MATH. The number left over after subtraction or division. L16. ▸†**b** The unpaid balance of a sum of money. *rare*. Only in L16.
5 The copies of a book remaining unsold when demand has fallen off, often disposed of at a reduced price. M18.

📖 **2** GIBBON To pass the remainder of his life in . . exile. A. J. CRONIN Half the roses in the . . jug and the remainder in the tooth-brush holder. **3** P. L. FERMOR The word 'coach' is a remainder of the Hungarian town . . Kocs. **5** M. KINGTON It markets . . remainders, that is, books . . the publishers could not sell.

Comb.: **remainder man** LAW the person to whom a remainder is devised; **remainder theorem** MATH.: that if a polynomial $f(x)$ is divided by $(x - a)$ the remainder will be $f(a)$.
▸ **B** *verb trans.* Dispose of (an unsold part of an edition of a book) at a reduced price; treat as a remainder (sense A.5). E20.

remake /ˈriːmeɪk/ *noun.* M19.
[from the verb.]
The action or an instance of remaking something; something remade; *esp.* (the making of) a new version of an old film with different actors etc.
¶ Rare before M20.

remake /riːˈmeɪk/ *verb trans.* Pa. t. & pple **-made** /-ˈmeɪd/. M17.
[from RE- + MAKE *verb*.]
Make again or differently.

reman /riːˈman/ *verb trans.* Infl. **-nn-**. M17.
[from RE- + MAN *verb*.]
1 Equip with fresh men; man anew. M17.
2 Make manly or courageous again. *poet.* E19.

remancipate /riːˈmansɪpeɪt/ *verb trans.* M17.
[Latin *remancipat-* pa. ppl stem of *remancipare*, formed as RE- + *mancipare* MANCIPATE.]
ROMAN LAW. Reconvey to the previous owner.
■ **remanciˈpation** *noun* M17.

remand /rɪˈmɑːnd/ *noun.* L18.
[from the verb.]
1 The action or process of remanding; the fact of being remanded. Now *spec.* recommittal of an accused person to custody. L18.
2 A remanded prisoner. L19.
1 on remand in custody pending trial.
Comb.: **remand centre** an institution to which accused people are remanded pending trial; **remand home** an institution to which young people are remanded or committed for detention.

remand /rɪˈmɑːnd/ *verb trans.* LME.
[Late Latin *remandare*, formed as RE- + Latin *mandare* command, send word.]
1 a Send back again (*to*); order to return (*to*); reconsign; remit, consign. Now *rare*. LME. ▸**b** Of a court etc.: send back (a prisoner) into custody, esp. to allow further enquiries to be made. Also ***remand in custody***. M17.
†**2** Call back, recall. E16–E19.
†**3** Demand back from a person. Only in 17.

remanence /ˈrɛmənəns/ *noun.* M16.
[medieval Latin *remanentia*, formed as next: see -ENCE.]
1 The fact of remaining; permanence. M16.
2 a *gen.* The remaining part; a residuum. *rare.* M16. ▸**b** PHYSICS. Magnetism remaining after removal of the magnetizing field, residual magnetism. Also, retentivity. L19.

remanent /ˈrɛmənənt/ *adjective.* LME.
[Latin *remanent-* pres. ppl stem of *remanere* REMAIN *verb*: see -ENT.]
1 *gen.* Left behind, remaining, residual; (chiefly *Scot.*) remaining over and above, additional. Now *rare*. LME.
2 PHYSICS. Of magnetism: remaining in a substance or specimen after removal of the magnetizing field. M19.

remanet /ˈrɛmənɛt/ *noun.* E16.
[App. from medieval Latin use as noun of Latin = there, or it, remains, 3rd person sing. pres. indic. of *remanere* REMAIN *verb*.]
1 A remainder. E16.
2 a LAW. A case or suit of which the hearing has been postponed. M18. ▸**b** A parliamentary bill left over until another session. L19.

remanié /rəmanje/ *adjective.* L19.
[French, pa. pple of *remanier* rehandle, reshape.]
GEOLOGY. Derived from an older stratum or structure.

remaniement /rəmanimɑ̃/ *noun.* Pl. pronounced same. E20.
[French, formed as prec. + -MENT.]
A rearrangement, a reconstruction.

remark /rɪˈmɑːk/ *noun¹.* M17.
[French *remarque*, formed as the verb.]
†**1** The fact or quality of being worthy of notice or comment. Only in ***of remark***, ***of great remark***, etc. M17–E18.
2 a An act of observing or noticing something. Now *rare*. M17. ▸**b** Observation, notice; comment. L17. ▸**c** A verbal or written observation; a comment; something said. (Foll. by *on*, *about*.) (Now the usual sense.) L17.
3 A sign or mark indicating something notable; an indication *of*, a trace *of*. Long *rare* or *obsolete*. M17.

📖 **2b** J. GALSWORTHY Nothing calls for remark except the payment. **c** A. J. CRONIN Forced himself to make a few conventional remarks. V. S. PRITCHETT The clerks . . made sly remarks about . . her corset. ***pass a remark***: see PASS *verb*.

remark *noun²* var. of REMARQUE.

remark /rɪˈmɑːk/ *verb.* L16.
[French *remarquer*, formed as RE- + *marquer* MARK *verb*.]
1 *verb trans.* Take notice of, perceive; regard with attention. L16.
†**2** *verb trans.* Mark out, distinguish; point out, indicate. M17–M18.
3 *verb trans.* Say by way of observation or comment. L17. ▸**b** *verb intrans.* Make a remark or remarks (*on*). M19.

📖 **1** THACKERAY The looks of gloom . . which . . Mr Morgan had remarked. **2** MILTON His manacles remark him, there he is. **3** B. JOWETT The modern philosopher would remark that the indefinite is equally real with the definite. J. CONRAD 'Willie's eyes bulged . . .' 'They always do,' remarked Renouard. **b** C. DARWIN The singular fact remarked on by several observers.

■ **remarker** *noun* (now *rare*) a person who makes or publishes remarks; orig. *spec.*, a reviewer, a critic: L17.

re-mark /riːˈmɑːk/ *verb trans.* L16.
[from RE- + MARK *verb*.]
Mark again.

remarkable /rɪˈmɑːkəb(ə)l/ *adjective, noun, & adverb.* E17.
[French *remarquable*, formed as REMARK *verb* + -ABLE.]
▸ **A** *adjective.* **1** Worthy of notice or observation; extraordinary, unusual, striking. E17.
†**2** Perceptible; noticeable. Also, likely to attract attention, conspicuous. E17–E19.

📖 **1** J. K. JEROME There was nothing . . remarkable about the apartment, and my friend wondered why he had been brought there. F. TOMLIN Someone as remarkable as Eliot commands attention.

▸ **B** *noun.* A remarkable thing or circumstance; something or someone extraordinary. Usu. in *pl. arch.* M17.
▸ **C** *adverb.* Remarkably. *non-standard.* L18.
■ **remarkaˈbility** *noun* M19. **remarkableness** *noun* M17. **remarkably** *adverb* in a remarkable manner, to a remarkable extent, notably, strikingly E17.

remarque /rɪˈmɑːk, *foreign* rəmark (*pl. same*)/ *noun.* Also **-k**. L19.
[French.]
ENGRAVING. A distinguishing feature indicating the state of the plate, freq. taking the form of a sketch in the margin.

remarry /riːˈmari/ *verb trans. & intrans.* E16.
[from RE- + MARRY *verb*.]
Marry again; marry a second or subsequent time.
■ **remarriage** *noun* a second or subsequent marriage E17.

remaster /riːˈmɑːstə/ *verb trans.* M20.
[from RE- + MASTER *verb*.]
Make a new master of (a recording), esp. to improve the sound quality; issue (a recording) from a new master. Chiefly as ***remastered*** *ppl adjective*, ***remastering*** *verbal noun*.

rematch /ˈriːmatʃ/ *noun.* M20.
[from RE- + MATCH *noun¹*.]
A return match or game.

rematch /riːˈmatʃ/ *verb trans.* M19.
[from RE- + MATCH *verb¹*.]
Match again.

rematerialize /riːməˈtɪərɪəlʌɪz/ *verb intrans.* Also **-ise**. L19.
[from RE- + MATERIALIZE.]
Materialize again or differently.
■ **rematerialiˈzation** *noun* M20.

remblai /rɑ̃blɛ/ *noun.* Also ***-ais*** (pronounced same). L18.
[French, from *remblayer* embank, formed as RE- + *emblayer* heap up.]
1 FORTIFICATION. The earth used to form a rampart, mound, or embankment. L18.
2 MINING. Material used to fill excavations made in a thick seam of coal. M19.

remboîtage /rɑ̃bwataʒ/ *noun.* Pl. pronounced same. M20.
[French, from *remboîter* re-case (a book).]
The action or an act of transferring a book into new binding, esp. of superior quality.

Rembrandt /ˈrɛmbrant/ *noun.* E20.
[See next.]
In full ***Rembrandt tulip***. A Darwin tulip of a class with streaked or variegated flowers.

Rembrandtesque /rɛmbranˈtɛsk/ *adjective.* M19.
[from *Rembrandt* (see below) + -ESQUE.]
Pertaining to or resembling the style of the Dutch painter and etcher Rembrandt Harmensz van Rijn (1606–69).
■ **Remˈbrandtian** *adjective* = REMBRANDTESQUE M20. **Rembrandtish** *adjective* somewhat resembling the style of Rembrandt M19. **Rembrandtism** *noun* the style of Rembrandt M19.

REME /ˈriːmi/ *abbreviation.*
(Corps of) Royal Electrical and Mechanical Engineers.

remede /rɪˈmiːd/ *noun.* Chiefly *Scot. arch.* Also **remeid** & other variants. LME.
[Old & mod. French *remède* from Latin *remedium* REMEDY *noun*.]
Remedy, redress.

remede /rɪˈmiːd/ *verb trans.* *Scot. arch.* Also **remeid** & other variants. LME.
[Old & mod. French *remédier* REMEDY *verb*.]
Remedy, redress, amend.

remediable /rɪˈmiːdɪəb(ə)l/ *adjective.* LME.
[Old & mod. French *remédiable* or Latin *remediabilis* curable, (later) curative, from *remediare*: see REMEDY *verb*, -ABLE.]
†**1** Capable of remedying something; remedial. LME–L16.
2 Able to be remedied or redressed. LME.

remedial /rɪˈmiːdɪəl/ *adjective.* M17.
[Late Latin *remedialis*, from Latin *remedium* REMEDY *noun*: see -AL¹.]
1 Affording a remedy, tending to relieve or redress something. M17.
2 a Designating or pertaining to teaching for children with learning difficulties. E20. ▸**b** Of a child: receiving or requiring remedial teaching. M20.
3 Concerned with or aimed at overcoming muscular disabilities or postural defects by means of special exercises. E20.

📖 **1** E. M. GOULBURN Suffering is a medicine, remedial but bitter. **2a** LADY BIRD JOHNSON One intern was giving remedial reading.

■ **remedially** *adverb* L18.

remediate /rɪˈmiːdɪət/ *adjective.* Long *rare* or *obsolete*. E17.
[Latin *remediat-* pa. ppl stem of *remediare* REMEDY *verb*: see -ATE².]
Remedial.

📖 SHAKES. *Lear* All you unpublished virtues of the earth Spring with my tears; be aidant and remediate.

¶ Perh. orig. an error for *remedial*.

remediate /rɪˈmiːdɪeɪt/ *verb trans.* M20.
[Back-form. from next.]
Remedy, redress.

remediation /rɪˌmiːdɪˈeɪʃ(ə)n/ *noun.* E19.
[Latin *remediatio(n-)*, from *remediare* REMEDY *verb*: see -ATION.]
The action of remedying something; *esp.* the giving of remedial teaching or therapy.

remediless /ˈrɛmɪdɪlɪs/ *adjective.* L15.
[from next + -LESS.]
1 Unable to be relieved, having no prospect of aid or rescue. Now *rare* or *obsolete*. L15.

2 Of trouble, disease, etc.: unable to be remedied, having no cure. E16.
▪ **remedilessly** *adverb* (now *rare*) M16. **remedilessness** *noun* (now *rare*) E17.

remedy /ˈrɛmɪdi/ *noun*. ME.
[Anglo-Norman *remedie* = Old & mod. French *remède* from Latin *remedium* medicine, means of relief, (in medieval Latin) concession, formed as RE- + *med*- stem of *mederi* heal.]
1 A cure for a disease or other physical or mental illness; any medicine or treatment which alleviates pain and promotes restoration to health. ME.
2 A means of counteracting or removing something undesirable; redress, relief. ME. ▸**b** *spec.* Legal redress. LME.
3 The small margin within which coins when minted are allowed to vary from the standard fineness and weight. LME.
4 A period of relaxation; *spec.* at some schools, a time specially granted for recreation, a half-holiday. LME.
📖 **1** B. PYM Reluctant to prescribe new drugs . . prefers homely remedies. **2** B. WEBB Social philosophy . . does not provide any remedies for racial wars. †**no remedy** unavoidably. **there is no remedy but** there is no alternative but.

remedy /ˈrɛmɪdi/ *verb trans*. LME.
[Old & mod. French *remédier* or Latin *remediare*, from *remedium* REMEDY *noun*.]
1 Heal, cure, (a person, diseased part, etc.). Now *rare*. LME.
2 Put right, reform, (a state of things); rectify, make good. LME.
†**3** Grant (a person) legal remedy. LME–M17.
📖 **2** J. K. GALBRAITH We must find a way to remedy . . poverty. P. CAREY You've never read Conrad? We must remedy that.

remeid *noun*, *verb* vars. of REMEDE *noun*, *verb*.

remember /rɪˈmɛmbə/ *verb*. ME.
[Old French *remembrer* from late Latin *rememorari* call to mind, formed as RE- + *memor* mindful.]
▸ **I 1** *verb trans.* Retain a memory of (something or someone); bring back into one's thoughts, recollect, recall, (a person, fact, etc.); keep in mind, not forget, (a duty, commitment, etc., *that*, *to do*). ME.
2 *verb refl.* Recollect, reflect to oneself. (Foll. by †*of*, *that*.) Now *rare*. ME.
3 *verb intrans.* Retain a memory of something or someone; recall a fact, knowledge, etc.; not forget to do something. (Foll. by *about*, (now *Scot. & US*) *of*). ME.
4 *verb trans.* **a** Think of, recall the memory of, (a person) with some feeling or intention. LME. ▸**b** Bear (a person) in mind as entitled to a gift, recompense, etc., or in making one's will. Also, reward, tip. L15.
5 *verb trans.* **a** Orig., record, mention (a thing, person, etc.). Later *spec.*, mention (a person etc.) in prayer. LME. ▸†**b** Commemorate. LME–M17.
📖 **1** R. CAMPBELL Though I had been to England as a baby I did not remember it. G. VIDAL He remembered him clearly; he was proud of his memory. V. BRAMWELL Remember that the best beauty bonus is a smile. A. GHOSH I can remember when I first learnt to tell the time. *Choice:* Remember to fill out a Customs form declaring the contents of your parcel. **it remembers me**, **it remembers you**, etc. *arch.* I, you, etc., recollect. †**remember one's courtesy** cover one's head. **remember oneself** (*a*) recover one's manners or intentions after a lapse; (*b*) see sense 2 above. **3** G. GREENE The wish to remember . . became too acute for silence. A. PILLING 'Go on,' wheedled Henry, hoping he'd remember about the spark plugs. J. NEEL That is literally all I can remember about them. **4a** G. S. HAIGHT Mary Anne was especially remembered at Miss Franklin's for English composition. **b** D. H. LAWRENCE He remembered Clifford handsomely in his will. **5b** SHAKES. *Temp.* The ditty does remember my drown'd father.
▸ **II 6** *verb trans.* Remind (a person). Usu. foll. by *of*, *that*, *to do*. Now *arch.* & *dial.* LME.
†**7** *verb trans.* Recall (a thing or person) to someone. LME–L17.
8 *verb trans.* Convey greetings from (a person). Usu. foll. by *to*. M16.
📖 **8** O. WILDE Remember me most warmly to your husband.
▪ **remembeˈbility** *noun* the fact of being rememberable M19. **rememberable** *adjective* able to be remembered; worthy of being remembered, memorable: LME. **rememberably** *adverb* (*rare*) E19. **rememberer** *noun* a person who or thing which remembers LME.

remembrance /rɪˈmɛmbr(ə)ns/ *noun & verb*. ME.
[Old French (Anglo-Norman *remembraunce*), from *remembrer*: see prec., -ANCE.]
▸ **A** *noun*. **1 a** The action of remembering; the process or fact of being remembered; memory or recollection concerning a particular person or thing (foll. by *of*); a particular memory or recollection, a reminiscence. ME. ▸**b** A person's faculty or power of remembering. LME. ▸**c** The point at which a person's memory of events begins, or the period over which it extends. M16. ▸**d** The surviving memory of a person. L16. ▸**e** In *pl.* Greetings, esp. conveyed through a third person. L18.
†**2 a** Mention, notice. LME–M17. ▸**b** A commemorative discourse or mention; a memorial inscription. Only in 16.
3 The action of reminding a person; a note providing a record or reminder, a memorandum. Later also, anything used to remind a person of something. Now *rare*. LME. ▸†**b** A reminder given by one person to another. L16–M17.
4 a An object serving to remind one person of another; a keepsake, a souvenir. LME. ▸**b** A memorial or record of some fact, person, etc. L15.
📖 **1a** M. TWAIN The remembrance of poor Susy's . . hayride . . brings me a pang. **2b** SHAKES. *Hen. V* Lay these bones in an unworthy urn, Tombless, with no remembrance over them.
Phrases: †**book of remembrance** a memorandum book, a record. **garden of remembrance** a garden commemorating the dead, esp. those killed in the wars of 1914–18 and 1939–45. **in remembrance of** in memory of.
Comb.: **Remembrance Day** (*a*) = *Remembrance Sunday* below; (*b*) *Hist.* = Armistice Day; **Remembrance Service**: held on Remembrance Sunday; **Remembrance Sunday** the Sunday nearest to 11 November, when those killed in the wars of 1914–18 and 1939–45 are commemorated; **Remembrancetide** the period immediately preceding Remembrance Sunday, considered as part of the liturgical year.
▸ **B** *verb trans.* Remind; remember. Chiefly as ***remembrancing*** *verbal noun*. *rare*. LME.

remembrancer /rɪˈmɛmbr(ə)nsə/ *noun*. LME.
[Anglo-Norman *remembrauncer*, from *remembraunce*: see prec., -ER².]
1 a Any of various officials of the Court of Exchequer. LME. ▸**b** An official of the Corporation of the City of London, appointed to represent that body before parliamentary committees and at Council and Treasury Boards. E18.
2 A person who reminds another, formerly *esp.* one appointed for that purpose. Also, a memoirist, a chronicler. E16.
3 a A thing serving as a reminder of something; a memento, a souvenir. L16. ▸**b** A book or pamphlet recording facts or information. L16.
1a King's Remembrancer, **Queen's Remembrancer** an officer (now of the Supreme Court) responsible for the collection of debts due to the Crown.
▪ **remembrancership** *noun* (*rare*) the office or position of remembrancer L19.

†**rememorate** *verb trans. & intrans.* LME–L17.
[Late Latin *rememorat-* pa. ppl stem of *rememorari*: see RE-, MEMORATE.]
Remind (a person); remember.

rememoration /rɪˌmɛməˈreɪʃ(ə)n/ *noun*. Long *rare*. LME.
[Late Latin *rememoratio(n-)*: see prec., -ATION.]
The action of remembering; an instance of this. Formerly also, the action of reminding someone.

remen /ˈrɛmɛn/ *noun*. M20.
[Egyptian.]
Hist. An ancient Egyptian measure of length.

†**remenant** *noun*. ME.
[Old French (also *remanant*), pres. pple of *remenoir*, *remanoir* REMAIN *verb*: see -ANT¹. See also REMNANT.]
1 *sing.* & in *pl.* = REMNANT *noun* 1. ME–L16.
2 = REMNANT 2b. Only in LME.

†**remercy** *verb trans.* L15–L16.
[Old & mod. French *remercier*, formed as RE-, MERCY.]
Thank.
📖 SPENSER She him remercied as the Patrone of her life.
▪ †**remerciments** *noun pl.* (*rare*) thanks M17–L18.

remex /ˈriːmɛks/ *noun*. Pl. **remiges** /ˈrɛmɪdʒiːz/. L17.
[Latin, from *remus* oar.]
†**1** A rower. *rare*. Only in L17.
2 ORNITHOLOGY. Any of the main flight feathers of a bird's wing; a primary or secondary feather. Usu. in *pl.* M18.

remicle /ˈrɛmɪk(ə)l/ *noun*. L19.
[from Latin *remig-*, *remex*: see prec., -CLE.]
ORNITHOLOGY. A small vestigial feather on the wing of some birds, attached to the second digit.

remiform /ˈrɛmɪfɔːm/ *adjective*. *rare*. L18.
[from Latin *remus* oar + -I- + -FORM.]
Shaped like an oar.

remigate /ˈrɛmɪgeɪt/ *verb intrans.* *rare*. E17.
[Latin *remigat-* pa. ppl stem of *remigare*, from *remex* REMEX: see -ATE³.]
Row.
▪ **remiˈgation** *noun* the action or an act of rowing E17.

remiges *noun* pl. of REMEX.

remigrate /riːmʌɪˈgreɪt/ *verb intrans.* E17.
[Orig. from Latin *remigrat-* pa. ppl stem of *remigrare* journey back: see -ATE³. Later from RE- + MIGRATE.]
†**1** Change back again. Only in 17.
2 Migrate again or back. E17.
▪ **remigration** *noun* E17.

remind /rɪˈmʌɪnd/ *verb trans.* M17.
[from RE- + MIND *verb*, prob. after REMEMORATE.]
1 Recall, remember, recollect. Now *rare* or *obsolete*. M17.
2 Cause (a person) to remember (*that*, *to do*); cause to think *of*. Also with direct speech as obj. M17.
📖 **2** I. MCEWAN 'We're on holiday,' Mary reminded him. D. MAY Her lined face reminded him of a Rembrandt portrait. M. MARRIN I kept reminding myself that I should be more careful.

reminder /rɪˈmʌɪndə/ *noun*. M17.
[from prec. + -ER¹.]
A thing that reminds or is intended to remind a person of something; *spec.* (*a*) a letter reminding a person of something that he she must do; (*b*) a memento, a souvenir.
📖 R. FRASER Mr Brontë . . seems to have found his children's presence a painful reminder of his wife. *Which?* You'd probably be sent a gentle reminder, instead of a stern . . letter.

remindful /rɪˈmʌɪn(d)fʊl, -f(ə)l/ *adjective*. E19.
[formed as prec. + -FUL.]
1 Mindful or retaining the memory *of*. E19.
2 Reminiscent or reviving the memory *of*. M19.

remineralize /riːˈmɪn(ə)r(ə)lʌɪz/ *verb*. Also **-ise**. M20.
[from RE- + MINERALIZE.]
MEDICINE. **1** *verb trans.* Restore the depleted mineral content of (bones, teeth, etc.). M20.
2 *verb intrans.* Undergo remineralization. M20.
▪ **remineraliˈzation** *noun* the natural restoration of the depleted content of bones, teeth, etc. M20.

Remington /ˈrɛmɪŋt(ə)n/ *noun*. M19.
[Eliphalet *Remington* (1793–1861) and his son Philo (1816–89), gunsmiths of Ilion, New York, the original manufacturers.]
(Proprietary name for) a make of firearm or a make of typewriter.

reminisce /rɛmɪˈnɪs/ *verb*. E19.
[Back-form. from next.]
1 *verb trans.* Recollect, remember; *esp.* say as a recollection. E19.
2 *verb intrans.* Indulge in reminiscences. M19.
📖 **1** A. GLYN 'I remember when the whole thing was eighteenth century,' he reminisced. **2** J. C. OATES Reminiscing about the early days of the department.
▪ **reminiscer** *noun* M20.

reminiscence /rɛmɪˈnɪs(ə)ns/ *noun*. L16.
[Late Latin *reminiscentia*, from Latin *reminisci* remember, formed as RE- + base of MIND *noun*¹: see -ENCE.]
1 The action or process of remembering; *spec.* the recovery of knowledge by mental effort. L16. ▸**b** PHILOSOPHY. Esp. in Platonism, the theory of the recovery of things known to the soul in previous existences. M17.
2 A recollection, a memory, *esp.* a recollection of a past fact or experience recounted to others (usu. in *pl.*); *spec.* (in *pl.*) a person's collective memories or experiences put into literary form. E19.
3 An expression, feature, fact, etc., which recalls or is suggestive of something else. M19.
4 PSYCHOLOGY. An improvement in the memory or performance of something partially learned, occurring after the learning has ceased. E20.
📖 **1** P. H. JOHNSON Her . . youth came back to her in a rush of reminiscence. **2** A. C. BOULT We were very happy to meet and exchange reminiscences. E. YOUNG-BRUEHL Published memoirs and reminiscences have been very valuable.
▪ †**reminiscency** *noun* the faculty of remembering M17–M18.

reminiscent /rɛmɪˈnɪs(ə)nt/ *adjective & noun*. M18.
[Latin *reminiscent-* pres. ppl stem of *reminisci*: see prec., -ENT.]
▸ **A** *adjective*. **1** Characterized by reminiscence; given to reminiscing. M18. ▸**b** Having a recollection *of* something. *rare*. M19.
2 Of the nature of reminiscence or reminiscences; evoking a reminiscence *of* a person or thing. M19.
📖 **1** E. NORTH Phylis . . was in a reminiscent mood, mostly about her early married life. **2** *Sunday Times* Dark blue braided uniforms reminiscent of hussars.
▸ **B** *noun*. A recounter or writer of reminiscences. Now *rare*. E19.
▪ **reminiscently** *adverb* L19.

reminiscential /ˌrɛmɪnɪˈsɛnʃ(ə)l/ *adjective*. M17.
[from REMINISCENCE after *essential*.]
Of the nature of or pertaining to reminiscence.

remise /rɪˈmiːz/ *noun*. L15.
[Old & mod. French, from *remis(e)* pa. pple of *remettre* put back or up.]
▸ **I** †**1** LAW. A transfer or surrender of property. L15–M18.
†**2** The action of remitting money; a remittance. M–L17.
▸ **II 3** *Hist.* **a** A shelter for a carriage; a coach-house. L17. ▸**b** A hired carriage of a better class than an ordinary hackney-coach. L17.

4 *FENCING.* A second thrust made after the first has missed and while still on the lunge. **E19.**
5 A specially planted shelter for partridges. **E20.**

remise /rɪˈmiːz/ *verb.* **L15.**
[Old & mod. French *remis(e)*: see prec.]
▶ **I** †**1** *verb trans.* Replace, put back *in* or *into* a place, state, etc.; convert again *into*; send back *to*. **L15–E17.**
2 *verb trans. & intrans. LAW.* Surrender or make over (a right, property, etc.). **L15.**
▶ **II 3** *verb intrans. FENCING.* Make a remise. **L19.**

remiss /rɪˈmɪs/ *adjective.* **LME.**
[Latin *remissus* pa. pple of *remittere* **REMIT** *verb*.]
†**1 a** *MEDICINE.* Weakened in consistency or colour; dilute. **LME–E17.** ▸**b** Esp. of a sound: weak, soft, faint. **M16–M17.**
2 (Of a person) careless of duty, negligent; (of conduct, an action, etc.) characterized by carelessness or negligence. **LME.**
3 Characterized by a lack of strictness; unrestrained, lax, lenient. Long *rare* or *obsolete*. **LME.**
4 Free from violence; lacking in force or energy. **M16.** ▸†**b** Esp. of heat or cold: not intense or strong; moderate, slight. **L16–L17.**
†**5** Diminished in tension; slack, loose, relaxed. **E–M17.**

🕮 **2** L. BLUE What! You haven't got a bottle of Pernod handy? How remiss of you!

■ **remissly** *adverb* **LME.** **remissness** *noun* **L16.**

remiss /rɪˈmɪs/ *verb trans.* **LME.**
[Latin *remiss-* pa. ppl stem of *remittere* **REMIT** *verb*.]
†**1** Remit; mitigate; pardon, pass over. **LME–M17.**
2 *LAW.* = **REMISE** *verb* 2. *rare.* **E19.**

remissful /rɪˈmɪsfʊl, -f(ə)l/ *adjective. rare.* **E17.**
[from **REMISS** *verb* or *adjective* + **-FUL.**]
†**1** Full of remission; merciful. Only in **E17.**
2 Remiss, careless, negligent. **M19.**

remissible /rɪˈmɪsɪb(ə)l/ *adjective.* **L16.**
[French *rémissible* or late Latin *remissibilis*, formed as **REMISS** *verb*: see **-IBLE.**]
Capable of remission; able to be remitted.
■ **remissiˈbility** *noun* (*rare*) **L17.**

remission /rɪˈmɪʃ(ə)n/ *noun.* **ME.**
[Old & mod. French *rémission* or Latin *remissio(n-)*, formed as **REMISS** *verb*: see **-ION.**]
1 Forgiveness or pardon of or *of* a sin or other offence; deliverance from guilt or punishment. **ME.** ▸†**b** An inclination towards pardon. *rare* (Shakes.). Only in **E17.**
†**2 a** Release from a debt or payment. **LME–E17.** ▸**b** Release from captivity, liberation; respite. **LME–M18.**
3 The action of giving up or reducing a debt, tax, punishment, etc.; *spec.* the reduction of a prison sentence on account of good behaviour. **LME.**
4 a A reduction in force or intensity; a decrease or abatement of a condition or quality, esp. of heat or cold. **LME.** ▸**b** *MEDICINE.* A lessening in the degree or intensity of an illness; the temporary disappearance of symptoms. **L17.**
†**5** Relaxation; a lessening of tension; a slackening of energy or application. **L16–M18.**
6 The action of sending back a person or thing; a remittal. *rare.* **E17.**

🕮 **1** BROWNING Children punished by mistake are promised a remission of next offence. **2a** SHAKES. *Coriol.* Though I owe My revenge properly, my remission lies In Volscian breasts. **3** C. ANGIER Max earned full remission of his sentence, but he still spent two whole years in prison. **4a** WORDSWORTH Darkness fell Without remission of the blast or shower. **b** G. DALY His cancer had gone into remission, but the respite was . . brief.

remissive /rɪˈmɪsɪv/ *adjective.* **LME.**
[medieval Latin *remissivus*, formed as **REMISS** *verb*: see **-IVE.**]
†**1** Producing or allowing a decrease *of* something; causing relaxation. **LME–E18.**
†**2** Remiss, careless, negligent. *rare.* **L15–M17.**
3 Characterized by remission or abatement. **L15.**
4 Inclined to or of the nature of remission or pardon. **E17.**

🕮 **4** J. CARROLL The . . intellectual role in the rise of the remissive attitude to crime.

■ **remissively** *adverb* (*rare*) **L15.**

remissory /rɪˈmɪs(ə)ri/ *adjective. rare.* **M16.**
[medieval Latin *remissorius*, formed as **REMISS** *verb*: see **-ORY[2].**]
Of the nature of remission.

remit /ˈriːmɪt, rɪˈmɪt/ *noun.* **LME.**
[from the verb.]
†**1** Remission, pardon. Chiefly *Scot. rare.* **LME–E17.**
2 Reference of a matter to another person or authority for settlement; *esp.* in *LAW*, the transfer of a case from one court or judge to another. Chiefly *Scot.* **M17.**
3 An item submitted for consideration at a conference etc. Chiefly *NZ.* **E20.**
4 A set of instructions, a brief; an area of authority or responsibility. **M20.**

🕮 **4** *Television Week* Mellersh . . was appointed . . with a remit to win new franchises. *Country Walking* Included within the remit of the tourist office is a . . nature reserve.

remit /rɪˈmɪt/ *verb.* Infl. **-tt-**. **LME.**
[Latin *remittere* send back, slacken, relax, postpone, formed as **RE-** + *mittere* send.]
▶ **I 1** *verb trans.* Forgive, pardon, (a sin or other offence). **LME.**
†**2** *verb trans.* Give up, surrender, (a right or possession). **LME–L17.**
3 *verb trans.* Refrain from exacting (a payment or service) or inflicting (a punishment); withdraw, cancel; grant remission of (suffering, a sentence). **LME.**
†**4** *verb trans.* Discharge, set free, release, (a person). Also foll. by *of*, *to*. **LME–M17.**

🕮 **3** C. V. WEDGWOOD The death sentence . . was remitted to life imprisonment. K. AMIS Pray to God to remit some part of your dreadful punishment.

▶ **II** †**5** *verb trans.* Relax, relieve from tension. **LME–E18.**
6 *verb trans.* Lay aside, mitigate, (anger, displeasure, etc.). **LME.** ▸**b** *verb trans. & intrans.* Give up, abandon, (a pursuit, occupation, etc.). **L16.**
7 a *verb trans.* Allow (one's diligence, attention, etc.) to slacken or diminish. **E16.** ▸**b** *verb intrans.* Abate, diminish, slacken. **E16.** ▸**c** *verb intrans.* Manifest a diminishing *of* some quality. Long *rare* or *obsolete*. **E17.**

🕮 **6b** A. W. KINGLAKE Engaged . . in a siege they could not remit. **7b** *British Medical Journal* Phobias may . . remit spontaneously without any treatment.

▶ **III 8** *verb trans.* Refer (a matter) *to* a person or authority for settlement; *spec.* in *LAW*, send back (a case) to an inferior court. **LME.** ▸**b** Send (a person) from one tribunal *to* another for trial or hearing. **M16.** ▸†**c** Commit (a person, oneself) *to* the charge of another. **L17–M18.**
9 *verb trans.* Refer (a person) *to* a book, person, etc., for information. **LME.**
10 *verb trans.* Send (a person) back to prison or other custody; recommit. Now *rare.* **LME.**
11 *verb trans.* †**a** *LAW.* Restore to a former and more valid title. (Cf. **REMITTER** *noun[1]* 1a). **M16–M18.** ▸**b** Put back *into* a previous position; consign again *to* a former state or condition. **L16.**
12 *verb trans.* Postpone, defer. **M16.**
13 *verb trans.* Send, transmit, (money or articles of value) to a person or place. Usu. foll. by *to*. **M16.**
14 *verb trans.* Refer, assign, or transfer *to* a thing or person. **L16.**

🕮 **8b** *Daily Telegraph* A youth was fined . . and two others remitted to juvenile court. **11b** JOHN BRIGHT You propose to remit to slavery three millions of negroes. **12** *Times* The movers refused Mr Tierney's request to remit the motion. **13** E. HUXLEY At least £2½ millions were remitted to Barbados.

■ **remitment** *noun* †(*a*) remission, pardon; (*b*) the remitting of money; remittance: **E17.** **remittable** *adjective* able to be remitted **E17.** **remittal** *noun* (*a*) a remission *for* sin or *of* a debt, penalty, etc.; (*b*) *LAW* the action of referring a case from one court to another: **L16.** **remiˈttee** *noun* a person to whom a remittance is made or sent **M18.**

remittance /rɪˈmɪt(ə)ns/ *noun.* **E18.**
[from prec. + **-ANCE.**]
A sum of money sent, esp. by post, from one place or person to another for goods or services or as an allowance; a quantity of goods sent in this way; the action of sending money etc. to another place.
Comb.: **remittance man** (chiefly *Hist.*) an emigrant who is supported or assisted by money sent from home.

remittent /rɪˈmɪt(ə)nt/ *adjective & noun.* **L17.**
[Latin *remittent-* pres. ppl stem of *remittere*, formed as **REMIT** *verb*: see **-ENT.**]
▶ **A** *adjective.* That remits or abates for a time; *spec.* in *MEDICINE*, (of a fever) characterized by fluctuating body temperature. **L17.**
▶ **B** *noun.* **1** *MEDICINE.* A remittent fever. **L17.**
2 A person who remits money. *rare.* **M19.**
■ **remittence** *noun* the quality of being remittent **E20.** **remittency** *noun* = **REMITTENCE E19.**

remitter /rɪˈmɪtə/ *noun[1].* **LME.**
[from **REMIT** *verb* + **-ER[4].**]
1 *LAW.* **a** A principle by which a person having two titles to an estate, and entering on it by the later or more defective of these, is adjudged to hold it by the earlier or more valid one. **LME.** ▸**b** An act of remitting a case to another court. **E18.**
2 Restoration to rights or privileges, or to a previous state. Now *rare.* **L16.**

remitter /rɪˈmɪtə/ *noun[2].* **M16.**
[from **REMIT** *verb* + **-ER[1].**]
1 A person who forgives or pardons a sin. *rare.* **M16.**
2 A person who sends a remittance. **L17.**

remittitur /rɪˈmɪtɪtəː/ *noun.* **L18.**
[Latin, 3rd person sing. pass. of *remittere* **REMIT** *verb*.]
LAW. **1** The remission of excessive damages awarded to a plaintiff; a formal statement of this. **L18.**
2 The action of sending the transcript of a case back from an appellate to a trial court; a formal notice of this. **L18.**

remix /ˈriːmɪks/ *noun.* **M20.**
[from the verb.]
A new version of a musical recording in which the separate tracks are combined in a different way; *loosely* a re-recording.

remix /riːˈmɪks/ *verb trans.* **M17.**
[from **RE-** + **MIX** *verb*.]
1 Mix again. **M17.**
2 *spec.* Create a different version of (a musical recording) by altering the balance of the separate tracks. **M20.**
■ **remixture** *noun* the action or an act of remixing something **E19.**

remnant /ˈrɛmnənt/ *noun & adjective.* **ME.**
[Contr. of **REMENANT.**]
▶ **A** *noun.* **1** *sing.* & in *pl.* That which remains of a thing, group of people, etc.; the remainder, the rest. Now *spec.* a small remaining amount or number; *Hist.* a small number of Jews surviving a period of persecution. **ME.** ▸**b** A survivor *of* something. *rare.* **L16.** ▸**c** *PHYSICAL GEOGRAPHY.* = **RESIDUAL** *noun* 5. **L19.**
2 A fragment, a small portion, a scrap. **LME.** ▸**b** *spec.* An end of a piece of cloth etc. left over after the main portion has been used or sold. **LME.**
3 A remaining trace *of* some quality, belief, condition, etc. **M16.**

🕮 **1** W. COWPER Rejoice That yet a remnant of your race survives. W. S. CHURCHILL On December 5 Napoleon abandoned the remnant of his armies on the Russian frontier. I. MURDOCH Ludens had cleared away the remnants of supper. **2** GEO. ELIOT That remnant of a human being. **b** *Country Living* Transform inexpensive straw hats . . with . . a bouquet cut from a remnant. **3** G. DALY Somehow he summoned a last remnant of strength.

▶ **B** *adjective.* Remaining. **M16.**
■ **remnantal** *adjective* (*PHYSICAL GEOGRAPHY*) of or pertaining to a remnant **E20.**

remodel /ˈriːmɒd(ə)l/ *noun.* **M20.**
[from the verb.]
ARCHITECTURE. An act of modelling or constructing a building again; a remodelled building.

remodel /riːˈmɒd(ə)l/ *verb trans.* Infl. **-ll-**, ***-l-**. **L18.**
[from **RE-** + **MODEL** *verb*.]
Model again, reconstruct.
■ **remodeller** *noun* **M19.**

remodify /riːˈmɒdɪfʌɪ/ *verb trans.* **M19.**
[from **RE-** + **MODIFY** *verb*.]
Modify (again), make a change in.
■ **remodifiˈcation** *noun* (a) further modification **M19.**

remolade /ˈrɛməlɑːd/ *noun. rare.* **E18.**
[French †*rémolade*, **RÉMOULADE.**]
An ointment used in farriery.

remold *noun, verb* see **REMOULD** *noun, verb.*

remonstrance /rɪˈmɒnstr(ə)ns/ *noun.* **L15.**
[Old French *remonstrance* (mod. *remontrance*) or medieval Latin *remonstrantia*, from *remonstrant-* pres. ppl stem of *remonstrare*: see **REMONSTRATE, -ANCE.**]
†**1** An appeal, a request. *rare.* Only in **L15.**
†**2** Proof, evidence; demonstration *of* some fact, quality, etc. **L16–L18.**
3 †**a** A written or spoken demonstration, statement, or account (*of* some matter). **L16–M18.** ▸**b** *Hist.* A formal statement of a grievance or similar matter of public importance; *esp.* (***the Grand Remonstrance***) that presented by the House of Commons to the Crown in 1641. **E17.** ▸†**c** *ECCLESIASTICAL HISTORY.* (**R-**.) A document presented in 1610 to the States of Holland by the Dutch Arminians, concerning the differences between themselves and the strict Calvinists. **M17–E18.**
4 The action of remonstrating; expostulation; an instance of this. **E17.**
5 *ROMAN CATHOLIC CHURCH.* = **MONSTRANCE** *noun* 2. **M17.**

🕮 **4** M. SEYMOUR The time had gone for gentle remonstrance. A. BROOKNER Remonstrances, reprobations, would be greeted with a storm of tears.

remonstrant /rɪˈmɒnstr(ə)nt/ *noun & adjective.* **E17.**
[medieval Latin *remonstrant-* pres. ppl stem of *remonstrare*: see next, **-ANT[1].**]
▶ **A** *noun.* **1** *ECCLESIASTICAL HISTORY.* (**R-**.) A member of the Arminian party in the Dutch Reformed Church, so called from the Remonstrance of 1610. **E17.**
2 A person who remonstrates. Formerly also, the author or a supporter of a formal remonstrance. **M17.**
▶ **B** *adjective.* **1** *ECCLESIASTICAL HISTORY.* (**R-**.) Of or belonging to the Arminian party in the Dutch Reformed Church. **E17.**
2 Remonstrating, expostulating. **M17.**

▪ **remonstrantly** *adverb* L19.

remonstrate /ˈrɛmənstreɪt/ *verb.* L16.
[medieval Latin *remonstrat-* pa. ppl stem of *remonstrare* demonstrate, formed as RE- + Latin *monstrare* show: see -ATE³.]
†**1** *verb trans.* **a** Make plain, demonstrate, show. Also foll. by *to* a person. L16–M18. ▸**b** Declare *that.* M17–M18.
†**2** *verb trans.* **a** Point out (a fault etc.) *to* someone by way of reproof or complaint; protest against (a wrong). E17–M18. ▸**b** Point out or represent (a grievance etc.) to some authority. Also foll. by *to.* M17–M18.
†**3** *verb intrans.* Raise an objection *to* a thing; address a remonstrance *to* a person. M17–L18.
4 *verb intrans.* Urge strong reasons *against* a course of action; expostulate *with* a person; argue, protest. L17.
5 *verb trans.* Say or plead in remonstrance. Also foll. by *that.* M18.

> **4** E. SIMPSON He had remonstrated with her for setting traps for the mice. P. ACKROYD He remonstrated with me for my absurd pride. **5** D. H. LAWRENCE 'You'll only break the thing down altogether, Clifford,' she remonstrated.

▪ **remonstratingly** *adverb* in a remonstrating manner E19. **reˈmonstrative** *adjective* of or characterized by remonstrance, expostulatory E17. **remonstrator** *noun* a person who remonstrates M17. **remonstratory** *adjective* (*rare*) = REMONSTRATIVE E19.

remonstration /rɛmənˈstreɪʃ(ə)n/ *noun.* L15.
[medieval Latin *remonstratio(n-)*, formed as prec.: see -ATION.]
The action of remonstrating; an instance of this.

remontant /rɪˈmɒnt(ə)nt/ *adjective & noun.* L19.
[French, pres. pple of *remonter* REMOUNT *verb*: see -ANT¹.]
▸ **A** *adjective.* (Esp. of a rose) blooming more than once in a season; (of a strawberry plant) bearing several crops in one season. Cf. PERPETUAL *adjective* 2c. L19.
▸ **B** *noun.* A remontant rose or strawberry. L19.

remontoir /rɛmənˈtwɑː/ *noun.* Also **-re.** E19.
[French, from *remonter* REMOUNT *verb.*]
HOROLOGY. A device by which a uniform impulse is given to the pendulum or balance at regular intervals.

remora /ˈrɛmərə/ *noun.* M16.
[Latin = delay, hindrance, formed as RE- + *mora* delay.]
1 Any of various slender marine fishes of the family Echeneidae, with the dorsal fin modified to form a large sucker for attachment to sharks etc., formerly believed to hinder the progress of any sailing ship to which it attached itself. M16.
2 An obstacle, a hindrance, an impediment. E17.
3 SURGERY. An instrument used to keep bones etc. in place. *rare.* L17.

remord /rɪˈmɔːd/ *verb.* Long *arch. rare.* LME.
[Old & mod. French *remordre* from Proto-Romance alt. of Latin *remordere*: see next.]
1 *verb trans.* Afflict (a person, one's conscience, oneself, etc.) with remorse. LME.
2 *verb intrans.* Feel remorse. LME.
†**3** *verb trans.* Recall with remorse. LME–L16.
†**4** *verb trans.* Blame, rebuke. L15–E17.

remorse /rɪˈmɔːs/ *noun.* LME.
[Old French *remors* (mod. *remords*) from medieval Latin *remorsus*, from Latin *remors-* pa. ppl stem of *remordere* vex, torment, formed as RE- + *mordere* bite, sting, etc.]
1 Deep regret and repentance for a wrong committed; compunction. Also, compassionate reluctance to inflict pain (chiefly in ***without remorse***). LME. ▸†**b** An instance of such feeling. M17–M18.
†**2** **a** Regretful remembrance *of* a thing. LME–L17. ▸**b** A solemn obligation. *rare* (Shakes.). Only in E17.
†**3** Sorrow, pity, compassion; in *pl.*, signs of tender feeling. M16–E18.
†**4** Biting or cutting force. *rare* (Spenser). Only in L16.

> **1** SHELLEY We were slaying still without remorse. B. CHATWIN He felt remorse for having left her.

Phrases: **without remorse** †(*a*) without mitigation or intermission; (*b*) see sense 1 above.

remorseful /rɪˈmɔːsfʊl, -f(ə)l/ *adjective.* L16.
[from prec. + -FUL.]
1 Affected with or characterized by remorse; repentant. L16.
†**2** Compassionate, full of pity. L16–E17.

> **1** M. E. BRADDON Such comfort as the Church can give to the remorseful sinner. **2** SHAKES. *Two Gent.* Thou art a gentleman.. Valiant, wise, remorseful, well accomplish'd.

▪ **remorsefully** *adverb* M19. **remorsefulness** *noun* E17.

remorseless /rɪˈmɔːslɪs/ *adjective & adverb.* L16.
[formed as prec. + -LESS.]
▸ **A** *adjective.* Without compassion or compunction, pitiless; relentless, unabating. L16.

> M. CREIGHTON His remorseless harrying of the north. *Times* The remorseless parade of whey-faced classic lovelies, each indistinguishable from the other.

▸ **B** *adverb.* Remorselessly. *rare.* L16.
▪ **remorselessly** *adverb* in a remorseless manner E17. **remorselessness** *noun* M17.

remortgage /riːˈmɔːɡɪdʒ/ *verb & noun.* M20.
[from RE- + MORTGAGE.]
▸ **A** *verb trans.* Mortgage again; revise the terms of an existing mortgage on (a property). M20.
▸ **B** *noun.* A different or revised mortgage. M20.

remote /rɪˈməʊt/ *adjective, noun, & adverb.* LME.
[Latin *remotus* pa. pple of *removere* REMOVE *verb.*]
▸ **A** *adjective.* **1** Situated at a distance or interval from each other; far apart. *arch.* LME.
2 **a** Far away, distant, (*from* some place, thing, or person); removed, set apart. L16. ▸**b** Out of the way, secluded; situated away from the main centres of population, society, etc. E17. ▸**c** Distant in time. E18. ▸**d** Situated, occurring, or performed at a (not necessarily great) distance. Esp. in ***remote control*** below. E20.
3 **a** Not closely connected with or affecting a person or thing. L16. ▸**b** Widely different or divergent *from* something else. M17. ▸†**c** Far-fetched; unusual. *rare.* L17–L18. ▸**d** Not closely related by blood or kinship. M18. ▸**e** Of a person: distant from others in manner; withdrawn, aloof. L19.
4 Slight, faint. E18.

> **1** SHAKES. *Phoenix* Hearts remote, yet not asunder. **2a** SIR W. SCOTT For our separate use.. We'll hold this hut's remoter end. E. M. FORSTER A small thing at hand is greater than a great thing remote. **b** M. RICHLER His family lived in a remote town perched atop a rocky hilltop. **c** G. L. HARDING In remote geological times parts.. of East Jordan were under the sea. **d** *Telelink* The micro's real-time clock can be used ..to provide remote, unattended operation. **3a** M. L. KING Many whites to whom the horror of slavery had been emotionally remote. M. LEITCH A place as remote from her own concerns as Siberia. **b** LD MACAULAY This calculation was not remote from the truth. **d** A. PRYCE-JONES Uncle Freddy, as I called him—he was in reality a very remote cousin. **e** J. B. PRIESTLEY Miss Trant seemed so dreamy and remote these days that she was considered unapproachable. **4** G. B. SHAW Paquito has not the remotest idea of what it is to be exploited. E. BOWEN The possibility of their ever falling in love remained.. remote.

▸ **B** *noun.* **1** A remote person or thing. *rare.* E16.
2 = ***remote control*** below. M20.
3 BROADCASTING. An outside broadcast. *US.* M20.
▸ **C** *adverb.* **1** At a great distance, far off. Chiefly *poet.* M17.
2 At or from a (not necessarily great) distance. Only in comb., as ***remote mounted*** etc. M20.
Special collocations & comb.: **remote control** (*a*) control of a machine or apparatus from a distance, esp. by signals transmitted from a radio or electronic device; (*b*) a usu. hand-held device for operating a television etc. by this means. **remote-controlled** *adjective* operated by remote control. **remote sensing** the scanning of the earth or another planet by satellite or high-flying craft in order to obtain information about it. **remote sensor** a recording device (as a camera on a satellite) which carries out remote sensing.
▪ **remotely** *adverb* in a remote manner, distantly; at or from a (not necessarily great) distance: L16. **remoteness** *noun* the state of being remote E17.

remotion /rɪˈməʊʃ(ə)n/ *noun.* Now *rare.* LME.
[Old French, or Latin *remotio(n-)*: see RE-, MOTION.]
1 Remoteness. LME.
2 The action of removing something; removal. LME.
†**3** The action of leaving or departing. Only in 17.

> **3** SHAKES. *Lear* This act persuades me That this remotion of the Duke and her Is practice only.

remotive /rɪˈməʊtɪv/ *adjective. rare.* L15.
[from Latin *remot-* pa. ppl stem of *removere* REMOVE *verb* + -IVE.]
That may be removed.

†**remoue** *verb* see REMOVE *verb.*

rémoulade /ˈrɛmʊlɑːd, *foreign* remulad (*pl. same*)/ *noun.* Also **re-.** M19.
[French from Italian *remolata*, of unkn. origin. Cf. earlier REMOLADE.]
A salad dressing made with hard-boiled egg-yolks, oil, vinegar, herbs, etc.

remould /ˈriːməʊld/ *noun.* Also ***-mold.** M20.
[from the verb.]
A worn tyre on to which a new tread has been moulded.

remould /riːˈməʊld/ *verb trans.* Also ***-mold.** L17.
[from RE- + MOULD *verb*².]
Mould again, shape differently, refashion; *spec.* re-form the tread of (a tyre).

remount /ˈriːmaʊnt/ *noun.* L18.
[from the verb.]
MILITARY. **1** A supply of fresh horses for a regiment. L18.
2 A horse used to replace another which is tired or has been killed. E19.

remount /riːˈmaʊnt/ *verb.* LME.
[In early use from Old & mod. French *remonter*, formed as RE- + *monter* MOUNT *verb*; later directly from RE- + MOUNT *verb.*]
▸ **I** *verb trans.* **1** †**a** Raise or lift up again; restore to a former state. LME–L16. ▸**b** Set up in place or put together again; *esp.* mount (a gun) again. Now *rare.* E17.
2 **a** Replace on horseback, help (a person) to mount again. LME. ▸**b** Provide (cavalry) with fresh horses. L17.
3 †**a** Rise again to or regain (a state or point). L15–M17. ▸**b** Climb or go up (a place or thing) again. E17. ▸**c** Mount or get on (a horse etc.) again. L18.
▸ **II** *verb intrans.* **4** Mount, rise, or move upwards again (*to*). LME.
5 Get on horseback again. (Foll. by †*to.*) L16.
6 Go back in the course of an investigation *to* a certain point, period, etc. M18. ▸**b** Go back in time *to* a certain date. M19. ▸**c** Go back *to* a source. M19.

removable /rɪˈmuːvəb(ə)l/ *adjective & noun.* M16.
[from REMOVE *verb* + -ABLE.]
▸ **A** *adjective.* **1** Subject to removal from an office, jurisdiction, holding, etc. M16.
2 Able to be removed. M16.
▸ **B** *noun.* A removable resident magistrate in Ireland. L19.
▪ **removaˈbility** *noun* L18.

removal /rɪˈmuːv(ə)l/ *noun.* E16.
[from REMOVE *verb* + -AL¹.]
1 **a** The action of changing one's place or position; *esp.* change of residence. Also, an instance of this. E16. ▸**b** The action of moving a person or thing to another place, post, etc.; the fact of being so moved; *spec.* the transfer of furniture and other household effects on moving house. Also, an instance of this. M17. ▸**c** In full ***removal of remains.*** The formal procedure of taking a body from the house to the church for the funeral service. *Anglo-Irish.* L19.
2 The action of taking a thing off or away; the action of getting rid of a person; *spec.* (*a*) dismissal from an office or post; (*b*) murder. Also, an instance of this. M16.

> **1a** J. AGATE Sorting out my papers before the removal to Fairfax Road. **b** *attrib.*: *Times* The Patels.. are worried that the removal men may damage their temple. **2** D. F. GALOUYE The simple removal of four screws would unfasten the grating.

▪ **removalist** *noun* (*Austral.*) a person or firm engaged in household or business removals M20.

remove /rɪˈmuːv/ *noun.* E16.
[from the verb.]
1 The action or an act of dismissing a person from a position or office. Now *rare.* E16. ▸†**b** The action of getting rid of a person by killing; murder. L16–M17. ▸†**c** The raising of a siege. *rare* (Shakes.). Only in E17.
2 †**a** The action of taking away or getting rid of a thing. L16–L17. ▸**b** FARRIERY. A procedure in which a horse's shoe is taken off, the hoof trimmed or dressed, and the shoe replaced; (now *dial.*) an old shoe used over again. L16. ▸**c** The action or an act of taking away a dish or course at a meal in order to bring on another in its place; *esp.* a dish taken away or brought on in this way. *arch.* L18.
3 The action of moving a thing from one place to another. Now *rare.* L16.
4 The action or an act of changing one's place, esp. one's residence; departure to another place. Now *rare.* L16. ▸†**b** A period of absence from a place. *rare* (Shakes.). Only in E17.
5 †**a** The action or an act of transferring a person from one office or post to another; the fact of being so transferred. E17–M18. ▸**b** A promotion of a pupil to a higher form or division in some schools. M17. ▸**c** A certain form or division of a form in some schools. M18.
6 **a** A space or interval by which one person or thing is remote from another in time, place, condition, etc.; a distance. E17. ▸**b** A stage in gradation; a degree (away). M17. ▸**c** A degree in descent or blood relationship. M18. ▸**d** TYPOGRAPHY. The number of sizes by which the type of a footnote or side-note is smaller than that of the text; *transf.* a footnote, a side-note. L19.

> **5b** A. BRAZIL I make up my mind every term I'm going to win a double remove. **6a** *Listener* At this remove I cannot recall many of the variations. V. GORNICK I became.. a prisoner yearning down at the street below, my sense of remove then overpowering. **b** L. MACNEICE The people the hero wants to get at.. are always at several removes. **c** M. FITZHERBERT A first cousin to Aubrey at one remove.

remove /rɪˈmuːv/ *verb.* Also (earlier) †**rem(o)ue.** ME.
[Old French *remeuv-*, *remov-* stressed and unstressed stems respectively of *removeir* (mod. *remouvoir*) from Latin *removere*: see RE-, MOVE *verb.* Some early forms are indistinguishable from those from Old & mod. French *remuer* (from *re-* RE- + *muer* from Latin *mutare* change), whence the vars. *rem(o)ue.*]
▸ **I** *verb trans.* **1** Move away from the position occupied; lift or push aside; take off or out; take away or withdraw from a place, person, etc. (*lit. & fig.*); *refl.* go away. ME. ▸**b** Get rid of (a person); assassinate, kill. Now *colloq.* M17. ▸**c** In *pass.* Of a dish or course in a meal: be followed *by.* M19. ▸**d** CRICKET. Of a bowler or ball: dismiss (a batsman). M20.
2 Move or transfer from one place to another; change the place or situation of; move; *formal* conduct the removal of (furniture etc.) as an occupation. ME.

▸†**b** Move or stir (a part of the body). L15–L16. ▸**c** *LAW.* Transfer (a case, formerly also, a person) for trial from one court of law to another. *obsolete* exc. *US.* E16.

3 a Send (a person) away; compel to leave a place; *spec.* in *SCOTS LAW*, compel (a tenant) to leave. ME. ▸**b** Dismiss (a person) from office; depose. ME. ▸†**c** Raise (a siege). ME–M17.

4 Relieve or free a person from (some (esp. bad) feeling, condition, etc.); eliminate. (Foll. by *from*.) LME. ▸†**b** Set aside (a feeling, thought, etc.). (Foll. by *from*.) LME–E18.

†**5** Dissuade (*from*). L15–M17.

> **1** B. PYM She removed the half-finished page from the typewriter. A. COHEN He removed his hat gallantly and bowed slightly. P. ROAZEN She had had trouble with her gall bladder until it was removed. R. FRASER Branwell had to be removed from Haworth Grammar School because of a nervous breakdown. *Sanity* Decision by Defence Secretary .. to remove commoners' rights at base. **c** THACKERAY Boiled haddock, removed by hashed mutton. **2** J. MOXON Then removing the string the space of 15 degrees in the Quadrant. J. MARQUAND The young lady had better be removed at once to the safe place. **4** P. TILLICH One cannot remove anxiety by arguing it away.

▸ **II** *verb intrans.* **6** Orig., shift one's place or position. Later, go away, depart, (*to*); *spec.* (*a*) change one's place of residence; (*b*) *SCOTS LAW* (of a tenant) leave a house or holding. Now *formal.* ME.

7 Of a thing: change place; move off or away; disappear. ME.

†**8** Move, stir; be in motion. ME–E17.

> **6** E. B. BROWNING I removed to our present residence just in time.

▪ **removement** *noun* (*arch.*) the action of removing something; the fact of being removed; removal: M17.

removed /rɪˈmuːvd/ *ppl adjective.* M16.
[from prec. + -ED¹.]
1 Esp. of cousins: distant in relationship by a certain number of degrees of descent. M16.
2 Lifted, taken away; *spec.* taken away by death. E17.
3 Distant, remote, separated, set apart. Now only foll. by *from.* E17.

> **1** *cousin once removed, cousin twice removed*, etc. **3** H. BELLOC Rooms removed from the other rooms of a house. *fig.*: S. ROSENBERG How far removed from their dream was the daily activity of Soviet society.

▪ **removedness** *noun* E17.

remover /rɪˈmuːvə/ *noun.* L16.
[from REMOVE *verb* + -ER¹.]
1 A person who or thing which removes or takes away something; *spec.* a person who conducts the removal of furniture etc. as an occupation. L16.
2 A person who changes place; a restless person. *rare.* L16.

> **1** B. VINE The furniture still stood about where the removers had stuck it. **2** SHAKES. *Sonn.* Love is not love which .. bends with the remover to remove.

remplaçant /rɑ̃plasɑ̃/ *noun.* Also (fem.) ***-ante*** /-ɑ̃ːt/. Pl. pronounced same. M19.
[French, pres. ppl adjective of *remplacer* replace: see -ANT¹.]
A person who replaces another; a substitute.

rempli /ˈrɒmˈpliː/ *adjective.* Also (earlier) †**-ply**. E18.
[French, pa. pple of *remplir* fill up.]
HERALDRY. Of an ordinary etc.: filled in with another colour leaving only a border round the outside.

remskoen /ˈrɛmskʊn/ *noun.* Also **riem-** /ˈriːm-/ & other vars. Pl. **-e** /-ə/. E19.
[Afrikaans, from Dutch *remschoen*, from *rem* brake + *schoen* SHOE *noun.*]
S. AFR. HISTORY. A wooden or metal shoe used to prevent a wheel from revolving; *fig.* an impediment to progress.

remuage /rəmɥaːʒ, rɛmjʊˈɑːʒ/ *noun.* E20.
[French, lit. 'moving about'.]
The periodic turning or shaking of bottled wine, esp. champagne, to move sediment towards the cork.

remuda /rəˈmuːdə/ *noun.* L19.
[Amer. Spanish from Spanish = exchange, replacement.]
A herd or collection of saddle-horses kept for remounts.

†**remue** *verb* see REMOVE *verb.*

remueur /rəmɥœːr/ *noun.* Pl. pronounced same. E20.
[French, lit. 'mover'.]
A person who engages in *remuage.*

remunerate /rɪˈmjuːnəreɪt/ *verb trans.* E16.
[Latin *remunerat-* pa. ppl stem of *remunerari* (later *-are*), formed as RE- + *munerari*, *-are*, from *munus*, *muner-* gift: see -ATE³.]
1 Make a repayment or return for (a service etc.). E16.
2 Reward; pay (a person) for services rendered or work done. L16. ▸**b** Of a thing: recompense (a person). E19.

> **2** J. M. KEYNES Workers are remunerated in strict proportion to their efficiency.

▪ **remunerable** *adjective* (*rare*) that may be rewarded; deserving reward: L16. **remuneˈration** *noun* reward, recompense; payment, pay: LME. **remunerator** *noun* (*rare*) a person who remunerates or rewards something or someone L17. **remuneratory** *adjective* serving to remunerate; affording remuneration: L16.

remunerative /rɪˈmjuːn(ə)rətɪv/ *adjective.* E17.
[In early use from medieval Latin *remunerativus*; later directly from prec.: see -IVE.]
†**1** Inclined to remunerate a service. *rare.* Only in E17.
2 That remunerates or rewards a person; profitable. L17.
▪ **remuneratively** *adverb* M17. **remunerativeness** *noun* L19.

remurmur /rɪˈməːmə/ *verb.* Chiefly *poet.* L17.
[Latin *remurmurare*, formed as RE- + *murmurare* MURMUR *verb.*]
1 *verb intrans.* **a** Give back or give out a murmuring sound; resound with murmurs; murmur in answer *to* a sound. L17. ▸**b** Of a sound: echo in murmurs. E18.
2 *verb trans.* Repeat in murmurs. E18.

remuster /riːˈmʌstə/ *verb intrans.* Orig. *Military slang.* M20.
[from RE- + MUSTER *verb.*]
1 Be assigned to other duties. M20.
2 Assemble again. M20.

remythologize /riːmɪˈθɒlədʒʌɪz/ *verb trans.* Also **-ise**. M20.
[from RE- + MYTHOLOGIZE, after *demythologize.*]
Provide with a new mythological system; reinterpret the elements of (an older mythology) in terms of a newer one.
▪ **remythologiˈzation** *noun* L20.

renable /ˈrɛnəb(ə)l/ *adjective. obsolete* exc. *dial.* ME.
[Old French *re(s)nable* from Latin *rationabilis*: see REASONABLE.]
(Of a person) eloquent, speaking or reading fluently or distinctly; (of speech etc.) fluent, clear.
▪ **renably** *adverb* ME.

Renaissance /rɪˈneɪs(ə)ns, *foreign* rənɛsɑ̃s/ *noun.* Also (esp. in sense 2) **r-**. M19.
[French (in spec. use short for *renaissance des arts*, *renaissance des lettres*), formed as RE- + *naissance* birth from Latin *nascentia*, from *nasci* be born, or from French *naiss-* pres. stem of *naître* from Proto-Romance: see -ANCE. Cf. RENASCENCE.]
1 a The revival of art and literature under the influence of classical models between the 14th and 16th cents., begun in Italy; the period of this movement. M19. ▸**b** The style of art, architecture, etc., developed in and characteristic of this period. M19.
2 Any revival or period of significant improvement and new life in cultural, scientific, economic, or other areas of activity. L19.

> **2** P. KAVANAGH New poets and writers who were bringing about a Renaissance in Irish letters. *San Francisco Focus* The .. hope that the current revival of business and employment .. will bloom into a full-scale Renaissance. ***Negro Renaissance***: see NEGRO *adjective.*

Comb.: **Renaissance humanism** = HUMANISM *noun* 3; **Renaissance man** a man who exhibits the virtues of an idealized man of the Renaissance; a man of varied talent and learning.
▪ **Renaissancer**, **Renaissancist** *nouns* a writer, thinker, etc., of the Renaissance; an advocate or student of a renaissance: L19.

Renaissant /rɪˈneɪs(ə)nt/ *adjective. rare.* M19.
[French, pres. pple of *renaître*: see prec., -ANT¹.]
1 Designating or pertaining to the Renaissance. M19.
2 = RENASCENT *adjective.* L20.

renal /ˈriːn(ə)l/ *adjective.* M17.
[French *rénal* from late Latin *renalis*, from Latin *renes* REINS: see -AL¹.]
Of or pertaining to the kidneys; affecting or arising from the kidneys.
renal colic colicky pain caused by any of various kidney conditions, esp. the passage of a renal calculus. **renal dialysis** dialysis performed artificially as a substitute for normal kidney function. **renal osteodystrophy**: due to the failure of the kidneys to convert dietary vitamin D to a more active form. ***renal pelvis***: see PELVIS 2. ***renal portal vein***: see PORTAL *adjective.* ***renal pyramid***: see PYRAMID *noun* 7.

renascence /rɪˈnas(ə)ns/ *noun.* E18.
[from next: see -ENCE.]
1 The process or fact of being born again; rebirth, renewal, revival. E18.
2 = RENAISSANCE *noun* 1. M19.

renascent /rɪˈnas(ə)nt/ *adjective & noun.* E18.
[Latin *renascent-* pres. ppl stem of *renasci*, formed as RE- + *nasci* be born: see -ENT.]
▸ **A** *adjective.* Being reborn, reviving, springing up afresh. E18.

> *Nature* The sudden change in political climate .. has produced a renascent fervour for learning.

▸ **B** *noun.* A person who takes part in a renaissance. *rare.* L19.

renationalize /riːˈnaʃ(ə)n(ə)lʌɪz/ *verb trans.* Also **-ise**. E20.
[from RE- + NATIONALIZE.]
1 Reinvest with national character. *rare.* E20.
2 Transfer (a formerly nationalized industry etc.) from private to State control or ownership again. M20.
▪ **renationaliˈzation** *noun* E20.

renature /riːˈneɪtʃə/ *verb.* M20.
[from RE- + NATURE *noun*, after *denature.*]
1 *verb trans.* Restore the nature or properties of (what has been denatured). M20.
2 *verb intrans.* Chiefly *BIOCHEMISTRY.* Undergo renaturation. M20.
▪ **renatuˈration** *noun* the action or process of renaturing; *spec.* (*BIOCHEMISTRY*) restoration of the conformation and hence the properties of a denatured macromolecule or macromolecular structure: M20.

rencontre /rɛnˈkɒntə, *foreign* rɑ̃kɔ̃tr (*pl. same*)/ *noun.* E17.
[French: see next.]
1 = RENCOUNTER *noun.* E17.
2 An organized but informal meeting, esp. of scientists. L20.

rencounter /rɛnˈkaʊntə/ *noun. arch.* E16.
[Old & mod. French *rencontre*, from *rencontrer*: see next. Cf. RE-ENCOUNTER *noun.*]
1 An encounter between two opposing forces; a battle, a conflict. E16. ▸**b** A hostile meeting between two adversaries; a duel. L16. ▸**c** A contest, orig. esp. in wit or argument. M17.
†**2** An unpleasant experience. Only in 17.
3 A chance meeting, usu. of two people. M17. ▸**b** A meeting of two things or bodies; an impact, a collision. Now *rare* or *obsolete.* M17.

rencounter /rɛnˈkaʊntə/ *verb.* Now *rare.* E16.
[Old & mod. French *rencontrer*, formed as RE- + Old French *encontrer*: see ENCOUNTER *verb.* Cf. RE-ENCOUNTER *noun.*]
1 *verb trans.* Meet or encounter (an army etc.) in a hostile manner; fight (a person). E16.
2 *verb trans.* Meet (a person etc.). M16. ▸†**b** *verb intrans.* Meet a person. Foll. by *with.* M–L17.
†**3** *verb trans.* Come into contact or collision with. Only in L17. ▸**b** *verb intrans.* Come together, collide. Only in 18.

rend /rɛnd/ *noun.* L16.
[from the verb.]
Orig. *gen.*, a rent, a split, a division. Later *spec.*, an open split in timber, caused by exposure to wind and sun.

rend /rɛnd/ *verb. arch. & literary.* Pa. t. & pple **rent** /rɛnt/, †**rended**. See also RENT *ppl adjective.*
[Old English *rendan* = Old Frisian *renda* rel. to Middle Low German *rende.*]
1 *verb trans.* **a** Tear, pull violently, wrench. Foll. by *away*, *off*, *out of*, *up*, etc. OE. ▸**b** Take (a thing) forcibly away *from* a person. E17.
2 *verb trans.* Tear apart or in pieces; split, divide. Later also (*fig.*), divide *into* or into factions etc. OE. ▸**b** Tear (one's clothes or hair) out of rage, grief, horror, or despair. ME. ▸†**c** Wear *out* (clothes) by tearing. *rare* (Shakes.). Only in L16. ▸**d** Make (laths) by splitting wood along the grain into thin strips. Also, strip (a tree) of bark. L17.
3 *verb intrans.* Burst, split, break, tear. ME.
4 *verb trans.* **a** Cause emotional pain to (a person, the heart, etc.). M16. ▸**b** Sound piercingly in (the air, sky, etc.). E17.

> **1a** G. K. CHESTERTON He rent the branch out of the tree. *absol.*: SHELLEY The dagger heals not, but may rend again. **2** E. WAUGH Navvies .. were rending the road with mechanical drills. W. S. CHURCHILL American society was rent by strong conflicting interests. G. DALY Ned's affair with Mary rent their life in two. **4b** A. MCCOWEN Shrieks of 'Darling!' rend the air.

render /ˈrɛndə/ *noun.* LME.
[from the verb.]
†**1** A recitation of a lesson. *rare.* Only in LME.
†**2** The action of making something over to another; surrender of a person or place. M16–L17.
3 *LAW.* **a** A return made by the cognizee to the cognizor in a fine; a conveyance of this nature. L16. ▸**b** *Hist.* A payment in money, goods, or services, made by a tenant to a landlord. M17. ▸**c** The action of performing a service. *rare.* M19.
†**4** An act of rendering an account or statement; an account of expenses. E17–M18.
5 A first coat of rendering or plaster applied to a brick or stone surface. M19.

render /ˈrɛndə/ *verb.* LME.
[Anglo-Norman, from Old & mod. French *rendre* from Proto-Romance alt. (repr. also in RENT *noun*¹) of Latin *reddere* give back, formed as RE- + *dare* give. For the unusual retention in English of the French inf. ending cf. TENDER *verb*².]
▸ **I** †**1** *verb trans.* Repeat (something learned); say over, recite. LME–M16.
2 *verb trans.* Reproduce or express in another language, translate. Also foll. by *into.* LME.
3 *verb trans.* Give in return, make return of; return (thanks); give *back*, restore. L15. ▸**b** *LAW.* Of a cognizee: make over as a return to the cognizor in a fine. L16. ▸**c** Return (a sound, image, etc.) by reflection or repercussion. Also foll. by *back.* Chiefly *poet.* L16.

4 *verb trans.* Reproduce, represent, esp. by artistic means; depict. L16. ▸**b** Play or perform (music). L17.
†**5** *verb trans.* Represent or describe as being of a certain character or in a certain state; make (a person) out to be. L16–E18.

📖 **2** H. CARPENTER Mornings of lessons rendering La Fontaine into English. **3** B. JOWETT Ought we to render evil for evil at all..? J. BRONOWSKI Every machine consumes more energy than it renders. **4** J. HUTCHINSON Hieroglyphs ..were rendered in..low or high relief. **b** R. TRAVERS Maggie rendered the ballads with true Victorian fervour.

▸**II 6** *verb trans.* Hand over, deliver *to* a person. LME. ▸**b** LAW. Of a judge or jury: deliver formally (a judgement or verdict). E19.
7 *verb trans.* Give *up*; resign, relinquish; *spec.* surrender (a stronghold, town, etc.) to the enemy. *arch.* L15. ▸**b** *verb refl.* & †*intrans.* Give (oneself) up; surrender. *arch.* E16.
8 *verb trans.* Give out, emit, discharge. Now *rare* or *obsolete.* L15.
9 *verb trans.* Present (an account, reason, answer, etc.); submit *to* a person for consideration or approval. L15. ▸†**b** Declare, state. *rare* (Shakes.). Only in E17.
10 *verb trans.* Pay as a rent, tax, or tribute. E16.
11 *verb trans.* Show (obedience, honour, attention, etc.); do (a service); give (assistance). L16.
12 *verb refl.* & *intrans.* Present (oneself), be present (*at* a certain place). *arch.* E17.

📖 **6** H. GREEN We are obliged to render a Report of behaviour to our Superior Authority. **9** *render an account*: see ACCOUNT *noun*. **11** A. GRAY A doctor who had rendered them skilled and faithful service. ***for services rendered***: see SERVICE *noun*[1]. ***render homage***: see HOMAGE *noun* 1. **12** J. CARLYLE I rendered myself at Paddington Station.

▸**III 13** *verb trans.* Bring (a person) *into* a state or condition; cause to be *in* a certain state. *rare.* LME.
14 *verb trans.* Cause to be or become; make of a certain nature, quality, condition etc. (Foll. by †*to be*.) E16.

📖 **14** D. LEAVITT When she sang, he was rendered speechless with pride. *refl.*: ISAIAH BERLIN We..render ourselves ridiculous by arriving at conclusions on too little evidence.

▸**IV 15** *verb trans.* Melt (fat); obtain or extract (fat) by melting; clarify; extract fat from (meat etc.). LME.
16 *verb trans.* Cover (stone or brickwork) with a first coating of plaster. M18.
17 NAUTICAL. **a** *verb trans.* Pass (a rope or line) through a place. M19. ▸**b** *verb intrans.* Of a rope or line: move freely round or through anything. M19.

📖 **15** G. LORD Garth..rendered down pork fat for paté. **16** *Holiday Which?* The buildings are rendered in discoloured cement.

Comb.: **render-set** *verb, noun,* & *adjective* (*a*) *verb trans.* cover (a wall etc.) with two coats of plaster; (*b*) *noun* (a) plastering of two coats; (*c*) *adjective* (of plastering) consisting of two coats.
▪ **renderable** *adjective* M18. **renderer** *noun* a person who renders something LME.

rendering /ˈrɛnd(ə)rɪŋ/ *noun.* LME.
[from prec. + -ING[1].]
1 The action of restoring, surrendering, giving, or returning something; that which is yielded or given. LME.
2 a (A) translation, or (an) interpretation of something. M17. ▸**b** Reproduction, representation, depiction, performance; an instance of this. M19.
3 a The action of plastering stone or brickwork with a first coat; the plaster thus applied. In Ireland also, a coating of mortar used under slating to keep the slates firm. M17. ▸**b** NAUTICAL. The free running or slipping of a rope or line. M18. ▸**c** The process of extracting, melting, or clarifying fat; the fat thus obtained and used in cooking. L18.

📖 **2b** *New Musical Express* This impeccably produced rendering of a fine Willie Nelson song. M. BERGMANN In *The Magic Mountain*, Freud's theories found artistic rendering. **3a** E. KUZWAYO These two houses were..finished with a cement rendering.

rendezvous /ˈrɒndɪvuː, -deɪvuː/ *noun.* Pl. same /-z/. L16.
[French, use as noun of *rendez-vous* 'present yourselves', from *rendre*: see RENDER *verb*.]
1 MILITARY. **a** A place appointed for the assembling of troops or armed forces. L16. ▸**b** A place or port used or suitable for the assembling of a fleet or number of ships. Also, instructions concerning such a place. E17.
2 *gen.* Any appointed or habitual meeting-place. L16.
†**3 a** A place of solitary retreat; a refuge. L16–M17. ▸**b** A last resort. *rare* (Shakes.). Only in L16.
4 A meeting or assembly held by appointment or arrangement. Formerly also, a group of people thus assembled. E17. ▸†**b** An assemblage of things. M–L17. ▸**c** The prearranged meeting in space between a spacecraft and another spacecraft or a celestial body; an instance of this. M20.

📖 **2** S. ROSENBERG The cellar of our house was turned into a rendezvous for revolutionaries. †***make one's rendezvous***, †***keep one's rendezvous*** meet (habitually) in or at a place. **3a** SHAKES. *1 Hen. IV* A rendezvous, a home to fly unto. **4** L. EDEL He has a rendezvous with an actress.

rendezvous /ˈrɒndɪvuː, -deɪvuː/ *verb.* M17.
[from the noun.]
1 *verb intrans.* Assemble at an appointed place; *gen.* come together, meet. M17. ▸**b** Of a spacecraft or its crew: effect a meeting in space; *spec.* dock with another spacecraft. M20.
†**2** *verb intrans.* Of a commander: assemble one's troops or fleet. M17–M18.
3 *verb trans.* **a** Bring together (troops or ships) at a fixed place. Now *US.* M17. ▸**b** *gen.* Gather; collect, assemble. Long *rare* or *obsolete.* L17.

📖 **1** C. RYAN In wave after wave they rendezvoused above the town of March. D. A. THOMAS Sturdee rendezvoused with Rear Admiral Stoddart.

rendition /rɛnˈdɪʃ(ə)n/ *noun.* E17.
[French †*rendition*, from *rendre* RENDER *verb*: see -ITION.]
1 a The surrender of a place, garrison, or possession. E17. ▸**b** The surrender of a person. M17. ▸**c** The action of giving up or returning something. *rare.* M17.
2 (A) translation. M17.
3 a The action of rendering, representing, or performing something; a dramatic or musical performance. M19. ▸**b** (A) visual representation *of* something. M20.

📖 **2** B. BETTELHEIM The English renditions of Freud's writings distort..the originals. **3a** J. THURBER A ragged rendition of the old song. **b** *Times* A near life-sized rendition of a naked girl.

rendu /rɑ̃dy/ *adjective.* M20.
[French = rendered, delivered.]
Designating a price on imported goods which includes tariffs and delivery costs.

rendzina /rɛndˈziːnə/ *noun.* E20.
[Russian from Polish *rędzina.*]
SOIL SCIENCE. A fertile lime-rich soil characterized by a dark friable humus-rich surface layer above a softer pale calcareous layer, occurring esp. under grassland on soft limestone.

renegade /ˈrɛnɪɡeɪd/ *noun* & *adjective.* L15.
[Anglicized from RENEGADO: see -ADE.]
▸**A** *noun.* **1** A person who abandons one religious faith for another, *esp.* a Christian who becomes a Muslim; an apostate. Now *rare.* L15.
2 A person who deserts a party or his or her principles; a person who changes his or her allegiance; a turncoat. M17.
▸**B** *adjective.* Of a person: abandoning one religious faith for another; deserting one's principles, changing one's allegiance. E18.
▪ **renegadism** *noun* the practice of deserting one's religion, principles, or party E19.

renegade /ˈrɛnɪɡeɪd/ *verb intrans.* E17.
[from prec.]
Turn renegade; abandon one's religion, principles, party, etc.

renegado /rɛnɪˈɡeɪdəʊ/ *noun* & *adjective. arch.* Pl. **-o(e)s.** L16.
[Spanish from medieval Latin *renegatus* use as noun of pa. pple of *renegare*: see RENEGE, -ADO.]
= RENEGADE *noun* & *adjective.*

renegate /ˈrɛnɪɡeɪt/ *noun* & *adjective. obsolete* exc. *dial.* LME.
[medieval Latin *renegatus*: see prec. Cf. RUNAGATE.]
▸**A** *noun.* A renegade, a deserter. LME.
▸**B** *adjective.* Renegade, unfaithful. LME.

renegation /rɛnɪˈɡeɪʃ(ə)n/ *noun. rare.* E17.
[from next + -ATION.]
The action of renouncing or renegading.

renege /rɪˈniːɡ, rɪˈneɪɡ/ *verb* & *noun.* Also **renegue.** M16.
[medieval Latin *renegare*, formed as RE- + *negare* deny, NEGATE.]
▸**A** *verb.* **1** *verb trans.* Renounce, abandon, desert (a person, faith, etc.). M16.
†**2** *verb intrans.* Make denial. M16–L17.
3 *verb intrans.* Refuse, decline. *rare.* L16.
4 *verb intrans.* CARDS. Refuse or fail to follow suit (permissible in certain games); revoke. L17.
5 *verb intrans.* Change one's mind, recant; go back *on* one's word, a contract, or an undertaking. Orig. *US.* L18.

📖 **2** SHAKES. *Lear* Such..rogues..Renege, affirm, and turn their halcyon beaks. **5** J. M. SYNGE I swear..I'll wed him, and I'll not renege. A. BLOND Publishers who offer contracts ..and then..renege on the deal.

▸**B** *noun.* CARDS. An instance of reneging. M17.
▪ **reneger** *noun* (*rare*) L16.

renew /rɪˈnjuː/ *verb.* LME.
[from RE- + NEW *adjective*, after earlier RENOVEL, Latin *renovare* RENOVATE *verb*.]
▸**I** *verb trans.* **1** Make new again; restore to the same condition as when new, young, or fresh. LME. ▸**b** Esp. of the Holy Spirit: make spiritually new; regenerate. LME. ▸**c** Assume again, recover (one's original strength, youth, etc.). L15.
2 Restore, re-establish, bring back into use or existence. LME.
3 Take up or begin again; resume (a speech, subject, etc.). LME.
4 †**a** Go over again, relate afresh. LME–L16. ▸**b** Repeat (a promise, vow, etc.); utter again. E16. ▸**c** Do over again, repeat (an action). *rare.* L16.
5 Replace; replenish; fill (a vessel) again. LME. ▸**b** Repair, make up for. Long *rare* or *obsolete.* M18.
6 Revive, reawaken (a feeling); resuscitate. LME.
7 Grant anew, reaffirm, reinstitute; *esp.* extend the period or application of (a lease, licence, subscription, etc.). LME.

📖 **1** S. ROGERS His..suit..renewed in patches Till it has almost ceased to be the old one. B. BAINBRIDGE Leaving her to renew her crumpled face. **2** *Spy* The renewed vogue for home delivery of bottled, unhomogenized milk. **3** B. JOWETT Socrates renews the attack from another side. L. GORDON Separated since..his impulsive marriage, they renewed steady contact. **4a** SPENSER Then gan he all this storie to renew. **5** *Pilot* A cracked cylinder was..repaired,..switches, filters, etc. renewed. **6** SHELLEY Quenching a thirst ever to be renewed. *USA Today* Renewed war fears cause jump in oil ..prices. **7** G. SAYER Joy's permit to..work in England would not be renewed. *Holiday Which?* A certificate of airworthiness is..renewed every year.

▸**II** *verb intrans.* **8** Grow afresh, become new again. LME.
†**9** Begin a fresh attack upon; return (*to* or *upon*); renew a fight. LME–L17.
10 Begin again, recommence. E16.
11 Grant a fresh lease or licence. L17.

📖 **8** POPE Thus while he sung, Ulysses' griefs renew. **10** M. MOORE Their intimacy renewed, and Mrs Carisbrooke was..communicative.

▪ **renewedly** *adverb* in a fresh or renewed manner M18. **renewedness** *noun* the state of being renewed M17. **renewer** *noun* a person who or thing which renews or restores something LME. **renewment** *noun* (now *rare* or *obsolete*) renewal L16.

renewable /rɪˈnjuːəb(ə)l/ *adjective* & *noun.* E18.
[from prec. + -ABLE.]
▸**A** *adjective.* **1** Able to be renewed. E18.
2 Of a source of material or energy: not depleted by utilization. L20.
▸**B** *noun.* A renewable source of material or energy. L20.
¶ Earlier (M16) in UNRENEWABLE.
▪ **renewaˈbility** *noun* M19.

renewal /rɪˈnjuːəl/ *noun.* L17.
[formed as prec. + -AL[1].]
1 The action of renewing something or the state of being renewed; an instance of this. L17. ▸**b** A planned urban redevelopment. Freq. in ***urban renewal*** s.v. URBAN *adjective.* M20.
2 Among charismatic Christians, the state or process of being renewed in the Holy Spirit. L20.
Comb.: **renewal theory** STATISTICS the branch of probability theory which considers populations of objects which fail and need renewal at random intervals.
▪ **renewalism** *noun* the beliefs and practices of the movement for charismatic renewal L20. **renewalist** *noun* an adherent of renewalism L20.

†**renfierce** *verb trans. rare* (Spenser). Only in L16.
[App. from FIERCE on the analogy of next.]
Make fierce.

†**renforce** *verb trans.* E16.
[Old & mod. French *renforcer*, formed as RE- + Old French *enforcier* ENFORCE *verb*. Cf. REINFORCE *verb*.]
1 Reinforce, strengthen. E16–M17.
2 Compel (a person) again *to do. rare* (Spenser). Only in L16.

reng /rɛŋ/ *noun.* E20.
[Persian *rang* colour, dye.]
A colouring, *esp.* a hair-dye.

renga /ˈrɛŋɡə/ *noun.* Pl. same, **-s.** L19.
[Japanese, from *ren* linking + *ga* from *ka* poetry.]
A Japanese poem in the form of a tanka (or series of tanka) with the first three lines composed by one person and the second two by another.

rengas /ˈrɛŋɡəs/ *noun.* M19.
[Malay.]
Any of several Malayan trees of the family Anacardiaceae, esp. *Gluta renghas*, containing a sap which often produces allergic reactions in those touching it; the wood or sap of such a tree.

renguerra /rɛnˈɡwɛːrə/ *noun.* E20.
[S. Amer. Spanish *renguera* limping, lameness, from *renguear* (Spanish *renquear*) to limp.]
VETERINARY MEDICINE. = SWAY-BACK *noun* 2.

reniform /ˈriːnɪfɔːm/ *adjective.* M18.
[from Latin *ren* kidney + -I- + -FORM.]
Having the form of a kidney; kidney-shaped.

renin /ˈriːnɪn/ *noun*. L19.
[formed as prec. + -IN[1].]
†**1** MEDICINE. A therapeutic extract prepared from animals' kidneys. L19–E20.
2 BIOCHEMISTRY. A proteolytic enzyme secreted by and stored in the kidneys, which catalyses the production of angiotensin from its inactive precursor. E20.

renish /ˈrɛnɪʃ/ *adjective*. *obsolete* exc. *dial*. LME.
[Origin unkn.]
Strange, uncouth; fierce, wild.

renitence /rɪˈnʌɪt(ə)ns, ˈrɛnɪt(ə)ns/ *noun*. *rare*. M17.
[French *rénitence*: see RENITENT, -ENCE.]
= next.

renitency /rɪˈnʌɪt(ə)nsi, ˈrɛnɪt(ə)nsi/ *noun*. Now *rare*. E17.
[formed as prec.: see -ENCY.]
†**1** Physical resistance, *esp.* the resistance of a body to pressure. E17–E18.
2 Resistance to constraint or compulsion; opposition, (a) reluctance. E17.

renitent /rɪˈnʌɪt(ə)nt, ˈrɛnɪt(ə)nt/ *adjective*. Now *rare*. E18.
[French *rénitent*, later from Latin *renitent-* pres. ppl stem of *reniti* struggle against, resist: see -ENT.]
1 Offering physical resistance; resisting pressure, hard. E18.
2 Recalcitrant, reluctant. M19.

renminbi /ˈrɛnmɪnbi/ *noun*. Pl. same. M20.
[Chinese *rénmínbì*, from *rénmín* people + *bì* currency.]
The currency introduced in China in 1948. Also, the yuan, the basic monetary unit of China.

rennet /ˈrɛnɪt/ *noun*[1]. LME.
[Prob. dial. repr. of unrecorded Old English form rel. to RUN *verb*. Cf. RUNNET.]
†**1** = BEESTINGS. Only in LME.
2 Curdled milk from the abomasum of an unweaned calf or other ruminant, containing rennin and used in curdling milk for cheese, junket, etc. Also, a preparation of the inner membrane of the abomasum similarly used. L15.
3 A plant or other substitute for animal rennet used to curdle milk, *esp.* lady's bedstraw, *Galium verum*. Cf. ***cheese-rennet*** s.v. CHEESE *noun*[1]. L16.
Comb.: †**rennet-bag** the abomasum of a calf used as rennet.

rennet /ˈrɛnɪt/ *noun*[2]. M16.
[French REINETTE.]
= REINETTE.

renneting /ˈrɛnɪtɪŋ/ *noun*. L19.
[from RENNET *noun*[1] + -ING[1].]
The action or process of adding rennet in order to curdle milk in cheese-making.

rennin /ˈrɛnɪn/ *noun*. L19.
[from RENN(ET *noun*[1] + -IN[1].]
BIOCHEMISTRY. An endopeptidase enzyme secreted by the abomasum of young ruminants which breaks down casein during the digestion of milk.

reno- /ˈriːnəʊ/ *combining form*.
[from Latin *ren* kidney + -O-.]
Chiefly MEDICINE. Of or pertaining to a kidney or the kidneys.
■ **renogram** *noun* (*a*) a graphical record of the varying radioactivity of a kidney into which a radioactive substance has been injected; (*b*) a radiograph or autoradiograph of a kidney: M20. **reˈnography** *noun* renal angiography or autoradiography E20. **renoˈvascular** *adjective* pertaining to the blood-vessels of the kidneys M20.

Renoiresque /rɛnwɑːˈrɛsk/ *adjective*. M20.
[from *Renoir* (see below) + -ESQUE.]
Of, pertaining to, or characteristic of the work of the French painter Pierre Auguste Renoir (1841–1919).

renormalization /riːˌnɔːm(ə)lʌɪˈzeɪʃ(ə)n/ *noun*. Also **-isation**. M20.
[from RE- + NORMALIZATION.]
A method used in quantum mechanics of removing unwanted infinities from the solutions of equations by redefining parameters such as the mass and charge of subatomic particles. Freq. *attrib.* Cf. NORMALIZE *verb* 4.
■ **reˌnormalizaˈbility** *noun* the quality of being renormalizable M20. **reˈnormalizable** *adjective* that permits of renormalization M20. **reˈnormalize** *verb trans.* apply renormalization to (freq. as ***renormalized*** *ppl adjective*) M20.

renosterbos /rɛˈnɒstəbɒs/ *noun*. *S. Afr.* Also **-bosch** /-bɒʃ/, **-bush** /-bʊʃ/, **rhen-**. E19.
[Afrikaans, from *renoster* rhinoceros + *bos* bush.]
A southern African shrub with greyish foliage, *Elytropappus rhinocerotis*, of the composite family, liable to invade large tracts of veld esp. after burning. Also called ***rhinoceros bush***.

†**renoume** *noun* & *verb* var. of RENOWN *noun*, *verb*.

renounce /rɪˈnaʊns/ *noun*. M18.
[French *renonce*, formed as next.]
1 CARDS. An act or instance of renouncing. Also, a chance of renouncing, by having no cards of the suit led. M18.
†**2** Renunciation. *rare*. Only in L18.

renounce /rɪˈnaʊns/ *verb*. LME.
[Old & mod. French *renoncer* from Latin *renuntiare* announce, proclaim, renounce, protest against, formed as RE- + *nuntiare* bring news.]
▶**I 1** *verb trans.* **a** Give up, resign, surrender (a claim, right, or possession). LME. ▶**b** Cast off, repudiate (a thing); decline to recognize, observe, etc. Formerly also, disclaim obedience or allegiance to (a person). LME. ▶**c** Decline further association with (a person); disclaim relationship to or acquaintance with; disown. L16.
2 *verb intrans.* **a** Make a renunciation of something. (Foll. by †*to*.) LME. ▶**b** LAW. Surrender formally some right or trust, esp. one's position as heir or executor. E17.
3 *verb trans.* Abandon, forsake, discontinue (an action, habit, intention, etc.). Also, abandon or reject (a belief or opinion) by open declaration. LME.
4 *verb intrans.* CARDS. Fail to follow suit; play a card of a different suit when having no card of the suit led. Cf. REVOKE *verb* 8. M17.

> **1a** C. FRANCIS Magellan renounced his Portuguese citizenship. A. S. BYATT A .. man of letters who had inherited and renounced a baronetcy. **b** BURKE To drive the Pope to extremities by .. renouncing his authority. **renounce the world** withdraw from society or material affairs in order to lead a spiritual life. **c** E. S. PERSON Rick .. renounces her out of his sense of honour. **3** H. ADAMS He had renounced his homage to King Louis. G. BATTISCOMBE If she refused him she renounced all hope of marriage.

▶†**II 5** *verb trans.* Announce, declare, proclaim. LME–E17.
■ **renounceable** *adjective* M19. **renouncement** *noun* the action of renouncing someone or something; a renunciation: L15. **renouncer** *noun* a person who renounces someone or something M16.

renovate /ˈrɛnəvət/ *pa. pple & ppl adjective*. Now *rare*. LME.
[Latin *renovatus* pa. pple of *renovare*: see next, -ATE[2].]
Renewed, revived.

renovate /ˈrɛnəveɪt/ *verb*. E16.
[Latin *renovat-* pa. ppl stem of *renovare*, formed as RE- + *novare* make new, from *novus* new: see -ATE[3].]
1 *verb trans.* Repair; restore by replacing lost or damaged parts; make new again. E16. ▶**b** Reinvigorate; refresh. L17. ▶**c** Renew on a higher level; regenerate. E19.
†**2** *verb trans.* Renew, resume (an action or purpose). M16–L18.
3 *verb intrans.* Revive, recover. Long *rare* or *obsolete*. L18.

> **1** G. NAYLOR The city should .. renovate the housing .. already there. **c** T. CHALMERS The Gospel .. will renovate the soul.

■ **renovative** *adjective* renovating M19. **renovator** *noun* a person who renovates something M19.

renovation /rɛnəˈveɪʃ(ə)n/ *noun*. LME.
[French *rénovation* or Latin *renovatio(n-)*, formed as prec.: see -ATION.]
1 The action of renovating something, or the condition of having been renovated; renewal, restoration; an instance of this, a change effected by renovating. LME. ▶†**b** CHRISTIAN THEOLOGY. Renewal of the body when the dead arise at the Last Judgement. E16–M17.
2 CHRISTIAN THEOLOGY. Renewal effected by the Holy Spirit; spiritual rebirth. LME.
†**3** The renewal or resumption *of* an action, agreement, condition, etc. E16–L18.

> **1** L. GRANT-ADAMSON The restaurant had closed for renovations. *attrib.*: *Independent* Renovation work is about to begin at Oulton Chapel.

renovationist /rɛnəˈveɪʃ(ə)nɪst/ *adjective & noun*. M20.
[from prec. + -IST.]
▶**A** *adjective*. Characterized by or favouring renovation; of or pertaining to (esp. political) renewal or reform. M20.
▶**B** *noun*. An advocate of renovation or (esp. political) renewal or reform. L20.

†**renovel** *verb trans. & intrans.* Infl. **-l(l)-**. ME–M16.
[Old French *renoveler* (mod. *renouveler*), formed as RE- + Latin *novellus* young, new, from *novus* new: see NOVEL *adjective*.]
Renew.
¶ Partial model for RENEW.

renovize /ˈrɛnə(ʊ)vʌɪz/ *verb trans.* *US*. *rare*. Also **-ise**. M20.
[Blend of RENOVATE *verb* and MODERNIZE.]
Restore and modernize.

renown /rɪˈnaʊn/ *noun*. Also †**renoume**. ME.
[Anglo-Norman *ren(o)un*, Old French *renon*, Old & mod. French *renom*, from *renomer* make famous, formed as RE- + *nomer* to name from Latin *nominare* NOMINATE *verb*.]
1 The fact or condition of being widely celebrated or held in high repute; glory, fame, honourable distinction. ME. ▶†**b** Report, rumour. ME–E17.
†**2** Reputation, *esp.* a good reputation. *rare*. ME–E17.

> **1** W. DE LA MARE Great deeds with sweet renown. A. LIVINGSTONE He won his renown as a Positivist. **of renown**, **of great renown**, **of high renown**, etc., famous, distinguished, widely known or celebrated. **2** SHAKES. *All's Well* A young gentlewoman .. of a most chaste renown.

■ **renownful** *adjective* (*rare*) renowned E17. **renownless** *adjective* (*rare*) unrenowned M16.

renown /rɪˈnaʊn/ *verb trans.* Now *rare*. Also †**renoume**. L15.
[Old French *renoumer* var. of *renomer*: see prec. The form *renown* has been assim. to the noun.]
Make famous, spread the fame of; celebrate.
■ **renowner** *noun* a person who renowns someone or something E17.

renowned /rɪˈnaʊnd/ *adjective*. LME.
[formed as prec. + -ED[1], after Old French *renomé* (mod. *renommé*).]
Celebrated, famous; full of renown.

> K. VONNEGUT Dr. Mintouchian is a renowned Shakespeare scholar. F. SPALDING North London Collegiate School was renowned for its academic excellence.

■ **renownedly** *adverb* (*rare*) E17.

renseignement /rɑ̃sɛɲəmɑ̃/ *noun*. Pl. pronounced same. M19.
[French.]
(A piece of) information. Also, a letter of introduction.

Renshaw cell /ˈrɛnʃɔː sɛl/ *noun phr.* M20.
[from Birdsey *Renshaw* (1911–48), US neurologist.]
PHYSIOLOGY. A nerve cell in the spinal cord that forms synapses between adjacent motor neurones so as to provide an inhibitory feedback path.

Renshaw smash /ˈrɛnʃɔː smaʃ/ *noun phr.* L19.
[from *Renshaw* (see below) + SMASH *noun*[1].]
TENNIS. A fast overhead volley associated with William Charles Renshaw (1861–1904) and his twin brother Ernest (1861–99).

rent /rɛnt/ *noun*[1]. ME.
[Old & mod. French RENTE, from Proto-Romance base repr. also by RENDER *verb*.]
†**1 a** In *pl.* Sources of revenue or income; separate pieces of property yielding a certain return to the owner. ME–E17. ▶**b** Revenue, income. ME–L18.
†**2** A tax or similar charge levied by or paid to a person. ME–L18.
3 A periodical payment made by a tenant to an owner or landlord for the use of land or buildings. Now also, the sum paid for the hire of machinery etc. for a certain time. ME. ▶**b** A piece of property for which rent is charged or paid; (esp. in *pl.*) a number of buildings let out to others. LME. ▶**c** *Hist.* A portion of the value of produce from land, which was paid to a landlord for use of the land. E19.
†**4** In France: a sum paid as interest on a public debt. L17–M18.
5 Money, cash, *esp.* that acquired by criminal means or in exchange for homosexual favours. Also = ***rent boy*** below. E19.

> **3** R. CROSSMAN Questions about rateable value and .. the fair-rent clauses. E. FEINSTEIN They were seriously behind with the rent. **b** R. KIPLING Rents lay .. two miles from Gunnison Street.

Phrases: ECONOMIC ***rent***. **for rent** (chiefly *N. Amer.*) available to be rented. ***quit-rent***: see QUIT *adjective*. RACK-RENT. **rent of ability** ECONOMICS financial gain resulting from a particular skill or ability. ***rent of assise***: see ASSIZE *noun* 1. ***wet rent***: see WET *adjective*. ***white rent***: see WHITE *adjective*.
Comb.: **rent boy** *slang* a young male prostitute; **rent car** *US* a hire-car; **rent-charge** LAW a rent forming a charge on lands etc., granted or reserved by deed in favour of a person, with a clause of distress in case of arrears (cf. RENT-SECK); **rent-charger** a person who receives or benefits from a rent-charge; **rent-free** *adjective* with exemption from rent; **rent party** *US*: at which the guests pay money towards the host's rent; **rent-roll** a register of lands and buildings owned by a person, together with the rents due from them; the sum of a person's income from rent; **rent-service** personal service by which lands or buildings are held in addition to, or in lieu of, money payment; **rent strike** a refusal to pay rent, usu. by a number of people as a protest; **rent table** an 18th-cent. office table.
■ **rentage** *noun* rent, rental; something which is rented: M17. **rentless** *adjective*[1] (*a*) producing no rent; (*b*) rent-free: M17.

rent /rɛnt/ *noun*[2]. M16.
[from RENT *verb*[1].]
1 The result of rending or tearing apart; *esp.* a large tear in a garment etc. M16.
2 A breach or dissension in a society or party, or between two people. Now *rare* or *obsolete*. E17.
3 A cleft, a fissure; a deep narrow gorge. E18.
4 The act of tearing or rending; the fact of being torn. *rare*. M19.

> **1** L. DURRELL Arm-chairs whose stuffing used to leak .. out of .. rents in their sides.

■ **rentless** *adjective*[2] (*rare*) without rents, untorn E17.

rent /rɛnt/ *ppl adjective*. LME.
[pa. pple of REND *verb*.]
Torn. Formerly also (*rare*), wearing torn or ragged clothing.

For other words beginning with *re-* see the entry for **re-**

rent /rɛnt/ *verb*[1]. *obsolete* exc. *Scot.* & *dial.* ME.
[Var. of REND *verb* based on pa. t. & pple *rent*.]
1 *verb trans.* Rend, lacerate, tear; pull to pieces. (Foll. by *from*, *off*.) ME.
2 *verb intrans.* Tear; give way or separate by tearing. E16.

rent /rɛnt/ *verb*[2]. LME.
[Old & mod. French *renter*, from *rente*: see RENT *noun*[1].]
†**1** *verb trans.* Provide with revenues; endow. LME–L15.
2 *verb trans.* Let (property) for rent or payment; hire *out*. LME.
3 *verb trans.* & *intrans.* Pay rent for (land, buildings, etc.); occupy or use by payment of rent. M16.
4 *verb intrans.* Be let *at* or *for* a certain rent. Now chiefly *N. Amer.* L18.
5 *verb trans.* Charge (a person) rent. *rare.* L19.
6 *verb trans.* Obtain money from (a person) by criminal means or in exchange for homosexual favours. L19.

📖 **2** R. P. JHABVALA The sea captains' houses were rented out for the season. K. VONNEGUT I persuaded her to rent their . . potato barn to me. **3** R. BERTHOUD They would sometimes rent a cottage at Sizewell. *She* He rented videos for me to watch. *New York Review of Books* New Yorkers rent They don't buy.

Comb.: **rent-a-car**, **rent-a-cop**, **rent-a-crowd**, **rent-a-room**, etc., a car, policeman, crowd, room, etc., that is readily available for hire or (*joc.* or *derog.*) easily or instantly acquired.
■ **renta'bility** *noun* the fact or condition of being rentable E19. **rentable** *adjective* (*a*) *rare* liable to pay rent; (*b*) available or suitable for renting; (*c*) ECONOMICS giving an adequate ratio of profit to capital: M17. **rented** *adjective* (*a*) (now *rare*) having or endowed with property yielding a revenue; (*b*) let for rent; leased, tenanted: LME.

rent *verb*[3] *pa. t.* & *pple*: see REND *verb*.

rental /'rɛnt(ə)l/ *noun* & *adjective*. LME.
[Anglo-Norman, or Anglo-Latin *rentale*: formed as RENT *noun*[1] + -AL[1].]
▶ **A** *noun*. **1 a** A register of the rents owed by tenants to a landlord; a rent-roll. Now chiefly *Scot.* LME. ▸**b** An income arising from rents received. LME.
2 a An amount paid or received as rent. LME. ▸**b** A house, car, etc., let out for rent. Chiefly *N. Amer.* M20.
3 SCOTTISH HISTORY. A lease granted by a landlord to a tenant so entitled by right of birth or inheritance. M16.
4 The fact or process of renting or letting property etc. E20.

📖 **2a** *Money Management* When tenant demand outstrips supply, rentals shoot up. **b** J. DIDION The apartment . . a one-bedroom rental.

▶ **B** *attrib.* or as *adjective*. Of or relating to renting. LME.

📖 P. AUSTER The rental agencies carry on a sort of business.

Comb.: **rental library** (chiefly *US*) a library at which a charge is made for the loan of books.

rentalsman /'rɛnt(ə)lzmən/ *noun*. *Canad.* Pl. **-men**. L20.
[from prec. on the analogy of *ombudsman*.]
An official responsible for the equitable letting and administration of rented property.

rente /rɑ̃t/ *noun*. Pl. pronounced same. L19.
[French.]
Stock, *esp.* French government stock; the interest or income accruing from such stock.

Rentenmark /'rɛnt(ə)nmɑːk/ *noun*. E20.
[German, from *Renten* securities: see MARK *noun*[2].]
Hist. In Germany, a monetary unit tied to industrial and agricultural resources, introduced in November 1923 and replaced by the Reichsmark in 1924.

renter /'rɛntə/ *noun*[1]. LME.
[from RENT *verb*[2] + -ER[1].]
†**1** A person who lets land, buildings, etc.; a landlord. *rare.* LME–L15.
2 A person who collects rents, taxes, or tribute. Now *rare.* M16.
3 A farmer of tolls or taxes. *rare.* L16.
4 A person who pays rent for land, a house, etc. M17. ▸**b** *spec.* A tenant-farmer. M17.
5 A shareholder in a theatre. *rare.* E19.
6 A male prostitute. *slang.* L19.
7 A distributor of films to cinemas. E20.
8 Something that is rented or hired out, *esp.* a rented car. Chiefly *US.* L20.

renter /'rɛntə/ *noun*[2]. Long *rare.* M16.
[from RENT *verb*[1] + -ER[1].]
A person who or thing which rends or tears.

renter /'rɛntə/ *verb trans.* & *intrans.* E18.
[French *rentrer*, *rentraire*. Cf. RANTER *verb*.]
Sew together (two pieces of cloth) with fine stitching so that the join is barely perceptible.

rentier /rɑ̃tje, 'rɒntɪeɪ/ *noun*. Pl. pronounced same. M19.
[French, from RENTE: see -IER.]
A person who makes an income from property or investment.

rentrée /'rɒntreɪ, *foreign* rɑ̃tre (*pl. same*)/ *noun*. L19.
[French.]
A return, *esp.* a return home after an annual holiday.

rent-seck /'rɛntsɛk/ *noun*. L15.
[Anglo-Norman *rente secque* lit. 'dry rent'.]
LAW. A rent reserved by deed in favour of a person, without a clause of distress in case of arrears. Cf. ***rent-charge*** s.v. RENT *noun*[1].

renule /'rɛnjuːl/ *noun*. Now *rare.* M19.
[from Latin *ren* kidney + -ULE.]
ZOOLOGY. Each of the separate lobules of which the kidneys in some mammals are composed.

renunciant /rɪ'nʌnsɪənt/ *noun* & *adjective*. M19.
[from Latin *renuntiant-*, *-ans* pres. pple of *renuntiare*: see RENUNCIATION, -ANT[1].]
▶ **A** *noun*. A person who renounces something. M19.
▶ **B** *adjective*. Renouncing. L19.

renunciate /rɪ'nʌnsɪeɪt/ *verb*. *rare.* M17.
[Back-form. from next.]
†**1** *verb trans.* & *intrans.* Declare or deny (something) openly. M–L17
2 *verb trans.* Renounce, give up. E19.

renunciation /rɪnʌnsɪ'eɪʃ(ə)n/ *noun*. LME.
[Old & mod. French *renonciation* or late Latin *renuntiatio(n-)* (classical Latin = announcement etc.), from Latin *renuntiat-* pa. ppl stem of *renuntiare* announce: see RENOUNCE *verb*, -ATION.]
1 The action of renouncing or giving up a possession, right, or claim; an instance of this. Also, a document expressing this. LME.
2 The action of rejecting or abandoning a belief, habit, etc.; the action of declining further association with a person; repudiation of a person or thing. LME. ▸**b** *spec.* (CHRISTIAN THEOLOGY) The action of renouncing the Devil, the world, and the flesh, at baptism. L19.
3 The action of forsaking something attractive; self-denial. E16.

📖 **1** H. HALLAM The queen's renunciation of her right of succession was invalid in . . his court. **2** A. J. AYER Hope for peace lay in . . renunciation of atomic weapons.

renunciative /rɪ'nʌnsɪətɪv/ *adjective*. LME.
[In sense 1 perh. from Latin *renuntiat-* pa. ppl stem of *renuntiare* announce (see RENOUNCE *verb*); in sense 2 from prec.: see -ATIVE.]
†**1** Serving to announce or enunciate. LME–E17.
2 Characterized by renunciation. M19.
■ Also **renunciatory** *adjective* M19.

renvers /rɑ̃vɛːrs, 'rɛnvəs/ *noun*. Pl. same. L19.
[French, formed as next.]
HORSEMANSHIP. A movement in which a horse walks parallel to a wall with its head and neck facing forward and its hindquarters curved towards the wall.

†**renverse** *verb trans.* E16.
[Old & mod. French *renverser*, formed as RE- + *enverser* overturn.]
1 Overturn, overthrow; throw into confusion. E16–L18.
2 Reverse; turn upside down, turn back. L16–L17.

renversé /rɒn'vəːseɪ/ *adjective*. Now *rare.* E18.
[French, pa. pple of *renverser*: see prec.]
HERALDRY. Inverted; reversed.

renversement /rɑ̃vɛrsəmɑ̃ (*pl. same*), rɒn'vəːs(ə)m(ə)nt/ *noun*. E17.
[French, formed as RENVERSE: see -MENT.]
Orig., the action of reversing or inverting; the result of this. Now usu. *spec.*, an aeroplane manoeuvre consisting of a half-loop effected simultaneously with a half-turn.
¶ Formerly naturalized.

renvoi /'rɒnvwɑː, *foreign* rɑ̃vwa (*pl. same*)/ *noun*. L19.
[French, from *renvoyer* send back, formed as RE- + *envoyer* send: see ENVOY *noun*[1].]
INTERNATIONAL LAW. The process by which a case, dispute, etc., is referred by a court of one country to the jurisdiction of another, and under that is referred back to the first country.

reopen /riː'əʊp(ə)n/ *verb*. M18.
[from RE- + OPEN *verb*.]
1 *verb trans.* Open or open up again. M18. ▸**b** Resume the discussion of (something settled). M19. ▸**c** Recommence (firing). M19.
2 *verb intrans.* Open again. M18.
1b reopening clause = REOPENER.

reopener /riː'əʊp(ə)nə/ *noun*. M20.
[from prec. + -ER[1].]
A clause in a contract between union and management which allows for the reopening of negotiations within the term of the contract. Also ***reopener clause***.

reorder /riː'ɔːdə/ *verb* & *noun*. L16.
[from RE- + ORDER *verb*.]
▶ **A** *verb trans.* †**1** Reordain (a person). *rare.* Only in L16.
2 Set in order again; re-establish, rearrange. E17.
3 Repeat an order for (a thing). E19.
▶ **B** *noun*. A renewed or repeated order for goods. E20.

reorg /riː'ɔːg/ *noun*. M20.
[Abbreviation.]
A reorganization.

reorganize /riː'ɔːg(ə)nʌɪz/ *verb trans.* & *intrans.* Also **-ise**. L17.
[from RE- + ORGANIZE.]
Organize again or differently.
■ **reorgani'zation** *noun* the action or process of reorganizing; (an instance of) fresh organization: E19. ˌ**reorgani'zational** *adjective* of or pertaining to reorganization L20. ˌ**reorgani'zationist** *noun* a person who favours (esp. political) reorganization M20. **reorganizer** *noun* a person who reorganizes M19.

reorient /riː'ɔːrɪɛnt, -'ɒr-/ *verb*. M20.
[from RE- + ORIENT *verb*.]
1 *verb trans.* Rearrange, redirect, give a new orientation to (an idea etc.); help (a person) to find his or her bearings again. M20.
2 *verb refl.* & *intrans.* Adjust (oneself) *to* something; come to terms with something; adopt a new direction. M20.

📖 **1** *Investors Chronicle* Macarthy . . owns 173 pharmacies and . . reoriented them to fit . . different markets. **2** P. QUILLIN Members of the health community . . reorient themselves to using new therapies.

reorientate /riː'ɔːrɪənteɪt, -'ɒr-/ *verb trans.* & *intrans.* M20.
[from RE- + ORIENTATE.]
= prec.
■ ˌ**reorien'tation** *noun* the action or process of reorienting; (a) fresh orientation: E20

reovirus /'riːəʊvʌɪrəs/ *noun*. M20.
[from initial letters of respiratory, enteric, and orphan (with ref. to those not identified, when discovered, with any known disease) + VIRUS.]
BIOLOGY. Any of a group of double-stranded RNA viruses that are sometimes associated with disease in animals, including respiratory and enteric infection in man.

reoxidize /riː'ɒksɪdʌɪz/ *verb*. Also **-ise**. M19.
[from RE- + OXIDIZE.]
1 *verb intrans.* Take up or combine with oxygen again. M19.
2 *verb trans.* Oxidize again. M20.
■ **reoxi'dation** *noun* the process of reoxidizing or of being reoxidized M19.

reoxygenate /riː'ɒksɪdʒəneɪt/ *verb trans.* M19.
[from RE- + OXYGENATE.]
Oxygenate afresh.
■ **reoxyge'nation** *noun* the action of reoxygenating something; the condition of being reoxygenated: M20.

rep /rɛp/ *noun*[1]. *colloq.* (now chiefly *US*). E18.
[Abbreviation.]
= REPUTATION.

rep /rɛp/ *noun*[2]. Now *rare.* M18.
[Perh. abbreviation of REPROBATE *noun*. The relation to DEMI-REP is not clear. Cf. RIP *noun*[6].]
1 An immoral person; a rip. M18.
2 An inferior or worthless article. L18.

rep /rɛp/ *noun*[3] & *adjective*. Also **repp**. M19.
[French *reps*, of unkn. origin.]
(Made of) a textile fabric of wool, silk, or cotton, with a corded surface.

rep /rɛp/ *noun*[4]. M19.
[Abbreviation.]
1 = REPETITION *noun* 2. *School slang.* M19.
2 = REPETITION *noun* 4d. Usu. in *pl.* M20.

rep /rɛp/ *noun*[5]. *colloq.* L19.
[Abbreviation.]
A (sales) representative.

rep /rɛp/ *noun*[6]. *colloq.* E20.
[Abbreviation.]
Repertory; a repertory company or theatre.

📖 S. BRETT When I was in rep I learned Iago in three days.

rep /rɛp/ *noun*[7]. Now *rare.* M20.
[Acronym, from roentgen equivalent physical.]
PHYSICS. A quantity of ionizing radiation that will release the same amount of energy in human tissue as one rad (formerly roentgen) of X-rays. Cf. REM *noun*[1].

rep /rɛp/ *verb intrans.* & *trans. colloq.* Infl. **-pp-**. M20.
[from REP *noun*[5].]
Act as a representative for (a company, product, etc.).

Rep. *abbreviation*. *US.*
1 Representative.
2 Republican.

repaid *verb pa. t.* & *pple* of REPAY *verb*.

repaint /'riːpeɪnt/ *noun*. L19.
[from RE- + PAINT *noun*.]
1 A substance used in repainting; a layer of colour put on in repainting. L19.
2 The act of repainting something; the fact of being repainted. L19.
3 Something repainted, esp. a golf ball. E20.

For other words beginning with *re-* see the entry for **re-**

repaint /riːˈpeɪnt/ *verb trans.* L17.
[from RE- + PAINT *verb*.]
Paint again or differently; restore the paint or colouring of.

repair /rɪˈpɛː/ *noun*¹. *arch.* ME.
[Old French *repaire*, *repeire* (mod. *repaire*, *repère*), from *repairer*: see REPAIR *verb*¹.]
1 Resort, habitual going *to* a place; temporary residence *in* a place. Chiefly in ***have repair***, ***make repair***. ME.
2 Concourse or gathering of people in or at a place; frequent coming or going *to* a place. Now *rare* or *obsolete*. ME.
3 A place to which one repairs; *esp.* a haunt, a person's usual abode. LME.
4 The action of going *to* or to a place; a visit. Now chiefly in ***make repair to***, ***make one's repair to***. LME.

repair /rɪˈpɛː/ *noun*². LME.
[from REPAIR *verb*².]
1 *sing.* & in *pl.* The action or process of restoring something to unimpaired condition by replacing or fixing worn or damaged parts; the result of this. LME.
2 Relative state or condition, esp. of a structure, machine, etc. L16.

📖 **1** G. SAYER Jack was incapable of doing . . household repairs. *fig.*: M. GARDINER Friendships were . . fractured . . beyond repair. ***running repairs***: see RUNNING *ppl adjective*. **2** M. FORSTER The . . house was in a shocking state of repair. **in bad repair** in poor condition. **in good repair**, **in repair** in good or proper condition. **out of repair** in bad condition, requiring repairs.

Comb.: **repairman** a man who repairs something.

repair /rɪˈpɛː/ *verb*¹. ME.
[Old French *repair(i)er* (mod. *repairer*, *repérer*) from late Latin *repatriare* return to one's country: see REPATRIATE *verb*.]
1 *verb intrans.* Go, make one's way *to*, *from*, etc., a place or person (*for* a thing). ME. ▸**b** Resort habitually *to* a place or person; go frequently or in numbers. LME.
†**2** *verb intrans.* Return (*again*), go back *to* or *from* a place, person, etc. LME–M17.
†**3** *verb intrans.* Be present in a place temporarily or habitually; live, reside. LME–L16.
†**4** *verb trans.* Draw *back*. *rare* (Spenser). Only in L16.

📖 **1** *Bicycle* I . . repaired to a cafe for some food. **2** SHAKES. *Mids. N. D.* Awaking when the other do May all to Athens back again repair.

repair /rɪˈpɛː/ *verb*². LME.
[Old & mod. French *réparer* from Latin *reparare*, formed as RE- + *parare* make ready, put in order.]
†**1** *verb trans.* **a** Adorn, ornament. LME–E16. ▸**b** Provide *with* something. M16–E17.
2 *verb trans.* Restore (a structure, machine, etc.) to unimpaired condition by replacing or fixing worn or damaged parts; mend. Also, renovate or renew by compensating for loss or exhaustion. LME. ▸**b** *verb trans.* & *intrans.* Heal, cure. L16. ▸†**c** *verb trans.* Revive, recreate (a person). *rare* (Shakes.). L16–E17.
3 *verb trans.* Remedy, put right (loss, damage, etc.); make up for, make amends for. L15. ▸**b** *verb intrans.* Make reparation *for* something. *rare*. L19.
†**4** *verb trans.* Restore (a person) to a former state; reinstate, re-establish, rehabilitate. M16–M18. ▸**b** Make amends to, compensate (a person). L16–L17.

📖 **2** H. L. PIOZZI The Baths . . will, I hope, repair my strength. D. DUNN A builder is repairing someone's leaking roof. *fig.*: M. LANE The damage done to Maria in infancy took a lifetime to repair. **b** G. SWIFT The . . surgeon's duty to repair the lightly wounded. **3** GIBBON The emperor seemed impatient to repair his injustice.

■ **repaira'bility** *noun* the state or quality of being repairable M20. **repairable** *adjective* able to be repaired L15. **repairer** *noun* a person who or thing which restores or mends something E16.

repand /rɪˈpand/ *adjective*. Now *rare*. M18.
[Latin *repandus* bent backwards, formed as RE- + *pandus* bent.]
BOTANY & ZOOLOGY. Having a weakly sinuate margin; wavy-edged.

reparable /ˈrɛp(ə)rəb(ə)l/ *adjective*. L16.
[Old & mod. French *réparable* from Latin *reparabilis*, from *reparare*: see REPAIR *verb*², -ABLE.]
Able or liable to be repaired, mended, or put right again; now *esp.* (of a loss etc.) that can be made good.
■ **repara'bility** *noun* L19. **reparably** *adverb* M18.

reparation /rɛpəˈreɪʃ(ə)n/ *noun*. LME.
[Old & mod. French *réparation* from late Latin *reparatio(n-)*, from Latin *reparat-* pa. ppl stem of *reparare*: see REPAIR *verb*², -ATION.]
1 a The action of restoring something to a proper or former state; restoration, renewal; maintenance (*of* a thing). LME. ▸†**b** Spiritual restoration, salvation; an instance of this. LME–E18.
2 The action of repairing or mending something; the fact of being repaired; repair of a structure etc. by replacing or fixing worn or damaged parts. Now *rare*. LME.
3 In *pl.* Repairs. Formerly also, sums spent on repairs. Now *rare*. LME.
4 a The action of making amends for a wrong or loss; compensation. LME. ▸**b** Healing of a physical injury. M19. ▸**c** Compensation for war damage owed by a defeated State. Usu. in *pl.* E20.

📖 **1a** SIR W. SCOTT You owe me something for reparation of honour. **4a** H. JAMES Would there . . be time for reparation? . . for the injury done his character. **c** *Daily Mail* The . . German payments for reparations.

reparative /rɪˈparətɪv, ˈrɛp(ə)rətɪv/ *adjective*. M17.
[formed as prec.: see -ATIVE.]
1 Capable of repairing; tending to repair; pertaining to repair. M17.
2 Pertaining to the making of amends; compensatory. L17.
■ Also **re'paratory** *adjective* M19.

†**repart** *verb trans.* M16–M18.
[Old & mod. French *répartir*, formed as RE- + *partir* PART *verb*.]
Distribute, divide between a number of people.

repartee /rɛpɑːˈtiː/ *noun*. M17.
[Old & mod. French *repartie* use as noun of fem. pa. pple of *repartir* set out again, reply readily, formed as RE- + *partir* PART *verb*.]
1 A witty reply; a quick and clever retort. M17.
2 The practice or faculty of making witty retorts; such retorts collectively. M17.

📖 **2** *Arena* The cabbie . . kept up a steady stream of . . rapid-fire repartee.

repartee /rɛpɑːˈtiː/ *verb*. Pa. t. & pple **-teed**. M17.
[from the noun.]
1 *verb intrans.* Make witty or clever retorts. Also foll. by *to*. Now *rare*. M17.
†**2** *verb trans.* Answer (a person or something said) with a repartee or retort. *rare*. E–M18.

repartition /riːpɑːˈtɪʃ(ə)n/ *noun*. M16.
[from RE- + PARTITION *noun*.]
1 Partition, distribution, formerly esp. of troops or military quarters; an instance of this. M16.
2 A fresh partition or distribution. M19.

repartition /riːpɑːˈtɪʃ(ə)n/ *verb trans.* E19.
[from RE- + PARTITION *verb*.]
Partition again.

repass /riːˈpɑːs/ *verb*. LME.
[Old & mod. French *repasser*: see RE-, PASS *verb*.]
1 *verb intrans.* Pass again, return; *esp.* go back in the opposite direction. Freq. in ***pass and repass***. LME.
2 *verb trans.* Cross (the sea, a river, etc.) again in the opposite direction. L15. ▸**b** Pass again over, through, etc.; go past again. E17.
3 *verb trans.* Cause to pass again; put *through* again. M16. ▸**b** Pass (a bill, resolution, etc.) again. L18.
4 *verb trans.* Cause (an object) to pass back from one place to another as if by magic. L16.
■ **repassage** *noun* [French] the action of repassing; the right to repass: LME.

repassant /rɪˈpas(ə)nt/ *adjective*. E19.
[from RE- + PASSANT.]
HERALDRY. Of an animal: depicted as passant towards the sinister side when another animal is passant towards the dexter.

repast /rɪˈpɑːst/ *noun*. LME.
[Old French (mod. *repas*), from *repaistre* (mod. *repaître*) from late Latin *repascere*, formed as RE- + Latin *pascere* feed. Cf. PASTURE *noun*.]
1 A quantity of food and drink forming or intended for a meal or feast (freq. with specifying word); an occasion when food is eaten; a meal. LME.
†**2** Food, a supply of food. LME–M18.
†**3** Refreshment; rest, repose. LME–E17.
†**4** A kind of food or drink. L15–L17.
5 The action or fact of eating food; refreshment in the form of food. *arch.* L16.

📖 **1** *Monitor (Texas)* The repast . . will open with chowder and clam cakes. **3** SPENSER His guest . . gan now to take more sound repast.

repast /rɪˈpɑːst/ *verb*. Now *rare*. LME.
[from the noun.]
†**1** *verb refl.* Refresh (oneself) with food. LME–E17.
†**2** *verb trans.* Feed, supply with food. L15–M17.
3 *verb intrans.* Feed, feast (*on*, *upon*). E16.

📖 **2** SHAKES. *Haml.* I'll . . like the . . pelican, Repast them with my blood. **3** *Daily Telegraph* Desperate Dan, . . who . . repasted upon cow pie.

†**repasture** *noun*. *rare*. L16–E17.
[from prec. + -URE.]
Food; a repast.

📖 SHAKES. *L.L.L.* What art thou then? Food for his rage, repasture for his den.

repat /ˈriːpat, riːˈpat/ *noun*. *colloq.* M20.
[Abbreviation.]
A repatriate. Also, repatriation.

repatriate /riːˈpatrɪeɪt, -ˈpeɪ-/ *noun*. E20.
[from the verb.]
A repatriated person.

repatriate /riːˈpatrɪeɪt, -ˈpeɪ-/ *verb*. E17.
[Late Latin *repatriat-* pa. ppl stem of *repatriare* go back home (in medieval Latin causative), formed as RE- + Latin *patria* native land: see -ATE³.]
1 *verb trans.* **a** Restore (a person) to his or her native country. E17. ▸**b** Devolve or return (legislation) to the constitutional authority of an autonomous country. *Canad.* M20.
2 *verb intrans.* Return to one's native country. M17.

📖 **1a** P. B. CLARKE The emperor was preparing to repatriate blacks to their homeland. *transf.*: *Westminster Gazette* A definite step . . to repatriate the United States silver coin.

■ **repatri'ation** *noun* (**a**) return or restoration to one's native country; (**b**) *Canad.* devolution or return of legislation to the constitutional authority of an autonomous country: L16.

repay /riːˈpeɪ, rɪ-/ *verb* & *noun*. LME.
[Old French *repaier*: see RE-, PAY *verb*¹.]
▸ **A** *verb*. Pa. t. & pple **-paid** /-ˈpeɪd/.
1 *verb trans.* Refund, pay back (money etc.); give in return or recompense (*for* something). LME. ▸**b** Return (a blow, visit, etc.). L16.
2 *verb trans.* Make repayment or return to (a person); pay (a person) back. M16.
3 *verb intrans.* Make repayment or return. M16.
4 *verb trans.* Make return or recompense for, requite (an action, service, etc.). (Foll. by *by*, *with*.) L16.

📖 **1** E. LONGFORD No one thought of repaying a loan. **2** P. CHAPLIN He was happy . . and wanted to repay her. **4** SHAKES. *Tam. Shr.* The poorest service is repaid with thanks.

▸†**B** *noun*. Repayment, return. L16–E19.
■ **repayable** *adjective* able or liable to be repaid E19. **repayer** *noun* a person who repays someone or something M17.

repayment /riːˈpeɪm(ə)nt, rɪ-/ *noun*. LME.
[from prec. + -MENT.]
1 An act of repaying someone or something; payment back of money etc. LME.
2 Requital or return of an action, service, etc. L16.
Comb.: **repayment mortgage**: in which the borrower repays the capital and interest combined.

repeal /rɪˈpiːl/ *noun*. L15.
[Anglo-Norman *repel* = Old French *rapel* (mod. *rappel*), from *rapeler*: see next.]
†**1** Recall of a person, esp. from exile. L15–M17.
2 The action or an act of repealing a law, sentence, etc.; annulment, revocation, withdrawal. E16. ▸**b** *spec.* (*Hist.*) Cancellation of the parliamentary Union between Great Britain and Ireland as an Irish political demand, esp. in 1830 and the 1840s. M19.
3 Means or possibility of release. *rare*. L16.

repeal /rɪˈpiːl/ *verb trans.* LME.
[Anglo-Norman *repeler* for Old French *rapeler* (mod. *rappeler*), formed as RE- + *ap(p)eler* APPEAL *verb*.]
1 Annul, rescind (a law, sentence, etc.); revoke, withdraw. LME.
†**2** Retract (a statement); give up, abandon (a thought, feeling, etc.). LME–M17.
†**3 a** Recall to a proper state or course; call on (a person) *to do*. *rare*. LME–L16. ▸**b** Recall (a person) from exile. L15–M17. ▸**c** Call or summon back. L16–E18. ▸**d** Try to get (a person) restored. *rare* (Shakes.). Only in E17.

📖 **1** W. GELDART The work of the Law Commission has . . led to much obsolete legislation being repealed. **2** MILTON Adam . . repeal'd The doubts that in his heart arose. **3b** *refl.*: SHAKES. *Rich. II* The banish'd Bolingbroke repeals himself.

■ **repeala'bility** *noun* the fact or condition of being repealable M19. **repealable** *adjective* able to be repealed or revoked L16. **repealer** *noun* a person who repeals something or who advocates repeal; *spec.* (*Hist.*) an advocate of the repeal of the Union between Great Britain and Ireland: M18.

repeat /rɪˈpiːt/ *noun*. LME.
[from the verb.]
1 MUSIC. **a** A passage (to be) repeated; the repetition of a passage. LME. ▸**b** A sign directing such a repetition. Also ***repeat mark***, ***repeat sign***. M17.
2 *gen.* A thing repeated; *esp.* †(**a**) a refrain to a poem; (**b**) a repeated broadcast of a television or radio programme; (**c**) a repetition of a musical piece or performance. L15.
3 The action or an act of repeating; repetition. M16.
4 a A duplicate of something. M19. ▸**b** A pattern on cloth, paper, etc., which is repeated uniformly over the surface. Also ***repeat pattern***. M19. ▸**c** COMMERCE. A fresh supply of goods similar to one already received; an order for such a supply. L19.

📖 **2** attrib.: *repeat order, repeat performance, repeat visit,* etc. **3a** L. GRANT-ADAMSON Today would bring a repeat of yesterday's sunshine. **d** J. G. BALLARD Watch the Horizon repeat on the video. **4c** *Lancashire Life* It is . . difficult . . for the shops to get repeats from the manufacturers.

Comb.: **repeat buying** the persistent buying of brands with which a consumer is familiar; **repeat fee**: paid to a radio or television artist each time his or her performance is rebroadcast; ***repeat mark***: see sense 1b above; ***repeat pattern***: see sense 4b above; ***repeat sign***: see sense 1b above.

repeat /rɪˈpiːt/ *verb*. LME.
[Old & mod. French *répéter* from Latin *repetere*, formed as RE- + *petere* attack, make for, demand, seek, etc.]
▶ **I 1** *verb trans.* Say again (something which one has already said); reiterate; *spec.* say again (part of a message, instruction, etc.) for emphasis or clarification. LME. ▸**b** *refl.* Say again what one has already said. M19.
2 *verb trans.* Recite or rehearse (something previously learned or composed); say formally in public; relate, recount. LME.
3 *verb trans.* Say again (something said by another or others). Freq. with direct speech as obj. L16.

📖 **1** B. PYM Nobody, repeat *nobody*, is to tamper with the . . heating apparatus. L. HELLMAN He hadn't answered and so I repeated the question. *absol.*: C. SANDBURG Why repeat? I heard you the first time. **2** H. JAMES Childish voices repeating the multiplication table. **3** W. GOLDING I beg you will not repeat my opinion to the common sort of passenger.

▶ **II †4** *verb trans.* Seek again, return to, encounter again. LME–L17.
5 a *verb trans.* Do, make, or perform again. M16. ▸**b** *verb trans.* Cause to recur or appear again; *spec.* broadcast (a radio or television programme) again. Freq. in *pass.* E18. ▸**c** *verb intrans.* Recur, appear again. E18. ▸**d** *verb refl.* Reproduce or present (oneself) again; recur in the same form. M19. ▸**e** *verb intrans.* Vote illegally more than once in an election. *US. rare.* L19. ▸**f** *verb trans.* Take (an educational course) again. M20.
6 *verb trans. & intrans.* Of a clock etc.: strike (the last hour or quarter) again. E18.
7 *verb trans. & intrans.* NAUTICAL. Of a ship: reproduce (a signal made by an admiral). M18.
8 Of a firearm: fire several shots without reloading. E19.
9 *verb intrans.* Of food: be tasted intermittently for some time after being swallowed as a result of belching or indigestion. L19.

📖 **5a** R. H. MOTTRAM She had to repeat her knock . . before it was answered. **c** *Listener* A . . rugged . . shape tends to repeat throughout the picture. **d** *Irish Democrat* History does not repeat itself. **f** *Independent* Students who do not pass have to repeat the year. **9** P. H. JOHNSON I hope these aren't cucumber sandwiches . . . Cucumber always repeats. HELEN FIELDING The problem . . with smoked salmon is that it repeats on me.

■ **repeata'bility** *noun* ability to be repeated; *spec.* the extent to which consistent results are obtained on repeated measurement (cf. REPRODUCIBILITY): E20. **repeatable** *adjective* (esp. of a scientific experiment or result) able to be repeated E19.

repeated /rɪˈpiːtɪd/ *adjective*. E17.
[from prec. + -ED[1].]
1 Reiterated; renewed; frequent. E17.
2 Recited, said again, or related, esp. in a specified manner. E18.
¶ Cf. earlier UNREPEATED.
■ **repeatedly** *adverb* again and again, frequently L17.

repeater /rɪˈpiːtə/ *noun*. L16.
[from REPEAT *verb* + -ER[1].]
†1 A person who teaches by rehearsal or recitation of lessons. *rare.* Only in L16.
2 A person who repeats something heard or learned; a relater, a reciter. L16.
3 a A clock etc. which can be made to repeat its last strike. E18. ▸**b** NAUTICAL. A ship which reproduces an admiral's signals. L18. ▸**c** A firearm which fires several shots without reloading. M19. ▸**d** A device for automatically reproducing signals at an increased strength for onward transmission in a telegraph or telephone circuit; a relay installation or satellite. M19.
4 MATH. A recurring decimal. *rare.* L18.
5 a A person who repeats an action, as voting at a particular election, taking a particular educational course, staying at a particular hotel etc., or achieving success in athletics etc. Chiefly *N. Amer.* M19. ▸**b** A person who is frequently committed to prison; a person who repeats an offence, a recidivist. Chiefly *US.* L19.
■ **repeatered** *adjective* equipped with automatic repeaters M20.

repeating /rɪˈpiːtɪŋ/ *ppl adjective*. E17.
[from REPEAT *verb* + -ING[2].]
1 That repeats. E17. ▸**b** Of a firearm: capable of firing several shots in succession without reloading. E19. ▸**c** Of a pattern: recurring uniformly over a surface. M20.
2 MATH. Of a decimal: recurring. *rare.* L18.
Special collocations: **repeating back** PHOTOGRAPHY a former type of camera back enabling two separate exposures to be made on one plate. **repeating circle** an instrument for accurately measuring angles by repeated measurements on a graduated circle. **repeating coil** TELEGRAPHY a transformer used to transmit a signal from one circuit to another without alteration.

repêchage /ˈrɛpəʃɑːʒ/ *noun*. E20.
[French, from *repêcher* lit. 'fish out, rescue'.]
An extra contest, esp. in rowing and cycling, in which the runners-up in the eliminating heats compete for a place in the final.

repel /rɪˈpɛl/ *verb trans.* Infl. **-ll-**. LME.
[Latin *repellere*, formed as RE- + *pellere* drive.]
†1 Remove, extinguish, quench. LME–L16.
2 Drive or force back (an invader, an attack, etc.); repulse. Also foll. by *from*, *†out of*. LME. ▸**b** Resist, repress, (a feeling etc.) as invalid. L16. ▸**†c** MEDICINE. Force back into the blood or system; repress (an infection, eruption, etc.). E18–M19.
3 Refuse to accept or admit; *esp.* reject (an argument, plea, etc.) as invalid. LME. ▸**b** Confute, disprove. Now *rare* or *obsolete.* M17.
†4 Reject or debar (a person) from an office, privilege, etc. LME–M18. ▸**b** Stop, hinder, or restrain (a person) *from* doing something. L15–E17.
5 Turn back, ward off (a weapon, blow, etc.); *fig.* resist, ward off (an evil). M16.
6 a Repulse the approaches of (a person) with harsh words or treatment, or by denial; reject (a suitor). L16. ▸**b** Be repellent or distasteful to. E19.
7 (Tend to) drive or force back or away (something moving or advancing), esp. by physical resistance, force of a magnetic or electric field, resistance to mixing of dissimilar substances, etc. E17.

📖 **2** G. SAYER Recruited to repel German troops. **3** *Times* His Lordship repelled the defenders' plea. **6a** P. GARDINER He decided to repel her with . . indifference. **b** R. GITTINGS She alternately repelled and attracted him. A. LIVINGSTONE All literary production repelled him.

■ **repellingly** *adverb* in a repelling manner E19.

repellent /rɪˈpɛl(ə)nt/ *adjective & noun*. Also **-ant**. M17.
[Latin *repellent-* pres. ppl stem of *repellere*: see prec., -ENT.]
▶ **A** *adjective.* **1** Of medicines or medical applications: having the effect of repressing an infection, eruption, etc. (Cf. REPEL *verb* 2c.) Now *rare* or *obsolete.* M17.
2 a Having the power of repelling other objects; characterized by repulsion. M18. ▸**b** Impervious to moisture. E19. ▸**c** Repelling or warding off attack. L19. ▸**d** Causing certain insects not to settle or approach. L20.
3 Repelling by some disagreeable feature; distasteful, disgusting, repulsive. L18.
▶ **B** *noun.* **1** MEDICINE. An application serving to repress an infection, eruption, etc. Now *rare* or *obsolete.* M17.
2 A repelling power or influence. E19.
3 A substance that causes certain insects not to settle or approach. Freq. in ***insect repellent***. E20.
■ **repellence** *noun* = REPELLENCY M18. **repellency** *noun* the quality of being repellent; repelling power: M18. **repellently** *adverb* L19.

repeller /rɪˈpɛlə/ *noun*. E17.
[from REPEL + -ER[1].]
1 A person who repels someone or something. E17.
†2 = REPELLENT *noun* 1. M17–M18.

†repent *noun*. L16–E17.
[from the verb.]
(An act of) repentance.

📖 SPENSER Reproch the first, Shame next, Repent behinde.

repent /ˈriːp(ə)nt/ *adjective*. M17.
[Latin *repent-* pres. ppl stem of *repere* creep: see -ENT.]
BOTANY. Creeping; *spec.* prostrate and rooting.

repent /rɪˈpɛnt/ *verb*. ME.
[Old & mod. French *repentir*, formed as RE- + *pentir*, from Proto-Romance alt. of Latin *paenitere*: see PENITENT.]
1 *verb intrans.* & (*arch.*) *refl.* Feel contrition or regret for something one has done or omitted to do; change one's mind through regret about past action or conduct. (Foll. by *of*, *†on*.) ME. ▸**b** *verb trans.* Cause to feel contrition or regret. Usu. *impers.* in ***(it) repents*** etc. *arch.* ME. ▸**†c** *verb intrans.* Mourn for an event. *rare* (Spenser). Only in L16.
2 *verb trans.* View or think of (an action etc.) with dissatisfaction and regret; *spec.* feel regret or contrition for (a fault, sin, etc.). ME.
†3 *verb trans.* Live *out* in repentance. *rare* (Shakes.). Only in E17.

📖 **1** M. MITCHELL The black sheep of the Butler family had repented of his evil ways. **b** A. C. SWINBURNE Will it not one day in heaven repent you? **2** LD MACAULAY His Majesty would soon have reason to repent his goodness.

■ **repenter** *noun* a person who repents, a penitent E17. **repentingly** *adverb* in a repenting manner E17.

repentance /rɪˈpɛnt(ə)ns/ *noun*. ME.
[Old & mod. French: see next, -ANCE.]
The act of repenting or the state of being repentant; regret or contrition for past action; an instance of this.
stool of repentance SCOTTISH HISTORY a stool formerly placed in a conspicuous position in a church on which offenders were to sit to make public repentance; a cutty-stool.

repentant /rɪˈpɛnt(ə)nt/ *adjective & noun*. ME.
[Old & mod. French, pres. pple of *repentir*: see REPENT *verb*, -ANT[1].]
▶ **A** *adjective.* **1** Of a person: experiencing repentance; regretful for past sins, penitent. (Foll. by *of*, *for*). ME.
2 Of an action: expressing or indicating repentance. M16.

📖 **1** L. KENNEDY He . . was repentant for his share of guilt.

▶ **B** *noun.* A person who repents, a penitent. Long *rare.* ME.
■ **repentantly** *adverb* in a repentant manner M16.

repeople /riːˈpiːp(ə)l/ *verb trans.* L15.
[French *repeupler*, formed as RE- + PEOPLE *verb*.]
1 Provide with a fresh population; repopulate. L15.
2 Restock with bees, fish, etc. Now *rare.* L17.

repercuss /riːpəˈkʌs/ *verb*. LME.
[Latin *repercuss-* pa. ppl stem of *repercutere*, formed as RE- + *percutere* PERCUSS. In sense 3, back-form. from REPERCUSSION.]
†1 *verb trans.* **a** Beat or drive back (air, a fluid, etc.); reduce (a swelling). LME–L18. ▸**b** Return, reverberate, (a sound). *rare.* L16–E18. ▸**c** Reflect (a ray of light). Only in 17.
†2 *verb trans.* Of light: impinge on (a reflecting surface). *rare.* LME–L16.
3 *verb intrans.* Have a repercussion or an indirect effect (*on*). E20.

repercussion /riːpəˈkʌʃ(ə)n/ *noun*. LME.
[Old & mod. French *répercussion* or Latin *repercussio(n-)*, formed as prec.: see -ION.]
†1 MEDICINE. The action of repressing infections, eruptions, etc. LME–E18.
2 The action or power of driving back an advancing force. Now *rare* or *obsolete.* M16.
3 Repulse or recoil of a thing after impact; the fact of being forced back by a resisting body. M16. ▸**b** MEDICINE. = BALLOTTEMENT. M19.
4 a Reflection of a sound; (an) echo, (a) reverberation. M16. ▸**b** MUSIC. In a fugue: the reentrance of the subject and answer after an episode. L19.
5 Reflection of or *of* light. Now *rare.* E17.
6 A blow given in return; *fig.* a return of any kind of action, a responsive act. E17.
7 An effect, *esp.* one distant from the event which caused it; an unintended or indirect consequence. Usu. in *pl.* E20.

📖 **5** *fig.*: COLERIDGE Our election from God is the repercussion of the beams of his love shining upon us. **6** S. JOHNSON Tenderness once excited will be . . increased by the . . repercussion of communicated pleasure. **7** J. BERGER Political and diplomatic repercussions of . . frontier incidents might . . prove disastrous. M. LANE These beginnings were to have . . repercussions on Maria's later life.

repercussive /riːpəˈkʌsɪv/ *adjective & noun*. LME.
[Old & mod. French *répercussif*, *-ive* or medieval Latin *repercussivus*, formed as prec. + -IVE.]
▶ **A** *adjective.* **†1** Of a medicine, application, etc.: serving to repel harmful bodily fluids or reduce swellings. LME–L17.
2 a Of a sound: reverberating, reverberated; echoing; repeated. L16. ▸**b** Of a place etc.: returning a sound. L17.
†3 Of light: reflected. L16–E18.
4 *fig.* Of an action, decision, etc.: having repercussions or indirect effects. L20.
▶**†B** *noun.* A repercussive medicine or application. LME–E18.

reperforator /riːˈpəːfəreɪtə/ *noun*. E20.
[from RE(CEIVING *adjective* + PERFORATOR.]
COMPUTING & TELEGRAPHY (now chiefly *Hist.*). A machine which perforates paper tape to record incoming signals or computer output.

reperible /ˈrɛp(ə)rɪb(ə)l/ *adjective. rare.* LME.
[from Latin *reperire* to find: see -IBLE.]
Discoverable.

repertoire /ˈrɛpətwɑː, *foreign* rəpɛrtwar (*pl. same*)/ *noun*. Also (earlier) **ré-**. M19.
[French *répertoire* from late Latin REPERTORIUM.]
A stock of dramatic parts, tunes, songs, etc., which a performer or company knows or is prepared to perform; *fig.* a stock of regularly performed actions, regularly used techniques, etc.

📖 Y. MENUHIN My repertoire expanded . . to include . . Brahms' Sonata in D Minor. I. MURDOCH That cat . . had a larger repertoire of attitudes than any . . Tim had ever drawn.

repertorial /rɛpəˈtɔːrɪəl/ *adjective*. L19.
[from REPERTORY + -AL[1].]
Of or pertaining to (a) repertory.

repertorium /rɛpəˈtɔːrɪəm/ *noun. rare.* M17.
[Late Latin: see next.]
Orig., a catalogue. Later, a store, a repository.

repertory /ˈrɛpət(ə)ri/ *noun.* M16.
[Late Latin *repertorium* inventory, from Latin *repert-* pa. ppl stem of *reperire* discover: see -ORY[1].]
†**1** An index; a catalogue; a calendar. M16–L18.
2 A store, a repository, esp. of retrievable examples or information. L16.
3 a A repertoire. M19. ▸**b** The performance of plays, operas, ballets, etc., by a company at regular short intervals; repertory theatres collectively. L19. ▸**c** In full ***repertory company***. A theatrical, operatic, or ballet company that performs works from a repertoire. E20.

📖 **3a** *New York Times* I reduced my repertory of facial expressions to two. **b** *Twenty Twenty* This California . . vision of Mozart's fairy-tale is in repertory until June.

reperuse /riːpəˈruːz/ *verb trans.* E17.
[from RE- + PERUSE.]
Peruse again or repeatedly.
■ **reperusal** *noun* a second perusal L17.

repetend /ˈrɛpɪtɛnd, rɛpɪˈtɛnd/ *noun.* E18.
[Latin *repetendum* neut. gerundive of *repetere* REPEAT *verb*: see -END.]
1 MATH. The repeating figure or figures in a recurring decimal fraction. Now *rare.* E18.
2 A recurring note, word, or phrase; a refrain. L19.

répétiteur /repetitœːr (*pl. same*); rɛˌpɛtɪˈtəː/ *noun.* M20.
[French = tutor, coach.]
1 A person who teaches musicians and singers, esp. opera singers, their parts. M20.
2 A person who supervises ballet rehearsals etc. M20.

repetition /rɛpɪˈtɪʃ(ə)n/ *noun.* LME.
[Old & mod. French *répétition*, or Latin *repetitio(n-)*, from *repetit-* pa. ppl stem of *repetere* REPEAT *verb*.]
▶ **I 1** The action of repeating something that has already been said or written, esp. in order to retain it in the memory, or as a literary device; an instance of this. LME.
2 The recitation, esp. in school, of something learned by heart; a piece to be learned and recited. L16.
3 Mention, narration. Now *rare.* L16.
4 The action of doing something again; repeated performance or application. L16. ▸**b** MUSIC. The repeating of a passage or note. Cf. REPEAT *noun* 1a, 1b. L16. ▸**c** MUSIC. The ability of an instrument to repeat a note quickly. L19. ▸**d** SPORT. A training exercise which is repeated; *spec.* (*a*) in athletics, any of the set distances run in repetition training; (*b*) in weight-training, any of a series of repeated raisings and lowerings of the weight. M20.
5 A copy, a replica. M19.

📖 **1** GEO. ELIOT Of the new details . . he could only retain a few . . by continual repetition. V. BRITTAIN I began to cry 'Edward! Oh, Edward!' in dazed repetition. **3** SHAKES. *Coriol.* A name Whose repetition will be dogg'd with Curses. **4** DICKENS These glances seemed to increase her confidence at every repetition.

▶ **II 6** (An instance of) claiming restitution or repayment; restitution, repayment. Chiefly *Scot.* LME.
Comb.: **repetition compulsion** *Psychoanal.* a powerful instinct to repeat a response regardless of the result; **repetition training** ATHLETICS: in which a runner alternately runs and rests over set distances (cf. ***interval training*** s.v. INTERVAL *noun*); **repetition work** the occupation of making the same article over and over again.
■ **repetitional** *adjective* = REPETITIONARY E18. **repetitionary** *adjective* characterized by or of the nature of repetition E18.

repetitious /rɛpɪˈtɪʃəs/ *adjective.* L17.
[formed as prec. + -IOUS.]
Characterized by (esp. tedious or unnecessary) repetition.
■ **repetitiously** *adverb* M19. **repetitiousness** *noun* L19.

repetitive /rɪˈpɛtɪtɪv/ *adjective.* M19.
[formed as REPETITION + -IVE.]
= REPETITIOUS.
repetitive strain injury injury arising from the continued repeated use of particular muscles during keyboarding; abbreviation *RSI*.
■ **repetitively** *adverb* M20. **repetitiveness** *noun* L19.

Repetitor /repeˈtiːtor/ *noun.* L18.
[German from medieval Latin = repeater (classical Latin = person who claims back), from Latin *repetere* REPEAT *verb*.]
In Germany, a private tutor of university students, esp. in law.

rephrase /riːˈfreɪz/ *verb trans.* L19.
[from RE- + PHRASE *verb*.]
Express in different words.

📖 L. NKOSI He asks the same questions . . rephrasing them to avoid monotony.

†**repine** *noun.* M16–E17.
[from the verb.]
The action or an act of repining.

repine /rɪˈpʌɪn/ *verb.* Now *literary.* LME.
[from RE- + PINE *verb*, after *repent*.]
†**1** *verb trans.* Cause trouble to. *rare.* Only in LME.
2 *verb intrans.* Feel or express regretful dissatisfaction; fret, complain. (Foll. by *against, at, that.*) E16. ▸**b** Long discontentedly *for. rare.* M18.
†**3** *verb trans.* Regard with regretful dissatisfaction; complain at. L16–L18.

📖 **2** C. P. SNOW I don't say this isn't a . . nuisance . . . Still, repining won't get us anywhere. W. GOLDING Why should anyone repine at the more luxurious fate of another? **b** T. GRAY These Ears . . for other notes repine.

■ **repinement** *noun* (*rare*) repining, discontent M18. **repiner** *noun* M16. **repiningly** *adverb* in a repining manner L16.

repique /rɪˈpiːk/ *noun & verb.* M17.
[French *repic* = Italian ripicco: see RE-, PIQUE *noun*[2].]
▶ **A** *noun.* In piquet: the winning of thirty points on cards alone before beginning to play, entitling a player to begin his or her score at ninety. Cf. PIQUE *noun*[2]. M17.
▶ **B** *verb.* **1** *verb trans. & intrans.* In piquet: score a repique against (an opponent). M17.
†**2** *verb trans. fig.* Repel, resist. *rare.* L17–E19.

repla *noun* pl. of REPLUM.

replace /rɪˈpleɪs/ *verb trans.* L16.
[from RE- + PLACE *verb*, prob. after French *remplacer*.]
1 Put back in a previous place or position. (Foll. by *in*.) L16.
2 Take the place of, become a substitute for, (a person or thing). Freq. in *pass.* (foll. by *by*). M18.
3 Fill the place of (a person or thing) *with* or *by* a substitute. M18. ▸**b** Provide or find a substitute for (a person or thing). L18.

📖 **1** M. WESLEY 'Your time is up,' said the operator . . . Rose replaced the receiver. **2** M. FRAYN The tramping died away and . . was replaced by . . silence. P. AUSTER There are always new people to replace the ones who have vanished. **3** SCOTT FITZGERALD Gatsby had dismissed every servant . . and replaced them with . . others. **b** B. VINE The light bulbs . . needed replacing.

■ **replaceaˈbility** *noun* replaceable quality L19. **replaceable** *adjective* able to be replaced; CHEMISTRY (of a hydrogen atom in an acid) able to be replaced by a base: E19. **replacer** *noun* a person who or thing which replaces another, a substitute L19.

replacement /rɪˈpleɪsm(ə)nt/ *noun.* L18.
[from prec. + -MENT.]
1 The action of replacing a person or thing; the fact of being replaced. L18. ▸**b** GEOLOGY & PALAEONTOLOGY. The dissolution of one mineral and the simultaneous deposition of another in its place; metasomatism; a process of fossilization in which organic constituents are replaced by inorganic material. Freq. *attrib.* E20.
2 A thing which or a person who replaces another. L19.

📖 **2** A. BISHOP His housekeeper gave notice; Mary . . found a replacement.

Comb.: **replacement therapy** MEDICINE therapy aimed at making up a deficit of a substance normally present in the body.

replacive /rɪˈpleɪsɪv/ *adjective & noun.* M20.
[from REPLACE *verb* + -IVE.]
▶ **A** *adjective.* That replaces something else; *spec.* (LINGUISTICS) (of a morph or morpheme) that consists of or is realized by the replacement of one form by another. M20.
▶ **B** *noun.* LINGUISTICS. A replacive morph or morpheme. M20.

replan /riːˈplan/ *verb trans.* Infl. **-nn-**. L19.
[from RE- + PLAN *verb*.]
Plan again or differently.

replant /riːˈplɑːnt/ *verb.* L16.
[from RE- + PLANT *verb*, perh. after French *replanter*.]
1 *verb trans.* Transfer (a tree, plant, etc.) to a new site, a larger pot, etc. L16. ▸**b** *transf.* Re-establish, resettle, (a person or thing). L16.
2 *verb trans. & intrans.* Provide (ground etc.) with new plants. M17.
■ **replanˈtation** *noun* (*a*) a second or fresh plantation; (*b*) SURGERY permanent reattachment to the body of a part which has been removed or severed: E17.

replate /riːˈpleɪt/ *verb.* M19.
[from RE- + PLATE *verb*.]
1 *verb trans.* Plate afresh; renew the plating on. M19.
2 *verb trans. & intrans.* PRINTING. Take a further cast of (a forme of type) to insert new material. *obsolete* exc. *Hist.* M20.

replay /ˈriːpleɪ/ *noun.* L19.
[from the verb.]
1 A replayed match. L19.
2 The action or an instance of replaying a sound recording, piece of film, etc. M20.
2 ***action replay***: see ACTION *noun*. ***instant replay***: see INSTANT *adjective*.

replay /riːˈpleɪ/ *verb trans.* L19.
[from RE- + PLAY *verb*.]
1 Play (a match etc.) again. L19.
2 Play back (a sound recording, piece of film, etc.). E20.

📖 **2** *fig.*: H. KAPLAN He replayed . . events . . over and over in his mind.

replead /riːˈpliːd/ *verb. rare.* L15.
[from RE- + PLEAD. Cf. Old French *repledoier*, French *replaider*.]
1 *verb intrans.* LAW. Raise a second plea (formerly, any plea). L15.
†**2** *verb trans.* Use as a further plea. Only in M18.
■ **repleader** *noun* (LAW) the action of or right to a second pleading E17.

repledge /rɪˈplɛdʒ/ *verb*[1] *trans.* LME.
[Old French *repleger*, -*eer*, -*ier* or medieval Latin *replegiare* give or become surety for (a person), formed as RE- + *plegier* PLEDGE *verb*.]
SCOTS LAW (now *Hist.*).
1 Withdraw (a person or cause) from the jurisdiction of another court to one's own, on giving a pledge that justice will be done. LME.
†**2** Take back (something forfeited or impounded) on proper security; replevy. M16–M17.
■ **repledger** *noun* M17.

repledge /riːˈplɛdʒ/ *verb*[2] *trans.* M18.
[from RE- + PLEDGE *verb*.]
Pledge again.

†**replegiation** *noun.* E16–E18.
[medieval Latin *replegiatio(n-)*, from *replegiare* REPLEDGE *verb*[1]: see -ATION.]
SCOTS LAW. The action of repledging a person or cause.

replenish /rɪˈplɛnɪʃ/ *noun. rare.* E19.
[from the verb.]
A fresh supply, esp. of money; a refill.

replenish /rɪˈplɛnɪʃ/ *verb.* LME.
[from Old French *repleniss-* lengthened stem of *replenir*, formed as RE- + *plenir* PLENISH.]
▶ **I** *verb trans.* **1** Supply or stock abundantly *with* things, animals, etc. Chiefly (in later use only) as ***replenished*** *ppl adjective.* Now *rare* or *obsolete.* LME.
2 †**a** Occupy (a place) as an inhabitant or settler; people. LME–L18. ▸**b** Occupy the whole of (a space or thing). Now *rare.* M16.
†**3** Fill with food; satisfy, satiate. LME–M17.
†**4** Imbue or fill abundantly *with* a quality, feeling, etc. Chiefly as ***replenished*** *ppl adjective.* LME–E18.
5 Fill physically or materially with or *with* a thing or things, people, etc. Chiefly (in later use only) as ***replenished*** *ppl adjective.* Now *rare* or *obsolete.* L15.
6 Fill up again; restore to the former amount or condition. E17.

📖 **2a** GIBBON Vacant habitations were replenished by a new colony. **b** W. S. LANDOR A light, the radiance of which cheered and replenished the . . heart. **5** SWIFT 'Twas still replenish'd to the top, As if they ne'er had touched a drop. **6** E. WAUGH We hope to replenish our stocks at the next port. C. GEBLER My uncle took the . . bottle and replenished my glass.

▶ **II** *verb intrans.* **7** Become filled; increase. *rare.* L16.
■ **replenisher** *noun* (*a*) a person who replenishes something; (*b*) (now *rare*) a device for increasing or maintaining an electric charge: L16. **replenishment** *noun* (*a*) the action of replenishing something; *rare* the fact of being replenished; (*b*) a thing that replenishes something; a fresh supply: E16.

replete /rɪˈpliːt/ *adjective & noun.* LME.
[Old & mod. French *replet*, fem. -*ète*, or Latin *repletus* pa. pple of *replere*, formed as RE- + *plere* fill.]
▶ **A** *adjective.* **1** Filled or abundantly supplied *with* or with a thing or things. Formerly also, crowded *with* people. LME.
2 Filled to satisfaction with or *with* food or drink; gorged, sated. LME. ▸†**b** Plethoric, stout. E17–M18.
3 Imbued or filled abundantly with a quality, feeling, etc. LME.
4 Full, perfect, complete. Now *arch. rare.* L15.

📖 **1** E. F. BENSON With . . nothing but her own replete engagement book to read. **2** E. BOWEN Van Winkle was . . replete but his eye continued to travel . . over the muffin dish. **3** A. STORR His letters . . are replete with vindictiveness and contempt. N. F. DIXON Survival of the individual . . is a task replete with problems.

▶ **B** *noun.* A thing that is replete; *spec.* a honey-pot ant distended with stored food. E20.
■ **repleteness** *noun* E17.

replete /rɪˈpliːt/ *verb trans.* Now *rare.* LME.
[Latin *replet-* pa. ppl stem of *replere*: see prec.]
†**1** Fill, supply, or imbue with something; cram, crowd. (Foll. by *with*.) LME–M17.
2 Replenish; fill again. E18.

repletion /rɪˈpliːʃ(ə)n/ *noun.* LME.
[Old & mod. French *réplétion*, or late Latin *repletio(n-)*, from Latin *replet-* pa. ppl stem of *replere*: see REPLETE *adjective & noun*, -ION.]
1 The action of eating or drinking to satisfaction or excess; surfeit; the condition of body arising from this. LME.

2 The action of filling something up; the state of being filled up or crowded. Freq. in ***fill to repletion***. LME.
3 The satisfaction of a desire or want. M17.

> 🕮 **1** F. TOMLIN I in my repletion had refused the cheese.

†repletive *adjective*. E17–M18.
[Old & mod. French *réplétif*, formed as prec.: see -IVE.]
Causing repletion, replenishing.

repleviable /rɪˈplɛvɪəb(ə)l/ *adjective*. M18.
[from REPLEVY *verb* + -ABLE.]
LAW. = REPLEVISABLE.

replevin /rɪˈplɛvɪn/ *noun*. LME.
[Anglo-Norman = Old French *replevir* recover: see REPLEVY *verb*.]
LAW. **1** The provisional restoration to, or recovery by, the owner of goods invalidly distrained, on his or her giving security to have the matter tried in court and to abide by the court's decision. LME. ▸**†b** Conditional release of a prisoner under a writ of mainprize. L16–M17.
2 A writ empowering a person to recover his or her goods by replevin. LME.
3 An action for recovering distrained goods by replevin. E16.

replevin /rɪˈplɛvɪn/ *verb trans*. M17.
[from the noun.]
LAW. **†1** = REPLEVY *verb* 1. *rare*. Only in M17.
2 = REPLEVY *verb* 2. Now chiefly *US*. L17.

replevisable /rɪˈplɛvɪsəb(ə)l/ *adjective*. LME.
[Anglo-Norman *replevis(s)able*, from *repleviss-* lengthened stem of *replevir* REPLEVY *verb*: see -ABLE.]
LAW. Able to be replevied.

replevy /rɪˈplɛvi/ *noun*. Now *rare*. LME.
[from the verb.]
LAW. **1** A writ of replevin. LME.
2 = REPLEVIN *noun* 1. M16. ▸**b** = REPLEVIN *noun* 1b. E17.

replevy /rɪˈplɛvi/ *verb*. M16.
[Old French *replevir* recover, formed as RE- + *plevir* app. from Germanic base also of PLEDGE *noun*.]
LAW. **1** *verb trans*. Conditionally release (a prisoner) by mainprize. Now *Hist*. M16.
2 *verb trans*. **a** Of a magistrate etc.: restore (goods) to the owner by replevin. Now *rare*. L16. ▸**b** Recover (distrained goods) by replevin. E17.
3 *verb intrans*. Bring an action for replevin. E17.

replica /ˈrɛplɪkə/ *noun*. M18.
[Italian, from Latin *replicare*: see REPLICATE *verb*.]
1 *MUSIC*. A repeat. M18.
2 A duplicate of a work of art, *esp*. one made by the original artist. E19.
3 A reproduction, a facsimile. Also, a copy or model, esp. on a smaller scale. M19.

> 🕮 **2** H. MOORE The founder . . makes a wax replica of the sculptor's original work. **3** P. G. WODEHOUSE Frances . . was a feminine replica of her . . brother. *attrib.*: *House & Garden* Replica furniture in styles ranging from Jacobean to Regency.

Comb.: **replica method** *METALLURGY* = ***replica technique*** below; **replica plate** *MICROBIOLOGY* a plate of selective culture medium which has been inoculated with bacteria transferred from a culture grown on a non-selective master plate using a piece of velvet to preserve the distribution of colonies; **replica plating** *MICROBIOLOGY* the technique of using replica plates, esp. to isolate specific bacterial mutations; **replica technique** a method of making a thin plastic film cast of an etched surface for examination in an electron microscope.

replicable /ˈrɛplɪkəb(ə)l/ *adjective*. E16.
[formed as REPLICATE *verb* + -ABLE.]
†1 Able to be replied to. *rare*. Only in E16.
2 Able to be repeated experimentally. M20.
■ **replicaˈbility** *noun* the state, condition, or property of being experimentally replicable M20. **replicably** *adverb* M20.

replicant /ˈrɛplɪk(ə)nt/ *noun*. E17.
[Latin *replicant-* pres. ppl stem of *replicare*: see REPLICATE *verb*, -ANT[1].]
†1 A fresh applicant. *rare*. Only in E17.
†2 A person who replies. M17–M18.
3 A person who or thing which replicates or copies someone or something; *esp*. (in science fiction) a genetically engineered or artificial being. L20.

replicar /ˈrɛplɪkɑː/ *noun*. Orig. *US*. L20.
[Blend of REPLICA and CAR.]
A motor car which is a full-size, functional replica of a vintage or classic model; *esp*. one custom-built from a kit.

replicase /ˈrɛplɪkeɪz/ *noun*. M20.
[from REPLIC(ATE *verb* + -ASE.]
BIOCHEMISTRY. A polymerase which catalyses the synthesis of a complementary RNA molecule using an RNA template.

replicate /ˈrɛplɪkət/ *noun*. L18.
[formed as next.]
1 *MUSIC*. A tone one or more octaves above or below a given tone. L18.
2 *SCIENCE*. A repetition of an experiment or trial; each of a number of similar parts or procedures which constitute an experiment or trial. E20.
3 *gen*. A copy; a replica. M20.

replicate /ˈrɛplɪkət/ *adjective*. M19.
[Latin *replicatus* pa. pple, formed as next: see -ATE[2].]
1 *BIOLOGY*. Of a leaf, insect wing, etc.: folded back on itself. M19.
2 *SCIENCE*. That is a replicate or repetition of an experiment or trial. M20.
3 *gen*. Of the nature of a replica or copy. L20.

replicate /ˈrɛplɪkeɪt/ *verb*. LME.
[Latin *replicat-* pa. ppl stem of *replicare* unfold, (later) reply, formed as RE- + *plicare* to fold: see -ATE[3]. Cf. PLY *verb*[1], REPLY *verb*.]
1 *verb trans*. Do or say again, repeat. *rare*. LME. ▸**b** *SCIENCE*. Repeat (an experiment or trial) to obtain a consistent result. E20.
2 *verb trans*. Answer, reply; say in answer. *rare*. M16.
3 *verb trans*. Fold or bend back. Chiefly as ***replicated*** *ppl adjective*. L17.
4 *verb trans*. Make a replica of (a picture etc.). L19. ▸**b** *verb refl. & intrans*. *BIOLOGY*. Of genetic material or a living organism: reproduce or give rise to a copy of (itself). M20. ▸**c** *verb trans*. Imitate; make or be a model or replica of. M20. ▸**d** *verb trans*. Copy or reproduce exactly. L20.

> 🕮 **1b** J. BOWLBY Earlier findings have been replicated on samples of diverse origin. **4b** C. PRIEST Brain cells never replicate, so . . mental ability . . declines. **c** *Times* The gallery is to have . . rooms that replicate rooms at Hutton Castle.

■ **replicative** *adjective* (*a*) *BOTANY* = REPLICATE *adjective* 1; (*b*) *BIOLOGY* pertaining to or involved in replication (REPLICATION 5b): M19. **replicatively** *adverb* (*a*) with regard to replication; †(*b*) *rare* with relation of a part to the whole, so as to be equally diffused: E18. **replicatory** *adjective* (*a*) *rare* of the nature of a reply; (*b*) *BIOLOGY* = REPLICATIVE (b): E19.

replication /rɛplɪˈkeɪʃ(ə)n/ *noun*. LME.
[Old French *replicacion* from Latin *replicatio(n-)*, formed as REPLICATE *verb*: see -ATION.]
1 The action of folding something up or back; a fold resulting from this. *rare*. LME.
2 (A) reply, (an) answer, *esp*. a reply to an answer. LME. ▸**b** *LAW*. A plaintiff's reply to the plea of the defendant. LME.
3 **†a** Repetition. LME–L17. ▸**b** *SCIENCE*. Repetition of an experiment or trial to obtain a consistent result. E20.
4 Return of a sound; (a) reverberation, (an) echo. Chiefly *poet*. E17.
5 **a** A copy, a reproduction; the action of reproducing something. L17. ▸**b** *BIOLOGY*. The process by which genetic material or a living organism produces a copy of itself. M20.
5b ***saltatory replication***: see SALTATORY *adjective*.

replicator /ˈrɛplɪkeɪtə/ *noun*. M20.
[In sense 1 from French *réplicateur*, formed as REPLICON + *-eur* -OR. In sense 2, agent-noun from REPLICATE *verb*: see -OR.]
1 *BIOLOGY*. A structural gene at which replication of a specific replicon is believed to be initiated. M20.
2 A thing which replicates something. M20.

replicon /ˈrɛplɪkɒn/ *noun*. M20.
[from REPLIC(ATION + -ON.]
BIOLOGY. (Part of) a nucleic acid molecule which replicates as a unit, beginning at a specific site within it.

réplique /replik/ *noun*. Also **re-**. Pl. pronounced same. L15.
[French, from *répliquer* from Latin *replicare*: see REPLICATE *verb*.]
A reply, a rejoinder.
¶ Formerly fully Anglicized.

replum /ˈrɛpləm, ˈriː-/ *noun*. Pl. **-pla** /-plə/. M19.
[Latin, app. = a covering moulding, formerly interpreted as 'door-frame'.]
BOTANY. A framework consisting of the placentae and the septum extending between them, found in certain fruits, esp. the siliquae and siliculae of cruciferous plants, in which the valves fall away by dehiscence.

replunge /riːˈplʌn(d)ʒ/ *verb & noun*. E17.
[from RE- + PLUNGE *verb*.]
▸ **A** *verb trans. & intrans*. Plunge again. E17.
▸ **B** *noun*. An act of replunging. E19.

reply /rɪˈplʌɪ/ *noun*. M16.
[from the verb.]
1 (An) answer in words or writing; *transf*. a response made by a gesture, action, etc. M16.
2 **a** Chiefly *SCOTS LAW*. A response to an answer; a replication. Now *rare* or *obsolete*. M16. ▸**b** *LAW*. A pleading by counsel for the prosecution or plaintiff after the final speech for the defence. M19.
3 A radar signal sent by a transponder in response to interrogation. M20.

> 🕮 **1** D. CARNEGIE Cubellis answered the advertisement, sending his reply to a box number. J. MARQUAND I had no adequate reply to the question. *Times* Her Majesty was . . pleased to make reply. G. BOYCOTT Trinidad's reply to our total . . was to make 392 for eight.

reply /rɪˈplʌɪ/ *verb*. LME.
[Old French *replier* from Latin *replicare*: see REPLICATE *verb*.]
▸ **I 1** *verb intrans*. Answer or respond in words or writing. Freq. foll. by *to*. LME. ▸**b** Respond by a gesture or action; return gunfire. E19.
2 *verb intrans. & trans*. Return or re-echo (a sound). *poet*. LME.
3 *verb intrans*. Respond to an answer; *spec*. in *LAW*, answer a defendant's plea, make a replication. LME.
4 *verb trans*. Return as an answer; say in reply (*that*). Also with direct speech as obj. LME.

> 🕮 **1** M. PATTISON Milton replies to these . . charges by a lengthy account. W. STYRON I thought I would . . reply to my father's letter. **b** *Daily News* Lancashire scored 189 . . Somersetshire . . replied with 90 for three. **2** TENNYSON Blow, let us hear the purple glens replying. **4** T. HARDY When questioned she . . replied that she was . . well.

▸**† II 5** *verb trans*. Fold or bend back. *rare*. LME–L16.
6 *verb trans*. Repeat. *rare*. LME–L16.
■ **replier** *noun* a person who replies LME.

repo /ˈriːpəʊ/ *noun*[1]. *colloq*. (chiefly *US*). Pl. **-os**. M20.
[Abbreviation: see -O.]
= REPURCHASE ***agreement***.

repo /ˈriːpəʊ/ *noun*[2] *& verb*. *colloq*. (chiefly *N. Amer.*). L20.
[Abbreviation: see -O.]
▸ **A** *noun*. Pl. **-os**. (An instance of) repossession of goods, a property, etc., when a purchaser defaults; a car etc. which has been repossessed. Chiefly in ***repo man*** = REPOSSESSOR. L20.
▸ **B** *verb trans*. Infl. **repo'd**, **repo's**. Repossess when a purchaser defaults. L20.

repoint /riːˈpɔɪnt/ *verb trans*. M19.
[from RE- + POINT *verb*[1].]
Point (brickwork, a wall, etc.) again.

repone /rɪˈpəʊn/ *verb trans*. *Scot*. E16.
[Latin *reponere*: see REPOSE *verb*[1].]
1 *LAW*. Restore to a position or office previously held; *spec*. restore to the ministry or a ministerial charge. E16. ▸**b** Restore the legal status of or rehabilitate pending retrial. (Foll. by *against* a decree or sentence.) L16.
†2 Put back *in* a place. *rare*. M16–M17.
3 Reply. *rare*. M17.

repopulate /riːˈpɒpjʊleɪt/ *verb trans*. L16.
[from RE- + POPULATE *verb*.]
Populate again.
■ **repopuˈlation** *noun* M18.

report /rɪˈpɔːt/ *noun*. LME.
[Old French, formed as the verb.]
1 **a** Rumour, gossip. Now *rare*. LME. ▸**b** A rumour; a way in which a person or thing is spoken of. LME. ▸**c** Repute, fame, reputation. Usu. with *good*, *bad*, etc. LME. ▸**†d** Testimony *to*, commendation. *rare* (Shakes.). L16–E17.
2 An account given or opinion expressed on some particular matter, esp. after investigation or consideration; a more or less formal account *of* some matter; a formal statement of the results of an investigation carried out by a person or appointed body. LME. ▸**b** The account of a bill etc. given in Parliament by the committee appointed to consider it. E17. ▸**c** *LAW*. A detailed formal account of a case heard in a court, esp. as prepared for publication. Freq. in *pl*. E17. ▸**d** A more or less detailed description of any event, proceeding, meeting, etc., *esp*. one intended for publication or broadcasting. E19. ▸**e** A statement in which an accusation is made against a serviceman or -woman; the charge itself. Freq. in ***on report***, on a charge. M19. ▸**f** A teacher's official periodical written statement about the work and behaviour of a pupil. L19.
†3 Relation, reference, bearing, connection. *rare*. E16–E18.
†4 *MUSIC*. A response; a note or part answering to another; a note, a sound. E16–M17.
5 A sudden loud noise as of an explosion or gunfire. L16. ▸**b** (A case containing) a pyrotechnic charge which makes a loud noise when set off. L18.
6 An employee who reports to another. L20.

> 🕮 **1** A. RADCLIFFE I do not lightly give faith to report. **b** SIR W. SCOTT There are bad reports of him among the Dominicans. **c** S. SMILES He . . held to his purpose, through good and through evil report. **2** SHAKES. *Two Gent.* We know, on Valentine's report, you are already Love's firm votary. W. COWPER My soul is sick with every day's report Of wrong and outrage. *Daily Mirror* In its report the Commission . . says that corruption is a . . grave offence. *Which?* For this report we tested 104 brands of . . emulsion paint. **make report** *arch.* give a report or account. **d** M. L. KING People . . followed reports of the bus protest in the newspapers. **f** R. BROOKE My term's report . . has come in, & is very bad. **5** J. B. MORTON His braces burst with a report like a sporting-gun.

Comb.: **report stage** the stage in a bill's passage through the British Parliament following the report of a committee and preceding the third reading.

report /rɪˈpɔːt/ *verb*. LME.
[Old French *reporter* from Latin *reportare* carry back, bear away, formed as RE- + *portare* carry. In usual sense closer to Old French *raporter* (mod. *rapporter*), ult. formed as RE- + AP-¹ + Latin *portare*.]
▸ **I** *verb trans*. †**1 a** Entrust or commit (oneself) *to* a person or thing for support or confirmation. LME–M17. ▸**b** Refer *to*, esp. for information. E16–M17.
†**2 a** Bring or convey; carry (news). LME–L16. ▸**b** Bring in return; obtain. *Scot*. E16–E17.
3 Bring back or give an account of (an event, circumstance, etc.) (*to* a person); convey (a message), repeat (something heard); relate (*that*); in *pass*., be stated (*to be*). LME. ▸†**b** Describe (a person). E–M17. ▸**c** Prepare a written account of (a meeting, event, etc.), esp. for publication in a newspaper, official journal, etc.; cover (an event) as a reporter. E17. ▸**d** Say factually. E20.
4 a Give in or make a more or less formal statement concerning (some matter or thing); make a report on; (of a parliamentary committee chairman) announce that the committee has dealt with (a bill). L16. ▸**b** Relate or announce, esp. as the result of special observation or investigation; inform those concerned of (an occurrence, fact, etc.). M17. ▸**c** *refl*. = sense 7c below. Now *rare*. E19. ▸**d** Name (a person) to a superior authority as having offended in some way. L19.
†**5** Cause to resound; re-echo (a sound). *rare*. L16–L17.
6 Fit (a firework) with a report or charge. Usu. in *pass*. L19.

> 🕮 **3** J. A. FROUDE The refugee friars were reported to be well supplied with money. W. C. BRYANT Report my words To royal Neptune. E. YOUNG-BRUEHL She reported her dreams, and her father replied with . . an interpretation. **reported speech** indirect speech. **reporting verb** any of the class of verbs which can convey the action of speaking and are used with both direct and reported speech. **c** L. KOPPETT Some 35 years of being paid to . . report baseball for daily newspapers. **4a** T. HARDY Oak came in to report progress for the day. B. HEAD We'd keep minutes and then report our decisions . . to a general meeting. **b** A. BRINK He reported it to the police. ANTHONY SMITH Researchers have reported a general decline in intellectual function. **d** E. WAUGH Stanley has reported Lionel Tennyson for being drunk. A. EDEN The doctor . . threatened to report me to the colonel for disobeying his warning.

▸ **II** *verb intrans*. **7 a** Give an account of, speak in a certain way *of*; give a report to convey that one is well, badly, etc., impressed. Freq. foll. by *of*. LME–E17. ▸**b** Draw up, make, or submit a report (*on*). Also, act as a reporter. LME. ▸**c** Inform authority of one's arrival or presence; present oneself *to* a person etc. on arrival. Also foll. by *in*. M19. ▸**d** Be responsible or account for one's activities *to* a superior, supervisor, etc. L19.

> 🕮 **7a** SHAKES. *All's Well* A gentleman that serves the Count Reports but coarsely of her. **b** J. GILMOUR Has any one . . seen these things, and come back . . to report on them? G. GREENE Keep your eyes open . . and then report direct to him. **report back** return with or make a report to or *to* one's principal etc. **c** D. BEATY Having to report in at the African Airways counter. **d** *Guardian* Reporting to the Promotions Manager, you will be responsible for the . . promotion of selected titles.

■ **reportative** *adjective* that presents or introduces reported speech L20. **reportedly** *adverb* according to report E20. †**reportingly** *adverb* (*rare*) (*a*) by hearsay; (*b*) correspondingly: L16–E17.

reportable /rɪˈpɔːtəb(ə)l/ *adjective*. M19.
[from prec. + -ABLE.]
1 Able or worthy to be reported. M19.
2 That should or must be reported to some authority. M20.

> 🕮 **2** *New York Times* Health officials are making Lyme a nationally reportable disease.

■ **reportaˈbility** *noun* M20.

reportage /rɛpɔːˈtɑːʒ, rɪˈpɔːtɪdʒ/ *noun*. E17.
[formed as prec. + -AGE. In later use after French Cf. RAPPORTAGE.]
†**1** Report, repute. *rare*. Only in E17.
2 Reported matter; gossip. L19.
3 The describing of events; *spec*. the reporting of events for the press or for broadcasting, esp. with reference to reporting style. Also, an instance of this, a piece of journalistic or factual writing. L19.

> 🕮 **3** *Listener* Imposing the techniques of popular . . journalism or television reportage. A. T. ELLIS I don't imagine . . what I told you is straight reportage.

reporter /rɪˈpɔːtə/ *noun*. LME.
[Anglo-Norman = Old French *reporteur* (mod. RAPPORTEUR), formed as REPORT *verb*: see -ER¹.]
1 A person who reports or relates; a recounter or narrator. LME. ▸**b** A person appointed to make a report or provide information on something. Also (SCOTS LAW), an official who receives and presents reports on juvenile offenders or juveniles in care. E17.
2 A person employed to prepare reports of legal cases, debates, meetings, etc., for publication; *spec*. a person employed to report news for a newspaper, magazine, television or radio network, etc. Also in titles of newspapers etc. E17.
†**3** A kind of firework. Also, a pistol. L17–M19.
4 CHEMISTRY & BIOCHEMISTRY. A molecule or gene used as a means of obtaining information about the system in which it occurs. Freq. *attrib*. L20.

> 🕮 **1** *fig*.: R. L. STEVENSON Looks and gestures . . are often the most clear reporters of the heart. **2** M. COREN Reporters were . . clamouring to interview him. *Sports Illustrated* Channel 7 sports reporter Bill Buckner.

reportorial /rɛpəˈtɔːrɪəl/ *adjective*. Orig. *US*. M19.
[Irreg. from prec. + -IAL, after *editorial*.]
Of, pertaining to, or characteristic of reporters; written in the style of a (newspaper) report.
■ **reportorially** *adverb* M19.

reposado /rɛpɒˈsɑːdəʊ/ *noun*. Pl. **-os**. L20.
[Spanish, lit. 'rested'.]
Tequila which has been aged in oak for between two months and a year.

reposal /rɪˈpəʊz(ə)l/ *noun*. Long *rare* or *obsolete*. E17.
[from REPOSE *verb*¹, *verb*² + -AL¹.]
1 The act of reposing (trust, confidence, etc.). Formerly also, trust or reliance *in* something. E17.
†**2** The fact or state of reposing or resting *in* a place. E–M17.

repose /rɪˈpəʊz/ *noun*. LME.
[from REPOSE *verb*² or from Old & mod. French *repos*, from *reposer* REPOSE *verb*².]
1 Temporary rest or cessation from activity, esp. in order to refresh physical or mental powers; *spec*. sleep, the rest given by sleep. LME.
†**2** A place of rest or safe-keeping. Formerly also, a thing to rest on. *rare*. LME–E18.
3 Relief or respite from exertion or excitement. Also foll. by *from*. E16.
4 a A state of peace or quiescence; quiet, calmness, tranquillity; stillness. M17. ▸**b** Absence of activity in a natural process. M18. ▸**c** Composure, ease of manner. M19.
5 ART. **a** Harmonious arrangement of figures or colours; a restful visual effect. L17. ▸†**b** A contrasting area of light and shade in a painting. *rare*. L17–E18.

> 🕮 **1** T. COLLINS A . . cat jumped on his knees, and settled itself for repose. H. BELLOC He slept the last few hours . . in a profound repose. **3** P. P. READ The frenzy of a week in London could be followed by some repose. **4a** V. SACKVILLE-WEST You . . looked so tragic when your face was in repose. M. BINCHY A special Mass . . for the repose of his soul. **b** J. RUSKIN Vesuvius was virtually in repose. **c** *Illustrated London News* An unhurried . . person, with a scholar's repose.

Phrases: **angle of repose** the greatest angle between two planes which is consistent with stability. **seek repose**, **take repose** rest.
■ **reposeful** *adjective* full of repose; having an air of repose; quiet: M19. **reposefully** *adverb* (*rare*) L19. **reposefulness** *noun* (*rare*) L19.

repose /rɪˈpəʊz/ *verb*¹ *trans*. LME.
[from RE- + POSE *verb*¹, after Latin *reponere* replace, restore, store up, lay aside or to rest, formed as RE- + *ponere* to place.]
†**1** Replace; put back in the same position. LME–M17. ▸**b** Restore. Also (SCOTS LAW) = REPONE *verb* 1. *rare*. LME–M17.
2 Place, put; *esp*. deposit *in* a place. Now *rare*. LME.
3 Set or place (confidence, trust, etc.) *in* a thing or person. Cf. REPOSE *verb*² 5. M16. ▸**b** Place or leave (something) *in* the control or management of another. L16.

> 🕮 **3** A. PRICE David reposes confidence in Elizabeth's . . loyalty.

repose /rɪˈpəʊz/ *verb*². LME.
[Old & mod. French *reposer* (earlier *repauser*) from late Latin *repausare*, formed as RE- + Latin *pausare* PAUSE *verb*.]
1 *verb refl*. Rest (oneself); lay (oneself) to rest. LME. ▸**b** *fig*. Settle (oneself) confidently *on* something. Now *rare* or *obsolete*. L16.
2 *verb intrans*. Take rest; cease from activity, exertion, or excitement. LME. ▸**b** Sit or lie down in rest. Also, lie or be laid, esp. in sleep or death. (Foll. by *in*, *on*.) M16. ▸**c** Remain still; lie in quiet. E19.
3 *verb trans*. Lay to rest *on* or *in* something. Now only *fig*. M16.
4 *verb trans*. Give rest to, refresh by rest. M16.
†**5** *verb intrans*. Confide or place one's trust *in* or rely *on* a thing or person. Cf. REPOSE *verb*¹ 3. M16–L18.
6 *verb intrans*. Be supported or based *on* or *upon*. Also, dwell *on* in thought. E17.

> 🕮 **1** J. BERESFORD A beast who . . proceeds . . to repose himself in the middle of the pond. **2** H. MAUNDRELL At Tripoli we repos'd a full week. ***repose on one's laurels***: see LAUREL *noun* 2. **b** *Irish Press* Remains reposing in St. Brigid's church. *transf*.: JO GRIMOND In his workshop . . reposed numerous bits of furniture. **3** GOLDSMITH I'll go to him, and repose our distresses on his . . bosom. **4** G. BANCROFT He . . halted . . to repose his wayworn soldiers. **6** BYRON On such things the memory reposes with tenderness.

■ **reposedness** *noun* the state or condition of repose or of being in repose E17.

reposit /rɪˈpɒzɪt/ *verb trans*. M17.
[Latin *reposit-* pa. ppl stem of *reponere* REPONE.]
1 Put or deposit (a thing) *in* a place; lay up, store. M17.
2 Replace. *rare*. E19.

reposition /riːpəˈzɪʃ(ə)n/ *noun*. LME.
[Late Latin *repositio(n-)* storage, formed as prec. + -ITION, perh. through REPOSIT and REPOSITORY *noun*. In sense 1 prob. from RE- + POSITION *noun* (but cf. medieval Latin *repositio(n-)* placing, arranging).]
1 SURGERY. The operation of restoring a bone, organ, etc., to the normal position; replacement. LME.
2 Reinstatement of a person to a position or office. Also, restoration to the possession of a thing. *Scot. arch*. M16.
3 The action of repositing or storing something. E17.

reposition /riːpəˈzɪʃ(ə)n/ *verb*. M20.
[from RE- + POSITION *verb*.]
1 *verb trans*. Put in a different position. Now also (*spec*.), change the image of (a company, product, etc.) to target a new or wider market. M20.
2 *verb intrans*. Adjust or alter one's position. M20.

repositor /rɪˈpɒzɪtə/ *noun*. L19.
[from REPOSIT + -OR.]
SURGERY. An instrument used in returning displaced organs etc. to the normal position.

repository /rɪˈpɒzɪt(ə)ri/ *noun*. L15.
[French †*repositoire* or Latin *repositorium*, from *reposit-*: see REPOSIT, -ORY¹.]
1 A receptacle, building, or other place, in which things are or may be deposited or stored; a part or place in which something is accumulated or exists in quantities. L15. ▸**b** *spec*. A place, room, or building, in which specimens, curiosities, or works of art are collected; a museum. Now *rare*. M17. ▸**c** A place where things are kept or offered for sale; a warehouse, a store, a shop. M18.
2 †**a** CHRISTIAN THEOLOGY. A transitional place of existence for the soul before incarnation. M17–E18. ▸**b** A place in which a dead body is deposited; a vault, a sepulchre. M17.
3 A place or thing in which something immaterial is held to be deposited or contained; a thing or person regarded as a store of information. M17. ▸**b** A person to whom some matter is entrusted or confided. L17.

> 🕮 **1** T. HILLERMAN The back porch was . . a repository for stored items. *Independent* A site for a nuclear waste repository. *American Horticulturist* The . . bog . . was a rich repository of such plants as pitcher plant. **3** S. NAIPAUL California became . . the New World's . . last repository of hope. **b** A. BROOKNER Lautner is the repository of the family's secrets.

repository /rɪˈpɒzɪt(ə)ri/ *adjective*. *rare*. L17.
[from prec. or from REPOSITION *verb*: see -ORY².]
†**1** Providing storage. Only in L17.
2 Pertaining or relating to repositioning, esp. to the replacing and reassembling of heavy ordnance during military manoeuvres. L19.

repossess /riːpəˈzɛs/ *verb trans*. L15.
[from RE- + POSSESS.]
1 Regain or recover possession of (a place, property, a right, etc.); reoccupy. Also (*spec*.), regain or retake possession of (property or goods being paid for by instalments) when a purchaser defaults on the payments. L15.
2 Restore (a person) †*to* or reinstate *in* possession of something. *Scot*. L16.
3 Put (a person) in possession *of* something again. L16.

> 🕮 **1** *Which?* If you don't keep up . . repayments the lender could repossess your home. **3** *refl*.: K. TENNANT Lago repossessed himself of the pearls.

■ **repossessed** *ppl adjective* (chiefly *US*) that has been regained or taken back, esp. by a vendor; second hand: M20. **repossession** *noun* (*a*) recovery; renewed possession; (*b*) *spec*. the recovery of property or goods being paid for by instalments when a purchaser defaults on the payments; legal proceedings to effect this: L16. **repossessor** *noun* a person who repossesses goods; *spec*. a person employed by a credit company to repossess an item when a purchaser defaults on the payments: M20.

repost *noun* see RIPOSTE *noun*.

repost /riːˈpəʊst/ *verb*¹ *trans*. M20.
[from RE- + POST *verb*².]
Put into or send through the post again.

For other words beginning with *re-* see the entry for **re-**

repost /riːˈpəʊst/ *verb*² *trans.* L20.
[from RE- + POST *verb*³.]
Appoint to a new post; station at a new post. Chiefly as ***reposting*** *verbal noun*.

repost *verb*³ see RIPOSTE *verb*.

repot /riːˈpɒt/ *verb trans. & intrans.* Infl. **-tt-**. M19.
[from RE- + POT *verb*¹.]
Put (a plant) into another, esp. larger, flowerpot.

repoussé /rəˈpuːseɪ/ *adjective & noun*. M19.
[French, pa. pple of *repousser*, formed as RE- + *pousser* PUSH *verb*.]
▸ **A** *adjective*. Of metalwork: raised into or ornamented in relief by means of hammering from the reverse side. M19.
▸ **B** *noun*. Ornamental metalwork fashioned by the repoussé method; the process of hammering into relief. M19.

repoussoir /rəpuswaːr/ *noun*. Pl. pronounced same. L19.
[French, from *repoussé*: see prec. Cf. -ORY².]
An object in the foreground of a painting serving to emphasize the principal figure or scene.

repp *noun & adjective* var. of REP *noun*³ *& adjective*.

repple depple /ˈrɛp(ə)l ˌdɛp(ə)l/ *noun*. *US Military slang*. M20.
[from REPL(ACEMENT + DEP(OT, modified by redupl. and respelling.]
A replacement depot, where soldiers based overseas gather before going home.

repr. *abbreviation*.
1 Represent(ed).
2 Reprint(ed).

†**repref** *noun* var. of REPROOF *noun*.

reprehend /rɛprɪˈhɛnd/ *verb*. ME.
[Latin *reprehendere*, formed as RE- + *prehendere* seize.]
1 *verb trans.* Reprove, rebuke, blame, find fault with. ME.
2 *verb intrans.* Find fault. Now *rare* or *obsolete*. L16.

> 📖 **1** E. MELLOR A . . recklessness which cannot be too severely reprehended. **2** SHAKES. *Mids. N. D.* Gentles, do not reprehend If you pardon, we will mend.

reprehensible /rɛprɪˈhɛnsɪb(ə)l/ *adjective*. LME.
[Late Latin *reprehensibilis*, from Latin *reprehens-* pa. ppl stem of *reprehendere*: see prec., -IBLE.]
Deserving of reprehension, censure, or rebuke; reprovable; blameworthy.

> 📖 A. S. NEILL It's . . reprehensible to cheat the grocer.

■ ˌ**reprehensiˈbility** *noun* L19. **reprehensibleness** *noun* (*rare*) E18. **reprehensibly** *adverb* M17.

reprehension /rɛprɪˈhɛnʃ(ə)n/ *noun*. LME.
[Latin *reprehensio(n-)*, from *reprehens-*: see prec., -ION.]
The action of reprehending a person or thing; censure, rebuke, reprimand. Also, an instance of this.

reprehensive /rɛprɪˈhɛnsɪv/ *adjective*. Now *rare*. L16.
[French *répréhensif* or medieval Latin *reprehensivus*, formed as prec.: see -IVE.]
Of the nature of reprehension; containing reproof.
■ Also **reprehensory** *adjective* L16.

represent /rɛprɪˈzɛnt/ *verb*. LME.
[Old & mod. French *représenter* or Latin *repraesentare*, formed as RE- + *praesentare* PRESENT *verb*.]
†**1** *verb trans.* Bring into the presence of someone or something; *esp.* present (oneself or another) *to* or *before*. LME–M17.
2 a *verb trans.* Bring clearly and distinctly to mind, esp. by description or imagination. LME. ▸**b** *verb trans.* State or point out (a fact) clearly or seriously *to* another, esp. by expostulation or persuasion; bring home *to* with the aim of influencing action or conduct. L16. ▸**c** *verb intrans.* Make representations or objections *against* something; protest. Now *rare*. E18.
3 *verb trans.* **a** Show or display to the eye; make visible or manifest. Formerly also, display in one's bearing or manner. Now *rare*. LME. ▸**b** *spec.* Exhibit through art; portray, depict, delineate. LME. ▸**c** Of a picture, image, etc.: exhibit by artificial resemblance or delineation. LME.
4 a *verb trans.* Exhibit or reproduce in action or show; perform or produce (a play etc.) on stage. LME. ▸**b** *verb intrans.* Appear on stage; act, perform. Now *rare*. M16. ▸**c** *verb trans.* Play or act the part of on stage. M17.
5 *verb trans.* **a** Symbolize; act as a visible or concrete embodiment of. LME. ▸**b** Of a quantity: indicate or imply (another quantity). M19.
6 *verb trans.* **a** Of a thing: stand for or in place of (a person or thing); act as an image of (something). Also, (of a person) denote (something) *by* a substitute. LME. ▸**b** Be an equivalent of, correspond to, replace (esp. another animal or plant in a given region). M19.
7 *verb trans.* **a** Take the place of (another); be a substitute in some capacity for; act or speak for (another) by a deputed right. LME. ▸**b** *spec.* Be an accredited deputy or substitute for (a number of people) in a legislative or deliberative assembly; be an elected Member of Parliament for (a certain constituency). Also in *pass.*, be acted for in this way (*by* someone). M17.
8 *verb trans.* **a** Describe or depict as having a specified character or quality; declare to be. (Foll. by *as*, *to be*.) E16. ▸**b** Give out, allege *that*. L19.
9 *verb trans.* Serve as a specimen or example of (a class or kind); exemplify. Freq. in *pass.* M19.

> 📖 **2b** LYTTON I have . . represented to my . . brother the necessity of sending my sons to school. **3b** A. KOESTLER Posters on which youth was . . represented with a laughing face. P. TILLICH In . . Renaissance art fate is sometimes represented as the wind. **5** SCOTT FITZGERALD To young Gatz . . that yacht represented all the beauty . . in the world. E. ROOSEVELT Ambassadors representing all . . their . . country stands for. **6a** J. N. LOCKYER If we represent the Sun by a globe. K. CROSSLEY-HOLLAND While Odin stood for violence . . Thor represented order. **7a** V. SACKVILLE-WEST The king would be represented at the funeral by the Duke of Gloucester. E. BOWEN Minors had been represented . . by their mothers. **b** M. DAS Kusumpur . . deserves a man of . . stature to represent it in the legislature. **8a** E. WAUGH To represent Elizabeth as . . blind to what her servants were doing. ISAIAH BERLIN Tolstoy . . represents them as . . feeble-witted creatures. **9** N. HAWTHORNE A soup in which twenty . . vegetables were represented.

■ ˌ**representaˈbility** *noun* the state or quality of being representable M19. **representable** *adjective* M17. ˌ**represenˈtee** *noun* (*rare*) †(*a*) a person who is represented; †(*b*) a (parliamentary) representative; (*c*) LAW a person to whom a representation is made: E17. **representment** *noun* (now *rare*) the action of representing in some form or figure; the fact of being so represented; a representation: L16. **representor** *noun* = REPRESENTER; *spec.* (LAW) a person on whose behalf a representation is made: M16.

re-present /riːprɪˈzɛnt/ *verb trans.* M16.
[from RE- + PRESENT *verb*.]
Present again or a second time; give back.

representant /rɛprɪˈzɛnt(ə)nt/ *noun*. E17.
[French *représentant* pres. pple of *représenter*: see REPRESENT, -ANT¹.]
1 A person representing another or others; a representative. *rare*. E17.
2 An equivalent, a counterpart. M19.

representation /ˌrɛprɪzɛnˈteɪʃ(ə)n/ *noun*. LME.
[Old & mod. French *représentation* or Latin *repraesentatio(n-)*, from *repraesentat-* pa. ppl stem of *repraesentare*: see REPRESENT, -ATION.]
1 a An image, likeness, or reproduction *of* a thing; *spec.* a reproduction in some material or tangible form, as a drawing or painting. LME. ▸**b** The action or fact of exhibiting or producing in some visible image or form. L15. ▸**c** The fact of expressing or denoting by means of a figure or symbol; symbolic action. Also in *pl.* E16. ▸**d** MATH. (The image of) a homomorphism from a given (abstract) group to a group or other structure having some further meaning or significance. L19.
2 a The action of presenting a fact etc. before another or others; an account, *esp.* one intended to convey a particular view and to influence opinion or action. M16. ▸**b** A formal and serious statement of facts, reasons, or arguments, made with the aim of influencing action, conduct, etc.; a remonstrance, a protest, an expostulation. Freq. in *pl.* L17.
3 A performance of a play or depiction of a character on stage. L16.
4 a The fact of standing for, or in place of, another, esp. with authority to act on that other's account; substitution of one thing or person for another. E17. ▸**b** LAW. The assumption by an heir of the position, rights, and obligations of his or her predecessor. L17.
5 a The action of presenting to the mind or imagination; an image or idea thus presented. M17. ▸**b** The mental process or faculty of forming a clear image or idea. M19.
6 a The fact of representing or being represented in a legislative or deliberative assembly, esp. in Parliament; the position, principle, or system implied by this. M18. ▸**b** The aggregate of those who represent an electorate. L18.

> 📖 **1** A. KNOX The representation of very heaven upon earth. *Athenaeum* An allegorical representation of the triumph . . at Philippi. **2a** J. PRIESTLEY Different representations of the Platonic doctrine. **b** D. BREWSTER Ferdinand . . instructed his ambassador to make . . representations to the Pope. **3** J. BERESFORD The last . . scene of the tragedy . . is too dreadful for representation. **4b right of representation** the right whereby the son of an elder son deceased succeeds to his grandfather in preference to the latter's immediate issue. **5a** J. LOCKE Lively representations set before their minds of the . . joys of Heaven. **6a** A. TOFFLER Techniques for guaranteeing equal representation for all. ***proportional representation***: see PROPORTIONAL *adjective* 1.

re-presentation /ˌriːprɛz(ə)nˈteɪʃ(ə)n/ *noun*. E19.
[from RE- + PRESENTATION.]
A renewed or different presentation.

representational /ˌrɛprɪzɛnˈteɪʃ(ə)n(ə)l/ *adjective*. M19.
[from REPRESENTATION + -AL¹.]
1 Pertaining to, or of the nature of, representation. Also, holding or pertaining to the doctrine of representationism. M19.
2 *spec.* Of a work of art or artistic style: that aims to depict things as they actually appear to the eye. E20.
■ **representationalism** *noun* (*a*) = REPRESENTATIONISM; (*b*) representational art: L19. **representationalist** *adjective & noun* (*a*) *adjective* of or pertaining to representationism; (*b*) *noun* a representationist: M19. **representationally** *adverb* M19.

representationism /ˌrɛprɪzɛnˈteɪʃ(ə)nɪz(ə)m/ *noun*. M19.
[formed as prec. + -ISM.]
The doctrine that a perceived object is a representation of the real external object.
■ **representationist** *noun* a supporter or advocate of representationism M19.

representative /rɛprɪˈzɛntətɪv/ *adjective & noun*. LME.
[Old & mod. French *représentatif*, *-ive* or medieval Latin *repraesentativus*, formed as REPRESENTATION: see -IVE.]
▸ **A** *adjective*. **1 a** Serving to represent, figure, portray, or symbolize. Also foll. by *of*. LME. ▸**b** Presenting or able to present ideas to the mind. Also, (of art) representational. M18. ▸**c** Relating to mental representation. M19.
2 a Standing for or in place of another or others, esp. in a prominent or comprehensive manner. E17. ▸**b** *spec.* Acting on behalf of a larger body of people in governing or legislating; pertaining to or based on a system of representation by elected deputies. Also, consisting of such deputies. E17.
3 Typical of a class or category; conveying an adequate idea or containing a typical specimen of others of the kind. L18.
4 Taking the place of allied forms or species found elsewhere. M19.

> 📖 **1a** D. WATERLAND Not merely as representative of God . . but as strictly and truly God. J. BARTH This story . . representative of . . many features of my boyhood. **2a** G. BURNET The Nation, of which the King was . . the representative head. **b** *Encycl. Brit.* An elected council representative of the . . Igbirra clans. **3** *Times* Twelve competitors out of a representative international field qualified. S. BIKO Who can be regarded as representative of black opinion? R. DINNAGE An absolutely representative sample of people to be interviewed.

Special collocations: **representative fraction** the ratio of a distance on a map to the distance it represents on the ground.
▸ **B** *noun*. **1** A person or thing representing a larger number or class; a sample, a specimen. Also, a typical embodiment *of* some quality or concept. M17.
2 A person who represents another or others in some special or particular capacity; *spec.* (*a*) a person who represents a section of the community as an elected member of a legislative body; (*b*) a person appointed to represent a monarch or government in another country; (*c*) an agent of a company or another person; (*d*) a delegate, a substitute; (*e*) a successor, an heir. M17.
†**3** A representative body or assembly. M17–M18.
4 A thing which symbolizes, stands for, or corresponds to some other thing. L18.

> 📖 **1** R. W. DALE He [Christ] is the great Representative of our religious life. R. LYDEKKER The sole British representative of this Family is the . . Mole. **2** *Saturday Review* The representatives of the press were deputising in the absence of their chiefs. G. F. KENNAN The Soviet Government . . had its own representative . . in Berlin. *Times* Labour's elected representatives . . mouth . . capitalism. J. RABAN He was the Gulf representative of a firm of electrical engineers in London. **4** J. PRIESTLEY Money is only a . . representative of the commodities . . purchased with it.

Phrases: **House of Representatives** the lower or popular legislative house of the United States Congress; a similar legislative body in Australia or New Zealand. ***personal representative***: see PERSONAL *adjective*.
■ **representatively** *adverb* LME. **representativeness** *noun* M17. ˌ**representaˈtivity** *noun* E20.

representer /rɛprɪˈzɛntə/ *noun*. LME.
[formed as prec. + -ER¹.]
†**1** A representative of a person or thing; *spec.* an elected representative. LME–E18.
2 †**a** A person who or thing which exhibits or shows; an exhibitor. L16–L17. ▸**b** A person who represents by acting; a performer, an impersonator. L16.
3 A person who makes a representation or who states a matter in a certain light. Now *rare* or *obsolete*. M17.

repress /rɪˈprɛs/ *verb trans.* ME.
[Latin *repress-* pa. ppl stem of *reprimere* repress: see RE-. Cf. PRESS *verb*¹.]
1 a Check, restrain, keep down (something bad or objectionable). ME. ▸**b** Check by special treatment; cure, stanch. L15.
2 a Hold back or withstand (passion, emotion, etc. in another) by opposition or control. LME. ▸**b** Keep down, suppress, control (one's own desires, feelings, etc.). LME. ▸**c** PSYCHOANALYSIS. Actively (but unknowingly) exclude

from the conscious mind or suppress into the unconscious (an unacceptable memory, impulse, or desire). **E20.**
3 Reduce (a person or persons) to subjection or quiet; put down by force; keep back or restrain from action. Also, quell (a riot etc.). **LME.**
4 Prevent from natural development, manifestation, etc. **L15.**

> **1a** M. L. King No society can . . repress an ugly past. **2a** N. Wanley Tiberius . . repressed the . . boldness of the proud Persian. H. T. Lane To repress the aggressiveness of a child will make him . . anti-social. **b** J. Conrad Renouard . . repressed an impulse to jump up. M. Forster He repressed his grief for their sake. **c** W. McDougall The function of the 'ego-complex' . . in . . repressing the sexual tendencies. **3** H. T. Buckle A hopeless undertaking . . to try to repress such powerful subjects.

■ **repressed** *ppl adjective* (earlier in **UNREPRESSED**) (*a*) restrained, checked, suppressed; (*b*) *spec.* in *PSYCHOANALYSIS* (of a person) that suppresses in his or her unconscious unwelcome thoughts and impulses; (of an unwelcome impulse etc.) suppressed into a person's unconscious: **M17. represser** *noun* = **REPRESSOR LME. repressible** *adjective* (earlier in **IRREPRESSIBLE**) able to be repressed; *BIOCHEMISTRY* susceptible to the action of a repressor: **M20.**

repressing /riːˈprɛsɪŋ/ *noun.* **M20.**
[from **RE-** + **PRESSING** *noun*.]
A new impression of a gramophone record or compact disc made from an old sound recording.

repression /rɪˈprɛʃ(ə)n/ *noun.* **LME.**
[Late Latin *repressio(n-)*, formed as **REPRESS**: see **-ION**.]
†**1** Ability to repress. Only in **LME.**
2 a The action of repressing; an instance of this. **M16.** ▸**b** *spec.* in *PSYCHOANALYSIS.* The action, process, or result of suppressing into the unconscious or of actively excluding from the conscious mind unacceptable memories, impulses, or desires. Cf. **SUPPRESSION** 7b. **E20.**
3 *BIOCHEMISTRY.* The inhibition of enzyme synthesis by the action of a repressor on an operon. **M20.**
■ **repressionist** *noun* an advocate of repression or repressive measures **L19.**

repressive /rɪˈprɛsɪv/ *adjective.* **LME.**
[from **REPRESS** + **-IVE**.]
Of the nature of or tending to repression.
■ **repressively** *adverb* **M19. repressiveness** *noun* **L19.**

repressor /rɪˈprɛsə/ *noun.* **E17.**
[Latin, agent-noun from *reprimere* **REPRESS**.]
1 A person who or thing which represses something. *rare.* **E17.**
2 *BIOCHEMISTRY.* A substance which by its action on an operon can inhibit the synthesis of a specific enzyme or set of enzymes. **M20.**
■ **repressory** *adjective* **E20.**

†**repreve** *noun, verb* vars. of **REPROOF** *noun*, **REPROVE.**

reprieval /rɪˈpriːv(ə)l/ *noun.* Now *rare.* **L16.**
[from **REPRIEVE** *verb*[1] + **-AL**[1].]
= **REPRIEVE** *noun.*

reprieve /rɪˈpriːv/ *noun.* **M16.**
[from next.]
1 a The action of reprieving a person; an instance of this; *esp.* a formal suspension or remission of the execution of a sentence on a condemned person. **M16.** ▸**b** A warrant granting the suspension or remission of a sentence. **E17.** ▸†**c** The time during which one is reprieved. Only in **E17.**
2 *transf.* **a** A respite or temporary escape from some trouble, calamity, etc. **M16.** ▸**b** Respite from a natural or violent death. **M17.**

> **2b** W. C. Bryant With those who flee Is neither glory nor reprieve from death.

reprieve /rɪˈpriːv/ *verb*[1] *trans.* Orig. †**repry. L15.**
[Earliest in pa. pple from Anglo-Norman, Old French *repris* pa. pple of *reprendre*: see **REPRISE** *verb.* The vowel change and development of *-v-* in the 2nd syll. are unexpl.]
†**1** Take or send back *to* prison; remand. **L15–L16.**
†**2** Postpone, delay, put off. *rare.* **M16–M17.**
3 Relieve or rescue (a person) from impending punishment; *esp.* suspend or delay the execution of (a condemned person). Also foll. by *from.* **L16.**

> **3** E. A. Kendall He may reprieve a condemned malefactor.

†**reprieve** *verb*[2] var. of **REPROVE.**

reprimand /ˈrɛprɪmɑːnd/ *noun.* **M17.**
[French *réprimande*, †*-ende* from Spanish *reprimenda* from Latin, neut. pl. gerundive of *reprimere* **REPRESS.**]
A sharp rebuke or censure, *esp.* one given by a person or body in authority, as by a judge to an offender.

reprimand /rɛprɪˈmɑːnd/ *verb trans.* **L17.**
[French *réprimander*, from *réprimande*: see prec.]
Rebuke or censure sharply.
■ **reprimander** *noun* (*rare*) **M19. reprimandingly** *adverb* (*rare*) **M18.**

reprime /rɪˈprʌɪm/ *verb*[1] *trans. rare.* **E16.**
[Latin *reprimere* **REPRESS.**]
Repress.

reprime /riːˈprʌɪm/ *verb*[2] *trans. & intrans. rare.* **M19.**
[from **RE-** + **PRIME** *verb*[2].]
Prime again.

reprint /ˈriːprɪnt/ *noun.* **E17.**
[from **RE-** + **PRINT** *noun*.]
The action or process of reprinting a book etc.; a reproduction in print of a book etc. already printed; the quantity reprinted.

reprint /riːˈprɪnt/ *verb trans. & intrans.* **M16.**
[from **RE-** + **PRINT** *verb*.]
Print (a work) again in a new edition; print (matter) a second time.
■ **reprinter** *noun* a publisher etc. who reprints or publishes a reprint **L17.**

reprisal /rɪˈprʌɪz(ə)l/ *noun.* **LME.**
[Anglo-Norman *reprisaille* from medieval Latin *reprisalia*, *represalia* neut. pl. (also *-alie* fem. pl.) contr. of *reprae(h)ensalia*, *-aliae*, from Latin *repraehens-* pa. ppl stem of *repraehendere*, formed as **RE-** + *praehendere* take: see **-AL**[1].]
▸**I 1** *Hist.* The practice of seizing by force property or people belonging to another State in retaliation or as recompense for loss sustained; an instance of this. Chiefly in ***letter of marque and reprisal*** s.v. **MARQUE** *noun*[1]. **LME.**
2 †**a** The taking *of* a thing as a prize. Also, a prize. *rare.* **L16–E17.** ▸**b** Regaining, recapture. Now *rare* or *obsolete.* **M17.**
3 An act of retaliation for injury or attack; *spec.* in war, the inflicting of a similar or more severe injury or punishment on an enemy. **E18.**

> **3** P. H. Gibbs Shooting up . . villages as reprisals for ambushes. W. S. Churchill Burnt in reprisal for the conduct of American militiamen.

▸**II 4** Compensation; an amount paid or received as compensation. Usu. in *pl.* Now *rare.* **M17.**
Phrases: **by way of reprisal, in reprisal** in retaliation, as reparation. ***letter of marque and reprisal***: see ***letter of marque*** (a) s.v. **MARQUE** *noun*[1]. **make reprisal(s)** retaliate so as to seek reparation.

reprise /rɪˈprʌɪz; *chiefly in sense 6* rɪˈpriːz/ *noun.* **LME.**
[Old & mod. French, use as noun of pa. pple fem. of *reprendre*: see next.]
▸**I** †**1** The fact of taking back something for one's own advantage; an amount taken back; loss, expense, cost. Only in **LME.**
2 A charge or payment falling due annually from a manor or estate. Usu. in *pl.* **LME.**
†**3 a** = **REPRISAL** *noun* 4. **M16–M18.** ▸**b** The action of taking something by way of retaliation. **M17–E18.**
4 A renewal or repetition of an action; a separate occasion of doing something. **L17.**

> **4** M. R. James The . . tower fell, not all at once, but in two reprises.

▸**II 5** *ARCHITECTURE.* A return of mouldings etc. in an internal angle. **E16.**
6 a *MUSIC.* The repetition of the first theme of a movement after the close of the development; *esp.* the recapitulation section of a movement in sonata form. Formerly also, a refrain. **E18.** ▸**b** *LINGUISTICS.* The repetition of a word or word group occurring in a preceding phrase. **M20.** ▸**c** A repetition of a theatrical performance; a restaging or rewriting of a play, esp. for television; a rerun, a replay. Also more widely, a further performance of any kind. **M20.**

> **6a** *Theatre Research International* The . . final section was a reprise with . . variations. **c** *Time* A locally televised reprise of his successful . . call-in program.

reprise /rɪˈprʌɪz; *in sense 1c* rɪˈpriːz/ *verb.* **LME.**
[Old & mod. French *repris* pa. pple of *reprendre*, from *re-* **RE-** + *prendre* take.]
†**1** *verb trans.* Reprehend, reprove (a person). *rare.* **LME–L15.**
2 †**a** *verb intrans. & trans.* Begin again, recommence. **LME–E17.** ▸†**b** *verb trans.* Take anew, gain afresh. *rare.* Only in **L16.** ▸**c** Repeat (a dramatic performance, song, etc.); restage, rewrite. Cf. **REPRISE** *noun* 6c. **M20.**
3 *verb trans.* Take back again, esp. by force; recapture, recover. Also, buy back. Now *rare* or *obsolete.* **LME.**
†**4** *verb trans.* Take or hold back out of a sum. **M16–E18.**
5 *verb trans.* Compensate (a person). Now *rare* or *obsolete.* **M17.**

> **2c** *Blitz* Nielsen reprises his TV role as . . Lieutenant Drebin.

repristinate /riːˈprɪstɪneɪt/ *verb trans.* **M17.**
[from **RE-** + **PRISTINE**: see **-ATE**[3].]
Restore to an original condition or position; revive.
■ **repristiˈnation** *noun* **M19.**

reprivatize /riːˈprʌɪvətʌɪz/ *verb trans.* Also **-ise. M20.**
[from **RE-** + **PRIVATIZE.**]
Make (an industry etc.) private again; denationalize.
■ **reprivatiˈzation** *noun* **M20.**

repro /ˈriːprəʊ/ *noun. colloq.* Pl. **-os. M20.**
[Abbreviation of **REPRODUCTION.**]
1 *PRINTING & PHOTOGRAPHY.* = **REPRODUCTION** 1e. Also (more fully ***repro proof***) = ***REPRODUCTION proof.*** **M20.**
2 A reproduction or copy, usu. of a piece of furniture. Usu. *attrib.* or in *comb.* **M20.**

> **2** *Morecambe Guardian* Good antique and repro furniture.

reproach /rɪˈprəʊtʃ/ *noun.* **ME.**
[Old & mod. French *reproche*, from *reprocher*: see next.]
1 (An expression of) blame or censure directed against a person; a rebuke, a reproof. **ME.** ▸†**b** An insult in act or deed. *rare.* **ME–E17.** ▸**c** *ROMAN CATHOLIC CHURCH*, in *pl.* A series of antiphons and responses, in which Christ is represented as reproaching his people, sung on Good Friday. **L19.**
2 A source or cause of disgrace or shame (*to* a person etc.); a fact, thing, or quality bringing disgrace or discredit on a person. **LME.**
3 Shame, disgrace, or blame falling on a person or thing. **L15.**

> **1** P. de Vries His bloodhound eyes sad with reproach. E. S. Person Letters of rejected lovers . . filled . . with reproaches. **3** Ld Macaulay He tried gentler means than those which had brought so much reproach on his predecessor.

Phrases: **above reproach, beyond reproach** perfect, faultless. **term of reproach**: expr. strong censure or condemnation.
■ **reproachless** *adjective* irreproachable **E19. reproachlessness** *noun* **M19.**

reproach /rɪˈprəʊtʃ/ *verb trans.* **ME.**
[Old French *reprochier* (mod. *reprocher*) from Proto-Romance verb meaning 'bring back near', from *re-* **RE-** + Latin *prope* near.]
1 Express disapproval to (a person); upbraid, rebuke. Also foll. by *with* a thing. **ME.** ▸**b** Censure (a thing, act, etc.). *arch.* **M17.**
2 Criticize or find fault with (a person's action etc.). Foll. by *against*, *to* a person. Now *rare.* **L15.**
3 Bring (a thing) into reproach or disrepute; be a reproach to (a person). Now *rare.* **L16.**

> **1** A. MacLean You didn't come . . to reproach me with my tactlessness. A. Brookner She reproaches him for being selfish.

■ **reproachable** *adjective* **M16. reproacher** *noun* a person who reproaches another **M16. reproachingly** *adverb* in a reproaching manner, reproachfully **L18.**

reproachful /rɪˈprəʊtʃfʊl, -f(ə)l/ *adjective.* **M16.**
[from **REPROACH** *noun* + **-FUL.**]
†**1** Shameful, disgraceful; deserving of censure; blameworthy. **M16–L18.**
2 Full of or expressing reproach; reproving, censuring, upbraiding. **M16.**

> **2** E. Longford Audrey wrote me a deeply reproachful letter.

■ **reproachfully** *adverb* **M16. reproachfulness** *noun* **M16.**

reprobacy /ˈrɛprəbəsi/ *noun.* **L16.**
[from **REPROBATE** *adjective*: see **-ACY.**]
The state or condition of being reprobate.
■ Also **reprobance** *noun* (*rare*) **E17.**

reprobate /ˈrɛprəbeɪt/ *noun.* **M16.**
[Late Latin *reprobatus* use as noun of pa. pple of Latin *reprobare*: see **REPROBATE** *verb*, **-ATE**[1]. In sense 1b absol. use of next.]
1 A person rejected by God; a person who has fallen from grace. **M16.** ▸**b** *collect. pl.* *The* people rejected by God and thus denied salvation. **M16.**
2 An unprincipled person; a person of loose or immoral character. **L16.**

> **2** S. O'Casey Gimme me money, y'oul' reprobate!

reprobate /ˈrɛprəbeɪt/ *adjective.* **L15.**
[Late Latin *reprobatus* pa. pple of Latin *reprobare*: see next, **-ATE**[2].]
1 Rejected by God; hardened in sin. **L15.** ▸**b** Lacking religious or moral obligation; abandoned, unprincipled. **M17.**
2 Rejected or condemned as worthless, inferior, or impure. Now *rare.* **M16.**
†**3** Depraved, degraded, morally corrupt. Also foll. by *to.* **M16–M18.**
†**4** Deserving of condemnation or reproof; appropriate to reprobates. **E17–L18.**

> **2** J. Spencer A great deal of reprobate Silver which . . looks like Sterling.

reprobate /ˈrɛprəbeɪt/ *verb trans.* **LME.**
[Latin *reprobat-* pa. ppl stem of *reprobare* disapprove, formed as **RE-** + *probare* approve: see **PROVE** *verb*, **-ATE**[3].]
1 Disapprove of, censure, condemn. **LME.**
2 Of God: reject or condemn (a person); exclude from salvation. **L15.**
3 Reject, refuse, put aside. **E17.** ▸**b** *LAW* (chiefly *Scot.*). Reject (an instrument or deed) as not binding. **E18.**

📖 **1** H. L. WILSON Especially reprobated by the matrons of the correct set. G. GORER Whether pre-marital experience is advocated or reprobated. **2** G. LAVINGTON Look upon themselves as reprobated, and forsaken of God. **3b** ***approbate and reprobate***: see APPROBATE 2.

■ **reprobater** *noun* (*rare*) E19. **reprobative** *adjective* conveying or expressing disapproval or reprobation M19. **reprobatory** *adjective* reprobative E19.

reprobation /rɛprəˈbeɪʃ(ə)n/ *noun*. LME.
[Old & mod. French *réprobation* or late Latin *reprobatio(n-)*, formed as prec.: see -ATION.]
†**1** Reproof, shame. *rare*. Only in LME.
2 Rejection of a person or thing; condemnation as worthless or spurious. Also, disapproval, censure, reproof. LME.
3 *THEOLOGY*. Rejection by God; the state of being so rejected and thus condemned to eternal misery. L15.
4 The action of raising objections (*against* a person or thing); a legal objection or exception. *rare*. L15.

📖 **2** H. JAMES He had never felt . . so chilling a blast of reprobation as this cold disgust.

reprobator /ˈrɛprəbeɪtə/ *noun*. M17.
[formed as REPROBATE *verb*, after *declarator* etc.: see -ORY².]
SCOTS LAW (now *Hist.*). An action to invalidate evidence by proving a witness liable to objections or to a charge of perjury. Also more fully ***action of reprobator***.

reproduce /riːprəˈdjuːs/ *verb*. E17.
[from RE- + PRODUCE *verb*, after French *reproduire*.]
1 a *verb trans*. Bring again into existence; create or form anew; *spec.* in *BIOLOGY*, regenerate (a lost limb or organ); generate (new individuals). E17. ▸**b** *verb intrans. & refl.* Produce further individuals like oneself or itself by sexual or asexual means. L19.
2 *verb trans*. Produce again by means of combination or change. M17.
3 a *verb trans*. Cause to be seen, heard, or otherwise effected again; present anew; repeat in some way. L17. ▸**b** *verb trans*. Repeat in a more or less exact copy; produce a copy or representation of (a work of art, picture, drawing, etc.). M19. ▸**c** *verb intrans*. Give a specified quality or result when copied. L19.
4 *verb trans*. Present again in writing or print. M19.
5 *verb trans*. Create again by mental effort; represent clearly to the mind. M19.

📖 **1a** D. MORRIS The primary function of sexual behaviour is to reproduce the species. **b** *Daily Telegraph* The use of sterile mutant strains which cannot reproduce is expected to be recommended for . . research. **3a** C. MUNGOSHI Sunlight . . is reproduced . . on the floor. *Gramophone* Enclosed headphones . . can . . reproduce extreme bass frequencies. *Paragraph* Diagrams . . reproduced from the original manuscript. **4** J. TYNDALL A letter . . so interesting I do not hesitate to reproduce it here.

■ **reproduceable** *adjective* (*rare*) = REPRODUCIBLE M19. **reproducer** *noun* a person who or thing which reproduces; *spec.* the pick-up of a gramophone; the replay head of a tape recorder: L18. ˌ**reproduciˈbility** *noun* the capacity to be produced again; the quality of being reproducible; *spec.* the extent to which consistent results are obtained when produced repeatedly (cf. REPEATABILITY): E20. **reproducible** *adjective* able to be reproduced M19. **reproducibly** *adverb* M20.

reproduction /riːprəˈdʌkʃ(ə)n/ *noun*. M17.
[from prec. after PRODUCTION.]
1 The action or process of forming, creating or bringing into existence again. M17. ▸**b** *MEDICINE & BIOLOGY*. = REGENERATION 3. E18. ▸**c** The production of new organisms by or from existing ones; the power of reproducing in this way. L18. ▸**d** The action or process of bringing an idea etc. to mind again in the same form. E19. ▸**e** Chiefly *PRINTING & PHOTOGRAPHY*. The action or process of copying a document or image. M19. ▸**f** *ECONOMICS*. In Marxist theory, the process by which given capital is maintained for further production by the conversion of part of its product into capital. L19. ▸**g** The process of reproducing sound; the degree of fidelity with which this is done. E20.
2 a A copy, esp. of a work of art; a print or photograph of a painting. Also, (usu. *attrib.*) a piece of furniture etc. made in imitation of a particular style or period. E19. ▸**b** A representation in some form or by some means of the essential features of a thing. M19.

📖 **1c** ***net reproduction rate***: see NET *adjective*² & *adverb*. ***vegetative reproduction***: see VEGETATIVE *adjective*. ***virgin reproduction***: see VIRGIN *noun & adjective*. **e** W. A. COPINGER Copyright may be infringed . . by reproduction. **f** **enlarged reproduction**, **expanded reproduction**, etc., reproduction in which the amount of capital is increased by conversion of part of the surplus value into additional means of production. **simple reproduction** reproduction in which the amount of capital remains constant, any surplus value being consumed. **g** *Times* Research . . on ways of improving reproduction from discs. **2a** J. BRAINE The Medici reproduction of Olympe. B. CHATWIN Furnished with reproduction Louis Seize furniture.

Comb.: **reproduction constant**, **reproduction factor** *NUCLEAR PHYSICS* = ***multiplication constant*** s.v. MULTIPLICATION; **reproduction proof** *PRINTING & PHOTOGRAPHY* a printed proof usable as an original for further reproduction.

reproductive /riːprəˈdʌktɪv/ *adjective & noun*. M18.
[formed as prec., after PRODUCTIVE.]
▶ **A** *adjective*. Of, pertaining to, or effecting reproduction. M18.
▶ **B** *noun*. *ENTOMOLOGY*. A sexually fertile individual in a colony of social insects. M20.
■ **reproductively** *adverb* L19. **reproductiveness** *noun* M19. ˌ**reproducˈtivity** *noun* E19.

reproductory /riːprəˈdʌkt(ə)ri/ *adjective*. M19.
[from REPRODUCT(IVE *adjective* + -ORY².]
= REPRODUCTIVE *adjective*.

reprogram /riːˈprəʊgram/ *verb trans*. Also **-gramme**. Infl. **-mm-**, *-**m-**. M20.
[from RE- + PROGRAMME *verb*.]
Program (esp. a computer) again or differently.
■ **reˈprogrammable** *adjective* L20.

reprography /rɪˈprɒgrəfi/ *noun*. M20.
[German *Reprographie*, from *Repro(duktion* reproduction + *Photo)graphie* photography.]
The science and practice of copying and reproducing documents or graphic material by photography, xerography, etc.
■ **reprographer** *noun* a person who makes copies of documents M20. **reproˈgraphic** *adjective* of or pertaining to reprography M20. **reproˈgraphics** *noun* reprography M20.

reproof /rɪˈpruːf/ *noun*. Also †**repref**, †**repreve**. ME.
[Old French *reprove*, from *reprover* REPROVE.]
†**1** Personal shame, disgrace, or ignominy resulting from some fact, event, conduct, etc. ME–M17.
†**2** Insulting or opprobrious language or action used against a person; insult, scorn. Also, an instance of this; an insult. ME–L16.
3 Censure, rebuke, reprehension; an instance of this, a rebuke. ME.
4 Disproof, refutation. Now *rare* or *obsolete*. E16.

📖 **3** A. C. CLARKE He pretended to blame Franklin, who accepted the reproof.

reproof /riːˈpruːf/ *verb trans*. E20.
[from RE- + PROOF *verb*.]
1 Make (a coat etc.) waterproof again. E20.
2 Make a fresh proof of (printed matter etc.). L20.

reprove /rɪˈpruːv/ *verb*. Also †**repreve**, †**reprieve**. ME.
[Old French *reprover* (mod. *réprouver*) from Latin *reprobare*: see REPROBATE *verb*.]
†**1** *verb trans*. Reject. ME–E17.
2 *verb trans*. Express disapproval of (conduct, an action, a belief, etc.); censure, condemn. Now *rare*. ME.
3 *verb trans*. Reprehend, blame, chide (a person). ME.
4 *verb intrans*. Express disapproval, make rebukes. ME.
†**5** *verb trans*. Prove to be false or erroneous; disprove. LME–L17.

📖 **3** M. GARDINER 'Really, Maya,' René reproved her, 'you ought to be more careful.'

■ **reprovable** *adjective* deserving of reproof or censure; blameworthy, reprehensible: ME. **reproval** *noun* reproof M19. **reprover** *noun* LME. **reprovingly** *adverb* in a reproving manner LME.

re-prove /riːˈpruːv/ *verb trans*. E16.
[from RE- + PROVE *verb*.]
Prove again.

†**repry** *verb* see REPRIEVE *verb*¹.

reptant /ˈrɛpt(ə)nt/ *adjective*. Now *rare*. M17.
[Latin *reptant-* pres. ppl stem of *reptare* creep: see -ANT¹.]
BOTANY & ZOOLOGY. Creeping, crawling.

reptation /rɛpˈteɪʃ(ə)n/ *noun*. Now *rare*. M19.
[Latin *reptatio(n-)*, from *rept-*: see REPTILE *adjective*, -ATION.]
BOTANY & ZOOLOGY. The action of creeping or crawling.

reptile /ˈrɛptʌɪl/ *noun*¹. LME.
[Old & mod. French, or late Latin (Vulgate), neut. of *reptilis*: see REPTILE *adjective*.]
1 A creeping or crawling animal; *spec.* an amniote animal of the vertebrate class Reptilia, characterized (in living forms) by scaly impermeable skin, poikilothermy, and oviparous (or ovoviviparous) reproduction, and including snakes, lizards, turtles, crocodiles, etc. LME.
2 A person of a mean, grovelling, or contemptible character. M18.
Comb.: **reptile house** a building at a zoo etc. in which reptiles are kept.
■ **repˈtiliary** *noun* a building or enclosure in which reptiles are kept E20. **reptiˈliferous** *adjective* (of rock) containing fossil reptiles M19. **repˈtiliform** *adjective & noun* (*a*) *adjective* having the form of a reptile; (*b*) *noun* (*rare*) an animal of this kind: M19. **repˈtilious** *adjective* (*rare*) resembling a reptile L19. **reptiˈlivorous** *adjective* feeding on reptiles M19.

reptile /ˈrɛptʌɪl/ *noun*². M20.
[from *rep(licating) tile* with a pun on prec.]
MATH. A two-dimensional figure of which two or more can be grouped together to form a larger figure having the same shape.

reptile /ˈrɛptʌɪl/ *adjective*. E17.
[Late Latin *reptilis*, from Latin *rept-* pa. ppl stem of *repere* creep, crawl: see -ILE.]
†**1** Of an animal: creeping, crawling. E17–L18.
2 Mean, grovelling, contemptible. M17.
3 Of the nature of, characterized by, or pertaining to the action of creeping or crawling. Now *rare* or *obsolete*. E18.

Reptilia /rɛpˈtɪlɪə/ *noun pl.* Also **r-**. E17.
[Latin, pl. of *reptile* REPTILE *noun*¹: see -IA².]
ZOOLOGY. Orig., those animals which creep or crawl. Now, a class of vertebrate animals comprising the reptiles.

reptilian /rɛpˈtɪlɪən/ *adjective & noun*. M19.
[from prec. + -IAN.]
▶ **A** *adjective*. **1** Resembling a reptile; of, pertaining to, or characteristic of the class Reptilia or a reptile. M19.
2 Mean, malignant, contemptible, underhand. M19.

📖 **1** I. MCEWAN Tourists . . moved along . . in reptilian slow motion. **2** G. GREENE The American racketeer, quick and cold and reptilian.

▶ **B** *noun*. = REPTILE *noun*¹ 1. *rare*. M19.

republic /rɪˈpʌblɪk/ *noun & adjective*. L16.
[French *république* from Latin *respublica*, from *res* affair, thing + fem. of *publicus* PUBLIC *adjective*.]
▶ **A** *noun*. †**1** The State, the general good. L16–L17.
2 (Also **R-**.) Any State in which supreme power is held by the people or their elected representatives as opp. to by a monarch etc.; a commonwealth. Also, a period during which a State has such a constitution. L16.
3 *transf.* Any community of people, animals, etc., with equality between its members. L17.

📖 **2** *Pall Mall Gazette* The distracted and faction ridden Republic of France. *New Yorker* During the first few years of the Republic. *BANANA* ***republic***. **3** ***republic of letters***: see LETTER *noun*¹.

▶ **B** *attrib.* or as *adjective*. Of the nature of or pertaining to a republic or republics; republican. Now *rare* or *obsolete*. M17.

republican /rɪˈpʌblɪk(ə)n/ *adjective & noun*. L17.
[from prec. + -AN, partly after French *républicain*.]
▶ **A** *adjective*. †**1** Belonging to the commonwealth or community. *rare*. Only in L17.
2 a Of, belonging to, or characteristic of a republic; having the form or constitution of a republic. E18. ▸**b** Of a person or party: advocating or upholding the form of State or government called a republic. L18.
3 (**R-**.) Of or pertaining to a political party styled 'Republican', *spec.* the US Republican Party (see below). E19.
4 Nesting in large colonies. Only in names of birds. E19.

3 Republican Party one of the two main US political parties (the other being ***Democratic***) which generally favours only a moderate degree of central power. **4 republican swallow** = *CLIFF* ***swallow***. **republican weaver** = ***sociable weaver*** s.v. SOCIABLE *adjective*.

▶ **B** *noun*. †**1** A person attached to the interests of the commonwealth or community. *rare*. Only in L17.
2 An advocate or supporter of a republican form of government. L17.
3 (**R-**.) A member of the Republican Party of the US, or more widely, of any political party styled 'Republican'. L18.
■ **republicanism** *noun* republican spirit; adherence to republican principles; republican government, institutions, etc.: L17. **republicanly** *adverb* (*rare*) in a republican manner M17.

republicanize /rɪˈpʌblɪk(ə)nʌɪz/ *verb*. Also **-ise**. L18.
[French *républicaniser*, formed as prec.: see -IZE.]
1 *verb trans*. Make republican in principles or character, convert into a republican form; *transf.* alter or recast on republican principles. L18.
2 *verb intrans*. Show republican tendencies. *rare*. M19.
■ **republicaniˈzation** *noun* L18.

republication /ˌriːpʌblɪˈkeɪʃ(ə)n/ *noun*. M18.
[from RE- + PUBLICATION.]
1 A fresh promulgation of a religion or law. M18.
2 A fresh publication of a will. M18.
3 The action of republishing a work; the fact of being republished; a fresh publication of a literary work. M18.

Republicrat /rɪˈpʌblɪkrat/ *noun*. M20.
[Blend of REPUBLICAN *noun* and DEMOCRAT *noun*.]
A member of a US political faction that includes both Republicans and Democrats. Also, a conservative Democrat with Republican sympathies.

republish /riːˈpʌblɪʃ/ *verb trans*. L16.
[from RE- + PUBLISH.]
Publish again or in a new edition etc.
■ **republisher** *noun* a person who republishes a work or works M18.

For other words beginning with *re-* see the entry for **re-**

repudiate /rɪˈpjuːdɪeɪt/ *verb trans.* Pa. pple & ppl adjective **-ated**, (orig.) †**-ate**. LME.
[Orig. pa. pple, from Latin *repudiatus* pa. pple of *repudiare*, from *repudium* divorce: see -ATE², -ATE³.]
1 a Orig. *spec.*, (of a husband) divorce, disown (one's wife). Later also *gen.*, abandon, disown (a person). LME. ▸**b** Discard, abandon (a thing). L17.
2 Refuse to accept (a thing) or deal with (a person); reject. M16. ▸**b** Condemn (an opinion, action, etc.), reject with abhorrence. E19. ▸**c** Deny (a charge etc.), reject as unfounded or inapplicable. M19.
3 Reject as unauthorized, refuse to recognize or obey. M17. ▸**b** Refuse to discharge or acknowledge (a debt etc.). M19.

1a P. H. GIBBS President Wilson had been repudiated by his own people. **b** J. MCPHEE He came north to repudiate one kind of life and to try another. **3** H. MACMILLAN Iraq . . repudiated her military agreements with Britain.

■ **repudiable** *adjective* that may be repudiated E17. **repudiant** *adjective* (rare) = REPUDIATIVE M20. **repudiative** *adjective* characterized by repudiation or rejection M19. **repudiator** *noun* a person who repudiates someone or something M19. **repudiatory** *adjective* of, pertaining to, or favouring repudiation (of a debt etc.) L19.

repudiation /rɪˌpjuːdɪˈeɪʃ(ə)n/ *noun.* M16.
[Latin *repudiatio(n-)*, formed as prec.: see -ATION.]
1 Divorce (of a wife). M16.
2 The action of repudiating someone or something; the fact of being repudiated; rejection, disownment, disavowal. M19. ▸**b** LAW. Refusal or failure to meet with the terms of a contract; a denial or serious breach of contract. E20.
■ **repudiationist** *noun & adjective* (a person) advocating repudiation, *spec.* (US) repudiation of a public debt M19.

repugn /rɪˈpjuːn/ *verb.* LME.
[Latin *repugnare*, formed as RE- + *pugnare* fight.]
1 *verb intrans.* Be contradictory or inconsistent; be contrary or opposed to a thing. Formerly also foll. by *to*. Now *rare* or *obsolete*. LME.
2 *verb intrans.* Offer opposition; resist, object. Formerly also foll. by *at*, *to*. Now *rare*. LME. ▸**b** Fight or contend *against*. Now *rare*. LME.
3 *verb trans.* †**a** Fight against, resist, repel (a person). LME–M17. ▸**b** Oppose, resist, contend against (a thing); reject, refute. LME.
†**4** *verb trans.* Be contrary or opposed to (a thing). LME–L17.
5 *verb trans. & intrans.* Affect (a person) with repugnance or aversion. M19.

3b R. C. HUTCHINSON Foolish masculine notions about repugning weakness. **5** *Harper's Magazine* Afraid of saying nothing: no term repugned her.

■ **repugner** *noun* (rare) a person who repugns LME.

repugnance /rɪˈpʌɡnəns/ *noun.* LME.
[Old & mod. French *répugnance* or Latin *repugnantia*, from *repugnant-*: see next, -ANCE.]
1 Contradiction, inconsistency; opposition or disagreement of ideas, statements, etc. LME.
†**2** Resistance or opposition offered to a thing or person. LME–M16.
3 A strong dislike of something; antipathy, aversion. M17.
■ Also **repugnancy** *noun* LME.

repugnant /rɪˈpʌɡnənt/ *adjective & noun.* LME.
[French *répugnant* or Latin *repugnant-* pres. ppl stem of *repugnare*: see REPUGN, -ANT¹.]
▶**A** *adjective.* **1** Contrary or contradictory (*to*), inconsistent or incompatible (*with*). LME.
2 Offering resistance (*to*); opposing, hostile, antagonistic. LME.
3 Distasteful or objectionable *to* a person; offensive, repulsive. L18.

1 W. CRUISE The clause was void, because it was repugnant to the . . act. **2** BYRON The drill'd dull lesson, forced down . . In my repugnant youth. **3** S. ROSENBERG A marriage of convenience was repugnant to her.

▶†**B** *noun.* **1** LOGIC. A term or proposition forming the contrary or contradictory of another. L15–L17.
2 A recusant, a resister. *rare*. Only in E17.
■ **repugnantly** *adverb* in a repugnant manner M16.

repugnatorial /rɪˌpʌɡnəˈtɔːrɪəl/ *adjective.* L19.
[Latin *repugnatorius*: see -AL¹.]
ZOOLOGY. Serving for defence; *spec.* designating glands in some insects and millipedes from which a repellent fluid can be emitted.

repullulate /rɪˈpʌljʊleɪt/ *verb intrans. rare.* E17.
[Latin *repullulat-* pa. ppl stem of *repullulare* sprout again: see RE-, PULLULATE.]
Bud or sprout again.
■ **repulluˈlation** *noun* E17.

repulse /rɪˈpʌls/ *noun.* LME.
[Latin *repulsus*, *repulsa*, from *repuls-*: see next.]
1 Refusal of a request etc., rejection; a rebuff. LME.
2 The action of repelling or forcing back an assailant etc.; the fact of being driven back. M16.

repulse /rɪˈpʌls/ *verb trans.* LME.
[Latin *repuls-* pa. ppl stem of *repellere* REPEL.]
1 Force back, drive away (an assailant etc.); repel by force of arms. LME.
2 Reject, refuse, rebuff. LME.
3 Affect (a person) with repulsion; disgust, appal. M19.

1 D. MAY The Russians were repulsed, with terrible losses, at the Battle of Tannenburg. **2** E. TEMPLETON Men tried to make her acquaintance and . . she repulsed their advances. **3** P. CAREY He was repulsed by the . . signs of cunning he saw.

■ **repulser** *noun* (rare) E17.

repulsion /rɪˈpʌlʃ(ə)n/ *noun.* LME.
[Late Latin *repulsio(n-)*, formed as prec.: see -ION.]
†**1** Repudiation, divorce. *rare*. Only in LME.
2 a The action of forcing back or driving away. LME. ▸**b** MEDICINE. The action of repressing an infection, eruption, etc. Now *rare* or *obsolete*. E18.
3 The action of one body in repelling another by some physical force such as magnetism; the tendency for this to occur. Opp. ***attraction***. E18. ▸**b** *transf.* Tendency to separate, introduce division or difference, etc. M19. ▸**c** GENETICS. The condition of two genes when the dominant allele of one occurs on the same chromosome as the recessive allele of the other. Cf. LINKAGE 2. E20.
4 Dislike, aversion, disgust. M18.
3 ***capillary repulsion***: see CAPILLARY *adjective* 3.
Comb.: **repulsion motor** ELECTRICITY an a.c. commutator motor for single-phase operation in which current is supplied to the stator only, the armature being short-circuited through the brushes and its current induced from the stator winding.

repulsive /rɪˈpʌlsɪv/ *adjective & noun.* LME.
[Old & mod. French *répulsif*, *-ive* or from REPULSE *verb* + -IVE.]
▶**A** *adjective.* **1** Having the property of physically repelling or resisting a person or thing; forcing back, driving away, etc. (Foll. by *of*, *to*.) LME.
2 Tending to repel a person by denial, coldness of manner, etc.; disconcerting. L16.
3 PHYSICS. Of the nature of, characterized by, or causing repulsion. Opp. ***attractive***. E18.
4 Repellent to the mind; disgusting, loathsome. E19.

2 V. WOOLF That sense of moral virtue . . so repulsive in good women. **4** DYLAN THOMAS Suddenly cornered by three repulsive looking . . men. *Observer* Producers won't make repulsive films if the public don't go to see them.

▶†**B** *noun.* A medicine or application that represses an infection, eruption, etc. LME–L17.
■ **repulsively** *adverb* M18. **repulsiveness** *noun* the state or quality of being repulsive E19.

repunit /ˈrɛpjuːnɪt/ *noun.* M20.
[from *rep*eated *unit*.]
MATH. A number consisting of a sequence of 1s or the single digit 1.

repurchase /riːˈpəːtʃɪs/ *verb & noun.* L16.
[from RE- + PURCHASE *noun*, *verb*.]
▶**A** *verb trans.* Purchase again, buy back. L16.
▶**B** *noun.* The action of buying back; an instance of this. E17.
Comb.: **repurchase agreement** a contract in which the vendor of (esp. government) securities agrees to repurchase them from the buyer.
■ **repurchaser** *noun* (rare) L16.

†**repure** *verb trans. rare.* E–M17.
[from RE- + PURE *verb*.]
Purify again.

SHAKES. *Tr. & Cr.* When that the wat'ry palate tastes indeed Love's thrice-repured nectar.

reputable /ˈrɛpjʊtəb(ə)l/ *adjective.* E17.
[French †*reputable* or medieval Latin *reputabilis*, formed as REPUTE *verb*: see -ABLE.]
†**1** That may be regarded or taken into account. *rare*. Only in E17.
2 Having a good reputation; of good repute, honoured, respectable. L17.

2 R. GITTINGS A reputable firm of family doctors. D. JACOBSON Paintings by reputable modern artists.

■ **reputaˈbility** *noun* M19. **reputably** *adverb* M18.

reputation /rɛpjʊˈteɪʃ(ə)n/ *noun.* ME.
[Latin *reputatio(n-)* computation, consideration, from *reputat-* pa. ppl stem of *reputare*: see REPUTE *verb*, -ATION.]
1 The condition or fact of being highly regarded or esteemed; distinction, respect, fame. Later also, a person of note or distinction. ME.
2 The general opinion or estimate of a person's character, behaviour, etc.; the relative esteem in which a person or thing is held. LME.
3 The honour, credit, or good name of a person or thing. M16.
4 The fame, credit, or notoriety of being, doing, or possessing something. M16.

1 R. HUSSEY A writer of reputation at that time. R. G. COLLINGWOOD Rugby . . had a high reputation owing . . to . . one first-rate teacher. **2** F. KAPLAN Dickens . . knew him by reputation as a dazzling speaker. **3** ANNE STEVENSON *Lupercal*, published in March . . , confirmed his growing reputation. G. DALY Modeling in the nude . . would ruin a girl's reputation. ***grave of reputations***: see GRAVE *noun*¹ 4. **4** J. GALSWORTHY She had quite a reputation for saying the wrong thing. B. BAINBRIDGE He bore the reputation of being a . . great classical scholar.

■ **reputational** *adjective* of or pertaining to reputation E20.

reputative /rɪˈpjuːtətɪv/ *adjective.* M17.
[medieval Latin *reputativus*, formed as prec.: see -ATIVE.]
Considered or regarded as such; putative, reputed.
■ **reputatively** *adverb* by repute or reckoning, reputedly; putatively: E17.

repute /rɪˈpjuːt/ *noun.* M16.
[from the verb.]
†**1** Opinion, estimate. *rare*. M16–E18.
2 Reputation of a specified kind. M16.
†**3** Relative estimation; rank, position. E17–E18.
4 Distinction, honour, credit. E17.
5 The reputation of a person. M17.

2 P. DALLY He was held in high repute on all sides. ***ill repute***: see ILL *adjective & adverb*. **5** H. BELLOC His repute had gone through all the north of Gaul.

■ †**reputeless** *adjective* (rare, Shakes.) devoid of repute; inglorious: only in L16.

repute /rɪˈpjuːt/ *verb.* LME.
[Old & mod. French *réputer* or Latin *reputare*, formed as RE- + *putare* reckon.]
1 *verb trans.* Consider, regard, reckon as being something. Usu. in *pass.* (Foll. by †*as*, †*for*, *to be*.) LME.
†**2** *verb trans.* Attribute to a person; assign. LME–M17.
†**3** *verb trans.* Hold (a person) in esteem; think well of, value. LME–M17.
†**4** *verb intrans.* Think (highly etc.) *of* a thing or person. L16–L17.

1 S. BEDFORD Three elder brothers, all reputed brilliant. M. MEYER Donat was reputed in the profession to be neurotic. **4** SHAKES. *2 Hen. VI* By reputing of his high descent . . As next the King he was successive heir.

reputed /rɪˈpjuːtɪd/ *ppl adjective.* M16.
[from prec. + -ED¹.]
1 Held in repute, respected. M16.
2 Supposed, reckoned, alleged. L16.

1 *Daily Telegraph* An internationally reputed geologist. *India Today* A reputed physician . . who wields high popularity. **2** SHAKES. *John* The reputed son of Coeur-de-Lion. **reputed quart** a measure of liquid, esp. of wine, beer, etc., containing a sixth of a gallon.

■ **reputedly** *adverb* by repute or common estimation; supposedly, allegedly: L17.

request /rɪˈkwɛst/ *noun.* ME.
[Old French *requeste* (mod. *requête*) from Proto-Romance use as noun of Latin *requisita* fem. of pa. pple of *requirere* REQUIRE *verb*.]
1 The action or an instance of asking or calling for something; the fact of being asked for something; a petition, *esp.* a written one; an expressed wish or desire. Also, a thing asked for. ME. ▸**b** *spec.* A nomination of a particular record etc. to be played on a radio programme or of a song etc. to be performed, often accompanied by a personal message; a record, song, etc., played or performed in response to a request. E20.
†**2** MATH. A postulate. *rare*. M16–E18.
3 The fact or condition of being sought after; demand. Formerly also, vogue, fashion. M16.

1 V. BRITTAIN I was bombarded . . with . . requests to help with jumble sales. E. CRISPIN A request for a glass of . . fruit juice. **b** *Zigzag* Playing requests in a bar. *attrib.*: *Radio Times* A request programme of records. **3** W. T. WATTS-DUNTON She was in request as a face model.

Phrases: **at a person's request**, **by request**, **on request** in response to a person's expressed wish. **Court of Request(s)** *Hist.* orig., a court held by the Lord Privy Seal chiefly to deal with petitions put forward by poor people; later, a local court for the recovery of small debts. **make request** *arch.* ask, beg. **Master of Request(s)**, **Master of the Request(s)** *Hist.* a leading officer of the Court of Requests. ***no flowers by request***: see FLOWER *noun* 2. ***on request*** see ***at a person's request*** above. **request for proposal** *N. Amer.* a detailed specification of goods or services required by an organization, sent to potential contractors or suppliers.
Comb.: **requestman** NAUTICAL a seaman making a written request to an officer; in *pl.* (treated as *sing.*), the occasion appointed for the presentation of such requests; **request programme** a radio etc. programme composed of items requested by the audience; **request stop** a stop at which a bus etc. halts only on request from a passenger or intending passenger.

request /rɪˈkwɛst/ *verb trans.* LME.
[from the noun, or from Old French *requester*.]
Ask to be favoured with or given (a thing), ask for; express a wish or desire *that*, *to do*; ask to be allowed *to do*; ask (a person) *to do* something.

W. GOLDING The captain requests . . your company at dinner. N. F. DIXON Drivers were requested to stop. A. BROOKNER Requesting Martine's permission and receiving it.

■ **requester** *noun* M16.

requeté /reke'te/ *noun.* M20.
[Spanish, perh. abbreviation of *requetefiel*, from *requete-* intensive prefix + *fiel* loyal.]
Hist. A member of a Carlist militia that took the Nationalist side during the Spanish Civil War of 1936–9.

requiem /'rɛkwɪəm, -ɪɛm/ *noun*[1]. ME.
[Latin, accus. of *requies* rest, first word of the introit in the mass for the dead, *Requiem aeternam dona eis, Domine* Give them eternal rest, O Lord.]
1 (Freq. **R-**.) ROMAN CATHOLIC CHURCH. A special mass said or sung for the repose of the soul of a dead person. Also ***mass of requiem***, ***requiem mass***. ME. ▸**b** A musical setting of a mass for the dead. L18.
2 Any dirge, solemn chant, etc., for the repose of the dead; *fig.* a memorial, a commemoration. E17.
3 Rest, peace, quiet; a period of this. Now *rare.* E17.

2 R. BURNS Ev'ry bird thy requiem sings. *Nature* His last book provides a fitting requiem.

requiem /'rɛkwɪəm, -ɪɛm/ *noun*[2]. M17.
[French, obsolete var. of *requin* shark, infl. by prec.]
More fully ***requiem shark***. A member of the large family Carcharhinidae which includes many of the larger voracious sharks, as the bull shark, the tiger shark, the blue shark, etc.

requiescat /rɛkwɪ'ɛskat/ *noun.* E19.
[Latin, from *requiescat in pace* may he or she rest in peace.]
A wish for the repose of a dead person.

requiescence /rɛkwɪ'ɛs(ə)ns/ *noun.* M17.
[from Latin *requiescere* to rest, from *requies* rest, after QUIESCENCE: see RE-, -ENCE.]
A state of rest or repose; peace, quiet.

requinto /re'kinto/ *noun.* Pl. ***-os*** /-ɔs/. Also ***-te*** /-te/. M20.
[Spanish, lit. 'second fifth subtracted from a quantity'.]
In Spain and Spanish-speaking countries, a small guitar tuned a fifth higher than a standard guitar.

†**requirant** *noun.* LME–E19.
[from REQUIRE *verb* + -ANT[1]. Cf. Old & mod. French *requérant*.]
A person making a request or demand; *spec.* a suitor, a wooer.

†**require** *noun. rare.* E16–M19.
[from the verb.]
(A) demand; the action of requiring.

require /rɪ'kwʌɪə/ *verb.* LME.
[Old French *requer-*, *requier-* stem of *requere* (mod. *requérir*) from Proto-Romance from Latin *requirere*, formed as RE- + *quaerere* seek, ask.]
†**1** *verb trans.* Ask (a person) a question, inquire of (someone) *if*, *why*, etc.; request something from or *of* (a person). Also foll. by *that*, *to do*. LME–E17. ▸**b** Seek, search for; inquire after. Also, invite or summon to something. LME–L18.
2 *verb trans.* Demand (a thing) authoritatively or as a right, insist on having (freq. foll. by *from*, *of*); order or instruct (a person etc.) *to do* something. LME. ▸**b** Ask or wish for (a thing) as a favour; desire or request *to do*. Now *rare.* LME.
3 *verb intrans.* Make a request or demand. LME.
4 *verb trans.* Demand (a thing, *that*) or call on (a person *to do*), in order to comply with a law, regulation, custom, etc. Also foll. by *from*, *of*. LME.
5 *verb trans.* Need (a thing or person) for a particular purpose; depend on for success or fulfilment. Now also, need *to be done*, *to do*. LME. ▸**b** Be necessary *to do* something. Now *rare.* L15.
6 *verb trans.* Feel a wish *to do* something; wish to have (a thing). E19.

2 I. MURDOCH A nominal faith . . was required . . in any candidate. M. AMIS The . . factory . . requires him to be at its premises. **4** G. VIDAL Protocol required his presence. M. COX Doing what was required of him officially. *Times* Coaches will be required to be fitted with limiters. **5** W. IRVING It does not require a palace to be happy. J. N. LOCKYER More than 1,200,000 Earths would be required to make one Sun. W. W. JACOBS His . . services would no longer be required. A. S. NEILL A child requires to know how to . . write correctly. A. CROSS Work . . requiring youthful energy. **6** *Melody Maker* Band requires record company.

■ **requirable** *adjective* (now *rare*) LME. **requirer** *noun* (now *rare*) L15.

required /rɪ'kwʌɪəd/ *adjective.* E17.
[from prec. + -ED[1].]
That is required, requisite, necessary.
required reading literature etc. which must be read for an educational course or in order to gain an understanding of a subject.
¶ Earlier (LME) in UNREQUIRED.
■ **requiredness** *noun* M20.

requirement /rɪ'kwʌɪəm(ə)nt/ *noun.* M16.
[formed as prec. + -MENT.]
†**1** The action of requiring something; a request. Only in M16.
2 A thing required or needed, a want, a need (freq. in *pl.*). Also, the action or an instance of needing or wanting something. M17.
3 Something called for or demanded; a condition which must be complied with. Freq. in *pl.* M19.

2 G. BOURNE Our food requirements reduced to one small pill. **3** W. C. WILLIAMS To satisfy the college entrance requirements. E. FEINSTEIN *She* needed to excel . . ; Anastasia was given love without any such requirement.

requisite /'rɛkwɪzɪt/ *adjective & noun.* LME.
[Latin *requisit-* pa. ppl stem of *requirere* search for, (pass.) be necessary: see REQUIRE *verb*, -ITE[2].]
▶**A** *adjective.* Required by circumstances; appropriate; necessary for a purpose, indispensable. LME.

W. S. JEVONS Capital is as requisite to production as land. A. SETON The requisite doleful pang at parting. **requisite variety** the variety necessary in a system for it to be able to control another system in which there is variety.

▶**B** *noun.* A required or necessary thing; a thing needed for a purpose. Freq. in *pl.* L15.

A. BEVAN Requisites for heavy industry; coal, iron ore. I. MURDOCH He could lend . . a razor. He handed over this requisite.

■ **requisitely** *adverb* M17. **requisiteness** *noun* E17.

requisition /rɛkwɪ'zɪʃ(ə)n/ *noun & verb.* LME.
[Old & mod. French *réquisition* or Latin *requisitio(n-)*, formed as prec.: see -ION.]
▶**A** *noun.* **1** The action of requiring something; a demand. LME. ▸**b** A requirement, a necessary condition. M19.
2 The action or an act of formally requiring or demanding that a duty etc. be performed; a written demand of this nature. L15. ▸**b** SCOTS LAW. The demand of a creditor for a debt to be paid or an obligation fulfilled. L17.
3 The action or an act of requiring a certain amount or number of something to be supplied; *esp.* an official demand or order made on a town, district, etc., to supply or lend something required for military purposes; a thing taken by this means. L18.
4 The state or condition of being called or pressed into service or use. L18.

3 *attrib.*: P. GORE-BOOTH Requisition notices on the doors. **4** SOUTHEY Horses . . in requisition for the French armies.

▶**B** *verb trans.* **1** Require (a thing or person) to be supplied or lent for military purposes; demand the use of; acquire by requisition. M19. ▸**b** Make demands for supplies etc. on (a place). L19.
2 *gen.* Take over the use of; press (a thing) into service; request to have (a thing). L19.

1 C. RYAN The Germans . . requisitioned the hotel. **2** CONAN DOYLE I had requisitioned the carriage for the day.

■ **requisitionally** *adverb* (*rare*) by means of military requisition L18. **requisitioner** *noun* = REQUISITIONIST M20. **requisitionist** *noun* a person making a requisition E19.

requisitor /rɪ'kwɪzɪtə/ *noun. rare.* L18.
[formed as REQUISITE + -OR.]
= REQUISITIONIST.

requisitory /rɪ'kwɪzɪt(ə)ri/ *noun. rare.* E19.
[French *réquisitoire* (cf. next): see -ORY[1].]
In French law, a formal charge made against an accused person by a public prosecutor.

requisitory /rɪ'kwɪzɪt(ə)ri/ *adjective. rare.* LME.
[medieval Latin *requisitorius* or Old French *réquisitoire*, formed as REQUISITE: see -ORY[2].]
1 Of the nature of, expressing, or conveying a request or requisition. LME.
2 Capable of making a requisition. E19.

requit /rɪ'kwɪt/ *verb & noun.* M16.
[from RE- + QUIT *verb*, or from REQUITE.]
▶†**A** *verb trans.* Infl. **-tt-**. Repay, requite. M16–E17.
▶**B** *noun.* Requital. *Scot.* L18.

requital /rɪ'kwʌɪt(ə)l/ *noun.* L16.
[from next + -AL[1].]
1 Return or recompense for a service, effort, etc.; a reward, a repayment. L16.
2 Return or repayment of an injury etc.; retaliation, revenge. L16.

1 H. H. WILSON An ungrateful requital of the . . services of the Company. **2** *Manchester Examiner* In requital of that shameful act.

requite /rɪ'kwʌɪt/ *verb & noun.* E16.
[from RE- + *quite* var. of QUIT *verb.*]
▶**A** *verb trans.* **1** Make return or recompense for (a service etc.); repay or reward (a person) for a kindness etc. E16.
2 Retaliate for, avenge (a wrong etc.); pay back or take revenge on (a person) for an injury etc. M16.
3 Give or do (a thing) in return *for* something; reciprocate (a feeling, action, etc.). M16.
†**4** Take the place of, make up or compensate for. Only in 17.

3 E. FEINSTEIN A love . . never . . equally requited.

▶**B** *noun.* Requital. Long *Scot. rare.* M16.
■ **requiter** *noun* L16.

reran *verb pa. t.*: see RERUN *verb.*

re-rate /riː'reɪt/ *verb trans.* M19.
[from RE- + RATE *verb*[1].]
Rate or assess again; *spec.* (STOCK EXCHANGE) reassess the worth or prospects of (a company or stock).

rerd /rəːd/ *noun & verb.* Long *obsolete* exc. *dial.* (chiefly *Scot.*). Also **rerde**.
[Old English *reord* = Old High German *rarta* voice, melody, Gothic *razda* speech, voice, language, Old Norse *rǫdd*, *radd-* voice, song.]
▶**A** *noun.* †**1** Voice; an utterance, a cry. OE–LME.
2 A loud cry; noise, *esp.* that made by crying, roaring, etc. ME.
▶**B** *verb intrans.* †**1** Speak, discourse. OE–ME.
2 Make a noise; roar, resound. LME.

rere *adjective, noun, & adverb* see REAR *adjective*[1], *noun, & adverb.*

reread /'riːriːd/ *noun.* L20.
[from RE- + READ *noun*[2].]
An act or instance of reading something again.

reread /riː'riːd/ *verb trans.* Also **re-read**. Pa. t. & pple **-read** /-'rɛd/. L18.
[from RE- + READ *verb.*]
Read (a book etc.) again.

F. HARRISON Immortal poets . . are to be read and re-read.

■ **rereadable** *adjective* (esp. of a book) able to be reread (with pleasure) M20. **re-reader** *noun* M20. **re-reading** *noun* the action of the verb; an instance of this; a new version or interpretation of something: L19.

rere-arch *noun* var. of REAR-ARCH.

rere-brace /'rɪəbreɪs/ *noun. obsolete* exc. *Hist.* ME.
[from Anglo-Norman word, from *rere-* back + *bras* arm.]
A piece of armour, orig. covering only the upper arm but later extending to the shoulder and the elbow.

rere-dorter /'rɪədɔːtə/ *noun. rare.* L15.
[formed as REAR *adjective*[1] + DORTER.]
Chiefly *Hist.* A privy or lavatory situated at the back of the dormitory in a convent or monastery.

reredos /'rɪədɒs/ *noun.* LME.
[from Anglo-Norman word from Old French *areredos*, from *arere* behind (see ARREAR *adverb*) + *dos* back.]
1 ECCLESIASTICAL. An ornamental facing or screen of stone or wood covering the wall at the back of an altar. LME. ▸**b** A choir screen. LME.
†**2** ECCLESIASTICAL. A velvet or silk hanging covering the wall behind an altar. LME–M16.
3 The brick or stone back of a fireplace or open hearth; a metal plate forming a fireback. *arch.* LME.

re-release /riːrɪ'liːs/ *verb & noun.* M20.
[from RE- + RELEASE *verb, noun.*]
▶**A** *verb trans.* Release (a film, record, etc.) again. M20.
▶**B** *noun.* A re-released film, record, etc. M20.

Guardian Weekly With re-releases, he has had 117 singles on sale.

reremouse *noun* var. of REARMOUSE.

rere-supper /'rɪəsʌpə/ *noun.* Long *arch.* ME.
[Anglo-Norman *rere-super*, formed as REAR *adjective*[1] + SUPPER *noun*[1].]
A (usu. sumptuous) supper eaten late after the evening meal.

reride /*as verb* riː'rʌɪd, *as noun* 'riːrʌɪd/ *verb & noun.* L19.
[from RE- + RIDE *verb, noun.*]
▶**A** *verb trans.* Pa. t. **-rode**/-'rəʊd/, pa. pple **-ridden** /-'rɪd(ə)n/. Ride (a route, contest, etc.) again. L19.
▶**B** *noun.* A second or further ride. L20.

re-route /riː'ruːt/ *verb trans.* Pres. pple **-teing**, **-ting**. E20.
[from RE- + ROUTE *verb.*]
Send or carry by a different route, redirect.

re-row /*as verb* riː'rəʊ, *as noun* 'riːrəʊ/ *verb & noun.* L19.
[from RE- + ROW *verb*[1], *noun*[3].]
▶**A** *verb trans. & intrans.* Row (a race, course, etc.) again. L19.
▶**B** *noun.* A second or further rowing of a race etc. E20.

rerun /*as verb* riː'rʌn, *as noun* 'riːrʌn/ *verb & noun.* Also **re-run**. E19.
[from RE- + RUN *verb, noun.*]
▶**A** *verb trans.* Infl. as RUN *verb*; pa. t. usu. **-ran** /-'ran/, pa. pple **-run**. Run (a thing) again; *spec.* show (a film, television programme, etc.) again; subject again to an experimental or computational procedure. E19.

Punch A . . race had to be rerun. *fig.*: E. JONG Isadora . . can only . . rerun the accident again and again in her brain.

For other words beginning with *re-* see the entry for **re-**

▶**B** *noun.* The action or an instance of rerunning something; a repeated film, television programme, etc.; the repeated performance of a computer program; *gen.* a repeated occurrence or attempt. **M20.**

Daily Telegraph A re-run of last year's rebellion. *Listener* Television addicts can watch . . endless reruns of situation comedies.

res /reɪz, riːz/ *noun*¹. Pl. same. **E17.**
[Latin = thing.]
A thing, a matter: chiefly in Latin phrs. Now also, the condition of something; the matter in hand, the point at issue, the crux.
res cogitans /ˈkɒɡɪtanz, ˈkɒdʒ-/ PHILOSOPHY a human regarded as a thinking being. **res communis** /kəˈmjuːnɪs/, pl. **-nes** /-neɪz/, LAW common property; something incapable of appropriation. **res extensa** /ɪkˈstɛnsə/, pl. **-sae** /-siː/, PHILOSOPHY a material thing considered as extended substance. **res gestae** /ˈɡɛstʌɪ, ˈdʒɛstiː/ *pl.* (an account of) things done, (a person's) achievements; events in the past; LAW (an account, esp. a spoken one, of) the facts of the case. **res integra** /ˈɪntɪɡrə/, pl. **-grae** /-ɡrʌɪ, -ɡriː/, [Latin = untouched] LAW a case or question not covered by a law or precedent. **res ipsa loquitur** /ˌɪpsə ˈlɒkwɪtə/, [Latin = the thing speaks for itself] LAW the principle that the occurrence of an accident implies negligence. **res judicata** /dʒuːdɪˈkɑːtə/, pl. **-tae** /-tʌɪ, -tiː/, LAW a matter that has been adjudicated by a competent court and which therefore may not be pursued further by the same parties. **res non verba** /nɒn ˈvəːbə/ *pl.* things not words, fact or action as opp. to mere talk. **res nullius** /ˈnʌlɪəs/ LAW no one's property; a thing or things that can belong to no one. **res publica** /ˈpʊblɪkə, ˈpʌblɪkə/, the state, republic, or commonwealth.

res /rɛz/ *noun*². *colloq.* Also **res.** (point). **L19.**
[Abbreviation.]
= RESIDENCE *noun*¹ 5a, b.

resail /*as verb* riːˈseɪl, *as noun* ˈriːseɪl/ *verb & noun.* **L16.**
[from RE- + SAIL *verb*¹, *noun*³.]
▶**A** *verb.* **1** *verb intrans.* Sail back again; set sail again. **L16.**
2 *verb trans.* Sail (a race etc.) again. **L19.**
▶**B** *noun.* A second or subsequent sailing of a race etc. **M20.**

resait *verb* see RECEIPT *verb*¹.

resalable *adjective* var. of RESALEABLE.

resale /riːˈseɪl, *esp. attrib.* ˈriːseɪl/ *noun.* **E17.**
[from RE- + SALE *noun.*]
The selling, as by a wholesaler to a retailer, of a thing previously bought.
Comb.: **resale price** the price at which a commodity is sold again; ***resale price maintenance***, the setting by a manufacturer of a minimum or fixed price for the retailing of its goods.

resaleable /riːˈseɪləb(ə)l/ *adjective.* Also **-salable**. **M19.**
[from RE- + SALEABLE.]
Able or fit to be resold.

†**resalgar** *noun.* Also **rosalger**. **LME–M17.**
[Ult. from Arab. *rahj al-ġār*: see REALGAR. Cf. ROSAKER.]
= REALGAR.

resam /rɛˈsam/ *noun.* **E20.**
[Malay.]
A thicket-forming Malaysian fern, *Dicranopteris linearis*, with creeping rhizomes and leathery pinnate leaves.

resarcelée /rəsɑːsəˈleɪ/ *adjective.* **E18.**
[Old & mod. French *recercelé* hooped, curled, formed as RECERCELÉE. Cf. SARCELLY.]
HERALDRY. = RECERCELÉE. Also, (of a cross) placed on or behind a cross of another colour. Usu. *postpositive.*
■ Also **reˈsarcelled** *adjective* (now *rare*) **L16.**

resat *verb pa. t. & pple* of RESIT *verb.*

resaw /*as verb* riːˈsɔː, *as noun* ˈriːsɔː/ *verb & noun.* **E17.**
[from RE- + SAW *verb*¹, *noun*¹.]
▶**A** *verb trans.* Saw further, cut up (sawn wood). Chiefly as ***resawing*** *verbal noun.* **E17.**
▶**B** *noun.* A machine used for the further cutting of sawn wood; wood cut by such a machine. **E20.**

reschedule /riːˈʃɛdjuːl, -ˈskɛd-/ *verb trans.* **M20.**
[from RE- + SCHEDULE *verb.*]
Replan in accordance with a different timetable, change the time of (a planned event etc.); *spec.* arrange a new scheme of repayments of (an international debt).

rescind /rɪˈsɪnd/ *verb trans.* **M16.**
[Latin *rescindere*, formed as RE- + *scindere* split, divide.]
1 Annul, repeal (a law, decree, etc.); revoke, cancel. **M16.**
2 Take away, remove. **M17.**
■ **rescindable** *adjective* **M19.** **rescinder** *noun* **L19.**

†**rescindent** *adjective. rare.* **L16–L18.**
[Latin *rescindent-* pres. ppl stem of *rescindere*: see prec., -ENT.]
Of a tool etc.: that cuts.

rescission /rɪˈsɪʒ(ə)n/ *noun.* **E17.**
[Late Latin *rescissio(n-)*, from Latin *resciss-* pa. ppl stem of *rescindere* RESCIND: see -ION.]
†**1** The action of cutting something off. *rare.* Only in **E17.**
2 The action or an act of annulling or repealing a law, decree, etc. **M17.**

rescissory /rɪˈsɪs(ə)ri/ *adjective.* **E17.**
[Late Latin *rescissorius*, from Latin *resciss-*: see prec., -ORY².]
Having the effect or power of rescinding or revoking something; connected with or characterized by rescission.

†**rescounter** *noun.* **M16.**
[Italian *riscontro* comparison, balancing, from *ri-* RE- + *scontro* encounter.]
1 Encounter; a hostile meeting. *rare.* Only in **M16.**
2 *sing.* & in *pl.* (The time for) settlement or payment of differences on accounts, *spec.* on a stock exchange. **E17–L18.**

rescous /ˈrɛskəs/ *noun & verb.* Long *arch.* **ME.**
[Old French *rescousse*, from *rescoure* RESCUE *verb.*]
▶**A** *noun.* †**1** Rescue, assistance, aid. **ME–E17.**
2 LAW. = RESCUE *noun* 2. **LME.**
▶†**B** *verb trans.* Rescue. **ME–E17.**

rescribe /rɪˈskrʌɪb/ *verb.* Now *rare.* **LME.**
[Latin *rescribere*, formed as RE- + *scribere* write.]
†**1** *verb intrans.* Write back, write in reply. **LME–E18.**
2 *verb trans.* Write (a letter etc.) again, rewrite. **M16.**

rescript /ˈriːskrɪpt/ *noun.* **LME.**
[Latin *rescriptum* neut. pa. pple of *rescribere*: see prec.]
1 a An epistle from the Pope replying to a query, petition, etc.; any papal decision, decree, or edict. **LME.** ▸**b** A Roman emperor's written reply to a magistrate etc. consulting him for guidance, esp. on a point of law. **E17.**
2 Any official edict, decree, or announcement. **M16.**
3 The action or an act of rewriting something; something written again; a copy. **E19.**

†**rescription** *noun.* **L16.**
[Old & mod. French (esp. sense 3), or late Latin *rescriptio(n-)* var. of Latin *rescriptum* RESCRIPT: see -ION.]
1 The action or an act of rewriting something. **L16–L17.**
2 The action of replying in writing; a written reply. **L16–M17.**
3 A promissory note issued by a government. Only in **L18.**

rescuable /ˈrɛskjʊəb(ə)l/ *adjective.* **E17.**
[from RESCUE *verb* + -ABLE.]
Able to be rescued.
■ **rescuaˈbility** *noun* **L20.**

rescue /ˈrɛskjuː/ *noun.* **LME.**
[from the verb, superseding RESCOUS.]
1 The action or an act of rescuing a person or thing; the fact of being rescued; succour, deliverance. **LME.** ▸**b** BRIDGE. In full ***rescue bid***. A bid made to help one's partner out of a difficult situation, as when his or her bid has been doubled. **E20.**
2 LAW. The forcible unlawful taking of a person out of legal custody; forcible recovery by the owner of goods distrained; an instance of this. **LME.**

1 W. MAXWELL Nobody ever came to my rescue. *attrib.*: *Royal Air Force News* St Athan's mountain rescue team . . were asked to help.

Comb.: **rescue archaeology** emergency excavation of archaeological sites in the face of projected building or road development; ***rescue bid***: see sense 1b above; **rescue breathing** mouth-to-mouth resuscitation; **rescue excavation** = ***rescue archaeology*** above; **rescue mission** *US* a mission established by a religious group to help the underprivileged etc., esp. in a city.

rescue /ˈrɛskjuː/ *verb.* **ME.**
[Old French *rescoure*, *reskeure* from Proto-Romance, formed as RE- + Latin *excutere* shake out, discard, formed as EX-¹ + *quatere* shake.]
1 *verb trans.* Save or bring away from danger, privation, corruption, etc.; set free or deliver (a person) from attack, harm, or custody; liberate (a town etc.) from siege etc.; salvage (a thing). **ME.**
2 *verb trans.* LAW. Recover or take back (property) by force; liberate (a person) from legal custody by unlawful force. **LME.**
3 BRIDGE. **a** *verb trans.* Aid (a partner) with a rescue bid. **E20.** ▸**b** *verb intrans.* Make a rescue bid. **M20.**

1 F. H. A. SCRIVENER Fragments rescued from the ruins. *Guardian* A war-time . . organization which rescued thousands of . . Jews. *Liverpool Echo* 17 days at sea . . before he was rescued. B. CHATWIN She . . rescued other women from the tyranny of the corset. G. DALY Study of nature might rescue art from . . artificiality.

■ **rescuˈee** *noun* a person who is rescued **M20.** **rescuer** *noun* **M16.**

reseal /riːˈsiːl/ *verb trans.* **L17.**
[from RE- + SEAL *verb*¹.]
Seal again.
■ **resealable** *adjective* (of a container etc.) able to be resealed, esp. so as to preserve the freshness of contents **M20.**

research /rɪˈsəːtʃ, ˈriːsəːtʃ/ *noun*¹. **L16.**
[French †*recerche* (now *recherche*), from *re-* RE- + *cerche* SEARCH *noun*¹.]
1 The action or an instance of searching carefully for a specified thing or person. Freq. foll. by *after.* Now *rare.* **L16.**
2 A search or investigation undertaken to discover facts and reach new conclusions by the critical study of a subject or by a course of scientific inquiry. Usu. in *pl.* **M17.**
3 Systematic investigation into and study of materials, sources, etc., to establish facts, collate information, etc.; formal postgraduate study or investigation; surveying of opinions or background information relevant to a project etc. Also (now *rare*), aptitude for or application to such investigation. **M17.**

2 B. PYM He . . despised Tom's researches into the subject. **3** P. DAVIES Research . . by physicists . . to discover situations in which negative energy might arise. E. SIMPSON He would . . finish the research and write the book. ***audience research***, ***cancer research***, ***consumer research***, ***market research***, etc. OPERATIONAL ***research***. **research and development** in industry etc., work directed towards the innovation, introduction, and improvement of products and processes; abbreviation ***R & D***. attrib.: ***research assistant***, ***research degree***, ***research department***, ***research fellow***, ***research grant***, ***research programme***, ***research student***, etc.

■ **researchful** *adjective* devoted to, characterized by, or full of research **E19.**

research /ˈriːsəːtʃ/ *noun*². *rare.* Also **re-search**. **M18.**
[from RE- + SEARCH *noun*¹.]
A second or repeated search.

research /rɪˈsəːtʃ, ˈriːsəːtʃ/ *verb*¹. **L16.**
[Old French *recercher* (mod. *rechercher*), from *re-* RE- + *cerchier* SEARCH *verb*¹.]
1 *verb trans.* **a** Engage in research on (a subject, person, etc.); investigate or study closely. **L16.** ▸**b** Engage in research for (a book etc.). **M20.**
2 *verb intrans.* Make researches; pursue a course of research. (Foll. by *in(to)*, *on.*) **L18.**

1a *Times* A team . . has researched the phenomenon of 'jet lag'. **2** *Nature* A biochemist who has researched in many areas. *Navy News* Winton has researched into sea ballads.

■ **researchable** *adjective* worthy of being researched, suitable for researching **M20.** **researchist** *noun* = RESEARCHER **E20.**

research /ˈriːsəːtʃ, riːˈsəːtʃ/ *verb*² *trans. & intrans.* Also **re-search**. **M18.**
[from RE- + SEARCH *verb*¹.]
Search again or repeatedly.

researcher /rɪˈsəːtʃə, ˈriːsəːtʃə/ *noun.* **E17.**
[from RESEARCH *verb*¹ + -ER¹.]
A person who researches; someone studying or investigating a subject, now freq. to provide background information for a politician, broadcaster, etc.; an academic etc. engaged chiefly in scientific or literary research rather than teaching.

P. QUILLIN Researchers . . wanted to see how diabetes relates to lifestyle. *Woman* Employing a researcher to check the manuscript.

reseat /riːˈsiːt/ *verb trans.* **M17.**
[from RE- + SEAT *verb.*]
1 Seat (a person, oneself) in a different or former chair; replace in a former position or office. **M17.**
2 Provide with a fresh seat or seats. **M19.**

réseau /ˈreɪzəʊ, *foreign* rezo/ *noun.* Pl. **-eaux** /-əʊ, *foreign* -o/. Also **rézel** /ˈreɪzɛl, *foreign* rezɛl (*pl. same*)/. **L16.**
[French = net, web.]
1 A plain net ground used in lace-making. **L16.**
2 A network, a grid, *esp.* one superimposed as a reference marking on a photograph in astronomy, surveying, etc. **E20.**
3 A spy or intelligence network, esp. in the French resistance movement during the German occupation (1940–5). **M20.**
1 réseau à l'aiguille /a: leɪɡwiː, *foreign* a leɡɥij/ [*aiguille* needle] handmade net ground in needlepoint lace. **réseau ordinaire** /ɔːdɪˈnɛː, *foreign* ɔrdinɛːr/ [= ordinary] standard machine-made net ground. **réseau rosacé** /rəʊˈzaseɪ, *foreign* rozase/ [= rosaceous] a mesh ground with a flower pattern.
¶ See also VRAI RÉSEAU.

resect /rɪˈsɛkt/ *verb trans.* **M17.**
[Latin *resect-* pa. ppl stem of *resecare* cut off, formed as RE- + *secare* cut.]
†**1** Cut off or away; remove. **M–L17.**
2 MEDICINE. Surgically remove a portion of (an organ or tissue). **M19.**
3 SURVEYING. Locate by resection. **L19.**
■ **resectaˈbility** *noun* ability to be resected **M20.** **resectable** *adjective* **M20.**

resection /rɪˈsɛkʃ(ə)n/ *noun.* **E17.**
[Latin *resectio(n-)*, formed as prec.: see -ION.]
†**1** The action of cutting something off or away. **E–M17.**
2 MEDICINE. The operation of surgically removing (a portion of) an organ or tissue. **L18.**
3 SURVEYING. The process of determining the position of a point by taking bearings from points already mapped. **L19.**
■ **resectional** *adjective* **L19.** **resectionist** *noun* (MEDICINE) a surgeon who carries out resection **M20.**

resectoscope /rɪˈsɛktəskəʊp/ *noun*. **E20**.
[from RESECT + -O- + -SCOPE.]
MEDICINE. A surgical instrument for transurethral resection (of the prostate).

reseda /ˈrɛsɪdə, rɪˈsiːdə, *esp. in senses A.2, B.* ˈrɛzɪdə/ *noun & adjective*. In senses A.2, B. also (earlier) **réséda**. **M18**.
[Latin, interpreted in classical times as imper. of *resedare* assuage, allay, with ref. to the plant's supposed curative powers. In senses A.2, B. orig. from French.]
▶ **A** *noun*. **1** Any of various chiefly Mediterranean plants constituting the genus *Reseda* (family Resedaceae), which have small greenish or whitish flowers in spikelike racemes and include the mignonette, *R. odorata*, and weld, *R. luteola*. **M18**.
2 A pale green colour similar to that of mignonette. Also ***reseda green***. **L19**.
▶ **B** *attrib.* or as *adjective*. Of the colour of reseda, pale green. **L19**.

reseize /riːˈsiːz/ *verb trans*. Also **-seise**. **ME**.
[from RE- + SEIZE *verb*.]
†**1** Put (a person) in possession *of* something again; replace *in* or restore to a former position or dignity. **ME–M17**.
2 Seize or take possession of (a thing or person) again. **M16**.

reselect /riːsɪˈlɛkt/ *verb trans*. **M20**.
[from RE- + SELECT *verb*.]
Select again; now *esp.* confirm (a sitting Member of Parliament) as constituency candidate at a forthcoming election.
▪ **reselection** *noun* the action or an instance of reselecting a thing or person, now esp. a sitting Member of Parliament **M20**.

resell /riːˈsɛl/ *verb trans*. Pa. t. & pple **-sold** /-ˈsəʊld/. **L16**.
[from RE- + SELL *verb*.]
Sell (a thing) again, esp. commercially.
▪ **reseller** *noun* a person or organization reselling something **L19**.

resemblance /rɪˈzɛmbl(ə)ns/ *noun*. **ME**.
[Anglo-Norman, Old French (mod. *ress-*): see RESEMBLE, -ANCE.]
1 The quality or fact of being like or similar in appearance, nature etc.; a likeness, a similarity. **ME**.
2 The characteristic appearance or look of a person or thing; semblance. *arch.* **LME**.
†**3** A thing resembling or similar to another; a thing compared to another; a simile, a comparison. **LME–L17**.
4 A likeness, image, or representation of a person or thing. *arch.* **LME**. ▸†**b** A symbol or figure of something. **M16–M17**. ▸†**c** An appearance or show of a quality; *spec.* a demonstration of affection. Also, a likelihood, a probability. **M16–E17**.

📖 **1** *Encycl. Brit.* A convergent resemblance . . results from the action of similar forces of natural selection . . on unrelated organisms. J. RABAN In her red slacks . . she bore a strong resemblance to a . . pillarbox. E. REVELEY She was . . rich like them, but there the resemblance ended. **2** DISRAELI A garden . . had the resemblance of a vast mosaic.

resemblant /rɪˈzɛmbl(ə)nt/ *adjective & noun*. Now *rare*. **LME**.
[Old French (mod. *ress-*), formed as next: see -ANT[1].]
▶ **A** *adjective*. **1** Similar, having a resemblance or likeness *to* a person or thing. Formerly also foll. by *of*. **LME**.
2 Characterized by a resemblance or similarity to a person or thing; accurate. **L16**.
▶ **B** *noun*. †**1** A semblance; a show. *rare*. **L15–M16**.
2 A counterpart, an equivalent. **L19**.

resemble /rɪˈzɛmb(ə)l/ *verb*. **ME**.
[Old French *resembler* (mod. *ress-*), formed as RE- + *sembler* seem from Latin *similare*, from *similis* like.]
1 *verb trans*. Be like, have a likeness or similarity to, have a feature or property in common with. **ME**.
2 *verb trans*. Compare, liken (a person or thing) *to* another. Formerly also foll. by *together*, *with*. *arch.* **LME**.
†**3** *verb trans*. Make an image or likeness of, represent, depict (a person or thing). **LME–E18**.
4 *verb trans*. Make (a person or thing) similar *to* another. Chiefly as ***resembled*** *ppl adjective*. Now *rare*. **LME**.
†**5** *verb intrans*. Seem, appear. Freq. foll. by *to be*. **LME–E16**.
6 *verb intrans*. Be similar *to*. Now *rare*. **LME**. ▸**b** Of a number of people or things: have a mutual likeness; be like or similar to each other. Now *rare*. **M18**.

📖 **1** SCOTT FITZGERALD She resembled a small Teddy bear. ISAIAH BERLIN Tolstoy resembles Maistre in being . . curious about first causes. E. FEINSTEIN She had begun to resemble her father.

▪ **resembler** *noun* **L16**. **resembling** *adjective* (*a*) that resembles or corresponds to something, similar, like; (*b*) (now *rare*) similar to each other, alike: **M16**.

resent /rɪˈzɛnt/ *verb*. **L16**.
[French †*resentir* (now *ress-*), from *re-* RE- + *sentir* feel.]
▶ **I** †**1** *verb trans*. Feel, experience (an emotion or sensation). **L16–M18**.
†**2** *verb trans*. Feel (something) as a cause of depression or sorrow, feel deeply or sharply; *refl.* have a feeling *of* pain, feel distress or regret. **E17–E18**. ▸**b** Repent, regret (an action). **M–L17**.
3 *verb trans*. Feel injured or insulted by (an act, circumstance, etc.); be aggrieved at, esp. through jealousy; begrudge; feel bitterness or indignation towards (a person). Also, show dipleasure or anger at. **E17**.
†**4** *verb trans*. Take or receive (an action etc.) in a certain way or with certain feelings, respond to. **M17–M18**. ▸†**b** Take favourably, approve of. *rare*. Only in **M17**.
†**5** *verb trans*. Appreciate, be grateful for (a favour etc.). **M17–M19**.

📖 **3** N. PODHORETZ I began to resent . . a purposeless infringement of my freedom. M. GORDON Resenting . . women who successfully took care of their children. M. FORSTER Instead of becoming reconciled to his treatment of her, she was resenting it.

▶ **II** †**6** *verb trans*. Give out, exhale (a perfume etc.); have a suggestion of, show traces of (a quality etc.). *rare*. **E–M17**.
†**7** *verb intrans*. Savour *of*, be characteristic or suggestive *of*. **M17–E19**.
▪ **resenter** *noun* **M17**. **resentingly** *adverb* in a resenting manner, resentfully **E17**. †**resentive** *adjective* apt or inclined to resent **M17–M18**.

resentful /rɪˈzɛntfʊl, -f(ə)l/ *adjective*. **M17**.
[from prec. + -FUL.]
Full of or inspired by resentment; bitter, aggrieved, begrudging.

📖 B. VINE Resentful of him . . seeing him as an oppressive . . husband.

▪ **resentfully** *adverb* **M19**. **resentfulness** *noun* **M19**.

resentment /rɪˈzɛntm(ə)nt/ *noun*. **E17**.
[French †*resentiment* (now *ress-*), formed as RESENT: see -MENT.]
1 An indignant sense of injury or insult received or perceived, a sense of grievance; (a feeling of) ill will, bitterness, or anger against a person or thing. Also, the manifestation of such feeling. **E17**. ▸**b** *spec.* A negative attitude towards society or authority arising, often unconsciously, from aggressive envy and hostility, frustrated by a feeling of inferiority or impotence. **L19**.
†**2** A sentiment felt towards another; susceptibility to physical or mental impressions; a feeling, an emotion, a sensation. **M17–M18**.
†**3** An appreciation or understanding of something; interest in or care for a thing. **M17–M18**.
†**4** Gratitude; a feeling or expression of this. **M17–M19**.
†**5** Reception of an idea etc. in a particular way; an idea, an opinion, a view. *rare*. **M17–M18**.
†**6** Change of mind; regret. *rare*. **M17–E18**.

📖 **1** SWIFT Rolling resentments in my mind and framing schemes of revenge. DAY LEWIS Sadness . . would have hardened into resentment. P. ACKROYD The old resentment came up in him again.

resequent /ˈriːsɪkwənt, rɪˈsiːk-/ *adjective & noun*. **E20**.
[from RE- + *-sequent* after *consequent*, *obsequent*, etc.]
PHYSICAL GEOGRAPHY. ▶**A** *adjective*. **1** Of a stream, valley, etc.: whose direction of flow or drainage has by erosion come to follow the original slope of the land but at a lower stratigraphic level than the original surface. **E20**.
2 Of a fault-line scarp or related feature: having a relief similar to that originally produced by the faulting, esp. by erosion of an obsequent scarp. **E20**.
▶ **B** *noun*. A resequent stream. **E20**.

†**reserate** *verb trans*. **L16–E18**.
[Latin *reserat-* pa. ppl stem of *reserare* unlock, formed as RE- + *sera* bar, bolt: see -ATE[3].]
Open up.
▪ †**reseration** *noun* the action of opening something up; a thing which opens something: **L16–M17**.

reserpine /rɪˈsəːpiːn/ *noun*. **M20**.
[from mod. Latin *Rauvolfia serpentina* (see below), with inserted *-e-*, + -INE[5].]
PHARMACOLOGY. A colourless alkaloid obtained from the roots of several plants of the genus *Rauvolfia*, esp. *R. serpentina*, and used to treat hypertension and formerly as a sedative. Cf. RAUWOLFIA.

reservable /rɪˈzəːvəb(ə)l/ *adjective*. **M17**.
[from RESERVE *verb* + -ABLE.]
That may be reserved.

reservation /rɛzəˈveɪʃ(ə)n/ *noun*. **LME**.
[Old & mod. French *réservation* or late Latin *reservatio(n-)*, from Latin *reservat-* pa. ppl stem of *reservare*: see RESERVE *verb*, -ATION.]
1 *ECCLESIASTICAL*. **a** The action of reserving something as a tithe. *obsolete* exc. *Hist.* **LME**. ▸**b** *ROMAN CATHOLIC CHURCH*. The action of the Pope in reserving to himself the right of nomination to a vacant benefice; an act of exercising this right; the fact of this being exercised. Usu. in *pl.* **LME**. ▸**c** The action or practice of retaining a portion of the Eucharistic elements (esp. the bread) after celebration of the sacrament. **M16**. ▸**d** *ROMAN CATHOLIC CHURCH*. The action or fact of a superior reserving to himself the power of absolution. **E17**.
2 *LAW*. The action or fact of retaining a right or interest in property being conveyed, rented, etc., to another; an instance of this; a right or interest so retained; the clause or part of a deed reserving this. **L15**.
†**3** **a** The action or an act of keeping back or concealing something from others; something concealed, a secret. **L16–M17**. ▸**b** Reticence, reserve. *rare*. **M–L17**.
†**4** The action or fact of keeping something back for further action or consideration. **L16–M17**.
5 (The making of) an expressed or tacit limitation, qualification, or exception to an agreement etc.; a feeling of uncertainty about a project, principle, etc. Freq. in *pl.* **E17**.
6 The action or fact of reserving a right, privilege, etc.; an instance of this; a right etc. thus reserved. **E17**. ▸**b** The action or fact of booking a seat, room, etc., in advance; an instance of this; something reserved in advance, as a hotel room. Orig. *US*. **E20**. ▸**c** (An) exemption from military service because of an important civilian occupation. **E20**.
7 **a** An area of land set apart for a special purpose, esp. for occupation by N. American Indians, black South Africans, Australian Aboriginals, etc. Orig. *US*. **L18**. ▸**b** In full ***central reservation***. A strip of land between the carriageways of a dual carriageway. **M20**.

📖 **5** T. ROETHKE I wouldn't hesitate to recommend it . . without reservation. R. BERTHOUD He had had reservations about tackling *West Wind*. **6b** SLOAN WILSON Reservations booked on Flight 227. *attrib.*: E. LEONARD Past the reservation desk to the foyer. **7a** *Life* The . . Indian Reservation in North Carolina.

▪ **reservationist** *noun* (chiefly *US*) (*a*) a person who puts limitations on an agreement etc.; (*b*) a person who makes advance bookings for transport etc.: **E20**.

†**reservatory** *noun*. **M17**.
[medieval Latin *reservatorium*, from Latin *reservat-*: see prec., -ORY[1].]
1 A receptacle for food; a cupboard, a storeroom, a storehouse. **M17–E19**. ▸**b** A vessel for liquids. *rare*. **M17–E18**.
2 A reservoir for water etc. **M17–M18**. ▸**b** A receptacle for fluid in an animal or plant. **L17–M18**.

reserve /rɪˈzəːv/ *noun & adjective*. **E17**.
[from the verb.]
▶ **A** *noun*. †**1** **a** A place or thing in which something is preserved or stored. **E–M17**. ▸**b** A remnant or residue *of* a quality, feeling, etc. *rare*. **M17–E18**. ▸**c** A thing or means to which one may have recourse. *rare*. **L17–E18**.
2 Something kept back or stored for future use; a store, a stock, an extra quantity. **M17**. ▸**b** In *pl.* & (occas.) *sing.* Funds kept available by a bank, insurance company, etc., to meet ordinary or probable demand; resources in gold etc. held by a nation. Also (chiefly *sing.*), the part of a company's profit added to its capital rather than being paid as a dividend. **M19**. ▸**c** An amount of oil, gas, a mineral, etc., known to exist in the ground in a particular region and to admit of being exploited. Usu. in *pl.* **E20**. ▸**d** Extra energy; a supply of energy or resilience. Usu. in *pl.* **E20**.
3 **a** *MILITARY*. In *pl.* & *sing.* Troops or parts of a force withheld from action to serve as later reinforcements or cover. **M17**. ▸**b** *MILITARY*. In *pl.* & *sing.* Forces kept in addition to a nation's regular army, navy, air force, etc., to be called on in emergency. Now also *sing.*, a member of this force, a reservist. **M19**. ▸**c** *SPORT*. A player who is second choice for a team or is kept to replace another if required; a substitute. Also *pl.*, the reserve or second team. **E20**.
4 A thing or place set apart for a specific purpose; *spec.* an area of land reserved as a safe habitat for wildlife, for occupation by a people, etc.; *Austral.* a public park. **M17**. ▸**b** A distinction given to an exhibit at a show etc., indicating that it will receive a prize if another is disqualified; an exhibit winning such an award. **M19**. ▸**c** In full ***central reserve***. = RESERVATION 7b. **M20**.
5 = RESERVATION 5. **M17**. ▸**b** More fully ***reserve price***. The price stipulated as the lowest acceptable for an item sold at auction. **M19**.
6 **a** Self-control, restraint; (in art, literature, etc.) avoidance of exaggeration or excessive effects. **M17**. ▸**b** Avoidance of plain speaking or openness; reticence; intentional withholding of the truth. Also, lack of cordiality, coolness or distance of manner, formality. **E18**.
†**7** An instance of keeping some knowledge from another person; a fact etc. kept back or disguised; a secret. **L17–E19**.
8 In textile or pottery decoration, electroplating, etc.: a substance or preparation used as a resist during the application of dyes, glazes and lustres, etching acids, etc. Cf. RESIST *noun* 2. Now *rare*. **M19**. ▸**b** In textile or pottery

decoration, an area left the original colour of the material or the colour of the background. **L19.**

2 S. UNWIN Mother had saved . . a few hundred pounds as a reserve for any emergency. R. GITTINGS Such remarks . . draw on the reserve of early experience. **b** F. TUOHY Large reserves of foreign currency. **c** *Times* The known reserves of coal . . and natural gas. **3b** F. FITZGERALD 525,000 men . . without calling up the reserves. ***naval reserve***, ***Royal Naval Reserve***, etc. **c** E. DUNPHY All you have got to look forward to is Aldershot reserves away next Wednesday. **4** J. G. BENNETT The game reserves in Kenya. **6b** E. LONGFORD Her reserve I did not find chilling since my own family were . . undemonstrative.

Phrases: **army of reserve** [French *armée de réserve*] MILITARY = sense 3a above. ***central reserve***: see sense 4c above. ***dip into one's reserves***: see DIP *verb*. ***Federal Reserve Bank***, ***Federal Reserve Board***, ***Federal Reserve System***: see FEDERAL *adjective*. ***hidden reserves***: see HIDDEN *ppl adjective*. ***INNER reserve***. **in reserve** kept or remaining unused but available if required. ***spinning reserve***: see SPINNING *adjective*. **with all reserve**, **with all proper reserve** without endorsing or committing oneself to something. **without reserve** openly, frankly; without limitation or restriction; *spec.* (in an auction) without a reserve price.

▶ **B** *attrib.* or as *adjective*. Of or pertaining to a reserve or reserves; kept in reserve, constituting a reserve. **E18.**

J. GROSS A . . hint about him of . . reserve power. *Evening Telegraph (Grimsby)* Reserve winger Kevin Brown.

Special collocations & comb.: **reserve bank** a central bank holding currency reserves; *spec.* (*US*) = ***Federal Reserve Bank*** s.v. FEDERAL *adjective*. **reserve buoyancy** NAUTICAL buoyancy available to a craft in excess of its weight. **reserve cell** MEDICINE a cell by whose division and differentiation adjacent tissue is renewed. **reserve currency** a foreign currency widely used in international trade, which a central bank is prepared to hold as part of its foreign exchange reserves. **reserve-grade** *adjective* (chiefly *Austral.*) (of a sports team) second grade. ***reserve price***: see sense 5b above.

reserve /rɪˈzəːv/ *verb trans.* **ME.**
[Old & mod. French *réserver* from Latin *reservare*, formed as RE- + *servare* keep, save.]

1 a Keep back or set aside for future use or for a later occasion, put by. (Foll. by *for*, †*to*.) **ME.** ▸**b** Postpone the making of (a decision, judgement, etc.), esp. in order to consider a case or await evidence; defer discussion of (a matter). (Foll. by *for*, *to*.) **LME.**

2 Retain or secure as one's own, esp. by formal or legal stipulation; keep *to* or *for* oneself; LAW make a reservation of in a lease etc. **LME.** ▸**b** Set apart (a portion of rent) for payment *in* corn etc. Now *rare* or *obsolete*. **L16.**

3 Set apart or keep for a person or for a special use (foll. by *for*, *to*); in *pass.*, (of an achievement) be fated *for*, fall to. **LME.** ▸**b** Set (a person) apart *for* a particular fate or end. Formerly also foll. by *to*. Now *rare*. **LME.** ▸†**c** Make an exception of; except or exempt (a thing or person) *from* something. **L15–E19.** ▸**d** In textile or pottery decoration, leave in the original colour of the material or the colour of the background. Usu. in *pass.* **L19.** ▸**e** Exempt (a person) from military service on the grounds of holding an important civilian occupation. Also, class (a civilian occupation) as high priority (usu. in *pass.*). **E20.**

4 ECCLESIASTICAL. **a** Set apart or keep back (a case for absolution) to be dealt with by a superior authority. Foll. by *for*, *to*. **LME.** ▸**b** Retain or preserve (a portion of the Eucharistic elements) after celebration of the sacrament. **M16.**

5 a Preserve (a person), keep alive; save *from* death. Now *rare*. **LME.** ▸†**b** Keep in store, save (a commodity etc.); preserve (food, a relic, etc.) from decay or destruction. **LME–M18.** ▸†**c** Keep or maintain in a certain state or condition. **E16–M17.** ▸†**d** Keep in one's possession. **M16–E17.** ▸†**e** Continue to have, retain (a characteristic, quality, etc.). **L16–E18.**

6 Engage (a seat, ticket, etc.) in advance, book; order (a thing) to be specially retained, usu. for a particular length of time. **M19.**

1a C. CONRAN Squeeze the lemon and reserve the juice. **b** N. COWARD I shall reserve my opinion . . until I've met . . Victor. *Times* Mr Justice Boreham reserved judgement. **2** *Socialist Leader* Government says it reserves the right. **3** G. BERKELEY This discovery was reserved to our times. J. BARZUN A difficult task reserved for the few. E. J. HOWARD Pie reserved for Hanwell's elevenses. D. ROWE We reserve our best behaviour for strangers. **6** B. CHATWIN He reserved a table at a restaurant.

■ **reserver** *noun* (*a*) *rare* a person who reserves something; †(*b*) = RESERVOIR *noun* 1: **E17.**

re-serve /riːˈsəːv, ˈriːsəːv/ *verb trans. & intrans.* **M19.**
[from RE- + SERVE *verb*[1].]
Serve again.

reserved /rɪˈzəːvd/ *adjective.* **M16.**
[from RESERVE *verb* + -ED[1].]

†**1** Preserved; remaining undestroyed. **M16–M17.**

2 Averse to showing familiarity, slow to reveal emotion or opinions; cold or distant in manner, formal; reticent, uncommunicative. Also, restrained, restricted, having reservations. **E17.**

3 That has been reserved; set apart, destined for a particular use etc.; booked in advance. **E17.**

2 A. KOESTLER They spoke . . with a . . reserved politeness. G. BODDY She appeared reserved, remote. **3 Reserved List** a list of naval officers removed from active service but kept in reserve in case of being required. **reserved occupation** a high-priority civilian occupation from which a person will not be taken for military service. **reserved seats** seats at an entertainment, on a means of transport, etc., which may be or have been specially engaged in advance. **reserved word** COMPUTING a word in a programming language which has a fixed meaning and cannot be redefined by the programmer.

■ **reservedly** /-vɪdli/ *adverb* in a reserved manner, with reserve or reservations **E17.** **reservedness** *noun* **E17.**

reservist /rɪˈzəːvɪst/ *noun.* **L19.**
[from RESERVE *noun* + -IST, after French *réserviste*.]
A member of a military reserve force.

reservoir /ˈrɛzəvwɑː/ *noun & verb.* **M17.**
[French *réservoir*, formed as RESERVE *verb* + *-oir* -ORY[1].]

▶ **A** *noun.* **1** A large natural or man-made lake or pool used for collecting and storing water for public and industrial use, irrigation, etc. Also, a large water tank. **M17.** ▸**b** A body of porous rock holding a large quantity of oil or natural gas. **E20.**

2 A source of supply, a store *of* (usu. immaterial) things; a reserve, a fund, a pool. **L17.** ▸**b** MEDICINE. A population which is chronically infested with the causative agent of a disease and can infect other populations. **E20.**

3 a A part of an animal or plant in which a fluid or secretion is collected or retained. **E18.** ▸**b** A part of an apparatus in which a fluid or liquid is contained; *spec.* in a closed hydraulic system, a tank containing fluid able to be supplied to the system as needed to compensate for small losses. **L18.**

4 Orig. *gen.*, a place of storage, a repository. Now only *spec.*, a receptacle for fluid or vapour. **M18.**

2 *Spectator* The vast reservoir of facts. P. H. GIBBS An enormous reservoir of emotion among the people.

Comb.: **reservoir engineering** the study and exploitation of natural oil and gas reservoirs; **reservoir rock** rock (capable of) forming a reservoir for oil or natural gas.

▶ **B** *verb trans.* Keep (as) in a reservoir, store. Now *rare*. **M19.**

reset /rɪˈsɛt/ *noun*[1]. **ME.**
[Old French *recet* from Latin *receptum*, from *recipere* RECEIVE.]

1 (A place of) refuge, (a) shelter. Now *rare* or *obsolete*. **ME.** ▸†**b** A person sheltering another, *esp.* one harbouring a criminal. **LME–E18.**

2 LAW (now *Scot.*). ▸**a** Shelter given to another, esp. to a criminal or proscribed person; the harbouring of criminals. *arch.* **LME.** ▸**b** The action or practice of receiving stolen goods. **L18.**

reset /riːˈsɛt, ˈriːsɛt/ *noun*[2]. Also **re-set**. **M19.**
[from RE- + SET *noun*[1].]
The action or an act of resetting something; a thing reset; a device for resetting an instrument etc.

reset /rɪˈsɛt/ *verb*[1] *trans.* Long *obsolete* exc. *Scot.* Infl. **-tt-**. **ME.**
[Old French *recet(t)er* from Latin *receptare*, from *recept-* pa. ppl stem of *recipere* RECEIVE.]

1 Harbour or shelter (a person, esp. a criminal). *arch.* **ME.**

2 Receive (stolen goods) from a thief with intent to cover up or profit by theft. **LME.**

■ **resetter** *noun* **LME.**

reset /riːˈsɛt/ *verb*[2]. Also **re-set**. Infl. **-tt-**. Pa. t. & pple **-set**. **M17.**
[from RE- + SET *verb*[1].]

▶ **I** *verb trans.* **1** Put (gems, a play, etc.) into a former or new setting; set (a broken limb, hair, etc.) again or differently. **M17.**

2 Plant again, replant. **E18.**

3 Typeset (a book) again or differently, recompose; set up (type) again. **M19.**

4 Cause (a device) to return to a former state, esp. to a condition of readiness; return (a counting device) *to* a specified value, esp. zero; COMPUTING set (a binary cell) to zero. **E20.**

3 *Bookman* Both books have been entirely reset for this edition. **4** N. LOWNDES Sashe forgot to re-set the alarm clock.

▶ **II** *verb intrans.* **5** Set again or differently, return to a previous setting. **L19.** ▸**b** Of a device: return to an initial state. **L20.**

■ **resetta'bility** *noun* ability to be reset **L20.** **resettable** *adjective* able to be reset **L19.**

resettle /riːˈsɛt(ə)l/ *verb.* Also **re-settle**. **M16.**
[from RE- + SETTLE *verb*.]

1 a *verb trans.* Settle (a thing or person) again in a new or former place, replace, re-establish; *spec.* establish (a homeless etc. person) again in a house or community; *S. Afr. Hist.* evict and settle (a black person) in a different area, often in a supposed homeland. **M16.** ▸**b** *verb intrans.* Settle down again. **L17.** ▸**c** *verb refl.* Settle again in one's seat or position. **E19.**

2 *verb trans.* **a** Bring to order again, restore to a settled state or condition. **E17.** ▸**b** Arrange again; make a new settlement of (a situation etc.). **M19.**

3 *verb trans.* Settle or people (a country) again. **E18.**

4 *verb trans.* Assign by a new settlement. **M19.**

1a A. BRINK Whole societies uprooted and resettled. I. MURDOCH He . . cleaned his glasses . . and resettled them firmly before his eyes. **c** DAY LEWIS The hens re-settled themselves in their straw.

resettlement /riːˈsɛt(ə)lm(ə)nt/ *noun.* **M17.**
[from RE- + SETTLEMENT.]

1 The action or fact of resettling a person, place, etc.; a fresh settlement; now *spec.* (*a*) the action of resettling demobilized military personnel into civilian life; (*b*) *S. Afr. Hist.* the action of resettling black people in a different area, often in a supposed homeland. **M17.**

2 The process of settling down again; the result of a person, place, etc., being resettled. **L17.**

1 *attrib.*: C. HOPE Resettlement camps fortified with foot patrols.

Resh Galuta /reɪʃ gəluːˈtɑː/ *noun phr.* **E19.**
[Aramaic *rēš gālūṯā* lit. 'chief of the exile'.]
= EXILARCH.

Resht /rɛʃt/ *adjective.* **L19.**
[A province and town in NW Iran.]
Designating a type of patchwork of a mosaic pattern traditionally made in Resht.

†**resiance** *noun.* **L16–M17.**
[French †*res(s)eance*, formed as next: see -ANCE.]
Abode, residence.

■ †**resiancy** *noun* **L16–L17.**

resiant /ˈrɛzɪənt/ *adjective & noun.* Now *arch. rare.* **LME.**
[Old French *reseant* pres. pple of *reseoir* from Latin *residere*: see next, -ANT[1].]

▶†**A** *adjective.* Resident, dwelling; abiding. Usu. *pred.* **LME–M18.**

▶ **B** *noun.* A resident. **LME.**

reside /rɪˈzʌɪd/ *verb*[1] *intrans.* **LME.**
[Prob. back-form. from RESIDENT, later infl. by French *résider* and Latin *residere* remain behind, rest, formed as RE- + *sedere* settle, sit.]

†**1** Settle; take up one's station. *rare.* **LME–M17.**

2 a Of a person holding an official position: occupy a specified place for the performance of official duties; be in residence. **LME.** ▸**b** Dwell permanently or for a considerable time, have one's regular home *in* or *at* a particular place. **L16.**

†**3** Remain or continue *in* a certain place or position; be placed or stationed. **L15–L18.**

4 Of power, a right, a quality, etc.: be vested, present, or inherent *in* a person etc. **E17.** ▸**b** Be physically present *in* or *on* a thing. **E17.**

2a *London Gazette* James Jefferyes, Esq., to reside for His Majesty's Service with the King of Sweden. **4** E. M. FORSTER A woman's power and charm reside in mystery. H. J. LASKI It is in the king in Parliament that British sovereignty resides. **b** S. P. THOMPSON Electricity may . . reside upon the surface of bodies as a charge. *Scientific American* That determinant must reside on the *a* antigen.

■ **resider** *noun* a resident **M17.** **residing** *noun* (*a*) residence; †(*b*) a dwelling-place: **L16.**

†**reside** *verb*[2] *intrans.* **L16.**
[Latin *residere* subside, formed as RE- + *sidere* sink.]

1 Subside. **L16–E18.**

2 Settle down to form a deposit. Only in **17.**

residence /ˈrɛzɪd(ə)ns/ *noun*[1]. **LME.**
[Old & mod. French *résidence* or medieval Latin *residentia*, from *resident-*: see RESIDENT *adjective*, -ENCE.]

1 The circumstance or fact of having one's permanent or usual abode in or at a certain place; the fact of residing or being resident. Freq. in ***have one's residence***, ***take up one's residence*** below. **LME.** ▸**b** ANTHROPOLOGY. The place in which it is customary for a couple to settle after marriage, according to the prevailing kinship system. **M19.**

2 The fact of living or staying regularly at or in a specified place for the performance of official duties or for work; a period of time required for this. Now freq. in ***in residence*** below. Also, a residential post held esp. for teaching purposes by an artist, writer, etc., within an institution (freq. as 3rd elem. of comb., as ***artist-in-residence***, ***writer-in-residence***, etc.). **LME.**

†**3** Continuance in some course or action. **LME–E17.**

†**4** The action of remaining in a place for a limited period of time; lingering; procrastination. Esp. in ***make residence***. Chiefly *Scot.* **LME–L16.**

5 a The place where a person resides; the abode *of* a person. **E16.** ▸**b** A dwelling, a house, *esp.* an impressive, official, or superior one; a mansion. **E17.** ▸**c** A settlement, esp. of traders. Long *obsolete* exc. *Hist. rare.* **E17.** ▸**d** = RESIDENCY 2b. **M20.**

6 *fig.* The seat *of* power, a particular quality, etc. **M16.**

7 The time during which a person resides in or at a place; a period of residing; a stay. L17.

📖 **1** G. SWIFT Longer and longer periods, which eventually merged into a permanent residence. **2** A. C. GRAYLING He could submit the *Tractatus* for the . . Ph.D. after one further year's residence. I. MURDOCH Patrick continued in his position of . . poet in residence. **5a** M. FORSTER Taking a lease . . while he looked for a more permanent residence. **7** *attrib.*: *Guardian* The cancellation of his residence permit.

Phrases: ***hall of residence***: see HALL *noun* 6b. **have one's residence** have one's usual dwelling-place or abode. **in residence** dwelling in or occupying a specific place, esp. for the performance of official duties or work. ***make residence***: see sense 4 above. ***private residence***: see PRIVATE *adjective*. **take up one's residence** establish oneself; settle.
Comb.: **residence city** [translating German *Residenzstadt*] (chiefly *Hist.*) a seat of a royal or princely court; **residence counsellor** *US* a psychiatric adviser attached to a residential block in a university; **residence time** (chiefly *SCIENCE*) the (average) length of time during which a substance, a portion of material, an object, etc., is in a given location or condition (esp. of adsorption, suspension, etc.).

†residence *noun*². M16.
[from RESIDE *verb*² + -ENCE.]
1 That which settles as a deposit; sediment; the deposit remaining after a chemical process has taken place. M16–L17.
2 The settling of sediment in a liquid. E17–E18.

residency /ˈrɛzɪd(ə)nsi/ *noun*. L16.
[formed as RESIDENCE *noun*¹: see -ENCY.]
1 = RESIDENCE *noun*¹ (now chiefly *N. Amer.*); *spec.* a musician's or a band's permanent or regular engagement at a club etc. L16.
2 a *Hist.* The official residence of a representative of the Governor-General or Viceroy (or formerly of the East India Company) at the court of an Indian State. E19. ▸**b** A group or organization of intelligence agents in a foreign country. L20.
3 *Hist.* An administrative division in Indonesia. E19.
4 The position or station of a medical graduate under supervision in a hospital; the period of specialized medical training during which this position is held. *N. Amer.* E20.

📖 **1** A. BROWNJOHN The university . . set up residencies for a sculptor . . , a composer and a poet. **4** R. JAFFE Med school . . then I'll be interning, and then residency.

resident /ˈrɛzɪd(ə)nt/ *adjective & noun*. ME.
[Old & mod. French *résident* or Latin *resident-* pres. ppl stem of *residere* RESIDE *verb*¹: see -ENT.]
▸ **A** *adjective*. **1** Residing, dwelling, or having an abode in a place. ME. ▸**b** Of a (species of) bird or animal: remaining in a specified place or region throughout the year. Also *occas.*, breeding regularly in a place or region. E19.
2 Staying regularly in or at a place for the performance of official duties or to work, study, etc. LME.
3 Of a thing: situated, lying. (Foll. by *in*.) LME.
4 Of a quality, power, etc.: abiding, present, inherent, established. E16.
5 *COMPUTING*. Of a program, file, etc.: occupying a permanent place in memory. M20.

📖 **1** S. BUTLER The deceased was . . resident in the parish. **2** E. YOUNG-BRUEHL A kind of informal resident tutor for their little daughter. ***resident AMBASSADOR***. **resident commissioner** *US* a delegate elected to represent Puerto Rico in the US House of Representatives, able to speak in the House and serve on committees but not to vote. **4** COLERIDGE Liberty of the Press (a power resident in the people).

▸ **B** *noun*. **1** A person who resides permanently in a place; a permanent or settled inhabitant of a town, district, etc. Also, a guest staying one or more nights at a hotel etc. LME. ▸**b** A bird belonging to a non-migratory species; *occas.* (more fully ***summer resident***) a bird which breeds regularly in a particular place or region. L19.
2 *Hist.* **a** A diplomatic representative, inferior in rank to an ambassador, residing at a foreign court. E17. ▸**b** Orig. a representative of the East India Company residing at a commercial outpost. Later, a representative of the Governor-General residing at the court of an Indian State; a British government agent in a semi-independent State. L18. ▸**c** The governor of a residency in Indonesia. E19.
3 A medical graduate who has completed an internship and is engaged in specialized practice under supervision in a hospital. *N. Amer.* L19.
4 [translating Russian *rezident*.] An intelligence agent in a foreign country. M20.

📖 **2a** C. V. WEDGWOOD The French resident in London presented a letter from the Queen.

■ **†residenting** *ppl adjective* (*rare*) residing, resident M17–E18. **residentship** *noun* the office or post of a resident L16.

residenter /ˈrɛzɪdɛntə/ *noun*. LME.
[Anglo-Norman *residencer*, Old French *-cier* from medieval Latin *residentiarius* RESIDENTIARY: see -ER².]
†1 *ECCLESIASTICAL*. A residentiary. *rare*. LME–E18.
2 A resident, an inhabitant. *Scot. & US*. M17.

residential /rɛzɪˈdɛnʃ(ə)l/ *adjective & noun*. M17.
[from RESIDENCE *noun*¹ + -IAL, after *presidential*.]
▸ **A** *adjective*. **1 a** Serving or used as a residence. M17. ▸**b** Suitable for or characterized by private houses. L19.
2 Connected with, entailing, or based on residence. M19.
3 Of or belonging to a British Government agent in a semi-independent State. *rare*. L19.

📖 **1a** J. CAREY The Inns of Court . . operated like residential clubs. **b** J. HELLER A luxurious urban mansion . . in a choice residential area. **2** *Which?* Residential care for elderly people.

▸ **B** *noun*. A residential hotel. Chiefly *Austral*. M20.
■ **residentially** *adverb* E20.

residentiary /rɛzɪˈdɛnʃ(ə)ri/ *noun & adjective*. E16.
[medieval Latin *residentiarius*, from *residentia* RESIDENCE *noun*¹: see -ARY¹.]
▸ **A** *noun*. **1** An ecclesiastic who is required to live in the place in which he is authorized to minister, *esp.* a canon of a cathedral or collegiate church. E16.
2 A person who or thing which is resident. E17.
▸ **B** *adjective*. **1** Involving, requiring, or pertaining to, official residence. Freq. *postpositive* in ***canon residentiary***. M17.
2 Residing or resident in a place; connected with residence. M17.
■ **residentiaryship** *noun* the office of a (canon) residentiary E17.

residentura /ˌrɪzɪdɛnˈturə, ˌrɛzɪdɛnˈtʊərə/ *noun*. M20.
[Russian *rezidentura*. Cf. RESIDENT *noun* 4.]
= RESIDENCY 2b.

Residenz /rɛzɪˈdɛnts/ *noun*. M19.
[German, lit. 'residence'.]
Chiefly *Hist*. The building in which a German princely court resided before 1918; a town which was the seat of a princely court.

residua *noun* pl. of RESIDUUM.

residual /rɪˈzɪdjʊəl/ *noun*. M16.
[formed as next.]
1 *MATH. & SCIENCE*. A quantity resulting from subtraction of one quantity from another; now usu., the difference between an observed or measured value of a quantity and its true, theoretical, or notional value. M16.
2 A remainder; an amount remaining after the main part is subtracted or accounted for. M19. ▸**b** The part of a gravitational or magnetic anomaly that remains after subtraction of the regional. M20.
3 A substance or product of the nature of a residue. L19.
4 A royalty paid to an actor, musician, etc., for a repeat of a play, television commercial, etc. M20.
5 *PHYSICAL GEOGRAPHY*. A portion of rocky or high ground remaining after erosion. M20.

📖 **2** *Oxford Economic Papers* A large residual in the market for graduates.

residual /rɪˈzɪdjʊəl/ *adjective*. L16.
[from RESIDUE + -AL¹.]
1 *MATH*. Resulting from the subtraction of one quantity from another. L16.
2 a Remaining; still left; left over. E17. ▸**b** *SCIENCE*. Left as a residue, esp. at the end of some process. M18. ▸**c** Left unexplained or uncorrected. M19. ▸**d** Of a state or property: retained after the removal of a causative agent or process; present in the absence of such an agent or process. M19. ▸**e** *PHYSICAL GEOGRAPHY*. (Of a deposit or feature) formed *in situ* by the weathering of rock; (of a soil) composed largely of such material. L19.

📖 **2a** R. SCRUTON The residual Hegelianism that all modern criticism betrays. **d** ***residual activity***, ***residual charge***, ***residual magnetism***, etc. **residual current**: which flows briefly in a circuit after the voltage is reduced to zero, due to the momentum of the charge carriers; ***residual current device***, a current-activated circuit-breaker used as a safety device for mains-operated electrical tools, appliances, etc. **residual stress** stress present in an object in the absence of any external load or force.

■ **residually** *adverb* to a residual extent; in a residual degree: M20.

residuary /rɪˈzɪdjʊəri/ *adjective & noun*. E18.
[from RESIDUUM + -ARY¹.]
▸ **A** *adjective*. **1** *LAW*. Of the nature of or pertaining to the residue of an estate. E18.
2 Of the nature of a residue or remainder; still remaining; residual. L18.

📖 **1 residuary devisee**, **residuary legatee** a beneficiary of the residue of an estate. **2** H. BUSHNELL Mere residuary substances of a dry and fruitless life. **residuary powers** powers remaining with one political group after other powers have been allocated to another group, as between a federal government and a province.

▸ **B** *noun*. A residuary legatee. E19.

residue /ˈrɛzɪdjuː/ *noun*. LME.
[Old & mod. French *résidu* from Latin RESIDUUM.]
1 The remainder, the rest; that which is left. LME. ▸**b** *SOCIOLOGY*. Any of the fundamental impulses which motivate human conduct, and which are not the product of rational deliberation. M20.
2 *LAW*. That which remains of an estate after the payment of all charges, debts, and bequests. LME.
3 *CHEMISTRY* etc. A substance left after combustion, evaporation, etc.; a deposit, a sediment; a waste product. LME.
4 *MATH*. A remainder. Now *spec.* a remainder left when an integer is divided by a given number; a number congruent to a given number modulo a third number; cf. CONGRUENT 2b, MODULUS 3. M19.
5 *BIOCHEMISTRY & CHEMISTRY*. A radical; a molecule (esp. an amino acid, sugar, etc.) incorporated without major alteration in a larger one. M19.

📖 **1** B. UNSWORTH His lips had stiffened with some residue of the old pain. M. WESLEY The dandelion root . . snapped, leaving a residue of root in the soil. **3** T. THOMSON The liquid being . . evaporated to dryness, left a residue. **5** R. F. CHAPMAN The common disaccharides . . all contain a glucose residue.

Phrases & comb.: **quadratic residue**, **cubic residue**, **biquadratic residue**, etc., a remainder left when a given number is divided into the square, cube, fourth power, etc., of some integer. **residue class** a class of integers congruent to one another modulo a given number (e.g. 2, 5, 8, 11, etc., are members of a residue class modulo 3).

residuous /rɪˈzɪdjʊəs/ *adjective*. Now *rare* or *obsolete*. E17.
[from Latin *residuus*: see next, -OUS.]
Remaining.

residuum /rɪˈzɪdjʊəm/ *noun*. Pl. **-dua** /-djʊə/. L17.
[Latin, use as noun of neut. of *residuus* remaining, from *residere* RESIDE *verb*¹.]
1 That which remains; a residue. L17. ▸**b** The masses; the poor. M19.
2 *LAW*. The residue of an estate. M18.
3 *CHEMISTRY* etc. = RESIDUE 3. M18.

resign /rɪˈzʌɪn/ *noun*. *rare*. LME.
[from the verb.]
Resignation.

resign /rɪˈzʌɪn/ *verb*. LME.
[Old & mod. French *résigner* from Latin *resignare* unseal, cancel, give up, formed as RE- + *signare* SIGN *verb*.]
▸ **I** *verb trans.* **1** Relinquish, surrender, or hand over (esp. a right, claim, obligation, or an official position). Also foll. by *into*, *to*, *up* (now *rare*). LME.
2 a Abandon or consign (something) *to* a person or thing; yield up (oneself etc.) *to* another's care or guidance. LME. ▸**b** Subordinate (one's will, reason, etc.) to another person, higher power, etc. L16. ▸**c** Reconcile (oneself, one's mind, etc.) *to* a condition, an inevitable event, etc. Also foll. by *to do*. E18.
†3 Refrain from. LME–L16.

📖 **1** P. WARNER Richard was glad to sign a treaty resigning Ascalon. E. YOUNG-BRUEHL When the school year ended, she resigned her post. **2a** J. MARTINEAU He . . vows to resign himself to her direction. **b** W. COWPER Resign our own and seek our Maker's will. **c** B. CHATWIN I resigned myself to lunching with a tearful palaeontologist.

▸ **II** *verb intrans.* **4** Give up one's employment, an official position etc.; retire. Formerly also, abdicate. Freq. foll. by *from* (orig. *US*). LME.
5 Submit *to* a person or thing. Now *rare*. LME.
6 Make surrender or relinquishment; *CHESS* discontinue play and admit defeat. M18.

📖 **4** G. BROWN Sir Stafford Cripps resigned as Chancellor of the Exchequer because of illness.

■ **resignee** *noun* †(*a*) a person to whom something is resigned; (*b*) a resigner: E17. **resigner** *noun* a person who resigns, esp. from employment, an official position, etc. M16. **resignment** *noun* (now *rare*) the action of resigning; resignation: LME.

re-sign /riːˈsʌɪn/ *verb*. E19.
[from RE- + SIGN *verb*.]
1 *verb trans.* Sign again; *spec.* sign the contract of (a person) for a further period. E19.
2 *verb intrans.* Of a sportsman etc.: sign a contract for a further period. M20.

resignant /rɪˈsɪgnənt/ *adjective*. Now *rare* or *obsolete*. L16.
[French *résignant* or from Latin *resignant-* pres. ppl stem of *resignare*: see RESIGN *verb*, -ANT¹.]
HERALDRY. Of the tail of an animal, esp. a lion: concealed.

resignation /rɛzɪgˈneɪʃ(ə)n/ *noun*. LME.
[Old & mod. French *résignation* from medieval Latin *resignatio(n-)*, from Latin *resignat-* pa. ppl stem of *resignare*: see RESIGN *verb*, -ATION.]
1 The action or an act of resigning, esp. from one's employment, an official position, etc.; an intention to do this. Also, a document etc. stating this intention. LME.
2 *SCOTS LAW* (now *Hist.*). The mode in which a vassal returned lands held to a feudal superior. LME.
†3 A giving up *of* oneself, esp. to God. L15–M17.

For other words beginning with *re-* see the entry for **re-**

4 The fact of resigning oneself or of being resigned *to* something; acquiescence, submission, uncomplaining endurance of adversity. **M17.**

> 🕮 **1** M. GARDINER Teaching wasn't my vocation . . . I sent in my resignation. *attrib.*: H. NICOLSON Duff Cooper making his resignation speech. **4** M. LANE She approached death with dignity and resignation.

■ **resignationism** *noun* the principles and practice of resignation; the state or quality of being resigned to one's fate: **L19.** **resignationist** *noun* (*rare*) an adherent of resignationism **M20.**

resigned /rɪˈzʌɪnd/ *adjective.* **M17.**
[from **RESIGN** *verb* + **-ED**[1].]
†**1** Abandoned, surrendered. Foll. by *up*. Only in **M17.**
2 Full of or characterized by resignation; submissive, acquiescent. Freq. foll. by *to*. **L17.**
3 Having given up an official position, one's employment, etc. **L19.**

> 🕮 **2** H. KISSINGER Neither anxious nor confident, but rather resigned to events.

■ **resignedly** /-nɪdli/ *adverb* in a resigned manner; submissively: **L17.** **resignedness** *noun* **M17.**

resile /rɪˈzʌɪl/ *verb intrans.* **E16.**
[French †*resilir* or Latin *resilire* leap back, recoil, formed as **RE-** + *salire* leap. In sense 1 = medieval Latin *resilire* (*ab*) repudiate.]
1 Draw back *from* an agreement, contract, etc.; retract. **E16.**
2 Draw back or withdraw *from* a course of action etc. **M17.**
3 Recoil or retreat *from* something with aversion. **L17.**
4 (Of a material thing) recoil or rebound after contact; (of something stretched or compressed) resume an original position, size, shape etc.; spring back. **E18.**
5 Turn back from a point reached; return to one's original position. *rare*. **L19.**

> 🕮 **1** *Financial Times* The club had not resiled from its agreement. **3** D. HUME I resiled from their excessive civilities.

resilia *noun* pl. of **RESILIUM.**

resilience /rɪˈzɪlɪəns/ *noun.* **E17.**
[formed as **RESILIENT**: see **-ENCE.**]
1 a The action or an act of rebounding or springing back. **E17.** ▸**b** Recoil *from* something; revolt. **M19.**
2 Elasticity; *spec.* the amount of energy per unit volume that a material absorbs when subjected to strain, or the maximum value of this when the elastic limit is not exceeded. **E19.**
3 The ability to recover readily from, or resist being affected by, a setback, illness, etc. **L19.**

> 🕮 **2** F. KING The paper . . had the toughness and resilience of plastic. **3** F. KAPLAN Their stubborn . . resilience helped them to survive their continuing embarrassments.

resiliency /rɪˈzɪlɪənsi/ *noun.* **M17.**
[formed as prec.: see **-ENCY.**]
1 Tendency to rebound, recoil, or return to a state. **M17.**
2 Elasticity. **M19.**
3 Power of recovery; resistance to adversity. **M19.**

resilient /rɪˈzɪlɪənt/ *adjective.* **M17.**
[Latin *resilient-* pres. ppl stem of *resilire*: see **RESILE, -ENT.**]
1 Returning to an original position; springing back, recoiling, etc. Also, looking back. **M17.**
2 Elastic; resuming an original shape or position after compression, stretching, etc. **L17.**
3 Of a person: readily recovering from illness, shock, etc.; resistant to setbacks or adversity. **M19.**

> 🕮 **2** *Which?* Resilient plugs are made of rubber . . to take the rougher treatment. **3** F. TOMLIN Although he knew he had cancer, Joad was as mentally resilient as ever.

■ **resiliently** *adverb* **M20.**

resilin /ˈrɛzɪlɪn/ *noun.* **M20.**
[from Latin *resilire* jump back, recoil, **RESILE** + **-IN**[1].]
BIOLOGY. An elastic material formed of cross-linked protein chains, found in the cuticles of many kinds of insect, esp. in the hinges and ligaments of wings.

†**resilition** *noun.* **M17–E18.**
[from **RESILE** *verb* + **-ITION.**]
The action or an act of springing back; recoil, rebound, resilience.

resilium /rɪˈzɪlɪəm/ *noun.* Pl. **-lia** /-lɪə/. **L19.**
[mod. Latin, formed as **RESILIN** + **-IUM.**]
ZOOLOGY. The resilient central part of the hinge of a bivalve shell, which tends to force apart the two valves.

resin /ˈrɛzɪn/ *noun & verb.* **LME.**
[Latin *resina*, medieval Latin *rosinum*, *rosina* cogn. with Greek *rhētinē* resin from a pine. Cf. **ROSIN.**]
▶ **A** *noun.* **1** Any hard, sticky, flammable, freq. aromatic substance containing organic polymers and terpenoids, secreted by various trees and other plants, often extracted by incision esp. from fir and pine, and, unlike a gum, insoluble in water; a kind of this. **LME.**
2 A resinous precipitate obtained by chemical treatment of various natural products. *rare*. **L17.**
3 Any synthetic material resembling a natural resin; now usu., any of a large and varied class of synthetic organic polymers (solid or liquid) that are thermosetting or thermoplastic and are used esp. as the chief ingredients of plastics (more fully ***synthetic resin***). Freq. with other specifying words. **L19.**

Comb.: **resin-bush** = **HARPUISBOS**; **resin canal** an intercellular resin-containing duct found in the wood and leaves of conifers; **resin-weed** = ***rosinweed*** s.v. **ROSIN** *noun*.

▶ **B** *verb trans.* Rub or treat with resin. **M19.**
■ **resiˈnaceous** *adjective* (*rare*) of the nature of or yielding resin; resinous: **M17.** **resined** *adjective* (**a**) treated with resin; (**b**) (of wood) having had the resin extracted: **L19.** **reˈsinic** *adjective* of, belonging to, or derived from resin **L19.** **resiˈniferous** *adjective* yielding or containing resin **L17.** **resiny** *adjective* resinous **L16.**

resinate /ˈrɛzɪneɪt/ *verb trans.* **L19.**
[from **RESIN** *noun* + **-ATE**[3].]
Flavour with resin; impregnate (fabric etc.) with resin.

resinify /ˈrɛzɪnɪfʌɪ/ *verb.* **E19.**
[French *résinifier*, from *résine* formed as prec.: see **-I-, -FY.**]
1 *verb trans.* Change (a substance) into resin. **E19.**
2 *verb intrans.* Become resinous; become a resin. **M19.**
■ **resinifiˈcation** *noun* (**a**) the process of making a substance resinous; the fact of becoming resinous; (**b**) a chemical reaction in which a synthetic resin is formed; conversion into a synthetic resin: **E19.**

resinize /ˈrɛzɪnʌɪz/ *verb trans.* Also **-ise**. **L19.**
[formed as next + **-IZE.**]
Treat with resin. Chiefly as ***resinized*** *ppl adjective.*

resinography /rɛzɪˈnɒgrəfi/ *noun.* **M20.**
[from **RESIN** *noun* + **-OGRAPHY.**]
The study of the structure, form, and properties of synthetic resins.
■ **resinographer** *noun* an expert in resinography **M20.** ˌ**resinoˈgraphic** *adjective* **M20.** ˌ**resinoˈgraphically** *adverb* **M20.**

resinoid /ˈrɛzɪnɔɪd/ *adjective & noun.* **M19.**
[from **RESIN** *noun* + **-OID.**]
▶ **A** *adjective.* Resembling resin. **M19.**
▶ **B** *noun.* A resinous substance; now usu., a synthetic resin; *spec.* one that is thermosetting, or is not permanently soluble and fusible. **L19.**

resinosis /rɛzɪˈnəʊsɪs/ *noun.* **E20.**
[from **RESIN** *noun* + **-OSIS.**]
FORESTRY. In coniferous trees: excessive flow of resin.

resinous /ˈrɛzɪnəs/ *adjective.* **M17.**
[French *résineux* from Latin *resinosus*, from *resina*: see **RESIN, -OUS.**]
▶ **I 1** Of the nature of resin. **M17.**
2 Of a plant, plant tissue, etc.: containing resin. **M17.**
3 Of an odour, lustre, etc.: characteristic of resin. **E19.**
4 Made with resin; having the odour of (esp. burnt) resin. **E19.**

> 🕮 **1** *fig.*: B. GILROY Days when a resinous silence seized the house. **4** DICKENS I can smell the heavy resinous incense as I pass the church.

▶ **II** †**5** *ELECTRICITY.* Designating electricity of the form produced by friction on resin (see **NEGATIVE** *adjective* 7). Opp. ***vitreous***. **M18–L19.**

resipiscence /rɛsɪˈpɪs(ə)ns/ *noun. arch.* **L16.**
[French *résipiscence* or late Latin *resipiscentia*, from Latin *resipiscere* come to oneself again, formed as **RE-** + *sapere* know: see **-ENCE.**]
Repentance for misconduct; recognition of past errors.

resist /rɪˈzɪst/ *verb & noun.* **LME.**
[Old & mod. French *résister* or Latin *resistere*, formed as **RE-** + *sistere* stop, redupl. of *stare* stand.]
▶ **A** *verb.* **1** *verb trans.* Stop or hinder the progress or course of; prevent (a weapon etc.) from penetrating. **LME.** ▸**b** Withstand the action or effect of. **M16.**
2 *verb trans.* Strive against, oppose, refuse to yield to, (a person, illness, influence, hostile action, etc.); refrain from (temptation); refuse to comply with (an order, a law, etc.). **LME.**
3 *verb intrans.* Withstand a person or thing; offer opposition, refuse to yield. Formerly also foll. by *against*, *to*. **LME.**
†**4** *verb intrans.* Stop; rest. **LME–M16.**
†**5** *verb trans.* Prevent (*from*). Only in **16.**
†**6** *verb trans.* Repel, disgust. *rare* (Shakes.). Only in **E17.**

> 🕮 **1** E. F. BENSON The pastry resisted the most determined assaults. **b** A. LOVELL A white soft Rock . . does not long resist the Sea Winds . . that eat it away. **2** T. BARLING He was shot resisting arrest. R. FRASER It was . . very hard to resist Bramwell's charm and brilliance. **cannot resist**, **could not resist**, etc., cannot etc. help (*doing* something); is etc. certain to be attracted by. **3** A. TOFFLER We can resist when the salesman tells us it's time to trade in our automobile.

▶ **B** *noun.* †**1** Resistance. **M16–M17.**
2 A protective coating of a resistant substance, applied esp. to parts of a fabric which are not to take dye, parts of pottery which are not to take glaze or lustre, or to provide protection against the etchant or solvent in photo-engraving, photogravure, or photolithography. **M19.**
2 attrib.: ***resist decoration***, ***resist-dyed***, ***resist pattern***, ***resist varnish***, etc.
■ **resistable** *adjective* (now *rare* or *obsolete*) = **RESISTIBLE** (earlier in **UNRESISTABLE**) **E17.** **resister** *noun* a person who or thing which resists something; *spec.* a member of a resistance movement: **LME.** **resistful** *adjective* = **RESISTIVE** **E17.**

resistance /rɪˈzɪst(ə)ns/ *noun.* **LME.**
[French *résistance* (earlier †*résistence*) from late Latin *resistentia*, from Latin *resistent-* pres. ppl stem of *resistere* **RESIST** *verb*: see **-ANCE.** Cf. **RESISTENCE.**]
1 a The action or an act of resisting, opposing, or withstanding. Foll. by *to*, †*of*. **LME.** ▸**b** Organized covert opposition to an occupying or ruling power; a secret organization resisting authority; *spec.* (usu. **R-**) *the* underground movement formed in France at the beginning of the war of 1939–45 to fight the German occupying forces and the Vichy government. **M20.**
2 a Power or capacity of resisting; ability to withstand something. Freq. with specifying word. **LME.** ▸**b** *PSYCHOANALYSIS.* Opposition, freq. unconscious, to the emergence into consciousness of repressed memories or desires. **E20.** ▸**c** *MEDICINE & BIOLOGY.* Lack of sensitivity to a drug, insecticide, etc., esp. due to continued exposure. **M20.**
3 Opposition of one material thing to another or to a force etc.; *esp.* the opposition offered by a body or fluid to the pressure or movement of another body or fluid. **LME.**
4 a The tendency to slow or hinder the conduction of electricity, magnetism, or heat; *spec.* (a measure of) the degree to which a substance or device slows or hinders the passage of an electric current. **M18.** ▸**b** An electrical component considered with respect to its resistance; *esp.* a resistor. **L19.**

> 🕮 **1a** *Daily News* The hillmen offered a stubborn resistance to the advance. **b** ***resistance fighter***, ***resistance movement***, etc. **2a** P. BOWLES You just happened to get infected because your resistance was low. ***crease resistance***, ***flame resistance***, etc. **c** *Which?* A strain of typhoid that had developed a resistance to chloramphenicol. **3** *Discovery* To diminish air-resistance by . . streamlining. A. MASON The knife had encountered a strange resistance, a substance hard as cedar.

Phrases: **line of least resistance** (**a**) the shortest distance between a buried explosive charge and the surface of the ground; (**b**) *fig.* the easiest method or course of action. ***multiple resistance***: see **MULTIPLE** *adjective*. ***negative resistance***: see **NEGATIVE** *adjective*. ***passive resistance***: see **PASSIVE** *adjective*. **piece of resistance** = **PIÈCE DE RÉSISTANCE.** **specific resistance** = **RESISTIVITY.** ***thermal resistance***: see **THERMAL** *adjective*.

Comb.: **resistance thermometer** an instrument used to measure a change in temperature by its effect on the electrical resistance of a metallic (usu. platinum) wire; **resistance welding** a method of welding in which the heat to cause fusion of the metals is produced by passing an electric current across the contact between two surfaces held together by mechanical pressure.
■ **resistanceless** *adjective* marked by a total lack of (esp. electrical) resistance **M20.**

resistant /rɪˈzɪst(ə)nt/ *adjective & noun.* **L15.**
[French *résistant* pres. pple of *résister* **RESIST** *verb*: see **-ANT**[1].]
▶ **A** *adjective.* That makes resistance or offers opposition; that is not overcome by a disease or drug. **L15.**

> 🕮 R. D. LAING Those with the most unacceptable beliefs are often most resistant to attempts to change them. M. STOTT Nearly all modern furniture is heat- and stain-resistant.

▶ **B** *noun.* A person who or thing which resists; *spec.* a member of a resistance movement. **E17.**
■ **resistantly** *adverb* **E17.**

résistant /rezistɑ̃/ *noun.* Pl. pronounced same. **M20.**
[French.]
A member of the French Resistance movement in the war of 1939–45.

†**resistence** *noun.* **LME–E18.**
[Old French *résistence*: see **RESISTANCE, -ENCE.**]
= **RESISTANCE.**
¶ In common use to *c* 1530.

resistent /rɪˈzɪst(ə)nt/ *adjective & noun.* **LME.**
[Latin *resistent-*, *ens* pres. pple of *resistere* **RESIST** *verb*: see **-ENT.**]
▶ **A** *adjective.* = **RESISTANT** *adjective*. **LME.**
▶†**B** *noun.* = **RESISTANT** *noun*. **E17–M17.**

resistentialism /rɛzɪˈstɛnʃ(ə)lɪz(ə)m/ *noun.* **M20.**
[Joc. blend of Latin *res* thing(s) + French *résister* **RESIST** *verb* with **EXISTENTIALISM.**]
A mock philosophy maintaining that inanimate objects are hostile to humans or seek to thwart human endeavours.
■ **resistentialist** *noun & adjective* (**a**) *noun* an adherent of the theory of resistentialism; (**b**) *adjective* of or pertaining to resistentialism: **M20.**

resistible /rɪˈzɪstəb(ə)l/ *adjective.* **M17.**
[from **RESIST** *verb* + **-IBLE.**]
Able to be resisted; to which opposition can be offered.

New Yorker Conversation . . about how resistible women seemed to be finding fashion these days.

¶ Earlier in IRRESISTIBLE, UNRESISTIBLE.
■ **resisti'bility** *noun* (*a*) the quality of being resistible; (*b*) power of offering opposition: E17.

resistive /rɪˈzɪstɪv/ *adjective*. E17.
[Orig. from medieval Latin *resistivus*, later from RESIST *verb*: see -IVE.]
1 Capable of, or liable to offer, resistance. E17.
2 ELECTRICITY. Pertaining to, possessing, or resulting from electrical resistance; *spec.* pertaining to or connected with resistance as a component of impedance (opp. *reactive*). E20.

1 *Nature* How to construct a building . . reasonably resistive to the most serious earthquake anticipated.

■ **resistively** *adverb* L19. **resistiveness** *noun* E19.

resistivity /ˌriːzɪˈstɪvɪti/ *noun*. L19.
[from prec. + -ITY.]
PHYSICS. The specific (electrical or thermal) resistance of a substance, now usu. defined as the resistance of a conductor of unit length and unit cross-sectional area. Also *specific resistivity*.
Comb.: **resistivity surveying** measurement of the current passing between electrodes embedded in the ground at a series of positions over a given area, in order to locate buried structural features by their differing resistivity.

resistless /rɪˈzɪs(t)lɪs/ *adjective*. Now *arch.* & *poet.* L16.
[from RESIST + -LESS.]
1 That cannot be withstood; irresistible. L16.
2 Powerless to resist; unresisting. L16.
■ **resistlessly** *adverb* E18. **resistlessness** *noun* L19.

resistor /rɪˈzɪstə/ *noun*. E20.
[from RESIST *verb* + -OR.]
ELECTRICITY. A passive device of known or variable resistance used to develop a voltage drop across itself or to limit current flow.

resit /*as verb* riːˈsɪt, *as noun* ˈriːsɪt/ *verb* & *noun*. M20.
[from RE- + SIT *verb*.]
► **A** *verb trans.* & *intrans.* Infl. **-tt-**. Pa. t. & pple **-sat** /-ˈsat/. Sit (an examination) again, usu. after failing or in order to improve one's grade. M20.
► **B** *noun*. The action or an instance of resitting an examination; an examination held specifically to enable candidates to resit. M20.

resite /ˈrɛzʌɪt/ *noun*. E20.
[from RESIN *noun* + -ITE[1].]
CHEMISTRY. A hard insoluble infusible plastic that is the final product of a phenol-aldehyde copolymerization.

re-site /riːˈsʌɪt/ *verb trans*. M20.
[from RE- + SITE *verb*.]
Place on another site; relocate.

resitol /ˈrɛzɪtɒl/ *noun*. E20.
[from RESITE + -OL.]
CHEMISTRY. A rubbery insoluble resin produced as an intermediate stage between resol and resite.

resitting /riːˈsɪtɪŋ/ *noun*. M17.
[from RE- + SITTING *noun*.]
1 A second sitting. M17.
2 The action of RESIT *verb*; an instance of this. *rare*. M20.

resize /riːˈsʌɪz/ *verb trans.* Orig. *US*. E20.
[from RE- + SIZE *verb*[1].]
Alter the size of, make larger or smaller; *spec.* (*a*) SHOOTING restore (a misshapen cartridge case) to a correct shape; (*b*) COMMERCE increase or (esp.) reduce the size of (a business operation or company) to accommodate changing requirements.
■ **resizable** *adjective* (esp. of a window on a computer screen) able to be resized L20.

resmethrin /ˈrɛzmɪθrɪn/ *noun*. L20.
[from unkn. 1st elem. + *-ethrin* after *pyrethrin*.]
A synthetic pyrethroid used in insecticidal sprays.

resol /ˈrɛzɒl/ *noun*. Also **-ole** /-əʊl/. E20.
[from RESIN *noun* + -OL.]
CHEMISTRY. An alcohol-soluble, usu. fluid resin formed as the first stage in a phenol-aldehyde copolymerization.

resold *verb pa. t.* & *pple* of RESELL *verb*.

resoluble /rɪˈzɒljʊb(ə)l/ *adjective*. E17.
[French *résoluble* or late Latin *resolubilis*, formed as RE- + SOLUBLE.]
Able to be resolved; resolvable.

Times I do not believe that the problems . . are resoluble by intellectual horsepower.

■ **resolu'bility** *noun* M19.

re-soluble /riːˈsɒljʊb(ə)l/ *adjective*. LME.
[from RE- + SOLUBLE.]
Able to be dissolved again.

†**resolute** *noun*. M16.
[Use as noun of next.]
1 A payment. M16–E17.
2 A resolute or determined person. L16–E19.

resolute /ˈrɛzəluːt/ *adjective*. LME.
[Latin *resolutus* pa. pple of *resolvere* RESOLVE *verb*.]
†**1** Dissolved. Also, friable. *rare*. Only in LME.
†**2 a** Morally lax, dissolute. *rare*. Only in LME. ▸**b** Weak, infirm. *rare*. Only in E17.
†**3** Of a rent: paid, rendered. LME–L17.
†**4** Determinate, positive, absolute, final. E16–M17.
5 Of a person, a person's mind, etc.: determined, purposeful, steadfast. E16.
†**6** Of a person: decided with regard to matters open to doubt. *rare*. M16–M17.
7 Of an action etc.: characterized by constancy or firmness of purpose. E17.

4 SIR T. MORE If he woulde geue them a resolute aunswere to the contrarye. **5** C. CHAPLIN I tried to scare her into backing out, but she was resolute. A. GRAY His face took on a resolute, slightly wolfish look. **7** J. BUCHAN His duty . . desperate defence conducted with a resolute ferocity.

■ **resolutely** *adverb* M16. **resoluteness** *noun* L16.

resolute /ˈrɛzəluːt/ *verb*. M16.
[Orig. from Latin *resolut-* pa. ppl stem of *resolvere* RESOLVE *verb*; in mod. use back-form. from next.]
†**1** *verb refl.* Decide *upon* a person. *rare*. Only in M16.
†**2** *verb trans.* Dissolve *into* something. *rare*. Only in E18.
3 *verb intrans.* Make or pass a resolution or resolutions. *US*. M19.

3 J. BRYCE The discontented . . flocked . . to 'resolute' against the rich.

resolution /rɛzəˈluːʃ(ə)n/ *noun*. LME.
[Latin *resolutio(n-)*, from *resolut-*: see prec., -ION.]
► **I** †**1** Death; a state of dissolution or decay. *rare*. LME–L16.
2 The process of reducing or separating a material object into or *into* constituent parts; a result of this; CHEMISTRY separation of a compound or mixture into or *into* component substances, elements, optical isomers, etc. Also, conversion *into* a different form or substance. LME. ▸**b** CHEMISTRY. Liquefaction. Long *rare*. M17. ▸**c** Orig. *spec.* the effect of an optical instrument (esp. an astronomical telescope) in making separate parts of an object distinguishable by the eye. Now also, the act, process, or capability of making distinguishable any objects or parts of an object, closely adjacent images, measurements, etc. in space or time; the smallest quantity which is measurable by such a process. M19.
3 MEDICINE. Orig., dissolution or dispersal of humours or accumulated matter in or from the body; *occas.* suppuration. Now *spec.*, disappearance of a growth or inflammation without suppuration or permanent tissue damage. LME.
4 Relaxation or weakening of an organ or part of the body. Now *rare* or *obsolete*. M16.
► **II 5 a** The process of reducing a non-material object into a simpler form or forms, or of converting it into or *into* some other thing or form; an instance of this. LME. ▸**b** PROSODY. The substitution of two short syllables for a long one. L19.
†**6** MATH. & LOGIC. The examination of the truth or falsehood of a proposition by moving from a particular known truth to a more general principle. M16–E18.
7 MUSIC. †**a** The separation of the parts of a canon so that they are given on separate staves instead of being written on a single stave. M16–E19. ▸**b** The action or process of causing discord to pass into concord; an instance of this. E18.
8 MECHANICS. The separation of a force into two or more forces of which it is the resultant. L18.

5a B. JOWETT The resolution of justice into two unconnected precepts.

► **III 9** Determination; firmness or steadfastness of purpose; a resolute or unyielding temper. LME.
10 The action or an act of resolving or making up one's mind; anything resolved on; a positive intention. M16.
†**11** The removal of doubt from a person's mind; confidence; certainty. *rare*. L16–M17.

9 C. C. TRENCH He lacked the resolution . . to press on to the enemy's destruction. **10** E. SIMPSON A list of resolutions for the New Year.

► **IV 12** The answering of a question; the solving *of* doubt or a problem; the settlement *of* a dispute. Formerly also, an explanation, a solution; the supplying *of* an answer. L15.
13 A formal decision or expression of opinion by a legislative assembly, committee, public meeting, etc.; a formulation of this. Also *gen.* (now *rare*), a statement; a decision, a verdict. M16.
†**14** An explanatory account *of* something. L16–M17.

12 N. SMITH This type of story . . from its opening to its crisis and resolution. **13** J. F. KENNEDY The . . committee . . adopted a resolution which deplored Germany's withdrawal. *Oxford Journal of Legal Studies* Considerations too complex for judicial resolution.

■ **resolutioner** *noun* (*a*) *Hist.* (**R-**) a Scottish supporter of the resolutions passed in 1650 for rehabilitating those who had not participated in the struggle against Cromwell; (*b*) *gen.* a person who formulates or supports a resolution: M17. **resolutionist** *noun* a resolutioner M19.

re-solution /riːsəˈluːʃ(ə)n/ *noun*. E19.
[from RE- + SOLUTION.]
Return to a state or condition of solution.

resolutive /ˈrɛzəluːtɪv/ *adjective* & *noun*. LME.
[medieval Latin *resolutivus*, from Latin *resolu-*: see RESOLUTE *verb*, -IVE.]
► **A** *adjective*. **1** Having the power to dissolve. LME.
2 LAW. Serving to dispel or terminate an obligation, right, etc. Chiefly in *resolutive clause*, *resolutive condition* below. E17.
2 resolutive clause SCOTS LAW a clause in an agreement whereby the agreement becomes void if the conditions specified are contravened. **resolutive condition** LAW a condition whose fulfilment teminates a contract etc.
► **B** *noun*. A medical application or drug which resolves inflammation or swelling. LME.

resolutory /rɛzəˈluːt(ə)ri/ *adjective*. *rare*. M16.
[from late Latin *resolutorius*, formed as prec.; in sense 2 from prec. with irreg. substitution of suffix: see -ORY[2].]
†**1** Explanatory, enlightening. M16–M17.
2 LAW. Of a condition: = RESOLUTIVE 2. E19.

resolvable /rɪˈzɒlvəb(ə)l/ *adjective*. M17.
[from RESOLVE *verb* + -ABLE.]
Able to be resolved.

L. HUDSON Rilke's sonnet, in which ambiguities are posed . . but are not resolvable.

¶ Earlier in UNRESOLVABLE.
■ **resolva'bility** *noun* M19.

resolve /rɪˈzɒlv/ *noun*. L16.
[from the verb.]
1 A firm intention, a resolution. L16.
2 Firmness or steadfastness of purpose. L16.
†**3** An answer, a solution. Only in 17.
4 A formal resolution of a legislative body, meeting, etc. Now *US*. M17.

1 V. BRITTAIN I made a mental resolve never again to appear officially dressed as a V.A.D. **2** M. FRAYN To advise her and strengthen her resolve.

resolve /rɪˈzɒlv/ *verb*. LME.
[Latin *resolvere*, formed as RE- + *solvere* loosen, dissolve.]
► **I** *verb trans.* **1** Melt, dissolve. *obsolete* exc. *dial.* LME.
2 a Disintegrate, decompose; separate (a thing) into constituent parts or elements. Now *rare* or *obsolete*. LME. ▸†**b** MATH. Solve (an equation). M–L18. ▸**c** PHYSICS. Analyse (a force or velocity) into components acting in particular directions. L18. ▸**d** Orig. *spec.*, perceive or reveal (a nebula) as a cluster of distinct stars. Now more widely, distinguish the parts of components of (an object, a group of objects, events, etc. closely adjacent in space or time); separately distinguish (peaks in a graph, spectrum, etc.). Cf. RESOLUTION 2C. L18.
3 MEDICINE. Soften (a hard growth); disperse or dissipate (accumulated matter, a swelling, etc.); remove (inflammation) by resolution. Formerly also, dissipate or allay (pain etc.). LME.
†**4** Relax (a limb etc.); weaken. Formerly also, cause to become lax or frivolous in behaviour. LME–E18.
5 †**a** Cause (strife) to cease. Only in E16. ▸**b** MUSIC. Cause (a discord) to pass into a concord. E18.

1 R. EDEN Cleopatra resolved a pearle in vineger & drunke it. **2a** H. M. MANCHESTER His bodie by death becomes putrid, resolved and crumbled to nothing.
d resolving power (a measure of) the ability of an optical, photographic, spectrometric, or analogous system to separate or distinguish closely adjacent images, peaks, etc.

► **II** *verb trans.* **6 a** Decompose or dissolve (a thing) *into* another form; reduce (a thing) *into* separate parts. LME. ▸**b** Convert or alter (a thing) *into* another thing or form. Also (now *rare*) foll. by *to*. M16.
7 a Reduce (a subject, statement, etc.) by mental analysis *into* a more elementary form, a set of principles, etc. LME. ▸†**b** Convert (a quantity) *into* another denomination. L16–L17.
8 *refl.* **a** Of a thing: dissolve, separate, or change (itself) *into* another (freq. less complex) form. E17. ▸**b** Of a legislative assembly, meeting, etc.: convert (itself) *into* a committee. E18.

6a *Spectator* A . . campaign intended . . to resolve the German Empire back again into its elements. **b** DICKENS The spectral figure . . seemed all resolved into a ghastly stare. **7a** R. H. TAWNEY The synthesis is resolved into its elements—politics, business, and spiritual exercises. **8a** E. FEINSTEIN The civil war was beginning to resolve itself into a Bolshevik victory.

► **III** *verb trans.* **9 a** Answer (a question, argument, etc.); solve (a problem). LME. ▸**b** Explain; make clear. L16.
10 a Determine or decide on (a course of action etc.). Freq. foll. by obj. clause E16. ▸**b** Of a legislative assembly,

meeting, etc.: adopt (a decision etc.) formally, pass (a resolution). Chiefly foll. by obj. clause. **M16.**

11 *refl.* **†a** Make up one's mind; *rare* free (oneself) *of* a doubt. **E16–E17.** ▸**b** Assure or satisfy (oneself) on a question, matter, etc. **L16.**

†12 Untie, loosen. *rare.* **M16–E17.**

†13 Free (a person) from doubt or perplexity; bring to a clear understanding *of* a doubtful point, matter, etc. Also foll. by subord. clause (passing into sense 14a). **M16–M18.**

†14 a Inform, tell (a person) *of* a thing. Also foll. by subord. clause. Freq. in *imper.* **M16–L17.** ▸**b** Tell (a person) in answer to a question. Usu. in *imper.* **E17–E19.**

15 Remove, dispel (a doubt, difficulty, etc.). Formerly also (*rare*), dispel (fear). **L16.**

16 Decide, determine (a doubtful point); settle (something) in one's mind. Freq. foll. by subord. clause expr. the decision reached. **L16.**

†17 Convince (a person) *of* something. Formerly also, assure (a person) *that.* **L16–M18.**

18 †a Advise (a person) on a decision. Only in **M17.** ▸**b** Of circumstances etc.: cause (a person) to decide *on* a course of action. Also foll. by *to do.* **M19.**

> 📖 **9a** SHAKES. *Tit. A.* Resolve me this: Was it well done . . To slay his daughter? A. S. BYATT He's not resolved the old . . problem. **10a** E. M. FORSTER She resolved that she would . . be at home to no one. **13** G. WASHINGTON I wish your Honor would resolve me, whether the militia . . must be supplied out of the public stocks. **14a** JONSON Resolue mee, why giue you that heauenly prayse, to this earthly banquet? **b** SIR W. SCOTT Resolve me . . , hast thou never practised such a pastime? **15** E. HEATH Going to meet . . to try to resolve their differences. **16** M. PUZO It was the last chance to resolve an affair without bloodshed. **18b** W. C. RUSSELL This marriage resolved Lord and Lady C . . . to send their son abroad.

▸ **IV** *verb intrans.* **†19** Of a river: have its source. *rare.* Only in **LME.**

20 a Become liquid, dissolve. Now *rare* or *obsolete.* **LME.** ▸**b** Undergo separation into constituent parts or elements; pass *into*, return or change *to*, another form. **LME.** ▸**c** *MEDICINE.* Undergo resolution. **E19.** ▸**d** *LAW.* Lapse; become void. **M19.** ▸**e** *MUSIC.* Be changed from discord to concord. **L19.**

21 a Make up one's mind; take a firm decision. Freq. foll. by *to do, on, upon.* **L16.** ▸**†b** Determine to set out *for* a place. **L16–M18.**

†22 a Be satisfied or convinced. **L16–M17.** ▸**b** Consult, take counsel. **L16–E18.**

> 📖 **20a** JONSON May my brain Resolve to water. **b** C. BRONTË The roof resolved to clouds. **21a** W. TREVOR He resolved to become a new man. E. JOHNSON Charles had resolved upon and taken a bold step. **b** SHAKES. *2 Hen. IV* I will resolve for Scotland. **22a** H. HAMMOND I have allwayes . . resolved of the truth of it. **b** DEFOE We will resolve further.

resolved /rɪˈzɒlvd/ *adjective.* **L15.**
[from prec. + -ED[1].]

1 †a Of the mind etc.: freed from doubt or uncertainty; fixed, settled. **L15–M17.** ▸**b** Of an action, state of mind, etc.: fully determined on, deliberate. **L16.**

2 Of a person: determined, decided. **E16.**

3 Separated, broken up, analysed. **M16.**

†4 Convinced, satisfied. **L16–E18.**

5 Of a person, the mind, etc.: characterized by determination or firmness of purpose; resolute. **L16.** ▸**†b** Confirmed; openly or sincerely adhering to a party, religious belief, etc. **E17–M18.**

†6 Melted, dissolved. **L16–M17.**

†7 Of a limb or part of the body: soft, relaxed. **L16–M17.**

■ **resolvedly** /-vɪdli/ *adverb* in a determined manner; resolutely: **L16.** **resolvedness** /-vɪdnɪs/ *noun* **E17.**

resolvent /rɪˈzɒlv(ə)nt/ *adjective & noun.* **L17.**
[Latin *resolvent-* pres. ppl stem of *resolvere* RESOLVE *verb*: see -ENT.]

▸ **A** *adjective.* **1** Chiefly *MEDICINE.* Able to cause resolution. Also foll. by *of.* **L17.**

2 Of a proposition: only asserting that which is already included in the conception of the subject. **M19.**

3 *MATH.* Designating an equation, function, expression, etc., which is introduced in order to reach or complete a solution. **M19.**

▸ **B** *noun.* **1** *MEDICINE.* A medicine applied to reduce swelling. **L17.**

2 A solvent. Now *rare.* **E18.**

3 A means of removing a difficulty, settling a problem, etc. **M19.**

4 *MATH.* A resolvent equation, function, etc. **M19.**

> 📖 **3** R. G. WHITE A coin which would serve as a common resolvent of all accounts.

resolver /rɪˈzɒlvə/ *noun.* **LME.**
[from RESOLVE *verb* + -ER[1].]

†1 A resolvent substance. **LME–M18.**

2 A person who or thing which answers a question, solves a doubt or difficulty, etc. **E17.**

3 A person who makes a resolve; a person who supports a resolution. **L17.**

4 *ELECTRICITY.* An electronic device which resolves an input signal into components. **M20.**

resolvible /rɪˈzɒlvɪb(ə)l/ *adjective.* **L17.**
[formed as prec. + -IBLE.]
= RESOLVABLE.

resonance /ˈrɛz(ə)nəns/ *noun.* **LME.**
[French †*reson(n)ance* (mod. *résonance*) from Latin *resonantia* echo, from *resonant-*: see next, -ANCE.]

1 a The reinforcement or prolongation of sound by reflection, as from the walls of a hollow space, or by the synchronous vibration of a neighbouring object; a sound so prolonged, a resonant sound. **LME.** ▸**b** The property of an object of giving rise to this. **M17.** ▸**c** The amplification of the sound of the voice by the bones and cavities of the head and chest. Also *MEDICINE*, the sound produced by tapping parts of the body, used as an aid to diagnosis. **E19.** ▸**d** *MECHANICS.* A condition in which an object or system is subjected to an oscillating force having a frequency at or close to that of a natural vibration of the object or system; the resulting amplification of the natural vibration. **L19.** ▸**e** *PHYSICS* etc. A condition in which a particle is subjected to an oscillating influence (as an electromagnetic field or another particle) of such a frequency that energy transfer occurs or reaches a maximum; an instance of this. **L19.** ▸**f** *ELECTRICITY.* The condition in which a circuit or device produces the largest possible response to an applied oscillating signal, esp. when its inductive and its capacitative reactances are balanced. **L19.** ▸**g** *ASTRONOMY.* The occurrence of a simple ratio between the periods of revolution of two bodies about a single primary. **E20.** ▸**h** *CHEMISTRY.* = MESOMERISM. **E20.** ▸**i** *PHYSICS & CHEMISTRY.* The transition of a particle possessing a magnetic moment between different quantum states in the presence of a magnetic field and electromagnetic radiation of an appropriate frequency; a spectroscopic technique in which such phenomena are observed. **M20.** ▸**j** *NUCLEAR PHYSICS.* A short-lived particle or excited state of a particle, manifested as an increased probability of capture, excitation, etc. at certain defined energies. **M20.**

2 *fig.* **a** A response in parallel or sympathy; a shared feeling or sense; an allusion, connotation, or feature reminiscent of another person or thing, an overtone in thought, art, language, etc. **E17.** ▸**b** The enhancement or enrichment of a colour in juxtaposition to a contrasting colour or colours. **M20.**

> 📖 **1a** H. ALLEN The last prolonged resonance of the bell . . died away. **b** Y. MENUHIN The resonance of those vaulting walls . . aided the single violin. **d** *Encycl. Brit.* Mechanical resonance . . built up to such large proportions as to be destructive, as in . . the Tacoma Narrows Bridge. **2a** F. KAPLAN In the portraits of the young women . . there are resonances of Georgina. **b** *Burlington Magazine* He could evoke from his blues and crimsons their fullest . . resonance.

Phrases: ***electron spin resonance***: see ELECTRON *noun*[2]. ***morphic resonance***: see MORPHIC 1. ***nuclear magnetic resonance***: see NUCLEAR *adjective*. ***tympanitic resonance***: see TYMPANITIC 1.

Comb.: **resonance absorption** *NUCLEAR PHYSICS* absorption of energy or of a particle under conditions of resonance; *spec.* resonance capture; **resonance capture** *NUCLEAR PHYSICS* absorption of a particle by an atomic nucleus which occurs only for certain well-defined values of particle energy; **resonance chamber** = RESONATOR 2; **resonance energy** (*a*) an energy value at which resonance occurs; (*b*) *CHEMISTRY* the extent of stabilization of a molecular structure attributed to mesomerism; **resonance fluorescence**: in which the light emitted has the same wavelength as that which excites the emission; **resonance hybrid** *CHEMISTRY* a molecular structure which is a combination of a number of mesomeric forms; **resonance radiation** (the radiation emitted in) resonance fluorescence; **resonance scattering** *NUCLEAR PHYSICS* elastic scattering of a particle by an atomic nucleus at an energy of the incident particle for which the scattering cross-section is large compared with that for adjacent energy values (cf. ***potential scattering*** s.v. POTENTIAL *noun*); **resonance stabilization** *CHEMISTRY* = ***resonance energy*** (b) above.

resonant /ˈrɛz(ə)nənt/ *adjective & noun.* **L16.**
[Old & mod. French *résonnant* or Latin *resonant-* pres. ppl stem of *resonare*: see RESOUND *verb*, -ANT[1].]

▸ **A** *adjective.* **1 a** Of a sound: echoing, resounding; continuing to sound or ring. **L16.** ▸**b** *PHONETICS.* Of a consonant: liquid, nasal. **M20.**

2 a Of a body, room, etc.: causing reinforcement or prolongation of sound, esp. by synchronous vibration. **L16.** ▸**b** Of a colour: enhancing or enriching another colour or colours by contrast. **L19.**

3 Of a place: echoing or resounding *with* something. **E19.**

4 *SCIENCE.* Pertaining to, exhibiting, or bringing about resonance in a circuit, atom, etc. **L19.**

> 📖 **1a** A. PRYCE-JONES His voice was dark and resonant. **2a** J. TYNDALL Upon their resonant cases, . . sounding the same musical note. **3** DISRAELI Resonant with the fall of statued fountains.

Special collocations: **resonant cavity** = RESONATOR 3b. **resonant frequency** a frequency at which resonance (of any kind) takes place. **resonant scattering** *NUCLEAR PHYSICS* = ***resonance scattering*** s.v. RESONANCE.

▸ **B** *noun. PHONETICS.* A liquid or nasal consonant. **L19.**

■ **resonantly** *adverb* **L17.**

resonate /ˈrɛz(ə)neɪt/ *verb.* **L19.**
[Latin *resonat-* pa. ppl stem of *resonare*: see RESOUND *verb*, -ATE[3].]

1 *verb intrans.* Produce or manifest resonance; resound. **L19.** ▸**b** *spec.* in *CHEMISTRY.* Exhibit mesomerism (cf. RESONANCE 1h). Foll. by *among* or *between* different hypothetical structures. **M20.**

2 *verb trans.* Act as a resonator for; amplify (a sound etc.) by resonance. **E20.**

> 📖 **1** *fig.*: L. GORDON A letter that resonates with personal implications.

■ **resonatory** *adjective* (*rare*) producing resonance **L19.**

resonator /ˈrɛz(ə)neɪtə/ *noun.* **M19.**
[from prec. + -OR.]

1 *ACOUSTICS.* A device responding to a specific vibration frequency, and used for detecting it when it occurs in combination with other sounds. **M19.**

2 A structure or device which reinforces or amplifies sound by resonance, *esp.* an acoustical chamber of a musical instrument, such as the hollow body of a stringed instrument. **L19.**

3 *ELECTRICITY.* **a** A device which displays electrical resonance, *esp.* one used for the detection of radio waves. **L19.** ▸**b** A hollow enclosure with conducting walls capable of containing electromagnetic fields having particular frequencies of oscillation, and exchanging electrical energy with them, esp. as used to detect or amplify microwaves. Also ***cavity resonator.*** **M20.**

4 An object or system which resonates, in any other sense. **L19.**

> 📖 **4** *attrib.*: A. KOESTLER The theory of memory traces as selective resonator systems.

resorb /rɪˈsɔːb/ *verb trans.* **M17.**
[Latin *resorbere*, formed as RE- + *sorbere* drink in.]
Absorb again, reabsorb; *esp.* in *PHYSIOLOGY*, absorb into the circulation (material already in the body, esp. that has been incorporated into the tissue).

> 📖 J. S. MARSHALL Bone is resorbed through the action of the osteoclast cells. *Nature* Because the bubbles could not be lost by migration, they must have been resorbed.

■ **resorbence** *noun* **L19.** **resorbent** *adjective* **L18.**

resorcin /rɪˈzɔːsɪn/ *noun.* Also **†-ine.** **M19.**
[from RES(IN *noun* + ORCIN.]
CHEMISTRY. = next. Freq. *attrib.*, esp. in names of dyes.

resorcinol /rɪˈzɔːsɪnɒl/ *noun.* **L19.**
[from prec. + -OL.]
CHEMISTRY. A crystalline phenol formerly obtained from galbanum and other resins but now made synthetically, and used in the manufacture of dyes, resins, etc., and in lotions and ointments to promote exfoliation of the skin; 1,3-dihydroxybenzene, $C_6H_4(OH)_2$.

■ **resorˈcylic** *adjective* pertaining to or derived from resorcinol **L19.**

resorption /rɪˈzɔːpʃ(ə)n, -ˈsɔːp-/ *noun.* **E19.**
[from RESORB after *absorb, absorption.*]
Chiefly *PHYSIOLOGY.* The fact or process of reabsorption, esp. of an organ or tissue, or of a material previously excreted. Cf. RESORB *verb.*

■ **resorptive** *adjective* **L19.**

resort /rɪˈzɔːt/ *noun.* **LME.**
[Old French, from *resortir*: see next.]

▸ **I 1** A thing to which one has recourse; the use of something as an aid, to give assistance, or as a means to an end. **LME.**

2 A tendency to frequent or be frequented. Chiefly in ***make resort of***, ***make resort to*** and ***of resort***, ***of great resort***, ***of public resort*** below. Now *rare.* **LME.**

†3 A gathering, a throng, a crowd. Formerly also, the coming together of people. **LME–E19.**

4 †a The right or privilege of having a final decision or appeal vested in one. **L15–E16.** ▸**b** Recourse *to* a person, expedient, etc., for aid, assistance, or the attainment of some end. **L15.**

†5 A person's staying at or frequenting of a place. **M16–L17.**

6 A place frequented or visited esp. for holidays, recreation, or a specific feature. Now freq. with specifying word. **M18.**

> 📖 **1** G. A. BIRMINGHAM A letter to *The Times*, the usual resort of an Englishman with a grievance. **2** H. H. WILSON An . . unregulated resort of persons to India for religious purposes. **3** H. BROOKE A promiscuous resort of swords-men. **4b** *Argosy* The matter was patched up . . without resort to the police. **5** MILTON Nor from the Heav'n of Heav'ns Hath he excluded my resort sometimes. **6** ***health resort***, ***holiday resort***, ***seaside resort***, etc.

▸**† II 7** A channel or arm of the sea. *rare.* Only in **L15.**

8 *Music.* A concourse of musical sounds. *rare.* Only in E16.
9 [French *ressort.*] A mechanical spring. L16–E18.
Phrases: **as a last resort**, **in the last resort** [after French *en dernier ressort*] orig., as a judge or court from which no appeal is possible; now, as a final expedient, when all else has failed, ultimately. LENDER *of last resort.* †**make resort of**, †**make resort to** visit or associate with habitually. **of resort**, **of great resort**, **of public resort**, etc., (of a place) much frequented, publicly accessible.

resort /rɪˈzɔːt/ *verb.* LME.
[Old French *resortir* (mod. *ressortir*), from *re-* RE- + *sortir* go out.]
†**1** *verb intrans.* Issue or emerge again. *rare.* LME–L15.
†**2** *verb intrans.* Return or revert *to* a former condition, habit, subject, etc.; return *to* a place. LME–M18.
†**3** *verb intrans.* Direct one's attention *to* a subject. LME–L16.
4 *verb intrans.* Go *to* a person for help; refer or turn *to* a book, author, etc., for information or guidance. *obsolete* exc. as passing into sense b. LME. ▸**b** Have recourse *to* something for aid, assistance, or as the means to an end. M17.
5 *verb intrans.* Make one's way, come *to* a person. Formerly also, go *to* a person habitually. LME.
6 *verb intrans.* Go regularly or frequently *to* a place. LME.
7 *verb intrans.* Proceed or *towards* a place; go in response *to* a summons. LME. ▸†**b** Of blood: flow *to* a part of the body. M16–E17.
†**8** *verb intrans.* Stay in a place; have one's abode. LME–L18.
†**9** *verb trans.* Frequent (a place). LME–M18.

> **4b** T. ROETHKE A . . boy who . . resorts to alcohol for peace of mind. **5** W. S. CHURCHILL Many officers . . resorted to him and loudly expressed their resentment. **6** J. T. FOWLER A cave . . whither Irish pilgrims still resort. **7** F. L. OLMSTED He resorted to Italy.

■ **resorter** *noun* (*a*) a person who resorts *to* a place or person; a holiday-maker, a visitor; (*b*) *US* a person running a business in a holiday resort: M16.

re-sort /riːˈsɔːt/ *verb trans.* L19.
[from RE- + SORT *verb.*]
Sort again or differently.

†**resound** *noun.* LME–M19.
[from the verb.]
A re-echoed sound; a resonance.

resound /rɪˈzaʊnd/ *verb.* LME.
[from RE- + SOUND *verb*¹, after Old French *resoner* or Latin *resonare*, formed as RE- + *sonare* sound.]
▶ **I** *verb intrans.* **1** Of a place: ring, re-echo. Freq. foll. by *to*, *with*. LME.
2 a Of a sound: echo, ring. E16. ▸†**b** Answer *to* something. *rare.* M16–M18. ▸**c** (Of a person, a person's reputation, etc.) be much mentioned, be renowned; (of an event etc.) cause a stir. L16.
3 Of a thing: make an echoing sound; continue sounding. M16.

> **1** A. LURIE The house . . resounded with frenzied thumping. **2a** G. SANTAYANA His last words . . resounded through the narrow passage. **c** G. M. TREVELYAN The event resounded through Italy. **3** T. HARDY There resounded from the smithy the ring of a hammer.

▶ **II** *verb trans.* **4** Proclaim or repeat loudly (the praises etc.) *of* a person or thing; celebrate. LME.
5 Repeat or utter (words etc.) in a loud or echoing manner. Now *rare.* E16.
6 a Of a place: re-echo, repeat (a sound) again. L16. ▸†**b** Return (a response or answer) *to* something. *rare.* Only in 17.

> **4** C. MERIVALE Horace resounds the praises of Italy. **5** P. SCHAFF They resound the creed and the doxology. **6a** WORDSWORTH Cliffs, woods and caves, her viewless steps resound.

■ **resounding** *ppl adjective* that resounds or re-echoes; *fig.* decisive, emphatic: LME. **resoundingly** *adverb* E17.

re-sound /riːˈsaʊnd/ *verb intrans.* L19.
[from RE- + SOUND *verb*¹.]
Sound again.

resource /rɪˈsɔːs, rɪˈzɔːs/ *noun & verb.* E17.
[French *ressource*, †*-ourse* use as noun of fem. pa. pple of Old French dial. *resourdre* rise again, recover from Latin *resurgere*: see RESURGE.]
▶ **A** *noun.* **1 a** A means of supplying a deficiency; a stock or reserve which can be drawn on when necessary; *N. Amer.* available assets. Now usu. in *pl.* E17. ▸**b** In *pl.* The collective means possessed by a country for its own support or defence. L18.
2 Possibility of aid or assistance. Chiefly in *without resource. arch.* L17.
3 An action or strategy which may be resorted to in a difficulty or emergency; an expedient, a device. L17.
4 A means of relaxation; a leisure occupation. L18.
5 Capability in devising expedients or in meeting difficulties; practical ingenuity. M19.

> **1a** P. ROAZEN A woman's greatest resource is her . . inner perceptiveness. P. AUSTER We pooled our resources. *resource allocation*, *resource planning*, etc. *human resources*: see HUMAN *adjective*. LEARNING *resource*. **b** *Times* Countries with . . large natural resources. **2** J. S. C. ABBOTT The French army was lost without resource. **3** GEO. ELIOT Flight was his only resource. **one's own resources** one's personal capabilities, ingenuity. **4** L. C. KNIGHTS Her other occupations and resources: visiting . . and small talk. **5** P. G. WODEHOUSE Resource in moments of crisis is largely a matter of preparedness.

Comb.: **resource centre** a library or other centre which houses a collection of resources for educational purposes; such a collection of educational materials; **resource industry** *N. Amer.* an industry, the raw materials of which occur as natural resources; **resource person** (chiefly *N. Amer.*) a person kept in reserve and called upon as necessary to perform a certain task; a person whose function it is to obtain resources.
▶ **B** *verb trans.* Provide or supply (a person etc.) with resources. Chiefly as *resourced ppl adjective.* L20.

> *Times* An inadequately resourced service.

resourceful /rɪˈzɔːsfʊl, -f(ə)l/ *adjective.* M19.
[from prec. + -FUL.]
1 Capable, full of practical ingenuity. M19.
2 Rich in reserves or natural resources. *rare.* L19.

> **1** H. MACMILLAN Resourceful in proposing solutions.

■ **resourcefully** *adverb* L20. **resourcefulness** *noun* M19.

resourceless /rɪˈzɔːslɪs/ *adjective.* L18.
[formed as prec. + -LESS.]
Without resource; lacking resources.
■ **resourcelessness** *noun* E19.

respect /rɪˈspɛkt/ *noun.* LME.
[Old & mod. French, or Latin *respectus*, from *respect-* pa. ppl stem of *respicere* look (back) at, regard, consider, formed as RE- + *specere* look.]
▶ **I 1** Relation, connection, reference, regard. Earliest in *have respect to*; now chiefly in *with respect to*, *in respect to*, & in *in respect of*, *in respect that* below. LME.
2 Attention, heed, consideration. (Foll. by *of*, *to*.) LME.
3 Comparison. Only in *in respect to*, †*in respect of*. Now *rare.* LME.
4 Orig., an aspect of a thing. Later, a particular, a point, a detail, (only after *in*, as *in some respects*, *in this respect*, etc.). LME.
5 Deferential esteem felt or shown towards a person, thing, or quality; a feeling of deferential esteem; the state of being esteemed or honoured. E16. ▸†**b** (High) social status. E–M17.
6 Discrimination, partiality, favour. Foll. by *of*. M16.
7 A relationship *to*, a reference *to*. M16.
8 A significant fact, a motive, a reason, a consideration, an aim. *arch.* M16.
9 In *pl.* Deferential or polite attentions or messages. Now only with *possess.*, chiefly in *give a person's respects to*, *pay one's respects* below. E17.
†**10** In *pl.* (Acts of) consideration of each of a number of things. E–M17.
11 Compliments, good wishes. Chiefly as *interjection*, indicating the speaker's approval. Orig. & chiefly *Black English*. L20.

> **1** C. S. LEWIS Recovery (in respect of one human being) of that vision . . common to all. H. J. EYSENCK Some . . concede the force of this argument with respect to colour. **2** COLERIDGE Have no respect to what nation a man is of. J. H. NEWMAN One ought to have respect to the intention of the party. **3** H. JAMES She had struck him, in respect to the beautiful world, as one of . . the most beautiful things. **4** S. JOHNSON Whatever has various respects, must have various appearances of good and evil. M. LANE In every important respect Fanny was . . an asset. **5** H. BELLOC Stolen . . from St. Giles without respect for the shrine. A. E. STEVENSON A decent respect for the opinions of others. E. L. DOCTOROW He had great respect for her personal courage. **8** R. C. TRENCH Higher respects than those of flesh and blood. **11** *Face* For services to British fashion, this season's . . award winner: Lionel Blair. Respect!

▶†**II 12** A respite. LME–M16.
Phrases: **give a person's respects to** convey a person's polite greetings to (another). **in respect of** as concerns; with reference to. **in respect that** considering that, since, because. **pay one's last respects** show respect towards a dead person by attending the funeral. **pay one's respects** show polite attention or sympathy (*to*) by presenting oneself or by making a call. **with respect**, **with all due respect**: a polite preface to an expression of disagreement with another person's views.
■ **respectless** *adjective* (now *rare*) M16.

respect /rɪˈspɛkt/ *verb.* L15.
[Latin *respect-* (see prec.), or from its frequentative deriv. *respectare.*]
†**1** *verb trans.* Postpone, put off, neglect. L15–E17.
2 *verb trans.* Regard, consider, take into account; pay attention to. Long *rare.* M16.
3 *verb trans.* Be directed to; refer to, relate to; deal with, be concerned with. M16. ▸†**b** Have an effect on. E17–E18.
4 *verb trans.* Treat or regard with deferential esteem, feel or show respect for. M16. ▸†**b** Prize, value, (a thing). L16–M17. ▸**c** Refrain from injuring, harming, insulting, interfering with, or interrupting. E17.
5 a *verb trans.* Front towards, face. Earliest & now only in HERALDRY (of a creature). M16. ▸**b** *verb intrans.* Front, face. Foll. by *to*, *towards*. *rare.* L16.
4 *respect persons*, *respect the person of*: see PERSON *noun*.
■ **respecter** *noun* E17.

respectabilise *verb* var. of RESPECTABILIZE.

respectability /rɪˌspɛktəˈbɪlɪti/ *noun.* L18.
[from RESPECTABLE: see -ABILITY.]
1 The state or quality of being respectable. L18.
2 The class of respectable people. E19.
3 A respectable person; a respectable feature of life or conduct. Now *rare.* M19.

> **1** W. PLOMER A quiet . . place of the utmost respectability. E. BLISHEN It was part of general respectability . . to go to Sunday School. H. LEVENSTEIN Academic respectability was particularly important.

respectabilize /rɪˈspɛktəb(ə)lʌɪz/ *verb trans.* Also **-ise**. M19.
[from next + -IZE.]
Make respectable.

respectable /rɪˈspɛktəb(ə)l/ *adjective & noun.* L16.
[from RESPECT *noun* + -ABLE. Cf. French *respectable.*]
▶ **A** *adjective.* †**1** Deserving notice, observation, or consideration. *rare.* L16–E17.
2 Deserving respect. L16.
3 Of a person: of good or fair social status, having qualities associated with such status; honest and decent in character or conduct; conventional in behaviour and attitudes. M18. ▸**b** Characteristic of or associated with people of such status or character; socially acceptable, conventional. M18. ▸**c** Of decent or presentable appearance. L18.
†**4** Commendatory; creditable; of a good or superior kind. M18–E19.
5 Considerable in number, size, quantity, etc. M18.
6 Of comparative excellence; tolerable, passable, fairly good or competent. L18.

> **2** J. LANGHORNE Thucydides was a great and respectable man. GIBBON Rendered his administration respectable in the eyes of . . his subjects. **3** DAY LEWIS A Welsh pirate who . . became a respectable wine-merchant. D. MACDONALD The young Joyce was considered immoral by respectable Dublin. L. WOOLF No respectable printer would have anything to do with it. **b** J. MARSH The Old Kent Road, although respectable, was not a high-class area. F. KAPLAN He had elevated himself to a respectable position. **c** N. BLAKE He . . puts on more respectable clothes. **5** P. G. WODEHOUSE That extra . . raised his salary to a very respectable figure. **6** N. HAWTHORNE It is at best but a respectable production.

▶ **B** *noun.* A respectable person. E19.
■ **respectably** *adverb* in a respectable manner; to a respectable degree: L18.

respectant /rɪˈspɛkt(ə)nt/ *adjective. rare.* L17.
[from RESPECT *verb* + -ANT¹.]
HERALDRY. Of animals: facing each other.

respectful /rɪˈspɛktfʊl, -f(ə)l/ *adjective.* L16.
[from RESPECT *noun* + -FUL.]
†**1** Mindful, heedful, careful, (*of*). L16–M17.
2 Full of, exhibiting, or marked by respect; deferential. (Foll. by *of*.) L16.
†**3** Deserving or commanding respect. M17–E18.
■ **respectfully** *adverb* L16. **respectfulness** *noun* E17.

respecting /rɪˈspɛktɪŋ/ *preposition.* M18.
[pres. pple of RESPECT *verb.*]
With reference to, with regard to, concerning.

respective /rɪˈspɛktɪv/ *adjective.* LME.
[medieval Latin *respectivus*, formed as RESPECT *verb*: see -IVE. Partly from French *respectif*, *-ive.*]
▶ **I 1** Relative, comparative. Long *rare.* LME. ▸†**b** Having reference *to*, corresponding *to*. L16–L17.
2 Properly pertaining to or connected with each of those in question individually; separate, several, own, particular. Usu. with possess. pronoun or *the*. Cf. earlier RESPECTIVE *adverb*, RESPECTIVELY 2. M17.

> **2** E. A. FREEMAN The respective amounts of truth and falsehood. S. BEDFORD They got engaged. To the . . approval of their . . respective families.

▶ **II** †**3** Attentive, considerate. Foll. by *of*, †*to*. Long *rare.* E16.
4 Marked by care or attention; heedful. Also, discriminating, partial. Long *rare.* L16.
†**5** Respectful, courteous, (*to*, *towards*). L16–L18.
†**6** Deserving respect. L16–M17.
■ †**respectiveness** *noun* L16–E18.

†**respective** *adverb. Scot.* M16–E18.
[Prob. from medieval Latin, abl. of *respectivus* (see prec.), but perh. postpositive use of the adjective.]
Respectively.

respectively /rɪˈspɛktɪvli/ *adverb.* LME.
[from RESPECTIVE *adjective* + -LY[2].]
▶ **I** †**1** Relatively; comparatively. (Foll. by *to*.) LME–M18.
2 Relatively to each of those in question individually; singly, separately; each individually or in turn, and in the order mentioned. Cf. earlier RESPECTIVE *adverb.* E17.

📖 **2** SCOTT FITZGERALD The crowd had split into two sections, following, respectively, the man on a stretcher and the girl. N. MANDELA The last men to be sentenced . . received twelve and seven years respectively.

▶ **II** †**3** Carefully, attentively; with due consideration. M16–L17.
4 Respectfully; deferentially. Now *rare.* L16.

respectuous /rɪˈspɛktjʊəs/ *adjective.* Long *arch. rare.* E17.
[from RESPECT *noun* + -UOUS, after French *respectueux*.]
†**1** Deserving respect. Only in 17.
2 Respectful, deferential. E17.

respirable /ˈrɛsp(ə)rəb(ə)l, rɪˈspʌɪ-/ *adjective.* L18.
[French, or late Latin *respirabilis*, from *respirare*: see RESPIRE, -ABLE.]
1 (Of air, a gas) able to be respired, breathable; (of a particle) able to be breathed in. L18.
2 Capable of respiring. *rare.* E19.
■ **respiraˈbility** *noun* L18.

respirate /ˈrɛspəreɪt/ *verb.* M17.
[Sense 1 from Latin *respirat-* pa. ppl stem of *respirare* RESPIRE; sense 2 back-form. from next: see -ATE[3].]
1 *verb intrans.* Respire, breathe. Chiefly as ***respirating*** *ppl adjective.* M17.
2 *verb trans.* Cause to respire; subject to artificial respiration. M20.

📖 **2** *Nature* The animals were respirated artificially with a Harvard respirator.

respiration /rɛspəˈreɪʃ(ə)n/ *noun.* LME.
[French, or Latin *respiratio(n-)*, from *respirat-*: see prec., -ATION.]
1 The action of breathing, the inspiration and expiration of air. In early use also, the supposed passage of air, vapours, etc. through the skin. LME. ▶**b** BIOLOGY. The process by which an organism absorbs oxygen from air, water, etc. and gives out carbon dioxide. M19. ▶**c** BIOCHEMISTRY & BIOLOGY. The complex biochemical process by which absorbed oxygen is combined with carbon in a cell or organism to form carbon dioxide and generate energy; any metabolic process in which energy is produced, esp. by a transfer of electrons to an external oxidant. M19.
2 A single act of breathing. LME.
†**3** Opportunity for breathing again; a breathing-space; a respite. E17–M18.
Phrases: **aerobic respiration** BIOCHEMISTRY & BIOLOGY: in which the oxidant is free oxygen. **anaerobic respiration** BIOCHEMISTRY & BIOLOGY: in which the oxidant is not free oxygen. ***artificial respiration***: see ARTIFICIAL *adjective* 1. **external respiration** = sense 1b above. **internal respiration** = sense 1c above.

respirator /ˈrɛspəreɪtə/ *noun.* L18.
[from RESPIRE + -ATOR.]
†**1** CHEMISTRY. An apparatus used for testing the composition of exhaled air. Only in L18.
2 A filtering device covering the mouth, or mouth and nose, or incorporated in a mask or helmet, to prevent the inhalation of dust, smoke, or other noxious substances in the air. Formerly also, a small mask of gauze or other material intended to warm inhaled air. M19.
3 MEDICINE. An apparatus for the artificial maintenance of respiration esp. in an unconscious or paralysed person. Also, an oxygen mask. E20.

respiratory /ˈrɛsp(ə)rət(ə)ri, rɪˈspʌɪ-, rɪˈspɪ-/ *adjective.* L18.
[mod. Latin *respiratorius*, from Latin *respirat-* (see RESPIRATE), or from French *respiratoire*: see -ORY[2].]
Of, pertaining to, affecting, or serving for respiration.
respiratory distress syndrome = HYALINE ***membrane disease***. **respiratory pigment** a protein with a pigmented prosthetic group in its molecule, involved in the transfer of oxygen or electrons in organisms. **respiratory quotient** PHYSIOLOGY the ratio of the volume of carbon dioxide evolved to that of oxygen consumed. **respiratory syncytial virus** a paramyxovirus which causes disease of the respiratory tract. **respiratory tract** the passage of the mouth, nose, throat, and lungs, through which air passes in respiration. ***respiratory tree***: see TREE *noun* 7(c). ***respiratory tuft***: see TUFT *noun* 1a.

respire /rɪˈspʌɪə/ *verb.* LME.
[Old & mod. French *respirer* or Latin *respirare*, formed as RE- + *spirare* breathe.]
▶ **I** *verb intrans.* **1** Breathe; inhale and exhale air. LME. ▶**b** Carry out or exhibit the biochemical processes of respiration. E20.
2 Breathe again; recover breath; get rest, enjoy a respite; recover hope, courage, or strength. LME.
†**3 a** Of wind: blow. *rare.* LME–M18. ▶**b** Of smell or vapour: be given off, exhale. LME–E16.
▶ **II** *verb trans.* **4** Breathe; inhale and exhale (air etc.). LME.
5 Give off, exhale (an odour etc.). L16.

respirometer /rɛspɪˈrɒmɪtə/ *noun.* L19.
[from RESPIRATION + -OMETER.]
1 MEDICINE. A spirometer. L19.
2 PHYSIOLOGY. A device which measures the rate of consumption of oxygen by a living or organic system. E20.
■ **respiroˈmetric** *adjective* M20. **respirometry** *noun* the measurement of rates of oxygen consumption M20.

respite /ˈrɛspʌɪt, -spɪt/ *noun.* ME.
[Old French *respit* (mod. *répit*) from Latin *respectus* RESPECT *noun*.]
1 A delay, or extension of time, asked or granted for some reason (orig. for further consideration of a matter); *spec.* a delay granted in the carrying out of a death sentence, a reprieve. ME.
2 (A period of) rest or relief from labour, suffering, war, responsibility, etc.; an interval of rest. (Foll. by *from*.) ME.
†**3** Delay in action. LME–L16.
†**4** Leisure; opportunity for action. E16–E17.

📖 **2** N. MONSARRAT A short respite in the bombing. G. DALY A respite from guilt.

Comb.: **respite care** temporary institutional care of a dependent elderly, ill, or handicapped person, granting a respite to the usual carer(s).

respite /ˈrɛspʌɪt, -spɪt/ *verb.* ME.
[Old French *respiter* from Latin *respectare*: see RESPECT *verb*.]
1 *verb trans.* Grant a delay or extension of time to; *spec.* reprieve from death or execution. ME. ▶†**b** Save or prolong (a life). L15–E17.
2 *verb trans.* Delay, postpone; *spec.* postpone the execution or exaction of (a sentence, punishment, obligation, etc.). LME. ▶†**b** Allow to remain unpaid for a time. M17–M18.
3 *verb trans.* Orig., cease from, give up; suspend. Now, give temporary relief from. LME.
4 *verb trans.* Relieve by an interval of rest; give temporary relief to. M16.
†**5** *verb intrans.* Rest; recover *from*. L16–M18.
6 *verb trans.* MILITARY. Suspend (a soldier) from pay; withhold (pay). Now *rare* or *obsolete*. E18.

resplend /rɪˈsplɛnd/ *verb intrans.* Now *literary.* L15.
[Latin *resplendere*, formed as RE- + *splendere* shine.]
Be resplendent or radiant; shine brightly.

resplendence /rɪˈsplɛnd(ə)ns/ *noun.* LME.
[Late Latin *resplendentia*, formed as next: see -ENCE.]
Dazzling or glorious brightness; brilliance, lustre, splendour.
■ Also **resplendency** *noun* E17.

resplendent /rɪˈsplɛnd(ə)nt/ *adjective.* LME.
[Latin *resplendent-* pres. ppl stem of *resplendere*: see RESPLEND, -ENT.]
Dazzlingly or gloriously bright; brilliant, lustrous, splendid.
■ **resplendently** *adverb* M18.

responaut /ˈrɛspənɔːt/ *noun.* M20.
[Irreg. from RESPIRATOR after *astronaut* etc.]
A person dependent on a mechanical respirator to maintain breathing.

respond /rɪˈspɒnd/ *noun.* LME.
[Old French, from *respondre* (mod. *répondre*) from Proto-Romance from Latin *respondere*: see next.]
1 ECCLESIASTICAL. **a** A responsory. LME. ▶**b** A response to a versicle. M16.
2 ARCHITECTURE. A half-pillar or half-pier attached to a wall to support an arch, esp. at the end of an arcade. LME.
3 An answer, a response. Now *rare.* E17.

respond /rɪˈspɒnd/ *verb.* M16.
[Latin *respondere*, formed as RE- + *spondere* make a solemn engagement.]
▶ **I** *verb intrans.* **1** Answer, give a reply; (of a congregation) say or sing the response in reply to a priest etc. M16.
2 Correspond to. *rare.* L16.
3 Act or behave in an answering or corresponding manner; act in response or responsively (*to*); BRIDGE make a bid on the basis of a partner's preceding bid. E18.

📖 **3** B. PYM It was so good of you to respond to my appeal. P. H. NEWBY He didn't respond to the drugs. V. GORNICK She would not laugh, respond, or participate.

▶ **II** *verb trans.* †**4** Answer or correspond to; reciprocate. E17–E19.
5 Say in response, reply. E19.
6 BRIDGE. Respond with (a bid). M20.

respondence /rɪˈspɒnd(ə)ns/ *noun.* L16.
[formed as prec. + -ENCE. Cf. French †*respondence*.]
1 The action of answering, replying, or responding; response. (Foll. by *to*.) L16.
2 Correspondence, agreement, concord. L16.
1 ***writ of*** INTENDENCE ***and respondence***.
■ **respondency** *noun* = RESPONDENCE 2 E17.

respondent /rɪˈspɒnd(ə)nt/ *noun & adjective.* E16.
[Latin *respondent-* pres. ppl stem of *respondere* RESPOND *verb*: see -ENT. Cf. French †*respondant* (now *répondant*).]
▶ **A** *noun.* **1** A person who answers; a person who responds to questioning etc.; *spec.* (*a*) a person who defends a thesis; (*b*) a person who supplies information for a survey. E16.
2 A defendant in a lawsuit, now *spec.* in an appeal or a divorce case. M16.
3 PSYCHOLOGY. A response to a specific prior stimulus. Opp. OPERANT *noun* 2. L20.
▶ **B** *adjective.* †**1** Corresponding (*to*). M16–E18.
2 That answers or replies; having the position of defendant in a lawsuit. E18.
3 a Responsive (*to*). M18. ▶**b** PSYCHOLOGY. Responsive; involving or designating a response, esp. a conditioned reflex, to some specific stimulus. M20.

respondentia /rɪspɒnˈdɛnʃə/ *noun.* E18.
[mod. Latin, formed as prec.]
A loan on the cargo of a vessel, to be repaid (with maritime interest) only if the goods arrive safe at their destination.

responder /rɪˈspɒndə/ *noun.* L19.
[from RESPOND *verb* + -ER[1].]
1 A person who responds or replies; a respondent. L19. ▶**b** BRIDGE. The partner of the opening bidder. M20.
2 †**a** An early form of radio receiver involving an electrolytic cell. Only in E20. ▶**b** RADAR etc. = TRANSPONDER. Also ***responder beacon***. M20.
3 BIOLOGY & MEDICINE. An individual, structure, etc., that responds or reacts to some stimulus or treatment. M20.

responsa *noun* pl. of RESPONSUM.

†**responsable** *adjective.* Chiefly *Scot.* E16.
[French, or medieval Latin *responsabilis*, from *responsare* reply, from Latin *respons-*: see RESPONSE, -ABLE.]
1 = RESPONSIBLE 2. E16–L17.
2 = RESPONSIBLE 3. M16–L17.

†**responsal** *noun & adjective.* LME.
[Late Latin *responsalis* (noun & adjective), from Latin *respons-*: see RESPONSE, -AL[1].]
▶ **A** *noun.* **1** A response, a reply. Latterly *spec.* a liturgical response or respond. LME–L19.
2 A respondent in a disputation. L15–L16.
3 A person appointed by a prelate to provide replies to questions. L16–E17.
▶ **B** *adjective.* **1** Answerable, responsible. M16–E18.
2 Responsive; of the nature of responses. E17–M18.

responsa prudentum /rɪˌspɒnsə pruːˈdɛntəm/ *noun phr. pl.* L17.
[Latin = the answers of the learned.]
LAW (now *Hist.*). The opinions and judgements of learned lawyers, orig. as forming part of Roman civil law.

responsary /rɪˈspɒns(ə)ri/ *noun. rare.* M16.
[medieval Latin *responsarium*, from Latin *respons-*: see next, -ARY[1].]
= RESPONSORY *noun*.

response /rɪˈspɒns/ *noun.* ME.
[Old French *respons* (mod. *répons*) or *response* (mod. *réponse*), or Latin *responsum*, from *respons-* pa. ppl stem of *respondere* RESPOND *verb*.]
1 An answer, a reply. ME. ▶**b** An answer given by an oracle; an answer attibuted to a supernatural source. L15. ▶**c** BRIDGE. A bid made on the basis of a partner's preceding bid. M20.
2 ECCLESIASTICAL. = RESPONSORY *noun*. Also, a part of the liturgy said or sung by a congregation in reply to the priest. LME.
3 MUSIC. A repetition of the subject of a fugue by another part. L18.
4 An action or feeling caused by a stimulus or influence; a reaction; *spec.* (chiefly PSYCHOLOGY) an excitation of a nerve impulse caused by any change or event; a physical reaction to a specific stimulus or situation; the action or fact of reacting to a stimulus. E19. ▶**b** The way in which an apparatus responds to a stimulus or range of stimuli. E20.

📖 **4** N. TINBERGEN Stimuli that influenced the chick's begging response. D. MORRIS Equipped with a set of instinctive responses to . . sexual signals. S. BELLOW My response was dead silence.

Phrases: **in response** in reply (*to*), by way of reaction (*to*).
Comb.: **response time** ELECTRICITY the time taken for a circuit or measuring device, when subjected to a change in input signal, to change its state by a specified fraction of its total response to that change.
■ **responseless** *adjective* M19. **responser** *noun* (*rare*) a person who makes a response M19.

responsibility /rɪˌspɒnsɪˈbɪlɪti/ *noun.* M18.
[from next + -ITY.]
1 A charge, trust, or duty, for which one is responsible; a person for whom or thing for which one is responsible. M18.
2 The state or fact of being responsible; the opportunity or necessity to be responsible. Foll. by *for*, *of*. L18.

📖 **1** J. FRAME I had the responsibility of looking after her. A. MACLEAN I have responsibilities towards both passengers and crew. **2** B. MAGEE Accepting responsibility for our lives. P. FITZGERALD Civil servants with responsibility for the arts. P. AUSTER Fatherhood had sobered him into a new sense of responsibility. J. BARNES The Voyage . . turned him into a soak. He just couldn't handle the responsibility. ***diminished responsibility***: see DIMINISHED 1. **on one's own responsibility** without authorization.

responsible /rɪˈspɒnsɪb(ə)l/ *adjective*. L16.
[French †*responsible*, from Latin *respons-*: see RESPONSE, -IBLE. Cf. earlier RESPONSABLE.]
†**1** Correspondent, answering, *to*. L16–L17.
2 Answerable, accountable, (*to*); liable to be called to account; having authority or control; being the cause. (Foll. by *for*.) M17. ▸**b** Accountable for one's actions; capable of rational conduct. M19.
3 Capable of fulfilling an obligation or trust; reliable, trustworthy; of good credit, social position, or reputation. L17. ▸**b** Of respectable appearance. *arch.* L18.
4 Involving responsibility or obligation. M19.

📖 **2** JOYCE He was not responsible, . . he had come on the scene by . . accident. L. WOOLF A . . useless war for which the . . governments were mainly responsible. E. YOUNG-BRUEHL Freud was financially responsible for his parents. **3** F. WELDON He was large, handsome and responsible. **4** A. MILLER You don't raise a guy to a responsible job who whistles in the elevator!

■ **responsibleness** *noun* E18. **responsibly** *adverb* M19.

responsion /rɪˈspɒnʃ(ə)n/ *noun*. LME.
[French †*responsion* or Latin *responsio(n-)*, from *respons-*: see RESPONSE, -ION.]
†**1** A sum falling to be paid; *esp.* an annual payment required from knights of a military order. LME–E18.
2 An answer, a reply; a response. Now *rare*. L15.
3 *Hist.* In *pl.* The first of three examinations which BA students at Oxford were required to pass until 1960. E19.

responsive /rɪˈspɒnsɪv/ *adjective*. LME.
[Old & mod. French *responsif*, *-ive* or late Latin *responsivus*, from Latin *respons-*: see RESPONSE, -IVE.]
1 Answering, making answer or reply. Orig. *spec.*, written in reply. (Foll. by *to*.) LME. ▸**b** *BRIDGE*. Of a double: used to invite a change to an unbid suit in response to a partner's take-out double. M20.
2 Correspondent, corresponding. *rare*. E17.
3 Responding readily to some stimulus or influence; sympathetic; impressionable. (Foll. by *to*.) M18.
4 Characterized by the use of (liturgical) responses. L18.
■ **responsively** *adverb* L18. **responsiveness** *noun* M19. **Responsivist** *noun & adjective* (*Indian Hist.*) (*a*) *noun* an advocate of working within the diarchical administrative system introduced in Indian provinces during British rule; (*b*) *adjective* of or pertaining to the Responsivists: E20. **responˈsivity** *noun* M19.

responsor /rɪˈspɒnsə/ *noun*. M20.
[from RESPONSE + -OR.]
RADAR etc. A device that receives and processes the reply from a transponder, usu. incorporated in the same unit as the interrogator.

responsorial /rɪspɒnˈsɔːrɪəl/ *noun*. M19.
[medieval Latin *responsoriale*, formed as RESPONSORY *noun*: see -AL[1].]
A book of responsories.

responsorial /rɪspɒnˈsɔːrɪəl/ *adjective*. E19.
[from (the same root as) next + -AL[1].]
1 Making answer or reply; responsive. E19.
2 Pertaining to, involving, or of the nature of (liturgical) responses. M19.
2 responsorial psalm: recited in parts, with a congregational response between each part.
■ **responsorially** *adverb* E20.

responsory /rɪˈspɒns(ə)ri/ *noun*. LME.
[Late Latin *responsorium* use as noun of neut. of *responsorius*: see next, -ORY[1].]
ECCLESIASTICAL. An anthem said or sung after a lesson by a soloist and choir alternately.

†**responsory** *adjective*. L16–M18.
[Late Latin *responsorius*, from Latin *respons-*: see RESPONSE, -ORY[2].]
Of the nature of an answer, reply, or response; of or pertaining to answering.

responsum /rɪˈspɒnsəm/ *noun*. Pl. **-sa** /-sə/. L19.
[Latin = reply.]
A written reply by a rabbi or Talmudic scholar to an inquiry on some matter of Jewish law.

respray /*as verb* riːˈspreɪ, *as noun* ˈriːspreɪ/ *verb & noun*. M20.
[from RE- + SPRAY *verb*[2].]
▸ **A** *verb trans.* Spray again or afresh, esp. with a different colour of paint. M20.
▸ **B** *noun*. The action or an act of respraying something. M20.

ressala(h) *nouns* vars. of RISSALA.

ressaldar *noun* var. of RISSALDAR.

ressentiment /rəsɑ̃timɑ̃/ *noun*. M20.
[German *Ressentiment* from French *ressentiment*, from *ressentir* RESENT.]
SOCIAL PSYCHOLOGY. = RESENTMENT 1b.
¶ Term introduced by Nietzsche.

rest /rɛst/ *noun*[1].
[Old English *ræst*, *rest* corresp. to Old Frisian *rasta*, Old Saxon *rasta* place of rest, Old High German *rasta* rest, league (German *Rast*), Old Norse *rǫst*, Gothic *rasta* mile.]
†**1** A bed, a couch. OE–ME.
2 The natural repose or relief from daily activity obtained by sleep. OE.
3 (Temporary) freedom from, cessation of, or absence of labour, exertion, or activity; repose obtained by ceasing to exert oneself; an instance of this; a period of resting. OE. ▸**b** Freedom from distress, trouble, molestation, or aggression; peace of mind; quietness, tranquillity. OE. ▸**c** The repose of death or of the grave. Chiefly in ***go to rest***, ***go to one's rest***, ***be laid to rest*** below. ME. ▸†**d** Restored vigour or strength. *rare* (Shakes.). L16–E17.
4 A place to rest or stay; a residence, an abode. Now *spec.* an establishment providing shelter or lodging for sailors or fishermen. OE.
5 Absence, loss, or cessation of motion; continuance in the same position or place. In early use also, absence of sound, silence. LME.
6 a *MUSIC*. An interval of silence of a specified duration. Also, the character or sign denoting such an interval. E16. ▸**b** A pause in elocution; a caesura in verse. E17.
7 A thing on which something else rests, a support or prop for holding or steadying something, as (*a*) a support for a firearm, employed in steadying the barrel to ensure accuracy of aim, *esp.* that used for a heavy musket; (*b*) a support for a cue in billiards, snooker, etc.; (*c*) a support or hook for a telephone receiver when not in use, incorporating a switch that is automatically closed when the receiver is lifted; (*d*) a projecting part of a removable denture that gives it support by lying against a tooth. E16.

📖 **3** MILTON And post o'er Land and Ocean without rest. W. COWPER From toilsome life to never-ending rest. S. BELLOW We ascended . . , often stopping for a rest. **b** H. F. CARY The truth, wherein rest is For every mind. C. KINGSLEY The impression of vastness and of solemn rest. **7** ***bedrest***, ***book rest***, ***foot-rest***, ***head-rest***, ***knife-rest***, ***leg-rest***, etc.

Phrases: **at rest** (*a*) dead; (*b*) in a state of (physical or mental) repose, quiescence, or inactivity; untroubled; (*c*) settled. ***chapel of rest***: see CHAPEL *noun*. ***day of rest***: see DAY *noun*. **give something a rest**, **give someone a rest**: stop thinking or talking about something or someone. **go to one's rest**, **go to rest** *arch.* (*a*) go to bed for the night; (*b*) die. ***lay to rest***: see LAY *verb*[1]. ***no rest for the wicked***: see WICKED *noun* 1. **set at rest** satisfy, assure; settle, decide finally. **take one's rest**, **take rest** *arch.* (go to) sleep.

Comb.: **rest-balk** a ridge left unploughed between two furrows; **rest-cure** a rest, esp. of some weeks, as a medical treatment; **rest-day** (*a*) (now *rare*) = ***day of rest*** s.v. DAY *noun*; (*b*) a day spent in or set aside for rest; **rest energy** *PHYSICS* the energy inherent in a body by virtue of its possession of rest mass; **rest frame** *PHYSICS* a frame of reference relative to which a given body is at rest; **rest gown** *Hist.* a gown used for evening wear at home; **rest-home** a place where old or frail people can live and be cared for; **rest-house** (*a*) in the Indian subcontinent, SE Asia, and Africa, a building for travellers to rest and shelter in; (*b*) an establishment catering for people requiring rest and recreation; **rest level** *GEOLOGY* the natural level of water in an aquifer or on the ground surface; **rest mass** *PHYSICS* the mass of a body measured when it is at rest; **rest room** (*a*) a room (esp. in a public building) set aside for rest and quiet; (*b*) *US* a lavatory.

rest /rɛst/ *noun*[2]. ME.
[Aphet. from (the same root as) ARREST *noun*.]
†**1** Fixed purpose; resolve. Only in ME.
†**2** A means of stopping or checking a horse. LME–E16.
†**3** Arrest of persons or goods. LME–L16.
4 In medieval armour, a contrivance fixed to the right side of a cuirass to receive and resist impact from the butt-end of a couched lance. LME.

rest /rɛst/ *noun*[3]. LME.
[Old & mod. French *reste*, formed as REST *verb*[3].]
1 That which remains over; a remainder, a remnant, a relic. Freq. in *pl.* Long *rare*. LME.
2 †**a** A sum remaining to be paid; balance or arrears of money due. Chiefly *Scot.* LME–L16. ▸**b** The balance of an account; a periodic balancing of accounts. E19. ▸**c** The reserve or surplus fund of a bank, esp. of the Bank of England. M19.
3 The remainder or remaining part(s), the residue, (*of*); *pl.* the remaining persons, animals, or things, the others. M16.
†**4** In primero, the stakes kept in reserve, the loss of which terminated the game; the venture of such stakes. M16–L17.
5 In real tennis and battledore: a spell of quick and continuous returning of the ball maintained by the players, a rally. L16.
6 *MEDICINE*. A small detached part of an organ, surrounded by tissue of another character; *esp.* (in full ***adrenal rest***) a small displaced part of the adrenal cortex. L19.

📖 **3** R. G. COLLINGWOOD One . . reads a paper, and the rest discuss it. DAY LEWIS The rest of the flat cart was filled with hens. JAN MORRIS They are only human, like the rest of us. W. M. CLARKE Both met women who were to fashion the rest of their lives.

Phrases: **and all the rest (of it)**, **and the rest (of it)** and everything else which might be mentioned or included. **as to the rest** in other respects, otherwise. **for the rest** as regards anything else. †**set one's rest**, **set up one's rest** (*a*) venture one's final stake or reserve; stake, hazard, or venture one's all (*up*)*on*; set one's final hope or trust *upon* or *in*; (*b*) have or take a resolution; be resolved or determined; fix or settle *upon*, decide *for*, place one's whole aim or end *in*; (*c*) take up one's (permanent) abode.

rest /rɛst/ *verb*[1].
[Old English *ræstan*, *restan* = Old Frisian *resta*, Old High German *restan*.]
▸ **I** *verb intrans.* **1** Take rest by lying down, and esp. by going to sleep; lie still to refresh oneself, lie asleep. With adverbs, sleep *well* etc. OE. ▸**b** Lie in death, lie in the grave. OE. ▸**c** Of the body of a dead person: remain at an undertaker's, a chapel, etc., before burial or cremation. Usu. in the progressive, ***be resting***. M20.
2 Take rest by cessation of or freedom from labour, exertion, or activity, desist or refrain from effort or activity; become or remain inactive. OE. ▸**b** Cease *from*, †*to do*; take a rest *from*. LME. ▸**c** Of land: lie fallow. M19. ▸**d** *THEATRICAL*. Of an actor: be (temporarily) out of work, be unemployed. Usu. in the progressive, ***be resting***. L19.
3 Be at ease, be in quiet; have peace of mind; continue without change of state or place; remain. OE. ▸**b** Stop or cease at a certain point and remain thereafter inoperative or inactive; (of a problem etc.) stop being pursued or discussed. L16. ▸**c** Voluntarily conclude presenting evidence in a law case. *US*. M19.
4 Come to have a place or position, settle, alight, lie, *on*, *upon*; lie or lean *on*, *upon*, or *against* a person or thing to obtain rest or support; be supported or spread out *on*, *upon*; be propped *against*. OE. ▸**b** Of the eyes, a look, etc.: come to be directed steadily *on*, *upon*. E19.
5 a Rely *on*, *upon*; (now *rare*) trust *to*. ME. ▸**b** Depend *on*, *upon*; be based or founded *on*. M16.
6 Remain confident or hopeful; put trust *in*. LME.
7 †**a** Be vested *in*; consist *in*, lie *in*. L15–M17. ▸**b** Lie *in* or remain *with* a person, as something to be accomplished or determined. L16.

📖 **1** C. BRONTË Too feverish to rest, I rose as . . day dawned. **b** C. KINGSLEY Let her rest in peace. F. O'CONNOR Mother would rest easier in her grave, knowing it was guarded. **2** MILTON The Harp Had work and rested not. E. M. FORSTER Instead of resting . . , I paid a round of calls. C. P. SNOW Mother could not rest until my father got a job. **b** *Guardian* Resting from his labours. **3** F. BURNEY I could not rest till I had the honour of assuring you. SCOTT FITZGERALD In the ditch . . rested a new coupé. **b** R. P. GRAVES There the matter rested. M. SPARK I'd let it rest . . I wouldn't take that risk. **c** *Tucson (Arizona) Citizen* A department attorney intoned, 'The government rests'. **4** SIR W. SCOTT The roof . . rested upon four . . arches. R. C. HUTCHINSON One hand resting on the trunk. G. GREENE He slid the plank . . so that one end rested on a large stone. R. DAHL Never . . resting on one thing for . . a moment. *Scientific American* The . . piston rests against the . . plate. **b** A. J. CRONIN His eyes searching, rested finally . . upon Andrew. **5b** K. TYNAN The inference . . rests on a few ambiguous lines. G. S. HAIGHT Miss Lewis's . . evangelicalism rested on diligent study of the Scriptures. **7b** R. W. CLARK The decision . . rested with the individual.

▸ **II** *verb trans.* **8** *refl.* **a** Take a rest. OE. ▸**b** With adjective compl.: continue being, remain. *arch.* LME. ▸†**c** Rely *upon*. *rare*. E–M17.
9 Give or allow rest or repose to; relieve or refresh by rest; lay to rest. ME. ▸**b** Allow to remain undisturbed, quiescent, or inactive; leave to lie fallow. L16. ▸**c** Voluntarily conclude presenting evidence pertinent to (a law case etc.). *US*. E20.
10 Place, lay, or set *on* or *upon* something for support or restraint; place (the weight of something) *on*. ME. ▸**b** Make or allow to depend *on*. M18.
11 Place or settle *in*. LME.

📖 **8a** M. W. MONTAGU Glad to stay there a day to rest myself. **b** TENNYSON Rest thee sure That I shall love thee. **c** AV *2 Chron.* 32:8 The people rested themselues vpon the words of Hezekiah. **9** SHAKES. *Merch. V.* Is my boy—God rest his soul!—alive or dead? D. DUNN He kneels upright to rest his back. **b** J. L. HARPER The sward was then rested from grazing. **c** *New Yorker* The prosecution rested the government's case. **10** J. M. COETZEE I rest my hand on his shoulder. **11** S. WEINTRAUB Lehzen, . . in whom the Princess could rest her confidence.

Phrases, & with adverbs in specialized senses: ***rest on one's laurels***: see LAUREL *noun* 2. ***rest on one's oars***: see OAR *noun*. **rest up** (*a*) recover one's strength by resting; (*b*) = sense 9 above.
■ **rester** *noun* LME.

rest /rɛst/ *verb*². Now *dial.* ME.
[Aphet. from (the same root as) ARREST *verb*.]
1 *verb trans.* Apprehend, seize, arrest. ME.
†**2** *verb intrans.* Stop; come to a decision. LME–M16.

rest /rɛst/ *verb*³. LME.
[Old & mod. French *rester* from Latin *restare*, formed as RE- + *stare* stand.]
1 *verb intrans.* **a** Remain due or unpaid. Chiefly *Scot.* LME. ▸**b** Remain or be left still undestroyed or unremoved. Now *rare.* L15. ▸†**c** Remain or be left over after subtraction, diminution, etc. M16–E18.
2 *verb intrans.* With compl.: remain or be left in a specified condition, continue to be. Freq. in ***rest assured***. LME.
†**3** *verb intrans.* Remain to be done or dealt with. Freq. *impers.* in ***it rests*** etc. LME–E18.
†**4** *verb trans.* Owe. Chiefly *Scot.* L16–E19.

🕮 **2** SHAKES. *Hen. VIII* My Lord, I rest your servant. B. JOWETT Rest assured that the more wise . . you are, the happier you will be. K. GIBBONS Folks can . . rest sure that their money is well spent.

†**restagnate** *verb.* M17.
[Latin *restagnat-* pa. ppl stem of *restagnare* overflow.]
1 *verb intrans.* Stagnate. M–L17.
2 *verb intrans. & trans.* (Cause to) overflow. L17–E18.
▪ †**restagnation** *noun* E17–E18.

restant /ˈrɛst(ə)nt/ *adjective.* LME.
[Latin *restant-* pres. ppl stem of *restare*: see REST *verb*³, -ANT¹. Partly from French *restant*.]
†**1** Temporarily resident. *rare.* Only in LME.
†**2** Remaining. *rare.* Only in L17.
3 BOTANY. Persistent. *rare.* E19.

restart /riːˈstɑːt, ˈriːstɑːt/ *noun.* L19.
[from RE- + START *noun*².]
A fresh start; a new beginning.

restart /riːˈstɑːt/ *verb trans. & intrans.* M19.
[from RE- + START *verb*.]
Start again.

restate /riːˈsteɪt/ *verb trans.* E18.
[from RE- + STATE *verb*.]
State or express over again or in a new way, esp. more clearly or convincingly.
▪ **restatement** *noun* E19.

restaurant /ˈrɛst(ə)rɒnt, -r(ə)nt, -rɔ̃ː, -rɒ̃, -rɑ̃ː/ *noun.* E19.
[French, use as noun of pres. pple of *restaurer* RESTORE *verb*: see -ANT¹.]
A public establishment where meals or refreshments may be obtained.
Comb.: **restaurant car** a dining-car on a train.
▪ **restauranter** *noun* (*US*) = RESTAURATEUR 1 L19. **restauranteur** /-ˈtəː/ *noun* [after RESTAURATEUR] = RESTAURATEUR 1 M20.

restaurate /ˈrɛstɔːreɪt/ *verb. rare.* L16.
[Latin *restaurat-* pa. ppl stem of *restaurare* RESTORE *verb*: see -ATE³.]
†**1** *verb trans.* Restore. L16–M17.
2 *verb intrans.* Take refreshments, have a meal. L19.

restaurateur /rɛst(ə)rəˈtəː, ˌrɛstɒr-/ *noun.* L18.
[French, from *restaurer* RESTORE *verb* + *-ateur* -ATOR.]
1 A keeper of a restaurant. L18.
2 A restaurant in France. Now *rare.* E19.

restauration /rɛstɔːˈreɪʃ(ə)n/ *noun.* Now *rare.* LME.
[Old & mod. French, or late Latin *restauratio(n-)*, formed as RESTAURATE: see -ATION. In branch II after German *Restauration*. See also RESTORATION.]
▸**I 1** = RESTORATION 1. Orig. *spec.* (THEOLOGY), the reinstatement of humankind in divine favour or in a state of innocence. LME.
†**2** = RESTORATION 2. Only in LME.
3 = RESTORATION 4. LME.
†**4** = RESTORATION 3. M16–L17.
▸**II 5** A restaurant in Continental Europe. M19.

†**restaurative** *adjective & noun* var. of RESTORATIVE.

restenosis /riːstɛˈnəʊsɪs/ *noun.* Pl. **-noses** /-ˈnəʊsiːz/. M20.
[from RE- + STENOSIS.]
MEDICINE. A recurrence of stenosis, esp. of a heart valve after surgery to correct it.

restful /ˈrɛstfʊl, -f(ə)l/ *adjective.* ME.
[from REST *noun*¹ + -FUL.]
Characterized by, of the nature of, or favourable to rest or repose; free from strife or disturbance; quiet, peaceful; soothing.

🕮 B. BAINBRIDGE Brenda felt more restful in her mind now. A. MCCOWEN It was not a restful household. V. BRAMWELL Green script is . . more restful on the eyes than white.

▪ **restfully** *adverb* LME. **restfulness** *noun* LME.

rest-harrow /ˈrɛstharəʊ/ *noun.* M16.
[from REST *verb*² + HARROW *noun*.]
Any plant of the leguminous genus *Ononis*; *esp.* either of two shrubby pink-flowered kinds with tough roots occurring as weeds in grassland, the usu. spiny *O. spinosa* and the usu. spineless *O. repens*.

restiff /ˈrɛstɪf/ *adjective.* Now *rare.* LME.
[Old French *restif* (mod. *rétif*) from Proto-Romance, from Latin *restare* REST *verb*³ + *-ivus* -IVE. See also RESTY *adjective*².]
Restive.
▪ **restiffness** *noun* E17.

restiform /ˈrɛstɪfɔːm/ *adjective.* M19.
[mod. Latin *restiformis*, from Latin *restis* cord: see -FORM.]
ANATOMY. Cordlike; *spec.* designating or pertaining to either of two rounded bundles of nerve fibres on each side of the medulla oblongata, connecting it with the cerebellum.
restiform body, ***restiform column***, ***restiform tract***.

resting /ˈrɛstɪŋ/ *noun.* ME.
[from REST *verb*¹ + -ING¹.]
1 The action of REST *verb*¹; taking rest; rest, repose, inactivity; peace of mind; reliance, confidence. ME.
2 A place where a person rests or may rest, a resting-place. Now *rare.* ME.
3 A pause, a stop for rest. *rare.* LME.
Comb.: **resting-place** (*a*) a place where a person rests or may rest, a place to rest; ***last resting-place***, the grave; (*b*) a break or landing in a staircase; **resting potential** BIOLOGY the electric potential of a cell relative to its surroundings when not stimulated or involved in passage of an impulse.

resting /ˈrɛstɪŋ/ *ppl adjective.* LME.
[from REST *verb*¹ + -ING².]
1 That rests, that is taking a rest. LME. ▸**b** BIOLOGY. (Of a bud, cell, etc.) not in the process of growth or division; (of an egg, spore, etc.) formed as an inactive stage to survive the winter or other unfavourable period. M19. ▸**c** THEATRICAL. Between acting jobs; unemployed. M20.
2 Remaining stationary. *rare.* E17.

restipulate /riːˈstɪpjʊleɪt/ *verb.* Now *rare.* M17.
[Latin *restipulat-* pa. ppl stem of *restipulari*, formed as RE- + *stipulare* STIPULATE *verb*.]
1 *verb trans.* Promise or engage in return. M17.
2 *verb intrans.* Make a promise in return. L17.
▪ **restipuˈlation** *noun* E17.

restitute /ˈrɛstɪtjuːt/ *verb.* Pa. pple **-tuted**, †**-tute**. LME.
[Latin *restitut-* pa. ppl stem of *restituere* restore, formed as RE- + *statuere* set up, establish.]
1 *verb trans.* Restore to a position or status; reinstate, rehabilitate. Now *rare.* LME.
2 *verb trans. & intrans.* Hand back, refund, return, (something). E18.
3 *verb intrans.* GENETICS. Of a break in a chromosome or chromatid: be rejoined. M20.

restitutio in integrum /rɛstɪˌtjuːtɪəʊ ɪn ɪnˈtɛgrəm/ *noun phr.* E18.
[Latin = restoration to the uninjured state.]
LAW. Placement of an injured party in the situation which would have prevailed had no injury been sustained; restoration of the status quo ante.

restitution /rɛstɪˈtjuːʃ(ə)n/ *noun.* ME.
[Old & mod. French, or Latin *restitutio(n-)*, formed as RESTITUTE: see -ION.]
1 The action or an act of restoring or giving back something to its proper owner; (an act of) reparation for loss or injury previously inflicted (freq. in ***make restitution***). (Foll. by *of*.) ME.
2 The action or an act of restoring a person or persons to a previous status or position; the fact of being restored or reinstated. Now *rare.* LME.
3 The action or an act of restoring a thing or institution to its original state or form, now *spec.* (THEOLOGY) to perfection (with ref. to *Acts* 3:21). LME.
†**4** Reposition, replacement. *rare.* L16–M17.
5 Resumption of a previous shape or position by virtue of elasticity or resilience. M17.
6 GENETICS. The rejoining of two parts of a broken chromosome or chromatid. M20.

🕮 **1** SHAKES. *2 Hen. VI* Many a pound . . Have I dispursed . . And never ask'd for restitution. J. A. FROUDE He had been promised restitution of his property. R. A. KNOX We must . . make restitution if we have defrauded people. **2** DEFOE The Restitution of King Charles the Second. **3** AV *Acts* 3:21 The times of restitution of all things.

Comb.: **restitution nucleus** GENETICS a cell or gamete nucleus having twice the normal chromosome number due to a defect in the spindle during cell division.
▪ **restitutionism** *noun* (*rare*) = RESTORATIONISM L19. **restitutionist** *noun* (THEOLOGY, chiefly *US*) = RESTORATIONIST *noun* 1 L18.

restitutive /ˈrɛstɪtjuːtɪv/ *adjective.* M17.
[from (the same root as) RESTITUTE + -IVE.]
†**1** Of a character consequent or dependent on restoration to a former status. *rare.* Only in M17.
2 Tending to restore a former state or position. L18.

restitutory /rɛstɪˈtjuːt(ə)ri/ *adjective.* L19.
[Latin *restitutorius*, formed as RESTITUTE: see -ORY².]
Of or pertaining to restitution.

restive /ˈrɛstɪv/ *adjective.* L16.
[Alt. of RESTIFF after adjectives in -IVE.]
†**1** Inclined to rest or remain still; inactive, inert. L16–M19.
†**2** Persistent, obstinate, settled or fixed, *in* an opinion or course of action. M17–E19.
3 (Orig. of a horse) refusing to go forward, stubbornly standing still, obstinately moving backwards or to the side; unmanageable, resisting control, intractable, refractory. Now also, restless, fidgety. M17.

🕮 **3** SIR W. SCOTT The . . man yielded a . . restive compliance. OUIDA He turned restive at the least attempt at coercion. *Law Times* His lordship's horse became restive. J. B. PRIESTLEY The audiences were . . apt to be restive. R. HOLMES I became increasingly restive in my attic room.

▪ **restively** *adverb* M19. **restiveness** *noun* E17.

restless /ˈrɛs(t)lɪs/ *adjective.* OE.
[from REST *noun*¹ + -LESS.]
1 Unable to rest; deprived of rest; finding no rest; uneasy in mind or spirit; fidgety; averse to being quiet or settled. OE.
2 Unceasing, continuous. Now *rare.* LME.
3 Constantly in motion, continually operating; never ceasing or pausing. L16.
4 Characterized by unrest; affording no rest. E17.

🕮 **1** T. HARDY The horse had become restless. H. JAMES Too restless to do anything but walk. M. CONEY Siervo was restless, twisting and turning. J. UPDIKE He was . . nervous . . and restless. **3** A. L. DU TOIT A pulsating restless earth. I. MURDOCH Bright restless eyes darting quick glances. E. SHOWALTER A restless and adventurous mind. **4** T. S. ELIOT Restless nights in . . cheap hotels. E. BOWEN A bleak restless place where nobody ever settled.

Special collocations: **restless flycatcher** a black and white Australian flycatcher, *Myiagra inquieta*, which hovers above the ground making a whirring noise; also called ***scissors-grinder***.
▪ **restlessly** *adverb* M16. **restlessness** *noun* M17.

restock /riːˈstɒk/ *verb*¹. L17.
[from RE- + STOCK *verb*¹.]
1 *verb trans.* Stock again or differently; replenish. L17.
2 *verb intrans.* Replenish or replace a stock. E20.

restock /riːˈstɒk/ *verb*² *trans.* L19.
[from RE- + STOCK *noun*¹.]
Fit (a gun etc.) with a new stock.

restorable /rɪˈstɔːrəb(ə)l/ *adjective.* E17.
[from RESTORE *verb* + -ABLE.]
Able to be restored or brought back to a former condition.

restoral /rɪˈstɔːr(ə)l/ *noun.* E17.
[formed as prec. + -AL¹.]
Restoration, restitution.

restoration /rɛstəˈreɪʃ(ə)n/ *noun.* L15.
[In isolated early use from Old French *restoration* var. of *restauration*; later (17) alt. of RESTAURATION after RESTORE *verb*.]
1 The action of restoring someone or something to a former state or position; *spec.* the restoring of a hereditary monarch to a throne; the fact of being restored or reinstated. (Foll. by *to*.) L15. ▸**b** *Hist.* (**R-**.) The re-establishment of monarchy in England with the return of Charles II in 1660; the period immediately following this (freq. *attrib.*). E18.
2 The action of restoring a person to health or consciousness; recovery of physical strength. Now *rare.* E17.
3 The action of restoring something to a person previously deprived of it; return of something lost or stolen. L18.
4 The action or process of restoring something to an unimpaired or perfect condition; the process of carrying out alterations and repairs with the idea of restoring a building, work of art, etc., to something like its original form; a general renovation. E19.
5 A model or drawing representing the supposed original form of a ruined building, extinct animal, etc. M19.
6 DENTISTRY. Any structure provided to replace or repair dental tissue so as to restore its form and function, such as a filling, a crown, or a bridge. M20.

🕮 **1** B. F. WESTCOTT The restoration of man and . . of nature are placed side by side. C. V. WEDGWOOD From the king's death until the bloodless Restoration of his son. *Listener* The restoration and maintenance of free institutions. **b** ***Restoration comedy***, ***Restoration drama***, ***Restoration dramatist***, etc. **4** J. STAINER The muniment-room was . . removed for the purposes of restoration. E. M. FORSTER Frescoes—now . . ruined by restoration.

restorationism /rɛstəˈreɪʃ(ə)nɪz(ə)m/ *noun.* Also **R-**. M19.
[from prec. + -ISM.]
CHRISTIAN CHURCH. **1** The doctrine that all people will ultimately be restored to a state of happiness in the future life. M19.
2 A charismatic movement seeking to restore the beliefs and practices of the early Church; the doctrine and principles of this movement. L20.

For other words beginning with *re-* see the entry for **re-**

restorationist /rɛstəˈreɪʃ(ə)nɪst/ *noun & adjective.* In sense A.1 & corresp. uses of the adjective also **R-**. **M19.**
[formed as prec. + -IST.]
▶ **A** *noun.* **1** CHRISTIAN CHURCH. A believer in restorationism with regard to the future life. **M19.** ▸**b** An adherent of charismatic restorationism. **L20.**
2 A restorer of dilapidated buildings etc. **L19.**
3 A person who seeks to restore a former practice or institution, *spec.* capital punishment. Cf. sense 1b above. **L20.**
▶ **B** *attrib.* or as *adjective.* Of or pertaining to restorationism or restorationists. **L20.**

restorative /rɪˈstɒrətɪv/ *adjective & noun.* Also †**restaur-**. **LME.**
[Old French *restoratif, -ive, restaur-*, formed as RESTORE *verb*: see -ATIVE.]
▶ **A** *adjective.* **1** Tending to restore strength, health, or (less commonly) consciousness or spirits. **LME.**
2 DENTISTRY. Pertaining to or used in dental restorations. **M20.**
▶ **B** *noun.* A restorative food, cordial, medicine, etc. **LME.**
■ **restoratively** *adverb* (*rare*) **M19.**

†**restore** *noun.* **LME–M17.**
[from the verb.]
Restoration, restitution.
SPENSER Till he had made amends, and full restore For all the damage which he had him doen afore.

restore /rɪˈstɔː/ *verb trans.* **ME.**
[Old French *restorer* (mod. *restaurer*) from Latin *restaurare*, formed as RE- + *-staurare* (also in *instaurare* renew).]
1 Give back, return, make restitution of (something previously taken away or lost). **ME.**
2 Make amends for; compensate for, make good (loss or damage); set right, repair (decay etc.). Now *rare*. **ME.**
3 Build up again; re-erect, reconstruct; bring back to the original state; *spec.* repair and alter (a building, work of art, etc.) so as to bring back something like the original form or condition. **ME.** ▸**b** Make a model or drawing representing the supposed original form of (a ruined building, extinct animal, etc.). **L18.**
4 a Reinstate or replace (a person) in a former office, dignity, or estate. Orig. *spec.* (THEOLOGY), replace (humankind) in a state of grace, free from the effects of sin. **ME.** ▸**b** Bring back to health, strength, or vigour; (now *rare*) bring back to mental calm. **LME.**
5 a Renew; set up or bring into existence again; re-establish, bring back into use. **ME.** ▸**b** *refl.* Return to the original position. **M17.** ▸**c** Replace or insert by conjecture (words or letters missing or illegible in a text, etc.). **M19.**
6 Bring back *to* a previous, original, or normal condition; reinstate *to* a former rank, office, or possession; take or put back *into*, convey or hand back *to*, a place. **ME.**
1 B. MONTGOMERY The victories . . had restored public confidence. **3** G. SANTAYANA Restore the ground floor in the style of the period. *Early Music* The harpsichord is the Italian one . . restored . . by Frank Hubbard. S. WEINTRAUB Wyatville . . restored Windsor Castle for George IV. **4a** ***restore in blood, restore to blood***: see BLOOD *noun*. **b** O. MANNING Sleep had restored her. **5a** B. ENGLAND They must . . restore the older man's circulation. R. DAVIES Spencer tried to restore order. **6** D. CECIL She was restored to health.
■ **restorer** *noun* **LME.**

restrain /rɪˈstreɪn/ *verb.* **ME.**
[Old French *restrei(g)n-, -ai(g)ne-* pres. stem of *restreindre, -aindre* from Latin *restringere* bind fast, confine, formed as RE- + *stringere* draw tight (see STRAIN *verb*[1]).]
▶ **I** *verb trans.* **1** Hold back or prevent *from* some course of action. **ME.**
2 Put a check or stop on, repress, keep down; keep in check, under control, or within bounds; hold in place. **ME.** ▸**b** Deprive of (or †*of*) liberty or freedom of action or movement; confine, imprison. **L15.** ▸**c** Of a seat belt: restrict movement of (part of the body), hold (a person) down and back. **M20.**
3 Restrict, limit, (*to*). **ME.**
†**4** Withhold (*from*). **LME–L16.**
†**5** Draw or bind tightly; compel, constrain. **LME–M17.**
†**6** Forbid or prohibit (a thing, a person *to do*). **L15–M17.**
1 E. L. DOCTOROW Grandfather had to be restrained from lifting the bags. J. HELLER Aristotle . . could hardly restrain himself from jumping up. **2** W. S. CHURCHILL The soldiery, whom their officers could no longer restrain. J. HERRIOT The rings were . . necessary to restrain the big animals. R. GRAVES A visiting sea Which no door could restrain. F. KING I wanted to shout . . . But I restrained myself. P. MAILLOUX It was difficult for them to restrain their tears. **3** E. WILSON Restrain your drawing to . . silhouette shapes. *Japan Times* Is your life-style restrained by the layout . . of your home?
▶ **II** *verb intrans.* **7** Act as a restraint. **LME.**
8 Refrain (*from*). Now *rare*. **L16.**
■ **restrainable** *adjective* **LME.** **restrainer** *noun* **M16.** **restrainingly** *adverb* in a restraining manner, so as to act as a restraint **M19.**

re-strain /riːˈstreɪn/ *verb trans.* **L19.**
[from RE- + STRAIN *verb*[1].]
Strain again.

restrained /rɪˈstreɪnd/ *adjective.* **L16.**
[from RESTRAIN + -ED[1].]
That has been restrained; repressed; kept under control or within bounds; confined; held in place, as by a safety belt or harness; characterized by restraint or reserve, not excessive or extravagant.
■ **restrainedly** /-nɪdli/ *adverb* in a restrained manner, with restraint **L16.** **restrainedness** *noun* (*rare*) **L16.**

restraint /rɪˈstreɪnt/ *noun.* **LME.**
[Old & mod. French *restreinte* fem. pa. pple of *restreindre*: see RESTRAIN.]
1 The action or an act of restraining something or someone. **LME.**
2 A means of or device for restraining someone or something; a force or influence having a restraining effect. **LME.**
3 †**a** A prohibition. **LME–E17.** ▸**b** More fully ***restraint of princes***. = EMBARGO *noun* 1. **L15.**
4 Restraining action or influence; (self-)control; the ability to restrain oneself; reserve; absence of excess or extravagance. **M16.**
5 Deprivation or restriction of liberty or freedom of action or movement; confinement, imprisonment. **M16.**
†**6** Restriction, limitation. **L16–M18.**
2 B. BAINBRIDGE We can . . behave without the restraints imposed by society. *Times* Seat belt sales are soaring, especially restraints for children. ***head restraint*** etc. **4** P. LARKIN She now had no restraint and was crying. LYNDON B. JOHNSON Unrealistic to expect restraint in wage increases. E. H. GOMBRICH This restraint of Chinese art, . . its deliberate limitation to a few simple motifs. **5** W. S. CHURCHILL Never been under restraint . . and never known what it was to be a captive.
Phrases: ***restraint of princes***: see sense 3b above. **restraint of trade** interference with free-market conditions, action aimed at this. **without restraint** freely, copiously, without inhibition.

restrict /rɪˈstrɪkt/ *verb trans.* Pa. pple & ppl adjective **-ed**, (earlier) †**restrict**. See also RESTRICTED. **LME.**
[Orig. pa. pple, from Latin *restrictus* pa. pple of *restringere* RESTRAIN.]
†**1** Staunch (blood). Only in **LME.**
2 Limit, bound, confine, (*to, within*). **M16.**
3 Restrain by prohibition, prevent *from*. **M19.**
2 Y. MENUHIN My arrival restricted . . these lessons. S. ROSENBERG They are . . restricted in their movements. P. DALLY Heavy . . curtains . . restricted the light. **3** P. MAILLOUX His Jewishness would not restrict him from working on Saturday.
¶ Described by Samuel Johnson (1755) as 'a word scarce English'. In earlier use chiefly Sc.
■ **restrictable** *adjective* **L19.** **restrictee** /rɪstrɪkˈtiː/ *noun* a person whose freedom of movement is restricted, esp. for political reasons **M20.** **restrictor** *noun* (*a*) a person who restricts someone or who advocates restriction; (*b*) a device for restricting the flow of a fluid: **E19.**

restricted /rɪˈstrɪktɪd/ *adjective.* **M16.**
[from prec. + -ED[1].]
1 *gen.* Limited, confined. Orig. *Scot.* **M16.**
2 In which a speed limit is operative. **M20.**
3 Of a document, information, etc.: for limited circulation only, not to be revealed to the general public for reasons of national security. **M20.**
4 Limited to use by a certain group, *spec.* (*a*) non-Jews, (*b*) non-military personnel. *US.* **M20.**
5 BIOLOGY. (Of a virus) unable to reproduce at its normal rate in certain hosts; (of DNA) subject to degradation by a restriction enzyme. **M20.**
6 Of a language system: having a limited syntax and lexicon. **M20.**
7 Of a person: not allowed freedom of movement, esp. for political reasons. **L20.**
■ **restrictedly** *adverb* (earlier in UNRESTRICTEDLY) **L19.** **restrictedness** *noun* **M19.**

restriction /rɪˈstrɪkʃ(ə)n/ *noun.* **LME.**
[Old French, or Latin *restrictio(n-)*, formed as prec.: see -ION.]
1 A thing which restricts someone or something, a limitation on action, a limiting condition or regulation. **LME.**
2 Constriction, compression, contraction. Formerly also, constipation. Now *rare*. **L15.**
3 The action or fact of limiting or restricting someone or something. **M16.** ▸**b** *spec.* Deliberate limitation of industrial output. **L19.**
4 LOGIC. = SUBALTERNATION 3. **M16.**
5 More fully ***mental restriction***. A tacitly introduced reservation. **L17.**
6 BIOLOGY. Limitation of the rate of reproduction of a virus in certain hosts, owing to the destruction of viral DNA by a restriction enzyme. **M20.**
Comb.: **restriction endonuclease**, **restriction enzyme** BIOCHEMISTRY an enzyme which divides DNA molecules at or close to a specific short sequence of nucleotides; **restriction fragment** BIOCHEMISTRY a fragment of a DNA molecule that has been cleaved by a restriction enzyme; ***restriction fragment length polymorphism*** (GENETICS) a variation in the length of restriction fragments produced by a given restriction enzyme in a sample of DNA, used in forensic investigations and to map hereditary disease.
■ **restrictionism** *noun* the policy of restricting some practice, institution, etc. **M20.** **restrictionist** *noun & adjective* (*a*) *noun* an advocate of restrictionism; (*b*) *adjective* of or pertaining to restrictionism or restrictionists: **E19.**

restrictive /rɪˈstrɪktɪv/ *adjective & noun.* **LME.**
[Old & mod. French *restrictif, -ive* or medieval Latin *restrictivus*, formed as RESTRICT: see -IVE.]
▶ **A** *adjective.* †**1** = RESTRINGENT *adjective.* **LME–E18.**
2 Implying, conveying, or expressing restriction or limitation; GRAMMAR (of a relative clause) delimiting the meaning or reference of a modified noun phrase or other element. **L16.**
3 Having the nature or effect of a restriction; imposing a restriction. **E17.**
3 restrictive covenant LAW a covenant imposing a restriction on the use of land; an obligation created by deed not to use land in a certain way. **restrictive practice** an arrangement in industry or trade aimed at restricting or controlling competition or output.
▶ **B** *noun.* †**1** = RESTRINGENT *noun* 2. **LME–L17.**
2 A term or expression having the force of, or implying, a restriction or qualification. **L17.**
■ **restrictively** *adverb* **E17.** **restrictiveness** *noun* **L17.** **restrictivist** *adjective* characterized by restriction, limiting **M20.**

restrike /*as verb* riːˈstrʌɪk, *as noun* ˈriːstrʌɪk/ *verb & noun.* **L19.**
[from RE- + STRIKE *verb*.]
▶ **A** *verb.* Infl. as STRIKE *verb*; pa. t. & pple usu. **-struck** /-ˈstrʌk/.
1 *verb trans.* Strike again; *esp.* stamp (a coin) afresh. **L19.**
2 ELECTRICITY. **a** *verb intrans.* Of an arc: strike again. **M20.** ▸**b** *verb trans.* Cause (an arc) to strike again. **L20.**
▶ **B** *noun.* **1** A reimpression of a coin, print, or medal. **E20.**
2 ELECTRICITY. The re-ignition of an arc. **M20.**

restring /riːˈstrɪŋ/ *verb trans.* Pa. t. & pple **-strung** /-ˈstrʌŋ/. **E19.**
[from RE- + STRING *verb*.]
String again; fit (a musical instrument) with new strings; thread (beads etc.) on a new string.

restringe /rɪˈstrɪn(d)ʒ/ *verb.* Long *rare*. **M16.**
[Latin *restringere*: see RESTRAIN.]
†**1** *verb trans. & intrans.* Have a constipating or astringent effect (on). **M16–M18.**
2 *verb trans.* Confine, limit, restrict. **M16.**

†**restringent** *adjective & noun.* **L16.**
[Latin *restringent-* pres. ppl stem of *restringere*: see RESTRAIN, -ENT.]
▶ **A** *adjective.* Having astringent properties; tending to prevent evacuation of the bowels; styptic. **L16–E19.**
▶ **B** *noun.* **1** A word having a limitative or restricting force. Only in **17.**
2 A medicine or application having astringent or styptic properties. **M17–L18.**
■ †**restringency** *noun* **M17–L18.**

restruck *verb pa. t. & pple*: see RESTRIKE *verb*.

restructure /riːˈstrʌktʃə/ *verb trans.* **M20.**
[from RE- + STRUCTURE *verb*.]
Give a new structure to; rebuild, rearrange.

restrung *verb pa. t. & pple* of RESTRING.

restudy /*as verb* riːˈstʌdi, *as noun* ˈriːstʌdi/ *verb & noun.* **E19.**
[from RE- + STUDY *verb*.]
▶ **A** *verb trans.* Study again. **E19.**
▶ **B** *noun.* The action or an act of restudying something. **M20.**

†**resty** *adjective*[1]. **ME–L17.**
[Old & mod. French *resté* left over, pa. pple of *rester* REST *verb*[3]: see -Y[5]. Cf. REASTY, REESED, REEST *verb*[1].]
Rancid.

resty /ˈrɛsti/ *adjective*[2]. Now *dial.* **E16.**
[Var. of RESTIFF: see -Y[7]. Cf. HASTY, TARDY *adjective*, RUSTY *adjective*[3].]
1 Restive. **E16.**
†**2** Sluggish, lazy; inactive. **M16–E18.**
■ †**restiness** *noun* **M16–E18.**

restyle /riːˈstʌɪl/ *verb trans.* **M20.**
[from RE- + STYLE *verb*.]
Style again; give a new style to; give a new designation or title to.

resuing /rɪˈsjuːɪŋ/ *noun.* **E20.**
[Origin unkn.]
MINING. A method of stoping in which the rock wall adjacent to a narrow vein is removed before the vein itself, so that the ore can be extracted in a cleaner condition.

result /rɪˈzʌlt/ *noun.* **E17.**
[from the verb.]
†**1** The action of springing back again *to* a former position or place. *rare*. Only in **E17.**

†**2** An impulse, an inclination. Only in M17.
3 A decision or resolution, esp. of a council or assembly. Now *US*. M17.
4 The effect, consequence, issue, or outcome of some action, process, or design. M17. ▸**b** A quantity, formula, etc., obtained by calculation; an item of information obtained by experiment or some other scientific method. L18. ▸**c** In *pl.* The outcome of trading over a given period, expressed as a statement of profit or loss announced by a business. L19. ▸**d** A final mark, score, or placing in an examination or a sporting event. Usu. in *pl.* E20. ▸**e** In *pl.* Satisfactory or favourable consequences (freq. in ***get results***). Also *sing.*, a successful performance against an opponent, esp. in a sporting event; a game which ends with an outright winner as opp. to being drawn. E20.

3 *New York Law Journal* Munder . . concurs in the result. **4** *Law Times* The result being that his profits diminished. T. CAPOTE Hospitalized as a result of his . . accident. **b** H. S. M. COXETER The result is 52, 5, 3. **c** *Daily Telegraph* Reed's first-half results . . are a little disappointing. E. WAUGH I have a list of the results . . Percy has done extremely well. **d** D. CUSACK Their results in other subjects . . are very disappointing. **e** E. O'NEILL Kept my nose to the grindstone . . . And I got results. J. SNOW The wicket most likely to produce a result. *Tennis World* It was a big win because I didn't have any results before.

■ **resultative** *adjective & noun* (GRAMMAR) (*a*) *adjective* expressing result; (*b*) *noun* a resultative verb: E20. **resultful** *adjective* having many results; fruitful: L19. **resultless** *adjective* M19.

result /rɪˈzʌlt/ *verb intrans.* LME.
[Latin *resultare* spring back, reverberate, (in medieval Latin) result, formed as RE- + *saltare* leap.]
1 Arise as an effect, issue, or outcome *from* some action, process, or design; end or conclude *in* a specified manner. LME.
†**2** Recoil; rebound, spring back. L16–L18.
3 LAW. Revert *to* a person. Now *rare*. M18.

1 E. JOHNSON All his sufferings had resulted from the . . marriage. J. N. ISBISTER Anti-Semitism . . had resulted in his not receiving academic recognition. **2** POPE The huge round stone resulting with a bound Thunders . . down. **3** W. CRUISE The use resulted to the feoffor.

resultance /rɪˈzʌlt(ə)ns/ *noun*. Now *rare*. LME.
[from (the same root as) prec. + -ANCE.]
†**1** Origin, beginning. *rare*. Only in LME.
†**2** The sum or gist of or *of* something. E–M17.
3 †**a** A thing issuing, proceeding, or emanating from another thing. Only in 17. ▸†**b** A reflection, an image in a mirror etc. E–M17. ▸**c** A result, an effect, an outcome. M17.
†**4** The fact of issuing or resulting (*from* something). Chiefly in ***by resultance***, derivatively. M–L17.

†**resultancy** *noun*. E17.
[formed as prec.: see -ANCY.]
1 = RESULTANCE 3a. E17–E18. ▸**b** = RESULTANCE 3b. E–M17.
2 = RESULTANCE 4. M–L17.
3 = RESULTANCE 2. M–L17.

resultant /rɪˈzʌlt(ə)nt/ *noun*. LME.
[Use as noun of Latin *resultant-*: see next.]
†**1** MATH. The total, the sum. *rare*. Only in LME.
2 MECHANICS. That force which is the equivalent or sum of two or more forces acting in different directions at one point; more widely, the composite or final effect of any two or more physical forces, agencies, etc. E19. ▸**b** The product or outcome *of* something. M19.

2 W. WHEWELL If two forces act in opposite directions, the resultant will be the difference . . in the direction of the greater. **b** F. R. LEAVIS The poem is the resultant of diverse suggestions.

¶ Rare before E19.

resultant /rɪˈzʌlt(ə)nt/ *adjective*. E17.
[Latin *resultant-* pres. ppl stem of *resultare*: see RESULT *verb*, -ANT[1].]
†**1** Reflecting, shining by reflection. E–M17.
2 That results, resulting, esp. as the total outcome of more or less opposed forces; consequent. M17.

2 F. W. FARRAR The overthrow of the . . city, and the resultant terror. *Times* The resultant mapping will be used in the general development. **resultant tone** MUSIC = COMBINATION *tone*.

■ **resultantly** *adverb* M19.

resume /rɪˈzjuːm/ *verb*. LME.
[Old & mod. French *résumer* or Latin *resumere*, formed as RE- + *sumere* take.]
▸ **I** *verb trans.* **1** Assume or put on again (something, esp. an emotion, faculty, or state) esp. after loss, relinquishment, or discard. LME. ▸**b** Reoccupy (a place or seat). M17.
2 a Begin again, recommence, (a practice or occupation) esp. after interruption; *esp.* go on again with, continue, (a discussion, statement, remark, etc.); (freq. with direct speech as obj.) go on to say. LME. ▸**b** Reassemble or bring together again for the transaction of business. *rare*. L15.
3 Take back into one's own possession, reassume possession of, (something, esp. lands, rights, etc., previously given or granted to another). LME.
4 a Repeat (a sentence or word). *rare*. LME. ▸**b** Recapitulate or summarize (facts etc.). L15.
5 a Take back (a person) to or into a specified state or relation. *arch*. L15. ▸**b** Take or pick up (a thing) to use again; return to the use of. L16.

1 E. BOWEN The two . . had resumed that air they wore on their wedding day. I. MURDOCH They both . . resumed their former postures. **b** DRYDEN Reason resum'd her place, and passion fled. D. L. SAYERS The jury returned; . . the judge resumed his seat. **2a** V. WOOLF The grey nurse resumed her knitting. J. B. MORTON Determined to resume his old life of careless gaiety. A. CARTER 'As I was saying,' she resumed. **3** T. SHERLOCK Why should God resume this Authority out of the Hands of His Son? H. J. S. MAINE In the case of . . villeins the lord did not resume their land. **4a** G. JOYE He resumeth the same sentence yet agen. **b** E. DOWDEN A philosophy which should resume all his views. **5a** H. VAUGHAN Resume thy spirit from this world. SHELLEY If Heaven should resume thee. **b** SPENSER My former shield I may resume againe. C. V. WEDGWOOD He . . resumed his cloak.

▸ **II** *verb intrans.* **6** Take a thing back into one's possession; reassume possession of something. Now *rare*. M16.
7 Give a résumé or summary. Long *rare* or *obsolete*. L18.
8 Recommence an interrupted practice or occupation; *esp.* go on again with or continue a discussion, statement, remark, etc.; go on to say something. E19.

6 J. WESLEY Love that lends our Joys, And Love resumes again. **8** W. GERHARDIE Firing subsided and then resumed. *Sunday Express* The concert is ready to resume. S. BEDFORD Things resumed much as they had been.

■ **resumable** *adjective* M17.

résumé /ˈrɛzjʊmeɪ/ *noun & verb*. Also **resumé**, in sense A.2 **resume**. E19.
[French, pa. pple of *résumer* RESUME.]
▸ **A** *noun*. **1** A summary, an epitome. E19.
2 A curriculum vitae. Chiefly *N. Amer.* M20.

1 A. BRINK Ben gave a resumé of Gordon's story. **2** *attrib.*: *New Musical Express* His most impressive résumé entry being a stint as a hired gun.

▸ **B** *verb trans.* Make a résumé of. *rare*. L19.

resummon /riːˈsʌmən/ *verb trans.* L16.
[from RE- + SUMMON *verb*.]
†**1** Issue (a writ) again. *rare*. Only in L16.
†**2** Recall (a thing) to mind. *rare*. Only in E17.
3 Convene (an assembly) again; summon (a person) again. E17.

resummons /riːˈsʌmənz/ *noun*. L15.
[Anglo-Norman *resomons*, from *re-* RE- + SUMMONS *noun*.]
LAW. A second or renewed summons.

resumption /rɪˈzʌm(p)ʃ(ə)n/ *noun*. LME.
[Old & mod. French *résumption* or late Latin *resumptio(n-)*, from Latin *resumpt-* pa. ppl stem of *resumere* RESUME *verb*: see -ION.]
1 LAW. The action, on the part of the Crown or other authority, of reassuming possession of lands, rights, etc., previously given or granted to another; an instance of this. LME. ▸**b** *gen.* The action or an act of taking something back into one's own possession. E18.
2 The action or an act of resuming, taking up, or commencing something again. L16. ▸**b** A return to specie payments. M19.
3 Recapitulation; a summary. *rare*. E18.

resumptive /rɪˈzʌm(p)tɪv/ *adjective & noun*. LME.
[In sense 1 from late Latin *resumptivus*, from Latin *resumpt-* (see prec.); in sense 2 from prec. after *presumptive*, *consumptive*, etc.: see -IVE.]
▸ **A** *adjective*. †**1** Of a medicine or medical preparation: restorative. *rare*. LME–M17.
2 That resumes, repeats, or summarizes something; GRAMMAR indicating resumption of a topic etc., having previous reference. M19.
▸ **B** *noun*. †**1** A restorative medicine. M16–M18.
2 GRAMMAR. A resumed topic etc. having previous reference. M20.
■ **resumptively** *adverb* E18.

resupinate /rɪˈsuːpɪneɪt, -ˈsjuː-/ *adjective*. L18.
[Latin *resupinatus* pa. pple of *resupinare* bend back, formed as RE- + SUPINE *adjective* + -ATE[2].]
Chiefly BOTANY. Inverted; *esp.* (of a flower) appearing by a twist of the stalk or ovary to be upside down.

resupination /rɪsuːpɪˈneɪʃ(ə)n, -sjuː-/ *noun*. E17.
[from Latin *resupinat-* pa. ppl stem of *resupinare*: see prec., -ATION.]
†**1 a** The effect of height on the proportions of a standing figure. *rare*. E–M17. ▸**b** The action of putting a part of the body etc. into an inverted position. Also, the fact of lying on, or the action of turning on, the back. *rare*. Only in M17.
2 BOTANY. Inversion of a flower etc. M18.

resupine /riːsuːˈpʌɪn, -sjuː-/ *adjective*. E17.
[Latin *resupinus*, formed as RE- + SUPINE *adjective*.]
†**1** Listless, apathetic. *rare*. E–M17.
2 Lying on the back; inclined backwards. M17.

resurgam /rɪˈsəːgam/ *interjection*. M17.
[Latin, lit. 'I shall rise again'.]
Proclaiming one's Christian faith in the resurrection of the dead.

resurge /rɪˈsəːdʒ/ *verb intrans.* L16.
[Latin *resurgere*, formed as RE- + *surgere* rise.]
Rise again.

re-surge /riːˈsəːdʒ/ *verb intrans.* L19.
[from RE- + SURGE *verb*.]
Surge back again.

resurgence /rɪˈsəːdʒ(ə)ns/ *noun*. M19.
[from Latin *resurgent-* pres. ppl stem of *resurgere*: see next, -ENCE.]
1 The action of rising again. M19.
2 The fissure through which a stream re-emerges at the end of an underground part of its course; the re-emergence of such a stream. M20.

resurgent /rɪˈsəːdʒ(ə)nt/ *noun & adjective*. L18.
[Latin *resurgent-* pres. ppl stem of *resurgere*: see RESURGE, -ENT.]
▸ **A** *noun*. **1** A person who has risen again. L18.
2 = RESURGENCE 2. M20.
▸ **B** *adjective*. **1** That rises, or tends to rise, again. E19.
2 GEOLOGY. Of or pertaining to steam and other gases which after being absorbed by volcanic magma from groundwater and native rock are subsequently released into the atmosphere. E20.

resurrect /rɛzəˈrɛkt/ *verb*. L18.
[Back-form. from next.]
1 *verb trans.* Raise (a person) from the dead; take from the grave, exhume; restore to life or view again; *fig.* revive the practice or memory of. L18.
2 *verb intrans.* Rise from the dead; be resurrected. E19.
3 *verb trans.* PHYSICAL GEOGRAPHY. Uncover by erosion (a landform formerly covered by deposition). Chiefly as ***resurrected*** *ppl adjective*. E20.

1 D. HEWETT Old bikes Stan had resurrected off the tip. R. TRAVERS Every failure . . of the detective's past was resurrected in a scathing attack. **2** P. PORTER Christians can resurrect anywhere.

■ **resurrector** *noun* (*rare*) (*a*) = RESURRECTIONIST (a); (*b*) a person who resurrects a person or thing: M19.

resurrection /rɛzəˈrɛkʃ(ə)n/ *noun & verb*. ME.
[Old & mod. French *résurrection* from late Latin *resurrectio(n-)*, from Latin *resurrect-* pa. ppl stem of *resurgere*: see RESURGE, -ION.]
▸ **A** *noun*. **1** CHRISTIAN CHURCH. (Also **R-**.) The rising of Christ from the dead. Also (chiefly *Hist.*), a church-festival commemorating this. ME. ▸**b** A dramatic, pictorial, or other representation of the resurrection of Christ. ME.
2 CHRISTIAN CHURCH. The rising of the dead at the Last Judgement. ME.
3 Revival from disuse, inactivity, or decay; restoration to vogue or memory; an instance of this. LME.
4 A resurrected thing. *rare*. L18.
5 Exhumation. Chiefly in ***resurrection man*** below. L18.

1 J. TAIT The men that condemned Christ were the first to be made aware of His resurrection. **2** P. CAREY Mrs. Cousins believed in the resurrection of the dead. **3** S. RUSHDIE Played in the room . . , this conversation overwhelms her, this electronic resurrection.

Comb.: **resurrection body** CHRISTIAN CHURCH the form in which a person will appear at the Last Judgement; **resurrection fern** any of several ferns which survive drought, esp. *Polypodium polypodioides*, of tropical and warm-temperate America; **resurrection man** *Hist.* = ***body-snatcher*** s.v. BODY *noun*; **resurrection plant** any of several plants which appear dead during drought but revive when moistened; *esp.* (*a*) a Californian clubmoss, *Selaginella lepidophylla*; (*b*) the rose of Jericho, *Anastatica hierochuntica*.

▸ **B** *verb trans.* Cause to resurrect. *rare*. M17.
■ **resurrectional** *adjective* of, pertaining to, or concerned with resurrection M19. **resurrectioner** *noun* (*rare*) = RESURRECTIONIST (a) E19. **resurrectionist** *noun* (*a*) *Hist.* a body-snatcher; a resurrection man; (*b*) *gen.* a person who resurrects something (*lit. & fig.*); (*c*) a believer in resurrection: L18. **resurrectionize** *verb trans.* (now *rare*) resurrect E19.

resurrective /rɛzəˈrɛktɪv/ *adjective*. *rare*. M17.
[from Latin *resurrect-* (see prec.) + -IVE.]
Of, pertaining to, or causing resurrection.

resurvey /riːˈsəːveɪ/ *noun*. M17.
[from RE- + SURVEY *noun*.]
A fresh survey.

resurvey /riːsəˈveɪ/ *verb trans.* L16.
[from RE- + SURVEY *verb*.]
1 Read over again; examine or consider afresh. L16.
2 Make a survey of (land etc.) again. M18.

resuscitable /rɪˈsʌsɪtəb(ə)l/ *adjective*. L17.
[Irreg. from next: see -ABLE.]
Able to be resuscitated.
■ **resuscitaˈbility** *noun* E20.

resuscitate /rɪˈsʌsɪteɪt/ *verb*. Pa. pple & ppl adjective **-ated**, (earlier) †**-ate**. E16.
[Orig. pa. pple, from Latin *resuscitatus* pa. pple of *resuscitare*, formed as RE- + *suscitare* raise, revive: see -ATE³.]
1 *verb trans.* Revive (a person) from apparent death or unconsciousness. E16.
2 *verb trans.* Revive, renew, or restore (a thing). E16.
3 *verb intrans.* Revive, be resuscitated. M17.

1 P. D. JAMES Try to resuscitate her, give her the kiss of life. **2** *New Statesman* She resuscitates one of the master themes of Conservative politics.

■ **resuscitative** *adjective* tending to resuscitate; revivifying, reviving: E17. **resuscitator** *noun* M19.

resuscitation /rɪˌsʌsɪˈteɪʃ(ə)n/ *noun*. L15.
[Late Latin *resuscitatio(n-)*, from Latin *resuscitat-* pa. ppl stem of *resuscitare*: see prec., -ATION.]
1 Revival of a person from apparent death or unconsciousness; an instance of this. L15.
2 Revival, renewal, or restoration of something; an instance of this. M17.

1 *New York Times* A near-drowned man being given mouth-to-mouth resuscitation. **2** E. JONES The patient's 'resistance' against the resuscitation of buried memories.

†**resverie** *noun* var. of REVERIE *noun*.

ret /rɛt/ *noun*¹. M19.
[from the verb.]
Retting; an instance of this.

ret /rɛt/ *noun*². *colloq. rare*. L19.
[Abbreviation of REITERATION.]
PRINTING. A form used to perfect a sheet of paper. Also, the second side of a printed sheet.

ret /rɛt/ *verb*. Infl. **-tt-**. LME.
[Rel. to ROT *verb*, corresp. to Middle Dutch *reeten*, (also mod.) *reten*, Middle Low German *röten*, Middle Dutch *ro(o)ten*.]
1 *verb trans.* Soften (esp. flax or hemp) by soaking in water or by exposure to moisture to encourage partial rotting. LME.
2 *verb trans.* Spoil (hay etc.) by wet or rot. Usu. in *pass.* M17.
3 *verb trans. & intrans.* Rot. M19.

ret. *abbreviation*.
1 Retired.
2 Returned.

retable /rɪˈteɪb(ə)l/ *noun*. E19.
[French *rétable*, *retable* from Spanish *retablo* from medieval Latin *retrotabulum*, from Latin RETRO- + *tabula* TABLE *noun*.]
A frame enclosing painted or decorated panels or a shelf or ledge for ornaments, raised above the back of an altar.

retablo /rɪˈtɑːbləʊ/ *noun*. Pl. **-os**. M19.
[Spanish: see prec.]
= prec. Also, a votive picture displayed in a church.

retail /ˈriːteɪl/ *noun, adjective, & adverb*. LME.
[Anglo-Norman (Anglo-Latin *retallia*, also in *ad retalliam vendere* sell by retail), spec. use of Old French *retaille* piece cut off, shred, from *retaillier*, from *re-* RE- + *taillier* cut (see TAIL *verb*¹).]
▸ **A** *noun*. **1** The sale to the public of goods in relatively small quantities, and usu. not for resale. Freq. opp. ***wholesale***. LME.
†**2** A detail. M–L17.
3 A retailer, a retail dealer. M19.
▸ **B** *attrib.* or as *adjective*. **1** Of or pertaining to the retailing of goods; sold by retail. E17.
2 Parcelled out; piecemeal. Also, petty, trivial. Long *rare* or *obsolete*. M17.
Special collocations & comb.: **retail park** (orig. *US*) an out-of-town shopping development, usu. containing a number of large chain stores. **retail price index** an index of the variation in the prices of retail goods. **retail price maintenance** = *RESALE price maintenance*. **retail therapy** *joc.* the practice of shopping in order to make oneself more cheerful.
▸ **C** *adverb*. By retail; at a retail price. L18.

retail /ˈriːteɪl, *esp. in sense* 2 rɪˈteɪl/ *verb*. LME.
[from prec.]
1 *verb trans.* Sell (goods) by retail. LME. ▸**b** *verb intrans.* Of goods: be sold by retail, esp. for a specified price. Freq. foll. by *at*, *for*. L19.
2 *verb trans.* Recount; relate in detail; repeat to another. L16.
■ **retailer** *noun* LME. **retailment** *noun* (now *rare*) the action or an act of retailing news etc. M19.

retain /rɪˈteɪn/ *verb*. LME.
[Anglo-Norman *reteig(n)-* repr. tonic stem of Old & mod. French *retenir* from Proto-Romance from Latin *retinere*, formed as RE- + *tenere* hold.]
▸ **I** *verb trans.* **1** †**a** Restrain; hold back, stop; prevent, hinder. LME–M18. ▸**b** Orig., keep in custody or under control. Later, keep in place, hold fixed. Freq. as ***retaining** ppl adjective*. M16.
2 †**a** Entertain, give hospitality to. *rare*. LME–L16. ▸**b** Keep attached to one's person or engaged in one's service. LME. ▸**c** Orig. *gen.*, (*rare*) engage, hire. Later *spec.*, secure the services of (esp. a barrister) by engagement and preliminary payment. M16.
3 **a** Keep hold or possession of; continue to have, keep, or possess. LME. ▸**b** Continue to use, practise, or recognize. M16. ▸**c** Allow to remain or prevail; preserve. E19.
4 Keep or bear in mind; remember. L15.

1b A. HENRY Skin, which alone retained his hand to his arm. **retaining wall** a wall supporting or confining a mass of earth or water. **2b** *Scholarly Publishing* Consultants had to be retained to redesign it. **c** J. BARTH The nurses and the minister retained separate attorneys. A. HAILEY The firm had been retained on the advice of . . lawyers. **retaining fee** a fee paid to secure the services of someone, esp. a barrister. **3a** W. COBBETT It seems to me to . . retain the water. M. STOTT Michael Foot's failure to retain the leadership. **b** B. JOWETT Better . . to retain the order in which Plato . . has arranged this. P. P. READ Authority he still retained from the old days. **c** LYTTON To this day are retained the massive walls. **retained object** *rare* (GRAMMAR) an object of a passive verb. **retained profit** profit retained in a business as opp. to being distributed to owners or shareholders. **4** H. WACE Unable to retain any but the simplest thought. A. BROOKNER They both retained a happy memory of . . Toto.

▸ **II** *verb intrans.* †**5** Refrain *from* something. M16–E17.
†**6** Adhere, belong, be attached *to*. M16–E18.
7 Remember. L16.
†**8** Continue, remain. *rare*. Only in M17.

7 E. B. TITCHENER The quick learner appears to retain as well as the slow.

■ **retainaˈbility** *noun* ability to be retained M19. **retainable** *adjective* †(**a**) (of a court action) able to be heard; (**b**) able to be retained: LME. **retainment** *noun* (**a**) the action or an act of retaining something; retention; †(**b**) entertainment, maintenance: LME.

retainer /rɪˈteɪnə/ *noun*¹. LME.
[from prec. + -ER⁴.]
1 Chiefly LAW. The action or fact of retaining something for oneself; an authorization to do this. Now *rare*. LME.
2 †**a** Engagement of a person esp. as a servant; entertainment or maintenance of a dependant or adherent. LME–M17. ▸**b** The fact of being retained in a particular capacity. L18. ▸**c** An authorization given to an attorney to act in a case. Chiefly *US*. E19.
3 **a** A fee paid to secure the services of someone, esp. a barrister; engagement by such a fee. L18. ▸**b** A sum paid to secure a particular service or facility; *spec.* a reduced rent paid to retain accommodation during a period of non-occupancy. M19.

retainer /rɪˈteɪnə/ *noun*². E16.
[formed as prec. + -ER¹.]
1 A dependant or follower of a person of rank or position (*Hist.*). Also (chiefly *joc.*), an old or faithful friend or servant (also ***old retainer***). E16.
2 **a** A person who or thing which retains or holds something. M16. ▸**b** DENTISTRY. A structure cemented to a tooth and connected to a bridge to hold it in place. L19.
■ **retainership** *noun* the state or position of being a retainer; the system of having retainers: L16.

retake /ˈriːteɪk/ *noun*. E20.
[from the verb.]
1 The action or an act of filming a scene etc. or recording music etc. again; a scene, recording, etc., obtained in this way. E20.
2 *gen.* The action or an act of retaking something; an examination or test (to be) taken again. M20.

1 S. BRETT The whole six minutes ran . . and no retakes were required. **2** *Times* 'Crammers' who promise good coaching for re-takes.

retake /riːˈteɪk/ *verb*. Pa. t. **-took** /-ˈtʊk/; pa. pple **-taken** /-ˈteɪk(ə)n/. LME.
[from RE- + TAKE *verb*.]
1 *verb trans.* Take again; take back. LME.
2 *verb trans.* Recapture. M17.
3 *verb intrans. & trans.* CHESS. Capture in return (a piece which has just made a capture). M19.
4 *verb intrans. & trans.* Take (esp. an examination or test) over again. M20.

1 F. BURNEY The expectations . . retook possession of her heart. J. AUSTEN She retook her . . place at the . . table. **2** *Spectator* The siege had been raised and Berber retaken. **4** *Horse & Hound* One . . week's preparation course for A1 (suitable for those retaking). P. FARMER I failed my exams. and . . had to spend . . last year retaking them.

■ **retaker** *noun* a person who retakes something L17.

retaliate /rɪˈtalɪeɪt/ *verb*. E17.
[Latin *retaliat-* pa. ppl stem of *retaliare*, formed as RE- + *talis* of such a kind: see -ATE³.]
1 *verb trans.* Requite, repay in kind (esp. an injury or insult). Also, cast (a charge or accusation) back *on* a person. Cf. earlier RETALIATION. E17.
†**2** *verb trans.* Give (something) in return or reply. Also, repay or requite (a person). *rare*. Only in M17.
3 *verb intrans.* Make requital or repayment in kind for something, esp. an injury or insult; attack in return; take reprisals. M17.

1 JAS. MILL Authority for retaliating some of the indignities. H. T. BUCKLE They used their abilities to retaliate the injury. **3** P. WARNER The English began hanging their prisoners . . ; the French retaliated by drowning theirs. *Daily Telegraph* He retaliated yesterday by defeating Connors.

■ **retaliative** *adjective* tending to retaliate; of the nature of retaliation: E19. **retaliator** *noun* a person who retaliates L18. **retaliatory** *adjective* of, pertaining to, or characteristic of retaliation E19.

retaliation /rɪˌtalɪˈeɪʃ(ə)n/ *noun*. L16.
[Prob. from (the same root as) prec.: see -ATION. Perh. partly from RE- + TALIATION.]
The action or an act of retaliating; requital or repayment in kind, esp. for injury or insult.

A. BLOND In retaliation for the American's piracy of Charles Dickens. P. CASEMENT The therapist has to . . respond to the patient's attacks, . . without . . retaliation.

retama /rəˈtɑːmə/ *noun*. M19.
[Spanish *retama* from Arab. *ratam(a)*.]
1 Any of various brooms and similar leguminous shrubs characteristic of arid regions of the western Mediterranean, including *Genista monosperma* and Spanish broom, *Spartium junceum*. M19.
2 Any of various thorny leguminous shrubs of the south-western US, esp. Jerusalem thorn (*Parkinsonia aculeata*) and palo verde. L19.

retard /rɪˈtɑːd, *in sense* 3 ˈriːtɑːd/ *noun*. L18.
[French, from *retarder*: see next.]
1 Retardation, delay. L18. ▸**b** = RETARDATION 2b(b). *rare*. M19.
2 In a motor vehicle, an adjustment for retarding the ignition spark. M20.
3 A person with a mental handicap. Also used as a term of abuse. *N. Amer. slang*. L20.

1 T. JEFFERSON A single day's retard. **in retard** retarded, delayed; ***in retard of***, behind (*lit. & fig.*). **3** G. C. CHESBRO Their dwarf son is a retard with a big nose.

retard /rɪˈtɑːd/ *verb*. L15.
[Old & mod. French *retarder* from Latin *retardare*, formed as RE- + *tardus* slow.]
1 *verb trans.* Keep back, delay, hinder; make slow or late; delay the progress, development, or accomplishment of. L15. ▸**b** Defer, postpone, put off. *rare*. M18.
2 *verb intrans.* Be or become delayed; come, appear, or happen later; undergo retardation. Now *rare*. M17.

1 F. CLISSOLD We had been much retarded by difficulties. P. QUILLIN Malnutrition . . retards healing. *Times* Men's drinking may retard unborn sons. **b** SIR W. SCOTT Now either to advance or retard the hour. **2** SIR T. BROWNE Putrefaction . . shall retard or accelerate according to the . . season. J. F. W. HERSCHEL The force retards, and the moon approaches.

■ **retardative** *adjective* tending or having the ability to retard M19. **retardatory** *adjective* having a retarding effect or influence M19. **retardive** *adjective* (*rare*) retardative L18. **retardment** *noun* the action or an act of retarding; (a) retardation; (a) delay: M17. **retardure** *noun* (long *rare* or *obsolete*) retardment M18.

retardance /rɪˈtɑːd(ə)ns/ *noun*. M16.
[Obsolete French, formed as prec.: see -ANCE.]
†**1** Retardation. M–L16.
2 The action of retarding; retardancy. Chiefly as 2nd elem. of comb., as ***fire retardance***, ***flame retardance***. M20.

retardancy /rɪˈtɑːd(ə)nsi/ *noun*. M20.
[formed as prec.: see -ANCY.]
The ability to retard. Chiefly as 2nd elem. of comb., as ***fire retardancy***, ***flame retardancy***.

retardant /rɪˈtɑːd(ə)nt/ *adjective & noun*. M17.
[from RETARD *verb* + -ANT¹.]
▸ **A** *adjective*. Retarding, tending to retard. Now chiefly as 2nd elem. of comb., as ***fire-retardant***, ***flame-retardant***. M17.
▸ **B** *noun*. A retarding agent, *esp.* a substance that reduces or inhibits a specified phenomenon (chiefly as 2nd elem. of comb., as ***fire retardant***, ***flame retardant***). M20.

retardataire /rətardatɛːr/ *noun & adjective*. Pl. of noun pronounced same. E20.
[French.]
Chiefly ART. ▸**A** *noun*. A work of art executed in the style of an earlier period. E20.
▸ **B** *adjective*. Behind the times; characterized by the style of an earlier period. M20.

retardate /rɪˈtɑːdeɪt/ *adjective & noun*. L16.
[Latin *retardatus* pa. pple of *retardare* RETARD *verb*: see -ATE².]
▸ **A** *adjective*. †**1** That has been retarded; slow; late. *rare*. Only in L16.
2 *spec.* Of a person: handicapped, esp. mentally or physically. *N. Amer.* M20.
▸ **B** *noun*. A person with a handicap. *N. Amer.* M20.
¶ Not recorded between L16 and M20.

retardation /riːtɑːˈdeɪʃ(ə)n/ *noun*. LME.
[Old & mod. French, or late Latin *retardatio(n-)*, from *retardat-* pa. ppl stem of *retardare* RETARD *verb*: see -ATION.]
1 The action or an act of retarding; the result of this; *spec.* backwardness in mental, physical, educational, or social development. LME.
2 SCIENCE. **a** Slowing, deceleration. M17. ▸**b** The lagging of the cycle of high and low tides behind (*a*) the cycle of day and night; (*b*) the period of the moon's transit across the meridian (cf. ESTABLISHMENT 7). L18.
3 MUSIC. A form of suspension in which resolution is achieved by rising a degree to a note forming a real part of the second chord. E19.

> **1** B. STILLINGFLEET Determine . . the acceleration or retardation of the winter. *Nature* Growth retardation occurs in rabbits congenitally infected with rubella. G. SERENY Psychopathy is not generally identified with mental retardation.

retarded /rɪˈtɑːdɪd/ *adjective & noun*. E19.
[from RETARD *verb* + -ED[1].]
▶ **A** *adjective*. **1** That has been retarded; *spec.* backward in mental, physical, educational, or social development (now considered *offensive*). E19.
2 PHYSICS. Designating parameters of an electromagnetic field which allow for the finite speed of wave propagation, so that the potential due to a distant source is expressed in terms of the state of the source at some time in the past. E20.

> **1** E. PAWEL Slow, if not downright retarded, in his sexual development. A. BRIEN How *backward* I was, *she* feared possibly *retarded*.

▶ **B** *noun pl.* *The* class of retarded people. *offensive*. M20.

retardee /riːtɑːˈdiː/ *noun*. *US*. *offensive*. L20.
[formed as prec. + -EE[1].]
A person with a mental handicap.

retarder /rɪˈtɑːdə/ *noun*. M17.
[formed as prec. + -ER[1].]
1 *gen.* A person who or thing which retards someone or something. M17.
2 A substance or device which acts as a retarding agent to a reaction or process. L19.

retch /rɛtʃ/ *verb*[1] *& noun*[1]. *obsolete* exc. *dial.* LME.
[Var. of REACH *verb*[1].]
▶ **A** *verb*. **1** *verb intrans.* Stretch; extend; reach. LME.
2 *verb trans.* Stretch or draw (a thing) *out*; *esp.* stretch (leather) in tanning. L15.
▶ **B** *noun*. †**1** Reach, grasp (*lit. & fig.*). LME–E17.
2 A (long) stretch of a river. M17.

retch /rɛtʃ, riːtʃ/ *verb*[2] *& noun*[2]. M16.
[Var. of REACH *verb*[2].]
▶ **A** *verb*. †**1** *verb intrans.* Hawk, bring *up* phlegm. M16–E17.
2 *verb intrans.* Make a motion of vomiting, esp. involuntarily and without effect. M19.
3 *verb trans.* Vomit (matter). L19.

> **2** D. WELCH I began to . . retch and be sick. **3** S. RAVEN Retching out little bursts of vomit.

▶ **B** *noun*. An act or instance of retching. M16.

> J. LE CARRÉ She began coughing . . , one hacking retch after another.

†**retchless** *adjective & adverb* var. of RECKLESS.

retd. *abbreviation*.
1 Retired.
2 Returned.

rete /ˈriːti/ *noun*. Pl. **retia** /ˈriːtɪə, ˈriːʃɪə/. LME.
[Latin = net.]
1 a An openwork metal plate fixed to an astrolabe, serving to indicate the positions of the principal fixed stars. LME. ▸†**b** A graduated scale affixed to an astronomical telescope. M–L17.
2 ANATOMY & ZOOLOGY. A network or plexus of vessels, fibres, or strands of tissue; *spec.* in full ***rete mirabile*** /mɪˈrɑːbɪli/, pl. ***rete mirabilia*** /mɪrəˈbɪlɪə/, [= wonderful] an elaborate network of fine blood-vessels, esp. diverging and converging arterioles, as that which controls the supply of gas to the swim bladder of many fishes. M16. ▸**b** The lower layer of the epidermis, containing the pigment cells. Also more fully ***rete Malpighii*** /malˈpɪɡɪʌɪ/ [= of Malpighi: see MALPIGHIAN], ***rete mucosum*** /mjʊˈkəʊsəm/ [= mucous]. L18. ▸**c** In full ***rete testis*** [= of the testis]. A network of vessels by which sperm pass from the seminiferous tubules to the vasa efferentia. L18.

retell /riːˈtɛl/ *verb trans.* Pa. t. & pple **-told** /-ˈtəʊld/. L16.
[from RE- + TELL *verb*.]
Tell (esp. a story) again. Also (*rare*), count again.

> *Athenaeum* It has lost nothing of its horror in the retelling.

retene /ˈrɛtiːn/ *noun*. M19.
[from Greek *rhētinē* resin + -ENE.]
CHEMISTRY. A polycyclic hydrocarbon, $C_{18}H_{18}$, related to abietic acid and occurring in resins; 7-isopropyl-1-methylphenanthrene.

retentate /rɪˈtɛnteɪt/ *noun*. M20.
[from Latin *retent-* (see next) + -ATE[2].]
Material which fails to pass through a semipermeable membrane during dialysis.

retention /rɪˈtɛnʃ(ə)n/ *noun*. LME.
[Old & mod. French, or Latin *retentio(n-)*, from *retent-* pa. ppl stem of *retinere*: see RETAIN, -ION.]
1 Power to retain something; capacity for holding or keeping something. LME.
2 MEDICINE. Failure to eliminate secreted or excreted matter (esp. urine) from the body; an instance of this. LME.
3 a The fact of keeping or bearing a thing in mind; the ability to do this; memory; *esp.* in PSYCHOLOGY, the faculty of retaining specific previously learned tasks or information in the memory (freq. distinguished from ***encoding*** and ***retrieval***). LME. ▸**b** The fact of maintaining, keeping up, or continuing to use something. E17. ▸**c** In phenomenology, the continued consciousness of or existence in the present of a previous act or event. M20.
4 The action or fact of keeping a thing in one's own possession or control. M16. ▸**b** Something that is kept back or retained. E20.
5 The action or fact of holding a thing fast or keeping a thing fixed in a place or position; the fact or condition of being kept, or of remaining, in place. Formerly also, detention of a person by forcible or other means. L16. ▸**b** Self-restraint, control. Formerly also, (a) restraint, (a) check. *rare*. E17.

> **1** J. BADCOCK Its ready absorption and retention of water. **3b** B. MOORE Your congregation might . . be served by retention of the Latin Mass. **4** J. R. GREEN The House . . insisted on the retention of its power. H. WILLIAMSON Two copies . . will be sent . . , one for your retention. **b** *Daily Mail* Ilderton . . looked a cheap retention at 100 gs. **5** J. TYNDALL A northern aspect . . causes . . the retention of the snow. **b** W. GIFFORD The retention with which he speaks of them . . is to be admired.

Comb.: **retention money**: withheld for an agreed period by a purchaser or contractee as security against the failure to fulfil a contract.

▪ **retentional** *adjective* of or pertaining to retention M20. **retentionist** *noun & adjective* (*a*) *noun* a person who advocates the retention of something; *esp.* an advocate of the retention of capital punishment; (*b*) *adjective* of or pertaining to retentionists: L19.

†**retentive** *noun*. LME.
[French, formed as next.]
1 Retention; *spec.* the power of retaining something in the mind; recollection, memory. LME–L15.
2 A restraining force; a means of restraint. E–M17.
3 *euphem.* In *pl.* The organs which regulate excretion. L17–E18.

retentive /rɪˈtɛntɪv/ *adjective*. LME.
[Old & mod. French *retentif*, *-ive* or medieval Latin *retentivus*, from Latin *retent-*: see RETENTION, -IVE.]
1 Of a person, the memory: good at remembering; tenacious. LME.
†**2** Sparing, niggardly, disinclined to spend money. Formerly also, restrained, cautious, reticent. LME–L17.
3 MEDICINE. Of a ligature etc.: serving to keep something in place. Also *gen.*, holding or confining something, keeping a firm hold (now *rare*). LME.
4 Having the property of retaining, tending to retain, a quality etc.; (esp. of a substance) apt to retain or hold moisture. Freq. foll. by *of*. M16.

> **1** F. TOMLIN Recording TSE's conversation . . from notes or from a fairly retentive memory. **4** DEFOE Woolen manufactures are . . retentive of infection. T. H. HUXLEY The chalk . . becomes stiff and retentive.

▪ **retentively** *adverb* (*rare*) E19. **retentiveness** *noun* (*a*) the state or quality of being retentive; (*b*) PHYSICS = RETENTIVITY: L17.

retentivity /riːtɛnˈtɪvɪti/ *noun*. L19.
[formed as prec. + -ITY.]
1 The ability of a substance to resist or (esp.) retain magnetization, freq. measured as the strength of the magnetic field that remains in a sample after removal of an inducing field. L19.
2 PSYCHOLOGY. (Degree of) retention in the memory. E20.
3 GEOLOGY. The property of a rock or mineral of retaining gases, esp. radiogenic ones. M20.

retenue /rət(ə)ny/ *noun*. *literary*. M19.
[French: see RETINUE.]
Reserve, restraint, caution, self-control.

retest /ˈriːtɛst/ *noun*. L19.
[from RE- + TEST *noun*[1].]
A renewed test.

retest /riːˈtɛst/ *verb trans.* M19.
[from RE- + TEST *verb*[2].]
Test again.

†**rethe** *adjective*. OE.
[Origin unkn.]
1 Of a person, a disposition: fierce, cruel, harsh; stern, severe; strict. OE–LME. ▸**b** Keen, eager, zealous. *rare*. Only in E19.
2 Of a thing, esp. rain, the sea, etc.: severe, terrible, furious. OE–LME.

rethink /ˈriːθɪŋk/ *noun*. M20.
[from the verb.]
An act of rethinking; a reappraisal; a result of this.

rethink /riːˈθɪŋk/ *verb trans. & intrans.* Pa. t. & pple **-thought** /-ˈθɔːt/. M18.
[from RE- + THINK *verb*[2].]
Think again, consider afresh, esp. with a view to changing one's intentions or attitudes.

> T. T. LYNCH You must . . re-think and re-observe. *Daily Telegraph* Mrs Thatcher . . promised to rethink methods of awarding grants.

▪ **rethinker** *noun* M20.

retia *noun* pl. of RETE.

retiarius /rɛtɪˈɑːrɪəs, -ˈɛːrɪəs/ *noun*. Pl. **-ii** /-ɪʌɪ, -iiː/. M17.
[Latin, from *rete* net + *-arius* -ARY[1].]
ROMAN HISTORY. A gladiator who fought using a net with which to entangle his adversary.
▪ **retiarian** /-ˈɛːrɪən/ *adjective & noun* (*rare*) (*a*) *adjective* of or pertaining to a retiarius; composed of retiarii; (*b*) *noun* a retiarius: M18.

retiary /ˈriːʃɪəri/ *noun & adjective*. M17.
[from prec.: see -ARY[1].]
▶ **A** *noun*. *rare*.
†**1** = prec. Only in M17.
2 A retiary spider (see below). M19.
▶ **B** *adjective*. **1** Of or relating to the making of webs, nets, or netlike structures. M17.
2 Fighting with a net, using a net, esp. in the manner of a retiarius. M17.
1 retiary spider a spider which constructs an orb-web.

reticella /rɛtɪˈtʃɛlə/ *noun & adjective*. M19.
[Italian, dim. of *rete* net: see RETE.]
▶ **A** *noun*. A lacelike fabric with a characteristic geometric pattern produced esp. in Venice from the 15th to the 17th cent. M19.
▶ **B** *attrib.* or as *adjective*. Of, pertaining to, or characteristic of reticella. M20.

reticello /rɛtɪˈtʃɛləʊ/ *noun*. Pl. **-lli** /-li/. L19.
[Italian, formed as prec.]
1 A network of fine glass threads embedded in some Venetian glass. Also (more fully ***reticello glass***), glass made with this type of decoration. L19.
2 = RETICELLA *noun*. *rare*. M20.

reticence /ˈrɛtɪs(ə)ns/ *noun*. E17.
[Latin *reticentia*, from *reticere* keep silent, formed as RE- + *tacere* be silent: see -ENCE.]
1 Maintenance of silence; avoidance of saying too much or of speaking freely, reserve in speech; disposition to say little, taciturnity; an instance of this. E17.
2 Abstinence from overemphasis; restricted use *of* something. *rare*. M19.

> **1** A. LEWIS The . . reticence with which this odd man was concealing his board result. S. WEINTRAUB Former reticences about matters once deemed private . . can be discarded. **2** D. M. MULOCK Surprised at her unusual reticence of epithets.

reticency /ˈrɛtɪs(ə)nsi/ *noun*. E17.
[formed as prec.: see -ENCY.]
= RETICENCE.

reticent /ˈrɛtɪs(ə)nt/ *adjective*. M19.
[Latin *reticent-* pres. ppl stem of *reticere*: see RETICENCE, -ENT.]
Disinclined to speak freely; characterized by reticence; reserved.

> E. M. FORSTER I was reticent, and she did not press me. J. GALSWORTHY A splendid listener, sympathetic, reticent about himself.

▪ **reticently** *adverb* M19.

reticle /ˈrɛtɪk(ə)l/ *noun*. M17.
[Latin RETICULUM: cf. RETICULE.]
†**1** A little net, a casting-net. Also, a structure resembling a net. *rare*. M17–L18.
2 A grid of fine threads or lines set in the focal plane or eyepiece of an optical instrument to facilitate observation and measurement. Also called ***reticule***. Cf. GRATICULE. M18.
3 A disc etc. with a pattern of opaque and transparent portions which can be rotated in the path of a beam of light or other radiation so as to interrupt it periodically. M20.

reticula *noun* pl. of RETICULUM.

For other words beginning with *re-* see the entry for **re-**

reticular /rɪˈtɪkjʊlə/ *adjective*. L16.
[mod. Latin *reticularis*, from Latin RETICULUM: see -AR¹.]
1 Resembling a net in appearance or construction; consisting of closely interwoven fibres or filaments; netlike. L16.
2 *ARCHITECTURE*. Of masonry, panelling, etc.: constructed of lozenge-shaped pieces or of square pieces set diagonally instead of vertically. *rare*. L18.
3 Resembling a net in effect or operation; intricate, tending to entangle. E19.
4 Of or pertaining to the reticulum of a ruminant. E20.
Special collocations: **reticular activating system** = *reticular formation* below. **reticular cell** a fibroblast or other unspecialized cell; *esp*. a fixed phagocytic cell of the reticuloendothelial system. **reticular fibres** microscopic branching fibres of reticulin forming a fine supporting network esp. around muscle and nerve fibres, blood-vessels, and in glandular and reticular tissue. **reticular formation** a diffuse network of nerve pathways in the brainstem connecting the spinal cord, cerebrum, and cerebellum, and mediating the overall level of consciousness. **reticular system** = *reticular formation* above. **reticular tissue** tissue of the reticuloendothelial system which forms part of the framework of lymphatic tissue, bone marrow, and the tissue of the spleen and liver.
■ **reticularly** *adverb* like a net M19.

reticulate /rɪˈtɪkjʊlət/ *adjective*. M17.
[Latin *reticulatus*, from RETICULUM: see -ATE².]
Reticulated, reticular; *BOTANY* having a conspicuous network of veins; *BIOLOGY* (of evolution) characterized by repeated hybridization between related lineages.
reticulate python = *reticulated python* s.v. RETICULATED 1. **reticulate thickening** *BOTANY* (in the tracheary elements of the xylem, esp. the metaxylem) a thickening of the cell wall in which the secondary wall is laid down as a network of transverse meshes.
■ **reticulately** *adverb* E19.

reticulate /rɪˈtɪkjʊleɪt/ *verb*. L18.
[Back-form. from next.]
1 *verb trans*. Divide into a network or something resembling this; arrange in small squares or intersecting lines. L18. ▸**b** Form or make (a net). *rare*. M19.
2 *verb intrans*. Be or become reticulated. M19.

reticulated /rɪˈtɪkjʊleɪtɪd/ *ppl adjective*. E18.
[from RETICULATE *adjective* + -ED¹.]
1 Constructed or arranged like a net; made or marked in a manner resembling a net or network. E18. ▸**b** *spec*. Of porcelain etc.: having a pattern of interlacing lines esp. of pierced work, forming a net or web. L19.
2 *ARCHITECTURE*. **a** = RETICULAR *adjective* 2. *rare*. E19. ▸**b** Designating or displaying a style of Decorated tracery characterized by circular shapes drawn at top and bottom into ogees, resulting in a netlike framework. M19.
3 Divided into small squares; (of an optical instrument) having a reticle to facilitate observation etc. M19.
1 reticulated python a python, *Python reticulatus*, of SE Asia, which can exceed 9 m. in length and is freq. regarded as the world's largest snake.

reticulation /rɪˌtɪkjʊˈleɪʃ(ə)n/ *noun*. L17.
[from RETICULATE *adjective*: see -ATION.]
1 A network; an arrangement of interlacing lines etc. resembling a net; reticulated structure or appearance; *PHOTOGRAPHY* (the formation of) a network of wrinkles or cracks in a photographic emulsion. L17.
2 A network of pipes used in irrigation and water supply. Chiefly *Austral. & NZ*. M20.

reticule /ˈrɛtɪkjuːl/ *noun*. E18.
[French *réticule* from Latin RETICULUM. Cf. RIDICULE *noun*².]
1 = RETICLE 2. E18.
2 A woman's small netted or other bag, esp. with a drawstring, carried or worn to serve the purpose of a pocket. E19.
3 *ASTRONOMY*. = RETICULUM 3. M19.

reticulin /rɪˈtɪkjʊlɪn/ *noun*. L19.
[from RETICULAR + -IN¹.]
A structural protein resembling collagen and distributed sparsely through connective tissue as reticular fibres.

reticulitis /rɪˌtɪkjʊˈlʌɪtɪs/ *noun*. E20.
[from RETICULUM + -ITIS.]
VETERINARY MEDICINE. Inflammation of the reticulum of a ruminant.

reticulocyte /rɪˈtɪkjʊlə(ʊ)sʌɪt/ *noun*. E20.
[from RETICUL(ATED + -O- + -CYTE.]
PHYSIOLOGY. An immature but enucleate red blood cell, having a granular or reticulated appearance when suitably stained.
Comb.: **reticulocyte count** the proportion or concentration of reticulocytes in the blood.
■ **reticulocytosis** /-sʌɪˈtəʊsɪs/ *noun* the presence in the blood of more than the normal percentage of reticulocytes due to increased bone marrow activity E20.

reticuloendothelial /rɪˌtɪkjʊləʊɛndə(ʊ)ˈθiːlɪəl/ *adjective*. E20.
[from RETICUL(UM + -O- + ENDOTHELIAL.]
MEDICINE. Of, pertaining to, or designating a diverse system of fixed and circulating phagocytic cells involved in the immune response, common esp. in the liver, spleen, and lymphatic system (usu. held to include the monocytes of the blood but not polymorphonuclear leucocytes).
■ **reticuloendotheliˈosis** *noun* overgrowth of some part of the reticuloendothelial system E20.

reticulosarcoma /rɪˌtɪkjʊləʊsɑːˈkəʊmə/ *noun*. Pl. **-mas**, **-mata** /-mətə/. M20.
[formed as prec. + SARCOMA.]
MEDICINE. A sarcoma arising from the reticuloendothelial system.

reticulose /rɪˈtɪkjʊləʊs/ *adjective*. E19.
[formed as prec. + -OSE¹.]
Chiefly *ZOOLOGY*. Designating or possessing a structure or pattern resembling a network.

reticulosis /rɪˌtɪkjʊˈləʊsɪs/ *noun*. Pl. **-loses** /-ˈləʊsiːz/. M20.
[from RETICUL(AR + -OSIS.]
MEDICINE. Abnormal, esp. malignant, proliferation of reticuloendothelial cells, esp. of the lymphatic system.

reticulum /rɪˈtɪkjʊləm/ *noun*. Pl. **-la** /-lə/. M17.
[Latin, dim. of *rete* net: see -CULE.]
1 *ANATOMY*. The second stomach of a ruminant. M17.
2 *ARCHITECTURE*. Reticular masonry. *rare*. L18.
3 (Usu. **R-**.) (The name of) a small constellation of the southern hemisphere between Dorado and Hydrus; the Net. E19.
4 Chiefly *BIOLOGY*. A netlike structure; a fine network of fibres, vessels, etc. M19. ▸**b** *ANATOMY*. Reticular tissue. L19. ▸**c** *CYTOLOGY*. A fine network within the cytoplasm of a cell. Now only in ***ENDOPLASMIC reticulum***, ***SARCOPLASMIC reticulum***. L19. ▸**d** = RETICULIN. Now *rare* or *obsolete*. E20.
Comb.: **reticulum cell** a cell of the reticuloendothelial system.

retiform /ˈriːtɪfɔːm/ *adjective*. L17.
[from Latin *rete* net + -I- + -FORM.]
Having the form of a net; netlike.

retina /ˈrɛtɪnə/ *noun*. LME.
[medieval Latin from Latin *rete* net.]
The light-sensitive layer which lines much of the inside of the eyeball, in which nerve impulses are triggered and pass via the optic nerve to the brain where a visual image is formed.

retinaculum /rɛtɪˈnakjʊləm/ *noun*. Pl. **-la** /-lə/. M18.
[Latin, from *retinere* hold back: see -CULE.]
1 *MEDICINE*. A surgical retractor (now *rare*); *ANATOMY* a structure which holds an organ or tissue in place (chiefly in mod. Latin phrs.). M18.
2 *ENTOMOLOGY*. **a** An arrangement of hooks, or hooks and bristles, which interlocks the fore and hindwings of various insects during flight. M19. ▸**b** In collembolans, a fused pair of appendages which hold back the furcula before releasing it for a spring. E20.
3 *BOTANY*. The viscidium of an orchid. Now *rare*. M19.
■ **retinacular** *adjective* L19.

retinal /ˈrɛtɪnal/ *noun*. M20.
[from RETINA + -AL².]
BIOCHEMISTRY. Either of two closely related yellow carotenoids which are the aldehydes of vitamins A_1 and A_2 (retinol) and occur in the retina combined with opsin as the visual pigment rhodopsin; *esp*. the aldehyde of vitamin A_1. Also called ***retinene***.
■ Also **retiˈnaldehyde** *noun* M20.

retinal /ˈrɛtɪn(ə)l/ *adjective*. M19.
[from RETINA + -AL¹.]
Of or relating to the retina.
■ **retinally** *adverb* with respect to or by means of the retina L20.

retinalite /ˈrɛtɪnəlʌɪt/ *noun*. M19.
[from Greek *rhētinē* resin + -LITE.]
MINERALOGY. A waxy serpentine with a resinous lustre.

retinence /ˈrɛtɪnəns/ *noun*. Long *rare* or *obsolete*. M17.
[Latin *retinentia*, from *retinent-* pres. ppl stem of *retinere* RETAIN: see -ENCE.]
Power of coherence. Also, control, restraint; an instance of this.

†**retinency** *noun*. *rare*. M17–E18.
[formed as prec.: see -ENCY.]
Retentiveness; an instance of this.

retinene /ˈrɛtɪniːn/ *noun*. M20.
[from RETINA + -ENE.]
BIOCHEMISTRY. = RETINAL *noun*.

retinispora *noun* var. of RETINOSPORA.

retinitis /rɛtɪˈnʌɪtɪs/ *noun*. M19.
[from RETINA + -ITIS.]
MEDICINE. Inflammation or apparent inflammation of the retina.
retinitis pigmentosa /pɪgmɛnˈtəʊzə/ a chronic hereditary retinopathy characterized by black pigmentation and gradual degeneration of the retina.

retino- /ˈrɛtɪnəʊ/ *combining form* of RETINA, forming terms in *ANATOMY & MEDICINE*: see -O-.
■ **retinoblaˈstoma** *noun*, pl. **-mas**, **-mata** /-mətə/, a rare malignant familial tumour of the retina in young children E20. **retinopathy** /rɛtɪˈnɒpəθi/ *noun* any (esp. non-inflammatory) disease of the retina M20. **retinoˈpathic** *adjective* of, pertaining to, or suffering from retinopathy M20. **retinoˈtopic** *adjective* [Greek *topikos* of or pertaining to place] that preserves the spatial relations of the sensory receptors of the retina M20.

retinoic /rɛtɪˈnəʊɪk/ *adjective*. M20.
[from RETIN(A + -OIC.]
BIOCHEMISTRY. ***retinoic acid***, a carboxylic acid, $C_{19}H_{27}COOH$, obtained from retinol by oxidation and used in ointments to treat acne.

retinoid /ˈrɛtɪnɔɪd/ *noun*. L20.
[from RETINOL *noun*² + -OID.]
BIOCHEMISTRY. Any substance with effects in the body like those of vitamin A.

†**retinol** *noun*¹. M–L19.
[from Greek *rhētinē* resin + -OL.]
CHEMISTRY. A liquid hydrocarbon extracted from resins.

retinol /ˈrɛtɪnɒl/ *noun*². M20.
[from RETINA + -OL.]
BIOCHEMISTRY. Either of two yellow carotenoid alcohols, $C_{20}H_{29}OH$ (vitamin A_1), found in egg-yolk, liver, etc., and $C_{20}H_{27}OH$ (vitamin A_2), found esp. in fish liver, which are essential for growth and (as the precursors of retinal) for vision in dim light.
■ **retinyl** /-nʌɪl, -nɪl/ *noun* the radical formed from retinol (chiefly in ***retinyl ester***) M20.

retinoscope /ˈrɛtɪnəskəʊp/ *noun*. L19.
[from RETINA + -O- + -SCOPE.]
An ophthalmoscope used to examine the refractive power of the eye by shining a beam of light into it and observing the movement of shadows on the retina.
■ **retinoˈscopic** *adjective* of or pertaining to the retinoscope or its use L19. **retinoˈscopically** *adverb* E20. **retinoscopy** /rɛtɪˈnɒskəpi/ *noun* examination of the eye with a retinoscope L19.

retinospora /rɛtɪˈnɒsp(ə)rə/ *noun*. Also **-nisp-** /-ˈnɪsp-/. L19.
[mod. Latin (see below), from Greek *rhētinē* resin + *spora* seed, from the resinous channels on the outer surface of the seeds.]
Any of various cypresses constituting the former genus *Retinospora* (or *Retinispora*), which was based on juvenile forms of *Chamaecyparis* (false cypresses) and *Thuja*.

retinue /ˈrɛtɪnjuː/ *noun & verb*. LME.
[Old French *retenue* use as noun of fem. of pa. pple of *retenir* restrain. Cf. RETENUE.]
▶ **A** *noun*. †**1** The fact of being in a person's service; a relationship of service or dependency. LME–E17.
2 A number or body of people in the service of or accompanying someone, esp. an important person; a train, a suite; the members of such a body collectively. LME.
†**3** The action of retaining or keeping something. Also, restraint, restraining force. *rare*. L15–M17.
†**4** Tenor, purport. *rare*. Only in L15.
📖 **2** J. L. WATEN An old . . woman followed by a retinue of women . . like herself. M. IGNATIEFF A mad, tattered King, abandoned by retinue.
▶ **B** *verb trans*. Provide with a retinue; accompany as a retinue. E19.

retinula /rɛˈtɪnjʊlə/ *noun*. Pl. **-lae** /-liː/. L19.
[mod. Latin, formed as RETINA + -ULE.]
ZOOLOGY. A pigmented cell in some arthropod compound eyes, from which the rhabdom arises.
■ **retinular** *adjective* of, pertaining to, or forming a retinula L19. **retinulate** *adjective* having retinulae L19.

retiracy /rɪˈtʌɪərəsi/ *noun*. *US*. E19.
[from RETIRE *verb* + -ACY, after *privacy*.]
Retirement, seclusion, privacy.

†**retirade** *noun*. L17–E19.
[French = Spanish, Portuguese *retirada*, Italian *ritirata* retreat, from *ritirare* retire.]
FORTIFICATION. A kind of retrenchment constructed within a bastion.

retiral /rɪˈtʌɪər(ə)l/ *noun*. Now chiefly *Scot*. E17.
[from RETIRE *verb* + -AL¹.]
1 The action or an act of retreating or withdrawing. E17.
2 Retirement, esp. from an office or position. L19.
📖 **1** J. D. MACKIE The retiral which followed the departure of Agricola. **2** *Lochaber News* Person required . . to fill vacancy due to retiral.

retire /rɪˈtʌɪə/ *noun*. Now *rare*. M16.
[from the verb.]
1 Retirement; withdrawal from the world or the society of others. M16.
†**2 a** Return to a place. M16–E17. ▸**b** The action of retiring or withdrawing to or from a place or position. L16–L17.
3 The action of drawing back or yielding ground in battle; retreat. *obsolete* exc. in ***sound retire***, ***sound a retire***, ***sound the retire***. M16.

4 A place of retirement; a retreat. L16.

1 KEATS He made retire From his companions, and set forth. 3 *Daily News* We heard the 'Cease fire' and 'Retire' sounded by buglers. 4 L. GIDLEY Forests . . in whose cool retire Are sombre glades.

retire /rɪˈtʌɪə/ *verb*. M16.
[Old & mod. French *retirer*, from *re-* RE- + *tirer* draw.]
▶ I *verb intrans.* 1 Withdraw, esp. *to* or *from* a specified place, position, or occupation, or to seek seclusion or shelter; *spec.* (*a*) leave office or employment, esp. on reaching the normal age for leaving service; (*b*) go to bed; (*c*) SPORT cease to compete; leave the field; *spec.* in CRICKET, voluntarily terminate or be compelled to suspend one's innings, usu. because of injury (freq. in ***retire hurt***). M16.
2 (Esp. of a military force) retreat before or *from* an enemy, fall back from or *from* an attacking position or an object of attack; FENCING give ground before one's adversary; take one or more steps backward; *gen.* move back or away; appear to recede; disappear *from* sight. M16.
†3 Return; come back. M16–L17.

1 E. WAUGH No. 28 overturned and . . retired from the race. E. LANGLEY They retired early and lay in their beds. G. GREENE The doctor in disgust . . had retired to the country. E. PAWEL His illness . . finally forced him to retire. ***retire on one's laurels***: see LAUREL *noun* 2. 2 W. S. CHURCHILL Lack of numbers . . compelled the British force to retire. A. MOOREHEAD When this sea retired a great lake remained. 3 T. DRANT Expulse nature with a forke Yet she will still retire.

▶ II *verb refl.* 4 Withdraw, leave, go away. Now *rare*. M16.

4 S. JOHNSON My desire . . to retire myself to some of our American plantations.

▶ III *verb trans.* 5 Cause to retire; *spec.* (*a*) order (a military force) to retreat, esp. before an enemy or from an attacking position or an object of attack; (*b*) compel (a person) to leave office or employment, esp. before reaching the normal age for leaving service; (*c*) BASEBALL cause (a batter or team) to retire; put out. M16. ▸†b Rally (troops). *Scot. rare*. L16–M17. ▸c Withdraw (a bill or note) from operation or currency; pay (a debt). L17.
6 Orig., put away; remove (a person or thing) *from* or *to* a place; withdraw (the mind, the thoughts) *from* an object or sphere. Later, withdraw (a thing) from notice; conceal, obscure. Now *rare* or *obsolete*. L16.
7 Draw or pull (a thing) back to a former position. Long *rare* or *obsolete*. L16. ▸†b Hold (a person) back *from* some course; dissuade, restrain. *rare*. L16–E17. ▸†c Get back; regain, recover. Only in 17.

5 C. J. LEVER The French were . . seen to retire their . . guns. *Times* One idea . . is that Sir Charles Villiers . . should be retired early. 6 EVELYN Retire your . . rarest Plants . . into your Conservatory. *Harper's Magazine* To retire your comely features in . . a veil. 7 P. LOWE Retire the needle the way that it went in. c W. WARBURTON Inheritance given to rent may be retired, or redeemed.

■ **retiˈree** *noun* (chiefly *US*) a person who has retired from office or employment, esp. on reaching the normal age for leaving service; a pensioner: M20. **retirer** *noun* a person who retires or retreats L16.

retiré /rətire/ *noun*. Pl. pronounced same. M20.
[French, pa. pple of *retirer*: see prec.]
BALLET. A movement in which one leg is raised until the toes touch the knee of the supporting leg, both legs being turned out in the hip sockets.

retired /rɪˈtʌɪəd/ *adjective*. L16.
[from RETIRE *verb* + -ED[1].]
1 Withdrawn from society or observation; secluded, sequestered. L16.
2 Orig., that has receded or subsided; contracted, shrunk. Later, that recedes; receding. *rare*. L16.
3 Of a person: not communicative of thoughts or opinions; reserved. Now *rare*. E17.
†4 Of thought etc.: carried on in seclusion or quiet; private. Also, inward, inner, recondite, hidden. E17–L18.
5 Of a person: having retired from office or employment, esp. on reaching the normal age for leaving service. E19.

1 L. STEPHEN Swiss enterprise has begun to penetrate these retired valleys. R. G. COLLINGWOOD He lived a very retired life; . . I never . . set eyes on him. 2 SHAKES. *John* We will . . like a bated and retired flood . . Stoop low. 3 BURKE Judges . . ought to be of a reserved and retired character. 4 W. PENN A Subject that requires your retired Consideration. D. WATERLAND In its retired mystical meaning. 5 *absol.*: *Country Life* There is good . . mackerel fishing for the retired.

Special collocations: **retired flank** FORTIFICATION: constructed towards the rear of a work. **retired list** MILITARY a list of retired officers. **retired pay** the pension given to a retired officer or official.

■ **retiredly** *adverb* (*rare*) in a secluded manner, privately L16. **retiredness** *noun* seclusion, privacy; reserve: L16.

retirement /rɪˈtʌɪəm(ə)nt/ *noun*. L16.
[formed as prec. + -MENT.]
1 The action or fact of retiring; an instance of this. L16.
2 The state or condition of having retired, esp. from office or employment on reaching the normal age for leaving service. Also, seclusion, privacy. E17.
3 A time, place, or abode characterized by seclusion or privacy; *esp.* a secluded place, a retreat. M17.

1 G. GROTE On the retirement of the Lacedaemonian force, the . . exiles were left destitute. *Manchester Examiner* The retirement of Mr Beith from the chairmanship. ***early retirement***: see EARLY *adjective*. 2 B. JOWETT Drawn from his retirement to defend his old master. *attrib.*: P. AUSTER He reached retirement age. 3 J. WILKES Exmouth; where he has . . a sweet country retirement.

Comb.: **retirement pension** = *old age pension* s.v. OLD *adjective*.

retiring /rɪˈtʌɪərɪŋ/ *adjective*. L16.
[formed as prec. + -ING[2].]
1 *gen.* That retires. L16.
2 Of a person: unassertive, reserved, shy. M18.

1 C. GROSS The retiring mayor of the town. 2 M. PUZO He was too retiring a person, did not have enough force.

■ **retiringly** *adverb* M19. **retiringness** *noun* E19.

retold *verb pa. t.* & *pple* of RETELL.

retook *verb pa. t.* of RETAKE *verb*.

retornado /retur'nadu/ *noun*. Pl. **-os** /-uʃ/. L20.
[Portuguese, from pa. pple of *retornar* return.]
A Portuguese citizen returning to settle in Portugal after living in a Portuguese colony.

retorsion /rɪˈtɔːʃ(ə)n/ *noun*. Now *rare*. M17.
[Old & mod. French *rétorsion* from medieval Latin: see RE-, -ION. Cf. TORSION.]
Retortion of an argument etc.

retort /rɪˈtɔːt/ *noun*[1]. L16.
[from RETORT *verb*[1].]
1 A sharp, witty, or angry reply, *esp.* one turning a charge or argument against its originator; a retaliation. L16.
2 The action or practice of making a sharp etc. reply or retaliation. L18.

1 A. EDEN 'I hate begging' . . which brought the . . retort ' . . I hate giving.' 2 BOSWELL Johnson's dexterity in retort . . was very remarkable. W. IRVING Nothing is so . . inviting as the retort of abuse.

retort /rɪˈtɔːt/ *noun*[2]. E17.
[French *retorte* from medieval Latin *retorta* use as noun of fem. pa. pple of Latin *retorquere*: see next.]
1 A vessel, usu. of glass, having a bulb and a long recurved neck and used for distilling liquids. E17.
2 A large clay or metal receptacle, vessel, or furnace in which a mineral substance can be heated, esp. to extract metals, oil, or gas, to separate mercury from amalgams, or to produce steel from iron and carbon. L17.
3 A machine which sterilizes canned or packaged foodstuffs by heating them directly or under pressure. L19.

Comb.: **retort carbon**: which remains as a residue in the retort when gas has been extracted from coal; **retort pouch** a type of flexible packaging in which food is sterilized by heating in a retort; **retort stand** a stand to which chemical equipment is fixed, usu. a vertical metal rod fixed to a heavy base.

retort /rɪˈtɔːt/ *verb*[1]. L15.
[Latin *retort-* pa. ppl stem of *retorquere*, formed as RE- + *torquere* twist.]
▶ I 1 *verb trans.* Turn or hurl back (an insult, accusation, attack, etc.). Also foll. by *against*, *on*, *upon*. L15.
2 *verb trans.* Repay, pay back, requite (something received, esp. an injury); reply in kind to (an insult etc.). Also foll. by *on*. M16.
3 a *verb trans.* Say by way of a retort, respond sharply *that*. E17. ▸b *verb intrans.* Make a retort or retorts. E19.
4 *verb trans.* Answer (an argument etc.) by a similar argument to the contrary; turn (an argument made) back *against* an opponent. E17.

3a *Sun* Landlord Robin, 43, retorted 'It's a load of tosh.' b A. LIVINGSTONE Her way of retorting to accusations.

▶ II †5 *verb trans.* Throw back (a weapon), turn back (a blow) on a striker. (Foll. by *upon*.) L16–L18.
†6 *verb trans.* Reflect (heat or light); echo (a sound); transmit by reflection. E17–E18.
†7 *verb trans.* Reject, refuse (an appeal). Only in E17.
†8 a *verb trans.* Turn or bend (a thing) back. E17–E18. ▸b *verb intrans.* Spring back, rebound, recoil; twist. M17–E18.

■ **retorter** *noun*[1] (now *rare* or *obsolete*) L16.

retort /rɪˈtɔːt/ *verb*[2] *trans.* M19.
[from RETORT *noun*[2].]
Heat (mercury etc.) in a retort.

■ **retorter** *noun*[2] a person retorting metal etc. L19.

For other words beginning with *re-* see the entry for **re-**

retorted /rɪˈtɔːtɪd/ *adjective*. L16.
[from RETORT *verb*[1] + -ED[1].]
1 Twisted or bent backwards, recurved. L16.
2 Esp. of an insult, charge, etc.: thrown or cast back, returned. E17.
3 Turned or facing backwards. E18.

retortion /rɪˈtɔːʃ(ə)n/ *noun*. L16.
[from RETORT *verb*[1]; perh. infl. in sense 1 by *contortion*: see -ION.]
1 The action or fact of bending or turning backwards; an instance of this. L16.
†2 The turning back of an argument against its originator; a sharp reply, a retort. E17–M18.
3 Return for something done; retaliation. Now *spec.* in INTERNATIONAL LAW, (a) retaliation by a State against subjects of another. M17.

retortive /rɪˈtɔːtɪv/ *adjective*. *rare*. M17.
[formed as RETORT *verb*[1] + -IVE.]
†1 Of the nature of squeezing. *rare*. Only in M17.
2 Turned backwards. E19.
3 Of the nature of a retort or sharp reply; characterized by retorts. E19.

retouch /riːˈtʌtʃ/ *verb* & *noun*. L17.
[Prob. from Old & mod. French *retoucher*: see RE-, TOUCH *verb*.]
▶ A *verb trans.* 1 Improve or repair (a painting, book, photographic negative or print, etc.) by small alterations or fresh touches; touch up; ARCHAEOLOGY apply secondary trimming or shaping to (a stone implement) at some period after initial manufacture. L17.
2 Touch upon, speak of, or introduce (a subject etc.) again. *rare*. E18.
▶ B *noun*. 1 The action or an instance of retouching a picture, composition, etc. E18.
2 ARCHAEOLOGY. Secondary trimming or shaping applied to a stone implement at some period after initial manufacture; an instance of this. E20.

■ **retoucher** *noun* a person who retouches something, esp. a photograph L19. **retouching** *noun* the action of the verb; a case or instance of this: M18.

retour /rɪˈtʊə/ *noun* & *verb*. ME.
[Old French, from *retourner* to return. Later readopted from mod. French.]
▶ A *noun*. 1 Return to a place. *Scot. arch.* ME.
2 SCOTS LAW (now *Hist.*). A return made to Chancery in response to a brieve of inquest concerning the ownership and value of land, stating the verdict of the jury; a return giving the value of land; an extract or copy of the return. LME.
3 A returned part; a vehicle to be returned to its starting-place (chiefly in ***retour ship***, ***retour wagon***, etc.). M18.
▶ B *verb*. Chiefly *Scot.*
†1 *verb intrans.* Of land etc.: return or revert *to* a person. LME–M16.
2 *verb intrans.* Return to or *to* a place. Long *arch.* LME.
3 *verb trans.* SCOTS LAW (now *Hist.*). ▸a Return or send in (a brieve, verdict, etc.) to Chancery. LME. ▸b Return (a person) as heir. E16. ▸c Deal with or state the value of (land etc.) in a retour. L16.

■ **retourable** *adjective* M18.

retrace /rɪˈtreɪs/ *verb trans.* L17.
[French *retracer*: see RE-, TRACE *verb*[1].]
1 Trace back to an origin or source. L17.
2 a Trace again with the eyes, look over again with care or close attention. E18. ▸b Trace again in memory, recall. M18.
3 Go back over (one's steps, way, etc.). L18.

3 B. UNSWORTH The alley simply terminated . . . He had to retrace his steps.

re-trace /riːˈtreɪs/ *verb trans.* M18.
[from RE- + TRACE *verb*[1].]
Trace or go over (a design etc.) again with a pen, pencil, etc.

retract /rɪˈtrakt/ *verb*[1]. LME.
[Latin *retract-* pa. ppl stem of *retrahere*, formed as RE- + *trahere* draw, pull.]
▶ I *verb trans.* 1 Draw or pull (a thing) back in; *spec.* (*a*) (of an animal) pull back (a part) into the body; (*b*) draw (an undercarriage etc.) up into the body of an aircraft. LME. ▸b PHONETICS. Pronounce (a sound) with the tongue drawn back; *spec.* pronounce (esp. a vowel) with the tongue in a position between front and central. Freq. as ***retracted ppl adjective***. L19.
†2 Delay (a person); restrain, hold back or prevent *from* something. E16–L17.
†3 Withdraw, remove, take away. M16–E18.

1 J. G. FARRELL The lips of the wound were retracted and gaping.

▶ II *verb intrans.* †4 Retire, retreat. *rare*. Only in M16.
5 Admit of being drawn back, undergo retraction, withdraw. L18.

5 *Do-It-Yourself* The movable blade guard will retract as the blade starts to cut.

retract /rɪˈtrakt/ *verb*[2]. **M16.**
[Old & mod. French *rétracter* or Latin *retractare*, formed as RE- + *tractare* frequentative of *trahere*: see prec.]
1 *verb trans.* Withdraw, recall, rescind (a decree, declaration, promise, etc.); withdraw or take back (a statement, accusation, etc.) as being erroneous or unjustified. (Implied earlier in RETRACTION 1.) **M16.** ▸†**b** *CHESS.* Take back or unmake (a move). **L19–E20.**
2 *verb intrans.* Withdraw or disavow a statement etc.; draw back from or go back on a promise, resolve, etc. (Foll. by *from*.) **M17.** ▸**b** *CARDS.* Change one's mind after having agreed or declined to play with a certain hand. **M19.**

> 🕮 **1** V. WOOLF I must retract some of the things I have said against them. J. JONES A false confession which he later retracted. **2** C. PETERS A later letter retracts and apologizes for the outburst.

■ Also †**retractate** *verb trans.* (*rare*): only in **E17.**

retractable /rɪˈtraktəb(ə)l/ *adjective.* Also **-ible.** **E17.**
[from RETRACT *verb*[1], *verb*[2] + -ABLE.]
1 That may be retracted or disavowed. **E17.**
2 Able to be drawn in, retractile. **M18.** ▸**b** Of an object: allowing the retraction of a component part. **M20.**
■ **retractaˈbility** *noun* capacity for retraction **L18.**

retractation /riːtrakˈteɪʃ(ə)n/ *noun.* **LME.**
[Latin *retractatio(n-)*, from *retractat-* pa. ppl stem of *retractare* RETRACT *verb*[2]: see -ATION.]
1 In *pl.* Further treatment and corrections of matters treated in former writings. Orig. & chiefly with ref. to the title of a book written by St Augustine. **LME.**
2 = RETRACTION 1. **EME.**

retractible *adjective* var. of RETRACTABLE.

retractile /rɪˈtraktʌɪl/ *adjective*[1]. **L18.**
[from RETRACT *verb*[1] + -ILE, after *contractile*.]
Esp. of parts of animals: capable of or producing retraction, retractable.
retractile testis *MEDICINE* a testis that has been or can be retracted into the inguinal region.
■ **retracˈtility** *noun* the quality, fact, or extent of being retractile **M19.**

retractile /rɪˈtraktʌɪl/ *adjective*[2]. *rare.* **L19.**
[from RETRACT *verb*[2] + -ILE, after prec.]
Characterized by or prone to the retraction of statements etc.

retraction /rɪˈtrakʃ(ə)n/ *noun.* **LME.**
[Latin *retractio(n-)*, formed as RETRACT *verb*[1]: see -ION.]
1 Recantation or withdrawal of a statement, accusation, etc., with admission of error; withdrawal from a promise etc. or *of* something decreed or declared; an instance of this. **LME.**
2 The action of drawing or pulling something back or in; the fact or condition of being drawn in or retracted. **LME.** ▸**b** *PHONETICS.* The drawing back of the tongue in the articulation of speech sounds; articulation thus effected. **L19.**
†**3** In *pl.* = RETRACTATION 1. **E16–M18.**

> 🕮 **1** L. HUDSON He demanded formal retractions at the least . . criticism. **2** *Nature* The emission and retraction of its tongue.

retractive /rɪˈtraktɪv/ *adjective.* **LME.**
[In sense 1 from medieval Latin *retractivus*; later from RETRACT *verb*[1], *verb*[2] + -IVE.]
1 Serving to retract or pull back something. **LME.**
2 Inclined to draw back; backsliding. *rare.* **E16.**
†**3** *CHESS.* Of a problem: involving the retracting of a move or moves. Only in **L19.**

retractor /rɪˈtraktə/ *noun.* **M19.**
[from RETRACT *verb*[1], *verb*[2] + -OR.]
1 *MEDICINE.* An instrument or appliance used in surgical operations to hold back skin, tissues, etc. from the area of the operation. **M19.**
2 *ANATOMY.* A muscle which serves to retract a limb or member. Also ***retractor muscle***. **M19.**
3 *CHESS.* A problem which involves the retraction of an assumed move or moves. **E20.**

†**retrait** *noun*[1] & *verb.* **L15.**
[Old & mod. French *retrait* (masc.), *retraite* (fem.) use as noun of pa. pple of *retraire*: see RETREAT *noun*. Cf. RETRAITE.]
▸ **A** *noun.* **1** = RETREAT *noun* 4. **L15–E17.**
2 = RETREAT *noun* 2. **L15–M17.**
3 = RETREAT *noun* 3. **E16–M17.**
4 = RETREAT *noun* 5. **M16–M17.**
▸ **B** *verb.* **1** *verb intrans.* Retreat, retire; resort *to*. **M16–M17.**
2 *verb trans.* Remove, take away, withdraw. **L16–E17.**

†**retrait** *noun*[2]. *rare* (Spenser). Only in **L16.**
[Alt. of Italian RITRATTO, perh. after *portrait* or infl. by prec.]
Portraiture; a portrait.

retraite /rətrɛt/ *noun.* Pl. pronounced same. **M19.**
[French: see RETRAIT *noun*[1].]
1 Retirement, seclusion, retreat. **M19.**
2 *MILITARY.* The signal for retreating. **L19.**
1 EN RETRAITE.

retral /ˈriːtr(ə)l/ *adjective.* **L19.**
[from RETRO- + -AL[1].]
1 Situated at or towards the back; directed backwards; posterior. **L19.**
2 Taking a backward direction. **L19.**
■ **retrally** *adverb* **M19.**

retravirus *noun* see RETROVIRUS.

†**retraxit** *noun.* **L16–E19.**
[Latin, 3rd person sing. perf. indic. of *retrahere* RETRACT *verb*[1].]
LAW. The formal withdrawal of a suit by a plaintiff.

retread /ˈriːtrɛd/ *noun.* **E20.**
[from RETREAD *verb*[2].]
1 A tyre supplied with a fresh tread, a remould. **E20.**
2 Orig. (*slang*), a retired soldier recalled for (temporary) service; a person retrained for new work. Now, a thing or person superficially altered but essentially the same as a predecessor; a revamp, a rehash. **M20.**

> 🕮 **2** *Express (Pennsylvania)* Fashions of today are just . . retreads of . . 30 years ago.

retread /riːˈtrɛd/ *verb*[1] *trans.* & *intrans.* Infl. as TREAD *verb*; pa. t. usu. **-trod** /-ˈtrɒd/, pa. pple **-trodden** /-ˈtrɒd(ə)n/, **-trod**. **L16.**
[from RE- + TREAD *verb*.]
Tread (a path etc.) again.

> 🕮 *Saturday Review* Their life is one of perpetual change. They never re-tread the same ground.

retread /riːˈtrɛd/ *verb*[2] *trans.* **E20.**
[from RE- + TREAD *noun*.]
1 Supply (a tyre) with a new tread. **E20.**
2 Provide (a person) with retraining or fresh employment, esp. after initial retirement. *US slang.* **M20.**
■ **retreader** *noun* **E20.**

retreat /rɪˈtriːt/ *noun.* **ME.**
[Old French *retret* (masc.), *retrete* (fem.), vars. of *retrait(e)* use as noun of pa. pple of Old & mod. French *retraire* from Latin *retrahere* RETRACT *verb*[1].]
†**1** A backhanded blow. *rare.* Only in **ME.**
2 *MILITARY.* The signal to withdraw from battle etc. (chiefly in ***blow the retreat***, ***sound the retreat***, ***blow a retreat***, ***sound a retreat***). Now also, a bugle call followed by drumming at sunset; a flag-lowering ceremony including this. **LME.** ▸†**b** The recall of a pursuing force. Only in **L16.**
3 The action or an act of retiring or withdrawing in the face of opposition, difficulty, or danger, esp. on the part of an army, combatant, etc., after defeat or to avoid an engagement. Now also, (a) decline in the value of shares etc. **LME.** ▸**b** The action of receding or sloping back, recession. **L18.**
4 A place of seclusion, privacy, or contemplation; a retired place or residence, *spec.* a second or further home. Also, a place of refuge; a hiding place, a lair, a den. **LME.** ▸**b** An establishment or institution for the care of the mentally ill, the elderly, etc. **L18.**
5 The action of retiring into privacy or security; withdrawal from public life, office, etc.; retirement, seclusion. **L15.** ▸**b** (A period of) complete seclusion for religious observance and contemplation. **M18.**
6 *ARCHITECTURE.* Recessed work; a recess or recessed part in a wall etc. **L17.**

> 🕮 **3** M. R. D. FOOT To harass the . . German retreat by . . ambushing. J. ARCHER The dollar was on the retreat. *Time* The intruders were in retreat. S. RUSHDIE There can be no retreat from the truth. ***beat a retreat***: see BEAT *verb*[1] 17. **b** F. J. MONKHOUSE The retreat of the continental ice-sheet. **4** HENRY MILLER A cosy retreat in which everything is offered you gratis. R. L. FOX A peaceful retreat of grottoes and shaded walks. **5** J. UPDIKE Physical frailty compelled retreat from social excitements.

retreat /rɪˈtriːt/ *verb*[1]. **LME.**
[formed as prec. or Old & mod. French *retraiter*.]
1 *verb intrans.* Withdraw or draw back, as from opposition, difficulty, etc., or into seclusion; *esp.* (of an army, combatant, etc.) retire before superior force or after a defeat, relinquish a position. Now also (of shares etc.), decline in value. **LME.** ▸**b** Recede, slope back. **M19.**
2 †**a** *verb refl.* Retire, withdraw. *rare.* **LME–L16.** ▸**b** *verb trans.* Cause to withdraw, lead back; remove, take away. Now chiefly *CHESS*, move (a piece) back from a forward or threatened position. **E16.**
†**3** *verb trans.* Retract, revoke. *Scot.* **LME–L17.**

> 🕮 **1** H. H. WILSON He saw his troops retreat from the field. W. SANSOM Footsteps . . retreated on the pavement. J. BRIGGS She would retreat to Crowlink. G. DALY Ned retreated into a private world. **b** N. HAWTHORNE The forehead . . retreats somewhat.

■ **retreater** *noun* **M17.** **retreatism** *noun* (*a*) a policy of retreat, advocacy of (military) withdrawal; (*b*) *SOCIOLOGY* a state of passive withdrawal from society induced by a sense of inability to attain or resist its norms: **M20.** **retreatist** *noun* & *adjective* (*a*) *noun* a person advocating a policy of retreat or (military) withdrawal; *SOCIOLOGY* a person suffering from retreatism; (*b*) *adjective* of, pertaining to, or characterized by retreatism: **M20.** **retreative** *adjective* pertaining to or suggestive of retreat; tending to withdraw: **L19.**

retreat /riːˈtriːt/ *verb*[2]. Also **re-treat.** **L19.**
[from RE- + TREAT *verb*.]
Treat again.
■ **retreatment** *noun* (a) further or renewed treatment **M19.**

retreatal /rɪˈtriːt(ə)l/ *adjective.* **L19.**
[from RETREAT *verb*[1] + -AL[1].]
GEOLOGY. Of or pertaining to the contraction and retreat of a sea or esp. of ice sheets and glaciers.

retreatant /rɪˈtriːt(ə)nt/ *noun.* **L19.**
[formed as prec. + -ANT[1].]
A person taking part in a religious retreat.

retree /rɪˈtriː/ *noun.* **E19.**
[formed as RETREAT *noun*, or French *retiré* pa. pple of *retirer* RETIRE *verb*.]
PAPER-MAKING. Damaged or defective sheets of paper.

retrench /rɪˈtrɛn(t)ʃ/ *verb.* **L16.**
[French †*retrencher* var. of *retrancher*, from *re-* RE- + TRENCH *verb*.]
▸ **I 1** *verb trans.* Diminish in extent, amount, or number; cut down, reduce. Formerly also, shorten, reduce in size. **L16.** ▸**b** *spec.* Reduce or curtail (expenditure etc.) by exercising economy. **E18.**
2 *verb trans.* Remove, take away, cut off. **E17.** ▸**b** Do away with (an item of expense); economize on, go without. **M17.** ▸**c** Cut out, excise, delete (part of a book etc.) **M17.** ▸**d** *euphem.* Make (an employee) redundant, sack. Chiefly *Austral.* **L20.**
3 *verb intrans.* Economize, reduce expenses. **M17.** ▸**b** Make reductions or excisions. *rare.* **E18.**

> 🕮 **3** E. BOWEN To retrench . . was now the object; money went . . farther at home.

▸ **II 4** *verb trans.* Protect (as) with a retrenchment or retrenchments, provide with fortifications. **L16.**
■ **retrencher** *noun* **E19.**

retrenchment /rɪˈtrɛn(t)ʃm(ə)nt/ *noun.* **L16.**
[French †*retrenchement* var. of *retranchement*, formed as prec.: see -MENT.]
▸ **I 1** The action of cutting something down, off, or out; (a) curtailment, (a) reduction. **L16.** ▸**b** The action of excising or deleting something; an instance of this. **L17.**
2 The action of economizing or cutting down expenditure; an economy. **M17.**
▸ **II 3** A fortification usu. consisting of a trench and parapet, esp. an inner line of defence within a large work. **L16.**

retribute /ˈrɛtrɪbjuːt, rɪˈtrɪbjuːt/ *verb.* Now *rare.* **L16.**
[Latin *retribut-* pa. ppl stem of *retribuere*, formed as RE- + *tribuere* assign: see TRIBUTE.]
1 *verb trans.* Give in return or as repayment; make return for, repay. **L16.**
2 *verb intrans.* Make a return or requital. **E17.**

retribution /rɛtrɪˈbjuːʃ(ə)n/ *noun.* **LME.**
[Christian Latin *retributio(n-)*, formed as prec.: see -ION. Cf. Old & mod. French *rétribution*.]
1 Recompense or return for a service, merit, etc. Now *rare.* **LME.** ▸†**b** Repayment or restitution of something given or lent. *rare.* **L16–M19.**
2 Return or requital of a crime, injury, sin, etc.; punishment, vengeance; an instance of this. Also, supposed requital or recompense in another life for one's good or bad deeds in this world. **LME.**

> 🕮 **2** P. L. FERMOR He was devoured . . in retribution for his tyranny. R. FRASER Fear of divine retribution. **day of retribution** the day on which divine reward or punishment will supposedly be assigned to humans; *gen.* a day of punishment or nemesis.

■ **retributionist** *noun* = RETRIBUTIVIST *noun* **M20.**

retributive /rɪˈtrɪbjʊtɪv/ *adjective.* **L17.**
[formed as RETRIBUTE + -IVE.]
Characterized by or of the nature of retribution, recompense, or punishment. Freq. in ***retributive justice***.
■ **retributively** *adverb* **M19.** **retributivism** *noun* (belief in or advocacy of) the policy or theory of retributive justice **M20.** **retributivist** *noun* & *adjective* (a person) believing in or advocating retributive justice **M20.**

retributor /rɪˈtrɪbjʊtə/ *noun.* **E17.**
[Latin, formed as RETRIBUTE: see -OR.]
A person who makes retribution; a repayer.

retributory /rɪˈtrɪbjʊt(ə)ri/ *adjective.* **E17.**
[formed as prec. + -ORY[2].]
Involving, producing, or characterized by retribution, recompense, or punishment.

retrieval /rɪˈtriːv(ə)l/ *noun.* **M17.**
[from RETRIEVE *verb* + -AL[1].]
1 The action of retrieving, recovering, or recalling something; an instance of this. **M17.** ▸**b** *spec.* The obtaining or consulting of material stored in a computer system, in books, on tape, etc. Freq. in ***data retrieval***, ***information retrieval***. **M20.**
2 Possibility of recovery. Chiefly in ***beyond retrieval***, ***past retrieval***. **E18.**

📖 **1** A. STORR Most elderly people find the retrieval of names . . difficult. **b** *attrib.*: *Which?* No part of this publication may be . . stored in a retrieval system. **2** J. A. FROUDE The debts . . were past retrieval.

retrieve /rɪˈtriːv/ *noun*. **L16**.
[from the verb.]
†**1** FALCONRY etc. The second discovery and flight of a previously disturbed bird. **L16–L17**.
2 a = RETRIEVAL 2. **L17**. ▸**b** = RETRIEVAL 1. Now *rare*. **E18**. ▸**c** A controlled exercise for a gun dog simulating the retrieval of game; the object retrieved. **M20**. ▸**d** SPORT. The action or an act of intercepting or otherwise regaining possession of the ball, or (in tennis etc.) of returning the ball successfully into court. *US*. **M20**. ▸**e** ANGLING. The action or an act of reeling or drawing in a line. **L20**.
■ **retrieveless** *adjective* (*rare*) that is past retrieval **M19**.

retrieve /rɪˈtriːv/ *verb*. **LME**.
[Old French *retroev-*, *-euv-* tonic stem of *retrover* (mod. *retrouver*), from *re-* RE- + *trover* (mod. *trouver*) find.]
1 *verb trans. & intrans.* Of a dog etc.: find or discover again (game temporarily lost); *esp.* flush or set up (a partridge) a second time. Now also, find and bring in (a killed or wounded bird, etc.). **LME**.
2 *verb trans.* **a** Recover (information etc.) by study or investigation, esp. of the past. Now *rare*. **M16**. ▸**b** Recover by an effort of memory, recall to mind. **M17**. ▸**c** Obtain (stored information) again from a computer etc. **M20**.
3 *verb trans.* Take possession of (a thing) again, recover, regain; *gen.* fetch, pick up. **L16**.
4 *verb trans.* Bring (a thing or person) back *from* or *out of* (†*into*, †*to*) a place or state; rescue, save. **L16**. ▸**b** Save (time) from another occupation. **L17**.
5 *verb trans.* Restore (esp. fortunes or honour) to a flourishing condition, revive. **L17**.
6 *verb trans.* Make good, repair, set right again (a loss, error, etc.). **L17**.
7 *verb intrans.* Recuperate, recover. Now *rare*. **L17**.
8 *verb trans. & intrans.* ANGLING. Reel in (a line). **M20**.

📖 **2b** J. ELLIOTT To the old man parts of the past were . . retrieved only with . . difficulty. **3** E. WELTY She stooped and . . retrieved a red apple she had hidden. E. FEINSTEIN Tsvetayev managed to retrieve . . the stolen prints. **4** G. SWIFT Retrieving the body . . from the River Leem. **5** M. LANE Mary Russell Mitford . . wrote to retrieve a fortune lost by her father. **6** H. JAMES This . . woman . . retrieved an insignificant appearance by a distinguished manner.

■ **retrievaˈbility** *noun* ability to be (easily) retrieved **L19**. **retrievable** *adjective* that may be retrieved; facilitating retrieval: **E18**. **retrievement** *noun* (*rare*) retrieval **L17**.

retriever /rɪˈtriːvə/ *noun*. **L15**.
[from prec. + -ER¹]
1 †**a** A dog used to set up game again. **L15–M17**. ▸**b** (An animal of) any of various breeds of medium-sized dog developed to find and bring in killed or wounded game; any dog used to retrieve game. **M19**.
2 A person who retrieves or recovers something. **M17**.
1b *golden retriever*, *Labrador retriever*, etc.

retro /ˈrɛtrəʊ/ *noun*¹. Pl. **-os**. **M20**.
[Abbreviation.]
= RETRO-ROCKET 2.

retro /ˈrɛtrəʊ/ *noun*² & *adjective*. **L20**.
[French *rétro* abbreviation of *rétrograde*, infl. by RETRO-.]
▶ **A** *noun*. Pl. **-os**. A thing imitating or reviving something from the past, *esp.* a nostalgic or revivalist style or fashion in dress, music, etc.; such things collectively. **L20**.

📖 *Times* Innovators mixed . . 1970s retro with dandyish frock coats.

▶ **B** *adjective*. Imitative or characteristic of a style, fashion, etc., from the past; nostalgic, revivalist. **L20**.

📖 *Face* Art Deco . . , dutifully retro but also fantastically modern.

retro /ˈrɛtrəʊ/ *adverb*. *rare*. **L18**.
[Latin.]
LAW. Backwards, retrospectively.

retro- /ˈrɛtrəʊ, ˈriːtrəʊ/ *combining form*.
[Latin *retro* backwards: see -O-.]
Forming words denoting action, motion, or effect back or in return, or position behind.
■ **retroaˈnalysis** *noun* (CHESS) analysis of a position so as to reconstruct the moves of the game leading to that position (earlier called *retrograde analysis*) **M20**. **retroanaˈlytical** *adjective* CHESS of the nature of or characterized by retroanalysis **M20**. **retro-ˈbulbar** *adjective* (ANATOMY & MEDICINE) situated or occurring behind the eyeball **L19**. **retrochoir** *noun* (ECCLESIASTICAL) the part of a cathedral or large church situated behind the high altar **M19**. **retrocogˈnition** *noun* (*a*) knowledge of the past supernaturally acquired; (*b*) PSYCHOLOGY paranormal cognition of events in someone or something else's past: **E20**. **retroˈcognitive** *adjective* involving or pertaining to retrocognition **L19**. **retro-engine** *noun* = RETRO-ROCKET 2 **M20**. **retro-fire** *verb & noun* (*a*) *verb trans.* ignite or fire (a retro-rocket); fire a rocket engine so as to give (a spacecraft) backward thrust; (*b*) *noun* the process or action of firing a retro-rocket: **M20**. **retrofit** *noun & verb* (orig. *US*) (*a*) *noun* a modification made to a product, esp. an aircraft, to incorporate changes and developments introduced after manufacture and freq. found in later products of the same type or model; (*b*) *verb trans.* subject to a retrofit: **M20**. **retrofocus** *adjective* PHOTOGRAPHY designating an optical system in which the distance of the rear surface from the image of an object at infinity exceeds the focal length, usu. achieved by placing a diverging group of lenses before a converging group **M20**. **retroˈject** *verb trans.* cast or throw back (opp. *project*) **M19**. **retroˈjection** *noun* (*rare*) the action of putting something back to an earlier date **E20**. **retroˈlental** *adjective* (MEDICINE) situated or occurring behind the lens of the eye; *retrolental fibroplasia*, proliferation of vessels in the eye, sometimes leading to blindness, in (esp. premature) infants, caused by high concentrations of oxygen: **M20**. **retroˈmingent** *noun & adjective* (an animal) that urinates backwards **M17**. **retroperitoˈneal** *adjective* (ANATOMY & MEDICINE) occurring or situated behind the peritoneum; *esp.* designating fibrosis which surrounds and obstructs the ureters causing kidney failure: **L19**. **retrophaˈryngeal** *adjective* (ANATOMY & MEDICINE) at the back of or behind the pharynx **M19**. **retroreˈflective** *adjective* (*a*) capable of looking back and reflecting (on a matter etc.); (*b*) having or being the property of a retroreflector: **M19**. **retroreflector** *noun* a device which reflects light back along the incident path, irrespective of its angle of incidence **M20**.

retroact /rɛtrəʊˈakt/ *verb intrans*. **L18**.
[from prec. + ACT *verb*.]
React. Also, operate in a backward direction or with retrospective effect.

retroaction /rɛtrəʊˈakʃ(ə)n/ *noun*. **L16**.
[formed as prec. + ACTION. Cf. French *rétroaction*.]
1 (A) return action, (a) reaction, (a) response. **L16**. ▸**b** PSYCHOLOGY. The (usu. deleterious) effect of later learning on the memory of what was learned previously. **M20**.
2 A retrospective action. Now *rare*. **E18**.
¶ Sense 1 in isolated use before **E19**.

retroactive /rɛtrəʊˈaktɪv/ *adjective*. **E17**.
[formed as prec. + ACTIVE (cf. *retrospective*), prob. after French *rétroactif*.]
1 Of legislation etc.: extending in scope or effect to the past, retrospective; backdated. (Foll. by *to*.) **E17**.
2 Operating in a backward direction. *rare*. **E17**.
3 PSYCHOLOGY. That affects the remembering of what has been previously learned. Esp. in *retroactive inhibition*, the impairment of memory of some learned material or task by subsequent learning of a similar kind. **E20**.
■ **retroactively** *adverb* **E19**. **ˌretroacˈtivity** *noun* the condition or fact of being retroactive or retrospective **E19**.

retrocede /ˈrɛtrə(ʊ)siːd/ *verb*¹ *intrans*. **M17**.
[Latin *retrocedere*, formed as RETRO- + CEDE.]
Move back, recede.

retrocede /rɛtrə(ʊ)ˈsiːd/ *verb*² *trans*. **E19**.
[French *rétrocéder*: cf. RETRO-, CEDE.]
Cede (territory) back again *to* a country or government.

retrocedent /rɛtrə(ʊ)ˈsiːd(ə)nt/ *adjective*. *rare*. **L16**.
[Latin *retrocedent-* pa. ppl stem of *retrocedere*: see RETROCEDE *verb*¹, -ENT. Cf. RECEDE *verb*¹.]
†**1** ASTRONOMY. = RETROGRADE *adjective* 1. **L16–L17**.
2 MEDICINE. (Of a condition) receding; (of gout) appearing to withdraw to the internal organs. **L18**.
■ **retrocedence** *noun* recedence, retrocession **L18**.

retrocession /rɛtrə(ʊ)ˈsɛʃ(ə)n/ *noun*¹. **L16**.
[Prob. from French *rétrocession*, formed as RETROCEDE *verb*²: see -ION.]
1 SCOTS LAW. A returning of a right to the person who granted it. **L16**.
2 The action or fact of ceding territory back to a country or government; an instance of this. **L18**.

retrocession /rɛtrə(ʊ)ˈsɛʃ(ə)n/ *noun*². **M17**.
[Late Latin *retrocessio(n-)*, formed as RETRO- + CESSION.]
1 The action or fact of moving backwards or receding, recedence. **M17**.
2 MEDICINE. The action of a disease striking inward to affect the internal organs. Now *rare* or *obsolete*. **L18**.
3 MEDICINE. Backward displacement or replacement of an organ. **E19**.

retrod, **retrodden** *verbs pa. t. & pple*: see RETREAD *verb*¹.

retrodict /rɛtrə(ʊ)ˈdɪkt/ *verb trans*. **M20**.
[Back-form. from next.]
Infer by retrodiction.
■ **retrodictable** *adjective* **M20**. **retrodictive** *adjective* of the nature of or involving retrodiction **M20**. **retrodictively** *adverb* **M20**.

retrodiction /rɛtrə(ʊ)ˈdɪkʃ(ə)n/ *noun*. **L19**.
[from RETRO- + DICTION, after *prediction*.]
The explanation or interpretation of past actions or events inferred from the laws that are assumed to have governed them; an instance of this.

retroduction /rɛtrə(ʊ)ˈdʌkʃ(ə)n/ *noun*. **M17**.
[formed as prec. + DE)DUCTION OR IN)DUCTION.]
†**1** The action or an act of bringing or drawing something back. Only in **M17**.
†**2** An afterword or postscript in a book etc. Only in **L18**.
3 PHILOSOPHY. A type of logical reasoning that develops from a commonly accepted proposition until reasons are found to alter the acceptance or understanding of the original proposition. **E20**.
■ **retroductive** *adjective* pertaining to or characterized by retroduction **E20**. **retroductively** *adverb* **M20**.

retroflected /rɛtrə(ʊ)ˈflɛktɪd/ *adjective*. **L18**.
[from Latin *retroflectere* bend back: see next, -ED¹.]
Bent, directed, or turned backwards.

retroflex /ˈrɛtrə(ʊ)flɛks/ *adjective & verb*. **L18**.
[from Latin *retroflex-* pa. ppl stem of *retroflectere* bend back, formed as RETRO- + *flectere* bend.]
▶ **A** *adjective*. **1** Chiefly ANATOMY & MEDICINE. Bent or turned backwards. **L18**.
2 PHONETICS. Pronounced with the tongue-tip curled back; cacuminal. **E20**.
▶ **B** *verb trans. & intrans*. Turn or fold back. **L19**.
■ **retroflexed** *adjective* = RETROFLEX *adjective* **E19**.

retroflexion /rɛtrə(ʊ)ˈflɛkʃ(ə)n/ *noun*. **E19**.
[from RETRO- + FLEXION.]
1 Chiefly MEDICINE. The fact or state of being turned or folded back. **E19**.
2 PHONETICS. Articulation of a sound with the tongue-tip curled back. **M20**.

retrogradation /ˌrɛtrəʊgrəˈdeɪʃ(ə)n/ *noun*. **M16**.
[Late Latin *retrogradatio(n-)*: see RETRO-, GRADATION.]
1 ASTRONOMY & ASTROLOGY. Retrograde motion, *esp.* that of a superior planet close to opposition. Opp. *progression*. **M16**. ▸**b** The backward movement of the lunar nodes on the ecliptic. Now *rare* or *obsolete*. **E18**.
2 The action or an act of going back towards some point in investigation or reasoning. **L16**.
3 The action or fact of moving back or backwards; retirement, retreat; *fig.* falling back in development, retrogression, decline; an instance of this, a retrograde step. **L16**. ▸**b** PHYSICAL GEOGRAPHY. The landward retreat of a beach or coastline caused by wave erosion. **E20**.

retrograde /ˈrɛtrəgreɪd/ *adjective, noun, & adverb*. **LME**.
[Latin *retrogradus*, formed as RETRO- + *gradus* step: see GRADE *noun*.]
▶ **A** *adjective*. **1** ASTRONOMY & ASTROLOGY. Of a planet etc.: (apparently) moving against the prevailing direction, esp. backward in the zodiac, i.e. from east to west, as when a superior planet is overtaken by the earth. **LME**.
2 a ASTRONOMY. (Of apparent motion in the sky) contrary to the order of the signs of the zodiac, from east to west; (of actual motion) contrary to the direction prevailing in the solar system, clockwise as seen from above the north pole. Opp. *direct*. **LME**. ▸**b** Directed or moving backwards; in a direction contrary to the previous motion; retreating. **E17**.
3 Tending or inclined to fall back or revert towards an inferior or less developed (former) condition; declining, deteriorating; reactionary. **E16**. ▸†**b** Backward; slow. *rare*. **L17–M18**. ▸**c** PETROGRAPHY. Of a metamorphic change: resulting from a decrease in temperature or pressure. Opp. PROGRADE *adjective* 1. **M20**.
4 a Going back on the previous course, doubled back. **M16**. ▸**b** Of order in enumeration etc.: inverse, reversed. **M17**. ▸**c** MUSIC. Of imitation etc.: having a sequence of notes played backwards. **E18**.
†**5** Opposed, contrary, or repugnant *to* something. **E17–L18**.
6 Of amnesia: pertaining to incidents preceding the causal event. **M20**.

📖 **3** J. WAINWRIGHT To them the abolition of hanging was a retrograde step.

Special collocations: **retrograde analysis** CHESS = RETROANALYSIS.
▶ **B** *noun*. **1** A person who falls back from a standard etc.; a degenerate or reactionary person. **L16**.
2 A backward movement or tendency. *rare*. **E17**.
▶ **C** *adverb*. In a backward or reverse direction. **E17**.
■ **retrogradely** *adverb* **M17**. **retrogradism** *noun* (*rare*) adoption of reactionary principles **M19**. **retrogradist** *noun* (*rare*) a reactionary **M19**.

retrograde /ˈrɛtrəgreɪd/ *verb*. **L16**.
[Latin *retrogradi*, later *retogradare*, formed as RETRO- + *gradi* proceed, walk.]
1 *verb trans.* Cause to become retrograde; turn back, reverse. Now *rare*. **L16**. ▸**b** Cause to move backwards. **E20**.
2 *verb intrans.* ASTRONOMY & ASTROLOGY. Of a planet, etc.: move in a retrograde manner, go (apparently) backward. **E17**.
3 *verb intrans.* Move backwards, go back in position or time; retire, recede. **E17**.
4 *verb intrans.* Fall back or revert towards an inferior or less developed (former) condition; regress, decline. **E17**.

retrogress /*as verb* rɛtrə(ʊ)ˈgrɛs, *as noun* ˈrɛtrəgrɛs/ *verb & noun*. **E19**.
[After *progress* by prefix-substitution: see RETRO-.]
▶ **A** *verb intrans.* Move backwards, go back; deteriorate, decline. **E19**.
▶ **B** *noun*. (A) retrogression. *rare*. **E19**.

retrogression /rɛtrə(ʊ)ˈgrɛʃ(ə)n/ *noun*. **M17**.
[from RETRO- + PRO)GRESSION, perh. as a var. of RETROGRADATION.]
1 ASTRONOMY & ASTROLOGY. = RETROGRADATION 1. **M17**.

2 Movement in a backward or reverse direction. E18. ▸**b** *MUSIC.* Retrograde imitation. M19.
3 The action or fact of going back or reverting towards an inferior or less developed (former) condition; decline, regression; a case or instance of this. M18.
■ **retrogressional** *adjective* of a retrograde character, retrogressive L19. **retrogressionist** *noun* a person inclined to be retrograde, a reactionary M19.

retrogressive /rɛtrə(ʊ)ˈɡrɛsɪv/ *adjective & noun.* E19.
[After *progressive* by prefix-substitution: see RETRO-.]
▸ **A** *adjective.* **1** Working back in investigation or reasoning. E19.
2 = RETROGRADE *adjective* 3. E19. ▸**b** *PETROGRAPHY.* = RETROGRADE *adjective* 3c. M20.
3 = RETROGRADE *adjective* 2b. M19.
▸ **B** *noun.* A retrograde or reactionary person. L19.
■ **retrogressively** *adverb* M19.

retropulsion /rɛtrə(ʊ)ˈpʌlʃ(ə)n/ *noun.* L18.
[from RETRO- + PULSION, after *propulsion.*]
MEDICINE. **1** Transference of an external disease to some internal part or organ. Now *rare* or *obsolete.* L18.
2 A moving or pushing back or backwards; *spec.* a tendency to walk backwards. L19.
■ **retropulsive** *adjective* (*rare*) causing backward or reverse movement E19.

retro-rocket /ˈrɛtrəʊrɒkɪt/ *noun.* M20.
[from RETRO- + ROCKET *noun*[3].]
†**1** An anti-submarine rocket fired backwards with a velocity equal to that of the launching aircraft, so as to fall vertically. *rare.* Only in M20.
2 A forward-directed auxiliary rocket used to slow down a spacecraft etc., as when re-entering the earth's atmosphere. M20.

retrorse /rɪˈtrɔːs/ *adjective.* E19.
[Latin *retrorsus* contr. of *retroversus*: see RETROVERSE.]
Chiefly *BOTANY & ZOOLOGY.* Turned or pointing backwards, reverted.
■ **retrorsely** *adverb* E19.

retrospect /ˈrɛtrəspɛkt/ *noun.* E17.
[After PROSPECT *noun* by substitution of prefix: see RETRO-.]
1 (A) regard or reference *to* a fact, authority, precedent, etc. E17. ▸**b** Application to past time. E18.
2 A survey or review of past times or events, esp. those relating to a particular subject or within one's own life or experience; the action of surveying the past thus. M17. ▸**b** A backward look or view. *rare.* L17.

> 🕮 **2** E. POUND Recapitulation and retrospect. **in retrospect** on reflection, when looked back on, with hindsight.

retrospect /ˈrɛtrəspɛkt/ *verb.* M17.
[App. from the noun: cf. PROSPECT *verb.*]
1 *verb intrans.* Indulge in retrospection. M17. ▸**b** Look or refer back *to*; reflect *on.* L17.
2 *verb trans.* Consider or think of retrospectively. M18.

retrospection /rɛtrə(ʊ)ˈspɛkʃ(ə)n/ *noun.* M17.
[Prob. from prec. + -ION: cf. PROSPECTION.]
1 The action of looking back or referring *to* something (usu. immaterial); reference or allusion to past events. M17.
2 The action or fact of looking back on or surveying past time or events; an instance of this, *esp.* a survey of one's past life or experiences or of a particular event or matter. L17.

retrospective /rɛtrə(ʊ)ˈspɛktɪv/ *adjective & noun.* M17.
[from RETROSPECT *noun* + -IVE.]
▸ **A** *adjective.* **1** Looking back on or dealing with the past. M17. ▸**b** Of an exhibition, compilation, etc.: showing the development of the work produced by an artist, musician, etc., over a period. E20.
2 Of a statute etc.: applying to the past as well as the present or future; retroactive. L18.
3 Esp. of a view: lying to the rear. L18.

> 🕮 **1** A. MASSIE All her work was retrospective. **2** *Times* The decision was retrospective to April 1.

▸ **B** *noun.* **1** A rear prospect or outlook. *rare.* E19.
2 A retrospective exhibition, compilation, etc. M20.

> 🕮 **2** F. SPALDING John Millais's retrospective at the Grosvenor Gallery.

■ **retrospectively** *adverb* by or with retrospection on past time; with retrospective effect or force: M17. **retrospectiveness** *noun* L19.

retrospectus /rɛtrə(ʊ)ˈspɛktəs/ *noun.* M20.
[Latin, pa. pple of *retrospicere* look back, after CONSPECTUS, PROSPECTUS.]
A retrospective review or summary.

retrotransposon /ˌrɛtrəʊtransˈpəʊzɒn, -trɑː-, -nz-/ *noun.* L20.
[from RETRO(VIRUS + TRANSPOSON.]
GENETICS. A transposon whose sequence shows homology with that of a retrovirus.

retroussage /rətrusaːʒ/ *noun.* M20.
[French, from *retrousser*: see next, -AGE.]
In etching, the action of drawing a fine cloth across an inked plate to draw out some ink and smear it irregularly across the plate.

retroussé /rəˈtruːseɪ, *foreign* rətruse/ *adjective.* E19.
[French, pa. pple of *retrousser* turn up, from *re-* RE- + *trousser* TRUSS *verb.*]
Usu. of the nose: turned up at the tip.

> 🕮 M. E. BRADDON The pert little *retroussé* nose.

retroverse /rɛtrə(ʊ)ˈvəːs/ *adjective. rare.* M19.
[Latin *retroversus*, formed as RETRO- + *versus* turned. Cf. RETRORSE.]
Turned or directed backwards, reversed.

retroversion /rɛtrə(ʊ)ˈvəːʃ(ə)n/ *noun.* L16.
[In senses 1, 4 from RETRO- + VERSION, after *reversion*; in sense 2 from RETROVERTED; in sense 3 app. from RETROVERT *verb*: see -ION.]
†**1** *SCOTS LAW.* Reversal, rescission. *rare.* Only in L16.
2 *MEDICINE.* The action or state of being turned backward or retroverted. L18.
3 The action of turning or looking back. E19.
4 Retranslation into the original language. L19.

retrovert /ˈrɛtrəvəːt/ *noun. rare.* L19.
[from RETRO- after *convert, pervert*: cf. REVERT *noun.*]
A person who reverts to his or her former faith.

retrovert /ˈrɛtrəvəːt/ *verb intrans. & trans. rare.* M17.
[Late Latin *retrovertere*, formed as RETRO- + *vertere* turn.]
Turn back; revert.

retroverted /ˈrɛtrəvəːtɪd/ *ppl adjective.* L18.
[from prec. + -ED[1].]
Turned backwards, reverted; *esp.* (*MEDICINE*) (of the uterus) tilted backwards towards the rectum.

Retrovir /ˈrɛtrəvɪə/ *noun.* L20.
[from next.]
PHARMACOLOGY. (Proprietary name for) the drug azidothymidine.

retrovirus /ˈrɛtrəʊvʌɪrəs/ *noun.* Also (*rare*) **retra-**. L20.
[mod. Latin, from *reverse transcriptase* + -O- + VIRUS.]
BIOLOGY. Any of a group of RNA viruses, including lentiviruses and various oncogenic viruses, which produce reverse transcriptase to transfer their own genome into a host's DNA for replication.
■ **retroviral** *adjective* L20.

retrusion /rɪˈtruːʒ(ə)n/ *noun. rare.* M17.
[Orig. from medieval Latin *retrusio(n-)*, from Latin *retrus-* pa. ppl stem of *retrudere* thrust back; later app. after *protrusion* or *intrusion*: see -ION.]
The action of putting or moving something away or back.

retsina /rɛtˈsiːnə/ *noun.* E20.
[mod.Greek, from *retsini* from Greek *rhētinē* pine resin.]
A Greek white wine flavoured with resin.

retter /ˈrɛtə/ *noun. rare.* E19.
[from RET *verb* + -ER[1].]
A person engaged in retting timber, flax, etc.

rettery /ˈrɛtəri/ *noun.* M19.
[formed as prec. + -ERY.]
A place where flax etc. is retted.

†**retund** *verb trans.* M17.
[Latin *retundere*, formed as RE- + *tundere* beat.]
1 Weaken physically; diminish the strength or effect of. M17–M18.
2 Drive or force back; repel; repress; refute. M17–M18.
3 Dull or blunt (the edge of a weapon). L17–L18.

retune /riːˈtjuːn/ *verb trans. & intrans.* E17.
[from RE- + TUNE *verb.*]
1 Put (a musical instrument) in tune again; alter the musical pitch of. E17.
2 Tune (a radio receiver etc.) to a different wavelength or frequency. M20.
3 Alter the tuning of (an engine) to improve smoothness and efficiency. L20.

return /rɪˈtəːn/ *noun.* LME.
[Anglo-Norman *retorn, return*, formed as next.]
▸ **I 1** The action or an act of coming back to or from a place, person, or condition. LME. ▸**b** In full ***return ticket***. A ticket for a journey to a place and back to the starting-point. M19. ▸**c** *CHRISTIAN THEOLOGY.* = PAROUSIA. E20.
2 Profit or income from investment of money or the expenditure of effort or skill; a profit made; in *pl.*, proceeds, profits, results. Also (*Hist.*), a consignment, a cargo, etc., taken back in exchange for merchandise sent out as a trading venture. Cf. sense 6b below. LME. ▸**b** A production of profit, the fact of being profitable. M18.
3 The action, on the part of a sheriff, of sending back a writ of execution to the issuing court, together with a report on it; a sheriff's report on a writ of execution; a form for making such a report (usu. in *pl.*). LME. ▸**b** The time at which a writ of execution is to be returned. L16.
4 a An official report made by a returning officer (originally a sheriff) as to the election of a member or members of Parliament; the fact of being elected to sit in Parliament. LME. ▸**b** A report of a formal or official character giving (esp. statistical) information, compiled or submitted by order of some authority; a form for making such a report; a set of statistics; *CRICKET* a summary of bowling figures at the end of play. M18.
5 †**a** Recovery *of* something taken. Only in M16. ▸**b** Restoration *of* something to a person. E17.
6 a A thing given or received by way of recompense, acknowledgement, or reciprocity. Also occas., the act of so giving something. M16. ▸**b** The yield of some productive thing considered in relation to the original amount or expenditure. Cf. sense 2 above. E17.
7 †**a** A reply, an answer, a retort. L16–L18. ▸**b** A thrust, stroke, volley, etc., given in reply to one from an opponent or enemy. E18.
8 (A) recurrence; (a) repetition of an occasion or event; the recurrence or renewal of some condition, as illness or indisposition. L16. ▸**b** In full ***return game***, ***return match***, etc. A second or further game, match etc., between the same opponents. L18.
9 The action or an act of bringing or sending a thing back to a former position. M17. ▸**b** A mechanism which effects this; *spec.* (***a***) ***carriage return***, a typewriter mechanism which returns the carriage to a fixed position; (in full ***carriage return key***) a key pressed to operate this; (***b***) (in full ***return key***) a key pressed on a computer keyboard to simulate a carriage return (esp. in a word-processing program) or to transfer data from an input buffer. L18. ▸**c** The action or an act of returning (a ball) to an opponent or to another player; skill in doing this. M19. ▸**d** *ELECTRICITY.* The route or means by which a current returns to its source. L19. ▸**e** *COMPUTING.* An instruction or process which causes a computer to revert to a main routine after executing a subroutine. M20.
10 *CARDS.* The action or an act of leading a suit previously led or bid by a partner. M18.
11 In *pl.* Orig., refuse tobacco. Later, mild light-coloured tobacco made from recut shag. L18.
12 A thing sent or given back. Usu. in *pl.* L19.

> 🕮 **1** J. R. GREEN His return was the signal for . . national joy. V. BRITTAIN Going back felt disturbingly like a return to school. **b** ***day return, period return***, etc. **2** ADAM SMITH The returns of the foreign trade of consumption are very seldom so quick as those of the home trade. **b** C. FRANCIS The oil companies want a fast return on investment.
> **4b** A. E. HOUSMAN Trouble in filling up my income Tax return. M. BELL The registrar's returns of births and deaths. **6b** C. SAGAN The cost . . seems . . modest compared with its potential returns. B. BAINBRIDGE Difficult to devote my time . . for so little return.

▸ **II 13** *ARCHITECTURE.* A side or part receding, esp. at right angles, from the front or direct line of a structure, as of a cornice, window, wall, etc. LME. ▸**b** A wing or side of a building. E17.
14 A bend or turn in a line or, formerly, in a stream, trench, etc.; a portion extending between two bends. Now *rare.* M17.
Phrases: **by return (of post)** †(***a***) by return of the courier who brought the original message; (***b***) by the next mail in the opposite direction. **in return** in exchange (*for*), as recompense or acknowledgement (*for*); as a reciprocal action. ***law of diminishing returns***: see DIMINISH. ***many happy returns (of the day)***: see HAPPY *adjective.* ***point of no return***: see POINT *noun*[1]. **return to nature** the abandonment of urban life in favour of rustic simplicity. ***sale or return***: see SALE *noun.* ***small profits and quick returns***: see SMALL *adjective.*
Comb.: **return crease** *CRICKET* either of two lines joining the popping-crease and bowling-crease at right angles to the bowling-crease and extending beyond it; **return date** *US LAW* the date on which a specified person is required to appear in court; **return-day** *LAW* the day on which a writ of execution is appointed to be returned; the day specified in a summons for when the summons will be heard; **return envelope** *US* an addressed envelope enclosed with a letter for the recipient's reply; **return fare** the fare for a return ticket; **return flight** an aircraft flight back to the starting-point; ***return game***: see sense 8b above. ***return key***: see sense 9b above; ***return match***: see sense 8b above; **return room** a mezzanine room at the turn of a flight of stairs; ***return ticket***: see sense 1b above.
■ **returnless** *adjective* (*literary*) E17.

return /rɪˈtəːn/ *verb.* ME.
[Old & mod. French *retorner, returner* (mod. *retourner*) from Proto-Romance, from Latin RE- + *tornare* TURN *verb.*]
1 *verb intrans.* Come or go back to a place, person, or condition. ME. ▸†**b** *verb trans.* Come or go back by way of. *rare* (Shakes.). Only in L16.
†**2** *verb intrans. & refl.* Turn away; go away again. LME–E17.
3 *verb trans.* †**a** Reverse or direct back (one's course); cause to face the other way; cause to turn away. LME–E18. ▸**b** Cause to turn back towards something; take or lead back in the former direction; cause to turn at an angle to the previous course; *ARCHITECTURE* continue (a wall etc.) in a changed direction, esp. at right angles. E16. ▸†**c** Induce (a person) to come back; recall, summon back. E16–E17.

4 *verb trans.* Bring back, convey back, or restore to a place, person, or condition; put back in or into a receptacle or other place. LME. ▸**b** *MILITARY.* Replace (arms etc.) in the usual receptacle. L17.

5 *verb trans.* Send back again; hit (a ball) back to an opponent. LME. ▸**b** *verb trans.* Turn back, force to go back; visit *(up)on* a person. Now *rare.* M16. ▸**c** *verb trans. & intrans.* Make a retort to (a charge, argument, etc.). Foll. by *to, upon* a person. Long *rare.* M16.

6 *verb trans.* **a** Report in answer to a writ or to some official demand for (esp. statistical) information; state by way of a report or verdict; report or announce the starting-price of (a horse etc.) in a race. LME. ▸**b** Orig., (of a sheriff) report as having been appointed to serve on a jury or to sit in Parliament. Later, (of an electorate) elect as a member of a Parliament or other administrative body or as a government. LME. ▸**c** *CRICKET.* Of a bowler: achieve (bowling figures) in an innings or other session of play. M20.

7 *verb trans.* Repay or pay back, esp. with something similar; respond to by a similar feeling or action; give or send in return or response; reply or reciprocate with. LME. ▸**b** Say or state in reply, retort. L16.

8 *verb trans.* Bring back in exchange; yield (profit etc.) in return; supply as the result of work or effort. L16.

9 *verb trans. CARDS.* Lead (a suit) previously led or bid by a partner; lead (a suit or card) after taking a trick. M18.

📖 **1** AV *1 Kings* 2:33 Their blood shall . . returne vpon the head of Ioab. J. LINGARD Till the earl . . was returned from Bologna. J. A. FROUDE The subject is one to which . . I shall . . return. TENNYSON Man's love once gone never returns. E. WAUGH Sounds of battle began to return. D. C. PEATTIE What grows on the desert returns as dust to dust. M. L. KING She was returning home. P. SCOTT Ministers had arrived . . by train but were returning . . by air. S. WEINTRAUB From Earl's Court they returned directly to Paddington. ***return empty***: see EMPTY *adjective* 4. **return to nature** abandon urban life in favour of rustic simplicity. ***return to one's muttons***: see MUTTON. ***return to one's vomit***: see VOMIT *noun.* ***return to the charge***: see CHARGE *noun.* **4** DEFOE These cases . . return me back to the advice above. J. C. POWYS Returning the volume to the bookcase. *Scientific American* Samples returned to the earth by the Apollo missions. **5** POPE Autolycus . . With added gifts return'd him [Ulysses] glorious home. SIR W. SCOTT Lake and fell . . return'd the martial yell. *Field* He did . . now and then return balls. **6b** R. P. JHABVALA If I . . stand for Parliament, they'd return me like a shot. **returning officer** an official whose duty it is to conduct or preside at an election (esp. in a constituency), and to report the result. **7** STEELE If any one returns me an Answer to a Letter. E. M. FORSTER Your son will return our calls. K. AMIS Having to return hospitality he never wanted. M. DAS He wished he could return the love. **return thanks** express thanks, esp. in a grace at a meal or in response to a toast or a condolence. ***return the compliment***: see COMPLIMENT *noun.* **b** M. DE LA ROCHE 'I've been blooded!' she cried . . . 'And so have I,' he returned. **8** *Your Business* An average petrol van engine . . might return 25 mpg. **9** *Bridge Magazine* East played the ace and returned a trump. ***return the lead***: see LEAD *noun*[2].

■ **returner** *noun* E17. **returning** *noun* (*a*) the action of the verb; (*b*) a return; a backward turn or bend: LME.

re-turn /riːˈtəːn/ *verb.* LME.
[from RE- + TURN *verb.*]
1 *verb trans.* Turn over, round, or back again. LME.
2 *verb intrans.* Turn again; turn back. LME.

returnable /rɪˈtəːnəb(ə)l/ *adjective.* LME.
[Anglo-Norman *retornable*, Old French *retournable*, formed as RETURN *verb*: see -ABLE.]
1 Of a writ of execution, etc.: appointed to be returned to the issuing court with a report. LME.
2 Likely to return; able to return. *rare.* LME.
3 Able to be returned; intended to be returned. M16.
■ **returnaˈbility** *noun* L19.

returned /rɪˈtəːnd/ *adjective.* LME.
[from RETURN *verb* + -ED[1].]
1 Bent or turned back; *ARCHITECTURE* made with a return. LME.
2 That has returned or come back. L16. ▸**b** Of a member of the armed services: discharged after (active) service, esp. abroad. *Canad., Austral., & NZ.* E20.
3 To be returned. *rare.* E18.
4 That has been returned; sent or brought back. M18.

returnee /rɪtəːˈniː/ *noun.* M20.
[from RETURN *verb* + -EE[1].]
A person who returns or is returned home from abroad esp. after war service or exile.

returnik /rɪˈtəːnɪk/ *noun.* L20.
[from RETURN *noun, verb* + -NIK.]
An emigré from an East European country who has returned to it, esp. following a change of regime.

retuse /rɪˈtjuːs/ *adjective.* M18.
[Latin *retusus* pa. pple of *retundere* RETUND.]
BOTANY & ENTOMOLOGY. Having a broad or rounded end with a shallow central notch.

retype /riːˈtʌɪp/ *verb trans.* M19.
[from RE- + TYPE *verb*[1].]
1 Typify anew. *rare.* M19.
2 Type again or afresh, esp. to correct errors. L19.

reub *noun* var. of RUBE.

Reuben /ˈruːb(ə)n/ *noun.* L19.
[Male forename.]
1 = RUBE 1. *N. Amer. slang.* L19.
2 In full ***Reuben sandwich***. A large sandwich containing cheese, meat, and sauerkraut, usu. made with rye bread and served hot. M20.

reune /riːˈjuːn/ *verb intrans. US colloq.* E20.
[Back-form. from REUNION.]
Hold a reunion.

reunification /ˌriːjuːnɪfɪˈkeɪʃ(ə)n/ *noun.* L19.
[from RE- + UNIFICATION.]
The action of reunifying; the state of being reunified.
■ **reunificationist** *noun* a supporter or advocate of reunification L20.

reunify /riːˈjuːnɪfʌɪ/ *verb trans. & intrans.* L19.
[from RE- + UNIFY.]
Unify again or afresh; unify after a division or separation.

reunion /riːˈjuːnɪən/ *noun.* In sense 3 also (now *rare*) ***réunion*** /reynjɔ̃ (*pl. same*)/. E17.
[French *réunion*, from *réunir* unite, or Anglo-Latin *reunio(n-)*, from *reunire*: see next, -ION.]
1 The action or an act of reuniting or coming together again; the state of being reunited. E17.
2 The fact or condition of meeting again after separation. E18.
3 A meeting or social gathering of people having some previous acquaintance or connection. E19.
■ **reunionism** *noun* advocacy of the reunion of the Anglican with the Roman Catholic Church L19. **reunionist** *noun* an advocate of the reunion of the Anglican with the Roman Catholic Church M19. **reunioˈnistic** *adjective* aiming at or desirous of the reunion of the Anglican with the Roman Catholic Church M19.

reunite /riːjʊˈnʌɪt/ *verb.* Pa. pple **-ited**, (earlier) †**-ite**. L15.
[Orig. pa. pple, from Anglo-Latin *reunitus* pa. pple of *reunire*, from Latin RE- + *unire* UNITE *verb.*]
1 *verb trans.* Unite or bring together again; join together after separation. L15.
2 *verb intrans.* Come together again and unite. M17.
■ **reunitable** *adjective* M17. **reuniter** *noun* M19. **reunition** /riːjʊˈnɪʃ(ə)n/ *noun* (*rare*) the action or an act of reuniting, (a) reunion M17.

re-up /ˈriːʌp/ *verb intrans. US slang.* Infl. **-pp-**. E20.
[from RE- + UP *verb.*]
Re-enlist.

reupholster /riːʌpˈhəʊlstə/ *verb trans.* M20.
[from RE- + UPHOLSTER *verb.*]
Upholster again or afresh.
■ **reupholstery** *noun* L20.

reuse /riːˈjuːs/ *noun.* Also **re-use**. M19.
[from RE- + USE *noun.*]
Further use; using over again; a second or further use.

reuse /riːˈjuːz/ *verb trans.* Also **re-use**. M19.
[from RE- + USE *verb.*]
Use again; use more than once.
■ **reusaˈbility** *noun* the quality or state of being reusable L20. **reusable** *adjective* able to be reused; suitable for a second or further use: M20.

réussi /reysi/ *adjective.* M20.
[French, pa. pple of *réussir* turn out, result, succeed.]
Fine, excellent, successful.

reutilize /riːˈjuːtɪlʌɪz/ *verb trans.* Also **-ise**. L19.
[from RE- + UTILIZE.]
Utilize again or for a different purpose.
■ **reutiliˈzation** *noun* M20.

rev /rɛv/ *noun*[1] & *verb.* E20.
[Abbreviation of REVOLUTION *noun.*]
▶ **A** *noun.* A revolution of an engine; chiefly *ellipt.* in *pl.*, revolutions per minute. Also, an act of revving an engine etc. E20.
Comb.: **rev counter** an instrument that measures and displays a rate of rotation, esp. the number of revolutions of an engine per minute.
▶ **B** *verb.* Infl. **-vv-**.
1 *verb trans. & intrans.* Increase the speed of revolution of (an internal-combustion engine) or the speed of revolution of the engine of (a vehicle), with the clutch disengaged. Also foll. by *up.* E20.
2 *verb intrans.* (Of an internal-combustion engine) revolve with increasing speed, (of a vehicle) operate with increasing revolution of the engine, esp. with the clutch disengaged. Also foll. by *up.* E20.

Rev *noun*[2] var. of REV. *noun.*

Rev. *abbreviation.*
1 Revelations (New Testament).
2 Reverend (see next).

Rev. /rɛv/ *adjective & noun.* As noun also **Rev** (no point). E18.
[Abbreviation of REVEREND *adjective & noun.*]
▶ **A** *adjective.* As a title of a member of the clergy: Reverend. Chiefly as a written form. E18.
▶ **B** *noun.* A member of the clergy, a person entitled 'Reverend'. *colloq.* M20.
¶ See note s.v. REVEREND.

revaccinate /riːˈvaksɪneɪt/ *verb trans.* M19.
[from RE- + VACCINATE.]
Vaccinate again; use a different vaccine on.
■ **revacciˈnation** *noun* M19.

†**revail** *verb trans.* Also **-ale**. LME.
[Old French *revaler*, from *re-* RE- + *avaler*: see AVALE.]
1 Lower, bring down, depress. *rare.* LME–L15.
2 Provide with a reveal or reveals. Chiefly as ***revailed*** *ppl adjective.* M17–E18.

revalorisation *noun*, **revalorise** *verb* vars. of REVALORIZATION, REVALORIZE.

revalorization /ˌriːvalərʌɪˈzeɪʃ(ə)n/ *noun.* Also **-isation**. E20.
[French *révalorisation*, from *ré-* RE- + *valorisation* VALORIZATION.]
The action or process of establishing a fresh price or value for something; revaluation.

revalorize /riːˈvalərʌɪz/ *verb trans.* Also **-ise**. E20.
[Back-form. from prec.]
Establish a fresh price or value for; revalue.

revaluate /riːˈvaljʊeɪt/ *verb trans.* M20.
[Back-form. from next.]
Reassess, form a new valuation of.

revaluation /riːˌvaljʊˈeɪʃ(ə)n/ *noun.* E17.
[from RE- + VALUATION.]
A second or revised valuation; the action or an act of revaluing something or someone.

revalue /riːˈvaljuː/ *verb trans.* L16.
[from RE- + VALUE *verb.*]
Value again or afresh; revise the value of; *spec.* adjust the value of (a currency) in relation to gold or another currency, esp. upwards.

📖 *Financial Times* The . . dinar was revalued by 2 per cent against the . . dollar.

revamp /*as verb* riːˈvamp, *as noun* ˈriːvamp/ *verb & noun.* M19.
[from RE- + VAMP *verb*[1].]
▶ **A** *verb trans.* Vamp or patch up again; rewrite in a new form; renovate, overhaul, revise. M19.
▶ **B** *noun.* A revamped version; a renovation, an overhaul, a revision; an act of revamping something. L19.

revanche /rəvɑ̃ʃ/ *noun.* M19.
[French, earlier *revenche*, from *revencher*: see REVENGE *verb.*]
Revenge; retaliation; *spec.* a nation's policy of seeking the return of lost territory.
¶ Earlier in EN REVANCHE.

revanchism /rɪˈvan(t)ʃɪz(ə)m/ *noun.* M20.
[from prec. + -ISM.]
A policy of seeking retaliation or revenge; *spec.* a nation's policy of seeking the return of lost territory.

revanchist /rɪˈvan(t)ʃɪst/ *noun & adjective.* E20.
[formed as prec. + -IST.]
▶ **A** *noun.* A person who seeks retaliation or revenge; *spec.* a person who seeks the return of a nation's lost territory. E20.
▶ **B** *adjective.* Of or pertaining to revanchism or revanchists; characterized by a policy of retaliation or revenge. M20.
■ **revanˈchistic** *adjective* of the nature of or characterized by revanchism M20.

revarnish /riːˈvɑːnɪʃ/ *verb trans.* M19.
[from RE- + VARNISH *verb.*]
Varnish again or afresh.

Revd *abbreviation.*
Reverend.

reveal /rɪˈviːl/ *noun*[1]. *rare.* E17.
[from the verb.]
A revelation, a disclosure.

reveal /rɪˈviːl/ *noun*[2]. Also **revel** /rɪˈvɛl/. L17.
[from REVAIL, later alt. after next.]
An internal side of an opening or recess, at right angles to the face of the work; *esp.* the vertical side of a doorway or window-opening.

reveal /rɪˈviːl/ *verb trans.* LME.
[Old & mod. French *révéler* or Latin *revelare*, formed as RE- + *velum* VEIL *noun.*]
1 *THEOLOGY.* Make known in a divine or supernatural manner. LME.
2 Make known by discourse or communication; divulge. LME.
3 Display, show, make clear or visible, exhibit. L15.

📖 **1** R. STRANGE The birth of Jesus reveals to us .. the meaning of being human. **revealed religion** (a) religion accepting or based on revelation, as opp. to natural religion. **2** S. UNWIN He entrusted me .. to reveal its contents to no one. I. MURDOCH The story .. will reveal .. what sort of person I am. F. WELDON Inspection of their birth certificates would reveal the girls to be illegitimate. L. HUDSON One must .. expect points of difference to be as revealing as points of similarity. **3** A. MACLEAN A quick search .. revealed nothing. M. M. KAYE Objects that .. had been unidentifiable were beginning to .. reveal themselves. A. PRICE Trousers rucked up to reveal .. an inch of hairy white leg. D. LODGE Skimpy swimsuits or revealing underwear.

■ **revealable** *adjective* (earlier in UNREVEALABLE) L17. **revealer** *noun* L15. **revealingly** *adverb* in a revealing manner M19. **revealment** *noun* the action of revealing something; (a) disclosure, (a) revelation: L16.

revegetate /riːˈvɛdʒɪteɪt/ *verb*. M18.
[from RE- + VEGETATE.]
1 *verb intrans.* Vegetate or grow again. M18.
2 *verb trans.* Produce a new growth of vegetation on (disturbed or barren ground). M20.
■ **revegeˈtation** *noun* M19.

reveille /rɪˈvali/ *noun*. Also (now *rare*) **-llé** /-leɪ/. M17.
[French *réveillez* imper. pl. of *réveiller* awaken, from *ré-* RE- + *veiller* from Latin *vigilare* keep watch.]
A signal given in the morning, usu. on a drum or bugle, to waken soldiers and indicate that it is time to rise; (the time of) the sounding of this signal.

📖 T. HEGGEN Any man caught in his bunk after reveille. *transf.*: H. ALLEN He .. warbled a melodious reveille to his love still asleep.

réveillon /revɛjɔ̃/ *noun*. Pl. pronounced same. E19.
[French, from *réveiller* (see prec.) + *-on* -OON.]
In France: a night-time feast or celebration, orig. one after midnight on Christmas morning.

revel /ˈrɛv(ə)l/ *noun*[1]. LME.
[Old French, formed as REVEL *verb*[1].]
1 Riotous or noisy mirth or merrymaking. LME.
2 An occasion or course of merrymaking or noisy festivity, esp. with dancing, games, or other forms of lively entertainment. LME. ▸**b** *spec.* A parish festival or feast; a fair. *dial.* L15.
2 master of the revels *Hist.* a person (permanently or temporarily) appointed to organize or lead revels.
Comb.: †**revel-rout** (*a*) uproarious revelry, boisterous merriment; (*b*) an occasion of revelling, a revel.
■ **revelment** *noun* (*rare*) the action of revelling, revelry E19.

revel *noun*[2] var. of REVEAL *noun*[2].

revel /ˈrɛv(ə)l/ *verb*[1]. Infl. **-ll-**, ***-l-**. LME.
[Old French *reveler* (refl.) from Latin *rebellare* REBEL *verb*.]
1 *verb intrans.* & (*arch.*) *trans.* with *it*. Make merry; engage in riotous or noisy festivities; take part in a revel. LME.
2 *verb trans.* Spend or waste (time or money) in revelry. Also foll. by *away*. E17.
3 *verb intrans.* Take intense pleasure or delight *in*. M18.

📖 **3** INA TAYLOR Despite being married .. he revelled in his reputation as a rake.

†**revel** *verb*[2] *trans.* Infl. **-ll-**. L16–M18.
[Latin *revellere*, formed as RE- + *vellere* pull.]
Draw back (humours or blood) from a part of the body. Cf. REVULSION 1.

revelation /rɛvəˈleɪʃ(ə)n/ *noun*. ME.
[Old & mod. French *révélation* or ecclesiastical Latin *revelatio(n-)*, from Latin *revelat-* pa. ppl stem of *revelare* REVEAL *verb*: see -ATION.]
1 THEOLOGY. The disclosure or communication of knowledge by a divine or supernatural agency; an instance of this; a thing disclosed or made known by divine or supernatural means. ME.
2 A striking disclosure of something previously unknown or not realized. M19.

📖 **1 the Revelation (of St John the Divine), (the Book of) Revelations** (names of) the last book of the New Testament, the Apocalypse. **2** A. J. AYER A sudden revelation of 'the loneliness of the human soul'. M. SEYMOUR No revelations had been made, but he was uneasily aware that something was afoot. P. ACKROYD I didn't know .. astronomy could be so delightful. Quite a revelation.

■ **revelational** *adjective* E18. **revelationist** *noun* (*a*) (now *rare*) a person who makes a revelation, esp. *the* author of the Apocalypse; (*b*) a believer in divine revelation: M17.

revelative /ˈrɛv(ə)lətɪv/ *adjective*. M19.
[from Latin *revelat-* (see prec.) + -IVE.]
Conveying a revelation.

revelator /rɛvəˈleɪtə/ *noun*. LME.
[Late Latin, from Latin *revelat-*: see REVELATION, -OR.]
A person who or thing which makes a revelation, esp. a divine revelation; a revealer.
¶ In isolated use before 19.

revelatory /rɛvəˈleɪt(ə)ri, ˈrɛv(ə)lət(ə)ri/ *adjective*. L19.
[from Latin *revelat-* (see REVELATION) + -ORY[2]. Cf. late Latin *revelatorius*.]
Serving to reveal something, esp. something significant; yielding a revelation.

📖 J. COE Somehow he had been anticipating this: the news was numbing, rather than revelatory.

reveler *noun* see REVELLER.

†**revellent** *noun & adjective*. M17.
[from Latin *revellent-* pres. ppl stem of *revellere*: see REVEL *verb*[2], -ENT.]
MEDICINE. ▸**A** *noun*. = REVULSIVE *noun*. M17–M19.
▸**B** *adjective*. = REVULSIVE *adjective*. E–M19.

reveller /ˈrɛv(ə)lə/ *noun*. Also ***-eler**. LME.
[from REVEL *verb*[1] + -ER[1].]
1 A participant in a revel, merrymaking, or festivity; a person given to revelling. LME.
2 A person who takes intense pleasure or delight *in* something. M19.

revelous /ˈrɛv(ə)ləs/ *adjective*. *rare*. LME.
[Old French, formed as REVEL *noun*[1]: see -OUS.]
Given to or marked by revelling.

revelry /ˈrɛv(ə)lri/ *noun*. LME.
[from REVEL *noun*[1] + -RY.]
The action of revelling, merrymaking; boisterous gaiety or mirth.

revenant /ˈrɛv(ə)nənt; *foreign* rəvənɑ̃ (*pl. of noun same*)/ *noun & adjective*. E19.
[French, pres. pple of *revenir* return: see REVENUE, -ANT[1].]
▸**A** *noun*. A person who has returned, esp. supposedly from the dead; a ghost. E19.
▸**B** *adjective*. Returned, esp. supposedly from the dead. E20.

revendication /rɪˌvɛndɪˈkeɪʃ(ə)n/ *noun*. M18.
[French, from *revendiquer* claim back, from *re-* RE- + *vendiquer* from Latin *vindicare*: see VINDICATE, -ATION.]
The action of claiming back or recovering something by a formal claim.

revenge /rɪˈvɛn(d)ʒ/ *noun*. LME.
[from the verb. Cf. French †*revenge*, †*revenche* (mod. REVANCHE).]
1 The action or an act of doing hurt or harm to another in return for wrong or injury suffered; satisfaction obtained by repayment of a wrong or injury; the desire for such action or satisfaction. LME. ▸**b** With *possess.* An individual's desire for such action or satisfaction; an act of gratifying this. M16. ▸†**c** The avenging of a person. *rare*. L16–M17.
2 Repayment *of* some wrong, injury, etc., by the infliction of hurt or harm. *arch.* L16.
†**3** Punishment; chastisement. L16–L17.
4 An opportunity for retaliation; a chance to win after an earlier defeat; *spec.* a return game. L17.

📖 **1** SHELLEY I have taken A full revenge for your unnatural feast. C. GEIKIE Plato held that revenge was wrong. J. MALCOLM People who write against Freud are motivated by a desire for revenge. M. MARRIN The murder might .. have to do with revenge. **b** RIDER HAGGARD I shook my fist .. and vowed to have my revenge. ***Aztec revenge*, MONTEZUMA'S REVENGE. 2 in revenge for, in revenge of** in return or retaliation for.

Comb.: **revenge tragedy** a drama based on a quest for vengeance; *spec.* a style of drama popular in England during the late 16th and 17th centuries and typically featuring scenes of carnage and mutilation.
■ **revengeless** *adjective* (now *rare*) free from or devoid of revengefulness or vindictiveness E17.

revenge /rɪˈvɛn(d)ʒ/ *verb*. LME.
[Old French *revenger*, *revencher* (mod. *revancher*) from late Latin *revindicare*, from Latin RE- + *vindicare*: see VINDICATE.]
1 *verb trans. refl.* & in *pass.* Avenge oneself; take revenge. (Foll. by *on* or *upon* (rarely *of*) a person, *for* or †*of* a wrong, injury, insult, etc., received or resented.) LME.
2 *verb trans.* Inflict punishment or exact retribution in retaliation for (an injury, harm, wrong, etc., done to oneself or another). (Foll. by *on* or *upon* a person.) LME. ▸**b** Maintain, uphold, or vindicate (a cause, quarrel, etc.) by some act of retribution or punishment. Now *rare* or *obsolete*. E16.
3 *verb trans.* Avenge an injury to (a person etc.). LME.
4 *verb intrans.* Take vengeance or revenge. LME.
†**5** *verb trans.* Punish. M16–E18.
■ **revengement** *noun* (long *rare*) (*a*) revenge, retribution; †(*b*) punishment: L15. **revenger** *noun* E16. **revengingly** *adverb* (*rare*) in a revenging manner, so as to take revenge E17. †**revengive** *adjective* (*rare*, Shakes.) revenging, vindictive: only in E17.

revengeful /rɪˈvɛn(d)ʒfʊl, -f(ə)l/ *adjective*. L16.
[from REVENGE *noun* + -FUL.]
Eager for revenge; vindictive.
■ **revengefully** *adverb* M17. **revengefulness** *noun* L16.

revenue /ˈrɛvənjuː/ *noun*. LME.
[Old & mod. French *revenu*, †*-ue* uses as noun of masc. & fem. pa. pple of *revenir* from Latin *revenire*, formed as RE- + *venire* come.]
†**1** Return to a place. *rare*. LME–M16.
2 Income, *spec.* from property, possessions, or investment, esp. of an extensive kind. Formerly also foll. by *of* the source of income. LME. ▸**b** *spec.* The annual income of a government or State, from all sources, out of which public expenses are met; the government department responsible for the collection of this. L17.
3 In *pl.* The collective items or amounts constituting such an income. Formerly also foll. by *of* the source. LME.
4 An income; a separate source or item of (private or public) income. LME.

📖 **2** ADAM SMITH The revenue derived from labour is called wages. J. R. MCCULLOCH It is .. from revenue that .. taxes should be derived. A. LOMAX The revenue from the .. gambling games. *Economist* Its revenue is likely to be less than 1% of .. TV advertising. **b *inland revenue***: see INLAND *adjective*. ***internal revenue***: see INTERNAL *adjective*. **3** J. K. GALBRAITH Inflation does not automatically bring added revenues. **4** H. MACMILLAN How to match .. expenditure with an adequate revenue.

Comb.: **revenue bond** a bond issued to finance a specific building etc. project and payable only from revenue deriving from that project; **revenue tax** a tax imposed to raise revenue, rather than to affect trade etc.
¶ Formerly also commonly stressed on 2nd syll.
■ **revenuer** *noun* (*US*) an agent of the internal revenue L19.

reverb /ˈriːvəːb, rɪˈvəːb/ *noun*. *colloq.* M20.
[Abbreviation of REVERBERATION.]
1 Reverberation of sound, *spec.* as produced by an electronic musical instrument or amplifier. M20.
2 A device for producing this. L20.

reverb /rɪˈvəːb/ *verb trans. & intrans. literary*. E17.
[Irreg. from Latin *reverberare*: see REVERBERATE. Cf. REVERBER.]
Reverberate, re-echo.
¶ In and after Shakes. *Lear*.

reverbatory /rɪˈvəːbət(ə)ri/ *adjective*. L16.
[Contr.]
= REVERBERATORY *adjective* 2.

reverber /rɪˈvəːbə/ *verb trans. & intrans. rare*. L17.
[Latin *reverberare*: see REVERBERATE. Cf. REVERB *verb*.]
Reverberate. Chiefly as ***reverbering*** *ppl adjective*.

reverberant /rɪˈvəːb(ə)r(ə)nt/ *adjective*. L16.
[In sense 1 from French *réverbérant* pres. pple of *réverbérer* from Latin *reverberare*: see REVERBERATE, -ANT[1]. In sense 2 from REVERBERATE + -ANT[1].]
1 HERALDRY. Of a lion's tail: turned up like the letter S, with the end outwards. Now *rare*. L16.
2 Reverberating; resonant. E19.
■ **reverberantly** *adverb* M20.

reverberate /rɪˈvəːbəreɪt/ *verb*. Pa. pple & ppl adjective **-ated**, (*arch.*) **-ate** /-ət/. L15.
[Latin *reverberat-* pa. ppl stem of *reverberare*, formed as RE- + *verberare* strike, beat, from *verbera* rods, scourge: see -ATE[3].]
▸**I** *verb trans.* †**1** Beat, drive, or force back; dissipate, dispel. L15–L18.
†**2** Of light: dazzle, light up. *rare*. L15–M16.
3 Cause to re-echo or resound, reflect (light, heat, etc.), esp. repeatedly. L16.
4 Direct, deflect, or force (flame, heat, etc.) back (*up*)*on*. E17.
5 Subject to the heat of a reverberatory furnace. E17.

📖 **3** J. RUSKIN The full glory of a tropical sunset, reverberated from the sea. N. HAWTHORNE The .. gun thundered .. and was reverberated from the heights. *Nature* The intensity of the radiation being reverberated in the cavity.

▸**II** *verb intrans.* **6** Shine or reflect (*from* a surface etc.), esp. repeatedly. Now *rare*. L16.
7 Resound, re-echo; continue sounding as if being re-echoed; *fig.* have continued effects, be heard much or repeatedly. E17.
8 Recoil, rebound, now esp. with a reverberating sound. E18.
9 Of flame etc.: be directed, deflected, or forced back *on*, *over*, etc. E18.

📖 **7** W. S. CHURCHILL Bright's thundering speeches .. reverberated through the nation. P. ACKROYD The shouts and cries of the prison reverberate around him. P. GARDINER The traumatic incidents .. continued to reverberate in his memory. **8** D. LEAVITT Louise throws down her fork; it .. reverberates against the table.

Phrases: **reverberating furnace** a reverberatory furnace.

reverberation /rɪˌvəːbəˈreɪʃ(ə)n/ *noun*. LME.
[Old & mod. French *réverbération* or medieval Latin *reverberatio(n-)*, formed as prec.: see -ATION.]
†**1** The fact (on the part *of* a thing) of being driven or forced back, esp. after impact; repulse of or *of* something. LME–L18.
†**2** The action *of* an agent in reverberating something. LME–L17.
3 a Reflection of or *of* light, heat, etc.; an instance of this. Now *rare*. LME. ▸**b** Re-echoing or reverberating of or *of* sounds; *spec.* prolongation of sound without perceptible distinct echoes, produced by repeated reflection from nearby surfaces, or artificially. Also, an instance of this. E17.

4 Subjection to heat in a reverberatory furnace. Now *rare*. **LME.**
5 a A re-echoing or reverberating sound; *fig.* a continued or repeated effect, a thing much heard or repeated. **M19.** ▸**b** A reflection of light or colour. Now *rare*. **M19.**

📖 **3b** E. BIRNEY Reverberation of boots . . where . . staff were trooping out. **5a** N. YOUNG Reverberations of the . . Vietnam Day demonstrations . . were felt in Britain. R. RENDELL A metal door whose clanging reverberations could still be heard.

Comb.: **reverberation chamber** a room specially designed to reflect sounds produced within it; **reverberation time** *ACOUSTICS* the time taken, after cessation of production of a steady sound, for the average sound intensity at a given frequency in a room or enclosure to die away, *spec.* to decrease by 60 decibels.

reverberative /rɪˈvəːbərətɪv/ *adjective.* **E18.**
[from REVERBERATE + -IVE.]
Inclined or disposed to reverberate; of the nature of a reverberation.

reverberator /rɪˈvəːbəreɪtə/ *noun.* **L18.**
[formed as prec. + -OR.]
1 A reflector; a reflecting lamp. Now *rare*. **L18.**
2 A thing which produces or undergoes reverberation. **E19.**

reverberatory /rɪˈvəːb(ə)rət(ə)ri/ *adjective & noun.* **E17.**
[from REVERBERATE: see -ORY², -ORY¹.]
▸ **A** *adjective.* **1** Designating or produced by fire forced or driven back by some contrivance on to the substance which is subjected to its operation. Now *rare*. **E17.**
2 Of a furnace, kiln, etc.: so constructed that the flame or heat is forced back on to the substance exposed to it. **L17.**
▸ **B** *noun.* A reverberatory furnace or kiln. **M17.**

reverdie /rəvɛrdi/ *noun.* Pl. pronounced same. **M20.**
[French, use as noun of fem. pa. pple of *reverdir* grow, turn green again.]
A medieval French song celebrating the return of spring.

Revere /rɪˈvɪə/ *adjective.* Chiefly *US*. **L20.**
[See PAUL REVERE.]
= PAUL REVERE.

revere /rɪˈvɪə/ *verb.* **M17.**
[French *révérer* or Latin *revereri*, formed as RE- + *vereri* be in awe of, fear.]
1 *verb trans.* Hold in or regard with deep respect or veneration. **M17.**
2 *verb intrans.* Be reverent. **L18.**
■ **reverable** *adjective* (*rare*) deserving reverence **E18.** **reverer** *noun* **L17.**

reverence /ˈrɛv(ə)r(ə)ns/ *noun.* In sense 3 now also ***révérence*** /reverɑ̃s (*pl. same*)/. **ME.**
[Old & mod. French *révérence* from Latin *reverentia*, from *reverent-* pres. ppl stem of *revereri* REVERE *verb*: see -ENCE.]
1 Deep respect or veneration, now esp. on account of the object's sacred or exalted character; the capacity for feeling or showing this; a feeling or manifestation of this. **ME.**
2 The condition or state of being deeply respected or venerated. **LME.**
3 A gesture indicative of respect; an obeisance; a bow or curtsy, now esp. as a dance movement. **LME.**
4 With possess. adjective (as ***your reverence*** etc.): a title of respect given to a member of the clergy, now esp. a priest in Ireland. **LME.**

📖 **1** LYTTON I hold the church in holy reverence. G. HEYER A . . public-school man with a reverence for good form. N. SHERRY Close contact with Vivien . . seemed to reduce his reverence for her.

Phrases: **do reverence to**, **pay reverence to** show deep respect or veneration for (a person or thing) by some action. †**save one's reverence**, †**saving one's reverence**: apologetically introducing a criticism, contradiction, or some remark that might offend the hearer.

reverence /ˈrɛv(ə)r(ə)ns/ *verb trans.* **ME.**
[Anglo-Norman *reverencer*, formed as prec.]
1 Regard with reverence, revere. Formerly also, worship. **ME.**
†**2** Salute (a person) with deep respect; make an obeisance to, curtsy or bow to; treat with respect or deference. **LME–L17.**
■ **reverencer** *noun* **L16.**

reverend /ˈrɛv(ə)r(ə)nd/ *adjective & noun.* Also (esp. in titles) **R-**. **LME.**
[Old & mod. French *révérend* or Latin *reverendus* gerundive of *revereri* REVERE *verb*: see -END. See also REV.]
▸ **A** *adjective.* **1** Of a person: deserving deep respect or reverence on account of advanced age, character, or (formerly) social status, personal ability, or great learning. Used *spec.* as a title of or form of address to members of the clergy. **LME.** ▸**b** Of, pertaining to, or characteristic of the clergy. **M17.**
2 = REVERENT 2. Now *rare*. **E16.**
3 Of a thing, place, etc.: deserving or inspiring reverence. Formerly also, sacred, hallowed, holy. **M16.**

📖 **1** SHAKES. *Merch. V.* I pray you, let me look upon the bond . . . Here 'tis, most reverend Doctor. J. WILSON He takes His reverend mother on his filial breast. ISAAC TAYLOR These bishops and reverend Fathers. *Church Times* Its diocesan leaflet lists . . women deacons equally with their male colleagues as 'The Reverend'. W. BOYD He saw . . the Reverend Norman Espie.

▸ **B** *noun.* A member of the clergy; a cleric, a divine, a preacher. Now also used as a form of address. *colloq.* **E17.**

📖 O. L. JACKSON Heard a very good sermon—from a Reverend from Pittsburgh. *New Scientist* He is a reverend of St Stephen's Church.

Phrases: **Most Reverend** (a title of or form of address to) an archbishop or an Irish Roman Catholic bishop. **Reverend Mother** (a title of or form of address to) the Mother Superior of a convent. **Right Reverend** (a title of or form of address to) certain religious dignitaries, esp. a bishop in the Anglican Church or the Moderator of the Church of Scotland. **Very Reverend** (a title of or form of address to) certain religious dignitaries, esp. a dean in the Anglican Church or an Irish Roman Catholic parish priest.
¶ It is commonly considered unacceptable to use *Reverend* (in full or abbreviated *Rev.* or *Revd*) with a surname alone (rather than with a forename, initial, other title, or some combination of these) or without preceding *the*: thus *the Reverend Joseph Brown, the Reverend J. B. Brown, the Reverend Dr Brown*, but not *(the) Reverend Brown*, and not *Reverend* as a form of address, either spoken (*Hello, Reverend (Brown)*) or to begin a letter (*Dear Reverend (Dr Brown)*).
■ **reverendly** *adverb* †(*a*) reverently; (*b*) in a way or to a degree that inspires reverence: **LME.** **reverendship** *noun* reverend or clerical character or standing; ***Your Reverendship***, ***His Reverendship***, a form of address used to or of a member of the clergy: **E17.**

reverent /ˈrɛv(ə)r(ə)nt/ *adjective.* **LME.**
[In sense 1 from Old French *reverent* or after medieval Latin *reverentissimus* most reverend (of bishops); in sense 2 from Latin *reverent-* pres. ppl stem of *revereri* REVERE *verb*: see -ENT.]
1 = REVEREND *adjective* 1, 3. Now *rare*. **LME.**
2 Characterized by reverence; feeling or showing reverence; deeply respectful. **LME.**
■ **reverently** *adverb* **LME.**

reverential /rɛvəˈrɛnʃ(ə)l/ *adjective.* **M16.**
[French †*révérencial*, *-tiel*, (now *-ciel*) or medieval Latin *reverentialis*, from Latin *reverent-*: see prec., -IAL.]
1 Of the nature of reverence; inspired or characterized by reverence; reverent. **M16.**
2 Inspiring reverence; venerable, reverend. *rare*. **E17.**
■ **reverentially** *adverb* **M17.** **reverentialness** *noun* (*rare*) **M19.**

reverie /ˈrɛv(ə)ri/ *noun.* Also **-ry**, †**resv-**. **ME.**
[In branch I from Old French *reverie* rejoicing, revelry, from *rever* be delirious (mod. *rêver* dream), of unkn. origin; in branch II from later French *resverie* (now *rêverie*): see -ERY.]
▸†**I 1** Joy, delight; revelry; wantonness, wildness. *rare*. **ME–M16.**
▸ **II 2** A fantastic, fanciful, or unpractical notion; a delusion. *arch.* **E17.**
3 A fit of abstracted musing; a daydream. **M17.** ▸**b** *MUSIC.* An instrumental composition suggestive of a dreamy or musing state. **L19.**
4 The fact, state, or condition of being lost in thought or engaged in musing. **M18.**

📖 **3** B. CHATWIN Letting the book fall . . she allowed herself to slide into a reverie. D. CECIL Wandering about by himself, absorbed in his reveries. **4** A. STORR States of reverie halfway between sleep and waking. S. HAZZARD Caroline . . would fall into long reverie, remembering though not pondering sights, episodes, and sensations.

reverie /ˈrɛv(ə)ri/ *verb intrans.* **L19.**
[from the noun.]
Indulge in reveries, daydream.

revers /rɪˈvɪə/ *noun.* Pl. same /rɪˈvɪəz/. **M19.**
[French: see REVERSE *noun*.]
A turned-back edge of a garment revealing the undersurface; the material covering such an edge. Usu. *pl.*

reversal /rɪˈvəːs(ə)l/ *noun.* **L15.**
[from REVERSE *verb* + -AL¹.]
1 *LAW.* The action of setting aside or annulling a judgement, sentence, decree, etc.; the fact of being set aside or annulled. **L15.**
2 The action or process of reversing something; an instance of this. **L17.**
3 Reversion *to* some practice etc. *rare*. **M19.**
4 *PHOTOGRAPHY.* Interconversion of positive and negative images; *spec.* direct production of a positive image from an exposed film or plate; direct reproduction of a positive or negative image. **L19.**
Comb.: **reversal film** photographic film that gives a positive image directly when processed; **reversal process** = sense 4 above; **reversal-process** *verb trans.* subject to the reversal process; **reversal speed** *AERONAUTICS* the air speed above which the effect of a control surface is reversed by the counteracting effect of distortion of the aircraft caused by operation of the surface.

reverse /rɪˈvəːs/ *noun.* **LME.**
[Old & mod. French *revers*, †*reverse*, from uses as noun of Latin *reversus*: see next.]
▸ **I 1** The opposite, the contrary. (Foll. by *of*, (now *rare*) *to*.) **LME.** ▸**b** The contrary of the usual manner. Chiefly in ***in reverse***. **L19.** ▸**c** *CONTRACT BRIDGE.* A rebid in a suit of higher rank than that which one has previously bid. **M20.**
2 The side of a coin, medal, seal, etc., which does not bear the main device or inscription; the design etc. on this side. Opp. OBVERSE *noun* 1. **E17.**
3 The side facing away; a side or face not seen or not intended to be seen. **L18.**
4 The verso of a leaf (in a book etc.). **E19.**

📖 **1** E. BLISHEN If my father's relatives were hard . . , my mother's were the reverse: all gentle. D. HALBERSTAM What was . . printed represented the reverse of his views. **2 the reverse of the medal**, **the reverse of the shield** *fig.* the opposite view of a matter (cf. ***the other side of the coin*** s.v. COIN *noun*).

▸ **II 5** = REVERS. *rare*. **LME.**
†**6** A back-handed stroke or cut with a sword etc. **L15–M17.**
†**7** = REVERSAL 2. **L15–L17.**
8 An adverse change of or *of* fortune; a disaster, a setback, now *esp.* a defeat in battle or a sports match. **E16.**
9 A complete change or alteration (*of*); a movement in the opposite direction. **E18.** ▸**b** *AMER. FOOTBALL.* A play in which a player reverses the direction of attack by passing the ball to a team-mate moving in the opposite direction. **M20.**
10 The action of reversing in dancing. **L19.**
11 Reverse gear; the position of a gear lever or selector corresponding to this. **L19.**

📖 **8** J. COLVILLE The withdrawal from . . Norway . . is admitted to be a reverse. **9** *Nature* Temperatures have been rising since the . . seventeenth century . . with reverses lasting several decades. **11** G. MOFFAT The car . . was in neutral instead of . . reverse.

reverse /rɪˈvəːs/ *adjective & adverb.* **ME.**
[Old French *revers(e)* from Latin *reversus*, *-sa* pa. pple (masc. & fem.) of *revertere* REVERT *verb*.]
▸ **A** *adjective.* **1** Opposite or contrary (*to* something else, or to each other) in character, order, succession, position, etc. **ME.** ▸**b** Lying behind or to the back. **M19.** ▸**c** *GEOLOGY.* Designating a fault or faulting in which relative downward movement has occurred in the strata situated on the underside of the fault plane. Opp. NORMAL *adjective* 6. **L19.**
†**2** Of a blow etc.: back-handed. **L16–M17.**
3 *MILITARY.* Connected with, commanding, or facing towards the rear. **E18.**
4 Acting in a way contrary or opposite to that which is usual or customary. **L19.**
▸ **B** *adverb.* In a reverse way; reversely. Now *rare*. **LME.**
Special collocations & comb.: **reverse angle** *CINEMATOGRAPHY & TELEVISION* the opposite angle from which the subject was seen in the preceding shot. **reverse bid** *CONTRACT BRIDGE* = REVERSE *noun* 1c. **reverse-charge** *adjective* designating a telephone call for which the charges have been reversed. **reverse dictionary** (*a*) a dictionary in which the words are arranged so that they are in alphabetical order when read backwards rather than forwards; (*b*) a dictionary in which terms or synonyms are given for concepts or definitions. **reverse discrimination** = ***positive discrimination*** s.v. POSITIVE *adjective*. **reverse engineering** the reproduction of another manufacturer's product following detailed examination of its construction or composition. **reverse fire** *MILITARY* gunfire from the rear. **reverse gear** a gear wheel or mechanism which enables a vehicle or vessel to travel in reverse without reversing the rotation of its engine. **reverse lever** a lever by means of which the reverse gear of an engine may be brought into use. **reverse osmosis** *PHYSICAL CHEMISTRY* the process by which a solvent (usu. water) passes through a porous membrane in the direction opposite to that for natural osmosis when subjected to a hydrostatic pressure greater than the osmotic pressure. **reverse plate** *PRINTING* a plate in which the usual colour arrangement is reversed, *esp.* one producing white type on a black background; matter printed with such a plate. ***reverse Polish***: see POLISH *adjective*. **reverse takeover** *COMMERCE*: in which a small esp. private company assumes control over a larger public one. **reverse thrust** thrust used to retard the forward motion of an aircraft, rocket, etc. ***reverse*** *TRANSCRIPTASE*. ***reverse transcription***: see TRANSCRIPTION 4. **reverse video** (the effect of) the reversal of the usual highlighting or coloration of characters and background on a VDU.
■ **reversely** *adverb* **M17.**

reverse /rɪˈvəːs/ *verb.* **ME.**
[Old French *reverser* (mod. *ren-*) from late Latin *reversare* from Latin *reversus*: see prec.]
▸ **I** *verb trans.* †**1 a** Bring back *to* or *into*. **ME–L16.** ▸**b** Remove; divert or turn away. *rare*. **L16–M17.**
†**2** Overthrow, overturn, upset, cast down. **LME–M17.**
3 Turn or place upside down; invert. **LME.** ▸**b** Hold or carry (a weapon) in the position of unreadiness for use. **M17.** ▸**c** *HERALDRY.* As ***reversed*** *ppl adjective*: (of a charge) used upside down. **M17.**
†**4** Turn back or trim (a garment) *with* some other material. **LME–E16.**

For other words beginning with *re-* see the entry for **re-**

5 Set aside, revoke, annul, (a judgement, decree, act, measure, etc.). **LME.**
6 Turn the other way round, transpose, turn inside out. **LME.**
7 Turn in the opposite direction; send on a course contrary to the previous or usual one. **LME.** ▸**b** Cause (an engine etc.) to work or revolve in the contrary direction; put (a motor vehicle) into reverse gear; drive (a motor vehicle) backwards. **M19.**
8 Convert into something of an opposite character or tendency; alter or change completely. **L15.** ▸**b** Employ, perform, etc., in a way opposite to the former or usual method. **E18.**

> 5 R. SCRUTON Judicial decisions cannot be reversed by Parliament. **6** E. HEMINGWAY He took the . . oar . . and reversed it so he could hold it by the blade. **7 reverse charges, reverse the charges** make the recipient of a telephone call responsible for paying for the call. **7b** J. G. BALLARD Jeremy has reversed the . . Porsche out of the garage.

▸ **II** *verb intrans.* †**9** Draw back or away; move backwards; go *back*, return *home*. **LME–L17.**
†**10** Fall over, fall down. **LME–M16.**
11 a In dancing, esp. waltzing: move or turn in the contrary direction. **M19.** ▸**b** (Of an engine) work or revolve in the contrary direction; move in reverse gear; drive or be driven backwards. **M19.**
12 *CONTRACT BRIDGE.* Rebid in a suit of higher rank than that which one has previously bid. **M20.**

> **11b** K. AMIS The taxi . . was . . beginning to reverse cautiously. A. CHRISTIE I don't think I can reverse . . The car never seems to go. **reversing light** a white light at the rear of a motor vehicle which lights up when it is in reverse gear.

reversement /rɪˈvəːsm(ə)nt/ *noun.* Now *rare.* **L16.**
[from prec. + -MENT.]
The action of reversing something, the fact of being reversed; reversal.

reverser /rɪˈvəːsə/ *noun.* **M17.**
[from REVERSE *verb* + -ER¹.]
1 *SCOTS LAW* (now *Hist.*). A person who borrows money on security of land. **M17.**
2 A person who or thing which reverses something; *spec.* a control used to put a vehicle in reverse, esp. a switch in an electric motor. **M18.**

reversi /rɪˈvəːsi/ *noun.* **E19.**
[French, alt., after *revers* REVERSE *noun*, of earlier *reversin* from Italian *rovescina*, from *rovesciare* to reverse. See also REVERSIS.]
1 *Hist.* = REVERSIS 1. **E19.**
2 A game played on a draughtboard with counters having one side different in colour from the other, the object being to enclose as many of the opponent's counters as possible between one's own in order to have the right to reverse them and make them one's own. **L19.**

reversible /rɪˈvəːsɪb(ə)l/ *adjective & noun.* **M17.**
[from REVERSE *verb* + -IBLE.]
▸ **A** *adjective.* **1** Able to be reversed; capable of reversing; *spec.* (of cloth) faced on both sides, so as to allow of being turned, (of a garment) faced on both sides, so as to be wearable with either outside. **M17.** ▸**b** Of a propeller: capable of providing reverse thrust, usu. by reversal of the pitch of the blades while the direction of rotation remains unchanged. **E20.**
2 *PHYSICS.* Of a change or process: that is capable of complete and detailed reversal; *spec.* designating or undergoing an ideal change in which a system is in thermodynamic equilibrium at all times. **M19.**
3 *CHEMISTRY.* Of a reaction: that occurs together with its converse, and so yields an equilibrium mixture of reactants and products. **L19.**
4 *PHYSICAL CHEMISTRY.* Designating an electrochemical cell in which the chemical reaction can be reversed by the application of a sufficiently large opposing electromotive force; pertaining to a state in which the electromotive force of the cell is balanced by an applied emf and no current is flowing. **L19.**
5 *PHYSICAL CHEMISTRY.* Of a colloid or colloidal system: able to be changed from a gelatinous state into a sol by a reversal of the treatment which turns the sol into a gel or gelatinous precipitate. **L19.**
▸ **B** *noun.* A reversible cloth or garment. **M19.**
■ **reversiˈbility** *noun* **M19.** **reversibly** *adverb* **L19.**

reversing /rɪˈvəːsɪŋ/ *ppl adjective.* **E19.**
[formed as prec. + -ING².]
1 Esp. of part of a machine: that reverses or causes reversal. **E19.**
2 Of the nature of or characterized by reversal (of an action, process, etc.). **L19.**
Special collocations: **reversing falls** a waterfall or rapid in a narrow river mouth over which water flows backwards as the tide comes in. **reversing layer** (now *rare*) a region of the solar atmosphere above the photosphere, formerly thought to be responsible for bringing about reversal of emission lines in the solar spectrum to absorption lines. **reversing mill** a rolling-mill in which sheet metal may be passed between the same rollers in both directions. **reversing propeller** a reversible propeller. **reversing stratum** = *reversing layer* above. **reversing thermometer** a thermometer the mercury thread of which breaks when inverted, so retaining the registered reading, used esp. for deep-water measurements.

reversion /rɪˈvəːʃ(ə)n/ *noun.* **LME.**
[Old & mod. French *réversion* or Latin *reversio(n-)*, from *revers-* pa. ppl stem of *revertere* REVERT *verb*: see -ION.]
▸ **I 1 a** *LAW.* The return of an estate to the donor or grantor, or his or her heirs, after the expiry of the grant; an estate which returns to the donor etc. in this way; *spec.* one granted or transferable to another party, esp. on the death of the original grantee; the right of succeeding to, or next occupying, an estate. **LME.** ▸**b** *SCOTS LAW.* A right of redemption operative in the case of a legal adjudication or a wadset. **L15.**
2 *transf.* **a** The right of succeeding to the possession of something, or of obtaining something at a future time (foll. by *of*); a thing or possession which a person expects to obtain. **E16.** ▸**b** The right of succession to an office or emolument, after the death or retirement of the holder. Foll. by *of*. **L16.**
3 A sum payable on a person's death, esp. as a result of life insurance. **L18.**
▸ **II** †**4** The remains of a dish, drink, or meal; *gen.* the rest, residue, or remainder *of*. **LME–E19.**
5 †**a** The action or fact of returning to or from a place. **LME–M18.** ▸**b** The action or fact of returning to a certain condition, practice, or belief; an instance of this. **L16.** ▸**c** *BIOLOGY.* The action or fact of reverting to a primitive, former, or ancestral type or condition; an instance of this. **M19.**
6 The fact of being turned the reverse way; the action or an act of turning something the reverse way. **LME.** ▸**b** *MATH.* In full ***reversion of a series, reversion of series***. Determination, from an expression of a variable *y* as a series of powers of another variable *x*, of an expression of *x* as a series of functions of *y*. **L17.**
Phrases: **in reversion** conditional on the expiry of a grant or the death of a person. ***reversion of a series, reversion of series***: see sense 6b above.
■ **reversional** *adjective* **L17.** **reversionist** *noun* = REVERSIONER **E19.**

reversionary /rɪˈvəːʃ(ə)n(ə)ri/ *adjective & noun.* **M17.**
[from prec. + -ARY¹.]
▸ **A** *adjective.* **1** Entitled to the reversion of something. *rare.* **M17.**
2 Of, pertaining to, or of the nature of a reversion. **E18.**
3 *BIOLOGY.* Relating to reversion to an ancestral type; tending to revert; atavistic. **L19.**
2 reversionary bonus an increase in the amount of an insurance policy payable at the maturation of the policy or the death of the person insured.
▸ **B** *noun.* = REVERSIONER. *rare.* **M17.**

reversioner /rɪˈvəːʃ(ə)nə/ *noun.* **E17.**
[formed as prec. + -ER¹.]
LAW. A person who possesses the reversion to an estate, office, etc.

reversis /rɪˈvəːsi/ *noun.* **L18.**
[French, var. of REVERSI.]
CARDS (now *Hist.*).
1 An obsolete game in which the object was to avoid winning the tricks. **L18.**
2 The taking of every trick by the same player. Only in ***make reversis, make the reversis***. **M19.**

revert /rɪˈvəːt, *in sense 2 also* ˈriːvəːt/ *noun.* **L16.**
[from the verb. In sense 2 after *convert* etc.]
†**1** *MUSIC.* A phrase in which the notes of the preceding phrase are repeated reversed with respect to ascending or descending the scale. **L16–E17.**
2 A person who returns to his or her previous religious faith. **M17.**
3 A return *to* some means etc. **L19.**

revert /rɪˈvəːt/ *verb.* **ME.**
[Old French *revertir* or Latin *revertere*, formed as RE- + *vertere* turn.]
▸ **I** *verb intrans.* †**1 a** Recover consciousness; come to oneself again. **ME–E18.** ▸**b** Improve, recover, revive; (of a plant etc.) spring up afresh. **LME–L16.**
2 Return, come or go back, to or from a place or position. Now *rare.* **LME.**
3 *LAW.* Return by reversion (*to*). **LME.**
†**4** Return to or *to* a person or party after estrangement or separation. **LME–M16.**
5 Return *to* a former subject of discourse or thought. **L16.**
6 Return to or *to* a former condition, custom, practice, idea, etc. **E17.** ▸**b** Chiefly *BIOLOGY.* Return *to* an earlier, original, or primitive state or condition; reproduce the characteristics of an ancestral form. Freq. in ***revert to type***. **M19.**

> 3 CONAN DOYLE The place . . is only a life interest and reverts to her husband's brother. **5** G. DALY He reverted to a theme that had stood him in good stead. **6** *Zigzag* He has reverted back on this tour to being completely solo. F. WELDON Sometimes widows like to revert to their maiden names. E. P. THOMPSON All Howard's . . work . . left little lasting impression, as conditions reverted after his death. P. ACKROYD In her sickness she reverted to the helpless condition of a child.

▸ **II** *verb trans.* **7** †**a** Recall. Only in **ME.** ▸†**b** Restore (*to*). **LME–M17.** ▸**c** Cause to return *to* a former condition or practice. **L20.**
8 †**a** Turn away; turn, force, or drive back; withdraw. **ME–M17.** ▸**b** Turn (one's eyes or steps) back; direct backwards. **M17.**
9 a Turn the other way; reverse, invert, turn up. Now *rare.* **LME.** ▸**b** *MATH.* Subject (a series) to reversion. **M18.**
†**10** Revoke, recall, annul. **M16–M17.**
■ **revertible** *adjective* capable of reverting, admitting of reversion, (*to*) **L15.**

revertant /rɪˈvəːt(ə)nt/ *adjective & noun.* **L17.**
[from prec. + -ANT¹, after French pres. pples in *-ant*.]
▸ **A** *adjective.* **1** *HERALDRY.* Bending, *spec.* in the form of an S. *rare.* **L17.**
2 *BIOLOGY.* Having reverted to the normal phenotype from a mutant or abnormal state. **M20.**
▸ **B** *noun. BIOLOGY.* A revertant cell, organism, strain, etc. **M20.**

reverter /rɪˈvəːtə/ *noun*¹. **L15.**
[formed as prec. + -ER⁴.]
LAW. Reversion (of land etc.).

reverter /rɪˈvəːtə/ *noun*². *rare.* **L19.**
[formed as prec. + -ER¹.]
A person who or thing which reverts.

revery *noun* var. of REVERIE *noun.*

†**revest** *verb*¹. **ME.**
[Old French *revestir* (mod. *revêtir*) from late Latin *revestire*, from Latin RE- + *vestire* clothe.]
1 *verb trans.* **a** Clothe (a priest etc.) in ecclesiastical vestments. Usu. in *pass.* **ME–E17.** ▸**b** *gen.* Clothe, dress, attire. **L15–M17.**
2 *verb refl.* Clothe oneself, esp. in ecclesiastical vestments. **ME–M17.**
3 *verb trans.* Invest or endow (a person) *with* property. *rare.* Only in **L15.**
4 *verb trans.* Put on (clothing) again. **L16–M19.**
5 *verb intrans.* Clothe oneself again. **E–M17.**
6 *verb trans.* = REVET *verb*¹. Chiefly as ***revested*** *ppl adjective.* **L17–M18.**

revest /riːˈvɛst/ *verb*². **M16.**
[from RE- + VEST *verb.*]
1 *verb trans.* Reinvest (a person) with authority, ownership, or office; reinstate. **M16.**
2 *verb intrans.* Be or become reinvested *in* a person. **M17.**
3 *verb trans.* Vest (something) again *in* a person etc. **L17.**

revestiary /rɪˈvɛstɪəri/ *noun.* Now *rare* or *obsolete.* **LME.**
[Old & mod. French *revestiaire* or medieval Latin *revestiarium*, from *re-* RE- + *vestiarium*: see VESTIARY.]
= REVESTRY.

revestry /rɪˈvɛstri/ *noun.* Now *rare.* **LME.**
[formed as prec. after VESTRY.]
The vestry of a church.

revet /rɪˈvɛt/ *verb*¹ *trans.* Infl. **-tt-**. Also **-vête** /-veɪt, -vɛt/. **E19.**
[French *revêtir*: see REVEST *verb*¹.]
Chiefly *FORTIFICATION.* Face (a rampart, wall, etc.) with masonry or other material; provide with a revetment. Usu. in *pass.*

revet /riːˈvɛt/ *verb*² *trans.* Infl. **-tt-**. **M20.**
[from RE- + VET *verb.*]
Vet again; recheck, re-examine.

revetment /rɪˈvɛtm(ə)nt/ *noun.* Also **-vête-** /-veɪt-, -vɛt-/. **L18.**
[French *revêtement*, formed as REVET *verb*¹: see -MENT.]
1 Chiefly *FORTIFICATION.* A retaining wall or facing of masonry or other material supporting or protecting a rampart, wall, etc. **L18.**
2 *ARCHITECTURE.* A facing of stone or other hard material over a less durable substance. *rare.* **M19.**

†**revie** *verb.* **LME.**
[Old & mod. French *renvier*, from *re-* RE- + *envier*: see ENVY *verb*².]
1 *verb trans.* Return (an invitation). *rare.* Only in **LME.**
2 *verb trans. & intrans.* Challenge (a person) in return. *rare.* **LME–L15.**
3 *verb trans. & intrans. CARDS.* Hazard a larger stake than that proposed by an opponent on (a card, trick, etc.). **L16–L17.**
4 *verb intrans.* Retort, retaliate. **E17–M18.**

review /rɪˈvjuː, *in sense 7* ˈriːvjuː/ *noun*. In sense 7 also **re-view**. LME.
[French †*reveue* (now *revue*), from *revoir*, from *re-* RE- + *voir*: see VIEW *noun*.]
1 An inspection of military or naval forces; *esp.* a display and formal inspection of troops or the fleet by the monarch, the commander-in-chief, a high-ranking visitor, etc. LME.
2 The action of looking over a book etc. for the purpose of correction or improvement; revision; an instance of this. Now *rare*. M16.
3 An inspection, an examination. Freq. in ***in review***. E17.
4 A general survey or reconsideration of some subject or thing (freq. in ***in review***, ***under review***); a retrospect, a survey of the past. E17.
5 LAW. Consideration of a judgement, sentence, etc., by some higher court or authority. M17.
6 An account or criticism of a (new or recent) book, play, film, product, etc., esp. as forming (part of) an article in a newspaper or periodical. M17. ▸**b** A periodical publication consisting mainly of articles on current events, new books, art, etc. Freq. in titles of periodicals. E18.
7 A second or repeated view. Formerly also (*rare*), the fact of seeing a place or person again. M17.
8 A facility for playing a tape recording during a fast rewind, so that it can be stopped when a particular point is reached. L20.

> **1** PRINCESS ALICE The Sultan . . in whose honour a great naval review . . was held. *attrib.*: A. DUGGAN We fell in on parade in review order. **2** BURKE What we have left standing in our . . reviews and reformations. **3** J. F. W. HERSCHEL Uranus was discovered . . in the course of a review of the heavens. **4** W. COWPER Mem'ry's . . wand That calls the past to our exact review. J. F. KENNEDY The programme would be kept constantly under review. J. BOWLBY My aim in this lecture has been to present a review of these findings. **5** W. BLACKSTONE Their sentence is final . . not even a review can be had. R. C. A. WHITE Supervisory jurisdiction is exercised . . on application for judicial review. **6** J. AGATE A delightful review of *Ego 5* in the *Manchester Guardian*. H. ROSENTHAL My first real reviews . . appeared in . . *Ballet and Opera*. **b** G. BODDY Murry and Lawrence planned a new review to be called the *Signature*. **7** F. ATTERBURY The Works of Nature will bear a Thousand Views, and Reviews.

Phrases: **bill of review** LAW: brought to procure examination and reversal of a decision made on an earlier bill. **court of review** LAW: before which judgements, sentences, etc., come for possible revision. ***cue and review***: see CUE *noun*[2]. **in review** under examination. ***judicial review***: see JUDICIAL *adjective*.

review /rɪˈvjuː, *in sense 2 also* riːˈvjuː/ *verb trans*. In sense 2 also **re-view**. L16.
[from RE- + VIEW *verb*, or from prec., after French *revoir*.]
1 Hold a review of (military or naval forces). L16.
2 View, inspect, or examine a second time or again. Formerly also, see again. L16.
3 Survey; take a survey of; look back on; survey in retrospect. L16.
4 LAW. Submit (a sentence, decision, etc.) to review. L16.
†**5** Look over or through (a book etc.) in order to correct or improve; revise. Also (*rare*), re-examine; reconsider. E17–E18.
6 Write a review of (a (new or recent) book, play, film, product, etc.). L18.

> **1** J. DOS PASSOS General Miles . . reviewed the parade. **2** L. STERNE How they viewed and re-viewed us as we passed over the rivulet! W. FALCONER Anxious to review his native shore. **3** T. JEFFERSON When I review his dispositions, and . . his conduct, I have little hope. J. GALSWORTHY He reviewed the revolution which had restored his Party to power. K. AMIS He decided not to review his financial position. **4** *Law Times* The court . . can review the exercise of his discretion by the County Court Judge. **5** W. PETTY Those who think 154,000 were . . destroyed ought to review the grounds of their Opinion. J. EDWARDS Ezra . . reviewed the copies and amended all errata's. **6** E. WAUGH I am reviewing an American book of etiquette for the *Atlantic Monthly*. M. FORSTER *Paracelsus* had been published . . and . . been well reviewed.

■ **reviewaˈbility** *noun* the quality or state of being (esp. judicially) reviewable E20. **reviewable** *adjective* (*a*) that may be reviewed; (*b*) *spec.* subject to judicial review: L18. **reviewal** *noun* the action or an act of reviewing something; an instance of this, a review: M17.

reviewer /rɪˈvjuːə/ *noun*. E17.
[from prec. + -ER[1].]
†**1** A person who revises a book etc.; a reviser. E17–E18.
2 Orig., the author of a special pamphlet criticizing another work. Now, a person who reviews a (new or recent) book, play, film, product, etc.; a writer of reviews. M17.

> **2** A. LIVINGSTONE The book was highly praised by reviewers.

†**revification** *noun*. *rare*. L17–E18.
[Alt. Cf. REVIVICATION.]
= REVIVIFICATION.

revigorate /riːˈvɪgəreɪt/ *verb trans*. E17.
[medieval Latin *revigorat-* pa. ppl stem of *revigorare*, from Latin RE- + *vigorare* make strong: see -ATE[3].]
Reinvigorate.

revile /rɪˈvʌɪl/ *verb*. ME.
[Old French *reviler*, from *re-* RE- + *vil* VILE *adjective*.]
†**1** *verb trans*. Degrade, abase. *rare*. Only in ME.
2 *verb trans*. Subject to insult or abuse; talk abusively to; criticize abusively, rail at. ME.
3 *verb intrans*. Talk abusively; criticize abusively, rail *at*. E16.

> **2** H. MARTINEAU He reviled heaven and earth when he saw his wife sinking from want. A. SETON Molly . . defended her mistress when she heard . . others reviling her. **3** AV 1 *Pet.* 2:23 Who when he was reuiled, reuiled not againe.

■ **revilement** *noun* the action or fact of reviling; an instance of this; a reviling speech: L16. **reviler** *noun* L16. **reviling** *verbal noun* the action of the verb; a reviling remark or speech: M16.

revirement /rəvirmɑ̃/ *noun*. Pl. pronounced same. E20.
[French.]
An alteration of one's plans; a complete change of attitude or opinion.

revirescence /riːvɪˈrɛs(ə)ns/ *noun*. *rare*. M18.
[formed as next: see -ESCENCE.]
Return to a youthful or flourishing condition.

revirescent /riːvɪˈrɛs(ə)nt/ *adjective*. *rare*. M17.
[Latin *revirescent-* pres. ppl stem of *revirescere*, formed as RE- + *viridis* green: see -ESCENT.]
Flourishing anew.

revise /rɪˈvʌɪz/ *noun*. L16.
[from the verb.]
†**1** The fact of being seen again. Only in L16.
2 a The action or an act of revising; a revision, a re-examination. L16. ▸**b** A revised version or form. M19.
3 PRINTING. A revised or corrected form of proof-sheet, including corrections made to an earlier proof; a second stage in proofing. E17.

> **2a** R. L'ESTRANGE The Book might be subjected to a careful Examination and Revise. **b** W. GARNER Here's the revise . . retyped with the new ending. **3** J. RUSKIN The revise of the last sheet was sent to printer.

revise /rɪˈvʌɪz/ *verb*. M16.
[Old & mod. French *réviser*, †*reviser* or Latin *revisere*, formed as RE- + *visere* examine, desiderative and intensive of *videre*, *vis-* see.]
†**1 a** *verb intrans*. Look again or repeatedly *at*, look back or reflect *on*. M16–M17. ▸**b** *verb trans*. See or look at again. E17–M18.
2 a *verb trans*. Orig. (*rare*), condense (esp. a written text) *into* a more concise form. Later, examine or re-examine and improve or amend (esp. written or printed matter); consider and alter (an opinion, plan, etc.). E17. ▸**b** *verb trans. & intrans*. Go over or read again (work already learned or done), esp. in preparation for an examination. M20.

> **1a** CHRISTOPHER LEVER Waking, or not, I oft reuise thereon. **b** H. BROOKE To revise it, to gaze and dwell upon it in secret. **2a** G. VIDAL I was later to revise the system of taxation. V. S. PRITCHETT He was continuously revising what he had written. **Revised Standard Version** a revision made in 1946–52 of the Authorized Version of the Bible. **Revised Version** a revision made in 1881–5 of the Authorized Version of the Bible. **b** C. FREMLIN What about her revising? . . How could she ever get through her Mocks?

■ **revisable** *adjective* able to be revised; liable to revision: L19. **revisal** *noun* the action or an act of revising; a revision, a re-examination: E17. **reviser** *noun* a person who revises something L17. **revisor** *noun* a reviser L16. **revisory** *adjective* capable of revising; engaged in or of the nature of revision: M19.

revision /rɪˈvɪʒ(ə)n/ *noun*. E17.
[Old & mod. French *révision* or late Latin *revisio(n-)*, from Latin *revisere*: see prec., -ION.]
1 The action of revising, esp. in preparation for an examination. E17. ▸**b** The result of revising; a revised version. M19. ▸**c** MEDICINE. (A) surgical operation to make good any deterioration (esp. of an artificial joint or other prosthetic appliance) following a previous operation. M20.
2 The fact of seeing a person or thing again; an instance of this. Now *rare*. L18.
3 A retrospective survey. *rare*. M19.

> **1** C. PRIEST I began a process of revision, going back through . . completed pages and rewriting . . passages. **b** J. KITTO A revision . . is now wanted, or rather, a new translation. **2** E. L. ARNOLD A sweet revision of Blodwin, my . . British wife! **3** W. C. MACREADY Let my revision of this day enable me to be more resolute.

■ **revisionary** *adjective* E19.

revisionism /rɪˈvɪʒ(ə)nɪz(ə)m/ *noun*. Freq. *derog*. E20.
[from prec. + -ISM.]
POLITICS. **1** A policy of revision or modification, esp. of Marxist–Leninist doctrine on evolutionary socialist (rather than revolutionary) or pluralist principles. E20.
2 The theory or practice of revising one's attitude to a previously accepted political situation, doctrine, or point of view. E20.

revisionist /rɪˈvɪʒ(ə)nɪst/ *noun & adjective*. M19.
[formed as prec. + -IST.]
▸**A** *noun*. **1** An advocate or supporter of revisionism. M19.
2 A reviser. *rare*. L19.
▸**B** *adjective*. That advocates or supports revisionism; of or pertaining to revisionism or revisionists. M19.

revivable /rɪˈvʌɪvəb(ə)l/ *adjective*. E19.
[from REVIVE + -ABLE.]
Able to be revived.
■ **revivaˈbility** *noun* M19.

revival /rɪˈvʌɪv(ə)l/ *noun*. E17.
[from REVIVE + -AL[1].]
1 a The action or an act of reviving something; restoration esp. of a former custom or practice to general use, acceptance, etc.; a result of this. E17. ▸**b** (The action of staging) a new production of an old play etc. M17. ▸**c** ARCHITECTURE. More fully ***Gothic revival***. The reintroduction of a Gothic style of architecture towards the middle of the 19th cent. M19.
2 A reawakening of religious fervour, esp. as resulting in a series of religious meetings held by a particular Church or community. E18.
3 Restoration or return to esp. bodily or mental vigour or activity or to life or consciousness. M18.

> **1a** J. T. MICKLETHWAITE The modern revival of extempore preaching. N. SHERRY There had been a revival of drama at the school. **revival of learning**, **revival of letters** the Renaissance in its literary aspect. **b** R. LUDLUM The Plaza Movie Theatre . . was showing a revival of *A Knife in the Water*. **c** *attrib.*: R. LIDDELL A Gothic revival school building. **2** G. M. TREVELYAN The Evangelical revival . . breathed fresh power into Scottish religion. *attrib.*: *New Yorker* One took up pentecostalism and died . . at a revival meeting. **3** GIBBON On his revival from the swoon . . he recovered his speech. G. MACDONALD This was the first time he had shown such a revival of energy. M. LOWRY Not so much asleep as lifeless, beyond hope of revival.

■ **revivalism** *noun* (*a*) belief in or the promotion of a revival of religious fervour; (*b*) tendency or desire to revive esp. a former custom or practice: E19. **revivalist** *noun* an advocate or adherent of revivalism E19. **revivaˈlistic** *adjective* of, pertaining to, or characteristic of revivalists or revivalism L19.

revive /rɪˈvʌɪv/ *verb*. LME.
[Old & mod. French *revivre* or late Latin *revivere*, from Latin RE- + *vivere* live.]
▸**I** *verb intrans*. **1** Return to consciousness; recover from a faint. LME.
2 Become active or operative again; return to a flourishing state; assume fresh life or vigour; (esp. of a former custom or practice) be restored to current use. Also, become valid again. L15. ▸**b** Return or come back again after a period of abeyance. M18. ▸**c** Of a play etc.: be revived. E20.
3 Return or come back to life; live again. E16

> **1** H. B. STOWE St Clare had fainted . . but as Miss Ophelia applied restoratives, he revived. D. PAE 'She is reviving,' exclaimed Eustace. **2** MILTON If . . the radiant Sun . . Extend his ev'ning beam, the fields revive. *Observer* The old religions of Buddhism and Confucianism are reviving in China. S. WEINTRAUB Her spirits revived with the reappearance . . of Feodora. G. GREENE Tired of hack journalism . . my desire to be a writer revived. **3** SHAKES. 1 *Hen. VI* Henry is dead and never shall revive. *Popular Science Monthly* Emotionally we revive in our children.

▸**II** *verb trans*. **4** Restore to consciousness; bring back from a faint. LME.
5 Restore to life; bring back *from* death or the grave. LME.
6 Make active or operative again; return to a flourishing state; give fresh life or vigour to; restore (esp. a former custom or practice) to current use. Also, re-enact, revalidate, (a law etc.) L15. ▸**b** Put on a new production of (an old play etc.) L18.
7 CHEMISTRY. Convert or restore (a metal, esp. mercury) to or into its normal or pure form; regenerate *from* a mixture or compound. *obsolete* exc. *Hist*. L15.
8 Restore to clearness or freshness; renovate. M19.

> **4** DEFOE This Water reviv'd his Father more than . . the . . Spirits I had given him. **5** T. FULLER I remember not in Scripture that God ever revived a brute Beast. **6** R. LEHMANN Colours revived her spirits, textures soothed her. W. S. CHURCHILL Reviving the obsolete claim to suzerainty, Henry denounced the Scots as rebels. P. H. JOHNSON I was much revived: the smell of coffee was stimulating. G. THOMAS Two military bands the town had once had were to be revived. **b** G. GREENE An old silent film . . *The New Babylon*, which the Forum recently revived. L. GORDON *Murder in the Cathedral* was revived successfully.

■ **revivement** *noun* (now *rare*) (*a*) a reviving or restoring influence; (*b*) the action or an act of reviving; revival: L16. **revivingly** *adverb* in a reviving manner M19.

For other words beginning with *re-* see the entry for **re-**

reviver /rɪˈvʌɪvə/ *noun*¹. M16.
[from prec. + -ER¹.]
1 A thing which revives something or someone. M16. ▸**b** A preparation for restoring a faded colour, polish, or lustre. M19. ▸**c** A stimulating drink. Chiefly in ***corpse-reviver*** (US), an alcoholic drink, *esp.* one taken for a hang-over. *slang*. L19.
2 A person who revives something. E17.

†**reviver** *noun*². E17.
[formed as prec. + -ER⁴.]
1 Revival, restoration, re-establishment. E–M17.
2 Law. ***bill of reviver***, a bill of revivor (cf. REVIVOR 3). M17–E18.

revivication /rɪˌvɪvɪˈkeɪʃ(ə)n/ *noun*. Now *rare*. M19.
[Alt. Cf. REVIFICATION.]
= REVIVIFICATION.

revivification /rɪˌvɪvɪfɪˈkeɪʃ(ə)n/ *noun*. M17.
[from late Latin *revivificat-* pa. ppl stem of *revivificare*: see next, -ATION.]
1 Restoration or return from death to life; an instance of this. M17. ▸**b** Recovery from a state of dormancy or suspended animation. E19.
2 *CHEMISTRY*. Reduction or restoration of a metal etc., after combination, to its original state. *obsolete* exc. *Hist.* M17.
3 Revival, restoration; renewal of vigour or activity; an instance of this. M18.

revivify /rɪˈvɪvɪfʌɪ/ *verb*. L17.
[French *revivifier* or late Latin *revivificare*, formed as RE- + VIVIFY.]
1 *verb trans.* Restore to animation or activity; revive, reinvigorate; put new life into. L17.
2 *CHEMISTRY*. **a** *verb trans.* = REVIVE 7. *obsolete* exc. *Hist.* E18. ▸**b** *verb intrans.* Return to the metallic or uncombined state. Long *rare* or *obsolete*. E18.
3 *verb trans.* Restore to life; make alive again. M18.

> 🕮 **1** W. S. CHURCHILL On the coasts of Newfoundland English fishermen had revivified the earliest colony of the Crown. J. BARZUN Old habits return, revivified by a word or .. incident. **3** J. C. MANGAN I would spring up revivified, reborn, a living soul again. H. DRUMMOND The biologist cannot devitalise a plant .. and revivify it again.

reviviscence /rɛvɪˈvɪs(ə)ns/ *noun*. E17.
[Late Latin *reviviscentia*, formed as next: see -ENCE.]
Revival; return to life or animation; restoration to a flourishing or vigorous condition.
■ Also **reviviscency** *noun* (*rare*) M17.

reviviscent /rɛvɪˈvɪs(ə)nt/ *adjective*. L18.
[Latin *reviviscent-* pres. ppl stem of *reviviscere* inceptive of *revivere* REVIVE: see -ENT.]
Reviving; returning to life or animation; giving renewed life.

revivor /rɪˈvʌɪvə/ *noun*. M16.
[from REVIVE + -OR.]
1 A person who revives something; a reviver. *rare*. M16.
†**2** Renewal, revival; an instance of this. E17–M19.
3 *LAW* (now *Hist.*). A proceeding for the revival of a suit or action abated by the death of one of the parties or by some other circumstance. Chiefly in ***bill of revivor***. Cf. REVIVER *noun*² 2. E18.

revocable /ˈrɛvəkəb(ə)l/ *adjective*. L15.
[Old French (mod. *ré-*) or Latin *revocabilis*, from *revocare*: see next, -ABLE. Cf. earlier IRREVOCABLE.]
Able to be revoked or recalled.

> 🕮 T. TAYLOR The decree of God had been absolute, and so not revocable.

■ **revocaˈbility** *noun* the quality of being revocable M19. **revocableness** *noun* L17. **revocably** *adverb* M19.

revocation /rɛvəˈkeɪʃ(ə)n/ *noun*. LME.
[Old & mod. French *révocation* or Latin *revocatio(n-)*, from *revocat-* pa. ppl stem of *revocare*: see REVOKE *verb*, -ION.]
1 The action of recalling someone or something: recall of a person, a call or summons to return. Now *rare* or *obsolete*. LME.
2 The action of revoking or annulling something; cancellation of a decree etc. LME.
†**3** Recantation; retraction of an opinion, statement, etc. LME–L17.

> 🕮 **1** *London Gazette* The Envoy delivered his Letters of Revocation, and is preparing to leave this Court. **2** *Philadelphia Inquirer* Richardson was arrested .. and charged with driving despite the revocation of his licence.

revocatory /ˈrɛvəkət(ə)ri/ *adjective & noun*. LME.
[Late Latin *revocatorius*, formed as prec.: see -ORY¹, -ORY².]
▸ **A** *adjective*. Pertaining to or expressive of revocation. LME.

> 🕮 F. A. KEMBLE She would (instead of rewriting it) tack on .. a sort of revocatory codicil.

▸† **B** *noun*. (A) revocation. *rare*. Only in M17.

revokable /rɪˈvəʊkəb(ə)l/ *adjective*. Also **revokeable**. L16.
[from REVOKE *verb* + -ABLE.]
Revocable.

revoke /rɪˈvəʊk/ *verb & noun*. LME.
[Old & mod. French *révoquer* or Latin *revocare*, formed as RE- + *vocare* call.]
▸ **A** *verb*. **I** *verb trans.* †**1** Bring (a person etc.) back to a belief, way of life, etc. (Foll. by *to*.) LME–L17. ▸**b** Draw (a person etc.) back or away *from* some belief, practice, etc., esp. a wrong or wicked one. LME–E17. ▸**c** Induce (a person) to refrain *from* a course of action etc.; restrain or prevent (a person) *from* something. L15–E17. ▸**d** Check, restrain. *rare*. L16–M17.
2 †**a** Bring (a person) back *into* life; restore to consciousness. LME–M17. ▸**b** Call (something) back to memory. Now *rare*. M16. ▸†**c** Revive (a custom, practice, etc.). L16–M17.
3 Annul, repeal, cancel, (a decree, promise, etc.); rescind. LME.
†**4** Retract, withdraw, recant. LME–L17.
5 Call or summon (a person) back, esp. from exile or from a position of responsibility abroad. Now *rare*. L15.
†**6** Take (something) back to oneself. E16–E17. ▸**b** Withdraw, draw back, (something). *rare*. L16–M17.

> 🕮 **1** SIR T. MORE Reuoking them that erred, setting vp agayne those that were ouerthrowen. **c** P. HOLLAND He could not be revoked from battaile. **2b** J. HAWKINS Reuoking to minde the former talk between the captaine and him. **3** M. BERLINS A will is automatically revoked when the person who made it gets married. G. DALY He would humiliate Annie and revoke her claim on him. **5** J. STRYPE The English forces were revoked from the marches of Scotland. *fig.*: W. COWPER We wish time spent revok'd, That we might try the ground again.

▸ **II** *verb intrans.* **7** Make revocation. LME.
8 *CARDS*. Fail to follow suit when able and required to do so. L16.

> 🕮 **7** G. CRABBE I make a promise, and will not revoke.

▸ **B** *noun*. **1** †**a** The right to have a decision repealed. *Scot.* Only in L15. ▸**b** Revocation, recall. *rare*. L19.
2 *CARDS*. (A) failure to follow suit when able and required to do so. E18.
■ †**revokement** *noun* (*rare*) the action of revoking, revocation E–M17. **revoker** *noun* (*CARDS*) a person who revokes L19.

revokeable *adjective* var. of REVOKABLE.

revolera /revoˈlera/ *noun*. M20.
[Spanish.]
BULLFIGHTING. A movement in which the bullfighter swirls the cape above his head.

revolt /rɪˈvəʊlt/ *noun*. M16.
[French *révolte* from Italian *rivolta*, from *rivoltare*: see next.]
1 A mass insurrection, an uprising, a rebellion. M16. ▸**b** An act of protest or defiance by an individual; *esp.* a refusal to submit to a lawful authority or established custom and practice. L16. ▸**c** A change of attitude; a switch of loyalties. L16.
2 The action of rebelling or protesting. L16.
3 Revulsion; a sense of loathing or disgust. *rare*. E17.

> 🕮 **1** R. H. TAWNEY Hardly a decade .. passed without a peasant's revolt. **b** *Harper's Magazine* The political philosophy of .. Jefferson was a product of .. infantile revolt against his father. **2** C. PANKHURST Unless the vote were granted to women .. a fiercer spirit of revolt would be awakened. **in revolt** in a state of rebellion.

revolt /rɪˈvəʊlt/ *verb*. M16.
[French (*se*) *révolter* from Italian *rivoltare* from Proto-Romance intensive of Latin *revolvere* REVOLVE.]
▸ **I** *verb intrans.* **1** Rise in rebellion against established authority; withdraw one's support from a leader etc. (Foll. by *against*, *from*.) M16. ▸†**b** Change one's loyalty or allegiance. Freq. foll. by *to*. M16–L17.
†**2** **a** Go over *to* another religion; stray *from* a faith etc. M16–L17. ▸**b** Withdraw from a course of action etc. Usu. foll. by *from*. L16–E17.
3 Feel revulsion or disgust *at*; react with repugnance *against*, turn in loathing *from*. M18.

> 🕮 **1** DE QUINCEY Other armies had revolted, and the rebellion was spreading. *Listener* She .. revolted in revenge against her family. **b** T. MANLEY Hopes of .. plunder allured many to revolt to the Enemy. **2b** C. MARLOWE Revolt, or I'll in piecemeal tear thy flesh. **3** B. MONTGOMERY My soul revolted against this way of doing business.

▸ **II** *verb trans.* †**4** **a** Turn (a thing) back. *rare* (Spenser). Only in L16. ▸**b** Cause to revolt. *rare*. L16–E17.
5 Affect (a person etc.) with disgust or repugnance; nauseate, disgust. M18.

> 🕮 **4b** W. BEDELL Pope Constantine .. reuolted Italie from the Greeke Emperours obedience. **5** BROWNING Obscenity .. slunk away, revolted at itself. O. STAPLEDON Strangers were often revolted by his uncouth proportions.

■ **revolted** *adjective* (**a**) that has rebelled, rebellious; (**b**) disgusted, nauseated: L16. **revolter** *noun* E17.

revolte /reɪˈvəʊlteɪ/ *noun*. Also ***révolté***, (fem.) ***-ée***, /revolte (*pl. same*)/. L19.
[French.]
A person who revolts; a rebel; a nonconformist.

revolting /rɪˈvəʊltɪŋ/ *adjective*. L16.
[from REVOLT *verb* + -ING².]
1 That revolts; rebellious. L16.
2 Disgusting, nauseating, horrible. E19.

> 🕮 **1** SHAKES. *John* Let the church .. breathe her curse .. on her revolting son. **2** P. BOWLES What revolting water .. I don't think I shall drink it.

■ **revoltingly** *adverb* M19. **revoltingness** *noun* M18.

revoluble /rɪˈvɒljʊb(ə)l/ *adjective*. Long *rare*. L16.
[Latin *revolubilis*, from *revolvere* REVOLVE: see -UBLE.]
Revolving; rolling.
■ **revoluˈbility** *noun* (*rare*) a tendency to roll back M19.

revolute /ˈrɛvəluːt/ *adjective*. LME.
[Latin *revolutus* pa. pple of *revolvere* REVOLVE.]
†**1** Having completed a full revolution. Only in LME.
2 Chiefly *BOTANY*. Rolled backwards at the edges. M18.

revolute /rɛvəˈluːt/ *verb intrans.* L19.
[Back-form. from next.]
Engage in rebellion or revolution.

revolution /rɛvəˈluːʃ(ə)n/ *noun & verb*. In senses 7a, b also **R-**. LME.
[Old & mod. French *révolution* or late Latin *revolutio(n-)*, from Latin *revolut-* pa. ppl stem of *revolvere* REVOLVE: see -ION.]
▸ **A** *noun*. **I** **1** *ASTRONOMY*. The action of a celestial object of moving in a circular or elliptical orbit or course around another; the apparent movement of the sun, stars, etc., round the earth; a single circuit of this nature. LME. ▸**b** The time in which a planet etc. completes a full circuit of its orbit. LME.
2 **a** The regular recurrence of a point or period of time; the lapse of a certain time. LME. ▸†**b** A cyclic period of time; an epoch. L16–E18. ▸†**c** The recurrence or repetition *of* esp. an event; an anniversary. M17–L18.
†**3** A twist; a convolution; a bend. LME–M18.
4 **a** The action of turning round or of revolving round a point; *esp.* motion round an axis or centre, rotation. LME. ▸**b** A completion of a single rotation. E18.

> 🕮 **2a** E. HOPKINS Naturalists affirm .. that the revolution of .. years gradually wears away the former body. **c** W. COWPER The constant revolution .. of the same repeated joys .. palls and satiates. **3** T. RAYNALDE Vaynes infynytely intricate and writhid with a thousand reuolutions. **4a** A. S. EDDINGTON The revolution of an electron around a nucleus. ***surface of revolution***: see SURFACE *noun* 3. **b** A. HIGGINS Turning the pump wheel .. so many revolutions per minute.

▸ **II** †**5** **a** The action of examining a matter through debate; discussion. *rare*. LME–M16. ▸**b** Consideration, reflection. L16–L18.

> 🕮 **5b** R. ORME Thoughts that by long revolution .. have been formed and polished.

▸ **III** **6** †**a** Alteration, change, mutation. LME–E18. ▸**b** A period or instance of significant change or radical alteration of a particular condition, state of affairs, etc. LME. ▸**c** *GEOLOGY*. A major mountain-building episode, *esp.* one extending over a whole continent or occurring at the close of a geological era. E19.
7 **a** The complete overthrow of an established government or social order by those previously subject to it; an instance of this; a forcible substitution of a new form of government. Freq. with specifying word. E17. ▸**b** In Marxism, the violent overthrow of the ruling class and the seizure of power through control of the means of production by a class to whom such control was previously denied; the historically inevitable transition from one system of production to another and the political change which ensues, leading to the eventual triumph of Communism. M19.

> 🕮 **6b** C. FRANCIS Carriage of .. cargo in containers is bringing about a revolution in trade by sea. ***green revolution***, ***Industrial Revolution***, ***scientific revolution***, ***sexual revolution***, ***social revolution***, etc. **7a** L. STRACHEY The .. tenacity of the reactionaries and the .. fury of their enemies could have no other issue but revolution. J. GALSWORTHY The revolution which had restored his Party to power. R. BERTHOUD The chaos and bloodshed of the 1917 Revolution. *attrib.*: F. BURNEY I am .. alarmed to find this County filled with .. Revolution Societies. ***American Revolution***, ***French Revolution***, ***Glorious Revolution***, ***Russian Revolution***, etc. **b** ***permanent revolution***: see PERMANENT *adjective*. ***proletarian revolution***: see PROLETARIAN *adjective*.

▸ **B** *verb trans.* = REVOLUTIONIZE 1. Usu. in *pass.* *rare*. E19.

> 🕮 A. WEST That country has been .. revolutioned, and counter-revolutioned, .. three or four times.

Comb.: **revolution counter** = ***rev counter*** s.v. REV *noun*¹.
■ **revolutional** *adjective* †(**a**) *ASTRONOMY* Pertaining to the revolution of the planets; (**b**) pertaining to or supporting revolution or a particular revolution; revolutionary: M17. **ˌrevolutionˈeering** *verbal noun* (*rare*) the practice and theory of revolution; agitation for revolution: E19. **revolutioner** *noun* a supporter of revolution; a participant in a particular revolution; a revolutionary: L17. **revolutionism** *noun* the theory or advocacy of revolutionary action M19. **revolutionist** *noun* an advocate of revolution; a revolutionary: E18. **ˌrevolutionˈology** *noun* (*rare*) the science or study of revolution E20.

revolutionary /rɛvəˈluːʃ(ə)n(ə)ri/ *adjective & noun*. In sense A.1 also **R-**. L18.
[from prec. + -ARY[1], partly after French *révolutionnaire*.]
▶ **A** *adjective*. **1** Pertaining to, characterized by, or of the nature of revolution; involving or constituting radical change; pertaining to or advocating political revolution. L18.
2 Revolving; marked by rotation. M19.

📖 **1** H. MACMILLAN A new and more far-reaching—almost revolutionary—project was about to be launched. A. PRICE Geoff's always been pathological about the Communists and the Revolutionary Left.

▶ **B** *noun*. A person who instigates or supports revolution; a participant in a particular revolution. M19.

📖 E. LONGFORD When governments become traitors, honest men become revolutionaries.

Phrases etc.: COUNTER-***revolutionary***. ***social revolutionary***: see SOCIAL *adjective*.
▪ **revolutionarily** *adverb* M19. **revolutionariness** *noun* M19.

revolutionize /rɛvəˈluːʃ(ə)nʌɪz/ *verb*. Also **-ise**. L18.
[from prec. + -IZE 3, after French *révolutionner*.]
1 *verb trans*. Bring (a country etc.) under a revolutionary form of government. L18.
2 *verb trans*. Convert (a person etc.) to revolutionism; change (existing procedures etc.) to accord with revolutionary principles. L18.
3 *verb trans*. Change (a thing) significantly or completely; reorganize or reconstruct (a thing) on new or radical lines. L18.
4 *verb intrans*. Engage in revolutions. *rare*. M19.

📖 **1** M. E. G. DUFF The object of these invaders has been to revolutionize Bulgaria. **2** SOUTHEY Sometimes the poet is called a Jacobin; at others it is said . . his opinions are revolutionised. **3** D. LODGE Three things . . have revolutionized academic life.

revolve /rɪˈvɒlv/ *verb & noun*. LME.
[Latin *revolvere*, formed as RE- + *volvere* roll, turn.]
▶ **A** *verb*. **I** *verb trans*. †**1** Turn (the eyes or one's gaze) back or round. LME–L17.
†**2** Roll; move by rolling. *rare*. LME–M16.
†**3** Restore; turn or bring (a thing) back to a place, position, or condition. Usu. foll. by *into*. LME–L17.
4 Turn over (something) *in* the mind, thoughts, etc. LME. ▸**b** Consider or meditate on (something). LME.
†**5** Bind (a limb etc.), tie or wrap up. LME–M17.
6 Search through, study repeatedly, or read (a book etc.). Now *rare* or *obsolete*. L15.
7 Cause (something) to move in a circle or to travel in an orbit around a central point; rotate (a thing) on an axis. M17.

📖 **4** V. WOOLF He had often revolved these questions in his mind. **b** H. MANTEL Her mind revolved the possibilities. **6** T. NASHE From thy byrth to thys moment . . reuolue the diarie of thy memory. **7** SCOTT FITZGERALD The touch of . . leaves revolved it slowly.

▶ **II** *verb intrans*. †**8** Deliberate; think *on*. M16–L18.
†**9** Return *to*. L16–M18.
10 Perform a circular motion; move in an orbit *about* or *round* a central point; rotate on an axis. L16.
11 Come round again, move round. M18.

📖 **8** W. PALEY A mind revolving upon the subject of . . jurisprudence. **9** HOR. WALPOLE You will smile at seeing Doddington again revolved to the court. **10** C. S. FORESTER The electric motor began to revolve. *fig.*: *Japan Times* His life revolved around the British Museum Reading Room. **11** G. CRABBE The year revolves, and I again explore The . . annals of my parish poor.

▶ **B** *noun*. †**1** Contemplation, determination. *rare*. Only in L16.
2 A rotation; a revolution. M17.
3 THEATRICAL. A revolving stage. E20.

📖 **2** B. W. PROCTER The stars Went round . . their circles lessening At each revolve. **3** *Listener* They are . . on a revolve which keeps whisking them away from us.

▪ **revolvable** *adjective* L19. **revolvency** *noun* (*rare*) tendency to revolve; capacity for revolution: L18.

revolver /rɪˈvɒlvə/ *noun*. M16.
[from REVOLVE *verb* + -ER[1].]
1 A person who or thing which revolves; *spec*. †(*a*) a person who considers or meditates on something; (*b*) a revolving mechanism or piece of machinery. M16.
2 A pistol with revolving chambers which are presented in succession before the hammer, enabling several shots to be fired without reloading. M19.

📖 **2** *attrib.*: G. M. FRASER The thunderous boom-boom-boom of revolver-fire.

▪ **revolvered** *adjective* provided with or carrying a revolver or revolvers E20.

revolving /rɪˈvɒlvɪŋ/ *ppl adjective*. L16.
[formed as prec. + -ING[2].]
That revolves; rotating; travelling in orbit; *poet.* (of time, the seasons, etc.) recurring, elapsing.

📖 W. COWPER Revolving seasons, fruitless as they pass. **revolving credit**: that is automatically renewed as debts are cleared. **revolving door** (*a*) a door with usu. four partitions set at right angles radiating out from, and revolving on, a central vertical axis; (*b*) *fig.* a situation in which the same events recur in a continuous cycle; a place or organization that people tend to enter and leave very quickly; *US* a situation in which someone moves from an influential government position to a private company, or vice versa. **revolving fund**: that is continually replenished as withdrawals are made. **revolving stage** a turntable set into a stage floor on which scenery is placed, enabling one setting to turn out of sight as the next one appears.

revue /rɪˈvjuː/ *noun*. L19.
[French = REVIEW *noun*.]
A light theatrical entertainment consisting of a series of short (usu. satirical) sketches, comic turns, songs, etc. Also, the genre comprising such entertainments.

📖 *Guardian* He became . . highly successful . . in light comedy and revue. *attrib.*: M. ALLINGHAM She washed and changed with the speed of a revue star.

▪ **revu'ette** *noun* a short revue M20.

revulsion /rɪˈvʌlʃ(ə)n/ *noun*. M16.
[French *révulsion* or Latin *revulsio(n-)*, from *revuls-* pa. ppl stem of *revellere*, formed as RE- + *vellere* pull: see -ION.]
1 MEDICINE. The drawing of blood from one part to another, as by counterirritation; lessening of a condition in one part of the body by irritation of another. Now *rare*. M16.
2 The action of drawing or the fact of being drawn back or away (*lit.* & *fig.*). Also, an instance of this. Now chiefly as passing into sense 3. E17.
3 A sudden violent change of feeling; a strong reaction in taste; abhorrence, repugnance; a sense of loathing. E19.
4 A sudden reaction or reversal in trade, fortune, etc. *rare*. E19.

📖 **2** P. RYCAUT There . . followed a Revulsion of the Forces from Dalmatia. **3** H. JAMES He had . . a revulsion in Mamies's favour. G. BODDY For her fellow guests . . she could feel only revulsion. **4** W. S. JEVONS A revulsion occasioned by a failure of . . capital must cause . . a collapse of credit.

▪ **revulsant** *noun* (now *rare*) MEDICINE a revulsive, a counterirritant L19. **revulsionary** *adjective* (*rare*) E19. **revulsive** *adjective* & *noun* (now *rare*) MEDICINE (an agent) capable of producing or tending to produce revulsion E17.

revusical /rɪˈvjuːzɪk(ə)l/ *noun*. *slang*. Chiefly *US*. M20.
[from REVU(E + MU)SICAL *noun*.]
A light theatrical entertainment combining elements of the revue and musical.

rew /ruː/ *noun*. *obsolete* exc. *dial.*
[Old English *rǣw* var. of *rāw* ROW *noun*[1].]
1 a A hedgerow. OE. ▸†**b** A row or line of persons or things; a rank, a series. ME–M17. ▸**c** A long heap or ridge of scythed grass. L19.
†**2** A streak, a stripe. *rare*. ME–L17.
¶ Sense 1a not recorded between OE and M19.

reward /rɪˈwɔːd/ *noun*. ME.
[Anglo-Norman, Old Northern French = Old French *reguard*, *regard* REGARD *noun*.]
▶ **I** †**1** Regard, consideration, heed. Chiefly in ***have reward***, ***take reward***, ***give reward***. ME–L15.
†**2** Estimation, worth. *rare*. Only in ME.

📖 **1** H. LOVELICH Owre lord . . took Reward to his Good lyf.

▶ **II 3** A return or recompense, esp. for service or merit. Also, retribution or punishment for wrongdoing. ME. ▸†**b** HUNTING & FALCONRY. A part of the carcass of the quarry, given to a hound or a hawk directly after a kill. LME–L17. ▸†**c** Remuneration; wages; a bonus. LME–L18. ▸**d** A sum of money offered for the capture or detection of a criminal, recovery of lost or stolen property, etc. L16. ▸**e** PSYCHOLOGY. A pleasant stimulus following a particular response which increases the probability of recurrence of that response in a similar situation. Freq. *attrib.*, esp. as ***reward cell***, ***reward centre***, ***reward system***, with ref. to areas of the brain in or near the hypothalamus which, when stimulated, produce sensations of pleasure. Cf. PUNISHMENT 1b. E20.
†**4** An extra supply or allowance of food; an extra dish. LME–M16.

📖 **3** W. STUBBS Hanging was the reward of treason. ANNE STEVENSON Work . . brought Sylvia the rewards she coveted. **go to one's reward**, **pass to one's reward** (orig. *US*) go to heaven, die. **d** *attrib.*: D. E. WESTLAKE The reward money our new government gave you.

▪ **rewardful** *adjective* yielding or producing reward L16. **rewardless** *adjective* LME.

reward /rɪˈwɔːd/ *verb*. ME.
[Anglo-Norman, Old Northern French *rewarder* = Old French *reguarder*, *regarder* REGARD *verb*.]
▶ **I** †**1** *verb trans*. Regard, heed, consider; observe. ME–E17.
†**2** *verb trans*. Agree; determine, decide. Only in LME.
†**3** *verb intrans*. Look; give heed. *rare*. Only in LME.
▶ **II** †**4** *verb trans*. Assign or give (a thing) to a person as a reward or recompense. ME–M17.
5 *verb trans*. Repay or recompense (a person) for service, merit, etc. ME. ▸†**b** HUNTING & FALCONRY. Give (a hound or hawk) part of the carcass of the quarry directly after a kill. LME–E17. ▸†**c** Give (a person) something from another person's legacy. LME–E17.
6 *verb trans*. †**a** Compensate for (a deficiency). Only in LME. ▸**b** Requite, make return for, (a service, a person's efforts, etc.). M16.
†**7** *verb trans*. **a** Pay back (harm or evil) to a person. *rare*. LME–M16. ▸**b** Repay (a person) for wrongdoing; punish. L15–L17.

📖 **4** AV *1 Sam.* 24:17 Thou hast rewarded mee good, whereas I haue rewarded thee euill. **5** B. VINE Her husband . . had been rewarded with a knighthood for some . . merchant-banking service. **6b** *Asian Art* Asia rewards our attention as does no other part of the world. **7b** AV *2 Sam.* 3:39 The LORD shall reward the doer of euill, according to his wickednesse.

▪ **rewardable** *adjective* able to be rewarded; worthy or deserving of reward: LME. **rewardableness** *noun* M17. **rewardably** *adverb* LME. **rewarder** *noun* a person who rewards someone or something; a repayer *of* a person or thing: ME.

rewarding /rɪˈwɔːdɪŋ/ *adjective*. L17.
[from prec. + -ING[2].]
That rewards someone or something. Now *esp.* gratifying, worthwhile; providing satisfaction.

📖 *Woman* We are always busy . . and it is such rewarding work.

¶ Earlier in UNREWARDING.
▪ **rewardingly** *adverb* M19. **rewardingness** *noun* M20.

rewarewa /ˈreɪwəreɪwə, *foreign* ˈriwariwa/ *noun*. M19.
[Maori, from *rewa* to float.]
A tall New Zealand tree, *Knightia excelsa* (family Proteaceae), with long narrow toothed leaves, reddish flowers, and downy twigs; the light easily split wood of this tree, used for furniture.

rewind /*as verb* riːˈwʌɪnd, *as noun* ˈriːwʌɪnd/ *verb & noun*. E18.
[from RE- + WIND *verb*[1].]
▶ **A** *verb*. Pa. t. & pple **-wound** /-ˈwaʊnd/.
1 *verb trans*. Wind (thread etc.) again. Also, wind (film, tape, etc.) backwards or back on to its original spool. E18.
2 *verb intrans*. Wind around; double back. *rare*. M19.

📖 **1** *fig.*: A. BURGESS You cannot rewind history as if it was a film.

▶ **B** *noun*. **1** A mechanism for rewinding film, tape, etc. M20.
2 The action or process of rewinding film, tape, etc. M20.

📖 **2** *attrib.*: *Which?* Most of the players in our test have a rewind facility. *fig.*: P. MONETTE A business acquaintance . . started to gossip . . . I put him on fast rewind.

▪ **rewinder** *noun* M19.

rewire /riːˈwʌɪə/ *verb & noun*. E20.
[from RE- + WIRE *verb*.]
▶ **A** *verb trans*. Provide (a building etc.) with new wiring. E20.
▶ **B** *noun*. An installation of new wiring. M20.
▪ **rewirable**, **-eable** *adjective* M20.

reword /riːˈwəːd/ *verb trans*. L16.
[from RE- + WORD *verb*.]
†**1** Re-echo. *rare* (Shakes.). Only in L16.
2 Put into words again; repeat. E17.
3 Change the wording of. L19.
▪ **rewording** *noun* the action of the verb; an instance of this, a reworded version: M19.

rework /riːˈwəːk/ *verb trans*. M19.
[from RE- + WORK *verb*.]
1 Work (a thing) again; resubmit or represent in revised or altered form, remake, refashion. M19. ▸**b** *spec.* in GEOLOGY. Of a natural agent: alter, *esp.* remove and redeposit (rock, sediment, etc.). L19.
2 Change the variety of (a plant) by grafting. M20.

📖 **1** *National Observer (US)* The garages have either refunded the money or reworked repairs. *Artist* The trellis work was strengthened . . the horse in the . . corner reworked.

▪ **reworker** *noun* L20. **reworking** *noun* the action of the verb; an instance of this, a new or revised version: L19.

rewound /riːˈwuːnd/ *verb*[1] *trans*. *rare*. E17.
[from RE- + WOUND *verb*[1].]
Wound again.

rewound *verb*[2] *pa. t. & pple* of REWIND *verb*.

rewrite /*as verb* riːˈrʌɪt, *as noun* ˈriːrʌɪt/ *verb & noun*. M16.
[from RE- + WRITE *verb*.]
▶ **A** *verb trans*. Pa. t. **-wrote** /-ˈrəʊt/, pa. pple **-written** /-ˈrɪt(ə)n/.
†**1** Write back, reply in writing, (*that*). Only in M16.

2 Write again or differently; revise or rework (a text). M18. ▸**b** LINGUISTICS. Write (an analysis of a phrase or sentence structure) in a different form, usu. by expansion. M20.

> 📖 **2** M. FRAYN I rewrote the letter without the . . personal touches. *fig.*: C. HEILBRUN Lives must be rewritten with . . new intellectual constructs.

▶ **B** *noun*. **1** The action or an act of rewriting or revising a text; a revised text. Orig. *US slang*. E20.

2 LINGUISTICS. The action or process of writing an analysis of a phrase or sentence structure in a different form, usu. by expansion. Chiefly in ***rewrite rule*** below. M20.

> 📖 **1** P. MAILLOUX He had completed a rewrite of the first chapter.

Comb.: **rewrite man** a person employed to rewrite newspaper copy for publication; **rewrite rule** a rule governing the rewriting of a structural analysis.

▪ **rewritable** *adjective* (COMPUTING & ELECTRONICS) (of an optical storage medium such as a compact disc) on which data can be written, and subsequently erased and rewritten, by the user L20. **rewriter** *noun* E20. **rewriting** *verbal noun* the action of the verb; an instance of this: ***rewriting rule*** = ***rewrite rule*** above: M19.

Rex /rɛks/ *noun*. Also (in sense 2) **r-**. E17.
[Latin = king.]
1 A king; the prosecution, as representing a reigning king, in criminal proceedings. Cf. REGINA. E17.
2 a (An animal of) a variety of rabbit or mouse in which the guard hairs are reduced and wavy, or absent, giving the fur a soft plushy texture; the genetic mutation which causes this. E20. ▸**b** (An animal of) a breed of cat with curly hair. M20.

> 📖 **1** E. W. COX *Rex* v. *Webb* is no authority for that distinction.

Rexine /ˈrɛksiːn/ *noun*. E20.
[Origin unkn.]
(Proprietary name for) a kind of artificial leather used esp. in upholstery and bookbinding.

> 📖 A. DESAI His parents slid off the slippery rexine seat.

Rexism /ˈrɛksɪz(ə)m/ *noun*. M20.
[from Latin (*Christus*) *Rex* (Christ) the King: see -ISM.]
Hist. A right-wing Roman Catholic political movement established in 1935 in Belgium.
▪ **Rexist** *noun* a supporter of Rexism M20.

Reye's syndrome /ˈreɪz sɪndrəʊm, ˈrʌɪz/ *noun phr*. M20.
[R. D. K. *Reye* (1912–78), Austral. paediatrician.]
MEDICINE. A frequently fatal metabolic disorder in young children, of uncertain cause but sometimes precipitated by aspirin and involving encephalitis and degeneration of the liver.

Reynard /ˈrɛnɑːd, ˈreɪ-/ *noun*. LME.
[Old & mod. French *renard*, †*-art*, the fox in the *Roman de Renart*: infl. in spelling by Middle Dutch *Reynaerd*, *-aert*.]
A fox (esp. as a proper name in stories).

> 📖 *Country Living* Reynard does not show: instead he shifts to a deeper part of the burrow.

Reynolds /ˈrɛn(ə)ldz/ *noun*. E20.
[Osborne *Reynolds* (1842–1912), Irish engineer and physicist.]
PHYSICS. **1** ***Reynolds number***, ***Reynolds' number***, a dimensionless number used in fluid mechanics as a criterion to determine whether fluid flow past a body or in a duct is steady or turbulent, evaluated as $l\upsilon\rho/\nu$, where l is a characteristic length of the system, υ is a typical speed, ρ is the fluid density, and ν is the kinematic viscosity of the fluid; ***magnetic Reynolds number***, an analogous number used in the description of the dynamic behaviour of a magnetized plasma. E20.
2 ***Reynolds stress***, the net rate of transfer of momentum across a surface in a fluid resulting from turbulence in the fluid. M20.

rezai /rəzɑːˈiː/ *noun*. E19.
[Persian & Urdu *razāī*.]
In the Indian subcontinent, a quilted counterpane or coverlet.

rez-de-chaussée /redʃose/ *noun*. E19.
[French, lit. 'level with the street'.]
The ground floor of a building.

rezident /rɛzɪˈdɛnt/ *noun*. Pl. **-y** /-i/. M20.
[Russian.]
= RESIDENT *noun* 4.

RF *abbreviation*.
1 (Also **rf**.) Radio-frequency.
2 Representative fraction (of a map).

Rf *symbol*.
CHEMISTRY. Rutherfordium.

RFA *abbreviation*.
1 Royal Field Artillery.
2 Royal Fleet Auxiliary.

RFC *abbreviation*.
1 COMPUTING. Request for comment, a document circulated on the Internet which forms the basis of a technical standard.
2 *Hist.* Royal Flying Corps.
3 Rugby Football Club.

RFD *abbreviation*. *US*.
Rural free delivery (of letters).

RFLP *abbreviation*.
GENETICS. Restriction fragment length polymorphism.

RFP *abbreviation*. *N. Amer.*
Request for proposal.

RGN *abbreviation*.
Registered General Nurse.

RGS *abbreviation*.
Royal Geographical Society.

RH *abbreviation*[1].
Royal Highness.

Rh *abbreviation*[2].
Rhesus (blood group).

Rh *symbol*.
CHEMISTRY. Rhodium.

r.h. *abbreviation*.
Right-hand.

RHA *abbreviation*.
Royal Horse Artillery.

rhabarbarum /rəˈbɑːb(ə)rəm/ *noun*. Long *rare* or *obsolete*. L16.
[medieval Latin, lit. 'foreign rhubarb', from late Latin *rha* rhubarb (perh. from *Rha* ancient name of the Volga) + Latin *barbarus* foreign, BARBAROUS. Cf. RHUBARB *noun & adjective*.]
= RHUBARB *noun* 1.

rhabdite /ˈrabdʌɪt/ *noun*. L19.
[from Greek *rhabdos* rod + -ITE[1].]
1 ZOOLOGY. A rhabdoid, *esp.* one having a lamellate structure. L19.
2 MINERALOGY. A form of schreibersite occurring as small esp. rod-shaped crystals. L19.

rhabditid /ˈrabdɪtɪd/ *adjective & noun*. M20.
[from mod. Latin *Rhabditida* (see below), formed as next + -ID[3].]
ZOOLOGY. ▶**A** *adjective*. Of, pertaining to, or belonging to the order Rhabditida of mainly free-living nematodes characterized by a rhabditiform oesophagus. M20.
▶ **B** *noun*. A rhabditid nematode. M20.

rhabditis /rabˈdʌɪtɪs/ *noun*. L19.
[mod. Latin *Rhabditis* (see below), from Greek *rhabdos* rod.]
A nematode of the genus *Rhabditis*, found in soil, water, and detritus, and in the larval stage possibly a facultative parasite of mammals. Now chiefly as mod. Latin genus name.
▪ **rhabˈditic**, **rhabˈditiform** *adjectives* characteristic or of the form of a rhabditis; *spec.* having or designating a short thick oesophagus with one or more bulbs, as in rhabditids and some other nematode larvae: L19. **rhabditoid** *adjective & noun* (*a*) *adjective* = RHABDITIFORM; (*b*) *noun* a nematode with a rhabditiform oesophagus: L19.

rhabdo- /ˈrabdəʊ/ *combining form*.
[from Greek *rhabdos* rod: see -O-.]
Chiefly SCIENCE. Of, pertaining to, or designating a rodlike structure.
▪ **rhabdocoel** /ˈrabdəsiːl/ *adjective & noun* (ZOOLOGY) (of, pertaining to, or designating) a turbellarian worm of the order Rhabdocoela, having a straight gut L19. **rhabdolith** *noun* (ZOOLOGY) a calcareous rod similar to a coccolith L19. **rhabdomyˈolysis** *noun* (MEDICINE) destruction of striated muscle cells, caused by disease M20. **rhabdomyˈoma** *noun*, pl. **-mas**, **-mata** /-mətə/, MEDICINE a benign tumour of striated muscle L19. **rhabdomyosarˈcoma** *noun*, pl. **-mas**, **-mata** /-mətə/, MEDICINE a malignant tumour originating in or showing features of striated muscle L19. **rhabdovirus** *noun* (BIOLOGY) any of a group of rod-shaped RNA viruses including the rabies virus M20.

rhabdoid /ˈrabdɔɪd/ *adjective & noun*. M19.
[formed as prec. + -OID.]
▶ **A** *adjective*. Rod-shaped; rodlike. *rare*. M19.
▶ **B** *noun*. A rod-shaped structure; *spec.* (ZOOLOGY) any of the small rodlike structures which are secreted by the epidermis of turbellarian worms and dissolve to form a mucus. E20.

rhabdom /ˈrabdəʊm/ *noun*. Also **-ome**. L19.
[Late Greek *rhabdōma*, from *rhabdos* rod: see -OME.]
ZOOLOGY. A translucent cylinder forming part of the light-sensitive receptor in an arthropod eye and consisting of fused rhabdomeres from adjacent cells.
▪ **rhabdomere** /-mɪə/ *noun* a regular array of microvilli in an arthropod visual cell L19. **rhabdomeric** /-ˈmɛrɪk/ *adjective* of or pertaining to a rhabdomere or rhabdomeres M20.

rhabdomancy /ˈrabdəmansi/ *noun*. M17.
[Greek *rhabdomanteia*, formed as RHABDO-, -MANCY.]
Divination by means of a rod or wand; *spec.* the use of a divining-rod to discover mineral ore, underground water, etc.
▪ **rhabdomancer** *noun* E19.

rhachi- *combining form*, **rhachilla** *noun*, **rhachio-** *combining form*, **rhachis** *noun*, etc., vars. of RACHI-, RACHILLA, etc.

Rhadamanthus /radəˈmanθəs/ *noun*. L16.
[Latin from Greek *Rhadamanthos*, a son of Zeus and Europa and one of the judges in the underworld.]
An inflexible or incorruptible judge; a severe master.

> 📖 *American Poetry Review* A poet . . who throughout the darkest nights of fascism had sat, a mute Rhadamanthus.

▪ **Rhadamanthine** *adjective* severe and incorruptible in judgement M17.

Rhaetian /ˈriːʃ(ə)n/ *adjective & noun*. L16.
[from *Rhaetia* (see below) + -IAN.]
▶ **A** *adjective*. **1** Designating, of, or pertaining to a chain of the Alps in SE Switzerland and the Tyrol; *Hist.* of or pertaining to an ancient Roman province comprising the region around this chain, called Rhaetia. L16.
2 GEOLOGY. Of, pertaining to, or designating the uppermost (youngest) stage of the Triassic in Europe (occas. classified as Jurassic or as a separate period). M20.
▶ **B** *noun*. **1** A native or inhabitant of the Rhaetian Alps or (*Hist.*) Rhaetia. L16.
2 = RHAETO-ROMANCE *noun*. Also = RHAETIC *noun* 2. L18.
3 GEOLOGY. The Rhaetian stage. M20.

Rhaetic /ˈriːtɪk/ *adjective & noun*. Also (in senses A.1, B.1) **Rhet-**, (in senses A.2, B.2) **Raet-**. M19.
[Latin *Rhaeticus*, formed as prec. + -IC.]
▶ **A** *adjective*. **1** GEOLOGY. = RHAETIAN *adjective* 2. M19.
2 Of or pertaining to the language Rhaetic. M20.
▶ **B** *noun*. **1** GEOLOGY. = RHAETIAN *noun* 3. L19.
2 The pre-Italic language of the Rhaetian Alps and the area to the south of them. M20.

Rhaeto- /ˈriːtəʊ/ *combining form*.
[from Latin *Rhaetus* RHAETIAN + -O-.]
Forming adjectives and nouns with the senses 'of Rhaetia', 'Rhaetian and —', as ***Rhaeto-Etruscan***.
▪ **Rhaeto-Liˈassic** *adjective* (GEOLOGY) of or pertaining to the Rhaetian and Liassic stages or series M20. **Rhaeto-ˈRoman** *adjective & noun* (*a*) *adjective* = RHAETO-ROMANCE *adjective*; (*b*) *noun* a speaker of Rhaeto-Romance: M20. **Rhaeto-Roˈmanic** *adjective* = RHAETO-ROMANCE *adjective* M19.

Rhaeto-Romance /ˌriːtə(ʊ)rə(ʊ)ˈmans/ *noun & adjective*. L19.
[from RHAETO- + ROMANCE *noun & adjective*.]
▶ **A** *noun*. The group of Romance dialects spoken in SE Switzerland and the Tyrol, including Romansh and Ladin. L19.
▶ **B** *adjective*. Of or pertaining to this group of dialects. L19.

rhagades /ˈragədiːz/ *noun pl*. OE.
[Latin from Greek, pl. of *rhagas* fissure.]
MEDICINE. Cracks, fissures, or thin scars in the skin, esp. around the mouth or anus.

Rhages /ˈrɑːdʒiːz/ *adjective*. E20.
[Former name of a city (now called Rayy) in Persia (Iran).]
Designating a type of pottery made in Rhages from the 11th to the 13th cent., characterized by polychrome enamelling.

rhagon /ˈragɒn/ *noun*. L19.
[mod. Latin, from Greek *rhag-*, *rhax* grape (with ref. to the appearance of the flagellated chambers).]
ZOOLOGY. A stage in the development of some sponges having the form of a flat pyramid with an osculum at the apex; a colony of this form.

rhamn /ram/ *noun*. Now *rare*. ME.
[Late Latin RHAMNUS.]
The Christ's thorn, *Paliurus spina-christi*. Cf. RHAMNUS.

rhamno- /ˈramnəʊ/ *combining form*.
[from RHAMNUS + -O-.]
CHEMISTRY. Forming names of compounds derived from rhamnose or its glycosides, or isolated from plants of the genus *Rhamnus*, as ***rhamnoglycoside*** etc.

rhamnose /ˈramnəʊz, -s/ *noun*. L19.
[from next + -OSE[2].]
CHEMISTRY. A hexose, $C_6H_{12}O_5$, which occurs widely in plants, esp. in berries of the buckthorn (genus *Rhamnus*).

rhamnus /ˈramnəs/ *noun*. M16.
[Late Latin from Greek *rhamnos*; later a modern application of the name by Linnaeus. Cf. RHAMN.]
Orig., the Christ's thorn, *Paliurus spina-christi*. Now, any of various allied shrubs constituting the genus *Rhamnus* (family Rhamnaceae), esp. the buckthorn, *R. cathartica*.

rhamphotheca /ramfə(ʊ)ˈθiːkə/ *noun*. L19.
[from Greek *rhamphos* beak + *thēkē* sheath.]
ORNITHOLOGY. The horny or leathery outer layer of a bird's bill.

rhapidosome /ˈrapɪdəsəʊm/ *noun*. M20.
[from Greek *rhapid-*, *rhapis* rod + -O- + -SOME[3].]
MICROBIOLOGY. In certain bacterial cells, a cylindrical body of unknown function.

rhapontic /rəˈpɒntɪk/ *noun*. Also **rap-**. M16.
[mod. Latin *rha Ponticum* Pontic rhubarb: see RHABARBARUM, PONTIC *adjective*[1].]
†**1** An alpine plant, *Leuzea rhapontica*, allied to the knapweeds. M16–E17.
2 A Bulgarian kind of rhubarb, *Rheum rhaponticum*; the astringent root of this. L16.

rhapsode /ˈrapsəʊd/ *noun*. M19.
[Greek *rhapsōidos*, from *rhapsōidia* RHAPSODY.]
GREEK HISTORY. A reciter of epic poems, *esp.* one of a group whose profession it was to recite the Homeric poems.

†**rhapsoder** *noun*. *rare*. E17–E18.
[formed as prec. + -ER[1].]
= RHAPSODIST 1.

rhapsodic /rapˈsɒdɪk/ *adjective*. L18.
[Greek *rhapsōidikos*, from *rhapsōidos* RHAPSODE or *rhapsōidia* RHAPSODY: see -IC.]
1 Exaggeratedly enthusiastic or ecstatic in language, manner, etc. L18.
2 Consisting of the recitation of rhapsodies. *rare*. M19.

> **1** *Times* His star-crossed lovers . . extol . . their love in passages of rhapsodic flimflam.

rhapsodical /rapˈsɒdɪk(ə)l/ *adjective*. M17.
[formed as prec.: see -ICAL.]
†**1** Of a literary work: consisting of a medley of narratives etc.; disconnected in style. M17–M18.
2 = RHAPSODIC 1. L18.

rhapsodically /rapˈsɒdɪk(ə)li/ *adverb*. E17.
[from RHAPSODIC + -ALLY.]
In a rhapsodic manner.

rhapsodise *verb* var. of RHAPSODIZE.

rhapsodist /ˈrapsədɪst/ *noun*. M17.
[from RHAPSODY + -IST.]
†**1** A collector of literary pieces. Cf. RHAPSODER. *rare*. M–L17.
2 a GREEK HISTORY. = RHAPSODE. M17. **▸b** *gen*. A reciter of poems. M18.
3 A person who uses rhapsodic language. M18.

rhapsodize /ˈrapsədʌɪz/ *verb*. Also **-ise**. E17.
[formed as prec. + -IZE.]
†**1** *verb trans*. Piece (narratives etc.) together to form a medley; relate (a story) disconnectedly. E17–M18.
2 *verb trans*. Recite (an epic poem) as or in the manner of a rhapsody. E19.
3 *verb intrans*. Talk or write rhapsodically. E19.

> **2** F. B. JEVONS We do know . . that the *Iliad* was rhapsodized. **3** A. BROOKNER He regarded those who rhapsodized about their childhoods with amusement.

rhapsody /ˈrapsədi/ *noun & verb*. M16.
[Latin *rhapsodia* from Greek *rhapsōidia* from *rhapsōidos* RHAPSODE, from *rhaptein* to stitch + *ōidē* song, ODE: see -Y[3].]
▸ A *noun*. **1** GREEK HISTORY. An epic poem, or part of one, of a suitable length for recitation at one time. M16.
†**2** A miscellaneous collection; a medley (*of* words, ideas, narratives, etc.); *spec*. a literary work consisting of miscellaneous or disconnected pieces; a written composition without a fixed plan. M16–M19.
†**3 a** The stringing together of unconnected poems. Only in E17. **▸b** The recitation of epic poetry. Only in E19.
4 An exaggeratedly enthusiastic or ecstatic expression of feeling; an effusive utterance or written work, often disconnected or lacking sound argument. M17.
5 MUSIC. A free instrumental composition in one extended movement, usu. emotional or exuberant in character. L19.

> **2** R. SANDERSON A rhapsody of uncircumcised nations. H. HALLAM A rhapsody of wild theory. **4** D. CECIL A Ruskinian rhapsody of lyrical ecstasy.

▸ B *verb*. *rare*.
1 *verb trans*. = RHAPSODIZE 2. E19.
2 *verb intrans*. = RHAPSODIZE 3. L19.

> **2** W. J. LOCKE He had rhapsodied over the vision.

rhatany /ˈratəni/ *noun*. E19.
[mod. Latin *rhatania* from RATANHIA.]
A S. American shrub, *Krameria triandra* (family Krameriaceae); an astringent extract from the root of this.

RHD *abbreviation*.
Right-hand drive.

rhe /reɪ/ *noun*. E20.
[from Greek *rhein* to flow: see RHEO-.]
PHYSICS. A unit of fluidity in the cgs system, defined variously as the reciprocal of the poise, the centipoise, or the centistokes.

rhea /ˈriːə/ *noun*[1]. E19.
[mod. Latin use as genus name of Latin, Greek *Rhea*, mother of Zeus (Jupiter) in class. mythol.]
Either of two S. American flightless birds of the family Rheidae, the grey *Rhea americana* (more fully ***common rhea***, ***grey rhea***, ***greater rhea***) and the brown *Pterocnemia pennata* (more fully ***lesser rhea***), resembling but smaller than the ostrich.

rhea /ˈriːə/ *noun*[2]. M19.
[Assamese *rihā*.]
Ramie, *Boehmeria nivea*.

rhebok /ˈriːbɒk/ *noun*. Also **ree-**, **-buck** /-bʌk/, (*S. Afr.*) **ribbok** /ˈrɪbɒk/. L18.
[Dutch *reebok* ROEBUCK.]
1 A small southern African antelope, *Pelea capreolus*, having a long slender neck and short straight horns. Also ***grey rhebok***. L18.
2 In full ***red rhebok***. The mountain reedbuck, *Redunca fulvorufula*. *S. Afr.* M19.

rheid /ˈriːɪd/ *noun & adjective*. M20.
[from Greek *rhein* to flow + *-id* after *liquid*.]
▸ A *noun*. A substance which undergoes viscous flow at a temperature below its melting point. M20.
▸ B *adjective*. Characteristic of a rheid; that is a rheid. M20.

> J. G. DENNIS A material is rheid by virtue of the time of observation. Rocks . . are so during geological deformation.

■ **rheˈidity** *noun* the phenomenon of rheid behaviour; a measure of this: M20.

rhematic /riːˈmatɪk/ *adjective*. E19.
[Greek *rhēmatikos*, from *rhēmat-*, *rhēma* word, verb: see -IC.]
1 Of or pertaining to the construction of sentences or the formation of words. *rare*. E19.
2 LINGUISTICS. Of, pertaining to, or of the nature of a rheme. M20.

rhematize /ˈriːmətʌɪz/ *verb trans*. Also **-ise**. M20.
[from RHEMAT(IC *adjective* + -IZE.]
LINGUISTICS. Make (a part of a sentence) rhematic.
■ **rhematiˈzation** *noun* M20.

rheme /riːm/ *noun*. L19.
[Greek *rhēma*, *-atos* that which is said, word, saying.]
1 LOGIC. An utterance that has the property of signification, as distinct from its identity as sound and form. Also, the part of a proposition or sentence which expresses a single idea. L19.
2 LINGUISTICS. The part of a sentence giving new information about the theme or topic of an utterance or discourse. Cf. COMMENT *noun* 5. M20.

Rhemish /ˈriːmɪʃ/ *adjective*. L16.
[from *Rhemes* former English spelling of *Rheims* (see below) + -ISH[1].]
Of or pertaining to Rheims, a city in NE France; *spec*. designating an English translation of the New Testament by Roman Catholics of the English college at Rheims, published in 1582.
■ **Rhemist** *noun* an author of the Rhemish translation of the New Testament L16.

rhenate /ˈriːneɪt/ *noun*. E20.
[from RHENIUM + -ATE[1].]
CHEMISTRY. A salt of the anion ReO_4^{2-}.
■ **rhenic** *adjective*: ***rhenic acid***, H_2ReO_4, the unstable parent acid of rhenates, known only in solution M20.

Rhenish /ˈrɛnɪʃ/ *adjective & noun*. LME.
[Anglo-Norman *reneis*, Old French *rinois*, *rainois* from medieval Latin alt. of Latin *Rhenanus*, from *Rhenus* RHINE *noun*[1]: see -ISH[1].]
▸ A *adjective*. **1** Of or pertaining to the River Rhine, or the regions bordering on it; ARCHAEOLOGY designating a type of pottery made in the Rhineland in the Roman period. LME.
†**2** Of, pertaining to, or designating a gold coin or gulden formerly current in Germany and the Netherlands. L15–L18.
1 Rhenish fan PHILOLOGY a fan-shaped bundle of isoglosses in the Rhine valley, separating Low German from High German. **Rhenish stoneware** stoneware, usu. salt-glazed, manufactured in the Rhineland. **Rhenish wine** wine produced in the Rhine region.
▸ B *noun*. Rhenish wine. LME.

rhenium /ˈriːnɪəm/ *noun*. E20.
[from Latin *Rhenus* RHINE *noun*[1] + -IUM.]
A rare heavy refractory metal which is a chemical element of the transition series, atomic no. 75, that occurs naturally in molybdenum ores and is used in superconducting alloys. (Symbol Re.)

rhenosterbos, **rhenosterbosch**, **rhenosterbush** *nouns* vars. of RENOSTERBOS.

rheo- /ˈriːəʊ/ *combining form*.
[from Greek *rheos* stream, current, thing that flows, from *rhein* to flow: see -O-.]
SCIENCE. Of or pertaining to flow or (esp. electric) current.
■ **rheobase** *noun* (PHYSIOLOGY) the minimum electrical stimulus which can excite a nerve or muscle E20. **rheoˈbasic** *adjective* (PHYSIOLOGY) designating or pertaining to a rheobase M20. **rheogoniˈometer** *noun* (PHYSICS) a goniometer used to measure shearing stresses in fluids M20. **rheogram** *noun* a diagram of the results of a rheological experiment M20. **rheoˈmorphic** *adjective* (GEOLOGY) of, pertaining to, or exhibiting (the result of) rheomorphism M20. **rheoˈmorphism** *noun* (GEOLOGY) the process by which a rock becomes plastic, usu. from partial melting or diffusion of magma M20. **rheophile** *noun & adjective* (ZOOLOGY) (an organism) that prefers or inhabits an environment of flowing water M20. **rheoˈphilic**, **rheˈophilous** *adjectives* (ZOOLOGY) rheophile M20. **rheophobe** *noun* (ZOOLOGY) a rheophobic organism M20. **rheoˈphobic** *adjective* (ZOOLOGY) that prefers or inhabits an environment of still rather than flowing water M20. **rheophyte** *noun* (BOTANY) a plant confined to flowing water M20. **rheophytic** /-ˈfɪtɪk/ *adjective* (BOTANY) that is a rheophyte L20. **rheoreˈceptive** *adjective* (ZOOLOGY) that is a rheoreceptor M20. **rheoreceptor** *noun* (ZOOLOGY) a receptor that senses the flow of surrounding water M20. **rheoscope** *noun* (now *rare* or *obsolete*) = GALVANOSCOPE M19. **rheoˈscopic** *adjective* (now *rare* or *obsolete*) pertaining to or acting like a rheoscope M19. **rheoˈtactic** *adjective* (BIOLOGY) pertaining to or exhibiting rheotaxis E20. **rheoˈtaxis** *noun* (BIOLOGY) the movement of an organism in response to a current of water E20. †**rheotome** *noun* (ELECTRICITY) a circuit-breaker M–L19. **rheotropic** /-ˈtrəʊpɪk, -ˈtrɒpɪk/ *adjective* (BIOLOGY) exhibiting or pertaining to rheotropism L19. **rheotropism** /riːˈɒtrəpɪzəm, riːə(ʊ)ˈtrəʊpɪz(ə)m/ *noun* (BIOLOGY) the orientation or movement of a plant or sessile animal in response to or esp. in the direction of a current of water L19.

rheology /rɪˈɒlədʒi/ *noun*. E20.
[from RHEO- + -LOGY.]
PHYSICS. **1** The branch of science that deals with the deformation and flow of matter, esp. the non-Newtonian flow of liquids and the plastic flow of solids. E20.
2 The rheological properties *of* a substance. M20.
■ **rheoˈlogical** *adjective* of or pertaining to the deformation and flow properties of matter M20. **rheoˈlogically** *adverb* as regards rheology M20. **rheologist** *noun* M20.

rheometer /rɪˈɒmɪtə/ *noun*. M19.
[from RHEO- + -METER.]
1 ELECTRICITY. = GALVANOMETER. M19.
2 a An instrument for measuring the force or velocity of a current, esp. of the flow of blood. L19. **▸b** An instrument for measuring rheological properties of matter, esp. the viscous stress of a fluid. M20.
■ **rheoˈmetric** *adjective* of or pertaining to a rheometer or rheometry M19. **rheometry** *noun* the measurement of flow or current by means of a rheometer M19.

rheopexy /ˈriːə(ʊ)pɛksi/ *noun*. M20.
[from RHEO- + -PEXY.]
PHYSICS. The property, possessed by some sols, of gelling rapidly when gently agitated. Cf. THIXOTROPY.
■ **rheoˈpectic** *adjective* M20.

rheostat /ˈriːəstat/ *noun*. M19.
[from RHEO- + -STAT.]
ELECTRICITY. A device, esp. of variable resistance, which allows the current in a circuit to be adjusted; *spec*. a variable resistor with a wire-wound core along which a contact can be slid.
liquid rheostat: see LIQUID *adjective & noun*.

rheostatic /riːəˈstatɪk/ *adjective*. L19.
[formed as prec. + -IC.]
†**1** Designating a machine producing continuous static electrical effects. Only in L19.
2 Of, pertaining to, or involving a rheostat or rheostats; *spec*. designating a form of brake used in electric vehicles, in which the motors are made to act as generators, the resulting power being dissipated in the starting rheostats. E20.

rhesis /ˈriːsɪs/ *noun*. *rare*. L19.
[Greek *rhēsis* word, speech.]
A set speech or discourse.

rhesus /ˈriːsəs/ *noun*. E19.
[mod. Latin (*Simia*) *rhesus* former taxonomic name of *Macaca mulatta* (see sense 1 below), from Latin *Rhesus*, Greek *Rhēsos*, a mythical king of Thrace.]
1 More fully ***rhesus monkey***, ***rhesus macaque***. A macaque, *Macaca mulatta*, of southern Asia, widely used in medical research. E19.
2 MEDICINE. Used *attrib*. and in *comb*. with ref. to a major blood group (first discovered in the rhesus monkey) consisting of three main antigens to which naturally occurring antibodies are rare, and which are usu. implicated in haemolytic disease of the newborn (see ***rhesus baby*** below). (Symbol Rh.) M20.
2 ***rhesus agglutinogen***, ***rhesus antibody***, ***rhesus antigen***, ***rhesus incompatibility***, ***rhesus system***, etc. **rhesus baby** an infant with haemolytic disease of the newborn owing to destruction of its rhesus-positive blood cells by its rhesus-negative mother's antibodies. **rhesus factor** any or all of the rhesus antigens, esp. the most important and common one. **rhesus negative** *adjective* lacking the main rhesus antigen, and therefore able to produce antibodies to it. **rhesus positive** *adjective* having the main rhesus antigen.

rhetic /ˈriːtɪk/ *adjective*[1]. M20.
[from Greek *rhētos* stated + -IC.]
LOGIC. Designating or pertaining to an act of uttering a rheme.

Rhetic *adjective*[2] & *noun* see RHAETIC *adjective & noun*.

rhetor /ˈriːtə/ *noun*. ME.
[Late Latin *rethor* var. of Latin *rhetor* from Greek *rhētōr*.]
1 CLASSICAL HISTORY. A teacher of rhetoric. ME. **▸**†**b** *transf*. A master of eloquence or literary expression. LME–E16.
2 An orator, *esp*. a professional one. Freq. *derog*. L16.

rhetoric /ˈrɛtərɪk/ *noun*. ME.
[Old French *rethorique* (mod. *rhétorique*) from medieval Latin *rethorica* var. of Latin *rhetorica* from Greek *rhētorikē* (sc. *tekhnē* art), from *rhētōr* RHETOR: see -IC.]
1 The art of using language so as to persuade or influence others; the body of rules to be observed by a speaker or writer in order to achieve effective or eloquent expression. Formerly also, a treatise on or textbook of this subject. ME. ▸**b** (Usu. **R-**.) (The name of) a class in a Roman Catholic school, college, or seminary, now only *spec.* the seventh and most senior class, immediately above Poetry, in certain Jesuit schools. L16. ▸**c** Literary prose composition, esp. as a school exercise. E19.
2 Orig., elegance or eloquence of language. Later, language calculated to persuade or impress; (freq. *derog.* or *joc.*) artificial, insincere, or extravagant language; in *pl.*, elegant expressions, rhetorical flourishes. LME. ▸**b** *transf.* & *fig.* Expressiveness; persuasiveness; *spec.* †(*a*) eloquence of gestures, facial expressions, etc.; (*b*) expressiveness or extravagance of artistic style or technique. M16.
†**3** Skill in using eloquent and persuasive language. LME–M18.

📖 **2** *Punch* Nigel Lawson last year startled his . . audience with some sparkling rhetoric. C. EASTON His rhetoric, rife with *sweethearts* and *darlings*. **b** SHAKES. *L.L.L.* The heavenly rhetoric of thine eye. J. N. SUMMERSON Buildings which . . demonstrate . . the 'rhetoric' of the Baroque.

rhetoric /rɪˈtɒrɪk/ *adjective*. *rare*. LME.
[formed as next: see -IC.]
= next.

rhetorical /rɪˈtɒrɪk(ə)l/ *adjective*. LME.
[Latin *rhetoricus*, formed as RHETOR: see -ICAL.]
1 Orig., eloquent, eloquently expressed. Later, expressed in terms to persuade or impress; (freq. *derog.*) expressed in artificial, insincere, or extravagant language. LME. ▸**b** Designating a rhythm of prose less regular than metrical. *rare*. E18.
2 Of, pertaining to, or concerned with the art of rhetoric. LME.
3 Of a person: apt to use rhetoric. M17.

📖 **1** *Rolling Stone* The article lacked description, interpretation and evaluation; in short, rhetorical criticism. **rhetorical question** a question, often implicitly assuming a preferred (usu. negative) answer, asked so as to produce an effect rather than to gain information. **2** G. PHELPS The author's command of the rhetorical devices. **3** J. DENNIS The rhetorical author . . makes use of his tropes and figures . . to cheat us.

■ **rhetoricalness** *noun* (*rare*) E18.

rhetorically /rɪˈtɒrɪk(ə)li/ *adverb*. LME.
[from RHETORIC *adjective* or prec.: see -ICALLY.]
In a rhetorical manner.

†**rhetoricate** *verb intrans*. E17–E18.
[Latin *rhetoricat-* pa. ppl stem of *rhetoricari*, formed as RHETORICAL: see -ATE[3].]
Use rhetorical language.
■ †**rhetorication** *noun* the use of rhetorical language; a piece of rhetoric, a rhetorical flourish: E17–L18.

rhetorician /rɛtəˈrɪʃ(ə)n/ *noun*. LME.
[Old French *rethoricien* (mod. *rhétoricien*), formed as RHETORIC *noun*: see -IAN.]
1 Chiefly CLASSICAL HISTORY. A teacher of rhetoric; a professional orator. LME.
2 Orig., an eloquent or elegant writer. Later, a person who uses rhetorical language; *esp.* (freq. *derog.*) a public speaker whose language is artificial, insincere, or extravagant. LME.
3 (**R-**.) In certain English Roman Catholic schools and colleges, a scholar in the class of Rhetoric. L17.

rhetoricize /rɪˈtɒrɪsʌɪz/ *verb*. Also **-ise**. L17.
[from RHETORIC *noun* + -IZE.]
1 *verb intrans*. Use rhetorical language. L17.
2 *verb trans*. Characterize with rhetoric; make rhetorical. Chiefly as ***rhetoricized*** *ppl adjective*. M20.

rhetorize /ˈrɛtərʌɪz/ *verb intrans*. Now *rare*. Also **-ise**. E17.
[App. from RHETOR + -IZE, perh. after late Latin *rhetoricare* in same sense.]
= RHETORICIZE 1.

rheum /ruːm/ *noun*[1]. Now chiefly *arch*. LME.
[Old French *reume* (mod. *rhume*) from late Latin *rheuma* bodily humour, flow from Greek, from *rhein* to flow.]
1 A watery substance secreted by a mucous membrane, esp. as collecting in or dripping from the nose, eyes, etc. Formerly also, (a flow of) any abnormal, harmful, or unhealthy moisture or 'humour' (freq. *fig.*). LME. ▸**b** *collect. sing.* Tears. *poet.* L16.
2 *spec.* A mucous discharge caused by infection with a cold. Also, a cold in the head; catarrh. Usu. in *pl.* LME.

rheum /ˈriːəm/ *noun*[2]. M18.
[mod. Latin (see below), from Greek *rhēon*. Cf. RHUBARB *noun* & *adjective*.]
A plant of the genus *Rheum*, of the knotgrass family; a rhubarb.

rheumatic /rʊˈmatɪk/ *adjective* & *noun*. LME.
[Old French *reumatique* (mod. *rhu-*) or Latin *rheumaticus* from Greek *rheumatikos*, from *rheuma* RHEUM *noun*[1]: see -ATIC.]
▶ **A** *adjective*. †**1** Consisting or of the nature of rheum. LME–L17.
2 Of a disease, symptom, etc.: orig., characterized by rheumy or catarrhal discharges; now, pertaining to, of the nature of, or characteristic of rheumatism. LME. ▸†**b** *transf.* & *fig.* Tearful. Also, phlegmatic. Only in 17.
3 Of weather, a place: orig., inducing catarrhal infections; later, tending to induce or exacerbate rheumatism. LME.
†**4** Full of or dripping with rheum; suffering from a discharge of rheum or catarrh. L16–M17.
5 Affected with or liable to be affected with rheumatism or rheumatic pain. E18.

📖 **2 rheumatic fever** an acute fever, chiefly of young people, caused by a streptococcal infection and marked by acute inflammation and pain of the joints. **4** T. NASHE Rumatique sore eyes that ran alwaies. **5** *fig.*: J. PRESS The entire movement of the syntax is rheumatic and muscle-bound.

▶ **B** *noun*. **1** In *pl.* Rheumatic pains, rheumatism. *colloq.* L18.
2 A person suffering from rheumatism. L19.
■ **rheumatical** *adjective* rheumatic E18. **rheumatically** *adverb* M19. **rheumaticky** *adjective* (*colloq.*) suffering from rheumatism M19.

rheumatise *noun*, *verb* vars. of RHEUMATIZ, RHEUMATIZE.

rheumatism /ˈruːmətɪz(ə)m/ *noun*. E17.
[French *rhumatisme* or Latin *rheumatismus* from Greek *rheumatismos*, from *rheumatizein*, from *rheuma* RHEUM *noun*[1]: see -ISM.]
†**1** A watery discharge. Only in E17.
2 Any disease in which inflammation and pain in joints and connective tissue are prominent features (orig. supposed to be caused by the internal flow of watery 'humours'), including rheumatic fever, arthritis, and gout. Formerly also, an attack of such a disease. L17.

rheumatiz /ˈruːmətɪz/ *noun*. Long *dial.* & *colloq.* Also **-ise**, **-ize** /-ʌɪz/. LME.
[Perh. from next. In later use from RHEUMATISM.]
Orig., a disease or pain caused by rheum. Now, rheumatism.

rheumatize /ˈruːmətʌɪz/ *verb trans*. Also **-ise**. LME.
[medieval Latin *rheumatisare* snuffle or Greek *rheumatizein*, from *rheuma* RHEUM *noun*[1]: see -IZE.]
†**1** Cause to flow like rheum. *rare*. Only in LME.
†**2** Bring rheum or tears to (the eyes). Only in L16.
3 Make rheumatic, affect with rheumatism. M19.

rheumatoid /ˈruːmətɔɪd/ *adjective*. M19.
[from RHEUMATISM + -OID.]
Resembling rheumatism; *spec.* in ***rheumatoid arthritis***, ***rheumatoid disease***, a chronic inflammatory disease characterized by changes in the synovial membranes etc., and resulting in painful deformity and immobility of the joints; of, pertaining to, or affected by this disease.
rheumatoid factor any of a group of auto-antibodies which are present in the blood of people with rheumatoid arthritis.

rheumatology /ruːməˈtɒlədʒi/ *noun*. M20.
[from RHEUMATISM + -OLOGY.]
MEDICINE. The branch of medicine that deals with rheumatism, arthritis, and other disorders of the joints, muscles, ligaments, etc.
■ **rheumatologist** *noun* M20.

rheumy /ˈruːmi/ *adjective*. L16.
[from RHEUM *noun*[1] + -Y[1].]
1 Of the nature of rheum. L16.
2 Esp. of the eyes: full of rheum, watery. L16.
3 Esp. of the air: moist, damp. *literary*. E17.

rhexia /ˈrɛksɪə/ *noun*. E19.
[mod. Latin (see below), use as genus name of Latin = viper's bugloss.]
A plant of the N. American genus *Rhexia* (family Melastomataceae), which includes the meadow beauties.

rhexis /ˈrɛksɪs/ *noun*. LME.
[mod. Latin from Greek *rhēxis*, from *rhēgnunai* break.]
1 MEDICINE. Rupture of an organ or (esp.) of a blood-vessel. Now *rare* or *obsolete*. LME.
2 BIOLOGY. The fragmentation of a cell or cellular component. M20.
■ **rhexigenous** /rɛkˈsɪdʒɪnəs/ *adjective* (of an intercellular space in plant tissue) formed by the cells being ruptured (cf. LYSIGENOUS) M20.

RHG *abbreviation*.
Royal Horse Guards.

rhinal /ˈrʌɪn(ə)l/ *adjective*. M19.
[from Greek *rhin-*, *rhis* nose + -AL[1].]
ANATOMY. Of or pertaining to the nose or the rhinencephalon.

rhinarium /rʌɪˈnɛːrɪəm/ *noun*. E19.
[formed as prec. + -ARIUM.]
1 ENTOMOLOGY. In various insects: a part of the clypeus; a sensory receptor at the base of an antenna. E19.
2 A hairless moist area at the tip of the nose in mammals. E20.
■ **rhinarial** *adjective* E20.

Rhine /rʌɪn/ *noun*[1] & *adjective*. LME.
[German *Rhein*, a river of western Europe, flowing mainly through Germany.]
▶†**A** *noun*. = ***Rhine wine*** below. Cf. RHENISH *noun* Only in LME.
▶ **B** *attrib.* or as *adjective*. Designating people connected with the River Rhine or the region bordering on it. LME.
Rhine daughter [translating German *Rheintochter*] = ***Rhine maiden*** below. **Rhineland** the region bordering the Rhine in Germany; ***Rhineland foot*** (*Hist.*), a measure of length used in fortifications, equivalent to two fathoms. **Rhinelander** (*a*) a native or inhabitant of the Rhineland; (*b*) a type of slow polka. **Rhine maiden** [formed as ***Rhine daughter*** above] (*a*) each of three water maidens in Wagner's opera *Der Ring des Nibelungen*; (*b*) a woman with the fair hair and large physique with which the Rhine maidens are usually portrayed. **Rhine wine** wine made from grapes grown in the Rhine valley.

rhine /rʌɪn/ *noun*[2]. Also (earlier) †**rine**. M17.
[German *Reinhanf* lit. 'clean hemp'.]
More fully ***Riga rhine (hemp)***. A fine quality of Russian hemp.

rhine /riːn/ *noun*[3]. Chiefly *dial.* Also **reen**. L17.
[Perh. ult. rel. to RUN *verb*.]
A large open ditch or drain.

Rhinegrave /ˈrʌɪngreɪv/ *noun*. In sense 2 also **r-**. M16.
[Middle Dutch *Rijngrave* (mod. *-graaf*), German *Rheingraf*, from *Rhein* (see RHINE *noun*[1]) + *Graf* GRAVE *noun*[2].]
Hist. **1** A count with a domain bordering on the River Rhine. M16.
2 [through French *rhingrave*] = PETTICOAT ***breeches***. L19.

†**rhinehurst** *noun*. E18–E19.
[Dutch *rhynseharst* from German *Rheinharz*, from *Rhein* (see RHINE *noun*[1]) + *Harz* resin.]
Burgundy pitch.

rhinencephalon /rʌɪnɛnˈsɛfəlɒn, -ˈkɛf-/ *noun*. M19.
[formed as RHINAL + ENCEPHALON.]
ANATOMY. The part of the brain (thought to be) primitively concerned with the sense of smell, largely coextensive with the limbic system.
■ **rhinenceˈphalic** *adjective* M19.

rhinestone /ˈrʌɪnstəʊn/ *noun*. L19.
[from RHINE *noun*[1] + STONE *noun*, translating French *caillou du Rhin*.]
A variety of rock crystal. Also, an artificial gem cut to imitate a diamond.
■ **rhinestoned** *adjective* wearing rhinestones; decorated or adorned with rhinestones: M20.

rhinitis /rʌɪˈnʌɪtɪs, rɪ-/ *noun*. L19.
[from RHIN(O- + -ITIS.]
Inflammation of the membranes of the nose.

rhino /ˈrʌɪnəʊ/ *noun*[1]. *slang*. E17.
[Origin unkn.]
Money. Freq. in ***ready rhino***.

rhino /ˈrʌɪnəʊ/ *noun*[2]. *colloq.* Pl. **-os**. L19.
[Abbreviation.]
= RHINOCEROS.

rhino- /ˈrʌɪnəʊ/ *combining form*.
[from Greek *rhin-*, *rhis* nose: see -O-.]
Of or pertaining to the nose.
■ **rhinoˈbatid** *noun* = ***guitar-fish*** s.v. GUITAR *noun* M19. **rhinolarynˈgitis** *noun* (MEDICINE) inflammation of the nose and larynx E20. **rhinolarynˈgologist** *noun* (MEDICINE) a specialist in rhinolaryngology M20. **rhinolarynˈgology** *noun* (MEDICINE) the branch of medicine that deals with the nose and larynx E20. **rhinoˈlogical** *adjective* of or pertaining to rhinology M19. **rhiˈnologist** *noun* an expert in or student of rhinology M19. **rhiˈnology** *noun* the branch of knowledge, esp. of medicine, that deals with the nose M19. **rhinopharynˈgitis** *noun* (MEDICINE) inflammation of the nose and pharynx L19. **rhinopharynx** *noun* = NASOPHARYNX L19. **rhinophore** *noun* (ZOOLOGY) an external olfactory organ, esp. as on a second pair of tentacles in opisthobranch molluscs L19. **rhinophyma** /-ˈfʌɪmə/ *noun*, pl. **-mas**, **-mata** /-mətə/, MEDICINE (a) chronic swelling and reddening of the nose, freq. associated with rosacea L19. **rhinoˈplastic** *adjective* of or pertaining to rhinoplasty M19. **rhinoplasty** *noun* plastic surgery of the nose M19. **rhinoˈrrhoea** *noun* discharge of fluid, esp. watery mucus, from the nose M19. **rhinoscope** *noun* (MEDICINE) an instrument for examining the nasal cavity M19. **rhinoˈscopic** *adjective* (MEDICINE) of or pertaining to rhinoscopy M19. **rhiˈnoscopy** *noun* (MEDICINE) examination of the nasal cavity, esp. with a rhinoscope M19.

rhinoceral /rʌɪˈnɒs(ə)r(ə)l/ *adjective*. *slang*. M19.
[from RHINOCEROS + -AL[1], with ref. to RHINO *noun*[1]. Cf. next.]
Rich.

†**rhinocerical** *adjective*. L17.
[from RHINOCEROS + -ICAL; in sense 2 with ref. to RHINO *noun*[1].]
1 a Heavy or cumbersome like a rhinoceros. Only in L17. ▸**b** Of a nose: resembling a rhinoceros's horn. Only in E18.
2 Rich. *slang*. L17–L18.

rhinocerine /rʌɪˈnɒsərʌɪn/ *adjective.* L19.
[from RHINOCEROS + -INE[1].]
Rhinocerotic.

rhinoceros /rʌɪˈnɒs(ə)rəs/ *noun.* Pl. same, **-es**. ME.
[Latin (pl. *-otes*) from Greek *rhinokerōs*, from *rhin-*, *rhis* nose + *keras* horn.]
1 A large heavy ungulate mammal of the perissodactyl family Rhinocerotidae, now restricted to Africa and SE Asia, having one or two horns on the nose and a thick folded hide. ME. ▸**b** *transf.* A large cumbersome person. E17.
2 *ellipt.* A rhinoceros beetle; a rhinoceros bird. Now *rare* or *obsolete*. E17.
1 black rhinoceros a two-horned rhinoceros, *Diceros bicornis*, of savannahs in sub-Saharan Africa. **Indian rhinoceros** a large one-horned rhinoceros, *Rhinoceros unicornis*, with prominent skin folds and a prehensile upper lip, found in NE India and Nepal. **square-lipped rhinoceros**, **white rhinoceros** a large two-horned rhinoceros, *Ceratotherium simum*, of eastern and southern Africa. ***woolly rhinoceros***: see WOOLLY *adjective*.
Comb.: **rhinoceros auklet** a mainly blackish-brown auk, *Cerorhinca monocerata*, of N. Pacific coasts, with a yellowish horn at the base of the bill; **rhinoceros beetle** any of various very large horned scarab beetles of the subfamily Dynastinae; **rhinoceros bird** †(*a*) = ***rhinoceros hornbill*** below; (*b*) an ox-pecker; **rhinoceros bush** the renosterbos, *Elytropappus rhinocerotis*; **rhinoceros horn** the keratinous horn of a rhinoceros, used ornamentally or for its supposed aphrodisiac properties; **rhinoceros hornbill** a hornbill, *Buceros rhinoceros*, of SE Asia.
¶ Pl. forms in Latin pl. form *-otes* have been regarded as belonging to next.

rhinocerot /rʌɪˈnɒsərɒt/ *noun.* Now *rare*. Pl. **-rotes** /-rəti:z/, **-rots**. M16.
[Back-form. from Latin *rhinocerotes* pl. of RHINOCEROS.]
= prec.

rhinocerotic /rʌɪˌnɒsəˈrɒtɪk/ *adjective.* M18.
[Late Latin *rhinoceroticus* formed as RHINOCEROS: see -IC.]
Of, pertaining to, characteristic of, or resembling (that of) a rhinoceros.

rhinocerotid /ˌrʌɪnə(ʊ)səˈrɒtɪd/ *noun.* M20.
[mod. Latin *Rhinocerotidae* (see below), formed as RHINOCEROS: see -ID[3].]
ZOOLOGY & PALAEONTOLOGY. A rhinoceros or other (extinct) mammal of the family Rhinocerotidae.

rhinosporidiosis /ˌrʌɪnəʊspərɪdɪˈəʊsɪs/ *noun.* Pl. **-oses** /-ˈəʊsi:z/. E20.
[from mod. Latin *Rhinosporidium* (see below), from RHINO- + SPORIDIUM: see -OSIS.]
MEDICINE. Chronic infection esp. of the nasal membranes by the fungus *Rhinosporidium seeberi*.
▪ **rhinospoˈridial** *adjective* pertaining to or caused by rhinosporidiosis E20.

rhinovirus /ˈrʌɪnəʊvʌɪrəs/ *noun.* M20.
[from RHINO- + VIRUS.]
BIOLOGY. Any of a group of picornaviruses including those which cause some forms of the common cold.

rhipidistian /rɪpɪˈdɪstɪən/ *noun & adjective.* E20.
[from mod. Latin *Rhipidistia* (see below), from Greek *rhipid-*, *rhipis* fan + *histia* pl. of *histion* sail + -AN.]
▸**A** *noun.* A fossil crossopterygian fish of the group Rhipidistia, which flourished from late Devonian to early Permian times. E20.
▸**B** *adjective.* Of or pertaining to (a fish of) the group Rhipidistia. E20.

rhipiphorid /rɪˈpɪf(ə)rɪd/ *noun & adjective.* L19.
[mod. Latin *Rhipiphoridae* (see below), from *Rhipiphorus* genus name, from Greek *rhipis* fan: see -PHOROUS, -ID[3].]
ENTOMOLOGY. ▸**A** *noun.* A beetle of the family Rhipiphoridae, whose larvae are endoparasites in other insects, esp. wasps. L19.
▸**B** *adjective.* Of, pertaining to, or designating this family. E20.

rhipsalis /rɪpˈseɪlɪs/ *noun.* Pl. **-lides** /-lɪdi:z/, **-lises**. M19.
[mod. Latin (see below), from Greek *rhips* wickerwork, mat + Latin *-alis* (see -AL[1]).]
An epiphytic cactus of the genus *Rhipsalis*. Cf. ***MISTLETOE cactus***.

rhizine /ˈrʌɪzɪn/ *noun.* Also **rhizina** /rɪˈzʌɪnə/, pl. **-nae** /-ni:/. M19.
[from Greek *rhiza* root + -INE[4].]
BOTANY. A hyphal strand attaching the thallus of a foliose lichen to the substrate.

rhizo- /ˈrʌɪzəʊ/ *combining form* of Greek *rhiza* root: see -O-.
▪ **rhizocarp** *noun* (*BOTANY*) a rhizocarpous plant L19. **rhizoˈcarpic**, **rhizoˈcarpous** *adjectives* (*BOTANY*) having a perennial root but a stem which dies down each year M19. **rhizoˈcephalan** *noun* (*ZOOLOGY*) any parasitic cirripede crustacean of the order Rhizocephala (e.g. the crab parasite *Sacculina carcini*), having most adult organs reduced or absent, and sending root-like absorptive processes into the host's body L20. **rhizoˈcephalous** *adjective* of, pertaining to, or belonging to the order Rhizocephala of parasitic cirripedes (cf. RHIZOCEPHALAN) L19. **rhizoˈgenic** *adjective* (of a cell etc.) root-forming L19. **rhizoˈmania** (*a*) *rare* an abnormal development of roots; (*b*) a viral disease attacking the roots of the sugar beet: M19. **rhizomorph** *noun* (*BOTANY*) a rootlike aggregation of hyphae in certain fungi M19. **rhizoˈmorphous** *adjective* (*BOTANY*) rootlike, resembling a root or a rhizomorph M19. **rhiˈzophagous** *adjective* feeding on roots M19. **rhizoplane** *noun* (*ECOLOGY*) the interface between a plant root and the soil M20. **rhizoplast** *noun* (*MICROBIOLOGY*) a fibrous or contractile structure at the lower end of a cilium or flagellum in a protozoan E20. **rhizosphere** *noun* (*ECOLOGY*) the sphere of chemical and bacteriological influence of the roots of a plant E20. **rhiˈzotomy** *noun* (an instance of) surgical cutting of a spinal nerve root E20. **rhizotron** *noun* a glass-walled underground chamber for the observation of plant roots *in situ* M20.

rhizobium /rʌɪˈzəʊbɪəm/ *noun.* Pl. **-ia** /-ɪə/. E20.
[mod. Latin *Rhizobium* (see below), from RHIZO- + Greek *bios* life + -IUM.]
An aerobic nitrogen-fixing bacterium of the genus *Rhizobium*, found in soil and esp. as a symbiont, in root nodules of leguminous plants.
▪ **rhizobial** *adjective* M20. **rhizobially** *adverb* L20.

Rhizoctonia /rʌɪzɒkˈtəʊnɪə/ *noun.* L19.
[mod. Latin form-genus name, from RHIZO- + Greek *ktonos* murder + -IA[1].]
BOTANY & AGRICULTURE. The asexual state of any of various fungi, some of which cause disease in plants.

rhizoid /ˈrʌɪzɔɪd/ *adjective & noun.* M19.
[from Greek *rhiza* root + -OID.]
BOTANY. ▸**A** *adjective.* Resembling a root. *rare.* M19.
▸**B** *noun.* A filamentous outgrowth on the underside of the thallus in various lower plants, esp. bryophytes, which serves both to anchor the plant and to conduct water. M19.
▪ **rhiˈzoidal** *adjective* pertaining to or of the nature of a rhizoid L19.

rhizome /ˈrʌɪzəʊm/ *noun.* Also (now *rare*) in Latin form **rhizoma** /rʌɪˈzəʊmə/, pl. **-mata** /-mətə/. M19.
[Greek *rhizōma*, from *rhizousthai* take root, from *rhiza* root: see -OME.]
BOTANY. A continuously growing, usu. horizontal, underground stem, which puts out lateral shoots and adventitious roots at intervals.
▪ **rhiˈzomatous** *adjective* consisting of or of the nature of a rhizome; having rhizomes: M19.

rhizophora /rʌɪˈzɒf(ə)rə/ *noun.* M19.
[mod. Latin (see below), from Greek *rhiza* root + fem. of *-phoros* bearing: cf. next.]
A mangrove of the genus *Rhizophora* (family Rhizophoraceae).

rhizophore /ˈrʌɪzə(ʊ)fɔ:/ *noun.* L19.
[from RHIZO- + -PHORE.]
BOTANY. A leafless branch in selaginellas, arising from a fork in the stem, which grows downwards and puts out roots at its tip on contact with the ground.

rhizopod /ˈrʌɪzə(ʊ)pɒd/ *noun.* M19.
[from RHIZO- + -POD.]
ZOOLOGY. **1** A protozoan of the superclass Rhizopoda, characterized by extensible pseudopodia and including amoebas, foraminifera, and (in some classifications) radiolarians. M19.
2 = RHIZOPODIUM. M20.
▪ **rhizopodous** /rʌɪˈzɒpədəs/ *adjective* belonging to or characteristic of the Rhizopoda M19.

rhizopodium /rʌɪzə(ʊ)ˈpəʊdɪəm/ *noun.* Pl. **-ia** /-ɪə/. M19.
[from prec. + PODIUM.]
1 *BOTANY.* The mycelium of a fungus. Now *rare* or *obsolete*. M19.
2 *BIOLOGY.* In protists, a pseudopodium that branches and anastomoses to form a network. M20.

rho /rəʊ/ *noun.* Pl. **rhos**. LME.
[Greek *rhō*.]
1 The seventeenth letter (P, ρ) of the Greek alphabet. LME.
2 *STATISTICS.* A correlation coefficient; *spec.* Spearman's coefficient of rank correlation. M20.
3 *PHYSICS.* In full ***rho meson***. A meson with isospin and spin of one and a mass of 770 MeV. M20.
¶ See also *CHI-rho*, RHO-THETA.

rhod- *combining form* see RHODO-.

rhodamine /ˈrəʊdəmi:n/ *noun.* L19.
[from Greek *rhodon* rose + AMINE.]
CHEMISTRY. Any of a class of synthetic xanthene dyes, chiefly pinks and reds. Usu. with following cap. letter.
rhodamine B, ***rhodamine G***, etc.

rhodanthe /rə(ʊ)ˈdanθi/ *noun.* M19.
[mod. Latin (see below), from Greek *rhodon* rose + *anthos* flower.]
An Australian plant of the composite family, *Helipterum* (formerly *Rhodanthe*) *manglesii*, bearing pink daisy-like everlasting flower-heads.

Rhode Island /rəʊd ˈʌɪlənd/ *noun phr.* L18.
[A State in the north-eastern US.]
Used *attrib.* to designate plants or animals associated with Rhode Island.
Rhode Island bent (grass) the lawn and pasture grass *Agrostis capillaris*. ***Rhode Island GREENING***. **Rhode Island Red** (a bird of) a breed of domestic fowl of American origin, typically having brownish-red plumage. **Rhode Island White** (a bird of) a white variety of Rhode Island Red.

Rhodes /rəʊdz/ *noun.* E20.
[Cecil John *Rhodes* (1853–1902), Brit. financier and S. African statesman.]
1 a ***Rhodes Scholarship***, any of several scholarships established by Rhodes and awarded annually since 1902 to students from certain foreign and Commonwealth countries for study at Oxford University. E20. ▸**b** ***Rhodes Scholar***, a person in receipt of such a scholarship. E20.
2 ***Rhodes grass***, a perennial grass, *Chloris gayana*, native to Africa and widely cultivated elsewhere as a pasture grass. E20.

Rhodesian /rə(ʊ)ˈdi:ʃ(ə)n, -ʒ(ə)n/ *adjective & noun.* L19.
[In sense A.1 formed as prec. + -IAN; in other senses from *Rhodesia* (see below) + -AN.]
▸**A** *adjective.* †**1** Of or pertaining to Cecil Rhodes (see prec.). Only in L19.
2 Chiefly *Hist.* Of, pertaining to, or characteristic of Rhodesia, a country in southern Africa comprising Northern Rhodesia (which became Zambia on independence in 1964) and Southern Rhodesia (which became Zimbabwe on independence in 1980). L19.
2 ***Rhodesian ridgeback***: see RIDGE *noun*[1].
▸**B** *noun. Hist.* A native or inhabitant of Rhodesia, *esp.* (until independence) a white one. L19.

Rhodian /ˈrəʊdɪən/ *noun & adjective.* M16.
[from Latin *Rhodius*, from *Rhodos*, *-us* = Greek *Rhodos* Rhodes, the largest of the Dodecanese Islands in the SE Aegean and from 1309 to 1522 the headquarters of the order of the Knights of the Hospital of St John at Jerusalem: see -AN.]
▸**A** *noun.* †**1** = HOSPITALLER 1. Only in M16.
2 A native or inhabitant of Rhodes. L16.
▸**B** *adjective.* **1** Of or pertaining to the order of the Knights Hospitallers. *rare.* L16.
2 Of or pertaining to Rhodes; inhabiting Rhodes. E17.
3 Designating a rhetorical style, less florid than the Asiatic, characteristic of the ancient Rhodian school of oratory. L18.
4 Designating a type of pottery characterized by brilliant pigments (esp. red), formerly thought to derive from Rhodes but now known to be a variety of later Isnik ware. L19.

📖 **3** DISRAELI A dashing speech . . worthy of the historical society in . . its Rhodian eloquence.

rhodic /ˈrəʊdɪk/ *adjective.* M19.
[from RHODIUM *noun*[2] + -IC.]
CHEMISTRY. Containing rhodium, esp. in the tetravalent state. Cf. RHODOUS.

rhodinol /ˈrəʊdɪnɒl/ *noun.* L19.
[from Greek *rhodinos* of or from roses, from *rhodon* rose: see -OL.]
CHEMISTRY. A liquid alcohol first isolated from rose oil, now known to be identical with citronellol but having different proportions of its isomers.
▪ **rhodinal** *noun* the aldehyde corresponding to rhodinol, citronellal E20.

rhodium /ˈrəʊdɪəm/ *noun*[1]. M17.
[mod. Latin (sc. *lignum* wood), neut. of *rhodius* roselike, from Greek *rhodon* rose.]
1 ***wood of rhodium***, ***rhodium-wood***, the sweet-scented wood of two bindweeds, *Convolvulus floridus* and *C. scoparius*, of the Canary Islands. Also called ***rosewood***. M17.
2 ***oil of rhodium***, the oil obtained from this wood; rosewood oil. L17.

rhodium /ˈrəʊdɪəm/ *noun*[2]. E19.
[from Greek *rhodos* rose (from the pink colour of its compounds) + -IUM.]
A very hard silvery-white metallic chemical element, atomic no. 45, belonging to the platinum group and used chiefly in corrosion-resistant alloys. (Symbol Rh.)

rhodo /ˈrəʊdəʊ/ *noun. colloq.* Pl. **-os**. E20.
[Abbreviation.]
= RHODODENDRON 2.

rhodo- /ˈrəʊdəʊ/ *combining form.* Before a vowel also **rhod-**.
[Greek, from *rhodon* rose: see -O-.]
Of or from roses; *spec.* rose-coloured, pink, red.
▪ **rhodoˈchrosite** *noun* [Greek *rhodokhrōs* rose-coloured] *MINERALOGY* manganese carbonate occurring as pink, brown, or grey crystals of the hexagonal system M19. **rhodophyte** *noun* (*BOTANY*) any alga of the division Rhodophyta, which comprises the red algae M20. **rhodoplast** *noun* (*BOTANY*) a plastid containing a red pigment, phycoerythrin, found in red algae L19.

rhododendron /rəʊdəˈdɛndr(ə)n/ *noun.* Pl. **-drons**, **-dra** /-drə/. E17.
[Latin from Greek, from *rhodon* rose + *dendron* tree.]
†**1** The oleander, *Nerium oleander*. Only in E17.
2 Any of numerous shrubs or low trees constituting the genus *Rhododendron*, of the heath family, widely cultivated for their showy, clustered, funnel-shaped or bell-shaped flowers of varied colours; *spec.* an evergreen

shrub or tree of this kind, *esp.* the purple-flowered *R. ponticum* of Asia Minor etc. (Cf. AZALEA.) E17.

Rhodoid /ˈrəʊdɔɪd/ *noun.* E20.
[French *Rhodoïd* from Latin *Rhod(anus* River Rhône + *-oïd(e* -OID.]
(Proprietary name for) an incombustible thermoplastic derived from cellulose acetate.

rhodolite /ˈrəʊd(ə)lʌɪt/ *noun.* L19.
[from RHODO- + -LITE.]
MINERALOGY. A pale violet or red variety of garnet, intermediate between pyrope and almandite

rhodologist /rə(ʊ)ˈdɒlədʒɪst/ *noun.* L19.
[from Greek *rhodon* rose + -OLOGIST.]
A botanist who specializes in the taxonomy of the genus *Rosa*.

rhodomontade *noun* var. of RODOMONTADE.

rhodonite /ˈrəʊd(ə)nʌɪt/ *noun.* E19.
[from Greek *rhodon* rose + -ITE[1].]
MINERALOGY. Manganese silicate, often with some iron, magnesium, or calcium, occurring as triclinic crystals of a brownish or (when pure) rose-pink colour, and used esp. as a decorative stone.

rhodopsin /rə(ʊ)ˈdɒpsɪn/ *noun.* L19.
[from RHODO- + Greek *opsis* sight, vision + -IN[1].]
BIOCHEMISTRY. A purplish-red light-sensitive pigment found in the retina of humans and in many other animal groups, consisting of a protein (opsin) bonded to a prosthetic group (retinal) which is liberated by the action of light. Also called ***visual purple***.

rhodora /rə(ʊ)ˈdɔːrə/ *noun.* L18.
[mod. Latin (see below), from Greek *rhodon* rose.]
A N. American azalea, *Rhododendron canadense* (formerly classified separately in a genus *Rhodora*), bearing rose-purple flowers before the leaves.

rhodous /ˈrəʊdəs/ *adjective. rare.* M19.
[from RHODIUM *noun*[2] + -OUS, after *ferrous* etc.]
CHEMISTRY. Containing rhodium, esp. in a lower valency state. Cf. RHODIC.

rhody /ˈrɒdi/ *noun. colloq.* M19.
[from RHOD(ODENDRON + -Y[6].]
= RHODODENDRON 2.

rhomb /rɒm(b)/ *noun.* L16.
[French *rhombe* or Latin RHOMBUS.]
1 *GEOMETRY.* = RHOMBUS 1. L16.
†**2** A wheel; a magic circle. *rare.* M–L17.
3 *CRYSTALLOGRAPHY.* A rhombohedron, a rhombohedral crystal. E19.

rhombencephalon /rɒmbɛnˈsɛfəlɒn, -ˈkɛf-/ *noun.* L19.
[from prec. + ENCEPHALON.]
ANATOMY. The hindbrain.
■ ˌrhombenceˈphalic *adjective* M20.

rhombi *noun pl.* see RHOMBUS.

rhombic /ˈrɒmbɪk/ *adjective & noun.* L17.
[from RHOMB + -IC.]
▶ **A** *adjective.* **1** Of a solid figure: having a rhombus as base or section plane; (esp. of a dodecahedron) bounded by equal rhombs; *CRYSTALLOGRAPHY* = ORTHORHOMBIC. L17.
2 **a** Having the shape of a rhombus; *spec.* (of a radio aerial) having a horizontal rhombic shape. E18. ▸**b** *ZOOLOGY & BOTANY.* Having the shape of a lozenge or diamond, often with rounded corners. E19.
▶ **B** *noun.* A rhombic radio aerial. M20.

rhombo- /ˈrɒmbəʊ/ *combining form* of RHOMB, RHOMBUS: see -O-.
■ **rhombogen** *noun* (*ZOOLOGY*) a sexual adult form in some mesozoans which gives rise to a free-living infusoriform larva (cf. NEMATOGEN) L19.

rhombohedron /rɒmbə(ʊ)ˈhiːdr(ə)n, -ˈhɛd-/ *noun.* Pl. **-dra** /-drə/, **-drons**. M19.
[from RHOMBO- + -HEDRON.]
Chiefly *CRYSTALLOGRAPHY.* A solid figure or object bounded by six equal rhombuses; *esp.* a crystal of this form.
■ **rhombohedral** *adjective* having the form of a rhombohedron; having a unit cell which is a rhombohedron: M19. **rhombohedric** *adjective* (*rare*) = RHOMBOHEDRAL M19.

rhomboid /ˈrɒmbɔɪd/ *noun & adjective.* L16.
[French *rhomboïde* or late Latin RHOMBOIDES.]
▶ **A** *noun.* **1** A shape resembling a rhombus; a parallelogram with adjacent sides unequal. L16.
2 *CRYSTALLOGRAPHY.* A rhombohedron. E19.
3 *ANATOMY.* = RHOMBOIDEUS. M19.
▶ **B** *adjective.* †**1** = RHOMBIC *adjective* 1. L17–M19.
2 *CRYSTALLOGRAPHY.* = RHOMBIC *adjective* 2. L17.
3 *ANATOMY.* Designating or pertaining to a rhomboideus muscle. M19.

rhomboidal /rɒmˈbɔɪd(ə)l/ *adjective.* M17.
[from prec. + -AL[1].]
1 = RHOMBIC *adjective* 2. M17.
2 = RHOMBIC *adjective* 1. E18.
1 ***Rhomboidal Net***: see NET *noun*[1] 6c.
■ **rhomboidally** *adverb* so as to form a rhomboid M19.

†**rhomboides** *noun.* L16.
[Late Latin from Greek *rhomboeides*, from *rhombos* RHOMBUS: see -OID.]
1 *GEOMETRY.* = RHOMBOID *noun* 1. L16–M18.
2 *ANATOMY.* = RHOMBOIDEUS. L16–M19.

rhomboideus /rɒmˈbɔɪdɪəs/ *noun.* Pl. **-ei** /-ɪʌɪ/. M19.
[mod. Latin (sc. *musculus* muscle), from prec.]
ANATOMY. Either of two muscles connecting the last cervical and the upper dorsal vertebrae with the scapula. Also ***rhomboideus muscle***.

rhombus /ˈrɒmbəs/ *noun.* Pl. **-buses**, **-bi** /-bʌɪ/. M16.
[Latin from Greek *rhombos*.]
1 *GEOMETRY.* A plane figure having four equal sides and equal opposite angles (two acute and two obtuse); an oblique equilateral parallelogram. M16.
2 A lozenge-shaped object, part, marking, etc. E17.
3 A flatfish of the former genus *Rhombus*; a turbot, a brill. Now *rare* or *obsolete.* M18.

rhonchus /ˈrɒŋkəs/ *noun.* Also **ron-**. Pl. **-chi** /-kʌɪ/. E19.
[Latin, from var. of Greek *rhegkhos* snoring.]
MEDICINE. An abnormal whistling or rasping sound produced by the passage of air through narrowed or partly blocked bronchi.
■ **rhonchal** *adjective* of or pertaining to a rhonchus; *joc.* of or pertaining to snoring: M19.

Rhône /rəʊn/ *noun.* Also **Rhone**. M19.
[A river rising in Switzerland and flowing through SE France.]
A (red or white) wine made from grapes grown in the Rhône valley (esp. the stretch between Lyons and Avignon) (also more fully ***Rhône wine***); a drink of this.

Rhoosian /ˈruːʃ(ə)n/ *noun & adjective. joc.* M19.
[Alt.]
= RUSSIAN *noun & adjective.*

rhopalia *noun* pl. of RHOPALIUM.

rhopalic /rə(ʊ)ˈpalɪk/ *adjective & noun.* L17.
[Late Latin *rhopalicus*, from Greek *rhopalos* club, tapered cudgel: see -IC.]
PROSODY. ▶**A** *adjective.* Of a passage or line of verse: in which each word contains one syllable more than the word immediately preceding it. L17.
▶ **B** *noun.* A rhopalic line or passage. M20.

rhopalium /rə(ʊ)ˈpeɪlɪəm/ *noun.* Pl. **-ia** /-ɪə/. L19.
[from Greek *rhopalos* club, tapered cudgel + -IUM.]
ZOOLOGY. Any of a number of marginal sensory structures in various jellyfish.
■ **rhopalial** *adjective* pertaining to or associated with a rhopalium L20.

rhopalocerous /rəʊpəˈlɒs(ə)rəs/ *adjective.* L19.
[from mod. Latin *Rhopalocera*, formed as prec. + Greek *keras* horn: see -OUS.]
ENTOMOLOGY. Of, characteristic of, or belonging to the lepidopteran suborder Rhopalocera, comprising butterflies (which are characterized by clubbed antennae).
■ **rhopaloceral** *adjective* (*rare*) L19.

rhopheocytosis /rə(ʊ),fiːəʊsʌɪˈtəʊsɪs/ *noun.* Pl. **-toses** /-ˈtəʊsiːz/. M20.
[from Greek *rhophein* gulp down + *-cytosis* after PINOCYTOSIS.]
BIOLOGY. A form of pinocytosis in which initial cytoplasmic projections are not formed.

rhotacise *verb* var. of RHOTACIZE.

rhotacism /ˈrəʊtəsɪz(ə)m/ *noun.* M19.
[mod. Latin *rhotacismus* ult. from Greek *rhōtakizein* make excessive or wrong use of the letter r, formed as RHO + *-izein* -IZE with hiatus-filling *k*: see -ISM.]
1 *LINGUISTICS.* Excessive use or distinctive pronunciation of the phoneme /r/ (repr. by the letter r); *spec.* use of the burr or uvular r. M19.
2 *PHILOLOGY.* Conversion of another sound, esp. the phoneme /s/ (repr. by the letter s), into the phoneme /r/ (repr. by the letter r). M19.

rhotacize /ˈrəʊtəsʌɪz/ *verb.* Also **-ise**. L19.
[Greek *rhōtakizein*: see prec., -IZE.]
PHILOLOGY. **1** *verb intrans.* Of a dialect: be characterized or marked by rhotacism. L19.
2 *verb trans.* Convert (a sound, esp. the phoneme /s/ repr. by the letter s) into the phoneme /r/ (repr. by the letter r). M20.
■ **rhotaciˈzation** *noun* (*a*) = RHOTACISM 2; (*b*) modification of a vowel sound caused by a following *r*: L20.

rho-theta /rəʊˈθiːtə/ *noun & adjective.* M20.
[from RHO (repr. distance) + THETA (repr. bearing).]
RADAR. ▶**A** *noun.* A position measured as range and bearing from a single ground station. M20.
▶ **B** *attrib.* or as *adjective.* Designating or involving a radar system which measures positions in this way. M20.

rhotic /ˈrəʊtɪk/ *adjective.* M20.
[from RHOT(ACISM + -IC.]
LINGUISTICS. Of, pertaining to, or designating a variety or dialect of English in which *r* is not only pronounced before a vowel but also before a consonant or word-finally.

Rhovyl /ˈrəʊvɪl/ *noun.* M20.
[Origin unkn.]
(Proprietary name for) a type of polyvinyl chloride fibre.

RHS *abbreviation.*
1 Royal Historical Society.
2 Royal Horticultural Society.
3 Royal Humane Society.

rhubarb /ˈruːbɑːb/ *noun & adjective.* LME.
[Old French *rubarbe*, *reubarbe* (mod. *rhubarbe*) from Proto-Romance shortening of medieval Latin *r(h)eubarbarum* alt. (by assoc. with RHEUM *noun*[2]) of RHABARBARUM.]
▶ **A** *noun.* **1** A plant of the genus *Rheum*, of the knotgrass family, having very large leaves. Also (with specifying word), any of several similar plants. LME.
2 The purgative and astringent rootstock of any of several plants of the genus *Rheum*, esp. *R. officinale* of W. China and Tibet, and *R. palmatum* of NE Asia. Also ***rhubarb root***. LME.
3 The long, fleshy, usu. pale red, acid leaf-stalks of a garden rheum, *Rheum* × *hybridum* (prob. a hybrid derivative of the rhapontic, *R. rhaponticum*), used when cooked as food; the plant producing these. L18.
4 A murmurous background noise, an indistinct conversation; *esp.* the repetition of the word 'rhubarb' by actors to represent an indistinct conversation or the noise of a crowd. *colloq.* M20. ▸**b** A low-level flight for opportune strafing. *Military slang.* M20. ▸**c** A heated dispute, a row. *US slang.* M20. ▸**d** Nonsense, worthless stuff. *slang.* M20.

> 📖 **1** ***monk's rhubarb***: see MONK *noun*[1]. PRICKLY ***rhubarb***.
> **4d** *Number One* And what is all this rhubarb about crabs being sexy?

▶ **B** *attrib.* or as *adjective.* **1** Bitter, tart. L16.
2 Made from or containing rhubarb. L17.
3 Of the colour of rhubarb; yellowish-brown (as of rhubarb root) or pale red (as of garden rhubarb). E19.

> 📖 **2** L. BLOCK I seemed to be developing a definite taste for the rhubarb jam.

■ **rhubarby** *adjective* resembling (that of) rhubarb; *esp.* tasting like rhubarb: M19.

rhubarb /ˈruːbɑːb/ *verb intrans. colloq.* M20.
[from prec.]
Orig., (of an actor) repeat the word 'rhubarb' to represent an indistinct conversation or the noise of a crowd. Now *gen.*, make a murmurous background noise, converse indistinctly. Also redupl.

> 📖 B. MASON The amorphous, rhubarbing hubbub of the audience.

rhumb /rʌm/ *noun.* L16.
[French *rumb*, †*rum*, earlier *ryn* (*de vent* of wind) point of the compass, prob. from Dutch *ruim* space, room; alt. later by assoc. with Latin RHOMBUS.]
NAUTICAL. **1** More fully ***rhumb-line***. The line followed by a ship sailing in a fixed direction; an imaginary line on the earth's surface intersecting all meridians at the same angle and used as the standard method of plotting a ship's course on a chart. L16. ▸†**b** *fig.* A course of action. M17–L18.
2 **a** Any of the 32 points of the compass. L16. ▸**b** The angle between two successive points of the compass. E17.

rhumba *noun & verb* var. of RUMBA.

rhumbatron /ˈrʌmbətrɒn/ *noun.* M20.
[Irreg. from Greek *rhumbos* whirling motion + -TRON.]
ELECTRONICS. A cavity resonator in which bunching of an electron beam is produced by a radio-frequency field, or in which a pulsed beam produces a radio-frequency voltage across a gap.

rhus /rʌs/ *noun.* E17.
[Late Latin from Greek *rhous*.]
Any of numerous shrubs and trees constituting the genus *Rhus* (family Anacardiaceae), which includes sumacs and poison ivies.

rhyme /rʌɪm/ *noun.* E17.
[Var. of RIME *noun*[2], by assoc. with the ult. source, Latin *rhythmus* RHYTHM *noun*.]
1 A piece of poetry or verse marked by corresponding terminal sounds. E17.
2 *sing.* & in *pl.* Poetry or verse marked by correspondence of terminal sounds. Freq. in ***in rhyme***, composed with such correspondence of sounds. M17.
3 Correspondence of the terminal sounds of two or more words or metrical lines, in English prosody strictly extending from the end to the last stressed vowel and no further, as *which, rich; grew, too; peace, increase; leather, together*; an instance of such correspondence of sound; a word so corresponding in sound with another. M17.

> 📖 **2** J. RUSKIN There is no such thing as a dialect for rhyme, or a language for verse. **3** *Punch* Metre and rhyme, however,

have been returning to poetry. ***double rhyme, eye rhyme, imperfect rhyme, treble rhyme***, etc.

Phrases: **rhyme royal** a form of verse consisting of stanzas of seven lines of iambic pentameters, rhyming *ababbcc*; also called ***ballade royal***. **without rhyme or reason** lacking sense or logic.
Comb.: **rhyme scheme** the ordered patterning of end-rhymes in poetry or verse; **rhyme sheet** a broadsheet printed with verses for display on a wall.
■ **rhymeless** *adjective* L16.

rhyme /rʌɪm/ *verb*. M17.
[Var. of RIME *verb*². Cf. prec.]
1 *verb trans.* Compose injurious or scurrilous rhymes about; destroy the reputation of (a person etc.) in verse; pester (a person) with verses. Chiefly in ***rhyme to death***. Now *arch. & poet.* M17.
2 *verb trans.* Put (a piece of writing) into rhyme; compose (a verse) in rhyme. Earliest as ***rhymed*** *ppl adjective*. M17. ▸**b** Foll. by *up*: improvise (a blues composition). *US Black slang*. M20.
3 *verb intrans.* Make or write rhymes or verses; versify. M17.
4 a *verb intrans.* (Of words or metrical lines) terminate in sounds that correspond; (of a word) act as a rhyme *with* or *to* (another word). L17. ▸**b** *verb trans.* Make (a word) act as a rhyme *with* another word. E19.
5 *verb intrans.* Use rhyme; find or provide a rhyme *to* (a word). L17.

📖 **3** SIR W. SCOTT I am going to Ashestiel . . to fish and rhyme. **4a** M. AMIS He thinks that halibut rhymes with Malibu. *fig.*: *Sunday Telegraph* This film . . rhymes with his fourth . . as an exercise in feyness. **rhyming dictionary**: in which words are arranged in groups according to the correspondence of their terminal sounds. **rhyming slang** a type of slang (orig. Cockney) in which a word is replaced by words or phrases which rhyme with the word substituted, often with the rhyming element omitted. **b** DAY LEWIS Holding the bread-knife poised over cottage loaf . . Uncle Willie ejaculates the word *pain*, rhyming it with 'rain'.

■ **rhymable** *adjective* (*rare*) L19. **rhymer** *noun* a person who writes rhymes or verses, esp. of an inferior quality E17. **rhymester** *noun* = RHYMER E18. **rhymist** *noun* a versifier; a person who uses rhymes: M18.

rhymic /ˈrʌɪmɪk/ *adjective*. *rare*. E19.
[from RHYME *noun* + -IC.]
1 Rhythmic. E19.
2 Of, pertaining to, or involving rhyme. M19.
■ **rhymical** *adjective* = RHYMIC 2 M18.

rhyncho- /ˈrɪŋkəʊ/ *combining form*.
[mod. Latin, from Greek *rhugkhos* snout, beak: see -O-.]
Forming chiefly scientific terms with the sense 'possessing or relating to a snout, proboscis, or beak'.
■ **rhynchocoel(e)** *noun* (ZOOLOGY) (*a*) *rare* a nemertean worm; (*b*) a body cavity in nemerteans containing the introverted proboscis: L19. **rhynchodaeum** /-ˈdiːəm/ *noun*, pl. **-daea** /-ˈdiːə/, [Greek *hodaion* that is by the way] ZOOLOGY a cavity anterior to and partly containing the proboscis of nemerteans, whelks, etc. L19. **rhynchostome** *noun* (ZOOLOGY) the anterior opening of the rhynchodaeum in whelks and related gastropods L19.

rhynchocephalian /ˌrɪŋkəʊsɪˈfeɪlɪən/ *adjective*. M19.
[from mod. Latin *Rhyncocephalia* (see below), formed as RHYNCHO- + *kephalē* head: see -AN.]
ZOOLOGY & PALAEONTOLOGY. ▶**A** *adjective*. Of or belonging to the reptilian order Rhynchocephalia, including the modern tuatara and various Mesozoic fossil forms. M19.
▶**B** *noun*. A rhynchocephalian reptile. L19.

rhynchokinesis /ˌrɪŋkə(ʊ)kɪˈniːsɪs, -kʌɪ-/ *noun*. M20.
[from RHYNCHO- + (AS) KINESIS.]
ZOOLOGY. In some birds and lizards, raising of the upper bill or jaw by bending of an extensive area of the cranium. Cf. PROKINESIS.
■ **rhynchokinetic** /-ˈnɛtɪk/ *adjective* M20.

rhynchophorous /rɪŋˈkɒf(ə)rəs/ *adjective*. E19.
[from mod. Latin *Rhynchophora* (see below): see RHYNCHO-, -PHOROUS.]
ENTOMOLOGY. Of or belonging to the former group Rhynchophora (now the superfamily Curculionoidea) of beetles having the head prolonged into a beak or snout.

rhynchosaur /ˈrɪŋkəsɔː/ *noun*. Also **rhynchosaurus** /rɪŋkə(ʊ)ˈsɔːrəs/, pl. **-ruses**, **-ri** /-rʌɪ, -riː/. M19.
[mod. Latin *Rhynchosaurus* genus name, formed as RHYNCHO- + Greek *sauros* lizard.]
PALAEONTOLOGY. Any of a group of tusked herbivorous diapsid reptiles of the late Triassic.
■ **rhyncho'saurian** *adjective & noun* (*a*) *adjective* of, pertaining to, or characteristic of a rhynchosaur; (*b*) *noun* a rhynchosaur: M19.

rhynchosporium /rɪŋkə(ʊ)ˈspɔːrɪəm/ *noun*. E20.
[mod. Latin *Rhynchosporium* (see below), formed as RHYNCHO- + SPORE + -IUM.]
BOTANY & AGRICULTURE. A fungus of the genus *Rhynchosporium*, members of which cause barley and rye leaf blotch; a disease caused by such a fungus.

rhyolite /ˈrʌɪəlʌɪt/ *noun*. M19.
[Irreg. from Greek *rhuax* stream (of lava) + -LITE.]
GEOLOGY. Orig., a variety of trachyte containing quartz; later, any volcanic rock showing a fluidal texture. Now, an acidic extrusive volcanic rock, usu. pale and of porphyritic texture, with phenocrysts esp. of quartz or potassium-feldspar in a fine-grained or glassy groundmass commonly showing fluidal structure.
■ **rhyodacite** /rʌɪəˈdeɪsʌɪt/ *noun* a porphyritic igneous rock intermediate in composition between rhyolite and dacite E20. **rhyolitic** /-ˈlɪtɪk/ *adjective* pertaining to, resembling, or related to rhyolite M19.

rhyparographer /rɪpəˈrɒgrəfə/ *noun*. M17.
[from Latin *rhyparographos* = Greek *rhuparographos*, from *rhuparos* filthy: see -GRAPHER.]
A painter of distasteful or sordid subjects. Later also, a painter of genre scenes or still life.
■ **rhyparographist** *noun* (*rare*) = RHYPAROGRAPHER L19. **rhyparo'graphic** *adjective* (*rare*) of, pertaining to, or characteristic of a rhyparographer or rhyparography L19. **rhyparography** *noun* (*a*) the painting of distasteful or sordid subjects; (*b*) still life or genre painting: L17.

rhyta *noun pl.* see RHYTON.

rhythm /ˈrɪð(ə)m/ *noun & verb*. M16.
[In branch I var. of RIME *noun*² (cf. RHYME *noun*) assim. to Latin *rhythmus* or French *rhythme*. In branch II from Latin *rhythmus* or French *rhythme* from Greek *rhuthmos* rel. to *rhein* to flow.]
▶**A** *noun*. **I** †**1** = RHYME *noun* 2. M16–L17.
†**2** = RHYME *noun* 1. L16–L17.
†**3** = RHYME *noun* 3. L16–L17.
▶**II 4 a** The measured flow of words or phrases in verse forming various patterns of sound as determined by the relation of long and short or stressed and unstressed syllables in a metrical foot or a line. M16. ▸**b** Rhythmical or metrical form. M17. ▸**c** The measured flow of words or phrases in prose; an instance of this. M19.
5 Regularity in the repetition in time or space of an action, process, feature, opposing or different conditions, events, etc.; (a) periodic or cyclical change or movement. E18. ▸**b** *spec.* in GEOLOGY & PHYSICAL GEOGRAPHY. Regularity in a feature of deposition etc.; a feature repeated at regular intervals in space. E20.
6 MUSIC. **a** The systematic grouping of musical sounds, principally according to duration and periodical stress; an instance of this, a specific arrangement of such groupings; the feeling for this. M18. ▸**b** *ellipt.* A rhythm instrument, musician, or section. M20.
7 ART & ARCHITECTURE. The harmonious sequence or correlation of colours, elements, or masses. L18.

📖 **4** S. R. DRIVER Though there was always rhythm, there was . . no metre in the strict sense. **c** GEO. ELIOT The church service . . , its recurrent responses and the familiar rhythm of its collects. **5** J. HAWKES The mind of an agricultural society . . rocked by the comforting seasonal rhythm. **6a** A. GRAY The rhythm excited him and his body moved to it easily. JAN MORRIS The excursion boats hoot their whistles . . in a Strauss-like rhythm. **7** M. GIROUARD Three slightly projecting bays, which . . supply a gently regular rhythm in a building otherwise asymmetrical.

Comb.: **rhythm and blues** any of various kinds of (originally black American) popular music with a strong rhythm derived from or influenced by the blues; **rhythm guitar** a guitar part in a group, consisting of the chord sequences of a song etc.; **rhythm instrument** an instrument constituting part of a band's rhythm section; **rhythm method** a method of avoiding conception by restricting sexual intercourse to the times of a woman's menstrual cycle when ovulation is least likely to occur; **rhythm section** the part of a popular or jazz group that principally provides the rhythm, usu. consisting of bass, drums, and sometimes piano.
▶**B** *verb*. †**1** *verb intrans.* = RHYME *verb* 3. Only in M16.
2 *verb trans. fig.* Bring (a person, oneself) into a specified condition by responding to rhythm. *rare*. M20.
■ **rhythmed** *adjective* †(*a*) rhymed; (*b*) characterized by rhythm; rhythmical: L17. **rhythmless** *adjective* E19.

†**rhythmer** *noun*. L16–L18.
[Var. of RIMER *noun*¹.]
A writer of rhymes or verses; a rhymer.

rhythmetic /rɪðˈmɛtɪk/ *adjective*. *rare*. E17.
[from RHYTHM *noun*, modelled on Greek adjectives in *-etikos*: see -IC.]
Rhythmical.
■ **rhythmetical** *adjective* M19.

rhythmi *noun pl.* of RHYTHMUS.

rhythmic /ˈrɪðmɪk/ *adjective & noun*. E17.
[Fr *rhythmique* or Latin *rhythmicus* from Greek *rhuthmikos*, from *rhuthmos* RHYTHM: see -IC. Cf. earlier RHYTHMICAL.]
▶**A** *adjective*. **1** Of or pertaining to rhythm. E17.
2 a Of language, verse, music, etc.: characterized by rhythm, having a pleasant or flowing rhythm. M17. ▸**b** Of a movement, sound, event, etc.: having a marked or recurrent pattern, regularly occurring. M19.
3 GEOLOGY & PHYSICAL GEOGRAPHY. Exhibiting or characterized by a spatial rhythm or periodic alternation. E20.

📖 **2a** G. M. FRASER It was a slow, rhythmic, rather graceful dance. **b** L. T. C. ROLT The rhythmic tread of . . troops marching over the Broughton bridge.

▶**B** *noun*. The science or theory of rhythm. Now *rare*. E17.

rhythmical /ˈrɪðmɪk(ə)l/ *adjective*. M16.
[formed as prec.: see -ICAL.]
†**1** Versifying. Only in M16.
†**2** Written in rhyming verse. L16–E18.
3 a = RHYTHMIC *adjective* 2a. L16. ▸**b** = RHYTHMIC *adjective* 2b. E17.
4 = RHYTHMIC *adjective* 1. E17.
■ **rhythmi'cality** *noun* the quality of being rhythmical L19.

rhythmically /ˈrɪðmɪk(ə)li/ *adverb*. E18.
[from RHYTHMIC *adjective* or prec.: see -ICALLY.]
†**1** So as to rhyme. *rare*. Only in E18.
2 In a rhythmic manner; in rhythm. L18.

rhythmicise *verb* var. of RHYTHMICIZE.

rhythmicity /rɪðˈmɪsɪti/ *noun*. E20.
[from RHYTHMIC *adjective* + -ITY.]
The quality of being rhythmic; the capacity for maintaining a rhythm.

rhythmicize /ˈrɪðmɪsʌɪz/ *verb trans.* *rare*. Also **-ise**. E20.
[from RHYTHMIC *adjective* + -IZE.]
Make (a song) rhythmical; provide or enrich with rhythm.
■ **rhythmici'zation** *noun* L20.

rhythmise *verb* var. of RHYTHMIZE.

rhythmist /ˈrɪðmɪst/ *noun*. M19.
[from RHYTHM *noun* + -IST.]
A person who is knowledgeable in or has a true sense of rhythm.

rhythmite /ˈrɪðmʌɪt/ *noun*. M20.
[from RHYTHMIC *adjective* + -ITE¹.]
GEOLOGY & PHYSICAL GEOGRAPHY. Each of the repeated units in a rhythmic sedimentary formation; *spec.* a varve.

rhythmize /ˈrɪðmʌɪz/ *verb*. Also **-ise**. L19.
[Greek *rhuthmizein*, from *rhuthmos* RHYTHM *noun*, or directly from RHYTHM *noun*: see -IZE.]
1 *verb trans.* Put into rhythm. L19.
2 *verb intrans.* Establish a regular rhythm. L19.
■ **rhythmi'zation** *noun* E20.

rhythmometer /rɪðˈmɒmɪtə/ *noun*. E19.
[from Greek *rhuthmos* RHYTHM *noun* + -METER.]
A simple kind of metronome.

rhythmopoeia /rɪðmə(ʊ)ˈpiːə/ *noun*. Also ***-peia**. M18.
[Latin from Greek *rhuthmopoiia*, from *rhuthmos* RHYTHM + *poiia* making, from *poiein* make.]
Rhythmical composition.

rhythmus /ˈrɪðməs/ *noun*. Pl. **-mi** /-mʌɪ/. M16.
[Latin from Greek *rhuthmos*: see RHYTHM.]
1 = RHYTHM *noun* 4a, 4b. M16.
†**2** MEDICINE. Regularity in the beat of a pulse. L17–E18.
3 MUSIC. = RHYTHM *noun* 6a. M18.

rhytidectomy /rʌɪtɪˈdɛktəmi/ *noun*. M20.
[from Greek *rhutid-*, *rhutis* wrinkle + -ECTOMY.]
Surgical removal of wrinkles, esp. from the face; face-lifting; an instance of this.

rhytidome /ˈrɪtɪdəʊm/ *noun*. L19.
[mod. Latin *rhytidoma* from Greek *rhutidōma*, from *rhutidoun* to wrinkle, from *rhutid-*, *rhutis* a wrinkle.]
BOTANY. The dead outer part of bark, composed of layers of periderm, phloem, and cortex.

rhytina /rʌɪˈtiːnə/ *noun*. Now *rare* or *obsolete*. M19.
[mod. Latin *Rhytina* (see below), from Greek *rhutis* wrinkle.]
An extinct sirenian, *Hydrodamalis gigas* (formerly *Rhytina stelleri*); = ***STELLER's sea cow***.

rhyton /ˈrʌɪtɒn, ˈrɪtɒn/ *noun*. Pl. **-tons**, **-ta** /-tə/. M19.
[Greek *rhuton* neut. of *rhutos* flowing rel. to *rhein* to flow.]
GREEK ANTIQUITIES. A type of drinking-vessel, often in the form of an animal's head, with one or more holes at the bottom through which liquid can flow.

RI *abbreviation*.
1 Religious instruction.
2 Latin *rex et imperator* King and Emperor, *regina et imperatrix* Queen and Empress.
3 Rhode Island.
4 Royal Institution.

ri /riː/ *noun*. Pl. same. M19.
[Japanese.]
1 A traditional Japanese unit of length, now equal to approx. 4 km (2.5 miles). M19.
2 In ancient Japan and in N. and S. Korea, the smallest subdivision of rural administration. M20.

ria /ˈriːə/ *noun*. L19.
[Spanish *ría* estuary.]
PHYSICAL GEOGRAPHY. A long narrow inlet of the sea formed by partial submergence of an unglaciated river valley.
Comb.: **ria coast** a coast marked by numerous rias.

RIAA *abbreviation*.
Record (since 1970, Recording) Industry Association of America.

rial /ˈrʌɪəl, *in sense 4* ˈriːɑːl/ *noun*. In sense 4 also **riyal**. **LME**.
[Orig. from next after French and (later) Spanish models: cf. **REAL** *noun*[1], *noun*[2]. Sense 4 from Persian from Arab. *riyāl* from Spanish *real* **REAL** *noun*[1].]
†**1** A royal person; a prince. **LME–L15**.
2 †**a** A French gold coin struck by Philip IV and his successors, current in Scotland in the 15th and 16th cents. **LME–L15**. ▸**b** *Hist.* An English gold coin equivalent to ten shillings, first issued by Edward IV in 1465. **L15**.
3 *Hist.* = **REAL** *noun*[1]. **E16**.
4 The basic monetary unit of Iran, Saudi Arabia (***riyal***), Oman, Qatar (***riyal***), and Yemen (***riyal***), equal to 100 dinars in Iran, 20 qursh or 100 halalas in Saudi Arabia, 1,000 baiza in Oman, 100 dirhams in Qatar, and 100 fils in Yemen. **M20**.

†**rial** *adjective*. **ME–E17**.
[Old French, var. of *real* **REAL** *adjective*[1].]
Royal, regal; sumptuous, magnificent, splendid.

Rialto /rɪˈaltəʊ/ *noun*. Also **r-**. **M16**.
[The part of Venice in which the Exchange was situated.]
A market, an exchange.

riant /ˈrʌɪənt, ˈriːənt/ *adjective*. Also ***riante*** /rjɑ̃ːt/. **M16**.
[French, pres. pple of *rire* from Latin *ridere* laugh: see **-ANT**[1].]
Of a person: smiling, cheerful. Of a landscape, scene, etc.: pleasing, cheering, attractive.
▪ **riantly** *adverb* **L19**.

†**riat** *noun* see **RYOT**.

riata /rɪˈɑːtə/ *noun*. Also **reata**. **M19**.
[Spanish *reata*: see **LARIAT**.]
= **LARIAT**.

rib /rɪb/ *noun*.
[Old English *rib(b)* corresp. to Old Frisian *ribb*, *rebb*, Old Saxon *ribbi* (Dutch *rib(be)*), Old High German *rippi*, *rippa* (German *Rippe*), Old Norse *rif*, from Germanic.]
▸ **I 1 a** Each of the series of thin curved bones connected in pairs to the spine in humans and other vertebrates and wholly or partly enclosing the thoracic or upper body cavity and its main organs. **OE**. ▸**b** *POTTERY*. An implement, orig. of bone, for shaping and smoothing an object being thrown. **E19** ▸**c** A joke; a teasing or joking remark. Chiefly *US*. **E20**.
2 A rib of an animal with meat adhering to it, used as food; a joint or cut from the ribs of an animal. **LME**.
3 [After *Genesis* 2:21.] A wife; a woman. *slang*. Now *rare*. **L16**.
1 ***floating rib***, ***movable rib***, etc. ***smite under the FIFTH rib***. **2** ***middle rib***, ***spare-rib***, etc.
▸ **II 4** *BIOLOGY*. A thickened strip of tissue extending through an organ or structure; *spec.* (***a***) a vein in a leaf, *esp.* the central vein, the midrib; (***b***) the shaft of a feather. **LME**.
5 A ridge of hard or dense rock (orig. *poet.*); *esp.* (the densest part of) a vein of ore, a dyke of hard stone. **L15**. ▸**b** *MINING*. A wall of coal left standing to support the roof of the workings. **M19**.
6 A narrow ridge or strip of land, as that between furrows or that separating a roadway from a ditch; *dial.* a furrow. **L17**.
7 A ridge raised on an object; *spec.* (***a***) (now *rare* or *obsolete*) an edge separating two faces of a cut diamond; (***b***) a raised band or flange on a metal plate etc.; a bar or ridge on a gun barrel, used to facilitate alignment of the sights or to join the barrels of a double-barrelled gun; (***c***) *KNITTING* a combination of alternate plain and purl stiches producing a ridged somewhat elastic fabric; a band of knitting so produced, esp. at the bottom or top edge of a part of a garment; (***d***) *BOOKBINDING* each of the raised bands on the spine of a book covering the lining. **M18**.
7 ***fisherman's rib***: see **FISHERMAN** 1.
▸ **III 8 a** A piece of timber etc. forming part of the framework or roof of a building; *dial.* a purlin. **LME**. ▸**b** *ARCHITECTURE*. A curved member supporting a vault or defining its form; each of the curved pieces of stone, timber, or metal strips forming the framework of a dome. Later also, a structural or decorative beam or moulding on a ceiling etc. **E18**. ▸**c** An arched or flat beam or girder supporting a bridge. **M18**.
9 Any of a the curved transverse struts of metal, timber, etc., in a ship, extending up from the keel and forming the framework of the hull. **LME**.
10 A bar or rod serving to strengthen or support a structure; *spec.* (***a***) (now *Scot. & north.*) a bar of a grate; (***b***) each of the curved pieces of wood forming the body of a lute or the sides of a violin; (***c***) either of the two horizontal iron bars of a printing-press on which the carriage supporting the bed slides; (***d***) each of the hinged rods supporting the fabric of an umbrella; (***e***) *AERONAUTICS* a structural member in an aerofoil, extending back from the leading edge and serving to define the contour of the aerofoil. **LME**.
Comb.: **rib-bender** *colloq.* a severe blow on the ribs; **rib-digger** *colloq.* a person given to light-hearted banter; **rib-digging** *adjective* (*colloq.*) bantering, teasing; **rib-eye** *N. Amer.* a cut of beef from the outer side of the ribs; **rib-grass** the ribwort plantain, *Plantago lanceolata*; **rib-joint** *US slang* (***a***) a brothel; (***b***) a cheap restaurant specializing in pork ribs; **rib-roast** *verb trans.* (*arch. slang*) beat severely with a stick etc., thrash; **rib-roasting** a beating, a thrashing; **rib-tickler** an amusing joke, situation, etc.; **rib-tickling** *adjective* amusing; **ribwork** a framework or arrangement suggestive of ribs.
▪ **riblike** *adjective* resembling a rib or ribs in shape **L19**.

rib /rɪb/ *verb*. Infl. **-bb-**. **M16**.
[from the noun.]
1 *verb trans.* Provide or strengthen with ribs; enclose as with ribs. **M16**. ▸**b** Form or act as the ribs of (a ship etc.). **L18**.
2 *verb trans.* Mark with ribs or bands; form or shape into ridges. **M16**. ▸**b** Plough (land) leaving a space between the furrows. **M18**.
3 *verb trans.* Beat (a person) on the ribs. Now *dial.* **E18**.
4 *verb trans. & intrans.* Knit (a row, a number of stitches, or part of a garment) in rib. **L19**.
5 *verb trans.* **a** Discredit, incriminate, put pressure on, (a person). Also, fool, dupe. *US slang*. Now *rare*. **E20**. ▸**b** Tease, make fun of. *colloq.* **M20**.

📖 **2** C. MORGAN The path was ribbed by moon, thinly and at . . intervals. **5b** R. COBB They . . made fun of his accent . . ribbed him incessantly.

RIBA *abbreviation*.
Royal Institute of British Architects.

ribald /ˈrɪb(ə)ld/ *noun & adjective*. **ME**.
[Old French *ribau(l)t*, *-auld*, (also mod. *-aud*), from *riber* pursue licentious pleasures from Germanic base repr. by Old High German *hrība* prostitute.]
▸ **A** *noun*. †**1** A member of a class of retainers also used as irregular troops; a menial, a serf. **ME–M17**.
2 A low-born or worthless person, a knave, a wretch. Long *arch.* **ME**.
†**3** A wicked, dissolute, or licentious person. **ME–L16**.
4 A person using offensively impious or lewd language; an irreverent or scurrilous person. *arch.* **ME**.
▸ **B** *adjective*. Of language, humour, etc., or a person: lewd, coarse, scurrilous; irreverent, impious. **E16**.

📖 *Globe & Mail (Toronto)* Ribald and unprintable jokes about working with Rita Hayworth. R. W. CLARK He was the model of iconoclastic youth, ribald about the Emperor.

▪ **ribaldrous** *adjective* (now *rare* or *obsolete*) = **RIBALD** *adjective* **M16**.

ribaldry /ˈrɪb(ə)ldri/ *noun & adjective*. **LME**.
[Old French *ribau(l)derie*, *re-*, formed as prec.: see **-RY**.]
▸ **A** *noun*. †**1** Debauchery, lasciviousness, vice. **LME–M17**.
2 Ribald language, behaviour, etc.; coarseness, lewdness; scurrilous jesting; irreverent mockery; an instance of this. **LME**.
▸†**B** *attrib.* or as *adjective*. Ribald. **E16–M17**.

riband /ˈrɪb(ə)nd/ *noun*[1] & *verb*[1]. Also (the usual form in sense 2) **ribband**. See also **RIBBON** *noun*. **ME**.
[Old French *riban* (now dial.), *reuban*, (also mod.) *ruban*, prob. from Germanic compound of **BAND** *noun*[2].]
▸ **A** *noun*. **1** = **RIBBON** *noun* 1b. **ME**. ▸**b** = **RIBBON** *noun* 1a. *arch.* **ME**.
2 *HERALDRY*. A sub-ordinary, in width one eighth of the bend, and one half of the cost, usually borne couped. **M16**.
3 = **RIBBON** *noun* 2. **M18**.
4 A narrow strip *of* something. *arch.* **E19**. ▸**b** In *pl.* = **RIBBON** *noun* 8. *arch.* **E19**.
5 In *pl.* = **RIBBON** *noun* 3b. *arch. slang*. **M19**.
3 ***blue riband***: see **BLUE** *adjective*. ***red riband***: see **RED** *adjective*.
Comb.: **riband-fish** = ***ribbonfish*** s.v. **RIBBON** *noun*; **Ribandman** *Hist.* = ***Ribbonman*** s.v. **RIBBON** *noun*; **riband wave** a greyish-white or ochreous geometrid moth, *Idaea aversata*, with a dark band running from front to back of each wing.
▸ **B** *verb trans.* Adorn or trim (as) with a riband or ribands. **LME**.
▪ **ribanding** *noun* ribbons collectively; (an instance of) decoration with ribbons: **LME**. **Ribandism** *noun* (*rare*, *Hist.*) = **RIBBONISM** **M19**. **Ribandist** *noun* (*rare*, *Hist.*) = ***Ribbonman*** s.v. **RIBBON** *noun* **E19**. **ribandry** *noun* (*rare*) ribbons collectively **E19**.

riband *noun*[2] & *verb*[2] var. of **RIBBAND** *noun*[1] & *verb*[1].

ribaudequin /rɪˈbəʊdəkɪn/ *noun*. Also **-kin**. **LME**.
[Old French, app. dim. of *ribaud* **RIBALD**.]
Hist. A kind of multi-barrelled cannon used in medieval warfare.

ribavirin /rʌɪbəˈvʌɪrɪn/ *noun*. **L20**.
[from *riba-* (prob. from *ribonucleic acid*) + **VIRUS** + **-IN**[1].]
PHARMACOLOGY. A synthetic guanosine analogue, $C_8H_{12}N_4O_5$, which interferes with the synthesis of viral nucleic acids and is used to treat viral infections.

ribband /ˈrɪb(ə)nd/ *noun*[1] & *verb*[1]. Also **riband**. **E18**.
[from **RIB** *noun* + **BAND** *noun*[2], or from **RIBBON** *noun*.]
▸ **A** *noun*. **1** *SHIPBUILDING*. Any of the long narrow strips of timber etc. fixed longitudinally to the ribs of a ship to keep them in position until the external planking or plating is added. Also, a square timber fastened on the outer side of the launch cradle to stop it slipping outwards. **E18**.
2 A light spar or beam used in the construction of a gun platform, pontoon bridge, etc. **L19**.
▸ **B** *verb trans.* Secure or provide with a ribband or ribbands. **M19**.

ribband *noun*[2] & *verb*[2] var. of **RIBAND** *noun*[1] & *verb*[1].

ribbed /rɪbd/ *adjective*. **E16**.
[from **RIB** *noun*, *verb*: see **-ED**[2], **-ED**[1].]
That has been ribbed; having ribs or ridges (of a specified kind or number); having riblike markings, banded.

📖 DICKENS A waistcoat of ribbed black satin. T. HOOD Lean-ribbed tigers.

ribber /ˈrɪbə/ *noun*. **E19**.
[from **RIB** *noun*, *verb* + **-ER**[1].]
1 A blow on the ribs. *slang*. Now *rare*. **E19**.
2 An attachment on a knitting-machine for producing rib. **L19**.

ribbing /ˈrɪbɪŋ/ *noun*. **M16**.
[from **RIB** *noun*, *verb* + **-ING**[1].]
1 Ribs collectively; riblike markings or ridges, a riblike structure or pattern; *spec.* a band of knitting in rib. **M16**.
2 The action of **RIB** *verb*; an instance of this. **M18**. ▸**b** *spec.* The action or an act of teasing or making fun of a person. *colloq.* **M20**.

📖 **1** P. WENTWORTH She had begun Johnny's second stocking and almost finished the ribbing at the top. *Practical Woodworking* The main frame is . . made with strong ribbing to maintain rigidity. **2b** *Sport* Stan had to contend with a good deal of ribbing from his team-mates.

ribbit /ˈrɪbɪt/ *interjection & noun*. Also **ribit**. **M20**.
[Imit.]
(Repr.) the croak of a frog.

ribble-rabble /ˈrɪb(ə)lrab(ə)l/ *adverb & noun*. **LME**.
[Redupl. of **RABBLE** *noun*[1].]
▸ **A** *adverb*. In great confusion. *rare*. Long *obsolete* exc. *Scot. dial.* **LME**.
▸ **B** *noun*. **1** Confused meaningless language, babble. *arch.* **L16**.
2 = **RABBLE** *noun*[1] 2. Now *dial.* **E17**.

ribbok *noun* see **RHEBOK**.

ribbon /ˈrɪb(ə)n/ *noun*. **E16**.
[Var. of **RIBAND** *noun*[1].]
1 a Fine fabric in the form of a narrow strip or band, used for trimming or decoration or to fasten a garment etc. **E16**. ▸**b** A narrow strip or band of such fabric. **E17**.
2 A ribbon of a special design or colour, worn to indicate the holding of an honour, membership of a group, etc.; *spec.* (***a***) the badge of an order of knighthood; (***b***) a small multicoloured piece of ribbon worn in place of the medal it represents. Also (in *pl.*), prizes or decorations awarded to the winners of a contest etc. (chiefly in ***in the ribbons***, ***into the ribbons***, among the prize-winners). **M17**.
3 †**a** A bell-pull. *slang*. Only in **L17**. ▸**b** In *pl.* Reins. *slang*. **E19**. ▸**c** Gin; spirits. *slang*. Now *rare* or *obsolete*. **E19**.
4 *HERALDRY*. = **RIBAND** *noun*[1] 2. Now *rare*. **E18**.
5 = **RIBBAND** *noun*[1] 1. **E18**.
6 A long thin flexible strip of anything; *spec.* a narrow band of impregnated fabric or coated plastic wound on a spool, used as the inking agent in a typewriter etc. **M18**. ▸**b** A strip of land or ground; *esp.* a path, a road. **M19**.
7 *ANATOMY & ZOOLOGY* etc. A ribbon-like tissue or structure. **E19**.
8 In *pl.* Torn strips of something; tatters, shreds. **E19**.

📖 **1a** M. MEYER A small bundle of papers tied with ribbon. **b** P. AUSTER Small presents . . an apple, for example, or a ribbon for my hair. E. NORTH A breeze arose, causing ribbons on women's hats to flutter. **2** ***blue ribbon***: see **BLUE** *adjective*. ***medal ribbon***: see **MEDAL** *noun*. ***red ribbon***: see **RED** *adjective*. **6** CONAN DOYLE From the end of Whitehall to Victoria Street, the black ribbon of traffic whirled and circled. M. G. EBERHART A ribbon of toothpaste emerged from its uncapped tube. ***paper ribbon***: see **PAPER** *noun & adjective*. **b** K. AMIS He looked . . at the ribbon of road ahead of them. **7** ***lingual ribbon***: see **LINGUAL** *adjective* 2. **8** *fig.*: C. LASCH This female cuts men to ribbons or swallows them whole.

Comb.: **ribbon-building** = ***ribbon development*** below; **ribbon cane** a variety of sugar cane whose mature stalks have red or purplish longitudinal stripes; **ribbon cartridge** (***a***) a pickup cartridge working on the same principle as a ribbon microphone; (***b***) a cartridge containing a spooled typewriter ribbon for easy and clean insertion into and removal from a typewriter; **ribbon chute** *colloq.* = ***ribbon parachute*** below; **ribbon copy** *US* the top copy of a typed letter or document; **ribbon development** the building of houses in a line along a main road, usu. one leading out of a town or village; **ribbon-fern** any of several cultivated ferns with narrow simply divided fronds, esp. *Pteris cretica*; **ribbon figure** a striped pattern of grain seen in some quarter-sawn hardwoods; **ribbonfish** any of various fishes having a very long slender flattened body; *esp.* (*a*) a scabbard-fish, *Lepidopus caudatus*; (*b*) the oarfish, *Regalecus glesne*; (*c*) a fish of the family Trachipteridae, related to the oarfish; **ribbon grain** = ***ribbon figure*** above; **ribbon-grass** a form of reed-grass with variegated leaves, *Phalaris arundinacea* var. *picta*, grown for ornament; **Ribbonman** *Hist.* a member of the Ribbon Society; **ribbon microphone**, (*colloq.*) **ribbon mike** a directional microphone deriving its electrical output from the vibration of a thin metal ribbon mounted between the poles of a permanent magnet; **ribbon parachute** a parachute having a canopy consisting of an arrangement of closely spaced tapes; **ribbon plant** the spider plant, *Chlorophytum comosum*; **ribbon snake** either of two N. American garter snakes, *Thamnophis sauritus* and *T. proximus*, with very thin bodies; **Ribbon Society** *Hist.* a Catholic secret society in Ireland formed to oppose Protestant supremacy and associated with agrarian disorders; **ribbonwood** any of several New Zealand trees of the mallow family whose bark is a source of fibre, esp. *Plagianthus regius* and the houhere, *Hoheria populnea*.

■ **ribboner** *noun* a person who wears a ribbon (only with specifying word); ***white ribboner***: see WHITE *adjective*: L19. **Ribbonism** *noun* (*Hist.*) the principles or policy of the Ribbon Society E19. **ribbon-like** *adjective* resembling a ribbon in shape or form E19. **ribbonry** *noun* ribbons collectively E19. **ribbony** *adjective* decked with ribbons; resembling a ribbon or ribbons: M19.

ribbon /ˈrɪb(ə)n/ *verb*. LME.
[from the noun.]
†**1** *verb trans.* Set around like a ribbon. Only in LME.
2 *verb trans.* Adorn or tie with ribbon or ribbons; mark or stripe as if with ribbons. Chiefly as ***ribboned*** *ppl adjective*. E16. ▸**b** Separate into thin narrow strips; tear into ribbons. M19.
3 *verb intrans.* Of melted wax etc.: form into long thin strips. L19.
4 *verb intrans.* Of a road etc.: extend or continue like a ribbon. Freq. foll. by *out*. E20.

📖 **2** F. WELDON The car was piled high with presents, beautifully wrapped and ribboned. **4** R. V. BESTE A queue of customers ribboned out through the door. I. MURDOCH The Roman Road . . ribboned over the hills and dales.

ribby /ˈrɪbi/ *adjective*. M19.
[from RIB *noun* + -Y¹.]
1 Having prominent ribs; suggestive of or resembling ribs, ridged, banded. M19.
2 Dirty, shabby; seedy, run-down; unpleasant, nasty. *slang*. M20.

ribcage /ˈrɪbkeɪdʒ/ *noun*. E20.
[formed as prec. + CAGE *noun*.]
The wall or chamber formed by the ribs around the chest.

ribes /ˈrʌɪbiːz/ *noun*. Pl. same. M16.
[medieval Latin from Arab. *rībās* sorrel, shrub of the genus *Ribes*.]
†**1** In *pl.* Berries of any of the shrubs of the genus *Ribes*, currants. M16–E17.
2 Any of various shrubs constituting the genus *Ribes* (family Grossulariaceae), which includes the redcurrant, *R. rubrum*, the blackcurrant, *R. nigrum*, and the gooseberry, *R. grossularia*. M16.

ribible /rɪˈbɪb(ə)l/ *noun*. *obsolete* exc. *Hist.* ME.
[Old French *rebebe*, Old Spanish *rabel* from Arab. *rabāb* stringed instrument resembling a fiddle.]
= REBEC.

ribit *interjection* & *noun* var. of RIBBIT.

ribitol /ˈrʌɪbɪtɒl, ˈrɪb-/ *noun*. M20.
[from RIBOSE + -ITOL.]
CHEMISTRY. A colourless crystalline pentahydric alcohol, $HOCH_2(CHOH)_3CH_2OH$, obtained by reduction of ribose and found uncombined in certain plants.
■ **ribityl** *noun* the radical $HOCH_2(CHOH)_3CH_2\cdot$ M20.

ribless /ˈrɪblɪs/ *adjective*. L18.
[from RIB *noun* + -LESS.]
Having no ribs.

riblet /ˈrɪblɪt/ *noun*. L19.
[formed as prec. + -LET.]
A small rib or ridge, esp. as used to reduce drag on a boat or aircraft.

riboflavin /rʌɪbə(ʊ)ˈfleɪvɪn/ *noun*. Also **-ine** /-iːn/. M20.
[from RIBOSE + FLAVIN.]
A yellow flavin with a ribityl sidechain, essential for metabolic energy production, present in many foods, esp. milk, liver, eggs, and green vegetables, and also synthesized by the intestinal flora; vitamin B_2. Also called ***lactoflavin***.

ribonucleic /ˌrʌɪbəʊnjuːˈkleɪɪk, -ˈkliːɪk, -ˈnjuː-/ *adjective*. M20.
[from RIBOSE + NUCLEIC.]
BIOCHEMISTRY. ***ribonucleic acid***, = RNA.
■ **riboˈnuclease** *noun* an enzyme which catalyses the hydrolysis of RNA into oligonucleotides and smaller molecules (also called ***RNase***) M20. **ribonucleoˈprotein** *noun* a nucleoprotein in which the nucleic acid is RNA M20. **riboˈnucleoside** *noun* a nucleoside containing ribose M20. **riboˈnucleotide** *noun* a nucleotide containing ribose E20.

ribophorin /rʌɪbə(ʊ)ˈfɒrɪn/ *noun*. L20.
[from RIBOSOME + -PHORE + -IN¹.]
BIOCHEMISTRY. Any of several membrane proteins thought to bind ribosomes to the endoplasmic reticulum.

ribose /ˈrʌɪbəʊz, -s/ *noun*. L19.
[Arbitrary alt. of ARABINOSE: see -OSE².]
BIOCHEMISTRY. A pentose occurring widely in nature as a constituent of nucleosides and several vitamins and enzymes.
Comb.: **ribosenucleic** *adjective*: ***ribose acid*** = ***RIBONUCLEIC acid***.

ribosome /ˈrʌɪbəsəʊm/ *noun*. M20.
[from RIBONUCLEIC + -SOME³.]
BIOLOGY. Each of the ribonucleoprotein particles in the cytoplasm of living cells, free or attached to endoplasmic reticulum, which bind messenger RNA and transfer RNA to synthesize polypeptides and proteins.
■ **ribosomal** *adjective* of or pertaining to a ribosome; ***ribosomal RNA***, the RNA of a ribosome: M20.

ribosyl /ˈrʌɪbə(ʊ)sʌɪl, -sɪl/ *noun*. M20.
[from RIBOSE + -YL.]
BIOCHEMISTRY. A monovalent radical derived from ribose by the loss of a hydroxyl group. Usu. in *comb.*

ribozyme /ˈrʌɪbə(ʊ)zʌɪm/ *noun*. L20.
[from RIBO(NUCLEIC + EN)ZYME.]
BIOCHEMISTRY. An RNA molecule capable of acting as an enzyme.
■ **riboˈzymal** *adjective* L20.

Ribston /ˈrɪbst(ə)n/ *noun*. Also **-stone**. M18.
[*Ribston* Park, between Knaresborough and Wetherby in N. Yorkshire.]
In full ***Ribston pippin***. A variety of eating apple, introduced from Normandy about 1707; the tree that bears this.

ribulose /ˈrʌɪbjʊləʊz, -s/ *noun*. M20.
[from RIBOSE + -ULOSE².]
BIOCHEMISTRY. A pentose which in the form of phosphate esters is an important intermediate in carbohydrate metabolism and photosynthesis.

ribwort /ˈrɪbwəːt/ *noun*. LME.
[from RIB *noun* + WORT *noun*¹.]
1 More fully ***ribwort plantain***. A plantain, *Plantago lanceolata*, with lanceolate prominently veined leaves, common in grassland. LME.
2 Any plant of the family Plantaginaceae. *rare*. M19.

RIC *abbreviation*.
Royal Irish Constabulary.

Ricard /ˈriːkɑː/ *noun*. M20.
[Name of the manufacturers.]
(Proprietary name for) an aniseed-flavoured aperitif; a drink of this.

Ricardian /rɪˈkɑːdɪən/ *adjective*¹ & *noun*¹. M19.
[from *Ricardo* (see below) + -IAN.]
▶ **A** *adjective*. Of, pertaining to, or accepting the doctrines of the political economist David Ricardo (1772–1823). M19.
▶ **B** *noun*. A follower or adherent of Ricardo. L19.
■ **Ricardianism** *noun*¹ (the holding of) the doctrines of Ricardo L19.

Ricardian /rɪˈkɑːdɪən/ *adjective*² & *noun*². M20.
[from medieval Latin *Ricardus* Richard + -IAN.]
▶ **A** *adjective*. Of or pertaining to Richard I (reigned 1189–99), Richard II (reigned 1377–99), or Richard III (reigned 1483–5), kings of England; (characteristic) of their times; *spec.* pertaining or adhering to the view that Richard III was a just and misrepresented king. M20.
▶ **B** *noun*. A contemporary or supporter of Richard I, II, or (*spec.*) III of England. L20.
■ **Ricardianism** *noun*² support for or advocacy of Richard III L20.

ricasso /rɪˈkasəʊ/ *noun*. Pl. **-os**. L19.
[Italian.]
The part of the blade of a sword next to the hilt.

Riccadonna /rɪkəˈdɒnə/ *noun*. E20.
[Italian, lit. 'rich lady'.]
(Proprietary name for) a type of Italian vermouth; a drink of this.

Ricci tensor /ˈriːtʃɪ ˌtɛnsə, -sɔː/ *noun phr.* E20.
[C. G. *Ricci* (1853–1925), Italian mathematician.]
MATH. A symmetric second-order tensor which describes the curvature of space-time, obtained by contracting the Riemann–Christoffel tensor.

rice /rʌɪs/ *noun*¹. *obsolete* exc. *dial.*
[Old English *-hris* (in comb.) = Frisian *riis*, *rys*, Middle & mod. Dutch *rijs*, Old High German *hriis*, Old Norse *hrís*; stem perh. from Gothic *hrisjan* to shake.]
1 *collect.* †**a** Twigs or small branches on a growing tree or bush. OE. ▸**b** Twigs, small branches, or brushwood cut and used for various purposes. ME.
2 A single twig or small branch. ME.
3 A reel, a winder. E17.

rice /rʌɪs/ *noun*². ME.
[Old French *ris* (mod. *riz*) from Italian *riso* from Proto-Romance from Latin *oryza* from Greek *oruza*, *-on*, of Eastern origin.]
1 a The grain of the grass *Oryza sativa*, a major world cereal. ME. ▸**b** The plant producing this grain, grown in warmer parts of the world, usu. in standing water. M16.
2 More fully ***wild rice***, ***Indian rice***. A N. American aquatic grass, *Zizania aquatica*; *collect. sing.* the edible seeds of this. L18.
3 With specifying word: any of several other grasses used as grain. M19.
1a ***brown rice***, ***saffron rice***, etc. **3** ***hungry rice***, ***mountain rice***, etc.
Comb.: **rice-bird** any of several small birds common in rice-fields, esp. the Java sparrow, and in America, the bobolink; **rice bowl** (*a*) a dish out of which rice is eaten; (*b*) *transf.* an area in which abundant quantities of rice are grown; **rice-bunting** the rice-bird or bobolink; **rice-burner** *US colloq.* (*derog.*) a Japanese motorcycle; **rice Christian**, **rice convert** *derog.* a person, esp. an Asian, adopting Christianity for material benefits; **rice-field** = PADDY *noun*¹ 2; **rice-flower** any of various shrubs constituting the Australian genus *Pimelea* (family Thymelaeaceae), with heads of white, yellow, or pink flowers; **rice-grain** *noun* & *adjective* (*a*) *noun* (ASTRONOMY, in *pl.*) granular markings observed on the surface of the sun; (*b*) *adjective* designating a type of decoration on porcelain in which perforations are made and allowed to fill with melted glaze; **rice-grass** any of various grasses allied to or resembling rice; esp. (*a*) (chiefly *Austral.*) a tall rhizomatous grass of wet places, *Leersia hexandra*; (*b*) a cord-grass native to southern England and western France, *Spartina* × *townsendii*; **rice-milk** milk boiled and thickened with rice and other ingredients; **rice-paper** (*a*) thin semi-transparent edible paper made from the flattened and dried pith of the Taiwanese shrub *Tetrapanax papyriferus* (family Araliaceae) and the Indo-Pacific shrub *Scaevola sericea* (family Goodeniaceae), used in (esp. oriental) painting and in baking biscuits etc.; (*b*) paper made partly or wholly from the straw of rice; **rice powder** (now *rare*) a face-powder made with pulverized rice; **rice-rat** any of a group of New World rodents, mainly arboreal or semi-aquatic, of the genus *Oryzomys* and related genera, esp. *O. palustris* of Central America and the south-eastern US; **rice stitch** a type of cross-stitch having a small stitch at right angles across each of the cross's limbs; **rice table** = RIJSTTAFEL; **rice-water** the liquid in which rice has been boiled, used as a drink, remedy, etc.
■ **ricey** *adjective* of or pertaining to rice; covered with rice; resembling rice in appearance or flavour: L18.

rice /rʌɪs/ *verb trans.* Chiefly *N. Amer.* E20.
[from RICE *noun*².]
COOKERY. Press (esp. cooked potatoes) through a coarse sieve to produce granular shapes, or thin strings.
■ **ricer** *noun* a utensil for ricing food L19.

ricercar /riːtʃəˈkɑː, ˈriːtʃəkɑː/ *noun*. Also **-re** /-ri/, pl. **-ri** /-ri/. L18.
[Italian *ricercare* search out, seek.]
MUSIC. Any of a variety of musical forms found between the 16th and 18th cents.; *esp.* an elaborate contrapuntal instrumental composition in fugal or canonic style.
■ Also **ricercata** /riːtʃəˈkɑːtə/ *noun*, pl. **-te** /-ti/, M18.

rich /rɪtʃ/ *adjective*, *noun*, & *adverb*.
[Old English *rīce* = Old Frisian *rīk(e)*, Old Saxon *rīki*, Old High German *rīchi* (Dutch *rijk*, German *reich*), Old Norse *ríkr*, Gothic *reiks*, from Germanic from Celtic *rix* = Latin *rex*, Old & mod. Irish *rí* king (cf. RAJA *noun*¹); reinforced in Middle English by Old & mod. French *riche* (orig. = powerful), from Germanic.]
▶ **A** *adjective*. †**1** Of a person: powerful, noble, great. Of a thing: sturdy, strong. OE–M16.
2 Having much wealth or abundant means; wealthy, moneyed, affluent. Opp. ***poor***. OE. ▸**b** Of a country, region, etc.: having valuable natural resources or successful industry or business, prosperous. ME.
3 Foll. by *in*, *with*, †*of*, and as 2nd elem. of comb.: having an abundance of, having much, filled or amply provided with, something specified. ME.
4 Of great worth or value, valuable. ME.
5 Of expensive or fine materials or workmanship; splendid, costly; sumptuous, luxurious; elaborate. ME. ▸†**b** Fine, magnificent. ME–L16.
6 a (Of food) containing much fat, flavour, spice, etc.; (of diet) consisting of such food; (of drink) full-bodied. Also, wholesome, nourishing. ME. ▸**b** Of colour, sound, or smell: strong and full, mellow and deep. ME.
7 Plentiful, abundant, ample; productive, rewarding, fulfilling; highly developed or cultivated. LME. ▸**b** Highly entertaining or amusing; absurd, outrageous; ironic; (of humour) earthy. M18.
8 a Of a mine, ore, etc.: yielding a large quantity or proportion of precious metal. M16. ▸**b** Of soil or an area of land: having the qualities necessary to produce good vegetation, fertile. L16. ▸**c** Of the mixture in an internal-combustion engine: containing a high proportion of fuel to air. E20.

📖 **2** *Times* The .. selfish .. 'get rich quick' society. P. ANGADI He's quite rich, so he can pay his way easily. G. DALY He was wonderfully rich, the son of a man who had made a fortune. I. MURDOCH He was a well-known painter and had even become a rich one. ***poor little rich boy, poor little rich girl***: see POOR *adjective*. ***the rich glutton***: see GLUTTON *noun*. **3** E. BOWEN Everyone .. thought well of them, so their ten years of marriage had been rich with society. B. SPOCK The mother's diet is rich in citrus fruits and .. vegetables. *Railway Magazine* Scotland is .. rich in abandoned .. railways. *Fortune* From Australia to the oil-rich sultanate of Brunei. **4** W. DAMPIER The Portuguese .. put their richest Goods into a Boat. **5** TENNYSON Flowerage That stood out from a rich brocade. **6a** R. POSTGATE A chocolate gâteau .. far too rich, but delicious. ***rich tea (biscuit)***: see TEA *noun*. **b** ALDOUS HUXLEY A rich, port-winey, cigary voice. G. DALY Her hair glinted a rich red. **7** M. TIPPETT Schönberg's imaginative life was unusually rich. M. MARRIN There's a great deal in the archives, they're .. very rich. *Social History of Medicine* The potato is not noted as a rich source of vitamin C. **rich rhyme** (a) rhyme in which not only the final vowels but also the preceding and following consonants of the rhyming words sound alike, as *rain, rein, taken, mistaken*. **b** N. COWARD Me, grumble! .. That's rich, that is. **8** ***strike it rich***: see STRIKE *verb*.

▶ **B** *absol.* as *noun*. **1** *collect. pl.* The class of rich people; *the* wealthy. OE.

2 A rich person. Long *rare*. ME.

📖 **1** C. SANDBURG The rich get richer and the poor get children. ***new rich***: see NEW *adjective*. ***soak-the-rich***: see SOAK *verb*.

▶ **C** *adverb*. Richly. Chiefly in comb., as ***rich-laden***, ***rich-toned***, etc. ME.

■ **richish** *adjective* (*rare*) somewhat rich L19.

rich /rɪtʃ/ *verb*. ME.

[from the adjective.]

1 *verb trans.* Enrich, make rich. ME.

†**2** *verb intrans.* Become rich. LME–E18.

-rich /rɪtʃ/ *suffix*.

[from RICH *adjective*.]

Forming adjectives with the sense 'rich in (the first element)', as ***oil-rich***, ***oxygen-rich***, ***protein-rich***.

Richard /ˈrɪtʃəd/ *noun*. M17.

[Male forename; in sense 2 joc. back-form. from DICK *noun*[3], in sense 3 rhyming slang for BIRD *noun*.]

†**1** A kind of apple. *rare*. M17–E18.

2 A detective. *slang*. E20.

3 A girl, a woman. Also more fully ***Richard the Third***. *rhyming slang*. M20.

Comb.: **Richard Roe** LAW (now *US*) an anonymous party, usu. the defendant, in a legal action, formerly *spec.* (ENGLISH LAW) in the now obsolete action of ejectment (cf. ***JOHN** Doe* (a)).

richardia /rɪˈtʃɑːdɪə/ *noun*. M19.

[mod. Latin (see below), from L. C. M. *Richard* (1754–1821), French botanist + -IA[1].]

A plant of the genus *Zantedeschia* (formerly *Richardia*), of the arum family; *esp.* the arum lily, *Z. aethiopica*.

Richardson /ˈrɪtʃəds(ə)n/ *noun*[1]. M19.

[Sir John *Richardson* (1787–1865), Scot. naturalist and explorer.]

Used *attrib.* and in *possess.* to designate birds or animals collected by Richardson or named in his honour.

Richardson's ground squirrel, **Richardson ground squirrel** the picket-pin gopher, *Spermophilus richardsoni*, of brush and grassland in central N. America. **Richardson's grouse**, **Richardson grouse** the spruce grouse. **Richardson's skua** the Arctic skua. **Richardson's squirrel**, **Richardson squirrel** = ***Richardson's ground squirrel*** above.

Richardson /ˈrɪtʃəds(ə)n/ *noun*[2]. M20.

[L. F. *Richardson* (1881–1953), English physicist.]

1 ***Richardson number***, ***Richardson's number***, with ref. to fluid motion, a dimensionless number given, essentially, by the ratio of the fluid density gradient to the square of the velocity gradient. M20.

2 ***Richardson criterion***, ***Richardson's criterion***, a criterion, depending on the value of the Richardson number, used to determine whether flow in a stratified fluid will be turbulent or laminar. M20.

Richardsonian /rɪtʃədˈsəʊnɪən/ *adjective & noun*. L18.

[from *Richardson* (see below) + -IAN.]

▶ **A** *adjective*. Of, pertaining to, or characteristic of the works or style of the English novelist Samuel Richardson (1689–1761). L18.

▶ **B** *noun*. An admirer, student, or imitator of Richardson or his writing. L19.

Richardson's equation /ˈrɪtʃəds(ə)nz ɪˌkweɪʒ(ə)n/ *noun phr.* E20.

[Sir Owen W. *Richardson* (1879–1959), English physicist.]

PHYSICS. An equation, $j = AT^2 e^{-\phi/kT}$, giving the maximum current density j of electrons emitted by a hot metal surface in terms of its temperature T and work function ϕ (where the constant A depends on the material and k is Boltzmann's constant). Also ***Richardson equation***, ***Richardson–Dushman equation*** [S. *Dushman* (1883–1954), US physicist].

Richard's pipit /ˌrɪtʃədz ˈpɪpɪt/ *noun phr.* M19.

[from *Richard*, surname of 19th-cent. French amateur ornithologist.]

A large pipit, *Anthus novaeseelandiae*, found throughout the Old World, mainly in wetlands.

Richelieu /ˈriːʃljəː/ *adjective*. L19.

[Origin uncertain: perh. from Cardinal *Richelieu* (1585–1642).]

EMBROIDERY. Designating a form of cutwork in which the spaces are connected by picoted bars.

richen /ˈrɪtʃ(ə)n/ *verb*. L19.

[from RICH *adjective* + -EN[5].]

1 *verb trans.* Make richer, enrich. L19.

2 *verb intrans.* Become richer. L19.

riches /ˈrɪtʃɪz/ *noun pl.* (orig. *sing.*). ME.

[Orig. var. of next; later analysed as pl.]

Abundant means, valuable possessions or resources, wealth. Formerly also, the possession of wealth, the condition of being rich; (treated as *sing.*) a particular form of wealth.

📖 J. R. GREEN The .. baronage turned greedily on the riches of the Church. G. GREENE Astonished that such riches could exist in sight of such poverty. *fig.*: M. GEE The riches I'd been promised, those feasts and satisfactions of the mind, were not there. ***rags to riches***: see RAG *noun*[1].

richesse /ˈrɪtʃɛs/ *noun*. Long *arch*. ME.

[Old French *richeise*, *-esce* (mod. *-esse*), from *riche* RICH *adjective* + *-esse* -ESS[2]. Cf. prec.]

†**1** *sing.* & in *pl.* Wealth; richness; riches. ME–L17.

2 A number or group of martens. L15.

richie /ˈrɪtʃi/ *noun*. *slang* (chiefly *US*). *derog.* Also **richy**. M20.

[from RICH *adjective* + -IE.]

A wealthy person, *esp.* a young one.

richly /ˈrɪtʃli/ *adverb*. OE.

[*rīclīce* = Middle Dutch *rikelike*, Middle Low German *rīk(e)līken*, Old High German *rīchlīche*, *rīh-*, Old Norse *ríkulega*, from Germanic base of RICH *adjective*, -LY[2].]

†**1** With great authority or power. Only in OE.

2 In a rich manner. OE.

3 So as to be rich. ME.

4 Fully, thoroughly. M16.

📖 **2** O. MANNING The sinking sun lit everything .. as richly pink as the heart of a pumpkin. *Early Music* Richly dressed men and women .. feasting. M. SEYMOUR His portraits of local characters are richly humorous and vivid. **4** G. BATTISCOMBE *Sing-Song* won the success it so richly deserved.

richness /ˈrɪtʃnɪs/ *noun*. ME.

[from RICH *adjective* + -NESS.]

The state or quality of being rich.

Richter /ˈrɪktə, ˈrɪxtə/ *noun*. M20.

[Charles Francis *Richter* (1900–85), US seismologist.]

GEOPHYSICS. Used *attrib.* with ref. to a logarithmic scale devised by Richter for expressing the magnitude of an earthquake from seismograph oscillations, the more destructive earthquakes having magnitudes between about 5.5 and 8.9. Chiefly in ***Richter magnitude***, ***Richter scale***.

📖 *fig.*: H. GREENE The news .. was a shock on the level of six or seven on the diplomatic Richter scale.

richweed /ˈrɪtʃwiːd/ *noun*. L18.

[from RICH *adjective* + WEED *noun*[1].]

Any of several N. American plants; *esp.* (***a***) horse-balm, *Collinsonia canadensis*; (***b***) clearweed, *Pilea pumila*.

richy *noun* var. of RICHIE.

ricin /ˈrʌɪsɪn/ *noun*. L19.

[from mod. Latin *Ricinus* (see below) + -IN[1].]

CHEMISTRY. A highly toxic polypeptide which is obtained from the pressed seeds of the castor oil plant, *Ricinus communis*, and has haemagglutinating properties.

ricinoleic /ˌrʌɪsɪnə(ʊ)ˈleɪɪk/ *adjective*. M19.

[formed as RICIN + OLEIC.]

Chem. ***ricinoleic acid***, a long-chain unsaturated fatty acid, the 7-hydroxy derivative of oleic acid, whose glyceride is the chief component of castor oil.

ricinus /ˈrɪsɪnəs/ *noun*. L17.

[Latin.]

The castor oil plant, *Ricinus communis*.

rick /rɪk/ *noun*[1].

[Old English *hrēac* = Middle Dutch *rooc*, *roke* (Dutch *rook*), Old Norse *hraukr*, of unkn. origin.]

A stack of hay, corn, etc., *esp.* one built in a regular shape and thatched; *transf.* a heap, a pile.

Comb.: **rickyard** a farmyard or enclosure where ricks are stored.

rick /rɪk/ *noun*[2]. M19.

[Prob. from RICK *verb*[2]. Cf. WRICK.]

A slight sprain or strain, esp. in the neck or back.

rick /rɪk/ *noun*[3]. *slang*. Also **'rick**. L19.

[Abbreviation.]

= RICKSHAW.

rick /rɪk/ *noun*[4] & *adjective*. *slang*. E20.

[Origin unkn.]

▶ **A** *noun*. = GEE *noun*[3]. E20.

▶ **B** *attrib.* or as *adjective*. Fictitious, spurious. M20.

rick /rɪk/ *verb*[1] *trans.* E17.

[from RICK *noun*[1]. Cf. REEK *verb*[2].]

Form or stack (hay, corn, etc.) into a rick or ricks. Also foll. by *up*.

rick /rɪk/ *verb*[2] *trans.* L18.

[Prob. var. of WRICK *verb* (though recorded earlier). Cf. RICK *noun*[2].]

Sprain, strain, or wrench slightly (a limb, joint, etc., esp. the back or neck).

ricker /ˈrɪkə/ *noun*. Orig. NAUTICAL. E19.

[Prob. from German *Rick* (pl. *Ricke*) fence, pole.]

A spar or pole made from the stem of a young tree.

ricket /ˈrɪkɪt/ *noun*[1]. *slang*. M20.

[Origin unkn.]

A blunder, a mistake.

ricket *noun*[2] see RICKETS.

ricket /ˈrɪkɪt/ *verb intrans.* *rare*. L19.

[Back-form. from RICKETY.]

Move in a tottering or shaky manner, lurch.

ricketed /ˈrɪkɪtɪd/ *adjective*. L17.

[from RICKET(S + -ED[2].]

Affected by rickets; *fig.* crippled, impaired.

ricketic /rɪˈkɛtɪk/ *adjective*. *rare*. L20.

[from RICKET(S + -IC.]

MEDICINE. Rachitic; = RICKETY *adjective* 1.

rickets /ˈrɪkɪts/ *noun pl.* (treated as *sing.* or *pl.*). Also (only in attrib. use & in comb.) in sing. **ricket**. M17.

[Origin uncertain: perh. orig. West Country dial., or alt. of Greek *rhakhitis* RACHITIS.]

A disease, esp. of children, caused by vitamin D deficiency, and characterized by imperfect calcification, softening, and distortion of the bones, typically resulting in bow-legs, and freq. associated with other signs of malnutrition.

rickettsia /rɪˈkɛtsɪə/ *noun*. Pl. **-iae** /-ɪiː/, **-ias**. E20.

[mod. Latin *Rickettsia* genus name, from H. T. *Ricketts* (1871–1910), US pathologist + -IA[1].]

MEDICINE & MICROBIOLOGY. Any of a group of very small rod-shaped or coccoid micro-organisms that are mostly intracellular parasites in vertebrates, including the causative agents of typhus and various other febrile diseases in humans, and are freq. transmitted by mites, ticks, or lice.

■ **rickettsial** *adjective* of, pertaining to, or caused by rickettsiae M20.

rickety /ˈrɪkɪti/ *adjective*. Also **-tty**. L17.

[from RICKET(S + -Y[1].]

1 Affected by or suffering from rickets; subject to rickets. L17. ▸**b** Of the nature of or pertaining to rickets; rachitic. E19.

2 Unsafe in construction, likely to collapse; unsteady; (of the mind etc.) feeble, lacking firmness. M18.

📖 **1b rickety rosary** a line of swellings on either side of the chest, reminiscent of a string of beads and symptomatic of rickets. **2** J. L. WATEN Three rickety wooden chairs, the legs tied with wire.

■ **ricketily** *adverb* M19. **ricketiness** *noun* the condition of being rickety M19.

rickety-rackety /ˈrɪkətɪˌrakəti/ *adjective*. L19.

[Redupl. of prec.]

Unsteady, shaky, tottering.

rickey /ˈrɪki/ *noun*. Orig. *US*. L19.

[Prob. from the surname *Rickey*.]

A drink consisting of a spirit, esp. gin, mixed with lime or lemon juice, ice, and carbonated water. Freq. with specifying word, as ***gin rickey***, ***whiskey rickey***, etc.

rickle /ˈrɪk(ə)l/ *noun & verb*. *Scot., Anglo-Irish, & north.* L15.

[Perh. from Norwegian dial. *rikl*, or from RICK *noun*[1].]

▶ **A** *noun*. **1** A heap, a pile, a mound, *esp.* one loosely built up. L15. ▸**b** A ramshackle or broken-down object. L19.

2 A heap of corn, hay, etc.; a pile of sheaves; a pile or stack of peats. L16.

▶ **B** *verb trans.* Make or form (corn, peat, etc.) into a heap, pile, or stack. M16.

rickrack *noun & verb* var. of RICRAC.

rickshaw /ˈrɪkʃɔː/ *noun*. Also **-sha** /-ʃə/. L19.

[Abbreviation of JINRICKSHA.]

A light two-wheeled hooded vehicle drawn by one or more persons.

ricky-tick /rɪkɪˈtɪk/ *noun & adjective*. *slang* (chiefly *US*). M20.

[Imit. Cf. RINKY-DINK, RINKY-TINK.]

▶ **A** *noun*. An even, repetitive, or monotonous rhythm, as in early jazz; old-fashioned straight jazz or ragtime. M20.

▶ **B** *adjective*. Of a rhythm etc.: even, repetitive, monotonous. Of music: trite, old-fashioned, unsophisticated. M20.

■ **ricky-ticky** *adjective* = RICKY-TICK *adjective* M20.

RICO *abbreviation.*
US LAW. Racketeering-influenced and Corrupt Organizations.

ricochet /ˈrɪkəʃeɪ, -ʃɛt/ *noun.* M18.
[French = the skipping of a shot or of a flat stone on water, of unkn. origin.]
Orig. *MILITARY.* The action of a projectile, esp. a bullet or shell, in rebounding at an angle off a surface or surfaces after being fired; a hit made after such a rebound. Also (now *rare*), a method of firing by which a shell etc. is made to rebound; the subjecting *of* a target to this kind of firing.

R. L. STEVENSON The shot buried itself in the . . sand. We had no ricochet to fear.

ricochet /ˈrɪkəʃeɪ, -ʃɛt/ *verb.* Pa. t. **-cheted** /-ʃeɪd/, **-chetted** /-ʃeɪd, -ʃɛtɪd/, pa. pple **-cheting** /-ʃeɪɪŋ/, **-chetting** /-ʃeɪɪŋ, -ʃɛtɪŋ/. M18.
[from the noun.]
Orig. *MILITARY.* **1** *verb trans.* Subject to ricochet firing. M18.
2 *verb intrans.* Of a projectile etc.: rebound from a surface or surfaces; move with a series of ricochets. (Foll. by *off, from, on,* etc.) E19.

2 J. KOSINSKI The bullet ricocheted off the ground and whizzed by. D. E. WESTLAKE Rosa . . slammed on the brakes, causing . . Vito to ricochet around the back seat.

ricordo /riˈkɔrdo/ *noun.* Pl. **-di** /-di/. E20.
[Italian, lit. 'memory'.]
A token of remembrance, a souvenir; *ART* a copy made by a painter of another's composition.

ricotta /rɪˈkɒtə/ *noun.* L19.
[Italian = recooked, from Latin *recocta* fem. pa. pple of *recoquere*, formed as RE- + *coquere* cook.]
A kind of soft white unsalted Italian cheese. Also ***ricotta cheese***.

ricrac /ˈrɪkrak/ *noun & verb.* Also **rickrack**. L19.
[Origin uncertain: perh. redupl. of RACK *verb*[1] or RICK *verb*[2].]
▶ **A** *noun.* A decorative zigzag braid used as a trimming for garments. L19.
▶ **B** *verb trans.* Infl. **-ck-**. Decorate (as) with ricrac. L20.

RICS *abbreviation.*
Royal Institution of Chartered Surveyors.

rictus /ˈrɪktəs/ *noun.* M18.
[Latin, lit. 'open mouth', from *rict-* pa. ppl stem of *ringi* gape.]
1 *BOTANY.* The throat of a two-lipped corolla. Cf. RINGENT. *rare.* M18.
2 The expanse or gape of the mouth, or of the beak or jaws of a bird, fish, etc.; *transf.* a fixed grin or grimace. E19.

2 N. BAWDEN Desperately smiling. A rictus of fear.

■ **rictal** *adjective* E19.

rid /rɪd/ *noun.* M17.
[from the verb. Cf. REDD *noun*[1].]
1 Progress, dispatch, speed. Now *dial.* M17.
2 Soil overlying stone or marl, needing to be removed to allow digging. E19.

rid /rɪd/ *verb*[1]. Infl. **-dd-**. Pa. t. & pple **rid**, (*arch.*) **ridded**. ME.
[Old Norse *ryðja*. Cf. REDD *verb*[1], *verb*[2].]
▶ **I 1** *verb trans.* Free from obstacles or encumbrances; *esp.* (**a**) (now *dial.*) clear (land, a path, etc.) of undergrowth etc.; (**b**) (now *dial. & US*) clear (a table) of food and dishes; tidy or clear *up* (a room etc.), set in order. ME.
2 *verb trans.* Set free, rescue, or save *from* or *out of*. Now *rare.* ME.
3 *verb trans.* Make (a person, place, or oneself) free *of* a troublesome or unwanted thing or person; relieve *of* or (now *rare*) *from*. M16.

3 W. MARCH She . . blew on it to rid it of dust. L. C. KNIGHTS Dorimant . . is trying to rid himself of an old mistress. M. HUNTER The champion who will rid the kingdom of its danger.

▶ **II 4** *verb trans.* Part or separate (combatants). *obsolete* exc. *dial.* LME.
5 a *verb trans.* Accomplish or get through (work). Also foll. by *off, away.* Now *dial.* LME. ▶**b** *verb intrans.* Of work: be accomplished. Now *dial.* E17.
6 a *verb trans.* Remove or dispose of (a troublesome or unwanted thing or person). (Foll. by *from, out of, off, away.*) L15. ▶†**b** Remove by violence; kill, destroy. L15–M17.
Phrases: **be rid of** be freed or relieved from (a troublesome or unwanted thing or person). **get rid of** remove, dispose of, (a troublesome or unwanted thing or person). †**rid ground**, †**rid space**, †**rid way** cover ground, make progress.

rid *verb*[2] *pa. t. & pple*: see RIDE *verb.*

ridable /ˈrʌɪdəb(ə)l/ *adjective.* Also **rideable**. E17.
[from prec. + -ABLE.]
1 Able to be ridden or used for riding. E17.
2 Able to be ridden through, over, etc. M17.
3 Suitable for being hunted on horseback. *rare.* E20.

■ **ridaˈbility** *noun* L19.

riddance /ˈrɪd(ə)ns/ *noun.* M16.
[from prec. + -ANCE.]
1 The action or an act of getting rid of something or someone. Formerly freq. in ***make riddance of***, ***make clean riddance of***. M16.
2 A deliverance or relief consisting in getting rid of something or someone. Chiefly in ***good riddance***, †***fair riddance***, †***gentle riddance***, †***happy riddance***, (foll. by *to, of*), a welcome relief or freedom from a troublesome or unwanted thing or person. M16.
†**3 a** Efficiency or speed in work. L16–M18. ▶**b** Progress or advance in movement. L16–M17.
4 Deliverance or rescue *from* something. L16.

2 M. RENAULT He might sack Jeepers, and good riddance too. *Times* The War of Independence . . can be seen . . as good riddance to bad rubbish.

riddel *noun* var. of RIDEL.

ridden /ˈrɪd(ə)n/ *adjective.* LME.
[from RIDE *verb* + -EN[6].]
†**1** ***room-ridden***, far-travelled. Only in LME.
2 Of a horse: that has been ridden, broken-in. E16.
3 Oppressed, harassed, troubled; infested, afflicted. Long only foll. by *with* or as 2nd elem. of comb., as ***cliché-ridden***, ***guilt-ridden***, ***poverty-ridden***, ***vermin-ridden***, etc. M17.

3 *Observer* We're ridden with guilt . . God bothers us.

ridden *verb pa. pple* of RIDE *verb.*

ridder /ˈrɪdə/ *noun*[1]. Now *dial.*
[Old English *hrid(d)er* = Old High German *rît(e)ra*, Middle High German *rîter(e)*, (German *Reiter*), from Germanic: see -ER[1]. Cf. RIDDLE *noun*[2].]
A sieve, a strainer.

ridder /ˈrɪdə/ *noun*[2]. *rare.* E16.
[from RID *verb*[1] + -ER[1].]
1 A person who gets rid *of* something; a deliverer. E16.
2 A person separating combatants. Cf. REDDER. *Scot.* E17.

ridder /ˈrɪdə/ *verb trans.* Long *obsolete* exc. *dial.* OE.
[from RIDDER *noun*[1].]
Sift, sieve, (corn etc.).

ridding /ˈrɪdɪŋ/ *noun.* ME.
[from RID *verb*[1] + -ING[1].]
1 The action of RID *verb*[1]; an act or instance of this. ME.
2 A cleared piece of ground, a clearing. *dial.* (freq. in place-names). ME.

riddle /ˈrɪd(ə)l/ *noun*[1].
[Old English *rǣdels(e)* corresp. to Old Frisian *riedsel*, Old Saxon *rādisli, rādislo* (Dutch *raadsel*), Old High German base of German *Rätsel*, from Germanic base READ *verb*, REDE *noun, verb*[1]: see -LE[1].]
1 A question or statement intentionally phrased to require ingenuity in ascertaining its answer or meaning, freq. as a game or pastime; a conundrum. Formerly also, advice; opinion, conjecture. OE.
2 A puzzling or perplexing thing; a difficult or insoluble problem; a mystery. LME.
3 A mysterious or enigmatic person. *literary.* M17.

1 P. H. JOHNSON Her crackers contained riddles, and she made us all guess them. B. KOPS What do you mean, Sam? You talk in riddles. **2** J. G. HOLLAND The riddle of life is unsolved. J. AGATE Desiring immensely to know the answer to the Shakespeare–Bacon riddle. *Daily Mirror* The 23-year-old riddle of what happened to the controversial painting.

Phrases: ***Jimmy Riddle***: see JIMMY *noun*[2] 5. ***riddle me a riddle***, ***riddle my riddle***: see RIDDLE *verb*[1] 2.

riddle /ˈrɪd(ə)l/ *noun*[2]. LOE.
[Alt. of RIDDER *noun*[1]: see -LE[1]. Cf. RUDDLE *noun*[2].]
1 A large coarse sieve for separating corn from chaff, sand from gravel, ashes from cinders, etc.; a similar part of a mechanism. LOE.
2 A board or metal plate set with pins, used in straightening wire. M19.
1 riddle of claret (chiefly *Scot.*) a case of thirteen bottles of claret (twelve quarts and a magnum).

riddle /ˈrɪd(ə)l/ *verb*[1]. LME.
[from RIDDLE *noun*[1].]
1 a *verb intrans.* Orig., puzzle, ponder, (*on*). Now, speak in riddles, be enigmatic; propound a riddle. LME. ▶**b** *verb trans.* Propound a riddle to (a person). E17.
2 *verb trans.* Interpret, solve, (a riddle or question). Also foll. by *out.* L16.
2 riddle me a riddle, **riddle my riddle** = ***riddle-me-ree*** (a) below.
Comb.: **riddle-me-ree** *interjection & noun* (**a**) *interjection* here's a riddle!, answer this puzzle!; (**b**) *noun* nonsense, rigmarole; also, a written or spoken charade or clue by which the letters of a word may be guessed.
■ **riddler** *noun*[1] a person speaking in or posing riddles E17.

riddle /ˈrɪd(ə)l/ *verb*[2] *trans.* ME.
[from RIDDLE *noun*[2].]
1 Pass through a riddle, sieve or separate with a riddle (also foll. by *out*); remove ashes or other unwanted material from with a riddle. ME.
2 Make many holes in, esp. with gunshot; *fig.* fill, pervade, or permeate (usu. with something undesirable). Chiefly as ***riddled ppl adjective.*** E16.

1 J. FOWLES Three fires . . had to be stoked . . and riddled twice a day. **2** J. COLVILLE We would sweep down on German trucks . . and riddle them with shot and shell. B. CHATWIN She wore . . green jerseys . . all . . riddled with holes. E. LONGFORD The Morris Motor . . and Pressed Steel works were riddled with communists. P. CAREY His life was riddled with sin and compromise.

■ **riddler** *noun*[2] a person who riddles corn, ashes, etc. E17.

riddling /ˈrɪdlɪŋ/ *noun*[1]. L15.
[from RIDDLE *verb*[1] + -ING[1].]
The propounding of a riddle or riddles; an instance of this. Formerly also, a riddle.

riddling /ˈrɪdlɪŋ/ *noun*[2]. M16.
[from RIDDLE *verb*[2] + -ING[1].]
1 The action of RIDDLE *verb*[2]; an instance of this. M16.
2 In *pl.* The coarser or less valuable parts of something separated by a riddle; siftings. M16.
3 = REMUAGE. M20.

riddling /ˈrɪdlɪŋ/ *adjective.* L16.
[from RIDDLE *verb*[1] + -ING[2].]
1 Speaking or expressed in riddles; enigmatic, obscure, puzzling. L16.
2 Interpreting or solving riddles. L16.
■ **riddlingly** *adverb* L16.

ride /rʌɪd/ *noun.* M18.
[from the verb.]
1 An act of riding; a journey or trip on horseback or in a vehicle, freq. a public one; *spec.* (**a**) a spell of riding, esp. for pleasure, on a horse, vehicle, person's back, etc.; (**b**) a passenger's conveyance in a car etc. without charge, a lift. M18. ▶**b** An act of sexual intercourse. *slang.* M20.
2 a A horse for riding. Freq. with qualifying adjective. L18. ▶**b** A motor vehicle. *N. Amer. slang.* M20. ▶**c** A roundabout, roller-coaster, etc., to be ridden at an amusement park or fair. Orig. *US.* M20.
3 A path or track made for riding on horseback, esp. through a wood; a riding. E19.
4 a A surging motion. E19. ▶**b** In jazz etc., an easily flowing or swinging rhythm; an improvised passage in such a rhythm. *slang.* M20. ▶**c** In full ***ride cymbal***. A cymbal in a drum kit used for keeping up a continuous rhythm. M20.
5 A batch of mounted recruits (*MILITARY*). Also *gen.*, a group of riders under instruction. M19.
6 a A vehicle's quality of comfort and smoothness as perceived by a driver or passenger. M20. ▶**b** The quality of a horse's gait when being ridden. M20.

1 C. CANNING A charming ride round jungly lanes. R. BRAUTIGAN A farmer gave me a ride in a truck. E. WELTY A half hour's ride . . on the city's . . streetcar line. P. AUSTER Those train rides up north. **2a** *Your Horse* I took her hunting regularly . . and she is now a super general purpose ride. **3** I. COLEGATE The wide grassy rides which . . had been cut through the wood. **6a** *Which?* Its ride, refinement and roadholding are not up to modern standards.

Phrases: **for the ride** *colloq.* for fun, as an observer only. ***musical ride***: see MUSICAL *adjective.* ***rough ride***: see ROUGH *adjective.* **take for a ride** (orig. *US*) (**a**) *colloq.* tease; mislead deliberately, hoax, cheat; (**b**) *slang* take on a car journey with the intention of murdering or kidnapping.

ride /rʌɪd/ *verb.* Pa. t. **rode** /rəʊd/, (*arch.*) **rid** /rɪd/, pa. pple **ridden** /ˈrɪd(ə)n/, (*arch.*) **rid** /rɪd/.
[Old English *rīdan* = Old Frisian *rīda*, Old Saxon *-rīdan* (Dutch *rijden*), Old High German *rītan* (German *reiten*), Old Norse *ríða*. Cf. ROAD *noun & adjective.*]
▶ **I** *verb intrans.* **1** Sit on and direct the movement of a horse, mule, camel, elephant, etc., or a cycle; travel on a horse etc. or cycle (foll. by *on*). Also, have the skill to sit on and direct the movement of a horse etc. OE. ▶**b** Go on horseback on a warlike raid or foray, *spec.* (*Hist.*) in the Scottish Borders in the 16th and 17th cents. ME. ▶**c** Go in procession on horseback to open a fair, market, etc. *Scot.* (now *Hist.*). LME. ▶**d** Serve in a cavalry regiment. E18. ▶**e** Of a person: weigh a specified amount when mounted on a horse. M19. ▶**f** In jazz etc., play with an easily flowing or swinging rhythm. *slang.* E20.
2 Move or be carried as if on horseback, esp. smoothly or lightly; glide; (of a ship etc.) float or sail buoyantly. (Foll. by *on, upon.*) OE. ▶**b** Of a ship etc.: lie or float at anchor. (Foll. by *at,* †*on.*) OE. ▶**c** Of a celestial object: appear to float in space. M17.
3 Have sexual intercourse, copulate. Now *coarse slang.* ME.
4 Be conveyed or travel in a vehicle, esp. a public one. (Foll. by *in, on.*) ME. ▶**b** Be carried about on a cart, rail, etc., to be mocked. (Foll. by *on,* †*in.*) *obsolete* exc. *Hist.* M16.

5 a Of a horse etc.: admit of being ridden, carry a rider, esp. in a specified way. L15. ▸**b** Of a stream, river, etc.: admit of being crossed on horseback. *Scot.* L18. ▸**c** Of land: be of a specified character for riding on, bear being ridden on. M19. ▸**d** Of a vehicle: admit of being driven, progress, in respect of comfort and smoothness. L20.
6 Rest or turn (as) on a pivot, axle, etc.; *fig.* rely or depend on something. (Foll. by *on, upon.*) L16. ▸**b** Extend or project *over* something; protrude; overlap. E17.

🕮 **1** S. O'FAOLÁIN Mounting my bicycle I . . rode on happily. M. MITCHELL They had a horse now and . . could ride instead of walk. E. COXHEAD She apparently had only one criterion 'Does he ride?' **2** R. MUDIE The bird rides lightly on the wing. C. BOWEN Safely and swiftly the fleet rides over the wave. *fig.: Sport* Cambridge United this season are riding on the crest of a wave. **b** G. DEARMER Rolling battleships at anchor ride. **c** E. MANNIN The moon rode high in the sky. **4** B. PYM They could have ridden on top of a bus together. **5d** *Milestones* The car rode quite well, handling bad surfaces with aplomb. **6** *Sunday Express* The hopes of British chess-players are riding on this match.

▸**II** *verb trans.* **7** Sit on and direct the movement of (a horse, mule, camel, elephant, etc., or a cycle). ME. ▸**b** RACING. Urge (a horse etc.) to excessive speed. M19. ▸**c** Travel in or on (a vehicle, freq. a public one), be a passenger on or in. Chiefly *N. Amer.* E20.
8 Ride over or through (land, a road, etc.) on a horse etc. or cycle; traverse (a certain distance) on a horse etc. or a cycle. ME. ▸**b** Take part in (a race) or complete (a race, course, etc.) on a horse etc. or a cycle. LME. ▸**c** Traverse on horseback in order to revive knowledge of or confirm (a boundary). LME. ▸**d** Ford or cross (a stream, river etc.) on horseback. *Scot. & north.* E16. ▸**e** Go in procession on horseback to open (Parliament, a market, a fair, etc.). *Scot.* (now *Hist.*). E17.
9 Have sexual intercourse with. Now *coarse slang.* LME.
10 Rest on, esp. by projecting or overlapping. LME.
11 (Of a ship etc.) withstand (a storm) without significant damage; *fig.* endure, survive, (pressure etc.); yield to so as to reduce the impact of (a blow etc.). Freq. foll. by *out.* E16.
12 Oppress, harass, trouble; tyrannize over, dominate completely. Orig. *spec.* (of a nightmare or witch), sit on a (person), use as a horse. Freq. as RIDDEN *adjective.* L16. ▸**b** Annoy, worry, pester. *colloq.* (orig. *US*). E20.
13 Be carried along or supported on, esp. lightly or smoothly. L16.
14 Convey in a cart or other vehicle. Chiefly *US.* L17.
15 Cause (a person) to ride, give a ride to; (of a rider) cause (a horse etc.) to move forward; drive *out of* a place on horseback. Formerly freq. in ***ride on a rail***, ***ride out of town on a rail*** s.v. RAIL *noun*[2]. E18. ▸**b** Keep (a ship) moored; secure or maintain at anchor. E18.

🕮 **7** M. W. MONTAGU I never rid a horse so much at my command in my life. D. LEAVITT He is . . riding his bicycle to the shopping mall. **c** *Publishers Weekly* You could ride the subway for a nickel. **8** W. MORRIS They ride the lealand highways, they ride the desert plain. P. GUEDALLA An obliging innkeeper rode twenty miles to tell him . . Clausel was safely lodged. **11** K. O'HARA He could have . . ridden the publicity. C. FRANCIS The offshore sailor must be prepared to . . ride out gales at sea. *Philadelphia Inquirer* There's always going to be prejudice . . but we have to ride it out. **13** *Daily News* She rides the waves instead of labouring through them. **15** SEBA SMITH Others . . proposed . . riding him out of town on a rail. I. SHAW I'll ride you over to the YMCA.

Phrases: **let a thing ride** let a thing take its natural course, leave a thing alone. **ride a hobby** pursue a favourite occupation or subject to an excessive degree. **ride and tie** (usu. of two people) travel with one horse by alternately riding and walking, each person riding ahead for some distance and tying up the horse for the one following. ***ride a tiger***: see TIGER *noun*. ***ride bodkin***: see BODKIN 4. ***ride cushions***: see ***ride the cushions*** below. **ride for a fall** act recklessly or arrogantly risking failure or defeat. ***ride herd on***: see HERD *noun*[1] 1. ***ride off into the sunset***: see SUNSET *noun* 1. ***ride on a rail***: see RAIL *noun*[2]. ***ride one's luck***: see LUCK *noun*. ***ride out of town on a rail***: see RAIL *noun*[2]. ***ride pillion***: see PILLION *noun*. ***ride roughshod over***: see ROUGH *adverb*. ***ride rusty***: see RUSTY *adjective*[3] 1. ***ride short***: see SHORT *adverb*. **ride shotgun** (chiefly *N. Amer.*) travel as an (armed) guard in the seat next to the driver of a vehicle; ride in the passenger seat of a vehicle; act as a protector. ***ride switch and spur***: see SPUR *noun*[1]. **ride the blind(s)** *US slang* travel on a blind baggage car without paying one's fare. **ride the clutch** keep one's foot too long on the clutch pedal of a motor vehicle, keeping it partially engaged. **ride the cushions**, **ride cushions** *US slang* travel on a train as a paying passenger. **ride the fade**, **ride the gain** BROADCASTING reduce or increase the gain when the input signal becomes too large or too small, in order to keep the output within the limits of succeeding equipment. **ride the lightning** *US slang* suffer execution on the electric chair. ***ride the line***: see LINE *noun*[2]. **ride the rails** *N. Amer. slang* travel by rail, esp. without a ticket. **ride the rods** *N. Amer. slang* travel on a bar underneath a railway carriage or wagon. ***ride the*** SKIMMINGTON. ***ride the stang***: see STANG *noun*[1]. ***ride to hounds***: see HOUND *noun*[1] 2. ***ride to scale***: see SCALE *noun*[1]. ***ride whip and spur***: see SPUR *noun*[1]. **ride work** exercise a racehorse.
With adverbs in specialized senses: **ride again** reappear, esp. unexpectedly and reinvigorated or modified (esp. in — *rides again*). **ride down** overtake on horseback; trample with a horse; exhaust (a horse) by excessive riding. **ride high** be ambitious, successful, or celebrated. **ride off** (*a*) cut (an animal) off from a herd by skilful riding; (*b*) *transf.* lead (a person) away from a subject etc., sidetrack; (*c*) POLO edge *off* (an opponent). **ride out** = ***ride off*** (a) above; (see also sense 11 above). **ride up** (of a garment etc.) move out of the proper position; work up the body so as to form folds or creases, ruck up.
Comb.: **ride-off** in an equestrian competition, a round or phase of competition to resolve a tie or determine qualifiers for a later stage; **ride-on** *adjective & noun* (designating) a power-driven lawnmower etc. on which the operator rides.

rideable *adjective* var. of RIDABLE.

rided /ˈrʌɪdɪd/ *adjective. rare.* L19.
[from RIDE *noun* + -ED[2].]
Having rides or woodland tracks.

ridel /ˈrʌɪd(ə)l/ *noun. arch.* Also **riddel** /ˈrɪd(ə)l/. ME.
[Old French (mod. *rideau*): see -EL[2].]
A curtain, now *esp.* an altar curtain.

rideman /ˈrʌɪdmən/ *noun.* Pl. **-men**. ME.
[from RIDE *verb, noun* + MAN *noun*.]
†**1** A riding bailiff. Only in ME.
2 An operator of a roundabout, roller-coaster, etc., at an amusement park or fair. *US slang.* E20.
3 In jazz etc., a musician playing in an easily flowing or swinging rhythm. *slang.* M20.

rident /ˈrʌɪd(ə)nt/ *adjective. rare.* E17.
[Latin *rident-* pres. ppl stem of *ridere* laugh: see -ENT.]
Radiantly cheerful, riant.

rideout /ˈrʌɪdaʊt/ *noun.* Also **ride-out**. M18.
[from RIDE *verb* + OUT *adverb*.]
†**1** = RIDER *noun* 6. Only in M18.
2 In jazz etc., a final chorus. *slang.* M20.

rider /ˈrʌɪdə/ *noun.* LOE.
[from RIDE *verb* + -ER[1].]
▸**I 1 a** A mounted warrior, a knight. Long *arch.* LOE. ▸**b** A mounted bandit or raider, formerly *spec.*, in the Scottish Borders in the 16th and 17th cents.; a moss-trooper. M16.
2 *gen.* A person who rides, *esp.* a person riding a horse, mule, camel, elephant, etc., or a cycle. Freq. with specifying word. ME. ▸**b** SCOTS LAW. A creditor having a claim on a person who in turn is claiming in a multiplepoinding. E19. ▸**c** A passenger, esp. on public transport. Chiefly *N. Amer.* L19.
†**3** A forest ranger. LME–E18.
4 *Hist.* A gold coin of Flanders and the Netherlands having a horseman on its obverse. Also, a gold coin current in Scotland during the 15th and 16th cents. LME.
5 †**a** A riding master; a horse trainer. M16–L17. ▸**b** A jockey. L18.
6 A commercial traveller. Now *rare* or *obsolete.* M18.
7 A horse (of a specified kind) for riding on. M19.
2 *boundary-rider*, ***dispatch-rider***, ***stock-rider***, etc.
▸**II 8** In *pl.* An additional set of timbers or iron plates used to strengthen the frame of a ship etc. internally or externally. E17.
9 a MINING. = HORSE *noun* 10a. M17. ▸**b** GEOLOGY. A thin seam of coal or deposit of ore overlying a principal seam or lode. L19.
10 a An additional clause or codicil amending or supplementing a drafted document; *esp.* an addition or amendment attached to a legislative bill at its final reading. M17. ▸**b** A corollary from or addition to something said or written; a qualification, a provision. E19. ▸**c** A subsidiary question in an examination (orig. esp. in mathematics). M19. ▸**d** An additional fee paid in kind to a performer etc., usu. in the form of food and drink. Also, a supplementary clause in a performer etc.'s contract specifying particular requirements for accommodation, food, drink, etc. M19. ▸**e** A recommendation or comment added by the jury to a judicial verdict. L19.
11 Any of various objects, components, machine parts, etc., surmounting, bridging, or working on or over others. E18.
12 OPHTHALMOLOGY. Each of a set of opaque lines extending radially outward from the main disc of a cataract. L19.
Phrases etc.: ***easy rider***: see EASY *adjective*. ***rough-rider***: see ROUGH *adjective*. ***stake and rider (fence)***: see STAKE *noun*[1].
■ **rideress** *noun* (*rare*) a female rider, a horsewoman M19. **riderless** *adjective* M19. **ridership** *noun* †(*a*) a rangership; (*b*) (orig. *N. Amer.*) the number of passengers using a particular form of public transport: LME.

rider /ˈrʌɪdə/ *verb trans. US.* M18.
[from the noun.]
Strengthen (a fence) with riders or braces.

ridered /ˈrʌɪdəd/ *adjective.* M19.
[from RIDER *noun, verb*: see -ED[2], -ED[1].]
1 GEOLOGY. Of a rock: traversed by riders. M19.
2 Of a fence: strengthened with riders or braces. Also (*rare*), having a ridered fence. *US.* M19.

ridge /rɪdʒ/ *noun*[1].
[Old English *hrycg* = Old Frisian *hregg*, Old Saxon *hruggi* (Middle Dutch *ruc*, Dutch *rug*), Old High German *hrucki* (German *Rücken*), Old Norse *hryggr*, from Germanic. Cf. RIG *noun*[1].]
1 The back or spine of a human or animal. Long *rare* or *obsolete.* OE.
2 The line or edge formed, *spec.* on a roof, by the junction of two surfaces sloping upwards towards each other; the long and narrow crest or top *of* anything. OE.
3 A long and narrow hilltop, mountain range, or watershed; a range or chain *of* hills or mountains; a line or reef of rocks. OE. ▸**b** METEOROLOGY. An elongated region of high barometric pressure. L19.
4 a AGRICULTURE. A raised strip of arable land, usu. one of a series, separated by furrows, into which a field is divided; *Hist.* this used as a measure of land. ME. ▸**b** HORTICULTURE. A raised hotbed on which cucumbers, melons, etc., are planted. E18.
5 A narrow elevation or raised band running along or across a surface; a raised line or strip *of* something. LME. ▸**b** = BAR *noun*[1] 7. E18. ▸**c** Any of the many raised lines on the skin esp. noticeable on the fingers, the palm of the hand, and the sole of the foot. M19.

🕮 **2** *Harper's Magazine* I made out the . . ridge of the back of a tremendous old bull. V. SACKVILLE-WEST Anquetil went up . . the sloping tiles. Cautiously he got astride the ridge. ***alveolar ridge***, ***brow ridge***, ***milk ridge***, etc. **3** GIBBON A ridge of hills, rising from the Danube, and called the Carpathian mountains. G. SAYER The Malvern Hills consist of a single ridge about ten miles long. **5** C. MUNGOSHI The grandfather carefully pinched . . the ridge of flesh just above the bridge of his nose. **c** E. WALLACE Line for line, ridge for ridge . . it is Millburgh's thumbprint.

Comb.: **ridgeback** (an animal of) a breed of dog having a short light-brown coat and a ridge of hair along the middle of the back, growing in the opposite direction to the rest of the coat; also more fully ***Rhodesian ridgeback***; **ridge-band** (now *dial.*) = ***backband*** s.v. BACK-; **ridge-bone** (now *rare* or *obsolete*) the spine, the backbone; **ridge cucumber** a variety of cucumber which is grown outside in temperate climates, freq. on ridges of soil (cf. sense 4b above) and is shorter than the greenhouse variety; **ridge-piece** a horizontal beam along the ridge of a roof, into which the rafters are fastened; **ridge-pole** (*a*) the horizontal pole of a ridge tent; (*b*) = ***ridge-piece*** above; **ridge runner** *US slang* a southern mountain farmer, a hillbilly; **ridge stone** (*a*) a curbstone for a well; (*b*) a coping-stone for the ridge of a house; **ridge tent** a tent having a central ridge supported by a pole or frame at each end; **ridge-tile** a (freq. decorative) tile of semicircular or curved section covering the ridge and sometimes the hips of a roof; **ridge-tree** = ***ridge-piece*** above.
■ **ridgewise** *adverb* in the manner or form of a ridge E18.

ridge /ˈrɪdʒ/ *noun*[2]. *slang* (now *US*). M17.
[Origin unkn.]
Gold; (a) gold coin; (a) metal coin.

ridge /rɪdʒ/ *adjective. Austral. slang.* M20.
[from RIDGE *noun*[2].]
Good, all right, genuine.

ridge /rɪdʒ/ *verb.* ME.
[from RIDGE *noun*[1]. Cf. RIG *verb*[1].]
1 *verb trans.* AGRICULTURE. Break up (land, a field, etc.) into ridges. Freq. foll. by *up.* ME.
2 *verb trans.* Provide (a building etc.) with a ridge or a covering for this; make or renew the ridge of (a house etc.). LME.
3 *verb trans.* Mark (as) with a ridge or ridges; raise ridges, bands, or ripples on (a surface). L17.
4 *verb trans.* HORTICULTURE. Plant (cucumbers, melons, etc.) in ridges or hotbeds. Freq. foll. by *out.* M18. ▸**b** Cover with soil *in* ridges; arrange in ridges. E19.
5 *verb intrans.* Form ridges; rise (*up*) in ridges. M19.
■ **ridger** *noun* (*a*) *dial.* = ***ridge-band*** s.v. RIDGE *noun*[1]; (*b*) AGRICULTURE an implement for ridging soil: M18. **ridging** *noun* (*a*) the action of the verb; (*b*) the ridge of a building: LME.

ridged /rɪdʒd/ *adjective.* ME.
[from RIDGE *noun*[1], *verb*: see -ED[2], -ED[1].]
Provided with a ridge or ridges, that has been ridged.

ridgel /ˈrɪdʒ(ə)l/ *noun.* Now *dial.* L16.
[App. from RIDGE *noun*[1], the testicle being thought of as remaining near the animal's back: see -EL[1]. Cf. earlier RIG *noun*[1] 2, RIDGELING.]
An animal imperfectly castrated or having genitals not properly developed; *esp.* a male ram, bull, or horse, with only one testicle.

ridgelet /ˈrɪdʒlɪt/ *noun.* Also **ridglet**. L18.
[from RIDGE *noun*[1] + -LET.]
A small ridge, esp. of earth.

ridgeling /ˈrɪdʒlɪŋ/ *noun.* Now *rare.* M16.
[from (the same root as) RIDGEL: see -ING[3], -LING[1].]
= RIDGEL.

ridgeway /ˈrɪdʒweɪ/ *noun.* OE.
[from RIDGE *noun*[1] + WAY *noun*.]
A track or road along a ridge, *esp.* one following the ridge of downs or low hills.

ridglet *noun* var. of RIDGELET.

ridgy /ˈrɪdʒi/ *adjective.* L17.
[from RIDGE *noun*[1] + -Y[1].]
Rising in or covered with ridges; having the form of a ridge.

🕮 I. MURDOCH He felt the ridgy densely textured bark of the tree.

ridgy-didge /rɪdʒɪˈdɪdʒ/ *adjective. Austral. slang.* M20.
[Redupl. of RIDGE *adjective.*]
= RIDGE *adjective.*

ridicule /ˈrɪdɪkjuːl/ *noun*[1]. L17.
[French, or its source Latin *ridiculum* use as noun of neut. sing. of *ridiculus* laughable, from *ridere* laugh.]
1 A ridiculous or absurd thing, characteristic, or habit; an absurdity. Now *rare.* L17.
2 Subjection to mocking and dismissive language or behaviour; the action or practice of ridiculing a person or thing; mockery, derision. L17.
3 Ridiculous nature or character (*of* a thing), ridiculousness; that which is ridiculous. E18.
†**4** A piece of derisive mirth or light mockery. E18–E19.

📖 **2** J. KLEIN Adults are often very disrespectful toward children's expression of feeling, showing amusement or ridicule. M. LANE She bravely bore the ridicule of the male establishment.

■ †**ridicle** *noun* = RIDICULE *noun*[1] 1: only in L16.

ridicule /ˈrɪdɪkjuːl/ *noun*[2]. *obsolete* exc. *dial.* E19.
[French, alt. of *réticule* RETICULE.]
= RETICULE 2.

ridicule /ˈrɪdɪkjuːl/ *verb trans.* L17.
[from RIDICULE *noun*[1].]
Subject to ridicule or mockery; make fun of, deride, laugh at. Formerly also (*rare*), make ridiculous.

📖 R. MACAULAY He ridiculed . . the ideals of those who cried for improvement. M. SEYMOUR He had seized on the chance to ridicule her in public.

■ **ridiculer** *noun* E18.

ridiculize /rɪˈdɪkjʊlʌɪz/ *verb trans. rare.* Also **-ise**. E17.
[formed as prec. + -IZE.]
Make ridiculous, ridicule.

ridiculosity /rɪˌdɪkjʊˈlɒsɪti/ *noun. rare.* E18.
[from next + -ITY.]
A ridiculous matter; ridiculousness.

ridiculous /rɪˈdɪkjʊləs/ *adjective, noun, & adverb.* M16.
[Latin (*ridiculosus* from) *ridiculus*: see RIDICULE *noun*[1], -OUS. Cf. French †*ridiculeux*.]
▶ **A** *adjective.* **1** Deserving or inviting ridicule or derisive laughter; absurd, preposterous, laughable. M16. ▸**b** Outrageous, scandalous, shameful (now *dial.* & *US*). Also (*colloq.*), unbelievable, astounding; outstanding, excellent. M19.
†**2** Derisive, mocking. *rare.* E17–L18.

📖 **1** V. BRITTAIN A realistic sense of humour always saved her from becoming ridiculous. O. MANNING Inchcape spoke as though marriage were some ridiculous custom of primitive tribes. M. MUGGERIDGE A ridiculous looking man, with tiny legs, . . a protruding stomach, and a large head. **b** J. B. MORTON The ridiculous speed with which big boats butt through the waves. *Melody Maker* But his swing is ridiculous He's got everything going for him.

▶ **B** *absol.* as *noun.* ***the ridiculous***, that which is ridiculous. M18.

📖 *Westminster Review* There is but one step, said Napoleon, from the sublime to the ridiculous.

▶ **C** *adverb.* Ridiculously. *non-standard.* M19.

📖 *Daily Mirror* Don't talk ridiculous!

■ **ridiculously** *adverb* M16. **ridiculousness** *noun* E17.

riding /ˈrʌɪdɪŋ/ *noun*[1]. OE.
[Old Norse *þriðjungr* third part, from *þriði* third, with early assim. of initial consonant to last of *east, west, north*: see -ING[3]. Cf. TRITHING.]
1 Each of the three administrative districts (***East Riding***, ***West Riding***, ***North Riding***) into which the county of Yorkshire in N. England was formerly divided. OE.
2 A similar division of other counties or districts in Britain or its former colonies. L17. ▸**b** *spec.* An electoral district in Canada. L18.

riding /ˈrʌɪdɪŋ/ *noun*[2]. ME.
[from RIDE *verb* + -ING[1].]
1 The action of RIDE *verb*; an instance of this; practice or skill of sitting on and directing the movement of a horse, mule, camel, elephant, etc.; a journey or expedition made on horseback. ME. ▸**b** A procession or parade in mockery of an instance of marital violence or disharmony, infidelity, etc. *obsolete* exc. *Hist.* M17.
2 A path or track specially intended for riding on horseback; *esp.* a green lane cut through a wood, a ride. ME.
3 NAUTICAL. The fact of a ship's lying at anchor; opportunity for doing so; anchorage. M16.
Attrib. & comb.: In the sense 'used or worn in or for horse-riding', as ***riding boot***, ***riding-breeches***, ***riding cane***, ***riding glove***, etc. Special combs., as **riding-coat** a coat worn for riding, *esp.* an overcoat to protect the rider from wet; ***riding-crop***: see CROP *noun* 4; **riding habit** a costume worn for riding; *spec.* = HABIT *noun* 3; **riding-hood** a large hood worn orig. for riding but later by women and children as a general outdoor garment (cf. *Red Riding Hood* s.v. RED *adjective*); **riding-house** *arch.* a large building for practising riding in; a riding-school; **riding lamp**, **riding light** a light shown by a ship when riding at anchor; **riding-master** a teacher of riding or horsemanship; *spec.* (*Hist.*) an officer responsible for the instruction of troopers in a cavalry regiment; **riding sail** a small sail set to keep a vessel steady when riding at anchor; **riding-school** a school or establishment teaching skills in riding or horsemanship.

riding rhyme /ˈrʌɪdɪŋ rʌɪm/ *noun phr.* L16.
[from RIDING *noun*[2] or *riding* ppl adjective of RIDE *verb* + RHYME *noun.*]
A form of verse (the heroic couplet), used esp. by Chaucer in his *Canterbury Tales*.

ridley /ˈrɪdli/ *noun.* E20.
[Origin unkn.]
Either of two marine turtles, the olive-coloured *L. olivacea* of the Indo-Pacific and S. Atlantic, and the rare grey *Lepidochelys kempii* of the N. Atlantic.

ridotto /rɪˈdɒtəʊ/ *noun.* Now *arch.* or *Hist.* Pl. **-os**. E18.
[Italian = French *réduit* from medieval Latin *reductus* use as noun of pa. pple of Latin *reducere* REDUCE.]
An entertainment or ball with music and dancing, freq. in masquerade, popular in the 18th cent.

riebeckite /ˈriːbɛkʌɪt/ *noun.* L19.
[from Emil *Riebeck* (d. 1885), German explorer + -ITE[1].]
MINERALOGY. Any of a group of sodium-containing monoclinic amphiboles, often containing magnesium, found as dark blue or black prismatic crystals, chiefly in alkaline igneous rocks, or as blue asbestos (crocidolite).

riegel /ˈriːg(ə)l/ *noun.* E20.
[German from Middle High German *rigel* crossbar, Old High German *rigil* bar: see RAIL *noun*[2].]
PHYSICAL GEOGRAPHY. A low transverse ridge of resistant bedrock on the floor of a glacial valley, a rock bar.

riel /ˈriːəl/ *noun.* M20.
[Khmer.]
The basic monetary unit of Cambodia, equal to 100 sen.

riem /rɪm, riːm/ *noun. S. Afr.* E19.
[Dutch: see RIM *noun*[2].]
A long strip or thong of dressed softened leather.

Riemann /ˈriːmən/ *noun.* E20.
[G. F. Bernhard *Riemann* (1826–66), German mathematician.]
MATH. Used *attrib.* and in *possess.* to designate various concepts developed by Riemann or arising out of his work.
Riemann–Christoffel tensor [E. B. *Christoffel* (1829–1900), German mathematician] a kind of fourth-order tensor used in describing curved space-time. **Riemann geometry** Riemannian geometry. ***Riemann hypothesis***: see ***Riemann's hypothesis*** below. **Riemann integral** a definite integral calculated by dividing an area under a curve into a number of rectangular intervals of equal width, summing these rectangles, and then taking the limit of the sum as the size of the intervals tends to zero. **Riemann's hypothesis**, **Riemann hypothesis** the hypothesis (as yet unproved) that all the zeros of the Riemann zeta function, except those on the real line, have a real part equal to ½. ***Riemann ZETA function***.

Riemannian /riːˈmanɪən/ *adjective.* L19.
[from prec. + -IAN.]
MATH. Designating, of, or pertaining to (*a*) a general system of differential geometry developed by Riemann and having applications in relativity theory; (*b*) *spec.* a non-Euclidean (elliptic) geometry in which space is everywhere positively curved (cf. LOBACHEVSKIAN).

riempie /ˈrɪmpi, ˈriːmpi/ *noun & adjective. S. Afr.* Also ***riempje***. M19.
[Dutch *riempje*, formed as RIEM + Afrikaans *-ie* dim. suffix.]
▶ **A** *noun.* A fine narrow *riem* or leather thong. M19.
▶ **B** *attrib.* or as *adjective.* Of furniture: having a seat or bottom of criss-crossed fine narrow *riems* or leather thongs. E20.
Comb.: ***riempiestoel*** /-stʊl/ [Afrikaans *stoel* stool] *S. Afr.* a chair with a *riempie* seat.

riemskoen *noun* see REMSKOEN.

rien ne va plus /rjɛ̃ nə va ply/ *interjection.* Also ***rien n'va plus***. L19.
[French.]
In roulette, the call made by the croupier while the wheel is spinning: no more bets!

Riesling /ˈriːzlɪŋ, -slɪŋ/ *noun.* M19.
[German.]
A dry white wine produced in Germany, Austria, Alsace, and elsewhere; the variety of vine and grape from which this is produced.

rietbok /ˈrɪtbɒk, *foreign* ritbɔk/ *noun.* Chiefly *S. Afr.* Also **reit-, -buck** /-bʌk/. L18.
[Dutch *rietbok*, from *riet* REED *noun*[1] + *bok* BUCK *noun*[1].]
= REEDBUCK.

Rif *noun & adjective* var. of RIFF *noun*[3] *& adjective.*

rifacimento /rɪˌfatʃɪˈmɛntəʊ, *foreign* rifatʃiˈmento/ *noun.* Pl. **-ti** /-ti/. L18.
[Italian, from *rifac-* stem of *rifare* remake.]
A remodelling or recasting of a literary work.

rifampicin /rɪˈfampɪsɪn/ *noun.* M20.
[from next with inserted *pi-* from *piperazine*.]
PHARMACOLOGY. A reddish-brown crystalline powder, a member of the rifamycin group of antibiotics, which is given orally to treat a range of diseases, esp. tuberculosis.
■ Also **rifampin** *noun* (chiefly *N. Amer.*) M20.

rifamycin /riːfəˈmʌɪsɪn/ *noun.* Also (earlier) **rifo-**. M20.
[Prob. from Italian *riformare* reform + -MYCIN.]
PHARMACOLOGY. Any of a class of natural and semisynthetic antibiotics first isolated from the bacterium *Streptomyces mediterranei*.

rife /rʌɪf/ *pred. adjective & adverb.*
[Late Old English *rȳfe*, prob. from Old Norse *rífr* good, acceptable = West Frisian *rju*, Middle Low German *rīve*, Middle Dutch *rīve*, *rijf* abundant, from Germanic: cf. Old Norse *reifa* enrich, *reifr* glad, cheerful.]
▶ **A** *adjective.* **1** Esp. of something regarded as undesirable or harmful: of common or frequent occurrence, prevalent, widespread. LOE. ▸†**b** Customary or common *to* or *with* a person. LME–M17.
2 Of a rumour, report, etc.: generally circulating, abroad, current. ME. ▸**b** Of a word or phrase: commonly used or heard. Esp. in ***rife in mouth***, ***rife in one's mouth***. Now *rare.* E16.
†**3** Famous, renowned. ME–L15.
4 Abundant, plentiful; numerous. ME.
5 Foll. by *with*, (now *rare*) *in*, *of*: having much or many, rich with, full of. ME.
6 Disposed, inclined; ready, prompt; quick. (Foll. by *for*.) Now *dial.* LME.

📖 **1** T. H. HUXLEY Volcanic action must have been rife on an enormous scale. C. FRANCIS Disease was rife and thirteen times as many . . died from illness as from battle injury. **2** J. A. FROUDE A rumour of the queen's arrest was rife in London. *Economist* Speculation was rife that a . . meeting was being arranged. **5** R. BROOKE All the shade Is rife with magic and movement.

▶ **B** *adverb.* †**1** Numerously, in large numbers. Only in ME.
2 Abundantly, copiously, plentifully. ME.
†**3** Frequently, often. ME–E17.
†**4** Promptly, speedily, readily. ME–E16.
■ †**rifely** *adverb* ME–M17. **rifeness** *noun* (*rare*) LME.

†**riff** *noun*[1]. Only in ME.
[Old French *rif* (*et raf*), ult. of Germanic origin. Cf. RAFF *noun*[1].]
riff and raff, all persons and things collectively, everybody, everything.
¶ Survives as 1st elem. of RIFF-RAFF.

riff /rɪf/ *noun*[2]. *obsolete* exc. *dial.* L16.
[Perh. repr. Old English *hrifþo*, from *hrēof* scabbed, leprous, or from Old French *rifle*, French dial. *riffle* in same sense.]
A cutaneous eruption; scabies, mange.

Riff /rɪf/ *noun*[3] *& adjective.* Also **Rif**. E20.
[*Rīf* an area of NE Morocco.]
▶ **A** *noun.* Pl. same, **-s**. A Berber of the Rīf area of Morocco; the Hamito-Semitic language of the Berbers of this area. E20.
▶ **B** *attrib.* or as *adjective.* Of or pertaining to the Riff or their language. E20.

riff /rɪf/ *noun*[4] *& verb.* E20.
[Abbreviation of RIFFLE *noun.*]
▶ **A** *noun.* **1** In popular music, jazz, etc., a short repeated phrase, freq. played over changing chords or harmonies or used as a background to a solo improvisation. E20.
2 *transf.* & *fig.* A repeated phrase, idea, or situation. L20.

📖 **1** M. BOOTH Mel's violin scrawking against the drums and the low riff of the electronic piano.

▶ **B** *verb intrans.* In popular music, jazz, etc.: play riffs. M20.

†**riff** *noun*[5] see REEF *noun*[2].

Riffian /ˈrɪfɪən/ *noun & adjective.* M19.
[formed as RIFF *noun*[3] *& adjective* + -IAN.]
= RIFF *noun*[3] *& adjective.*

riffle /ˈrɪf(ə)l/ *noun.* M17.
[from the verb.]
▶ **I** †**1** A scratch, a slight abrasion. *Scot.* Only in M17.
2 An act or instance of riffling something; a quick skim or leaf through a book, papers, etc.; a shuffle performed by riffling playing-cards (also ***riffle-shuffle***). L19.

📖 **2** *Guardian* I skimmed the book in a first riffle.

▶ **II 3** A rocky or shallow part of a river or stream where the water flows brokenly; a rapid; a patch of ripples or waves. Chiefly *N. Amer.* L18. ▸**b** A ripple, a ruffle. M20.
4 A slat, groove, or channel set across a trough or sluice to break the flow of a liquid or to filter (orig. esp. gold) particles from water. Orig. *US.* M19.

📖 **3 make the riffle** succeed in crossing a rapid; *fig.* be successful in an undertaking. **b** P. GALLICO A riffle of wind that swept down the valley from Hermon.

Comb.: **riffle beetle** any of various small aquatic beetles constituting the family Elmidae, which live in fast-flowing water.
■ **riffled** *adjective* having or provided with riffles **E20.**

riffle /ˈrɪf(ə)l/ *verb.* **M17.**
[Perh. partly a var. of RUFFLE *verb*[1], partly from French †*riffler* = Old & mod. French *rifler* RIFLE *verb*[1]. Infl. by RIPPLE *verb*[1].]
1 †**a** *verb intrans.* Caress one another. *rare.* Only in **M17.** ▸**b** *verb trans.* Handle tentatively or gently; caress; ruffle in a light or rippling manner. **M19.**
2 *verb intrans.* Of water: form a ripple or a rapid. *US. rare.* **M18.**
3 a *verb trans.* CARDS. Shuffle (cards) by flicking up and releasing the corners or sides of two piles of cards so that they intermingle and may be slid together to form a single pile. **L19.** ▸**b** *verb trans.* Flick through (a book, pages, papers etc.); thumb through (a book etc.), releasing the leaves in (esp. rapid) succession. **E20.** ▸**c** *verb intrans.* Thumb or leaf *through*, search quickly *through*. **M20.**

> **1b** P. THEROUX A stiff breeze riffling the Lombardy poplars. **3b** J. TUSA The officer . . riffles the passport pages. **c** M. LEAPMAN Riffling through books of etiquette. P. AUSTER I ransacked the closet . . riffling through drawers.

riffler /ˈrɪflə/ *noun*[1]. **L18.**
[French *rifloir*, formed as RIFLE *verb*[1]: see -ER[2].]
A tool with a curved file-surface at each end, used in carving, metalworking, etc.

riffler /ˈrɪflə/ *noun*[2]. **E19.**
[from RIFFLE *noun or verb* + -ER[1].]
1 A horse-hoe, a scuffler. *dial.* **E19.**
2 A trough or sluice containing one or more transverse strips or slats to break or slow the flow of a liquid. **M19.**

riffling /ˈrɪflɪŋ/ *noun.* **E20.**
[from RIFFLE *noun, verb* + -ING[1].]
1 An arrangement or system of riffles or filters. **E20.**
2 The action of RIFFLE *verb*; an instance of this. **M20.**

riffling /ˈrɪflɪŋ/ *ppl adjective.* **M18.**
[from RIFFLE *verb* + -ING[2].]
That riffles; *spec.* (of water) moving in riffles, agitated.

riff-raff /ˈrɪfraf/ *noun & adjective.* Also **riffraff**. **L15.**
[from *riff and raff* s.v. RIFF *noun*[1]. Cf. RAFF *noun*[1].]
▸ **A** *noun.* **1** *collect.* Disreputable or undesirable people, people of low social class; *the* lowest element *of* a community, class, etc., the rabble. **L15.** ▸**b** A disreputable person, a member of the rabble. *rare.* **E17.**
2 *collect.* Worthless stuff, odds and ends, rubbish. Now *dial.* **E16.**

> **1** W. S. MAUGHAM The riff-raff that frequents the bars of London. M. RENAULT Not even with decent people, but with people . . I consider absolute riff-raff. M. BINCHY A lot of riff-raff have been coming recently, and *loud* people. **b** W. SOYINKA Why do you mix with these gutter boys, these riff-raffs.

▸ **B** *attrib.* or as *adjective.* **1** Of a person: disreputable, low, belonging to the rabble. Now *rare.* **L16.**
2 Of a thing: worthless, rubbishy. Now *dial.* **E17.**
■ **riff-raffy** *adjective* having the character of riff-raff, disreputable **E20.**

riffy /ˈrɪfi/ *adjective.* **M20.**
[from RIFF *noun*[4] + -Y[1].]
Of popular music, jazz, etc.: full of riffs, repetitive.

rifle /ˈrʌɪf(ə)l/ *noun*[1]. Now *dial. & US.* **LME.**
[Old French *riffle* stick, piece of wood. Cf. mod. Norman French *rifle* in same sense as English.]
1 A piece of wood used for sharpening scythes. **LME.**
2 A bent stick attached to the butt of a scythe for laying corn in rows. **L16.**

rifle /ˈrʌɪf(ə)l/ *noun*[2]. **L17.**
[from RIFLE *verb*[3].]
1 Each of a set of spiral grooves cut on the interior surface of the barrel or bore of a gun. Earliest in ***rifle gun*** below. **L17.**
2 A gun, *esp.* one fired from shoulder-level, having a long spirally grooved barrel intended to make a bullet etc. spin and thereby have greater accuracy over a longer distance. Freq. with specifying word. **L18.** ▸**b** In *pl.* Troops armed with rifles, riflemen. **M19.** ▸**c** A hunter armed with a rifle. Cf. GUN *noun* 4. **M20.**
2 ***Enfield rifle, Garand rifle, Kentucky rifle, Mannlicher rifle, Martini rifle, Springfield rifle***, etc. ***express rifle***: see EXPRESS *adjective.* ***telescopic-rifle***: see TELESCOPIC 1.
Comb.: **rifle-green** *adjective & noun* (of) the dark green colour of a rifleman's uniform; **rifle-gun** (now *arch. & US dial.*): = sense 2 above; **rifle microphone**, (*colloq.*) **rifle mike** *US* = ***gun microphone*** s.v. GUN *noun*; **rifle-range** (*a*) the distance able to be reached by a bullet from a rifle; (*b*) a place for practising shooting with a rifle; **rifle regiment** a regiment of troops armed with rifles; **rifle-shot** (*a*) = ***rifle-range*** (a) above; (*b*) a person skilled (to a specified degree) in shooting with a rifle; (*c*) a shot fired with a rifle.
■ **riflery** /ˈrʌɪf(ə)lri/ *noun* (chiefly *US*) rifles collectively; firing from or shooting with rifles: **M19. riflescope** *noun* (*US*) a telescopic rifle sight **M20.**

rifle /ˈrʌɪf(ə)l/ *verb*[1]. **ME.**
[Old & mod. French *rifler*, †*riffler* scrape, scratch, plunder, ult. of Germanic origin. Cf. RIFLE *verb*[3].]
1 a *verb trans.* Rob (a person) methodically, esp. by searching pockets or clothes; ransack, plunder, or pillage (a receptacle, place, etc.) thoroughly with intent to steal; rob or strip bare *of* something. **ME.** ▸**b** *verb intrans.* Make a vigorous search *through.* **M20.**
2 *verb trans.* Carry off as booty; plunder, steal. **LME.**
†**3** *verb trans.* Affect strongly or injuriously; break or strip off. **E17–L18.**

> **1a** GOLDSMITH We'll rifle the spring of its earliest bloom. DISRAELI The most skilful plunderer that ever rifled the dying. J. MALCOLM The danger of a . . bank being rifled. *Times* The officer went into the shop, and found him rifling the till. **b** A. ALVAREZ He began to search, rifling through the shirts . . in the chest of drawers. **2** F. W. ROBERTSON The bodies have been rifled from their mausoleum.

rifle /ˈrʌɪf(ə)l/ *verb*[2]. *obsolete* exc. *dial.* **L16.**
[Dutch *rijfelen* rel. to French *rafler* RAFFLE *verb*[1].]
1 *verb intrans.* Play at dice; gamble (*for* a stake). **L16.**
2 *verb trans.* Dispose of by dicing or raffling; gamble *away.* **E17.**

rifle /ˈrʌɪf(ə)l/ *verb*[3]. **M17.**
[In sense 1 formed as RIFLE *verb*[1], in senses 2, 3 from RIFLE *noun*[2] 1.]
1 *verb trans.* Form spiral grooves in (a gun or the barrel or bore of a gun) to make a bullet etc. spin and thereby have greater accuracy over a longer distance. **M17.**
2 *verb trans. & intrans.* Shoot (*at*) with a rifle. **E19.**
3 *verb trans.* Hit or kick (a ball etc.) hard and straight. **M20.**

> **3** *Guardian* Robson . . seized on a rebound . . and joyfully rifled the equaliser past Shilton.

rifle bird /ˈrʌɪf(ə)l bəːd/ *noun phr.* **M19.**
[App. from RIFLE *noun*[2], either imit., or from a resemblance of the plumage to a military uniform.]
Each of three birds of paradise of the genus *Ptiloris*, having velvety black plumage with bright coloured patches, and a long bill.
magnificent rifle bird *Ptiloris magnificus*, of northern Queensland and New Guinea. **paradise rifle bird** *Ptiloris paradiseus*, of eastern Australia. **Queen Victoria rifle bird, Queen Victoria's rifle bird, Victoria's rifle bird** *Ptiloris victoriae*, of Queensland.

rifled /ˈrʌɪf(ə)ld/ *adjective*[1]. **E17.**
[from RIFLE *verb*[1] + -ED[1].]
Plundered, pillaged, ransacked. Formerly also, disordered, disarranged, ruffled.
¶ Earliest in UNRIFLED *adjective*[1].

rifled /ˈrʌɪf(ə)ld/ *adjective*[2]. **E17.**
[from RIFLE *verb*[3] + -ED[1].]
1 Of a gun: having a spirally grooved bore. **E17.**
2 Of a bullet etc.: having projecting studs or ribs fitting into corresponding grooves in a gun barrel; (of a shotgun cartridge) grooved. **M18.**

rifleman /ˈrʌɪf(ə)lmən/ *noun.* Pl. **-men**. **M18.**
[from RIFLE *noun*[2] + MAN *noun.*]
1 A soldier armed with a rifle; a member, esp. a private, of a rifle regiment; a person skilled with or using a rifle. **M18.**
2 †**a** = RIFLE BIRD. Only in **19.** ▸**b** A small green and yellow New Zealand wren, *Acanthisitta chloris.* **L19.**

rifler /ˈrʌɪflə/ *noun*[1]. **ME.**
[from RIFLE *verb*[1] + -ER[1].]
1 A robber, a thief; a plunderer. **ME.**
2 FALCONRY. A hawk that grasps only feathers in striking at the quarry. Long *arch.* **L15.**

rifler /ˈrʌɪflə/ *noun*[2]. Now *rare* or *obsolete.* **L18.**
[from RIFLE *noun*[2] or *verb*[3] + -ER[1].]
= RIFLEMAN 1.

rifling /ˈrʌɪflɪŋ/ *noun*[1]. **ME.**
[from RIFLE *verb*[1] + -ING[1].]
The action of RIFLE *verb*[1]; an instance of this, a robbery, a sacking.

rifling /ˈrʌɪflɪŋ/ *noun*[2]. **L18.**
[from RIFLE *verb*[3] + -ING[1].]
The arrangement of spiral grooves on the inside of a gun barrel; the making of these grooves.

rifomycin *noun* see RIFAMYCIN.

rift /rɪft/ *noun*[1]. **ME.**
[Of Scandinavian origin (cf. Old Norse *ript* breach of contract, Norwegian, Danish *rift* cleft, chink): rel. to RIVE *verb.* Cf. RIFT *verb*[1], REFT *noun.*]
†**1** An act of tearing or rending, a splitting. Only in **ME.**
2 A cleft or fissure in the earth, a rock, etc.; an opening or break in a cloud or mist; a crack or split in an object. **LME.** ▸**b** QUARRYING. Any of a series of parallel planes along which (esp. igneous) rock may be split most easily, freq. distinct from the natural bedding planes; the property of rock capable of splitting in this way. Chiefly *US.* **L19.** ▸**c** A large fault running parallel to the major regional relief, esp. one bounding a rift valley. Also, a rift valley. **E20.**
3 Oak timber split into strips or boards, rather than being sawn. Also ***rift timber***. Now *rare.* **L16.**
4 A break in friendly relations between individuals, groups, nations, etc.; a division, a schism, a dissension. **E17.**

> **2** G. HUNTINGTON Though the rain had been stopping . . there was still no rift in the clouds. F. HOYLE The ice . . sometimes cracks open, forming a narrow rift.
> **4** JO GRIMOND The only way to heal the rift in industry was partnership between workers and management. F. SPALDING The divergence of opinion inevitably created a rift between the sisters.

Comb.: **rift block** GEOLOGY a horst or a graben; **rift-sawn** *adjective* (of timber) sawn radially, across the annual rings; quarter-sawn; **rift valley** a large elongated valley with steep walls formed by the depression of a block of the earth's surface between nearly parallel faults or fault-zones (cf. GRABEN); ***Great Rift Valley***, an extensive system of rift valleys running from the Jordan Valley through the Red Sea to E. Africa; ***Rift Valley fever***, a disease of animals in E. Africa, caused by an arbovirus, which can affect humans as a mild fever.
■ **riftless** *adjective* **L18. rifty** *adjective* having rifts, full of rifts or chinks **M16.**

rift /rɪft/ *noun*[2]. Long *obsolete* exc. *Scot. & north.* **LME.**
[from RIFT *verb*[2].]
An act of belching, a belch.

rift /rɪft/ *noun*[3]. *US.* **E18.**
[Perh. alt. of †*riff* var. of REEF *noun*[2].]
1 A rapid, a cataract, *esp.* one formed by the protrusion of rocks in the bed of a stream. **E18.**
2 The wash of the surf on a beach or shore. **M19.**

rift /rɪft/ *verb*[1]. Pa. pple **rifted**, †**rift**. **ME.**
[Of Scandinavian origin (cf. Old Norse *ripta* make void, invalidate). Cf. RIFT *noun*[1].]
1 *verb intrans.* Form fissures or clefts; gape open, split; move or drift apart. **ME.**
2 *verb trans.* Tear or split (a thing) apart, cleave, rend. Freq. as ***rifted ppl adjective.*** **M16.** ▸**b** Form or force by cleaving. **M19.**

> **1** *Scientific American* They rift apart over millions of years. **2** SHELLEY New fire From earthquake-rifted mountains of bright snow Shook its portentous hair.

rift /rɪft/ *verb*[2]. Long *obsolete* exc. *Scot. & north.* **ME.**
[Old Norse *rypta.*]
1 *verb trans.* Belch out (wind etc.); emit or utter (as) by belching. **ME.**
2 *verb intrans.* Belch. **ME.** ▸**b** Rise *up* on the stomach; *fig.* come back unpleasantly to the memory. **M17.** ▸**c** Boast, brag. *Scot.* **E18.**

rifting /ˈrɪftɪŋ/ *verbal noun.* **L19.**
[from RIFT *noun*[1] or *verb*[1] + -ING[1].]
1 The presence of rifts or cleavage planes in rock; the action of splitting rock, esp. mica, into thick slabs or sheets. **L19.**
2 GEOLOGY. The formation of rifts dividing the earth's crust into distinct blocks or plates. **E20.**

rig /rɪɡ/ *noun*[1]. *dial.* **ME.**
[Var. of RIDGE *noun*[1].]
1 = RIDGE *noun*[1]. *Scot. & north.* **ME.**
2 = RIDGEL. **LME.**

rig /rɪɡ/ *noun*[2]. *obsolete* exc. *dial.* **LME.**
[Prob. from Old Norse *hregg* storm.]
A storm, a tempest, a strong wind.

rig /rɪɡ/ *noun*[3]. *obsolete* exc. *dial.* **L16.**
[Origin unkn.: rel. to RIG *verb*[3].]
A promiscuous, licentious, or immoral girl or woman.

rig /rɪɡ/ *noun*[4]. **E18.**
[Origin unkn.: rel. to RIG *verb*[4].]
1 Sport, banter, ridicule; a frolic, a prank, a mischievous act. Now *dial.* **E18.**
2 A trick, a scheme, a dodge; a method of cheating or swindling. *colloq.* **L18.**

rig /rɪɡ/ *noun*[5]. **E19.**
[from RIG *verb*[2].]
1 NAUTICAL. The arrangement of masts, sails, etc., on a vessel. Also, rigging. **E19.**
2 A costume, an outfit, a style of dress. Cf. earlier RIG-OUT. *colloq.* **M19.**
3 Orig., an equipage, a horse-drawn vehicle. Later, any vehicle; *spec.* a lorry, a truck, a semi-trailer. Chiefly *N. Amer. & Austral.* **M19.**
4 An apparatus or device used for a specific purpose; *spec.* (*a*) = ***oil rig*** s.v. OIL *noun*; (*b*) an amateur's radio transmitter and receiver. **M19.**
5 The penis. *coarse slang.* **M20.**

> **2** G. DALY This rig included a frock coat with a velvet collar. **in full rig** smartly or ceremonially dressed. **4** ***JACK-UP rig.***

rig /rɪg/ *verb*¹ *trans. Scot. & north.* Infl. **-gg-**. LME.
[Var. of RIDGE *verb*.]
1 = RIDGE *verb* 2. LME.
2 = RIDGE *verb* 1. M19.

rig /rɪg/ *verb*² *trans.* Infl. **-gg-**. L15.
[Perh. of Scandinavian origin: cf. Norwegian *rigga* bind or wrap up, Swedish dial. *rigga på* harness.]
1 *verb trans.* Make (a sailing ship) ready for the sea; equip with sails, rigging, and other necessary tackle. Also foll. by *out*, *up*, (arch.) *forth*. (Earlier as RIGGING *noun*² 1.) L15. ▸**b** *verb intrans.* Of a sailing ship: be rigged, get rigged. M16.
†**2** *verb trans.* Provide (an army) with equipment for battle. Only in E16.
3 *verb trans.* Dress, clothe, fit out or provide with clothes. Also foll. by *out*. Now *colloq.* M16.
4 *verb trans. gen.* ▸**a** Furnish or provide (*with*). Usu. foll. by *up*. L16. ▸**b** Fit *out* in some way. L17.
5 *verb trans.* Chiefly NAUTICAL & AERONAUTICS. Set in proper order for working; assemble and adjust the parts of. E17. ▸**b** NAUTICAL. Run *out*, draw *in*, (a boom or stay). M18.
6 *verb trans.* Set or fit up, esp. hastily or as an expedient or makeshift. Also foll. by *up*. E19.

> 📖 **1** *Cruising* She was rigged . . with a taller mast and . . more sail area. **3** E. TEMPLETON The kitchenmaid, rigged up in black and white for the occasion. **5** *Windsurf* The board is supplied with a basic sail which is easy to rig. **6** C. MACKENZIE We've rigged a rope-ladder to get down into the hold. K. HULME A shower–there's one rigged up at the back of the boatshed.

rig /rɪg/ *verb*³ *intrans. obsolete* exc. *dial.* Infl. **-gg-**. L16.
[Origin unkn.: rel. to RIG *noun*³.]
Behave promiscuously or licentiously; romp or climb about.

rig /rɪg/ *verb*⁴ *trans.* Infl. **-gg-**. E19.
[Origin unkn.: rel. to RIG *noun*⁴.]
1 Hoax, play tricks on; *US* rag, tease. *dial.* E19.
2 Manage or manipulate in an underhand or fraudulent manner. M19.

> 📖 **2** K. WATERHOUSE I was trapped without time to think . . or to rig the facts. C. CAUSLEY They rigged a trial and shot him dead. E. SHOWALTER To contact his friends in the government and to rig the medical board.

Phrases: **rig the market** cause an artificial rise or fall of prices with a view to personal profit.

Riga /ˈriːgə/ *noun*¹. M18.
[Capital of Latvia.]
Used *attrib.* in the names of certain products exported from Riga.
Riga balsam an essential oil obtained from the Swiss stone pine, *Pinus cembra*. ***Riga rhine (hemp)***: see RHINE *noun*².

riga /ˈriːgə/ *noun*². E20.
[Hausa.]
A man's loose-fitting robe, worn in W. Africa.

rigadoon /rɪgəˈduːn/ *noun & verb*. As noun also ***rigaudon*** /ˈrigɔdɔ̃ (*pl. same*)/. L17.
[French *rigodon*, *rigaudon* said to be from *Rigaud* a dancing-master who devised it.]
▸ **A** *noun*. **1** A lively dance for couples, in duple or quadruple time, of Provençal origin. L17.
2 A piece of music for this dance. M18.
▸ **B** *verb intrans.* Dance a rigadoon E19.

rigaree /rɪgəˈriː/ *adjective*. E20.
[Perh. from Italian *rigare*: see RIGATONI.]
GLASS-MAKING. Designating or pertaining to a pattern of raised bands on a glass vessel, produced by applying threads of softened glass.

†**rigation** *noun*. M17–L18.
[Latin *rigatio(n-)*, from *rigat-* pa. ppl stem of *rigare* wet, water: see -ATION.]
Irrigation; (a) moistening.

rigatoni /rɪgəˈtəuni/ *noun*. M20.
[Italian, from *rigato* pa. pple of *rigare* draw a line, make fluting, from *riga* a line.]
Pasta in the form of short hollow fluted tubes; an Italian dish consisting largely of this and usu. a sauce.

rigaudon *noun* see RIGADOON.

rigescent /rɪˈdʒɛs(ə)nt/ *adjective*. L19.
[Latin *rigescent-* pres. ppl stem of *rigescere*, from *rigere* be stiff: see -ESCENT.]
Tending to be rigid or stiff.
■ **rigescence** *noun* stiffening M18.

riggal *noun* see RIGOL.

rigger /ˈrɪgə/ *noun*¹. E17.
[from RIG *verb*², *noun*⁵ + -ER¹. In sense 6 abbreviation of OUTRIGGER.]
▸ **I 1 a** A person who rigs ships. E17. ▸**b** A person who attends to the rigging of aircraft. E20.
2 A belt-driven wheel. L18.
3 As 2nd elem. of comb.: a ship rigged in a specified way. L19.
4 A person who works with lifting-tackle; a person who erects and maintains scaffolding etc. E20.
5 A worker on an oil rig. M20.
3 ***full-rigger***, ***square-rigger***, etc.
▸ **II 6** = OUTRIGGER 5. E20.

rigger /ˈrɪgə/ *noun*². E19.
[from RIG *verb*⁴ + -ER¹.]
A trickster; a fraudulent manipulator; a person who rigs a market etc.
¶ See also THIMBLERIGGER.

rigging /ˈrɪgɪŋ/ *noun*¹. *Scot. & north.* LME.
[from RIG *noun*¹ or *verb*¹ + -ING¹. Cf. RIDGING.]
1 The ridge or roof of a building. Also (*rare*), the making of a ridge or ridges. LME.
2 A person's or animal's back. E16.
3 The ridge or top of an elevated stretch of ground or raised path. M16.

rigging /ˈrɪgɪŋ/ *noun*². LME.
[from RIG *verb*² + -ING¹.]
1 The action of RIG *verb*²; *spec.* (NAUTICAL) the action of equipping a sailing ship with the necessary shrouds, stays, braces, etc. LME.
2 a The system of ropes or chains employed to support a ship's masts (***standing rigging***) and to control or set the yards, sails, etc. (***running rigging***). L16. ▸**b** The system of ropes and wires used to support the structure of and distribute the load of an airship, biplane, etc. M19.
3 Clothing, dress; *rare* an item of clothing. M17.
4 (An) apparatus for lifting, lifting-tackle. M19.
Comb.: **rigging lines** the cords which join the canopy of a parachute to the harness; **rigging-loft** (*a*) a loft or long room where rigging is prepared before fitting to a ship; (*b*) *US* a space above a theatre-stage from which scenery is manipulated.

riggish /ˈrɪgɪʃ/ *adjective*. Now chiefly *dial.* L16.
[from RIG *noun*³ + -ISH¹]
Esp. of a woman or girl: promiscuous, licentious, immoral.

riggot /ˈrɪgət/ *noun*. *obsolete* exc. *dial.* M17.
[Alt. of RIGOL.]
A groove, a furrow, a channel. In later use *spec.* a channel for surface water, a gutter.

Riggs's disease /ˈrɪgzɪz dɪˌziːz/ *noun phr.* Also **Riggs disease**. L19.
[J. M. *Riggs* (1810–85), US dentist.]
MEDICINE. Periodontitis.

right /rʌɪt/ *noun*¹.
[Old English *riht* = Old Frisian *riuht*, Old Saxon, Old High German *reht* (Dutch, German *Recht*), Old Norse *réttr*, from Germanic base also of RIGHT *adjective*.]
▸ **I** †**1** The standard of permitted and forbidden action; law. OE–E17.
†**2** One's duty. OE–ME.
3 a That which is consonant with justice, goodness, or reason; that which is morally or socially correct; just or equitable treatment; fairness in decision; justice. OE. ▸**b** Consonance with fact; correctness. L18. ▸**c** In *pl.* The just, good, equitable, or correct points or aspects of something; the arguments in favour. Chiefly in ***the rights and wrongs of***. M19.
4 Entitlement or justifiable claim, on legal or moral grounds, to have or obtain something, or to act in a certain way. OE.
5 A legal, equitable, or moral title or claim to the possession of property or authority, the enjoyment of privileges or immunities, etc. Also, (*dial.*) an obligation (usu. in neg. contexts.) Foll. by *to*, *to do*, (now chiefly LAW) *of (doing)*; also freq. with specifying word (when usu. in *pl.*). OE. ▸**b** A document substantiating a claim or title. M16. ▸**c** In *pl.* A title or authority to perform, publish, film, or televise a particular work, event, etc. L19.
6 A thing that justly accrues or falls to someone; what one may properly claim; one's due. OE. ▸†**b** *sing.* & (usu.) in *pl.* The last sacraments of the Church. Cf. RIGHT *noun*². ME–E16. ▸**c** In *pl.* A stag's full complement of antlers. LME.
7 In *pl.* & (earlier) †*sing.* The true account or interpretation *of* a matter. M18.

> 📖 **3a** J. WYNDHAM So young, Terry. So sure of right and wrong. **c** G. W. TARGET No intention of discussing the rights and wrongs of corporal punishment. **5** W. SPALDING A certain part of the senators . . possessed votes without the right of addressing the assembly. S. RAVEN Hugo had taken money from them which he had no right to. B. FRIEDAN A cliché . . that women spent half a century fighting for 'rights'. B. CASTLE The right of an employee to withdraw his labour. M. BERLINS Those residents with a right of abode are free from immigration control and cannot be deported. ***animal rights*** etc. **c** M. SPARK The Triad [Press] sold the American rights, the paperback rights, the film rights.

▸ **II 8** The right hand part, side, region, or direction. ME.
9 MILITARY. The right wing of an army. Also (in *pl.*), soldiers whose place is on the right. E18.
10 POLITICS. (Also **R-**.) Orig., those members of comparatively conservative opinions in a Continental legislature, by custom seated on the right of the president. Now, (the views and aims of) any party or political group favouring conservative views. Also, the more conservative section of a philosophical, religious, etc., group. E19.
11 A shoe etc. for the right foot; a glove etc. for the right hand. E19.
12 FOOTBALL & HOCKEY etc. (The position of) a player who plays primarily on the right side of the pitch. Chiefly in ***inside right***, ***outside right***. M19.
13 A shot fired at game with the right barrel of a double-barrelled shotgun; a creature hit by such a shot. (Earliest in ***right-and-left*** below.) M19.
14 Chiefly BOXING. (A blow dealt with) the right hand. L19.
15 A right turn. M20.

> 📖 **8** *Autocar* With the gearchange switched from the left of the cockpit to the right. S. WEINTRAUB On the Queen's right was the King of Denmark; on her left was the King of Greece. **14** *Ring* Floored . . by a terrific right to the jaw.

Phrases etc.: **as of right** by virtue or reason of a legal or moral entitlement. **bang to rights**, **banged to rights** *slang* (caught) red-handed, in the act. **be in the right** have justice, reason, or fact on one's side. **Bill of Rights** (*a*) ENGLISH HISTORY the bill establishing the constitutional settlement of 1689; (*b*) US HISTORY the bill establishing the constitutional amendments of 1791; (*c*) a bill stating and establishing the rights of individuals or of a class of people. **by right** †(*a*) = ***by rights*** below; (*b*) = ***as of right*** above. **by rights** if right were done. ***civil rights***: see CIVIL *adjective*. ***conjugal rights***. **dead to rights** *slang* (*a*) completely, certainly; (*b*) = ***bang to rights*** above. **Declaration of Rights** ENGLISH HISTORY the declaration of the constitutional settlement of 1689. ***divine right (of kings)***: see DIVINE *adjective* 2. **do right by**, (now *rare*) **do right to** treat justly or fairly, act dutifully towards (a person). ***equal rights***: see EQUAL *adjective*. ***hang a right***: see HANG *verb*. **have right** (now *rare*) have justice or reason on one's side. **have the right** (now *rare*) have justice, reason, or the law on one's side. ***human rights***: see HUMAN *adjective*. **in one's own right** through one's own (legal) position or effort, independently of one's relationship with others. **in right of** *arch.* on the grounds of or through the legal or moral entitlement of (a person). ***Latin rights***: see LATIN *adjective*. ***mere right***: see MERE *adjective*. ***miner's right***: see MINER 1. ***natural right***: see NATURAL *adjective*. ***New Right***: see NEW *adjective*. **of right** = ***as of right*** above. ***petition of right***: see PETITION *noun*. ***performing rights***: see PERFORM. ***Public Lending Right***: see PUBLIC *adjective* & *noun*. ***radical right***: see RADICAL *adjective* 2c. RAGGED ***right***. **right-and-left** a shot fired at game with both barrels of a double-barrelled shotgun; a creature hit by such a shot. ***right of*** ANGARY. ***right of representation***: see REPRESENTATION 4b. ***right of search***: see SEARCH *noun*¹ 1. ***right of visit***: see VISIT *noun* 4. ***right of visitation***: see VISITATION *noun* 1b. **right of way** (*a*) the legal right, established by usage or grant, to pass through grounds or property belonging to another; a path or thoroughfare subject to such a right; (*b*) *N. Amer.* the right to build and operate a railway line on land belonging to another; the land on which a railway line is built; (*c*) the legal right of a pedestrian, rider, or driver to proceed with precedence over other road-users at a particular point; the right of a ship, boat, aeroplane, etc., to proceed with precedence over others in a particular situation. **rights issue** an issue of shares offered at a special price by a company to its existing shareholders. ***rights of man***: see MAN *noun*. **right-to-life** *adjective* of or pertaining to opposition to the abortion of the unborn foetus. **right-to-lifer** an opponent of abortion of the unborn foetus. **right-to-work** *spec.* (*US*) a worker's right not to be required to join a trade union. ***serial rights***: see SERIAL *adjective*. ***special drawing rights***: see SPECIAL *adjective*. **to rights** (*a*) to or into a proper condition or order (chiefly in ***bring to rights***, ***put to rights***, ***set to rights***); (*b*) (now *US*) at once, straightaway. **to the right about** = ***right about*** s.v. RIGHT *adverb*; ***send to the right about*** (*arch.*), cause to retreat or flee, send away or dismiss unceremoniously. ***true right***: see TRUE *adjective*, *noun*, & *adverb*. **within one's rights** not exceeding one's authority or entitlement.
¶ In most senses of branch II opp. ***left***, in some also opp. ***centre***.
■ **rightism** *noun* the political, philosophical, etc., views or principles of the right M20. **rightist** *noun* & *adjective* (*a*) *noun* an adherent of the right; (*b*) *adjective* of or pertaining to rightism or the right; (***New Rightist*** *noun* & *adjective*: see NEW *adjective*): M20. **rightless** *adjective* †(*a*) wrongful, lawless; (*b*) without rights, deprived of rights: L16.

right /rʌɪt/ *noun*². Now considered *erron.* L16.
[Var. of RITE *noun*, infl. by RIGHT *noun*¹. Cf. earlier RIGHT *noun*¹ 6b.]
= RITE *noun*.

right /rʌɪt/ *adjective*.
[Old English *riht* = Old Frisian *riuht*, Old Saxon, Old High German *reht* (Dutch, German *recht*), Old Norse *réttr*, Gothic *raihts*, from Germanic base rel. to Latin *rectus*, from Indo-European.]
▸ **I 1** Straight; not bent, curved, or crooked; direct, going straight towards its destination; directed straight forwards. Now only in ***right line***, a straight line. OE.
2 Formed by or with reference to a straight line or plane perpendicular to another straight line or plane. LME. ▸**b** Of a solid figure: having the ends or base at right angles with the axis. L17.
▸ **II 3** Of a person, disposition, etc.: disposed to do what is just or good; upright, righteous. Now *rare*. OE.
4 Consonant with justice, goodness, or reason; equitable; morally or socially correct. Latterly chiefly *pred.* OE.
5 Agreeing with some standard or principle; correct, proper. Also, agreeing with facts; true. OE. ▸**b** Leading in the proper direction, leading towards the place one wishes to reach (*lit.* & *fig.*). E18.

6 Fitting, appropriate; exactly answering to what is required or suitable; to be preferred. OE. ▸**b** Regarded with approval; socially acceptable; potentially influential. M19. ▸**c** Reliable or trustworthy (from the criminal's point of view); friendly or sympathetic to criminals. Cf. WRONG *adjective* 4b. *Criminals' slang*. M19.

7 Properly pertaining or attached to a person or thing. ME.

8 Of the mind or mental faculties: healthy, normal, sound; such that one can think and act competently. Chiefly in ***in one's right mind***, ***in one's right senses***. ME.

9 Of a person: correct in opinion, judgement, or procedure. E16. ▸**b** Appended as an interrogative to the end of a statement, inviting agreement or approval: am I right? M20.

10 Mentally healthy, sane; competent to think and act. Usu. in neg. contexts, esp. (*colloq.*) in ***not right in one's head***, ***not right in the head***. M17.

11 In a satisfactory or proper state; in good order. M17.

12 In good health and spirits; sound, well, comfortable. *colloq.* Now chiefly *Austral. & NZ* (infl. by ALL RIGHT), exc. in various compar. phrs., as ***(as) right as rain***. M19.

📖 **4** J. BENTHAM It is right that men should be . . upon a par with one another. *Encounter* I know what I'm doing is right. **5** SHAKES. *L.L.L.* A right description of our sport, my lord. B. JOWETT His notion of educating by a right use of pleasure. G. GREENE 'So he was at your school.' 'That's right'. P. FITZGERALD 'I've never read any Wordsworth.' 'Is that right?' **b** C. S. LEWIS If you're on the wrong road, progress means doing an about-turn and walking back to the right road. *Glasgow Herald* Extensions of the fishing limits . . are a step in the right direction. **6** I. MURDOCH I'll have to break it to my father first—and I'll have somehow to find the right moment. D. CAMERON The difficulties of having the boat in the right place at the right time. **b** D. HALLIDAY He had been to all the right schools and belonged to all the right clubs. J. CAREY Goodyer knew the right people. **7** R. TRAVERS The gallant Starlight, dying of his wounds, refused to give his right name. **8** M. SPARK They hoped to contest Lisa's will . . on the grounds that Lisa, when she made it, was not in her right mind. **9** *New Scientist* Right in insisting on adequate insurance cover. J. SIMMS If she looked a little . . doubtful, I was probably right to be worried. **b** G. V. HIGGINS You been here before, right? **10** M. L. ROBY He ain't right in the head. Got a few marbles missing. **11** MRS H. WARD Don't mix up my silks, Lucy; I shall never get them right again. **12** *Listener* I gave him a drink . . and he was right.

▸**III 13** Rightful, legitimate, lawful. *arch.* OE.

14 Justly entitled to the name or attribution; having the true character of; true, real, genuine, veritable. OE.

📖 **14** *Times* Lord Emsworth must have looked a right nana . . wearing 'coronet and ermine'.

▸**IV 15** Designating that side of the body which is usually the stronger of the two and which is in the position of east if one is facing north, its individual parts, and (*occas.*) their clothing; designating the corresponding side of any other body or object. OE.

16 That has the relative position of the right side with respect to the left. (Sometimes with ref. to the direction in which an object is considered to face, sometimes with ref. to an object's appearance to a spectator.) In pred. use usu. foll. by *of*; in attrib. use now chiefly replaced by RIGHT HAND. ME. ▸**b** *MATH.* Designating an entity whose definition involves two elements in a conventionally defined order, opposite to that designated as left. M20.

17 (Also **R-**.) Of or pertaining to the right in politics, philosophy, etc. See RIGHT *noun*[1] 10. L18.

Special collocations, phrases, & comb.: ALL RIGHT *adjectival phr.* **a right one** *colloq.* a fool, an extremely stupid or awkward person. ***a right understanding***: see UNDERSTANDING *noun*. ***as right as a trivet***: see TRIVET *noun* 1. **as right as rain** perfectly sound and healthy. ***come to the right shop***: see SHOP *noun*. ***get the right end of the stick***: see STICK *noun*[1]. ***get the right sow by the ear***: see SOW *noun*[1]. ***have one's head screwed on the right way***: see SCREW *verb*. ***have one's heart in the right place***: see HEART *noun*. ***have the right end of the stick***: see STICK *noun*[1]. ***have the right sow by the ear***: see SOW *noun*[1]. ***hit the right note***: see NOTE *noun*[2]. ***lay the saddle upon the right horse***: see SADDLE *noun*. ***Miss Right***: see MISS *noun*[2]. ***Mr Right***. ***on the right foot***: see FOOT *noun*. ***on the right track***: see TRACK *noun*. **put right** restore to order, health, etc.; correct the mistaken impression of (a person); direct properly. **right angle** the angle formed by two perpendicular lines, as in the corner of a square or in a quarter circle, equivalent to ninety degrees; ***at right angles*** perpendicularly (*to* another line, etc.), so as to form an angle of 90 degrees. **right-angle** *adjective* right-angled. **right-angled** *adjective* containing or forming a right angle or right angles; characterized by right angles; lying at right angles *to* another thing. **right arm** (*a*) a mainstay, a chief executive agent, one's most reliable helper; (*b*) *CRICKET* a player who bowls with the right arm. ***right ascension***: see ASCENSION 2. **right back** in *FOOTBALL & HOCKEY* etc., (the position of) a back who plays primarily on the right of the pitch. ***right bank***: see BANK *noun*[1] 1. ***right bower***: see BOWER *noun*[5]. **right brain** the right-hand side of the human brain, believed to be associated with creative thought and the emotions. **right-brained** *adjective* having the right as the dominant or more efficient part of the brain. **right centre** in *FOOTBALL & HOCKEY* etc., (the position of) a player who plays primarily to the right of the centre of the pitch. ***right circular cone***, ***right cone***: see CONE *noun* 3. **right defender** in *FOOTBALL & HOCKEY* etc., a right half who plays deep. **right-eye** *adjective* having both eyes on the right-hand side of the head; *spec.* designating flatfish (flounders) of the family Pleuronectidae. **right-eyed** *adjective* (*a*) having the right as the dominant or more efficient eye; (*b*) = ***right-eye*** above. **right field** *BASEBALL* (a fielder in) the part of the outfield to the right of the batter when facing the pitcher. **right-fielder** *BASEBALL* a fielder in the right field. **right flank** = RIGHT WING *noun phr.* 2. **right-footed** *adjective* having the right as the dominant or more efficient foot. **right half(-back)** in *FOOTBALL & HOCKEY* etc., (the position of) a half-back who plays primarily on the right of the pitch. ***right line***: see sense 1 above. **right-lined** *adjective* (now *rare*) = RECTILINEAR *adjective*. **right midfield** in *FOOTBALL & HOCKEY* etc., the midfield players who play primarily on the right of the pitch. **right-minded** *adjective* naturally disposed to think rightly, having sound views or principles. **right-mindedness** the quality or state of being right-minded. ***right NANTZ***. **right side** *spec.* (*a*) the principal side, the side naturally turned forwards, the side intended to be uppermost or foremost; (*b*) ***on the right side***, in the better or more commendable way; (*c*) ***on the right side of***, on the safe, advantageous, appropriate, desirable, etc., side of (something), of an age less than (the age specified), in a position to be viewed with favour by (a person). **right-sided** *adjective* (*a*) *MEDICINE* located in or affecting the right side of the body; (*b*) having the limbs of the right side of the body more serviceable than those of the left, using the right arm and leg by preference. **right sphere** *ASTRONOMY* the celestial sphere as seen by an observer at the earth's equator. **the right stuff** *colloq.* (*a*) money; (*b*) (orig. *US*) the necessary qualities for a given job or task; (*c*) alcoholic drink. **right triangle** a right-angled triangle. **right turn** a turn that brings a person's front to face as his or her right side did before; a turn or turning to the right. **right whale** each of three baleen whales of the family Balaenidae, of Arctic and temperate waters, having long baleen plates and a deeply curved jaw, esp. the widespread *Balaena glacialis* (see also ***GREENLAND right whale***). **right you are!** *colloq.*: expr. agreement or assent. **see a person right** look after a person, protect the interests of a person. **set right** = ***put right*** above. ***set the saddle upon the right horse***: see SADDLE *noun*. **she's right**, **she'll be right** *Austral. & NZ colloq.* everything is (or will be) all right, that is (or will be) fine. ***strike the right note***: see NOTE *noun*[2]. ***THAT'S right***. **too right** *colloq.*: expr. agreement or approval. ***touch the right chord***: see CHORD *noun*[2] 4.

¶ In branch II freq. opp. ***wrong***. In most senses of branch IV opp. ***left***, in some also opp. ***centre***.

■ **rightmost** *adjective* situated furthest to the right M20.

right /rʌɪt/ *verb*.

[Old English *rihtan*, formed as RIGHT *adjective*.]

†**1** *verb trans.* Make straight (a path, way, etc.); straighten. OE–LME.

†**2** *verb trans.* Guide, direct; govern, rule, judge. OE–E16.

3 *verb trans.* Set upright or (formerly) up; raise, rear, erect. Also foll. by *up*. Long *obsolete* exc. *dial.* OE.

4 *verb trans.* Do justice to; make reparation to (a person) or for (an injury); avenge; vindicate, justify, rehabilitate, (esp. oneself). OE.

†**5** *verb trans.* Correct or amend (a person, one's life, etc.). OE–L16.

6 *verb trans.* Bring into accordance with truth; correct or render exact (accounts etc.); give correct information to (a person). Also foll. by *up*. OE.

7 *verb trans.* Set in order, adjust, set or put right; rectify; (now *dial. & US*) clear or clean *up*. OE.

8 *verb trans.* Restore, *refl.* return, to a straight or vertical, or the proper position; *refl.* recover one's balance or equilibrium, correct a false step, (*lit. & fig.*). M17.

9 *verb intrans.* Recover or reassume a straight or vertical position. M18.

10 *verb refl.* Restore, return, to a proper or normal condition. M19.

📖 **7** P. AUSTER To sacrifice his own life . . to right the wrong. **8** G. GREENE The table rocked and righted itself. M. BRAGG When his balance left him and he staggered . . he would right himself. N. SHAVE Righting a canoe after capsize without getting out. **right the helm** *NAUTICAL* put the helm straight in line with the keel.

■ **rightable** *adjective* L19.

right /rʌɪt/ *adverb*.

[Old English *rihte*, formed as RIGHT *adjective*.]

▸**I 1** Straight; in a direct course or line. Latterly chiefly with prepositions & adverbs, as *on*, *from*, *to*, etc. OE. ▸**b** In the proper course. *arch.* ME.

2 (With prepositions & adverbs.) All the way *to*, *from*, *into*, *round*, *through*, etc., *down*, *along*, *back*, etc., quite or completely *off*, *out*, *round*, etc. LOE.

3 a Immediately *after* some event. ME. ▸**b** (With adverbs) Without delay, straightaway, immediately. *colloq.* M19.

📖 **2** V. WOOLF They had climbed right up on to the top of the cliff. W. GOLDING The fire was right out, smokeless and dead. A. SILLITOE Never happy about our life together, right from the start. I. COLEGATE Pulling her cloak round her with the hood right over her head. I. WATSON They're inland; right inland, as far away . . as they can get. **3b** P. CASEMENT He had told her to come right over.

▸**II 4** Precisely, exactly, just, altogether, to the full. Now *arch. & dial.* exc. with adverbs of time, esp. *now*, or of place, as *at*, *in*, *on*, etc. OE.

5 Very. Now chiefly *arch. & dial.* OE.

†**6** In neg. contexts: at all; whatever. ME–E17.

📖 **4** R. DAHL He didn't hammer them right home. A. TYLER I was born right here in Clarion. **5** B. HINES Hawks are right nervous. ***Right Honourable***, ***Right Reverend***, etc.

▸**III 7** In accordance with justice, goodness, reason, or (now *rare*) righteousness; in a morally or socially correct manner. OE.

8 In a proper, fitting, or appropriate manner; in the required or necessary way; in due or proper order, satisfactorily. OE.

9 In accordance with facts or the truth; accurately, correctly, exactly. ME.

📖 **8** SHAKES. *Meas. for M.* When once our grace we have forgot, Nothing goes right. J. LOCKE The first thing should be taught him is to hold his Pen right. L. OLIVIER If I played it right . . I might be taken on. **9** I. MURDOCH Her words; I was not even sure I had heard them right.

▸**IV 10** On or towards the right side; in the direction of the right; (of rotatory motion) clockwise. ME.

Phrases & comb.: ALL RIGHT *adverb* ***eyes right***: see EYE *noun*. ***left, right, and centre***: see LEFT *adverb*. **right about** [earlier ***to the right about*** S.V. RIGHT *noun*[1]] to the right through 180 degrees so as to face in the opposite direction (orig. as a military command, and freq. with imper. of verb as ***right about face***, ***right about turn***, etc.). **right-about-face**, **right-about-turn** *noun & verb intrans.* (make) a turn to the right through 180 degrees so as to face in the opposite direction; (make) a retreat or hasty departure; (make) a reversal of policy, opinion, or behaviour. ***right and left***: see ***left, right, and centre*** S.V. LEFT *adverb*. **right away** immediately, without delay. ***right down one's street***: see STREET *noun*. **right enough** *colloq.* certainly, indeed, undeniably, sure enough. ***right, left, and centre***: see LEFT *adverb*. **right now** (*a*) at this particular moment; (*b*) = ***right away*** above. **right off** = ***right away*** above. ***right off the bat***: see BAT *noun*[1] 2. **right on!** *slang*: expr. enthusiastic agreement, approval, or encouragement. **right-on** *adjective* (*US slang*) greatly approved of, up to date, relevant. ***right on the SCHNOZZ***. **right out** (now *arch. & dial.*) = OUTRIGHT *adverb* 2, 3. **right-thinking** *adjective* having sound views and principles. **right-up** *adjective* (*a*) (now *rare*) steep, rising straight up; fixed upright; †(*b*) honest, upright. ***right up one's street***: see STREET *noun*. ***serve a person right***: see SERVE *verb*[1]. ***stage right***: see STAGE *noun* 4.

-right /rʌɪt/ *suffix* (not productive).

[from RIGHT *adjective*, *adverb*.]

Forming a few adjectives and adverbs with the sense 'straight, direct(ly)', as ***forthright***, ***outright***, ***upright***, etc.

right-down /ˈrʌɪtdaʊn/ *adverb & adjective*. L16.

[from RIGHT *adverb* + DOWN *adverb*.]

Downright; positive(ly); thorough(ly), complete(ly).

righten /ˈrʌɪt(ə)n/ *verb trans.* ME.

[from RIGHT *adjective* + -EN[5].]

Set or put right; set in order; restore to a straight or vertical, or the proper position.

righteous /ˈrʌɪtʃəs/ *adjective, noun, & adverb*.

[Old English *rihtwīs*, formed as RIGHT *noun*[1] + -WISE or RIGHT *adjective* + WISE *noun*[1], assim. to *bounteous*, *plenteous*, etc. Cf. WRONGOUS.]

▸**A** *adjective*. **1** Of a person: just, upright, virtuous; guiltless, sinless; conforming to the precepts of divine law or accepted standards of morality; acting rightly or justly. OE.

2 Of an action etc.: characterized by justice or uprightness; morally right or justifiable. OE.

†**3** Rightful, lawful, legitimate; *rare* genuine. Chiefly *Scot.* LME–M18.

4 Fine, excellent; of good quality; of the preferred type. *US slang* (chiefly *Black English*). M20.

▸**B** *absol.* as *noun*. **1** Righteous people as a class. Now usu. with *the*. OE.

†**2** A righteous person. OE–M17.

▸†**C** *adverb*. Righteously; rightfully. ME–E16.

■ **righteously** *adverb* OE.

righteousness /ˈrʌɪtʃəsnɪs/ *noun*. OE.

[from RIGHTEOUS *adjective* + -NESS.]

1 The quality or state of being righteous; uprightness, rectitude; virtue, integrity. OE.

†**2** A righteous act. Usu. in *pl.* OE–L17.

righter /ˈrʌɪtə/ *noun*[1]. OE.

[from RIGHT *verb* + -ER[1].]

†**1** A person who arranges or regulates something. *rare*. OE–L16.

†**2** An executioner. *rare*. Only in L15.

3 A person who sets right wrongs, grievances etc.; a redresser, a vindicator. L16.

righter /ˈrʌɪtə/ *noun*[2]. L19.

[from RIGHT *noun*[1] + -ER[1].]

As 2nd elem. of comb.: an advocate of rights of the specified kind, as ***equal-righter***.

rightful /ˈrʌɪtfʊl, -f(ə)l/ *adjective*. LOE.

[from RIGHT *noun*[1] + -FUL.]

†**1** = RIGHTEOUS *adjective* 1. LOE–E19.

2 Of an action etc.: in conformity with what is right or just; equitable, thoroughly fair. ME.

3 Having a legal or morally just claim; legitimately claimed; lawful. ME.

4 Proper, fitting, appropriate; correct. ME.

📖 **3** MILTON Every Soule in Heav'n Shall . . Confess him rightful King. LD MACAULAY An innocent boy, . . kept out of his rightful inheritance. **4** M. AMIS A certain toy . . abducted from its rightful nook.

■ **rightfully** *adverb* ME. **rightfulness** *noun* ME.

right hand /rʌɪt 'hand/ *noun & adjectival phr.* As adjective also **right-hand**. OE.
[from RIGHT *adjective* + HAND *noun*.]
▶**A** *noun phr.* **1** The hand of the right side. OE. ▸**b** A person of usefulness or importance; an efficient or indispensable helper or aid. E16.
2 (The region or direction of) the right side of a person or thing. OE. ▸†**b** The position of honour; a position of precedence. M17–E18.

📖 **1b** N. SAHGAL Suddenly he was indispensable, . . the right hand . . of the Prime Minister and her household.

▶**B** *adjectival phr.* On or to the right side; done with the right hand. L16.

📖 A. CROSS She eased into the right hand lane on the Triborough bridge. **right-hand drive** a motor-vehicle steering-system with the steering-wheel and other controls fitted on the right side; a vehicle with such steering. **right-hand man** †(*a*) a soldier holding a position of responsibility or command on the right of a troop of horse; (*b*) = sense A.1b above. **right-hand rule** PHYSICS = *Fleming's right-hand rule* s.v. FLEMING *noun*². **right-hand screw** a screw which rotates clockwise when inserted; any equivalent spiral.

right-handed /rʌɪt'handɪd, *esp. attrib.* 'rʌɪthandɪd/ *adjective & adverb.* LME.
[from prec. + -ED².]
▶**A** *adjective.* **1** Having the right hand more serviceable than the left; using the right hand by preference. LME.
2 *fig.* Skilful, dexterous. *rare.* M17.
3 Of or pertaining to the right hand; *spec.* (*a*) (of an action) performed with the right hand; (*b*) (of an implement etc.) adapted or designed for use by a right-handed person. E18.
4 Characterized by rightward direction or rotation. Of a shell: †(*a*) sinistral; (*b*) dextral. L18.
▶**B** *adverb.* Towards the right; with the right hand. M19.
■ **right-handedly** *adverb* L19. **right-handedness** *noun* M19.

right-hander /rʌɪt'handə/ *noun.* M19.
[formed as prec. + -ER¹.]
1 A blow delivered with the right hand. M19.
2 A right-handed person. L19.
3 A right-hand turn or bend. L20.

right-ho *interjection* var. of RIGHTO.

rightie *noun* var. of RIGHTY.

rightly /'rʌɪtli/ *adverb.*
[Old English *rihtlīce*, formed as RIGHT *adjective* + -LY².]
▶**I 1** In accordance with justice, goodness, or reason; fairly, uprightly; in conformity with moral or social correctness. OE.
2 In accordance with some standard or principle; properly; in the right manner. OE.
3 In accordance with truth or fact; exactly, accurately. Formerly also, precisely. OE.
4 With good reason; justifiably. M19.

📖 **1** D. ROWE He had *acted rightly* and . . he had no reason to feel ashamed. **2** G. SAYER If rightly used, England's suffering could be for her ultimate good. **3** *Punch* If I remember rightly, they were mostly ballet photographs. **4** G. GREENE Why aren't they afraid of fish then, you may rightly ask.

▶†**II 5** Directly, straight. ME–M17.

rightness /'rʌɪtnɪs/ *noun.*
[Old English *rehtnisse*, *rihtnesse*, formed as RIGHT *adjective* + -NESS.]
▶**I 1** The quality or state of being right. OE.
†**2** Straightness. OE–E17.
▶**II 3** The condition of being on the right. L19.

righto /'rʌɪtəʊ, rʌɪt'əʊ/ *interjection.* Also **right-ho**, **right-o(h)**. L19.
[from RIGHT *adjective* + HO *interjection*¹. Cf. RIGHTY-HO *interjection*.]
Expressing agreement with or acquiescence in an opinion, proposal, etc., or compliance with a request.

rightward /'rʌɪtwəd/ *adverb & adjective.* E19.
[from RIGHT *adjective* + -WARD.]
▶**A** *adverb.* On or in the direction of the right side; towards the right. E19.
▶**B** *adjective.* Situated on the right; directed or tending towards the right; executed from left to right. E19.

📖 G. ORWELL The recent rightward swing means . . we are being regimented by wealthy men. *Scientific American* Usually a reader . . moves his eyes . . in a rightward and downward direction.

■ Also **rightwards** *adverb* M19.

right wing /rʌɪt 'wɪŋ/ *noun & adjectival phr.* As adjective also **right-wing**. L16.
[from RIGHT *adjective* + WING *noun*.]
▶**A** *noun phr.* **1** The division on the right side of an army or fleet in battle array. L16.
2 FOOTBALL, HOCKEY, etc. (The position of) a player on the right side of the centre(s); the part of the field in which a right wing normally plays. L19.
3 The conservative or reactionary section of a group or political party; the less liberal or progressive section of a left-wing or socialist group or political party. E20.

📖 **3** *Labour Monthly* The point where the right wing advocates dictatorship of the proletariat.

▶**B** *adjective.* Of or pertaining to the right wing, esp in politics. E20.

📖 M. ARGYLE Protestants support right-wing parties, Jews support the left and have radical attitudes.

■ **right-'winger** *noun* (*a*) POLITICS an adherent of the right wing; (*b*) a player on the right wing: E20. **right-'wingery** *noun* (POLITICS) (*a*) adherents of the right wing collectively; (*b*) = RIGHT-WINGISM: M20. **right-'wingism** *noun* (POLITICS) adherence to the right wing, the beliefs or practices of the right wing M20.

righty /'rʌɪti/ *noun. colloq.* Also **rightie**. M20.
[from RIGHT *noun*¹ + -Y⁶.]
1 A right-handed person, esp. a sportsperson. M20.
2 POLITICS. An adherent of the right. M20.

righty-ho /'rʌɪtɪhəʊ, rʌɪtɪ'həʊ/ *interjection.* Also **righty-oh** /'rʌɪtɪ(j)əʊ, rʌɪtɪ'(j)əʊ/. E20.
[from RIGHT *adjective* + -Y⁶ + HO *interjection*¹.]
= RIGHTO.

rigid /'rɪdʒɪd/ *adjective & noun.* LME.
[(French *rigide* from) Latin *rigidus*, from *rigere* be stiff: see -ID¹.]
▶**A** *adjective.* **1** Stiff, unyielding; unable to bend or be bent, not pliant or flexible; fixed in position. LME. ▸**b** Of an airship: of the type whose shape is maintained by a framework. E20.
2 Strict in opinion, observance, procedure, or method; admitting or allowing of no deviation; scrupulously exact or precise. L16.
3 Harsh, severe, inflexible, unchanging, unvarying; not adaptable in outlook or response. M17.

📖 **1** P. H. NEWBY A bridge that was rigid would snap if it carried too much traffic. S. COOPER Cally felt cold with fright; she stood rigid. **2** J. TYNDALL The fossils . . were subjected to rigid scrutiny. J. R. GREEN The Lennoxes had remained rigid Catholics. J. BUCHAN She respected Mr. Craw for his rigid seclusion. H. MOORE Rigid adherence to the doctrine results in domination of the sculpture by the material. **rigid designator** LOGIC a term that identifies the same object or individual in every possible world. **3** W. LIPPMANN Industry . . must be flexible, not rigid; change must be possible. A. BISHOP Mrs Ogilvie was rigid, a disciplinarian. V. BRAMWELL In a rigid schedule allow yourself a treat occasionally.

Phrases: **bore rigid**, **scare rigid**, etc., *colloq.* bore, frighten, etc., (a person) excessively.
▶**B** *noun.* **1** A strict or precise person. *rare.* E18.
2 A rigid airship. E20.
3 A lorry etc. with a rigid chassis, a lorry etc. which is not articulated. L20.
■ **rigidize** *verb trans.* make rigid (chiefly as ***rigidized*** *ppl adjective*) M20. **rigidly** *adverb* M17. **rigidness** *noun* rigidity M17.

rigidify /rɪ'dʒɪdɪfʌɪ/ *verb.* M19.
[from RIGID *adjective*: see -FY.]
1 *verb trans.* Make rigid. M19.
2 *verb intrans.* Become rigid. L19.
■ **rigidifi'cation** *noun* M20.

rigidity /rɪ'dʒɪdɪti/ *noun.* E17.
[Latin *rigiditas*, from *rigidus*: see RIGID, -ITY.]
1 The state of being physically rigid; stiffness, (an) inability to bend or be bent. E17.
2 Strictness, severity, harshness, inflexibility; (an) inability to adapt in outlook or response. M17.
Phrases: **modulus of rigidity** a measure of the resistance of an object to deformation without change in volume.

†**riglet** *noun* var. of REGLET.

rigmarole /'rɪgmərəʊl/ *noun, adjective, & verb.* M18.
[App. colloq. alt. of RAGMAN ROLL.]
▶**A** *noun.* **1** A succession of incoherent statements; an unconnected or rambling account or tale; a long-winded harangue of little meaning or importance. M18.
2 Incoherent, rambling, or long-winded language. E19.
3 A succession of tiresome duties; a lengthy and complicated procedure; a fuss. M20.

📖 **1** D. WELCH Difficult to stop this rigmarole of explanation. A. POWELL This story of yours is becoming rather a rigmarole. **2** J. WAIN A brown envelope containing some meaningless piece of rigmarole from a government office. **3** J. HARVEY A rigmarole of wedging the newspaper so it hung out over the dartboard. M. SCAMMELL The rigmarole of form-filling that hospital admission entailed.

▶**B** *attrib.* or as *adjective.* Incoherent, rambling, long-winded. Now *rare.* M18.
▶**C** *verb trans. & intrans.* Talk incoherently or long-windedly (to). *rare.* E19.
■ **rigmarolery** *noun* = RIGMAROLE *noun* 2 E19. **rigmarolish** *adjective* E19.

rigol /'rɪg(ə)l/ *noun.* In sense 1 also (earlier) †**regal**, **riggal**. LME.
[French *rigole* watercourse, furrow, groove. See also RIGGOT.]
1 A groove in wood or stone; a slot. *obsolete* exc. *dial.* LME.
2 A ring, a circle. Now only with ref. or allusion to Shakes. *2 Hen. IV.* L16.
3 a A small channel or gutter. *dial.* L19. ▸**b** NAUTICAL. A projecting strip above a porthole to prevent water from entering. M20.

📖 **2** SHAKES. *2 Hen. IV* A sleep That from this golden rigol hath divorc'd So many English kings.

rigor /'rɪgɔː, 'rʌɪgɔː, -gə/ *noun*¹. LME.
[Latin = numbness, stiffness. Cf. RIGOUR.]
1 MEDICINE. A sudden feeling of chill, accompanied by a bout of shivering, marking a rise in body temperature, as at the onset or the height of a fever. LME.
2 In full ***rigor mortis*** /'mɔːtɪs/ [= of death]. The stiffening of the joints and muscles of a body a few hours after death, usu. lasting from one to four days. M19.

rigor *noun*² see RIGOUR.

rigorism /'rɪgərɪz(ə)m/ *noun.* Also (now *rare*) **rigour-**. E18.
[from RIGOUR + -ISM, assim. to Latin RIGOR *noun*¹.]
1 Extreme strictness in interpreting or enforcing a law, precept, etc. E18.
2 ROMAN CATHOLIC THEOLOGY. The doctrine that in doubtful cases of conscience the strict course is always to be followed. L19.

rigorist /'rɪgərɪst/ *noun & adjective.* Also (now *rare*) **rigour-**. E18.
[formed as prec. + -IST.]
▶**A** *noun.* **1** A person who favours or insists on the severest or strictest interpretation or enforcement of a law, precept, etc. Cf. LAXIST. E18.
2 ROMAN CATHOLIC THEOLOGY. A person who holds that in doubtful cases of conscience the strict course is always to be followed. Cf. TUTIORIST. E18.
▶**B** *attrib.* or as *adjective.* Of or pertaining to rigorists or rigorism. L19.
■ **rigo'ristic** *adjective* of, pertaining to, or characteristic of a rigorist, of the nature of rigorism E20.

rigorous /'rɪg(ə)rəs/ *adjective.* LME.
[Old French (*rigoureux*), or late Latin *rigorosus*, from Latin RIGOR *noun*¹: see -OUS.]
▶**I 1** Rigidly severe or unbending; austere, stern; extremely strict in application. LME.
2 Severely exact, rigidly accurate or logical, scrupulous. LME.
3 Strictly adhered to, unswerving. *rare.* M17.

📖 **1** S. JOHNSON I . . hope she will not be too rigorous with the young ones. GEO. ELIOT He wanted a refuge from a standard disagreebly rigorous. F. NORRIS Dressed in a white organdy frock of the most rigorous simplicity. **2** G. BERKELEY Truth and convenience are very different things to the rigorous eye of a philosoper. H. GUNTRIP A rigorous training in philosophy.

▶**II 4** Of the weather etc.: severe; bitterly cold. Formerly also of heat: excessive, violent. E16.

📖 **4** A. COWLEY When rigorous Winter binds you up with Frost. *Times* South-westerly winds between force 5 and force 6 . . meant rigorous yachting conditions.

■ **rigorously** *adverb* LME. **rigorousness** *noun* LME.

rigour /'rɪgə/ *noun.* Also *-**or**. LME.
[Old French (mod. *rigueur*) from Latin RIGOR *noun*¹: see -OUR.]
▶**I 1** Severity in dealing with a person or persons; extreme strictness; harshness. LME.
2 The strict application or enforcement *of* a law, rule, etc. LME. ▸†**b** *ellipt.* The rigour of the law. LME–E18.
3 Strictness *of* discipline etc.; austerity of life; puritanical severity or strictness; rigorism. LME.
4 Severity of weather or climate; extremity or excess of cold. LME. ▸**b** Extreme distress or hardship. M18.
5 Strict accuracy, severe exactitude. L15.
6 An instance of rigour; a harsh or severe action, proceeding, or state; a hardship, an exacting requirement. Usu. in *pl.* M16.

📖 **1** E. PAWEL He judged Brod, with merciless rigour. **3** S. RICHARDSON Rigour makes it difficult for sliding virtue to recover. L. RITCHIE The rigour of the monastic discipline speedily terminated her life. **4** T. GRAY The rigour Of bleak Germania's snows. **b** DICKENS Alleviating the rigour of her conditions by pecuniary donations for her comfort. **5** D. R. HOFSTADTER Euclid's lack of absolute rigor was the cause of some . . path-breaking in mathematics. **6** J. HILTON Only seven out of . . a hundred survived the rigours of the climate. P. ACKROYD The rigours of my post exhausted me.

▶**II 7** = RIGOR *noun*¹ 1. Now *rare.* M16.
†**8** Physical stiffness or hardness. L16–E18.

rigourism *noun*, **rigourist** *noun & adjective* see RIGORISM, RIGORIST.

rig-out /'rɪgaʊt/ *noun. colloq.* E19.
[from RIG *verb*² + OUT *adverb*.]
An outfit, a suit of clothes, a costume, a style of dress. Cf. RIG *noun*⁵ 2.

Rigsmaal /ˈriːgzmɔːl/ *noun.* Now *rare.* **E20.**
[Danish, from genit. of *rige* realm + *mål* (formerly *maal*) language.]
= **Bokmål**, esp. from a Danish perspective. Cf. **Riksmål**.

Rig-veda /rɪgˈveɪdə, -ˈviːdə/ *noun.* **L18.**
[Sanskrit *ṛgveda*, from *ṛc* sacred stanza + *veda* **Veda**.]
The oldest and principal of the Hindu Vedas.
■ **Rig-vedic** *adjective & noun* (*a*) *adjective* of or pertaining to the Rig-veda; (*b*) *noun* Rig-vedic Sanskrit: **L19.**

rigwiddy /ˈrɪgwɪdi/ *noun & adjective. Scot.* (now *dial.*) & †*north.* Also **-woodie** /-wʊdi/. **LME.**
[from **rig** *noun*[1] + **widdy** *noun*[1].]
► **A** *noun.* A backband or ridgeband for a cart-horse, orig. one made of twisted withes or twigs. **LME.**
► **B** *attrib.* or as *adjective.* Ugly, wizened, misshapen. Also as a vague term of abuse. **M17.**

rijsttafel /ˈrʌɪstɑːf(ə)l/ *noun.* **L19.**
[Dutch, from *rijst* **rice** *noun*[2] + *tafel* table.]
A meal of SE Asian food consisting of a selection of different (usu. spiced) rice dishes.

rikishi /ˈrɪkɪʃi/ *noun.* Pl. same. **E20.**
[Japanese, from *riki* strength + *shi* warrior.]
= **sumotori**.

rikka /ˈrɪka/ *noun.* **L19.**
[Japanese, lit. 'standing flowers', from *ritsu* stand + *ka* flower(s).]
A traditional and formal style of Japanese flower arrangement, used esp. to decorate Buddhist temples.

Riksmål /ˈriːksmɔːl/ *noun.* **E20.**
[Norwegian, from genit. of *rike* realm + *mål* language.]
= **Dano-Norwegian** *noun*, *spec.* in Norway. Cf. **Bokmål**, **Landsmål**, **Rigsmaal**.

rilawa /ˈrɪləwɑː/ *noun. rare.* **M19.**
[Sinhalese *rilavā*. Cf. earlier **rillow**.]
The toque macaque, *Macaca sinica*, of Sri Lanka.

rile /rʌɪl/ *verb & noun.* **E19.**
[Var. of **roil** *verb*[2].]
► **A** *verb.* **1 a** *verb trans.* Excite, irritate, make angry. Also foll. by *up. colloq.* **E19.** ▸**b** *verb intrans.* Become angry. Foll. by *up. colloq.* **M19.**
2 *verb trans.* Make (a liquid) turbid by stirring up the sediment; muddy. Chiefly *US.* **M19.**

> 🕮 **1** P. Angadi She really riles me. She's such a fool.

► **B** *noun.* A turbid or muddy condition of liquid. *rare.* **M19.**
■ **riley** *adjective* (*US*) (*a*) turbid, muddy; (*b*) angry, irritable: **E19.**

Riley /ˈrʌɪli/ *noun. colloq.* (orig. *US*). Also **Reilly**. **E20.**
[Unexpl. use of surname.]
the life of Riley, a comfortable pleasant carefree existence.

rilievo *noun* var. of **relievo** *noun*[1].

Rilkean /ˈrɪlkɪən/ *adjective.* **M20.**
[from *Rilke* (see below) + **-an**.]
Of, pertaining to, or characteristic of the German poet and writer Rainer Maria Rilke (1875–1926) or his work.

rill /rɪl/ *noun.* **M16.**
[Prob. of Low Dutch origin: cf. Low German *ril(le)*, Dutch, East Frisian *ril* (whence German *Rille*). Cf. medieval Latin (Norman) *rilla*.]
1 A small stream; a rivulet. Also, a small temporary channel formed on the surface of soil or sand after rain or tidal ebb; such a channel or pattern of channels as preserved in rock by fossilization. **M16.**
2 A small narrow furrow in which seeds are sown, a drill. Now *dial.* **M17.**
3 *Astronomy.* = **rille**. **L19.**
4 *Phonetics.* [Danish *rille*.] More fully ***rill spirant***. A fricative produced by forcing air through a narrow aperture formed by the tongue and the roof of the mouth. **E20.**

> 🕮 **1** *transf.*: D. Jacobson At these words rills of tears and blood ran . . back into my nose and mouth. *attrib.*: B. W. Sparks In the wet season . . the slope may be under the influence of concentrated rill action.

■ **rillet** *noun* a small rill or rivulet **M16.** **rillock** *noun* (*rare*) a rillet **L19.** **rilly** *adjective* (now *rare* or *obsolete*) having many rills **E18.**

rill /rɪl/ *verb.* **E17.**
[from the noun.]
1 *verb intrans.* Flow in a small stream. Chiefly *poet.* **E17.**
†**2** *verb trans.* Make small narrow furrows in (soil). *rare.* Only in **M17.**
3 *verb trans.* **a** Utter (words, a song, etc.) in liquid notes. *rare.* **L18.** ▸**b** Form by flowing. *rare.* **M19.**

> 🕮 **1** W. de la Mare Fast though he baled, the water rilled in faster.

rille /rɪl/ *noun.* **M19.**
[German: see **rill** *noun*.]
Astronomy. A long narrow trench or valley on the surface of the moon.

rilled /rɪld/ *adjective*[1]. **E20.**
[from **rill** *noun*, *verb*: see **-ed**[2], **-ed**[1].]
Marked by or having a rill or rills.

rilled /rɪld/ *adjective*[2]. **L20.**
[from **rille** + **-ed**[2].]
Astronomy. Characterized by or having a rille or rilles.

rillettes /ˈriːjɛt/ *noun* (treated as *sing.* or *pl.*). **L19.**
[French.]
Pâté made of minced pork, chicken, etc., seasoned and combined with fat.

rilling /ˈrɪlɪŋ/ *noun.* **E17.**
[from **rill** *noun* or *verb* + **-ing**[1].]
1 The formation of a rill or small narrow channel; a furrow. **E17.**
2 *Archaeology.* Pottery decoration or marking consisting of fine grooves. **M20.**

†**rillow** *noun.* **L17–L18.**
[formed as **rilawa**.]
= **rilawa**.

Rilsan /ˈrɪlsan/ *noun.* **M20.**
[Arbitrary formation from French *ricin* castor oil plant: see **ricinus**.]
(Proprietary name for) a kind of nylon used esp. as a fibre.

rim /rɪm/ *noun*[1].
[Old English *rima* = Old Norse *rimi* a strip of land. No other cognates are known.]
†**1** A border, a bank, a coast. Only in **OE.**
2 The surface *of* a stretch of water. Now chiefly *US.* **ME.**
3 a The outer edge of a wheel, connected by the spokes to the hub, on which a tyre may be fitted. **LME.** ▸**b** A hoop-shaped band of wood forming the outer frame of a sieve, musical instrument, etc. **M17.** ▸**c** The part of a frame of a pair of spectacles surrounding the lens (usu. in *pl.*); *colloq.* (in *pl.*) spectacles. **M19.** ▸**d** Any circular object or mark. **M19.**
4 a The outer limit or margin of an object, esp. of something circular. **E17.** ▸**b** The visible limit or margin of the horizon, the landscape, etc. (Foll. by *of.*) **M19.** ▸**c** The outer edge of a semi-circular desk around which a newspaper's subeditors work. *US slang.* **E20.**
5 a A raised edge or border; *esp.* a circular one. **M17.** ▸**b** A margin or boundary line of land etc.; a narrow strip. **L18.** ▸**c** *ellipt.* = **rimrock** (a) below. *N. Amer.* **M19.**

> 🕮 **2a** *Bicycle* Braking hard can make rims very hot. **d** M. Spark One accusing another of leaving a rim round the edge of the bath. **4a** M. Sinclair Now and then her eyelids shook, fluttered red rims. ***Pacific rim***: see **pacific** *adjective*. **b** J. L. Waten The sun . . peered over the red rim of the horizon. **5a** *Asian Art* Flowers . . fill the background and are repeated on the underside of the rim. **b** D. Lessing A big, cool empty sky . . above a rim of dark mountains.

Comb.: **rim-brake** a brake acting on the rim of a wheel; **rim drive** a method of driving the turntable of a record-player by means of frictional contact between the motor shaft and the inner rim of the turntable; **rimfire** *adjective* (*a*) (of a cartridge) having the primer around the edge of the base; (*b*) (of a rifle) adapted for such cartridges; **rimland** a peripheral region with political or strategic significance; **rim light** *Photography & Cinematography* a light placed behind the subject in order to give the appearance of a halo of light; the light produced by a lamp in such a position; **rim lock** a lock that is fitted to the surface of a door etc., as opposed to a mortise lock; **rim man** *US slang* a newspaper subeditor; **rimrock** *noun & verb* (*N. Amer.*) (*a*) *noun* (*Geology*) an outcrop of resistant rock, *esp.* one forming a cliff at the edge of a plateau; the bedrock around and above the edge of a gravel deposit or placer; (*b*) *verb trans.* (*slang*) drive a (sheep) over a cliff; **rimrocker** *N. Amer. slang* a person who drives sheep over a cliff; **rim-shot** a drum-stroke in which the stick strikes the rim and the head of the drum simultaneously; **rimstone** *Geology* a layer of calcite deposited by evaporation round the rim of a pool of water, characteristic of karst land.
■ **rimless** *adjective* (esp. of spectacles) without a rim **E19.**

rim /rɪm/ *noun*[2]. *obsolete* exc. *dial.*
[Old English *rēoma* = Middle Dutch *rieme* (Dutch *riem*) leather strap or thong. Cf. **riem**.]
†**1** A membrane, a thin layer of skin. **OE–M17.** ▸**b** A scale or film over the eye. **OE–L16.**
2 In full ***rim of the belly***. The peritoneum. **M16**

> 🕮 **2** Shakes. *Hen. V* I will fetch thy rim out at thy throat.

rim /rɪm/ *verb*[1]. Infl. **-mm-**. **L18.**
[from **rim** *noun*[1].]
1 *verb trans.* Provide with a rim; be a rim to; border, edge, encircle. **L18.**
2 *verb intrans.* Of a steel ingot: form an outer rim of relatively pure steel. **M20.**

> 🕮 **1** W. Boyd Her fingernails were rimmed with what looked like brown ink. *Footloose* Climbing on the gritstone crags that rim the moors. **2 rimming steel** a low-carbon steel in which deoxidation has been controlled to produce ingots having an outer rim relatively free from carbon and impurities.

rim /rɪm/ *verb*[2]. Infl. **-mm-**. **E20.**
[Perh. var. of **ream** *verb*[3].]
1 a *verb intrans.* Wish to have sexual intercourse. *US dial.* **E20.** ▸**b** *verb trans.* Lick or suck (a person's anus), usu. as a preliminary to sexual intercourse. *coarse slang* (orig. *US*). **M20.**
2 *verb trans.* Cheat, swindle, (a person). *N. Amer. slang.* **M20.**

rima /ˈrʌɪmə/ *noun.* **M19.**
[Latin.]
Anatomy. In full ***rima glottidis*** /glɒˈtʌɪdɪs/. The passage in the glottis between the vocal cords.

rimaye /riːˈmeɪ/ *noun.* **E20.**
[French, from Latin *rima* fissure + French *-aye* collect. suffix.]
= **bergschrund**.

Rimbaldian /rɪmˈbaldɪən/ *adjective.* Also **Rimbaudian** /-ˈbəʊdɪən/. **E20.**
[French *Rimbaldien*, from *Rimbaud* (see below) + *-ien* **-ian**.]
Of, pertaining to, or characteristic of the French poet Arthur Rimbaud (1854–91) or his work.

rime /rʌɪm/ *noun*[1].
[Old English *hrīm* = Middle & mod. Dutch *rijm*, Old Norse *hrím*.]
1 Hoar-frost (now *poet.*). Also (*dial.*), a chill mist or fog. **OE.**
2 *Meteorology.* Frost formed on cold objects by the rapid freezing of supercooled water vapour in cloud or fog. **L19.**

> 🕮 **1** *transf.*: D. Hewett Face . . clean of make-up, a rime of salt on her blonde lashes.

rime /rʌɪm; *in branch II foreign* rim/ *noun*[2]. **ME.**
[Old & mod. French from medieval Latin *rithmus*, *rythmus* (used spec. of accentual verse which was usu. rhymed) for Latin *rhythmus* **rhythm** *noun*. See also **rhyme** *noun*, **rhythm**.]
► **I 1** = **rhyme** *noun* 1, 2, 3. Formerly also, metre, measure. *arch.* **ME.**
► **II 2** ***rime couée*** /kue/, = ***tail-rhyme*** s.v. **tail** *noun*[1]. **ME.**
3 ***rime riche*** /riʃ/, = ***rich rhyme*** s.v. **rich** *adjective* 7. **E20.**
■ **rimeless** *adjective* **M16.**

rime /rʌɪm/ *verb*[1].
[Old English *rȳman* = Old Frisian *rēma*, Middle Dutch *rūmen*, *ruymen* (Dutch *ruimen*), Old Saxon *rūmian*, Old High German *rūmen* (German *räumen*), Old Norse (Icelandic) *rýma*, ult. from Germanic base also of **room** *adjective*. Cf. **ream** *verb*[3].]
1 *verb trans.* †**a** Clear (a way); vacate, give up. **OE–ME.** ▸**b** Remove. *dial.* **M19.**
2 *verb intrans.* †**a** Withdraw, leave. **OE–LME.** ▸**b** Move house. *dial.* **M19.**
3 *verb trans.* †**a** Extend, increase, enlarge. Only in **OE.** ▸†**b** *verb refl.* Stretch (oneself). **OE–LME.** ▸**c** Widen *out* (a hole). *techn.* **E19.**

rime /rʌɪm/ *verb*[2]. *arch.* See also **rhyme** *verb.* **ME.**
[Old French *rimer*, formed as **rime** *noun*[2].]
1 *verb intrans.* = **rhyme** *verb* 3. *obsolete* exc. *Scot.* **ME.**
2 *verb trans.* = **rhyme** *verb* 2. Now *rare.* **ME.**
†**3** *verb intrans.* = **rhyme** *verb* 4. **LME–M17.**
4 *verb trans.* = **rhyme** *verb* 1. **L16.**
†**5** *verb intrans.* Use rime. Cf. **rhyme** *verb* 5. Only in **17.**
6 *verb trans.* = **rhyme** *verb* 4b. *rare.* **L19.**
■ **rimester** *noun* a writer of inferior verses: **L16.**

rime /rʌɪm/ *verb*[3]. **M18.**
[from **rime** *noun*[1].]
1 *verb trans.* Cover (an object) with rime or hoar-frost. **M18.**
2 *verb intrans.* Become rimed. **M20.**

rimed /rʌɪmd/ *adjective.* **L19.**
[from **rime** *noun*[1], *verb*[3]: see **-ed**[2], **-ed**[1].]
Covered with rime.

rime-frost /ˈrʌɪmfrɒst/ *noun.* Long *arch. rare.* **ME.**
[from **rime** *noun*[1] + **frost** *noun*, corresp. to Icelandic *hrímfrost*, Old Swedish *hrimfrost*.]
Hoar-frost, rime. Also, an instance of this; a frosty morning.

rimer /ˈrʌɪmə/ *noun*[1]. *arch.* See also **rhymer**. **ME.**
[from **rime** *verb*[2] + **-er**[1].]
A person who writes rhymes; a rhymer.

rimer /ˈrʌɪmə/ *noun*[2]. Now *rare.* **E19.**
[from **rime** *verb*[1] + **-er**[1].]
= **reamer** *noun*.

rimer *noun*[3] var. of **rymer**.

rimestock /ˈrʌɪmstɒk/ *noun. rare.* **M17.**
[Norwegian *rimstok* var. of *rimstaf* = Old Norse *prímastafr* (Swedish *primstaf*), from *prim* **prime** *noun*[1] + *stafr* stave, letter.]
= ***clog-almanac*** s.v. **clog** *noun*.

rimmed /rɪmd/ *adjective.* **E18.**
[from **rim** *noun*[1], *verb*[1]: see **-ed**[2], **-ed**[1].]
Having or provided with a rim, esp. one of a specified colour, form, material, etc.

rimming /ˈrɪmɪŋ/ *noun.* **M17.**
[from **rim** *noun*[1], *verb*[1] + **-ing**[1].]
The action of **rim** *verb*[1]. Also, a rim, a border.

rimmon /rɪˈmɔːn/ *noun*. Also **rimon**. Pl. **-im** /-ɪm/. **M20.**
[Hebrew *rimmōn* lit. 'pomegranate'.]
A pomegranate-shaped ornament or decorative cover for each of the bars at either end of a Jewish law-scroll.

rimose /rʌɪˈməʊs/ *adjective*. **E18.**
[Latin *rimosus*, from **RIMA**: see **-OSE**[1].]
Chiefly *BOTANY*. Full of or marked by fissures or chinks.
■ **rimosity** *noun* **E18.** ˈ**rimous** *adjective* = **RIMOSE E18.**

rimple /ˈrɪmp(ə)l/ *noun & verb*. **LME.**
[Corresp. in sense to Middle & mod. Dutch and Middle & mod. Low German *rimpel*. Cf. **RUMPLE** *noun*.]
► **A** *noun*. A wrinkle. Also, a ripple. Now *Scot. & dial.* **LME.**
► **B** *verb intrans. & trans.* Wrinkle, ripple. *rare*. **LME.**
■ **rimpled** *adjective* (now *dial. & US*) **LME.**

rimu /ˈrɪmʊ, ˈriːmuː/ *noun*. **M19.**
[Maori.]
A tall evergreen coniferous tree of New Zealand, *Dacrydium cupressinum*; the wood of this tree. Also called ***red pine***.

rimy /ˈrʌɪmi/ *adjective*. **OE.**
[from **RIME** *noun*[1] + **-Y**[1].]
Covered with rime; frosty.

rin /rɪn/ *noun*. Pl. same. **L19.**
[Japanese.]
A monetary unit of Japan, equal to one-tenth of a sen; a former coin of this value.

rin *verb* see **RUN** *verb*.

rinceau /rɛ̃so/ *noun*. Pl. ***-eaux*** /-o/. **L18.**
[French.]
A moulded, carved, or painted decoration on furniture etc., often in the form of scrolls or acanthus leaves.

rind /rʌɪnd/ *noun*[1] & *verb*.
[Old English *rind*, *rinde*, corresp. to Old Saxon *rinda*, Middle Dutch *rinde*, *rende*, *runde* (Dutch *run*), Old High German *rinta*, *rinda* (German *Rinde*), of unkn. origin.]
► **A** *noun*. **1** The (outer) bark of a tree or plant. Also (now *rare*), a piece of bark. **OE.** ▸**b** *BOTANY*. The hard outer layer of a rhizomorph or other part of a fungus. **L19.**
2 The tough outer layer or covering of something; *spec*. (***a***) the peel or skin of a fruit or vegetable (now esp. of a citrus fruit); (***b***) the outer crust of a cheese; (***c***) the skin of a person or animal (now esp. of bacon). **OE.** ▸**b** The edge or rim of something; the border of a country or piece of land. *obsolete* exc. *Scot.* **M16.** ▸†**c** A membrane, a pellicle; *esp*. (***a***) the pia mater; (***b***) the peritoneum. **L16–L17.**
3 *fig*. The external or superficial aspect of something, as opp. to its inner or true nature. **OE.** ▸**b** A person's body or outward appearance. *rare*. **LME.** ▸**c** Impudence, effrontery. Cf. **CRUST** *noun* 9. *slang*. **E20.**

📖 **2** *She* Steep six blackcurrant leaves . . with the rind of half a lemon. **3** COLERIDGE No dullard, But one that strips the outward rind of things.

Comb.: **rind graft** = ***crown graft*** s.v. **CROWN** *noun*.
► **B** *verb trans*. Remove the rind from; *spec*. strip the bark from (a tree). **LME.**
■ **rinded** *adjective* having a rind, esp. of a specified kind **M16.** **rindless** *adjective* (esp. of bacon) having no rind **ME.** **rindy** *adjective* having a tough rind **E18.**

rind /rʌɪnd/ *noun*[2]. **ME.**
[Prob. from Middle & mod. Low German *rīn*, Middle & mod. Dutch *rijn*, †*rine*, Flemish *rijne*, with parasitic *d*.]
= **INK** *noun*[2] 1.

rinderpest /ˈrɪndəpɛst/ *noun*. **M19.**
[German, from *Rinder* cattle (pl. of *Rind*) + *Pest* plague.]
An infectious disease of ruminants, esp. oxen, caused by a paramyxovirus and characterized by fever, dysentery, and inflammation of the mucous membranes; cattle-plague.

rindle /ˈrɪnd(ə)l/ *noun & verb*. Now chiefly *Scot. & dial.* Also (earlier) †**rinnel**.
[Old English *rinnelle*, *rynele* fem., *rynel* masc., from stem of **RUN** *verb*. See also **RUNNEL**.]
► **A** *noun*. A small watercourse or stream; a runnel. **OE.**
► **B** *verb intrans*. Stream, flow. **M19**

†**rine** *noun* see **RHINE** *noun*[2].

rine /rʌɪn/ *verb*. *obsolete* exc. *dial.*
[Old English *hrinan* = Old Saxon, Old High German *hrinan* (Middle Dutch, Middle High German *rinen*) touch, Old Norse *hrína* (Norwegian *rina*) take effect on.]
1 *verb trans*. Touch; affect. **OE.**
†**2** *verb intrans*. Reach for, lay one's hand or fingers *on*, something. Only in **ME.**
†**3** *verb intrans*. Belong or pertain *to* a person or thing; tend *to* something. Chiefly *Scot.* **ME–M16.**

riner /ˈrʌɪnə/ *noun*. **L17.**
[from prec. + **-ER**[1].]
In the game of quoits, a touch of the peg by the quoit.

rinforzando /rɪnfɔːtˈsandəʊ/ *adverb, adjective, & noun*. **E19.**
[Italian, pres. pple of *rinforzare* strengthen.]
MUSIC. ►**A** *adverb & adjective*. A direction: with a sudden stress or crescendo. **E19.**
► **B** *noun*. Pl. **-dos**, **-di** /-di/. A sudden stress or crescendo made on a short phrase. **M19.**

ring /rɪŋ/ *noun*[1].
[Old English *hring* = (Old) Frisian *(h)ring*, Old Saxon, Old High German *hring* (Dutch, German *Ring*), Old Norse *hringr*, from Germanic (whence also **RANK** *noun*, Finnish *rengas*).]
► **I 1 a** A small circular band, usu. of precious metal and frequently set with precious stones, worn on the finger as an ornament or as a token of betrothal, marriage, etc. **OE.** ▸**b** Orig., an ornamental band, esp. of precious metal, for the arm or neck. Later (freq. as 2nd elem. of comb.), a small circular band of esp. precious metal hung from or encircling a part of the body other than a finger. **OE.**
2 *Hist*. Any of a number of small iron circles which interlaced to form chain-mail. Usu. in *pl.* **OE.**
3 a A circular band of any material used as a link, for fastening, etc. **OE.** ▸†**b** A circular door-knocker. **LME–L17.** ▸**c** = ***curtain-ring*** s.v. **CURTAIN** *noun*. **E19.** ▸**d** = ***leg-ring*** s.v. **LEG** *noun*. **E20.** ▸**e** A circular device, usu. forming part of a gas or electric cooker or hob, providing heat from below and used for cooking. **E20.** ▸**f** A bottomless cylindrical vessel used for growing plants by the ring culture method (see below). **M20.**
4 *Hist*. A circlet of metal suspended from a post which each of a number of riders attempted to carry off on the point of a lance. Chiefly in ***run at the ring***, ***ride at the ring***. **E16.**
5 Any of a number of raised metal bands cast in the body of a cannon (now *Hist.*); *ARCHITECTURE* a raised decorative band forming part of the moulding on the capital of a column. **E17.**

📖 **1a** E. LANGLEY On his little finger gleamed the heavy signet ring. **b** ***ankle-ring***, ***ear-ring***, ***nose-ring***, etc. **3a** F. H. JOYNSON One course of bricks, strongly bound together by stout iron rings. ***O-ring***, ***Raschig ring***, ***split ring***, etc. **e** I. MCEWAN The cooker . . was of the kind found in caravans, with two rings, no oven.

► **II 6** Orig., the visible limit of the horizon. Later, the border, rim, or outer part of a circular object, esp. of a coin or a wheel. **OE.**
7 A thing or mark having the form of a circular band; a circular piece or part of an object; a coil. **LME.**
8 *spec*. **a** *ASTRONOMY*. A thin band of particles etc. round a planet; a halo round the moon. **M17.** ▸**b** Each of a series of concentric circles seen in a cross-section of a tree-trunk, representing a layer of secondary xylem added to the wood in a single period of growth, esp. one year. Cf. ***growth ring*** s.v. **GROWTH. L17.** ▸**c** Any of a number of raised circular marks at the base of the horns of an animal, varying in number according to the animal's age. **E18.** ▸**d** *BOTANY*. The annulus of a fungus. **L18.** ▸**e** *ARCHAEOLOGY*. A circular prehistoric earthwork, usu. consisting of a rampart or bank and a ditch. Usu. *attrib.*, as ***ring-bank***, ***ring-ditch***, etc. **L18.** ▸**f** Any of a number of widening concentric circular ripples caused by an object's dropping into water. **E19.** ▸**g** A gold-coloured band worn on the sleeve to designate rank in the armed services. **M20.** ▸**h** The anus. Freq. in ***spew one's ring*** below. *coarse slang*. **M20.**

📖 **7** SHELLEY Sometimes the Snake around his enemy's neck Locked in stiff rings his adamantine coil. E. BOWEN Have I got blue rings under my eyes? T. BARLING I'll bet you . . leave a ring around the bath.

► **III 9** A group of people or things arranged in a circle; such an arrangement. **OE.** ▸**b** *CHEMISTRY*. A number of atoms bonded together to form a closed loop. **M19.** ▸**c** *CYTOLOGY*. A chromosome, group of chromosomes, or part of a chromosome in the form of a loop, without free ends. **E20.**
10 A combination of people drawn together due to a shared interest or goal and often acting unscrupulously or illicitly; *spec*. (***a***) an organization attempting to manipulate political affairs; (***b***) a group or network of dealers, traders, etc., seeking to monopolize and control a particular market by cooperation in trading at agreed price-levels; (***c***) an organization or network of people engaged in espionage. Usu. with specifying word. **M19.**
11 *MATH*. A set of elements which is a group under (a binary operation analogous to) addition and closed under (another analogous to) multiplication, with the property that multiplication is distributive over addition and associative. **M20.**

📖 **9** *Amateur Stage* As each character enters the ring of spectators he introduces himself. *New York Times* Everyone sat in a ring, holding hands, eyes closed. **10** R. H. TAWNEY The exactions of rings and monopolies . . drove weaker competitors out of the field. *Spectator* They . . were . . charged with being part of a sex ring which traded each other's . . children.

► **IV 12 a** An enclosed, usu. circular, space used for a circus performance, bullfight, etc. **ME.** ▸**b** A space, orig. within a circle of spectators, now within a roped square on a raised platform, for a boxing or wrestling match. Also, *the* institution or profession of boxing. **L17.** ▸**c** An enclosed space at a racecourse where bookmakers gather to take bets. Also, *the* bookmaking profession. **L18.** ▸**d** An enclosed or clear space at an auction, used for displaying livestock prior to sale. **L19.**
13 A circular or spiral course. Chiefly in ***in a ring***, ***make rings round***, ***run rings round*** below. **L16.**

📖 **13** W. COWPER They sport like wanton doves in airy rings.

Phrases: **get the ring** become engaged to be married. **hold the ring**, **keep the ring** (***a***) be a bystander or onlooker while others fight or quarrel; (***b***) *fig*. refrain from action; monitor a dispute without involvement in it. †**lead the ring** take the lead, be foremost, instigate a course of action, esp. an illicit or illegal one. **make rings round** = ***run rings round*** below. **ring-a-ring o' roses** a game played by children holding hands and dancing in a circle. **Ring of Fire** *GEOLOGY* a zone of high seismic and volcanic activity surrounding the Pacific Ocean. **run rings round** *colloq.* surpass (a person) with the greatest ease; beat easily; outclass; outwit. **spew one's ring** *coarse slang* vomit violently. ***THREE-ring circus***. ***throw one's hat into the ring***: see **HAT** *noun*.
Comb.: **ring armature** *ELECTRICITY* an armature having a ring winding; **ring-armour** = ***chain-armour*** s.v. **CHAIN** *noun*; **ring-billed** *adjective* having a band of colour around the bill; ***ring-billed gull***, an American gull, *Larus delawarensis*; **ring binder** a loose-leaf binder with ring-shaped hinged metal clasps which can be opened to pass through holes punched in the paper; **ring binding**: using ring-shaped metal clasps to hold sheets of paper together; **ring blackbird** = ***ring ouzel*** below; **ringbolt** (orig. *NAUTICAL*) a bolt with an eye at one end, to which a ring is attached; **ringbone** *FARRIERY* (***a***) a deposit of bony matter on the pastern-bones of a horse; (***b***) the growth of such bony matter, as a specific disease of horses; **ring book** a notebook having the form of a ring binder; **ring-bound** *adjective* having a ring binding; **ring-building** *ARCHAEOLOGY* the forming of pottery vessels by adding successive layers of ring-shaped pieces of clay; **ring burner** a ring on a gas cooker or hob, a gas ring; **ring-canal** *ZOOLOGY* a circular canal around the mouth, esp. forming part of the digestive system of some coelenterates or the water-vascular system of echinoderms; †**ring-carrier** (*rare*, Shakes.) a go-between; **ring circuit** (***a***) *ELECTRONICS* = ***ring counter*** below; (***b***) *ELECTRICITY* a wiring arrangement for power distribution in a house etc., in which sockets and appliances are connected to a single loop of cable which starts from and returns to a fuse-box; **ring complex** *GEOLOGY* an association of cone-sheets and ring dykes; **ring counter** *ELECTRONICS* a counting circuit consisting of a number of flip-flops or other bistable devices wired in a closed loop; **ringcraft** skill in boxing; **ring-cross** a design consisting of a cross enclosed in a circle; **ring culture** the technique of growing plants, esp. tomatoes, using a bottomless cylindrical vessel which contains nutrients and rests on an inert bed through which water is provided; **ring dance** a dance, often a traditional one, in which dancers form a circle; **ring-dial** *Hist.* a small portable sundial with a graduated brass ring; **ring dyke** *GEOLOGY* a dyke that is arcuate or roughly circular in plan, formed by upwelling of magma along ring fractures; **ring dotterel** = ***RINGED plover***; **ring-dove** (***a***) the woodpigeon, *Columba palumbus*; (***b***) a domesticated or feral African collared dove, *Streptopelia roseogrisea* ('*risoria*'); **ring-fence** *noun & verb* (***a***) *noun* a fence completely enclosing an estate, piece of land, etc.; *transf. & fig.* an effective or comprehensive barrier or means of segregation; (***b***) *verb trans.* enclose (a piece of land etc.) with a ring-fence; *transf. & fig.* treat as if enclosed by a ring-fence, segregate, keep separate; **ring finger** the finger next to the little finger, esp. of the left hand, on which the wedding ring is usu. worn; **ring flash** *PHOTOGRAPHY* a circular electronic flash tube that fits round the camera lens to give shadowless lighting of a subject near the lens; **ring-fort** *ARCHAEOLOGY* a fort or other position defended by circular ramparts and ditches; **ring fracture** a fracture in the form of a circle; *GEOLOGY* a conical or nearly cylindrical fault associated with cauldron subsidence; **ring-frame** a spinning machine in which the thread is wound by means of a traveller running on a horizontal ring; **ring gear** a crown wheel; **ring gland** *ZOOLOGY* a gland in dipteran larvae which secretes ecdysone; **ring-junction** a road junction at which traffic is channelled in two directions round a central island, entering and leaving by smaller islands; **ring light** = ***ring flash*** above; **ring main** (***a***) an electric main that starts from and returns to a particular power station or sub-station, so that each consumer has an alternative path for supply in the event of a failure; (***b***) = ***ring circuit*** (b) above; (***c***) an arrangement of pipes forming a closed loop into which steam, water, or sewage may be fed and whose points of draw-off are supplied by flow from two directions; **ring-man** (***a***) (*obsolete* exc. *dial.*) the ring finger; (***b***) a sporting man; a bookmaker; **ring modulator** *ELECTRONICS* a circuit that incorporates a closed loop of four diodes and can be used for balanced mixing and modulation of signals; **ring-neck** *adjective & noun* (***a***) *adjective* ring-necked; (***b***) *noun* any of various ring-necked animals or birds; **ring-necked** *adjective* (of an animal) having a band of colour round the neck; ***ring-necked parakeet***, a pale green parakeet, *Psittacula krameri*, native to central Africa and southern Asia but introduced to parts of Britain and Europe; ***ring-necked pheasant***, the common Asian pheasant *Phasianus colchicus*, now widely introduced; **ring-oiled** *adjective* lubricated by a ring oiler; **ring oiler** in a machine, a metal ring which rests on and turns with a journal and dips into a reservoir of lubricant, so automatically lubricating the bearings; **ring-opener** = ***ring-pull*** (a) below; **ring ouzel** a thrush, *Turdus torquatus*, of the western Palaearctic, the male of which has black plumage with a white bar on the breast, the female being more brown; **ring pheasant** a ring-necked pheasant; **ring pigeon** = ***ring-dove*** above; **ring plover** = ***RINGED plover***; **ring-pull** *noun & adjective* (***a***) *noun* a ring attached to the seal of a tin which breaks the seal when pulled; (***b***) *adjective* (of a tin) having a ring-pull; **ring-road** a bypass encircling a town or urban area; **ring-rope** (in *pl.*) the ropes surrounding a boxing or wrestling ring; **ring rot** a disease of potato tubers, caused by the bacterium *Corynebacterium sepedonicum*; **ring scaler** *ELECTRONICS* = ***ring counter*** above; **ring shake** *FORESTRY* a

partial or complete split between two or more consecutive rings in a tree; **ring-snake** any of various snakes with bands of colour around the body; *esp.* (*a*) the Eurasian grass snake; (*b*) *US* a snake of the genus *Diadophis*, esp. *Diadophis punctatus*; **ring spanner**: in which the jaws form a ring with internal serrations which fit completely around a nut, putting pressure on all its faces; **ringspot** (*a*) any of several plant diseases characterized by annular spots on the leaves; (*b*) an annular mark on a plant or animal; **ring-thrush** = *ring ouzel* above; †**ring-time** (*rare*, Shakes.) a time of giving or exchanging rings; **ring velvet**: of so fine a quality that a width of it can be drawn through a ring; **ring-walk** *arch.* a circuitous walk undertaken by a hunter in order to check the intended course prior to a hunt; **ring-wall** (*a*) a wall completely surrounding or encircling a certain area; (*b*) a roughly circular rock wall surrounding a crater or mare on the moon or a similar formation on the earth, freq. of volcanic origin; **ringway** a circular system of major roads round a town or urban area; **ring winding** ELECTRICITY a form of armature winding in which each turn of the winding passes through the centre of the hollow armature core; **ring-work** a circular entrenchment.

■ **ringie** *noun* (*Austral. slang*) the keeper of the ring in a game of two-up M20. **ringless** *adjective* M19. **ringlike** *adjective* resembling a ring; having the form of a circular line: L19. **ringwise** *adverb* in the manner or form of a ring or rings L19. **ringy** *adjective*[1] (*a*) resembling a ring; marked with rings; (*b*) *N. Amer. slang* irritable, angry: L17.

ring /rɪŋ/ *noun*[2]. M16.

[from RING *verb*[1].]

1 A set or peal *of* (church) bells. M16.

2 a A ringing sound or noise; *spec.* (*a*) the sound produced by ringing a bell, esp. a doorbell; (*b*) each of a series of ringing sounds signalling that a telephone is receiving a call. E17. ▸**b** A ringing tone or quality in the voice. M19. ▸**c** The resonance of a coin or glass vessel by which its genuineness or inherent purity is tested; *fig.* a specified inherent quality, esp. of a statement or utterance. M19. ▸**d** ELECTRONICS. A sequence of damped oscillations at the resonant frequency of a circuit; an individual oscillation in such a sequence. M20.

†**3** Money obtained by begging or extortion. *slang.* L17–L18.

4 a An act of ringing a bell, esp. a doorbell. E18. ▸**b** An act of ringing a coin to test its genuineness. *rare.* L19. ▸**c** A telephone call. Freq. in ***give a person a ring***, make a telephone call to a person. *colloq.* E20.

5 ***ring-in***, a fraudulent substitution. Cf. RING *verb*[1] 13. *Austral. & NZ slang.* M20.

> **1** T. HEARNE The Church is very . . handsome, and hath a Ring of eight very good Bells. **2a** ELLIS PETERS The ring of harnesses and hooves . . entered ahead of the cavalcade, a lively sound. **b** F. NORRIS Bewildered at the truculent ring in Annixter's voice. **c** G. SANTAYANA When Oliver protested . . the words had a familiar ring. **4a** J. WAINWRIGHT Beth . . answered Bowling's ring, led him to the kitchen.

Phrases: ***give a person a ring***: see sense 4c above. **ring of truth** a convincing impression of truthfulness. **the dead ring (of)** *Austral. & NZ slang* a striking resemblance (to).

■ **ringy** *adjective*[2] having a ringing quality or tone M19.

ring /rɪŋ/ *verb*[1]. Pa. t. **rang** /raŋ/, (*arch. & non-standard*) **rung** /rʌŋ/. Pa. pple **rung**.

[Old English *hringan* corresp. to Old Norse *hringja*.]

▸**I** *verb intrans.* **1 a** Give out a clear resonant or vibrating sound as of a hard metal object being struck. OE. ▸**b** *fig.* Convey a specified impression or inherent quality. Freq. in ***ring true***, ***ring false*** below. E17. ▸**c** Of an electric circuit or a solid body: undergo damped oscillation at its resonant frequency. M20.

2 a Of a bell: give out a clear metallic note under the impact of the clapper. ME. ▸**b** Of a bell: convey a summons *to* prayers, church, etc. E16. ▸**c** Of a telephone: produce a series of resonant or vibrating sounds signalling that a call is being received. E20.

3 a Of a place: resound or reverberate with a sound or noise. Freq. foll. by *with*, †*of* a sound. ME. ▸**b** Be filled with talk *of*, resound *with* the renown or fame of, an event, person, etc. E17.

4 a Cause a bell to sound; *spec.* summon or send for a person, esp. a servant, or a thing. ME. ▸†**b** Summon people to church, prayers, etc., by means of ringing a bell. LME–L17. ▸**c** Call a person by telephone. Also foll. by *up*. E20.

5 Of a sound: be loud or resonant; resound, re-echo. Freq. foll. by *out*. LME.

6 Of the ears: be affected by a sensation of buzzing or resonance; be filled *with* a sound. LME.

> **1a** P. D. JAMES Their footsteps rang on the marble floor. *Guitar Player* Lift your left hand slightly after each chord so that the second string rings clearly. **b** JONSON But Crassus, and this Caesar here ring hollow. **3a** G. S. HAIGHT The children, who made Bird Grove ring with happy laughter. **b** ADDISON She . . has made the Country ring with several imaginary Exploits which are palmed upon her. **4a** E. M. FORSTER Lucy could ring for the maid. N. MARSH Marco came in . . . He said: 'You rang, sir?' **5** M. SHADBOLT He began to chop wood. The crisp sounds rang against the trees.

▸**II** *verb trans.* **7** Make (a bell) sound. OE.

8 Of a bell: indicate (the hour etc.) by ringing. OE.

9 Sound (a peal, knell, etc.) on a bell. OE.

10 Utter resoundingly, shout (a name etc.) aloud. ME. ▸†**b** Instil (a lesson etc.) *in* a person's mind by constant repetition. M17–E18.

11 a Cause to give out a ringing sound. Now *rare.* LME. ▸**b** Test the resonance of (a coin etc.) to demonstrate genuine quality. L17.

12 a Usher *in* or *out* with the sound of bells. M16. ▸**b** Summon (a person) by ringing a bell. Also foll. by *down*, *in*, *up*, etc. M16. ▸**c** Foll. by *up*, *down*: direct (a theatre-curtain) to be raised or lowered by ringing a bell. L18. ▸**d** Call (a person) by telephone. Also foll. by *up*. L19.

13 Change, substitute; *spec.* fraudulently change the identity of (a motor vehicle). *slang.* E19.

> **8** R. H. DANA The city bells were just ringing one. **12a** BROWNING Scorns to have the old year end Without a present shall ring in the new.

Phrases, & with adverbs in specialized senses: ***ring a bell***: see BELL *noun*[1]. **ring back** make a return telephone call (to). ***ring false***: see ***ring true*** below. **ring in** (*a*) report (something) by telephone; *fig.* include, bring into an operation; (*b*) make contact by telephone; (*c*) *Austral. & NZ slang* substitute fraudulently; (see also senses 12a, b above). **ring in one's ears**, **ring in one's heart** linger persistently in one's memory. **ring off** finish a telephone conversation by replacing the receiver. ***ring the bell***: see BELL *noun*[1]. ***ring the bells backward(s)***: see BACKWARD *adverb*. ***ring the changes***: see CHANGE *noun*. **ring round** *verb phr. trans. & intrans.* call (a succession of people) by telephone. **ring true**, **ring false** convey a convincing impression of truth, falsehood. **ring up** record (a sale) on a cash register; (see also senses 4c, 12a, c, d above).

ring /rɪŋ/ *verb*[2]. Pa. t. & pple **ringed**. LME.

[from RING *noun*[1].]

▸**I 1** *verb trans.* **a** Put a ring through the nose of (an animal) to control its behaviour. LME. ▸**b** Put a ring on the leg of (a bird etc.) to aid subsequent identification. E20.

2 *verb trans.* Adorn (a finger etc.) with a ring or rings. *rare.* LME.

†**3** *verb trans.* Attach rings to (a mare) in such a way as to prevent covering by a stallion. E17–E18.

4 *verb trans.* **a** Mark (a tree) with a ring of colour. M18. ▸**b** Strip (a tree) of a band of bark, in order to kill the tree or to check rapid growth. E19.

5 *verb trans.* Provide (a wheel) with an iron tyre. Now *rare* or *obsolete* exc. *Scot.* E19.

6 *verb trans.* Cut (a vegetable, fruit, etc.) into rings. M19.

7 *verb trans.* Draw a circle round (a printed date etc.) so as to focus attention on it. L20.

> **2** *fig.*: SHAKES. *John* I will . . ring these fingers with thy household worms. **7** *Times* She . . has probably already ringed a date . . for the election.

▸**II 8** *verb intrans.* **a** Make a circle; gather in a ring. Usu. foll. by *about*, *round*. Now *rare.* L15. ▸**b** Of cattle: move or mill round in a circle. *Austral. & S. Afr.* M19. ▸**c** (Of a bird) rise spirally in flight; (of a stag, fox, etc.) take a circular course when hunted. L19.

9 *verb trans.* Surround, encircle; form a ring round the edge of; hem *in*. Also foll. by *round*, *about*. L16. ▸**b** Enclose (cattle or game) in a circle by riding or beating round them. M19.

10 *verb trans.* Place or fasten (a ring or ring-shaped object) *round* something. *rare.* L18.

> **8a** E. B. BROWNING We should see the spirits ringing Round thee. **c** B. HINES The hawk . . began to ring up high over the hawthorn hedge. **9** M. HOLROYD An aggressive shyness ringed him about like some fortress. G. DALY The ballroom was ringed with chairs. *Japan Times* The presidential building, ringed by barbed wire and hundreds of police.

Phrases: **ring the shed** *Austral. slang* beat all the shearers of a particular shed at sheep-shearing.

Comb.: **ringbark** *verb trans. & intrans.* remove a ring of bark from (a tree) in order to kill the tree or to check rapid growth.

ringe /rɪn(d)ʒ/ *noun. dial.* E18.

[Var. of RANGE *noun*[1].]

A row, line, or elongated heap of something.

ringed /rɪŋd/ *adjective.* OE.

[from RING *noun*[1], *verb*[2]: see -ED[1], -ED[2].]

1 Of armour: made of rings. *rare.* OE.

2 a (Of a person) wearing a ring or rings on the fingers; (of the fingers etc.) adorned with a ring or rings. LME. ▸**b** Of a bird: bearing a ring or rings on one or both legs. E20.

3 Marked or encircled (as) by a ring or rings. E16.

4 a Having the form of a ring. L16. ▸**b** ZOOLOGY. Composed of rings or ringlike segments. Now *rare.* M19.

> **2a** A. LURIE A bulky man with . . plump white ringed hands.

Special collocations: **ringed dove** = *ring-dove* s.v. RING *noun*[1]. **ringed perch** the American yellow perch, *Perca flavescens*. **ringed plover** either of two small plovers having a black ring across the chest, *Charadrius hiaticula* and the smaller *C. dubius*. **ringed seal** an Arctic seal, *Phoca hispida*, with irregular ring-shaped markings. **ringed snake** = *ring-snake* s.v. RING *noun*[1]. **ringed thrush** = *ring ouzel* s.v. RING *noun*[1].

Ringelmann /ˈrɪŋg(ə)lmən/ *noun.* L19.

[Origin uncertain: perh. from Maximilien *Ringelmann* (1861–1931), French scientist.]

Used *attrib.*, and formerly in *possess.*, with ref. to the estimation of the darkness and density of smoke by visual comparison with a chart bearing different shades of grey (formed by lines ruled with different spacings on a white card), as ***Ringelmann card***, ***Ringelmann chart***, ***Ringelmann scale***.

ringent /ˈrɪn(d)ʒ(ə)nt/ *adjective.* M18.

[Latin *ringent-* pres. ppl stem of *ringi* to gape: see -ENT. Cf. RICTUS.]

Widely gaping. Chiefly BOTANY, of a two-lipped corolla: having the lips widely separate (opp. ***personate***).

ringer /ˈrɪŋə/ *noun*[1]. LME.

[from RING *verb*[1] + -ER[1].]

1 A person who rings, *esp.* a bell-ringer. LME.

2 A thing which rings; a device for ringing a bell. L19.

3 A horse, athlete, etc., fraudulently substituted for another in a competition or event; a person engaging in such a fraud. *colloq.* (chiefly *US*). L19.

4 An outsider, an intruder; an impostor, *spec.* a person who attaches himself or herself to a group to which he or she does not belong. *colloq.* (chiefly *US*). L19.

5 An exact counterpart; a person's or thing's double. Chiefly in ***be a ringer for***, ***be a ringer of***, ***be a dead ringer for***, ***be a dead ringer of***, resemble closely or exactly. *colloq.* (orig. *US*). L19.

6 A false registration plate attached to a stolen motor vehicle; a criminal who uses these. *slang.* M20.

7 ***ringer-up***, a person making a telephone call. M20.

¶ Recorded earlier in ME as a surname.

ringer /ˈrɪŋə/ *noun*[2]. L17.

[from RING *noun*[1], *verb*[2] + -ER[1].]

1 a In full ***hog ringer***. A person who fastens rings in pigs' snouts. Chiefly *US*. Now *rare.* L17. ▸**b** A person who rings the legs of birds. E20.

2 CURLING. A stone positioned within the circle drawn round either tee. E19.

3 A quoit thrown so as to enclose the pin aimed at; such a throw. M19.

4 A crowbar, *esp.* one used in mining, plate-laying, etc. M19.

5 a An expert. *Austral. slang.* M19. ▸**b** The fastest sheep-shearer in a shed. *Austral. & NZ.* L19.

6 A fox or other animal which runs in a circle when hunted. L19.

7 A stockman; a station hand. *Austral.* E20.

8 An air force officer. Freq. with numeral specifying rank. Cf. RING *noun*[1] 8g. *colloq.* M20.

8 ***half-ringer***, ***two-ringer***, etc.

¶ Rare before E19.

Ringer /ˈrɪŋə/ *noun*[3]. L19.

[Sydney *Ringer* (1834–1910), English physician.]

BIOLOGY. In full ***Ringer solution***, ***Ringer's solution***. A physiological saline solution of a type introduced by Ringer, usu. containing, in addition to sodium chloride, salts of potassium and calcium.

Ringerike /ˈrɪŋəriːkə/ *noun.* E20.

[A district centred on Honefoss, north of Oslo in Norway.]

Used **attrib.** to designate a style of late Viking decorative art, characterized by abundant use of foliage patterns.

ringette /rɪŋˈɛt/ *noun.* L20.

[from RING *noun*[1] + -ETTE.]

A form of ice hockey played (usu. by women or girls) with a rubber ring instead of a puck, and in which no intentional body contact is allowed.

ringgit /ˈrɪŋgɪt/ *noun.* M20.

[Malay = milled coin, (as adjective) milled, serrated.]

The principal monetary unit of Malaysia, formerly also known as a dollar, consisting of 100 sen; a coin or note of this value.

ringhals *noun* see RINKHALS.

ringing /ˈrɪŋɪŋ/ *noun.* ME.

[from RING *verb*[1] + -ING[1].]

1 The action of RING *verb*[1]; an instance of this; a sound produced (as) by a bell or bells. ME.

2 A sensation in the ears similar to that produced by the sound of bells etc. LME.

3 ELECTRONICS. Transient damped oscillation occurring in a circuit at its resonant frequency as a result of a sudden change in voltage level; in TELEVISION, the occurrence on the screen of black lines to the right of a white object, caused by transient oscillation in the video amplifier. M20.

Comb.: **ringing floor** the place below a belfry where bell-ringers stand; **ringing tone** a sound heard by a telephone caller indicating that the number dialled is ringing.

ringing /ˈrɪŋɪŋ/ *ppl adjective.* ME.

[from RING *verb*[1] + -ING[2].]

1 Having or giving out the sound of a bell etc.; resounding, resonant. ME.

2 Of frost: severe, so that the ground rings under the feet. E19.

📖 1 N. GORDIMER We went down the ringing iron steps of the fire escape. *fig.*: M. SEYMOUR Lucy . . spoke her mind with ringing sincerity.

■ **ringingly** *adverb* M19. **ringingness** *noun* L19.

ringle /ˈrɪŋg(ə)l/ *noun*[1] *& verb*[1]. LME.
[from RING *noun*[1] + -LE[1].]
▶ **A** *noun.* **1** A metal, esp. iron, ring. Now chiefly, *spec.* one for a pig's nose or a horse's harness. Now *dial.* LME. ▸†**b** A door-knocker. M17–E18.
2 A circular band; a circle. *obsolete* exc. *Scot.* L16.
▶ **B** *verb trans.* **1** = RING *verb*[2] 1a. Now *dial.* L16.
†**2** = RING *verb*[2] 3. L17–E18.

ringle /ˈrɪŋg(ə)l/ *verb*[2] *& noun*[2]. Now *Scot. & dial.* E17.
[from RING *verb*[1] + -LE[3].]
▶ **A** *verb intrans.* Ring, jingle. E17.
▶ **B** *noun.* A ringing or jingling sound. E19.

ringlead /ˈrɪŋliːd/ *verb trans. rare.* Pa. t. & pple **-led** /-lɛd/. L16.
[Back-form. from next.]
Instigate (a course of action); manage (people) as ringleader.

ringleader /ˈrɪŋliːdə/ *noun.* E16.
[from RING *noun*[1] + LEADER: see ***lead the ring*** s.v. RING *noun*[1].]
A person who takes a leading role amongst a group of people engaged in an illicit or illegal activity; an instigator or organizer of a conspiracy etc. Also (now *rare* or *obsolete*), a leader; a chief authority.

📖 M. LEITCH He was the ringleader, evil genius at the back of the business.

ringled *verb pa. t. & pple* of RINGLEAD.

ringlet /ˈrɪŋlɪt/ *noun.* M16.
[from RING *noun*[1] + -LET.]
1 A small ring. M16.
2 A circular dance or course; a circular marking, formation, or part; *spec.* a fairy-ring. L16.
3 A lock of hair hanging in a corkscrew-shaped curl. M17.
4 ENTOMOLOGY. Any of several brown (satyrid) butterflies marked with small rings; *esp.* the common *Aphantopus hyperantus.* E19.

📖 **1** BURKE This deficiency is made up by strengthening the first ringlet of the chain. *New Scientist* Saturn's rings are composed of thousands of narrow 'ringlets'. **3** J. KEROUAC A pretty blonde with immense ringlets of hair.

■ **ringleted** *adjective* (*a*) (of the hair) worn in ringlets; (*b*) (of a person) wearing the hair in ringlets: E19. **ringlety** *adjective* (of hair) tending to curl in ringlets E19.

ringmaster /ˈrɪŋmɑːstə/ *noun & verb.* L19.
[from RING *noun*[1] + MASTER *noun*[1].]
▶ **A** *noun.* A person directing the performances in a circus ring. L19.

📖 *transf.*: *Times* He holds the stage at press conferences, ever the ringmaster.

▶ **B** *verb trans.* Direct (people, events, etc.) in the manner of a ringmaster. *rare.* M20.

■ **ringmastership** *noun* the skill or position of a ringmaster M20.

ring-net /ˈrɪŋnɛt/ *noun & verb.* OE.
[from RING *noun*[1] + NET *noun*[1].]
▶ **A** *noun.* †**1** A coat of chain-mail. Only in OE.
2 a A form of salmon-net. *obsolete* exc. *dial.* E16. ▸**b** A long seine-net supported at the ends by separate boats, one of which circles round towards the other, trapping the fish within the net, used esp. in the Scottish herring fishing industry. M20.
▶ **B** *verb trans.* Infl. **-tt-**. Catch (fish, esp. herring) using a ring-net. Chiefly as ***ring-netting*** *verbal noun.* M20.

ringside /ˈrɪŋsʌɪd/ *noun.* M19.
[from RING *noun*[1] + SIDE *noun*.]
The area immediately surrounding a boxing ring or other sports arena; *gen.* an area designated for spectators.

📖 *attrib.*: L. KENNEDY A ringside view of the contours of my cousin Cynthia.

Comb.: **ringside seat** (*a*) a seat immediately adjacent to a boxing contest or other sporting event; (*b*) *transf. & fig.* a place affording a clear view; an advantageous or privileged position from which to observe or monitor something.

■ **ringsider** *noun* a person occupying a position at a ringside; a spectator: L19.

ringster /ˈrɪŋstə/ *noun.* L19.
[from RING *noun*[1] + -STER.]
1 A member of a political or price-fixing ring. *US.* L19.
2 A boxer. E20.

ring-straked /ˈrɪŋstreɪkt/ *adjective.* Now *poet.* E17.
[from RING *noun*[1] + STRAKE *noun* + -ED[2].]
Of an animal, insect, etc.: having bands of colour round the body.

ringtail /ˈrɪŋteɪl/ *noun.* Also **ring-tail**, (in sense 4) **ring tail** /*also* rɪŋ ˈteɪl/. M16.
[from RING *noun*[1] + TAIL *noun*[1].]
1 a A female harrier (formerly mistaken for a separate species). M16. ▸**b** More fully ***ringtail eagle.*** = RING-TAILED *eagle.* L18.
2 NAUTICAL. A small triangular gaff topsail; a small triangular sail set on the stern of a vessel to form a self-steering device. M18.
3 A ring-tailed animal; *spec.* (more fully ***ringtail possum***) any of several possums of Australia and New Guinea of the genus *Pseudocheirus* and related genera, which have a prehensile tail. L18.
4 A dog's tail which is curled so as to form nearly a complete circle. L19.
5 A worthless or irritable person; a hobo. *US slang.* E20.
2 attrib.: ***ringtail boom, ringtail sail*** etc.

ring-tailed /ˈrɪŋteɪld/ *adjective.* E18.
[formed as prec. + -ED[2].]
Chiefly ZOOLOGY & ORNITHOLOGY. **1 a** Having a band of colour around or across the tail. E18. ▸**b** Having the tail ringed with alternating colours. E18.
2 Having the tail curled at the end. M19.
Special collocations: **ring-tailed eagle** an immature golden eagle, having a single light band across the tail (formerly mistaken for a separate species). **ring-tailed lemur** a lemur with a black and white striped tail, *Lemur catta.* **ring-tailed possum** = ***ringtail possum*** s.v. RINGTAIL 3. **ring-tailed roarer** *US* an imaginary animal; an exceptionally strong or noisy person.

ringworm /ˈrɪŋwəːm/ *noun.* LME.
[from RING *noun*[1] + WORM *noun*, prob. after Du *ringworm*, Norwegian, Danish *ringorm*.]
A contagious itching skin-disease occurring in small circular patches, caused by any of several fungi and affecting esp. the scalp or the feet; tinea, athlete's foot.
honeycomb ringworm: see HONEYCOMB *noun & adjective.*
Comb.: **ringworm bush, ringworm shrub** a tropical American leguminous shrub, *Cassia alata*, used as a remedy for ringworm.

rink /rɪŋk/ *noun & verb.* Orig. *Scot.* LME.
[Origin uncertain: perh. ult. from Old French *renc* (mod. *rang*) RANK *noun*.]
▶ **A** *noun.* **1** *Scot.* †**a** An area of ground set aside for jousting or racing; a course marked out for riding, running, or jousting. LME–M17. ▸**b** A spell of running, a run; a race; the action of running. Formerly also, the course or way followed by a person. Now *arch. rare.* L15.
2 A stretch of natural or artificial ice measured off or marked out for the game of curling. L18. ▸**b** A team in curling or quoits. E19.
3 A sheet of ice for skating or ice hockey, *esp.* one artificially prepared and roofed over (more fully ***ice rink***); a smooth floor, usu. of asphalt or wood, for roller-skating. Also, a building containing either of these. M19.
4 A measured strip of bowling-green on which a match is played. Also, a team in bowls. M19.
▶ **B** *verb intrans.* Skate on or as on a rink. L19.

rinkhals /ˈrɪŋk(h)als/ *noun.* Chiefly *S. Afr.* Also (earlier) **ring-** /ˈrɪŋ-/. Pl. same. L18.
[Afrikaans, from *ring* ring + *hals* neck.]
A large venomous hooded spitting cobra of southern Africa, *Hemachatus haemachatus*, of the family Elapidae, having a brown or black skin with one or two white rings across the neck.

rinky-dink /rɪŋkɪˈdɪŋk/ *noun & adjective. slang* (chiefly *N. Amer.*). L19.
[Origin unkn. Cf. next, RICKY-TICK.]
▶ **A** *noun.* Something worn out or antiquated; a worthless object. Also, a cheap place of entertainment. L19.
give the rinky-dink to, hand the rinky-dink to cheat or swindle (a person).
▶ **B** *adjective.* Worthless worn-out; old-fashioned. L19.

rinky-tink /rɪŋkɪˈtɪŋk/ *adjective. slang* (chiefly *US*). M20.
[Imit. Cf. prec., RICKY-TICK, TINK *noun*[1] *& interjection.*]
Designating a jazz or ragtime piano on which simple repetitive tunes are played; tinkling, jangling.

Rinne /ˈrɪnə/ *noun.* L19.
[H. A. *Rinne* (1819–68), German otologist.]
MEDICINE. Used in *possess.* and *attrib.* with ref. to a test for partial deafness in which a sounding tuning-fork is placed against the skull until the note is no longer heard, then held near to the ear, to compare perception of sound conducted through bone and through air. Freq. in ***Rinne test, Rinne's test.***

Rinpoche /ˈrɪmpɒtʃeɪ/ *noun.* L18.
[Tibetan, lit. 'precious (jewel)'.]
(An honorific title given to) a religious teacher held in high regard among Tibetan Buddhists. Cf. PANCHEN.

†**rinrig** *noun, adverb, & adjective* var. of RUNRIG.

rinse /rɪns/ *noun.* E18.
[from the verb.]
1 A small bundle of (esp. heather) twigs for cleaning out pots or other vessels. *Scot.* E18.
2 a The action or an act of rinsing something; *colloq.* a wash. M19. ▸**b** A solution for cleansing the mouth. L19. ▸**c** A preparation for temporarily tinting or conditioning the hair; an application of this. E20.

📖 **2a** E. DAVID A rinse in a colander under running cold water. **c** *Independent* Elderly ladies with blue rinses.

rinse /rɪns/ *verb.* ME.
[Old & mod. French *rincer*, †*raincier*, †*reincier*, ult. origin unkn.]
†**1** *verb trans.* Clear, make clean, by removal. Only in ME.
†**2** *verb intrans.* Of a priest: clean the chalice and fingers with wine and water after the Eucharist. Only in ME.
3 *verb trans.* Wash (a thing) with or in esp. clean water in order to remove impurities; *spec.* (*a*) wash out or clean esp. dregs from (a cup, glass, etc.) by pouring in, agitating, and emptying out water or other liquid; (*b*) wash lightly by immersion and gentle agitation in or pouring over of water; (*c*) put (clothes, crockery, the hair, etc.) through or in clean water after washing to remove soap or detergent; (*d*) clean (the mouth) by taking in, swilling round, and emitting again a mouthful of water or mouthwash. Freq. foll. by *out.* LME. ▸**b** Treat (hair) with a tinting or conditioning rinse. M20.
4 *verb trans.* Remove, take *away*, clear *out*, by rinsing. M16.
5 *verb trans.* Wash *down* with liquor. *obsolete* exc. *Scot. rare.* E19.

📖 **3** ADDISON He rins'd the wound, And washed away the . . blood. M. MILLAR Can't you rinse out your own socks? T. BERGER He began to find tumblers in the soapy liquid . . and rinse them with hot water in the adjoining sink. N. LOWNDES She rinsed her hands under the tap. **b** *absol.*: M. KELLY Louise's hair seemed to go an elegant grey all at once (she rinses a bit). **4** *Practical Hairstyling & Beauty* Rinse salt or chlorine out of your hair immediately you come out of the sea or pool.

■ **rinser** *noun* (*rare*) E17. **rinsing** *noun* (*a*) the action of the verb; (*b*) (usu. in *pl.*) the liquid with which something has been rinsed: ME.

Rinzai /rɪnˈzʌɪ/ *noun.* L19.
[Japanese from Chinese *Lin-ji* a Zen master (d. 867), its founder.]
One of the three branches of Zen Buddhism, the others being Soto and Obaku.

rio /ˈriːəʊ, *foreign* ˈriːo/ *noun.* Pl. **rios**, ***rii*** /ˈriːiː/. M19.
[Italian = stream.]
In Venice, a small side canal.

Rioja /rɪˈɒhə, *foreign* riˈoxa/ *noun.* E20.
[See below.]
(A) wine produced in Rioja, a district of northern Spain.
■ **Riojan** *adjective* of or pertaining to Rioja (the place or the wine) M20.

riometer /riːˈɒmɪtə, ˈrʌɪəʊmiːtə/ *noun.* M20.
[from relative ionospheric opacity + -METER.]
GEOPHYSICS. An instrument for measuring the absorption of cosmic radio waves by the ionosphere.

rione /riˈoːne/ *noun.* Pl. **-ni** /-ni/. E20.
[Italian.]
A district or administrative division of Rome.

riot /ˈrʌɪət/ *noun.* ME.
[Old French *riot(e)* (mod. *riotte*) debate, quarrel, from Old French *r(u)ihoter* to quarrel. Cf. ROYET.]
1 a Dissolute or wasteful living; debauchery, dissipation, extravagance. Now *rare.* ME. ▸**b** Unrestrained revelry, mirth, or noise. E18.
2 a An instance or course of dissolute or wasteful living; a feast, a revel, *esp.* a noisy or unrestrained one; a disturbance arising from this. Now *rare.* ME. ▸**b** A vivid or lavish display *of* colour, sound, etc. L19.
3 HUNTING. A hound's indiscriminate following of any scent other than that of the quarry. Freq. in ***hunt riot, run riot*** below. ME.
4 a Violence, tumult, public disorder. LME. ▸**b** An instance of this; a violent disturbance of the peace by a crowd; an occurrence of public disorder. Formerly also, a hostile attack or encounter. LME.
5 Orig. THEATRICAL. A very amusing person or thing; *spec.* an uproariously successful performance or show. *colloq.* E20.

📖 **1a** JAS. MILL The pleasures of voluptuous indolence and riot. **b** J. THOMSON To swell the riot of th'autumnal feast. W. H. DIXON With bray of snorting horns and riot of exploding guns. **2b** J. TROLLOPE A violently healthy plumbago cascaded in a riot of . . pale blue flowers. H. WILLIAMSON The next picture was a riot of fun and laughter. **4b** E. PAWEL The demonstrations tended to get out of hand and turn into . . riots. **5** *New Yorker* He's such a clown—a riot with people.

Phrases: **hunt riot** = ***run riot*** (a) below. **run riot** (*a*) HUNTING (of a hound) follow indiscriminately any scent other than that of the quarry; (*b*) *fig.* throw off all restraint or control; (of a plant) grow luxuriantly or wildly.
Attrib. & comb.: In the senses 'concerned, esp. as representing lawful authority, with the suppression of riot', as ***riot police***; 'used or carried, esp. by the representatives of lawful authority, in the suppression of riot', as ***riot gun, riot shield.*** Special

combs., as **Riot Act** (*a*) *Hist.* an Act, passed in 1715 and repealed in 1967, making it a felony for an assembly of more than twelve people to refuse to disperse after the reading of a specified portion of it by lawful authority; (*b*) ***read the Riot Act*** (now chiefly *joc.*), insist that noise, disobedience, etc., must cease, reprimand or caution sternly; ***riot grrrl***: see GRRRL.

riot /ˈrʌɪət/ *verb*. LME.
[Old & mod. French *rio(t)ter*, formed as prec.]
▶ **I 1** *verb intrans.* & †*trans.* with *it*. ▸**a** Live in a dissolute or wasteful manner; indulge to excess *in* something. Now *rare*. LME. ▸**b** Revel or take great delight or pleasure *in* something. *arch.* M17.
2 *verb trans.* Spend or waste (money, time, etc.) in dissolute, wasteful, or luxurious living. Also foll. by *away*, *out*. L16.

📖 **1** AV *2 Pet.* 2:13 They that count it pleasure to riot in the day time. **b** DICKENS Vaunting and, as it were, rioting in, her huge unworthiness. **2** TENNYSON He.. Had rioted his life out, and made an end.

▶ **II** †**3** *verb trans.* Ravage, harry, or spoil (a country etc.). *Scot. & north. rare.* Only in LME.
4 a *verb intrans.* Take part in a riot, esp. one constituting a violent disturbance of the peace by a crowd. M18. ▸**b** *verb trans.* Attack (a person or property) in the course of a riot. *rare.* L19.
5 *verb intrans.* HUNTING. = ***run riot*** (a) s.v. RIOT *noun*. Also foll. by *after*, *on*. M20.

📖 **4** *Japan Times* Venezuela exploded into.. days of rioting and looting. **b** *Daily News* S.K.T. Station has been rioted and.. destroyed.

■ **rioter** *noun* a person who riots; *spec.* a person taking part in a violent disturbance of the peace by a crowd: LME. **riotry** *noun* (*a*) rioting, riotous conduct, riotousness; (*b*) *rare* riotous people collectively: ME.

†**riotise** *noun*. L16–M17.
[from RIOT *noun* + -ISE¹.]
Riotous life or conduct.

riotous /ˈrʌɪətəs/ *adjective*. ME.
[Old French, formed as RIOT *noun*: see -OUS.]
†**1** Troublesome, difficult. *rare.* ME–L16.
2 Of a person: given to dissolute or wasteful living; prodigal, extravagant. Now *rare*. LME.
3 Of a way of life, conduct, etc.: dissolute, extravagant; characterized by excessive revelry. LME. ▸**b** Noisy, tumultuous, unrestrained. Also, vivid, lavish. L15.
4 Characterized by rioting, esp. by a violent disturbance of the peace by a crowd; taking part in a riot; inciting others to riot. LME.

📖 **3** H. H. WILSON The dissolute and riotous conduct of.. its inhabitants. F. HUME He spent all her wealth in riotous living. **b** A. SILLITOE A cry.. stopped everyone's riotous catcalls. G. KEILLOR Back to school after a riotous week of Easter break. **4** *Connecticut* A riotous display of bright red, green and yellow vegetables.

■ **riotously** *adverb* LME. **riotousness** *noun* M16.

RIP *abbreviation*.
Rest in peace; (orig.) Latin *Requiescat*, or *requiescant*, *in pace* may he or she, or they, rest in peace.

rip /rɪp/ *noun*¹. Long *Scot.* & *dial.* ME.
[Old Norse *hrip*.]
1 A wicker basket or pannier, used esp. for carrying fish. ME.
2 A hen or pheasant coop. M19.

rip /rɪp/ *noun*². *Scot.* M17.
[Origin uncertain: perh. formed as RIP *noun*⁴. Cf. RIP *noun*⁵.]
A handful of unthreshed grain or of hay; *spec.* the last handful of grain remaining to be cut in a harvest-field.

rip /rɪp/ *noun*³. Long *dial.* L17.
[Origin unkn.]
A strickle for a scythe.

rip /rɪp/ *noun*⁴. E18.
[from RIP *verb*¹. Cf. next, RIP *noun*².]
1 A rent made by ripping; a long tear. Also, an act of ripping something. E18.
2 *ellipt.* = ***ripsaw*** (a) s.v. RIP *verb*¹. Freq. in ***half-rip***. M19.
3 A rapid rush; a quick run (now chiefly *dial.*). Also MUSIC (*US*), a series of sounds comprising a fast glissando played up to a strongly accented note. M19.
4 A fine imposed on a member of the police for an infraction of regulations. *US slang.* M20.

📖 **1** H. WILLIAMSON He lifted.. his tunic and with a rip of stitches opened his field dressing. P. O'DONNELL A long rip gaped in the knee of her slacks.

Comb.: **rip cord** (*a*) a cord fastened to a strip of fabric sewn into and forming part of the skin of a balloon, causing rapid deflation when the cord is pulled and the strip torn away; (*b*) a cord holding a parachute pack closed, causing the parachute to unfold and inflate when the cord is pulled and the pack opened; **rip line** = ***rip cord*** (a) above.

rip /rɪp/ *noun*⁵. L18.
[App. rel. to RIP *verb*¹. Cf. prec., RIP *noun*².]
1 a A stretch of rough water in the sea, caused by the meeting of currents; an overfall. L18. ▸**b** *ellipt.* = ***rip current*** below. M20.
2 A stretch of rough water in a river. Chiefly *US*. E19.
Comb.: **rip current** an intermittent strong surface current flowing out from the shore; **rip tide** (*a*) = ***rip current*** above; (*b*) = sense 1a above; (*c*) *fig.* a state of conflicting psychological forces.

rip /rɪp/ *noun*⁶. L18.
[Perh. var. of REP *noun*².]
1 An inferior, worthless, or worn-out horse. L18.
2 A dissolute immoral person, esp. a man; a rake; *colloq.* a wretch. L18.
3 A person or thing of little or no value. E19.

📖 **1** G. J. WHYTE-MELVILLE Those thorough-bred rips never have courage to face large fences. **2** G. B. SHAW The mother a most deplorable old rip. L. STRACHEY The old rip.. with his jewelled mistress by his side.

rip /rɪp/ *verb*¹. Infl. **-pp-**. LME.
[Origin unkn. Cf. REAP *verb*², RIP *noun*⁵.]
▶ **I** *verb trans.* **1** Cut, pull, or tear (a thing) quickly or forcibly away from something. Freq. foll. by *off*, *from*, *out*. LME. ▸**b** Steal. *slang.* E20. ▸**c** Defeat overwhelmingly, esp. in a sporting event. *US slang.* L20.
2 Cut, slash, or tear (a thing) apart or open, esp. with a sharp instrument. Freq. foll. by *apart*, *open*, *through*, *up*, etc. M16. ▸**b** Split or cleave (timber); saw (wood) in the direction of the grain. M16. ▸**c** Strip (a building or roof) of tiles or slates and laths, esp. in the process of repair or renovation. L16. ▸**d** Take out or cut away by quarrying etc.; clear of surface-soil. E19. ▸**e** Pull the rip-cord of (a parachute or balloon). E20.
3 Disclose, make known; search into, examine. Now chiefly *fig.* (foll. by *up*), reopen (a discussion, esp. an unwelcome one), revive the memory of (esp. a grievance or a discreditable action). L16.
4 Form or make (esp. a hole) by tearing or slashing, esp. violently or forcibly. Also foll. by *up*. L19.
5 Annoy intensely. Chiefly in ***wouldn't it rip you***. *Austral. slang.* M20.
6 Attack verbally; criticize severely. *N. Amer. colloq.* L20.

📖 **1** G. ORWELL Posters were ripped from the walls, banners torn to shreds. G. GREENE Summers.. was ripping out the skirting-boards in the.. dining room. R. INGALLS He got out the cigarettes, ripped off the cellophane. **b** *Telegraph (Brisbane)* Some have ripped millions of dollars from Medibank. **c** *Arizona Daily Star* The Tucson.. All-Stars ripped Prescott for 15 hits. **2** K. WATERHOUSE I.. ripped the piece of paper into four. P. MORTIMER I ripped open the mauve envelope, tearing it carelessly with my thumb. T. KENEALLY Ripping their clothes and tearing their flesh on the barbs. **3** HAZLITT We do not want to rip up old grievances. M. E. BRADDON Why do you come.. to rip up the secrets of the past? **4** A. DJOLETO Mensa had managed to rip a hole in the wire fence. B. HINES She nipped this skin and pulled, ripping a hole in it. *Miami Herald* The guy who ripped ABC for its big-name.. extravaganzas.

▶ **II** *verb intrans.* **7 a** Progress, move *along*, by cutting or slashing. *rare.* L18. ▸**b** Come violently apart; split, tear. M19.
8 a Use strong language; swear, curse. Now *dial.* L18. ▸**b** Break or burst *out* angrily. M19.
9 Rush along with violence or great speed. Freq. in ***let rip*** below. Orig. *US*. M19.

📖 **7** R. BLOOMFIELD The sweeping Scythe now rips along. **b** R. H. DANA The sail ripped from head to foot. *New Yorker* The banner.. had blown down in the wind and ripped. **8a** J. ADAMS Your secretary will rip about this measure. **b** R. L. STEVENSON 'You may leave..' he added, his temper ripping out. **9** G. B. SHAW Rip ahead, old son. *On Board International* The speed sailors.. were ripping up and down at Ma'alea, taking advantage of the flat waters.

Phrases, & with adverbs in specialized senses: **let rip** *colloq.* (*a*) act or proceed without restraint; speak violently; (*b*) not check the speed of or interfere with (freq. in ***let her rip***). **rip and tear** *US & dial.* rage, rave; go raging *about*. **rip into** unleash a verbal attack on, criticize sharply, castigate. **rip off** (*a*) *colloq.* steal (from); embezzle; exploit financially; cheat, defraud; rob; deceive; (*b*) *colloq.* copy; plagiarize; (*c*) *US slang* have sexual intercourse with; *esp.* rape. **rip out** utter (esp. an oath or curse) abruptly or violently; (see also senses 1, 8b above). **rip up** reopen (a wound or sore) roughly; (see also senses 2, 3, 4 above).
Comb.: **rip-and-tear** *adjective* (*US*) of or pertaining to crude and violent criminal methods; **rip-off** *adjective* & *noun* (*colloq.*) (*a*) (designating or pertaining to) a fraud, swindle, or instance of esp. financial exploitation; (*b*) (designating or pertaining to) an imitation or plagiarism, esp. one intended to exploit a current public interest; **ripsaw** *noun* & *verb* (*a*) *noun* a coarse saw for cutting wood along the grain; (*b*) *verb trans.* cut (wood) with a ripsaw; **rip-stop** *adjective* (of nylon clothing or equipment) woven in such a way that a tear will not spread; **rip track** *N. Amer.* a section of railway line used as a site for repairs to carriages.
■ **ripped** *adjective* (*a*) that has been ripped; (*b*) *N. Amer. slang* intoxicated by a drug; (*c*) *slang* (foll. by *off*) robbed; exploited; stolen; (*d*) *slang* having the muscles showing prominently: E19.

†**rip** *verb*² var. of REAP *verb*¹.

riparial /rʌɪˈpɛːrɪəl/ *adjective*. L19.
[formed as next + -AL¹.]
= RIPARIAN *adjective*.

riparian /rʌɪˈpɛːrɪən/ *adjective* & *noun*. M19.
[from Latin *riparius*, from *ripa* bank: see -ARIAN.]
▶ **A** *adjective.* Of, pertaining to, situated on, or inhabiting the banks of a river; riverine. M19.
▶ **B** *noun.* A riparian proprietor. L19.

riparious /rʌɪˈpɛːrɪəs/ *adjective*. *rare*. M17.
[formed as prec.: see -ARIOUS.]
= RIPARIAN *adjective*.

ripe /rʌɪp/ *noun*. Now *rare*. ME.
[Latin *ripa* bank.]
The bank of a river; the seashore.

ripe /rʌɪp/ *adjective*.
[Old English *ripe* = Old Saxon *ripi* (Dutch *rijp*), Old High German *rīfi* (German *reif*), from West Germanic.]
1 (Esp. of grain or fruit) developed to the point of readiness for harvesting, at the full point of natural growth; (of cheese, wine, etc.) complete in natural development, fully matured; ready to be used or consumed. OE. ▸**b** Of a boil etc.: fully maturated, come to a head. LME. ▸**c** Esp. of the complexion: red and full, resembling ripe fruit. L16.
2 (Of a person or animal) fully grown; *spec.* (*a*) (of an animal) ready to be killed and used as food; (*b*) (of a person) fully developed mentally and physically. *arch.* ME. ▸†**b** Of a foetus: ready to be born. *rare.* M16–M18. ▸**c** Of a female insect, fish, etc.: ready to lay eggs or spawn. M19.
3 Of a person, the mind: of mature judgement or knowledge; fully informed; fully developed *in* a personal quality. ME.
†**4** Properly considered or deliberated; matured by reflection or study. ME–M17.
5 Of a person's age: mature, adult; *esp.* advanced but characterized by mental and physical health and strength. LME.
6 a Fully prepared, ready, or able *to do*; ready, fit, or prepared *for*; arrived at the fitting stage or time for a specified action or purpose. LME. ▸**b** Of time: sufficiently advanced, esp. for a particular action or purpose. M16.
7 a Drunk. *arch. slang.* E19. ▸**b** Fine, excellent; thoroughgoing. Also, beyond reasonable bounds, esp. of propriety; excessive. *slang.* E20.

📖 **1** A. SILLITOE Blackberries were big and ripe. V. BRAMWELL Choosing ripe fruit will avoid the need to balance the acidity. *Country Homes* Even runnier than a ripe Brie. **c** TENNYSON An underlip.. a little too ripe, too full. **2** WORDSWORTH Ripe men, or blooming in life's spring. H. STEPHENS A ripe sheep.. is easily known.. by the fulness exhibited in all the external parts. **3** G. SANDYS As sound in judgement as ripe in experience. A. TROLLOPE Mr. Crawley.. had been a ripe scholar. **5** J. TYNDALL Simplicity of treatment,.. out of place.. for a reader of riper years. E. WAUGH Now in ripe age, with his triumphs behind him. **6a** WORDSWORTH The inly-working North Was ripe to send its thousands forth. L. M. MONTGOMERY Ripe for any enticing form of mischief. *Auckland Metro* Two other inner city hotels are ripe for redevelopment. **b** B. WEBB The time is ripe for bold.. leadership. R. V. JONES A man thinks of an idea and tries it before the time is really ripe. **7b** J. FRASER 'What the bloody hell are you playing at?' 'That's ripe considering you.. near broke my arm.'

■ **ripely** *adverb* LME. **ripeness** *noun* OE.

ripe /rʌɪp/ *verb*¹. *arch.*
[Old English *rīpian* (= Old Saxon *rīpon* (Dutch *rijpen*), Old High German *rīfēn* (German *reifen*)), from the adjective Largely superseded by RIPEN.]
1 *verb intrans.* Grow or become ripe. OE.
2 *verb trans.* Make ripe, bring to ripeness. Formerly also *spec.*, cause (a boil etc.) to come to a head. OE.
†**3** *verb trans.* **a** Prepare (a matter) by careful consideration. OE–M16. ▸**b** Make (a person) ripe in knowledge. E–M16.

📖 **2** J. SYLVESTER On Trees.. they ripe the Plum and Pear.

ripe /rʌɪp/ *verb*². Long *obsolete* exc. *Scot.* & *north.*
[Old English *rȳpan*, app. rel. to Gothic *raupjan*, Old High German *roufen* (German *raufen*), and Low German *ruppen* (German *rupfen*) pluck, pull.]
†**1 a** *verb intrans.* Engage in robbery. OE–ME. ▸**b** *verb trans.* Rob, plunder. Only in OE.
2 *verb intrans.* Grope; search, esp. *for* or *after* something hidden. ME.
3 *verb trans.* Search (a place, receptacle, etc.) thoroughly; rifle, ransack. ME.
4 *verb trans.* Examine thoroughly; investigate, scrutinize, look into. ME.
5 *verb trans.* Break, dig, or plough up (ground). Now usu. foll. by *up*. LME.
6 *verb trans.* Cleanse, clear out. E18.

ripen /ˈrʌɪp(ə)n/ *verb*. LME.
[from RIPE *adjective* + -EN⁵.]
1 *verb trans.* Make ripe; bring to the full point of natural growth or development; bring to maturity. Earliest as

***ripening** ppl adjective.* **LME.** ▸**b** Cause (a boil etc.) to come to a head or maturate. **L16.**

2 *verb intrans.* Grow ripe; reach the full point of natural growth or development; come to maturity; *fig.* develop *into.* **M16.** ▸**b** Of a boil etc.: come to a head, maturate. **E18.** ▸**c** Bring (a material, esp. rayon) to a required state by any of various usu. gradual industrial processes. Chiefly as ***ripening** verbal noun.* **E20.**

> **1** J. TRAPP Age clarifies wine and ripens it. POPE The blooming boy is ripen'd into man. **2** H. MARTINEAU The acquaintance had ripened into friendship. S. TROTT I doubted that the last tomatoes were going to ripen. M. KEANE The stones . . seemed to ripen in the hot sunshine.

■ **ripener** *noun* (*a*) a person who or thing which ripens; (*b*) *spec.* a device in which honey is allowed to stand until it is ready to be put in jars: **M16.**

ripicolous /rʌɪˈpɪkələs/ *adjective. rare.* **M19.**
[from Latin *ripa* bank + -I- + -COLOUS.]
Inhabiting or frequenting river-banks; riparian.

ripieno /rɪpɪˈeɪnəʊ/ *adjective & noun.* **E18.**
[Italian, from *ri-* RE- + *pieno* full.]
MUSIC. ▸**A** *attrib. adjective.* Orig., supplementary, re-enforcing. Now chiefly, of or pertaining to a ripieno. **E18.**
▸**B** *noun.* Pl. **-nos**, **-ni** /-ni/. Orig., a supplementary player or instrument. Now chiefly, the body of instruments accompanying the concertino in baroque concerto music. **M18.**

riposte /rɪˈpɒst/ *noun.* Also (*arch.*) **repost**. **E18.**
[French (earlier †*risposte*) from Italian *risposta* use as noun of fem. pa. pple of *rispondere*, formed as RESPOND *verb.*]
1 *FENCING.* A quick thrust given after parrying a lunge; a return thrust. **E18.**
2 A retaliatory action; a quick sharp reply or retort. **M19.**

> **2** F. SPALDING She loved it if she found another guest equally good at the quick riposte.

riposte /rɪˈpɒst/ *verb.* Also (*arch.*) **repost**. **E18.**
[French *riposter* (earlier †*risposter*), formed as prec.]
1 *verb intrans. & (rare)* †*trans. FENCING.* Make a riposte in reply to (an opponent). **E18.**
2 *verb intrans.* Retaliate; make a quick sharp reply or retort. **M19** ▸**b** *verb trans.* Utter as a riposte. **L19.**

> **2** K. TYNAN When a master slapped his face . . he . . riposted by slapping the master. **b** *Daily Telegraph* 'I don't care if you are Basil Brush,' ripostes the sergeant-major.

ripper /ˈrɪpə/ *noun.* **E17.**
[from RIP *verb*[1] + -ER[1].]
1 A person who rips something. **E17.** ▸**b** *spec.* A murderer who rips or mutilates the victims' bodies. **L19.**
2 A thing, esp. a tool or apparatus, which rips something. **L18.** ▸**b** *spec.* An implement that is attached to a tractor to break up concrete or hard soil. **M20.**
3 A person or thing of particular excellence; *spec.* an attractive young woman. *slang* (now chiefly *Austral.*). **M19.**
4 A bill abolishing a State or city office or commission. *US colloq.* **L19.**
5 A kind of illegal fishing tackle comprising a line with a heavy metal bar attached to it fitted with hooks. *Scot.* **E20.**

rippier /ˈrɪpɪə/ *noun.* Long *obsolete* exc. *Hist.* **LME.**
[from RIP *noun*[1] + -IER.]
A person carrying fish inland to sell.

ripping /ˈrɪpɪŋ/ *noun.* **M16.**
[from RIP *verb*[1] + -ING[1].]
The action of RIP *verb*[1]; an instance of this. Also, something that has been removed by ripping.
Comb.: **ripping-chisel** (*a*) a chisel for separating two joined pieces of wood; (*b*) a crowbar; **ripping cord**, **ripping line** = *rip cord* (a) s.v. RIP *noun*[4]; **ripping-saw** = *ripsaw* s.v. RIP *verb*[1].

ripping /ˈrɪpɪŋ/ *adjective.* **E18.**
[from RIP *verb*[1] + -ING[2].]
1 That rips or tears something. **E18.**
2 †**a** Very fast or rapid. Only in **19.** ▸**b** Excellent, splendid. *arch. slang.* **M19.**

> **2b** D. MACKAIL 'Thanks awfully', said Rex. 'That'll be ripping.'

■ **rippingly** *adverb* **L19.**

ripple /ˈrɪp(ə)l/ *noun*[1]. **LME.**
[Corresp. to Frisian *ripel*, Dutch, Middle & mod. Low German *repel*, Old High German *riffila* (German *Riffel*). Cf. RIPPLE *verb*[1].]
A toothed or hooked implement; *spec.* one resembling a comb, for removing seeds from flax or hemp.

ripple /ˈrɪp(ə)l/ *noun*[2]. Long *north.* **M17.**
[from RIPPLE *verb*[2].]
A slight cut, scratch, or mark; a graze.

ripple /ˈrɪp(ə)l/ *noun*[3]. **M18.**
[from RIPPLE *verb*[3].]
1 A stretch of shallow broken water in a river obstructed by rocks or sand bars; a shoal. *US.* **M18.**
2 A light ruffling of the surface of water; a series of small waves; a small wave. Also *spec.* in *PHYSICS*, a wave on a fluid surface the restoring force for which is provided by surface tension rather than gravity, and which consequently has a wavelength shorter than that corresponding to the minimum speed of propagation. **L18.** ▸**b** *transf.* Something resembling or suggestive of a ripple on water, esp. as having a wavy or crinkled appearance; a gentle lively sound, esp. of talk or laughter, that rises and falls. **M19.** ▸**c** Chiefly *GEOLOGY.* In full ***ripple mark***. A ridge or ridged surface left on sand, mud, or rock by the action of water or wind. **M19.** ▸**d** (Also **R-**.) (US proprietary name for) a kind of ice-cream interlayered with wavy bands of coloured flavoured syrup. **M20.**
3 = RIFFLE *noun* 4. **M19.**
4 *ELECTRICITY.* Small periodic (usu. undesirable) variations in voltage superposed on a direct voltage or on an alternating voltage of lower frequency. Freq. *attrib.* **E20.**
5 A method of firing or discharging missiles etc. in succession or at intervals. **M20.**

> **2** A. KOESTLER Like a pebble dropped into a pond, spreading its ripples. *fig.*: *Economist* The . . budget cuts might have produced a ripple of no confidence across the private sector. **b** L. MACNEICE The half-grown wheat in the wind is a ripple of satin. A. R. AMMONS The snake shed himself in ripples / across a lake of sand. B. PYM There was a ripple of laughter from the audience. **d** J. WINTERSON Ida was . . eating raspberry ripple.

Comb.: **ripple cloth** cloth having a rippled appearance; **ripple control** *ELECTRICITY* control of simple operations, such as switching of street lights, by superposition of a high-frequency switching signal on the mains supply; **ripple counter** *ELECTRONICS* a binary counter consisting of a series of bistable circuits wired in cascade, so that each changes its state only after all the preceding ones have done so; **ripple effect** the continuous and spreading results of an event or action; **ripple-fired** *adjective* (of missiles) fired in rapid succession or at intervals; **ripple-flaking** *ARCHAEOLOGY* in shaping a flint implement, the removal of flakes in such a way as to give the surface the appearance of ripples; *ripple mark*: see sense 2c above; **ripple-marked** *adjective* that has ripple marks; **ripple sole** a kind of rubber sole having thick wavy ripple-shaped ridges; **ripple-through counter** = *ripple counter* above.

■ **rippleless** /-l-l-/ *adjective* **M19.** **ripplet** *noun* a small ripple **E19.** **ripply** *adjective* marked or characterized by ripples **L18.**

ripple /ˈrɪp(ə)l/ *noun*[4]. *Scot. arch.* **L15.**
[Origin unkn.]
A disease, possibly of venereal origin, affecting the back and loins. Usu. in *pl.*

ripple /ˈrɪp(ə)l/ *verb*[1] *trans.* **ME.**
[Corresp. to Frisian *ripelje*, Middle & mod. Dutch, Middle Low German, Dutch *repelen*, Old High German *rifilōn* (German *riffeln*). Cf. RIFFLE *verb*, RIPPLE *noun*[1].]
1 Remove seeds from (flax or hemp) with a ripple. **ME.**
2 Remove (seeds) from flax or hemp with a ripple. Freq. foll. by *off.* **L15.**
■ **rippler** *noun* **M18.**

ripple /ˈrɪp(ə)l/ *verb*[2] *trans.* Now *Scot. & north.* **LME.**
[Prob. of Scandinavian origin: cf. Norwegian *ripie* to scratch.]
1 Scratch slightly; graze. **LME.**
2 Break up (ground) lightly. **M18.**

ripple /ˈrɪp(ə)l/ *verb*[3]. **L17.**
[Origin unkn.]
1 *verb intrans.* Have or show a lightly ruffled, crinkled, or waved surface; be covered with ripples; form ripples, undulate lightly. **L17.** ▸**b** Flow or progress in ripples. **M18.** ▸**c** Pass quickly *through* each of a series in turn. **M20.**
2 *verb trans.* Cause to ripple; form ripples in or on; mark (as) with ripples; cause to undulate lightly. **L18.** ▸**b** Produce or utter with a rising and falling sound. Also foll. by *out.* **L19.**

> **1** A. B. EDWARDS The young barley rippling for miles in the sun. V. WOOLF The sea was rippling faintly, . . lines of green and blue . . beginning to stripe it. **b** TENNYSON The rivulet . . Ripples on in light and shadow. **c** P. L. FERMOR Applause rippled through the gathered crowd. **2** T. S. ELIOT The brisk swell Rippled both shores. F. MUIR Photographed in the nude, rippling his muscles. **b** A. E. W. MASON The girl . . rippled out a laugh of gladness.

■ **rippling** *noun* (*a*) the action of the verb; an instance of this; (*b*) *US* = RIPPLE *noun*[3] 1; (*c*) the sound of water in motion: **M17.** **ripplingly** *adverb* in a rippling manner **M19.**

rippled /ˈrɪp(ə)ld/ *adjective.* **M19.**
[from RIPPLE *noun*[3], *verb*[3]: see -ED[2], -ED[1].]
That has been rippled; having ripples.
¶ Earlier in UNRIPPLED.

ripple-grass /ˈrɪp(ə)lgrɑːs/ *noun. Scot. & US.* **E19.**
[App. from RIPPLE *noun*[2] + GRASS *noun.*]
Either of two plantains, the ribwort plantain, *Plantago lanceolata*, and greater plantain, *P. major.*

Rippon /ˈrɪp(ə)n/ *noun. obsolete* exc. *Hist.* **E17.**
[*Ripon* (see below).]
(In full ***Rippon spur***) a spur manufactured in the town of Ripon in N. Yorkshire; any spur. Usu. in *pl.*

riprap /ˈrɪprap/ *noun & verb.* **L16.**
[Redupl. of RAP *noun*[1], *verb*[1].]
▸**A** *noun.* **1** †**a** A sound resembling that caused by a rapid succession of blows; a sharp blow. **L16–E17.** ▸**b** A kind of detonating firework. Also, the sound of fireworks detonating. **L19.**
2 Loose stone used to form a foundation for a breakwater or other structure; a structure made of this. Orig. *US.* **M19.**
▸**B** *verb trans.* Infl. **-pp-**.
1 Construct a breakwater or other work with a foundation of loose stone. **M19.**
2 Of a curling-stone: knock against (another stone). *Scot. rare.* **M19.**

ripresa /riˈpreːsa/ *noun.* Pl. ***-se*** /-se/. **M18.**
[Italian.]
MUSIC. A repeat; a refrain.

rip-roaring /ˈrɪprɔːrɪŋ/ *adjective* (chiefly *attrib.*). *colloq.* (orig. *US*). **M19.**
[from RIP *verb*[1] + ROARING *adjective.* Cf. next.]
Full of vigour or spirit; boisterous, wildly noisy; excellent, first-rate.

> *Times* A rip-roaring . . affair of incessant movement and high good spirits. B. CHATWIN Its members were in a rip-roaring mood.

■ **rip-roaringly** *adverb* **M20.**

riproarious /rɪpˈrɔːrɪəs/ *adjective. colloq.* (orig. *US*). **M19.**
[from RIP *verb*[1] + UP)ROARIOUS. Cf. prec.]
Boisterous, violent.
■ **riproariously** *adverb* (*rare*) **M19.**

ripsnorter /ˈrɪpsnɔːtə/ *noun. colloq.* (orig. *US*). **M19.**
[from RIP *verb*[1] + SNORTER *noun*[1].]
A person or thing of exceptionally remarkable appearance, quality, strength, etc.; *spec.* a storm, a gale.

ripsnorting /ˈrɪpsnɔːtɪŋ/ *adjective. colloq.* (orig. *US*). **M19.**
[from prec. after *rip-roaring.*]
= RIP-ROARING.
■ **ripsnortingly** *adverb* **L20.**

Ripuarian /rɪpjʊˈɛːrɪən/ *adjective & noun.* **L18.**
[from medieval Latin *Ripuarius*: see -ARIAN.]
▸**A** *adjective.* **1** *Hist.* Of, pertaining to, or designating the ancient Franks living on the Rhine between the Moselle and Meuse; *spec.* designating the code of law prevailing among them. **L18.**
2 Designating a northern dialect of Middle Franconian German. **E20.**
▸**B** *noun.* **1** *Hist.* A member of the Ripuarian Franks. Usu. in *pl.* **L18.**
2 A northern dialect of Middle Franconian German. **E20.**

Ripuary /ˈrɪpjʊəri/ *adjective. rare.* **E17.**
[formed as prec. + -ARY[1].]
Hist. Of, pertaining to, or designating the Ripuarian code of law.

Rip Van Winkle /rɪp van ˈwɪŋk(ə)l/ *noun.* **E19.**
[Hero of a story in Washington Irving's *Sketch Book* (1819–20), who fell asleep in the Catskill Mountains in New York State and awoke after 20 years to find the world completely changed.]
A person who has been asleep or unperceptive for a long time; *esp.* one who has remained oblivious to fundamental social and political changes over an extended period.
■ **Rip-Van-Winkledom** *noun* (*a*) the Catskill Mountains in New York State; (*b*) a state of prolonged sleep (*lit. & fig.*): **L19.** **Rip-Van-Winkleish** *adjective* characteristic of or resembling Rip Van Winkle, ignorant of present (esp. social and political) conditions **E19.** **Rip-Van-Winkleism** *noun* (*a*) an outmoded custom, opinion, or expression; (*b*) the state of being a Rip Van Winkle: **M19.**

riroriro /ˈriːrəʊriːrəʊ/ *noun. NZ.* Also **riro-riro**. **M19.**
[Maori: imit.]
A small grey fly-eater of New Zealand, *Gerygone igata.* Also called ***rainbird***.

ris *verb pa. pple*: see RISE *verb.*

†**risagon** *noun.* **L17–M19.**
[Origin unkn.]
PHARMACOLOGY. = ZEDOARY.

risbank /ˈrɪzbaŋk/ *noun.* Long *obsolete* exc. *dial. rare.* Also (earlier) †**rice-bank**. **M17.**
[Dutch *rijsbank*, from *rijs* RICE *noun*[1] + *bank* BANK *noun*[1].]
A man-made bank, *esp.* one faced or strengthened with brushwood.

Risc /rɪsk/ *noun.* Also **RISC**, **risc**. **L20.**
[Acronym, from reduced instruction set computer (or computing).]
COMPUTING. A type of microprocessor capable of a limited set of operations and able to perform basic tasks quickly using relatively simple circuitry; computing using such microprocessors.

ris de veau /ri də vo/ *noun phr.* **E19.**
[French.]
Sweetbread of veal prepared as a dish.

rise /rʌɪz/ *noun*. LME.
[from the verb. In sense 1 perh. erron. for RUSE.]
▶ **I** †**1** An act of turning or doubling by a hunted hare, to elude a pursuer. Only in LME.
†**2** A revolt, a rebellion. Earliest in ***make a rise***, revolt, rebel. *rare*. LME–M19.
3 (The time of) the rising of the sun, moon, etc., above the horizon. Also, the direction of sunrise, the east. Earliest in SUNRISE, and now chiefly in this and parallel formations, as ***moonrise*** etc. LME.
4 Upward movement; ascent; transference to a higher level. Also, an instance of this. L16. ▸**b** Capacity for or power of rising. E18. ▸**c** *CRICKET*. The upward movement of a ball after pitching. M19. ▸**d** *THEATRICAL*. The raising of the curtain at the beginning of a scene. Freq. in ***at rise***. E20. ▸**e** An erection of the penis. Freq. in ***get a rise***. *slang*. M20.
†**5 a** A spring or bound upwards; *esp.* one made at the outset of an extended jump or leap. Only in 17. ▸**b** A start or aid towards rising in a leap; a place from which to rise or soar. M17–E18.
6 Upward movement to a position of power or prosperity; elevation in fortune or rank; advance towards a flourishing or prosperous condition. Formerly also (*rare*), an occasion or means of achieving this. M17. ▸**b** The action of rising from or *from* a specified condition; *spec.* (*CHRISTIAN THEOLOGY*) the resurrection of Christ. *arch*. M18.
7 *ANGLING*. The movement of a fish to the surface of the water to take a fly or bait; an instance of this. M17.

🕮 **2** BOSWELL The Genoese, eager to repress the rise of 1734. **3** J. K. JAMES To her at rise, to her at sunset hour. R. BRIDGES She . . Lookt left and right to rise and set of day. **4** SIR W. SCOTT The steed along the drawbridge flies, Just as it trembled on the rise. **d** J. OSBORNE At rise of curtain Jimmy and Cliff are seated in . . armchairs. **6** W. SPALDING The rise of the Medici . . furnished liberal patrons to art. J. BRYCE The rise and fall of the Whig party. **7** *New Yorker* They nipped at the fly and disappeared . . I got no more rises.

▶ **II 8** A piece of rising ground; a hill. LME. ▸**b** A long, broad, gently sloping elevation rising from the seabed, *esp.* that at the edge of a continental shelf. E20.
9 The vertical height of a step, arch, inclined surface, etc., measured from the base to the highest point. M17.
10 An upward slope or direction, esp. of a stratum, bed, or vein. L17. ▸**b** *MINING*. An excavation or working on the up side of a shaft. M19.
11 A flight *of* steps. Also = RISER 2. E18.

🕮 **8** C. MACLEOD Helen mounted the not inconsiderable rise towards the residential area. W. SOYINKA On a misty day, the steep rise towards Itoko would join the sky. **10** T. H. HUXLEY A very sharp rise leads from the Pacific to the . . Andes. **11** *Lancashire Life* From the entrance-hall an eight-rise flight of stairs takes you to a . . landing.

▶ **III 12** An increase in something that can be measured or quantified, as the height of the sea, pressure, temperature, value, price, etc.; the amount of this increase. E17.
13 A raising of pitch in a tone or voice. E17.
14 *spec.* An increase in the amount of wages or salary. M19.

🕮 **12** C. LYELL The perpendicular rise and fall of . . spring-tides is fifteen feet. B. STEWART Heat is . . absorbed by the ice without producing any rise of temperature. *Law Times* A great rise . . in the value of the . . property. M. BERESFORD This . . would put the beginning of the population rise at about 1460. **14** F. CHICHESTER I asked for a rise from fifteen . . to twenty-five shillings a week.

▶ **IV 15** An origin, a source; a beginning; a start. M17.
16 An occasion; a ground, a basis. *obsolete* exc. in ***give rise to*** below. M17.
17 The action of coming into existence or notice. M17.

🕮 **15** J. WESLEY Nor Plague of unknown Rise. P. GALLICO It was here that the brook . . had its rise. **16** L. STERNE The rise of this sudden demigration was as follows. **17** W. JONES The rise of a poet in their tribe. J. MARTINEAU Concurrent with the rise of new questions.

Phrases: **get a rise out of**, **take a rise out of** provoke into a display of temper or indignation, esp. by teasing. **give rise to** bring about, cause. ***Irishman's rise***: see IRISHMAN. **make a rise** (*a*) succeed in striking gold etc. by mining; (*b*) see sense 2 above. **on the rise** becoming more valuable or dearer; increasing. ***take a rise out of***: see ***get a rise out of*** above. †**take one's rise (from)** start or begin with in narration. **the rise of** *US* (now *rare*) more than (a specified amount).
Comb.: **rise time** *ELECTRONICS* the time required for a pulse to rise from 10 per cent to 90 per cent of its steady value.
¶ Recorded earlier in ME in surname and place-name.

rise /rʌɪz/ *verb*. Pa. t. **rose** /rəʊz/; pa. pple **risen** /ˈrɪz(ə)n/; (*dial.*) **ris** /rɪz/.
[Old English *risan* = Old French *risa*, Old Saxon, Old High German *risan* (Dutch *rijzen*, German *reisen* (of the sun), Old Norse *rísa*, Gothic (*ur*)*reisan*), from Germanic strong verb without known cognates.]
▶ **I** *verb intrans.* **1** †**a** Make an attack, take hostile measures. (Foll. by *on*, *against*.) OE–M17. ▸**b** Rebel, revolt; take up arms; cease to be quiet or submissive. Also foll. by *against*, *on*, *up*. ME.
2 Get out of bed, wake *up*, esp. in the morning. OE.
3 Return to life; come back from the dead. Also foll. by *up*. ME.
4 Get up from sitting, kneeling, or lying; stand up; get to one's feet. Also foll. by *up*. Cf. sense 5 below. ME. ▸†**b** Of an animal, esp. one hunted as game: come out of, emerge from, cover. LME–M17. ▸**c** Become erect or stiff; resume an upright position; (of a person's hair) stand on end (*lit.* & *fig.*). E16. ▸**d** Of an animal, esp. a horse: raise itself *on* the hind legs; rear. *rare*. M17. ▸**e** Depart *from* a table, meal, etc., esp. on finishing eating; *dial.* (of a funeral party in Wales) leave the home of the deceased or bereaved prior to the interment. M18.
5 Get up, recover one's upright position, after a fall (*lit.* & *fig.*). Cf. sense 4 above. ME.
6 Of a legislature, court of law, etc.: cease to sit for business, adjourn, esp. for a vacation or recess. E16. ▸†**b** *MILITARY*. Break up camp; retire or draw off *from* a siege. M16–M18.

🕮 **1b** A. S. NEILL The whole village would rise up against me. D. FRASER On the night of 23rd October the native Irish rose. **2** AV *Gen.* 22:3 Abraham rose vp early in the morning. O. MANNING He rose and dressed. **4** L. DURRELL He did not rise however but sat on in his uncomfortable high-backed chair. G. GREENE He rose uncertainly to his feet. **b** SPENSER A Tigre forth out of the wood did rise. **c** SHELLEY The sheaths . . Rose like the crest of cobra-dicapel. **d** TENNYSON On his haunches rose the steed. **5** W. COWPER Pride falls unpitied, never more to rise. **5** *Gentleman's Magazine* Were their Forefathers to rise up and . . see . . their Descendants. N. MARSH If you cut off my head I'll rise from the dead. **6** *Times* Parliament has risen till October 25. N. GORDIMER An important State witness was due to be called for cross-examination before the court rose for the day.

▶ **II** *verb intrans.* **7** Come or go upwards, move or be carried upwards; ascend into the air. ME. ▸**b** Of a bird: fly up from the ground or out of covert. E16. ▸**c** Of a tree etc.: grow to a (usu. specified) height. E17. ▸**d** Of a horse: spring up from the ground in preparation for jumping an obstacle. Also foll. by *to*. M19.
8 Of the sun, moon, etc.: appear above the horizon. Also, (of the day etc.) dawn, begin. ME.
9 Increase by an amount that can be measured or quantified; (of the sea, a river, etc.) increase in height to a (usu. specified) level, esp. through tidal action or flooding. ME. ▸**b** Reach a greater height or size; swell up; *spec.* (of dough or pastry) swell by the action of yeast etc. LME. ▸**c** (Of liquid in a measuring instrument) reach a higher level; (of a measuring instrument) register an increase of pressure or temperature. M17. ▸**d** Of a liquid or molten metal: boil. M19.
10 a Of an emotion, esp. indignation or anger: be experienced or felt suddenly. Also foll. by *against*. ME. ▸**b** Esp. of a person's spirits: be raised by joy or hope; become more cheerful. LME. ▸**c** Of the stomach: become nauseated (*at*). Freq. in ***one's gorge rises at*** below. E16.
11 Extend directly upwards or away from the ground; form an elevation from the level. ME. ▸**b** Have an upward slant or curve; slope or incline upwards. M17.
12 Come up to the surface of the ground or water. LME. ▸**b** *spec.* (Of a fish) come to the surface of the water for food; *fig.* (of a person) react to provocation (chiefly in ***rise to the bait***). M17.

🕮 **7** T. GRAY Rise, my soul! on wings of fire. I. MURDOCH Steam was rising from the pavement. S. BRETT I will be making an announcement to the audience before the curtain rises. **b** J. BUCHAN A brace of black-game . . rose at my approach. R. WARNER A heron rose flapping from the river. **c** J. MILLS This tree seldom rises higher than . . thirty feet. D. JOHNSON Sugar cane rises up out of its own stubble. **d** C. J. LEVER Sir Roger when within two yards of the brink rose to it, and cleared it. **8** MILTON The Moon Rising in clouded Majestie. R. HUGHES The next day the sun rose . . large, round and red. **9** F. MORYSON When the river riseth, it . . overfloweth the fields. A. R. WALLACE The river sometimes rose 30 feet in eight hours. **b** R. JAMES The blister . . rose well, and discharged plentifully. D. STOREY The loaves, rising, were standing in the hearth. **10a** LD MACAULAY I . . feel my soul rise against oppression. H. ROTH He could feel dread rising within him. **b** A. FINE Their heads felt clearer, their spirits rose. **11** J. R. GREEN To the west . . rose one of the stateliest of English castles. H. E. BATES A great spire . . rises up for two hundred and seventy feet from a churchyard. **b** G. MACDONALD Looking up the lane, which rose considerably towards the other end. TOLKIEN The land rose, swelling up towards a line of low humpbacked downs. **12** J. STEINBECK His body rose to the surface. **b** E. HEMINGWAY Trout would rise in the pool when there was a hatch of fly.

▶ **III** *verb intrans.* **13** Develop a greater power of action, feeling, thought, or expression. ME. ▸**b** Become capable of a specified action; prove equal to a particular need (freq. in ***rise to the occasion***). Foll. by *to*. E19.
14 a Become more important or influential; achieve increased wealth or status; rise to a higher social position. ME. ▸**b** Become more appealing. Chiefly in ***rise in a person's estimation***. Also foll. by †*on* a person. M17.
15 a Increase in amount, number, or degree; amount *to* a specified sum. ME. ▸**b** Become dearer or more valuable; increase *in* price, value, etc. E16.
16 a Of the voice etc.: increase in volume; become higher in pitch, ascend in the musical scale. LME. ▸**b** Become stronger or more intense; increase in strength *to* a certain point; *spec.* (of the wind) increase in force, blow more strongly. L16.

🕮 **13** B. JOWETT Thoughts and expressions in which he rises to the highest level. **b** F. W. ROBERTSON We do not rise to philanthropy all at once. J. HIGGINS Better to rise to a challenge than go for the easy choice. **14a** H. J. LASKI A . . bishop . . who rose from humble circumstances to the wealthy bishopric of Winchester. *Blackwood's Magazine* He had risen . . in the world by Turkish standards. M. PUZO By that time McCluskey was rising from sergeant to lieutenant. **b** LD MACAULAY The character of Socrates does not rise upon me. M. BISHOP Paisley began to rise higher in Sam's estimation. **15** *Daily Telegraph* Demand for steel is continuing to rise. *City Limits* 500 . . are made and devoured on weekdays, rising to 1000 on Saturdays. **b** G. ROSE The Funds rose 1 per cent on the news. *Christian Science Monitor* The dollar rose . . against other currencies during the first half of 1991. **16a** E. PROUT The bass rises to the third of the tonic chord. D. HAMMETT Her voice gradually rising until towards the end she was screaming into my face. J. MARQUAND His voice had risen to a high treble. **b** W. WILKIE Command the winds in bolder gusts to rise. C. MACKENZIE Elsie feared that tempers were rising, and . . drew her father's fire upon herself. I. MURDOCH A murmur . . rose to a roar and re-echoed from the façades. E. ALBEE His cheeks went red and the colour rose in his neck.

▶ **IV** *verb intrans.* **17** Come into existence, appear; *spec.* (*a*) (of a person) come on the scene; *arch.* be born (esp. *of* or *from* a particular person or family); (*b*) (of a tree etc.) begin to grow; (*c*) (of the wind etc.) begin to blow, get up; (*d*) (of a blister etc.) form. Also foll. by *up*. ME. ▸**b** Come before the eye or mind. Also foll. by *up*. E18.
18 Originate, result. (Foll. by *of*, *from*, *out of*.) ME. ▸**b** Of a river etc.: have its spring or source, esp. *in* a specified place. LME. ▸†**c** Be produced or derived. M16–E18.
19 a Come to pass, occur, happen, take place. ME. ▸**b** Of a report, rumour, etc.: come into circulation; become current. ME. ▸†**c** Come *to* hand. *rare* (Spenser). Only in L16.
20 Be built; undergo construction from the foundations. L16.

🕮 **17** MILTON Of the Royal Stock . . shall rise A Son. W. COWPER Elysian scenes disclose His bright perfections at whose word they rose. W. MORRIS Month-long no breeze . . Rose up o'er the sea. **b** M. BARING Many little absurd incidents . . rose up clearly before me. **18** T. GRAY Tell me, whence their sorrows rose. G. CRABBE From study will no comforts rise? **19a** MILTON Lest a question rise Whether he durst accept the offer. TENNYSON Then rose a . . feud betwixt the two. **b** TENNYSON A rumour rose about the Queen, Touching her guilty love for Lancelot. **20** SHELLEY Beside the . . Nile, The Pyramids have risen. LD MACAULAY Streets and alleys . . were rising on that site.

▶ **V** *verb trans.* **21** Cause to rise; *spec.* (*a*) *rare* bring (the dead) back to life; (*b*) cause (game) to emerge from cover; (*c*) cause (a fish) to come to the surface of the water for food. Now *arch.* & *dial.* LME.
22 Increase; make higher or dearer. Now *rare* exc. *dial.* E17. ▸**b** Exceed in number or amount. *US*. M19.
23 a *NAUTICAL*. = RAISE *verb* 19. M17. ▸**b** Lift up; cause to ascend or mount up. *arch.* E18. ▸**c** Promote (a person) in rank, position, or salary. *rare*. E19.
24 Get, procure, obtain. Now chiefly *dial.* M18.
25 Surmount, gain the top of, (a hill or slope); ascend. Chiefly *US*. E19.

🕮 **21** C. J. LEVER The clatter of my equipage . . might have risen the dead. *Country Living* If they rise a fox on the . . hill, they may run it for . . miles. **22** W. DOUGLASS Their recoinings . . did rise the price of Goods. **23a** F. MARRYAT She had risen her hull out of the water. **25** *Country Life* They rose the hill . . and ran on.

▶ **VI** *verb trans.* **26** As ***rising*** *pres. pple*. Approaching (a specified age). M18.

🕮 **26** N. STREATFEILD Pauline rising four and Petrova sixteen months. *Dressage Review* Dynasty is rising ten and a Hanoverian.

Phrases: ***one's gorge rises at***: see GORGE *noun*[1]. **rise above** (*a*) be or become superior to (petty feelings etc.); (*b*) show dignity or strength in the face of (difficulty, poor conditions, etc.). **rise and shine** *colloq.* (usu. in *imper.*) get out of bed smartly, esp. in the morning; wake up. ***rise from the ashes***: see ASH *noun*[2]. ***rise from the ranks***: see RANK *noun*. **rise in the world** attain a higher social position. ***rise with the lark***: see LARK *noun*[1]. ***rise with the sun***: see SUN *noun*[1].

risen *verb pa. pple* of RISE *verb*.

riser /ˈrʌɪzə/ *noun*. LME.
[from RISE *verb* + -ER[1].]
1 A person who or thing which rises; *esp.* a person who gets up early, late, etc., in the morning (freq. with specifying word). LME.

2 The upright part of a step; the vertical piece connecting two treads in a stair. M16. ▸**b** *PHYSICAL GEOGRAPHY.* Each of the steeply sloping parts of a glacial stairway or similar stepped landform. M20. ▸**c** A low platform on a stage or in an auditorium, used to give greater prominence to a speaker or performer; any of a group of similar platforms arranged in steplike fashion. M20.
3 *PRINTING* (now *Hist.*). Wooden or metal blocks on which stereotype and other plates are fastened. E19.
4 A fish that rises to the surface of the water for food. M19.
5 *MINING.* An upward dislocation of a seam. M19.
6 *FOUNDING.* A vertical channel in a mould in which molten metal rises. L19.
7 a = *rising main* (b) s.v. RISING *adjective.* L19. ▸**b** A vertical pipe for the upward flow of liquid or gas; *spec.* (**a**) one carrying water or steam from one floor to another in a central heating system; (**b**) one extending from an offshore drilling or production platform to the seabed, through which drilling may be done or oil or gas may flow. E20.
8 = *lift-web* s.v. LIFT *noun*². E20.

rishi /ˈrɪʃi/ *noun.* Pl. same, **-s**. M18.
[Sanskrit *ṛṣi.*]
In Hinduism: (the title of) an inspired poet or sage; a holy seer; an ascetic, a saint.

rishitin /rɪˈʃiːtɪn/ *noun.* M20.
[from Japanese *Rishiri*, a variety of potato + euphonic *-t-* + -IN¹.]
BIOCHEMISTRY. A terpenoid which is an antifungal phytoalexin found in the tubers of some varieties of white potato.

rishon /ˈrɪʃɒn/ *noun.* L20.
[Hebrew *ri'šōn* primary, first: cf. -ON.]
PARTICLE PHYSICS. A hypothetical particle postulated as a constituent of quarks and leptons.

risible /ˈrɪzɪb(ə)l/ *adjective & noun.* M16.
[Late Latin *risibilis*, from Latin *ris-* pa. ppl stem of *ridere* laugh: see -IBLE.]
▸ **A** *adjective.* **1** Having the faculty or power of laughing; inclined or given to laughter. Now *rare.* M16.
2 Capable of exciting laughter; laughable, ludicrous. E18.
3 Pertaining to or used in laughter. M18.

> 🕮 **1** A. HILL What must risible Foreigners have thought of the Court of King William? **2** J. GILCHRIST Foreigners . . get laughed at as if . . guilty of some risible blunder. P. BAILEY An account can be opened with a pittance, with the risible contents of a begging bowl. **3** R. MACAULAY The risible muscles of her face were sore with exertion.

▸ **B** *noun.* In *pl.* The risible faculties or muscles. Chiefly *US.* L18.
■ **risi'bility** *noun* (**a**) the state or condition of being risible; a disposition to laugh; (**b**) in *pl.* (*US*) = RISIBLE *noun*: E17.

rising /ˈrʌɪzɪŋ/ *noun.* ME.
[from RISE *verb* + -ING¹.]
1 The action of RISE *verb*; an instance of this. ME.
2 The action of taking up arms, rebellion; an insurrection, a revolt. ME.
3 a A swelling, an abscess, a tumour, a boil. Now *dial.* & *US.* LME. ▸**b** A part or thing standing out above its surroundings; a prominence, a projection. L16.
4 The upward slope of a hill; a piece of rising ground; a hill, a mound. M16.
5 Yeast, leaven; a fermenting agent. *dial.* & *N. Amer.* L16.
6 *NAUTICAL.* A narrow strake used as a support for the thwarts in a small rowing boat. E17.
Phrases: **rising of the lights** (long *dial.*) an illness characterized by difficulty in breathing.

rising /ˈrʌɪzɪŋ/ *adjective & adverb.* LME.
[from RISE *verb* + -ING².]
▸ **A** *adjective.* **1** That rises; (of ground) sloping upward; (of a person) advancing in fortune, influence, or dignity, coming to prominence. LME.
2 *HERALDRY.* Of a bird or winged creature: shown preparing for flight or taking wing. E17.
Special collocations: **rising damp** moisture absorbed from the ground into a wall. *rising diphthong*: see DIPHTHONG 1. **rising five** [strictly the pres. pple: see RISE *verb* 26] a child approaching his or her fifth birthday, *esp.* one who may thus be qualified to start school (usu. in *pl.*). **rising line** a curved line on the plan of a ship showing the heights of the floor-timbers. **rising main** (**a**) the vertical pipe of a pump; (**b**) an electricity main passing from one floor of a building to another. **rising sign** *ASTROLOGY* an ascendant sign. *rising sun*: see SUN *noun*¹ (*land of the rising sun*: see LAND *noun*¹).
▸ **B** *adverb.* Upwards *of*, in excess *of*, (*rare*). Also, fully as much as; rather more than. *US.* E19.

risk /rɪsk/ *noun.* Also (earlier) †**risque**. M17.
[French *risque* from Italian †*risco*, *rischio*, from *rischiare* run into danger.]
1 Danger; (exposure to) the possibility of loss, injury, or other adverse circumstance. (Foll. by *of*.) M17. ▸**b** (Exposure to) the possibility of commercial loss, *spec.* (**a**) in the case of insured property or goods, (**b**) as part of economic enterprise and the source of entrepreneurial profit. L17.
2 A chance or possibility of danger, commercial loss, or other risk. (Foll. by *of*.) M17.
3 A person considered a liability or danger; a person exposed to risk. Freq. with specifying word. M20.

> 🕮 **1** LD MACAULAY There would be great risk of lamentable change in the character of our public men. P. LOMAS I notice that you always avoid risk But a full life involves risk. **b** ADAM SMITH The ordinary rate of profit always rises . . with the risk. M. BRETT Unit trusts pool the money of individual investors to provide a spread of risk. **2** R. LYND The ordinary pedestrian . . takes extraordinary risks in crossing the roads. A. CAIRNCROSS The tendency to spread risks and steady production by diversifying output. G. GREENE Easier to run the risk of death than ridicule. **3** D. LEAVITT We're such good credit risks.

Phrases: **at one's own risk**, **at one's risk** agreeing to make no claims; accepting responsibility for loss, injury, etc. **at risk** (**a**) in danger, exposed to a risk, (*of*); (**b**) liable to repay loss or damage. *OCCUPATIONAL risk.*
Comb.: **risk analysis** the systematic investigation and forecasting of risks in business and commerce; **risk capital** money put up for speculative business investment; **risk money** (**a**) money allowed to a cashier to cover accidental deficits; (**b**) = *risk capital* above.
■ **riskful** *adjective* risky L18. **riskless** *adjective* M19.

risk /rɪsk/ *verb trans.* Also (earlier) †**risque**. M17.
[French *risquer*, formed as prec., or from Italian †*riscare*, *rischiare*: see prec.]
1 Endanger, put at risk, expose to the chance of injury or loss. M17.
2 Venture on; accept the chance of (a thing, *doing*). E18.

> 🕮 **1** C. S. FORESTER Those Galicians risked their lives to save him. R. DAVIES I never bet, and I wouldn't have risked money on that. H. KISSINGER Unconstrained rivalry could risk everything . . in a nuclear holocaust. *risk one's neck*: see NECK *noun*¹. **2** W. S. CHURCHILL Speed was essential, but disaster could not be risked. D. M. THOMAS The memory . . is too precious to risk losing.

■ **risker** *noun* (*rare*) L17.

risky /ˈrɪski/ *adjective.* E19.
[from RISK *noun* + -Y¹.]
1 Involving risk, dangerous, hazardous. E19.
2 = RISQUÉ. L19.
1 risky shift *SOCIAL PSYCHOLOGY* in decision-making, a shift of opinion towards an option involving greater risk that may take place when responsibility for a decision rests with a group rather than an individual.
■ **riskily** *adverb* L19. **riskiness** *noun* L19.

Risley /ˈrɪzli/ *noun.* M19.
[Richard *Risley* Carlisle (d. 1874), US gymnast and circus performer.]
Used *attrib.* (chiefly in *Risley act*) to designate an act in which a supine acrobat juggles another with his or her feet.

risoluto /rɪzəˈluːtəʊ/ *adjective & adverb.* M18.
[Italian.]
MUSIC. ▸†**A** *adjective.* Resolved into a concord. Only in M18.
▸ **B** *adverb.* A direction: with resolution or emphasis. M19.

Risorgimento /rɪˌsɔːdʒɪˈmɛntəʊ/ *noun.* Pl. **-ti** /-ti/, **-tos**. L19.
[Italian = renewal, renaissance.]
1 *Hist.* The movement which led to the unification of Italy as an independent State in 1870. L19.
2 A revitalization or renewal of activity in any sphere. M20.

risorius /rɪˈzɔːrɪəs, rɪˈsɔː-/ *noun.* E19.
[mod. Latin (sc. *musculus*) *risorius*, from Latin *risor* laugher + *-ius* adjectival suffix.]
ANATOMY. A muscle of facial expression running from the corner of the mouth, variable in form and absent in some individuals. Also *risorius muscle*.

risotto /rɪˈzɒtəʊ/ *noun.* Pl. **-os**. M19.
[Italian, from *riso* rice.]
An Italian dish of rice cooked in stock with various other ingredients, as meat, onions, etc.

risp /rɪsp/ *verb & noun.* Chiefly *Scot.* LME.
[Old Norse *rispa* to scratch, score (Icelandic, Swedish *rispa*, Norwegian *rispe*). Cf. Danish *rispe* plough for the first time.]
▸ **A** *verb.* **1** *verb trans.* Rub; grate together; file, rasp. LME.
2 *verb intrans.* Make a harsh, rasping, or grating sound. E19.
▸ **B** *noun.* **1** A carpenter's file; a rasp. E16.
2 *Hist.* A small serrated bar fixed upright on a house-door, with a ring attached, which was forcibly rubbed up and down the bar to attract the attention of those inside. E19.
3 A grating or rasping sound. M19.

risposta /riˈsposta, rɪˈspɒstə/ *noun.* Pl. **-ste** /-ste/. L19.
[Italian = a reply.]
MUSIC. A fugal response.

†**risque** *noun, verb* see RISK *noun, verb.*

risqué /ˈriːskeɪ, ˈrɪskeɪ, rɪˈskeɪ/ *adjective.* M19.
[French, pa. pple of *risquer* RISK *verb.*]
Of a joke, story, etc.: slightly indecent, liable to shock slightly.

Riss /rɪs/ *adjective & noun.* E20.
[A tributary of the River Danube in Germany.]
GEOLOGY. (Designating or pertaining to) the penultimate Pleistocene glaciation in the Alps, possibly corresponding to the Saale of northern Europe.

rissala /rɪˈsɑːlə/ *noun.* Also **ress-**, **-ah**. M18.
[Urdu *risālah*, from Persian *risāla* troop of horse from Arab. *risāla* mission.]
Hist. A squadron of Indian cavalry in the Anglo-Indian army.

rissaldar /rɪsɑːlˈdɑː/ *noun. Anglo-Indian.* Also (now *rare*) **ress-** /rɛs-/. E19.
[Urdu *risāl(ā)dār*, from Persian *risāla* RISSALA + *-dār* holding, holder.]
An Indian officer in a cavalry regiment, of a rank usu. corresponding to captain or (*rissaldar-major*) major.

rissole /ˈrɪsəʊl/ *noun.* E18.
[French, later form of Old French *ruissole* dial. var. of *roisole*, *roussole* from Proto-Romance use as noun of fem. of late Latin *russeolus* reddish, from Latin *russus* red.]
A ball or small cake of chopped meat etc. coated with breadcrumbs, cooked by frying.

Risso's dolphin /ˈrɪsəʊz ˈdɒlfɪn/ *noun phr.* L19.
[Giovanni Antonio *Risso* (1777–1845), Italian naturalist.]
A pale grey dolphin, *Grampus griseus*, with dark grey fins and a rounded beakless snout, found in temperate seas. Also called *grampus*.

ristorante /ristoˈrante/ *noun.* Pl. **-ti** /-ti/. E20.
[Italian.]
An Italian restaurant.

ristra /ˈriːstrə/ *noun.* L20.
[Spanish = string.]
A string or wreath of dried red chilli peppers, often hung as a decoration in Mexico and the south-western US.

risus sardonicus /ˌrʌɪsəs sɑːˈdɒnɪkəs/ *noun phr.* L17.
[mod. Latin, from Latin *risus* laugh (from *ridere* to laugh) + medieval or mod. Latin *sardonicus*: cf. SARDONIC.]
MEDICINE. An involuntary grinning expression resulting from chronic abnormal contraction of the facial muscles, as in tetanus.

rit /rɪt/ *verb & noun.* Long *obsolete* exc. *Scot.* & *north.* ME.
[Corresp. to Old High German *rizzan*, Middle & mod. High German *ritzen.*]
▸ **A** *verb trans.* Infl. **-tt-**. Rip or cut with a sharp instrument; tear; scratch; make an incision in. ME.
▸ **B** *noun.* **1** A scratch; a slight incision. E18.
2 A rut made by a cartwheel. E19.

rit. *abbreviation.*
MUSIC. Ritardando.

Ritalin /ˈrɪtəlɪn/ *noun.* M20.
[Origin unkn.]
PHARMACOLOGY. (Proprietary name for) methylphenidate.

ritard /rɪˈtɑːd, ˈriːtɑːd/ *adverb, adjective, & noun.* L19.
[Abbreviation of next.]
MUSIC. = RALLENTANDO.

ritardando /rɪtɑːˈdandəʊ/ *adverb, adjective, & noun.* Pl. of noun **-dos**, **-di** /-di/. E19.
[Italian, pres. pple of *ritardare* slow down.]
MUSIC. = RALLENTANDO.

rite /rʌɪt/ *noun.* ME.
[Old & mod. French †*rit*, later *rite*, or from Latin *ritus* (religious) usage. See also RIGHT *noun*².]
1 A formal procedure or act in a religious or other solemn observance. ME.
†**2** The custom or practice of a country, people, etc. LME–M16.
†**3** A religion. LME–M16.
4 A custom or practice of a formal kind, a social observance. L16.
5 A body of liturgical etc. observances characteristic of a religious denomination. E18.
Phrases: *CONJUGAL rites. last rites*: see LAST *adjective. Latin rite*: see LATIN *adjective.* **rite of intensification** *ANTHROPOLOGY* a rite marking a special event affecting a social group and tending towards strengthening the bonds uniting its members (usu. in *pl.*). **rite of passage** [translating French RITE DE PASSAGE] a rite marking a new defined stage in a person's life, as the beginning of adulthood.
■ **riteless** *adjective* E17.

rite de passage /rit də pasaːʒ, riːt də paˈsɑːʒ/ *noun phr.* Pl. ***rites de passage*** (pronounced same). E20.
[French.]
ANTHROPOLOGY. = RITE *of passage*.

ritenuto /rɪtəˈnuːtəʊ/ *adverb, adjective, & noun.* E19.
[Italian, pa. pple of *ritenere* from Latin *retinere*: see RETAIN *verb.*]
MUSIC. ▸**A** *adverb & adjective.* A direction: with immediate reduction of speed, restrained, held back in tempo. E19.

▶**B** *noun*. Pl. **-ti** /-ti/, **-tos**. A ritenuto phrase or passage. **E19**.

rites de passage *noun phr.* pl. of RITE DE PASSAGE.

rithe /rʌɪθ/ *noun*. Long *obsolete* exc. *dial.*
[Old English *rīþ(e)* = Frisian *ryd*, *ride*, Middle Low German *rīd(e)* etc.]
A small stream; a brooklet.

ritodrine /ˈrɪtədriːn/ *noun*. **L20**.
[from *ri-*, of unkn. origin + *-to-*, perh. from TOCO- + EPHE)DRINE.]
PHARMACOLOGY. A bicyclic derivative of ephedrine used during labour as a uterine relaxant and to treat foetal asphyxia.

ritornel /rɪtɔːˈnɛl/ *noun*. **L17**.
[Anglicized from next.]
MUSIC. = next.

ritornello /rɪtɔːˈnɛləʊ/ *noun*. Pl. **-llos**, **-lli** /-li/. **L17**.
[Italian, dim. of *ritorno* RETURN *noun*.]
MUSIC. An instrumental refrain, interlude, or prelude, esp. in a vocal work.

ritournelle /rɪtʊəˈnɛl/ *noun*. **M19**.
[French, formed as prec.]
MUSIC. = prec.

ritratto /rɪˈtratəʊ/ *noun*. Long *rare*. Pl. **-ttos**, **-tti** /-ti/. **E18**.
[Italian Cf. RETRAIT *noun*².]
A picture, a portrait.

Ritschlian /ˈrɪtʃlɪən/ *adjective & noun*. **L19**.
[from *Ritschl* (see below) + -IAN.]
▶**A** *adjective*. Of or pertaining to the German Protestant theologian Albrecht Ritschl (1822–89) or his doctrines. **L19**.
▶**B** *noun*. An adherent of Ritschl or his doctrines. **L19**.
■ **Ritschlianism** *noun* **L19**.

ritter /ˈrɪtə/ *noun*. *obsolete* exc. *Hist.* **E19**.
[German, var. of REITER *noun*¹.]
A German or Austrian knight or mounted warrior; a member of the German or Austrian minor nobility.

Ritterkreuz /ˈrɪtərkrɔyts, ˈrɪtəkrɔɪts/ *noun*. Pl. **-e** /-ə/. **M20**.
[German, formed as prec. + *Kreuz* CROSS *noun*.]
The Knight's Cross of the Iron Cross, a German decoration instituted by Adolf Hitler and awarded for distinguished service in war.

Ritter's disease /ˈrɪtəz dɪˌziːz/ *noun phr.* **L19**.
[Gottfried *Ritter* von Rittershain (1820–83), Bohemian physician.]
MEDICINE. A severe form of staphylococcal infection in newborn babies, involving generalized inflammation of the skin.

rittmaster /ˈrɪtmɑːstə/ *noun*. *obsolete* exc. *Hist.* **M17**.
[Anglicized from German RITTMEISTER.]
A captain in a Scottish cavalry regiment.

Rittmeister /ˈrɪtmʌɪstə/ *noun*. **M20**.
[German, from *Ritt* riding + *Meister* MASTER *noun*¹.]
A captain in a German or Austrian cavalry or (now) tank regiment.

ritual /ˈrɪtjʊəl/ *adjective & noun*. **L16**.
[Latin *ritualis*, from *ritus* RITE: see -AL¹.]
▶**A** *adjective*. **1** Of, pertaining to, or used in a solemn rite or solemn rites. **L16**.
2 Of the nature of or constituting a solemn rite or solemn rites; carried out as a solemn rite. **M17**.
3 Of, pertaining to, or constituting a social or psychological ritual; conventional, habitual. **M20**.

> 🕮 **1** WORDSWORTH The ritual year Of England's Church. T. PARSONS An . . elaborate system of ritual rules governing the preparation and consumption of food. DAY LEWIS Her father, who with ritual taper was lighting the altar. *Japan Times* Standing exhibition of . . ritual goods of world ethnic groups. **2** J. MCCLURE Back marked by long cuts . . . Those wounds suggest a ritual killing. A. BRINK The ritual washing of hands in the house of the bereaved. **3** B. PYM He offered her the bag of jelly babies, but this was only a ritual gesture. V. GORNICK 'Wouldn't it be wonderful if . . ' was her ritual beginning.

Special collocations: **ritual abuse** (esp. sexual) abuse of children by adults supposedly involved in satanic rituals. **ritual bath** a purificatory bath; *spec.* = MIKVA. **ritual choir** the part of a church in which choir-offices are performed.
▶**B** *noun*. **1 a** A prescribed order of performing religious or other devotional service. **M17**. ▸**b** A book containing details of the order, forms, or ceremonies to be observed in the celebration of religious or other solemn service. **M17**.
2 A ritual observance or act. Orig. only in *pl.* **M17**. ▸**b** PSYCHOLOGY. A series of actions compulsively performed under certain circumstances, the non-performance of which results in tension and anxiety. **M20**.
3 The performance of ritual acts. **M19**.

> 🕮 **2** M. PYKE The Zuni Indians observe most elaborate rituals in which . . formal dances are danced. N. GORDIMER The offerings that are part of the ritual of arrival. R. SCRUTON The old rituals and dogmas of the Church. **3** A. MARS-JONES Changed status must be marked by ritual.

■ **ritu'ality** *noun* (*rare*) †(**a**) a rite, a ceremony; (**b**) ritualism, attention to ritual: **M17**. **ritually** *adverb* **E17**.

ritualise *verb* var. of RITUALIZE.

ritualism /ˈrɪtjʊəlɪz(ə)m/ *noun*. **M19**.
[from RITUAL + -ISM.]
Regular observance or practice of ritual, esp. when excessive or without regard to its function; *spec.* (chiefly *Hist.*) the beliefs and practices of the High Church party in the Church of England.

ritualist /ˈrɪtjʊəlɪst/ *noun & adjective*. **M17**.
[from RITUAL + -IST.]
▶**A** *noun*. **1** A person versed in ritual; a student of liturgical rites and ceremonies. **M17**.
2 A person who advocates or practises the observance of symbolic religious rites, esp. to an excessive extent, *spec.* (chiefly *Hist.*) a member of the High Church party in the Church of England; a person whose behaviour is characterized by ritualism. **L17**. ▸**b** ANTHROPOLOGY. A person who performs a tribal ritual. **M20**.
2 Old Ritualist ECCLESIASTICAL HISTORY = ***Old Believer*** s.v. OLD *adjective*, *noun*², *& adverb*.
▶**B** *attrib.* or as *adjective*. Of or pertaining to ritualists or ritualism. **L19**.
■ **ritua'listic** *adjective* of, pertaining to, or characteristic of ritualists or ritualism; devoted to or fond of ritual; characteristic of ritual actions or behaviour: **M19**. **ritualistically** *adverb* **L19**.

ritualize /ˈrɪtjʊəlʌɪz/ *verb*. Also **-ise**. **M19**.
[from RITUAL + -IZE.]
▶**I** *verb intrans.* **1** Practise ritualism in religious observance. **M19**.
▶**II** *verb trans.* **2** Convert to ritualism in religious observance. **M19**.
3 Make into a ritual. **M20**.
4 ZOOLOGY. Cause (an action or behaviour pattern) to undergo ritualization. Freq. as ***ritualized*** *ppl adjective*. **M20**.
■ **rituali'zation** *noun* the action or process of ritualizing something; *spec.* (**a**) ZOOLOGY the evolutionary process by which an action or behaviour pattern in an animal loses its ostensible function but is retained for its role in social interaction; (**b**) PSYCHOLOGY the formalization of certain actions expressing a particular emotion or state of mind: **M20**.

ritz /rɪts/ *noun & verb*. *N. Amer. colloq.* Also **R-**. **E20**.
[from *Ritz* the name of some luxury hotels, from César *Ritz* (1850–1918), Swiss-born hotelier.]
▶**A** *noun*. ***put on the ritz***, assume an air of superiority, behave haughtily; dress up smartly, live luxuriously. **E20**.
▶**B** *verb trans.* Behave haughtily towards; snub. **E20**.

ritzy /ˈrɪtsi/ *adjective*. *colloq.* **E20**.
[formed as prec. + -Y¹.]
Having class, poise, or polish; luxurious, smart, stylish, glamorous. Also, pretentious, ostentatious, flashy, haughty.
■ **ritzily** *adverb* **E20**. **ritziness** *noun* **M20**.

riu *noun* var. of RYU.

Riu-kiu *noun & adjective* var. of RYUKYU.

riva /ˈriːvə/ *noun*. **L19**.
[Italian from Latin *ripa* bank.]
In Italy: a river-bank, a seashore, a quay.

rivage /ˈrʌɪvɪdʒ/ *noun*. Long *obsolete* exc. *poet.* **ME**.
[Old & mod. French, from *rive* from Latin *ripa* bank.]
A coast, a shore, a bank.

rival /ˈrʌɪv(ə)l/ *noun & adjective*. **L16**.
[Latin *rivalis* orig. 'a person using the same stream as another', from *rivus* stream: see -AL¹. Earlier in the verb.]
▶**A** *noun*. **1** A person competing for the same objective as another; a person striving to equal or outdo another. **L16**.
†**2** A person having the same objective as another, an associate. Only in **E17**.
3 A person who or thing which is arguably equal in quality or distinction to another. **M17**.

> 🕮 **1** G. BROWN Oscar was my rival for being top of the form. J. VIORST We ceased being rivals. We no longer ran the same races. **3** D. BREWSTER A man who has had no rival in . . times . . past.

▶**B** *attrib.* or as *adjective*. Holding the position of a rival or rivals, competing. **L16**.

> 🕮 W. S. CHURCHILL Experts dispute the population . . and rival estimates vary. G. VIDAL Huan was murdered by a rival faction.

■ **rivaless** *noun* (long *rare*) a female rival **L17**. **rivalize** *verb intrans.* (now *rare*) enter into rivalry, compete, *with* **E19**. **rivalless** /-l-l-/ *adjective* **E19**. **rivalship** *noun* the state or character of a rival; competition, rivalry: **E17**.

rival /ˈrʌɪv(ə)l/ *verb*. Infl. **-ll-**, ***-l-**. **L15**.
[from the noun.]
1 *verb intrans.* Act as a rival, be a competitor. **L15**.
2 *verb trans.* Be the rival of, compete with; be arguably equal in quality or distinction to. **E17**.

> 🕮 **1** SHAKES. *Lear* You, who with this king Hath rivall'd for our daughter. **2** C. EASTON Her musical talent rivalled her sister's. R. BERTHOUD London rivalled Paris as a focal point of all-round creativity.

¶ In isolated use before **17**.

rivality /rʌɪˈvalɪti/ *noun*. Now *rare*. **L16**.
[Latin *rivalitas*, formed as RIVAL *noun*: see -ITY.]
Rivalry.

rivalrous /ˈrʌɪv(ə)lrəs/ *adjective*. **E19**.
[from next + -OUS.]
1 Of the nature of rivalry. **E19**.
2 Given to rivalry; acting as a rival. **E20**.

rivalry /ˈrʌɪv(ə)lri/ *noun*. **L16**.
[from RIVAL *noun* + -RY.]
1 The action of rivalling someone; the state of rivalling someone or something; competition. **L16**.
2 PSYCHOLOGY. Alternation of perception between (parts of) different images presented separately but simultaneously to each eye. **L19**.

rive /rʌɪv/ *noun*. Chiefly *Scot.* **E16**.
[from the verb.]
A pull, a tug, a tear, a rent, a crack.

rive /rʌɪv/ *verb*. Now chiefly *arch.*, *poet.*, & *Scot.* Pa. t. **rived**; pa. pple **rived**, **riven** /ˈrɪv(ə)n/. **ME**.
[Old Norse *rífa* = Old Frisian *riva*, of unkn. origin.]
▶**I** *verb trans.* **1** Tear apart or in pieces by pulling or tugging; cause to split open, make a rent in. **ME**. ▸†**b** Tear up (a letter, document, etc.). Chiefly *Scot.* **LME–M17**.
2 Tear or pull *off* or *away*; tear or wrench away *from*; tear, drag, or pull *down*, *up*, or *out*; pull *to* the ground. **ME**.
3 Sever, cleave, divide, or open up by means of a knife or weapon; split or cleave (wood, stone, etc.) by appropriate means (also foll. by *up*, *off*). **ME**. ▸†**b** Drive (a weapon) *through* the heart etc.; thrust *into*. **LME–L15**.
4 Rend (the heart, soul, etc.) with painful thoughts or feelings. **ME**.
5 Plough (untilled ground); break *up* with the plough. Also foll. by *out*. *Scot. & north.* **M16**.
▶**II** *verb intrans.* **6** Be split, cleave, crack, open up. **ME**. ▸**b** Of the heart: break or burst with sorrow. **LME**.
†**7** Pierce, cut, or shear *through* or *into* the body. **ME–L15**.
8 Commit robbery; pillage, plunder, take away *from*. Chiefly *Scot.* **L15**.
9 Tear voraciously, tug, (*at*). **E16**.

†**rivel** *noun*. **ME–M17**.
[Origin unkn. App. repr. earlier in RIVELLED.]
A wrinkle, a fold, a pucker.

rivel /ˈrɪv(ə)l/ *verb*¹. Now *arch.* & *dial.* Infl. **-ll-**, ***-l-**. **ME**.
[from the noun.]
1 *verb intrans.* Become wrinkled or shrivelled; form wrinkles or small folds. **ME**.
2 *verb trans.* Cause (the skin) to wrinkle or pucker; shrivel *up*. **M16**.

rivel /ˈrɪv(ə)l/ *verb*². Long *obsolete* exc. *Canad. dial.* Infl. **-l(l)-**. **ME**.
[French †*rivler*.]
†**1** *verb intrans.* **a** Become entangled. Only in **ME**. ▸**b** Ravel or fray *out*. Only in **M16**.
2 *verb trans.* Open *out* by unravelling, unweave. **M17**.

riveling /ˈrɪv(ə)lɪŋ/ *noun*. Chiefly *Scot.* *obsolete* exc. *Hist.* **OE**.
[Origin uncertain: perh. rel. to RIVEL *noun* etc.]
A shoe of raw hide.

rivelled /ˈrɪv(ə)ld/ *adjective*. Now *arch.* & *dial.* **LOE**.
[App. from RIVEL *noun* + -ED². Cf. WRITHLED.]
1 Wrinkled; full of wrinkles or small folds; corrugated, furrowed. **LOE**.
†**2** Pleated or gathered in small folds. **L15–L16**.
3 Shrunken, shrivelled, esp. by heat. Also foll. by *up*. **E17**.

riven *verb pa. pple*: see RIVE *verb*.

river /ˈrɪvə/ *noun*¹. **ME**.
[Anglo-Norman *river(e)*, Old & mod. French *rivière* †river-bank, river from Proto-Romance use as noun (sc. *terra* land) of fem. of Latin *riparius*, from *ripa* bank: see -ER².]
1 A copious stream of water flowing naturally in a channel towards the sea, a lake, or another stream. **ME**. ▸**b** *transf.* & *fig.* A copious stream or flow *of*. **LME**.
†**2** A stream, or the banks of a stream, as a place frequented for hawking; the sport of hawking. **ME–E17**.
3 (Usu. **R-**.) *The* constellation Eridanus. **M16**.
4 TYPOGRAPHY. More fully ***river of white***. A white line or streak down a printed page where spaces between words on consecutive lines are close together. **L19**.
5 The finest grade of diamond. **M20**.

> 🕮 **1** *fig.*: R. BURNS And hast thou crost that unknown river, Life's dreary bound?

Phrases etc.: ***down-river***: see DOWN *preposition*. **down the river** *colloq.* finished, past, over and done with. ***head of the river***: see HEAD *noun*. ***lost river***: see LOST *adjective*. ***Old Man River***: see OLD

MAN *adjectival phr. red river hog*: see RED *adjective. river of white*: see sense 4 above. *sabbatical river*: see SABBATICAL *adjective*. **sell down the river** *colloq.* [orig. of selling a troublesome slave to the owner of a sugar cane plantation on the lower Mississippi, where conditions were harsher than in the northern slave States] let down, betray. *tidal river*: see TIDAL *adjective*. UP-RIVER. **up the river** *colloq.* [orig. to Sing Sing prison, situated up the Hudson River from the city of New York] to or in prison.

Comb.: **river-bank** the raised or sloping edge or border of a river, the bank or ground adjacent to a river; **river-bed** the bed or channel in which a river flows; **river birch** the red birch, *Betula nigra*, of N. America; **river blindness** (blindness due to) onchocerciasis; **riverboat** a boat designed for use on rivers; **river-bottoms** *US* low-lying alluvial land along the banks of a river; **river bullhead** the miller's thumb, *Cottus gobio*; **river capture** PHYSICAL GEOGRAPHY the natural diversion of the headwaters of one stream into the channel of another, freq. resulting from rapid headward erosion of the latter stream; **river crab** (*a*) a crab which inhabits freshwater; (*b*) *rare* a crayfish; **river-diggings** gold or diamond diggings in the neighbourhood of a river or stream, or in a dried-up river-bed; *river dolphin*: see DOLPHIN 1; **river-drift** alluvium; **river-drive** *N. Amer.* a drive of logs down a river; **river-driver** *N. Amer.* a lumberman who keeps logs moving on a drive down a river; **river-driving** *N. Amer.* the action of driving logs down a river; **river duck** a duck which frequents rivers; *spec.* = *dabbling duck* s.v. DABBLE *verb*; **river engineering** the branch of civil engineering that deals with the improvement and control of rivers; **river fish** a fish which inhabits rivers and streams; **river-god** MYTHOLOGY a tutelary god supposed to live in and to preside over a river; **river gravel** gravel that was formed on the bed of a river; **river gum** *Austral.* the most widespread of the red gums, *Eucalyptus camaldulensis*, which occurs near streams; **river herring** (chiefly *US*) any of several freshwater fishes resembling herring, esp. the alewife and the moon-eye; **river hog** (*a*) a capybara; (*b*) a bush pig; **river-horse** (*a*) a hippopotamus; (*b*) = KELPIE *noun*[1]; **river lamprey** a freshwater lamprey, esp. the lampern, *Lampetra fluviatilis*; **river limpet** a freshwater limpet, *Ancylus fluviatilis*, having an elliptical shell with a curved conical tip; **riverman** a waterman; **river mussel** a freshwater mussel; **river oak** *Austral.* any of several trees of the genus *Casuarina* (family Casuarinaceae) found by streams, esp. *C. cunninghamiana* of New South Wales; **river pearl** a pearl from a freshwater mussel, esp. *Margaritifera margaritifera*; *river pirate*: see PIRATE *noun* 5; **river runner** *N. Amer.* (*a*) a person who takes a vessel up and down a river; (*b*) a person who engages in river running; **river running** travelling down a river in a small craft (as a rubber dinghy), as a leisure activity; **river salmon** a freshwater salmon; **river-shrew** = OTTER *shrew*; **river snail** any of a group of prosobranch (gill-breathing) snails found in lakes and rivers, esp. a large one of the genus *Viviparus*; **river stone** a diamond found in river-diggings; **river trout** a freshwater trout; **river-water** water in, forming, or obtained from a river or stream; **river-weed** a plant growing naturally in rivers; *spec.* an underwater plant of the American genus *Podostemum* (family Podostemaceae), esp. *P. ceratophyllum* of clear fast streams in N. America.

■ **rivered** *adjective* watered by rivers; having a river or rivers: M17. **riverless** *adjective* M19. **riverlet** *noun* a small river, a brook, a stream, a rivulet L17. **river-like** *adverb & adjective* (*a*) *adverb* in the manner of or like a river; (*b*) *adjective* characteristic of or resembling a river: M17. **riverwise** *adverb* in the manner of a river; in relation to a river: E20. **rivery** *adjective* (*a*) resembling a river, river-like; (*b*) having many streams or rivers: E17.

river /ˈrʌɪvə/ *noun*[2]. Now chiefly *arch. & dial.* L15.
[from RIVE *verb* + -ER[1].]
1 A person who rives something. L15.
†**2** A robber, a pillager, a plunderer. Chiefly *Scot.* L15–E17.

river /ˈrɪvə/ *verb. rare.* LME.
[from RIVER *noun*[1].]
1 *verb intrans.* †**a** Pursue game beside a river. Only in LME. ▸**b** Sail or row on a river. L19.
†**2** *verb trans.* Wash (wool or sheep) in a river. M16–E18.
3 *verb intrans.* Follow a river-like course. E20.

riverain /ˈrɪvəreɪn/ *adjective & noun.* M19.
[French, from *rivière* RIVER *noun*[1].]
▸ **A** *adjective.* = RIVERINE *adjective.* M19.
▸ **B** *noun.* A person who lives beside or near a river. M19.

riveret /ˈrɪvərɪt/ *noun.* Long *rare.* M16.
[French †*riveret* (now *rivièrette*) dim. of *rivière* RIVER *noun*[1]. See also RIVULET.]
A small river or stream; a rivulet, a rill, a brook.

riverine /ˈrɪvərʌɪn/ *adjective.* M19.
[from RIVER *noun*[1] + -INE[1].]
1 Situated or living on the banks of a river; riparian. M19.
2 Of or pertaining to a river; resembling a river. L19.

riverscape /ˈrɪvəskeɪp/ *noun.* E20.
[from RIVER *noun*[1] + SCAPE *noun*[3], after *landscape*.]
1 A picturesque view or prospect of a river. E20.
2 A painting of a river or riverside scene. M20.

riverside /ˈrɪvəsʌɪd/ *noun & adjective.* ME.
[from RIVER *noun*[1] + SIDE *noun*.]
▸ **A** *noun.* The side or bank of a river; the ground adjacent to or stretching along a river. ME.
▸ **B** *attrib.* or as *adjective.* Situated or taking place on a riverside. M18.

riverward /ˈrɪvəwəd/ *adverb & adjective.* M19.
[from RIVER *noun*[1] + -WARD.]
▸ **A** *adverb.* Towards a river; in the direction of a river. M19.
▸ **B** *adjective.* Facing or directed toward a river. L19.

■ Also **riverwards** *adverb* L19.

rivet /ˈrɪvɪt/ *noun*[1]. ME.
[Old French, from *river* clinch, of unkn. origin: see -ET[1].]
1 A burr or clinch on a nail or bolt. Long *rare*. ME.
2 A short nail or bolt for fastening together metal plates etc., the headless end of which is beaten out or pressed down after insertion. LME.
3 In *pl.* Money, coins. *slang.* M19.
2 *Almain rivets*: see ALMAIN *adjective. explosive rivet*: see EXPLOSIVE *adjective* 2. *pop-rivet*: see POP *verb*.
Comb.: **rivet gun** a hand-held tool for inserting rivets.

rivet /ˈrɪvɪt/ *noun*[2]. L16.
[Origin unkn.]
sing. & in *pl.* A kind of wheat, *Triticum turgidum*, now little grown, with heavily bearded ears and short plump grains having a dorsal hump (also *rivet-wheat*). Also called *cone wheat*.

rivet /ˈrɪvɪt/ *verb trans.* Infl. **-t-**, **-tt-**. LME.
[from RIVET *noun*[1]. Repr. earlier in RIVETER.]
1 Secure (a nail or bolt) by hammering or beating out the projecting end of the shank into a head or knob; clinch. LME.
2 Secure or fasten with or as with rivets; fix, fasten, or secure firmly; make immovable. LME.
3 Direct intently (the eye or the mind) *on* or *upon*; command or engross (the attention). E17. ▸**b** Engross the attention of (a person). Usu. in *pass.* M18.

> 📖 **2** SIR W. SCOTT Warriors, who, arming for the fight, Rivet and clasp their harness light. E. B. BROWNING Seize him, . . Rivet him to the rock. F. M. FORD It riveted on him the idea that he might find some other woman. I. MURDOCH It was my duty to stay: that harsh word riveted me to the spot. *Time* His legs riveted in a professional gunman's solid stance. **3** V. WOOLF Her eyes were riveted on the camellia. G. STEINER There are many scenes which rivet the imagination. **b** M. GORDON Sarah was riveted; she sat at Mrs. Davenport's knee, asking questions.

■ **riveting** *adjective* that rivets something or someone; *esp.* engrossing, enthralling: L17. **rivetingly** *adverb* L20.

riveter /ˈrɪvɪtə/ *noun.* Also **-tt-**. ME.
[from prec. + -ER[1].]
1 A person who inserts rivets. In early use also, a maker of rivets. ME.
2 A machine for inserting rivets. L19.
¶ Not recorded between LME and E19.

riviera /rɪvɪˈɛːrə/ *noun.* Also **R-**. M18.
[Italian = seashore, coast.]
A coastal region with a warm climate and popularity as a holiday resort, orig. *spec.* one around Genoa in Italy, later also the Mediterranean coast from Marseilles in France to La Spezia in Italy.

rivière /rivjɛːr (*pl. same*), rɪvɪˈɛː/ *noun.* M19.
[French: see RIVER *noun*[1].]
1 NEEDLEWORK. A row of openwork. M19.
2 A necklace of diamonds or other gems, *esp.* one consisting of more than one string. L19.

†**rivo** *interjection.* L16–E17.
[App. of Spanish origin.]
An exclamation used at revels or drinking-bouts.

rivulet /ˈrɪvjʊlɪt/ *noun.* L16.
[Alt. of RIVERET, perh. after Italian *rivoletto* dim. of *rivolo* dim. of *rivo* from Latin *rivus* stream: see -LET.]
1 A small stream or river; a streamlet. L16.
2 Any of several brownish geometrid moths with wavy markings, of the genus *Perizoma*. M19.

> 📖 **1** L. D. STAMP Rain . . collects to form tiny temporary rivulets. WILBUR SMITH Sweat . . streamed in rivulets down jet-black cheeks.

rivulose /ˈrɪvjʊləʊs/ *adjective.* L19.
[from Latin *rivulus* small stream + -OSE[1].]
BOTANY. Marked with irregular sinuous lines.

rix-dollar /ˈrɪksdɒlə/ *noun.* L16.
[Dutch †*rijksdaler*, from genit. of *rijk* empire, State, kingdom + Low German *daler* DOLLAR.]
Hist. **1** A silver coin and monetary unit of various European countries (as the Netherlands, Germany, Austria, Denmark, Sweden), used in their commerce with the East etc. L16.
2 A monetary unit of Cape Province. L18.

riyal *noun* see RIAL *noun*.

riza /ˈriːzə/ *noun.* E20.
[Russian from Old Church Slavonic = garment.]
A metal shield or plaque framing the painted face and other features of a Russian icon, and engraved with the lines of the completed picture.

rizzar /ˈrɪzə/ *verb trans. Scot.* M18.
[French †*ressoré* parched, from *re-* RE- + †*sorer* smoke, dry, etc., from Old French *sor* yellowish: see SORREL *adjective & noun*[2].]
Dry, parch, or cure (esp. haddocks) in the sun. Freq. as *rizzared ppl adjective*.

RK *abbreviation.*
Religious knowledge.

RL *abbreviation.*
Rugby League.

rly. *abbreviation.*
Railway.

RM *abbreviation.*
1 *Hist.* Reichsmark.
2 Resident Magistrate.
3 Royal Mail.
4 Royal Marines.

rm. *abbreviation.*
Room.

RMA *abbreviation.*
Royal Military Academy.

RMP *abbreviation.*
Royal Military Police.

RMS *abbreviation*[1].
Royal Mail Steamer (also Ship).

rms *abbreviation*[2].
Chiefly ELECTRICITY. Root-mean-square.

RMT *abbreviation.*
National Union of Rail, Maritime, and Transport Workers.

RN *abbreviation.*
1 Registered Nurse.
2 Royal Navy.

Rn *symbol.*
CHEMISTRY. Radon.

RNA /ɑːrɛnˈeɪ/ *noun.* M20.
[Abbreviation of RIBONUCLEIC *acid*.]
BIOLOGY. Any of the nucleic acids which yield ribose on hydrolysis, occurring chiefly in the cytoplasm of cells, where they direct the synthesis of proteins, and as the genetic material in some viruses. Freq. with specifying word or letter, as *mRNA*, *tRNA*. Cf. DNA.
MESSENGER *RNA*. RIBOSOMAL *RNA*. *transfer RNA*: see TRANSFER *noun*.
Comb.: **RNA virus** a virus in which the genetic information is stored in the form of RNA.

■ **RNase** /ɑːrɛnˈeɪz/ *noun* an enzyme which breaks RNA up into smaller molecules, a ribonuclease M20.

RNAS *abbreviation.*
Hist. Royal Naval Air Service.

r'n'b *abbreviation.*
Rhythm and blues. Cf. R & B.

RNLI *abbreviation.*
Royal National Lifeboat Institution.

RNR *abbreviation.*
Royal Naval Reserve.

r'n'r *abbreviation.*
Rock and roll. Cf. R & R.

RNVR *abbreviation.*
Royal Naval Volunteer Reserve.

RNZAF *abbreviation.*
Royal New Zealand Air Force.

RNZN *abbreviation.*
Royal New Zealand Navy.

roach /rəʊtʃ/ *noun*[1]. ME.
[Old French *roche*, *roce*, also *ro(c)que*, of unkn. origin.]
A small freshwater fish of the carp family, *Rutilus rutilus*, common in rivers of Europe and western Asia; any of various small fishes resembling this, esp. (*US*) *Hesperoleucus symmetricus* (more fully *California roach*), and (chiefly *Anglo-Irish*) the rudd.
(as) sound as a roach in excellent health.
Comb.: **roach-backed** *adjective* (of a quadruped, esp. a horse) having an upwardly curving back; **roach pole** a type of rod used in fishing for roach.

roach /rəʊtʃ/ *noun*[2]. M17.
[Var. of ROCHE *noun*[1].]
†**1** = ROCHE *noun*[1] 1. Only in M17.
†**2** MINING. Ore to the side of the main vein. M17–M19.
†**3** A seam or bed of coal. L17–E18.
4 A rough variety of Portland stone. E19.

roach /rəʊtʃ/ *noun*[3], *adjective, & verb.* L18.
[Perh. a use of ROACH *noun*[1]. Cf. *roach-backed* s.v. ROACH *noun*[1].]
▸ **A** *noun.* **1** NAUTICAL. An upward curve in the leech of a sail. L18.
2 An upward curve or upward curvature in the back of a quadruped. L19.
3 A roll of hair brushed upwards and back from the face; a topknot. *US.* L19.
▸ **B** *attrib.* or as *adjective.* Of a horse's mane: clipped or trimmed short so that the hair stands on end. *US.* L18.
▸ **C** *verb trans.* **1** Clip or trim (a horse's mane) short so that the hair stands on end. *US.* E19.
2 Of a person: brush or cut (the hair) in a roach. Also foll. by *up*. *US.* M19.

3 NAUTICAL. Cut (a sail) with a roach. M19.
■ **roached** *adjective* (chiefly *US*) (*a*) having an upward curve; (*b*) that has been roached: L18.

roach /rəʊtʃ/ *noun*⁴. M19.
[Abbreviation of COCKROACH. In sense 4 perh. a different word.]
1 A cockroach. Chiefly *N. Amer.* M19.
2 A police officer. *US slang.* M20.
3 A despicable person; *esp.* an unattractive or immoral woman. *US slang.* M20.
4 The butt of a cigarette, *spec.* a marijuana cigarette. *slang.* M20.
■ **roachy** *adjective* (*a*) infested with cockroaches; *transf.* badly prepared or looked after; (*b*) of or pertaining to cockroaches, suggestive of cockroaches: E20.

road /rəʊd/ *noun & adjective.* See also RAID *noun.*
[Old English *rād* = Old Frisian *rēd*, Middle Dutch *rede*, Old Norse *reið* rel. to RIDE *verb.*]
▶ **A** *noun.* †**1** Riding on horseback; a journey on horseback. OE–E17.
†**2** *spec.* Riding with hostile intent; a hostile incursion; a foray, a raid. Cf. INROAD *noun.* OE–L17.
3 A sheltered piece of water near a shore where ships may ride at anchor in safety; a roadstead. ME.
4 A path or way between different places, usu. one wide enough for vehicles as well as pedestrians and with a specially prepared surface. Also, the part of such a way intended for vehicles, the roadway. L16. ▸**b** An underground passage or gallery in a mine. M19. ▸**c** A railway. (Cf. earlier RAILROAD *noun*) Chiefly *US.* M19. ▸**d** *spec.* With specifying word: a common trade route, now freq. for illicit goods. M20.
5 *transf. & fig.* A route, a course, a means, a mode of access. L16.
6 A way or direction taken or pursued; a course followed in a journey. Freq. with possess. prons. E17.
7 Way, manner. Chiefly *dial.* L19.

> 🕮 **4** M. WEBB Going across fields, not being able to find the road. I. MCEWAN Colin and Mary had to leave the pavement and walk in the road. *Proverb*: The road to hell is paved with good intentions. ***byroad***, ***cart-road***, ***dirt road***, ***high road***, ***main road***, ***open road***, ***slip-road***, etc. **d** J. W. GREGORY The northern silk road . . crossed Persia and Kashgar to the Tarim Basin in Chinese Turkestan. **5** ISAIAH BERLIN Education and legislation as the roads to happiness.

Phrases etc.: **any road** (chiefly *north.*) = ANYWAY 2. **by road** using transport along roads, travelling along roads. **capitalist road** [translating Chinese *zīběn zhǔyì dàolù*] in Communist China, esp. during the cultural revolution, an observable tendency to adopt political ideals and practices leading towards capitalism (cf. ROADER *noun*¹ 2). GENTLEMAN ***of the road***. ***get the show on the road***: see SHOW *noun*¹. ***hit the road***: see HIT *verb*. **in one's road** *colloq.* in one's way, obstructing or inconveniencing one. **in the road** *colloq.* in the way, causing an obstruction or inconvenience. ***knight of the road***: see KNIGHT *noun*. ***last across the road***: see LAST *adjective*. ***middle of the road***: see MIDDLE *adjective & noun*. ***no through road***: see THROUGH *preposition & adverb*. ***off-road***, ***off-the-road***: see OFF *adverb* etc. ***one for the road***: see ONE *adjective, noun, & pronoun*. **on the road** (*a*) travelling, journeying, on or during a journey etc.; (esp. of a musical or theatrical group) on tour; travelling as a firm's representative or as a tramp; (*b*) (of or with reference to the price of a vehicle) including the cost of licence plates, tax, etc., fully ready for use on public roads. ***open road***: see OPEN *adjective*. **out of one's road** *colloq.* where one is not obstructed or inconvenienced. **out of the road** (*a*) *colloq.* out of the way, where no obstruction or inconvenience is caused; (*b*) *arch.* away from the usual course, way, or practice *of*. ***royal road***: see ROYAL *adjective*. **rule of the road** the fixed custom or law regulating the side to be taken by vehicles and riders or by ships etc. in progressing or passing each other. ***secondary road***: see SECONDARY *adjective*. **take the road** set out. **take to the road** (now *arch.* or *Hist.*) become a highwayman. ***tertiary road***: see TERTIARY *adjective*. ***the end of the road***: see END *noun*. ***tram-road***: see TRAM *noun*². ***turnpike road***: see TURNPIKE *noun* 5a.

Comb.: **road allowance** *Canad.* (*a*) a strip of land retained by government authorities for the construction of a road; (*b*) an area at either side of a road which remains a public right of way; **road apples** *N. Amer. slang* horse droppings; **road band** a touring group of musicians; **roadbed** (*a*) the foundation structure of a railway; (*b*) the material laid down to form a road; (*c*) *US* the part of a road on which vehicles travel; **roadblock** *noun & verb* (*a*) *noun* an obstruction or barrier across a road, *esp.* one set up by police etc. to check vehicles and their occupants; *transf. & fig.* any obstruction; (*b*) *verb trans.* obstruct with a roadblock; **road-book** (*a*) a book giving maps of or describing the roads of a district or country; (*b*) a book describing a journey by road; a driver's logbook; **road brand** *N. Amer.* a temporary brand given to cattle in transit; **road-brand** *verb trans.* (*N. Amer.*) give a road brand to; **road breaker** a person or mechanical tool which breaks up a road surface prior to repair etc.; **road bridge** a bridge that carries a road; **road company** *US* a travelling theatrical company; **roadcraft** knowledge of or skill in the use of the road; **roadfarer** a person who travels by road; **road fund** (*a*) *Hist.* a fund, esp. that established by the Roads Act of 1920, to meet the cost of building and maintaining roads and bridges; (*b*) ***road fund licence***, a licence allowing a particular vehicle to be driven on public roads; **road hand** *Austral.* a man hired to assist in driving cattle etc.; **road-head** (*a*) the part of a roadway in a mine between the last support and the face; (*b*) the end of a road; **road-holding** the ability of a vehicle to retain its stability when moving, esp. when cornering at high speeds; **roadhouse** a roadside inn or hotel; any roadside establishment providing refreshment or entertainment; **road hump** a hump or ramp created in a road to make traffic reduce its speed; **road kid** *slang* a boy tramp or hobo; **road-kill** *colloq.* (chiefly *N. Amer.*) the killing of an animal by a vehicle on a road; an animal or animals killed in this way; *fig.* a person or thing that is useless or moribund; **road manager** an organizer of tour details and supervisor of equipment etc. for touring musicians; **road-map** a map showing the roads of a country or area; ***road-metal***: see METAL *noun* 10; **road movie** a film of a genre in which the main character is travelling, either in flight or on a journey of self-discovery; **road oil** *N. Amer.* oil sprinkled on the roads to lay dust; **road rage** violent anger caused by the stress and frustration involved in driving a motor vehicle; **road roller** a heavy mechanical roller used for flattening road surfaces; **roadrunner** either of two sturdy fast-running birds of the cuckoo family, found in arid regions, *Geococcyx californiana* of the southern US and Mexico (***greater road-runner***) and *G. velox* of Central America (***lesser road-runner***); **roadscape** (*a*) a view or prospect of a road, a picture of a road; (*b*) landscaping of a road; **road sense** capacity for intelligent handling of vehicles or coping with traffic on the road; **road show** (*a*) a show given by touring actors or musicians, usu. with the minimum of equipment and preparation; (*b*) a company giving such shows; (*c*) a radio or television programme done on location, esp. each of a series done in different locations; **road sign** a sign giving information or instruction to road-users; **roadsman** (*a*) *rare* a driver of vehicles; (*b*) = ROADMAN 1; **road tax** a periodic tax payable on motor vehicles using public roads; **road test** a test of the performance of a vehicle on the road; **road-test** *verb trans.* test the performance of (a vehicle) on the road; **road-tester** a person who conducts a road test; **road train** a large lorry pulling one or more trailers; **road tunnel** a tunnel through which a road passes; **road warrior** *US colloq.* a person who travels frequently as part of his or her job and does much work while travelling.
▶ **B** *attrib.* or as *adjective*. = AWAY *adjective. N. Amer.* M20.
■ **roadless** *adjective* M19.

road /rəʊd/ *verb*¹. E17.
[from the noun.]
▶ **I** *verb intrans.* †**1** Make raids. *rare.* E17–E18.
2 Travel on a road, start out on a journey. *Scot.* L19.
▶ **II** *verb trans.* †**3** Traverse (a way). Only in E17.
4 Provide or lay out with roads. Chiefly as ***roaded*** *ppl adjective.* L18.
5 Make a road through. *Scot.* M19.

road /rəʊd/ *verb*² *trans. & intrans.* Earlier as ROADER *noun*². M19.
[Origin unkn.]
Of a dog: follow up (game) by the scent of the trail.

roadability /rəʊdəˈbɪlɪti/ *noun.* E20.
[from ROAD *noun* + -ABILITY.]
Suitability for being driven on public roads; roadworthiness; road-holding ability.

roadable /ˈrəʊdəb(ə)l/ *adjective.* E20.
[from ROAD *noun* + -ABLE.]
Suited to being driven on public roads.

roadeo /ˈrəʊdɪəʊ/ *noun. N. Amer.* Pl. **-os**. M20.
[from ROAD *noun* after *rodeo*.]
A gathering of lorry drivers for competitive events in and exhibitions of driving skill.

roader /ˈrəʊdə/ *noun*¹. M16.
[from ROAD *noun* or *verb*¹ + -ER¹.]
1 A ship lying at anchor in a road. Now *rare.* M16.
2 ***capitalist roader*** [translating Chinese *zǒuzīpài*], in Communist China, esp. during the Cultural Revolution, a party official allegedly having capitalist tendencies. M20.

roader /ˈrəʊdə/ *noun*². E19.
[from ROAD *verb*² + -ER¹.]
A dog which pursues game by the scent of the trail.

road-goose *noun* var. of RAT-GOOSE.

road-hog /ˈrəʊdhɒg/ *noun & verb. colloq.* L19.
[from ROAD *noun* + HOG *noun.*]
▶ **A** *noun.* A reckless or inconsiderate road-user, esp. a motorist. L19.
▶ **B** *verb intrans.* Infl. **-gg-**. Be or act like a road-hog. Chiefly as ***road-hogging*** *verbal noun.* E20.
■ **road-hoggery** *noun* behaviour characteristic of a road-hog M20. **road-hoggish** *adjective* M20.

roadie /ˈrəʊdi/ *noun. colloq.* M20.
[from ROAD *noun* + -IE.]
An assistant employed by a touring band of musicians to erect and maintain equipment.

roadman /ˈrəʊdmən/ *noun.* Pl. **-men**. E19.
[from ROAD *noun* + MAN *noun.*]
1 A workman engaged in the making or upkeep of roads. E19.
2 A frequent user of roads; a person who is on the road, as a tramp or a firm's travelling representative. E20.
3 A competitor in road races, a person who specializes in road racing. M20.
■ **roadmanship** *noun* ability to drive on public roads; skill in using roads: M20.

roadside /ˈrəʊdsʌɪd/ *noun & adjective.* E18.
[from ROAD *noun* + SIDE *noun.*]
▶ **A** *noun.* **1** The side next to a road. *rare.* E18.
2 The side or border of a road; the strip of land beside a road. M18.
▶ **B** *attrib.* or as *adjective*. Situated beside a road. E19.

roadstead /ˈrəʊdstɛd/ *noun.* M16.
[from ROAD *noun* + STEAD *noun.*]
= ROAD *noun* 3.

roadster /ˈrəʊdstə/ *noun.* M18.
[from ROAD *noun* + -STER.]
▶ **I 1** A ship etc. riding, or able to ride, at anchor in a road. M18.
▶ **II 2** A horse for riding (or driving) on roads. E19.
3 A cycle for use on roads. L19.
4 A light horse-drawn carriage. *US.* L19.
5 An open two-seater motor car. Orig. *US.* E20.
▶ **III 6** A person accustomed to roads, a traveller. Now *rare* in *gen.* sense. M19.
7 A person with no fixed abode, a tramp. Orig. *US.* L19.

roadway /ˈrəʊdweɪ/ *noun.* L16.
[from ROAD *noun* + WAY *noun.*]
1 A way used as a road. Formerly also, a highway. Now passing into sense 2. L16.
2 The main or central portion of a road, *esp.* that intended for use by vehicles, in contrast to side-paths. E19.
3 The portion of a bridge, railway, etc., used by traffic. M19.

roadwork /ˈrəʊdwəːk/ *noun.* M19.
[from ROAD *noun* + WORK *noun.*]
1 a Work done in building or repairing roads. M19. ▸**b** In *pl.* Repairs to roads or to utilities under roads. M20.
2 The management of vehicles, cattle, etc., on roads. L19.
3 Physical exercise or training undertaken along roads. E20.

roadworthy /ˈrəʊdwəːði/ *adjective.* E19.
[from ROAD *noun* + -WORTHY.]
1 Fit for the road; in a suitable condition for using on public roads. E19.
2 Of a person: fit to travel. *rare.* M19.
■ **roadworthiness** *noun* E20.

roam /rəʊm/ *verb & noun.* ME.
[Origin unkn.]
▶ **A** *verb.* **1** *verb intrans.* Wander, rove, ramble; move about aimlessly or unsystematically, esp. over a wide area. ME.
2 *verb trans.* Wander or move aimlessly or unsystematically over, through, or about (a place). E17.
3 *verb trans.* Cause (the eyes) to rove. *rare.* E20.

> 🕮 **1** D. CECIL How she delighted to roam solitary by stream and pasture. D. H. LAWRENCE Outside she saw the dog . . roaming round. K. LINES He roamed about the hills, looking for the beautiful girls. B. EMECHETA Their eyes roaming this way and that way in childish terror. **2** W. CATHER At night the coyotes roam the wintry waste. D. LESSING Gangs of boys . . were roaming the townships. A. BROOKNER Tote would be . . roaming the kitchen in search of his breakfast. **3** M. ANGELOU I . . roamed my eyes around for his walking stick.

▶ **B** *noun.* An act of roaming; a ramble. M17.
■ **roamer** *noun* LME.

roan /rəʊn/ *noun*¹. ME.
[Sense 2, and perh. also senses 1 and 3, from *Roan* old name of Rouen in Normandy, France.]
†**1** Used *attrib.* to designate a skin tanned perh. by a method originating in Rouen. ME–L16.
†**2** Used *attrib.* to designate things made in or associated with Rouen; *spec.* (designating) a linen cloth. LME–L17.
3 Soft flexible leather made of sheepskin, used in bookbinding as a substitute for morocco. E19.

roan /rəʊn/ *adjective & noun*². M16.
[Old French (mod. *rouan*), of unkn. origin.]
▶ **A** *adjective.* (Of an animal, orig. and esp. a horse, or an animal's coat) having the prevailing colour thickly interspersed with some other, *esp.* bay, sorrel, or chestnut mixed with white or grey; designating the colour effect of such a coat. (Earlier as ROANED.) M16.
roan antelope a rare antelope, *Hippotragus equinus*, of African savannahs.
▶ **B** *noun.* **1** Roan colour. L16.
2 A roan animal. L16. ▸**b** A roan antelope. L19.
Phrases: **blue roan** (an animal having a coat of) black mixed with white or grey. **red roan** (an animal having a coat of) bay mixed with white or grey. **strawberry roan** (an animal having a coat of) chestnut mixed with white or grey.

roaned /rəʊnd/ *adjective.* Long *obsolete* exc. *Scot.* L15.
[from ROAN *adjective* + -ED¹.]
Roan-coloured.

roanoke /ˈrəʊənəʊk/ *noun.* E17.
[from Virginia Algonquian *rawranoke*.]
Wampum, esp. as made and used by Indians of Virginia.

roar /rɔː/ *noun*¹. LME.
[from the verb.]
1 A full deep prolonged cry uttered by a lion or other large wild animal; a loud and deep sound uttered by one or more persons, esp. as an expression of pain or anger. LME. ▸**b** A boisterous outburst of or *of* laughter. L18.

2 *transf.* A loud prolonged sound of cannon, thunder, wind, the sea, or other inanimate agent. ME.

> 1 TENNYSON The panther's roar came muffled, while I sat Low in the valley. J. G. FARRELL The volume of cheering below in the street increased to a deafening roar. **b** P. FITZGERALD His remarks were greeted with roars of laughter. **2** J. BERGER We .. sped up the mountain, deafened by the roar of the engine. P. MATTHIESSEN The flood's roar is oppressive, drowning the voice.

Phrases: **go with a roar** *colloq.* make uninterrupted progress, be a conspicuous success.

†roar *noun*². LME.
[Middle Dutch *roer*, Low German *rōr* = Old Saxon *hrōra*, Old High German *ruora* (German *Ruhr*) motion. Cf. UPROAR *noun*. In sense 2 perh. assoc. with ROAR *noun*¹.]
1 An uproar, a tumult, a disturbance. Only in ***in a roar, on a roar, upon a roar***. LME–E17.
2 A wild outburst of mirth. *rare* (Shakes.). Only in E17.

roar /rɔː/ *verb*.
[Old English *rārian* corresp. to Middle Low German *rāren*, *rēren*, Middle Dutch *reeren*, Old High German *rērēn* (German *röhren*), from West Germanic, of imit. origin.]
▶ **I** *verb intrans.* **1** Of a person: utter a very loud and deep or hoarse cry or cries, esp. under the influence of pain, anger, or great excitement; shout, yell. OE. ▸**†b** Shout in revelry; behave in a noisy riotous manner. L16–M18. ▸**c** Shout *with* or *with* laughter; laugh boisterously, loudly, or without restraint. E19.
2 Of a lion or other large wild animal: utter a full deep prolonged cry. ME. ▸**b** Of a horse: make an unusually loud sound in breathing, esp. during and after exertion, due to strain or other disorder of the larynx. Freq. as ***roaring*** *verbal noun*. E19.
3 Of cannon, thunder, wind, the sea, or another inanimate agent: make a loud prolonged noise or din. ME. ▸**b** Of a place: resound or echo with noise. *rare*. LME.
4 CURLING. Send a stone with great speed. L18.
5 Travel on or in a vehicle which is making a loud noise; motor rapidly; *fig.* move rapidly or without restraint. E20.

> 1 G. VIDAL When he spoke at all, he roared at everyone. *Evening News (Worcester)* One of the events sure to get the crowds roaring. **c** A. TURNBULL Sitting quietly during the funny bits and roaring when the house was still. L. WOOLF People .. roared with laughter at the pictures. **3** DAY LEWIS The cart, its iron-shod wheels roaring on the metalled road, leapt and swayed. B. EMECHETA Taxis, motor bikes .. would roar into action. *New Yorker* After dark the surf roars on the cliffs. **5** B. EMECHETA He jumped into his car and roared out of the palace compound. *Banker* Inflation has roared to over 80%.

▶ **II** *verb trans.* **6** Utter or proclaim loudly; shout (*out*). LME.
7 With compl.: force, call, bring, make, etc., to do or be something, by roaring. E17.
8 Foll. by *up*: abuse, reprimand. *slang* (chiefly *Austral.*). E20.

roarer /ˈrɔːrə/ *noun*. LME.
[from prec. + -ER¹.]
1 A person who or animal or thing which roars. LME.
†2 A noisy riotous bully or reveller. L16–E18.
3 A superlatively good thing. *slang* (chiefly *US*). E19.
1 RING-TAILED ***roarer***.

roaring /ˈrɔːrɪŋ/ *adjective & adverb*. LME.
[from ROAR *verb* + -ING².]
▶ **A** *adjective*. **1** That roars. LME.
2 Behaving or living in a noisy riotous manner. Now chiefly in ***roaring boy***. L16.
3 Characterized by riotous or noisy revelry; full of din or noise. E18.
4 Of trade: very brisk, highly successful. M18.
5 Boisterous, exuberant; full-blooded, wholehearted, unqualified, out-and-out. *colloq.* M19.

> 2 *Sunday Times* Devlin is a roaring boy of 39 .. given to inspired lunacy and sometimes great acting. **5** *Listener* Psychiatric treatment has not proved a roaring success.

Special collocations: ***roaring forties***: see FORTY *noun* 5. **roaring game** *the* game of curling. ***roaring twenties***: see TWENTY *noun* 5.
▶ **B** *adverb*. Excessively and noisily. Chiefly qualifying *drunk* and its synonyms. *colloq.* L17.
■ **roaringly** *adverb* M19.

roast /rəʊst/ *noun*. ME.
[In sense 1 from Old French *rost* masc. (mod. *rôt*) or *roste* fem., roasting, roast meat, from *rostir* (see ROAST *verb*); in sense 2 from ROAST *adjective*; in other senses from the verb.]
1 A piece of meat etc. roasted for food; a joint of roast meat; a part of an animal prepared or intended for roasting. ME.
2 Roast meat; roast beef. LME.
3 An operation or act of roasting something. L16. ▸**b** A social gathering at which a (usu. specified) food is roasted and eaten. Chiefly *US*. L19.
4 An act of criticizing or ridiculing someone unmercifully; a denunciation, a severe reprimand. Now chiefly *N. Amer.* M18.

Phrases: ***rule the roast***: see RULE *verb*.

roast /rəʊst/ *adjective*. ME.
[pa. pple (obs.) of ROAST *verb*.]
Roasted, prepared by roasting.
roast beef, roast potatoes, etc. †**cry roast meat** be foolish enough to announce to others a piece of private luck or good fortune. **roast-beef plant** the stinking iris, *Iris foetidissima*, whose crushed leaves emit an odour thought to resemble that of roast beef.

roast /rəʊst/ *verb*. Pa. pple **-ed**, †**roast**. ME.
[Old French *rostir* (mod. *rôtir*) from West Germanic, from base also of Old Saxon, Old High German *rōst* (Old High German also *rōsta*), *rōstisarn* grill, gridiron.]
▶ **I** *verb trans.* **1** Cook (meat or other food) by prolonged exposure to open heat or (now) in an oven. ME.
2 Torture by exposure to flame or heat. ME.
3 Warm (oneself or one's limbs) at a very hot fire. LME.
4 Expose (ores etc.) to protracted heat in a furnace, to remove impurities or make more easily workable; calcine. L16.
5 Expose (coffee beans) to heat in order to prepare for grinding. E18.
6 Ridicule or criticize unmercifully; denounce, reprimand severely. E18.
▶ **II** *verb intrans.* **7** Undergo the process of being roasted. ME.
8 Roast something. LME.

roaster /ˈrəʊstə/ *noun*. LME.
[from ROAST *verb* + -ER¹.]
▶ **I 1** A person who roasts something. LME. ▸**b** *spec.* An industrial processor of raw coffee beans. L19.
2 a A pan or dish in which meat etc. may be roasted, a roasting-tin. M17. ▸**b** A kind of oven in which meat etc. can be roasted. L18.
3 A furnace used in roasting ore. M19.
4 An apparatus for roasting coffee beans. M19.
5 A very hot day with a scorching sun. *colloq.* L19.
▶ **II 6** A pig, fowl, or other article of food fit for roasting. L15.

roasting /ˈrəʊstɪŋ/ *noun*. ME.
[from ROAST *verb* + -ING¹.]
1 The action of ROAST *verb*. ME.
2 An act of severely criticizing or ridiculing someone; a denunciation, a severe reprimand. E18.
Comb.: ***roasting-jack***: see JACK *noun*¹ 5; ***roasting-spit***: see SPIT *noun*¹ 1.

roasting /ˈrəʊstɪŋ/ *adjective*. L16.
[from ROAST *verb* + -ING².]
1 That is being roasted. L16.
2 That roasts meat etc. E17.
3 Exceedingly hot or warm; blazing, scorching. *colloq.* L18.

rob /rɒb/ *noun*. Now *rare*. LME.
[medieval Latin from Arab. *rub*.]
A syrup made from fruit juice and sugar.

rob /rɒb/ *verb*. Infl. **-bb-**. ME.
[Old French *rob(b)er* from Germanic from base repr. also by REAVE *verb*¹. Cf. ROBE *noun*¹.]
1 *verb trans.* Unlawfully deprive (a person) of or *of* something, esp. by force or the threat of force; *transf.* deprive *of* what is due or normal. ME. ▸**b** SOCCER. Deprive (an opposing player) of the ball. L19.
†2 *verb trans.* With double obj: deprive of. ME–E17.
3 *verb trans.* Plunder, pillage, rifle, (a place); ARCHAEOLOGY remove stones from (a site) (also foll. by *out*). (Foll. by *of* what is taken.) ME.
4 *verb intrans.* Commit robbery. ME.
5 *verb trans.* Steal. Now chiefly *slang & dial.* ME. ▸**b** *fig.* Orig. (*rare*), remove, take *away*, cut off *from*. Now (ARCHAEOLOGY), remove (stones) from a site for use as building material. LME.

> 1 A. TROLLOPE The troubles of life had .. robbed the elder lady of her beauty. I. MURDOCH An enterprising thief could rob her of all her money. V. S. PRITCHETT His bailiff has been robbing him for years. *fig.*: *Sunday Express* My Chanel suit cost 70 quid, and even then .. I was robbed. ***rob Peter to pay Paul***: see PETER *noun*¹. ***rob the spittle***: see SPITTLE *noun*².

■ **robbing** *noun* the action of the verb; an instance of this, a robbery: ME.

roband /ˈrəʊband/ *noun*. ME.
[Prob. from Old Norse: cf. Old Irish *rā* sailyard, BAND *noun*¹. Cf. ROBBIN.]
NAUTICAL. A length of rope passed through eyelet-holes in the head of a sail and used to secure the sail to the yard above.

robber /ˈrɒbə/ *noun*. ME.
[Anglo-Norman, Old French *rob(b)ere*, formed as ROB *verb*: see -ER².]
A person who commits robbery.
the CORSICAN ***robber***.
Comb.: **robber baron** (**a**) *Hist.* a feudal lord who engaged in plundering; (**b**) *transf.* (chiefly *US*) a financial or industrial magnate who behaves with ruthless and irresponsible acquisitiveness; **robber crab** = COCONUT ***crab***; **robber-fly** a fly of the family Asilidae, which takes other insects as prey in mid-flight; **robber trench** ARCHAEOLOGY a trench representing the foundations of a wall, the stones having been removed.
■ **robberhood** *noun* brigandage, robbery M19.

robbery /ˈrɒb(ə)ri/ *noun*. ME.
[Anglo-Norman, Old French *rob(b)erie*, formed as ROB *verb*: see -ERY.]
1 The action or practice of unlawfully seizing property belonging to another, esp. by force or the threat of force; an instance of this. ME.
†2 Plunder, spoil, booty. ME–M16.
3 *fig.* More fully ***daylight robbery, highway robbery***. Unashamed swindling or overcharging; blatant sharp practice. M19.

> 1 *Listener* More street crimes—robberies and rapes—than in any other State.

robbin /ˈrɒbɪn/ *noun*. Now *rare* or *obsolete*. L15.
[Alt.]
NAUTICAL. = ROBAND.

robe /rəʊb, *foreign* rɔb (*pl. same*)/ *noun*¹. ME.
[Old & mod. French from Proto-Romance from Germanic base of ROB *verb*, the orig. sense being 'booty', (hence) clothes, regarded as booty.]
1 A long loose outer garment reaching to the ankles; *spec.* such a garment worn by a baby, esp. at a christening. ME. ▸**b** A dressing-gown. Chiefly *N. Amer.* M19. ▸**c** A woman's gown. L19.
2 *sing.* & in *pl.* A long outer garment of a special form and material worn in virtue of a person's rank, office, profession, etc. Freq. with specifying word. ME. ▸**b** ***the Robe***, the legal profession. Freq. in ***of the robe***, ***of the long robe***. *arch.* M17.
3 In *pl.* Outer clothes in general. Now *rare* or *obsolete*. ME.
4 *fig.* A covering compared to a long enveloping garment. E17.
5 Orig., the dressed skin of a buffalo used as a garment or rug. Now, a blanket or wrap to cover the lower part of the body out of doors. *N. Amer.* E19.

> 2 S. WEINTRAUB She had already sat .. as Empress of India in state robes .. for a photograph. **4** F. W. ROBERTSON Before the world has put on its .. robe of light.

Phrases: ***Mistress of the Robes***: see MISTRESS *noun* 3. ***Nessus robe***. ***robe de chambre*** /rɔb də ʃɑ̃ːbr/, pl. ***robes de chambre*** (pronounced same), a dressing-gown, a negligée. ***robe de nuit*** /rɔb də nɥi/, pl. ***robes de nuit*** (pronounced same), a nightdress. ***robe de style*** /rɔb də stil/, pl. ***robes de style*** (pronounced same), a woman's formal dress with a tight bodice and a long bouffant skirt. ***the short robe***: see SHORT *adjective*.
■ **robeless** *adjective* M17.

robe /rəʊb/ *noun*². Also **'robe**. M20.
[Abbreviation.]
A wardrobe.

robe /rəʊb/ *verb*. ME.
[from ROBE *noun*¹.]
1 *verb trans.* Clothe in a robe or robes. ME.
2 *verb intrans.* Put on robes. E17.

> 1 *fig.*: M. L. KING Citizens whose ideas are robed in the garments of patriotism. **2** J. HIGGINS In the sacristy .. he robed for evening mass.

robed /rəʊbd/ *adjective*. ME.
[from ROBE *noun*¹, *verb*: see -ED², -ED¹.]
Wearing a robe or robes. (Foll. by *in*.)

†Roberdsmen *noun pl.* ME–L18.
[from next (with unkn. significance) + MEN.]
Marauding vagrants or outlaws of 14th-cent. England.

Robert /ˈrɒbət/ *noun*. LME.
[Male forename, of Germanic origin.]
†1 A robin. Only in LME.
2 = HERB ***Robert***. M19.
3 A policeman. Cf. BOBBY *noun*¹. *colloq.* (now *rare*). L19.

Robertian /rəˈbəːtɪən/ *adjective & noun*. E20.
[from *Robert* (see below) + -IAN.]
Hist. ▶**A** *adjective*. Of or pertaining to Robert the Strong (d. 866), count of Anjou and Blois, or his descendants, who became kings of France. E20.
▶ **B** *noun*. A follower or successor of Robert the Strong. M20.

Robertine /ˈrɒbətiːn, -tʌɪn/ *noun & adjective*. M19.
[from *Robert* (see below, prec.) + -INE¹.]
▶ **A** *noun*. A follower of the English-born scholastic theologian Robert of Melun (d. 1167). M19.
▶ **B** *adjective*. = ROBERTIAN *adjective*. M20.

Robertsonian /rɒbətˈsəʊnɪən/ *adjective*. M20.
[from William R. B. *Robertson* (1881–1941), US biologist + -IAN.]
CYTOLOGY. Designating the formation of a metacentric chromosome from two heterologous acrocentric chromosomes by the fusion of their centromeres (or by a translocation with the loss of a small fragment); (of a karyotypic change) brought about by this process.

> *British Medical Journal* Down's syndrome due to Robertsonian translocation between chromosomes 14 and 21.

Robespierrist /ˈrəʊbspɪəːrɪst/ *noun & adjective.* M19.
[from *Robespierre* (see below) + -IST.]
Hist. ▶**A** *noun.* A follower or adherent of Robespierre (1758–94), one of the leaders in the French revolution; a Jacobin. M19.
▶**B** *adjective.* Associated with or supporting Robespierre. M20.

robin /ˈrɒbɪn/ *noun*[1]. M16.
[Old French male forename, alt. of *Robert*.]
1 A small brown passerine bird of Europe and Asia Minor, *Erithacus rubecula*, of the family Turdidae (thrushes and chats), the adult of which has an orange-red throat and breast. (Earlier in ROBIN REDBREAST.) M16. ▸**b** Any of various related or similar birds of this family; *esp.* (*N. Amer.*) the red-breasted thrush, *Turdus migratorius* (also ***American robin***). E18. ▸**c** Any of various similar but unrelated birds; *esp.* (*Austral. & NZ*) any of the Australasian family Eopsaltridae, allied to flycatchers and whistlers. E19.
2 Any of various fishes. E17.
3 Any of several red-flowered or red-tinged plants, *esp.* red campion, *Silene dioica*, and herb Robert, *Geranium robertianum*. *dial.* L17.
1b ***magpie-robin***, ***scrub-robin***, etc. **c** ***New Zealand robin***, ***Peking robin***, ***yellow robin***, etc.
Comb. & phrases: ***American robin***: see sense 1b above; ***ragged robin***: see RAGGED *adjective*; **robin-chat** any of several African chats of the genera *Cossypha* and *Dryocichloides*; ***robin huss***: see HUSS (b); **Robin ruddock** (now *dial.*) = sense 1 above; **Robin-run-in-the-hedge**, **Robin-run-the-hedge** *dial.* any of several creeping hedge plants, esp. ground ivy, *Glechoma hederacea*, and cleavers, *Galium aparine*; **robin's egg (blue)** *US* a greenish-blue colour; **robin-snow** *US* a light fall of snow coming before the departure or after the return of the American robin; **robin's pincushion** a mosslike gall on a rose bush; a bedeguar; **robin's plantain** *US* (*a*) any of several early-flowering fleabanes, esp. *Erigeron pulchellus*; (*b*) = ***rattlesnake weed*** s.v. RATTLESNAKE *noun*; ***round robin***: see ROUND *adjective*; ***searobin***: see SEA *noun*.

†**robin** *noun*[2]. M–L18.
[Var.]
= ROBING 2.

†**Robine** *noun.* Only in 18.
[French.]
An early variety of pear.

robinet /ˈrɒbɪnɛt/ *noun.* LME.
[Old French, dim. of male forename *Robin*: see ROBIN *noun*[1], -ET[1]. Cf. RABINET.]
1 A robin. Now *north.* LME.
†**2** A hoisting-tackle. LME–E16.
†**3** **a** A siege engine that threw stones. LME–E16. ▸**b** A kind of small cannon. M16–L17.
4 A tap or valve in a pipe. M19.

robing /ˈrəʊbɪŋ/ *noun.* See also ROBIN *noun*[2]. LME.
[from ROBE *verb* + -ING[1].]
1 Clothing; a robe, a gown. LME.
2 A trimming of bands or stripes on a gown or robe. LME.
3 The action of putting on robes. M19.
Comb.: **robing room**: for the putting on of official robes.

Robin Goodfellow /rɒbɪn ˈgʊdfɛləʊ/ *noun.* M16.
[Personal name: see below.]
The mischievous sprite or goblin believed to haunt the English countryside in the 16th and 17th cents. (also called ***Hobgoblin***, ***Puck***). Formerly also, a hobgoblin, a sprite.

Robin Hood /rɒbɪn ˈhʊd/ *noun.* L15.
[A popular English outlaw traditionally famous from medieval times.]
†**1** A person who acted the part of Robin Hood in a mummer's play or yearly festival. L15–E17.
2 An outlaw, a bandit, a leader of outlaws, *esp.* a gallant one. Also, a person who acts irregularly for the benefit of the poor, esp. against the rich. L16.
3 A robin. *dial.* M19.
4 More fully ***Robin Hood hat***. A high-crowned hat with the brim turned up at the back and down at the front, and trimmed with a feather. L19.
Phrases: **Robin Hood's barn** an out-of-the-way place.
■ **Robin-Hood** *verb intrans.* live or behave like a Robin Hood M19. **Robin-Hoodish** *adjective* characteristic or reminiscent of a Robin Hood E19. **Robin-Hoodism** *noun* behaviour characteristic of a Robin Hood L19.

robinia /rəˈbɪnɪə/ *noun.* M18.
[mod. Latin (see below), from Jean and Vespasien *Robin*, royal gardeners in Paris in the late 16th and early 17th cents.]
Any of several N. American leguminous trees and shrubs of the genus *Robinia*, with pinnate leaves and flowers in pendulous racemes; *esp.* the false acacia or black locust, *R. pseudoacacia*, often planted in Europe.

Robinocracy /rɒbɪˈnɒkrəsi/ *noun.* E18.
[from male forename *Robin* (put for Robert: see below) + -O- + -CRACY.]
Hist. The regime of Sir Robert Walpole (1676–1745), the predominant figure in British politics between 1721 and 1742; the clique led by Walpole; the period of Walpole's supremacy.

robin redbreast /rɒbɪn ˈrɛdbrɛst/ *noun phr.* LME.
[from male forename *Robin* (see ROBIN *noun*[1]) + REDBREAST, as an alliterative formation.]
1 The (European or American) robin. LME.
2 A Bow Street runner. *slang.* Now *rare* or *obsolete.* M19.

Robinsonade /ˌrɒbɪnsəˈneɪd, -ˈnɑːd/ *noun.* M19.
[German, from *Robinson* (see below) + *-ade* -AD[1].]
A novel with a subject similar to that of *Robinson Crusoe*; a story about shipwreck on a desert island.

Robinson Crusoe /ˌrɒbɪns(ə)n ˈkruːsəʊ/ *verb & noun.* M18.
[The eponymous hero of Daniel Defoe's novel (1719), who survives shipwreck on a desert island.]
▶**A** *verb trans.* Maroon on a desert island. *rare.* M18.
▶**B** *noun.* = CRUSOE *noun.* M19.

roble /ˈrəʊb(ə)l/ *noun.* M19.
[Spanish & Portuguese = Italian *rovere*, French *rouvre*, from Latin ROBUR.]
The Californian white oak, *Quercus lobata*; any of several trees resembling this in the quality of their timber, e.g. the S. American leguminous tree, *Platymiscium pinnatum*, and the W. Indian tree *Catalpa longissima* (family Bignoniaceae). Also, the wood of these trees.

roborant /ˈrəʊb(ə)r(ə)nt, ˈrɒb-/ *noun & adjective.* Now *rare.* M17.
[Latin *roborant-* pres. ppl stem of *roborare* strengthen, from *robor-*, *robur* strength: see -ANT[1].]
MEDICINE. ▶**A** *noun.* A strengthening or restorative medicine. M17.
▶**B** *adjective.* Strengthening; restorative. M19.

†**roborate** *verb trans.* Pa. pple **-ate(d)**. LME.
[Latin *roborat-* pa. ppl stem of *roborare*: see prec., -ATE[3].]
1 Ratify, confirm, (a charter etc.). LME–M17.
2 Strengthen, invigorate; fortify. M16–E18.

robot /ˈrəʊbɒt/ *noun.* E20.
[Czech (in K. Čapek's play *R.U.R.* ('Rossum's Universal Robots'), 1920), from *robota* forced labour = Polish, Ukrainian *robota* (whence German †*Robot* forced labour), Russian *rabota* work.]
1 A machine (sometimes resembling a human being in appearance) designed to function in place of a living agent; a machine which carries out a variety of tasks automatically or with a minimum of external impulse, *esp.* one that is programmable. E20. ▸**b** = AUTOMATON 3. E20.
2 An automatic traffic light. Chiefly *S. Afr.* M20.
Comb.: **robot bomb** = ***flying bomb*** s.v. FLYING *ppl adjective*.
■ **robotism** *noun* mechanical or unthinking behaviour or character E20. **roboti'zation** *noun* the action or process of robotizing something E20. **robotize** *verb trans.* automate; *fig.* make mechanical or lifeless, cause to act as if lacking will or consciousness: E20. **robo'tology** *noun* robotics M20. **roboto'morphic** *adjective* designating or pertaining to a view of man as a robot or an automaton M20. **robotry** *noun* the condition or behaviour of robots E20.

robotic /rəʊˈbɒtɪk/ *adjective & noun.* M20.
[from prec. + -IC, -ICS.]
▶**A** *adjective.* Of or pertaining to robots; characteristic of or resembling a robot. M20.
▶**B** *noun.* **1** In *pl.* (treated as *sing.*). The branch of technology that deals with the design, construction, operation, and application of robots. M20.
2 A robot. *rare.* M20.
■ **robotical** *adjective* M20. **roboticist** *noun* an expert in making and operating robots M20. **roboticized** *adjective* robotized M20.

Rob Roy /rɒb ˈrɔɪ/ *noun.* L19.
[A famous Highland freebooter (1671–1734).]
1 In full ***Rob Roy canoe***. A light canoe for a single person, propelled by alternate strokes of a double-bladed paddle. L19.
2 A cocktail made of Scotch whisky and vermouth. M20.

robur /ˈrəʊbə/ *noun.* *rare.* E17.
[Latin.]
A hard-wooded variety of oak, esp. the English or pedunculate oak, *Quercus robur*. Also ***robur-oak***.

robust /rə(ʊ)ˈbʌst/ *adjective.* M16.
[(Old & mod. French *robuste* from) Latin *robustus* oaken, firm and hard, solid, from *robus* older form of *robur* oak, strength.]
1 Strong and sturdy in physique or construction; ZOOLOGY & ANTHROPOLOGY (of a bodily part) stout, thickset, strong. M16.
2 Coarse, rough, rude. Now *rare.* M16.
3 Involving or requiring bodily or mental strength or hardiness. L17.
4 *fig.* Strong, vigorous, healthy; not readily damaged or weakened. Also, uncompromising, bold, direct; firm, unyielding. L18.
5 Designating a statistical test that yields approximately correct results despite the falsity of certain of the assumptions on which it is based; designating a calculation, process, or result where the result is largely independent of certain aspects of the input. M20.
6 Of wine, food, etc.: full-bodied; strong in taste or smell, hearty. M20.

> **1** V. WOOLF They did not look robust They were weedy for the most part. C. DAY A good robust instrument, . . which he was in no danger of breaking. J. G. BALLARD The children were well-nourished and enjoyed robust good health. **3** W. RAEPER George was a delicate boy despite his robust interests. **4** *Times* Mates is known for his blunt speaking and is expected to give a robust response.

■ **robustic** *adjective* (long *obsolete* exc. *Canad. dial.*) robust, boisterous, violent M17. **robus'ticity** *noun* (chiefly ZOOLOGY & ANTHROPOLOGY) robustness L18. **robustly** *adverb* L17. **robustness** *noun* L16. †**robustous** *adjective* robust L16–E19.

robusta /rə(ʊ)ˈbʌstə/ *noun.* E20.
[Latin, fem. of *robustus* ROBUST, former specific epithet of the plant.]
More fully ***robusta coffee***. A coffee-plant of a widely grown African species, *Coffea canephora*, more disease-resistant than arabica but yielding coffee of a less high quality; beans or coffee obtained from such a plant.

robustious /rə(ʊ)ˈbʌstʃəs/ *adjective.* *arch.* M16.
[from ROBUST + -IOUS. Cf. RUMBUSTIOUS.]
1 Robust; big and strong, massive. M16.
2 Boisterous, noisy, strongly self-assertive; violent. M16.
■ **robustiously** *adverb* E17. **robustiousness** *noun* E17.

ROC *abbreviation.*
Royal Observer Corps.

roc /rɒk/ *noun.* Also (earlier) †**roche**, †**rock**, †**ruc(k)**, †**rukh**. L16.
[Spanish *rocho*, *ruc* from Arab. *ruḵḵ*, from Persian *ruḵ*.]
A mythical bird of Eastern legend, imagined as being of enormous size and strength.

rocaille /rə(ʊ)ˈkʌɪ, *foreign* rɔkaj/ *noun.* M19.
[French.]
An artistic or architectural style of decoration characterized by ornate rock- and shell-work; a rococo style.

rocambole /ˈrɒk(ə)mbəʊl/ *noun.* L17.
[French from German *Rockenbolle*.]
A cultivated variety of sand leek, *Allium scorodoprasum*, with bulbs and bulbils which are used like garlic but have a milder flavour; also, the edible part of this plant. Also called ***Spanish garlic***.

rocambolesque /rɒˌkambɒˈlɛsk/ *adjective.* M20.
[from *Rocambole* (see below) + -ESQUE.]
Of or resembling Rocambole, a character in the novels of Ponson du Terrail (1829–71) who had improbable and fantastic adventures; incredible, fantastic.

roche /rəʊtʃ/ *noun*[1]. See also ROACH *noun*[2]. ME.
[Old & mod. French: see ROCK *noun*[1].]
†**1** A cliff; a rocky height. ME–M17.
†**2** A rock, a boulder. ME–L16.
3 Rock, stone. Long *obsolete* exc. *dial.* ME.
4 More fully (now the only form) ***roche alum***. Rock alum. LME.
†**5** = ROACH *noun*[2] 2. *dial.* M18–M19.
Comb.: ***roche alum***: see sense 4 above; **roche lime** unslaked lime.

Roche /rəʊʃ/ *noun*[2]. L19.
[Edouard Albert *Roche* (1820–83), French mathematician.]
ASTRONOMY. Used *attrib.* & in *possess.* to designate concepts arising from Roche's work.
Roche limit (*a*) the closest distance to which a self-gravitating body can approach a more massive body without being pulled apart by the gravitational field of the latter; (*b*) the smallest continuous equipotential surface (having the form of two lobes meeting at a point) which can exist around both members of a system of two gravitating bodies, e.g. a binary star system. **Roche lobe** either of the two volumes of space bounded by the Roche limit around a binary system. **Roche's limit** = ***Roche limit*** above. **Roche zone** the region of space within the Roche limit of a single massive body.

†**roche** *noun*[3] see ROC.

roche /rəʊtʃ/ *verb.* See also ROCK *verb*[3]. L16.
[from ROCHE *noun*[1].]
†**1** *verb trans.* Make hard like a rock. Only in L16.
2 †**a** *verb intrans.* Form crystals. M–L17. ▸**b** *verb trans.* Purify (alum) by recrystallizing it after previously dissolving it. L17.

rochea /ˈrəʊʃɪə/ *noun.* M20.
[mod. Latin (see below), from François de la *Roche* (1743–1812), Swiss botanist + -A[1].]
A succulent plant of the southern African genus *Rochea* (family Crassulaceae); esp. *R. coccinea*, with showy heads of crimson flowers, grown as a house-plant.

Rochelle /rɒˈʃɛl/ *adjective.* LME.
[See sense 1 below.]
†**1** Designating wine exported from La Rochelle, a seaport of western France. LME–M18.

2 *Rochelle* **salt**, potassium sodium tartrate tetrahydrate, a salt whose crystals are strongly piezo-electric. L16.

roche moutonnée /rɒʃ muːtɒne, rɒʃ muːˈtɒneɪ/ *noun phr.* Pl. **-s -s** (pronounced same). M19.
[French, formed as ROCHE *noun*[1] + *moutonnée*: see MOUTONNÉED.]
PHYSICAL GEOGRAPHY. A bare rock outcrop which has been shaped by glacial erosion, characteristically smoothed and rounded by abrasion but often displaying one side which is rougher and steeper.
■ ***roche moutonnéed*** /rɒʃ muːˈtɒneɪd/ *adjective* containing many *roches moutonnées* E20.

rocher /ˈrɒtʃə/ *noun.* Long *obsolete* exc. *dial.* ME.
[Old French *rochier* (mod. *rocher*), formed as ROCHE *noun*[1].]
A rock; a stony or rocky bank.

roches moutonnées *noun phr.* pl. of ROCHE MOUTONNÉE.

rochet /ˈrɒtʃɪt/ *noun*[1]. ME.
[Old & mod. French var. of *roquet* corresp. to medieval Latin *rochetum* dim. of Germanic base repr. also by Old English *rocc*, Old Saxon, Middle & mod. Dutch *rok*, Old High German *roch* (German *Rock*) coat: see -ET[1].]
1 a An ecclesiastical vestment similar to a surplice, worn chiefly by bishops and abbots. ME. ▸†**b** A bishop. L16–L17.
2 An outer garment of the nature of a smock or cloak. Now *dial.* ME.
■ **rocheted** *adjective* wearing a rochet M19.

rochet /ˈrɒtʃɪt/ *noun*[2]. Now *local.* Also †**rocket**. ME.
[Old French *rouget*, formed as ROUGE *adjective & noun*[1]: see -ET[1].]
The red gurnard, *Aspitrida cuculus*.

†**rochet** *noun*[3] *& verb* see RATCHET.

†**rochetta** *noun.* M17–E18.
[Italian *rocchetta*.]
= POLVERINE.

rock /rɒk/ *noun*[1]. ME.
[Old French *ro(c)que* var. of Old & mod. French *roche* = medieval Latin *rocca*, *rocha* of unkn. origin.]
1 A large rugged mass of stone forming a cliff, crag, or other natural feature. ME. ▸**b** A large stone, a boulder; *US* a stone of any size. E18. ▸**c** A curling-stone. *Canad.* E20.
2 *transf. & fig.* **a** *sing.* & in *pl.* A source of danger or destruction. E16. ▸**b** A thing providing a sure foundation or support; a source of shelter or protection; *spec.* Jesus Christ. Cf. STONE *noun* 7a. E16. ▸**c** A coin, *spec.* a dollar; in *pl.*, money. *US slang.* M19. ▸**d** A precious stone, *spec.* a diamond. *slang* (orig. *US*). E20. ▸**e** An ice-cube; in *pl.*, cubed or crushed ice for use in a drink. *slang* (orig. *US*). M20. ▸**f** In *pl.* The testicles. *coarse slang.* M20. ▸**g** The drug crack. Also, a small piece of crack or of crystallized cocaine. Cf. CRACK *noun* 13. *slang* (orig. *US*). L20.
3 Stone occurring in bulk as part of the earth's fabric, either exposed at the surface or lying underneath soil, water, etc.; similar material on any other planet. L16. ▸**b** GEOLOGY. Any of the mineral constituents of which the earth's crust is composed, including sands, clays, etc. L18. ▸**c** Mineral ore. *US.* M19.
4 In full ***rockfish***. Any of various fishes frequenting rocks or rocky bottoms. L16. ▸**b** = ***rock-salmon*** (c) below. L20.
5 In full ***rock-dove***, ***rock-pigeon***. A wild pigeon, *Columba livia*, which roosts in caves and on cliff ledges and is the ancestor of many breeds of domestic pigeon. E17.
6 A kind of hard confectionery usually made in cylindrical peppermint-flavoured sticks. M18.
7 A mistake made by a baseball player. Freq. in ***pull a rock***, make such a mistake. *US slang.* M20.

📖 **2b** JANET MORGAN Her father . . was 'the rock' on which the family rested.

Phrases: **between a rock and a hard place** *N. Amer. colloq.* without a satisfactory alternative, in difficulty. **blue rock** a blue variety of rock-dove. ***cock-of-the-rock***: see COCK *noun*[1]. **get one's rocks off** *coarse slang* (*a*) achieve sexual satisfaction; (*b*) obtain enjoyment or satisfaction. ***like a shag on a rock***: see SHAG *noun*[2]. **on the rocks** *colloq.* (*a*) short of money; destitute; (*b*) (esp. of a marriage) on the point of dissolution, in danger of breaking up; (*c*) (of a drink) served undiluted with ice. ***pull a rock***: see sense 7 above. ***red rock***, ***red rock-cod***, ***red rock fault***, ***red rockfish***: see RED *adjective*. **rock of ages** *rhyming slang* wages. ***schooner on the rocks***: see SCHOONER *noun*[1]. ***serpentine rock***: see SERPENTINE *noun* 3. **the Rock** Gibraltar. ***trap rock***: see TRAP *noun*[4].
Comb.: **rock alum** alum prepared from Italian alunite; **rock badger** = *rock hyrax* below; **rock bar** PHYSICAL GEOGRAPHY = RIEGEL; **rock-basin** a basin-shaped hollow in a rock, *esp.* one of natural origin; GEOLOGY a large depression in a rocky area, attributed to the action of ice; **rock bass** a red-eyed N. American fish, *Ambloplites rupestris*, of the sunfish family Centrarchidae, found chiefly in rocky streams; **rock beauty** (*a*) a small dark brown and yellow Caribbean reef fish, *Holacanthus tricolor*; (*b*) an ornamental cruciferous rock-plant, *Petrocallis pyrenaica*, of the Alps and Pyrenees, with lilac flowers; **rock-bed** a base of rock, a rocky bottom; **rock-bird** a bird that lives in or frequents rocky places; *esp.* a puffin; **rock bolt** MINING a tensioned rod passing through a bed of rock and anchoring it to the body of rock behind; **rock-bottom** *noun & adjective* (*a*) *noun* bedrock; *fig.* the lowest possible level; (*b*) *adjective* lowest possible, (of a price) unbeatable; fundamental, firmly grounded; **rock-bound** *adjective* (of a coast) rocky and inaccessible by sea; **rock brake** the parsley fern, *Cryptogramma crispa*; **rock-bun** = *rock-cake* below; **rockburst** a sudden violent rupture or collapse of highly stressed rock in a mine; **rock-cake** a small currant cake with a hard uneven surface; **rock-candy** *N. Amer.* = sense 6 above; **rock cavy** a cavy, *Kerodon rupestris*, of dry rocky parts of eastern Brazil; also called *moco*; **rock chuck** the N. American yellow-bellied marmot, *Marmota flaviventris*; **rock coal** *US* anthracite; **rock cod** any of a number of marine fishes, chiefly in the families Scorpaenidae and Serranidae, that frequent rocky habitats, esp. in Australian waters; **rock cook** a wrasse, *Centrolabrus exoletus*, found off European coasts and occasionally in intertidal pools; **rock cress** any of various chiefly white-flowered plants belonging to or formerly included in the genus *Arabis*; **rock-crusher** (*a*) a machine used to break down rocks; (*b*) BRIDGE a superlative hand; **rock crystal** quartz in the form of transparent colourless crystals; a piece of this; **rock cycle** GEOLOGY an idealized cycle of processes undergone by rocks in the earth's crust, involving igneous intrusion, uplift, erosion, transportation, deposition as sedimentary rock, metamorphism, remelting, and further igneous intrusion; ***rock-dove***: see sense 5 above; **rock duck** = *harlequin duck* s.v. HARLEQUIN *noun & adjective*; **rock-dust** *noun & verb* (*N. Amer.*) (*a*) *noun* pulverized stone used to prevent explosions in coalmines; (*b*) *verb trans.* treat (a mine) with this; **rock-face** a vertical expanse of natural rock; **rockfall** a descent of loose rocks; a mass of fallen rock; **rock fan** PHYSICAL GEOGRAPHY an eroded rock surface similar in shape to an alluvial fan, with a convex profile in transverse section; **rock-fill** ENGINEERING large rock fragments used to form the bulk of the material of a dam; ***rockfish***: see sense 4 above; **rock-flour** finely powdered rock, *esp.* that formed as a result of glacial erosion; **rockfoil** [from FOIL *noun*[1]] = SAXIFRAGE; **rock-garden** a mound or bank built of earth and stones and planted with rock-plants; a garden in which rockeries are the chief feature; **rock glacier** a large mass of rock debris, in some cases mingled with ice, which moves gradually downhill; **rock goat** the ibex; **rock grouse** the ptarmigan; **rock hair** any of several pendent lichens of the genus *Alectoria*; **rock-hewn** *adjective* cut out of the rock; **rock-hog** *slang* a labourer engaged in tunnelling through rock; **rockhopper (penguin)** a small penguin, *Eudyptes crestatus*, found in the Falkland Islands, New Zealand, and Tristan de Cunha and having a crest of feathers on the forehead; **rock hound** *N. Amer. colloq.* a geologist; an amateur mineralogist; **rock-hounding** *N. Amer. colloq.* the hobby or activity of an amateur mineralogist; **rock-house** (*a*) a house built of stone or quarried rock; (*b*) a shady place under overhanging rocks providing a habitat for ferns; **rock hyrax** a hyrax of the genus *Procavia*, which inhabits rock outcrops; **rock jock** [JOCK *noun*[5]] *slang* a mountaineer; **rock kangaroo** (*a*) = *rock wallaby* below; (*b*) = WALLAROO; **rock lizard** any of various small climbing lizards living in mountains and arid rocky habitats; **rock lobster** = ***spiny lobster***; **rockman** (*a*) *Scot.* a person who captures birds on rocks or cliffs; (*b*) a quarryman who gets out slate from a slate quarry; **rock maple** *US* (the wood of) the sugar maple, *Acer saccharum*; **rock martin** a martin, *Ptyonoprogne fuligula*, found in many parts of Africa; **rock mechanics** the branch of science and engineering that deals with the mechanical properties and behaviour of rock; **rock melon** = CANTALOUP; **rock oak** *N. Amer.* the chestnut oak *Quercus prinus*; **rock-oil** petroleum, crude oil; **rock ouzel** the ring ouzel; **rock pebbler** *Austral.* the regent parrot, *Polytelis anthopeplus*; **rock phosphate** a sedimentary rock rich in phosphates; phosphorite; ***rock-pigeon***: see sense 5 above; **rock pile** *US slang* a prison; **rock pipit** a dark-coloured pipit, *Anthus petrosus*, of rocky shores of NW Europe; **rock pitch** MOUNTAINEERING an expanse of rock between belays; **rock-plant** a plant that grows on or among rocks; **rock python** any of several large snakes of the family Boidae, esp. the African *Python sebae*; **rock rabbit** (*a*) = *rock hyrax* above; (*b*) = PIKA; **rock-ribbed** *adjective* having ribs of rock; *fig.* resolute, uncompromising, esp. in political allegiance; **rock rose** (*a*) any of various chiefly yellow-flowered dwarf shrubs and herbaceous plants constituting the genera *Helianthemum* and *Tuberaria* (family Cistaceae), esp. *H. nummularium*, a frequent plant of calcareous grassland; occas., a cistus; (*b*) *N. Amer.* the bitter-root, *Lewisia rediviva*; (*c*) an aggregate of tabular crystals of a mineral suggestive of the petals of a rose; **rock-salmon** (*a*) the saithe; (*b*) *US* = ***amberjack*** s.v. AMBER *adjective*; (*c*) a catfish (genus *Anarhichas*) or dogfish (genus *Scyliorhinus*) as sold for food; **rock-salt** common salt occurring naturally in bulk; ***rock samphire***: see SAMPHIRE 1; ***Rock-SCORP***; ***Rock scorpion***: see SCORPION 6. **rock skipper** a small marine fish of the blenny family, Blenniidae, which can survive out of water for a limited time; **rock-slide** a slippage of rock; a mass of rock fragments that has subsided; **rock sparrow** any of several brownish-grey Old World sparrows of the genus *Petronia* which frequent rocky country; **rock-stone** stone obtained by quarrying or cutting from the rock; (now chiefly *W. Indies*) a stone, a pebble; **rock stream** = *rock glacier* above; **rock thrush** any of various thrushes of the genus *Monticola*, esp. *M. saxatilis* of parts of southern Europe and Asia; **rock tripe** any of several edible lichens of the genus *Umbilicaria*; **rock wallaby** a wallaby of the genus *Petrogale*, frequenting rocky ground; **rock warbler** a small songbird, *Origma solitaria* (family Acanthizidae), of rocky habitats in New South Wales, Australia; **rock waste** fragments of rock produced by weathering; **rock-water** spring water coming from a rock; **rock-weed** any of various seaweeds growing on tide-washed rocks; **rock whiting** (*a*) a fish of the Australasian family Odacidae, resembling a wrasse; (*b*) = STRANGER *noun* 9b; **rock wool** = ***mineral wool*** s.v. MINERAL *adjective*; **rock-work** (*a*) a natural mass of rocks or stones; (*b*) stones piled together in a rockery; rough stonework resembling or imitating natural rocks; **rock worm** a marine polychaete worm of the family Eunicidae; **rock wren** (*a*) a wren, *Salpinctes obsoletus*, found in western N. America and in Central America; (*b*) a New Zealand wren, *Xenicus gilviventris* (family Xenicidae).
■ **rockless** *adjective* M17. **rocklet** *noun* a small rock M19. **rocklike** *adjective* resembling a rock; possessing the qualities of rock; hard or firm as rock (*lit. & fig.*): L16.

rock /rɒk/ *noun*[2]. Now *arch.* or *Hist.* ME.
[Middle Low German *rocken*, Middle Dutch *rocke* (Dutch *rok*, *rokken*) or Old Norse *rokkr* = Old High German *rocko* (German *Rocken*), from Germanic. Cf. RATCHET.]
A distaff; the quantity of wool or flax placed on a distaff for spinning.
have tow on one's rock: see TOW *noun*[1] 1.
Comb.: **Rock Day**, **Rock Monday** the Monday after 6 January.

rock /rɒk/ *noun*[3]. E19.
[from ROCK *verb*[1].]
1 The action of ROCK *verb*[1]; swaying to and fro; a spell of this, a to-and-fro movement. E19.
2 a Musical rhythm characterized by a strong beat. M20. ▸**b** Orig. = ***rock and roll*** below. Now usu., modern popular music derived from this and characterized by a strong beat, esp. when regarded as more serious and complex than pop; any of various styles of this. Also ***rock music***. M20.
2b ***acid rock***, ***folk rock***, ***heavy rock***, ***punk rock***, etc.
Phrases: **rock and roll** a type of popular dance-music originating in the 1950s, characterized by a fast strong beat and simple melodies and chord structures, derived from rhythm and blues and country music; a dance to this music. **rock and roller** a devotee of rock and roll. **rock 'n' roll** = ***rock and roll*** above; **rock 'n' roller** = ***rock and roller*** above.
Comb.: **rock festival** a festival, often held outdoors, at which rock music etc. is performed; **rockfest** *N. Amer. colloq.* = ***rock festival*** above; ***rock music***: see sense 2b above; **rock-shaft** a shaft which oscillates about its axis rather than making complete revolutions; *esp.* one working the levers connected with certain valves in an engine; **rock star** a famous and successful singer or performer of rock music.
■ **rockish** *adjective* characteristic or reminiscent of rock music L20. **rockster** *noun* a performer of rock music M20.

†**rock** *noun*[4] see ROC.

rock /rɒk/ *verb*[1].
[Late Old English *roccian*, prob. from Germanic base meaning 'move, remove', repr. also by Middle Low German, Middle Dutch *rukken*, *rocken* (Dutch *rukken*), Old High German *rucchan* (German *rücken* move, push), Old Norse *rykkja* pull, tug.]
1 *verb trans.* Move (esp. a person or cradle) gently to and fro; bring *to* or *into* a state of sleep or rest by this means. LOE.
2 *verb trans.* Cause to sway to and fro or from side to side. ME
3 *verb intrans.* **a** Sway to and fro under some impact or stress; shake, vibrate; *dial.* stagger, reel. LME. ▸**b** Swing oneself to and fro, esp. while sitting in a rocking-chair. L18.
4 *verb intrans.* **a** Of popular music: possess a strong beat, esp. in 2/4 or 4/4 time; exhibit the characteristics of rock music. M20. ▸**b** Dance vigorously to or perform such music. M20.
5 *verb trans.* Distress, perturb; surprise, dumbfound. *colloq.* M20.

📖 **1** J. STEINBECK He rocked himself back and forth in his sorrow. H. E. BATES She pushed the pram, rocking it up and down. **2** *Sunday Mail (New Delhi)* Two bomb blasts rocked a students' meeting. **3a** G. A. BIRMINGHAM The Major started so violently that the punt rocked. P. ANGADI Maggie and Mum rocked with laughter. **b** J. C. OATES She wept, rocking from side to side. **5** *Observer* New sex scandals rock Washington.

Phrases: **rock along** *US colloq.* continue in typical fashion. **rock out** *colloq.* perform rock music loudly and vigorously; enjoy oneself enthusiastically, esp. by dancing to rock music. **rock the boat** disturb the equilibrium of a situation.

rock /rɒk/ *verb*[2] *trans.* E17.
[from ROCK *noun*[1].]
†**1** Surround or wall with or as with rocks. *rare.* E–M17.
2 Throw stones at. *US slang.* M19.
3 Remove the fur from the inside of (a kettle). *dial.* L19.

rock /rɒk/ *verb*[3]. L17.
[Var.]
= ROCHE *verb.*

rockabilly /ˈrɒkəbɪli/ *noun.* Orig. *US.* M20.
[Blend of *rock and roll* and *hillbilly*.]
1 A type of popular music originating in the south-eastern US, combining elements of rock and roll and hillbilly music. M20.
2 A performer or devotee of this music. M20.

rockaboogie /ˈrɒkəˌbuːgi/ *noun.* M20.
[Blend of *rock and roll* and *boogie-woogie*.]
A type of popular music combining elements of rock and roll and boogie-woogie.

rock-a-bye /ˈrɒkəbʌɪ/ *interjection.* E19.
[from ROCK *verb*[1] + *-a-* + *-bye* as in BYE-BYE *interjection*. Cf. LULLABY.]
Used in lulling a child while rocking him or her to sleep.

rockahominy /rɒkəˈhɒmɪni/ *noun. US.* E17.
[Virginia Algonquian *rokohamin*. Cf. HOMINY.]
Maize roasted and finely ground.

Rockaway /ˈrɒkəweɪ/ *noun. US.* M19.
[A town in New Jersey, USA.]
A four-wheeled horse-drawn carriage, open at the sides, with two or three seats and a standing top that projects over the driver's seat.

Rockefeller /ˈrɒkəfɛlə/ *noun.* M20.
[John D. *Rockefeller* (1839–1937), US financier and philanthropist.]
An immensely rich person, a millionaire.

rocker /ˈrɒkə/ *noun.* ME.
[from ROCK *verb*[1] + -ER[1].]
1 A person who rocks a cradle. ME.
2 A curved support on which a rocking-chair, cradle, etc., rocks. M18.
3 A beam fixed to the body of a horse-drawn coach to support the floorboards. L18.
4 A rocking-chair; a rocking-horse. M19.
5 = CRADLE *noun* 10. M19.
6 SKATING. **a** A skate with a curved blade. M19. ▸**b** A figure similar to a counter (COUNTER *noun*[3] 5). L19.
7 A rocking device forming part of a mechanism; *esp.* (*a*) a device for controlling the positions of brushes in a dynamo; (*b*) a rocker arm in an internal-combustion engine. L19.
8 ENGRAVING. = CRADLE *noun* 9. Also ***mezzotint rocker***. L19.
9 A tanning vat in which hides are rocked to and fro. L19.
10 A popular song that rocks; a rock song. M20.
11 A person who performs, dances to, or enjoys rock music; *spec.* one associated with long hair, leather jackets, and motorcycles (freq. opp. MOD *noun*[3]). M20.
12 A curved stripe under the three chevrons of a sergeant's badge (*US* MILITARY); any similar badge bearing a slogan or device. M20.
Phrases: **off one's rocker** *colloq.* crazy, mad. ***shoofly rocker***: see SHOOFLY 3.
Comb.: **rocker arm** a rocking lever in an engine; *esp.* one in an internal-combustion engine which serves to work a valve and is operated by a pushrod from the camshaft; **rocker-bottom foot** MEDICINE = ***rocker foot*** below; **rocker box** ASTRONOMY a simple altazimuth mount as used with a Dobsonian telescope; **rocker foot** MEDICINE a foot with the sole curved downwards; **rocker panel** in a motor vehicle, a panel forming part of the bodywork below the level of the passenger door; **rocker switch** an electrical on/off switch incorporating a spring-loaded rocker.

rockery /ˈrɒk(ə)ri/ *noun.* M19.
[from ROCK *noun*[1] + -ERY.]
A heap of rough stones and soil used for the ornamental growing of rock-plants.

rocket /ˈrɒkɪt/ *noun*[1]. Now *rare.* ME.
[Old French *roket* var. of *roquet*: see ROCHET *noun*[1].]
1 = ROCHET *noun*[1] 2. Now *dial.* ME.
2 ECCLESIASTICAL. = ROCHET *noun*[1] 1a. Chiefly *Scot.* ME.

rocket /ˈrɒkɪt/ *noun*[2]. L15.
[French *roquette* from Italian *rochetta* var. of *ruchetta* dim. of *ruca* from Latin *eruca*: see -ET[1].]
1 A cruciferous plant, *Eruca vesicaria* subsp. *sativa*, having purple-veined pale yellow or white flowers and acrid leaves, eaten esp. in the Mediterranean as a salad. Also ***garden rocket***. Cf. ROQUETTE. L15.
2 With specifying word: any of various other cruciferous plants; *spec.* any of several plants of the genus *Sisymbrium*, resembling mustard plants. Also, any of several plants of other families. E17.
3 More fully ***dame's rocket***, ***sweet rocket*** = ***dame's violet*** s.v. DAME *noun*. M18.
2 ***dyer's rocket***, ***London rocket***, ***sea rocket***, ***yellow rocket***, etc.
Comb.: **rocket larkspur** the larkspur commonly cultivated, *Consolida ajacis*.

rocket /ˈrɒkɪt/ *noun*[3]. E17.
[Old & mod. French *roquette* from Italian *rocchetto* dim. of *rocca* ROCK *noun*[2], with ref. to the cylindrical shape: see -ET[1].]
1 A cylindrical projectile that can be propelled to a great height or distance by the combustion of its contents and the backward ejection of waste gases, usu. giving a burst of light and used for signalling or entertainment. E17.
2 More fully ***rocket engine***, ***rocket motor***. An engine operating on the same principle, providing thrust as in a jet engine but without depending on atmospheric air for combustion. E20.
3 An elongated device or craft (as a flying bomb, a missile, a spacecraft) in which a rocket engine is the means of propulsion. E20.
4 A severe reprimand. *colloq.* M20.
1 ***Congreve rocket***, ***signal rocket***, etc. **2** ***booster rocket***, ***ion rocket***, ***vernier rocket***, etc. **3** ***ballistic rocket***, ***sounding rocket***, ***space rocket***, etc.
Phrases: **off one's rocket** *colloq.* = ***off one's*** ROCKER. **rise like a rocket (and fall like a stick)** rise suddenly and dramatically (and subsequently fall equally suddenly).
Comb.: **rocket-bomb** = ***flying bomb*** s.v. FLYING *ppl adjective*; **rocket chamber** the combustion chamber of a rocket engine; **rocket launcher** a device or structure for launching rockets, esp. missiles or space rockets; **rocket net** a net with small rockets attached round the edge, which is laid on the ground and then propelled so as to envelop a group of feeding birds for ringing; **rocket-net** *verb trans.* trap with a rocket net; **rocket pad** a launching pad for a rocket; **rocket plane** (*a*) an aircraft powered by a rocket motor; (*b*) an aircraft armed with rockets; **rocket projector** = ***rocket launcher*** above; **rocket range** a rocket-launching range; **rocket science** *colloq.* (orig. *US*) something very complex or hard to understand (usu. with neg.); **rocket scientist** (*a*) a scientist who builds rockets; (*b*) *colloq.* (chiefly *N. Amer.*) a very intelligent person (usu. with neg.); **rocket ship** (*a*) a spaceship powered by rockets; (*b*) a warship armed with rockets; ***rocket sled***: see SLED *noun* 2; **rocketsonde** [after RADIOSONDE] a package of scientific instruments which is released from a rocket in the upper atmosphere and floats down by parachute, transmitting automatic radio measurements of the atmosphere etc.
▪ **rocketry** *noun* the branch of science that deals with rockets and rocket propulsion; the use of rockets: M20.

†**rocket** *noun*[4] var. of ROCHET *noun*[2].

rocket /ˈrɒkɪt/ *verb.* E19.
[from ROCKET *noun*[3].]
1 *verb trans.* Discharge rockets at; bombard with rockets. E19.
2 *verb trans.* Propel (someone) at speed; send by or as by rocket. M19.
3 *verb intrans.* Of a game-bird: fly up almost vertically when flushed; fly fast and high overhead. M19.
4 *verb intrans.* Move like a rocket, move very fast up or away; (of prices etc.) increase substantially, soar. L19.
5 *verb trans.* Reprimand severely. *colloq.* M20.
📖 **4** N. MANDELA The cost of living is rocketing. V. GLENDINNING An empty train rocketing . . through the night.
▪ **rocketer** *noun* a thing that rockets M19. **rocketing** *noun* (*a*) the action or practice of the verb; (*b*) *colloq.* a severe reprimand: E20.

rocketeer /rɒkɪˈtɪə/ *noun.* M19.
[from ROCKET *noun*[3] + -EER.]
1 A person who discharges rockets. M19.
2 A person who experiments or works with rockets. E20.
▪ **rocketeering** *noun* = ROCKETRY M20.

rockier /ˈrɒkɪə/ *noun. dial.* L18.
[from ROCK *noun*[1] + -IER.]
The rock-dove.

rocking /ˈrɒkɪŋ/ *verbal noun*[1]. LME.
[from ROCK *verb*[1] + -ING[1].]
1 The action of ROCK *verb*[1]. LME.
2 The action of using a cradle or rocker in gold-mining or engraving. M19.
Comb.: **rocking-chair** *noun & adjective* (*a*) *noun* a chair mounted on curved supports or on springs so that the sitter can gently rock to and fro in it; (*b*) *adjective* (*US*) lacking or not involving first-hand experience; **rocking-horse** a model of a horse mounted on curved supports or on springs, for a child to rock on.

rocking /ˈrɒkɪŋ/ *noun*[2]. *Scot.* Now *rare* or *obsolete.* L18.
[from ROCK *noun*[2] + -ING[1].]
A social gathering of a kind formerly held on winter evenings in the country districts of Scotland.

rocking /ˈrɒkɪŋ/ *ppl adjective.* LME.
[from ROCK *verb*[1] + -ING[2].]
1 That rocks. LME.
2 PROSODY. Designating a metre in which each foot consists of a stressed syllable standing between two unstressed syllables. L19.
📖 **1** *Melody Maker* A rocking version of . . 'Sweet Sixteen'.
rocking stone a logan.

Rockingham /ˈrɒkɪŋəm/ *adjective.* M19.
[See below.]
Designating earthenware, china, glaze, etc., produced on the estate of the second Marquess of Rockingham (1730–82) at Swinton, S. Yorks., from *c* 1745 to 1842, and products (esp. tea-services) resembling these.

Rockite /ˈrɒkʌɪt/ *noun.* E19.
[from Captain *Rock*, an assumed name + -ITE[1].]
Hist. A member of an Irish organization associated with agrarian disorders in the earlier part of the 19th cent.
▪ **Rockism** *noun* M19.

rockling /ˈrɒklɪŋ/ *noun.* E17.
[from ROCK *noun*[1] + -LING[1].]
Any of several small gadid fishes of Atlantic coasts, *esp.* one of the genus *Rhinonemus* or the genus *Ciliata*.

rockoon /rɒˈkuːn/ *noun.* M20.
[Blend of ROCKET *noun*[3] and BALLOON.]
A rocket fired from a balloon; a balloon carrying a rocket to be fired in the upper atmosphere.

rocksteady /rɒkˈstɛdi/ *noun.* Also **rock steady**. M20.
[from ROCK *noun*[3] + STEADY *adjective*.]
A style of popular music originating in Jamaica, characterized by a slow tempo and accentuated offbeat; a dance to such music. Cf. REGGAE, SKA.

Rockwell /ˈrɒkwɛl/ *noun.* E20.
[Stanley P. *Rockwell*, 20th-cent. US metallurgist.]
Rockwell test, a hardness test in which the depth of penetration of the material (usu. a metal) by a steel ball or a diamond cone is measured; ***Rockwell hardness***, relative hardness determined in this way.

rocky /ˈrɒki/ *noun*[1]. *Nautical slang.* E20.
[Origin uncertain: perh. with allus. to ROCKY *adjective*[2] 1.]
A member of the Royal Naval Reserve.

rocky /ˈrɒki/ *adjective*[1] & *noun*[2]. L15.
[from ROCK *noun*[1] + -Y[1].]
▸ **A** *adjective.* **1** Containing many rocks; consisting or formed of rock; having the character of rock. L15.
2 *fig.* **a** Of the heart or disposition: hard, unfeeling, unyielding. L16. ▸**b** Firm as a rock; unflinching, steadfast. E17.
3 Growing on or among rocks. *rare.* M17.
📖 **1** F. O'BRIEN Riding iron bicycles over rocky roads.
▸ **B** *noun.* ***the Rockies***, the Rocky Mountains. E19.
▪ **rockily** *adverb*[1] L20. **rockiness** *noun* E17.

rocky /ˈrɒki/ *adjective*[2]. *colloq.* M18.
[from ROCK *verb*[1] + -Y[1]. In sense 3 sometimes interpreted as *fig.* use of ROCKY *adjective*[1].]
1 Unsteady, tottering; shaky; tipsy, drunken. M18.
2 In poor health; ill, unwell. L18.
3 Difficult, hard. L19.
📖 **1** H. BAILEY The marriage . . got off to a rocky start. **2** N. MAILER 'You must be in a state of shock.' 'I'm a little rocky'. **3** G. KENDALL This has been a rocky year for . . us.
▪ **rockily** *adverb*[2] L20.

Rocky Mountain /rɒkɪ ˈmaʊntɪn/ *noun phr.* E19.
[See below.]
Used *attrib.* to designate things found in or associated with the Rocky Mountains, a mountain range in western N. America.
Rocky Mountain bee plant = ***bee plant*** s.v. BEE *noun*[1]. ***Rocky Mountain fever***: see ***Rocky Mountain spotted fever*** below. **Rocky Mountain goat** a goat of the north-western US and southern Alaska, *Oreamnos americanus*; also called ***mountain goat***. **Rocky Mountain grasshopper**, **Rocky Mountain locust** a migratory N. American grasshopper, *Melanoplus spretus*. **Rocky Mountain oyster** lamb's fry. **Rocky Mountain sheep** = ***bighorn*** s.v. BIG *adjective*. **Rocky Mountain spotted fever**, **Rocky Mountain fever** a sometimes fatal rickettsial disease transmitted by ticks. **Rocky Mountain spotted fever tick**, **Rocky Mountain spotted tick**, **Rocky Mountain wood tick** a tick, *Dermacentor andersoni*, of western N. America, where it is the vector of Rocky Mountain fever.

rococo /rəˈkəʊkəʊ/ *adjective & noun.* M19.
[French, fanciful alt. of *rocaille* pebble- or shell-work from *roc* ROCK *noun*[1].]
▸ **A** *adjective.* **1** Old-fashioned, antiquated. M19.
2 (Of furniture or architecture) of or characterized by an elaborately ornamental late baroque style of decoration prevalent in 18th-cent. Continental Europe, with asymmetrical patterns involving motifs, scroll-work, etc.; (of music, literature, etc.) highly ornamented, florid; *gen.* extravagantly or excessively ornate. M19.
📖 **2** *Country Life* Delicate rococo plaster ceilings . . in . . pastel shades. *Antiquarian Horology* Rococo designs inspired by rocks and water forms. B. CHATWIN A Swan Service tureen: a Rococo fantasy on legs of intertwined fishes.
Special collocations: **rococo embroidery** a form of cutwork outlined in buttonhole stitch, used for table linen, cushion covers, etc. **rococo stitch** canvas stitch formed with bundles of four straight stitches crossed with short slanting stitches, worked in diagonal lines.
▸ **B** *noun.* The rococo style of art, decoration, etc. M19.
📖 W. S. MAUGHAM The frivolous ornament of rococo. A. EINSTEIN The Rococo had been a last tremulous echo of the . . Baroque.

rod /rɒd/ *noun & verb.*
[Late Old English *rodd*, prob. rel. to Old Norse *rudda* club.]
▸ **A** *noun.* **I 1** A straight slender shoot or stick, growing on or cut from a tree or bush. LOE. ▸**b** *fig.* In biblical translations and allusions: an offshoot, a descendant. LME
2 a A straight stick or a bundle of twigs bound together for use in caning or flogging. Also *fig.*, a means or instrument of punishment; punishment, chastisement. LOE. ▸**b** BASKET-MAKING. A long straight pliant stick. E16.
3 a A stick carried in the hand by a walker, shepherd, rider, magician, etc. *arch.* ME. ▸**b** A dowsing-rod. E17.
4 A wand or staff (carried) as a symbol of office, authority, power, etc.; the holder of such an office. LME.
5 a A long slender tapering, usu. sectioned, length of wood, cane, metal, plastic, etc., to which a reel and line are attached for fishing. LME. ▸**b** *transf.* An angler. L19. ▸**c** A right or permit to fish a length of river. M20.
6 a A stick used for measuring. L15. ▸**b** A small piece of wood, bone, etc., marked with figures and used in calculating. *obsolete* exc. *Hist.* E17.
📖 **2a** L. STRACHEY He was . . sentenced to . . twenty strokes of the birch rod. M. L. KING Negroes have been battered by the iron rod of oppression.
▸ **II 7 a** As a measure of length: = PERCH *noun*[2] 2. Now *rare* exc. *Hist.* LME. ▸**b** More fully ***square rod***. As a measure of

area: = PERCH *noun*[2] 2b. Cf. ROOD *noun* 5. Now *rare* exc. *Hist.* L15.

▶ **III 8** A slender connecting part or shaft; *dial.* the shaft of a cart or wagon. Also, a straight narrow bar of metal. L17. ▸**b** In full ***fuel rod***. A long slender piece of fuel for a nuclear reactor. M20.

9 An animal or plant structure with an elongated slender form; *esp.* a bacillus. M19. ▸**b** *ANATOMY.* Each of the elongated light-sensitive cells in the retina responsible primarily for monochrome vision in poor light. Cf. CONE *noun* 8. M19.

10 *CARPENTRY.* A board on which a working drawing of a joinery assembly is set out in full size, usually in horizontal and vertical section. M20.

📖 **8** D. LARDNER This plunger hangs from a rod. J. CONRAD Green . . curtains which ran on a brass rod. ***levelling rod***, ***piston-rod***, ***radius rod***, etc. *fig.*: C. STORR The rain . . coming down . . in steady, steel-grey rods.

▶ **IV** *slang.* **11** The penis, esp. when erect. E20.

12 A pistol, a revolver. Chiefly *US.* E20.

13 The rod connecting the drawbars of a railway carriage or truck. *N. Amer.* E20.

14 A hot rod. Chiefly *US.* M20.

Phrases: **a rod in pickle** (*a*) a punishment in store; (*b*) *Austral. slang* a racehorse being unobtrusively prepared for a win and betting coup. ***Black Rod***: see BLACK *adjective*. ***blue rod***: see BLUE *adjective*. ***kiss the rod***: see KISS *verb*. **make a rod for oneself**, **make a rod for one's own back** act in a way that will bring one trouble later. ***ride the rods***: see RIDE *verb*. **rod and gun** fishing and shooting. ***white rod***: see WHITE *adjective*.

Comb.: **rodman** (*a*) (chiefly *US*) a surveyor's assistant who holds the levelling rod; (*b*) an angler; (*c*) *slang* a gunman; **rod-mill** a workshop where iron is rolled into rods; **rod puppet**: operated and supported by rods.

▶ **B** *verb.* Infl. **-dd-**.

†**1** *verb trans.* Provide with rods or laths. Only in L16.

2 *verb trans.* Beat (a person) with a rod; cane. Chiefly as RODDING *noun*. M17.

3 Fit with lightning-conductors. *US.* L19.

4 *verb trans.* Push a rod through (a drain or pipe) in order to clear obstructions. L19.

5 *verb intrans.* Foll. by *up*: arm oneself with a gun or guns. *US slang.* E20.

■ **rodder** *noun* (*slang*, chiefly *US*) a hot-rodder, a person who converts cars into hot rods M20. **rodless** *adjective* M19. **rodlet** *noun* a little rod or rod-shaped object L19. **rodlike** *adjective* resembling or shaped like a rod; long, thin, and straight: E17.

rodded /ˈrɒdɪd/ *adjective*. M16.

[from ROD *noun*, *verb*: see -ED[2], -ED[1].]

†**1** Formed into rounded pleats. *rare.* Only in M16.

2 Made or provided with rods. M16.

3 Shaped like a rod. M19.

4 Foll. by *up*: armed with a gun or guns. *US slang.* E20.

rodding /ˈrɒdɪŋ/ *noun*. M17.

[from ROD *noun*, *verb* + -ING[1].]

1 The action of ROD *verb*. M17.

2 Metal in the form of rods; an arrangement of rods. L19.

3 *GEOLOGY.* A coarse linear structure in deformed metamorphic rocks characterized by the arrangement of grains of constituent minerals in parallel rods. Also ***rodding structure***. E20.

†**roddle** *noun* & *verb* see RUDDLE *noun*[1] & *verb*.

rode /rəʊd/ *noun*. *N. Amer.* E17.

[Origin unkn.]

A rope, *esp.* one securing an anchor or trawl.

rode /rəʊd/ *verb*[1] *trans.* E17.

[Prob. from older Dutch *ro(e)den* = Low German *roden*, *raden*, Old Frisian *rotha* root out, extirpate.]

Clear (a stream, dyke, etc.) of weeds.

rode /rəʊd/ *verb*[2] *intrans.* M18.

[Origin unkn.]

1 Of a wildfowl: fly landward in the evening. M18.

2 Of a woodcock: perform a regular evening territorial flight during the breeding season. M19.

rode *verb*[3] *pa. t.* of RIDE *verb*.

rodent /ˈrəʊd(ə)nt/ *noun* & *adjective*. M19.

[Latin *rodent-* pres. ppl stem of *rodere* gnaw: see -ENT.]

▶ **A** *noun. ZOOLOGY.* A mammal of the order Rodentia, characterized by strong continuously-growing incisor teeth and no canines, and including rats, mice, squirrels, voles, and beavers. M19.

Comb.: **rodent officer** an official employed to deal with rodent pests; **rodent-run** a distraction display of some birds, esp. waders, in which they resemble a running rodent.

▶ **B** *adjective*. **1** *ZOOLOGY.* Gnawing; that is a rodent. M19.

2 *MEDICINE.* Of a facial ulcer: consisting of a slow-growing malignant tumour. M19.

■ **rodential** /rə(ʊ)ˈdɛnʃ(ə)l/ *adjective* (*rare*) of, pertaining to, or resembling a rodent L19. **rodentian** /rə(ʊ)ˈdɛnʃ(ə)n/ *adjective* (*rare*) of, pertaining to, or consisting of rodents M19. **rodentiˈcidal** *adjective* pertaining to or of the nature of a rodenticide M20. **roˈdenticide** *noun* a poison used to kill rodents M20.

rodeo /ˈrəʊdɪəʊ, rəˈdeɪəʊ/ *noun* & *verb*. Orig. *US.* M19.

[Spanish, from *rodear* go round, based on Latin *rotare* ROTATE *verb*.]

▶ **A** *noun*. Pl. **-os**.

1 A round-up of cattle for counting, inspecting, branding, etc.; a place where cattle are rounded up. M19.

2 A display or competition exhibiting the skills of riding broncos, roping calves, wrestling steers, etc. E20. ▸**b** *transf.* A similar (usu. competitive) exhibition of other skills, as motorcycle riding, fishing, etc. Cf. ROADEO. E20.

▶ **B** *verb intrans.* Compete in a rodeo. M20.

rodgersia /rɒˈdʒəːzɪə/ *noun*. E20.

[mod. Latin (see below), from John *Rodgers* (1812–82), US admiral + -IA[1].]

Any of several large mostly Chinese plants constituting the genus *Rodgersia*, of the saxifrage family, grown for their showy often palmately lobed leaves and panicles of starry flowers.

rodham /ˈrɒdəm/ *noun*. M20.

[Origin unkn.]

In the Fen district of East Anglia, a raised bank formed on the bed of a dry river-course by the deposition of silt and by compaction and lowering of the adjacent peat soil.

Rodinesque /rəʊdəˈnɛsk/ *adjective*. E20.

[from *Rodin* (see below) + -ESQUE.]

Of, pertaining to, or reminiscent of the French Romantic School sculptor Auguste Rodin (1840–1917) or his work.

rodingite /ˈrəʊdɪŋʌɪt/ *noun*. E20.

[from River *Roding*, New Zealand + -ITE[1].]

GEOLOGY. A crystalline rock consisting of diallage, grossular, etc., formed by the calcium metasomatism of basic or ultrabasic igneous rocks.

rodney /ˈrɒdni/ *noun*[1] & *adjective*[1]. M19.

[Perh. from male forename *Rodney*. Sense A.2 perh. a different word.]

▶ **A** *noun*. **1** An idler, a loafer; a casual worker; a disreputable character. Now also, a stupid or awkward person. *dial.* & *colloq.* M19.

2 A small fishing boat or punt. *Canad.* L19.

▶ **B** *attrib.* or as *adjective*. Hulking, rough. Chiefly *dial.* M19.

Rodney /ˈrɒdni/ *noun*[2] & *adjective*[2]. M20.

[George Brydges, Lord *Rodney* (1718–92), English admiral.]

(Designating) a type of decanter designed with a wide base for use on shipboard.

rodomont /ˈrɒdəmɒnt/ *noun*. *arch.* L16.

[French, from Italian *rodomonte* from a boastful character in the *Orlando* epics.]

A great bragger or boaster.

rodomontade /ˌrɒdə(ʊ)mɒnˈteɪd/ *noun*, *verb*, & *adjective*. Also **rh-**. E17.

[French from Italian †*rodomontada*, *-ata*, from *rodomonte*: see prec., -ADE.]

▶ **A** *noun*. **1** A brag, a boast; an extravagantly boastful or arrogant remark or speech. E17.

2 Boastful or inflated language or behaviour; extravagant bragging. M17.

▶ **B** *verb intrans.* Boast, brag; rant. L17.

▶ **C** *adjective*. Bragging, boastful; ranting. M18.

■ **rodomontader** *noun* a braggart M19.

†**rodomontado** *noun* & *adjective*. L16.

[formed as prec.: see -ADO.]

▶ **A** *noun*. Pl. **-oes**.

1 = RODOMONTADE *noun*. L16–E18.

2 = RODOMONT. E17–L18.

▶ **B** *adjective*. = RODOMONTADE *adjective*. M–L17.

Rodriguan /rɒˈdriːg(ə)n/ *adjective* & *noun*. L20.

[from *Rodrigues* (see below) + -AN.]

▶ **A** *adjective*. Of, pertaining to, or characteristic of (the people of) the island of Rodrigues, a dependency of Mauritius in the western Indian Ocean. L20.

▶ **B** *noun*. A native or inhabitant of Rodrigues. L20.

rodster /ˈrɒdstə/ *noun*. *rare.* L19.

[from ROD *noun* + -STER.]

An angler.

roe /rəʊ/ *noun*[1].

[Old English *rā*, earlier *rāa*, *rāha* (also *rāhdēor*) = Old Saxon, Old High German *rēho* (Dutch *ree*, German *Reh*), Old Norse *rá*.]

A small Eurasian deer, *Capreolus capreolus*, having short pointed antlers and no visible tail. Also ***roe-deer***.

Comb.: **roe ring** a track worn by roe-deer running in circles prior to mating.

roe /rəʊ/ *noun*[2]. LME.

[Middle Low German, Middle Dutch *roge* = Old High German *rogo*: cf. Middle Low German *rogen*, Old Norse *hrogn* = Old High German *rogen* (German *Rogen*). Cf. ROWN.]

(The mass of eggs or spawn contained in) the ovaries of a female fish, esp. when ripe. Also ***hard roe***.

soft roe the ripe testes of a male fish.

■ **roed** *adjective* having roe; full of spawn (chiefly as 2nd elem. of comb., as ***hard-roed***, ***soft-roed***): E17.

roe /rəʊ/ *noun*[3]. M19.

[Perh. transf. use of prec.]

The patterned alternation of light and dark streaks in the grain of wood, esp. mahogany.

roebuck /ˈrəʊbʌk/ *noun*. LME.

[from ROE *noun*[1] + BUCK *noun*[1].]

The male of the roe-deer.

Comb.: **roebuck-berry** *Scot.* (the fruit of) the stone bramble, *Rubus saxatilis*.

Roedean /ˈrəʊdiːn/ *adjective*. M20.

[See below.]

Of a (young) woman's speech, accent, etc.: (excessively) refined in the manner popularly associated with Roedean, an independent public school for girls in Brighton, on the south coast of England.

roemer /ˈrəːmə/ *noun*. L19.

[Dutch, or German *Römer*: cf. RUMMER.]

A type of decorated German or Dutch wineglass with knobs or prunts on the stem.

Roentgen /ˈrʌntjən; ˈrəːnt-, ˈrɒnt-; -g(ə)n, -ʒ(ə)n/ *noun*. Also **Rönt-**. L19.

[Wilhelm Conrad *Roentgen* (1845–1923), German physicist, discoverer of X-rays.]

1 Used *attrib.* with ref. to Roentgen's work on X-rays. L19.

2 (**r-**.) More fully ***Roentgen unit***. The former unit of exposure to X- or gamma radiation, equal to the quantity of radiation that gives rise to ions carrying a total charge of 2.58×10^{-4} coulombs per kilogram of air. Abbreviation ***R***. Cf. REM *noun*[1]. E20.

1 Roentgen rays *Hist.* X-rays.

■ †**Roentgenization** *noun* subjection to X-rays: only in E20. †**Roentgenized** *adjective* subjected to X-rays L19–E20.

roentgeno- /ˈrʌntjənəʊ; ˈrəːnt-, ˈrɒnt-; -gənəʊ, -ʒənəʊ/ *combining form* of prec.: see -O-. In some words **roentgen-**.

■ **roentgenˈkymogram** *noun* a recording made with a kymograph (KYMOGRAPH 2) E20. **roentgenˈkymograph** *noun* = KYMOGRAPH 2 E20. **roentgenkymoˈgraphic** *adjective* of, pertaining to, or involving the roentgenkymograph M20. **roentgenkyˈmography** *noun* the process or technique of using a kymograph (KYMOGRAPH 2); kymography: E20. **roentgenogram** *noun* an X-ray photograph E20. **roentgenograph** *noun* & *verb* (*a*) *noun* a roentgenogram; (*b*) *verb trans.* radiograph: E20. **roentgenoˈgraphic** *adjective* pertaining to or involving roentgenography E20. **roentgenoˈgraphically** *adverb* by means of roentgenography E20. **roentgeˈnography** *noun* radiography carried out by means of X-rays E20. **roentgenoˈlogic**, **roentgenoˈlogical** *adjectives* of, pertaining to, or involving roentgenology E20. **roentgenoˈlogically** *adverb* by means of roentgenology E20. **roentgeˈnologist** *noun* a person who practises roentgenology E20. **roentgeˈnology** *noun* (the branch of science that deals with) the medical use of X-rays, esp. as a diagnostic tool E20. **roentgenoscope** *noun* & *verb* (*a*) *noun* = FLUOROSCOPE; (*b*) *verb trans.* examine by means of a fluoroscope: E20. **roentgenoˈscopic** *adjective* fluoroscopic E20. **roentgeˈnoscopy** *noun* fluoroscopy E20. **roentgenoˈtherapy** *noun* radiotherapy carried out by means of X-rays E20.

roer /ruə/ *noun*. E19.

[Dutch from German *Rohr* gun barrel, pipe, reed.]

In South Africa, a long-barrelled smooth-bore gun used in hunting big game.

roesti /ˈrøsti/ *noun pl.* (treated as *sing.* or *pl.*). Also **rösti**. M20.

[Swiss German.]

A Swiss dish of grated potatoes, formed into a pancake and fried.

roestone /ˈrəʊstəʊn/ *noun*. Now *rare.* E19.

[from ROE *noun*[2] + STONE *noun*.]

= OOLITE 1.

rofia *noun* see RAFFIA.

rog /rɒg/ *verb trans.* & *intrans.* Long *obsolete* exc. *dial.* Infl. **-gg-**. LME.

[Perh. rel. to RUG *verb*[1].]

Shake; move to and fro.

rog /rɒdʒ/ *interjection*. *colloq.* M20.

[Abbreviation.]

= ROGER *interjection*.

Rogallo /rə(ʊ)ˈgaləʊ/ *adjective* & *noun*. M20.

[Francis M. *Rogallo*, 20th-cent. US engineer.]

(Designating) a light flexible triangular wing deployed by means of tension lines or rigid tubes and used on spacecraft and for hang-gliding.

rogan /ˈrəʊg(ə)n, ˈrɒg(ə)n/ *noun*. *Canad.* M18.

[Canad. French *(h)ouragan* from early Algonquian or Montagnais *ora:kan* dish.]

A watertight container made of birch-bark.

rogan josh /rəʊg(ə)n ˈdʒəʊʃ/ *noun phr.* Also **roghan josh**. M20.

[Urdu *rogan još*, *raugan-još* (preparation of mutton) stewed in ghee, from Urdu *roġan*, *rauġan* from Persian *rauġan* oil, ghee + Urdu, Persian *-još* act of braising or stewing.]

A dish of curried meat (usu. lamb) cooked in a rich sauce.

Rogatian /rə(ʊ)ˈgeɪʃ(ə)n/ *noun.* M16.
[formed as ROGATIST: see -IAN.]
= ROGATIST.

rogation /rə(ʊ)ˈgeɪʃ(ə)n/ *noun.* LME.
[Latin *rogatio(n-)*, from *rogat-* pa. ppl stem of *rogare* ask.]
1 ECCLESIASTICAL *sing.* & (usu.) in *pl.* Solemn prayers consisting of the litany of the saints chanted on the three days before Ascension Day. Also, the days set aside for these prayers. LME. ▸†**b** *transf.* Begging for alms. M16–E17.
2 ROMAN HISTORY. The submission by a consul or tribune of a proposed law for acceptance by the people. Also, a law so submitted and accepted. LME.
†**3** A formal request. L16–L17.
Comb.: **Rogation day** each of the three days preceding Ascension Day (usu. in *pl.*); **rogation flower** the milkwort, *Polygala vulgaris*, which was carried in procession in Rogation week; **Rogation Sunday** the Sunday before Ascension Day; **Rogationtide** the period of the Rogation days; **Rogation week** the week in which Ascension Day falls.

Rogatist /ˈrəʊgətɪst/ *noun.* M16.
[from *Rogatus* (see below) + -IST.]
ECCLESIASTICAL HISTORY. A member of a Donatist sect led by Rogatus, who flourished in the 4th cent. AD.

rogatory /ˈrəʊgət(ə)ri/ *adjective.* M19.
[French *rogatoire* from medieval Latin *rogatorius*, from Latin *rogat-*: see ROGATION, -ORY[2]. Cf. INTERROGATORY.]
LAW. Making or pertaining to a request through a foreign court for the obtaining of information or evidence from a specified person within the jurisdiction of that court. Chiefly in ***letters rogatory***.

†**roger** *noun*[1]. *slang.* Only in M16.
[Perh. rel. to ROGUE *noun*.]
A begging vagrant pretending to be a poor Oxford or Cambridge scholar.

Roger /ˈrɒdʒə/ *noun*[2] & *interjection.* M16.
[Male forename, from Old French *Rog(i)er*, of Germanic origin.]
▶ **A** *noun.* **1** †**a** A goose. *slang.* M16–E17. ▸**b** The penis. *coarse slang.* M17.
2 A man; a lad, a chap. *colloq.* (now *rare*). M17.
3 = *Roger's blast* below. *dial.* L19.
Phrases & comb.: ***Jolly Roger***: see JOLLY *adjective*. ***Roger de Coverley***: see ***Sir Roger de Coverley*** below. **Roger's blast** *dial.* a sudden small localized whirlwind. **Sir Roger de Coverley**, **Roger de Coverley** /-də ˈkʌvəli/ (the tune of) an English country dance. STINKING *Roger*.
▶ **B** *interjection.* Acknowledging a radio message etc. as received. Also (*slang*), expr. assent or agreement. M20.

roger /ˈrɒdʒə/ *verb.* E18.
[from prec.]
1 *verb trans.* & *intrans.* Copulate with (a woman); have sexual intercourse (with). *coarse slang.* E18.
2 *verb trans.* Acknowledge (a radio message etc.) as received. *US.* M20.

Rogerene /ˈrɒdʒəriːn/ *noun. US.* M18.
[from *Rogers* (see below) + *-ene*, after NAZARENE.]
A member of a small religious sect founded by John Rogers (1648–1721) in Connecticut, opposed to various formal practices of Churches and participation in military service. Also more fully ***Rogerene Quaker***.

roghan josh *noun phr.* var. of ROGAN JOSH.

rognon /rɔɲɔ̃/ *noun.* Pl. pronounced same. E19.
[French.]
1 A kidney, used as food. Usu. in *pl.* E19.
2 MOUNTAINEERING. A rounded outcrop of rock or stones surrounded by a glacier or an ice-field. M20.

rogue /rəʊg/ *noun* & *adjective.* M16.
[Perh. rel. to ROGER *noun*[1], prob. from Latin *rogare* ask, beg.]
▶ **A** *noun.* **1** An idle vagrant, a vagabond. *obsolete* exc. *Hist.*. M16.
2 A dishonest or unprincipled person; a rascal. L16. ▸†**b** A servant. *derog.* L16–L18.
3 A mischievous person, now esp. a child. Freq. as a playful term of reproof or reproach. L16.
4 A seedling or plant regarded as undesirable in a crop, *esp.* one deviating from the standard variety. M19.
5 An elephant or other large wild animal driven away or living apart from the herd and having savage or destructive tendencies. M19.
6 A horse inclined to shirk on the racecourse or when hunting. L19.

> **2** J. ALMON Fox was rogue enough to do anything. D. LESSING Each country has its own type of rogue. **3** J. POTTER That sly rogue Cupid has pierced your heart. **5** H. O. FORBES No elephant, unless a rogue, would trample us down.

Comb. & phrases: **rogue and villain** *rhyming slang* (now *Hist.*) a shilling; **rogue's badge** *the* blinkers of a horse; **rogue's gallery** a collection of photographs of known criminals, used to identify suspects; *transf.* any collection of people notable for a certain shared quality or characteristic, esp. a disreputable one.
▶ **B** *attrib.* or as *adjective.* **1** Of an elephant or other large wild animal: living apart from the herd and having savage or destructive tendencies. M19.
2 *transf.* & *fig.* Inexplicably aberrant, faulty, or defective; misplaced, occurring (esp. in isolation) at an unexpected place or time; uncontrolled, undisciplined, irresponsible. M20.

> **1** G. S. FORBES A very hazardous meeting with a rogue elephant. **2** L. P. HARTLEY He distrusted . . imagination; it was a rogue quality that jumped the queue. S. TROTT Four rogue roses . . The last roses of summer in January. *Which Video?* This was a rogue machine and not likely to happen on my one.

■ **roguery** *noun* (*a*) conduct characteristic of a rogue; an instance of this, a roguish act; (*b*) playful mischief, fun: L16. **rogueship** *noun* (*arch.*) (with possess. adjective, as ***your rogueship*** etc.) a mock title of respect given to a rogue L16. †**roguy** *adjective* = ROGUISH L16–M18.

rogue /rəʊg/ *verb.* L16.
[from the noun.]
1 *verb intrans.* Wander about, live, or act like a rogue. Now *rare.* L16.
†**2** *verb trans.* Denounce as a rogue; accuse of roguery. M–L17.
3 *verb trans.* Free (a crop) from inferior or undesirable plants or seedlings; weed *out* (such plants) from a crop. M18.
4 *verb trans.* Deal dishonestly with, swindle. M19.
■ **roguer** *noun* a person employed to identify and eliminate inferior plants in a crop, esp. of potatoes M20.

roguish /ˈrəʊgɪʃ/ *adjective.* L16.
[from ROGUE *noun* + -ISH[1].]
1 Pertaining to or characteristic of a rogue. L16.
2 Acting like a rogue; unprincipled, dishonest. L16.
3 Playfully mischievous; waggish. L17.

> **3** J. A. SYMONDS He made himself a favourite by roguish ways and ready wit.

■ **roguishly** *adverb* E17. **roguishness** *noun* L16.

Rohilla /rə(ʊ)ˈhɪlə, ˈrəʊhɪlə/ *noun* & *adjective.* L18.
[Pashto *Rōhēlah*, from *Rōh* a district of Afghanistan.]
▶ **A** *noun.* Pl. **-s**, same. A member of a people of Afghan origin inhabiting the Bareilly district of northern India. L18.
▶ **B** *attrib.* or as *adjective.* Of or pertaining to this people. L18.

Rohrflöte /ˈroːrfløːtə/ *noun.* Pl. ***-ten*** /-tən/. L18.
[German, from *Rohr* tube + *Flöte* flue-stop.]
MUSIC. An organ-stop with partly closed pipes, the stopper at the top of each pipe being pierced by a thin tube.

rohun /ˈrəʊən/ *noun.* Also **rohuna** /ˈrəʊənə/. M19.
[Hindi *rohan*, *rohan(a)*.]
A tree of India and Sri Lanka, *Soymida febrifuga* (family Meliaceae), valued for its medicinal bark. Chiefly in ***rohun bark***.

Rohypnol /rəʊˈhɪpnɒl/ *noun.* L20.
[Origin uncertain: perh. from *ro-* (from the name of the manufacturer, Hoffman–La *Roche*) + HYPNO- + -OL.]
(Proprietary name for) the drug flunitrazepam.

roid /rɔɪd/ *adjective.* Long *obsolete* exc. *dial.* LME.
[Old French *roide*, *rode* from Latin *rigidus* RIGID, or perh. in some cases alt. of RUDE.]
1 Stout, strong; violent, rough. LME.
2 Rude; large, unwieldy. LME.

roi fainéant /rwa fɛneɑ̃/ *noun phr.* Pl. ***-s -s*** (pronounced same). M19.
[French, lit. 'sluggard king': see FAINÉANT.]
Any of the later Merovingian kings of France, whose power was merely nominal; *gen.* any person with merely nominal power.

†**roil** *noun*[1]. LME.
[Origin unkn.]
1 Orig., a large powerful horse. Later, an inferior or spiritless horse. LME–L16.
2 *transf.* A large ungainly woman. M16–L18.

roil /rɔɪl/ *noun*[2]. Now chiefly *US.* L17.
[from ROIL *verb*[2].]
Agitation; disturbance; *spec.* a turbulent stretch of water; *fig.* a confused mass.

> D. HARSENT Where trees scattered the glare, a roil of leaves flowing along the bough.

■ **roily** *adjective* muddy, turbid; turbulent; ***roily oil***, petroleum containing much emulsified water: E19.

roil /rɔɪl/ *verb*[1] *intrans. obsolete* exc. *dial.* ME.
[Prob. from Old French *roillier*, *roeillier* roll, rel. to *roelle* wheel.]
†**1** Roam or rove about. ME–E17.
†**2** Of the eyes: roll. *rare.* Only in LME.
3 Play or frolic, *esp.* in a rough manner; romp. L18.

roil /rɔɪl/ *verb*[2]. Now *US* & *dial.* L16.
[Perh. from Old French *ruiler* mix mortar from late Latin *regulare* REGULATE. See also RILE *verb* & *noun*.]
1 *verb trans.* Make (liquid) turbid or muddy by disturbing the sediment; *fig.* disturb, disorder. Cf. RILE *verb* 2. L16. ▸**b** *verb trans.* Disturb in temper; irritate, make angry. Cf. RILE *verb* 1a. M18.
2 *verb intrans.* Move in a confused or turbulent manner. M20.

> **1** *Wall Street Journal* Inflation fears have roiled the stock . . markets in recent months. **2** *Scientific American* Suddenly . . a large ash cloud began to roil up from the mountain. *fig.*: C. MCCULLOUGH In that state where the words were roiling inside her.

†**roin** *noun.* Only in LME.
[Old French *roigne*.]
A scab; scurf.
¶ Survived in ROINISH.

†**roin** *verb intrans.* LME–E17.
[Prob. from Old French *rongier*: cf. Old French *grognir*, *grogner* GROIN *verb*[1].]
Growl.

roinish /ˈrɔɪnɪʃ/ *adjective.* Long *arch.* LME.
[from ROIN *noun* + -ISH[1].]
Scabby, scurvy; *fig.* mean, base.

rois fainéants *noun phr.* pl. of ROI FAINÉANT.

roi soleil /rwa sɔlɛːj/ *noun phr.* Pl. ***-s -s*** (pronounced same). L19.
[French, lit. 'sun king', (the heraldic device of) Louis XIV of France.]
A pre-eminent person or thing.

†**roist** *verb intrans.* M16–E17.
[Back-form. from next.]
= ROISTER *verb*.
■ †**roisting** *adjective* = ROISTERING *adjective* M16–E19.

roister /ˈrɔɪstə/ *noun. arch.* M16.
[Old & mod. French *rustre* ruffian, alt. of *ruste*, from Latin *rusticus* RUSTIC.]
A roisterer. Also †***roister-doister***.

roister /ˈrɔɪstə/ *verb intrans.* L16.
[from the noun.]
Enjoy oneself noisily or boisterously; behave uproariously; revel.

> F. HERBERT Shouting and roistering like students returning from vacation.

■ **roisterer** *noun* a noisy reveller (cf. ROISTER *noun*) E19. **roistering** *noun* (*a*) the action of the verb; (*b*) an instance of this, a revel: M19. **roistering** *adjective* characterized by or given to noisy revelry, boisterous, uproarious: L16. **roisteringly** *adverb* M17. **roisterous** *adjective* = ROISTERING *adjective* L16.

roitelet /ˈrɔɪtəlɛt, *foreign* rwatlɛ (*pl. same*)/ *noun. arch.* E17.
[French, from Old French *roitel* dim. of *roi* king: see -ET[1].]
A petty or minor king.

roke /rəʊk/ *noun*[1] & *verb.* Now *Scot.* & *dial.* See also ROOK *noun*[3], ROUK. ME.
[Prob. of Scandinavian origin. Cf. REEK *noun*[1].]
▶ **A** *noun.* Smoke; steam; mist, fog; drizzle. ME.
▶ **B** *verb intrans.* Smoke; steam; be foggy or misty; drizzle. E17.
■ **roky** *adjective*[1] LME.

roke /rəʊk/ *noun*[2]. L19.
[Alt. of RAUK, with specialized application.]
METALLURGY. A fault in steel.
■ **roky** *adjective*[2] characterized by rokes M20.

rokelay /ˈrɒkəleɪ/ *noun. Scot.* E18.
[Alt. of French ROQUELAURE.]
Hist. A woman's short cloak worn in the 18th cent.

roker /ˈrəʊkə/ *noun.* L19.
[Perh. from Danish *rokke*, Swedish *rocka* ray.]
The thornback (ray), *Raja clavata*.

rolag /ˈrəʊlag/ *noun.* M20.
[Gaelic, dim. of *rola* a roll.]
A roll of carded wool ready for spinning.

Roland /ˈrəʊlənd/ *noun.* E16.
[The legendary nephew of Charlemagne, celebrated with his comrade Oliver in the *Chanson de Roland*, a medieval romance.]
A person comparable to Roland in respect of courage; a person who is a full match for another.
a Roland for an Oliver an effective retort; an effective retaliatory blow; a quid pro quo.

Rolandic /rəʊˈlandɪk/ *adjective.* L19.
[formed as next + -IC.]
ANATOMY. Designating various parts of the central nervous system investigated by Rolando (see next), esp. the motor area of the cerebral cortex.
Rolandic fissure = ***fissure of*** ROLANDO.

Rolando /rəʊˈlandəʊ/ *noun.* M19.
[Luigi *Rolando* (1773–1831), Italian anatomist.]
ANATOMY. Used after *of*, and *attrib.*, to designate various features of the central nervous system.
fissure of Rolando a groove in the brain separating the frontal lobe from the parietal lobe. **Rolando substance** the translucent gelatinous substance which fills the ends of the posterior grey horns of the spinal medulla; also called ***substantia gelatinosa of Rolando***. **sulcus of Rolando** = ***fissure of Rolando*** above.

role /rəʊl/ *noun.* Also **rôle**. E17.
[French †*roule*, †*rolle*, *rôle* ROLL *noun*[1], orig. the roll or paper containing an actor's part.]
1 An actor's part in a play, film, etc.; *fig.* the part played or assumed by a person in society, life, etc. E17.
2 The characteristic or expected function of a person or thing, esp. (PSYCHOLOGY) in a particular setting or environment. L19.
3 COMPUTING. A symbol or series of symbols expressing the function or meaning of a term in an index or thesaurus, esp. in relation to other terms. Usu. *attrib.* M20.

1 L. DURRELL Increasingly critical of the French rôle during the war. *Dateline Magazine* She . . was the . . choice to play the title role of Patty Hearst. **2** B. MAYO The role of reasoning in moral argument. J. KLEIN Divorce of role from self destroys the integrity of the personality. W. M. CLARKE She slipped easily into the role of housekeeper.

Comb.: **role model** a person looked to by others as an example in a particular role; **role reversal** the assumption of a role which is the reverse of that normally performed.

roleo /ˈrəʊlɪəʊ/ *noun. US.* Pl. **-os**. M20.
[from ROLL *verb* + ROD)EO.]
A logrolling contest.

role-play /ˈrəʊlpleɪ/ *verb & noun.* M20.
[Back-form. from next; as noun from ROLE + PLAY *noun*, after next.]
▸ **A** *verb trans. & intrans.* Chiefly PSYCHOLOGY. Recreate or represent (a situation, event, etc.) by means of role-playing; portray (a person or characteristic) in this way. M20.
▸ **B** *noun.* Chiefly PSYCHOLOGY. Role-playing; an instance of this. L20.
■ **role player** *noun* (*a*) a person who plays a role or who participates in role-playing; *spec.* (BASKETBALL) a player who performs a specific function and is only brought on when required; (*b*) a player of role-playing games: M20.

role-playing /ˈrəʊlpleɪɪŋ/ *verbal noun.* M20.
[from ROLE + PLAYING.]
1 Chiefly PSYCHOLOGY. The acting out or performance of a particular role, either consciously, as a technique in psychotherapy, training, etc., or unconsciously, in accordance with the perceived expectations of society as regards a person's behaviour in a particular position. M20.
2 Participation in a role-playing game; the playing of such games. L20.
Comb.: **role-playing game** a game in which players take on the roles of imaginary characters, usu. in a setting created by a referee, and thereby vicariously experience the imagined adventures of these characters.

Rolf /rɒlf/ *adjective & verb.* M20.
[Ida P. *Rolf* (1897–1979), US physiotherapist.]
▸ **A** *adjective.* Designating a technique of deep massage for reducing muscular and mental tension. M20.
▸ **B** *verb trans.* Use the Rolf technique on. Chiefly as ***Rolfing*** *verbal noun.* L20.

roll /rəʊl/ *noun*[1]. ME.
[Old French *rolle*, *roulle* (mod. *rôle*) from Latin *rotulus* var. of *rotula* dim. of *rota* wheel. Cf. ROLE, SCROLL *noun*.]
▸ **I 1** A piece of parchment or paper (intended to be) written on and rolled up for convenient handling, carrying, or storage; a scroll. ME.
2 *spec.* A document, esp. an official record, in a rolled form. Freq. with specifying word or phr. ME.
3 a A list or catalogue of names, deeds, etc. Chiefly *fig.* ME. ▸**b** An official list or register; *spec.* (*a*) a muster-roll; (*b*) a school register; (*c*) SCOTS LAW a list of cases coming before a judge or court; (*d*) the list of those qualified to practise as solicitors (usu. in *pl.*). Also, the total numbers on such an official list. LME.
▸ **II 4** A cylinder formed by turning flexible material (esp. cloth or paper) over and over on itself without folding; this as a definite measure. LME. ▸**b** A quantity of banknotes rolled together; *transf.* the money a person possesses. *US & Austral.* M19. ▸**c** A quantity of photographic or cinematographic film supplied rolled up. L19. ▸**d** = ***music-roll*** (b) s.v. MUSIC *noun.* E20.
5 a An item of food that is rolled up, esp. round a filling, before being cooked. Usu. with specifying word. LME. ▸**b** A small individual loaf of bread, properly one rolled or doubled over before baking (also ***bread roll***); this with a specified filling. L16.
6 A cylindrical or semicylindrical mass of or *of* something. LME. ▸**b** ARCHITECTURE. A spiral scroll as in an Ionic capital; a moulding of convex section. E17. ▸**c** BUILDING. A rounded strip of wood to which the flashing is attached on the ridge or the lateral joints of a roof. M19.
7 †**a** A small quantity of cloth, wool, etc., rolled up to form an ornamental band. LME–E18. ▸†**b** A bandage; = ROLLER *noun*[1] 6. LME–L16. ▸**c** A round cushion or pad, *esp.* one forming part of a woman's head-dress. Now only *spec.* (*dial.*), an annular pad to ease the carrying of heavy articles on the head. LME.
8 A part of something which is rolled or turned over. E16.
9 GEOLOGY. An orebody in sedimentary rock that has a C- or S-shaped cross-section cutting across bedding. Freq. *attrib.* M20.

5b B. MALAMUD Poured . . milk into his tea and ate a buttered roll. **6** M. H. KINGSTON Her rolls of fat bounce . . and rub together.

▸ **III 10** A cylinder or roller, *esp.* one used to shape metal in a rolling-mill. LME. ▸**b** BOOKBINDING. A revolving patterned tool used in impressing and gilding; the pattern produced by this. M17.
Phrases: **a roll Jack Rice couldn't jump over** *Austral. slang* a large quantity of money. ***bread roll***: see sense 5b above. **call the roll** take a roll-call. ***crescent roll***: see CRESCENT *adjective* 2. ***Dutch roll***: see DUTCH *adjective.* ***French roll***: see FRENCH *adjective & noun.* ***jelly roll***: see JELLY *noun*[1] & *verb.* **Master of the Rolls** a judge who presides over the Civil Division of the Court of Appeal in England and Wales, originally being the keeper of the public records. ***porteous roll***: see PORTEOUS 2. **roll of honour** a list of those honoured, esp. the dead in war. **strike off the rolls** debar (esp. a solicitor) from practising after dishonesty etc. ***Swiss roll.*** **the Rolls** *Hist.* the former buildings in Chancery Lane in which the records in the custody of the Master of the Rolls were kept.
Comb.: **roll-call** *noun & verb* (*a*) *noun* a calling out of names from a list in order to establish who is present; *US* a calling out of a list of members of a legislative body to establish how each wishes to vote; (*b*) *verb trans.* call the roll for (a group of people); **roll-collar** a turned-over collar on a garment; **roll feed** a feed mechanism supplying paper, strip metal, etc., by means of rollers; **roll-formed** *adjective* formed by roll-forming; **roll-forming** cold forming of metal by repeated passing between rollers; ***roll latten***: see LATTEN 1; **roll mark**: produced on sheet metal flattened by an imperfect set of rollers; **roll-neck** *noun & adjective* (*a*) *noun* a high loosely turned-over collar; a garment with such a collar; (*b*) *adjective* (of a garment) having a roll-neck; **roll-necked** *adjective* = ***roll-neck*** (b) above.

roll /rəʊl/ *noun*[2]. L17.
[from the verb.]
1 A rapid succession of notes, esp. on a drum, producing an almost continuous sound; *transf.* any almost continuous reverberating sound. L17. ▸**b** PHONETICS. A trill. M20.
2 The action or an act of rolling. M18. ▸**b** A rolling gait or motion; a swagger. M19. ▸**c** (A) full or partial rotation by a vehicle, aircraft, or boat about its longitudinal axis. M19. ▸**d** A gymnastic exercise in which the body is rolled into a tucked position and turned in a forward or backward circle. L19. ▸**e** A throw of a die or dice. E20. ▸**f** An act of sexual intercourse or erotic fondling. Chiefly in ***a roll in the hay*** s.v. HAY *noun*[1]. *colloq.* M20.
3 A sonorous or rhythmical flow of words in verse or prose. M18.
4 An undulation or swell on the surface of land. M19.

1 S. T. FELSTEAD The drums . . played a murderously fast roll. E. WELTY The house shook . . after a long roll of thunder. **2** H. WILLIAMSON The roll of the earth from darkness into light was brief. **b** C. EKWENSI She walked with a roll of her hips. **c** C. FRANCIS Lack of stability may produce more than a bad roll. *Buses* To steer so quickly as to induce a certain amount of roll.

Phrases: ***a roll in the hay***: see HAY *noun*[1]. **on a roll** *slang* (chiefly *N. Amer.*) (*a*) enjoying a series of successes or a run of luck; (*b*) engaged in a period of intense activity. ***western roll***: see WESTERN *adjective.*
Comb.: **roll axis** the axis about which a vehicle, aircraft, or boat rolls; **roll bar** an overhead metal bar strengthening the frame of a motor vehicle (esp. in racing) and protecting the occupants if the vehicle overturns; **roll cage** a centre box section in a motor vehicle for protecting the occupants if the vehicle overturns; **roll cast** *verb trans. & intrans.* (ANGLING) cast (a line) without throwing it behind; **roll rate** the angular velocity of a vehicle, aircraft, or boat about its roll axis.

roll /rəʊl/ *verb.* Also (*Scot. & north.*) **row** /rəʊ/. ME.
[Old French *rol(l)er*, (also mod.) *rouler* from Proto-Romance, from Latin *rotulus* ROLL *noun*[1].]
1 a *verb intrans.* Turn over and over; revolve (as) on an axis; *spec.* (*N. Amer.*) (of a car etc.) overturn. Freq. with adverbs. ME. ▸**b** *verb trans.* Turn over and over; turn over and over *in* something or between two surfaces; cause to revolve (as) on an axis; *spec.* (*N. Amer.*) overturn (a car etc.). LME. ▸**c** *verb trans. & intrans.* Turn over in the mind. LME. ▸**d** *verb trans. & intrans.* (Cause to) change direction by a rotary movement, rotate partially. LME. ▸**e** *verb intrans.* Wallow or luxuriate in; have plenty of (esp. money). Foll. by *in*. L15. ▸**f** *verb intrans.* Centre *on* a subject etc. E18.
2 a *verb intrans.* Move or go forward by turning over and over or revolving (as) on an axis. Freq. with adverbs. LME. ▸**b** *verb trans.* Cause to move or go forward by turning over and over or by revolving (as) on an axis; *spec.* throw (a die or dice), obtain (a specified score) in doing this. LME. ▸**c** *verb trans.* Drive, push, or draw (a wheeled vehicle); convey in a wheeled vehicle (now *Scot.*); move by means of rollers. E16. ▸**d** *verb intrans.* (Of a vehicle) move or run on wheels; (of a person etc.) be conveyed in a wheeled vehicle; *fig.* (of time etc.) go by, elapse. Also (*colloq.*), start moving. E16. ▸**e** *verb intrans. & trans.* Of a celestial object: perform a periodical revolution; traverse (a distance) in doing this. E17. ▸**f** *verb trans. & intrans.* Esp. in CINEMATOGRAPHY. (Cause to) begin action or operation. M20. ▸**g** *verb trans. & intrans.* Display or be displayed moving on a cinema or television screen (as) on a roller. M20.
3 *verb intrans.* (Of the sea, a river, etc.) flow with an undulating motion, heave or surge onwards; move or advance with an undulating or a wavelike motion; (of smoke etc.) ascend or descend in rolls or curls. LME. ▸**b** *verb trans.* Carry or propel with an undulating motion; cause (smoke etc.) to ascend or descend in rolls. M17. ▸**c** *verb intrans. fig.* Pour in; flow *in* plentifully. E18. ▸**d** *verb intrans.* Of land: undulate; extend in gentle falls and rises. Chiefly as ROLLING *adjective.* E19.
4 *verb intrans.* Wander, roam. LME.
5 *verb trans.* Turn (a thing) round on itself or about an axis; form into a more or less cylindrical or spherical shape by doing this; make by forming material into a cylinder or ball. Also foll. by *up*. LME. ▸**b** *verb intrans.* Form into a roll; curl up *into* a specified shape. Also foll. by *up*. LME. ▸**c** *verb trans.* Form into a mass. M16.
6 *verb trans.* Wrap or envelop *in* something. Also foll. by *up*. LME.
7 *verb trans.* Flatten, level, or form by passing a roller etc. over or by passing between rollers. Also foll. by *out*. LME. ▸**b** *verb trans.* Of flowing water: make (stone or rock) smooth and round by attrition. Chiefly as ***rolled*** *ppl adjective.* E19. ▸**c** *verb intrans.* Turn out or *out* after being flattened or levelled. E19.
8 a *verb intrans.* Move or sail with an irregular, swaying, or rocking motion; *transf.* walk with an unsteady swaying gait. L15. ▸**b** *verb intrans.* (Of a boat or vehicle) sway to and fro on an axis parallel to the direction of motion. (Of an aircraft) turn about its longitudinal axis. E17. ▸**c** *verb trans.* Cause to sway to and fro. E19. ▸**d** *verb trans.* Rob (esp. someone drunk, drugged, or sleeping). *slang.* L19.
9 a *verb intrans.* (Of thunder etc.) reverberate; produce a deep continuous reverberating sound; (of language, sound, etc.) flow in deep or mellow tones. E16. ▸**b** *verb trans.* Utter or articulate with a reverberating, vibratory, or trilling effect; *spec.* pronounce (a consonant, esp. *r*) with a trill. M16.
†**10** *verb intrans.* [translating Hebrew *gālal.*] In biblical use: rely *on* God. M16–M17.
11 *US.* **a** *verb intrans.* Play bowls. M19. ▸**b** *verb trans.* Bowl (a game making a specified score, a number of strikes). L20.

1a B. BAINBRIDGE She wasn't rolling about in the gutter with a bottle of meths. P. CAREY As the . . car slid sideways, she thought . . it would roll. S. COOPER She rolled over in the still water. M. FORSTER She liked her baby to have . . liberty to roll around. **b** J. DICKEY I went back to the man on the ground . . and rolled him on to his back. **d** H. B. STOWE Rolling up his eyes, and giving . . droll glances. J. IRVING Her eyes were almost completely rolled up into her head. **2a** J. STEINBECK Candy rolled to the edge of his bunk. J. M. COETZEE He knocked over an empty bottle which rolled away. F. KAPLAN Tears rolled down his cheeks. **b** N. TINBERGEN A gull rolls a misplaced egg back into its nest. **c** G. VIDAL His secretary rolled a portable bar toward us. **d** M. L. KING We waited for the next bus. In fifteen minutes it rolled down the street. **g** R. RAYNER The camera shows . . the fear on her face, and the end credits roll. **3** J. RABAN Breakers were rolling in from the open Atlantic. P. D. JAMES Storm clouds . . were rolling in from the West. **5** A. CARTER Her sleeves were rolled up, revealing forearms of great strength. *Rolling Stone* Loretta wets her hair . . and rolls it on . . curlers. M. MOORCOCK He tries to roll a cigarette out of newspaper and tea-leaves. **b** T. HOOD The wood-louse dropped and rolled into a ball. **c** E. WAUGH He rolled the cable . . into a ball and threw it into the corner. **6** C. READE Gerard rolled himself in the bed-clothes. **7** E. BOWEN The curate, rolling the cricket-pitch in the Rectory field. BETTY SMITH Sissy took a ball of . . dough, rolled it flat with the rolling-pin. **8a** B. BAINBRIDGE He rolled walrus-fashion along the path. **b** E. WAUGH The ship rolled heavily in an apparently calm sea. **9a** M. MUGGERIDGE The . . Scottish voice with the R's rolling . . like thunder. N. SAHGAL Fluent phrases . . rolled off his tongue. W. HORWOOD Behind him distant thunder rolled. **b** HUGH WALPOLE Although she rolled her r's her Glebeshire accent was not . . strong. W. GASS I roll the words on my . . tongue.

Phrases: **be rolling (in it)** *colloq.* be very rich. ***have people rolling in the aisles***: see AISLE 2. ***heads will roll***: see HEAD *noun.* ***keep the ball rolling***: see BALL *noun*[1] 2. **rolled gold**: in the form of a thin coating applied to a baser metal by rolling. ***roll in the hay***: see HAY *noun*[1]. **rolled into one** combined into one person or thing. **rolled oats**: which have been husked and crushed. **roll the bones** *US slang* play dice. **roll with the punches** (of a boxer) move the body away from an opponents's blows in order to lessen the impact; *fig.* adapt oneself to difficult circumstances. ***start the ball rolling***: see BALL *noun*[1] 2.
With adverbs in specialized senses: **roll back** *N. Amer.* reduce, cause (esp. prices) to decrease. **roll in** (*a*) COMPUTING transfer (data) from an auxiliary store to a main memory when required; (cf. ***roll out*** below); (*b*) (of audio apparatus) exhibit a response increasing smoothly from zero with increasing signal frequency; (cf. ***roll off*** below). **roll off** (*a*) (of audio apparatus) exhibit a response decreasing smoothly to zero with increasing signal frequency; (*b*) cause (the frequency response of audio apparatus) to decrease smoothly at the end of its range; (cf. ***roll in*** above). **roll on** (*a*) put on or apply by rolling; (*b*) ***roll on*** —, may — come or happen soon; (see also sense 2d above). **roll out** (*a*) *US colloq.* get out of bed, get up; (*b*) COMPUTING transfer (data) from a main memory to an

auxiliary store when a program of greater priority requires the former; (cf. *roll in* above). **roll over** (*a*) send (a person) sprawling or rolling; (*b*) ECONOMICS finance the repayment of (maturing stock etc.) by the issue of new stock. **roll up** (*a*) *colloq.* congregate, assemble; arrive, appear on the scene; (*b*) MILITARY drive the flank of (an enemy line) back and round so that the line is shortened or surrounded; (*c*) **roll up one's sleeves**: see SLEEVE *noun*; (see also senses 5, 5b, 6 above).

Comb.: **rollaway** *noun & adjective* (a bed) that may be removed on wheels or castors; **roll-back** (*a*) the action or an act of rolling backwards; (*b*) *N. Amer.* a reduction or decrease, esp. in price; **roll-in/roll-out** COMPUTING the process of switching data between main and auxiliary memories in order to process several tasks simultaneously; paging; **roll-off** (*a*) in ten-pin bowling, a game to resolve a tie; (*b*) the smooth fall of response with frequency of a piece of audio equipment at the end of its range; (cf. *roll off* above); **roll-out** (*a*) the official wheeling out of a new aircraft or spacecraft; *transf.* the official introduction of new equipment etc.; (*b*) the part of a landing during which an aircraft travels along the runway losing speed; (*c*) AMER. FOOTBALL a play in which a quarterback moves out from the blockers before attempting to pass; **roll-over** (*a*) *colloq.* the overturning of a vehicle etc.; (*b*) ECONOMICS the extension or transfer of a debt or other financial relationship; *spec.* reinvestment of money realized on the maturing of stocks etc.; (*c*) a facility on an electronic keyboard enabling one or several keystrokes to be registered correctly while another key is depressed; **roll-top** *adjective & noun* (*a*) *adjective* (esp. of a desk) having a flexible cover sliding in curved grooves; (*b*) *noun* (the flexible cover of) a roll-top desk; **rollway** *US* (*a*) a slope made for rolling logs down into water; (*b*) a pile of logs on a river-bank awaiting transportation; **roll-your-own** *colloq.* a hand-rolled cigarette.

■ **rolla'bility** *noun* ability to roll, ease of rolling L20. **rollable** *adjective* able to be rolled E18. **rolly** *adjective* (*rare*) characterized by rolling L19.

roller /ˈrəʊlə/ *noun*[1] & *verb*. Also (*Scot.*) **rower** /ˈrəʊə/. ME.
[from prec. + -ER[1].]
▶ **A** *noun*. **I 1** A hard revolving cylinder used to lessen the friction of anything passed over it; each of a set of these used to move a heavy object. ME. ▸**b** The revolvable barrel of a winch or windlass. M17. ▸**c** *gen.* Any revolving cylinder, *esp.* one forming part of a driving mechanism; a short cylinder serving as a wheel. M17.
2 A heavy, now usu. metal, cylinder fitted in a frame, used for flattening, levelling, stamping, crushing, or rolling; each of a set of these for forming metal etc. into bars or sheets; *spec.* (long *obsolete* exc. *Scot. dial.*) a rolling-pin. LME.
3 A person who rolls something; *spec.* (*Austral.*) a person who trims and rolls fleeces in a shearing shed. LME. ▸**b** An insect which causes leaves to roll up, *esp.* the larva of any of various tortricid moths. M19. ▸**c** A thief, *esp.* one whose victims are drugged, sleeping, or drunk. Chiefly *N. Amer. slang.* E20.
4 a A cylindrical piece of wood, metal, or plastic, *esp.* one on which cloth or other material is rolled up. M16. ▸**b** Orig., a curl-paper. Now usu., a small metal or plastic cylinder round which the hair is rolled for curling. Usu. in *pl.* L18.
5 A revolving cylinder of some absorbent material, mounted on an axis and used to ink a forme etc. in printing or to apply paint to a flat surface. L18.
▶ **II 6** More fully ***roller-bandage***. A long surgical bandage formed into a roll for easy and firm application. LME. ▸**b** A swaddling-band. Now *arch. & dial.* M17. ▸**c** A broad padded girth for a horse. L17. ▸**d** A roll of carded wool; a long heap of hay etc. *dial.* M19.
7 A long swelling wave, moving with a steady sweep or roll. E19.
8 †**a** In *pl.* The London horse and foot police patrol. *slang. rare.* Only in E19. ▸**b** A police officer. *US slang.* M20.
9 A variety of tumbler pigeon. M19.
10 A person who rolls or sways from side to side; *esp.* = ***holy roller*** s.v. HOLY *adjective*. M19. ▸**b** A ship that rolls. L19. ▸**c** BASEBALL. A ball that rolls along the ground after being hit. L19.
11 A control in an aircraft for regulating roll. M20.
Phrases: ***high roller***: see HIGH *adjective, adverb, & noun*. ***holy roller***: see HOLY *adjective*.
Comb.: **roller arena** a roller-skating rink; **rollerball** a ball-point pen using relatively thin ink; ***roller bandage***: see sense 6 above; **roller bearing**: like a ball-bearing but with small cylinders instead of balls; **roller bit** OIL INDUSTRY a drilling bit in which the cutting teeth are on rotating conical or circular cutters; **rollerblade** *noun & verb* (*a*) *noun* (**R-**) (proprietary name for) a boot shaped like an ice-skating boot but with a set of small wheels fixed underneath, one behind the other, for roller-skating in the manner of ice-skating; (*b*) *verb intrans.* skate on such a pair of boots; **rollerblader** a person who skates on Rollerblades; **roller-board** MUSIC: carrying the rollers in an organ; **roller-coast** *verb intrans.* = ***roller-coaster*** (*c*) below; **roller-coaster** *noun, adjective, & verb* (*a*) *noun* a switchback railway at a fairground or amusement park; (*b*) *adjective* that goes up and down, or changes repeatedly or suddenly; (*c*) *verb intrans.* go up and down or change repeatedly or suddenly; **roller-coat** *verb trans.* apply (paint) with a roller; **roller derby** a type of speed-skating competition on roller-skates; **roller disco**: at which the dancers wear roller-skates; disco-dancing on roller-skates; **roller drier** a heated drum in which milk is dried to produce milk powder; **roller-gin** a cotton-gin in which cleaning is effected by rollers; **roller hockey**: played on roller-skates; **roller-skate** *noun & verb* (*a*) *noun* a metal frame with four small wheels, fitted to a shoe for gliding across a hard surface; a skate with wheels instead of a blade; (*b*) *verb intrans.* move on roller-skates; **roller-skater** a person who roller-skates; **roller steady** ENGINEERING a device consisting of two rollers which grip an article being turned on a lathe; **roller-towel** a towel with the ends joined, hung on a roller; **roller tube** BIOLOGY a tube which is continually rotated so as to moisten with nutrient solution the cells or tissue being grown in it.
▶ **B** *verb trans.* Form into rolls. Chiefly *dial.* E19.

roller /ˈrəʊlə/ *noun*[2]. L17.
[German, from *rollen* to roll.]
Any of various brightly coloured crow-sized birds of the genera *Coracias* and *Eurystomus*, constituting the family Coraciidae, *esp.* (more fully ***common roller***) *C. garrulus* of southern Europe and central Asia. Also (with specifying word), any bird of certain related families.
cuckoo roller a large, mainly grey bird, *Leptosomus discolor*, of Madagascar and the Comoro Islands, sole member of the family Leptosomatidae. **ground roller** any of various short-winged Madagascan birds of the family Brachypteracidae.

Roller /ˈrəʊlə/ *noun*[3]. *colloq.* L20.
[from ROLL(S-ROYCE + -ER[6].]
A car made by Rolls-Royce.

rollick /ˈrɒlɪk/ *verb & noun*. E19.
[Prob. of dial. origin; perh. blend of ROMP *verb* and FROLIC *verb*.]
▶ **A** *verb intrans.* Be high-spirited or exuberant; romp, revel. E19.
> 📖 P. H. NEWBY The porpoises .. played around, rollicked.

▶ **B** *noun*. **1** Exuberant gaiety. M19.
2 A romp, an escapade. L19.
■ **rollicker** *noun* E19. **rollicky** *adjective* (*rare*) given to rollicking L19.

rollicking /ˈrɒlɪkɪŋ/ *noun*. In sense 2 also **rollock-** /ˈrɒlək-/. M19.
[from prec. + -ING[1]. In sense 2 euphem. alt. of *bollocking*.]
1 The action of ROLLICK *verb*. M19.
2 A telling-off, a severe reprimand. *colloq.* M20.

rollicking /ˈrɒlɪkɪŋ/ *adjective*. E19.
[from ROLLICK *verb* + -ING[2].]
Exuberant, high-spirited; lively.
> 📖 M. SEYMOUR A rollicking novel set in Ireland.

rolling /ˈrəʊlɪŋ/ *noun*. LME.
[from ROLL *verb* + -ING[1].]
1 The action of ROLL *verb*; an instance of this. LME. ▸**b** = LOGROLLING 2a. *US.* E19.
†**2** The action or an act of bandaging; a bandage. LME–L17.
3 A curve; a turn, a fold. L16. ▸**b** In *pl.*, paper and tobacco for rolling a cigarette; a hand-rolled cigarette (usu. in *pl.*). *N. Amer. colloq.* E20.
Comb.: **rolling chamber** a compartment for water-ballast extending across the beam of a ship; **rolling-mill** a machine or factory by or in which metal etc. is rolled into shape; **rolling moment** the moment acting on an aircraft about its longitudinal axis; **rolling paper** *US* a cigarette paper (usu. in *pl.*); **rolling-pin** a cylinder of esp. wood, for rolling out pastry, dough, etc., to the required thickness; **rolling-press** (*a*) a copperplate-printers' press in which the plate passes in a bed under a revolving cylinder; (*b*) a press which flattens, smooths, etc., by means of rollers.

rolling /ˈrəʊlɪŋ/ *adjective*. LME.
[from ROLL *verb* + -ING[2].]
1 That rolls. LME.
2 *transf.* †**a** Of a person, personal opinions, etc.: changeable, shifting, inconstant. M16–L18. ▸**b** Progressive; increasing; subject to periodic review. E18. ▸**c** Staggered; *esp.* (of strikes etc.) taking place in different places in succession. M20.
> 📖 **1** *Proverb*: A rolling stone gathers no moss. **2b** *Times* The Post Office .. has a five-year rolling programme .. to spend £3,000m.

Special collocations: **rolling barrage** = CREEPING *barrage*. **rolling boil** COOKERY a continuous boil, above a simmer. **rolling drunk** *adjective* swaying or staggering from drunkenness. **rolling hitch** a kind of hitch used to attach a rope to a spar or larger rope. **rolling lift bridge** a type of bascule bridge. **rolling news** a broadcast news service in which a channel or station is dedicated entirely to news reports, which are broadcast 24 hours a day. **rolling-stock** (*a*) the locomotives, carriages, or other vehicles, used on a railway; (*b*) *US* the road vehicles of a company. **rolling stone** *fig.* a person unwilling to settle for long in one place.
■ **rollingly** *adverb* (now *rare*) M16.

rollio /ˈrɒlɪəʊ/ *noun*. Pl. **-os**. E19.
[Alt.]
= ROULEAU 3.

rollmop /ˈrəʊlmɒp/ *noun*. Also **-mops** /-mɒps/. E20.
[German *Rollmops*.]
A rolled uncooked pickled herring fillet.

rollocking *noun* see ROLLICKING *noun*.

rollocks /ˈrɒləks/ *noun pl. slang.* M20.
[Euphem. alt. of BOLLOCK *noun*. Cf. ROLLICKING *noun* 2.]
= BOLLOCK *noun* 2.

roll-on /ˈrəʊlɒn/ *adjective & noun*. M20.
[from *roll on* s.v. ROLL *verb*.]
▶ **A** *adjective*. That rolls on; *esp.* (of a deodorant, cosmetic, etc.) applied by means of a rotating ball in the neck of the container. M20.
▶ **B** *noun*. **1** A roll-on deodorant, cosmetic, etc. M20.
2 A light elastic corset. M20.
Comb.: **roll-on roll-off** *adjectival phr.* designating a ship (esp. a passenger ferry), a method of transport, etc., in which vehicles are driven directly on at the start of the voyage and off at the end (abbreviation *ro-ro*).

roll-over /ˈrəʊləʊvə/ *noun*. Orig. *US.* M20.
[from *roll over* s.v. ROLL *verb*.]
1 An overturning, a turning upside down; a complete revolution. M20.
2 ECONOMICS. The extension or transfer of a debt or other financial relationship; *spec.* reinvestment of money realized on the maturing of stocks, bonds, etc.; an issue of stocks or bonds replacing one which matures. M20.
3 A facility on an electronic keyboard enabling one or several keystrokes to be registered correctly while another key is still depressed, thereby facilitating rapid typing. L20.
4 In a lottery: the cumulative carry-over of prize money from one draw to the next, typically added to the value of the jackpot; an accumulated jackpot, or a lottery draw with such a jackpot. L20.

Rolls-Royce /rəʊlzˈrɔɪs/ *noun*. E20.
[Proprietary name for a type of luxury motor car, from Charles Stewart *Rolls* (1877–1910), English motorist and aviator + Sir (Frederick) Henry *Royce* (1863–1933), English engineer and founder of the Rolls-Royce company.]
A thing considered to be of the highest quality.
> 📖 P. CAREY She made her famous .. crumble and sweetened it with the Rolls Royce of honeys.

roll-up /ˈrəʊlʌp/ *noun & adjective*. M18.
[from *roll up* s.v. ROLL *verb*.]
▶ **A** *noun*. †**1** In *pl.* Stockings with tops designed to be rolled up or down the legs. M18–E19.
2 a = ROLY-POLY *noun* 3. Also (*N. Amer.*), an article of food rolled up into a cylinder and stuffed with a filling. M19. ▸**b** An article of luggage rolled up and secured by means of a strap. M19. ▸**c** A hand-rolled cigarette. *slang.* M20.
3 An assembly, a meeting. *Austral. slang.* M19.
4 = ***roll-up fund*** below. L20.
▶ **B** *adjective*. That can be rolled up; made by rolling up. E20.
roll-up fund an investment fund in which the return is reinvested to attract capital gains tax rather than income tax.

Rolodex /ˈrəʊlə(ʊ)dɛks/ *noun*. *N. Amer.* M20.
[Invented name.]
(Proprietary name for) a desktop card index for addresses and telephone numbers, in the form of a rotating spindle or small tray to which removable cards are attached.

roloway /ˈrəʊləweɪ/ *noun*. L18.
[W. African name.]
A diana monkey of a race distinguished by its long white beard.

rolwagen /ˈrəʊlwag(ə)n/ *noun*. Also (earlier) †**row-wagon**. M18.
[Dutch, lit. 'roll-wagon'.]
A kind of Chinese K'ang-Hsi blue and white cylindrical porcelain vase; a Dutch imitation of this.

roly-poly /rəʊlɪˈpəʊli/ *noun & adjective*. E17.
[Fanciful formation from ROLL *verb*.]
▶ **A** *noun*. †**1** A worthless person; a rascal. Only in E17.
2 a Any of various games involving the rolling of a ball at a target. E18. ▸**b** An act of rolling over and over down a bank or grassy slope; a children's game involving this. E19.
3 A pudding made of a sheet of suet pastry covered with jam etc., formed into a roll and steamed or baked. M19.
4 Any of several bushy plants of arid regions of Australia which break off and are rolled by the wind; esp. *Sclerolaena muricata*, of the goosefoot family. M19.
▶ **B** *adjective*. †**1** Trifling, worthless. Only in L17.
2 Esp. of a child: podgy, dumpy, plump. E19.
Special collocations: **roly-poly pudding** = sense A.3 above.

ROM *abbreviation*.
COMPUTING. Read-only memory.

Rom /rɒm/ *noun*. Pl. ***Roma*** /ˈrɒmə/, same. M19.
[Romany = man, husband, cogn. with DOM *noun*[2] & *adjective*.]
A (male) Gypsy, a Romany.

Rom. *abbreviation*[1].
Romans (New Testament).

rom. *abbreviation*[2].
Roman (type).

Romagnol /rəʊmə'njɒl/ *noun & adjective*. Also **-ole** /-əʊl/. E19.
[Italian *Romagnolo*, from *Romagna* (see below).]
▶ **A** *noun*. A native or inhabitant of the Romagna, a district of northern Italy (now part of the region of Emilia-Romagna). E19.
▶ **B** *adjective*. Of or pertaining to the Romagna or its inhabitants. E19.
■ **Romagnese** *adjective* = ROMAGNOL *adjective* M20. **Romagnola** /rəʊmə'njəʊlə, *foreign* roma'ɲo:la/ *noun* (an animal of) an Italian breed of large cattle characterized by a silver-grey hide with a white dorsal stripe M20.

Romaic /rə(ʊ)'meɪɪk/ *adjective & noun*. E19.
[mod. Greek *romaiikos*, from mod. Greek, Greek *Rhōmaikos* Roman, from *Rhōmē* Rome (used spec. of the Eastern empire): see -IC.]
(Of or pertaining to) the vernacular language of modern Greece.

Romaika /rə(ʊ)'meɪkə/ *noun*. E17.
[mod.Greek *rhomaikē* from fem. of *Rhōmaikos*: see prec.]
†**1** = ROMAIC *noun*. Only in E17.
2 A modern Greek folk-dance. E19.

romaine /rə(ʊ)'meɪn/ *noun*. E20.
[French, fem. of *romain* Roman.]
1 A cos lettuce. Also more fully ***romaine lettuce***. Chiefly *N. Amer.* E20.
2 Any of various crêpe fabrics; *spec.* (more fully ***Romaine crêpe***) a semi-sheer crêpe fabric of silk, rayon, or acetate. E20.
¶ *Romaine crêpe* is a US proprietary name.

romaji /'rəʊmədʒi/ *noun*. E20.
[Japanese, from *rōma* Roman + *ji* letter(s).]
A system of Romanized spelling for transliterating Japanese.

romal /rəʊ'mɑ:l/ *noun*. Also **ru-** /ru:-/. L17.
[Persian, Urdu *rūmāl*, from *rū* face + *māl* (base of Persian *mālidan* wipe) wiping.]
1 A silk or cotton square or handkerchief, sometimes worn in the Indian sub-continent as a head-dress; a thin, often checked, silk or cotton fabric made in the Indian sub-continent. L17.
2 *Hist*. The handkerchief or bandage used by Indian Thugs to strangle their victims. M19.

Romalis /rəʊ'mɑ:lɪs/ *noun*. M19.
[Spanish.]
A Spanish Gypsy dance; a piece of music for this dance.

Roman /'rəʊmən/ *noun*[1]. OE.
[In sense 1 directly from Latin *Romanus* (see ROMAN *adjective*); in other senses formed as ROMAN *adjective*.]
1 a A native or inhabitant of ancient Rome; a citizen, soldier, etc., belonging to the ancient Roman Republic or Empire. OE. ▸**b** A native or inhabitant of medieval or modern Rome. M16.
2 In *pl*. The Christians of ancient Rome; in *pl*. (treated as *sing*.), St Paul's Epistle to the Romans, a book of the New Testament. LME.
3 A member of the Roman Catholic Church. M16.
4 a The Italian dialect of modern Rome. L16. ▸**b** Latin. *rare*. M17.
5 (**r-**.) Roman type; in *pl*., letters of a roman font. Cf. ROMAN *adjective* 3. L16.
Phrases: **Emperor of the Romans**, **King of the Romans** *Hist*. the sovereign head of the Holy Roman Empire.

roman /rɔmɑ̃, rəʊ'mɑ:n/ *noun*[2]. Pl. pronounced same. M18.
[French.]
The French for 'a romance, a novel', occurring in various phrases used in English
■ ***roman-à-clef*** /a kle, ɑ: 'kleɪ/, pl. ***romans-à-clef*** (pronounced same), [lit. 'novel with a key'] a novel in which actual people or events appear under fictitious names L19. ***roman à thèse*** /a 'tɛ:z/, pl. ***romans à thèse*** (pronounced same), [lit. 'novel with a thesis'] a novel that seeks to expound or promote a theory M19. ***roman de geste*** /də 'ʒɛst/, pl. ***romans de geste*** (pronounced same) = CHANSON ***de geste*** M19. ***roman-fleuve*** /-flœ:v/, pl. ***romans-fleuves*** (pronounced same), [lit. 'river novel'] a novel featuring the leisurely description of the lives and members of a family; a sequence of self-contained novels: M20. ***roman noir*** /nwa:r/, pl. ***-s -s*** (pronounced same), [lit. 'black novel'] a Gothic novel, a thriller M20. ***roman policier*** /pɔlisje/, pl. ***-s -s*** (pronounced same), a detective novel or story E20.

roman /'rəʊmən/ *noun*[3]. *S. Afr*. Pl. same. L18.
[from Afrikaans *rooi* red + *man* man.]
ZOOLOGY. **1** A marine fish, *Chrysoblephus laticeps* (family Sparidae), having reddish skin. L18.
2 A large nocturnal sun-spider (solifugid) with a reddish body. E20.

Roman /'rəʊmən/ *noun*[4]. M19.
[from ROMANY.]
A Romany.

Roman /'rəʊmən/ *adjective*. See also ROMAYNE. ME.
[Old & mod. French *Romain* from Latin *Romanus*, from *Roma* ROME: see -AN.]
1 Of, pertaining or belonging to, connected with, or originating from ancient Rome, its territory, or its inhabitants; holding the position of an ancient Roman citizen; current among the ancient Romans. ME. ▸**b** Of language, speech, etc.: Latin. ME.
†**2** = ROMANCE *adjective* 1. LME–E19.
3 (Now usu. **r-**.) (Of printed type) of a plain upright kind resembling that of ancient Roman inscriptions and manuscripts, esp. as distinguished from Gothic and italic; (of handwriting) round and bold. E16.
4 Of antiquities etc.: belonging to or surviving from the time of the ancient Romans. M16.
5 Of, pertaining to, or characteristic of the Church in Rome; Roman Catholic. M16.
6 Of a character exemplified by or ascribed to the ancient Romans. L16. ▸**b** Of a nose: having a high bridge; aquiline. E17.
7 Of, pertaining to, or originating from medieval or modern Rome or its inhabitants. L16. ▸**b** *BRIDGE*. Designating, of, or pertaining to a bidding system introduced by certain Italian players. M20.
8 *ARCHITECTURE*. = COMPOSITE *adjective* 2. E17.
9 Of, designating, or occurring in the alphabet developed by the ancient Romans or any modern alphabet based on it with letters A–Z. E18.
10 Engaged in the study of Roman law, antiquities, history, etc. M19.

> 📖 **1** MILTON To rescue Israel from the Roman yoke. J. RUSKIN Just where the Roman galleys used to be moored. **3** *Library* The use of Roman punctuation marks immediately following italicized words. **5** GLADSTONE The . . doctrine of the Roman theologians.

Special collocations, comb., & phrases: **Holy Roman Empire** *Hist*. the Western part of the Roman Empire as revived by Charlemagne in 800. ***Prince of the Holy Roman Church***: see PRINCE *noun*. **Roman alum** a reddish native alum found in Italy; a manufactured imitation of this. **Roman balance** = STEELYARD *noun*[2]. **Roman candle** (*a*) a firework discharging a succession of flaming coloured balls, sparks, etc.; (*b*) *slang* a parachute jump on which the parachute fails to open; (*c*) *slang* a Roman Catholic. **Roman cement** = PARKER'S CEMENT. **Roman Empire** *Hist*. the empire established by Augustus in 27 BC and divided by Theodosius in AD 395 into the Western or Latin and Eastern or Greek Empires. **Roman father** a dominating head of a family. **Roman fever** (*a*) *Hist*. a type of malaria formerly prevalent at Rome; (*b*) *fig*. (*derog*.) a strongly felt attraction towards the Roman Catholic Church, its ritual, beliefs, etc., on the part of an Anglican or other non-Catholic. **Roman foot** an ancient Roman unit of length, equal to 11.64 inches (approx. 296 mm). **Roman holiday** (an event occasioning) enjoyment or profit derived from the suffering or discomfiture of others; a pitiable spectacle. ***Roman HYACINTH***. **Roman law** the code of law developed by the ancient Romans and forming the basis of many modern codes. **Roman mile** an ancient Roman unit of length, equal to approx. 1620 yards (1480 m). **Roman nettle** a severely stinging nettle of southern Europe, *Urtica pilulifera*, which bears the female flowers in globose heads. **Roman-nosed** *adjective* having a Roman nose. **Roman numeral** any of the letters representing numbers in the Roman numerical system: I = 1, V = 5, X = 10, L = 50, C = 100, D = 500, M = 1000. **Roman snail** a large European snail, *Helix pomatia*, long valued as food. **Roman tub** *US* a large sunken bathtub. **Roman uncial** = ***half-uncial*** s.v. HALF-. **Roman vitriol** *arch*. copper sulphate. **Roman wormwood** (*a*) a wormwood of central and eastern Europe, *Artemisia pontica*, used in making absinthe; (*b*) the ragweed *Ambrosia artemisiifolia*, a N. American plant with similar leaves.
■ **Romanly** *adverb* in a Roman manner, after the Roman fashion E17.

Romanaccio /rəʊmə'natʃəʊ, *foreign* roma'nattʃo/ *noun*. M20.
[Italian, from *Romano* Roman + pejorative suffix *-accio*.]
A modern popular Italian dialect spoken in Rome.

Roman Catholic /rəʊmən 'kaθ(ə)lɪk/ *adjectival & noun phr*. L16.
[from ROMAN *adjective* + CATHOLIC.]
▶ **A** *adjectival phr*. Designating or pertaining to the Christian Church which acknowledges the Bishop of Rome (the Pope) as its head. Freq. opp. ***Protestant***. L16.
▶ **B** *noun phr*. A member of the Roman Catholic Church. Freq. opp. ***Protestant***. L16.
■ **Roman Ca'tholicism**, **Roman Catho'licity** *nouns* (adherence to) Roman Catholic doctrine and practice E19.

romance /rə(ʊ)'mans, 'rəʊmans/ *noun & adjective*. ME.
[Old French *romanz*, *-ans* (fem. *-ance*) the vernacular tongue, a work composed in this, from popular Latin adverb formed on Latin *Romanicus*: see ROMANIC, -ANCE.]
▶ **A** *noun*. **1** (**R-**.) Orig., the vernacular language of France, as opp. to Latin. Later also, any of various related languages, as (*a*) Provençal; (*b*) Spanish. Now *esp*., the languages descended from Latin collectively. ME.
2 A medieval vernacular verse, or later prose, narrative relating the legendary or extraordinary adventures of some hero of chivalry. ME.
3 An extravagant fiction; (a) wild exaggeration; (an) inventive falsehood. L15.
4 A Spanish historical ballad or short epic poem. E17.
5 A fictitious usu. prose narrative depicting a setting and events remote from everyday life; *esp*. one of a kind prevalent in the 16th and 17th cents., overlaid with long digressions from the plot. M17.
6 a A literary genre with romantic love or highly imaginative events or adventures forming the central theme; romantic fiction. Also, a work of this genre; a romantic novel or narrative; now *esp*. a love story. M17. ▸**b** Romantic or imaginative character, quality, atmosphere, etc.; *spec*. (*a*) a prevailing sense of wonder or mystery surrounding the mutual attraction in a love affair; (*b*) redolence or suggestion of, or association with the adventurous, chivalrous, or extraordinary. Also, sentimental or idealized love; a love affair. E19.
7 *MUSIC*. A short vocal or instrumental piece of a simple or informal character. L18.

> 📖 **2** K. CLARK Chivalrous romances of the Gothic time . . with their allegories . . and their endless journeys. **3** LD MACAULAY This romance rests on no evidence, and . . seems hardly to deserve confutation. **6a** H. REED Scott . . the great writer of historical romance. **b** A. PHILLIPS The idea of being a country doctor . . still had a romance of its own. L. SPALDING She loved him but the whole romance was fated from the start. C. HEILBRUN Marriage has owed too much to romance, too little to friendship.

▶ **B** *attrib*. or as *adjective*. **1** (**R-**.) Derived or descended from Latin; designating or pertaining to any of the languages descended from Latin; of or pertaining to these languages collectively. LME.
2 Having the character of or attributes associated with romance; chivalrous; romantic. M17.

> 📖 **2** R. BOLDREWOOD An occasional romance gleam through the . . prosaic mist of his ordinary day-dreams.

¶ See also GALLO-ROMANCE, PROTO-ROMANCE, RHAETO-ROMANCE.
■ **romanceishness** *noun* (*rare*) a tendency towards what is romantic M19. **romancical** *adjective* (*rare*) (*a*) of the nature of romances, romantic; (*b*) writing or composing romances: M17. **romancist** *noun* (*rare*) a writer or composer of romances; a romantic novelist: M17.

romance /rə(ʊ)'mans/ *verb*. LME.
[from prec.]
†**1** *verb intrans*. Recite a romance. Only in LME.
2 *verb intrans*. **a** Exaggerate or distort the truth, esp. fantastically; talk hyperbolically. L17. ▸**b** Have romantic or fantastic ideas; use romantic or extravagant language. M19.
3 *verb trans*. Have a romance or love affair with; court, woo. Also, seek to persuade (a rival, client, etc.), esp. by attentiveness or flattery; court the favour of. M20.

> 📖 **2a** SMOLLETT The fellow romanced a little, . . to render the adventure the more marvellous. **3** B. HOLIDAY I was accused of romancing everyone in the band. *Daily Telegraph* Investors . . romanced with . . the glitz and glamour that attend privatisation campaigns.

■ **romancer** *noun* (*a*) a writer of a romance or romances, esp. in the medieval period; (*b*) an inventor of extravagant fictions, a fantastic liar; (*c*) *rare* a romantic person: ME. **romancing** *verbal noun* the action of the verb; *esp*. the use of extravagant fiction or invention: LME.

romancé /rɔmɑ̃se/ *adjective*. *rare*. M20.
[French, from *romancer* fictionalize.]
Esp. of a biography: fictionalized, written in the form of a novel.

romancy /rə(ʊ)'mansi/ *noun*. E17.
[Alt. of ROMANCE *noun*, perh. after Spanish *romance* or Italian *romanzo*.]
†**1** A romance, a romantic narrative. E17–E18.
2 Romance language. *rare*. M19.

romancy /rə(ʊ)'mansi/ *adjective*. M17.
[from ROMANCE *noun* + -Y[1].]
Associated with or redolent of romance; romantic.

Romanensian /rəʊmə'nɛnsɪən/ *adjective & noun*. *rare*. L19.
[from mod. Latin *Romanensis* Roman, from Latin *Romanus* (see ROMAN *adjective*) + *-ensis* belonging to, -ESE + -IAN.]
▶ **A** *adjective*. Tending towards or supporting the Roman Catholic Church. L19.
▶ **B** *noun*. A supporter of the Roman Catholic Church; a Roman Catholic. L19.

Romanes /'rɒmənɪz/ *noun*. M19.
[Romany, adverb from *Romano*: see ROMANY.]
The Romany language.

Romanesco /rəʊmə'nɛskəʊ/ *adjective & noun*. M20.
[Italian, from *Romano* Roman + *-esco* -ESQUE.]
(Of or pertaining to) the main modern dialect of Rome.

Romanese /rəʊmə'ni:z/ *noun*. *rare*. M19
[from ROMAN *noun*[1], *adjective* + -ESE.]
= ROMANSH *noun*.

Romanesque /rəʊmə'nɛsk/ *adjective & noun*. E18.
[French, from *roman* ROMANCE *noun & adjective*: see -ESQUE.]
▶ **A** *adjective*. **1** = ROMANCE *adjective* 1. E18.
†**2** Romantic. L18–M19.
3 Designating or belonging to a style of architecture prevalent in Europe from the 10th to the 12th cent., characterized by massive vaulting and round arches. Cf. NORMAN *adjective* 2. E19.
▶ **B** *noun*. The Romanesque style of architecture. M19.

Romani *noun & adjective* var. of ROMANY.

Romanian /rə(ʊ)ˈmeɪnɪən, rʊ-/ *noun & adjective.* Also **Rou-, Ru-,** /rʊ-/. M19.
[from *Romania* (see below) + -AN.]
▶ **A** *noun.* **1** A native or inhabitant of Romania, a country in SE Europe. M19.
2 The Romance language of Romania. L19.
▶ **B** *adjective.* Of or pertaining to Romania, its inhabitants, or their language. M19.
Romanian stitch = *oriental stitch* s.v. ORIENTAL *adjective.*

Romanic /rəʊˈmanɪk/ *adjective & noun.* E18.
[Latin *Romanicus* from *Romanus* Roman: see -IC.]
▶ **A** *adjective.* **1** = ROMANCE *adjective* 1; *spec.* Proto-Romance. Also, using a Romance language. E18.
2 Derived or descended from the ancient Romans, inheriting aspects of ancient Roman social or political life. M19.
▶ **B** *noun.* = ROMANCE *noun* 1; *spec.* Proto-Romance. E18.
■ **Romanicist** /-nɪsɪst/ *noun* a student of or scholar in Romance languages or literature M20.

romanise *verb* var. of ROMANIZE.

Romanish /ˈrəʊmənɪʃ, *as noun also* rəʊˈmanɪʃ/ *adjective & noun.* OE.
[from (the same root as) ROMAN *adjective* + -ISH¹. As noun perh. from ROMANSH after *English.*]
▶ **A** *adjective.* †**1** = ROMAN *adjective* 1. OE–ME.
2 Belonging to or characteristic of the Roman Catholic Church. L16.
▶ **B** *noun.* = ROMANSH. L17.

Romanism /ˈrəʊmənɪz(ə)m/ *noun.* L17.
[from ROMAN *adjective* + -ISM.]
1 Roman Catholicism. Freq. *derog.* L17.
2 A feature characteristic of classical Roman architecture. E19.
3 (Attachment to) the spirit, people, laws, etc., of the ancient Roman world. L19.

Romanist /ˈrəʊmənɪst/ *noun & adjective.* E16.
[mod. Latin *Romanista*, from ROMAN *adjective* + -IST.]
▶ **A** *noun.* **1** A member or supporter of the Roman Catholic Church. Freq. *derog.* E16.
2 An expert in or student of Roman Law. M17.
3 An expert in or student of Roman antiquities or the Romance languages. M19.
4 Any of several 16th-cent. Dutch and Flemish painters influenced by the techniques of Italian Renaissance artists, esp. those of Raphael and Michelangelo. L19.
▶ **B** *attrib.* or as *adjective.* Belonging or adhering to the Roman Catholic Church. Freq. *derog.* M17.
■ **Romaˈnistic** *adjective* inclining to, tending towards, or characteristic of Roman Catholicism E19.

romanità /romaniˈtaː/ *noun. rare.* E20.
[Italian, from next.]
1 = next. E20.
2 The spirit or influence of the central Roman Catholic authorities; acceptance of papal policy. M20.

romanitas /rəʊˈmaːnɪtaːs, -ˈman-/ *noun.* M20.
[Late Latin from Latin *Romanus* (see ROMAN *adjective*) + *-itas* -ITY. Cf. next.]
The spirit or ideals of ancient Rome.

Romanity /rə(ʊ)ˈmanɪti/ *noun.* M18.
[from ROMAN *adjective* + -ITY. Cf. prec.]
†**1** A Latinism. *rare.* Only in M18.
2 = ROMANITAS. M19.

romanize /ˈrəʊmənʌɪz/ *verb.* Also **-ise.** E17.
[from ROMAN *adjective* + -IZE, or from French *romaniser.*]
1 *verb trans.* Make Roman or Roman Catholic in character; bring under the influence or authority of Rome. E17.
2 *verb intrans.* Follow Roman custom or practice. E17.
3 *verb intrans.* Follow or imitate the practices of Roman Catholicism; become Roman Catholic. M17.
4 *verb trans.* Transliterate into the Roman alphabet; put into roman type. M19.
■ **romaniˈzation** *noun* (*a*) assimilation to Roman customs or models; (*b*) transliteration into Roman characters; a system or example of romanized spelling: L19. **Romanizer** *noun* a person, esp. an Anglican, who favours or adopts practices of the Roman Catholic Church M19.

Romano /rə(ʊ)ˈmaːnəʊ/ *noun.* E20.
[Italian = Roman.]
A strong-tasting hard cheese, originally made in Italy. Also more fully ***Romano cheese.***

Romano- /rə(ʊ)ˈmaːnəʊ/ *combining form.* M19.
[from ROMAN *adjective* + -O-.]
Forming adjective and noun combs. with the sense 'Roman (and)' as ***Romano-British, Romano-Briton, Romano-Germanic.***

Romanowsky /rəʊməˈnɒfski/ *noun.* E20.
[D. L. *Romanowsky* (1861–1921), Russian physician.]
BIOLOGY & MEDICINE. Used *attrib.* and in *possess.* to designate a class of stains and techniques for the detection of parasites in blood.

Romansh /rə(ʊ)ˈmanʃ, -ˈmaːnʃ/ *noun & adjective.* Also **Ru-** /rʊ-/, **-sch, -tsch** /-(t)ʃ/. M17.
[Romansh *Ruman(t)sch, Roman(t)sch*, from medieval Latin *romanice*, formed as ROMANIC.]
(Designating or pertaining to) a group of Rhaeto-Romance dialects spoken in the Swiss canton of Grisons.

romantic /rə(ʊ)ˈmantɪk/ *adjective & noun.* M17.
[from ROMAUNT + -IC.]
▶ **A** *adjective.* **1 a** Of a narrative etc.: having the nature or qualities of romance in form or content. M17. ▸**b** Tending towards or characterized by romance as a stylistic basis or principle of literature, art, or music (freq. as opp. to ***classical***); *spec.* (usu. **R-**) designating or pertaining to a movement or style during the late 18th and early 19th cents. in Europe marked by an emphasis on feeling, individuality, and passion rather than classical form and order, and preferring grandeur or picturesqueness to finish and proportion. E19. ▸**c** Of a story, novel, film, etc.; having romance or a love affair as its subject. M20.
2 Of, characterized by, or suggestive of, an idealized, fantastic, or sentimental view of life, love, or reality; appealing to the imagination and feelings. M17. ▸**b** Inclined towards romance; readily influenced by the imagination; imaginative; idealistic. E18.
3 a Of a statement, story, etc.: fabulous, fictitious; unfounded. M17. ▸†**b** Unreal; purely imaginary. M17–E18.
4 Of a project etc.: fantastic, quixotic; impractical. L17.

> 🕮 **1b** *Literary Review* In theory, avant gardism is romantic individualism taken to its extreme conclusion. *Country Walking* Attracting . . tourists in the days of Wordsworth and the Romantic Movement. **2** C. M. YONGE Wedded affection was not lacking, but romantic love was thought an unnecessary preliminary. J. R. GREEN The romantic daring of Drake's voyage . . roused a general enthusiasm throughout England. M. MOORCOCK I enjoyed Esmé's company as an equal but felt nothing romantic towards her. **4** J. PLAMENATZ A romantic side to his talk about revolution . . in the abstract.

▶ **B** *noun.* **1** In *pl.* Features, ideas, etc., characteristic or suggestive of romance. Now *rare.* L17.
2 (Freq. **R-**.) An adherent or practitioner of romanticism in the arts; a romanticist. Also, a romantic, sentimental, or idealistic person. E19.
■ **romantical** *adjective* (now *rare*) having a romantic character or tendency L17. **romantiˈcality** *noun* (*rare*) a romantic thing or characteristic M19. **romantically** *adverb* (*a*) in a romantic manner; (*b*) picturesquely: L17. **romanticalness** *noun* (*rare*) romantic quality or character L18. **romanˈticity** *noun* (now *rare* or *obsolete*) romantic quality or character L18. †**romanticly** *adverb* romantically L17–E19. **romanticness** *noun* (*rare*) romantic quality or character M18.

romanticise *verb* var. of ROMANTICIZE.

romanticism /rə(ʊ)ˈmantɪsɪz(ə)m/ *noun.* In sense 1 also **R-.** E19.
[from prec. + -ISM.]
1 The romantic movement or style in art, literature, or music; (adherence to) the spirit of this movement. E19.
2 A tendency towards romance or romantic views. M19.

> 🕮 **1** J. M. ROBERTS That profound welling-up of human energies and creativity which we call Romanticism. **2** N. SHERRY Fortune . . turned him from romanticism to a cynical realism.

■ **romanticist** *noun & adjective* (*a*) *noun* an exponent or admirer of romanticism in literature, art, or music; (*b*) *adjective* of or pertaining to romanticism or romanticists: E19.

romanticize /rə(ʊ)ˈmantɪsʌɪz/ *verb.* Also **-ise.** E19.
[from ROMANTIC *adjective* + -IZE.]
1 *verb trans.* Make romantic or unrealistic in character; describe or portray in a romantic fashion. E19.
2 *verb intrans.* Indulge in romantic thoughts, words, or actions. M19.

> 🕮 **1** G. GREENE If we romanticize the horrible end of the Archduke . . we lose all sense of tragedy. **2** *Daily Telegraph* Too willing to romanticize about the past.

■ **romanticiˈzation** *noun* the action of romanticizing; an instance of this: M20.

romantism /rə(ʊ)ˈmantɪz(ə)m/ *noun. rare.* L19.
[French *romantisme*, from *romantique* ROMANTIC + *-isme* -ISM.]
Romanticism; romance-writing.
■ **romantist** *noun* (*rare*) a romanticist L19.

Romantsch *noun & adjective* var. of ROMANSH.

Romany /ˈrɒməni, ˈrəʊ-/ *noun & adjective.* Also **-ni.** E19.
[Romany *Romani* fem. and pl. of *Romano* adjective, from ROM.]
▶ **A** *noun.* Pl. **-nies, -nis.**
1 A Gypsy. E19.
2 The language of the Gypsies, prob. of Indo-Aryan origin but with regional variations reflecting contact with other languages. E19.
▶ **B** *adjective.* Of or pertaining to the Gypsies or their language. M19.
Romany chal a male Gypsy. **Romany chi** /tʃʌɪ/ [Romany *chai* girl] a Gypsy girl. **Romany rye** a man, not a Gypsy, who associates with Gypsies.

romanza /roˈmanθa, -tsa, -zə/ *noun.* M19.
[Spanish or Italian, from popular Latin adverb whence also ROMANCE *noun.*]
MUSIC. A romantic song or melody; a lyrical piece of music; = ROMANCE *noun* 7.

Romanze /roˈmantsə/ *noun.* Pl. ***-zen*** /-tsən/. L19.
[German, lit. 'romance'.]
MUSIC. A composition of a tender or lyrical character; *spec.* a slow romantic instrumental piece or movement.

romaunt /rə(ʊ)ˈmɔːnt/ *noun & adjective. arch.* M16.
[Old French *roma(u)nt* (later *roman*) analogical var. of *roma(u)nz* ROMANCE *noun.*]
▶ **A** *noun.* **1** A romance; a romantic narrative or poem. M16.
2 A Romance form of speech. *rare.* M16.
▶ **B** *attrib.* or as *adjective.* Of a word or form: Romance, Romanic. *rare.* M16.

Romayne /rə(ʊ)ˈmeɪn/ *adjective.* LME.
[Var. of ROMAN *adjective.*]
†**1** Roman. LME–L16.
2 Designating carving etc. with a motif of heads in medallions, introduced into England from Italy in the early 16th cent. E20.

Romberg /ˈrɒmbəːg/ *noun.* L19.
[Moritz Heinrich *Romberg* (1795–1873), German physician.]
MEDICINE. Used *attrib.* and in *possess.* to designate the test of requiring a patient to stand with feet together and eyes closed, and the sign or symptom, diagnostic of sensory ataxia, shown by a patient who then sways or falls.

rombowline /rɒmˈbəʊlɪn/ *noun.* M19.
[Origin unkn.]
NAUTICAL. Old rope or canvas used for temporary purposes not requiring strength.

rom-com /ˈrɒmkɒm/ *noun. colloq.* L20.
[Abbreviation.]
A romantic comedy.

Rome /rəʊm/ *noun.* ME.
[Old & mod. French, or Latin *Roma* Rome, a city in (now the capital of) Italy.]
1 The Roman Empire. ME.
2 The Roman Catholic Church, its influence, institutions, central authorities, etc. M16.
Phrases: ***Court of Rome***: see COURT *noun*¹.
Comb.: **Rome-penny** (*obsolete* exc. *Hist.*) = ***Peter's pence*** (a) s.v. PETER *noun*¹; **Rome-runner** (long *obsolete* exc. *Hist.*) a person, esp. a cleric, constantly journeying to Rome to obtain benefices etc.; **Rome-scot** (*obsolete* exc. *Hist.*) = ***Peter's pence*** (a) s.v. PETER *noun*¹; ***see of Rome***: see SEE *noun*¹ 2b.

Romeo /ˈrəʊmɪəʊ/ *noun.* Pl. **-os.** M18.
[The hero of Shakespeare's *Romeo & Juliet.*]
1 A lover, a passionate admirer; a seducer of women; a womanizer. M18.
2 (**r-**.) A type of high slipper, usu. of felt, now worn only by men. *US.* L19.

romer /ˈrəʊmə/ *noun.* M20.
[Carrol *Romer* (1883–1951), Brit. barrister and the inventor.]
A small piece of plastic or card bearing perpendicularly aligned scales or (if transparent) a grid, used to determine the precise reference of a point within the grid printed on a map.

Romeward /ˈrəʊmwəd/ *adverb & adjective.* ME.
[from ROME + -WARD.]
▶ **A** *adverb.* **1** In the direction of the city of Rome. ME.
2 Towards the Roman Catholic Church or Roman Catholicism. M19.
▶ **B** *adjective.* **1** Directed towards or facing the city of Rome. M19.
2 Directed or tending towards the Roman Catholic Church or Roman Catholicism. M19.
■ Also **Romewards** *adverb* M19.

Romish /ˈrəʊmɪʃ/ *adjective.* M16.
[from ROME + -ISH¹, prob. after Dutch *roomsch*, German *römisch.*]
1 Roman Catholic. Chiefly *derog.* M16.
2 = ROMAN *adjective* 1. *arch.* M16.
†**3** = ROMAN *adjective* 5. Only in ***Romish Catholic.*** E17–E19.
■ **Romishness** *noun* M19.

†**Romist** *noun.* L16–E19.
[from ROME + -IST.]
A Roman Catholic.

rommelpot /ˈrɒm(ə)lpɒt/ *noun.* M19.
[Dutch, lit. 'rumble pot'.]
A type of drum found chiefly in the Low Countries, consisting of an earthenware pot covered at the top by a bladder pierced by a stick that is pushed up and down or rotated.

Romney /ˈrʌmni, ˈrɒm-/ *noun.* M19.
[*Romney* Marsh, an area of rich grazing land on the coast of Kent in S. England.]
In full ***Romney Marsh***. (An animal of) a breed of stocky long-woolled sheep originally bred in Kent and now common in New Zealand. Also ***Romney sheep***, ***Romney Marsh sheep***.

Romney /ˈrɒmni/ *adjective.* E20.
[from *Romney* (see below).]
Designating a garment or fashion resembling those worn in portraits of women by the English portrait painter George Romney (1734–1802).

romneya /ˈrɒmnɪə/ *noun.* L20.
[mod. Latin (see below), from T. *Romney* Robinson (1792–1882), Irish astronomer.]
Either of two Californian shrubby poppies of the genus *Romneya*, *R. coulteri* and *R. trichocalyx*, grown for their showy white flowers. Also called ***Californian poppy***.

romp /rɒmp/ *noun.* E18.
[Perh. alt. of RAMP *noun*¹.]
1 A person who romps; *esp.* a lively playful girl. E18.
2 A spell of lively boisterous play. Now also, a playful or light-hearted journey or excursion. M18.
3 SPORT. A victory by a substantial margin; an easily-won game. *colloq.* M20.

📖 **1** DE QUINCEY Such a girl . . you might call a romp; but not a hoyden. **2** F. BURNEY My little rogue soon engaged him in a romp. C. EASTON A lovely country walk together, sort of a romp across the country. **3** *Rugby World & Post* Ten tries . . scored against the Royal Navy . . in a 44–3 romp.

Phrases: **in a romp** with the greatest ease.
■ **rompish** *adjective* inclined to romp, playful E18. **rompishness** *noun* E18. **rompy** *adjective* characterized by romps or romping M19.

romp /rɒmp/ *verb.* E18.
[Perh. alt. of RAMP *verb*¹.]
1 *verb intrans.* Play about in a lively, light-hearted, or boisterous manner. E18.
2 *verb intrans.* **a** Proceed easily and rapidly. *colloq.* L19. ▸**b** Get *in* (or *home*) with ease; win a race, contest, etc. with ease. *colloq.* L19.
3 *verb trans.* Drive or convey in a romping fashion. *rare.* L19.
4 *verb trans.* with *it*. Win a contest, esp. an election, easily. *colloq.* M20.

📖 **1** M. SEYMOUR Both families could romp unselfconsciously through games of animal grab. **2a** *Times* He and Davies romped to a 5–1 lead. *Times* The prospect of more tasty takeover bids sent food shares romping ahead. **b** *Autosport* He romped home to win in the first two rounds.

■ **romping** *adjective* (*a*) (of a person) that romps, given to romping; (*b*) (of an action etc.) having the character of a romp or romps: E18. **rompingly** *adverb* E19.

romper /ˈrɒmpə/ *noun.* M19.
[from ROMP *verb* + -ER¹.]
1 A person who romps. M19.
2 A one-piece garment covering the legs and trunk, worn esp. by a young child. Usu in *pl.* E20.
Comb.: **romper room** a playroom for very young children; **romper suit** = sense 2 above.

romulea /rɒˈmjuːlɪə/ *noun.* L19.
[mod. Latin (see below), from *Romulus*: see next.]
Any of various small bulbous plants constituting the genus *Romulea*, of the iris family, native to southern Europe and southern Africa, with lilac, yellow, or white flowers resembling a crocus.

Romulian /rɒˈmjuːlɪən/ *adjective. rare.* M19.
[from *Romulus* (see below) + -IAN.]
Derived from or connected with Romulus, the mythical founder of Rome.

†**ron** *verb* see RUN *verb*.

roncador /ˈrɒŋkədɔː/ *noun. US.* L19.
[Spanish, from *roncar* snore, snort.]
Any of various croakers of the Pacific coast of N. America; *spec.* a large croaker, *Roncador stearnsi*, that is blue above and silver below and popular as a game-fish. **yellowfin roncador** the yellowfin croaker, *Umbrina roncador*.

ronchus *noun* var. of RHONCHUS.

rond /rɒnd/ *noun. obsolete* exc. *dial.* LME.
[Var. of RAND *noun*¹.]
†**1** = RAND *noun*¹ 2. LME–E17.
2 In East Anglia, a marshy, reed-covered strip of land between a natural river-bank and a man-made embankment. Cf. RAND *noun*¹ 1. M19.

rondache /rɒnˈdaʃ; *foreign* rɔ̃daʃ (*pl. same*)/ *noun.* Now *arch.* or *Hist.* E17.
[French, from *rond* ROUND *adjective*.]
A small circular shield or buckler.

rondavel /rɒnˈdɑːv(ə)l/ *noun. S. Afr.* L19.
[Afrikaans *rondawel*.]
A round tribal hut usu. with a thatched conical roof. Also, a similar building used esp. as a holiday cottage or an outbuilding on a farm.

rond de cuir /rɔ̃ də kɥir/ *noun phr.* Pl. ***ronds de cuir*** (pronounced same). E20.
[French, lit. 'circle of leather'.]
A round leather cushion, often used on office chairs in France. Also *transf.*, a bureaucrat.

ronde /rɒnd/ *noun.* M19.
[French, fem. of *rond* ROUND *adjective*.]
1 A style of script with gothic characteristics used in France from the 18th cent.; printing type imitating or based on this writing. M19.
2 A dance in which the participants move in a circle or ring. M20.
3 A round or course of talk, activity, etc.; *fig.* a treadmill. M20.

rondeau /ˈrɒndəʊ/ *noun.* Pl. **-eaux** /-əʊ, -əʊz/. E16.
[Old & mod. French, later form of *rondel*: see next. Cf. ROUNDEL.]
1 A poem of ten or thirteen lines with only two rhymes throughout and with the opening words used twice as a refrain. E16.
2 MUSIC. = RONDO 1. L18.

rondel /ˈrɒnd(ə)l/ *noun.* ME.
[Old French, from *rond* ROUND *adjective*: see prec., -EL². Cf. ROUNDEL.]
1 A circle; a circular object. *arch.* ME. ▸†**b** A rung of a ladder. E17–E18.
2 A rondeau, *esp.* one of a special form. LME.
■ **rondelet** /ˈrɒndəlɛt/ *noun* a short poem or song, usu. of seven lines, in the form of a rondeau L16.

rondeletia /rɒndəˈliːʃə/ *noun.* L18.
[mod. Latin (see below), from G. *Rondelet* (1507–66), French physician and naturalist + -IA¹.]
1 Any of various tropical American trees and shrubs constituting the genus *Rondeletia*, of the madder family, several of which are grown for their large, freq. fragrant, flowers. L18.
2 An artificial perfume resembling the scent of these flowers. M19.

rondelle /rɒnˈdɛl/ *noun.* M19.
[French, from *rond* ROUND *adjective*.]
A circular piece of something.

rondeña /ronˈdeɲa/ *noun.* L19.
[Spanish, from *Ronda* (see below).]
A type of song or dance native to Ronda in Andalusia in Spain.

rondeurs /rɔ̃dœːr/ *noun pl. rare.* M20.
[French.]
Rounded forms or lines; *spec.* the curves of the female body.

rondo /ˈrɒndəʊ/ *noun.* Pl. **-os**. L18.
[Italian from French RONDEAU.]
1 A piece of music with a recurring leading theme, often as the final movement of a concerto, sonata, etc. L18.
2 A game of chance played with balls on a table. M19.

rond-point /rɔ̃pwɛ̃/ *noun.* Pl. ***ronds-points*** (pronounced same). L19.
[French, from *rond* ROUND *adjective* + *point* centre.]
A circular space in a garden from which paths radiate; a roundabout where roads converge.

ronds de cuir *noun phr.* pl. of ROND DE CUIR.

ronds-points *noun* pl. of ROND-POINT.

rondure /ˈrɒndjʊə/ *noun. arch. rare.* L16.
[French *rondeur* with ending assim. to -URE. Cf. ROUNDURE.]
A circle, a round object; roundness.

rone /rəʊn/ *noun*¹. *obsolete* exc. *dial.* ME.
[Prob. of Scandinavian origin: cf. Norwegian dial. *rune*, Old Norse *runnr* (Icelandic *runnur*) in same sense.]
A thicket; thick bush or undergrowth.

rone /rəʊn/ *noun*². *Scot.* L16.
[Origin unkn.]
†**1** The pipe of a boat's pump. L16–M18.
2 A pipe or gutter at the eaves of a roof for carrying off rainwater. M18.

Roneo /ˈrəʊnɪəʊ/ *noun & verb.* As verb also **r-**. E20.
[from *ro(tary* + *Neo(style*.]
▶**A** *noun.* (Proprietary name for) any of various kinds of office equipment, esp. a duplicating machine. E20.
▶**B** *verb trans.* Copy or reproduce with a Roneo duplicating machine. Chiefly as ***roneoed*** *ppl adjective.* E20.

Rong /rɒŋ/ *noun & adjective.* Pl. of noun same. M19.
[Tibetan.]
= LEPCHA.

Ronga /ˈrɒŋgə/ *noun & adjective.* E20.
[Ronga.]
▶**A** *noun.* Pl. same, **-s**.
1 A member of a Bantu-speaking people of southern Mozambique. E20.
2 The Bantu language of this people. E20.
▶**B** *attrib.* or as *adjective.* Of or pertaining to the Ronga or their language. E20.

ronge /rɒn(d)ʒ/ *verb.* Long *obsolete* exc. *dial.* Also †**rounge**. ME.
[Old French *ro(u)ngier* (mod. *ronger*), ult. rel. to Latin *rodere*: see RODENT.]
†**1** *verb intrans.* Gnash the teeth. Only in ME.
2 *verb trans. & intrans.* Gnaw (at). LME. ▸†**b** *verb intrans.* Chew the cud. LME–L15.
†**3** *verb trans.* Clip (coin). *Scot.* M16–L17.

rongeur /rɔ̃ˈʒəː/ *noun.* L19.
[French = gnawing, a rodent, from *ronger*: see prec.]
SURGERY. Strong surgical forceps with a biting action, used for removing small pieces from bone. Also ***rongeur forceps***.

ronggeng /ˈrɒŋgɛŋ/ *noun.* E19.
[Malay.]
1 A dancing-girl in Malaysia. E19.
2 A form of Malaysian popular dance, often accompanied by singing. E20.

rongo-rongo /rɒŋgəʊˈrɒŋgəʊ/ *noun.* E20.
[Easter Island name.]
ARCHAEOLOGY. Hieroglyphic signs or script found on wooden tablets on Easter Island in the eastern Pacific Ocean; the art of incising these.

ronin /ˈrəʊnɪn/ *noun.* Pl. same, **-s**. L19.
[Japanese.]
In feudal Japan, a lordless wandering samurai; an outlaw. Now also *transf.*, a Japanese student who has failed and is permitted to retake a university (entrance) examination.

ronquil /ˈrɒŋkɪl/ *noun.* L19.
[from Spanish *ronquillo* slightly hoarse, from *ronco* hoarse.]
Any of various N. Pacific coastal perciform fishes of the family Bathymasteridae, with a continuous dorsal fin and broad pectoral fins.

Ronsardist /ˈrɒnsɑːdɪst/ *noun.* L19.
[from *Ronsard* (see below) + -IST.]
A poet who writes in the style of the French poet Pierre de Ronsard (1524–85).

Röntgen *noun* var. of ROENTGEN.

Ronuk /ˈrɒnʌk/ *noun & verb.* As verb also **r-**. L19.
[Origin unkn.]
▶**A** *noun.* (Proprietary name for) a polish; *spec.* a floor polish. L19.
▶**B** *verb trans.* Polish with Ronuk. E20.

roo /ruː/ *noun. Austral. colloq.* Also **'roo**. L19.
[Abbreviation.]
= KANGAROO *noun* 1.
Comb.: **roo-bar**: fitted to the front of a motor vehicle to protect the radiator in the event of collision with a kangaroo etc.

rood /ruːd/ *noun.*
[Old English *rōd* = Old Frisian *rōd(e)*, Old Saxon *rōda*. In branch II rel. to Old Saxon *rōda*, Middle & mod. Dutch *ro(o)de* (also mod. *roede*), Old High German *ruota* (German *Rute*).]
▶**I** †**1** A cross as an instrument of execution; = CROSS *noun* 2. OE–LME.
2 *The* Cross on which Jesus suffered; *the* cross as the symbol of the Christian faith. *arch.* OE.
3 A crucifix, *esp.* one stationed above the middle of a rood-screen; *rare* a figure of the Cross of Jesus as a religious object. OE.
▶**II 4** A former measure of length for land, usu. equal to a perch. OE.
5 a A former measure of area for land, later standardized at a quarter of an acre (40 square perches, approx. 0.1012 hectare); a plot of land of this size. OE. ▸†**b** A measure of area for land, paving, timber, masonry, etc., usu. equal to a square perch. LME–M19.
Comb. & phrases: **by the rood!** *arch.* expr. asseveration; **Holy Rood**: see HOLY *adjective*. **rood-beam** a transverse beam supporting a rood, usu. forming the head of a rood-screen; **Rood day** (*obsolete* exc. *Hist.*) Holy Rood Day; **rood-loft** a loft or gallery at the top of a rood-screen; **rood-screen** a screen, usu. of richly carved wood or stone, separating the nave from the chancel of a church.

roodge /ruːdʒ/ *verb trans. obsolete* exc. *dial.* L17.
[Origin unkn.]
Push, lift; move with effort.

rood goose *noun* var. of RAT-GOOSE.

roof /ruːf/ *noun & verb.*
[Old English *hrōf* = Old Frisian *hrōf*, Middle & mod. Low German *rōf*, Middle Dutch *roof* (Dutch *roef* cabin, coffin lid), Old Norse *hróf* boat shed.]
▶**A** *noun.* Pl. **roofs**, **rooves** /ruːvz/.
1 The outside upper covering of a building, esp. a house; the framing structure on top of a building sup-

porting this. OE. ▸**b** The overhead interior surface of a room or other compartment; the ceiling. ME. ▸**c** *transf.* A dwelling-place, a house; a home, a household. ME.

2 A thing which forms a shelter or covering; a lid, a top; *fig.* the highest point or upper limit. OE. ▸**b** The upper air, the sky; heaven. Also ***roof of heaven***. *poet.* OE. ▸**c** In full ***roof of the mouth***. The palate. OE. ▸**d** *MINING*. The stratum lying immediately over a bed of coal etc.; the top of a working or gallery. L17. ▸**e** The top of a covered vehicle, now esp. a motor vehicle. E18. ▸**f** The highest mountain range or plateau within a particular region. M19. ▸**g** A hat. *slang*. M19. ▸**h** *AERONAUTICS*. = CEILING 5a. Now *rare* or *obsolete*. E20. ▸**i** *MOUNTAINEERING*. The underside of a rock overhang. M20.

🕮 **1** F. KING The shed, with its roof of .. corrugated iron. H. MANTEL I wished I could tear the roof off and let some light into the flat. **c** D. L. SAYERS He .. has not a .. cent or a roof. **2** *New Statesman* Starting salary £2,185 .. rising to a roof of £2,835. B. HINES Above .. the trees .. the rooves of their foliage stretched round him. **b** SHELLEY Under the roof of blue Ionian weather. **c** E. MANNIN Linton clicked his tongue against the roof of his mouth. **e** G. V. HIGGINS A small .. open car with a canvas roof. **f** *Listener* If you want .. a test of stamina .. you can walk the Roof of Wales.

Phrases: ***French roof***: see FRENCH *adjective*. **go through the roof** (of a price etc.) reach extreme or unexpected heights, become exorbitant. **hit the roof** *colloq.* become very angry. ***Italian roof***: see ITALIAN *adjective*. **lift the roof** = ***raise the roof*** s.v. RAISE *verb*. ***mansard roof***: see MANSARD 1. ***M-roof***: see M, M 2. ***raise the roof***: see RAISE *verb*. ***roof of heaven***: see sense 3b above. ***roof of the mouth***: see sense 3c above. **roof of the world** orig., the Pamirs; later also, Tibet, the Himalayas. **roof over one's head** a place to live, a house. **the roof falls in** *colloq.* a disaster occurs, everything goes wrong. **under a person's roof** in a person's house (esp. with ref. to hospitality). **under one roof**, **under the same roof** within the same house or other building.

Comb.: **roof bolt** *MINING* a tensioned rod anchoring the roof of a working to the strata above; **roof-brain** the cerebral cortex; **roof-climb** *verb intrans.* climb over the roofs of buildings; **roof-garden** an area, usu. with plants etc., built on the flat roof of a building for outdoor eating or entertainment; **roof light** (*a*) a flashing warning light on top of a motor vehicle; (*b*) a small interior light on the inside roof of a motor vehicle; (*c*) a window panel built into a roof; **roofline** the outline or silhouette of a roof or a collection of roofs; **roof pendant** *GEOLOGY* a mass of country rock projecting downwards into a batholith; **roof prism** a triangular prism in which the reflecting surface is in two parts that are angled like two parts of a pitched roof; in *pl.* (in full ***roof-prism binoculars***) a pair of binoculars using such prisms; **roof-rack** a framework fitted to the roof of a motor vehicle for carrying luggage; **roof rail** a longitudinal or transverse structural member at the edge of the roof of a road vehicle; **roof rat** a variety of the black rat having a brownish back and greyish underparts; **roofscape** (a view presented by) an expanse of roofs; **roof-slate** (a) slate used as roofing; **roof tax** *derog.* a property-based tax proposed as an alternative to the community charge in the UK; **roof-tile** a tile used as roofing; a ridge-tile; **rooftop** *adjective & noun* (situated on) the outer surface of a roof; **roof-tree** (*a*) = ***ridge-piece*** s.v. RIDGE *noun*[1]; (*b*) *NAUTICAL Hist.* a jackstay or piece of wood used to hold or support netting etc.; **roof-water** rainwater collected from or falling from a roof.

▸ **B** *verb trans.* **1** Provide or cover with a roof. Also foll. by *in*, *over*. LME.

2 Be or form a roof over. Also foll. by *in*, *over*. Chiefly *literary*. E17. ▸**b** Shelter, house. *rare*. *literary*. E19.

🕮 **1** A. DJOLETO The house was roofed with asbestos. M. M. KAYE The durbar hall .. had been roofed in by an awning. Z. TOMIN John .. cleaned up the well and roofed it over. **2** D. HAMMETT Where Bush Street roofed Stockton before slipping downhill to Chinatown. R. ADAMS The orderly rows of beans .. roofing them over.

▪ **roofage** *noun* = ROOFING (b), (c) M19. **roofed** *adjective* having or covered (as) with a roof; having a roof of a specified kind: L15. **roofer** *noun* (*a*) a person who builds or repairs roofs; (*b*) *slang* = ROOF *noun* 2g; (*c*) a letter of thanks for hospitality etc.: M19. **roofing** *noun* (*a*) the action of covering a building with a roof; (*b*) that which forms a roof or roofs; (*c*) material used for building a roof: LME. **roofless** *adjective* having no roof; (of a person) homeless: E17. **rooflet** *noun* a small roof or covering M19. **rooflike** *adjective & adverb* (in a manner) characteristic of a roof or roofs L18. **roofy** *adjective* (*rare*) (*a*) *poet.* covered with a roof; (*b*) having many roofs: L17.

rooi-aas /ˈrɔɪɑːs/ *noun*. *S. Afr.* L19.
[Afrikaans, from *rooi* red + *aas* bait.]
= ***red-bait*** noun s.v. RED *adjective*.

rooibaadjie /ˈrɔɪbʌɪki, -bʌɪtʃi/ *noun*. *S. Afr.* M19.
[Afrikaans, from *rooi* red + *baadjie* jacket.]
1 A British regular soldier; *Hist.* a redcoat. M19.
2 A red nymph of the southern African locust *Locustana pardalina* in its gregarious phase. M19.

rooibekkie /ˈrɔɪbɛki/ *noun*. *S. Afr.* L18.
[Afrikaans, from *rooi* red + *bek* beak + *-ie* dim. suffix.]
Any of various waxbills with red beaks; *esp.* (*a*) (more fully ***common rooibekkie***) the common waxbill, *Estrilda astrild*; (*b*) (more fully ***king rooibekkie***) the pin-tailed whydah, *Vidua macroura*.

rooibok /ˈrɔɪbɒk/ *noun*. *S. Afr.* E19.
[Afrikaans, from *rooi* red + *bok* buck.]
An impala.

rooibos /ˈrɔɪbɒs/ *noun*. *S. Afr.* E20.
[Afrikaans, from *rooi* red + *bos* bush.]
1 Any of several southern African leguminous shrubs of the genus *Aspalathus*. E20.
2 A shrub or small tree, *Combretum apiculatum* (family Combretaceae), of central and southern Africa, bearing red or yellow foliage in winter, and spikes of scented yellow flowers. M20.
Comb.: **rooibos tea** an infusion of the dried leaves of a rooibos plant, esp. *Aspalathus linearis*, credited with tonic properties.

rooi-els /ˈrɔɪɛls/ *noun*. *S. Afr.* E19.
[Afrikaans, from *rooi* red + *els* alder.]
An evergreen tree of southern Africa, *Cunonia capensis* (family Cunoniaceae), bearing compound leaves and racemes of fragrant cream flowers; the reddish wood of this tree. Also called ***red alder***.

rooigras /ˈrɔɪxras/ *noun*. *S. Afr.* L19.
[Afrikaans, from *rooi* red + *gras* grass.]
A southern African grass, *Themeda triandra*, which turns a reddish colour in winter.

rooihout /ˈrɔɪhəʊt/ *noun*. *S. Afr.* L18.
[Afrikaans, from *rooi* red + *hout* wood.]
Any of several southern African trees with reddish wood, esp. the Cape plane, *Ochna arborea*; the wood of these trees.

rooikat /ˈrɔɪkat/ *noun*. *S. Afr.* L18.
[Afrikaans, from *rooi* red + *kat* cat.]
= CARACAL.

rooikrans /ˈrɔɪkrans/ *noun*. *S. Afr.* E20.
[Afrikaans, from *rooi* red + *krans* wreath, in ref. to the red aril of the seed.]
An Australian wattle, *Acacia cyclops*, introduced into southern Africa as a sand-binder and used as fodder.

rooinek /ˈrɔɪnɛk/ *noun*. *S. Afr. slang. joc.* or *derog.* L19.
[Afrikaans, from *rooi* red + *nek* neck.]
A British or English-speaking South African.

rooirhebok /rɔɪˈriəbɒk, -ˈriːbɒk/ *noun*. *S. Afr.* M19.
[Afrikaans, from *rooi* red + RHEBOK.]
The mountain reedbuck, *Redunca fulvorufula*; red rhebok.

rook /rʊk/ *noun*[1].
[Old English *hrōc* = Middle & mod. Low German *rōk*, Middle Dutch *roec* (Dutch *roek*), Old High German *hruoh*, Old Norse *hrókr*, from Germanic, prob. of imit. origin.]
1 A black raucous-voiced Eurasian bird of the crow family, *Corvus frugilegus*, which nests in colonies. OE.
2 a A greedy or grasping person. *derog.* E16. ▸**b** A cheat, a swindler, esp. at gambling. *slang*. L16. ▸†**c** A foolish person, a gull. L16–M17.
3 A crowbar. *slang & dial.* L18.
Comb.: **rook-pie**: made with (young) rooks; **rook rifle** (chiefly *Hist.*) a small-bore rifle for shooting rooks; **rook-worm** a worm eaten by rooks; *esp.* the larva of the cockchafer.
▪ **rookish** *adjective* of, pertaining to, or resembling a rook or rooks M18.

rook /rʊk/ *noun*[2]. ME.
[Old French *rok*, *roc*, *rock*, ult. from Arab. *rukk* of uncertain original meaning.]
CHESS. Each of the four pieces set in the corner squares at the beginning of a game, moving in a straight line forwards, backwards, or laterally over any number of unoccupied squares; a castle.

rook /rʊk/ *noun*[3]. *Scot. & north.* L17.
[Var.]
= ROKE *noun*[1].

rook /rʊk/ *noun*[4]. Chiefly *US*. E20.
[Abbreviation.]
= ROOKIE.

rook /rʊk/ *verb*. M16.
[from ROOK *noun*[1].]
1 *verb trans.* & (now *rare*) *intrans.* Cheat, swindle; *esp.* win or extract money from (a person) by fraud; charge (a person) extortionately. *slang*. M16.
†**2** *verb trans.* Win or take by fraud. M–L17.

🕮 **1** R. C. HUTCHINSON They rook you frightfully at those .. places, it's a racket. J. KEROUAC Rooking them with all those .. carnival tricks.

▪ **rooker** *noun* L17.

rookery /ˈrʊk(ə)ri/ *noun*. E18.
[from ROOK *noun*[1] + -ERY.]
1 A collection of rooks' nests, esp. in a clump of trees; a colony of rooks. E18. ▸**b** *fig.* A dense collection of housing, esp. in a slum area. L18.
2 A row, a disturbance. *dial. & slang*. E19.
3 A colony of sea birds or marine mammals, esp. seals; a place where sea birds etc. breed. M19.

🕮 **1b** *Literary Review* The .. nightlife .. among the squares and rookeries of Victorian London.

rookie /ˈrʊki/ *noun*. *slang*. Also **-ky**. L19.
[Origin uncertain: perh. alt. of RECRUIT *noun*.]
1 A raw recruit, esp. in an army or police force; *transf.* a novice in a particular field or profession. L19.
2 *spec.* A new member of a sports team, *esp.* one playing in his or her first major league or championship. Chiefly *N. Amer.* E20.

🕮 **1** B. FORBES We're not two rookies in the police force. **2** CLIVE JAMES I was a rookie for the L. A. Rams.

rookus /ˈrʊkəs/ *noun*. *US slang*. L19.
[Var.]
= RUCKUS.
Comb.: **rookus-juice** alcoholic liquor.

rooky *noun* var. of ROOKIE.

rooky /ˈrʊki/ *adjective*[1]. E17.
[from ROOK *noun*[1] + -Y[1].]
Consisting of or having many rooks.

rooky /ˈrʊki/ *adjective*[2]. *Scot. & north.* L17.
[from ROOK *noun*[3] + -Y[1].]
Smoky; steamy; foggy, misty; drizzly.

room /ruːm, rʊm/ *noun*[1].
[Old English *rūm* = Old Frisian, Old Saxon, Old High German, Old Norse, Gothic *rūm* (Dutch *ruim*, German *Raum*), from Germanic base of ROOM *adjective*.]
▸ **I 1** The amount of space that is or may be occupied by a thing. OE.
2 Capacity to accommodate a person or thing or allow a particular action; sufficient space (*for*, *to do*). Freq. with specifying word. OE. ▸**b** *fig.* Opportunity or allowance for something to occur, develop, etc.; scope (*for*, *to do*). OE.

🕮 **1** *Westminster Gazette* Customers who need garage room for .. vehicles. R. P. BISSELL The economy size tube .. takes up more room. **2** E. NESBIT There's no room to make the chapters any longer. E. WAUGH I will stay a little ... Will there be room for me? M. MITCHELL There was no room on the narrow sidewalks. **b** W. BRONK Awake, our invention finds more room to move. *Classical Review* A. admits some room for doubt. *Japan Times* There is always room for improvement.

▸ **II 3** A particular portion of space; a specific space or area. ME. ▸†**b** In *pl.* Domains, dominions, territories. *Scot.* LME–L16. ▸**c** A piece of rented land; a farm holding. *Scot.* Now chiefly *Hist.* E16.
4 †**a** A place or spot of unspecified extent. ME–L17. ▸**b** A place in a series or sequence. *Scot.* Now *rare* or *obsolete*. L16. ▸**c** A fishing station. *N. Amer.* E17.
5 A place or seat occupied by or assigned to a person or thing. Later *spec.*, (contrasted with ***company***) a place or seat as opp. to a person's actual presence. Now *rare*. LME. ▸†**b** A place or seat in the theatre. L16–E17. ▸†**c** *transf.* A place *in* a person's affection etc. L16–L17.
†**6 a** An office, an appointment, a position, *esp.* one held by right or inheritance. LME–M18. ▸**b** Position, authority. L15–L16.

🕮 **3** R. BRIDGES A Zephyr straying out of heaven's wide room Rush'd down. **5** SHAKES. *Rich. II* Go thou and fill another room in hell. HANNAH MORE I had rather have their room than their Company.

▸ **III 7** A compartment within a building enclosed by walls or partitions, floor and ceiling, *esp.* (freq. with specifying word) one set aside for a specified purpose; (with *possess.*) a person's private chamber or office within a house, workplace, etc. ME. ▸**b** *transf.* The people present in a room; the company. E18. ▸**c** ***the room***, a room or rooms for public gatherings or business; an assembly room; *spec.* (*a*) an auction room; (*b*) a gambling room. Usu. in *pl.* M18. ▸**d** The main room of a house; the living-room. *Scot.*, *N. Amer.*, *& dial.* L18. ▸**e** In *pl.* A set of rooms occupied by a person or persons, an institution, etc.; lodgings. Freq. with *possess.* L18.
8 a *MINING*. A working space left between pillars of coal. L17. ▸**b** A space or compartment lying between the timbers of a ship's frame, the thwarts of a boat, etc. E18. ▸**c** A capacity measure for coals, equivalent to 5¼ chaldrons. E19.

🕮 **7** P. AUSTER A large hall, a vast and impressive room. P. DALLY He .. confined her to her room. ***baggage room***, ***changing room***, ***common-room***, ***control room***, ***darkroom***, ***dining-room***, ***locker room***, ***news room***, ***sitting-room***, ***waiting-room***, etc. **b** ADDISON His .. Figure drew upon us the Eyes of the whole Room. **c** A. CHRISTIE In the Rooms, jauntily placing the minimum stake on the even numbers. **e** C. E. PASCOE The rooms of the Society of Arts .. are in John Street. ALDOUS HUXLEY Bernard had to slink back .. to his rooms.

Phrases: ***double room***: see DOUBLE *adjective & adverb*. ***elbow room***: see ELBOW *noun*. ***FLORIDA room***. ***green room***: see GREEN *adjective*. **in room of**, **in the room of** (now *rare*) in (the) place of, in lieu of. ***ladies' room***: see LADY *noun & adjective*. ***leave the room***: see LEAVE *verb*[1]. ***little boys' room***, ***little girls' room***: see LITTLE *adjective*. ***long room***: see LONG *adjective*[1]. **make room (for)** (*a*) make way or draw back to allow (another) to enter or pass; (*b*) clear a space for (something) by moving other things. ***men's room***: see MAN *noun*. **no room to swing a cat in**, **not room to swing a cat in** very little space. **room at the top** opportunity to join an élite, the top ranks of a profession, etc. ***white room***: see WHITE *adjective*.

Comb.: **room clerk** a hotel clerk who assigns rooms to guests; ***room-divider***: see DIVIDER 2b; **room-mate** a person occupying the same room or rooms as another; ***room-ridden***: see RIDDEN *adjective* 1; **room service** (the department providing) service of food or drink taken to a guest's room in a hotel etc.; **roomstead** (now *rare* or *obsolete*) a room, a compartment; a certain area or space; **room temperature** a comfortable ambient temperature, usu. taken as approx. 20°C; **room-to-room** *adjective* (of a telephone) connecting rooms within the same building.

■ **roomage** *noun* (*US*, *rare*) space, internal capacity M19. **roomed** *adjective* having rooms of a specified number or kind M16. **roomer** *noun* (*a*) a house with a specified number of rooms; (*b*) *N. Amer.* a lodger occupying a room or rooms without board: M19. **roo'mette** *noun* (chiefly *N. Amer.*) (*a*) a private single compartment in a sleeping-car; (*b*) a small bedroom for letting: M20. **roomful** *adjective & noun* (*a*) *adjective* (*rare*, *poet.*) roomy; (*b*) *noun* as much or as many as a room will contain: E17. **roomie** *noun* (*N. Amer. colloq.*) a room-mate E20. **roomless** *adjective* (*rare*) M16. **roomlet** *noun* a small room L19.

room /ruːm/ *noun*². Long *dial.* L16.
[Origin unkn.]
Dandruff.

room /ruːm/ *adjective & adverb.*
[Old English *rūm* = Old Frisian *rūm*, Middle Dutch *ruum* (Dutch *ruim*), Middle & mod. Low German *rūm*, Old High German *rumi*, Old Norse *rúmr*, Gothic *rums*, from Germanic.]
▶ **A** *adjective.* **1** Spacious, roomy; wide, extensive. Long *Scot. rare.* OE.
†**2** Clear, unobstructed, empty; (of land) unoccupied, uninhabited. Long *Scot.* ME–E19. ▸**b** Of the wind: favourable for sailing. Chiefly *Scot.* M17–E20.
▶ **B** *adverb.* †**1** Widely; to or at a distance. OE–LME.
2 Amply; fully. Now *dial.* OE.
3 NAUTICAL. = LARGE *adverb* 5. M16.

room /ruːm/ *verb*¹.
[Old English *rūmian*, formed as prec.; perh. formed anew in Middle English.]
†**1 a** *verb intrans.* Become clear of obstructions. Only in OE. ▸**b** *verb trans.* Clear (esp. the chest or throat) of obstruction or congestion. LME–L15.
2 *verb trans.* Extend, enlarge. Long *obsolete* exc. *dial.* ME.
†**3** *verb intrans. & trans.* Vacate or leave (a place); depart (from). ME–M16.
4 *verb trans.* Clear (a space); make room or space in. Long *arch.* exc. *Scot. dial.* LME.

room /ruːm/ *verb*². M16.
[from ROOM *noun*¹.]
1 *verb trans.* †**a** Install. *Scot. rare.* M16–M17. ▸**b** SCOTTISH HISTORY. Allocate (an area of common pasture) to a tenant farmer on an estate. M17.
2 Chiefly *N. Amer.* ▸**a** *verb intrans. & trans.* (with *it*). Occupy a room or rooms as a lodger; share a room or rooms with another (foll. by *together*, *with*). E19. ▸**b** *verb trans.* Accommodate or lodge (a person) as a guest. Now *rare.* M19.

📖 **2a** T. C. WOLFE I think I shall room alone hereafter. R. JAFFE Go to Harvard . . and room together. *Philadelphia Inquirer* I wouldn't want to room with him.

rooming /ˈruːmɪŋ/ *verbal noun.* M20.
[from prec. + -ING¹.]
The action of ROOM *verb*²; an instance of this.
Comb.: **rooming-house** *N. Amer. & Austral.* a building divided into furnished rooms or apartments for rent; **rooming-in** *noun & adjective* (designating) a hospital scheme whereby a newborn baby is kept beside and cared for as much as possible by the mother.

roomth /ruːmθ/ *noun.* Long *obsolete* exc. *dial.* E16.
[from ROOM *adjective* + -TH¹.]
†**1** = ROOM *noun*¹ 6a. E16–E17.
2 = ROOM *noun*¹ 2. M16.
†**3** = ROOM *noun*¹ 3. M16–M17.
4 = ROOM *noun*¹ 7. L16.
†**5** = ROOM *noun*¹ 1. Only in 17.
■ **roomthy** *adjective* roomy L16.

roomy /ˈruːmi/ *adjective.* L16.
[from ROOM *noun*¹ + -Y¹.]
1 Having much room; spacious; capacious. L16.
2 Of a female animal: wide-hipped. L18.

📖 **1** A. CROSS It was a nice roomy apartment. *Motorway Express* Not particularly roomy in estate car terms.

■ **roomily** *adverb* E19. **roominess** *noun* M19.

roon /ruːn/ *noun. Scot.* Now *rare.* M17.
[Origin unkn.]
The border or selvage of a piece of cloth; a strip of cloth.

roop *noun*, *verb* vars. of ROUP *noun*¹, *verb*.

roorback /ˈruːəbak/ *noun. US.* M19.
[Baron von *Roorback*, fictitious author.]
A political slander or false report.

Roorkee chair /ˈruəkiː ˈtʃɛː/ *noun phr.* E20.
[A town in Uttar Pradesh, India.]
A collapsible chair with a wooden frame and canvas back and seat, originally produced in Roorkee.

roosa /ˈruːsə/ *noun.* Also **rusa**, **rusha** /ˈruːʃə/. M19.
[Hindi *rūsā*, Marathi *rośē* from Sanskrit *rohiṣa*.]
More fully ***roosa grass***. An Indian grass, *Cymbopogon martinii*, which yields an essential oil.

roose /ruːz/ *verb & noun.* Long *obsolete* exc. *Scot.* & *north.* Also (*Scot.*) **ruise**. ME.
[As verb from Old Norse *hrósa*, as noun from Old Norse *hrós* boast.]
▶ **A** *verb.* †**1** *verb refl. & (rare) intrans.* Boast or be proud of something. Usu. foll. by *of*. ME–M17.
2 *verb trans.* Commend, praise; flatter. ME.
▶ **B** *noun.* **1** Boasting, bragging; a boast, a brag. ME.
2 Commendation, praise; flattery. ME.

Roosevelt /ˈrəʊz(ə)vɛlt, ˈruː-/ *noun.* L19.
[Theodore *Roosevelt*: see next.]
Roosevelt elk, ***Roosevelt wapiti***, ***Roosevelt's elk***, ***Roosevelt's wapiti***, a wapiti of a large, dark-coloured race found in coastal forests of north-western N. America.

Rooseveltian /ˈrəʊz(ə)vɛltɪən, ˈruː-/ *adjective.* E20.
[from family name *Roosevelt* + -IAN.]
Of, pertaining to, or characteristic of (a member of) the Roosevelt family, esp. Theodore Roosevelt (1858–1919), US president 1901–9, or his relative and nephew-in-law Franklin D. Roosevelt (1882–1945), US president 1933–45.

roost /ruːst/ *noun*¹ & *verb.*
[Old English *hrōst* = Middle & mod. Dutch *roest* (cf. also Old Saxon *hrōst* spars of a roof), of unkn. origin.]
▶ **A** *noun.* **1** A support, esp. a branch, on which a bird perches; a place where a bird or group of birds or bats regularly settles to sleep. OE. ▸**b** A hen-house; the part of a hen-house in which the birds perch at night. L16.
2 The underside of a roof; a loft. *local.* L18.
3 *fig.* A resting-place; *esp.* a place offering temporary sleeping accommodation. E19.

📖 **3** O. W. HOLMES A million roosts for man, but only one nest.

Phrases: **at roost** roosting, perched. **come home to roost** *fig.* (of an action etc.) recoil unfavourably upon the originator. **go to roost** retire to rest. ***rule the roost***: see RULE *verb*. **take roost** perch.
Comb.: **roost-cock** (now *dial.*) a domestic cock.
▶ **B** *verb.* **1** *verb intrans.* Of a bird: perch or settle on a roost; sleep or rest in a roost. Also foll. by *in*, *on*. M16.
2 *verb intrans. fig.* ▸**a** Lodge oneself; settle to rest; *esp.* pass the night. Also foll. by *at*, *in*. Chiefly *literary.* M16. ▸**b** Seat oneself; be seated. Foll. by *at*, *on*. *colloq.* E19.
3 *verb trans.* Provide with a resting-place, esp. sleeping accommodation. M19.

📖 **2a** THACKERAY Stopped to roost at Terracina. **b** P. DE VRIES I found myself roosting at a local diner counter.

■ **roosted** *adjective* (*poet.*) perched on or settled in a roost M18. **roosting** *noun* (*a*) the action of the verb; an instance of this; (*b*) a place suitable for roosting: E17.

roost *noun*² var. of ROUST *noun*².

rooster /ˈruːstə/ *noun.* L18.
[from ROOST *noun*¹ + -ER¹.]
1 A domestic cock. Chiefly *dial.* & *N. Amer.* L18.
2 A person likened to a rooster; *spec.* (*a*) an informer; (*b*) a conceited or lascivious person. *slang* (now chiefly *US*). L18.
3 A N. American violet, *Viola palmata*, esp. as used in a children's game resembling conkers. Chiefly in ***fight roosters***. L19.
Comb.: **rooster comb**, **rooster-heads** *US* the shooting-star, *Dodecatheon meadia*; **rooster tail** *N. Amer.* the spray of water thrown up behind a speedboat or surfboard.

root /ruːt/ *noun*¹ & *adjective.* LOE.
[Old Norse *rót* from Scandinavian base obscurely rel. to Latin *radix* root, *ramus* branch, and WORT *noun*¹.]
▶ **A** *noun.* **I 1** The colourless, usu. underground, part of a vascular plant (developed from the radicle) which serves to anchor it, convey nourishment, etc.; in *pl.*, such an organ with any accompanying branches, rootlets, or fibres. LOE.
2 The underground part of a plant used as food or in medicine. Now chiefly, this part when fleshy and enlarged, used as a vegetable; a plant grown for its fleshy edible underground part. LOE. ▸**b** The penis. *coarse slang.* L16.
3 The permanent underground stock of a plant from which the stems or leaves are produced. Also (now *rare*), a (growing) plant. ME.
4 ANATOMY. The embedded or basal part of a bodily organ or structure, such as a hair, the tongue, a tooth, a nail, etc. ME. ▸**b** Either of two short paired nerves which arise from the spinal cord and unite to form each spinal nerve. L19.
5 The bottom or base *of* something material; *esp.* the foot of a hill (usu. in *pl.*). ME. ▸**b** The bottom of the groove of a screw thread. L19.
6 a That part of anything by or at which it is attached to something else. M17. ▸**b** The opaque base of a precious stone, esp. an emerald. L17.

📖 **1** W. CATHER The . . trees of the desert, whose roots are always seeking water. ***adventitious root***, ***aerial root***, ***tap root***, ***tuberous root***, etc. **2** *Farmer's Magazine* Very few turnips . . this season; this root having generally failed. **3** J. ABERCROMBIE The propagation of bulbous and tuberous roots for general supply. **4** J. BINGHAM Her dyed fair hair, the brown showing at the roots on the scalp. **5** N. CALDER Eclogite, a material found . . in the roots of mountains.

▶ **II 7** The source or origin of or *of* some quality, condition, action, etc. ME.
8 A person or family forming the source of a lineage. ME. ▸**b** A scion, an offshoot. Chiefly in biblical use. ME.
9 The basis or means of continuance or growth of a thing. ME.
10 The bottom or real basis of a thing; the inner or essential part. Formerly also *spec.*, the bottom *of* the heart. ME.
11 †**a** A hold on a person's affections or favour. E–M18. ▸**b** In *pl.* Social, cultural, or ethnic origins, esp. as the reasons for a person's long-standing emotional attachment to a place. E20.

📖 **7** SHELLEY The root of all this ill is prelacy. J. KLEIN Our need for others has its roots in our earliest experiences. **9** A. ALISON This prodigious change . . laid the axe to the root of the aristocracy. **10** F. W. ROBERTSON The root of the matter has not been reached. E. BLISHEN She had been at the root of so much pain and enmity. **11b** L. R. BANKS The things that stopped him; the claims of his business, his wife, his kids, his *roots*. C. POTOK He wandered from city to city, never finding roots anywhere.

▶ **III 12** ASTROLOGY. = RADIX 2. Long *rare* or *obsolete.* LME.
13 MATH. **a** A number which, when multiplied by itself a requisite number of times, produces a given expression. LME. ▸**b** A value of an unknown quantity which will satisfy a given equation. E18. ▸**c** A unique node or vertex of a graph from which every other node can be reached. Also ***root node***. M19.
14 LINGUISTICS. An ultimate unanalysable element of language; a (not necessarily surviving) morphological element as a base from which words are formed by means of affixation or other modification. M16.
15 MUSIC. The fundamental note of a chord. E19.
16 A forceful kick. *slang.* E20.
17 An act of sexual intercourse; a (usu. female) sexual partner. *Austral. coarse slang.* M20.
Phrases: ***cube root***: see CUBE *adjective* 1. **digital root** the digit obtained when all the digits of a number are added and the process repeated until the result is a single digit. ***motor root***: see MOTOR *noun & adjective*. **on its own roots**, **on own roots** (of a plant) having its tissues all developed from the same embryo, not grafted or budded. **pull up by the roots** (*a*) uproot; (*b*) eradicate, destroy. **put down roots** (*a*) begin to draw nourishment from the soil; (*b*) *fig.* become settled or established. **root and branch** *adjectival & adverbial phr.* thorough(ly), radical(ly). ***root of scarcity***, ***scarcity root***. ***serpentary root***: see SERPENTARY 2. **strike at the root of**, **strike at the roots of** set about destroying. **take root**, **strike root** (*a*) begin to grow and draw nourishment from the soil; (*b*) *fig.* become fixed or established, settle down *in* a place etc. **third root** cube root.
Comb.: **root-aorist** PHILOLOGY in certain Indo-European languages, an aorist formed by adding personal endings directly to the root-syllable of the verb; **root-ball** the mass formed by the roots of a plant and the soil surrounding them; **root-balled** *adjective* (of a plant, esp. a tree) having the root-ball wrapped in sacking etc. for protection during transportation etc.; **root beer** *N. Amer.* an effervescent drink made from an extract of roots; **root-bound** *adjective* (of a plant) pot-bound; **root canal** the pulp-filled cavity within the root of a tooth; **root-cap** BOTANY = CALYPTRA (a); **root cellar** *N. Amer.*: a cellar in a house for storing root vegetables etc. **root-climber** a plant which climbs by means of rootlets developed on the stem; **root crop**: consisting of a vegetable with an edible root, as beet, carrot, potato, etc.; **root cutting**: taken from the root of a plant; **root digger** (*a*) a tool for digging up edible roots; (*b*) a member of a N. American Indian people who subsisted chiefly on roots (cf. DIGGER 1d); **root directory** COMPUTING the directory at the highest level of a hierarchy; **root doctor** *US dial.*: who treats ailments using roots; **root-fallen** *adjective* (of a grain-crop) fallen due to frost-damaged roots; **root fly** any of numerous dark slender flies of the family Anthomyiidae whose larvae can cause serious damage to the roots of crops; **root gall** a gall on the root of a plant caused by an insect, nematode, etc.; **root ginger**: in its raw unprepared state; **root-graft** *noun & verb* (*a*) *noun* a graft of a scion on to a root; a naturally occurring graft between the roots of neighbouring trees; (*b*) *verb trans.* graft by means of a root-graft; **root-hair** BOTANY any of the unicellular outgrowths from the outer layer of cells of a root, whose function is to absorb moisture from the soil; **root-house** (*a*) an ornamental building made chiefly of tree-roots, esp. in a garden; (*b*) a house or barn for storing roots; **root-knot** a plant disease caused by infestation of the roots by nematodes of the genus *Meloidogyne*, producing characteristic swellings; **root-leaf** a radical leaf; **root-mean-square** PHYSICS the square root of the mean of the squares of a set of values; abbreviation *rms*; ***root node***: see sense 13c above; ***root nodule***: see NODULE 4; **root position** MUSIC: of a chord whose lowest note is the root (sense 15); **root pressure** BOTANY the hydrostatic pressure generated in the roots of a plant, which helps the sap to rise in the xylem; **root-prune** *verb trans.* prune (a tree) by cutting its roots; **root rot** a plant disease that attacks roots; **rootstock** (*a*) BOTANY a

rhizome; *esp.* a short erect rhizome or underground stem from which new leaves and shoots are produced annually; (*b*) a stock on to which another variety has been grafted or budded; (*c*) a primary form from which offshoots have arisen; a primitive form; **root swell**, **root swelling** an outgrowth of a tree above a root; **root-weed**: which propagates itself by roots rather than seeds; **root-worm** any of various nematodes that infest the roots of plants.

▶**B** *adjective.* Of an idea etc.: from which another or others originated; fundamental. **M17.**

■ **rootless** *adjective* devoid of roots **LME.** **rootlessly** *adverb* (*fig.*) **E20.** **rootlessness** *noun* (*fig.*) **M19.** **rootlet** *noun* (*a*) a slender root or division of a root; any of the secondary roots thrown out laterally for support by ivy and other climbing plants; (*b*) PHYSIOLOGY (now *rare*) a slender branch, fibre, etc., of a structure, esp. a vein or nerve: **L18.** **rootlike** *adjective* resembling (that of) a root **M19.** **rootling** *noun* a rootlet, a subsidiary root **E18.**

root /ruːt/ *noun*[2]. *colloq.* **M19.**
[from ROOT *verb*[2].]
The action or an act of rooting or rummaging.

root /ruːt/ *verb*[1]. **ME.**
[from ROOT *noun*[1]. Cf. ROUT *verb*[5].]
1 *verb trans.* Fix or attach (as) by means of a root or roots; establish firmly; implant deeply. Chiefly *fig.* Also foll. by *in, into, to,* etc. **ME.**
2 *verb intrans.* Grow roots, take root; *fig.* settle, establish oneself (freq. foll. by *in*). **ME.** ▸**b** *verb trans.* Cause (a cutting) to grow roots. **E19.** ▸**c** *verb intrans.* Have a basis or origin *in* something. **L19.**
3 *verb trans.* Pull, drag, or dig up by the roots; *fig.* remove, eradicate, destroy. Usu. foll. by *out, up.* **ME.** ▸**b** Clear *away* completely. **LME.**
4 *verb trans. & intrans.* Kick (a person) esp. in the buttocks. *slang.* **L19.**
5 *Austral. coarse slang.* **a** *verb trans. & intrans.* Have sexual intercourse (with). **M20.** ▸**b** *verb trans.* Ruin; exhaust; frustrate. **M20.**

> 1 J. B. PRIESTLEY What roots them there . . is their work. K. LINES As though terror had rooted her white feet to the ground. M. HUNTER True fantasy . . is always firmly rooted in fact. 2 K. MOORE To tug at some couch-grass rooting in the lily bed. *Garden News* Side shoots root better than . . terminal shoots. 3 R. LINDNER Anton went into hiding . . but the F.B.I. finally rooted him out.

■ **rooter** *noun*[1] (*a*) an eradicator *of* something (usu. foll. by *-out, -up*); (*b*) *spec.* (*Hist.*) an advocate of the total abolition of episcopal government: **M16.** **rooting** *noun* (*a*) the action of the verb; an instance of this; (*b*) a root; roots collectively; a firm attachment by means of roots: **ME.**

root /ruːt/ *verb*[2]. In sense 1 also (earlier) †**wroot**. See also ROUT *verb*[4].
[Old English *wrōtan* = Old Norse *róta*, Middle & mod. Low German *wrōten*, Middle & mod. Dutch *wroeten*, Old High German *ruozzen* rel. to Old English *wrōt*, Low German *wrōte*, German *Rüssel* snout, and perh. ult. Latin *rodere* gnaw. Partly directly from Old Norse.]
1 *verb intrans. & trans.* Of an animal, esp. a pig: turn up (the ground etc.) with the snout, beak, etc., in search of food. **OE.**
2 a *verb intrans.* Poke about, rummage. Also foll. by *about, around.* Cf. earlier ROUT *verb*[4] 1b. **M19.** ▸**b** *verb trans.* Find or extract by rummaging. Foll. by *out, up.* **M19.**
3 *verb intrans.* Foll. by *for*: cheer or applaud (a sports team etc.); *gen.* support. *colloq.* (orig. *US*). **L19.** ▸**b** *verb trans.* Cheer or spur *on. colloq.* (chiefly *US*). **M20.**

> 1 R. MACAULAY The lean pigs scuffled and rooted in the dark forest. 2a *New Yorker* Bomb-squad officers . . were . . rooting through nearby trash cans. K. AMIS Victor began to root clumsily in a cupboard. P. LIVELY What's he been doing rooting around in Daddy's stuff? 3 *Golf World* The fans, rooting for a British victory, cheered his bunkered ball. *K.O.* I'm rooting for him in his multi-charge lawsuit.

Phrases: **rootin' tootin'** *adjectival phr.* (*slang*, chiefly *N. Amer.*) noisy, boisterous; rip-roaring, lively.
■ **rooter** *noun*[2] (*colloq.*, chiefly *US*) (*a*) a person or animal (esp. a pig) which roots; (*b*) a machine for loosening the surface of the ground: **M17.**

rootage /ˈruːtɪdʒ/ *noun.* **L16.**
[from ROOT *noun*[1], *verb*[1] + -AGE.]
†**1** The action of rooting *out* or eradicating something. *rare.* Only in **L16.**
2 A place to take root. **L19.**
3 A system of roots. **L19.**

rooted /ˈruːtɪd/ *adjective.* **ME.**
[from ROOT *verb*[1], *noun*[1]: see -ED[1], -ED[2].]
1 That has (been) rooted (*lit. & fig.*). **ME.** ▸**b** Of a disease: chronic. *rare.* **LME.**
2 Esp. of a plant: having a root or roots, *spec.* of a specified kind or number. **M16.**

> 1 GEO. ELIOT There's no more moving you than the rooted tree. A. THIRKELL People . . had a rooted objection to taking responsibility. E. J. HOWARD Everybody . . seemed rooted or frozen in their various positions. ***deep-rooted***: see DEEP *adverb.* 2 P. THROWER Give the rooted cuttings as much light as possible.

■ **rootedly** *adverb* in a rooted or firmly established manner **E17.** **rootedness** *noun* the quality of being rooted or firmly established **M17.**

rootfast /ˈruːtfɑːst/ *adjective. rare.* **LOE.**
[Old Norse *rótfastr* (Norwegian, Swedish *rotfast*), from *rót* ROOT *noun*[1] + *fastr* FAST *adjective*.]
Firmly held (as) by the roots.
■ **rootfastness** *noun* **E16.**

rootle /ˈruːt(ə)l/ *verb intrans. & trans.* **E19.**
[from ROOT *verb*[2] + -LE[3].]
= ROOT *verb*[2] 1, 2a, b.

roots /ruːts/ *adjective.* **L20.**
[from ROOT *noun*[1] + -S[1].]
Esp. of music: expressive of a distinctive ethnic or cultural (esp. West Indian) identity; traditional, authentic, unadulterated.

> *Q* American artists who slipped without fuss from roots music to the cabaret bar.

rootsy /ˈruːtsi/ *adjective. colloq.* **L20.**
[formed as prec. + -Y[1].]
Of music: uncommercialized, unadulterated; full-blooded; *gen.* traditional, ethnic.

rooty /ˈruːti/ *noun. Military slang.* **L19.**
[formed as ROTI.]
Bread.

rooty /ˈruːti/ *adjective.* **L15.**
[from ROOT *noun*[1] + -Y[1].]
Full of roots; consisting of roots; of or suggestive of roots.
■ **rootiness** *noun* **E19.**

rooty-toot /ruːtɪˈtuːt/ *noun & adjective. slang* (chiefly *US*). **L19.**
[Imit. of the sound of a trumpet.]
▶**A** *noun.* Something, esp. an early style of jazz, that is noisy or lively. **L19.**
▶**B** *adjective.* Of music, esp. early jazz: noisy and lively. **L20.**

rooves *noun pl.* see ROOF *noun.*

ropable *adjective* var. of ROPEABLE.

rope /rəʊp/ *noun*[1]. See also RAPE *noun*[1].
[Old English *rāp* = Old Frisian *rāp*, Middle & mod. Low German *rēp*, Middle & mod. Dutch *reep*, Old & mod. High German *reif*, Old Norse *reip*, Gothic *raip* (in *skaudaraip* shoe-thong), from Germanic (adopted in Finnish as *raippa* rod, twig).]
▶**I 1** (A piece of) stout cord made of twisted strands of hemp, sisal, flax, cotton, nylon, wire, or other similar material. **OE.**
2 *spec.* **a** A stout line used for measuring; a sounding-line. Later, a specific measure of length. Now *local.* **OE.** ▸**b** *sing.* & in *pl.* A tightrope. **LME.** ▸**c** In *pl.* The cords marking off a boxing- or wrestling-ring or a cricket ground. **E19.** ▸**d** A clothes-line. Now *Scot. dial.* **M19.** ▸**e** A lasso. *US.* **M19.** ▸**f** A skipping-rope. **L19.** ▸**g** MOUNTAINEERING. A climbing-rope; *transf.* a group of climbers roped together. **L19.**
3 A rope or halter for hanging a person; *transf.* execution by hanging. **ME.**

> 3 B. BEHAN Some of them had left the cell for the rope or the firing squad.

▶**II 4** A quantity of some material twisted together in the form of a rope; a thing resembling a rope in shape. **OE.** ▸**b** ASTRONOMY. A group of magnetic lines of force twisted together. **M20.** ▸**c** ANTHROPOLOGY. A system of descent or inheritance in which the link is formed from father or mother to the children of the opposite sex. **M20.** ▸**d** A cigar. *US slang.* **M20.** ▸**e** Marijuana. *slang.* **M20.**
5 A number of or *of* onions, ova, pearls, etc., strung together. **LME.**
6 A viscid strand in drink or food, esp. beer, milk, or bread, caused by bacterial or fungal contamination. **M18.**

> 4 T. HARDY An immense rope of hair like a ship's cable. 5 B. CHATWIN Three ropes of pearls fell into the ruffles of her . . blouse.

Phrases: **at the end of one's rope** (chiefly *N. Amer.*) at the end of one's tether, at the extreme limit of one's patience, resources, abilities, etc. **give a person enough rope**, **give a person plenty of rope** give a person enough freedom of action to bring about his or her own downfall. ***jump rope***: see JUMP *verb.* **know the ropes**, **learn the ropes** be or become experienced in or familiar with some customary action, practice, etc. ***left-hand rope***: see LEFT HAND *noun & adjectival phr.* ***long rope***: see LONG *adjective*[1]. ***money for old rope***: see MONEY *noun.* ***old rope***: see OLD *adjective.* **on the high ropes** elated; enraged; disdainful. **on the rope** MOUNTAINEERING roped together. **on the ropes** (*a*) BOXING forced against the ropes by the opponent's attack; (*b*) *fig.* near defeat. **rope of sand** a thing having no binding power; deceptive security. **show a person the ropes** teach a person about some customary action, practice, etc. ***skip rope***: see SKIP *verb*[1]. ***standing ropes***: see STANDING *adjective.*
Comb.: **rope-a-dope** *US slang* a tactic in boxing whereby a boxer rests against the ropes and protects himself with his arms and gloves, goading an opponent to throw tiring ineffective punches; **rope-barrel** = ***rope-roll*** below; **rope border** (esp. in BASKET-MAKING) a border resembling twisted strands of rope; **rope brown** a type of strong brown paper originally made from old rope; **rope burn**: caused by the friction of a rope; **rope-dancer** = ***rope-walker*** below; **rope-dancing** = ***rope-walking*** below; **rope-end** *noun & verb* = ROPE'S END; **rope horse** *US*: ridden by a person roping an animal; **rope-house** a building in which ropes are made and stored; **rope ladder**: made of two long ropes connected at intervals by short crosspieces of rope, wood, or metal; **rope-maker** a person who makes ropes; ***rope-maker's eye*** (NAUTICAL), a special eye made at the end of a rope; **rope-moulding**: cut spirally in imitation of strands of rope; **rope-roll** a cylinder on which drawing-ropes are wound; **rope-sight** CAMPANOLOGY facility in judging when to pull a rope, from the position and movement of others; **rope stitch** an ornamental embroidery stitch producing a ropelike effect by a series of slanted overlapping stitches; **rope-trick** a trick with a rope; *spec.* = ***INDIAN rope-trick***; **rope-walk** a long stretch of ground where ropes are made; **rope-walker** a performer on a tightrope; **rope-walking** the action of performing on a tightrope; **rope-way** (*a*) a cable railway; (*b*) a rope used as a means of transport; **rope-work** (*a*) a place where ropes are made; (*b*) an arrangement of ropes; (*c*) use of ropes in climbing; **rope-yard**: where ropes are made.
■ **ropelike** *adjective* resembling a rope **M19.** **ropery** *adjective* (*a*) a place where ropes are made; (*b*) *arch.* trickery, roguery: **LME.**

rope /rəʊp/ *noun*[2]. Now *dial.*
[Old English (*h*)*rop* = Middle Dutch *rop*, of unkn. origin.]
An entrail, an intestine. Usu. in *pl.*

rope /rəʊp/ *verb.* **ME.**
[from ROPE *noun*[1].]
1 *verb trans.* Tie, fasten, or secure with a rope. Also foll. by *up.* **ME.**
2 *verb intrans.* (Of a liquid) become viscid, form ropes; be drawn out into a filament. **LME.** ▸**b** *verb trans.* Draw out or twist into the shape of a rope. **M19.**
3 *verb trans.* Enclose or mark off (a space) with a rope. Usu. foll. by *in, off.* **M18.**
4 *verb trans.* Catch with a rope; lasso. *N. Amer. & Austral.* **E19.**
5 MOUNTAINEERING. **a** *verb trans.* Attach (a person) to another with a rope; connect (a party of climbers) with a rope. **M19.** ▸**b** *verb intrans.* Of a party of climbers: connect each other together with a rope. Usu. foll. by *up.* **M19.** ▸**c** *verb trans.* Assist with ropes. **L19.**
6 *verb trans.* NAUTICAL. Sew a bolt-rope to (a sail). **M19.**
7 *slang.* **a** *verb trans.* Pull back (a horse) so as to intentionally lose a race. **M19.** ▸**b** *verb intrans.* Lose a race intentionally by holding back. **L19.**

> 1 DAY LEWIS He roped the wheelbarrow on top of the ass cart. L. SPALDING Lights moved on the water . . , roped to night fishermen. 3 *South Wales Echo* A section of the centre had to be roped off. 5a DOUGLAS CLARK Redruth was climbing solo . . . Silk was roped to a partner. b C. BONINGTON We soon roped up, fearful of hidden crevasses.

With adverbs & prepositions in specialized senses: **rope down** MOUNTAINEERING abseil. **rope in** persuade to take part. **rope into** persuade to take part in.

ropeable /ˈrəʊpəb(ə)l/ *adjective.* Also **ropable**. **L19.**
[from prec. + -ABLE.]
1 Able to be roped. **L19.**
2 (Of a horse etc.) intractable, wild; (of a person) angry. *Austral. & NZ slang.* **L19.**

rope-band /ˈrəʊ(p)band/ *noun.* **ME.**
[Alt. by popular etym.]
= ROBAND.

ropemanship /ˈrəʊpmənʃɪp/ *noun.* **M19.**
[from ROPE *noun*[1] after *horsemanship* etc.]
Skill in walking along or climbing up a rope.

roper /ˈrəʊpə/ *noun.* **ME.**
[from ROPE *noun*[1], *verb* + -ER[1].]
1 A person who makes ropes. **ME.**
2 A person who uses a lasso. Chiefly *US.* **E19.**
3 A gambling-house decoy. Also ***roper-in***. **M19.**
4 A jockey who prevents a horse from winning by holding it back; a person who intentionally loses a race. **L19.**

rope's end /rəʊps ˈɛnd/ *noun & verb phr.* Also (the usual form as verb) **rope's-end**. **LME.**
[from ROPE *noun*[1] + -'S[1] + END *noun*.]
▶**A** *noun phr.* **1** The end of a rope; *esp.* (*Hist.*) a short piece of rope used for flogging, esp. for flogging a sailor. **LME.**
2 A hangman's noose. **E19.**
▶**B** *verb trans.* Flog with a rope's end. **E19.**

ropey *adjective* var. of ROPY.

rope-yarn /ˈrəʊpjɑːn/ *noun & adjective.* **E17.**
[from ROPE *noun*[1] + YARN *noun*.]
Chiefly NAUTICAL. ▶**A** *noun.* **1** A single yarn forming part of a strand in a rope; a piece of yarn obtained by unpicking an old rope. **E17.**
2 Yarn obtained by untwisting rope-strands, or used for making them. **E17.**
3 A small or trifling thing. **E19.**
▶**B** *adjective.* Designating a day given as a holiday or (esp.) a half-holiday. Chiefly *Nautical slang.* **L19.**

roping /ˈrəʊpɪŋ/ *noun.* **M16.**
[from ROPE *noun*[1], *verb* + -ING[1].]
1 Ropes collectively; a set or arrangement of ropes. **M16.**

2 A ropelike formation. **M17.**
3 The action of ROPE *verb.* **M19.**
Comb.: **roping-pole**, **roping-stick** *Austral.* a long pole with a noosed rope attached to the end, used for catching cattle and unbroken horses.

ropy /ˈrəʊpi/ *adjective.* Also **ropey**. **L15.**
[from ROPE *noun*¹ + -Y¹.]
1 Of a liquid or bread: forming viscid or slimy threads; sticky and stringy. **L15.**
2 Having the form or tenacity of a rope. **M18.**
3 Poor in quality; unwell. *colloq.* **E19.**

> **2** M. ANGELOU A long, ropy, peach-tree switch. **3** L. R. BANKS I wrote half the night, and my writing got ropier and my spelling got weirder. *Listener* Felt ropy last night . . bad stomach upset and temperature this a.m. N. HORNBY Paul's gone to see whether there's any ropy holiday liqueurs mouldering in the back of a cupboard.

■ **ropily** *adverb* **M19.** **ropiness** *noun* **M17.**

roque /rəʊk/ *noun.* **L19.**
[Alt. of CROQUET.]
A form of croquet played in the US on a court surrounded by a bank and using ten hoops and short-handled mallets.

Roquefort /ˈrɒkfɔː/ *noun.* **M19.**
[A village in SW France.]
1 (Proprietary name for) a soft blue cheese made from ewes' milk at Roquefort. **M19.**
2 In full ***Roquefort dressing***. A salad-dressing made with Roquefort. Chiefly *N. Amer.* **M20.**

roquelaure /ˈrɒkələː/ *noun.* **E18.**
[Antoine-Gaston, Duc de *Roquelaure* (1656–1738), Marshal of France. Cf. ROKELAY.]
Hist. A man's knee-length cloak with a cape collar, fashionable during the 18th cent.

roquet /ˈrəʊkeɪ/ *verb & noun.* **M19.**
[App. arbitrary alt. of CROQUET.]
CROQUET. ▶**A** *verb.* **1** *verb trans.* Of a ball: strike (another ball). **M19.**
2 *verb trans. & intrans.* Strike (another player's ball) with one's own. **M19.**
▶**B** *noun.* An act of hitting another player's ball with one's own. **M19.**

roquette /rɒˈkɛt/ *noun.* **E20.**
[French: see ROCKET *noun*².]
= ROCKET *noun*² 1.

roral /ˈrɔːr(ə)l/ *adjective. rare.* **M17.**
[Latin *ror-*, *ros* dew + -AL¹.]
Dewy.

†**rorid** *adjective.* **LME–E18.**
[Latin *roridus*, formed as prec.: see -ID¹.]
Dewy.

roriferous /rɔːˈrɪf(ə)rəs/ *adjective. rare.* **M17.**
[from Latin *rorifer*, formed as RORAL + -OUS.]
Bringing or bearing dew.

ro-ro /ˈrəʊrəʊ/ *adjective.* **M20.**
[Abbreviation.]
= ROLL-ON ***roll-off***.

rorqual /ˈrɔːkw(ə)l/ *noun.* **E19.**
[French from Norwegian *røyrkval* from Old Norse *reyðarhvalr*, from *reyðr* specific name + *hvalr* whale.]
Any of various baleen whales of the family Balaenopteridae, characterized by a pleated throat and small dorsal fin; *esp.* (*a*) (more fully ***common rorqual***) the fin whale; (*b*) (more fully ***lesser rorqual***) the minke whale.

Rorschach /ˈrɔːʃɑːk/ *adjective & noun.* **E20.**
[Hermann *Rorschach* (1884–1922), Swiss psychiatrist.]
▶**A** *adjective.* Designating or pertaining to a type of personality test in which a standard set of ink blots of different shapes and colours is presented one by one to a subject, who is asked to describe what they suggest or resemble. **E20.**
▶**B** *noun.* A Rorschach test. **M20.**

Rörstrand /ˈrəːstraːnd/ *noun & adjective.* **L19.**
[Name of a ceramics factory opened in 1725 near Stockholm, Sweden.]
(Designating) the varieties of pottery and porcelain manufactured at Rörstrand.

rort /rɔːt/ *noun. Austral. slang.* **E20.**
[Back-form. from RORTY.]
1 A trick, a fraud, a dishonest practice. **E20.**
2 A wild party. **M20.**

rort /rɔːt/ *verb intrans. slang.* **E20.**
[Back-form. from next.]
1 Engage in fraud or dishonest practices. Chiefly as ***rorting*** *verbal noun. Austral.* **E20.**
2 Shout or complain loudly (*at*). Also, call the odds at a race meeting. **M20.**
■ **rorter** *noun* (*Austral.*) **E20.**

rorty /ˈrɔːti/ *adjective. slang.* **M19.**
[Origin unkn.]
1 Boisterous, rowdy; jolly, splendid. **M19.**
2 Coarse, earthy. **L19.**

Rory /ˈrɔːri/ *noun. rhyming slang.* **M19.**
[*Rory O'More*, a legendary Irish rebel, hero of a popular 19th-cent. ballad.]
In full ***Rory O'More***.
1 A floor. **M19.**
2 A door. **L19.**
1 on the Rory poor, penniless.

rosace /ˈrəʊzeɪs/ *noun.* **M19.**
[French formed as ROSACEOUS.]
1 A rose window. **M19.**
2 A rose-shaped ornament or design. **L19.**

rosacea /rəʊˈzeɪʃɪə/ *noun.* **L19.**
[Latin, fem. of *rosaceus*, in the sense of 'rose-coloured': see next.]
MEDICINE. A condition in which certain facial blood-vessels enlarge, giving the cheeks and nose a flushed appearance. Also ***acne rosacea***.

rosaceous /rəʊˈzeɪʃəs/ *adjective.* **M18.**
[from Latin *rosaceus*, from *rosa* ROSE *noun*: see -ACEOUS.]
1 BOTANY. Of or pertaining to the Rosaceae or rose family. **M18.**
2 Rose-shaped. **L18.**

rosaker /ˈrəʊseɪkə/ *noun.* Long *obsolete* exc. *Hist.* **L16.**
[Alt. of next.]
= REALGAR.

rosalger *noun* var. of RESALGAR.

rosalia /rəʊˈzɑːlɪə/ *noun.* **E19.**
[Italian female forename in *Rosalia, mia cara* title of an Italian song using this device.]
MUSIC. The repetition of a phrase or melody one note higher, with the retention of the same intervals and a consequent change of key.

rosaline /ˈrəʊzəliːn/ *noun.* **E20.**
[Prob. from French.]
In full ***rosaline point***. A type of fine needlepoint or pillow-lace.

rosaniline /rəʊˈzanɪliːn, -lɪn/ *noun.* **M19.**
[from ROSE *noun* + ANILINE.]
CHEMISTRY. A tricyclic amine derived from aniline, used as a magenta dye and (usu. as fuchsine) a medical fungicide.

rosarian /rəʊˈzɛːrɪən/ *noun.* **M19.**
[from Latin *rosarium*: see ROSARY, -IAN.]
1 A person interested or engaged in the cultivation of roses. **M19.**
2 ROMAN CATHOLIC CHURCH. A member of a Confraternity of the Rosary. **M19.**

rosarium /rəʊˈzɛːrɪəm/ *noun.* Pl. **-iums**, **-ia** /-ɪə/. **M19.**
[Latin: see next.]
A rose-garden.

rosary /ˈrəʊz(ə)ri/ *noun.* **ME.**
[Latin *rosarium* rose-garden, Anglo-Latin *rosarius* (sc. *nummus* penny), uses as noun of neut. and masc. of adjective from *rosa* ROSE *noun*: see -ARY¹.]
†**1** A customary rent. *rare.* Only in **ME.**
2 *Hist.* A counterfeit penny of foreign origin, current during the 13th cent. and declared illegal by Edward I. **LME.**
3 A piece of ground set apart for the cultivation of roses; a rose-garden. Formerly also, a rose bush. **LME.**
4 ROMAN CATHOLIC CHURCH. A form of devotion accompanying the contemplation of fifteen mysteries (now usu. in groups of five), in which fifteen decades of Hail Marys are recited, each decade preceded by an Our Father and followed by a Glory Be; a book containing this devotion. **E16.**
5 a ROMAN CATHOLIC CHURCH. A string of 165 beads divided into fifteen sets (each having ten small and one large bead), used for keeping count in the recital of this or a similar devotion; now *esp.* a similar set of 55 beads (also more fully ***the lesser rosary***). **L16.** ▶**b** A string of beads or knotted cord used similarly in other religious traditions. **M19.**
Comb. & phrases: **rickety rosary**: see RICKETY 1b; **rosary pea** (a seed of) the jequirity, *Abrus precatorius*; **Rosary-Sunday** ROMAN CATHOLIC CHURCH the first Sunday in October, when the victory over the Turks in 1571 is sometimes celebrated.

†**rosa solis** *noun phr.* **M16.**
[mod. Latin, lit. 'rose of the sun', alt. of ROS SOLIS.]
1 The sundew, *Drosera rotundifolia*. **M16–L18.**
2 A cordial or liqueur originally made with the juice of the sundew plant, later from spiced and flavoured spirits. **M16–E19.**

roscid /ˈrɒsɪd/ *adjective.* Now *rare.* **E17.**
[Latin *roscidus* dewy, from *ros* dew: see -ID¹.]
Dewy, moist; falling like dew.

Roscius /ˈrɒsɪəs, ˈrɒʃɪəs/ *noun.* **M17.**
[Quintus *Roscius* Gallus (d. 62 BC), a famous Roman actor.]
An actor of outstanding ability, success, or fame.
■ **Roscian** *adjective* characteristic of Roscius; famous for acting: **M17.**

roscoe /ˈrɒskəʊ/ *noun. US slang.* **E20.**
[The surname *Roscoe*.]
A gun, *esp.* a pistol or revolver. Also ***John Roscoe***.

roscoelite /ˈrɒskəʊlʌɪt/ *noun.* **L19.**
[Sir Henry *Roscoe* (1833–1915), English chemist + -LITE.]
MINERALOGY. A vanadium ore that is an analogue of muscovite, occurring as minute green or brown scales.

rose /rəʊz/ *noun & adjective.*
[Old English *rōse* corresp. to Middle Dutch *rōse* (Dutch *roos*), Old High German *rōsa* (German *Rose*), Old Norse *rósa*, from Germanic from Latin *rosa* rel. to Greek *rhodon*; reinforced in Middle English from Old & mod. French *rose*.]
▶**A** *noun.* **I 1** The flower, freq. fragrant and (in cultivated forms) double, of the rose (sense 2). **OE.**
2 Any plant of the genus *Rosa* (family Rosaceae), which comprises pinnate-leaved, usu. prickly, freq. climbing shrubs bearing large usu. pink, white, yellow, or crimson flowers and includes many species, varieties, and hybrids grown for ornament; a rose bush. **LME.**
3 Any of various plants resembling the rose, esp. in the beauty of their flower. Chiefly in phrs. (see below) or with specifying word. **LME.**
2 ***burnet rose***, ***cabbage rose***, ***damask rose***, ***Japanese rose***, ***moss rose***, ***tea rose***, etc. **3** ***Alpine rose***, ***Christmas rose***, ***guelder rose***, ***rock rose***, etc.
▶**II 4** A rose as a symbol of beauty, virtue, perfection, etc.; a thing or person (esp. a woman) of great beauty, virtue, perfection, etc.; a paragon. **OE.** ▶**b** In *pl.* Favourable circumstances; ease, success, comfort, pleasure, etc. **M19.**
5 Secrecy; confidence; privacy. Chiefly in ***under the rose*** below. **M16.**

> **4** LONGFELLOW The Rose in which the Word Divine Became incarnate. C. WILLIAMS Hell is a funnel; heaven is a rose. J. FOWLES I hear she's the rose of the season. **b** R. CHURCH Life had been all roses . . in the infants' school.

▶**III 6** HERALDRY. A conventionalized representation of a rose, usu. with five lobes or petals. **ME.**
7 (A representation of) a rose as the emblem of either of the Houses of York (***white rose***) or Lancaster (***red rose***), or of England. Now also, this as the emblem of any of various rival sports teams of Yorkshire and Lancashire. **LME.** ▶**b** A representation of a rose in painting, needlework, etc. **LME.**
8 a A figure of a rose, carved or moulded in plaster etc.; *spec.* (ARCHITECTURE) = ROSETTE *noun* 4a. **LME.** ▶**b** A rose-shaped ornamental knot of ribbon etc. freq. worn on a shoe-front, hat, bodice, etc.; *spec.* this worn on a clergyman's hat. Cf. ROSETTE *noun* 2. **E17.** ▶**c** MUSIC. An ornamental device inserted in the sound-hole or the table of certain stringed instruments. **L17.**
9 a A circular pattern showing the thirty-two points of the compass; *spec.* the card of a compass or barometer. Cf. ***compass rose*** s.v. COMPASS *noun*, ***rose diagram*** below. **E16.** ▶**b** A circular mounting through which the shaft of a door-handle or the wiring of an electric light may pass. **M19.** ▶**c** A movement in sword dancing, in which the dancers form a circle and each sets his or her hilt under his or her neighbour's point to create an interlocked pentagon, octagon, etc. **E20.**
10 A natural structure or formation resembling or suggesting a rose in shape; *spec.* (*a*) a circular protuberance round the base of a deer's antler; (*b*) a circular pattern of feathers on the crown of a fancy pigeon's head; (*c*) GEOLOGY. = ***rock rose*** (c) s.v. ROCK *noun*¹; (*d*) the rounded end of a (sprouting) potato. **M17.**
11 a More fully ***rose diamond***. A rose-cut diamond. **L17.** ▶**b** In full ***rose window***. A circular window, *esp.* one with tracery radiating like the spokes of a wheel or the petals of a flower. **E19.** ▶**c** In full ***rose nail***. A nail with a rounded head cut into triangular facets. **M19.**
12 A perforated cap or nozzle attached to the spout of a watering-can, hose, etc., as a sprinkler or strainer. **E18.**

> **7** JOYCE Bravo Lancaster! The red rose wins. *Western Mail (Cardiff)* Those who have worn the white jersey with the red rose. **8a** C. MACKENZIE From the heart of every oaken rose . . peered . . a deadly sin. P. FUSSELL The 'bar' to the Military Cross . . is a . . silver rose. **9b** *Practical Householder* Two extra cables . . one to the ceiling rose. **12** *Good Housekeeping* Watering can . . with a choice of detachable roses.

▶**IV 13** A pink or light crimson; the colour of a red or pink rose. **ME.**
14 †**a** A rose-coloured wine. Only in **LME.** ▶**b** A rose-coloured or reddish variety of apple, pear, potato, etc. **L17.**
15 A fresh pink or blushing complexion. Usu. in *pl.* **L16.**
16 ***the Rose***, a local inflammation of the skin, *esp.* erysipelas. **L16.**

13 C. MACKENZIE The setting sun . . flushing with rose the . . tops of the Alps. 15 B. BAINBRIDGE The roses left her cheeks.

Phrases: *ash of roses*, *ashes of roses*: see ASH *noun*[2] 1. *bed of roses*: see BED *noun*. **golden rose** an ornament, usu. consisting of or incorporating a wrought-gold rose, blessed and presented by the Pope on the fourth Sunday of Lent as a mark of favour to some notable Roman Catholic person, church, or city. *moonlight and roses*: see MOONLIGHT *noun* 1. **not the rose but near it** not ideal but approaching or near this. **oil of roses** (an) oil extracted from roses. *Persian Yellow rose*: see PERSIAN *adjective*. *pluck a rose*: see PLUCK *verb*. *red rose*: see sense 5 above. *ring-a-ring o'roses*: see RING *noun*[1]. **rose du Barry** [Comtesse *du Barry* (1746–93), a patron of the Sèvres porcelain factory] = *rose Pompadour* below. **rose of heaven** a Mediterranean campion, *Silene coeli-rosa*, with rose-purple flowers, grown for ornament. **rose of Jericho** a cruciferous plant, *Anastatica hierochuntica*, of deserts in N. Africa and the Middle East; also called *resurrection plant*. **rose of Sharon** [translating Hebrew (*S. of S.* 2:1) = an unidentified flower] (*a*) *N. Amer.* the common garden hibiscus, *Hibiscus syriacus*; (*b*) a shrubby St John's wort, *Hypericum calycinum*, freq. planted as ground cover; (*c*) (chiefly *N. Amer.*) a variety of floral quilt pattern. **smell of roses** seem to be flawless or faultless. *south sea rose*: see SOUTH *adverb, adjective, noun, & verb*. **the last rose** the last flowering *of* an era, art form, etc. *Tudor rose*: see TUDOR *adjective*. **under the rose** in secret, in strict confidence; = SUB ROSA. **Wars of the Roses** the 15th-cent. civil wars between the Yorkists and Lancastrians (cf. sense 5 above). *white rose*: see sense 5 above.

▶ **B** *attrib.* or as *adjective*. **1** Having, containing, or covered or decorated with roses. OE.
2 Of or pertaining to a rose or roses. ME.
3 Made from, or flavoured or scented with, roses. LME.
4 Having the shape of a rose. E16.
5 Of the colour of a red or pink rose; delicate red, light crimson. L16.

1 *rose-bed*, *rose-bower*, *rose-walk*, etc. **2** *rose blossom*, *rose-dust*, *rose-grower*, *rose-petal*, etc. **3** *rose-crystal*, *rose-powder*, etc. **4** *rose boss*, *rose knot*, *rose ornament*, etc. **5** J. HAY A sky . . Blushed rose o'er the minster-glades.

Comb. & special collocations: **rose acacia** a false acacia, *Robinia hispida*, with rose-coloured flowers, native to mountains in the US; **rose aphid** any of various aphids that affect roses, esp. *Macrosiphum rosae*; **rose-apple** (the fragrant edible fruit of) any of several Malayan trees of the genus *Syzygium*, of the myrtle family, esp. *S. jambos* and *S. malaccensis*, much grown in the tropics; **rosebay** (*a*) the oleander, *Nerium oleander*; (*b*) (more fully *rosebay willowherb*) an ornamental willowherb, *Chamerion angustifolium*, of woodland clearings etc., with long lanceolate leaves and showy rose-purple flowers; (*c*) any of several N. American azaleas, esp. *Rhododendron maximum*; **rose-beetle** a rose-chafer, esp. *Cetonia aurata*; **rose-berry** a rose-hip; **rose bit** a countersink bit having a conical head with radial cutting teeth that meet at the tip; **rosebowl** (*a*) a bowl for holding cut roses; *spec.* this as a prize in a competition; (*b*) the annual New Year's Day final of the American college football tournament, in the Rose Bowl Stadium in Pasadena, California (freq. *attrib.*); **rose box** (*a*) a box for holding roses; (*b*) NAUTICAL the strainer at the end of the suction pipe of a bilge pump; **rose-breasted** *adjective* having a rosy or carmine-coloured breast; *rose-breasted cockatoo*, the galah, *Eolophus roseicapillus*; *rose-breasted finch* = *rosefinch* below; *rose-breasted grosbeak*, an American grosbeak, *Pheucticus ludovicianus*, the male of which is black and white with a red breast-patch; **rose-bug** *US* a rose-chafer, esp. *Macrodactylus supspinosus*; **rose bush** a rose plant; †**rose-cake** (*a*) a cake of compressed rose-petals, used as a perfume; (*b*) a kind of sweet flavoured with oil of roses; **rose-campion** an ornamental garden campion, *Lychnis coronaria*, with woolly leaves and magenta flowers; **rose-chafer** any of various burnished green or copper chafers of the genus *Cetonia*, esp. *C. aurata*, which feed on the flowers of roses etc. as adults; *US* a reddish-brown chafer, *Macrodactylus subspinosus*; **rose cockatoo** = GALAH; **rose comb** a flat flesh-coloured comb on the head of certain fowls; a bird having this; **rose copper** copper which has been repeatedly melted, highly refined, or purified; **rose-cut** *noun & adjective* (*a*) *noun* a style of cutting a diamond into a flat-bottomed hemisphere with a curved upper surface covered with triangular facets; (*b*) *adjective* (of a diamond) cut in this style; **rose diagram**: in which values of a quantity in various directions are shown graphically according to compass bearing, as on a wind-rose; *rose diamond*: see sense A.11a above. **rose-drop** (*a*) MEDICINE = ROSACEA; cf. *rosy drop* s.v. ROSY *adjective*; (*b*) a kind of sweet flavoured with essence of roses; **rose-engine** an arm on a lathe for engraving intricate curved patterns; **rosefinch** any of various small Eurasian finches of the genus *Carpodacus*, the males of which have red or pink plumage; **rose-fish** any of various Atlantic scorpaenid redfishes of the genus *Sebastes*, esp. *S. marinus*; **rose-gall** = BEDEGUAR; **rose gall-fly**, **rose gall-wasp** any of various gall-wasps of the genus *Diplolepis*, which produce galls on rose-leaves; **rose geranium** any of several pelargoniums, esp. *Pelargonium graveolens*, with rose-scented leaves and pink flowers; a perfume resembling the scent of such a plant; **rose gold** gold alloyed with a little copper, having a reddish tinge; **rose-grub** = *rose-maggot* below; **rose-hip** the fruit of the rose; = HIP *noun*[2]; **rose-hopper** = *rose leafhopper* below; **rose-leaf** the leaf or (usu.) petal of a rose; **rose leafhopper** a greenish-yellow leafhopper, *Edwardsiana rosae*, which attacks the foliage of roses; **rose linnet**, (*Scot.*) **rose lintie** (*a*) the linnet in summer plumage; (*b*) the redpoll; **rose madder** the rose colour produced by madder dye or pigment; **rose-maggot** the larva of any of various rose-infesting insects, *esp.* tortricid leaf-rollers; **rose mahogany** an Australian timber tree, *Dysoxylum fraserianum* (family Meliaceae); its fragrant reddish wood; **rose-mallow** any ornamental hibiscus; **rose-mole** a reddish mark or mole; *rose nail*: see sense A.11c above; **rose-noble** (*obsolete* exc. *Hist.*) a gold coin of variable value current in the 15th and 16th cents., being a type of noble stamped with a rose; **rosepath** a pattern used in weaving; **rose plantain** a sport of the greater plantain, *Plantago major*, in which the flowering spike is replaced by a rosette of leafy bracts; **rose-point** point lace having a raised pattern of a conventionalized rose; **rose Pompadour** [Marquise de *Pompadour* (1721–64), mistress of Louis XV of France] a soft shade of pink or pale crimson developed *c* 1757 as a ground colour for Sèvres porcelain; **rose quartz** MINERALOGY a translucent pink variety of quartz; **rose-rash** = ROSEOLA; **rose rial** (*obsolete* exc. *Hist.*) a gold coin stamped with a rose, having a value of thirty shillings, coined by James I; **roseroot** a tall glaucous stonecrop of mountains and sea-cliffs, *Sedum* (or *Rhodiola*) *rosea*, which has greenish-yellow flowers and a root smelling of roses when bruised; **rose sawfly** any of various sawflies with larvae that feed on rose-leaves; **rose show** an exhibition mainly or entirely of roses; **rose-spot** MEDICINE a red spot characteristic of certain fevers, esp. typhoid; **Rose Sunday** (*obsolete* exc. *Hist.*) the fourth Sunday in Lent; **rose-temple** a raised turret or summer-house over which climbing roses may be trained; **rose-tinted** *adjective* rose-coloured; **rose tree** a rose bush; *esp.* a standard rose; **rose vine** *US* a climbing rose; *rose window*: see sense A.11b above; **rose-work** a pattern produced by a rose-engine; the process by which this is produced; **rosewort** (now *rare*) = *roseroot* above.

■ **roseless** *adjective* without roses; pale, colourless: M19. **roselet**, **-lette** *noun* a small rose; a figure or representation of this: L15. **roselike** *adjective* resembling a rose in appearance or scent M16. **rosery** *noun* a rose-garden; a cluster or plantation of rose bushes: L16.

rose /rəʊz/ *verb*[1]. M16.
[from ROSE *noun*.]
†**1** *verb intrans.* Blossom like a rose. *rare*. Only in M16.
2 *verb trans.* Colour like a rose; make rosy. Chiefly as *rosed ppl adjective*. E17. ▸**b** *verb intrans.* Become rosy; blush. *rare*. E20.
3 *verb trans.* Perfume with rose-scent. *poet. rare*. L19.

rose *verb*[2] *pa. t.* of RISE *verb*.

rosé /ˈrəʊzeɪ, *foreign* roze/ *noun & adjective*. L19.
[French = pink.]
(Designating) any light red or pink wine, coloured by brief contact with red grape skins.

roseal /ˈrəʊzɪəl/ *adjective*. *arch*. M16.
[from Latin *roseus*, from *rosa* ROSE *noun*, + -AL[1].]
1 = ROSEATE *adjective* 1. M16.
2 = ROSEATE *adjective* 2. L16.
3 = ROSEATE *adjective* 3. Long *rare* or *obsolete*. E17.

rose-a-ruby /rəʊzəˈruːbi/ *noun*. Now *rare* or *obsolete*. L16.
[App. from ROSE *noun* + RUBY *noun*.]
The pheasant's-eye, *Adonis annua*.

roseate /*as adjective* ˈrəʊzɪət, *as verb* ˈrəʊzɪeɪt/ *adjective & verb*. LME.
[from Latin *roseus* rosy + -ATE[2], -ATE[3].]
▶ **A** *adjective*. **1** Rose-coloured, rose-red, rosy. LME.
†**2** Formed or consisting of roses. E17–L18.
†**3** Rose-scented. *rare*. M17–E18.
4 *fig.* Happy; optimistic; promising. M19.

1 R. BRADBURY The strawberry glass . . bathed the town in roseate warmth. **roseate spoonbill** an American spoonbill, *Ajaia ajaja*, which has a pink body with red markings. **roseate tern** a tern, *Sterna dougallii*, with a pale pink breast and long tail streamers, of worldwide distribution. **4** P. G. WODEHOUSE He . . plunged into pleasant, roseate dreams about Flick. *Times* Former colleagues . . took the roseate path to television reporting.

▶ **B** *verb*. †**1** *verb intrans.* Flower or bud like a rose. *rare* (only in Dicts.). Only in E17.
2 *verb trans.* Make roseate or rosy. *rare*. M19.

rosebud /ˈrəʊzbʌd/ *noun*. L15.
[from ROSE *noun* + BUD *noun*[1].]
1 The bud or unopened flower of a rose; *fig.* a thing likened to this, esp. for its beauty, delicateness, or pale red or pink colour. Freq. *attrib.* L15.
2 (A term of endearment for) a pretty young woman. L18. ▸**b** A débutante. *US*. L19. ▸**c** *Hist.* A member of the junior branch of the Guides (now called a *Brownie*). E20.

1 *attrib.*: E. PAUL She had . . a rosebud mouth with petulant corners.

rose-color *noun & verb*, **rose-colored** *adjective* see ROSE-COLOUR, ROSE-COLOURED.

rose-colour /ˈrəʊzkʌlə/ *noun & verb*. Also *-**color**. LME.
[from ROSE *noun & adjective* + COLOUR *noun*.]
▶ **A** *noun*. **1** The colour of a rose; a pink or light crimson. LME.
2 *fig.* Ease, success, comfort, pleasure, etc. Also, optimism. M19.
▶ **B** *verb trans.* Make red or rosy; *fig.* make (a thing, circumstance, event, etc.) seem pleasant or attractive. *rare*. M16.

rose-coloured /ˈrəʊzkʌləd/ *adjective*. Also *-**colored**. E16.
[from ROSE *noun* + COLOURED.]
1 Of the pink or light crimson colour of a rose. E16.
2 *fig.* Cheerfully optimistic; tending to view everything in a highly favourable light. M19.

1 *rose-coloured pastor*: see PASTOR *noun* 4. **rose-coloured starling** = *rose-coloured pastor* s.v. PASTOR *noun* 4. **2 see through rose-coloured spectacles** regard (circumstances etc.) with unfounded favour or optimism, have an idealistic view of.

rosed /rəʊzd/ *adjective*. M16.
[from ROSE *noun*, *verb*[1]: see -ED[2], -ED[1].]
†**1** Made, flavoured, or scented with roses or rose-petals. M16–M17.
2 Made red or rosy in colour; rose-coloured. L16.
3 Of a watering-can: having a specified kind of rose. M19.
4 Decorated with (representations of) roses. L19.

roselite /ˈrəʊzəlʌɪt/ *noun*. M19.
[from Gustav *Rose* (1798–1873), German mineralogist + -LITE.]
MINERALOGY. A rare rose-red monoclinic arsenate of cobalt and calcium related to erythrite.

rosella /rə(ʊ)ˈzɛlə/ *noun*[1]. E19.
[App. from *Rose-hiller*, from *Rose-hill*, Parramatta, near Sydney, Australia.]
1 Any of various brightly coloured seed-eating Australian parrots of the genus *Platycercus*, *esp.* the very common *P. eximius* (more fully *eastern rosella*). E19.
2 A sheep whose wool is beginning to fall off naturally and is therefore easy to shear. *Austral. & NZ*. M19.

rosella /rə(ʊ)ˈzɛlə/ *noun*[2]. Also **roselle** /-ˈzɛl/, **roz-**. M19.
[Perh. alt. of the French name *l'oseille de Guinée* sorrel of Guinea, infl. by ROSE *noun & adjective*.]
The Jamaica sorrel, *Hibiscus sabdariffa* (see SORREL *noun*[1] 2). Also, an allied Australian plant, *H. heterophyllus*, similarly used in food.

rosemaling /ˈrəʊsəmɑːlɪŋ, -mɔːlɪŋ/ *noun*. M20.
[Norwegian = rose-painting.]
The art of painting (wooden objects) with flower motifs; flower motifs, esp. painted on wood.
■ **rosemaled** /-mɑːld/ *adjective* decorated with rosemaling L20. **rosemalt** /-mɑːlt/ *adjective* [Norwegian *-malt* pa. pple of *male* to paint] = ROSEMALED M20.

rosemary /ˈrəʊzm(ə)ri/ *noun*. LME.
[Alt. of ROSMARINE *noun*[1] by assoc. with ROSE *noun* and MARY.]
1 A linear-leaved aromatic dwarf labiate shrub, *Rosmarinus officinalis*, native to southern Europe, much grown as a culinary herb and for use in perfumery; the leaves of this plant as used to flavour roast meat, stews, etc. LME.
2 Any of several plants resembling rosemary, esp. in having narrow leaves; esp. *bog rosemary* (see BOG *noun*[1]). Usu. with specifying word. L16.

Rosenmüller /ˈrəʊz(ə)nmʊlə/ *noun*. L19.
[J. C. *Rosenmüller* (1771–1820), German anatomist.]
ANATOMY. *organ of Rosenmüller*, = PAROVARIUM.

Rosenthal /ˈrəʊz(ə)ntɑːl/ *adjective*. M20.
[Philipp *Rosenthal* (1855–1937), founder of a porcelain factory at Selb in Bavaria, *c* 1880.]
Designating pottery made in Rosenthal's factory.

roseola /rə(ʊ)ˈziːələ, rəʊzɪˈəʊlə/ *noun*. E19.
[from Latin *roseus* rose-coloured + dim. suffix *-ola*, after *rubeola*.]
MEDICINE. A rose-coloured rash occurring in measles, syphilis, typhoid fever, etc. Formerly also, rubella.
■ **roseolar** *adjective* of, pertaining to, or of the nature of roseola L19. **roseolous** *adjective* roseolar M19.

rose-pink /ˈrəʊzpɪŋk, *esp. as adjective* rəʊzˈpɪŋk/ *noun & adjective*. M18.
[from ROSE *noun* + PINK *noun*[4], *noun*[6].]
▶ **A** *noun*. **1** A pinkish pigment made by colouring whiting or chalk with an extract of Brazil-wood etc. M18.
2 A pink colour like that of a rose; *fig.* sentimentality, esp. in writing. M19.
3 An ornamental N. American plant, *Sabatia angularis*, of the gentian family, having yellow-centred pink flowers. L19.
▶ **B** *adjective*. **1** Of a pink colour like that of a rose. M19.
2 *fig.* = ROSE-COLOURED *adjective* 2. M19.

rose-red /ˈrəʊzrɛd, *esp. as adjective* rəʊzˈrɛd/ *adjective & noun*. ME.
[from ROSE *noun* + RED *noun*.]
▶ **A** *adjective*. Red like a rose; rose-coloured. ME.
▶ **B** *noun*. A red colour like that of a rose. LME.

roset /rə(ʊ)ˈzɛt/ *noun*. LME.
[Prob. from ROSE *noun*.]
†**1** A rose-coloured pigment; the colour produced by this. LME–L17.
2 = ROSETTE *noun*. E19.

Rosetta stone /rə(ʊ)ˈzɛtə stəʊn/ *noun phr.* E20.
[A stone discovered in 1799 near Rosetta, Egypt, bearing a 2nd cent. BC trilingual inscription in Greek, demotic Egyptian, and Egyptian hieroglyphs which provided the key for deciphering hieroglyphs.]
fig. & allus. A key to some previously indecipherable mystery, unattainable understanding, etc.

rosette /rə(ʊ)ˈzɛt/ *noun & verb*. M18.
[French, dim. of *rose* ROSE *noun*: see -ETTE.]
▶ **A** *noun*. **1** An object or arrangement of things resembling a rose in shape; *spec.* (*a*) a circular roselike pattern, esp. on a rose-engine; (*b*) a rose diamond; (*c*) a circular mounting, esp. on a ceiling, through which the wiring of

an electric light may pass (cf. ROSE *noun* 9b); (*d*) GEOLOGY = ***rock rose*** (c) s.v. ROCK *noun*[1]; (*e*) ENGINEERING a coplanar arrangement of lines about a point that represents the axes of strain gauges used to determine the strain existing in a structure or material at that point. **M18.**

2 A rose-shaped arrangement of ribbon etc., worn esp. as an ornament, a badge of membership or support, or a symbol of a prize won in a competition. **L18.** ▸**b** A rose-shaped or star-shaped symbol used in hotel and restaurant guides to indicate the standard of service or cuisine provided. **M20.**

3 METALLURGY. Any of the disclike plates formed by successive sprinklings of water over the molten copper in a crucible. Now *rare*. **L18.**

4 ARCHITECTURE. **a** A painted, carved, or moulded ornament resembling or representing a rose on a wall or other surface. **E19.** ▸**b** A rose-window. **M19.**

5 BIOLOGY. **a** A cluster of organs or parts, or a marking or group of markings (e.g. on a leopard's skin), resembling a rose in form or arrangement. **M19.** ▸**b** A naturally occurring circular arrangement of horizontally spreading leaves, esp. about the base of a stem. Also, an abnormal similar cluster of leaves on the stem resulting from shortening of the internodes, a symptom of disease. **M19.** ▸**c** Any of various plant diseases in which the leaves form a radial cluster on the stem. Also ***rosette disease***. **L19.** ▸**d** MEDICINE. A group of erythrocytes adhering to a macrophage bearing complementary surface receptors produced in tests for antibodies etc. **M20.**

📖 **1** *Flowers* For a round tray, a central rosette of flowers would be . . appropriate. **2** *Horse & Rider* I decided to keep my initial placings, and hand out the rosettes.

Comb.: **rosette disease**: see sense 5c above; **rosette gauge** ENGINEERING an assembly of strain gauges whose axes correspond to the lines of a rosette (see sense 1(e) above); **rosette plant** a plant having most or all of its leaves in a basal rosette.

▶ **B** *verb*. **1** *verb intrans*. MEDICINE. Of a cell or group of cells: form a rosette. **M20.**

2 *verb trans*. Award a rosette to, as a mark of excellence. **L20.**

▪ **rosetted** *adjective* (*a*) having, formed into, or marked with rosettes; (*b*) having been awarded a rosette; (*c*) affected with rosette disease: **M19.** **rosetting** *noun* development of abnormal leaf clusters due to plant disease **M20.**

rose-water /ˈrəʊzwɔːtə/ *noun & adjective*. **LME.**
[from ROSE *noun* + WATER *noun*.]

▶ **A** *noun*. **1** Water distilled from roses, or scented with essence of roses, used as a perfume etc. Also (*rare*), a particular variety of this. **LME.**

2 *fig*. Something pleasant, refined, gentle, or sentimental; pleasantness, gentleness, sentimentality. **L16.**

▶ **B** *attrib*. or as *adjective*. **1 a** Pleasant; socially refined or sophisticated. **L16.** ▸**b** Gentle; sentimental. Also, comfortable. **M19.**

2 Of or pertaining to rose-water. **M17.**

Comb. & special collocations: **rose-water pipe** an oriental tobacco-pipe in which the smoke passes through rose-water before reaching the mouth; **rose-water still**: for making rose-water.

▪ **rose-watered** *adjective* (having been made) pleasant, refined, gentle, or sentimental **E17.**

rosewood /ˈrəʊzwʊd/ *noun*. **M17.**
[from ROSE *noun* + WOOD *noun*[1].]

1 The fragrant dark-coloured wood, valued in cabinet-work, of any of several tropical leguminous trees of the genus *Dalbergia*, esp. *D. nigra* (more fully ***Brazilian rosewood***), *D. stevensonii* (more fully ***Honduras rosewood***), and *D. latifolia* (more fully ***Indian rosewood***); a tree yielding such wood. **M17.**

2 Any of various similar woods or the trees producing them, esp. (*a*) *W. Indies* torchwood, *Amyris balsamifera*, and (*b*) (*Austral.*) *Dysoxylon fraserianum* and *Synoum glandulosum* (family Meliaceae). Also = ***rhodium-wood*** s.v. RHODIUM *noun*[1] 1. **L17.**

3 A shade or tint resembling that of rosewood. **M19.**

2 Burmese rosewood (*a*) amboyna wood (from *Pterocarpus indicus*); (*b*) padouk (from *P. macrocarpus*).

Rosh Chodesh *noun phr*. var. of ROSH HODESH.

Rosh Hashana /rɒʃ həˈʃɑːnə, *foreign* roʃ haʃaˈna/ *noun phr*. Also **Rosh Hashanah**. **M18.**
[Hebrew *rōʾš haššānāh* lit. 'head of the year'.]

Jewish New Year, celebrated on the first (and sometimes second) day of the month Tishri.

Rosh Hodesh /rɒʃ ˈxəʊdəʃ, *foreign* roʃ ˈxodɛʃ/ *noun phr*. Also **Rosh Chodesh**. **L19.**
[Hebrew *rōʾš ḥōdeš* lit. 'head of the month'.]

A Jewish half-holiday observed at the appearance of the new moon, the beginning of the Jewish month.

Roshi /ˈrəʊʃi/ *noun*. **M20.**
[Japanese, from *rō* old + *shi* teacher.]

The spiritual leader of a community of Zen Buddhist monks; an advanced Zen master.

Rosicrucian /rəʊzɪˈkruːʃ(ə)n/ *noun & adjective*. **E17.**
[from mod. Latin *rosa crucis* (or *crux*), translating German *Rosenkreuz*: see -IAN.]

▶ **A** *noun*. A member of a 17th- and 18th-cent. society, reputedly founded by Christian Rosenkreuz in 1484, devoted to metaphysical and mystical lore, as that concerning transmutation of metals, prolongation of life, and power over the elements and elemental spirits (*Hist.*); a member of any of various modern organizations deriving from this. **E17.**

▶ **B** *adjective*. Belonging to, connected with, or characteristic of this society or any deriving or said to derive from it. **E17.**

▪ **Rosicrucianism** *noun* **M18.**

Rosie *noun* var. of ROSY.

rosier /ˈrəʊzɪə/ *noun*. *obsolete* exc. *poet*. **E16.**
[Old & mod. French from Latin *rosarium* rose-garden, from *rosa* ROSE *noun*.]

A rose tree, a rose bush.

rosin /ˈrɒzɪn/ *noun & verb*. **ME.**
[Alt. of RESIN *noun*.]

▶ **A** *noun*. **1** = RESIN *noun*; *spec*. the solid amber residue obtained after the distillation of crude turpentine oleoresin (also ***gum rosin***), or of naphtha extract from pine stumps (also ***wood rosin***), used in adhesives, varnishes, inks, etc., and for treating the bows of stringed instruments. **ME.**

2 Alcoholic drink. *slang*. **M18.**

Comb.: **rosin-back** *slang* (a horse used by) a bareback rider or acrobat; **rosin oil**: obtained by the fractional distillation of rosin, with similar uses; **rosinweed** *US* any of various coarse gum-exuding yellow-rayed plants constituting the genus *Silphium* of the composite family.

▶ **B** *verb*. **1** *verb trans*. Smear or seal with rosin; rub (esp. a violin bow or string) with rosin. **LME.**

2 *verb trans. & intrans*. Drink (liquor). Now *dial*. **E18.**

▪ **rosiner** *noun* (*Anglo-Irish & Austral. slang*) an alcoholic drink, esp. a strong one **M20.** †**rosinous** *adjective* resinous **M17–L18.** **rosiny** *adjective* resinous **M16.**

Rosinante /rɒzɪˈnanti/ *noun*. Also **r-**. **M18.**
[Spanish *Rocinante* (from *rocín* horse, jade), the hero's horse in Cervantes' *Don Quixote*.]

(A name for) a worn-out or ill-conditioned horse; a hack.

†**rosmarine** *noun*[1]. **OE–M18.**
[Old French *rosmarin* (mod. *romarin*) or Middle Dutch *rosemarine* (Dutch *ros(e)marijn*, or immed. from Latin *ros marinus*, lit. 'sea dew', late Latin *rosmarinum*. See also ROSEMARY.]

Rosemary.

†**rosmarine** *noun*[2]. *rare* (Spenser). Only in **L16.**
[mod. Latin *rosmarus*, or Italian, Spanish *rosmaro*, Portuguese *rosmar*; perh. infl. by MARINE.]

The walrus.

Rosminian /rɒzˈmɪnɪən/ *noun & adjective*. **M19.**
[from Antonio *Rosmini*- Serbati (1797–1855), its Italian founder + -IAN.]

▶ **A** *noun*. A member of the Institute of Charity, a religious congregation founded in 1828. **M19.**

▶ **B** *adjective*. Of or pertaining to Rosmini, his philosophy, or the Institute of Charity. **M19.**

rosoglio *noun* var. of ROSOLIO.

rosolic /rəʊˈzɒlɪk/ *adjective*. **M19.**
[from Latin *rosa* ROSE *noun* + -OL + -IC.]

CHEMISTRY. ***rosolic acid***, = AURIN.

rosolio /rəʊˈzəʊlɪəʊ/ *noun*. Also **-glio**. Pl. **-os**. **E19.**
[Italian, var. of *rosoli*, from Latin *ros* dew + *solis* genit. of *sol* sun: cf. ROS SOLIS.]

A sweet cordial made esp. in Italy from alcohol, raisins, sugar, rose-petals, cloves, cinnamon, etc.

RoSPA /ˈrɒspə/ *abbreviation*.
Royal Society for the Prevention of Accidents.

ross /rɒs/ *noun*[1]. **L16.**
[App. of Scandinavian origin, corresp. to Norwegian dial. *ros* (*rus*) scrapings.]

†**1** Rubbish, refuse; dregs. **L16–M17.**

2 The scaly outer portion of the bark of a tree. Chiefly *US*. **L18.**

Ross /rɒs/ *noun*[2]. **E20.**
[Sir James Clark *Ross* (1800–62), Scot. polar explorer.]

Used *attrib*. and in *possess*. to designate certain polar birds and mammals.

Ross seal a small, large-eyed seal, *Ommatophoca rossi*, which breeds on the Antarctic pack ice. **Ross's gull** a pinkish-white Arctic gull, *Rhodostethia rosea*.

Ross /rɒs/ *noun*[3]. **E20.**
[Sir Charles A. F. L. *Ross*, (1864–1930), Scottish-born engineer and soldier.]

Used *attrib*. to designate a type of .303 rifle developed in the 1890s and used by the Canadian Army, esp. in the war of 1914–18.

ross /rɒs/ *verb trans*. Chiefly *N. Amer*. **M19.**
[from ROSS *noun*[1].]

Remove the bark from (a tree).

▪ **rosser** *noun* a machine for removing the bark from a tree **L19.**

Rossby wave /ˈrɒsbɪ weɪv/ *noun phr*. **M20.**
[Carl-Gustaf Arvid *Rossby* (1898–1957), Swedish meteorologist.]

PHYSICS & METEOROLOGY. A long-wavelength fluctuation of a current in a fluid system having no divergence and subject to Coriolis force; *esp*. a lateral fluctuation of a jet stream.

Rossettian /rəˈzɛtɪən/ *adjective*. **L19.**
[*Rossetti* (see below) + -AN.]

Pertaining to or characteristic of the English poet and Pre-Raphaelite artist Dante Gabriel Rossetti (1828–82) or his work.

▪ **Rossettiˈana** *noun pl*. relics of or information about Rossetti **E20.**

rossie /ˈrɒsi/ *noun*. *Anglo-Irish* (*derog*.). **E20.**
[Irish *rásaidhe*, *rásaí* runner, racer; wanderer.]

A woman who travels or wanders about; a female Gypsy; a promiscuous woman.

Rossi–Forel scale /ˌrɒsɪfɒˈrɛl skeɪl/ *noun phr*. **L19.**
[from Michele Stefano Conte de *Rossi* (1834–98), Italian geologist + François-Alphonse *Forel* (1841–1912), Swiss physician and limnologist.]

A ten-point scale used to measure the local intensity of an earthquake.

Rossinian /rɒˈsiːnɪən/ *adjective*. **M19.**
[*Rossini* (see below) + -AN.]

Pertaining to or characteristic of the Italian operatic composer Gioacchino Antonio Rossini (1792–1868) or his music.

rosso antico /ˌrɒsəʊ anˈtiːkəʊ/ *noun phr*. **L18.**
[Italian, lit. 'ancient red'.]

1 A red stoneware produced at Josiah Wedgwood's Staffordshire factories. **L18.**

2 A rich red Italian marble used for decoration. **L19.**

ros solis /rɒs ˈsəʊlɪs/ *noun phr*. Now *rare* or *obsolete*. **L16.**
[mod. Latin use of Latin *ros* dew + *solis* genit. of *sol* sun: cf. ROSA SOLIS, ROSOLIO.]

= ROSA SOLIS.

Ross River /rɒs ˈrɪvə/ *noun phr*. **M20.**
[A river near Townsville, Queensland, Australia.]

MEDICINE. ***Ross River fever***, a mosquito-borne disease characterized by a rash, and joint and muscle pain, occurring throughout Australia; also called ***epidemic polyarthritis***. Hence ***Ross River virus***, the virus causing this.

Ross's goose /ˈrɒsɪz ˈguːs/ *noun phr*. **L19.**
[Bernard Rogan *Ross* (1827–74), Irish fur-trader with the Hudson's Bay Company.]

A small Arctic goose, *Anser rossi*, which breeds in northern Canada.

rostellum /rɒˈstɛləm/ *noun*. Pl. **-lla** /-lə/, **-llums**. In sense 1a formerly also Anglicized as †**rostel**. **M18.**
[Latin = small beak or snout, dim. of ROSTRUM.]

1 BOTANY. †**a** The radicle of a seed. **M18–L19.** ▸**b** A beaklike process (a sterile stigma) in the column of an orchid flower between the fertile stigmas and the anther. **M19.**

2 ZOOLOGY. **a** The piercing mouthparts of a louse (now *rare*). Also, a projection on the male genitals of certain butterflies. **E19.** ▸**b** The protruding forepart of the head of a tapeworm, armed with hooklets or spines. **M19.**

▪ **rostellar** *adjective* pertaining to, or constituting, a rostellum **L19.** **rostellate** /ˈrɒstəleɪt, rɒˈstɛleɪt/ *adjective* having a rostellum; of the form or shape of a rostellum: **E19.**

roster /ˈrɒstə, ˈrəʊst-/ *noun & verb*. **E18.**
[Dutch *rooster* (i) gridiron, (ii) table, list (with ref. to its parallel lines), from *roosten* roast: see -ER[1].]

▶ **A** *noun*. A list or plan showing the rotation of duties and leave for individuals or groups in any organization, orig. a military force; *transf*. a group of people considered as being on a list or roster. **E18.**

📖 C. THUBRON The roster for washing up . . caused acrimony. S. QUINN An impressive roster of speakers.

▶ **B** *verb trans*. Place on a roster. **E20.**

📖 N. F. DIXON Two inexperienced co-pilots had been rostered to fly together.

rösti *noun* var. of ROESTI.

rostra *noun pl*. see ROSTRUM.

rostral /ˈrɒstr(ə)l/ *noun & adjective*. **LME.**
[Partly from medieval Latin deriv. of Latin ROSTRUM; partly immed. from ROSTRUM + -AL[1]; in sense B.2 alt. of next, perh. after French *rostral(e)*.]

▶†**A** *noun*. A bony process resembling a bird's beak, *esp*. the coracoid process of the scapula. **LME–M16.**

▶ **B** *adjective*. †**1** Designating the coracoid process. Only in **LME.**

2 Of a column, pillar, etc.: decorated with (representations of) the beak-heads of ancient warships. **LME.**

3 *ZOOLOGY.* Of, pertaining to, or situated in or on the rostrum (**ROSTRUM** 3). **E19.**

4 *ANATOMY.* Situated or occurring near the front end, esp. in the region of the nose and mouth or, in an embryo, near the hypophysial region. **L19.**

■ **rostrally** *adverb* (*ANATOMY*) towards the rostral part **M20.**

rostrate /ˈrɒstrət/ *adjective.* **LME.**
[Latin *rostratus*, formed as **ROSTRUM**: see **-ATE**[2].]
†**1** Curved like a bird's beak: designating the coracoid process of the scapula. Only in **LME.**
†**2** = **ROSTRAL** *adjective* 2. Only in **17.**
3 a *BOTANY.* Bearing an elongated process like a bird's beak. **E19.** ▸**b** *ZOOLOGY.* Having a rostrum; terminating in a rostrum. **E19.**
■ **roˈstrated** *adjective* (*a*) = **ROSTRAL** *adjective* 2; also, (of an ancient warship) having a beak-head; (*b*) = **ROSTRATE** *adjective* 3: **E18.**

rostriform /ˈrɒstrɪfɔːm/ *adjective.* **E19.**
[mod. Latin *rostriformis*, formed as **ROSTRUM**: see **-I-**, **-FORM.**]
Shaped like a beak or rostrum; beaklike.

rostro- /ˈrɒstrəʊ/ *combining form* of **ROSTRUM**: see **-O-.**
■ **rostro-ˈcarinate** *adjective* (*ARCHAEOLOGY*) of or pertaining to stone implements of a keeled and beaked shape, esp. of the African Pleistocene, and to certain flint objects from East Anglia, now believed to be natural **E20. rostroˈcaudally** *adverb* along the axis from the rostral end to the caudal end **M20.**

rostrum /ˈrɒstrəm/ *noun.* Pl. **-tra** /-trə/, (*rare*) **-trums. M16.**
[Latin = beak, beak-head, from *rodere* gnaw.]
1 *ROMAN ANTIQUITIES.* A platform or stand for speakers in the Forum of ancient Rome, decorated with the beak-heads of captured warships. Usu. in *pl.* (**rostra**), treated as *sing.*, the part of the Forum in which this was situated. **M16.** ▸**b** *transf.* A platform, stage, stand, etc., esp. for public speaking; *spec.* (*a*) a pulpit; (*b*) a conductor's platform facing the orchestra; (*c*) a platform for supporting a film or television camera. **M18.**
2 *ROMAN ANTIQUITIES.* A beaklike projection from the prow of a warship; a beak-head. **E17.**
3 *ANATOMY & ZOOLOGY.* **a** A beak, a snout; an anterior prolongation of the head, as in a weevil; the elongated mouthparts of certain insects. **M18.** ▸**b** A process or formation resembling a beak. **E19.**
4 *BOTANY.* A beaklike process; *esp.* (in the flower of certain plants of the Asclepiadaceae) any of the segments of the corona. **M19.**

> 🕮 **1b** HOR. WALPOLE Making an oration from the rostrum to the citizens of Westminster. JEREMY COOPER Christie . . sold fifty-five musical clocks from his London rostrum.

rosulate /ˈrɒzjʊlət/ *adjective.* **M19.**
[from late Latin *rosula* dim. of *rosa* **ROSE** *noun* + **-ATE**[2].]
BOTANY. Arranged like the petals of a double rose; forming a close rosette.

Rosy /ˈrəʊzi/ *noun. slang.* Also **-ie, r-. E20.**
[Rhyming slang.]
In full *Rosy Lee*. Tea.

rosy /ˈrəʊzi/ *adjective & verb.* **LME.**
[from **ROSE** *noun* + **-Y**[1].]
▸ **A** *adjective.* **1** Of or having the pink or light crimson colour of a rose; rose-coloured. **LME.** ▸**b** Of a person, the complexion, etc.: bright, glowing; healthy. **L16.** ▸**c** Blushing. **M17.** ▸**d** Drunk; tipsy. *slang.* **E20.**
2 Having many roses; composed of or decorated with roses. **L16.**
3 Resembling a rose; *esp.* rose-scented, fragrant. **L16.**
4 Of an event, circumstance, etc.: bringing happiness; promising, hopeful. **L18.**

> 🕮 **1** E. L. ORTIZ For underdone meat . . the juices will run rosy. **b** R. C. HUTCHINSON The children came, rosy from their baths. *rosy about the gills*: see **GILL** *noun*[1] 2. **3** U. HOLDEN Face cream . . smelling . . like Mamma's rosy scent. **4** G. F. NEWMAN She . . considered her prospects . . ; they didn't appear very rosy.

Special collocations & comb.: **rosybill** (more fully *rosybill pochard*) a S. American pochard, *Netta peposaca*, which has a pink bill. **rosy-billed** *adjective* having a pink or light crimson bill; *rosy-billed pochard* = *rosybill* above. **rosy cross** the emblem of the Rosicrucians. **rosy drop** a red swelling on the face; cf. *rose-drop* s.v. **ROSE** *noun & adjective.* **rosy finch** any of various finches of the genus *Leucosticte*, with partly pinkish plumage, occurring in Asia and western N. America.
▸ **B** *verb trans. & intrans.* Make or become rosy. *rare.* **M17.**
■ **rosied** *adjective* (*rare*) made rosy; decorated with roses: **M19. rosily** *adverb* with a rosy colour; in a rosy manner: **E19. rosiness** *noun* **M17.**

rot /rɒt/ *noun.* **ME.**
[Perh. of Scandinavian origin: cf. Icelandic, Norwegian *rot*, Swedish dial. *råt*.]
1 The process of rotting; the state of being rotten; decay, putrefaction. Also, rotten or decayed matter. **ME.**
2 a Any of various parasitic diseases, mainly of sheep, characterized by tissue necrosis, esp. of the liver; a particular form, instance, or epidemic, of this. **LME.** ▸**b** *MEDICINE.* Any of various human diseases characterized by tissue necrosis or emaciation. Now *rare.* **LME.**
3 *CRICKET.* A rapid fall of wickets during an innings; *transf.* a rapid succession of (usu. unaccountable) failures, a sudden decline or breakdown in standards or behaviour. Chiefly in *stop the rot*, *the rot set in*. **M19.**
4 Nonsense, rubbish. Also as *interjection*, expr. incredulity or ridicule. *colloq.* **M19.**

> 🕮 **1** C. MUNGOSHI His father's teeth were all black with rot. P. CAREY The thatch was full of rot and the walls were seeping. **3** J. B. PRIESTLEY He could not pretend . . that such pitiful economies . . could stop the rot. *Times* The rot began when Appleyard came into the attack. M. WOODHOUSE I went up to London . . and that . . is where the rot set in. **4** P. G. WODEHOUSE Cutting short some rot at the other end . . I hung up the receiver. C. MUNGOSHI He . . talked and believed so much rot and superstition.

Phrases etc.: *dry rot*: see **DRY** *adjective. foot-rot*: see **FOOT** *noun. soft rot*: see **SOFT** *adjective. tommy-rot*: see **TOMMY** *noun*[1]. *wet rot*: see **WET** *adjective. white rot*: see **WHITE** *adjective.*
Comb.: **rot-grass** = *white rot* (b) s.v. **WHITE** *adjective*; **rotproof** *adjective & verb trans.* (treat so as to make) resistant to rot.

rot /rɒt/ *verb & adjective.*
[Old English *rotian* = Old Frisian *rotia*, Old Saxon *roton*, Middle Dutch *roten*, Old High German *rōzzēn*; rel. to Old High German *rōten*, Middle High German *rœzen*. Cf. **RET** *verb*.]
▸ **A** *verb.* Infl. **-tt-.**
1 *verb intrans.* Of animal or vegetable matter: decompose by the action of bacteria, fungi, etc.; decay, putrefy; (of stone) disintegrate through weathering or chemical action. **OE.** ▸**b** *fig.* Diminish, esp. towards extinction; decay morally or socially, become corrupt. **ME.** ▸**c** Of sea ice: thaw. *N. Amer.* **L19.**
2 *verb intrans.* Of a person: waste away, esp. because of imprisonment; languish *in* a place, esp. a prison. **ME.** ▸**b** Of a sheep: develop the rot. **E16.**
3 *verb trans.* Cause (animal or vegetable matter) to decompose or decay; make putrid. Also (now *arch. & dial.*) in imprecations in imper. or optative form, expr. anger, irritation, impatience, etc. **LME.** ▸**b** *fig.* Spoil or ruin (an action, plan, etc.) Also foll. by *up*. *slang.* **E20.**
4 *verb intrans. & trans.* (Cause to) diminish or disappear by decomposition (foll. by *away*, *down*); (cause to) drop *off* through decomposition. **LME.**
5 *verb trans.* Cause (a sheep) to develop the rot. **LME.**
6 a *verb trans.* Ridicule; denigrate. *arch. slang.* **L19.** ▸**b** *verb intrans.* Talk nonsense, joke; fool *about*. *arch. slang.* **L19.**

> 🕮 **1** W. MORRIS Dead men rotting to nothing. E. MUIR The red fruit . . fell at last and rotted where it fell. **b** ISAIAH BERLIN The western world . . 'rotting' . . in rapid decay. **2** J. DICKEY I saw myself . . rotting for weeks in some county jail. P. P. READ The . . officers investigating . . decided to let him rot in self-imposed exile. **3** G. HEYER 'It's gone too far now. Rot that nephew of yours!' *Embroidery* Dyeing . . with vitriol . . often rotted the silk. A. CARTER Rain has rotted all the corn. **4** SHAKES. *Timon* Thy lips rot off! F. WELDON Last autumn's chrysanthemum stems had . . rotted away to slime. *fig.*: J. GALSWORTHY The nation is being rotted down. **6a** F. DONALDSON 'We shall get rotted by those kids in Dexter's,' moaned Harvey. **b** E. WAUGH 'Do you play . . well?' . . 'Do you really, or are you rotting?'

Comb.: **rot-gut** *noun & adjective* (*slang*) (designating) adulterated or inferior alcoholic liquor, esp. beer or whisky.
▸†**B** *adjective.* Rotten, rotted; decayed. **L16–E18.**
■ **rotter** *noun* (*a*) a thing which is rotting or which causes rot; (*b*) *slang* an (esp. morally) objectionable or reprehensible person: **E17.**

rota /ˈrəʊtə/ *noun.* **E17.**
[Latin = wheel.]
1 *the Rota*, the supreme ecclesiastical and secular court of the Roman Catholic Church. **E17.**
2 *the Rota*, a political club founded in 1659 advocating rotation of those in government. *obsolete* exc. *Hist.* **M17.**
3 A rotational order of people, duties to be done, etc.; a list of these; a roster. **L17.**
4 *MEDIEVAL MUSIC.* = **ROUND** *noun*[1] 15b. **L19.**

> 🕮 **3** A. S. BYATT A shared family rota and it was his go to wash up. F. HOYLE Joe Stoddard was on the rota . . Joe's watch fell on . . 27th August.

Comb.: **rota cut** a rotational rationing of power or water supplies in time of shortage.

rota- *combining form* var. of **ROTO-.**

rotal /ˈrəʊt(ə)l/ *adjective.* **M17.**
[from **ROTA** + **-AL**[1].]
1 Of or pertaining to a wheel or wheels. *rare.* **M17.**
2 Of or pertaining to the Roman Catholic Rota. **E20.**

rotamer /ˈrəʊtəmə/ *noun.* **M20.**
[from **ROTA(TIONAL** + **-MER.**]
CHEMISTRY. Any of a number of isomers of a molecule which can be interconverted by rotation of part of the molecule about a particular bond.

Rotameter /rəʊˈtamɪtə, ˈrəʊtəmiːtə/ *noun.* Also **r-. E20.**
[from **ROTA(TION** + **-METER.**]
1 (Proprietary name for) a device with a transparent wall that is fitted into a pipe or tube and indicates the rate of flow of fluid through it. **E20.**
2 (**r-.**) = **ROTOMETER. E20.**

rotan(g) *nouns* see **RATTAN** *noun*[1].

rotary /ˈrəʊt(ə)ri/ *adjective & noun.* **M18.**
[medieval Latin *rotarius*, formed as **ROTA**: see **-ARY**[1].]
▸ **A** *adjective.* **1** Of motion: revolving around a centre or axis; rotational. **M18.**
2 Of a thing: acting by means of rotation; *esp.* (of a machine) operating through the rotation of some part. **M19.** ▸**b** *OIL INDUSTRY.* Designating, of, or pertaining to a system of drilling in which the drilling string is rotated. **E20**
3 (**R-.**) Designating or pertaining to a worldwide organization of charitable societies for business and professional men, founded in Chicago in 1905 to promote unselfish service and international goodwill, meetings originally being hosted by members in rotation. **E20.**
2 *rotary blade*, *rotary chopper*, *rotary grill*, *rotary kiln*, *rotary mower*, *rotary pump*, *rotary valve*, etc.
Special collocations: **rotary beater** = *rotary egg-beater* below. **rotary camera**: in which the photographic subject (esp. a document) is moved automatically past the lens in synchrony with the film. **rotary clothes-drier**, **rotary clothes-line** an approximately square frame around which clothes-line is wound, attached to a central pole and rotated by the wind. **Rotary Club** a local branch of the Rotary organization. **rotary converter** an electric motor adapted for use with either alternating or direct current and capable of converting one to the other. **rotary cutter** a machine which produces veneer by rotating a log longitudinally against a blade. **rotary cutting** the method of producing veneer using a rotary cutter. **rotary egg-beater**: for beating eggs etc. by hand. **rotary engine** any engine which produces rotary motion or which has a rotating part or parts; *spec.* (*a*) an aircraft engine with a fixed crankshaft around which cylinders and propeller rotate; (*b*) a Wankel engine. **rotary machine** *PRINTING* = *rotary press* below. **rotary press** *PRINTING*: that prints from a rotating cylindrical surface on to paper forced against it by another cylinder. **rotary printing** the method of printing using a rotary press. **rotary quern** *ARCHAEOLOGY*: in which one stone is rotated on top of another by hand, water-power, etc. **rotary shutter** a continuously rotating shutter used in cine cameras and projectors. **rotary switch** *ELECTRICITY* a switch operated by rotary action, esp. where two or more circuits are controlled. **rotary table** *OIL INDUSTRY* in rotary drilling, a power-driven steel turntable which rotates the drilling column. **rotary-wing** *AERONAUTICS* an aerofoil rotating in an approximately horizontal plane, providing all or most of the lift in a helicopter, autogiro, etc.
▸ **B** *noun.* **1** A rotary machine or device; *spec.* = *rotary press* above. **L19.**
2 (**R-.**) The Rotary organization (since 1922 officially *Rotary International*) or its principles; an individual Rotary Club. **E20.**
3 = **ROUNDABOUT** *noun* 5. *N. Amer.* **M20.**

> 🕮 **2** H. FAST I'm due to speak to Rotary in thirty-five minutes. **3** A. CROSS Rotaries which seemed . . designed to enable cars going in opposite directions to meet head-on.

■ **Roˈtarian** *adjective & noun* (*a*) *adjective* of, pertaining to, or characteristic of the Rotary organization or its members; (*b*) *noun* a member of a Rotary Club: **E20. Roˈtarianism** *noun* the Rotarian system; the principles or ideals of the Rotary organization: **E20.**

rotascope /ˈrəʊtəskəʊp/ *noun.* **M19.**
[from Latin *rota* wheel + **-SCOPE.**]
Hist. A type of gyroscope used for demonstration purposes.

rotate /ˈrəʊteɪt/ *adjective.* **L18.**
[from Latin *rota* wheel + **-ATE**[2].]
BOTANY. Wheel-shaped; *esp.* (of a corolla) monopetalous with a short tube and spreading limb.
■ Also †**rotated** *adjective* **M–L18.**

rotate /rə(ʊ)ˈteɪt/ *verb.* **L17.**
[Latin *rotat-* pa. ppl stem of *rotare*, formed as **ROTA**: see **-ATE**[3].]
1 *verb intrans. & trans.* Change in position, responsibility, office, ownership, etc., in a regularly recurring order. Earliest as *rotating ppl adjective.* **L17.** ▸**b** *verb trans. spec.* Grow (different crops, plants, etc.) successively on the same piece of ground in a regular order to avoid exhausting the soil; change the position of (tyres) on a motor vehicle to distribute wear. **M19.**
2 *verb intrans. & trans.* Turn around a centre or axis (also foll. by *about*, *around*); (cause to) revolve on or *on* a centre or axis. **E19.**
3 *verb trans.* Foll. by *out*: dismiss (staff) from office or employment in turn. Usu. in *pass.* **L19.**
4 *verb trans. MILITARY.* Recall (a unit etc.) from overseas or combat service to a home base or less active area. Also foll. by *back*. Usu. in *pass. US.* **M20.**

> 🕮 **1** *Holiday Which?* We are . . going to rotate seats so . . we all have a chance to sit near the guide. *Wall Street Journal* In the six months that Spain holds the rotating EC presidency. **2** B. HINES He . . rotated his fist to look at his watch on the underside of his wrist. *Scientific American* Each star . . may be rotating on its axis. **3** P. FRIEDMAN Put in all new people . . everybody . . on the embassy-based staff now is being rotated out.

■ **rotatable** *adjective* **L19. rotatory** /ˈrəʊtət(ə)ri, -ˈteɪt(ə)ri/ *adjective* (*a*) = **ROTARY** *adjective* 1, 2; (*b*) recurring in rotation: **M18.**

rotation /rə(ʊ)ˈteɪʃ(ə)n/ *noun.* L15.
[Old French *rotation* or from Latin *rotatio(n-)*, formed as prec.: see -ATION.]
†**1** *ALCHEMY.* The transmutation of the four elements into one another. Only in L15.
2 The action or an act of rotating around an axis etc.; the fact of being so rotated. M16 ▸**b** *CRYSTALLOGRAPHY, MATH., & PHYSICS.* The conceptual operation of turning a system about an axis. L19. ▸**c** *MATH.* = CURL *noun* 6. E20. ▸**d** *STATISTICS.* The mathematical rearrangement of a body of data, regarded as representing a set of points in a space, so that the axes of the space come to lie in directions of particular relevance. M20.
3 The action or an act of rotating in position, responsibility, office, etc.; a regularly recurring series or order. E17. ▸**b** The action or an act of rotating crops etc.; the system or method of farming using this. L18. ▸**c** *FORESTRY.* The cycle of planting, felling, and replanting; the actual or planned time which this cycle takes. L19. ▸**d** *BASEBALL.* The order of play assigned to pitchers for the matches of a particular series. M20.
Phrases: **by rotation**, **in rotation** in a recurring order; in turn, in succession.

rotational /rə(ʊ)ˈteɪʃ(ə)n(ə)l/ *adjective.* M19.
[from prec. + -AL¹.]
1 Of or pertaining to rotation; acting in rotation. M19.
2 *PHYSICS.* Of, pertaining to, or designating the (quantized) energy possessed by a body, esp. a molecule, by virtue of its rotation. E20.
3 *AGRICULTURE.* Designating a method of land management in which animals are grazed on different areas of land successively. M20.
■ **rotationally** *adverb* in a rotational manner; by or with respect to rotation: L19.

rotative /ˈrəʊtətɪv/ *adjective.* L18.
[from ROTATE *verb* + -IVE.]
That rotates; rotating, rotary.

rotativism /ˈrəʊtətɪˌvɪz(ə)m, rə(ʊ)ˈteɪt-/ *noun.* Also **R-**. E20.
[from prec. + -ISM.]
POLITICS. An autocratic system of government whereby people and political parties rotate in office by mutual arrangement rather than electoral authority.
■ **rotativist** *adjective & noun* (*a*) *adjective* of, pertaining to, or advocating rotativism; (*b*) *noun* an advocate of rotativism: E20.

rotator /rə(ʊ)ˈteɪtə/ *noun.* L17.
[Orig. from Latin (formed as ROTATE *verb*); later from ROTATE *verb*: see -OR.]
1 *ANATOMY & ZOOLOGY.* A muscle by which a limb or part can be moved circularly. L17.
2 A thing which rotates or which causes something to rotate; *esp.* a laboratory device for rotating bottles etc. so as to mix the contents. L18.
1 rotator cuff *ANATOMY* (the muscles associated with) a capsule with fused tendons that supports the arm at the shoulder joint.

Rotavator /ˈrəʊtəveɪtə/ *noun.* Also **Roto-** /ˈrəʊtəʊ-/, **r-**. M20.
[from ROTA(RY *adjective* + CULTI)VATOR.]
(Proprietary name for) a machine with rotating blades for breaking up soil.
■ **rotavate** *verb trans.* [back-form.] (*a*) break up (soil) with a Rotavator; (*b*) work (a substance) into soil with a Rotavator: M20.

rotavirus /ˈrəʊtəvʌɪrəs/ *noun.* L20.
[mod. Latin, from Latin *rota* wheel + VIRUS.]
BIOLOGY. Any of a class of wheel-shaped double-stranded RNA viruses, some of which cause acute enteritis in man.

ROTC *abbreviation. US.*
Reserve Officers' Training Corps.

rotche /rɒtʃ/ *noun.* Now *rare* exc. *dial.* Also **rotchie** /ˈrɒtʃi/. E19.
[Alt. of ROTGE.]
The little auk; = ROTGE.

rote /rəʊt/ *noun*¹. ME.
[Old French = Provençal, medieval Latin *rot(t)a* ROTTA.]
MEDIEVAL MUSIC. = ROTTA.

rote /rəʊt/ *noun*² & *verb*¹. ME.
[Origin unkn.]
▸ **A** *noun.* †**1** (A) custom, (a) habit. Only in ME.
2 (A) mechanical practice or performance; (an instance of) mere form or routine. *obsolete* exc. as below. ME.
2 by rote in a mechanical or repetitious manner; *esp.* (of learning etc.) acquired through memorization without proper understanding or reflection.
Comb.: **rote learning** learning by rote; *spec.* (*PSYCHOLOGY*) the learning by rote of a series of items, as part of the study of learning.
▸ **B** *verb.* **1** *verb trans. & intrans.* Repeat or recite (a passage etc.) by rote. Now *rare.* L16.
†**2** *verb trans.* In *pass.* Be remembered or fixed through repetition. Foll. by *in*, *on*. *rare.* E17–L18.
■ **roter** *noun* (*rare*) a person who learns or recites by rote E17.

rote /rəʊt/ *noun*³. E16.
[French, or directly from Latin ROTA.]
†**1** *ROMAN CATHOLIC CHURCH.* = ROTA 1. E16–L18.
2 Rotation; turn. *rare.* M19.

rote /rəʊt/ *noun*⁴. Now *Scot. & N. Amer.* E17.
[Var.]
= RUT *noun*³.

rote /rəʊt/ *verb*². *rare.* L16.
[Latin *rotare*: see ROTATE *verb*.]
†**1** *verb trans.* = ROTATE *verb* 2. Only in L16.
2 *verb intrans.* Leave or resign from office, employment, etc., in turn. Foll. by *out*. Cf. ROTATE *verb* 3. L17.

rotenone /ˈrəʊtənəʊn/ *noun.* E20.
[from supposed Japanese *roten* derris + -ONE.]
CHEMISTRY. A toxic crystalline polycyclic ketone, $C_{23}H_{22}O_6$, obtained from the roots of several leguminous plants (esp. derris, cube, and timbo), and widely used as an insecticide.

rotge /ˈrɒtdʒi/ *noun.* Now *rare* exc. *dial.* Also **-gee**. L17.
[Prob. imit., but perh. misunderstanding of Frisian *rotgies* brent goose.]
The little auk; = ROTCHE.

rother /ˈrɒðə/ *noun.* Long *dial.*
[Old English *hrīþer*, *hrȳþer* = Old Frisian *hrither*, from *hrīth*, Old High German *hrind* (German *Rind*).]
An ox; *gen.* any horned animal. Also ***rother-beast***.

Rotherham plough /ˈrɒð(ə)rəm plaʊ/ *noun phr.* M18.
[from *Rotherham* a town in S. Yorkshire.]
A type of plough, prob. introduced from the Netherlands in the mid 18th cent.

Rothschild /ˈrɒθstʃʌɪld/ *noun.* M19.
[Mayer Amschel *Rothschild* (1744–1812) and his descendants, proprietors of an international banking company.]
An extremely wealthy person; a millionaire.
come the Rothschild *colloq.* pretend to be extremely wealthy.

roti /ˈrəʊtiː/ *noun.* E20.
[Hindi, Urdu *roṭī*. Cf. ROOTY *noun*.]
A type of unleavened bread originally from the Indian subcontinent.

rôti /roti/ *noun & postpositive adjective.* Pl. of noun pronounced same. L18.
[French, from *rôtir*: see ROTISSERIE.]
COOKERY. ▸**A** *noun.* A dish or main course of roasted meat. L18.
▸ **B** *postpositive adjective.* Of food: roasted. M19.

rotifer /ˈrəʊtɪfə/ *noun.* L18.
[mod. Latin, from Latin *rota* wheel + -I- + -FER.]
ZOOLOGY. Any of various mainly microscopic invertebrate animals constituting the phylum Rotifera, characterized by an anterior ciliated organ or corona, and common in fresh water. Also called ***wheel animalcule***.
■ **roˈtiferous** *adjective* of or belonging to this phylum M19.

rotisserie /rə(ʊ)ˈtɪs(ə)ri/ *noun.* M19.
[French *rôtisserie*, from *rôtir* roast.]
1 A restaurant or shop specializing in roasted or barbecued meat etc. M19.
2 A type of roasting oven with a power-driven rotating spit. Also ***rotisserie oven***. M20.
■ **rotisse** *verb trans. & intrans.* (chiefly *US*) [back-form.] cook (meat) using a rotisserie M20.

rôtisseur /rotisœːr/ *noun.* Pl. pronounced same. M18.
[French, from *rôtir* (see prec.) + *-eur* -OR.]
A chef in charge of all roasting, and usu. grilling and frying, in a restaurant etc.

Rotissomat /rə(ʊ)ˈtiːsə(ʊ)mat/ *noun.* Also **r-**. M20.
[from ROTISS(ERIE + -O- + -MAT.]
(Proprietary name for) a kind of rotisserie oven.

rotl /ˈrɒt(ə)l/ *noun.* E17.
[Arab. *raṭl*, perh. alt. of Greek *litra*.]
A unit of weight in some Middle Eastern and eastern Mediterranean countries, varying locally and equivalent to between 1 and 5 lb (approx. 0.45 and 2.3 kg).

roto /ˈrəʊtəʊ/ *noun. N. Amer.* Pl. **-os**. M20.
[Abbreviation of ROTOGRAVURE.]
A pictorial (section of a) newspaper or magazine.

roto- /ˈrəʊtəʊ/ *combining form.* Also **rota-** /ˈrəʊtə/.
[Repr. Latin *rota* wheel, or ROTARY *adjective*: see -O-.]
= ROTARY *adjective* 2.
■ **rotochute** *noun* a device with rotating blades that is attached to an object to function like a high-speed parachute M20.

rotogravure /rəʊtəgrəˈvjʊə/ *noun.* E20.
[*Rotogravur* Deutsche Tiefdrück Gesellschaft, German company, assim. to PHOTOGRAVURE.]
PRINTING. **1** A method of gravure printing using a rotary press, esp. used for long print runs of magazines, stamps, etc. E20.
2 A sheet or (esp.) a section of a magazine printed by this method. E20.

rotolo /rə(ʊ)ˈtəʊləʊ, ˈrɒtələʊ/ *noun.* Pl. **-li** /-li/, **-los**. E17.
[Italian, formed as ROTL.]
= ROTL.

rotometer /rə(ʊ)ˈtɒmɪtə, ˈrəʊtəmiːtə/ *noun.* Also **rota-** /rə(ʊ)ˈta-, ˈrəʊtə-/. E20.
[from ROTO- + -METER.]
A hand-held measuring device incorporating a small wheel whose revolutions are registered in terms of distance travelled, e.g. on a map or plan.

roton /ˈrəʊtɒn/ *noun.* M20.
[from ROT(ATION + -ON.]
PHYSICS. A quantum or quasiparticle associated with vortex motion in a liquid, esp. in liquid helium.

rotonda *noun* see ROTUNDA.

rotor /ˈrəʊtə/ *noun.* L19.
[Irreg. for ROTATOR.]
1 *MATH.* A vector quantity representing a rotation rather than a linear displacement. Now *rare.* L19.
2 A rotating part in a motor or dynamo, *esp.* a rotor arm. E20.
3 A rotating vertical cylinder that can be mounted on a ship, using the Magnus effect to provide auxiliary propulsion. E20.
4 A hub with a number of radiating aerofoils that is rotated in an approximately horizontal plane to provide the lift for a rotary-wing aircraft. M20.
5 The rotating vessel in a centrifuge. M20.
6 A part of an encoding or decoding machine, rotation of which changes numerous electric circuits and thereby the code. M20.
7 A large eddy in which the air circulates about a horizontal axis, esp. in the lee of a mountain. M20.
Comb.: **rotor arm** the rotating part of the distributor of an internal-combustion engine which successively makes and breaks electrical contacts so that each spark-plug fires in turn; **rotor blade** each of the radiating aerofoils of the rotor of a rotary-wing aircraft; **rotor cloud** a turbulent cloud in a rotor (sense 7); **rotor disc** (*a*) the space swept out by rotor blades as they rotate; (*b*) a rotor head; **rotor head**, **rotor hub** the rotating structure at the upper end of a shaft of a rotary-wing aircraft, to which the rotor blades are attached; **rotor ship** a ship whose auxiliary motive power is derived from cylindrical rotors (sense 3).

rotorcraft /ˈrəʊtəkrɑːft/ *noun.* Pl same. M20.
[from ROTOR + CRAFT *noun*.]
A rotary-wing aircraft.

Rototiller /ˈrəʊtəʊtɪlə/ *noun.* Chiefly *N. Amer.* Also **r-**. E20.
[from ROTO- + TILLER *noun*¹.]
= ROTAVATOR.
¶ Proprietary name.
■ **rototill** *verb intrans.* [back-form.] prepare soil with a Rototiller M20.

roto-tom /ˈrəʊtəʊtɒm/ *noun.* M20.
[from ROTO- + TOM-)TOM *noun*.]
A small shell-less drum tuneable by rotation usu. within a range of an octave.

Rotovator *noun* var. of ROTAVATOR.

rotta /ˈrɒtə/ *noun.* L19.
[medieval Latin, prob. from late Latin *chrotta*, formed as CRWTH. Cf. earlier ROTE *noun*¹.]
MEDIEVAL MUSIC. Any of various stringed instruments similar to a psaltery.

rottack /ˈrɒtək/ *noun.* Long *obsolete* exc. *Scot.* Also †**rottock**. LME.
[from ROT *verb* + -OCK.]
Decayed or musty matter; an old or decayed thing.

rottan /ˈrɒt(ə)n/ *noun.* Now *Scot. & dial.* L15.
[Var. of RATTON.]
A rat.

†**rottang** *noun* see RATTAN *noun*¹.

rotten /ˈrɒt(ə)n/ *adjective, verb, noun, & adverb.* ME.
[Old Norse *rotinn* prob. pa. pple of (unrecorded) verb corresp. to ROT *verb*.]
▸ **A** *adjective.* **I 1** In a state of rotting or decomposition; that has rotted; decayed, putrid; *esp.* made soft, friable, or liable to disintegrate because of rotting (also foll. by *with*). ME. ▸**b** Of air, water, etc.: contaminated, foul. ME. ▸**c** Of weather: damp, wet, rainy. Now chiefly as passing into sense A.4b. L16.
2 Of a sheep: affected with the rot. LME.

📖 **1** V. WOOLF We tread on rotten oak apples, red with age and slippery. *She* The bacteria which lurk in rotten teeth and gums.

▸ **II** *fig.* **3** Morally, socially, or politically corrupt. LME.
4 a Weak, unsound. E17. ▸**b** Disagreeable, unpleasant; (of a person) disagreeably ill; (of a plan, idea, etc.) worthless, unsatisfactory. *colloq.* L19. ▸**c** Drunk. *Scot. dial. & Austral. slang.* M20.

📖 **3** R. W. Emerson The war or revolution . . that shatters a rotten system. J. Wainwright He was a lousy Mafioso—because he wasn't all rotten. **4b** L. Gould She would not . . dampen one more Kleenex from his rotten box. D. Nabokov She was feeling rotten, in bed with a hot-water bottle. T. Parks It was a rotten childhood. ***rotten excuse***, ***rotten idea***, ***rotten scheme***, etc.

▸ **B** *verb trans. & intrans.* Make or become rotten. *rare.* LME.
▸ **C** *noun.* Rotting or rotted matter; the rotted part of something. Now *rare* or *obsolete.* E17.
▸ **D** *adverb.* As intensifier: to an extreme degree, absolutely. *slang.* L19.

📖 M. Twain I'm most rotten certain 'bout that. *Jackie* I'd fancied him rotten ever since. **knock rotten** *Austral.* kill, stun. **spoil a person rotten** spoil or indulge a person excessively.

Special collocations & comb.: **rotten apple** a bad person, *esp.* a morally corrupt person. ***rotten borough***: see BOROUGH 3. **rotten-hearted** *adjective* thoroughly corrupt. **Rotten Row** (*a*) a road in Hyde Park in London used for horse or (formerly) carriage exercise; (*b*) NAUTICAL a place in a naval shipyard for storing old or ageing ships. **rotten-stone** a decomposed siliceous limestone used as a powder for polishing metals; also called ***tripoli***.

■ **rottenly** *adverb* M19. **rottenness** /-n-n-/ *noun* (*a*) the state or condition of being rotten (*lit.* & *fig.*); (*b*) rotten or decayed matter: ME.

rottle /ˈrɒt(ə)l/ *verb intrans.* Now *dial.* LME.
[Middle Dutch, Middle Low German *rotelen*, German *rosseln*, prob. of imit. origin. Cf. RATTLE *verb*[1], RUTTLE.]
Rattle.

†**rottock** *noun* var. of ROTTACK.

Rottweiler /ˈrɒtvʌɪlə, -wʌɪlə/ *noun.* E20.
[German, from *Rottweil* a town in SW Germany.]
(An animal of) a large powerful breed of dog having short coarse hair and a broad head with pendent ears.

rotula /ˈrɒtjʊlə/ *noun.* Pl. **-lae** /-liː/. LME.
[Latin, dim. of *rota* wheel: see -ULE.]
1 ANATOMY. **a** The kneecap, the patella. Now *rare* or *obsolete.* LME. ▸**b** A disclike bony process, *esp.* the point of the elbow. Now *rare* or *obsolete.* M18.
2 A mechanical device showing the apparent motions and phases of the sun and moon. *rare.* M18.
3 ZOOLOGY. Each of five radial calcareous plates or pyramids which form the Aristotle's lantern in sea urchins. L19.
■ **rotular** *adjective* (ANATOMY, now *rare* or *obsolete*) patellar E19.

rotulet /ˈrɒtjʊlɪt/ *noun. rare.* M19.
[from Latin *rotulus* roll + -ET[1].]
A small roll or part of a larger roll of parchment etc.

rotund /rə(ʊ)ˈtʌnd/ *noun.* Now *rare.* M16.
[Use as noun of Latin *rotundus*: see next.]
1 A circular or spherical object. M16.
†**2** *spec.* = ROTUNDA 1. M–L18.

rotund /rə(ʊ)ˈtʌnd/ *adjective.* L15.
[Latin *rotundus*, from *rotare* ROTATE *verb.*]
1 Now chiefly BOTANY & ZOOLOGY. Round, circular, spherical. L15.
2 Of speech, literary style, etc.: sonorous, grandiloquent. M19.
3 Of a person, part of the body, etc.: plump, podgy. M19.

📖 **2** De Quincey The style of Latin they affect is . . too florid, too rotund. **3** A. Koestler A piece of check waistcoat over the slightly rotund belly. I. Murdoch He has become so rotund . . even his head has become fat.

¶ Rare before 18.
■ **rotundate** *adjective* (BOTANY & ZOOLOGY) rounded off L18. **rotundly** *adverb* L16. **rotundness** *noun* (*rare*) E18.

rotund /rə(ʊ)ˈtʌnd/ *verb trans. rare.* M17.
[from (the same root as) ROTUND *adjective.*]
Make rotund.

rotunda /rə(ʊ)ˈtʌndə/ *noun.* In sense 1 also (earlier, long *rare*) ***rotonda*** /rəˈtɒndə/. E17.
[Alt., after Latin *rotundus*, of Italian *rotonda* fem. of *rotondo* round. Cf. ROTUNDO.]
1 A building with a circular interior and plan, *esp.* one with a dome; *spec.* (***the Rotunda***) the Pantheon in Rome. E17.
2 a A circular hall or room. L18. ▸**b** The main hall of a public building; a concourse. *N. Amer.* E20.
3 A rounded formal gothic script used esp. in Italy from the 13th cent.; printing type based on this style. E20.

rotundity /rə(ʊ)ˈtʌndɪti/ *noun.* LME.
[Old & mod. French *rotondité* or Latin *rotunditas*, formed as ROTUND *adjective*: see -ITY.]
1 A rotund person or thing. LME.
2 The state or condition of being rotund; roundness, sphericity. L16.

rotundo /rə(ʊ)ˈtʌndəʊ/ *noun.* Now *rare* or *obsolete.* Pl. **-o(e)s.** E17.
[Alt. of ROTUNDA.]
A circular form or thing; *spec.* = ROTUNDA 1, 2a.

roture /rɔtyːr/ *noun.* L17.
[Old & mod. French.]
1 LAW (now *Hist.*). Tenure of land (esp. in France) subject to payment of rent as opp. to feudal duties. L17.
2 Low social rank. Now chiefly *Hist.* L18.

roturier /rɔtyrje/ *noun & adjective.* Now chiefly *Hist.* Fem. ***-ière*** /-jɛːr/. Pl. of noun pronounced same. L16.
[French, formed as prec.: see -IER.]
(Designating, or pertaining to) a person of low social rank.

Rotwelsch /ˈroːtvɛlʃ/ *noun.* M19.
[German, from Middle High German *rot* beggar or *rôt* red + *welsch* WELSH *adjective & noun.*]
In Germany and Austria, a form of criminals' slang.

rouble /ˈruːb(ə)l/ *noun.* Also **ruble.** M16.
[French from Russian *rubl'*.]
The basic monetary unit of Russia, the USSR (*Hist.*), and some other former republics of the USSR, equal to 100 kopeks; a coin or note representing this.

roucou /ruːˈkuː/ *noun.* M17.
[French *ro(u)cou* from Galibi *rucu* var. of Tupi *urucú* URUCU.]
1 A tropical American tree, *Bixa orellana* (family Bixaceae), which yields the dye annatto. M17.
2 = ANNATTO. M17.

roucoulement /rukulmɑ̃/ *noun. rare.* M19.
[French.]
A soft cooing sound (as) of a dove.

roué /ˈruːeɪ/ *noun.* E19.
[French, use as noun of pa. pple of *rouer* break on the wheel (the punishment said to be deserved by such a debauchee).]
A debauchee, a rake.

📖 *Times* He plays the Don as a middle-aged roué.

■ **rouéism** *noun* (*rare*) debauchery, dissipation M19.

Rouen /ˈruːɒ̃, *foreign* rwɑ̃/ *noun.* E18.
[A city in northern France. Cf. ROAN *noun*[1].]
1 Used ***attrib.*** to designate things made in or associated with Rouen. E18. ▸**b** In full ***Rouen ware***. A kind of earthenware made in Rouen, esp. in the 16th and 17th cents. M19.
2 In full ***Rouen duck***. (A bird of) a breed of large duck resembling the wild mallard in colouring. M19.

rouf /rəʊf/ *adjective & noun. slang* (chiefly *Criminals'*). M19.
[Reversal of FOUR.]
▸ **A** *adjective.* Four. M19.
▸ **B** *noun.* Four things; *spec.* (*a*) four pounds (or, formerly, shillings); (*b*) a four-year prison sentence. M20.

rouge /ruːʒ/ *noun*[1] *& adjective.* LME.
[Old & mod. French from Latin *rubeus* red.]
▸ **A** *adjective.* Red. *obsolete* exc. as below. LME.
Rouge Croix /krwɒ/, †**Rouge Cross** one of the four Pursuivants of the English College of Arms, with reference to the red cross of St George. **Rouge Dragon** one of the four Pursuivants of the English College of Arms, with reference to the red dragon of Cadwallader, the royal badge of Henry VII. **rouge royal** a reddish Belgian marble.
▸ **B** *noun.* †**1** The colour red. *rare.* Only in LME.
2 A red powder or cream used as a cosmetic to add colour to the lips or esp. the cheeks. M18.
3 Red as one of the two colours of divisions in rouge-et-noir and roulette. Earliest in ***rouge-et-noir***. L18.
4 A radical; a republican; a socialist. Now chiefly (*Canad.*), a member of the Quebec Liberal Party. Cf. RED *noun* 5b. E19.
5 Any of various metallic oxides etc. used as polishing powders; *esp.* (in full ***jeweller's rouge***) a fine preparation of ferric oxide used as a metal polish. Usu. with specifying word. M19.
6 French red wine; = RED *noun* 4b. M20.
Phrases etc.: **rouge de fer** /də ˈfɛː/ an orange-red enamel used on Chinese porcelain, made from a ferric oxide base. **rouge-et-noir** /ruːʒeɪˈnwɑː/ a gambling game in which stakes are placed on a table marked with red and black diamonds. **rouge flambé** /ˈflɒmbeɪ/ a bright red Chinese porcelain glaze, made from copper oxide.

rouge /ruː(d)ʒ/ *noun*[2]. M19.
[Origin unkn.]
1 In the Eton College field game, a score awarded when an attacker touches a ball that has been kicked or deflected over the goal-line by the defending team. M19.
2 CANAD. FOOTBALL. A single point awarded when the receiving team fails to run a kick out of its own end zone. L19.

rouge /ruːʒ/ *verb trans. & intrans.* L18.
[from ROUGE *noun*[1].]
1 Apply rouge (to). L18.
2 *fig.* (Cause to) colour or blush. L18.

📖 **1** W. Boyd His lips were . . pink, almost as if he had rouged them. **2** H. Gold You should have seen me rouge all over.

rouget /ruʒɛ/ *noun.* Pl. pronounced same. L19.
[French.]
A red mullet, esp. as used in cooking.

Rouget cell /ˈruːʒeɪ sɛl/ *noun phr.* E20.
[C. M. B. *Rouget* (1824–1904), French physiologist.]
ANATOMY. = PERICYTE.

rough /rʌf/ *noun.* ME.
[from the adjective.]
▸ **I** †**1** *The* rough or uneven part or surface *of* something. *rare.* Only in ME.
2 a Rough or broken ground. *poet.* LME. ▸**b** An area of rough or untilled ground, *esp.* one covered with undergrowth, small trees, etc. Also ***the roughs***. E17. ▸**c** GOLF. *The* unmowed ground off the fairway between tee and green. E20.
3 *transf. The* hard or disagreeable part or aspect of or *of* something (esp. life); rough treatment, hardship. Also, an instance of this. Freq. contrasted with ***smooth***. LME. ▸**b** Heavy housework. Freq. in ***do the rough***. M20.
4 A nail driven into a horse's shoe to prevent slipping. Chiefly *Scot.* L19.

📖 **2a** Wordsworth O'er rough and smooth she trips along. **b** *Caravan Life* Mountain bikes . . are . . for riders who want to take to the rough. *Mandy* Into the roughs, the marshy land below the stream. **c** *Times* He missed the green . . taking three from out of the fluffy rough. **3** C. Mackenzie Living far from the . . crowd you have to take the rough with the smooth. **b** M. Dickens Cosy discussions on clothes . . and women to do the rough.

▸ **II 5** *sing.* & in *pl.* Unrefined or refuse material left after a technical process, as the working of minerals or the threshing of corn. L17.
6 a A rough or provisional draft, sketch, etc. L17. ▸**b** *gen.* The unfinished, provisional, or natural state of something. L18. ▸**c** (An) uncut precious stone; *esp.* an uncut diamond. E20.
7 In *pl.* (treated as *sing.*). Alum used as an adulterant in bread. Now *rare.* M19.
8 A person of a rough or unrefined character; a violent or disorderly person; a ruffian. M19.

📖 **6a** *Campaign* The work should be run as roughs rather than being typeset. **8** A. Paton A gang of . . roughs broke in.

Phrases: **bit of rough** *slang* a (usu. male) sexual partner whose lack of sophistication or toughness is a source of physical attraction. **in the rough** (*a*) in a rough, unfinished, or provisional state; (*b*) in a natural state; in an everyday condition.

rough /rʌf/ *adjective & adverb.* Also †**ruff.** See also ROW *adjective*[1].
[Old English *rūh* = Middle Low German, Middle Dutch *rūch*, *rū* (Dutch *ruig*, *ruw*), Old High German *rūh* (German *rauh*), from West Germanic. Cf. RUFF *noun*[1].]
▸ **A** *adjective.* **I 1** Having an uneven or irregular surface; not level or smooth; unpolished. OE. ▸**b** Of cloth, hair, vegetation, etc.: coarse in texture. OE. ▸**c** Of a bone: having meat on it. *Scot.* L18. ▸**d** Designating the side of a tennis, squash, etc., racket opposite to the smooth side (SMOOTH *adjective* 1c), from which the loops of twisted string project, esp. used as a call when the racket is spun to decide on the server or choose ends. L19. ▸**e** BACTERIOLOGY. Of a bacterial phenotype: characterized by corrugated and irregular colonies, and by cells lacking polysaccharide capsules. E20.
2 Covered with (esp. long) hair; hairy, shaggy; unclipped, unshorn. OE. ▸†**b** (Of a hide) undressed, untanned; *rare* made of undressed hide. OE–M17.
3 Of ground etc.: uneven, rugged; uncultivated, wild. OE.
4 Of the sea or weather: stormy, turbulent, violent. LME. ▸**b** Of a journey: undertaken during or accompanied by stormy weather. M19.

📖 **1** G. Vidal The rough granite surface of the column. G. Swift I felt its rough lip against my bare arm. **b** R. West The fringe of rough grass. ***rough-coated***, ***rough-haired***, etc. **2** Milton Rough Satyrs danc'd, and Fauns with clov'n heel. **3** D. H. Lawrence We stumbled over the rough path. **4b** Richard Doyle After a rough passage . . landed at Ostend.

▸ **II 5 a** Of an action: violent, harsh; insensitive, inconsiderate. ME. ▸**b** (Of a place) occupied or frequented by rough or violent people; (of a time) characterized by violent events, riotous. M19. ▸**c** Of an experience or occurrence: troublesome, unpleasant; unreasonable, unfair. M19.
6 Of language or facial expression: harsh, uncompromising; impolite, offensive. ME.
7 Of a person, disposition, etc.: inclined to be violent or harsh; ungentle, unkind. LME. ▸**b** Of a horse: unbroken; not easily ridden or uncomfortable to ride due to an irregular pace. L16.
8 Of a medicine: strong or powerful in effect. *rare.* L17.
9 Foll. by *on*: hard or unfair towards. *colloq.* L19.
10 Unwell, ill; miserable, dejected. *colloq.* (orig. *dial.*). L19.

5a A. BURGESS The lovemaking . . had been rough at first but later more tender. **b** G. PALEY A busy man selling discount furniture in a rough neighbourhood. **c** U. SINCLAIR You had been having a rough time of it. A. LURIE It's rough to be cursed out like that. **6** L. STRACHEY She even liked . . his rough unaccommodating speech. **7** S. SPENDER Children who were rough . . threw words like stones and wore torn clothes. U. LE GUIN They get rough with him, beat him up. **9** C. SIMMONS His first wife had been very rough on him. **10** *Times* She . . pretended to feel rough when she surfaced around lunch-time.

▶**III 11** Rudimentary, crude, imperfect; not requiring or accomplished with skill. **ME.** ▸**b** Of accommodation etc.: lacking in comfort or refinement; basic. **M19.**

12 Of materials, esp. stone: in a natural or crude state; undressed, unworked. **LME.**

13 Approximately accurate or adequate; generally sufficient; preliminary, provisional. **L16.** ▸**b** Ignoring or incapable of fine distinctions. Now chiefly in ***rough justice*** below. **E19.** ▸**c** Of stationery etc.: used for writing preliminary notes or records. **M19.** ▸**d** Of a vacuum: produced by a relatively low degree of evacuation. **E20.**

14 Plentifully supplied. Chiefly in ***rough and round*** below. *Scot.* **E18.**

11 F. H. JOYNSON The iron . . run into rough moulds. **13** J. B. PRIESTLEY How many Members of Parliament could give even the roughest description of . . a coal-mine? H. J. EYSENCK A rough idea . . of the kinds of topic psychologists . . study. A. SILLITOE He . . pencilled rough calculations into his notebook. **c** R. K. NARAYAN I want a rough notebook.

▶**IV 15** Of alcoholic drink: harsh to the taste; not smooth; sharp, acid. **LME.**

16 (Of a sound) discordant, harsh, grating; (of the voice) hoarse. **LME.** ▸**b** Of a speech sound: aspirated. **M18.**

17 a Of diction or style: graceless, unrefined, unpolished. **M16.** ▸**b** Of language: coarse, vulgar. **M20.**

18 Of a person, disposition, etc.: uncultured, uncultivated, unrefined. **L16.**

19 Of a task etc.: requiring strength; heavy, manual. **E18.**

16 A. PRICE Weston's voice was rough with . . tension. **18** C. V. WEDGWOOD Training transformed . . rough rural recruits into disciplined soldiers. B. EMECHETA She was rough, not as cultivated as the sleek, younger woman. **19** A. THIRKELL The rough work and . . washing were done by Effie.

Phrases: **get rough (with)** begin to act violently (towards). ***give a person a rough ride***: see RIDE *noun*. **rough-and-ready** *adjective* rough or crude but effective; unelaborate, not over-particular. **rough and round** *Scot.* (*a*) (of food) plain but substantial; (*b*) (of a person) homely, unsophisticated. **rough as bags**, **rough as guts**, **rough as sacks** *slang* (chiefly *Austral.* & *NZ*) coarse, uncouth. ***the rough edge of one's tongue***: see EDGE *noun*. **the rougher sex** the male sex. **the rough side of one's tongue** = ***the rough edge of one's tongue*** s.v. EDGE *noun*.

Special collocations & comb.: **roughback** = ***rough dab*** below. **rough bent** a N. American bent-grass, *Agrostis scabra*; also called ***tickle-grass***. **rough bounds** *Scot.* [Gaelic *Garbh-chriochan*] the mountainous area between the Sound of Mull and Loch Duich. ***rough breathing***: see BREATHING 5. **rough calf** BOOKBINDING dressed calfskin used with the flesh side outermost. ***rough*** CHERVIL. **rough coal** *dial.* a free coal which is mined in large blocks. **rough coat** a preliminary coat of plaster applied to a surface. **rough collie** (an animal of) a breed of long-coated black and white, or black, tan, and white collie. **rough copy** (*a*) a first or original draft; (*b*) a copy of a picture etc. comprising only the essential details. **rough cut** the first version of a film after preliminary editing. **rough dab** (more fully ***long rough dab***) a N. Atlantic flatfish, *Hippoglossoides platessoides*, of the family Pleuronectidae, with a rough skin; also called ***American plaice***, ***roughback***. ***rough deal***: see DEAL *noun*³ 3. **rough diamond** (*a*) an uncut diamond; (*b*) a person of good nature but rough manners. **Rough Fell** (an animal of) a breed of large long-woolled sheep found in parts of the Pennine area of England. **rough file**: having coarse cutting ridges. **rough-footed** *adjective* (*a*) (of a bird, esp. a domestic pigeon) having feathered feet; (*b*) *arch.* wearing shoes of undressed hide. **rough grazing** (an area of) uncultivated land used for grazing livestock. **rough green snake** = ***rough-scaled green snake*** below. **rough greyhound** = DEER-*hound*. **rough horsetail** a rough-stemmed horsetail, *Equisetum hyemale*, formerly used for scouring; also called ***pewterwort***, ***scouring rush***, ***shavegrass***. **rough hound** any of various dogfishes, *esp.* the lesser-spotted dogfish, *Scyliorhinus canicula*. **rough house** *slang* an uproar, a disturbance; boisterous or violent behaviour. **rough-house** *verb* (*slang*) (*a*) *verb intrans.* cause an uproar or disturbance; behave boisterously or violently; (*b*) *verb trans.* handle (a person) roughly or violently. **rough justice** (*a*) treatment that is approximately fair; (*b*) very unfair treatment. **rough leaf** (now *rare*) (*a*) the first true leaf of a plant, as distinguished from the cotyledons; (*b*) the stage of growth when the true leaves have appeared. **rough-legged** *adjective* having hairy or feathered legs; ***rough-legged buzzard***, a migratory holarctic buzzard, *Buteo lagopus*, which breeds in the subarctic tundra. **rough-lock** *noun* & *verb* (*N. Amer.*) (*a*) *noun* a device (esp. a chain) for slowing the downward passage of a vehicle, logs, etc.; (*b*) *verb trans.* slow (a vehicle etc.) with such a device. **rough log**, **rough logbook**: containing notes to be written up later in the main logbook. **rough mix** a preliminary blend of separate soundtracks of a piece of music. **rough music** *slang* (now *Hist.*) noisy uproar, esp. as intended to display public outrage or discontent at the behaviour of others. **roughneck** *colloq.* (*a*) a rough or rowdy person; (*b*) a worker on an oil rig. **roughneck** *verb intrans.* (*colloq.*) work as a roughneck on an oil rig. **rough passage** (*a*) a sea-crossing undertaken during rough weather; (*b*) a difficult time or experience. **rough pâté**: made with coarsely-chopped or -minced ingredients. **rough puff pastry**: made without allowing the pastry to rest between each turning. **rough ride** *colloq.* a difficult time or experience. **rough-scaled** *adjective* having rough scales; ***rough-scaled green snake***, a colubrid snake, *Opheodrys aestivus*, of the eastern US and Mexico; ***rough-scaled snake***, a small highly venomous elapid snake, *Tropidechis carinatus*, of tropical Queensland. **rough scuff**, **rough scruff** *US slang* a rough or disreputable person; *collect.* *the* riffraff, *the* rabble. **rough seal** = RINGED *seal*. **rough shoot**, **rough shooting** (*a*) the action or an act of shooting game without beaters; (*b*) an area where this is permissible. **rough spin** *Austral. slang* a piece of bad luck. **rough stuff** *colloq.* unruliness, violent behaviour. **rough-tail** = ***shieldtail*** s.v. SHIELD *noun*¹. **rough timber**: partly dressed, having only the branches removed. **rough-tonguing** verbal abuse; a scolding. **rough trade** *slang* a rough or esp. a lower-class person engaged in or solicited for homosexual prostitution; (the activities of) such people collectively. **rough-tree** NAUTICAL *Hist.* (*a*) = ***roof-tree*** (b) s.v. ROOF *noun*; (*b*) an unfinished mast or spar. **rough-winged swallow** a brown-backed American swallow, *Stelgidopteryx ruficollis*. **rough work** (*a*) preliminary or provisional work; (*b*) *colloq.* violence; (*c*) a task requiring the use of force.

▶**B** *adverb.* In a rough manner; roughly, crudely. **ME.**

Phrases: **live rough** habitually sleep rough, have no proper home. **sleep rough**, (now *rare*) **lie rough** sleep outdoors or not in a proper bed, esp. habitually as having no home.

Comb.: **rough-dry** *verb trans.* dry (clothes) roughly, esp. without ironing; **rough-handle** *verb trans.* treat roughly or violently; **rough-hew** *verb trans.* form or shape out roughly; **rough-hewn** *adjective* (*a*) formed or shaped out roughly; (*b*) (of a person) unrefined, uncultivated, uncouth; **roughshod** *adjective* (of a horse) having shoes with nail-heads projecting to prevent slipping; ***ride roughshod over*** (*fig.*) domineer over, treat inconsiderately or arrogantly.

■ **roughish** *adjective* somewhat rough **M18.** **roughly** *adverb* (*a*) in a rough manner; (*b*) approximately, in an approximate sense: **ME.** **roughness** *noun* (*a*) the quality of being rough; (*b*) a rough part or place; (*c*) (*dial.*, chiefly *US*) hay, corn-husks, etc., as opp. to grain, used as animal fodder: **LME.** **roughsome** *adjective* (*Scot.*) roughish; rough-mannered, uncouth: **M17.**

rough /rʌf/ *verb.* **L15.**
[from the adjective.]

1 *verb trans.* Make rough by pulling, scraping, rubbing, etc.; *spec.* ruffle (feathers, hair, etc.) by rubbing in the wrong direction. Usu. foll. by *up*. **L15.** ▸**b** Make (a horse's shoe) rough by inserting nails, to prevent slipping. **E19.**

2 *verb trans.* †**a** Offend or grate on (the ear). *rare.* Only in **E17.** ▸**b** Use rough language to. Now *rare* or *obsolete.* **M19.** ▸**c** Treat roughly or harshly; *esp.* (foll. by *up*) assault violently, beat up. *colloq.* **M19.**

3 *verb intrans.* & *trans.* with *it*. Live outdoors or in rough accommodation etc.; do without basic conveniences or comforts. **M18.**

4 *verb trans.* Work on or form in a rough or preliminary fashion (also foll. by *off*); plan or sketch *out* roughly, fill or sketch *in* roughly; *spec.* plane (wood) *down* roughly. **L18.** ▸**b** Break in (a horse). Usu. foll. by *off*. Chiefly *Austral.* **E19.** ▸**c** Shear (a sheep) roughly or inadequately. *Austral.* & *NZ.* **L19.** ▸**d** Subject (a vacuum system) to partial or preliminary evacuation. Also foll. by *down*, *out*. **M20.**

1 R. JEFFERIES The hurricane roughs up the straw on . . the ricks. E. CHILDERS If he roughed my suit, so much the better: I intend to rough his. **2c** *Daily Mail* He will be roughed and bustled around for the first few rounds. T. O'BRIEN They don't talk and our interrogation teams rough them up. **3** M. RENAULT He was keen on adventure, and roughing it. *Scouting* Some scouters . . like a bit of home comfort at camp, rather than 'roughing it'. **4** G. GREENE He roughs in very well the atmosphere of commercial travelling. F. MUIR I had a synopsis roughed out. *Practical Householder* Rough down . . a small section of the workpiece.

Comb.: **rough-out** *noun* & *adjective* (*a*) *noun* (ARCHAEOLOGY) an artefact left or abandoned at a preparatory stage of manufacture, the intended final form being clear; (*b*) *adjective* (*US*) designating informal outdoor clothing; **rough-up** *slang* (*a*) an informal trial or contest; (*b*) a fight, a brawl.

■ **rougher** *noun* a person who carries out rough or provisional work **L19.**

roughage /ˈrʌfɪdʒ/ *noun.* **L19.**
[from ROUGH *adjective* + -AGE.]

1 The unused or refuse part of a crop; rough grass or weeds. *dial.*, *US*, & *NZ.* **L19.**

2 The fibrous matter in vegetable foodstuffs which aids digestion though itself indigestible. **E20.**

2 *fig.*: C. S. LEWIS There is no roughage in a Kipling story—it is all unrelieved vitamins.

rough-and-tumble /rʌf(ə)nˈtʌmb(ə)l/ *noun, adverb,* & *adjective.* Orig. *Boxing slang.* **E19.**
[from ROUGH *adjective* + AND *conjunction*¹ + TUMBLE *noun.*]

▶**A** *noun.* Haphazard or random fighting; an instance of this; (a) scuffle, (a) scramble. **E19.**

B. EMECHETA Dirty and wet from the rough and tumble of the match. *transf.*: M. MEYER Strindberg hated the rough-and-tumble of open debate.

▶**B** *adverb.* In an irregular or disorderly manner. **E19.**

Z. N. HURSTON Mr. Allen might have eaten by the rules but . . I went at it rough-and-tumble.

▶**C** *adjective.* **1** Disregarding the rules, irregular; haphazard; scrambling, riotous, disorderly. **M19.**

2 Of a person: practising irregular methods of fighting etc.; inclined to be rough or violent. **M19.**

1 *National Observer (US)* Sandwiches are . . self-contained lunches that can withstand a good deal of rough-and-tumble action.

roughcast /ˈrʌfkɑːst/ *adjective, noun,* & *verb.* Also **rough-cast**. **E16.**
[from ROUGH *adjective* & *adverb*: see CAST *ppl adjective*, *noun*¹, *verb*.]

▶**A** *adjective.* **1** Of a wall etc.: coated with plaster consisting of a mixture of lime and gravel. **E16.**

2 Formed roughly; crude, preliminary. **L16.**

▶**B** *noun.* **1** Plaster composed of lime and gravel, used on an outside wall. **L16.**

†**2** A rough sketch or outline. **L16–M17.**

▶**C** *verb trans.* Pa. t. & pple **-cast**.

1 Coat with roughcast. **M16.**

2 Form roughly or crudely; prepare a preliminary version of (a plan etc.). **L16.**

■ **roughcaster** *noun* a plasterer who applies roughcast **L16.** **roughcasting** *noun* (*a*) the action or an act of coating with roughcast; (*b*) = ROUGHCAST *noun* 1: **M16.**

roughen /ˈrʌf(ə)n/ *verb.* **L16.**
[from ROUGH *adjective* + -EN⁵.]

1 *verb trans.* Make rough. Also foll. by *up*. **L16.** ▸**b** *fig.* Irritate; ruffle. **M19.**

2 *verb intrans.* Become rough. **M18.**

1 SHELLEY Its rude hair Roughens the wind that lifts it. G. DODD The nap of the cloth is roughened up by a brush. *refl.*: DICKENS That girl's . . nature seemed to roughen itself against seeing us so bound up in Pet. **2** A. TYLER His voice was furry and dark, roughening on vowels. R. FRAME The lawn . . furthest from the house roughened to long grass. G. R. TURNER Her skin was roughening and would become lined.

roughie /ˈrʌfi/ *noun. slang.* **E20.**
[from ROUGH *noun* + -IE.]

1 = ROUGH *noun* 8. Chiefly *Scot.* & *Austral.* **E20.**

2 a An outsider in a horse-race etc. *Austral.* **E20.** ▸**b** An unfair or unreasonable act. Chiefly in ***put a roughie over***, commit such an act. *Austral.* **E20.**

roughing /ˈrʌfɪŋ/ *noun.* **M18.**
[from ROUGH *verb* + -ING¹.]

1 The action of ROUGH *verb.* **M18.** ▸**b** A roughened surface. **M19.**

2 The action or fact of living under rough or uncomfortable conditions. Also ***roughing it***. **E19.**

3 SPORT. Foul handling or tackling. Chiefly *N. Amer.* **M19.**

Comb.: **roughing pump** a pump for evacuating a system from atmospheric pressure to a lower pressure at which a second pump can operate.

roughometer /rʌˈfɒmɪtə/ *noun. US.* **E20.**
[from ROUGH *adjective* + -OMETER.]

= PROFILOMETER 2(b).

rough-rider /ˈrʌfrʌɪdə/ *noun.* **M18.**
[from ROUGH *adjective* + RIDER *noun.*]

1 A person who breaks in horses; a person who can ride an unbroken horse. **M18.**

2 A rough-mannered horse-rider. **E19.** ▸**b** MILITARY. An irregular cavalryman; *spec.* (*US Hist.*) a member of the Volunteer Cavalry regiment in the Spanish-American War of 1898. **L19.**

■ **rough-ride** *verb intrans.* [back-form.] ride an unbroken horse; *fig.* domineer *over*: **L19.**

roughy /ˈrʌfi/ *noun*¹. *Austral.* & *NZ.* **M19.**
[Perh. from ROUGH *adjective* + -Y¹.]

Either of two small fishes, the ruff, *Arripis georgianus*, and *Trachichthys australis*, a brown fish with rough-edged scales.

roughy *noun*² var. of RUFFY.

rouille /ruj/ *noun.* **M20.**
[French, lit. 'rust'.]

A Provençal sauce made from pounded red chillies, garlic, breadcrumbs, etc., blended with stock, freq. added to bouillabaisse.

rouk /raʊk, rʊk/ *noun. Scot.* & *north.* **L15.**
[Var.]

= ROKE *noun*¹.

■ **rouky** *adjective* **E19.**

roulade /rʊˈlɑːd/ *noun.* **E18.**
[French, from *rouler* to roll: see -ADE.]

1 MUSIC. A florid passage of runs etc. in solo vocal music, *esp.* one sung to one syllable. **E18.**

2 Any of various dishes prepared by spreading a filling on to a base of meat, sponge, etc., which is then rolled up and freq. served sliced. **L19.**

rouleau /ruˈləʊ/ *noun*. Pl. **-eaux** /-əʊ/, **-eaus**. L17.
[French formed as ROLE.]
1 A cylindrical packet of gold coins. L17. ▸**b** A stack of disc-shaped objects, esp. red blood cells. M19.
2 A roll or a coil *of* something, esp. hair. L18.
3 A turned tube or length of rolled fabric used as trimming or to form a belt on a garment etc. E19.
4 In full ***rouleau vase***. A type of narrow-necked cylindrical vase originally made in China in the late 17th cent. E20.

roulement /rulmɑ̃/ *noun*. Pl. pronounced same. E20.
[French, lit. 'roll, roster'.]
MILITARY. (A) movement of troops or equipment, esp. from a reserve force to provide relief.

roulette /ruˈlɛt/ *noun*. M18.
[French, dim. of *rouelle* wheel, from late Latin *rotella* dim. of *rota* wheel.]
†**1** *gen.* A small wheel. *rare*. Only in M18.
2 A gambling game in which a ball is dropped on to a revolving wheel with numbered compartments in the centre of a table, players betting on (the colour, height, or parity of) the number at which the ball comes to rest. M18. ▸**b** The wheel used in this game. Now *rare*. M19.
3 A revolving toothed wheel; *spec.* (**a**) one for making dotted lines in etching and engraving; (**b**) one for perforating a sheet of postage stamps. M19.
4 A hair curler. Now *rare* or *obsolete*. M19.
5 MATH. A curve generated by a point on a rolling curve. Now *rare*. M19.
2 RUSSIAN *roulette*. VATICAN *roulette*.
■ **rouletted** *adjective* (**a**) (of a postage stamp) having a perforated edge; (**b**) ARCHAEOLOGY (of pottery etc.) indented with decorative lines or dots by means of a roulette or comb: M19. **rouletting** *noun* (chiefly ARCHAEOLOGY) (**a**) the action or an act of perforating or indenting a surface with a roulette or comb; (**b**) ornamentation produced in this way: L19.

Rouman /ˈruːmən/ *noun & adjective*. Now *rare*. M19.
[French *Roumain* from Romanian *Român*, from Latin *Romanus* ROMAN *adjective*.]
= ROMANIAN *noun & adjective*.

Roumanian *noun & adjective* var. of ROMANIAN.

Roumelian /ruˈmɛlɪən, -ˈmiːl-/ *adjective & noun*. E19.
[from *Roumelia* (see below) + -AN.]
▸**A** *adjective*. Of or pertaining to Roumelia, an area in the south of the Balkan peninsula, now divided between Greece and Bulgaria; of or pertaining to the form of Greek spoken there. E19.
▸**B** *noun*. = ROUMELIOTE *noun*. M20.

Roumeliote /ruˈmiːlɪəʊt/ *noun & adjective*. M19.
[mod.Greek *Roumeliōtēs*, formed as prec.: see -OT².]
▸**A** *noun*. A native or inhabitant of Roumelia. M19.
▸**B** *adjective*. = ROUMELIAN *adjective*. M19.

roumi /ˈruːmi/ *noun*. Fem. ***-ia*** /-ɪə/. L16.
[Arab. *rūmī* adjective, from *(al-)Rūm* inhabitants of the late Roman or Byzantine Empire.]
In Arabic-speaking countries: a foreigner, *esp.* a European.

roun /ruːn/ *noun*. Long *obsolete* exc. *Scot.* Also †**rune**. See also RUNE *noun*.
[Old English *rūn* = Middle Dutch *rune*, *ruun*, Old Saxon *rūna*, Old High German *rūna* (German *Raun*, dial. *Rûn*), Old Norse *rúnar*, *rúnir* (pl.) Gothic *rūna*.]
▸†**I 1** See RUNE *noun*. OE.
▸**II** †**2** A secret, a mystery. OE–ME.
†**3** Advice, counsel; private consultation. OE–ME.
†**4** (A piece of) writing. OE–ME.
5 †**a** Discourse, speech; rumour; an instance of this. ME–M16. ▸**b** An utterance; *esp.* a whisper. ME.
†**6** A song; a cry. Only in ME.

roun *verb* see ROUND *verb*¹.

rounce /raʊns/ *noun*¹. L17.
[Dutch *ronse*, *ronds*, *rondse*.]
PRINTING. The (curved) handle of the winch by which the bed of a hand printing-press is run in and out; the whole of this winch.

rounce /raʊns/ *noun*². *US*. M19.
[Perh. alt. of RAMSCH.]
A card or domino game in which winning points are subtracted from an initial score.

rouncing /ˈraʊnsɪŋ/ *adjective*. Long *dial.* L16.
[Prob. imit.]
Roaring, noisy.

rouncival /ˈraʊnsɪv(ə)l/ *noun & adjective*. L16.
[Perh. from Spanish *Roncesvalles*, French *Roncevaux* a village in northern Spain. Cf. RUNCIBLE SPOON.]
▸**A** *noun*. **1** (In full ***rouncival pea***) a large variety of garden or field pea; in *pl.*, peas of this variety. L16.
†**2** *transf.* A large and boisterous woman. Freq. *derog.* L16–M17.
▸†**B** *adjective*. Of large proportions or capacity. L16–L17.

rouncy /ˈraʊnsi/ *noun*. Long *arch*. ME.
[Old French *ronci*, *roncin*, medieval Latin *roncinus*, *runcinus*, of unkn. origin.]
A horse, *esp.* one of cob type for riding.

round /raʊnd/ *noun*¹. ME.
[from the adjective.]
▸**I 1** A spherical object; a planet. *rare*. ME. ▸**b** *fig.* The vault of the sky, heaven. L16.
2 A circular or cylindrical object. ME.
3 *spec.* **a** A rung of a ladder. LME. ▸**b** A large cylindrical cut *of* beef, usu. from the haunch. M17. ▸**c** BREWING. A large cask used in the final process of fermentation. E19. ▸**d** A slice across a loaf of bread; a sandwich made from whole slices of bread. M19. ▸**e** A crossbar connecting the legs of a chair etc. L19.
4 †**a** A piece of sculpture modelled clear of any ground. M–L17. ▸**b** ARCHITECTURE. A rounded moulding. L17. ▸**c** A plane with a convex bottom and iron, for working hollows or grooves. M19.
5 ***the round***: ▸**a** A form of sculpture in which the figure stands clear of any ground and can be seen from all aspects (cf. RELIEF *noun*² 1). Chiefly in ***in the round*** below. E19. ▸**b** The natural unsquared form of timber. E19.

> 📖 **1** T. S. ELIOT In the hollow round of my skull. **b** SIR W. SCOTT The wild birds carol to the round. **2** R. L. STEVENSON Close to his hand . . was a little round of paper.

▸**II 6** A circle, a ring, a coil. ME. ▸**b** A single turn of yarn etc. as wound on a reel. M18.
7 The circumference, bounds, or extent *of* a circular object. LME.
8 A natural feature or man-made structure with a circular form. E16. ▸**b** A curve or bend in a river etc. E17.
9 A circular group or arrangement of people or things. L16.

> 📖 **6** SHAKES. *Macb.* What . . wears upon his baby brow the round And top of sovereignty? **7** TENNYSON The dark round of the dripping wheel.

▸**III 10 a** MILITARY. A watch that makes a regular inspection of sentries or that patrols a town etc.; a circuit made by such a watch. LME. ▸**b** Any customary circuit or route followed for the inspection or supervision of people or things; *spec.* (**a**) a visit by a doctor to each of the patients in a ward or to those patients unable to visit a surgery etc.; (**b**) a fixed route on which things are regularly delivered (usu. with specifying word). E17. ▸**c** A recreational walk or drive round a place or places, a tour. *arch.* E17. ▸**d** The circuit of a place etc. Now only with *of*. E17. ▸**e** GOLF. A spell of play in which the player plays all the holes in the course once. L18. ▸**f** NAUTICAL. In *pl.* Inspection. E20.
†**11** A swinging stroke or thrust with a sword. L15–E17.
12 A ring dance. E16.
13 A revolving motion, a circular or recurring course. E17.
14 a A regularly recurring series of or *of* events, activities, etc.; (now *poet.*) a recurring or revolving course *of* time. M17. ▸**b** *spec.* A recurring succession or series of or *of* meetings for discussion or negotiation; a stage in such a series. M20.

> 📖 **10b** DYLAN THOMAS Ocky Milkman on his round. P. ROAZEN On rounds he remembered which patient was suffering most. ***milk round***, ***paper-round***. **13** SHELLEY The earth in its dismal round. **14a** M. SPARK Nurses . . on their daily round of washing . . and prettifying the patients. *People* The social round . . was fabulously costly in clothes. **b** *Economist* Two months into the current wage round. *EuroBusiness* A round of negotiations . . scheduled to last for four years.

▸**IV 15** MUSIC. †**a** A type of song sung by two or more people, each taking up the strain in turn. E16–L17. ▸**b** A short unaccompanied canon in which three or more voices singing at the same pitch or in octaves enter in turn. M18.
16 A single provision of drinks to each member of a group. M17.
17 A single shot or discharge from a firearm or piece of artillery; a single charge of ammunition to fire one shot. E18.
18 a A single turn of play by all the players in a card-game. M18. ▸**b** A single stroke in succession from each bell of a set or peal. E19. ▸**c** A single bout in a boxing- or wrestling-match. E19. ▸**d** ARCHERY. A fixed number of arrows shot from a fixed distance. L19. ▸**e** A stage in a sporting competition. Freq. with specifying word. E20.
19 A single distinct outburst *of* applause. L18.

> 📖 **16** *Argosy* Dennim paid for another round of drinks. J. PORTER The local chap . . proved . . willing to stand his round. **18e** *TV Times* The . . British clubs . . drew Belgian opposition in the second round of the UEFA Cup.

Phrases: **go one's rounds** take one's customary route for delivery, inspection, etc. **go the round**, (now usu.) **go the rounds** (of news etc.) be passed on from person to person. **in the round** (**a**) (of sculpture) with all sides shown, not in relief; (**b**) THEATRICAL with the audience round at least three sides of the stage; esp. in ***theatre-in-the-round*** s.v. THEATRE *noun*; (**c**) *fig.* with all features shown; all things considered. **make one's rounds** = ***go one's rounds*** above. **make the round of** go to each in turn, go round. **make the rounds** = ***go the rounds*** above. **out-of-round** *noun & adjective* (**a**) *noun* the extent to which an object departs from being circular in cross-section; (**b**) *adjective* (of an object) not perfectly circular. **this earthly round** *poet.* the earth.

round /raʊnd/ *noun*². M18.
[from ROUND *verb*².]
Chiefly NAUTICAL. The action of rounding; a curved part or structure.

round /raʊnd/ *adjective*. ME.
[Old French *ro(u)nd-* inflectional stem of *ro(o)nt*, earlier *reont* (mod. *rond*), from Proto-Romance var. of Latin *rotundus* ROTUND *adjective*.]
▸**I 1** Having all parts of the surface equidistant from the centre; spherical, like a ball. ME.
2 Cylindrical; having a convex surface or outline, curved. ME. ▸**b** Of a garment: enveloping the body completely, not open at the front; cut circularly at the bottom, so as to have no train; full. LME. ▸†**c** Of cloth: made of thick thread. *Scot.* L15–L16. ▸**d** Of the shoulders: bent forward from the line of the back. E18. ▸**e** Of a fish: not gutted. L19.
3 Having all parts of the circumference equidistant from the centre; circular. ME. ▸**b** Going round in or tracing out a circle. M16. ▸**c** PHONETICS. Of a sound, esp. a vowel: enunciated by contracting the lips to form a circular shape. L16. ▸**d** Of a blow: delivered with a swing of the arm. E19.
4 Plump, free from angularity; well-fleshed. ME.

> 📖 **1** D. H. LAWRENCE A great round globe of iron. J. STEINBECK Her head was small and round. **2** J. CONRAD The . . jetty with the squat round tower. DAY LEWIS He is wearing his round, shallow clerical hat. ***a round peg in a square hole***, ***a square peg in a round hole***: see PEG *noun*¹. **3** R. WEST The loch . . was a dark shining circle, perfectly round. B. EMECHETA The . . woman had a face as round as a perfect O. **4** TENNYSON An armlet for the roundest arm on earth.

▸**II 5** Of a number: full, complete, entire (freq. in ***round dozen***); *esp.* expressed for convenience or as an estimate in few significant numerals (as in tens, hundreds, etc.) or with a fraction removed. ME. ▸**b** Of a calculation etc.: approximate, rough. *rare*. M17.
6 a Brought to a perfect finish; perfect; neatly turned or finished off. Formerly also, (of work) carried out to a proper finish. LME. ▸**b** Of a voice, sound, etc.: full and mellow; not harsh. M16. ▸**c** Of a wine or spirit: having a good balance between taste, smell, and alcoholic strength. L20.
7 Of a sum of money or (long only *Scot.*) an amount: large, considerable. L16.

> 📖 **5** H. ADAMS The . . line . . measures in round numbers one hundred feet. C. N. PARKINSON He distrusts that round figure of £10,000,000. **6a** P. J. BAILEY Ere yet he could . . foresee Life's round career accomplished in the skies.

▸**III** †**8** (Of a blow, measure, etc.) heavy, hard, severe; (of fighting) vigorous. LME–M18.
9 Outspoken, uncompromising, or severe in speech *with*; (of a statement etc.) categorical, blunt. LME. ▸**b** Plain, honest, straightforward. *arch.* E16.
10 Of movement: quick, brisk, smart. Chiefly in ***a round pace***, ***a good round pace***. M16. ▸†**b** Of speech: flowing. M16–M18.

> 📖 **8** J. ARBUTHNOT A good round Whipping. **9** DICKENS The lady . . rated him in good round terms. A. TROLLOPE Must he not be round with her, . . give her to understand in plain words?

Special collocations & comb.: **round-arch**, **round-arched** *adjectives* (ARCHITECTURE) characterized by or having rounded or semi-circular arches. **roundball** *US* †(**a**) baseball; (**b**) basketball. **round barrow** ARCHAEOLOGY a circular grave-mound common in (but not confined to) the Bronze Age of Europe. **round bilge** NAUTICAL a curved, as opp. to an angular or stepped, hull. **round bracket**: of the form ( ). **round-celled** *adjective* (MEDICINE) (of a sarcoma) characterized by round, undifferentiated cells. ***round clam***: see CLAM *noun*² 1. **round coal**: in large lumps. **round dance** (**a**) a ring dance; (**b**) a dance in which couples revolve around the floor. **round-eared** *adjective* (of a cap) having round flaps at the ears. **roundeye** *slang*, *derog.* a European, as opp. to an Oriental. **round-faced** *adjective* having a round face. **round fish** (**a**) fish of a rounded form (opp. ***flatfish***). **round-fish** = ***pilot-fish*** s.v. PILOT *noun* 3. **round game** a game (esp. at cards) for three or more players in which each player plays as an individual as opp. to as part of a team. **round hand** a style of handwriting in which the letters are round and bold. **round heel** (chiefly *US slang*) [with ref. to worn heels allowing the wearer to fall backwards easily] (**a**) in *pl.* a tendency to be promiscuous; (**b**) *sing.* & in *pl.* a promiscuous person, esp. a woman. **round-heeled** *adjective* (chiefly *US slang*) sexually promiscuous. ***round* HERRING**. **round log** *US*: felled but not hewn. **round lot** *US* a standard unit of trading in a particular security. **round meal** coarse oatmeal. **round-mouthed** *adjective* (chiefly ZOOLOGY) having a round mouth; ***round-mouthed snail***, a terrestrial prosobranch snail, *Pomatias elegans*, characteristic of chalk downland. **round-nosed** *adjective* (of a tool) having the end formed so as to produce a rounded cut or surface. **round-off** *noun & adjective* (**a**) *noun* an act of rounding off a number; (**b**) *adjective* (of a file) used to round or blunt a point. **round pin** on an electrical plug, a pin with a circular rather than a rectangular cross-section. ***round rape***: see RAPE *noun*[3] 1. **round robin** (*a*) a petition, *esp.* one with the signatures written in a circle to conceal the order of writing; (*b*) *N. Amer.* a tournament in which each competitor competes once with each of the others; (*c*) *HORSE-RACING* a form of multiple bet involving three horses, adding up to ten bets; (*d*) a sequence, a series. **round seam** *NAUTICAL*: joining two edges without lapping. **round seizing** *NAUTICAL*: used to lash two ropes together with a series of turns. **round shot** *Hist.* cast-iron or steel spherical balls for firing from cannon. **round-shouldered** *adjective* having the shoulders bent forward so that the back is rounded. **round text** large round-hand. **round timber** *US*: felled but not hewn. **round-top** *noun & adjective* (*a*) *noun* (*NAUTICAL*) a (formerly circular) platform around a mast-head of a sailing ship; (*b*) *adjective* having a rounded top. **round towel** (now *rare*) a roller towel. **round tower** *ARCHAEOLOGY* a high tower of circular plan tapering from the base to a conical roofed top, found esp. in Ireland. **round trip** a trip to one or more places and back again, esp. by a circular route; (***round-trip ticket*** (N. Amer.), a return ticket). **round-tripper** (*a*) a traveller who makes a round trip; (*b*) *BASEBALL* a home run. **round-tripping** *ECONOMICS* the practice of earning profit by borrowing on overdraft and relending in money markets. **round turn** (*a*) *NAUTICAL* a complete turn of a rope around another rope, a bollard, etc.; (*b*) ***bring up with a round turn*** (colloq.), check or stop suddenly. **round-winged** *adjective* having round wings; ***round-winged muslin***, a small whitish European moth, *Thumatha senex*, of the family Arctiidae; ***round-winged hawk*** (chiefly *FALCONRY*), any of various birds of prey of the family Accipitridae, esp. a hawk of the genus *Accipiter*. **round wood** short logs of small diameter from the tops of pine and spruce trees, used for furniture.

■ **roundish** *adjective* M16. **roundward** *adjective* (*rare*) circular L19. **roundways** *adverb* (*rare*) = roundwise M17. **roundwise** *adverb & adjective* (now *rare*) (*a*) *adverb* in a circular form or arrangement; (*b*) *adjective* circular: L16. **roundy** *adjective* (now *dial.*) (*a*) rounded, of a round shape; (*b*) (of coal) lumpy: L16.

round /raʊnd/ *verb*[1]. *arch.* Also (earlier) **roun** /raʊn/.
[Old English *rūnian* = Old Saxon *rūnon*, Middle Low German, Middle Dutch *rūnen*, Old High German *rūnēn* (German *raunen*), Old Swedish *runa*, from RUNE *noun*. For the parasitic *d* cf. BOUND *adjective*[1].]

1 *verb intrans.* Whisper; converse or talk privately. OE.

2 *verb trans.* Whisper (something), utter in a whisper. OE. ▸**b** Address in a whisper; tell (a person) in a whisper (something, *that*); later *esp.* reprimand in private. Freq. in ***round a person in the ear***. LME.

†**3** *verb intrans.* Speak, talk, converse. Only in ME. ▸**b** *verb trans.* Say or tell (something). ME–L15.

†**4** *verb intrans.* Take counsel, deliberate. Only in ME. ▸**b** *verb trans.* Talk about, discuss. ME–M17.

round /raʊnd/ *verb*[2]. LME.
[from the adjective; in early use perh. after Old French *rondir*.]

▸ **I** *verb trans.* **1** Make round; give a circular, spherical, or curved form to. LME. ▸**b** Make convex or curving in outline; form into a cylinder; fill out to a rounded form. L17. ▸**c** Enunciate (a sound) with rounded lips. M19.

2 †**a** Deface (coin) by cutting or paring. LME–E17. ▸†**b** Cut (the hair) short round the head; cut the hair of (a person) in this way. Also, tonsure. LME–L18. ▸**c** Crop (the ears of a dog). L18.

3 Surround or encircle (*with*). *arch.* E16. ▸**b** Hem *in*. *rare.* E17.

4 **a** Make a complete circuit of, travel round. L16. ▸**b** Walk around, take a turn round. Now *rare* or *obsolete*. E17. ▸**c** Cause to turn to an opposite position or move in a circle. E18. ▸**d** Pass round so as to get to the opposite side of. M18. ▸**e** Collect or bring together (members of a group or esp. a herd of cattle), esp. by going round. Usu. foll. by *up*. M19.

5 Finish off, bring to completion, esp. satisfactorily or appropriately. Freq. foll. by *off*, *out*. E17. ▸**b** Bring (a sentence etc.) to a neat close; end (a sentence etc.) *with* something. M18. ▸**c** Express (a number) in few significant figures for convenience. Freq. foll. by *off*. E20.

> 🕮 **1** E. DIEHL Rounding the backs of books . . to produce a smooth . . surface. A. TYLER She carried her books clutched to her chest, rounding her shoulders. **b** W. M. PRAED Slender arms . . Are rounded with a statue's grace. **4a** J. M. COETZEE The marshland begins to curve back . . and we know that we have rounded the lake. **d** J. MCPHEE A boat rounds a bend from the west. D. ATTENBOROUGH *The Beagle* . . rounded Cape Horn and came north again. **e** J. A. MICHENER Men . . would . . round up cattle. S. TOWNSEND They took hours to round up all the pensioners. **5** M. ANGELOU I like a serious man . . to laugh. Rounds out the personality. V. BROME Jones's letter . . appeared to round off . . the interminable story.

▸ **II** *verb intrans.* **6** Have or assume a curved or full shape; become round, circular, or spherical. LME.

7 **a** Walk about; *spec.* (of a guard) go the rounds. Now *rare*. M16. ▸**b** Take a circular or winding course; make a turn; turn round. E17. ▸**c** Curve *off*. L17.

> 🕮 **6** *Chambers's Journal* The little . . apples grew and rounded and yellowed.

With adverbs & prepositions in specialized senses: **round down** (*a*) decrease (a number) when rounding it; (*b*) *NAUTICAL* overhaul (a rope). **round in** *NAUTICAL* haul in. **round off** (*a*) make round, convex, or curved by trimming off edges or angles; (*b*) complete (an estate etc.) by adding adjacent lands; (see also senses 5, 5c above). **round on** (*a*) make a sudden verbal attack on or unexpected retort to (a person); (*b*) *slang* inform on. **round out** (*a*) *verb phr. intrans.* (*AERONAUTICS*) flare; (*b*) *verb phr. trans.* see sense 5 above. **round to** *NAUTICAL* sail closer to the wind. **round up** (*a*) increase (a number) when rounding it; (*b*) *NAUTICAL* sail closer to the wind; (*c*) *NAUTICAL* take up the slack of (a rope running through a block); (see also sense 4e above).

Comb.: **round-out** *AERONAUTICS* = FLARE *noun*[1] 3b.

round /raʊnd/ *adverb & preposition*. ME.
[As adverb from ROUND *adjective*; preposition perh. aphet. of AROUND.]

▸ **A** *adverb*. **I 1** With a circular course; so as to return again to the starting-point. ME. ▸**b** To each in turn of a group, number of places, etc.; with (successive) inclusion of all members of a group etc. E17. ▸†**c** From all sides; all over. *rare*. M17–M18. ▸†**d** Of a horse: with all four feet shod. L17–M18. ▸**e** Throughout; from beginning to end. Chiefly in ***the year round***, ***all the year round***. M18. ▸**f** = ABOUT *adverb* 2b. Chiefly *US*. M19.

2 In a ring or circle; so as to encircle or enclose something; in every direction from a centre or within a (specified) radius; on all or most sides; *loosely* somewhere near, about. ME.

3 By a circuitous or indirect route. M17. ▸**b** To a specific or specified place. L17. ▸**c** *CRICKET*. In the direction lying behind the batsman. M19.

> 🕮 **1** C. BAX We'll go round from right to left. J. MITCHELL He felt weak, but the blood pumped loudly round. V. GLENDINNING Before Charlotte knew it spring had come round again. **b** S. DOWELL Employing . . men to go round with samples. T. HARDY The business of handing round refreshments. J. GRENFELL Would there be enough lifejackets to go round? **2** H. MARTINEAU They will wake up all the sheep . . for a mile round. A. RANSOME A last look round to see that nothing had been forgotten. K. TENNANT Don't keep a man standing round in the cold. **3** S. PEPYS We are fain to go round by Newgate because of Fleet-bridge being under rebuilding. **b** E. M. FORSTER After tea . . he went round to see Hamidullah. N. SHUTE I slept round at Honey's house.

▸ **II 4** With a rotatory movement. ME.

5 **a** With change to the opposite direction or position. M18. ▸**b** With change to an opposite opinion etc. E19.

> 🕮 **4** W. COWPER Smack went the whip, round went the wheels. G. GREENE The pigeon swivelled round in circles unable to rise. **5a** C. MCCULLOUGH Sat down in a . . chair . . pulling it round so she could see. H. SECOMBE Hopkins turned round, saw the weapon and froze. **b** O. MANNING I had to talk her round, but now we're agreed.

▸ **III** †**6** With a round or full utterance; bluntly; plainly. LME–L18.

†**7** With a free or easy motion. LME–L16. ▸**b** Straightforwardly. *rare*. E–M17.

▸ **B** *preposition*. **1** So as to encircle or make a (complete) circuit of. E16. ▸**b** So as to include, visit, etc., in turn or successively; to various points or places in. E17. ▸**c** Throughout; from the beginning to the end of (a period of time). E18.

2 On or along the circuit or periphery of; at points on the circumference of. M17. ▸**b** So as to surround or envelop. E18. ▸**c** Around; about; near; approximately. *colloq.* E20.

3 In all or various directions from; on all sides of. E18.

4 So as to revolve about (a centre or axis). E18. ▸**b** Concerning; about. L19.

5 So as to make a partial circuit about or reach the other side of; on or to the other side of. M18.

> 🕮 **1** T. HARDY Streams of . . meteors racing round . . the planet. I. MCEWAN Flies gyrated slowly round the ceiling light. **b** G. GREENE He would follow his mother round the stalls. B. NEIL I went with him round the police stations and the hospitals. **2** V. WOOLF Sitting round a table after tea. W. S. MAUGHAM There were settees round the walls. **b** E. WAUGH A bandolier of cartridges round his waist. M. FRAYN Sasha struggled out of his overcoat and pulled it round Manning's shoulders. **c** D. ABSE We hung round Lydia Pike's house. D. NORDEN There weren't many items . . for bulk-buying round our way. **3** G. GREENE Smashing London to bits all round me. **5** G. B. SHAW Turning to watch him until he passes out of sight round the corner. V. WOOLF The man steering the plough round the . . rocks.

Phrases & comb.: ***round the bend***: see BEND *noun*[3]. ***round the clock***: see CLOCK *noun*[1]. **round-the-houses** *adjective & noun* (*a*) *adjective* (of a motor race) following the streets of a city etc.; cf. ***go round the houses*** s.v. HOUSE *noun*[1]; (*b*) *noun* (*rhyming slang*) trousers. ***round the twist***: see TWIST *noun*[1]. **round the wicket** *CRICKET* with delivery of the ball from the hand further away from the bowler's wicket.

roundabout /ˈraʊndəbaʊt/ *adjective & noun*. ME.
[from next.]

▸ **A** *adjective*. †**1** Circular in cross-section. Only in ME.

2 Circuitous, indirect; circumlocutory. E17.

3 **a** = ROUND *adjective* 2b. E18. ▸**b** Designating a type of chair with a circular seat and semi-circular back. M18.

4 Plump, stout. Now *rare*. E19.

5 Of a fireplace: allowing people to sit all round. *Scot.* E19.

▸ **B** *noun*. **1** A circular course or object; *spec.* a circular fort, esp. a prehistoric one. Now *dial.* M16. ▸**b** A round oatcake. *Scot.* (*obsolete* exc. *dial.*). E18.

2 †**a** A farthingale; a hoop. *rare*. M16–M19. ▸**b** A short jacket. *US*. E19. ▸**c** An armchair with a rounded back. *US*. M19. ▸†**d** A woman's loose dressing-gown. *US*. M–L19.

3 An indirect or evasive utterance; a circumlocution. Now *rare*. L17. ▸**b** A circuitous route; a detour. Now *rare*. M18.

4 †**a** A kind of ring dance. M18–E19. ▸**b** A merry-go-round; now *esp.* a large revolving device in a playground for children to ride on. M18.

5 A road junction at which traffic moves in one direction round a central island. E20.

4b swings and roundabouts: see SWING *noun*[1].

■ **roundabou'tation** *noun* (*rare*) (a) circumlocution E19. **roundaboutly** *adverb* in a circuitous or circumlocutory manner L19. **roundaboutness** *noun* the quality of being circuitous or circumlocutory E19.

round about /raʊnd əˈbaʊt/ *adverbial & prepositional phr.* ME.
[from ROUND *adverb* + ABOUT.]

▸ **A** *adverbial phr.* **1** In a circle; on all sides or in all directions. ME.

2 With a rotatory movement; so as to pass or turn right round. LME.

3 = ROUND *adverb* 5a. L16.

4 By a circuitous route. L19.

> 🕮 **1** BROWNING Yon hollow, crusted roundabout With copper where the clamp was. DOUGLAS CLARK Bob . . does a circular tour of all the villages round about.

▸ **B** *prepositional phr.* **1** = ROUND *preposition* 1. LME.

2 In a circle about; on all sides of; in all directions from. LME.

3 Approximately; about; around. E20.

> 🕮 **2** SCOTT FITZGERALD Egotism tended . . to blind him to what was going on round about him. **3** *Harper's Magazine* His association with the magazine started round about 1936.

round-arm /ˈraʊndɑːm/ *adjective & adverb*. Also **roundarm**. M19.
[from ROUND *adjective* + ARM *noun*[1].]

▸ **A** *adjective*. **1** *CRICKET*. Performed with an outward horizontal swing of the arm; (of a bowler) using such an action in bowling. M19.

2 Of a blow: dealt with an outward swing of the arm. L19.

▸ **B** *adverb*. With a round-arm action. L19.

■ **round-armed** *adjective* (*CRICKET*) = ROUND-ARM *adjective* 1 M19. **round-armer** *noun* (*CRICKET*) a round-arm delivery M20.

rounded /ˈraʊndɪd/ *adjective*. LME.
[from ROUND *verb*[2] + -ED[1].]

1 That has been rounded. LME.

2 Having a circular, spherical, or curving form. E18.

3 Of a sound or the voice: sonorous, mellow, full; *spec.* (*PHONETICS*) (of a vowel etc.) enunciated by contracting the lips to form a circular shape. M19.

■ **roundedness** *noun* M19.

roundel /ˈraʊnd(ə)l/ *noun*. Also **roundle**. See also RUNDLE *noun*[1]. ME.
[Old French *rondel(le)*, formed as ROUND *adjective*: see -EL[2]. Cf. RONDEAU, RONDEL, RUNLET *noun*[1].]

▸ **I 1** **a** A small circular object, a disc, *esp.* a decorative one. ME. ▸**b** *HERALDRY*. Any of various circular charges distinguished by their tincture. ME. ▸**c** A small round pane or window. M19. ▸**d** A circular identification mark painted on military aircraft, *esp.* that of the Royal Air Force, comprising a design of concentric red, white, and blue circles. M20.

2 A circle marked out or formed in some way; a ring of people or things. Now *rare*. ME. ▸†**b** The outer circuit or rim *of* a thing. M16–M17. ▸†**c** A round hole or hollow. L16–E17.

3 †**a** A sphere, a globe; *spec.* the ball of the elbow- or knee-joint. LME–L17. ▸**b** *ARCHITECTURE*. A bead-moulding. M16.

4 †**a** A small round table. *Scot.* L15–M16. ▸†**b** A round mat for a dish etc. to stand on. M16–E18. ▸**c** *Hist.* A small round shield. M16. ▸**d** *Hist.* A round wooden trencher. L18.

5 †**a** A rung of a ladder. Cf. RUNDLE *noun*[1] 4a. L16–M17. ▸**b** A round turret. *Scot.* M18.

▸ **II 6** A poem of eleven lines in three stanzas; a rondeau. LME.

7 A ring dance. L16.

roundelay /ˈraʊndəleɪ/ *noun*. LME.
[Old & mod. French *rondelet* ROUNDLET, from *rondel* ROUNDEL, with ending assim. to VIRELAY or LAY *noun*[2].]

1 A short simple song with a refrain; *poet.* a bird's song. LME.

2 A piece of music for such a song. L16.

3 A ring dance. L16.

†**roundelet** *noun* var. of ROUNDLET.

rounder /ˈraʊndə/ *noun*. E17.
[from ROUND *noun*[1], *verb*[2] + -ER[1].]

▸ **I 1** †**a** A person (esp. a soldier) who makes the round of sentries etc. E17–L18. ▸**b** A Methodist local preacher travelling a circuit. E19. ▸**c** A person who makes the round of prisons or bars; a habitual criminal or drunkard. *N. Amer. slang*. M19. ▸**d** A transient railway worker. *US slang*. E20.

2 In *pl.* (treated as *sing.*). A game played with a bat and ball between two teams, in which players hit the ball and run to a base or through a round of bases in advance of the fielded ball. E19. ▸**b** A complete run of a player round all the bases as a unit of scoring in rounders. M19.

▸**II 3** A round tower. *rare*. L18.

▸**III 4 a** A tool for boring. M19. ▸**b** A tool for giving a rounded form to something. M19.

5 A person, esp. a shoemaker, who gives something a rounded form. L19.

Roundhead /ˈraʊndhɛd/ *noun & adjective*. M17.
[from ROUND *adjective* + HEAD *noun*.]
▸**A** *noun*. **1** *Hist.* [From their custom of wearing the hair cut short.] A member or supporter of the parliamentary party in the English Civil War; a 17th-cent. parliamentarian. M17. ▸**b** An immigrant from northern Europe, *spec.* a Swede. *N. Amer. slang. derog.* L19. ▸**c** ANTHROPOLOGY. (**r-**.) A brachycephalic person. L19.
†**2** (**r-**.) A long-handled weapon fitted at the end with a ring of sharp spikes. Only in M17.
▸**B** *adjective*. (**r-**.) Round-headed; parliamentarian. M19.

round-headed /raʊndˈhɛdɪd/ *adjective*. M17.
[from ROUND *adjective* + HEADED *adjective*.]
1 Having a round head or top. M17. ▸**b** ANTHROPOLOGY. Brachycephalic. L19.
2 *Hist.* Belonging to the parliamentary party in the English Civil War. M17.
1 round-headed borer *US* the wood-boring larva of any of various longhorn beetles. ***round-headed rampion***: see RAMPION 2.

roundhouse /ˈraʊndhaʊs/ *noun*. LME.
[In sense 1 app. from ROUND *noun*[1]; other senses from ROUND *adjective*: see HOUSE *noun*[1].]
1 *Hist.* A prison; a place of detention. LME.
2 NAUTICAL. A cabin or set of cabins on the after part of the quarterdeck, esp. on a sailing ship. E17.
3 A round building in which machinery is worked by circular movement. M17. ▸**b** ARCHAEOLOGY. A circular domestic structure, usu. of Bronze Age or Iron Age date. M20.
4 A circular repair-shed for railway locomotives, with a turntable in the centre. M19.
5 a BASEBALL. A pitch made with a sweeping sidearm motion. *US*. E20. ▸**b** A blow given with a wide sweep of the arm. *slang*. E20.

rounding /ˈraʊndɪŋ/ *noun*. M16.
[from ROUND *verb*[2] + -ING[1].]
1 The action of ROUND *verb*[2]. Also foll. by adverb. M16.
2 A rounded edge or surface; a curved outline or part. Formerly also, a tonsure. M16.
3 NAUTICAL. (A piece of) narrow rope for winding round a cable etc. to prevent chafing. M18.

rounding /ˈraʊndɪŋ/ *adjective & adverb*. E17.
[from ROUND *verb*[2] + -ING[2].]
▸**A** *adjective*. **1** That rounds. E17.
2 Circular; circuitous. E18.
▸**B** *adverb*. So as to have a rounded form. L17.

roundle *noun* see ROUNDEL.

roundlet /ˈraʊndlɪt/ *noun*. Also †**roundelet**. ME.
[Old & mod. French *rondelet* dim. of *rondel* ROUNDEL: see -LET.]
1 A small roundel. ME. ▸**b** HERALDRY. A roundel. ME.
†**2** A small cask. Cf. RUNLET *noun*[1]. ME–M18.

roundly /ˈraʊndli/ *adverb*. LME.
[from ROUND *adjective* + -LY[2].]
1 In a circular manner; in a circle. LME.
2 Completely, thoroughly; in a thoroughgoing manner. LME.
3 Plainly, bluntly; frankly, openly; without qualification. E16. ▸†**b** Fluently; glibly. M16–L17.
4 Quickly, briskly, promptly. M16.
5 Sharply, severely. L16.

roundness /ˈraʊn(d)nɪs/ *noun*. LME.
[from ROUND *adjective* + -NESS.]
1 The quality of being round. LME.
2 Compass; circumference. Now *rare* or *obsolete*. LME.
3 †**a** A circular course, an orbit; a spiral. LME–L16. ▸**b** A round object or formation. Now *rare*. LME.
1 out-of-roundness the quality of being out-of-round.

roundsman /ˈraʊn(d)zmən/ *noun*. Pl. **-men**. L18.
[from ROUND *noun*[1] + -S[1] + MAN *noun*.]
1 *Hist.* A labourer in need of parochial relief, employed in turn by a number of farmers. L18.
2 A person who makes rounds of inspection; *esp.* (*US*) a police officer in charge of a patrol. M19.
3 A trader's employee who goes round customers taking orders and making deliveries. L19.
4 A journalist covering a specified subject. *Austral.* L20.

Round Table /raʊnd ˈteɪb(ə)l/ *noun phr.* ME.
[from ROUND *adjective* + TABLE *noun*.]
1 The round table at which the legendary British King Arthur and his chosen knights sat so that none should have precedence; the order comprising these knights; this body of knights. ME. ▸†**b** A meeting or assembly of King Arthur's knights. ME–L15.
2 *Hist.* An assembly of knights for the purpose of holding a tournament and festival, *esp.* that instituted by Edward III in 1345. LME.
3 Any of various natural or man-made formations reputedly associated with King Arthur. LME.
4 (Usu. with lower-case initials.) An assembly of people around a table; *esp.* an assembly for discussion, esp. at a conference at which all participants are accorded equal status. Freq. ***attrib.*** E19.
5 A formal association meeting regularly for discussion; *esp.* (a branch of) an international charitable association founded in 1927, which holds discussions, debates, etc., and undertakes community service. E20.
■ **Round Tabler** *noun* (***a***) (with lower-case initials) *rare* a participant in a discussion; (***b***) a member of the Round Table association: L19.

round-up /ˈraʊndʌp/ *noun*. Also **roundup**. M18.
[from ***round up*** s.v. ROUND *verb*[2].]
1 NAUTICAL. The upward curvature or convexity to which the transoms or beams of a ship are shaped. M18.
2 The rounding up of cattle etc. usu. for the purpose of registering ownership, counting, etc.; the group of men and horses engaged in this. M19. ▸**b** The systematic rounding up of people or things; *spec.* the arrest of people suspected of a particular crime or crimes. L19. ▸**c** A social gathering of acquaintances or friends. L19.
3 A summary or résumé of facts or events; *spec.* (BROADCASTING) a summary of newsworthy items. L19.

> 🕮 **2b** E. PAWEL Occupation forces began the roundup . . of Czechoslovakia's Jews. **3** *Radio Times* Commentary . . together with a round-up of the day's play.

roundure /ˈraʊndjʊə/ *noun. arch.* E17.
[Var. of RONDURE with assim. to ROUND *adjective*; later from ROUND *adjective* + -URE.]
Roundness.

roundworm /ˈraʊndwəːm/ *noun*. M16.
[from ROUND *adjective* + WORM *noun*.]
A nematode worm, *esp.* a parasitic one infesting the gut of a mammal or bird, as *Ascaris lumbricoides* (which infests humans).

†**rounge** *verb* var. of RONGE.

roup /raʊp/ *noun*[1]. Also **roop** /ruːp/. ME.
[from the verb.]
▸**I** †**1** Clamour, crying. Only in ME.
2 An auction; the action of selling or letting by auction. *Scot. & north.* L17.
▸**II 3** Any of various respiratory diseases of poultry, *esp.* avian mycoplasmosis and advanced coryza. M16.
4 ***the roup***, hoarseness, huskiness; an inflammation of the throat. *Scot. & north.* L16.
■ **rouped** *adjective* (*Scot. & north.*) hoarse L17. **roupy** *adjective*[1] (***a***) *Scot. & north.* hoarse; (***b***) (of poultry) affected with the roup; pertaining to the roup: L17.

roup /ruːp/ *noun*[2]. Now *rare* or *obsolete*. E17.
[Origin unkn.]
A disease of poultry characterized by inflammation of the rump.
■ **roupy** *adjective*[2] (of poultry) affected with this disease E18.

roup /raʊp/ *verb. Scot. & north.* Also **roop** /ruːp/. ME.
[Of Scandinavian origin: cf. Old Norse *raupa* boast, brag.]
1 *verb intrans.* Shout, roar; croak. ME. ▸†**b** *verb trans.* Proclaim; utter loudly. Only in 16.
2 *verb trans. & intrans.* Sell or let (something) by auction. L15. ▸**b** *verb trans.* Sell up (a person). E19.
■ **rouper** *noun* M16. **rouping** *noun* (***a***) the action of the verb; (***b***) an auction: E16.

Rous /raʊs/ *noun*. E20.
[Francis Peyton *Rous* (1879–1970), US physician.]
Used ***attrib.*** to designate a type of sarcoma which affects birds, esp. poultry, and the RNA virus which causes this.

rous /raʊs/ *adverb. rare*. L17.
[Imit.]
With a bang.

rousant /ˈraʊz(ə)nt/ *adjective. rare*. LME.
[from ROUSE *verb*[1] + -ANT[1].]
HERALDRY. Of a bird: rising, preparing for flight.

rouse /raʊz/ *noun*[1]. L16.
[from ROUSE *verb*[1].]
†**1** A shake, esp. of a bird's feathers. L16–L17.
2 MILITARY. The reveille. E19.
3 A violent action; an instance of vigorous agitation. E19.

rouse /raʊz/ *noun*[2]. *arch.* E17.
[Prob. aphet. from CAROUSE, by division of *drink carouse* as *drink a rouse*.]
1 A full draught of wine, beer, etc.; a whole glassful. E17.
2 A drinking-bout. E17.

rouse /raʊz/ *verb*[1]. Also †**rouze**. LME.
[Prob. from Anglo-Norman. Cf. AROUSE.]
1 a *verb intrans.* Of game: rise from cover. *rare*. LME. ▸**b** *verb trans.* Cause (game) to rise or issue from cover or a lair. M16.
2 *verb intrans.* & (*rare*) †*refl.* FALCONRY. Of a hawk: raise and shake the feathers. L15.
3 †**a** *verb trans.* Raise, lift up. L16–M17. ▸**b** *verb trans.* Of a hawk: raise and shake (the feathers). L16. ▸†**c** *verb intrans.* Rise up, stand on end. *rare* (Shakes.). Only in E17.
4 *verb trans.* Cause to start up from sleep or repose; wake. Freq. foll. by *from, out of*. L16. ▸**b** *verb intrans.* Get up from sleep or repose; wake up. E17. ▸†**c** *verb trans.* Chase away (sleep). *rare* (Milton). Only in M17.
5 *verb trans. fig.* Startle (a person) out of a state of inactivity, security; etc.; provoke to activity, excite; *refl.* overcome one's indolence. L16. ▸**b** *verb intrans.* Become active; stir oneself. Freq. foll. by *up*. L16. ▸**c** *verb trans.* Provoke to anger. M19.
6 *verb trans.* Evoke or excite (a feeling). L16.
7 *verb trans.* **a** Stir up, agitate, or put in motion (a thing). Now *rare*. L16. ▸**b** Stir (a liquid, *esp.* beer while brewing). E19.
8 a *verb intrans.* Move violently; rush. *rare* (now *Canad. dial.*). L16. ▸**b** *verb trans.* NAUTICAL. Haul *in*, *out*, or *up* with force. E17.

> 🕮 **4** W. GOLDING I was roused . . from a too brief . . sleep. J. M. COETZEE Before dawn . . K roused his mother. P. ACKROYD He had been roused from his reverie by voices chanting. **5** D. H. LAWRENCE Kate had to rouse her into getting some . . medicine. C. P. SNOW It roused me to . . savage, tearful love. J. GLASSCO Nothing could rouse us from the delicious lethargy of the Parisian spring. G. KENDALL Rousing himself from . . a stupor. **6** N. SHERRY Cancer and leprosy . . terms which rouse the greatest fear.

■ **rousable** *adjective* (earlier in UNROUSABLE) E20. **rousement** *noun* (*US*) a rousing up of religious fervour L19. **rousing** *adjective* (***a***) that rouses; *esp.* exciting, stirring; (***b***) (of a fire) roaring, blazing strongly; (***c***) *arch.* (of a lie) outrageous: LME. **rousingly** *adverb* M17.

rouse /raʊz/ *verb*[2] *trans.* M17.
[Aphet. from ARROUSE.]
1 Sprinkle (herring etc.) with salt in the process of curing. M17.
2 Sprinkle with water. *Scot.* L18.

rouse /raʊs/ *verb*[3] *intrans. Austral. & NZ colloq.* L19.
[Cf. ROUST *verb*[1], *verb*[3].]
Scold; (foll. by *at, on*) speak chidingly to a person.

rouseabout /ˈraʊzəbaʊt/ *noun & verb*. M18.
[from ROUSE *verb*[1] + ABOUT.]
▸**A** *noun*. **1** A bustling, roaming, or active person. *dial.* M18.
2 a A general hand employed on a farm, sheep station, etc.; *esp.* one handling the wool in a shearing-shed, from the board to the table. *Austral. & NZ.* M19. ▸**b** *transf.* A general worker; a casual labourer. *Austral. & NZ.* E20.
▸**B** *verb intrans.* Work as a rouseabout. *Austral.* L19.

rouser /ˈraʊzə/ *noun*. E17.
[from ROUSE *verb*[1] + -ER[1].]
1 A person who or thing which rouses someone or something; *spec.* an instrument used for stirring beer in brewing. E17. ▸**b** A person or thing remarkable in some respect; an outrageous lie. *colloq.* E19.
2 A loud noise; a noisy person or thing. M18.
3 = ROUSEABOUT *noun* 2a. *Austral.* L19.

> 🕮 **1** W. C. WILLIAMS He was a grand rouser of a child's imagination.

rousette /ruˈzɛt/ *noun*. L18.
[French *roussette* fem. of Old French *rousset* reddish, from *roux* red: see -ETTE.]
Any of various Old World fruit-bats of the genus *Rousettus*, which form large cave-dwelling colonies and feed mainly on nectar and pollen. Also ***rousette bat***, ***rousette fruit-bat***.

rousie /ˈraʊzi/ *noun. Austral. & NZ colloq.* E20.
[Abbreviation: see -IE.]
= ROUSEABOUT *noun* 2a.

Rousseauan /ruˈsəʊən/ *adjective & noun*. L19.
[from Jean Jacques *Rousseau* (1712–78), French philosopher and novelist + -AN.]
▸**A** *adjective*. Of or pertaining to Rousseau or his views on religion, politics, etc.; characteristic of Rousseau or his style. L19.
▸**B** *noun*. An admirer, student, or adherent of Rousseau or Rousseauism. E20.
■ **Rousseau'esque** *adjective* = ROUSSEAUAN *adjective* M20. **Rousseauian** *adjective* L19. **Rousseauish** *adjective* L19. **Rousseauism** *noun* the principles or doctrines of Rousseau M19.

Rousseauist *noun & adjective* = ROUSSEAUAN L19. **Rousseau'istic** *adjective* M19. **Rousseauite** *noun & adjective* L19. **Rousseauvian** *adjective* E19.

Roussillon /ˈruːsɪjɒn, *foreign* rusijɔ̃/ *noun*. M18.
[See below.]
A red wine made in the former province of Roussillon (now the department of Pyrénées-Orientales) in southern France.

roust /raʊst/ *noun*[1] & *verb*[1]. Long *obsolete* exc. *Scot.* ME.
[Old Norse *raust* voice.]
▶ **A** *noun.* A cry, a shout, a roar. ME.
▶ **B** *verb intrans.* Shout, roar. *Scot.* LME.

roust /ruːst/ *noun*[2]. Also **roost**. M17.
[Old Norse *røst* (Norwegian *røst*).]
A turbulent tidal race formed by the meeting of conflicting currents, esp. in the sea between Orkney and Shetland.

roust /raʊst/ *noun*[3]. *N. Amer. slang.* M20.
[from ROUST *verb*[2].]
Harassment, beating up, esp. by the police; a police raid.

roust /raʊst/ *verb*[2]. M17.
[Perh. alt. of ROUSE *verb*[1].]
1 *verb trans.* Rouse *from*; stir *up*. M17. ▸**b** *verb intrans.* Get up (foll. by *up, out*); rummage *around*. L19.
2 *verb trans.* Jostle; (esp. of the police) harass, beat up. *N. Amer. slang.* E20.

> 🕮 **1** D. BAGLEY To roust the Lieutenant from whatever corner he was sleeping in. G. BOYCOTT No sooner do you sit down . . than the captain is rousting you out again. **2** N. THORNBURG Detectives who had rousted him the night of the murder.

■ **rouster** *noun* (*colloq.*) (**a**) *US* = ROUSTABOUT *noun* 1; (**b**) *US & Austral.* = ROUSTABOUT *noun* 2: L19. **rousting** *noun* (*US colloq.*) the action of the verb; an instance of this, a police raid: M20.

roust /raʊst/ *verb*[3] *intrans. Austral. colloq.* E20.
[Alt.]
= ROUSE *verb*[3].

roustabout /ˈraʊstəbaʊt/ *noun & verb.* M19.
[from ROUST *verb*[2].]
▶ **A** *noun.* **1** A dock labourer; a deck hand. *US.* M19.
2 A casual or unskilled labourer; *spec.* (**a**) *N. Amer.* a casual labourer in a circus; (**b**) *Austral.* = ROUSEABOUT *noun* 2. Also, a layabout. L19.
3 A labourer on an oil rig. M20.
▶ **B** *verb intrans.* Work as a roustabout. *US.* E20.

rout /raʊt/ *noun*[1]. ME.
[Anglo-Norman *rute*, Old French *route* from Proto-Romance word meaning 'broken or fractional company', use as noun (sc. *turba, turma* band, crowd) of fem. of Latin *ruptus* pa. pple of *rumpere* break. Cf. next, ROUTE.]
▶ **I 1** A company, band, or troop of people. Now *rare* exc. as in sense 4 below. ME. ▸**b** A pack, flock, or herd of animals. Formerly also, a large number or group of anything. Now *rare*. ME.
†**2** Assemblage, array. ME–E17.
3 An attendant company; a retinue, a train. Now *rare*. ME.
▶ **II 4** A disorderly or tumultuous crowd of people. ME. ▸**b** LAW. An assemblage of three or more people who have made a move towards committing an illegal act. LME. ▸†**c** *The* rabble, *the* masses. LME–M18.
5 Riot, tumult, disturbance, uproar; fuss, clamour. LME. ▸†**b** Sway, influence. Only in ***bear a rout***. M16–E17.
6 A large evening party or reception. Cf. DRUM *noun*[1] 4. *arch.* M18.
Comb.: **rout-chair**, **rout-seat** *arch.* a light cane chair or bench available for hire for parties etc.

rout /raʊt, rʌt/ *noun*[2]. Chiefly *Scot.* E16.
[from ROUT *verb*[2].]
A loud noise or shout; *Scot.* a bellow or low of a cow etc.

rout /raʊt/ *noun*[3]. L16.
[French †*route* (cf. *déroute* DEROUT *noun*) prob. from Italian *rotta* breakage, discomfiture of an army, from Proto-Romance: see prec.]
1 (A) disorderly or precipitate retreat by a defeated army, body of troops, etc. L16.
2 A defeated and fleeing army. Now *rare*. E17.

> 🕮 **1** C. RYAN The movement of the Germans . . assumed the characteristics of a rout—a frenzied exodus. *fig.*: *Ice Hockey News Review* Pennycook hit a hat-trick in the 11-1 rout. **put to the rout** put to flight, defeat utterly.

rout /raʊt/ *noun*[4]. E19.
[from ROUT *verb*[4].]
The action or an act of searching or turning something out.

†**rout** *noun*[5] var. of ROUTE *noun*.

rout /raʊt/ *verb*[1] *intrans. obsolete* exc. *dial.*
[Old English *hrūtan* = Old Frisian *hrūta*, Old Saxon *hrūtan*, Old High German *hrūzzan*, prob. of imit. origin.]
Snore.

†**rout** *verb*[2].
[Old English *hrūtan*, of unkn. origin.]
1 *verb intrans.* Rush, dash. OE–LME.
2 *verb trans.* Throw, hurl. Only in LME.
3 *verb trans.* Beat severely. Long only *Scot.* LME–E19.

rout /raʊt/ *verb*[3]. Chiefly *Scot. & north.* ME.
[Old Norse *rauta, rjóta*.]
1 *verb intrans.* Of a cow: bellow, roar, low. ME.
2 *transf.* **a** *verb intrans.* Of a person: roar or cry loudly. ME. ▸**b** *verb trans.* Utter in a roar; shout *out*. E19.
3 *verb intrans.* Of the sea, wind, etc.: roar, make a loud noise. Now *rare*. ME.

rout /raʊt/ *verb*[4]. M16.
[Var. of ROOT *verb*[2].]
1 a *verb intrans. & trans.* = ROOT *verb*[2] 1. Now chiefly *dial.* M16. ▸**b** *verb intrans.* = ROOT *verb*[2] 2a. E18.
2 *verb trans.* Tear *up*, scoop *out*; *spec.* cut a groove, or any pattern not extending to the edges, in (a wooden or metal surface). E18.
3 *verb trans.* Fetch or force (a person) *out* of bed or from a house or hiding place. Usu. foll. by *out*. L18.

> 🕮 **1b** A. P. HERBERT Jane heard him routing about there. **3** *Practical Woodworking* Rout these out using a dovetail cutter. **4** R. L. STEVENSON Foraging about . . I routed out some biscuit . . and a piece of cheese. J. BUCHAN I routed out Geordie Hamilton from his room.

rout /raʊt/ *verb*[5] *trans.* L16.
[Alt. of ROOT *verb*[1]. Cf. Middle Dutch *rūten* (now *ruiten*).]
Root *out*, remove, eradicate.

rout /raʊt/ *verb*[6]. L16.
[from ROUT *noun*[3].]
1 *verb trans.* Compel (an army, body of troops, etc.) to retreat in disorder. L16. ▸**b** *fig.* Disperse, dispel; discomfit, defeat. M17.
†**2** *verb intrans. & refl.* Retreat in disorder. M17–L17.

> 🕮 **1** N. MONSARRAT The remnants of its defending army had been routed by 30,000 . . legionaries. **b** E. LONGFORD With a . . majority of 140 against them, the Tories were utterly routed.

route /ruːt, *US & Mil. also* raʊt/ *noun & verb.* As noun also †**rout**. ME.
[Old French *rute*, (also mod.) *route*, from Proto-Romance use as noun (sc. *via* way) of fem. of Latin *ruptus* pa. pple of *rumpere* break. Cf. ROUT *noun*[1], *noun*[2].]
▶ **A** *noun.* **1** A way, road, or course of (esp. regular) travel or passage from one place to another; (with following numeral) a specific highway, esp. in the US and France. ME. ▸**b** A round travelled regularly for the collection, delivery, or sale of goods. *N. Amer.* M19.
2 Routine; regular course. *rare.* E18.
3 MILITARY. The order to march. *arch.* exc. in ***column of route*** below. M18.

> 🕮 **1** H. WOUK The winter route for ships bringing us . . iron ore lay along the . . coast. A. N. WILSON Part of the security arrangements that the Tsar should always return . . by a different route. *fig.*: *City Limits* Rather than take the 'Star Wars' route his films . . deal with accessible technology.

Phrases: **column of route** the formation assumed by troops when on the march. **en route**. **go the route** *US* (**a**) BASEBALL pitch for an entire game; (**b**) *fig.* go all the way.
Comb.: **route-goer** BASEBALL a pitcher who goes the route; **routeman** *N. Amer.* (**a**) = ROUNDSMAN 3; (**b**) a salesman who works a particular route; **route march** *noun & verb* (**a**) *noun* a training march for troops in which the required distance and interval must be kept but other rules are relaxed; (**b**) *verb intrans.* go on a route march; **route sheet** *N. Amer.* an engagement itinerary for a touring company or artist; **route taxi** *W. Indies*: following a fixed route.

▶ **B** *verb trans.* Pres. pple & verbal noun **routeing**, **routing**.
1 Orig., mark (a ticket) for use on a certain route. Later, send, forward, or direct to be sent by a certain route. L19. ▸**b** Direct (an electrical signal or transmission) over a particular circuit or path, or *to* a particular location. M20.
2 Schedule, bill, (an entertainment). *rare.* E20.

> 🕮 **1** *Truck* One in three goods vehicles is being routed away from the motorway. *Garbage* Air is routed through a duct and . . blown out of the building.

router /ˈraʊtə/ *noun*[1]. Now *rare* or *obsolete.* M17.
[from ROUT *noun*[1] + -ER[1].]
A person who takes part in a rout, a rioter.

router /ˈraʊtə/ *noun*[2] & *verb.* E19.
[from ROUT *verb*[4] + -ER[1].]
▶ **A** *noun.* **1** A cutter used to form a groove, recess, etc. E19.
2 (In full ***router plane***) a two-handled plane with a cutter projecting below the sole used to form and plane a groove or recess; an electrically powered machine similar to this, with a rotating cutter. M19.
▶ **B** *verb trans.* Hollow out (a groove etc.) with a router. L19.

routh /raʊθ/ *noun. Scot. & north.* L17.
[Origin unkn.]
Abundance, plenty.
■ **routhy** *adjective* (*Scot.*) = ROUTH *adjective* L18.

routh /raʊθ/ *adjective. Scot.* L18.
[Cf. prec.]
Abundant, plentiful; well supplied.

routier /rutje/ *noun.* Pl. pronounced same. M17.
[French, formed as ROUTE.]
1 *Hist.* = RUTTER *noun*[2]. M17.
2 *Hist.* A member of any of numerous bands of mercenaries active in France during the later Middle Ages. M19.
3 In France, a long-distance lorry driver. M20.

routine /ruːˈtiːn/ *noun, adjective, & verb.* L17.
[French, formed as ROUTE.]
▶ **A** *noun.* **1** A regular course of procedure; an unvarying performance of certain acts; regular or unvarying procedure or performance. L17. ▸**b** A set form, esp. of speech; a series of set words or phrases. *rare.* L17.
2 THEATRICAL. A set sequence of actions forming an entertainment or performance, *esp.* a dance, a comedy act, etc. Also, a set sequence of exercises in gymnastics, keep-fit, etc. E20.
3 COMPUTING. A set of stored instructions which performs a specific task; *esp.* one which may be part of a longer, self-contained program. M20.

> 🕮 **1** N. WEST His regular routine, working ten hours . . sleeping the rest. W. PLOMER Ageing people . . are apt to become preoccupied . . with routine. J. BRIGGS Neither . . was . . suited to the routine of office life. **2** J. FONDA Namby-pamby . . routines that don't speed up your heart beat aren't . . worth your while. *Punch* You do a high-kicking dance routine on Cannon and Ball's Xmas Show.

▶ **B** *adjective.* **1** Performed as part of a routine; unvarying, mechanical. E19.
2 Customary, standard, usual. M20.

> 🕮 **2** L. DEIGHTON I shouldn't worry about it. It's just a routine check. *Scientific American* It has become routine in many . . hospitals to record evoked potentials.

▶ **C** *verb trans.* Organize according to a routine; incorporate into a routine. L19.
■ **routinary** *adjective* = ROUTINE *adjective* L19. **routi'neer** *noun* a person who adheres to (a) routine L19. **routinely** *adverb* as a matter of course or of routine; according to (a) routine: E20. **routiner** *noun* †(**a**) *rare* = ROUTINEER; (**b**) a set of equipment for testing circuits and switching apparatus in a telephone exchange: L19. **routinish** *adjective* routine, usual M19. **routinism** *noun* the prevalence of or adherence to (a) routine L19. **routinist** *noun & adjective* (**a**) *noun* a person who adheres to (a) routine; (**b**) *adjective* routine: M19.

routing *pres. pple & verbal noun*: see ROUTE *verb*.

routinier /rutinje/ *noun. rare.* Pl. pronounced same. E19.
[French.]
A person who adheres to (a) routine; *esp.* (MUSIC) a conductor who performs in a mechanically correct but uninspiring way.

routinize /ruːˈtiːnʌɪz/ *verb trans.* Also **-ise**. E20.
[from ROUTINE + -IZE.]
Subject to (a) routine; make into a matter of routine.
■ **routini'zation** *noun* M20.

routous /ˈraʊtəs/ *adjective. arch.* M17.
[from ROUT *noun*[1] + -OUS.]
LAW. Of the nature of, concerned in, or constituting a rout.
■ **routously** *adverb* E17.

roux /ruː/ *noun.* E19.
[French = browned (sc. butter).]
A mixture of melted fat (esp. butter) and flour used as a thickener in making sauces etc.

†**rouze** *verb* var. of ROUSE *verb*[1].

ROV *abbreviation.*
Remotely operated vehicle.

rov *noun* see RAV.

rove /rəʊv/ *noun*[1]. ME.
[from Old Norse *ró*, with parasitic *v*.]
A small metal plate or ring through which a rivet or nail is passed and clinched, esp. in boat-building; a burr.

rove /rʌv/ *noun*[2]. Now *dial.* LME.
[Old Norse *hrufa* or Middle Dutch *rove* (Dutch *roof*), Middle High German, German *rove* rel. to Old High German *riob*, Old Norse *hrjufr*, Old English *hrēof* scabby, leprous. Cf. DANDRUFF, ORF *noun*.]
1 †**a** A scabby or scurfy condition of the skin. Only in LME. ▸**b** A scab. L16.
†**2** A rind; a crust. *rare.* LME–E17.

†**rove** *noun*[3]. L16–E18.
[French †*arrove* var. of *arrobe*, formed as ARROBA.]
= ARROBA.

rove /rəʊv/ *noun*[4]. E17.
[from ROVE *verb*[1].]
1 A ramble, a wander. E17.
2 A method of light ploughing. *dial.* E18.

rove /rəʊv/ *noun*[5]. **L18.**
[Rel. to ROVE *verb*[2]. Cf. ROW *noun*[2].]
(A sliver of) fibrous material (esp. cotton or wool) drawn out and slightly twisted.

rove /rəʊv/ *verb*[1]. **L15.**
[Prob. ult. of Scandinavian origin.]
▶ **I** †**1** *verb intrans.* Shoot with arrows at or *at* a random target with the range not determined. **L15–M17.** ▸**b** *fig.* Guess (*at*). **M16–L17.**
†**2** *verb intrans.* Shoot wide of a mark; *fig.* diverge, digress. Usu. foll. by *from*. **M16–M17.**
†**3** *verb trans.* **a** Aim at (a target). Only in **M16.** ▸**b** Shoot (an arrow) at random. Chiefly *fig.* **L16–E17.**
4 *verb intrans.* ANGLING. Troll with live bait. **M17.**
▶ **II 5** *verb intrans.* **a** Wander about with no fixed destination; roam, ramble. **M16.** ▸**b** Of the eyes: look in changing directions; wander. **M17.** ▸**c** Wander in the mind, rave. *Scot. & dial.* **L17.**
6 *verb trans.* Wander over or through, traverse. **M17.**

🕮 **5** T. HARDY Roving freely from room to room. **b** R. C. HUTCHINSON His eyes roved no longer, but looked straight to the . . distance. H. ROTH His gaze roved about the room. **6** H. L. MENCKEN Children at play . . roved the open streets. R. LINDNER He roved the world during the next few years.

Comb.: **rove-beetle** any of numerous beetles constituting the large family Staphylinidae, having short elytra which leave most of the abdomen visible.

rove /rəʊv/ *verb*[2] *trans.* **L18.**
[Origin unkn. Cf. ROVE *noun*[5].]
Form (slivers of wool or cotton) into roves.

rove /rəʊv/ *verb*[3] *trans. rare.* **M19.**
[Origin unkn.]
Reduce the diameter of (a grindstone). Only as ***roving*** *verbal noun*.

rove *verb*[4] *pa. t.*: see REEVE *verb*[1].

rover /ˈrəʊvə/ *noun*[1]. **ME.**
[Middle Low German, Middle Dutch *röver*, from *röven* (Dutch *rooven*) rob: see REAVE *verb*[1]. Cf. REAVER.]
1 A pirate. **ME.** ▸†**b** A pirate ship; a privateer. **L16–E18.**
†**2** A marauder, a robber. **E16–E18.**

rover /ˈrəʊvə/ *noun*[2]. **LME.**
[from ROVE *verb*[1] + -ER[1].]
1 ARCHERY. A target chosen at random, and at an undetermined range. Later also, a mark for long-distance shooting. Chiefly in ***shoot at rovers***. **LME.** ▸†**b** An arrow used in roving. **L16–E17.**
2 A person who roves or wanders. **E17.** ▸†**b** An inconstant male lover. **L17–E18.** ▸**c** In AUSTRAL. RULES FOOTBALL, a player forming part of the ruck, usu. small, fast, and skilful at receiving the ball; in AMER. FOOTBALL, a defensive linebacker assigned to move about to anticipate opponents' plays. **L19.** ▸**d** (**R-**.) *Hist.* A senior Scout (cf. ***Venture Scout*** s.v. VENTURE *noun*). Also ***Rover Scout***. **E20.** ▸**e** A remote-controlled surface vehicle for extraterrestrial exploration. **L20.**
3 CROQUET. A ball that has passed through all the hoops but not pegged out; a player whose ball has done this. **M19.**

1 †**at rovers** without definite aim or object; at random.
Comb.: ***Rover Scout***: see sense 2d above; **rover ticket**: giving unlimited travel by bus or railway for a specified time or within a specified region.

rover /ˈrəʊvə/ *noun*[3]. **M18.**
[from ROVE *verb*[2] + -ER[1].]
A person who makes slivers of cotton or other fibrous material into roves.

roving /ˈrəʊvɪŋ/ *verbal noun*[1]. **L15.**
[from ROVE *verb*[1] + -ING[1].]
The action of ROVE *verb*[1]; an instance of this.
Comb.: **roving commission** authority given to a person or group (orig., a ship) conducting an inquiry to travel as may be necessary.

roving /ˈrəʊvɪŋ/ *noun*[2]. **L18.**
[from ROVE *verb*[2] + -ING[1].]
1 The action of ROVE *verb*[2]. **L18.**
2 A rove; roves collectively. **E19.**

roving /ˈrəʊvɪŋ/ *adjective*. **L16.**
[from ROVE *verb*[1] + -ING[2].]
1 That roves; wandering; roaming. **L16.** ▸**b** Of a journalist etc.: required to travel to various locations to deal with events as they occur. **M20.**
†**2** Random; conjectural. **M–L17.**
3 Characterized by wandering; inclined to rove. **E18.**

🕮 **1** *Antiquity* The *ad hoc* cooking places of the roving hunters. *fig.*: I. MURDOCH Millie would never . . contain her roving affections. **3** W. R. D. FAIRBAIRN He lived a roving and unsettled life.

Special collocations: **roving eye** a tendency to ogle or towards infidelity. **roving sailor** *dial.* any of several creeping plants esp. ivy-leaved toadflax, *Cymbalaria muralis*.
■ **rovingly** *adverb* †(*a*) randomly, without definite aim; (*b*) in a roving or wandering manner: **E17.**

row /rəʊ/ *noun*[1].
[Old English *rāw* prob. rel. to Middle Dutch *rie* (Dutch *rij*), Middle High German *rīhe* (German *Reihe*), from Germanic: cf. Sanskrit *rekhā* stroke, line. See also REW.]
1 A number of people or things in a more or less straight line. Formerly also *transf.*, a series *of* things. Freq. foll. by *of*. **OE.** ▸**b** A rank on a chessboard or draughtboard. **L15.** ▸**c** A number of people or things in a circle. *rare.* **L16.** ▸**d** The alphabet; = ***cross-row*** s.v. CROSS-. **L16–E17.**
2 a A set of people (or things) of a certain kind; a class. Now *rare.* **ME.** ▸**b** MUSIC. = ***tone-row*** s.v. TONE *noun*. **M20.**
†**3** A ray, a beam. **ME–E16.** ▸**b** A line of written or printed text. **LME–L16.**
4 a A street (esp. a narrow one) with a continuous line of houses along one or both sides. Now chiefly in street-names. **LME.** ▸**b** A line of cells in a prison. Chiefly in ***death row*** s.v. DEATH. Chiefly *US*. **M20.**
5 a A line of seats across a theatre etc. **E18.** ▸**b** A line of plants in a field or garden. **M18.** ▸**c** A complete line of stitches in knitting or crochet. **E19.**

🕮 **1** J. M. BARRIE A row of . . newspapers lying against each other like fallen soldiers. A. WILSON Silly boys who join the back row of the chorus every year. D. PROFUMO A row of . . sea-fish, . . drying along the top of the fence. **2a** M. CUTLER An only daughter, . . who is . . approaching the old-maid's row. **4** E. LAX Seas crashing up along the shore by rows of apartments. **5a** S. PLATH We slipped out of our seats . . down the length of our row while the people grumbled. **b** S. TROTT With the harvest of chard in my arms, I stood pondering the depleted rows.

Phrases: **a hard row to hoe**, **a long row to hoe**, etc., a difficult task to perform. **in a row** (*a*) so as to form a row; (*b*) *colloq.* in succession. ***Millionaires' Row***: see MILLIONAIRE. ***Rotten Row***: see ROTTEN *adjective, verb, noun, & adverb.* ***skid row***: see SKID *noun*.
Comb.: **row crop**: planted in rows; **row house** *N. Amer.* a terrace house; **row matrix** MATH.: consisting of a single row of elements; **row vector** MATH.: represented by a row matrix.
¶ Sense 1b not recorded between **L15** and **20**.
■ **rowed** *adjective* †(*a*) having stripes of a specified colour; (*b*) having a specified number of rows: **E16.**

row /rəʊ/ *noun*[2]. *rare.* **L17.**
[Origin unkn. Cf. ROVE *noun*[5].]
= ROVE *noun*[5].

row /raʊ/ *noun*[3]. **M18.**
[Origin unkn.]
1 A loud noise or commotion; a din; noise, clamour. **M18.**
2 A heated dispute, a quarrel. **M18.**
3 A severe reprimand; the condition of being reprimanded. **L20.**

🕮 **2** D. ARKELL One of their most painful rows, during which he . . threw . . earth at her. JOAN SMITH Several MPs were embroiled in the row.

Phrases & comb.: **kick up a row**, **make a row** *colloq.* (*a*) make a considerable noise; (*b*) make a vigorous protest. **row-de-dow** *arch.* noise, din; commotion.

row /rəʊ/ *noun*[4]. **M19.**
[from ROW *verb*[1].]
A spell of rowing; a journey or trip in a rowing boat.

row /raʊ/ *adjective*[1]. Now *arch. & dial.* **OE.**
[Inflectional var.]
= ROUGH *adjective*.

row /raʊ/ *adjective*[2]. *obsolete* exc. *north.*
[Old English *hrēow* app. ablaut var. of *hrēaw* RAW *adjective*.]
Raw, uncooked; untanned.

row /rəʊ/ *verb*[1].
[Old English *rōwan* = Middle Low German *rojen* (Dutch *roeijen*), Old Norse *róa* rel. to Latin *remus*, Greek *eretmon* oar. Cf. RUDDER.]
1 *verb intrans.* Use oars to propel a boat through water. **OE.**
2 *verb intrans.* Of a boat: move along the surface of water by means of oars. **ME.** ▸**b** *verb trans.* Of a boat: be fitted with (a specified number of oars). **M18.**
3 *verb intrans.* Of an animal: swim, paddle. Now *poet.* **ME.**
4 *verb trans.* Propel (a boat) by means of oars. **ME.** ▸**b** Make (a stroke) or achieve (a rate of striking) in the course of rowing. **M19.**
5 *verb trans.* Convey or transport (as) in a boat propelled by oars. **LME.**
6 *verb trans.* Make (one's way), cross, (as) by rowing. *rare.* **L15.**
7 *verb trans.* **a** Take up oars in (a specified rowing position in a crew). **M19.** ▸**b** Take part in (a rowing race); compete against (another person or crew) in such a race. **L19.** ▸**c** Have or make use of in a rowing-race. **L19.**

🕮 **1** C. ISHERWOOD Otto kept splashing with his oars . . because he couldn't row properly. **4** L. HELLMAN I rowed the dinghy out to the boat. **5** D. H. LAWRENCE After breakfast, Kate was rowed home down the lake.

Comb.: **row-barge** *Hist.*: propelled by oars; **rowboat** (now *N. Amer.*) = ***rowing boat*** s.v. ROWING *verbal noun*[1]; **row-galley** *Hist.*: propelled by oars; **row-port** *Hist.* a hole near the water-line in the side of a small sailing ship, to allow for the use of oars in calm weather.

Phrases: **row against the stream**, **row against the wind and tide** undertake a difficult task; work in the face of opposition. **row down** overtake in a rowing, esp. bumping, race. **row in** *slang* conspire *with*. **row out** exhaust by rowing. **row over** complete the course of a rowing race with little effort, owing to the absence or inferiority of competitors.
■ **rowable** *adjective* (*rare*) able to be rowed (on) **L16.** **rowage** *noun* †(*a*) the charge for rowing; (*b*) *rare* equipment for rowing: **L16.**

row /rəʊ/ *verb*[2]. *obsolete* exc. *dial.* **ME.**
[from ROW *noun*[1].]
†**1** *verb intrans.* Send out rays; dawn. Only in **ME.**
2 *verb trans.* Arrange or put in a row; in *pass.*, be set *with* something in a row or rows. **M17.** ▸**b** *verb intrans.* Form a row or rows. **E19.**

row /raʊ/ *verb*[3]. *obsolete* exc. *dial.* **ME.**
[Origin unkn.]
†**1 a** *verb trans.* Pierce. Only in **ME.** ▸**b** *verb intrans.* Poke the fingers *in* something. **L15–E17.**
2 *verb trans.* Stir; rake about. Freq. foll. by *up*. **LME.**

row /raʊ/ *verb*[4] *trans.* Now *dial.* **LME.**
[from ROW *adjective*[1].]
Raise a nap on (cloth).

row /raʊ/ *verb*[5]. **L18.**
[from ROW *noun*[3].]
†**1** *verb trans.* Attack; assail; create disorder in. *slang.* **L18–M19.**
2 *verb intrans.* Make a row or loud commotion. Now usu., have a row, quarrel heatedly. **L18.**
3 *verb trans.* Reprimand severely. **E19.**

🕮 **2** U. HOLDEN How happy they were. She and Ches never rowed. **3** H. L. WILSON It had been all his own doing, . . so why should he row me about it?

row *verb*[6] see ROLL *verb*.

rowan /ˈrəʊən, ˈraʊən/ *noun*. Orig. *Scot. & north.* **L15.**
[Of Scandinavian origin: cf. Old Norse *reynir*, Norwegian *rogn*, *raun*.]
1 = ***mountain ash*** (a) s.v. MOUNTAIN *noun*. Also ***rowan tree***. **L15.**
2 In full ***rowan-berry***. The red berry of this tree. **L16.**

rowdy /ˈraʊdi/ *noun, adjective, & verb*. Orig. *US*. **E19.**
[Perh. rel. to ROW *adjective*[1].]
▶ **A** *noun*. Orig., a rough and lawless backwoodsman. Later, any rough disorderly person. **E19.**

🕮 K. KESEY This . . rowdy . . serving time for gambling and battery.

▶ **B** *adjective*. **1** Rough, disorderly, noisy. **E19.** ▸**b** *transf.* Of an animal: refractory. **L19.**
2 Characterized by noise and disorder. **M19.**

🕮 **1** P. L. FERMOR One rowdy tableful, riotously calling for . . stronger wine. **2** F. KAPLAN Some . . elections were rowdy, most of them corrupt.

▶ **C** *verb*. **1** *verb trans.* Treat in a rowdy manner. *rare.* **E19.**
2 *verb intrans.* Act in a noisy disorderly manner. **L19.**
Comb.: **rowdy-dow** *slang* boisterous noise, uproar; **rowdy-dowdy** *adjective* (*slang*) characterized by boisterous noise.
■ **rowdily** *adverb* **L20.** **rowdiness** *noun* **M19.** **rowdyish** *adjective* somewhat rowdy **M19.** **rowdyism** *noun* rowdy behaviour or conduct **M19.**

rowel /ˈraʊ(ə)l/ *noun & verb*. **ME.**
[Old French *roel(e)* from late Latin *rotella* dim. of Latin *rota* wheel.]
▶ **A** *noun*. †**1** A small wheel. **ME–L16.**
2 A small spiked revolving wheel or disc at the end of a spur. **LME.** ▸**b** The head or top of this. **M19.**
†**3** ECCLESIASTICAL. A wheel-shaped chandelier. **LME–M16.**
†**4** The kneecap. **LME–L16.** ▸**b** A small knob on a scourge or a horse's bit. **M16–E17.**
5 A circular piece of material (esp. leather) inserted between the flesh and skin of an animal, esp. a horse, supposedly to discharge an exudate. Now *Hist.* **L16.**
▶ **B** *verb*. Infl. **-ll-**, ***-l-**.
1 a *verb intrans. & trans.* (with *it*). Use rowels to spur a horse. *rare.* **L16.** ▸**b** *verb trans.* Spur (a horse) with a rowel. **M19.** ▸**c** *verb trans.* Prick with rowels. Chiefly *fig.* **L19.**
2 *verb trans.* Insert a rowel (sense 5) in (an animal). Now *Hist.* **L16.**
■ **rowelled** *adjective* (*rare*) (*a*) that has been rowelled; (*b*) provided with a rowel or rowels: **L16.**

rowen /ˈraʊən/ *noun*. Now chiefly *dial. & US.* **ME.**
[Old Northern French var. of Old & mod. French *regain*, from Old French *regaaignier*, from *re-* + *gaaignier*: see GAIN *verb*[2].]
sing. & in *pl.* A second growth or crop of grass in a season; = AFTERMATH 1.

rower /ˈrəʊə/ *noun*[1]. **LME.**
[from ROW *verb*[1] + -ER[1].]
A person who rows a boat; a competitor in a rowing race.

rower *noun*[2] see ROLLER *noun*[1] & *verb*.

rowet /ˈraʊɪt/ *noun*. *dial.* **M18.**
[App. from ROW *adjective*[1].]
Rowen. Also, rough coarse grass growing on wasteland etc.

rowing /ˈrəʊɪŋ/ *verbal noun*[1]. **OE.**
[from ROW *verb*[1] + -ING[1].]
The action of **ROW** *verb*[1]; this as a sport or pastime.
Comb.: **rowing boat** a small boat propelled by oars; **rowing-machine** an exercise machine for simulating the action of rowing; **rowing race** a race between rowing boats; **rowing tank** a tank of water containing a static boat, in which a rower's technique can be monitored.

rowing /ˈraʊɪŋ/ *noun*[2]. **M19.**
[from ROW *verb*[5] + -ING[1].]
The action of **ROW** *verb*[5]; an instance of this, a severe reprimand.

Rowland /ˈrəʊlənd/ *noun*. **E20.**
[H. A. *Rowland* (1848–1901), US physicist.]
PHYSICS. Used *attrib.* and in *possess.* to designate devices and concepts associated with Rowland.
Rowland circle a circle on which must lie the slit, (concave) grating, and photographic plate of a spectrograph if all the spectral lines are to be brought to a focus on the plate. **Rowland ghost** a spurious spectral line produced by a periodic error in the spacing of the lines of a diffraction grating (usu. in *pl.*). **Rowland grating** a concave diffraction grating ruled on a machine designed by Rowland. **Rowland mounting** a device for holding a camera and a diffraction grating, which are connected by a bar forming a diameter of the Rowland circle. **Rowland ring** a torus made of a magnetic material whose properties it is wished to investigate and linked with a coil of current-carrying wire. **Rowland's circle** = *Rowland circle* above. **Rowland's mounting** = *Rowland mounting* above.

rowlock /ˈrɒlək, ˈrʌlək/ *noun*. **M18.**
[Alt. of OARLOCK by substitution of ROW *verb*[1] for the 1st syll.]
A device on a boat's gunwale, usu. consisting of two thole-pins or a rounded fork, serving as a fulcrum for an oar and keeping it in place.

rown /raʊn/ *noun*. Now *dial.* **LME.**
[Old Norse *hrogn* (Norwegian *rogn*, Swedish *rom*) = Old High German *rogan* (German *Rogen*): cf. ROE *noun*[2].]
The roe of a fish.

Rowton house /ˈraʊt(ə)n ˈhaʊs/ *noun phr.* **L19.**
[Montague William Lowry-Corry, 1st Lord *Rowton* (1838–1903), English social reformer.]
Hist. A type of cheap lodging-house aiming to provide accommodation of a decent standard for poor single men.

rowty /ˈraʊti/ *adjective*. Now *north.* **L16.**
[Rel. to ROWET.]
Of grass etc.: coarse, rank.

†row-wagon *noun* see ROLWAGEN.

rowy /ˈrəʊi/ *adjective*. Now *dial.* **M16.**
[from ROW *noun*[1] + -Y[1].]
1 Of cloth: having an uneven texture. **M16.**
2 Esp. of bacon: streaky, streaked. **M18.**
■ **rowiness** *noun* **L19.**

Roxbury russet /rɒksb(ə)rɪ ˈrʌsɪt/ *noun phr.* **E19.**
[*Roxbury*, a town in Massachusetts, USA.]
An old US variety of apple, green-skinned with russet markings.

royal /ˈrɔɪəl/ *adjective & noun*. **LME.**
[Old French *roial* (mod. *royal*) from Latin *regalis* REGAL *noun*[1] & *adjective*.]
► **A** *adjective* (*postpositive* in certain fixed collocations).
► **I 1** Originating or derived from a king, queen, emperor, or other monarch, or from a line of such monarchs. **LME.**
2 Pertaining to a monarch, or the dignity or office of a monarch; pertaining to a monarch as head of State or the armed forces. **LME.**
3 Of, belonging to, or used by a monarch; in the service of a monarch. **LME.** ►**b** Proceeding from, or issued under the authority of, a monarch. **E17.**
4 Of a person: having the rank of a monarch; belonging to the family of a monarch (freq. in honorific titles). Also, having rank comparable to that of a monarch. **LME.**
5 Founded by or under the patronage of a royal person. **E16.**

📖 **1** T. GRAY High potentates, and dames of royal birth. G. VIDAL The . . story . . reflects no credit on our royal house. **2** MILTON On a Throne of Royal State. W. BLACKSTONE Seamen in the royal fleet. **3** LD MACAULAY Two royal messengers were in attendance. J. RUSKIN The power of the royal hand. G. BLACK The Royal Enclosure at Ascot. **4** SHAKES. *Merch. V.* How doth that royal merchant, good Antonio? GIBBON The royal youth was commanded to take the crown. *Your Royal Highness* etc. **5** J. RUSKIN I hope . . royal or national libraries will be founded. *Royal Air Force News* The Royal British Legion Honorary Association.

► **II 6** Befitting or appropriate to a monarch; stately, magnificent, resplendent; grand, imposing; of great size, strength, or quality. **LME.** ►**b** Excellent, first-rate. Also (*US*) as an intensifier, freq. with ironic force. *colloq.* **L16.**
7 Having the character appropriate to a monarch; noble, majestic; generous, munificent. **LME.**

📖 **6** R. KIPLING There would . . be a royal fight between . . Badalia and Jenny. **7** BROWNING A stag-hunt gives the royal creature law. R. BROOKE Honour has . . paid his subjects with a royal wage.

Special collocations & phrases: ***Astronomer Royal***: see ASTRONOMER 1. ***ballade royal***: see BALLADE noun 1. ***battle royal***: see BATTLE noun. ***chapel royal***: see CHAPEL noun. ***James Royal***: see JAMES 1a. ***osmund royal***: see OSMUND noun[2]. ***pair royal***: see PAIR noun[1]. ***prince royal***: see PRINCE noun. ***princess royal***: see PRINCESS noun. ***rhyme royal***: see RHYME noun. **Royal Air Force** the air force of the UK; ***Marshal of the Royal Air Force***: see MARSHAL noun[1]. **Royal Ann(e)** *US* = NAPOLEON 7. **royal antelope** a tiny antelope, *Neotragus pygmaeus*, found in forested areas of W. Africa. ***royal assent***: see ASSENT noun 2. ***royal Bengal (tiger)***: see BENGAL noun & adjective. **royal binding** a binding with the royal arms on the cover. **royal blue** a deep vivid blue. **Royal British Legion** an association of former members of the British armed forces, formed in 1921. **royal burgh** a Scottish burgh which derives its charter directly from the Crown. ***Royal Commission***: see COMMISSION noun. ***royal demesne***: see DEMESNE noun. ***royal duke***: see DUKE noun. **Royal Engineers** the engineering branch of the British army. **royal family** the group of people closely related by birth or marriage to a monarch, *spec.* the British monarch. **royal fern** a large fern of boggy places, *Osmunda regalis*, with fronds densely covered with sporangia so as to resemble a flowering panicle; also called ***flowering fern***. ***royal fish***: see FISH noun[1]. ***royal flush***: see FLUSH noun[3]. **royal icing** a hard shiny icing made from egg-white (and icing sugar). **Royal Institution** a British society founded in 1799 for the spreading of scientific knowledge among the population at large. ***royal jelly***: see JELLY noun[1]. **Royal Marine** a member of a body of marines in the British navy. **royal mast** a mast fixed on top of a topgallant mast; cf. ***royal sail*** below. ***Royal Maundy***: see MAUNDY 1c. **Royal Navy** the navy of the UK and its predecessors. **royal oak** a sprig of oak formerly worn on oak-apple day to commemorate the restoration of Charles II in 1660. **royal octavo** octavo on royal paper. **royal palm** a palm of the American genus *Roystonea*, esp. *R. regia*, widely cultivated as an avenue tree. **royal paper** paper 24 by 19 inches for writing or 25 by 20 inches (now, 636 by 480 mm) for printing. ***royal peculiar***: see PECULIAR noun. **royal plural** = ***royal we*** below. ***royal prerogative***: see PREROGATIVE noun 1. **royal quarto** quarto on royal paper. **royal road** a smooth or easy way *to* learning etc.; a way of attaining knowledge, understanding, etc., without trouble. **royal sail** a small sail hoisted above the topgallant sail; cf. ***royal mast*** above. **Royal Sappers and Miners** *Hist.* = ***Royal Engineers*** above. **Royal Society (of London)** a British learned society founded in 1662 to promote scientific discussion. **Royal Sovereign** a variety of early-ripening strawberry. **royal stag**: with a head of 12 or more points. **royal standard** a banner bearing the royal arms and flown when a member of the royal family is present. **royal straight** CARDS a royal flush. **royal tennis** = ***real tennis*** s.v. TENNIS noun 1. **Royal Victorian Chain** a British order of chivalry founded by Edward VII in 1902 and conferred by the monarch, chiefly on members of royal families. **Royal Victorian Order** a British order of chivalry founded by Queen Victoria in 1896 and conferred by the monarch, usu. for great personal service. **royal warrant** a warrant authorizing a company to be the supplier of a particular category of goods to a particular member of the British royal family. **royal we** *the* pronoun 'we' as used by a monarch, esp. in formal pronouncements and declarations, or (chiefly *joc.*) by any individual in place of 'I'. ***Royal Worcester***: see WORCESTER 2. ***ship-royal***: see SHIP noun 1. ***suit royal***: see SUIT noun 1b. ***voyage royal***: see VOYAGE noun.
► **B** *noun*. **1 †a** A king, a prince. **LME–L15.** ►**b** A member of the royal family; a royal personage. *colloq.* **M18.**
†2 Any of various coins. **L15–M18.**
3 †a = BAY *noun*[8]. Also, a branch above this. **L16–E17.** ►**b** A stag with a head of twelve points or more. **M19.**
4 *NAUTICAL*. A royal sail; a royal mast. **M18.**
5 ***the Royals***, the Royal Marines; *Hist.* the 1st Dragoons; *Hist.* the 1st Regiment of Foot. **M18.**
6 Royal blue. **L19.**
7 ***the Royal***, the Royal Society; the Royal Show (of the Royal Agricultural Society). **M20.**
Phrases: ***Blues and Royals***: see BLUE noun 6.

royale /rwajal/ *noun*. Pl. pronounced same. **M19.**
[French, lit. 'royal', in same sense.]
= IMPERIAL *noun* 7.

royalet /ˈrɔɪəlɛt/ *noun*. Now *rare*. **M17.**
[from ROYAL noun + -ET[1], perh. after French *roitelet*.]
A petty king or chieftain.

royalise *verb* var. of ROYALIZE.

royalist /ˈrɔɪəlɪst/ *noun & adjective*. Also **R-**. **M17.**
[from ROYAL + -IST, perh. after French *royaliste*.]
► **A** *noun*. A supporter or adherent of a monarch or a monarch's rights, esp. in times of civil war, rebellion, or secession, *spec.* (*Hist.*) a supporter of the King against Parliament in the English Civil War; a monarchist. **M17.**
► **B** *attrib.* or as *adjective*. Of or pertaining to royalists or royalism. **M17.**
■ **royalism** *noun* attachment or adherence to the monarchy or to the principle of monarchical government **L18.** **roya'listic** *adjective* **M19.**

royalize /ˈrɔɪəlʌɪz/ *verb*. Also **-ise**. **L16.**
[from ROYAL + -IZE.]
1 *verb trans.* Make royal; give a royal character or standing to. **L16.** ►**b** Make famous, celebrate. Long *rare*. **L16.**
2 *verb intrans. & trans.* (with *it*). Bear rule as a monarch; act the king or queen. **E17.**

royally /ˈrɔɪəli/ *adverb*. **LME.**
[from ROYAL + -LY[2].]
1 With the splendour or pomp appropriate to a monarch; magnificently, splendidly. **LME.**
2 With the power or authority of a monarch; in a manner befitting a monarch. **LME.** ►**b** Exceedingly, very; well and truly. *colloq.* **M19.**
†3 In a monarchical manner. **LME–E17.**
4 With royal munificence or liberality. **E17.**

📖 **2b** *Underground Grammarian* I've been suckered, royally suckered.

royalty /ˈrɔɪəlti/ *noun*. **LME.**
[Old French *roialte* (mod. *royauté*), formed as ROYAL: see -TY[1].]
1 a The position or office of a monarch; royal dignity; royal power, sovereignty. **LME.** ►**†b** With possess. adjective (as ***your royalty*** etc.): = MAJESTY 2. **L16–E17.** ►**†c** The sovereignty or sovereign rule *of* a State. Only in **L16.**
†2 Magnificence, splendour, pomp. **LME–M17.**
3 a A right or privilege pertaining to or enjoyed by a monarch. Usu. in *pl.* **LME.** ►**†b** In *pl.* Emblems or insignia of sovereignty. **E17–M18.**
4 *sing.* & in *pl.* Royal persons; members of a royal family. **L15.**
5 A prerogative or right granted by a monarch, esp. in respect of jurisdiction or over minerals. **L15.** ►**b** A payment made by a person working a mine, obtaining oil, etc., to the owner of the site or of the mineral rights over it; a payment made for the use of a patent or a technical process; a payment made to an author, editor, or composer for each copy of a work sold or performed; a payment for the right to use specialist or privilaged information. **M19.**
6 Kinglike or majestic character or quality; lordliness; munificence, generosity. **M16.**
7 a *SCOTTISH HISTORY*. A district held directly of the king or queen. **L16.** ►**b** A domain, manor, etc., in possession of royal rights or privileges. Now *rare* or *obsolete*. **M17.**
8 a A kingdom, a realm; a monarchical state. **M17.** ►**b** Monarchical government. **L19.**

📖 **4** C. EASTON They were received like royalty. **6b** V. S. PRITCHETT He is kept going financially by . . royalties from a one-act 'vaudeville'.

royet /ˈrɔɪət/ *adjective, noun, & verb*. *Scot.* **M16.**
[Origin uncertain: perh. rel. to RIOT noun.]
► **A** *adjective*. **†1** Extravagant, nonsensical. Only in **M16.**
2 Riotous, wild; disorderly, incoherent. **E18.**
► **B** *noun*. **1** Extravagance, dissipation; disorderly behaviour; a riot. **M16.**
2 A troublesome or quarrelsome person. **M19.**
► **C** *verb intrans.* Riot, be riotous, live riotously. **L16.**
■ **royetness** *noun* wildness; romping: **E16.**

Royston crow /rɔɪstən ˈkrəʊ/ *noun phr.* **E17.**
[*Royston*, a town in Hertfordshire, England.]
The hooded crow.

rozella, **rozelle** *nouns* vars. of ROSELLA *noun*[2].

rozzer /ˈrɒzə/ *noun*. *slang*. **L19.**
[Origin unkn.]
A police officer, a detective.

RP *abbreviation*.
Received pronunciation.

RPI *abbreviation*.
Retail price index.

rpm *abbreviation*.
Revolution(s) per minute.

RPV *abbreviation*.
Remotely piloted vehicle.

RR *abbreviation*. *US*.
1 Railroad.
2 Rural route.

-rrhagia /ˈreɪdʒɪə/ *suffix*.
[mod. Latin from Greek, from base of *rhēgnunai* break, burst: cf. HAEMORRHAGY.]
MEDICINE. Forming nouns with the sense 'flow, discharge, of an abnormal or excessive character', as ***blennorrhagia***, ***menorrhagia***, ***metrorrhagia***.

-rrhoea /ˈriːə/ *suffix*. Also ***-rrhea**.
[from Greek *rhoia* flux, flow.]
Chiefly *MEDICINE*. Forming nouns with the sense 'flow, discharge, esp. of an abnormal character', as ***diarrhoea***, ***gonorrhoea***, ***logorrhoea***.

rRNA *abbreviation*.
BIOCHEMISTRY. Ribosomal RNA.

RRP *abbreviation*.
Recommended retail price.

RS *abbreviation*.
1 Received standard; (formerly) received speech.
2 Royal Scots.
3 Royal Society.

Rs. *abbreviation.*
Rupee(s).

RSA *abbreviation.*
1 Royal Scottish Academy; Royal Scottish Academician.
2 Royal Society of Arts.

RSC *abbreviation.*
1 Royal Shakespeare Company.
2 Royal Society of Chemistry.

RSFSR *abbreviation.*
Hist. Russian Soviet Federative Socialist Republic.

RSI *abbreviation.*
Repetitive strain injury.

RSJ *abbreviation.*
Rolled steel joist.

RSM *abbreviation.*
Regimental Sergeant-Major.

RSNC *abbreviation.*
Royal Society for Nature Conservation.

RSPB *abbreviation.*
Royal Society for the Protection of Birds.

RSPCA *abbreviation.*
Royal Society for the Prevention of Cruelty to Animals.

RSV *abbreviation.*
Revised Standard Version (of the Bible).

RSVP *abbreviation.*
French *Répondez, s'il vous plaît* please reply.

rt. *abbreviation.*
Right.

R/T *abbreviation.* Also **RT**.
Radio-telegraph, radio-telephone.

RTA *abbreviation.*
Road traffic accident.

RTE *abbreviation.*
Radio Telefís Éireann (the official broadcasting authority of the Republic of Ireland).

RTFM *abbreviation.*
COMPUTING (*slang*). Read the fucking manual.

Rt. Hon. *abbreviation.*
Right Honourable.

Rt. Rev. *abbreviation.* Also **Rt Revd**.
Right Reverend.

RU *abbreviation.*
1 Rugby Union.
2 (**RU-486**.) [from *Roussel-Uclaf*, the French firm which first manufactured the drug.] PHARMACOLOGY. (Proprietary name for) the drug mifepristone.

Ru *symbol.*
CHEMISTRY. Ruthenium.

Rualla /ruː'alə/ *noun & adjective.* M19.
[Arab. *Ruwalā*.]
▶ **A** *noun.* Pl. same. A member of a Bedouin people. M19.
▶ **B** *attrib.* or as *adjective.* Of or pertaining to the Rualla. L19.

ruana /ruː'ɑːnə/ *noun.* M20.
[Amer. Spanish from Spanish (*manta*) *ruana* lit. 'poor man's cloak', from *rúa* street from late Latin *ruga* furrow, street from Latin *ruga* wrinkle.]
A S. American cape or poncho, worn esp. in Colombia and Peru.

Ruanda *noun & adjective* see RWANDA.

rub /rʌb/ *noun*[1]. L16.
[from RUB *verb*.]
1 A thing that slows or diverts a bowl in its course; the fact of being so slowed or diverted. L16. ▸†**b** Any physical obstacle or impediment to movement. L17–E19.
2 An impediment, hindrance, or difficulty of a non-material nature. Now *rare* exc. in ***there's the rub*** & vars. L16.
3 An act or spell of rubbing. E17.
†**4** An unevenness; a mark or flaw in a surface. E17–M18.
5 a An intentional wound given to the feelings of another; *esp.* a slight reproof, a tease. M17. ▸**b** An encounter with something annoying or disagreeable; an unpleasant experience in one's relations with others. M17.
6 A mower's whetstone. *dial.* E19.
7 A sound as of rubbing. E20.
8 A loan *of*. *Nautical slang.* E20.
Phrases: **rub of the green**, **rub on the green** an accidental interference with the course or position of a golf ball.
Comb.: **rub resistance** the degree to which print will withstand rubbing without becoming smudged or detached.

rub /rʌb/ *noun*[2]. M19.
[Abbreviation.]
= RUBBER *noun*[2] 1.

rub /rʌb/ *verb.* Infl. **-bb-**. ME.
[Perh. from Low German *rubben* of unkn. origin.]
1 *verb intrans.* Move and at the same time press on or against something. ME.
2 *verb trans.* Subject (a surface or substance) to the action of something moving over it with pressure and friction (foll. by *with*); subject to pressure and friction in order to clean, polish, make smooth, etc.; treat *with* a substance applied in this way. LME. ▸**b** Reproduce the design of (a monumental brass or stone) by placing a sheet of paper over it and rubbing it with heelball or coloured chalk. M19.
3 *verb trans.* Move (one thing) to and fro over another with pressure and friction (foll. by *against, over*). Foll. by *together*: move (two things) against each other in this way. LME. ▸**b** Bring (corresponding parts of the bodies of two people) into mutual contact. Chiefly in ***rub elbows***, ***rub shoulders*** below. M17.
4 *verb intrans.* Foll. by *along, on* (also *through, out*): continue with more or less difficulty; contrive, make shift; manage, get by; get along. *colloq.* LME.
5 *verb trans.* Orig. (*Scot.*), grind (grain etc.) to meal by friction; produce (meal) by this process. Later also (*gen.*), reduce *to* powder by friction. E16.
6 *verb trans.* **a** Affect painfully or disagreeably; annoy, irritate. Cf. ***rub the wrong way***, ***rub up the wrong way*** below. Now *rare.* E16. ▸†**b** Impede, hinder. *rare* (Shakes.). Only in E17.
7 *verb trans.* Remove, take away, by rubbing. Foll. by *from, off, out of*. E16.
8 *verb intrans.* Go, make off. Usu. foll. by *off*. Now *rare* or *obsolete.* M16.
9 *verb intrans.* Of a bowl: be slowed or diverted by unevenness of the ground, an obstacle, etc. L16.
10 *verb trans.* Revive in the memory; recall to mind. Now usu. foll. by *up*. L16. ▸**b** Foll. by *up*: refresh (one's memory); brush up (a subject). M17.
11 *verb trans.* Force *into* or *through*, spread *over*, a surface by rubbing. L16.
12 *verb intrans.* Bear rubbing; admit of being rubbed (*off, out*, etc.). L17.
13 *verb trans.* Chafe, abrade. E19.

📖 **1** K. MANSFIELD The . . cat . . rubbed against her knees. **2** JOYCE They . . rubbed him all over with spermaceti oil. J. STEINBECK He rubbed his . . cheek with his knuckles. G. SWIFT He took off his glasses and began to rub them . . with a handkerchief. **3** J. M. BARRIE You can obtain a light by rubbing two pieces of stick together. S. COOPER Westerly rubbed a hand over his own eyes. A. CARTER I'd rub my back against . . chairs, as cats do. **4** R. W. CLARK Most . . rubbed along well enough with their neighbours. **6** J. GALSWORTHY He did not wish to rub his nieces, he had no quarrel with them. **7** C. E. RIDDELL London . . has begun to rub the sleepy dust out of her . . eyes. **10b** N. MITFORD He had gone to Barcelona to rub up his Spanish. **11** M. KEANE She could . . rub methylated spirit . . into his heel. **12** C. H. SPURGEON Dirt will rub off when it is dry.

Phrases: **not have two pennies to rub together** & vars., lack money, be poor. ***rub a person's nose in it***: see NOSE *noun*. **rub elbows** (chiefly *US*) = ***rub shoulders*** below. **rub noses** (of two people) touch noses in greeting, as a sign of friendship in some societies. **rub one's hands** move one's hands to and fro against each other, usu. to signify keen satisfaction or to generate warmth. ***rub salt in a person's wound(s)***, ***rub salt in the wound(s)***: see SALT *noun*[1]. **rub shoulders** come into contact (*with*). **rub the wrong way** annoy, irritate (cf. ***rub up the wrong way*** below).
With adverbs in specialized senses: **rub away** remove by rubbing. **rub down** (*a*) clean (a horse) from dust and sweat by rubbing; (*b*) make smooth, grind down, etc., by rubbing; (*c*) *colloq.* search (a person) by passing one's hand all over the body. **rub in** (*a*) apply (dry colours) by rubbing; draw or sketch in this way; (*b*) apply (an ointment etc.) by means of continued rubbing; (*c*) *slang* emphasize, reiterate, (esp. something disagreeable); freq. in ***rub it in***. **rub off** (of a quality) have an effect (*on* a person) through close or continued contact; (see also senses 6, 7, 10 above). **rub out** erase by rubbing; *fig.* (*N. Amer.*) kill, eliminate (see also senses 4, 10 above). **rub over** go over (with the hand, a tool, etc.) in the process of rubbing. **rub up** (*a*) mix or prepare by rubbing; (*b*) *slang* caress in order to excite sexually; (*c*) *slang* masturbate; (*d*) make clean, clear, or bright (again) by rubbing; (*e*) (in full ***rub up the wrong way***) annoy, irritate (cf. ***rub the wrong way*** above); (see also sense 9b above).
Comb.: **rub-board** (*a*) a board fitted with teeth between which linen is drawn; (*b*) *N. Amer.* a washboard; **rub-down** an act of rubbing down; **rub-out** *US slang* a murder, an assassination, esp. of one gangster by another; **rub-rail** a rail to protect a vehicle etc. against rubbing; **rubstone** a stone for sharpening or smoothing a surface by rubbing, *esp.* a kind of whetstone; **rub-up** an act of rubbing up.

rub-a-dub /'rʌbədʌb/ *noun.* L18.
[Imit.]
1 The sound of a drum being beaten; a drumming sound. L18.
2 A pub, a hotel. *rhyming slang.* L19.
■ Also **rub-a-dub-'dub** *noun* E19.

rubai /ru'bɑːiː/ *noun.* Pl. ***rubaiyat*** /'ruːbʌɪ(j)at, -bʌɪ-/. M19.
[Arab. *rubāʿī* (pl. *rubāʿiyāt*), from *rubāʿī* quadripartite.]
In Persian poetry, a quatrain.

†**ruban** *noun.* L15–L18.
[French: see RIBAND *noun*[1].]
A ribbon.

Rubarth's disease /'ruːbɑːts dɪˌziːz/ *noun phr.* M20.
[C. S. *Rubarth* (b. 1905), Swedish veterinary scientist.]
VETERINARY MEDICINE. An infectious virus disease of dogs that affects the liver and is sometimes fatal; infectious canine hepatitis.

rubashka /rʊ'baʃkə/ *noun.* Pl. **-ki** /-ki/, **-kas**. E20.
[Russian.]
A type of blouse or tunic worn in Russia.

rubato /rʊ'bɑːtəʊ/ *adjective & noun.* L18.
[Italian, lit. 'robbed'.]
MUSIC. ▶**A** *adjective.* ***tempo rubato***, rubato. L18.
▶ **B** *noun.* Pl. **-tos**, **-ti** /-ti/. The action or practice of temporarily disregarding strict tempo during performance; an instance of this. L19.

†**rubb** *noun.* L17–E18.
[Low German *rubbe* = Dutch *rob* (hence German *Robbe*).]
A seal (the animal).

rubbaboo /rʌbə'buː/ *noun.* E19.
[Ult. from Algonquian.]
N. AMER. HISTORY. A kind of soup or broth made from pemmican.

†**rubbage** *noun & adjective* see RUBBISH *noun & adjective.*

rubbedy /'rʌbədi/ *noun. Austral. slang.* Also **rubberdy**. L19.
[Alt.]
= RUB-A-DUB 2. Cf. RUBBITY.

rubber /'rʌbə/ *noun*[1] *& adjective.* M16.
[from RUB *verb* + -ER[1].]
▶ **A** *noun.* **I 1 a** A hard brush, cloth, etc. used for rubbing things clean. Now *rare.* M16. ▸**b** An implement of metal or stone used for rubbing, esp. in order to smooth or flatten a surface. M17. ▸**c** A pad or roll of soft material used for rubbing and polishing; an article for erasing chalk from a blackboard, usu. consisting of a soft pad attached to a wooden handle. L19.
2 A whetstone. Now *dial.* M16.
†**3** A dentifrice. *rare.* M–L16.
4 †**a** A strigil. L16–E17. ▸**b** A bath towel. L16.
5 A large coarse file. L17.
6 A machine or machine part which acts by rubbing. Formerly also, a friction brake. L18.
7 A brick which is rubbed smooth. E19.
▶ **II 8** A person who rubs something; *spec.* (*a*) a worker engaged in rubbing in order to smooth or polish something; (*b*) a person who takes brass-rubbings. L16. ▸**b** A person who applies massage, *esp.* (*N. Amer.*) one who massages sportsmen or athletes; an attendant who rubs the bathers at a Turkish bath. E17.
9 *fig.* A rebuke, an irritating remark; a source of annoyance. Now *rare.* E18.
▶ **III 10** An organic substance made from the coagulated latex of various plants, esp. *Hevea brasiliensis*, which in its natural state is thermoplastic and tacky and after vulcanization tough and elastic; any of various artificial polymeric substances similar to this. Formerly *spec.*, caoutchouc as used for rubbing out pencil marks. L18.
11 In *pl.* Overshoes or galoshes made of rubber; plimsolls, *esp.* ones worn for climbing. M19.
12 A rubber tyre; the tyres of a vehicle collectively; a car. *US.* L19.
13 BASEBALL. The pitcher's plate. Also, the home plate. *US.* L19.
14 A piece of rubber for erasing pencil or ink marks; an eraser. E20.
15 A condom. *slang.* M20.
10 ***butyl rubber***, ***crêpe rubber***, ***indiarubber***, ***Pará rubber***, ***sponge rubber***, etc.
▶ **B** *attrib.* or as *adjective.* Made of rubber. M19.
Comb. & special collocations: **rubber band**: see BAND *noun*[2] 2; **rubber boa** a short brown snake, *Charina bottae*, of the family Boidae, found in western N. America; **rubber cement** a cement or adhesive containing rubber in a solvent; **rubber cheque** *slang* a cheque that bounces; **rubber-chicken circuit** (chiefly *N. Amer. slang*) an after-dinner-speaking circuit; ***rubber dam***: see DAM *noun*[1] 4b; **rubber fetishism** sexual fetishism which is centred on objects made of rubber; **rubber goods** articles made of rubber; *spec.* contraceptive devices; **rubber heel** (*a*) a shoe heel made of rubber; (*b*) *slang* a person who investigates the conduct of members of his own organization; *spec.* an internal police investigator; **rubber-heel** *verb intrans. & trans.* (*slang*) investigate (a colleague), keep (an associate) under surveillance, spy *on*; **rubber-heeler** *slang* = ***rubber heel*** (b) above; **rubber ice** *N. Amer.* thin flexible ice; ***rubber johnny***: see JOHNNY 4; **rubber plant** a tree of SE Asia, *Ficus elastica*, of the mulberry family, formerly used as a source of rubber, and now popular as a house-plant for its large glossy dark green leaves; **rubber-proofed** *adjective* coated or treated with rubber for water-proofing; **rubber snake** = ***rubber boa*** above; **rubber solution** a solution of rubber, *spec.* one used as an adhesive in mending rubber articles; **rubber stamp** (*a*) a hand-held device which can be brought down firmly on to a surface to apply an inked impression; an impression so made; (*b*) a person or institution that gives uncritical endorsement or agreement; **rubber-stamp** *verb trans.* (*a*) mark using a

rubber stamp; make (an impression) with a rubber stamp; (*b*) endorse or approve uncritically; pass routinely or automatically; **rubber-tapper** a person who taps a tree, esp. *Hevea brasiliensis*, for rubber; **rubber-tapping** the collection of rubber by tapping trees; **rubberware** rubber goods; **rubberwear** rubber clothing.

■ **rubberiness** *noun* the state or condition of being rubbery M20. **rubberize** *verb trans.* treat, coat, or impregnate with rubber E20. **rubberless** *adjective* lacking rubber or rubber tyres L19. **rubbery** *adjective* resembling or suggestive of rubber E20.

rubber /ˈrʌbə/ *noun*[2]. L16.
[Origin uncertain: perh. a specific application of prec.]
1 A set of three (or five) games between the same sides or persons in cards, bowls, cricket, etc., the overall winner being the one who wins the greater number of games; a set of two (or three) games won by the same side or person (making further play unnecessary). L16.
†**2 a** A spell, a round, a turn. M–L17. ▸**b** A quarrel; a bout of quarrelling or recrimination. L17–E18.
Comb.: **rubber bridge** a type of bridge scored in rubbers, in which the hands are not replayed (cf. ***duplicate bridge*** s.v. DUPLICATE *adjective*); **rubber game**, **rubber match**: played to determine the winner of a series.

rubber /ˈrʌbə/ *verb.* L19.
[from RUBBER *noun*[1]. In sense 1 from RUBBERNECK.]
1 *verb intrans.* **a** Turn the head round in order to look at something. Also foll. by *around*, *for*. *US slang*. L19. ▸**b** Listen (*in*) on a party telephone line. *N. Amer. colloq.* E20.
2 *verb trans.* Coat or cover with rubber. E20.

rubberdy *noun* var. of RUBBEDY.

rubberneck /ˈrʌbənɛk/ *verb & noun. colloq.* (orig. *US*). L19.
[from RUBBER *noun*[1] & *adjective* + NECK *noun*[1].]
▶ **A** *verb.* **1** *verb intrans.* Crane the neck in curiosity, gape; look around, sightsee. L19.
2 *verb trans.* Stare at. M20.
▶ **B** *noun.* A person who stares; an inquisitive person; a sightseer, a tourist. L19.
■ **rubbernecker** *noun* = RUBBERNECK *noun* M20.

rubberoid /ˈrʌb(ə)rɔɪd/ *noun & adjective.* L19.
[from RUBBER *noun*[1] & *adjective* + -OID.]
▶ **A** *noun.* A substitute for rubber. L19.
▶ **B** *adjective.* Resembling rubber; made of such a substance. M20.

†**rubbidge** *noun & adjective* see RUBBISH *noun & adjective*.

rubbing /ˈrʌbɪŋ/ *noun.* LME.
[from RUB *verb* + -ING[1].]
1 The action of RUB *verb*; an instance of this. LME.
2 An impression or copy made by rubbing. M19.
Comb.: **rubbing alcohol** denatured, usu. perfumed alcohol used in massaging; **rubbing stone** a rubstone.

rubbish /ˈrʌbɪʃ/ *noun & adjective.* Also †**-idge**, †**-age**. LME.
[Anglo-Norman *rubbous*, perh. alt. of pl. of Anglo-Norman deriv. of Old French *robe* spoils (see RUBBLE); assim. to *-ish* (and *-idge*).]
▶ **A** *noun.* **1** Waste material; rejected and useless matter of any kind; debris, litter, refuse. LME.
2 Worthless material or articles, trash; worthless or absurd ideas, talk, or writing, nonsense. Also as *interjection*. E17.

📖 **1** ***rubbish bin***, ***rubbish dump***, ***rubbish tip***, etc. **2** L. NKOSI You . . are not to drink until the others arrive! . . Rubbish! We have priority claims! K. ISHIGURO How you can sit and watch rubbish . . You hardly used to watch television.

▶ **B** *attrib.* or as *adjective.* Of the nature of rubbish, rubbishy; worthless. L16.
■ **rubbishly** *adjective* (*rare*) worthless, rubbishy L18.

rubbish /ˈrʌbɪʃ/ *verb trans.* Orig. *Austral. & NZ slang.* M20.
[from prec.]
Disparage, reject as worthless; criticize severely.

📖 *Times* His second book was also rubbished.

■ **rubbisher** *noun* L20.

rubbishing /ˈrʌbɪʃɪŋ/ *noun.* L20.
[from prec. + -ING[1].]
The action or an act of rubbishing something or someone; a severe criticism.

rubbishing /ˈrʌbɪʃɪŋ/ *adjective.* E19.
[from RUBBISH *noun & adjective* + -ING[2].]
Paltry, worthless, rubbishy.

rubbishy /ˈrʌbɪʃi/ *adjective.* L18.
[from RUBBISH *noun* + -Y[1].]
1 Covered with rubbish. L18.
2 Of the nature of rubbish; paltry, contemptible, worthless. E19.

📖 **2** *Liverpool Daily Post* Why don't you get rid of that rubbishy old furniture.

rubbity /ˈrʌbɪti/ *noun. Austral.* M20.
[Alt.]
= RUB-A-DUB 2. Cf. RUBBEDY.
■ Also **rubbity-ˈdub** *noun* E20.

rubble /ˈrʌb(ə)l/ *noun & verb.* LME.
[Perh. from Anglo-Norman alt. of Old French *robe* spoils: see ROBE *noun*[1]. Cf. RUBBISH *noun & adjective*.]
▶ **A** *noun.* **1** Waste fragments of stone, brick, etc., esp. as the rubbish of decayed or demolished buildings. Formerly also, rubbish or refuse in general. LME.
2 Pieces of undressed stone used in building walls, as hard core, etc. M16. ▸**b** Masonry made of rubble. Also ***rubble-work***. E19.
3 GEOLOGY. Loose angular stones or fragments of broken material forming a mantle over some rocks, and found beneath alluvium or soil. L18.
4 Floating piles of ice fragments. L19.

📖 **1** K. CROSSLEY-HOLLAND They . . reduced the . . walls of Asgard to rubble.

Comb.: **rubble-stone** (*a*) = senses 2, 3 above; (*b*) in *pl.*, stones of the nature of rubble; ***rubble-work***: see sense 2b above.
▶ **B** *verb.* †**1** *verb trans.* **a** Crush, bring to ruin. Only in LME. ▸**b** Cure (an ailment). Only in LME.
2 *verb intrans.* Poke or crawl about among rubbish or refuse. Now *dial.* M17.
3 *verb trans.* Reduce to rubble. Usu. in *pass.* E20.
■ **rubbler** *noun* a young or casual worker in a slate quarry M19. **rubbly** *adjective* containing a lot of rubble; consisting of rubble, of the nature of rubble: M18.

rubby /ˈrʌbi/ *noun. Canad. colloq.* M20.
[from *rub(bing alcohol* s.v. RUBBING *noun* + -Y[6].]
1 A habitual drinker of rubbing alcohol. M20.
2 Rubbing alcohol, sometimes mixed with wine etc., used as an intoxicant. M20.
Comb.: **rubby-dub** = sense 1 above.

rubby-dubby /ˈrʌbɪdʌbi/ *noun.* M20.
[Perh. from RUB *verb* + DUB *verb*[1] + -Y[6].]
ANGLING. Minced fish such as pilchards, mackerel, etc., placed in a net bag and used as a lure for shark and other large fish.

rube /ruːb/ *noun. N. Amer. slang.* Also **reub**, **R-**. L19.
[Pet-form of *Reuben*.]
1 A farmer, a rustic, a country bumpkin. *derog.* L19.
2 ***hey Rube!***: a rallying call or cry for help, used by circus people. L19.

rubeanic /ruːbɪˈanɪk/ *adjective.* L19.
[from Latin *rubeus* red + CY)AN + -IC.]
CHEMISTRY. ***rubeanic acid***, an orange-red solid, $CS(NH_2)_2$, formed by reaction of cyanogen and hydrogen sulphide and used as a reagent to detect copper.

rubefacient /ruːbɪˈfeɪʃ(ə)nt/ *adjective & noun.* E19.
[Latin *rubefacient-* pres. ppl stem of *rubefacere* make red, from *rubeus* red + *facere* make: see -ENT.]
MEDICINE. ▶**A** *adjective.* Producing redness or slight inflammation. E19.
▶ **B** *noun.* An agent, esp. a counterirritant, producing redness of the skin. E19.

rubefaction /ruːbɪˈfakʃ(ə)n/ *noun.* LME.
[Anglo-Latin *rubefactio(n-)*, from Latin *rubefact-* pa. ppl stem of *rubefacere*: see prec., -FACTION.]
Reddening or redness of the skin, esp. as produced artificially.

†**rubefy** *verb* var. of RUBIFY.

Rube Goldberg /ruːb ˈgəʊl(d)bəːg/ *adjective. N. Amer.* M20.
[Reuben ('*Rube*') Lucius *Goldberg* (1883–1970), US humorous artist, whose illustrations often depicted such devices.]
Designating a device that is unnecessarily complicated, impracticable, or ingenious. Cf. HEATH ROBINSON.
■ Also **Rube Goldˈbergian** *adjective* M20.

rubella /rʊˈbɛlə/ *noun.* L19.
[Use as noun of neut. pl. of Latin *rubellus* reddish, from *rubeus* red: see -EL[2].]
German measles.
■ **rubelliform** *adjective* resembling the characteristic rash of rubella M20.

rubellite /ˈruːbəlʌɪt/ *noun.* L18.
[from Latin *rubellus*: see prec., -ITE[1].]
A red variety of the mineral tourmaline.

Rubenist /ˈruːbɪnɪst/ *noun.* Also ***Rubéniste*** /rybenist/. M20.
[French *Rubéniste*, from *Rubens* (see below) + *-iste* -IST.]
An admirer, student, or imitator of the Flemish painter Sir Peter Paul Rubens (1577–1640) or his work, *esp.* one of a group of 17th-cent. French artists who followed Rubens.

Rubens /ˈruːbɪnz/ *noun.* L18.
[See RUBENIST.]
▶ **I 1** More fully ***Rubens hat***. A hat with a high crown and a brim turned up at one side. L18.
2 a ***Rubens brown***, a brown earth-colour. M19. ▸**b** ***Rubens madder***, madder brown. L19.
▶ **II 3** Used *attrib.* to designate someone or something Rubensesque. M19.
■ **Rubeˈnesque** *adjective* E20. **Rubensˈesque** *adjective* characteristic or suggestive of the paintings of Rubens; (of a woman's figure) full and rounded: E20. **Ruˈbensian** *adjective* of, pertaining to, or characteristic of Rubens or his work L19.

rubeola /rʊˈbiːələ/ *noun.* L17.
[Use as noun of fem. of medieval Latin dim. (after *variola*) of Latin *rubeus* red.]
†**1** A rash of red spots or pimples. Only in L17.
2 Measles. E19.
3 German measles. Now *rare* or *obsolete*. M19.
■ **rubeolar** *adjective* of the nature of or characteristic of rubeola L19. **rubeoloid** *adjective & noun* (a disease) resembling rubeola M19. **rubeolous** *adjective* rubeolar E19.

rubeosis /ruːbɪˈəʊsɪs/ *noun.* Pl. **-oses** /-ˈəʊsiːz/. M20.
[from Latin *rubeus* red + -OSIS.]
MEDICINE. Reddening of the iris as a result of vascular proliferation, occurring esp. in diabetics. Also ***rubeosis iridis*** /ˈʌɪrɪdɪs/ [Latin = of the iris].

rubescent /rʊˈbɛs(ə)nt/ *adjective.* M18.
[Latin *rubescent-* pres. ppl stem of *rubescere* redden, from *ruber* red: see -ESCENT.]
Tending to redness; reddening, blushing.

📖 J. TORRINGTON We lay in silence watching the rubescent dramas . . projected onto the walls by the firelight.

rubiaceous /ruːbɪˈeɪʃəs/ *adjective.* M19.
[from mod. Latin *Rubiaceae* (see below), from *Rubia* the genus madder (Latin *rubia* madder): see -ACEOUS.]
BOTANY. Of or pertaining to the Rubiaceae or madder family.

rubicelle /ˈruːbɪsɛl/ *noun.* L17.
[French, dim. of *rubis* RUBY: see -EL[2].]
A yellow or orange-red variety of spinel.

Rubicon /ˈruːbɪk(ə)n, -ɒn/ *noun.* Also (esp. in sense 2) **r-**. E17.
[A stream in NE Italy marking the ancient boundary between Italy and Cisalpine Gaul. By taking his army across it (i.e. outside his own province) in 49 BC Julius Caesar committed himself to war against the Senate and Pompey.]
1 A boundary, a limit; *esp.* one which once crossed betokens irrevocable commitment; a point of no return. Freq. in ***cross the Rubicon***. E17.
2 CARDS. A target score which increases the penalty of a losing player who fails to reach it, *spec.* the score of 100 as a critical score in piquet; the failure of a loser to reach this score. L19.

rubicund /ˈruːbɪk(ə)nd/ *adjective.* LME.
[Latin *rubicundus*, from *rubere* be red, from *ruber* red.]
1 Inclined to redness; red. LME.
2 Of the face, complexion, etc.: reddish, flushed, highly coloured, esp. as the result of good living. Of a person: having such a complexion. L17.

📖 **1** M. AMIS From the country, where everything was good: the sack of wheat, the rubicund apple-rack. **2** I. RANKIN A rubicund man, hot and jacketless . . , was dispensing the drinks.

■ **rubiˈcundity** *noun* L16. **rubicundly** *adverb* L16.

rubidium /rʊˈbɪdɪəm/ *noun.* M19.
[from Latin *rubidus* red, with ref. to two spectral lines in the red part of the spectrum: see -IUM.]
A soft, silvery-white, highly reactive chemical element, atomic no. 37, belonging to the alkali metal group and found in a few minerals. (Symbol Rb.)
Comb.: **rubidium-strontium dating**: based on measurement of the relative amounts in rock of rubidium-87 and its beta decay product, strontium-87.

rubied /ˈruːbɪd/ *adjective.* E17.
[from RUBY *noun* + -ED[2].]
Coloured like a ruby; ornamented with rubies.

rubify /ˈruːbɪfʌɪ/ *verb trans.* Now *rare*. Also †**rubefy**. LME.
[Old French *rubifier*, *rube-* (mod. *rubéfier*) from medieval Latin *rubificare* from Latin *rubefacere*, from *rubeus* red: see -FY.]
Make red, redden.
■ **rubifiˈcation** *noun* the process of causing redness or becoming red L19.

rubiginous /rʊˈbɪdʒɪnəs/ *adjective.* M17.
[from Latin *rubigin-* rust, blight + -OUS.]
†**1** Of a plant: affected by rust. *rare*. Only in M17.
2 Rusty; rust-coloured. L17.

Rubik's cube /ˌruːbɪks ˈkjuːb/ *noun phr.* Also **Rubik cube**. L20.
[E. *Rubik* (b. 1944), Hungarian teacher.]
(Proprietary name for) a puzzle consisting of a cube seemingly formed by 26 smaller cubes of which each visible face shows one of six colours, the aim being to make each side of the larger cube of a uniform colour by rotating its horizontal and vertical layers.

†**rubine** *noun.* E16.
[Alt. of RUBY after Old French *rubin*, Spanish *rubin*, medieval Latin *rubinus*: see -INE[1].]
1 A ruby. E16–L17.
2 A ruby colour. Only in E18.

rubinglimmer /ˈruːbɪnɡlɪmə/ *noun.* M19.
[German, from *Rubin* ruby + *Glimmer* mica, GLIMMER *noun*^{2}.]
MINERALOGY. = LEPIDOCROCITE.

rubio /ˈruːbɪəʊ/ *noun.* L19.
[Spanish, lit. 'fair, blond, golden'.]
Limonite mined in N. Spain.

rubious /ˈruːbɪəs/ *adjective.* E17.
[from RUBY + -OUS.]
Ruby-coloured.

rubisco /rʊˈbɪskəʊ/ *noun.* Pl. **-os.** L20.
[from R(IB)U(LOSE + BIS- + C(ARB)O(XYL.]
BIOCHEMISTRY. An enzyme, ribulose 1,5-bisphosphate carboxylase, present in plant chloroplasts, and involved in fixing atmospheric carbon dioxide in photosynthesis and in oxygenation of the resulting compound in photorespiration.

ruble *noun* var. of ROUBLE.

rub-off /ˈrʌbɒf/ *noun.* M20.
[from *rub off* s.v. RUB *verb*.]
1 An act of masturbation. *slang.* M20.
2 A thing that rubs off on someone or something; *spec.* a (usu. beneficial) secondary effect or consequence; influence. L20.

rubor /ˈruːbə/ *noun.* LME.
[Latin, rel. to *ruber* red.]
Redness, ruddiness.

rubral /ˈruːbr(ə)l/ *adjective.* M20.
[from Latin *rubr-*, *ruber* red + -AL^{1}.]
ANATOMY. Of or pertaining to the red nucleus of the brain.

rubredoxin /ruːbrɪˈdɒksɪn/ *noun.* M20.
[from Latin *rubr-*, *ruber* red + REDOX + -IN^{1}. Cf. FERREDOXIN.]
BIOCHEMISTRY. Any of a class of proteins having an iron atom coordinated to the sulphur atoms of four cysteine residues, and concerned in intracellular electron-transfer processes.

rubric /ˈruːbrɪk/ *noun, adjective, & verb.* In sense A.1 also †**rubrish.** ME.
[Old French *rubrique*, *-bric(h)e* or its source Latin *rubrica* use as noun (sc. *terra* earth or ochre as writing material) of adjective from base of *rubeus*, *ruber* red. Cf. RUBY.]
▶ **A** *noun.* **1** A written or printed text in distinctive (esp. red) lettering; *spec.* (*a*) a heading of a chapter or other section in a book or manuscript; (*b*) *CHRISTIAN CHURCH* a liturgical direction for the conduct of divine service; †(*c*) *CHRISTIAN CHURCH* a calendar of saints; an entry in red letters of a name in such a calendar; (*d*) *LAW* the heading of a statute or section of a legal code; (*e*) an explanatory or prescriptive note introducing an examination paper etc. ME. ▸**b** *transf.* A designation, a category; an injunction; a general rule; an established custom. M19.
2 Red ochre, ruddle. *arch.* LME.
3 A decorative flourish attached to a signature. *rare.* L19.

> 📖 **1** R. V. JONES The rubric advised candidates to spend . . an hour on the first part. A. KENNY The . . 'rubrics' prescribed whether he should stand or kneel, open or close his hands. ***black rubric***: see BLACK *adjective*. **b** J. P. STERN His writings are too rich and too varied to be brought under one common rubric. E. JONG That Bloody Rogue, Ralph Griffiths (hiding behind the preposterous Rubrick of G. Fenton).

▶ **B** *adjective.* **1** Containing or inscribed with a rubric; (of lettering) written or printed in red. L15.
2 Red, ruddy. *poet.* E17.
▶ **C** *verb trans.* Infl. **-ck-.** = RUBRICATE 1, 2. Now *rare.* L15.
■ **rubrical** *adjective* (*a*) *rare* marked by red letters; (*b*) of, pertaining to, or in accordance with a rubric or rubrics, esp. in liturgy: M17. **rubrically** *adverb* L17. **rubrician** /rʊˈbrɪʃ(ə)n/ *noun* a student or follower of liturgical rubrics M19. **rubricism** /-sɪz(ə)m/*noun* a strict or overzealous observance of liturgical rubrics M19. **rubricist** /-sɪst/ *noun* strict or overzealous observer of liturgical rubrics M19. **rubricity** /rʊˈbrɪsɪti/ *noun* (*a*) *rare* assumption of a red colour; (*b*) observance of liturgical rubrics: E19.

rubricate /ˈruːbrɪkeɪt/ *verb.* L16.
[Latin *rubricat-* pa. ppl stem of *rubricare*, from *rubrica*: see prec., -ATE^{3}.]
1 *verb trans.* Write, print, or mark in red. Formerly also (*CHRISTIAN CHURCH*), enter (a name) in red letters in a calendar of saints. L16.
2 *verb trans.* Provide (a text) with a rubric or rubrics. M19.
3 *verb intrans.* Sign one's name with a rubric. *rare.* M19.
■ **rubriˈcation** *noun* (*a*) the action or an act of rubricating something, esp. of marking a text etc. in red; (*b*) a rubricated passage or text: L19. **rubricator** *noun* (*Hist.*) a person employed to rubricate parts of a manuscript or early printed book M19.

†**rubrish** *noun* see RUBRIC.

rubro- /ˈruːbrəʊ/ *combining form.*
[from Latin *rubr-*, *ruber* red: see -O-.]
ANATOMY. Forming adjectives with the senses 'relating to the red nucleus of the brain and', 'passing from the red nucleus to', as ***rubro-oculomotor***, ***rubro-reticular***, ***rubro-spinal***.

ruby /ˈruːbi/ *noun, adjective, & verb.* ME.
[Old French *rubi* (mod. *rubis*) from medieval Latin *rubinus* use as noun of adjective from base of Latin *rubeus*, *ruber* red.]
▶ **A** *noun.* **1** A rare and valuable precious stone varying from deep crimson or purple to pale rose-red, now recognized as a variety of corundum. Also (now usu. with specifying word), a red spinel (formerly confused with this). ME.
†**2** A person (esp. a woman) of great worth or beauty. ME–L16.
3 †**a** *ALCHEMY.* The red form of the philosopher's stone. L15–E17. ▸**b** *CHEMISTRY.* A red compound of an element or elements. Usu. foll. by *of*. Long *obsolete* exc. *Hist.* L17.
4 a A red facial spot or pimple. M16. ▸**b** In *pl.* The lips. Chiefly *poet.* L16.
5 The colour of a ruby; a glowing purplish red; *HERALDRY* (long *obsolete* exc. *Hist.*) the tincture gules in the fanciful blazon of arms of peers. L16.
6 a Red wine. Chiefly *poet.* L17. ▸**b** Blood. *slang.* M19.
7 A size of type (equal to 5½ points) intermediate between nonpareil and pearl. L18.
8 *ellipt.* Ruby glass; ruby port. M19.
1 ***BALAS-ruby***. ***spinel ruby***: see SPINEL 1.
▶ **B** *adjective.* **1** Of the colour of a ruby, of a glowing purplish red; *HERALDRY* (long *obsolete* exc. *Hist.*) of the tincture gules in the fanciful blazon of arms of peers. L15.
2 Of or pertaining to a ruby or rubies; set or provided with a ruby or rubies. E16.

> 📖 **1** *Lady* One lady had a ruby velvet, trimmed with costly lace. **2** ***ruby mine***, ***ruby ring***, ***ruby stone***, etc.

Special collocations & comb. (of noun & adjective): **ruby anniversary** = ***ruby wedding*** below. **ruby-back**, **ruby-backed** *adjectives* designating fine Chinese porcelain backed with pink or crimson enamel. **ruby blende** a reddish-brown transparent variety of sphalerite. **ruby copper** cuprous oxide. **ruby-dazzler** *Austral. & NZ slang* a thing of exceptional quality. **ruby glass** glass coloured by various metallic oxides. **ruby port** a deep red port, *esp.* one matured in wood for only a few years and then fined. **ruby-red** (of) the colour of a ruby, (of) a glowing purplish red. **ruby silver** (*a*) proustite; (*b*) pyrargyrite. **ruby spinel** = SPINEL 1. **ruby-tail** (more fully ***ruby-tail fly***, ***ruby-tail wasp***) = ***ruby-tailed fly*** below. **ruby-tailed** *adjective* having a red tail; ***ruby-tailed fly***, ***ruby-tailed wasp***, any of various cuckoo wasps which have part of the abdomen a metallic red colour; *esp.* any European species of the genus *Chrysis*. **rubythroat** (*a*) (in full ***Siberian rubythroat***) a small bird, *Luscinia calliope*, related to the European robin, which breeds in Siberia, and the male of which has a red throat; (*b*) = ***ruby-throated hummingbird*** below. **ruby-throated** *adjective* (of a bird) having a red throat; ***ruby-throated hummingbird***, a hummingbird, *Archilochus colubris*, that has a metallic green back and is the commonest hummingbird in much of N. America; ***ruby-throated warbler*** = ***rubythroat*** (a) above. **ruby wedding** the fortieth (or forty-fifth) anniversary of a wedding. **ruby zinc** (*a*) = ***ruby blende*** above; (*b*) zincite.
▶ **C** *verb trans.* Dye or tinge with a ruby colour. Chiefly as ***rubied*** *ppl adjective. poet.* E18.

RUC *abbreviation.*
Royal Ulster Constabulary.

†**ruc** *noun* see ROC.

rucervine /ruːˈsəːvʌɪn/ *adjective.* L19.
[from mod. Latin *Rucervus* former genus name, from RUSA *noun*^{1} + Latin *cervus* deer: see CERVINE.]
ZOOLOGY. Of or belonging to a group of SE Asian deer comprising the swamp deer, the thamin, and the recently extinct *Cervus schomburgki* of Thailand.

ruche /ruːʃ/ *noun & verb.* E19.
[Old & mod. French from medieval Latin *rusca* tree bark, of Celtic origin.]
▶ **A** *noun.* A frill of gathered ribbon, lace, etc., used esp. as a trimming. E19.
▶ **B** *verb trans.* Trim with a ruche or ruches. L19.
■ **ruched** *adjective* trimmed with a ruche or ruches; gathered into a ruche or ruches: M19. **ruching** *noun* (a) trimming made of ruches M19.

ruck /rʌk/ *noun*^{1} *& verb*^{1}. ME.
[App. of Scandinavian origin, corresp. to Norwegian *ruka*.]
▶ **A** *noun.* **1** A gathered heap or stack of fuel or other combustible material. ME. ▸†**b** A measure of capacity *spec.* of coal. ME–M17.
2 A haystack, a corn-stack. Now *Scot. & dial.* LME.
3 a A large number or quantity; a multitude, a crowd. LME. ▸**b** A rough heap or pile of anything, a bundle, a cluster. Now *Scot. & dial.* L17. ▸**c** *AUSTRAL. RULES FOOTBALL.* A group of three players who follow the play without fixed positions. L19. ▸**d** *RUGBY FOOTBALL.* A loose scrum in which the ball is on the ground. E20.
4 Nonsense, rubbish. *US colloq.* L19.
Phrases: **in a ruck** in one group, in a cluster. **the ruck** (*a*) the main body of competitors in a race etc. not likely to overtake the leaders; (*b*) a grouping of undistinguished people or things; the ordinary or general mass of.
Comb.: **ruckman** *AUSTRAL. RULES FOOTBALL* a member of a ruck whose function is esp. to knock the ball to the ruck-rover; **ruck-rover** *AUSTRAL. RULES FOOTBALL* a mobile member of a ruck.
▶ **B** *verb.* **1** *verb trans.* Stack or pile up (hay etc.). Also foll. by *up*. *Scot. & dial.* E18.
2 *verb intrans.* **a** *RUGBY FOOTBALL.* Form a ruck. M20. ▸**b** *AUSTRAL. RULES FOOTBALL.* Play as one of the members of a ruck. M20.

ruck /rʌk/ *noun*^{2} *& verb*^{2}. L18.
[Old Norse *hrukka* (Norwegian *hrukka*) rel. to Norwegian *rukla*, *rukka*, Middle Swedish *rynkia*. Cf. RUCKLE *noun*^{3}, RUNKLE.]
▶ **A** *noun.* A ridge, a wrinkle; *esp.* a crease or fold in fabric, a carpet, etc. L18.

> 📖 R. C. HUTCHINSON A ruck in the under-blanket which pressed into her side.

▶ **B** *verb intrans. & trans.* (Cause to) form a ruck or rucks; (cause to) crease or wrinkle. Also foll. by *up*. E19.

> 📖 D. WELCH The rugs on the floor were rucked up . . as if someone had been skidding . . about. S. MIDDLETON With her hands between her knees, rucking her dress.

■ **rucky** *adjective* (*rare*) having many rucks or creases E19.

ruck /rʌk/ *noun*^{3}. *colloq.* M20.
[Perh. from RUCK *verb*^{5}, or shortening of RUCTION or RUCKUS.]
A quarrel; a row; a fight, *esp.* one involving a number of people.

†**ruck** *noun*^{4} see ROC.

ruck /rʌk/ *verb*^{3} *intrans. & †refl.* Now *dial.* ME.
[Perh. of Scandinavian origin: cf. Norwegian dial. *ruka*.]
Squat, crouch, cower.

ruck /rʌk/ *verb*^{4} *intrans. slang.* L19.
[Origin unkn.]
Give information about a crime or criminal; inform *on*. Also, reject or disown a person (foll. by *on*).

ruck /rʌk/ *verb*^{5} *trans. slang.* L19.
[Origin unkn.]
Rebuke; reprimand.

> 📖 P. WILLMOTT The governor . . rucks you if you take more than ten minutes for a quarter of an hour's job.

ruckle /ˈrʌk(ə)l/ *noun*^{1}. *Scot. & north.* E19.
[from RUCK *noun*^{1} + -LE^{1}.]
A heap, a stack, esp. of hay or of peat.

ruckle /ˈrʌk(ə)l/ *noun*^{2}. Chiefly *Scot.* E19.
[Of Scandinavian origin: cf. Norwegian dial. *rukl*.]
A rattling or gurgling noise; *esp.* a death-rattle.

ruckle /ˈrʌk(ə)l/ *noun*^{3}. M19.
[from RUCK *noun*^{2} + -LE^{1}. Cf. RUNKLE.]
= RUCK *noun*^{2}.

ruckle /ˈrʌk(ə)l/ *verb*^{1} *trans.* Now *Scot. & dial.* ME.
[from RUCK *verb*^{1} + -LE^{3}.]
= RUCK *verb*^{1} 1.

ruckle /ˈrʌk(ə)l/ *verb*^{2} *intrans.* Chiefly *Scot.* M16.
[Of Scandinavian origin: cf. Norwegian dial. *rukla*.]
Make a rattling or gurgling sound, esp. a death-rattle.

ruckle /ˈrʌk(ə)l/ *verb*^{3} *trans. & intrans.* M19.
[from RUCK *verb*^{2} + -LE^{3}.]
= RUCK *verb*^{2}.

rucksack /ˈrʌksak, ˈrʊk-/ *noun.* M19.
[German, from *Rucken* dial. var. of *Rücken* back + *Sack* SACK *noun*^{1}.]
A bag or knapsack to be carried on the back by means of shoulder-straps, used esp. by walkers and climbers.
■ **rucksacked** *adjective* provided with or carrying a rucksack E20. **rucksackful** *noun* the contents of a rucksack; as much as a rucksack will hold: L20.

ruckus /ˈrʌkəs/ *noun.* Orig. & chiefly *N. Amer.* L19.
[Origin uncertain: perh. rel. to RUCTION, RUMPUS. See also ROOKUS.]
An uproar, a disturbance; a row, a commotion.

†**ructation** *noun.* E17–L18.
[Late Latin *ructatio(n-)*, from *ructat-* pa. ppl stem of *ructare*: see -ATION.]
= ERUCTATION.

ruction /ˈrʌkʃ(ə)n/ *noun. dial. & colloq.* E19.
[Origin unkn.]
A disturbance; a disorderly dispute or quarrel; a row; in *pl.*, unpleasant arguments or reactions.

rud /rʌd/ *noun*^{1}. Long *arch. & dial.*
[Old English *rudu* rel. to RED *adjective, noun*. Cf. RUDDY.]
1 Red, redness; ruddiness. OE.
2 Facial complexion, esp. when reddish or ruddy. OE.
3 †**a** A red cosmetic. Only in OE. ▸**b** = RUDDLE *noun*^{1}. M17.

rud /rʌd/ *noun*^{2}. *obsolete* exc. *dial.* Also **ruds** /rʌdz/, pl. same. LME.
[Origin unkn.]
Pot marigold, *Calendula officinalis*.

rud /rʌd/ *verb trans.* Infl. **-dd-.** ME.
[Rel. to RUD *noun*^{1}, RUDDY.]
†**1** Make red or ruddy. ME–L17.
2 = RUDDLE *verb. dial.* L17.

rudaceous /rʊˈdeɪʃəs/ *adjective.* E20.
[from Latin *rudus* rubble + -ACEOUS.]
GEOLOGY. Of a rock: composed of larger grains than is an arenaceous rock.

rudas /ˈruːdəs/ *noun & adjective. Scot.* E18.
[Origin unkn.]
▶ **A** *noun.* An ill-natured or cantankerous woman; a hag. E18.
▶ **B** *adjective.* Esp. of a woman: cantankerous, resembling or like a hag. E19.

rudbeckia /rʌdˈbɛkɪə, ruːd-/ *noun.* M18.
[mod. Latin (see below), from Olaf *Rudbeck* (1660–1740), Swedish botanist + -IA[1].]
Any of various tall plants constituting the genus *Rudbeckia* of the composite family, native to N. America and much grown for ornament, which bear yellow or orange flowers with a prominent conical dark-coloured disc, and include black-eyed Susan, *R. hirta*, and various coneflowers.

rudd /rʌd/ *noun*[1]. E16.
[App. from RUD *noun*[1].]
A European freshwater fish of the carp family, *Scardinius erythrophthalmus*, resembling the roach but with redder fins and a golden iris.

Rudd /rʌd/ *noun*[2]. L18.
[Perh. from Margaret Caroline *Rudd* (d. 1779), famous courtesan for whom it may have been invented.]
Chiefly *Hist.* An elaborately fitted lady's dressing-table of a kind fashionable in the late 18th cent. Also more fully ***Rudd table***.

rudder /ˈrʌdə/ *noun & verb.*
[Old English *rōþer* = Old Frisian *rōther*, Middle Low German, Middle Dutch *rōder* (Dutch *roer*), Old High German *ruodar* (German *Ruder*), from West Germanic, rel. to ROW *verb*[1].]
▶ **A** *noun.* †**1** A paddle; an oar. OE–E17.
2 A broad flat piece of wood or metal, hinged vertically to the stern of a boat or ship and pivoted by means of a tiller or wheel to steer the vessel. ME. ▸**b** A similar device used to steer an aircraft; now *esp.* a vertical aerofoil pivoted on its leading edge from the tailplane by means of a pedal or bar. E19. ▸**c** The use of a rudder; the extent to which a rudder is or may be turned. E20.
3 *fig.* A person who or thing which guides or directs; a guiding principle or rule. LME.
4 BREWING. A paddle for stirring malt in a mash-tub. LME.
5 The tail of an otter. E20.

🕮 **2c** D. GARNETT I overbanked and didn't use enough rudder.

Comb.: **rudder-bar** a foot-operated bar which controls an aircraft rudder; **rudder-bird**, **rudder-duck** = RUDDY *duck*. **rudder-fish** (chiefly *US*) any of various perciform marine fishes which often follow vessels; *esp.* (**a**) a fish of the sea chub family Kyphosidae, esp. *Kyphosus sectatrix*; (**b**) the pilot-fish, *Naucrates ductor*; (**c**) any of several stromateoid fishes, esp. the barrel-fish (more fully ***black rudder-fish***) and the medusa-fish (more fully ***brown rudder-fish***); (**d**) (in full ***banded rudder-fish***) a bluish carangid fish, *Seriola zonata*.
▶ **B** *verb trans. & intrans.* Steer by means of a rudder. M19.

🕮 N. SHUTE He glanced quickly at the cruiser to check the direction, ruddering slightly to maintain his course. C. A. LINDBERGH I rudder the *Spirit of St. Louis* back on course.

■ **ruddered** *adjective* provided with a rudder; steered by means of a rudder: M19. **rudderless** *adjective* E17.

ruddervator /ˈrʌdəveɪtə/ *noun.* M20.
[from RUDDER + ELE)VATOR.]
A control surface on an aircraft designed to act as both rudder and elevator.

ruddle /ˈrʌd(ə)l/ *noun*[1] *& verb.* Also (earlier) †**rod-**. LME.
[Rel. to RUD *noun*[1], *verb*: see -LE[1]. Cf. RADDLE *noun*[1] *& verb*[1], REDDLE *noun*.]
▶ **A** *noun.* Red ochre used as a colouring, esp. for marking sheep. LME.
▶ **B** *verb trans.* Mark or colour (as) with ruddle. Usu. in *pass.* E18.
Comb.: **ruddleman** a digger of or dealer in ruddle.

ruddle /ˈrʌd(ə)l/ *noun*[2]. Long *dial.* L16.
[Var.]
= RIDDLE *noun*[2] 1.

ruddock /ˈrʌdək/ *noun.*
[Old English *rudduc* rel. to RUD *noun*[1], RUDDY *adjective*: see -OCK.]
1 The robin. Now *dial.* OE.
†**2** A gold coin; in *pl.*, gold, money. *slang.* M16–E17.
†**3** A toad. M17–M18.

ruddy /ˈrʌdi/ *adjective*[1], *noun, verb, & adverb.*
[Late Old English *rudig* from base of RUD *noun*[1]: see -Y[1].]
▶ **A** *adjective.* **1** Of the face, complexion, etc.: naturally suffused with red; freshly or healthily red. LOE. ▸**b** Of a person: having such a complexion. ME. ▸**c** Characterized by or producing such a complexion or colouring. E19.
2 *gen.* Red; suffused or tinged with red; reddish. LME.
3 Bloody, cursed. *colloq.* E20.

🕮 **1** QUILLER-COUCH A sharp ruddy face like a frozen pippin. F. PARTRIDGE With the ruddy cheeks of a gardener. **b** P. FARMER A white-haired yet ruddy and vigorous woman. **c** J. L. MOTLEY A figure . . instinct with ruddy vigorous life. **2** P. D. JAMES In the ruddy glow of the flames his whole body gleamed. **3** D. BOGARDE Quoted the ruddy *Oxford Dictionary* at us.

Special collocations: **ruddy duck** a New World stiff-tail duck, *Oxyura jamaicensis*, the breeding males of which have deep red-brown plumage with white cheeks and a blue bill. **ruddy goose** = ***ruddy shelduck*** below. **ruddy plover** *US & dial.* the sanderling, *esp.* the male in summer plumage. **ruddy sheldrake**, **ruddy shelduck** a shelduck, *Tadorna ferruginea*, with an orange-chestnut body, found from SE Europe to central Asia. **ruddy turnstone** the New World race of the common turnstone, breeding on the Arctic coastal tundra.
▶ **B** *noun.* Ruddiness, esp. in facial complexion. *arch.* ME.
▶ **C** *verb trans.* & (*rare*) *intrans.* Make or become ruddy; redden. L17.
▶ **D** *adverb.* Bloody, cursed(ly). *colloq.* E20.

🕮 H. WOUK The Jerries are fine pilots and ruddy good shots.

■ **ruddily** *adverb* E19. **ruddiness** *noun* LME.

rude /ruːd/ *adjective, noun, & adverb.* ME.
[Old & mod. French from Latin *rudis* unworked, uncultivated, (orig. used of handicraft etc.), rel. to *rudus* broken stone (cf. RUDERA). Cf. ROID.]
▶ **A** *adjective.* **I 1** Uneducated, unlearned; ignorant; characterized by ignorance or lack of learning. ME.
2 Uncultured, unrefined, unsophisticated; characterized by lack of culture or sophistication. Also, uncivilized, primitive. ME.
3 Inexperienced; inexpert, unskilled. Also foll. by *in*, †*of*. Now *arch. rare.* LME.
4 Ill-mannered, impolite; offensive or discourteous, esp. intentionally. LME. ▸**b** Indecent, lewd; dirty. *colloq.* M20.
5 Rough, harsh; ungentle, unkind; characterized by rough or violent behaviour. Now also, abrupt, startling, sudden. LME. ▸**b** Of a sound: discordant, harsh, unmusical. *literary.* LME.
6 a Of weather, the sea, etc.: turbulent, rough. LME. ▸**b** Of health: robust, vigorous. L18.

🕮 **3** D. L. SAYERS If it's not a rude question, who's paying you, Biggy? JOAN SMITH How rude of me, I should have offered you some tea or coffee. **b *rude joke***, ***rude picture***, ***rude word***, etc. **4** BYRON Hands more rude than wintry sky. M. PATTISON We have lately had some rude reminders.

▶ **II 7** Roughly made or done; lacking finish or accuracy; coarse, inelegant; imperfect. ME. ▸**b** Of appearance: large and coarse or inelegant; rugged. LME.
8 In a natural or original state; lacking shape or order. Now *spec.* (**a**) (of natural material) crude, raw, untreated; (**b**) (of landscape etc.) uncultivated, wild. LME. ▸**b** In an early or primitive state of development. E17.
†**9** Of cost or expenses: large in amount. *Scot.* L15–M16.

🕮 **7** CONAN DOYLE He had been scribbling in a rude schoolboy hand. J. REED These were rude boxes, made of unplaned wood and daubed with crimson. **8** WORDSWORTH Three pillars of rude stone. S. LEACOCK The rude grass and the roots that Nature furnishes. **b** B. JOWETT He has traced the growth of states from their rude beginning.

Special collocations: **rude awakening** a sudden and severe disillusionment or arousal from complacency. **rude boy** *colloq.* (**a**) a young unemployed black man inhabiting the poorer areas of Jamaica; (**b**) a young person with an enthusiasm for ska or reggae music and an unconventional style of smart dress.
▶ **B** *noun.* **1 a** *collect. pl.* The class of rude people, the ignorant or unsophisticated. LME. ▸**b** A rude or unsophisticated person. *colloq.* M20.
2 = ***rude boy*** above. *colloq.* L20.
▶ **C** *adverb.* In a rude manner; rudely. *rare.* L15.
■ **rudely** *adverb* LME. **rudeness** *noun* LME. **rudery** *noun* (**a**) rudeness, esp. in speech or behaviour; (**b**) an instance of this; a rude remark, joke, etc.: M20. **rudesby** *noun* (*arch.*) an insolent or ill-mannered person M16. **rudie** *noun* (*colloq.*) = ***rude boy*** above M20. **rudish** *adjective* LME.

†**rudera** *noun pl.* E17–L18.
[Latin, pl. of *rudus*: see RUDE *adjective* etc..]
Fragments or ruins of a building.

ruderal /ˈruːd(ə)r(ə)l/ *adjective & noun.* M19.
[formed as prec. + -AL[1].]
BOTANY. ▶**A** *adjective.* Growing on waste ground or among rubbish. M19.
▶ **B** *noun.* A ruderal plant. E20.

ruderate /ˈruːdəreɪt/ *verb trans.* Now *rare.* E17.
[Latin *ruderat-* pa. ppl stem of *ruderare*, from *rudus*: see RUDE *adjective* etc., -ATE[3].]
Pave with broken stone or rubble.
■ **rudeˈration** *noun* M18.

Rudesheimer /ˈruːdəshʌɪmə/ *noun.* L18.
[German *Rüdesheimer*, from *Rüdesheim*: see below.]
A fine white wine produced in the area of Rüdesheim, a town on the Rhine in Germany.

rudiment /ˈruːdɪm(ə)nt/ *noun.* M16.
[French, or Latin *rudimentum*, from *rudis* RUDE *adjective*, after *elementum* ELEMENT *noun*.]
1 In *pl.* *The* first principles or elements of a subject; *the* basic knowledge or skills required before further progress in a subject is possible. Usu. foll. by *of*. M16. ▸**b** A first or basic principle. *rare.* M16. ▸**c** (Usu. **R-**.) In *pl.* (The name of) a class in a Roman Catholic school, college, or seminary, now only *spec.* the third class, immediately above Figures and below Grammar, in certain Jesuit schools. E18.
2 In *pl.* *The* imperfect beginnings of something; *the* preliminary stages; *the* foundations. Usu. foll. by *of*. M16.
3 A preliminary stage; an undeveloped or immature form; *spec.* in BIOLOGY, the earliest identifiable structure in an embryo which will develop into an organ, limb, leaf, etc. E17.

🕮 **1** E. WAUGH Lessons in the rudiments of theology. P. AUSTER Victor learned some of the rudiments of speech, but he never progressed. **2** R. L. STEVENSON The rudiments of a notion of the rules of health. P. V. WHITE Mother . . hadn't the rudiments of a religious faith.

■ **rudiˈmental** *adjective* = RUDIMENTARY L16.

rudimentary /ruːdɪˈmɛnt(ə)ri/ *adjective.* M19.
[from RUDIMENT + -ARY[1].]
1 Of or pertaining to basic principles; fundamental; *esp.* (of knowledge, teaching, etc.) limited to the rudiments of a subject. M19.
2 Of, pertaining to, or constituting a preliminary stage or form; undeveloped, immature. M19.

🕮 **1** R. MACAULAY A little conversation in . . my rudimentary Greek. **2** D. ACHESON Prior to the Second World War the United States had the most rudimentary foreign intelligence service.

■ **rudimentarily** *adverb* L20. **rudimentariness** *noun* L19.

rudist /ˈruːdɪst/ *noun & adjective.* Orig. in mod. Latin form †**Rudista**, pl. **-stae**. L19.
[mod. Latin *Rudista* former family name, from Latin *rudis* RUDE *adjective*: see -IST.]
PALAEONTOLOGY. ▶**A** *noun.* Any of various cone-shaped fossil bivalve molluscs of the superfamily Rudistacea, which formed colonies resembling reefs in the Cretaceous period. L19.
▶ **B** *adjective.* Of, pertaining to, or designating the Rudistacea. L20.
■ Also **ruˈdistid** *adjective & noun* E20.

rudite /ˈruːdʌɪt/ *noun.* E20.
[from Latin *rudus*: see RUDE *adjective* etc., -ITE[1].]
GEOLOGY. A consolidated sedimentary rock, esp. breccia or conglomerate, consisting of particles coarser than sand grains. Cf. PSEPHITE.

Rudolphine /rʊˈdɒlfʌɪn/ *adjective.* M17.
[from *Rudolph* II (1552–1612), Holy Roman Emperor + -INE[1].]
Designating (in ***Rudolphine tables***, ***Rudolphine numbers***) a series of astronomical calculations published by Kepler (of whom Rudolph II was patron).

ruds *noun* var. of RUD *noun*[2].

rue /ruː/ *noun*[1]. Now *arch.* exc. *Scot.*
[Old English *hrēow* = Middle Low German, Middle Dutch *rouwe*, Dutch *rouw*, Old High German *(h)riuwa* (German *Reue*), rel. to RUE *verb*.]
1 Repentance, regret; sorrow, dejection. OE.
2 Pity, compassion. ME.

🕮 **1** A. E. HOUSMAN With rue my heart is laden For golden friends I had. **take the rue** *Scot.* repent; take offence.

rue /ruː/ *noun*[2]. ME.
[Old & mod. French from Latin *ruta* from Greek *rhutē*.]
1 Any of various Mediterranean dwarf shrubs constituting the genus *Ruta* (family Rutaceae), with bipinnate or tripinnate glaucous leaves and yellow flowers; *esp.* the bitter aromatic herb *R. graveolens*, formerly much used in medicine. ME.
2 With specifying word: any of various plants of other genera and families resembling rue in some way, esp. in having much-divided leaves. M16.
2 *goat's rue*, ***meadow-rue***, ***wall rue***, etc.

rue /ruː/ *verb.* Pres. pple **rueing**, **ruing**.
[Old English *hrēowan* = Old Frisian *hriōwa*, Old Saxon *hreuwan* (Dutch *rouwen*), Old High German *(h)riuwan* (German *reuen*), from Germanic.]
▶†**I 1** *verb trans.* Cause (a person) to repent of sin or wrongdoing. OE–LME.
2 *verb trans.* Cause (a person) to regret a past action, *that*, etc. OE–LME.
3 *verb trans.* Cause to feel sorrow or distress; grieve. OE–M16.
4 *verb trans.* Cause to feel pity or compassion. ME–L16.
▶ **II 5** *verb trans. & intrans.* Repent of (sin or wrongdoing); feel contrition (for). ME.
6 a *verb trans.* Regret or repent of (a past action), esp. because of its consequences; wish (a past action) undone or altered. ME. ▸**b** *verb intrans.* Feel regret or dissatisfac-

tion at a past action; repent of or *of* a promise or contract made (chiefly *Scot.*). ME.

7 *verb trans. & intrans.* Feel sorrow or distress at (a past event, fact, etc.), esp. because of consequent suffering; lament (of). ME.

8 a *verb intrans.* Feel pity or compassion. Usu. foll. by †*of, on, upon. arch.* exc. *Scot.* ME. ▸†**b** *verb trans.* Feel pity or compassion for. ME–E17.

📖 **5** SIR W. SCOTT Conscience, anticipating time, Already rues the enacted crime. **6a** G. P. R. JAMES If they hurt a hair of his head they shall rue it. L. M. MONTGOMERY Mark my words . . Marilla Cuthbert'll live to rue the step she's took. **b** P. THOMPSON Avoid green gooseberries, or you will have cause to rue. **7** T. HOOD I promis'd myself an hour should come To make him rue his birth. **8a** R. BURNS Rue on thy despairing lover!

Phrases: **rue the day**, **rue the hour**, etc., regret or lament the action of a particular day, hour, etc., because of its consequences.

rueful /ˈruːfʊl, -f(ə)l/ *adjective.* ME.
[from RUE *noun*¹ + -FUL.]

1 Exciting sorrow or compassion; pitiable, lamentable. ME.

†**2** Full of pity or compassion. Only in ME.

3 Expressing or accompanied by sorrow or regret; remorseful; doleful. ME.

📖 **1** *Manchester Weekly Times* In a rueful plight, crushed by a great defeat. **3** W. STYRON We parted . . in a spirit of grave though rueful affection. P. LIVELY He turned on her a rueful expression . . like a boy caught out in a misdemeanour.

■ **ruefully** *adverb* ME. **ruefulness** *noun* L16.

rueing *verb pres. pple*: see RUE *verb.*

ruelle /ryɛl (*pl. same*), ˈruːɛl/ *noun.* LME.
[Old & mod. French = lane, dim. of *rue* street.]

1 The space between a bed and the wall; the part of a bed next the wall. LME.

2 Chiefly *Hist.* A ladies' bedroom used to hold fashionable morning receptions, esp. in 17th and 18th cent. France. Also, a reception held in such a room. L17.

3 In France and French-speaking countries: a small street; a lane, an alley. E20.

ruellia /rʊˈɛlɪə/ *noun.* M18.
[mod. Latin (see below), from Jean *Ruel* (1479–1539), French botanist + -IA¹.]

Any of various plants with trumpet-shaped flowers constituting the genus *Ruellia* (family Acanthaceae), of tropical America and including several grown for ornament.

Rueping process /ˈruːpɪŋ ˌprəʊsɛs/ *noun phr.* E20.
[from Max *Rueping* (fl. 1902), German timber engineer.]

A method of preserving wood by applying creosote to it after subjecting it to high air pressure.

Rufai /rʊˈfɑːiː/ *noun.* Pl. same, -S. M19.
[Turkish *rūfai* from Arab. *rifāʿī* from Aḥmad al-*Rifāʿī* founder of the order d. 1183.]

A dervish belonging to an order practising the repeated calling out of chants to induce trance etc. Also called ***howling dervish***.

rufescent /rʊˈfɛs(ə)nt/ *adjective.* E19.
[Latin *rufescent-* pres. ppl stem of *rufescere*, from *rufus* reddish: see -ESCENT.]

Of a somewhat reddish or rufous colour.

ruff /rʌf/ *noun*¹. Also †**ruffe**. E16.
[Prob. use as noun of var. of ROUGH *adjective.* Cf. earlier RUFFE *noun*².]

†**1** A ruffle or frill around a garment sleeve. E16–M17.

2 A decorative frill worn around the neck; *esp.* a projecting frill of fluted and starched linen etc. fashionable in the Elizabethan and Jacobean periods. M16. ▸**b** A fringe of fur round the hood or along the edges of a jacket or parka. *N. Amer.* E20.

3 *transf.* A projecting ring of some material resembling a ruff; *spec.* a projecting or distinctively coloured ring of feathers or hair round a bird's or animal's neck. L16.

4 A Eurasian bird of the sandpiper family, *Philomachus pugnax*; *esp.* the male, which has a large ruff and ear-tufts in the breeding season. Cf. REE *noun*¹, REEVE *noun*². M17.

5 A variety of the domestic pigeon resembling the jacobin. M18.

ruff /rʌf/ *noun*². L16.
[Old French *roffle, rouffle*, earlier *ronfle, romfle*, corresp. to Italian *ronfa*, perh. alt. of *trionfo* TRUMP *noun*².]

†**1** A card-game resembling whist. L16–L17.

†**2** A trump card or suit. Only in 17.

3 The action or an act of trumping a card, suit, etc. M19.

3 ruff and discard *BRIDGE* the winning of a trick by ruffing in one hand while discarding a loser from the other.

ruff /rʌf/ *noun*³. L17.
[Perh. imit. Cf. RUFFLE *noun*⁴.]
= RUFFLE *noun*⁴.

ruff *noun*⁴ see RUFFE *noun*¹.

†**ruff** *adjective* var. of ROUGH *adjective & adverb.*

ruff /rʌf/ *verb*¹ *trans.* M16.
[Perh. from RUFF *noun*¹. Cf. RUFFLE *verb*¹.]

1 Form (material etc.) into a ruff or ruffs; provide with a ruff or ruffs. Chiefly as RUFFED *adjective.* Now *rare.* M16.

2 = RUFFLE *verb*¹ 2. Long *obsolete* exc. *Scot.* L16.

†**3** *FALCONRY.* Of a hawk: strike at without securing (a quarry). L16–M17.

ruff /rʌf/ *verb*². L16.
[Rel. to RUFF *noun*².]

CARDS. **1** *verb intrans.* Play a trump, trump a card, suit, etc. Formerly also, draw one or more cards from a stock while discarding in exchange. L16.

2 *verb trans.* Lay a trump on, trump (a card, suit, etc.). M18.

2 ruff out *BRIDGE* defeat (a card or suit) by trumping, so as to establish master cards in the suit led.

■ **ruffer** *noun* a card that ruffs or trumps another E17.

†**ruff-coat** *noun.* M17–M19.
[Prob. formed as RUFF *noun*¹ + COAT *noun.*]

ANGLING. The caddis-fly larva in its case.

ruffe /rʌf/ *noun*¹. Also (the only form in senses 3, 4) **ruff**. LME.
[formed as RUFF *noun*¹.]

†**1** A sea bream. LME–M17.

2 A small Eurasian freshwater fish, *Gymnocephalus cernua*, of the perch family, olive-brown in colour with dark spots and rough prickly scales. LME.

3 An Australian marine food fish, *Arripis georgianus*, of the family Arripididae. L19.

4 Either of two marine butterfishes of the genus *Centrolophus*. Also, the pumpkinseed. *US.* M20.

†**ruffe** *noun*² var. of RUFF *noun*¹.

ruffed /rʌft/ *adjective.* L16.
[from RUFF *noun*¹, *verb*¹: see -ED², -ED¹.]

1 Wearing a ruff; provided with a ruff or ruffs. L16.

2 Of an animal, bird, etc.: having thick or raised feathers, fur, scales, etc., around the neck like a ruff; having markings suggestive of a ruff. L18.

2 ruffed bustard the houbara. **ruffed grouse** a N. American woodland grouse, *Bonasa umbellus*, which has a black ruff on the sides of the neck. **ruffed lemur** the largest lemur, *Varecia variegata*, varying from black and white to deep red in colour.

ruffian /ˈrʌfɪən/ *noun, adjective, & verb.* L15.
[Old & mod. French *ruffian, rufian* (mod. also *rufien*), from Italian *ruffiano*, prob. from dial. *rofia* scab, scurf, from Germanic (whence also Old High German *ruf* scurf).]

▶ **A** *noun.* **1** A violent lawless person; a rough, a rowdy. L15.

†**2** A dissolute person; *esp.* one distinguished as such by dress or appearance. M16–L17.

†**3** A prostitute's pimp. M16–M17.

▶ **B** *adjective.* Of or pertaining to a ruffian or ruffians; having the character or appearance of a ruffian. M16.

▶ **C** *verb intrans. &* †*trans.* (with *it*). Behave like a ruffian; *poet.* (of wind etc.) rage, bluster. M16.

■ **ruffianage** *noun* (*rare*) = RUFFIANISM M19. **ruffiandom** *noun* the domain of ruffians; ruffians collectively: L19. **ruffianish** *adjective* (*rare*) = RUFFIANLY L16. **ruffianism** *noun* (**a**) the conduct characteristic of a ruffian or ruffians; violence, lawlessness; (**b**) ruffians collectively: L16. **ruffianize** *verb* †(**a**) *verb intrans.* pimp; (**b**) *verb trans.* make ruffian in character or appearance: L16. **ruffian-like** *adjective & adverb* (**a**) *adjective* = RUFFIANLY; (**b**) *adverb* (*rare*) in the manner or a ruffian or ruffians: M16. **ruffianly** *adjective* (**a**) having the character or appearance of a ruffian; (**b**) characteristic of or appropriate to a ruffian or ruffians: L16.

†**ruffin** *noun.* L16–E17.
[from RUFFE *noun*¹, with obscure ending.]
= RUFFE *noun*¹ 1.

Ruffini /rʊˈfiːni/ *noun.* E20.
[Angelo *Ruffini* (1864–1929), Italian anatomist.]

ANATOMY. Used **attrib.** and with *of* to designate certain dermal sensory organs.

ruffle /ˈrʌf(ə)l/ *noun*¹. E16.
[from RUFFLE *verb*¹.]

▶ **I** †**1 a** Impairment *of* one's reputation. *rare.* Only in E16. ▸**b** Disorder, confusion. (Not always clearly distinguishable from RUFFLE *noun*².) M16–E18.

2 A state of mental or emotional disturbance; agitation, perturbation, an instance of this. E18. ▸**b** A disturbing or annoying experience or encounter; annoyance, vexation, a cause of this. E18.

3 A break or change in the smoothness or evenness of something; a fold or wrinkle produced by ruffling. E18.

4 The action of ruffling cards. L19.

📖 **3** A. JESSOPP Never . . a ruffle on the gently heaving water.

▶ **II** †**5** A loose fold or turned-down top of a high-topped boot. Only in L16.

6 A strip of lace etc. gathered along one edge to make an ornamental frill, esp. for the wrist or neck of a garment; a fold of material gathered for decoration (usu. in *pl.*). L17. ▸†**b** In *pl.* Handcuffs. *slang.* L18–E20. ▸**c** An object resembling a ruffle; *esp.* the ruff of a bird. M19.

📖 **3** J. TROLLOPE There was . . Lady Unwin, swimming forwards in a tide of green silk ruffles.

Comb.: **ruffle shirt** *N. Amer.* (**a**) a shirt decorated with ruffles; (**b**) *transf.* an aristocrat, a wealthy person.

■ **ruffly** *adjective* (*rare*) slightly ruffled or curled; having a ruffle or ruffles: L19.

ruffle /ˈrʌf(ə)l/ *noun*². *arch.* M16.
[from RUFFLE *verb*².]

1 A disturbance or tumult; a fight, a skirmish; a dispute. M16.

†**2** Ostentation; display. *rare.* L16–L17.

ruffle /ˈrʌf(ə)l/ *noun*³. *rare.* E17.
[Prob. rel. to RUFFE *noun*¹: cf. -LE¹.]

A sea bream. Cf. RUFFE *noun*¹ 1.

ruffle /ˈrʌf(ə)l/ *noun*⁴. E19.
[from RUFFLE *verb*³.]

A rapid vibrating drum beat.

ruffle /ˈrʌf(ə)l/ *verb*¹. ME.
[Origin unkn. Cf. RAFFLE *verb*², RIFFLE *verb.*]

1 *verb trans.* Disturb the smoothness or evenness of; spoil the neat arrangement of; cause to form or fall into folds or wrinkles. Formerly also, crease, crumple. ME. ▸**b** Roughen (skin etc.) by abrasion. E17. ▸**c** *verb trans.* Gather into a ruffle or ruffles; trim with ruffles. Usu. in *pass.* M17.

2 *verb trans.* Disorder or disarrange (hair or feathers); cause to stick up or out irregularly. LME. ▸**b** Of a bird: erect (the feathers) in anger, display, etc. Also foll. by *up*. M17.

†**3** *verb trans.* Throw into disarray or confusion, tangle, ravel. LME–M17. ▸**b** Involve in obscurity or perplexity, confuse or bewilder (a person). LME–L17.

†**4** *verb intrans.* Search through something, ransack. Also foll. by *up. rare.* LME–L16.

†**5** *verb trans.* Fold, bundle, or heap *up* together carelessly. M16–M17.

6 *verb intrans.* Rise and fall irregularly; form or fall into folds; flutter in this manner. L16.

7 †**a** *verb trans.* Stir *up* to indignation. *rare* (Shakes.). Only in E17. ▸**b** *verb trans.* Annoy, vex, discompose, disturb; make angry, irritated, etc. M17. ▸**c** *verb intrans.* Be or become ruffled. E18.

8 *verb trans.* Turn over (the pages of a book, etc.) hurriedly, riffle (cards). E17.

📖 **1** R. L. STEVENSON The sea breeze was . . ruffling the . . surface of the anchorage. B. CHATWIN A . . breeze ruffled the net curtains. **2** P. G. WODEHOUSE She ruffled his hair lightly with . . her fingers. **7b** CONAN DOYLE Holmes had . . ruffled our visitor whose chubby face had assumed a . . less amiable expression. *Astrology* Soothe people whose feelings you have ruffled.

■ **ruffler** *noun*¹ an attachment to a sewing-machine, for making ruffles L19.

ruffle /ˈrʌf(ə)l/ *verb*². *arch.* LME.
[Origin unkn.]

1 *verb intrans.* Contend or struggle *with*; do battle *for*. LME.

2 *verb intrans. & trans.* (with *it*). Behave with conspicuous arrogance, boastfulness, etc.; make a great display; swagger. LME. ▸**b** *verb intrans.* Of wind, water, etc.: be turbulent, swirl, rage. L16.

†**3** *verb trans.* Handle roughly; attack, beat; bully. LME–E18. ▸**b** Kiss, embrace, or touch (a woman) without consent. E17–E18. ▸**c** Take or snatch rudely or roughly. E17–E18.

■ **ruffler** *noun*² (**a**) a boastful, swaggering, or arrogant person; †(**b**) a vagrant or vagabond, *esp.* one posing as an injured war veteran: M16.

ruffle /ˈrʌf(ə)l/ *verb*³ *intrans.* Chiefly *Scot.* Long *rare* or *obsolete.* E18.
[Perh. imit. Cf. RUFFLE *noun*⁴.]

Of a drum: sound a rapid vibrating beat.

ruffled /ˈrʌf(ə)ld/ *adjective.* M16.
[from RUFFLE *noun*¹, *verb*¹: see -ED², -ED¹.]

That has been ruffled; having or decorated with a ruffle or ruffles.

📖 V. GORNICK To . . mollify her ruffled spirits. A. LURIE Her ruffled pink flannel nightgown. ***smooth a person's ruffled feathers***: see FEATHER *noun.*

Rufflette /ˈrʌflɛt/ *noun.* Also **r-**. M20.
[from RUFFLE *noun*¹ + -ETTE.]

(Proprietary name for) a kind of facing tape threaded with cord to be sewn to the top of a curtain, enabling the tape and curtain to be gathered into ruffles when the curtain is drawn back.

ruffling /ˈrʌflɪŋ/ *noun.* LME.
[from RUFFLE *noun*¹, *verb*¹: see -ING¹.]

The action of RUFFLE *verb*¹, an instance of this, the result of this. Also, lace or other material used for making ruffles.

ruffy /ˈrʌfi/ *noun. Scot.* Also **roughy**. L18.
[Origin unkn.]

A torch made of wood or rags; a firebrand.

rufiyaa /ˈruːfiːjɑː/ *noun.* Pl. same. **L20.**
[Sinhalese (Maldivian), from (the same root as) RUPEE.]
The basic monetary unit of the Maldives, equal to one hundred laris.

rufo- /ˈruːfəʊ/ *combining form.*
[from Latin *rufus* red: see -O-.]
BOTANY & ZOOLOGY. Forming adjectives denoting colour, with the sense 'rufous and —', as ***rufo-fulvous***.

rufous /ˈruːfəs/ *adjective & noun.* **L18.**
[from Latin *rufus* red, reddish + -OUS.]
▶ **A** *adjective.* Reddish-brown; rust-coloured. **L18.** ***rufous hornero***, ***rufous scrub-bird***, ***rufous whistler***, etc.
▶ **B** *noun.* **1** A reddish-brown colour. **L18.**
2 Either of two reddish-brown moths, the geometrid *Coenocalpe lapidata* (more fully ***slender-striped rufous***), and the noctuid *Coenobia rufa* (more fully ***small rufous***). **M19.**

rufter-hood /ˈrʌftəhʊd/ *noun.* **L16.**
[from unkn. 1st elem. + HOOD *noun*¹.]
FALCONRY. A type of hood used for a newly captured hawk.

rug /rʌɡ/ *noun*¹. *Scot.* **LME.**
[from RUG *verb*¹.]
1 A pull, a tug. **LME.**
2 A (torn-off) portion *of* something; a catch, an acquisition. **LME.**

rug /rʌɡ/ *noun*². **M16.**
[Prob. of Scandinavian origin and rel. to RAG *noun*¹. Cf. Norwegian dial. *rugga* coverlet, Swedish *rugg* ruffled hair.]
†**1** A type of frieze or coarse woollen cloth; a particular variety of this. Also, a cloak etc. made of this. **M16–E18.**
2 A thick woollen coverlet or wrap, used esp. while travelling. Also, a piece of protective (esp. waterproof) material used as a covering for a horse, dog, etc. **L16.**
3 A piece of thick material, usu. with a deep or shaggy pile or woven in a pattern of colours, or a piece of dressed animal skin, to be placed as a covering or decoration on part of a floor. **E19.** ▸**b** A toupee, a wig. *N. Amer. slang.* **M20.**

> 📖 **2** ***railway rug***, ***travelling rug***, etc. ***New Zealand rug***: see NEW ZEALAND 1. **3** M. HOCKING The floor was stone-flagged with rugs cast about here and there. ***hearthrug***, ***oriental rug***, ***prayer rug***, ***scatter rug***, ***sheepskin rug***, etc. ***Dagestan rug***, ***Kurdistan rug***, ***rya rug***, ***Saraband rug***, etc.

Comb.: **rug brick**: having a rough surface; **rug-cutter** *arch. slang* a dancer, *esp.* an energetic or accomplished one; **rug-cutting** *arch. slang* dancing, esp. of an energetic or accomplished kind; **rug-headed** *adjective* (*rare*) having coarse unkempt hair; **rug-rat** *N. Amer. slang* a child.
Phrases: **cut a rug**, **cut the rug** *slang* (now chiefly *N. Amer.*) dance, esp. in an energetic or accomplished manner. ***pull the rug from under***, ***pull the rug out from under***: see PULL *verb*. ***sweep a thing under the rug***: see SWEEP *verb*.
■ **rugging** *noun* a coarse woollen cloth (cf. RUG *noun*² 1) **M19.**

†**rug** *adjective. slang* (esp. GAMBLING). **L17–M19.**
[Origin unkn.]
Safe, secure.

rug /rʌɡ/ *verb*¹. *Scot. & north.* Infl. **-gg-**. **ME.**
[Prob. of Scandinavian origin. Cf. Norwegian *rugge*, Danish †*rugge* rock (a cradle), sway.]
1 *verb trans.* Pull, tug, or tear (a thing). Also, seize. (Foll. by *down*, *out*, *up*, etc.) **ME.**
2 *verb intrans.* Pull or tear (*at*); struggle. **ME.**

rug /rʌɡ/ *verb*² *trans.* Infl. **-gg-**. **E19.**
[from RUG *noun*².]
Cover (*up*) with a rug.

ruga /ˈruːɡə/ *noun.* Pl. **rugae** /ˈruːdʒiː/. **L18.**
[Latin.]
Chiefly ANATOMY, BOTANY, & ZOOLOGY. A wrinkle, a fold, a ridge. Usu. in *pl.*
■ **rugal** *adjective* = RUGOSE *adjective* **M20.** **rugate** *adjective* = RUGOSE *adjective* **M19.** **rugately** *adverb* rugosely **M19.**

rugby /ˈrʌɡbi/ *noun.* Also **R-**. **M19.**
[*Rugby*, English public school in Warwickshire.]
1 A form of football, in which points are scored by carrying (and grounding) an elliptical ball across the opponents' goal-line or by kicking it between the two posts and over the crossbar of the opponents' goal. Also ***rugby football***. **M19.**
2 ***Rugby fives***, a form of fives played with the gloved hands between two or four players in a four-walled court. **L19.**
Comb.: ***Rugby fives***: see sense 2 above. ***rugby football***: see sense 1 above. **Rugby League** an association of rugby football clubs formed in 1922 (formerly called Northern Union); rugby played according to Rugby League rules, with a team of 13; **rugby tackle**: in which the arms are used to bring an opposing player down, as in rugby football; **Rugby Union** an association of rugby football clubs formed in 1871; rugby played according to Rugby Union rules, with a team of 15.
■ **Rugbeian** /-ˈbiːən/ *noun* a person educated at Rugby School **E18.**

†**ruge** *noun. rare.* **LME–L18.**
[Latin RUGA.]
A wrinkle, a fold.

†**ruge** *verb trans. & intrans. rare.* **L17–L19.**
[Latin *rugare*, formed as prec.]
Make or become wrinkled.

rugged /ˈrʌɡɪd/ *adjective.* **ME.**
[Prob. of Scandinavian origin. Cf. RUG *noun*², Swedish *rugga* roughen.]
†**1** Hairy, shaggy; (of a horse) rough-coated. Cf. RAGGED *adjective* 1. **ME–E18.** ▸**b** Of cloth etc.: woven with a rough surface. **M16–E19.**
2 Having irregular projections, broken into irregular prominences; (of the ground) broken, uneven, rough. **M16.** ▸**b** (Of the face etc.) wrinkled, furrowed; frowning; (of the features) irregular, strongly marked. **L16.**
3 a Of weather etc.: rough, stormy, tempestuous. Now *rare.* **M16.** ▸**b** Involving great effort, hardship, etc.; difficult. **M18.**
4 Rough or harsh in sound. **L16.**
5 Of a person, character, etc.: austere, severe, not gentle. **L16.**
6 Uncultured, unsophisticated; unrefined; undeveloped. **E17.**
7 Strong, sturdy; robust, vigorous. **M18.** ▸**b** Of a machine etc.: strongly constructed, capable of withstanding rough usage. **E20.**

> 📖 **2** W. ROBERTSON Clambering up the rugged track with infinite fatigue. W. BLACK The curious convolutions of this rugged coast. **b** P. D. JAMES The rugged, weatherbeaten face, with its look of . . fortitude. **3b** J. PATTINSON If things get really rugged I just put the bite on my old man. **6** *Taste* A simple meal with rugged wine or beer. **7** SIR W. SCOTT Rugged foresters of the old . . breed. S. NAIPAUL The rugged individualism of the frontiersmen. **b** *Australian Financial Review* A rugged all-metal . . die-cast body.

■ **ruggediˈzation** *noun* the action or process of making something rugged **M20.** **ruggedized** *adjective* made rugged **M20.** **ruggedly** *adverb* **LME.** **ruggedness** *noun* **M16.**

rugger /ˈrʌɡə/ *noun*¹. *arch.* **LME.**
[from RUG *verb*¹ + -ER¹.]
A plunderer, a robber.

rugger /ˈrʌɡə/ *noun*². *colloq.* **L19.**
[from RUGBY: see -ER⁶.]
Rugby football.
Comb.: **rugger bugger** *slang* (orig. *S. Afr.*) a rugby player or fan, esp. a boorish or boisterous one.

ruggle /ˈrʌɡ(ə)l/ *noun. obsolete* exc. *dial.* **L16.**
[Origin unkn.]
A plaything, a toy.

ruggy /ˈrʌɡi/ *adjective.* Now *dial.* **LME.**
[Alt. of RUGGED *adjective*: see -Y¹.]
Rugged, rough; wild, stormy.

Rugian /ˈruːdʒɪən/ *noun & adjective.* **E17.**
[from Latin *Rugii* Rugians + -AN.]
▶ **A** *noun.* A member of an ancient Germanic tribe; the East Germanic language of this tribe. **E17.**
▶ **B** *adjective.* Of or pertaining to the Rugians or their language. **L19.**

†**rugine** *noun.* **LME–M18.**
[French from medieval Latin *rugina*, prob. alt. of Latin *runcina* plane.]
A surgeon's rasp.

rugosa /ruːˈɡəʊzə/ *noun.* **L19.**
[Latin, fem. of *rugosus* (see next), used as a specific epithet.]
The Japanese or ramanas rose, *Rosa rugosa*, which has dark green, wrinkled leaves, deep pink flowers, and large orange-red hips; a variety or hybrid of this.

rugose /ruːˈɡəʊs/ *adjective.* **LME.**
[Latin *rugosus*, formed as RUGA: see -OSE¹. In sense 2 from mod. Latin order name *Rugosa* use as noun of neut. pl. of *rugosus*.]
1 BOTANY, ZOOLOGY, & ANATOMY. Marked by rugae; wrinkled, corrugated, ridged. **LME.**
2 Of, pertaining to, or designating a fossil coral of the Palaeozoic order Rugosa, which includes horn-shaped corals with ridged surfaces. **L19.**
1 rugose mosaic a mosaic disease of potatoes marked by esp. strong wrinkling of the leaves.
■ **rugosely** *adverb* **M19.**

rugosity /ruːˈɡɒsɪti/ *noun.* **L16.**
[French *rugosité* or late Latin *rugositas*, formed as prec.: see -ITY.]
1 Chiefly ANATOMY, BOTANY, & ZOOLOGY. The state of being rugose or wrinkled. **L16.**
2 A corrugation, a wrinkle; a slight roughness. Usu. in *pl.* **M17.**

rugous /ˈruːɡəs/ *adjective.* Now *rare.* **E17.**
[formed as RUGOSE: see -OUS.]
= RUGOSE.

rugulose /ˈruːɡjʊləʊs/ *adjective.* **E19.**
[from RUGA + -ULOSE¹.]
Chiefly ZOOLOGY & BOTANY. Having small wrinkles; finely rugose.
■ **rugulosity** /-ˈlɒs-/ *noun* **L19.**

Ruhmkorff coil /ˈruːmkɔːf kɔɪl/ *noun phr. obsolete* exc. *Hist.* **M19.**
[Heinrich Daniel *Ruhmkorff* (1803–77), German-born inventor.]
PHYSICS. A powerful type of induction coil.

ruin /ˈruːɪn/ *noun.* **ME.**
[Old & mod. French *ruine* from Latin *ruina*, from *ruere* fall.]
1 The action on the part of a fabric or structure of giving way and falling down; *esp.* the collapse of a building. Now *rare.* **ME.** ▸**b** The action of falling to the ground or from a height. Long *rare* or *obsolete.* **L15.**
2 The state of a fabric or structure which has given way and fallen down; *esp.* the collapsed condition of a building. **LME.**
3 In *pl.* & (*rare*) *sing.* The remains of a fabric or structure which has given way and fallen down; *esp.* the remains of a decayed and fallen building, town, etc. **LME.**
4 The decay or downfall of a person, society, etc.; complete loss of resources, wealth, or (social) position. **LME.**
5 The condition of a person, society, etc., having suffered decay or downfall; *esp.* the condition of a person reduced to abject poverty. **LME.**
6 A cause of destruction or downfall; a destructive influence or agent. **LME.**
7 Destruction; complete overthrow or devastation (of a person or thing). **LME.**
8 In *pl.* Damage or injury done to a thing. **M16.**
9 A ruined person or thing. **E17.**
10 Gin, esp. of a poor quality. *slang.* **E19.**

> 📖 **1** WORDSWORTH The crash of ruin fitfully resounds. **2** M. W. MONTAGU In a few years they all fall to ruin. **3** *Daily Telegraph* The handsome ruins of Warkworth castle. *Atlantic* Ancient Mayan ruins. **4** A. L. ROWSE Putting it across large sections of the middle classes that Labour's economics meant financial ruin. **6** SIR W. SCOTT By a quarrel you would become the ruin of me. **7** T. GRAY Ruin seize thee, ruthless King! TENNYSON Sword and fire, Red ruin, and the breaking up of laws. **8** J. RAY Secured from all Ruins and Concussions. **9** R. DAVIES His career . . would be a ruin. J. CASEY The old undermined seawall, a ruin for twenty-five years.

Phrases: ***blue ruin***: see BLUE *adjective*. **in ruins** in a state of ruin, completely wrecked; ***lie in ruins***: see LIE *verb*¹. ***mother's ruin***: see MOTHER *noun*¹ & *adjective*.

ruin /ˈruːɪn/ *verb.* **M16.**
[Old & mod. French *ruiner* or medieval Latin *ruinare*, from Latin *ruina*: see prec.]
†**1** *verb trans.* Destroy, extirpate, eradicate; get rid of by a destructive process. **M16–E18.**
2 *verb trans.* Devastate; reduce (a building, town, etc.) to ruins; *fig.* defeat or overthrow (a kingdom, power, etc.) completely. **M16.**
3 *verb trans.* Inflict irredeemable damage or loss on; deprive of resources, wealth, (social) position, etc.; seduce and abandon (a woman). **L16.**
4 *verb trans.* Involve in disaster or failure, make entirely abortive; injure; spoil; wreck completely. **L16.**
5 *verb intrans.* Come to ruin; be damaged, impoverished, outcast, etc.; fail. Long *rare.* **L16.**
6 *verb intrans.* Fall into ruins; decay, crumble; collapse. Now *rare* exc. *poet.* **E17.**

> 📖 **2** EARL OF CHATHAM To have the power of that House reduced, but not . . absolutely ruined. *Examiner* Our batteries continued to ruin the works. **3** W. COWPER To catch renown by ruining mankind. R. MACAULAY I would soon be ruined . . what with the rent and the bills. V. S. PRITCHETT He has almost ruined himself . . to pay for her extravagance. **4** M. E. HERBERT The contents of his pack . . were irretrievably ruined. J. DOS PASSOS Peace would ruin his plans for an American army.

■ **ruinable** *adjective* (*rare*) **E18.** **ruiner** *noun* **L16.**

ruinate /ˈruːɪneɪt/ *adjective.* **M16.**
[medieval Latin *ruinatus* pa. pple, formed as next: see -ATE².]
1 Of a building, town, etc.: ruined, ruinous. **M16.** ▸**b** Of land: exhausted, abandoned. **M19.**
2 Injured; spoiled; wrecked. Now *rare.* **L16.**

ruinate /ˈruːɪneɪt/ *verb.* **M16.**
[medieval Latin *ruinat-* pa. ppl stem of *ruinare*: see RUIN *verb*, -ATE³.]
▶ **I** *verb trans.* **1** = RUIN *verb* 2. **M16.**
2 Impoverish; deprive of resources, status, etc. **M16.**
†**3** = RUIN *verb* 1. **M16–M18.**
4 Damage or change irrevocably; spoil, wreck. *arch.* **L16.**
▶ **II** *verb intrans.* **5** Go or fall to ruin. **M16.**
†**6** Fall with a crash. *rare* (Spenser). Only in **L16.**
■ **ruinated** *adjective* (*a*) (now *rare*) decayed, fallen down, in ruins; †(*b*) impoverished; subverted; brought into decline: **M16.** **ruiˈnatious** *adjective* (*US*) ruinous **M19.** **ruinator** *noun* (*rare*) a person who ruins someone or something **M17.**

ruination /ruːɪˈneɪʃ(ə)n/ *noun.* **M17.**
[from RUINATE *verb*: see -ATION.]
The action of ruining someone or something; the fact or condition of being ruined.

> 📖 A. STORR Witches . . were also seen as causing the . . ruination of crops by poisoning.

ruinosity /ruːɪˈnɒsɪti/ *noun. rare.* LME.
[medieval Latin *ruinositas*, formed as next: see -ITY.]
Decay, dilapidation; a decayed or dilapidated thing.

ruinous /ˈruːɪnəs/ *adjective.* LME.
[Latin *ruinosus*, from *ruina*: see RUIN *noun*, -OUS.]
1 Falling or fallen down; decayed, dilapidated. LME.
2 Disastrous, destructive, pernicious; *transf.* excessively expensive. LME.
3 Brought to ruin, sunk into decline. *rare.* L16.
†**4** Pertaining to a fall or crash. *rare.* Only in M17.

📖 **1** J. TYNDALL The weather had broken up the mountains into ruinous heaps **2** A. HIGGINS The heat of the sun quite ruinous to the ladies' complexions. E. FEINSTEIN Yakov was . . able to secure her release by paying a ruinous amount of money.

■ **ruinously** *adverb* M16. **ruinousness** *noun* M17.

ruise *verb & noun* see ROOSE.

†**ruiter** *noun.* L16–E18.
[Dutch.]
= RUTTER *noun*[1].

rukh /rʊk/ *noun.* L19.
[Hindi *rūkh* from Sanskrit *vṛkṣa* tree.]
In the Indian subcontinent: a forest; a forest reserve.

rulable /ˈruːləb(ə)l/ *adjective.* Long *rare.* LME.
[from RULE *noun, verb* + -ABLE.]
Able to be ruled; governable.

rule /ruːl/ *noun.* ME.
[Old French *riule, reule, ruile* from Proto-Romance from Latin *regula* straight stick, bar, pattern, rel. to *regere* rule, REX.]
▶ **I 1** A principle, regulation, or maxim governing individual conduct (also foll. by *of*); a principle governing scholarly or scientific procedure or method (cf. ***rule of thumb*** below). ME. ▸**b** A principle governing a regular feature of a language (orig. *spec.* word form or position in a sentence); now usu. as a statement forming part of a formal grammar. L15. ▸**c** MATH. A prescribed method or process for finding unknown numbers or values, or solving particular problems. M16.
2 A fact, or the statement of a fact, which holds generally good; the normal or usual state of things. ME. ▸**b** A standard of discrimination or estimation; a criterion, a test, a measure. LME.
3 *transf.* An exemplary person or thing; a guiding example. *rare.* LME.

📖 **1** J. A. FROUDE His object . . was . . to find a rule by which to govern his own actions. T. S. ELIOT My rule is to remember that I understand nobody. A. J. AYER The function of an empirical hypothesis is to provide a rule for the anticipation of experience. **b** N. CHOMSKY The rules in question are not laws of nature. **c** ***Cardan's rule, trapezoidal rule***, etc. **2** *New Scientist* The rule is that lightning is dangerous. **b** *Law Times* No hard and fast rule by which to construe . . commercial agreements.

▶ **II 4** (Also R-.) The code of discipline or body of regulations observed by a religious order or congregation; *occas.* an order or congregation observing a particular rule. Freq. with specifying word. ME.
5 A principle regulating practice or procedure; a dominant custom or habit. Also, accepted or prescribed principles, method, practice, custom, etc.; *rare* rigid system or routine. LME. ▸**b** In *pl.* (Also R-.) Any of various codes of practice or sets of regulations, esp. governing the playing of a (specified) sport; *spec.* = ***Australian Rules*** s.v. AUSTRALIAN *adjective.* L17.
6 A regulation governing individual and collective practice set or adopted by (the members of) a corporate body. LME.
7 LAW. An order made by a judge or court, the application of which is limited to the case in connection with which it is granted. LME. ▸**b** A formal order or regulation governing the procedure or decisions of a court of law; a decision or decree forming part of the common law, or having the force of law. M16.
8 *Hist.* **a** ***the rules***, a defined area around or near any of various prisons, esp. those of the Fleet and King's or Queen's Bench, within which certain prisoners, esp. debtors, were allowed to live on giving proper security. M17. ▸**b** (The) freedom of movement and action allowed within such an area. M18.

📖 **4** ***Benedictine rule, Cistercian rule, Franciscan rule***, etc. **5** J. H. NEWMAN They speak by rule and by book. M. GORDON At Oxford there's a rule: No serious conversation at table. **6** C. ISHERWOOD Hyperconscious of all bylaws . . rules and petty regulations. *Flight International* The airfield is protected by Rule 36 airspace.

▶ **III 9** The control or government exercised by or over a person or thing. Freq. foll. by *of.* ME.
10 Control, government, dominion. LME.
†**11** Order; discipline; the state or condition of being settled or regulated. LME–E17.
†**12 a** Conduct, behaviour, manner of acting. LME–E17. ▸**b** Disorder, riot. M16–E18.

📖 **9** E. A. FREEMAN The rule of the conquered land was entrusted to William Fitz-Osbern. L. CHAMBERLAIN Only under Soviet rule has the international caviare industry really been organised. **10** J. RUSKIN The woman's power is for rule, not for battle.

▶ **IV 13** A strip of wood, metal, plastic, etc., usu. marked with units of linear measurement (as centimetres, inches, etc.), used for measuring length or marking straight lines. ME. ▸†**b** A straight line drawn on paper, esp. on which to transcribe music. L15–M17. ▸**c** (Official or accepted) measurement; *fig.* careful, accepted, or official practice. E17.
†**14** Array; marshalled or hierarchical order. LME–E16.
15 TYPOGRAPHY. A thin strip of metal (usu. brass) used to separate headings, columns of type, articles, etc., and to ornament text. Also, a short or long dash, used for punctuation etc. L17. ▸**b** A strip of metal used to keep type level and in place during setting or printing. L17.
16 (Usu. R-.) (The name of) *the* constellation Norma. M19.

📖 **13** *Practical Woodworking* A quick check with a rule . . confirmed that . . the fences extend about the same distance. **15** ***em rule, en rule***.

Phrases & comb.: ***as a general rule***: see GENERAL *adjective.* ***as a rule***: see AS *adverb* etc. ***Australian Rules (football)***: see AUSTRALIAN *adjective.* **bend the rules** interpret the rules leniently; overlook infringement of the rules. **brass rule** TYPOGRAPHY thin strips of brass from which ornamental figures etc. may be made. **by rule** in a regular manner; mechanically. ***by rule and line***: see LINE *noun*[2]. ***direct rule***: see DIRECT *adjective.* ***Freedom of the Rule***: see FREEDOM. ***golden rule***: see GOLDEN *adjective.* ***home rule***: see HOME *noun & adjective.* INDIRECT ***rule***. ***Judge's Rules***: see JUDGE *noun.* ***left-hand rule***: see LEFT HAND *adjective* 1. ***Lesbian rule***: see LESBIAN *adjective* 1. **out of rule** contrary to custom. **particular rule** = sense 7 above. ***rewrite rule***: see REWRITE *verb & noun.* **Rule 43** in the United Kingdom, a clause in the rules for prison governance whereby a prisoner considered to be at risk from the rest of the prison community may be placed in protective solitary confinement. **rule-joint** a movable joint resembling that used in a folding rule for measuring lengths. **rule of court** (**a**) = sense 7 above; (**b**) = sense 7b above. **rule of law** (**a**) any valid legal proposition; (**b**) *the* doctrine that arbitrary exercise of power is controlled by subordinating (governmental, military, economic, etc.) power to well-defined and impartial principles of law; *spec.* (ENGLISH LAW) *the* concept that ordinary exercise of governmental power must conform to general principles as administered by the ordinary courts. ***rule of false position, rule of position***: see POSITION *noun* 2c. ***rule of proportion***: see PROPORTION *noun.* ***rule of the road***: see ROAD *noun.* **rule of three** MATH. a method of finding a fourth number from three given numbers, of which the first is in the same proportion to the second as the third is to the unknown fourth. **rule of thumb** a general principle or a method derived from practice or experience rather than theory. **rule-right** *adjective* (*rare*) †(**a**) *Scot.* as straight or exact as a rule for measuring lengths or marking lines; (**b**) according to an established rule, regular. **Rules Committee**: of a house of a US federal or state legislature responsible for expediting the passage of bills. **rules of evidence** the legal rules governing the admissibility of evidence. **rules of the game** *transf.* conventions in political or social relations etc. **run the rule over** investigate; examine (esp. cursorily) for correctness, consistency, etc. ***sliding rule***. **standing rule of court** = sense 7b above (cf. ***rule of court*** (b) above). **stretch the rules** = ***bend the rules*** above. ***ten-minute rule, ten-minutes rule***: see TEN *adjective.* ***the rules***: see sense 8a above. **work to rule** perform occupational duties exactly as officially or formally stated in a job description or code of practice, in order to reduce output and efficiency, usu. as a form of industrial action.

■ **ruleless** /-l-l-/ *adjective* (**a**) lawless; unrestrained; (**b**) having no rules, irregular: LME. **rulelessness** *noun* L19.

rule /ruːl/ *verb.* ME.
[Old French *reuler* from late Latin *regulare* REGULATE *verb.*]
▶ **I 1** *verb trans.* Guide, influence, manage, control; moderate or restrain (oneself, one's desires, actions, etc.). ME. ▸**b** In *pass.* Allow oneself to be advised, guided, directed (*by*). LME.
†**2** *verb trans.* Exercise or administer (some power or authority). LME–L16.
3 *verb trans. & intrans.* Govern; exercise authority or sovereignty over (a person or thing); *transf.* dominate; be superior (to). LME.
4 *verb trans. & intrans.* Decide, determine, pronounce authoritatively, (a person or thing *to be, that*). LME.
5 *verb intrans.* COMMERCE. Of a price, trade, goods, etc.: maintain a (specified) rate, value, quality, etc. E17. ▸**b** *transf.* Proceed in a certain way; have a specified character or quality. L17.

📖 **1** SIR W. SCOTT The . . Abbot . . commanded Halbert to rule his temper. E. GASKELL One who rules himself to . . sobriety of conduct. E. WAUGH Great brewing families which rule London. R. RENDELL We were ruled by the clock. **3** C. HILL England . . should be ruled by a representative assembly. *Sunday Times* The showroom was ruled by . . Mademoiselle Renée. **4** ANTHONY SMITH Someone could be ruled dead if . . the brain would never be able to resume control. P. MAILLOUX The Nazis ruled that Jewish writers . . be published by Jewish publishers.

▶ **II 6** *verb trans.* Mark (paper etc.) with parallel straight lines. LME. ▸**b** Make (a line) with or as with a ruler. L16.
Phrases, & with adverbs & prepositions in specialized senses: ***divide and rule***: see DIVIDE *verb.* **rule off** COMMERCE (**a**) *verb phr. trans.* close (account-books) for the day; (**b**) *verb phr. intrans.* cease trading or other business for the day. **rule out** exclude or eliminate (esp. formally or officially); decide against. **rule over** govern, exercise authority or sovereignty over. **rule the roost, rule the roast** be in control.

ruler /ˈruːlə/ *noun & verb.* LME.
[from RULE *verb* + -ER[1].]
▶ **A** *noun.* **1** A person who or thing which governs or exercises authority or sovereignty. Freq. foll. by *of.* LME.
2 A person who controls, manages, administers, or influences something. Now *arch. rare.* LME.
3 A straight-edged strip or cylinder of wood, metal, plastic, etc., usu. marked with units of linear measurement (as centimetres, inches, etc.), used for measuring length or marking straight lines. LME.

📖 **1** C. S. LEWIS The principal aim of rulers . . was to keep their subjects quiet. **2** *Reader* The rulers of the British Museum are an irresponsible corporation. **ruler of the choir** *arch.* a cantor. **3** ***parallel ruler(s)***: see PARALLEL *adjective.*

▶ **B** *verb trans.* Hit or beat with a ruler. *colloq.* M19.

📖 DICKENS Caned every day . . except on holiday Monday, when he was only ruler'd.

■ **ruleress** *noun* (*rare*) a female ruler LME. **rulership** *noun* (**a**) the office or quality of a ruler; sovereignty; (**b**) a province; a government: M17.

ruling /ˈruːlɪŋ/ *noun.* ME.
[from RULE *verb* + -ING[1].]
1 The action of governing or exercising authority; the exercise of government, authority, control, influence, etc. ME.
2 An authoritative pronouncement; *spec.* a judicial decision. LME.
3 The action of using a ruler; the action of marking parallel straight lines on paper, textiles, etc. L16. ▸**b** A ruled line or ruled lines; *spec.* (PALAEOGRAPHY) lines ruled in preparation for writing a manuscript. L19.

📖 **2** J. B. MORTON A ruling was changed recently from 'guilty' to 'innocent'.

ruling /ˈruːlɪŋ/ *adjective.* L16.
[from RULE *verb* + -ING[2].]
1 That rules; exercising control, authority, influence, etc.; governing, reigning. L16.
2 Dominant; prevalent. M18.
3 Of a price etc.: current, prevailing. M19.

📖 **1** LD MACAULAY He belonged half to the ruling and half to the subject caste. T. B. BOTTOMORE A potential ruling elite is . . constituted by . . managers of industry. **Ruling Elder** a nominated or elected lay official of any of various Christian Churches, esp. of the Presbyterian Church. **ruling planet** ASTROLOGY a planet which is held to have a particular influence over a specific sign of the zodiac, house, aspect of life, etc. **2** LD MACAULAY Hatred had become one of the ruling passions of the community.

rullion /ˈrʌlɪən/ *noun.* Chiefly *Scot.* M17.
[Var. of RIVELING.]
A shoe made of undressed hide.

ruly /ˈruːli/ *adjective.* Now *arch. & poet.* LME.
[Orig. from RULE *noun* + -Y[1]; in later use prob. back-form. from UNRULY *adjective.*]
Observing rules; amenable to rule; law-abiding, disciplined, orderly.

rum /rʌm/ *noun*[1]. M17.
[Perh. abbreviation of RUMBULLION *noun*[1].]
1 A spirit distilled from various products of the sugar cane, esp. molasses and dunder. M17.
2 Intoxicating liquor in general. *N. Amer.* E19.
1 ***navy rum, pineapple rum, white rum***, etc.
Comb.: ***rum baba***: see BABA *noun*[1]; **rum baron** a magnate in illegal liquor traffic; ***rum butter***: see BUTTER *noun*[1] 1; **rum-cherry** (the fruit of) a N. American wild cherry, *Prunus serotina*, resembling the bird cherry; **rum cocktail**: in which rum is the principal ingredient; **rum-hound** *slang* (**a**) = ***rumpot*** below; (**b**) *US* a prohibition agent; **rum-jar** *slang* (now *Hist.*) a type of German trench mortar bomb; **rumpot** *N. Amer. slang* a habitual heavy drinker; **rum-runner** (**a**) a person who smuggles or lands illicit liquor; (**b**) = ***rum ship*** below; **rum-running** the smuggling or landing of illicit liquor; **rum ship** a ship engaged in rum-running; **rum shop** *US & W. Indies* a shop or tavern selling liquor, a saloon.

†**rum** *noun*[2]. *slang.* E18.
[In sense 2 from RUM *adjective*[2]. Sense 1 may be a different word.]
1 A poor country clergyman in Ireland. Only in E18.
2 [Ellipt. for *rum customer.*] A strange person. E–M19.

rum /rʌm/ *noun*[3]. *US.* E20.
[Abbreviation of RUMMY *noun*[1].]
A form of the card-game rummy.

rum /rʌm/ *adjective*[1]. *slang.* Now *rare* or *obsolete.* M16.
[Origin unkn.]
Good, fine, excellent; great.
rum booze good liquor; wine. **rum pad** the highway.

rum /rʌm/ *adjective*[2]. *colloq.* Compar. & superl. **-mm-**. L18.
[Origin unkn.]
Odd, strange, queer; bad, difficult.

H. JAMES People do live in rum places when they come abroad. B. BAINBRIDGE Ashburner's behaviour was a bit rum, rambling on about his grandma. **rum customer** an odd or strange person. **rum go**, **rum start** a surprising occurrence, an unforeseen turn of events.

■ **rumness** *noun* M19.

rumaki /ruːˈmɑːki/ *noun*. Pl. same, **-s**. M20.
[Perh. alt. of Japanese *harumaki* spring roll.]
An appetizer, of oriental origin, consisting chiefly of chicken livers, water chestnuts, and bacon, marinated and broiled.

rumal *noun* var. of ROMAL.

Rumanian *noun & adjective* var. of ROMANIAN.

rumänite /ruːˈmeɪnʌɪt, ˈruːmənʌɪt/ *noun*. L19.
[from German *Rumänien* Romania: see -ITE[1].]
MINERALOGY. A variety of amber found in Romania, containing sulphur and succinic acid.

Rumansh, **Rumansch**, **Rumantsch**, *nouns & adjectives* vars. of ROMANSH.

rumba /ˈrʌmbə/ *noun & verb*. Also **rh-**. E20.
[Amer. Spanish.]
▶ **A** *noun*. An Afro-Cuban dance; a ballroom dance imitative of this, danced on the spot with a pronounced movement of the hips; the dance rhythm of this, usu. in 2/4 time; a piece of music with this rhythm. E20.
▶ **B** *verb intrans*. Dance the rumba. M20.

rumbelow /ˈrʌmbələʊ/ *noun*. Now *rare*. LME.
[Arbitrary combination of syllables.]
A refrain, orig. sung by sailors when rowing.

rumble /ˈrʌmb(ə)l/ *noun*. LME.
[from RUMBLE *verb*[1]. Sense 5 may be a different word (cf. RUMBLE *verb*[1] 7).]
1 A rumbling sound. LME. ▸**b** AUDIO. Low-frequency noise originating as mechanical vibration in a turntable. M20. ▸**c** A rumour. *US colloq.* M20.
2 †**a** Commotion, bustle, uproar. LME–L17. ▸**b** A severe blow. *Scot. dial.* LME. ▸**c** A fight, esp. in the street. *slang* (chiefly *N. Amer.*). M20.
3 The rear part of a horse-drawn carriage when arranged to provide sitting accommodation or to carry luggage; *N. Amer.* (in full ***rumble seat***) = DICKY *noun* 5b. E19.
4 A rotating cylinder in which iron castings are tumbled and cleaned of adhering sand. M19.
5 An interruption in the course of a crime; an alarm; a tip-off. *Criminals' slang.* E20.
Comb.: **rumble seat**: see sense 3 above; **rumble strip** a strip across a road where the surface causes a rumbling or vibration in passing vehicles, used to slow traffic.
■ **rumbly** *adjective* of a rumbling character L19.

rumble /ˈrʌmb(ə)l/ *verb*[1]. LME.
[Prob. from Middle Dutch *rommelen*, *rumm-* (Dutch *romm-*), of imit. origin. Sense 7 may be a different word (cf. RUMBLE *noun* 5).]
1 *verb intrans.* Make a low, heavy, continuous but varying sound, as of distant thunder. LME.
2 *verb intrans.* Move with such a sound; (of people) be carried in a rumbling vehicle. (Foll. by *up*, *down*, *round*, *by*, etc.) LME.
3 *verb intrans.* **a** Make a noise or disturbance. Long *obsolete* exc. *Scot.* LME. ▸**b** Produce a rumbling noise by agitating or moving something. *rare.* LME. ▸**c** Toss about in bed or on the ground. Long *obsolete* exc. *Scot. dial.* L16.
4 *verb trans.* Cause to move or travel with a rumbling sound; *dial.* scramble (eggs), mash (potatoes), stir, agitate. E16.
5 *verb trans.* Utter, say, or give out, with a rumbling sound. (Foll. by *out*.) L16.
6 *verb trans.* Put *out* unceremoniously; handle roughly. *slang.* E19.
7 *verb trans.* Get to the bottom of; see through, understand; recognize or discover the wrongdoing or misbehaviour of (a person). *slang.* L19.
8 *verb trans.* Clean (iron castings) in a rumble. E20.
9 *verb intrans.* Take part in a fight, esp. in the street. *slang* (chiefly *N. Amer.*). M20.

1 H. JOBSON My stomach was rumbling, yet I still couldn't face the idea of food. **2** P. G. WODEHOUSE In the street . . a . . waggon rumbled past. **7** P. D. JAMES She worked for . . something . . sinister and they rumbled her.

■ **rumblement** *noun* (*rare*) a rumbling E18. **rumbler** *noun* a person who or thing which rumbles; *spec.* (***a***) a resounding line of poetry; (***b***) a cart, a carriage; (***c***) a type of round bell on a harness etc.: E17. **rumbling** *noun* (***a***) the action of the verb; (***b***) a rumbling noise; in *pl.*, early indications of a forthcoming or likely event; grumblings of discontent: LME. **rumbling** *adjective* (***a***) that rumbles; of the nature of a rumble; (***b***) (of a drain) formed of loose stones: M16.

†**rumble** *verb*[2] *intrans.* LME–E18.
[Origin uncertain: perh. rel. to RAMBLE *verb*, ROAM.]
Ramble.

rumblegumption /rʌmb(ə)lˈgʌm(p)ʃ(ə)n/ *noun*. *Scot.* M18.
[Origin uncertain: cf. GUMPTION, RUMGUMPTION.]
1 Common sense, gumption. M18.
2 Disturbance, commotion. M19.

rumble-tumble /rʌmb(ə)lˈtʌmb(ə)l/ *noun*. E19.
[from RUMBLE *verb*[1] + TUMBLE *verb*.]
1 a The rumble of a horse-drawn carriage. *obsolete* exc. *Hist.* E19. ▸**b** A horse-drawn coach, carriage, or cart. *obsolete* exc. *Hist.* E19.
2 In the Indian subcontinent: scrambled eggs. L19.

rumbo /ˈrʌmbəʊ/ *noun*. *arch.* M18.
[App. from RUM *noun*[1].]
A kind of strong punch, made chiefly of rum.

rumbullion /rʌmˈbʌlɪən/ *noun*[1]. *obsolete* exc. *Hist.* M17.
[Origin unkn.]
Rum; a drink of rum.

rumbullion /rʌmˈbʌlɪən/ *noun*[2]. Now *rare* or *obsolete*. E18.
[Alt. of *Rambouillet*: see RAMBOUILLET.]
1 A variety of peach. E18.
2 A variety of gooseberry. L18.

rumbustical /rʌmˈbʌstɪk(ə)l/ *adjective*. *dial. & colloq.* L18.
[Prob. from alt. of ROBUSTIC + -AL[1].]
= RUMBUSTIOUS.

rumbustious /rʌmˈbʌstʃəs, -tɪəs/ *adjective*. L18.
[Prob. alt. of ROBUSTIOUS.]
Boisterous, noisy, unruly; turbulent, rough.

Q. BELL A jolly rumbustious extrovert. O. MANNING Acclimatised to Cairo's . . rumbustious vitality.

■ **rumbustiously** *adverb* M20. **rumbustiousness** *noun* rumbustious character; boisterous behaviour: E20.

rumdum /ˈrʌmdʌm/ *adjective & noun*. *N. Amer. slang.* Also **-dumb**. L19.
[from RUM *noun*[1] + DUMB *adjective & noun*.]
▶ **A** *adjective*. Stupefied through drink; unconscious; stupid. L19.
▶ **B** *noun*. A habitual drunkard; a stupid person. L19.

rumen /ˈruːmɛn/ *noun*. E18.
[Latin *rumen*, *rumin-* throat, gullet.]
The first and largest stomach of a ruminant, in which food, esp. cellulose, is partly digested by bacteria.
■ **rumeˈnitis** *noun* inflammation of an animal's rumen E20. **rumeˈnotomy** *noun* (an instance of) surgical incision into an animal's rumen L19.

rumenal *adjective* var. of RUMINAL.

rumex /ˈruːmɛks/ *noun*. Pl. **rumices** /ˈruːmɪsiːz/. L18.
[Latin = sorrel.]
A dock, sorrel, or other plant of the genus *Rumex*, of the knotgrass family.

Rumford /ˈrʌmfəd/ *adjective & noun*. *obsolete* exc. *Hist.* E19.
[Sir Benjamin Thompson, Count von *Rumford* (1753–1814), American-born Brit. physicist.]
▶ **A** *adjective*. Designating ovens and fireplaces designed by Rumford or improved according to systems devised by him. E19.
▶ **B** *noun*. A Rumford oven or fireplace. E19.

rumfustian /rʌmˈfʌstɪən/ *noun*. E19.
[from RUM *noun*[1] + FUSTIAN.]
Hist. A drink similar to egg-nog.

rumgumption /rʌmˈgʌm(p)ʃ(ə)n/ *noun*. Chiefly *Scot. & north.* L17.
[Origin uncertain: cf. GUMPTION, RUMBLEGUMPTION.]
Common sense, gumption.

rumices *noun* pl. of RUMEX.

ruminal /ˈruːmɪn(ə)l/ *adjective*. Also **rumenal**. M19.
[formed as RUMEN + -AL[1].]
†**1** Ruminant. Only in Dicts. Only in M19.
2 Of or pertaining to the rumen of an animal. E20.

ruminant /ˈruːmɪnənt/ *noun & adjective*. M17.
[Latin *ruminant-* pres. ppl stem of *ruminari*: see RUMINATE *verb*, -ANT[1].]
▶ **A** *noun*. An animal that chews the cud; any of a group of artiodactyl mammals (including bovids, camels, and deer) that have four (or three) stomachs and can digest cellulose. M17.
▶ **B** *adjective*. **1** That is a ruminant. L17.
2 Contemplative; given to or engaged in meditation. M19.

ruminate /ˈruːmɪnət/ *adjective*. M19.
[Latin *ruminatus* pa. pple, formed as next: see -ATE[2].]
BOTANY. Of the endosperm of a seed, e.g. the nutmeg: having an irregular pattern of ridges and furrows, so as to appear chewed.

ruminate /ˈruːmɪneɪt/ *verb*. M16.
[Latin *ruminat-* pa. ppl stem of *ruminari*, *-are*, formed as RUMEN: see -ATE[3].]
1 *verb trans.* Turn over in the mind; meditate deeply on. M16.
2 *verb intrans.* Chew the cud. M16.
3 *verb intrans.* Meditate, ponder. L16.
4 *verb trans.* Chew or turn over in the mouth again. E17.

3 J. SYMONS They found Cassidy . . ruminating over a glass of beer.

■ **ruminatingly** *adverb* thoughtfully L19. **ruminative** *adjective* contemplative, meditative M19. **ruminatively** *adverb* L19. **ruminator** *noun* a person who ruminates L16.

ruminated /ˈruːmɪneɪtɪd/ *adjective*. E17.
[from RUMINATE *verb*, *adjective* + -ED[1].]
1 Meditated, considered. E17.
2 BOTANY. = RUMINATE *adjective*. M19.

rumination /ruːmɪˈneɪʃ(ə)n/ *noun*. E17.
[from RUMINATE *verb*: see -ATION.]
1 Contemplation, meditation; in *pl.*, meditations, thoughts, reflections. E17.
2 The action of chewing the cud; MEDICINE. = MERYCISM. M17.

rumkin /ˈrʌmkɪn/ *noun*[1]. *arch.* M17.
[from Dutch *roemer* RUMMER + unexpl. -KIN.]
A kind of drinking-vessel.

rumkin /ˈrʌmkɪn/ *noun*[2]. L17.
[App. from RUMP *noun* + -KIN.]
A tailless cock or hen. Cf. RUMPY *noun*.

rummage /ˈrʌmɪdʒ/ *noun*. L15.
[Old French *arrumage* (mod. *arrimage*), from *arrumer* var. of *arimer*, *aruner*, *ariner*, from AR- + *run* ship's hold from Middle & mod. Dutch *ruim* space: see ROOM *noun*[1], -AGE. Cf. medieval Latin *rumagium*.]
†**1 a** NAUTICAL. The arranging of casks etc. in the hold of a vessel. L15–L17. ▸**b** Place of stowage or storage; storage capacity. L16–M17.
2 Bustle, commotion, turmoil. *obsolete* exc. *Scot.* L16.
3 Miscellaneous articles, lumber; rubbish. L16.
4 A thorough but unsystematic search; an act of rummaging. M18. ▸**b** A thorough search of a vessel by a Customs officer. M19.

4 C. KEENE Have a rummage for it among the old music-book shops.

Comb.: **rummage goods** goods unclaimed or out of date in a warehouse; **rummage sale** (***a***) a sale of rummage goods; (***b***) (esp. *N. Amer.*) a jumble sale.

rummage /ˈrʌmɪdʒ/ *verb*. L15.
[from the noun.]
▶ **I** *verb trans.* †**1** NAUTICAL. Arrange or rearrange (goods) in the hold of a ship; arrange, put in order, set straight. L15–E18.
2 Disarrange, disorder; make untidy by searching. Also (*rare*), knock about, stir; drive out. L16.
3 Make a thorough search of (a vessel etc.) (NAUTICAL); ransack; search untidily and unsystematically. Also foll. by *over*, *out*, *up*. E17.
4 Fish *out* or dig *up* by searching. E18.
5 Scrutinize, examine minutely, investigate. Also foll. by *over*. E18.
▶ **II** *verb intrans.* **6** NAUTICAL. Make search, or (formerly) arrange or rearrange goods, in a ship. L16.
7 *gen.* Engage in a search, esp. an untidy and unsystematic one. Also foll. by *about*, *around*. E17.

7 K. WATERHOUSE Rummaging around . . for the smelling salts. D. ADAMS He rummaged feverishly amongst the debris . . all about him.

■ **rummager** *noun* M16.

rummer /ˈrʌmə/ *noun*. M17.
[Of Low Dutch origin: cf. Dutch *roemer*, Low German (whence German) *römer*, from *roemen* etc. extol, praise, boast. Cf. ROEMER.]
A kind of large drinking-glass. Also ***rummer glass***.

rummery /ˈrʌm(ə)ri/ *noun*. *US* (now *rare*). L19.
[from RUM *noun*[1] + -ERY.]
A liquor shop.

rummish /ˈrʌmɪʃ/ *adjective*. *slang*. M18.
[from RUM *adjective*[2] + -ISH[1].]
Somewhat odd or strange.

rummy /ˈrʌmi/ *noun*[1] & *verb*. Orig. *US*. E20.
[Origin unkn.]
▶ **A** *noun*. Any of a group of card-games whose main object is to acquire sets of three or more cards of the same rank, or three or more cards in suit and sequence, and which is played by drawing from a common stock and discarding on to a waste pile. E20.
gin rummy: see GIN *noun*[2] 2. ***OKLAHOMA rummy***.
▶ **B** *verb intrans.* Obtain a hand that can be laid down at rummy; say 'rummy' signifying this. Also foll. by *out*. E20.

rummy /ˈrʌmi/ *adjective*[1] & *noun*[2]. *colloq.* E19.
[from RUM *adjective*[2] + -Y[1].]
▶ **A** *adjective*. = RUM *adjective*[2]. E19.
▶ **B** *noun*. An odd or unconventional person. L20.
■ **rummily** *adverb* E19. **rumminess** *noun* L19.

rummy /ˈrʌmi/ *adjective*² & *noun*³. M19.
[from RUM *noun*¹ + -Y¹.]
▶ **A** *adjective.* Of, pertaining to, or suggestive of rum. M19.
▶ **B** *noun.* **1** *US HISTORY.* A political opponent of temperance or prohibition. M19.
2 a A habitual heavy drinker. *slang* (chiefly *US*). M19. ▸**b** A stupid or gullible person. *US slang.* E20.

rumor *noun & verb* see RUMOUR.

rumorous /ˈruːm(ə)rəs/ *adjective.* M16.
[from next + -OUS.]
1 Making a loud confused sound; resounding. *arch.* M16.
†**2** Of the nature of rumour; rumoured. *rare.* E–M17.

rumour /ˈruːmə/ *noun & verb.* Also *-**or**. LME.
[Old French *rumur*, *-or* (mod. *-eur*) from Latin *rumor* noise, din: see -OUR.]
▶ **A** *noun.* **1** †**a** A (widespread) report of a favourable or laudatory nature. Only in LME. ▸**b** Talk or report *of* a person or thing in some way noted or distinguished. *arch.* LME.
2 a General talk or hearsay not based on definite knowledge. LME. ▸**b** An unverified or unconfirmed statement or report circulating in a community. LME.
3 †**a** Loud expression or manifestation of disapproval; uproar, tumult, disturbance. LME–M17. ▸**b** Clamour, outcry; noise, din. *arch.* LME.

> 🕮 **2a** B. WEBB We are a prey to rumour . . as to what is happening. **rumour has it** it is rumoured (*that*). **b** M. WEBB Rumours came to us of battles over sea. A. CROSS I want you . . to settle the rumors forever. **3b** A. ROOK Tomorrow the guns will renew their rumour.

▶ **B** *verb.* †**1** *verb intrans.* Resound with disapproval. Only in LME.
2 *verb trans.* Spread or report (*that*) by way of rumour. Also with pers. obj. & inf. Usu. in *pass.* L16.

> 🕮 **2** L. DURRELL He is rumoured to be fantastically attractive to women. M. MEYER It was openly rumoured that Henrik was not Knud Ibsen's son. A. CARTER The girl was rumoured to have started her career in freak shows.

▪ **rumoured** *ppl adjective* announced by rumour; commonly reported: E17. **rumourer** *noun* (*rare*) a person who spreads rumours E17.

rump /rʌmp/ *noun & verb.* LME.
[Prob. of Scandinavian origin: cf. Middle & mod. Danish *rumpe*, Middle & mod. Swedish *rumpa*, Icelandic *rumpur*.]
▶ **A** *noun.* **1** The part of an animal's body from which the tail springs; an animal's hindquarters or buttocks. Formerly also, an animal tail. LME. ▸†**b** The part *of* a tail which is next to the body. E17–M18. ▸†**c** A kind of bustle. L18–E19.
2 A cut of meat from an animal's hindquarters. L15.
3 A small, unimportant, or contemptible remnant or remainder of a parliament or similar body. M17. ▸**b** Any remainder or remnant. M20.

> 🕮 **1** ***stump and rump***: see STUMP *noun*¹. **2 rump and dozen** *arch.* a rump of beef and a dozen of claret; *fig.* corporal punishment administered on the buttocks. **3 The Rump** = ***Rump Parliament*** s.v. PARLIAMENT *noun*. **b** *Modern Railways* A new connection to the rump of the . . coastal line.

Comb.: **rump-bone** (now *rare* or *obsolete*) the coccyx; ***Rump Parliament***: see PARLIAMENT *noun*; **rumpsprung** *adjective* baggy in the seat; **rump steak** a cut of beef from the rump.
▶ **B** *verb trans.* **1** Turn one's back on (a person), esp. as a mode of snubbing. Now *rare* or *obsolete.* M18.
2 Plunder completely; clean (a person) of money. *Scot.* E19.
¶ Earlier in ME as a surname.
▪ **rumped** *adjective* †(*a*) having a bustle or false rump; (*b*) *ZOOLOGY* having a rump of a specified form, colour, etc.: E18. **Rumper** *noun* (*Hist.*) a member or supporter of the Rump Parliament M17. **Rumpish** *adjective* (*Hist.*, *rare*) of or belonging to the Rump Parliament M17.

rumple /ˈrʌmp(ə)l/ *noun.* E16.
[Middle & mod. Dutch *rompel* from Middle Dutch *rompe*, Middle Low German *rumpe*, or from Middle Dutch, Middle Low German *rumpelen*, *rompelen* rumple (verb). Cf. RIMPLE *noun*.]
A wrinkle, a fold, a crease; a rumpled state or appearance.

rumple /ˈrʌmp(ə)l/ *verb trans.* E17.
[from the noun.]
1 Introduce irregular folds into, make no longer smooth; wrinkle, crumple, tousle. Also foll. by *up.* E17.
†**2** Squeeze together, distort. M–L17.

> 🕮 **1** G. GREENE The girl rumpled his thin streaky hair. P. AUSTER A tall . . fellow . . with rumpled clothes and a two-day beard.

rumpless /ˈrʌmplɪs/ *adjective.* M17.
[from RUMP *noun* + -LESS.]
Having no rump or tail; tailless.
▪ **rumplessness** *noun* M20.

rumply /ˈrʌmpli/ *adjective.* M19.
[from RUMPLE *noun* + -Y¹.]
Full of rumples, uneven.

rumpo /ˈrʌmpəʊ/ *noun. slang.* L20.
[from RUMP + -O.]
Sexual intercourse. Cf. RUMPY-PUMPY.

rumption /ˈrʌm(p)ʃ(ə)n/ *noun. Scot. & north.* E19.
[Blend of RUMPUS and RUCTION. Cf. earlier POLRUMPTIOUS.]
A rumpus, an uproar.

rumpus /ˈrʌmpəs/ *noun & verb. colloq.* M18.
[Prob. fanciful. Cf. RUCKUS.]
▶ **A** *noun.* A disturbance, a commotion; a row, a dispute. Also, noise, disagreement, controversy. M18.

> 🕮 W. S. MAUGHAM You're afraid of Betty . . kicking up a rumpus. R. H. MORRIESON A rumpus about Herbert not having . . a job.

Comb.: **rumpus room** *N. Amer.*, *Austral.*, & *NZ* a room in a house for recreation, which does not need to be kept tidy; a play-room.
▶ **B** *verb trans.* Create a disturbance. M19.

rumpy /ˈrʌmpi/ *noun.* M19.
[from RUMP *noun* + -Y⁶.]
1 A Manx cat. M19.
2 = RUMKIN *noun*². L19.
▪ **rumpy-ˈpumpy** *noun* (*joc.*) sexual intercourse (cf. RUMPO) M20.

rumti- /ˈrʌmti/ *combining form.* E19.
[Arbitrary.]
A meaningless combination of syllables used in refrains or imitations of sounds, as ***rumti-tum***, ***rumti-tumty***.
▪ **rumti-ˈtoo** *adjective* (*colloq.*) commonplace E20.

rum-tum /ˈrʌmtʌm/ *noun & adjective.* L19.
[Fanciful.]
▶ **A** *noun.* **1** A light-hearted diversion or prank. *dial.* L19.
2 A light racing-boat for one sculler, with outriggers and sliding seat, used on the lower Thames. L19.
3 A regular rhythmic musical sound. E20.
▶ **B** *attrib.* or as *adjective.* Designating or characterized by a regular rhythmic musical sound. L19.

run /rʌn/ *noun.* ME.
[from the verb.]
▶ **I 1** An act or spell of running. ME. ▸**b** The distance covered or the time taken by a run. Also, a race (esp. in hunting); the course of a race. L16. ▸**c** An act of running away, a bolt. M19. ▸**d** ***the runs***, an attack of diarrhoea. *colloq.* M20.
2 A trip or journey made by a ship, train, aircraft, etc., *esp.* one made regularly; a short trip or excursion made by car etc., esp. for pleasure. Also, the distance of such a trip. E18. ▸**b** A single trip on a toboggan etc. down a course. L19. ▸**c** A regular delivery round. Usu. with specifying word. E20. ▸**d** *MILITARY.* An offensive operation; a short flight by an aircraft on a straight and even course at a constant speed before or while dropping bombs. E20.
3 a *CRICKET.* A point scored by the batsmen each running to the other's wicket; an equivalent point awarded for some other reason. M18. ▸**b** *BASEBALL* etc. A point scored by the batter returning to the plate after touching the other bases; an equivalent point awarded for some other reason. M19.
4 †**a** The total amount of the cargo carried by a ship on a single voyage. Only in L18. ▸**b** A landing of smuggled goods. M19.
5 A rapid fall. Chiefly in ***with a run***. E19.

> 🕮 **1** DICKENS Mr. Pickwick . . took two or three short runs . . and went slowly and gravely down the slide. *Trout & Salmon* The spring salmon run is the most important. **b** E. W. LANE The run seldom exceeds three or four miles. *Horse & Hound* A fox . . gave a short but fast run to the earth. **c** N. F. DIXON Simple decisions as to whether to hide or make a run for it. **2** P. GALLICO A . . locomotive engaged in making the first run from San Francisco to Oregon City. R. DAHL It would knock thirty miles off the day's run. *Ships Monthly* Most speedy of the 21-knot . . series, *FEV* was preferred for the Calais run.

▶ **II 6** The action of running, esp. in rapid retreat or flight. Chiefly in ***on the run*** below. ME. ▸**b** A running pace. M19. ▸**c** Capacity for running; *spec.* (*GOLF*) capacity of a ball for onward movement after pitching. M19.
7 a The flow or onward movement *of* water, air, etc.; a (strong) current of water; a swell; (chiefly *MINING*) a landslide; a downward trickle of paint when applied too thickly. ME. ▸**b** A small stream, a rivulet. Chiefly *north.* & *US dial.* ME. ▸**c** The flow or melody *of* verse. L17. ▸**d** *MUSIC.* A rapid scale passage; a roulade. M19.
8 *NAUTICAL.* The after part of a ship's bottom where it rises and narrows towards the stern. E17.
9 A general tendency of movement or development; the course *of* something immaterial; the line or lie *of* a thing, the grain. M18.
10 Free use of or access to a place. Foll. by *of.* M18. ▸**b** The pasture of an animal for a certain period. M19.

> 🕮 **6b** W. GOLDING It was . . Alfred, pale, sweating, trembling, coming at a run. **7a** G. W. THORNBURY The run of the waves and their . . leaps are beautifully given in these sketches. *Coarse Angler* The roots . . slow down the flow to make fishable slacks and steady runs. **9** J. H. NEWMAN The general run of things . . as I have represented it. **10** M. HASTINGS They had the complete run of the house. M. HUNTER I had the run of my grandfather's library.

▶ **III 11 a** A large open stretch of land for pasturage; a sheep or cattle station. Chiefly *Austral.* & *NZ.* M17. ▸**b** A regular track made by an animal. E19. ▸**c** An enclosure for domestic animals or fowls. M19.
12 A slope down which something may run by impetus. Now only, a slope of snow used for tobogganing or skiing. M19. ▸**b** A track or support along or on which something may move. L19. ▸**c** In *pl.* A place for loading or unloading wagons. *US.* L19.
13 A pipe or trough along or down which water may run. M19.

> 🕮 **12** *Skiing Today* Runs high enough . . to guarantee . . some good skiing.

▶ **IV 14 a** A continuous stretch *of* something; *spec.* (*a*) a continuous vein of rock or ore; (*b*) a length of electric cable. L17. ▸**b** A continued spell or course *of* some condition or state of things; a spell of good or bad luck. L17. ▸**c** A ladder in a knitted garment (esp. hosiery). E20.
15 a A sudden demand for repayment from a bank made by a large number of customers. Freq. foll. by *on.* L17. ▸**b** *transf.* An extensive or well-sustained demand for a commodity, currency, etc. Foll. by *on.* E19.
16 A series, a sequence, esp. of cards in a specified suit; *spec.* a set of consecutive numbers of a periodical. E18. ▸†**b** A persistent attack *against* or *upon* a person or thing. Only in 18. ▸**c** (Pl. same.) A pair *of* millstones. *US.* L18. ▸**d** A group of animals in motion or migration; *esp.* a shoal of fish ascending a river from the sea for spawning. L18.
17 A continuous period of being presented on the stage etc. E18. ▸**b** *transf.* A success with the public. E18.
18 a A spell of making or allowing a liquid to run; the amount run off at one time; *spec.* the amount of sap drawn off when sugar maples are tapped; the amount of maple sugar produced at one time. E18. ▸**b** A measure of yarn for spinning. M18. ▸**c** A spell of making or allowing machinery to run, esp. for manufacture or experimentation; a quantity produced, treated, etc., in one period of production or manufacture. L19. ▸**d** A spell of sheep-shearing; a period of employment as a shearer. *Austral.* & *NZ.* E20.
19 *The* usual, ordinary, or average type or class. Usu. with specifying adjective. E18. ▸**b** A number of animals born or reared at the same time. M19. ▸**c** A line or class of goods. L19.

> 🕮 **14a** *Which?* Expansion is most noticeable in long runs of pipe. **b** J. MCCARTHY Hardly ever . . has a minister had so long a run of power. *Lancaster & Morecambe Guardian* Because of the . . club's good cup run the fixture will . . be rearranged. N. F. DIXON A run of bad luck . . followed by one of good luck. **15b** S. UNWIN There has been such a run on their books that they have sold out. S. BRITTAN Thorneycroft responded to the run on the pound with his . . deflationary package. **16** E. P. THOMPSON Population increase was supported by a long run of good harvests. **17** R. HOLMES An opera . . which had a short and unsuccessful run. **b** LD MACAULAY The history of . . publications which have had a run. **18c** *Nature* The difference . . was found . . in different electrophoretic runs. *Graphics World* These badges are produced in ones and twos—the only run limit is time. **19** A. STORR The patients who most interested Jung were a . . group . . unlike the usual run of neurotics. D. PIPER Several . . portraits of him are . . above the average run.

Phrases: **a good run for one's money**, **a run for one's money** (*a*) vigorous competition; (*b*) pleasure derived from an activity. **get the run** *slang* (chiefly *Austral.*) be dismissed from one's employment. ***home run***: see HOME *adjective*. ***long run***; ***long-run***: see LONG *adjective*¹. **on the run** (*a*) hurrying about from place to place; (*b*) fleeing from justice, an enemy, etc. ***paper run***: see PAPER *noun & adjective*. **run of the mill** the material produced from a mill before sorting; *fig.* the ordinary or undistinguished type. **run-of-the-mill** *adjective* ordinary, undistinguished. ***short run***: see SHORT *adjective*. ***ski run***: see SKI *noun & adjective*. ***split run***: see SPLIT *adjective*. **the run of one's teeth**, **the run of one's knife** free board, usu. in return for work done.
Comb.: **run-boat** *US*: which collects or transports the catch made by fishing boats at sea; **run holder** *Austral.* & *NZ* the owner or manager of a sheep or cattle run; **run-of-river** *adjective* (of a hydroelectric plant) using water taken directly from a river with little or no regulation of the flow. **run time** *noun & adjective* (*COMPUTING*) (*a*) *noun* the length of time a program takes to run; the time at which the program is run; (*b*) *adjective* (***run-time***) (of software) in a reduced version that can be run but not changed.
▪ **runless** *adjective* (*CRICKET & BASEBALL* etc.) devoid of runs; unable to score: E20.

run /rʌn/ *adjective.* L15.
[pa. pple of RUN *verb*.]
1 That has run; that has been run. Also foll. by adverb. L15.
2 *MINING.* Of coal: botryoidal. M18.
3 Complete, utter. *Scot. rare.* L18.

Special collocations & comb.: **run lace**: having a design embroidered on it after making. **run metal**, **run steel** a form of cast iron. **run-with-bull**, **run-with-ram** *NZ* (of a cow or ewe) given the chance to mate.

run /rʌn/ *verb.* Also (earlier, *obsolete* exc. *Scot.*) **rin** /rɪn/, †**ron**, (now *dial.*) **urn** /ɜːn/. Pres. pple **running**; pa. t. **ran** /ran/; pa. pple **run**, (now *dial.*) **runned**. See also RUN *adjective*.

[Old English *rinnan* = Old Frisian *rinna*, *renna*, Old Saxon, Old High German *rinnan*, Old Norse *rinna*, Gothic *rinnan*, from Germanic strong verb of unkn. origin. In Old English and early Middle English the metath. *urn* was the prevailing form; *run* (rare before 16) resulted from levelling of forms. See also EARN *verb*[2].]

▶ **I 1** *verb intrans.* Go with quick steps on alternate feet, never having both or all feet on the ground at the same time. Freq. with prepositions and adverbs. OE. ▸**b** Go or travel hurriedly; *fig.* hasten *to* a person, esp. for help, resort *to*. ME. ▸†**c** Ride on horseback, *spec.* in a tournament. ME–L17.

2 *verb intrans.* Go about freely without restraint or check; (of livestock) graze. OE. ▸†**b** Move rapidly *through* or *over* a country etc. causing destruction. ME–L17.

3 *verb intrans.* Retreat rapidly, flee, abscond, (now chiefly in ***run for it*** below); *colloq.* leave, depart, (also foll. by *along*, *away*). ME. ▸**b** *verb trans.* Flee or escape from (a place, country, etc.). E17.

4 *verb intrans.* Compete in a running race; finish such a race in a specified position. ME. ▸**b** *verb trans.* Compete in (a running race); contend with (a person) in a race. M16. ▸**c** *verb intrans.* Stand as a candidate *for* an elected post; seek election. E19.

5 *verb intrans.* Of a fish: swim rapidly; *spec.* migrate up river from the sea, esp. to spawn. ME.

🕮 **1** R. C. HUTCHINSON He ran faster now, sweating and panting. G. GREENE Running fast on long . . legs across the . . playground. I. COLEGATE Carley turned . . and ran out of the flat. M. WESLEY The train was puffing into the station; they had to run to catch it. **b** BOSWELL Obliged to run half over London, in order to fix a date correctly. *transf.*: C. READE I did . . glimpse why folk in trouble run to drink so. **2** B. JOWETT We are resolved . . not to let them run about as they like. *Country Life* The Prescelly sheep run together on the Castlemartin range. *fig.*: L. M. MONTGOMERY I just let my thoughts run. **3** THACKERAY He did not care to . . own . . that he was about to run. N. MITCHISON I must run or the . . party will miss me. **4b** S. TROTT What marathon are you going to run? *Money Management* A . . rosette . . for running Capability a very close second. **c** S. BELLOW Her second husband . . went to Congress and even ran in . . presidential primaries.

▶ **II 6** *verb intrans.* Pass, spread, or move quickly from point to point; (of a plant) climb; (of a sound) be repeated in quick succession; MUSIC sing or play quickly. OE. ▸**b** Of a weapon: pass easily and quickly *through*. ME. ▸**c** Of a thought etc.: come *into* or pass *through* the mind suddenly; revolve *in* the mind, recur persistently. ME. ▸**d** Of the eye: glance, look quickly or cursorily. Foll. by *down*, *along*, etc. E17.

7 *verb intrans.* (Of a thing, esp. a vehicle) move rapidly, easily, or smoothly, (freq. with prepositions or adverbs); move (as) by rolling or on wheels; (of a person) slide or move forward on skis, a sleigh, etc. OE. ▸**b** Of the tongue: wag excessively. M16. ▸**c** Of a plant: shoot up to produce seed, bolt. E18. ▸**d** Of bark: peel off easily from a tree. M18. ▸**e** Of a knitted garment, esp. hosiery: ladder. L19.

8 *verb intrans.* Of a ship or its crew etc.: sail straight and fast; sail or be driven *on to* the shore, rocks, etc.; come *aground* or *ashore*. OE.

9 *verb intrans.* (Of a machine) operate, be in action or operation; (of a film, tape, etc.) pass between spools, be shown or played. M16. ▸**b** *transf.* Of a business etc.: function, operate. E20.

10 *verb intrans.* (Of a vehicle, ship, etc.) make a regular journey between (two) places, travel or be travelling a route; (of a person) make a (rapid) journey. L18.

🕮 **6** CARLYLE There run reports that make me shudder. C. M. YONGE A whisper ran through the congregation. D. M. THOMAS She broke into a . . pleasant hum, running up and down the . . semi-quavers. H. ROTH A faint thrill of disquiet ran through him. **c** J. TYNDALL Extravagant analogies . . ran through my brain. **7** I. MURDOCH Trains run on rails. DAY LEWIS Through the cornfields the . . local trains ran. M. AYRTON Wire along which the chain runs with a . . rattling sound. **8** E. HEMINGWAY Sailing barges running with the wind for Venice. I. FLEMING They ran out westwards from the harbour. **9** M. LAVIN The driver was at the wheel and the engine was running. E. BLISHEN It was the eve of publication, I guess, for the presses were running. P. AUSTER He had adapted the engine to run on methane gas. **10** A. J. CRONIN Sometimes she must run down to Cardiff . . in the car. P. H. NEWBY The ferry to Port Fouad was still running. P. THEROUX The frozen switch . . the snow: we were running very late. *Bus Fayre* Running hourly in each direction the service is maintained by . . Morris Bros. coaches.

▶ **III 11** *verb intrans.* Of a liquid, sand, etc.: flow; course. Also with compl. OE. ▸**b** Spread over a surface; *spec.* (of a colour in a fabric) spread from the dyed parts, diffuse. E17.

12 *verb intrans.* Flow, stream, or be wet *with*. ME.

13 *verb intrans.* Discharge or carry off a liquid; *spec.* (of the nose, eyes, etc.) exude liquid matter. ME. ▸**b** *verb trans.* Flow with (a specified liquid). ME.

14 *verb intrans.* **a** Of a vessel: overflow, leak. ME. ▸**b** Of an hourglass: allow the sand to pass from one compartment to another. E16. ▸**c** Of a bath: be in the process of being filled with water. Usu. in the progressive, ***be running***. M20.

15 *verb intrans.* Flow as the result of melting; *spec.* (of a candle) gutter. LME. ▸**b** *verb trans.* Smelt (metal); form *into* bars etc. by allowing to flow into moulds; cast. M17. ▸**c** *verb trans.* Fasten *together* with molten metal. M17.

16 *verb intrans.* **a** Coagulate; curdle. Now *dial.* LME. ▸**b** Unite or combine, esp. when moist or melted. Usu. foll. by *together*. LME.

🕮 **11** R. WARNER The river . . is narrow and runs fast. I. MURDOCH Perspiration was running . . like tears down . . his face. A. PRICE Swine Brook was running red again, with the wounded . . laid out along its banks. E. DAVID Cook the mulberries with the sugar until the juice runs. *Country Walking* If a good sea is running, the waves . . can be spectacular. **12** J. REED Workers in the pit, exhausted and running with sweat. K. LINES Rivers ran with milk and wine. **14c** G. SWIFT I can hear the sounds of Marian's bath running.

▶ **IV 17** *verb intrans.* Of a period of time: pass or go by, elapse. Now *rare*. OE.

18 *verb intrans.* Continue, go on; be current or operative. ME. ▸**b** (Of money) have currency, be in circulation; (of a writ etc.) have legal force or effect; (of a practice) be generally prevalent. ME. ▸**c** Of a play, broadcast, exhibition, etc.: be presented. E19.

19 *verb intrans.* Have course; extend, stretch; form a continuous line; (of the memory) go back. ME. ▸**b** Of a quality: be common *in* a family. L18. ▸**c** Of a newspaper article etc.: be published, appear. E20.

20 *verb intrans.* Pass into a specified state as by running; get; become. Now chiefly in phrs. LME.

21 *verb intrans.* Of a document etc.: have a specified content, wording, or tenor. L16. ▸**b** Be constituted. E18.

22 *verb intrans.* Have a specified character, quality, arrangement, etc.; be of a specified size, number, etc. Freq. foll. by *at*, *to*. M17.

🕮 **17** W. GOLDING What . . days must run before the body uses all the fat and flesh? **18** *Strand Magazine* Her contract . . had two years more to run. F. SPALDING Lessons ran from nine until one-thirty. **b** J. I. M. STEWART A comedy of mine was then running in a London theatre. **19** I. MURDOCH The lawn . . ran the whole length of the Hospital. J. T. STORY The . . Gallery which runs around two sides of the restaurant. **b** V. WOOLF The collecting mania tends to run in families. **20** GOLDSMITH He ran into debt with everybody that would trust him. *Daily Mirror* When an eighteen-year-old . . decided to impersonate his brother . . he ran into trouble right away. *Sunday Gleaner* They . . ran into difficulties on the way back. A. HOLLINGHURST The conversation did run a bit thin. **21** B. MONTGOMERY It was . . issued on . . 6th August. It ran as follows. H. CARPENTER 'I went to a marvellous party,' runs the first line. **22** *Guardian* The . . operetta which runs to a bothersome two . . hours. M. EDWARDES Losses were running at millions of pounds. *Literature & Theology* These readings . . run contrary to the . . argument of the rest of the book.

▶ **V 23** *verb trans.* Keep to (a certain course); follow (a scent) in hunting; *Austral.* follow (the tracks of a person or animal). OE.

24 *verb trans.* Traverse or cover (a distance, course, etc.) by running; navigate (a stretch of water, esp. a dangerous one); run about in (a place). ME. ▸**b** CRICKET. Score (a run or bye); score (a run or runs) by running between the wickets; score from (a stroke) in this way. M18. ▸**c** CROQUET. Play through (a hoop). L19. ▸**d** Drive past or fail to stop at (a red traffic light etc.). *colloq.* (chiefly *N. Amer.*). M20.

25 *verb trans.* Chase or hunt (game), esp. on horseback or with a vehicle. LME.

26 *verb trans.* Perform (an errand). E16.

27 *verb trans.* Expose oneself to or incur (a risk etc.). L16.

28 *verb trans.* Sew (fabric) loosely or hastily with running stitches. E18.

🕮 **23** M. BERGMANN Infatuation, like a disease, runs a certain course. **24** *Annual Register* Powell . . started from Lee-Bridge, to run two miles in ten minutes. E. BLUNDEN Boys run miles for the raree-show. *Scientific American* Adult rats . . also learn to run a maze. *National Observer (US)* Their daughters are too busy running the streets. **27** G. GREENE Sometimes it seems easier to run the risk of death than ridicule.

▶ **VI 29** *verb trans.* **a** Make (a horse etc.) move quickly, esp. when riding it. OE. ▸**b** Enter (a horse) for a race. M18. ▸**c** Put forward as a candidate for an elected post. L18. ▸**d** Graze (sheep, cattle, etc.); raise (livestock). Chiefly *Austral.* E19.

30 *verb trans.* **a** Drive (a sword etc.) *through* or *into* a person; stab or pierce (a person) deeply with a sword etc. (usu. foll. by *through* (the body)). ME. ▸**b** Drive or cause to strike *against*, *into*, or *through*; force or drive *out of* or *off*. ME.

31 *verb trans.* Cause to move, esp. rapidly, easily, or smoothly; GOLF play (a ball) along the ground; THEATRICAL move (a piece of scenery, esp. a flat) about the stage, esp. along a groove. LME. ▸**b** Transport or convey in a vehicle, ship, etc.; *spec.* smuggle (illicit goods). E18. ▸**c** Pass (the eye, a hand, etc.) rapidly *along*, *over*, etc.; pass (a ribbon etc.) *through*; NAUTICAL suspend (a rope) between two points. E18. ▸**d** Allow (an account) to accumulate for a time without making any payment. M19.

32 *verb trans.* **a** Cause to coagulate or curdle. Now chiefly *dial.* LME. ▸**b** *fig.* Unite or combine *into* or *together*; convert *into*. E18.

33 *verb trans.* Bring into a specified state (as) by running. Chiefly in phrs. M16.

34 *verb trans.* Cause (a liquid etc.) to flow *into* a vessel, *through* a strainer, etc.; discharge; let water escape through (a tap) etc. M16. ▸**b** Cause water to flow over (a thing) held *under* a tap etc. E20. ▸**c** Fill (a bath) with water. M20.

35 *verb trans.* **a** Draw or trace (a line); *spec.* mark off (a boundary line); *fig.* draw (a parallel, distinction, etc.). M17. ▸**b** Cause to extend in a specified direction or take a specified course; form (a cornice etc.); cover (a space) with plaster. E18. ▸**c** Publish (an article etc.) in a newspaper or magazine. L19. ▸**d** BRIDGE. Take an uninterrupted succession of tricks in (a suit); take (a number of tricks) in this way. E20.

36 *verb trans.* **a** Cause (a vehicle, ship, etc.) to travel a regular route. M18. ▸**b** Cause (a machine or vehicle) to operate; show (a film etc.); perform (a test, experiment, etc.) using a particular procedure; own and use (a car). E19. ▸**c** Direct or manage (a business etc.); *transf.* control (a person, *esp.* a spy). M19. ▸**d** Be suffering from (a fever or high temperature). E20.

37 *verb trans.* **a** Tease, nag; harass. *arch. US & Austral. colloq.* M19. ▸**b** Report or hand over to the police; MILITARY bring a charge against. *slang.* E20.

🕮 **30a** ADDISON He received a challenge . . and before Twelve a Clock was run through the Body. **b** A. S. NEILL An engine-driver ran his express into a goods. C. EGLETON A truck-driver ran us off the road. E. WELTY The coward, he ought to be run out of town. **31** W. BLACK The boat was run in to her moorings. SCOTT FITZGERALD I ran the car under its shed. *Observer* David Craig ran the ball past his own keeper. **b** P. FITZGERALD He was going to run . . the sea scouts up to London. *Listener* Two boats suspected of running drugs. **c** E. BOWEN He ran a comb through his hair. J. HIGGINS Running his hands . . over the body, searching for a weapon. **33** *Field* He had almost run himself to a standstill. J. STUART Some say whiskey will run a man crazy. **34** W. A. MILLER Water, run through a fine sieve. J. CANNAN The women . . had been running the taps. **b** C. CONRAN Hard-boil the . . eggs . . . Run them under cold water. **c** M. ALLEN Begin by running me a hot bath. **35** A. CARNEGIE We ran lines across the hillside. **b** M. MACHLIN Boats running absorbent booms around the ship. **c** *New Yorker* The papers . . ran editorials applauding it. **36a** *Reader's Digest* They run planes . . in and out of Chicago. **b** G. B. SHAW Motor oil. The stuff you run . . aeroplanes on. J. RULE Patients . . needing their temperatures taken, needing tests run. D. LEAVITT He . . cleaned the kitchen and ran the dishwasher. **c** J. T. STORY English hotels are run entirely for the convenience of English hoteliers. M. MUGGERIDGE They planned to take over the . . economic system and run it better. B. FORBES 'Who's running you?' he said. **d** M. CONEY He was running a slight fever. *transf.*: *Forbes* The School of Arts . . is running a $5 million deficit.

Phrases: (A selection of cross-refs. only is included: see esp. other nouns.) ***cut and run***: see CUT *verb*. ***run a blockade***: see BLOCKADE *noun* 1. ***one's writ runs***: see WRIT *noun* 1. **run a game (on)** *US Black slang* obtain money (from) by deceit or trickery. **run a mile** *fig.* flee; be evasive through fear, reluctance, etc. ***run amok***: see AMOK *adverb*. **run-and-gun** *adjective* (BASKETBALL) denoting fast, free-flowing play without emphasis on set plays or defence. **run-and-shoot (offence)** AMER. FOOTBALL a style of offence featuring a fast-paced quarterback throwing quick, short passes while evading tacklers. ***run (a person) hard***: see HARD *adverb*. **run a person off his or her feet** occupy or overwork a person to the point of exhaustion (usu. in *pass.*). **run a thing by a person**, **run a thing past a person** check a person's reactions to an idea or proposition. ***run athwart***: see ATHWART *preposition* 2. **run a voyage** (of a ship) risk an unaccompanied voyage during a time of war. **run dry** (*a*) cease to flow; (*b*) *fig.* be exhausted. **run for it** seek safety by fleeing. ***run foul of***: see FOUL *adverb*. ***run heel***: see HEEL *noun*[1]. ***run high***: see HIGH *adverb*. ***run idle***: see IDLE *adjective*. **run interference** AMER. FOOTBALL move in such a way as to cause interference. **run into the ground** exhaust or defeat by constant pursuit or pressure. ***run it fine***: see FINE *adjective*. ***run its course***: see COURSE *noun*[1]. **run low** become depleted; have too little. ***run mad***: see MAD *adjective*. ***run mute***: see MUTE *adjective* 6. **run one's mouth** *US & Black slang* talk profusely or excessively, chatter; complain. ***run one's own show***: see SHOW *noun*[1]. **run out of steam** become weary; lose impetus. ***run out of town on a rail***: see RAIL *noun*[2]. **run out on** abandon, desert. ***run ragged***: see RAGGED *adjective* 6. ***run rings round***: see RING *noun*[1]. ***run riot***: see RIOT *noun*. **run scared** (*a*) *US* stand for office in a manner indicating or suggesting a fear of losing; (*b*) be frightened, panic. **run short** (*a*) = *run low* above; (*b*) run out (*of*). ***run the blockade***: see BLOCKADE *noun* 1. ***run the gantlope***: see GANTLOPE. ***run the gauntlet***: see GAUNTLET *noun*[2]. ***run the rule over***: see RULE *noun*. ***run the show***: see SHOW *noun*[1]. ***run to earth***: see EARTH *noun*[1]. **run to meet** *fig.* anticipate (troubles etc.). ***run to seed***: see SEED *noun*. ***run to waste***: see WASTE *noun*. ***run up against***: see AGAINST *preposition*. **run wild** grow or stray unchecked or undisciplined or untrained. ***run with the ball***: see BALL *noun*[1] 2. ***walk before one can run***: see WALK *verb*[1].

With adverbs in specialized senses: (See also Phrases above.) **run around** (*a*) take from place to place by car etc.; (*b*) go about hurriedly with no fixed goal; (*c*) deceive or evade repeatedly; (*d*) *slang* associate or consort *with*; engage in esp. casual or illicit sexual relations *with*. **run away** (*a*) flee in the face of danger or opposition; (*b*) abscond; depart surreptitiously; *spec.* elope; (*c*) ***run away with***: carry off (stolen property etc.); accept or believe (an idea etc.) without due reflection; win (a prize) easily; (of an expense etc.) consume or exhaust (a supply of money); (*d*) (of a horse) bolt (*with* rider, a carriage or its occupants); (*e*) get away *from*, outdistance, esp. in a race; (see also sense 3 above). **run down** (*a*) (of a clock, battery, etc.) cease to function through gradual loss of power; (*b*) (of a person or a person's health) become feeble through overwork, lack of nourishment, etc. (chiefly as RUN-DOWN *adjective*); (*c*) (cause to) diminish or decrease; (*d*) reduce or bring gradually to a halt (the activities of an organization etc.); (*e*) deteriorate; fall into disuse or decay; (*f*) (of a vehicle or driver) knock down (a person); NAUTICAL collide with and sink (a vessel); (*g*) pursue (game) until caught or killed; (*h*) discover after a search; (*i*) disparage; (*j*) *US slang* perform (a piece of music etc.), esp. in rehearsal; (*k*) ***run it down*** (*US (esp. Black) slang*), describe or explain a situation in full. **run in** (*a*) (now *rare*) agree *with*; (*b*) (of a combatant) rush to close quarters; (*c*) *Austral.* pursue and confine (cattle or horses); (*d*) *colloq.* pay a short visit (*to* a person); (*e*) *colloq.* arrest; (*f*) operate (new machinery, esp. a motor vehicle or its engine) at reduced speed in the early stages; (*g*) insert, slip in; (*h*) fix *with* (molten lead etc.). **run off** (*a*) flee, abscond, elope; (*b*) *US* steal; (*c*) SPORT decide (a race) after a series of heats or in the event of a tie; (*d*) (cause to) flow away; (*e*) produce (a copy or copies) on a machine; (*f*) write or recite rapidly, dash off; (*g*) *US slang* digress suddenly; ***run off at the mouth***, talk excessively; (*h*) *arch.* become smaller, diminish. **run on** (*a*) continue in operation; (*b*) (of time) pass, elapse; (*c*) continue speaking; talk incessantly, chatter; (*d*) (of written characters) be joined together; (*e*) TYPOGRAPHY continue on the same line as the preceding matter. **run out** (*a*) (of a period of time, lease, etc.) expire, come to an end; (*b*) (of a liquid etc.) escape from a containing vessel; (*c*) exhaust or use up one's stock (*of*); (of a stock) become exhausted or used up; (*d*) (of a crop variety) lose its distinguishing characteristics in successive generations; (*e*) (now *rare* or *obsolete*) squander (a fortune); (*f*) (of a rope) be paid out; (*g*) produce; (*h*) extend, jut out; (*i*) advance (a gun etc.) so as to project the muzzle etc.; (*j*) TYPOGRAPHY expand, fill out; *spec.* set with a hanging indentation; (*k*) emerge from a contest in a specified manner or position; win by achieving a required score etc.; (*l*) finish (a race etc.); (*m*) CRICKET dismiss (a batsman) by knocking down the wicket with the ball while the batsman is running; cause (oneself, one's partner) to be dismissed in this way; (*n*) exhaust (oneself) by running; (*o*) ***run out on*** (*colloq.*), desert or abandon (a person). **run over** (*a*) overflow; (*b*) (now *rare* or *obsolete*) glance over, read hurriedly; (*c*) (of a vehicle or its driver) knock down, *spec.* knock down and pass over. **run through** draw a line through (written words); (see also sense 30a above). **run up** (*a*) shoot up, grow rapidly; (*b*) increase, mount up; (*c*) rise in price *to*; amount *to*; (*d*) accumulate (a number of things, a debt, etc.); (*e*) force (a rival bidder) to bid higher at an auction; (*f*) cause (a price) to rise; cause to rise in price; (*g*) cause to ascend or rise; *esp.* raise (a flag) to the top of a mast; (*h*) build or make rapidly or hurriedly; *spec.* make (a garment) by sewing quickly or simply; (*i*) add up (a column of figures) rapidly; (*j*) be runner-up in a race etc. (*k*) run (an aircraft engine) quickly while out of gear in order to warm it up; (*l*) (of an aircraft engine) warm up; (*m*) *Austral.* bring in (a horse etc.) from pasture; (*n*) trace or follow up in some way; (*o*) *arch.* go back in time or memory; (*p*) ***run up against***, meet with or encounter (a difficulty etc.).

With prepositions in specialized senses: (See also Phrases above.) **run across** — happen to meet or encounter. **run after** — (*a*) pursue at a run; (*b*) seek the society of; pursue with admiration or attentions; (*c*) give much time to (a pursuit etc.). **run against** — (*a*) act, operate, or be directed against; (*b*) happen to meet or encounter. **run before** — keep ahead of, anticipate. **run in** — †(*a*) incur, expose oneself to (blame, loss, danger, etc.); (*b*) lapse or fall into arrears of (payment etc.); (see also senses 6c, 19b above). **run into** — (*a*) incur (blame, displeasure, expenses, etc.); (*b*) rush or fall into (a practice, absurdity, etc.); (*c*) reach as many as, amount to; (*d*) *arch.* change or develop into; (*e*) merge into; be continuous or coalesce with; (*f*) collide with, esp. by accident; (*g*) encounter, happen to meet; (see also senses 6c, 30a, 32b, 34 above). **run on** — (*a*) refer or relate to; be concerned with; (*b*) (of the mind) be engrossed or occupied with (a subject). **run over** — (*a*) glance or look over; survey or scan rapidly; deal with hastily or superficially; (*b*) repeat quickly; recapitulate; (*c*) touch (the keys of a piano etc.) in quick succession; (*d*) *US colloq.* impose upon, treat with contempt; (see also senses 2b, 31c above). **run through** — (*a*) examine or peruse rapidly; deal with rapidly or successively; (*b*) consume or spend (esp. a fortune) rapidly or recklessly; (*c*) pervade; (*d*) rehearse or repeat (a procedure etc.), esp. briefly; (see also senses 2b, 6b, 6c, 30a, 31c above); (*e*) (now *rare*) undergo, experience. **run to** — (*a*) reach, amount or extend to, (a specified quantity etc.); (*b*) have the money for; cover the expense of, be sufficient for; (*c*) manage to provide, have the resources or capacity for; (*d*) fall into (ruin etc.); (*e*) (of land) produce naturally; (*f*) (of a plant) tend to the development of (now chiefly in ***run to seed***); (*g*) (of a person) show a tendency to; (see also senses 1b, 22 above). **run upon** — (*a*) *arch.* have a tendency to, favour; (*b*) (of the mind etc.) dwell upon; be engrossed by; (*c*) (now *rare* or *obsolete*) engage in (a practice etc.). **run with** — (*a*) accompany; (of land) march with; (*b*) agree with; (*c*) (chiefly *US*) associate with (a person).

Comb.: **runabout** (*a*) a person who runs or roves about from place to place; *colloq.* an assistant, a dogsbody; (*b*) a small light car, aircraft, or (chiefly *US*) motor-boat; **run and fell** (designating) a type of seam in which two pieces of a garment are sewn together at the edges with one then turned over and stitched to the other; **run-and-read** *adjective* given to hasty reading; **run-around** (*a*) *colloq.* (an instance of) deceit or evasion; (esp. in ***give the run-around***); (*b*) *colloq.* a short journey or excursion; (*c*) TYPOGRAPHY type set in shorter measure so as to fit at the side of an illustration; (*d*) *US colloq.* a whitlow; **run-back** (*a*) an act of running backwards; (*b*) AMER. FOOTBALL a forward run made after catching a kick or intercepting a pass; (*c*) the additional space located at either end of a tennis-court; **run-flat** *adjective* designating a kind of tyre which does not deflate after puncturing; **run-over** (*a*) an act of running over; *esp.* a hasty perusal; (*b*) the action or an act of continuing printed matter into a margin or on to a subsequent line or page; **run-through** (*a*) a (freq. hasty or cursory) rehearsal of a play etc.; (*b*) a brief outline or summary.

runability /rʌnəˈbɪlɪti/ *noun*. Also **-nn-**. M20.
[from RUN *verb* + -ABILITY. Cf. RUNNABLE.]
The capacity for running; ability to be run; *spec.* (PAPER-MAKING & PRINTING) the degree of ease with which paper passes through a machine.

runagate /ˈrʌnəgeɪt/ *noun & adjective*. *arch.* E16.
[Alt. of RENEGATE by assoc. with RUN *verb*, AGATE *adverb*.]
▶ **A** *noun*. †**1** = RENEGADE *noun* 1. E16–L17.
2 A deserter; a fugitive. M16.
3 A vagabond, a wanderer. M16.
▶ **B** *adjective*. = RENEGADE *adjective*. M16.

runanga /ˈrʌnaŋa/ *noun*. M19.
[Maori.]
A Maori assembly or council.

runaway /ˈrʌnəweɪ/ *noun & adjective*. M16.
[from *run away* s.v. RUN *verb*.]
▶ **A** *noun*. **1** A fugitive; a deserter. M16. ▸†**b** An apostate. M16–M17. ▸**c** An animal (esp. a horse) or vehicle which is running out of control. E17.
2 An act of running away or out of control. Chiefly *US*. E18. ▸**b** = RUNWAY 1. *colloq.* (chiefly *US*). M19. ▸**c** Uncontrolled departure of a system, esp. a nuclear reactor, from its usual or intended equilibrium. M20.
▶ **B** *attrib.* or as *adjective*. **1** That has run away; fugitive. M16. ▸**b** Done or performed after running away. M18.
2 That is running away or out of control. E17. ▸**b** *fig.* Developing at an ever-increasing rate; unrestrained, rampant; (of success etc.) immeasurable, overwhelming. M19.

runch /rʌn(t)ʃ/ *noun*. *Scot. & north.* M16.
[Origin unkn.]
Either of two common cruciferous weeds, charlock, *Sinapis arvensis*, and wild radish, *Raphanus raphanistrum*.
▪ Also **runchie** *noun* E18.

runcible spoon /ˌrʌnsɪb(ə)l ˈspuːn/ *noun phr*. L19.
[Nonsense word used by Edward Lear (1812–88), English humorist: prob. fanciful alt. of ROUNCIVAL.]
A fork curved like a spoon and having three broad prongs, one of which has a slightly sharp edge.

runcinate /ˈrʌnsɪnət/ *adjective*. L18.
[mod. Latin *runcinatus*, from Latin *runcina* carpenter's plane (formerly taken to mean a saw) + -ATE[2].]
BOTANY. Of a leaf: strongly lobed or toothed, with the lobes or teeth curved towards the base. Freq. in ***runcinate-pinnatifid***.
▪ Also **runcinated** *adjective* (now *rare*) L18.

rundale /ˈrʌndeɪl/ *adverb, noun, & adjective*. LME.
[from RUN *verb* + *dale* Scot. & north. var. of DOLE *noun*[1]. Cf. RUNRIG.]
Hist. ▶**A** *adverb*. With reference to the holding of land: in separate strips cultivated by different occupiers. LME.
▶ **B** *noun*. **1** A land-tenure system used esp. in Scotland and Ireland, similar to runrig but involving larger sections of land. Chiefly in ***in rundale***. L15.
2 (A strip of) land occupied and cultivated under this system. E19.
▶ **C** *adjective*. Held under or designating this system. E17.

rundle /ˈrʌnd(ə)l/ *noun*[1]. ME.
[Var. of ROUNDEL. In sense 5 perh. alt. of RUNNEL *noun*.]
1 a = ROUNDEL 2. *arch.* ME. ▸**b** A circular or spherical object. Formerly *spec.* = ROUNDEL 4b. *arch.* LME. ▸**c** A circular enclosure or field. Now *dial.* L16.
†**2 a** A coil; a curve. M16–M17. ▸**b** BOTANY. A circular arrangement of flowers or leaves; an umbel, a whorl. L16–E19.
3 HERALDRY. = ROUNDEL 1b. Now *rare* or *obsolete*. M16.
4 a A cylinder of wood. Formerly *spec.* a rung of a ladder. Cf. ROUNDEL 5a. Now *rare*. M16. ▸**b** A solid wheel or barrel. Now *rare*. E17.
5 A pollard tree. *dial.* L17.

rundle /ˈrʌnd(ə)l/ *noun*[2]. Long *dial.* L16.
[Var. of RUNNEL *noun* with intrusive *d*.]
A small stream.

rundlet *noun* see RUNLET *noun*[1].

run-down /*as adjective* rʌnˈdaʊn, *as noun* ˈrʌndaʊn/ *adjective & noun*. Also **run down**, **rundown**. L17.
[from *run down* s.v. RUN *verb*.]
▶ **A** *adjective*. †**1** Downtrodden, oppressed. *rare*. Only in L17.
2 In a low state of health; weak or ill through overwork etc. M19.
3 Dilapidated; *esp.* (of a district etc.) decayed, shabby, seedy. L19.
4 (Of a clock etc.) completely unwound; no longer functioning through lack of power. L19.

> 📖 **2** J. R. ACKERLEY I had made no actual plans for a holiday, but I was terribly run down. R. P. GRAVES Alfred had an unpleasant sore throat and felt . . run-down. **3** R. INGALLS A quiet, slightly run-down neighbourhood. F. RAPHAEL A life of penurious self-indulgence on his rundown estate. **4** E. AMBLER Leads for attaching the thing to a run-down battery.

▶ **B** *noun*. **1** BASEBALL. An action whereby defending players attempt to tag out a runner caught off base between them. E20.
2 HORSE-RACING. A list of entries and betting odds. Freq. *attrib.* *US slang*. M20.
3 A (usu. verbal) listing of items of information; a summary; a brief account. M20.
4 A gradual reduction in the size or scope of an organization etc. M20.

> 📖 **3** W. GOLDING I gave him a run-down of the virtues . . of the boat. **4** *Observer* The growing run-down of necessary social services.

▪ **run-downness** /-n-n-/ *noun* E20.

rune /ruːn/ *noun & verb*. Also †**roun**. OE.
[Var. of ROUN *noun*. In sense 1 not recorded between ME and L17; reintroduced in 17 as rendering of late Latin *runa*, infl. by Old Norse *rúnar*, *rúnir* (pl.), secret or hidden lore, runes, magical signs.]
▶ **A** *noun*. **I 1** Any of the letters of the earliest Germanic alphabet, used esp. by the Scandinavians and Anglo-Saxons from around the 3rd cent. AD, and formed by modifying Roman or Greek characters to facilitate carving on wood or stone; a similar character or mark believed to have magical power or significance. Also, a character of a non-Germanic or esp. ancient alphabet resembling this. OE.
2 An incantation, a charm, *esp.* one denoted by magic or cryptic signs; a magic word. L18.
3 (A division of) an ancient Finnish poem; *esp.* any of the songs of the Kalevala. M19.

> 📖 **2** K. CROSSLEY-HOLLAND He murmured the runes, the magic words, and turned Idun into a nut.

▶†**II** See ROUN *noun*.
Comb.: **rune-ribbon** a carved area on a stone within which runes were engraved; **rune-row** a runic alphabet; **rune-staff** (*a*) a magic wand inscribed with runes; (*b*) a runic calendar; **rune-stave** *arch.* a runic letter or symbol; **rune-stone** (*a*) a large stone carved with runes; (*b*) a small stone, piece of bone, etc., marked with a rune and used in divination; **rune-tree** = ***tree-rune*** s.v. TREE *noun*.
▶ **B** *verb intrans.* Compose or recite poetry etc.; chant. *rare*. *literary*. M20.

rung /rʌŋ/ *noun*.
[Old English *hrung* = Middle Low German *runge* (Dutch *rong*), Old High German *runga* (German *Runge* from Low German), Gothic *hrugga* (rendering Greek *rhabdos*).]
1 A strong rounded stick, *esp.* one used as a strengthening crosspiece or rail in a cart, chair, etc. OE.
2 Each of the horizontal supports or crossbars of a ladder. ME.
3 A cudgel; a stout staff. *Scot. & north.* M16.
4 SHIPBUILDING. A floor-timber. Cf. WRONG *noun*[1] 1. Now *rare*. E17.
▪ **runged** *adjective* having rungs L17. **rungless** *adjective* L19.

rung *verb pa. t. & pple*: see RING *verb*[1].

Runge–Kutta /rʊŋəˈkʊtə/ *noun*. M20.
[from C. D. T. *Runge* (1856–1927) + M. W. *Kutta* (1867–1944), German mathematicians.]
MATH. Used *attrib.* to designate a method of approximating to solutions of differential equations.

runic /ˈruːnɪk/ *adjective & noun*. M17.
[mod. Latin *runicus*, from Old Norse: see RUNE, -IC.]
▶ **A** *adjective*. **1** Consisting of runes; carved or written in runes. M17. ▸**b** Inscribed with runes. E18. ▸**c** Of, pertaining to, or concerned with runes. M19.
2 a Of or pertaining to ancient Scandinavia; *transf.* (of literature) contemporaneous with that of ancient Scandinavia. *arch.* M17. ▸**b** Of an ornamental design: having an interlacing geometric form characteristic of rune-bearing monuments etc. M19.
▶ **B** *noun*. †**1** Old Norse. M–L17.
2 A runic alphabet. M19.
3 TYPOGRAPHY. A style of display lettering with a thickened face and often a condensed form. L19.

run-in /ˈrʌnɪn/ *noun*. M19.
[from *run in* s.v. RUN *verb*.]
1 An act of running in; *spec.* (RUGBY FOOTBALL) an act of running over the touch-line of the opposite side with the ball. M19.
2 A quarrel, a row; a fight. Chiefly in ***have a run-in (with)***. *colloq.* E20.
3 The approach of an aircraft to a dropping-point or landing-place. M20.

4 *transf.* An introductory statement or event. Also = **RUN-UP** 2d. **M20.**

5 A place for storing stolen goods. *Criminals' slang.* **M20.**

Comb.: **run-in groove** on a gramophone record, the blank groove traversing the annular area outside the grooves carrying the recording; **run-in shed** *US* an open-fronted shelter in which horses are housed.

runkle /ˈrʌŋk(ə)l/ *noun & verb.* **ME.**
[Prob. of Scandinavian origin: cf. **RUCKLE** *noun*².]
▶ **A** *noun.* A wrinkle, a crease. Now *Scot.* **ME.**
▶ **B** *verb intrans. & trans.* Wrinkle, rumple. *colloq.* (orig. *Scot.*). **ME.**

runlet /ˈrʌnlɪt/ *noun*¹. *arch.* Also (earlier) **rund-** /ˈrʌnd-/. **LME.**
[Old French *rondelet* dim. of *rondelle*, formed as **ROUND** *adjective*. Cf. **ROUNDEL**.]
A cask of varying capacity; the quantity of liquor contained in this.

runlet /ˈrʌnlɪt/ *noun*². **L17.**
[from **RUN** *noun* + **-LET**.]
A little stream; a runnel.

runnability *noun* var. of **RUNABILITY**.

runnable /ˈrʌnəb(ə)l/ *adjective.* **L19.**
[from **RUN** *verb* + **-ABLE**.]
1 *HUNTING.* Of a deer: warrantable. **L19.**
2 Able to be run; manageable; operable; *spec.* (*a*) *COMPUTING* (of a program) able to be executed; (*b*) (of a river etc.) sufficiently deep to be navigable, esp. by a small boat. **L20.**

runnage /ˈrʌnɪdʒ/ *noun.* **M19.**
[from **RUN** *verb* + **-AGE**.]
1 Flow or quantity of water in a river. *rare.* **M19.**
2 The length of a unit weight of twine, thread, etc. (as a measure of its bulk). **M20.**

runnel /ˈrʌn(ə)l/ *noun & verb.* **L16.**
[Var. of **RINDLE** infl. by **RUN** *verb*.]
▶ **A** *noun.* **1** A small stream; a brook, a rill. **L16.**
2 A small watercourse or channel; a gutter. **M17.**
▶ **B** *verb trans.* Infl. **-ll-**, *-**l-**. Form streams or channels in (a surface). **M19.**

runner /ˈrʌnə/ *noun.* **ME.**
[from **RUN** *verb* + **-ER**¹.]
▶ **I 1** A person who runs, esp. in a race. **ME.** ▸**b** *BASEBALL.* = ***base-runner*** s.v. **BASE** *noun*¹. **M19.** ▸**c** *CRICKET.* A person who runs on behalf of an injured batsman. **M19.** ▸**d** A person who runs ahead of a dog-sledge in order to find or clear a path in snow. *N. Amer.* **M19.** ▸**e** *AMER. FOOTBALL.* A player who runs with the ball on an attacking play. **L19.** ▸**f** A wounded game-bird which can run but not fly. **M20.**
2 a A messenger, a courier; a scout; a person employed to fetch and carry things, an assistant; *MILITARY* an orderly. **ME.** ▸†**b** A spy for a gambling-den, gang of thieves, etc. Only in **18.** ▸**c** A person employed or acting as a collector or agent for a bank, broker, or bookmaker; a person who solicits trade for a hotel, lawyer, etc. **M18.** ▸**d** A police officer. Chiefly in ***Bow Street runner***. Now *arch.* or *Hist.* **L18.** ▸**e** A freelance antique dealer. *slang.* **M20.**
3 A fugitive; a deserter. Long *rare.* **ME.**
4 a A horse capable of running well; *spec.* a horse taking part in a race. **L15.** ▸**b** A fast-sailing ship; *spec.* (*US*) = ***run-boat*** s.v. **RUN** *noun.* **L17.** ▸**c** A roadworthy motor vehicle. **M20.**
5 a Any of various birds that run and hide rather than fly, *esp.* the water rail. Now *rare.* **M17.** ▸**b** = **RACER** 2b. *US.* **L18.** ▸**c** Any of various carangid fishes of tropical or temperate seas, esp. *Elagatis pinnulata* (more fully ***rainbow runner***) and *Caranx crysos* (more fully ***blue runner***, ***hardtail runner***). Also, the cobia. **L19.** ▸**d** In full ***Indian runner***. (A bird of) a breed of duck, either white, fawn, or coloured as a wild mallard, distinguished by an erect posture and kept for egg-laying. **L19.**
6 a A smuggler. Now chiefly with specifying word. **E18.** ▸**b** = ***blockade-runner*** s.v. **BLOCKADE** *noun.* **M19.** ▸**c** A sailor engaged for a single short voyage. *Nautical slang.* **L19.**
7 A person who operates a machine or manages an institution etc.; *spec.* an engine-driver; *slang* the leader of a street gang. Chiefly *US.* **L19.**
▶ **II 8** †**a** A strainer. *rare.* **L15–E16.** ▸**b** A small stream; a brook. *Scot. & north.* **M16.** ▸**c** *FOUNDING.* A channel along which molten metal runs from the furnace to the mould. **M19.** ▸**d** = **RUN** *noun* 14c. **E20.**
9 A revolving millstone, usu. the upper one of a pair; any stone used for grinding or polishing. **M16.** ▸**b** A tool used in decorating a revolving piece of pottery. **L19.** ▸**c** The rotor of a turbine. **E20.**
10 A ring capable of sliding on a rod etc. to facilitate movement, or through which something may be drawn; *spec.* (*MOUNTAINEERING*) = ***running belay*** s.v. **RUNNING** *ppl adjective.* **M16.** ▸**b** *MINING.* A device connecting the loose end of a pulley-rope to the boring-rods. **M19.**
11 *NAUTICAL.* A rope in a single block, with one end passed round a tackle-block and the other having a hook attached. **E17.**
12 a A long creeping stem arising from an axillary bud, which roots at the nodes and forms new plants. Cf. **STOLON** 1. **M17.** ▸**b** In full ***runner bean***. Any of several cultivated varieties of beans which twine round stakes for support, *esp.* (more fully ***scarlet runner***) *Phaseolus coccineus*, with red flowers and long pods; the pods of this bean, eaten young as a vegetable. **L18.**
13 A cut of beef. *Scot.* **L17.**
14 Each of the long pieces (usu. curved at the ends) on which a sledge etc. slides; the blade of a skate. **M18.**
15 a A support or groove along or in which something slides; a roller for moving a heavy object. **E19.** ▸**b** *BUILDING.* A long horizontal beam or girder. **L19.**
16 *BOOKBINDING.* A board used in cutting the edges of a book. **E19.**
17 A long narrow ornamental strip of cloth, usu. placed along a table; a long narrow rug, esp. for a hall or staircase. **L19.**
18 *TYPOGRAPHY.* A marginal figure or letter denoting the line number, used for reference purposes esp. in plays etc. Usu. in *pl.* **L19.**
19 A lightweight soft-soled sports or leisure shoe. Usu. in *pl. Austral. colloq.* **L20.**

Phrases & comb.: **do a runner** *slang* (*a*) escape by running away, abscond; (*b*) depart hastily and unceremoniously. ***front runner***: see **FRONT** *noun, adjective, & adverb.* ***ROME-runner***. ***runner bean***: see sense 12b above. **runner-up**, pl. **runners-up**, **runner-ups**, a competitor or team taking second place in a contest or race.

■ **runnered** *adjective* (of a sledge etc.) having runners **L19.** **runnerless** *adjective* (esp. of a strawberry plant) not producing runners **M20.**

runnet /ˈrʌnɪt/ *noun. obsolete* exc. *dial.* **L15.**
[Var. of **RENNET** *noun*¹.]
1 = **RENNET** *noun*¹ 2. **L15.**
2 = **RENNET** *noun*¹ 3. **L17.**

running /ˈrʌnɪŋ/ *noun.* **OE.**
[from **RUN** *verb* + **-ING**¹.]
▶ **I 1** The action of **RUN** *verb*; an instance of this; *spec.* racing. Also foll. by adverb. **OE.** ▸**b** Capacity for running. **M19.**
2 The discharge of mucus, blood, or other matter from the body; a sore which discharges matter. **OE.** ▸**b** A leakage of air from a musical instrument, esp. an organ. **L18.**
3 A channel, a watercourse; a stream. *rare.* **ME.**
4 A course, a direction. *rare.* **M16.**
5 A stage in the production of beer, wine, or spirits; the liquor obtained at a specified stage. **E17.** ▸**b** The result of a smelting process. **M17.** ▸**c** An act of tapping a tree for sap; the amount of sap produced from this. **M18.**
6 A line of running stitches. **M19.**
▶ **II 7** Rennet. Now *dial.* **OE.**

Phrases: **in the running** (of a competitor) having a good chance of winning. **make the running** take the lead; set the pace. **out of the running** (of a competitor) having a poor chance of winning. †**running of the reins** a venereal discharge, as in gonorrhoea. **take up the running** = ***make the running*** above.

Comb.: **running-board** a footboard extending along either side of a vehicle; **running brand** *US* a cattle brand made with a running iron; **running iron** *US* a straight branding iron used for altering cattle brands; **running light** (*a*) *NAUTICAL* = ***NAVIGATION light***; (*b*) a small light on a motor vehicle that remains illuminated while the vehicle is running; **running off** = **RUN-OFF** 3; **running shoe** a (freq. spiked) shoe for running (usu. in *pl.*); ***give a person his or her running shoes***, dismiss a person.

running /ˈrʌnɪŋ/ *adjective.* **ME.**
[from **RUN** *verb* + **-ING**².]
▶ **I 1** That runs. **ME.** ▸†**b** Volatile, flighty, giddy. **L16–M17.** ▸**c** Employed as an attendant on foot or to run as a messenger. *obsolete* exc. *Hist.* **E17.**
2 Fluid, liquid; melting readily; (of sand, soil, etc.) having no coherence, slipping or falling readily; *fig.* (of metre, music, etc.) of a smooth, flowing, or rapid character. **LME.**
3 a Of a disease: passing from one part of the body to another; *esp.* spreading over the skin. Now *rare* or *obsolete.* **LME.** ▸**b** Of a plant: spreading by creeping stems or runners. **M16.**
4 Current, prevalent, general; existing; in progress. **LME.** ▸†**b** Of cash: available for use. **L17–E19.**
5 Chiefly *NAUTICAL.* ▸**a** Of a rope etc.: capable of moving when pulled; *esp.* moving freely through a block, ring, etc. **L15.** ▸**b** Of a knot: slipping easily along a rope and so adjusting the size of a noose. **L16.**
6 Continuous, sustained; constantly repeated or recurring. **L15.** ▸**b** Of a lease etc.: allowed to run on for a certain specified or indefinite time. **M18.**
7 Of a measurement: linear. **M17.**
8 *postpositive.* Consecutive; in succession. **M17.**
9 Of a ship: sailing in time of war without a convoy. **E19.**
10 *MEDICINE.* Of the pulse: weak, rapid, and irregular. **L19.**

> 📖 **8** N. STREATFEILD I disapprove . . of you being allowed out two Sundays running.

▶ **II 11** Performed with or accompanied by a run; rapid, hasty. **ME.**
†**12** Of a meal: eaten hurriedly; slight. **E17–L18.**

> 📖 **11** L. KOPPETT To stop a running attack, a defensive line must hold.

Special collocations: **running account** a current account. **running back** *AMER. FOOTBALL* (the position of) a back whose primary function is to run carrying the ball. ***running banquet***: see **BANQUET** *noun* 2. **running battle** (*a*) a battle (esp. a naval one) carried on while one side flees and the other pursues; (*b*) a military engagement which constantly changes its location. **running belay** *MOUNTAINEERING*: through which the climbing rope runs freely, acting as a pulley if the climber falls. **running bowline** a bowline knot adapted to form a noose. **running commentary** an oral description of events as they occur; *spec.* a broadcast report of a sporting contest etc. **running dog** *slang* [translating Chinese *zǒugǒu*, from *zǒu* to run + *gǒu* dog] a servile political follower. **running fight** = ***running battle*** above. **running fire** a rapid successive discharge of firearms by each of a line of troops. **running fit** *MECHANICS*: allowing freedom of movement of the parts. **running fix** a fix obtained by determining bearings at different times and making allowance for the distance covered by the observer in the interval. ***running footman***: see **FOOTMAN** 3. **running gear** (*a*) the moving parts of a machine; *esp.* the wheels, steering, and suspension of a vehicle; (*b*) the rope and tackle used in handling (part of) a boat. **running hand** writing in which the pen etc. is not lifted after each letter. **running head**, **running headline** a heading printed at the top of a number of consecutive pages of a book. **running ice** *N. Amer.*: which moves downstream in blocks and sheets. **running jump**: preceded and augmented by a run; ***take a running jump (at yourself)*** (*colloq.*) go away, be off, (usu. as *interjection*). **running martingale** a form of martingale consisting of a strap fastened at one end to a horse's girth, and divided at the other end into two branches fitted with rings through which the reins are passed. **running mate** (chiefly *US*) (*a*) a horse entered in a race in order to set the pace for another horse from the same stable which is intended to win; (*b*) a candidate for a subordinate office in an election, *spec.* the vice-presidential candidate in US presidential elections. **running moss** *dial.* the stag's-horn clubmoss, *Lycopodium clavatum*. **running mould** *PLASTERING*: moving on fixed guides and used to shape cornices etc. **running noose**: formed with a running knot. **running pine** *N. Amer.* = ***running moss*** above. **running repairs** hurried, minor, or temporary repairs made to machinery etc. while in use. ***running rigging***: see **RIGGING** *noun*² 2a. **running set** a country dance in which the dancers perform a number of figures in quick succession. **running sore** a suppurating sore; *fig.* a constant nuisance or irritation. **running stitch** (any of) a line of loose, open stitches for gathering etc. **running title** = ***running head*** above. **running toad** = **NATTERJACK**. **running total**: continually adjusted to take account of further items. **running water** (*a*) water flowing in a stream or river; (*b*) a constant supply of water from a tap etc.

■ **runningly** *adverb* (*arch.*) †(*a*) concurrently; (*b*) rapidly, readily: **LME.**

†**runnion** *noun. rare.* Also **ronyon**. **L16.**
[Origin unkn.]
1 A coarse unpleasant woman. *derog.* **L16–E17.**
2 The penis. Only in **M17.**

> 📖 **1** SHAKES. *Macb.* 'Aroint thee, witch!' the rump-fed ronyon cries.

runny /ˈrʌni/ *adjective.* **E19.**
[from **RUN** *verb* + **-Y**¹.]
1 Tending to run or flow; (excessively) fluid, not set; (of an egg) lightly cooked so as to have a soft centre. **E19.**
2 Of the nose: running, discharging mucus. **M20.**

runo /ˈruːnəʊ/ *noun.* Pl. **-not** /-nɒt/, **-nos**. **L19.**
[Finnish.]
An ancient Finnish poem or song on an epic or legendary subject; *spec.* any of the songs of the Kalevala. Cf. **RUNE** *noun* 3.

run-off /ˈrʌnɒf/ *noun.* **M19.**
[from ***run off*** s.v. **RUN** *verb*.]
1 The action or an act of running off something; a quantity run off, esp. by a mechanical process. **M19.**
2 *spec.* **a** A final deciding competition, election, race, etc., held after a tie. **L19.** ▸**b** (The amount of) water that is carried off an area by streams and rivers after having fallen as rain; the action or an instance of water running off from an area; *N. Amer.* the period when this occurs, *esp.* the spring thaw. **L19.**
3 The dropping of fruit before it is ripe. **E20.**
4 A separate area of land where young animals etc. are kept. *NZ.* **M20.**
5 An act of urinating. *slang.* **M20.**

runology /ruːˈnɒlədʒi/ *noun.* **M19.**
[from **RUNE** + **-OLOGY**.]
The branch of knowledge that deals with runes.
■ **runoˈlogical** *adjective* **M20.** **runologist** *noun* **M19.**

runot *noun pl.* see **RUNO**.

run-out /ˈrʌnaʊt/ *noun.* **E19.**
[from ***run out*** s.v. **RUN** *verb*.]
1 a *FOUNDING.* The action of running or flowing out. Now *spec.* leakage of molten metal from a cupola or a mould. **E19.** ▸**b** An act of running out or fleeing; an escape. *slang.* **E20.**
2 *CRICKET.* An instance of a batsman being dismissed by being run out. **M19.**

3 *MOUNTAINEERING.* The length of rope required to climb a single pitch; a pitch climbed by means of a single length of rope. **E20.**
4 A mock auction. Freq. *attrib. slang.* **M20.**
5 *ENGINEERING.* Deviation of a wheel, drill, etc., from its proper course; the extent of this. **M20.**
6 = OUT-RUN 3. **M20.**
7 (The blank groove traversing) the annular area between the label and the grooves carrying the recording on a gramophone record. Freq. in ***run-out groove.*** **M20.**
1b ***take a run-out powder***: see POWDER *noun*[1].

runrig /ˈrʌnrɪɡ/ *noun, adverb, & adjective. Scot.* Also †**rin-**. **LME.**
[from RUN *verb* + RIG *noun*[1]. Cf. RUNDALE.]
Hist. ▶**A** *noun.* A land-tenure system in which land was divided into thin strips with a (not necessarily contiguous) number being occupied and cultivated by each of the joint holders (chiefly in ***in runrig***); a strip of land occupied and cultivated under this system. **LME.**
▶**B** *adverb.* With reference to the holding of land: in separate strips cultivated by different occupiers. **E16.**
▶**C** *adjective.* Held under or designating this system. **M18.**
■ **runrigged** *adjective* = RUNRIG *adjective* **L17.**

runt /rʌnt/ *noun.* **E16.**
[Origin unkn.]
1 a An old or decayed tree stump. Now *dial.* **E16.** ▸**b** A hardened stem or stalk of a plant, esp. a cabbage. *Scot. & north.* **E17.**
2 a A small ox or cow, *esp.* one of any of various Scottish Highland or Welsh breeds. **M16.** ▸**b** An old ox or cow. Now *dial.* **M17.** ▸**c** A small or inferior pig or other animal, *esp.* the smallest or weakest in a litter. Also, a small or inferior object. **E18.**
3 *transf.* **a** An ignorant or uncouth person. *arch.* **E17.** ▸**b** An old woman; a hag. Now *Scot. & dial.* **M17.** ▸**c** A small or undersized person; a short stocky person. Usu. *derog.* **L17.**
4 (A bird of) a large stout variety of the domestic pigeon. **M17.**

> 🕮 **3c** E. BAKER He'd been such a skinny little runt.

■ **runted** *adjective* stunted, undersized **L17.** **runting** *noun* the birth or development of laboratory animals that are small for their kind **M20.** **runtish** *adjective* stunted, undersized **M17.** **runty** *adjective* (*a*) stunted, undersized; small and stocky; (*b*) *dial.* surly; obstinate: **E19.**

run-up /ˈrʌnʌp/ *noun.* **M19.**
[from ***run up*** s.v. RUN *verb.*]
1 The action of running up to a certain point. **M19.**
2 *spec.* **a** *SPORT.* A run made in preparation for a jump, throw, bowl, etc. **L19.** ▸**b** *GOLF.* A low approach shot. **L19.** ▸**c** = RUN-IN 3. **M20.** ▸**d** The period of time preceding an important event. **M20.**
3 *BOOKBINDING.* A design made on the spine of a book by running a roll along each joint. Freq. *attrib.* **L19.**
4 A rapid increase in the price or value of a commodity. *US.* **M20.**
5 The warming up of a motor, esp. an aircraft engine. **M20.**

> 🕮 **2a** *Cricketer* Daniel bowled . . off a short run-up. **d** *Marketing Week* In the run-up to Christmas.

runway /ˈrʌnweɪ/ *noun.* **M19.**
[from RUN *verb* + WAY *noun.*]
1 a A track made by an animal, *spec.* a deer; *esp.* one made to a watering-place. **M19.** ▸**b** A place for fowls to run in. **L19.**
2 a A raised (sloping or horizontal) ramp or gangway; *esp.* a projecting platform in a theatre etc., a catwalk. **L19.** ▸**b** A specially prepared surface on an airfield along which aircraft take off and land. **E20.**
3 A groove in which something slides; *spec.* (*a*) a groove in the casing of a sash-window; (*b*) an incline down which logs are slid. **L19.**
Comb.: **runway light** each of a series of lights marking the course of a runway.

Runyonesque /rʌnjəˈnɛsk/ *adjective.* **M20.**
[from *Runyon* (see below) + -ESQUE.]
Characteristic of or resembling the American journalist and author (Alfred) Damon Runyon (1884–1946), or his writings.
■ **Runyonese** *noun* slang characteristic of that used in the writings of Runyon **M20.**

rupee /ruːˈpiː/ *noun.* **E17.**
[Hindi *rupiyā*, *rūp-* from Sanskrit *rūpya* wrought silver.]
The basic monetary unit of India, Pakistan, Nepal, Bhutan, Sri Lanka, Mauritius, and the Seychelles, equal to 100 paise in India, 100 paisa in Pakistan and Nepal, and 100 cents in Sri Lanka, Mauritius, and the Seychelles.
sicca rupee: see SICCA *noun*[1].

rupestral /ruːˈpɛstr(ə)l/ *adjective & noun.* **M19.**
[from mod. Latin *rupestris*, from Latin *rupes* rock: see -AL[1].]
BOTANY. ▶**A** *adjective.* Growing on rocks. **M19.**
▶**B** *noun.* A rupestral plant. **E20.**

rupestrian /ruːˈpɛstrɪən/ *adjective.* Also (earlier, *rare*) **-ean**. **L18.**
[formed as prec. + -AN.]
Of painting etc.: done on rock or cave walls.

rupia /ˈruːpɪə/ *noun.* **E19.**
[mod. Latin from Greek *rhupos* filth, dirt: see -IA[1].]
MEDICINE. Thick lamellated scabs on the skin, as in secondary syphilis.
■ **rupial** *adjective* pertaining to, of the nature of, or affected with rupia **M19.**

rupiah /ruːˈpiːə/ *noun.* **M20.**
[Indonesian, formed as RUPEE.]
The basic monetary unit of Indonesia, equal to 100 sen.

rupicapra /ruːpɪˈkaprə/ *noun.* **L17.**
[Latin, from *rupes* rock + *capra* she-goat.]
ZOOLOGY. The chamois. Now only as mod. Latin genus name.
■ **rupicaprine** *adjective* of, pertaining to, or designating bovids of the subfamily Caprinae and tribe Rupicaprini, e.g. chamois, mountain goats, gorals, and serows **E19.**

rupp /rʌp/ *noun.* **M20.**
[Acronym, from road used as a public path.]
In Britain, a public right of way designated as a road and used esp. as a footpath or bridleway.

rupt /rʌpt/ *verb trans. poet. rare.* Pa. pple **-ed**, same. **L15.**
[Latin *rupt-*: see RUPTURE.]
Break, rupture. Chiefly as ***rupt ppl adjective.***

ruption /ˈrʌpʃ(ə)n/ *noun.* Now *rare* or *obsolete.* **L15.**
[Obsolete French, or late Latin *ruptio(n-)*, from Latin *rupt-*: see RUPTURE, -ION.]
1 (A) breach of the peace; (a) disturbance. *rare.* **L15.**
2 *ZOOLOGY & MEDICINE.* (A) breaking or rupture of a membrane or tissue. **M16.**

†**ruptory** *noun.* **LME–E18.**
[medieval Latin *ruptorium*, from Latin *ruptor* agent-noun from *rumpere* to break: see -ORY[1].]
MEDICINE. An application which causes a swelling to come to a head and break.

rupture /ˈrʌptʃə/ *noun & verb.* **LME.**
[Old & mod. French, or Latin *ruptura*, from *rupt-* pa. ppl stem of *rumpere* to break: see -URE.]
▶**A** *noun.* **1** *gen.* The action or an act of breaking or bursting, esp. on the part of a bodily organ or tissue; the fact of being broken or burst. **LME.** ▸**b** *MEDICINE.* (A) hernia, *esp.* (an) inguinal hernia. **LME.**
2 †**a** (A) breach or violation of a treaty, contract, etc. Freq. foll. by *of.* **LME–M17.** ▸**b** A breach of harmonious relations; *esp.* a disagreement between two parties followed by separation. **L16.** ▸**c** (A) breach of continuity; (an) interruption. Long *rare.* **M17.**
3 a A break or split in a surface, esp. the skin. **LME.** ▸**b** A fissure in the earth's surface; a ravine, a chasm. **L15.**

> 🕮 **1** *Times* In zones of secondary damage rupture of welding was rare. **2b** J. F. HENDRY To add to the difficulties, there was a rupture with Paula.

Comb.: **rupturewort** any of several small prostrate plants constituting the genus *Herniaria*, of the pink family, esp. *H. glabra*, formerly reputed to cure hernia.
▶**B** *verb.* **1** *verb trans.* Cause a rupture in; break or burst (a bodily organ or tissue etc.); breach or sever (a connection etc.). **M18.**
2 *verb intrans.* Undergo or suffer a rupture. **M19.**

> 🕮 **1** L. URIS The French had taken a stand . . , even at the risk of rupturing relations with the British. L. WHISTLER He had ruptured himself with coughing. ***rupture a gut***: see GUT *noun.* **ruptured duck** *US Military slang* (*a*) a damaged aircraft; (*b*) [with ref. to its eagle motif] the discharge button given to ex-servicemen.

Comb.: **rupturing capacity** *ELECTRICAL ENGINEERING* a measure of the ability of a circuit-breaker to withstand the surge produced by its operation.
■ **rupturable** *adjective* **L19.**

rural /ˈrʊər(ə)l/ *adjective & noun.* **LME.**
[Old & mod. French, or late Latin *ruralis*, from Latin *rur-*, *rus* the country: see -AL[1].]
▶**A** *adjective.* **1** Of, pertaining to, or characteristic of the country or country life; existing or performed in the country; agricultural, pastoral. **LME.**
2 Of a person: resident or working in the country. **LME.** ▸**b** Of an official, an official body, etc.: having authority or jurisdiction over a country area. **LME.**
3 Characteristic or suggestive of country people; rustic; simple. Freq. *derog.* **LME.** ▸**b** Of art, literary style, etc.: befitting the country or a pastoral subject; unpolished, plain. **LME.**

> 🕮 **1** A. BURGESS A modified form of the Lancashire rural dialect. W. M. CLARKE Linnell . . slipped into rural life with enthusiasm, growing fruit, building garden sheds. **2** A. STORR Rural folk are . . often better mannered than their urban counterparts. **3** V. SACKVILLE-WEST She must be hating . . Norfolk! How intolerably rural George would become. **b** MILTON I . . began . . To meditate my rural minstrelsie.

Special collocations & phrases: ***rural dean***: see DEAN *noun*[1] 2. **rural delivery** *NZ* = ***rural free delivery*** below. **rural district** *Hist.* in Britain, a group of country parishes governed by an elected council. **rural free delivery** *US* a postal service providing deliveries to remote areas not served directly by a post office. **Rural Institute** *Scot.* a Women's Institute. **rural school** *US* a local elementary school in a rural area. **Women's Rural Institute** *Scot.* = ***Rural Institute*** above.
▶**B** *noun.* **1** A resident of the country; a country person, a rustic. Long *arch.* **LME.**
2 *ellipt.* = ***(Women's) Rural Institute*** above. *Scot.* **M20.**
■ **ruralism** *noun* (*a*) = RURALITY (a); (*b*) a country idiom or expression; a rusticism: **M19.** **ruralist** *noun* (*a*) a country person; (*b*) an advocate of rural as opp. to urban life: **M18.** **ruˈrality** *noun* (*a*) rural quality or character; rural life, scenery, etc.; (*b*) a rural characteristic or feature; a rural object: **M18.** **rurally** *adverb* **L18.** **ruralness** *noun* (*rare*) **M18.**

ruralize /ˈrʊər(ə)lʌɪz/ *verb.* Also **-ise**. **E19.**
[from RURAL *adjective* + -IZE.]
1 *verb trans.* Make rural in character. **E19.**
2 *verb intrans.* Go into or spend time in the country. **E19.**
■ **ruraliˈzation** *noun* **M19.**

rurban /ˈrəːb(ə)n/ *adjective.* **E20.**
[from R(URAL *adjective* + URBAN.]
Combining the characteristics of rural and urban life.
■ **rurbanism** *noun* belief in the interaction and inseparability of urban and rural life **E20.** **rurbanist** *noun* an adherent of rurbanism **E20.** **rurbaniˈzation** *noun* the action of rural influences on urban life **M20.**

ruridecanal /ˌrʊərɪdɪˈkeɪn(ə)l, -ˈdɛk(ə)n(ə)l/ *adjective.* **M19.**
[from Latin *ruri-* combining form from *rur-*, *rus* (see RURAL) + DECANAL.]
Of or pertaining to a rural dean or deanery.

Ruritania /rʊərɪˈteɪnɪə/ *noun.* **L19.**
[An imaginary kingdom in SE Europe in the novels of Anthony Hope (1863–1933).]
A state or country seen as a setting for romantic adventure and intrigue; a petty state; *gen.* any imaginary country.

> 🕮 *New Statesman* Let's not kid ourselves about a renaissance. This is national senescence, the Road to Ruritania.

■ **Ruritanian** *adjective & noun* (*a*) *adjective* of, pertaining to, or characteristic of romantic adventure and intrigue or its setting; (*b*) *noun* a native or inhabitant of a Ruritania; a person associated with romantic adventure and intrigue: **L19.**

rurp /rəːp/ *noun.* **M20.**
[from realized ultimate reality piton.]
MOUNTAINEERING. A type of very small piton.

ruru /ˈruːruː/ *noun. NZ.* **M19.**
[Maori.]
The boobook owl.

Rus /rʌs, ruːs/ *noun & adjective.* **E20.**
[formed as Russ.]
Hist. ▶**A** *noun pl.* A people of Scandinavian or perhaps Slavonic origin whose settlement around Kiev and the Dnieper in the 9th cent. gave rise to the Russian principalities. See also (earlier) RUSS *noun* 3. **E20.**
▶**B** *adjective.* Of or pertaining to this people. **M20.**

rusa /ˈruːsə/ *noun*[1]. **L18.**
[mod. Latin *Rusa* former genus name, from Malay.]
More fully ***rusa deer***. A large deer, *Cervus timorensis*, of the Indonesian archipelago (also called ***Timor deer***). Formerly also, the sambar.
■ **rusine** *adjective* of, belonging to, or characteristic of the former genus *Rusa*, which included the rusa deer and the sambar **M19.**

rusa *noun*[2] var. of ROOSA.

rusbank /ˈrəːsbaŋk/ *noun. S. Afr.* **L19.**
[Afrikaans, from *rus*(t rest + *bank* bench.]
A wooden settle, usu. with a seat of woven leather thongs.

ruscus /ˈrʌskəs/ *noun.* **L16.**
[Latin.]
A plant of the genus *Ruscus*, of the lily family; *esp.* butcher's broom, *R. aculeatus*.

ruse /ruːz/ *noun.* **LME.**
[Old & mod. French, from *ruser* use trickery, (formerly) drive back, perh. ult. from Latin *rursus* back(wards). Cf. RUSH *verb*[2], RISE *noun*.]
†**1** A detour or doubling back of a hunted animal to elude capture. Only in **LME.**
2 A trick, a stratagem. **L16.** ▸**b** Artifice, trickery. **E19.**

> 🕮 **2** L. P. HARTLEY The tentative booking was fictitious, a ruse for gaining time.

rusé /ryze/ *adjective.* Fem. **-ée**. **M18.**
[French.]
Inclined to use ruses; deceitful, sly, cunning.

ruse de guerre /ryːz də ɡɛːr/ *noun phr.* Pl. ***ruses de guerre*** (pronounced same). **E19.**
[French, lit. 'ruse of war'.]
A stratagem intended to deceive an enemy in war; *transf.* a justifiable trick.

rusée *adjective* see RUSÉ.

ruses de guerre *noun phr.* pl. of RUSE DE GUERRE.

rush /rʌʃ/ *noun*[1].

[Old English *rysc(e)* (recorded chiefly in place-names) corresp. to Middle Low German, Middle High German (Dutch, German) *rusch*.]

1 Any of numerous plants constituting the genus *Juncus* (family Juncaceae), with slender cylindrical pith-filled stems (properly leaves) and inconspicuous greenish or brownish flowers, chiefly growing in marshy ground or by water. Also, the stem of such a plant; such stems collectively as a material in basketry, for making chair-bottoms, etc., and formerly for strewing floors. OE. **2** A worthless or unimportant thing. Chiefly in ***not care a rush***, ***not be worth a rush***. ME. **3** With specifying word: any of various rushlike plants of other genera and families. L17.

3 ***club-rush***, ***Dutch rush***, ***flowering rush***, ***spike-rush***, etc.

Comb.: **rush-bearing** *Hist.* an annual ceremony in parts of northern England of carrying rushes and garlands to a church to strew the floor or decorate the walls; **rush-bush** a tuft of rushes; **rush-candle** *Hist.*: made from the pith of a rush dipped in tallow etc.; **rushlight** (*a*) *Hist.* (the light of) a rush-candle; (*b*) *fig.* an insignificant person or thing; **rush-nut** the edible tuber of the tiger-nut, *Cyperus esculentus*; **rush-toad** the natterjack.

■ **rushlike** *adjective* resembling (that of) a rush L16. **rushy** *adjective*[1] (*a*) = RUSHEN; (*b*) producing or having many rushes; (*c*) rushlike: LME.

rush /rʌʃ/ *noun*[2] *& adjective*. LME.

[from RUSH *verb*[2].]

▶ **A** *noun*. **1** The action or an act of rushing; *esp.* an unusual or excessive amount of activity, the movement of large numbers of people or things (freq. with specifying word); *gen.* haste, urgency. LME. **2** A sound or sensation (as) of rushing; a thrill *of* fear, pleasure, etc.; *slang* a drug-induced euphoria. LME. **3** Dysentery in cattle. Chiefly *dial.* L18. **4 a** RUGBY & AMER. FOOTBALL. An attempt by one or more players to force the ball through a line of defenders. M19. ▸**b** A contest of strength between first- and second-year university students. *US. obsolete* exc. *Hist.* M19. ▸**c** A round of social events organized for prospective new members by a fraternity or sorority. *US.* L19. **5 a** A sudden large migration of people, esp. to a new goldfield; the destination of such a migration. Freq. in ***gold-rush***. M19. ▸**b** A migratory flock or flight of birds. L19. ▸**c** A stampede of horses or cattle. *Austral.* L19. **6** A sudden strong demand for a commodity. Foll. by *for*, *on*. M19. **7** CINEMATOGRAPHY, in *pl.* The first prints of a film after a period of shooting; the preliminary showing of such a film. E20.

> 🕮 **1** D. CUSACK If people did their work properly there wouldn't be any last-minute rush. *Evening Post (Nottingham)* Providing his registration forms are not held up in the Christmas postal rush! J. SCOTT The lunch-time rush for snackbar sandwiches. **2** *Rupert* He hears a rush of wings . . as a great eagle swoops down. I. MURDOCH Franca, looking at him, felt the old familiar rush of feeling.

Phrases: **all in a rush**, **in a rush** in a hurry, rapidly, briskly. **get a rush** *US colloq.* (of a person, esp. a woman) receive frequent attentions from another. **give a person a rush** *US colloq.* lavish attention on a person. ***in a rush***: see ***all in a rush*** above. ***the bum's rush***: see BUM *noun*[2] 1. **with a rush** with a sudden and rapid onset.

Comb.: **rush hour** *noun & adjective* (of or pertaining to) a period of the day when the movement of people or esp. traffic is at its heaviest; **rush line** AMER. FOOTBALL a defensive line of players; **rush-release** *noun & verb* (*a*) *noun* the action of releasing a record etc. in the shortest possible time; a record etc. so released; (*b*) *verb trans.* release (a record etc.) in this way.

▶ **B** *attrib.* or as *adjective*. Characterized by rushing; involving the movement of large numbers of people or things; done with or necessitating haste or urgency. L19.

rush election, ***rush job***, ***rush order***, ***rush work***, etc.

■ **rushy** *adjective*[2] (*rare*) quick, hurried, rushed E20.

rush /rʌʃ/ *verb*[1]. ME.

[from RUSH *noun*[1].]

1 *verb trans.* **a** Strew (a floor) with rushes. ME. ▸**b** Bind or make with rushes. M19. **2** *verb intrans.* Gather rushes. *rare.* M16.

rush /rʌʃ/ *verb*[2]. LME.

[Anglo-Norman *russher* var. of Old French *russer*, (also mod.) *ruser*: see RUSE.]

▶ **I** *verb intrans.* **1** Of a thing: move with great force and speed; flow, fall, spread, etc., rapidly and forcefully. Usu. foll. by adverb or preposition. LME. **2** Of a person or animal: run or charge quickly or impetuously. Formerly also, fall (*down*) violently. Usu. foll. by adverb or preposition. LME. ▸**b** Make an attack or assault (*lit. & fig.*). Foll. by *on*, *upon*. M16. ▸**c** Hurry about or around; hasten; travel rapidly. Usu. foll. by adverb or preposition. M19. ▸**d** AMER. FOOTBALL. Run carrying the ball; gain ground by this action. M20. **3** *fig.* Act hastily or rashly; begin or enter *into* an undertaking etc. hastily or rashly. M16.

> 🕮 **1** E. BOWEN The colder air from the lounge rushed in from behind her. Z. TOMIN I was walking upstream on a river bank, the water was rushing by. **2** D. H. LAWRENCE Alvina . . overturned her chair as Cicio rushed past her. A. MACLEAN The door was kicked open and the men rushed inside. G. PRIESTLAND The other three rushed at me begging me not to broadcast the passage. **c** N. F. DIXON Political leaders . . rush about getting things done. M. SEYMOUR He could rely on Persse to come rushing down to London. ***rush round in circles***: see CIRCLE *noun*. **3** S. BELLOW He rushed into marriage without talking it over with me.

▶ **II** *verb trans.* †**4** Knock or drive out of position. Usu. foll. by adverb or preposition. LME–L17. **5** Impel or cause to move rapidly and forcefully. Usu. foll. by adverb or preposition. Now *rare* exc. as passing into sense 6. LME. **6** Convey or transport rapidly or urgently (usu. foll. by *into*, *out of*, *to*); send or post (a thing) to (a person) as soon as possible. M16. ▸**b** *transf.* Process, work through, or produce rapidly or urgently. Also foll. by *off*, *out*, *through*. M19. **7** Force the pace or speed of; hurry, hustle. Also foll. by *on*, *through*. E19. ▸**b** Hurry or pressure (a person); hurry (a person) *into* an ill-considered action or undertaking; in *pass.*, have much to do in a limited time, be hard-pressed. L19. ▸**c** Defraud by overcharging; *slang* charge (a person) a specified, esp. excessive, amount *for* something. L19. ▸**d** Court the affection of (a person, esp. a woman) by means of frequent entertainment etc. *colloq.* (chiefly *US*). L19. ▸**e** Entertain (an applicant) in order to assess suitability for membership of a fraternity or sorority, or to give inducement to join. *US.* L19. **8** Run at (as) in an attack; (attempt to) negotiate or overcome by a sudden assault. M19. ▸**b** In *pass.* Of land: be occupied rapidly during a gold-rush. M19.

> 🕮 **6** *Star (Sheffield)* My husband to be was rushed into hospital. *Femina* Rush us your opinion . . on a subject you feel strongly about. **b** R. INGALLS She and Don . . rushed out invitations. **7** R. C. HUTCHINSON I know only one thing about marriage—that it's no damn good rushing the business. *Times* The CBI was 'rushing' a council meeting . . to consider Mr Heath's letter. **b** JILLY COOPER The Teales would breakfast very early because they don't like to be rushed. D. DU MAURIER I rushed you into it. I never gave you a chance to think it over. **rush a person off his or her feet** (usu. in *pass.*) = ***run a person off his or her feet*** s.v. RUN *verb*. **d** C. PORTER What a joy supreme! To be rushed by all you dear men. **8** X. HERBERT A huge roan beast turned and rushed him. C. RYAN Frost's men had tried to rush the southern end of the bridge. **rush one's fences** act with undue haste.

■ **ru'shee** *noun* (*US colloq.*) a candidate for membership of a fraternity or sorority E20. **rushingly** *adverb* in a rushing manner; rapidly, impetuously: LME.

rusha *noun* var. of ROOSA.

rushen /ˈrʌʃ(ə)n/ *adjective*. Now *arch. & dial.* OE.

[from RUSH *noun*[1] + -EN[4].]

Made of a rush or rushes.

rusher /ˈrʌʃə/ *noun*. M17.

[from RUSH *verb*[2] + -ER[1].]

1 A person who or thing which rushes. M17. ▸**b** AMER. FOOTBALL. A player who rushes; *esp.* a forward. L19. **2** A participant in a gold-rush. *Austral. & US.* M19.

rus in urbe /ruːs ɪn ˈəːbeɪ/ *noun phr.* M18.

[Latin, lit. 'country in city'.]

An illusion of countryside created by a building, garden, etc., within a city; an urban building etc. which has this effect.

rusk /rʌsk/ *noun*. L16.

[Spanish & Portuguese *rosca* twist, coil, twisted roll of bread, of unkn. origin.]

1 Bread broken into small pieces and hardened by rebaking, formerly used esp. on sea voyages. Chiefly *Hist.* L16. **2** A piece of bread prepared in this way to form a light biscuit, esp. for use as baby food. M18.

rusk /rʌsk/ *verb trans.* Long *obsolete* exc. *Scot.* ME.

[Of Scandinavian origin: cf. Icelandic *ruska*, Norwegian, Danish *ruske*.]

Disturb violently; ruffle (hair, feathers, etc.).

†**ruskin** *noun*. L17.

[Irish *rúscán* from *rúsc* bark.]

1 In Ireland, a tub made usu. of bark for preserving butter. L17–E18. **2** Butter preserved in such a tub. Only in 18.

Ruskinian /rʌˈskɪnɪən/ *noun & adjective*. M19.

[from *Ruskin* (see below) + -IAN.]

▶ **A** *noun*. An adherent or admirer of the English art and social critic John Ruskin (1819–1900) or his artistic and social theories. M19.

▶ **B** *adjective*. Of, pertaining to, or characteristic of Ruskin or his writings. L19.

■ **Ruski'nese** *noun & adjective* (*a*) *noun* the literary style and characteristics of Ruskin; (*b*) *adjective* = RUSKINIAN *adjective*: M19. **Ruski'nesque** *adjective & noun* (*a*) *adjective* characteristic of Ruskin or his writings; (*b*) *noun* the style of art or architecture favoured by Ruskin: M19. **'Ruskinism** *noun* the principles and theories of Ruskin M19. **'Ruskinite** *noun & adjective* = RUSKINIAN L19.

rusma /ˈrʌzmə/ *noun*. Now *rare*. E17.

[App. from Turkish *hirizma* from Greek *khrisma* ointment (see CHRISM *noun*).]

A depilatory composed of lime and orpiment, formerly used in tanning.

Russ /rʌs/ *adjective & noun*. Now *rare*. E16.

[Russian *Rus'* old name for Russia and the Russian people before the 16th cent. Cf. medieval Latin *Russus*.]

▶ **A** *adjective*. Russian. E16.

▶ **B** *noun*. **1** A Russian. M16. **2** The Russian language. L16. †**3** = RUS *noun*. M–L19.

■ **Russic** *adjective* (*arch.*) Russian L17.

†**russel** *noun & adjective*. L15–E19.

[Prob. from Flemish *Rijsel* Lille.]

(Made of) a kind of woollen clothing fabric used esp. in the 16th cent.

†**russelet** *noun*. L17–E19.

[French *rousselet*, from Old French *r(o)ussel* (mod. *rousseau*) reddish, red-haired.]

Any of several varieties of pear having a russet skin or russet specks.

Russell /ˈrʌs(ə)l/ *noun*. M19.

[Origin unkn.]

More fully ***Russell cord***. A type of ribbed or corded fabric, usu. having a cotton warp and woollen weft.

Russell body /ˈrʌs(ə)l bɒdi/ *noun phr.* E20.

[from William *Russell* (1852–1940), Scot. pathologist.]

MEDICINE. A hyaline mass of immunoglobulin produced in quantity in, and sometimes extruded by, plasma cells in excessive response to challenge by antibodies.

Russell fence /ˈrʌs(ə)l fɛns/ *noun phr. Canad.* M20.

[Said to be from a Mr *Russell*, its inventor.]

A fence in which the top rail lies in the crux of crossed posts and the lower rails hang suspended from it.

Russellian /rʌˈsɛlɪən/ *adjective & noun*. E20.

[from Bertrand *Russell* (see RUSSELL'S PARADOX) + -IAN.]

▶ **A** *adjective*. Of, pertaining to, or characteristic of Bertrand Russell or his mathematical or philosophical theories. E20.

▶ **B** *noun*. An advocate or adherent of Russell's theories. M20.

Russellite /ˈrʌs(ə)lʌɪt/ *noun*. E20.

[from *Russell* (see below) + -ITE[1].]

An advocate or adherent of the political views of the Irish Unionist politician (and later supporter of Home Rule) Thomas W. Russell (1841–1920).

Russell lupin /ˈrʌs(ə)l ˈluːpɪn/ *noun phr.* M20.

[George *Russell* (1857–1951), Brit. horticulturist.]

A lupin of a kind developed by George Russell, with long racemes of often bicoloured flowers, probably by hybridization between *Lupinus polyphyllus* and *L. arboreus*.

Russell paradox *noun phr.* var. of RUSSELL'S PARADOX.

Russell–Saunders coupling /rʌs(ə)lˈsɔːndəz ˈkʌplɪŋ/ *noun phr.* E20.

[from Henry Norris *Russell* (1877–1957), US astrophysicist, and Frederick Albert *Saunders* (1875–1963), US physicist.]

PHYSICS. An approximation employed in a procedure for combining the orbital and spin angular momenta of a set of electrons in an atom to describe the possible energy states which they may adopt.

Russell's paradox /ˌrʌs(ə)lz ˈparədɒks/ *noun phr.* Also **Russell paradox**. E20.

[from Bertrand *Russell*, 3rd Earl Russell (1872–1970), English mathematician and philosopher.]

A paradox concerning the set of all sets that do not contain themselves as members, viz. that the condition for it to contain itself is that it should not contain itself.

Russell's viper /ˈrʌs(ə)lz ˈvʌɪpə/ *noun phr.* E20.

[from Patrick *Russell* (1727–1805), Scot. physician and naturalist.]

A large venomous snake, *Vipera russelli*, found from India to Indonesia, and having a yellowish-brown body marked with black rings or spots.

Russenorsk /ˈruːsənɔːsk/ *noun*. Now chiefly *Hist.* M20.

[Norwegian, from *Russe* Russian + *Norsk* Norwegian.]

A pidgin formerly used by Russian and Norwegian fishermen. Also called ***Russonorsk***.

russet /ˈrʌsɪt/ *noun, adjective, & verb*. ME.

[Anglo-Norman var. of Old French *ro(u)sset* dim. of *rous* (mod. *roux*) from Portuguese *ros*, Italian *rosso*, from Latin *russus* red: see -ET[1].]

▶ **A** *noun*. **1** A coarse woollen cloth of a reddish-brown or subdued colour, formerly used for clothing esp. by country people and the poor. Now *arch.* or *Hist.* ME. ▸†**b** In *pl.* Garments made of such cloth. M16–M17. **2** A reddish-brown colour. LME. **3** A variety of fruit or vegetable with a reddish-brown usu. rough skin; *spec.* (*a*) a variety of eating apple with a reddish- or yellowish-brown or brown-spotted skin; (*b*) a variety of potato with a reddish skin. E18.

2 E. M. FORSTER Autumn approached .. touching the .. beech-trees with russet. 3 R. FIRBANK Fuller of wrinkles than a withered russet.

▶ **B** *adjective.* **1** Of a reddish-brown colour. ME. ▶**b** Of a fruit or vegetable: that is a russet. E17.

2 Of a garment: made of russet. Now *arch.* or *Hist.* LME. ▶**b** *transf.* Rustic, homely, simple. Now *rare.* L16.

3 Of footwear: made of unblackened leather; tan, brown. M17.

1b *Bon Appetit* 2 medium russet potatoes, peeled. **2** R. BURNS Be thou clad in russet weed, Be thou deckt in silken stole.

Special collocations & comb.: **russet coat** (*a*) a coat made of russet cloth; a russet-coloured coat; (*b*) a russet apple. **russet-coated** *adjective* (now *rare*) wearing a russet coat; rustic, homely.

▶ **C** *verb.* **1** *verb trans.* Make russet in colour. L16.

2 *verb intrans.* Become russet in colour; *spec.* (of an apple etc.) develop a rough reddish- or yellowish-brown skin. L17.

■ **russeted** *adjective* = RUSSET *adjective* 1 L19. **russeting** *noun* (*a*) the action or process of making or becoming russet; †(*b*) a rustic, a peasant; (*c*) a russet apple: L16. **russety** *adjective* inclining to a russet colour L18.

Russia /ˈrʌʃə/ *noun.* M17.

[medieval Latin, from *Russi* the Russian people. Cf. RUSS.]

▶ **I 1** Used *attrib.* to designate things obtained from or associated with Russia, a country in eastern Europe and northern Asia, or (more widely) the tsarist Russian empire, the former USSR, or the republics associated with Russia in the Commonwealth of Independent States. M17.

1 Russia braid = SOUTACHE. **Russia duck** *Hist.* a strong coarse linen formerly used for men's clothing. **Russia leather**: made of skins impregnated with oil distilled from birch-bark, used esp. in bookbinding.

▶ **II 2** *ellipt.* = ***Russia leather*** above. E19.

Russian /ˈrʌʃ(ə)n/ *noun & adjective.* M16.

[medieval Latin *Russianus*, formed as prec.: see -AN.]

▶ **A** *noun.* **1** A native or inhabitant of Russia or (more widely) its former empire, the former USSR, or the republics associated with Russia in the Commonwealth of Independent States; a person of Russian descent. M16. ▶**b** A member of the Russian Orthodox Church. L16. ▶**c** An untamed animal. *Austral. arch.* M19.

2 The Slavonic language of Russia, the official language of the former USSR. E18.

3 *ellipt.* = ***Russian cigarette*** below. M20.

▶ **B** *adjective.* **1** Of, pertaining to, or characteristic of Russia or the former USSR; inhabiting or native to Russia or the former USSR. L16.

2 Of, pertaining to, or written in the Russian language. L18.

Phrases: ***Great Russian***: see GREAT *adjective.* ***Little Russian***: see LITTLE *adjective.* WHITE RUSSIAN.

Special collocations: **Russian bagatelle** = COCKAMAROO. **Russian ballet** a style of ballet developed at the Russian Imperial Ballet Academy, popularized in the West by Sergei Diaghilev's Ballet Russe from 1909. **Russian Bank** a card-game for two people, similar to solitaire. **Russian bath** a type of steam bath. **Russian Blue** (an animal of) a breed of cat with short greyish-blue fur, green eyes, and large pointed ears. **Russian boot** a leather boot loosely enclosing the calf. **Russian cigarette**: having a hollow pasteboard filter. **Russian dinner**: in which fruit and wine are placed at the table centre and courses served from a sideboard. **Russian doll** each of a set of brightly painted hollow wooden dolls of varying sizes, designed to fit inside each other. **Russian dressing** a salad dressing with a mayonnaise base. **Russian Easter egg** an egg-shaped usu. highly decorated container for Easter presents. **Russian egg**: poached and served with mayonnaise on a lettuce leaf. **Russian encephalitis** = ***Russian spring–summer encephalitis*** below. **Russian longhair** (an animal of) a stocky long-haired breed of cat with a relatively short tail. **Russian olive** *N. Amer.* a silvery-leaved spiny shrub, *Elaeagnus angustifolia* (family Elaeagnaceae), of SE Europe and W. Asia, naturalized in parts of N. America. **Russian pony** (an animal of) a breed of small hardy roan pony originating in Russia. **Russian Revolution** the revolution of 1917, in which the Tsar was eventually overthrown and replaced by Bolshevik government (cf. ***OCTOBER Revolution***). **Russian roulette** an act of daring comprising squeezing the trigger of a revolver held to the head after loading one chamber and spinning the cylinder; *fig.* a dangerously unpredictable situation or enterprise. ***Russian sable***: see SABLE *noun*[2] 2a. **Russian salad**: consisting of diced cooked vegetables mixed with mayonnaise. **Russian scandal** = ***Chinese whispers*** s.v. CHINESE *adjective.* **Russian spring–summer encephalitis** a form of viral encephalitis resembling influenza, transmitted to humans by wood ticks or by drinking the milk of infected goats. **Russian stitch** = ***herring-bone stitch*** s.v. HERRING-BONE *noun & adjective.* **Russian tea** (*a*) (a drink of) tea grown in the Caucasus; (*b*) (a drink of) tea laced with rum or served with lemon. **Russian thistle** *N. Amer.* a prickly tumbleweed, *Salsola kali* subsp. *ruthenica*, an inland form of saltwort, native to Russia. **Russian vine** an ornamental climbing plant of the knotgrass family, *Fallopia baldschuanica*, of central Asia, bearing long racemes of white or pink flowers. **Russian wolfhound** = BORZOI.

■ **Russianism** *noun* (*a*) attachment to or sympathy with Russia or the former USSR; (*b*) (chiefly *Hist.*) the form of Communism associated with Russia or the USSR; (*c*) a Russian characteristic or expression: M19. **Russianist** *noun* a student of or expert in subjects pertaining to Russia or the former USSR, esp. Russian language and literature L20. **Russianiˈzation** *noun* the action of making or process of becoming Russian in character L19. **Russianize** *verb trans.* make Russian in character, Russify M19. **Russianness** /-n-n-/ *noun* M20.

Russify /ˈrʌsɪfʌɪ/ *verb trans.* M19.

[from RUSS *adjective* + -I- + -FY.]

Make Russian in character, Russianize.

■ **russifiˈcation** *noun* M19.

Russki /ˈrʌski/ *noun & adjective. colloq.* Chiefly *joc.* or *derog.* Pl. **-s**, **-es**. Also **Russky**. M19.

[Russian *russkiĭ*, or from RUSS(IAN after Russian surnames ending with *-skiĭ*.]

(A) Russian.

Russniak /rʊsˈnjak/ *noun & adjective.* E19.

[Russniak *Rusn(y)ak*, Ukrainian *Rusnak*. Cf. Czech *Rusňak*, Polish *Rusniak*.]

▶ **A** *noun.* A member of the Ukrainian people inhabiting Galicia in east central Europe; the Ukrainian dialect of this people. Cf. RUTHENIAN *noun.* E19.

▶ **B** *adjective.* Of or pertaining to this people or their dialect. E19.

Russo- /ˈrʌsəʊ/ *combining form.*

[from RUSS + -O-.]

Forming adjective and noun combs. with the meaning 'Russian, of Russia' or 'Russian and', as ***Russo-American***, ***Russo-Chinese***, ***Russo-Slavonic***, etc.

■ **Russophil(e)** *adjective & noun* (a person who is) friendly towards Russia or fond of Russia and things Russian L19. **Russophobe** *adjective & noun* (a person who is) affected with Russophobia M19. **Russoˈphobia** *noun* irrational fear or dislike of Russia or things Russian M19.

Russonorsk /ˈrʌsəʊnɔːsk/ *noun.* Now chiefly *Hist.* M20.

[from RUSSO- + NORSK.]

= RUSSENORSK.

russula /ˈrʌsələ/ *noun.* L19.

[mod. Latin (see below), from Latin *russus* red (because many have a red cap).]

Any of numerous woodland toadstools of the genus *Russula*, typically having a brightly coloured flattened cap and a white stem and gills.

rust /rʌst/ *noun*[1] *& verb.*

[Old English *rūst* = Old Saxon, Old & mod. High German *rost*, Middle & mod. Dutch *roest*, from Germanic base also of RED *adjective.*]

▶ **A** *noun.* **1** A reddish-brown or brownish-orange coating formed on iron or steel by oxidation, esp. due to contact with moisture; a similar coating formed on any other metal; any coating, stain, etc., resembling rust. OE.

2 *fig.* (A state of) deterioration or impairment, esp. due to inactivity or neglect. Also, inactivity, neglect; age. OE. ▶**b** Moral decline or decay; corruption, esp. of a specified kind. Long *rare* or *obsolete.* OE.

3 a A reddish-brown discoloration of foliage; *spec.* any of various plant diseases caused by fungi of the class Urediniomycetes or of the unrelated genus *Albugo*, and characterized by dusty patches of various colours. Also ***rust disease***. ME. ▶**b** Any of various parasitic fungi causing rust in plants. Also ***rust fungus***. E19.

4 The colour of rust; reddish-brown, brownish-orange. E18.

1 H. DOUGLAS The .. wires .. had become corroded by rust. D. PROFUMO A metal roof, eaten in places by rust. **2** *Sunday Express* A tutor .. after the long holidays .. is to take a bit of the rust off. **3a** ***crown rust***, ***stem rust***, ***white rust***, etc. **4** *Lancashire Life* This .. jersey dress in a rich shade of rust.

Attrib. & comb.: In the sense 'of the colour of rust', as ***rust-brown***, ***rust-red***, ***rust-yellow***, etc. Special combs., as **rust-belt** (chiefly *US*) a declining or inactive major industrial area, orig. *spec.* the steel-producing region of the American Midwest and North-East; **rust bucket** *colloq.* an old rusty ship, car, etc.; **rust-coloured** *adjective* of the colour of rust, reddish-brown, brownish-orange; ***rust disease***: see sense 3a above; ***rust fungus***: see sense 3b above; **rust-resistance** resistance to developing or forming rust; **rust-resistant**, **rust-resisting** *adjectives* (of a metal) made so as not to rust; (of a plant) not liable to rust disease.

▶ **B** *verb.* **1 a** *verb intrans.* Of metal, esp. iron or steel: develop or form rust, become rusty; oxidize. ME. ▶**b** *verb trans.* Cause to develop or form rust. L16. ▶†**c** *verb intrans. fig.* Become rust. *rare* (Shakes.). Only in L16.

2 a *verb intrans.* Deteriorate or become spoiled, esp. through inactivity or neglect (freq. foll. by *out*). Also, become stuck, lodged, or fixed due to rust (freq. foll. by *in, into, out, up*). ME. ▶**b** *verb trans.* Waste *away* (oneself, one's life, etc.) through idleness. M19.

3 *verb intrans.* & (*rare*) *trans.* Become or make rust-coloured. M16.

4 *verb trans.* Make morally corrupt. Now *rare.* L17.

5 *verb trans. & intrans.* Affect or become affected with rust or blight. M18.

1a E. WILSON Gleaming suits of armor .. rusting in the rain. **b** *New Scientist* A corrosive mist that rusted .. aluminium. **2a** *New Scientist* Rusted-out tanks hold sentinel beside .. fruit trees. M. ATWOOD I find the lid of an old maple syrup, the lid rusted shut. **3** P. MORTIMER Early September .. the leaves rusting.

■ **rusting** *adjective* (*a*) causing rust; (*b*) becoming rusty, developing rust: M18. **rustless** *adjective* (*a*) free from rust; (*b*) not susceptible to rust: M19.

rust /rʌst/ *noun*[2]. *dial. & colloq.* L18.

[Back-form. from RUSTY *adjective*[3].]

An offended, restive, or rebellious attitude, condition, or state. Chiefly as below.

nab the rust: see NAB *verb*[1]. **take rust**, **take the rust** (of a horse) become restive; (of a person) take offence.

rustic /ˈrʌstɪk/ *adjective & noun.* LME.

[Latin *rusticus*, from *rus* country: see -IC.]

▶ **A** *adjective.* **1** Of, found in, or associated with the country; rural. LME. ▶**b** Of a person: living in the country; employed or involved in rural work, as farming, hunting, etc.; of peasant or farming stock or background. E17.

2 Made in a plain, simple, or rough form or style; *spec.* made of untrimmed branches or rough timber; ARCHITECTURE having a rough or roughened surface or deeply sunk or chamfered joints. Formerly also (ARCHITECTURE), of, resembling, or associated with Tuscan style. M16. ▶**b** Of lettering: freely formed. L18.

3 Plain, simple, unsophisticated; unrefined, uneducated. Also (*rare*), rough, unmannerly, ill-bred. L16.

1 *Early Music* A tambourine lends rustic spice to the .. refrains. *Japan Times* The interior of a rustic cottage. **rustic bunting** a bunting, *Emberiza rustica*, of northern Eurasia. **b** *Royal Air Force Journal* Some rustic policeman in the wilds of the north-west. **2 rustic work** rough or pitted masonry. **3** E. BOWEN To look .. rustic in London .. Gera wore a large chip straw hat. P. L. FERMOR They make one feel .. rustic and dowdy.

▶ **B** *noun.* **1** A person from or living in the country; a peasant; a rustic person, *esp.* a simple unsophisticated one. LME.

2 ARCHITECTURE. Rough or pitted masonry; a stone or (formerly) joint resembling or used with this (usu. in *pl.*). E18.

3 Any of various mottled brown noctuid moths, as *Hoplodrina blanda* and (in full ***common rustic***) *Mesapamea secalis*. E19.

■ **rusticism** /-sɪz(ə)m/ *noun* (*rare*) a rustic idiom or expression L19. **rusticize** /-sʌɪz/ *verb* (*a*) *verb intrans.* speak in a country dialect; (*b*) *verb trans.* send to the country; (*c*) *verb trans.* make rustic in appearance: E19. **rusticly** *adverb* (now *rare*) E17. **rusticness** *noun* (*rare*) L17.

rustical /ˈrʌstɪk(ə)l/ *adjective & noun. arch.* LME.

[Old French, or medieval Latin *rusticalis* RUSTIC *adjective*: see -ICAL.]

▶ **A** *adjective.* **1** = RUSTIC *adjective* 1b. LME.

2 Made in a plain, simple, or rough form or style; *spec.* made of untrimmed branches or rough timber. Cf. RUSTIC *adjective* 2. L15. ▶†**b** Physically strong; robust. L16–L17.

3 = RUSTIC *adjective* 1. M16.

4 = RUSTIC *adjective* 3. M16.

▶ **B** *noun.* = RUSTIC *noun* 1. M16.

rustically /ˈrʌstɪk(ə)li/ *adverb.* M16.

[from RUSTIC *adjective* or RUSTICAL *adjective*: see -ICALLY.]

In a rustic manner, style, or state.

rusticate /ˈrʌstɪkeɪt/ *verb.* L15.

[Latin *rusticat-* pa. ppl stem of *rusticari* live in the country, from *rusticus* RUSTIC: see -ATE[3].]

1 a *verb trans.* Imbue with rural ways or practices; countrify. L15. ▶**b** *verb intrans.* Go to, live in, or spend time in the country; adopt rural ways or practices. M17.

2 *verb trans.* **a** Send down or dismiss (a student) temporarily from a university as a punishment. E18. ▶**b** Send to or settle in the country. M18.

3 *verb trans.* Roughen the surface of (masonry, pottery, etc.); make rustic in appearance or style; ARCHITECTURE fashion or form (masonry) by rustication. E18.

1b C. KEENE I .. heard .. you were going to rusticate on some riverside. **2a** HARPER LEE I was rusticated for .. painting the college pump scarlet.

■ **rusticater**, **-or** *noun* L19.

rustication /rʌstɪˈkeɪʃ(ə)n/ *noun.* E17.

[Latin *rusticatio(n-)*, formed as prec.: see -ATION.]

1 The action of going to, spending time in, or living in the country; a stay in the country. Formerly also, a rural pastime, practice, or occupation. E17. ▶**b** = RUSTICITY 2. L18.

2 a Temporary dismissal from a university; an instance or period of this. M18. ▶**b** The action of sending a person to the country; the state of being sent to the country. M18.

3 ARCHITECTURE. A style of masonry in which the surface of the blocks is roughened; masonry cut in massive blocks separated from each other by deep joints; the action or practice of producing this. E19. ▸**b** A rustic feature or element. M19.

📖 **2a** E. LONGFORD The stiff sentence of a year's rustication. **b** *Daily Telegraph* Mao's rustication programme under which . . young people have been sent from the cities.

rusticity /rʌˈstɪsɪti/ *noun*. M16.
[French *rusticité* or Latin *rusticitas*, formed as RUSTIC: see -ICITY.]
1 Lack of refinement, sophistication, or education; ignorance; lack of verbal polish; social awkwardness. M16. ▸**b** An instance of this; a rustic expression or mannerism. *rare*. E18.
2 The condition or character of or associated with living in the country; a state of rural quiet, simplicity, etc. M17. ▸**b** A rustic feature, characteristic, or thing. M17.

📖 **2** N. PINKNEY The town . . had an air of rusticity and recluseness.

rustle /ˈrʌs(ə)l/ *verb & noun*. LME.
[Imit.: cf. Frisian *russelje*, *risselje*, Flemish †*ruysselen*, *rijsselen*, Dutch *ridselen*, *ritselen*. See also REESLE.]
▶ **A** *verb*. **1** *verb intrans*. Make a succession of rapid, light, crisp sounds, as the result of movement. LME.
2 *verb intrans*. Move with a rustling sound. Foll. by adverb or preposition. L16.
3 *verb trans*. Cause (a thing) to move with or make a rustling sound. M17.
4 a *verb trans*. Pick up or move (a thing) quickly; gather or round up; produce or acquire (something) quickly when needed. Usu. foll. by *up*. *colloq*. M19. ▸**b** *verb intrans*. Move or work energetically; hustle. *US colloq*. L19. ▸**c** *verb trans. & intrans*. Of an animal: forage (for). *US colloq*. L19. ▸**d** *verb trans. & intrans*. Round up and steal (esp. cattle or horses). E20.

📖 **1** A. UTTLEY Something rustled in the ivy bushes. I. MCEWAN Dry . . leaves stirred and rustled. **2** M. SINCLAIR Miss Kendal rustled in . . in black silk. **3** J. RATHBONE A breeze in a wood rustling the leaves. **4a** J. RABAN The Council rustled up a scratch crew. J. BRIGGS Rustling up picnics, arranging outings and excursions. **b** D. WELCH A nurse rustled by busily. J. KEROUAC Rustle around the kitchen see what there is.

▶ **B** *noun*. A rustling sound or movement. M18.

📖 B. UNSWORTH I heard the rustle of her clothes. M. WESLEY The rustle of the reeds as they swayed.

■ **rustler** *noun* a person who or thing which rustles; *spec*. a cattle-thief: E19. **rustling** *noun* (*a*) the action of the verb; an instance of this; (*b*) a rustling sound: LME. **rustling** *adjective* (*a*) making a rustle or rustles; (*b*) of the nature of a rustle; (*c*) *US colloq*. bustling, energetic, active: M16. **rustlingly** *adverb* with a rustling noise; so as to rustle: L18. **rustly** *adjective* tending to rustle E16.

rustproof /ˈrʌs(t)pruːf/ *adjective & verb*. L17.
[from RUST *noun*[1] + PROOF *adjective*.]
▶ **A** *adjective*. Resistant or not susceptible to rust. L17.
▶ **B** *verb trans*. Make rustproof. E20.
■ **rustproofing** *noun* the action or process of making something rustproof; a substance used for this: E20.

rustre /ˈrʌstə/ *noun*. E18.
[French.]
HERALDRY. A lozenge-shaped charge with a round hole in cut in the centre disclosing the field.
■ **rustred** *adjective* having rustres E19.

rusty /ˈrʌsti/ *adjective*[1]. OE.
[from RUST *noun*[1] + -Y[1].]
1 Covered or affected with rust; rusted. OE. ▸**b** Of a plant: affected with rust or blight. E16.
†**2** Morally corrupt. LME–E17.
3 a Of a person: old, worn-out, or decrepit in appearance. LME. ▸**b** No longer skilled or practised in a particular accomplishment through age or inactivity; *spec*. (of knowledge, an ability, etc.) deteriorated or impaired by neglect. E16. ▸**c** Old; antiquated, obsolete. M16.
4 Rust-coloured; of or tending toward a reddish-brown or brownish-orange. LME. ▸**b** Of (esp. dark) clothing: shabby, worn, or faded with age or use. E18.
5 Rugged; rough; unrefined; *spec*. (*a*) socially awkward, unmannerly; (*b*) (of a sound, the voice, etc.) hoarse, harsh, grating; †(*c*) (chiefly *Scot*.) lacking verbal polish. LME.

📖 **1** N. CALDER The rusty eyesores of scrapyards. **3a** W. IRVING A little rusty, musty old fellow. **b** C. A. LINDBERGH I . . was . . a little rusty from not flying recently. W. S. MAUGHAM Our wits . . grow rusty because there is no occasion to use them. **4** G. GREENE The handkerchief rusty with blood. **b** ELLIS PETERS A man . . in a rusty black cassock.

Special collocations & comb.: **rusty dab** *US* = YELLOWTAIL *flounder*. **rustyback (fern)** a European dwarf fern of rocks and walls, *Ceterach officinarum*, with simply lobed fronds densely covered below with whitish then rust-coloured scales.
■ **rustily** *adverb* L16. **rustiness** *noun*[1] LME.

rusty /ˈrʌsti/ *adjective*[2]. Now *dial*. E16.
[Var. of REASTY, RESTY *adjective*[1].]
Rancid.

rusty /ˈrʌsti/ *adjective*[3]. M16.
[Var. of RESTY *adjective*[2], perh. infl. by RUSTY *adjective*[1].]
1 Intractable, obstinate; angry, annoyed, impatient; offended; *spec*. (of a horse) restive. Freq. in ***ride rusty***, ***run rusty***, be or become intractable, impatient, or restive. Now *dial. & colloq*. E18.
2 Bad-tempered, cross; nasty. *colloq*. E19.
■ **rustiness** *noun*[2] (*colloq*.) bad temper, crossness M19.

rut /rʌt/ *noun*[1] *& verb*[1]. LME.
[Old & mod. French *rut*, †*ruit*, from Proto-Romance from Latin *rugitus*, from *rugire* roar.]
▶ **A** *noun*. **1** The periodic sexual excitement or activity of male deer, antelope, goats, etc.; the season or time during which this occurs. LME.
†**2** The company of deer among which a particular stag is sexually dominant. LME–M17.
▶ **B** *verb*. Infl. **-tt-**.
1 *verb intrans*. Of a male deer etc.: be in a state of periodic sexual excitement, be in rut. LME.
2 *verb intrans. & (rare) trans*. Copulate (with). *rare*. E17.

rut /rʌt/ *noun*[2] *& verb*[2]. L16.
[Prob. from Old French *rote*, *rute* ROUTE.]
▶ **A** *noun*. **1** A (deep) furrow or track made in the ground by the passage of a wheeled vehicle or other traffic. L16. ▸**b** A track or passage in the ground, as dug out by an animal or created by running water. E17.
2 *transf*. A deep line or depression in the skin, flesh, or bone. Now *rare*. E17.
3 *fig*. An unchanging habit, procedure, or method, *esp*. a tedious or dreary one; a narrow undeviating course of thought, action, or life. M19.

📖 **1** M. M. KAYE Granite . . worn into ruts . . by the passing of generations of men. B. PYM The mud in the lanes dried into hard ruts. **b** N. GORDIMER The road has ruts . . from the rains. **3** *Woman* Hector . . was in a rut At one o'clock every day . . Hector reached for his hat. V. G. KIERNAN The rut of private egotism.

▶ **B** *verb trans*. Infl. **-tt-**. Mark (the ground etc.) with ruts; furrow. Chiefly as ***rutted ppl adjective***. L16.

rut /rʌt/ *noun*[3]. Now *N. Amer. & dial*. See also ROTE *noun*[4]. E17.
[Origin unkn. Cf. RUT *noun*[1].]
The roaring of the sea, esp. in breaking on the shore.

rut /rʌt/ *verb*[3]. Now *Scot*. Infl. **-tt-**. LME.
[Var. of RIT *verb*.]
†**1** *verb trans. & intrans*. Cut or pierce with a weapon. Only in LME.
2 *verb trans*. Cut or make a furrow in (earth, turf, etc.). E19.

rutabaga /ruːtəˈbeɪɡə/ *noun*. Chiefly *N. Amer*. L18.
[Swedish dial. *rotabagge*.]
(The edible root of) the swede, *Brassica napus* var. *napobrassica*.

rutaceous /ruːˈteɪʃəs/ *adjective*. M19.
[from mod. Latin *Rutaceae* (see below), from Latin *ruta* rue: see -ACEOUS.]
Of or pertaining to the Rutaceae or rue family; resembling rue.

ruth /ruːθ/ *noun*[1]. *arch*. ME.
[from RUE *verb*, prob. after Old Norse *hrygð*: see -TH[1]. Cf. WROATH.]
1 Compassion, pity; the feeling of sorrow for another. ME.
2 Contrition, repentance; remorse. Now *rare*. ME.
3 Sorrow, grief, distress. Formerly also, an instance or expression of this. ME.
†**4 a** A cause of or reason for sorrow or regret. ME–E17. ▸†**b** Mischief; calamity; ruin. ME–M17.
■ **ruthful** *adjective* (*a*) compassionate, pitying; (*b*) that engenders compassion or pity, pitiable; (*c*) (esp. of a sound, action, etc.) expressing grief or sorrow; (*d*) (of a person or emotion) sad, dejected: ME. **ruthfully** *adverb* (now *rare*) (*a*) in a pitiable way, piteously, dolefully; †(*b*) compassionately: ME. **ruthfulness** *noun* (*rare*) (*a*) sorrow, grief; (*b*) compassion: L16.

ruth /rʌt/ *noun*[2]. Also (earlier) **rutt**. E19.
[Sanskrit *ratha* chariot, carriage, coach.]
In the Indian subcontinent, a vehicle, a carriage.

ruthenate /ˈruːθ(ə)neɪt/ *noun*. L19.
[from RUTHENIUM + -ATE[1].]
CHEMISTRY. A salt of an anion containing ruthenium and oxygen.

Ruthenian /ruːˈθiːnɪən/ *noun & adjective*. M16.
[from *Ruthenia* a former region of east central Europe (from medieval Latin *Rut(h)eni* pl., rel. to *Ruzi*, *Russi* Russians) + -AN. Cf. RUSSIAN.]
▶ **A** *noun*. **1** A Ukrainian, esp. of Galicia and neighbouring regions of east central Europe, a Russniak. Also, a member of the Uniat Church of the Ruthenians. M16.
2 The language of the Ruthenians, a dialect of Ukrainian. M19.
▶ **B** *attrib*. or as *adjective*. Of or pertaining to the Ruthenians, their liturgy, or their language. M19.
■ Also **Ruthene** *noun & adjective* (now *rare*) M16.

ruthenium /rʊˈθiːnɪəm/ *noun*. M19.
[from medieval Latin *Ruthenia* Russia (having been first found in ores from the Urals) + -IUM.]
A rare silvery-white metallic chemical element, atomic no. 44, belonging to the platinum group, which is harder and more refractory than platinum and is used as a chemical catalyst, a hardener in alloys, etc. (Symbol Ru.)
Comb.: **ruthenium red** an intensely coloured red mixed-valence complex salt of ruthenium, used as a microscopic stain.
■ **rutheniate** *noun* = RUTHENATE M19. **ruthenic** /-ˈθɛn-/ *adjective* of, pertaining to, or containing ruthenium, esp. in a state in which it has a valency of three or more M19. **ruthenious** *adjective* of or containing ruthenium in the divalent state M19.

ruther /ˈrʌðə/ *adverb*. *US colloq. & dial*. L19.
[Repr. a pronunc.]
= RATHER *adverb*.

Rutherford /ˈrʌðəfəd/ *noun*. M20.
[Ernest *Rutherford* (1871–1937), New Zealand-born Brit. physicist.]
PHYSICS. **I 1** Used *attrib*. and in *possess*. to designate concepts developed by Rutherford. M20.
Rutherford formula, **Rutherford law** a mathematical expression of Rutherford scattering. **Rutherford model** a model of the atom in which all positive charge is concentrated in a nucleus, devised to account for Rutherford scattering. **Rutherford scattering** elastic scattering of charged particles by the electric fields of atomic nuclei. **Rutherford's formula**, **Rutherford's law**, **Rutherford's scattering formula**, **Rutherford's scattering law** = ***Rutherford formula***.
▶ **II 2** (Usu. **r-**.) A unit of radioactivity orig. equal to one million disintegrations per second; a quantity of radioactive material with this degree of activity. M20.

rutherfordium /rʌðəˈfɔːdɪəm/ *noun*. M20.
[from prec. + -IUM.]
(A name proposed for) a very unstable radioactive transuranic chemical element, atomic no. 104, produced artificially. (Symbol Rf.) Cf. KURCHATOVIUM.

ruthless /ˈruːθlɪs/ *adjective*. ME.
[from RUTH *noun*[1] + -LESS.]
Having no pity or compassion; pitiless, merciless.

📖 J. AGATE A ruthless capacity to trample on . . competing talents. E. WAUGH A man of ruthless ambition who has reached . . eminence by betraying his friends.

■ **ruthlessly** *adverb* L16. **ruthlessness** *noun* L18.

rutilant /ˈruːtɪl(ə)nt/ *adjective*. Now *literary*. LME.
[Latin *rutilant-* pres. ppl stem of *rutilare*, from *rutilus* reddish: see -ANT[1].]
Glowing or glittering with red or golden light.

rutile /ˈruːtɪl/ *noun*. E19.
[from Latin *rutilus* reddish.]
MINERALOGY. A tetragonal, usu. reddish-brown, mineral, titanium dioxide, that is an important ore of titanium. Cf. TITANITE 1.
■ **rutilated** *adjective* (of quartz) containing needles of rutile L19.

rutilous /ˈruːtɪləs/ *adjective*. *rare*. M17.
[formed as prec. + -OUS.]
Shining with red light; reddish.

rutin /ˈruːtɪn/ *noun*. M19.
[from Latin *ruta* RUE *noun*[2]: see -IN[1].]
CHEMISTRY. A phenolic glycoside, $C_{27}H_{30}O_{16}$, found esp. in common rue, buckwheat, and capers.

rutt *noun* see RUTH *noun*[2].

ruttee /ˈrʌtiː/ *noun*. Also †**rati**. E17.
[Hindi *ratt(ī)* from Sanskrit *raktikā* the seed of the jequirity.]
In the Indian subcontinent, a small weight (about 0.11 gram, 1.75 grains) used for weighing gems.

rutter /ˈrʌtə/ *noun*[1]. Also **-ier** /-ɪə/. L15.
[Middle Dutch var. of *ruter*, *ruyter* (Dutch *ruiter*, whence German *reuter*), from Old French *routier*, *routeur*: see ROUTER *noun*[1].]
1 *Hist*. A (German) cavalry soldier of the 16th and 17th cents. Formerly also *transf*., a dashing cavalier, a gallant. Cf. RUITER. L15.
2 One of a party of swindlers. Long *rare* or *obsolete*. L16.

rutter /ˈrʌtə/ *noun*[2]. *arch*. Also †**-ier**. L15.
[Old & mod. French *routier*, from *route* ROUTE *noun*.]
A mariner's (esp. a pilot's) guide to sea routes, tides, etc., esp. for a particular journey or destination. Cf. ROUTIER 1.

📖 J. CLAVELL He took out his . . rutter to check some bearings.

rutter /ˈrʌtə/ *noun*[3]. E20.
[from RUT *verb*[3] + -ER[1].]
A spade for cutting peat turf.

ruttier *noun*[1], **ruttier** *noun*[2] vars. of RUTTER *noun*[1], *noun*[2].

ruttish /ˈrʌtɪʃ/ *adjective*. E17.
[from RUT *verb*[1] + -ISH[1].]
Lustful, lascivious; of or pertaining to sexual excitement.

ruttle /ˈrʌt(ə)l/ *verb & noun.* Now *dial.* LME.
[Corresp. to Middle Low German *rutelen*, prob. of imit. origin. Cf. RATTLE *verb*[1], ROTTLE.]
▶ **A** *verb intrans.* Rattle; make a rattling noise in the throat. LME.
▶ **B** *noun.* A rattling noise in the throat. E18.

rutty /ˈrʌti/ *adjective.* L16.
[from RUT *noun*[2] + -Y[1].]
1 Marked by or having many ruts. L16.
2 Deeply sunk or furrowed. L19.

ruvid /ˈruːvɪd/ *adjective. rare.* M17.
[Italian *ruvido*, app. repr. Latin *ruidus*.]
†**1** Rude, barbarous. Only in M17.
2 Rough, rugged. M19.

rux /rʌks/ *noun. Nautical slang.* E20.
[Origin unkn. Cf. RUCK *verb*[5], RUCKUS.]
A disturbance, an uproar.

Ruy Lopez /ruːɪ ˈləʊpɛz/ *noun.* L19.
[*Ruy López* de Segura (fl. 1560), Spanish priest and chess expert, who developed this opening.]
CHESS. A chess opening in which White moves the king's bishop to the fifth rank usually on the third move.

RV *abbreviation*[1].
1 Recreational vehicle, as a motorized caravan. *US.*
2 Revised Version (of the Bible).

rv *abbreviation*[2].
Rendezvous.

Rwanda /ˈrwandə, rʊˈandə/ *noun & adjective.* Also (earlier) **Ruanda**. E20.
[Bantu.]
▶ **A** *noun.* Pl. same. A native or inhabitant of Rwanda, an E. African republic (formerly a kingdom) bordered by the Democratic Republic of Congo (Zaire), Uganda, Tanzania, and Burundi; the Bantu language of Rwanda. E20.
▶ **B** *attrib.* or as *adjective.* Of, pertaining to, or designating the Rwanda or their language. E20.
▪ Also **Rwandan** *adjective & noun* L20.

Ry. *abbreviation.*
Railway.

-ry /ri/ *suffix.*
[Aphet. form of -ERY.]
1 = -ERY. Occurring chiefly after an unstressed syllable ending in *d, t, l, n,* or *sh,* or (occas.) a stressed vowel or diphthong, as ***heraldry***, ***infantry***, ***rivalry***, ***yeomanry***, etc.
2 Repr. Old French *-rie, -erie,* as **ancestry**, ***carpentry***, ***castelry***, ***falconry***, etc.

rya /ˈriːə/ *noun.* M20.
[Swedish.]
In full ***rya rug***. A Scandinavian type of knotted pile rug.

Rydberg /ˈrɪdbəːg/ *noun.* E20.
[Johannes Robert *Rydberg* (1854–1919), Swedish physicist.]
PHYSICS. **I 1** Used *attrib.* and in *possess.* to designate concepts developed by Rydberg. E20.
Rydberg constant, **Rydberg's constant** a constant, 1.097 × 10^7 m^{-1} (symbol *R*), which appears in the formulae for the wave numbers of lines in atomic spectra and is a function of the rest mass and charge of the electron, the speed of light, and Planck's constant. **Rydberg formula**, **Rydberg's formula** an empirical formula giving the wave numbers of frequencies of the lines in the spectral series of atoms and simple molecules.
▶ **II 2** (Also **r-**.) In full ***Rydberg unit***. A unit of energy given by $e^2/2a_0$ (approximately 2.425 × 10^{-28} joule), where *e* is the electronic charge and a_0 is the radius of the first Bohr orbit for a nucleus of infinite mass. M20.

rye /rʌɪ/ *noun*[1].
[Old English *ryġe* = Old Norse *rugr* from Germanic forms repr. by Old Frisian *rogga*, Old Saxon *roggo* (Dutch *rogge, rog*), Old High German *rokko*.]
1 An awned cereal grass, *Secale cereale*, resembling barley, grown esp. in colder parts of Eurasia; the grain of this cereal, used to make coarse bread, beer, spirits, etc. OE.
2 *ellipt.* Rye whiskey. *N. Amer.* M19.
3 *ellipt.* Rye bread. M20.
Phrases: **rye and Indian (bread)** *US* bread made from a mixture of rye and (Indian) cornmeal. ***wild rye***: see WILD *adjective, noun, & adverb.*
Comb.: **rye bread**: made from rye flour; **rye brome(-grass)** a brome found as a cornfield weed, *Bromus secalinus*, in which the caryopsis becomes tightly enwrapped by the lemma when ripe; **rye coffee** *US* a drink resembling coffee, made from roasted rye; **rye-land** (usu. inferior) land, suitable for cultivating rye; **rye whiskey**: distilled from fermented rye; **rye-worm** the larva of the gout-fly.

†**rye** *noun*[2]. LME–M18.
[Prob. from Anglo-Norman.]
A disease of hawks.

rye /rʌɪ/ *noun*[3]. M19.
[Romany *rai* from Sanskrit *rājan* RAJA *noun*[1].]
Among Gypsies: a man; a gentleman.
ROMANY rye.

ryebuck /ˈrʌɪbʌk/ *adverb & adjective. slang* (chiefly *Austral.*). Now *rare.* M19.
[Origin uncertain: perh. from German *Reibach* var. of *Rebbach* profit.]
▶ **A** *adverb.* Well; suitably. M19.
▶ **B** *adjective.* Good, excellent; genuine. Also as *interjection*, expr. agreement or assent. M19.

ryegrass /ˈrʌɪgrɑːs/ *noun.* M17.
[In sense 1 from RYE *noun*[1] + GRASS *noun.* In sense 2 alt. of *ray-grass* s.v. RAY *noun*[5].]
1 = ***wild rye*** s.v. WILD *adjective, noun, & adverb. rare.* M17.
2 Any of several grasses constituting the genus *Lolium*, with flattened sessile spikelets pressed close to the rachis; *esp.* the perennial *L. perenne* (in full ***common ryegrass***) and the annual or biennial *L. multiflorum* (in full ***Italian ryegrass***), both much grown as fodder grasses. E18.

Ryeland /ˈrʌɪlənd/ *noun.* E19.
[A district in Herefordshire, England, where the breed was first developed.]
(An animal of) a small hornless versatile breed of sheep producing both wool and meat. Freq. *attrib.*

ryepeck /ˈrʌɪpɛk/ *noun.* M19.
[Origin unkn.]
An iron-tipped pole for mooring a punt or marking the course in a water race.

Rylean /ˈrʌɪlɪən/ *adjective.* M20.
[from *Ryle* (see below) + -AN.]
PHILOSOPHY. Of, pertaining to, or characteristic of the English philosopher Gilbert Ryle (1900–76) or his theories on linguistic philosophy and philosophical behaviourism.

rymer /ˈrʌɪmə/ *noun.* Also **rimer**. L18.
[Origin unkn.]
A post in or on which a paddle moves up and down, forming part of the mechanism which opens and closes a weir or lock.

ryo /rɪˈəʊ/ *noun.* Pl. same, **-s**. L19.
[Japanese.]
Hist. A former Japanese monetary unit.

ryokan /rɪˈəʊkan/ *noun.* Pl. same, **-s**. M20.
[Japanese, from *ryo* travel + *kan* building.]
A traditional Japanese inn or hostelry.

ryot /ˈrʌɪət/ *noun.* Also (earlier) †**riat**. E17.
[Persian & Urdu *ra'īyat*, Urdu *raiyat* from Arab. *ra'iyya(t)* flock, herd, subjects of a ruler, from *ra'ā* to pasture. Cf. RAYAH.]
In the Indian subcontinent, a peasant, a farming tenant.

ryotti /rʌɪˈɒti/ *adjective. rare.* L18.
[Persian & Urdu *ra'īyatī* from Urdu *raiyat* RYOT.]
In the Indian subcontinent, *spec.* Bengal: (of land) held on permanent tenure in return for an established rent.

ryotwar /ˈrʌɪətwɑː/ *adjective.* E19.
[Urdu *raiyatwār*, from *raiyat* RYOT + *-wār* pertaining to.]
= RYOTWARY *adjective.* Chiefly in ***ryotwar system***.

ryotwary /ˈrʌɪətwɑːri/ *adjective & noun.* M19.
[Persian & Urdu *ra'īyatwārī*, formed as prec.]
▶ **A** *adjective.* In the Indian subcontinent, designating a system of land tenure agreed directly between the government and farmers without intervention by a landlord. M19.
▶ **B** *noun.* The ryotwary system. M19.

rype /ˈruːpə/ *noun.* Also **ryper**. Pl. **ryper**. M18.
[Norwegian, var. of *rjupe, rjupa*, Icelandic (Old Norse) *rjúpa*.]
The ptarmigan.

ryu /rɪˈuː/ *noun.* Also **riu**. Pl. same. L19.
[Japanese *-ryū* school, style, system.]
Any Japanese school or style of art.

Ryukyu /rɪˈuːkjuː/ *noun & adjective.* Also **Riu-kiu**. E19.
[formed as next.]
= RYUKYUAN.

Ryukyuan /rɪˈuːkjʊən/ *noun & adjective.* M20.
[from Japanese *Ryūkyū* (see below) + -AN.]
▶ **A** *noun.* A native or inhabitant of the Ryukyu Islands, south of mainland Japan; any of the Japanese dialects spoken there. M20.
▶ **B** *adjective.* Of, pertaining to, or characteristic of the Ryukyu Islands, the Ryukyuans, or their dialects. L20.

Ss

S, s /ɛs/.
The nineteenth letter of the modern English alphabet and the eighteenth of the ancient Roman one, derived from a Semitic (Phoenician) character, which represented a voiceless sibilant, /s/, /ʃ/. Mod. English pronunciation is according to the following general rules: S is pronounced /s/ at the beginning of a word or of the second elem. of a compound, and when doubled or in contact with a voiceless consonant; between vowels, and when phonetically final, a single s is usu. pronounced /z/. However, there are many anomalies, esp. in words derived from Latin or Greek: e.g. ***absurd***, ***observe***, ***evasive***, ***dissolve***, ***possess***. In some words mod. English has /ʃ/, /ʒ/, developed from earlier English /sj/, /zj/, written either as *s* (before diphthongal *u*) or as *si*, which when rapidly pronounced are similar to /ʃ/, /ʒ/: e.g. ***sure***, ***sugar***, ***censure***, ***mission***, ***treasure***, ***evasion***. In a few words adopted from Old French S is silent, as in ***aisle***, ***isle***. Pl. **S's**, **Ss**, **ss**, /ˈɛsɪz/. See also **ESS** *noun*[1].
▶ **I 1** The letter and its sound.
2 The shape of the letter. ▸**b** One of the two directions of twist in spinning yarn. Usu. *attrib.* Cf. **Z, z** 2b.
1 s-aorist PHILOLOGY an aorist formed in certain Indo-European languages by adding *s* and the ending to the verbal stem. ***2 collar of SS***: see **COLLAR** *noun*. **S-bend** an S-shaped bend (in a road, waste pipe, etc.). **S-shaped** *adjective* having a shape or a cross-section like the capital letter S.
▶ **II** Symbolical uses.
3 Used to denote serial order; applied e.g. to the nineteenth (or often the eighteenth, I or J being omitted) group or section, sheet of a book, etc.
4 [Initial letter of secondary.] ***S wave***, an earthquake wave which is a shear wave or secondary wave (cf. ***P wave*** s.v. **P, P**).
5 PHYSICS. Denoting the quantum number of spin angular momentum of one electron (*s*) or an assemblage of electrons (*S*).
6 RADIO. ***S meter***, a meter that indicates the strength of a received signal.
7 ASTRONOMY. [Initial letter of *slow*] ***s-process***, a process believed to occur in giant stars by which heavy atomic nuclei are produced from other nuclei by a combination of neutron captures and beta decays.
8 PHYSICS. ***S-matrix***, a scattering matrix, i.e. a matrix of probability amplitudes that occurs in the expression of the initial wave functions in a scattering process in terms of all the possible final wave functions.
9 ***S-band***, the range of microwave frequencies between 1550 and 5200 megahertz, used for radio communication and radar.
10 CHEMISTRY. [Abbreviation of Latin *sinister* left] (Cap. S.) Designating (compounds having) a configuration about an asymmetric carbon atom in which the substituents, placed in order according to certain rules, form an anticlockwise sequence when viewed from a particular direction. Opp. **R, R** 7.
▶ **III 11** Abbrevs.: (A small selection only is given here. Those all in caps. or small caps. also occur with a full stop after each letter; some of those all in caps. also occur (i) with initial cap. only, (ii) in small caps.) **S.** = (ANATOMY & ZOOLOGY) sacral (in vertebral formulae); Society. **S** = Saint; (ELECTRICITY) siemens; small; (BACTERIOLOGY) smooth; South(ern); special (in ***S level***, of the General Certificate of Education examination); strain (of virus etc.); (PARTICLE PHYSICS) strangeness (quantum number); (CHEMISTRY) sulphur; (BIOCHEMISTRY) Svedberg unit. **s** = second(s); (PHYSICS & CHEMISTRY) sharp (orig. designating one of the four main series (S, P, D, F) of lines in atomic spectra, now more frequently applied to electronic orbitals, states, etc., possessing zero angular momentum and total symmetry (as ***s-electron***, ***s-orbital***, etc.)); (in former British currency) [Latin] *solidus*, *-di* shilling(s); (GRAMMAR) singular; son; (PHYSICS) strange quark; succeeded.

s' *adverb, conjunction, & adjective* see **SO** *adverb, conjunction, & adjective*.

's *pronoun* see **US** *pronoun*.

's *verb* see **BE**, **DO** *verb*, **HAVE** *verb*.

's *adverb* see **AS** *adverb*.

's- /s/ *prefix* (not productive). Chiefly *arch.*
[Euphem. abbreviation.]
In oaths and forcible exclamations: God's, as ***'sblood***, ***'sdeath***, ***'strewth***.

-s /ɪz, z, s (*see below*)/ *suffix*[1]. Also (see below) **-es**, **-'s** /ɪz, z/.
[In branch I Old English *-as*; in branch II from **-S**[3].]
▶ **I 1** Forming pl. of nouns, in mod. English usage according to the following rules (cf. **-S**[2]): (i) /ɪz/ after a sibilant or affricate, *-es* being added if the sing. is not spelt with a final silent *-e*, as *boxes*, *cases*, *mazes*, *porches*; (ii) /z/ after a vowel or voiced consonant other than /z, ʒ, dʒ/, *-es* being added in certain cases when the sing. is spelt with final *o*, as *beds*, *gigolos*, *hoods*, *potatoes*, *tomatoes*, *tubs*; (iii) /s/ after a voiceless consonant other than /s, ʃ, tʃ/, as *bets*, *books*, *cats*, *cliffs*.
2 Forming the pl. of abbreviations, letters, and symbols: /ɪz, z/ written *-s* or *-'s*, as *C's*, *Cs*, *MPs*, *1960s*.
▶ **II 3** Forming adverbs: see **-S**[3].
¶ In a few cases sing. nouns ending in a final voiceless fricative /θ, f, s/ may have voicing to /ð, v, z/ respectively, as *bath*, *baths*, *calf*, *calves*, *house*, *houses*, or a final consonant after a vowel may be doubled, as *fez*, *fezzes*, *quiz*, *quizzes*. Sing. nouns with final *y* after a consonant generally form the pl. in *-ies*, as *country*, *countries*, *spy*, *spies*, *worry*, *worries*. Cf. **-ER**[3].

-s /ɪz, z, s (*see below*)/ *suffix*[2]. Also (see below) **-es** /ɪz, z/.
[Old English dial., prob. from Old English 2nd person sing. pres. ending *-es*, *-as*.]
Forming 3rd person sing. pres. indic. of verbs, in mod. English usage according to the following rules (cf. **-S**[1]): (i) /ɪz/ after a sibilant or affricate, *-es* being added if the verb is not spelt with a final silent *e*, as ***grazes***, ***lunches***, ***places***, ***pushes***; (ii) /z/ after a vowel or voiced consonant other than /z, ʒ, dʒ/, *-es* being added in certain cases when the verb is spelt with final *o*, as ***dies***, ***fades***, ***goes***, ***lassoes***, ***rubs***, ***wallows***; (iii) /s/ after a voiceless consonant other than /s, ʃ, tʃ/, as ***bakes***, ***cuts***, ***puffs***, ***wants***.
¶ Verbs with final *y* after a consonant generally form the 3rd person sing. in *-ies*, as *dry*, *dries*, *hurry*, *hurries*, *try*, *tries*.

-s /s, *after vowel or voiced consonant* z/ *suffix*[3] (not productive).
[Old English *-es* masc. and neut. genit. sing. ending.]
Forming adverbs from nouns, adjectives, and (later, by analogy) adverbs, as *afterwards*, *besides*; (with changed spelling) *hence*, *once*. In later use some words were identified with **-S**[1] from their formal coincidence with pl. nouns, as *days*, *mornings*, *needs*, *Sundays*.

-s /s, *after vowel or voiced consonant* z/ *suffix*[4].
[After **-S**[1].]
Forming nicknames (as *Carrots*, *Fats*) or pet names (as *Babs*, *ducks*, *Pops*).

-s *suffix*[5] see **-'S**[1] 2.

-'s /ɪz, s, z, (*see below*)/ *suffix*[1]. In sense 2 **-s** /z, s/.
[formed as **-S**[3].]
1 Forming the possessive case of nouns, in mod. English usage according to the following rules (cf. **-S**[1], **-S**[2]): (i) /ɪz/ following a sibilant or affricate, as ***fox's***, ***goose's***, ***witch's***; (ii) /z/ following a vowel or voiced consonant other than /z, ʒ, dʒ/, as ***children's***, ***dog's***, ***girl's***, ***tiger's***, ***women's***; (iii) /s/ following a voiceless consonant other than /s, ʃ, tʃ/, as ***book's***, ***calf's***, ***cat's***, ***sheep's***.
2 (**-s.**) (Not productive.) Forming the possessive prons. ***hers***, ***its***, ***ours***, ***theirs***, ***yours***.
¶ In certain instances there is no change in pronunciation for the possessive, and its written representation is by an additional apostrophe only: (i) pl. nouns spelt with final *s*, as *books'*, *cats'*, *girls'*, *tigers'*; (ii) a few nouns with final sibilant in fixed phrs., as *for conscience' sake*, *for goodness' sake*. An additional apostrophe only is also usual with the possessive of classical names of more than one syllable spelt with final *s*, as *Moses'*, *Venus'*, *Socrates'*, *Xerxes'*; English names with final *s* may take either *'s* /ɪz/ or an apostrophe only, as *Charles's* or *Charles'*, *Dickens's* or *Dickens'*.

-'s *suffix*[2] see **-S**[1] 2.

SA *abbreviation.*
1 Salvation Army.
2 Sex appeal.
3 MEDICINE. Sino-auricular or -atrial.
4 MILITARY. Small arms.
5 South Africa(n).
6 South America(n).
7 South Australia(n).
8 *Hist.* [German.] *Sturmabteilung.*

SAA *abbreviation.*
Small arm(s) ammunition.

Sa'dī /ˈsɑːdi/ *adjective.* **L19.**
[Arab., from Banū *Sa'd* a people claiming descent from Muhammad.]
Hist. Designating or pertaining to a dynasty of Moroccan sharifs of the 16th and 17th cents.

Saadian /ˈsɑːdɪən/ *adjective.* Also **Sa'dian**. **M20.**
[formed as **SA'DĪ** + **-AN**.]
Hist. Of or pertaining to the Sa'dī dynasty.

saag /sɑːɡ/ *noun.* Also **sag**. **L20.**
[Hindi *sāg*.]
In Indian cookery: spinach.

saaidam /ˈsʌɪdam/ *noun. S. Afr.* **E20.**
[Afrikaans, from *saai* sow + *dam* dam.]
A basin of land enclosed by earthen walls, built to receive flood-water for its irrigation.

Saale /ˈzɑːlə/ *adjective & noun.* **M20.**
[A river in Germany.]
GEOLOGY. ▶**A** *adjective.* Designating or pertaining to the penultimate Pleistocene glaciation in northern Europe, perhaps corresponding to the Riss glaciation of the Alps. **M20.**
▶ **B** *noun.* The Saale glaciation. **M20.**

Saalian /ˈzɑːlɪən/ *adjective & noun.* **M20.**
[formed as prec. + **-IAN**.]
GEOLOGY. ▶**A** *adjective.* **1** Designating or pertaining to a minor orogenic episode in the late Permian of Europe. **M20.**
2 = **SAALE** *adjective.* **M20.**
▶ **B** *noun.* **1** The Saalian orogenic episode. **M20.**
2 = **SAALE** *noun.* **M20.**

Saanen /ˈsɑːnən/ *noun.* **E20.**
[A small town in the canton of Berne, Switzerland.]
(An animal of) a breed of hornless white dairy goat, first developed in the region of Saanen.

Saarlander /ˈzɑːlandə/ *noun & adjective.* **M20.**
[German, from *Saarland* (see below).]
▶ **A** *noun.* A native or inhabitant of Saarland, a State in western Germany. **M20.**
▶ **B** *adjective.* Of or pertaining to Saarland or the Saarlanders. **L20.**

sabadilla /sabəˈdɪlə/ *noun.* **E19.**
[Spanish *cebadilla* dim. of *cebada* barley.]
A Mexican plant, *Schoenocaulon officinale*, of the lily family; a preparation of its seeds, used as an insecticide and (formerly) as an anthelmintic.

Sabaean /saˈbiːən/ *adjective & noun.* Also **Sabean**. **L16.**
[from Latin *Sabaeus*, Greek *Sabaios*, from *Saba* from Arab. *Sabā'* = Hebrew *šᵉḇā* (see below): see **-AN**.]
Hist. ▶**A** *adjective.* Of or pertaining to Saba (Sheba), an ancient kingdom of the SW part of the Arabian peninsula, its people, or their language. **L16.**
▶ **B** *noun.* **1** A native or inhabitant of ancient Saba (Sheba). **E17.**
2 The Semitic language of the Sabaeans. **E20.**
■ **Sabaic** /saˈbeɪɪk/ *noun & adjective* (of) the Semitic language of the Sabaeans **L20.**

Sabaism /ˈseɪbeɪɪz(ə)m/ *noun.* **E18.**
[French *sabaïsme*, from Hebrew *ṣāḇā'* hosts (of heaven), after presumed etym. of **SABIAN**: see **-ISM**.]
1 The worship of stars or of spirits in them, esp. as practised in ancient Arabia and Mesopotamia. **E18.**
2 = **SABIANISM** 1. **M19.**

sabal /ˈseɪb(ə)l/ *noun.* **E19.**
[Perh. from an Amer. Indian name.]
Any of various tropical American fan palms constituting the genus *Sabal*, which includes the cabbage palmetto, *S. palmetto*.

sabalo /ˈsabələʊ/ *noun. US.* Pl. **-os**. **L19.**
[Spanish *sábalo* shad.]
The tarpon, *Megalops atlanticus*.

Sabaoth /ˈsabeɪɒθ, saˈbeɪɒθ/ *noun.* **ME.**
[Latin from Greek *Sabaōth* from Hebrew *ṣᵉḇā'ōṯ* pl. of *ṣāḇā'*: see **SABAISM**.]
1 *pl.* Heavenly hosts. Only in ***Lord of Sabaoth*** (chiefly in the New Testament and the *Te Deum*) = ***Lord of hosts*** s.v. **HOST** *noun*[1]. **ME.**
†**2** As *sing.* = **SABBATH**. **ME–M19.**

†**sabat** *noun* see **SABBATH**.

sabatia *noun* var. of **SABBATIA**.

Sabatier effect /saˈbatɪə ɪˌfɛkt/ *noun phr.* **L19.**
[from Armand *Sabatier* (1834–1910), French physician and scientist.]
PHOTOGRAPHY. Partial or complete reversal of an image on film or paper, resulting from exposure to unsafe light after partial development.

sabaton /ˈsabətɒn/ *noun.* LME.
[Old Provençal *sabató* (mod. *sabatoun*) augm. of *sabata* = French *savate*, Spanish *zapata* boot, *zapato* shoe.]
Hist. **1** A type of shoe worn in the Middle Ages. LME.
2 A piece of armour for the upper side of the foot. LME.

sabayon /ˈsabʌɪjɒn/ *noun.* E20.
[French from Italian *zabaione* var. of ZABAGLIONE.]
Zabaglione.

Sabba-day /ˈsabədeɪ/ *noun. US colloq.* Now *rare.* L18.
[Repr. a pronunc.]
= ***Sabbath day*** s.v. SABBATH.
Comb.: **Sabba-day house**: used for rest between church services.

sabbat *noun* see SABBATH.

Sabbatarian /sabəˈtɛːrɪən/ *noun & adjective.* E17.
[from late Latin *sabbatarius*, from Latin *sabbatum*: see next, -ARIAN.]
▶ **A** *noun.* **1** A Jew who (strictly) observes the (Saturday) Sabbath. E17.
2 A Christian who (strictly) observes the (Sunday) Sabbath. E17.
3 A Christian who observes Saturday as the Sabbath. M17.
▶ **B** *adjective.* Of or pertaining to the Sabbath or its (esp. strict) observance; holding the tenets of the Sabbatarians. M17.
■ **Sabbatarianism** *noun* sabbatarian principles or practice L17.

sabbath /ˈsabəθ/ *noun.* Also (earlier) †**sabat**, (in sense 3) **sabbat** /ˈsabət/. OE.
[Old & mod. French *sabbat*, †*sabat* or its source Latin *sabbatum* from Greek *sabbaton* from Hebrew *šabbāṯ*, from *šāḇaṯ* rest. The spelling with *th* and the consequent pronunc. are after the Hebrew form and pronunc.]
1 (Usu. **S-**.) ▸**a** *The* seventh day of the week (Saturday) set aside for religious observance and rest from work by Jews and some Christian sects. OE. ▸**b** *The* first day of the week (Sunday) set aside by Christians for religious observance and rest from work. LME. ▸**c** *The* sixth day of the week (Friday) set aside for religous observance and rest from work by Muslims. E17.
2 *transf.* A period of rest from work, pain, etc. LME.
3 A midnight meeting of sorcerers and witches, allegedly presided over by the Devil and attended by demons, involving satanic rites. Also ***witches' sabbath***. M17.
Comb.: **Sabbath candle**: lit shortly before dusk on the eve of the Jewish Sabbath; **Sabbath day** = sense 1 above; (***Sabbath day's journey*** (*a*) *Hist.* the distance a Jew might travel on the Sabbath (approx. ⅔ mile); (*b*) *fig.* an easy journey); **Sabbath goy** a Gentile who performs for Orthodox Jews tasks forbidden to the latter on the Sabbath; **Sabbath lamp**: lit on the eve of the Jewish Sabbath; **Sabbath loaf** a plaited loaf eaten on the Jewish Sabbath; **Sabbath school** a Sunday-school.
■ **sabbathize** *verb intrans.* (now *rare*) [alt. of SABBATIZE after SABBATH] observe the Sabbath E17. **Sabbathless** *adjective* observing no Sabbath E17. **Sabbathly** *adverb & adjective* (*a*) *adverb* every Sabbath; (*b*) *adjective* recurring every Sabbath: L16.

sabbatia /saˈbeɪʃə/ *noun.* Also **sabatia**. E19.
[mod. Latin (see below), from Constantino and Liberato *Sabbati*, 18th-cent. Italian botanists + -IA¹.]
Any of various N. American plants constituting the genus *Sabatia*, of the gentian family, resembling centaury and having pink flowers with a yellow eye. Also called ***marsh pink***.

Sabbatian /saˈbeɪʃ(ə)n/ *noun*¹. E18.
[from *Sabbatius* (see below) + -AN.]
Hist. A member of a 4th-cent. Christian sect founded by a former Novationist, Sabbatius, who held Quartodeciman views.

Sabbatian /saˈbeɪʃ(ə)n/ *noun*² *& adjective.* L19.
[from Latinized form of Hebrew *Šabbĕṯāi Ṣĕḇī* Shabbatai Tzevi (see below).]
Hist. ▶**A** *noun.* A member of the religious sect founded by Shabbatai Tzevi, a Jewish Messianic pretender (1626–76). L19.
▶ **B** *adjective.* Of or pertaining to Sabbatians or Sabbatianism. L19.
■ **Sabbatianism** *noun* the doctrine or religion of the Sabbatians L19.

sabbatical /səˈbatɪk(ə)l/ *adjective & noun.* L16.
[from Late Latin *sabbaticus* seventh, of sabbath from Greek *sabbatikos*, from *sabbaton* SABBATH: see -AL¹, -ICAL.]
▶ **A** *adjective.* **1** Of the nature of a sabbath or period of rest. Chiefly in ***sabbatical year*** below. L16. ▸**b** *spec.* Designating (a period of) leave from duty granted at intervals (orig. every seven years) to a teacher in a university etc. for study and travel. L19.
2 Of, pertaining to, or appropriate to the Sabbath. M17.
Special collocations: **sabbatical millenary, sabbatical millennium** the last of the seven thousands of years which (on the analogy of the seven days of the creation) were supposed to form the destined term of the world's existence. **sabbatical officer** a person granted sabbatical leave for the performance of a certain office. **Sabbatical river** an imaginary river celebrated in Jewish legend, said to stop flowing on the Sabbath. **sabbatical year** (*a*) every seventh year, prescribed by the Mosaic law to be observed as a 'sabbath', during which the land was to be fallow and all debtors were to be released; (*b*) a year's sabbatical leave.
▶ **B** *noun.* A period (esp. a year) of sabbatical leave. Freq. in ***on sabbatical***. M20.
■ **sabbatic** *adjective* (now *rare*) = SABBATICAL *adjective* M17. **sabbatically** *adverb* M19. **sabbaticalness** *noun* E18.

sabbatise *verb* var. of SABBATIZE.

Sabbatism /ˈsabətɪz(ə)m/ *noun. rare.* L16.
[Late Latin *sabbatismus* from Greek *sabbatismos*, from *sabbatizein* keep the Sabbath, from *sabbaton* SABBATH: see -ISM.]
1 A sabbatical rest (with allus. to *Hebrew* 4:9). L16.
2 Formal observance of the Sabbath. E17.

sabbatize /ˈsabətʌɪz/ *verb.* Also **-ise**. LME.
[Late Latin *sabbatizare* from Greek *sabbatizein*, from *sabbaton* SABBATH: see -IZE.]
1 *verb intrans.* **a** Enjoy or undergo a period of rest. LME. ▸**b** Observe the Sabbath. E17.
2 *verb trans.* Observe (a specified day) as the Sabbath. E17.
■ **sabbatiˈzation** *noun* the action of sabbatizing M17.

sabe /ˈsɑːbeɪ/ *verb & noun. slang* (chiefly *US*). M19.
[Spanish *sabe* (*usted*) do you know. Cf. SAVVY.]
▶ **A** *verb trans. & intrans.* Pres. pple & verbal noun **-eing**. = SAVVY *verb.* M19.
▶ **B** *noun.* = SAVVY *noun.* L19.

Sabean *adjective & noun* var. of SABAEAN.

†**sabeline** *noun. rare.* Also **-ll-**. ME–L19.
[Old French from medieval Latin *sabelina* (*pellis*) sable (fur), from *sabel* SABLE *noun*²: see -INE¹.]
The fur of the sable.

sabella /səˈbɛlə/ *noun.* M19.
[mod. Latin (see below), perh. from Latin *sabulum* sand + -ELLA.]
ZOOLOGY. A sabellid, *esp.* one of the genus *Sabella*. Now only as mod. Latin genus name.

Sabellian /səˈbɛlɪən/ *noun*¹ *& adjective*¹. LME.
[ecclesiastical Latin *Sabellianus*, from *Sabellius* (see below) + -AN.]
CHRISTIAN THEOLOGY. ▶**A** *noun.* A person who holds the doctrine held by Sabellius (a 3rd-cent. African heresiarch) that the persons of the Trinity are merely aspects of one; a modalist. LME.
▶ **B** *adjective.* Of or pertaining to the Sabellians or their doctrine. L16.
■ **Sabellianism** *noun* (belief in) the Sabellian doctrine E18.

Sabellian /səˈbɛlɪən/ *noun*² *& adjective*². E17.
[from Latin *Sabellus* + -IAN.]
Hist. ▶**A** *noun.* A member of a group of peoples who inhabited parts of ancient Italy, comprising (amongst others) the Sabines and the Samnites; the Italic language of these peoples. E17.
▶ **B** *adjective.* Of or pertaining to the Sabellians or their language. E17.
■ **Sabellic** *adjective* = SABELLIAN *adjective*² L19.

sabellid /səˈbɛlɪd/ *noun & adjective.* L19.
[from mod. Latin *Sabellidae* (see below), formed as SABELLA: see -ID³.]
ZOOLOGY. ▶**A** *noun.* A member of the polychaete family Sabellidae of small marine worms living in tubes often made of sand grains etc. and having fanlike retractable tentacles for filter-feeding. L19.
▶ **B** *adjective.* Of, pertaining to, or designating this family. E20.

†**sabelline** *noun* var. of SABELINE.

saber *noun & verb* see SABRE *noun*¹ *& verb.*

sabha /səˈbɑː/ *noun.* E20.
[Sanskrit *sabhā*.]
In the Indian subcontinent: an assembly; a council; a society. Cf. LOK SABHA, RAJYA SABHA.

sabi /ˈsabi/ *noun.* M20.
[Japanese, lit. 'loneliness'.]
In Japanese art, a quality of simple and mellow beauty expressing a mood of spiritual solitude recognized in Zen Buddhist philosophy. Cf. WABI.

Sabian /ˈseɪbɪən/ *noun & adjective.* E17.
[from Arab. *ṣābiʼ* + -AN.]
▶ **A** *noun.* **1 a** A member of a religious sect classed in the Koran with Muslims, Jews, and Christians, as believers in the true God. E17. ▸**b** = MANDAEAN *noun.* L18.
2 A star-worshipper (cf. SABIANISM 2). E18.
▶ **B** *adjective.* Of or pertaining to the Sabians. M18.

Sabianism /ˈseɪbɪənɪz(ə)m/ *noun.* L18.
[from prec. + -ISM.]
1 The religion of the Sabians. L18.
2 = SABAISM 1. E19.

sabicu /sabɪˈkuː/ *noun.* M19.
[Cuban Spanish *sabicú*.]
A leguminous tree, *Lysiloma latisiliqua*, of the W. Indies and Florida; the timber of this tree, resembling mahogany.

sabin /ˈseɪbɪn/ *noun.* Also **-ine** /-iːn/. M20.
[from Wallace Clement *Sabine* (1868–1919), US physicist.]
ACOUSTICS. A unit of sound absorption equal to the absorbing power of one square foot of perfectly absorbing surface. Also called ***open window unit***.

Sabine /ˈsabʌɪn/ *noun*¹ *& adjective.* OE.
[from Latin *Sabinus*: see -INE¹.]
Hist. ▶**A** *noun.* **1** A member of a people who inhabited the central region of ancient Italy. OE.
2 The Italic language of this people. M19.
▶ **B** *adjective.* Of or pertaining to the Sabines or their language. M16.

sabine *noun*² var. of SABIN.

sabinene /ˈseɪbɪniːn/ *noun.* E20.
[from mod. Latin (*Juniperus*) *sabina* (see SAVIN) + -ENE.]
CHEMISTRY. A colourless liquid bicyclic terpene, $C_{10}H_{16}$, found in oil of savin and some other essential oils.

Sabine's gull /ˈsabʌɪnz ˈgʌl/ *noun phr.* M19.
[from Sir Edward *Sabine* (1788–1883), Brit. explorer, soldier, and President of the Royal Society.]
An Arctic gull, *Larus sabini*, with a forked tail, dark grey head, and black and yellow bill.

Sabinian /səˈbɪnɪən/ *noun & adjective.* M19.
[Latin *Sabinianus*, from *Sabinus* (see below).]
ROMAN LAW. ▶**A** *noun.* A member of the school of law partly founded by Massurius Sabinus, a celebrated jurist in the time of the emperor Tiberius. M19.
▶ **B** *adjective.* Of or pertaining to Sabinus or the school of law founded by him. E20.

Sabin vaccine /ˈseɪbɪn ˈvaksiːn/ *noun phr.* M20.
[from Albert Bruce *Sabin* (1906–93), Russian-born US microbiologist.]
MEDICINE. A poliomyelitis vaccine made from attenuated viruses of the three serological types and administered orally.

Sabir /səˈbɪə/ *noun.* M19.
[French, from *sabir* 'know' in the language invented by Molière for *Le bourgeois gentilhomme*, prob. from Spanish *saber* know.]
1 A French-based pidgin language used in parts of N. Africa. M19.
2 (**s-**.) A lingua franca. M19.

sabji *noun* var. of SABZI.

sabkha /ˈsabkə, -xə/ *noun.* Also **seb-** /ˈsɛb-/. L19.
[Arab. *sabḵa* a saline infiltration, salt flat.]
GEOGRAPHY. An area of coastal flats subject to periodic flooding and evaporation, resulting in accumulation of aeolian clays, evaporites, and salts, found esp. in N. Africa and Arabia.

sable /ˈseɪb(ə)l/ *noun*¹, *adjective*¹, *& verb.* ME.
[Old French (as heraldic term), gen. identified with next, although sable fur is dark brown.]
▶ **A** *noun.* **1** HERALDRY. Black (represented in engraving by horizontal and vertical lines crossing each other). ME.
2 The colour black; blackness; black clothing, esp. as a symbol of mourning. *poet.* LME.
3 In *pl.* Mourning clothes. *poet.* E17.
4 *ellipt.* The sable antelope (see sense B.2 below). L19.
▶ **B** *adjective.* **1** HERALDRY. Black. LME.
2 *gen.* Black. Chiefly *poet.* LME.
†**3** Mournful. LME–L18.
2 sable antelope a large grazing antelope with long curved horns, *Hippotragus niger*, of southern and eastern Africa, the male of which has a black coat and white belly.
▶ **C** *verb trans.* Blacken. Also, clothe in sables. Chiefly *poet.* Now *rare.* E17.
■ **sableness** *noun* (*a*) *poet.* blackness; †(*b*) mournfulness: E17. **sably** *adverb* (*poet.*) blackly M19.

sable /ˈseɪb(ə)l/ *noun*² *& adjective*². LME.
[Old French = sable fur, also in *martre sable* 'sable-marten' (animal and its fur) from medieval Latin *sabelum*, of Slavonic origin.]
▶ **A** *noun.* **1** A small carnivorous mustelid, *Martes zibellina*, allied to the martens, occurring in Siberia and on Hokkaido, and yielding a valuable dark brown fur. Formerly also, any of various similar mustelids, *esp.* the American marten *Martes americana*. Cf. ***red sable*** s.v. RED *adjective.* LME.
2 a The skin or fur of the sable, esp. as dressed and used for clothing. Also ***Russian sable***. LME. ▸**b** A garment, esp. a coat, made of this fur. L20.
†**3** ***old sable***, Russian iron of a superior quality (so called from being originally stamped with a representation of a sable). L18–M19.
4 A fine paintbrush made from the hair of the sable. L19.
▶ **B** *attrib.* or as *adjective.* Made of the fur of the sable. M18.

†sable *noun*³. E17–E18.
[Prob. Dutch *sabel*, German †*Sabel* (now *Säbel*): see SABRE *noun*¹.]
= SABRE *noun*¹.

sablefish /ˈseɪb(ə)lfɪʃ/ *noun*. Pl. **-es** /-ɪz/, (usu.) same. M20.
[from SABLE *adjective*¹ + FISH *noun*¹.]
A large marine fish, *Anoplopoma fimbria* (family Anoplopomatidae), found throughout the N. Pacific, with a slaty-blue to black back.

sabot /ˈsabəʊ/ *noun*. E17.
[French from Old French *çabot* blend of *çavate* (mod. SAVATE) and *bote* (mod. *botte*) BOOT *noun*².]
1 a A shoe made of a single piece of wood shaped and hollowed out to fit the foot. E17. ▸**b** A heavy shoe with a thick wooden sole. M19. ▸**c** A decorative metal foot-cover for a piece of wooden furniture. M20.
2 MILITARY. **a** A wooden disc attached to a spherical projectile to keep it in place in the bore when discharged. M19. ▸**b** A metal cup or ring fixed to a conical projectile to make it conform to the grooves of the rifling. M19. ▸**c** A device fitted inside the muzzle of a gun to hold the projectile to be fired. M20.
3 In baccarat and *chemin de fer*, a box for dealing the cards, a shoe. M20.
4 A small snub-nosed yacht. *Austral*. M20.
■ **saboted** *adjective* wearing sabots M19.

sabotage /ˈsabətɑːʒ/ *noun & verb*. E20.
[French, from *saboter* make a noise with sabots, execute badly, destroy, formed as prec.: see -AGE.]
▶ **A** *noun*. Deliberate damage to or destruction of property, esp. in order to disrupt the production of goods or as a political or military act. E20.

📖 H. MACMILLAN Sabotage and wrecking operations such as a cutting of the pipelines.

▶ **B** *verb trans*. Commit sabotage on; destroy; spoil; make useless. E20.

📖 *Peace News* Merseyside NVDA group sabotaged a generator by putting sugar into the diesel tank. P. MAILLOUX Once more he had sabotaged his own hopes.

sabota lark /səˈbəʊtə lɑːk/ *noun phr*. L19.
[from Bantu *sabota*.]
Either of two buff-coloured larks, *Mirafra sabota* and *M. naevius*, found in southern Africa.

saboteur /sabəˈtəː/ *noun*. E20.
[French, from *saboter* (see SABOTAGE) + *-eur* -OR.]
A person who commits sabotage.

sabra /ˈsabrə/ *noun*. Also **S-**. M20.
[mod. Hebrew *ṣabbār* or its source Arab. *ṣabr* prickly pear.]
A Jew born in the region of the modern State of Israel; an Israeli born in Israel.

sabre /ˈseɪbə/ *noun*¹ & *verb*. Also ***-ber**. L17.
[French, alt. of †*sable* from German *Sabel* local var. of *Säbel* from Hungarian *szablya*.]
▶ **A** *noun*. **1** A cavalry sword with a curved blade specially adapted for cutting. L17. ▸**b** A light (curved or straight) fencing sword with a flattened blade and blunted cutting edge; the exercise of fencing with these. E20.
2 A soldier armed with a sabre; *transf*. military force. E19.

📖 **1** ***rattle the sabre***: see RATTLE *verb*¹. **2** P. M. M. KEMP Three troops—in total about a hundred sabres.

Comb.: **sabre-bayonet** a weapon which can be used either as a sabre or a bayonet; **sabre-cut** (*a*) a blow with a sabre; (*b*) a cut made or scar left by this; **sabre leg** a leg on a piece of furniture which curves inwards and is usu. square in cross-section; **sabre-rattler** a person who engages in sabre-rattling; **sabre-rattling** the display or threat of military force; **sabre saw** a portable electric saw with a narrow reciprocating blade, used for cutting curves; **sabretooth** (in full ***sabretooth cat***, ***sabretooth tiger***) = ***sabre-toothed cat*** below; **sabre-toothed** *adjective* designating various large extinct carnivorous mammals bearing long sabre-shaped upper canines; ***sabre-toothed cat***, ***sabre-toothed tiger***, any of various extinct sabre-toothed felids of the subfamily Machairodontinae, esp. *Smilodon* of the American Pleistocene; cf. MACHAIRODONT; **sabrewing** any of various Central and S. American hummingbirds of the genus *Campylopterus*, which have mainly shining green plumage.
▶ **B** *verb trans*. Strike, cut down, or wound with a sabre. E18.
■ **sabred** *adjective* armed with a sabre M18.

†sabre *noun*² see SAMBAR *noun*¹.

sabretache /ˈsabətaʃ/ *noun*. E19.
[French from German *Säbeltasche*, from *Säbel* sabre + *Tasche* pocket.]
A flat satchel suspended by long straps from the left side of the sword-belt of some cavalry officers.

sabreur /saˈbrəː/ *noun*. M19.
[French, from *sabrer* to sabre + *-eur* -OR.]
1 A person, esp. a cavalry soldier, who fights with a sabre. M19.
2 A person who fences using a sabre. E20.

sabulous /ˈsabjʊləs/ *adjective*. M17.
[from Latin *sabulosus*, from *sabulum* sand: see -ULOUS.]
1 Sandy; consisting or of the nature of sand. M17.
2 MEDICINE. Designating a gritty or sandy secretion or excretion, esp. in the urinary system. Now *rare* or *obsolete*. L17.

sabzi /ˈsʌbziː/ *noun*. Pl. **-is**. Also **sabji** /ˈsʌbdʒiː/. L19.
[Hindi, Urdu *sabzī*: see SUBJEE.]
1 = SUBJEE. L19.
2 In Indian cookery: vegetables; a dish of cooked vegetables. L20.

SAC *abbreviation*.
1 Senior Aircraftman.
2 Strategic Air Command. *US*.

sac /sak/ *noun*¹.
[Old English *saca* accus. & genit. pl. of *sacu* SAKE *noun*¹.]
Hist. A right of local jurisdiction; *spec*. in ***sac and soc***, in pre-Conquest England, the rights of jurisdiction included in the grant of a manor by the crown.

sac /sak/ *noun*². M18.
[French, or mod. Latin use of Latin *saccus*: see SACK *noun*¹.]
1 BIOLOGY. A natural baglike cavity in an organism; the membrane or other structure enclosing this. M18.
2 MEDICINE. A pouch formed by the pathological dilatation or protrusion of a part; the membranous envelope of a hernia, cyst, tumour, etc. E19.
3 A bag. *rare*. E19.
1 ***embryo sac***. ***pollen-sac***: see POLLEN *noun*.
Comb.: **sacbrood** a fatal disease of honeybee larvae, caused by an RNA virus; **sac-winged bat** a tropical American bat belonging to any of several genera of the family Emballonuridae, distinguished by a pouchlike scent gland in the wing membrane of the males; esp. *Saccopteryx bilineata*.
■ **saclike** *adjective* M19.

sac /sak/ *noun*³. *slang*. M20.
[Abbreviation of SACCHARINE.]
A saccharine tablet.

sac /sak/ *noun*⁴. CHESS *slang*. M20.
[Abbreviation.]
= SACRIFICE *noun* 4C.

Sac *noun*⁵ & *adjective* var. of SAUK.

sac-à-lait /ˈsakəleɪ, sakəˈleɪ/ *noun*. *US*. L19.
[Louisiana French, lit. 'bag for milk', by folk etym. from Choctaw *sakli* trout.]
Any of various fishes of the genera *Pomoxis* and *Fundulus*, esp. the white crappie, *P. annularis*.

sacate /səˈkɑːteɪ, zə-/ *noun*. Also **z-** /z-/. M19.
[Mexican Spanish *zacate* grass, hay from Nahuatl *zacatl*. Cf. next.]
Any of several grasses grown in Mexico, the southern US, and the Philippines, and used for hay or fresh forage; fodder made from such a grass.

sacaton /ˈsakətəʊn, ˈza-/ *noun*. Also **za-** /ˈza-/. M19.
[Mexican Spanish *zacatón* augmentative of *zacate*: see prec.]
Any of several tough drought-resistant grasses of Mexico and the southern US which are used for hay, esp. *Sporobolus wrightii* and (more fully ***alkali sacaton***) *S. airoides*.

saccade /səˈkɑːd/ *noun*. E18.
[French.]
1 A jerking movement. Now *rare* exc. as passing into sense 2. E18.
2 A brief rapid movement of the eye from one position of rest to another, whether voluntary or involuntary. M20.
■ **saccadic** *adjective* of or pertaining to a saccade or saccades; jerky, discontinuous: E20. **saccadically** *adverb* M20.

saccate /ˈsakeɪt/ *adjective*. E19.
[from SAC *noun*² + -ATE².]
1 BOTANY. Dilated into the form of a sac; pouch-shaped. E19.
2 MEDICINE. Encysted. L19.
■ **saˈccated** *adjective* encysted M19.

saccharase /ˈsakəreɪz/ *noun*. E20.
[formed as SACCHARINE + -ASE.]
BIOCHEMISTRY. = INVERTASE.

saccharated /ˈsakəreɪtɪd/ *adjective*. L18.
[formed as SACCHARINE + -ATE² + -ED¹.]
Containing or made with sugar; sweetened.

saccharic /səˈkarɪk/ *adjective*. E19.
[formed as SACCHARINE + -IC.]
CHEMISTRY. Of or derived from a sugar or saccharin.
saccharic acid a dicarboxylic acid obtained by the oxidation of a monosaccharide; *spec*. that formed from glucose, HOOC$(CHOH)_4$COOH.
■ **saccharate** /ˈsakəreɪt/ *noun* a salt or ester of (a) saccharic acid E19.

saccharide /ˈsakərʌɪd/ *noun*. M19.
[formed as SACCHARINE + -IDE.]
CHEMISTRY. †**1** A substance formed in the fermentation of melted sugar. Only in M19.
†**2** A compound formed by the action of an acid on a sugar. Only in M19.
3 A sugar, *esp*. a monosaccharide or oligosaccharide; a simple derivative of such a compound. L19.

sacchariferous /sakəˈrɪf(ə)rəs/ *adjective*. M18.
[formed as SACCHARINE + -I- + -FEROUS.]
Yielding or containing sugar.

saccharify /səˈkarɪfʌɪ, ˈsak(ə)rɪfʌɪ/ *verb trans*. M19.
[from SACCHARINE + -I- + -FY.]
Chiefly BREWING. Convert (starch etc.) into sugar.
■ **saccharifiˈcation** *noun* the natural process by which starch etc. is converted into sugar M19.

saccharimeter /sakəˈrɪmɪtə/ *noun*. M19.
[formed as SACCHARINE + -I- + -METER.]
A polarimeter for measuring the optical activity of sugars.
■ **saccharimetry** *noun* the process of estimating the quantity of sugar in a solution, esp. by measuring optical activity; saccharometry: M19. **sacchariˈmetric** *adjective* L19. **sacchariˈmetrical** *adjective* M19.

saccharin /ˈsakərɪn/ *noun*. L19.
[formed as next + -IN¹. See also next.]
CHEMISTRY. **1** The anhydride of saccharic acid. Now *rare* or *obsolete*. L19.
2 An intensely sweet substance, *o*-sulphobenzoic imide, $C_7H_5NO_3S$, used as a non-fattening sweetener for food and drink; a pill of this. L19.
■ **saccharinize** *verb trans*. sweeten by adding saccharin; *fig*. make agreeable or inoffensive: L20.

saccharine /ˈsakərʌɪn, -ɪn, -iːn/ *adjective & noun*. L17.
[from mod. Latin SACCHARUM + -INE¹.]
▶ **A** *adjective*. **1** Of, pertaining to, or of the nature of sugar; characteristic of sugar; sugary. L17.
2 Containing a high proportion of sugar. E18.
3 Resembling sugar; *spec*. (GEOLOGY) = SACCHAROIDAL *adjective*. M19.
4 *fig*. Excessively sweet. Chiefly *joc*. & *iron*. M19.
Special collocations: **saccharine diabetes** = DIABETES ***mellitus***. **saccharine fermentation** = SACCHARIFICATION.
▶ **B** *noun*. **1** Sugar. Now *rare* or *obsolete*. M19.
2 = SACCHARIN. L19.
■ **saccharined** *adjective* (of a voice etc.) excessively sweet or sugary in tone M20. **sacchaˈrinity** *noun* sweetness M19.

saccharize /ˈsakərʌɪz/ *verb*. Also **-ise**. M18.
[formed as prec. + -IZE.]
1 *verb intrans*. Of starch etc.: undergo conversion into sugar. *rare*. M18.
2 *verb trans*. Convert (esp. starch etc.) into sugar, esp. during the mashing of grain before fermentation. L19.
■ **ˈsacchariˌzation** *noun* conversion into sugar E20.

saccharo- /ˈsakərəʊ/ *combining form* of mod. Latin SACCHARUM sugar: see -O-.
■ **saccharoˈlytic** *adjective* (BIOCHEMISTRY) of or pertaining to the chemical breakdown of carbohydrates; capable of effecting this: E20. **sacchaˈrometer** *noun* (chiefly BREWING) a hydrometer for estimating the amount of sugar in a solution L18. **sacchaˈrometry** *noun* = SACCHARIMETRY L19.

saccharoid /ˈsakərɔɪd/ *adjective & noun*. M19.
[formed as SACCHARINE + -OID.]
▶ **A** *adjective*. GEOLOGY. = SACCHAROIDAL. M19.
▶ **B** *noun*. CHEMISTRY.
†**1** An unidentified sweetish substance. Only in M19.
2 Orig., = SACCHARIDE 3. Now *spec*. any of various polysaccharides that resemble sugars in certain properties. L19.

saccharoidal /sakəˈrɔɪd(ə)l/ *adjective*. M19.
[formed as prec. + -AL¹.]
GEOLOGY. Having or designating a granular texture resembling that of loaf sugar.

saccharomycete /sakərəʊˈmʌɪsiːt/ *noun*. Orig. only in pl. **-mycetes** /-ˈmʌɪsiːts, -mʌɪˈsiːtiːz/. L19.
[Anglicized sing. of mod. Latin *saccharomycetes*, formed as SACCHARO- + Greek *mukētes* pl. of *mukēs* fungus.]
A true yeast of the family Saccharomycetaceae; *loosely* any of various similar fungi.

saccharose /ˈsakərəʊz, -s/ *noun*. L19.
[formed as SACCHARINE + -OSE².]
CHEMISTRY. †**1** *gen*. A disaccharide, *esp*. one of the general formula $C_{12}H_{22}O_{11}$. L19–E20.
2 *spec*. = SUCROSE 2. L19.

saccharum /ˈsakərəm/ *noun*. M19.
[mod. Latin from medieval Latin from Greek *sakkharon* sugar: see SUGAR *noun & adjective*.]
Sugar, *esp*. invert sugar. Formerly also *spec*., sucrose.

sacciform /ˈsaksɪfɔːm/ *adjective*. M19.
[from Latin *saccus* (see SACK *noun*¹) + -I- + -FORM.]
BIOLOGY & ANATOMY. Shaped like a sac or pouch.

saccoon /səˈkuːn/ *noun*. *arch*. Also **segoon** /səˈguːn/. E18.
[Alt. of SECONDE.]
FENCING. = SECONDE 2.

saccular /ˈsakjʊlə/ *adjective*. M19.
[from SACCULUS + -AR¹.]
Of the nature of a sac; *spec*. in MEDICINE (of an aneurysm) formed by a localized bulge on the side of an artery.

sacculated /ˈsakjʊleɪtɪd/ *adjective*. M19.
[from SACCULUS + -ATE² + -ED¹.]
Composed of or divided into saccules; possessing a saccule or sacculus.
■ **sacculate** *adjective* (now *rare*) = SACCULATED L19. **saccuˈlation** *noun* (an instance of) the formation of or division into saccules M19.

saccule /ˈsakjuːl/ *noun*. M19.
[Anglicized from next: see -ULE.]
A small sac, cyst, or pouch; *spec.* in ANATOMY, the smaller of the two divisions of the membranous labyrinth of the inner ear.

sacculus /ˈsakjʊləs/ *noun*. Pl. **-li** /-lʌɪ, -liː/. M16.
[Latin, dim. of *saccus*: see SACK *noun*¹, -CULE.]
†**1** A small bag containing medicaments, applied to an affected part. M16–L17.
2 a ANATOMY & BIOLOGY. A small sac; a pouchlike dilatation of an organ. M18. ▸**b** MICROBIOLOGY. A hollow network of cross-linked murein forming the cell wall in some bacteria. M20.

sac de nuit /sak də nɥi/ *noun phr*. Now *rare*. Pl. ***sacs de nuit*** (pronounced same). E19.
[French.]
An overnight bag.

sacellum /səˈsɛləm/ *noun*. Pl. **-lla** /-lə/. E19.
[Latin, dim. of *sacrum* shrine, from *sacer* holy.]
ARCHITECTURE. **1** CHRISTIAN CHURCH. A chapel, esp. a sepulchral one, within a church. E19.
2 A small roofless Roman temple. M19.

sacerdoce /ˈsasədəʊs, ˈsakə-/ *noun*. *rare*. E17.
[French, formed as next.]
= SACERDOCY.

sacerdocy /ˈsasədəʊsi, ˈsakə-/ *noun*. Also in Latin form ***sacerdotium*** /sasəˈdəʊsɪəm, sakəˈdəʊtɪəm/, pl. **-ia** /-ɪə/. M17.
[Latin *sacerdotium*, from *sacerdot-* (see SACERDOTAL): see -CY.]
The function, office, or character of a priest; the sacerdotal system.

sacerdotage /sasəˈdəʊtɪdʒ, sakə-/ *noun*. *joc. derog.* M19.
[from Latin *sacerdot-* (see next), with allus. to *dotage*.]
Sacerdotalism or sacerdotalists collectively, considered as characteristic of a religion in decline.

sacerdotal /sasəˈdəʊt(ə)l, sakə-/ *adjective*. LME.
[Old & mod. French, or Latin *sacerdotalis*, from *sacerdot-*, *sacerdos* priest: see -AL¹.]
CHRISTIAN CHURCH. **1** Of or pertaining to a priest or the priesthood; befitting or characteristic of a priest; priestly. LME. ▸**b** Holding the office of priest. L17.
2 Of a doctrine etc.: ascribing sacrificial functions and supernatural powers to ordained priests; *derog.* claiming excessive authority for the priesthood. L19.
■ **sacerdotalism** *noun* (*a*) sacerdotal principles or practice; the sacerdotal system; *esp.* (*derog.*) assumption of excessive authority by the priesthood; (*b*) the assertion of or belief in the sacerdotal doctrine: M19. **sacerdotalist** *noun* an advocate or defender of sacerdotalism M19. **sacerdotalize** *verb trans.* (chiefly *derog.*) make subservient to sacerdotalism M19. **sacerdotally** *adverb* M19.

sacerdotium *noun* see SACERDOCY.

SACEUR /ˈsakjʊə/ *abbreviation*.
Supreme Allied Commander Europe.

sachaline /ˈsakəlɪn, -iːn/ *noun*. *N. Amer.* E20.
[from the specific epithet of the plant, from *Sakhalin* an island north of Japan.]
A tall perennial knotweed, *Fallopia sachalinensis*, resembling bamboo but with large cordate leaves, native to Japan and Sakhalin and grown for ornament.

sachem /ˈseɪtʃəm, ˈsatʃəm/ *noun*. E17.
[Massachusetts Algonquian *sontim*.]
1 The supreme chief of some N. American Indians. E17.
2 A prominent member of a society etc.; a political leader. *joc.* (chiefly *N. Amer.*). L17.
■ **sachemdom** *noun* (*a*) the position of sachem; (*b*) the territory ruled by a sachem: M18. **sachemship** *noun* = SACHEMDOM L18.

Sachertorte /ˈzaxərtɔrtə/ *noun*. Pl. ***-ten*** /-t(ə)n/. E20.
[German, from Franz *Sacher* pastry-chef, its creator + *Torte* tart, pastry, cake. Cf. TORTE.]
A Viennese chocolate gateau with apricot jam filling and chocolate icing.

sachet /ˈsaʃeɪ/ *noun*. L15.
[Old & mod. French, dim. of *sac*: see SACK *noun*¹, -ET¹.]
†**1** A small carrying bag. *rare*. Only in L15.
2 a A small scented bag, esp. for holding handkerchiefs. M19. ▸**b** (A small bag or packet containing) dry perfume for placing among clothing etc. M19.
3 A small sealed bag or packet, now freq. of plastic, containing a small portion of a substance, esp. shampoo. E20.

> 📖 **3** C. PHILLIPS The after-dinner coffee was of the do-it-yourself variety; a jug of hot water and a sachet of powder.

Sachlichkeit /ˈzaxlɪçkaɪt/ *noun*. M20.
[German, lit. 'objectivity'.]
Objectivism, realism. Also *spec.*, = NEUE SACHLICHKEIT.

Sachverhalt /ˈzaxfɛrhalt/ *noun*. Pl. ***-e*** /-ə/. E20.
[German.]
PHILOSOPHY. Esp. in phenomenology, a state of affairs, an objective fact.

†**sacietie** *noun* see SATIETY.

sack /sak/ *noun*¹.
[Old English *sæc* = Middle Dutch *sak* (Dutch *zak*), Old High German *sac* (German *Sack*), Old Norse *sekkr*, Gothic *sakkus*, from Latin *saccus* (whence also Old & mod. French SAC *noun*²) corresp. to Greek *sakkos*, of Semitic origin. Cf. next.]
1 A large bag, usu. oblong and open at one end, made of a strong material as hessian, canvas, thick paper, or plastic, and used to store and carry foodstuffs, coal, mail, etc. OE. ▸**b** A coat pocket. *Criminals' slang*. L17. ▸**c** Orig., a hammock, a bunk. Later also *gen.*, a bed (only in ***the sack*** (b) below). *slang* (chiefly *N. Amer.*). E19. ▸**d** A paper bag. *US*. E20. ▸**e** = BAG *noun* 10. *US*. E20. ▸**f** AMER. FOOTBALL. An act of tackling a quarterback behind the scrimmage line. L20.
2 (A piece or garment of) sackcloth. Cf. ***Sack-friar*** below, ***Sacked Friar*** s.v. SACKED *adjective*. Now *rare*. OE.
3 A sack with its contents; the quantity contained in a sack; a sackful. ME.
4 ***the sack***, dismissal from employment or office. Chiefly in ***get the sack***, ***give the sack to*** below. E19.
Phrases: **get the sack** *slang* receive one's dismissal from employment or office. **give the sack to** *slang* dismiss (a person) from employment or office; *transf.* discard (a lover). **hit the sack** *slang* (chiefly *N. Amer.*) (*a*) go to bed, sleep; (*b*) have sexual intercourse *with*. **hold the sack** *US* bear an unwelcome responsibility. ***paper sack***: see PAPER *noun* & *adjective*. ***sad sack***: see SAD *adjective*. **the sack** (*a*) ROMAN HISTORY the punishment (for parricide) of being sewn in a sack and drowned; (*b*) *slang* (chiefly *N. Amer.*) bed (freq. in ***hit the sack*** above); (*c*) see sense 4 above.
Comb.: **sack-bearer** the larva of any of various American moths of the family Lacosomidae, which make cases from leaves; **sack chair** a loosely filled bag for use as a chair; **sack drill**, **sack duty** *US Nautical slang* = ***sack time*** below; **Sack-friar** *Hist.* = ***Sacked Friar*** s.v. SACKED *adjective*; **sack lunch** *N. Amer.* a packed lunch, esp. in a paper bag; **sack paper** strong brown paper; **sack race** a running race between competitors in sacks up to the waist or neck; **sack ship** *Hist.* in Newfoundland, a large ship for transporting fish; **sack time** *slang* (chiefly *US*) sleep; time spent in bed.
■ **sacked** *adjective* wearing sackcloth, dressed in sackcloth; ***Sacked Friar*** (*obsolete* exc. *Hist.*), a member of a medieval mendicant order of the 13th and 14th cents who wore sackcloth: LME. **sacken** *adjective* (*obsolete* exc. *Scot.*) made of sackcloth LME. **sacker** *noun*¹ (*N. Amer.*) = ***baseman*** s.v. BASE *noun*¹ E20. **sackful** *noun* as much as a sack will hold; *fig.* a large amount: L15. **sacking** *noun* †(*a*) *rare* a material used for women's dresses; (*b*) (a piece of) material for making a sack, esp. sackcloth: L16. **sacklet** *noun* (*rare*) a little sack LME. **sacklike** *adjective* resembling (that of) a sack E19. **sacky** *adjective* (*a*) resembling a sack; (*b*) *Scot.* made of sackcloth: L19.

sack /sak/ *noun*². Also (earlier) †**seck**. E16.
[from French (*vin*) *sec* dry (wine). Cf. SEC *adjective*.]
Hist. A white wine formerly imported from Spain and the Canaries. Also (with specifying word), indicating place of origin or exportation.
Canary sack, ***Malaga sack***, ***sherris sack***, etc.

sack /sak/ *noun*³. M16.
[French *sac* (in *mettre à sac* put to sack) from Italian *sacco* sack, bag (in *fare il sacco* etc., perh. orig. referring to filling a sack with plunder) from Latin *saccus*: see prec. & cf. SAC *noun*². Partly directly from SACK *verb*².]
The action or an act of sacking or plundering a captured town etc. Orig. in †***put to sack***, sack, plunder.

sack /sak/ *noun*⁴. L16.
[Prob. orig. a use of SACK *noun*¹, later assoc. with French SAC *noun*².]
1 Orig., a woman's loose gown. Later *spec.*, a gown falling loosely at the back in a train from the shoulders. L16.
2 A loosely hanging coat not shaped to the back. M19.
3 A (style of) woman's short unwaisted dress, usu. narrowing at the hem, popular esp. in the late 1950's. Also more fully ***sack dress***. M20.
Comb.: ***sack dress***: see sense 3 above; **sack suit** (chiefly *US*): having a straight loose-fitting jacket.

sack /sak/ *verb*¹. LME.
[from SACK *noun*¹; in sense 1 partly after medieval Latin *saccare*, Middle Dutch *sacken*, etc.]
1 *verb trans.* Put into a sack; *esp.* pack or store (goods) in a sack or sacks. Also foll. by *up*. LME. ▸†**b** Heap up (as) in a sack. L16–E17. ▸**c** = POCKET *verb* 3. *slang*. E19. ▸**d** AMER. FOOTBALL. Tackle (a quarterback) behind the scrimmage line. M20.
2 *verb trans.* **a** Beat in a contest. E19. ▸**b** Dismiss from employment or office; *transf.* (*a*) jilt (a lover etc.); (*b*) expel from school. Freq. in *pass. colloq.* M19.
3 *verb trans.* Return (stray logs) to a slide. *US*. M19.
4 *verb intrans.* **a** Foll. by *down*, *out*: go to bed; sleep. *slang* (chiefly *US*). M20. ▸**b** Foll. by *in*: go to bed; lie in. *slang* (chiefly *US*). M20.

> 📖 **1** F. NORRIS A small part of his wheat . . had been sacked. **2b** N. F. DIXON Trench was sacked from the police. **4a** E. V. CUNNINGHAM Lost a night's sleep . . . How about I sack down for a few hours? W. WHARTON At nine o'clock I sack out. **b** D. F. GALOUYE I let you sack in this morning.

■ **sackable** *adjective* (of an action etc.) liable to incur dismissal from employment or office L20.

sack /sak/ *verb*² *trans.* M16.
[from SACK *noun*³.]
Plunder and destroy (a captured town etc.); strip of possessions or goods; despoil, pillage.

> 📖 C. HILL The town refused to surrender, and after an eight days' siege it was sacked.

■ **sacker** *noun*² L16.

sackage /ˈsakɪdʒ/ *noun*. *arch.* M16.
[French *saccage*, from *saccager* from Italian *saccheggiare*, from *sacco* SACK *noun*³.]
= SACK *noun*³.

sackalever /sakəˈliːvə/ *noun*. E19.
[Italian *saccaleva*.]
Chiefly *Hist.* A small sailing ship formerly used in the eastern Mediterranean.

sackbut /ˈsakbʌt/ *noun*. L15.
[French *sa(c)quebute* from earlier †*saqueboute*, †-*bot(t)e*, hooked lance for pulling a man off a horse, from *saquer* var. of Old French *sachier* pull + *bouter* BUTT *verb*¹.]
MUSIC. **1** An early form of trombone, of the Renaissance period. L15.
†**2** = SACKBUTTER. L15–M17.
■ **sackbutter** *noun* (*Hist.*) a player on the sackbut E16.

sackcloth /ˈsakklɒθ/ *noun*. ME.
[from SACK *noun*¹ + CLOTH.]
A coarse fabric (now of flax or hemp) used to make sacks, wrap bales, etc., and (esp.) formerly worn as a sign of penitence or mourning. Also, a penitential garment made of this.
in sackcloth and ashes wearing sackcloth and having ashes sprinkled on the head as a sign of mourning or penitence.
■ **sackclothed** *adjective* wearing sackcloth; *esp.* mourning, penitent M17.

sacket /ˈsakɪt/ *noun*. LME.
[Old French *saquet* var. of *sachet* SACHET.]
1 A small bag. *obsolete* exc. *Scot.* & *dial.* LME.
2 As a term of reproach or abuse: a wretched, despicable, or undeserving person. *Scot.* & *dial.* M19.

sackie /ˈsaki/ *noun*. M20.
[Guyanese name.]
Any of various small tropical S. American parrots, *esp.* the black-headed caique, *Pionites melanocephala*.

sackless /ˈsaklɪs/ *adjective*.
[Old English *saclēas* from Old Norse *saklauss*, from *sak-*, *sǫk*: see -LESS. Cf. SAC *noun*¹.]
1 Unchallenged, undisputed; unmolested. Long *arch.* OE.
2 Not guilty, innocent. Usu. foll. by *of*. *arch.* exc. *Scot.* OE. ▸**b** Inoffensive; guileless, simple; feeble-minded. *Scot.* & *north.* L16.
†**3** Of an accusation or penalty: without just cause. ME–L16.
¶ In sense 1 obsolete after 16; revived by Sir Walter Scott in 19.

sacra /ˈsakrə/ *noun*¹ *pl.* E19.
[Latin, pl. of *sacrum*: see SACRAL *adjective*².]
Sacred objects. Formerly also, writings on a sacred subject.

sacra *noun*² *pl.* see SACRUM.

sacral /ˈseɪkr(ə)l/ *adjective*¹ & *noun*. M18.
[from SACRUM + -AL¹.]
ANATOMY. ▸**A** *adjective*. Pertaining to the sacrum. M18.
▸**B** *noun*. A vertebra, nerve, etc., situated in the sacral region. M19.

sacral /ˈseɪkr(ə)l, ˈsak-/ *adjective*². L19.
[from Latin *sacrum* sacred thing, rite, etc., use as noun of neut. sing. of *sacer* sacred + -AL¹.]
Chiefly ANTHROPOLOGY. Of or pertaining to a sacred rite or rites; having a sacred purpose or significance.
■ **sacrality** /-ˈkral-/ *noun* sacral character or quality M20. **sacraliˈzation** *noun* the action or an act of endowing a thing with sacred significance, esp. through ritual E20. **sacralize** *verb trans.* endow with sacred significance, esp. through ritual E20.

sacrament /ˈsakrəm(ə)nt/ *noun* & *verb*. ME.
[Old & mod. French *sacrement* from Latin *sacramentum* solemn oath or engagement, from *sacrare* hallow, from *sacer* sacred; used in Christian Latin as translation of Greek *mustērion* MYSTERY *noun*¹.]
▸**A** *noun*. Also (in sense 5) in Latin form **sacramentum** /ˈsakrəmɛntəm/.
1 CHRISTIAN CHURCH. A religious ceremony or act regarded as imparting spiritual grace to the participants or having spiritual benefits; *spec.* (*a*) in the Orthodox, pre-Reformation Western, and Roman Catholic Churches, each of the seven rites of baptism, confirmation, the

Eucharist, penance, extreme unction, ordination, and matrimony; (*b*) in Protestant Churches, either of the rites of baptism and the Eucharist. ME.

2 *spec.* *The* Eucharist; *the* consecrated elements; *esp.* the host. ME.

3 An oath, a solemn engagement; *esp.* one confirmed by ritual. ME.

4 *transf.* **a** A thing of sacred character or significance; a sacred pledge, a covenant. ME. ▸**b** A mystery; a secret. Now *rare*. LME. ▸**c** A type or symbol *of* something. M16.

5 ROMAN LAW (now *Hist.*). An oath given by each party to a suit for the forfeiture by the unsuccessful litigant of a sum of money deposited as a pledge; the sum of money so deposited. L19.

Phrases: ***last sacraments***: see LAST *adjective*. **receive the sacrament** communicate; ***receive the sacrament upon*** (*arch.*), confirm (one's word etc.) by taking the sacrament. **sacrament of reconciliation** (chiefly ROMAN CATHOLIC CHURCH) the practice of private confession of sins to a priest and the receiving of absolution. **sacrament of the present moment** every moment regarded as an opportunity to receive divine grace. **sacrament of the sick** ROMAN CATHOLIC CHURCH extreme unction. **take the sacrament**, **take the sacrament upon** (*arch.*) = ***receive the sacrament***, ***receive the sacrament upon*** above. **the Blessed Sacrament**, **the Holy Sacrament** = sense 2 above.

Comb.: **sacrament day**: on which the Eucharist is celebrated; **sacrament house** a tabernacle; **sacrament-money** money collected at the Eucharist; **Sacrament Sabbath**, **Sacrament Sunday**: on which the Eucharist is celebrated (in the Presbyterian Church and esp. in Scotland formerly only once or twice a year).

▶ **B** *verb*. †**1** *verb intrans.* Participate in a sacrament. *rare*. Only in LME.

2 *verb trans.* Bind (as) by an oath or sacrament. Freq. foll. by *to*, *to do*. LME.

3 Consecrate. E19.

sacramental /sakrəˈmɛnt(ə)l/ *adjective & noun*. LME.
[French *sacramental*, *-tel* from late Latin *sacramentalis*, from Latin *sacramentum*: see prec., -AL¹.]

▶ **A** *adjective*. **1** Of or pertaining to a sacrament or the sacraments; *spec.* (of an oath etc.) confirmed by a sacrament, sacred. LME.

2 Of a doctrine etc.: based on or attaching importance to the sacraments. L19.

▶ **B** *noun*. CHRISTIAN CHURCH. An observance analogous to a sacrament, but not reckoned among the sacraments, as the use of holy water, the sign of the cross, etc. LME.

■ **sacramentalism** *noun* (*a*) = SACRAMENTARIANISM; (*b*) the theory that the natural world is a reflection of an ideal supernatural world: M19. **sacramentality** /-ˈtal-/ *noun* sacramental character or quality M17. **sacramentally** *adverb* LME.

sacramentarian /sakrəm(ə)nˈtɛːrɪən/ *noun & adjective*. M16.
[mod. Latin *sacramentarius*, from *sacramentum*: see SACRAMENT, -ARIAN.]

▶ **A** *noun*. **1** ECCLESIASTICAL HISTORY. (Usu. **S-**.) Orig., any of the early Protestant theologians who rejected the doctrine of the real presence of Christ in the Eucharist. Later also *gen.*, any believer in the metaphorical as opp. to the real presence of Christ in the Eucharist. M16.

2 A person believing in the impartation of spiritual grace through the sacraments. M17.

3 *Hist.* (A nickname for) a Methodist. M18.

▶ **B** *adjective*. **1** ECCLESIASTICAL HISTORY. Of or pertaining to the Sacramentarians or their beliefs. M17.

2 Of or pertaining to the sacraments or sacramental doctrine. M19.

■ **sacramentarianism** *noun* sacramentarian principles and practices; sacramental doctrine: L19.

sacramentary /sakrəˈmɛnt(ə)ri/ *adjective & noun*. Now *rare*. M16.
[formed as SACRAMENTARIAN: see -ARY¹; in sense B.2 from medieval Latin *sacramentarium*.]

▶ **A** *adjective*. **1** *Hist.* = SACRAMENTARIAN *adjective* 1. M16.

2 = SACRAMENTARIAN *adjective* 2. M16.

▶ **B** *noun*. *Hist.*

1 = SACRAMENTARIAN *noun* 1. M16.

2 In the Western Church, a book giving the appropriate rites and prayers for each sacrament. E17.

sacramentum *noun* see SACRAMENT *noun*.

sacrarium /səˈkrɛːrɪəm/ *noun*¹. Pl. **-ria** /-rɪə/. E18.
[Latin, from *sacer* sacred: see -ARIUM.]

1 ECCLESIASTICAL. **a** = SANCTUARY *noun* 2b. E18. ▸**b** = PISCINA 2. M19.

2 ROMAN ANTIQUITIES. A sacred repository, a shrine; *esp.* a room in a house containing the images of the penates. M18.

†**sacrary** *noun*. LME.
[Old French *sacrarie*, *-raire*, formed as SACRARIUM.]

1 A sacred repository; a shrine, a sanctuary. LME–M17.

2 ECCLESIASTICAL. = SANCTUARY *noun* 2b. LME–E18.

†**sacrate** *verb trans. rare*. M17–M18.
[Latin *sacrat-* pa. ppl stem of *sacrare*: see SACRE *verb*, -ATE³.]
Consecrate, dedicate.

sacre /ˈseɪkə/ *verb*. Now *arch. rare*. ME.
[Old & mod. French *sacrer* from Latin *sacrare* consecrate, dedicate to a divinity, from *sacer* consecrated, holy.]

†**1** *verb trans. & intrans.* Consecrate (the Eucharistic elements); celebrate (the Eucharist). ME–M16.

2 *verb trans.* **a** Consecrate (a monarch, bishop, etc.) to office. Usu. in *pass.* ME. ▸†**b** Unite in the sacrament of marriage; solemnize (a marriage). LME–L15.

†**3** *verb trans.* Offer up or dedicate to a god (usu. in *pass.*); *transf.* dedicate to a particular person or purpose. Usu. foll. by *to*, *unto*. ME–M17.

†**4** Sanctify, bless. LME–M17.

sacré bleu /sakre blø/ *interjection*. Freq. *joc.* M19.
[French, alt. of *sacré Dieu* holy God.]
Expr. surprise, dismay, etc. Freq. in literal renderings of French speech.

sacred /ˈseɪkrɪd/ *adjective & noun*. LME.
[pa. pple of SACRE: see -ED¹.]

▶ **A** *adjective*. **1** Consecrated to or considered especially dear to a god or supernatural being. Foll. by *to*. LME. ▸**b** *transf.* Dedicated or appropriated exclusively to a particular person or purpose. M17.

2 Set apart for or dedicated to a religious purpose and so deserving veneration or respect; consecrated, hallowed (in names of animals and plants indicating ancient or traditional veneration). LME.

3 *transf.* Regarded with or deserving veneration or respect as of something holy, esp. (now *arch. & Hist.*) as an epithet of royalty. M16.

4 Protected (as) by religious sanction or reverence from violation, interference, incursion, etc., sacrosanct, inviolable. Also foll. by *from*. M16.

5 Accursed. Now *rare* or *obsolete*. L16.

> 🕮 **1** E. O. M. DEUTSCH The dove sacred to Venus. P. KAVANAGH Forts which everyone regarded as sacred to the fairies. **b** J. WAIN Chairs which were sacred to their use. **2** J. CONRAD Bearers of a spark from the sacred fire. **3** L. M. MONTGOMERY Such an affecting farewell . . will be sacred in my memory forever. **4** C. MACKENZIE Compelled to take the sacred meerschaum from his mouth. J. B. YEATS People will do and say anything, and . . nothing is sacred. P. G. WODEHOUSE He had lightly betrayed a sacred trust which had been reposed in him.

Special collocations: **sacred axe** a Chinese porcelain mark, supposedly designating a warrior. **sacred band** GREEK HISTORY an élite corps of 300 men within the Theban army, comprising 150 pairs of lovers chosen from noble families. **Sacred Blood** the blood of Christ. **sacred book**: embodying the laws and teachings of a particular religion. **sacred circle** an exclusive company, an élite. ***Sacred College***: see COLLEGE *noun* 1; (***Dean of the Sacred College***: see DEAN *noun*¹ 6). **sacred concert**: comprising sacred music. **sacred cow** *colloq.* (chiefly *derog.*) (with ref. to the Hindu veneration of the cow as a sacred animal) a person, idea, institution, etc., unreasonably held to be above questioning or criticism. **sacred egoism** = SACRO EGOISMO. **Sacred Heart** ROMAN CATHOLIC CHURCH (*a*) (an image representing) the heart of Christ as an object of devotion; (*b*) a private prayer devoted to the heart of Christ. **sacred history**: that contained in the Bible. ***sacred ibis***. **sacred music**: accompanying sacred words; having a sacred theme or purpose. **sacred number** a number (esp. seven) considered significant in religious symbolism. **sacred orders** *rare* = ***holy orders*** s.v. ORDER *noun* 2a. **sacred poetry**: concerned with religious themes. ***sacred scarab***: see SCARAB 1a. ***Sacred War***: see WAR *noun*¹. **sacred way** a route used (esp. habitually) for religious processions or pilgrimages. ***Sacred Writ***: see WRIT *noun* 1. **sacred writing** = ***sacred book*** above.

▶†**B** *noun*. In *pl.* Sacred rites or observances. E17–M18.

■ **sacredly** *adverb* (*a*) with strict observance, inviolably; (*b*) in a sacred or religious manner: M16. **sacredness** *noun* L17.

sacrificable /səˈkrɪfɪkəb(ə)l, sakrɪˈfɪkəb(ə)l/ *adjective*. *rare*. M17.
[from Latin *sacrificare*, from *sacrificus* (see SACRIFICE *noun*): see -ABLE.]
Able to be sacrificed.

†**sacrifical** *adjective*. E17–L18.
[Latin *sacrificalis*, from *sacrificus*: see SACRIFICE *noun*, -AL¹.]
= SACRIFICIAL 1.

sacrificant /səˈkrɪfɪk(ə)nt/ *noun*. *rare*. M17.
[Latin *sacrificant-* pres. ppl stem of *sacrificare*: see SACRIFICABLE, -ANT¹.]
= SACRIFICER.

sacrificator /ˈsakrɪfɪkeɪtə/ *noun*. Now *rare* or *obsolete*. M16.
[Latin, agent-noun from *sacrificare*: see prec., -OR.]
= SACRIFICER.

■ †**sacrificatory** *adjective* = SACRIFICIAL 1 L16–L17. †**sacrificature** *noun* the system or practice of sacrificing L18–E19.

sacrifice /ˈsakrɪfʌɪs/ *noun*. ME.
[Old & mod. French from Latin *sacrificium* rel. to *sacrificus*, from *sacer* sacred, holy + *-ficus* -FIC.]

1 The ritual killing (and freq. burning of the body) of an animal or person, or the offering of a material possession to a god, in propitiation or homage; the practice of so doing. ME.

2 A person or thing offered in sacrifice. ME.

3 THEOLOGY. **a** The Crucifixion as Christ's offering of himself in propitiation for human redemption. LME. ▸**b** The Eucharist regarded as an offering of the bread and wine in union with the body and blood of Christ, or as an act of thanksgiving. E16.

4 The surrender of something valued or desired, esp. one's life, for the sake of something regarded as more important or worthy, or in order to avoid a greater loss, reduce expenditure, etc.; the loss entailed by this action. Also foll. by *of*. L16. ▸**b** A loss incurred in underselling an item to get rid of it. M19. ▸**c** CHESS. The surrender of a chessman, esp. a pawn, in order to facilitate an immediate attack or to gain a future advantage. L19. ▸**d** BASEBALL. Any of various plays which put out the batter while allowing a base runner to advance. L19. ▸**e** BRIDGE. A bid made higher than the expected fulfillable contract to prevent an opponent making a score greater than the penalty one is likely to incur. Also ***sacrifice bid***. M20.

> 🕮 **1** J. G. FARRELL The river could be persuaded not to flood by the sacrifice of a black goat. **4** LD MACAULAY Not likely to gain anything by the sacrifice of his principles. S. LEACOCK From their sacrifice shall come a . . better world for all. A. BROOKNER He would not ask her to make sacrifices. **b** DICKENS Its patterns were Last Year's and going at a sacrifice.

Phrases: **fall a sacrifice to** be overcome or destroyed by. ***passive sacrifice***: see PASSIVE *adjective*. **sacrifice of praise (and thanksgiving)** [with ref. to *Leviticus* 7:12 etc.] CHRISTIAN CHURCH an offering of praise to God. ***the supreme sacrifice***: see SUPREME *adjective*.

Comb.: ***sacrifice bid***: see sense 4e above; **sacrifice bidding** BRIDGE the action or an act of making a sacrifice bid; **sacrifice market**: in which goods are sold below cost price; **sacrifice price**: entailing loss on the seller.

sacrifice /ˈsakrɪfʌɪs/ *verb*. ME.
[from the noun.]

1 a *verb trans.* Kill (an animal or person) as a sacrifice; make an offering or sacrifice of. Foll. by *to*. ME. ▸**b** *verb intrans.* Kill an animal or person as a sacrifice; offer up a sacrifice. ME.

2 *verb trans.* Surrender or make a sacrifice of (something valued or desired etc.); devote or give over (one's life, time, etc.) to. Freq. foll. by *for*, *to*. E18. ▸**b** *verb trans. & intrans.* Sell (goods) at a sacrifice. M19. ▸**c** *verb intrans. & trans.* BASEBALL. Advance (another player) by making a sacrifice. E20. ▸**d** *verb trans.* CHESS. Make a sacrifice of (a chessman, esp. a pawn). E20. ▸**e** *verb intrans.* BRIDGE. Make a sacrifice bid. M20.

3 *verb trans.* Kill (an experimental animal) for scientific purposes. E20.

> 🕮 **1** J. G. FRAZER The Spartans . . sacrificed horses to him. **2** *Observer* No American President will sacrifice New York . . to save Berlin. E. BOWEN The . . mansion was to be sacrificed to the family's passion for town-planning. S. BELLOW Men sacrificed their lives for one another.

■ **sacrificer** *noun* a person, esp. a priest, who sacrifices something M16.

sacrificial /sakrɪˈfɪʃ(ə)l/ *adjective*. E17.
[from Latin *sacrificium* SACRIFICE *noun* + -AL¹.]

1 Of or pertaining to sacrifice; constituting a sacrifice. E17.

2 Involving or designating a metal anode that is used up when protecting another metal against electrolytic corrosion. M19.

■ **sacrificially** *adverb* M20.

sacrilege /ˈsakrɪlɪdʒ/ *noun*¹ & *verb*. ME.
[Old & mod. French *sacrilège* from Latin *sacrilegium*, from *sacrilegus* stealer of sacred things, from *sacer* sacred + *legere* take possession of.]

▶ **A** *noun*. **1** Orig., the crime of stealing or misappropriating a sacred object or objects, esp. from a church. Later also *gen.*, any offence against a consecrated person, or violation or misuse of what is recognized as sacred or under Church protection. Also, an instance of this. ME.

2 *transf.* (An instance of) profanation of anything held sacred or dear. ME.

> 🕮 **1** D. LODGE It was sacrilege to tell anything other than the strict truth in Confession. P. CAREY She took communion without being confirmed. This was a sacrilege. **2** SLOAN WILSON Time was given us . . to spend, and it's . . sacrilege to wish it away.

▶ **B** *verb trans.* Commit sacrilege on. *rare*. M16.

■ **sacrileger** *noun* (*arch.*) a person who commits or has committed sacrilege LME. **sacriˈlegious** *adjective* (*a*) involving or constituting sacrilege; (*b*) committing or guilty of sacrilege: LME. **sacriˈlegiously** *adverb* E17. **sacriˈlegist** = SACRILEGER E17.

†**sacrilege** *noun*². Long only *poet.* ME–E19.
[Latin *sacrilegus*: see SACRILEGE *noun*¹.]
= SACRILEGER.

sacring /ˈseɪkrɪŋ/ *noun*. *arch.* ME.
[from SACRE *verb* + -ING¹.]

1 *The* consecration of the Eucharistic elements. Also more fully ***the sacring of mass***, ***the sacring of the mass***. ME. ▸†**b** The consecrated elements. *rare*. Only in ME.

2 The ordination and consecration of a monarch, bishop, etc. ME.

Comb.: **sacring bell** (*a*) a small bell rung at the elevation of the eucharistic elements; †(*b*) a small bell rung to summon parishioners to morning prayers.

sacrist /ˈsakrɪst, ˈseɪ-/ *noun*. L16.
[Old & mod. French *sacriste*, or medieval Latin *sacrista*, from Latin *sacer* sacred + *-ista* -IST.]
1 A sacristan. L16.
2 In Aberdeen University, either of two college officials, orig. responsible for furnishing the church, later acting as chief porter or mace-bearer. M17.

sacristan /ˈsakrɪst(ə)n/ *noun*. ME.
[medieval Latin *sacristanus*, from *sacrista*: see prec., -AN.]
A person in charge of a sacristy and its contents. Also, the sexton of a parish church (*arch.*).
■ **sacristaness** *noun* (*rare*) a female sacristan M19.

sacristy /ˈsakrɪsti/ *noun*. LME.
[French *sacristie*, Italian *sacrestia*, or medieval Latin *sacristia*, from *sacrista*: see -Y³.]
A room in a religious house or church for keeping the vestments, sacred vessels, etc., and used by a celebrant preparing for a service.

sacro- /ˈseɪkrəʊ/ *combining form*.
[from Latin (*os*) *sacrum* SACRUM: see -O-.]
ANATOMY. Forming adjectives with the sense 'pertaining to the sacrum and', as ***sacro-iliac***, ***sacro-sciatic***, ***sacro-spinous***, ***sacro-tuberous***.
■ **sacro-iliitis** /-ɪlɪˈʌɪtɪs/ *noun* (MEDICINE) inflammation of the sacro-iliac joint M20.

sacro egoismo /ˈsakro ɛɡoˈizmo/ *noun phr. derog.* M20.
[Italian, lit. ' sacred egoism'.]
Egocentric nationalism, esp. in dealing with foreign States.

sacrosanct /ˈsakrə(ʊ)saŋkt, ˈseɪkrə(ʊ)-/ *adjective*. L15.
[Latin *sacrosanctus*, orig. two words, *sacro* abl. of *sacrum* sacred rite, and *sanctus* pa. pple of *sancire* make sacred.]
Secured from violation or infringement (as) by religious sanction; (of a person, institution, law, etc.) exempt from charge or criticism; inviolable, sacred.

> K. HULME People's houses are private and sacrosanct. N. SHERRY To many people, Big Ben and the news at nine were sacrosanct.

■ **sacroˈsanctity** *noun* the state or condition of being sacrosanct M17.

sacrum /ˈseɪkrəm/ *noun*. Pl. **sacrums**, **sacra** /ˈseɪkrə/. M18.
[Short for late Latin *os sacrum*, translating Greek *hieron osteon* sacred bone (from the belief that the soul resides in it).]
ANATOMY. A triangular bone which is wedged between the two hip-bones, forming the back of the pelvis and resulting from the fusing of (usu. five) vertebrae.

sacs de nuit *noun phr.* pl. of SAC DE NUIT.

SACW *abbreviation*.
Senior Aircraftwoman.

SAD *abbreviation*.
MEDICINE. Seasonal affective disorder.

sad /sad/ *adjective, adverb, & verb*.
[Old English *sæd* = Old Saxon *sad* (Dutch *zat*), Old High German *sat* (German *satt*), Old Norse *saðr*, Gothic *saþs*, from Germanic word rel. to Latin *sat*, *satis* enough. Cf. SADE *verb*.]
▶ **A** *adjective*. Compar. & superl. **-dd-**.
▶ **I** †**1** Satisfied; sated, weary, tired. Foll. by *of*, *to do*. OE–LME.
†**2** Settled in purpose or condition; steadfast, firm, constant. ME–M17.
3 Dignified, grave; sober, mature, serious. Also, trustworthy; orderly and regular in conduct. Now *arch. & dial.* ME. ▶†**b** Profoundly learned (*in*). ME–E16. ▶†**c** Strong; resolute. LME–L15.
4 a Feeling, expressing, or characterized by sorrow; sorrowful, mournful. ME. ▶**b** Causing sorrow; distressing, calamitous. LME.
5 Exceptionally bad; deplorable; shameful; regrettable, unfortunate. L17.
6 Very unfashionable or inadequate; socially inept, esp. through being studious or obsessive. Cf. SADDO. *colloq.* M20.

> **4a** A. WILSON Eric is sad because his idol has feet of clay. B. PYM A sad autumn day with the leaves nearly all fallen . . with no promise of brightness. **b** E. BOWEN It is sad that so many years . . have gone by without your promised visit. *Guardian* I have had the sad task of identifying the corpse of a Muntjac. **5** DICKENS The lady . . being a sad invalid, has been ill three days. *Listener* A wander-witted granddad, a sad bore to his family. **6** *Daily Express* The show is very tongue in cheek, anyone who takes it too seriously is a bit sad. *Glasgow Herald* I . . used to list jumble sales as one of my hobbies. (Sad I know.)

▶ **II 7** †**a** Massive, weighty; solid, dense; forming a compact body. Also (*rare*), firmly fixed. OE–M17. ▶**b** Of soil: stiff, heavy, difficult to work. *obsolete* exc. *dial.* LME. ▶**c** Of dough etc.: heavy, having failed to rise. L17.
†**8** Of sleep: sound, deep. ME–L15.
†**9** Falling heavily, delivered with force, heavy. ME–M17.
10 Of a colour: dark, deep; dull, sober, neutral-tinted. Formerly also, dark or sober in colour. LME.
Special collocations & comb.: **sad-iron** a solid flat-iron. **sad sack** *US colloq.* a very inept person, orig. an inept soldier.
▶ **B** *adverb*. Compar. & superl. **-dd-**.
†**1** Firmly, strongly, fixedly. ME–L15.
†**2** Thoroughly; truly, certainly. LME–L15.
3 Heavily; with force. *obsolete* exc. *dial.* LME.
4 Sorrowfully. *poet.* L15.
▶ **C** *verb trans.* Infl. **-dd-**.
1 Make solid or firm; compress. *obsolete* exc. *dial.* LME.
†**2** Make steadfast, establish, confirm (*in*). LME–M17.
†**3** Make dull; darken (a colour). L16–M17.
†**4** Make sorrowful; sadden. E17–E19.
■ **saddish** *adjective* M17.

sadden /ˈsad(ə)n/ *verb*. LME.
[from SAD *adjective* + -EN⁵.]
1 *verb trans.* Make solid or firm; compress, compact (foll. by *down*); make cohesive. Now *dial.* LME. ▶†**b** *verb intrans.* Become stiff or solid. M17–M18.
2 *verb trans. & intrans.* Make or become sad or gloomy in feeling or (occas.) appearance. E17.
3 *verb trans.* Dull or tone down (a colour on cloth) by applying certain chemicals. L18.

> **2** D. MADDEN It saddens his daughter very much to see him so lonely.

saddle /ˈsad(ə)l/ *noun*.
[Old English *sadol*, *-ul* = Middle Dutch *sadel* (Dutch *zadel*, *zaal*), Old High German *satal*, *-ul* (German *Sattel*), Old Norse *sǫðull*, from Germanic word perh. ult. rel. to Indo-European base also of SIT *verb*, repr. in Gothic *sitls*, Latin *sella* seat.]
▶ **I 1** A seat for a rider, usu. made of leather, raised at the front and rear, and fitted with stirrups, to be fastened on the back of a horse etc. by means of a girth passing under the body. Also, a support for packs to be similarly fastened on the back of a horse etc. (cf. ***pack-saddle*** s.v. PACK *noun*). OE. ▶**b** A permanently fixed seat for the rider of a bicycle, motorcycle, etc. L19.
2 The part of a draught horse's harness which attaches to the shafts of a vehicle. L18.
1 ***side-saddle***, ***war-saddle***, ***Western saddle***, etc.
▶ **II 3** A support, *esp.* one that is concave or resembles a saddle in shape; *spec.* (***a***) NAUTICAL a wooden block hollowed out above and below and fixed between two spars so that one may rest on and attach to the other; (***b***) a block etc. for supporting a cable or wire on a suspension bridge, pier, telegraph-pole, etc.; (***c***) each of the supports of a fixed horizontal steam boiler; the forward projection of a steamroller's boiler, supporting its weight over the front rolls; (***d***) a fireclay bar for supporting ceramic ware in a kiln; (***e***) the guided movable base of a slide rest, drilling head, etc.; (***f***) a device fitted around a segment of electrical wire or a conduit to insulate and fix it in place; (***g***) DENTISTRY the base of a denture, covering the gums and bearing the artificial teeth; (***h***) the (adjustable) ridge near the broad base of a guitar, etc., over which the strings pass. E16.
4 A depression in a line of hills, a col; a broad pass with gently sloping approaches; a ridge that rises to a higher ground at each end; GEOLOGY a depression along the axis of an anticline, concave in longitudinal section and convex in transverse section. M16. ▶**b** MINING & GEOLOGY. In full ***saddle reef***. A reef or vein of ore following the bedding planes in the curve of an anticline or syncline; *spec.* one that is anticlinal. M19.
5 A joint of meat consisting of the two loins and conjoining vertebrae. M18.
6 a A saddle-like marking on the back of a mammal or bird, as a harp seal, pig, etc. M18. ▶**b** CONCHOLOGY. An elevation in a folded septum in a mollusc shell; a forward-facing convexity in a suture line in the shell of an ammonite etc. E19. ▶**c** The lower part of the back of a domestic fowl or game-bird; *esp.* that of a cock, which bears long feathers. M19.
7 MATH. In full ***saddle point***. A point at which a curved surface is locally level but at which its curvature in two directions differs in sign. Also, (in game theory) the joint outcome of the two parties following unmixed optimal strategies in a zero-sum game. E20.
8 A piece of leather stitched across the instep of a shoe, often in a contrasting colour. M20.
Phrases: †**beside the saddle** off the mark; out of action or competition. ***boot and saddle***: see BOOT *noun*². **in the saddle** (***a***) on horseback; (***b***) in control, in office; ready for work. **lay the saddle upon the right horse**, **set the saddle upon the right horse** lay blame on the guilty person. †**win the saddle or lose the horse** realize great profit or suffer great loss in a risky venture.
Attrib. & comb.: In the senses 'shaped like a saddle, concave', as ***saddle-nose***, ***saddle-plate***, ***saddle-stone***, etc., 'used for riding', as ***saddle-ass***, ***saddle-ox***, ***saddle-pony***, etc. Special combs., as **saddle-bag** a bag carried beside or behind a saddle; *esp.* either of a pair of bags connected by a strap etc. and carried across a horse's back behind the saddle or (*N. Amer.*) across a rack over the rear wheel of a bicycle; **saddle-bar** (***a***) any of the horizontal bars crossing upright stanchions in a framework supporting or securing individual panels of a leaded window; (***b***) SADDLERY either of the side pieces of a saddle-tree which connect the pommel and cantle; **saddlebill** (more fully ***saddlebill stork***) a large black and white African stork, *Ephippiorhynchus senegalensis*, which has a yellow saddle-shaped frontal shield on top of the bill; also called ***jabiru***, ***African jabiru***; **saddle-blanket** *US* a small blanket for folding and using as a saddle-cloth; **saddle block** MEDICINE anaesthetization of the perineal region by a low spinal injection; **saddle-bow** the arched front or rear of a saddle; **saddlebred** *noun & adjective* (a horse) bred to have the gaits of an American saddle horse; **saddle bronco** *US* a bronco ridden with a saddle in a rodeo; **saddle brown** *noun & adjective* (of) the tan colour of saddle-leather; **saddle-cloth** laid on a horse's back beneath the saddle; **saddle-coloured** *adjective* (of complexion) saddle brown, tanned; **saddle embolus** MEDICINE: which straddles a bifurcation in an artery, esp. the lower aorta, blocking both branches; **saddle feather** = ***saddle hackle*** below; **saddle-gall**: on a horse's back, caused by the chafing of a saddle; **saddle-galled** *adjective* chafed by a saddle; having a saddle-gall; **saddle-grafting**: in which the top of the stock is cut in a wedge-shaped form and the split scion is fitted closely over it; **saddle hackle (feather)** any of the long feathers growing backwards from the saddle of a cock; **saddle-hackled** *adjective* (of a cock) having saddle hackles; **saddle horse** (***a***) a horse used for riding; (***b***) a wooden frame or stand on which saddles are cleaned, repaired, etc.; **saddle-house** a building for storing saddlery; **saddle-joint** ANATOMY: in which the articulating surfaces are reciprocally saddle-shaped; **saddle oyster** (a shell of) any of various saddle-shaped bivalves of the super family Anomiacea, esp. *Anomia ephippium* of the Atlantic, and *Placuna sella* of the Indo-Pacific; ***saddle point***: see sense 6 above; **saddle quern**: having a fixed, slightly concave lower stone and a large movable oval upper stone; ***saddle reef***: see sense 3b above; **saddle scabbard** *N. Amer.* a holster fixed to a saddle, for carrying a rifle or shotgun when riding; **saddle seat** (***a***) the seat of a saddle; (***b***) (a chair with) a concave or centrally depressed seat; **saddle-shaped** *adjective* shaped like a saddle, having a concave central section; **saddle-shell** = ***saddle oyster*** above; **saddle shoe**: with a piece of leather stitched across the instep, often in a contrasting colour; **saddle shoulder** on a garment, a square-cut shoulder formed by an extension of the sleeve to the neckline; **saddle-skirts** the small flaps covering stirrup bars; **saddle soap** soft soap containing neat's-foot oil, used for cleaning leather; **saddle-sore** *adjective* chafed by a saddle; **saddle stitch** (***a***) BOOKBINDING a stitch of thread or a wire staple passed through the centre fold of a booklet, magazine, etc.; (***b***) a decorative top stitch made with long stitches on the upper side alternated with short stitches on the underside of cloth, a garment, etc.; **saddle-stitch** *verb trans.* sew (cloth etc.) with saddle stitches; **saddle-stitching** (***a***) the making of saddle stitches; (***b***) a row or series of saddle stitches; **saddle-tank** a water tank which fits over the top and sides of a railway engine; a locomotive with a saddle-tank; **saddle thrombus** MEDICINE = ***saddle embolus*** above; **saddle tramp** *N. Amer. slang* an itinerant cowboy; **saddle-tree** the frame of a saddle; **saddle vein** MINING = ***saddle reef*** above; **saddle wire** BOOKBINDING a wire staple passed through the back fold of a single gathering.
■ **saddleless** /-l-l-/ *adjective* (***a***) (of a horse) without a saddle; †(***b***) *rare* (of a rider) out of the saddle: L15. **saddle-like** *adjective* resembling a saddle, esp. in shape; concave in one direction and convex in the other: L18.

saddle /ˈsad(ə)l/ *verb*. OE.
[from the noun.]
1 *verb trans.* Put a saddle on (a horse etc.). Also foll. by *up*. OE. ▶†**b** *verb trans.* Ride (a horse etc.). M16–E18. ▶**c** *verb intrans.* Mount a saddled horse etc. (now *rare*); put a saddle on a horse etc. (also foll. by *up*). M19. ▶**d** *verb trans.* Enter (a horse) in a race. E20.
2 *verb trans.* **a** Burden (a person) *with* a load, task, responsibility, etc. OE. ▶**b** *verb trans.* Impose (a burden) *on*. E19.
3 *verb trans.* Bend (a thing) downwards in the middle, make saddle-shaped, make concave. E19.
4 *verb trans.* Place or fit firmly on or over a supporting structure. Usu. in *pass. US.* M19.

> **1 saddling paddock** (***a***) a paddock in which horses are prepared for a race; (***b***) *Austral. slang* a place where sexual contacts are known to be easily made, orig. the bar of Melbourne's Theatre Royal, frequented by prostitutes in the 19th cent. **2a** *World Soccer* Officials in faraway Moscow saddled the Ukraine club . . with all the national team fixtures. *Punch* Her escort is saddled with another job . . to transport another uncontrollable passenger.

saddleback /ˈsad(ə)lbak/ *noun & adjective*. M16.
[from SADDLE *noun* + BACK *noun*¹.]
▶ **A** *noun*. **1** A thing, now esp. a hill or ridge, having a concavely curved or depressed upper outline. M16.
2 Any of various animals or birds with saddle-like markings on the back, as a black-backed gull, a hooded crow, a saddleback seal, dolphin, shrew, etc.; *esp.* a New Zealand wattlebird, *Creadion carunculatus*. L18. ▶**b** (An animal of) each of three breeds of black pig having a white band running across the shoulders and down to the forelegs. E20.
3 ARCHITECTURE. A tower roof having two opposite gables connected by a ridged-roof. M19.
4 GEOLOGY. An anticline. L19.
2b ***Wessex saddleback***.
▶ **B** *adjective*. = SADDLEBACKED *adjective*; *esp.* (of an animal) having saddle-like markings on the back. L17.
saddleback caterpillar the larva of the N. American moth *Sibine stimulea* (family Limacodidae), which has stinging hairs. **saddleback crow** the hooded crow. **saddleback dolphin** the

common dolphin. **saddleback gull** a black-backed gull, esp. *Larus marinus*. **saddleback jackal** an African black-backed jackal, *Canis mesomelas*. **saddleback pig** = sense A.2b above. **saddleback seal** a mature male harp seal. **saddleback shrew** the Arctic shrew of N. America, *Sorex arcticus*.

saddlebacked /ˈsad(ə)lbakt/ *adjective*. **M16.**
[formed as prec. + -ED².]
1 Having a concavely curved or depressed upper surface, outline, or edge. **M16.**
2 Of a horse: having a markedly concave or depressed back; sway-backed. **L17.**
3 ARCHITECTURE. Of a tower: having a saddleback. **M19.**
4 Of an animal: having saddle-like markings on the back. Cf. SADDLEBACK *noun* 2. **M19.**
4 saddlebacked crow = ***saddleback crow*** s.v. SADDLEBACK *adjective*. **saddlebacked shrew** = ***saddleback shrew*** s.v. SADDLEBACK *adjective*.

saddler /ˈsadlə/ *noun*. **ME.**
[from SADDLE *noun* + -ER¹.]
1 A maker or seller of saddles or saddlery. **ME.**
2 MILITARY. An officer responsible for the saddlery of a cavalry regiment. **M19.**
3 A saddle-horse. *US colloq.* **L19.**
4 a = ***saddleback seal*** s.v. SADDLEBACK *adjective*. **L19.** ▸**b** = ***saddleback gull*** s.v. SADDLEBACK *adjective*. **L19.**

saddlery /ˈsadləri/ *noun*. **LME.**
[from prec. + -Y³. Cf. -ERY.]
1 The making or selling of saddles and other equipment for horses; the craft or business of a saddler. **LME.**
2 *collect.* Saddles and other equipment for horses; articles made or sold by a saddler. **E18.**
3 A place where saddles and other equipment for horses are made, sold, or stored. **M19.**

saddo /ˈsadəʊ/ *noun*. *colloq.* Pl. **-os**, **-oes**. **L20.**
[from SAD *adjective* + -O.]
A person perceived as socially inadequate, unfashionable, or otherwise contemptible. Cf. SAD *adjective* 6.

Sadducaean *noun & adjective* var. of SADDUCEAN.

Sadducaic /sadjʊˈkeɪɪk/ *adjective*. **M19.**
[from late Greek *Saddoukaios* SADDUCEE, after *Pharisaic*.]
Sadducean.
■ Also †**Sadducaical** *adjective* (*rare*) **E17–E18.**

Sadducean /sadjʊˈsiːən/ *noun & adjective*. Also **-caean**. **M16.**
[from late Latin *Sadducaeus* SADDUCEE + -AN.]
▸†**A** *noun*. = SADDUCEE. **M16–L17.**
▸**B** *adjective*. Of, pertaining to, or characteristic of the Sadducees. **L16.**

Sadducee /ˈsadjʊsiː/ *noun*. **OE.**
[Late Latin *Sadducaeus* from late Greek *Saddoukaios* from post-biblical Hebrew *ṣĕdūqī* from the personal name *ṣādōq* Zadok.]
1 *Hist.* A member of a Jewish sect in the time of Jesus, which denied the resurrection of the dead, the existence of angels, and the authority of the traditional Mosaic oral law. **OE.**
2 *transf.* A materialist; THEOLOGY a person who denies the resurrection. *rare*. **L17.**
■ **Sadduceeism** *noun* (**a**) the doctrine or beliefs of the Sadducees; (**b**) the materialist scepticism and denial of immortality considered as characteristic of the Sadducees: **M17.** †**Sadducism** *noun* [mod. Latin *Sadducismus*] = SADDUCEEISM **M17–L18.** **Sadducize** *verb intrans.* (*rare*) hold the doctrines of the Sadducees **E18.**

sade /seɪd/ *verb*. *obsolete* exc. *dial.*
[Old English *sadian* from West Germanic verb from Germanic base of SAD *adjective*. Cf. SATE *verb*.]
†**1** *verb intrans.* Become sated or weary. **OE–LME.**
2 *verb trans.* Glut, satiate; make weary (*of*). **OE.**

Sadeian /ˈseɪdiːən, ˈsɑːd-/ *adjective*. **M20.**
[from de *Sade* (see SADISM) + -IAN.]
Of, pertaining to, or characteristic of de Sade.
■ Also **Sadean** *adjective* **L20.**

sadful /ˈsadfʊl, -f(ə)l/ *adjective*. *rare*. **M17.**
[from SAD *adjective* + -FUL.]
Sorrowful.

sadhu /ˈsɑːdhuː/ *noun*. Also **S-**. **M19.**
[Sanskrit *sādhu* adjective, good, (as noun) good man, holy man.]
HINDUISM. A holy man, a sage.
■ **sadhuism** *noun* the principles and practices of a sadhu **E20.**

Sadie Hawkins /seɪdi ˈhɔːkɪnz/ *noun*. *N. Amer.* **M20.**
[A character in the cartoon strip *Li'l Abner* by Alfred Gerald Caplin (1909–79), US cartoonist.]
Used *attrib.* to designate a day early in November on which, by a fictional tradition, a woman may propose marriage to a man.

sadism /ˈseɪdɪz(ə)m/ *noun*. **L19.**
[French *sadisme*, from Donatien-Alphonse-François, Comte (known as Marquis) de *Sade* (1740–1814), French novelist and pornographer: see -ISM.]
The condition or state of deriving (esp. sexual) pleasure from inflicting pain, suffering, humiliation, etc.; *colloq.* enjoyment of cruelty to others. Cf. MASOCHISM.
■ **sadic** *adjective* = SADISTIC *adjective* **E20.**

sadist /ˈseɪdɪst, sɑːd-/ *noun & adjective*. **E20.**
[formed as prec. + -IST.]
▸**A** *noun*. A person who derives (esp. sexual) pleasure from inflicting pain, suffering, humiliation, etc.; *colloq.* a cruel or merciless person. **E20.**

> 🕮 J. POYER Slow, painful death at the hands of sadists who delight in inflicting the worst possible pain. G. SWIFT This sadist, this power-monger, this refiner of cruelties.

▸**B** *adjective*. = SADISTIC *adjective*. **E20.**
■ **saˈdistic** *adjective* of, pertaining to, or characteristic of sadism or a sadist: **L19.** **saˈdistically** *adverb* **E20.**

saditty /ˈsadɪti/ *adjective*. *US Black slang*. **M20.**
[Origin unkn.]
Affecting an air of superiority.

sadly /ˈsadli/ *adverb & adjective*. **ME.**
[from SAD *adjective* + -LY².]
▸**A** *adverb*. †**1** Heavily. **ME–M17.** ▸**b** Solidly, fully; completely, to the utmost. Only in **LME.**
†**2 a** Strongly, resolutely. **ME–L15.** ▸**b** Steadfastly; firmly, constantly. **ME–E17.** ▸**c** Firmly, tightly, closely. **LME–L15.**
†**3** Gravely; soberly, seriously. **ME–L18.** ▸**b** Steadily, quietly, calmly. Only in **ME.**
4 Sorrowfully, mournfully. **ME.**
5 So as to cause sadness; distressingly, calamitously; grievously; deplorably, regrettably. **M17.** ▸**b** Modifying a sentence: deplorably; shamefully; regrettably, unfortunately. **L20.**

> 🕮 **4** *Punch* 'I have a lot of trouble being tall,' said Superman sadly. **5** H. JAMES It had sadly begun to rain. I. MURDOCH A jocular tone . . sadly out of key with the solemnity of the young people. **b** *Which?* Sadly, these were cost-cutting measures.

▸**B** *pred. adjective*. In ill health; unwell. Cf. POORLY *adjective*. Now *dial.* **E18.**

sadness /ˈsadnɪs/ *noun*. **ME.**
[from SAD *adjective* + -NESS.]
The condition or quality of being sad.

sado- /ˈseɪdəʊ/ *combining form*.
[from SADISM, SADISTIC: see -O-.]
Forming nouns and adjectives with the sense 'sadism and', or 'sadistic and', as ***sado-necrophilia***, ***sado-erotic***.

sado-maso /seɪdəʊˈmasəʊ/ *adjective & noun*. *slang* (chiefly *US*). **L20.**
[Abbreviation.]
▸**A** *adjective*. = SADO-MASOCHISTIC. **L20.**
▸**B** *noun*. Pl. **-os**. = SADO-MASOCHIST. **L20.**

sado-masochism /seɪdəʊˈmasəkɪz(ə)m/ *noun*. **M20.**
[from SADO- + MASOCHISM.]
PSYCHOLOGY. A combination of sadism and masochism; the simultaneous presence of sadistic and masochistic elements.
■ **sado-masochist** *noun* a person with both sadistic and masochistic impulses **M20** **sado-masoˈchistic** *adjective* of, pertaining to, or characteristic of sado-masochism or sado-masochists **M20.**

sadza /ˈsadzə/ *noun*. **M20.**
[Shona.]
In southern and eastern Africa, a porridge made of ground maize or millet.

SAE *abbreviation*.
Society of Automotive Engineers (used *spec.* to designate a scale of viscosity used for lubrication oils).

s.a.e. *abbreviation*.
Stamped addressed envelope.

Saengerfest *noun* var. of SÄNGERFEST.

saeta /saˈeta/ *noun*. **E20.**
[Spanish, lit. 'arrow'.]
Esp. in southern Spain, an unaccompanied Andalusian folk-song, sung during religious processions.

saeter /ˈseɪtə, ˈsɛtə/ *noun*. Also **setter** /ˈsɛtə/. **L16.**
[Old Norse *sætr* mountain pasture: cf. Norwegian *sæter*, *seter*, Swedish *säter*. In sense 2a directly from Norwegian.]
1 In Orkney and Shetland, a meadow associated with a dwelling; a summer pasture in the outfield. **L16.**
2 a In Scandinavia, a mountain pasture where cattle remain in summer. **L18.** ▸**b** A dairy or farm on such a pasture. **E20.**

saeva indignatio /ˌsʌɪvə ɪndɪɡˈnɑːtɪəʊ/ *noun phr.* **M19.**
[Latin, lit. 'savage indignation'.]
An intense feeling of contemptuous anger at human folly.

Safaitic /safəˈɪtɪk/ *adjective*. **E20.**
[from *Safa*, a place in Syria SE of Damascus + -ITIC.]
Of, pertaining to, or designating an ancient Semitic language known only from inscriptions discovered near Safa, probably of the first centuries AD.

safari /səˈfɑːri/ *noun, verb, & adjective*. **L19.**
[Kiswahili from Arab. *safar* journey, trip, tour.]
▸**A** *noun*. **1** A hunter's or traveller's party or caravan, esp. in E. Africa. **L19.**
2 A journey; a cross-country expedition on foot or in vehicles, orig. and esp. in E. Africa, for hunting, tourism, or scientific investigation. Freq. in ***on safari***. **E20.**

> 🕮 **2** *transf.*: P. HILL His educated hands went on safari down her stomach.

Comb.: **safari ant** an African driver ant, *esp.* one of the genus *Anomma*; **safari camp** *Austral.* a camp in the outback; **safari jacket** a belted lightweight jacket, typically having short sleeves and four patch pockets; **safari look** a fashion of clothes resembling those traditionally worn on safari; **safari park** an area of parkland where wild animals are kept in the open and through which visitors may drive; **safari supper** a social occasion at which the different courses of a meal are eaten at different people's houses.
▸**B** *verb intrans.* Go on safari. **E20.**
▸**C** *attrib.* or as *adjective*. Sandy brown or beige; of the colour of clothes traditionally worn on safari. **L20.**

Safavid /ˈsafəvɪd/ *adjective & noun*. **E20.**
[from Arab. *ṣafawī* descended from *Ṣafī al Dīn*: see SOPHY *noun*, -ID³.]
Hist. ▸**A** *adjective*. Of, pertaining to, or designating a ruling dynasty of Persia, *c* 1500–1736. **E20.**
▸**B** *noun*. A member of this dynasty. **L20.**

safe /seɪf/ *noun*. **LME.**
[from SAVE *verb*; later assim. to next.]
1 A receptacle for the safe storage of articles; *esp.* (**a**) a ventilated chest or cupboard for protecting provisions from insects etc.; (**b**) a strong fireproof lockable container for money or other valuables. **LME.**
2 A tray laid under plumbing fixtures to receive spilled water. Also ***safe-tray***. **M19.**
3 A contraceptive sheath. *colloq.* **L19.**
4 The operative position of a firearm's safety device; the state in which a gun cannot be fired. **E20.**
1 *meat safe*, ***night safe***, etc.
Comb.: **safe-blower** (orig. *US*) a robber who uses explosive material to burst open a safe; **safe-breaker**, **safe-cracker** (orig. *US*) a robber who breaks open safes; ***safe-tray***: see sense 2 above.

safe /seɪf/ *adjective*. **ME.**
[Old & mod. French *sauf* (Anglo-Norman *saf*) from Latin *salvus* uninjured, entire, healthy.]
▸**I 1** Uninjured, unharmed; having escaped or avoided injury or damage. Freq. in ***safe and sound***. **ME.**
†**2** In sound health, well; *esp.* healed, cured, restored to health. Also foll. by *of*. **ME–E16.**
†**3** THEOLOGY. Delivered from sin or condemnation, saved; in a state of salvation. **ME–E17.**
†**4** Mentally or morally sound or sane. **LME–E19.**

> 🕮 **1** C. BRONTË We arrived safe at home. B. MONTGOMERY The certainty . . of the safe arrival of our reinforcements. J. WYNDHAM They'll be back safe and sound, you'll see.

▸**II 5** Not exposed to danger; not liable to be harmed or lost; secure. (Foll. by *from*, †*of*.) **ME.**
6 Of a place or thing: affording security or immunity; not dangerous, not likely to cause harm or injury. Also foll. by *for*. **LME.**
7 Of an action, procedure, etc.: free from risk, not involving danger or mishap, guaranteed against failure. **L16.**
8 Secured, kept in custody; unable to escape. Also, not likely to intervene or do harm. **L16.**
9 Sure in procedure; not liable to fail or mislead; trustworthy, dependable. Also, cautious, avoiding risk. **E17.** ▸**b** LAW. Of evidence, a verdict, etc.: convincing, sustainable. Freq. in ***safe and satisfactory***. **M20.**
10 a Foll. by *of*: sure to obtain. Now *rare* or *obsolete*. **M17.** ▸**b** Certain *to do* a thing, certain of being something. **L18.**
11 Good, excellent. *slang*. **L20.**

> 🕮 **5** G. GREENE He had the papers safe in his pocket. J. BETJEMAN Safe in her sitting room Sister is putting her feet up. **6** S. BELLOW This is a safe building, guards and doormen round the clock. **7** *Liverpool Mercury* One is perfectly safe in saying that the position of the defendants has . . improved. J. G. FARRELL With the country in such an uproar, it was not safe to go far afield. **9** *Guardian* They chose the safe middleroad candidate. G. BOYCOTT Holding . . has a safe pair of hands and made the catch. *Motorway Express* The safest drivers are those aged 64 to 68. **10b** I. T. THURSTON If anyone blundered, it was safe to be Baum. **11** V. WALTERS 'Safe, er, I mean that's fine,' said Janice.

Phrases: **a safe pair of hands** (in sport) a good catcher of the ball; *gen.* someone considered trustworthy and reliable. ***as safe as houses***: see HOUSE *noun*¹. ***fail safe***: see FAIL *verb*. **in safe hands** protected by someone trustworthy from harm or damage. **on the safe side** with a margin of security against error or risk. ***play safe***: see PLAY *verb*. ***safe as houses***: see HOUSE *noun*¹.
Special collocations & comb.: **safe area** in the war of 1939–45, an area not liable to be attacked or invaded. **safe bet** a bet that is certain to succeed; a virtual certainty. **safe deposit** a place in which valuables are stored. **safe edge** a smooth edge of a file. **Safehand** (proprietary name for) a courier service for confidential documents. **safe hit** BASEBALL = ***base hit*** s.v. BASE *noun*¹. **safe-hold** a place of safety from attack. **safe house** a place of refuge or rendezvous for spies, terrorists, etc. **safekeep** *verb trans.* (*rare*) keep safe, protect. **safe keeping** the action of keeping some-

thing safe; protection, preservation. **safe lamp**, **safelight** PHOTOGRAPHY a dim darkroom lamp, usu. with a filter which is coloured according to the sensitivity of the materials used. **safe load** a load which leaves a required margin of security against causing breakage or injury to a structure. **safe period** the part of the menstrual cycle during which conception is least likely. **safe seat** a parliamentary seat which is likely to be retained at an election with a large majority. **safe sex**: engaged in by people who have taken precautions to protect themselves against sexually transmitted diseases such as Aids.

■ **safeness** *noun* LME.

safe /seɪf/ *verb*. E17.

[from the adjective.]

1 *verb trans.* Make safe or secure. Also, conduct safely *out of*. *rare*. E17.

2 *verb intrans.* & *trans.* MOUNTAINEERING. = BELAY *verb* 3b. M20.

safe-conduct /seɪfˈkɒndʌkt/ *noun*. ME.

[Old & mod. French *sauf-conduit*, medieval Latin *salvus conductus*, from Latin *salvus* SAFE *adjective* + *conductus* CONDUCT *noun*[1].]

1 The privilege, granted by a monarch or other authority, of being protected from arrest or harm while making a particular journey or travelling within a certain region. ME.

2 A document by which this privilege is conveyed. LME.

> **1** A. MASON Inviting their chief to a meeting under guarantee of safe-conduct. *fig.*: J. R. LOWELL A great controlling reason in whose safe-conduct we trust.

safeguard /ˈseɪfgɑːd/ *noun* & *verb*. LME.

[Anglo-Norman *salve garde*, Old & mod. French *sauve garde* (Anglo-Latin *salva gardia*), from *sauve* SAFE *adjective* + *garde* GUARD *noun*. Cf. SAGGAR.]

▶ **A** *noun*. **1** Protection, safety, security. Now *rare* or *obsolete*. LME. ▸†**b** Custody, safe keeping. E16–E19.

2 †**a** Guarantee of safety or safe passage given by a person in authority; safe-conduct. LME–E17. ▸**b** A permit for safe passage; a safe-conduct. Also, a guard or escort granted for the same purpose. M17.

3 *gen.* Anything that offers security from danger; a defence, a protection. L15.

4 An outer skirt worn by a woman to protect her dress when riding. *obsolete* exc. *Hist.* L16.

†**5** A picket or outpost of soldiers. L17–E18.

6 A warrant granted by a military commander to protect a place from pillage. Also, a detachment of soldiers sent to guard a place protected by such a warrant. Long *rare*. E18.

7 Any of various technical devices for ensuring safety. E19.

> **1** †**in safeguard** in safety or security. **2a** SHAKES. *Coriol.* On safeguard he came to me. **3** A. E. STEVENSON An effective system of arms reductions with adequate safeguards. P. H. GIBBS Isn't the League of Nations the safeguard of peace?

▶ **B** *verb trans.* **1** Keep secure from danger or attack; guard, protect, defend. LME.

†**2** Send or conduct in safety. E–M17.

3 Protect (a native product or industry) against foreign imports. E20.

> **1** J. T. STORY People .. who safeguard .. the country against our enemies. A. BROOKNER It was up to him to safeguard their honour.

safely /ˈseɪfli/ *adverb*. ME.

[from SAFE *adjective* + -LY[2].]

1 In a safe manner; *spec.* (*a*) without harm or injury caused; (*b*) in a manner free from danger, securely; (*c*) without risk of error. ME.

†**2** In safe confinement or custody. ME–E17.

†**3** With confidence. LME–L17.

> **1** T. W. HIGGINSON We can safely assume .. more than this. J. BUCHAN One spot where .. I might safely lie hidden. *Sunday Times* What you can safely let your horse eat. **2** SHAKES. *All's Well* I'll keep him dark and safely lock'd.

safener /ˈseɪf(ə)nə/ *noun*. M20.

[from SAFE *adjective* + -EN[5] + -ER[1].]

A substance that reduces the harmfulness to plants of other substances, esp. in an insecticide, fungicide, etc.

safety /ˈseɪfti/ *noun* & *adjective*. ME.

[Old & mod. French *sauveté* from medieval Latin *salvitas*, from Latin *salvus*: see SAFE *adjective*, -TY[1].]

▶ **A** *noun*. **1** The state of being protected from or guarded against hurt or injury; freedom from danger. With possess.: the safety of a specified person or (formerly also in *pl.*) persons. ME. ▸†**b** Salvation. LME–L17.

†**2** Close custody or confinement. ME–L16.

†**3** A means or instrument of safety; a protection, a safeguard. LME–L18.

4 The quality of being unlikely to cause hurt or injury; the quality of not being dangerous or presenting a risk. E18.

5 *Hist.* ***Patent Safety***, the original hansom cab, which had a device to prevent its overturning if it tilted. M19.

6 *ellipt.* A safety bicycle, a safety-catch, a safety match, a safety razor, etc. L19.

7 a AMER. FOOTBALL. An act of advancing the ball in one's own end zone by a down; a score of two points awarded against a team for this. Also (more fully ***safety man***), a defensive back who plays in the deepest position. L19. ▸**b** POLO. An act of hitting the ball over one's own goal-line. E20. ▸**c** BASEBALL. A safe hit. E20.

8 A metal-ringed outlet for a stove-pipe in the roof of a tent etc. *N. Amer.* M20.

> **1a** V. PYKE He crossed the river in safety. *Daily Telegraph* To secure the safety of men working underground. G. DALY A gunboat .. waiting to move British subjects to safety. **c** SIR W. SCOTT The weary watch their safeties ask. **2** SHAKES. *John* Imprison him .. Deliver him to safety. **4** *Daily Telegraph* A drug .. to be referred to the Committee on Safety of Drugs. **6** T. O'BRIEN I flicked the safety back and forth, making certain it wouldn't jam.

Phrases: **coefficient of safety**, **factor of safety** = *safety factor* below. ***margin of safety***: see MARGIN *noun*. ***Patent Safety***: see sense 5 above. ***play for safety***: see PLAY *verb*.

▶ **B** *attrib.* or as *adjective*. Designed to reduce any risk of injury or damage incurred during use or operation. E19.

Comb. & special collocations: **safety belt** (*a*) = ***seat belt*** s.v. SEAT *noun*; (*b*) a belt or strap worn by a person working at a height to prevent a fall; **safety bicycle** *Hist.* a bicycle of a type differing from the earliest models in the lower and hence safer position of the saddle; **safety boat** a lifeboat; **safety bolt** a device for locking the trigger of a gun; **safety cab** a tractor cab designed with a view to safety in use; **safety cage** a protective metal cage; *spec.* a framework of reinforced struts protecting a car's passenger cabin against crash damage; **safety-catch** a catch or stop attached to a mechanical device as a safeguard, esp. in hoisting apparatus or on the trigger of a gun; **safety chain** (*a*) a subsidiary chain connecting railway cars etc. together; (*b*) a chain securing a watch, bracelet, etc., to prevent it falling off if the fastening opens accidentally; (*c*) a chain on a door preventing opening beyond a certain point; **safety-critical** *adjective* designed or made to be fail-safe; **safety curtain** a fireproof curtain which can be lowered to protect the main body of a theatre from fire on or behind the stage; **safety deposit** = ***safe deposit*** s.v. SAFE *adjective*; **safety engineer** a person trained in accident prevention and the organization and implementation of measures to ensure (esp. industrial) safety; **safety factor** the ratio of total strength to working strength for a material or structure; **safety film** PHOTOGRAPHY film with a non-flammable or slow-burning base; **safety first** a maxim or slogan emphasizing the necessity of taking precautions to avoid accidents; **safety-firster** a person unwilling to take risks; **safety fuse** (*a*) a fuse (FUSE *noun*[1]) which can be ignited at a safe distance from the charge; (*b*) an electrical fuse (FUSE *noun*[2]); **safety glass** toughened or laminated glass; ***safety island***: see ISLAND *noun*[1] 2b; **safety lamp** a miner's lamp in which the flame is protected so as not to ignite firedamp; ***safety man***: see sense 7a above; **safety match** a match which can be ignited only by striking on the specially prepared surface provided; **safety net**: used to prevent injury to an acrobat etc. in case of a fall from a height; *fig.* any means of protection against difficulty or loss; **safety officer** a person responsible for safety in a factory etc.; **safety paper**: specially prepared to guard against the counterfeiting of banknotes etc.; **safety play** (*a*) (BILLIARDS & SNOOKER etc.) play that aims to leave a position in which one's opponent is unable to score; (*b*) BRIDGE play that risks the loss of one trick in order to prevent the loss of a greater number; †**safety plug** (*a*) = ***fusible plug***; (*b*) an electrical fuse; **safety razor** a razor with a guard close to the blade to reduce the risk of cutting the skin; **safety rod** NUCLEAR ENGINEERING a rod of a neutron-absorbing material which can be inserted into a reactor in an emergency to slow or stop the reaction; **safety valve** (*a*) a valve in a steam boiler which automatically opens to release steam when the pressure exceeds a pre-set amount; (*b*) *fig.* a means of giving harmless vent to excitement, energy, etc.; **safety vent** an outlet affording safety; *spec.* = sense 8 above; **safety zone** *US* an area of a road marked off for pedestrians to wait in safety for buses etc.

safety /ˈseɪfti/ *verb trans.* Orig. & chiefly *US*. E20.

[from the noun.]

Make safe; *spec.* (*a*) secure (an aircraft component, esp. a nut) against loosening due to vibration; (*b*) apply the safety-bolt or safety-catch of (a gun etc.).

safety pin /ˈseɪfti pɪn/ *noun phr.* & *verb*. Also (the usual form as verb) **safety-pin**. M19.

[from SAFETY *noun* + PIN *noun*[1], *verb*.]

▶ **A** *noun*. **1** A pin for fastening clothing, bent back on itself so as to form a spring, and with a guard covering the point when closed to prevent its accidental unfastening. M19.

2 A pin used for fastening, locking, or securing some part of a machine. L19.

▶ **B** *verb trans.* Infl. **-nn-**. Pin *on* or attach with a safety pin. Also, attach a safety pin or safety pins to. E20.

†**saffer** *noun* var. of ZAFFRE.

saffian /ˈsafɪən/ *noun*. L16.

[Russian *saf'yan* alt. of Romanian *saftian* ult. from Persian *saktiyān*.]

Leather made from goatskin or sheepskin tanned with sumac and dyed in bright colours; an example of this. Also ***saffian leather***.

safflower /ˈsaflaʊə/ *noun*. LME.

[Dutch *saffloer* or German *Saflor* from Old French *saffleur* from Italian †*saffiore* var. of *asfiore*, *asfrole*, *zaffrole* from Arab. *asfar* a yellow plant: infl. by assoc. with *saffron* and *flower*.]

1 The dried florets of *Carthamus tinctorius* (see below); a red dye produced from these, used in rouge etc. LME.

2 A plant of the composite family, *Carthamus tinctorius*, with orange-yellow thistle-like flower-heads, cultivated in Egypt, Asia, etc., for the dye obtained from its florets and for the oil from its seeds, used esp. in cooking. L17.

saffraan /səˈfrɑːn/ *noun*. Also **saffran**. E19.

[Afrikaans from Dutch saffron-yellow, formed as SAFFRON *noun*.]

A large southern African evergreen tree, *Cassine crocea*, of the spindle tree family, with deep yellow inner bark and clusters of greenish flowers followed by white plum-shaped fruit; the hard, light brown wood of this tree.

saffranon /ˈsafrənən/ *noun*. M18.

[App. alt. of French *safran* or its source medieval Latin *safranum* SAFFRON *noun*.]

= SAFFLOWER 1.

saffron /ˈsafrən/ *noun* & *adjective*. ME.

[Old & mod. French *safran* from medieval Latin *safranum* from Arab. *za'farān*.]

▶ **A** *noun*. **1** The dried stigmas of an autumn-flowering crocus, *Crocus sativus*, used for giving an orange-yellow colour to food and as a flavouring; (more fully ***saffron crocus***) this plant. ME. ▸**b** With specifying word: any of several similar yellow colourings or plants yielding them; any of several plants resembling the saffron crocus in appearance. M16.

2 The orange-yellow colour imparted by saffron. LME.

3 CHEMISTRY. = CROCUS *noun*[1] 3. *obsolete* exc. *Hist.* L17.

4 = ***clouded yellow*** s.v. CLOUD *verb* 3. Now *rare*. E19.

1b bastard saffron safflower. **Indian saffron** turmeric. ***meadow saffron***: see MEADOW *noun*.

▶ **B** *adjective*. Of an orange-yellow colour. LME.

Comb. & special collocations: **saffron bun**: made with saffron; **saffron butterfly** (now *rare*) = sense A.4 above; ***saffron crocus***: see sense A.1 above; **saffron cake**: made with saffron; **saffron milk cap** an edible orange-coloured funnel-shaped agaric (mushroom), *Lactarius deliciosus*; **saffron plum** a small tree of the W. Indies and Florida, *Bumelia angustifolia* (family Sapotaceae), having a sweet edible yellow fruit. **saffron rice**: cooked with saffron; **saffron-thistle** = SAFFLOWER 2; **saffron-wood** = SAFFRAAN; **saffron-yellow** (of) an orange-yellow colour.

■ **saffrony** *adjective* (*rare*) resembling saffron M17.

saffron /ˈsafrən/ *verb trans. rare*. ME.

[from the noun.]

Season or dye with saffron; give an orange-yellow colour to.

safranine /ˈsafrəniːn/ *noun*. Also **-in** /-ɪn/. M19.

[French, formed as SAFFRON *noun* + -INE[5].]

CHEMISTRY. †**1** The yellow colouring matter in saffron. Only in M19.

2 A coal tar derivative which dyes yellowish red; any of a related class of chiefly red azine dyes obtained typically by coupling of diazotized aromatic monoamines with aromatic diamines. L19.

safrole /ˈsafrəʊl/ *noun*. M19.

[from SAS)SAFR(AS + -OLE[2].]

CHEMISTRY. A liquid bicyclic aromatic ether, $C_{10}H_{10}O_2$, which occurs in oil of sassafras and some other essential oils.

sag /sag/ *noun*[1]. L16.

[from the verb.]

1 NAUTICAL. A movement or tendency to leeward. L16.

2 An act of sagging; a sinking, a subsidence; a place where a surface has subsided, a depression. E18. ▸**b** A temporary commercial decline, a temporary slump in business activity, a temporary fall in profits or prices. L19.

3 The dip below the horizontal line of a rope, wire, etc. supported at two points; the perpendicular distance from its lowest point to the straight line between the points of support. M19.

Comb.: **Sagbag** (proprietary name for) a bean-bag chair; **sag pond**: whose basin is the result of subsidence associated with a fault; **sag wagon** *slang* a van that follows a cycle race and picks up exhausted riders.

sag *noun*[2] var. of SEDGE.

sag *noun*[3] var. of SAAG.

sag /sag/ *verb*. Infl. **-gg-**. LME.

[Middle & mod. Low German *sacken* = Dutch *zakken* in same sense.]

1 *verb intrans.* **a** Sink or subside gradually under weight or pressure; droop, hang *down* loosely or unevenly. LME. ▸**b** Of a rope, ship, etc., supported at two points: bend or curve downwards in the middle as a result of weight or pressure. L18. ▸**c** Bulge (*out*). Chiefly *dial.* M19.

2 *verb intrans.* Decline, esp. temporarily, to a lower level, through lack of strength or effort; weaken, diminish. LME. ▸**b** Show a temporary commercial decline, (of business activity) experience a temporary slump; (of profits or prices) fall temporarily. Also foll. by *away*, *down*. LME.

3 *verb intrans.* Drag oneself along wearily or feebly. L16.

4 *verb intrans.* NAUTICAL. Of a vessel: drift, be carried off course. Chiefly in ***sag to leeward***. M17.

5 *verb trans.* Cause to bend downwards in the middle. **M18.**

> 📖 **1a** G. GREENE The skin of his face . . sagged and hung in pouches. R. FRAME The trees are heavy with apples . . , sagging with them. G. KEILLOR He sagged in Don's arms and went limp. P. FARMER His jeans . . sagged off his buttocks. **b** L. DEIGHTON Posts between which telegraph wire sagged low enough . . to decapitate a horseman. B. BAINBRIDGE Their mattress sagged in the middle. **2** F. KING Her voice, previously sagging, had . . tautened and sharpened. *New York Times* After . . trading opened . . the dollar sagged to another record low. *International Business Week* Productivity . . begins to sag as the economy slows.

saga /ˈseɪɡə/ *noun*¹. *rare.* **L16.**
[Latin.]
A witch.

saga /ˈsɑːɡə/ *noun*². **E18.**
[Old Norse (Icelandic) = SAW *noun*².]
1 a An Old Norse prose narrative of Iceland or Norway, *esp.* one which recounts the traditional history of Icelandic families or of the kings of Norway. **E18.** ▸**b** *transf.* A narrative regarded as having the traditional characteristics of the Icelandic sagas; a story of heroic achievement. Also, a novel or series of novels recounting the history of a family through several generations; *loosely* a long and complicated account of a series of events. **M19.**
2 [Partly after German *Sage*.] A story which has been handed down by oral tradition and added to or adapted in the course of time; historical or heroic legend. **M19.**

> 📖 **1b** E. HUXLEY The saga of their trek on foot . . is a fantastic epic. *Dance* This singular saga of dance history. **2** GEO. ELIOT The old German saga of the Venusberg. R. W. CHAMBERS How much of this is history, and how much saga, it is not easy to say.

Comb.: **saga boy** *W. Indies* a well-dressed lounger, a playboy; **saga-man** [Old Norse *sǫgu-maðr*] a narrator of sagas; the hero of a saga.

saga *noun*³ pl. of SAGUM.

sagaciate /səˈɡeɪʃɪeɪt/ *verb intrans. US dial.* **M19.**
[App. joc. from SAGACI(OUS + -ATE³.]
Thrive, prosper.

sagacious /səˈɡeɪʃəs/ *adjective.* **E17.**
[from Latin *sagac-*, *sagax* + -IOUS.]
1 Acute in perception, esp. of smell. (Foll. by *of*.) Now *rare* or *obsolete*. **E17.**
2 Gifted with acute mental discernment; able to make good judgements, penetrating, shrewd. **M17.** ▸**b** Resulting from or exhibiting mental acuteness; characterized by sagacity. **M19.**
3 Of an animal: intelligent. **M18.**
■ **sagaciously** *adverb* **M17.** **sagaciousness** *noun* **L17.**

sagacity /səˈɡasɪti/ *noun.* **L15.**
[French *sagacité* or Latin *sagacitas*, formed as prec.: see -ACITY.]
1 Acuteness of mental discernment; soundness of judgement, shrewdness. **L15.** ▸**b** A sagacious observation. Usu. in *pl.* **M19.**
2 Exceptional intelligence in an animal; skill in adaptation. **E16.**
†**3** Acute sense of smell. **E17–L18.**

> 📖 **1** C. C. TRENCH His reputation for financial sagacity . . gave his views great weight. **2** W. IRVING The sagacity of the beaver in cutting down trees.

sagakomi /səˈɡakəmi/ *noun. N. Amer.* **E18.**
[Ojibwa *sakākkomin*.]
The bearberry, *Arctostaphylos uva-ursi*; the leaves of this plant, used with, or as a substitute for, tobacco.

sagamité /saɡɑːmiːˈteɪ/ *noun.* **M17.**
[French, repr. Cree *kisa:kamite:w* lit. 'it is a hot liquid'.]
Gruel or porridge made from coarse hominy.

sagamore /ˈsaɡəmɔː/ *noun.* **E17.**
[Eastern Abnaki *sàkəma*.]
= SACHEM *noun* 1.

Sagan /ˈseɪɡ(ə)n/ *noun.* **E17.**
[Late use of Hebrew *sāgān* from Akkadian *šaknu* governor. In the Bible the Hebrew word denotes a civil governor.]
JEWISH ANTIQUITIES. The deputy of the Jewish high priest; the captain of the Temple.

saganaki /saɡəˈnɑːki/ *noun.* **M20.**
[mod. Greek = small two-handled frying-pan (traditionally used to prepare the dish).]
A Greek dish consisting of breaded or floured cheese fried in butter, often with lemon juice, served as an appetizer.

sagapenum /saɡəˈpiːnəm/ *noun.* Formerly Anglicized as †**sagapene**. **M16.**
[Late Latin from Greek *sagapēnon*.]
An oleoresin from a kind of giant fennel, *Ferula persica*, formerly used esp. to stimulate menstruation and relieve spasms of smooth muscles. Also, the plant from which this is obtained.

sagaris /ˈsaɡ(ə)rɪs/ *noun.* **E17.**
[Greek, of unkn. origin.]
ANTIQUITIES. A single-edged battleaxe used by Scythians, Persians, Amazons, etc.

sagathy /ˈsaɡəθi/ *noun & adjective. obsolete* exc. *Hist.* **E18.**
[French *sagatis*, Spanish *sagatí*, ult. origin unkn.]
(Made of) a worsted fabric orig. woven in Amiens.

sagbend /ˈsaɡbɛnd/ *noun.* **M20.**
[from SAG *noun*¹ + BEND *noun*³.]
The curved stretch of pipe below the point of inflection in an S-shaped length of pipeline being lowered on to the seabed from a barge. Cf. OVERBEND *noun*.

sage /seɪdʒ/ *noun*¹. **ME.**
[Old & mod. French *sauge* from Latin *salvia* 'the healing plant', from *salvus* SAFE *adjective*.]
1 Any plant of the genus *Salvia*, of the labiate family; spec. *S. officinalis*, a greyish-leaved aromatic culinary herb; the leaves of this plant, used as a flavouring. **ME.** ▸**b** With specifying word: any of various plants of other genera and families resembling sage, esp. in having grey hoary leaves. **LME.**
2 The colour of sage, grey-green. **L18.**
3 = *sagebrush* below. **E19.**
1b *bitter sage*: see BITTER *adjective*. **black sage** a labiate plant of California, *Trichostema lanatum*. *JERUSALEM sage.* **white sage** any of several hoary shrubby plants of the western US, esp. *Krascheninnikovia lanata*, of the goosefoot family, and a type of sagebrush, *Artemisia ludoviciana*. **wood sage**: see WOOD *noun*¹ & *adjective*¹.
Phrases: **sage and onion (stuffing)** a stuffing made chiefly of sage and onions, used with poultry, pork, etc.
Comb.: **sagebrush** (an area covered by) any of several downy artemisias, esp. *Artemisia tridentata*, freq. abundant in arid regions of western N. America; *Sagebrush State*, (a popular name for) Nevada; **sagebush** = *sagebrush* above; **sage cheese** = *sage Derby* below; **sage cock** = *sage grouse* below; **sage Derby** a cheese flavoured and mottled by an infusion of leaves of sage, traditionally made in Derbyshire; **sage-green** *noun & adjective* (of) a shade of dull greyish green resembling that of the foliage of sage, *Salvia officinalis*; **sage grouse** a large grouse, *Centrocercus urophasianus*, of the sagebrush regions of western N. America, noted for the courtship display in which the male fans its tail and inflates air sacs on its breast; **sage hare** = *sage rabbit* below; **sage hen** = *sage grouse* above; **sage rabbit** a small cottontail, *Sylvilagus nuttalli*, of western N. America; **sage sparrow** a grey-headed sparrow, *Amphispiza belli* of the family Emberizidae, of western N. America; **sage tea** an infusion of leaves of sage, used as a stomachic and slight stimulant; **sage thrasher** a streaked mockingbird, *Oreoscoptes montanus*, of western N. America; **sage-wood** a southern African buddleia, *Buddleja salviifolia* (family Loganiaceae), with leaves like those of sage and racemes of white or purple flowers; the hard, heavy wood of this tree.
■ **sagey** *adjective* (*rare*) pertaining to or of the nature of sage **M18.**

sage /seɪdʒ/ *noun*². **LME.**
[from SAGE *adjective*¹.]
A person of profound wisdom and discretion, a wise person; *esp.* any of those men of ancient history or legend traditionally regarded as the wisest of humankind.
Seven Sages: see SEVEN *adjective*.
■ **sageship** *noun* (*rare*) the quality of being a sage; (with possess. adjective, as *his sageship* etc.) a title of respect given to a sage: **M19.**

SAGE /seɪdʒ/ *noun*³. Also **Sage**. **M20.**
[Acronym, from Semi-Automatic Ground Environment.]
MILITARY. An early warning and air defence control system covering the US and Canada.

sage /seɪdʒ/ *adjective*¹. **ME.**
[Old & mod. French from Proto-Gallo-Romance, from Latin *sapere* be wise.]
1 Of a person: wise, discreet, judicious, now esp. through experience. **ME.** ▸**b** Of advice, behaviour, etc.: characterized by profound wisdom; based on sound judgement. **M16.** ▸**c** Of an expression, bearing, etc.: exhibiting profound wisdom. Now freq. *iron.* **E19.**
†**2** Grave, dignified, solemn. **M16–M17.**

> 📖 **1b** P. G. WODEHOUSE The venerable old man was whispering sage counsel. **2** SHAKES. *Haml.* We should profane the service of the dead To sing sage requiem to her.

■ **sagely** *adverb* **LME.** **sageness** *noun* the quality of being sage; profound wisdom: **E16.**

sage /seɪdʒ/ *adjective*². **L18.**
[from SAGE *noun*¹.]
Of the colour of sage, of a grey-green colour.

sagene /ˈsaʒɛn/ *noun*¹. **M18.**
[Russian *sazhen'*.]
Hist. A unit of length formerly used in Russia, equal to 7 feet (2.13 m).

sagene /səˈdʒiːn/ *noun*². *rare.* **M19.**
[Latin from Greek *sagēnē*.]
A fishing net; *fig.* a network of railways etc.

saggar /ˈsaɡə/ *noun & verb.* Also **sagger**. **M18.**
[Prob. contr. of SAFEGUARD *noun*.]
▸**A** *noun.* A protective case of baked fireproof clay in which fragile ceramic wares are enclosed while being fired in a kiln; any case used to protect objects in a furnace. **M18.**
Comb.: **saggar clay**: from which saggars are made.
▸**B** *verb trans.* Place in or on a saggar. **M19.**

saggy /ˈsaɡi/ *adjective. colloq.* **M19.**
[from SAG *verb* + -Y¹.]
Apt to sag.
■ **sagginess** *noun* **M20.**

sagina /səˈdʒʌɪnə/ *noun.* **M20.**
[mod. Latin (see below), use as genus name of Latin *sagina*: see next.]
Any of various small low-growing plants constituting the genus *Sagina*, of the pink family, esp. *S. subulata* and *S. procumbens*, sometimes used instead of grass to form lawns. Also called *pearlwort*.

saginate /ˈsadʒɪneɪt/ *verb trans. rare.* **E17.**
[Latin *saginat-* pa. ppl stem of *saginare*, from *sagina* process or means of fattening: see -ATE³.]
Fatten (an animal) for food.
■ **sagiˈnation** *noun* **E17.**

sagitta /səˈdʒɪtə/, (*esp. in sense 1*) -ˈɡɪt-, (*esp. in sense 2*) ˈsadʒ-/ *noun.* **M16.**
[Latin, lit. 'an arrow'.]
1 (Usu. **S-**.) (The name of) a small constellation of the northern hemisphere, lying in the Milky Way north of Aquila; the Arrow. **M16.**
2 †**a** *GEOMETRY.* The versed sine of an arc. **E18–M19.** ▸**b** *GEOMETRY & OPTICS.* The line from the midpoint of a circular arc to the midpoint of its chord. **E20.**
3 *ARCHITECTURE.* The keystone of an arch. **E18.**
4 The middle horizontal stroke in the Greek letter ε. **M19.**

sagittal /ˈsadʒɪt(ə)l, səˈdʒɪ-/ *adjective.* **LME.**
[medieval Latin *sagittalis*, formed as prec.: see -AL¹.]
1 *ANATOMY & ZOOLOGY.* **a** Designating or pertaining to the convoluted suture on the top of the skull between the two parietal bones. Formerly also, designating or pertaining to other arrow-shaped bone sutures and processes. **LME.** ▸**b** Designating, pertaining to, or lying in a plane parallel to the sagittal suture, esp. that which divides the body in the midline into right and left halves. **M19.**
2 Pertaining to or resembling an arrow or an arrowhead. *rare.* **M17.**
3 *OPTICS.* Pertaining to or designating the equatorial plane of an astigmatic system. **E20.**
Special collocations: **sagittal crest** *ZOOLOGY* a bony ridge on the top of the skull to which the jaw muscles are attached in many mammals, esp. carnivores, apes, etc. **sagittal focal line**, **sagittal focus** *OPTICS* the focus formed by rays outside the sagittal plane. **sagittal ray** *OPTICS* a ray in the sagittal plane. **sagittal section** (*ANATOMY & ZOOLOGY*) a section taken in the sagittal plane.
■ **sagittally** *adverb* (*ANATOMY*) in a sagittal plane **L19.**

Sagittarian /sadʒɪˈtɛːrɪən/ *noun & adjective.* **E20.**
[from SAGITTARI(US + -AN.]
ASTROLOGY. ▸**A** *noun.* A person born under the sign Sagittarius. **E20.**
▸**B** *adjective.* Of or pertaining to Sagittarius; born under Sagittarius. **E20.**

Sagittarius /sadʒɪˈtɛːrɪəs/ *noun.* **OE.**
[Latin = archer, Sagittarius, formed as SAGITTA: see -ARY¹.]
1 (The name of) a constellation on the ecliptic in the southern hemisphere, between Scorpius and Capricorn; *ASTROLOGY* (the name of) the ninth zodiacal sign, usu. associated with the period 22 November to 21 December (see note s.v. ZODIAC); the Archer. **OE.** ▸**b** *ASTROLOGY.* = SAGITTARIAN *noun.* **M20.**
2 *HERALDRY.* A charge representing an archer, esp. in the form of a centaur, with a drawn bow. **E17.**

sagittary /ˈsadʒɪtəri/ *noun.* **LME.**
[Latin *sagittarius* pertaining to arrows, formed as SAGITTA: see -ARY¹.]
1 = SAGITTARIUS 1. Now *rare.* **LME.**
2 A centaur; *spec.* the one which, according to medieval romance, fought in the Trojan army against the Greeks. **E16.**
3 A representation of a centaur or mounted archer; *spec.* in *HERALDRY*, = SAGITTARIUS 2. **E17.**
4 An archer. *arch.* **M19.**

sagittate /ˈsadʒɪteɪt/ *adjective.* **M18.**
[formed as SAGITTA + -ATE².]
BOTANY & ZOOLOGY. Shaped like an arrowhead.
■ **sagittated** *adjective* (now *rare*) **M18.**

sagittiform /saˈdʒɪtɪfɔːm/ *adjective. rare.* **L19.**
[mod. Latin *saggitiformis*, formed as SAGITTA: see -FORM.]
Having the shape of an arrow or arrowhead.

sago /ˈseɪɡəʊ/ *noun.* Pl. **-os**. **M16.**
[Malay *sagu* (orig. through Portuguese).]
The starch prepared from the pith of several palms and cycads, used as an article of food; an example of this; (more fully *sago palm*) any of the palms yielding this starch, esp. *Metroxylon sagu* and *M. rumphii*, of swamps in SE Asia.
Comb.: **sago-grass** an Australian forage-grass, *Paspalidium globoideum*; **sago pudding** a pudding made by boiling sago in

milk; **sago spleen** MEDICINE (now *rare*) amyloid degeneration of the Malpighian corpuscles of the spleen, resembling boiled sago.

sagoin /sə'gɔɪn/ *noun*. E17.
[French †*sagoin*, *sagouin* from Portuguese *saguim*, *sagui* from Tupi *saui*: cf. SAKI *noun*[1].]
A marmoset.

saguaro /sə'gwɑːrəʊ, sə'wɑːrəʊ/ *noun*. Also **sahuaro**. Pl. **-os**. M19.
[Mexican Spanish, prob. from Uto-Aztecan.]
A tree-sized branching cactus, *Carnegiea gigantea*, found in desert regions of Mexico and the south-western US.

sagum /'seɪgəm/ *noun*. Pl. **-ga** /-gə/. E18.
[Latin (also *sagus* = late Greek *sagos*), of Gaulish origin.]
ANTIQUITIES. A Roman military cloak; a woollen cloak worn by the ancient Gauls, Germans, and Spaniards.

sagwire /'sagwʌɪə/ *noun*. L17.
[App. from Portuguese *sagueiro*, from *sagu* SAGO.]
The sugar-palm, *Arenga saccharifera*, of Indonesia and Malaysia; the palm wine obtained from this tree.

sah /sɑː/ *noun*. L19.
[Repr. a pronunc.]
In representations of black speech: sir.

sa-ha /'sɑːhɑː/ *interjection*. E17.
[Perh. rel. to SEE-HO, SOHO *interjection*.]
A cry used in coursing.

Sahaptian /sə'haptɪən/ *noun & adjective*. M20.
[from prec. + -AN.]
(Of) the language family consisting (chiefly) of Nez Percé and Sahaptin.

Sahaptin /sə'haptɪn/ *noun & adjective*. Also **Shahaptan** /ʃə'haptan/. M19.
[Salish *S'aptnx*, of unkn. origin.]
▶ **A** *noun*. **1** Orig., a Nez Percé; a member of any of several groupings of the Nez Percé and other linguistically related peoples. Now, a member of any of various closely related N. American Indian peoples of the Columbia River basin. M19.
2 The language or language group of any of these peoples. M19.
▶ **B** *adjective*. Of or pertaining to (the language of) any of these peoples. M19.

Sahara /sə'hɑːrə/ *noun*. E17.
[Arab. *ṣaḥrā'*, pl. *ṣaḥārā* desert.]
1 (The name of) the great desert extending across northern Africa. Also ***Sahara Desert***. E17. ▸**b** *transf.* & *fig.* A desert, a wilderness. M19.
2 A shade of brown or yellow. Freq. *attrib.* E20.

📖 **1b** J. WAINWRIGHT It was . . as desolate as a moonscape; a Sahara of snow.

Saharan /sə'hɑːrən/ *adjective & noun*. M19.
[from prec. + -AN.]
▶ **A** *adjective*. Pertaining to or characteristic of the Sahara; of the language Saharan. M19.
▶ **B** *noun*. **1** One of the languages of the eastern Sahara. M20.
2 A member of a people living in the Sahara; *spec.* one of the former Spanish Sahara on the Atlantic coast. L20.

Saharaui, **Saharwi** *nouns & adjectives* vars. of SAHRAWI.

sahel /sə'hɛl/ *noun*. *rare*. E20.
[The *Sahel* in W. Africa: see next.]
A semi-arid region occurring as a transitional area between desert and savannah; terrain characteristic of such a region.

Sahelian /sə'hiːlɪən/ *adjective*. L20.
[from *Sahel* (see below) + -IAN.]
Of, pertaining to, or designating the Sahel, a belt of land in W. Africa south of the Sahara, comprising parts of Senegal, Mauritania, Mali, Niger, and Chad and consisting mostly of savannah.

sahib /'sɑː(h)ɪb, sɑːb/ *noun*. *Anglo-Indian*. Also **saab** /sɑːb/. L17.
[Urdu, through Persian from Arab. *ṣāḥib* friend, lord, master.]
1 An Englishman or other European as addressed or spoken of by Indians. Also as a title affixed to a person's name or office. L17.
2 *transf.* A gentleman; a person considered socially acceptable. E20.
1 MEMSAHIB. **2** ***miss sahib***: see MISS *noun*[2]. ***pukka sahib***: see PUKKA *adjective* 3.
Comb.: **sahib-log** [Urdu *log* people] Europeans in India collectively.
■ **sahiba** *noun* mistress, lady M19. **sahibdom** *noun* = SAHIBHOOD E20. **sahibhood** *noun* the quality or condition of being a sahib M20.

Sahidic /sə'hɪdɪk/ *noun & adjective*. M19.
[from Arab. *ṣa'īdī* upper + -IC.]
(Of or pertaining to) the dialect of Coptic spoken in Thebes and Upper Egypt, in which a version of the Bible is extant.

sahitya /'sɑːhɪtjə/ *noun*. M20.
[Sanskrit *sāhitya* combination, composition.]
The text of an Indian song accompanying a dance.

Sahiwal /'sɑːhɪvɑːl, -wɑːl/ *noun*. E20.
[The name of a town in the central Punjab, Pakistan.]
(An animal of) a breed of cattle, originally native to Pakistan but now used in tropical regions elsewhere, distinguished by small horns and a hump on the back of the neck.

Sahli /'sɑːli/ *noun*. E20.
[Hermann *Sahli* (1856–1933), Swiss physician.]
MEDICINE. Used *attrib.* and in *possess.* with ref. to a method for determining the haemoglobin content of the blood by converting a sample into acid haematin and determining it colorimetrically.

Saho /'sɑːhəʊ/ *noun & adjective*. Also (earlier) †**Shiho**, †**Shoho**. L18.
[Saho, or Amharic *šoho*, from Cushitic.]
▶ **A** *noun*. Pl. same.
1 A member of a Cushitic-speaking people of Eritrea in Ethiopia. L18.
2 The language or dialect of this people. L19.
▶ **B** *attrib.* or as *adjective*. Of or pertaining to the Saho or their language. M19.

Sahrawi /sə'rɑːwi/ *noun & adjective*. Also **Saharaui** /sahə'raʊi/, **Saharwi** /sə'hɑːwi/. L20.
[Arab. *ṣaḥrāwī* (whence Spanish *saharaui*) of the desert, formed as SAHARA: see -I[2].]
▶ **A** *noun*. A native or inhabitant of the western (formerly Spanish) Sahara, a Saharan. L20.
▶ **B** *adjective*. Of or pertaining to the Sahrawis. L20.

sahuaro *noun* var. of SAGUARO.

sai /sʌɪ/ *noun*[1]. L18.
[French *saï* from Portuguese from Tupi *sai*.]
A capuchin monkey, *esp.* the weeper capuchin.

sai /sʌɪ/ *noun*[2]. Pl. same. L20.
[Japanese, from Okinawa dial.]
A dagger of Okinawan origin characterized by two sharp prongs curving outward from the hilt, often used as one of a pair.

saic /'seɪɪk/ *noun*. M17.
[French *saïque*, from Turkish *şayka*.]
A kind of sailing boat resembling a ketch, formerly common in the eastern Mediterranean and the Black Sea.

said /sɛd/ *adjective*. ME.
[pa. pple of SAY *verb*[1].]
1 Already named or mentioned. ME.
†**2** Spoken, uttered; recited, not sung. Chiefly in ***said saw***, ***old said saw***, a traditional proverb. L15–E19.

said *verb pa. t.* & *pple* of SAY *verb*[1].

saiga /'seɪgə, 'sʌɪgə/ *noun*. E19.
[Russian, prob. from a Finnic lang. (cf. Finnish *saija*, Estonian *sai*).]
A central Asian gazelle, *Saiga tartarica*, occurring on the cold steppe, and distinguished by an inflated snout. Also ***saiga antelope***.

Saigonese /sʌɪgɒ'niːz/ *noun*. Pl. same. M20.
[from *Saigon* (see below) + -ESE.]
Hist. A native or inhabitant of Saigon (now Ho Chi Minh City), formerly the capital of S. Vietnam.

sail /seɪl/ *noun*[1].
[Old English *seg(e)l* = Old Frisian *seil*, Old Saxon *segel* (Dutch *zeil*), Old High German *segal* (German *Segel*), Old Norse *segl*, from Germanic.]
1 A shaped piece of material (orig. canvas, now usu. nylon etc.) extended on the rigging of a vessel so as to catch the wind and cause it to propel the vessel through the water. Also *occas.*, a similar device for propelling a wind-driven vehicle over land. OE. ▸**b** *transf.* A thing resembling a sail in shape or function; *spec.* (***a***) a wind-catching apparatus, now usu. a set of boards, attached to each arm of a windmill; (***b***) the wing of a bird; †(***c***) AERONAUTICS a flat aerodynamically structured part of a balloon etc. ME.
2 The sails of a vessel etc. collectively. LME.
3 a *collect. sing.* & †in *pl.* Sailing vessels. Usu. preceded by a numeral. LME. ▸**b** A sailing vessel, esp. as discerned from its sails. E16.
4 ZOOLOGY. A part of a marine animal that resembles a sail, or is imagined to act as a sail, as (***a***) the dorsal fin of a sailfish; (***b***) either of the two large tentacles of a paper nautilus; (***c***) the float of a Portuguese man-of-war. E19.
5 A sheet of canvas, nylon, etc. for covering the load in a wagon. Chiefly *S. Afr.* M19.
6 In *pl.* (treated as *sing.*). (A nickname for) a ship's sailmaker. *Nautical slang.* M19.
7 (Usu. **S-**.) In *pl. The* constellation Vela. M19.
8 The conning tower of a submarine. M20.

📖 **1** ***head-sail***, ***mainsail***, ***mizzen-sail***, ***topsail***, etc. **2** ***hoist sail***, ***lower sail***, etc. **3a** H. COX The . . navy comprised . . twenty-seven sail.

Phrases: **at full sail** (***a***) (sailing) with a strong favourable wind or at full speed; (***b***) *fig.* making easy rapid progress. ***carry sail***: see CARRY *verb*. ***come with a wet sail***: see WET *adjective*. ***crowd of sail***: see CROWD *noun*[2]. ***crowd on sail***, ***crowd sail***: see CROWD *verb*[1]. ***flowing sail***: see FLOWING *ppl adjective*. **full sail** (***a***) (the condition of a ship with) sails filled or distended by the wind; (***b***) = ***at full sail*** above. ***make sail***: see MAKE *verb*. ***pack on all sail***: see PACK *verb*[1]. ***press of sail***: see PRESS *noun*[1]. ***set sail***: see SET *verb*[1]. ***SHORTEN sail(s)*** **take in sail** (***a***) furl the sail or sails of a vessel; (***b***) *fig.* moderate one's ambitions. ***take the wind out of a person's sails***: see WIND *noun*[1]. **under sail** having the sails set.
Comb.: **sail-arm** a radiating arm of a windmill to which a sail is attached; **sailboard** *noun & verb* (orig. *US*) (***a***) *noun* a board with a mast and sail, used in windsurfing; (***b***) *verb intrans.* ride on a sailboard; **sailboarder** a windsurfer; **sail-boat** (chiefly *N. Amer.*) a sailing boat; **sailfish** (***a***) a billfish, *Istiophorus platypterus*, with a very tall and long dorsal fin, found in warm seas worldwide; (***b***) the basking shark, which has a tall dorsal fin; **sail-fluke** a European edible flatfish, *Lepidorhombus whiffiagonis*, of the turbot family; also called *whiff*; **sail-flying** = SAILPLANING *noun*; **sail loft** a large room in which sails are made; **sailmaker** a person who makes, repairs, or alters sails; **sail-needle** a large needle used in sewing canvas; **sail plan** a scale diagram of the masts, spars, rigging, and sails of a sailing vessel; **sailsman** a sailor; a person who manages a sailing boat; **sail wing** the sail of a hang glider with its framework; **sailyard** (***a***) NAUTICAL any of the yards or spars on which sails are spread; †(***b***) any of the radiating beams bearing the sails of a windmill.
■ **sailage** *noun* †(***a***) the speed of a ship under sail; (***b***) the sails of a ship collectively: M17. **sailed** *adjective* (of a vessel) fitted with sails, esp. of a specified kind L16. **sailless** /-l-l-/ *adjective* (***a***) (of a boat, rigging, etc.) having no sails; (***b***) (of the sea) devoid of ships etc.: E17.

sail /seɪl/ *noun*[2]. ME.
[Prob. from SAIL *verb*[2].]
1 ARCHITECTURE. A projecting piece above or below a window. ME.
2 An amount of projection from a surface. E17.

sail /seɪl/ *noun*[3]. E16.
[from SAIL *verb*[1].]
1 An act of sailing; a voyage or trip in a sailing vessel. Earliest in *comb.* E16. ▸**b** *transf.* A ride in a cart, wagon, etc. *Scot. & Anglo-Irish.* M19.
†**2** A number (of ships) sailing. *rare* (Shakes.). Only in E17.
3 Sailing qualities; speed in sailing. Long *rare* or *obsolete*. E17.

📖 **1** W. IRVING We . . had a magnificent sail . . down Lake Champlain. **2** SHAKES. *Per.* We have descried . . A portly sail of ships make hitherward.

sail /seɪl/ *verb*[1].
[Old English *segl(i)an* from Germanic.]
▶ **I** *verb intrans.* **1** Of a person: travel on water in a vessel propelled by means of sails or engine-power; navigate a vessel in a specified direction. OE.
2 Of a vessel: move or travel on water by means of sails or engine-power. ME.
3 Of a person or vessel: begin or resume a journey by water; set sail. ME.
4 Glide over water or through the sky, either driven by the wind or with no visible effort. ME.
5 Move in a stately or dignified manner, suggestive of that of a ship under sail. Also, move or pass rapidly or smoothly. E19.

📖 **4** DRYDEN Swans that sail along the Silver Flood. BYRON The high moon sails upon her beauteous way. **5** C. EGLETON He sailed through Immigration and collected his suitcases. S. TROTT The first . . miles of the . . Marathon were terrific. I sailed along. K. MOORE Mrs Baxter sailed into the room like a duchess.

▶ **II** *verb trans.* **6** Sail over, navigate, (a sea, river, etc.). Formerly also, sail on (a course, voyage, etc.). LME.
7 a Navigate (a ship or other vessel). LME. ▸**b** Set afloat and manoeuvre (a toy boat). M19.
8 Glide through (the air). E18.
9 Send (an object) sailing through the air; throw, propel. M20.

📖 **9** *Washington Post* He sailed his racquet into the stands, with no . . casualties.

Phrases: ***sail by the log***: see LOG *noun*[1]. **sail in** proceed boldly to action. **sail into** launch into, attack. ***sail off into the sunset***: see SUNSET *noun* 1.
■ **sailable** *adjective* (now *rare*) (of a ship, river, etc.) able to be sailed or navigated M16. **sailing** *adjective* †(***a***) spreading out like a full sail; (***b***) that travels on water by means of sails: LME.

sail /seɪl/ *verb*[2] *intrans.* ME.
[Old French *saillir* from Latin *salire* leap.]
†**1** Dance. Only in ME.
2 ARCHITECTURE. Project from a surface. Now only as ***sailing ppl adjective***. LME.
2 sailing course a projecting course, esp. in the upper part of a lighthouse or other tall building.

sailab /'sʌɪlɑːb/ *noun*. E20.
[Urdu from Persian *saylāb* torrent, from Arab. *sayl* flood, torrent + Persian *'āb* water.]
A method of cultivation used in the Indus basin in Pakistan and northern India in which the land is irrigated by flood-water from the rivers.

sailcloth /ˈseɪlklɒθ/ *noun*. ME.
[from SAIL *noun*[1] + CLOTH *noun*.]
†**1** A piece of cloth used as part of a sail (on a ship or windmill). ME–L19.
2 a Canvas or other fabric used for sails. E17. ▸**b** A fabric like thin canvas used for dresses, other garments, upholstery, etc. L19.

sailer /ˈseɪlə/ *noun*. LME.
[from SAIL *verb*[1] + -ER[1].]
†**1** A person who sails; a sailor. LME–E17.
2 A sailing vessel, *esp.* one that sails in a specified way. LME.
3 BASEBALL. A fast pitched ball that sails through the air. M20.

> **2** DEFOE A very strong . . ship, and a pretty good sailer.

sailing /ˈseɪlɪŋ/ *noun*[1]. OE.
[from SAIL *verb*[1] + -ING[1].]
1 The action of sailing in or directing the course of a vessel. OE. ▸**b** A voyage. M16. ▸**c** (A) departure of a ship etc. from port. M18.
2 The speed or style of progression of a vessel. L17. ▸**b** *fig.* Progress or success in some activity. Usu. with specifying word. E19.

> **1** *New York Times* Windsurfing . . started life as a simple and inexpensive alternative to sailing. **b** *Sea Breezes* Made a number of sailings between the . . ports. **c** D. A. THOMAS Troops . . were disembarked and all sailings cancelled. **2b** A. MAUPIN The past was so much dead weight, excess baggage, to be cast overboard when the sailing got tough.

Phrases: ***plain sailing***: see PLAIN *adjective*[1] & *adverb*. ***plane sailing***: see PLANE *adjective*.
Attrib. & comb.: Esp. designating a vessel propelled by means of a sail or sails, as ***sailing boat***, ***sailing-dinghy***, ***sailing ship***, ***sailing vessel***, etc. Special combs., as **sailing-master** an officer responsible for the navigation of a vessel, esp. a yacht; **sailing orders**: given to the captain of a vessel regarding time of departure, destination, etc.; **sailing rule** a rule governing maritime traffic, intended to prevent the collision of ships etc.

sailing /ˈseɪlɪŋ/ *noun*[2]. M16.
[from SAIL *verb*[2] + -ING[1].]
ARCHITECTURE. The condition or fact of projecting from a surface; (a) projection.

sail-off /ˈseɪlɒf/ *noun*. Chiefly *N. Amer*. M20.
[from SAIL *verb*[1] + OFF *adverb*.]
An additional sailing contest to decide a tie. Also, a series of sailing contests or races held to decide a championship.

sailor /ˈseɪlə/ *noun*. M17.
[Alt. of SAILER: see -OR.]
1 A person occupied (esp. professionally) with navigation; a mariner, *esp.* one below the rank of officer. M17. ▸**b** With specifying word: a person considered in respect of his or her liability to seasickness. L18.
2 = SAILER 2. *arch*. M17.
3 †**a** The paper nautilus. L18–E19. ▸**b** A soldier beetle. M19.
4 *ellipt*. A sailor hat. L19.

> **1b** M. BRIDGMAN People who were bad sailors would not travel.

Phrases: ***roving sailor***: see ROVING *ppl adjective*. ***wandering sailor***: see WANDERING *ppl adjective*.
Comb.: **sailor collar** a collar cut deep and square at the back, tapering to a V-neck at the front; **sailor-fish** = ***sailfish*** s.v. SAIL *noun*[1]; **sailor hat** (*a*) a straw hat with a straight narrow brim and flat top; (*b*) a hat with a turned-up brim in imitation of a sailor's, worn by women and children; **sailor knot** = ***sailor's knot*** below; **sailor-man** (now chiefly *joc*.) a seaman; **sailor pants** *US* flared trousers such as those worn by sailors; **sailor's choice** *US* (*a*) any of various W. Atlantic grunts, esp. *Haemulon parrai*; (*b*) the pinfish, *Lagodon rhomboides*; **sailor's farewell** *Nautical slang* an abusive farewell (cf. ***soldier's farewell*** s.v. SOLDIER *noun*); **sailor's knot** (*a*) any of various kinds of knot used by sailors; (*b*) a kind of knot used in tying a neck-tie; **sailor's pleasure** *Nautical slang* (a time for) the overhauling of personal possessions, airing clothes, etc., esp. with a view to going ashore; **sailor suit**: resembling that of an ordinary seaman, worn mainly by small boys; **sailor-suited** *adjective* wearing a sailor suit; **sailor top** (*a*) a jerkin resembling a type worn by sailors; (*b*) a ladies' blouse of similar design;
■ **sailoress** *noun* a female sailor L19. **sailoring** *noun* the work of a sailor M19. **sailorizing** *noun* (*colloq*.) the pursuits or work of sailors L19. **sailorless** *adjective* having no sailors E19. **sailorly** *adjective* having the characteristics of or befitting a sailor M19. **sailorship** *noun* (*rare*) seamanship E19.

sailplane /ˈseɪlpleɪn/ *noun*. E20.
[from SAIL *noun*[1] + PLANE *noun*[4].]
An engineless aeroplane, a glider designed for sustained flight; an aeroplane with a small engine normally used only at take-off.
■ **sailplaning** *noun* the flying of sailplanes, gliding E20.

saimiri /sʌɪˈmɪəri/ *noun*. L18.
[Portuguese *saimirim*, from Tupi SAI *noun*[1] + *mirī* small.]
= ***squirrel monkey*** s.v. SQUIRREL *noun*.

sain /seɪn/ *verb*. Now *arch*. & *dial*.
[Old English *seġnian* = Old Saxon *segnon* (Dutch *zegenen*), Old High German *seganōn* (German *segnen* bless), Old Norse *signa*, from Latin *signare* sign (with the cross), from *signum* SIGN *noun*.]
1 *verb trans*. Make the sign of the cross on or over (a thing or person) in an act of consecration, blessing, exorcism, etc. OE. ▸**b** *verb intrans*. Make the sign of the cross. Long *obsolete* exc. *Scot*. LME.
2 *verb trans*. Bless. ME. ▸**b** [Infl. by Latin *sanare*.] Heal. M19.
3 *verb trans*. Secure (a person) by prayer or enchantment *from* evil influence. L17.

sainfoin /ˈseɪnfɔɪn, ˈsan-/ *noun*. Also **san-**. M17.
[French †*saintfoin* (mod. *sainfoin*) orig. lucerne, from mod. Latin *sanctum foenum* lit. 'holy hay', alt. of *sanum foenum* wholesome hay, based on Latin *herba medica* erron. alt. of *herba Medica* lit. 'Median grass', translating Greek *Mēdikē poa*.]
A leguminous plant, *Onobrychis viciifolia*, with pinnate leaves and bright pink flowers in dense racemes, formerly much grown for fodder.

saint /seɪnt, *before a name usu.* s(ə)nt/ *noun* & *adjective*. Before a name also **St**.
[Old English *sanct* from Latin *sanctus* use as noun of pa. pple of *sancire* confirm, ratify, consecrate; re-formed early in Middle English from Old French *seint(e)*, (also mod.) *saint(e)* holy, sacred, from Latin *sanctus*.]
▶ **A** *noun*. **1** ECCLESIASTICAL. (The title of) a holy person formally recognized by the Church as living with God in heaven after death and regarded as eligible for veneration by the faithful; *spec*. a canonized person. Abbreviation ***St***, ***S***. OE. ▸**b** A representation or image of a saint. LME. ▸**c** *transf*. In religions other than Christianity, a person who is an object of posthumous veneration. Formerly also, a pagan god or demigod. LME.
2 Any of the blessed dead in Heaven. OE.
3 a A member of God's chosen people; a member of the Church, a Christian; (chiefly in biblical use). Also, (a name used by themselves for) a member of any of certain Christian denominations or sects. ME. ▸**b** In biblical use, an angel. LME.
4 A very holy person; *colloq*. a very good or long-suffering person. ME. ▸**b** (A nickname for) a member of a morally or religiously zealous group; *spec*. (now *Hist*.) a member of a 19th-cent. party campaigning against slavery in England. L18.

> **2** H. E. MANNING Not . . canonised on earth, though they are saints in heaven. **3a** AV *Acts* 9:32 Peter . . came downe also to the Saints, which dwelt at Lydda. **4** B. RUBENS They were the family saints, suspected for their virtues. A. LIVINGSTONE Devoted himself to the poor and . . became known locally as a saint.

▶ **B** *adjective*. **1** Of a person (or angel): that is a saint. ME.
2 Of a thing: holy. Long *obsolete* exc. in dedications of churches. ME.

> **1** S. CISNEROS Saint Jude, patron saint of lost causes. *Life* The other depicts Saint Michael and his sword. **2** SHAKES. *Haml*. By Gis and by Saint Charity, Alack, and fie for shame! ***St Faith***, ***St Saviour***, etc.

Phrases, special collocations, & comb.: ***All Saints' (Day)***: see ALL *adjective* 2. **communion of saints** the unity and fellowship between all members of the Church, living or dead. ***Latter-day Saint***: see ***latter-day*** s.v. LATTER *adjective*. ***patron saint***: see PATRON *noun* 2. **St Andrew's cross** an X-shaped cross. **St Anthony cross**, **St Anthony's cross** = ***tau cross*** s.v. TAU *noun*[1] 2(b). **St Anthony's fire** (*a*) inflammation of the skin due to ergot poisoning; cf. ERGOTISM 1; †(*b*) erysipelas. ***St Barnaby's thistle***: see BARNABY 2. **St Bernard (dog)** (an animal of) a breed of very large dog orig. kept by the monks of the Hospice of the Great St Bernard pass (in the Alps between Switzerland and Italy) for rescuing travellers in distress. **St Bernard lily**, **St Bernard's lily** a plant of Continental Europe, *Anthericum liliago*, of the lily family, which bears racemes of white flowers. **St Brigid anemone**, **St Brigid's anemone** an anemone of a double or semi-double garden race of *Anemone coronaria*. **St Bruno lily**, **St Bruno's lily** a plant of the Alps, *Paradisea liliastrum*, which resembles St Bernard's lily but has larger flowers. **St Cross** (*obsolete* exc. in the dedication of churches etc.) the Cross on which Jesus died. ***St Cuthbert's beads***, ***St Cuthbert's duck***: see CUTHBERT 1, 2. **St Dabeoc's heath** an Irish heath, *Daboecia cantabrica*, which bears large purple flowers. ***St Distaff's day***: see DISTAFF *noun*. **St Elmo's fire** a corposant. **St George's cross** a red +-shaped cross on a white background. **St George's day** 23 April. **St George's mushroom** a white edible fungus, *Tricholoma gambosum*, which first appears about St George's day. **St Germain pear** a fine dessert pear. ***St Ignatius's bean***, ***St Ignatius' bean***: see IGNATIUS'S BEAN. **St John's bread** (the fruit of) the carob tree, *Ceratonia siliqua*. **St John's wort** any of various plants constituting the genus *Hypericum* (family Guttiferae), members of which commonly have pentamerous yellow flowers; *esp*. (more fully ***common St John's wort***) *H. perforatum*, said to come into flower on the feast of St John the Baptist, 24 June. **St Leger** a horse-race for three-year-olds run at Doncaster in northern England. **St Lucie cherry** [translating French *bois de Ste Lucie*] the mahaleb, *Prunus mahaleb*. **St Luke's summer** a period of fine weather occurring about the feast of St Luke, 18 October. **St Mark's fly** a dark fly, *Bibio marci*, which flies slowly with the legs hanging down and first appears around St Mark's Day (April 25th). **St Martin's summer** a period of fine weather occurring about Martinmas (11 November). ***St Monday***: see MONDAY *noun*. †**St Nicholas' clerk**, †**St Nicholas's clerk** (*a*) a poor scholar; (*b*) a highwayman, a thief. **St Patrick's cabbage** a saxifrage of shady places in southern and western Ireland, *Saxifraga spathularis* (one of the parents of London pride). **St Peter's fish** (*a*) [with allus. to *Matthew* 17:27] any of several fishes with a mark on each side near the pectoral fin; (*b*) a cichlid fish, *Sarotherodon galilaeus*, of the Middle East and northern and central Africa. **St Peter's wort** a St John's wort, *Hypericum tetrapterum*, which occurs in damp places and is said to flower about the feast of St Peter, 29 June. **saint's day** an annual day on which a Church celebrates the memory of a saint. **St Vitus's dance**, **St Vitus' dance** Sydenham's chorea.
¶ As adjective now felt to be an appositional use of the noun. Main entries of the type *St Cloud*, *St Kilda* are placed among other words beginning *st-*, as if they began *stc-*, *stk-*, etc.
■ **saintdom** *noun* saints collectively M19. **saintess** *noun* a female saint LME. **sainthood** *noun* (*a*) the condition, status, or dignity of a saint; (*b*) saints collectively: M16. **saintish** *adjective* (chiefly *derog*.) saintlike E16. **saintless** *adjective* (*rare*) †(*a*) that is no saint; (*b*) that has no patron saint: E17. **saintlike** *adjective* resembling or characteristic of a saint; saintly: L16. **saintling** *noun* (chiefly *derog*.) a small or insignificant saint E17. **sainˈtology** *noun* hagiology M19.

saint /seɪnt/ *verb*. ME.
[from the noun.]
†**1** *verb trans*. In *pass*. Be or become a saint in heaven. ME–M19.
2 *verb trans*. Call (a person) a saint, treat as a saint; canonize. LME.
3 *verb intrans*. & *trans*. (with *it*). Act like a saint; live a saintly life. LME.
4 *verb trans*. Cause to be regarded as a saint; represent as a saint. Now *rare*. E17.

sainted /ˈseɪntɪd/ *adjective*. L16.
[from SAINT *verb* + -ED[1].]
1 Befitting a saint; sacred. *arch*. L16.
2 Of saintly life or character; enrolled among the saints; canonized. *arch*. E17.
2 my sainted aunt!, **my sainted mother!**: expr. surprise, disbelief, etc.

†**saint-errant** *noun*. Freq. *iron*. Pl. **saints-errant**. L17–M19.
[from SAINT *noun* + ERRANT, after *knight errant*.]
A person who travelled in search of spiritual adventures.
■ †**saint-errantry** *noun* the character, practice, or spirit of such a person L17–E19.

saintly /ˈseɪntli/ *adjective*. E16.
[from SAINT *noun* + -LY[1].]
Characteristic of or befitting a saint or saints; very holy or virtuous.

> J. DISKI Their lives depended on the good sense and saintly forbearance of other users of the road. J. UPDIKE His saintly face . . was unable to conceal, quite, his murderous pride.

■ **saintliness** *noun* M19.

saintpaulia /s(ə)ntˈpɔːlɪə/ *noun*. L19.
[from Baron Walter von *Saint-Paul* (1860–1910), German explorer + -IA[1].]
Any of various dwarf plants of E. Africa constituting the genus *Saintpaulia* (family Gesneriaceae), having hairy leaves and clusters of violet, pink, or white flowers; esp. *S. ionantha*, popular as a house-plant. Also called ***African violet***.

†**saints-errant** *noun* pl. of SAINT-ERRANT.

saintship /ˈseɪntʃɪp/ *noun*. E17.
[from SAINT *noun* + -SHIP.]
1 The condition of being a saintly person; saintliness. Also (freq. *iron*.) as a title. E17.
2 The condition or status of a canonized saint. M17.

> **1** BYRON Whose . . eyes . . Might shake the saintship of an anchorite.

Saint-Simonian /seɪntsɪˈməʊnɪən/ *adjective* & *noun*. Also **St-**. M19.
[from *Saint-Simon* (see below) + -IAN.]
▶ **A** *adjective*. Belonging to or characteristic of the socialist system of the Comte de Saint-Simon (1760–1825), who advocated State control of all property and a distribution of produce according to individual vocation and capacity. M19.
▶ **B** *noun*. A supporter of the political ideas or system of Saint-Simon. M19.
■ **Saint-Simonianism**, **Saint-Simonism** /-ˈsʌɪm(ə)nɪz(ə)m/ *nouns* support for or adherence to the political system advocated by Saint-Simon M19. **Saint-Simonist** /-ˈsʌɪm(ə)nɪst/ *noun* a Saint-Simonian E19.

sais *noun* var. of SYCE.

Saite /ˈseɪʌɪt/ *noun* & *adjective*. L17.
[Latin *Saites* from Greek *Saïtēs*, from *Saïs* Sais: see -ITE[1].]
▶ **A** *noun*. A native or inhabitant of Sais (see SAITIC). L17.
▶ **B** *adjective*. Of or pertaining to Sais; = SAITIC. M19.

saith *verb* see SAY *verb*[1].

saithe /seɪθ/ *noun*. M16.
[from Old Norse *seiðr*.]
A common N. Atlantic gadid fish, *Pollachius virens*, which is an important food fish; the flesh of this as food. Also called ***coalfish***, ***coley***.

Saitic /seɪˈɪtɪk/ *adjective*. L17.
[Latin *Saiticus* from Greek *Saitikos*, from *Saitēs*: see SAITE, -IC.]
Of or pertaining to Sais, an ancient capital of Lower Egypt on the Nile Delta, or the 26th dynasty of the kings of Egypt (664–525 BC).

Saiva /ˈʃʌɪvə/ *noun & adjective*. L18.
[Sanskrit *śaiva* pertaining to or sacred to Siva, a worshipper or follower of Siva.]
HINDUISM. ▶**A** *noun*. A member of one of the three great divisions of modern Hinduism, exclusively devoted to the worship of the god Siva as the supreme being. L18.
▶**B** *adjective*. Of or pertaining to this division of Hinduism. M19.
■ **Saivism** *noun* = SIVAISM L19. **Saivite** *noun & adjective* = SIVAITE M19.

saiyid *noun* var. of SAYYID.

saj /sɑːdʒ/ *noun*. M19.
[Persian & Urdu *sāj* from Arab.: cf. Sanskrit *śāka*.]
The teak tree, *Tectona grandis*; the wood of this tree, teak.

sajou /saʒu/ *noun*. L18.
[French, abbreviation of *sajouassu* alt. of *cayouassou*, from Tupi SAI *noun*[1] + *guassú* large.]
A capuchin monkey.

Saka /ˈʃakə/ *noun*[1] *& adjective*[1]. E17.
[Old Persian *Saka*: cf. Greek *Sakai* pl., Latin *Sacae* pl.]
Of or pertaining to, a member of, an Iranian (Scythian) people of central Asia (AD *c* 300–1000); (of) their language.
■ **Sakian** *noun & adjective* (of) the Saka language M20.

Saka /ˈʃakə, ˈʃɑːkə/ *noun*[2] *& adjective*[2]. L19.
[Sanskrit *Śaka* noun, *Śāka* adjective, from Iranian, formed as prec.]
▶**A** *noun*. Pl. **-s**, same. A member of an ancient Scythian people that entered India about the 1st cent. BC. L19.
▶**B** *attrib*. or as *adjective*. **1** Of or pertaining to the Sakas or their language. L19.
2 Designating or pertaining to an era in Indian chronology reckoned from AD 78. L19.

sakabula /sakəˈbuːlə/ *noun*. *S. Afr.* L19.
[Xhosa *isakabula*.]
The long-tailed widow-bird, *Euplectes progne*, a common bird of the veld in SE Africa.

Sakai /ˈsɑːkʌɪ/ *noun & adjective*. M19.
[Malay, lit. 'subject, dependent'.]
▶**A** *noun*. Pl. same, **-s**.
1 A member of an aboriginal people of the Malay peninsula; any Malayan aboriginal. M19.
2 The Austro-Asiatic language of the Sakai. E20.
▶**B** *attrib*. or as *adjective*. Of or pertaining to the Sakai or their language. L19.

sakawinki /sakəˈwɪŋki/ *noun*. M18.
[Alt. of Dutch *sagwijntje*.]
Any of various small S. American monkeys, *esp*. a squirrel monkey or a marmoset.

sake /seɪk/ *noun*[1]. *obsolete* exc. in phrs.
[Old English *sacu* = Old Frisian *sake*, Old Saxon *saka* (Dutch *zaak*), Old High German *sahha* (German *Sache*), Old Norse *sǫk*, from Germanic word meaning 'affair, thing, cause, legal action, accusation, crime', repr. also by Old English *sacan* quarrel, accuse, from base rel. to that of SEEK *verb*.]
†**1** Contention, strife; a quarrel. OE–ME.
†**2** Guilt, sin; an offence, a crime. OE–LME.
†**3** A charge, an accusation of guilt; grounds for accusation. Only in ME.
†**4** Regard or consideration for someone. *rare* (Spenser). Only in L16.
Phrases: ***for conscience sake***: see CONSCIENCE. **for God's sake**, **for goodness sake**, **for heaven's sake**, **for Pete's sake**, etc.: expr. exasperation, impatience, etc. ***for mercy's sake***: see MERCY *noun* 3. **for old sake's sake** for the sake of old friendship. **for old times' sake**, **for old time's sake** in memory of former times. †**for one's name sake**, †**for one's name's sake** out of regard for one's name. ***for pity's sake***: see PITY *noun*. †**for sake's sake** for God's sake; for its own sake. †**for that sake** on that account, for that reason. **for the sake of** out of consideration for; in the interest of, because of; in order to please or honour (a person) or attain (a thing). ***mercy sakes***: see MERCY *noun*. **sakes!**, **sakes alive!** (*dial. & N. Amer.*) expr. surprise.

sake /ˈsɑːki, ˈsakeɪ/ *noun*[2]. Also **saké**, **saki**. L17.
[Japanese.]
A Japanese alcoholic drink made from fermented rice.

Sakellaridis /sakəˈlarɪdɪs/ *noun*. Also **-ides** /-ɪdiːz/. E20.
[*Sakellaridēs*, a Greek cotton-grower who originated the variety.]
A superior variety of Egyptian cotton, widely grown in the early 20th cent.
■ Also ˈ**Sakel** *noun* E20.

saker /ˈseɪkə/ *noun*. LME.
[Old & mod. French *sacre* from Arab. *ṣakr* hawk, falcon.]
1 A large migratory Eurasian falcon, *Falco cherrug*, with a dark brown back and pale head, popular for falconry. LME.
2 *Hist*. An old form of cannon smaller than a demiculverin, formerly much used in sieges and on ships. E16.

saki /ˈsɑːki/ *noun*[1]. L18.
[French, alt. of mod. Latin †*cagui* from Tupi *saui* (see SAGOIN).]
Any of various S. American cebid monkeys of the genera *Pithecia* and *Chiropotes*, with coarse coats and bushy tails.

saki *noun*[2] var. of SAKE *noun*[2].

sakia /ˈsɑːkɪə/ *noun*. L17.
[Arab. *sākiya* use as noun of fem. active pple of *sakā* irrigate.]
A machine for drawing water for irrigation, consisting of a large vertical wheel to which earthen pots are attached and moved by means of a horizontal wheel turned by oxen or asses.

Sakta /ˈʃɑːktə/ *noun*. E19.
[Sanskrit, from *śākta* relating to power or the Sakti.]
A member of one of the principal Hindu sects which worships the Sakti or divine energy, esp. as this is identified with Durga, the wife of Siva.
■ **Saktism** *noun* worship of the Sakti L19.

Sakti /ˈʃakti/ *noun*. Also **Sh-**. E19.
[Sanskrit *śakti* power, divine energy.]
HINDUISM. The female principle, esp. when personified as the wife of a god, as Durga is the Sakti of Siva; supernatural energy embodied in the female principle.

sakura /səˈkʊərə/ *noun*. L19.
[Japanese.]
Any of several Japanese flowering cherries, *esp*. a cultivar of *Prunus serrulata*; the wood of these trees.

sal /sal/ *noun*[1]. ME.
[Latin = salt.]
CHEMISTRY, ALCHEMY, & PHARMACOLOGY. = SALT *noun*[1] (in various senses). Long only with specifying word, in names of particular salts.
sal ammoniac: see AMMONIAC *adjective* 1. †**sal marine** common salt. **sal mirabilis** [mod. Latin = wonderful] Glauber's salt (cf. MIRABILITE). **sal soda** crystallized sodium carbonate.

sal /sɑːl/ *noun*[2]. L18.
[Hindi *sāl* from Sanskrit *śāla*.]
An important timber tree of India, *Shorea robusta* (family Dipterocarpaceae), which yields the resin dammar (also ***sal-tree***); the wood of this tree (also ***sal-wood***).

†**sal** *noun*[3]. *Theatrical slang*. M–L19.
[Abbreviation.]
= SALARY *noun* 1.

sala /ˈsɑːlə/ *noun*[1]. E17.
[Italian, Spanish = SALLE.]
A hall, a large room; *spec*. a dining-hall.

sala /ˈsɑːlɑː/ *noun*[2]. L19.
[Sanskrit *śālā* public building.]
In the Indian subcontinent: a rest-house, an inn.

salaam /səˈlɑːm/ *noun*. E17.
[Arab. *salām* = Hebrew *šālōm*.]
1 An oriental greeting, meaning 'Peace', used chiefly in Muslim countries; a ceremonial obeisance sometimes accompanying this salutation, consisting in the Indian subcontinent of a low bow with the right palm on the forehead. E17.
2 In *pl*. Respectful compliments. L18.

salaam /səˈlɑːm/ *verb intrans. & trans*. E17.
[from the noun.]
Make a salaam (to).
📖 E. MANNIN Welcomed on board by salaaming waiters.

salable *adjective* var. of SALEABLE.

salacious /səˈleɪʃəs/ *adjective*. M17.
[Latin *salac-*, *salax*, from *salire* to leap: see -OUS, -IOUS.]
1 Lustful, lecherous; erotic, lewd. M17.
2 Tending to provoke lust. *rare*. M17.
📖 **1** V. NABOKOV I touched her . . lips with the utmost piety, . . nothing salacious.
■ **salaciously** *adverb* M18. **salaciousness** *noun* E18.

salacity /səˈlasɪti/ *noun*. E17.
[French *salacité* or Latin *salacitas*, formed as prec.: see -ACITY.]
The quality or condition of being salacious; lustfulness, lecherousness, lewdness.

salad /ˈsaləd/ *noun*. Also (now *arch. & dial*.) **sallet** /ˈsalɪt/. LME.
[Old & mod. French *salade* from Provençal *salada* from Proto-Romance, from Latin SAL *noun*[1].]
1 a A cold dish of vegetables such as lettuce and cucumber, usu. raw, chopped, and seasoned with oil, vinegar, herbs, etc., and often combined with egg, cold meat, fish, etc. LME. ▸**b** *fig*. A mixture. E17.
2 A vegetable or herb that can be eaten raw. LME. ▸**b** *spec*. Lettuce. *dial. & US*. M19.
📖 **1a** ***cheese salad***, ***chicken salad***, ***ham salad***, ***prawn salad***, etc. **b** *Nation* The building is an entertaining salad of styles. **2** ***corn-salad***: see CORN *noun*[1].
Phrases: ***fruit salad***: see FRUIT *noun*. ***green salad***: see GREEN *adjective*. †**pick a salad** make a selection. ***SHAWNEE salad***.
Comb.: **salad bar** a servery from which salad may be obtained; **salad basket** (*a*) a wire basket in which water is shaken from salad ingredients after washing; (*b*) *slang* [translating French *panier à salade*] a police van, a Black Maria; ***salad burnet***: see BURNET *noun* 2; **salad cream** creamy salad-dressing; **salad days** a period of youthful inexperience; **salad-dressing** a sauce for salad, such as oil and vinegar, mayonnaise, etc.; **salad-oil** olive oil of superior quality, such as is used in dressing salads; **salad servers** a large spoon and fork for serving salads.
■ **salading** *noun* herbs and vegetables used for salad M17.

salade *noun* var. of SALLET.

salade niçoise /salad niswaz/ *noun phr*. Pl. **-s -s** (pronounced same). E20.
[French = salad from Nice (in southern France).]
A salad usu. made from hard-boiled eggs, anchovies, black olives, tomatoes, etc.

saladero /saləˈdɛːrəʊ, *foreign* salaˈðero/ *noun*. Pl. **-os** /-əʊz, *foreign* -ɔs/. L19.
[Spanish.]
In Spain and Latin America, a slaughterhouse where meat is also prepared by drying or salting.

salades niçoises *noun phr*. pl. of SALADE NIÇOISE.

saladine *noun* see CELANDINE.

salagrama /ʃɑːləˈgrɑːmə/ *noun*. E19.
[Sanskrit *śālagrāma*: see SHALGRAM.]
= SHALGRAM.

salak /səˈlak/ *noun*. E19.
[Malay.]
Any of various thorny palm trees constituting the genus *Salacca*, of SE Asia, esp. *S. zalacca*; the edible pear-shaped fruit of *S. zalacca*.

salal /səˈlal/ *noun*. E19.
[Chinook Jargon *sallal*.]
A N. American gaultheria, *Gaultheria shallon*, with racemes of pink or white flowers and edible purple-black berries.

salamander /ˈsaləmandə/ *noun & adjective*. ME.
[Old & mod. French *salamandre* from Latin *salamandra* from Greek.]
▶**A** *noun*. **1 a** A mythical animal like a lizard supposed to live in, or to be able to endure, fire. Later also, a figure of this animal used as an emblem. ME. ▸**b** Any of the tailed amphibians which together with newts constitute the class Urodela; *esp*. a terrestrial member of the family Salamandridae. E17.
2 A person etc. capable of existing in or enduring fire; *spec*. (***a***) a spirit supposed to live in fire; †(***b***) *fig*. a woman who lives chastely in the midst of temptations; (***c***) a soldier who exposes himself to fire in battle; (***d***) a fire-eating juggler. L16.
3 An object or material used in fire or capable of withstanding great heat; *spec*. †(***a***) asbestos; (***b***) an iron or poker used red-hot for lighting a pipe, igniting gunpowder, etc.; (***c***) COOKERY a circular iron plate which is heated and placed over food to brown it; (***d***) METALLURGY a mass of metal etc. found below the hearth of a blast-furnace; (***e***) *N. Amer*. a brazier. M17.
4 A pocket gopher, esp. *Geomys pinetis*. *US local*. E19.
5 A drinking toast common among German students. M19.
1b ***spectacled salamander***: see SPECTACLED 2.
▶**B** *attrib*. or as *adjective*. = SALAMANDRINE *adjective* 1. E18.
Comb. & special collocations: †**salamander safe** *US* a fireproof safe; **salamander-stove** *US* a small portable stove for heating a room.
■ **salaˈmandrian** *adjective & noun* (***a***) *adjective* resembling (that of) a salamander; ZOOLOGY of, pertaining to, or designating a urodele amphibian, esp. of the family Salamandridae; (***b***) *noun* a salamandrian amphibian: E17. **salaˈmandrid** *noun & adjective* (***a***) *noun* a urodele amphibian of the family Salamandridae; (***b***) *adjective* of, pertaining to, or designating this family: M19. **salaˈmandroid** *adjective & noun* (***a***) *adjective* resembling a salamander; (***b***) *noun* a urodele amphibian, *esp*. one of the superfamily Salamandroidea: M19. **salaˈmandrous** *adjective* (*rare*) existing in fire; fiery, passionate: E18.

salamander /ˈsaləmandə/ *verb*. *rare*. M19.
[from the noun.]
1 *verb intrans*. Live or exist in fire. M19.
2 *verb trans*. COOKERY. Brown (food) by means of a salamander. L19.
3 *verb trans*. Submit to great heat. E20.

salamandrine /saləˈmandrɪn/ *adjective & noun*. E18.
[from Latin *salamandra* SALAMANDER *noun* + -INE[1].]
▶**A** *adjective*. **1** Capable of living in or enduring fire. E18.
2 ZOOLOGY. Of, pertaining to, or designating a urodele amphibian, esp. of the family Salamandridae or the subfamily Salamandrinae. M19.
▶**B** *noun*. **1** A spirit supposed to live in fire. L18.
2 = SALAMANDER *noun* 1b. L19.

salami /sə'lɑːmi/ *noun.* **M19.**
[Italian, pl. of *salame*, repr. popular Latin word from verb meaning 'salt'.]
1 An orig. Italian variety of sausage, highly seasoned and often flavoured with garlic. **M19.**
2 In full ***salami technique***. A way of carrying out a plan by means of a series of small or imperceptible steps; *spec.* computer fraud in which small amounts of money are transferred from numerous customer accounts into another account. **L20.**
Comb.: **salami tactics** a piecemeal attack on or elimination of (esp. political) opposition; ***salami technique***: see sense 2 above.

Salam–Weinberg /səlɑːm'wʌɪnbəːg/ *noun.* **L20.**
[See WEINBERG–SALAM.]
PARTICLE PHYSICS. = WEINBERG–SALAM.

salangane /'salənɡeɪn/ *noun.* **L18.**
[French from *salamga*, name of the bird in the Philippines.]
Any of various swiftlets of the genus *Collocalia*, which make edible nests.

salarian /sə'lɛːrɪən/ *adjective.* **M17.**
[from Latin *salarius*: see SALARY *noun*, -IAN.]
†**1** Pertaining to salt. Only in **M17.**
2 ***Salarian Way*** [translating Latin *Via Salaria*], an ancient road running from Rome north-east to Reate (now Rieti) and later extended to the Adriatic. **M19.**

salariat /sə'lɛːrɪət/ *noun.* **E20.**
[French, from *salaire* SALARY *noun*, after *prolétariat*.]
The salaried class; salary-earners collectively.

salaried /'salərɪd/ *ppl adjective.* **E17.**
[from SALARY *noun*, *verb*: see -ED[2], -ED[1].]
1 Having or receiving a salary. **E17.**
2 Of a position or post: having a salary attached. **M19.**

🕮 **2** A. MILLER Some dull salaried job where you could never hope to make a killing.

salary /'saləri/ *noun.* **ME.**
[Anglo-Norman *salarie* = Old & mod. French *salaire* from Latin *salarium* (orig.) money allowed to Roman soldiers for the purchase of salt, (later) pay, stipend, use as noun (sc. *argentum* money) of *salarius* pertaining to salt, formed as SAL *noun*[1]: see -ARY[1].]
1 Fixed regular payment made by an employer to an employee in return for work; now *spec.* payment made for professional or non-manual work (cf. WAGE *noun* 2). **ME.**
†**2** Reward, recompense; a fee, an honorarium. **LME–L17.**

🕮 **1** H. ROSENTHAL At the end of April Steuart left . . though remaining on salary until September. C. HARMAN The . . project ensured her a salary of three pounds a week. **2** SHAKES. *Haml.* Why, this is hire and salary, not revenge.

Comb.: **salaryman** a white-collar worker in Japan.

salary /'saləri/ *verb trans.* **L15.**
[Chiefly from the noun; in early use from French *salarier*.]
Recompense, reward; pay a regular salary to.

salat /sa'lɑːt/ *noun.* Also (earlier) **salah** /sa'lɑː/. **E17.**
[Arab. *ṣalā*, pl. *ṣalāt*, prayer, worship.]
Ritual prayer, the second of the Five Pillars of Islam; *spec.* the five ritual prayers which a Muslim is obliged to perform daily, consisting of set movements and spoken or silent recitations.

salaud /salo/ *noun.* Pl. pronounced same. **M20.**
[French, from *sale* dirty.]
As a term of abuse: a contemptible or objectionable person.

salband /'sɑːlband/ *noun.* **E19.**
[German, earlier *Sahlband*, from *selbe* SELF *pronoun* etc. + *Ende* end.]
GEOLOGY. A thin crust of different character on an igneous mass or mineral vein.

salbutamol /sal'bjuːtəmɒl/ *noun.* **M20.**
[from SAL(ICYL + BUT(YL + AM(INE + -OL.]
PHARMACOLOGY. A sympathomimetic agent used esp. as a bronchodilator in the treatment of asthma.
¶ A proprietary name for this drug is VENTOLIN.

salchow /'salkəʊ/ *noun.* **E20.**
[Ulrich *Salchow* (1877–1949), Swedish figure-skater.]
SKATING. A full-turn jump from the inside back edge of one skate to the outside back edge of the other. Also more fully ***salchow jump***.

Saldanier /saldə'nɪə/ *noun. S. Afr. Hist.* **M19.**
[Afrikaans, from *Saldanha*: see below.]
A Nama of the region of Saldanha Bay, Cape Province, South Africa, in the 17th cent.

sale /seɪl/ *noun.* **LOE.**
[Old Norse *sala* = Old High German *sala*, from base of Germanic verb meaning 'sell'.]
1 The action or an act of giving or agreeing to give something to a person in exchange for money; in *pl.*, the quantity or amount sold. **LOE.** ▸**b** With specifying word: an opportunity for being sold; demand. **L16.**
2 An event at which goods are sold publicly; a public auction. **L17.**
3 A special disposal of shop goods at reduced prices in order to sell them rapidly, esp. at the end of a season. **M19.**
4 BOOKSELLING. The ordinary trade rate. **E20.**

🕮 **1** *Times* A substantial increase in the sales of filter-tip cigarettes. *New Scientist* Most countries have banned the sale of irradiated food. **b** S. UNWIN Publications with a continuous and profitable sale. **2** *Antique* Christie's announced a whole sale of such works. **3** *Times* Many retailers have brought forward the start of their summer sales.

Phrases: ***bargain and sale***: see BARGAIN *noun* 2. ***bill of sale***: see BILL *noun*[3]. **for sale** intended to be sold, offered for purchase. **on sale** = *for sale* above. **sale and leaseback** a transaction in which a property is sold and the vendor takes a lease on it from the buyer. **sale of work** a sale of handiwork, esp. of articles made by members of an association, society, etc., and held on behalf of a charitable or political cause. **sale or return** an arrangement by which a purchaser takes a quantity of goods with the right to return them without payment. †**to sale** = *for sale* above. **up for sale** (esp. of a property) for sale. †**upon sale** = *for sale* above.
Comb.: **sale day** (*a*) the day on which a sale is held; (*b*) *Austral. & NZ* a market-day; **sale-leaseback** = *sale and leaseback* above; **sale price** (*a*) a retail price; (*b*) a price fetched at auction; (*c*) a price reduced in a sale; **sale ring** a circle of buyers at an auction; **saleroom**: where objects are displayed and sold, esp. at an auction; **sales clerk** *N. Amer.* a shop assistant; **sales department** the section of a firm concerned with selling its products as opp. to manufacturing or dispatching them; **sales drive** an energetic effort to sell goods extensively; **sales engineer** a salesperson with technical knowledge of his or her goods and their market; **salesgirl** a young saleswoman; **saleslady** a saleswoman; **salesperson** a salesman, a saleswoman; **sales pitch** = *sales talk* below; **sales representative**, (*colloq.*) **sales rep** a person who represents a commercial firm to prospective customers and solicits orders; **sales resistance** the ability or disposition to resist buying something offered for sale; **salesroom** *US* = *saleroom* above; **sales talk** persuasive argument intended to promote the sale of goods or the acceptance of an idea; **sales tax**: levied on retail sales or receipts from sales; **sale-yard** *Austral. & NZ* an enclosure in which livestock is sold.

sale /seɪl/ *verb.* Pres. pple **saleing**, **saling**. **E19.**
[from the noun.]
1 *verb intrans. & trans.* Sell. *rare.* **E19.**
2 *verb intrans.* Shop at a sale. Also, hold a sale. Now *rare.* **E20.**

saleable /'seɪləb(ə)l/ *adjective.* Also **salable**. **M16.**
[from SALE *noun* + -ABLE.]
1 Able to be sold; fit for sale. **M16.** ▸**b** Designating the price which an article is on sale. **L18.**
†**2** Venal, mercenary. **L16–L18.**

🕮 **1** A. BLOND The agent . . will not accept a manuscript unless he thinks it is saleable.

■ **salea'bility** *noun* **L18.** **saleableness** *noun* **E18.** **saleably** *adverb* **M17.**

sale Boche /sal bɔʃ/ *noun phr.* Also ***sale boche***. Pl. **-s -s** (pronounced same). **E20.**
[French, from *sale* dirty + BOCHE.]
(A French term of abuse for) a German.

Salem /'seɪləm/ *noun.* Now chiefly *Hist.* **M19.**
[Place-name in *Genesis* 14:18 (Hebrew *Šālēm*), understood to be another name for Jerusalem and to mean 'peace' (Hebrew *šālōm*).]
(A name for) a particular Nonconformist chapel or meeting-house; *transf.* a Nonconformist chapel.

Salempore /'saləmpɔː/ *noun.* **L16.**
[French *salempouri*, Dutch *salamporij*, of unkn. origin.]
A coloured cotton cloth (often blue) formerly made at Nellore in India and largely exported to the W. Indies.

salep /'saləp/ *noun.* **M18.**
[French from Turkish *sālep* from Arab. *ṯaʻlab* fox, shortening of *kusā 't-taʻlab* orchid (lit. 'fox's testicles'): cf. SALOOP.]
A starchy preparation of the dried tubers of various orchids, esp. of the genus *Orchis*, used in cookery and formerly as a tonic.

†**saler** *noun.* **ME–E16.**
[Anglo-Norman = Old French *sal(l)ier(e* (mod. *salière*) from medieval Latin *salarium*, *salaria*, from Latin SAL *noun*[1]: see -ER[2].]
A salt-cellar.
¶ The source of the 2nd elem. of *salt-cellar*.

saleratus /salə'reɪtəs/ *noun. US.* **M19.**
[mod. Latin *sal aeratus* lit. 'aerated salt'.]
Orig., impure potassium bicarbonate used in baking-powder. Later, sodium bicarbonate (baking soda).

Salernitan /sə'ləːnɪt(ə)n/ *adjective & noun.* **E17.**
[Latin *Salernitanus*, from *Salernum* Salerno: see -AN.]
▶ **A** *adjective.* Of or pertaining to Salerno, an Italian maritime town near Naples, or the medical school which formerly flourished there. **E17.**
▶ **B** *noun.* A native or inhabitant of Salerno; a physician of the Salernitan school. **E17.**

sales Boches *noun phr.* pl. of SALE BOCHE.

Salesian /sə'liːzj(ə)n, -liːʒ(ə)n/ *adjective & noun.* **M19.**
[French *salésien*, from St François de *Sales*: see -IAN.]
▶ **A** *adjective.* Of or pertaining to the French devotional writer and bishop St Francis de Sales (1567–1622), or a community founded by him or under his patronage, esp. the order founded in Italy in 1859 by St John Bosco for the education of boys and young men. **M19.**
▶ **B** *noun.* A follower of St Francis de Sales; *esp.* a member of a Salesian order. **L19.**

salesman /'seɪlzmən/ *noun.* Pl. **-men**. **E16.**
[from SALE *noun* + -'S[1] + MAN *noun*.]
A man who sells goods or conducts sales; *spec.* (*a*) one who sells produce or services for another; (*b*) (orig. *US*) a commercial traveller.
travelling salesman: see TRAVELLING *ppl adjective*.
■ **salesmanship** *noun* the work or position of a salesman; the technique or skill of selling: **L19.**

saleswoman /'seɪlzwʊmən/ *noun.* Pl. **-women** /-wɪmɪn/. **E18.**
[formed as prec. + WOMAN *noun*.]
A woman who sells goods or conducts sales, esp. on behalf of another.
■ **saleswomanship** *noun* the work or position of a saleswoman; the technique or skill of being a saleswoman: **L20.**

†**sal-gem** *noun.* **ME–M19.**
[medieval Latin *sal gemma* or *gemmae* lit. 'gemlike salt'.]
Native sodium chloride; rock-salt.

salgram *noun* see SHALGRAM.

Salian /'seɪlɪən/ *noun*[1] *& adjective*[1]. **E17.**
[from late Latin *Salii* Salian Franks: see -IAN.]
▶ **A** *noun.* A member of a Frankish people who inhabited a region near the Zuyder Zee in the 4th cent. AD, and to whom the ancestors of the Merovingian dynasty belonged. **E17.**
▶ **B** *adjective.* Of or belonging to the Salians. **E18.**

Salian /'seɪlɪən/ *adjective*[2] *& noun*[2]. **E17.**
[formed as SALII + -AN.]
ROMAN HISTORY. ▶**A** *adjective.* Pertaining to or designating an association of priests who performed ritual dances. **E17.**
▶ **B** *noun.* A Salian priest. **L18.**

†**saliaunce** *noun. rare* (Spenser). Only in **L16.**
[Rel. to SALIENT: see -ANCE.]
An assault, a sally.

Salic /'salɪk, 'seɪlɪk/ *adjective*[1]. In sense 1 also **Salique** /sə'liːk/. **M16.**
[French *salique* or medieval Latin *Salicus*, from late Latin *Salii*: see SALIAN *noun*[1] *& adjective*[1], -IC.]
1 ***Salic law***, orig., an alleged law of succession of the French monarchy, by which females were excluded from the crown; later *gen.*, any law excluding females from dynastic succession. **M16.**
2 Of or pertaining to the Salian Franks. Chiefly in ***Salic code***, ***Salic law***, a Frankish law-book written in Latin. **L18.**

salic /'salɪk/ *adjective*[2]. **E20.**
[from S(ILICON + AL(UMINIUM + -IC.]
PETROGRAPHY. Designating, belonging to, or characteristic of a large category of igneous rocks that broadly includes those rich in non-ferromagnesian aluminous and siliceous minerals such as quartz, feldspars, and feldspathoids.

salic /'seɪlɪk/ *adjective*[3]. **M20.**
[from Latin *sal* salt + -IC.]
SOIL SCIENCE. Designating a soil horizon which is at least 15 cm (approx. 6 inches) thick and enriched with salts more soluble in water than gypsum.

salicaceous /salɪ'keɪʃəs/ *adjective.* **M19.**
[from mod. Latin *salicaceus*, from Latin *salic-*, *salix* willow: see -ACEOUS.]
BOTANY. Of or pertaining to the Salicaceae or willow family.

salices *noun pl.* see SALIX.

salicet /'salɪsɛt/ *noun.* **M19.**
[German, from Latin *salic-*: see next, -ET[1].]
MUSIC. = SALICIONAL.

salicetum /salɪ'siːtəm/ *noun.* Also (earlier) **salictum** /sə'lɪktəm/. Pl. **-ta** /-tə/, **-tums**. **L18.**
[(Alt. of) Latin *salictum*, from *salic-*, *salix* willow: see -ETUM.]
A plantation of willows, *esp.* one containing many different species and varieties.

salicin /'salɪsɪn/ *noun.* **M19.**
[French *salicine*, from Latin *salic-*: see prec., -IN[1].]
A water-soluble glucoside, $C_{13}H_{18}O_7$, obtained from the bark of willows (genus *Salix*), formerly used as an analgesic.

salicional /sə'lɪʃ(ə)n(ə)l/ *noun.* **M19.**
[German *Salicional*, from Latin *salic-*, *salix* willow, with obscure suffix.]
An organ-stop with a soft reedy tone resembling that of a willow pipe.

salicologist /salɪ'kɒlədʒɪst/ *noun.* **L19.**
[from Latin *salic-*: see SALICACEOUS, -OLOGIST.]
An expert in or student of willows, esp. their taxonomic relationships.

salictum *noun* var. of SALICETUM.

salicyl /ˈsalɪsʌɪl, -sɪl/ *noun.* M19.
[French *salicyle*, formed as SALICOLOGIST: see -YL.]
CHEMISTRY. The radical, $C_6H_4(OH)(CO\cdot)$, of salicylic acid. Usu. in *comb.*
Comb.: **salicylaldehyde** *o*-hydroxybenzaldehyde, $C_7H_6O_2$, a colourless volatile liquid smelling of bitter almonds, found in oil from meadowsweet etc., and used in perfumery and flavouring.

salicylate /səˈlɪsɪleɪt/ *noun.* M19.
[from prec. + -ATE¹.]
CHEMISTRY. A salt or ester of salicylic acid.

salicylic /salɪˈsɪlɪk/ *adjective.* M19.
[from SALICYL + -IC.]
1 *CHEMISTRY.* ***salicylic acid***, a bitter-tasting derivative, $HO\cdot C_6H_4\cdot COOH$, of phenol that is used in making aspirin and dyes and as a fungicide. M19.
2 *MEDICINE.* Made from, impregnated with, or involving the use of salicylic acid. L19.
■ **salicylism** /səˈlɪsɪlɪz(ə)m/ *noun* a toxic condition produced by excessive dosage with aspirin or salicylates L19.

salie /ˈsali/ *noun.* E19.
[Afrikaans from Dutch = sage.]
= ***sage-wood*** s.v. SAGE *noun*¹.

salience /ˈseɪlɪəns/ *noun.* M19.
[from next: see -ENCE.]
1 The fact or condition of projecting outwards; prominence, conspicuousness, esp. (*SOCIOLOGY*) in consciousness. M19.
2 A salient or projecting feature or object. M19.
3 The quality of leaping or springing up. *rare.* M19.
📖 **1** F. R. LEAVIS His patterns . . lack definition and salience. *Guardian Weekly* Immigration had remained an issue of what the sociologists call low salience.
■ Also **saliency** *noun* M17.

salient /ˈseɪlɪənt/ *adjective & noun.* M16.
[Latin *salient-* pres. ppl stem of *salire* to leap: see -ENT.]
▶ **A** *adjective.* **1** *HERALDRY.* Of a lion, stag, etc.: having the hind legs in the sinister base and the forelegs raised close together in the dexter chief, as if leaping. M16.
2 a Leaping, jumping; *ZOOLOGY* saltatorial. M17. ▸**b** Of water: jetting forth; rushing upwards. M17.
3 Of an angle: pointing outwards, like an ordinary angle of a polygon (opp. ***re-entrant***); (of a fortification) formed by two lines of works meeting and pointing away from the centre of the fortification. L17.
4 Projecting above or beyond a surface or outline, jutting out; prominent, noticeable, conspicuous; *SOCIOLOGY* standing out or prominent in consciousness. L18.
📖 **4** W. J. LOCKE A deep red silk peignoir . . which clung to every salient curve of her figure. M. M. R. KHAN A brief recapitulation of the salient features of Bill's life.
Special collocations: **salient point** †(*a*) the heart as it first appears in the embryo; (*b*) *arch.* the starting-point of something; (*c*) a significant or conspicuous factor or item.
▶ **B** *noun. FORTIFICATION.*
1 A salient angle or part of a work. E19.
2 A narrow projection of land, *esp.* one held by a military line of attack or defence; *spec.* (usu. **S-**), the projection of the military line at Ypres in western Belgium in the war of 1914–18 (the scene of severe fighting). M19.
📖 **2** *Independent* A salient which pokes a little of Honduras into Nicaragua. *fig.*: *Discovery* There are too many salients in the front line of social progress.
■ **saliently** *adverb* M19.

salientian /seɪlɪˈɛnʃɪən, -ˈɛnt-/ *adjective & noun.* M20.
[from mod. Latin *Salientia* (see below), from Latin *salient-* (see prec.) + -IA¹: see -AN.]
ZOOLOGY. ▶**A** *adjective.* Of, pertaining to, or designating a tailless amphibian of the superorder Salientia, which comprises the anurans and some extinct orders. M20.
▶ **B** *noun.* An amphibian belonging to this superorder. M20.

saliferous /səˈlɪf(ə)rəs/ *adjective.* E19.
[from Latin *sal* salt + -I- + -FEROUS.]
Of strata etc.: containing or yielding salt.

salification /ˌsalɪfɪˈkeɪʃ(ə)n/ *noun.* L17.
[mod. Latin *salificatio(n-)*, from *salificare*: see next, -ATION.]
Conversion into a salt; the action or condition of being so converted.

salify /ˈsalɪfʌɪ/ *verb trans.* Now *rare.* L18.
[French *salifier* from mod. Latin *salificare*, from Latin SAL *noun*¹: see -I-, -FY.]
CHEMISTRY. Convert into a salt.
■ **salifiable** *adjective* L18.

saligenin /səˈlɪdʒənɪn/ *noun.* M19.
[from SALI(CIN + -GEN + -IN¹.]
CHEMISTRY. A crystalline aromatic alcohol, *o*-hydroxybenzyl alcohol, $C_6H_4(OH)(CH_2OH)$, used as a local anaesthetic.

saligot /ˈsalɪgɒt/ *noun.* L16.
[Old French.]
A water chestnut, *Trapa natans.*

Salii /ˈseɪlɪʌɪ/ *noun pl.* E16.
[Latin, from *salire* leap: see SALIENT.]
ROMAN HISTORY. Members of a sodality of priests (at Rome usu. associated with Mars) who performed ritual dances on certain occasions.

salina /səˈlʌɪnə/ *noun.* L16.
[Spanish from medieval Latin = salt pit; in Latin only as pl. *salinae* salt-pans.]
A salt lake, spring, or marsh; a salt-pan, a salt-works. Also (orig. *Jamaican*), a low marshy area of land near the coast.

salinator /ˈsalɪneɪtə/ *noun.* Long *rare.* E18.
[Latin, from *salinae*: see prec., -ATOR.]
A salter.

saline /ˈseɪlʌɪn/ *adjective & noun.* L15.
[from Latin SAL *noun*¹ + -INE¹.]
▶ **A** *adjective.* **1** Of the nature of salt; containing salt, impregnated with salt. Formerly also, made of salt. L15.
2 Like that of salt; like salt, salty. M17.
3 Of or pertaining to a chemical salt; of the nature of a salt. L18.
4 *MEDICINE.* Consisting of or based on salts of the alkali metals or magnesium, esp. sodium chloride. L18.
5 Of a plant etc.: growing in or inhabiting salt plains or salt-marshes. *rare.* E19.
📖 **1** J. PLAYFAIR The water would gain admission to the saline strata. C. MERIVALE Mehadia, long celebrated for its saline baths. **2** C. DARWIN The solution was sufficiently strong to taste saline. **4 saline solution** an aqueous solution of sodium chloride, *esp.* physiological saline.
▶ **B** *noun.* **1** [medieval Latin *salina.*] = SALINA. L15.
2 A saline residue obtained by the evaporation or calcination of a substance. Now *rare.* M17.
3 *MEDICINE & BIOLOGY.* An aqueous solution of sodium chloride, *esp.* (more fully ***physiological saline***) one made to have the same concentration of the salt as blood. L19.
■ **salinely** *adverb* (*rare*) E20. **salineness** *noun* (*rare*) salinity L17.

salinification /səˌlɪnɪfɪˈkeɪʃ(ə)n/ *noun.* E20.
[from SALINE: see -FICATION.]
The action or process of becoming or making saline.

salinisation *noun* var. of SALINIZATION.

salinity /səˈlɪnɪti/ *noun.* M17.
[from SALINE + -ITY.]
The quality of being saline; the concentration of dissolved salts in water etc., usu. expressed in parts per thousand by weight.
Comb.: **salinity crisis** *GEOLOGY* a period of greatly increased evaporation and salinity in the Mediterranean in the late Miocene.

salinization /ˌsalɪnʌɪˈzeɪʃ(ə)n/ *noun.* Also **-isation.** E20.
[formed as prec. + -IZATION.]
The accumulation of salts in the soil.

salino- /səˈlʌɪnəʊ/ *combining form.* Now *rare.* L17.
[from SALINE: see -O-.]
Forming adjectives with the sense 'consisting of salt and —', as ***salinosulphureous***.

salinometer /salɪˈnɒmɪtə/ *noun.* M19.
[from SALINE + -OMETER.]
An instrument for measuring the salinity of water.
■ **salinometry** *noun* the use of a salinometer; measurement of the salinity of water: E20.

Salique *adjective* see SALIC *adjective*¹.

Salisbury steak /ˈsɔːlzb(ə)ri steɪk/ *noun phr. N. Amer.* L19.
[J. H. *Salisbury* (1823–1905), US physician specializing in the chemistry of foods.]
A patty of minced beef mixed with milk, breadcrumbs, and seasoning, and cooked.

Salish /ˈseɪlɪʃ/ *noun & adjective.* M19.
[Salish *séˀlišˀ* Flatheads.]
▶ **A** *noun.* Pl. same, **-es.**
1 Orig., a member of a N. American Indian people of NW Montana. Now, a member of a group of N. American Indian peoples including them and inhabiting the northwestern US and SW Canada. M19.
2 A group of languages spoken by the Salish. M19.
▶ **B** *attrib.* or as *adjective.* Of or pertaining to the Salish or their languages. M19.
■ **Salishan** *adjective & noun* (of or pertaining to) Salish M20.

salita /səˈliːtə, *foreign* saˈliːta/ *noun.* Pl. **-te** /-ti, *foreign* -te/, **-tas.** E20.
[Italian.]
In Italy: an upward slope, a stretch of rising ground.

salitrose /ˈsalɪtrəʊs/ *adjective.* M19.
[Spanish *salitroso*, from *salitre*, from medieval Latin *sal nitri* salt of nitre, formed as SAL *noun*¹ + NITRE: see -OSE¹.]
Containing sodium nitrate.

saliva /səˈlʌɪvə/ *noun.* LME.
[Latin.]
1 A colourless liquid secreted by the salivary and mucous glands of the mouth, which becomes mixed with food during chewing and facilitates swallowing; spittle. LME.
2 Unwanted small bubbles occurring together in glass. M20.
Comb.: **saliva ejector** *DENTISTRY* a suction device for removing saliva from the mouth during a dental operation; **saliva test** a scientific test performed on a sample of saliva.
■ **salival** *adjective* (now *rare*) = SALIVARY LME. **salivant** /ˈsalɪv(ə)nt/ *adjective & noun* (a substance) promoting salivation M19.

salivaria *noun* pl. of SALIVARIUM.

salivarian /salɪˈvɛːrɪən/ *adjective.* M20.
[from mod. Latin *Salivaria* subgenus name, use as noun of fem. of Latin *salivarius*: see SALIVARY, -AN.]
BIOLOGY. Designating trypanosomes which occur in the bloodstream of the secondary host, and are transmitted via its mouth when it bites a vertebrate. Cf. STERCORARIAN *adjective.*

salivarium /salɪˈvɛːrɪəm/ *noun.* Pl. **-ria** /-rɪə/. L19.
[from SALIVA + -ARIUM.]
A spittoon, *esp.* one disguised with a lid, ornamental casing, etc.

salivary /ˈsalɪv(ə)ri/ *adjective.* E18.
[Latin *salivarius*, formed as SALIVA: see -ARY¹.]
1 Of a gland etc.: secreting or conveying saliva. E18.
2 Of, pertaining to, or existing in the saliva or salivary glands. E19.

salivate /ˈsalɪveɪt/ *verb.* M17.
[Latin *salivat-* pa. ppl stem of *salivare*, formed as SALIVA: see -ATE³.]
1 *verb trans.* Produce an unusual secretion of saliva in (a person). Now *rare.* M17.
2 *verb intrans.* **a** Secrete saliva, esp. in excess. Also, spit. L17. ▸**b** *fig.* Display relish *at* or *over* some prospect or anticipated event. L20.
📖 **2b** *Times* Pye, who are marketing the records . . , are salivating at the sales prospects.
■ **saliˈvation** *noun* (*a*) the action or (formerly) an act of salivating; †(*b*) saliva; an excretion resembling saliva: L16.

salix /ˈseɪlɪks, ˈsalɪks/ *noun.* Pl. **-ices** /-ɪsiːz/, **-ixes.** L18.
[Latin.]
Any of various small trees and shrubs constituting the genus *Salix* (family Salicaceae); a willow.

Salk vaccine /ˈsɔːlk vaksiːn/ *noun phr.* M20.
[Jonas Edward *Salk* (1914–95), US virologist.]
MEDICINE. The first vaccine developed against polio, made from viruses of the three immunological types inactivated with formalin.

salle /*in sense 1 foreign* sal (*pl. same*); *in sense 2* sɑːl, sɔːl/ *noun.* In sense 2 also †**saul.** M18.
[French: cf. SALA *noun*¹.]
1 a A hall, a large room, esp. in France. *rare.* M18. ▸**b** A gambling house or room. Also ***salle de jeux*** /də ʒø/. L19. ▸**c** A fencing school or room. Also more fully ***salle d'armes*** /darm/. M20.
2 The finishing department of a papermill, in which finished sheets are examined, sorted, and packed. E19.
1a *salle-à-manger* /-amɑ̃ʒe/ a dining-hall, a dining-room. ***salle d'attente*** /datɑ̃t/ a waiting-room, esp. at a station. ***salle d'eau*** /do/ a washroom, a shower-room. ***salle des pas perdus*** /de pɑ pɛrdy/ [lit. 'of the lost footsteps'] a waiting-hall at a court of law, station, etc.; a lobby. ***salle privée*** /prive/ a private gambling room in a casino.

sallee *noun* see SALLY *noun*².

Sallee-man /ˈsalɪman/ *noun.* Also **Sally-man.** Pl. **-men** /-mɛn/. M17.
[*Sallee*, a Moroccan seaport formerly of piratical repute.]
1 A Moorish pirate ship. Also ***Sallee rover.*** *obsolete* exc. *Hist.* M17.
2 *ZOOLOGY.* A chondrophore of the genus *Velella.* M18.

sallenders /ˈsaləndəz/ *noun.* Also (earlier) †**-der.** E16.
[Origin unkn.: cf. French *solandre.*]
VETERINARY MEDICINE. A dry scabby eruption affecting the back of the hock in horses. Cf. MALLENDERS.

sallet /ˈsalɪt/ *noun.* Also **salade** /səˈlɑːd/. LME.
[French *salade* from Provençal *salada*, Italian *celata*, or Spanish *celada*, from Proto-Romance use as noun (sc. *cassis*, *galea* helmet) of *caelata* fem. pa. pple of Latin *caelare* engrave, from *caelum* chisel. The form in *-et* arose from reduction of the final syll. due to initial stress.]
▶ **I 1** *ANTIQUITIES.* A light round helmet without a crest and with the lower part curving outwards behind, worn as part of medieval armour. LME.
▶ **II 2** See SALAD.

sallow /ˈsaləʊ/ *noun.*
[Old English (Anglian) *salh*, infl. *salg-* (repr. directly by dial. SAUGH) from Germanic, rel. to Old High German *salaha*, Old Norse *selja*, and to Latin SALIX, Greek *helikē*.]

1 A willow; *esp.* a pussy willow, as distinguished from the flexible willows or osiers. Also, a branch of such a willow. OE. ▸†**b** = SALLY *noun*[2] 2. *Austral.* E–M19.
2 The wood of a sallow tree. LME.
3 Any of various noctuid moths whose larvae feed on sallow or willow, esp. *Xanthia icteritia*. Also more fully ***sallow moth***. E19.
■ **sallowy** *adjective* having many sallows M19.

sallow /ˈsaləʊ/ *adjective.*
[Old English *salo* = Middle Dutch *salu, saluwe* discoloured, dirty, Old High German *salo* dark-coloured (German dial. *sal*), Old Norse *sǫlr* yellow, from Germanic.]
Of a person or the complexion: having an unhealthy yellow or pale brown colour.
> *transf.*: CARLYLE Their faith is no sallow plant of darkness. **sallow kitten (moth)** a kitten-moth, *Furcula furcula*.

■ **sallowish** *adjective* M18. **sallowness** *noun* E18.

sallow /ˈsaləʊ/ *verb trans.* M19.
[from the adjective.]
Make sallow.

sally /ˈsali/ *noun*[1]. LME.
[Old & mod. French *saillie* use as noun of fem. pa. pple of *saillir* to leap, alt. of Old French *salir* from Latin *salire*.]
▶ **I 1** A sudden charge out of a besieged place against the enemy, a sortie (esp. in ***make a sally***). Formerly also, a place from which a sally may be made. LME.
2 A leaping or rushing movement. Now only NAUTICAL, a sudden rush by crew from one part of a vessel to another, usu. to free it when aground. L16.
3 A sudden start into activity. E17.
4 An excursion, an expedition. M17.
5 A sudden departure from the bounds of custom, prudence, or propriety; an audacious or adventurous act, an escapade. Now *rare*. M17.
6 A breaking forth from restraint; an outburst *of* emotion or expression. L17.
7 A sprightly or audacious utterance or literary composition; a brilliant remark, a witticism; a piece of banter. M18.
> **1** R. L. FOX Stone-throwers . . used to repel army sallies. **3** *Daily Telegraph* A . . sally against the credit industry would choke off . . demand. **4** P. P. READ The elegant suit . . for sallies into the West End. *fig.*: L. EDEL Faulkner's bold sally into the consciousness of an idiot. **6** D. HUME It is difficult to abstain from some sally of panegyric. **7** W. S. MAUGHAM Laughter at the sallies of the local wag.

▶ **II 8** ARCHITECTURE. A deviation from the alignment of a surface; a projection, a prominence, esp. on the end of a timber. M16.

sally /ˈsali/ *noun*[2]. In sense 2 also **sallee**. M16.
[Alt. of SALLOW *noun*.]
1 = SALLOW *noun* 1. *dial.* M16.
2 Any of several eucalypts and acacias resembling willows in habit or appearance. *Austral.* L19.

sally /ˈsali/ *noun*[3]. M17.
[Perh. from SALLY *noun*[1] 2.]
CAMPANOLOGY. **1** The first movement of a bell when set for ringing; the position of a bell when set. M17.
2 The part of a bell-rope near the lower end which has coloured wool woven into it to provide a grip for the hands. E19.

Sally /ˈsali/ *noun*[4]. *colloq.* E20.
[Alt. of *Salvation Army* s.v. SALVATION.]
1 a *The* Salvation Army. Also ***Sally Ann(e)***, ***Sally Army***. E20. ▸**b** A member of the Salvation Army. M20.
2 A Salvation Army hostel. Also ***Sally Ann(e)***. M20.

sally /ˈsali/ *verb.* LME.
[from SALLY *noun*[1].]
1 †**a** *verb trans.* Mount an attack against, assault. *Scot.* LME–L16. ▸**b** *verb intrans.* Of a military force etc.: rush *out* from a place of defence or retreat in order to attack; *spec.* (of a besieged force) make a sortie. LME.
2 *verb intrans.* Set *out* on a journey or expedition; go *forth* from a place. L16.
3 *verb intrans.* Of a thing: come out suddenly, break out, burst forth. M17.
4 a *verb intrans.* Move or run from side to side; progress by rocking. NAUTICAL & *dial.* E19. ▸**b** *verb trans.* Rock (a vessel) by running from side to side, usu. to free it when aground. NAUTICAL. E20.
> **2** D. ARKELL Eliot would sally forth . . to savour the Paris night. **3** J. BARZUN Self-assertiveness can sally forth when cloaked in humour.

■ **sallier** *noun* (*rare*) a person who takes part in a sally L17.

Sally Lunn /salɪ ˈlʌn/ *noun.* L18.
[Perh. name of a woman who first sold such cakes in Bath in the late 18th cent.]
1 A sweet light teacake, usu. served hot. L18.
2 Any of several varieties of yeast and soda bread, esp. in the southern US. E20.

Sally-man *noun* var. of SALLEE-MAN.

sallyport /ˈsalɪpɔːt/ *noun.* M17.
[from SALLY *noun*[1] + PORT *noun*[3].]
1 FORTIFICATION. An opening in a fortified place from which troops may make a sally; a postern. M17.
2 *Hist.* An opening in each quarter of a fire-ship for the escape of the crew after the ship has been ignited. M18.
3 A landing-place at Portsmouth orig. reserved for the use of men-of-war's boats. E19.

salmagundi /salməˈgʌndi/ *noun.* L17.
[French *salmigondis*, †-*gondin*, of unkn. origin.]
1 COOKERY. A cold dish made from chopped meat, anchovies, eggs, onions, etc. L17.
2 A hotchpotch, a miscellany. M18.
> **2** *Maledicta* Linguistic salmagundi spoken by . . personnel who served in South Vietnam.

Salmanazar /salməˈneɪzə/ *noun.* M20.
[*Salmanasar* late Latin (Vulgate) form of *Shalmaneser* King of Assyria (*2 Kings* 17–18).]
A very large wine bottle.

salmi /ˈsalmi/ *noun.* Also **-s**. Pl. pronounced same. M18.
[Abbreviation of French *salmigondis* SALMAGUNDI.]
A ragout of game stewed in a rich sauce.

salmiac /ˈsalmɪak/ *noun.* L18.
[German *Salmiak* contr. of Latin *sal ammoniacum*.]
MINERALOGY. Native ammonium chloride.

salmine /ˈsalmiːn/ *noun.* L19.
[from Latin *salmo* salmon + -INE[5].]
BIOCHEMISTRY. A protein, one of the protamines, isolated from the sperm of salmon etc.

salmon /ˈsamən/ *noun*[1] & *adjective.* ME.
[Anglo-Norman *sa(u)moun*, Old & mod. French *saumon* from Latin *salmo(n-)*.]
▶ **A** *noun.* Pl. same, **-s**: see note below.
1 Any of various large migratory fishes of the family Salmonidae having pink flesh and much esteemed as game-fish and food; the flesh of any of these as food; *esp.* (***a***) (also ***Atlantic salmon***) *Salmo salar*; (***b***) (more fully ***Pacific salmon***) any fish of the genus *Oncorhynchus*. ME. ▸**b** Any of various fishes resembling the true salmons but not related to them, *esp.* (***a***) *US* a sciaenid sea trout of the genus *Cynoscion*; also = ***pikeperch*** s.v. PIKE *noun*[3]; (***b***) *Austral.* & *NZ.* = ***Australian salmon*** s.v. AUSTRALIAN *adjective*; also = ***threadfin*** (a) s.v. THREAD *noun*. L18.
2 The colour of the flesh of salmon; a yellowish- or orange-pink colour. L19.
1 ***Chinook salmon***, ***chum salmon***, ***humpback salmon***, ***silver salmon***, ***sockeye salmon***, etc.
Comb.: **salmon bass** *S. Afr.* = KABELJOU; **salmonberry** *N. Amer.* any of several pink-fruited N. American brambles, *esp.* the pink-flowered *R. spectabilis*; the fruit of such a shrub; **salmon-coloured** *adjective* of salmon colour; **salmon disease** (***a***) an infectious skin disease of salmon etc., freq. with secondary fungal infection; also called ***ulcerative dermal necrosis***; (***b***) = ***salmon poisoning*** below; ***salmon fry***: see FRY *noun*[1] 1; **salmon ladder** a fish ladder for use by migrating salmon etc.; **salmon leap** a stony slope or cascade in a river up which salmon etc. leap to swim further upstream; **salmon louse** = ***gill maggot*** s.v. GILL *noun*[1]; **salmon pass** = ***salmon ladder*** above; ***salmon peal***: see PEAL *noun*[2]; **salmon-pink** the light pink colour of salmon flesh; **salmon poisoning** a fatal disease of dogs on the Pacific coast of N. America, caused by rickettsias present in flukes infesting ingested salmon; **salmon run** a migration of salmon up a river from the sea; **salmon stair** = ***salmon ladder*** above; **salmon trout** = ***sea trout*** (a) s.v. SEA; any of various similar fishes, *esp.* (***a***) *US* the rainbow trout; (***b***) *US* the N. American lake trout; (***c***) *Austral.* the Australian salmon.
▶ **B** *attrib.* or as *adjective.* Of the colour of the flesh of salmon; light yellowish- or orange-pink. L18.
> S. MINOT Tennis hats and faded salmon shorts.

¶ The pl. *-s* is now used only *techn.* to denote different species of salmon.
■ **salmonet** *noun* (now *rare* or *obsolete*) a young salmon L16. **salmonid** /ˈsalmənɪd, salˈmɒnɪd/ *noun* & *adjective* (***a***) *noun* a fish of the family Salmonidae, which includes salmon and trout; (***b***) *adjective* of, pertaining to, or designating this family: M19. **salmoniform** /salˈmɒnɪfɔːm/ *adjective* of or resembling the salmons; *spec.* of or belonging to the order Salmoniformes to which the family Salmonidae belongs L19. **salmonoid** /ˈsal-/ *noun* & *adjective* (***a***) *noun* a fish of the family Salmonidae or the super-family Salmonoidea; (***b***) *adjective* of or resembling the salmons; *spec.* of or belonging to this family or superfamily: M19. **salmony** *adjective* somewhat salmon-coloured M20.

†**salmon** *noun*[2]. M16–M19.
[Origin unkn.]
In phrs. expressive of asseveration or adjuration, as ***by salmon***, ***by the salmon***.

salmonella /salməˈnɛlə/ *noun.* Pl. **-llae** /-liː/, **-llas**. E20.
[mod. Latin *Salmonella* (see below), from Daniel Elmer *Salmon* (1850–1914), US pathologist + -ELLA.]
BACTERIOLOGY. **1** A bacterium of the genus *Salmonella*, comprising pathogenic, Gram-negative, rod-shaped forms, some of which cause food poisoning, typhoid, and paratyphoid in people and various diseases in animals. E20.
2 = SALMONELLOSIS. M20.
■ **salmoneˈllosis** *noun*, pl. **-lloses** /-ˈləʊsiːz/, infection with, or a disease caused by, salmonellae E20.

salol /ˈsalɒl/ *noun.* L19.
[from SAL(ICYL + -OL.]
PHARMACOLOGY. Phenyl salicylate, $C_6H_4(OH)(COOC_6H_5)$, a compound used as a mild analgesic and antipyretic.

†**Salomon** *noun* see SOLOMON.

Salomonic /saləˈmɒnɪk/ *adjective.* *rare.* L19.
[from Latin *Salomon* Solomon + -IC.]
Of or pertaining to King Solomon.

salon /ˈsalɒn, *foreign* salɔ̃ (*pl. same*)/ *noun* & *adjective.* L17.
[French: see SALOON.]
▶ **A** *noun.* **1** A reception room in a palace or large house, esp. in France or other Continental country; a drawing-room. L17.
2 *spec.* The reception room of a lady of fashion, esp. in Paris; a social gathering of eminent people in such a room. E19.
3 An establishment in which the business of hairdresser, beautician, etc., is conducted. E20.
> **2** J. PEYSER She held salons, one for painters . . and one for writers.

Phrases: ***salon des refusés*** /de rəfyze/ [French = exhibition of rejected works] an exhibition ordered by Napoleon III in 1863 to display pictures rejected by the Salon. **the Salon** an annual exhibition in Paris of painting, sculpture, etc., by living artists.
▶ **B** *attrib.* or as *adjective.* Designating light music as played in a fashionable salon. Occas. *derog.* E20.

salone /saˈloːne/ *noun.* Pl. ***-ni*** /-ni/. E20.
[Italian: see SALOON.]
A reception room in a palace or large house, esp. in Italy.

salonnière /salɒnɪˈɛː/ *noun.* E20.
[French, formed as SALON *noun*.]
A woman who holds a salon; a society hostess.

saloon /səˈluːn/ *noun.* E18.
[French *salon* from Italian *salone* augm. of SALA *noun*[1]: see -OON.]
1 a = SALON *noun* 1. Now *US*. E18. ▸**b** = SALON *noun* 2. Now *rare*. E19.
2 A large room or hall used for meetings, exhibitions, etc., esp. in a hotel or public building. M18.
3 a A large cabin on a passenger ship for the common use of all passengers or only for those paying first-class fares. Formerly also, the passenger cabin of an aeroplane. M19. ▸**b** A railway carriage without compartments, furnished luxuriously as a drawing-room or for a specific purpose. Also ***saloon car***, ***saloon carriage***. M19. ▸**c** A car with a closed body and no partition behind the driver, for four or more people. Also ***saloon car***. E20.
4 a Any large public room used for a specified purpose. M19. ▸**b** *Hist.* A music hall; the type of entertainment provided at such halls. Also ***saloon theatre***. M19.
5 A place where alcoholic drinks are served, a bar. *US.* M19. ▸**b** A refreshment bar in a theatre; a lounge bar in a public house (also ***saloon bar***). E20.
3b ***dining saloon***, ***sleeping saloon***, etc. **4a** ***billiard saloon***, ***dancing saloon***, ***shooting saloon***, etc.
Comb.: ***saloon bar***: see sense 5b above; ***saloon car***: see senses 3b, c above; ***saloon carriage***: see sense 3b above; **saloon deck**: for passengers on a ship using the saloon; **saloon girl** a prostitute; **saloon-keeper** *US* a person who keeps a bar, a bartender; **saloon pistol**, **saloon rifle**: adapted for firing at short range as in a shooting saloon; ***saloon theatre***: see sense 4b above.
■ **saloonist** *noun* (*US*) = ***saloon-keeper*** above L19.

saloop /səˈluːp/ *noun.* E18.
[Alt. of French SALEP.]
1 = SALEP. E18.
2 A hot drink consisting of an infusion of powdered salep or (later) sassafras, with milk and sugar, formerly sold on the streets of London as a tonic. E18.

salopette /saləˈpɛt/ *noun.* L20.
[French.]
sing. & (usu.) in *pl.* Trousers with a high waist and shoulder-straps, worn esp. as a skiing garment and as a Frenchman's overalls.

Salopian /səˈləʊpɪən/ *adjective* & *noun.* E17.
[from *Salop*, a name for Shropshire, evolved from *Salopesberia* and *Salopescire* Anglo-Norman alt. of Middle English forms of Old English *Scrobbesbyriġ* Shrewsbury and *Scrobbesbyriġscīr* Shropshire: see -IAN.]
▶ **A** *adjective.* **1** Of or belonging to Shropshire, a county in central England. E17.
2 Designating a variety of porcelain made at the Caughley factory near Broseley, Shropshire in the late 18th and early 19th cents. M19.
▶ **B** *noun.* **1** A native or inhabitant of Shropshire. L17.
2 A pupil of Shrewsbury School. M19.

salotto /sa'lɒtəʊ/ *noun*. Pl. **-tti** /-tti/. **E20**.
[Italian, dim. of SALA *noun*[1].]
In Italy: a drawing-room, a reception room; a lounge.

salp /salp/ *noun*. **M19**.
[French *salpe* formed as next.]
ZOOLOGY. Any of various free-swimming pelagic tunicates of the class Thaliacea, frequently colonial and with transparent bodies.

salpa /'salpə/ *noun*. Pl. **-pae** /-piː/, **-pas**. **M19**.
[mod. Latin, prob. from classical Latin from Greek *salpē* fish.]
ZOOLOGY. Any of various salps of the family Salpidae. Now only as mod. Latin genus name.

Salpausselkä /'salpaʊsɛlkə/ *noun*. **E20**.
[Finnish.]
PHYSICAL GEOGRAPHY. Either of two steep recessional moraines in southern Finland, usu. regarded as a series of end moraines marking the last glacial readvance.

salpicon /'salpɪkɒn/ *noun*. **E18**.
[French from Spanish, from *salpicar* sprinkle (with salt).]
COOKERY. A stuffing for veal, beef, or mutton, also used as a garnish.

salpiglossis /salpɪ'glɒsɪs/ *noun*. **E19**.
[mod. Latin (see below), from Greek *salpigx* trumpet + *glōssa* tongue, from the shape of the corolla.]
Any of various garden annuals constituting the genus *Salpiglossis*, of the nightshade family, grown for their funnel-shaped flowers.

salpinges *noun* pl. of SALPINX.

salpingo- /sal'pɪŋgəʊ/ *combining form*. Before a vowel also **salping-**.
[from Greek *salpigg-*, *salpigx* trumpet: see -O-.]
MEDICINE. Of the Fallopian (or, formerly, the Eustachian) tubes.
■ **salpin'gectomy** *noun* (an instance of) surgical removal of a Fallopian tube (also called *tubectomy*) **L19**. **salpin'gitis** *noun* inflammation of the Fallopian (or, formerly, the Eustachian) tubes caused by bacterial infection **M19**. **salpingogram** *noun* an image of the Fallopian tubes obtained with X-rays or ultrasound **E20**. **salpingo'graphic** *adjective* of or pertaining to salpingography **E20**. **salpin'gography** *noun* the process or technique of obtaining salpingograms **M20**. **salpin'golysis** *noun* the removal of adhesions that hold the Fallopian tubes in abnormal positions with respect to the ovaries and hence prevent conception **M20**. **salpingo-oopho'rectomy** *noun* (an instance of) surgical removal of a Fallopian tube and an ovary **L19**. **salpingo-oopho'ritis** *noun* inflammation of a Fallopian tube and an ovary **E20**. **salpingo-pha'ryngeal** *adjective* of or pertaining to the Eustachian tube and the pharynx **L19**. **salpin'gostomy** *noun* a surgical operation to restore free passage through a blocked Fallopian tube **L19**. **salpin'gotomy** *noun* (an instance of) surgical incision into a Fallopian tube **L19**.

salpinx /'salpɪŋks/ *noun*. Pl. **salpinges** /sal'pɪndʒiːz/. **M19**.
[formed as prec.]
ANTIQUITIES. An ancient Greek trumpet with a straight tube.

sal-prunella /salprʊ'nɛlə/ *noun*. **L17**.
[mod. Latin, from SAL *noun*[1] + PRUNELLA *noun*[3].]
Potassium nitrate cast into cakes or balls.

salsa /'salsə/ *noun*. **M19**.
[Spanish, Italian = sauce.]
1 Esp. in Latin American cookery: a spicy tomato sauce. **M19**.
2 [Amer. Spanish.] Contemporary dance music of Caribbean origin which incorporates jazz and rock elements; a dance to this music. **L20**.
1 salsa verde [= green] (*a*) an Italian sauce made with olive oil, garlic, capers, anchovies, vinegar or lemon juice, and parsley; (*b*) a Mexican sauce of finely chopped onion, garlic, coriander, parsley, and hot peppers.

salse /sals/ *noun*. Now *rare*. **M19**.
[French from Italian *salsa*, orig. the name of a mud volcano near Modena.]
GEOLOGY. A mud volcano.

salsify /'salsɪfi/ *noun*. **L17**.
[French *salsifis* (also †*salsefie*, †*-fique*) from Italian †*salsefica* (mod. *sassefrica*), earlier †*erba salsefica*, of unkn. origin.]
A purple-flowered plant of the composite family, *Tragopogon porrifolius*, allied to the scorzoneras and grown for its similar-tasting root; the root of this plant, eaten as a vegetable.
black salsify (the root of) the cultivated scorzonera, *Scorzonera hispanicus*.

salsola /sal'səʊlə, 'salsələ/ *noun*. **E19**.
[mod. Latin (see below) from Italian †*salsola* dim. of *salso* salty.]
Any of various sodium-rich plants constituting the genus *Salsola*, of the goosefoot family, which grow on sea-coasts and in inland saline habitats, e.g. saltwort, *S. kali*.
■ **salso'laceous** *adjective* belonging to the genus *Salsola*, resembling a salsola **M19**.

salsuginous /sal'sjuːdʒɪnəs/ *adjective*. **M17**.
[from Latin *salsugin-*, *salsugo* saltness, from *salsus* salty: see -OUS.]
†**1** Impregnated with salt; brackish. **M17–M18**.
2 Of a plant: growing in salt-impregnated soil. *rare*. **L19**.

salt /sɔːlt, sɒlt/ *noun*[1] & *adjective*[1].
[Old English *s(e)alt* = Old Saxon *salt* (Dutch *zout*), Old & mod. High German *salz*, Old Norse *salt* noun, *saltr* adjective, from Germanic, from Indo-European base repr. also by Latin *sal*, Greek *hals*.]
▶**A** *noun*. **1** The substance (sodium chloride, NaCl), which gives seawater its characteristic taste, a white or (when impure) reddish-brown mineral crystallizing in the cubic system; this substance as obtained by mining or by evaporation of seawater and used esp. for seasoning and preserving food. Also ***common salt***. **OE**.
2 a A substance resembling common salt in its properties, esp. in being a soluble non-flammable solid having a distinct taste and obtained by evaporation of a solution. *obsolete* exc. as repr. by senses c, d below. **ME**. ▸**b** ALCHEMY. One of the elementary principles of which all substances were supposed to be compounded. **L16**. ▸**c** In *pl*. A crystalline compound used as a medicine, cosmetic, etc. (usu. with specifying word); *spec*. = ***Epsom salt(s)*** s.v. EPSOM 2. **M18**. ▸**d** CHEMISTRY. A compound formed by the combination of an acid radical or positive ion with a basic radical or negative ion, esp. by the replacement of all or part of the hydrogen in an acid by a metallic element. **L18**.
3 A place in which salt is abundant or from which it is dug; *esp*. a salt-pit, a salt-marsh. **LME**.
4 A salt-cellar. **LME**.
5 a That which gives liveliness, freshness, or individual quality to a person's character, life, etc. Freq. (after Shakes.) in ***salt of youth***. **L16**. ▸**b** That which gives life or pungency to speech, writing, etc.; sting, piquancy, wit. **L16**.
6 In *pl*. Salt water entering a river from the sea, esp. in an exceptional rush during storms. **M17**.
7 Money collected at the Eton College Montem. *obsolete* exc. *Hist*. **M18**.
8 A sailor, *esp*. one of great experience. Also ***old salt***. *colloq*. **M19**.

📖 **1 *bay salt*, *celery salt*, *rock salt*, *solar salt*, etc. *spirit of salt*, *spirits of salt*:** see SPIRIT *noun*. **2c** S. RICHARDSON Mrs. Jewkes held her Salts to my Nose, and I did not faint. ***bath salts*, *fruit salts*, *smelling-salts***, etc. ***d acid salt***: see ACID *adjective* 2. ***basic salt***: see BASIC *adjective* 2. ***double salt***: see DOUBLE *adjective* & *adverb*. ***microcosmic salt***. **salt of lemon** potassium hydrogen oxalate, used to remove stains and mould from linen. ***salt of sorrel***: see SORREL *noun*[1]. ***salt of steel***: see STEEL *noun*[1]. ***salt of tartar***: see TARTAR *noun*[1]. ***salt of wormwood***: see WORMWOOD *noun* 1. ***triple salt***: see TRIPLE *adjective* & *adverb*. **4** *Daily Telegraph* Silver salts made before 1700 fetch thousands of pounds. ***standing salt***: see STANDING *adjective*. **5a** SHAKES. *Merry W*. We have some salt of our youth in us. **b *Attic salt***: see ATTIC *adjective*[1].

Other phrases: **above the salt**, **below the salt** among the more honoured, less honoured, guests (with ref. to the former custom of placing a salt-cellar in the middle of a table with the host at one end); of greater, lesser, worth, dignity, social standing, etc. ***a dose of salts***: see DOSE *noun* 1. **eat a person's salt**, **eat salt with** accept a person's hospitality and the resulting obligations of honour and respect; be a guest of. **in salt** sprinkled with salt or immersed in brine as a preservative. ***like a dose of salts***: see DOSE *noun* 1. **not made of salt**, **not made of sugar or salt** not disconcerted by wet weather. **put salt on the tail of** capture (with ref. to jocular advice given to children for catching a bird). **rub salt in a person's wound(s)**, **rub salt in the wound(s)** behave or speak so as to aggravate a hurt already inflicted. **take with a grain of salt**, **take with a pinch of salt** accept with a certain amount of reserve, regard as incredible or exaggerated. **the salt of the earth** [*Matthew* 5:13] a person or persons of great excellence, virtue, worthiness, etc.; those whose qualities are a model for the rest; *iron*. the aristocracy, the wealthy. **worth one's salt** efficient, competent, capable.

▶**B** *adjective*. **1** Impregnated with or containing salt; having the characteristic taste of salt; saline; = SALTY *adjective*[1] 1. **OE**.
2 Treated with salt as a preservative or seasoning; salted. **OE**.
3 †**a** Of fish: marine. **ME–L16**. ▸**b** Of plants: growing in the sea or on salt-marshes. **M17**.
4 Of experience, etc.: bitter, painful, vexatious. Long *rare* exc. *Scot*. **L15**.
5 Of speech, wit, etc.: pungent, stinging. Now *rare*. **L16**.
6 Costly, dear; (of cost) excessive. *slang & dial*. **E18**.

📖 **1** H. SMART She wept salt tears in the solitude of her . . chamber. G. E. HUTCHINSON The lagoon . . apparently is salter than the sea. **b *salt beef*, *salt pork***, etc.

Comb. & special collocations: **salt bath** a bath of a molten salt or salts, as used in annealing; **salt-box** (*a*) a box for keeping salt for domestic use; (*b*) *US* a frame-house having two storeys at the front and one at the back (also ***salt-box frame***, ***salt-box house***, etc.); **salt bridge** CHEMISTRY (*a*) a tube containing an electrolyte (freq. in the form of a gel) which provides electrical contact between two solutions; (*b*) an electrostatic link between parts of a large molecule, esp. between an acidic and a basic group; **salt-burn** = ***salt-sore*** below; **saltbush** *noun* & *adjective* (*a*) *noun* shrubs and plants of the genus *Atriplex* and related genera of the goosefoot family, characteristic of arid alkaline regions esp. in inland Australia; any of these plants; (*b*) *adjective* (of land) dominated by saltbush; **salt-cake** (*a*) common salt in the form of a cake; (*b*) sodium sulphate; **salt-cat** a mass of salt, or of salt mixed with another material; *spec*. a mixture of salt, gravel, old mortar or lime, cumin seed, and stale urine, used to attract pigeons and keep them at home; **salt cedar** *US* an introduced European tamarisk, *Tamarix gallica*; **salt chuck** *N. Amer. colloq*. the sea, the ocean; **salt dome** an anticline resulting from the forcing of a salt plug into overlying strata, sometimes forming a trap for gas, oil, etc.; also = ***salt plug*** below; †**salt eel** *colloq*. the end of a rope, esp. when used as a whip; **saltfat** [FAT *noun*[1]] (chiefly *Scot*.) a salt-cellar; **salt finger** each of a number of alternating columns of rising and descending water produced when a layer of water is overlain by a denser, saltier layer; **salt fingering** the occurrence of salt fingers; **salt fish** (a) fish preserved in salt; *esp*. (*W. Indies*) preserved cod; **salt flat** a flat expanse of land covered with a layer of salt (freq. in *pl*.); **salt-glaze** *noun* & *verb* (*a*) *noun* a hard stoneware glaze produced by throwing salt into the kiln during firing; *collect*. ceramic objects to which salt-glaze has been applied; (*b*) *verb trans*. apply salt-glaze to; **salt-glazing** (the application of) salt-glaze; **salt grass** *US* a grass that grows in salt meadows or alkaline plains, *esp*. (*a*) *Distichlis spicata*; (*b*) a spartina; **salt hay** *US*: made from salt grass; **salt horse** *Nautical slang* (*a*) salted beef; (*b*) a naval officer with general duties; **salt-house** a building in which salt is made or stored; ***salt junk***: see JUNK *noun*[2] 1c; **salt lake** a saline lake, usu. with no outlet to the sea so that salts brought in by rivers accumulate in it; ***salt-lick***: see LICK *noun* 1b; **salt-making** the production of salt, esp. by evaporation of salt water; **salt-marsh** (a tract of) marsh liable to be flooded by salt water (sometimes used for pasture or for collecting seawater to make salt); **salt meadow** (chiefly *N. Amer*.) a meadow liable to be flooded by salt water; **salt-mine** a mine yielding rock salt; *joc*. (usu. in *pl*.), a place of hard labour; *spec*. a person's work or place of employment; **salt-pan** (*a*) a shallow depression in the ground in which salt water evaporates to leave a deposit of salt; (*b*) a shallow vessel in which brine is evaporated in salt-making; **salt-pit**: from which salt is obtained; **salt plug** a roughly cylindrical mass of salt, typically 1–2 km (0.5–1 mile) in diameter and several kilometres deep, which has been forced upwards so as to distort the overlying strata and form a salt dome; **salt-pond** a pool of salt water; *spec*. a natural or man-made pond into which seawater is run to be evaporated; **salt rising** *N. Amer*. a yeastless raising agent for bread, containing salt, milk, and soda; also, sourdough; ***salt sea***: see SEA *noun*; **salt-shaker** (chiefly *N. Amer*.) a salt-cellar that is shaken; **salt side** *US* salt pork; **salt sore** a sore caused by exposure to salt water; **salt-spoon** a small spoon for taking table salt, usu. with a short handle and a round deep bowl; **salt spray**: consisting of salt water; **salt-spreader** a vehicle that spreads salt on roads to thaw snow and ice; **salt spring** a natural flow of salt water or brine out of the earth; **salt tablet** a tablet of salt to be swallowed, esp. to replace salt lost in perspiration; **salt-tax** a tax imposed on trade in salt; **salt water** water containing dissolved salt, *esp*. seawater; *colloq*. the sea; *joc*. tears; **salt-water** *adjective* (*a*) of, pertaining to, consisting of, or living in salt water; (*b*) *US* & *W. Indies* designating a recent, usu. black, immigrant; (*c*) ***salt-water taffy*** (*US*), a confectionery made chiefly from corn syrup and sugar, sold at seaside resorts in the north-eastern USA; **salt-weed** *US* American pennyroyal, *Hedeoma pulegiodes*; **salt-well** a salt spring, a salt-pan; *esp*. a bored well from which brine is obtained for salt-making; **salt-works** a building or place in which salt is produced. See also SALT-CELLAR.
■ **saltish** *adjective* **L15**. **saltishness** *noun* **M16**. **saltless** *adjective* **LME**. **saltlike** *adjective* resembling (that of) salt; CHEMISTRY ionic; (of a hydride) containing the anion H^-: **E20**. **saltly** *adverb* with the taste or smell of salt **L16**. **saltness** *noun* **OE**.

SALT /sɒlt, sɔːlt/ *noun*[2]. **M20**.
[Acronym, from strategic arms limitation talks (or treaty).]
A series of negotiations between the superpowers (begun in 1969) aimed at the limitation or reduction of nuclear armaments. Usu. *attrib*.

salt /sɔːlt, sɒlt/ *adjective*[2]. **M16**.
[Aphet. from French *à saut* lit. 'to leaping', from Latin *saltus* a leap, from *salire* to leap.]
†**1** Of a female animal: in heat. Cf. SALTY *adjective*[2]. **M16–M18**.
2 Lecherous, salacious. **L16**.

📖 **2** SHAKES. *Meas. for M*. Whose salt imagination yet hath wrong'd Your well-defended honour. C. S. LEWIS There's your lover, child. Either a monster . . or a salt villain.

¶ Rare between 17 and 20.

salt /sɔːlt, sɒlt/ *verb trans*.
[Old English *s(e)altan* = Middle Low German *solten*, Dutch *zouten*, Old High German *salzan*, Old Norse *salta*, Gothic *saltan*, from Germanic: cf. SALT *noun*[1].]
1 Treat with or store in salt as a preservative; cure or preserve (esp. meat or fish) with salt or salt water (brine). Also foll. by *down*, †*up*. **OE**. ▸**b** Foll. by *away*, *down*: put by, store away, (money, stock, etc.). *colloq*. **M19**.
2 Season with salt. Freq. as ***salted*** *ppl adjective*. **OE**. ▸**b** *fig*. Flavour as with salt; make biting, piquant, or less bland. **L16**. ▸**c** Make (a horse) resistant to disease through having survived attacks; make (a person) seasoned by experience; acclimatize. Chiefly as ***salted*** *ppl adjective*. **M19**.
3 a In biblical use: sprinkle salt on (a sacrifice); rub (a newborn child) with salt; spread salt on (land) to make barren. Now *rare*. **ME**. ▸**b** Rub salt into (a wound). *rare*. **ME**.
4 Provide (livestock) with salt. *N. Amer*. **L18**.
5 Make (a river etc.) salty; *fig*. (*Scot*.) embitter. **L18**.
6 Make (a mine etc.) appear to be more valuable a source than it is by introducing extraneous ore, material, etc., into it. *colloq*. **M19**. ▸**b** Fraudulently increase the

apparent value of (an invoice, account, etc.). *Commercial slang*. M19.

7 Foll. by *out*: (in soap-making) cause (soap) to separate from the lye by adding salt after saponification; CHEMISTRY reduce the solubility of (an organic substance) by adding an electrolyte to the solution, causing precipitation. M19. ▸**b** Foll. by *in*: increase the solubility of (an organic compound) by adding an electrolyte to the solvent. M20.

8 Sprinkle (a road etc.) with salt to thaw lying snow or ice; sprinkle (snow or ice) with salt in order to thaw it. L19.

9 Treat with chemical salts. L19.

1b *Economist* Members of previous governments . . have salted away enormous sums. **c** *Westminster Gazette* An expert and thoroughly 'salted' journalist. **2** ***salted almonds, salted peanuts***, etc. **b** G. MEREDITH He salted his language in a manner I cannot repeat.

salta /ˈsaltə/ *noun*. E20.
[from Latin *saltire* leap, perh. after HALMA.]
A game resembling draughts played on a chequer-board of 100 squares by two people with fifteen pieces each.

salt-and-pepper /sɔːlt(ə)ndˈpɛpə, sɒlt-/ *adjective*. E20.
[from SALT *noun*¹ + AND *conjunction*² + PEPPER *noun*.]
Esp. of hair: of two or more colours, one of which is light. Cf. PEPPER-AND-SALT *adjective*.

saltant /ˈsalt(ə)nt/ *adjective*. E17.
[Latin *saltant-*, *saltans* pres. pple of *saltare* to dance, frequentative of *salire* leap: see -ANT¹.]
1 Leaping, jumping, dancing. Now *rare* or *obsolete*. E17.
2 HERALDRY. Of a small animal: salient. *rare*. M19.

saltarello /saltəˈrɛləʊ/ *noun*. Pl. **-llos**, **-lli** /-liː/. L16.
[Italian *salterello*, Spanish *salterelo* rel. to Italian *saltare*, Spanish *saltar* to leap, dance, from Latin *saltare* (see prec.).]
1 The jack of a spinet or harpischord. *rare*. L16.
2 *Hist*. An animated Italian and Spanish dance for a couple involving numerous sudden skips or jumps; a piece of music for this dance or in its rhythm. E18.

Saltash luck /ˈsɔːltaʃ ˈlʌk/ *noun phr*. *Nautical slang*. E20.
[*Saltash*, a fishing port in Cornwall.]
A thankless or fruitless task that involves getting wet through.

saltate /ˈsalteɪt, ˈsɔː-, ˈsɒ-/ *verb*. E17.
[Latin *saltat-* pa. ppl stem of *saltare* dance: see SALTANT, -ATE³.]
1 *verb intrans*. Leap, jump, skip. *rare*. E17.
2 *verb trans*. & *intrans*. PHYSICAL GEOGRAPHY. Move by saltation. Chiefly as ***saltating*** *ppl adjective*. M20.

saltation /salˈteɪʃ(ə)n, sɔː-, sɒ-/ *noun*. E17.
[Latin *saltatio(n-)*, formed as prec.: see -ATION.]
1 a Dancing; a dance. E17. ▸**b** Leaping, jumping; a leap, a jump. M17. ▸**c** *fig*. An abrupt transition, a *saltus*. M19.
2 BIOLOGY. A sudden large-scale mutation; an abrupt evolutionary change. L19.
3 PHYSICAL GEOGRAPHY. A mode of transport of hard particles over an uneven surface in a turbulent flow of air, water, etc., in which they are lifted sharply up and accelerated forward by the flow, then fall back. E20.
■ **saltational** *adjective* of, pertaining to, or occurring by means of saltation M20. **saltationism** *noun* (BIOLOGY) the theory that new species arise suddenly as a result of major mutations L20. **saltationist** *adjective* & *noun* (BIOLOGY) of or pertaining to, an advocate of, saltationism M20.

saltative /ˈsaltətɪv, sɔː-, sɒ-/ *adjective*. *rare*. E19.
[from SALTATE *verb* + -IVE.]
= SALTATORY *adjective* 1.

saltatorial /saltəˈtɔːrɪəl, sɔː-, sɒ-/ *adjective*. L18.
[from Latin *saltatorius* SALTATORY + -AL¹.]
Of, pertaining to, or characterized by leaping (or dancing); BIOLOGY adapted for leaping; *spec*. belonging to the orthopteran suborder Saltatoria, which includes locusts, crickets, and grasshoppers.

saltatory /ˈsaltət(ə)ri, sɔː-, sɒ-/ *noun* & *adjective*. E17.
[from Latin *saltatorius* adjective, from *saltator* agent-noun of *saltare*: see SALTANT, -ORY².]
▸†**A** *noun*. A dancer. *rare*. Only in E17.
▸**B** *adjective*. **1** Of, pertaining to, or characterized by dancing or leaping; adapted for leaping. M17.
2 Proceeding by abrupt movements or transitions; progressing by saltation. M19.
2 saltatory replication BIOLOGY the rapid duplication of a short section of DNA to give a series of very many identical copies within the genome.

salt-cellar /ˈsɔːltsɛlə, ˈsɒ-/ *noun*. LME.
[from SALT *noun*¹ + SALER: spelling assim. to CELLAR *noun*.]
1 A small container used on the table for holding salt. LME.
2 An unusually deep hollow above the collar-bone, esp. in a young woman. Usu. in *pl*. *colloq*. M19.

saltee /ˈsɔːltiː/ *noun*. *slang*. Now *rare* or *obsolete*. M19.
[App. from Italian *soldi* pl. of *soldo* SOU.]
A penny.

salten /ˈsɔːlt(ə)n, ˈsɒ-/ *adjective*. *rare*. M17.
[from SALT *noun*¹ + -EN⁴.]
1 Salted. M17.
2 Made of salt. L19.

salter /ˈsɔːltə, ˈsɒ-/ *noun*. OE.
[from SALT *verb* + -ER¹.]
1 A manufacturer of or dealer in salt; also = ***dry-salter*** s.v. DRY *adjective* & *adverb*. OE.
2 A workman involved in salt-making. E17.
3 A person who preserves meat, fish, etc., in salt. E17.

saltern /ˈsɔːltən, ˈsɒ-/ *noun*. Now chiefly *Hist*. OE.
[from SALT *noun*¹ + Old English *ærn* building, place (cf. BARN *noun*¹ & *verb*).]
A building in which salt is obtained by boiling or evaporation; a salt-works. Also, an area of land laid out with pools in which seawater is allowed to evaporate.
¶ Between OE and L17 recorded chiefly in place-names.

saltery /ˈsɔːltəri, ˈsɒ-/ *noun*. E17.
[from SALTER: see -ERY.]
†**1** The goods dealt in by salters or dry-salters. Only in ***saltery wares***. E–M17.
2 A salt-works. L19.
3 A factory where fish is prepared for storage by salting. *N. Amer*. (now chiefly *Hist*.). E20.

salti *noun pl*. see SALTO.

saltie *noun* var. of SALTY *noun*.

saltier *noun* var. of SALTIRE.

saltigrade /ˈsaltɪgreɪd, ˈsɔː-, ˈsɒ-/ *noun* & *adjective*. M19.
[mod. Latin *Saltigradae* (see below), from Latin *saltus* a leap + -I- + -*gradus* walking.]
ZOOLOGY. ▸**A** *noun*. A jumping spider. M19.
▸**B** *adjective*. Specialized for movement by leaping; *spec*. designating or pertaining to the jumping spiders (formerly classified together as the group Saltigradae). M19.

saltimbanco /saltɪmˈbaŋkəʊ/ *noun*. Pl. **-os**. Also in French form **-banque** /-baŋk/. M17.
[Italian, from *saltare* to leap + *in* on + *banco* bench.]
A mountebank; a quack.

saltimbocca /saltɪmˈbɒkə/ *noun*. M20.
[Italian, from *saltare* to leap + *in* in, into + *bocca* mouth.]
COOKERY. A dish consisting of rolled pieces of veal and ham cooked with herbs.

saltine /sɔːlˈtiːn, sɒ-/ *noun*. Chiefly *US*. E20.
[from SALT *noun*¹ + -INE⁴.]
A salted cracker, a thin crisp biscuit.

salting /ˈsɔːltɪŋ, ˈsɒ-/ *noun*. ME.
[from SALT *verb* + -ING¹.]
1 The action of SALT *verb*. ME.
2 *sing*. & (usu.) in *pl*. Salt land; *esp*. land other than marshland regularly covered by the tide. *local*. E18.

saltire /ˈsaltʌɪə, ˈsɔː-/ *noun*. Also **saltier**. LME.
[Old French *saut(e)our*, *sau(l)toir* stirrup cord, stile with crosspiece, saltire, from medieval Latin *saltatorium* use as noun of neut. of Latin *saltatorius* SALTATORY.]
HERALDRY. An ordinary in the form of an X-shaped or St Andrew's cross; a cross of this shape.
in saltire diagonally crossed, arranged in an X-shape. **per saltire** divided into four by two crossed diagonal lines.
■ **saltireways** *adverb* = SALTIREWISE M16. **saltirewise** *adverb* in the form or manner of a saltire, in saltire E18.

salto /ˈsaltəʊ, ˈsɔː-; *in sense 1 also foreign* ˈsalto/ *noun*. Pl. **-tos**, (in sense 1) **-*ti*** /-ti/. L19.
[Italian = leap, from Latin *saltus*.]
1 ***salto mortale*** /mɔːˈtɑːleɪ, *foreign* morˈtaːle/ [= fatal leap], a daring or flying leap; *fig*. a risky step, an unjustified inference, a leap of faith. L19.
2 A somersault. L20.

Saltoun /ˈsɔːltən/ *noun*. L19.
[from Lord *Saltoun* (prob. the 17th Lord Saltoun, d. 1886).]
ANGLING. A kind of artificial fly.

saltpetre /sɔːltˈpiːtə, sɒ-/ *noun*. Also ***saltpeter**. LME.
[Old & mod. French *salpêtre*, medieval Latin *salpetra* prob. for *sal petrae* salt of rock; alt. by assim. to SALT *noun*¹.]
Potassium nitrate, occurring as a white crystalline substance with a saline taste and used in preserving meat and as the chief constituent of gunpowder.
Phrases: **Chile saltpetre**: see CHILE *noun*¹.

saltus /ˈsaltəs/ *noun*. *literary*. Pl. same. M17.
[Latin = a leap.]
A leap, a sudden transition; a breach of continuity, esp. in reasoning.

saltwort /ˈsɔːltwəːt/ *noun*. M16.
[from SALT *noun*¹ + WORT *noun*¹.]
1 Any of several plants rich in alkali that belong to the genus *Salsola*, of the goosefoot family; *esp*. (in full ***prickly saltwort***) *S. kali*, a prickly plant of sandy coasts. M16.
2 ***black saltwort***, sea milkwort, *Glaux maritima*. L16.
3 = ***glasswort*** (a) s.v. GLASS *noun* & *adjective*. L16.

salty /ˈsɔːlti, ˈsɒ-/ *adjective*¹ & *noun*. LME.
[from SALT *noun*¹ + -Y¹.]
▸**A** *adjective*. **1** Containing or impregnated with salt; tasting of salt; = SALT *adjective*¹ 1. LME.
2 Consisting of salt. *rare*. E17.
3 Piquant; racy. M19.
4 Esp. of a sailor: tough, hard-bitten, aggressive. *US slang*. E20.
5 Angry, irritated; hostile. *US slang*. M20.
5 jump salty *US slang* (suddenly) become annoyed or angry.
▸**B** *noun*. Also **saltie**. A seagoing ship. *N. Amer*. M20.
■ **saltily** *adverb* E20. **saltiness** *noun* L17.

†**salty** *adjective*². E17–L18.
[from SALT *adjective*² + -Y¹.]
= SALT *adjective*² 1.

salubrious /səˈluːbrɪəs/ *adjective*. M16.
[from Latin *salubris*, from *salus* health: see -OUS.]
1 Favourable to health; healthy, health-giving. M16.
2 Esp. of surroundings, a place, etc.: pleasant, agreeable. E20.

2 *Vanity Fair* Winnie . . had moved into a more salubrious house, complete with Jacuzzi.

■ **salubriously** *adverb* L18. **salubriousness** *noun* L17.

salubrity /səˈluːbrɪti/ *noun*. LME.
[Latin *salubritas*, from *salubris*: see prec., -ITY.]
The quality of being salubrious, healthiness, wholesomeness.

salud /saˈluː, *foreign* saˈluð/ *interjection*. M20.
[Spanish = (good) health.]
Expr. good wishes, esp. before drinking: cheers! good health!

†**salue** *verb* & *noun*. ME.
[As verb from Old & mod. French *saluer*, from Latin *salutare* SALUTE *verb*; as noun from Old French *salu* (mod. *salut*) SALUTE *noun*¹.]
▸**A** *verb*. **1** *verb trans*. Greet, salute. ME–E17.
2 *verb intrans*. Give a greeting. ME–L16.
▸**B** *noun*. A greeting. ME–L15.

saluki /səˈluːki/ *noun*. Also **sloug(h)i** /ˈsluːgi/. E19.
[Arab. *salūkī*, from *Salūk* a town in Arabia.]
(An animal of) a breed of medium-sized, lightly built gaze-hound with large pendent ears. Also called ***Persian greyhound***.

salumeria /ˌsal(j)ʊməˈriːə, *foreign* ˌsalumeˈriːa/ *noun*. E20.
[Italian = grocer's, or pork-butcher's shop, from *salume* salted meat, from *sale* formed as SAL *noun*¹.]
An Italian delicatessen.

saluresis /saljʊˈriːsɪs/ *noun*. M20.
[formed as next + DI)URESIS.]
MEDICINE. Excretion by the kidneys of a greater than usual quantity of salts.

saluretic /saljʊˈrɛtɪk/ *adjective* & *noun*. M20.
[formed as SAL *noun*¹ + DI)URETIC.]
MEDICINE. ▸**A** *adjective*. Promoting the renal excretion of salts. M20.
▸**B** *noun*. A saluretic drug. L20.

salut /saly/ *noun*. Pl. pronounced same. L17.
[French, ellipt. for *salut du Saint Sacrament* salutation (or benediction) of the Blessed Sacrament.]
ROMAN CATHOLIC CHURCH. In France and French-speaking countries, the service of benediction.

salut /saly/ *interjection*. M20.
[French, lit. 'health'.]
Used as a toast: cheers! good health!

salutary /ˈsaljʊt(ə)ri/ *noun* & *adjective*. LME.
[Old & mod. French *salutaire* or Latin *salutaris*, from *salut-*, *salus* health, welfare, greeting, salutation, rel. to *salvus* safe: see -ARY².]
▸**A** *noun*. A remedy. *rare*. LME.
▸**B** *adjective*. **1** Conducive to well-being; producing good effects, beneficial, wholesome. Also (CHRISTIAN THEOLOGY), bringing or aiding salvation. L15.
2 *spec*. Health-giving; promoting recovery from disease. *arch*. M17.

1 V. BRITTAIN I did not forget the debate, for it had taught me a salutary lesson. C. CHAPLIN Prohibition has had a salutary effect on the public's health.

■ **salutarily** *adverb* M16. **salutariness** *noun* E18.

salutation /saljʊˈteɪʃ(ə)n/ *noun*. LME.
[Old & mod. French, or directly from Latin *salutatio(n-)*, from *salutat-* pa. ppl stem of *salutare*: see SALUTE *verb*, -ATION.]
1 The action or an act of giving a greeting or saluting; a manner of saluting; an utterance, form of words, or gesture by which one person greets another on meeting, at the beginning of a letter, etc. LME. ▸**b** CHRISTIAN CHURCH. A liturgical formula of greeting between minister and people. LME. ▸**c** NAUTICAL. The action of saluting by firing guns, lowering flags, etc.; an instance of this, a salute. Now *rare*. L16.
2 *ellipt*. Used as a greeting: 'I offer salutation.' *arch*. M16.
3 ROMAN HISTORY. A ceremonial visit paid to a Roman in his house. L17.

1 the angelic salutation, **the salutation** (*a*) the angel's greeting to the Virgin Mary (cf. *Luke* 1:28–9), which forms the first part of the Ave Maria; (*b*) (a representation of) the Annunciation.

salutatory /sə'lju:tət(ə)ri/ *noun & adjective*. **M17.**
[Latin *salutatorius*, from *salutare* SALUTE *verb*: see -ORY[1], -ORY[2].]
▶ **A** *noun*. †**1** An audience-chamber; *spec*. a chamber in a church or monastery where visitors were received. Only in **M17.**
2 a A salutatory oration. *US*. **L18.** ▸**b** A greeting addressed to readers of the first issue of a periodical. *US*. **M19.**
▶ **B** *adjective*. **1** Designating or pertaining to an address of welcome, *spec*. one given as an oration by a member of a graduating class at an American college or university. *US*. **L17.**
2 *gen*. Pertaining to or of the nature of a salutation. **L19.**
▪ **saluta'torily** *adverb* (*rare*) by way of greeting or salutation **M19.** **salutatorian** /-'tɔ:rɪən/ *noun* (*US*) a student who delivers a salutatory **M19.**

salute /sə'lu:t, sə'lju:t/ *noun*[1]. **LME.**
[Partly from Old & mod. French *salut* (as noun corresp. to *saluer* SALUE), partly from SALUTE *verb*. Cf. next.]
▶ **I** An act of saluting.
1 An utterance or (now more usu.) a gesture or action by which one person expresses respect, homage, or courteous recognition to another when arriving or departing; a greeting, a salutation. **LME.**
2 *spec*. A kiss given in greeting. **L16.**
3 Chiefly MILITARY & NAUTICAL. ▸**a** A formal or ceremonial sign of respect or celebration, as marked by the discharge of guns, lowering of flags or sails, sounding of pipes, etc. **L17.** ▸**b** A prescribed or specified movement of the hand or a weapon as a sign of respect, recognition, or allegiance. **M19.** ▸**c** *The* position assumed by an individual in saluting. **M19.**
4 FENCING. The formal performance of certain guards etc. by fencers about to engage. **E19.**

> 🕮 **1** R. P. JHABVALA With his hands joined in the Indian salute. **3a** *Sun (Baltimore)* The plane waggled its wings in salute to the troops.

▶†**II 5** Safety, well-being, salvation. **L15–E16.** ▸**b** *ellipt*. At the start of a letter: greetings. Only in **M16.**
Phrases: **clenched fist salute** a salute made with the fist raised and clenched, palm forward (used esp. by Communists). ***Nazi salute***: see NAZI *adjective*. **raised-arm salute** a salute made with the arm outstretched in front at an angle of about 45° from the vertical. **take the salute** (*a*) MILITARY & NAUTICAL gesture in acknowledgement of a salute, as the highest officer present; (*b*) receive ceremonial salutes by members of a procession.

salute /sə'lu:t, sə'lju:t/ *noun*[2]. Long *obsolete* exc. *Hist*. **LME.**
[Spec. use of Old & mod. French *salut*: see prec.]
A gold coin bearing a representation of the Annunciation that circulated in France in the 15th cent.

salute /sə'lu:t, sə'lju:t/ *verb*. **LME.**
[Latin *salutare*, from *salut-*, *salus* health.]
1 *verb trans*. Greet in words; address on meeting, esp. courteously or respectfully. **LME.** ▸**b** Hail or greet as king etc. Usu. with double obj. *arch*. **M16.**
2 *verb trans*. Greet with a conventional gesture of respect or courteous recognition; greet *with* an action or gesture. **LME.** ▸**b** MILITARY & NAUTICAL. Pay respect to, greet, or acknowledge with a formal salute. **LME.** ▸†**c** Honour (a person) *with* a gift etc. **L16–M17.** ▸**d** Kiss, greet with a kiss. *arch*. **E17.**
3 *verb trans*. **a** Appear, meet, or present itself as if in welcome of or respect to. *arch. & poet*. **LME.** ▸**b** Of a sound or sight: meet or strike (the eye or ear). Now *rare*. **L16.**
4 *verb intrans*. Give a salute; *arch*. make a salutation, give a greeting. Also foll. by *to*. **L16.**
†**5** *verb trans*. Pay one's respects to; pay a complimentary visit to. **L16–L17.**
†**6** *verb trans*. *fig*. Begin acquaintance with. *rare*. **M17–E18.**

> 🕮 **1** E. SEGAL He wandered into his backyard and was saluted by an unfamiliar voice. **b** F. MORYSON King Henrie was saluted Lord of Ireland. **2** A. S. BYATT He saluted Frederica . . with his rolled umbrella. **b** H. ALLEN The thunder of the cannon of the . . British fleet saluting the Tuscan flag. **3a** SHAKES. *Tit. A.* As when the golden sun salutes the morn. **4** M. MOORCOCK I saluted in military fashion.

Phrases: **salute the judge** *Austral. colloq*. win a race.
▪ **saluter** *noun* **M16.**

salutiferous /saljʊ'tɪf(ə)rəs/ *adjective*. Now *rare* or *obsolete*. **M16.**
[from Latin *salutifer*, from *salut-*: see prec., -FEROUS.]
1 Conducive to safety or salvation. **M16.**
2 Health-giving, wholesome. **E17.**

salvable /'salvəb(ə)l/ *adjective*. **LME.**
[In sense 1 from late Latin *salvare* SAVE *verb*; in sense 2 from SALVE *verb*[3]: see -ABLE.]
1 THEOLOGY. †**a** Capable of saving. Only in **LME.** ▸**b** Able to be saved. **M17.**
2 Of a ship, cargo, etc.: able to be salvaged. **L18.**
▪ **salva'bility** *noun* **M17.**

Salvadorean /salvə'dɔ:rɪən/ *adjective & noun*. **L19.**
[from *El Salvador* (see below) + -EAN.]
▶ **A** *adjective*. Of or pertaining to El Salvador, a republic in Central America. **L19.**
▶ **B** *noun*. A native or inhabitant of El Salvador. **M20.**
▪ **Salvadoran** *adjective & noun* = SALVADOREAN **M20.** **Salvadorian** *adjective & noun* = SALVADOREAN **L19.**

salvage /'salvɪdʒ/ *noun*[1] & *verb*[1]. **M17.**
[Old & mod. French from medieval Latin *salvagium*, from Latin *salvare* save: see -AGE.]
▶ **A** *noun*. **1** Compensation paid to those who have voluntarily saved a ship or its cargo from loss by shipwreck, enemy capture, fire, etc. **M17.**
2 a The action of saving a ship or its cargo from wreck, capture, permanent loss, etc. **E18.** ▸**b** *gen*. The saving of property from fire or other danger. **L19.** ▸**c** The saving and collection of waste material, esp. paper, for recycling. **E20.**
3 a Property salvaged; a thing salvaged. **M18.** ▸**b** Waste material, esp. paper, suitable for recycling. **M20.**

> 🕮 **1** *Scotsman* The Admiralty court . . awarded . . the Southampton tugs . . a total salvage of £10,372. **2a** *Skin Diver* Topics . . such as navigation, . . light salvage and deeper diving. **3b** R. CROMPTON We'll say we're collectin' salvage if anyone comes.

Comb.: **salvage archaeology**, **salvage excavation** *N. Amer*. = ***rescue archaeology***, ***rescue excavation*** s.v. RESCUE *noun*; **salvage yard** *N. Amer*. a place where disused machinery is broken up.
▶ **B** *verb trans*. **1** Save or rescue from shipwreck, fire, loss, or general destruction; *transf. & fig*. retrieve or preserve in adverse circumstances, rescue a remnant of. **L19.**
2 Take, esp. purloin, and make use of (unemployed or unattached property). *US & Austral. colloq*. **E20.**
3 Save and collect (waste) for reuse or recycling. **M20.**

> 🕮 **1** *Milton Keynes Express* Two of the later batsmen held on to salvage a draw. B. NEIL Wondering . . how to . . salvage a little dignity. D. A. THOMAS Three battleships were sunk . . though all were subsequently salvaged. **3** BETTY SMITH Katie salvaged the longer bits of discarded chalk.

▪ **salvageable** *adjective* **L20.** **salvager** *noun* a person who salvages something, a salvor **E19.**

salvage *adjective & noun*[2] see SAVAGE *adjective & noun*[2].

†**salvage** *verb*[2] see SAVAGE *verb*.

Salvarsan /'salvəsan/ *noun*. Now chiefly *Hist*. **E20.**
[German, from Latin *salvare* save + German *Ars*(*enik* arsenic + -AN.]
PHARMACOLOGY. = ARSPHENAMINE.

salvation /sal'veɪʃ(ə)n/ *noun*. **ME.**
[Old French *sauvacion*, *salv-* (mod. *salvation*) from ecclesiastical Latin *salvatio(n-)* (rendering Greek *sōtēria*) from *salvare* SAVE *verb*: see -ION.]
1 CHRISTIAN THEOLOGY. The saving of the soul; deliverance from sin and its consequences and admission to eternal life, brought about by Christ. **ME.**
2 *gen*. The action of saving something; the state of being saved; preservation or deliverance from destruction, ruin, loss, or harm. **LME.**
3 A source, cause, or means of salvation; a person who or thing which saves. Now chiefly in ***be the salvation of***. **LME.**

> 🕮 **1** D. CUPITT Doctrines asserting that baptism . . is universally necessary to salvation. R. FRASER Mr Brontë preferred to dwell on damnation rather than salvation. **2** M. L. KING There is no salvation for the Negro through isolation.

Phrases: **work out one's own salvation** strive for (spiritual) salvation (cf. *Philippians* 2:12); *transf*. be independent or self-reliant in striving towards a goal.
Comb.: **Salvation Army** a worldwide evangelical organization founded on quasi-military lines for the revival of Christianity and the service of the poor and homeless; **salvation history** = HEILSGESCHICHTE; **Salvation Jane** = PATERSON'S CURSE.
▪ **salvational** *adjective* pertaining to or concerned with salvation; able to mediate salvation: **M19.** **Salvationer** *noun* (*rare*) a member of the Salvation Army **L19.** **salvationism** *noun* (*a*) religious teaching which lays particular stress on individual salvation; (*b*) (usu. **S-**) the principles or methods of the Salvation Army: **L19.** **salvationist** *noun & adjective* (*a*) *noun* a member of the Salvation Army (usu. **S-**); an evangelical preacher; *rare* a saviour; (*b*) *adjective* of or pertaining to salvationism: **L19.** **salvationize** *verb trans*. preach salvation to, seek to convert or save **E20.**

†**salvator** *noun*. **LME–E18.**
[Late or ecclesiastical Latin, from *salvare* save: see -ATOR.]
A saviour; *spec*. Jesus Christ.

Salvatorian /salvə'tɔ:rɪən/ *noun & adjective*. **E20.**
[formed as prec. + -IAN.]
(A member) of the Society of the Divine Saviour, a Roman Catholic congregation founded in Rome in the late 19th cent.

salvatory /'salvət(ə)ri/ *noun*. **M16.**
[medieval Latin *salvatorium* place of preservation, from *salvare* SAVE *verb*: see -ORIUM.]
†**1** A box for holding ointment. **M16–E18.**
2 A repository for safe storage. *rare*. **L17.**

salvatory /'salvət(ə)ri/ *adjective*. **M19.**
[from SALVATION after *preservation*, *preservatory*, etc.]
Saving, imparting safety or salvation (*to*).

salva veritate /ˌsalvɑ: verɪ'tɑ:teɪ/ *adverbial phr*. **M20.**
[Latin = safe in truth.]
Chiefly LOGIC. Without infringement of truth.

salve /salv, sɑ:v/ *noun*[1].
[Old English *salf*, *sealf(e* = Old Saxon *salba* (Dutch *zalf*), Old High German *salba* (German *Salbe*), from Germanic: cf. SALVE *verb*[1].]
1 A healing ointment. **OE.** ▸**b** *spec*. A mixture, usu. of tar and grease, for use as an ointment for sheep. Now *rare*. **E16.**
2 *fig*. **a** A remedy for sin, sorrow, etc. Now *rare*. **ME.** ▸**b** A thing which soothes or consoles wounded feelings, an uneasy conscience, etc. **M18.** ▸**c** Flattery, ingratiation. *slang*. **M19.**

> 🕮 **1** R. SUTCLIFF The salves which the old field surgeon had shown him how to use. **2a** I. GURNEY Sorrow finds salve in you. **b** R. FRAME He has always bought her presents, and . . he doesn't do it merely as . . a salve to his conscience.

salve /'salveɪ, 'salvi:/ *noun*[2]. **LME.**
[Latin = hail, greetings, imper. of *salvere* be well; in sense 1 from the opening words of the antiphon *salve regina* hail (holy) queen.]
1 ROMAN CATHOLIC CHURCH. (Usu. **S-**.) More fully ***Salve Regina*** /rə'dʒi:nə/. A popular Marian antiphon, now said or sung esp. after compline, and after the divine office from Trinity Sunday to Advent; formerly also, the singing of this antiphon as a separate devotion. Also, a musical setting for this. **LME.**
2 An utterance of 'salve'; a greeting or salutation on meeting. Now *rare* or *obsolete*. **L16.**

salve /salv, sɑ:v/ *noun*[3]. Long *rare* or *obsolete*. **E17.**
[from SALVE *verb*[2].]
A thing that explains away a discrepancy or palliates a fault or defect. Cf. SALVO *noun*[2] 3, 4.

salve *noun*[4] see SALVO *noun*[1].

salve /salv, sɑ:v/ *verb*[1] *trans*.
[Old English *s(e)alfian* = Old Frisian *salvia*, Old Saxon *salbon* (Dutch *zalven*), Old High German *salbôn* (German *salben*), Gothic *salbōn*, from Germanic base also of SALVE *noun*[1].]
1 Anoint (a wound, sore, etc.) with salve or ointment. *arch. & poet*. **OE.** ▸**b** Smear (sheep) with a medicinal mixture esp. of tar, grease, etc. Now *rare*. **E16.**
2 †**a** Restore to health, cure (a person). Freq. foll. by *of* a sickness, sin, etc. **ME–L16.** ▸**b** Heal or remedy (a disease, sin, sorrow, etc.). Long *obsolete* exc. as passing into sense 4. **LME.**
†**3** *fig*. Make good, smooth over (a defect, a lack, an offence, a disgrace, a dispute, etc.). Also foll. by *up*. **L16–E18.**
4 *fig*. Soothe (wounded feelings, an uneasy conscience, etc.); console. Also foll. by *over*. **E19.**

> 🕮 **1** J. MASEFIELD They salved my cuts and stopped the bleeding. **4** W. DE LA MARE A sovereign skill A wounded heart to salve and heal. D. M. THOMAS The lavish gifts she brought home—as though to salve her conscience.

†**salve** *verb*[2] *trans*. **L16.**
[App. from late Latin *salvare* SAVE *verb*, infl. by SOLVE *verb*.]
1 Explain, account for (a difficulty, discrepancy, etc.); overcome (a doubt or objection). **L16–M18.** ▸**b** ASTRONOMY. Account for or explain by devising an appropriate theory or hypothesis. Only in **17.**
2 Make tenable or credible, obviate objections to (an opinion, hypothesis, etc.). **L16–E18.**
3 Preserve (a person's honour, reputation, etc.); make good (one's oath, etc.). Also, save the reputation of (a person). **L16–E19.**
1b ***salve the phenomena***: see PHENOMENON.

salve /salv/ *verb*[3] *trans*. **E18.**
[Back-form. from SALVAGE *noun*[1]. Cf. earlier SALVOR.]
Save (a ship or cargo) from loss at sea; salvage, make salvage of.

salver /'salvə/ *noun*. **M17.**
[French *salve* tray for presenting objects to the king, or its source Spanish *salva* orig., sampling of food or drink, tray on which sampled food was placed, from *salvar* save, make safe; the ending *-er* is due to assoc. with *platter*.]
A tray or flat dish, usu. of metal, on which drinks, letters, visiting-cards, etc., are offered.
Comb.: **salver-shaped** *adjective* (BOTANY) (of a corolla) having a flat spreading limb at right angles to a long cylindrical tube (in the periwinkle and phlox); = HYPOCRATERIFORM.

salverform /'salvəfɔ:m/ *adjective*. Chiefly *US*. **E19.**
[from SALVER *noun* + -FORM.]
BOTANY. Salver-shaped.

salvia /'salvɪə/ *noun*. **LME.**
[mod. Latin *Salvia* (see below) from Latin *salvia* SAGE *noun*[1].]
Any of numerous labiate plants constituting the genus *Salvia*, which includes sage and clary; *spec*. one of the ornamental kinds, esp. the scarlet-flowered *S. splendens*.

salvific /salˈvɪfɪk/ *adjective.* L16.
[Late Latin *salvificus* saving, from Latin *salvus*: see SAFE *adjective*, -FIC.]
Causing or able to cause salvation.

salvinia /salˈvɪnɪə/ *noun.* L19.
[mod. Latin (see below), from Antonio Maria *Salvini* (1653–1729), an Italian Greek scholar + -IA¹.]
Any of various small aquatic ferns constituting the genus *Salvinia* (family Salviniaceae), some of which are grown in aquaria; esp. *S. molesta*, now a serious weed in tropical waterways.

salvo /ˈsalvəʊ/ *noun*¹. Pl. **-o(e)s**. Also (earlier) †**salve**. L16.
[French *salve*, Italian *salva* salutation, with substitution of *-o* ending (cf. -ADO 2).]
1 A simultaneous discharge of artillery or other firearms, esp. in a battle or as a salute. L16. ▸**b** A number of bombs released simultaneously from one or more aircraft. M20.
2 *transf.* A number of similar things, actions, etc., appearing or occurring simultaneously or in rapid succession; a barrage, a volley, a sudden burst, esp. of applause. M17.

salvo /ˈsalvəʊ/ *noun*². Pl. **-os**. E17.
[Latin, ablative neut. sing. of *salvus* SAFE *adjective*, as in medieval Latin law phrs. like *salvo jure* without prejudice to the right of (a specified person) etc.]
1 A saving clause; a provision that a certain ordinance shall not be binding where it would interfere with a specified right or duty; a reservation, a qualification. (Foll. by *of*, *for*, †*to*.) E17.
2 A dishonest mental reservation; an evasion, an excuse. Now *rare*. M17.
†**3** A solution of a difficulty, an answer to an objection. Cf. SALVE *noun*³. M17–L18.
4 A thing intended to save a person's reputation or soothe offended pride or conscience. Cf. SALVE *noun*³. M18.

Salvo /ˈsalvəʊ/ *noun*³. *Austral. colloq.* Pl. **-os**. L19.
[Abbreviation: see -O.]
A member of the Salvation Army; in *pl.*, *the* Salvation Army.

salvo /ˈsalvəʊ/ *verb trans.* M19.
[from SALVO *noun*¹.]
Salute with a salvo or volley of shots etc.; drop a salvo of (bombs).

sal volatile /sal vəˈlatɪli/ *noun phr.* M17.
[mod. Latin = volatile salt.]
Ammonium carbonate, esp. in the form of an aromatic solution in alcohol to be sniffed as a restorative in faintness etc.; smelling-salts.

salvor /ˈsalvə, ˈsalvɔː/ *noun.* L17.
[formed as SALVE *verb*³ + -OR.]
NAUTICAL. **1** A person engaged in, assisting in, or attempting salvage. L17.
2 A ship used in salvage. E19.

salvy /ˈsalvi, ˈsɑːvi/ *adjective. dial. & US.* M19.
[from SALVE *noun*¹ + -Y¹.]
Of a greasy or soapy consistency. Also *derog.*, (of a person) unctuous or oily in manner, slimy.

salwar *noun* var. of SHALWAR.

Salzburger /ˈsaltsbəːgə, *foreign* ˈzaltsbʊrgər/ *adjective & noun.* M19.
[German.]
(A native or inhabitant) of Salzburg, a city in western Austria.
Salzburger nockerl a kind of small light sweet dumpling made with beaten eggs.

SAM /sam/ *abbreviation.*
Surface-to-air missile.

Sam /sam/ *noun*¹. *arch. slang.* E19.
[Origin uncertain: in sense 1 perh. from familiar dim. of male forename *Samuel* (cf. SAMMY *noun*); in sense 2 perh. from SALMON *noun*² or from SANG *noun*¹.]
1 ***stand Sam***, pay expenses, esp. for drinks, a meal, etc. E19.
2 ***upon my Sam***, expr. asseveration. *joc.* L19.

Sam /sam/ *noun*². *derog. & racially offensive.* M19.
[Abbreviation of SAMBO *noun*¹ 1.]
A black man.

sam /sam/ *verb*¹. *obsolete* exc. *dial.* Infl. **-mm-**.
[Old English *samnian* = Old Frisian *somnia*, Old Saxon *samnon*, Middle Low German, Middle Dutch *sam(e)nen* (Dutch *zamelen*), Old High German *samanōn* (German *sammeln*), Old Norse *samna*, *safna*, from Germanic base repr. also by Sanskrit *samanā* together.]
†**1 a** *verb trans.* Assemble (people). OE–LME. ▸**b** *verb trans.* Bring together, join, in marriage, friendship, love, etc. Only in ME. ▸**c** *verb intrans.* Assemble, come together. Only in ME.
2 *verb trans.* Bring or collect (things) together. Usu. foll. by *together*, *up*. OE.
3 *verb trans.* Orig. (foll. by *together*) coagulate. Now, curdle (milk) for cheese. E17.

sam /sam/ *verb*². Infl. **-mm-**. L19.
[Perh. from some word with SAM-. Cf. SAMMY *verb*.]
= SAMMY *verb*.

sam- /sam/ *prefix* (not productive). *obsolete* exc. *dial.*
[Old English *sam-* = Old Saxon, Old High German *sām-*, from Germanic from Indo-European base also of SEMI-.]
Forming adjectives with the sense 'half-'.
sam-sodden half cooked, half done; *fig.* half-baked, stupid.

Sam. *abbreviation.*
Samuel (in the Bible).

samaan *noun* var. of SAMAN *noun*².

samadh /səˈmɑːd/ *noun.* E19.
[Sanskrit *samādhi*: see next.]
In the Indian subcontinent: the tomb of a holy man or yogi who is assumed to have achieved *samadhi* rather than to have died.

samadhi /səˈmɑːdi/ *noun.* L18.
[Sanskrit *samādhi* contemplation, lit. 'a putting together, joining'.]
HINDUISM & BUDDHISM. **1** The state of union with creation into which a perfected yogi or holy man is said to pass at the time of apparent death. Also = SAMADH; a memorial constructed over this. L18.
2 A state of intense concentration induced by meditation, in which union with creation is attained; the last stage of yoga. E19.

samaj /səˈmɑːdʒ/ *noun.* L19.
[Sanskrit *samāja* meeting, society.]
In the Indian subcontinent: an assembly, a society; *esp.* a religious body or movement.

Samal /ˈsamal/ *noun & adjective.* E20.
[Samal.]
▸**A** *noun.* A member of a Muslim people inhabiting the Sulu archipelago in the Philippines; the Austronesian language of this people. E20.
▸**B** *attrib.* or as *adjective.* Of or pertaining to this people or their language. M20.

saman /ˈsɑːmən/ *noun*¹. L18.
[Sanskrit *sāman* chant.]
HINDUISM. A sacrificial chant or hymn of praise, usu. drawn from the Rig-veda.

saman /saˈmɑːn/ *noun*². Also **samaan**. L19.
[Amer. Spanish *samán* from Carib *zamang*.]
The guango or rain-tree, *Albizia saman*. Also ***saman tree***.

samango /saˈmaŋgəʊ/ *noun.* Pl. **-os**. L19.
[Bantu.]
In full ***samango guenon***, ***samango monkey***. An African monkey, *Cercopithecus mitis*, which has blue-grey fur with black markings. Also called ***diadem monkey***, ***diademed monkey***.

Samanid /səˈmɑːnɪd, ˈsamənɪd/ *noun & adjective.* Also †**-ide**. M19.
[from *Sāmān-Khodā*, founder of the dynasty + -ID³.]
▸**A** *noun.* A member of a Muslim dynasty which ruled in Persia in the 9th and 10th cents., the first native dynasty following the Muslim Arab conquest. M19.
▸**B** *adjective.* Pertaining to or designating this dynasty. E20.

samara /ˈsamərə, səˈmɑːrə/ *noun.* L16.
[mod. Latin use of Latin *samara* seed of the elm.]
BOTANY. A dry indehiscent fruit in which the pericarp is extended to form a wing, as in the elm and ash.

Samaritan /səˈmarɪt(ə)n/ *noun & adjective.* OE.
[Late Latin *Samaritanus*, from Greek *Samareitēs*, from *Samareia* Samaria (see below): see -ITE¹, -AN.]
▸**A** *noun.* **1** A native or inhabitant of Samaria, a region west of the River Jordan; *esp.* an adherent of a religious system resembling ancient Judaism accepting as scripture only the Pentateuch. OE. ▸**b** = ***Samaritan Pentateuch*** below. Long *rare*. E17. ▸**c** The Aramaic dialect used in Samaria; the script in which this is written. L18.
2 In full ***good Samaritan***. [After *Luke* 10:33.] A person who is compassionate and helpful, esp. to those in adversity. M17.
3 A member of an organization founded in London in 1953 that offers counselling, esp. by telephone, to people in emotional distress or contemplating suicide; in *pl.*, this organization. M20.
▸**B** *adjective.* Of or pertaining to Samaria or the Samaritans; used by the Samaritans; of or characteristic of a good Samaritan. LME.
Samaritan Pentateuch a recension of the Pentateuch used by the Samaritans, the manuscripts of which are written in archaic characters.
■ **Samaritanism** *noun* (*a*) the religious system of the Samaritans; (*b*) compassion, helpfulness: M17.

samarium /səˈmɛːrɪəm/ *noun.* L19.
[from SAMAR(SKITE + -IUM.]
A hard grey metallic chemical element, atomic no. 62, belonging to the lanthanide series, found in small quantities in monazite, samarskite, and other rare-earth minerals. (Symbol Sm.)

samarra /səˈmarə/ *noun*¹. M18.
[medieval Latin: cf. SIMAR.]
Hist. A rough outer garment painted with flames, devils, etc., worn on the way to execution by a person condemned by the Inquisition to be burnt.

Samarra /səˈmɑːrə/ *noun*². M20.
[A city in northern Iraq, featuring in a tale in a play by Somerset Maugham, in which a man sees Death in Baghdad and flees to distant Samarra to escape, not realizing that Death always intended meeting him that night in Samarra.]
appointment in Samarra, an unavoidable meeting with death or fate.

samarskite /ˈsamɑːskʌɪt/ *noun.* M19.
[from V. E. *Samarskiĭ*-Vykhovets (1803–70), Russian mining engineer + -ITE¹.]
MINERALOGY. A complex niobate and tantalate of yttrium, uranium, and iron, with other metals including lanthanides, found as velvet-black or dark brown monoclinic prisms in granite pegmatites.

samba /ˈsambə/ *noun*¹. L19.
[Portuguese, of African origin.]
A Brazilian dance of African origin; a Latin American and ballroom dance imitative of this; a piece of music for this dance, usu. in 2/4 or 4/4 time.

samba *noun*² var. of SAMBO *noun*¹.

samba *noun*³ var. of SAMBAR *noun*¹.

samba /ˈsambə/ *verb intrans.* Pa. t. & pple **sambaed**, **samba'd**. M20.
[from SAMBA *noun*¹.]
Dance the samba.

sambal /ˈsambal/ *noun.* E19.
[Malay.]
In Malayan and Indonesian cookery, a relish consisting of raw vegetables or fruit prepared with spices and vinegar.

sambaquí /sambaˈki/ *noun.* L19.
[Tupi-Guarani.]
ARCHAEOLOGY. A mound or midden of shells found on the S. Brazilian coast, in which remains of prehistoric and historic cultures have been found.

sambar /ˈsambə/ *noun*¹. Also (earlier) †**sabre**, **-bur**, **samba**. L17.
[Hindi *sāar*, *sābar* from Sanskrit *śambara*.]
A large deer, *Cervus unicolor*, of which there are several subspecies, native to southern Asia and introduced to Australia and New Zealand.

sambar /ˈsambɑː/ *noun*². M20.
[Tamil *cāmpār* from Marathi *sāb(h)ar* from Sanskrit *sambhāra* collection, materials.]
In southern Indian cookery, a highly seasoned lentil and vegetable dish.

sambo /ˈsambəʊ/ *noun*¹. In sense 2 also **zam-** /ˈzam-/. Pl. **-o(e)s**. In sense 1 also **samba** /ˈsambə/, pl. **-s**. E18.
[In sense 1 perh. from Fulfulde *sambo* uncle. In sense 2 from Amer. Spanish *zambo* = a kind of yellow monkey from Kikongo *nzambu* monkey; cf. Spanish *zambo* (adjective) bandy-legged.]
1 (Usu. **S-**.) (A nickname for) a black person. Also *attrib.*, esp. with ref. to a subservient manner or attitude supposed to be typical of black American slaves. *derog. & racially offensive.* E18.
2 *Hist.* A dark-skinned person of mixed descent, esp. having one black and one American Indian parent, or having one black and one mixed-race parent. M18.

sambo /ˈsambəʊ/ *noun*². M20.
[Russian, acronym, from *samozashchita bez oruzhiya*, lit. 'unarmed self-defence'.]
A type of wrestling resembling judo, originating in the former USSR. Also more fully ***sambo wrestling***.

sambok *noun & verb* var. of SJAMBOK.

Sam Browne /sam ˈbraʊn/ *noun.* E20.
[Sir Samuel J. *Browne* (1824–1901), Brit. military commander.]
In full ***Sam Browne belt***. A belt with a supporting strap passing over the right shoulder, esp. as worn by army and police officers.

sambuca /samˈb(j)uːkə/ *noun*¹. Also **sambuke** /-ˈbjuːk/. LME.
[Latin from Greek *sambukē*, cogn. with Aramaic *śabbĕkā*.]
ANCIENT HISTORY. **1** A triangular stringed instrument. LME.
2 A kind of siege-engine. *rare*. LME.

sambuca /samˈbʊkə/ *noun*². Also **-cca**. L20.
[Italian, from Latin *sambucus* elder tree.]
An Italian aniseed-flavoured liqueur; a drink of this.

sambuk /ˈsambuːk/ *noun*. Also **-buq**. L16.
[Origin unkn.]
A small sailing vessel used on the Arabian and Red Seas.

sambuke *noun* var. of SAMBUCA *noun*[1].

sambuq *noun* var. of SAMBUK.

sambur *noun* var. of SAMBAR *noun*[1].

Samburu /samˈbʊruː/ *noun & adjective*. L19.
[Nilotic.]
▶**A** *noun*. Pl. same. A member of a pastoral people of mixed Hamitic stock inhabiting northern Kenya. Also, the Nilotic language of this people. L19.
▶**B** *attrib*. or as *adjective*. Of or pertaining to the Samburu or their language. L19.

samcloth /ˈsamklɒθ/ *noun*. Long *obsolete* exc. *Hist*. LME.
[Perh. from SEAM *noun*[1] + CLOTH *noun*.]
A piece of canvas or other cloth for embroidering, a sampler.

same /seɪm/ *adjective, pronoun, noun, & adverb*. ME.
[Old Norse *same* masc., *sama* fem., neut. = Old High German, Gothic *sama* from Germanic adjective from Indo-European, whence also Sanskrit *sama*, Greek *homos* (see HOMO-). Superseded ILK *adjective*[1] & *pronoun*[1] and SELF *pronoun, adjective, & noun* in general use.]
Usu. preceded by *the*.
▶**A** *adjective*. **1** Identical with what is indicated in the following context. (Foll. by *as, that, when, where*, etc.; (*arch*.) *with*.) ME.
2 Identical with what has been indicated in the preceding context. ME. ▸**b** ***that same, this same, those same***, etc., (of a thing or person) previously alluded to, just mentioned, aforesaid. ME.
3 Of a thing or person: that is the one identical thing or person, although designated by different names, standing in different relations, or related to different subjects or objects. LME.
4 a Chiefly *pred*. Of a thing or person: sharing identical attributes with another, itself, or him- or herself at a different time; exactly agreeing *in* amount, quality, operation, etc. Also, unchanged, unvarying; uniform, monotonous. M17. ▸**b** Corresponding in relative position. L17.
5 *pred*. Equally acceptable or unacceptable; no different. Chiefly in ***all the same, just the same***. Foll. by *to*. E19.

> 📖 **1** T. HARDY She was intending to go back by the same carrier who had brought her. L. DURRELL He had made the same judgements . . as we were later to make. G. GREENE My father and mother were both killed on the same night that I lost my hand. A. THWAITE Wearing the same clothes he had worn . . earlier. **2** D. EDEN Wrap it up an post it the same way. *Daily Telegraph* Under the same amendment the Government has agreed that . . a list should be provided. **b** SIR W. SCOTT If this same Palmer will lead me From hence. **3** C. ISHERWOOD Let's hope they will . . die in the same hour of the same night. M. AMIS Mr. Riding and my father were the same age. D. LEAVITT They danced—the only same sex couple on the floor. **4a** W. H. PRESCOTT Bigotry is the same in every faith and every age. S. J. PERELMAN I am still the same springy kid. F. TUOHY Other blocks, all exactly the same, blotted out the distances. T. ROETHKE Nothing new here: the same themes, the same waitresses, the same jokes. *Traveller* Ghoul means the same in Arabic. **b** I. MURDOCH Company or no company, she came always at the same hour. **5** S. DELANEY If you want to go back there it's all the same to me.

Phrases: (A selection of cross-refs. only is included: see esp. other nouns.) ***at the same time***: see TIME *noun*. ***by the same token***: see TOKEN *noun*. ***from the same stable***: see STABLE *noun*[1] 2b. *INDIVIDUALLY* ***the same***. ***in the same boat***: see BOAT *noun* 1. ***in the same measure***: see MEASURE *noun*. **much the same** similar, approximately the same. ***not in the same street with***: see STREET *noun*. ***of the same leaven***: see LEAVEN *noun*. ***one and the same***: see ONE *adjective, noun, & pronoun*. **same but different** *colloq*. almost the same, subtly different. **same difference** *colloq*. no difference, the same thing. ***sing the same song***: see SING *verb*[1]. ***speak the same language***, ***talk the same language***: see LANGUAGE *noun*[1]. **the very same**, †**the same very** exactly or emphatically the same. ***under the same roof***: see ROOF *noun*.
▶**B** *pronoun & noun*. **1** *The* same person or persons. ME.
2 *The* same thing. ME.
3 The aforesaid person, thing, or things; the person, thing, or things in question; *loosely* he, she, it, they. Now chiefly *LAW & COMMERCE*. LME.
†**4** Used pleonastically for emphasis after a demonstrative. L16–E17.
5 *LINGUISTICS*. In *pl*. Utterances or parts of utterances that are identical. M20.

> 📖 **2** *New Scientist* The same holds for the . . habits of baboons. **3** S. WEYMAN To addressing one hundred circulars, one guinea . . To wafering the same, half a guinea. G. W. TURNER Put the tailboard up and secure same with a length of wire. **4** SHAKES. *Rom. & Jul.* What a pestilent knave is this same!

Phrases: **same again**, **the same again** another, esp. another drink, of the same kind as the last. **same here** *colloq*. I agree, my case is similar. **same to you**, **the same to you** may you do, have, find, etc., likewise.
▶**C** *adverb*. †**1** Together, mutually; with one accord; into one group. ME–L15.
2 In the same manner; similarly; just *as*. M18. ▸**b** ***the same***, = ***all the same*** below. *obsolete* exc. *poet*. L18.

> 📖 **2** GEO. ELIOT You'll never think the same of me again. M. LOWRY He knows bloody well same as myself it doesn't pay to shout and be unkind.

Phrases: **all the same** in spite of what has been mentioned; even if circumstances had been otherwise; nevertheless, notwithstanding. **just the same** (*a*) in an identical manner; (*b*) = ***all the same*** above. **same like** *dial*. or *joc*. just like, the same as, in the same manner as.

samel /ˈsam(ə)l/ *adjective*. M17.
[Origin uncertain: perh. repr. Old English form with the sense 'half burnt', from SAM- + pa. pple of *aelan* burn.]
Of a brick or tile: imperfectly burnt.

samely /ˈseɪmli/ *adjective*. L18.
[from SAME *adjective* + -LY[1].]
Lacking in variety, monotonous.
■ **sameliness** *noun* †(*a*) identity; (*b*) monotony: M17.

sameness /ˈseɪmnɪs/ *noun*. L16.
[from SAME *adjective* + -NESS.]
1 The quality of being the same; identity. L16.
2 Uniformity, monotony; an instance of this. M18.

samey /ˈseɪmi/ *adverb & adjective*. *colloq*. L19.
[from SAME *adverb, adjective* + -Y[1].]
▶**A** *adverb*. ***all the samey*** = ***all the same*** s.v. SAME *adverb*. L19.
▶**B** *adjective*. Identical; lacking in variety, monotonous. E20.

> 📖 M. LASKI They're always readable, if a bit samey.

■ **sameyness** *noun* M20.

samfu /ˈsamfuː/ *noun*. M20.
[Chinese (Cantonese) *shaam foò*, from *shaam* coat + *foò* trousers.]
A suit consisting of jacket and trousers worn by Chinese women and occas. men.

Samhain /saʊn; ˈsaʊɪn, ˈsawɪn/ *noun*. L19.
[Irish (Gaelic *samhuinn*) from Old Irish *samain*.]
The first day of November, celebrated by the ancient Celts as a festival marking the beginning of winter and their new year; All Saints' Day. Cf. BELTANE.

Sam Hill /sam ˈhɪl/ *noun*. *N. Amer. slang. euphem*. M19.
[Origin unkn.]
= HELL *noun* 2. Chiefly in exclamatory phrs. preceded by *in* or *the* with an interrogative word.

Samhita /ˈsamhɪtɑː/ *noun*. E19.
[Sanskrit *saṃhitā* union, connection.]
A continuous version of a Vedic text, involving phonetic liaison between, and alteration of, the words; *gen*. any of the basic collections of Vedic texts.

Sami /ˈsɑːmi, sɑːm/ *noun pl*. L18.
[Lappish (earlier *Sabme*, *Samek*): ult. origin unkn. Cf. Swedish, Norwegian *Same*.]
The Lapps collectively.
¶ The preferred native and scholarly term.

Samian /ˈseɪmɪən/ *adjective & noun*. L16.
[Latin *Samius*, Greek *Samios* (see below): see -AN.]
▶**A** *adjective*. Of or pertaining to Samos, an island in the Aegean Sea, the birthplace of Pythagoras. L16.
Samian earth earth from Samos, used to make pottery etc. **Samian letter** the letter Y, used by Pythagoras as an emblem of the different roads of Virtue and Vice. **Samian ware** (*a*) pottery made of Samian earth; (*b*) (also **s-**) a fine kind of reddish-brown pottery found extensively on Roman sites.
▶**B** *noun*. **1** A native or inhabitant of Samos. L16.
2 (Freq. **s-**.) Samian ware. M20.

samiel /ˈsɑːmɪəl/ *noun*. L17.
[Turkish *samyeli* hot wind, from Arab. *samm* poison + Turkish *yel* wind.]
The simoom.

samisen /ˈsamɪsɛn/ *noun*. Also **sham-** /ˈʃam-/. E17.
[Japanese from Chinese *sānxián* (Wade–Giles *sān-hsien*), from *sān* three + *xián* string.]
A long-necked three-stringed Japanese lute, played with a plectrum or the fingers. Cf. SAN-HSIEN.

samite /ˈsamʌɪt/ *noun*. ME.
[Old French *samit* ult. from medieval Latin *examitum* from medieval Greek *hexamiton*, from Greek *hexa-* HEXA- + *mitos* thread.]
Hist. A rich silk fabric, sometimes interwoven with gold, used in the Middle Ages esp. for ecclesiastical garments. Formerly also, a garment or cushion of this fabric.

samiti /ˈsamɪti/ *noun*. M20.
[Sanskrit = meeting, committee.]
In the Indian subcontinent, an assembly, a committee.

samizdat /ˈsamɪzdat, samɪzˈdat/ *noun*. Also **S-**. M20.
[Russian, from *sam(o-* self + *izdat(el'stvo* publishing house.]
The clandestine or illegal copying and distribution of literature, esp. in the former USSR; an underground press; a text or texts produced by this.

> 📖 *attrib*.: P. P. READ A samizdat story which had been smuggled out of Czechoslovakia. **in samizdat** in this form of publication.

samlet /ˈsamlɪt/ *noun*. M17.
[Contr. of SALMON *noun*[1] + -LET. Cf. earlier SALMONET.]
A young salmon.

samlor /ˈsamlɔː/ *noun*. M20.
[Thai.]
Chiefly in Thailand, a three-wheeled freq. motorized vehicle, used as a taxi.

sammen /ˈsamən/ *adjective*. E19.
[Alt.]
= SAMEL.

sammie /ˈsami/ *noun*. *Austral*. & *NZ slang*. L20.
[Repr. a pronunc. of 1st syll. of *sandwich* modified by following *w*: see -IE.]
A sandwich.
■ Also **sammo** *noun*, pl. **-os**, L20.

Sammy /ˈsami/ *noun*. *slang*. Now *rare* or *obsolete*. M19.
[Familiar dim. of male forename *Samuel*: see -Y[6].]
†**1** A ninny, a simpleton. M–L19.
2 [from ***Uncle Sam*** s.v. UNCLE *noun*.] An American soldier in the war of 1914–18. E20.

sammy /ˈsami/ *verb trans*. L19.
[Extended form of SAM *verb*[2].]
Partially dry (leather). Also, slightly dampen (dried leather).

samn /sam/ *noun*. L19.
[Arab.]
In the Middle East: a type of clarified butter, similar to ghee, from which the water has been extracted by boiling.

Samnite /ˈsamnʌɪt/ *noun & adjective*. LME.
[Latin *Samnites* pl., rel. to *Sabinus* SABINE *noun*[1] & *adjective*: see -ITE[1].]
Hist. ▶**A** *noun*. **1** A member of a people of ancient Italy, believed to be an offshoot of the Sabines, and often at war with republican Rome. LME.
2 A type of gladiator. E17.
3 The language of the Samnites. M19.
▶**B** *adjective*. Of, pertaining to, or used by the Samnites. E17.
■ **Samˈnitic** *adjective* [Latin *Samniticus*] M18.

†**Samnitis** *noun*. *rare* (Spenser). Only in L16.
[Origin unkn.]
A type of poisonous plant.

Samoan /səˈməʊən/ *adjective & noun*. M19.
[from *Samoa* (see below) + -AN.]
▶**A** *adjective*. Of or pertaining to Samoa, a group of islands in the Pacific, or its people, or their language. M19.
▶**B** *noun*. **1** A native or inhabitant of Samoa. M19.
2 The language of Samoa. M19.

samogon /ˈsaməgɒn/ *noun*. E20.
[Russian, from *samo-* self + *gon-* stem of *gnat'* distill.]
In countries of the former USSR, an illegally distilled spirit similar to vodka.

samolus /səˈməʊləs/ *noun*. L19.
[Latin, perh. from Celtic.]
Orig., a plant of wet places that was used by the Druids. Now, any plant of the genus *Samolus*, of the primrose family, *esp*. brookweed, *S. valerandi*.

Samorin /ˈsamərɪn/ *noun*. Also **Za-** /ˈza-/ & other vars. L16.
[Portuguese from Malayalam *sāmūri*.]
Hist. (The title of) the Hindu ruler of Calicut in southern India.

Samos /ˈseɪmɒs/ *noun*. M19.
[Greek: see SAMIAN.]
(A) fortified dessert wine produced in Samos.

samosa /səˈməʊsə/ *noun*. M20.
[Persian & Urdu *samosa(h)*.]
A triangular pastry fried in ghee or oil, containing spiced vegetables or meat.

Samosatenian /ˌsaməʊsəˈtiːnɪən/ *noun & adjective*. L16.
[Late Latin *Samosatenus*, Greek *Samosatēnos*, from *Samosata*: see -IAN.]
ECCLESIASTICAL HISTORY. ▶**A** *noun*. A follower of Paul of Samosata; = PAULIAN *noun*. L16.
▶**B** *adjective*. Of or pertaining to the Samosatenians or their beliefs. L17.

Samothracian /saməˈ(ʊ)θreɪʃɪən, -ʃ(ə)n/ *noun & adjective*. M17.
[from Latin *Samothrace*, Greek *Samothrakē* an island in the Aegean Sea + -IAN.]
▶**A** *noun*. A native or inhabitant of Samothrace. M17.
▶**B** *adjective*. Of or pertaining to Samothrace or its people. M18.

samovar /ˈsaməvɑː, saməˈvɑː/ *noun.* M19.
[Russian, from *samo-* self + *varit'* boil.]
A Russian tea urn, with an internal heating device to keep the water at boiling point.

Samoyed /ˈsaməjɛd/ *noun & adjective.* In sense 3 also **s-**. L16.
[Russian *samoed.*]
▶ **A** *noun.* **1** A member of any of several peoples inhabiting northern Siberia. L16.
2 (Any of) the Uralic group of languages of the Samoyeds. E19.
3 (An animal of) a white or buff breed of dog, once used for working in the Arctic, having a thick shaggy coat, stocky build, pricked ears, and a tail curling over the back. L19.
▶ **B** *adjective.* Of or pertaining to the Samoyeds. M17.
¶ See also OSTYAK *Samoyed*, YENISEI *Samoyed*.
■ **Samoˈyedic** *adjective & noun* (*a*) *adjective* = SAMOYED *adjective*; (*b*) *noun* = SAMOYED *noun* 2: E19.

samp /samp/ *noun. US & S. Afr.* M17.
[Algonquian (Massachusetts) *nasamp*.]
Coarsely-ground Indian corn; a kind of porridge made from this.

sampaguita /sampəˈgiːtə/ *noun.* E20.
[Filipino Spanish, from Tagalog *sampaga* Arabian jasmine + Spanish dim. suffix *-ita*.]
In the Philippines: (the fragrant white flowers of) the Arabian jasmine, *Jasminum sambac*.

sampan /ˈsampan/ *noun.* E17.
[Chinese *sānban* (Wade–Giles *san-pan*) boat, from *sān* three + *băn* board.]
A small boat used in the Far East, usu. with a stern-oar or stern-oars.

samphire /ˈsamfʌɪə/ *noun.* M16.
[French (*herbe de*) *Saint Pierre* lit. 'St Peter's herb'.]
1 An umbelliferous plant, *Crithmum maritimum*, of sea-cliffs and coasts, whose fleshy leaves are used in pickles (more fully ***rock samphire***). Also, any of several other maritime plants similarly used, *esp.* (in full ***marsh samphire***) glasswort (genus *Salicornia*). M16.
2 The leaves of samphire, used esp. in pickles. E17.
1 ***golden samphire***: see GOLDEN *adjective*.

sampi /ˈsampʌɪ/ *noun.* M19.
[Late Greek, prob. from *hōs an pi* like pi.]
An ancient Greek character representing the number 900, also hypothetically identified with any of several sibilants in early Greek alphabets.

sample /ˈsɑːmp(ə)l/ *noun & adjective.* ME.
[Aphet. from Anglo-Norman *assample* var. of Old French *essample* EXAMPLE *noun*.]
▶ **A** *noun.* †**1** A fact, incident, story, etc., serving to bear out some proposition or statement. Cf. EXAMPLE *noun* 1. ME–E16.
†**2** Action or conduct viewed as worthy of imitation; a person whose conduct deserves imitation; = EXAMPLE *noun* 5. ME–E17.
3 A relatively small part or quantity intended to show what the whole is like; a specimen; *spec.* (*a*) COMMERCE a small amount of a fabric, foodstuff, or other commodity, presented or shown to a prospective customer as a specimen of the goods offered for sale; (*b*) a specimen taken for scientific testing or analysis; (*c*) an illustrative or typical example; (*d*) STATISTICS a portion selected from a population, the study of which is intended to provide statistical estimates relating to the whole. LME.
4 A sound, esp. a piece of music, created by sampling (see SAMPLE *verb* 3c). L20.

> 📖 **3** *New York Times* 'Pushers' of narcotics . . sometimes offered free samples to beginners. N. CALDER To recover samples of the mud from the ocean floor. P. PARISH The size of the sample of patients must be statistically representative. *Which?* A sample of cells is gently scraped off the cervix with a spatula or brush. ***random sample***: see RANDOM *adjective*.

Comb.: **sample-bag** (*a*) (chiefly *Austral.*) a bag containing a commercial traveller's or advertiser's (orig. free) samples; (*b*) a small bag used by merchants and farmers to carry samples of corn etc.; **sample book**: containing samples of fabric, wallpaper, etc., for prospective buyers; **sample bottle**: in which samples of fluid esp. from the body may be collected; **sample card** a piece of cardboard to which is fastened a sample of fabric, wallpaper, etc.; a pattern card; **sample case**: containing samples carried by a commercial traveller; **sample point** STATISTICS a single possible observed value of a variable; **sample room**: in which samples are kept for inspection or displayed to prospective customers; **sample space** STATISTICS the range of values of a random variable.
▶ **B** *attrib.* or as *adjective.* Serving as a sample. E19.

> 📖 M. GORDON Lavinia did a sample interview with me. *American Speech* Murray accepted the editorship in 1878 on the basis of sample pages.

sample /ˈsɑːmp(ə)l/ *verb trans.* L16.
[from the noun.]
†**1** Be or find a match to; parallel; intend as a match *for*. L16–L17.
†**2** Illustrate, explain by examples; symbolize. Also, imitate, copy. Only in 17.
3 a Take a sample or samples of; assess or test the quality of (a thing) from a sample; get a representative experience of. M18. ▸**b** Present a sample or samples of. Also, serve as a sample of. L19. ▸**c** ELECTRONICS & AUDIO. Ascertain the momentary value of (an analogue signal) many times a second so that these values may be represented digitally (effectively converting the original analogue signal to a digital one); record (sound) digitally for subsequent electronic processing. Also, subject the music of (a composer, performer, etc.) to this process. M20.
4 Provide with samples. M20.

> 📖 **3a** W. CATHER Frank . . came in from the dining-room, where he had been sampling the Captain's French brandy. P. BOWLES She had sampled the tea several times and eventually found it to her liking.

Comb.: **sample-and-hold** *adjective* (ELECTRONICS) designating a circuit or technique in which a varying voltage is sampled periodically and the sampled voltage is retained in the interval until the next sampling.

sampler /ˈsɑːmplə/ *noun*¹. ME.
[Aphet. from Old French *essamplaire* var. of *essemplaire*, *exemplaire* EXEMPLAR *noun*.]
†**1** An example to be imitated; a model; an original from which a copy may be taken. ME–L17.
†**2** An illustrative or typical example; a representation, a symbol. ME–L17.
3 A beginner's exercise in embroidery; a piece of embroidery worked in various stitches as a specimen of skill, usu. containing the alphabet and some mottos, and often displayed on a wall etc. E16.
4 FORESTRY. A young tree left standing when others are cut down. Usu. in *pl.* M17.
5 A relatively small part or quantity intended to show what the whole is like. Cf. SAMPLE *noun* 3. E19. ▸**b** A thing which contains a sample; a collection of representative items; *spec.* a usu. promotional recording of examples of a performer, type of music, etc. Chiefly *US*. M20.

> 📖 **3** RACHEL ANDERSON A needlepoint sampler, the letters picked out in . . cross stitch. **5b** *Melody Maker* Jazz releases from A & M Records commencing . . with a jazz sampler.

■ **samplery** *noun* the making of samplers E17.

sampler /ˈsɑːmplə/ *noun*². L18.
[from SAMPLE *verb* + -ER¹.]
1 A person who samples something; *spec.* a person who tests the quality of something from a sample. L18.
2 A device for obtaining samples for scientific study. E20.
3 An electronic device used to sample sound. L20.
2 ***snapper sampler***: see SNAPPER *noun*¹ 2d.

sampling /ˈsɑːmplɪŋ/ *verbal noun.* M17.
[from SAMPLE *verb* + -ING¹.]
The action of SAMPLE *verb*; *spec.* (*a*) the action or process of testing the quality of something from a sample; (*b*) the process of sampling sounds.
Comb.: **sampling distribution** STATISTICS the theoretical frequency distribution of a statistic, based on a sample, over other similar samples; **sampling error** STATISTICS error due to the use of only a sample of a population.

sampot /sɑ̃po/ *noun.* M20.
[French from Khmer *sampuet*.]
A kind of sarong worn in Cambodia.

samprasarana /samprəˈsɑːrənə/ *noun.* M19.
[Sanskrit *samprasāraṇa* lit. 'stretching out, extension'.]
PHILOLOGY. Esp. in Sanskrit, the derivation of vowels from semi-vowels or of semi-vowels from vowels; the interchange between the vowels and semi-vowels.

†**Sampson** *noun* var. of SAMSON.

Samsam /ˈsamsam/ *noun.* M19.
[Malay.]
Chiefly *Hist.* A person of mixed Malayo-Thai origin from the west coast of the Malay peninsula.

samsara /səmˈsɑːrə/ *noun.* L19.
[Sanskrit *saṃsāra* a wandering through.]
HINDUISM & BUDDHISM. The endless cycle of death and rebirth to which life in the material world is bound.
■ ***samsaric*** *adjective* E20.

samshoo /ˈsamʃuː/ *noun.* Also **-shoe**, **-tchoo**, & other vars. L17.
[Pidgin English: ult. origin unkn.]
Chinese liquor distilled from rice or sorghum.

samskara /səmˈskɑːrə/ *noun.* E19.
[Sanskrit *saṃskāra* preparation, a making perfect.]
1 HINDUISM. A purificatory ceremony or rite marking a stage or an event in life; each of twelve such rites enjoined on the first three classes of the brahmin caste. E19.
2 BUDDHISM. A mental impression, instinct, or memory. E19.

Sam Slick /sam ˈslɪk/ *noun. US slang.* L19.
[The hero of a series of stories by T. C. Haliburton (1796–1865), Nova Scotian judge and political propagandist.]
A type of smooth-spoken sharp-practising New Englander; a resourceful trickster.

Samsoe /ˈsamsəʊ/ *noun.* M20.
[A Danish island.]
In full ***Samsoe cheese***. A firm buttery cheese from Samsoe.

Samson /ˈsams(ə)n/ *noun.* In senses 2, 3 also **s-**, †**Samp-**. M16.
[Latin *Sam(p)son*, Greek *Sampsōn* from Hebrew *šimšōn*, a blinded Hebrew hero of great strength (*Judges* 13–16).]
1 A person resembling Samson, esp. in great strength or in blindness. M16.
2 *Hist.* = CRAMP *noun*² 3. M19.
3 FORESTRY. A pole used to direct the fall of a tree being felled. E20.
Comb.: **Samson-fish** an Australian carangid fish, *Seriola hippos*, valued as a sporting fish. **Samson fox** a N. American variety of the red fox, in which the fur lacks guard hairs and so has a scorched appearance. **Samson's post**, **Samson post** †(*a*) a kind of mousetrap; (*b*) NAUTICAL a strong pillar passing through the hold of a ship or between decks; a post in a whaler to which a harpoon rope is attached.
■ **Samˈsonian** *adjective & noun* (*a*) *adjective* of, pertaining to, or resembling Samson; (*b*) *noun* a strong man: E17.

samsonite /ˈsams(ə)nʌɪt/ *noun.* In sense 2 usu. **S-**. E20.
[from prec. + -ITE¹.]
1 A variety of dynamite having an inert base of borax and salt. E20.
2 (Proprietary name for) a make of suitcase, briefcase, or other item of luggage. Usu. *attrib. US*. M20.

samtchoo *noun* var. of SAMSHOO.

Samuelite /ˈsamjʊəlʌɪt/ *noun.* M20.
[from *Samuel* (see below) + -ITE¹.]
Hist. ▶**A** *noun.* A supporter of Sir Herbert Samuel (1871–1963), British Liberal politician; *spec.* a member of the official Liberal Party which was led by Samuel after the secession in 1931 of the Liberal National Party under Sir John Simon (see SIMONITE). M20.
▶ **B** *adjective.* Of or pertaining to Samuel or his supporters. M20.

samurai /ˈsamʊrʌɪ, -jʊrʌɪ/ *noun & adjective.* E18.
[Japanese.]
▶ **A** *noun.* Pl. same. In feudal Japan, a member of a military caste, *esp.* a member of the class of military retainers of the daimyos. E18.
▶ **B** *attrib.* or as *adjective.* **1** Of or pertaining to the samurai. L19.
2 ***Samurai bond***, a bond in yen in the Japanese market, issued by a foreigner. L20.

> 📖 **1** I. MURDOCH Was it . . when I saw her cut the napkins in two with the Samurai sword?

samyama /ˈsamjəmə/ *noun.* E19.
[Sanskrit *saṃyama* restraint, control of the senses.]
HINDUISM & BUDDHISM. Collectively, the three final stages of meditation in yoga, which lead to *samadhi* or the state of union.

san /san/ *noun*¹. L16.
[Greek.]
An early Doric character representing a sibilant, later displaced by sigma.

San /sɑːn/ *noun*² *& adjective.* L19.
[Nama *sān* aborigines, settlers proper.]
▶ **A** *noun.* Pl. same.
1 = BUSHMAN *noun* 1. L19.
2 (Any of) the group of Khoisan languages of the Bushmen. M20.
▶ **B** *attrib.* or as *adjective.* Of or pertaining to the Bushmen or (any of) their languages. M20.

san /san/ *noun*³. L19.
[Japanese, contr. of more formal *sama*.]
In Japan, an honorific title used after a personal or family name as a mark of politeness. Also (*colloq.*), used after other names or titles (cf. MAMA-SAN).

san /san/ *noun*⁴. *colloq.* E20.
[Abbreviation.]
= SANATORIUM 3.

sanad /sanad/ *noun.* Also **sunnud** /ˈsʌnʌd/. M18.
[Urdu & Persian, from Arab. *sanad* document, legal instrument.]
In the Indian subcontinent, a charter, a patent, a warrant.

sanatarium /sanəˈtɛːrɪəm/ *noun.* Chiefly *US*. Pl. **-ria** /-rɪə/, **-riums**. M19.
[formed as SANATORIUM: see -ARIUM.]
= SANATORIUM 1, 2.

sanative /ˈsanətɪv/ *adjective.* LME.
[Old French *sanatif* or late Latin *sanativus*, from Latin *sanat-* pa. ppl stem of *sanare* heal: see -IVE.]
1 Conducive to or promoting (physical or moral) health; curative, healing. LME.

2 Of or concerned with healing. L17.

sanatorium /sanəˈtɔːrɪəm/ *noun*. Pl. **-riums**, **-ria** /-rɪə/. M19.
[mod. Latin, from *sanat-*: see prec., -ORIUM.]
1 An establishment for the medical treatment and recuperation of invalids, esp. convalescents or the chronically sick. M19.
2 A health resort. M19.
3 A room or building for sick people in a school etc. Cf. SAN *noun*⁴. M19.

> 1 ANNE STEVENSON He was . . suffering from tuberculosis and sent . . to a famous sanatorium. *Times* He had a nervous breakdown and spent three weeks in a sanatorium.

sanatory /ˈsanət(ə)ri/ *adjective*. L17.
[App. alt. of SANATIVE by substitution of -ORY².]
= SANATIVE.

sanbenito /sanbəˈniːtəʊ/ *noun*. Pl. **-os**. M16.
[Spanish *sambenito*, from *San Benito* St Benedict, so called iron. from its resemblance to the Benedictine scapular.]
In the Spanish Inquisition, a yellow scapular-shaped garment, with a red St Andrew's cross before and behind, worn by a confessed and penitent heretic. Also, a similar black garment with flames, devils, and other devices, worn by an impenitent confessed heretic at an auto-da-fê.

Sancerre /sɒnˈsɛː, *foreign* sɑ̃sɛːr (*pl. same*)/ *noun*. L18.
[A city in central France.]
A light white, occas. red, wine produced in the district around Sancerre.

sancho /ˈsaŋkəʊ/ *noun*¹. Also **sanko**. Pl. **-os**. E19.
[Twi *o-sanku*.]
A simple W. African guitar.

Sancho /ˈsan(t)ʃəʊ/ *noun*². Pl. **-os**. L19.
[*Sancho* Panza, the squire of Don QUIXOTE.]
A companion or foil to a quixotic person.

Sancho /ˈsan(t)ʃəʊ/ *noun*³. L19.
[from next.]
The nine of trumps in Sancho Pedro and similar games.

Sancho Pedro /san(t)ʃəʊ ˈpɛdrəʊ/ *noun*. L19.
[Spanish.]
A card-game like all fours or cinch, in which the nine and five of trumps have their face value and the ten of trumps wins the game. Cf. PEDRO.

sancocho /sanˈkotʃo/ *noun*. M20.
[Amer. Spanish, from Spanish = half-cooked meal, from *sancochar* parboil.]
In S. America and the Caribbean: a rich soup or stew of meat, fish, and vegetables.

sanct /saŋ(k)t/ *adjective*. *rare*. L19.
[Latin *sanctus*: see SAINT *noun & adjective*.]
Holy, sacred, consecrated.

sancta *noun pl.* see SANCTUM.

sanctanimity /saŋ(k)təˈnɪmɪti/ *noun*. *rare*. E19.
[from Latin *sanctus* holy + *animus* mind: see -ITY.]
Holiness of mind.

sancta sanctorum *noun phr.* pl. of SANCTUM SANCTORUM.

sancta simplicitas /saŋ(k)tə sɪmˈplɪsɪtɑːs/ *interjection*. M19.
[Latin, lit. 'holy simplicity'.]
Expr. astonishment at a person's naivety.

sanctificate /saŋ(k)ˈtɪfɪkeɪt/ *verb trans*. *rare*. L17.
[Christian Latin *sanctificat-* pa. ppl stem of *sanctificare*: see SANCTIFY, -ATE³.]
Sanctify.

sanctification /ˌsaŋ(k)tɪfɪˈkeɪʃ(ə)n/ *noun*. LME.
[Christian Latin *sanctificatio(n-)*, formed as prec.: see -ATION.]
1 CHRISTIAN THEOLOGY. The action of the Holy Spirit in making a believer holy by instilling grace and removing sin; the condition or process of being thus sanctified. LME.
2 The action of setting apart a thing as holy or sacred; hallowing, consecration. L15.
3 ECCLESIASTICAL. The action of making a person a saint; canonization. M19.
4 Blackmail, *esp.* the extortion of political favours from a diplomat. *slang*. L20.

sanctified /ˈsaŋ(k)tɪfʌɪd/ *ppl adjective*. LME.
[from next: see -ED¹.]
1 Of a person: made holy or saintly, esp. (CHRISTIAN THEOLOGY) by the divine grace of the Holy Spirit. LME.
2 (Of ground, a church, etc.) consecrated, hallowed; (of an action, quality, etc.) holy, spiritually profitable. E16.
3 Affecting holiness; sanctimonious. L16.

sanctify /ˈsaŋ(k)tɪfʌɪ/ *verb trans*. LME.
[In earliest use from Old French *saintifier*, later infl. by *sanctifier* from Christian Latin *sanctificare*, from Latin *sanctus* holy: see -FY.]
†**1** Set apart religiously for an office or function; consecrate (a king etc.). LME–M17.
†**2** Canonize, make a saint of. LME–M17.
†**3 a** Honour as holy; ascribe holiness to, hallow. LME–E17. ▸**b** Manifest (God etc.) as holy. M16–E17.
4 Make holy, impart sanctity to, (a thing, action, etc.); make legitimate or binding by a religious sanction. LME.
5 Make (a person) holy, purify, free from sin. LME.
6 a Consecrate (a thing); set apart as holy or sacred. L15. ▸**b** Keep or observe (a day etc.) as holy. L16.
7 Make productive of or conducive to holiness. L16.
8 Impart real or apparent sacredness to; entitle to reverence or respect; justify, sanction. Now *rare*. E17.
9 Blackmail (a person), esp. to extract political favours. *slang*. L20.

> 1 SHAKES. *2 Hen. IV* Let all the tears . . Be drops of balm to sanctify thy head. **3a** SHAKES. *All's Well* Whilst I from far His name with zealous fervour sanctify. **3b** AV *Ezek.* 36:23 I will sanctifie my great Name . . and the heathen shall know, that I *am* the Lord. **4** *Quest* Even the meanest performance could . . be sanctified by its reminder of God. **5** *absol.*: F. MYERS All truth ennobles and some sanctifies. **7** S. HAYWARD Sufferings . . are sanctified and made a means of preparing for heaven. **8** C. KINGSLEY He argued stoutly . . with his own conscience, that the means sanctify the end.

■ **sanctifiable** *adjective* (*rare*) able to be sanctified L19. **sanctifier** /ˈsaŋ(k)tɪfʌɪə/ *noun* a person who or thing which sanctifies something or someone; *spec.* (CHRISTIAN THEOLOGY) the Holy Spirit: M16.

sanctilogy *noun* var. of SANCTOLOGY.

sanctiloquent /saŋ(k)ˈtɪləkwənt/ *adjective*. *rare*. M17.
[from Latin *sanctus*, *sancti-* holy + *loquent-* pres. ppl stem of *loqui* speak: see -ENT.]
Speaking of holy or sacred things.

sanctimonial /saŋ(k)tɪˈməʊnɪəl/ *noun*. Now *rare* or *obsolete*. E16.
[Old French *sanctimoniale* or ecclesiastical Latin *sanctimonialis* nun, use as noun of late Latin *sanctimonialis*: see next.]
A nun.

†**sanctimonial** *adjective*. *rare*. Only in 18.
[Late Latin *sanctimonialis* holy, pious, from Latin *sanctimonia*: see SANCTIMONY, -IAL.]
= SANCTIMONIOUS *adjective* 1.

sanctimonious /saŋ(k)tɪˈməʊnɪəs/ *adjective*. E17.
[formed as next: see -OUS.]
†**1** Holy in character; sacred, consecrated. E17–E19.
2 Affecting piety, pretending sanctity. E17.

> 2 M. MEYER A sanctimonious chastiser of supposed indecencies.

■ **sanctimoniously** *adverb* E17. **sanctimoniousness** *noun* L17.

sanctimony /ˈsaŋ(k)tɪməni/ *noun*. M16.
[Latin *sanctimonia*, from *sanctus* holy: see -MONY.]
†**1** Holiness of life and character; religiousness, sanctity. M16–E18.
†**2** Sacredness; in *pl.*, sacred things. M16–L17.
3 Affected or hypocritical piety; pretence of sanctity. E17.

sanction /ˈsaŋ(k)ʃ(ə)n/ *noun*. LME.
[Old & mod. French from Latin *sanctio(n-)*, from *sanct-* pa. ppl stem of *sancire* make inviolable, from var. of base of *sacer* SACRED *adjective*.]
1 A law, a decree; *esp.* an ecclesiastical decree. *obsolete* exc. *Hist.* LME.
2 Orig., a solemn oath. Later, binding force given to an oath; a thing which makes an oath or engagement binding. E17.
3 a LAW. A penalty enacted in order to enforce obedience of a law. Later more widely, a punishment or reward for disobedience or obedience of a law. M17. ▸**b** The part or clause of a law or charter which declares the penalty attached to infringement. *obsolete* exc. *Hist.* M17. ▸**c** POLITICS. Military or economic action taken by a State or alliance of States to coerce another to conform to an international agreement or norms of conduct. Usu. in *pl.* E20.
4 The action of making something legally binding; solemn confirmation or ratification given by a supreme authority to a law, enactment, etc. M17.
5 ETHICS. A consideration which operates to enforce obedience to a rule of conduct; a recognized motive for conformity to moral or religious law, operating through a desire for some resultant good or fear of some resultant evil. L17.
6 Official permission (for an action etc.); authoritative acknowledgement or recognition (of a custom, institution, etc.). Also *loosely*, approval or encouragement given to an opinion or action by custom, tradition, etc. E18. ▸**b** In military intelligence, permission to kill a particular individual; killing resulting from this. *slang*. L20.
7 a A thing which serves to support or authorize an action, procedure, etc. E18. ▸†**b** A recommendation, a testimonial. L18–E19.

> 1 *pragmatic sanction*: see PRAGMATIC *adjective*. **3c** D. CAUTE The British Government should stop the international oil companies brazenly flouting sanctions. *transf.*: *Times Lit. Suppl.* It is difficult . . to imagine how sanctions against inchastity could be reimposed. *attrib.*: P. DRISCOLL Countries whose laissez-faire attitudes had encouraged sanctions-breaking. **6** H. J. LASKI Without the sanction of religion the full achievement of the social purpose is impossible. H. ARENDT To win sanction for the new loans he had been obliged to bribe the press.

■ **sanctionary** *adjective* (*rare*) pertaining to (esp. an ecclesiastical) law or decree M19. **sanctionative** *adjective* (LAW) pertaining to the imposition of sanctions M19. **sanctioˈneer** *noun* = SANCTIONIST *noun* M20. **sanctionism** *noun* (*rare*) the theory or advocacy of military or esp. economic sanctions M20. **sanctionist** *noun & adjective* (a person) advocating or supporting the use or imposition of sanctions M20. **sanctionless** *adjective* (*rare*) L19.

sanction /ˈsaŋ(k)ʃ(ə)n/ *verb trans*. L18.
[from the noun.]
1 Ratify; make legal, valid, or binding. L18.
2 Give official permission for, authorize; *loosely* encourage, give approval of, agree to. L18.
3 Enforce (a law, legal obligation, etc.) by attaching a penalty to transgression. E19.
4 Impose sanctions on (a person), penalize. M20.

> 2 E. F. BENSON Plays which the censor would not sanction for the London stage. M. L. KING A weary world, pleading . . for peace, has often found the church morally sanctioning war.

■ **sanctionable** *adjective* L19. **sanctioned** *ppl adjective* allowed by authority; LAW (of a right) defined or created by a sanction antecedently to any wrong: L18. **sanctioner** *noun* a person who sanctions something M19. **sanctionment** *noun* (*rare*) the action of sanctioning something E19.

sanctitude /ˈsaŋ(k)tɪtjuːd/ *noun*. *arch.* LME.
[Latin *sanctitudo(n-)*, from *sanctus* holy: see -TUDE.]
The quality of being holy or saintly; sanctity.

sanctity /ˈsaŋ(k)tɪti/ *noun*. LME.
[Partly from Old French *sain(c)tité* (mod. *sainteté*), partly directly from Latin *sanctitas*, from *sanctus* holy: see -ITY.]
1 Holiness of life, saintliness. LME. ▸**b** In *pl.* Qualities of holiness or saintliness. *rare*. L16.
2 The quality of being sacred or hallowed; sacredness, inviolability. E17. ▸**b** In *pl.* Sacred obligations, feelings, objects, etc. E19.
3 (Usu. **S-**.) = HOLINESS *noun* 3. *rare*. M17.

> 1 BURKE The blind reverence they bear to the sanctity of the Pope. ***odour of sanctity***: see ODOUR 1. **2** *Howard Journal* The judicial process should be . . less concerned with upholding the sanctity of the system. *Daily Telegraph* The 'sanctity of life' theory gave priority to life saving irrespective of quality of care.

sanctology /saŋ(k)ˈtɒlədʒi/ *noun*. *rare*. Also **-tilogy** /-ˈtɪlədʒi/. E19.
[from Latin *sanctus* (see SAINT *noun & adjective*) + -OLOGY.]
A catalogue of saints.

sanctoral /ˈsaŋ(k)t(ə)r(ə)l/ *noun*. M17.
[Anglicization: see -AL¹.]
= next.

sanctorale /saŋ(k)təˈreɪli, -ˈrɑːli/ *noun*. L19.
[medieval Latin, from Latin *sanctus* (see SAINT *noun & adjective*), after TEMPORAL *noun*¹.]
ECCLESIASTICAL. The part of the breviary and missal which contains the offices proper for saints' days.

sanctuary /ˈsaŋ(k)tjʊəri/ *noun*. Also †**sentuary**. ME.
[Anglo-Norman *sanctuarie*, Old & mod. French *sanctuaire* from Latin *sanctuarium*, from *sanctus* holy, after SACRARIUM: see -ARY¹.]
▸ **I** A holy place.
1 A building or place set apart for the worship of a god or gods; a church, a temple. Also (*arch.*), a church or body of believers; a priestly office or order. ME. ▸**b** Heaven. Long *rare* or *obsolete*. LME.
2 a JEWISH ANTIQUITIES. In the Jewish Temple: the holy place; the holy of holies. ME. ▸**b** The part of the chancel containing the high altar. Also, the chancel. LME. ▸**c** *gen.* The innermost or most sacred part of any temple. LME.
†**3** A shrine or box containing relics. LME–L15.
4 A piece of consecrated ground; a churchyard, a cemetery. Now *dial.* LME.

> 1 H. B. HACKETT Shiloh was one of the . . most sacred of the Hebrew sanctuaries. *transf.*: D. BREWSTER Admiring disciples crowded to this sanctuary of the sciences. **2c** *fig.*: SHELLEY Though ne'er yet Thou hast unveiled thy inmost sanctuary.

▸ **II** (A place of) protection.
5 a Orig., a church or other sacred place in which, by the law of the medieval church, a fugitive or debtor was immune from arrest. Later *gen.*, any place in which a similar immunity is granted to a fugitive; a place of refuge and safety. LME. ▸**b** Immunity from arrest or punishment, secured by taking refuge in a sanctuary; the right or privilege of such protection; shelter, refuge. LME.
6 HUNTING. Protection of game etc. from being killed. *rare*. E17.

7 An area of land where wild animals or plants are protected and encouraged to breed or grow. **L19.**

> 📖 **5a** J. TULLOCH His .. house was a sanctuary to the most eminent of the factious party. *Hongkong Standard* The sanctuary taken by his troops comprised two large camps on .. a hill. **b** SHAKES. *Rich. III* God in heaven forbid We should infringe the holy privilege Of blessed sanctuary! J. A. MICHENER Seeking sanctuary from the brothers of the man he had slain. **7** ***bird sanctuary***, ***nature sanctuary***, etc.

■ **sanctuaried** *adjective* (*rare*) made into or containing a sanctuary **M19.** **sanctuarize** *verb trans.* (*rare*) afford sanctuary to; shelter by means of a sanctuary or sacred privileges: **E17.**

sanctum /ˈsaŋ(k)təm/ *noun.* Pl. **-tums**, **-ta** /-tə/. **L16.**
[Latin, neut. of *sanctus* holy. Cf. next.]
1 A sacred place or shrine in a temple or church. **L16.**
2 A place where a person can be alone and free from intrusion; a private room, study, etc. **E19.**

sanctum sanctorum /saŋ(k)təm saŋ(k)ˈtɔːrəm/ *noun phr.* Pl. **sancta sanctorum** /saŋ(k)tə/. **LME.**
[Latin, neut. sing. and neut. genit. of *sanctus* holy, translating Hebrew *qōdeš haq-qŏdāšîm* holy of holies. Cf. prec.]
1 JEWISH ANTIQUITIES. The holy of holies in the Jewish Temple. **LME.**
2 = SANCTUM 1. **L16.**
3 = SANCTUM 2. **E18.**

sanctus /ˈsaŋ(k)təs/ *noun.* **LME.**
[Latin = holy, the first word of the hymn.]
1 CHRISTIAN CHURCH. (Also **S-**.) The hymn beginning *Sanctus, sanctus, sanctus* 'Holy, holy, holy', which forms the conclusion of the Eucharistic preface; a musical setting of this. **LME.**
†**2** ***black sanctus***, a burlesque hymn; a discord of harsh sounds expressive of contempt or dislike, formerly from a husband to an unfaithful wife. **L16–M19.**
Comb.: **sanctus bell** a bell, esp. one in a turret at the junction of the nave and the chancel, rung during the sanctus or formerly also before a service to summon people to church.

sand /sand/ *noun.*
[Old English *sand* = Old Frisian *sand*, *sond*, Old Saxon *sand*, Old High German *sant* (Dutch *zand*, German *Sand*), Old Norse *sandr*, from Germanic.]
1 Granular material consisting of small eroded fragments of (mainly siliceous) rocks, finer than gravel, forming the constituent of a beach, desert, or the bed of a river or sea and used for various purposes, as in smoothing stone, founding, or as an ingredient in mortar. **OE.** ▸†**b** A seashore; land as opp. to sea. *poet.* **ME–M16.** ▸**c** A sandy soil. Freq. in *pl.* **E17.** ▸**d** GEOLOGY & MINING. A stratum of sand or soft sandstone. **M19.** ▸**e** *collect.* Bunkers on a golf course. **M19.** ▸**f** SOIL SCIENCE. Material consisting of rock fragments whose sizes fall within a specified range, usu. approx. 0.02 to 2 mm in diameter. **L19.** ▸**g** A light yellowish-brown or beige colour resembling that of sand. **E20.**
2 A sandbank, a shoal, (usu. in *pl.*); in *pl.*, tracts of sand along a shore, estuary, etc., or forming the bed of a river or sea; sandy or desert wastes. **ME.**
3 A grain of sand, *spec.* in an hour-glass. Chiefly *fig.* **L16.**
4 ANATOMY & MEDICINE. Any of various substances resembling sand, present normally or as pathological products in organs or secretions. **L16.**
5 *slang.* **a** Sugar. **E19.** ▸**b** Firmness of purpose; courage; stamina. Chiefly *US.* **M19.** ▸**c** A fuss, a disturbance. Chiefly in ***raise sand*** below. *US.* **L19.**

> 📖 **1** ***black sand***, ***silver sand***, ***singing sand***, ***sinking sand***, etc. **2** L. LOCHHEAD Ariadne lay on the silver sands. **5** SHAKES. *Two Gent.* A heart As full of sorrows as the sea of sands. M. R. D. FOOT The sands of their luck were running out.

Phrases: **built on sand** *fig.* lacking a firm foundation; unstable; ephemeral. **bury one's head in the sand**, **hide one's head in the sand** ignore unpleasant realities, refuse to face facts. ***plough the sand(s)***: see PLOUGH *verb.* **raise sand** *US slang* create a disturbance, make a fuss. ***rope of sand***: see ROPE *noun*[1].
Comb.: **sandbank** a bank of sand formed in a shallow part of a river or sea by the action of tides and currents; **sand bar** a sandbank, esp. formed at the mouth of a river or harbour or (*US*) on the coast; **sand-barite** (barite formed into) a rock rose (crystal aggregate); **sand-bath** (*a*) a vessel containing heated sand for the even heating of retorts etc.; (*b*) (now *rare*) a medicinal bath of heated sand; **sand-bed** (*a*) a bed or stratum of sand; (*b*) FOUNDING a bed of sand into which the iron from a blast-furnace is run or in which castings are made; **sand-binder** a plant which helps to stabilize loose or shifting (esp. coastal) sand; **sand blow** the removal or deposit of large quantities of sand by the wind; a place where this has occurred; **sand boa** any of various burrowing snakes of the subfamily Boinae, of N. America, Africa and Asia; **sand boil** *US* an eruption of water through the surface of the ground; **sand-bur** *US* any of various plants with small clinging fruits, esp. several grasses of the genus *Cenchrus* and *Ambrosia acanthicarpa* of the composite family; the fruit of these plants; **sand-cast** *verb trans.* cast (metal, an object) using a sand-mould; **sand-casting** (*a*) the action or process of casting metal etc. in a sand-mould; (*b*) an object cast using a sand-mould; **sandcastle** a mass of sand formed into the shape of a castle, usu. by a child on the seashore; **sand cat** a small wild cat, *Felis margarita*, with a plain yellow to greyish coat, a dark-ringed tail, and large eyes, of the deserts of N. Africa and SW Asia; **sand cay** a small sandy island, usu. elongated parallel to the shore; *esp.* one found on a coral reef, composed of fine coral debris; **sand cherry** (the fruit of) either of two dwarf wild cherries, *Prunus pumila*, of central N. America, and *P. besseyi*, of the western US; **sand-clock** an hourglass; **sand-cloud** a cloudlike mass of sand accompanying a simoom; **sand-club** = ***sand-iron*** below; **sand core** a compact mass of sand dipped into molten glass and withdrawn so as to serve as a core in the making of a hollow vessel; **sand crab** any of various crabs which live on or burrow in sand, esp. any of the family Ocypodidae, which includes fiddler crabs and ghost crabs; **sand-crack** (*a*) a fissure in a horse's hoof; (*b*) a crack in the skin of a person's foot caused by walking on hot sand; (*c*) a crack in a brick due to imperfect mixing; **sand culture** a hydroponic method of plant cultivation using beds of purified sand supplied with nutrient solutions; **sand dab** any of various dabs of sandy coasts; *esp.* (*N. Amer.*) (*a*) the windowpane, *Scophthalmus aquosus*; (*b*) any of several fishes of the genus *Citharichthys*; **sand-devil** in Africa, a small whirlwind; **sand dollar** a roundish flat irregular sea urchin of the order Clypeasteroida; **sand drown** a magnesium deficiency disease of plants, esp. tobacco, grown in sandy soil; **sand-dune** a mound or ridge of sand formed by the wind; **sand eel** any of various small burrowing eel-like fishes of the family Ammodytidae, esp. of the genus *Ammodytes*, some species of which are abundant in northern oceans; **sand filter**: used in water purification and consisting of layers of sand arranged with coarseness of texture increasing downwards; **sand-fish** any of various fishes which habitually feed over or esp. burrow in sand, as the Australian *Crapatulus arenarius*, and *Trichodon trichodon* of the N. Pacific; **sand flea** (*a*) = JIGGER *noun*[2] 1; (*b*) *US* = ***sand-hopper*** below; **sandfly** any of various small bloodsucking flies; *esp.* (*a*) a tropical fly of the genus *Phlebotomus* and family Psychodidae, transmitting leishmaniasis and other diseases; (*b*) = ***blackfly*** (b) s.v. BLACK *adjective*; ***sandfly fever***, a mild viral disease resembling influenza and transmitted by sandflies of the genus *Phlebotomus*; **sand fox** a small fox, *Vulpes rueppellii*, with long ears and a thick coat, living in desert and steppe areas from Morocco to Afghanistan; **sand-gaper** the common soft-shelled clam, *Mya arenaria*; **sand garden** in Japanese landscape gardening, an open space covered with sand, the surface of which is raked into a pattern; **sand glacier** PHYSICAL GEOGRAPHY an extensive sheet or layer of loose sand formed by the wind and moving in the manner of a glacier, esp. out from a saddle in a ridge; **sand-glass** an hourglass; **sand goanna** an Australian monitor lizard, *Varanus gouldii*; also called ***bungarra***; **sand goby** a common goby, *Pomatoschistus minutus*; **sand-grain** an etching or other printing plate with a surface roughened by being pressed with a sheet of sandpaper; (usu. *attrib.*) a print produced from such a plate; **sand-groper** *Austral.* (*a*) *Hist.* a gold-rush pioneer; (*b*) *joc.* a Western Australian (see GROPER *noun*[1] 2); **sand-happy** *adjective* dazed or suffering stress as a result of a long period spent in the desert; **sandhog** *US* a person who works underground or under water laying foundations, constructing tunnels, etc.; **sand-hole** (*a*) a small hole or flaw in cast metal or glass; (*b*) a hole in sand, dry or water-filled; **sand-hopper** any of various small jumping amphipod crustaceans of sandy beaches, esp. of the genus *Orchestia*; **sand-iron** = ***sand wedge*** below; **sand key** *US* = ***sand cay*** above; ***sand lance***: see LANCE *noun* 5; **sand lark** (*a*) (*obsolete* exc. *dial.*) any of various small waders; (*b*) any of various larks of the genera *Ammomanes* and *Calandrella*, esp. *C. raytal* (in full ***Indian sand lark***); **sand leek** a European garlic, *Allium scorodoprasum*, of which the rocambole is a cultivated variety; **sand lily** (*a*) a stemless plant of the lily family, *Leucocrinum montanum*, of the western US, bearing clusters of fragrant white flowers; (*b*) the sea daffodil, *Pancratium maritimum*; **sand-lime** *adjective* designating a brick made by baking sand with slaked lime under pressure; **sand lizard** any of various lizards of sand-dunes or dry heathland, *esp.* the common Eurasian lizard *Lacerta agilis*; **sandman** (*a*) a man who digs sand; (*b*) [with allus. to the eyes' smarting from tiredness] a fictional person supposed to make children sleep by sprinkling sand in their eyes, a personification of sleep or tiredness; **sand martin** a small brown migratory martin, *Riparia riparia*, which nests in holes esp. in sandy banks and cliffs; any of several other birds of this genus; **sand-mason** a burrowing polychaete worm of the genus *Lanice*, which builds a flexible tube of grains of sand; **sand-mould** a mould for casting metal etc., made of sand; **sand-moulding** a process of moulding bricks in which the moulds are sprinkled with sand; **sand myrtle** a small chiefly white-flowered evergreen shrub, *Leiophyllum buxifolium*, of the heath family, native to sandy pine-barrens in eastern N. America; **sand-painting** (a picture made by) a technique of painting with coloured sands, used esp. by Navajo Indians; **sand pear** an ornamental Chinese pear tree, *Pyrus pyrifolia*; **sand perch** (*a*) *US* a small bass, *Roccus americanus*, of marine and fresh water in eastern N. America; (*b*) any of various elongated fishes of the Indo-Pacific family Mugiloididae, which burrow in sand in shallow inshore waters; **sand-picture**: formed by laying coloured sands on an adhesive background; *gen.* any design made in sand; **sand pie** wet sand formed into the shape of a pie, esp. by a child; **sandpit** (*a*) a pit from which sand is or has been excavated; (*b*) a hollow partially filled with sand for children to play in; **sand-plain** a plain covered in sand, or formed from sand deposited by melt water from a glacier; **sand plant** = ***sand-binder*** above; **sand plover** any of several plovers of the genus *Charadrius* which frequent beaches or other sandy areas; **sand-pump**: used to raise wet sand or silt from a drill-hole, oil-well, etc.; **sand rat** (chiefly *N. Amer.*) any of various desert rodents, as a gerbil, a pocket gopher, or a naked mole rat; **sand-reed** the marram-grass, *Ammophila arenaria*, a common sand-binder; **sand ripple** any of a series of small parallel ridges formed in the surface of sand by wind or water; **sand-rock** sandstone; **sand shadow** an accumulation of sand to the lee of an obstruction; **sand-shark** (*a*) a voracious brown-spotted shark of the Atlantic, *Odontaspis taurus*; (*b*) any of various mainly innocuous rays, dogfish, and sharks seen in shallow coastal waters; **sand-shoe**: suitable for use on sand, usu. made of canvas with a rubber or hemp sole; **sand-skipper** = ***sand-hopper*** above; **sand-smelt** a silverside; *spec.* the green and silver *Atherina presbyter* of the eastern Atlantic; **sandsoap** a heavy-duty gritty soap; **sand sole** a European sole (flatfish), *Pegusa lascaris*; **sand-spout** a pillar of sand raised by a whirlwind in a desert; ***sand spurrey***: see SPURREY *noun* 2; **sand-star** any of several starfish, esp. *Astropecten irregularis*; ***sand stargazer***: see STARGAZER 2; **sandstock** *adjective* designating a brick made with sand dusted on the surface; **sandstorm** a desert storm of wind with clouds of sand; **sand-sucker** (*a*) the American plaice, *Hippoglossoides platessoides*; (*b*) *US colloq.* any soft-bodied marine animal which burrows in sand; **sand-table** (*a*) a sand-covered surface on which letters, designs, or models can be placed and removed; *spec.* (MILITARY) a relief model in sand used to explain tactics etc.; (*b*) = ***sand-trap*** (a) below; **sand-trap** (*a*) a device for separating sand and other impurities from a stream of water or pulp, esp. in paper manufacture; (*b*) GOLF (chiefly *N. Amer.*) a bunker; **sand-tray** (*a*) = ***sand-table*** (a) above; (*b*) a sandbox for a cat to urinate or defecate in; **sand-verbena** any of various esp. coastal plants of the genus *Abronia* (family Nyctaginaceae), of western N. America, bearing clusters of fragrant red, yellow, or white flowers resembling verbena; **sand-wash** *US* a sloping surface of sand spread out by an intermittent stream; **sand-wasp** = DIGGER 3; **sand wave** a wavelike formation in sand; *spec.* in PHYSICAL GEOGRAPHY, an undulation similar to a megaripple but on a larger scale; **sand wedge** GOLF an iron adapted for lifting the ball out of sand; **sand-worm** a lugworm; **sand-yacht** a wind-driven vehicle with a sail (or wing) and a three-wheeled chassis, for use on sandy beaches etc.; a land-yacht; **sand-yachting** travel or racing in a sand-yacht.
■ **sandlike** *adjective* resembling sand, esp. in colour or appearance **M17.**

sand /sand/ *verb.* **LME.**
[from the noun.]
1 *verb trans.* Sprinkle with or as with sand. **LME.**
2 *verb trans.* Run (a ship) on to a sandbank; beach, run aground. Long *obsolete* exc. *Scot.* **M16.**
3 *verb trans.* **a** Overlay with sand, bury under sand. Also foll. by *over*, *up*. **E17.** ▸**b** AGRICULTURE. Put sand on (land) as a dressing. **E18.**
4 *verb trans.* Mix or adulterate with sand. **M18.**
5 *verb trans.* Smooth or polish with sand or sandpaper. **M19.**
6 *verb intrans.* Become clogged *up* with sand. **E20.**

> 📖 **1** J. GRIGSON Sand the top evenly with grated nutmeg. **5** R. LOWELL Houses kept being sanded down, repainted, or abandoned. U. LE GUIN He .. sanded the boards back to silky smoothness. **sand and canvas** (orig. *Nautical slang*) clean thoroughly. **sanding plate** a lap (LAP *noun*[4]) used with sand and water in grinding marble.

sandal /ˈsand(ə)l/ *noun*[1]. **LME.**
[Latin *sandalium* from Greek *sandalion* dim. of *sandalon* wooden shoe, prob. of Asiatic origin (cf. Persian *ṣandal* sandal).]
1 A light shoe having an openwork upper usu. fastened by straps over the instep or round the ankle, or having an upper consisting simply of such straps. **LME.**
2 A richly embroidered light shoe of red leather, silk, etc., forming part of the official dress of a bishop or monarch. **LME.**
3 A strap for fastening a low shoe, passing over the instep or round the ankle. **E19.**
1 ***open sandal***: see OPEN *adjective.*
Comb.: **sandal-foot** a stocking with a non-reinforced heel, suitable for wearing with sandals.

sandal /ˈsand(ə)l/ *noun*[2]. **LME.**
[medieval Latin *sandalum*, *santalum* (see SANTAL *noun*[1]), ult. from Sanskrit *candana* through Persian *chandal* mangrove, Arab. *ṣandal*, late Greek *sandanon*, *santalon*.]
= SANDALWOOD 1. Formerly also, ointment made of powdered sandalwood.
Comb.: **sandal-tree** any tree yielding sandalwood, *esp.* the white sandalwood tree.

sandal /ˈsand(ə)l/ *noun*[3]. **M18.**
[Turkish, Persian, Arab. *sandal* any of various kinds of boat, perh. from Greek *sandalion*, *sandalon*: see SANDAL *noun*[1].]
A long, narrow two-masted boat used in the eastern Mediterranean and off the north coast of Africa.

sandal /ˈsand(ə)l/ *verb trans.* Infl. **-ll-**, *-**l**-. **E18.**
[from SANDAL *noun*[1].]
1 Put sandals on (the feet), provide with sandals. Chiefly as ***sandalled*** ***ppl adjective.*** **E18.**
2 Fasten (a shoe) with a sandal. **L19.**

sandalwood /ˈsand(ə)lwʊd/ *noun.* **E16.**
[from SANDAL *noun*[2] + WOOD *noun*[1].]
1 The scented wood of any of several trees of the genus *Santalum* (family Santalaceae); *esp.* (more fully ***white sandalwood***) that of *S. album*, native to India. Also, a tree yielding this wood. **E16.**
2 Any of various trees of other genera whose wood resembles sandalwood in scent or appearance; *esp.* (*a*) *Austral.* the budda, *Eremophila mitchellii* (family Myoparaceae); (*b*) *W. Indies* the torchwood, *Amyris balsamifera*, of the rue family; the wood of such a tree. Freq. with specifying word. **E16.**
3 A perfume derived from sandalwood oil. **M19.**
4 A light yellowish-brown colour. **E20.**
2 ***bastard sandalwood***, ***red sandalwood***, etc.
Comb.: **Sandalwood English** = BISLAMA; **sandalwood oil** a yellowish aromatic oil distilled from sandalwood (sense 1), used in perfumes and cosmetics and formerly as an antiseptic.

sandar *noun pl.* see SANDUR.

sandarac /ˈsandərak/ *noun.* Also **-ach**. LME.
[Latin *sandaraca* from Greek *sandarakē*, *-akhē*, of Asiatic origin.]
1 = REALGAR. LME.
†**2** = ***bee-bread*** (b) s.v. BEE *noun*¹. E17–M18.
3 A resin obtained from either of two coniferous trees, *Tetraclinis articulata* of NW Africa and (more fully ***Australian sandarac***) *Callitris endlicheri* of Australia, which is used in the preparation of varnishes and (formerly) for blotting ink. Also ***gum sandarac***. M17.

Sandawe /sanˈdɑːweɪ/ *noun & adjective.* Also **-wi** /-wi/. E20.
[Sandawe.]
▶**A** *noun.* Pl. same. A member of a central Tanzanian people having physical, cultural, and linguistic affinities with the Nama; the language of this people. E20.
▶**B** *attrib.* or as *adjective.* Of or pertaining to the Sandawe or their language. E20.

sandbag /ˈsan(d)bag/ *noun & verb.* L16.
[from SAND *noun* + BAG *noun*.]
▶**A** *noun.* A bag filled with sand, used for various purposes, esp. (***a***) for making temporary fortifications or for protecting a building against blast and splinters or floodwaters; (***b***) as ballast, esp. for a boat or balloon; (***c***) as a weapon for inflicting a heavy blow without leaving a mark; (***d***) in ENGRAVING, as a support for the plate; (***e***) to stop a draught from a window or door. L16.
▶**B** *verb.* Infl. **-gg-**.
1 *verb trans.* Barricade or defend with sandbags; place sandbags against (a window, chink, etc.). M19.
2 *verb trans.* Fell with a blow from a sandbag. L19. ▸**b** *fig.* Bully, coerce by harsh means, (chiefly *N. Amer.*); criticize. L19.
3 *verb intrans. & trans.* POKER. Refrain from raising (another player) at the first opportunity in the hope of doing so by a greater amount later. M20.
4 *verb intrans.* Deliberately underperform in a race or competition to gain an unfair advantage. *slang.* L20.

> 🕮 **2b** *Globe & Mail (Toronto)* Each will attempt to sandbag the Liberals into adopting its policies.

■ **sandbagger** *noun* (chiefly *US*) (***a***) a person who uses a sandbag as a weapon; (***b***) a boat that uses sandbags as ballast; (***c***) POKER a person who sandbags; (***d***) *slang* a person who deliberately underperforms in a race etc.: L19.

sandblast /ˈsan(d)blɑːst/ *noun & verb.* E19.
[from SAND *noun* + BLAST *noun*¹.]
▶**A** *noun.* **1** A blast or jet of sand. E19.
2 A device for roughening, cleaning, or treating glass, stone, wood, or metal with a jet of sand driven by compressed air or steam. L19.
▶**B** *verb trans.* Subject to a blast of sand, esp. so as to clean or polish. L19.
■ **sandblaster** *noun* (***a***) a worker who uses a sandblast; (***b***) = SANDBLAST *noun* 2: L19.

sand-blind /ˈsan(d)blʌɪnd/ *adjective.* Now *arch., poet., & dial.* L15.
[Prob. alt. of Old English *samblind* (from SAM- + BLIND *adjective*), after SAND *noun*.]
Partially sighted.
■ **sand-blindness** *noun* M16.

sandbox /ˈsan(d)bɒks/ *noun.* L16.
[from SAND *noun* + BOX *noun*².]
1 A box with a perforated top for sprinkling sand on to wet ink. *obsolete* exc. *Hist.* L16.
2 A box or receptacle holding sand, used for various purposes; *esp.* (***a***) a box used on a locomotive for sprinkling sand on slippery rails; (***b***) GOLF (now *rare*) a container for the sand used in teeing; (***c***) (chiefly *N. Amer.*) a children's small low-sided sandpit; (***d***) a box kept indoors and filled with sand or other material for a cat to urinate or defecate in. L17.
Comb.: **sandbox tree** a W. Indian tree of the spurge family, *Hura crepitans*, whose dried seed-cases were formerly used to hold sand for blotting ink.

sandboy /ˈsan(d)bɔɪ/ *noun.* E19.
[from SAND *noun* + BOY *noun*, perh. orig. 'boy hawking sand for sale'.]
(as) happy as a sandboy, (as) jolly as a sandboy, etc., extremely happy or carefree.

Sande /ˈsandeɪ/ *noun.* Also **s-**. E19.
[Mende.]
A secret tribal tribal cult for women, based on secret rites of initiation etc., and widespread in Sierra Leone and Liberia. Cf. PORO.

sanded /ˈsandɪd/ *adjective.* L16.
[from SAND *noun, verb*: see -ED², -ED¹.]
†**1** Of the colour of sand; sandy. L16–L17.
†**2** Partially sighted. E17–L18.
3 Composed of or covered with sand; sandy. Now *rare.* E18.
4 That has been sanded; *esp.* made smooth by sanding. E18.

Sandemanian /sandɪˈmeɪnɪən/ *adjective & noun.* M18.
[from *Sandeman* (see below) + -IAN.]
▶**A** *adjective.* Of or pertaining to a religious sect developed from the Glassites by the Scottish sectarian Robert Sandeman (1718–71). M18.
▶**B** *noun.* A member of this sect. L18.
■ **Sandemanianism** *noun* M18.

sander /ˈsandə/ *noun.* E17.
[from SAND *verb* + -ER¹.]
1 A person who or thing which sprinkles sand, esp. on slippery roads or railways. E17.
2 A machine for smoothing surfaces with sandpaper or an abrasive disc. L19.

sanderling /ˈsandəlɪŋ/ *noun.* E17.
[Origin uncertain: cf. SAND *noun*, -LING¹.]
A small migratory sandpiper, *Calidris alba*, which breeds in the Arctic tundra.

sanders /ˈsɑːndəz, ˈsan-/ *noun*¹. Also **saund-** /ˈsɔːnd-/. ME.
[Old French *sandre* var. of *sandle* SANDAL *noun*².]
More fully ***sanders-wood***. Any of the several kinds of sandalwood or of the trees yielding such wood. Now *rare* exc. in ***red sanders(-wood)***, (the wood of) the red sandalwood, *Pterocarpus santalinus*.

sanders /ˈsɑːndəz, ˈsan-/ *noun*². E19.
[Origin unkn.]
A dish consisting of minced beef and layers of mashed potato.

sandesh /ˈsandɛʃ/ *noun.* E20.
[Bengali *sandeś*.]
A Bengali sweet made of curdled milk, sugar, and pistachios.

sandgrouse /ˈsan(d)graʊs/ *noun.* Pl. same. L18.
[from SAND *noun* + GROUSE *noun*¹.]
Any of various seed-eating ground birds constituting the genera *Pterocles* and *Syrrhaptes* and the family Pteroclididae, which are related to pigeons and occur in arid areas of the Old World.
Namaqua sandgrouse, ***pintailed sandgrouse***, etc.

sandhi /ˈsandi/ *noun.* E19.
[Sanskrit *saṃdhi* combination.]
LINGUISTICS. Modification in the sound (and form) of a morpheme under the influence of a following or preceding sound, either in a sentence (***external sandhi***), e.g. in English, the change from *a* to *an* before a vowel, or, in word formation, within a word (***internal sandhi***).

sand-hill /ˈsandhɪl/ *noun.* OE.
[from SAND *noun* + HILL *noun*.]
1 A hill or bank of sand; *esp.* a dune on the seashore. OE.
2 (**S-**.) In *pl.* A region of SE Alberta, Canada; in the mythology of Plains Indians, the abode of departed spirits. *Canad.* M20.
Comb.: **sand-hill crane** a rare N. American crane, *Grus canadensis*.
■ **sand-hiller** *noun* (*US slang*) a poor white person living in the sandy hills of Georgia and South Carolina M19.

sandhya /ˈsandjɑː/ *noun.* M19.
[Sanskrit *saṃdhyā* junction.]
HINDUISM. Either of the two daily devotions, morning or evening prayers. Also, the period preceding a *yuga*.

Sandinista /sandɪˈniːstə, -ˈnɪstə/ *noun.* Also **Sandinist** /ˈsandɪnɪst/. E20.
[Spanish, from Augusto César *Sandino* (1893–1934), Nicaraguan revolutionary leader + *-ista* -IST.]
Orig. (now *Hist.*), a member of a revolutionary Nicaraguan guerrilla organization founded by Sandino. Now, a leftwing revolutionary movement founded in his name, which overthrew the Nicaraguan president in 1979 and formed a government (cf. CONTRA *noun* 2).

sandiver /ˈsandɪvə/ *noun.* LME.
[App. from Old French *sain de verre* (mod. *suin de verre*) lit. 'grease of glass'.]
A saline scum found floating on molten glass; glass gall.

S & L *abbreviation. US.*
Savings and loan (association).

sandling /ˈsan(d)lɪŋ/ *noun.* LME.
[from SAND *noun* + -LING¹.]
1 A sand eel. Long *obsolete* exc. *Scot.* LME.
2 = DAB *noun*². E17.
3 (Usu. **S-**.) A sandy coastal district of Suffolk. Usu. in *pl.* L18.

sandlot /ˈsan(d)lɒt/ *noun & adjective. US.* L19.
[from SAND *noun* + LOT *noun*.]
▶**A** *noun.* A vacant plot of sandy land in a town, *esp.* one used by children for playing sport and games. L19.
▶**B** *attrib.* or as *adjective.* Played or playing on a sandlot. L19.

> 🕮 *First Base* Every sandlot kid who . . fantasised about becoming a major-league player.

■ **sandlotter** *noun* a member of a team playing in a sandlot L19.

S & M *abbreviation.*
Sado-masochism.

sandolo /ˈsandolo, ˈsandələʊ/ *noun.* Pl. ***-li*** /-li/, ***-los*** /-ləʊz/. E20.
[Italian.]
A small flat-bottomed rowing boat used in Venice.

Sandow /ˈsandəʊ/ *noun.* L19.
[Eugen *Sandow* (1867–1925), Russo-German exponent of physical culture.]
1 Used *attrib.* and in *possess.* to designate exercises, equipment, and societies endorsed by Sandow. L19.
2 A phenomenally strong man. E20.

sandpaper /ˈsan(d)peɪpə/ *noun, verb, & adjective.* E19.
[from SAND *noun* + PAPER *noun*.]
▶**A** *noun.* Paper with sand or other abrasive material stuck to it, used for smoothing or polishing woodwork etc. E19.
Comb.: **sandpaper tree** any of several tropical trees, the rough leaves of which are used for polishing, e.g. the sausage-tree, *Kigelia pinnata*.
▶**B** *verb trans.* Smooth (as) with sandpaper; *fig.* bring to perfection, refine. M19.
▶**C** *adjective.* Rough or abrasive in style etc. M20.
■ **sandpaperer** *noun* L19. **sandpapery** *adjective* resembling sandpaper, rough to the touch M20.

sandpiper /ˈsan(d)pʌɪpə/ *noun.* L17.
[from SAND *noun* + PIPER.]
Any of various smaller waders of the family Scolopacidae, esp. of the genera *Calidris* and *Tringa*.
green sandpiper, ***pectoral sandpiper***, ***solitary sandpiper***, ***Terek sandpiper***, ***wood sandpiper***, etc.

sandstone /ˈsan(d)stəʊn/ *noun.* M17.
[from SAND *noun* + STONE *noun*.]
Any of various sedimentary rocks composed of sand grains, esp. of quartz, cemented together, and red, yellow, brown, grey, or white in colour.
Red Sandstone either of two series of red sedimentary rocks, chiefly sandstones, belonging to the Permo-Triassic system (***New Red Sandstone***) or Devonian system (***Old Red Sandstone***) of NW Europe.

sandur /ˈsandə, -dəː/ *noun.* Pl. **-dar**, **-durs**. Also **sandr**, pl. same, **-s**. L19.
[Icelandic *sandur*, pl. *sandar*, (Old Norse *sandr*), SAND *noun*.]
PHYSICAL GEOGRAPHY. A broad, flat or gently sloping plain of glacial outwash.

sandveld /ˈsandvɛlt, -ntf-/ *noun. S. Afr.* E19.
[Afrikaans, formed as SAND *noun* + VELD.]
A region of light sandy soil; *spec.* a coastal region of the southern Cape.

Sandwich /ˈsanwɪtʃ, -wɪdʒ/ *noun*¹. Also **s-**. L15.
[A town in Kent, SE England.]
Used *attrib.* to designate things made in or associated with Sandwich.
Sandwich tern a moderately large crested tern, *Sterna sandvicensis*, found in both Old and New Worlds.

sandwich /ˈsanwɪdʒ, -wɪtʃ/ *noun*² *& adjective.* M18.
[John Montagu, 4th Earl of *Sandwich* (1718–92), said to have eaten food in this form so as to avoid having to leave the gaming-table.]
▶**A** *noun.* **1** A set of two or more (esp. buttered) slices of bread with a usu. savoury filling between them. Freq. with specifying word. M18.
2 = ***sandwich-man*** below. M19.
3 a In full ***sandwich-cake***. A cake consisting of two or more layers of sponge with jam, cream, etc., in between. E20. ▸**b** A laminated board or panel consisting of a layer of lightweight material bonded between two thin sheets of strong material, used esp. in aircraft. M20.
4 *ellipt.* A sandwich course (see sense B.1 below). M20.

> 🕮 **1** ***cheese sandwich***, ***club sandwich***, ***cucumber sandwich***, ***ham sandwich***, ***open sandwich***, ***Reuben sandwich***, etc. ***knuckle sandwich***: see KNUCKLE *noun*. ***two sandwiches short of a picnic***: see ***short of*** (b) s.v. SHORT *adverb*. *fig.*: E. LYALL The . . oddest day, a sort of sandwich of good and bad. **3a** ***Victoria sandwich***: see VICTORIA 6. **4** ***thick sandwich***: see THICK *adjective*.

Comb.: **sandwich-board** either of the advertising boards carried by a sandwich-man; **sandwich-boat** the boat which rows in two divisions of the bumping races at Oxford and Cambridge, occupying the last position in a higher division and the first position in a lower division; **sandwich box**: for carrying sandwiches; ***sandwich cake***: see sense A.3a above; **sandwich construction** the structure or method of fabrication of sandwich panels; **sandwich generation** (chiefly *US*) a generation of people, typically in their thirties or forties, responsible for bringing up their own children and for the care of their ageing parents; **sandwich-man** a man hired to advertise a thing by walking the streets with two sandwich-boards suspended from his shoulders, one in front and one behind; **sandwich panel** a panel constructed as a sandwich.
▶**B** *adjective.* **1** Of a training course etc.: consisting of alternating periods of theoretical instruction in a college etc. and practical experience with a firm etc. Of a student: taking part in such a course. E20.

2 CHEMISTRY. Pertaining to or designating (complexes having) a structure in which a metal atom is bonded between two parallel cyclic ligands in different planes. Chiefly in ***sandwich compound***. M20.
1 *thick sandwich course*: see THICK *adjective*.

Sandwich /ˈsanwɪtʃ/ *noun*³. L19.
[A town on Cape Cod, Massachusetts.]
Used *attrib.* to designate a glass factory at Sandwich and glass produced there from 1825 to 1888.

sandwich /ˈsanwɪtʃ, -wɪdʒ/ *verb*. E19.
[from SANDWICH *noun*².]
†**1** *verb intrans.* Have a meal of sandwiches. Only in E19.
2 *verb trans.* Put in a sandwich. E19.
3 *verb trans. fig.* Insert (a thing) between two other dissimilar ones, place (different elements) alternately; squeeze (*in*) between two others. M19. ▸**b** FOOTBALL. Trap or crush (an opposing player) between oneself and a player of one's own side. L20.

> 🕮 **3** F. M. FORD His love-affairs . . were sandwiched in at odd moments. *Time* He sits . . sandwiched between speakers blaring . . hard rock music. *Art & Artists* His descendant . . sandwiches the Wedgwood name between Tony and Benn.

sandwort /ˈsandwəːt/ *noun*. L16.
[from SAND *noun* + WORT *noun*¹.]
Any of various small white-flowered plants of the genus *Arenaria* and several related genera of the pink family; *esp.* (in full ***thyme-leaved sandwort***) *Arenaria serpyllifolia*, of walls, dry sandy ground, etc., and (in full ***three-nerved sandwort***) *Moehringia trinervia*, of shady places.
sea sandwort: see SEA *noun*.

Sandy /ˈsandi/ *noun*. *colloq.* L18.
[Scot. pet-form of male forename *Alexander*. Cf. SAWNEY.]
(A nickname for) a Scotsman.

sandy /ˈsandi/ *adjective*. OE.
[from SAND *noun* + -Y¹.]
1 Resembling sand, esp. in texture; composed of or containing a large proportion of sand. OE. ▸**b** Of or containing sand as used for measuring time (cf. *sand-glass* s.v. SAND *noun*). *poet.* L16.
2 Chiefly of hair: of a light brownish- or yellowish-red. Also, having hair of this colour. E16.
3 *fig.* Resembling sand in lacking cohesion or stability. L16.

> 🕮 **1b** SHAKES. *1 Hen. VI* Ere the glass . . Finish the process of his sandy hour.

Special collocations: **sandy blight** *Austral.* a painful form of conjunctivitis which feels as though it is caused by sand in the eye; **sandy laverock** (*obsolete exc. dial.*) = ***sand lark*** (a) s.v. SAND *noun*; **sandy ray** a ray, *Raja circularis*, of the NE Atlantic which has cream-coloured dorsal spots.
■ **sandiness** *noun* M17. **sandyish** *adjective* L18.

sandyx /ˈsandɪks/ *noun*. LME.
[Latin from Greek *sandux*.]
Hist. A red pigment derived from oxides of lead or iron.

sane /seɪn/ *adjective*. E17.
[Latin *sanus* healthy.]
1 Of sound mind, not mad; (of the mind) sound. E17.
2 Of the body, its organs or functions: healthy, not diseased. *rare*. M18.
3 Sensible, rational; moderate; free from misleading prejudices etc. M19.

> 🕮 **1** N. MAILER He certainly hadn't acted like a disorientated . . person but on the contrary, seemed altogether sane. **3** *Independent* The trust fostered a sane climate of discussion about Aids when others were calling for punishment and retribution.

■ **sanely** *adverb* E19. **saneness** *noun* E18.

san fairy ann /ˌsan fɛːri ˈan/ *interjection*. *slang*. E20.
[Joc. alt. of French *ça ne fait rien* it does not matter.]
Expr. indifference to or resigned acceptance of a state of affairs.

Sanfedista /sanfəˈdɪstə/ *noun*. Pl. **-sti** /-sti/. Also Anglicized as **Sanfedist** /ˈsanfɛdɪst/. M19.
[Italian, from (*Banda della*) *Sante Fede* (Society of the) holy faith + *-ista* -IST.]
Hist. A member of an Italian pro-papal anti-liberal association of the late 18th and early 19th cents.

Sanfilippo's syndrome /sanfɪˈliːpəʊz ˌsɪndrəʊm/ *noun phr.* Also **Sanfilippo syndrome**, **San Filippo('s) syndrome**, **Sanfillipo('s) syndrome**. M20.
[from Sylvester J. *Sanfilippo*, 20th-cent. US physician.]
MEDICINE. A form of mucopolysaccharidosis characterized by mental handicap, hepatosplenomegaly, and dwarfism.

sanfoin *noun* var. of SAINFOIN.

Sanforized /ˈsanfərʌɪzd/ *adjective*. Also **-ised**, **s-**. M20.
[from *Sanford* L. Cluett (1874–1968), US inventor of the process + -IZE + -ED¹.]
Of cotton or other fabrics: preshrunk by a special process.
¶ Proprietary name.

San Franciscan /san franˈsɪsk(ə)n/ *noun & adjective*. L19.
[from *San Francisco* (see below) + -AN.]
▸ **A** *noun*. A native or inhabitant of San Francisco, a city in California, US. L19.
▸ **B** *adjective*. Of or pertaining to San Francisco. L19.

sang /saŋ/ *noun*¹. *Scot. & north.* L18.
[Origin unkn. Cf. SAM *noun*¹.]
by my sang, expr. asseveration.

sang /saŋ/ *noun*² *& verb*¹. *US colloq.* M19.
[Aphet.]
▸ **A** *noun*. = GINSENG. M19.
▸ **B** *verb intrans.* Collect ginseng. Chiefly as ***sanging*** *verbal noun*. M19.

sang /sʌŋ/ *noun*³. Also **srang** /srʌŋ/. Pl. same, **-s**. E20.
[Tibetan *s(r)ang* ounce.]
Hist. A former Tibetan monetary unit, equal to 100 sho; a coin or note of this value.

sang *verb*² *pa. t.*: see SING *verb*¹.

Sanga /ˈsaŋgə/ *noun*¹. Pl. same. E19.
[Galla *sangaa* ox, or Amharic *sänga* steer.]
(An animal of) a breed of E. African cattle with large lyre-shaped horns.

sanga *noun*² var. of SUNGA.

sangam /ˈsaŋgəm/ *noun*. M19.
[Sanskrit *samgama*.]
In the Indian subcontinent, a river confluence.

sangar /ˈsaŋgə/ *noun & verb*. M19.
[Persian & Pashto, prob. from Persian *sang* stone.]
Chiefly MILITARY. ▸**A** *noun*. A parapet, a breastwork; a fortified lookout post. M19.
▸ **B** *verb trans.* Fortify with a sangar. E20.

sangaree /saŋgəˈriː/ *noun*. M18.
[Spanish *sangría* SANGRIA.]
A cold drink of diluted and spiced wine, drunk esp. in tropical countries.

sang-de-boeuf /sɑ̃dəbœf/ *noun*. L19.
[French, lit. 'ox's blood'.]
A deep red colour found on old Chinese porcelain; (porcelain bearing) a ceramic glaze of this colour.

Sängerfest /ˈsɛŋəfɛst/ *noun*. *US*. Also **Saeng-**. M19.
[German, from *Sänger* singer + FEST.]
A choral festival.

sang-froid /sɒŋˈfrwɑː/ *noun*. M18.
[French, lit. 'cold blood'.]
Coolness, self-possession, esp. in the face of danger or disturbing circumstances.

> 🕮 J. FOWLES He let himself be ribbed . . with a smiling sang-froid.

sangha /ˈsaŋgə/ *noun*. M19.
[Sanskrit *saṃgha*, from *sam* together + *han* come in contact.]
BUDDHISM. The Buddhist community, the Buddhist order of monks, nuns, and novices.

Sangiovese /ˌsandʒɪəˈveɪzi/ *noun*. E20.
[Italian.]
(A vine yielding) a black grape used in making Chianti and other Italian red wines; wine made from these grapes.

sanglier /sɑ̃gli(j)e/ *noun*. Pl. pronounced same. LME.
[Old French *sengler*, (also mod.) *sanglier* from Latin *singularis* solitary, SINGULAR, used as noun in late Latin = a boar separated from the herd, in medieval Latin = wild boar.]
A wild boar. Formerly *spec.*, one that is fully grown.
¶ Orig. fully naturalized.

Sango /ˈsaŋgəʊ/ *noun*. M20.
[Ngbandi.]
A dialect of Ngbandi; *spec.* a lingua franca developed from this and other dialects of Ngbandi, one of the official languages of the Central African Republic.

Sangoan /saŋˈgəʊən/ *adjective & noun*. M20.
[from *Sango* Bay, Uganda + -AN.]
ARCHAEOLOGY. (Designating or pertaining to) a palaeolithic cultural stage in central Africa, roughly contemporary with the Mousterian culture in Europe.

sangoma /saŋˈgɔːma/ *noun*. Also **isan-** /ɪsaŋ-/. L19.
[Nguni.]
In southern Africa, a witch-doctor, usu. a woman, claiming supernatural powers of divination and healing.

Sangrado /saŋˈgrɑːdəʊ/ *noun*. *arch.* Pl. **-os**. E19.
[In Le Sage's *Gil Blas*, a doctor whose sole remedies were bleeding and the drinking of hot water: cf. Spanish *sangrador* bleeder.]
A medical practitioner resembling Dr Sangrado; an ignorant pretender to medical knowledge.

sangrail /saŋˈgreɪl/ *noun*. *arch.* Also **sangreal** /saŋˈgriːəl, ˈsaŋgrɪəl/. LME.
[Old French *saint graal* Holy Grail: see SAINT *noun & adjective*, GRAIL *noun*². Var. by false etym. from French *sang real* (Christ's) real or royal blood.]
The Holy Grail.

sangre azul /ˌsangre aˈθul/ *noun phr.* M19.
[Spanish = blue blood.]
The purity of blood claimed by certain ancient Castilian families, which professed to be free from Moorish or Jewish ancestry. Cf. ***blue blood*** s.v. BLUE *adjective*.

Sangria /saŋˈgriːə/ *noun*. M20.
[Spanish *sangría* lit. 'bleeding'.]
A Spanish drink made of sweetened diluted red wine with spices and fruit.

sanguiferous /saŋˈgwɪf(ə)rəs/ *adjective*. L17.
[from Latin *sanguis* blood + -FEROUS.]
Bearing or conveying blood.

sanguification /ˌsaŋgwɪfɪˈkeɪʃ(ə)n/ *noun*. L16.
[mod. Latin *sanguificatio(n-)*, from *sanguificat-* pa. ppl stem of *sanguificare* form or convert into blood, from Latin *sanguis* blood: see -FICATION.]
The formation of blood; conversion into blood.

sanguinaria /saŋgwɪˈnɛːrɪə/ *noun*. E19.
[mod. Latin *Sanguinaria* (see below), use as noun of fem. of Latin *sanguinarius*: see next, -IA¹.]
BOTANY & MEDICINE. The bloodroot, *Sanguinaria canadensis*; the dried rhizome and root of this, used esp. to treat bronchial catarrh.
■ ˈ**sanguinarine** *noun* (CHEMISTRY) a toxic bitter alkaloid, $C_{20}H_{15}NO_5$, obtained esp. from bloodroot M19.

sanguinary /ˈsaŋgwɪn(ə)ri/ *noun & adjective*. ME.
[Latin *sanguinarius*, from *sanguis* blood: see -ARY¹.]
▸†**A** *noun*. **1** Any of several plants reputed to stop bleeding, esp. shepherd's purse, *Capsella bursa-pastoris*. ME–E16.
2 A bloodthirsty person. M16–M17.
▸ **B** *adjective*. **1** Of or pertaining to blood. *rare*. LME.
2 Involving or characterized by slaughter or bloodshed; (of a person) bloodthirsty. E17.
3 *euphem.* = BLOODY *adjective* 8a. *joc.* L19.

> 🕮 **2** J. HOWELL The . . most sanguinary Warrs are about Religion. **3** G. B. SHAW The inhabitants . . call one another sanguinary liars.

■ **sanguinarily** *adverb* M19. **sanguinariness** *noun* L17.

sanguine /ˈsaŋgwɪn/ *adjective & noun*. ME.
[Old & mod. French *sanguin(e)* from Latin *sanguineus*: see SANGUINEOUS.]
▸ **A** *adjective*. **1 a** Blood-red. Also ***sanguine red***. Now only *literary*, in HERALDRY, & in names of animals and plants. ME. ▸**b** Of the complexion: florid, ruddy. L17.
2 a Of or pertaining to blood; consisting of or containing blood. Now *rare*. LME. ▸**b** Causing or delighting in bloodshed; bloody, sanguinary. Now *poet. & rhet.* E18.
3 *Hist.* Having the constitution characterized by the predominance of blood over the other three bodily humours, believed to be indicated by a ruddy face and a brave and hopeful amorous disposition. LME.
4 Having the temperament attributed to people of this constitution (now *Hist.*); confident, optimistic. E16.

> 🕮 **4** D. H. LAWRENCE He was too healthy and sanguine to be wretched. JOHN BROOKE A marriage with the King . . was beyond her most sanguine expectations. D. FRASER Brooke had not been sanguine about Russian chances of holding out.

▸ **B** *noun*. †**1** (A piece of) blood-red cloth. Only in ME.
2 A blood-red colour. *obsolete* exc. HERALDRY. LME.
†**3** Sanguine constitution or temperament. M16–E18.
4 A crayon coloured red or flesh with iron oxide; a drawing executed with such a crayon. M19.
■ **sanguinely** *adverb* M17. **sanguineness** *noun* M16.

†**sanguine** *verb trans.* *rare*. L16.
[from the adjective.]
1 Stain or paint a blood-red colour. L16–L17.
2 Stain with blood. E17–E19.

sanguineous /saŋˈgwɪnɪəs/ *adjective*. E16.
[from Latin *sanguineus* (from *sanguin-*, *sanguis* blood) + -OUS.]
1 Chiefly ZOOLOGY & BOTANY. Blood-red. E16.
2 Characterized by bloodshed; (of a person) bloodthirsty. Now *rare*. E17.
3 Of or pertaining to blood; of the nature of or containing blood. M17. ▸†**b** Of an animal: having blood. M17–E18.
4 a Sanguine in constitution or temperament (now *Hist.*); full-blooded, plethoric. M18. ▸**b** Optimistic, sanguine. M19.
■ **sanguineousness** *noun* M19.

sanguinity /saŋˈgwɪnɪti/ *noun*. *rare*. LME.
[In sense 1 from Old French *sanguinité* or medieval Latin *sanguinitas*, formed as SANGUINEOUS. In sense 2 from SANGUINE *adjective* + -ITY.]
†**1** Consanguinity. LME–M18.
2 The quality of being optimistic or sanguine. M18.

sanguinivorous /saŋgwɪˈnɪv(ə)rəs/ *adjective*. E19.
[from Latin *sanguin-*, *sanguis* blood + -I- + -VOROUS.]
= SANGUIVOROUS.

sanguinolent /saŋˈgwɪn(ə)lənt/ *adjective*. LME.
[Latin *sanguinolentus*, from *sanguin-*, *sanguis* blood: see -ULENT.]
1 Full of, containing, or stained with blood. LME.
†**2** Blood-red. LME–E16.
3 Bloodthirsty, cruel. *rare*. L16.

sanguinous /ˈsaŋgwɪnəs/ *adjective*. *rare*. LME.
[Old French *sanguineux*, from late Latin *sanguinosus*, from Latin *sanguin-*, *sanguis* blood: see -OUS.]
1 Of or pertaining to blood. LME.
†**2** Involving bloodshed. Only in M18.

sanguivorous /saŋˈgwɪv(ə)rəs/ *adjective*. M19.
[from Latin *sanguis* blood + -VOROUS.]
Feeding on blood.

Sanhedrin /ˈsanɪdrɪn/ *noun*. Also **-im** /-ɪm/. L16.
[Post-biblical Hebrew *sanhedrīn* from Greek *sunedrion* council, from *sun-* SYN- + *hedra* seat.]
JEWISH HISTORY. (More fully ***Great Sanhedrin***) the supreme Jewish council and highest court of justice in ancient Jerusalem with 71 members. Also, any of certain lower courts of justice.
■ **Sanhedrist** *noun* a member of the Sanhedrin L16.

san-hsien /sanˈʃjɛn/ *noun*. Also **sanxian**. M19.
[Chinese *sānxián* (Wade–Giles *sān-hsien*), from *sān* three + *xián* string.]
MUSIC. A Chinese three-stringed lute. Cf. SAMISEN.

sanicle /ˈsanɪk(ə)l/ *noun*. LME.
[Old French from medieval Latin *sanicula*, *-culum*, prob. from Latin *sanus* healthy, SANE, with ref. to the plant's supposed healing powers.]
1 A palmate-leaved umbelliferous plant, *Sanicula europaea*, of rich woodland (more fully ***wood sanicle***); *gen.* any plant of the genus *Sanicula*, e.g. *S. marilandica*, black snakeroot. LME.
2 With specifying word: any of various plants of other genera thought to resemble *Sanicula* in form or healing properties. LME.
2 white sanicle *US* white snakeroot, *Eupatorium rugosum*.

sanidine /ˈsanɪdiːn/ *noun*. E19.
[from Greek *sanid-*, *sanis* board: see -INE[5].]
MINERALOGY. A glassy variety of orthoclase, occurring as flat crystals.
■ **saˈnidinite** *noun* (GEOLOGY) an igneous rock consisting largely of sanidine L19.

sanies /ˈseɪnɪiːz/ *noun*. LME.
[Latin.]
1 MEDICINE. A thin fetid discharge from a wound or ulcer, containing serum, pus, and blood. Now *rare*. LME.
†**2** *gen.* Any watery fluid of animal origin. M17–M19.

sanify /ˈsanɪfʌɪ/ *verb*. M19.
[from Latin *sanus* healthy, SANE + -FY.]
1 *verb intrans.* Become sane or reasonable. *rare*. M19.
2 *verb trans.* Make healthy; improve the sanitary conditions of (a city etc.). L19.
■ **sanifiˈcation** *noun* (*rare*) L19.

Sanio /ˈsanɪəʊ/ *noun*. L19.
[Gustav *Sanio* (1832–91), German botanist.]
BOTANY. **1** Used *attrib.*, in possess., and with *of*, to designate a bar of thickened material, consisting of primary wall and intercellular layer, between the pits of gymnosperm tracheids. Now *rare* or *obsolete*. L19.
2 ***Sanio's law***, each of a set of laws thought to govern the variation in size of gymnosperm tracheids. E20.

sanious /ˈseɪnɪəs/ *adjective*. Now *rare*. LME.
[Old & mod. French *sanieux* from Latin *saniosus*, formed as SANIES: see -OUS.]
Of the nature of or containing sanies; yielding a discharge of sanies.

sanitar /sanɪˈtɑː/ *noun*. E20.
[Russian.]
In Russia: a hospital attendant; *spec.* a medical orderly in the army.

sanitaria *noun pl.* see SANITARIUM.

sanitarian /sanɪˈtɛːrɪən/ *noun & adjective*. M19.
[from SANITARY: see -AN, -ARIAN.]
▶ **A** *noun*. **1** A person who studies sanitation; a person in favour of sanitary reform. M19.
2 A public health officer. *US*. M20.
▶ **B** *adjective*. Of or pertaining to sanitation; advocating sanitary reform. L19.
■ **sanitarianism** *noun* advocacy of sanitation or sanitary reform L19.

sanitarium /sanɪˈtɛːrɪəm/ *noun*. Chiefly *US*. Pl. **-riums**, **-ria** /-rɪə/. M19.
[from Latin *sanitas* health (see next) + -ARIUM.]
= SANATORIUM 1, 2.

sanitary /ˈsanɪt(ə)ri/ *adjective*. M19.
[French *sanitaire*, from Latin *sanitas* health, from *sanus* healthy: see -ARY[1].]
1 a Of or pertaining to the conditions affecting health, esp. with reference to cleanliness and protection against infection; concerning sanitation. M19. ▸**b** Designating an appliance, soap, etc., made especially with a view to health and hygiene; free from or designed to kill germs, infection, etc.; hygienic. M19.
2 Intended or tending to promote health. M19.

> **1a** *Social History of Medicine* Sanitary conditions deteriorated and outbreaks of infectious diseases became more and more common. **2** J. R. LOWELL Solitary communion with Nature does not seem to have been sanitary . . in its influence on Thoreau's character.

Special collocations: **sanitary belt** a belt worn to support a sanitary towel. **sanitary engineer** a person who works on the design, construction, or maintenance of sanitary appliances or sewerage; a plumber. **sanitary inspector** an officer appointed to inspect sanitary conditions, a public health inspector. **sanitary napkin** *N. Amer.* = ***sanitary towel*** below. **sanitary pad** = ***sanitary towel*** below. **sanitary protection** sanitary towels, tampons, etc., used by women during menstruation. **sanitary towel** a pad worn by women during menstruation to absorb menstrual flow. **sanitary ware** porcelain for lavatories etc.
■ **sanitarily** *adverb* with regard to sanitary condition L19. **sanitariness** *noun* the condition of being sanitary L19.

sanitate /ˈsanɪteɪt/ *verb trans*. L19.
[Back-form. from next.]
Put in a sanitary condition; provide with sanitary appliances.

sanitation /sanɪˈteɪʃ(ə)n/ *noun*. M19.
[Irreg. from SANITARY: see -ATION.]
Sanitary conditions; (study or planning of) the maintenance or improvement of these. Also *spec.*, toilet facilities.
Comb.: **sanitation man**, **sanitation truck** *US*: employed in the removal and disposal of domestic refuse.
■ **sanitationist** *noun* (*rare*) a person who is skilled in or advocates sanitation L19.

sanitize /ˈsanɪtʌɪz/ *verb trans*. Also **-ise**. M19.
[from SANITARY: see -IZE.]
1 Make sanitary or hygienic; disinfect. M19.
2 Make (information etc.) more acceptable by the removal of undesirable or improper material. M20.

> **1** *New Scientist* In the wine industry, sulphites are used . . to sanitise containers. **2** *Daily Telegraph* It is an offence . . for a user to sanitise his data before letting the subject see it. F. KAPLAN Sanitized images of a golden childhood.

■ **sanitiˈzation** *noun* M20. **sanitizer** *noun* a substance which sanitizes something; a disinfectant: M20.

sanity /ˈsanɪti/ *noun*. LME.
[Latin *sanitas*, from *sanus* healthy: see SANE, -ITY.]
1 Healthy condition, good health. *arch*. LME. ▸†**b** Wholesomeness. E17–M18.
2 The state of being sane; soundness of mind or judgement; mental health. E17.

sanjak /ˈsandʒak/ *noun*. M16.
[Turkish *sancak* lit. 'banner'.]
1 *Hist.* In the Ottoman Empire, any of the administrative districts into which a vilayet was divided. M16.
†**2** = next. M16–M19.
■ **sanjakate** /ˈsandʒəkət/ *noun* = SANJAK 1 L17. †**sanjakship** *noun* = SANJAK 1 M17–E19.

sanjakbeg /ˈsandʒakbɛg/ *noun*. Also **-bey** /-beɪ/. E16.
[Turkish, formed as prec., BEG *noun*[1].]
Hist. The governor of a sanjak.

San Joaquin Valley fever /san wɑːˌkiːn valɪ ˈfiːvə/ *noun phr*. M20.
[A river valley in S. California.]
= COCCIDIOIDOMYCOSIS.

sank *verb pa. t.*: see SINK *verb*.

Sanka /ˈsaŋkə/ *noun*. Chiefly *N. Amer.* E20.
[Repr. abbreviation of French *sans caffeine* without caffeine.]
(Proprietary name for) a make of decaffeinated coffee.

Sankaracharya /ʃaŋkərəˈtʃɑːrjə/ *noun*. M20.
[Sanskrit, from *Śaṅkara Ācārya*, famous teacher of Vedanta philosophy c 8th cent.]
(The title of) any of various Indian religious teachers and leaders.

Sankey /ˈsaŋki/ *adjective & noun*. M20.
[Ira David *Sankey* (1840–1908), US writer of popular mission hymns.]
(Designating) a style of gospel song popularized by Sankey, or a song in this style.

Sankhya /ˈsɑːŋkjə/ *noun*. L18.
[Sanskrit *sāṃkhya* lit. 'relating to number'.]
A leading system of Hindu philosophy, based on a dualism of matter and soul.

sanko *noun* var. of SANCHO *noun*[1].

San Luiseño *noun & adjective* see LUISEÑO.

sannah /ˈsanə/ *noun*. Also **sanna**. L17.
[Origin unkn.]
Hist. A cotton fabric formerly exported from the Indian subcontinent.

sannup /ˈsanəp/ *noun*. *N. Amer.* E17.
[Algonquian (Massachusetts) *sanomp*.]
A married male N. American Indian; the husband of a N. American Indian woman. Cf. SQUAW.

sannyasi /sənˈjɑːsi/ *noun*. Also **sanyasi**, **-sin** /-sɪn/. E17.
[Sanskrit *saṃnyāsī* nom. sing. of *saṃnyāsin* laying aside, abandoning, ascetic, from *saṃ* together + *ni* down + *as* throw.]
A brahmin in the fourth stage of his life; a wandering Hindu fakir.

Sanocrysin /seɪnəʊˈkrʌɪsɪn/ *noun*. E20.
[Irreg. from Latin *sanus* healthy, sane + -O- + Greek *khrusos* gold + -IN[1].]
PHARMACOLOGY. A complex salt of gold, trisodium (dithiosulphato)aurate(I), formerly used to treat tuberculosis.
¶ Proprietary name in the US.

sanpaku /sanˈpaku/ *noun*. M20.
[Japanese, lit. 'three white', from *san* three + *haku* white.]
Visibility of the white of the eye below the iris as well as on either side.

San Pellegrino /ˌsan pɛlɛˈgriːnəʊ/ *noun*. E20.
[See below.]
Mineral water obtained from springs in San Pellegrino, a village in Lombardy.

sanpro /ˈsanprəʊ/ *noun*. *colloq*. L20.
[Abbreviation.]
= SANITARY ***protection***.

sans /sanz/ *noun*. E20.
[Abbreviation.]
TYPOGRAPHY. = SANS SERIF.

sans /sanz, sɑ̃(z)/ *preposition*. Now chiefly *literary* (freq. *joc.*) exc. HERALDRY. ME.
[Old French *san*, *sanz* (mod. *sans*), earlier *sen(s* from Proto-Romance var. of Latin *sine*, partly infl. by Latin *absentia* absence. Cf. SENZA.]
Without.

> SHAKES. *A.Y.L.* Second childishness and mere oblivion; Sans teeth, sans eyes, sans taste, sans everything. *Publishers Weekly* 75 relevant illustrations, sans razzle-dazzle. ***sans blague!*** /blag/ [lit. 'without joking'] you don't say! I don't believe it! ***sans cérémonie*** /seremɔni/ unceremoniously; without the usual ceremony or formality. ***sans façon*** /fasɔ̃/ [lit. 'without manner'] = ***sans cérémonie*** above. ***sans-gêne*** /ʒɛ(ː)n/ [lit. 'without embarrassment'] disregard of the ordinary forms of civility or politeness. ***sans nombre*** /nɔ̃br/ HERALDRY innumerable, without a definite number. ***sans pareil*** /parɛːj/ [lit. 'not having its like'] unique, unequalled. ***sans peur*** /pœːr/ without fear, fearless; esp. in ***sans peur et sans reproche***. ***sans phrase*** /frɑːz/ without more words, without exceptions or qualifications. ***sans recours*** /rəkuːr, rəˈkʊə/ [lit. 'without recourse'] LAW an endorsement on a bill of exchange absolving the endorser or any other party from liability. ***sans reproche*** /rəprɔʃ/ without reproach, blameless; esp. in ***sans peur et sans reproche***.

¶ Formerly fully naturalized.

sansa /ˈsansə/ *noun*. M19.
[Bantu from Arab. *ṣanj*, Persian *sinj* cymbal(s).]
= MBIRA.

Sanscrit *noun & adjective* var. of SANSKRIT.

sansculotte /sanzkjuːˈlɒt, *foreign* sɑ̃kylɔt (*pl. same*)/ *noun*. L18.
[French, from *sans* without + *culotte* knee-breeches.]
1 A lower-class Parisian republican in the French Revolution (*Hist.*); *gen.* an extreme republican or revolutionary. L18.
2 *transf.* A shabbily dressed person, a ragamuffin. E19.
■ **sansculotterie** /-ˈlɒtəri, *foreign* -lɔtri/ *noun* (*Hist.*) the principles, spirit, or behaviour of sansculottes; sansculottes collectively: L18. **sansculottic** *adjective* (**a**) pertaining to the sansculottes or to sansculottism, revolutionary; (**b**) inadequately or improperly clothed: E19. **sansculottish** *adjective* = SANSCULOTTIC (a) L18. **sansculottism** *noun* (*Hist.*) the principles or practice of sansculottes L18. **sansculottist** *noun* (*Hist.*) an advocate or supporter of sansculottism M19. **sansculottize** *verb* (*rare*) (**a**) *verb trans.* make republican in character; (**b**) *verb intrans.* favour sansculottic or republican principles: L18.

sansculottid /sanzkjuːˈlɒtɪd/ *noun*. E19.
[French *sansculottide*, from prec.]
Hist. Each of the five (in leap years six) complementary days added at the end of the month Fructidor of the French Republican calendar (more fully ***sansculottid day***); in *pl.*, the festivities held during these days.

sansei /ˈsanseɪ/ *noun*. Pl. same. M20.
[Japanese, from *san* three, third + *sei* generation.]
An American whose grandparents were immigrants from Japan. Cf. NISEI.

sanserif *noun* var. of SANS SERIF.

sansevieria /sansɪˈvɪərɪə/ *noun*. Also **-sever-**. E19.
[mod. Latin (see below), from Raimondo di Sangro (1710–71), Prince of *Sanseviero* (now Sansevero) in Italy: see -IA[1].]
Any of various tropical African and Asian plants constituting the genus *Sansevieria*, of the agave family, having stiff erect leaves yielding a tough fibre and which include the house-plant mother-in-law's tongue, *S. trifasciata*. Also called ***bowstring hemp***.

Sansi /ˈsɑːnsi/ *noun*. L19.
[Origin unkn.]
A member of a low Hindu caste of the Punjab.

Sanskrit /ˈsanskrɪt/ *noun & adjective.* Also **Sanscrit**. **E17.**
[Sanskrit *saṃskṛta* prepared, elaborated, perfected. Cf. PRAKRIT.]
▸**A** *noun.* The ancient Indo-Aryan language of the Indian subcontinent, the principal language of religious writings and scholarship, the source of some of the modern languages of the area (as Hindi, Bengali, Nepali, Sinhalese), and now also one of the languages recognized for official use in the modern State of India. **E17.**
▸**B** *adjective.* Of, pertaining to, or written in Sanskrit. **L18.**
■ **Sanˈskritic** *adjective* pertaining to, derived from, resembling, or using Sanskrit **M19.** **Sanskritist** *noun* an expert in or student of Sanskrit or Sanskrit writings **M19.** **Sanskritize** *verb trans.* (**a**) translate into Sanskrit, introduce Sanskrit elements into; (**b**) adapt to the beliefs or practices of a high Hindu caste: **L19.** **Sanskritiˈzation** *noun* the action or process of Sanskritizing something **L19.**

sans serif /san ˈsɛrɪf/ *noun & adjective.* Also **sanserif**. **M19.**
[App. from SANS *preposition* + SERIF.]
TYPOGRAPHY. ▸**A** *noun.* A letterform, esp. a typeface, without serifs. **M19.**
▸**B** *adjective.* Having no serifs. **L19.**

Sant /sant/ *noun.* **E20.**
[Hindi, Panjabi, from Sanskrit *santah* (pl.) venerable men.]
An Indian holy man; (the title of) a Hindu or Sikh ascetic.

Santa /ˈsantə/ *noun. colloq.* **E20.**
[Abbreviation.]
= SANTA CLAUS 1.

Santa Ana /santə ˈanə/ *noun. US.* **L19.**
[Spanish = Saint Anne.]
A hot dry föhn-type wind of desert origin, usu. strong and dust-laden, which blows off the Santa Ana Mountains on to the coastal plain of southern California. Also ***Santa Ana wind***.

Santa Claus /ˈsantə klɔːz/ *noun.* Orig. *US.* **L18.**
[Dutch dial. *Sante Klaas* Saint Nicholas.]
1 An imaginary person said to bring presents for children on Christmas Eve; Father Christmas. **L18.**
2 *collect.* Christmas presents or delicacies. *US dial.* **E20.**

Santa Gertrudis /santə gəˈtruːdɪs/ *adjective & noun.* Pl. same. **M20.**
[A division of the King Ranch, Kingsville, Texas, where the breed was developed.]
Designating, an animal of, a breed of large red-coated beef cattle suitable for hot climates, developed by crossing brahmins and shorthorns.

santal /ˈsant(ə)l/ *noun*[1]. **E18.**
[French from medieval Latin *santalum* from late Greek *santalon*: see SANDAL *noun*[2].]
1 Sandalwood. Also ***santal-wood***. **E18.**
2 CHEMISTRY. Any of several carbohydrates obtained from sandalwood. **L19.**

Santal /ˈsantɑːl/ *noun*[2] *& adjective.* **M19.**
[Bengali *sāotāl*, from *Saont*, a place in Midnapur, India.]
▸**A** *noun.* Pl. **-s**, same.
1 A member of a Munda people of NE India. **M19.**
2 = SANTALI *noun.* **M19.**
▸**B** *attrib.* or as *adjective.* Of or pertaining to the Santals or Santali. **L19.**

santalaceous /santəˈleɪʃəs/ *adjective.* **M19.**
[from mod. Latin *Santalaceae*, from *Santalum* (see below): see -ACEOUS.]
BOTANY. Of or pertaining to the family Santalaceae, of which *Santalum* (sandalwood) is the type genus.

Santali /sanˈtɑːli/ *noun & adjective.* **L19.**
[from SANTAL *noun*[2] + -I[2].]
▸**A** *noun.* The Munda language of the Santals. **L19.**
▸**B** *attrib.* or as *adjective.* Of or pertaining to the Santals or their language. **L19.**

santalin /ˈsantəlɪn/ *noun.* **M19.**
[French *santaline*, from *sental*: see SANTAL *noun*[1], -IN[1].]
CHEMISTRY. The chief pigment of red sanders.

santalol /ˈsantəlɒl/ *noun.* **L19.**
[from SANTAL *noun*[1] + -OL.]
CHEMISTRY. Either of two isomeric terpenoid alcohols, $C_{15}H_{24}O$, which are fragrant liquids found in sandalwood oil.

Santa Maria /santə məˈriːə/ *noun.* **L17.**
[Spanish = Saint Mary.]
A tropical American tree, *Calophyllum brasiliense* (family Guttiferae); the wood of this tree.

santé /sɑ̃te/ *interjection.* **E20.**
[French, lit. 'health'.]
Expr. good wishes before drinking.

santeria /santeˈriə/ *noun.* **M20.**
[Spanish *santería* lit. 'holiness, sanctity'.]
An Afro-Cuban religious cult with many Yoruba elements.

santero /sanˈtero/ *noun.* Pl. ***-os*** /-ɔs/. **M20.**
[Spanish.]
1 In Mexico and Spanish-speaking areas of the south-western US: a maker of religious images. **M20.**
2 A priest of a religious cult, esp. of *santeria*. **M20.**

†**santie** *noun* var. of SANTY.

santim /ˈsantiːm/ *noun.* **E20.**
[Latvian *santims*, from French *centime* + the Latvian masculine ending *-s*.]
A monetary unit of Latvia, equal to one-hundredth of a lat.

santir /sanˈtɪə/ *noun.* Also **santoor**, **santour** /sanˈtʊə/. **M19.**
[Arab. *santīr*, *sintīr*, *santūr* (Persian *santūr*, Turkish *santur*), alt. of Greek *psaltērion* PSALTERY.]
A dulcimer of Arab and Persian origin.

santo /ˈsantəʊ/ *noun.* Pl. **-os**. **M17.**
[Spanish or Italian.]
1 = SANTON. **M17.**
2 A wooden representation of a saint or other religious symbol from Mexico, the south-western US, or elsewhere in Spanish-speaking parts of the Americas. **M19.**

Santobrite /ˈsantəbrʌɪt/ *noun.* **M20.**
[from the name of Mon*santo* Chemical Company + *-brite* (arbitrary ending).]
(Proprietary name for) a preparation of sodium pentachlorophenate used as a fungicide, wood preservative, insecticide, etc.

Santo Domingan /ˌsantəʊ dəˈmɪŋg(ə)n/ *adjective.* **M20.**
[from *Santo Domingo* (see below) + -AN.]
Of or pertaining to Santo Domingo, capital city (and former name) of the Dominican Republic.

santolina /santəˈliːnə/ *noun.* **L16.**
[mod. Latin (see below), perh. alt. of Latin SANTONICA.]
Any of various Mediterranean plants constituting the genus *Santolina*, of the composite family, aromatic usu. silvery-grey undershrubs allied to camomile; *esp.* lavender cotton, *S. chamaecyparissus*.

santon /ˈsantɒn/ *noun.* **L16.**
[French from Spanish, from *santo* SAINT *noun*: see -OON.]
1 A Muslim hermit or holy man, a marabout. Formerly also, a yogi, a Hindu ascetic. **L16.**
2 Chiefly in Provence: a figurine adorning a representation of the manger in which Jesus was laid. **E20.**

santonica /sanˈtɒnɪkə/ *noun.* **M17.**
[Latin *Santonica* (sc. *herba*) a kind of wormwood, fem. sing. of *Santonicus* pertaining to the Santoni, a Gallic tribe.]
collect. The dried flower-heads of several kinds of wormwood, esp. *Artemisia cina* of central Asia, used as an anthelmintic. Also called ***Levant wormseed***.
■ **ˈsantonin** *noun* a soluble toxic crystalline substance, $C_{15}H_{18}O_3$, obtained from santonica heads and used as an anthelmintic **M19.**

santoor *noun* var. of SANTIR.

santorin /santəˈriːn, ˈsantərɪn/ *noun.* Also **S-**, **-ini** /-iːni/. **M19.**
[Greek *Santorinē*, former name of Thira, from Italian *Sant' Irene* St Irene, Italian name for the island.]
In full ***Santorin earth***. A natural volcanic ash, similar to pozzolana, found on the island of Thira in the Cyclades.

Santos /ˈsantɒs/ *noun.* **L19.**
[A port in Brazil.]
Coffee exported from Santos.

santour *noun* var. of SANTIR.

san ts'ai /ˈsan tsʌɪ/ *noun phr.* **E20.**
[Chinese *sāncǎi* (Wade–Giles *sān-ts'ai*), from *sān* three + *cǎi* colour.]
Chinese pottery, esp. of the Tang dynasty, decorated in three colours; decoration in three enamel colours applied to pottery and porcelain.

†**santy** *noun.* Also **son-**, **-tie**. **M16–E17.**
[Origin uncertain: perh. formed as SANCTITY.]
Used in oaths and exclamations, esp. in ***God's santy***, ***God's sonties***.

Sanusi *noun & adjective* var. of SENUSSI.

sanxian *noun* var. of SAN-HSIEN.

sanyasi *noun* var. of SANNYASI.

saola /ˈʃaʊlɑː/ *noun.* **L20.**
[Vietnamese, lit. 'spindle horn'.]
A small two-horned mammal, *Pseudoryx nghetinhensis*, discovered in Vietnam in 1992, with similarities to both antelopes and oxen.

saouari /saʊˈɑːri/ *noun.* Also **souari** /suːˈɑːri/, **swarri** /ˈswɑːri/, & other vars. **E19.**
[French from Galibi *sawarra*.]
A tall Guyanese tree, *Caryocar amygdaliferum* (family Caryocaraceae).
saouari nut the edible oily nutlike seed of this tree.

sap /sap/ *noun*[1].
[Old English *sæp* corresp. to Middle & mod. Low German, Middle & mod. Dutch *sap*, Old High German *saf* (German *Saft*), prob. repr. Germanic form and rel. to Old Norse *safi*.]
1 The fluid, chiefly water with dissolved sugars and mineral salts, which circulates in the vascular system of a plant and is essential to its growth. **OE.** ▸**b** *transf.* Vigour, vitality. **E16.** ▸**c** Moisture in stone. **L19.** ▸**d** CYTOLOGY. The fluid component of a cell or organelle; *esp.* the contents of a plant cell vacuole. **L19.**
2 = ***sapwood*** below. **LME.**
3 Juice or fluid of any kind. Long *rare* exc. *Scot. & north.* **LME.**
4 [Abbreviation of *saphead*, **sapskull** below.] A simpleton, a fool. *colloq.* **E19.**
5 A club, a bludgeon, (orig. one made from a sapling). *US slang.* **L19.**

> 📖 **1b** LYTTON The sap of youth shrinks from our veins. **d** ***nuclear sap***: see NUCLEAR *adjective.* **3** *fig.*: SHAKES. *Hen. VIII* If with the sap of reason you would quench . . the fire of passion.

Comb.: **sap-beetle** any of various small beetles of the family Nitidulidae which frequent flowers and sap-runs; **sap-green** *noun & adjective* (*a*) *noun* a green pigment made from buckthorn berries; the colour of this; (*b*) *adjective* of the colour of sap-green; **saphead** *colloq.* = sense 4 above; **sap-headed** *adjective* (*colloq.*) foolish, stupid; **sap lath**: made of sapwood; **sap-rot** a disease of sapwood caused by fungi, esp. *Coltricia versicolor*; **sap-run** an increased flow of sap in a sugar maple; **sapskull** *colloq.* = sense 4 above; **sap spout**: through which sap is drawn from a sugar maple; **sap-stain** bluish discoloration of sapwood, caused esp. by fungi; **sapsucker** any of various small North and Central American woodpeckers of the genus *Sphyrapicus*, which drill holes and visit them for sap and insects, *esp.* (more fully ***yellow-bellied sapsucker***) the N. American *S. varius*, with a red head, a yellow belly, and otherwise black and white plumage; **sapwood** the outer wood of a tree, which contains the functioning vascular tissue and is usu. lighter in colour than the heartwood; the alburnum.
■ **sapful** *adjective* containing much sap or moisture **L17.**

sap /sap/ *noun*[2]. Also (earlier) †**sappe**, †**zappe**. **L16.**
[Italian *zappa*, French †*sappe*, †*zappe* (now *sape*) spade, spadework (cf. late Latin *sappa*), perh. from Arab. *sarab* burrow, underground passage, *sabora* probe a wound, explore.]
1 MILITARY. **a** Orig., the process of undermining a wall or defensive work. Later, the construction of covered trenches for approaching a besieged or fortified place without danger from enemy fire. **L16.** ▸**b** A covered trench or tunnel constructed for this purpose. **M17.**
2 Stealthy or insidious attack or destruction of something. **M18.**

> 📖 **1b** H. WILLIAMSON The 183rd Tunnelling Company had been mining Russian saps. **2** C. J. ELLICOTT An endeavour by slow sap to weaken the authority . . of the New Testament.

sap /sap/ *noun*[3]. *School slang.* **L18.**
[Cf. SAP *verb*[3].]
1 A person who studies hard or is absorbed in books. **L18.**
2 At Eton College: study, bookwork. **M19.**

sap /sap/ *verb*[1]. Infl. **-pp-**. **L16.**
[French *saper*, †*sapper* from Italian *zappare*, from *zappa*: see SAP *noun*[2].]
1 a *verb intrans.* MILITARY. Dig a sap or covered trench; approach a besieged or fortified place by means of a sap. **L16.** ▸**b** *verb intrans. & trans.* Make (one's way) in a stealthy or insidious manner. **M18.**
2 Dig under the foundations of (a wall etc.); *transf.* undermine, make insecure. **M17.** ▸**b** PHYSICAL GEOGRAPHY. Undermine by water or glacial action. Chiefly as ***sapping*** *verbal noun.* **M19.**
3 *verb trans. fig.* [freq. interpreted as fig. of SAP *verb*[2].] Weaken or destroy insidiously (health, strength, courage, etc.). **M18.**

> 📖 **2** DICKENS A crazy building, sapped and undermined by the rats. **3** G. GREENE Was the enemy trying to sap our confidence in our . . leaders? V. BROME Cancer had sapped his reserves of strength.

sap /sap/ *verb*[2]. Infl. **-pp-**. **E18.**
[from SAP *noun*[1].]
1 *verb trans.* Drain or dry (wood) of sap. **E18.**
2 *verb trans.* Remove the sapwood from (a log). Chiefly as ***sapping*** *verbal noun.* **L19.**
3 *US slang.* **a** *verb trans.* Hit (a person) with a club etc.; beat *up*. **E20.** ▸**b** *verb intrans.* Foll. by *up on*: Beat up, club. **E20.**

> 📖 **3a** L. ARMSTRONG He saw some big fellows sapping up a group of little kids. **b** M. ANGELOU We're not going down to Hang 'em High and let some cracker sheriff sap up on our heads.

¶ Cf. SAP *verb*[1] 3.

sap /sap/ *verb*[3] *intrans. School slang.* Infl. **-pp-**. **E19.**
[Cf. SAP *noun*[3].]
Pore over books; study hard. Chiefly as ***sapping*** *verbal noun.*

sapa /ˈseɪpə/ *noun.* M16.
[Latin.]
Orig., new wine boiled to a syrup. Later = ROB *noun.*

sapajou /ˈsapədʒuː/ *noun.* L17.
[French, perh. from Tupi.]
A capuchin monkey.

sapan *noun* var. of SAPPAN.

sapele /səˈpiːli/ *noun.* E20.
[A port on the Benin River, Nigeria.]
The reddish-brown timber of several tropical African trees of the genus *Entandophragma* (family Meliaceae), esp. *E. cylindricum.* Also ***sapele mahogany.***

saperavi /sapəˈrɑːvi/ *noun.* E20.
[Russian, from Georgian *sap'eravi* (adjective) of or pertaining to paint or dye, (noun) type of grape, wine made from this, from *p'eri* colour, painting, dyeing.]
A red wine from Georgia in the Caucasus.

saphena /səˈfiːnə/ *noun.* LME.
[medieval Latin from Arab. *ṣāfin.*]
ANATOMY. Either of the saphenous veins. Also ***saphena vein.***

saphenous /səˈfiːnəs/ *adjective.* M19.
[from prec. + -OUS.]
ANATOMY. Designating or pertaining to either of two large superficial veins in the leg; associated with either of these veins.

saphie /ˈsafiː/ *noun.* L18.
[Mande *safaye.*]
A N. African or Arabic charm.

saphir d'eau /safir do/ *noun.* E19.
[French, lit. 'sapphire of water'.]
= ***water sapphire*** (b) s.v. WATER *noun.*

sapid /ˈsapɪd/ *adjective. literary.* E17.
[Latin *sapidus,* from *sapere* have a taste: see -ID[1]. Cf. INSIPID, SIPID.]
1 Of food etc.: having a distinct (esp. pleasant) taste or flavour; savoury, palatable. E17.
2 Of talk, writing, etc.: agreeable, mentally stimulating. E17.
■ **saˈpidity** *noun* the quality of being sapid M17.

sapience /ˈseɪpɪəns/ *noun.* Now *rare.* ME.
[Old & mod. French from Latin *sapientia,* from *sapient-*: see next, -ENCE.]
1 Wisdom, understanding, formerly esp. as an attribute of God. ME. ▸†**b** Correct taste and judgement. M17–L18.
2 Assumed or apparent wisdom. *iron.* or *derog.* LME.

sapient /ˈseɪpɪənt/ *adjective & noun.* LME.
[Old French, or Latin *sapient-* pres. ppl stem of *sapere* have a taste, be sensible or wise: see -ENT.]
▶ **A** *adjective.* **1 a** Wise. Now only *iron.* or *literary.* LME. ▸**b** Having knowledge *of,* aware *of.* Long *rare.* M18.
2 ANTHROPOLOGY. Of, pertaining to, or characteristic of modern man, *Homo sapiens.* L20.
▶ **B** *noun.* †**1** = prec. Only in LME.
2 [= Latin *sapiens.*] A wise man, a sage. Now only *joc.* M16.
■ **sapiently** *adverb* LME.

sapiential /seɪpɪˈɛnʃ(ə)l/ *adjective. literary.* L15.
[Old & mod. French, or Christian Latin *sapientialis,* from Latin *sapientia*: see SAPIENCE, -AL[1].]
Pertaining to or characterized by wisdom, esp. the wisdom of God.
■ **sapientially** *adverb* (*rare*) M19.

sapin /sapɛ̃ (*pl. same*), ˈsapɪn/ *noun.* ME.
[Old & mod. French from Latin *sapinus.*]
A fir tree or allied tree. Also ***sapin tree.***
¶ Formerly fully naturalized.

sapindaceous /sapɪnˈdeɪʃəs/ *adjective.* M19.
[from mod. Latin *Sapindaceae,* from *Sapindus* (see below): see -ACEOUS.]
BOTANY. Of or pertaining to the family Sapindaceae, of which *Sapindus* (soapberry) is the type genus.

Sapiny /ˈsapɪni/ *noun & adjective.* Pl. of noun same. E20.
[Sebei.]
= SEBEI.

Sapir–Whorf hypothesis /səpɪəˈwɔːf hʌɪˌpɒθɪsɪs/ *noun phr.* M20.
[Edward *Sapir* (1884–1939) and Benjamin Lee *Whorf* (1897–1941), US linguists.]
LINGUISTICS. A hypothesis, first advanced by Sapir in 1929 and subsequently developed by Whorf, that the structure of a language partly determines a native speaker's categorization of experience. Cf. WHORFIAN.

sapless /ˈsaplɪs/ *adjective.* L16.
[from SAP *noun*[1] + -LESS.]
1 Of wood, a plant, etc.: devoid of sap, dry, withered. L16. ▸**b** Of soil: dry, lacking moisture; barren, unproductive. M17.
2 *transf. & fig.* Lacking vitality, energy, or vigour; characterless, insipid: (of an idea, saying, etc.) worthless, trivial, pointless. L16.

🕮 **2** SHAKES. *1 Hen. VI* When sapless age and weak unable limbs should bring thy father to his drooping chair. DRYDEN Now sapless on the verge of Death he stands.

■ **saplessness** *noun* M19.

sapling /ˈsaplɪŋ/ *noun & adjective.* ME.
[from SAP *noun*[1] + -LING[1].]
▶ **A** *noun.* **1** A young tree; *spec.* in FORESTRY, one with a trunk a few inches in diameter. ME.
2 A young or inexperienced person. L16.
3 A greyhound under one year of age. M19.
▶ **B** *attrib.* or as *adjective.* Designating or made out of a sapling. E18.

🕮 SIR W. SCOTT A small sapling stick, with a hooked head. W. HORWOOD Ivy entwines the sapling sycamore.

■ **saplinghood** *noun* (*rare*) the condition or state of being a sapling M19.

sapo /ˈsɑːpəʊ/ *noun. US.* Pl. **-os.** Also **sarpo.** M18.
[Spanish = toad.]
A toadfish, *esp.* an Atlantic toadfish of the genus *Opsanus.*

sapodilla /sapəˈdɪlə/ *noun.* L17.
[Spanish *zapotillo* dim. of *zapote* SAPOTA.]
A tropical American tree, *Manilkara zapota,* family Sapotaceae (also called ***naseberry, sapota***), which yields chicle; the edible sweet brownish fruit of this tree (also ***sapodilla plum***).

sapogenin /səˈpɒdʒɪnɪn/ *noun.* M19.
[from SAPO(NIN + -GEN + -IN[1].]
CHEMISTRY. Orig., a compound obtained by treating saponin with dilute mineral acids. Now, any of various steroid aglycones of the saponins.

saponaceous /sapəˈneɪʃəs/ *adjective.* E18.
[from mod. Latin *saponaceus,* from Latin *sapo(n-)*: see next, -ACEOUS.]
1 Of the nature of or resembling soap; consisting of or containing soap; soapy. E18.
2 Unctuous in manner, flattering; evasive. *joc.* M19.

saponaria /sapəˈnɛːrɪə/ *noun.* M19.
[mod. Latin use as genus name of fem. of medieval Latin *saponarius* adjective, from Latin *sapo(n-)* soap (late, in classical Latin a preparation for dyeing the hair): see -IA[1].]
A plant of the genus *Saponaria,* of the pink family, with clawed pink petals and opposite leaves; esp. *S. officinalis*; = ***soapwort*** (a) s.v. SOAP *noun*[1].

saponarin /sapəˈnɛːrɪn/ *noun.* E20.
[formed as prec. + -IN[1].]
CHEMISTRY. A white or pale yellow flavonoid diglycoside, $C_{27}H_{30}O_{15}$, first found in soapwort, *Saponaria officinalis.*
■ **saponaretin** /səpɒnəˈriːtɪn/ *noun* [-ETIN] a monoglycoside derived from saponarin by hydrolysis E20.

saponification /səˌpɒnɪfɪˈkeɪʃ(ə)n/ *noun.* E19.
[French, or from next: see -FICATION.]
CHEMISTRY. **1** The process of saponifying; orig., the alkaline hydrolysis of a fat to form a soap; now also, the alkaline hydrolysis of any ester to give a metal salt and an alcohol. E19.
2 The (natural) conversion of the soft parts of a corpse into adipocere. L19.
Comb.: **saponification equivalent, saponification number, saponification value** the amount of alkali required to saponify a particular quantity of fat etc., *spec.* the number of milligrams of potassium hydroxide required by one gram of fat etc.

saponify /səˈpɒnɪfʌɪ/ *verb.* E19.
[French *saponifier,* from Latin *sapo(n-)*: see SAPONARIA, -FY.]
CHEMISTRY. **1** *verb trans.* Orig., convert (a fat or oil) into soap by alkaline hydrolysis. Now also, hydrolyse (an ester) to form a metal salt and an alcohol. E19.
2 *verb intrans.* Orig., (of a fat or oil) become converted into soap. Now also, (of an ester) become hydrolysed to form a metal salt and an alcohol. E19.
■ **saponifiable** *adjective* able to be saponified or converted into soap M19. **saponifier** *noun* (a) (now *rare* or *obsolete*) an apparatus for isolating glycerine and fatty acids by saponification; (b) an alkali used in saponification: L19.

saponin /ˈsapənɪn/ *noun.* Also **-ine** /-iːn/. M19.
[French *saponine,* from Latin *sapo(n-)*: see SAPONARIA, -IN[1].]
CHEMISTRY. Any of various steroid or terpenoid glycosides obtained from certain plants, which are usu. toxic (esp. to fish), form foam in aqueous solution; and are used esp. as emulsifiers and detergents; *spec.* such a substance derived from soapwort, *Saponaria officinalis,* or the soapbark tree, *Quillaja saponaria.*

saponite /ˈsapənʌɪt/ *noun.* M19.
[from Latin *sapo(n-)* (see SAPONARIA) + -ITE[1].]
MINERALOGY. A magnesium-rich montmorillonoid mineral occurring as soft soapy amorphous masses filling veins and cavities in serpentine and basalt.

saponule /ˈsapənjuːl/ *noun.* Now *rare* or *obsolete.* L18.
[formed as prec. + -ULE.]
CHEMISTRY. A substance formed by the incomplete saponification of volatile oils.

sapor /ˈseɪpɔː, -pə/ *noun.* Now *rare.* Also **-pour.** LME.
[Latin, from *sapere* have a taste. Cf. SAVOUR *noun.*]
1 A quality perceptible by taste, as sweetness, bitterness, etc.; the distinctive taste of a substance. LME.
2 The sensation of taste. M17.
■ **sapoˈrific** *adjective* (*rare*) imparting flavour or taste E18.

saporous /ˈseɪpərəs/ *adjective. rare.* LME.
[Orig. from medieval Latin *saporosus,* later from prec.: see -OUS.]
Orig., pleasing to the taste, savoury. Later, of or pertaining to taste; having flavour or taste.
■ **sapoˈrosity** *noun* the quality of being saporous L18.

sapota /səˈpəʊtə/ *noun.* Also (esp. in sense 2) **-te** /-ti, -teɪ/. M16.
[Spanish ZAPOTE, Portuguese *sapota,* from Nahuatl *zapotl.*]
1 (The fruit of) the sapodilla, *Manilkara zapota* (formerly *Sapota achras*). M16.
2 = MAMMEE 2. Earliest in ***MAMMEE sapota.*** M17.
■ **sapoˈtaceous** *adjective* of or pertaining to the family Sapotaceae, or sapodilla M19.

sapotoxin /ˈsapətɒksɪn/ *noun.* L19.
[formed as SAPONIN + TOXIN.]
CHEMISTRY. Any markedly toxic saponin.

sapour *noun* var. of SAPOR.

sappan /ˈsapən/ *noun.* Also **sapan.** L16.
[Dutch from Malay *sapang,* of southern Indian origin.]
The wood of the leguminous tree *Caesalpinia sappan* and other Indo-Malayan trees of this genus, formerly used to provide a red dye. Now only ***sappanwood.***

†**sappe** *noun* see SAP *noun*[2].

sapper /ˈsapə/ *noun.* E17.
[from SAP *verb*[1] + -ER[1].]
A soldier who digs saps or builds and repairs fortifications, fieldworks, etc.; in the British army, a soldier (*spec.* a private) in the Royal Engineers, formerly called the ***Royal Sappers and Miners.***

sapperment /sapəˈmɛnt/ *interjection. rare.* E19.
[German, alt. of *Sakrament* SACRAMENT *noun.*]
Used as an oath by German-speakers.

Sapphic /ˈsafɪk/ *adjective & noun.* Also (esp. as noun) **s-.** E16.
[French *saphique,* †*sapphique* from Latin *Sapphicus* from Greek *Sapphikos,* from *Sapphō* (see below): see -IC.]
▶ **A** *adjective.* Of or pertaining to Sappho, an allegedly homosexual poetess of Lesbos (*c* 600 BC); *spec.* designating or pertaining to a poetic metre associated with Sappho. Also = LESBIAN *adjective* 2. E16.
▶ **B** *noun.* A metre associated with Sappho, *esp.* one consisting of a trochaic pentameter line with a dactyl in the third foot; in *pl.,* verses written in such a metre. L16.

sapphire /ˈsafʌɪə/ *noun & adjective.* ME.
[Old French *safir* (mod. *saphir*) from Latin *sapphirus, sapp(h)ir,* from Greek *sappheiros* (prob.) lapis lazuli.]
▶ **A** *noun.* **1** A transparent blue precious stone consisting of corundum; MINERALOGY any transparent variety of corundum of gem quality. ME.
2 a HERALDRY. The tincture azure in the fanciful blazon of arms of peers. Long *obsolete* exc. *Hist.* M16. ▸**b** The deep blue of a sapphire. L17.
3 Any of various bright blue hummingbirds, esp. of the genus *Hylocharis.* M19.
1 ***star sapphire***: see STAR *noun*[1] & *adjective.* ***water sapphire***: see WATER *noun.* ***white sapphire***: see WHITE *adjective.*
▶ **B** *attrib.* or as *adjective.* Made or consisting of sapphire; set or provided with a sapphire or sapphires; resembling a sapphire in colour, deep blue. LME.
Comb. & special collocations: **sapphire-blue** *adjective & noun* (of) a deep blue colour; **sapphire mink** a mink of a variety with blue-grey fur; the fur of such an animal; **sapphire quartz** a rare indigo-blue variety of quartz; **sapphire wedding** the forty-fifth anniversary of a wedding.
■ **sapphiric** /səˈfɪrɪk/ *adjective* (*rare*) of the nature of or resembling a sapphire E17.

sapphirine /ˈsafɪrʌɪn/ *noun.* E19.
[from prec. + -INE[5].]
MINERALOGY. Any of certain pale blue minerals; *esp.* a usu. granular monoclinic silicate of aluminium and magnesium, occurring esp. in metamorphic rocks.

sapphirine /ˈsafɪrʌɪn/ *adjective.* LME.
[Latin *sapphirinus* from Greek *sappheirinos,* from *sappheiros* SAPPHIRE: see -INE[1].]
Consisting of or resembling (that of) sapphire; *esp.* sapphire-blue.

sapphism /ˈsafɪz(ə)m/ *noun.* Also **S-.** L19.
[from *Sappho* (see SAPPHIC) + -ISM.]
Lesbianism.
■ **sapphist** *noun* a lesbian E20.

sapple /ˈsap(ə)l/ *verb trans. Scot.* M19.
[Frequentative of var. of SOP *verb*: see -LE[3]. Cf. next.]
Rinse, wash out; soak (clothes) in soapy water.

sapples /ˈsap(ə)lz/ *noun pl. Scot.* E19.
[from prec., although recorded earlier.]
Soap suds, bubbles.

sappy /ˈsapi/ *adjective.* LOE.
[from SAP *noun*[1] + -Y[1].]
1 Of a plant, tree, wood, etc.: full of sap. LOE. ▸**b** Consisting of or containing sapwood. *obsolete* exc. *dial.* LME.
2 Full of moisture; wet. Also (*obsolete* exc. *dial.*), (of meat, fruit, etc.) juicy, succulent. LME.
3 Full of vitality, young and vigorous. Also, full of goodness, substantial. M16.
4 Fat, plump. Now *Austral.* (esp. of livestock) & *dial.* L17.
5 Foolish, silly, soppy. *colloq.* L17.

📖 **3** F. R. LEAVIS *The Portrait of a Lady* belongs to the sappiest phase of James's art. **5** J. IRVING The passage about the 'gleams of sunshine'—okay, it's sappy.

■ **sappily** *adverb* L17. **sappiness** *noun* M16.

sapraemia /sapˈriːmɪə/ *noun.* Also ***sapremia**. L19.
[from Greek *sapros* putrid + -AEMIA.]
MEDICINE. Blood-poisoning due to toxins produced by putrefactive bacteria.
■ **sapraemic** *adjective* L19.

sapristi /sapristi, saˈpriːsti/ *interjection.* M19.
[French, alt. of *sacristi*.]
Expr. astonishment, exasperation, etc.

📖 P. MANN 'Soup,' he announced, rather as a magician might say 'Sapristi'.

sapro- /ˈsaprəʊ/ *combining form.*
[from Greek *sapros* putrid: see -O-.]
Used in *BIOLOGY* with the sense 'of decay or putrefaction'.
■ **saprobiˈology** *noun* the branch of science that deals with saprobic environments M20. **saprobiˈotic** *adjective* = SAPROBIC *adjective* 2 M20. **saproˈgenic**, **saprogenous** /səˈprɒdʒɪnəs/ *adjectives* causing decay or putrefaction; produced by putrefaction: L19. **saprophile** *noun & adjective* (a bacterium) that inhabits putrid matter L19. **saprophilous** /səˈprɒfɪləs/ *adjective* inhabiting putrid matter L19. **saproxylic** /saprəˈzɪlɪk, saprɒ(k)-/ *adjective* [Greek *xulon* wood] dependant on dead and decaying wood, or on organisms found only in such wood L20.

saprobe /ˈsaprəʊb/ *noun.* M20.
[from prec. after MICROBE etc.]
BIOLOGY. An organism, esp. a fungus, that derives its nourishment from decaying organic matter.

saprobic /səˈprəʊbɪk/ *adjective.* E20.
[from prec. + -IC.]
BIOLOGY. **1** Characterized by the prevalence of decaying organic material; *spec.* polysaprobic. E20.
2 Of, pertaining to, or characteristic of a saprobe; deriving nourishment from decaying organic matter. M20.
■ **saprobicity** /saprə(ʊ)ˈbɪsɪti/ *noun* = SAPROBITY M20.

saprobity /səˈprəʊbɪti/ *noun.* M20.
[from prec. + -ITY.]
ECOLOGY. The degree to which the decomposition of organic material is occurring in an aquatic environment.

saprolegnia /saprəˈlɛɡnɪə/ *noun.* M19.
[mod. Latin (see below), formed as SAPRO- + Greek *legnon* border: see -IA[1].]
A fungus of the genus *Saprolegnia*, which includes kinds infesting the bodies of fish; infestation with such a fungus.

saprolite /ˈsaprəlʌɪt/ *noun.* L19.
[from SAPRO- + -LITE.]
GEOLOGY. A soft clay-rich rock formed *in situ* by chemical weathering of igneous and metamorphic rocks.
■ **saprolitic** /saprəˈlɪtɪk/ *adjective* E20.

sapropel /ˈsaprəpɛl/ *noun.* E20.
[German, formed as SAPRO- + Greek *pēlos* mud, earth, clay.]
An unconsolidated nitrogen-rich sludge of decomposing aquatic micro-organisms that accumulates in anaerobic environments on the bottoms of lakes and seas.
■ **sapro'pelic** *adjective* E20.

saprophagous /səˈprɒfəɡəs/ *adjective.* E19.
[from SAPRO- + -PHAGOUS.]
BIOLOGY. Feeding on or deriving nourishment from dead or decaying matter.

saprophyte /ˈsaprə(ʊ)fʌɪt/ *noun.* L19.
[from SAPRO- + -PHYTE.]
A vegetable organism that derives its nutriment from decaying organic matter.
■ **saprophytic** /-ˈfɪtɪk/ *adjective* of, pertaining to, or of the nature of a saprophyte L19. **sapro'phytically** *adverb* E20. **saprophytism** *noun* the state of living as a saprophyte L19.

saprotrophic /saprə(ʊ)ˈtrəʊfɪk, -ˈtrɒf-/ *adjective.* M20.
[from SAPRO- + -TROPHIC.]
BIOLOGY. Of an organism: that feeds on or derives nourishment from decaying organic matter.
■ **ˈsaprotroph** *noun* a saprotrophic organism M20.

sapsago /sapˈseɪɡəʊ/ *noun.* Orig. & chiefly *US.* M19.
[Alt.]
= SCHABZIEGER.

sapucaia /sapuːˈkɑːjə/ *noun.* E17.
[Portuguese from Tupi *yasapukaya*.]
A S. American tree, *Lecythis zabucajo* (family Lecythidaceae), related to the Brazil nut; the oily edible seed of this (also ***sapucaia-nut***).

SAR *abbreviation.*
Search and rescue.

Sarabaite /sarəˈbeɪʌɪt/ *noun.* Also **Sarabite** /ˈsarəbʌɪt/. LME.
[ecclesiastical Latin *Sarabaita*, of unkn. origin: see -ITE[1].]
ECCLESIASTICAL HISTORY. Any of a class of monks in the early Christian Church who lived together in small bands without rule or superior.

saraband /ˈsarəband/ *noun*[1]. Also **sarabande** /sarəˈbɑːnd/. E17.
[French *sarabande* from Spanish, Italian *zarabanda*.]
A slow and stately Spanish dance in triple time; a piece of music for this dance or in its rhythm, often with a lengthened note on the second beat of the bar, *esp.* one which forms a movement of a suite.

📖 *fig.*: P. O'DONNELL Grotesque shadows of two men . . moved . . in an eerie saraband.

Saraband /ˈsarəband/ *noun*[2]. E20.
[*Saravand*, a district in western Iran.]
A kind of Persian rug characterized by a pattern of leaf or pear forms. Also ***Saraband rug***.

sarabande *noun* var. of SARABAND *noun*[1].

Sarabite *noun* var. of SARABAITE.

Saracen /ˈsarəs(ə)n/ *noun & adjective.* OE.
[Old French *Sar(r)azin*, *-cin* (mod. *Sarrasin*) from late Latin *Saracenus* from late Greek *sarakēnos*, perh. from Arab. *šarkī* eastern, from *šark* sunrise, east. Cf. SARSEN.]
▸ **A** *noun.* **1** *Hist.* Orig., a member of any of the nomadic peoples of the Syrian and Arabian deserts which harassed the borders of the Roman Empire. Later also, an Arab, a Turk, a Muslim, esp. at the time of the Crusades. OE.
†**2 a** A heathen, a pagan, an infidel. ME–M16. ▸**b** A boorish person, a barbarian. *rare.* E18–M19.
Comb.: **Saracen corn** *arch.* buckwheat, *Fagopyrum esculentum* (cf. SARRAZIN); †**Saracen's consound** a kind of ragwort, *Senecio fluviatilis*, said to have been used by the Saracens in healing wounds; **Saracen's corn** (*a*) = ***Saracen corn*** above; †(*b*) sorghum, *Sorghum vulgare*; **Saracen's head** the head of a Saracen or Turk, esp. as a heraldic charge or as an inn sign; †**Saracen's woundwort** = ***Saracen's consound*** above.
▸ **B** *adjective.* Saracenic. ME.
■ **Saracenism** *noun* (*Hist.*, *rare*) the political or religious organization of the Saracens M17.

Saracenic /sarəˈsɛnɪk/ *adjective.* M17.
[medieval Latin *Saracenicus*, from late Latin *Saracenus*: see prec., -IC.]
1 Of, pertaining to, or characteristic of the Saracens. M17.
2 *spec.* Designating (a building etc. in) a characteristically Islamic architectural style. Formerly also, designating a light Gothic style. M18.
3 Barbaric, heathenish. *rare.* M19.
■ **Saracenical** *adjective* (now *rare* or *obsolete*) = SARACENIC E17. †**Saracenican** *adjective* = SARACENIC E17–L18.

saraf /səˈrɑːf/ *noun.* L16.
[Persian & Urdu from Arab. *ṣarrāf*, from *ṣarafa* exchange money. Cf. SHROFF.]
A banker or money-changer in the East; = SHROFF.

sarafan /ˈsarəfan/ *noun.* L18.
[Russian.]
A long loose sleeveless dress worn over a blouse and forming part of the national costume of Russian peasant women.

Sarakatsan /sarəˈkats(ə)n/ *noun & adjective.* M20.
[mod.Greek *Sarakatsanoi* (pl.).]
▸ **A** *noun.* Pl. **-sani** /-sɑːni/, **-sans**, same. A member of a nomadic pastoral people of northern Greece. M20.
▸ **B** *attrib.* or as *adjective.* Of or pertaining to this people. M20.

Saramaccan /sarəˈmak(ə)n/ *noun & adjective.* Also **-kk-**. M20.
[from *Saramacca* (see below) + -AN.]
▸ **A** *noun.* A creole language spoken in the region of the upper reaches of the River Saramacca in Suriname, S. America. M20.
▸ **B** *adjective.* Of, pertaining to, or designating this language. M20.

Saran /səˈran/ *noun.* Orig. *US.* Also **s-**. M20.
[Origin unkn.]
(Proprietary name for) polyvinyl chloride (PVC), esp. as a film. Also ***Saran Wrap***.

sarang *noun* var. of SERANG.

sarangi /səˈraŋɡi, sɑːˈrʌŋɡi/ *noun.* M19.
[Sanskrit *sāraṅgī*.]
An Indian bowed stringed instrument. Cf. SARINDA.

sarape *noun* var. of SERAPE.

sarassin *noun* var. of SARRAZIN.

Saratoga /sarəˈtəʊɡə/ *noun.* Chiefly *US.* E19.
[*Saratoga* Springs, resort in New York State, USA.]
1 ***Saratoga water***, mineral water obtained from the springs at Saratoga. E19.
2 In full ***Saratoga trunk***. A large travelling trunk with a rounded top. M19.
3 ***Saratoga chips***, ***Saratoga potatoes***, potato crisps. L19.

sarazin *noun* var. of SARRAZIN.

sarbacane /ˈsɑːbəkeɪn/ *noun. obsolete* exc. *Hist.* M17.
[French (also †*sarbatenne*) from Spanish *cebratana*, from Arab. = blowpipe, ult. from Persian.]
†**1** An ear-trumpet. Only in M17.
2 A blowpipe for shooting with. M18.

sarcasm /ˈsɑːkaz(ə)m/ *noun.* Also (earlier) in Latin form †**sarcasmus**. M16.
[French *sarcasme* or late Latin *sarcasmus* from late Greek *sarkasmos*, from *sarkazein* tear flesh, gnash the teeth, speak bitterly, from *sark-*, *sarx* flesh.]
1 A bitter or wounding expression or remark, a taunt, *esp.* one ironically worded. M16.
2 The use of or the faculty of using such remarks; language consisting of such remarks. M16.

📖 **1** GEO. ELIOT Blows are sarcasms turned stupid. **2** P. P. READ 'I can imagine that you are kept very busy'. The sarcasm was unconcealed. C. HARMAN Ruth . . and Valentine . . became prime targets for Nora's scorn and sarcasm.

■ †**sarcasmous** *adjective* sarcastic M17–M18.

sarcast /ˈsɑːkast/ *noun.* M17.
[from prec. after *enthusiasm*/ *enthusiast* etc.]
A sarcastic writer or speaker.

sarcastic /sɑːˈkastɪk/ *adjective.* L17.
[French *sarcastique*, from *sarcasme* SARCASM after *enthusiasme*, *enthusiastique* etc.: see prec., -IC.]
Characterized by or involving sarcasm; given to the use of sarcasm; bitterly cutting or ironic.

📖 A. P. PRIMROSE Facts . . dismissed by a knowing wink or a sarcastic smile. P. CAREY She thought of sarcastic jokes about Rossetti.

■ **sarcastical** *adjective* (now *rare*) = SARCASTIC M17. **sarcastically** *adverb* M17.

Sarcee /ˈsɑːsiː/ *adjective & noun.* Also **Sarsi**. L18.
[Blackfoot *saahsiwa*, Cree *sa:si:w*.]
▸ **A** *adjective.* Designating or pertaining to an Athapaskan people of Alberta, Canada, or their language. L18.
▸ **B** *noun.* Pl. **-s**, same.
1 A member of this people. E19.
2 The language of this people. E20.

†**sarcelle** *noun.* LME–E19.
[Old French *cercelle* (mod. *sarcelle*) = Anglo-Latin *cercella* from popular Latin *cercedula* from classical Latin *querquedula*.]
A teal, garganey, or other small duck.

sarcelly /ˈsɑːsəli/ *adjective.* L15.
[Anglo-Norman *sercelé*, *cercelé* = Old French *cercelé* ringleted, curled, pa. pple of *cerceler*, from *cercel* from late Latin *circellus* dim. of Latin *circulus* dim. of *circus* circle: see -Y[5]. Cf. RESARCELÉE.]
HERALDRY. **1** Designating a variety of the cross moline in which the points are recurved or curled back. L15.
2 Of a cross, esp. a cross moline: voided and open at the ends. M17.
■ **sarcelled** *adjective* = SARCELLY 2 L17.

sarcenet *noun & adjective* var. of SARSENET.

sarcina /ˈsɑːsɪnə/ *noun.* Pl. **-nae** /-niː/. M19.
[mod. Latin (see below) from Latin = bundle, from *sarcire* patch, mend.]
MICROBIOLOGY. A bacterium of the genus *Sarcina* of anaerobic, Gram-positive, non-pathogenic cocci found in the gut and in various animal fluids. Also, a cubical cluster of cocci, typical of this genus.

sarcle /ˈsɑːk(ə)l/ *verb trans.* Long *obsolete* exc. *Hist.* M16.
[Old French *sarcler* from Latin *sarculare*, from *sarculum* hoe, from *sar(r)ire* to weed.]
Weed with a hoe.
■ **sarcler** *noun* a weeding or pruning implement LME.

sarco- /ˈsɑːkəʊ/ *combining form.*
[from Greek *sark-*, *sarx* flesh: see -O-.]
Used chiefly in *BIOLOGY & MEDICINE*, with the sense 'of flesh, fleshy tissue, or muscle'.
■ **sarcocarp** *noun* (*BOTANY*) the fleshy part of a drupaceous fruit between the epicarp and the endocarp, the part usually eaten E19. †**sarcocele** *noun* a fleshy tumour of the testicle E17–M19. **sarcocyst** *noun* a cyst in muscle tissue containing spores or sporoblasts of sarcosporidia L19. **sarcoˈlactate** *noun* a salt or ester of sarcolactic acid L19. **sarcoˈlactic** *adjective* (*CHEMISTRY*) ***sarcolactic acid***, the dextrorotatory form of lactic acid M19. **sarcoˈlemma** *noun* the fine transparent tubular sheath investing the fibres of skeletal muscles M19. **sarcoˈlemmal** *adjective* of or pertaining to the sarcolemma E20. †**sarcology** *noun* the branch of anatomy that deals with the fleshy parts of the body E18–L19. **sarcomere** *noun* [-MERE] a structural unit of a myofibril in striated muscle, consisting of a dark band and the nearer half of each adjacent pale band L19. **sarcoplasm**, †**-plasma** *noun* the

cytoplasm of muscle cells L19. **sarco'plasmic** *adjective* of, pertaining to, or containing sarcoplasm; ***sarcoplasmic reticulum***, the characteristic endoplasmic reticulum of striated muscle: L19. **sarcosome** *noun* a large mitochondrion found in striated muscle L19. **sarco'testa** *noun* (BOTANY) the fleshy, freq. brightly coloured, outer layer of the testa in some seeds (opp. ***sclerotesta***) L19.

sarcococca /sɑːkə(ʊ)'kɒksə/ *noun.* E20.
[mod. Latin (see below), formed as SARCO- + Greek *kokkos* berry.]
Any of several small ornamental winter-flowering shrubs of the genus *Sarcococca*, of the box family, native to eastern Asia, with white or pink, often fragrant, petalless flowers followed by black or red berries.

sarcocolla /sɑːkəʊ'kɒlə/ *noun.* Also (earlier, now *rare*) **-col(l)** /'sɑːkəkɒl/. LME.
[Latin from Greek *sarkokolla*, formed as SARCO- + *kolla* glue: so called because reputedly able to agglutinate wounds.]
A gum resin from Arabia and Iran, having the form of yellow or red grains.

sarcode /'sɑːkəʊd/ *noun & adjective.* Now *rare* or *obsolete.* M19.
[French, formed as SARCO-: see -ODE¹.]
BIOLOGY. ▶**A** *noun.* The protoplasm of animals. M19.
▶**B** *adjective.* Protoplasmic. M19.
■ **sar'codic** *adjective* M19.

sarcoid /'sɑːkɔɪd/ *adjective & noun.* M19.
[formed as SARCO- + -OID.]
▶**A** *adjective.* **1** ZOOLOGY etc. Resembling flesh. *rare.* M19.
2 MEDICINE. Of, pertaining to, or resembling sarcoidosis. M20.
▶**B** *noun.* MEDICINE. A granuloma of sarcoidosis; a fleshy tumour. L19.
■ **sar'coidal** *adjective* (MEDICINE) = SARCOID *adjective* 2 M20.

sarcoidosis /sɑːkɔɪ'dəʊsɪs/ *noun.* Pl. **-doses** /-'dəʊsiːz/. M20.
[from prec. + -OSIS.]
MEDICINE. A chronic disease characterized by the widespread appearance of granulomas derived from the reticuloendothelial system.

sarcolite /'sɑːkəlʌɪt/ *noun.* E19.
[from SARCO- + -LITE.]
MINERALOGY. A tetragonal basic aluminosilicate of sodium and calcium occurring as small flesh-coloured crystals in some igneous rocks.

sarcoma /sɑː'kəʊmə/ *noun.* Pl. **-mas**, **-mata** /-mətə/. M17.
[mod. Latin from Greek *sarkōma*, from *sarkoun* become fleshy, from *sark-*, *sarx* flesh: see -OMA.]
MEDICINE. †**1** A fleshy excrescence. M17–M18.
2 A malignant tumour of connective or other non-epithelial tissue. E19.
2 KAPOSI's *sarcoma*.
■ **sarcoma'tosis** *noun* a condition in which sarcomas occur disseminated in the body L19. **sarcomatous** *adjective* of, pertaining to, or of the nature of a sarcoma M18.

sarcophagus /sɑː'kɒfəgəs/ *noun & verb.* LME.
[Latin from Greek *sarkophagos* (adjective & noun), formed as SARCO- + *-phagos* eating.]
▶**A** *noun.* Pl. **-gi** /-gʌɪ, -dʒʌɪ/.
1 A stone coffin, *esp.* one adorned with sculpture, an inscription, etc. LME.
2 GREEK ANTIQUITIES. A stone fabled to be able to consume the flesh of dead bodies deposited in it, and used for coffins. Now *rare.* E17.
†**3** A flesh-eater; a cannibal. *rare.* E17–M19

> 🕮 **1** *fig.*: *New Scientist* The rogue reactor still . . discharging its radioactivity within its dense sarcophagus of concrete and steel.

▶**B** *verb trans.* Deposit or enclose in a sarcophagus. *rare.* M19.
■ **sarcophagal** *adjective* (*rare*) (*a*) flesh-eating; (*b*) represented on sarcophagi: E17. †**sarcophage** *noun* = SARCOPHAGUS E17–M19. **sarcophagous** *adjective* (*rare*) (*a*) flesh-eating, carnivorous; (*b*) resembling a sarcophagus: M18. **sarcophagy** *noun* (*rare*) [Greek *sarkophagia*] the practice of eating flesh M17.

sarcopside /sɑː'kɒpsɪd/ *noun.* L19.
[German *Sarkopsid*, irreg. from Greek *sark-*, *sarx* flesh + *opsis* sight.]
MINERALOGY. A monoclinic phosphate of ferrous iron, manganese, and magnesium, usu. occurring as flesh-red to brown fibrous masses.

sarcoptid /sɑː'kɒptɪd/ *noun & adjective.* L19.
[mod. Latin *Sarcoptidae* (see below), from *Sarcoptes* genus name, formed as SARCO- + Greek *koptein* to cut: see -ID³.]
▶**A** *noun.* Any member of the family Sarcoptidae of ectoparasitic mites. L19.
▶**B** *adjective.* Of, pertaining to, or designating this family. M20.
■ **'sarcopt** *noun* = SARCOPTID *noun* L19. **sarcoptic** *adjective* (of mange) caused by the itch-mite, *Sarcoptes scabiei* L19.

sarcosine /'sɑːkəsiːn/ *noun.* M19.
[from SARCO- + -S- + -INE⁵.]
BIOCHEMISTRY. A crystalline amino acid which occurs esp. as a product of the metabolism of creatine; *N*-methylglycine, CH_3NHCH_2COOH.

sarcosporidium /ˌsɑːkəʊspə'rɪdɪəm/ *noun.* Pl. **-dia** /-dɪə/. L19.
[formed as SARCO- + SPORIDIUM.]
MICROBIOLOGY. A spore-forming protozoan of the coccidian genus *Sarcocystis* that is a common parasite in muscle tissue, esp. of domestic and laboratory mammals.
■ **sarcosporidial** *adjective* of or pertaining to sarcosporidia E20. **sarcosporidi'osis** *noun* (disease caused by) infection with sarcosporidia L19.

sarcous /'sɑːkəs/ *adjective.* M19.
[formed as SARCO- + -OUS.]
Consisting of flesh or muscular tissue.

sard /sɑːd/ *noun*¹. LME.
[Old & mod. French *sarde* or Latin *sarda*, formed as SARDIUS.]
Yellow or orange-red cornelian.

Sard /sɑːd/ *noun*² *& adjective.* E19.
[(Italian *Sardo* from) Latin *Sardus*.]
= SARDINIAN.

sardana /sar'dana/ *noun.* E20.
[Catalan & Spanish.]
A Catalan dance performed to pipes and drum.

Sardanapalian /sɑːdənə'peɪlɪən/ *adjective.* M19.
[from Latin *Sardanapalus*, Greek *Sardanapalos*, name given by Greek historians to the proverbially decadent last king of Assyria *c* 627 BC (prob. not a historical character): see -IAN.]
Resembling Sardanapalus and his attributes; luxuriously effeminate.
■ Earlier †**Sardanapalical** *adjective*: only in M16.

sardar /sə'dɑː, 'səːdɑː/ *noun.* Also **sirdar**. L16.
[Persian & Urdu *sar-dār*, from Persian *sar* position of head or chief + *-dār* holder, holding.]
1 In the Indian subcontinent and other Eastern countries, a military or political leader; *spec.* (*Hist.*) the British commander-in-chief of the Egyptian army. L16. ▸**b** A Sikh. L20.
2 A personal servant. Also ***sardar-bearer***. *Anglo-Indian.* E19.

sardelle /sɑː'dɛl/ *noun.* L16.
[Italian *sardella* dim. of *sarda*, from Latin: see SARDINE *noun*².]
A sardine, anchovy, or other small fish similarly prepared for eating.

Sardian /'sɑːdɪən/ *adjective & noun.* M16.
[Latin *Sardianus* from Greek *Sardianos*, from *Sardeis* pl. (Latin *Sardis*, *Sardes*): see below, -IAN.]
▶**A** *adjective. Hist.* Of or pertaining to Sardis, capital of Lydia, an ancient country in Asia Minor. M16.
▶**B** *noun.* **1** *Hist.* A native or inhabitant of Sardis. L16.
2 = SARD *noun*¹. M18.

sardine /'sɑːdʌɪn/ *noun*¹. LME.
[Late Latin *sardinus* from Greek *sardinos* var. of *sardios* SARDIUS.]
ANTIQUITIES. = SARDIUS.

sardine /sɑː'diːn/ *noun*² *& verb.* LME.
[Old & mod. French, corresp. to Italian *sardina* from Latin, from *sarda* from Greek, prob. from *Sardō* Sardinia.]
▶**A** *noun.* **1** A young pilchard or similar small usu. clupeid marine fish, esp. when cured, preserved, and packed for use as food. LME.
2 In *pl.* (treated as *sing.*) A form of hide-and-seek in which each seeker joins the hider on discovery until one seeker remains. E20.
1 packed like sardines crowded or confined close together (as sardines are in a tin).
▶**B** *verb trans.* Pack closely as sardines in a tin; crowd, cram, press tightly. *colloq.* L19.

> 🕮 E. JONG There were five of us sardined into that tiny car.

Sardinian /sɑː'dɪnɪən/ *noun & adjective.* L16.
[from *Sardinia* (see below) + -AN.]
▶**A** *noun.* **1** A native or inhabitant of the Mediterranean island of Sardinia, now administratively part of Italy, or the former kingdom of Sardinia which included mainland territory in Italy besides the island. L16.
2 The Romance language (or group of dialects) of Sardinia. E19.
▶**B** *adjective.* **1** Of or pertaining to Sardinia. E17. ▸**b** Of, pertaining to, or designating the language (or group of dialects) of the Sardinians. M19.
†**2** Of laughter etc.: sardonic. E17–M18.
Special collocations: **Sardinian warbler** a black, brown, and white warbler, *Sylvia melanocephala*, common in the Mediterranean region.

sardius /'sɑːdɪəs/ *noun.* LME.
[Late Latin from Greek *sardios*, prob. from *Sardō* Sardinia. Cf. SARDINE *noun*¹.]
ANTIQUITIES. A red precious stone mentioned in the Bible (*Revelation* 4:3) and in classical writings, prob. a ruby or cornelian.

†**sardonian** *adjective.* L16–L18.
[French †*sardonien*, from Latin *sardonius* from late Greek *Sardonios* Sardinian, substituted for *sardanios* Homeric epithet of bitter or scornful laughter: see -AN, -IAN.]
= SARDONIC *adjective*.

sardonic /sɑː'dɒnɪk/ *adjective.* M17.
[French *sardonique* alt. of †*sardonien*: see prec., -IC.]
(Of laughter, a smile, etc.) bitter, scornful, mocking; characterized by or exhibiting bitterness, scorn, or mockery. Cf. also RISUS SARDONICUS.

> 🕮 ISAAC TAYLOR The sardonic historian, whose rule it is to exhibit human nature always as an object of mockery. J. STEINBECK The corners of his mouth were turned slightly up in a sardonic smile.

■ **sardonically** *adverb* M19. **sardonicism** /-sɪz(ə)m/ *noun* the quality or condition of being sardonic; an instance of this, a sardonic remark: E20. **'sardony** *noun* [after *irony*] the quality or condition of being sardonic M20.

sardonyx /'sɑːdənɪks/ *noun.* ME.
[Latin from Greek *sardonux*, prob. from *sardios* SARDIUS + *onux* ONYX.]
A variety of onyx or stratified chalcedony in which white layers alternate with layers of sard.

Sardoodledom /sɑː'duːd(ə)ldəm/ *noun.* L19.
[Fanciful formation from Victorien *Sardou* (1831–1908), French dramatist + DOODLE *noun* + -DOM.]
Well-written but trivial or morally objectionable plays considered collectively; the milieu in which these are admired.

> 🕮 G. B. SHAW Sailing the Lyceum ship into the shadows of Sardoodledom.

saree *noun* var. of SARI.

sargasso /sɑː'gasəʊ/ *noun.* Pl. **-o(e)s**. L16.
[Portuguese *sargaço*, of unkn. origin.]
Gulfweed, sargassum; a mass of this; *fig.* a confused or stagnant mass or region.
Comb.: **Sargasso Sea** the region of the western Atlantic ocean around 35° N., in which floating sargasso is prevalent; *fig.* a region of confusion, uncertainty, or stagnation.

sargassum /sɑː'gasəm/ *noun.* E20.
[mod. Latin (see below), from prec.]
Any brown alga of the genus *Sargassum*, the members of which are kept afloat by air-filled bladders and form dense floating masses in warmer parts of the Atlantic (also called ***gulfweed***, ***sargasso***); a mass of such alga.
Comb.: **sargassum fish** a small toadfish, *Histrio histrio*, which lives in clusters of sargassum; also called ***mouse-fish***.

sarge /sɑːdʒ/ *noun*¹. *colloq.* M19.
[Abbreviation.]
A sergeant. Chiefly as a form of address.

†**sarge** *noun*² *& adjective* see SERGE.

sargo /'sɑːgəʊ/ *noun.* Pl. **-os**. L19.
[Spanish from Latin SARGUS.]
A grunt (fish), *Anisotremus davidsoni*, of the N. American Pacific coast. Also (*rare*) = SARGUS.

Sargonid /'sɑːgənɪd/ *noun & adjective.* Also **-ide** /-ʌɪd/. L19.
[from Akkadian *Sargon* (see below) + -ID³.]
▶**A** *noun.* A member of the Assyrian dynasty founded by Sargon II (ruled 722–705 BC), in power until the fall of Assyria in 607 BC. L19.
▶**B** *adjective.* Of, pertaining to, or designating this dynasty. E20.

sargus /'sɑːgəs/ *noun.* Now *rare.* L16.
[Latin = Greek *sargos*.]
A sea bream.
¶ Formerly a genus name.

sari /'sɑːri/ *noun.* Also **saree**. L18.
[Hindi *sāṛī* from Sanskrit *śāṭikā*.]
A traditional garment of Indian women, worn over a choli and an underskirt, consisting of a length of cotton, silk, or other cloth wrapped around the waist and draped over one shoulder.
■ **saried**, **sareed** *adjective* clothed in a sari M20.

Sarik *noun & adjective* var. of SARYK.

sarin /'sɑːrɪn/ *noun.* M20.
[German, of unkn. origin.]
An organophosphorus nerve gas, $(C_3H_7O)(CH_3)FPO$.

sarinda /sə'rɪndə, 'sɑːrɪndɑː/ *noun.* M19.
[Hindi *sārindā*.]
A form of sarangi played by Indian folk musicians.

sarissa /sə'rɪsə/ *noun.* Pl. **-ssae** /-siː/. E17.
[Greek.]
GREEK ANTIQUITIES. A long lance used in the Macedonian phalanx.

sark /sɑːk/ *noun. Scot. & north.*
[Old English *serc*, *syrc* = Old Norse *serkr* from Germanic.]
A shirt, a chemise.

sark /sɑːk/ *verb trans.* LME.
[from the noun.]
1 BUILDING. Cover (the rafters of a roof) with sarking. Orig. *Scot. & north.* LME.
2 Provide with or clothe in a sark. *Scot. & north.* L15.
■ **sarking** *noun* (*a*) boarding fitted between the rafters of a roof under the tiles etc.; freq. *attrib.*; (*b*) *Scot. & north.* material for making shirts: LME.

sarkar /ˈsɑːkɑː/ *noun. Anglo-Indian.* Also **circar**, **sirkar**. E17.
[Persian & Urdu *sarkār*, from *sar* head, chief + *kār* agent, doer.]
†**1** The court or palace of an Indian king or prince. Only in E17.
2 A province; a revenue division. E17.
3 A State or government; *spec.* the State or Government of India. L18.
4 A house-steward. L18.
5 A writer, an accountant; a clerk employed in a merchant's office. E19.

Sarkese /sɑːˈkiːz/ *noun & adjective.* M19.
[from *Sark* (see below) + -ESE.]
▶ **A** *noun.* Pl. same. Also (pl.) **-kees**.
1 A native or inhabitant of the Channel Island of Sark. M19.
2 The variety of Norman French used on Sark. M20.
▶ **B** *adjective.* Of or pertaining to Sark. L19.

sarky /ˈsɑːki/ *adjective. colloq.* E20.
[from abbreviation of SARCASTIC + -Y[1].]
Sarcastic.
■ **sarkily** *adverb* M20. **sarkiness** *noun* M20.

sarlac /ˈsɑːlək/ *noun.* L18.
[Kalmuck *sarluk*.]
= YAK *noun*[1].

Sar-Major /sɑːˈmeɪdʒə/ *noun. colloq.* E20.
[Abbreviation.]
A sergeant-major. Freq. as a form of address.

sarmale /sarˈmale/ *noun pl.* M20.
[Romanian.]
A Romanian dish of forcemeat and other ingredients wrapped in esp. cabbage or vine leaves.

Sarmatian /sɑːˈmeɪʃ(ə)n/ *adjective & noun.* E17.
[Latin *Sarmatia* the land of the *Sarmatae* (Greek *Sarmatai*, *Sauromatai*: cf. SAUROMATIAN): see -AN.]
▶ **A** *adjective.* Of or pertaining to the region north of the Black Sea anciently known as Sarmatia, now included in Poland and southern Russia. E17.
▶ **B** *noun. Hist.*
1 A member of a nomadic people formerly inhabiting Sarmatia. E17.
2 The language of the Sarmatians. E20.

sarment /ˈsɑːm(ə)nt/ *noun.* In sense 2 also in Latin form **sarmentum** /sɑːˈmɛntəm/, pl. **-ta** /-tə/. LME.
[Latin *sarmentum*, orig. = cut twigs, from *sarpere* to prune.]
1 A twig. Formerly, a cutting. Now *rare*. LME.
2 BOTANY. A long whiplike runner, leafless except at the tip. M19.
■ **sarˈmentose** *adjective* (BOTANY) producing long leafless runners M18. **sarˈmentous** *adjective* (BOTANY) = SARMENTOSE E18.

sarnie /ˈsɑːni/ *noun. slang.* M20.
[Prob. repr. a colloq. or dial. pronunc. of 1st elem. of SANDWICH *noun*[2]: see -IE.]
= SANDWICH *noun*[2] 1.

Sarn't /sɑːnt/ *noun. colloq.* M20.
[Abbreviation.]
A military sergeant. Freq. as a form of address.

sarod /səˈrəʊd/ *noun.* M19.
[Urdu, from Persian *surod* song, melody.]
An Indian stringed musical instrument.

saron /ˈsɑːrɒn/ *noun.* E19.
[Javanese.]
An Indonesian musical instrument, normally having seven bronze bars which are struck with a mallet.

sarong /səˈrɒŋ/ *noun.* M19.
[Malay, lit. 'sheath, quiver'.]
1 A traditional skirtlike garment of the Malay archipelago, Java, and some Pacific islands, consisting of a long strip of (often striped) cloth worn tucked round the waist or under the armpits by both sexes; a woman's garment resembling this, worn esp. on the beach. M19.
2 A cloth used for such garments. *rare*. M19.
Comb.: **sarong kebaya** the traditional dress of Malay and Indonesian women, comprising a sarong and a kebaya.
■ **saronged** *adjective* wearing a sarong M20.

Saronic /səˈrɒnɪk/ *adjective.* M19.
[Latin *Saronicus*, Greek *Sarōnikos*: see -IC.]
Of, pertaining to, or designating a gulf in the Aegean Sea between Attica and the Peloponnese.
■ Also **Saronian** *adjective* (*rare*) E17.

saros /ˈsɛːrɒs/ *noun.* E17.
[Greek from Akkadian *šār(u)*.]
1 ANCIENT HISTORY. In Babylonia: the number 3600; a period of 3600 years. E17.
2 ASTRONOMY. A cycle of 6585.32 days (approx. 18 years) in which solar and lunar eclipses repeat themselves. E19.

Sarouk /saˈruːk/ *noun & adjective.* E20.
[A village near Arak in Iran.]
(Designating) any of various types of rug made in Sarouk.

sarpanch /ˈsɑːpʌn(t)ʃ/ *noun.* M20.
[Urdu *sar-panch*, from *sar* head + *panch* five (from Sanskrit *pañca*).]
In India: the head of a panchayat or village council.

sarplier /ˈsɑːplɪə/ *noun.* ME.
[Anglo-Norman *sarpler*, Old French *sarpillere* (mod. *serpillière* packing cloth).]
†**1** A large sack of coarse canvas for wool; a unit of weight of wool. ME–L18.
†**2** A wrapping of sackcloth or other coarse material for packing merchandise. M16–M19.
3 A large sack into which hops are gathered and carried to a kiln. *local*. L19.

sarpo *noun* var. of SAPO.

sarracenia /sarəˈsiːnɪə/ *noun.* M18.
[mod. Latin (see below), from D. *Sarrazin* 17th-cent. Canad. botanist + -IA[1].]
Any of the insectivorous plants constituting the genus *Sarracenia* (family Sarraceniaceae); = ***pitcher-plant*** (a) s.v. PITCHER *noun*[1].

sarrazin /ˈsarəzɪn/ *noun.* Also **sarassin** /-sɪn/, **sarazin**. M19.
[French *sarrasin*, for *blé sarrasin* lit. 'Saracen wheat'.]
Buckwheat, *Fagopyrum esculentum*. Cf. ***Saracen corn*** s.v. SARACEN.

sarrusophone /səˈrʌsəfəʊn/ *noun.* L19.
[from *Sarrus*, French bandmaster who invented it in 1856 + -O- + -PHONE.]
MUSIC. A brass instrument of the oboe family, played with a double reed.

sarsa /ˈsɑːsə/ *noun.* Also **sarza** /ˈsɑːzə/. E17.
[Abbreviation.]
= SARSAPARILLA *noun* 1.

sarsaparilla /sɑːs(ə)pəˈrɪlə/ *noun.* L16.
[Spanish *zarzaparilla*, from *zarza* bramble + dim. of Spanish *parra* vine, twining plant.]
1 Any of several tropical American kinds of smilax used medicinally, esp. *Smilax ornata* (in full ***Jamaica sarsaparilla***) and *S. regelii* (in full ***Honduras sarsaparilla***); the dried root of such a plant, used to treat rheumatism, skin complaints, and formerly also syphilis. Also, a carbonated drink flavoured with this root. L16.
2 Any of several plants of other genera which resemble sarsaparilla or have a root used similarly. Chiefly with specifying word. M19.
2 Indian sarsaparilla an Indo-Malayan asclepiad, *Hemidesmus indicus*. **wild sarsaparilla** a N. American plant, *Aralia nudicaulis* (family Araliaceae).

sarsen /ˈsɑːs(ə)n/ *noun.* L17.
[App. var. of SARACEN.]
In full ***sarsen stone***, ***sarsen boulder***. Any of the once numerous large boulders or blocks of grey Tertiary sandstone or silicified conglomerate found on chalk downs, esp. in Wiltshire where they were used to construct prehistoric stone monuments.

sarsenet /ˈsɑːsnɪt/ *noun & adjective.* Also **sarcenet**. LME.
[Anglo-Norman *sarzinett* perh. dim. of *sarzin* SARACEN, after Old French *drap sarrasinois*, medieval Latin *pannus saracenicus* Saracen cloth: see -ET[1].]
▶ **A** *noun.* A fine soft silk (later cotton) fabric, now used chiefly for linings; a dress made of this. LME.
▶ **B** *attrib.* or as *adjective.* **1** Made of sarsenet. E16.
†**2** *fig.* Of speech, manners, etc.: soft, gentle. L16–E19.

> 📖 **2** SIR W. SCOTT Such sarsenet chidings as tender mothers give to spoiled children.

Sarsi *adjective & noun* var. of SARCEE.

Sart /sɑːt/ *noun & adjective.* L19.
[Turkic, orig. = merchant from Sanskrit *sārtha*, prob. through Sogdian.]
▶ **A** *noun.* In Turkestan and parts of Afghanistan: a town-dweller as opp. to a nomad; *derog.* a person who speaks an Iranian as opp. to a Turkic language. L19.
▶ **B** *attrib.* or as *adjective.* Of or pertaining to the Sarts. L19.

sartage /ˈsɑːtɪdʒ/ *noun. US.* L19.
[French, from *sarter* clear ground: see -AGE.]
The clearing of woodland by setting fire to trees.

sartin /ˈsɑːtɪn/ *adjective & noun. colloq.* M18.
[Repr. a pronunc.]
= CERTAIN *adjective, noun*.

sartor /ˈsɑːtɔː/ *noun. joc.* M17.
[Latin, from *sart-* pa. ppl stem of *sarcire* patch, botch: see -OR.]
A tailor.

sartorial /sɑːˈtɔːrɪəl/ *adjective.* E19.
[formed as prec. + -IAL.]
Of or pertaining to a tailor or tailoring; of or pertaining to (esp. men's) clothes.

> 📖 *Spectator* A shop in . . Chelsea . . has neatly solved the male sartorial problem.

■ **sartorially** *adverb* with regard to clothes E20. **sartorian** *adjective* (*rare*) = SARTORIAL M17.

sartorius /sɑːˈtɔːrɪəs/ *noun.* E18.
[mod. Latin *sartorius* (*musculus*) lit. 'tailor's muscle' (from the cross-legged seating posture formerly adopted by tailors when sewing), formed as SARTOR.]
ANATOMY. A long narrow muscle in the thigh, used in flexing the knee.

Sartrean /ˈsɑːtrɪən/ *adjective & noun.* Also **-ian**. M20.
[from *Sartre* (see below) + -AN, -IAN.]
▶ **A** *adjective.* Of, pertaining to, or characteristic of the French writer and philosopher Jean-Paul Sartre (1905–80), his writing, or his existentialist philosophy. M20.
▶ **B** *noun.* An adherent or student of Sartre's ideas. M20.

Sarum /ˈsɛːrəm/ *adjective.* L16.
[from medieval Latin = Salisbury, perh. from Latin *Sarisburia*.]
ECCLESIASTICAL HISTORY. Designating or pertaining to the order of divine service used in the diocese of Salisbury from the 11th cent. to the Reformation. Chiefly in ***Sarum use***.

sarus /ˈsɛːrəs/ *noun.* M19.
[Sanskrit *sārasa*.]
In full ***sarus crane***. A large red-headed crane, *Grus antigone*, which is found from India to the Philippines.

sarvodaya /sɑːˈvəʊdəjə/ *noun.* E20.
[Sanskrit, from *sarva* all + *udaya* prosperity.]
The welfare of all; the new social order advocated in India by M. K. Gandhi and his followers.

Saryk /saˈriːk/ *noun & adjective.* Also **Sarik**. L19.
[Turkic.]
▶ **A** *noun.* Pl. **-s**, same. A member of a Turkic people inhabiting Turkmenistan in central Asia. L19.
▶ **B** *attrib.* or as *adjective.* **1** Of or pertaining to the Saryks. L19.
2 *spec.* Designating a carpet or rug made by the Saryks, similar in design to a Bokhara. L19.

sarza *noun* var. of SARSA.

SAS *abbreviation.*
Special Air Service.

†**sa sa** *interjection.* E17–E19.
[French *çà çà* redupl. of *çà* here, hither, exclam. formerly used in fencing when delivering a thrust. Cf. SESSA.]
Expr. encouragement or enthusiasm.

Sasak /ˈsɑːsak/ *adjective & noun.* E19.
[Sasak.]
▶ **A** *adjective.* Of or pertaining to a Malay people of the island of Lombok, Indonesia, or their language. E19.
▶ **B** *noun.* A member of this people; the language of this people. M19.

Sasanian *adjective & noun* var. of SASSANIAN.

sasanqua /səˈsaŋkwə, -kə/ *noun.* M19.
[Japanese †*sasank(w)a* (now *sazanka*).]
A Japanese camellia, *Camellia sasanqua*, having fragrant white or pink flowers and seeds which yield tea-seed oil.

s.a.s.e. *abbreviation. US.*
Self-addressed stamped envelope.

sash /saʃ/ *noun*[1]. Also (earlier) †**shash**. L16.
[Arab. *šāš* muslin, (length of cloth for) a turban.]
†**1** A length of fine fabric worn twisted round the head as a turban in some Middle-Eastern countries. L16–E18.
2 A long strip of fabric worn over one shoulder or round the waist, *spec.* as part of a uniform or insignia. L17.
■ **sashing** *noun* sashes collectively M19.

sash /saʃ/ *noun*[2]. L17.
[Alt. of CHASSIS, taken as pl.]
1 a A usu. wooden frame fitted with one or more panes of glass forming a window or part of a window; *esp.* such a frame or either of two such frames which may be slid up and down in grooves and held by cords and weights in a window aperture. L17. ▸†**b** A window frame covered with paper or linen. L17–E19. ▸**c** A glazed light of a glass-house or garden frame. E18.
2 A wooden frame in which a thin narrow saw blade is stretched. *US*. L19.
Comb.: **sash bar**: dividing the glass in a sash; **sash cord** a strong cord attaching a sash-weight to a sash; **sash cramp**: used for clamping sashes during gluing; **sash-door**: fitted with a glazed sash in the upper part; a French window; **sash frame**: fixed in the opening of a wall to receive the sash or sashes of a window; **sash saw** (*a*) a small tenon saw used in making sashes; (*b*) *US* = sense 2 above; **sash tool** a glazier's or painter's narrow brush suitable for work on sashes; **sash weight**: attached to either of the two cords of a sash to counterbalance it and hold it at any height; **sash-window** a window with a sash or sashes, *esp.* one with two sliding sashes.
■ **sashless** *adjective* M19.

sash /saʃ/ *verb trans.* E18.
[from SASH *noun*[2].]
Provide with sash-windows; construct or glaze as a sash-window.

sashay /saˈʃeɪ/ *noun. N. Amer.* E20.
[from the verb.]
1 A venture, a sally; an excursion, an expedition. E20.
2 A *chassé*, esp. in square dancing. M20.

sashay /saˈʃeɪ/ *verb. colloq.* (chiefly *N. Amer.*). M19.
[Alt. of CHASSÉ *verb*.]
1 *verb intrans.* **a** Perform a *chassé*, esp. in square dancing; *transf.* move with gliding steps, usu. in a casual or ostentatious manner; strut, parade. M19. ▸**b** Move diagonally or sideways; travel an irregular path; wander, saunter. M19.
2 *verb trans.* Cause to sashay; walk or parade (a person); carry or convey (an object), manoeuvre (a vehicle). E20.

> **1a** G. VIDAL She came sashaying into the office with her shirt hiked up. **2** K. GIBBONS My aunt sashays her large self out of the toilet.

sashed /saʃt/ *adjective*[1]. E18.
[from SASH *noun*[2], *verb*: see -ED[2], -ED[1].]
Provided or constructed with a sash or sash-windows.

sashed /saʃt/ *adjective*[2]. L18.
[from SASH *noun*[1] + -ED[2].]
Dressed or adorned with a sash.

sashimi /ˈsaʃɪmi/ *noun.* L19.
[Japanese, from *sashi* pierce + *mi* flesh.]
A Japanese dish of small pieces of raw fish served with grated horseradish and soy sauce.

sashoon /saˈʃuːn/ *noun. obsolete* exc. *US.* L17.
[Alt. of French *chausson*.]
A leather pad formerly worn inside the leg of a boot.

sasin /ˈsasɪn/ *noun.* M19.
[from local Himalayan word.]
= ***blackbuck*** s.v. BLACK *adjective*.

sasine /ˈseɪzɪn/ *noun.* M17.
[Alt. of SEISIN after law Latin *sasina*.]
SCOTS LAW. The action of giving legal possession of feudal property. Also, the instrument by which the possession of feudal property is proved.

Sask. *abbreviation.*
Saskatchewan.

saskatoon /saskəˈtuːn/ *noun.* Chiefly *Canad.* E19.
[Cree *misa:skwato:min*, from *misa:skwat* amelanchier + *min* berry.]
An amelanchier of western N. America, *Amelanchier alnifolia*; the sweet purple berry of this shrub.

sasquatch /ˈsaskwɒtʃ/ *noun. Canad.* E20.
[Salish.]
A large hairy manlike monster supposedly inhabiting Canada and the north-western US.

sass /sas/ *noun. colloq.* L18.
[Var. of SAUCE *noun*.]
1 Fresh or preserved vegetables or fruit eaten as part of a meal or as a relish. *US.* L18.
2 Sauciness, impertinence, cheek. *N. Amer.* M19.

> **2** G. PLIMPTON I never had the sass to join in the fun. T. MORRISON Slapped in the face . . for some sass she could not remember.

sass /sas/ *verb trans. & intrans. N. Amer. colloq.* M19.
[Var. of SAUCE *verb*.]
Speak impertinently to (a person); answer (someone) *back.* L19.

> *Sunday Times* I had sassed fellow-journalists with impunity.

sassaby /səˈseɪbi, ˈsasəbi/ *noun.* E19.
[formed as TSESSEBI.]
= TSESSEBI.

sassafras /ˈsasəfras/ *noun.* L16.
[Spanish *sasafrás*, perh. ult. from Latin *saxifraga* saxifrage.]
1 A tree of the genus *Sassafras*, of the laurel family, esp. *S. albidum* native to the eastern US, with greenish-yellow flowers, leaves, and bark with a spicy aroma. Also, the wood of this tree. L16. ▸**b** The dried bark of this tree, used as a medicine and flavouring; (more fully ***sassafras tea***) an infusion of this. L16. ▸**c** In full ***sassafras oil***. An oil extracted from (the bark of) the sassafras, used medicinally and in perfumery. Also ***oil of sassafras***. M18.
2 Any of various similarly aromatic and medicinal trees of other genera and families; *Austral.* any of several trees of the family Monimiaceae with aromatic bark, e.g. *Doryphora aromatica* and *D. sassafras*. Also, the wood or bark of such a tree. E19.
2 Brazilian sassafras either of two S. American trees of the laurel family, *Aniba panurensis* and *A. amazonica*, whose wood yields a fragrant oil. **swamp sassafras** the sweet bay, *Magnolia virginiana*.

Sassanian /saˈseɪnɪən/ *adjective & noun.* Also **Sasanian**. L18.
[from *Sasan* (Persian *Sāsān*): see below, -IAN.]
▸**A** *adjective.* Of or pertaining to the family of Sasan, whose grandson Ardashir I founded the dynasty which ruled the Persian Empire 224–651; pertaining to or characteristic of the period of this dynasty. L18.
▸**B** *noun.* A member of this family, esp. any of the Sassanian kings. M19.
■ **ˈSassanid** *noun & adjective* (**a**) *noun* a descendant of Sasan, *esp.* a king of the Sassanian dynasty; (**b**) *adjective* = SASSANIAN *adjective*: L18.

†**sasse** *noun.* M17–M19.
[Dutch *sas*, of unkn. origin.]
= LOCK *noun*[2] 8.

Sassella /saˈsɛlə/ *noun.* M20.
[Italian.]
A red wine from the Valtellina district in Lombardy, Italy.

Sassenach /ˈsasənax, -nak/ *noun & adjective. Scot. & Anglo-Irish.* Freq. *derog.* E18.
[Gaelic *Sassunach* = Irish *Sasanach*, from *Sasan-* (cf. Gaelic *Sasunn*, Irish *Sasana* England) from Latin *Saxones*, Old English *Seaxe*, *Seaxan* Saxons.]
▸**A** *noun.* An English person. Cf. SAXON *noun* 1b. E18.
▸**B** *attrib.* or as *adjective.* English. M19.

sassolite /ˈsasəlʌɪt/ *noun.* M19.
[from Lago del *Sasso* in Tuscany, western Italy + -*l*- + -ITE[1].]
MINERALOGY. A mineral consisting of native boracic acid, occurring as a scaly incrustation or as tabular crystals around fumaroles.
■ Also †**sassoline** *noun*: only in 19.

sassy /ˈsasi/ *noun.* M19.
[Prob. of African origin: cf. Twi *sese* plane tree.]
1 ***sassy-bark tree***, ***sassy tree***, a W. African leguminous tree, *Erythrophleum suavolens*. M19.
2 ***sassy bark***, ***sassy wood***, the poisonous bark of this tree. L19.

sassy /ˈsasi/ *adjective. colloq.* (orig. & chiefly *N. Amer.*). M19.
[Var. of SAUCY.]
Saucy, impudent, cheeky; bold, lively; stylish.

> J. AGEE It was a fast, sassy tune. *Blactress* Brighter colors used on the eyes . . compliment younger, sassier fashions. C. NOLAN Sassy rasps of schoolboy's humour.

■ **sassily** *adverb* L20. **sassiness** *noun* L20.

sastruga /saˈstruːgə/ *noun.* Also **z-** /z-/. Pl. **-gi** /-gi/. M19.
[German, from Russian *zastruga* small ridge, furrow in snow, from *zastrugat'* to plane or smooth, from *strug* plane (the tool).]
Any of a series of low irregular ridges formed on a level snow surface by wind erosion, often aligned parallel to the wind direction. Usu. in *pl.*

SAT *abbreviation.*
EDUCATION. **1** Scholastic aptitude test. *N. Amer.*
2 Standard assessment test.

sat *verb pa. t. & pple*: see SIT *verb*.

Sat. *abbreviation.*
Saturday.

Satan /ˈseɪt(ə)n/ *noun.* OE.
[Late Latin (Vulgate), Greek, from Hebrew *śāṭān* adversary, from *śāṭan* oppose, plot against.]
1 The supreme evil spirit, the Devil, Lucifer. OE.
2 †**a** A devil; an opponent, an adversary. LME–L17. ▸**b** A detestable person or animal. Now *rare.* L16.

> **1** ***limb of Satan***: see LIMB *noun*[1]. **2b** SHAKES. *1 Hen. IV* Falstaff, that old white-bearded Satan.

Comb.: **Satan monkey** the black-bearded saki, *Chiropotes satanas*.
■ **Saˈtanity** *noun* (*rare*) Satanic conduct or character M19. **Satanize** *verb trans.* (*rare*) make like Satan; make into or like a devil: L16. **Sataˈnology** *noun* beliefs or doctrine concerning Satan M19. **Sataˈnophany** *noun* the appearance or visible manifestation of Satan M19. **Satanoˈphobia** *noun* fear of Satan M19. **Satanship** *noun* (*rare*) the quality of being a Satan M17.

Satanas /ˈsatənas/ *noun. arch.* OE.
[Late Latin (Vulgate) from Greek, from Aramaic *sāṭānā* emph. form of *sāṭān* from Hebrew *śāṭān*: see prec.]
= SATAN 1.

satang /ˈsataŋ/ *noun.* Pl. same. L19.
[Thai from Pali *sata* hundred.]
A monetary unit of Thailand, equal to one-hundredth of a baht.

satanic /səˈtanɪk/ *adjective.* Also (esp. in sense 1) **S-**. M17.
[from SATAN + -IC.]
1 Of or pertaining to Satan. M17.
2 Characteristic of or befitting Satan; extremely wicked, diabolical, infernal. L18.
Phrases: **satanic abuse** = ***ritual abuse*** s.v. RITUAL *adjective*. **Satanic school** a group of writers (orig. Byron, Shelley, and imitators) accused of impiety and the portrayal of immorality.

satanical /səˈtanɪk(ə)l/ *adjective.* Now *rare.* Also **S-**. M16.
[formed as prec. + -ICAL.]
†**1** Resembling Satan, devilish. M16–M18.
2 = SATANIC. M16.

satanically /səˈtanɪk(ə)li/ *adverb.* Also **S-**. E17.
[from prec. + -LY[2].]
In a satanic manner.

Satanism /ˈseɪt(ə)nɪz(ə)m/ *noun.* M16.
[from SATAN + -ISM.]
1 Satanic or diabolical disposition or doctrine; evil practice, wickedness. M16.
2 The characteristics of the Satanic school. E19.
3 The worship of Satan, usu. including a travesty of Christian forms. L19.
■ **Satanist** *noun* (**a**) an adherent or worshipper of Satan; (**b**) a writer of the Satanic school: M16. **Sataˈnistic** *adjective* (*rare*) of or pertaining to Satanists; adhering to Satanism: L19.

satara /səˈtɑːrə/ *noun.* L19.
[A town and district in India.]
A woollen ribbed cloth.

satay /ˈsateɪ/ *noun.* Also **satai**, **saté**. M20.
[Malay *satai*, *sate*, Indonesian *sate*. Cf. SOSATIE.]
An Indonesian and Malaysian dish consisting of small pieces of meat grilled on a skewer and usu. served with a spiced peanut sauce.

SATB *abbreviation.*
MUSIC. Soprano, alto, tenor, and bass (as a combination of voices).

sat-bhai /ˈsɑːtbɑːi/ *noun.* Pl. same. M19.
[Hindi *sāt* seven + *bhāī* brothers, from their gregarious habits.]
The white-headed jungle babbler of India, *Turdoides striatus*, a large brown bird with a long tail and slightly curved bill. Also called ***seven sisters***.

satchel /ˈsatʃ(ə)l/ *noun.* ME.
[Old French *sachel* from Latin *sacellus* dim. of *saccus* SACK *noun*[1].]
A small bag; *esp.* a bag for carrying schoolbooks, usu. with a strap to hang over the shoulders.
Comb.: **satchel charge** explosive on a board fitted with a rope or wire loop for carrying and attaching.
■ **satchelled** *adjective* having or carrying a satchel M18.

satcom /ˈsatkɒm/ *noun.* Also **SATCOM**. L20.
[Blend of SATELLITE and *communications*.]
Satellite communications. Also in designations of particular communications satellites, as ***Satcom C4***.

sate /seɪt/ *noun.* E20.
[Var. of SET *noun*[1].]
A heavy chisel or punch used by a blacksmith for cutting metal.

sate /seɪt/ *verb trans.* E17.
[Prob. alt. of SADE by assoc. with SATIATE *verb*.]
1 Fill or satisfy to the full (with food); gratify fully by the satisfaction of a desire. Also, surfeit or cloy by gratification of appetite or desire; glut, satiate. Freq. in *pass.* E17.
†**2** Saturate. L17–M18.

> **1** J. BETJEMAN The robin waited To . . feed till it was sated. D. ATTENBOROUGH So many worms . . that even a mole's appetite is sated. G. KENDALL Hunger that wouldn't be sated by anything less than a full investigation.

■ **satedness** *noun* the state of being sated M19. **sateless** *adjective* (chiefly *poet.*) not to be sated, insatiable E18.

saté *noun* var. of SATAY.

sateen /saˈtiːn/ *noun.* L19.
[Alt. of SATIN *noun* after *velveteen*: see -EEN[1].]
A cotton or linen fabric woven like satin with a glossy surface.

satellise *verb* var. of SATELLIZE.

satellite /ˈsatəlʌɪt/ *noun & adjective.* M16.
[Old & mod. French, or Latin *satelles*, *satellit-*.]
▸**A** *noun.* **1** A member of an important person's staff or retinue; a follower, an (esp. obsequious) underling. M16.
2 **a** *ASTRONOMY.* A celestial object which orbits a larger one; *esp.* a moon orbiting a planet. M17. ▸**b** *transf.* A small or secondary building, island, etc., linked with a nearby larger and more important one. L18. ▸**c** An artificial object placed (or designed to be placed) in orbit round the earth or a celestial object. M20.
3 **a** A country or State politically or economically dependent on and subservient to another. Also ***satellite country***, ***satellite State***. E19. ▸**b** A community or town economically or otherwise dependent on a nearby larger town or city. Also ***satellite community***, ***satellite town***. E20.
4 A European noctuid moth, *Eupsilia transversa*, with a white crescent-shaped mark on the forewing. M19.
5 *PHYSICS.* A spurious or subordinate spectral line; *spec.* one caused by an irregularity in the positions of lines in a diffraction grating. Also ***satellite line***. E20.
6 *CYTOLOGY.* A short section of a chromosome demarcated from the rest by a constriction (if terminal) or by two constrictions (if intercalary). Cf. TRABANT 2. E20.
7 *ANATOMY.* More fully ***satellite cell***. Each of the cells that go to make up the membrane surrounding the nerve cell bodies in many ganglia. Formerly also, a Schwann cell. E20.
8 *BACTERIOLOGY.* A bacterial colony growing in culture near a second colony which is the source of a growth factor required by the first. Usu. *attrib.* M20.

9 *BIOLOGY.* A portion of the DNA of a genome with repeating base sequences and of different density from the main sequence. **M20.**

10 Used *attrib.* to designate a computer or computer terminal distant from, but connected to and serving or being served by, a main computer. **M20.**

> 🕮 **1** S. T. FELSTEAD His horde of flat-footed female satellites. **2b** T. PYNCHON The dining hall and its smaller private satellites. **c** I. MURDOCH A bright satellite, a man-made star . . crossed the sky in a great arc. **3a** A. E. STEVENSON Half of Indochina has become a . . Communist satellite.

Comb.: **satellite airfield**: auxiliary to and serving as a substitute for a larger airfield; **satellite broadcasting**: in which the signal is transmitted via an orbiting artificial satellite; ***satellite cell***: see sense 7 above; ***satellite community***: see sense 3b above; ***satellite country***: see sense 3a above; **satellite dish** a concave dish-shaped aerial for receiving broadcasting signals transmitted by satellite; **satellite feed** a live broadcast via satellite forming part of another programme; **satellite photo**, **satellite photograph**, **satellite picture** a photograph taken from an orbiting artificial satellite; ***satellite State***: see sense 3a above; **satellite station** (*a*) an orbiting artificial satellite; *spec.* a space station; (*b*) a secondary radio station which receives and retransmits programmes, so as to improve local reception; **satellite telescope**: in orbit beyond the range of atmospheric distortion; **satellite television**: in which the signal is transmitted via an artificial satellite; ***satellite town***: see sense 3b above. **satellite vein** a vein that closely accompanies an artery.

▶ **B** *adjective.* That is a satellite to something else; subsidiary, subordinate; associated; ancillary. Also, transmitted by satellite. **L19.**

■ **satellited** *adjective* (*a*) attended by a satellite; (*b*) *CYTOLOGY* (of a chromosome) having a satellite or satellites: **L19. satellitic** /-ˈlɪtɪk/ *adjective* pertaining to or of the nature of a satellite or lesser planet **E19.**

satellite /ˈsatəlʌɪt/ *verb.* **M20.**
[from the noun.]
1 *verb intrans.* Orbit like a satellite. *rare.* **M20.**
2 *verb trans.* Transmit by way of a communications satellite. **L20.**

satellitism /ˈsatəlʌɪtɪz(ə)m/ *noun.* **M20.**
[from SATELLITE *noun* + -ISM.]
1 *BACTERIOLOGY.* The occurrence of satellites (SATELLITE *noun* 8); the promotion of bacterial growth by the proximity of a colony of different bacteria. **M20.**
2 *POLITICS.* The fact or condition of being a satellite country or State; the role of a satellite. **M20.**

satellitium /satəˈlɪtɪəm/ *noun.* **L17.**
[Latin = bodyguard, retinue.]
ASTROLOGY. A grouping of several planets in a sign.

satellitosis /satəlʌɪˈtəʊsɪs/ *noun.* Pl. **-toses** /-ˈtəʊsiːz/. **E20.**
[formed as SATELLITE *noun* + -OSIS.]
MEDICINE. A proliferation of glial cells around nerve cells in the brain or spinal cord.

satellize /ˈsatəlʌɪz/ *verb.* Also **-ise**. **E20.**
[formed as prec.: see -IZE.]
1 *verb intrans.* Cluster *about*. *rare.* **E20.**
2 *verb trans.* Make (a country etc.) into a political or economic satellite. **M20.**
■ **satelliˈzation** *noun* the action of making into a satellite; the condition or process of being satellized: **M20.**

satelloid /ˈsatəlɔɪd/ *noun.* **M20.**
[formed as prec.: see -OID.]
A proposed type of satellite able to maintain a low orbit, and change course, by expending power.

satem /ˈsɑːtəm/ *adjective.* **E20.**
[Avestan *satəm* hundred: cf. CENTUM *adjective* exemplifying this distinction between the two groups.]
PHILOLOGY. Designating or pertaining to a chiefly eastern group of Indo-European languages having sibilants where cognate words in the western group have (voiceless) velar consonants.

sati *noun* var. of SUTTEE.

satiable /ˈseɪʃəb(ə)l/ *adjective.* **L15.**
[from next + -ABLE.]
†**1** Satiating, satisfying. Only in **L15.**
2 Able to be satiated. **L16.**

satiate /ˈseɪʃɪeɪt/ *verb.* Pa. pple **-ated**, (now *rare*) **-ate** /-ət/. **LME.**
[Latin *satiat-* pa. ppl stem of *satiare*, from *satis* enough: see -ATE³. Cf. SATE *verb*.]
1 *verb trans.* Fill or satisfy (with food); gratify to the full (a person, desire, etc.). (Foll. by *with*.) **LME.**
2 *verb trans.* Gratify beyond one's natural desire; weary or disgust by repletion; glut, cloy, surfeit. Freq. in *pass.* **L16.** ▸**b** *verb intrans.* Be gratified to the full. *rare.* **L18.**
†**3** *verb trans.* Saturate. **L17–L18.**

> 🕮 **1** D. ATTENBOROUGH There is usually enough fruit on a tree to satiate . . them. **2** A. POWELL One becomes satiated even with . . attractive prospects.

■ **satiˈation** *noun* (*a*) the action of satiating a person or thing; the fact of being satiated; (*b*) *PSYCHOLOGY* the point at which satisfaction of a need, or familiarity with a stimulus, reduces or ends an organism's responsiveness or motivation: **M17.**

satiety /səˈtʌɪɪti/ *noun.* Also (earlier) †**sacietie**. **M16.**
[Old French *sacieté* (mod. *satiété*) from Latin *satietas*: see -ITY.]
1 a The state of being glutted or satiated with food; a feeling of disgust or surfeit caused by excess of food. **M16.** ▸**b** The condition of having any desire gratified to excess; weariness or dislike of an object of desire caused by gratification or attainment. **M16.** ▸†**c** The condition of being pleasantly filled or fully gratified; full attainment of an object of desire. **M16–E18.** ▸**d** *PSYCHOLOGY.* Satisfaction of a need (esp. hunger) as it is registered physiologically. **M20.**
2 (A) sufficiency, (an) abundance. *rare.* **E17.**

> 🕮 **1b** BARONESS ORCZY Lust . . grows with its satisfaction, there is no satiety. **c** SPENSER Fairely shee attempered her feast, and pleasd them . . with meete satiety.

Phrases: **to satiety** to an amount or degree which satisfies or gluts desire.

Comb.: **satiety centre** an area of the brain concerned with the regulation of food intake.

satin /ˈsatɪn/ *noun & adjective.* **LME.**
[Old French, from Arab. *zaytūnī* pertaining to the town of Zaytun (identified with Tsinkiang (Chuanchow)). Cf. SATEEN.]
▶ **A** *noun.* **1** A fabric of silk, or various man-made fibres resembling silk, with a glossy surface on one side produced by a weave in which the threads of the warp are caught and looped by the weft only at certain intervals. **LME.** ▸**b** A garment, esp. a dress, made of satin. **L18.**
2 The plant honesty, *Lunaria annua*, so called from its lustrous white pods. Also ***white satin***. **L16.**
3 In full ***white satin***, ***satin moth***. A glossy white moth, *Leucoma salicis*, of the family Lymantriidae. **M18.**
4 Gin. Also more fully ***white satin***. *slang.* **M19.**
5 (An animal of) a breed of rabbit developed in America, having smooth fur with a satin-like sheen. **M20.**

> 🕮 **1** J. MARSH An eighteenth century . . gown of pale-blue satin. ***Denmark satin***: see DENMARK 1. ***duchesse satin***: see DUCHESSE 3. **satin de chine** a silk fabric. **b** J. CANNAN A high-waisted . . satin with gold lace sleeves.

▶ **B** *attrib.* or as *adjective.* **1** Made of satin; resembling satin in texture or surface. **LME.**
2 Clothed in satin. **E17.**

Comb. & special collocations: **satin beauté** /ˈbəʊteɪ/ [French = beauty] a soft finely woven material with a dull crêpe back and brilliant satin finish; **satin beauty** a Eurasian geometrid moth, *Deileptenia ribeata*, with mottled brownish wings; **satin bell** a white mariposa lily, *Calochortus albus*; **satin-bird**, **satin bowerbird** a common bowerbird of eastern Australia, *Ptilonorhynchus violaceus*, the male of which has iridescent blue-black plumage and decorates its bower with predominantly blue objects; ***satin duchesse***: see DUCHESSE 3; **satin finish** a polish given to silver etc. with a metallic brush; any finish resembling satin in texture or surface produced on materials in various ways; **satinflower** any of several plants whose flowers have a satiny sheen, e.g. greater stitchwort, *Stellaria holostea*; **satin flycatcher** a monarch flycatcher, *Myiagra cyanoleuca*, occurring in eastern Australia, the male of which has bluish upperparts; **satin leather** leather finished so as to resemble satin; ***satin moth***: see sense 3 above; **satin oil** = ***satin leather*** above; **satin-paper** a fine glossy writing paper; **satin spar** a fibrous variety of gypsum, with a pearly lustre; **satin stitch** a long straight embroidery stitch which produces an appearance like satin; ***satin sycamore***: see SYCAMORE 3b; **satin-top** an Australian fodder grass, *Bothriochloa erianthioides*; **satin-walnut** *US* (the wood of) the sweet gum, *Liquidambar styraciflua*; **satin weave** a fabric, or method of weaving fabric, in which either the warp or the weft predominates on the surface; **satin wire** a silk-covered thickly padded wire used in millinery; **satin white** a white pigment of calcium sulphate and alumina; **satinwood** any of various lustrous yellow woods used for cabinet-work, esp. (more fully ***Sri Lanka satinwood***) that of the Indian tree *Chloroxylon swietenia* and (more fully ***Jamaican satinwood***) that of the W. Indian *Zanthoxylum flavum*, both of the rue family; any of the trees producing this wood.

■ **satined** *adjective* (*rare*) having a satin-like surface or finish; clothed in satin: **E18. satinize** *verb trans.* impart a satin-like surface to **M19. satin-like** *adjective* **L17. satiny** *adjective* resembling satin **L18.**

satin /ˈsatɪn/ *verb trans.* **M19.**
[from prec.]
Give (paper) a glossy surface resembling satin.

satiné /satine, ˈsatɪneɪ/ *noun.* **M19.**
[French (*bois*) *satiné*.]
A kind of satinwood, derived from the tropical S. American tree *Brosimum rubescens*, of the mulberry family.

satinette /satɪˈnɛt, ˈsatɪnɪt/ *noun.* Also **satinet**. **E18.**
[from SATIN *noun & adjective* + -ETTE.]
1 A satin-like fabric usu. woven in silk and cotton or cotton and wool. **E18.**
2 (A bird of) a fancy breed of domestic pigeon. **L19.**

satire /ˈsatʌɪə/ *noun.* Also (earlier) †**satyr**. **E16.**
[Old & mod. French, or Latin *satira* later form of *satura* verse composition dealing with a variety of subjects, medley, mixture. Formerly assoc. with SATYR *noun*¹ and so spelt.]
1 A work or composition in prose or (orig.) verse which (usu. humorously) exposes prevailing vices or follies or ridicules an (esp. prominent) individual; a lampoon; a performance or broadcast of a similar nature; *ROMAN ANTIQUITIES* a poetic medley, esp. of a satirical nature. **E16.** ▸**b** *fig.* An object, fact, or circumstance that brings ridicule on some person or thing. **L17.**
†**2** A satirical person, a satirist. **E16–E18.**
3 a The branch of literature etc. constituted by satires; satirical composition. **L16.** ▸**b** The use of sarcasm, irony, ridicule, etc., to expose vice or folly or to lampoon an individual. **L17.**

> 🕮 **1** M. ELPHINSTONE Introducing satires on manners and domestic life into Asia. HARPER LEE Cather published . . a snide satire on Louise's brother. **b** B. TAYLOR An . . ungainly person, whose clothes were a . . satire on his professional skill. **3b** M. O. W. OLIPHANT A tone of satire in her voice when she noted the late marriage.

satire /ˈsatʌɪə/ *verb trans. rare.* **E20.**
[from prec.]
= SATIRIZE *verb* 2.

satiric /səˈtɪrɪk/ *noun & adjective.* **LME.**
[French *satirique* or late Latin *satiricus*, from Latin *satira*: see SATIRE *noun*, -IC.]
▶ **A** *noun.* †**1** A writer of satires; a satirist. *rare.* **LME–E17.**
2 In *pl.* Satiric writings. *rare.* **E17.**
▶ **B** *adjective.* **1** Of, pertaining to, or of the nature of satire; consisting of or containing satire; writing satire. **E16.**
†**2** Fond of or disposed to satire; satirical. **E17–M18.**

> 🕮 **1** THACKERAY Comedy . . full of bitter satiric strokes against a certain young lady.

satirical /səˈtɪrɪk(ə)l/ *adjective.* **E16.**
[formed as prec.: see -ICAL.]
1 Of, pertaining to, or of the nature of satire; containing satire; satiric. **E16.**
2 Disposed to or fond of indulging in satire; characterized by satire. **L16.**

> 🕮 **1** GIBBON Their satirical wit degenerated into . . angry invectives. *fig.*: D. HEWETT A . . fly-spotted fifteen-watt globe burnt dimly in satirical welcome. **2** DISRAELI Receiving some not very encouraging response, . . they voted her ladyship cursedly satirical.

■ **satirically** *adverb* **L16. satiricalness** *noun* **M17.**

satirise *verb* var. of SATIRIZE.

satirism /ˈsatɪrɪz(ə)m/ *noun. rare.* **L16.**
[from SATIRE *noun* + -ISM.]
Indulgence in satire; satirical utterance.

satirist /ˈsatɪrɪst/ *noun.* **L16.**
[from SATIRE *noun* + -IST.]
A writer of satires; a person who satirizes some person or thing.

satirize /ˈsatɪrʌɪz/ *verb.* Also **-ise**. **E17.**
[French *satiriser*, formed as SATIRE *noun*: see -IZE.]
1 *verb intrans.* Write satires; assail someone or something with satire. Now *rare.* **E17.**
2 *verb trans.* Assail with satire; make the object of or expose to satire; describe or ridicule satirically. **M17.**

> 🕮 **2** *American Speech* A lead article satirizing American temperance groups.

■ **satirizer** *noun* **M19.**

satisfaction /satɪsˈfakʃ(ə)n/ *noun.* **ME.**
[Old & mod. French, or Latin *satisfactio(n-)*, from *satisfact-* pa. ppl stem of *satisfacere*: see SATISFY, -FACTION.]
▶ **I** With ref. to debt or obligation.
1 *ECCLESIASTICAL.* The performance by a penitent of penal and meritorious acts in retribution for sin; such acts as the last part of the sacrament of penance. **ME.**
2 Now chiefly *LAW.* The payment of a debt or fulfilment of an obligation or claim; the atoning *for* an injury or offence by reparation, compensation, or the endurance of punishment. Also, the penalty or act by which an obligation is discharged or an offence atoned for. **LME.**
3 *CHRISTIAN THEOLOGY.* The atonement made by Christ for the sins of humankind. **LME.**
4 The opportunity to satisfy one's honour in a duel; the acceptance of a challenge to a duel from a supposedly injured party. Chiefly in ***demand satisfaction***, ***give satisfaction***. **E17.**

> 🕮 **2** W. BLACKSTONE Taking . . a personal chattel . . to procure satisfaction for the wrong committed.

▶ **II** With ref. to feelings or desires.
5 a The action of fulfilling a desire or expectation, or of contenting a person in this way; an instance of this. Also, the fact of having been thus fulfilled or contented. **LME.** ▸**b** Satisfied or contented state of mind; gratification or pleasure occasioned by something. Foll. by *at, with, that.* **L15.** ▸**c** *PSYCHOLOGY.* The satisfying of a need or desire so that it no longer affects or motivates behaviour. **E20.**
6 Sufficient information; proof or removal of doubt, conviction. **L16.**

> 🕮 **5a** L. M. MONTGOMERY A real satisfaction to see that poor child wearing something decent. E. FROMM Satisfaction of all desires is not conducive to *well-being.* **b** H. T. LANE Grinning with satisfaction at my evident confusion. P. D. JAMES She entered her flat . . with a sense of satisfaction.

Phrases: **make satisfaction** make reparation, pay compensation. **to one's satisfaction** to a sufficient or pleasing extent, so that one is satisfied. **to the satisfaction of** to the standard desired by; to the contentment of.

Comb.: **satisfaction note** an acknowledgement of satisfaction with repairs signed by someone claiming repair costs from an insurance company; **satisfaction piece** LAW a formal acknowledgement by someone who has received satisfaction of a mortgage or judgement, authorizing its entry on the record; **satisfaction theory** CHRISTIAN THEOLOGY the belief that Christ suffered punishment as satisfaction for the sins of humankind.

■ **satisfactionist** *noun* (CHRISTIAN THEOLOGY, *rare*) a person who believes in the satisfaction theory M17.

satisfactory /satɪsˈfakt(ə)ri/ *adjective.* LME.
[Old & mod. French *satisfactoire* or medieval Latin *satisfactorius*, from Latin *satisfact-*: see prec., -ORY[1], -ORY[2].]

1 ECCLESIASTICAL & CHRISTIAN THEOLOGY. Serving to make satisfaction or atonement for sin. Cf. SATISFACTION 1, 3. LME.
2 Serving to satisfy a debt or obligation. *rare.* E17.
3 Sufficient, adequate; (of an argument) convincing. Also, that causes or gives satisfaction; such as one may be content or pleased with. M17.

📖 **3** LD MACAULAY James . . eagerly challenged His Grace to produce . . a satisfactory reply. *Times* A baby with two heads . . was said . . to be in a satisfactory condition. *Which?* It needs bright lighting . . for satisfactory results.

■ **satisfactorily** *adverb* L16. **satisfactoriness** *noun* M17.

satisfiable /ˈsatɪsfʌɪəb(ə)l/ *adjective.* E17.
[from SATISFY + -ABLE.]
Able to be satisfied. Formerly also (*rare*), satisfactory.
■ **satisfiaˈbility** *noun* M20.

satisfice /ˈsatɪsfʌɪs/ *verb.* Also †**-fise**. M16.
[Alt. of SATISFY infl. by Latin *satisfacere*.]
1 *verb trans.* Satisfy. *obsolete* exc. *north.* M16.
2 *verb intrans.* Decide on and pursue a course of action that will satisfy the minimum requirements necessary to achieve a particular goal. M20.

📖 **2** *British Journal of Sociology* Prescriptions . . chosen to maximise (or satisfice) on both imperatives.

■ **satisficer** *noun* M20.

satisfy /ˈsatɪsfʌɪ/ *verb.* LME.
[Old French *satisfier* irreg. from Latin *satisfacere*, from *satis* enough: see -FY.]
▶ **I** With ref. to debt or obligation.
1 *verb trans.* Now chiefly LAW. Pay off or discharge fully; clear (a debt); adequately fulfil (an obligation) or comply with (a demand). Also, pay a debt to (a creditor). LME.
†**2** *verb trans.* Make reparation for (a wrong or injury); atone for (an offence). LME–E18. ▸**b** Make atonement or reparation to (a person, his or her honour, etc.). E17–M19.
3 *verb intrans.* Make full payment, reparation, or atonement (*for*); *spec.* in CHRISTIAN THEOLOGY, (of Christ) suffer punishment *for* the sins of humankind. *obsolete* exc. CHRISTIAN THEOLOGY. LME.

📖 **1** W. CRUISE The . . estate was not sufficient to satisfy the legacies.

▶ **II** With ref. to feelings or desires.
4 *verb trans.* **a** Fulfil the desire or expectation of; be accepted by (a person, his or her taste, judgement, etc.) as adequate; content. Also, fulfil (a desire or expectation). LME. ▸**b** In *pass.* Be content (*with*, *to do*); be well pleased (*with*). LME.
5 *verb trans.* Cause to have enough; supply fully the needs of; put an end to (an appetite or want) by fully supplying it. LME.
6 *verb trans.* Answer sufficiently (an objection or question); fulfil or comply with (a request); solve (a doubt or difficulty). LME.
7 *verb trans.* Provide with sufficient proof or information; free from doubt or uncertainty; convince. (Foll. by *of*, *that*.) L15.
8 *verb intrans.* Cause or give satisfaction or contentment. E17.
9 *verb trans.* Answer the requirements of (a state of things, a hypothesis, etc.); accord with (conditions). M17. ▸**b** MATH. Of a known quantity: fulfil the conditions of (an equation), be an admissible solution to (an equation). E19.

📖 **4a** C. P. SNOW Paul was satisfying his curiosity about Humphrey's family. J. DIDION He can satisfy his American History requirement with a three-unit course. **satisfy the examiners** attain the standard required to pass an examination. **b** N. SHERRY Not satisfied with simply editing the magazine, he took it over. **5** *Medical & Physical Journal* He takes . . food without being satisfied. **7** I. MURDOCH A glance round . . satisfied me that Hugo wasn't there. **8** D. CECIL Marianne . . satisfies on . . virtue but not on sense.

■ **satisfiedly** *adverb* in a satisfied manner L16. **satisfiedness** *noun* satisfied state or quality L16. **satisfier** *noun* LME. **satisfyingly** *adverb* in a satisfying manner M17. **satisfyingness** *noun* (*rare*) satisfying quality M19.

satispassion /satɪsˈpaʃ(ə)n/ *noun.* E17.
[medieval Latin *satispassio(n-)*, from Latin *satis pati* suffer enough, after *satisfactio(n-)*: see SATISFACTION, PASSION *noun*.]
CHRISTIAN THEOLOGY. Atonement by an adequate degree of suffering.

†**sative** *adjective.* L16–E18.
[Latin *sativus* that can be sown or planted, from stem of *serere* sow: see -IVE.]
Sown, planted; cultivated rather than wild.

satnav /ˈsatnav/ *noun.* L20.
[Acronym, from *satellite navigation*.]
Chiefly NAUTICAL. Navigation assisted by information from satellites; a navigation system capable of receiving such information.

satori /səˈtɔːri/ *noun.* E18.
[Japanese = awakening.]
ZEN BUDDHISM. A sudden inner experience of enlightenment.

satranji /ʃəˈtrandʒi/ *noun.* Also **sitringee** /sɪˈtrɪndʒiː/ & other vars. E17.
[Persian & Urdu *šatranjī* from Persian *šatranj* chess, ult. from Sanskrit *caturaṅga* army, chess, with ref. to the original chequered pattern.]
A carpet or floor-rug made of coloured cotton, now usu. with a striped pattern.

satrap /ˈsatrap/ *noun.* LME.
[Old & mod. French *satrape* or Latin *satrapa*, *satrapes* from Greek *satrapēs*, from Old Persian *kšatra-pāvan* protector of the country, from *kšatra-* country + *pā-* protect.]
1 A provincial governor in ancient Persia. LME.
2 *transf.* A subordinate ruler, *esp.* one who rules tyrannically or in ostentatious splendour. LME.
■ **satrapal** *adjective* L19. **saˈtrapic** *adjective* M16. **saˈtrapical** *adjective* E19.

satrapy /ˈsatrəpi/ *noun.* E17.
[French *satrapie* or Latin *satrapia* from Greek *satrapeia*: see prec., -Y[3].]
A province ruled over by a satrap.

satsang /ˈsatsaŋ/, *foreign* ˈsʌtsʌŋ/ *noun.* E20.
[Sanskrit *satsaṅga* association with good men, from *sat* good man + *saṅga* association.]
INDIAN PHILOSOPHY. A spiritual discourse, a sacred gathering.

satsuma /satˈsuːmə/, *in sense 1 also* ˈsatsjʊmə/ *noun.* Also (esp. in sense 1) **S-**. L19.
[A province in the island of Kyushu, Japan.]
1 In full ***Satsuma ware***. A kind of cream-coloured Japanese pottery. L19.
2 A variety of tangerine, orig. from Japan, with a sharper taste and freq. seedless or with undeveloped seeds; the tree bearing this fruit, *Citrus reticulata* cv. Owari. L19.

saturable /ˈsatʃʊrəb(ə)l, -tjʊr-/ *adjective.* L16.
[from SATURATE *verb*: see -ABLE. Cf. earlier INSATURABLE, UNSATURABLE.]
1 Able to be saturated. L16.
2 Of a magnetic system: capable of retaining a saturating magnetic field (see SATURATE *verb* 3b). M20.
2 saturable reactor an iron-cored coil whose impedance to alternating current can be varied by varying the direct current in an auxiliary winding so as to change the degree of magnetization of the core.
■ **saturaˈbility** *noun* E20.

saturate /ˈsatʃʊrət, -tjʊrət/ *noun.* M20.
[formed as prec.: see -ATE[1].]
CHEMISTRY. A saturated fat or fatty acid (see SATURATED 2).

saturate /ˈsatʃʊrət, -tjʊrət/ *adjective.* LME.
[Latin *saturatus* pa. pple of *saturare*: see next, -ATE[2].]
†**1** Satisfied, satiated. LME–E17.
2 = SATURATED 3. M17.
3 Soaked through, saturated; filled to capacity. Chiefly *poet.* L18.
†**4** CHEMISTRY. = SATURATED 2. L18–E19.

saturate /ˈsatʃʊreɪt, -tjʊreɪt/ *verb.* M16.
[Latin *saturat-* pa. ppl stem of *saturare*, from *satur* full, satiated: see -ATE[3].]
▶ **I** *verb trans.* †**1** Satisfy, satiate. M16–E19.
2 Cause (a substance) to combine with, dissolve, or hold the greatest possible quantity of another substance; foll. by *with* (freq. in *pass.*). Also (ORGANIC CHEMISTRY), cause to become saturated as regards bonding (SATURATED 2). L17.
3 Impregnate, soak thoroughly; fill to capacity; imbue with, steep in. (Foll. by *in*, *with*.) M18. ▸**b** PHYSICS. Magnetize or charge fully. M19. ▸**c** ELECTRONICS. Put (a device) into a state in which no further increase in current is achievable. E20.
4 MILITARY. Overwhelm (enemy defences, a target area, etc.) by aerial attack, esp. by intensive bombing. M20.
5 Supply (a market) beyond the point at which demand for a product is satisfied. M20.

📖 **3** E. PEACOCK The sleeve . . was saturated with blood. R. FRY Objects saturated . . with the most . . repulsive associations. **5** *Vanity Fair* Japan's . . electronics industry . . had begun to saturate the world markets with all its marvelous gadgets.

▶ **II** *verb intrans.* **6** Reach or show a condition of saturation; reach a state in which no further change or increase is possible. E20.

📖 **6** J. ROMER It was left for several days to . . saturate properly.

■ **saturator** *noun* a person who or thing which saturates something; *spec.* a device which saturates air or gas with the vapour of water or of a volatile liquid: L19.

saturated /ˈsatʃʊreɪtɪd, -tjʊr-/ *ppl adjective.* M17.
[from prec. + -ED[1].]
1 *gen.* That has been saturated; exhibiting saturation. M17. ▸**b** Of a solution: containing the greatest amount of solute that it can for the temperature it is at. L18.
2 CHEMISTRY. Orig., (of a compound) containing the greatest possible proportion of some element; (of an atom, radical, etc.) chemically combined to the maximum extent. Now, (of an organic compound, molecule, group, etc.) having a structure containing the greatest possible number of hydrogen atoms, and hence having no multiple bonds between carbon atoms; (of a carbon atom) singly bonded to four other atoms. M19. ▸**b** Of a mineral: containing the maximum possible amount of combined silica. Of an igneous rock: containing neither free silica nor any undersaturated minerals. E20.
3 Of a colour: free from admixture of white; intense, deep. M19.

📖 **1** P. BARKER Eating chips so saturated in vinegar that it leaked out. *Sunday Times* Heathrow and Gatwick—already operating almost at capacity—will become saturated. **3** A. LURIE It was almost night by now, the sky a saturated blue.

Special collocations: **saturated diving** = SATURATION *diving*. **saturated steam** steam containing the greatest amount of water that it can for the temperature it is at.

saturation /satʃʊˈreɪʃ(ə)n, -tjʊ-/ *noun.* M16.
[Late Latin *saturatio(n-)*, from Latin *saturat-*: see SATURATE *verb*, -ATION; later from the verb.]
†**1** Complete satisfaction of appetite; satiation. M16–M19.
2 The action or an act of saturating; the state of being saturated. M17.
3 Degree of intensity of a colour; relative freedom from admixture of white. L19. ▸**b** *transf.* A control on a television set used to adjust the colour quality of the picture. M20.
4 In full ***saturation dive***. A dive in which a diver's bloodstream is saturated with helium or other suitable gas at the pressure of the surrounding water, so that the decompression time afterwards is independent of the duration of the dive. L20.

Comb.: **saturation bombing** MILITARY intensive aerial bombing; **saturation current** the greatest current that can be carried by a gas or electronic device; ***saturation dive***: see sense 4 above; **saturation diving** the practice or action of performing a saturation dive; **saturation point** the state or condition at which saturation is reached; *fig.* the limit of acceptability; **saturation pressure**, **saturation vapour pressure** PHYSICS the pressure exerted by a vapour that is in equilibrium with its liquid or solid phase.

Saturday /ˈsatədeɪ, -di/ *noun, adverb, & adjective.*
[Old English *Sætern(es)dæg* corresp. to Old Frisian *saterdei*, Middle Low German *sater(s)dach*, Middle Dutch *saterdach* (Dutch *zaterdag*), translating Latin *Saturni dies* day of (the planet) Saturn.]
▶ **A** *noun.* The seventh day of the week, following Friday. OE.
Egg Saturday: see EGG *noun*. ***Holy Saturday***: see HOLY *adjective*. **Saturday-to-Monday** a period running from a Saturday to a Monday, often used with ref. to excursion tickets.
▶ **B** *adverb.* On Saturday. Now *colloq.* ME.
▶ **C** *attrib.* or as *adjective.* Of Saturday; characteristic of Saturday; taking place on Saturday(s). M16.
Saturday penny *arch.* a penny or small sum of money given to a child on a Saturday as pocket money.
■ **Saturdays** *adverb* (*colloq.*) on Saturdays, each Saturday LME.

Saturday night /ˈsatədeɪ nʌɪt, ˈsatədi/ *adjectival phr.* L19.
[from prec. + NIGHT *noun*.]
Designating activities, esp. entertainments or revelries, taking place on or as on a Saturday night.
Saturday night palsy, **Saturday night paralysis** *colloq.* temporary local paralysis of the arm after it has rested on a hard edge for a long time, as during a drunken sleep. **Saturday night special** *N. Amer. colloq.* a cheap low-calibre pistol or revolver such as might be used by a petty criminal.

Saturn /ˈsat(ə)n/ *noun.* OE.
[Latin *Saturnus*, perh. of Etruscan origin.]
1 ROMAN MYTHOLOGY. The god of agriculture, in classical times identified with Greek Kronos, ruler of the gods until deposed by his son Zeus (Jupiter). OE.
2 ASTRONOMY. The sixth planet in order of distance from the sun, a gas giant well known for its ring system, whose orbit lies between those of Jupiter and Uranus. OE.

▸**b** *ASTROLOGY.* Saturn as a supposed cause of coldness, sluggishness, and gloominess in those born under its influence, and in general as a malign force over human affairs. **LME.**
3 *ALCHEMY.* The metal lead. *obsolete* exc. *Hist.* **LME.**
4 *HERALDRY.* The tincture sable in the fanciful blazon of arms of sovereign houses. Long *obsolete* exc. *Hist.* **L16.**

saturnal /sə'tə:n(ə)l/ *noun & adjective.* Now *rare.* **L15.**
[Latin *Saturnalis*, from *Saturnus* SATURN: see -AL¹. As noun from French *saturnales* fem. pl.]
▸ **A** *noun.* In *pl.* = SATURNALIA. **L15.**
▸†**B** *adjective.* Of or pertaining to the planet Saturn or its astrological influence. **L16–L17.**

Saturnalia /satə'neɪlɪə/ *noun* (treated as *sing.* or *pl.*). In sense 2 also **s-**. **L16.**
[Latin, use as noun of neut. pl. of *Saturnalis*: see prec.]
1 *ROMAN HISTORY.* The festival of Saturn, held in mid December and characterized by general unrestrained merrymaking, the precursor of Christmas. **L16.**
2 *transf.* & *fig.* A period of unrestrained tumult and revelry; an orgy. **L18.**
■ **Saturnalian** *adjective* **E18.**

Saturnian /sə'tə:nɪən/ *adjective & noun.* **M16.**
[Latin *Saturnius* (from *Saturnus* SATURN) + -AN.]
▸ **A** *adjective.* **1 a** Of or pertaining to the planet Saturn; attributed to the malign influence of Saturn. **M16.** ▸**b** *PHYSICS.* Of or pertaining to a former model of the nuclear atom in which electrons are assumed to orbit in rings around a central nucleus, thus resembling the appearance of Saturn. Now *Hist.* **E20.**
2 Pertaining to the god Saturn, esp. with ref. to the supposed golden age of his reign. **E17.**
3 *PROSODY.* Designating the metre used in early Roman poetry, before the introduction of Greek metres. **L17.**
▸ **B** *noun.* †**1** A person born under the astrological influence of the planet Saturn; a person of saturnine temperament. Only in **L16.**
2 An (imagined) inhabitant of the planet Saturn. **M18.**
3 *PROSODY.* In *pl.* Saturnian verses. *rare.* **L19.**

saturnic /sə'tə:nɪk/ *adjective.* Now *rare.* **L19.**
[from SATURN + -IC.]
Affected with lead-poisoning.

saturnicentric /satə:nɪ'sɛntrɪk/ *adjective.* **L18.**
[from SATURN + -I- + -CENTRIC.]
Having or calculated with reference to Saturn as the centre.

saturniid /sə'tə:nɪɪd/ *adjective & noun.* **L19.**
[mod. Latin *Saturniidae* (see below), from *Saturnia* genus name: see -ID³.]
ENTOMOLOGY. ▸**A** *adjective.* Of, pertaining to, or designating the family Saturniidae of silk moths, which includes many large tropical species. **L19.**
▸ **B** *noun.* A silk moth of this family. **M20.**

saturnine /'satənʌɪn/ *adjective.* **LME.**
[Old & mod. French *saturnin* or medieval Latin *Saturninus*, from *Saturnus* SATURN: see -INE¹.]
1 a In *ASTROLOGY*, born under or affected by the influence of the planet Saturn. Now usu. *gen.*, of a cold, sluggish, and gloomy temperament. **LME.** ▸**b** Of dark and grim appearance. **L18.**
2 Of or pertaining to lead. Now *rare.* **M17.** ▸**b** *MEDICINE.* Of a disorder: caused by absorption of lead. Of a patient: suffering from lead-poisoning. Now *rare.* **E19.**

> 🕮 **1a** V. ACKLAND My father's saturnine moods. **b** O. WILDE How evil he looked! The face was saturnine and swarthy.

saturnism /'satənɪz(ə)m/ *noun.* Now *rare.* **M19.**
[from SATURN + -ISM.]
MEDICINE. Lead-poisoning.

satya /'sʌtjə/ *noun.* **M20.**
[Sanskrit.]
INDIAN PHILOSOPHY. Truth, truthfulness.

satyagraha /sʌ'tjɑ:grəhɑ:/ *noun.* **E20.**
[Sanskrit *satyāgraha* force born of truth, from *satya* truth + *āgraha* pertinacity.]
1 *Hist.* A policy of passive resistance to British rule in India formulated by M. K. Gandhi. **E20.**
2 *gen.* Any policy of non-violent resistance. **E20.**
■ **satyagrahi** *noun*, pl. **-is**, same, [mod. Sanskrit *satyāgrahī*] an exponent or practitioner of satyagraha **E20. satyagrahist** *noun* = SATYAGRAHI **M20.**

satyr /'satə/ *noun*¹. **LME.**
[Old & mod. French *satyre* or Latin *satyrus* from Greek *saturos*. Cf. SATIRE *noun.*]
1 a *MYTHOLOGY.* Any of a class of woodland gods supposed to be the companions of Bacchus, represented in early Greek art as a man with a horse's ears and tail, later in Roman art as a man with a goat's ears, tail, legs, and budding horns. **LME.** ▸**b** A lustful or sensual man. **L18.**
2 An ape; *spec.* the orang-utan. Now *rare* or *obsolete.* **LME.**
3 A butterfly of the genus *Satyrus*, having dark brown wings and found from southern Europe to central Asia. Formerly more widely, any satyrid butterfly. **L19.**
■ **satyress** *noun* a female satyr **M19. satyrish** *adjective* characteristic of a satyr; lustful, sensual: **M20.**

†**satyr** *noun*² see SATIRE *noun.*

satyral /'satɪr(ə)l/ *noun.* **L18.**
[Old French *satirel*, *-al* dim. of *satire* SATYR *noun*¹.]
HERALDRY. A monster with the body of a lion, the face of an old man, and short curved horns.

satyresque /satɪ'rɛsk/ *adjective.* **M18.**
[Italian *satiresco*, from *satiro* SATYR *noun*¹: see -ESQUE.]
Resembling a satyr; having the characteristics of a satyr.

satyriasis /satɪ'rʌɪəsɪs/ *noun.* **LME.**
[Late Latin from Greek *saturiasis*, from *saturos* SATYR *noun*¹: see -IASIS.]
MEDICINE. Excessive or uncontrollable sexual desire in a male; satyromania. Formerly also, priapism.

satyric /sə'tɪrɪk/ *adjective.* **E17.**
[Latin *satyricus*, Greek *saturikos*, from *saturos* SATYR *noun*¹: see -IC.]
Of or pertaining to satyrs; *esp.* designating a comic type of Greek drama in which the chorus dressed as satyrs.
■ **satyrical** *adjective* = SATYRIC **L16. satyrically** *adverb* (*rare*) in the manner of a satyr **L19.**

satyrid /sə'tɪrɪd/ *noun & adjective.* **E20.**
[mod. Latin *Satyridae* (see below), from use as mod. Latin genus name of Latin *satyrus*: see SATYR *noun*¹, -ID³.]
▸ **A** *noun.* A butterfly of the family Satyridae, typically brown with small eyespots. **E20.**
▸ **B** *adjective.* Of, pertaining to, or designating this family. **M20.**

satyrion /sə'tɪrɪən/ *noun.* Now *rare* or *obsolete.* **LME.**
[Old & mod. French or Latin from Greek *saturion*, from *saturos* SATYR *noun*¹, with ref. to the supposed aphrodisiac properties of the plants.]
Any of various kinds of tuberous-rooted orchid.

satyromania /ˌsatɪrə'meɪnɪə/ *noun.* **L19.**
[from SATYR *noun*¹ + -O- + -MANIA.]
Excessive or uncontrollable sexual desire in a male; satyriasis. Cf. NYMPHOMANIA.
■ **satyromaniac** *noun & adjective* (***a***) *noun* a man exhibiting satyromania; (***b***) *adjective* of, pertaining to, or exhibiting satyromania: **L19.**

sauba /'sɔ:bə, *foreign* sa'uba/ *noun.* **M19.**
[Portuguese *saúva* from Tupi *ysáuwa*.]
= ***leaf-cutter ant*** s.v. LEAF *noun*¹.

sauce /sɔ:s/ *noun.* See also SASS *noun.* **ME.**
[Old & mod. French from Proto-Romance use as noun of fem. of Latin *salsus* salted, salt. The etymological sense is identical with that of *salad*.]
1 Any liquid or semi-liquid preparation eaten as an accompaniment to food; the liquid constituent of a dish. Formerly also, any condiment for meat, fish, etc. **ME.**
2 *fig.* A thing which adds piquancy or excitement to a word, idea, action, etc. **L15.**
3 [Perh. from SAUCY.] ▸**a** A saucy or impudent person. Usu. as *voc.* Long *rare.* **M16.** ▸**b** Sauciness, impertinence, cheek. *colloq.* **M19.**
4 Fresh or preserved vegetables or fruit eaten as part of a meal or as a relish. Chiefly *US.* **E17.** ▸**b** Stewed fruit. *N. Amer.* **M19.**
5 A solution of salt etc. used in some manufacturing processes. Now *rare.* **M19.**
6 Alcohol. Also occas., a narcotic drug. *slang* (orig. *US*). **M20.**

> 🕮 **1** *Proverb*: What is sauce for the goose is sauce for the gander. ***brown sauce***, ***cheese sauce***, ***mint sauce***, ***tomato sauce***, ***white sauce***, etc. *transf.*: L. BLUE Greek food . . is . . served with the exhilaration of a party, and such a sauce cannot be imitated. **2** SIR W. SCOTT The piquant sauce of extreme danger. **3b** R. L. STEVENSON One more word of your sauce, and I'll . . fight you. **6** *Sun (Melbourne)* A month to live unless he gets off the sauce.

Phrases: †**pay sauce** pay dearly. **serve with the same sauce** subject to the same thing that has been inflicted on oneself or on another person.
Comb.: **sauce-alone** = *GARLIC-mustard*; **sauce-boat** a boat-shaped vessel for serving sauce; **saucebox** *colloq.* a saucy or impertinent person; ***sauce PÉRIGUEUX***; ***sauce Robert*** /sos rɔbɛr/: consisting of chopped onions cooked with butter and seasoned.
■ **sauceless** *adjective* having no sauce; *fig.* lacking piquancy: **L19.**

sauce /sɔ:s/ *verb trans.* See also SASS *verb.* **LME.**
[from the noun.]
1 Season, dress, or prepare (food) with sauce or condiments. **LME.**
2 *fig.* Provide a pleasing accompaniment to; make pleasant or agreeable, reduce the severity of; add piquancy or excitement to. **E16.**
3 †**a** Charge extortionate prices to. *rare* (Shakes.). Only in **L16.** ▸†**b** Beat, flog. **L16–E18.** ▸**c** Rebuke smartly. *obsolete* exc. *dial.* **L16.**
4 Speak impertinently to. *colloq.* **M19.**

> 🕮 **1** R. MILNER Spanish rice, thickly sauced. *transf.*: B. HOLYDAY He endeavour'd to sauce their dishes with his scurrility.

saucepan /'sɔ:spən/ *noun.* **L17.**
[from SAUCE *noun* + PAN *noun*¹.]
Orig., a small skillet with a long handle, used esp. for boiling sauce. Now, a pan, usu. round and made of metal with a lid and a long handle at the side, used for boiling or stewing food etc. on top of a cooker.
double saucepan = ***double boiler*** s.v. DOUBLE *adjective & adverb.*
Comb.: **saucepan lid** *rhyming slang* (***a***) one pound sterling (cf. QUID *noun*²); (***b***) a child (cf. KID *noun*¹ 4a).
■ **saucepanful** *noun* the amount that a saucepan will hold **M19.**

saucer /'sɔ:sə/ *noun.* **ME.**
[Old French *saussier*, *saussiere* (mod. *saucière*) sauce-boat, from *sauce* SAUCE *noun*, prob. after late Latin *salsarium*.]
†**1** A usu. metal receptacle for holding condiments or sauces at a meal. **ME–E18.**
2 *BOTANY.* Any of certain saucer-shaped parts of a plant, e.g. the cyathium of a spurge. **L16.**
3 A small circular dish or plate. Now *spec.* a round shallow dish used to support a cup and catch any liquid spilt. **E17.** ▸**b** = ***flying saucer*** s.v. FLYING *ppl adjective.* **M20.**
4 *MECHANICS.* Any of various kinds of iron bolt or socket. **M18.**

> 🕮 **3** B. BEHAN Cups and saucers instead of mugs. *fig.*: *Bulletin (Sydney)* Choom's eyes were saucers of awed interest. *attrib.*: *Architectural Review* The three saucer domes which form the roof.

Comb.: **saucer bath** (now chiefly *Hist.*) a wide shallow bath usu. kept in a bedroom and used for sponging oneself down; **saucer bug** a disc-shaped predatory water bug, *Ilyocoris cimicoides*, which breathes by means of an air bubble around its body; **saucer-burial** *US HISTORY* burial of a black person paid for by donations placed in a saucer laid on or near the corpse; **saucer eye**: that is large and round like a saucer; **saucer-eyed** *adjective* having saucer eyes; **saucerman** a being imagined or believed to be the pilot or passenger of a flying saucer.
■ **saucerful** *noun* as much as a saucer will hold **LME. saucerless** *adjective* **M19.**

saucer /'sɔ:sə/ *verb.* **E20.**
[from the noun.]
1 *verb intrans.* Take the shape of a saucer, be as shallow as a saucer. **E20.**
2 *verb trans.* Shape like a saucer. **M20.**
3 *verb trans.* Pour (a liquid) into a saucer, esp. from a cup. **M20.**

saucerian /sɔ:'sɪərɪən/ *adjective & noun.* **M20.**
[from SAUCER *noun* + -IAN.]
▸ **A** *adjective.* Of or pertaining to a flying saucer. **M20.**
▸ **B** *noun.* **1** A believer in the existence of flying saucers. **M20.**
2 A being imagined or believed to travel by flying saucer. **L20.**

saucerization /sɔ:sərʌɪ'zeɪʃ(ə)n/ *noun.* Also **-isation**. **E20.**
[from SAUCER *noun* + -IZATION.]
SURGERY. The excision of bone or flesh so as to leave a shallow saucer-shaped cavity.
■ **'saucerize** *verb trans.* excise (bone or flesh) in this manner **M20.**

saucery /'sɔ:səri/ *noun. obsolete* exc. *Hist.* **ME.**
[Old French *sausserie*, medieval Latin *salsaria*, from Old French *sausse*, medieval Latin *salsa* SAUCE *noun*: see -ERY.]
A section of servants in a household entrusted with the preparation of sauces; the part of a house in which sauces were prepared.

sauch *noun* var. of SAUGH.

†**saucht** *noun* var. of SAUGHT.

saucier /sosje/ *noun.* Pl. pronounced same. **M20.**
[French.]
A sauce cook.

†**saucisse** *noun.* **E17–L18.**
[French.]
Chiefly *MILITARY.* = SAUCISSON 1b, 2.

saucisson /sosisɔ̃/ *noun.* Pl. pronounced same. **M17.**
[French, augm. of *saucisse* SAUSAGE *noun*.]
1 a A firework consisting of a tube packed with gunpowder. **M17.** ▸**b** *Hist.* A long tube packed with gunpowder, formerly used as a fuse for firing a mine. **E19.**
2 *MILITARY.* A large fascine. **E18.**
3 A large thick sausage. **M18.**

saucy /'sɔ:si/ *adjective.* See also SASSY *adjective.* **E16.**
[from SAUCE *noun* + -Y¹.]
†**1** Flavoured with sauce; resembling sauce; savoury. **E16–M17.**
2 a Insolent, presumptuous; impertinent, rude, cheeky. **E16.** ▸**b** Of a ship or boat: orig. (*fig.*), presumptuous, rashly venturing; later, smart, stylish. **L16.** ▸**c** Orig., wanton, lascivious. Now (*colloq.*), smutty, suggestive. **E17.** ▸**d** Cheeky in an endearing way; pert, sprightly. **E18.**

3 Fastidious, particular, spoilt. *obsolete* exc. *dial.* L16. **4** Scornful, disdainful. *obsolete* exc. *Scot. & dial.* E18.

📖 **2a** J. IRVING Cushie Percy—a little too saucy with her mouth. **b** SHAKES. *Tr. & Cr.* The saucy boat, Whose weak untimber'd sides.. Co-rivalled greatness. **c** *Sun* The.. libel trial heard.. saucy revelations. **d** J. RUSKIN Some saucy puppies on their hind legs.

■ **saucily** *adverb* M16. **sauciness** *noun* M16.

saudade /sau'dadə/ *noun.* E20.
[Portuguese.]
Longing, melancholy, nostalgia, as a supposed characteristic of the Portuguese or Brazilian temperament.

Saudi /'saʊdi, 'sɔːdi/ *noun & adjective.* M20.
[Arab. *saʿūdī*, from *Saʿūd* name of a dynasty + -ī[2].]
▶ **A** *noun.* **1** A member of an Arabian dynasty which ruled Nejd from the 18th cent. and has ruled the kingdom of Saudi Arabia, comprising the greater part of the Arabian peninsula, since its foundation in 1932. M20.
2 A native or inhabitant of Saudi Arabia; a person of Saudi descent. M20.
▶ **B** *adjective.* **1** Of or pertaining to this dynasty. M20.
2 Of or pertaining to Saudi Arabia. M20.
Comb.: **Saudi Arabian** *noun & adjective* = senses A.2, B.2 above.
■ **Saudian**, **Saudite** *adjectives* = SAUDI *adjective* M20. **Saudiiˈzation** *noun* the process or result of rendering more Saudi in character, esp. by the transfer of posts in industry in Saudi Arabia from foreigners to Saudi nationals L20.

sauerbraten /'saʊəbrɑːt(ə)n, *foreign* 'zaʊərbraːtən/ *noun. N. Amer.* L19.
[German, from *sauer* sour + *Braten* roast meat.]
A dish of German origin consisting of beef marinaded in vinegar with peppercorns, onions, and other seasonings and then cooked.

sauerkraut /'saʊəkraʊt/ *noun.* M17.
[German (whence French *choucroute*), from *sauer* sour + *Kraut* vegetable, cabbage.]
1 Finely chopped pickled cabbage, a typical German dish. M17.
2 (Usu. **S-**.) A German. *US slang. derog.* M19.

sauf /sof/ *preposition. literary. rare.* M19.
[French. Cf. SAVE *preposition & conjunction*.]
Except for, apart from.

sauger /'sɔːgə/ *noun.* L19.
[Origin unkn.]
A small N. American pikeperch, *Stizostedion canadense*.

saugh /sɔːx, -k/ *noun. Scot. & north.* Also **sauch**. LME.
[Repr. Old English (Anglian) *salh* = West Saxon *sealh* SALLOW *noun*.]
= SALLOW *noun* 1, 2.

†**saught** *noun.* Long *Scot. & north.* Also **saucht**. LOE–E20.
[Prob. from Old Norse *sǽtt*, *sátt*, from Germanic.]
Agreement, peace, tranquillity.

saugrenu /sogrəny/ *adjective. literary. rare.* L19.
[French.]
Absurd, preposterous, ridiculous.

Sauk /sɔːk/ *noun & adjective.* Also **Sac** /sak/. E18.
[Canad. French *Saki* from Ojibwa *osākī*. Cf. Sauk *asākīwa* person of the outlet.]
▶ **A** *noun.* Pl. **-s**, same. A member of an Algonquian people inhabiting parts of the central US, formerly in Wisconsin, Illinois, and Iowa, now in Oklahoma and Kansas; the language of this people. E18.
▶ **B** *attrib.* or as *adjective.* Of or pertaining to the Sauks or their language. M18.

†**saul** *noun* see SALLE.

saulie /'sɔːli/ *noun. Scot. obsolete* exc. *Hist.* E17.
[Origin unkn.]
A hired mourner at a funeral.

sault /saʊ, *in sense 2 also* suː/ *noun.* ME.
[Old French, earlier spelling of Old & mod. French *saut* from Latin *saltus*, from *salire* leap.]
1 A leap, a jump, *spec.* by a horse. Long *obsolete* exc. *Scot.* ME.
2 A waterfall, a rapid. *N. Amer.* E17.

Saumur /'səʊmjʊə, *foreign* somyr/ *noun.* L19.
[A town in the department of Maine-et-Loire, France.]
A French white wine resembling champagne.

sauna /'sɔːnə/ *noun & verb.* L19.
[Finnish.]
▶ **A** *noun.* A room or building of a type originating in Finland in which the body is cleansed or relaxed in very hot air (in Finland produced by hot stones on to which liquid may be thrown); a bath or session in such a room or building. Also ***sauna bath***. L19.
facial sauna (a small apparatus providing) a steam bath as a beauty treatment for the face.
▶ **B** *verb intrans.* Take a sauna. M20.

saunders *noun* var. of SANDERS *noun*[1].

saunter /'sɔːntə/ *noun.* E18.
[from the verb.]
1 The habit of loafing or idling. *rare.* E18.
2 A sauntering manner of walking; a leisurely relaxed gait. E18.
3 A leisurely relaxed walk or ramble; a stroll. E19.

saunter /'sɔːntə/ *verb.* LME.
[Origin unkn.]
†**1** *verb intrans.* Muse, wonder. Also, chatter idly, babble. LME–L16.
2 *verb intrans.* Orig., wander aimlessly; travel as a vagrant. Later, walk with a leisurely relaxed gait; stroll; travel by vehicle in a slow and leisurely manner. M17.
3 *verb trans. & intrans.* Fritter *away* (time etc.); loiter over (one's work). Also, loiter or stroll around (a place). L17.

📖 **2** R. MACAULAY The children sauntered down Sloane Street, loitering at.. shop windows. *fig.*: W. S. MAUGHAM Pleasant reveries sauntered through her mind. **3** D. H. LAWRENCE Sauntering the day away.

■ **saunterer** *noun* L17. **saunteringly** *adverb* in a sauntering manner E19.

-saur /sɔː/ *suffix.*
[mod. Latin *-saurus* from Greek *sauros* lizard.]
PALAEONTOLOGY & ZOOLOGY. Forming names of (esp. extinct) animals, chiefly after mod. Latin genus names in ***-saurus***, indicating reptilian nature or affinities, as ***dinosaur***, ***ichthyosaur***, ***stegosaur***, etc.

saurel /sɒ'rɛl/ *noun.* L19.
[French from late Latin *saurus* from Greek *sauros* horse mackerel.]
Any of various elongated carangid fishes of the genus *Trachurus*, with bony plates along each side, *esp.* (***a***) the scad; (***b***) the jack mackerel.

saurian /'sɔːrɪən/ *noun & adjective.* E19.
[from mod. Latin *Sauria* (see below), from Greek *sauros* lizard: see -IAN.]
▶ **A** *noun.* **1** Orig., a reptile of the former order Sauria, which comprised the lizards and (orig.) the crocodiles. Now usu. *spec.* (***a***) a crocodile; (***b***) a large extinct Mesozoic reptile. E19.
2 *fig.* A person or thing resembling a dinosaur. E20.
▶ **B** *adjective.* **1** Designating, pertaining to, or characteristic of a saurian. E19.
2 *fig.* Resembling a lizard or a dinosaur in appearance, character, etc. M19.

saurischian /sɔː'rɪskɪən, -'rɪʃɪən, saʊ-/ *adjective & noun.* L19.
[from mod. Latin *Saurischia* (see below), from Greek *sauros* lizard + *iskhion* ISCHIUM: see -IA[2], -IAN.]
PALAEONTOLOGY. ▶ **A** *adjective.* Of, pertaining to, or designating the order Saurischia of dinosaurs, which includes forms having a lizard-like pelvic structure, and comprises the sauropods and theropods. L19.
▶ **B** *noun.* A dinosaur of this order. L19.

sauroid /'sɔːrɔɪd/ *adjective.* M19.
[from Greek *sauros* lizard + -OID.]
Resembling a saurian or lizard.

Sauromatian /sɔːrə'meɪʃ(ɪ)ən/ *noun. rare.* E17.
[from Greek *Sauromatai*: see SARMATIAN, -IAN.]
Hist. = SARMATIAN *noun* 1.

sauropod /'sɔːrəpɒd, saʊ-/ *noun & adjective.* L19.
[from mod. Latin *Sauropoda* (see below), from Greek *sauros* lizard: see -POD.]
▶ **A** *noun.* A member of the infraorder Sauropoda of gigantic herbivorous saurischian dinosaurs, characterized by massive bodies, small heads, and long necks and tails. L19.
▶ **B** *adjective.* Of, pertaining to, or designating a dinosaur of this suborder. L19.

saury /'sɔːri/ *noun.* L18.
[Perh. formed as SAUREL with different suffix.]
Any of various elongated marine fishes of the family Scomberesocidae, having narrow beaklike jaws, esp. *Scomberesox saurus* of the N. Atlantic and southern hemisphere. Also ***saury pike***.

sausage /'sɒsɪdʒ/ *noun.* LME.
[Old Northern French *saussiche* (var. of Old French *salsice*, mod. *saucisse*) from medieval Latin *salsicia* use as noun of neut. pl. of *salsicius* (sc. Latin *farta* neut. pl. of pa. pple of *farcire* stuff), from Latin *salsus* salted.]
1 Minced pork, beef, or other meat, seasoned and often mixed with other ingredients and usu. enclosed in a short length of animal intestine or synthetic casing so as to form a cylindrical roll; a length of this. LME.
2 *transf.* A thing shaped like a sausage; *spec.* (***a***) MILITARY. = SAUCISSON *noun* 2; (***b***) an elongated aeronautical balloon (also ***sausage balloon***); (***c***) *slang* (now *Hist.*) a German trench mortar bomb; (***d***) a length of padded fabric placed at the foot of a door to stop draughts; (***e***) NAUTICAL a tube-like fender suspended horizontally on a vessel or quayside. M17.
3 A German. *slang.* Now *rare* or *obsolete.* L19.
4 A person. Esp. in ***silly old sausage***. *colloq.* M20.

📖 **1** *Bologna sausage*, *Cumberland sausage*, *German sausage*, *polony sausage*, etc. **not a sausage** *colloq.* nothing at all. **2** F. O'CONNOR White hair stacked in sausages around her head. *Practical Householder* Place a sausage of mortar on the foundation.

Comb.: ***sausage balloon***: see sense 2 above; **sausage board** a surfboard rounded at both ends; **sausage curl** a curl in the hair resembling a sausage; **sausage dog** *colloq.* a dachshund; **sausage machine** a machine for making sausages; *fig.* an institution with a relentlessly uniform process or repetitive routine; **sausage meat** minced meat used in sausages or as a stuffing; **sausage roll** a roll of sausage meat enclosed in pastry; **sausage-tree** a tropical African tree, *Kigelia pinnata* (family Bignoniaceae), with red bell-shaped flowers and large pendulous sausage-shaped fruits.
■ **sausagey** *adjective* resembling a sausage E20.

sausage /'sɒsɪdʒ/ *verb trans. rare.* E20.
[from the noun.]
Treat in a manner reminiscent of the manufacture of a sausage; shape like a sausage.

Saussurean /səʊ'sjʊərɪən/ *adjective & noun.* M20.
[from *Saussure* (see below) + -AN.]
▶ **A** *adjective.* Of, pertaining to, or characteristic of the Swiss scholar Ferdinand de Saussure (1857–1913) or his linguistic theories. M20.
▶ **B** *noun.* An adherent of Saussure's theories. M20.
■ **Saussureanism** *noun* adherence to Saussure's theories M20.

saussurite /'sɔːsjʊərʌɪt/ *noun.* E19.
[from Horace Benedict de *Saussure* (1740–99), Swiss naturalist + -ITE[1].]
MINERALOGY. A very compact aggregate of albite, zoisite or epidote, and other minerals, produced by alteration of calcic plagioclase.
■ **sauˌssuritiˈzation** *noun* replacement by or conversion to saussurite; the formation of saussurite: L19. **sauˈssuritized** *adjective* wholly or partly replaced by or converted to saussurite E20.

saut /so/ *noun.* Pl. pronounced same. L19.
[French = leap.]
1 ***Saut Basque***, a dance of the French Basque provinces. L19.
2 BALLET. A leap in dancing. Esp. in ***saut de Basque***, a leap made while turning, holding one leg straight and the other at right angles to the body. L19.

sauté /'səʊteɪ/ *noun, adjective, & verb.* E19.
[French, pa. pple of *sauter* leap.]
COOKERY. ▶ **A** *noun.* A dish cooked by frying quickly in a little hot fat. E19.
▶ **B** *adjective.* Of meat, vegetables, etc.: fried quickly in a little hot fat. M19.
▶ **C** *verb trans.* Pa. t. & pple **-téd**, **-téed**. Fry (food) quickly in a little hot fat. M19.

Sauternes /sə(ʊ)'təːn/ *noun.* E18.
[A district near Bordeaux in France.]
A sweet white wine from Sauternes.

sautoir /'səʊtwɑː/ *noun.* M20.
[French: cf. SALTIRE.]
A long necklace consisting of a fine gold chain usu. set with jewels.

sauve qui peut /sovkipø/ *noun & verb phr.* E19.
[French, lit. 'save-who-can'.]
▶ **A** *noun phr.* A general stampede, a complete rout; panic, disorder. E19.
▶ **B** *verb phr. intrans.* (*inf.*). Stampede or scatter in flight. M20.

Sauveterrian /səʊv'tɛrɪən/ *adjective.* M20.
[French *Sauveterrien*, from *Sauveterre*: see below, -IAN.]
ARCHAEOLOGY. Designating or pertaining to a mesolithic culture of which remains were first discovered at Sauveterre-la-Lémance in Lot-et-Garonne, France.

Sauvignon /'səʊvɪnjɒn, *foreign* soviɲɔ̃ (*pl. same*)/ *noun.* M19.
[French.]
1 A white grape used in wine-making; a white wine made from this grape. M19.
2 = CABERNET ***Sauvignon***. M19.

sav /sav/ *noun. colloq.* M20.
[Abbreviation.]
= SAVELOY.

savable /'seɪvəb(ə)l/ *adjective.* Also **save-**. LME.
[from SAVE *verb* + -ABLE.]
Able to be saved; THEOLOGY salvable.

Savage /'savɪdʒ/ *noun*[1]. L19.
[Arthur *Savage* (1857–1938), US inventor.]
A repeating rifle produced by Savage in 1894; *gen.* any firearm produced by the Savage Arms Company.
¶ Proprietary name in the US.

savage /'savɪdʒ/ *adjective & noun*[2]. Also (*arch.*) **salvage** /'salvɪdʒ/. ME.
[Old & mod. French *sauvage* (Anglo-Norman also *savage*) from Proto-Romance alt. of Latin *silvaticus* of woodland, wild, from *silva* wood, forest: see -AGE.]
▶ **A** *adjective.* **I** **1** Of an animal: wild, undomesticated, untamed. *arch.* ME.

2 Orig. of land, a plant, etc.: wild, uncultivated. Later only of landscape: forbidding, impressively wild and rugged. *arch.* ME.
3 Of a noise, movement, etc.: wild, ungoverned; crude. *arch.* LME.
4 Now esp. of a people or lifestyle: primitive, uncivilized; uncouth. LME. ▸†**b** Remote from society, solitary. M–L17.

> 📖 **4** H. ARENDT The honesty . . of savage and uncivilised peoples. **savage man** (chiefly *HERALDRY*) a primitive person as represented in heraldry and pageantry; a human figure naked or surrounded by foliage. **b** MILTON O might I here In solitude live savage.

▸ **II** †**5** Indomitable, intrepid, bold, valiant. ME–L15.
6 Orig. of an animal, later also of a person, action, etc.: fierce, ferocious; cruel, harsh. ME.
7 Enraged, furious; coarse, brutal in speech. E19.

> 📖 **6** D. M. FRAME Our judicial torture . . is more savage than their cannibalism. G. BATTISCOMBE Bitten by a savage peccary. *transf.*: R. W. EMERSON The bellowing of the savage sea. **7** G. GREENE This . . author . . had anticipated failure but not this savage public execration.

▸ **B** *noun.* **1** A primitive or uncivilized person. LME. ▸**b** A cruel, fierce, or coarse and uncouth person. E17.
2 = *savage man* above. Also = JACK *noun*[1] 2. L16.
3 †**a** A wild animal. L17–M19. ▸**b** A bad-tempered horse. M19.

1 *the noble savage*: see NOBLE *adjective*.
■ **savagedom** *noun* the condition of being a savage; savage people collectively: M19. **savagely** *adverb* LME. **savageness** *noun* LME. **savagess** *noun* (*rare*) a female savage M17.

savage /ˈsavɪdʒ/ *verb*. Orig. †**salvage**. M16.
[from SAVAGE *adjective*.]
†**1** *verb intrans.* Act in a savage manner; be cruel or barbarous. *rare.* M16–M17.
2 *verb trans.* Make (a person or animal) savage or fierce. L16.
3 *verb trans.* Of a person: behave savagely towards; criticize brutally, treat harshly. L18.
4 *verb trans.* Of an animal, as a dog or horse: attack ferociously, injure severely. L19.

> 📖 **3** R. BERTHOUD Epstein's work was . . savaged for its 'debased Indo-Chinese style'. **4** R. COBB Nightmares about being savaged . . by enormous . . dogs.

savagerous /ˈsavɪdʒ(ə)rəs, səˈvadʒ(ə)rəs/ *adjective*. *US dial.* M19.
[formed as prec. + DANG)EROUS.]
Fierce, wild, violent, dangerous.

savagery /ˈsavɪdʒ(ə)ri/ *noun*. L16.
[formed as prec. + -ERY.]
1 The quality of being fierce or cruel; a cruel act. L16.
†**2** Wild vegetation. *rare* (Shakes.). Only in L16.
3 The condition of being primitive or uncivilized; a savage state of human society. E19.
4 Savage beasts or savages collectively. *rare.* M19.
5 Ruggedness of scenery. *arch.* L19.

savagism /ˈsavɪdʒɪz(ə)m/ *noun*. L18.
[formed as prec. + -ISM.]
= SAVAGERY 3.

SAVAK /ˈsavak/ *noun*. M20.
[Acronym, from Persian *Sāzmān-i-Attalāt Va Amnīyat-i-Keshvar* National Security and Intelligence Organization.]
Hist. The secret intelligence organization of Iran, established in 1957 and disbanded in 1979.

savannah /səˈvanə/ *noun*. Also **savanna**. M16.
[Spanish †*zavana*, †*çavana*, (now *sabana*) from Taino *zavana*.]
1 Orig., a treeless plain, esp. in tropical America. Now, an open grassy plain with few or no trees in a tropical or subtropical region; grassland or vegetation of this kind. M16.
2 A tract of low-lying damp or marshy ground. *US.* L17.
Comb.: **savannah flower** *W. Indies* any of several twining shrubs of the genus *Echites* (family Asclepiadaceae); **savannah forest** grassland similar to savannah but with a denser growth of trees; **savannah grass** a stoloniferous grass, *Axonopus compressus*, of tropical and subtropical America; **savannah monkey** a common African guenon, *Cercopithecus aethiops*, of which the green monkey, grivet, and vervet are different forms; **savannah sparrow** a small sparrow, *Passerculus sandwichensis*, of the family Emberizidae, common throughout most of N. America; **savannah woodland** = *savannah forest* above.

savant /ˈsav(ə)nt, *foreign* savɑ̃ (*pl. same*)/ *noun*. E18.
[French, use as noun of adjective, orig. pres. pple of *savoir* know.]
A learned person, *esp.* a distinguished scientist etc.
idiot savant: see IDIOT *noun*.

savante /ˈsav(ə)nt, *foreign* savɑ̃ːt (*pl. same*)/ *noun*. M18.
[French, fem. of prec.]
A learned (French) woman.

savarin /ˈsavərɪn; *foreign* savarɛ̃ (*pl. same*)/ *noun*. L19.
[Anthelme Brillat-*Savarin* (1755–1826), French gastronome.]
A light ring-shaped cake made with yeast and soaked in liqueur-flavoured syrup.

savate /səˈvɑːt, *foreign* savat/ *noun*. M19.
[French, orig. a kind of shoe: cf. SABOT.]
A form of boxing in which the feet and fists are used.

save /seɪv/ *noun*. LME.
[from the verb.]
†**1** A receptacle for storing food. *rare.* Only in LME.
2 An act of saving, a piece of economy. Chiefly *dial.* L19.
3 a *FOOTBALL & HOCKEY* etc. An act of preventing an opponent from scoring, esp. as performed by a goalkeeper. L19. ▸**b** *BASEBALL.* The credit given to a relief pitcher for maintaining a team's winning lead; the action of maintaining such a lead. M20.
4 *BRIDGE.* A sacrifice bid. Freq. in ***cheap save***. E20.
5 *COMPUTING.* The action of saving a file of data. L20.

> 📖 **3a** *Sun* The keeper made a series of brilliant . . saves.

save /seɪv/ *verb*. See also SALVE *verb*[2]. ME.
[Anglo-Norman *sa(u)ver*, Old French *salver*, (also mod.) *sauver* from late Latin *salvare* save, from Latin *salvus* SAFE *adjective*.]
▸ **I** Rescue, protect.
1 *verb trans.* Deliver, rescue, or protect (a person) from impending or potential danger, harm, or annoyance; make or keep safe, put in safety. (Foll. by *from*.) ME. ▸**b** Be a protection or means of deliverance to. LME.
2 *verb trans.* **a** *CHRISTIAN THEOLOGY.* Deliver (a person, the soul) from sin and its consequences; preserve from damnation. ME. ▸**b** *transf.* Reclaim from immorality, corruption, etc.; be the salvation of. L19.
†**3** *verb trans.* Choose not to kill (a person, animal, etc.); allow to live, spare. ME–M17.
4 *verb refl.* Protect or preserve oneself; get away, escape, (*from*). ME.
5 *verb trans.* Keep or protect (a thing) from damage, loss, or destruction. Formerly also, keep in safe possession. Now *spec.* in *COMPUTING*, keep (data) by moving a copy to a storage location, usu. on tape or disk. ME.
6 *verb trans.* Keep (honour, one's reputation, etc.) morally intact or unhurt; preserve, safeguard. ME.
7 *verb trans.* Rescue from a life-threatening illness or injury. Formerly also, heal, cure. ME.
†**8** *verb trans.* Store, preserve, keep in sound condition. ME–E18.
9 *verb trans.* Prevent the loss of (a game, match, bet, etc.). E17.
10 *verb trans.* Be in time for, manage to catch. M18.

> 📖 **1** *Medical & Physical Journal* A great many lives were saved by . . inoculation. H. B. STOWE 'Do save me—do hide me!' said Eliza. J. TYNDALL A sudden effort was necessary to save me from falling. *absol.*: POPE The same ambition can destroy or save. **2a** E. WAUGH I'd been worrying about my soul and whether I was saved. T. F. POWYS All men might be saved if they repented. **4** SIR W. SCOTT Save himself from degradation and disgrace. **5** E. LANGLEY How to save the knees of my trousers by sewing patches . . on them. D. FRASER The Battle of Britain had saved the country from invasion. *Amstrad PCW* You must save the files you want on to your disc before switching off. **7** S. MIDDLETON The child . . was rushed into hospital where antibiotics failed to save him.

▸ **II** Reserve, lay aside.
11 *verb trans.* Keep for a particular purpose or as potentially useful; set aside, reserve. LME.
12 *verb trans.* Store up or put by (money, goods, etc.) as an economy or for future use; keep instead of spending, consuming, or parting with. Also foll. by *up*. LME. ▸**b** *verb intrans.* Keep or store up money, esp. for future use. Also foll. by *up*. L16.
13 *verb trans.* Avoid spending, giving, or consuming (money, goods, etc.); keep in one's possession by not spending etc. Also, avoid spending or putting in (time, effort, etc.). LME.
14 *verb trans.* Be careful or economical in the use of; use or consume sparingly. E17.
15 *verb trans. spec.* ▸**a** Collect and keep (seed) in stock for sowing. M17. ▸**b** Dry (corn, hay, peat) by exposure to the air; harvest, stack. E18.
16 *verb trans.* Treat carefully so as to reduce or avoid fatigue, wear, or stress. L18.

> 📖 **11** B. SPOCK You can save what is left for the next day. L. SPALDING All the food . . saved in anticipation of his arrival has been eaten. **12** J. A. FROUDE He was able to save money for his son's education. P. D. JAMES He had been saving . . a small sum which would tide him over. **b** A. E. LINDOP I'm saving up to buy her a big book on birds. **13** J. K. JEROME We had dispensed with tea, so as to save time. G. GREENE He could easily have saved money by paying cash. **14** SWIFT To save your Master's Candles.

▸ **III** Avoid or prevent something undesirable.
17 *verb trans.* Avoid or enable another to avoid (a burden or inconvenience); *occas.* dispense with the need for. E17. ▸**b** *verb trans. FOOTBALL, HOCKEY, & CRICKET* etc. Prevent an opposing side from gaining (a run), scoring (a goal), etc. E19. ▸**c** *verb intrans. FOOTBALL & HOCKEY* etc. Prevent a goal from being scored. L19.

> 📖 **17** SIR W. SCOTT My letters lie there for me, as it saves their being sent down to Rosebank. **b** *Field* His shot was saved by the goal-keeper.

Phrases etc.: ***God save the mark***: see MARK *noun*[1]. **God save you, save you**: expr. greeting, good wishes, benediction, etc. **save a person's bacon** prevent a person from suffering loss, injury, or death; rescue a person from danger or crisis. ***save a person's life***: see LIFE *noun*. ***save appearances***: see APPEARANCE. **save-as-you-earn** a method of saving in Britain by regular deduction from earnings at source. ***saved by the bell***: see BELL *noun*[1]. ***save face***: see FACE *noun*. **save one's bacon** = *save one's hide* below. ***save one's BREATH (to cool one's porridge)***. **save oneself** avoid overdoing things. ***save one's face***: see FACE *noun*. **save one's hide, save one's skin** avoid loss, injury, or death; escape from danger or crisis. †**save one's longing** anticipate one's desire and so prevent it. **save one's neck** (*a*) escape death by hanging; (*b*) = ***save one's hide*** above. **save one's own hide, save one's own neck, save one's own skin** preserve one's own life or look after one's own interests, esp. at another's expense. **save one's pocket** avoid spending one's money. ***save one's skin***: see ***save one's hide*** above. **save the day** = ***save the situation*** below. ***save the mark***: see MARK *noun*[1]. ***save the phenomena***: see PHENOMENON. **save the situation** avert disaster. **save the tide** *NAUTICAL* get in and out of port etc. while the tide lasts. **save the trouble** avoid useless or pointless effort. ***save you***: see ***God save you*** above. ***save your reverence, saving your reverence***: see REVERENCE *noun*. **well saved** an applauding expression used when a rider has avoided a fall or a goalkeeper etc. has saved a goal.

save /seɪv/ *preposition & conjunction*. ME.
[Old French *sauf* (masc.), *sauve* (fem.), orig. varying with the gender of the accompanying noun (now only *sauf*), from Latin *salvo*, *salva* abl. sing. of masc. or neut. and fem. of *salvus* SAFE *adjective*, as used absol. as in *salvo jure*, *salva innocentia* without violation of right or innocence. Later prob. identified with imper. of SAVE *verb*. Cf. SAVING *preposition & conjunction*, SAUF.]
▸ **A** *preposition*. **1** Except, with the exception of, but. ME.
†**2** But for. *rare.* E16–E19.

> 📖 **1** M. DRABBLE Dances to which all other girls save Clara seemed to be invited. J. ARCHER No ornaments in the room save a crucifix. **2** KEATS She seem'd a splendid angel, newly drest, Save wings, for heaven.

▸ **B** *conjunction*. **1** = EXCEPT *conjunction* 1. Now only foll. by *that*. ME.
2 = EXCEPT *conjunction* 3. Also foll. by *for*. ME.
3 = EXCEPT *conjunction* 2. *arch.* or *poet.* LME. ▸†**b** But *that*, were it not *that*. *rare* (Shakes.). Only in L16.

> 📖 **1** R. COBB I cannot remember anything about his appearance, save that he had a morning coat. **2** M. J. HIGGINS Save and except in a dead calm she is utterly unseaworthy. *Chronicle* In no way formidable save from its enormous strength and bulk. E. J. BANFIELD Little for the population to do save eat, drink. D. H. LAWRENCE A small liqueur glass . . empty save for a tiny drop.

saveable *adjective* var. of SAVABLE.

save-all /ˈseɪvɔːl/ *noun*. M17.
[from SAVE *verb* + ALL *noun*.]
1 A means of preventing loss or waste; *spec.* a container for keeping something which would otherwise be lost or unused. M17.
2 *Hist.* A device for burning a candle-end, as a pan with a projecting spike on which to fix the candle-end. M17.
3 A stingy person, a miser. Now *dial.* L18.
4 *NAUTICAL HISTORY.* A sail set under another or between two others. L18.

saveloy /ˈsavəlɔɪ/ *noun*. M19.
[Alt. of French †*cervelat*, (also mod.) *-as* from Italian *cervellata*: see CERVELAT. Cf. SAV.]
A highly seasoned dried and smoked pork sausage, sold ready to eat.

saver /ˈseɪvə/ *noun*. ME.
[from SAVE *verb* + -ER[1].]
1 A person who saves, preserves, or rescues a person or thing from danger, harm, etc.; a saviour, a preserver. ME.
2 A person who saves esp. money; an economizer, a hoarder. M16.
†**3** A person who escapes financial loss, esp. in gambling. L16–L17.
4 A means of saving or economizing; *spec.* something that economizes on time, money, etc. (freq. as 2nd elem. of comb.). M17. ▸**b** A tariff or (esp. rail) fare promoted as saving money. L20.
5 A hedging bet. *Racing slang.* L19.

> 📖 **1** C. NESS Salvation is the work of the saved, not of the saver. **2** *Daily Telegraph* A linked policy can be encashed . . and the saver gets . . his savings returned. **4** ***money-saver***, ***space-saver***, ***time-saver***, etc.

Savile Row /savɪl ˈrəʊ/ *adjectival phr.* L19.
[A street in London.]
Designating a fashionable and expensive tailor with an establishment in Savile Row, or a style or item, esp. a man's suit, made in or associated with such an establishment.

savin /ˈsavɪn/ *noun.* Also **savine.** OE.
[Old French *savine* (mod. *sabine*) from Latin *sabina* use as noun (sc. *herba* plant) of fem. sing. of *Sabinus* SABINE *noun*[1] & *adjective.*]
1 A juniper, *Juniperus sabina*, of the mountains of southern Europe and western Asia, with scalelike adpressed leaves densely covering the branches. Also (*US*), the red cedar, *J. virginiana.* OE.
2 The dried tops of *Juniperus sabina*, an extract of which was formerly used to stimulate menstruation, as an anthelmintic, etc. OE.

saving /ˈseɪvɪŋ/ *noun.* ME.
[from SAVE *verb* + -ING[1].]
1 The action of SAVE *verb*; an instance of this; *spec.* (*a*) rescuing, deliverance; (*b*) economizing, an economy. ME.
2 A salvo, a reservation, a saving clause. *obsolete* exc. LAW. L15.
3 In *sing.* & (usu.) *pl.* Money saved; *spec.* sums of money saved on a regular basis, often by means of economizing. M18.

1 U. HOLDEN As important as . . the concealing of light was the saving of hot water. W. MCILVANNEY He was never given to saving, knowing there would always be another job. *Which?* The drawbacks outweigh the saving. **3** K. VONNEGUT His savings had been wiped out by the failure of the . . Loan Association. M. R. MITFORD All the savings of a month, the hoarded halfpence, the new farthings. ***dip into one's savings***: see DIP *verb.* ***National Savings***: see NATIONAL *adjective.* ***Premium Savings Bond***: see PREMIUM *noun.* **savings and loan** *US* (designating) a cooperative association which accepts savings at interest and lends money to savers for house or other purchases.

Comb.: **savings account** a deposit account; **savings bank** a bank which receives small deposits at interest and returns the profits to the depositors. **savings book** a book containing an official record of transactions on a savings account; **savings-box** a money box for savings; **savings certificate** an interest-bearing document issued by the British Government for the benefit of savers; **savings ratio** ECONOMICS the ratio of personal savings to disposable income in an economy.

saving /ˈseɪvɪŋ/ *ppl adjective.* ME.
[from SAVE *verb* + -ING[2].]
1 CHRISTIAN THEOLOGY. That delivers a person or soul from sin and its consequences. ME.
2 That saves, rescues, or protects a person or thing from danger, harm, etc. M16.
3 That preserves a person from moral or intellectual error. Also, (of a quality) redeeming. L16.
4 Accustomed to save, hoard up, or economize; parsimonious, economical. Also, that makes economical use of (freq. as 2nd elem. of comb.). L16.
5 Incurring neither loss nor gain; not winning or losing. Now *Canad. dial.* E17.

3 G. GREENE He still put off the saving lie: there was always the possibility of a miracle. **4** M. PENN They were a very saving couple and had a tidy bit put by. ***labour-saving, space-saving, time-saving***, etc.

Special collocations: **saving clause** LAW a clause containing a stipulation of exemption etc. **saving grace** (*a*) CHRISTIAN THEOLOGY the redeeming grace of God; (*b*) a redeeming quality or characteristic.
■ **savingly** *adverb* M16. **savingness** *noun* (*rare*) M17.

saving /ˈseɪvɪŋ/ *preposition & conjunction.* LME.
[Prob. modification of SAVE *preposition & conjunction* after TOUCHING *preposition.*]
▶ **A** *preposition.* **1** = SAVE *preposition* 1. LME.
2 Without prejudice or offence to. LME.
▶ **B** *conjunction.* = SAVE *conjunction.* Also foll. by *that*, (rare) *for.* LME.

saviour /ˈseɪvjə/ *noun.* Also ***-or.** ME.
[Old French *sauveour* (mod. *sauveur*) from Christian Latin *salvator* (rendering Greek *sōtēr* and ult. late Hebrew *yēšūaʿ* Jesus), from late Latin *salvare* SAVE *verb.*]
1 A person who saves, preserves, or rescues a person or thing from danger, harm, etc. ME.
2 (Now **S-**.) God or esp. Christ as the being who saves humankind from sin and its consequences. Freq. ***Our Saviour, The Saviour.*** ME.
■ **saviouress** *noun* a female saviour M16. **saviourhood** *noun* the quality or fact of being a saviour M19. **saviourship** *noun* (*rare*) = SAVIOURHOOD M17.

Savi's warbler /ˈsɑːvɪz ˈwɔːblə/ *noun phr.* M19.
[Paolo *Savi* (1798–1871), Italian zoologist and geologist.]
A Eurasian warbler, *Locustella luscinioides*, which frequents reed-beds, and has plain brown plumage and a song like that of a grasshopper.

savoir /savwar/ *noun.* E19.
[French, lit. 'know'.]
Knowledge. Also *ellipt.*, = SAVOIR FAIRE, SAVOIR VIVRE.

savoir faire /savwar fɛːr/ *noun.* E19.
[French, lit. 'know how to do'.]
The instinctive ability to act suitably in any situation; tact.

savoir vivre /savwar viːvr/ *noun.* M18.
[French, lit. 'know how to live'.]
Knowledge of the world and the ways of society, ability to conduct oneself well; worldly wisdom, sophistication.

Savonarola /sav(ə)nəˈrəʊlə/ *noun.* E20.
[Girolamo *Savonarola* (1452–98), a Dominican monk known for his fierce opposition to ecclesiastic, moral, and political licence and corruption.]
1 A person regarded as having a puritanical attitude, esp. towards the arts. E20.
2 In full ***Savonarola chair.*** A kind of folding chair typical of the Italian Renaissance. E20.
■ **Savonarolan** *adjective* M20.

savonette /ˈsavɒnɛt/ *noun.* E18.
[French (now *savonnette*), dim. of *savon* soap: see -ETTE.]
Soap, esp. in the form of a ball; a ball of soap.

Savonius rotor /səˈvəʊnɪəs ˈrəʊtə/ *noun phr.* E20.
[Sigurd J. *Savonius* (fl. 1930), Finnish engineer.]
A rotor consisting of two opposed semicylindrical blades, used to measure the speed of air and water currents and as a windmill rotor for the generation of electricity.

Savonnerie /ˈsavɒnri/ *noun & adjective.* L19.
[French, lit. 'soap factory', from *savon* soap + *-erie* -ERY.]
(Designating) a hand-knotted pile carpet made in a factory established in a former soap works in 17th-cent. Paris. Also, (designating) any similar French carpet.

Times The sale will contain . . 16 antique Oriental carpets and one Savonnerie.

savor *noun, verb* see SAVOUR *noun, verb.*

savorous /ˈseɪv(ə)rəs/ *adjective. arch.* LME.
[Old French *saverous, savorous* (mod. *savoureux*) from late Latin *saporosus*, from Latin *sapor*: see SAVOUR *noun*, -OUS.]
Having an appetizing flavour or smell, pleasant-tasting. Formerly also, delightful, enjoyable.

savory /ˈseɪv(ə)ri/ *noun*[1]. ME.
[Perh. repr. (with change of intervocalic *ð* to *v*) Old English *sæþerie* from Latin *satureia.*]
A plant of the labiate genus *Satureja*; *esp.* either of two kinds grown as herbs, the annual *S. hortensis* (more fully ***summer savory***) and the perennial *S. montana* (more fully ***winter savory***), natives of southern Europe. Also, the leaves of either of these plants used as a flavouring.

savory *adjective & noun*[2] see SAVOURY *adjective & noun.*

savour /ˈseɪvə/ *noun.* Also ***-or.** ME.
[Old French (mod. *saveur*) from Latin *sapor* taste, (occas.) smell, from *sapere* have a taste: see -OUR. Cf. SAPOR.]
1 Flavour, taste, *esp.* a distinctive or characteristic one; the power of affecting the sense of taste, esp. agreeably; tastiness. Also, a touch or hint of a flavour other than the prevailing one. ME.
2 A smell, a perfume, an aroma. Now *poet. & arch.* ME. ▸**b** *fig.* Repute, estimation. Now *poet.* M16.
†**3** **a** Attractive quality, merit. ME–L15. ▸**b** Character, style, sort. E–M17.
†**4** Relish or taste for something; delight, satisfaction. ME–M16.
†**5** Perception, understanding. LME–M17.
6 Essential virtue or quality. Also, interest, power to excite. M17.

1 R. MACAULAY The sparkle and glitter of good talk and good glass, the savour of delicate food. *fig.*: *Blackwood's Magazine* To get the savour of the Mir's table talk, you must hear . . about its setting. **2** C. LAMB The nostrils of the young rogues dilated at the savour. **b** TENNYSON Mark, A name of evil savour in the land. **3b** SHAKES. *Lear* This admiration . . is much o'th'savour Of other your new pranks. **6** M. PATTISON All the savour of life is departed.

■ **savourless** *adjective* without savour; tasteless, odourless; without interest, insipid: LME. **savoursome** *adjective* (*arch.*) full of savour L16.

savour /ˈseɪvə/ *verb.* Also ***-or.** ME.
[Old & mod. French *savourer* from late Latin *saporare*, from *sapor* SAVOUR *noun.*]
▶ **I** Have a savour.
1 *verb intrans.* Of food or drink: have a particular, esp. agreeable, taste. *obsolete* exc. *Scot. dial.* ME.
2 *verb intrans.* Emit a (specified) scent or odour; smell *of. arch.* ME.
3 *verb intrans. fig.* Be agreeable or *well* pleasing (*to*). Now *rare* or *obsolete.* ME.
4 *verb intrans.* & (*rare*) *trans.* Show traces of or *of*; have some of the characteristics of or *of.* ME.

4 R. L. STEVENSON I will not say that the . . family was Poor White, because the name savours of offence.

▶ **II** Give a savour to.
†**5** *verb trans.* Flavour with salt or spice. ME–L17.
6 *verb trans.* Season, flavour; give tone or character to. *rare.* L16.
▶ **III** Perceive a savour.
7 *verb trans.* Relish, like, care for. Now *rare* or *obsolete.* ME.
†**8** *verb trans.* Perceive, apprehend. Also, experience. ME–M17.
9 *verb trans.* Taste. Now *esp.* taste with relish, dwell on the taste of; *fig.* enjoy or appreciate (an experience, sensation, etc.). LME.
10 *verb trans.* Be aware of or smell (an odour, something with an odour). *arch.* LME.

9 E. TEMPLETON The excitement which she was determined to savour to the last drop. *Daily Mail* He . . savoured the flavour with great deliberation. F. FORSYTH He . . savoured the cool of the inner room after the heat . . of the taxi.

■ **savourer** *noun* LME. **savouringly** *adverb* in a savouring manner M17.

†**savourly** *adverb.* LME.
[from SAVOUR *noun* + -LY[2].]
1 With relish or enjoyment; agreeably; keenly. LME–L17. ▸**b** Of weeping: done with passion or bitterness. M17–E18.
2 With understanding or appreciation; wisely; effectively. LME–M17.

savoury /ˈseɪv(ə)ri/ *adjective & noun.* Also ***-ory.** ME.
[Old French *savouré* tasty, fragrant, from SAVOUR *noun* + *-é* -ATE[2] (see -Y[5]); the ending was assim. to -Y[1].]
▶ **A** *adjective.* **1** Having an appetizing taste or smell. Also, having a pleasant smell, fragrant (now usu. in neg. contexts). ME.
2 *fig.* **a** Pleasant; acceptable. ME. ▸†**b** THEOLOGY. Spiritual in character; spiritually delightful or edifying. Also, holy; saintly. LME–M19.
3 Of food: having a salty or piquant taste or flavour; not sweet. M17.

1 H. KELLER The savoury odour of the meat made me hungry. **3** G. A. SALA The rice fritters and savoury soups of the Lancashire vegetarians.

▶ **B** *noun.* A savoury dish, *esp.* one served at the beginning or end of a meal as a stimulant to appetite or digestion. M17.

A. P. HERBERT She had taken in the savoury and carried . . the meat-course back to the kitchen.

■ **savourily** *adverb* (*a*) in a savoury manner, appetizingly; †(*b*) *fig.* pleasurably; appreciatively: LME. **savouriness** *noun* LME.

Savoy /səˈvɔɪ/ *noun.* L16.
[French *Savoie* a region of SE France. In sense 3 from the *Savoy* Theatre in London.]
1 In full ***Savoy cabbage.*** A variety of cabbage with puckered leaves, grown for winter use. L16.
2 **a** In full ***Savoy biscuit.*** A kind of finger-shaped sponge-biscuit. E18. ▸**b** ***Savoy cake***, a large sponge cake baked in a mould. E19.
3 ***Savoy opera, Savoy operetta***, any of the Gilbert and Sullivan operas originally presented in the Savoy Theatre by the D'Oyly Carte company. L19.

Savoyard /səˈvɔɪɑːd, savɔɪˈɑːd/ *noun & adjective.* E17.
[French In senses A.1, B. from French *Savoie* (see prec.), in senses A.2, 3 from London place-names: see -ARD.]
▶ **A** *noun.* **1** A native or inhabitant of Savoy in France. E17.
2 *Hist.* A resident of the precinct of the Savoy Palace in London, which formerly had the right of sanctuary. *rare.* L17.
3 A member of the D'Oyly Carte company which originally presented Gilbert and Sullivan operas at the Savoy theatre in London. Also, a devotee of these operas. Cf. SAVOY 3. L19.
▶ **B** *adjective.* Of or belonging to Savoy in France or its inhabitants. M18.

savvy /ˈsavi/ *noun, verb, & adjective. slang.* L18.
[Orig. black & pidgin English after Spanish *sabe usted* you know. Cf. SABE.]
▶ **A** *noun.* Common sense, practical intelligence, shrewdness. L18.
▶ **B** *verb trans. & intrans.* Know; understand, comprehend. Freq. in interrog. following an explanation. L18.

X. HERBERT I want a spear . . A spe-ar or something, savvy? A. WARNER I savvied right enough that the petrol tank would keep me afloat.

▶ **C** *adjective.* Having or demonstrating common sense; knowledgeable, experienced; knowing, shrewd. Chiefly *US.* E20.

Scientific American Savvy customers, who prize performance, price and quick delivery. *New York Times* His success has . . been tied to a savvy choice of location. *Independent* The savviest cultural phenomenon in movie history.

saw /sɔː/ *noun*[1].
[Old English *saga* = Middle Low German, Middle Dutch *sage* (Dutch *zaag*), Old High German *saga* Old Norse *sǫg*, from Germanic.]
1 A hand tool with a toothed metal blade used to cut wood or other material by means of a to-and-fro motion; any of a variety of hand-operated or power-driven tools or devices used to cut through solid material by the continuous or to-and-fro motion of the edge of a blade, disc,

band, etc. OE. ▸**b** A flexible saw used as a musical instrument, played with a bow; a musical saw. M20.

2 *ZOOLOGY.* A serrated part or organ; *spec.* the toothed snout of a sawfish. M17.

3 *CARDS.* = ***cross-ruff*** (a) s.v. CROSS-. Cf. SEE-SAW *noun* 2b. M18.

1 ***band-saw***, ***bow-saw***, ***buzz-saw***, ***chain-saw***, ***circular saw***, ***compass-saw***, ***drag-saw***, ***fretsaw***, ***hacksaw***, ***handsaw***, ***keyhole saw***, ***lock-saw***, ***pit-saw***, ***ripsaw***, ***tenon saw***, etc. †**draw the saw of contention**, †**draw the saw of controversy**, †**draw the saw** keep up a fruitless dispute.

Comb.: **sawbench** a circular saw with a bench to support the material and advance it to the saw; **sawbill** any of various birds with serrated bills; *esp.* a merganser or other bird of the genus *Mergus*; **saw-billed** *adjective* having a serrated bill; **saw-doctor** (*a*) a machine for giving a saw a serrated edge; (*b*) a person responsible for maintaining saws; **saw-edged** *adjective* having a serrated edge like a saw; **saw-file**: for sharpening the teeth of saws; **sawfish** any of various cartilaginous fishes of the family Pristidae, which have a long flattened snout with toothlike projections along each edge; **sawfly** any of various hymenopteran insects mainly of the superfamily Tenthredinoidea, members of which have a serrated ovipositor, lack a constriction between the thorax and abdomen, and include many kinds whose larvae are injurious to plants; **saw-frame** the frame in which a saw-blade is held taut; **saw-gate** (*a*) [GATE *noun*[1]] a hole bored to allow the entrance of a fretsaw; (formerly) the channel cut by a saw; (*b*) [GATE *noun*[2]] = ***saw-frame*** above; **saw-gin** a cotton gin in which the fibres are separated by revolving toothed discs; **saw-grass** *US* either of two sedges, *Cladium mariscus* and *C. jamaicense*, noted for their sharp-edged leaves; **saw-handle** (*a*) the handle of a saw; †(*b*) *slang* a pistol (with a handle like that of a saw); **saw-horse** a frame or trestle for supporting wood that is being sawn; **saw-log** a (felled) tree-trunk suitable for cutting up into timber; **saw palmetto** either of two small palms of the southern US with toothed petiole margins, *Serenoa repens* and *Acoelorrhaphe wrightii*; **saw-pit** a pit in the ground in which the lower of two people working a pit-saw stands; **saw-scaled viper** a small venomous rough-scaled viper of the genus *Echis*, esp. *E. carinatus* of Africa and southern Asia; **saw-set** a tool for wrenching sawteeth in alternate directions to allow the saw to work freely; **saw-shark** any member of the family Pristiophoridae of small sharks with a sawlike flattened snout, found in Indo-Pacific seas; **saw-sharpener** (*a*) a person who sharpens saws; (*b*) *dial.* [from a characteristic grating call] the great tit, *Parus major*; **saw-timber**: suitable for sawing into boards or planks; **sawtooth** *noun & adjective* (*a*) *noun* a tooth of or like that of a saw, a serration; *ellipt.* a sawtooth waveform etc.; (*b*) *adjective* having a serrated profile; (of a roof) with a serrated profile incorporating windows in the steeper (usu. sunward-facing) sides; *ELECTRONICS* designating, pertaining to, or having a waveform showing a repeated slow linear rise and rapid linear fall, or the reverse; **saw-whet (owl)** a small brown American owl of the genus *Aegolius* with a characteristic grating call, esp. *A. acadicus* of eastern N. America; **saw-wort** a plant of the composite family, *Serratula tinctoria*, of pastures, woods, etc., with sharp-toothed leaves and purple flower-heads; ***alpine saw-wort***, a related mountain plant, *Saussurea alpina*; **saw-wrest** = ***saw-set*** above.

■ **sawlike** *adjective* resembling (that or those of) a saw E17.

saw /sɔː/ *noun*[2].

[Old English *sagu* = Old Frisian *sege*, Middle Low German, Middle Dutch *sage*, Old High German *saga* (German *Sage*), Old Norse SAGA *noun*[2], from Germanic, from base of SAY *verb*[1].]

†**1** A saying; discourse; speech. OE–E17.

†**2** A story, a tale, a recital. Only in ME.

†**3** A decree, a command. ME–L16.

4 A pithy saying; a maxim, a proverb. Freq. in ***old saw***. ME.

saw /sɔː/ *verb*[1]. Pa. t. **sawed**; pa. pple **sawed**, **sawn** /sɔːn/. ME.

[from SAW *noun*[1].]

▸ **I** *verb trans.* **1** Cut with a saw or with a to-and-fro action like that of a saw. ME.

2 Make or form by cutting (as) with a saw. M16.

3 Cause to move like a saw. E19.

📖 **1** J. A. FROUDE Trees were cut down and sawn into planks. G. VIDAL Sawing . . bacon in half with a blunt knife. D. JACOBSON He took out a knife . . and threatened to saw my head off. **saw gourds** *US slang* snore loudly. **saw the air** gesticulate with the hands as if sawing something invisible. **saw wood** *fig.* (*US slang*) (*a*) attend to one's own affairs, continue working steadily; (*b*) = ***saw gourds*** above. **2** *fig.*: J. TYNDALL This wonderful fissure . . sawn through the mountain by the waters of the Tamina.

▸ **II** *verb intrans.* **4** Use a saw; cut something (as) with a saw. ME.

5 Admit of being cut with a saw. E18.

6 Move something to and fro like a saw; *esp.* play a stringed instrument with a bow (freq. foll. by *away (at)*). M18.

📖 **4** *fig.*: DICKENS The grating wind sawed rather than blew. **6** A. CARTER The pit band . . began to saw away as best it could.

■ **sawed** *ppl adjective* (*a*) = SAWN *adjective*; (*b*) serrated: M16. **sawer** *noun* (now *rare*) a person who saws, a sawyer ME. **sawing** *noun* (*a*) the action of the verb; an instance of this; ***plain sawing***: see PLAIN *adjective*[1] & *adverb*; (*b*) in *pl.* (now only *Scot.*), sawdust: LME. **sawing** *ppl adjective* that saws; (of sound) rasping, harsh: LME. **sawn** *ppl adjective* that has undergone the operation of sawing; ***sawn-off*** (*a*) cut off or short by sawing; (of a shotgun) with a specially shortened barrel to make handling easier and give a wider field of fire; (*b*) *colloq.* (of a person etc.) short, undersized: M16.

saw *verb*[2] *pa. t.* of SEE *verb*.

sawah /ˈsɑːwə/ *noun.* Also ***sawa***. L18.

[Malay.]

In Malaysia and Indonesia: an irrigated rice-field.

sawbones /ˈsɔːbəʊnz/ *noun. slang.* M19.

[from SAW *verb*[1] + BONE *noun* + -S[1].]

(A name for) a surgeon or a doctor.

sawbuck /ˈsɔːbʌk/ *noun. US.* M19.

[Dutch *zaagbok*, formed as SAW *noun*[1] + BUCK *noun*[1]. Cf. BUCK *noun*[7].]

1 A saw-horse. Cf. BUCK *noun*[7] 1. M19. ▸**b** More fully ***sawbuck pack-saddle***, ***sawbuck saddle***. A pack-saddle shaped like a saw-horse. L19.

2 [With allus. to the X-shaped ends of a saw-horse.] Ten dollars; a ten-dollar note. Also, a ten-year prison sentence. *slang.* M19.

Sawbwa /ˈsɔːbwɑː/ *noun.* E19.

[Burmese.]

Hist. The hereditary ruler of a Shan state in eastern Burma (Myanmar).

sawder /ˈsɔːdə/ *noun & verb. colloq.* Now *rare* or *obsolete.* M19.

[App. var. of SOLDER.]

▸ **A** *noun.* In full ***soft sawder***. Flattery, blarney. M19.

▸ **B** *verb trans.* Flatter, butter up. M19.

sawdust /ˈsɔːdʌst/ *noun & verb.* E16.

[from SAW *noun*[1] + DUST *noun*.]

▸ **A** *noun.* Wood in a state of small particles, produced (as) in sawing; such material as typically used to cover the floor of a circus ring, public house, etc., or (formerly) as stuffing for dolls etc. E16.

spit and sawdust: see SPIT *noun*[2].

▸ **B** *verb trans.* Cover, sprinkle, or strew with sawdust. E19.

■ **sawdusty** *adjective* full of or covered in sawdust; savouring of or resembling sawdust; of the nature of sawdust: M19.

sawmill /ˈsɔːmɪl/ *noun.* M16.

[from SAW *noun*[1] + MILL *noun*[1].]

A factory in which wood is sawn into planks, boards, etc., by machinery.

■ **sawmiller** *noun* a person who owns or runs a sawmill M19. **sawmilling** *noun* the business of sawing wood in a sawmill E20.

sawn *pa. pple, ppl adjective* see SAW *verb*[1].

sawney /ˈsɔːni/ *noun, adjective, & verb. colloq.* L17.

[Local var. of SANDY *noun*.]

▸ **A** *noun.* **1** A simpleton, a fool. L17.

2 (Freq. **S-**.) (A nickname for) a Scotsman. *derog.* E18.

3 Bacon. Now *rare* or *obsolete.* E19.

▸ **B** *adjective.* Foolish, stupid; foolishly sentimental. E19.

▸ **C** *verb intrans.* Play the fool; wheedle. Now *rare.* E19.

sawyer /ˈsɔːjə/ *noun.* ME.

[from SAW *noun*[1] + -YER. Cf. SAWER.]

1 A worker whose business is to saw timber. ME.

2 Any of various large longhorn beetles of the genus *Monochamus*, the larvae of which bore in the wood of conifers. Also (esp. *NZ*), a wood-boring bush-cricket. L18

3 An uprooted tree held fast by one end in a river. *US.* L18.

sax /saks/ *noun*[1]. In sense 1 also **seax** /ˈsiːaks/; in sense 2 also **zax** /zaks/.

[Old English *seax*, Old Frisian *sax*, Old Saxon, Old High German *sahs*, Old Norse *sax*, from Germanic, from Indo-European base of Latin *secare* to cut.]

1 *Hist.* A (Saxon) knife, short sword, or dagger. OE.

2 A slater's chopper, with a point for making nail-holes. M17.

sax /saks/ *noun*[2]. *colloq.* E20.

[Abbreviation.]

A saxophone; a saxophonist.

alto sax, ***tenor sax***, etc.

Comb.: **saxman** a (male) saxophonist.

■ **saxist** *noun* a saxophonist M20.

saxatile /ˈsaksətʌɪl, -tɪl/ *adjective.* M17.

[French, or Latin *saxatilis*, from *saxum* rock, stone: see -ATILE.]

ZOOLOGY & BOTANY. Living or growing on or among rocks.

saxaul /ˈsaksɔːl/ *noun.* L19.

[Prob. name of the plant in Turkestan.]

A shrubby plant, *Haloxylon ammodendron*, of the steppes of Asia.

saxboard /ˈsaksbɔːd/ *noun.* M19.

[Prob. from SAX *noun*[1] + BOARD *noun*: cf. Old Norse use of *sax* = gunwale near the prow.]

NAUTICAL. The uppermost strake of an open boat's side.

Saxe /saks/ *adjective & noun.* With ref. to colour, usu. **s-**. M19.

[French from German *Sachsen* Saxony.]

▸ **A** *adjective.* From Saxony, Saxon. Also, saxe blue in colour. M19.

Saxe blue (of) a light blue colour with a greyish tinge, as produced by Saxony blue. **Saxe paper** an albuminized paper formerly used in photography.

▸ **B** *noun.* Saxe paper; saxe blue. M19.

saxeous /ˈsaksɪəs/ *adjective. rare.* L17.

[from Latin *saxeus*, from *saxum* rock, stone: see -OUS.]

Of stone, stony.

saxhorn /ˈsakshɔːn/ *noun.* M19.

[from Charles Joseph *Sax* (1791–1865) and his son Antoine Joseph 'Adolphe' *Sax* (1814–94), Belgian instrument-makers + HORN *noun*.]

Any of a group of valved brass wind instruments with a tube of conical bore.

saxicavous /sakˈsɪkəvəs/ *adjective. rare.* M19.

[from mod. Latin *saxicavus*, from *saxum* rock, stone + *cavare* to hollow: see -OUS.]

ZOOLOGY. Of a mollusc: that hollows out rock or stone.

saxicoline /sakˈsɪk(ə)lʌɪn/ *adjective.* L19.

[from mod. Latin *saxicola*, from *saxum* rock, stone + *colere* inhabit: see -INE[1].]

ZOOLOGY. Living among rocks; saxatile.

saxicolous /sakˈsɪk(ə)ləs/ *adjective.* M19.

[from mod. Latin *saxicola*: see prec., -COLOUS.]

BOTANY. Of a plant, esp. a lichen: growing on rocks. Cf. CORTICOLOUS.

saxifrage /ˈsaksɪfreɪdʒ/ *noun.* LME.

[Old & mod. French, or late Latin *saxifraga* (sc. *herba* plant), from *saxum* rock + *frag-* base of *frangere* to break, prob. in allus. to the habitat.]

1 Any of numerous freq. dwarf and rosette-forming plants with panicles of esp. white flowers constituting the genus *Saxifraga* (family Saxifragaceae), many of which grow in the crevices of (esp. alpine) rocks. LME.

2 With specifying word: any of several plants of other genera or families. M16.

2 ***burnet saxifrage***, ***golden saxifrage***, ***pepper saxifrage***.

■ **saxifraˈgaceous** *adjective* of or pertaining to the family Saxifragaceae M19.

saxitoxin /saksɪˈtɒksɪn/ *noun.* M20.

[from mod. Latin *Saxi(domus* a genus of clams (from Latin *saxum* rock, stone + *domus* home) + TOXIN.]

BIOLOGY. A toxic alkaloid which is synthesized by the dinoflagellates responsible for red tides and accumulates in molluscs which feed on these dinoflagellates.

Saxo- /ˈsaksəʊ/ *combining form.* L18.

[from SAXON: see -O-.]

Forming adjectives with the sense 'Saxon and —', as ***Saxo-Norman***.

Saxon /ˈsaks(ə)n/ *noun & adjective.* ME.

[Old & mod. French from Latin *Saxo(n-)*, pl. *Saxones* = Greek *Saxones* from West Germanic (whence Old English pl. *Seaxan*, *Seaxe*, Old Saxon, Old High German *Sahso*, German *Sachse*), perh. from base of SAX *noun*[1]. Cf. FRANK *noun*[1].]

▸ **A** *noun.* **1** A member of a Germanic people living in northern Germany in the early Christian era, of which one portion conquered and occupied parts of southern Britain in the 5th and 6th cents.; an Anglo-Saxon; *loosely* a member of any of the Germanic peoples that settled in Britain. ME. ▸**b** An English person who is presumed to be of Saxon descent; (esp. among Celtic speakers) an English person as distinct from a Welsh or Irish person, a Lowland Scot as distinct from a Highlander, (cf. SASSENACH). Also, any person of English or British descent, esp. as opp. to one of Latin descent. E19.

2 The language of the Saxons; Anglo-Saxon, Old English. LME.

3 A native or inhabitant of Saxony in Germany. M18.

4 A kind of firework. Now *rare* or *obsolete.* M19.

5 A noctuid moth, *Hyppa rectilinea*. M19.

▸ **B** *adjective.* **1** Designating, of, or pertaining to the Saxons or their language; Anglo-Saxon. LME. ▸**b** *ARCHITECTURE.* Designating, of, or pertaining to the Romanesque style used in England in the Saxon period. E18. ▸**c** Esp. among Celtic speakers: English as opp. to Welsh, Irish, or Gaelic. Also, of English or British descent, esp. as opp. to Latin. L18.

2 Of or pertaining to Saxony in Germany. M17.

Phrases: ***Norman Saxon***: see NORMAN *adjective* 1. **Old Saxon** a member of, of or pertaining to, the Saxon peoples who remained in Germany, as opp. to an Anglo-Saxon; (of) the language of the Old Saxons, esp. as exemplified in 9th-cent. poetry; **Saxon blue** = ***Saxony blue*** s.v. SAXONY *adjective*. **Saxon green** cobalt green.

■ **Saxondom** *noun* = ANGLO-SAXONDOM M19. **Saxonish** *adjective* of the Saxons; resembling what is Saxon: M16. **Saxonism** *noun* = ANGLO-SAXONISM L18. **Saxonist** *noun* (*a*) an expert in or student of Anglo-Saxon or the Anglo-Saxons; (*b*) an advocate of the use of English words of purely Anglo-Saxon origin: L16. **Saxonize** *verb trans. & intrans.* make or become Saxon or Anglo-Saxon E19. **Saxonly** *adverb* in a Saxon manner; in the Saxon tongue: LME.

Saxonian /sakˈsəʊnɪən/ *noun & adjective. rare.* L16.

[from late Latin *Saxonia* SAXONY + -AN.]

▸† **A** *noun.* A Protestant of Saxony. Only in L16.

▸ **B** *adjective.* Of Saxony. M18.

Saxonic /sakˈsɒnɪk/ *adjective.* M17.

[medieval Latin *Saxonicus*, from Latin *Saxon-*: see SAXON, -IC.]

1 Of or pertaining to Saxony. *rare.* M17.

2 Anglo-Saxon. L17.

■ †**Saxonical** *adjective* (*rare*) = SAXONIC L16–E17. **Saxonically** *adverb* (*rare*) in a Saxonic manner E17.

Saxony /ˈsaks(ə)ni/ *adjective & noun.* M19.
[A region of Germany (German *Sachsen*), formerly a kingdom, from late Latin *Saxonia*, from Latin *Saxon-* SAXON: see -Y³.]
▶ **A** *adjective.* Designating things from or originating in Saxony, esp. (material, a garment, etc., made from) a fine kind of wool or a similar artificial material. M19.
Saxony blue a solution of indigo in concentrated sulphuric acid, formerly used as a dye.
▶ **B** *noun.* Saxony wool; cloth or carpet material made from this. M19.

saxophone /ˈsaksəfəʊn/ *noun.* M19.
[from Adolphe *Sax* (see SAXHORN) + -O- + -PHONE.]
1 A keyed brass wind instrument with a reed mouthpiece, made in several sizes and registers, used esp. in jazz and popular music. M19.
2 A person who plays the saxophone; a saxophonist. E20.
1 *soprano saxophone*, *alto saxophone*, *tenor saxophone*, etc.
■ **saxophonic** /saksəˈfɒnɪk/ *adjective* E20. **saxophonist** /sakˈsɒf(ə)nɪst, saksəˈfəʊnɪst/ *noun* a person who plays the saxophone M19.

saxotromba /ˈsaksətrɒmbə/ *noun. obsolete* exc. *Hist.* M19.
[formed as prec. + Italian *tromba* trumpet.]
A brass wind instrument like a saxhorn but with a more cylindrical bore.

say /seɪ/ *noun¹ & adjective.* ME.
[Old & mod. French *saie* from Latin *saga* collect. pl. (used as sing.) of *sagum* coarse woollen blanket, military cloak.]
▶ **A** *noun.* A cloth of fine texture resembling serge, orig. containing silk, now usu. of wool. ME.
▶ **B** *attrib.* or as *adjective.* Made of this material. M16.

†**say** *noun².* ME.
[Aphet. from ASSAY *noun.*]
1 The trial or testing of virtue, fitness, etc. Latterly only *Scot.*, a probation. Cf. ASSAY *noun* 1. ME–M18. ▸**b** *HUNTING.* Testing of the fatness of a game animal. Also, a cut made in doing this. E17–M19.
2 The testing of food by taste or smell; *esp.* the tasting of food or drink before it is presented to a king, noble, etc. LME–L17.
3 An attempt; a feat. Cf. ASSAY *noun* 8. LME–M17.
4 The assaying of metals or ores. Also, temper of metal. Cf. ASSAY *noun* 2. L16–M17.

say /seɪ/ *noun³.* Long *obsolete* exc. *Scot.* LME.
[Old Norse *sár* cask. See also SOE.]
A bucket or tub, *esp.* one carried by two people using a pole.

say /seɪ/ *noun⁴.* L16.
[from SAY *verb¹.*]
1 What a person says; words as opp. to actions. Also, a remark. Now *poet. & dial.* L16.
2 A current saying, a proverb, a saw. *obsolete* exc. *Scot.* E17.
3 One's stated opinion; what one has intended to say; an opportunity for giving one's opinion, the power to influence a decision, the right to be consulted, (*in, on, over* a matter). E17.
4 A talk *to* or *with* a person. Now *dial.* L18.

📖 **3** *Sounds* The GLC have total say in who appears . . in London. A. BURGESS He says his say and then shuts up. *City Limits* If you give people a chance to have their say, ideas will come. **have the say** (orig. *US*) be in control or command.

say /seɪ/ *verb¹.* Pa. t. & pple **said** /sɛd/ (see also SAID *ppl adjective*). 2 sing. pres. (*arch.*) **sayest** /ˈseɪɪst/; 3 sing. pres. **says** /sɛz/, (*arch.*) **saith** /sɛθ, seɪθ/.
[Old English *secgan* = Old Frisian *sega*, *sedza*, Old Saxon *seggian* (Dutch *zeggen*), Old High German *sagēn* (German *sagen*), Old Norse *segja*, from Germanic.]
▶ **I** *verb trans.* **1** With simple obj. or direct speech: utter, pronounce, or speak (a word, words, an articulate sound); offer as a remark, put forward. Also, (of a book, letter, notice, author, etc.) state in the words specified, have as wording. OE. ▸†**b** In *pass.* Of a word: be derived (*of*). ME–L16. ▸**c** Of an object: represent esp. visually, display (a certain message); *esp.* (of a clock etc.) show (a certain time etc.). M20.
2 With clause, or with simple or pronominal obj.: declare or state in spoken words (a fact, thought, opinion, intention, etc.); promise, predict; *transf.* convey, communicate, mean, indicate. (Foll. by *to*; orig. with dative obj.) OE. ▸**b** Of a sum of money: support a specified bet or wager (*that*). *colloq.* M20. ▸**c** Of a thing: indicate by its very appearance, inherently suggest. *colloq.* L20.
3 †**a** Denote, signify. Latterly only *is to say*, *are to say*, etc. OE–E17. ▸†**b** With compl.: speak of, call, or describe (by a specified name or designation). Usu. in *pass.* LME–L17. ▸**c** In *pass.* with inf.: be alleged or reported; be described or referred to. E17.
4 †**a** With inf. or subjunctive clause, and dative obj.: tell (a person) to do something. OE–M16. ▸**b** In *pass.* Be ruled, submit to command or advice. Now *dial.* L16. ▸**c** With inf., and indirect obj. understood or introduced by *for*: tell someone to do something, say that one should do something. *colloq.* E20.
5 With clause: declare or make known *who, what, how, whether*, etc. OE. ▸**b** With clause: form and give an opinion, judge, decide. E18.
†**6** Deliver (a speech etc.), relate (a story); express (thanks, one's opinion, etc.); tell (truth, lies). OE–M17.
†**7** Speak of, enumerate, describe. Only in ME.
8 Recite or repeat (something of set form); speak the words of (a prayer, mass, etc.); recite from memory. ME.
9 In *imper.* with simple word or clause or parenthetically: select, assume, suppose; take (a number, description, etc.) as near enough for one's purpose. L16.

📖 **1** AV *Judg.* 12:6 Then said they vnto him, Say now, Shibboleth: and he said Sibboleth. A. H. RICE I don't want people to see you together; it makes them say things. H. G. WELLS Sit down, everyone . . . Who says steak-and-kidney pie? J. CONRAD I have said no word to him that was not strictly true. V. WOOLF 'Merchant of this city,' the tombstone said. E. BOWEN 'Fred,' she said, 'it was not as simple as that'. **c** W. J. BURLEY The perpetual calendar said Wednesday August 25th. **2** AV *Luke* 13:17 And when hee had said these things, all his adversaries were ashamed. K. H. DIGBY Gibbon says . . the French monarchy was created by the bishops. DICKENS The fever has left him, and the doctor says he will soon mend. GEO. ELIOT Your kindness makes you say I'm useful to you. A. HELPS Mauleverer only said that to tease you. H. JAMES Moments in life when even Beethoven has nothing to say to us. D. LESSING The set of his shoulders said that he was listening, so she went on. C. ISHERWOOD In a dialogue, you can say absolutely anything. A. DIMENT The light meter said I was okay on F2.8 at a thirtieth. **b** W. TUCKER A dollar says you won't come back. **c** *New Scientist* A lower second says lack of skill and uncreative. **3a** R. COPLAND Pigneum in Arabyke is to saye the ars hole. **b** P. BAYNE Thus all things are said created in or by Christ. **c** T. H. HUXLEY Rocks which thus allow water to filter through them are said to be permeable. L. P. HARTLEY She's said to be very fond of children. M. HOLROYD A . . witch whose salad dressings were said to contain spells. **4a** LD BERNERS Say vnto hym that he drynke to you in the name of good peace. **c** W. DENLINGER Without asking the price, the woman said to buy the dog. *Times* Father said for Chris to take one of the lanterns. **5** MILTON Say Goddess, what ensu'd. *Sunday Times* Hypothetical . . situations, such as . . not saying when you've been given too much change. **b** POPE Hard to say, if greater want of skill Appear in writing or in judging ill. **8** B. MOORE The Mass was said in Latin. L. P. WILKINSON Every boy . . had to learn a piece of poetry and say it in early school. **9** SHAKES. *Twel. N.* Say I do speak with her . . what then? DICKENS Early in the week, or say Wednesday. W. FAULKNER A lay brother in a twelfth-century monastery—a gardener, a pruner of vines, say. F. HOYLE If even a small proportion were retained, say one per cent.

▶ **II** *verb intrans.* **10** *absol.* or with adverbial compl.: make an utterance, speak, talk; say something unspecified or understood contextually. Freq. in phrs. (see below). OE. ▸†**b** Tell *of* something; speak *for* or *against*. OE–E18. ▸†**c** Recite a prayer, say mass etc. Freq. contrasted with *sing.* LME–L18.
11 a In *imper.*, introducing a question: tell me, tell us. (Orig. foll. by dative.) Now *poet.* ME. ▸**b** *interjection.* Expr. surprise, admiration, protest, etc., or drawing attention to one's next utterance (cf. *I say* below). *N. Amer.* M19.

📖 **10** DRYDEN If Fame say true, The wretched Swain his Sorrows did renew. SMOLLETT So saying, he drew his long rapier. B. JOWETT Be persuaded by me, and do as I say. A. P. HERBERT Ernest, as they say, 'saw red.' **c** BURKE Those who neither sing nor say. **11a** SHAKES. *Lear* Say, how is that? A. E. HOUSMAN Say, lad, have you things to do? **b** J. LONDON The galley stove kept going . . and hot coffee—say! B. SCHULBERG 'Say, I didn't expect all *this*,' the dope said.

Phrases: ***do you mean to say that —?***: see MEAN *verb¹*. **have nothing to say for oneself** (*a*) be unable to put forward anything as a justification or excuse for one's conduct; (*b*) be habitually reticent or lacking vivacity. **have nothing to say to** have no dealings with, have no bearing on. ***hear say***: see HEAR *verb*. **how say you?** *LAW* how do you find? (requesting the jury to give its verdict). **I'll say (so)**: expr. strong agreement or enthusiastic assent. ***I must say***: see MUST *aux. verb¹*. **I say** *interjection* expr. surprise, admiration, protest, etc., or drawing attention to one's next utterance (*I say, I say, I say*, a standard formula used to introduce a joke). **it is said**, **it was said**, etc., the rumour or general report is, was, etc. (*that*), people say, said, etc. (*that*). **it says** a (specified or understood) book or other source says (*that*). ***needless to say***: see NEEDLESS *adjective*. **not to say** and indeed, or possibly even. **say a lot for** = *say much for* below. **say a MOUTHFUL**. **say it with** — [after *say it with flowers*, an advertising slogan of the Society of American Florists] express one's feelings, make one's point, etc., by the use of —. **say little for** be little to the credit of. **say much for** be much to the credit of. ***say no***: see NO *noun¹* 2. **say on** in *imper.*, say what you wish to say. ***say one's beads***: see BEAD *noun*. **say one thing for** = *say that for* below. **say out** (*a*) say openly; †(*b*) finish saying, say to the end. **say over** repeat from memory. **says I**, **says he**, etc. *non-standard* I, he, etc., said. **says you**: expr. doubt about or rejection of the remark of a previous speaker (cf. SEZ). **say that for** concede the previous or following statement as one point in favour of. ***say the truth***: see TRUTH *noun*. ***say the word***: see WORD *noun*. ***say uncle***: see UNCLE *noun*. ***say when***: see WHEN *conjunction*. ***say yes***: see YES *noun*. **so to say** = *so to speak* s.v. SPEAK *verb*. ***suffice it to say***: see SUFFICE 1. ***THAT is to say***. ***THAT said***. ***the hell you say***: see HELL *noun*. **they say** it is rumoured or generally reported (*that*). ***to say nothing of***: see NOTHING *pronoun & noun*. ***to say the least (of it)***: see LEAST. **what do you say to —?**, **what would you say to —?** how would you like —?, how would — suit you? **when all is said and done** after all, in the long run, nevertheless. **you can say that again** *interjection* expr. strong agreement or assent. ***you don't mean to say that —?***: see MEAN *verb¹*. **you don't say (so)**: expr. surprise, disbelief, etc. **you said it**, **you've said it**: expr. strong agreement or assent.
■ **sayable** *adjective & noun* (*a*) *adjective* able to be said; (*b*) *noun* (a word or words) that can be said: M19.

†**say** *verb² trans.* ME.
[Aphet. from ASSAY *verb.*]
1 Put to the proof, test the quality or purity of; find out about. ME–M19.
2 *verb intrans.* Apply or set oneself *to do*. ME–L18.
3 Attempt, try to do. M16–E17.

sayall *noun* var. of SEYAL.

SAYE *abbreviation.*
Save-as-you-earn.

sayer /ˈseɪə/ *noun¹.* ME.
[from SAY *verb¹* + -ER¹.]
†**1** A reciter, a poet, a narrator. ME–E19.
2 A person who says something. Formerly also, a person who speaks in a specified manner (cf. SOOTHSAYER). LME.

sayer /ˈseɪə/ *noun².* Long *obsolete* exc. *Hist.* LME.
[Aphet.]
An assayer.

sayest *verb* see SAY *verb¹*.

saying /ˈseɪɪŋ/ *noun.* ME.
[from SAY *verb¹* + -ING¹.]
1 The action of SAY *verb¹*; utterance, enunciation; recitation. ME.
2 A thing said; *esp.* a thing said often or by a well-known person; an adage, a proverb, a maxim; a quotation. ME.

📖 **1** J. HEYWOOD Saying and doying, are twoo thinges, we say. I. MURDOCH Daily tasks of a priestly kind like the saying of a liturgy. **go without saying** be too well known or obvious to need mention. **there is no saying** it is impossible to know. **2** G. SAYER Such sayings as: 'Resist not evil.' **as the saying goes**, **as the saying is**: used to accompany a proverb or cliché.

sayonara /sʌɪəˈnɑːrə/ *interjection & noun.* L19.
[Japanese, lit. 'if it be so'.]
(The Japanese word for) goodbye.

says *verb* see SAY *verb¹*.

Say's law /ˈseɪz lɔː/ *noun phr.* M20.
[Jean Baptiste *Say* (1767–1832), French economist.]
ECONOMICS. The proposition that supply creates its own demand.

say-so /ˈseɪsəʊ/ *noun. colloq.* M17.
[from SAY *verb¹* + SO *adverb.*]
A person's mere word or affirmation; an arbitrary assertion; an authoritative decision; authority to make a decision, a voice in a decision.

📖 O. WISTER He was the cook that had the say-so in New York. J. LE CARRÉ They insisted on Kurtz's say-so before they went ahead. P. BARKER I don't chastise my lads on anybody else's say-so.

say-well /ˈseɪwɛl/ *noun. obsolete* exc. *dial.* LME.
[from SAY *verb¹* + WELL *adverb.*]
The use of fair words; virtuous or approving speech; verbal commendation. Freq. personified.

sayyid /ˈseɪjɪd/ *noun.* Also **saiyid**, **syed**, & other vars., **S-**. M17.
[Arab. = lord, prince.]
(A title of respect for) a Muslim claiming descent from Muhammad through Husain, the prophet's elder grandson. Also used, in Muslim countries, as a respectful form of address.

saz /saz/ *noun.* L19.
[Turkish from Persian *sāz* musical instrument.]
A stringed instrument similar to the tamboura, found in Turkey, N. Africa, and the Near East.

saza /ˈsaza/ *noun.* M20.
[Luganda *-saza.*]
In Uganda: an administrative area; a county.

Sazarac /ˈsazərak/ *noun.* Chiefly *US.* Also **Sazerac.** M19.
[Origin unkn.]
A cocktail consisting of bourbon, pernod or absinthe, bitters, and syrup, usu. with a slice of lemon. Also ***Sazarac cocktail***.

Sb *symbol.*
[Latin *stibium.*]
CHEMISTRY. Antimony.

SBA *abbreviation. US.*
Small Business Administration.

S-bahn /ˈɛsbaːn/ *noun.* M20.
[German, abbreviation of (*Stadt*) *Schnellbahn* (urban) fast railway.]
In some German cities, a fast (sub)urban railway line or system.

sbirro /'zbirro/ *noun*. Now *derog*. exc. *Hist*. Pl. **-rri** /-rri/. **M17.**
[Italian, now colloq.]
An Italian police officer.

'sblood /zblʌd/ *interjection. arch.* **L16.**
[from 'S- + BLOOD *noun*.]
God's blood!: an oath or forcible exclamation.

SBM *abbreviation.*
Single buoy mooring.

SBN *abbreviation.*
Hist. Standard book number (now **ISBN**).

'sbodikins /'zbɒdɪkɪnz/ *interjection. arch.* **L17.**
[from 'S- + pl. of BODIKIN.]
God's bodikins!: an oath.

SBR *abbreviation.*
Styrene-butadiene rubber.

SBS *abbreviation.*
Special Boat Service.

'sbud /zbʌd/ *interjection. arch.* Also **sbuds** /zbʌdz/. **L17.**
[Perh. alt. of 'SBLOOD.]
= 'SBLOOD.

SC *abbreviation.*
1 South Carolina.
2 Special constable.

Sc *symbol.*
CHEMISTRY. Scandium.

sc. *abbreviation.*
Scilicet (= that is to say).

s.c. *abbreviation.*
TYPOGRAPHY. Small capital(s).

scab /skab/ *noun & adjective.* **ME.**
[Old Norse *skabb* (Old Swedish *skabber*, Swedish *skabb*, (O)Da. *skab*) = Old English *sċeabb* (see SHAB *noun*). Its application to persons may have been due partly to Middle Dutch *schabbe* slut, scold.]
▶ **A** *noun*. †**1** A skin disease in which pustules or scales are formed; occas. *spec*., scabies, ringworm, or syphilis. **ME–L18.**
2 a A cutaneous disease in animals; itch, mange; *esp.* (more fully ***sheep scab***) an intensely itching disease caused in sheep by the parasitic mite *Psoroptes communis*. **LME.** ▸**b** Any of several fungal plant diseases causing rough patches, esp. in apples and potatoes. **M18.**
3 The protective crust which forms over a wound or sore during healing. **LME.** ▸**b** *FOUNDING.* A lump or blister on an iron casting caused by erosion of the wall of the mould. **L19.**
4 a A mean or contemptible person; a scoundrel. *colloq. derog.* **L16.** ▸**b** A worker who refuses to join a trade union; a person who refuses to join a strike or who takes over the work of a striker, a blackleg. *colloq. derog.* **L18.**
Comb.: **scab-mite** *US* the itch-mite, *Sarcoptes scabiei*; **scabweed** *NZ* a mat-forming downy plant of the composite family, *Raoulia australis*, allied to the cudweeds.
▶ **B** *attrib.* or as *adjective*. Working as a scab or blackleg; produced by or employing scabs. *colloq. derog.* **M19.**

> 📖 *Socialist Review* The Labour Press . . cannot descend to scab printing.

scab /skab/ *verb*. Infl. **-bb-**. **M17.**
[from the noun.]
1 *verb trans.* Encrust with a scab or scabs. Now only in *pass.* **M17.**
2 *verb intrans.* Of a wound or sore: form a scab or scabs; heal *over*. **E18.**
3 a *verb intrans. & trans.* (with *it*). Work as a scab or blackleg. *colloq.* **E19.** ▸**b** *verb trans.* Ostracize (a person) as a scab; boycott (a firm etc.) for employing scab labour. *colloq. rare.* **E19.** ▸**c** *verb trans.* Perform (a job) as a scab; have (a job) performed by a scab or scabs. *colloq.* **L19.**

> 📖 **3a** *Times* A driver who was prepared to scab as a special favour.

†**scabbado** *noun*. **M17–E18.**
[from SCAB *noun* + -ADO: cf. SCRUBBADO.]
Venereal disease, syphilis.

scabbard /'skabəd/ *noun*[1]. **ME.**
[Anglo-Norman *escauberge* (cf. Anglo-Latin *eschauberca*, *scarbegium*, etc.) prob. from Frankish compound of base rel. to SHEAR *noun*[1] + base meaning 'protect' (as in HAUBERK).]
1 A case or sheath, usu. of hide or leather bound with metal, which protects the blade of a sword, dagger, bayonet, etc., when not in use (chiefly *Hist.*). Also, a sheath in which a firearm, tool, etc., is kept. **ME.**
†**2** Any of various kinds of natural sheath or integument; a cocoon etc. **E17–M18.**

> 📖 **1** H. ALLEN The possessor of that ancient title loosened his . . sword in its scabbard. *Reader's Digest* Your Diary-Almanac comes . . with its own pencil, fitting . . into the scabbard on its spine. **throw away the scabbard** *fig.* abandon all thought of making peace.

Comb.: **scabbard-fish** any of various elongated marine fishes of the genera *Lepidopus* and *Aphanopus* (family Trichiuridae), having a long continuous dorsal fin and long jaws with large teeth; *esp.* the edible silver-coloured *Lepidopus caudatus*.
■ **scabbarded** *adjective* having a scabbard (of a specified kind) **L19.** **scabbardless** *adjective* **L16.**

scabbard /'skabəd/ *noun*[2]. *rare* (now *Scot.*). **LME.**
[from SCAB *noun* + -ARD: cf. Dutch *schobberd* beggar, rogue.]
A scabbed or contemptible person.

scabbard /'skabəd/ *noun*[3]. Now *rare* or *obsolete*. **M17.**
[Middle Low German *schalbort*, from *schale* shell, rind, etc. (German *Schale*: see SCALE *noun*[1], SHELL *noun*) + *bort* BOARD *noun*.]
= ***scale-board*** s.v. SCALE *noun*[3].
■ †**scabbarding** *noun* the spacing of lines of type **L18–E19.**

scabbard /'skabəd/ *verb trans.* **L16.**
[from SCABBARD *noun*[1].]
1 Put (a sword) into its scabbard; sheathe. **L16.**
2 *MILITARY.* Beat (a soldier) with a sword or bayonet scabbard as a punishment. Now *Hist.* **E19.**

scabbed /skabd/ *adjective.* Now *rare.* **ME.**
[from SCAB *noun* + -ED[2].]
1 Affected with a disease called scab. **ME.**
2 Mean, paltry, contemptible. Cf. SCALD *adjective*[1] 2. *derog. obsolete* exc. *Scot.* **ME.**
3 *FOUNDING.* Blistered with scabs. **L19.**

scabble /'skab(ə)l/ *verb trans.* **E17.**
[Later var. of SCAPPLE.]
= SCAPPLE.
■ **scabbler** *noun* a workman engaged in or hammer used for scabbling stone **M19.**

scabby /'skabi/ *adjective.* **LME.**
[from SCAB *noun* + -Y[1].]
1 Suffering from scab. **LME.** ▸**b** *FOUNDING.* = SCABBED *adjective* 3. **L19.** ▸**c** *PRINTING.* Blotchy, through uneven inking. *obsolete* exc. *Hist.* **L19.**
2 Contemptible, mean, vile. Now *colloq.* **E18.**

> 📖 **2** D. EDGAR You should quit the army . . and refuse to fight their scabby, skunky little war.

Special collocations: **scabby mouth** *Austral. & NZ* a contagious viral disease of sheep and goats, marked by ulceration round the mouth. **scabby sheep** *fig.* a corrupt or disreputable member of a family or group.
■ **scabbiness** *noun* **L16.**

scaberulous /skə'bɛr(j)ʊləs/ *adjective.* **L19.**
[from mod. Latin *scaberulus* dim. of *scaber* scabrid: see -ULOUS.]
BOTANY. Minutely scabrous.

scabies /'skeɪbiːz/ *noun.* **LME.**
[Latin, from *scabere* to scratch.]
MEDICINE. †**1** Any of various skin diseases characterized by a scabby or scaly eruption. **LME–M18.**
2 A contagious skin disease, marked by itching and red papules, caused by the itch-mite, *Sarcoptes scabiei*. **E19.**

scabious /'skeɪbɪəs/ *noun.* **LME.**
[medieval Latin *scabiosa* (sc. *herba* plant), use as noun of fem. sing. of Latin *scabiosus*: see next, -OUS. Cf. Old & mod. French *scabieuse*.]
Any of various plants of the genus *Scabiosa* and related genera of the teasel family, which bear numerous lilac, bluish, etc., flowers in shallowly convex heads and which were formerly believed effective against certain skin diseases.
devil's-bit scabious: see DEVIL *noun*. ***field scabious***: see FIELD *noun*. ***sheep's scabious***: see SHEEP *noun*. ***sweet scabious***: see SWEET *adjective & adverb*.

scabious /'skeɪbɪəs/ *adjective.* Now *rare.* **LME.**
[from French *scabieux* or Latin *scabiosus*, from SCABIES: see -OUS.]
Orig., scabbed, scabby. Later, of the nature of or pertaining to scabies.

scabish /'skeɪbɪʃ/ *noun. US.* **E19.**
[Alt. of SCABIOUS *noun*.]
Any of several evening primroses (genus *Oenothera*). Also, the field scabious, *Knautia arvensis*.

scabland /'skabland/ *noun.* Chiefly *US.* **E20.**
[from SCAB *noun* + LAND *noun*[1].]
PHYSICAL GEOGRAPHY. Flat elevated land consisting of patchy poor thin soil with little vegetation over igneous rock deeply scarred by channels of glacial or fluvioglacial origin; *spec.* that forming part of the Columbia Plateau, Washington State, USA. Freq. in *pl.*

scabrid /'skeɪbrɪd/ *adjective.* **M19.**
[Late Latin *scabridus*, from Latin *scaber*: see next, -ID[1].]
BOTANY. (Somewhat) scabrous.
■ **sca'bridity** *noun* **L19.**

scabrous /'skeɪbrəs, 'skabrəs/ *adjective.* **L16.**
[from French *scabreux* or late Latin *scabrosus*, from Latin *scaber* (rel. to *scabere* to scratch, SCABIES): see -OUS.]
†**1** Of an author, work, or style: harsh, unmusical, unpolished. **L16–L17.**
2 Chiefly *BOTANY & ZOOLOGY.* Rough to the touch on account of minute projections; bearing short stiff hairs. **M17.** ▸**b** Encrusted with dirt. Chiefly *US.* **M20.**
3 Full of obstacles; (of a subject or situation) difficult to deal with; requiring tactful handling. **M17.**
4 Marked by, suggestive of, or showing an interest in scandal or salacious detail; indecent, risqué. **L19.**

> 📖 **2b** E. BOWEN A once bewitching villa, now scabrous, awaits the knacker. **4** *Athenaeum* Mr Maude . . has chosen to write about . . adultery . . and many other potentially scabrous topics. *London Review of Books* His propaganda pieces grow more outrageously scabrous.

■ **scabrously** *adverb* **L16.** **scabrousness** *noun* **E18.**

scacchic /'skakɪk/ *adjective. rare.* **M19.**
[from Italian *scacchi* chess + -IC.]
Of or pertaining to chess.

scad /skad/ *noun*[1]. Now *dial.* **L16.**
[Origin unkn.: cf. SKEG *noun*[2].]
A wild black plum; *esp.* the bullace, *Prunus insititia*.

scad /skad/ *noun*[2]. **E17.**
[Origin unkn.]
Any of numerous carangid fishes, *esp.* one with a row of large scales along each side; a horse-mackerel; spec. *Trachurus trachurus*, which is caught for food (esp. in southern Africa) and for fishmeal and bait (in Europe).

scad /skad/ *noun*[3]. *colloq.* (orig. *US*). **M19.**
[Origin unkn.]
1 A dollar; *esp.* in *pl.*, money. **M19.**
2 *sing.* & (usu.) in *pl.* A large amount; lots, heaps. **M19.**

> 📖 **2** S. BELLOW At . . college I had time to read scads of books.

scaddle /'skad(ə)l/ *adjective.* Now *dial.* **L15.**
[Old High German *scad(h)al*, *scadel*, *scatal*, *-el*, Gothic *skaþuls*, from Germanic base also of SCATHE *noun*.]
1 Of an animal: wild, shy. **L15.**
2 Esp. of an animal: mischievous, troublesome; thievish. **L16.**

scaff /skaf/ *noun*[1]. Chiefly *Scot.* Also **skaff**. **LME.**
[Old French *scaphe* from Latin *scapha* from Greek *skaphē* trough, skiff.]
A light boat, a skiff; *spec.* (*Scot.*) = SCAFFIE.
■ **scaffie** *noun* (*Scot.*, now *Hist.*) a kind of large undecked fishing boat (also ***scaffie-boat***) **L19.**

scaff /skaf/ *noun*[2] *& verb.* **M18.**
[Origin unkn.: cf. SCOFF *verb*[2].]
▶ **A** *noun. Scot.*
1 Food, provisions. Cf. SCOFF *noun*[2]. **M18.**
2 Disreputable people collectively; riff-raff; scum. Also ***scaff and raff***, ***scaff-raff***. **E19.**
▶ **B** *verb trans.* Eat voraciously. *Scot. & dial.* **L18.**

scaffold /'skafəʊld, -f(ə)ld/ *noun.* **ME.**
[Old French *(e)schaffaut* (mod. *échafaud*) = Provençal *escadafalc*, from Proto-Romance compound of EX-[1] + source of CATAFALQUE.]
1 A temporary platform, usu. of planks supported on poles or suspended, for people engaged in the erection, repair, decoration, etc., of a building. Also *sing.* & in *pl.* = SCAFFOLDING. **ME.**
†**2** A movable wooden structure used in sieges. **LME–E16.**
†**3 a** A raised platform, stand, or temporary stage, on which a person is exhibited to public view or a play (esp. a mystery play) performed. **LME–L17.** ▸**b** A raised platform for spectators; a gallery in a theatre or church. **L15–L18.**
4 An elevated platform on which a criminal is executed (*Hist.*); *the* punishment of being executed. **M16.**
5 A raised wooden framework on which food or tobacco is laid or hung to dry, or, among N. American Indians (*Hist.*), corpses are exposed. **M16.**
6 *METALLURGY.* An obstruction in a blast-furnace caused by material adhering to the wall. **M19.**

> 📖 **4** CONAN DOYLE His destination is more likely to be Broadmoor than the scaffold. **go to the scaffold** be executed. **send to the scaffold** cause to be executed.

Comb.: **scaffold pole**: supporting scaffolding.

scaffold /'skafəʊld, -f(ə)ld/ *verb trans.* **LME.**
[from the noun.]
1 Surround (a building) with scaffolding; *transf. & fig.* prop up, support. **LME.**
†**2** Provide with a platform, stand, or gallery. **M16–M17.**
3 Place (food) on a raised framework of wood to be dried; *Hist.* among N. American Indians, expose (a corpse) on a scaffold. **L18.**

> 📖 **1** C. BLOUNT New Titles may be Scaffolded with Laws.

scaffoldage /'skafəʊldɪdʒ, -f(ə)ld-/ *noun. rare.* **E17.**
[from prec. + -AGE.]
= SCAFFOLDING *noun* 1.

scaffolder /'skafəʊldə, -f(ə)ld-/ *noun.* **L16.**
[from SCAFFOLD *noun*, *verb* + -ER[1].]
†**1** An occupant of the gallery at a theatre. *rare.* Only in **L16.**
2 A person whose business it is to erect scaffolding. **M19.**

scaffolding /'skafəʊldɪŋ, -f(ə)ld-/ *noun.* **ME.**
[from SCAFFOLD *noun* or *verb* + -ING[1].]
1 A temporary framework of wooden platforms and poles supporting people engaged in the erection, repair, or decoration of a building. **ME.** ▸**b** A wooden platform

or framework; = SCAFFOLD *noun* 3a, 5. Now *rare*. M16. ▸**c** A supporting framework (*lit. & fig.*); *esp.* a temporary conceptual framework used for constructing a theory etc. L19. ▸**d** *METALLURGY*. = SCAFFOLD *noun* 6. L19.
2 The action of SCAFFOLD *verb*; *METALLURGY* the formation of scaffolds in a blast-furnace. M19.

> **1c** L. AUCHINCLOSS Fantasy may have been the scaffolding that sustained me until I could develop my own character. J. COX A shoot fruits once, then becomes scaffolding for succeeding years' shoots.

scaffy /ˈskafi/ *noun. Scot. colloq.* M19.
[Dim. of SCAVENGER *noun*.]
A street sweeper; a refuse collector.

scag /skag/ *noun. US slang*. Also **skag**. E20.
[Origin unkn.]
1 A cigarette; a cigarette stub. E20.
2 Heroin. M20.

scaglia /ˈskɑːljə/ *noun*. L18.
[Italian = scale, chip of marble, from Germanic: see SCALE *noun*[3].]
GEOLOGY. A dark fine-grained shale found in the Alps and Apennines.

scagliola /skalˈjəʊlə/ *noun*. L16.
[Italian *scagli(u)ola* dim. of SCAGLIA.]
†**1** = SCAGLIA. L16–L18.
2 Plasterwork of Italian origin, designed to imitate marble and other kinds of stone. M18.
■ **scagliolist** *noun* a worker in scagliola E19.

scaife /skeɪf/ *noun*. L18.
[Perh. from Dutch *schijf* (German *Scheibe*) disc, wheel.]
1 A thin sharp-edged iron wheel used in some ploughs in place of or in front of the coulter. *local*. L18.
2 A revolving wheel used in polishing diamonds. L19.

scala /ˈskeɪlə/ *noun*. Pl. **-lae** /-liː, -lʌɪ/. E18.
[Latin = ladder.]
ANATOMY. Each of the three passages into which the cochlea of the inner ear is divided.
scala media /ˈmiːdɪə/ [= middle] the central duct of the cochlea, containing the sensory cells and separated from the other two passages by membranes. **scala tympani** /tɪmˈpɑːni/ [= of the tympanum] the lower bony passage of the cochlea. **scala vestibuli** /vɛˈstɪbjʊli/ [= of the vestibule] the upper bony passage of the cochlea.

scalable /ˈskeɪləb(ə)l/ *adjective*. L16.
[from SCALE *verb*[2] + -ABLE.]
1 Able to be scaled or climbed. L16.
2 Able to be measured or graded according to a scale. M20.
3 Able to be changed in scale. *rare*. L20.
■ **scalaˈbility** *noun* M20.

scalade /skəˈlɑːd/ *noun*. Now *rare* or *obsolete*. Also †**scalado**, pl. **-o(e)s**. L16.
[Italian *scalada* (now *scalata*), from medieval Latin *scalare* SCALE *verb*[2]: see ESCALADE *noun*.]
1 = ESCALADE *noun*. L16.
2 A scaling-ladder. *rare*. M17.

scala mobile /ˌskaːla ˈmoːbile/ *noun phr.* L20.
[Italian, lit. ' moving stair, escalator'.]
In Italy, a system of wage indexation by which earnings are linked by a sliding scale to the retail price index.

scalar /ˈskeɪlə/ *adjective & noun*. M17.
[Latin *scalaris*, from *scala* ladder: see SCALE *noun*[4], -AR[1].]
▸**A** *adjective*. **1** Resembling a ladder; *BOTANY* = SCALARIFORM. *rare*. M17.
2 *MATH*. Of the nature of a scalar; of or pertaining to a scalar or scalars. M19.
3 Of or pertaining to a musical scale. E20.
4 Of or pertaining to a graduated scale. M20.
2 scalar field a field defined at each point by a scalar quantity. **scalar product** a scalar function of two vectors, equal to the product of their magnitudes and the cosine of the angle between them; also called ***dot product***.
▸**B** *noun*. *MATH*. A real number; a quantity having magnitude but no direction, and representable by a single real number. Cf. VECTOR *noun* 2a. M19.

scalariform /skəˈlarɪfɔːm/ *adjective*. M19.
[from Latin *scalaris* (see SCALAR) + -FORM.]
BOTANY. Esp. of a plant cell: having bands of tissue etc., arranged in parallel formation like the rungs of a ladder.

scalawag *noun* var. of SCALLYWAG.

†**scald** *noun*[1]. M16–L17.
[Alt. of SCALL *noun* by assoc. with SCALD *adjective*[1].]
= SCALL *noun*.

scald /skɔːld/ *noun*[2]. E17.
[from SCALD *verb*.]
1 An injury to a body surface caused by direct exposure to hot liquid or steam. E17. ▸**b** Any of several diseases which produce a similar effect to that of scalding; *esp.* a disease of fruit marked by browning etc., usu. caused by excessive sunlight or bad storage conditions. L19.
2 The action or an act of scalding an article of food, a utensil, etc. M17.
3 A hot liquid or solution used for scalding. Now *rare*. L17.
4 A patch of land scorched by the sun. *local*. L18.

scald /skɔːld/ *adjective*[1] & *noun*[3]. Now *arch. & dial.* LME.
[Later spelling of SCALLED.]
▸**A** *adjective*. **1** Affected with scall; scabby. Cf. SCALD-HEAD. LME.
2 Mean, paltry, contemptible. Cf. SCABBED 2. *derog.* LME.
▸**B** *noun*. A contemptible person. *derog.* L16.

> G. B. SHAW You young scald: if I had you here I'd teach you manners.

scald /skɔːld/ *adjective*[2]. Chiefly *dial.* L18.
[pa. pple of SCALD *verb*.]
= SCALDED *adjective*[1].
scald cream clotted cream. **scald milk** skimmed milk.

scald /skɔːld/ *verb*. ME.
[Anglo-Norman, Old Northern French *escalder*, Old French *eschalder* (mod. *échauder*) from late Latin *excaldere* wash in hot water, formed as EX-[1] + *cal(i)dus* hot, from *calere* be warm.]
1 *verb trans.* Burn (a body surface) by direct exposure to very hot liquid or steam. ME. ▸**b** *verb intrans.* Suffer a scald. L16. ▸**c** *verb intrans.* Be hot enough to burn the skin. (Earlier as SCALDING *ppl adjective*) M17.
2 *verb trans. transf. & fig.* Of tears, words, etc.: produce a painful effect on (a part of the body) similar to that produced by boiling water. ME.
3 *verb trans.* **a** Wash and clean (the carcass of an animal) with boiling water, to remove hair, feathers, etc.; take *off* (hair, feathers, etc.) in this manner. ME. ▸**b** Rinse clean (a vessel etc.) in boiling water. Also foll. by *out*. M18. ▸**c** Apply a hot solution to. M18.
4 *verb trans. COOKERY*. ▸**a** Pour very hot liquid over. LME. ▸**b** Heat (liquid, esp. milk) to just short of boiling point. L15.
5 a *verb trans.* Of the sun, fire, etc.: scorch, burn. *obsolete* exc. *dial.* LME. ▸**b** *verb intrans.* Be scorched or burnt; (now *Scot.*) become inflamed, sore, or raw. E16.
6 *verb trans. & intrans.* Fill or be filled with painful emotion, burning desire, etc. Now *rare*. LME.

> **1** R. L. STEVENSON The springs . . hot enough to scald a child seriously. **c** H. DAVY Water scalds at 150°. **2** J. MARTINEAU Uttering falsehoods that should scald his lips. W. C. BRYANT The tears that scald the cheek. **3b** W. ELLIS Heat a . . Quantity of Water . . for scalding Pails. **4a** M. WEBB The kettle's boiling . . and all's done, only to scald the tea. **6** B. BEHAN Walton scalded my heart with regard to my religion.

scald-berry /ˈskɔːldb(ə)ri/ *noun. dial.* E18.
[from SCALD *noun*[1] + BERRY *noun*[1], from the belief that the berry caused ringworm.]
The fruit of the bramble, the blackberry.

scald-crow /ˈskɔːldkrəʊ/ *noun. Anglo-Irish.* E18.
[App. from SCALD *adjective*[1] + CROW *noun*[1], in ref. to the bird's grey body, compared to the blackness of the carrion crow.]
A hooded crow.

scalded /ˈskɔːldɪd/ *adjective*[1]. LME.
[from SCALD *verb* + -ED[1].]
1 That has been scalded. LME.
2 Of land: so poor as to support little if any vegetation. *Austral.* E20.
1 like a scalded cat at a very fast pace.

†**scalded** *adjective*[2]. E16–E18.
[from SCALD *noun*[1] + -ED[2].]
= SCALD *adjective*[1].

scalder /ˈskɒldə/ *verb trans.* Now *north.* E17.
[App. from SCALD *verb* + -ER[5].]
Scald, scorch.

scald-fish /ˈskɔːldfɪʃ/ *noun*. Pl. **-es** /-ɪz/, (usu.) same. E19.
[from SCALD *adjective*[1] + FISH *noun*[1].]
A flatfish of European seas, *Arnoglossus laterna* (family Bothidae), having fragile scales stripped off during trawling. Also called ***megrim***.

scald-head /ˈskɔːldhɛd/ *noun*. M16.
[from SCALD *adjective*[1] + HEAD *noun*.]
A head infected with ringworm or similar disease of the scalp; a person affected by this.
■ **scald-headed** *adjective* having a head infected with ringworm E19.

scald-hot /ˈskɔːldhɒt/ *adjective. obsolete* exc. *dial.* LME.
[from SCALD *verb* + HOT *adjective*.]
Scalding hot.

scalding /ˈskɔːldɪŋ/ *noun*[1]. ME.
[Prob. rel. to Old French *eskallin*, *escalin*, *escarlin*: see ESCALINE.]
Hist. A Flemish coin introduced into England and Ireland in the 13th cent.

scalding /ˈskɔːldɪŋ/ *noun*[2]. LME.
[from SCALD *verb* + -ING[1].]
1 The use of boiling or very hot liquid in the preparation of a carcass for food; the partial boiling of milk etc.; *sing.* & in *pl.*, a quantity of liquid thus heated. (Earliest in ***scalding-house*** below.) LME.
2 The action of burning with very hot liquid or steam. LME. ▸†**b** Inflamed or sore condition. LME–L16. ▸**c** A hot sensation as of scalding. L16. ▸**d** *HORTICULTURE*. Scorching of plants by the sun's heat after watering. M19.
Comb.: **scalding-house** a room in which utensils or the carcasses of animals are scalded.

scalding /ˈskɔːldɪŋ/ *ppl adjective & adverb*. ME.
[from SCALD *verb* + -ING[2].]
▸**A** *adjective*. **1** That scalds; very hot; burning. ME.
2 *transf. & fig.* Producing an effect or sensation like that of scalding. ME. ▸†**b** Of desire etc.: burning, fervent. LME–L16.

> **1** J. BALDWIN I stared at . . Paris, . . under the scalding sun. M. OLIVER Tea was brought to us scalding in white cups. **2** K. A. PORTER He shouted . . , and spoke outright some scalding and awful truths.

▸**B** *adverb*. ***scalding hot***, hot enough to burn the skin. LME.

scaldino /skalˈdiːno/ *noun*. Pl. **-ni** /-ni/. M19.
[Italian, from *scaldare* warm.]
In Italy, a small earthen brazier.

scale /skeɪl/ *noun*[1]. ME.
[Old Norse *skál* bowl, pl. weighing-scales = Old High German *scāla* (German *Schale*), from Germanic, rel. to base of Old English *sćealu* SHALE *noun*[1], Old Saxon *skala* cup (Dutch *schaal*), Old High German *scala* SHELL *noun*, husk (German *Schale*).]
▸**I 1** A drinking-bowl or cup (*obsolete* exc. *Scot.*). Now *esp.* (*S. Afr.*) a measuring pot in which sorghum or maize beer is sold or drunk. ME.
▸**II** Apparatus for weighing.
2 Either pan of a balance. Also ***scale-pan***. LME.
3 *sing.* (esp. *fig.*) & in *pl.* A weighing instrument; *esp.* one (more fully ***pair of scales***) consisting of a beam pivoted at its middle and having a dish, pan, etc., suspended at either end. LME.
4 (Usu. **S-**.) In *pl.* & †*sing. The* constellation or zodiacal sign Libra. M17.

> **3** C. PRIEST I weighed myself on her scales, and found I had lost weight. *fig.*: W. COWPER Providence . . weighs the nations in an even scale. J. HILTON In the balancing of probabilities . . the scales don't bump . . either way. W. R. GEDDES The scales are weighed heavily against him.

Phrases: ***Clerk of the Scales***: see CLERK *noun*. **go to scale**, **ride to scale** (of a jockey) ride to the weighing-room before or after a race. **throw into the scale** cause to be a factor in a contest, debate, etc. **tip the scale(s)**, **turn the scale(s)** cause one pan of a balance to outweigh the other *at* a certain weight; *fig.* (of a motive, circumstance, etc.) be decisive.
Comb.: **scale-beam** (***a***) the transverse bar of a balance; (***b***) a weighing instrument of the steelyard kind; **scale house** *US* a place in which large scales for weighing animals etc. are kept; **scale-pan** = sense 2 above; **scalesman** a person who uses scales in weighing.

scale /skeɪl/ *noun*[2]. Now *dial.* ME.
[Old Norse *skáli*, from Germanic base rel. to SCALE *noun*[1], SHELL *noun*. Cf. SHIEL, SHIELING.]
A hut, a shed.

scale /skeɪl/ *noun*[3]. ME.
[Aphet. from Old French *escale* (mod. *écale* husk, stone chip) from Germanic base also of SCALE *noun*[1].]
1 Any of the small thin hard outgrowths or modifications of the skin in many fishes and reptiles, and some mammals, usually overlapping, and forming a covering for the body. Also, a similar thin plate on the integument of an invertebrate; *esp.* any of the minute flat structures covering the wings of butterflies and moths. Occas. as *collect. sing.* ME.
2 A thin plate, lamina, or flake, esp. one detached from a surface; a small dry flake of the superficial part of the epidermis, such as is shed in certain skin diseases. ME. ▸**b** *BOTANY*. A flattened membranous plate of cellular tissue, usu. a rudimentary leaf or bract, protecting a leaf-bud, a flower in a catkin, etc.; any of the overlapping lignified bracts covering the seeds in the cone of a coniferous tree. L18. ▸**c** The protective covering of a scale insect; the insect itself. Also, the diseased condition of a plant infested with scale insects. E19.
3 a *Hist.* Any of the thin pieces of metal composing scale-armour (see below). LME. ▸**b** A coin; money. *Scot. & US slang.* L19.
4 Either of the plates of bone, horn, ivory, etc., forming the outside of the handle of a knife or razor; either of the metal sides to which such a plate is riveted. LME.
5 Now usu. *collect. sing.* Any of several kinds of flaky deposit; *spec.* (***a***) the film of oxide which forms on iron or other metal when heated and hammered or rolled; (***b***) tartar on teeth; (***c***) a thick hard whitish deposit of inorganic salts formed in a boiler, kettle, etc., by precipitation from water. E16.

6 Thin board. Now *dial.* **M17.**
7 *Hist.* A plate of metal worn instead of an epaulette by military and naval officers. **M19.**

📖 **2** R. FIRBANK An old green garden-seat with the paint peeling off in scales. **scales fall from a person's eyes** *fig.* [in allus. to *Acts* 9:18] a person receives sudden enlightenment or revelation.

Comb.: **scale-armour** *Hist.* armour consisting of small overlapping plates of metal, leather, or horn; **scale-bark** bark shed in scalelike pieces, as that of the plane tree; **scale-blight** the disease caused by scale insects; **scale-blue** the groundwork of royal blue with a scale-pattern characteristic of some Worcester china; **scale-board** thin board used as hatboxes, veneer, as backing for pictures, etc., and (*Hist.*) by printers for making register; **scale-bug** *US* = *scale insect* below; **scale carp** the typical form of the common carp, *Cyprinus carpio*; **scale-fern** the rustyback fern, *Ceterach officinarum*; **scale-fish** a true fish, having scales (esp. as distinct from a shellfish); **scale insect** any homopteran insect of the family Coccidae having a flattened scalelike protective covering, and infesting and injuring various plants; **scale leaf** a small modified leaf, esp. a colourless membranous one, as on a rhizome or forming part of a bulb; **scale-moss** a liverwort of the order Jungermanniales, characterized by a row of scaly leaves on either side of the stem; **scale-pattern** a pattern having a representation of scales; an imbricated pattern; **scale-reading** (an) examination of the pattern of scales on a fish as an indicator of its age, history, etc.; **scale-roof** a scaled roof (SCALED *adjective*[1] 2c); **scale-tailed** *adjective* having a scaly tail; ***scale-tailed squirrel***, = ***scaly-tailed squirrel*** s.v. SCALY *adjective*; **scale-work** work, decoration, etc., with a scale-pattern; **scale-worm** any of various marine polychaete worms which have protective disc-shaped growths from some parapodia, including sea mice.

■ **scaleless** /-l-l-/ *adjective* (esp. of a fish or reptile) having no scales **E17.** **scalelike** *adjective* resembling a scale; thin, flat, and somewhat rigid: **M19.**

scale /skeɪl/ *noun*[4]. **LME.**
[Latin *scala* staircase, ladder (usu. in pl.), from base of *scandere* to climb.]

▶ **I** †**1** A ladder. Formerly *spec.*, a scaling-ladder. Freq. *fig.*, esp. in ref. to Jacob's ladder (*Genesis* 28:12). **LME–E19.**
†**2** A rung of a ladder. **LME–L17.**
3 A flight of stairs. Usu. in ***scale-stairs*** below. *obsolete* exc. *Scot.* **L16.**

▶ **II 4** A series of graduated marks on a straight line or curve representing a series of numerical values, used to measure distance, temperature, quantity, etc.; *spec.* the equally divided line on a map, chart, or plan which indicates its scale (sense 8 below), and is used for finding the distance between two points. **LME.**
5 A strip of wood, ivory, metal, etc., having graduated and numbered spaces on it, used for measuring distances. **LME.**
6 Relative magnitude or extent; degree, proportion. Freq. in ***on a grand scale***, ***on a lavish scale***, ***on a small scale***. **E17.** ▸**b** *PHOTOGRAPHY.* The range of exposures over which a photographic material will give an acceptable variation in density. **M20.**
7 *fig.* A standard of measurement, calculation, or estimation. **E17.**
8 The ratio between a model and the object represented, between a map and the area represented, etc.; a system of representing objects etc. in a smaller or larger size in exact proportion. **M17.** ▸**b** The ratio of the width of an organ-pipe to its length, which determines the timbre. **L19.**

📖 **5** ***Gunter's scale***, ***marquois scale***, etc. **6** E. A. FREEMAN Its scale . . surpassed that of any church . . in England. G. F. KENNAN The . . intervention of foreign troops on a major scale. *Harper's Magazine* Our . . wish to preserve the planet must . . be reduced to the scale of our competence. ***full-scale***: see FULL *adjective*. ***large-scale***: see LARGE *adjective*. **7** W. EMPSON The human mind has two main scales on which to measure time. **8** A. C. CLARKE A foot ruler lay . . in the middle of the picture to give an idea of the scale. L. D. STAMP Mapping the geology of the country on the scale of one inch to one mile. attrib.: ***scale drawing***, ***scale model***, etc.

▶ **III 9** *MUSIC.* **a** A series of notes ascending or descending by fixed intervals, esp. one beginning on a certain note; *spec.* any of the graduated series of notes into which the octave is divided. **L16.** ▸**b** The notes of a scale played or sung as a musical exercise. Usu. in *pl.* **M19.**
10 A graduated series of steps or degrees, esp. as used in classification. **E17.** ▸**b** A series of tones of a given colour produced by mixing the colour with different proportions of white or black. **M19.** ▸**c** *PSYCHOLOGY.* A graded series in terms of which the measurements of such phenomena as sensations, attitudes, or mental attributes are expressed. **L19.**
11 *MATH.* **a** A number of terms included between two points in a progression or series. Now *rare.* **L17.** ▸**b** Any of the various conceivable systems of notation based on the principle that the value of a figure varies in geometrical progression according to its serial place, but distinguished by the number chosen as the radix, base, or unit of multiplication. **L18.**
12 a A graduated table of prices, charges, etc. **L18.** ▸**b** A graduated table of wage or salary rates; a wage or salary in accordance with this. **E20.**

📖 **9** A. HOPKINS 'Cellos . . declaim a . . theme based on a descending scale. ***chromatic scale***, ***diatonic scale***, ***harmonic scale***, ***Pythagorean scale***, etc. **10** A. BAIN A scale of degrees from . . opacity to . . transparency. *Daedalus* A huge earthquake whose magnitude must have been about 8.7 on the Richter scale. P. P. READ He . . felt contempt for anyone beneath him on the social scale. ***Beaufort scale***, ***Celsius scale***, ***Kelvin scale***, etc. **12a** JOCELYN BROOKE There was no fixed scale of punishments. **b** M. ANGELOU We would pay the performers . . union scale.

Phrases: ***economy of scale***: see ECONOMY *noun* 3. **in scale** (esp. of a detail in a drawing) in correct proportion to the background or surroundings; opp. ***out of scale***. ***out of scale***: see *in scale* above. **scale of two** etc., a scale of arithmetical notation having as radix or base the number given, esp. used *attrib.* & *absol.* to designate a scaler (electronic pulse-counter) in which an output pulse is produced when a number of input pulses equal to the specified radix has been received. ***SLIDING scale***. **to scale** so as to represent every part of the original in exact proportion.
Comb.: **scale effect**: occurring when the scale of something is changed, as a result of contributory factors not all varying in the same proportion; **scale factor** a numerical factor by which each of a set of quantities is multiplied; **scale height** the vertical distance over which an atmospheric parameter or other quantity decreases by a factor *e* (approx. 2.718); **scale-stairs** *Scot.* a straight flight of steps, as opp. to a spiral staircase.

scale /skeɪl/ *noun*[5]. **L16.**
[from SCALE *verb*[2].]
†**1** An escalade. **L16–M17.**
2 The estimation of an amount of timber standing or in logs; the amount of the estimate. *N. Amer.* **L19.**

scale /skeɪl/ *noun*[6]. Now *rare.* **E17.**
[Old French *scal(l)e*, *escal(l)e* (mod. *escale*, esp. in phr. *faire escale* go ashore) or Italian *scala* = Spanish, Portuguese *escala* seaport, harbour, from Latin *scala* ladder: see SCALE *noun*[4].]
1 A seaport town; a port forming a centre of trade. **E17.**
†**2** A landing-place; *occas.* a custom-house. *rare.* **L17–E19.**

scale /skeɪl/ *verb*[1]. **LME.**
[from SCALE *noun*[3].]
1 *verb trans.* **a** Remove the scales from (fish etc.). **LME.** ▸**b** Free the surface of (a thing) from any of various scaly deposits; *spec.* (*a*) (*Hist.*) clean the bore of (a cannon etc.) by exploding a small amount of powder; (*b*) remove tartar from (teeth). **E18.**
2 *verb trans.* Remove in the form of scales or flakes (foll. by *off*, *away*); in *pass.*, have the surface removed thus. **LME.**
3 *verb intrans.* Come off in scales or thin pieces; flake *off* or *away*. **LME.**

📖 **3** S. BELLOW The . . paint was scaling from the brick walls.

scale /skeɪl/ *verb*[2]. **LME.**
[Old French *escaler* or medieval Latin *scalare*, from Latin *scala* SCALE *noun*[4].]
▶ **I 1** *verb trans.* **a** *Hist.* Attack (a fortress etc.) with scaling-ladders. **LME.** ▸**b** Climb, get over (a wall or other obstacle); ascend, reach the top of, (a mountain etc.). Also, climb up to or into. **LME.**
2 *verb intrans.* Climb, ascend. **M16.** ▸**b** Rise high in pitch. **M19.**

📖 **1** H. M. FIELD The highest pass in Europe . . and . . it seemed as if we were scaling heaven itself. C. MORGAN A prisoner had escaped by scaling the roof. *fig.*: M. COREN Cecil . . never attained the literary heights which his brother so often scaled. **scaling-ladder**: (*a*) *Hist.* used in assaults on fortified places; (*b*) used by fire-fighters for scaling high buildings. **2** MILTON The . . stair That scal'd by steps of Gold to Heav'n Gate.

▶ **II** Measure or regulate by a scale.
3 a *verb trans.* Adjust the amount etc. of (a thing) according to a fixed scale. Chiefly in ***scale down***, reduce proportionately according to such a scale; ***scale up***, increase proportionately according to such a scale. Orig. *US.* **L18.** ▸**b** *verb trans.* Measure or represent (a thing) in exact proportion to its size or according to a given scale. **L19.** ▸**c** *verb trans.* Alter (a quantity or property) by changing the units in which it is measured. **M20.** ▸**d** *verb intrans.* Of a quantity or property: vary or be variable according to a defined rule or principle, esp. so as to keep some proportion constant. **L20.**
4 *verb trans.* *FORESTRY.* Estimate the amount of (standing timber); measure (a log). Of a tree: yield (a certain amount of timber). *N. Amer.* **M19.**
5 *verb trans.* Estimate the proportions of; provide a standard of proportion for. **L19.**
6 *verb trans.* & *intrans.* Of an electronic scaler: count (electrical pulses). **M20.**

📖 **3a** C. CHAPLIN The . . Company was scaling its terms according to . . seating capacity. *Company* You can scale down your ambition . . if costs soar. **b** C. FORD Photographs of lute roses . . which may be adapted and scaled as required.

scale /skeɪl/ *verb*[3]. **E17.**
[from SCALE *noun*[1].]
1 *verb trans.* Weigh (as) on a scale. **E17.** ▸**b** Weigh out (dough) in standard quantities for making into loaves. Usu. with *off.* **M19.**
2 a *verb trans.* Show a weight of (a certain amount), esp. in a sporting contest. **M19.** ▸**b** *verb intrans.* Of a jockey: be weighed; weigh *in* after a race. **M19.**

📖 **1** SHAKES. *Meas. for M.* By this, is . . the corrupt deputy scaled. **2a** *Muscle Power* Are there . . big neck measurements on men who scaled less than 90 pounds?

scale /skeɪl/ *verb*[4] *trans. US.* **L19.**
[Origin unkn.]
Send (a flat object, esp. a stone) skimming through the air, esp. close to the surface of water.

scale /skeɪl/ *verb*[5]. Chiefly *Austral.* & *NZ slang.* **E20.**
[Prob. use of SCALE *verb*[1] or *verb*[2].]
1 *verb trans.* Swindle, defraud, cheat (a person); steal (a thing). **E20.**
2 *verb trans.* & *intrans.* Ride on (public transport) without paying. **E20.**

scaled /skeɪld/ *adjective*[1]. **LME.**
[from SCALE *noun*[3] + -ED[2].]
1 Of a fish, snake, etc.: covered with scales; scaly. Now *rare* exc. as 2nd elem. of comb. and in *HERALDRY.* **LME.**
2 a *Hist.* Of armour: composed of metal scales. **M16.** ▸**b** = IMBRICATED 2, 3. **L18.** ▸**c** Covered with tiles in imitation of scales. **M19.**

scaled /skeɪld/ *adjective*[2]. **E20.**
[from SCALE *noun*[4] + -ED[2].]
Provided with a graduated scale.

scaledrake /ˈskeɪldreɪk/ *noun. Scot.* & *north.* **E17.**
[Var. of SHELDRAKE.]
= SHELDRAKE.

scalene /ˈskeɪliːn/ *noun* & *adjective.* **M17.**
[Late Latin *scalenus* from Greek *skalenos* uneven, unequal, scalene.]
▶ **A** *noun.* **1** *GEOMETRY.* A triangle with three unequal sides. *rare.* **M17.**
2 *ANATOMY.* = SCALENUS. **L19.**
▶ **B** *adjective.* **1** *GEOMETRY.* Of a triangle: having three unequal sides. **M18.**
2 *ANATOMY.* Of, pertaining to, or designating a scalenus muscle. **E19.**
1 scalene cone, **scalene cylinder**: of which the axis is not perpendicular to the base.

scaleni *noun* pl. of SCALENUS.

scalenohedron /skəˌliːnə(ʊ)ˈhiːdrən, -ˈhɛd-/ *noun.* Pl. **-dra** /-drə/, **-drons.** **M19.**
[from SCALENE + -O- + -HEDRON.]
CRYSTALLOGRAPHY. A closed crystal form in which the faces are similar scalene triangles.
■ **scalenohedral** *adjective* pertaining to or having the form of a scalenohedron **L19.**

scalenotomy /skeɪlɪˈnɒtəmi/ *noun.* **M20.**
[formed as prec. + -TOMY.]
Surgical cutting of a scalenus muscle; an instance of this.

scalenous /skəˈliːnəs/ *adjective.* Now *rare* or *obsolete.* **M17.**
[from late Latin *scalenus* SCALENE + -OUS.]
= SCALENE *adjective* 1.

†**scalenum** *noun.* **L16–L18.**
[Late Latin, use as noun (sc. *triangulum*) of neut. of *scalenus*: see SCALENE.]
GEOMETRY. A scalene triangle.

scalenus /skəˈliːnəs/ *noun.* Pl. **-ni** /-nʌɪ, -niː/. **E18.**
[mod. Latin, use as noun of masc. of late Latin *scalenus* (sc. *musculus* muscle): see SCALENE.]
ANATOMY. Each of four paired triangular muscles in the lower lateral region of the neck. Also ***scalenus muscle***.

scaler /ˈskeɪlə/ *noun*[1]. **M16.**
[from SCALE *verb*[2] + -ER[1].]
1 A person who scales a wall, mountain, etc. **M16.**
2 A person who uses a scale in surveying. **M19.**
3 *FORESTRY.* A person who scales or measures logs. *N. Amer.* **L19.**
4 An electronic pulse-counter, suitable for high count-rates, in which a display or recording device is actuated after a fixed number of pulses has been received and added electronically. **M20.**

scaler /ˈskeɪlə/ *noun*[2]. **E17.**
[from SCALE *verb*[1] + -ER[1].]
A person who removes scales from fish, scale from boilers, etc; an instrument for doing this.

scaler /ˈskeɪlə/ *noun*[3]. *Austral.* & *NZ slang.* **E20.**
[from SCALE *verb*[5] + -ER[1].]
A swindler, a fraud, a cheat; *esp.* a person who rides on public transport without paying.

scale-up /ˈskeɪlʌp/ *noun.* **M20.**
[from *scale up* s.v. SCALE *verb*[2].]
The action or result of increasing the scale of something.

scalewise /ˈskeɪlwʌɪz/ *adjective & adverb.* **M20.**
[from SCALE *noun*[4] + -WISE.]
▶ **A** *adjective.* = SCALAR *adjective* 3. **M20.**
▶ **B** *adverb.* In the manner of a musical scale. **M20.**

scaley *noun* see SCALY *noun.*

scalic /ˈskeɪlɪk/ *adjective.* **M20.**
[from SCALE *noun*[4] + -IC.]
Of or following a musical scale; scalar.

scaling /ˈskeɪlɪŋ/ *noun.* **L16.**
[from SCALE *verb*[1] + -ING[1].]
1 The action of SCALE *verb*[1]. **L16.** ▸**b** The material which scales off; scale, scales. **M17.**
2 Arrangement of scales. **E18.**

scall /skɔːl/ *noun & adjective. obsolete* exc. *Scot. & north.* **ME.**
[Old Norse *skalli* bald head, from Germanic: cf. SCALE *noun*[3], SHELL *noun.*]
▶ **A** *noun.* A scaly or scabby disease of the skin, *esp.* of the scalp. **ME.**
dry scall psoriasis. **humid scall**, **moist scall** eczema.
▶ †**B** *adjective.* = SCALLED. **L16–E17.**
■ **scalled** *adjective* (now *rare*) = SCALD *adjective*[1] **ME.**

scallawag *noun* var. of SCALLYWAG.

scallet /ˈskalɪt/ *noun. local.* Also **-ot** /-ət/. **E19.**
[Origin unkn.]
A bed of freestone in Wiltshire or Somerset.

scallion /ˈskalɪən/ *noun.* **LME.**
[Anglo-Norman *scal(o)un* = Old French *escalo(i)gne*, from Proto-Romance alt. of Latin *Ascalonia* (sc. *caepa* onion) shallot, from *Ascalo(n-)* Ascalon, a port in ancient Palestine.]
1 A spring onion; any of several varieties of onion or related plants which are used like the spring onion, as the Welsh onion, *Allium fistulosum*, and the shallot, *Allium cepa* var. *aggregatum*. Also, any long-necked onion with an undeveloped bulb. Now chiefly *dial. & N. Amer.* **LME.**
2 A leek. *Scot. & US.* **E19.**

scallom /ˈskaləm/ *noun.* **E20.**
[Origin unkn.]
BASKET-MAKING. A stake or rod, of which a thin or spliced end is wound round another stake to form a base or frame of a basket; the method of weaving baskets in this manner.

scallom /ˈskaləm/ *verb trans.* **L19.**
[Origin unkn.]
BASKET-MAKING. Plait or wind (a scallom) in forming the base or frame of a basket.

scallop /ˈskɒləp, ˈskaləp/ *noun & verb.* Also **scoll-** /ˈskɒl-/. **ME.**
[Aphet. from Old French *escalope* ESCALLOP.]
▶ **A** *noun.* **1** (A shell of) any of various marine bivalve molluscs of the family Pectinidae, with circular or fan-shaped shell valves. Also, the edible flesh of some of these molluscs, *esp.* the larger species of *Pecten*. **ME.** ▸**b** (A representation of) a scallop shell, *esp.* (*Hist.*) a valve of this shell worn by a pilgrim as a souvenir of the shrine of St James at Compostela. **ME.**
2 A vessel or other object shaped like a scallop shell, esp. a small pan or dish for baking or serving food. Also, a part or formation resembling a scallop shell. **LME.** ▸**b** Any of a series of convex rounded projections forming the scalloped edge of a garment or other object; a scalloped form. Also (in *pl.*), an ornamental edging cut in material in imitation of a scalloped edge. **E17.** ▸†**c** Lace or edging of a scalloped pattern; a scalloped lace band or collar. **E–M17.**
3 a An escalope. **E18.** ▸**b** A flat cake of potato cooked in batter. *Austral.* **L20.**

> 🕮 **2b** A. WILSON The . . silk dress fell round her ankles in scallops edged with blue velvet.

Comb.: **scallop shell** (*a*) (one valve of) the shell of a scallop, esp. (*Hist.*) as a pilgrim's badge; (*b*) a European geometrid moth, *Rheumaptera undulata*, with wing markings that resemble a scallop shell.
▶ **B** *verb trans.* **1** Shape or cut in the form of a scallop shell (freq. foll. by *out*); ornament or trim with scallops. **M18.**
2 Bake (food, esp. shellfish) in a scallop. **M18.**

> 🕮 **1** E. L. DOCTOROW The whole city was rock and you could . . scallop it out for subway tunnels.

■ **scalloped** *adjective* (*a*) having the border, edge, or outline cut into a series of semicircular segments resembling a scallop shell; (*b*) that has been baked in a scallop: **L17.** **scalloper** *noun* a person who or boat which gathers or dredges for scallops **L19.** **scalloping** *noun* (*a*) the action of the verb; (*b*) scalloped ornament, edging, marking, etc.: **L18.**

scallopini *noun* var. of SCALOPPINE.

scallot *noun* var. of SCALLET.

scally /ˈskali/ *noun. slang.* **L20.**
[Abbreviation of next.]
A roguish self-assured young man, esp. in Liverpool; a tearaway.

scallywag /ˈskalɪwag/ *noun.* Orig. *US.* Also **scala-**, **scalla-** /ˈskalə-/. **M19.**
[Origin unkn.]
1 A disreputable person, a rascal; a good-for-nothing, a shirker; a scamp. *colloq.* **M19.**
2 An impostor or intriguer, esp. in politics; *spec.* (*US* HISTORY) a Southern white person who supported Reconstruction. *slang.* **M19.**
3 An undersized or ill-conditioned cow. *US slang.* **M19.**

> 🕮 **1** T. PARKS It's . . time you young scallywags went to bed. *attrib.*: *Times Lit. Suppl.* A hard-drinking scallywag father.

■ **scallywaggery** *noun* (*colloq.*) (*a*) roguery; (*b*) political opportunism: **L19.**

scalogram /ˈskeɪlə(ʊ)gram/ *noun.* **M20.**
[from SCALE *noun*[4] + -O- + -GRAM, perh. after *cardiogram*.]
PSYCHOLOGY. (A diagram showing) a set of items in an attitude test, ranked so that a positive response to one item implies a positive response to all those below it on the scale.
Comb.: **scalogram analysis**: by means of a scalogram; **scalogram board** a board with movable slats on which results are recorded in scalogram analysis.

scaloppine /skalə(ʊ)ˈpiːni/ *noun.* Also **scallopini**. **M20.**
[Italian, pl. of *scaloppina* dim. of *scaloppa* escalope.]
A dish consisting of escalopes of meat (esp. veal) sautéed or fried.

scalp /skalp/ *noun*[1]. **ME.**
[Prob. of Scandinavian origin.]
1 a The top or crown of the head; the skull, the cranium. Now only *Scot. & north.* **ME.** ▸**b** The head or skull of a whale exclusive of the lower jaw. **L19.**
2 a The skin and connective tissue covering the cranium, usu. covered with hair. **L16.** ▸**b** The skin taken from the head of a dead animal (usu. in order to collect a reward). *US.* **E18.**
3 a *Hist.* The scalp with the hair belonging to it cut or torn from an enemy's head by a N. American Indian as a battle trophy. **E17.** ▸**b** *fig.* A trophy or symbol of victory, conquest, etc. **M18.**
4 a A bare rock or stone projecting above water or surrounding vegetation. *Scot. & north.* **E18.** ▸**b** The peak of a mountain. Chiefly *poet.* **E19.**
5 A wig made to cover part of the scalp. **E19.**

> 🕮 **3a** W. IRVING The chief . . had his scalps to show and . . battles to recount. **b** N. J. CRISP Cramer was . . her kind of scalp, a trophy she could never resist.

Comb.: **scalp-lock** *Hist.* a long lock of hair left on the shaved head by a N. American Indian as a challenge to enemies; **scalp yell**: celebrating the taking of a scalp.
■ **scalpless** *adjective* without a scalp **M18.**

scalp /skalp/ *noun*[2]. Chiefly *Scot. & north.* **E16.**
[Prob. same word as prec. See also SCAUP.]
A bank providing a bed for shellfish; an oyster-bed, a mussel-bed.

scalp /ˈskalp/ *verb*[1] *trans.* Now *rare* or *obsolete.* **M16.**
[Latin *scalpere*: cf. SCALPEL.]
Cut, engrave; scrape, scratch.

scalp /ˈskalp/ *verb*[2] *trans.* See also SCULP *verb*[2]. **L17.**
[from SCALP *noun*[1].]
1 a *Hist.* Cut off the scalp of (a person, esp. an enemy). **L17.** ▸**b** Criticize savagely or mercilessly; (chiefly *US*) inflict loss or defeat on, humiliate, or destroy the influence of. **M19.**
2 *transf.* Remove the top or surface of (an object, metal, soil, etc.). **L17.** ▸**b** In milling etc., separate different sizes of, remove unwanted parts from, (wheat etc.). **L19.**
3 Buy and resell (shares, tickets, etc.) for a high or quick profit; speculate for a small quick profit on (commodity or other markets). *colloq.* Orig. & chiefly *N. Amer.* **L19.**

> 🕮 **1a** J. A. MICHENER The Cheyenne . . knelt beside the corpse and scalped it. **scalping-knife** a knife used for scalping an enemy. **b** J. F. FERRIER Dr Reid and his followers, instead of scalping a doctrine, have merely tomahawked a word. A. BRIDGE He's always being scalped . . . he will chase women. D. KYLE He would be scalped on the cab fare. **2** A. FENTON This scalping of the moorland left great stretches bare. G. BENFORD Rising temperatures had scalped the hills of their snow.

■ **scalped** *adjective* (*a*) having the scalp torn off or torn bare or removed; (*b*) (of metal) having had the surface layer removed: **M18.**

scalp /skalp/ *verb*[3] *trans. rare.* **E18.**
[Origin unkn.]
= SCAPPLE *verb.*

scalpel /ˈskalp(ə)l/ *noun & verb.* **M18.**
[French, or Latin *scalpellum* dim. of *scalprum*, *scalper* cutting tool, chisel, knife, from base of *scalpere* scratch, carve: see -EL[2].]
▶ **A** *noun.* A small light knife shaped for holding like a pen, used in surgery, anatomy, etc. **M18.**

> 🕮 *fig.*: H. REED The most acute intellectual scalpel . . the metaphysician can handle.

▶ **B** *verb trans.* Infl. **-ll-**, *-**l-**. Cut with a scalpel. *rare.* **M18.**

scalper /ˈskalpə/ *noun*[1]. In sense 2 also **scaup-**, **scorp-** /ˈskɔːp-/. **LME.**
[Partly from Latin *scalper* (see prec.), partly from SCALP *verb*[1] + -ER[1].]
†**1** SURGERY. = SCALPRUM. **LME–M17.**
2 An engraving tool for hollowing out woodcut or linocut designs. **L17.**

scalper /ˈskalpə/ *noun*[2]. **M18.**
[from SCALP *verb*[2] + -ER[1].]
1 *Hist.* A person who removes scalps. **M18.**
2 a A ticket tout. *slang* (orig. *US*). **M19.** ▸**b** A person who makes a profit by selling at a discount cheaply bought unused portions of long-distance railway tickets. *US slang.* **L19.** ▸**c** A speculator on commodity or other markets who buys and resells for small quick profits. *colloq.* (orig. & chiefly *US*). **L19.**
3 A scalping-knife. *rare.* **M19.**
4 A machine for scalping wheat etc. Cf. SCALP *verb*[2] 2b. **L19.**

scalpette /skalˈpɛt/ *noun.* **L19.**
[from SCALP *noun*[1] + -ETTE.]
A kind of small wig used for covering a bald patch.

scalpriform /ˈskalprɪfɔːm/ *adjective.* **E19.**
[from Latin *scalprum* (see next) + -I- + -FORM.]
Esp. of the incisors of a rodent: chisel-shaped.

scalprum /ˈskalprəm/ *noun.* Now *rare* or *obsolete.* **L17.**
[Latin: see SCALPEL.]
SURGERY. A large scalpel; a raspatory.

scalpture /ˈskalptʃə/ *noun. rare.* **M17.**
[Latin *scalptura*, from *scalpt-* pa. ppl stem of *scalpere* SCALP *verb*[1]: see -URE. Cf. SCULPTURE.]
(A) carving, (an) engraving.

scaly /ˈskeɪli/ *adjective & noun.* As noun also **-ley**. **LME.**
[from SCALE *noun*[3] + -Y[1].]
▶ **A** *adjective.* **1** Covered with or consisting of scales or parts resembling scales; having many scales or flakes; having a surface that peels off in thin plates or layers. **LME.** ▸**b** Pertaining to or consisting of fish. *poet.* **E17.**
2 a Of skin diseases: in which the skin becomes scaly. **L16.** ▸**b** Of plants: infested with scale insects. **L19.**
3 Poor, shabby, despicable; *spec.* (of a person) mean, stingy. Also (*rare*), unwell, sickly. *arch. slang.* **L18.**

> 🕮 **4** P. G. WODEHOUSE The things you think are going to be the scaliest . . always turn out not so bad.

Special collocations: **scaly anteater** a pangolin. **scaly-bark (hickory)** the shagbark hickory, *Carya ovata*; the edible nut of this tree. **scaly dove** a small Central and S. American dove, *Scardafella squammata*, whose plumage has a scaled appearance. **scaly-foot** any of various snake lizards of the genus *Pygopus*, with no forelimbs, and hindlimbs reduced to flaps. **scaly francolin** an African francolin, *Francolinus squamatus*, with dun plumage having a scaled appearance. **scaly lizard** (now *rare*) a pangolin. **scaly-tail** a scaly-tailed squirrel. **scaly-tailed** *adjective* having a scaly tail; ***scaly-tailed squirrel***, any of various gliding rodents of the family Anomaluridae, found in the forests of west and central Africa, and having scales on the underside of the tail (also called ***anomalure***).
▶ **B** *noun.* A large yellow-fish, *Barbus natalensis*, found in rivers in Natal. **M20.**
¶ Perh. earlier in ME as a surname.
■ **scaliness** *noun* **E17.**

scam /skam/ *noun & verb. slang* (orig. & chiefly *US*). **M20.**
[Origin unkn.]
▶ **A** *noun.* **1** A trick, a ruse; a swindle, a fraud, a racket. **M20.**
2 A story; a rumour; information. **M20.**

> 🕮 **1** R. SILVERBERG I had a scam going, offering to send people to other planets. *Independent* Exposé of a billion-pound arms scam.

▶ **B** *verb.* Infl. **-mm-**.
1 *verb intrans.* Perpetrate a fraud. **M20.**
2 *verb trans.* Cheat, trick, or swindle (a person, firm, etc.). **L20.**
■ **scammer** *noun* a criminal, *esp.* a petty crook or swindler; a person who lives by his or her wits: **L20.**

scamander /skəˈmandə/ *verb intrans.* Now *arch. rare.* **M19.**
[App. from Greek *Skamandros* a river in Homer's *Iliad*, after MEANDER *verb.*]
Wander about, meander.

scamble /ˈskamb(ə)l/ *verb & noun.* **E16.**
[Origin unkn.: cf. SCRAMBLE *verb*, SHAMBLE *verb*[2].]
▶ **A** *verb.* †**1** *verb intrans.* Find the means for a meal. **E16–E17.**
2 †**a** *verb intrans.* Scramble for money, food, etc. lying on the ground or thrown to a crowd; struggle greedily and

indecorously to obtain something. Foll. by *for, after.* M16–L17. ▸**b** *verb trans.* Scatter (money or food) for a crowd to scramble for. *obsolete* exc. *dial.* L16.

†**3** *verb trans.* Seize in a scuffle; take *away* greedily or unscrupulously. L16–L17.

4 *verb intrans.* Stumble along (*lit. & fig.*). *obsolete* exc. *dial.* L16.

5 *verb trans.* Collect haphazardly. Usu. foll. by *up*. *obsolete* exc. *dial.* L16.

6 *verb intrans.* Throw out the limbs loosely and awkwardly in walking; shamble. *obsolete* exc. *dial.* M17.

7 *verb trans.* Remove piecemeal; cut *away*. *rare.* E18.

▸**B** *noun.* A scramble, a confused struggle; a mess. *rare.* Long *obsolete* exc. *dial.* E17.

■ **scambling** *noun* (*a*) (now *rare*) the action of the verb; an instance of this; (*b*) (*obsolete* exc. *dial.*) a makeshift meal: E16.

scambling /ˈskamblɪŋ/ *adjective.* Now *rare* or *dial.* L16.
[from prec. + -ING².]

†**1** Contentious; greedy, rapacious. L16–L17.

2 Clumsily executed; slipshod; makeshift. L16.

3 Irregular, rambling, scattered. L16.

4 Straddling; shambling. M17.

■ **scamblingly** *adverb* (*rare*) E17.

scammered /ˈskaməd/ *adjective. slang.* Now *rare* or *obsolete.* M19.
[Origin unkn.]
Intoxicated, drunk.

scammony /ˈskaməni/ *noun.* OE.
[from Old French *escamonie, scamonee* or Latin *scammonea, -ia*, from Greek *skammōnia, -ōnion*.]
A purgative drug obtained from the dried roots of the western Asian *Convolvulus scammonia* or (more fully ***Mexican scammony***) the Mexican *Ipomoea orizabensis*, both of the bindweed family. Also, either of these plants.

scamorza /skaˈmɔːtsə/ *noun.* L20.
[Italian, from *scamozzare* cut off: cf. MOZZARELLA.]
A white Italian cheese made from cow's or buffalo's milk, produced in small gourd-shaped balls.

scamp /skamp/ *noun & verb*¹. M18.
[Prob. from Middle Dutch *schampen* slip away, decamp from Old French *esc(h)amper* from Proto-Romance, from Latin *ex* EX-¹ + *campus* field.]

▸**A** *noun.* †**1** A highway robber. M18–M19.

2 A good-for-nothing, a worthless person; a rogue, a rascal. Now also, a mischievous person, esp. a child. E19.

> 🕮 **2** DICKENS Those are the cleverest scamps I ever had any thing to do with! H. MANTEL I was a raggedy scamp with a snivel nose and a hole in my breeks.

▸**B** *verb intrans.* †**1** Be a highwayman. Only in M18.

2 Go or wander *about* or *off*, esp. with mischievous intent. *Scot.* M19.

■ **scamphood** *noun* (*rare*) the quality of being a scamp M19. **scamping** *adjective* (*rare*) that behaves like a scamp; good-for-nothing: M19. **scampish** *adjective* having the character of a scamp; characteristic of a scamp: M19.

scamp /skamp/ *verb*² *trans.* M19.
[Perh. same word as prec., but allied in sense to SKIMP *verb*.]
Do (work, a job, etc.) carelessly, hurriedly, or inadequately.

> 🕮 V. WOOLF She had scamped her work . . not 'given her mind' to it.

scampavia /skampaˈviːa/ *noun.* Pl. ***-vie*** /-ˈviːe/. E18.
[Italian, from *scampare* run off, decamp + *via* way, away.]
Hist. A small fast warship used in the Mediterranean.

scamper /ˈskampə/ *noun*¹. L17.
[from the verb.]
The action of SCAMPER *verb*; an instance of this.

scamper /ˈskampə/ *noun*². M19.
[from SCAMP *verb*² + -ER¹.]
A person who scamps work.

scamper /ˈskampə/ *verb intrans.* L17.
[Prob. formed as SCAMP *noun & verb*¹ + -ER⁵.]

†**1** Run away, decamp. L17–M19.

2 Run or skip nimbly, playfully, or impulsively; go hastily from place to place. L17.

> 🕮 **2** H. MARTINEAU Children were scampering up and down these stairs at play. J. G. HOLLAND A black fox dashed across our way, and . . scampered into cover. M. LOWRY The . . dog came scampering up . . scuttling about in circles.

■ **scamperer** *noun* E18.

Scamperdale /ˈskampədeɪl/ *noun.* M20.
[Prob. from Lord *Scamperdale*, a character in R. S. Surtees's *Mr Sponge's Sporting Tour* (1853).]
A type of Pelham bit with the mouthpiece angled back to prevent chafing.

scampi /ˈskampi/ *noun pl.* (also treated as *sing.*). In sense 1 sing. **-po** /-pəʊ/. E19.
[Italian, pl. of *scampo*]

1 Norway lobsters. Also (*rare*) *sing.*, a Norway lobster. E19.

2 A dish of these lobsters, usu. fried in breadcrumbs or in a sauce. Usu. treated as *sing.* M20.

¶ Also called ***Dublin Bay prawn(s)*** in both senses.

†**scampsman** *noun. rare.* Pl. **-men**. L18–M19.
[from SCAMP *noun* + -'S¹ + MAN *noun*.]
A highwayman.

scan /skan/ *verb & noun.* LME.
[Late Latin use of Latin *scandere* climb, in the sense 'scan (a verse)', with allus. to raising and lowering the foot to mark rhythm.]

▸**A** *verb.* Infl. **-nn-**.

▸**I 1 a** *verb trans.* Analyse (a line etc. of verse) by determining the nature and number of the component feet or the number and prosodic value of the syllables; test the metrical correctness of (a verse) as by rhythmically emphatic recitation. Also (*rare*), describe prosodically (a word or sequence of words). LME. ▸**b** *verb intrans.* Admit of being scanned; be metrically correct. M19.

†**2** *verb trans.* Criticize; judge the correctness or value of. M16–E19.

3 *verb trans.* Investigate or consider minutely. M16.

†**4** *verb trans.* Interpret, assign a meaning to (a word, an action, etc.). M16–M17.

5 *verb trans.* Perceive, discern. Now *rare* or *obsolete.* M16.

6 *verb trans.* **a** Look at or over intently or quickly; *spec.* search through (a text, list, etc.) for particular information or features. L18. ▸**b** Cause (an area, object, or image) to be systematically traversed by a beam or detector; convert (an image) into a linear sequence of signals in this way for transmission or processing; *spec.* in MEDICINE, produce an image of a surface or cross-section of (the body or part of it) using a scanner; examine (a patient etc.) with a scanner. E20. ▸**c** Traverse or analyse (an element of an image etc.) as part of the scanning of the larger whole. M20. ▸**d** Cause (a beam etc.) systematically to traverse an area; cause (an aerial) to rotate or oscillate for this purpose. M20.

7 *verb intrans.* Carry out scanning. M20.

> 🕮 **1b** F. A. PALEY The lines will neither scan nor construe like ordinary verses. **3** C. DARWIN Man scans with scrupulous care, the . . pedigree of his horses before he matches them. **5** J. BEATTIE One part . . we dimly scan Through the dark medium of life's feverish dream. **6a** E. WHARTON Mr Rosedale stood scanning her with interest. J. BARTH Scanning the audience, I saw almost no unfamiliar faces. P. P. READ His eyes scanned the columns of criticism . . —and came to rest on a review. **7** N. SHUTE Every technical paper that one scans through quickly. *Physics Bulletin* The beam repeatedly scans across the faceplate.

▸**II** †**8** *verb trans.* Climb. *rare* (Spenser). Only in L16.

▸**B** *noun.* **1** The action or an instance of scanning; close scrutiny; a sweeping search through a text etc. Also (now *rare* or *obsolete*), perception, discernment. E18.

2 A single line or traverse of a beam, detector, etc., forming part of a systematic scanning action. Also, an entire raster. M20.

3 An image, diagram, etc., obtained by (esp. medical) scanning. M20.

> 🕮 **1** G. WASHINGTON What will be the end of these manoeuvres is beyond my scan. J. GARDNER His first duty of the day was . . a quick scan of all the British . . papers. L. DEIGHTON The preliminary scan . . showed Kleiber was a one-time employee of the CIA.

Comb.: **scan-column index** a tabular representation of coded information concerning or contained in a set of documents, for use in information retrieval.

scance /skɑːns/ *verb*¹. Chiefly *Scot.* (now *rare* or *obsolete*). L16.
[App. from Latin *scans-* pa. ppl stem of *scandere* climb, scan: see prec.]

1 *verb trans.* Examine critically, scrutinize, reflect on, (a thing). L16.

†**2** *verb intrans.* Reflect, comment. Foll. by *of, on, upon.* E17–E19.

†**3** *verb trans.* = SCAN *verb* 1a. *rare.* E18–E19.

scance /skɑːns/ *verb*² *intrans.* Chiefly *Scot.* E17.
[Perh. same word as prec., but cf. ASKANCE *adverb* etc.]
Glance, look with disdain. Foll. by *on, at.*

Scand /skand/ *noun. colloq.* M20.
[Abbreviation.]
A Scandinavian.

scandal /ˈskand(ə)l/ *noun & verb.* ME.
[Old & mod. French *scandale* from ecclesiastical Latin *scandalum* cause of offence from Hellenistic Greek *skandalon* snare for an enemy, cause of moral stumbling (orig. trap). Cf. SLANDER *noun*.]

▸**A** *noun.* **1** CHRISTIAN THEOLOGY. **a** Discredit to religion brought about by the conduct of a religious person; formerly also, conduct of this kind. Also, moral perplexity caused by the conduct of a person looked up to as an example. ME. ▸**b** An obstacle to faith in or obedience to God; an occasion of unbelief or moral lapse; a stumbling-block. L16.

2 (Rumour etc. causing) damage to reputation; defamatory talk; malicious gossip. L16. ▸†**b** A dishonourable imputation. Later *spec.*, a slander. E17–E19.

3 a A disgraceful circumstance, event, or situation, *esp.* one causing public offence or outrage. L16. ▸**b** A person whose conduct causes public outrage, indignation, etc., or brings his or her class, country, profession, etc., into disrepute. M17.

4 Offence or outrage to moral feeling or sense of decency, esp. as a subject of general discussion. E17.

5 LAW. An irrelevant or indecent statement made in court which detracts from its diginity. E18.

> 🕮 **1a** J. A. FROUDE Catholics . . could not appear in Protestant assemblies without causing scandal to the weaker brethren **b** T. SHERLOCK The Resurrection . . has wiped away the Scandal and Ignominy of the Cross. G. TYRRELL A . . scandal to the religious imagination of the masses. **scandal of particularity** the obstacle to faith of seeing a particular man, Jesus, as a universal saviour. **2** E. A. FREEMAN Scandal affirmed that neither of them was really of kingly birth. **3a** P. H. GIBBS I can't afford to get into any scandal with an attractive lady. *Economist* Most of the juicy scandals on the Westminster rumour-mill do not get printed. **4** LD MACAULAY The disclosure . . could not be made without great scandal.

Comb.: **scandalmonger** a person who spreads malicious scandal; **scandal sheet** *derog.* a newspaper etc. giving prominence to sensational stories, malicious gossip, etc.

▸**B** *verb trans.* Infl. **-ll-**, ***-l-**.

†**1** Disgrace, bring into disrepute. L16–L17.

2 Spread scandal concerning, defame, (a person). Formerly also, revile. Now *arch. & dial.* E17.

†**3** Shock the feelings of; scandalize. M17–E18.

■ †**scandalled** *adjective* (*a*) *rare* (Shakes.) disgraced, shameful; (*b*) slandered: E–M17.

scandala magnatum *noun phr.* pl. of SCANDALUM MAGNATUM.

scandalise *verb*¹, *verb*² vars. of SCANDALIZE *verb*¹, *verb*².

scandalize /ˈskand(ə)lʌɪz/ *verb*¹. Also **-ise**. L15.
[Old & mod. French *scandaliser* or ecclesiastical Latin *scandalizare*, from Greek *skandalizein*, from *skandalon*: see prec., -IZE.]

†**1** *verb trans.* Make a public scandal of (a discreditable secret). *rare.* Only in L15.

2 *verb trans.* CHRISTIAN THEOLOGY. Be an obstacle or stumbling-block to (a person's faith); injure spiritually by one's example. Now *rare.* M16.

3 a *verb trans.* Make false or malicious statements about (a person's character or conduct); slander, malign, (a person). Formerly also, treat with contempt. M16. ▸**b** *verb intrans.* Talk or spread scandal. M18.

4 *verb trans.* Bring shame or discredit on, disgrace, (a person). Now *rare.* L16.

5 *verb trans.* Offend the moral sensibilities of; horrify or shock by a (real or imagined) violation of morality or propriety. E17.

> 🕮 **3a** *New Zealand Herald* If a certain person . . does not stop scandalizing my name, legal action will be taken. **b** G. B. STERN She persecuted her, she scandalised about her. **5** N. CHOMSKY An act of aggression that scandalised the civilised world. *Premiere* The teen drama that scandalized Moscow with its sexual explicitness.

■ **scandaliˈzation** *noun* the action of scandalizing; the condition or fact of being scandalized: M16. **scandalized** *adjective* horrified, shocked M17. **scandalizer** *noun* a slanderer, a libeller M17.

scandalize /ˈskand(ə)lʌɪz/ *verb*² *trans.* Also **-ise**. M19.
[Alt. from SCANTLE *verb* + -IZE.]
NAUTICAL. Reduce the area of (a sail) by lowering the peak and tricing up the tack.

scandalon *noun* var. of SKANDALON.

scandalous /ˈskand(ə)ləs/ *adjective.* L16.
[French *scandaleux* or medieval Latin *scandalosus*, from ecclesiastical Latin *scandalum*: see SCANDAL, -OUS.]

1 Of the nature of a scandal; grossly disgraceful, outrageous, shameful; improper. Also (now *rare*) of a person: guilty of gross misconduct. L16. ▸†**b** Of the nature of or causing a stumbling-block or occasion of offence. L16–L17.

2 Of words, writing, etc.: defamatory, libellous. Also (now *rare*) of a person: addicted to or loving scandal. E17.

> 🕮 **1** LD MACAULAY He was indolent . . and worldly: but such failings . . are scandalous in a prelate. I. MURDOCH It's scandalous, wicked . . a society which allows it deserves to be blown to bits. *Pink Paper* Look at the scandalous state of AIDS treatment research in the UK. **2** HENRY FIELDING The most scandalous tongues . . never dared censure my reputation.

■ **scandalously** *adverb* E17. **scandalousness** *noun* M17.

scandalum magnatum /ˌskandələm magˈneɪtəm/ *noun phr.* Pl. ***scandala magnatum*** /ˌskandələ/. E17.
[medieval Latin, lit. 'scandal of magnates'.]
LAW (now *Hist.*). The utterance or publication of a malicious report against a dignitary. Also (*joc.*), something scandalous.

scandaroon /skandəˈruːn/ *noun.* M17.
[App. alt. of *Iskenderun*, a port in Turkey.]

†**1** A swindler, a fraudulent dealer. Only in M17.

2 A variety of domestic pigeon. M19.

scandent /ˈskandənt/ *adjective.* L17.
[Latin *scandent-* pres. ppl stem of *scandere* climb: see -ENT.]
BIOLOGY. Esp. of a plant: having a climbing habit.

Scandian /ˈskandɪən/ *adjective. rare.* M17.
[from Latin *Scandia* Scandinavia + -AN.]
Scandinavian.
■ Also †**Scandic** *adjective* (*rare*) E18–E19.

Scandihoovian /skandɪˈhuːvɪən/ *noun & adjective. slang* (chiefly *N. Amer.*). E20.
[Arbitrary joc. alt. of SCANDINAVIAN.]
(A) Scandinavian.

Scandinavian /skandɪˈneɪvɪən/ *adjective & noun.* E18.
[from (Latin) *Scandinavia* (see below) + -AN.]
▶ **A** *adjective.* **1** Of or pertaining to Scandinavia, an area including Norway, Sweden, Denmark (and Iceland), its people, or its languages. E18.
2 Of furnishing etc.: made in a Scandinavian style, esp. as characterized by simplicity of design and the use of pine. M20.
▶ **B** *noun.* **1** The languages of the Scandinavian peoples collectively; *spec.* North Germanic. E18.
2 A native or inhabitant of Scandinavia. M19.
■ **Scandinavianism** *noun* the characteristic spirit or ideas of the Scandinavians M19. **Scandinaviani'zation** *noun* the action or process of Scandinavianizing a place-name etc. M20. **Scandinavianize** *verb trans.* make (a place-name etc.) Scandinavian in form or character E20.

scandium /ˈskandɪəm/ *noun.* L19.
[from Latin *Scandia*, contr. of *Scandinavia*: see -IUM.]
A soft silvery chemical element, atomic no. 21, which is one of the transition metals and is found in small quantities in association with rare-earth elements (among which it is often classified) and in some tin and tungsten ores. (Symbol Sc.)
■ **scandia** *noun* scandium oxide, Sc_2O_3, a weakly basic white amorphous solid L19.

Scanian /ˈskeɪmɪən/ *adjective & noun.* L19.
[from medieval Latin *Scania* from Old Norse *Skáni* or *Skáney* Skåne (see below): see -AN.]
▶ **A** *adjective.* **1** Of or pertaining to the province of Skåne in southern Sweden. L19.
2 GEOLOGY. **a** = MENAPIAN *adjective.* Now *rare.* L19. ▸**b** Designating a cold stadial at the end of the last Pleistocene glaciation in northern Europe, and the resulting moraines. M20.
▶ **B** *noun.* GEOLOGY. = MENAPIAN *noun* (now *rare*); the Scanian stadial. E20.

scanmag /ˈskanmag/ *noun. slang.* Now *rare* or *obsolete.* L18.
[Abbreviation of SCANDALUM MAGNATUM.]
Scandal, *esp.* malicious gossip.

scannable /ˈskanəb(ə)l/ *adjective.* E19.
[from SCAN *verb* + -ABLE.]
Able to be scanned.

scanner /ˈskanə/ *noun.* M16.
[from SCAN *verb* + -ER¹.]
1 A person who scans or critically examines something. M16.
2 A person who scans verse. E19.
3 A device for scanning or systematically examining something, *esp.* a device for representing the intensities of an image in digitized form. E20. ▸**b** TELEVISION. Any of several devices that permit the sequential transmission of an image or its subsequent reconstruction in a receiver. E20. ▸**c** A radar aerial that scans a large area, esp. by rotating or oscillating. M20. ▸**d** MEDICINE. A machine for scanning (part of) the body and measuring the intensity of the radiation from different areas as a diagnostic aid after administration of a radioisotope. Also, a machine using ultrasound, magnetic resonance imaging, tomography, etc., to obtain a visual representation of internal organs. M20.

> 📖 **1** F. MAHONY The . . philosopher, the scanner of whate'er lies hidden in . . the human heart. B. VINE The dipper into magazines, the desultory scanner of newsprint.

scanning /ˈskanɪŋ/ *noun.* LME.
[from SCAN *verb* + -ING¹.]
1 PROSODY. = SCANSION 2. LME.
2 a Close investigation or consideration, critical examination or judgement; discernment. M16. ▸**b** The action of systematically traversing an object or image with a beam or detector; MEDICINE the examination of a patient, an organ, etc., using a scanner. E20. ▸**c** The rapid or systematic searching of textual material for particular information or features. M20.
Phrases: **auditory scanning** the system of echolocation thought to be used by dolphins, whales, etc., for the location and ranging of objects.
Comb.: **scanning coil** each of four coils around the neck of a cathode-ray tube or scanning electron microscope, which determine the raster pattern traced by the electron beam; **scanning disc** a rotating disc having a spiral of holes near the edge, used in mechanical systems of television to provide a sequential scan of a scene by optical means for transmission and reception; **scanning electron microscope** a form of electron microscope used to examine the surface of a specimen, which is scanned by an electron beam in a raster pattern, and an image derived from the secondary electrons emitted; abbreviation *SEM*; **scanning field** = RASTER *noun* 1; **scanning line** = LINE *noun*² 11g; *scanning raster*: see RASTER *noun* 1; **scanning spot** the spot where an incident beam (usu. of electrons or light) strikes the surface it is scanning; **scanning transmission electron microscope** a microscope similar to the scanning electron microscope, but in which the image is derived from electrons transmitted through the specimen; abbreviation *STEM*; **scanning tunnelling microscope** a type of high resolution microscope using neither light nor an electron beam, but with an ultra-fine tip able to reveal atomic and molecular details of surfaces; abbreviation *STM*.

scanning /ˈskanɪŋ/ *ppl adjective.* M19.
[from SCAN *verb* + -ING².]
1 That scans or closely examines (a person or thing); critical, searching. M19.
2 MEDICINE. Designating a slurred and measured form of speech with regular pauses between syllables, characteristic of some nervous diseases. M19.
■ **scanningly** *adverb* L19.

scansion /ˈskanʃ(ə)n/ *noun.* M17.
[Latin *scansio(n-)*, from *scans-* pa. ppl stem of *scandere* climb (for sense see SCAN): see ION.]
†**1** The action of climbing up. *rare.* Only in M17.
2 PROSODY. The metrical scanning of verse; the division of (a) verse into metrical feet; an example of this. L17.
■ **scansional** *adjective* (PROSODY) of or pertaining to scansion M19. **scansionist** *noun* (PROSODY) an expert in scansion M19.

scansorial /skanˈsɔːrɪəl/ *adjective.* E19.
[from Latin *scansorius*, from *scans-*: see prec., -IAL.]
1 Of or pertaining to climbing; *spec.* in ZOOLOGY, adapted for climbing. E19.
2 That climbs or is given to climbing; *spec.* belonging or pertaining to a group of climbing birds formerly classified together in an order Scansores. M19.

scant /skant/ *noun. obsolete* exc. *dial.* ME.
[Old Norse *skamt* use as noun of adjective: see next.]
Scanty supply; dearth, scarcity.

scant /skant/ *adjective & adverb.* ME.
[Old Norse *skamt* neut. of *skammr* short, brief = Old High German *scam*. Largely superseded by SCANTY.]
▶ **A** *adjective.* **1** Barely sufficient or adequate; limited; scarce; not abundant. Also, very little, less than enough. ME. ▸**b** Barely amounting to, hardly reaching (a specified quantity). M19.
2 Sparing, parsimonious. Also, careful, not lavish. Foll. by *of*. *obsolete* exc. *Scot. dial.* ME.
3 Limited in extent, narrow. *arch.* LME.
4 Having a scanty or limited supply *of*; short *of*. *arch.* L16.
5 Lacking in quality; poor, meagre. Foll. by *in*. *arch.* E17.
6 NAUTICAL. Of wind: too much ahead, so that a ship has to sail very close. Cf. SCANT *verb* 2. E17.

> 📖 **1** D. H. LAWRENCE Three days have I hidden, and eaten scant bread. *Listener* So-called evidence is more scant. I. WATSON He paid us scant heed, beyond a nod. **b** J. LONDON He slept a scant five hours. L. CHAMBERLAIN Strain the stock and make up with water to a scant ¼ litre. **4** R. L. STEVENSON Cold, naked and . . scant of wood.

▶ **B** *adverb.* Hardly, scarcely; barely. Now *Scot. & dial.* ME.

> 📖 SIR W. SCOTT Scant three miles the band had rode.

■ **scantity** *noun* (*rare*) scantiness, scarceness LME. **scantly** *adverb* (*a*) *arch.* scarcely, hardly, barely; (*b*) in scant measure; inadequately: LME. **scantness** *noun* LME.

scant /skant/ *verb.* LME.
[from SCANT *adjective.*]
▶ **I** *verb intrans.* **1** Become scant or scarce. *obsolete* exc. *Scot.* LME.
2 NAUTICAL. Of wind: become unfavourable, draw too much ahead. Cf. SCANT *adjective* 6. M16.
▶ **II** *verb trans.* **3** Provide (a person etc.) with an inadequate supply; stint, limit, restrict. Also, keep (a person) short *of* something; restrict (a person) *in* a commodity etc. *arch.* M16.
4 Make scant or small; reduce in size, diminish in amount. *arch.* L16.
5 Stint the supply of; provide grudgingly; deny, withhold. *arch.* L16.
6 Confine within narrow bounds; limit, hedge in. *obsolete* exc. *poet.* L16.
7 Slight, neglect. Now chiefly *US*. E17.

> 📖 **6** G. M. HOPKINS A dare-gale skylark scanted in a dull cage. **7** *New York Review of Books* No issue is scanted as too controversial.

†**scantillon** *noun.* ME.
[Aphet. from Old French *escantillon* (mod. *échantillon*) sample. Cf. SCANTLING.]
1 A measuring tool, a gauge. ME–E16.
2 Dimension, measured size. LME–E16.
3 A specimen, a sample. LME–E17.

scantle /ˈskant(ə)l/ *noun. rare.* E16.
[Prob. from next.]
†**1** Prescribed or measured size; scantling. Only in E16.
†**2** A small piece or portion, a scantling. L16–M17.
3 A gauge for sizing slates; a small or irregular slate. M19.

scantle /ˈskant(ə)l/ *verb trans.* L16.
[Perh. dim. of SCANT *verb*: see -LE³.]
†**1** Give scant provision to, stint; = SCANT *verb* 3. L16–M17.
2 Make scant or small; diminish; restrict. *obsolete* exc. as ***scantled*** *ppl adjective.* L16.
†**3** Adjust to a required measure; make proportionate *to*. E17–E18.

scantling /ˈskantlɪŋ/ *noun.* E16.
[Alt., by assoc. with -LING¹, of SCANTILLON.]
1 Measured or prescribed size; a set of standard dimensions, esp. for timber, stone, an aircraft, or a ship. E16. ▸†**b** *fig.* The measure or extent of an individual's capacity or ability. L16–M18.
†**2** A measuring-rod, a gauge; *fig.* a standard of measurement. M16–L17.
3 A sample, a specimen. Also, a sketch, a rough draft. *arch.* M16.
†**4** Limited measure, amount, or space; a limit; *spec.* in ARCHERY, the distance from the mark by which a shot may deviate and still be regarded as a hit. L16–L17.
5 A small or scanty portion or amount, a modicum. Formerly also, an abridgement, a small remnant. *arch.* L16.
6 A portion, an allowance. *arch.* M17.
7 a A timber beam of small cross-section, *esp.* one less than five inches square; *collect. sing.* timber cut to such a size. M17. ▸**b** A block of stone of a fixed size; *collect. sing.* stone cut to such a size. E18.
8 A trestle for holding casks. *rare.* M17.

> 📖 **1** *Wales* The scantling of the baulks varies from twelve to fourteen inches. **5** R. C. HUTCHINSON This scantling of slack muscles and impoverished flesh. *Times Lit. Suppl.* A scantling of the many [works] which might contain . . neologisms. **7a** F. P. GROVE The thinnest of box-lumber, held in place by poplar scantlings.

scanty /ˈskanti/ *adjective & noun.* L16.
[from SCANT *noun* or *adjective* + -Y¹.]
▶ **A** *adjective.* **1** Meagre, barely sufficient or adequate; not ample or copious. L16.
2 Existing in small or insufficient quantity; scarce, not abundant. L17.
†**3** Parsimonious; (of soil) yielding little. L17–L18.
4 Deficient in extent or size; small, brief. E18.

> 📖 **1** R. FRASER Breakfast was scanty—milk and . . dry bread. **2** *Sciences* Cartesian thinking . . often manifests itself as elegant theory backed by scanty evidence. **4** *New York Times* In every garage, there were girlie calendars . . —bikinis and scanty clothing, but no nudes.

▶ **B** *noun.* Underwear, esp. women's brief knickers or panties. Now only in *pl. colloq.* (chiefly *US*). E20.
■ **scantily** *adverb* E17. **scantiness** *noun* M16.

scape /skeɪp/ *noun*¹. ME.
[Aphet. from ESCAPE *noun.*]
1 An act of escaping. *arch.* ME.
†**2** A thoughtless transgression. Also, an immoral act, *esp.* one of an amorous or sexual nature. Cf. ESCAPE *noun* 3. LME–L17.
†**3** A mistake, *esp.* a clerical or printer's error; = ESCAPE *noun* 3b. M16–E18.

scape /skeɪp/ *noun*². E17.
[Latin *scapus* from Greek *skapos* rod, cogn. with *skēptron* SCEPTRE *noun.*]
1 BOTANY. Orig. *gen.*, a stem. Now, a leafless or almost leafless flowering stem arising directly from the rootstock. E17.
2 ARCHITECTURE. The shaft of a column. Also, an apophyge. M17.
3 ENTOMOLOGY. The basal segment of an insect's antenna, esp. when it is enlarged or lengthened. E19.
4 ORNITHOLOGY. The whole stem of a feather; the calamus and the rachis together. Now *rare.* L19.

scape /skeɪp/ *noun*³. L18.
[Back-form. from LANDSCAPE *noun.*]
A (representation of a) scenic view. Freq. as 2nd elem. of combs. (formed in imit. of ***landscape***), as ***cityscape***, ***lunarscape***, ***moonscape***, etc.

> 📖 G. GREENE Looked sadly . . over the monotonous repetitive scape of sea. *Modern Painters* Familiar, even cosy suburban scapes.

scape /skeɪp/ *noun*⁴. M19.
[Origin uncertain: perh. from SCAPE *noun*³: cf. INSCAPE.]
A reflection or impression of the essential unique quality of a thing or action, esp. as embodied in literary, artistic, etc., expression.
¶ In the poetic theory of Gerard Manley Hopkins (1844–89), English poet.

scape /skeɪp/ *noun*[5] & *interjection.* M19.
[Imit.]
▶ **A** *noun.* A snipe. M19.
▶ **B** *interjection.* Repr. the cry of the snipe when flushed from cover. L19.

scape /skeɪp/ *verb*[1] *trans. & intrans.* Now *arch. & poet.* Now also **'scape.** ME.
[Aphet.]
= ESCAPE *verb.*
Comb.: †**scape-gallows** a criminal who has escaped execution on the gallows; **scapethrift** *arch.* a spendthrift.

scape /skeɪp/ *verb*[2] *intrans.* M18.
[Back-form. from SCAPEMENT.]
HOROLOGY. Of (part of) an escapement: perform its function.

scapegoat /ˈskeɪpɡəʊt/ *noun & verb.* M16.
[from SCAPE *noun*[1] or *verb*[1] + GOAT.]
▶ **A** *noun.* **1** In the biblical ritual of the Day of Atonement (*Leviticus* 16), a goat chosen by lot to be sent into the wilderness, after the chief priest had symbolically laid the sins of the people on it (while another goat was appointed to be sacrificed). M16.
2 A person or thing blamed or punished for a mistake, fault, etc., of another or others. E19.

📖 **2** *Drew Magazine* Decaying, inner-city courthouses . . forced to serve as scapegoats for a skyrocketing crime rate.

▶ **B** *verb trans.* Make a scapegoat of (a person). M20.
■ **scapegoater** *noun* a person who scapegoats someone M20. **scapegoating** *noun* (**a**) the action or practice of making a scapegoat of someone; (**b**) *spec.* in PSYCHOLOGY, aggressively punitive behaviour directed against other, esp. weaker, people or groups: M20. **scapegoatism** *noun* = SCAPEGOATING (a) M20.

scapegrace /ˈskeɪpɡreɪs/ *noun*[1] & *adjective.* E19.
[from SCAPE *verb*[1] + GRACE *noun*, lit. 'person who escapes the grace of God'.]
▶ **A** *noun.* A rascal; a (young) scamp. E19.
▶ **B** *adjective.* That is a scapegrace; characteristic of a scapegrace. M19.

scapegrace /ˈskeɪpɡreɪs/ *noun*[2]. *N. Amer.* M19.
[Alt. of *cape race*, *Cape Racer*, from *Cape Race*, Newfoundland, after prec.]
The red-throated diver, *Gavia stellata*.

scapement /ˈskeɪpm(ə)nt/ *noun.* M18.
[Aphet. from ESCAPEMENT.]
= ESCAPEMENT 1.

scapho- /ˈskafəʊ/ *combining form* of Greek *skaphē* boat: see -O-.
■ **scaphoceˈphalic** *adjective & noun* (MEDICINE) (**a**) *adjective* pertaining to, characteristic of, or affected with scaphocephalus; (**b**) *noun* a person with scaphocephalus: M19. **scaphoˈcephalus** *noun* [from Greek *kephalē* head, after *hydrocephalus*] MEDICINE the condition of having an abnormally long and narrow skull due to premature ossification of the sagittal suture M19. **scaphoˈcephaly** *noun* (MEDICINE) = SCAPHOCEPHALUS E20. **scaˈphocerite** *noun* [from Greek *keras* horn + -ITE[1]] ZOOLOGY a boat-shaped appendage on each of the second antennae in decapod crustaceans L19. **scaphognathite** /skafəɡˈnaθʌɪt, -ˈneɪ-/ *noun* [from Greek *gnathos* jaw + -ITE[1]] ZOOLOGY a paddle-shaped appendage on each of the second maxillae in decapod crustaceans, which beats to produce a respiratory water current or to aid aerial ventilation L19. **scaphopod** *noun & adjective* [see -POD] ZOOLOGY (**a**) *noun* any of various burrowing marine molluscs of the class Scaphopoda, which have a tusk-shaped shell with both ends open; also called *tusk shell*; (**b**) *adjective* of, pertaining to, or designating this class: E20.

scaphoid /ˈskafɔɪd/ *adjective & noun.* M18.
[mod. Latin *scaphoides* from Greek *skaphoeidēs*, from *skaphē*: see prec., -OID.]
Chiefly ANATOMY & ZOOLOGY. ▶**A** *adjective.* Boat-shaped; navicular. M18.
scaphoid bone the first proximal carpal bone in the wrist; the corresponding carpal or tarsal bone in the foot of a mammal.
▶ **B** *noun.* The scaphoid bone. M19.

scapi *noun* pl. of SCAPUS.

scapigerous /skəˈpɪdʒ(ə)rəs/ *adjective.* M19.
[from SCAPE *noun*[2] + -I- + -GEROUS.]
BOTANY. Having a scape or (almost) leafless stem.

scapolite /ˈskapəlʌɪt/ *noun.* E19.
[from Greek *skapos* (see SCAPE *noun*[2]) + *lithos* stone: see -LITE.]
MINERALOGY. Any of a group of silicates of aluminium, calcium, and sodium, forming a series from marialite to meionite. Also called ***wernerite***.
■ **scapoliti'zation** *noun* the alteration of aluminosilicate minerals of igneous rocks into, or their replacement by, scapolites E20. **scaˈpolitize** *verb trans.* M20.

scapple /ˈskap(ə)l/ *verb trans.* LME.
[Aphet. from Old French *escapeler*, *eschapeler* dress timber. Cf. SCABBLE.]
Reduce the faces of (a block of stone or (formerly) timber) to a plane surface without working them smooth; = SCALP *verb*[3].

scapula /ˈskapjʊlə/ *noun.* Pl. **-lae** /-liː/, **-las.** L16.
[Late Latin, sing. of classical Latin *scapulae*.]
ANATOMY. The shoulder-blade of a mammal; the dorsal part of the pectoral girdle of a tetrapod.

scapular /ˈskapjʊlə/ *noun.* L15.
[Late Latin *scapulare*, from SCAPULA shoulder: see -AR[1].]
1 ECCLESIASTICAL. **a** A monastic cloak consisting of a piece of cloth covering the shoulders and extending in front and behind almost to the feet, which forms part of the regular habit of certain religious orders. L15. ▸**b** A symbol of affiliation to a religious order, consisting of two small rectangles of woollen cloth, joined by tapes passing over the shoulders. M19.
2 MEDICINE. = SCAPULARY *noun* 2. Long *rare* or *obsolete.* M18.
3 ORNITHOLOGY. Any feather covering the shoulder, above the place where the wing joins the body. Usu. in *pl.* M18.

scapular /ˈskapjʊlə/ *adjective.* L17.
[from SCAPULA + -AR[1].]
1 ORNITHOLOGY. Designating a shoulder feather. L17.
2 ANATOMY & ZOOLOGY. Of or pertaining to the scapula. E18.
2 scapular arch ZOOLOGY the part of the pectoral girdle formed by the scapulae and coracoids.

scapulary /ˈskapjʊləri/ *noun.* ME.
[Anglo-Norman, var. of Old French *eschapeloyre* from medieval Latin *scapelorium*, *scapularium*, var. of late Latin *scapulare* (see SCAPULAR *noun*) with ending assim. to -ARY[1].]
1 ECCLESIASTICAL. **a** = SCAPULAR *noun* 1a. ME. ▸**b** = SCAPULAR *noun* 1b. *rare.* L17.
2 MEDICINE. A bandage passing over and around the shoulders to support other bandages etc. M18.
3 = SCAPULAR *noun* 3. M19.

scapulary /ˈskapjʊləri/ *adjective.* M16.
[Sense 1 from Old French *eschapulaire*, sense 2 from SCAPULA + -ARY[1].]
†**1** Of a cloak: covering the shoulders. Only in M16.
2 = SCAPULAR *adjective* 2. L18.

scapulimancy /ˈskapjʊlɪˌmansi/ *noun.* L19.
[from SCAPULA + -I- + -MANCY.]
Divination by means of the cracks in a burned shoulder-blade bone.

scapulo- /ˈskapjʊləʊ/ *combining form* of Latin *scapula* shoulder: see -O-.
■ **scapuloˈcoracoid** *adjective & noun* (**a**) *adjective* (ANATOMY) of or belonging to the scapula and the coracoid; (**b**) *noun* (ZOOLOGY) a bone in some vertebrates formed by the fusion of the scapula and the coracoid: M19. **scapuloˈdynia** *noun* pain in the muscles of the shoulder M19.

scapus /ˈskeɪpəs/ *noun.* Now *rare.* Pl. **-pi** /-pʌɪ, -piː/. M16.
[Latin: see SCAPE *noun*[2].]
1 ARCHITECTURE. = SCAPE *noun*[2] 2. Now *rare* or *obsolete.* M16.
†**2** BOTANY. = SCAPE *noun*[2] 1. E–M18.
3 ORNITHOLOGY. = SCAPE *noun*[2] 4. L19.

scar /skɑː/ *noun*[1]. ME.
[Old Norse *sker* low reef. Cf. SCAUR, SKERRY *noun*[2].]
†**1** A rock, a crag. ME–M16.
2 A high steep rock-face on a hillside, esp. in the limestone of the English Yorkshire Dales etc.; a precipice, a cliff. L17.
3 A low or sunken rock in the sea; a rocky tract on the seabed. E18.

📖 **2** JOHN PHILLIPS Ranges of scars which begird the hills of Derbyshire.

■ **scarry** *adjective*[1] precipitous, rocky LME.

scar /skɑː/ *noun*[2]. LME.
[Aphet. from Old French *escharre* (later *escarre*, *eschare*) from late Latin *eschara* (also *scara*) scar, scab from Greek *eskhara* hearth, brazier, scab. Cf. ESCHAR.]
1 a A usu. permanent mark left on the skin after the healing of a wound, sore, or burn; a cicatrice. Also (*transf.*), a mark left on something after damage etc. LME. ▸**b** *fig.* A lasting effect on a thing or person of a former unfortunate experience, condition, etc. L16.
2 BOTANY. The mark left by the separation of a leaf, frond, etc.; the hilum of a seed. L18.

📖 **1** A. SETON A jagged purple scar puckered his right cheek. D. HIGHSMITH The suit bore the . . scars of a lifetime's responsibilities in its faded knees and elbows. **b** H. SACHEVERELL The Prosecution wou'd leave a Scar upon his good name. D. LODGE It is the fear, the shame, that leaves the scars.

Comb.: **scar tissue** the fibrous connective tissue of which scars are formed.
■ **scarless** *adjective* showing or leaving no scar M17. **scarry** *adjective*[2] (long *rare*) of the nature of a scar; marked with scars: M17.

scar /skɑː/ *noun*[3]. M18.
[Latin SCARUS.]
= SCARUS. Also ***scar-fish***.

scar /skɑː/ *adjective. Scot. & north.* ME.
[Old Norse *skiarr* (Norwegian *skerr*), whence also *skirra* SCARE *verb.*]
Of a person or animal, esp. a horse: shy, timid; nervous, excitable.

scar /skɑː/ *verb.* Infl. **-rr-.** M16.
[from SCAR *noun*[2].]
1 *verb trans.* Mark with a scar or scars; disfigure by inflicting a wound. M16.
2 a *verb trans.* Form a scar on; cover *up* (a wound) with a scar. E17. ▸**b** *verb intrans.* Heal *over* with a scar. M19.

📖 **1** C. G. SELIGMAN The Barabra scar their cheeks with vertical . . cuts. *transf.*: J. S. HUXLEY Trenches and barbed wire scarring the grassy slopes.

scarab /ˈskarəb/ *noun.* L16.
[Abbreviation of Latin SCARABAEUS.]
1 a ENTOMOLOGY. Orig., a beetle of any kind. Now, a scarabaeid or scarabaeoid beetle, *esp.* (in full ***sacred scarab***) *Scarabaeus sacer*, which was revered by the ancient Egyptians. L16. ▸†**b** *transf. & fig.* Used as a term of abuse. Only in 17.
2 ANTIQUITIES. An ancient Egyptian gem cut in the form of a scarab beetle, engraved with symbols on its flat underside, and worn as a signet-ring or on a chain round the neck. L19.
■ **scaˈrabidoid** *adjective* (US) = SCARABAEOID *adjective* E20. **ˈscaraboid** *noun & adjective* (ANTIQUITIES) (a gem etc.) resembling a scarab L19.

scarabaei *noun* pl. of SCARABAEUS.

scarabaeid /skarəˈbiːɪd/ *adjective & noun.* M19.
[mod. Latin *Scarabaeidae* (see below), from Latin SCARABAEUS: see -ID[3].]
ENTOMOLOGY. ▶**A** *adjective.* Of, pertaining to, or designating the beetle family Scarabaeidae, which includes the dung beetles, goliath beetles, chafers, etc. M19.
▶ **B** *noun.* A beetle of this family. M19.
■ **scarabaeidoid** *adjective* (now *rare*) = SCARABAEOID *adjective* L19.

scarabaeoid /skarəˈbiːɔɪd/ *adjective & noun.* L19.
[(mod. Latin *Scarabaeoidea*) formed as next: see -OID.]
▶ **A** *adjective.* Resembling a scarab; *spec.* in ENTOMOLOGY (**a**) designating the third-stage larva of hypermetamorphic oil-beetles; (**b**) of, pertaining to, or designating a beetle of the superfamily Scarabaeoidea, which includes stag beetles, dor-beetles, scarabaeids, etc. L19.
▶ **B** *noun.* A beetle resembling a scarab; *spec.* a beetle of the superfamily Scarabaeoidea. L19.

scarabaeus /skarəˈbiːəs/ *noun.* Pl. **-baei** /-ˈbiːʌɪ/. L16.
[Latin = beetle: cf. Greek *karabos* horned beetle.]
1 ENTOMOLOGY. A scarabaeid beetle. Now only as mod. Latin genus name. L16.
2 ANTIQUITIES. = SCARAB 2. L18.
■ **scarabaeiform** *adjective* (ENTOMOLOGY) designating a type of beetle larva having a C-shaped body, a fleshy abdomen, and limited mobility M20.

scarabee /ˈskarəbiː/ *noun. arch.* L16.
[Anglicized from prec.]
= SCARAB 1a.

scaramouch /ˈskarəmaʊtʃ, -muːtʃ/ *noun & verb.* M17.
[Orig. from Italian *Scaramuccia* (see below) from *scaramuccia* SKIRMISH *noun*, whence also French *Scaramouche*, source of the later and present form.]
▶ **A** *noun.* **1** (Usu. **S-**.) A stock character of the cowardly and foolish boaster in Italian *commedia dell'arte*, usu. represented as a Spanish don, wearing a black costume. M17.
2 A boastful coward, a braggart; a rascal, a scamp. *arch.* L17.
▶ **B** *verb intrans.* Act the part of or behave like a scaramouch. *rare.* M19.

Scarborough /ˈskɑːb(ə)rə/ *noun.* M16.
[A town on the Yorkshire coast, NE England.]
1 ***Scarborough warning***, very short notice, no notice at all. Now *rare.* M16.
2 ***Scarborough lily***, a southern African plant grown for ornament, *Cyrtanthus elatus* (family Amaryllidaceae), bearing a cluster of scarlet flowers on a leafless stem. L19.

scarce /skɛːs/ *adjective & adverb.* ME.
[Anglo-Norman, Old Northern French *scars* aphet. of *escars*, Old French *eschars*, mod. *échars* (of coin) below standard value, (of wind) slight, from Proto-Romance pa. pple with the sense 'plucked out', from verb corresp. to Latin *excerpere* select out, EXCERPT *verb.*]
▶ **A** *adjective.* †**1 a** Restricted in quantity, size, or amount; scanty. ME–L16. ▸**b** Of wind: slight, almost calm. LME–E17.
†**2** Of a person, a person's actions, etc.: stingy, niggardly, parsimonious. ME–M17.
3 Esp. of food or other commodities: existing or available in insufficient quantity. LME.
4 Existing in limited number; hard to find; rare. LME. ▸**b** In names of butterflies and moths: designating a species more rarely encountered than the nominate form. M19.
5 Poorly provided with; deficient in; short of. Foll. by *of*. Now *rare* or *obsolete.* M16.

📖 **3** DISRAELI Stocks fell . . the exchange turned, money became scarce. **4** S. TRUEMAN The . . long-billed curlew had beome extremely scarce, or extinct. *Garden* Lowland raised bogs are now relatively scarce in the UK and . . plants . . are under threat.

Phrases: **as scarce as hen's teeth**: see HEN *noun*. **make oneself scarce** *colloq.* go away, disappear, keep out of the way.

▶ **B** *adverb*. †**1** Scantily, sparsely. Cf. SCARCELY *adverb* 1. *rare*. Only in ME.

2 Barely, hardly; only just; not quite; = SCARCELY *adverb* 2. Freq., usu. with hyphen, before a ppl adjective used attrib. Now *arch.* or *literary*. LME.

†**3** Seldom, rarely. L16–M17.

4 With difficulty. *rare*. M17.

> 📖 **2** W. OWEN I shall scarce see much of you unless you arrive early. H. CRANE Scarce enough cash left to tip the conductor. W. DE LA MARE A scarce-heard utterance, followed by a sigh.

†**scarce** *verb trans. & intrans. rare.* LME–E17.
[from SCARCE *adjective*.]
Make or become less or scarce.

scarcely /ˈskɛːsli/ *adverb*. ME.
[from SCARCE *adjective* + -LY².]
†**1** Scantily; inadequately; parsimoniously. ME–M17.
2 Barely, hardly; only just; not quite; (freq. *iron.*) surely not. ME.

> 📖 **2** L. MURRAY It is scarcely possible to act otherwise. H. CONWAY He blamed my partner, who could scarcely believe his ears. A. S. BYATT Work on the edition . . had scarcely progressed. O. MANNING He could scarcely stifle his cry of pain. B. CHATWIN Her salary scarcely paid the rent.

scarcement /ˈskɛːsm(ə)nt/ *noun*. *Scot. & north.* E16.
[App. from SCARCE *verb* + -MENT.]
A plain flat set-off or rabbet in a wall, foundation, or bank of earth; *transf.* a flat ledge projecting from a rock-face.

scarceness /ˈskɛːsnɪs/ *noun*. Now *rare*. ME.
[from SCARCE *adjective* + -NESS.]
†**1** Niggardliness, stinginess; (of soil) infertility. ME–L17.
2 Insufficient supply, scarcity, shortage. LME.
3 Uncommonness, rarity. LME.

scarcity /ˈskɛːsɪti/ *noun*. ME.
[Old Northern French *escarceté*, Old French *eschar-*. (mod. *écharseté*) from *eschars*: see SCARCE *adjective*, -ITY.]
†**1** Frugality, parsimony; niggardliness, stinginess. ME–M16.
2 Insufficiency of supply; lack of availability, esp. of a commodity, in proportion to demand; shortage. Also, an instance of this, a period of scarcity. ME.
†**3** Want *of*, shortage *of*; penury, hardship. LME–E17.

> 📖 **2** P. MATTHIESSEN They'd been through scarcity before, and would always believe that something would turn up. *Sciences* The growing scarcity . . of water has generated heated arguments over water rights.

Comb. & phrases: **root of scarcity**, **scarcity root** [by erron. association of German *Mangoldwurzel* mangel-wurzel with *Mangel* dearth] the mangel-wurzel variety of beet; **scarcity value** an enhanced value of a commodity due to scarcity.

scare /skɛː/ *noun*¹. LME.
[from SCARE *verb*.]
†**1** Fear, dread. LME–E17.
2 An act of scaring or state of being scared; a sudden fright; *spec.* (**a**) a general or public fear of war, invasion, illness, etc., esp. a needless one occasioned by unsubstantiated or exaggerated rumour; (**b**) a financial panic causing share-selling etc.; M16.
3 A thing that scares or frightens a person or thing, *esp.* a scarecrow or other device for scaring birds from crops. M16.

> 📖 **2** W. S. CHURCHILL An invasion scare took a firm hold of the . . authorities. G. BODDY After one scare from intruders she had slept with a revolver . . on the bedside table. *Independent on Sunday* Food scares began erupting with frightening regularity, exposed . . by a new army of health specialists.

Comb.: **scare-buying** *US* = *panic buying* s.v. PANIC *adjective & noun*²; **scare-head**, **scare-heading** a shockingly sensational newspaper headline; **scare tactic** a strategy intended to influence public reaction by the exploitation of fear (usu. in *pl.*).
■ **scareful** *adjective* (now *rare*) terrifying, alarming M16.

scare /skɛː/ *noun*². *rare*. M19.
[Old Norse *skǫr* a joint.]
GOLF. The shank of a golf club.

scare /skɛː/ *verb*. ME.
[Old Norse *skirra* frighten, (also) avoid, prevent, refl. shrink from, from *skjarr* shy, timid.]
1 *verb trans.* **a** Frighten, make fearful or afraid. ME. ▸**b** Frighten away, drive off. Usu. with *away*, *off*, etc. LME.
2 *verb intrans.* Take fright; be alarmed (at). *obsolete* exc. *Scot. dial.* LME.
3 *verb intrans.* Be fearful or prone to fear; become frightened, esp. by unsubstantiated rumour etc. E20.

> 📖 **1a** A. F. DOUGLAS-HOME The curtained . . four-poster beds had . . scared them. **b** D. W. JERROLD A chap, with rags on him, not fit to scare birds. ALDOUS HUXLEY Flapping his hands at her as though . . to scare away some . . dangerous animal. **3** G. GREENE He scares easily . . any sound . . and he's off.

Phrases, & with adverbs in specialized senses: **scare out** = *scare up* (a) below. *scare rigid*: see RIGID *adjective*. *scare stiff*: see STIFF *adjective*. *scare the lights out of*, *scare the liver and lights out of*: see LIGHTS. *scare the living daylights out of*: see DAYLIGHT. *scare the pants off*. *scare the shit out of*: see SHIT *noun*. **scare up** (chiefly *N. Amer.*) (**a**) frighten (game) out of cover; (**b**) *colloq.* bring to light, discover; procure, rustle up.

Comb.: **scare-babe** (now *rare* or *obsolete*) something to frighten children, a bugbear, a bogey; **scare-quotes** quotation marks placed round a word or phrase to draw attention to an unusual or arguably inaccurate use.
■ **scarer** *noun* a person who or thing which scares someone or something; *spec.* (more fully *bird-scarer*) a person or thing, other than a scarecrow, for scaring birds from crops etc.: M18.

scarecrow /ˈskɛːkrəʊ/ *noun*. M16.
[from SCARE *verb* + CROW *noun*¹.]
1 A person whose occupation is to scare birds. *rare*. M16.
2 **a** A device, esp. a human figure dressed in old clothes, for scaring birds away from crops etc. L16. ▸**b** *fig.* Something, often not really alarming, that frightens or is intended to frighten; an object of groundless fear. L16. ▸**c** In the war of 1939–45, a weapon or manoeuvre which had a purely deterrent effect. *Military slang*. M20.
3 A badly dressed, grotesque-looking, or very thin person; someone who looks like a scarecrow. L16.

> 📖 **2b** *Nature* The prospect of world-wide famine, always something of a scarecrow, . . diminished.

scared /skɛːd/ *adjective*. L16.
[from SCARE *verb* + -ED¹.]
That has been scared; fearful; frightened, afraid. (Foll. by *of*, *at*, *by*, etc.).
scared shitless, *scared stiff*, *scared to death*, etc. *run scared*: see RUN *verb*.
■ **scaredly** *adverb* E20. **scaredy** *adjective & noun* (*colloq.*) (**a**) *adjective* timid, cowardly; only in *scaredy-cat*, a timid person, a coward; (**b**) *noun* = *scaredy-cat*: M20.

scaremonger /ˈskɛːmʌŋgə/ *noun & verb*. L19.
[from SCARE *noun*¹ + MONGER *noun*.]
▶ **A** *noun*. A person who spreads alarming rumours; an alarmist. L19.
▶ **B** *verb intrans.* Spread alarming rumours. Freq. as *scaremongering verbal noun & ppl adjective*. E20.

scarf /skɑːf/ *noun*¹. ME.
[Prob. from Old French (mod. *écart*, from *écarver*), perh. from an Old Norse base repr. by Swedish *skarf*, Norwegian *skarv* piece to lengthen a board or a garment, joint or seam effecting this, from Swedish *skarfva*, Norwegian *skarva* lengthen in this way.]
▶ **I 1 a** CARPENTRY & SHIPBUILDING. A joint by which two timbers are connected longitudinally, the ends being bevelled or notched so as to fit into each other with mutual overlapping. Also *scarf joint*. ME. ▸†**b** SHIPBUILDING. The overlapping of adjacent timbers in a ship's frame to ensure strength at the joints. Esp. in *give scarf*. E18–M19.
2 A flattened or grooved edge of metal prepared for welding. M19.
▶ **II 3** WHALING. A longitudinal cut made in a whale's body. M19.
4 FORESTRY. A V-shaped incision cut in a trunk during felling to govern the direction in which the tree falls; a sloping surface left by such an incision. *NZ*. M19.

scarf /skɑːf/ *noun*². Pl. **scarves** /skɑːvz/, **-s**. M16.
[Prob. alt. (by assoc. with prec.) of SCARP *noun*¹.]
1 a A broad band of material worn round the waist or diagonally across the body over one shoulder, esp. by a soldier or official; a sash. M16. ▸**b** ECCLESIASTICAL. A band of material worn round the neck with either end hanging down in front, as a part of clerical dress. M16.
2 a A square, triangular, or long narrow piece of silk or other fine material, worn usu. round the neck or head or over the shoulders for decoration; *spec.* a black scarf of this kind worn over the shoulder by mourners at a funeral. M16. ▸**b** A long strip of woollen or other warm material worn round the neck in cold weather. E19.
†**3** A sling for an injured limb. L16–E19.
4 HERALDRY. = SCARP *noun*¹. L17.

> 📖 **2a** H. MANTEL She folded the scarf into a triangle and slipped it over her head. *fig.*: R. L. STEVENSON The fogs . . crawl in scarves among the sandhills.

Comb.: **scarf-pin** a usu. ornamental pin for fastening a scarf; **scarf-ring**: for holding a scarf in position; **scarf-skin** (now *rare*) the outer layer of the skin; the epidermis, the cuticle.
■ **scarf-wise** *adverb* in a diagonal manner across the body from shoulder to hip L16.

scarf /skɑːf/ *noun*³. *Scot.* M17.
[Norn *skarf* from Old Norse *skarfr*.]
= SCART *noun*¹.

scarf /skɑːf/ *noun*⁴. *US slang*. M20.
[Var. of SCOFF *noun*².]
Food.

scarf /skɑːf/ *verb*¹ *trans.* L16.
[from SCARF *noun*².]
1 Cover with or as with a scarf or scarves; wrap, envelop. Chiefly *literary*. L16.
2 Wrap (a garment) *about* or *around* a person like a scarf. *rare*. E17.

> 📖 **1** I. GURNEY Still meadows . . Enwreathed and scarfed by phantom lines of white.

scarf /skɑːf/ *verb*². E17.
[from SCARF *noun*¹.]
▶ **I 1** *verb trans.* CARPENTRY & SHIPBUILDING. Join by a scarf joint. E17.
2 *verb intrans.* CARPENTRY & SHIPBUILDING. Be joined with a scarf (*to*). L18.
3 *verb trans.* Bevel or flatten (the edge of a piece of metal to be welded). M19.
1 scarfed joint = *scarf joint* s.v. SCARF *noun*¹ 1a.
▶ **II 4** *verb trans.* WHALING. Make an incision in the blubber of (a whale). M19.
5 *verb trans.* FORESTRY. Cut a scarf in (timber). *Austral. & NZ*. L19.

scarf /skɑːf/ *verb*³ *trans. & intrans. US slang*. M20.
[Var. of SCOFF *verb*².]
Scoff, eat greedily.

scari *noun* pl. of SCARUS.

scarification /ˌskarɪfɪˈkeɪʃ(ə)n, ˌskɛːrɪ-/ *noun*. LME.
[Old & mod. French, or late Latin *scarificatio(n-)*, from *scarificat-* pa. ppl stem of *scarificare*: see SCARIFY *verb*¹, -ATION.]
1 The action or process of scarifying something; an instance of this. LME.
2 A slight incision or group of incisions in the skin or a mucous membrane, esp. (in MEDICINE) made with a scarificator. M16.

scarificator /ˈskarɪfɪkeɪtə, ˈskɛːrɪ-/ *noun*. E17.
[Latinized form of French *scarificateur*, formed as prec. + *-eur*: see -ATOR.]
1 MEDICINE. An instrument used in scarification, *esp.* one which makes several incisions simultaneously. E17.
†**2** AGRICULTURE. = SCARIFIER *noun* 2a. L18–E19.

scarifier /ˈskarɪfʌɪə, ˈskɛːrɪ-/ *noun*. M16.
[from next + -ER¹.]
1 A person who or thing which scarifies something. Now *rare*. M16.
2 a AGRICULTURE. An implement or machine with prongs for loosening soil; a cultivator. Now chiefly *Austral.* L18. ▸**b** A machine with spikes attached to a roller or grader, for breaking up a road surface. L19. ▸**c** HORTICULTURE. An implement for cutting and removing debris from the turf of a lawn. L20.

scarify /ˈskarɪfʌɪ, ˈskɛːrɪ-/ *verb*¹ *trans.* LME.
[Old & mod. French *scarifier* from late Latin *scarificare* alt. of Latin *scarifare* from Greek *skariphasthai* scratch an outline, sketch lightly, from *skariphos* pencil, stylus: see -FY.]
1 a Make scratches or slight incisions in (the skin, a wound), esp. (in MEDICINE) with a scarificator for purposes of vaccination. Later also (*gen.*), cover with scratches or scars. LME. ▸**b** *fig.* Hurt, wound; subject to merciless criticism. L16.
2 Make incisions in the bark of (a tree); remove surplus branches from (a tree). LME.
3 a AGRICULTURE. Loosen (soil) with a scarifier. Now chiefly *Austral.* E19. ▸**b** Break up (a road surface) with a scarifier. E19. ▸**c** HORTICULTURE. Cut and remove (debris from the turf of a lawn) with a scarifier. L20.

scarify /ˈskɛːrɪfʌɪ/ *verb*² *trans. colloq.* (orig. *dial.*). L18.
[Irreg. from SCARE *verb* + -I- + -FY, perh. after TERRIFY.]
Scare, frighten; terrify.

†**scariole** *noun*. LME–E18.
[Italian *scariola*: see ESCAROLE.]
Broad-leaved endive, escarole. Also, a similar wild plant, perh. a wild lettuce, *Lactuca serriola*.

scarious /ˈskɛːrɪəs/ *adjective*. E19.
[French *scarieux* or mod. Latin *scariosus*.]
1 BOTANY. Of a bract etc.: dry and membranous in texture, and colourless. Opp. HERBACEOUS *adjective* 2. E19.
2 ZOOLOGY. Dry, not fleshy; covered with roughened scales. Now *rare*. M19.
■ Also (sense 1) **scariose** *adjective* L18.

scarlatina /skɑːləˈtiːnə/ *noun*. E19.
[mod. Latin, from Italian *scarlattina* fem. of *scarlattino* dim. of *scarlatto* scarlet.]
MEDICINE. = SCARLET FEVER.
■ **scarlatinal** *adjective* pertaining to, or resulting from, scarlet fever M19. **scarlatiniform** *adjective* (of a rash) resembling that seen in scarlet fever M19.

scarlet /ˈskɑːlət/ *noun & adjective*. ME.
[Aphet. from Old French *escarlate* fem. (mod. *écarlate*), from Hispano-Arab. *ʾeškarlāt*, *ʾeškelāt*, (cogn. with Hispano-Arab. *siklaṭūn*; cf. Spanish *ciclaton*) from Proto-Romance *escarlat*, ult. from Latin *sigillatus* adorned with small images.]
▶ **A** *noun*. **1** Orig., any rich or brightly coloured cloth. Later, (cloth of) a brilliant red colour tinged with orange. ME.
2 Official or ceremonial clothing of scarlet, as a soldier's uniform, a judge's gown, a huntsman's coat, etc.;

transf. the rank, dignity, or office signified by such clothing. L15.

3 †**a** A person who wears a uniform or insignia of scarlet. Only in E17. ▸**b** *collect.* People clothed in scarlet. *rare.* E19.

4 A pigment or dye of the colour of scarlet; *spec.* any of a group of coal tar colouring matters used in such pigments and dyes. M17.

5 Any of several cultivated varieties of a N. American strawberry, *Fragaria virginiana*. Now chiefly in ***little scarlet***, a variety grown for jam-making. E19.

▸ **B** *adjective*. **1 a** Of the colour scarlet. ME. ▸**b** Clothed in scarlet, wearing a scarlet uniform or insignia. L16. ▸**c** Red with shame or indignation. L16.

2 Of an offence, sin, etc.: wicked, heinous. Also, sinful, immoral; *esp.* promiscuous, unchaste. M17.

> 📖 **1a** D. L. SAYERS His scarlet robe clashed . . with the crimson of the roses. **c** I. MURDOCH His face . . flushed scarlet with emotion.

Special collocations: **scarlet-bean** = *scarlet runner* below. **scarlet day** an occasion observed in civic life etc. by the public wearing of official robes of scarlet. **scarlet grosbeak** a common rosefinch, *Carpodacus erythrinus*. **scarlet hat** ROMAN CATHOLIC CHURCH a cardinal's hat as a symbol of rank. **scarlet ibis** an ibis, *Eudocimus ruber*, of northern S. America, which is bright red with black wing tips. **scarlet king-snake** = *scarlet snake* below. **scarlet lady** *arch. derog.* the Roman Catholic Church, regarded as excessively devoted to showy ritual (with allus. to *Revelation* 17). **scarlet letter** US HISTORY a representation of the letter *A* in scarlet cloth which people convicted of adultery were condemned to wear. *scarlet* LYCHNIS. **scarlet macaw** a large Central and S. American parrot, *Ara macao*, which is mainly red with yellow and blue on the wings, tail, etc. **scarlet oak** a N. American oak, *Quercus coccinea*, whose leaves turn bright red in autumn. ***scarlet pimpernel***: see PIMPERNEL 3. **scarlet rosefinch** = ***scarlet grosbeak*** above. ***scarlet runner***: see RUNNER *noun* 12b. **scarlet snake** a small colubrid snake, *Cemophora coccinea*, found in the south-eastern US, which is red with black and yellow bands. **scarlet tanager** a tanager, *Piranga olivacea*, of eastern N. America, the breeding male of which is bright red with black wings and tail. **scarlet tiger (moth)** a brightly coloured European moth, *Callimorpha dominula*, with red and black hindwings. †**scarlet whore** *derog.* = ***scarlet lady*** above. **scarlet woman** *derog.* †(***a***) = ***scarlet lady*** above; (***b***) a notoriously promiscuous woman, a prostitute.

scarlet fever /skɑːlət ˈfiːvə/ *noun phr.* L17.
[SCARLET *adjective* + FEVER *noun*.]
A highly contagious disease, characterized by fever, sore throat, and a widespread scarlet rash, and caused by bacteria of the genus *Streptococcus*. Also called ***scarlatina***.

scarn *noun* var. of SKARN.

scaroid /ˈskarɔɪd, ˈskɛː-/ *adjective & noun.* L19.
[from SCARUS + -OID.]
▸ **A** *adjective*. Of or pertaining to the family Scaridae of tropical parrot-fishes. L19.
▸ **B** *noun*. A fish of this family. L19.

scarp /skɑːp/ *noun*[1]. Also **-e**. M16.
[Aphet. from Old Northern French *escarpe* = Old French *escherpe* (mod. *écharpe*), prob. identical with Old French *escharpe* pilgrim's scrip suspended from the neck (cf. Old Norse *skreppa* SCRIP *noun*[1]. Cf. SCARF *noun*[2].]
HERALDRY. A diminutive of the bend sinister, one-half its width.

scarp /skɑːp/ *noun*[2]. L16.
[Italian *scarpa* whence French *escarpe* ESCARP *noun*.]
1 FORTIFICATION. A bank or an inner slope of a ditch in front of and below a rampart. L16.
2 *gen.* Any steep bank or slope; *spec.* in GEOGRAPHY, the steep slope of a cuesta. E19.

scarp /skɑːp/ *verb*[1] *trans.* E19.
[from prec.]
1 Make (a slope) perpendicular or steep; cut to a steep slope. E19.
2 FORTIFICATION. Provide (a ditch) with a steep scarp. E19.
■ **scarped** *adjective* reduced to a steep face, cut away, steep E19.

scarp /skɑːp/ *verb*[2] *intrans.* M19.
[Origin uncertain: perh. same word as prec.]
AGRICULTURE. Of land: be torn up irregularly.

scarp-bolt /ˈskɑːpbəʊlt/ *noun.* M19.
[App. from Danish *skarpbolt* lit. 'sharp bolt'.]
A long pointed bolt used in shipbuilding.

scarpe *noun* var. of SCARP *noun*[1].

scarper /ˈskɑːpə/ *verb. slang.* M19.
[Prob. from Italian *scappare* escape, get away; reinforced during or after the war of 1914–18 by rhyming slang *Scapa flow* go.]
1 *verb intrans.* Leave in haste, run away; escape. M19.
2 *verb trans.* Leave or escape from (a place). Chiefly in ***scarper the letty***, leave one's lodgings without paying the rent. M20.

> 📖 **1** P. BARKER Go on, scarper! You know you're not supposed to be here.

scarpetti /skɑːˈpɛti/ *noun pl.* L19.
[Italian, pl. of *scarpetto* small shoe, from *scarpa*: see next.]
Rope-soled shoes worn for rock-climbing, esp. in the North Italian Alps.

scarpine /ˈskɑːpiːn/ *noun.* L16.
[Italian *scarpino* dim. of *scarpa* shoe.]
†**1** A light shoe. *rare.* L16–E17.
2 *Hist.* An instrument of torture for the feet. M19.

scarping /ˈskɑːpɪŋ/ *noun. rare.* M17.
[from SCARP *verb*[1] + -ING[1].]
A steep slope; the rocky face of a hill.

scarred /skɑːd/ *adjective.* ME.
[from SCAR *noun*[2], *verb*: see -ED[2], -ED[1].]
Bearing scars, traces of injury, marks, etc.

scart /skɑːt/ *noun*[1]. *Scot.* Also (earlier) †**-th**. LME.
[Alt. formed as SCARF *noun*[3].]
A cormorant; a shag.

scart /skɑːt/ *noun*[2]. *Scot.* L16.
[Metathetic var. of SCRAT *noun*[2].]
1 A scratch. L16.
2 A mark made by a pen. M18.

scart /skɑːt/ *noun*[3]. *rare.* M19.
[Perh. var. of SCAT *noun*[2].]
A gust (of wind); a strip (of cloud).

SCART /skɑːt/ *noun*[4]. Also **Scart**, **scart**. L20.
[French acronym, from Syndicat des Constructeurs des Appareils Radiorécepteurs et Téléviseurs, the committee which designed the connector.]
Used ***attrib.*** with ref. to a 21-pin socket used to connect video equipment.

scart /skɑːt/ *verb trans. Scot.* LME.
[Metathetic var. of SCRAT *verb*.]
1 Scratch, scrape. LME.
2 Gather together, accumulate. E17.
3 Scribble (over). E19.

scarth /skɑːθ/ *noun*[1]. ME.
[Old Norse *skarð* (Middle Swedish *skardh*) notch, cleft, mountain pass = Old English *sceard* SHARD *noun*[1].]
†**1** A fragment, a shard. ME–L15.
2 A cliff, a bare rock. *dial.* M19.

†**scarth** *noun*[2] see SCART *noun*[1].

scarus /ˈskɛːrəs/ *noun.* Pl. **-ri** /-rʌɪ/. E17.
[Latin from Greek *skaros*.]
Orig., a fish described by classical writers. Later, a parrot-fish. Now chiefly as mod. Latin genus name.

scarves *noun pl.* see SCARF *noun*[2].

scary /ˈskɛːri/ *adjective. colloq.* L16.
[from SCARE *noun*[1] + -Y[1].]
1 Terrifying, frightening. L16.
2 Frightened, timorous. Orig. & chiefly *N. Amer.* E19.

> 📖 **1** P. CHAPLIN She's a brave . . person . . to go on all the most scary rides at carnivals. **2** J. M. SYNGE I have been getting a little bit scary about your extravagance.

■ **scarily** *adverb* M19.

scat /skat/ *noun*[1]. ME.
[Old Norse *skattr* = Old English *scēat*, *scǣtt*, Old Frisian *skett* money, cattle, Old Saxon *skat* (Dutch *schat*), Old High German *scaz* (German *Schatz*) treasure, Gothic *skatts* (piece of) money, from Germanic. Cf. SCEATTA.]
1 A tax, a tribute. Orig. in †***scat haver***, oats taken in payment of scat. Now only *Hist.*, with ref. to countries under Scandinavian rule. ME.
2 *spec.* In Orkney and Shetland, land-tax paid to the Crown by a udal tenant. Also ***scat tax***. E16.

scat /skat/ *noun*[2]. *dial.* E18.
[Origin unkn.]
1 A sudden shower of rain. E18.
2 A blow, a buffet. L18.
3 A sharp sound, as of a bullet or something being burst. L19.
4 A brief spell of weather, activity, etc. L19.

scat /skat/ *noun*[3]. *US slang.* E20.
[Origin unkn.]
Whiskey.

scat /skat/ *noun*[4]. E20.
[Prob. imit.]
JAZZ. Improvised singing in which meaningless syllables, usu. imitating the sound of a musical instrument, are used instead of words. Freq. in ***scat-singer***, ***scat-singing***. Cf. VOCALESE.

scat /skat/ *noun*[5]. M20.
[Greek *skat-*, *skōr*: see SCATOLOGY.]
1 Dung, excrement; in *pl.*, droppings. M20.
2 Heroin. *slang.* L20.

> 📖 **1** J. UPDIKE The floor . . was covered with industrial carpeting the dull green of goose scat.

scat /skat/ *noun*[6]. M20.
[Abbreviation of mod. Latin *Scatophagidae* (see below), from Greek *skatophagos* dung-eating (because the fish is often found beside sewage outlets).]
Any of numerous small deep-bodied silvery fishes of the family Scatophagidae, occurring in inshore and estuarine waters of the Indo-Pacific.

scat /skat/ *verb*[1] *trans. dial.* Infl. **-tt-**. Pa. t. & pple **scatted**, **scat**. M19.
[Origin uncertain: cf. SCAT *noun*[2].]
Break in pieces, shatter.

scat /skat/ *verb*[2] *intrans. colloq.* Infl. **-tt-**. M19.
[Perh. from a hiss + *cat*, used to drive away cats, or abbreviation of SCATTER *verb*.]
Go away immediately, leave quickly. Usu. in *imper.* **quicker than scat** extremely quickly.

scat /skat/ *verb*[3]. Infl. **-tt-**. M20.
[from SCAT *noun*[4].]
JAZZ. **1** *verb intrans.* Perform scat-singing; sing or improvise with meaningless syllables. M20.
2 *verb trans.* Sing or improvise (a song) using meaningless syllables instead of words. M20.

scat /skat/ *adverb. dial.* M19.
[Origin uncertain: cf. SCAT *noun*[2].]
go scat, fall down; break in pieces; *fig.* become bankrupt.

scatback /ˈskatbak/ *noun.* M20.
[from SCAT *verb*[2] + BACK *noun*[1].]
AMER. FOOTBALL. A fast-running backfield player.

Scatchard /ˈskatʃɑːd/ *noun.* M20.
[George *Scatchard* (1892–1973), US physical chemist.]
BIOCHEMISTRY. **1** ***Scatchard plot***, a graph of the concentration of a solute absorbed by a protein, membrane, cell, etc., against its concentration in the surrounding medium. M20.
2 ***Scatchard analysis***, the use of Scatchard plots to deduce the number and nature of the binding sites on a protein etc. L20.

scathe /skeɪð/ *noun.* Now *arch. & dial.* Also (*Scot.*) **skaith**. OE.
[Old Norse *skaði* = Old English *sćeaþa* malefactor, (rarely) injury, Old Frisian *skatha* injury, Old Saxon *skaþo* malefactor, Old High German *skado* (German *Schade*) injury, harm, from Germanic, whence also Gothic *skaþis* harm.]
†**1** A person who does harm; a malefactor; a wretch, a fiend. OE–ME.
2 Harm, damage; an injury, a loss. OE. ▸**b** A thing which does harm. L16.
3 Cause for sorrow or regret; a pity, a shame. ME.

> 📖 **2** T. H. HUXLEY It was cheering . . to hear you got through winter . . without scathe. **do scathe**, **work scathe** do harm. **have scathe**, **take scathe** be harmed.

■ **scatheful** *adjective* harmful, hurtful OE.

scathe /skeɪð/ *verb trans.* Also (*Scot.*) **skaith**. ME.
[Old Norse *skaða* = Old English *sćeaþian*, Old Frisian *skathia*, Old Saxon *scaþon*, Old High German *skadōn* (Dutch, German *schaden*), from Germanic.]
1 Injure, harm, damage. Now chiefly as ***scathed ppl adjective***. ME.
2 Injure or destroy by fire, lightning, etc.; blast, scorch, sear. *poet. & rhet.* E19.
3 *fig.* Hurt or wither with sharp criticism etc. Chiefly as SCATHING *ppl adjective*. M19.

scatheless /ˈskeɪðlɪs/ *adjective.* ME.
[from SCATHE *noun* + -LESS.]
Unharmed, without injury.
■ **scathelessly** *adverb* M19.

scathing /ˈskeɪðɪŋ/ *ppl adjective.* L18.
[from SCATHE *verb* + -ING[2].]
1 That scathes or blasts. L18.
2 Harsh, sharp and hurtful; cutting, scornful. M19.

> 📖 **2** I. COLEGATE She could be . . scathing in her criticism. L. GRANT-ADAMSON His scathing rejection of violence.

■ **scathingly** *adverb* M19.

scatology /skəˈtɒlədʒi/ *noun.* L19.
[from Greek *skat-*, *skōr* dung (cf. SCORIA) + -OLOGY.]
1 (Preoccupation with) obscene literature, esp. concerning excretion or excrement. L19.
2 PALAEONTOLOGY. The branch of science that deals with fossil excrement or coprolites. L19.
3 The branch of medicine or zoology that deals with the study and analysis of faeces. Also called ***coprology***. L19.
■ **scatoˈlogic** *adjective* = SCATOLOGICAL L19. **scatoˈlogical** *adjective* of or pertaining to scatology; characterized by a preoccupation with obscenity: E20.

scatomancy /ˈskatə(ʊ)mansi/ *noun.* M16.
[mod. Latin *scatomantia*, formed as prec. + -MANCY.]
Divination or diagnosis based on the examination of faeces.

scatophagous /skəˈtɒfəgəs/ *adjective.* L19.
[from mod. Latin *scatophagus* from Greek *skatophagos*, formed as SCATOLOGY: see -PHAGOUS.]
Feeding on dung; coprophagous.

scattald /ˈskat(ə)ld/ *noun. Scot.* E17.
[Of Scandinavian origin: cf. Old Norse *skattr* SCAT *noun*[1], *hald* HOLD *noun*[1].]
In Orkney and Shetland, the common land of a district, used for pasture, peat, etc.
■ **scattalder** *noun* a person who shares in the scattald M18.

scatter /ˈskatə/ *noun.* M17.
[from the verb.]
1 The action or an act of scattering; wide or irregular distribution; dispersion. M17.
2 A quantity loosely distributed or interspersed; a scattering, a sprinkling. M19.
3 STATISTICS. The degree to which repeated measurements or observations of a quantity differ; that which is measured by the variance. E20.
4 The scattering of light or other radiation; *spec.* in RADIO, used *attrib.* to denote the use of scattering within the atmosphere to extend the range of radio communication. M20.

> **1** A. PRICE There was a scatter of clapping from the spectators. **2** J. GRIGSON Serve with a light scatter of parsley. *Modern Painters* His sketch of . . a scatter of boulders around the pothole mouth. **3** *Applied Linguistics* The results . . would clearly benefit from replication with samples of increased size and scatter.

Comb.: **scatter diagram**, **scatter plot** STATISTICS a diagram in which two variates are plotted for each of a number of subjects, so that the form of the association between the variates can be seen.
■ **scattergram**, **scattergraph** *nouns* (STATISTICS) = *scatter diagram* above M20. **scatteˈrometer** *noun* a radar designed to provide information about the roughness or the profile of a surface from the way it scatters the incident microwaves M20.

scatter /ˈskatə/ *verb.* ME.
[Prob. var. of SHATTER *verb*, with substitution of *sc* for *sh* under Scandinavian influence.]
1 *verb trans.* Squander (goods or possessions). *arch.* ME.
2 a *verb trans.* Separate (a collection of people or things); disperse, dissipate; dispel (clouds, matter, etc.). ME. ▸**b** *verb intrans.* Separate and disperse; move away in various directions. LME. ▸**c** *verb trans. fig.* Distract (the mind, thoughts, etc.); cause to wander. Long *rare* or *obsolete.* LME.
3 *verb trans.* **a** Throw about in disorder. ME. ▸†**b** Throw down (a thing) negligently; drop. L16–L18.
4 *verb trans.* **a** Distribute at sporadic intervals; place here and there, spread over a wide area. Chiefly as ***scattered*** *ppl adjective.* LME. ▸**b** BASEBALL. Of a pitcher: yield (hits) only at intervals and so restrict scoring. L19.
5 a *verb trans.* Throw or send out in various directions, distribute widely; sprinkle, strew; sow (seed etc.). Formerly also (*fig.*), spread (a rumour, prophecy, etc.). LME. ▸**b** *verb intrans.* Spread in various directions. L16. ▸**c** *verb intrans. & trans.* Of a gun or cartridge: fire (shot) diffusely. M18. ▸**d** *verb trans.* PHYSICS. Of a surface, semi-opaque substance: throw back (light) brokenly in all directions. More widely, deflect, diffuse, or reflect (radiation, particles, etc.) randomly. M19. ▸**e** *verb intrans.* PHYSICS. Of radiation, particles, etc.: undergo scattering. L20.
6 *verb trans.* Sprinkle or strew *with* something; cover (a surface etc.) by scattering. Chiefly as ***scattered*** *ppl adjective.* L16.

> **2a** A. BRINK The car, zigzagging down the road, scattering children and chickens. **b** A. BURGESS The . . Regiment fired over the heads of the crowds and the crowds scattered. **c** SIR W. SCOTT One word from Isaac . . recalled her scattered feelings. **4a** L. SPALDING Grass huts were still scattered along the beach. *Dance* Former company members, scattered around the globe. *transf.*: M. COREN Examples of anger against injustice are scattered throughout those early writings. **5a** P. L. FERMOR Women scattering grain in their yards to a rush of poultry. **6** M. GARDINER The big . . living-room was scattered with books.

Comb.: **scatter bomb**: that scatters its material over a wide area; **scatterbrain** a person incapable of serious thought or concentration; **scatterbrained** *adjective* that is a scatterbrain; characteristic of a scatterbrain; **scatter cushion**, **scatter rug**, etc., a small cushion, rug, etc., to be placed (apparently) randomly for decorative effect; **scattergood** *arch.* a person who squanders goods or possessions, a spendthrift; **scatter-gun** *noun & adjective* (orig. & chiefly *N. Amer.*) (*a*) *noun* a shotgun; (*b*) *adjective* = *scattershot adjective* below; *scatter rug*: see *scatter cushion* above; **scattershot** *noun & adjective* (orig. & chiefly *N. Amer.*) (*a*) *noun* shot loaded in a charge for a shotgun; (*b*) *adjective* random, haphazard, indiscriminate.
■ **scatterable** *adjective* E19. **scatteˈration** *noun* the action of scattering; the fact or condition of being scattered: L18. **scattered** *ppl adjective* that has been scattered; dispersed, spread out or occurring at sporadic intervals; straggling, disorganized: LME. **scatteredly** *adverb* in a scattered, disordered, or sporadic manner E17. **scatterer** *noun* a person who or thing which scatters something; *spec.* (*a*) a device for sowing seed; (*b*) PHYSICS anything which scatters radiation, particles, etc.: M16. **scatterling** *noun* (*arch.*) a vagabond, a vagrant L16. **scattery** *adjective* scattered; sparse; straggling: E19.

scattering /ˈskat(ə)rɪŋ/ *noun.* ME.
[from prec. + -ING[1].]
1 a A quantity scattered. ME. ▸**b** A small number or amount *of* something; a small proportion. E17.
2 The action of SCATTER *verb*; an instance of this. LME.

> **2** *Rayleigh scattering*, *Rutherford scattering*, *Thomson scattering*, etc.

Comb.: **scattering angle** PHYSICS the angle through which a scattered particle or beam is deflected.

scattering /ˈskat(ə)rɪŋ/ *ppl adjective.* LME.
[formed as prec. + -ING[2].]
1 a That scatters or disperses in all directions. LME. ▸**b** Scattered or spread out over a wide area; occurring sporadically; straggling. Now chiefly *US.* E17.
2 PHYSICS. That causes scattering (of light, radiation, particles, etc.). E19.

> **2** **scattering layer** OCEANOGRAPHY any of a number of layers in the sea which give rise to strong acoustic echoes due to a high plankton concentration.

■ **scatteringly** *adverb* in a scattering manner; intermittently: LME.

scatty /ˈskati/ *adjective*[1]. *US slang.* E20.
[Origin unkn.]
Bad-tempered.

scatty /ˈskati/ *adjective*[2]. *colloq.* E20.
[Prob. from *scatt(erbrained* s.v. SCATTER *verb* + -Y[1].]
Scatterbrained, disorganized; foolish, absurd.
■ **scattily** *adverb* L20. **scattiness** *noun* M20.

scaturient /skəˈtjʊərɪənt/ *adjective.* Chiefly *literary.* L17.
[Latin *scaturient-* pres. ppl stem of *scaturire*, from *scatere* flow out: see -ENT.]
That flows or gushes out.

scaum /skɔːm/ *noun. Scot. & dial.* E19.
[from the verb.]
1 A burn, a scorch; a mark made by burning. E19.
2 A thin haze or mist; a light, misty vapour. E19.

scaum /skɔːm/ *verb trans. Scot. & dial.* M17.
[Origin unkn.]
1 Burn slightly, scorch, char. M17.
2 Cover with a thin haze or mist. M19.

scaup /skɔːp/ *noun.* L17.
[Scot. var. of SCALP *noun*[2].]
Either of two diving ducks of the genus *Aythya*, the males having a dark head and breast and a white-sided body, *A. marila* (more fully ***greater scaup***) of Eurasia and Canada, and *A. affinis* (in full ***lesser scaup***) of N. America. Also more fully ***scaup-duck***.

scauper *noun* see SCALPER *noun*[1].

scaur /skɔː/ *noun.* Chiefly *Scot.* E18.
[Dial. var. of SCAR *noun*[1].]
A precipitous bank; a cliff; the ridge of a hill.

scavage /ˈskavɪdʒ/ *noun.* L15.
[Anglo-Norman *scawage* (whence Anglo-Latin *scawagium*) = Old Northern French *escauwage*, from *escauwer* inspect from Flemish *scauwen* = Old English *scēawian* SHOW *verb*.]
Hist. A toll formerly levied by the mayor, sheriff, or corporation of London and other towns on foreign merchants, on goods offered for sale within the town's precincts.

scavage /ˈskavɪdʒ/ *verb trans. & intrans. rare.* M19.
[Back-form. from next.]
= SCAVENGE *verb.*

scavager /ˈskavɪdʒə/ *noun.* L15.
[Anglo-Norman *scawager*, from *scawage* SCAVAGE *noun*: see -ER[2].]
Hist. An officer whose duty it was to collect scavage and later also to keep the streets clean.
■ **scavagery** *noun* (*rare*) = SCAVENGERY M19.

scavenage /ˈskav(ə)nɪdʒ/ *noun. rare.* L19.
[Irreg. from SCAVEN(GE *verb* + -AGE.]
The action or work of scavenging.

scavenge /ˈskavɪn(d)ʒ/ *verb & noun.* M17.
[Back-form. from next.]
▶ **A** *verb.* **1** *verb trans.* Clean *out* (dirt etc.). Long *rare.* M17.
2 *verb trans. & intrans.* Remove dirt from (the streets); remove waste from (the surface of a river). M19.
3 *verb intrans. & trans.* Search for and collect (anything usable) from amongst usu. discarded material (freq. foll. by *for*). Also (of an animal or bird) feed on (carrion). L19.
4 *verb trans. & intrans.* **a** Remove (the combustion products) from the cylinders of an internal-combustion engine during the return stroke of the pistons. L19. ▸**b** CHEMISTRY. Combine with or remove (free radicals, electrons, etc.). M20.

> **3** B. BETTELHEIM Starving prisoners . . scavenged for potato peelings in the refuse containers. A. CARTER Mangy dogs scavenged in an enormous midden. B. LOPEZ A . . rookery, beneath which the bear had scavenged dead birds.

▶ **B** *noun.* The action or process of scavenging, *esp.* the removal of combustion products from the cylinders of an internal-combustion engine; an act of scavenging. E20.

scavenger /ˈskavɪn(d)ʒə/ *noun.* M16.
[Alt. of SCAVAGER from Anglo-Norman *scawager*, from *scawage*: see SCAVAGE *noun*, -ER[1]. For the intrusive *noun* cf. *harbinger*, *messenger*, etc.]
1 *Hist.* **a** = SCAVAGER. M16. ▸**b** An official in the East India Company. E18.
2 a A person employed to clean streets. M16. ▸**b** *fig.* A person who does corrupt or disgusting work; a dishonourable person. M16. ▸**c** A thing, *esp.* an animal, that feeds on carrion or refuse. Now also, a phagocytic cell. L16.
3 A person who collects discarded things, esp. for reuse; *spec.* (*Hist.*) a child employed in a spinning-mill to collect loose cotton lying about the floor or machinery. M19.
4 CHEMISTRY. A substance or species which scavenges (sense 4b) free radicals or other species. M20.
Comb.: **scavenger cell** = PHAGOCYTE *noun.*; **scavenger hunt** a game in which people try to collect certain miscellaneous objects, usu. outdoors over a wide area; **Scavenger's daughter** = SKEVINGTON'S ***daughter***.
■ **scavengery** *noun* arrangements for cleaning streets and removing refuse etc.; the action of collecting and removing dirt: M17.

scavenger /ˈskavɪn(d)ʒə/ *verb. rare.* M17.
[from the noun.]
1 *verb trans.* Remove dirt from (the streets etc.); *fig.* cleanse, purify. Also, make dirty by scavenging. M17.
2 *verb intrans.* Work at scavenging. M19.

scaw /skɔː/ *noun.* E19.
[Shetland dial., repr. Old Norse *skage.*]
A promontory.

scazon /ˈskeɪz(ə)n, ˈska-/ *noun.* L17.
[Latin from Greek *skazōn* use as noun of masc. pres. pple of *skazein* limp, halt.]
PROSODY. A modification of the iambic trimeter, in which a spondee or trochee takes the place of the final iambus; = CHOLIAMB. Also ***scazon iambic***.
■ **scaˈzontic** *adjective* consisting of or written in scazons L19.

Sc. D. *abbreviation.*
Latin *Scientiae Doctor* Doctor of Science.

SCE *abbreviation.*
Scottish Certificate of Education.

sceatta /ˈʃatə/ *noun.* Also **sceat** /ʃat/.
[Old English *scéat*, *scǽtt*: see SCAT *noun*[1].]
1 Orig., an Anglo-Saxon coin or monetary unit. Later *spec.* in NUMISMATICS, a small Anglo-Saxon (usu. silver) coin. OE.
†**2** Treasure, money. OE–ME.

Sceaux /səʊ/ *noun & adjective.* L19.
[A town near Paris (see below).]
(Designating) a type of tin-enamelled faience made at Sceaux in the late 18th cent., often decoratively painted and modelled in the form of figures.

scelerate /ˈsɛlərət/ *adjective & noun.* Long *rare.* Also **-at.** E16.
[Latin *sceleratus* pa. pple of *scelerare*, from *sceler-*, *scelus* wickedness: see -ATE[2].]
▶ **A** *adjective.* Extremely wicked, villainous. E16.
▶ **B** *noun.* An extremely wicked person, a villain, a wretch. E18.

scelidosaur /ˈsɛlɪdə(ʊ)sɔː/ *noun.* M19.
[mod. Latin *Scelidosaurus* (see below), from *scelido-* used for stem of Greek *skelos* leg: see -SAUR.]
PALAEONTOLOGY. An armoured dinosaur of the Jurassic genus *Scelidosaurus*, an early ornithischian of uncertain relationship.

scena /ˈʃeɪnə/ *noun.* E19.
[Italian from Latin = SCENE.]
1 (The words and music of) a scene in an Italian opera. E19.
2 A vocal composition consisting largely of dramatic recitative of an operatic style. E19.

scenario /sɪˈnɑːrɪəʊ/ *noun & verb.* L19.
[Italian, from Latin *scena* SCENE.]
▶ **A** *noun.* Pl. **-os.**
1 a A sketch or outline of the plot of a play, ballet, novel, etc., with details of the scenes and situations. L19. ▸**b** CINEMATOGRAPHY. A film script with all the details of scenes, stage-directions, etc., necessary for shooting the film. E20.
2 A description of an imagined situation or a postulated sequence of events; an outline of an intended course of action; *spec.* a scientific description or speculative model intended to account for observable facts. Also *loosely*, a situation, a sequence of events. M20.

> **1a** *Dance* Selections from the ballet's original scenario. **2** *Times* A scenario was floated . . which suggests Mr Sterling being appointed chairman. M. PAFFARD The archetypal scenario—the scene of domestic bliss.

▶ **B** *verb trans.* Make a scenario of (a book, idea, etc.); sketch *out.* M20.
■ **scenarioize** *verb trans.* = SCENARIO *verb* E20. **scenarist** *noun* (CINEMATOGRAPHY) a scenario writer E20.

†scenary *noun.* L17.
[Italian *scenario*: see prec., -ARY[1].]
1 = SCENARIO *noun* 1a. L17–M18.
2 The scene of an action. E18–E19.
3 = SCENERY *noun* 3. E18–E19.

scend /sɛnd/ *verb & noun.* Also **send**. L15.
[Origin uncertain: perh. aphet. from DESCEND, or rel. to SEND *verb*[1].]
▶ **A** *verb intrans.* NAUTICAL. Of a vessel: pitch or surge up in a heavy sea. L15.
▶ **B** *noun.* **1** The driving impulse or surge of a wave or the sea. E18.
2 A sudden plunge or pitch of a vessel *aft*, *forward*, etc. M19.

scene /siːn/ *noun.* M16.
[Latin *scena*, *scaena* stage, scene from Greek *skēnē* tent, booth, stage, scene. Cf. SKENE *noun*[2].]
▶ **I** THEATRICAL. **1** A subdivision of (an act of) a play, in which the time is continuous and the setting fixed, marked in classic drama by the entrance or departure of one or more actors and in non-classic drama often by a change of setting; the action and dialogue comprised in any one of these subdivisions. M16.
2 Any of the pieces of scenery used in a play to depict its setting, consisting chiefly of backcloths and theatrical props at the back and sides of the stage; the setting thus presented to the audience. Also, the pieces of scenery collectively. M16.
3 The action or presentation of a dramatic piece on stage; a play in performance. *obsolete* exc. in ***the scene opens*** below. L16.
4 The place in which the action of (part of) a play is supposed to occur; the setting of a dialogue, novel, etc. L16.
5 = SKENE *noun*[2]. E17.
6 The stage seen as representing dramatic art or the acting profession. Now only *arch.* E17.

📖 **1** G. SWIFT Working on the big death-bed scene. **2** *attrib.*: M. FONTEYN Its stage mechanisms . . can make complete scene transformations in ten seconds. **4** SHAKES. *Rom. & Jul.* In fair Verona, where we lay our scene. R. L. STEVENSON The scene of this little book is on a high mountain.

▶ **II** *transf.* **7 a** The place where an action is carried on, business is being done, or events are happening. L16. ▸**b** A specified sphere of human activity or interest. M20. ▸**c** A place where people of common interests meet or where a particular activity is carried on. Also *loosely*, an (esp. fashionable) activity or pursuit; a situation, an experience; a way of life. *slang* (orig. *US*). M20. ▸**d** A social environment frequented predominantly by homosexuals. *slang.* M20.
8 An action, episode, situation, etc., forming a subject of narration or description or occurring in real life. E17.
9 A view or picture presented to the eye (or to the mind) of a place, a series of actions or events, a collection of objects, etc. M17.
10 A display of anger or other strong feeling, esp. in public; a row, a disturbance. M18.

📖 **7a** DAY LEWIS The scene of a battle long ago. *Scotsman* A rescue jet had been sent to the scene. **b** *Midweek Truth (Melbourne)* Joy is not involved in the music scene. *Accountancy* Students need to know about . . the contemporary financial scene. **c** J. LENNON Things . . I didn't know about before, because of the scene I was in. CLIVE JAMES The New York subway . . is a bad scene. **8** R. S. THOMAS The slow scene unfolds before his luckless eyes. **10** B. BAINBRIDGE Very polite to everyone. She never made a scene. A. AYCKBOURN Will you try . . not to start any more scenes or arguments?

Phrases etc.: **behind the scenes** among the actors and scenery offstage where the audience is not admitted. **behind-the-scenes** *adjective* not known to the public, secret. **change of scene** a change of one's surroundings through travel etc. **make the scene** *slang* participate in an event or activity. **not one's scene** *colloq.* not what one enjoys or finds interesting. **one's scene** *colloq.* what one enjoys or finds interesting. **on the scene** *slang* at the place where events are happening; involved in an activity. ***primal scene***: see PRIMAL *adjective*. **quit the scene** leave; die. **scene-of-crime**, **scenes-of-crime** *adjectives* designating (a member of) a civilian branch of the police force concerned with the collection of forensic evidence. ***set the scene***: see SET *verb*[1]. ***steal the scene***: see STEAL *verb*. **the scene of the crime** the place where a crime has been committed. **the scene opens** the action of (a scene of) a play begins. **this scene of things** the world considered as a theatre in which people are actors. ***transformation scene***: see TRANSFORMATION 3.
Comb.: ***scene-dock***: see DOCK *noun*[3] 8; **scene-painter** a person who paints stage scenery; **scene-plot** a list and description of the scenes in a play; **scene-room**: where scenery is stored; **scene-shifter** a person who moves the scenery on a theatre stage during a performance; **scene-steal** *verb intrans.* = ***steal the scene*** s.v. STEAL *verb*; **scene-stealer** an actor etc. who steals the scene.
■ **scenist** *noun* (long *rare* or *obsolete*) a person who moves or paints stage scenery E19.

scène à faire /sɛn a fɛːr/ *noun phr.* Pl. ***scènes à faire*** (pronounced same). L19.
[French, lit. 'scene for action'.]
THEATRICAL. The most important scene in a play or opera.

scenery /ˈsiːn(ə)ri/ *noun.* M18.
[Alt. of SCENARY *noun*, as if from SCENE + -ERY.]
†1 Dramatic action; a display of emotion. M18–E19.
2 a The decoration of a theatre stage or a film or television set, consisting of backcloths and theatrical props representing the scene of the action. L18. ▸**b** *transf.* The background, *the* setting, *the* surroundings. L18.
3 The general appearance of a place and its natural features, esp. with ref. to its picturesqueness. L18.
4 A view of a picturesque scene; (a pictorial representation of) a landscape. Now *rare*. L18.

📖 **2b** J. F. HENDRY To him Rilke was a friendly part of the scenery. **3** J. K. JEROME Round Clifton Hampden . . the river scenery is rich and beautiful.

scènes à faire *noun phr.* pl. of SCÈNE À FAIRE.

scenester /ˈsiːnstə/ *noun. colloq.* (orig. & chiefly *US*). L20.
[from SCENE *noun* + -STER.]
A person associated with or immersed in a particular fashionable cultural scene.

scenic /ˈsiːnɪk/ *noun.* L19.
[from the adjective.]
1 A scene, a setting. *rare.* L19.
2 A film or photograph of natural scenery. E20.
3 *ellipt.* Scenic wallpaper. M20.

scenic /ˈsiːnɪk/ *adjective.* E17.
[Latin *scenicus* from Greek *skēnikos* belonging to the stage, from *skēnē*: see SCENE, -IC.]
1 Of or pertaining to the theatre; dramatic, theatrical. E17. ▸**b** Represented on the stage. M18. ▸**c** Of or pertaining to stage scenery or stage effect. E19.
2 Of or pertaining to natural scenery. Now also, having much fine scenery, providing landscape views. M19.
3 a With ref. to painting or sculpture: representing a scene or incident involving several people. M19. ▸**b** Of wallpaper: creating a continuous scene or landscape on the walls of a room. E20.

📖 **1** H. PHILLIPS A scenic mask of Pan. *fig.*: A. MATHEWS Her charities were . . often spontaneous, though perhaps somewhat scenic. **c scenic artist** a painter or designer of stage scenery. **2** E. NORTH Branch off the A1 . . and take minor but much more scenic roads. L. ELLMANN Long car drives to scenic spots like Minster Lovell. **scenic railway** a miniature railway running through artificial scenery, used as an attraction at a fair, in a park, etc.

scenical /ˈsiːnɪk(ə)l/ *adjective.* LME.
[from (the same root as) SCENIC *adjective*: see -AL[1].]
1 = SCENIC *adjective* 1. LME.
2 Dramatic or theatrical in style or manner. Formerly also, fictitious; illusory; not genuine. Chiefly *derog.* M16.
3 Resembling a stage scene. E18.
■ **scenically** *adverb* M17.

Scenicruiser /ˈsiːnɪkruːzə/ *noun. US.* M20.
[from SCENI(C *adjective* + CRUISER.]
(Proprietary name for) a luxury coach equipped for long-distance travel, esp. for touring areas of scenic beauty.

scenite /ˈsiːnʌɪt/ *noun & adjective. rare.* E17.
[Latin *scenites* from Greek *skēnitēs* from *skēnē* tent: see -ITE[1].]
▶ **A** *noun.* A person who lives in a tent; a member of a nomad people living in tents. E17.
▶ **B** *attrib.* or as *adjective*. Of or pertaining to a scenite. M18.

scenographer /siːˈnɒɡrəfə/ *noun.* L16.
[Greek *skēnographos* scene-painter, from *skēnē*: see SCENE, -GRAPHER.]
A painter or designer of theatrical scenery; a person who draws buildings etc. in perspective.

scenography /siːˈnɒɡrəfi/ *noun.* M17.
[French *scénographie* or Latin *scenographia* from Greek *skēnographia* scene-painting, from *skēnē*: see SCENE, -GRAPHY.]
1 The representation of objects in perspective; a perspective elevation. M17.
2 The painting or design of theatrical scenery. M18.
■ **scenographic** /-ˈɡrafɪk/ *adjective* of or pertaining to scenography L17. **sceno'graphically** *adverb* (*rare*) E18.

scent /sɛnt/ *noun.* Also (earlier) **†sent**. LME.
[from the verb.]
1 a The faculty or sense of smell, esp. of a dog or other animal which finds objects or prey by this sense. LME. ▸**b** *fig.* The power of detecting or discovering a specified thing or things. L16.
2 a The odour of an animal or person, perceptible to a hound etc. and used as a means of pursuit; a trail as indicated by this odour. LME. ▸**b** *fig.* A set of clues that can be followed like a trail. E17. ▸**c** *transf.* In the game of hare and hounds, fragments of paper scattered on the ground by the quarry to serve as a track for the pursuers. M19.
3 *gen.* A distinctive, now esp. pleasant, odour, as of a flower etc. L15.
4 A sweet-smelling liquid prepared by distillation from a flower etc.; perfume. M18.

📖 **1a** N. ALGREN He shuffled on . . finding his way toward food more by scent than by sight. **b** J. G. HOLLAND All of them had a scent for heresy. **2a** J. MASEFIELD The hounds . . went nosing to the scent. **3** V. BRITTAIN The city was sweet with the scent of wallflowers. **4** *Times* I . . told the glamorous lady assistant that I wanted a bottle of scent.

Phrases: **false scent** a trail mistakenly believed to lead to the quarry, *esp.* one laid with the intention of deflecting pursuit or misleading or misdirecting an investigation. **lose the scent** (*a*) (of a pursuer) fail to follow a quarry's trail, be misled or misdirected; (*b*) (chiefly HUNTING) (of a quarry) deflect pursuit from the trail, mislead or misdirect a pursuer. **on the scent**, **on the right scent** following a trail which leads to the quarry, pursuing the correct line of investigation. **put off the scent**, **throw off the scent** cause to lose the line of the quarry's trail, mislead or misdirect (a pursuer or an investigation). **wrong scent** = ***false scent*** above.
Comb.: **scent-bag** a bag containing a strong-smelling substance, drawn over ground to make an artificial scent for hounds; **scent-bottle** a bottle for perfume, *esp.* an ornamental one; **scent gland** ZOOLOGY a gland which secretes an odorous pheromone or defensive substance; **scent marking** ZOOLOGY the deposition by a mammal of a secreted pheromone, esp. on prominent objects in the area; **scent scale** ENTOMOLOGY any of various pheromone-secreting scales found in some male Lepidoptera and Trichoptera, esp. on the wings; **scent tuft** ENTOMOLOGY a pheromone-secreting brush found in some male Lepidoptera; a hair pencil; **scent-wood** an Australian shrub with fragrant wood, *Alyxia buxifolia* (family Apocynaceae).
¶ See note under the verb.
■ **scentful** *adjective* (long *rare* or *obsolete*) full of perfume; fragrant: E17. **scenty** *adjective* (*rare*) smelling of scent; scented: M20.

scent /sɛnt/ *verb.* Also (earlier) **†sent**. LME.
[Old & mod. French *sentir* feel, perceive, smell, from Latin *sentire* feel, perceive.]
1 *verb trans.* Of a hound etc.: find or track (game, prey, etc.) by smell. Also more widely, become aware of the presence of, or recognize at a distance, by the sense of smell. LME. ▸**b** *fig.* Perceive, find out instinctively; recognize, detect. M16.
2 *verb intrans.* Of a hound etc.: orig., perceive the smell *of* a quarry; later, hunt by the sense of smell, sniff the air for a scent. Long *rare*. LME.
3 *verb intrans.* Exhale an odour, smell of something. Now *rare* or *obsolete*. LME.
4 *verb trans.* Impregnate with an odour; perfume. L17.

📖 **1** D. ATTENBOROUGH If it scents its prey, it swings its head . . to determine the direction. P. BENSON I could scent her tobacco. **b** E. BOWEN He had scented something fishy about this trip. *Times* NUM scents victory in ballot. **4** E. WAUGH The honeysuckle outside my . . window scents the room at night.

¶ Orig. a hunting term. The unexplained spelling *scent* is not recorded until 17.
■ **scenter** *noun* E17. **scenting** *ppl adjective* (*a*) that exhales an odour or perfume; (*b*) of or pertaining to hunting by scent: L16.

scented /ˈsɛntɪd/ *adjective.* Also (earlier) **†sented**. L16.
[from SCENT *verb*, *noun*: see -ED[1], -ED[2].]
†1 Endowed with the power of tracking by sense of smell. L16–M17.
2 That has a scent or perfume; impregnated with perfume, perfumed (*with*). M17.

📖 **2** R. K. NARAYAN She applied a little scented oil to her hair. P. FARMER Summer gardens scented with lilies and pinks.

scentless /ˈsɛntlɪs/ *adjective.* E17.
[from SCENT *noun* + -LESS.]
†1 Without the faculty of smell. *rare.* Only in E17.
2 Without odour or perfume. E17.
3 HUNTING. Having no scent for the hounds to follow. L19.
2 scentless MAYWEED.

scepsis /ˈskɛpsɪs/ *noun. rare.* L19.
[Greek *skepsis* inquiry, doubt, from *skeptesthai*: see SCEPTIC.]
A sceptical attitude in philosophy.

scepter *noun & verb* see SCEPTRE.

sceptic /ˈskɛptɪk/ *noun & adjective.* Also (*arch.* & *N. Amer.*) **sk-**. L16.
[French *sceptique* or Latin *scepticus*, in pl. *sceptici* followers of the Greek philosopher Pyrrho (see below), from Greek *skeptikos*, pl. *skeptikoi*, from *skeptesthai* look about, consider, observe, rel. to *skopein*, *skopos*: see SCOPE *noun*[1], -IC.]
▶ **A** *noun.* **1** PHILOSOPHY. A person who maintains the impossibility of real knowledge of any kind, orig. *spec.* (now *Hist.*), a follower of the Greek philosopher Pyrrho of Elis (*c* 300 BC), a Pyrrhonist; a person who holds that there are no adequate grounds for certainty as to the truth of any proposition whatever. L16.
2 A person who doubts the validity of accepted beliefs in a particular subject; a person inclined to doubt any assertion or apparent fact. E17.
3 A person seeking the truth; an inquirer who has not yet arrived at definite convictions. E17.
4 A person who doubts the truth of (important parts of) the Christian religion; *loosely* an unbeliever in Christianity. M17.

📖 **2** S. NAIPAUL Jones' psychic talents . . would have convinced the most hardened sceptic.

▸ **B** *adjective.* = SCEPTICAL *adjective.* Now *rare.* **L16.**

sceptical /ˈskɛptɪk(ə)l/ *adjective.* Also (*arch.* & *N. Amer.*) **sk-**. **E17.**
[formed as prec.: see -ICAL.]
1 Of a person: inclined to scepticism; dubious, incredulous. **E17.**
2 Of a doctrine, opinion, etc.: characteristic of a sceptic; of the nature of scepticism. **M18.**

📖 **1** A. BISHOP Russell was sceptical about . . vaccines . . to cure obscure diseases.

■ **sceptically** *adverb* **L17.**

scepticise *verb* var. of SCEPTICIZE.

scepticism /ˈskɛptɪsɪz(ə)m/ *noun.* Also (*arch.* & *N. Amer.*) **sk-**. **M17.**
[from SCEPTIC + -ISM.]
1 PHILOSOPHY. The doctrine of the sceptics, Pyrrhonism; the opinion that real knowledge of any kind is unattainable. **M17.**
2 A sceptical attitude in relation to a particular branch of knowledge; doubt as to the truth of some assertion or apparent fact. Also, mistrustfulness, doubting disposition. **M17.**
3 Doubt or unbelief with regard to the Christian religion. **E19.**
■ Also **sceptism** *noun* (*rare*) **M17.**

scepticize /ˈskɛptɪsʌɪz/ *verb.* Also **-ise**, (*arch.* & *N. Amer.*) **sk-**. **L17.**
[from SCEPTIC + -IZE.]
†**1** *verb trans.* Foll. by *away*: remove (a certainty), cast doubt on. Only in **L17.**
2 *verb intrans.* Act or behave as a sceptic; practise scepticism. **L17.**

sceptre /ˈsɛptə/ *noun* & *verb.* Also ***scepter**. **ME.**
[Old French *ceptre*, (also mod.) *sceptre* from Latin *sceptrum* from Greek *skēptron*, from *skēptein* alt. of *skēptesthai* prop oneself, lean (on). Cf. SCAPE *noun*[2].]
▸ **A** *noun.* **1** An ornamental rod held in the hand as a symbol of regal or imperial authority. **ME.** ▸**b** HERALDRY. A charge representing such a rod. **E17.**
2 The authority symbolized by a sceptre; royal or imperial dignity, sovereignty. **LME.**
3 *Hist.* A gold unite first coined in 1604. **L17.**
†**4** (Usu. **S-**.) (The name of) either of two former constellations in the northern and southern hemispheres. **E18–M19.**
▸ **B** *verb trans.* **1** Provide with a sceptre. **LME.**
2 Touch (with a sceptre) as a sign of royal assent or ratification. *rare.* **M19.**
■ **sceptral** *adjective* pertaining to or serving as a sceptre **M19.** **sceptred** *ppl adjective* provided with a sceptre, bearing a sceptre; invested with regal or imperial authority: **E16.** **sceptredom** *noun* (*rare*) †(**a**) a monarch's reign; (**b**) sovereign authority: **L16.** **sceptreless** *adjective* (*rare*) (**a**) not acknowledging any sovereign authority; (**b**) without a sceptre: **E19.**

†**scerne** *verb trans. rare* (Spenser). Only in **L16.**
[Aphet. from DISCERN, after Italian *scernere*.]
Perceive, discover.

scf *abbreviation.*
Standard cubic feet (i.e. cubic feet of gas at standard temperature and pressure).

sch. *abbreviation.*
1 Scholar.
2 School.
3 Schooner.

schaalstein *noun* see SCHALSTEIN.

Schabzieger /ˈʃaptsiːgər/ *noun.* **M19.**
[German *Schabziger*, from *schaben* grate + *Ziger* a kind of cheese. Cf. SAPSAGO.]
A hard green Swiss cheese for cooking, made from curds and flavoured with melilot.

schadchan *noun* var. of SHADCHAN.

Schadenfreude /ˈʃaːd(ə)nfrɔɪdə/ *noun.* Also **s-**. **L19.**
[German, from *Schaden* harm + *Freude* joy.]
Malicious enjoyment of another's misfortune.

📖 G. WILL The unpleasantness on Wall Street produced a satisfying surge of *schadenfreude* about Yuppies getting their comeuppances.

schalet /ˈʃalɪt, ʃaˈlɛt/ *noun.* **M20.**
[Yiddish *shalent*, *shalet* var. of *tsholnt* CHOLENT.]
1 = CHOLENT. **M20.**
2 A Jewish baked fruit pudding. **M20.**

schalstein /ˈʃaːlʃtʌɪn/ *noun.* Also in sense 1 **schaal-**. **E19.**
[German, from *Schale* skin, shell + *Stein* stone.]
†**1** MINERALOGY. = WOLLASTONITE. **E–M19.**
2 GEOLOGY. Any of various altered basic or calcareous tuffs, usu. laminated in structure. **M19.**

schans /skans/ *noun. S. Afr.* Also ***schanz*** & other vars. **L19.**
[Dutch *schans* = German *Schanze*.]
A heap or breastwork of stones used as a protection against rifle-fire.

schappe /ʃap, ˈʃapə/ *noun.* **L19.**
[German = silk waste.]
A fabric or yarn made from waste silk.
■ **schapping** *noun* fermentation of waste silk in order to remove gum **E20.**

schapska /ˈʃapskə/ *noun.* **L19.**
[French *chapska*, *schapska* from Polish *czapka* cap.]
A flat-topped cavalry helmet.

Schatz /ʃats/ *noun.* Pl. ***-en*** /-ən/. **E20.**
[German, lit. 'treasure'.]
A girlfriend, a sweetheart. Freq. as a term of endearment.

Schaumann's body /ˈʃaʊmənz bɒdi/ *noun phr.* Also **Schaumann body**. **M20.**
[Joergen *Schaumann* (1879–1953), Swedish dermatologist.]
MEDICINE. A rounded laminated body containing iron and often calcium, numbers of which are often found inside giant cells in sarcoidosis.

†**schediasm** *noun.* **M17–L18.**
[Greek *skhediasma*, from *skhediazein* do a thing in a casual or offhand manner.]
An extemporized work, a jotting.

schedule /ˈʃɛdjuːl, ˈskɛd-/ *noun.* Also (earlier) †**ced-**, †**sed-**. **LME.**
[Old & mod. French *cédule* from late Latin *schedula* small slip of paper, dim. of *scheda* from Greek *skhedē* leaf of papyrus: see -ULE. Cf. SKED *noun*.]
†**1** A slip or scroll of parchment or paper containing writing; a label; a short note. **LME–L17.**
2 Orig., a separate sheet of paper or parchment accompanying a document and containing explanatory or supplementary matter. Later, an appendix to a formal legal document, esp. in the form of tables or an inventory; any list, form, classification, or tabular statement, *esp.* one arranged under headings prescribed by official authority; *spec.* a list of rates or prices. **LME.**
†**3** [translating Spanish *cédula* or Italian *cedola*.] A royal writ or permit. **E17–M18.**
4 A timetable (orig. & chiefly *N. Amer.*); a programme or plan of events, operations, broadcasts, etc. **M19.**

📖 **2** SHAKES. *Twel. N.* Divers schedules of my beauty . . inventoried, and . . labell'd. *Daily Telegraph* Schedule Six of the Finance Bill. **4** I. SHAW He looked up the schedule of the planes flying out of Brussels to New York. F. KAPLAN With a heavy writing schedule, he . . worked nights as well as mornings. G. DALY She arranged her schedule so . . Georgie could visit her every Friday afternoon. **according to schedule** = *on schedule* below. *behind schedule*: see BEHIND *preposition*. **on schedule** as planned; on time.

■ **schedular** *adjective* of or pertaining to a schedule; (of a tax system) organized according to a schedule: **E20.**

schedule /ˈʃɛdjuːl, ˈskɛd-/ *verb trans.* **M19.**
[from prec. Cf. SKED *verb*.]
1 Put or enter in a schedule or list; *spec.* (**a**) put (something) on a timetable or on a programme of future events; (**b**) include (a building etc.) on a list of ancient monuments of national importance to be preserved and protected. Also, arrange for (a person or thing) to do something; arrange (an event), esp. for a particular time. **M19.**
2 Affix as a schedule (esp. to an Act of Parliament). **L19.**

📖 **1** A. TYLER The funeral was scheduled for ten-thirty Saturday morning. *Japan Times* The ship is scheduled to make eight cruises this year.

■ **scheduler** *noun* (**a**) a person who or machine which arranges a schedule or an appropriate order for the occurrence of planned activities, operations, etc.; (**b**) COMPUTING a program that arranges jobs or a computer's operations into an appropriate sequence; a part of the hardware designed to perform a similar function: **M20.** **scheduling** *verbal noun* the action of the verb; *spec.* the preparation of a timetable for the completion of each stage of a complex project; the coordination of many related actions or tasks into a single time-sequence: **L19.**

scheduled /ˈʃɛdjuːld, ˈskɛd-/ *adjective.* **L19.**
[from SCHEDULE *verb* + -ED[1].]
Entered on a schedule or list, included in a schedule; *spec.* (of a flight, sailing, etc.) forming part of a regular service, not specially chartered.

📖 *Holiday Which?* The cheapest scheduled air fare to Geneva, Paris and Brussels. **Scheduled Caste** in India, a caste officially regarded as socially disadvantaged. **scheduled flight**, **scheduled service**, etc. a public flight, service, etc., operated according to a regular timetable. **scheduled territory** = *sterling area* s.v. STERLING *noun*[1] & *adjective*. **Scheduled Tribe** in India, a category of people officially regarded as socially disadvantaged.

Scheele's green /ʃeɪləz ˈgriːn/ *noun phr.* **E19.**
[from Karl Wilhelm *Scheele* (1742–86), German-born Swedish chemist.]
A form of copper arsenite formerly used as a pigment in calico printing and wallpaper manufacture.

scheelite /ˈʃiːlʌɪt/ *noun.* **M19.**
[formed as prec. + -ITE[1].]
MINERALOGY. A tetragonal form of calcium tungstate, $CaWO_4$, usu. found in fluorescent white (or coloured) bipyramidal crystals in quartz veins and contact metamorphic zones, and an important ore of tungsten.

schefflera /ˈʃɛflərə/ *noun.* **M20.**
[mod. Latin (see below), from J. C. *Scheffler*, 18th-cent. botanist of Danzig.]
Any of various tropical or subtropical evergreen shrubs or small trees constituting the genus *Schefflera* (family Araliaceae), grown for their decorative foliage.

Scheherazade /ʃəhɛrəˈzaːd/ *noun.* **M19.**
[The female narrator of the linked stories of the *Arabian Nights' Entertainment*.]
A female teller of long or numerous stories, *esp.* one who is young and attractive.

Scheiner /ˈʃʌɪnə/ *noun.* **E20.**
[Julius *Scheiner* (1858–1913), German astrophysicist.]
PHOTOGRAPHY. Used *attrib.* with ref. to a method of measuring and expressing the speed of photographic emulsions.
Scheiner number a number depending on the logarithm of the least exposure that will give a visible image on development.

Scheiner's halo /ʃʌɪnəz ˈheɪləʊ/ *noun phr.* **L20.**
[Christoph *Scheiner* (c 1575–1650), German astronomer.]
ASTRONOMY. A faintly luminous halo occasionally seen around the sun or moon at an angle of 23–32°, due to refraction by pyramidal ice crystals in the upper atmosphere.

Scheitholt /ˈʃaɪthɔlt/ *noun.* **M20.**
[German, from *Scheit* log + dial. *Holt* wood.]
Hist. A stringed instrument of central Europe, resembling a primitive zither.

schelling /ˈskɛlɪŋ/ *noun.* Long *obsolete* exc. *Hist.* **M16.**
[Dutch: see SHILLING. Cf. SCHILLING, SKILLING *noun*[2].]
A silver coin formerly current in the Low Countries, of the value of 6 stivers.

Schellingian /ʃɛˈlɪŋɪən/ *noun* & *adjective.* **E19.**
[from *Schelling* (see below) + -IAN.]
▸ **A** *noun.* A follower of the German philosopher, Friedrich Wilhelm Joseph von Schelling (1775–1854). **E19.**
▸ **B** *adjective.* Of or pertaining to Schelling or his doctrines. **M19.**
■ **ˈSchellingism** *noun* the system of philosophy taught by Schelling **M19.**

schelm /ʃɛlm/ *noun.* Now *arch. rare.* **L16.**
[German: cf. SKELM.]
A rascal, a villain.

schema /ˈskiːmə/ *noun.* Pl. **-mata** /-mətə/, **-mas**. **L18.**
[(German from) Greek *skhēma*, *-mat-*: see SCHEME *noun*[1].]
1 In Kantian philosophy, a rule or procedure of the imagination enabling the understanding to apply a concept, esp. a category, to what is given in sense-perception. **L18.**
2 ECCLESIASTICAL. A draft canon or decree submitted to either of the Vatican Councils for discussion. **M19.**
3 A schematic representation of something; a hypothetical outline or plan; a theoretical construction; a draft, a synopsis, a design. **L19.**
4 PSYCHOLOGY. An (unconscious) organized mental model of something in terms of which new information can be interpreted or an appropriate response made. **E20.**

📖 **3** ALDOUS HUXLEY The substitution of simple intellectual schemata for the complexities of reality. ISAIAH BERLIN History is reducible to a natural science or a metaphysical or theological schema. E. H. GOMBRICH The schemata and patterns an artist has learned to handle.

schematic /skiːˈmatɪk/ *adjective* & *noun.* **E18.**
[from Latin *schemat-* (see SCHEME *noun*[1]) or directly from SCHEME *noun*[1]: see -ATIC.]
▸ **A** *adjective.* **1** Orig. (*rare*), corresponding to something in accordance with a scheme. Now, of or pertaining to a scheme or schema; of the nature of, or resembling, a diagrammatic representation or sketch; representing objects by symbols etc. **E18.**
2 ART. Following a conventional type. **M19.**
3 Suggested or modified by a preconceived system. **L19.**

📖 **1** W. JAMES A true account—so far as conceptions so schematic can claim truth at all. J. UPDIKE If . . the fruitful diagrams of Marx do schematic justice to the topology of a world.

▸ **B** *noun.* A schematic representation; a diagram, *esp.* one of electronic circuitry. **E20.**
■ **schematically** *adverb* **L19.**

†**schematical** *adjective. rare.* **L17.**
[formed as prec.: see -ICAL.]
1 Pertaining to a figure of speech. Only in **L17.**
2 Statistical. Only in **M18.**

schematise *verb* var. of SCHEMATIZE.

schematism /ˈskiːmətɪz(ə)m/ *noun*. **E17.**
[mod. Latin *schematismus* from Greek *skhēmatismos* the assumption of a certain form or appearance, from *skhēmat-*: see **SCHEMA**, **-ISM.**]
†**1** The use of a figure of speech. Only in **E17.**
2 A mode of arrangement of parts or particles; inner structure. Now *rare* or *obsolete*. **M17.**
3 A schematic or stereotyped arrangement, form, idea, or (method of) presentation. **E18.**
4 *PHILOSOPHY & PSYCHOLOGY.* The employment of a schema or schemata in cognition. Cf. **SCHEMA 1. L18.**

📖 **3** *Scientific American* A mental mechanics as precise . . as the innate schematism posited by Chomsky.

■ **schematist** *noun (rare)* the inventor of a doctrinal system **L17.**

schematize /ˈskiːmətʌɪz/ *verb*. Also **-ise. M17.**
[In branch I from Greek *skhēmatizein* assume a certain form, figure, etc., from *skhēmat-*; in branch II from *skhēmat-*: see **SCHEMA**, **-IZE.**]
▶ **I** *verb intrans.* †**1** Assume a new form or shape. *rare.* Only in **M17.**
▶ **II** *verb trans.* **2** Formulate in regular order; put or arrange in (a) schematic or conventional form; represent by a scheme or schema. **M19.**
3 Apply (a concept, esp. a category) to the data of sense-perception by means of a schema or schemata. **M19.**

📖 **2** J. CAREY Art simplifies and schematizes life . . while appearing to represent its complexity.

■ **schemati'zation** *noun* (*a*) the action or process of schematizing something; (*b*) a hypothetical organization of schemata; an analytical, tabular, or diagrammatic representation of data: **E20.**

scheme /skiːm/ *noun*[1]. **M16.**
[Latin *schema*, *-mat-* from Greek *skhēma* form, figure: cf. **SCHEMA.**]
†**1** A figure of speech. **M16–L17.**
†**2 a** *ASTROLOGY.* A representation of the positions of celestial objects at a particular time; *spec.* a horoscope. **L16–E19.** ▶**b** *gen.* A diagram; a figure illustrating or elucidating a proposition, description, design, etc., as a map of a town or an architect's drawing. **M17–E19.**
3 A schematic statement or analysis; *spec.* (*a*) a conspectus, an outline, an epitome of a book, argument, etc.; (*b*) a table, an orderly list, a system of classification. Now also, a timetable. **M17.**
4 A plan, a design; a project, an enterprise; a programme of work or action to attain an objective, a plan for regular contributions towards a pension etc. Now also *derog.*, a selfish, deceitful, or foolish project; a plot. **M17.** ▶**b** A comic or light-hearted escapade; an outing, an excursion. *obsolete* exc. *dial.* **M18.**
†**5** The form or appearance of something; a particular form. **M17–M18.**
6 †**a** A hypothesis, a theory. **L17–M19.** ▶**b** A body of related doctrines, a speculative system. **L17.**
7 A complex unity of elements cooperating and interacting according to a plan; (the mode of organization of) a system of correlated things, institutions, arrangements, etc. **M18.** ▶**b** In full ***scheme of colour***. A characteristic selection and arrangement of colours; *spec.* = ***colour scheme*** s.v. **COLOUR** *noun*. **L19.**

📖 **2b** J. RAY The Description . . would be tedious and difficult to understand without a Scheme. P. LUCKOMBE A great variety of mathematical schemes, maps, and other useful devices to embellish his works. **4** P. G. WODEHOUSE Marriage had . . rearranged his entire scheme of life. W. S. CHURCHILL He examined schemes for capturing the marvellous rock. J. BARZUN Man will invent a hundred schemes . . to satisfy his passions. ***South Sea scheme***: see **SOUTH** *adverb, adjective, noun, & verb*. **b** J. AUSTEN That glorious achievement, A Scheme to Town. **7 A.** STORR In Jung's scheme of things, the arts ranked very low. S. TROTT Of what importance was I . . in the scheme of the cosmos?

■ **schemeless** *adjective* **L19.**

†**scheme** *noun*[2]. **E18.**
[Origin unkn.]
ARCHITECTURE. The arc of larger radius in the middle of a three-centre arch or an arch of less than a semicircle, esp. a relieving arch of this form. Freq. more fully ***scheme-arch***.

scheme /skiːm/ *verb*. **E18.**
[from **SCHEME** *noun*[1].]
1 *verb trans.* Reduce to a schematic form or a formula. Also, plan *out* methodically. *rare.* **E18.**
2 a *verb trans.* Plan or contrive to bring about (an occurrence etc.), esp. artfully or deceitfully; plan or schedule (a thing). **M18.** ▶**b** *verb intrans.* Resort to contrivance; devise a scheme or plan, esp. secretly or deceitfully. **M19.**

📖 **2a** SIR W. SCOTT Offences which were wilfully and maliciously schemed. *Daily Telegraph* Most motorway repairs are schemed to end by mid-November. **b** C. KINGSLEY Half-a-dozen plans suggested themselves . . as he sat brooding and scheming. P. D. JAMES He was ambitious for the new job, had cleverly planned and schemed to get it.

■ **schemer** *noun* a person who schemes, a plotter **E18.** **scheming** *verbal noun* the action of the verb; an instance of this: **E19.** **scheming** *adjective* that schemes; cunning, artful, deceitful: **M19.** **schemingly** *adverb* **L19.**

schemist /ˈskiːmɪst/ *noun*. *arch.* **M17.**
[from **SCHEME** *noun*[1] + **-IST.**]
†**1** An astrologer. Cf. **SCHEME** *noun*[1] 2a. Only in **M17.**
†**2** An intriguer. **E18–E19.**
3 A planner. **M18.**

schemozzle *noun & verb* var. of **SHEMOZZLE.**

Schengen /ˈʃɛŋg(ə)n/ *noun*. **L20.**
[A town in Luxembourg, where the agreement was signed.]
In full ***Schengen agreement***. An agreement on the relaxation of border controls signed in 1985 by France, Belgium, the Netherlands, (West) Germany, and Luxembourg, and later by a number of other countries.

schepen /ˈskeɪp(ə)n/ *noun*. *obsolete* exc. *Hist.* **L15.**
[Dutch.]
A Dutch alderman or petty magistrate.

Scherbius /ˈʃəːbɪəs/ *noun*. **E20.**
[Arthur *Scherbius* (fl. 1906), German engineer.]
ELECTRICITY. Used *attrib.* with ref. to a method for regulating the speed of large a.c. induction motors, in which the voltage applied to the rotor is altered by means of a separate commutator motor and flywheel assembly.

Schering bridge /ˈʃɛːrɪŋ brɪdʒ/ *noun phr.* Also **Schering's bridge. E20.**
[from H. E. M. *Schering* (1880–1959), German engineer.]
ELECTRICITY. An a.c. bridge circuit for measuring the capacitance and power factor of insulating materials.

Schermuly /ˈʃəːmuːli/ *adjective*. **E20.**
[William *Schermuly* (1857–1929), English inventor.]
Designating (a component of) equipment comprising a line-carrying rocket fired from a pistol, used in life-saving at sea.
¶ Proprietary name.

scherzando /skɛːtˈsandəʊ/ *adverb, adjective, & noun*. **E19.**
[Italian, from *scherzare*, from **SCHERZO.**]
MUSIC. ▶**A** *adverb & adjective*. A direction: playful(ly). **E19.**
▶ **B** *noun*. Pl. **-dos**, **-di** /-di/. A movement or passage (to be) played playfully. **L19.**

scherzo /ˈskɛːtsəʊ/ *noun*. Pl. **-zos**, **-zi** /-tsi/. **M19.**
[Italian, lit. 'sport, jest'.]
MUSIC. A vigorous, light, or playful composition, esp. as a movement in a symphony or sonata.
■ **scherzetto** /-ˈsɛtəʊ/ *noun*, pl. **-ttos**, **-tti** /-ti/, a short passage or piece of music with the character of a scherzo **E20.** **scherzino** /-ˈsiːnəʊ/ *noun*, pl. **-nos**, **-ni** /-ni/, = **SCHERZETTO L19.**

schiacciato *noun* var. of **STIACCIATO.**

Schick /ʃɪk/ *noun*. **E20.**
[Bela *Schick* (1877–1967), Hungarian-born US paediatrician.]
MEDICINE. (Designating) a test for previously acquired immunity to diphtheria, using an intradermal injection of diphtheria toxin.
Comb.: **Schick-negative** *adjective* failing to show a positive reaction in the Schick test; **Schick-positive** *adjective* showing a positive reaction in the Schick test.

Schiedam /skɪˈdam/ *noun*. **E19.**
[A town in the Netherlands.]
A variety of gin.

Schiff /ʃɪf/ *noun*. **L19.**
[Hugo *Schiff* (1834–1915), German chemist.]
CHEMISTRY. Used *attrib.* and in *possess.* to designate compounds or reactions Schiff devised or investigated.
Schiff base, **Schiff's base** any organic compound having the structure $R^1R^2C{=}NR^3$ (where $R^{1,2,3}$ are alkyl groups and R^1 may be hydrogen). **Schiff reaction**, **Schiff's reaction** the action of aldehydes of restoring the magenta colour to Schiff's reagent. **Schiff reagent**, **Schiff's reagent** an acid solution of fuchsine decolorized by sulphur dioxide or potassium metabisulphite. **Schiff test**, **Schiff's test** the Schiff reaction used as a test for aldehydes.

schiffli /ˈʃɪfli/ *noun & adjective*. **L19.**
[Swiss German = German *Schiffchen* shuttle.]
(Designating) a type of embroidery machine with diagonal shuttles which work on fabric stretched on a movable frame; (designating) embroidery worked on such a machine.

Schilder's disease /ˈʃɪldəz dɪˌziːz/ *noun phr.* **M20.**
[from Paul Ferdinand *Schilder* (1886–1940), US neurologist and physiologist.]
MEDICINE. A disease of childhood characterized by degeneration of the white matter of the brain, esp. in the occipitotemporal lobes, leading to blindness, dementia, and spastic paralysis.

schiller /ˈʃɪlə/ *adjective & noun*. **E19.**
[German = play of colours.]
GEOLOGY. ▶**A** *attrib. adjective.* Designating minerals or rocks having a shining surface. **E19.**
schiller spar = **BASTITE.**
▶ **B** *noun*. An iridescent lustre, *spec.* that characteristic of certain minerals. **M19.**

schillerize /ˈʃɪlərʌɪz/ *verb trans.* Also **-ise. L19.**
[from prec. + **-IZE.**]
GEOLOGY. Cause (a crystal) to show schiller. Chiefly as ***schillerized*** *ppl adjective*.
■ **schilleri'zation** *noun* the process of becoming or fact of being schillerized **L19.**

schilling /ˈʃɪlɪŋ/ *noun*[1]. **M18.**
[German: see **SHILLING.** Cf. **SCHELLING, SKILLING** *noun*[2].]
1 *Hist.* A silver coin formerly used in Germany. **M18.**
2 The basic monetary unit of Austria until the introduction of the euro in 2002, equal to 100 groschen. **E20.**

Schilling /ˈʃɪlɪŋ/ *noun*[2]. **E20.**
[Victor *Schilling* (1883–1960), German haematologist.]
MEDICINE. Used *attrib.* and in *possess.* to designate a method of classifying and counting white blood cells, and the results so obtained.

Schilling test /ˈʃɪlɪŋ tɛst/ *noun phr.* **M20.**
[from Robert Frederick *Schilling* (b. 1919), US physician.]
MEDICINE. A test, used esp. for pernicious anaemia, involving measurement of the excretion of radioactively labelled vitamin B_{12} administered orally.

schimmel /ˈʃɪm(ə)l, ˈskɪm-/ *noun*. Chiefly *S. Afr.* **M19.**
[German or Dutch.]
A roan or dapple-grey horse.

Schimpfwort /ˈʃɪmpfvɔrt/ *noun*. Pl. **-wörter** /-vœrtər/. **M20.**
[German, from *Schimpf* insult + *Wort* word.]
An insulting epithet, a term of abuse.

schindylesis /skɪndɪˈliːsɪs/ *noun*. Pl. **-leses** /-ˈliːsiːz/. **M19.**
[mod. Latin from Greek *skhindulēsis*.]
ANATOMY. An articulation formed by the reception of a thin plate of one bone into a fissure or groove in another.

schinken /ˈʃɪŋkən/ *noun*. **M19.**
[German.]
German ham.
Comb.: ***schinkenwurst*** /-vʊrst/ ham sausage.

schipperke /ˈskɪpəki, ˈʃɪp-, -kə/ *noun*. **L19.**
[Dutch dial., lit. 'little boatman', from its use as a watchdog on barges.]
A (breed of) small black dog distinguished by pointed erect ears, a large ruff of longer fur on the neck and chest, and usu. a docked tail.

schism /ˈsɪz(ə)m, ˈskɪz(ə)m/ *noun*. Orig. †**scisme. LME.**
[Old French *s(c)isme* (mod. *schisme*) from ecclesiastical Latin *schisma* from Greek *skhisma* rent, cleft, (in the New Testament) division in the Church, from base of *skhizein* cleave, split. Cf. next.]
1 *ECCLESIASTICAL.* **a** A division, esp. a formal split within or the secession of a group from, the Church; the division of (part of) a Church into mutually opposed organizations; the state of or an instance of such division, esp. as caused by a dispute over discipline, the validity of an episcopal or papal election, etc. **LME.** ▶**b** The offence of causing or promoting (a) schismatic division in a Church, esp. the Established Church; the state of belonging to a schismatic body. **LME.** ▶**c** A sect or body formed by division within or secession from the Church; a body maintaining an ecclesiastical organization independent of that of the Catholic Church. *arch.* **E16.**
2 *gen.* Formerly, any state of dissension or mutual hostility. Now, any division of a previously united body of people into mutually opposing parties; (*arch.*) a party or faction formed as a result of such a division; any split or breach between people or things. **LME.**

📖 **1a** C. BURNEY The schism between the Greek and Latin churches . . in the ninth century. *Times Lit. Suppl.* The community of Old Believers, who upheld the schism in the Orthodox Church. **b** I. WALTON No such sin as Schism, if an adherence to some visible Church were not necessary. W. POPPLE Heresy relates to Errors in Faith, and Schism to those in Worship or Discipline. **2** LD MACAULAY The schism which had divided the Whig party was now completely healed. *Premiere* The schism with Hughes, which brought to an abrupt end what had been a mutually satisfying collaboration.

Comb.: **schism-house**, **schism-shop** *arch. derog.* a nonconformist place of worship.

schisma /ˈskɪzmə/ *noun*. Pl. **-mata** /-mətə/. **M17.**
[Late Latin, spec. use of Greek *skhisma* division: see prec.]
ACOUSTICS. Any of several very small intervals of musical pitch; now *esp.* the interval representing the excess over five octaves of eight fifths and a major third in just intonation, approximately one-hundredth of a tone.

schismatic /sɪzˈmatɪk, skɪz-/ *noun & adjective*. Orig. †**scismatik. LME.**
[Old French *scismatique* (mod. *schismatique*) from ecclesiastical Latin *schismaticus* from ecclesiastical Greek *skhismatikos*, from Greek *skhisma*, *-mat-*: see **SCHISM.**]
▶ **A** *noun*. **1** A person who promotes or is guilty of schism, esp. in the Church; a member or adherent of a schismatic body, faction, etc. **LME.**
2 *spec.* A Roman Catholic occasionally attending Church of England services to avoid the legal penalties against recusants. Long *obsolete* exc. *Hist.* **L16.**

1 W. BLACKSTONE Papists and protestant dissenters . . were supposed to be equally schismatics in departing from the national church.

► **B** *adjective.* Of or pertaining to schism or schismatics; of the nature of schism; guilty of or inclining to schism. LME.

▪ **schismatical** *adjective* = SCHISMATIC *adjective* M16. **schismatically** *adverb* M16. **schismaticalness** *noun* (now *rare*) the quality of being schismatic M17.

schismatize /ˈsɪzmətʌɪz, ˈskɪz-/ *verb intrans.* Also **-ise.** E17.
[French †*scismatiser* or medieval Latin *schismatizare* cause a schism, from ecclesiastical Greek *skhisma*, *-mat-*: see SCHISM, -IZE.]
Behave schismatically; favour or advocate schismatic principles; lead or belong to a schismatic body.
▪ **schismatist** *noun* (*rare*) a schismatic M18.

schismogenesis /sɪzməˈdʒɛnɪsɪs, skɪz-/ *noun.* M20.
[from SCHISM + -O- + -GENESIS.]
ANTHROPOLOGY. The origin or development of differentiation between groups or cultures due to the reciprocal exaggeration of behaviour patterns and responses that tend to destroy social stability.

schist /ʃɪst/ *noun.* L18.
[French *schiste*, from Latin (*lapis*) *schistos* fissile (stone) from Greek *skhistos* from base also of *skhizein*: see SCHISM.]
GEOLOGY. A coarse-grained pelitic metamorphic rock which has a structure marked by parallel layers of various minerals and can be split into thin irregular plates. Also, a component or texture of this type.

schistose /ˈʃɪstəʊs/ *adjective.* L18.
[from SCHIST + -OSE¹.]
GEOLOGY. Laminated; having a formation resembling a schist; formed of schist.
▪ **schistosity** /-ˈstɒsɪti/ *noun* a planar alignment or cleavage in a crystalline metamorphic rock; the direction or line of this: L19. **schistous** *adjective* = SCHISTOSE E19.

schistosome /ˈskɪstə(ʊ)səʊm/ *noun.* E20.
[mod. Latin *Schistosoma* (see below), from Greek *skhistos* (see SCHIST) + *sōma* body: see -SOME³.]
ZOOLOGY. Any of various parasitic trematodes of the genus *Schistosoma* and family Schistosomatidae of which the early stages occur in freshwater snails and the adults are parasitic in the blood vessels of birds and mammals including man; a blood fluke. Cf. BILHARZIA.
▪ **schistoˈsomal** *adjective* M20. **schistosomiasis** /-ˈmʌɪəsɪs/ *noun*, pl. **-ases** /-əsiːz/, (*MEDICINE*) disease caused by infection with blood flukes of the genus *Schistosoma*, characterized by chronic symptoms esp. of the digestive and urinary systems, and sometimes by fever E20. **schistosomiˈcidal** *adjective* M20. **schistoˈsomicide** *noun* (*PHARMACOLOGY*) a substance or drug that destroys schistosomes M20. **schistosomule** /-ˈsɒmjuːl/ *noun* = SCHISTOSOMULUM M20. **schistosomulum** /-ˈsɒmjʊləm/ *noun*, pl. **-ula**, a blood fluke of the genus *Schistosoma* which has entered its adult host but is not yet mature E20.

schitz *noun & adjective* see SCHIZ.

schitzy /ˈskɪtsi/ *adjective. slang.* Also **schizzy.** M20.
[formed as next + -Y¹.]
Schizophrenic; *spec.* exhibiting or suffering the effects of hallucinogenic drugs.

schiz /skɪts/ *noun & adjective. slang* (chiefly *N. Amer.*). Also (as adjective usu.) **-tz.** M20.
[Abbreviation of SCHIZOID or SCHIZOPHRENIC: cf. prec.]
► **A** *noun.* A schizophrenic; *spec.* a person who experiences a drug-induced hallucination. M20.
► **B** *adjective.* Schizophrenic. M20.

schizandra /skɪtˈsandrə/ *noun.* M19.
[mod. Latin *Schisandra* (see below), formed as SCHIZO- + Greek *andr-*, *anēr* man, on account of the divided stamens.]
A Chinese herb, *Schisandra chinensis*, whose berries are credited with various stimulant or medicinal properties.

schizanthus /skɪtˈsanθəs/ *noun.* E19.
[mod. Latin, formed as SCHIZO- + Greek *anthos* flower.]
= ***POOR MAN's orchid***.

schizo /ˈskɪtsəʊ/ *noun & adjective. colloq.* M20.
[Abbreviation.]
► **A** *noun.* Pl. **-os.** = SCHIZOPHRENIC *noun.* M20.
► **B** *adjective.* = SCHIZOPHRENIC *adjective.* M20.

schizo- /ˈskʌɪzəʊ, ˈʃʌɪz-, *in sense 2 usu.* ˈskɪtsəʊ, ˈskɪdzəʊ/ *combining form.*
[from Greek *skhizein* to split + -O-; in sense 2 repr. SCHIZOPHRENIA.]
1 *BOTANY & ZOOLOGY.* Forming words, usu. based on Greek, with the sense 'split, divided'.
2 *PSYCHIATRY & PSYCHOLOGY.* Forming words pertaining to schizophrenia.
▪ **schizo-aˈffective** *adjective & noun* (a person) exhibiting symptoms of both schizophrenia and manic-depressive psychosis M20. **schizocarp** *noun* a dry fruit which breaks up into two or more one-seeded mericarps when mature L19. **schizoˈcarpic**, **schizoˈcarpous** *adjectives* resembling or belonging to a schizocarp L19. **schizocoel(e)** /-siːl/ *noun* a perivisceral cavity formed by splitting of the embryonic mesoblast L19. **schizoˈcoelic** *adjective* = SCHIZOCOELOUS E20. **schizoˈcoelous** *adjective* of, pertaining to, or having a schizocoel L19. **schizocoely** *noun* development of a coelom by splitting of the mesoblast M20. **schizoˈgenic**, **schiˈzogenous** *adjectives* (of an intercellular space in a plant) formed by the splitting of the common wall of contiguous cells (cf. LYSIGENOUS) L19. **schiˈzogonic** *adjective* pertaining to schizogony; ***schizogonic cycle***, the second of the two stages in the life history of some sporozoans: E20. **schizogony** /-ˈzɒɡəni/ *noun* asexual reproduction by multiple fission, found in some protozoa, esp. parasitic forms L19. **schizomycete** /-ˈmʌɪsiːt/ *noun*, pl. **-mycetes** /-ˈmʌɪsiːts, -mʌɪˈsiːtiːz/, (now chiefly *Hist.*) a member of the class Schizomycetes, which comprises the bacteria when they are classified as fungi L19. **schizoˈrhinal** *adjective* (*ORNITHOLOGY*) having each nasal bone deeply cleft or forked L19. **schizoˈtaxia** *noun* a genetically determined defect in the functioning of the nervous system which may predispose to schizophrenia M20. **schizoˈtaxic** *adjective & noun* (*a*) *adjective* of or pertaining to schizotaxia; (*b*) *noun* a person with schizotaxia: M20. **schizothyme** *noun & adjective* (characteristic of) a person who exhibits a personality type with some schizophrenic characteristics, esp. introversion and withdrawal E20. **schizothymia** /-ˈθʌɪmɪə/ *noun* the constitution or temperament typical of a schizothyme M20. **schizoˈthymic** *adjective* of or pertaining to schizothymia M20. **schizoˈtypal** *adjective* of, pertaining to, or affected by schizotypy M20. **ˈschizotype** *noun* a personality type in which mild symptoms of schizophrenia are present M20. **schizoˈtypic** *adjective* = SCHIZOTYPAL M20. **schizotypy** *noun* the state or condition of being a schizotype M20.

schizoid /ˈskɪtsɔɪd, skɪdz-/ *adjective & noun.* E20.
[from SCHIZO(PHRENIA + -OID.]
► **A** *adjective.* **1** *PSYCHIATRY & PSYCHOLOGY.* Resembling or tending towards schizophrenia, but with milder or less developed symptoms; pertaining to or affected by a personality disorder marked by coldness and inability to form social relations. E20.
2 *transf. & fig.* = SCHIZOPHRENIC *adjective* 2. M20.
► **B** *noun.* A schizoid person. E20.
▪ **schiˈzoidal** *adjective* M20. **schiˈzoidia** *noun* the schizoid state, esp. when regarded as caused by the same genetic disorder as schizophrenia M20.

schizont /ˈskʌɪzɒnt/ *noun.* E20.
[formed as SCHIZO- + -ONT.]
ZOOLOGY. In protozoa, esp. sporozoans, a cell that divides by schizogony to form daughter cells or merozoites.
▪ **schizontiˈcidal** *adjective* that is a schizonticide M20. **schiˈzonticide** *noun* (*PHARMACOLOGY*) a substance or drug that kills schizonts M20. **schizontoˈcidal** *adjective* = SCHIZONTICIDAL M20. **schiˈzontocide** *noun* = SCHIZONTICIDE M20.

schizophrenia /skɪtsə(ʊ)ˈfriːnɪə, skɪdz-/ *noun.* E20.
[mod. Latin, from SCHIZO- + Greek *phrēn* mind: see -IA¹.]
1 *PSYCHIATRY.* A psychotic mental illness characterized by a breakdown in the relation between thoughts, feelings, and actions, usu. accompanied by withdrawal from social activity and the occurrence of delusions and hallucinations. E20.
2 *transf. & fig.* The maintenance of two apparently conflicting attitudes, opinions, etc. M20.
▪ **ˈschizophrene** *noun* a schizophrenic, a person with a predisposition towards schizophrenia E20. **schizophreniform** /-ˈfrɛn-/ *adjective* resembling schizophrenia M20. **ˌschizophrenoˈgenic** *adjective* tending to give rise to schizophrenia M20.

schizophrenic /skɪtsə(ʊ)ˈfrɛnɪk, skɪdz-/ *adjective & noun.* E20.
[from prec. + -IC.]
► **A** *adjective.* **1** *PSYCHIATRY.* Characteristic of or having schizophrenia. E20.
2 *transf. & fig.* Characterized by mutually contradictory or inconsistent elements, attitudes, etc. M20.
► **B** *noun.* A person with schizophrenia. E20.
▪ **schizoˈphrenically** *adverb* in a manner suggestive or characteristic of schizophrenia M20.

schizostylis /skɪzəʊˈstʌɪlɪs/ *noun.* Pl. same. M19.
[mod. Latin (see below), from SCHIZO- + Latin *stilus* STYLE *noun*, with ref. to the split styles of the plant.]
Either of two southern African plants of the genus *Schizostylis*, of the iris family; *spec.* the Kaffir lily, *S. coccinea*.

schizzy *noun* var. of SCHITZY.

schlag /ʃlaːk/ *noun.* M20.
[Abbreviation.]
= SCHLAGOBERS, SCHLAGSAHNE.

Schlagobers /ʃlaːkˈoːbərs/ *noun.* M20.
[German dial., from *schlagen* to beat + *Obers* cream.]
(Coffee with) whipped cream.

schlagsahne /ˈʃlaːkzaːnə/ *noun.* E20.
[German, from *schlagen* to beat + *Sahne* cream.]
Whipped cream.

Schlamperei /ˈʃlampərai/ *noun. derog.* M20.
[German.]
Indolent slovenliness, muddleheadedness.

schlemiel /ʃləˈmiːl/ *noun. colloq.* L19.
[Yiddish from German *Shlemihl.*]
An awkward clumsy person; a foolish or unlucky person.

M. BLONSKY Isn't it better to play the schlemiel than be the malfeasant?

schlenter /ˈʃlɛntə/ *noun & adjective.* Also (*Austral. & NZ*) **slan-** /slan-/ & other vars. M19.
[(Afrikaans from) Dutch *slenter* knavery, trick.]
► **A** *noun.* **1** A trick. *Austral. & NZ colloq.* M19.
2 A counterfeit diamond. *S. Afr.* L19.
► **B** *adjective.* Dishonest, crooked; counterfeit, fake. *Austral., NZ, & S. Afr. colloq.* L19.
¶ In Austral. & NZ usage, *slanter* now the usual form.

schlep /ʃlɛp/ *noun*¹. *US colloq.* M20.
[Abbreviation.]
= SCHLEPPER.

schlep /ʃlɛp/ *noun*². *colloq.* (chiefly *US*). M20.
[Yiddish, prob. formed as next.]
A troublesome business, (a piece of) hard work.

schlep /ʃlɛp/ *verb. colloq.* Also **-pp.** Infl. **-pp-.** E20.
[Yiddish *shlepn* from German *schleppen* drag.]
1 *verb trans.* Haul, carry, drag. E20.
2 *verb intrans.* Toil; move or go slowly or awkwardly. M20.

schlepper /ˈʃlɛpə/ *noun. colloq.* (chiefly *US*). M20.
[Yiddish, as prec.: see -ER¹.]
A person of little worth, a fool; a pauper, a beggar, a hanger-on.

schlich /ʃlɪk/ *noun.* L17.
[German: cf. SLICKENS.]
METALLURGY & MINING. Finely powdered ore esp. in a slurry.

schlicht function /ʃlɪçt ˈfʌŋ(k)ʃ(ə)n/ *noun phr.* M20.
[from German *schlicht* simple, plain.]
MATH. An injective function.

Schlieffen /ˈʃliːfən/ *adjective.* E20.
[Alfred, Graf von *Schlieffen* (1833–1913), German general.]
Hist. Designating a plan or model for the invasion and defeat of France formulated by von Schlieffen before 1905 and applied, with modifications, in 1914.

schliere /ˈʃlɪərə/ *noun.* Also **S-.** Usu. in pl. **-ren** /-rən/. L19.
[German = stria, streak from earlier *Schlier* marl from Middle High German *slier* mud, rel. to Middle High German *slier* ulcer from Old High German *sclierrun* (dative pl.).]
1 *PETROGRAPHY.* An irregular streak or mass in igneous rock differing transitionally from its surroundings in texture or composition, and usu. elongated by flow. L19.
2 A zone or stratum in a transparent medium which is detectable by refraction anomalies as a result of differences in pressure, temperature, or composition. L19.

schlimazel /ʃlɪˈmɒz(ə)l/ *noun. colloq.* (chiefly *US*). Also **sh-**, **-zl.** M20.
[Yiddish, from Middle High German *slim* crooked + Hebrew *mazzāl* luck.]
A consistently unlucky accident-prone person.

schlock /ʃlɒk/ *noun & adjective. colloq.* (chiefly *N. Amer.*). E20.
[App. from Yiddish *shlak* apoplectic stroke, *shlog* wretch, untidy person, apoplectic stroke, from *shlogn* to strike.]
► **A** *noun.* Cheap, shoddy, or defective goods; inferior material, trash. E20.
Comb.: **schlockmeister** [German *Meister* master] a purveyor of cheap or trashy goods.
► **B** *adjective.* Cheap, inferior, trashy. E20.
▪ **schlocky** *adjective* characterized by schlock; shoddy, trashy: M20.

schlong /ʃlɒŋ/ *noun. US slang.* M20.
[Yiddish *shlang*, from Middle High German *slange* (German *Schlange*) snake.]
The penis. Also, a contemptible person.

schloss /ʃlɒs/ *noun.* E19.
[German.]
A castle, *esp.* one in Germany or Austria.

schlub *noun* var. of SHLUB.

schlump /ʃlʊmp/ *noun. slang* (chiefly *US*). Also **shl-.** M20.
[App. rel. to Yiddish *shlumperdik* dowdy, cogn. with German *Schlumpe* slattern.]
A dull-witted, slow, or slovenly person; a slob; a fool, a chump.

schmaltz /ʃmɔːlts, ʃmalts/ *noun & verb.* M20.
[Yiddish from German *Schmalz* dripping, lard.]
► **A** *noun.* **1** Melted chicken fat. Chiefly in ***schmaltz herring***, a form of pickled herring. M20.
2 Sentimentality, emotionalism; excessively sentimental music, writing, drama, etc. *colloq.* M20.
► **B** *verb trans.* Impart a sentimental atmosphere to; play (music) in a sentimental manner. Freq. foll. by *up*. *colloq.* M20.
▪ **schmaltzy** *adjective* (*colloq.*) sentimentalized, overemotional M20

schmatte *noun* var. of SHMATTE.

schmear *noun* var. of SHMEAR.

schmeck /ʃmɛk/ *noun. slang.* M20.
[Yiddish, lit. 'a sniff, a smell'. Cf. SMACK *noun*⁴.]
A drug; *spec.* heroin.
▪ **schmecker** *noun* a drug addict, *esp.* a heroin addict M20.

schmeer *noun* var. of SHMEAR.

schmegegge /ʃmə'gɛgi/ *noun. US slang.* Also **shm-**, **-ggy**, & other vars. **M20.**
[Origin unkn.]
1 A contemptible person, an idiot. **M20.**
2 Rubbish, nonsense. **M20.**

Schmeisser /'ʃmʌɪsə/ *noun.* **M20.**
[Louis and Hugo *Schmeisser*, German small-arms designers.]
Any of various German types of sub-machine-gun in use from 1918 onwards.

schmelz /ʃmɛlts/ *noun.* **M19.**
[German = enamel.]
Any of several varieties of decorative glass; *spec.* one coloured red with a metallic salt, used to flash white glass.

Schmelzglas /'ʃmɛltsglaːs/ *noun.* **M20.**
[German.]
= prec.

schmendrik /'ʃmɛndrɪk/ *noun. US slang.* Also **shm-**, **-ck**. **M20.**
[A character in an operetta by Abraham Goldfaden (1840–1908), Yiddish dramatist.]
A contemptible, foolish, or immature person.

Schmerz /ʃmɛrts/ *noun.* **E20.**
[German = pain.]
Grief, sorrow, regret, pain.

Schmidt /ʃmɪt/ *noun.* **M20.**
[Bernhard Voldemar *Schmidt* (1879–1935), Estonian-born German optician.]
ASTRONOMY. **1** Used ***attrib.*** with ref. to an optical system invented by Schmidt. **M20.**
2 A Schmidt telescope. **M20.**
1 Schmidt camera = ***Schmidt telescope***. **Schmidt correcting plate**, **Schmidt corrector (plate)**, **Schmidt plate** an aspheric lens of complex figure used in the Schmidt telescope and other catadioptric systems that use the same principle. **Schmidt telescope** an astronomical telescope used exclusively for wide-field photography at the primary focus, having a Schmidt corrector plate at the centre of curvature of a spherical primary mirror.

Schmidt number /'ʃmɪt nʌmbə/ *noun phr.* **M20.**
[from E. H. W. *Schmidt* (1892–1975), German engineer.]
PHYSICS. A dimensionless number, analogous to the Prandtl number, used in the study of convective mass transfer and evaluated as the ratio of kinematic viscosity to mass diffusivity.

Schmidt reaction /'ʃmɪt rɪˌakʃ(ə)n/ *noun phr.* Also **Schmidt's reaction**. **M20.**
[from K. F. *Schmidt* (1887–1971), German organic chemist.]
ORGANIC CHEMISTRY. A synthesis in which a carbonyl compound is treated with hydrazoic acid in the presence of mineral acid to form nitriles, amides, or amines.

schmierkäse /'ʃmiːrkɛːzə/ *noun.* **E20.**
[German, from *schmieren* to smear + *Käse* cheese. Cf. **SMEARCASE.**]
A soft cheese, *spec.* cottage cheese.

Schmitt trigger /'ʃmɪt ˌtrɪgə/ *noun phr.* **M20.**
[from Otto H. *Schmitt* (1913–98), US biophysicist and electronics engineer.]
ELECTRONICS. More fully ***Schmitt trigger circuit***. A bistable circuit in which the output increases to a steady maximum when the input rises above a certain threshold, and decreases almost to zero when the input voltage falls below another threshold.

schmo /ʃməʊ/ *noun. N. Amer. slang.* Pl. **-o(e)s**. **M20.**
[Alt. of **SCHMUCK.**]
An idiot, a fool.

schmooze /ʃmuːz, ʃmuːs/ *noun. N. Amer. colloq.* **M20.**
[Yiddish *schmues* chat, gossip from Hebrew *šěmūʿōt* pl. of *šěmūʿāh* rumour.]
Chat; gossip; a long and intimate conversation.

schmooze /ʃmuːz, ʃmuːs/ *verb intrans. N. Amer. colloq.* **L19.**
[Yiddish *schmuesn* talk, converse, chat, formed as prec.]
Chat, gossip.

schmuck /ʃmʌk/ *noun. slang.* **L19.**
[Yiddish *shmok* penis.]
A contemptible or objectionable person; an idiot.
■ **schmucky** *adjective* contemptible; stupid: **M20.**

schmutter /'ʃmʌtə/ *noun. colloq.* **M20.**
[formed as **SHMATTE.**]
Clothing. Also *fig.*, rubbish (freq. in ***old schmutter***).

schmutz /ʃmʊts/ *noun. slang.* **M20.**
[Yiddish or German.]
Dirt, filth, rubbish.

schnapper /'snapə/ *noun.* Chiefly *Austral. & NZ.* **E19.**
[Alt. of **SNAPPER** *noun*[1], after German *Schnapper*.]
Any of various marine fishes of the family Sparidae, *esp.* an Australasian food fish of the genus *Chrysophrys*.

schnapps /ʃnaps/ *noun.* Also **schnaps**. **E19.**
[German *Schnaps* dram of drink, liquor (esp. gin) from Low German, Dutch *snaps* gulp, mouthful, from *snappen* seize, snatch, **SNAP** *verb*. Cf. **SNAPS.**]
Any of various strong spirits resembling genever gin.

schnauzer /'ʃnaʊtsə/ *noun.* **E20.**
[German.]
(A dog of) a breed of black or pepper-and-salt wire-haired terrier, having a stocky build, a blunt, bearded muzzle, and ears that droop forwards.

schnitzel /'ʃnɪtz(ə)l/ *noun.* **M19.**
[German.]
A veal cutlet or escalope. Esp. in ***Wiener schnitzel***, ***Vienna schnitzel***, one coated with egg and breadcrumbs and fried.

schnockered /'ʃnɒkəd/ *adjective. US colloq.* **M20.**
[Var. of **SNOCKERED.**]
Drunk.

schnook /ʃnʊk/ *noun. N. Amer. colloq.* **M20.**
[Perh. from German *Schnucke* a small sheep or Yiddish *shnuk* snout.]
A dupe, a sucker; a simpleton.

schnorkel *noun & verb* see **SNORKEL.**

schnorrer /'ʃnɒrə/ *noun.* Chiefly *US.* **L19.**
[Yiddish var. of German *Schnurrer*, from *schnurren* (slang) go begging.]
Orig. (*spec.*), a Jewish beggar. Now (*gen.*), a beggar, a layabout, a scrounger.
■ **schnorr** *verb trans.* obtain by begging **L19.**

schnozz /ʃnɒz/ *noun. N. Amer. slang.* **M20.**
[Yiddish *shnoytz* from German *Schnauze* snout. Cf. next.]
The nose; a nostril.
on the schnozz, **right on the schnozz** precisely, exactly on time, on the dot.

schnozzle /'ʃnɒz(ə)l/ *noun. slang* (orig. *US*). **M20.**
[Yiddish *shnoytzl* dim. of *shnoytz*: see prec. Cf. **SNOZZLE.**]
The nose.
■ Also **schnozzola** /ʃnɒ'zəʊlə/ *noun* **M20.**

Schnurkeramik /'ʃnuːrkeˌraːmɪk/ *noun.* **E20.**
[German, from *Schnur* string, cord + *Keramik* ceramics, pottery.]
ARCHAEOLOGY. = ***corded ware*** s.v. **CORDED** *adjective* 2.

Schoenbergian /ʃəːn'bəːgɪən/ *adjective & noun.* **E20.**
[from *Schoenberg* (see below) + **-IAN.**]
▶ **A** *adjective.* Of, pertaining to, or characteristic of the Austrian composer Arnold Schoenberg (1874–1951) or his music. **E20.**
▶ **B** *noun.* An admirer or adherent of Schoenberg; an exponent of Schoenberg's music. **M20.**

Schoenflies /'ʃøːnfliːs/ *noun.* **M20.**
[Arthur *Schoenflies* (1853–1928), German mathematician.]
CRYSTALLOGRAPHY. Used ***attrib.*** with ref. to a system of notation for space groups.

schol /skɒl/ *noun. colloq.* **L19.**
[Abbreviation.]
A scholarship.

schola cantorum /skəʊlə kan'tɔːrəm/ *noun phr.* Pl. **scholae cantorum** /'skəʊliː, -lʌɪ/. **L18.**
[medieval Latin = school of singers.]
1 A choir school attached to a cathedral or monastery; orig., the papal choir at Rome, established by Gregory the Great (*c* 540–604). **L18.**
2 *gen.* A group of singers. Freq. as the title of such a group. **E20.**

scholar /'skɒlə/ *noun.* Also (*dial.*) **scholard** /'skɒləd/. **OE.**
[Orig. directly from late Latin *scholaris*, later aphet. from Old French *escoler*, *-lier* (mod. *écolier*) from late Latin *scholaris* from Latin *schola* **SCHOOL** *noun*[1]: see **-AR**[1].]
1 A person receiving formal teaching from another, a pupil, *spec.* (***a***) a schoolchild; (***b***) a person taught by a particular teacher or instructor; (***c***) a student in a medieval university; (***d***) a junior or undergraduate member of a university. *arch.* **OE.** ▸**b** A person who regards another as his or her leader or teacher; a disciple. **L16.**
2 A learned or erudite person, orig. esp. in the classics, now in languages, literature, or any non-scientific subject, an academic. Also (now *arch. & dial.*), a person who is able to read and write. **ME.** ▸**b** With specifying adjective: a person with a specified aptitude for study. **E17.**
3 A student who in reward for academic merit is given financial support for education by a school, college, or university. **E16.**
4 *ROMAN HISTORY.* A member of one of the four companies into which the imperial guard was divided. **E20.**

📖 **1** J. HAMMOND And teach my lovely scholar all I know. **2** G. B. SHAW The training of the scholar and the sportsman may . . diverge as they adolesce. I. ORIGO The distinguished Leopardian scholar and critic. **b** O. MANNING Always was a poor scholar Never could remember anything. **3** ***Fulbright scholar***, ***King's Scholar***, ***Rhodes Scholar***, etc.

Phrases: ***Oxford Scholar***: see **OXFORD** *adjective*. **scholar's mate** *CHESS*: in which the second player is checkmated in the opponent's fourth move.
■ **scholardom** *noun* (*rare*) the realm of scholars or scholarship **L19.** **scholarhood** *noun* (*rare*) (***a***) the learned world; (***b***) the condition of being a scholar: **M19.** **scholarism** *noun* (now *rare*) scholarship, learning **L16.**

scholarch /'skəʊlɑːk/ *noun.* **M19.**
[Greek *skholarkhēs* from *skholē* **SCHOOL** *noun*[1]: see **-ARCH.**]
Hist. The head or ruler of a school: *spec.* (***a***) the head of an Athenian school of philosophy; (***b***) in parts of Germany, Switzerland, and France, an official formerly charged with the inspection of the schools within a city or district.
■ **scholarchate** *noun* the office of a scholarch; the body of scholarchs: **M18.**

scholard *noun* see **SCHOLAR.**

†**scholarity** *noun. rare.* **L16–L19.**
[Old French *sc(h)olarité* or medieval Latin *scholaritas* from late Latin *scholaris*: see **SCHOLAR**, **-ITY.**]
The status of a scholar.

scholarlike /'skɒləlʌɪk/ *adverb & adjective.* **M16.**
[from **SCHOLAR** + **-LIKE.**]
▶†**A** *adverb.* Like a scholar or learned person; in a manner befitting a scholar. **M16–E17.**
▶ **B** *adjective.* †**1** Pertaining to scholars; scholastic. Only in **L16.**
2 Resembling or befitting a scholar or learned person; scholarly. **L16.**

scholarly /'skɒləli/ *adjective.* **M17.**
[from **SCHOLAR** + **-LY**[1].]
Pertaining to, characterizing, or befitting a scholar; learned, erudite.

📖 P. L. FERMOR A . . scholarly man, living alone with his books. J. KLEIN I wrote in a . . scholarly manner: I quoted my sources.

■ **scholarliness** *noun* **E17.**

scholarly /'skɒləli/ *adverb. rare.* **L16.**
[from **SCHOLAR** + **-LY**[2].]
As befits a scholar; in a learned manner.

scholarship /'skɒləʃɪp/ *noun.* **M16.**
[from **SCHOLAR** + **-SHIP.**]
1 The status or emoluments of a scholar given financial support for education in reward for academic merit by a school, college, or university; an instance of this. **M16.**
2 Academic achievement or study; learning, erudition, orig. esp. the classics; (now *arch. & dial.*) literacy. Also, the world of learning, scholars collectively. **L16.**

📖 **1** A. J. AYER A minor scholarship in mathematics at Trinity College. ***Rhodes Scholarship*** etc. ***State Scholarship***, ***travelling scholarship***, etc. *attrib.*: R. HOGGART The scholarship boys and girls go off to the grammar-school. **2** F. O'CONNOR The lack of scholarship, the lack of intellectual honesty. K. CLARK The heroic age of scholarship when new texts were discovered.

scholastic /skə'lastɪk/ *adjective & noun.* **L16.**
[Latin *scholasticus* from Greek *skholastikos* studious, learned, (noun) scholar, from *skholazein* be at leisure, devote one's leisure to learning, from *skholē*: see **SCHOOL** *noun*[1], **-IC.**]
▶ **A** *adjective.* **1** Of, pertaining to, or designating the scholasticism of the universities of medieval Europe, of or pertaining to the schoolmen. **L16.**
2 Of or pertaining to scholarship or formal education; academic. **M17.**
3 Precise in a manner regarded as typical of medieval scholasticism; *derog.* pedantic, needlessly formal or subtle. **L18.**
▶ **B** *noun.* **1** A representative or adherent of the scholasticism of the universities of medieval Europe, a schoolman. **M17.**
2 A scholar, an erudite person, an academic. Now *rare.* **M17.**
3 *Hist.* In the Byzantine Empire, an advocate. *rare.* **M19.**
4 *ROMAN CATHOLIC CHURCH.* A member of any of several religious orders, esp. the Society of Jesus, who is at the stage between the novitiate and the priesthood. **L19.**
■ †**scholastical** *adjective & noun* (***a***) *adjective* = **SCHOLASTIC** *adjective*; (***b***) *noun* = **SCHOLASTIC** *noun* 1: **LME–L18.** **scholastically** *adverb* in a scholastic manner **M16.**

scholasticate /skə'lastɪkeɪt/ *noun.* **L19.**
[mod. Latin *scholasticatus*, formed as **SCHOLASTIC** *adjective*: see **-ATE**[1].]
ROMAN CATHOLIC CHURCH. A house of studies for scholastics, esp. of the Society of Jesus.

scholasticism /skə'lastɪsɪz(ə)m/ *noun.* **M18.**
[from **SCHOLASTIC** + **-ISM.**]
1 The educational tradition of the universities of medieval Europe, characterized esp. by a method of philosophical and theological speculation which aimed at a better understanding of the revealed truths of Christianity by defining, systematizing, and reasoning; the principles and practices of the schoolmen. **M18.**
2 Strict adherence to methods regarded as characteristic of the educational tradition of medieval Europe; narrow-minded insistence on traditional doctrines and forms of exposition; pedantry. **M19.**
■ **scholasticized** *ppl adjective* imbued with or influenced by scholasticism **E20.** **scholasticizing** *ppl adjective* inclining to or favouring scholastic principles **M19.**

scholia *noun* pl. of SCHOLIUM.

scholiast /ˈskəʊlɪast/ *noun*. L16.
[Late Greek *skholiastēs*, from *skholiazein*, formed as next.]
A person who writes explanatory notes on an author; *esp.* an ancient commentator on a classical writer.

scholion /ˈskəʊlɪən/ *noun*. L16.
[Greek: see next.]
= SCHOLIUM.

scholium /ˈskəʊlɪəm/ *noun*. Pl. **-lia** /-lɪə/. M16.
[mod. Latin, from Greek *skholion* from *skholē* learned discussion: see SCHOOL *noun*¹.]
An explanatory note or comment, *esp.* one made by an ancient commentator on a classical text.

Schönlein /ˈʃəːnlʌɪn/ *noun*. L19.
[J. L. *Schönlein* (1793–1864), German physician.]
MEDICINE. **1** ***Schönlein's disease***, a form of Henoch–Schönlein purpura associated esp. with pain in the joints. Cf. HENOCH 1. L19.
2 ***Schönlein–Henoch purpura***, ***Schönlein–Henoch's purpura***, = ***Henoch–Schönlein purpura*** s.v. HENOCH 2. M20.

school /skuːl/ *noun*¹.
[Old English *scōl*, *scolu*, corresp. to Middle Low German, Middle Dutch *schōle* (Dutch *school*), Old High German *scuola* (German *Schule*), from Germanic, from Latin *schola* from Greek *skholē* leisure, employment of leisure in disputation, lecture, (later) school; reinforced in Middle English by aphet. from Old French *escole* (mod. *école*) from Proto-Romance *scola*.]
▶ **I 1** An establishment in which children are given formal education. OE. ▸**b** Without article: instruction in or attendance at a school; the set time of attendance at a school. OE. ▸**c** *collect.* The pupils attending a school. ME. ▸**d** A division of a school, comprising several forms or classes. Freq. with specifying word. E17. ▸**e** The building or set of buildings occupied by a school. M19.
2 *Hist.* The place in which a philosopher in ancient Greece or Rome taught. OE.
3 An environment or situation in which instruction or training is obtained in a particular skill, virtue, etc.; a person or thing regarded as a source of such training. OE.
4 a An institution in which formal instruction in a specific skill or attribute is given; a course of instruction taking place at a specified time. Also without article: some institution or course providing instruction; attendance at such an institution or course of instruction. Usu. with specifying word. LME. ▸**b** A manual of instruction in a particular subject. Now only *spec.* (MUSIC), an instruction-book for a particular instrument. L17. ▸**c** A course of training given by an organization to its staff. *US.* M20.
5 A body of people who are or have been taught by a particular philosopher, scientist, artist, etc.; a group of people who are disciples of the same person, or who share some principle, method, style, etc. Also, a particular doctrine or practice as followed by such a body of people. Freq. with specifying word. E17.
6 a A group of gamblers or of people drinking together. E19. ▸**b** A gang of thieves or beggars working together. *slang. rare.* M19.

📖 **1** ***boarding school***, ***convent school***, ***elementary school***, ***grammar school***, ***high school***, ***independent school***, ***junior school***, ***prep school***, ***primary school***, ***private school***, ***public school***, ***secondary school***, etc. **b** I. MURDOCH Old friends, having been at school together. **d** ***lower school***, ***middle school***, ***upper school***, etc. **3** R. A. KNOX Railway travelling is the best . . school of human patience. **4a** J. VAN DRUTEN An . . actress who runs a school where she teaches the Pushkin method. ***charm school***, ***dancing school***, ***flying school***, ***music school***, ***riding school***, etc. ***evening school***, ***night school***, ***summer school***, ***Sunday school***, etc. **5** A. BEVAN The Marxist school of political thought. ***Cockney School***, ***Manchester School***, ***Newgate school***, ***Norwich school***, ***Oxford School***, ***Prague school***, ***Satanic school***, ***Umbrian School***, etc. **6** ***poker school*** etc.

▶ **II 7 a** Orig., an organized body of teachers and scholars in one of the higher branches of study cultivated in the medieval period, *esp.* such a body in medieval Europe constituting a university. Now, a department, faculty, or course of study in a college or university; an independent division of a university, for teaching and research in a particular subject. OE. ▸**b** In *pl.* The faculties composing a university; universities in general; the sphere of academic discussion or traditional academic methods. LME. ▸**c** A college, a university. Also without article: some college or university; attendance at a college or university. *N. Amer.* M18.
8 a The building or room used for the classes or lectures of a particular subject in a university. Now *Hist.* exc. in names in universities of early foundation. LME. ▸**b** In *pl.* A building belonging to a university, containing rooms serving for disputations, meetings of the academic body, examinations, etc. L16.
9 In *pl.* The periodical examinations for the degree of BA at Oxford University. E19.

📖 **7a** P. ROTH I *will* go to medical school. **9** J. DAWSON I never took schools. I was ill.

▶ **III** Repr. Latin *schola*, Greek *skholē*.
†**10** A hostelry for pilgrims in Rome. OE–LME.
†**11** A public building, gallery, etc. LME–E17.
12 ROMAN HISTORY. Any of the companies into which the imperial guard was divided. L18.

Phrases: ***approved school***: see APPROVE *verb*² 3. ***begin school***: see BEGIN *verb*. FIRST ***school***. ***free school***: see FREE *adjective*. ***Ionic school***: see IONIC *adjective*¹ 3. **keep a school**, **keep school** be the master or mistress of a school. ***military school***: see MILITARY *adjective*. ***new school***: see NEW *adjective*. ***normal school***: see NORMAL *adjective*. ***petty school***: see PETTY *adjective*. **put to school**: subject to teaching; presume to correct (one's superior). RAGGED ***school***. ***real school***: see REAL *adjective*². **school leaving age** the minimum age at which a school pupil may leave school. **school of hard knocks** *colloq.* (chiefly *N. Amer.*) the experience of a life of hardship, considered as a means of instruction. **School of the Air** a school or system of teaching using radio to broadcast education programmes, *esp.* that used to teach children in the Australian outback. **school of thought** a group of people sharing a cause, principle, attitude, etc. **set to school** (now *rare* or *obsolete*) = ***put to school*** above. ***start school***, ***start to school***: see START *verb*. **teach school** teach in a school. **tell tales out of school** betray secrets. **the schools** (*a*) the universities of medieval Europe, the teachers of these universities, the schoolmen collectively; (*b*) see sense 7b above.

Comb.: **school age**: at which a child is required to attend school; **school board** (*a*) *N. Amer.* a local board responsible for the provision and maintenance of schools; (*b*) *Hist.* in Britain from 1870 to 1902, a board elected by the rate-payers of a district and responsible for the provision and maintenance of local elementary schools; **School Certificate** (now only *NZ*) a public examination of proficiency for secondary school pupils; **schoolchild** a child attending school; **school colours** the distinctive colours of a school, esp. as conferred to denote selection to represent the school; **school committee** *NZ* a group of the parents of primary schoolchildren elected to assist the staff of the school; **schoolcraft** *arch.* knowledge taught in schools; **schoolday** (*a*) (in *pl.*) the period of life at which one is at school; (*b*) a day on which school is to be attended; **school district** *N. Amer.* a unit for the local administration of schools; **school-divine** *arch.* = ***schoolman*** (a) below; **school-divinity** *arch.* the religious principles and doctrines of medieval scholasticism; **schoolfellow** a present or past member of the same school as oneself; **schoolhouse** (*a*) a building used as a school; (*b*) a house usu. adjoining a school and lived in by a schoolmaster or schoolmistress, esp. by the head-teacher of the school; **school inspector** an officer appointed to inspect and report on the condition, teaching standards, etc., of schools; **schoolkeeper** (*a*) *arch.* a schoolteacher; (*b*) a caretaker in a school; **school land** *N. Amer.* land set apart for the financial support of schools; **school-leaver** a child who is about to leave or has just left school; **schoolman** (*a*) *Hist.* a teacher in any of the universities of medieval Europe, a medieval scholastic; (*b*) (now *rare* or *obsolete*) a person versed in the traditional philosophy and theology of medieval scholasticism; (*c*) a person engaged in scholastic pursuits; *US* a male teacher; **schoolmate** a friend or companion at school; **school milk** *Hist.* milk provided at reduced cost or free of charge to children in school; **school report** = REPORT *noun* 2f; **schoolroom** a room used for lessons in a school or private house; **schoolroomy** *adjective* characteristic of or resembling a schoolroom; **school section** *N. Amer.* a section of land set apart by the government for the maintenance of public schools; **schools broadcast** a radio or television programme for the instruction of children at school; **school-ship**: used for training in practical seamanship; **schools programme** = ***schools broadcast*** above; **school-time** (*a*) the time at which school begins, or during which school continues; (*b*) the period of life spent at school.
¶ See also OLD SCHOOL.
■ **schooldom** *noun* the domain of school or schools E19. **schoolery** *noun* (*rare*) that which is taught in a school L16. **schoolful** *noun* as many or as many as a school will hold L19. **schoolie** *noun*¹ (*colloq.*) (*a*) *north. & Austral.* a school teacher; (*b*) a classroom instructor in the navy: E20. **schoolless** /-l-l-/ *adjective* having or attending no school; untaught: LME.

school /skuːl/ *noun*². LME.
[Middle Low German, Middle Dutch *schōle* (Dutch *school*) troop, multitude, spec. 'school' of whales = Old Saxon *scola*, Old English *scolu* troop, from West Germanic word perh. orig. meaning division. Cf. SHOAL *noun*².]
1 A shoal or large number of fish, porpoises, whales, etc., swimming together, esp. whilst feeding or migrating. LME.
2 *transf.* A crowd, a large group, orig. of people or things, later of birds or mammals. Now *rare.* LME.
Comb.: **school shark** a small shark, *Galeorhinus australis*, occurring in Australian coastal waters and formerly much exploited for food and oil; also called ***tope***.
■ **schoolie** *noun*² (*colloq.*) any small fish normally found in a school or shoal L20.

school /skuːl/ *verb*¹. LME.
[from SCHOOL *noun*¹.]
1 *verb trans.* **a** Teach, train; educate or inform by instruction or discipline. Formerly also, admonish, reprimand. Also foll. by *in*, *to do*. Usu. in *pass.* LME. ▸**b** Discipline, bring under control, correct. Freq. *refl.* L16. ▸**c** Remove or subdue by instruction or discipline. Foll. by *away*, *down*. M19.
2 a *verb trans.* In *pass.* Be sent to school; be educated at school. L16. ▸**b** *verb intrans.* Attend school. *rare.* M20.
3 a *verb trans.* Train or exercise (a horse) in movements. M19. ▸**b** *verb intrans.* Ride straight across country. L19.
4 *verb trans.* Rear (a plant) in a nursery. E20.
5 *verb intrans.* Gamble in a school of gamblers. *slang.* M20.

📖 **1a** T. KENEALLY The boy was schooled to announce . . Smolders' innocence to all comers. G. DALY He was schooled at home until he went up to Oxford. **b** G. GREENE She had . . schooled herself to accept responsibility. I. COLEGATE We . . have to learn to school our emotions. **2a** *Columbus (Montana) News* Annin was . . schooled in Columbus, graduating in 1906.

school /skuːl/ *verb*² *intrans.* L16.
[from SCHOOL *noun*².]
Of fish, whales, etc.: collect or swim together in schools or shoals. (Foll. by *up*.)

schoolable /ˈskuːləb(ə)l/ *adjective*. *rare.* L16.
[from SCHOOL *verb*¹, *noun*¹: see -ABLE.]
†**1** Able to be schooled or trained. Only in L16.
2 Of an age to attend school, liable to compulsory education. M19.

schoolboy /ˈskuːlbɔɪ/ *noun & adjective*. L16.
[from SCHOOL *noun*¹ + BOY *noun*.]
▶ **A** *noun.* A boy attending school. L16.
every schoolboy knows it is a generally known fact (that).
▶ **B** *attrib.* or as *adjective.* Of or pertaining to schoolboys; characteristic of a schoolboy. L17.

📖 *Daily Telegraph* An odd blend of . . poetic phraseology and schoolboy humour.

■ **schoolboyhood** *noun* the state of being a schoolboy; schoolboys collectively: M19. **schoolboyish** *adjective* resembling or characteristic of a schoolboy L18. **schoolboyishly** *adverb* E20. **schoolboyishness** *noun* L19.

schooler /ˈskuːlə/ *noun*. Chiefly *US*. L20.
[from SCHOOL *noun*¹ + -ER¹.]
A person attending a school. Usu. in *comb.*, as ***grade schooler***, ***high schooler***, ***preschooler***.

schoolgirl /ˈskuːlgəːl/ *noun & adjective*. L18.
[from SCHOOL *noun*¹ + GIRL *noun*.]
▶ **A** *noun.* A girl attending school. L18.
▶ **B** *attrib.* or as *adjective.* Of or pertaining to schoolgirls; characteristic of a schoolgirl. M19.

📖 J. CLEARY I speak only schoolgirl French.

■ **schoolgirlhood** *noun* the state of being a schoolgirl L19. **schoolgirlish** *adjective* resembling or characteristic of a schoolgirl M19. **schoolgirlishness** *noun* L19. **schoolgirly** *adjective* schoolgirlish L19.

schooling /ˈskuːlɪŋ/ *verbal noun*. LME.
[from SCHOOL *verb*¹ + -ING¹.]
1 The action of teaching or the state of being taught; scholastic education. LME. ▸**b** The maintenance of a child at school; the cost of school education. M16. ▸**c** The employment or profession of teaching in school. *rare.* L18.
†**2** Disciplinary correction, punishment; admonition, reproof. M16–E19.
3 The training or exercising of a horse in a riding-school or over fences. M18.

school-marm /ˈskuːlmɑːm/ *noun & adjective*. *colloq.* (orig. *US*). Also **-ma'am**, **-ma'm**. M19.
[from SCHOOL *noun*¹ + MARM.]
▶ **A** *noun.* **1** A schoolmistress. M19.
2 A tree which has forked to form two trunks. *N. Amer. slang.* M20.
▶ **B** *adjective.* Like a school-mistress, prim and correct. M20.
■ **school-marming** *noun* the occupation of being a schoolmistress E20. **school-marmish** *adjective* like or suggestive of a school-mistress; prim and correct: L19. **school-marmishly** *adverb* M20. **school-marmy** *adjective* school-marmish M20.

schoolmaster /ˈskuːlmɑːstə/ *noun*¹ & *verb*. ME.
[from SCHOOL *noun*¹ + MASTER *noun*¹.]
▶ **A** *noun.* **1 a** A male teacher in a school; the headmaster of a school. ME. ▸†**b** A private tutor. E16–M17. ▸**c** An experienced horse used to train horses or riders at a riding-school or in competition or hunting. M20.
2 A tropical Atlantic snapper fish, *Lutjanus apodus*, found esp. in coastal waters of the Caribbean area. M18.
▶ **B** *verb.* **1** *verb trans.* Govern, regulate, or command in the manner of a schoolmaster. M19.
2 *verb intrans.* Be a schoolmaster. E20.
■ **schoolmasterish**, **schoolmasterly** *adjectives* characteristic of or resembling a schoolmaster M19. **schoolmastership** *noun* the position or work of a schoolmaster M16. **schoolmastery** *adjective* schoolmasterish E20.

schoolmaster /ˈskuːlmɑːstə/ *noun*². M19.
[from SCHOOL *noun*² + MASTER *noun*¹, after prec.]
The leader of a school of fishes etc.; *esp.* a bull whale.

schoolmistress /ˈskuːlmɪstrɪs/ *noun*. ME.
[from SCHOOL *noun*¹ + MISTRESS *noun*.]
A female teacher in a school; the headmistress of a school. Formerly also, a governess.
■ **schoolmistressy** *adjective* characteristic of or resembling a schoolmistress E20.

schoolward /ˈskuːlwəd/ *adverb & adjective.* **E19.**
[from SCHOOL *noun*[1] + -WARD.]
▶ **A** *adverb.* Towards school; in the direction of school. **E19.**
▶ **B** *adjective.* Directed or going towards school. **L19.**
■ Also **schoolwards** *adverb* **M19.**

schooly /ˈskuːli/ *adjective. colloq.* **M20.**
[from SCHOOL *noun*[1] + -Y[1].]
Suitable for or characteristic of a school.

schoon /skuːn/ *verb.* **M19.**
[Back-form. from next.]
1 *verb intrans.* Sail, skim, glide, esp. in the manner of a schooner. **M19.**
2 *verb trans.* Run (one's mind) *over* a thing. *rare.* **M20.**

schooner /ˈskuːnə/ *noun*[1]. **E18.**
[Origin uncertain: perh. ult. rel. to SCUN.]
1 A small seagoing fore-and-aft rigged vessel, orig. with two masts, later often with three or four, the foremast being equal to or smaller than the other masts. **E18.**
2 *US HISTORY.* In full ***prairie schooner***. A large covered wagon used by emigrants in the 19th cent. to cross the N. American plains. **M19.**
Phrases: *prairie schooner*: see sense 2 above. **schooner on the rocks** *slang* (orig. *NAUTICAL*) a joint of meat baked or roasted surrounded by potatoes or batter.
Comb.: **schooner barge** (*a*) *US* a short-masted vessel designed to be towed; (*b*) a flat-bottomed vessel rigged as a topsail schooner; **schooner-frigate**, **schooner-yacht**, etc.: resembling a schooner in build or rig; **schooner yawl** a variety of two-masted schooner.

schooner /ˈskuːnə/ *noun*[2]. **L19.**
[Origin uncertain: perh. fanciful use of prec.]
1 A large beer glass of locally variable capacity; the (measure of) beer contained in such a glass. Chiefly *US, Austral., & NZ.* **L19.**
2 A tall, waisted sherry glass; the measure contained by this. **M20.**

schoot *noun* see SCHUIT.

Schopenhauerism /ˈʃəʊpənhaʊərɪz(ə)m, ˈʃɒp-/ *noun.* **L19.**
[from Arthur *Schopenhauer* (1788–1860), German philosopher + -ISM.]
The pessimistic and atheistic philosophy of Schopenhauer, according to which the world is governed by a blind cosmic will entailing suffering from which man finds release only through knowledge, contemplation, and compassion.
■ **Schopenhauerian** *adjective & noun* (*a*) *adjective* characterized by the doctrines or ideas of Schopenhauer; (*b*) *noun* a follower of Schopenhauer or his doctrines: **L19.** **Schopenhauerist** *noun* = SCHOPENHAUERIAN *noun* **L19.**

schorl /ʃɔːl/ *noun.* **L18.**
[German *Schörl*, of unkn. origin.]
MINERALOGY. Tourmaline, esp. the black iron-rich variety. Formerly also (with specifying word), any of various other similar minerals.
schorl rock, *schorl-schist*, etc.
■ **schorˈlaceous** *adjective* of the nature of or resembling schorl; *esp.* occurring as columnar crystals: **L18.** **schorlite** *noun* (now *rare* or *obsolete*) any of several schorlaceous minerals, *esp.* pycnite **L18.**

Schotten–Baumann /ʃɒtənˈbaʊmən/ *noun.* **L19.**
[Carl Ludwig *Schotten* (1853–1910) and Eugen *Baumann* (1846–96), German chemists.]
ORGANIC CHEMISTRY. Used *attrib.* (esp. in ***Schotten–Baumann method***, ***Schotten–Baumann reaction***), with ref. to a type of reaction in which a primary or secondary amine or alcohol reacts with an acid halide in basic aqueous solution to form an amide or ester.

schottische /ʃɒˈtiːʃ, ˈʃɒtɪʃ/ *noun & verb.* **M19.**
[German (*der*) *Schottische*(*tanz*) (the) Scottish (dance).]
▶ **A** *noun.* **1** A dance resembling a slow polka; a piece of music for this dance. **M19.**
2 ***Highland Schottische***, a lively dance resembling the Highland fling. **L19.**
▶ **B** *verb intrans.* Dance a schottische. *rare.* **M19.**

Schottky /ˈʃɒtki/ *noun.* **M20.**
[Walter *Schottky* (1886–1976), German physicist.]
PHYSICS etc. Used *attrib.* to designate concepts, phenomena, etc. investigated or developed by Schottky.
Schottky barrier an electrostatic depletion layer formed at the junction of a metal and a semiconductor and causing it to act as an electrical rectifier. **Schottky defect** a vacancy in a crystal lattice in which the missing atom is not interstitial, and the number of anion and cation vacancies is such as to preserve electrical neutrality; the smallest possible group of such vacancies that preserves neutrality. **Schottky diagram** = *Schottky plot* below. **Schottky diode** a solid-state diode having a metal-semiconductor junction, used in fast switching applications. **Schottky effect** the increase in thermionic emission of a solid surface resulting from the lowering of its work function by the presence of an external electric field; *esp.* an increase in anode current in a thermionic valve due to the electric field produced by the anode at the surface of the cathode. **Schottky line** a straight line produced in a Schottky plot. **Schottky plot** a diagram used to illustrate the Schottky effect, obtained by plotting the logarithm of the current density against the square root of the applied electric field at constant emitter temperature, ideally to give a straight line of a particular gradient. **Schottky slope** the gradient of a Schottky line. **Schottky theory** the theoretical basis of the Schottky effect. **Schottky transistor** a solid-state transistor having a metal-semiconductor junction, used in fast switching applications.

schout /skaʊt, *foreign* sxɔut/ *noun.* **L15.**
[Dutch, rel. to German *Schulze*.]
Hist. In the Netherlands and Dutch colonies, a municipal or administrative officer, a bailiff.

schradan /ˈʃrɑːdən/ *noun.* **M20.**
[from Gerhard *Schrader* (b. 1903), German chemist + -AN.]
A viscous liquid organophosphorus compound, $([(CH_3)_2N]_2PO)_2O$, used in aqueous solution as a systemic insecticide.

Schrader /ˈʃreɪdə/ *noun.* **L19.**
[George H. F. *Schrader* (fl. 1895), US inventor.]
(Proprietary name for) a type of air valve used esp. on tyres.

Schrammel /ˈʃram(ə)l/ *noun.* **E20.**
[Johann (1850–97) and Josef (1852–94) *Schrammel*, Austrian musicians.]
1 ***Schrammel quartet*** [German *Schrammelquartett*], a Viennese light-music ensemble comprising two violins, guitar, and accordion (orig. clarinet), popularized by the Schrammels. **E20.**
2 ***Schrammel band***, ***Schrammel orchestra***, an enlarged Schrammel quartet. **M20.**
3 ***Schrammelmusik*** /-mjuːˈziːk/, music played by or arranged for a Schrammel quartet or orchestra. **M20.**

Schrecklichkeit /ˈʃrɛklɪçkaɪt/ *noun.* **E20.**
[German = frightfulness.]
Orig. *spec.*, a deliberate military policy of terrorizing an enemy, esp. the civilian population. Now freq. *gen.*, frightfulness, awfulness, an atmosphere of dread or fear.

schreibersite /ˈʃraɪbəzaɪt/ *noun.* **M19.**
[from Carl von *Schreibers*, 19th-cent. Viennese mineralogist + -ITE[1].]
MINERALOGY. A strongly magnetic white or (when tarnished) brownish phosphide of iron and nickel crystallizing in the tetragonal system and found in iron meteorites. Cf. RHABDITE 2.

schreierpfeife /ˈʃraɪə(p)faɪfə/ *noun.* Pl. **-fen** /-f(ə)n/. **M20.**
[German, lit. 'screamer pipe'. Cf. RAUSCHPFEIFE.]
MUSIC. A kind of shawm used in the 16th and 17th cents. Cf. SCHRYARI.

Schreiner /ˈʃraɪnə/ *noun & verb.* Also (esp. as verb) **s-**. **E20.**
[Ludwig *Schreiner* (fl. 1900), German textile manufacturer.]
TEXTILES. ▶**A** *noun.* Used *attrib.* with ref. to a method of giving lustre to mercerized fabrics by passing them through a calender which impresses many fine, evenly-spaced, parallel lines on to the material. **E20.**
Schreiner calender, *Schreiner finish*, etc.
▶ **B** *verb trans. & intrans.* Finish (fabric) by the Schreiner method. Chiefly as ***Schreinered*** *ppl adjective*, ***Schreinering*** *verbal noun.* **E20.**
■ **Schreinerize** *verb trans. & intrans.* = SCHREINER *verb* (chiefly as ***Schreinerizing*** *verbal noun*) **E20.**

Schröder /ˈʃrəːdə, *foreign* ˈʃrøːdər/ *noun.* Also **Schroeder**. **L19.**
[H. G. F. *Schröder* (1810–85), German mathematician and physicist.]
Used *attrib.* and in *possess.* (esp. in ***Schröder stairs***, ***Schröder's stairs***) to designate a line drawing of a staircase drawn with parallel lines, so that the perspective is ambiguous and the orientation of the staircase appears to alternate.
Schröder staircase, *Schröder stair-figure*, *Schröder's staircase*, *Schröder's stair-figure*, etc.

Schrödinger /ˈʃrəːdɪŋə, *foreign* ˈʃrøːdɪŋər/ *noun.* Also **Schroed-**. **E20.**
[Erwin *Schrödinger* (1887–1961), Austrian-born physicist.]
PHYSICS. ***Schrödinger equation***, ***Schrödinger wave equation***, ***Schrödinger's equation***, ***Schrödinger's wave equation***, a differential equation which forms the basis of the quantum-mechanical description of matter in terms of the wavelike properties of particles in a field, its solution being related to the probability density of a particle in space and time (also called ***wave equation***); ***Schrödinger function***, a solution of the Schrödinger equation.

Schroeder *noun* var. of SCHRÖDER.

Schroedinger *noun* var. of SCHRÖDINGER.

schrund /ʃrʊnt/ *noun.* **L19.**
[German = cleft, crevice.]
A crevasse; *spec.* = BERGSCHRUND.

schryari /ʃrɪˈɑːri/ *noun.* Pl. same. **M20.**
[Origin uncertain: perh. rel. to SCHREIERPFEIFE.]
= SCHREIERPFEIFE.

schtiebel *noun* var. of SHTIBL.

schtook *noun* var. of SHTOOK.

schtoom *adjective & verb* var. of SHTOOM.

Schubertiad /ʃuːˈbəːtɪad/ *noun.* **M19.**
[German *Schubertiade*: see next, -AD[1].]
A concert party or recital devoted solely to the performance of music and songs by Schubert.

Schubertian /ʃuːˈbəːtɪən/ *adjective & noun.* **M19.**
[from *Schubert* (see below) + -IAN.]
▶ **A** *adjective.* Of, pertaining to, or characteristic of the Austrian composer Franz Peter Schubert (1797–1828) or his music. **M19.**
▶ **B** *noun.* An interpreter, student, or admirer of Schubert or his music. **E20.**

Schuhplattler /ˈʃuːplatlər/ *noun.* **L19.**
[German, from *Schuh* shoe + southern German dial. *Plattler* (from *platteln* to slap).]
A lively Bavarian and Austrian folk-dance, characterized by the slapping of the thighs and heels.

schuit /skuːɪt, *foreign* sxœyt/ *noun.* Also **schoot** /ʃuːt/, **schuyt**. **M17.**
[Dutch. Cf. SCOUT *noun*[2], SHOUT *noun*[1].]
A Dutch flat-bottomed riverboat.

Schüller–Christian /ʃʊləˈkrɪstʃ(ə)n/ *noun.* **M20.**
[from Artur *Schüller* and H. A. *Christian*: see HAND–SCHÜLLER–CHRISTIAN.]
MEDICINE. ***Schüller–Christian disease***, ***Schüller–Christian syndrome***, ***Schüller–Christian's disease***, ***Schüller–Christian's syndrome***, = ***HAND–SCHÜLLER–CHRISTIAN disease***.

Schultz–Charlton /ʃʊltsˈtʃɑːlt(ə)n/ *noun.* **E20.**
[from Werner *Schultz* (1878–1948) and Willy *Charlton* (b. 1889), German physicians.]
MEDICINE. Used *attrib.* to denote (a diagnostic test based on) the phenomenon whereby a scarlet fever rash is locally extinguished by intradermal injection of (serum containing) antibody to the scarlet fever toxin.

Schumannesque /ʃuːməˈnɛsk/ *adjective.* **M20.**
[from *Schumann* (see below) + -ESQUE.]
Resembling the musical compositions or technique of the German composer Robert Alexander Schumann (1810–56).

Schumpeterian /ʃʊmpəˈtɪərɪən/ *adjective & noun.* **M20.**
[from J. A. *Schumpeter* (1883–1950), Moravian-born economist + -IAN.]
ECONOMICS. ▶**A** *adjective.* Designating or pertaining to the economic doctrines of Schumpeter, esp. dealing with the role of the entrepreneur, interest, and business cycles in the capitalist system. **M20.**
▶ **B** *noun.* A supporter or advocate of Schumpeter's doctrines. **M20.**

Schupo /ˈʃuːpəʊ/ *noun.* Pl. **-os**. **E20.**
[German, colloq. abbreviation of *Schutzpolizei*, *Schutzpolizist* security police (officer).]
In Germany: a police officer; *the* police force.

schuss /ʃʊs/ *noun & verb.* **M20.**
[German, lit. 'a shot'.]
▶ **A** *noun.* A straight downhill run on skis; the slope on which such a run is executed. Also *transf.*, a rapid downward slide. **M20.**
▶ **B** *verb.* **1** *verb trans.* Ski straight down (a slope etc.); cover (a certain distance) by means of a schuss. **M20.**
2 *verb intrans.* Ski straight down a slope. Also *transf.*, move rapidly (esp. downwards). **M20.**

Schutzstaffel /ˈʃʊtsʃtafəl/ *noun.* Pl. ***-eln*** /-əln/. **M20.**
[German, lit. 'defence squadron'.]
Hist. (A detachment of) the internal security force of Nazi Germany. Abbreviation ***SS***.

schuyt *noun* var. of SCHUIT.

schvartze, **schvartzer** *nouns* see SCHWARTZE.

schwa /ʃwɑː/ *noun.* Also **shwa**. **L19.**
[German: see SHEVA.]
PHONETICS. The neutral central vowel sound /ə/, typically occurring in unstressed syllables, as the final syllable of 'sofa' and the first syllable of 'along'. Also, the symbol ə representing this sound, as in the International Phonetic Alphabet. Also called ***sheva***.

Schwabacher /ˈʃvɑːbakə/ *noun.* **E20.**
[German, from *Schwabach* a town in central Bavaria + *-er* -ER[1].]
A German gothic typeface, based on a form of bastarda script, originating in the late 15th cent.

Schwann /ʃvan/ *noun.* **L19.**
[Theodor *Schwann* (1810–82), German physiologist.]
ANATOMY. **1** ***sheath of Schwann***, ***Schwann's sheath***, = NEURILEMMA 2. **L19.**
2 ***Schwann cell***, each of the cells which envelop the axons of peripheral nerve fibres, and form the myelin

sheath when it is present; formerly *spec.*, the parts of these cells containing the nucleus and cytoplasm. E20.

■ **Schwa'nnoma** *noun*, pl. **-mas**, **-mata** /-mətə/, MEDICINE a tumour (neurofibroma) derived from a Schwann cell M20.

schwarm /ʃvarm/ *noun*. E20.
[German.]
An enthusiasm, a craze, an infatuation. (Foll. by *for*.)

schwärm /ʃvɛrm/ *verb intrans.* (no inflected parts used). E20.
[Pseudo-German from German *schwärmen*: see next.]
Feel or display enthusiasm or passion (*for*).
■ ***schwärmer***, (fem.) ***schwärmerin*** *nouns* an enthusiast, a zealot L19.

schwärmerei /ʃvɛrməˈraɪ, ˈʃvɛrməraɪ/ *noun*. Pl. ***-reien*** /-raɪən/. M19.
[German, from *schwärmen* swarm, display enthusiasm, rave.]
Enthusiastic or fervent devotion to a person or a cause; schoolgirlish attachment, esp. to a person of the same sex; (an) infatuation, a crush.
■ ***schwärmerisch*** /ˈʃvɛrmərɪʃ/ *adjective* extravagantly enthusiastic, infatuated L19.

schwartze /ˈʃvɑːtsə/ *noun*. *slang* (usu. *derog.*). Also **schv-**, **-tzer**, & other vars. M20.
[Yiddish *shvartser* (masc.), *shvartse* (fem.), from *shvarts* black, formed as German *schwarz*: see SWART *adjective*.]
A black person.

Schwarz /ʃvɑːts/ *noun*. M20.
[H. A. *Schwarz* (1843–1921), German mathematician.]
MATH. ***Schwarz's inequality***, ***the Schwarz inequality***, a theorem which states that the square of the sum of a set of products of two quantities cannot exceed the sum of the squares of the first terms multiplied by the sum of the squares of the second terms.

schwarzlot /ˈʃvartsloːt/ *noun*. E20.
[German, lit. 'black lead'.]
(Decoration consisting wholly or chiefly of) black enamel, as used on Dutch and German glass of the 17th cent. and on later German and Austrian ceramics.

Schwarzschild /ˈʃvɑːtsʃiːlt, ˈʃwɔːtstʃʌɪld/ *noun*. E20.
[Karl *Schwarzschild* (1873–1916), German astronomer.]
1 ***Schwarzschild equation***, ***Schwarzschild's law***, a quantitative law of reciprocity failure in photographic emulsions. E20.
2 PHYSICS. Used *attrib.* to denote concepts arising out of the exact solution of Einstein's field equations for general relativity described by Schwarzschild. E20.
2 ***Schwarzschild coordinate***, ***Schwarzschild field***, ***Schwarzschild geometry***, ***Schwarzschild solution***, ***Schwarzschild surface***, etc. **Schwarzschild black hole** a black hole of a kind postulated to result from the complete gravitational collapse of an electrically neutral and non-rotating body, having a physical singularity at the centre to which infalling matter inevitably proceeds and at which the curvature of space–time is infinite. **Schwarzschild radius** the radius of the Schwarzschild sphere. **Schwarzschild singularity** a singularity in coordinates, but not a physical singularity in space–time, occurring at the Schwarzschild radius. **Schwarzschild sphere** the effective boundary or horizon of a Schwarzschild black hole, which infalling matter reaches in an infinite time as seen by an external observer but a finite time in the reference frame of the matter, and at which the escape velocity is infinite, so that the escape of matter or radiation from the inside is impossible except by some quantum-mechanical process.

Schweinerei /ʃvaɪnəˈraɪ, ˈʃvaɪnəraɪ/ *noun*. Pl. ***-reien*** /-raɪən/. E20.
[German, lit. 'piggishness'.]
Obnoxious behaviour, an instance of this; a repulsive incident or object, a scandal.

schweinhund /ˈʃvaɪnhʊnt/ *noun*. Also ***schweine-*** /ˈʃvaɪnə-/. Pl. ***-de*** /-də/. M20.
[German, lit. 'pig dog'.]
A German term of abuse: filthy dog, swine, bastard.

Schweizerdeutsch /ˈʃvʌɪtsərdɔɪtʃ/ *noun*. Pl. same. Also **Schwyzertütsch** /ˈʃviːtsərtuːtʃ/. M20.
[German *Schweizerdeutsch*, Swiss-German *Schwyzertütsch* Swiss-German.]
The German dialect of Switzerland, Swiss-German; a native or inhabitant of the part of Switzerland where Schweizerdeutsch is spoken, a Swiss-German.

Schwenkfeldian /ʃwɛŋkˈfɛldɪən/ *noun & adjective*. M16.
[from *Schwenkfeld* (see below) + -IAN.]
► **A** *noun*. A member of a Protestant Church founded by Caspar Schwenkfeld (1490–1561), a Silesian mystic, and surviving in Philadelphia, USA. M16.
► **B** *adjective*. Of, pertaining to, or designating this church. M16.
■ Also '**Schwenkfelder** *noun & adjective* L18.

schwerpunkt /ˈʃvɛːrpʊŋkt/ *noun*. M20.
[German = centre of gravity, focal point, from *schwer* hard, weighty + *Punkt* point.]
Focus, emphasis; strong point; area of concentrated (esp. military) effort.

Schwung /ʃvʊŋ/ *noun*. M20.
[German, lit. 'swinging motion'.]
Energy, verve, panache.

Schwyzertütsch *noun* var. of SCHWEIZERDEUTSCH.

sciaenid /sʌɪˈiːnɪd/ *noun & adjective*. E20.
[mod. Latin *Sciaenidae* (see below), from *Sciaena* genus name, from Greek *skiaina* a kind of fish, perh. the meagre: see -ID[3].]
ZOOLOGY. ► **A** *noun*. A member of the family Sciaenidae of tropical and temperate percoid fishes, including croakers, drums, and sculpins. E20.
► **B** *adjective*. Of, pertaining to, or designating this family. E20.
■ **sciaenoid** *noun & adjective* (*a*) *noun* = SCIAENID *noun*; (*b*) *adjective* of, pertaining to, or designating the family Sciaenidae or the genus *Sciaena*; resembling a fish of this kind: M19.

sciagraph /ˈsʌɪəgrɑːf/ *noun*. Now *rare*. Also †**scio-**. M17.
[Partly from SCIAGRAPHY, partly from (the same root as) SKIAGRAPH.]
1 = SCIAGRAPHY 1b. M17.
2 = SKIAGRAPH *noun*. L19.

sciagrapher /sʌɪˈagrəfə/ *noun*. Now *rare*. Also †**scio-**. L17.
[from SCIAGRAPHY: see -GRAPHER. Cf. SKIAGRAPHER.]
A person who practises sciagraphy.

sciagraphy /sʌɪˈagrəfi/ *noun*. Now *rare*. Also †**scio-**. L16.
[French *sciagraphie*, *scio-* from Latin *sciagraphia*, *scio-* from Greek *skiagraphia*, *skio-*, from *skia* shadow: see -GRAPHY. Cf. SKIAGRAPHY.]
1 DRAWING. The branch of perspective that deals with the projection of shadows; the delineation of an object in perspective showing gradations of light and shade. L16. ▸**b** A drawing in perspective, esp. of the cross-section of a building, showing gradations of light and shade. E17.
2 The art of making or using sundials or similar devices to tell the time from the angle of a shadow. Long only in Dicts. M17.
†**3** An outline, a sketch. Chiefly *transf.* & *fig.*, an overall perspective. L17–M18.
■ **scia'graphic** *adjective* E19. **scia'graphical** *adjective* L17.

sciamachy /sʌɪˈaməki/ *noun*. Also **ski-** /skʌɪ-/, **-om-** /-ˈɒm-/. E17.
[Greek *skiamakhia*, from *skia* shadow: see -MACHY.]
A sham fight, as for exercise or practice; fighting with shadows; *fig.* imaginary or futile combat.

sciapod /ˈsʌɪəpɒd/ *noun*. Pl. **sciapodes** /sʌɪˈapədiːz/, **sciapods**. Also **skia-** /ˈskiːə-/. L16.
[Latin *Sciapodes* pl. from Greek *skiapodes*, from *skia* shadow + *pod-*, *pous* foot.]
A monster having the form of a man with a single large foot, in medieval iconography freq. represented with the foot raised as a sunshade.

sciatic /sʌɪˈatɪk/ *noun & adjective*. E16.
[Old & mod. French *sciatique* from late Latin *sciaticus* alt. of medieval Latin *ischiaticus*: see ISCHIATIC. Cf. medieval Latin *scia* hip.]
ANATOMY & MEDICINE. ► **A** *noun*. †**1** = SCIATICA. E16–E19.
†**2** The hip. Only in M16.
3 *ellipt*. A sciatic nerve, vein, etc. M16.
► **B** *adjective*. **1** Of, belonging to, or associated with the ischium or hip. L16.
2 Of the nature of or pertaining to sciatica; affected with sciatica. L16.
1 **sciatic nerve** the largest nerve in the human body, which emerges from the pelvis on either side and passes down the back of the thigh. **sciatic notch** either of two notches on the posterior edge of the hip-bone.

sciatica /sʌɪˈatɪkə/ *noun*. LME.
[Late Latin *sciatica* (sc. *passio* passion, affliction), fem. of *sciaticus*: see prec.]
(A condition characterized by) pain in the back of the hip and thigh, formerly ascribed to inflammation of the sciatic nerve but now believed to be due usually to pressure of the lumbar vertebrae on the spinal nerve roots.

sciatical /sʌɪˈatɪk(ə)l/ *adjective*. Now *rare*. L16.
[from SCIATIC *adjective* + -AL[1].]
†**1** = SCIATIC *adjective* 2. *rare*. Only in L16.
2 = SCIATIC *adjective* 1. M17.

SCID *abbreviation*.
Severe combined immune deficiency, a rare genetic disorder in which affected children have no resistance to disease and must be kept isolated from infection from birth.

science /ˈsʌɪəns/ *noun*. ME.
[Old French from Latin *scientia* knowledge, from *scient-* pres. ppl stem of *scire* know: see -ENCE.]
1 a The state or fact of knowing; knowledge or cognizance *of* something specified or implied. Also, knowledge (more or less extensive) as a personal attribute. Now only THEOLOGY, chiefly rendering scholastic terms. ME. ▸†**b** Theoretical perception of a truth, as contrasted with moral conviction (conscience). E–M17.
2 a Knowledge acquired by study; acquaintance with or mastery of a department of learning. Formerly also in *pl.*, (a person's) various kinds of knowledge. Now *rare* or *obsolete*. ME. ▸**b** Skilful technique, esp. in a practical or sporting activity. Now *rare*. L18.
3 a A particular branch of knowledge or study; a recognized department of learning; *spec.* each of the seven medieval liberal arts (see ART *noun*[1] 4). Now *rare*. ME. ▸†**b** A craft, trade, or occupation requiring trained skill. L15–M17. ▸**c** An activity or discipline concerned with theory rather than method, or requiring the systematic application of principles rather than relying on traditional rules, intuition, and acquired skill. Freq. opp. ***art***. L16. ▸**d** A branch of study that deals either with a connected body of demonstrated truths or with observed facts systematically classified and more or less comprehended by general laws, and which includes reliable methods for the discovery of new truth in its own domain; *spec.*, any of the natural sciences (see sense 4a below). Freq. (*sing.* & in *pl.*) with specifying word. E17.
4 a The kind of organized knowledge or intellectual activity of which the various branches of learning are examples. Now usu. *spec.*, the intellectual and practical activity encompassing those branches of study that apply objective scientific method to the phenomena of the physical universe (the natural sciences), and the knowledge so gained; scientific doctrine or investigation; the collective understanding of scientists. Also (with specifying word), as sense 3d above. LME. ▸**b** (Usu. **S-**.) = ***Christian Science*** s.v. CHRISTIAN *adjective*. E20.

1a POPE My words no fancy'd woes relate: I speak from science. **2a** T. GRAY Be love my youth's pursuit, and science crown my Age. **3a** B. F. WESTCOTT Theology is the crown of all the sciences. *transf.*: C. LAMB Facts . . are trifles to a true adept in the science of dissatisfaction. **c** R. KIRWAN Previous to the year 1780, mineralogy . . could scarce be deemed a Science. **d** ***biological science***, ***exact science***, ***experimental science***, ***marine science***, ***mathematical science***, ***moral sciences***, ***natural science***, ***nuclear science***, ***physical science***, etc.; ***computer science***, ***earth science***, ***life science***, ***plant science***, ***soil science***, etc.; ***bioscience***, ***neuroscience***, ***pseudoscience***, etc. **4a** T. S. COBBOLD This species is new to science. *Nature* The technology born of science has catalysed stupendous economic growth. ***science book***, ***science laboratory***, ***science teacher***, etc.

Phrases: **blind with science** *colloq.* confuse by the use of long or technical words or involved explanations. ***dismal science***: see DISMAL *adjective* 4. **man of science** †(*a*) a man skilled or learned in any discipline, art, or craft; (*b*) a scientist. **Master of Science** (a person who has been awarded) a degree (usu. above a bachelor's degree) for a high level of proficiency in one or more scientific subjects. ***the noble science***: see NOBLE *adjective*.
Comb.: **science fantasy** science fiction, regarded as a kind of fantasy literature; **science park** an industrial estate devoted to science-based industry.

scienced /ˈsʌɪənst/ *adjective*. Now *rare* or *obsolete*. M17.
[from prec. + -ED[2].]
†**1** Learned. M17–M19.
2 Well versed in the skills of boxing. E19.

science fiction /sʌɪəns ˈfɪkʃ(ə)n/ *noun phr.* M19.
[from SCIENCE + FICTION *noun*. Cf. SCI-FI.]
Fiction based on imagined future scientific discoveries, major environmental or social changes, etc., freq. involving space or time travel or life on other planets.
¶ In general use only from E20.
■ **science-fictional** *adjective* pertaining to or characteristic of science fiction M20. **science-fictionalized** *adjective* made into science fiction M20. **science-fictio'neer**, **science-fictionist** *nouns* a writer or connoisseur of science fiction M20.

scient /ˈsʌɪənt/ *adjective & noun*. Now *rare* or *obsolete*. LME.
[Old French from Latin *scient-*: see SCIENCE, -ENT.]
► **A** *adjective*. Having science, knowledge, or skill. LME.
►† **B** *noun*. A scientist. Only in L19.

scienter /sʌɪˈɛntə/ *noun & adverb*. E19.
[from Latin = knowingly, formed as prec. with adverbial suffix.]
LAW. ► **A** *noun*. The fact of an act's having been done knowingly (esp. as a ground for criminal punishment or civil damages). E19.
► **B** *adverb*. Knowingly; intentionally. L19.

sciential /sʌɪˈɛnʃ(ə)l/ *adjective*. LME.
[Late Latin *scientialis*, from *scientia*: see SCIENCE, -AL[1].]
1 Of or pertaining to knowledge or science. LME.
2 Having knowledge. L15.

scientific /sʌɪənˈtɪfɪk/ *adjective & noun*. L16.
[Old & mod. French *scientifique* or late Latin *scientificus*, equiv. to *scientiam faciens* producing knowledge, translating Greek (Aristotle) *epistēmonikos*, from *scient-*: see SCIENCE, -FIC.]
► **A** *adjective*. **1** Of a person, book, institution, etc.: occupied in or concerned with (esp. natural) science. In early use, concerned with the liberal arts (opp. ***mechanical***). L16.
†**2** = SCIENTIFICAL *adjective* 1. Only in M17.
3 Of, pertaining to, or of the nature of science; based on, regulated by, or engaged in the application of science, as opp. to traditional rules or natural skill; valid according to the objective principles of scientific method. Also *loosely*, systematic, methodical. L17. ▸**b** Characterized by trained or methodical skill. *colloq.* L18.

4 Of, pertaining to, or inspired by Christian Science. **L19.**

1 *Guardian* The Kremlin's thought-police are moving in . . on the Soviet scientific community. **3** *Scientific American* There existed a very thorough international cooperation in scientific research. B. MAGEE There can be no empirical evidence for it, and therefore it cannot be held to be scientific. ***Site of Special Scientific Interest***: see SITE *noun*. **b** W. G. GRACE He was the most scientific batsman amongst the professionals.

Special collocations: **scientific creationism** (advocacy of) creation science. **scientific farming**: conducted according to scientific theories rather than traditional practice. **scientific fiction** (now *rare*) = SCIENCE FICTION. **scientific humanism** a doctrine that the future and welfare of the human race should be directed by the application of scientific methods. **scientific management** management of a business, industry, etc., according to principles of efficiency derived from experiments in methods of work, production, payment, etc., and esp. from time-and-motion studies. **scientific method** a method of procedure that has characterized natural science since the 17th cent., consisting in systematic observation, measurement, and experiment, and the formulation, testing, and modification of hypotheses (freq. in *pl.*). **scientific misconduct** action which wilfully compromises the integrity of scientific research, such as plagiarism or the falsification or fabrication of data. **scientific notation** a system of representing numbers as a product of a number between 1 and 10 (or −1 and −10, or 0.1 and 1) and a power of 10. **scientific revolution** a rapid and far-reaching development in science; *spec.* the developments in the 20th cent. involving the introduction of automation, atomic energy, electronics, etc.

▶†**B** *noun.* A scientist. *colloq.* **M–L19.**

scientifical /sʌɪənˈtɪfɪk(ə)l/ *adjective.* **L16.**
[formed as prec.: see -ICAL.]
†**1** Of a syllogism, a proof, evidence, etc.: demonstrative. Of a conclusion: demonstratively proved. **L16–M18.**
†**2** Designed for the furthering of knowledge. **L16–M17.**
3 Expert in or concerned with science. Now *rare*. **M17.**
4 Of or pertaining to science, scientific. *rare*. **L18.**
■ **scientifiˈcality** *noun* [orig. translating German (Nietzsche) *Wissenschaftlichkeit*] the property or quality of being scientifical, scientificity **E20.** **scientificalness** *noun* **M19.**

scientifically /sʌɪənˈtɪfɪk(ə)li/ *adverb.* **M17.**
[formed as prec.: see -ICALLY.]
1 In a scientific manner; according to the methods of science; formerly also, by means of demonstrative reasoning. Also occas., as regards science. **M17.**
2 Systematically, methodically, thoroughly. **E20.**

scientificity /sʌɪəntɪˈfɪsɪti/ *noun.* **L20.**
[from SCIENTIFIC *adjective* + -ITY.]
The quality of being scientific; scientific character.

scientifiction /sʌɪəntɪˈfɪkʃ(ə)n/ *noun.* Now *rare*. **E20.**
[Blend of SCIENTIFIC *adjective* and FICTION *noun*.]
= SCIENCE FICTION.
■ **scientifictional** *adjective* **L20.**

scientise *verb* var. of SCIENTIZE.

scientism /ˈsʌɪəntɪz(ə)m/ *noun.* **L19.**
[formed as next + -ISM.]
1 Thought or expression regarded as characteristic of scientists. *rare*. **L19.**
2 Excessive belief in the power of scientific knowledge and techniques, or in the applicability of the methods of physical science to other fields, esp. human behaviour and the social sciences. Freq. *depreciative*. **E20.**

scientist /ˈsʌɪəntɪst/ *noun.* **M19.**
[from Latin *scient(ia* (see SCIENCE) or SCIENT(IFIC + -IST.]
1 A person conducting research in or with expert knowledge of a (usu. physical or natural) science; a person using scientific methods; a student of science. **M19.**
2 (Usu. **S-**.) = ***Christian Scientist*** s.v. CHRISTIAN *adjective*. **L19.**

scientistic /sʌɪənˈtɪstɪk/ *adjective.* Usu. *depreciative*. **L19.**
[In sense 1 from SCIENTIST, in sense 2 from SCIENTISM: see -IC.]
1 Characteristic of, or having the attributes of, a scientist. *rare*. **L19.**
2 Of, pertaining to, or exhibiting scientism. **M20.**
■ **scientistically** *adverb* **L19.**

scientize /ˈsʌɪəntʌɪz/ *verb. rare.* Also **-ise**. **L19.**
[from (the same root as) SCIENT(IST + -IZE.]
1 *verb intrans.* Make scientific propositions, theorize. **L19.**
2 *verb trans.* Make scientific; give a scientific character or basis to; organize on scientific principles. **M20.**
■ **scientiˈzation** *noun* **L20.**

Scientology /sʌɪənˈtɒlədʒi/ *noun.* **M20.**
[from Latin *scient(ia* knowledge (see SCIENCE) + -OLOGY.]
A system of religious philosophy founded in 1951 by the American writer L. Ron Hubbard (1911–86), whose proponents seek self-knowledge and spiritual fulfilment through graded courses of study and training.
¶ Proprietary name.
■ **Scientologist** *noun* an adherent or practitioner of Scientology **M20.**

scientometrics /sʌɪəntəˈmɛtrɪks/ *noun.* **L20.**
[from Latin *scient(ia* (see SCIENCE) + -O- + METRIC *noun*[1]: see -ICS.]
The branch of information science that deals with the application of bibliometrics to the study of the spread of scientific ideas.
■ **scientometric**, **scientometrical** *adjectives* **L20.**

sci-fi /ˈsʌɪfʌɪ/ *noun. colloq.* **M20.**
[Abbreviation.]
= SCIENCE FICTION.
■ Also **sci-fic** /ˈsʌɪfɪk/ *noun* (*rare*) **M20.**

scilicet /ˈsʌɪlɪsɛt, ˈskiːlɪkɛt/ *adverb & noun.* **LME.**
[Latin, from *scire licet* one may understand or know. Cf. VIDELICET.]
▶**A** *adverb.* To wit; that is to say; namely (introducing a word to be supplied or an explanation of an ambiguity). Abbreviation ***scil.*** or ***sc.*** **LME.**
▶**B** *noun.* The word '*scilicet*' or its equivalent, introducing a specifying clause. **M17.**

scilla /ˈsɪlə/ *noun.* **E19.**
[Latin *scilla*, *squilla* sea onion from Greek *skilla*: cf. SQUILL.]
Any of various small bulbous blue-flowered plants of the genus *Scilla*, of the lily family, which includes the spring squill, *S. verna*, and several species grown for ornament.

Scillonian /sɪˈləʊnɪən/ *noun & adjective.* **L18.**
[from *Scilly* (see below) + *-onian*, perh. after *Devonian*.]
▶**A** *noun.* A native or inhabitant of the Scilly Isles off the coast of Cornwall. **L18.**
▶**B** *adjective.* Of or relating to the Scilly Isles or their inhabitants. **L19.**

scimitar /ˈsɪmɪtə/ *noun.* **M16.**
[Repr. French *cimeterre*, *cimiterre* or Italian *scimitarra*, †*cimitara*, etc., of unkn. origin.]
A short oriental sword with a curved single-edged blade, usu. broadening towards the end.
Comb.: **scimitar-babbler** any of several babblers of SE Asia with a long curved bill, chiefly of the genus *Pomatorhinus*; **scimitarbill** either of two mainly black, long-tailed birds of the E. African genus *Rhinopomastus* (of the wood hoopoe family Phoeniculidae), with a long slender downcurved bill; ***scimitar oryx***.
■ **scimitared** *adjective* carrying or armed with a scimitar **M19.**

scincoid /ˈsɪŋkɔɪd/ *adjective & noun.* **L18.**
[from mod. Latin *Scincoidea* (see below), from use as genus name of Latin *scincus* SKINK *noun*[1]: see -OID.]
▶**A** *adjective.* Resembling a skink; *spec.* belonging to the superfamily Scincoidea or the family Scincidae of skinks and similar lizards. **L18.**
▶**B** *noun.* A scincoid lizard. **M19.**
■ Also **scinˈcoidian** *adjective & noun* (now *rare*) **M19.**

scindapsus /sɪnˈdapsəs/ *noun.* **M20.**
[mod. Latin (see below), use as genus name of Greek *skindapsos* a climbing plant.]
Any of various tropical climbing plants constituting the genus *Scindapsus*, of the arum family, native esp. to SE Asia and including several, esp. *S. pictus*, grown as houseplants.

scintigram /ˈsɪntɪɡram/ *noun.* **M20.**
[from SCINTI(LLATION + -GRAM.]
MEDICINE. An image or other record of part of the body obtained by measuring radiation from an introduced radioactive tracer by scintillation or an analogous detection method.
■ **scintigraph** *noun* (*a*) a device for producing scintigrams; (*b*) a scintigram: **M20.** **scintiˈgraphic** *adjective* of, done by, or pertaining to scintigraphy **M20.** **scintiˈgraphically** *adverb* by means of scintigraphy **M20.** **scinˈtigraphy** *noun* the production and use of scintigrams **M20.**

†**scintil** *noun.* **L16–M19.**
[Anglicization.]
= next.

scintilla /sɪnˈtɪlə/ *noun.* **L17.**
[Latin.]
A spark; a trace, a tiny piece or amount.

Independent 'Not a shred, tittle or scintilla of evidence' of a conspiracy. **scintilla juris**, **scintilla iuris** /ˈdʒʊərɪs, ˈjʊ-/ [Latin, genit. of *jus* right, law] *LAW* (now *Hist.*) a doctrine of property law providing a possibility of seisin when a contingent interest was limited by an executory one.

scintillant /ˈsɪntɪl(ə)nt/ *adjective.* **E17.**
[Latin *scintillant-* pres. ppl stem of *scintillare*: see next, -ANT[1].]
1 *HERALDRY.* Of a firebrand or other burning object: emitting sparks. **E17.**
2 Scintillating (*lit.* & *fig.*). **M18.**
■ **scintillantly** *adverb* **E20.**

scintillate /ˈsɪntɪleɪt/ *verb.* **E17.**
[Latin *scintillat-* pa. ppl stem of *scintillare*, from *scintilla* a spark: see -ATE[3].]
1 *verb intrans.* Emit sparks or little flashes of light; sparkle, twinkle; *fig.* talk or write cleverly and wittily, be brilliant. **E17.** ▸**b** *NUCLEAR PHYSICS.* Of a phosphor: fluoresce momentarily when struck by a charged particle or high-energy photon. **M20.**
2 *verb trans.* Emit as a spark or sparks; flash forth. **E19.**

1 V. BRITTAIN Every leaf and flower seems to scintillate with light. L. WOOLF A fountain of words scintillating with wit and humour. **2** *Modern Maturity* A most beautiful dragonfly. It scintillated all the colors of the rainbow.

scintillating /ˈsɪntɪleɪtɪŋ/ *ppl adjective.* **L18.**
[from prec.: see -ING[2].]
That scintillates; brilliant, sparkling (*lit.* & *fig.*).
scintillating scotoma *MEDICINE* hallucinatory flickering patterns and gaps in the visual field as seen in migraine.
■ **scintillatingly** *adverb* **E20.**

scintillation /sɪntɪˈleɪʃ(ə)n/ *noun.* **E17.**
[Latin *scintillatio(n-)*, formed as SCINTILLATE: see -ATION.]
1 The action of scintillating; an instance of this; a flash, a spark, a brilliant display. **M17.**
2 *spec.* The twinkling of the light of the stars. **M17.**
3 *NUCLEAR PHYSICS.* A small flash of visible or ultraviolet light emitted by fluorescence in a phosphor when struck by a charged particle or high-energy photon. **E20.**

1 S. JOHNSON A man who . . dazzles the attention with sudden scintillations of conceit. DE QUINCEY The sudden scintillation of Kate's dress played upon by the morning sun.

Comb.: **scintillation counter** a particle counter consisting of a scintillation detector and an electronic counting circuit; **scintillation detector** a detector for charged particles and gamma rays in which scintillations produced in a phosphor are detected and amplified by a photomultiplier, giving an electrical output signal.

scintillator /ˈsɪntɪleɪtə/ *noun.* **L19.**
[from SCINTILLATE + -OR.]
1 A scintillating star. *rare*. **L19.**
2 *NUCLEAR PHYSICS.* **a** A material that fluoresces when struck by a charged particle or high-energy photon. **M20.** ▸**b** = *SCINTILLATION* ***detector***. **M20.**

scintillogram /sɪnˈtɪlə(ʊ)ɡram/ *noun.* **M20.**
[from SCINTILL(ATION + -O- + -GRAM.]
MEDICINE. A scintigram.
■ **scinˈtillograph** *noun* a scintigraph **M20.** **scintilloˈgraphic** *adjective* **M20.** **scintiˈllography** *noun* **M20.**

scintillometer /sɪntɪˈlɒmɪtə/ *noun.* **L19.**
[formed as prec. + -METER.]
†**1** An instrument for measuring the intensity of the scintillation of the stars. Only in **L19.**
2 *PHYSICS.* A device containing a scintillator for detecting and measuring low intensities of ionizing radiation. **M20.**
■ **scintillometry** *noun* the use of a scintillometer (sense 2) **M20.**

scintilloscope /sɪnˈtɪləskəʊp/ *noun.* **E20.**
[formed as prec. + -SCOPE.]
An instrument in which alpha particles are detected by the scintillation they induce in a fluorescent screen.

scintillous /sɪnˈtɪləs/ *adjective.* Now *rare* or *obsolete*. **E16.**
[from Latin *scintilla* spark: see -OUS.]
Scintillating.

scintiscanner /ˈsɪntɪskanə/ *noun.* **M20.**
[formed as SCINTIGRAM + SCANNER.]
MEDICINE. A device which scans the body or part of it and creates an image of the internal distribution of radioactivity.
■ **scintiscan** *noun* an autoradiograph obtained with a scintiscanner **M20.** **scintiscanning** *noun* the production and use of scintiscans **M20.**

†**sciograph**, †**sciographer**, †**sciography** *nouns* see SCIAGRAPH etc.

sciolism /ˈsʌɪəlɪz(ə)m/ *noun.* **E19.**
[from next: see -ISM.]
Pretentious superficiality of knowledge.

C. KINGSLEY Shallow and conceited sciolism, engendered by hearing popular lectures on all manner of subjects.

sciolist /ˈsʌɪəlɪst/ *noun.* **E17.**
[from late Latin *sciolus* dim. of Latin *scius* knowing, from *scire* know: see -IST.]
A superficial pretender to knowledge.
■ **scioˈlistic** *adjective* characteristic of a sciolist **M19.**

sciolous /ˈsʌɪələs/ *adjective.* Now *rare* or *obsolete*. **M17.**
[formed as prec. + -OUS.]
Having a smattering of knowledge, sciolistic.

sciomachy *noun* var. of SCIAMACHY.

sciomancy /ˈsʌɪəmansi/ *noun.* **E17.**
[mod. Latin *sciomantia*, from Greek *skia* shadow + *manteia*: see -MANCY.]
Divination by means of shadows; divination by communication with the ghosts of the dead.

scion /ˈsʌɪən/ *noun.* In sense 1 also ***cion**. **ME.**
[Old French *ciun*, *cion*, *sion* (mod. *scion*) twig, shoot, of unkn. origin.]
1 A shoot or twig, *esp.* one cut for grafting or planting. **ME.**
2 An heir, a descendant; a younger member of a (noble) family. (*rare* before **19.**) **ME.**

■ **scioness** *noun* (*joc.*, *rare*) a female heir or descendant **E20.**

sciophilous /sʌɪˈɒfɪləs/ *adjective.* **E20.**
[from Greek *skia* shadow + **-O-** + **-PHILOUS.**]
BOTANY. Of a plant: thriving best in shade or conditions of low light intensity.

sciophyte /ˈsʌɪəfʌɪt/ *noun.* **E20.**
[formed as prec. + **-PHYTE.**]
BOTANY. A sciophilous plant.

scioptric /sʌɪˈɒptrɪk/ *noun & adjective.* Now *rare* or *obsolete.* **E18.**
[from Greek *skia* shadow, after *catoptric*, *dioptric*.]
▶†**A** *noun.* A ball as described in sense B. below. Only in **E18.**
▶**B** *adjective.* Designating a ball of wood with a hole made through it in which a lens is placed, used in a camera obscura. **M18.**
■ Also **scioptic** *noun & adjective* **M18.**

Sciote /ˈʃiːəʊt/ *adjective & noun.* **E18.**
[from *Scio* Italian name of Chios + **-OTE.**]
▶**A** *adjective.* Of or pertaining to Chios, an island in the Aegean Sea. **E18.**
▶**B** *noun.* A native or inhabitant of Chios. **M19.**

scire facias /sʌɪriː ˈfeɪʃɪas/ *noun phr.* **LME.**
[Law Latin = let (him or her) know.]
LAW (now *Hist.*). A writ directing a sheriff to require a person to show why a judgement against him or her, esp. the revocation of a patent, should not be executed.

scirocco *noun* var. of **SIROCCO.**

scirrhi *noun pl.* see **SCIRRHUS.**

scirrhous /ˈsɪrəs, ˈskɪ-/ *adjective.* **M16.**
[French *scirr(h)eux* (now *squirreux*) from mod. Latin *scirrhosus*, formed as next: see **-OUS.**]
MEDICINE. Designating or pertaining to a growth, esp. a carcinoma, which is hard and strong due to dense fibrous tissue; *transf.* indurated; covered with hard excrescences.
■ **sciˈrrhosity** *noun* (now *rare*) a scirrhous growth; the state or condition of being scirrhous: **L16.**

scirrhus /ˈsɪrəs, ˈskɪ-/ *noun.* Pl. **scirrhi** /-riː, -rʌɪ/, **scirrhusses.** **LME.**
[mod. Latin, alt. of Latin *scirros* from Greek *skirros*, *skiros* hard coat or covering, a hardened swelling, rel. to *skiros* hard.]
MEDICINE. **1** A hard, firm, and almost painless swelling; *spec.* a scirrhous tumour. **LME.**
2 The condition characterized by the presence of a scirrhus; an instance of this. Now *rare.* **LME.**
■ Also †**scirrhe** *noun* **L16–M18.**

†**scismatik** *noun & adjective* see **SCHISMATIC.**

†**scisme** *noun* see **SCHISM.**

scissel /ˈsɪs(ə)l/ *noun.* **E17.**
[Old & mod. French *cisaille*, from *cisailler* clip with shears.]
Metal clippings; *esp.* the scrap metal remaining after coin blanks have been cut out of a metal sheet.

scissile /ˈsɪsʌɪl, -ɪl/ *adjective.* **E17.**
[Latin *scissilis*, from *sciss-*: see next, **-ILE.**]
Able to be cut or divided; *spec.* (***a***) *MINERALOGY* (esp. of alum) that splits into laminae; (***b***) *CHEMISTRY* (esp. of a bond) readily undergoing scission.

scission /ˈsɪʃ(ə)n/ *noun.* **LME.**
[Old & mod. French, or late Latin *scissio(n-)*, from Latin *sciss-* pa. ppl stem of *scindere* cut, cleave: see **-ION.**]
1 The action or an act of cutting or dividing; (a) division; a split. **LME.**
2 a *CHEMISTRY.* Breakage of a bond, esp. in a long chain polymer such that two smaller chains result. **E20.** ▸**b** *NUCLEAR PHYSICS.* The event of separation of the parts of a nucleus undergoing fission, as distinct from the process as a whole. **M20.**

> 🕮 **1** R. D. LAING There is a persistent scission between the self and the body.

scissiparity /sɪsɪˈparɪti/ *noun. rare.* **L19.**
[from Latin *sciss-* (see prec.), after *fissiparity* etc.]
BIOLOGY. Reproduction by fission of an individual; fissiparity, schizogenesis.
■ **scissiparous** /sɪˈsɪp(ə)rəs/ *adjective* = **FISSIPAROUS L19.**

scissor *noun* see **SCISSORS.**

scissor /ˈsɪzə/ *verb.* **E17.**
[from next.]
1 *verb trans.* Cut (*up*, *off*) with scissors; make (*into*) by cutting with scissors. **E17.**
2 *verb trans.* Clip out or *out* (a newspaper extract etc.); cut, expunge, (a passage or part of a book, play, etc.). **M19.**
3 *verb trans.* **a** Cause (the legs) to move like scissors. **M20.** ▸**b** Fix (a person, a part of a person's body) in a scissors hold or similar grip. **M20.**
4 *verb intrans. RUGBY FOOTBALL.* Execute a tactical move in which a player running diagonally takes the ball from the hands of a team-mate and runs on, thus changing the direction of attack. **L20.**

> 🕮 **1** D. C. MURRAY Each folio being scissored into half a dozen pieces. *Times* Katharine Hamnett . . scissored divided shorts out of powder pink denim. **2** *Time* The Finance Committee scissored the entire wellhead tax scheme out of the bill. **3b** C. LASCH Legs which can . . scissor victims to death.

■ **scissorer** *noun* (*US*) a person who scissors, a person who uses scissors **L19.**

scissors /ˈsɪzəz/ *noun pl.* In attrib. use & in comb. usu. in sing. **scissor** (otherwise long *rare*). Also (earlier) †**cy-**, †**si-**, & other vars. **LME.**
[Old & mod. French *cisoires* (now only = large shears), from pl. of late Latin *cisorium* cutting instrument, from Latin *cis-* (see **CHISEL** *noun*[1]); later assoc. with *sciss-* pa. ppl stem of *scindere* cut, cleave.]
1 Treated as *pl.* & (occas.) *sing.* A pair of pivoted blades attached to handles, each handle having a hole for fingers and thumb, used for cutting paper, fabric, hair, etc., and operated by bringing the handles together so that the sharp edges of the blades close on the material to be cut. Also ***pair of scissors.*** **LME.**
2 As *interjection.* Expr. disgust or impatience. *slang.* **M19.**
3 Treated as *sing.* Any of various movements suggestive of the action of a pair of scissors, as (***a***) a high jump in which the athlete, crossing the bar in a sitting position, brings the trailing leg up as the leading leg goes down on the other side of the bar; (***b***) *RUGBY FOOTBALL* a tactical move in which a player running diagonally takes the ball from the hands of a team-mate and runs on, thus changing the direction of attack; (***c***) *WRESTLING* a hold in which the legs grip a part of the adversary's body, esp. the head, and are then locked at the instep or ankles to apply pressure (also ***scissors hold***). **L19.**
4 Treated as *sing.* A progressive divergence between two kinds of price or income, esp. as shown on a graph of the two indices plotted against each other. **E20.**

> 🕮 **1** *Belfast Telegraph* A snip of the scissors or a shampoo and set. ***cutting-out scissors, embroidery scissors, kitchen scissors, nail scissors, pinking scissors, surgical scissors***, etc. *fig.*: CARLYLE Suddenly shorn through by the scissors of Destiny. **scissors and paste** (designating) a method of subediting or compiling an article, book, etc., by mere rearrangement or excerption of the work of others.

Comb.: **scissorbill** (***a***) a skimmer, *esp.* the Indian *Rynchops albicollis*; (***b***) *slang* a foolish or objectionable person, a gossip; **scissor bird** (***a***) = ***scissor-tail*** below; (***b***) = ***scissorbill*** above; **scissor-cut** a silhouette cut freehand with scissors; **scissor-kick** *FOOTBALL*: performed by a player turning in mid-air and sending the ball backwards over the head; **scissor-lift** a surface raised or lowered by the closing or opening of crossed supports pivoted like the two halves of a pair of scissors; **scissors-grinder** (***a***) a person who grinds or sharpens scissors; (***b***) *dial.* the nightjar; (***c***) see **GRINDER** 6; ***scissors hold***: see sense 3 above; **scissors-kick** in *SWIMMING*, a movement, esp. in the sidestroke, in which the legs are parted slowly and brought together forcefully; **scissor-tail** either of two American flycatchers having very long outer tail feathers, *Tyrannus forficatus* (more fully ***scissor-tailed flycatcher***) and *T. savana*; **scissor-tooth** a carnassial tooth of a carnivore.
■ **scissorwise** *adverb* in the form or manner of a (pair of) scissors **L19.**

†**scissure** *noun.* **LME–E19.**
[French, or Latin *scissura*, from *sciss-*: see **SCISSION, -URE.**]
1 *ANATOMY.* A natural cleft or opening in an organ or part. **LME–E19.**
2 A longitudinal cleft or opening made by cutting or division; a fissure. **LME–E19.**

scitamineous /sɪtəˈmɪnɪəs/ *adjective.* Now *rare.* **E19.**
[from mod. Latin *Scitamineae* (see below) + **-OUS.**]
Of or pertaining to the order Scitamineae (now called Zingiberales) of monocotyledonous tropical plants, which includes the families Musaceae and Zingiberaceae.

sciurine /ˈskjʊərʌɪn, ˈsʌɪjʊərɪn/ *adjective & noun.* **M19.**
[from Latin *sciurus* from Greek *skiouros* (from *skia* shadow + *oura* tail) + **-INE**[1].]
▶**A** *adjective.* Resembling or of the nature of a squirrel; *spec.* of, pertaining to, or designating the subfamily Sciurinae of squirrels. **M19.**
▶**B** *noun.* A sciurine rodent; a squirrel. **M19.**

sclaff /sklaf/ *noun.* **M19.**
[Prob. imit.: cf. next.]
1 A blow with the palm of the hand or with a flat instrument; a slap. *Scot.* **M19.**
2 A light loose-fitting shoe or slipper; an old worn-down shoe. *Scot.* **M19.**
3 *GOLF.* A stroke in which the club scrapes the ground before hitting the ball. **M19.**
■ **sclaffy** *adjective* (*GOLF*, *rare*) of the nature of a sclaff **L19.**

sclaff /sklaf/ *verb.* **E19.**
[Prob. imit.]
1 *verb intrans.* Walk in a flat-footed or shuffling way. *Scot.* **E19.**
2 *verb trans.* Strike with the open hand or a flat surface; slap. *Scot.* **M19.**
3 *verb trans. & intrans. GOLF.* Scrape (the ground behind the ball) with the club in making a shot; hit (a ball) after scraping the ground with the club. **L19.**

†**sclander** *noun, verb*, †**sclanderous** *adjective* see **SLANDER** *noun, verb*, etc.

sclareol /ˈsklɛːrɪɒl/ *noun.* **E20.**
[from medieval Latin *sclarea* **CLARY** *noun*[2] + **-OL.**]
CHEMISTRY. A colourless diterpenoid alcohol, $C_{20}H_{36}O_2$, found in the leaves of clary and tobacco, and used to counter rust fungus.

†**Sclav**, †**Sclave** *nouns & adjectives*, †**Sclavic** *adjective & noun*, vars. of **SLAV** etc.

†**Sclavon** *noun & adjective*, †**Sclavonian** *noun & adjective*, etc., vars. of **SLAVON** etc.

sclera /ˈsklɪərə/ *noun.* **L19.**
[mod. Latin, from Greek *sklēros* hard + **-A**[1].]
ANATOMY. The tough white outer layer of the eyeball, continuous with the cornea.

scleractinian /ˌsklɪərakˈtɪnɪən, sklɛ-/ *noun & adjective.* **E20.**
[mod. Latin *Scleractinia* (see below), formed as **SCLERO-** + Greek *aktin-*, *aktis* ray + **-IA**[1]: see **-AN.**]
ZOOLOGY. ▶**A** *noun.* A coral of the order Scleractinia characterized by a compact calcareous skeleton and including all living stony or true corals; madreporarian. **E20.**
▶**B** *adjective.* Of or pertaining to such a coral or the group as a whole. **E20.**

scleral /ˈsklɪər(ə)l/ *adjective.* **M19.**
[from **SCLERA** + **-AL**[1].]
ANATOMY. Of or pertaining to the sclera.

sclereid /ˈsklɪərɪɪd/ *noun.* **L19.**
[Irreg. from Greek *sklēros* hard + **-ID**[2], perh. after *tracheid*.]
BOTANY. Any of a group of thick-walled, freq. short and conspicuously pitted cells, one of the two groups making up the sclerenchyma.

sclerema /sklɪəˈriːmə, sklə-/ *noun.* **M19.**
[mod. Latin form of French *sclérème*, from Greek *sklēros* hard, after *œdème* oedema.]
MEDICINE. A hardening of the skin and subcutaneous tissue, esp. as a fatal condition in newborn infants.

sclerenchyma /sklɪəˈrɛŋkɪmə, sklə-/ *noun.* **M19.**
[mod. Latin, formed as **SCLERO-**, after *parenchyma*.]
†**1** *ZOOLOGY.* The hard calcareous substance of the skeleton of a stony coral. *rare.* Only in **M19.**
2 *BOTANY.* Strengthening tissue with thick or lignified secondary walls, consisting of long cells (fibres) and chiefly short cells (sclereids). **L19.**
■ **sclerenchymatous** /-ˈkɪmətəs/ *adjective* (now only *BOTANY*) consisting or of the nature of sclerenchyma **M19.**

scleriasis /sklɪəˈrʌɪəsɪs, sklə-/ *noun.* Now *rare* or *obsolete.* Pl. **-ases** /-əsiːz/. **L17.**
[mod. Latin, formed as **SCLERO-** + **-IASIS.**]
MEDICINE. Scleroderma.

sclerification /ˌsklɛrɪfɪˈkeɪʃ(ə)n/ *noun.* **M20.**
[from **SCLER(ENCHYMA** + **-I-** + **-FICATION.**]
The conversion of plant tissue into sclerenchyma.
■ **sclerified** *adjective* that has undergone sclerification **M20.**

sclerite /ˈsklɪərʌɪt, ˈsklɛ-/ *noun.* **M19.**
[from Greek *sklēros* hard + **-ITE**[1].]
ZOOLOGY. Each of the distinct units into which the exoskeleton of various animals is divided; *esp.* each of the chitinous plates joined by membranes to form the skeleton of an arthropod.

scleritis /sklɪəˈrʌɪtɪs, sklə-/ *noun.* **M19.**
[from **SCLERA** + **-ITIS.**]
MEDICINE. Inflammation of the sclera.

sclero- /ˈsklɪərəʊ, ˈsklɛrəʊ/ *combining form.*
[from Greek *sklēros* hard: see **-O-.**]
Forming nouns & adjectives with the senses 'pertaining to, involving, or exhibiting hardness or hardening' or (*spec.*) 'of or pertaining to the sclera of the eye', as ***sclerotomy.***
■ **scleroblast** *noun* (***a***) *BOTANY* a sclereid; (***b***) *ZOOLOGY* a spicule-forming cell in a sponge: **L19.** **scleroprotein** *noun* (*BIOCHEMISTRY*) a structural protein, as a collagen, elastin, keratin, fibroin, etc. **E20.** **scleroˈtesta** *noun* (*BOTANY*) the hard inner part of the testa in some seeds **E20.** **scleroˈtherapy** *noun* (*MEDICINE*) the treatment of varicose blood-vessels by the injection of a sclerosant. **M20.**

scleroderma /sklɪərəˈdəːmə/ *noun.* **M19.**
[mod. Latin, formed as **SCLERO-** + Greek *derma* skin.]
MEDICINE. A chronic hardened condition of the skin and connective tissue. Also, sclerema.
■ **sclerodermatous** *adjective* of or pertaining to scleroderma **L19.** **sclerodermia** /-ˈdəːmɪə/ *noun* scleroderma **M19.**

sclerogen /ˈsklɪərədʒ(ə)n, ˈsklɛ-/ *noun.* **M19.**
[from **SCLERO-** + **-GEN.**]
BOTANY. The hard lignified material on the inner surface of some plant cells.

sclerogenous /sklɪəˈrɒdʒɪnəs, sklə-/ *adjective.* **M19.**
[from **SCLERO-** + **-GENOUS.**]
BIOLOGY. Causing thickening of tissue.

scleroma /sklɪə'rəʊmə, sklə-/ *noun*. Now *rare*. Pl. **-mas**, **-mata** /-mətə/. **M19.**
[from SCLERO- + -OMA.]
MEDICINE. A hardened patch of granulation tissue in skin or membrane.

sclerophyll /'sklɪərəfɪl, 'sklɛ-/ *noun & adjective*. **E20.**
[German *Sklerophyll*, formed as next.]
BOTANY. ▶**A** *noun*. A sclerophyllous plant. **E20.**
▶**B** *adjective*. = SCLEROPHYLLOUS *adjective*. **E20.**

sclerophyllous /sklɪə'rɒfɪləs, sklə-/ *adjective*. **E20.**
[from SCLERO- + Greek *phullon* leaf + -OUS.]
BOTANY. Of woody evergreen vegetation: having leaves that are hard and tough, and usu. small and thick, so reducing the rate of loss of water. Also, characterized by such vegetation.
▪ **sclerophylly** *noun* the fact of being sclerophyllous **E20.**

sclerosant /sklɪə'rəʊz(ə)nt, sklə-, -s(ə)nt/ *noun & adjective*. **M20.**
[from SCLEROSIS + -ANT[1].]
MEDICINE. (Of, pertaining to, or designating) an agent producing sclerosis or hardening of tissue, or inducing thrombosis in varicose blood-vessels.

Scleroscope /'sklɪərəskəʊp, 'sklɛ-/ *noun*. Also **s-**. **E20.**
[from SCLERO- + -SCOPE.]
An instrument for determining the hardness of a material by measuring the height of rebound of a small diamond-tipped hammer dropped on to the material from a standard height.
¶ Proprietary name in the US.

sclerose /sklɪə'rəʊs, sklə-/ *verb trans*. *rare*. **L19.**
[Back-form. from next.]
Affect with sclerosis; harden. Usu. in *pass*.

sclerosed /sklɪə'rəʊst, sklə-/ *ppl adjective*. **L19.**
[from SCLEROSIS + -ED[2].]
1 *MEDICINE.* Affected with sclerosis. **L19.**
2 *BOTANY.* Of tissue or cell walls: exhibiting sclerosis; lignified. **L19.**

sclerosing /sklɪə'rəʊsɪŋ, sklə-/ *ppl adjective*. **L19.**
[from SCLEROSE *verb* + -ING[2].]
MEDICINE. Becoming affected with sclerosis; causing or involving sclerosis.

sclerosis /sklɪə'rəʊsɪs, sklə-/ *noun*. Pl. **-roses** /-'rəʊsiːz/. **LME.**
[mod. Latin, from Greek *sklērōsis*, from *sklēroun* harden: see -OSIS.]
1 *MEDICINE.* Orig., a hard external tumour. Now, a hardening of any tissue or structure, esp. of the circulatory or nervous system, freq. caused by diffuse scarring after inflammation. **LME.**
2 *BOTANY.* Hardening of cell walls by thickening or lignificaton. **L19.**
3 *fig.* Rigidity, excessive resistance to change. **M20.**
1 ***amyotrophic lateral sclerosis***, ***disseminated sclerosis***, ***multiple sclerosis***, etc.

sclerotal /sklɪə'rəʊt(ə)l, sklə-/ *noun*. **M19.**
[formed as next + -AL[1].]
ZOOLOGY. A sclerotic bone or plate.

sclerotia *noun* pl. of SCLEROTIUM.

sclerotic /sklɪə'rɒtɪk, sklə-/ *adjective & noun*. **M16.**
[from medieval Latin (*tela*) *sclerotica*, formed as SCLEROSIS: see -OTIC.]
▶**A** *adjective*. **1** *ANATOMY & ZOOLOGY.* **a** Designating the sclera of the eye. Chiefly in ***sclerotic coat***, ***sclerotic membrane***, ***sclerotic tunic***. **M16.** ▸**b** Of, pertaining to, or connected with the sclera of the eye. **E19.**
2 *MEDICINE.* Of or pertaining to sclerosis; affected with sclerosis. Now *rare*. **M16.**
3 *BOTANY.* Marked by sclerosis or thickening of the cell wall. **L19.**
4 *fig.* Unmoving, unchanging, rigid. **M20.**
1b sclerotic bone, **sclerotic plate** each of the thin bones forming a ring around each eye in some birds and reptiles. **sclerotic ring** the ring formed by the sclerotic bones.
▶**B** *noun*. The sclera of the eye. Now *rare*. **L17.**

sclerotin /'sklɪərətɪn, 'sklɛ-/ *noun*. **M20.**
[from SCLERO- + *-tin* after *chitin*, *keratin*, etc.]
BIOLOGY. Any of a class of structural proteins which form the exocuticles of insects and are hardened and darkened by a natural tanning process in which protein chains are cross-linked by quinone groups.

sclerotinia /sklɪərə'tɪnɪə, sklɛ-/ *noun*. **E20.**
[mod. Latin *Sclerotinia* (see below), from SCLEROTIUM + *-inia* arbitrary suffix.]
Any of various parasitic fungi constituting the genus *Sclerotinia*, with apothecia arising from a sclerotium, species of which cause rotting in fruit, vegetables, tubers, etc. Also ***sclerotinia disease***, ***sclerotinia rot***.

sclerotised *adjective* var. of SCLEROTIZED.

sclerotitis /sklɪərə'tʌɪtɪs, sklɛ-/ *noun*. Now *rare*. **E19.**
[from SCLEROTIC *noun* + -ITIS.]
MEDICINE. = SCLERITIS.

sclerotium /sklɪə'rəʊtɪəm, sklə-/ *noun*. Pl. **-tia** /-tɪə/. **M19.**
[mod. Latin, orig. a genus name (see sense 1 below), from Greek *sklēros* hard: see -IUM.]
1 Any of various hyphomycetous fungi, freq. pathogens, constituting the genus *Sclerotium*, which formerly included asexual states of certain ascomycetes. **M19.**
2 *MYCOLOGY.* The hard dark resting body of certain fungi, consisting of a mass of hyphal threads, which is capable of remaining dormant for long periods in unfavourable conditions. **L19.**
3 *ZOOLOGY.* A cystlike growth enclosing a portion of plasmodium of a myxomycete in its dormant stage. **L19.**
▪ **sclerotioid** *adjective* resembling a sclerotium **M19.**

sclerotized /'sklɪərətʌɪzd, 'sklɛ-/ *adjective*. Also **-ised**. **E20.**
[from SCLEROTIC + -IZE + -ED[1].]
ZOOLOGY. Hardened by conversion into sclerotin.
▪ **scleroti'zation** *noun* the process of becoming sclerotized; the state of being sclerotized: **M20.** **sclerotize** *verb trans.* harden by sclerotization **M20.**

sclerotome /'sklɪərətəʊm, 'sklɛ-/ *noun*. **M19.**
[from SCLERO- + -TOME.]
1 *ANATOMY & ZOOLOGY.* Each of the series of segments of the embryonic mesoderm which give rise to the vertebral column and associated structures. **M19.**
2 *SURGERY.* A knife used in sclerotomy. *rare*. **L19.**
▪ **sclero'tomal** *adjective* = SCLEROTOMIC **L20.** **sclero'tomic** *adjective* (*ANATOMY & ZOOLOGY*) of or pertaining to a sclerotome or sclerotomes **L19.**

sclerotomy /sklɪə'rɒtəmi, sklə-/ *noun*. **L19.**
[from SCLERO- + -TOMY.]
Surgical incision into the sclerotic coat of the eyeball; an instance of this.

sclerous /'sklɪərəs/ *adjective*. **M19.**
[from Greek *sklēros* hard + -OUS.]
1 Of animal tissue: hard, bony. **M19.**
2 *MEDICINE.* Affected by sclerosis, sclerosed. **M19.**

SCM *abbreviation*.
1 State Certified Midwife.
2 Student Christian Movement.

scob /skɒb/ *noun*. Long *rare*. **ME.**
[Origin unkn.]
Orig. *gen.*, a box, a chest. Later (*School slang*), a large wooden storage box also used as a school desk.
¶ First recorded as a surname.

scobberlotcher /'skɒbəlɒtʃə/ *noun*. **L17.**
[Origin unkn.]
An idler.

scobiform /'skəʊbɪfɔːm/ *adjective*. *rare*. **M18.**
[from Latin *scobis* sawdust, filings + -FORM.]
BOTANY. Like sawdust or filings in appearance.

scoff /skɒf/ *noun*[1]. **ME.**
[Perh. of Scandinavian origin. Cf. early mod.Danish *skof*, *skuf* jest, mockery, *skuffe* mock, jest, also (as now) deceive, disappoint, rel. to Old Frisian *skof* mockery, Old High German *skof*, *skopf* poet. Cf. SCOP.]
1 a Contemptuous ridicule, scorn, mockery. Now *rare* or *obsolete*. **ME.** ▸**b** A taunt, an expression of scorn or mockery. **L16.**
2 An object of contempt, ridicule, or scorn. **M17.**

> 🕮 **1a** T. TAYLOR As in nicknames taken up in scoffe. **b** JOHN BOYLE The scoffs . . of Swift . . more venomously dangerous, than the wounds of a common serpent. **2** LD MACAULAY The principles of liberty were the scoff of every grinning courtier.

scoff /skɒf/ *noun*[2]. *colloq.* (orig. *S. Afr.*). **M19.**
[Afrikaans *skof* repr. Dutch *schoft* quarter of a day, each of the four meals of the day.]
Food; a meal. Cf. SCARF *noun*[4].

> 🕮 *attrib.*: A. FUGARD They let him keep his scoff-tin.

scoff /skɒf/ *verb*[1]. **ME.**
[from SCOFF *noun*[1].]
1 *verb intrans.* Speak derisively, be scornful, esp. concerning something deserving serious consideration or treatment; mock. Usu. foll. by *at*. **ME.**
2 *verb trans.* **a** Deride, taunt, ridicule irreverently. Now chiefly *US*. **LME.** ▸**b** Utter scoffingly. **M19.**

> 🕮 **1** K. LINES They had been heard to scoff at the ancient statue. *Today* The Premier scoffed at the plan.

▪ **scoffer** *noun*[1] (*a*) a person who scoffs, esp. at religion or morality; †(*b*) *rare* a jester, a buffoon: **LME.** **scoffingly** *adverb* in a scoffing manner **M16.**

scoff /skɒf/ *verb*[2]. **L18.**
[Partly var. of SCAFF *verb*, partly from SCOFF *noun*[2].]
1 a *verb intrans.* Eat, feed; have one's food *with*. *colloq. & dial.* **L18.** ▸**b** *verb trans.* Eat (food etc.) greedily or quickly, gulp (food) *down*. Cf. SCARF *verb*[3]. *colloq. & dial.* **E19.**
2 *verb trans.* Seize, plunder. Now chiefly *Scot.* **L19.**

> 🕮 **1a** *Grocer* Ideas of healthy eating . . discarded as the executives prepared to spend the next 2½ hours scoffing. **b** M. GARDINER I handed him the chocolates . . . I bet he scoffed the lot.

▪ **scoffer** *noun*[2] **M20.**

scoffery /'skɒf(ə)ri/ *noun*. *rare*. **L16.**
[from SCOFF *noun*[1] + -ERY, after *mockery*.]
Mockery, ridicule, derision. Formerly also, a ridiculous piece of conduct.

scofflaw /'skɒflɔː/ *noun*. *colloq.* (chiefly *N. Amer.*). **E20.**
[from SCOFF *verb*[1] + LAW *noun*[1].]
A person who flouts the law, *esp.* a person not complying with various laws which are difficult to enforce effectively.

> 🕮 *Miami Herald* By putting a thumb print on the traffic ticket, the scofflaw might be more easy to trace.

scogger /'skɒɡə/ *noun*. *north.* **E17.**
[Origin unkn. Cf. COCKER *noun*[1] 2.]
A footless stocking worn either as a gaiter or as a sleeve to protect the arm; the foot of a stocking worn over a boot to give grip on icy surfaces.

scoinson /'skɔɪns(ə)n/ *noun*. **M19.**
[Refash. of SCUNCHEON after its source, Old French *escoinson*.]
ARCHITECTURE. In full ***scoinson arch***. = REAR-ARCH.

scoke /skəʊk/ *noun*. *US*. **L18.**
[Origin uncertain: cf. Eastern Abnaki *skókimin* pokeweed, lit. 'snake berry'.]
Pokeweed, *Phytolacca americana*.

scold /skəʊld/ *noun*. **ME.**
[Prob. from Old Norse *skáld* poet, SKALD.]
1 Orig., a ribald person, esp. a woman. Later, a persistently nagging or grumbling woman (rarely a man). **ME.**
2 An act of scolding; a scolding rebuke. Now chiefly *Scot. & US*. **E18.**

> 🕮 **1** SHAKES. *Tam. Shr.* I know she is an irksome brawling scold. **common scold** a woman who disturbs the peace of the neighbourhood by her constant scolding. **scold's bit**, **scold's bridle** *Hist.* = BRANKS 1. **2** *Time* An ancient scold . . [that] . . nations are not producing babies fast enough.

scold /skəʊld/ *verb*. **LME.**
[from the noun.]
1 *verb intrans.* Orig. (chiefly of a woman), behave as a scold; quarrel noisily; grumble or complain *at* someone; use violent or vituperative language. Now in milder sense, find fault persistently; utter continuous reproof. **LME.**
2 *verb trans.* Orig., †***scold it out***, continue wrangling to the end. Later, drive or force by scolding into a specified state or position (foll. by obj. & compl. or adverbial phr.) Now *rare*. **L16.**
3 *verb trans.* Rebuke (esp. a child) in a prolonged or continuous manner; chide. **E18.**

> 🕮 **1** DEFOE I scolded heartily at him. **2** W. COWPER No man was ever scolded out of his sins. **3** E. BLYTON Anne was severely scolded . . for falling asleep.

▪ **scolder** *noun* (*a*) a person who scolds; †(*b*) a common scold: **LME.** **scolding** *verbal noun* the action of the verb; an instance of this, a telling-off: **LME.** **scoldingly** *adverb* in a scolding manner **M16.**

scoleces *noun pl.* see SCOLEX.

scolecite /'skəʊlɪsʌɪt/ *noun*. **E19.**
[from Greek *skōlēk-*, *skōlēx* worm + -ITE[1].]
1 *MINERALOGY.* A calcium zeolite occurring in radiating groups of needle-shaped or fibrous crystals. **E19.**
2 *BOTANY.* In ascomycetous fungi: a coiled hypha at the centre of a young perithecium. **L19.**

scolecodont /'skəʊlɪkədɒnt/ *noun*. **M20.**
[from Greek *skōlēk(o)-*, *skōlēx* worm + -ODONT.]
PALAEONTOLOGY. The jaws of an annelid worm, found as a microfossil in some rocks.

scolecoid /skə(ʊ)'liːkɔɪd/ *adjective*. **M19.**
[from Greek *skōlēkoeidēs*, from *skōlēk-*, *skōlēx* worm: see -OID.]
Resembling a worm or a scolex.

scolex /'skəʊlɛks/ *noun*. Pl. **scoleces** /skə(ʊ)'liːsiːz/, **scolices** /'skəʊlɪsiːz/. **M19.**
[mod. Latin from Greek *skōlēk-*, *skōlēx* worm.]
The anterior end of a tapeworm, bearing suckers and hooks for attachment; the equivalent but invaginated structure in the cysticercus stage of a tapeworm.

scolia *noun* pl. of SCOLION.

Scoline /'skəʊliːn/ *noun*. **M20.**
[from S(UCCINYL)C(H)OLINE.]
PHARMACOLOGY. (Proprietary name for) the drug succinylcholine.

scolion /'skəʊlɪən/ *noun*. Pl. **-lia** /-lɪə/. **L16.**
[Greek *skolion*.]
GREEK HISTORY. A song consisting of verses sung in turn by the guests at a banquet; a festival song.

scoliosis /skɒlɪ'əʊsɪs, skəʊ-/ *noun*. Pl. **-oses** /-'əʊsiːz/. **E18.**
[Greek *skoliōsis*, from *skolios* bent, curved: see -OSIS.]
MEDICINE. Abnormal lateral curvature of the spine. Cf. LORDOSIS, KYPHOSIS.
▪ **scoliotic** /-'ɒtɪk/ *adjective* pertaining to or affected with scoliosis **M20.**

scollop /ˈskɒləp/ *noun*[1]. *Anglo-Irish*. E19.
[Irish *scolb*.]
A thatch-peg.

scollop *noun*[2] & *verb* var. of SCALLOP.

scoloc /ˈskɒləʊk/ *noun*. ME.
[Old Irish *scolóc*, from *scol* school. Cf. Irish *scológ* farmer, rustic.]
SCOTTISH HISTORY. A tenant of church land; a student in a monastery; a scholar.

scolopaceous /skɒlə(ʊ)ˈpeɪʃəs/ *adjective*. Now *rare*. L18.
[mod. Latin *scolopaceus*, from Latin *scolopac-*, *scolopax* snipe, woodcock from Greek *skolopax*: see -ACEOUS.]
ORNITHOLOGY. Resembling a snipe.

scolopale /ˈskɒləpeɪl/ *noun* & *adjective*. Pl. **-lia** /-lɪə/, **-s**. E20.
[from Greek *skolop-*, *skolops* spike + -AL[1].]
ENTOMOLOGY. ▶**A** *noun*. A cuticular sheath enclosing the dendrite in a sensillum or chemoreceptor; the rod of a scolopidium. E20.
▶**B** *adjective*. Designating the parts of a scolopidium or scolopale. E20.

scolopender /skɒlə(ʊ)ˈpɛndə/ *noun*. Now *rare*. LME.
[from next.]
†**1** = SCOLOPENDRIUM. LME–L17.
2 = SCOLOPENDRA 2. M16.

scolopendra /skɒlə(ʊ)ˈpɛndrə/ *noun*. L16.
[Latin from Greek *skolopendra*.]
†**1** A mythical marine fish. L16–M17.
2 A centipede. Now only as mod. Latin genus name. E17.
■ **scolopendrine** /-drɪn/ *adjective* resembling or pertaining to a centipede or centipedes L19.

scolopendrium /skɒlə(ʊ)ˈpɛndrɪəm/ *noun*. Also (earlier) †**-dria**. Pl. **-iums**, **-ia** /-ɪə/. LME.
[mod. Latin from late Latin *scolopendrion* from Greek *skolopendrion*, from its supposed resemblance to the scolopendra.]
The hart's tongue fern, *Phyllitis scolopendrium*.

scolopidium /skɒlə(ʊ)ˈpɪdɪəm/ *noun*. Pl. **-dia** /-dɪə/. M20.
[from Greek *skolop-*, *skolops* spike + -IDIUM.]
ENTOMOLOGY. A subunit of a chordotonal organ, consisting chiefly of the nucleus and dendrite of a sensory nerve cell and a tubular sheath and rod enclosing the dendrite.

scolopoid /ˈskɒləpɔɪd/ *adjective*. M20.
[formed as prec. + -OID.]
ENTOMOLOGY. = SCOLOPOPHOROUS.

scolopophore /ˈskɒləpəfɔː/ *noun*. L19.
[formed as prec. + -O- + -PHORE.]
ENTOMOLOGY. The sheath enclosing the terminal rod of certain cells; the chordotonal organ of which this sheath is part.
■ **scoloˈpophorous** *adjective* (of a sensory end-organ) having the elongated tubular form of a scolopidium M20.

scolops /ˈskɒlɒps/ *noun*. M20.
[Greek *skolops* spike.]
ENTOMOLOGY. The rodlike structure inside the sheath of a scolopidium.

scolytid /skəˈlʌɪtɪd, ˈskɒlɪtɪd/ *noun* & *adjective*. L19.
[mod. Latin *Scolytidae* (see below), from *Scolytus* genus name, from Greek *skolios* bent, curved: see -ID[3].]
(Of, pertaining to, or designating) any of various small cylindrical bark- or wood-boring beetles of the family Scolytidae; a bark beetle.
■ **scolytoid** *adjective* pertaining to or resembling this family; *esp.* designating or pertaining to a kind of fleshy apodous larva, as the final larval stage of insects which undergo hypermetamorphosis L19.

scomber /ˈskɒmbə/ *noun*. Pl. **-bri** /-briː, -brʌɪ/. E17.
[Latin from Greek *skombros* tuna or mackerel.]
A mackerel or other member of the family Scombridae. Now only as mod. Latin genus name.
■ **scombroid** *adjective* & *noun* (*a*) *adjective* resembling the mackerel; of or pertaining to the perciform family Scombridae, superfamily Scombroidea, or suborder Scombroidei; (*b*) *noun* a scombroid fish: M19.

scombrotoxic /skɒmbrəˈtɒksɪk/ *adjective*. M20.
[from prec. + -O- + TOXIC.]
MEDICINE. Involving or designating poisoning caused by eating the contaminated flesh of scombroid fish, which may contain high levels of histamine etc.

scomfish /ˈskʌmfɪʃ/ *verb trans*. *Scot.* & *north*. LME.
[Abbreviation of *discomfish* early Scot. var. of DISCOMFIT *verb*.]
†**1** Defeat, vanquish. Only in LME.
2 Suffocate, stifle, choke (with heat, smoke, etc.). Also, seriously injure. M18.

†**scomm** *noun*. E17–E18.
[Late Latin *scomma* from Greek *skōmma*, from *skōptein* jeer, scoff.]
A mocking or scoffing speech or action.

sconce /skɒns/ *noun*[1]. LME.
[Aphet. from Old French *esconse* hiding place, lantern, or from medieval Latin *sconsa* aphet. from *absconsa* (sc. *laterna*) dark (lantern), use as noun of fem. pa. pple of *abscondere* hide: see ABSCOND.]
†**1** A lantern or candlestick with a screen to protect the light from the wind, and a handle for carrying. LME–M18. ▶**b** A flat candlestick with a handle. M19.
2 A bracket for a candle or a light hung on or fixed to an interior wall; *esp.* an ornamental bracket for holding one or more candles etc. LME.
3 A street lamp or lantern attached to an exterior wall. *rare*. M19.

🕮 **2** J. D. MACDONALD The . . wall sconces held orange bulbs with orange shades.

sconce /skɒns/ *noun*[2]. LME.
[Dutch *schans*, †*schantze* brushwood, screen of brushwood for defence, earthwork of gabions, from Middle & mod. High German *schanze*, of unkn. origin. In sense 1 perh. from prec.]
1 A screen, an interior partition. Now *dial.* LME.
2 A small fort or earthwork, *esp.* one defending a ford, pass, etc. L16.
3 A screen or shelter affording protection from the weather, offering concealment, etc. *obsolete* exc. *Scot.* L16.
4 A fixed seat at the side of a fireplace. *Scot.* & *dial.* L18.
5 In full ***sconce-piece***. An ice floe, a water-washed iceberg. M19.

🕮 **2** *fig.*: T. FULLER One of the best bulwarks and sconces of Soveraignty. †**build a sconce** *slang* run up a score at an inn etc. **3** A. GORDON The fervent Heat of the Sun made some kind of Sconce . . necessary.

sconce /skɒns/ *noun*[3]. *joc. arch.* M16.
[Perh. joc. use of SCONCE *noun*[1].]
The head, *esp.* the crown or top of the head; *transf.* sense, brains, wit.

🕮 *Century Magazine* If she . . showed any sconce for the business.

sconce /skɒns/ *verb*[1] *trans*. Now *rare*. L16.
[Partly from SCONCE *noun*[2], partly aphet. from ENSCONCE.]
1 Fortify, entrench. Also, shelter, protect. L16.
†**2** Hide, screen from view. Only in M17.
3 = ENSCONCE 3. M19.

sconce /skɒns/ *verb*[2] & *noun*[4]. Chiefly *Oxford Univ. slang*. E17.
[Origin uncertain: perh. from SCONCE *noun*[3].]
▶**A** *verb trans*. **1** Orig., fine (a person) for a breach of college or university discipline. Now (of undergraduates dining in hall), challenge (a fellow undergraduate) to drink a tankard of beer etc. at one draught, as a penalty for a breach of etiquette or other minor misdemeanour. E17.
2 *gen.* Fine. M17.

🕮 **1** *Etonian* Hall dinner. Was sconced in a quart of ale for quoting Latin. **2** J. MORLEY A new minister, who . . did not shrink from sconcing the powerful landed phalanx.

▶**B** *noun*. **1** An act of sconcing; a tankard or mug used for this. M17.
†**2** A fine. L17–E18.

scone /skɒn, skəʊn/ *noun*. Orig. *Scot.* E16.
[Perh. a shortening of Middle Low German *schonbrot*, Middle Dutch *schoonbroot* fine bread.]
1 Orig., a large round cake made of wheat or barley-meal baked on a griddle; any of the quarters into which such a cake may often be cut. Now usu., a small sweet or savoury cake made of flour, milk, and a little fat, baked on a griddle or in an oven. Freq. with specifying word. E16.
2 In full ***scone cap***. A bonnet traditionally worn by men in the Scottish Lowlands. *Scot.* E19.
3 The head. Freq. in ***do one's scone***, lose one's head, lose one's temper. *Austral.* & *NZ slang*. M20.

🕮 **1** P. ANGADI Mary spread jam carefully on a scone. ***cheese scone***, ***sultana scone***, ***treacle scone***, etc. DROP-SCONE. ***dropped scone***: see DROPPED 2.

Comb.: ***scone cap***: see sense 2 above; **scone-hot** *adjective* (*Austral. slang*) (*a*) ***go a person scone-hot***, reprimand a person severely, lose one's temper at a person; (*b*) very good, very much.

scoop /skuːp/ *noun*. ME.
[Middle Low German, Middle Dutch *schōpe* (Du *schoep*) vessel for bailing, bucket of a water-wheel = Middle High German *schuofe* (German †*Schufe*), from West Germanic verb meaning 'draw water' rel. to SHAPE *verb*. In branch II directly from the verb.]
▶**I 1 a** A utensil for pouring or conveying liquids, *esp.* one in the form of a ladle with a long straight handle. Now chiefly NAUTICAL & *dial.* ME. ▶**b** The bucket of a water-wheel or of a dredging or draining machine. L16.
†**2** A basket. LME–L17.
3 a A shovel, esp. one with deep sides and a short handle, used for shovelling up and carrying materials of a loose nature such as grain, coins, or sugar. L15. ▶†**b** = LADLE *noun* 1C. E16–M17.
4 An instrument with a bowl- or gouge-shaped blade, used for cutting out a piece or core from an object or a soft substance; *spec.* †(*a*) a hollow garden trowel; (*b*) the bucket or excavating part of a digging-machine; (*c*) a small kitchen utensil with a deep bowl used for serving portions of ice-cream, mashed potato, etc.; (*d*) MEDICINE a surgical instrument resembling a long-handled spoon. E18.

🕮 **1a** *fig.*: DICKENS Some men . . made scoops of their two hands joined, and sipped. **3a** H. STEPHENS Wooden scoops . . to shovel up the corn in heaps.

▶**II 5 a** The action or an act of scooping; a thing which is scooped. Also, a quantity scooped up. M18. ▶**b** A scooped shot or stroke in hockey, cricket, etc. M19. ▶**c** MUSIC. Portamento. E20.
6 a A place scooped or hollowed out; a natural concavity or hollow. L18. ▶**b** A large light suspended from the ceiling of a film or TV studio. M20.
7 a An item of news acquired and published by a newspaper etc. in advance of its rivals; an exclusive; a sensational piece of news. Orig. *US*. L19. ▶**b** A sudden fall in stock market prices, enabling stocks to be bought at cheaper rates, followed by a rise in prices and thus a profit. *US slang*. L19. ▶**c** A lucky stroke of business. *colloq.* L19.

🕮 **5a** L. MCMURTRY Ladling himself a big scoop of beans. **6a** J. RABAN Bustard—they cook it in charcoal in scoops in the sand. **7a** A. FRATER I want murder, famine and armed insurrection. I want *scoops*!

Phrases: **give a person the scoop on** provide a person with the latest information on. **on the scoop** on a drunken spree.
Comb.: **scoop bonnet** a woman's bonnet shaped like a scoop; **scoop-neck** a rounded, low-cut neckline of a garment; **scoop-necked** *adjective* (of a garment) having a scoop-neck; **scoop stretcher** an adjustable stretcher with two separate longitudinal parts which may be placed underneath a casualty and clipped together.
■ **scoopful** *noun* a quantity that fills a scoop; as much or as many as a scoop can contain: E18.

scoop /skuːp/ *verb*. ME.
[from branch I of the noun.]
1 *verb trans*. Convey or pour (water) with or as with a scoop. Also foll. by *out*. ME.
2 *verb trans*. Remove or lift (a portion of a soft substance or part of a heap of objects) with or as with a scoop. Usu. foll. by *away*, *out*, *up*. E17.
3 *verb trans*. Hollow out (as) with a scoop. Freq. foll. by *out*. E18.
4 *verb trans*. Form by scooping or as if by scooping. Freq. foll. by *out*. M18.
5 a *verb trans*. Take or amass in large quantities, win (an award etc.). Freq. foll. by *in*, *up*. Also (*US slang*), defeat, get the better of. M19. ▶**b** Outdo (a rival reporter, newspaper, etc.) by obtaining and publishing an earlier or exclusive news item; obtain (a news item) as a scoop. Orig. *US*. L19.
6 *verb trans*. Propel or take (as) by a scooping movement. Freq. foll. by *up*. M19.
7 *verb intrans*. MUSIC. Perform a portamento or scoop. E20.

🕮 **1** E. L. DOCTOROW She bathed her with the warm water scooping it in her hands. **2** B. MASON Roy cupped his hand, scooped out a mass of pulpy berries. **3** L. STEPHEN The rocks below . . scooped out by the glacier in old days. **4** N. MOSLEY Steps scooped out like cooking spoons. **5a** *Daily Mirror* Public schoolboy . . scooped £100,000 in a McDonald's quiz. **scoop the kitty**, **scoop the pool** in gambling, win all the money that is staked; *transf.* gain everything, be completely successful. **b** *transf.*: P. LARKIN Why have British libraries allowed themselves to be so comprehensively scooped in this field? **6** E. FIGES Goodness, she said . . . Scooping up the crumpled remains.

■ **scooper** *noun* (*a*) a person who or thing which scoops something; (*b*) (now *rare*) the avocet; (*c*) a tool used esp. in engraving, for hollowing out portions of the surface worked: M17. **scooping** *noun* (*a*) the action of the verb; (*b*) a concavity, a hollow: M19.

scoop-net /ˈskuːpnɛt/ *noun*. M18.
[from SCOOP *noun* or *verb* + NET *noun*[1].]
A small long-handled fishing net; a large net for sweeping a river bottom.

scoopy /ˈskuːpi/ *adjective*. *colloq.* L20.
[formed as prec. + -Y[1].]
Of the neckline of a garment: rounded and low-cut; scoop-necked.

scoosh *noun* & *verb* var. of SKOOSH.

scoot /skuːt/ *noun*[1]. E19.
[from SCOOT *verb*[1].]
1 A sudden gush of water; a pipe or opening through which such a gush flows. *Scot.* E19.
2 The action or an act of scooting. *dial.* or *slang*. M19.
3 A bout of drunkenness, a drunken spree. Chiefly in ***on the scoot***. *Austral.* & *NZ colloq.* E20.

🕮 **2** L. A. G. STRONG The trot became an undignified scoot for safety.

scoot /skuːt/ *noun*[2]. *slang*. M20.
[Abbreviation.]
= SCOOTER *noun* 5b.

scoot /skuːt/ *verb*[1]. Also (earlier) †**scout**. M18.
[Origin unkn.]
1 a *verb intrans*. Go suddenly and swiftly, dart; run away hurriedly. Freq. foll. by *away*, *off*. Orig. *Nautical slang*. M18. ▶**b** *verb trans*. Move or convey suddenly or swiftly. E20.
2 *verb trans*. Eject (water) forcibly, squirt. *Scot.* E19.

3 *verb intrans.* Slide suddenly, skid. *Scot. & US.* **M19.**

1a *Which?* Young Jonathan . . scooted past his mother . . and pulled over a boiling kettle. **b** N. FREELING She scooted her wheelchair across the room.

scoot /skuːt/ *verb² intrans. colloq.* **M20.**
[Abbreviation.]
= SCOOTER *verb.*

scooter /ˈskuːtə/ *noun.* **E19.**
[from SCOOT *verb*¹ + -ER¹. In sense 3 perh. rel. to COULTER.]
1 A person who scoots or moves hurriedly. **E19.**
2 A syringe, a squirt. *Scot. & north.* **E19.**
3 A simple plough with a single handle used for marking furrows, making drills, etc. Also more fully ***scooter plough***. *US.* **E19.**
4 Any of various kinds of light fast boats; *spec.* (*a*) *N. Amer.* a sailing boat able to travel on both ice and water; (*b*) a fast motorboat, used in the war of 1914–18; (*c*) a motorized pleasure-boat resembling a motor scooter. Freq. with specifying word, as ***sea scooter***, ***water scooter***, etc. **E20.**
5 a A child's toy consisting of a footboard mounted on two tandem wheels with a long steering handle, propelled by resting one foot on the footboard and pushing the other against the ground. **E20.** ▸**b** A light two-wheeled open motor vehicle with a shieldlike protective front. Also ***motor scooter***. **E20.** ▸**c** Any of various kinds of small or light motor vehicle; *esp.* (*a*) *slang* a small car; (*b*) *slang* a single-decked bus. **E20.**
■ **scooterist** *noun* a person who drives or travels on a scooter **E20.**

scooter /ˈskuːtə/ *verb intrans.* **E20.**
[from the noun.]
Travel by or ride on a scooter.

scop /ʃɒp, skɒp/ *noun.*
[Old English *scóp*, *sćeop* = Old High German *scof*, *scopf* poet, Old Norse *skop* mocking, railing. Cf. SCOFF *noun*¹.]
Hist. A poet or minstrel during the Anglo-Saxon period.
¶ Obsolete after ME; revived in L18.

scopa /ˈskəʊpə/ *noun*¹. Pl. **-pae** /-piː/. **E19.**
[Latin, in class. use only in pl. *scopae* twigs, shoots, a broom or brush.]
ENTOMOLOGY. A brush or tuft of hairs found on various insects; *esp.* the pollen brush of a bee.

scopa /ˈskopa/ *noun*². **M20.**
[Italian, lit. 'broom, besom'.]
An Italian card-game similar to cassino.

scopae *noun* pl. of SCOPA *noun*¹.

scoparin /ˈskəʊpərɪn/ *noun.* **M19.**
[formed as next + -IN¹.]
A yellow crystalline pigment found in broom flowers, with diuretic properties.

scoparius /skəʊˈpɛːrɪəs/ *noun.* **L19.**
[mod. Latin (see below): cf. SCOPA *noun*¹.]
PHARMACOLOGY. The tops of common broom, *Cytisus scoparius*, containing sparteine and scoparin, used as a diuretic, purgative, and emetic.

scope /skəʊp/ *noun*¹. **M16.**
[Italian *scopo* aim, purpose from Greek *skopos* mark for shooting at, from *skop-*, *skep-* as in *skopein* observe, aim at, examine, *skeptesthai* look out.]
1 A target; a mark for shooting or aiming at. Chiefly *fig.* Long *obsolete* exc. as coinciding with sense 2 or 3. **M16.**
2 a A thing aimed at or desired; an end in view; a purpose, an aim. Now *rare.* **M16.** ▸†**b** A person who is an object of desire or pursuit. **L16–E18.**
3 a The main purpose, intention, or drift of a writer, book, etc. Formerly also, the subject or argument chosen for treatment. Now *rare.* **M16.** ▸†**b** The intention of a law; the drift or meaning of a proposal. *rare.* **M–L17.**
4 The range of a projectile. Now *rare* or *obsolete.* **M16.**
5 a Unhindered range, free play, opportunity or liberty *for* or *to do* something. Freq. in ***give scope to***, ***have scope (to do)***. **M16.** ▸†**b** An instance of liberty or licence. *rare* (Shakes.). Only in **E17.**
6 a Space or range for freedom of movement or activity. Freq. in ***give scope (to)***, ***have scope***. **M16.** ▸**b** The ability of a horse to extend its stride or jump. **L20.**
7 A tract of land; *esp.* a piece of land belonging to an individual owner. Now *rare. Anglo-Irish.* **M16.**
†**8** MEDICINE. A plan or method of treatment; = INTENTION 6. **L16–L17.**
9 a The reach or range of a person's mental activity or perception; extent of view, sweep of outlook. Freq. in ***beyond one's scope***, ***within one's scope***. **L16.** ▸**b** The sphere or area over which any activity operates; range of application; the field covered by a branch of knowledge, an inquiry, etc. Freq. in ***beyond the scope of***, ***within the scope of***. **L16.**
10 A space, an extent, an area, *esp.* a large one; spaciousness. **L16.**
11 NAUTICAL. The length of cable run out when a ship rides at anchor. **L16.**

2a M. ARNOLD Fluctuate idly without term or scope. †**to scope** (*rare*, Shakes.) to the purpose. **3a** J. REYNOLDS The main scope and principal end of this discourse. **5a** C. THUBRON The paper was expanding . . there would be scope for national investigative reporting. **6a** ROBERT JOHNSON In no place plants may take larger scope to spread their branches. **b** *Times* The . . fence of sloping poles . . required more scope than most of the contenders possessed. **9a** M. E. BRADDON Her intellect was rather limited in its scope. **b** G. M. TREVELYAN The scope of this work is confined to the social history of England.

■ **scopeless** *adjective* (*a*) aimless; (*b*) lacking scope or opportunity: **M17.** **scopy** *adjective* (of a horse) having plenty of scope, able to jump well **L20.**

scope /skəʊp/ *noun*². *colloq.* **E17.**
[Abbreviation.]
1 A shortened form of many words terminating in -SCOPE, as ***cystoscope***, ***horoscope***, ***microscope***, ***oscilloscope***, ***periscope***, ***radarscope***, ***telescope***, etc. **E17.** ▸**b** *spec.* A VDU; a radar screen. **M20.**
2 Also ***scope sight***. A telescopic sight for a gun. **M20.**

scope /skəʊp/ *verb.* **M17.**
[from SCOPE *noun*¹.]
†**1** *verb intrans.* Look *at*. *rare.* Only in **M17.**
†**2** *verb trans.* Assess the scope or range of. Only in **E19.**
3 Foll. by *out*: investigate or assess (a person or state of affairs); examine; check out. *US slang.* **L20.**

-scope /skəʊp/ *suffix.*
[mod. Latin *-scopium*, from Greek *skopein* look at, examine.]
Forming nouns denoting scientific instruments or devices for viewing, observing, or examining: formed on Greek bases, as ***autoscope***, ***chronoscope***, ***gyroscope***, ***helioscope***, ***laryngoscope***, ***ophthalmoscope***, etc., on Latin bases, as ***fluoroscope***, ***oscilloscope***, and on English bases, as ***radarscope***, ***sniperscope***.

Scophony /ˈskɒf(ə)ni/ *noun.* **M20.**
[Perh. from Greek *skopein* look at, examine + *-phony*, after *telephony* etc.]
TELEVISION. (Proprietary name for) an early projection television system employing a method of picture scanning using a Kerr cell and a mirrored cylinder.

scopiform /ˈskəʊpɪfɔːm/ *adjective.* Now *rare.* **L18.**
[from Latin *scopa* SCOPA *noun*¹ + -I- + -FORM.]
ZOOLOGY & MINERALOGY. Arranged in bundles; broom-shaped, fascicular.

scopine /ˈskəʊpiːn/ *noun.* **E20.**
[formed as next + -INE⁵.]
CHEMISTRY. A colourless crystalline alkaloid, $C_8H_{13}NO_2$, formed by hydrolysis of scopolamine.

scopolamine /skəˈpɒləmiːn/ *noun.* **L19.**
[from mod. Latin *Scopolia* genus name + AMINE.]
CHEMISTRY & PHARMACOLOGY. A syrupy liquid alkaloid, $C_{17}H_{21}NO_4$, with powerful narcotic and sedative properties, which is found in plants of the nightshade family, esp. the thorn-apple. Cf. HYOSCINE.
■ **scopoˈletin** *noun* a yellow crystalline derivative of coumarin, 7-hydroxy-6 methoxycoumarin, $C_{10}H_8O_4$, commonly found in higher plants **L19.** ˈ**scopolin** *noun* a glycoside of scopoletin **L19.** ˈ**scopoline** *noun* = OSCINE *noun* **L19.**

scopophilia /skɒpə(ʊ)ˈfɪlɪə/ *noun.* Also **scopto-**, **skopto-**, /skɒptə(ʊ)-/. **E20.**
[from Greek *skopia* observation + -PHILIA.]
PSYCHOLOGY. Sexual stimulation or satisfaction derived principally from looking; voyeurism.
■ **scopophiliac** *noun & adjective* (a) scopophilic **M20.** **scopophilic** *noun & adjective* (*a*) *noun* a person displaying scopophilia; (*b*) *adjective* of, pertaining to, or characterized by scopophilia: **M20.**

scopperil /ˈskɒpərɪl/ *noun.* **LME.**
[Origin uncertain. Cf. Icelandic *skoppara-kringla* spinning-top, from *skoppa* spin like a top.]
1 A small top consisting of a disc with a pointed peg passed through the centre and spun with the thumb and finger. *obsolete* exc. *dial.* **LME.** ▸**b** *transf.* An active restless child. Also, a squirrel. *dial.* **E19.**
†**2** HERALDRY. A disc-shaped badge. *rare.* **L15–M16.**
3 A seton. *dial.* **M19.**

scops /skɒps/ *noun.* **E18.**
[mod. Latin *Scops* former genus name from Greek *skōps*.]
More fully ***scops owl***. Any of various small owls of the genus *Otus*, distinguished by their ear-tufts; esp. *O. scops*, widespread in Eurasia and N. Africa.

scoptic /ˈskɒptɪk/ *noun & adjective.* *rare.* **M17.**
[Greek *skōptikos*, from *skōptein* mock, jeer.]
▸†**A** *noun.* In *pl.* Mocking or satirical writings. Only in **M17.**
▸**B** *adjective.* Mocking, satirical. **L17.**

scoptophilia *noun* var. of SCOPOPHILIA.

scopula /ˈskɒpjʊlə/ *noun.* **E19.**
[Late Latin, dim. of *scopa* broom, besom.]
Chiefly ENTOMOLOGY. A small, dense tuft of hairs, esp. on the tarsus; a scopa.
■ **scopulate** *adjective* bearing a scopula **E19.**

-scopy /skəpi/ *suffix.*
[from Greek *skopia* observation, from *skopein* examine, look at: see -Y³.]
Forming nouns denoting: (*a*) (formerly) divination by inspection of something (***ooscopy***, ***ornithoscopy***); (*b*) scientific examination by means of an instrument (***microscopy***, ***telescopy***); (*c*) medical examination of a part of the body (***gastroscopy***, ***peritoneoscopy***).

scorbutic /skɔːˈbjuːtɪk/ *adjective.* **M17.**
[mod. Latin *scorbuticus*, from medieval Latin *scorbutus* scurvy, perh. from Middle Low German *schorbūk*, Dutch *scheurbuik*, from Middle Low German, Middle Dutch *schoren* break, lacerate + *būk* (*buik*) belly.]
MEDICINE. **1** Of or pertaining to scurvy; symptomatic of, caused by, or affected with scurvy. **M17.**
†**2** Of food, remedies, etc.: good against scurvy, antiscorbutic. **L17–L18.**
■ †**scorbutical** *adjective* = SCORBUTIC 1, 2 **M17–M18.**

scorbutus /skɔːˈbjuːtəs/ *noun.* **M19.**
[medieval Latin: see prec.]
MEDICINE. Scurvy.

scorch /skɔːtʃ/ *noun.* **LME.**
[from next.]
1 More fully ***scorch mark***. A mark caused by scorching; a superficial burn. **LME.** ▸**b** BOTANY. A form of necrosis, esp. of fungal origin, marked by browning of leaf margins. **E20.**
2 The action or an act of scorching; a scorching effect. *lit. & fig.* **E17.**
3 A spell of fast driving. *colloq.* **L19.**

2 H. KING Shelters vs from the scorches of the last Judgement.

scorch /skɔːtʃ/ *verb*¹. **ME.**
[Perh. ult. rel to Old Norse *skorpna* be shrivelled.]
1 *verb trans.* **a** Heat or burn the surface of so as to char, parch, harm, or discolour; cause (a plant etc.) to wither or shrivel up through excessive heat or drought. Formerly also foll. by *away*, *up*. **ME.** ▸**b** *transf. & fig.* Affect with a burning sensation; affect, shrivel, or discolour as by excessive heat, proximity to flame, etc. **LME.** ▸**c** Subject (an area) to systematic burning so as to deny its crops and other resources to an invading enemy force. Chiefly in ***scorched earth policy*** below. **M20.**
2 *verb intrans.* Become discoloured, charred, or burnt as a result of heating, overcooking, etc. **LME.**
†**3** *verb trans.* Destroy or consume by fire. **L15–E17.**
4 *verb intrans.* Drive or go at high speed. Also foll. by *away*, *up*. *colloq.* **L19.**

1a E. F. BENSON A torrid August had scorched the lawn to a faded yellow. A. SILLITOE A meal of scorched streaky and broken sausages. **b** M. SPARK Gardnor's hushed confidence continued to scorch Freddy's ear-drums. *Practical Gardening* Fertilisers can sometimes scorch foliage. **c scorched earth policy** a military strategy of burning or destroying all the crops and other resources of an area that would otherwise sustain an invading enemy force. **2** A. AUSTIN Together we will watch the cakes, Nor let them scorch. **4** *Punch* The . . Renault Fuego GTX will scorch from 0–60 mph in just 10.1 seconds.

scorch /skɔːtʃ/ *verb*² *trans.* Now *rare* or *obsolete* exc. *dial.* **LME.**
[Alt. of SCORE *verb*, perh. after *scratch*.]
Slash or cut with a knife. Also (*dial.*), scratch, scarify.

scorcher /ˈskɔːtʃə/ *noun.* **M19.**
[from SCORCH *verb*¹ + -ER¹.]
1 A person who or thing which scorches; *fig.* a scathing or harsh rebuke or attack. **M19.**
2 A very hot day. *colloq.* **M19.**
3 A very attractive girl or woman. *colloq.* **L19.**
4 A person who drives at high speed. *colloq.* **L19.**
5 SPORT. An extremely fast shot or hit. *colloq.* **E20.**
6 A thing, esp. a book or play, that is licentious or risqué. *colloq.* **M20.**

scorching /ˈskɔːtʃɪŋ/ *ppl adjective.* **M16.**
[formed as prec. + -ING².]
That scorches; *spec.* (*colloq.*) (*a*) (of the weather) very hot; (*b*) (of a rebuke etc.) harsh, scathing; (*c*) (of a play etc.) sensational, risqué; (*d*) (of a shot or hit) exceedingly fast.
■ **scorchingly** *adverb* **L16.** **scorchingness** *noun* **L18.**

scordatura /skordaˈtuːra/ *noun.* Pl. **-re** /-re/. **L19.**
[Italian, from *scordare* be out of tune.]
MUSIC. Alteration of the normal tuning of a stringed instrument so as to produce particular effects for certain pieces or passages; an instance of this.

†**scordium** *noun*. Also **-ion**. LME–M19.
[mod. Latin (see below), from Greek *skordion*.]
The water germander, *Teucrium scordium*, formerly used as a diaphoretic, an antidote to poisons, etc.

score /skɔː/ *noun*. LOE.
[Partly from Old Norse *skor* notch, tally, twenty, from Germanic base of SHEAR *verb*, partly from the verb.]
► **I** Pl. in sense 1 same (after a numeral or quantifier), **-s**.
1 A group or set of twenty; approximately twenty (of a particular class). Also (*colloq.*) in *pl.*, a lot *of*, a great many. LOE. ▸**b** *ellipt.* Twenty years of age. Now *rare* exc. in ***threescore***, ***fourscore***, etc. *arch.* ME.
2 A weight of twenty or twenty-one pounds, esp. used in weighing livestock. *arch.* LME.
†**3** A distance of twenty paces. M16–L17.
4 A measure for coals of approximately 20 to 26 corves or tubs. *arch.* M18.
5 Twenty dollars, a twenty-dollar bill, (*US*). Also, twenty pounds sterling, esp. in banknotes. *slang*. E20.

📖 **1** A. E. HOUSMAN Take from seventy springs a score, It only leaves me fifty more. O. SITWELL The . . ground is covered with scores of . . wild flowers. M. KENYON Interviews with two score discovered clients. **b** H. SUTCLIFFE He died at two-score.

► **II 6** A drawn line, orig. one constituting a boundary (chiefly *fig.* in †***out of score***, beyond the limit, excessively, unreasonably); a stroke, a mark. ME.
7 a Orig., a crack, a crevice (*obsolete* exc. *Scot.*). Later, a cut, a notch, a scratch; a line incised with a sharp instrument. LME. ▸**b** NAUTICAL & MECHANICS. A notch or groove in which something is placed; *spec.* (**a**) the groove of a block or deadeye round which a rope passes; (**b**) a notch or groove made in a piece of timber or metal to allow the fitting in of another piece. L18. ▸**c** A narrow, steep path or street leading down to the sea. Also, a steep-sided valley, a cutting. *local*. L18.
8 a The line at which a marksman stands when shooting at a target, or on which competitors stand at the start of a race. Now *rare*. E16. ▸**b** CURLING. = ***hog-score*** s.v. HOG *noun*. M19.
9 MUSIC. A written or printed piece of a composition showing all the vocal and/or instrumental parts arranged one below the other. E18. ▸**b** *spec.* The music composed for a film or (esp.) a musical; the musical part of the soundtrack of a film. Also ***film score***. E20.

📖 **6** SIR W. SCOTT Draw a score through the tops of your t's. **7a** J. BELKNAP An incision is made by two scores . . two inches deep. **9** J. G. COZZENS On the piano . . are the scores of some . . carols. ***miniature score***, ***orchestral score***, ***piano score***, ***vocal score***, etc.

► **III 10** A list, an enumeration; a total. Long. *obsolete* exc. *Scot.* ME.
†**11 a** A notch cut in a stick or tally to record an item in an account; a tally so kept. LME–L16. ▸**b** A mark made to record a point scored in a game. L17–E19.
12 A running account kept by means of tallies or marks made with chalk etc.; a row of such marks, esp. as recording credit in a public house. LME.
13 A sum recorded as owed by a customer esp. in a public house; the amount of an innkeeper's bill or reckoning. E17.
14 Reason; a motive. Chiefly in ***on that score***, ***on the score of***, ***on this score***, below. M17.
15 The list or total of points made by a player or side in a game or awarded to a competitor in a match; the number of points made by a side or an individual. M18. ▸**b** PSYCHOLOGY. A numerical record of the marks allotted to individuals in the measurement of abilities, capacity to learn, or in the assessment of personality. E20. ▸**c** *fig.* The essential point or crux of a matter; the state of affairs; the full facts. Freq. in ***know the score*** s.v. KNOW *verb*. *colloq.* M20.

📖 **10** P. SIDNEY Thou would'st not sett me in their score Whom death to his cold boosome drawes. **11a** T. ELYOT The scores whiche men . . do make on styckes for their remembrance. **b** JOSEPH STRUTT One chalk, or score, is reckoned for every fair pin. **12** SHAKES. *2 Hen. VI* There shall be no money; all shall eat and drink on my score. T. BROWN Preach'd against . . rubbing out of Ale-house Scores. **13** L. P. HARTLEY 'Pay me,' the landlord said . . . The . . men settled their score. **15** C. POTOK Lose the game by a score of eight to seven. *Which Micro?* At the end . . you're given . . a score for enemy destroyed. **c** P. SCOTT 'What's the score about Havildar Baksh?' 'He's a prisoner.' N. STACEY He had the courage to tell me the score as far as I was concerned.

► **IV 16** An act of scoring (*lit.* & *fig.*); *esp.* an act or instance of scoring off another person. Also, a piece of good fortune. *colloq.* M19. ▸**b** The money or goods obtained by means of a successful crime. *slang*. E20. ▸**c** The action or process of obtaining a supply of narcotic drugs; a supplier of narcotic drugs. *slang* (orig. *US*). M20. ▸**d** A person who is the subject of a sexual advance; *esp.* a prostitute's client. *slang*. M20.

📖 **16** *Scotsman* A loud cheer signified that . . this was a distinct score. J. UPDIKE 'She ain't even taught you how to screw,' Esmeralda said, pleased to have an additional score on Candy. **b** *New Yorker* A million dollars from a computer crime is considered a respectable but not an extraordinary score. **d** G. BAXT I . . got my hot tail out of there. I heard the score yelling.

Phrases: ***full score***: see FULL *adjective*. **go off at score** start off vigorously or suddenly. **keep score**, **keep the score** register a score as it is made. ***know the score***: see sense 15c above. **on that score** so far as that is concerned. **on the score of** for the reason of, because of. **on this score** so far as this is concerned. ***open score***: see OPEN *adjective*. ***out of score***: see sense 6 above. **pay off old scores** avenge oneself for past offences. ***short score***: see SHORT *adjective*. **scores of** *colloq.* a lot of, a great many.
Comb.: **scoreboard** (**a**) *arch.* a blackboard in a public house, recording chalked-up debts; (**b**) esp. in CRICKET, a large board for publicly displaying the score in a match; **score-book**: prepared for entering esp. cricket scores in; **score-box** CRICKET a room or hut in which the official scorers work; **score-card** a printed card prepared for entering esp. cricket, baseball, or golf scores in; **score draw** a drawn game in football etc. in which goals are scored; **scoreline** (part of) a line in a newspaper etc. giving the intermediate or final score in a sports contest between two people or sides; **score-reader** a person who practises score-reading; **score-reading** the action or process of reading or playing the piano from a musical score; **score-sheet**: prepared for entering esp. cricket, baseball, or football scores in.
■ **scoreless** *adjective* E17.

score /skɔː/ *verb*. LME.
[Partly from Old Norse *skora* make an incision, count by tallies, from *skor* (see prec.), partly from the noun.]
► **I 1** *verb trans.* Cut the surface of (esp. the skin) with incisions, notches, or scratches; mark with a line or lines, esp. by drawing. LME. ▸**b** Make long parallel cuts on (meat etc.), esp. in preparation for roasting or baking. LME. ▸**c** GEOLOGY. Mark with scratches or furrows, esp. by glacial action. M19.
†**2** *verb trans.* Fracture. Also, wreck (a ship). *Scot.* E–M16.
3 *verb trans.* Form (marks, figures, etc.) by cutting or marking the surface of esp. the skin. L16. ▸†**b** Mark *out* (a path, boundary, etc.). E17–E18.
4 *verb trans.* Draw a line through (writing etc.) as a means of deletion. Freq. foll. by *out*. L17.
5 *verb trans.* NAUTICAL. Make a score or groove in; fix by means of a score. L18.
6 *verb trans.* Criticize (a person) severely. *N. Amer.* E19.
7 *verb trans.* MUSIC. ▸**a** Write out in a score; compose or arrange for orchestral performance, esp. by a specified instrument or instruments (freq. foll. by *for*). M19. ▸**b** Compose the score for (a film, musical, etc.). E20.

📖 **1** E. BOWEN The car . . turned . . , deeply scoring the gravel. A. UTTLEY It had always been a pasture, . . but it was scored by . . little footpaths. TOLKIEN The blade scored it with a dreadful gash, but those . . folds could not be pierced. **b** H. STEPHENS Some butchers . . score the fat . . of the hind quarter. **3** W. IRVING On the bark of the tree was scored the name. M. ROBERTS Nights of . . worry . . scored new lines on her forehead. H. WOUK The boat, scoring a green-white circle on the dark sea, picked up speed. **b** G. SANDYS Hast thou . . Scor'd out the . . Suns obliquer wayes? **4** H. MARTINEAU Scoring the lease from corner to corner, with his . . pen. *Daily Telegraph* The passage in the will containing the bequest . . was scored out. **6** T. R. LOUNSBURY Poor Lipscomb . . was soundly scored for his . . vulgarity. *Nation* He does not hesitate to score the Germans for their . . adherence to their own . . manners. **7a** W. IRVING He pretended to score down an air as the poet played it. *American* Gilchrist skilfully scored the cantata for full orchestra.

► **II 8** *verb trans.* Record as a debt, esp. by making notches on a tally. Also foll. by *up*. LME.
9 *verb trans.* †**a** Count and record the number of (members of a specified class), esp. by making notches on a tally; keep an account of. Also foll. by *up*. LME–L17. ▸**b** BIOLOGY & MEDICINE. Count and record the number of (experimentally treated cells, bacterial colonies, etc.) showing a particular character. M20.
10 †**a** *verb intrans.* Incur a number of debts; obtain drink, goods, etc., on credit. L16–L18. ▸**b** *verb trans.* Add (an item) to a list of debts; incur (a debt). *rare*. L17.
11 *verb trans.* Record (a person) as a debtor. Also foll. by *up*. Now *rare*. L16.
12 a *verb trans.* Set down in the score of a game or contest. Usu. in *pass.* M18. ▸**b** *verb intrans.* Keep the tally of points, runs, etc., in a game or contest; act as scorer. M19.
13 a *verb trans.* Add (a specified number of points) to one's score in a game or contest; count for (a specified number of points) added to a player's score in a game or contest. M18. ▸**b** *verb intrans.* Make a point or points in a game or contest. M19. ▸**c** *verb trans.* BASEBALL. Cause (a team-mate) to score. E20. ▸**d** *verb trans.* & *intrans.* PSYCHOLOGY. Obtain (results) in a test of abilities, capacities, or personality traits; record results in (a test). Cf. SCORE *noun* 15b. E20.
14 a *verb trans.* & *intrans.* Achieve (a success etc.); make (a hit). Freq. in ***score points off*** s.v. POINT *noun*¹. Chiefly *colloq.* L19. ▸**b** *verb trans.* & *intrans.* Make (a gain), esp. dishonestly; *slang* commit (a theft or robbery), steal (goods etc.), esp. from an open counter or display. L19. ▸**c** *verb intrans.* & *trans.* (Of a man) have intercourse with or *with* (a woman), esp. as a casual affair; (of a prostitute) obtain (a client). *slang*. E20. ▸**d** *verb intrans.* & *trans.* Obtain (a narcotic drug), esp. illegally; take (a dose of a narcotic drug). *slang*. M20.

📖 **8** SHAKES. *1 Hen. IV* Score a pint of bastard in the Half-moon. G. A. SALA Three-and-ninepence scored against me on the slate. **9a** A. COWLEY An hundred Loves at Athens score. DRYDEN A whole Hydra more Remains . . too long to score. **11** W. HUNTINGTON Thus I scored up my . . Master, who . . discharged my debts with honour. **12a** E. HOYLE If your Game is scored 1, 2, or 3, you must play the Reverse. **13a** A. TROLLOPE A great many sixpenny points [at whist] were scored. ***score a miss***: see MISS *noun*¹ 4b. **b** *Encycl. Brit.* The player whose ball is in hand cannot score. **c** C. MATHEWSON Schlei made a base hit . . and scored both men. **14a** *Athenaeum* Occasionally the . . editor scores a point. *Manchester Examiner* He scored two unequivocal successes. G. SAINTSBURY The Republic scores by its appeal to . . human weaknesses. **score off** *colloq.* = ***score points off*** s.v. POINT *noun*¹. **b** D. TOPOLSKI I spotted a sugar factory . . and scored a couple of kilos. **c** W. S. BURROUGHS I drifted along taking shots when I could score. **d** W. H. CANAWAY He would like to score with . . Cheryl.

► **III 15** *verb intrans.* Esp. of hounds on a scent: start off strongly and vigorously; go off at score. M19.
■ **scorable** *adjective* able to be scored; from which a score may be made: M20. **scorer** *noun* a person who or thing which scores; *spec.* a person who keeps a record of the score in a game or contest: LME.

scoria /ˈskɔːrɪə/ *noun* & *adjective*. Pl. **-riae** /-riːiː/, (*rare*) **-rias**. LME.
[Latin from Greek *skōria* refuse from *skōr* dung.]
► **A** *noun*. **1** The slag or dross remaining after the smelting out of a metal from its ore. LME.
2 GEOLOGY. Rough masses resembling clinker, formed by the cooling of volcanic ejecta, and of a light aerated texture. L18.
► **B** *adjective*. GEOLOGY. Composed of scoria. L19.
scoria cone = ***cinder-cone*** s.v. CINDER *noun*.
■ **scoriac** *adjective* = SCORIACEOUS M19. **scoriˈaceous** *adjective* of, pertaining to, or resembling scoria L18. **scoriform** *adjective* having the form of or resembling scoria L18.

scoriation /skɔːrɪˈeɪʃ(ə)n/ *noun*. Long *rare* or *obsolete*. L16.
[Aphet. from EXCORIATION.]
An excoriation (*lit.* & *fig.*).

scorify /ˈskɔːrɪfʌɪ/ *verb trans.* M18.
[from SCORIA + -FY.]
1 Reduce to scoria or slag; *esp.* refine or assay (precious metal) by treating in this way a portion of ore fused with lead and borax. M18.
2 Convert (lava) into scoria. *rare*. M19.
■ **scorifiˈcation** *noun* the process or result of scorifying, esp. as a method of refining or assaying M18. **scorifier** *noun* a thing which scorifies something; *spec.* a fireclay vessel used in the process of refining or assaying: M18.

scoring /ˈskɔːrɪŋ/ *verbal noun*. LME.
[from SCORE *verb* + -ING¹.]
The action of SCORE *verb*; an instance or result of this.
Comb.: **scoring block** CARDS a pad of printed score-sheets; **scoring board**: on which the state of the score at a match or contest is shown; **scoring-book**: in which the score of a match or contest is entered; **scoring-booth**, **scoring-box** CRICKET = ***score-box*** s.v. SCORE *noun*; **scoring-card** = ***score-card*** s.v. SCORE *noun*; **scoring-paper** (**a**) = ***score-sheet*** s.v. SCORE *noun*; (**b**) MUSIC printed paper on which a musical score may be entered.

scorious /ˈskɔːrɪəs/ *adjective*. M17.
[from SCORIA + -OUS.]
Of the nature of scoria; having much scoria.

scorn /skɔːn/ *noun*. ME.
[Old French *escarn* corresp. to Provençal *esquern*, from *escharnir*, *eschernir*: see next.]
1 Mockery, derision; contempt. ME.
2 A manifestation of contempt; a derisive utterance or gesture; a taunt, an insult. *arch.* ME.
3 Orig., matter for mockery or derision, something contemptible. Later, an object of mockery or contempt. ME.

📖 **1** M. MEYER Rosamond . . poured scorn on them, mockingly quoting things they had said. ANNE STEVENSON The children would be baptized . . despite her scorn for the rector. **2** TENNYSON I met with scoffs, I met with scorns. **3** MILTON Made of my Enemies the scorn and gaze. W. C. BRYANT A scandal and a scorn To all who look on thee.

Phrases: ***laugh to scorn***: see LAUGH *verb*. **think it scorn**, **think scorn** *arch.* disdain (foll. by *that*, *to do*). **think scorn of** *arch.* despise.
■ **scornful** *adjective* (**a**) full of scorn, contemptuous (*of*), derisive; †(**b**) regarded with scorn, contemptible: ME. **scornfully** *adverb* LME. **scornfulness** *noun* M16.

scorn /skɔːn/ *verb*. ME.
[Aphet. from Old French *escharnir*, *eschernir* from Proto-Romance from Germanic, from base of Old Saxon *skern* etc. jest, mockery.]
†**1** *verb intrans.* Speak or behave contemptuously; use derisive language, jeer. (Foll. by *at*, *with*.) Long *obsolete* exc. *Scot.* Now *rare*. ME.
†**2** *verb trans.* Treat with ridicule, show extreme contempt for, mock, deride. ME–M17.

3 *verb trans.* Hold in disdain or strong contempt, despise, (freq. foll. by *to do*); reject contemptuously. ME.

1 SIR W. SCOTT She gecked and scorned at my northern speech. 3 J. BALDWIN Her mother scorned to dignify these words with her attention. JO GRIMOND They .. scorned loud-speakers as new-fangled contraptions. A. CARTER Buffo, scorning a glass, .. tipped vodka straight .. down his throat.

■ **scorner** *noun* (*arch.*) a person who scorns or mocks something, esp. religion; ***chair of the scorner***, ***seat of the scorner***, etc., (with ref. to *Psalms* 1:1), the position of a mocker esp. of religion: ME.

scorodite /ˈskɒrədʌɪt/ *noun*. E19.
[German *Skorodit* from Greek *skorodon* garlic (so called from its smell when heated): see -ITE¹.]
MINERALOGY. An orthorhombic hydrous ferric arsenate occurring in pale green or greenish-brown crystals and crusts.

scorp /skɔːp/ *noun*. *Military slang*. E20.
[Abbreviation.]
= SCORPION 6. Also ***Rock-scorp***.

scorpaena /skɔːˈpiːnə/ *noun*. E18.
[Latin, from Greek *skorpaina* a kind of fish, app. irreg. fem. from *skorpios* SCORPION.]
Orig., any of various spiny fishes, chiefly of the families Scorpaenidae and Cottidae. Now only as mod. Latin genus name of scorpion fishes.
■ **scorpaenid** *noun* any of various fishes of the family Scorpaenidae, many of which have venomous spines L19. **scorpaenoid** *adjective & noun* (*a*) *adjective* of, pertaining to, or designating this family or the suborder Scorpaenoidei; (*b*) *noun* a scorpaenoid fish: M19.

scorpene /ˈskɔːpiːn/ *noun*. L18.
[Anglicized from prec.]
Orig., = prec. Now only (*US*), a Californian scorpion fish, *Scorpaena guttata*.

scorper *noun* see SCALPER *noun*¹.

Scorpio /ˈskɔːpɪəʊ/ *noun & adjective*. LME.
[Latin *scorpio(n-)*: see SCORPION.]
▶ **A** *noun*. Pl. **-os**.
1 = SCORPIUS; ASTROLOGY (the name of) the eighth zodiacal sign, usu. associated with the period 23 October to 21 November (see note s.v. ZODIAC); the Scorpion. LME.
2 A person born under the sign Scorpio. M20.
▶ **B** *attrib.* or as *adjective*. Of a person: born under the sign Scorpio. L19.
■ **Scorpian** *noun* = SCORPIO *noun* 2 M20.

scorpioid /ˈskɔːpɪɔɪd/ *adjective & noun*. M19.
[Greek *skorpioeidēs*, from *skorpios* SCORPION: see -OID.]
▶ **A** *adjective*. **1** BOTANY. Of a monochasial cyme: in which successive branches arise on opposite sides of the stem and the apical part of the inflorescence is coiled like a scorpion's tail. M19.
2 ZOOLOGY. Resembling a scorpion; belonging to the order Scorpiones. *rare*. M19.
▶ **B** *noun*. **1** BOTANY. A scorpioid cyme. *rare*. M19.
2 ZOOLOGY. A scorpion; a scorpion-like animal. L19.
■ **scorpiˈoidal** *adjective* (BOTANY) = SCORPIOID *adjective* 1 M19.

scorpion /ˈskɔːpɪən/ *noun*. ME.
[Old & mod. French from Latin *scorpio(n-)* extension of *scorpius* from Greek *skorpios*.]
1 Any of various arachnids constituting the order Scorpiones, characterized by the possession of two large pincers or pedipalps, and a long upwardly curved tail bearing a venomous sting. ME. ▸**b** HERALDRY. A charge representing a scorpion. E17. ▸**c** (With specifying word.) any of various other animals related to or resembling the scorpions. E18.
2 (Usu. **S-**.) *The* constellation Scorpius; (now *rare*) *the* zodiacal sign Scorpio. Cf. SCORPIO *noun* 1, SCORPIUS. LME.
3 In *pl.* A whip of torture made of knotted cords or armed with metal spikes (with allus. to 1 *Kings* 12:11). Freq. in ***lash of scorpions***, ***whip of scorpions***. LME. ▸**b** *gen.* Any ancient instrument of torture; ANTIQUITIES a medieval weapon. Usu. in *pl.* M16.
4 *Hist.* An ancient military engine for hurling missiles, used chiefly in the defence of the walls of a town. LME.
5 Any of various fishes armed with spines, *esp.* a scorpion fish. E16.
6 *Military slang.* (A nickname for) a civilian inhabitant of Gibraltar. Also ***Rock scorpion***. M19.
1c ***book scorpion***, ***whip scorpion***, etc.
Phrases: **false scorpion** = PSEUDOSCORPION. †**oil of scorpions** an oily substance prepared from scorpions, used as an antidote against the sting of a scorpion, and for other medicinal purposes. ***Rock scorpion***: see sense 6 above.
Comb.: **scorpion fish** any of various spiny fishes of the family Scorpaenidae, esp. of the genera *Scorpaena* and *Scorpaenodes*, many of which are venomous; **scorpion fly** any of various winged insects of the order Mecoptera, esp. of the genus *Panorpa*, the males of which have an upwardly curved abdomen resembling the tail of a scorpion; **scorpion grass** a plant of the genus *Myosotis*, a forget-me-not (so called from its scorpioid cymes); **scorpion orchid** any of various epiphytic orchids belonging to the genus constituting *Arachnis*, with spider-like flowers, native to eastern and SE Asia; **scorpion senna** a yellow-flowered leguminous shrub of southern Europe, *Hippocrepis emerus*; **scorpion shell** (a shell of) any of various Indo-Pacific gastropods of the genus *Lambis*, with long tubular spines along the outer lip of the aperture; **scorpion-spider** any of various arachnids, *esp.* a whip scorpion (see WHIP *noun*.).
■ **scorpiˈonic** *adjective* (*rare*) (*a*) pertaining to the scorpion; (*b*) ASTROLOGY (usu. **S-**) of, pertaining to, or characterized by the sign of Scorpio: E18. **scorpiˈonid** *adjective* of or pertaining to typical scorpions of the family Scorpionidae L19. **scorpion-like** *adjective* resembling (that of) a scorpion L16.

Scorpius /ˈskɔːpɪəs/ *noun*. OE.
[Latin *scorpius* scorpion, Scorpio from Greek *skorpios*.]
(The name of) a constellation of the southern hemisphere lying partly in the Milky Way, on the ecliptic between Libra and Sagittarius. Cf. SCORPIO *noun* 1, SCORPION 2.

†**scorse** *noun*. *rare* (Spenser). Only in L16.
[from next.]
Barter, exchange.

scorse /skɔːs/ *verb*¹. Long *obsolete* exc. *dial.* E16.
[Origin unkn. Cf. CORSE *verb*, COSS *verb*.]
1 *verb trans.* Barter, exchange. E16.
2 *verb intrans.* Make or effect a barter or exchange. L16.
■ †**scorser** *noun* M16–M18.

†**scorse** *verb*² *trans. rare* (Spenser). Only in L16.
[Italian *scorsa* a run, from *scorrere* from Latin *excurrere*: see EXCUR.]
Chase.

scortation /skɔːˈteɪʃ(ə)n/ *noun*. Now *arch. rare*. M16.
[Late Latin *scortatio(n-)*, from Latin *scortat-* pa. ppl stem of *scortari* associate with prostitutes, from *scortum* prostitute: see -ATION.]
Fornication.

scortatory /ˈskɔːtət(ə)ri/ *adjective*. *rare*. *literary*. L18.
[from Latin *scortat-*: see prec., -ORY².]
Of, pertaining to, or consisting in fornication or lewd behaviour.

scorzalite /ˈskɔːzəlʌɪt/ *noun*. M20.
[Evaristo Pena *Scorza* (b. 1899), Brazilian mineralogist: see -ITE¹.]
MINERALOGY. A hydrous phosphate of aluminium and magnesium, occurring in solid masses and in blue monoclinic crystals, and isomorphic with lazulite.

scorzonera /skɔːzə(ʊ)ˈnɪərə/ *noun*. E17.
[Italian, from *scorzone* from Proto-Romance alt. of medieval Latin *curtio(n-)* poisonous snake, against whose venom the plant may have been regarded as an antidote.]
Any of various plants constituting the genus *Scorzonera*, of the composite family, allied to the goat's-beard; esp. *S. hispanica*, cultivated in Europe for its tapering purple-brown root. Also, the root of *S. hispanica*, eaten as a vegetable.

Scot /skɒt/ *noun*¹.
[Old English *Scottas* (pl.) from medieval Latin *Scotus* from late Latin *Scottus*, whence also Old High German *Scotto* (German *Schotte*): ult. origin unkn.]
1 *Hist.* A member of an ancient Gaelic-speaking people who migrated from Ireland to the northern part of Great Britain around the 6th cent. AD, and from whom the name Scotland ultimately derives. Formerly also, a native or inhabitant of Ireland. OE.
2 A native or inhabitant of Scotland; a person of Scottish birth or descent. ME.
3 (An animal of) a breed of Scottish cattle. *dial.* L18.
4 An irritable or cross person. Also, a fit of irritation, temper. *colloq.* E19.
¶ See note s.v. SCOTCH *adjective & noun*³.

scot /skɒt/ *noun*². LOE.
[Partly from Old Norse *skot* SHOT *noun*¹, partly aphet. from Old French *escot* (mod. *écot*), of Germanic origin. Cf. SHOT *noun*¹.]
1 *Hist.* Orig., a customary tax levied on or contribution paid by a subject to a lord or ruler; a custom paid to a sheriff or bailiff; a local or municipal tax. Later, a payment corresponding to a modern tax, rate, or other assessed contribution (chiefly in ***lot and scot***, ***scot and lot***, below). LOE. ▸**b** *spec.* A tax levied on the inhabitants of the marshes and levels of Kent and Sussex. *local. rare.* L18.
2 A payment, a contribution, a reckoning, esp. for entertainment or at a public house; a share of this. Chiefly in ***pay for one's scot***, ***pay one's scot*** below. ME.
Phrases: **lot and scot** = *scot and lot* below. **pay for one's scot**, **pay one's scot** settle one's share of an account (*lit.* & *fig.*). **scot and lot** a tax levied by a municipal corporation in proportionate shares on its members for the defraying of municipal expenses; the financial burdens of a borough etc.
Comb.: **scotale** (*obsolete* exc. *Hist.*) a festival at which ale paid for by a forced contribution was drunk at the invitation of the lord of a manor or of a forester or bailiff; **scot-free** *adjective* not subject to the payment of scot; (now chiefly *fig.*) exempt from injury, punishment, etc., safe, unharmed (freq. in ***get off scot-free***, ***go scot-free***).

scot /skɒt/ *verb*. *rare*. Infl. **-tt-**. ME.
[from prec.]
†**1** *verb intrans.* Participate, share (*with* a person). Only in ME.
†**2** *verb intrans.* ***scot and lot***, ***lot and scot***, pay one's share of the financial burdens of a borough. *Scot.* LME–E18.
3 *verb trans.* Levy scot on (a person or property); assess for this purpose. M18.

Scot. *abbreviation*.
Scotland; Scottish.

scotch /skɒtʃ/ *noun*¹. LME.
[from SCOTCH *verb*¹.]
1 An incision, a cut, a score, a gash. Now *dial.* LME.
2 *spec.* A line scored or marked on the ground in the game of hopscotch. L17.

scotch /skɒtʃ/ *noun*². Now chiefly *Scot.* & *dial.* E17.
[Origin uncertain: perh. rel. to SKATE *noun*².]
A wedge or block placed under or against a wheel, cask, etc., to prevent movement or slippage.

Scotch /skɒtʃ/ *adjective & noun*³. L16.
[Contr. of SCOTTISH. Cf. SCOTS.]
▶ **A** *adjective*. **1** = SCOTTISH *adjective* 1b. L16. ▸**b** = SCOTS *adjective* 1b. L18. ▸**c** TYPOGRAPHY. Designating a typeface, orig. *gen.* any imported by the US from Scotland, later *spec.* a type of the early 19th cent. revived by the Edinburgh type foundry Miller & Richard. M19.
2 = SCOTS *adjective* 2. L18.
3 Having a quality or qualities attributed to Scottish things or people, esp. frugality or thrift. E19.

1 C. H. PEARSON Maud, the aunt of the Scotch king. A. G. GARDINER The old prides .. of the clans still linger in the forms of the Scotch names. 2 SIR W. SCOTT Able-bodied, and, as the Scotch phrase then went, *pretty* men. 3 E. DYSON He's touched me three times .., and I'm as Scotch as most people.

Special collocations & comb.: ***Scotch asphodel***: see ASPHODEL 2. ***Scotch argus***: see ARGUS 2. **Scotch attorney** *W. Indies* any of various strangler trees of the genus *Clusia* (family Guttiferae). ***Scotch baronial***: see BARONIAL 2. **Scotch Blackface** = ***Scottish Blackface*** s.v. SCOTTISH *adjective*. **Scotch boiler** a fire-tube boiler in which combustion takes place inside the shell. **Scotch bonnet** (*a*) the fairy-ring champignon, *Marasmius oreades*; (*b*) a small, very hot variety of chilli pepper; = HABANERO 2. **Scotch broth** a soup made from beef or mutton with pearl barley and vegetables. **Scotch cap** a man's brimless head-dress, made of firm woollen cloth and decorated with two tails or streamers at the back. **Scotch cart** (chiefly *S. Afr.*) a light strongly built two-wheeled cart, used chiefly for transporting gravel, manure, etc. **Scotch catch** MUSIC a Scotch snap. **Scotch coffee** *slang* hot water flavoured with burnt biscuit. **Scotch collops** (*a*) beef cut small and stewed; (*b*) steak and onions. †**Scotch cloth** a cheap fabric resembling lawn. **Scotch cousin** a distant relative. **Scotch cuddy**, **Scotch draper** (now *arch.* & *dial.*) = SCOTCHMAN 1b. **Scotch egg** a hard-boiled egg enclosed in sausage meat and fried, usu. served cold. **Scotch elm** the wych elm, *Ulmus glabra*. **Scotch fir** = ***Scots pine*** s.v. SCOTS *adjective*. **Scotch glue** an adhesive made from hide and other animal products, used (esp. formerly) in carpentry. **Scotch-Irish** *adjective & noun* (*a*) *adjective* of or pertaining to those inhabitants of Northern Ireland descended fron Scottish settlers or their immediate descendants in other countries; of mixed Scots and Irish descent; (*b*) *noun* Scotch-Irish people collectively. ***Scotch kale***: see KALE 1. ***Scotch*** LOVAGE. **Scotch marmalade** a kind of marmalade orig. made in Scotland, usu. with extra orange peel for richness. **Scotch mist** (*a*) a thick drizzly mist common in the Highlands; (*b*) an unreal or insubstantial thing (freq. used as a retort implying that someone has imagined or failed to understand something); (*c*) whisky served with a twist of lemon; a drink of this. **Scotch pancake** = DROP-SCONE. **Scotch pebble** an agate, jasper, cairngorm, or other semiprecious stone found as a pebble in a stream in Scotland. **Scotch peg** *rhyming slang* the leg. **Scotchprint** a type of coated plastic film used in lithographic printing. **Scotch rose** the burnet rose, *Rosa pimpinellifolia*. ***Scotch snap***: see SNAP *noun* 11. **Scotch spur** HERALDRY a charge representing a prick-spur. **Scotch tape** (proprietary name for) adhesive usu. transparent cellulose or plastic tape. **Scotch-tape** *verb trans.* affix or join with Scotch tape. **Scotch terrier** = ***Scottish terrier*** s.v. SCOTTISH *adjective*. **Scotch thistle** any of several thistles identified with the thistle forming the emblem of Scotland, esp. the spear thistle, *Cirsium vulgare*, and (now usu.) the cotton-thistle, *Onopordum acanthium*. ***Scotch warming-pan***: see WARMING-PAN 2a. **Scotch whisky** whisky distilled in Scotland, esp. from malted barley; a drink of this. ***Scotch*** WOODCOCK. **Scotch yoke** a mechanism by which circular motion is transformed into simple linear motion, consisting of a crank bearing a peg which slides to and fro along a straight slot.
▶ **B** *noun*. **1** = SCOTS *noun* 1. L17.
2 *collect. pl.* *The* Scottish people; the Scots. M18.
3 *ellipt.* (Pl. **-es**.) Something manufactured in, originating in, or associated with, Scotland; *spec.* (*a*) (also **s-**) = ***Scotch whisky*** above; (*b*) a Scotch typeface (sense A.1c above); (*c*) (also **s-**) = ***Scotch peg*** above. M19.

1 SIR W. SCOTT Which is to say, in plain Scotch, the gallows. 2 C. H. PEARSON The Scotch were divided by a quarrel. 3 M. PAGE 'A Scotch and soda,' Julie said to the steward. *attrib.*: D. MACKENZIE He poured another drink from the Scotch bottle.

¶ *Scots* or *Scottish* is generally preferred in Scotland or by people of Scottish descent, except in sense B.3 and the special collocations given above.
■ **Scotchery** *noun* (*rare*) Scotch characteristics M18. **Scotchify** *verb trans.* make Scottish in form, character, or manners L18. **Scotchifiˈcation** *noun* the action or an act of Scotchifying a person or thing M19. **Scotchness** *noun* Scotch quality or character M19.

scotch /skɒtʃ/ *verb*¹ *trans.* LME.
[Origin unkn.]
1 Make an incision or incisions in; cut, score, gash. Now *arch. & dial.* LME.
2 a [After Shakes. *Macb.*] Wound without killing, (temporarily) disable. L18. ▸**b** Stamp out, decisively put an end to, (esp. something dangerous); frustrate (a plan or hope); quash, bring to nothing. E19.

1 P. HOLLAND Many creekes doth scotch and cut Peloponnesus. T. BARKER Wash the Eele . . . Scotch it all along both the sides. **2a** C. MERIVALE The Arian heresy was scotched, if not actually killed. *absol.*: BYRON We will not scotch, But kill. **b** *Expositor* Fanaticism . . should be scotched. M. HOLROYD Any idea . . of marrying was scotched by her father.

scotch /skɒtʃ/ *verb*². E17.
[from SCOTCH *noun*².]
1 *verb intrans.* Hesitate, stick *at*; scruple *to do*. Also, haggle *with* a person *for* something. (Chiefly in neg. contexts.) *obsolete* exc. *dial.* E17.
2 *verb trans.* Block or wedge (a wheel, cast, etc.) with a scotch to prevent movement or slippage. Also foll. by *up*. M17.

Scotchgard /ˈskɒtʃɡɑːd/ *noun*. M20.
[from SCOTCH *adjective* after *Scotch tape* + G(U)ARD *noun*.]
(US proprietary name for) any of a series of organofluorine chemicals used as waterproof grease- and stain-resistant finishes for textiles, leather, etc.

Scotchlite /ˈskɒtʃlʌɪt/ *noun*. M20.
[formed as prec. + LITE *noun*².]
(Proprietary name for) a light-reflecting material containing a layer of minute glass lenses.

Scotchman /ˈskɒtʃmən/ *noun*. Pl. **-men**. LME.
[from SCOTCH *adjective* + MAN *noun*.]
1 = SCOTSMAN 1. LME. ▸**b** A travelling draper or pedlar. Now *arch. & dial.* E18. ▸**c** In full ***Flying Scotchman***. = SCOTSMAN 2. L19. ▸**d** A prickly, bushy pasture grass, *Aciphylla colensoi*. *NZ*. L19.
2 NAUTICAL. A piece of hide, wood, iron, etc., placed over a rope to prevent its being chafed. M19.
3 A two-shilling piece. *S. Afr. colloq.* L19.
4 = SCOTSMAN 3. *S. Afr.* E20.
Phrases: ***Flying Scotchman***: see sense 1c above. **Scotchman hugging a Creole** *W. Indies* = ***Scotch attorney*** s.v. SCOTCH *adjective & noun*³.

Scotchwoman /ˈskɒtʃwʊmən/ *noun*. Pl. **-women** /-wɪmɪn/. E19.
[formed as prec. + WOMAN *noun*.]
= SCOTSWOMAN.

Scotchy /ˈskɒtʃi/ *adjective & noun*. *colloq.* E19.
[from SCOTCH *adjective* + -Y⁶.]
▶ **A** *adjective*. Characteristic of what is Scottish; resembling something Scottish. E19.
▶ **B** *noun*. A Scottish person. M19.
■ **Scotchiness** *noun* E19.

scote /skəʊt/ *verb trans.* *obsolete* exc. *dial.* M17.
[Origin unkn.]
Set a drag on (the wheel of a wagon).

scoter /ˈskəʊtə/ *noun*. L17.
[Origin unkn.]
Each of three northern diving ducks of the genus *Melanitta*, which breed in the Arctic and subarctic and overwinter off coasts further south.
surf scoter, ***velvet scoter***, etc.

scotia /ˈskəʊʃə/ *noun*. M16.
[Latin from Greek *skotia* from *skotos* darkness (with ref. to the dark shadow within the cavity).]
ARCHITECTURE. A concave moulding, esp. at the base of a column; a casement.

†**Scotian** *adjective*. *rare*. E17–E19.
[from medieval Latin *Scotia* Scotland + -AN.]
Of or belonging to Scotland; Scottish.

Scotic /ˈskɒtɪk/ *adjective*. *rare*. M17.
[Late Latin *Scoticus*, formed as SCOT *noun*¹ + -IC.]
†**1** Designating the form of English used in (esp. the Lowlands of) Scotland. Only in M17.
2 *Hist.* Of or pertaining to the ancient Scots (SCOT *noun*¹ 1). L18.

Scotican /ˈskɒtɪk(ə)n/ *adjective*. *rare*. M17.
[formed as prec. + -AN, after *Anglican*.]
Of or pertaining to the reformed Church of Scotland.

Scoticise *verb* var. of SCOTTICIZE.

Scoticism *noun* var. of SCOTTICISM.

Scoticize *verb* var. of SCOTTICIZE.

Scotify *verb* var. of SCOTTIFY.

†**Scotise** *verb* var. of SCOTIZE.

†**Scotism** *noun*¹. *rare*. L16–M18.
[formed as SCOT *noun*¹ + -ISM.]
(A) Scotticism.

Scotism /ˈskəʊtɪz(ə)m/ *noun*². M17.
[formed as next + -ISM.]
†**1** A subtlety held to be characteristic of the Scotists; an instance of hair-splitting. Usu. in *pl.* Only in M17.
2 The teaching or beliefs of Scotus or the Scotists. L19.

Scotist /ˈskəʊtɪst/ *noun & adjective*. M16.
[from John Duns *Scotus* (see below) + -IST.]
Hist. ▶**A** *noun*. A follower or adherent of the scholastic theologian John Duns Scotus (*c* 1266–1308), whose teaching (in opposition to that of Aquinas) emphasized the limitation of reason and maintained that the Incarnation was not dependent on the Fall. M16.
▶ **B** *adjective*. Of, pertaining to, or characteristic of the Scotists or Scotism. M19.
■ †**Scotistical** *adjective* of, pertaining to, or characteristic of the Scotists or Scotism E17–E18.

†**Scotize** *verb*. Also **-ise**. L16.
[from SCOT *noun*¹ + -IZE.]
1 *verb intrans.* Become Scottish in customs, characteristics, etc., *esp.* adopt or favour the principles of the reformed Church of Scotland. L16–M17.
2 *verb trans.* Make Scottish in customs, characteristics, etc., *esp.* imbue with the principles of the reformed Church of Scotland. Chiefly as ***Scotized*** *ppl adjective*. M17–E18.

Scotland Yard /skɒtlənd ˈjɑːd/ *noun*. M19.
[The headquarters of the Metropolitan Police, situated from 1829 to 1890 in Great Scotland Yard, a short street off Whitehall in London, from then until 1967 in New Scotland Yard on the Thames Embankment, and from 1967 in New Scotland Yard, Broadway, Westminster.]
The Criminal Investigation Department of the London Metropolitan Police.

Scot Nat /skɒt ˈnat/ *noun & adjectival phr.* L20.
[Abbreviation.]
= ***Scottish Nationalist*** s.v. SCOTTISH *adjective*.

Scoto- /ˈskɒtəʊ, ˈskəʊtəʊ/ *combining form*¹. M17.
[from SCOT *noun*¹ + -O-.]
Forming adjective and noun combs. with the sense 'Scottish; Scottish and —, Scotland in connection with —', as ***Scoto-Irish***, ***Scoto-Norwegian***.

scoto- /ˈskəʊtəʊ/ *combining form*².
[from Greek *skotos* darkness: see -O-.]
Forming nouns with the sense 'darkness'.
■ **scotophase** *noun* (BIOLOGY) an artificially imposed period of darkness; an artificial night: L20. **scotophor**, **-phore** *noun* a substance which darkens when bombarded by electrons, used as a coating for the screens of cathode-ray tubes to provide the reverse of the imaging behaviour of phosphor coatings M20. **scotoscope** *noun* (*rare*) an instrument which enables the user to see in the dark M17.

scotoma /skɒˈtəʊmə, skə(ʊ)-/ *noun*. Pl. **-mas**, **-mata** /-mətə/. M16.
[Late Latin from Greek *skotōma* dizziness, from *skotoun* darken, from *skotos* darkness.]
MEDICINE. †**1** Dizziness accompanied by dimness of sight. M16–E19.
2 An obscuration of part of the visual field, due to lesion of the retina, the optic nerve, or the ophthalmic centres in the brain. L19.
2 *SCINTILLATING* ***scotoma***.
■ **scotomatous** *adjective* characterized by or affected by a scotoma or scotomata E20. **scotometer** *noun* (OPHTHALMOLOGY) an instrument for diagnosing and measuring scotomata L19. **scotoˈmetric** *adjective* by means of or pertaining to scotometry M20. **scotometry** *noun* the use of a scotometer E20. **scotomia** *noun* (MEDICINE) = SCOTOMA 1 M16.

scotomize /ˈskɒtəmʌɪz, ˈskəʊ-/ *verb trans.* Also **-ise**. E20.
[from Greek *skotoun* darken, make dim-sighted + -IZE.]
PSYCHOANALYSIS. Form a mental blind spot about something, esp. in an attempt to deny items of conflict.
■ **scotomiˈzation** *noun* E20.

†**scotomy** *noun*. LME–E18.
[mod. Latin *scotomia*, alt. of SCOTOMA after diseases in *-ia*: see -Y³.]
MEDICINE. = SCOTOMA 1.

scotophil /ˈskəʊtə(ʊ)fɪl/ *adjective*. Also **skoto-**, **-phile** /-fʌɪl/. M20.
[from SCOTO-² + -PHIL.]
BIOLOGY. Designating a phase of the circadian cycle of a plant or animal during which light inhibits, or does not influence, reproductive activity. Cf. ***photophil(e)*** s.v. PHOTO-.
■ **scotoˈphilic** *adjective* scotophil M20. **scoˈtophily** *noun* the state of an organism in a scotophil phase M20.

scotophobia /skəʊtə(ʊ)ˈfəʊbɪə/ *noun*¹. M20.
[from SCOTO-² + -PHOBIA.]
PSYCHOLOGY. Fear or dislike of the dark.
■ **scotophobic** *adjective* pertaining to or affected with scotophobia L20.

Scotophobia /skɒtə(ʊ)ˈfəʊbɪə, skəʊtə(ʊ)-/ *noun*². L20.
[from SCOTO-¹ + -PHOBIA.]
Dread or dislike of Scotland and things Scottish.

scotopic /skə(ʊ)ˈtɒpɪk/ *adjective*. E20.
[from SCOTO-² + -OPIA + -IC.]
PHYSIOLOGY. Of, pertaining to, or designating vision in dim light, which involves chiefly the rods of the retina. Cf. PHOTOPIC.
■ **scotopia** /-ˈtəʊpɪə/ *noun* dark-adapted vision E20.

Scots /skɒts/ *adjective & noun*. Orig. *Scot. & north*. LME.
[Var. of SCOTTISH. Cf. SCOTCH *adjective & noun*³.]
▶ **A** *adjective*. **1** = SCOTTISH *adjective* 1b. LME. ▸**b** *Hist.* Of the coinage or monetary units formerly used in Scotland (cf. STERLING *adjective* 2a) (usu. *postpositive*). Also, designating any of various weights and measures formerly used in Scotland and differing from the English standard. E16.
2 a Designating or characteristic of the form of northern English spoken in (esp. the Lowlands of) Scotland. M16. ▸**b** Scottish Gaelic. *rare*. M19.
3 = SCOTCH *adjective* 3. Now *rare* or *obsolete*. E17.
1b ***penny Scots***, ***pound Scots***, etc.
Special collocations & comb.: **Scots-Irish** = ***Scotch-Irish*** s.v. SCOTCH *adjective & noun*³. **Scots Nat** *colloq.* a member of the Scottish National Party. **Scots pine** a pine tree, *Pinus sylvestris*, native to the Scottish Highlands and the kind most commonly planted; also called ***Scotch fir***.
▶ **B** *noun*. **1** The form of northern English spoken in (esp. the Lowlands of) Scotland. E16.
2 Scottish Gaelic. Now *rare* or *obsolete*. M19.
¶ See note s.v. SCOTCH *adjective & noun*³.

Scotsman /ˈskɒtsmən/ *noun*. Pl. **-men**. LME.
[from SCOTS *adjective* + MAN *noun*.]
1 A man of Scottish birth or descent; a male Scot. LME.
2 In full ***Flying Scotsman***. An express train running between London and Edinburgh. L19.
3 An edible sea bream, *Polysteganus praeorbitalis*, of South African coasts. *S. Afr.* M20.
■ **Scotsmanship** *noun* the nature or quality of a Scotsman E19.

Scotswoman /ˈskɒtswʊmən/ *noun*. Pl. **-women** /-wɪmɪn/. E19.
[from SCOTS *adjective* + WOMAN *noun*.]
A woman of Scottish birth or descent; a female Scot.

Scott connection /skɒt kəˈnɛkʃ(ə)n/ *noun phr.* E20.
[Charles Felton *Scott* (1864–1944), US electrical engineer.]
ELECTRICAL ENGINEERING. A method of connecting two single-phase transformers to convert a three-phase voltage to a two-phase one (or to two single-phase ones), or vice versa.
■ **Scott-connected** *adjective* M20.

Scottice /ˈskɒtɪsi/ *adverb*. *rare*. E19.
[medieval Latin.]
In (plain) Scots.

Scotticise *verb* var. of SCOTTICIZE.

Scotticism /ˈskɒtɪsɪz(ə)m/ *noun*. Also **Scoticism**. E18.
[from late Latin *Scot(t)icus* + -ISM.]
1 A Scottish word, idiom, or grammatical feature. E18.
2 A (typically) Scottish outlook; adherence to or support for what is Scottish. *rare*. E19.

Scotticize /ˈskɒtɪsʌɪz/ *verb trans. & (rare) intrans.* Also **Scoti-**, **-ise**. M18.
[formed as prec. + -IZE.]
Make or become Scottish in speech, customs, characteristics, etc.
■ **Scotticiˈzation** *noun* L20.

Scottie /ˈskɒti/ *noun*. E20.
[Abbreviation.]
= ***Scottish terrier*** s.v. SCOTTISH *adjective*.

Scottify /ˈskɒtɪfʌɪ/ *verb trans.* Also **Scoti-**. M17.
[from next: see -FY.]
Make Scottish in form, character, or manners. Chiefly as ***Scottified*** *ppl adjective*.
■ **Scottifiˈcation** *noun* the action or process of Scottifying a thing or person; an instance or result of this: M19.

Scottish /ˈskɒtɪʃ/ *adjective & noun*. LOE.
[from SCOT *noun*¹ + -ISH¹, repl. Old English *Scyttisć*. Cf. SCOTCH *adjective & noun*³, SCOTS.]
▶ **A** *adjective*. **1** †**a** Of or pertaining to the ancient Scots (SCOT *noun*¹ 1). LOE–LME. ▸**b** Of, pertaining to, or native to Scotland, the northern part of Great Britain and the United Kingdom and before union with England an independent State; *esp.* (of a person) belonging to Scotland by birth or descent. LOE.
†**2** = SCOTCH *adjective* 3. M16–E17.
3 = SCOTS *adjective* 2. L16.
Special collocations & comb.: ***Scottish baronial***: see BARONIAL 2. **Scottish Blackface** (an animal of) a hardy breed of sheep developed in upland areas of northern Britain, with black legs and muzzle and long wool. **Scottish Chaucerian** any of a number of 15th- and 16th-cent. Scottish poets influenced by and imitating the work of Geoffrey Chaucer. **Scottish-French** *rare* French spoken by a Scot or with a Scottish accent. **Scottish Nationalism** the political programme or ideals of the Scottish National Party. **Scottish Nationalist** *adjective & noun* (*a*) *adjective* of or pertaining to the Scottish National Party or its programme; (*b*) *noun* a member of the Scottish National Party. **Scottish**

National Party a political party seeking autonomy for Scotland, formed in 1934 by an amalgamation of the National Party of Scotland and the Scottish Party. **Scottish terrier** (a dog of) a small stocky breed of terrier, usu. black or brindled, with thick shaggy fur, erect pointed ears and tail, and a square bearded muzzle.

▶**B** *noun*. **1** †**a** The language of the ancient Scots (SCOT *noun*¹ 1); Scottish Gaelic. *rare*. Only in LME. ▸**b** = SCOTS *noun* 1. E17.

2 *collect. pl.* *The* Scottish people; the Scots. *rare*. M17.

¶ See note s.v. SCOTCH *adjective & noun*³.

■ **Scottishly** *adverb* E19. **Scottishness** *noun* M19. **Scottishry** *noun* Scottish character or nationality; a Scottish trait: M20.

Scottishman /ˈskɒtɪʃmən/ *noun*. Long *rare*. Pl. **-men**. E16.
[from SCOTTISH *adjective* + MAN *noun*.]
= SCOTSMAN 1.

scotty /ˈskɒti/ *adjective*. In sense 1 also **S-**. M18.
[from SCOT *noun*¹ + -Y¹.]
1 Characteristically or distinctively Scottish. *rare*. M18.
2 Cross, irritable. *colloq*. L19.

scoundrel /ˈskaʊndr(ə)l/ *noun & adjective*. L16.
[Origin unkn.]
▶**A** *noun*. An unscrupulous villain; a rogue. L16.

> P. G. WODEHOUSE I consider you a scoundrel of the worst type.

▶**B** *adjective*. Of, pertaining to, or characteristic of a scoundrel; scoundrelly. Formerly also, base, degraded in character or type. Now *rare*. M17.

> T. HEARNE The Printer is that scoundrel Rascal. THACKERAY Coarse artifices and scoundrel flatteries.

■ **scoundreldom** *noun* the world of scoundrels, scoundrels collectively; scoundrelism: M19. **scoundrelism** *noun* the character, conduct, or practices of a scoundrel; a scoundrelly act or trait: E17. **scoundrelly** *adjective* that is a scoundrel; of, belonging to, or characteristic of a scoundrel; characterized by scoundrelism: L18.

scoup /skaʊp/ *verb intrans*. Chiefly *Scot*. LME.
[Origin unkn.]
Bound, caper, skip; (of an animal) progress with leaps and bounds.

scour /ˈskaʊə/ *noun*¹. *obsolete* exc. *Scot*. ME.
[Origin uncertain: cf. Old Norse *skúr* a shower, SCOUR *verb*².]
1 The action of scouring or moving hastily; an instance of this; a run, a rush. ME.
2 An onset, an attack. ME.
3 A gusty shower of rain; the blowing of a strong wind. L18.

scour /ˈskaʊə/ *noun*². E17.
[from SCOUR *verb*¹.]
1 An apparatus for washing auriferous earth or sand in order to separate the gold. E17.
2 A stretch of river or seabed where the bottom is scoured by the current; a shallow place in a river where the bed is of gravel. L17.
3 The action or an act of scouring; an instance of this; the state of being scoured, esp. by a swift water current. E18.
†**4** A hearty drink *of*; a swig. *Scot*. E18–E19.
5 Diarrhoea, esp. in cattle. Also in *pl*., an attack of this (chiefly *US*). M18.
6 A substance used for scouring. L19.
7 A building in which wool is scoured. *Austral. & NZ*. L19.
5 ***white scour(s)***: see WHITE *adjective*.

scour /ˈskaʊə/ *verb*¹. ME.
[Middle Low German, Middle Dutch *schüren* from Old French *escurer* (mod. *écurer*) from late Latin *excurare* (in medieval Latin (*e*)*scurare*), formed as EX-¹ + *curare* take care of, (medieval Latin) clean, from *cura* CURE *noun*¹.]
1 *verb trans*. Cleanse or polish (esp. metal) by hard rubbing with soap, chemicals, sand, etc. Also foll. by adjective compl., *from*, *of*. ME. ▸†**b** *verb trans*. Wear (fetters); sit in (the stocks). *slang*. LME–L17. ▸**c** *verb trans*. Thrust (a sword, knife, etc.) into a person's body. *hyperbol*. E17. ▸**d** *verb intrans*. Of a plough: pass easily through soil, without earth etc. adhering to the mould-board; *fig*., succeed. (Usu. in neg. contexts.) *US*. L19.
2 *verb trans*. Rid, clear, (a district, the sea, etc.) *of* or *from* an enemy or other unwanted occupant. ME.
3 *verb trans*. Remove grease or dirt from (cloth, wool, silk, etc.) by the use of soap, chemicals, etc. LME.
4 *verb trans*. Cleanse (a wound, a sore, an animal's carcass, etc.) with a medicament or other preparation. Now *rare*. LME.
5 *verb trans*. **a** Clear out or *out* (a ditch, drain, pipe, etc.) by the removal of clogging or blocking matter. Also, clear out or cleanse (a channel etc.), esp. by the natural action of water. LME. ▸**b** Clear or refresh (the throat) with liquor. *Scot*. L18.
6 a *verb trans*. Act as or administer a drastic purgative to; purge (the bowels) drastically; cleanse by purging. LME. ▸**b** *verb intrans*. Act as a purge. Also, be purged drastically; (of livestock) have diarrhoea. L16.
7 *verb trans*. Beat, scourge, (chiefly *fig*.). Also, punish, treat severely. *obsolete* exc. *Scot*. LME.
8 *verb trans*. Remove, get rid of, (esp. rust or dirt) by hard rubbing with soap, chemicals, sand, etc. Freq. foll. by *away*. LME. ▸†**b** Rid a district by force of (an enemy or other unwanted occupant). Also foll. by *from*, *out of*. L15–M18. ▸†**c** Discharge, evacuate, (pus or other morbid matter, excrement, etc.). L16–M18. ▸**d** Remove or clear away (esp. clogging or blocking matter) by the action of water. L16.
9 *verb trans*. Chiefly MILITARY. Subject (a position, body of men, etc.) to a burst of gunfire; command (a position etc.) with one's guns. M16.
10 *verb trans*. Wash (the hands, face, etc.) vigorously; scrub. Formerly also, cleanse (the teeth) by chewing a substance. Now *joc*. L16.

> **1** J. ARBUTHNOT Soap and Sand to scowre the Rooms. J. FULLER The basins were being scoured. *fig*.: T. FULLER Scoured bright an old holy-day with a new solemnitie. **c** SIR W. SCOTT I should scour my knife between your ribs. **2** ALBAN BUTLER He scoured the sea of pirates. **3** *New Zealand Herald* Half the New Zealand clip is scoured before export. **4** J. WOODALL To cleanse and scowre ulcers. H. GLASSE Take your eel and scour it well with salt. **5a** G. THORNLEY He scowred the Fountains, that the Water might be clear. G. SWIFT The less water a river conducts the less . . capacity to scour its channel. J. RABAN The Atlantic tide here . . was too feeble to scour the harbour clean. **6a** P. HOLLAND To feed Pikes . . and to scoure them from the . . muddy fennish taste. J. MINIFIE Water . . so alkaline as to be undrinkable, scouring both cattle and men. **b** W. COLES Great Celandine . . scowreth and cleanseth effectually. W. H. PARKER The cattle scour profusely after a time. **8** R. SANDERSON The stains will not easily . . be scoured off again. *transf*.: J. RABAN The sand . . will scour the skin from one's face. **b** T. FULLER King Saul . . scoured Witches out of all Israel. **c** T. VENNER It . . scowreth downwards crude and phlegmaticke humors. **d** C. LYELL The tide enters . . each channel, scouring out mud. **10** SWIFT British Midas' dirty Paws; Which . . the Senate strove to scour. R. ELLIS And teeth a native lotion hardly scours quite pure.

scour /ˈskaʊə/ *verb*². LME.
[Rel. to SCOUR *noun*¹. Cf. SKIRR.]
1 *verb intrans*. **a** Move *about* or range hastily or energetically, esp. in search or pursuit of something. LME. ▸**b** Move rapidly, go in haste, run, esp. in a specified direction. LME. ▸†**c** Depart in haste, run away, decamp. Chiefly *colloq*. L16–M18.
2 *verb trans*. **a** Pass rapidly over or along (a tract of land or water); *esp*. traverse in search or pursuit of something. LME. ▸**b** Look quickly over, consider, scan. L19.
†**3** *slang*. **a** *verb intrans*. Roister in the streets at night, causing damage to property and ill-treating or attacking the watch, travellers, etc. L17–M18. ▸**b** *verb trans*. Ill-treat or attack (the watch, travellers, etc.) while roistering in the streets at night. L17–E18. ▸**c** *verb trans*. Roister through (the streets) at night. L17–M18.

> **1a** R. KNOLLES Scouring alongst the coast of Italie. *Daily Telegraph* The . . authorities scoured fruitlessly about in quest of a new site. *Times* Forced to scour round local houses for a telephone. **b** SOUTHEY Through the red sky terrific meteors scour. **c** J. VANBRUGH The Regiment scours when the Collonel's a Prisoner. **2a** S. JOHNSON We may scour the country together. J. W. SCHULTZ The hunters scoured the foothills in quest of deer. **b** H. CARPENTER Davidson . . scoured the literary journals for anything that might interest Auden. A. GUINNESS I watched his sad eyes scour the Roman hills. **3a** M. PRIOR So thro' the Street at Midnight scow'rs. **b** DRYDEN Scowring the Watch grows out of fashion wit.

scourer /ˈskaʊərə/ *noun*¹. Now *rare*. LME.
[Orig. aphet. from Old French *descouvreor*, from *desco(u)vrir* DISCOVER, later from SCOUR *verb*²: see -ER¹.]
†**1** A person sent out to reconnoitre; a military scout or spy. LME–E19.
†**2** A person in the habit of roistering through the streets at night, causing damage to property and ill-treating or attacking the watch, travellers, etc. L17–M19.
3 A person who ranges over land or sea. L19.

scourer /ˈskaʊərə/ *noun*². LME.
[from SCOUR *verb*¹ + -ER¹.]
A person who or thing which scours something; *spec*. (*a*) a person who cleanses or polishes esp. metal by hard rubbing with soap, sand, chemicals, etc.; †(*b*) a wad or sponge for cleaning out the bore of a gun; a ramrod fitted with such a contrivance; (*c*) a purgative agent, a cathartic; (*d*) an implement or contrivance for scouring or scrubbing.

scourge /skəːdʒ/ *noun*. ME.
[Aphet. from Old French *escurge*, *escorge*, from *escorgier*: see next.]
1 A whip, a lash; *esp*. a whip used as an instrument of punishment. ME.
2 A person or thing seen as a figure of severe punishment or retributive justice. Also, a cause of calamity or suffering, esp. on a large scale. LME.
†**3** BOTANY. A runner, a creeping shoot. LME–L16.

> **1** G. WHITE The happy schoolboy brings . . forth His long forgotten scourge. TENNYSON Mortify Your flesh . . with scourges and with thorns. **2** SHELLEY Our poverty . . was God's scourge for disobedient sons. LYNDON B. JOHNSON The death rate from . . pneumonia and other traditional scourges declined. L. NKOSI He is known as the scourge of the Establishment. **the Scourge of God** [Latin *flagellum Dei*] Attila, the leader of the Huns in the 5th cent. AD. ***white scourge***: see WHITE *adjective*.

scourge /skəːdʒ/ *verb trans*. ME.
[Old French *escorgier* from Proto-Romance, from Latin EX-¹ + *corrigia* thong, whip.]
1 Beat with a scourge; whip severely, flog. ME. ▸**b** Drive or force (as) by the blows of a scourge. M17.
2 Punish severely, chastise; castigate with satire or invective; afflict; oppress; devastate. LME.
3 Exhaust the fertility of (land). *Scot*. M18.

> **1** J. AGEE To be scourged with a cat-o'-nine tails. *fig*.: J. BUCHAN Mudflats which were being scourged by a south-west gale. **b** MILTON Till the wrauth . . scourge that wisdom back to Hell. **2** AV *Heb*. 12:6 For whome the Lord loueth hee chasteneth, and scourgeth euery sonne whom he receiueth.

■ **scourger** *noun* (*a*) *gen*. a person who scourges someone or something (*lit. & fig*.); †(*b*) = FLAGELLANT 1: L15.

Scourian /ˈskʊrɪən, ˈskaʊrɪən/ *adjective*. M20.
[from *Scourie*, a village on the west coast of Sutherland, Scotland + -IAN.]
GEOLOGY. Of, pertaining to, designating, or formed by an early metamorphic episode undergone by the Lewisian rocks of NW Scotland.

scouring /ˈskaʊərɪŋ/ *noun*. ME.
[from SCOUR *verb*¹ + -ING¹.]
1 The action of SCOUR *verb*¹; an act or instance of this. ME.
2 Diarrhoea, esp. in livestock; (freq. in *pl*.) an attack of this. L16.
3 *sing*. & in *pl*. Dirt, refuse, etc., removed by scouring. L16.
Comb.: **scouring machine**, **scouring mill** an apparatus for scouring cloth after weaving; **scouring pad** a pad of abrasive material for cleaning kitchenware etc.; **scouring paper** emery-paper, glass-paper; **scouring powder** an abrasive powder for cleaning kitchenware etc.; **scouring rush** any of several horse-tails, esp. rough horsetail, *Equisetum hyemale*, having stems rough with silica, used for scouring and polishing; **scouring-stone** a stone used for cleaning paved floors.

Scouse /skaʊs/ *noun & adjective*. In sense 1 also **s-**. M19.
[Abbreviation of LOBSCOUSE.]
▶**A** *noun*. **1** = LOBSCOUSE. M19.
2 *slang*. **a** A native or inhabitant of Liverpool, a city in NW England. M20. ▸**b** The dialect of English spoken in Liverpool, the manner of pronunciation or accent characteristic of this. M20.
▶**B** *attrib*. or as *adjective*. Of or pertaining to Liverpool or its inhabitants or dialect. *slang*. M20.
■ **Scouser** *noun* (*slang*) = SCOUSE *noun* 2a M20.

scout /skaʊt/ *noun*¹. Long *obsolete* exc. *dial*. LME.
[Old Norse *skúte*: cf. *skúta* jut out, cogn. with *skjóta* SHOOT *verb*.]
A high overhanging rock.

scout /skaʊt/ *noun*². LME.
[Middle Dutch *schûte* (Dutch *schuit*) rel. to Old Norse *skúta* (Danish *skude*) light fast vessel, perh. from base also of SHOOT *verb*. Cf. SCHUIT, SHOUT *noun*¹.]
A flat-bottomed Dutch boat, galliot-rigged, used chiefly in rivers and coastal waters. Also, a vessel resembling this used in warfare.

scout /skaʊt/ *noun*³. M16.
[Old French *escoute*, from *escouter*: see SCOUT *verb*¹. Cf. earlier SCOUT-WATCH.]
1 The action of seeking (esp. military) information (freq. in ***on the scout***); an instance of this; a scouting or reconnoitring expedition. Also ***scout-round***. M16.
2 a Chiefly MILITARY. A person sent out ahead of a main force in order to get information about the enemy's position, movements, strength, etc. M16. ▸**b** More fully ***scout bee***. A bee searching for a new site for a swarm to settle or for a new food-source. M19. ▸**c** (Usu. **S-**.) A member of a youth organization now known as the Scout Association, founded for boys in 1908 by Lord Baden-Powell and since 1990 admitting girls, intended to develop character esp. by open-air activities. Also (chiefly *joc. & derog*.), a boy or man who is obtrusively honest and inexperienced. Also (orig.) ***Boy Scout***. E20. ▸**d** = ***talent scout*** s.v. TALENT *noun*¹. E20. ▸**e** A fellow, a chap, a person. Freq. in ***good scout***. *arch. colloq*. E20.
3 Chiefly MILITARY. A body of men sent out to gain information. Now *US*. L16.
4 a A person who keeps watch over the actions of another; *spec*. †(*a*) a mean spy, a sneak; (*b*) in oil-drilling operations, a person employed by a company to keep watch on the activities of other companies; (*c*) SPORT a person employed to observe and report on the performance of a rival team or club; (*d*) a police officer. L16. ▸†**b** A watch, a pocket timepiece. *slang*. L17–E19.

5 a A warship adapted for the purposes of reconnoitring. E18. ▸**b** An airship or aeroplane used for reconnoitring; a lightly-armed fighter aeroplane. Also ***scout plane***. E20.

6 CRICKET & BASEBALL etc. Orig., a fielder. Later, a person, esp. a boy, employed to run after the balls at practice. Now *rare* or *obsolete*. E19.

> **1** P. SCHUYLER Capt. Baker . . went upon a scout and . . was shot. P. DICKINSON Send a bloke to do a preliminary scout round. **2a** SHAKES. *1 Hen. VI* What tidings send our Scouts? W. IRVING Throwing out scouts in the advance. **b** T. HOOPER About 2 per cent of the bees reaching foraging age become scouts. **c** J. I. M. STEWART Mark's absolutely the Boy Scout. **d** M. RICHLER He played hockey well enough to interest professional scouts. **e** J. LE CARRÉ I've got nothing against old Adrian. He's a good scout. **3** I. ALLEN He sent a scout of about 300 . . to hunt at the mouth of Otter Creek. W. FAULKNER A scout of two or three would lurk about the Varner fence. **4a** *Athletic Journal* The scout should familiarize himself . . with the types of defense . . used by opponents. **5a** *London Gazette* A French Scout of 40 Guns. **b** E. BLUNDEN Bayonets and accoutrements not unnoticed by German flying Scouts. **6** J. A. GIBBS The famous Gloucestershire hitter has made things merry for spectators and scouts alike. N. CARDUS Great gaps between the leg-side scouts.

Phrases: ***Boy Scout***: see sense 2c above. ***Cub Scout***: see CUB *noun*[1] 4. **Girl Scout** *US* a member of an organization for girls founded in the US in 1912 on the model of the British Guide Association and known as the Girl Scout Association. ***King's Scout***: see ***Queen's Scout*** below. ***Lone Scout***: see LONE *adjective*. **Queen's Scout, King's Scout** a Scout who holds the highest award of proficiency during the reign of a queen (or king). ***talent scout***: see TALENT *noun*[1]. ***Venture Scout***: see VENTURE *noun*.

Comb.: ***scout bee***: see sense 2b above; **scout car** (*a*) *US* a police patrol car; (*b*) MILITARY a fast armoured vehicle used for reconnaissance and liaison; **Scout Law** a code of conduct enjoined on a Scout to which a member must promise obedience; ***scout plane***: see sense 5b above; **Scout's honour** the oath taken by a Scout, used as a protestation of honour and sincerity.

■ **Scoutery** *noun* (chiefly *joc.* & *derog.*) the characteristic attitude or activity of a Scout (only in ***Boy Scoutery***) M20. **Scoutish** *adjective* (chiefly *joc.* & *derog.*) characteristic of a Scout in attitude or activity (only in ***Boy Scoutish***) M20. **Scoutism** *noun* = SCOUTERY (only in ***Boy Scoutism***) M20.

scout /skaʊt/ *noun*[4]. *Scot. & north.* L16.
[Origin unkn.]
Any of various sea birds of British coasts, as the guillemot, the puffin, and the cormorant.

scout /skaʊt/ *noun*[5]. E18.
[Origin uncertain: perh. identical with SCOUT *noun*[3].]
A college servant, esp. at Oxford University.

scout /skaʊt/ *verb*[1]. LME.
[Aphet. from Old French *escouter* (mod. *écouter*) alt. of *ascolter* from Proto-Romance, from Latin *auscultare* listen.]
1 *verb intrans.* Act as a scout; move about in search of or look around for information. Also *colloq.* (freq. foll. by *about, around*), make a search. LME.
2 *verb intrans.* Skulk, lie concealed. *obsolete* exc. *dial.* L16.
†**3** *verb trans.* Watch or spy on (a person). Also foll. by *about, round*. *rare*. Only in 17.
4 *verb trans.* Explore, examine, get information about (territory etc.). E18.
†**5** *verb intrans.* Act as a fielder in cricket. L18–E20.
6 *verb trans.* & *intrans.* SPORT. Observe and report on the performance of (a rival team or club). Orig. & chiefly *US*. E20.
7 a *verb trans.* Observe (a team, company, or individual) with a view to identifying and recruiting to one's own organization suitably talented people. M20. ▸**b** *verb intrans.* Look for suitably talented people for recruitment to one's own organization; act as a talent scout. M20.

> **1** LD MACAULAY Keyes . . had been out scouting among his old comrades. *Art Line* They . . scout for 'great' pictures in the trouble-torn areas of the world. **4** B. RUBENS They had sent him . . to scout the lay of the land. C. RYAN To scout the area and bring back information about German positions. **6** *Sun (Baltimore)* Dick Jamerson . . scouted Fordham in its 16-10 win over Southern Methodist. **7a** *Rolling Stone* No one seems to have scouted him; he was offered no athletic scholarships. **b** *Washington Post* All had either coached or scouted for Denver after their playing days.

scout /skaʊt/ *verb*[2] *trans.* E17.
[Prob. of Scandinavian origin from base of Old Norse *skjóta* SHOOT *verb* (cf. *skúta*, *skúti* a taunt, *skútyrði*, *skotyrði* abusive language).]
†**1** Mock at, deride. E17–M18.
2 Reject (a suggestion etc.) with scorn; treat (an idea etc.) as absurd. E18.

> **2** S. LEACOCK Danger? pshaw! fiddlesticks! everybody scouted the idea. R. FIRBANK Audaciously scouting the Augustinian theory 'that the Blessed Virgin conceived our Lord through the Ears.'

†**scout** *verb*[3] see SCOOT *verb*[1].

scouter /ˈskaʊtə/ *noun*. M17.
[In sense 1 from SCOUT *verb*[1], in sense 2 from SCOUT *noun*[3]: see -ER[1].]
1 A person who scouts, a scout. M17.
2 (Usu. **S-**.) An adult leader of the Scouts (SCOUT *noun*[3] 2C). M20.

scouth /skaʊθ/ *noun*. *Scot.* L16.
[Origin unkn.]
Opportunity, scope. Also, abundance, plenty.

scouting /ˈskaʊtɪŋ/ *verbal noun*. M17.
[In sense 1 from SCOUT *verb*[1], in sense 2 from SCOUT *noun*[3]: see -ING[1].]
1 The action or practice of SCOUT *verb*[1]. M17.
2 The characteristic activity and occupation of a Scout (SCOUT *noun*[3] 2c); the Scout movement itself. E20.

scoutmaster /ˈskaʊtmɑːstə/ *noun*. L16.
[from SCOUT *noun*[3] + MASTER *noun*[1].]
A leader or captain of a band of scouts; *spec.* (usu. **S-**) the Scouter in charge of a group of Scouts.
Scoutmaster General *Hist.* the chief of the intelligence department of the Parliamentary army in the English Civil War.
■ **scoutmastering** *noun* the occupation of a scoutmaster M20. **scoutmasterly** *adjective* resembling or characteristic of a scoutmaster M20.

†**scout-watch** *noun*. LME.
[formed as SCOUT *noun*[3] + WATCH *noun*. Cf. SCOUT *noun*[3].]
1 A sentinel; a person who keeps watch, a guard. LME–E18.
2 The action of keeping watch and guard (freq. in ***make scout-watch***). LME–E17.
3 A body of men set to watch and keep guard. E16–E17.

scovan /ˈskəʊv(ə)n/ *noun*. L18.
[Cornish dial., of unkn. origin.]
MINING. Tin ore with few impurities.
scovan lode a vein of hard tin ore in which the metal occurs without gossan, usu. with quartz and chlorite.

scove /ˈskəʊv/ *noun*. L18.
[Cornish dial., of unkn. origin.]
In Cornish mining, = prec.

scovel /ˈskʌv(ə)l/ *noun*. Long *obsolete* exc. *dial.* M16.
[French †*escouvelle* (mod. *écouvillon*) dim. of †*escouve* (from Latin *scopa*) broom. Cf. next.]
A baker's malkin.

scovin /ˈskʌvɪn/ *noun*. *obsolete* exc. *dial.* M17.
[Alt.]
= prec.

scow /skaʊ/ *noun*[1]. *Scot.* E16.
[Origin uncertain: perh. rel. to next.]
A strip or stave of wood. Usu. in *pl.*

scow /skaʊ/ *noun*[2] & *verb*. M17.
[Dutch *schouw*, earlier *schouwe*, *schoude* = Low German *schalde* rel. to Old Saxon *skaldan* push (a boat) from the shore. Cf. SCOW *noun*[1], *noun*[3].]
▸ **A** *noun*. **1 a** A large flat-bottomed lighter or punt. Also (*joc.* & *derog.*), any boat of poor or inferior quality. Chiefly *Scot.* & *US*. M17. ▸**b** A small flat-bottomed racing yacht. *US*. E20.
2 *transf.* Any of various containers or vehicles used for transporting loads. *US*. M20.
▸ **B** *verb trans.* Transport, carry *over*, in a scow. Chiefly *Scot.* & *US*. M18.
1a ***sturgeon scow***: see STURGEON 2.

scow /skaʊ/ *noun*[3]. *slang*. *derog.* Orig. *Scot.* M19.
[Origin uncertain: perh. a transf. use of SCOW *noun*[1] or *noun*[2].]
A woman, *esp.* an ugly or ungainly one.

scowbanker /ˈskaʊbaŋkə/ *noun*. Now *slang* & *dial.* M18.
[Origin unkn.]
A loafer. Formerly also, a person engaging in unfair business practices, a dishonest or unscrupulous trader.
■ **scowbank** *verb* & *noun* (*a*) *verb intrans.* loaf; (*b*) *noun* = SCOWBANKER: M19.

scowder /ˈskaʊdə/ *verb* & *noun*. *Scot.* E16.
[Origin unkn.]
▸ **A** *verb trans.* & *intrans.* Scorch, burn slightly. E16.
▸ **B** *noun*. **1** Scorching, baked slight burning. L18.
2 A roughly baked oatcake; *fig.* an inexperienced or stupid person. *Anglo-Irish*. M19.
■ **scowdering** *ppl adjective* that scowders; (of cold etc.) withering, blighting: L18.

scowl /skaʊl/ *noun*. E16.
[from the verb.]
A gloomy, sullen, or threatening look; *esp.* a heavy frown expressing anger.

> F. NORRIS His frown had lowered to a scowl. S. MIDDLETON This child screwed his face into a scowl of hatred. *transf.*: BROWNING Sky—what a scowl of cloud.

scowl /skaʊl/ *verb*. LME.
[Prob. of Scandinavian origin (cf. Danish *skule* cast down one's eyes, give a sidelong look), perh. ult. rel. to Old English *scūlēgede* squint-eyed.]
1 *verb intrans.* Look with a scowl; look angry or sullen. Foll. by *at, on, upon*. LME. ▸**b** Be exhibited or expressed with a scowl. *poet.* E18.
2 *verb intrans.* Of a thing: present a gloomy, forbidding, or threatening aspect. L16.
3 *verb trans.* Direct or express with a scowl. *poet. rare.* M17.

> **1** C. STEAD You sit there scowling with a hangdog expression. P. FARMER Herr Professor . . scowled at the way I stumbled over every elementary phrase. M. ATWOOD I scowled at them. Their voices were way too loud. **b** W. IRVING A menace scowled upon the brow. **2** W. S. CHURCHILL Its . . stone structure which still scowls upon the roofs of Andelys. **3** T. GRAY Thirst and Famine scowl A baleful smile upon their baffled Guest.

■ **scowler** *noun* M19. **scowlingly** *adverb* in a scowling manner M18.

scowly /ˈskaʊli/ *adjective*. M20.
[from SCOWL *noun*, *verb*: see -Y[1].]
Given to scowling; sullen, morose.

SCP *abbreviation*.
Single cell protein.

SCPS *abbreviation*.
Society of Civil and Public Servants.

SCR *abbreviation*.
1 Senior Common (or Combination) Room.
2 ELECTRONICS. Silicon-controlled rectifier.

scr. *abbreviation*.
Hist. Scruple(s) (of weight).

scrab /skrab/ *noun*. *Scot.* & *north.* LME.
[Prob. of Scandinavian origin: cf. Swedish dial. *scrabba* and CRAB *noun*[2].]
The crab-apple; the tree bearing this, *Malus sylvestris* (also ***scrab-tree***).

scrab /skrab/ *verb trans.* *obsolete* exc. *Scot.* & *dial.* Infl. **-bb-**. L15.
[Dutch *schrabben*: see SCRABBLE *verb*.]
1 Scratch, claw. L15.
2 Snatch, grab. *rare*. M19.

scrabble /ˈskrab(ə)l/ *noun*[1]. L18.
[from SCRABBLE *verb*.]
1 A scramble; a confused struggle, a free-for-all. *N. Amer.* L18.
2 A scrawled written character; a piece of scrawled writing; a scrawl, a scribble. M19.
3 The action or an act of scrabbling. L19.

> **1** R. D. SAUNDERS The toughest scrabble you . . ever saw in Missouri politics. **2** P. F. TYTLER Peregrine's letters they could read, but the Duchess . . defied them . . with her fearful scrabbles. *Athenaeum* A composition . . executed in a scrabble of lines which wants repose. **3** T. B. ALDRICH The scrabble of the animal's four paws . . on the gravelled pathway.

Scrabble /ˈskrab(ə)l/ *noun*[2]. M20.
[Origin unkn.]
(Proprietary name for) a game in which players use lettered tiles to form words on a special board.
■ **Scrabbler** *noun* a person who plays Scrabble M20.

scrabble /ˈskrab(ə)l/ *verb*. M16.
[Middle Dutch *schrabbelen* frequentative of *schrabben* scratch, scrape, cf. synon. Middle Dutch *schrāven*. Cf. SCRAB *verb*, SCRUBBLE.]
1 *verb intrans.* Make marks at random; write in rambling or scrawling characters; scrawl, scribble. M16. ▸**b** *verb trans.* Write or depict (a thing) scrawlingly; scrawl on (a thing). Cf. earlier SCRABBLED *adjective*. M19.
2 *verb intrans.* Make hurried scratching movements; scratch or grope *about* hurriedly to find or collect something. L16. ▸**b** *verb trans.* Make hurried scratching movements with. *rare*. L19.
3 *verb intrans.* Scramble on hands and feet; stumble or struggle along. Freq. foll. by *up*. M17.
4 *verb trans.* Get, form, or move (a thing) by hurried scratching. Also foll. by *up*. M17.
5 *verb intrans.* Struggle or scramble *for*. *rare*. L17.

> **1** AV *1 Sam.* 21:13 He . . scrabled on the doores of the gate. **b** C. M. YONGE I do scrabble down things that tease me. HUGH MILLER To scrabble his initials with my fingers, in red paint. **2** R. WEST I went . . to scrabble for Nancy's shoes in the dark cupboard. P. BARKER He scrabbled at the slippery sides to save himself. P. CUTTING We could hear rats scrabbling in the rubbish piles. **b** W. DE LA MARE Scrabbling her forehoofs on the treacherous waste. **3** E. BOWEN All three scrabbled up a steep shingly incline. P. WYLIE I scrabbled back to the stern cockpit. **4** R. MOORE The kids scrabbled up the money off the floor. **5** J. VANBRUGH They have thrown it amongst the Women to scrabble for.

scrabbled /ˈskrab(ə)ld/ *adjective*. E17.
[from SCRABBLE *noun*[1], *verb*: see -ED[2], -ED[1].]
That has been scrabbled, having scrabbles; *spec.* inscribed with scrawling characters, written in a scrawling way.

scrag /skrag/ *noun*[1]. M16.
[Perh. alt. of CRAG *noun*[2]. In sense 4 from the verb.]
1 A skinny person or animal. *derog.* M16.
2 In full ***scrag-end***. The inferior end of a neck of mutton. M17.
3 The neck, esp. of a person. *colloq.* E19.

4 A rough tackle in rugby football. *slang. rare.* E20.

> 1 T. DEKKER Not so leane a hollow-cheekt Scrag as thou art. SIR W. SCOTT I had been . . on a little scrag of a Cossack. **2** C. LAMB Our scanty mutton scrags on Fridays. A. BURGESS She cooks tasty meals out of scrag end. **3** C. BRONTË Fastened round my bronze scrag under my cravat. **4** P. G. WODEHOUSE The difference between a decent tackle and a bally scrag.

scrag /skrag/ *noun*[2]. Now chiefly *dial.* M16.
[Origin uncertain: perh. alt. of CRAG *noun*[1]. Cf. SCRAGGED *adjective*[1], SCROG, SHRAG.]
1 A tree stump. Also, a roughly projecting branch, outcrop, etc. M16.
2 In full ***scrag-whale***. The grey whale, *Eschrichtius gibbosus*, which has a humped ridge in place of a dorsal fin. Now *rare*. E18.
3 Rough, rocky, and barren ground. *rare*. M19.

scrag /skrag/ *verb trans.* Infl. **-gg-**. M18.
[from SCRAG *noun*[1]. In sense 3 perh. back-form. from SCRAGGY *adjective*[1].]
1 *slang.* **a** Execute by hanging. Also, wring the neck of, strangle. M18. ▸**b** Seize roughly by the neck; treat (a person) roughly, manhandle. M19. ▸**c** Kill, murder. *US*. M20.
2 Subject (a spring or suspension system) to a process of overextension and compression in order to improve strength and set. Also, (foll. by *out*) shorten the normal length of a spring by a specified amount by this means. Freq. as ***scragging*** *verbal noun & ppl adjective*. E20.
3 Scrape or drag (esp. the hair) *back* or *up*. *rare*. M20.

> **3** L. DURRELL Their hair scragged up in ribbons and plaits.

■ **scragger** *noun* (*rare*) a person who or thing which scrags someone or something; *spec.* (*arch. colloq.*) a hangman: L19.

†**scragged** *adjective*[1]. E16–E18.
[App. alt. of CRAGGED. Cf. SCRAG *noun*[2].]
Rough and irregular in outline; (of ground) rugged, barren.

scragged /skragd/ *adjective*[2]. Now *rare*. L16.
[from SCRAG *noun*[1] + -ED[2].]
= SCRAGGY *adjective*[2].

scraggling /ˈskrag(ə)lɪŋ/ *adjective*. E17.
[Irreg. from SCRAG *noun*[1], *noun*[2] with intrusive *-l-* + -ING[2]. In sense 2 prob. after *straggling*.]
†**1** Scraggy, meagre. *rare*. Only in E17.
2 Straggling, irregular in outline or distribution. E18.

> **1** T. ADAMS A leane, scraggling, starued Creature. **2** N. HAWTHORNE The remains being somewhat scanty and scraggling.

scraggly /ˈskragli/ *adjective*. Chiefly *N. Amer.* M19.
[formed as prec. + -Y[1].]
Irregular or ragged in growth or form; scraggy.

> C. MCCULLERS A group of warehouse coloured boys and scraggly children. P. ROTH A thin, scraggly growth of beard. *comb.*: M. E. WILKINS The walls . . had a scraggly-patterned paper on them.

scraggy /ˈskragi/ *adjective*[1]. ME.
[from SCRAG *noun*[2] + -Y[1].]
Rough, irregular, or broken in outline or contour; (of a rock) rugged; (of a stem or branch) knotted; (of a tree) ragged, stunted.

> J. P. PHILIPS A scraggy Rock . . Half overshades the Ocean. CARLYLE There is game abundant in the scraggy woodlands.

¶ Rare before L16.
■ **scraggily** *adverb*[1] L19. **scragginess** *noun*[1] L19.

scraggy /ˈskragi/ *adjective*[2]. E17.
[from SCRAG *noun*[1] + -Y[1].]
1 Esp. of a person or animal: thin, skinny, bony. Chiefly *derog.* E17.
2 Of meat: lean. *rare*. E18.

> **1** R. K. NARAYAN It was harrowing to look at his thin, scraggy frame. **2** MORTIMER COLLINS He ate . . scraggy chops. **scraggy end** *rare* = SCRAG *noun*[1] 2.

■ **scraggily** *adverb*[2] M19. **scragginess** *noun*[2] M19.

scraich /skreɪk. -x/ *verb & noun*. *Scot.* Also **scraigh**. L18.
[Imit.: cf. SCRAUGH.]
▶ **A** *verb intrans.* Esp. of a bird: utter a harsh cry, screech. L18.
▶ **B** *noun*. A harsh cry, a screech, *esp.* that of a bird. L18.

scram /skram/ *noun*[1]. Chiefly *Anglo-Irish*. M19.
[Var. of SCRAN.]
= SCRAN 2.

scram /skram/ *noun*[2]. *slang*. M20.
[from SCRAM *verb*[3].]
NUCLEAR PHYSICS. The rapid shutting down of a nuclear reactor, usu. in an emergency. Freq. *attrib.*

scram /skram/ *verb*[1] *trans. dial.* Infl. **-mm-**. L17.
[Origin unkn.: parallel to SHRAM.]
Numb or paralyse with cold. Chiefly as ***scrammed*** *ppl adjective*.

scram /skram/ *verb*[2] *intrans. slang* (orig. *US*). Infl. **-mm-**. E20.
[Prob. abbreviation of SCRAMBLE *verb*.]
Go away quickly. Freq. in *imper.*

scram /skram/ *verb*[3]. *slang*. Infl. **-mm-**. M20.
[Origin uncertain: perh. from prec.]
NUCLEAR PHYSICS. **1** *verb trans.* Shut down (a nuclear reactor), usu. in an emergency. M20.
2 *verb intrans.* Of a nuclear reactor: shut down, usu. in an emergency. M20.

scramasax /ˈskraməsaks/ *noun*. M19.
[Old Frankish, from unexpl. 1st elem. + *sahs* SAX *noun*[1].]
ARCHAEOLOGY. A large knife with a single-edged blade used in hunting and fighting and freq. found among the grave-goods in Anglo-Saxon burials.

scramble /ˈskramb(ə)l/ *noun*. L17.
[from the verb.]
1 An eager or hasty struggle or competition for or *for* something. Also, a rushed, confused, or disorderly proceeding. L17.
2 a An act of scrambling; *esp.* a scrambling journey. M18. ▸**b** A motorcycle race across rough and hilly ground. E20. ▸**c** A rapid take-off in an emergency, esp. by a group of aircraft. *Military slang*. M20. ▸**d** *AMER. FOOTBALL.* An impromptu movement by a quarterback to evade tacklers. *US*. L20.
3 A dish composed of hastily-mixed ingredients. Also (*rare*), an informal meal of such dishes. L19.

> **1** C. M. YONGE Lessons were always rather a scramble. *New Yorker* The 'scramble' of the European powers for African territory. **2a** G. MACDONALD The rats made one frantic scramble. *Scots Magazine* I donned my climbing boots for a wee scramble on the . . cliffs. **c** *Flypast* The squadron made its first scramble, to patrol Narvik.

Comb.: **scramble net** (*a*) *NAUTICAL* a heavy net down which people may climb from a ship in an emergency; (*b*) the webbing of a child's climbing-frame.

scramble /ˈskramb(ə)l/ *verb*. L16.
[Imit.: cf. CRAMBLE, SCAMBLE.]
1 a *verb intrans.* Stand up, get into a specified place or position, by the struggling use of the hands and feet; make one's way by clambering, crawling, etc., over steep or rough ground; move hastily and awkwardly into a specified place or position. L16. ▸**b** *verb trans.* Collect or gather *up* hastily or clumsily; cause to move or deal with hastily or awkwardly (usu. foll. by *away, through*, etc.). E19. ▸**c** *verb intrans. AMER. FOOTBALL.* Of a quarterback: make an impromptu movement to evade tacklers. M20.
2 a *verb intrans.* Struggle or compete eagerly or hastily with others for or *for* something. L16. ▸†**b** *verb trans.* Struggle or compete eagerly or hastily with others for (something); seize rapaciously or unscrupulously. Only in M17. ▸**c** *verb trans.* Scatter (money etc.) to be struggled or competed for. M19.
3 *verb trans.* **a** Cook (egg) by breaking into a pan with butter, milk, etc., and stirring the mixture over heat; *fig.* jumble or muddle (something). M19. ▸**b** Make (a telephone conversation or broadcast transmission) unintelligible without an appropriate decoding device by altering the transmitted frequencies in a particular way. E20.
4 *Military slang.* **a** *verb intrans.* Of an aircraft, pilot, etc.: effect a rapid take-off in an emergency, esp. as part of a group; become airborne quickly. M20. ▸**b** *verb trans.* Cause (an aircraft, pilot, etc.) to effect a rapid take-off in an emergency; cause to become airborne quickly. M20.

> **1a** K. MANSFIELD She scrambled to her feet. J. WAIN So she was fit enough to scramble in and out of a canoe? G. LORD He increased his speed, scrambling up the slope. *fig.*: M. GARDINER Refugees were scrambling out of Germany . . as best they could. **scrambling net** = *scramble net* (a) s.v. SCRAMBLE *noun*. **b** T. HOOK He hastily scrambled up the papers. *Quarterly Review* Amendments hastily scrambled through committee. *Footloose* I . . scrambled my bike up the steep bank. **2a** R. KNOLLES Scrambling for the money that was cast abroad. H. ROBBINS They did not have to scramble with the crowds for a seat. **b** R. STAPYLTON A little basket . . to be scrambled by the poore. **3a** R. SILVERBERG She had been primed to come tomorrow, . . his wife . . had scrambled things up. A. LURIE Not at the cost of failing school, scrambling his brains . . with acid. **b** E. H. CLEMENTS We ought to scramble the telephone. *absol.*: G. GREENE One of them going back to normal transmission just when the other scrambled. **4a** *Royal Air Force News* A Wessex SAR helicopter . . was scrambling from Manston. **b** *Ships Monthly* Seven helicopters . . were scrambled to evacuate 150 passengers.

scrambled /ˈskramb(ə)ld/ *adjective*. E17.
[from prec. + -ED[1].]
That has been scrambled.
scrambled egg(s) (*a*) a dish of eggs cooked by scrambling (SCRAMBLE *verb* 3a); (*b*) *joc.* the gold braid or insignia worn on an officer's dress uniform, esp. on the cap.

scrambler /ˈskramblə/ *noun*. L17.
[formed as prec. + -ER[1].]
1 A person who scrambles. L17.
2 A thing which scrambles; *spec.* (*a*) a plant, often a climbing one, depending on the support of others; (*b*) an electronic device used to make a telephone conversation or broadcast transmission unintelligible without a corresponding decoding device, by altering the sound frequencies in a particular way; (*c*) (more fully ***scrambler bike***) a motorcycle for use over rough terrain, esp. in moto-cross riding; a trail-bike. M20.

scrambling /ˈskramblɪŋ/ *adjective*. E17.
[from SCRAMBLE *verb* + -ING[2].]
1 That scrambles. Also *fig.*, (of a meal) served or eaten hastily and informally; rushed and confused; irregular, unmethodical. E17.
2 Irregular or rambling in form or habit; (of a plant) of straggling or rambling growth. L17. ▸**b** Of a person: shambling, uncouth. M18.

> **1** J. PORTER We enjoyed our scrambling meal infinitely more than . . our dinner.

■ **scramblingly** *adverb* M17.

scrambly /ˈskrambli/ *adjective*. E20.
[formed as prec. + -Y[1].]
1 Tending to scramble, scrambling. E20.
2 Esp. of rough or steep ground: requiring to be traversed by scrambling; necessitating scrambling. E20.

> **1** *Time* Little scrambly front legs and big thumping back legs. **2** A. CHRISTIE A scrambly cliff path down to the sea.

scramjet /ˈskramdʒɛt/ *noun*. M20.
[from supersonic + combustion + RAMJET.]
AERONAUTICS. A ramjet in which combustion takes place in a stream of gas moving at supersonic speed.

scran /skran/ *noun*. *dial. & slang*. E18.
[Origin unkn.]
†**1** A reckoning at an inn, a bill. Only in E18.
2 Food, eatables, esp. consisting of broken pieces or scraps; provisions; *NAUTICAL* rations. E19.
3 The action of collecting broken pieces or scraps of food. M19.
2 bad scran to — (chiefly *Anglo-Irish*) bad luck to —.

scranch /skrɔːn(t)ʃ/ *verb & noun*. *obsolete* exc. *Scot. & dial.* Also **scraunch**. E17.
[Prob. imit.: cf. CRANCH.]
▶ **A** *verb trans.* Crunch or crush noisily. E17.
▶ **B** *noun*. A crunching noise or sound. E19.

scrannel /ˈskran(ə)l/ *adjective*. *literary*. M17.
[Prob. ult. from base repr. by Norwegian *skran* shrivelled, *skrank* lean large-boned figure. Cf. next.]
Thin, meagre; (of music) harsh, unmelodious.

> MILTON Their lean and flashy songs Grate on their scrannel Pipes of wretched straw. E. F. BENSON These scrannel staccato tinklings that . . made her wince.

scranny /ˈskrani/ *adjective*[1]. Chiefly *dial.* E19.
[Prob. formed as prec.: see -Y[1]. Cf. SCRAWNY.]
Lean, thin; (of diet) poor, meagre.

scranny /ˈskrani/ *adjective*[2]. Chiefly *dial.* M19.
[Origin unkn.]
Crazy, wild.

scrap /skrap/ *noun*[1]. LME.
[Old Norse *skrap* scraps, trifles, from base of *skrapa* SCRAPE *verb*.]
1 In *pl.* Fragments of uneaten food, esp. as constituting the remains of a meal; odds and ends; useless remnants. LME.
2 A remnant; a small detached piece of something; a fragmentary portion; (usu. in neg. contexts) the smallest piece or amount. L16. ▸**b** A picture, paragraph, etc., cut from a book or newspaper, esp. as to be kept in a collection. L19. ▸**c** A small person or animal. *colloq.* L19.
3 *sing.* & (usu.) in *pl.* The residue formed in the process of rendering fat or extracting oil from whalemeat, fish, etc. M17.
4 *sing.* & (now *rare*) in *pl.* Discarded metal for reprocessing. Also ***scrap-metal***. L18.

> **1** P. CHAPLIN Dogs nosed under the table for scraps. I. BANKS Seagulls . . crowding round an out-jutting building, where kitchen scraps are being thrown out. **2** D. CUSACK There's not a scrap of vice in her. A. LURIE She dressed her dolls in the scraps left from alterations. S. MIDDLETON He sat on a bench in the street, picking up scraps of conversation. **c** R. RENDELL The youngest child . . was ill . . . 'Poor little scrap'.

Phrases: **scrap of paper** [with ref. to an alleged statement by the German Chancellor, Bethmann-Hollweg (1856–1921), in connection with German violation of Belgian neutrality in August 1914] a document containing a treaty or pledge which one party does not intend to honour.

Comb.: **scrapbook** (*a*) a blank book for sticking pictures, newspaper cuttings, etc., in; (*b*) a loosely constructed documentary broadcast programme, esp. as covering a particular year or period; **scrap heap** a heap of scrap iron; an accumulation of discarded metal for reprocessing; ***on the scrap heap***, worn out, superseded; **scrap iron** (*a*) cast or wrought iron broken up and set aside for reprocessing; broken pieces and small articles of old and disused ironwork collectively; (*b*) *US slang* an alcoholic drink of poor quality; ***scrap-metal***: see sense 4 above; **scrap paper** (*a*) paper for repulping or reuse; (*b*) rough paper for casual jotting; **scrap screen** (chiefly *Hist.*) a screen decorated with cut-out pictures etc.; **scrapyard** the site of a scrap heap; *spec.* a place where scrap metal is collected.

■ **scraplet** *noun* a small scrap E16. **scrappet** *noun* a small quantity or amount, a little scrap E20.

scrap /skrap/ *noun*². *colloq.* L17.
[Perh. from SCRAPE *noun*¹.]
†**1** A plot, a sinister scheme. L17–E19.
2 A scrimmage, a tussle; a fight, a rough quarrel, esp. a spontaneous one. M19.

📖 **1** C. HATTON They are in great feare Sr Robt. Payton shou'd bring them into ye scrappe. **2** *Boxing News* The Fernandez scrap was billed as being for the vacant junior WBC title. G. DALY Ruskin loved a good scrap over aesthetic issues.

scrap /skrap/ *verb*¹. *colloq.* Infl. **-pp-**. L19.
[from prec.]
1 *verb intrans.* Take part in a scrap. Freq. foll. by *with*. L19.
2 *verb trans.* Have a scrap with. *rare.* L19.

📖 **1** R. PARK His cut chin . . would soon inform Ma . . that he had been scrapping. P. CHAPLIN Mother scrapped with Gerry by phone throughout the afternoon.

■ **scrapper** *noun* (*colloq.*) (*a*) a person who fights; *spec.* a boxer; (*b*) *N. Amer.* a fish that is hard to land once caught: L19.

scrap /skrap/ *verb*² *trans.* Infl. **-pp-**. L19.
[from SCRAP *noun*¹.]
Make scrap of (esp. worn-out or superseded machinery); consign to the scrap heap; discard as useless.

📖 *Times* Existing plans could be scrapped and fresh ones made. M. DIBDIN American warships of an obsolete type, waiting to be sold or scrapped. D. A. THOMAS *Benbow* . . Sold 1931 for scrapping at Rosyth.

scrape /skreɪp/ *noun*¹. LME.
[from SCRAPE *verb*.]
▶ **I 1** An instrument for scraping, a scraper. Long *rare* or *obsolete*. LME.
2 †**a** A piece scraped off. Only in LME. ▸**b** A place where soil etc. has been scraped away; a bare place on a hillside etc., a hollow formed by scraping; *spec.* a shallow pit dug in the ground by a bird, esp. during a courtship display. L18. ▸**c** A layer of thinly spread butter. Chiefly in ***bread and scrape*** below. M19. ▸**d** Crude turpentine obtained by scraping or cutting into the trunk of a pine or fir tree. *US*. M19. ▸**e** The part of the cane on a woodwind instrument that is scraped to a narrow edge in the production of a reed. M20.
3 *gen.* An act or sound of scraping. L15. ▸**b** An awkward or obsequious bow or salutation in which one foot is drawn backwards on the ground. E17. ▸**c** ***scrape of a pen***, ***scrape of the pen***, a hasty scribble, a small scrap of writing. *Scot.* L17. ▸**d** A drawing of a bow over the strings of a violin. E19. ▸**e** A shave. *joc.* M19. ▸**f** Dilatation of the cervix and curettage of the uterus; *spec.* an induced abortion. *colloq.* M20.
4 A person who uses excessive economy, a miser. *obsolete* exc. *Scot. & dial.* E18.

📖 **1** R. HOLME An Irone Scrape . . set in a wooden handle . . for the skullion to scrape . . the furnice hole. **2b** E. A. ARMSTRONG An unmated female red-necked phalarope makes scrapes in the herbage. P. MATTHIESSEN On the ledge path we find . . half a dozen scrapes . . in the snow. B. ODDIE Before Cley reserve acquired its . . scrapes and lagoons. **c** ***bread and scrape***: see BREAD *noun*¹. **e** *Early Music* There are 3 basic scrapes . . of which no.1 is the most common. **3** R. DAHL He heard . . the scrape . . of shovels digging into the soil. **b** S. LOVER To every one of these assurances . . Andy made a bow and a scrape. **d** J. AUSTEN No sound of a Ball but the first Scrape of one violin.

▶ **II 5** An embarrassing or awkward predicament or situation, esp. one resulting from an unwise escapade. E18.
6 A hand-to-hand fight, a skirmish, a brawl. *US colloq.* (now *rare*). E19.

📖 **5** R. MACAULAY I . . hope she won't get into some real scrape and land in a police court. A. BISHOP His liveliness got him into constant scrapes.

scrape /skreɪp/ *noun*². Long *dial.* E17.
[Origin unkn. Cf. SHRAPE *noun*.]
A device for bird-catching; = SHRAPE *noun*.

scrape /skreɪp/ *verb*. Also †**shrape**.
[Old English *scrapian* from Germanic, reinforced in Middle English by Old Norse *skrapa* or Middle & mod. Dutch *schrapen* to scratch.]
†**1** *verb intrans. & trans.* Scratch with the fingernails, claws, etc. OE–E17. ▸**b** *verb intrans.* Scratch lightly on a door as a request for admittance. Freq. foll. by *at*. E18–E19.
2 *verb trans.* †**a** Erase (writing etc.) with a knife, pen, or other instrument. Also foll. by *away*, *out*. ME–L17. ▸**b** *gen.* Remove (an outer layer, an excrescence, a stain, etc.) from an object by drawing a hard or sharp edge across the surface. Freq. foll. by *away*, *from*, *off*, *out* (*of*). LME.
3 *verb trans.* Remove an outer layer, an excrescence, a stain, etc., from (an object) by drawing a hard or sharp edge over the surface; abrade, clean, or make smooth by this process. LME. ▸**b** Form (an image) by drawing a hard or sharp edge across the surface of stone etc.; *spec.* produce (a mezzotint engraving) by treating the prepared copper plate in this way. M16. ▸**c** Clean (esp. a bowl, dish, or other utensil) out or *out* by drawing the edge of a spoon, knife, etc., across the inner surface. L19. ▸**d** Draw (hair) tightly *back* from the forehead. E20.
4 *verb trans.* **a** Of an animal: remove or replace (soil etc.) by scratching with the feet or claws; make (a hole) by this means. Also foll. by *out*. Now *rare*. LME. ▸†**b** *verb intrans.* Of an animal: scratch in the ground with the feet or claws. LME–M17.
5 a *verb trans.* Contrive with an effort to bring or provide; amass with great difficulty. Now only foll. by *together*, *up*. M16. ▸**b** *verb intrans.* Amass and keep a thing or things, esp. money, with difficulty; save, economize. M16.
6 *verb trans.* Draw or move (an object) roughly over a surface, draw or move roughly over (a surface), esp. so as to cause abrasion or produce a grating sound. M16. ▸†**b** *verb trans.* Insult or silence (a speaker) by drawing one's feet noisily over the floor. L16–M19. ▸**c** *verb intrans.* Graze *against* or *on*; progress roughly *over*. Also, emit a grating sound esp. as a result of this. L18.
7 *verb trans. & intrans.* Play (a violin); play (a tune etc.) on a violin. *joc. & derog.* L16.
8 †**a** *verb trans.* ***scrape a leg***, bow by drawing back one leg and bending the other. Only in 17. ▸**b** *verb intrans.* Draw back one foot in making a clumsy bow. Freq. in ***bow and scrape*** below. M17.
9 a *verb intrans.* Barely manage, just get by, (freq. foll. by *along*, *by*); *esp.* just achieve the minimum standard required to pass an examination (freq. foll. by *through*). L19. ▸**b** *verb trans.* Cause (a person) to achieve a specified result or reach a specified objective at the minimum level of performance possible; barely manage to achieve (a specified result) or reach (a specified objective). L19.

📖 **1** E. TOPSELL The little Dog . . ranne barking to the doore, . . fawning and scraping his Lord and maister. **b** LYTTON We came to the door . . at which Fleuri scraped gently. **2a** SIR T. MORE A . . learned priest, that . . scraped out *diabolus* and wrote *Iesus Christus*. **b** P. MORTIMER I scraped bits of butter off six saucers on to a plate. **3** B. BAINBRIDGE Scraping potatoes and chopping . . brussels sprouts. *Scientific American* The hull was merely scraped of marine growths and repainted. **b** THACKERAY The family arms were just new scraped in stone. **d** P. BARKER Red hair scraped back into a bun. **4a** P. H. GOSSE The females . . lay their eggs in holes . . . The sand is again scraped back over the eggs. **5a** MALCOLM X Somehow, Lansing-to-Boston bus fare had been scraped up by Shorty's old mother. M. LANE Funds were scraped together for Branwell to study in London. **b** GOLDSMITH She scraped and scraped at pleasure, till I was almost starved to death. L. P. HARTLEY Parents scrape and save and sacrifice themselves, and then their children look down on them. **6** W. SOYINKA He scraped his boots nervously on the marble floor. A. CARTER Spoons scraped the bottoms of earthenware bowls. **b** LD MACAULAY Another [orator] was coughed and scraped down. **c** J. HAWKES The roof of the van brushes then scrapes against the rotted eaves. **7** R. H. DANA The musicians were still there . . scraping and twanging away. **9a** B. BAINBRIDGE The way we scrape along. Never a penny over at the end of the week. V. BROME His examination results . . were poor, and he just scraped through. **b** C. M. FLANDRAU A futile effort to scrape Billy through an examination. D. MADDEN Kathy would scrape a minimal pass.

Phrases: ***bow and scrape***: see BOW *verb*¹ 6. **scrape acquaintance with** (chiefly *derog.*) contrive to get to know. ***scrape a leg***: see sense 8a above. **scrape an acquaintance with** (chiefly *derog.*) contrive to get to know. ***scrape the barrel***: see BARREL *noun* 1.

Comb.: **scrape ceremony** ORNITHOLOGY a display by a bird in which it digs a shallow pit in the ground and presses its breast into it, usu. during courtship; **scrape-trencher** (*obsolete* exc. *Hist.*) a servant employed to scrape the trenchers after use.

■ **scraping** *verbal noun* the action of the verb; an instance or result of this; *esp.* the grating noise produced by drawing something roughly over a surface: LME.

scraper /ˈskreɪpə/ *noun*. M16.
[from prec. + -ER¹.]
▶ **I 1** A person who scrapes; *spec.* (*a*) (chiefly *Scot.*) a person who scrapes together money, a money-grubber, a miser; (*b*) *derog.* = FIDDLER 1. Now *rare*. M16.
2 A bird that scratches in the soil; formerly *spec.* in ORNITHOLOGY, a member of the former order Rasores of gallinaceous birds. E17.
▶ **II 3** A thing which scrapes, a device for scraping esp. dirt from a surface; *spec.* (*a*) ANTIQUITIES = STRIGIL 1; (*b*) an instrument for scraping off the sweat from a horse; (*c*) a three-sided engraving tool used to remove burrs left by the graver, etching needle, or dry-point, or to obliterate a line; a similar instrument used in scraping mezzotint; (*d*) ARCHAEOLOGY a prehistoric flint implement with a sharpened edge used for scraping material such as hide or wood; (*e*) (more fully ***cabinet scraper***) a thin rectangular piece of metal whose sharpened long edge is pushed over the surface of wood to smooth it; (*f*) MUSIC a simple percussion instrument. M16.
4 A fixed appliance, usu. consisting of a metal blade with a horizontal upper edge, on which dirt from the soles of boots or shoes may be scraped off, esp. before entering a building. E18.
5 A foot. Chiefly in ***take to one's scrapers***, take to one's heels, decamp. *Anglo-Irish.* L18.
6 a Orig., a machine drawn by horses or oxen for ditch-digging, road-making, etc. Now *spec.* a mechanical earth-mover. E19. ▸**b** An instrument for scraping dirt, mud, etc., from a road or pedestrian surface. M19.
7 A cocked hat. *arch. slang.* E19.
8 = PIG *noun*¹ 8. L19.
9 = SKYSCRAPER 2. E20.

Comb.: **scraperboard** cardboard or board with a blackened surface which can be scraped off for making white-line drawings; a piece of this material; **scraper ring** a piston ring designed to scrape oil off the cylinder wall.

scrapiana /ˈskrapɪˈɑːnə/ *noun pl. rare.* L18.
[from SCRAP *noun*¹ or SCRAPE *verb*: see -ANA, -IANA.]
Literary scraps or cuttings.

scrapie /ˈskreɪpi/ *noun.* E20.
[from SCRAPE *verb* + -IE.]
A subacute fatal disease of sheep and goats, characterized by degeneration of the central nervous system, leading to uncoordinated gait and itching.

scrappage /ˈskrapɪdʒ/ *noun.* M20.
[from SCRAP *noun*¹, *verb*²: see -AGE.]
The action of discarding something as worn out or superseded.

scrapple /ˈskrap(ə)l/ *noun*¹ & *verb*. Long *dial.* LME.
[from SCRAPE *verb* + -LE¹.]
▶ **A** *noun.* A tool used for scraping or raking things up. LME.
▶ **B** *verb trans. & intrans.* Scrape. E16.

scrapple /ˈskrap(ə)l/ *noun*². *US.* M19.
[from SCRAP *noun*¹ + -LE².]
Scraps of pork etc. stewed with meal and shaped into large cakes; ponhaus.

scrappy /ˈskrapi/ *adjective*¹. M19.
[from SCRAP *noun*¹ + -Y¹.]
Consisting of scraps; made up of odds and ends; disjointed, unconnected. Also, (orig. & chiefly *US*) lean, scrawny; meagre.

📖 THACKERAY There is a dreadfully scrappy dinner, the evident remains of a party. M. KINGSLEY My classical knowledge is scrappy.

■ **scrappily** *adverb* L19. **scrappiness** *noun* M19.

scrappy /ˈskrapi/ *adjective*². Orig. *N. Amer.* L19.
[from SCRAP *noun*², *verb*¹: see -Y¹.]
Inclined to scrap or fight; aggressive, pugnacious, quarrelsome.

📖 *Rolling Stone* She was scrappy—her sister . . remembers her once beating up a bully.

scrapy /ˈskreɪpi/ *adjective.* L19.
[from SCRAPE *verb* + -Y¹.]
Tending to scrape; *spec.* having or producing a harsh grating noise.

scrat /skrat/ *noun*¹. Long *obsolete* exc. *dial.* OE.
[Old Norse *skrat(t)i* wizard, goblin, monster, rel. to Old High German *scrato* (German *Schrat*) satyr, sprite. Cf. SCRATCH *noun*².]
1 A hermaphrodite. OE.
2 A hobgoblin. Also, the Devil. LME.
¶ In sense 2, only in place-names before E19.

scrat /skrat/ *noun*². *obsolete* exc. *dial.* M16.
[from the verb. Cf. SCART *noun*².]
1 Orig., a weal made by a rod or whip. Later, an act or result of scratching, a scratch. M16.
2 A small portion or part. L16.
3 A person who scrapes or saves; a miserly person. L17.

scrat /skrat/ *verb. obsolete* exc. *dial.* Infl. **-tt-**. ME.
[Origin unkn. Cf. SCART *verb*, SCRATCH *verb*.]
1 a *verb intrans.* = SCRATCH *verb* 1c. ME. ▸**b** *verb trans.* = SCRATCH *verb* 1a. ME. ▸**c** *verb trans.* = SCRATCH *verb* 1b. L15.
2 *verb trans. & intrans.* = SCRATCH *verb* 4. M16.
3 *verb trans. & intrans.* = SCRATCH *verb* 2. M16.
4 *verb intrans.* = SCRATCH *verb* 3a, b. L16.

scratch /skratʃ/ *noun*¹ & *adjective*. L16.
[from SCRATCH *verb*.]
▶ **A** *noun.* **I 1** A long narrow superficial wound in the skin made by scratching; *colloq.* a trivial wound, a flesh-wound. L16.
2 a In *pl.* (A condition characterized by) scabby or suppurating cracks on a horse's pasterns, with acute soreness. Also called ***cratches***, ***rat's tails***. Freq. with *the*. L16. ▸**b** The mange. E19.
3 Any of various shallow linear abrasions on an object or substance produced by contact with a harder object or substance; a shallow linear incision. M17.
4 a A rough or irregular mark made by a pencil, paintbrush, etc.; a slight sketch, a scribble, a hasty scrawl. M17. ▸**b** Money, *esp.* paper money. *slang* (orig. *US*). E20.
5 In salt-making, a hard crust precipitated during boiling. E18.

6 A line or mark drawn as an indication of a boundary or starting-point; *spec.* †(*a*) CRICKET = CREASE *noun*[1] 3; (*b*) BOXING the line across the centre of the ring to which opponents are brought at the beginning of an encounter (now chiefly *fig.* in ***up to scratch*** below); (*c*) a line or mark from which competitors in a race, esp. those not receiving a handicap, start. L18. ▸**b** The starting-point in a handicap for a competitor receiving no odds; *spec.* in GOLF, a handicap of zero. Also, the number of strokes in which a golfer with such a handicap might be expected to complete a specified course. M19. ▸**c** A candidate or competitor withdrawn from a race or other competition. M20.

7 a The faint grating noise produced by scratching on a hard surface; a sound of scratching. L18. ▸**b** AUDIO. A rough hiss, caused by the friction of the stylus in the groove, heard when a record is played. E20. ▸**c** A technique of playing a record whereby the record is briefly moved backwards and forwards during play to produce a rhythmic scratching effect; the style of music characterized by this. L20.

> **1** SIR W. SCOTT Surely a few drops of blood from a scratch . . are not to part father and son. J. S. CORBETT The young ensign passed through the four months of . . fighting without a scratch. **4a** M. DELANY I send you a little scratch not worthy to be called a sketch. W. COWPER Every scratch of his pen was accounted a treasure. **b** *Private Eye* Putting even more scratch into the bulging wallets of the lawyers. **6** J. D. ASTLEY Some eight or ten toed the scratch, and I won very easily. **b** H. VARDON A player whose handicap was several strokes removed from scratch. **c** *Sun (Baltimore)* The overnight favorite . . was a late scratch. **7a** G. B. SHAW There is a scratch, and the flame of a match is seen.

▸ **II 8 a** An act of scratching; *spec.* a spell of scratching oneself to relieve itching. M18. ▸**b** A skirmish, a trivial fight. *rare.* M19.

> **8a** THOMAS HUGHES Lifting . . his short hat . . to make room for a scratch. H. C. WYLD Dogs enjoy a good scratch.

▸ **III 9** = ***scratch-wig*** below. M18.

10 BILLIARDS etc. Orig. (now *rare*), a lucky stroke, a fluke. Later, a shot incurring a penalty. M19.

11 *ellipt.* A scratch crew, a crew hastily assembled. *rare.* L19.

12 = ***scratch video*** below. L20.

Phrases: **from scratch** (*a*) from the beginning; (*b*) without help or advantage. **up to scratch** up to the required standard, able to do what is required.

Comb.: **scratch-build** *verb trans.* build (a model) from scratch, without using specially prepared components; **scratch card** a card with a section or sections coated in an opaque waxy substance which may be scraped away to reveal a symbol indicating whether a prize has been won in a competition; **scratch-coat** (chiefly *US*) a rough coating of plaster scratched before it is quite dry to ensure the adherence of the next coat; **scratch dial** ARCHAEOLOGY a set of marks found on the wall of a church and taken to be an ancient form of sundial; **scratch filter** AUDIO a filter designed to reduce the audibility of scratches and hiss in reproduced sound; **scratch-grass** any of several bristly or prickly plants; *esp.* (*a*) *dial.* cleavers, *Galium aparine*; (*b*) *US* tear-thumb, *Polygonum sagittatum*; **scratch hardness** the hardness of a metal or mineral as estimated by measuring the width of a scratch made on the material by a diamond point under a specified load; **scratch hit** BASEBALL a weakly made hit that allows the batter to reach first base; **scratch hole** a hole or trench scratched out of the ground; **scratch-mix** *adjective* of or pertaining to a style of music in which several records are intercut with each other, using the scratch technique, to create a collage of rhythmic sound; **scratch-mixing** the action of playing records in a scratch-mix style; **scratch pad** (*a*) (orig. & chiefly *N. Amer.*) a scribbling block; (*b*) COMPUTING a small, very fast memory for the temporary storage of data or for indirect addressing of the main memory; **scratch paper** *N. Amer.* scribbling paper; **scratchplate** a plastic or metal plate attached to the front of a guitar to protect it from being scratched by the pick; **scratch sheet** US SPORT a printed list of the entries in the day's races and their odds; **scratch stock** a tool for inlaying lines etc. along the grain of wood; **scratch video** a technique or genre of video-making in which a number of short, sharp images are cut and mixed into a single film and fitted to a synchronized soundtrack; a video made in this way; **scratch-weed** = *scratch-grass* (a) above; **scratch-wig** a wig covering only part of the head; **scratch-work** (*a*) sgraffito; (*b*) scratched lines on an engraving plate.

▸ **B** *attrib.* or as *adjective.* Collected or made hastily and from what is available, impromptu; heterogeneous; with no handicap given. M19.

> P. BROOK The group . . whether a scratch cast or a permanent company. R. GITTINGS Beef . . to build him up after the scratch meals of the last month. L. DEIGHTON Batting for the scratch team the village had put up.

■ **scratchless** *adjective* without a scratch; unscathed: E19.

Scratch /skratʃ/ *noun*[2]. *colloq.* & *dial.* Also **s-**. M18.
[Alt. of SCRAT *noun*[1].]
In full ***Old Scratch***. The Devil.

scratch /skratʃ/ *verb*. LME.
[Prob. blend of SCRAT *verb* and CRATCH *verb*.]

1 a *verb trans.* Make a long narrow superficial wound in the skin of, esp. by tearing with claws or fingernails. Also, score or mark the surface of by contact with a sharp pointed object. LME. ▸**b** *verb trans.* Tear or drag *out* or *off* with the claws or fingernails. E16. ▸**c** *verb intrans.* Attack or wound a person or animal with the claws or fingernails (foll. by *at*). Also, produce a long narrow superficial wound or abrasion with a sharp or pointed object. L16.

2 a *verb trans.* Of a bird or animal: extricate or get *out* with the claws; (foll. by *up*) move (soil etc.) with the claws. E16. ▸**b** *verb intrans.* Of a bird or animal: rake the surface of the ground with the claws, esp. in search of something; move soil etc. with the claws. M19.

3 a *verb intrans.* Struggle to make money, amass and keep money etc. with difficulty. Now chiefly *transf.* in ***scratch around for***, ***scratch for*** below. E16. ▸**b** *verb intrans.* Barely manage, get *along, on, through* with difficulty. M19. ▸**c** *verb intrans.* Depart in haste, make off with all speed. Freq. foll. by *for*. *US colloq.* M19. ▸**d** *verb trans.* Produce or get with difficulty, scrape *up*. E20.

4 *verb trans.* & *intrans.* Rub or scrape without marking (a part of the body) with the fingernails or claws, esp. to relieve itching. M16.

†**5 a** *verb trans.* Seize rapaciously (as) with the claws. L16–L17. ▸**b** *verb intrans.* Struggle fiercely *for*. L16–E17.

6 *verb trans.* **a** Make shallow linear abrasions on (a surface, esp. of a specified object or substance), as a result of contact with a harder object or substance; cause to be marked or damaged in this way. M17. ▸**b** Form or produce (an image etc.) by scratching. M17. ▸**c** Furrow (the soil) very lightly for the purpose of cultivation. L17. ▸**d** *verb trans.* = SCRATCH-BRUSH *verb*. M19.

7 a *verb trans.* Erase the name of (a person etc.) from a list; cancel or strike *out* (writing) with a pen, pencil, etc.; cross out. Also, expunge from a list of competitors or candidates; *spec.* withdraw (a competitor or candidate) from a race or other competition. L17. ▸**b** *verb trans.* & *intrans.* Of a voter: erase the name of (a candidate or candidates) from the party ticket. *US.* M19. ▸**c** *verb intrans.* Of a competitor or candidate: withdraw or be withdrawn from a race or other competition. Also *joc.*, withdraw one's acceptance of an invitation. M19. ▸**d** *verb trans.* Cancel or abandon (an undertaking or project). E20.

8 a *verb intrans.* Drag the fingernails or claws over a hard surface with a faint grating noise, esp. *at* a door as a signal for admittance. Also, (of a pen) move over the paper with a slight noise. E18. ▸**b** *verb trans.* Scrape or rub (an object) on a hard surface with a faint grating noise. L19. ▸**c** *verb intrans.* & *trans.* Play (a record) using the scratch technique (SCRATCH *noun*[1] 7c). L20.

9 *verb intrans.* Of a horse: contract scratches in the pasterns. *rare.* M18.

10 *verb intrans.* **a** Scribble, write hurriedly or carelessly. E19. ▸**b** Forge (banknotes or other papers). *US slang.* M19.

11 BILLIARDS etc. ▸**a** *verb intrans.* Make a stroke that incurs a penalty; *spec.* hit the cue-ball into a pocket. *US.* E20. ▸**b** *verb trans.* Hit (the cue-ball) badly, incurring a penalty; *spec.* hit (the cue-ball) into a pocket. *US.* M20.

> **1a** R. K. NARAYAN She and her sister had scratched each other's faces. G. GREENE Her thighs . . were scratched with briars. **b** SHAKES. *Two Gent.* This foolish love, That like a testy babe will scratch the nurse. **c** T. HOOD How the long brambles do scratch. H. MANTEL She would . . spit and scratch. **2a** F. MORYSON They [jackals] had scratched up the earth. **b** R. BROUGHTON Chanticleer scratching . . on the dunghill. **3a** V. PALMER We'll have to scratch for another year . . to pay off the new boat. **4** SHAKES. *Mids. N. D.* If my hair do but tickle me I must scratch. W. GOLDING She sniffed, scratched her nose. J. BARTH Scratching a fly bite on one leg. **5a** E. LUDLOW If we take the people's liberties . . , they will scratch them back. **6** R. J. SULLIVAN Marble is soft, and can be scratched with a knife. J. D. DANA The stones . . are sometimes scratched themselves. **b** C. MIDDLETON I had scratched . . some faint resemblance of an image. **c** DRYDEN The . . Swain Scratch'd with a Rake, a Furrow for his Grain. **7a** LD MACAULAY The butler refused to scratch Hough's name out of the buttery book. *Country Life* Savon, one of the Newmarket hopes, has now been scratched by his owner. **c** *Athletics Today* He pulled a muscle . . and had to scratch from both finals. **8a** *Daily News* He [a dog] scratched so persistently at the door. **b** F. T. BUCKLAND A match being scratched on a box for ignition. **10** SIR W. SCOTT I . . scratched down another ballad.

Phrases: **scratch a — and find a —** reveal the true or fundamental character of —. **scratch around for**, **scratch for** make arduous efforts to obtain or find. **scratch my back and I will scratch yours** do me a favour and I will return it (freq. with ref. to a state of mutual aid or flattery). **scratch one's head** be perplexed, show perplexity. **scratch the surface** deal with a matter only in the most superficial way.

Comb.: **scratch-back** (*a*) a back-scratcher, esp. in the form of a small ivory or metal hand on a long handle; (*b*) a toy which makes a sound of tearing cloth when rubbed on a person's back; **scratch blue** a decoration of incisions filled with blue pigment found on 18th-cent. stoneware; (also ***scratch blue ware***) stoneware so decorated; **scratchboard** = *scraperboard* s.v. SCRAPER.

■ **scratchable** *adjective* (*rare*) M19. **scratchingly** *adverb* (*rare*) in a scratching manner L16.

scratch-brush /ˈskratʃbrʌʃ/ *noun* & *verb*. L18.
[from SCRATCH *noun*[1], *verb* + BRUSH *noun*[2].]

▸ **A** *noun.* A brush of fine wire used in gilding, electroplating, etc., to polish or clean articles of metal. L18.

Comb.: **scratch-brush lathe** a lathe with a circular revolving scratch-brush.

▸ **B** *verb trans.* Polish or clean using a scratch-brush. L18.

■ **scratch-brusher** *noun* a person who uses a scratch-brush L19.

scratched /skratʃt/ *adjective*. M16.
[from SCRATCH *noun*[1], *verb*: see -ED[2], -ED[1].]
That has been scratched; having a scratch or scratches.

scratched figure TYPOGRAPHY a numeral figure with a slanting line drawn across it, used in printing examples of arithmetical operations involving cancelling. **scratched blue** = *scratch blue* s.v. SCRATCH *verb*.

scratcher /ˈskratʃə/ *noun*. M16.
[from SCRATCH *verb* + -ER[1].]

1 a A person who scratches; *spec.* (*a*) *US slang* a forger; (*b*) *US* a voter who crosses the name of a candidate or candidates from the party ticket; (*c*) a person who plays records using a scratch technique (SCRATCH *noun*[1] 7c). M16. ▸†**b** ORNITHOLOGY. A member of the former order Rasores; = SCRAPER 2. Only in M19.

2 A thing which scratches; *spec.* (*a*) a tool used in plastering to roughen the surface of the preliminary coating; (*b*) a device put down an oil or gas well to clear the bore or create turbulence mechanically. E19.

scratching /ˈskratʃɪŋ/ *noun*[1]. Now chiefly *dial.* LME.
[Origin unkn. Cf. CRACKLING.]
sing. & (usu.) in *pl.* The residue of tallow-melting. Also, the residue of pork fat left after rendering lard.

scratching /ˈskratʃɪŋ/ *verbal noun*[2]. M16.
[from SCRATCH *verb* + -ING[1].]
The action of SCRATCH *verb*; an instance of this; *esp.* a faint grating noise produced by scratching.

Comb.: **scratching post** a stake or post against which an animal rubs itself to relieve itching.

scratchy /ˈskratʃi/ *adjective*. E18.
[from SCRATCH *noun*[1] + -Y[1].]

†**1** Of a horse: affected with the scratches. E18–E19.

2 Of a drawing etc.: composed of scratches as opp. to bold, firm lines; done carelessly. E19.

3 a Tending to make scratches or a scratching noise. Also, (esp. of a garment) tending to cause itchiness; demanding relief (as if) by scratching, itchy. M19. ▸**b** (Of a sound) rough, grating; (of a sound recording) characterized by scratch (SCRATCH *noun*[1] 7b). L19. ▸**c** *fig.* Bad-tempered, peevish, irritable. E20.

4 SPORT. Of action or performance: ill-sustained, uneven, ragged. L19.

■ **scratchily** *adverb* E20.

scrattle /ˈskrat(ə)l/ *verb*. Long *dial.* ME.
[Frequentative of SCRAT *verb*: see -LE[3].]

1 a *verb intrans.* Scratch, esp. repeatedly. ME. ▸**b** *verb trans.* Scrape *away* or move (snow etc.) by scratching. L19.

2 *verb intrans.* Scramble, progress with difficulty. E19.

scraugh /skrɔːk, -x/ *noun* & *verb*. *Scot.* E19.
[Imit.: cf. SCRAICH.]

▸ **A** *noun.* A loud hoarse cry. E19.

▸ **B** *verb intrans.* Utter a loud hoarse cry. E19.

scraunch *verb* & *noun* var. of SCRANCH.

†**scraw** *noun*[1]. M16–M19.
[Perh. from Dutch *schraag* trestle.]
A frame for hanging textile fabrics on to dry.

scraw /skrɔː/ *noun*[2]. *Scot.* & *Anglo-Irish.* L17.
[Irish *scraith*, Gaelic *sgrath*.]

1 A turf used for covering a roof under thatch, or for burning. L17.

†**2** A thin covering of grass-grown soil formed on the surface of a bog. L18–E19.

scrawl /skrɔːl/ *noun*[1]. L17.
[from SCRAWL *verb*[2].]

1 A scrawled thing; a hastily and badly written letter, a careless sketch. Also, (usu. in *pl.*, now *rare*) a scrawled or illegible character. L17.

2 A careless, illegible style of handwriting. E18.

> **1** THACKERAY A scrawl from his pencil brings an enormous price. B. D. W. RAMSAY I received a scrawl in Sir Colin's own handwriting. B. EMECHETA The sheets were covered with red ink scrawls. **2** F. BURNEY Her hand-writing . . was a . . miserable scrawl.

scrawl /skrɔːl/ *noun*[2]. Chiefly *dial.* M19.
[Perh. from next.]
A young or small shore-crab, a hermit crab.

scrawl /skrɔːl/ *verb*[1] *intrans.* *obsolete* exc. *dial.* LME.
[App. alt. of CRAWL *verb*, perh. infl. by SPRAWL *verb*. Cf. next.]

†**1** Spread the limbs sprawlingly; gesticulate. LME–L16.

2 Move with a scrambling and shuffling motion; crawl. M16.

†**3** Teem; = CRAWL *verb* 2. M16–M17.

scrawl /skrɔːl/ *verb*[2]. E17.
[Perh. transf. use of prec.]
1 *verb trans.* Write or draw in a sprawling, untidy manner. E17. ▸**b** Cover (a surface) with scrawling inscriptions or marks. Also foll. by *over*. M17.
2 *verb intrans.* & †*trans.* (with *it*). Scribble, write carelessly or awkwardly. E17.

📖 **1** A. CARTER They all seized lipsticks and scrawled obscenities over every surface. H. CARPENTER A poem . . scrawled in his uneven . . handwriting. **b** SMOLLETT The windows . . are scrawled with doggrel rhimes. **2** BROWNING Splash and scrawl, . . swift penman Paul!

■ **scrawler** *noun* a person who writes carelessly M18. **scrawling** *noun* the action of the verb; an instance of this; scribbling, (a piece of) careless untidy writing: E17.

scrawly /ˈskrɔːli/ *adjective*. M19.
[from SCRAWL *noun*[1], *verb*[2]: see -Y[1].]
Badly or untidily written; irregularly designed.
■ **scrawliness** *noun* M19.

scrawny /ˈskrɔːni/ *adjective*. Orig. *US*. M19.
[Var. of SCRANNY *adjective*[1].]
Lean, scraggy.

📖 K. A. PORTER He was so scrawny all his bones showed. M. FORSTER She became . . whey-faced and scrawny.

■ **scrawniness** *noun* M19.

scray /skreɪ/ *noun*. Chiefly *dial.* M17.
[Origin unkn.]
The common tern, *Sterna hirundo*.

scraze /skreɪz/ *noun* & *verb*. Long *dial.* E18.
[App. a blend of SCRATCH *noun*[1] and GRAZE *noun*.]
▶ **A** *noun*. A scratch, a graze. E18.
▶ **B** *verb trans.* Scratch, graze. M19.

screak /skriːk/ *verb* & *noun*. Now chiefly *dial.* Also **skreek**. L15.
[Of Scandinavian origin: cf. Old Norse *skrækja*, Norwegian *skrika*, prob. imit. Cf. SCREECH *verb*, SHRIEK *verb*, SKRIKE, SKREIGH *noun*[1] & *verb*.]
▶ **A** *verb*. **1** *verb intrans.* Utter a shrill harsh cry; screech, scream. Also foll. by *out*. L15. ▸**b** Of an ungreased hinge etc.: make a shrill grating sound, creak. M16.
2 *verb trans.* Cry *out* or utter with a shrill harsh cry. M16.
▶ **B** *noun*. A shrill harsh cry; a shrill grating sound. E16.
screak of day *dial.* daybreak.
■ **screaking** *noun* the action of the verb; an instance of this, a shrill cry or grating sound: M16. **screaky** *adjective* apt to screak L19.

scream /skriːm/ *noun*. LME.
[from the verb.]
1 A loud high-pitched piercing cry characteristically expressing pain, alarm, fear, anger, etc.; the action of emitting such a cry. LME.
2 The shrill cry of certain birds and animals; any loud high-pitched piercing noise likened to a human or animal scream; *spec.* (JAZZ) the sound produced by a high note being played loudly on a wind instrument. LME.
3 A cause of laughter; an irresistibly funny person or situation. Cf. YELL *noun* 3. *colloq.* L19.
4 The giving of information or evidence, *spec.* against an accomplice in crime. *slang*. E20.
5 An urgent message. *slang*. E20.

📖 **1** SMOLLETT His wife . . seeing her husband in these dangerous circumstances, uttered a dreadful scream. C. ISHERWOOD Frau Nowak's shrill scolding rose to a scream. *Times* As the main body of demonstrators began to move away . . screams of 'Fascist pigs' continued. ***primal scream***: see PRIMAL *adjective*. **2** E. DE MAUNY The scream of the bandsaws on the breaking-down bench. P. ANGADI She . . heard the chirps of sparrows and the occasional scream of swifts. **3** *Jackie* Remember the year Sally . . convinced us Prince Charles was coming to our school? That was a scream.

scream /skriːm/ *verb*. ME.
[Perh. repr. an Old English word or from a related Middle Dutch word (cf. Middle Dutch *schreem* noun) or Old Frisian word (cf. West Frisian *skrieme* weep).]
1 *verb intrans.* **a** Utter a loud high-pitched piercing cry or scream in pain, alarm, fear, anger, etc.; cry out *for* with a scream. Also, play or sing unpleasantly loud and shrill notes; laugh uncontrollably, be convulsed *with* laughter. Also foll. by *out*, *away*. ME. ▸**b** Of a bird or animal: emit a characteristic shrill cry. ME. ▸**c** Of an inanimate thing: make a noise like a scream; travel swiftly (as) with a screaming noise. L18. ▸**d** Turn informer; give evidence against an accomplice in crime. *slang*. E20.
2 *verb trans.* Utter or emit (as) with a scream, speak or sing (words etc.) in a screaming tone. Also foll. by *out*. E18.
3 a *verb trans.* Bring or reduce to a specified state (as) by screaming. E19. ▸**b** *verb intrans.* Express oneself angrily, excitedly, etc., in speech or writing. Also, be blatantly obvious or conspicuous. L19. ▸**c** *verb intrans.* Have a great desire *for* a thing, *to do*. E20. ▸**d** *verb trans.* Communicate (a thing, *that*) strongly. M20. ▸**e** *verb trans.* Foll. by *on*: insult (a person) in playing the dozens (see DOZEN *noun* 1d). *US Black slang*. L20.

📖 **1** LD MACAULAY She screamed for help. R. L. STEVENSON One child, who had lost her parents, screamed steadily and with increasing shrillness. J. STEINBECK She screamed then, and Lennie's other hand closed over her mouth. C. EASTON Training and temperament kept Jacqueline smiling when she wanted to scream. **b** H. CAINE Under the cliffs, where the sea-birds scream. **c** *Sunday Mail (Brisbane)* Making U-turns at high speed to make their tyres scream. D. M. THOMAS A jet, presumably from the . . RAF station, screams across the sky. **2** SIR W. SCOTT 'He is dead!' screamed the agonized parent. *Athletics Today* 'One in Ten Olympic Stars on Drugs' screamed the headlines. **3a** N. COWARD If he comes near me I'll scream the place down. **b** S. BRETT This . . took me longest to work out. It's been screaming at me for days, but I just couldn't see it. *Forbes* Doctors would call up screaming, complaining about the delay in getting results. **c** R. D. ABRAHAMS I scream You scream We all scream For ice cream. J. WAINWRIGHT Inside his kinky little skull he was screaming to confess. **d** B. SCHULBERG He wore a new suit . . . His shoes screamed newness. W. CAMP There must be something about her . . which screams that she's beddable.

screamer /ˈskriːmə/ *noun*. E18.
[from prec. + -ER[1].]
1 A person who or thing which screams; a person prone to scream in alarm etc. E18.
2 Each of three gooselike S. American birds constituting the family Anhimidae, with heavy bodies, small heads, short hooked bills, and spurred wings. L18. ▸**b** = SERIEMA. L18. ▸**c** A swift. E19.
3 a A person, animal, or thing of exceptional size, attractiveness, etc.; a splendid specimen. *slang*. E19. ▸**b** A very amusing thing or person; a very frightening story. *slang*. M19. ▸**c** An exclamation mark. *slang*. L19. ▸**d** A thing moving (as) with or making a screaming sound; *spec.* (*a*) a very powerful shot in a game; (*b*) a bomb falling with a screaming noise; (*c*) JAZZ a passage featuring loud high notes played on a wind instrument; such a note. *slang*. L19. ▸**e** An informer; a complainer. *slang*. E20. ▸**f** In full ***screamer headline***. A large, freq. sensational, newspaper headline. *US slang*. E20. ▸**g** ***the screamers***, = ***screaming habdabs*** s.v. HABDABS. *slang*. M20.
1 two-pot screamer *Austral. slang* a person who easily shows the effects of alcohol.

screaming /ˈskriːmɪŋ/ *verbal noun*. LME.
[from SCREAM *verb* + -ING[1].]
The action of SCREAM *verb*; an instance of this.

screaming /ˈskriːmɪŋ/ *adjective*. E17.
[from SCREAM *verb* + -ING[2].]
1 That screams; sounding shrilly. E17.
2 a Very amusing, hysterically funny. *slang*. M19. ▸**b** Violent or startling in effect; glaring, blatant, obvious. M19. ▸**c** Very good, splendid. *slang*. M19.
1 screaming eagle *US Military slang* = ***ruptured duck*** s.v. RUPTURE *verb* 1. ***screaming*** HABDABS. ***screaming*** MEEMIE.
■ **screamingly** *adverb* in a screaming manner; *colloq.* extremely, exceedingly (esp. in ***screamingly funny***): L18.

screamy /ˈskriːmi/ *adjective*. *colloq.* L19.
[from SCREAM *noun* or *verb* + -Y[1].]
Given to screaming; having a screaming voice or sound; violent or exaggerated in expression, colour, etc.
■ **screaminess** *noun* L19.

scree /skriː/ *noun*. Orig. in *pl.* E18.
[Old Norse *skriða* landslip, rel. to *skriða* slide, glide = Old English *scrīþan*, Old High German *skrītan* (German *Schreiten*).]
A loose mass of stony detritus forming a precipitous slope on a mountainside. Also, the material composing such a slope.

screech /skriːtʃ/ *noun*[1]. M16.
[Alt. of SCRITCH *noun*. Cf. SCREECH *verb*.]
1 A loud harsh high piercing cry or scream characteristically expressing sudden intense pain, alarm, etc.; a shrill grating cry. M16. ▸**b** *transf.* a loud harsh squealing sound. M19.
2 Any of various birds having a harsh discordant cry, *esp.* the barn owl, swift, or mistle thrush. Now *dial.* M17.

📖 **1** N. HAWTHORNE We could hear . . a railway train . . and its discordant screech. R. PARK She gave a screech of astonishment.

Comb.: **screech beetle** a water beetle, *Hygrobia hermanni*, with large eyes, which can squeak by rubbing the tip of the abdomen against the wing cases; **screech owl** (*a*) the barn owl (from its discordant cry which is supposed to be an evil omen); (*b*) any of various small American owls of the genus *Otus*, allied to the Scops owls; esp. *O. asio* of N. America; (*c*) *fig.* a bearer of evil tidings; a person who presages misfortune.
■ **screechy** *adjective* given to screeching; loud, shrill, and discordant: E19.

screech /skriːtʃ/ *noun*[2]. *slang*. E20.
[Ult. from SCREIGH.]
Whisky; any strong alcoholic liquor, *esp.* one of inferior quality.

screech /skriːtʃ/ *verb*. L16.
[Alt. (with expressive lengthening of the vowel) of SCRITCH *verb*. Cf. SCREECH *noun*[1].]
1 *verb intrans.* Utter or emit a harsh high piercing cry or sound, call out shrilly; *transf.* complain or protest stridently. L16. ▸**b** *transf.* Emit or make a loud harsh squealing sound, esp. caused by friction; move with such a sound. M18.
2 *verb trans.* Utter or emit (words etc.) with a screech. M19.
3 *verb trans.* Cause to utter a shrill squeaking noise. *rare*. M19.

📖 **1** B. VINE Peacocks . . screech regularly at dawn. **b** L. DEIGHTON The tyres screeched like half-slaughtered dogs. M. DUFFY We screeched to a halt outside.

■ **screeching** *verbal noun* the action of the verb; an instance of this: E17. **screechingly** *adverb* in a screeching manner M19.

screecher /ˈskriːtʃə/ *noun*. M19.
[from prec. + -ER[1].]
A person who or thing which screeches.

screed /skriːd/ *noun*. ME.
[Prob. var. of SHRED *noun*. In sense 2, from the verb.]
1 A cut or broken fragment or piece; a torn strip, a shred, a tatter; a strip of land. *obsolete* exc. *dial.* ME. ▸**b** An edging or decorative border on a garment etc. *dial.* E19.
2 A rip, a tear; a tearing or scraping noise, a loud shrill sound. *Scot.* E18.
3 A long, esp. tedious, piece of writing or speech; a (dull) tract; in *pl.* (*colloq.*), great quantities *of*. M18. ▸†**b** A drinking-bout. *Scot.* E19–E20.
4 A strip of plaster or other material placed on a surface as a guide to the thickness of the coat of plaster, cement, etc., to be applied; a strip of wood etc. drawn across fresh plaster etc. to level it; a levelled layer of material, as cement, forming part of a floor, road, etc. E19.

📖 **3** J. BLACKWOOD Any news will be welcome and I will give you a screed in reply. M. SINCLAIR You send me some ghastly screed about Spinoza.

screed /skriːd/ *verb*. LME.
[Orig. var. of SHRED *verb*. Later from the noun.]
1 *verb trans.* & *intrans.* Shred, tear, rip. *obsolete* exc. *dial.* LME.
2 *verb intrans.* Make a sound as of tearing cloth; make a loud shrill sound. *Scot.* E18.
3 *verb trans.* Recite or relate (an account etc.) volubly or readily. Usu. foll. by *off*, *away*. *Scot.* L18.
4 *verb intrans.* Level (a surface) by means of a screed; apply (material) as a screed to a floor surface. L19.
4 screed in finish off a surface around (a frame etc.) by means of a screed. **screed off** remove (excess material) from a surface by means of a screed.
■ **screeder** *noun* a person employed to lay floor screeds L20. **screeding** *noun* (*a*) the action of the verb; (*b*) the material of a screed: E19.

screef /skriːf/ *noun* & *verb*. *Scot.* & FORESTRY. E19.
[Var. of SCRUFF *noun*[1].]
▶ **A** *noun*. A layer of vegetation on the surface of the ground. E19.
▶ **B** *verb trans.* Clear (surface vegetation) from the ground. E20.

screel /skriːl/ *verb* & *noun*. *Scot.*, *dial.*, & *Barbados*. Also **skreel**. L19.
[Imit., or rel. to SKIRL *verb*[1].]
▶ **A** *verb intrans.* Utter or emit a high-pitched or a discordant cry or sound; screech, scream. L19.
▶ **B** *noun*. A high-pitched cry or sound. L19.

screen /skriːn/ *noun*[1]. ME.
[Aphet. from Old Northern French *escren* var. of *escran* (mod. *écran*) from Old Frankish = Old High German *skrank* (German *Schrank* cupboard) bar, barrier, fence.]
1 A light upright freq. decorative structure, rigid or consisting of hinged boards or panels, used to give shelter from heat, light, or draughts or to provide concealment or privacy. ME. ▸**b** A small hand-held disc or plate of cloth, wood, paper, etc., for shading one's face from fire. M16. ▸**c** A wooden seat or settle with a high back to keep away draughts. *dial.* E19. ▸**d** Any thin extended surface set up to intercept shot in gunnery trials. L19. ▸**e** A frame covered with fine wire netting, used in a window or doorway to keep out flies, mosquitoes, etc. L19.
2 A partition, sometimes having a door or doors, dividing a room or building into different areas. LME. ▸**b** ECCLESIASTICAL. A usu. decorated partition of wood, stone, etc., separating the nave from the chancel, choir, or sanctuary. M17. ▸**c** A wall set in front of a building and masking the façade. M19. ▸**d** GEOLOGY. A roughly tabular body of older rock separating two intrusions. E20.
3 *transf.* A thing giving shelter, protection, or concealment; shelter or concealment provided thus. M16. ▸**b** A line or belt of trees planted to give protection from wind. M17. ▸**c** MILITARY. A small body of troops, ships, etc., detached to cover the movements of the main body. L19. ▸**d** METEOROLOGY. = STEVENSON SCREEN. L19. ▸**e** CRICKET. A large white usu. wooden screen on wheels placed outside the boundary behind the bowler, to act as a shield against

visual distraction and help the batsman see the ball. Also ***sight-screen***. L19. ▸**f** A windscreen. E20. ▸**g** In N. American football, basketball, etc., a manoeuvre in which an attacking player is protected by a group of team-mates. M20.

4 A large sieve or riddle used for sorting or grading grain, coal, etc., into different sizes. L16.

5 *fig.* A measure adopted to avoid attack, encroachment, censure, etc.; the protection afforded by this. E17.

6 a A part of an electrical or other instrument which serves to shield it from external electromagnetic effects etc. Cf. SHIELD *noun*[1] 10(d). E19. ▸**b** *RADIO.* An arrangement of parallel wires located over the ground below a transmitting aerial, serving to reduce loss of power to the earth. E20. ▸**c** *ELECTRONICS.* = ***screen grid*** below. E20.

7 A flat usu. white or silver surface on which moving or still photographic pictures or images can be projected; the surface of a cathode-ray tube or similar electronic device, esp. of a television, VDU, monitor, etc., on which pictures or images appear; a television, a monitor; (freq. with *the*) films collectively, the cinema or television industry. E19. ▸**b** A notice-board, a display stand; a photograph frame resembling a folding screen. M19. ▸**c** *PHOTOGRAPHY.* More fully ***focusing screen***. A flat piece of ground glass on which the image formed by a camera lens is focused. M19.

8 a In *PRINTING*, a transparent plate or film covered with a pattern of crossed lines, dots, etc., behind which a photosensitive surface is exposed to obtain a halftone image; the pattern of dots etc. in a print so produced. In *PHOTOGRAPHY*, a patterned transparent plate or film combined with a negative during printing to give a textured appearance to the finished print. L19. ▸**b** *PRINTING.* A framed sheet of fine gauze or mesh, orig. silk, through which ink is forced in screen printing. Cf. ***silk screen*** s.v. SILK *adjective*. M20.

9 An instance or act of checking or examining a thing or person for the presence or absence of a disease, quality, substance, etc. M20.

> 🕮 **1** D. M. THOMAS Screens round a bed by the door. **2b *chancel-screen*, *choir-screen*, *rood-screen*.** **3** T. HARDY A screen of ivy . . across the front of the recess. D. ATTENBOROUGH Oxygen in the atmosphere forms a screen . . which cuts off most of the ultraviolet rays of the sun. **5** J. S. NORTHCOTE They furnished a real and legal screen for the protection of the Christian Society. G. BATTISCOMBE She . . shuts herself away . . behind a screen of shyness. **7** I. MURDOCH Violence, except on the screen, is always pathetic, ludicrous and beastly. *Listener* Valentino was the great heart-throb of the silent screen. *Daily Telegraph* National Westminster Bank is planning to put screens displaying . . stock market information into a select number of branches. ***off-screen***: see OFF *adverb* etc. ***on-screen***: see ON *adverb* etc.. ***silver screen***: see SILVER *noun & adjective*. **the big screen** cinema. **the small screen** television. ***wide screen***: see WIDE *adjective*.

Attrib. & comb.: Esp. with ref. to the cinema or television, as ***screen actor***, ***screen adaptation***, ***screen beauty***, ***screen credit***, ***screen début***, ***screen kiss***, ***screen rights***, ***screen story***, ***screen version***, etc. Special combs., as **screen current** *ELECTRONICS* the current flowing in the screen grid of a valve; **screen door** the outer door of a pair, used for protection against insects, weather, etc.; **screen dump** the process or an instance of causing what is displayed on a VDU screen to be printed out; a resulting printout; **screen editing** the editing of material displayed on a VDU screen; **screen editor** a program enabling material displayed on a VDU screen to be edited; **screen grid** *ELECTRONICS* a grid placed between the control grid and the anode of a valve to reduce the capacitance between these electrodes; **screen-memory** *PSYCHOLOGY* a childhood memory of an insignificant event recalled to block the recall of a (usu. previous) significant emotional event; **screen pass** *AMER. FOOTBALL* a forward pass to a player protected by a screen of team-mates; **screen-perch** an indoor perch for a hawk, with a weighted curtain of material hanging below it to prevent the hawk tangling the jesses; **screen plate** *PHOTOGRAPHY* (*Hist.*) a form of colour plate incorporating minute filters in primary colours; **screenplay** the script of a television or cinema film together with acting instructions, scene direction, etc.; **screen porch** *N. Amer.* a veranda protected by a screen against insects; **screen print** (*a*) a picture or design produced by screen printing; screen-printed fabric; (*b*) a facility for producing a printout of material displayed on a VDU screen; **screen-print** *verb trans.* print (a surface or a design) by screen printing; **screen printer** a person engaged or skilled in screen printing; **screen printing**, **screen process** a printing process in which ink is transferred to the surface to be printed through a screen (sense 8b), the non-printing parts of the screen having been blanked out; **screen saver** *COMPUTING* a program which replaces an unchanging screen display with a moving image, in order to prevent damage to the phosphor; **screenshot** *COMPUTING* an image of the display on a computer screen, used in demonstrating the operation of a program; **screen temperature** *METEOROLOGY* the shade temperature as measured by a thermometer in a screen (sense 3d); **screen test** a filmed audition of a prospective film or television actor; the film etc. shot on such an occasion; **screen-test** *verb trans.* give a screen test to (an actor); **screen time** the time allotted to or occupied by a production, subject, etc., on film or television; **screen voltage** *ELECTRONICS* the voltage applied to the screen grid of a valve; **screen-washer** = ***windscreen washer*** s.v. WIND *noun*[1]; **screenwriter** a person who writes a film script or a screenplay.

■ **screenful** *noun* as much or as many as can be shown at one time on a cinema, television, or VDU screen M20. **screenless** *adjective* E20.

screen /skriːn/ *noun*[2]. *slang*. Now *rare*. L18.
[Origin uncertain: perh. rel. to SCREEN *noun*, *verb*[2].]
A banknote. Chiefly in ***queer screen***, a forged banknote.

screen /skriːn/ *verb*. L15.
[from SCREEN *noun*[1].]
1 *verb trans.* Shelter, protect, or conceal (as) with a screen; cover or provide with a screen; hide partially or completely; shield from danger, punishment, detection, etc. (Foll. by *from*.) L15. ▸**b** Shut or close *off* or *in* (as) with a screen. E18. ▸**c** *MILITARY.* Cover the movements of (an army etc. or an enemy force) with a body of troops, ships, etc. L19. ▸**d** Surround (a nuclear reactor or other source of ionizing radiation) with a mass of material to absorb the radiation. E20. ▸**e** *ELECTRICITY.* Protect from external electric or magnetic fields; cover (a wire or circuit) in order to prevent it from radiating electrical interference. E20. ▸**f** In American football, basketball, etc.: shield (a team-mate) from an opponent; act as a shield against (an opponent). E20.
2 *verb trans.* **a** Pass (grain, coal, etc.) through a screen or large sieve. E17. ▸**b** Examine or check (a person, group, etc.) for the presence or absence of a quality (esp. reliability or loyalty), substance, disease, etc.; vet; test for suitability for a particular application; evaluate or analyse (data etc.) for interest or relevance. M20. ▸**c** Select, separate, or (foll. by *out*) exclude by means of such examination, checking, or analysis. M20.
3 *verb trans.* In an Inn of Court, post on a screen or notice-board. L19.
4 a *verb trans.* Project on a screen; show (a film etc.) on a screen; broadcast (a programme etc.) on television. E20. ▸**b** *verb intrans.* Be (well or badly) suited for reproduction on a cinema or television screen; (of a film or a television programme) be shown or broadcast. E20.
5 *verb trans.* *PRINTING.* Process (a picture etc.) with a lined or otherwise patterned screen to allow halftone reproduction; print by squeezing ink through a gauze or mesh screen. M20.

> 🕮 **1** W. IRVING Great exertions were made to screen him from justice. J. GALSWORTHY Under a . . Japanese sunshade . . visitors could be screened from the eyes of the curious. R. CHANDLER The drive curved and tall moulded hedges . . screened it from the street. R. INGALLS The silk walls had been screened by a . . fence of carved jade flowers. **b** J. WAINWRIGHT They led him . . to the ward, and pointed out the screened-off bed. **2b** *Daily Telegraph* Electronic equipment at airports to 'screen' passengers for weapons. D. BARLOW Less than one case in a hundred is picked up when pregnant mothers are randomly screened. **c** *New Yorker* An employment policy . . screening out people who might harbor tendencies towards nonconformist intellectualising. **4a** *Guardian* Czech television screened the invasion. *Listener* Children are sometimes known to see . . horror films screened later on. **b** H. L. WILSON She'll screen well, and . . can turn on the tears.

■ **screenable** *adjective* M20. **screener** *noun* E19.

screenage /ˈskriːnɪdʒ/ *noun*. E20.
[from SCREEN *noun*[1] + -AGE.]
The material used as a screen for ionizing radiation; such screens collectively; the action or efficiency of screening.

screenager /ˈskriːneɪdʒə/ *noun*. *colloq.* L20.
[Blend of SCREEN *noun*[1] and TEENAGER.]
A person in his or her teens or twenties who is at ease with new technology, esp. computers.

screening /ˈskriːnɪŋ/ *noun*. E18.
[from SCREEN *verb* + -ING[1].]
1 The action of SCREEN *verb*; an instance of this; *spec.* a showing of a film or television programme. E18.
2 In *pl.* Refuse separated from sifted or screened grain etc.; *spec.* an inferior grade of wheat or polished rice. M18.
3 The blocking of broadcast signals by an obstruction, as a hill or building. E20.
4 *PHYSICS.* The reduction of the electric field about an atomic nucleus by the space charge of the surrounding electrons. E20.

> 🕮 **1** D. O. SELZNICK Private screenings of . . one of the greatest motion pictures. *Nature* Screening for HIV is available to all. *attrib.*: *Hansard* The efficiency of the screening methods of M.I.5.

Comb.: **screening constant** *PHYSICS* the difference between the atomic number of a nucleus and its effective charge, reduced by screening.

screeve /skriːv/ *noun*. *Scot. & slang*. L18.
[Prob. from SCREEVE *verb*[2].]
A piece of writing; *spec.* a begging letter. Also, a banknote.

screeve /skriːv/ *verb*[1] *intrans.* Now *dial.* LME.
[Aphet. from Old French *escrever*, formed as ES- + Latin *crepare* crackle, crack.]
Orig. of a wound: discharge matter or moisture, ooze.

screeve /skriːv/ *verb*[2]. *slang*. M19.
[Perh. from Italian *scrivere* from Latin *scribere* write.]
1 *verb trans.* Write. M19.
2 *verb intrans.* Draw on a pavement with coloured chalks. M19.
■ **screever** *noun* M19.

screigh /skriːk, -x/ *noun*. *Scot. dial.* E19.
[Perh. from SKREIGH *noun*[1] & *verb*. Cf. SCREECH *noun*[2].]
Whisky.

screw /skruː/ *noun*[1]. LME.
[Old French *escroue* fem. (mod. *écrou* masc.), either from West Germanic = Middle High German *schrūbe* (German *Schraube*), corresp. to Middle Dutch *schrūve*, or directly from Latin *scrofa* sow, (in medieval Latin) female screw. Cf. Spanish *puerca* sow, screw. In branch II from the verb.]
▸ **I 1** A rod or pin having a spiral ridge or thread running around the outside (***male screw***), fitting by rotation into a round socket bored with a corresponding groove or thread (***female screw***), and used to raise a weight, apply pressure, or regulate or measure longitudinal movement. LME. ▸**b** *MECHANICS.* A modification of the inclined plane. L16. ▸**c** An instrument of torture for crushing the thumbs, *the* thumbscrews. Usu. in *pl.* M17.
2 The rotating spirally ridged or spiral-shaped end of an instrument designed to bore a hole or draw something out; the worm of a corkscrew etc.; such an instrument, *spec.* †(***a***) a gimlet; (***b***) a corkscrew. L16.
3 A metal male screw, usu. tapering and with a sharp point and a slotted head, used esp. in carpentry to fasten things by being driven into wood etc. and rotated to form a thread; a similar male screw rotated into a female screw to fasten things. Also = ***screw-bolt*** below. E17. ▸**b** Helical grooving or ridging. L19.
4 *fig.* A means or instance of applying pressure or coercion. Freq. in ***put on the screw(s)***, ***turn the screw(s)*** below. M17.
5 Each of the component parts of a screw-joint. M17.
6 A thing having a spiral course or shape. M17. ▸**b** = ***screw-stone*** below. E18.
7 *slang*. **a** A key, *esp.* a skeleton key. M17. ▸**b** A prison warder. E19.
8 More fully ***screw-propeller***. A propeller consisting of a set of three or four blades set at an angle on a central shaft or boss, used esp. for propelling a ship or aircraft. M19. ▸**b** In full ***screw-steamer***. A ship driven by a propeller or propellers. M19.

> 🕮 **1 *Archimedean screw*, *bench screw*, *Jack screw*, *levelling screw*, *water-screw***, etc. **3 *Allen screw*, *lag screw*, *wood-screw***, etc. **6** R. D. BLACKMORE There was scarcely the screw of his tail to be seen.

▸ **II 9** An act of screwing something; a turn of a screw. E18. ▸**b** *BILLIARDS & SNOOKER* etc. A stroke giving spin to the cue-ball by striking it below its centre; the oblique curling motion resulting from this stroke. M19. ▸**c** *CRICKET & TENNIS* etc. Spin imparted to the ball on delivery; a ball to which spin has been imparted. M19.
10 a A person, esp. a woman, considered in sexual terms; a (*good*, *bad*, etc.) sexual partner. Also, a prostitute. *coarse slang*. E18. ▸**b** An act of sexual intercourse. *coarse slang*. E20.
11 The state of being twisted awry; a contortion of the body or features. E18. ▸**b** ***the screws***, rheumatism. *slang*. L19.
12 A severe tutor; a rigorous examination. *US College slang*. E19.
13 An unhealthy or worn-out horse. *slang*. E19.
14 A small amount *of* a commodity, as tobacco, wrapped up in a small twisted piece of paper; a wrapper of this kind. M19.
15 *slang*. **a** A person forcing down a price by haggling; a stingy miserly person. M19. ▸**b** Salary, wages. M19.
16 A look, a stare, *esp.* an aggressive one. *slang* (orig. *Austral.*). E20.

> 🕮 **10a** M. MACHLIN He's not such a great screw. **14** *Woman's Illustrated* The children pack the basket. 'Don't forget the screw of salt'.

Phrases: **a screw loose** *colloq.* a dangerous weakness in an arrangement etc., something amiss; (***have a screw loose***, be eccentric or slightly mentally disturbed). **put on the screw(s)**, **turn the screw(s)** *colloq.* apply moral or psychological pressure, esp. to extort or intimidate.

Comb.: **screw axis** *CRYSTALLOGRAPHY* an axis such that a combination of rotation about it and translation along it constitutes a symmetry operation, but neither does so alone; **screw-bean** a mesquite of the south-western US, etc., *Prosopis pubescens*, with spirally twisted pods; **screw-bolt** *noun & verb* (*a*) a metal male screw with a blunt end on which a nut is threaded to bolt things together; (*b*) *verb trans.* fasten with a screw-bolt; **screw cap** = ***screw top*** below; **screw-capped** *adjective* = ***screw-topped*** below; **screw-coupling** a female screw with threads at each end for joining lengths of pipe or rods; **screw-die** = DIE *noun*[1] 5(a); **screw dislocation** *CRYSTALLOGRAPHY* a form of crystal defect characterized by a unit distortion of the lattice in a particular direction such that the lattice planes perpendicular to that direction form continuous spiral sheets; **screw eye** a screw having a loop or eye for passing cord etc. through rather than a slotted head; **screw fly** *US* = *screw-worm fly* below; **screwgate (karabiner)** a type of lockable karabiner; **screw-gear** gear consisting of a screw with an endless thread and a cog-wheel or pinion; **screw hook** a hook for hanging things on, with a threaded point for fastening it to a wall etc.; **screw-jack** a vehicle jack worked by a screw device; **screw-joint** a joint formed by screwing together the ends of piping etc.; **screw-nail** a wood-screw; **screw pile** a foundation pile with a screw at its lower end adapted for screwing instead of driving; **screw-pin** (*a*) a threaded, esp. adjustable, pin or bolt, as on a vice; (*b*) the pin or rod forming the foundation of a screw; **screw pine** = PANDANUS 1; **screw-plate** a hardened steel plate with threaded holes for making male screws; **screw-press** a machine in which pressure is applied by means of a screw; *screw-propeller*: see sense 8 above; **screw-pump** = ARCHIMEDEAN *screw*; **screw-rate** the number of screw-threads of a screw per unit length; *screw-steamer*: see sense 8b above; **screw stock** = DIE *noun*[1] 5(a); **screw-stone** a stone containing the hollow cast of an encrinite; **screw tail** a dog's tail which is twisted or crooked; **screw-tap** a tool used for cutting female screws; **screw-thread** the helical ridge of a screw; **screw top** a round cap or lid that can be screwed on to a bottle, jar, etc.; **screw-top, screw-topped** *adjectives* (of a bottle etc.) having a screw top; **screw-up** *colloq.* (orig. *US*) a blunder, a muddle, a mess; a state or situation of confusion or emotional disturbance; **screw valve** a stopcock opened and shut with a screw; **screw worm** *US* the larva of any of various blowflies which develop in the wounds or nostrils of animals and man, esp. *Cochliomyia hominivorax*, the larva of which has spiny hairs encircling each segment; **screw-worm fly** *US* the adult of the screw worm.

■ **screwish** *adjective* (*rare*) of the nature of a screw L16. **screwless** *adjective* E20. **screw-wise** *adverb* in the manner or form of a screw M18.

†screw *noun*[2]. Also **scrow**. L17–M19.

[Prob. from French: cf. French *escrouelle*, now *écrouelle*.]

Any of various freshwater shrimps (gammarids).

screw /skruː/ *verb*. L16.

[from SCREW *noun*[1].]

▶ **I 1** *verb trans.* Twist, contort, (the features, body, etc.); wrench (one's head, oneself) *round*. L16.

2 *verb trans.* Propel by a spiral movement; force or squeeze tortuously *into, through*, etc. M17.

3 a *verb trans.* Twist violently so as to alter in shape. E18. ▶**b** *verb trans.* = *screw up* (f) below. Cf. FUCK *verb* 2b. *US colloq.* M20.

4 *coarse slang.* **a** *verb intrans.* = FUCK *verb* 1. E18. ▶**b** *verb trans.* = FUCK *verb* 2. E18. ▶**c** *verb trans. & intrans.* = FUCK *verb* 3. M20.

5 *verb intrans.* Wind spirally, twist or turn *around* like a screw, follow a curling course. E19.

6 a *verb trans. & intrans.* In various ball-games: impart spin or curl to (a ball etc.); swerve, spin, curl. M19. ▶**b** *verb trans.* RUGBY FOOTBALL. Cause (a scrum) to twist round by pushing in a body. L19.

7 *verb intrans.* Depart hastily, go away. Freq. foll. by *out, off. slang* (orig. & chiefly *US*). L19.

8 a *verb trans.* Look at, watch (a person); *spec.* stare at (a person) before a fight. *slang* (orig. & chiefly *Austral.*). E20. ▶**b** *verb intrans.* Look. *Austral. slang.* E20.

> 📖 **1** G. MANVILLE FENN Screwing his . . face into a state of rigid determination. C. PHILLIPS The man screwed himself around in his seat. **2** C. NESS If the . . serpent can but see a hole . . he will easily screw in his whole body. **3a** V. WOOLF Cam screwed her handkerchief round her finger. **b** W. GADDIS She got fed up with him screwing the Sunday roast, so she shot herself. J. IRVING He said that women's lib had screwed up his wife so much that she divorced him. **c** M. J. BOSSE Did I screw up by admitting . . you knew about the package? **4c** E. REVELEY Screw the lawyers and court orders—I'm doing this my own way!

▶ **II 9** *verb trans.* Attach or fix (as) with an inserted screw or screws. E17.

10 *verb trans.* Compress or force (as) with a screw or vice; stretch or tighten (as) by turning a screw; adjust or operate (an instrument etc.) by tightening a screw. Freq. foll. by *up*. E17. ▶**b** *fig.* Make more tense; work up (*in, into*). Also foll. by *up*. E17.

11 *verb trans.* Extort, force, or draw (information, money, consent, etc.) *out of* a person, esp. by psychological pressure. E17.

12 *verb trans.* Examine rigorously. *obsolete* exc. *US College slang.* E17.

13 a *verb trans.* Oppress, exploit; cheat *out of* money etc., defraud, deceive. Also foll. by *down*. Now *colloq.* M17. ▶**b** *verb trans.* Force (a seller) to lower a price, beat down. L17. ▶**c** *verb intrans.* Be mean or parsimonious. M19.

14 *verb trans.* Produce, attain, or elicit with an effort. Also foll. by *out, up*. L17.

> 📖 **9** JAMES SMITH A square piece of wood . . being firmly screwed . . to the board. **10** P. N. HASLUCK Screw the book into the press. TENNYSON Screw not the chord too sharply lest it snap. M. WOODHOUSE Screwing up the throttle control rod . . to raise the idling speed. **b** SHAKES. *Macb.* But screw your courage to the sticking place, And we'll not fail. **11** *Times* By screwing more money out of tax-payers he diminishes their savings. **13a** *Tucson Magazine* It's all right to screw the people.

▶ **III 15 a** *verb trans.* Rotate (a thing) so as to insert or fix it into or on to a surface or object (as) by means of a spiral thread or screw; attach (two things) *together* in this way. E17. ▶**†b** *fig.* Gradually implant (an idea etc.); insinuate (esp. oneself) into favour etc. E17–E19. ▶**c** *verb trans.* Take *out* (a screw) by turning, unscrew. *rare.* E17. ▶**d** *verb intrans.* Be adapted or designed for joining or taking apart by means of a screw or screws. Usu. foll. by *off, on*. L17.

16 *verb intrans.* Move or penetrate with a winding course; *fig.* worm one's way *into*. E17.

17 *verb trans.* Tighten (a screw etc.) by turning. M17.

18 *verb trans.* Provide with a spiral groove or ridge; cut a thread on or in. M17.

19 *verb trans.* Break into (a house etc.) with a skeleton key; *gen.* burgle. *slang.* E19.

20 *verb intrans.* Travel on water by means of a propeller or propellers. M19.

21 *verb trans.* Wear out (a horse) with hard work. *Austral. slang.* L19.

> 📖 **15** C. GEBLER Maureen screwed the top on to the mustard jar. P. D. JAMES Hooks had been screwed into the lower shelf. **d** *Which?* Round filters simply screw on the front of the camera lens.

With adverbs in specialized senses, & phrases: **have one's head screwed on (the right way)** *colloq.* have common sense, be level-headed. **screw a person's neck** throttle or strangle a person. **screw around** *colloq.* (orig. *US*) (*a*) *coarse slang* be promiscuous; (*b*) *slang* fool about. **screw up** (*a*) raise (a payment, rent, etc.) to an exacting or extortionate figure; (*b*) contract the surrounding parts of (the mouth or eyes); contort (the face); (*c*) summon up (one's courage etc.); (*d*) contract and crush (a piece of paper etc.) into a tight mass; (*e*) *colloq.* (chiefly *N. Amer.*) blunder, make an error, esp. through incompetence; (*f*) *colloq.* (orig. *US*) spoil, ruin, bungle, mismanage (an event, opportunity, etc.); upset, disturb mentally; (see also senses 3b, 10, 14 above).

Comb.: **screw-down** *adjective* adapted or designed to be closed by screwing; **screw-in, screw-on** *adjectives* adapted or designed to be attached by screwing into or on to something.

■ **screwable** *adjective* able to be screwed; *coarse slang* (of a woman) sexually attractive: L19. **screwer** *noun* (*a*) a person who or thing which screws; (*b*) *slang* a burglar, a housebreaker: M17.

screwball /ˈskruːbɔːl/ *noun, adjective, & verb.* Chiefly *N. Amer.* M19.

[from SCREW *noun*[1] + BALL *noun*[1]. Cf. **oddball** s.v. ODD *adjective.*]

▶ **A** *noun.* **1** Orig. in CRICKET, a ball bowled with spin. Now in BASEBALL, a ball pitched with reverse spin against the natural curve. M19.

2 An eccentric or mad person. *slang.* M20.

3 JAZZ. Fast improvisation, unrestrained swing. *slang.* M20.

> 📖 **2** J. STEINBECK Whether brilliant or a screwball nobody ever knew.

▶ **B** *adjective.* Eccentric, mad; *spec.* designating or pertaining to a style of zany fast-moving comedy film involving eccentric characters or ridiculous situations. *slang.* M20.

> 📖 *Time* Screwball fantasy about a . . quarterback . . who dies and comes back to life as an eccentric millionaire.

▶ **C** *verb intrans.* Pitch a screwball in baseball; travel like a screwball. *rare.* M20.

screwdriver /ˈskruːdrʌɪvə/ *noun.* L18.

[from SCREW *noun*[1] + DRIVER.]

1 A tool consisting of a handle attached to a shaft with a tip shaped to fit the head of a screw so as to turn it. L18.

2 A cocktail made of vodka and orange juice. Orig. *US.* M20.

screwed /skruːd/ *adjective.* E17.

[from SCREW *verb, noun*[1]: see -ED[1], -ED[2].]

1 That has been screwed; provided with a screw or screws; twisted, contorted, contracted; *slang* ruined. E17.

2 Partly intoxicated, tipsy. *slang.* M19.

Comb.: **screwed-up** *adjective* (*colloq.*) (of a condition, situation, etc.) excessively intense or complicated; (of a person) confused, upset; neurotic, slightly emotionally disturbed.

screwing /ˈskruːɪŋ/ *noun.* L17.

[from SCREW *verb* + -ING[1].]

The action of SCREW *verb*; an instance or act of this.

> 📖 A. WILSON Married to an old man. You've never had a proper screwing.

Comb.: **screwing die, screwing stock** = DIE *noun*[1] 5(a).

screwmatic /skruːˈmatɪk/ *adjective & noun. joc.* L19.

[Alt. of *rheumatic* after SCREW *noun*[1].]

▶ **A** *adjective.* Rheumatic. *rare.* L19.

▶ **B** *noun.* In *pl.* = RHEUMATIC *noun* 1. L19.

screwsman /ˈskruːzmən/ *noun. slang.* Pl. **-men**. E19.

[from SCREW *noun*[1] + -'S[1] + MAN *noun*.]

A burgler, a housebreaker; a safe-cracker.

screwy /ˈskruːi/ *adjective. slang.* E19.

[from SCREW *noun*[1] or *verb* + -Y[1].]

1 Slightly intoxicated, tipsy. E19.

2 Of a person: mean, parsimonious. M19.

3 Of a horse: worn out, unhealthy. M19.

4 Of a track etc.: winding. L19.

5 Mad, eccentric; absurd, ridiculous. Orig. *US.* L19.

■ **screwiness** *noun* L19.

scrib /skrɪb/ *noun*[1]. Now *rare* or *obsolete.* E17.

[Perh. var. of SCRUB *noun*[1].]

A miser.

scrib /skrɪb/ *noun*[2]. *rare.* L18.

[Abbreviation.]

= SCRIBBLE *noun* 1.

scribable /ˈskrʌɪbəb(ə)l/ *adjective. arch.* LME.

[from SCRIBE *verb* + -ABLE. Cf. medieval Latin *scrivabilis*.]

Suitable for being written on.

scribacious /skrʌɪˈbeɪʃəs/ *adjective. rare.* L17.

[from Latin *scribere* write + -ACIOUS.]

Given to or fond of writing.

■ **scribaciousness** *noun* L19.

†scribbet *noun.* L17–E18.

[Perh. from SCRIBE *verb* + -ET[1].]

A charcoal crayon or pencil.

scribble /ˈskrɪb(ə)l/ *verb*[1] *& noun.* LME.

[from medieval Latin dim. of Latin *scribere* write: see -LE[3].]

▶ **A** *verb.* **1** *verb trans.* **a** Write in an untidy or illegible hand through haste or carelessness; write hurriedly, resulting in an inferior composition. Also, draw or portray (an object) by rapid and irregular marks similar to hurried handwriting. Freq. foll. by *away, down, out.* LME. ▶**b** Cover with untidy or illegible writing or irregular marks. Usu. foll. by *over.* M16.

2 a *verb intrans.* Write something hastily or carelessly; produce inferior writing; (freq. *derog.* or *joc.*) be an author or writer. Also, make meaningless or irregular marks resembling hurried writing. E16. ▶**b** *verb trans.* With obj. & compl.: bring into a specified state by scribbling. *rare.* E18.

> 📖 **1a** S. BEDFORD Before sailing, Louis had found time to scribble a postcard. **b** A. CARTER The city was scribbled all over with graffiti. **2a** J. GRENFELL I used to scribble a bit. Poetry.

▶ **B** *noun.* **1** A hastily or carelessly written letter, note, etc. Also, an inferior or trivial composition. L16.

2 Hurried or careless and untidy handwriting; an example of this. Also, a figure etc. drawn with irregular and meaningless marks similar to hurried hand writing. E18.

> 📖 **1** D. M. THOMAS Her last word from me had been one of my indifferent scribbles. **2** M. KEANE The envelope was covered with doodling scribbles . . making no kind of sense.

■ **scribblative** /ˈskrɪblətɪv/ *adjective* (*rare*) of or pertaining to scribbling E19. **scribblement** *noun* = SCRIBBLE *noun* 1 E17. **scribbler** *noun*[1] (*a*) a person who scribbles; a writer or author, *esp.* an inferior one; (*b*) (chiefly *N. Amer.*) a scribbling block or pad: M16. **scribblingly** *adverb* in a scribbling manner L16.

scribble /ˈskrɪb(ə)l/ *verb*[2] *trans.* L17.

[Prob. from Low German. Cf. German *schrubbeln, schrobbeln* frequentative from Middle Low German, Middle Dutch *schrubben, schrobben* SCRUB *verb.*]

Card (wool, cotton), etc. coarsely.

■ **scribbler** *noun*[2] a person who or machine which scribbles wool L17.

scribbleomania /ˌskrɪbləˈmeɪnɪə/ *noun. rare.* L18.

[from SCRIBBLE *verb*[1] + -O- + -MANIA.]

A craze or passion for scribbling.

scribble-scrabble /ˈskrɪb(ə)lskrab(ə)l/ *adverb & noun. colloq.* L16.

[Redupl. of SCRIBBLE *verb*[1].]

▶**† A** *adverb.* In a scribbling manner. *rare.* Only in L16.

▶ **B** *noun.* **†1** A scribbler. Also, a reckless person. M17–E18.

2 A piece of hurried or careless writing. M18.

scribbling /ˈskrɪblɪŋ/ *noun.* M16.

[from SCRIBBLE *verb*[1] + -ING[1].]

1 The action of SCRIBBLE *verb*[1]. M16.

2 A scribbled thing; a scrawl, a scribbled mark. L16.

Comb.: **scribbling block, scribbling pad** a pad of scribbling paper; **scribbling paper** paper used for rough drafts, jottings, etc.

scribbly /ˈskrɪbli/ *adjective.* L19.

[from SCRIBBLE *verb*[1] + -Y[1].]

Characterized by scribbling; resembling a scribble. Chiefly in ***scribbly gum***, any of several Australian eucalypts, esp. *Eucalyptus haemastoma*, with irregular marks on the bark formed by the burrowing larvae of a moth, *Ogmograptus scribula*.

scribe /skrʌɪb/ *noun*[1]. ME.

[Latin *scriba* official or public writer (in Vulgate translating Greek *grammateus*, Hebrew *sōpēr*), from *scribere* write.]

1 JEWISH HISTORY. Orig., a member of the class of professional copyists, editors and interpreters of Scripture and the law. Later, such a person chiefly serving as a jurist and in the Gospels often coupled with the Pharisees as upholders of ancestral tradition. ME.

2 *Hist.* A public official concerned with writing or keeping records, accounts, etc.; a secretary, a clerk. LME.

3 A person who writes at another's dictation; an amanuensis. Now *rare*. **L15.**
4 Chiefly *Hist.* A transcriber of documents; *esp.* an ancient or medieval copyist of manuscripts. **M16.**
5 A person skilled in handwriting. *arch.* **L16.**
6a A person who writes or is in the habit of writing; an author; the writer of a particular letter etc. Freq. *joc.* **L16.** ▸**b** A journalist. *colloq.* (now *N. Amer.*). **E19.**

📖 **5** DICKENS No great scribe; rather handling the pen like the pocket-staff he carries about with him.

■ **scribal** *adjective* (chiefly *Hist.*) of, pertaining to, or characteristic of (the work of) a scribe **M19.** **scribeship** *noun* (*rare*) the office or function of a scribe **E17.** **scribism** *noun* (*rare*) the teaching and literature of the Jewish scribes **M17.**

scribe /skrʌɪb/ *noun*[2]. **E18.**
[from the verb.]
1 A written mark; a letter, a piece of writing. Chiefly in ***scribe o' the pen***. Cf. SCRIP *noun*[2]. Chiefly *Scot.* & *dial.* **E18.**
2 More fully ***scribe awl***. A pointed tool for marking wood, stone, metal, etc. to guide a saw, or in sign-writing. **E19.**
Comb.: ***scribe-awl***: see sense 2 above; **scribe-mark** a guide mark made with a scribing tool.

scribe /skrʌɪb/ *verb.* **LME.**
[In sense 1 partly from Latin *scribere* write, partly from SCRIBE *noun*[1]; in sense 2 perh. aphet. from DESCRIBE. Cf. SCRIVE.]
1 a *verb trans.* Write down. Chiefly *Scot.* & *dial.*. **LME.** ▸**b** *verb intrans.* Act as a scribe, write. Now chiefly *Scot.* & *dial.* **M17.**
2 *verb trans.* Orig. in CARPENTRY, mark the intended outline of (a piece of timber) with one point of a pair of compasses, the other point being drawn along the edge of the piece to which the marked piece is to be fitted. Now, mark or score (a piece of wood, metal, stone, etc.) with a pointed instrument or a laser beam in order to indicate the outline to which the piece is to be cut or shaped; draw (a line etc.) in this way. **L17.** ▸**b** Shape the edge of (a piece of wood, metal, stone, etc.) to fit the profile of another piece or an uneven surface. **L17.**
3 Make identifying marks on. **M19.**

📖 **2** *fig.*: M. AYRTON This patch . . scribed with tracks cut through scrub . . by men with wheel-barrows.

■ **scriber** *noun* a tool or appliance for scribing; = SCRIBE *noun*[2] 2: **M19.** **scribing** *noun* (*a*) the action of the verb; (*b*) an identifying mark; (*c*) in *pl.*, incised markings on stone etc.; writings, scribblings: **E18.**

Scriblerian /skrɪˈblɪərɪən/ *noun* & *adjective.* **M20.**
[from Martinus *Scriblerus*, a character invented by the Scriblerus Club (see below) + -IAN. Cf. SCRIBBLER *noun*[1].]
▶ **A** *noun. Hist.* A member of the Scriblerus Club formed *c* 1713 by Pope, Swift, Arbuthnot, and others, who published the *Memoirs of Martinus Scriblerus* in 1741 in order to ridicule lack of taste in learning. **M20.**
▶ **B** *adjective.* Of, pertaining to, or characteristic of the Scriblerus Club or its members. **M20.**

scried *verb*[1], *verb*[2] *pa. t.* & *pple* of SCRY *verb*[1], *verb*[2].

scrieve /skriːv/ *verb*[1] *intrans. Scot.* **L18.**
[App. from Old Norse *skrefa* to stride.]
Move or glide along swiftly.

scrieve /skriːv/ *verb*[2] *trans.* **L19.**
[Var. of SCRIVE *verb*.]
Scribe, mark; *esp.* mark the outline of a ship to be built. Freq. foll. by *in*. Chiefly in ***scrieve board***, a scrive-board.

scriggle /ˈskrɪg(ə)l/ *verb* & *noun.* Chiefly *dial.* **E19.**
[App. a blend of WRIGGLE *verb* and STRUGGLE *verb*.]
▶ **A** *verb intrans.* Wriggle, struggle. **E19.**
▶ **B** *noun.* A wriggle; a scrawly piece of writing; a squiggle. **M19.**

scrim /skrɪm/ *noun* & *adjective.* **L18.**
[Origin unkn.]
▶ **A** *noun.* **1** Open-weave fabric (orig., thin canvas; now also, loosely woven cotton, hessian, or linen) of various thicknesses, used chiefly for upholstery, and for lining in the building and other industries. **L18.**
2 THEATRICAL & CINEMATOGRAPHY. Gauze cloth used for screens or as a lens filter; a screen or filter made of this. Orig. & chiefly *N. Amer.* **E20.**
3 *transf.* & *fig.* A veil, a screen; something that conceals what is happening. **M20.**

📖 **3** *Time* The vast . . shuffle area is a stage, with theatrical lighting, scrims and backdrops.

▶ **B** *attrib.* or as *adjective.* Made of scrim. **L19.**

📖 F. FORSYTH Dressed from head to toe in camouflage green, his face masked with scrim netting.

†**scrimer** *noun. rare* (Shakes.). Only in **E17.**
[Aphet. from French *escrimeur*, from *escrimer* to fence.]
A fencer, a sword-fighter.

scrimish /ˈskrɪmɪʃ/ *noun.* Long *obsolete* exc. *dial.* **E16.**
[Var. of SKIRMISH *noun*. Cf. next.]
†**1** An alarm, an outcry. *rare.* Only in **E16.**
2 A skirmish. **M16.**

scrimmage /ˈskrɪmɪdʒ/ *noun* & *verb.* See also SCRUMMAGE. **LME.**
[Alt. of prec. with assim. to -AGE. Cf. SCRUM.]
▶ **A** *noun.* **1** A skirmish. Also, a fencing bout. *obsolete* exc. *US.* **LME.**
2a A noisy dispute or tussle; a rough or confused struggle; a scuffle; = SCRUMMAGE *noun* 1. *colloq.* **L18.** ▸**b** A confused noisy proceeding, *esp.* a thorough search roughly or noisily carried out. *Scot.* & *dial.* **M19.**
3 In RUGBY FOOTBALL, = SCRUM *noun* 1 (now *rare*). In various other sports, *spec.* Australian Rules football, a (confused) tussle for possession of the ball. **M19.**
4 In AMER. FOOTBALL, a sequence of play beginning with a backward pass from the centre to put the ball in play and continuing until the ball is declared dead. Also, (*N. Amer.*) a session in which a sports team's various squads practise plays against each other. **L19.**

📖 **2a** J. C. LINCOLN Likely 'twould end in his bein' killed in some rumshop scrimmage. *fig.*: L. BLUE Guests at this type of gastronomic scrimmage enjoy milling around the kitchen. **4 line of scrimmage** the imaginary line separating two teams at the beginning of a scrimmage.

Comb.: **scrimmage line** = ***line of scrimmage*** above.
▶ **B** *verb.* **1** *verb intrans.* Skirmish, quarrel, fight. Chiefly *dial.* **E19.**
2 *verb intrans.* Bustle about; search thoroughly or noisily. **M19.**
3 *verb trans.* RUGBY, AUSTRAL. RULES, & AMER. FOOTBALL. Put (the ball) in a scrum or scrimmage; propel or take along in a scrum or scrimmage. **E20.**
4 *verb intrans.* AMER. FOOTBALL. Engage in a scrimmage. **E20.**
■ **scrimmager** *noun* **L19.**

scrimmy /ˈskrɪmi/ *interjection. colloq. rare.* **L19.**
[Origin unkn.]
Expr. astonishment.

scrimp /skrɪmp/ *adjective* & *adverb.* Orig. & chiefly *Scot.* **L17.**
[Perh. rel. to SHRIMP *noun* & *adjective*. Cf. SHRIMPED.]
▶ **A** *adjective.* Scant, scanty, meagre. **L17.**

📖 R. C. HUTCHINSON A city man by his appearance, scrimp and bald.

▶ **B** *adverb.* Scarcely, barely. Now *rare.* **M18.**
■ **scrimply** *adverb* (*a*) parsimoniously; (*b*) scarcely, barely: **E18.**

scrimp /skrɪmp/ *verb* & *noun.* **M18.**
[from prec.]
▶ **A** *verb.* **1** *verb trans.* Restrict (a person) in supplies, esp. of food. **M18.**
2 *verb trans.* Cut short in amount; use sparingly. **L18.**
3 *verb intrans.* Economize, be parsimonious. Freq. in ***scrimp and save***. **M19.**

📖 **1** TENNYSON The Master scrimps his haggard sempstress of her daily bread. **3** B. T. BRADFORD David . . scrimped and scraped . . yet was always beset by the most acute financial worries.

▶ **B** *noun.* The action or process of scrimping; meagre allowance; economy. Also, an instance of this; a small amount *of* something. **M19.**

📖 J. KELMAN Nothing at all in the house bar a scrimp of cheese.

■ **scrimped** *adjective* that has been scrimped; meagre, contracted, narrow: **E18.**

scrimpy /ˈskrɪmpi/ *adjective*[1]. **M19.**
[from SCRIMP *adjective* + -Y[1].]
Small, meagre, scanty.

📖 *Time* Never throws away a line, even the scrimpiest, that he hasn't impeccably polished.

■ **scrimpiness** *noun* **M19.**

scrimpy /ˈskrɪmpi/ *adjective*[2]. **E20.**
[from SCRIMP *verb* + -Y[1].]
Of a person: inclined to scrimp or economize; mean, parsimonious.

scrimshander /ˈskrɪmʃandə/ *verb* & *noun.* Also **skr-**, (in sense B.1) **-dy** /-di/. **M19.**
[from var. of SCRIMSHAW + -ER[1].]
▶ **A** *verb trans.* & *intrans.* = SCRIMSHAW *verb.* **M19.**
▶ **B** *noun.* **1** = SCRIMSHAW *noun.* **M19.**
2 A person who scrimshaws. Cf. earlier SCRIMSHONER. **L20.**

scrimshank /ˈskrɪmʃaŋk/ *verb* & *noun. slang.* Also **skr-**. **L19.**
[Origin unkn.]
Orig. & chiefly MILITARY. ▶**A** *verb intrans.* Shirk duty. **L19.**
▶ **B** *noun.* **1** An act or period of scrimshanking. **E20.**
2 A scrimshanker. **E20.**
■ **scrimshanker** *noun* a shirker **E20.**

scrimshaw /ˈskrɪmʃɔː/ *verb* & *noun.* Also (earlier) †**-shont** & other vars.; **skr-**. **E19.**
[Origin unkn. Later perh. infl. by the surname *Scrimshaw*. Cf. SCRIMSHANDER.]
▶ **A** *verb trans.* & *intrans.* Decorate (bone, ivory, shells, etc.) with carved or coloured designs, as a craft or pastime originally practised by sailors during long voyages. **E19.**
▶ **B** *noun.* Decoration of bone, ivory, shells, etc., with carved or coloured designs. Also, an item of work produced in this way; *spec.* a piece of carved or decorated bone, ivory, shell, etc. **M19.**
■ **scrimshoner** *noun* = SCRIMSHANDER 2 **L19.**

scrin /skrɪn/ *noun.* Chiefly *dial.* **M18.**
[Cf. Middle Dutch *schrinde*, *schrunde* = Old High German *scrunta* (German *Schrunde*) fissure, crack.]
A small or lesser vein of ore in a lead-mine.

scrinch /skrɪn(t)ʃ/ *verb intrans. rare* (chiefly *US*). **M19.**
[Cf. SCRINGE *verb*[1], SCRUNCH *verb*.]
Sit closely or bunch together.

scringe /skrɪn(d)ʒ/ *verb*[1]. *obsolete* exc. *Scot.* & *dial.* **E17.**
[Alt. of CRINGE *verb*. Cf. SCROUNGE *verb*.]
1 *verb trans.* Screw up (one's face); cause (the back or shoulders) to flinch from cold. **E17.**
2 *verb trans.* Squeeze violently. **L18.**
3 *verb intrans.* Flinch, cower. **E19.**
4 Wander or prowl about. **M19.**

scringe /skrɪn(d)ʒ/ *verb*[2] & *noun.* Chiefly *Scot.* & *dial.* **L18.**
[Origin unkn.]
▶ **A** *verb.* **1** *verb trans.* Whip, flog; *fig.* castigate, lash (a person) with the tongue. **L18.**
2 *verb intrans.* Fish with a scringe net. **E19.**
3 *verb trans.* Catch (fish) with a scringe net. **L19.**
▶ **B** *noun.* In full ***scringe net***. A kind of seine-net. **M19.**

scrip /skrɪp/ *noun*[1]. *arch.* **ME.**
[Aphet. from Old French *escrep(p)e* purse, bag for alms, var. of *escherpe* (mod. *écharpe*), or Old Norse *skreppa* (perh. also from Old French). Cf. SCARP *noun*[1].]
A small bag, wallet, or satchel, *esp.* one carried by a pilgrim, shepherd, or beggar.

scrip /skrɪp/ *noun*[2]. **L16.**
[Perh. alt. of SCRIPT *noun*[1] by assoc. with SCRAP *noun*[1]. In sense 2, prob. infl. by SCRIP *noun*[3].]
1 A small piece, a scrap, *esp.* a scrap of paper, usu. with writing on it (cf. SCRIBE *noun*[2]); (in full ***scrip of a pen***) a scrap of writing, a brief note. *obsolete* exc. *dial.* **L16.**
2 *US.* **a** Documentation certifying indebtedness issued as currency or in lieu of money; a document certifying this. **L18.** ▸**b** More fully ***land scrip***. A certificate entitling the holder to acquire possession of certain portions of public land. **M19.** ▸**c** Fractional paper currency. **L19.**

scrip /skrɪp/ *noun*[3]. **M18.**
[Abbreviation of ***subscription receipt*** s.v. SUBSCRIPTION.]
Orig., a receipt for a share or shares in a loan or a commercial venture. Now *spec.* a provisional certificate of money subscribed to a bank or company entitling the holder to a formal certificate and dividends after completion of the necessary payments; *collect.* such certificates; *gen.* any share certificates.
Comb.: **scrip issue** the issue of additional shares to shareholders instead of a dividend in proportion to the shares already held; an instance of this.

scrip /skrɪp/ *noun*[4]. *slang.* **M20.**
[Abbreviation.]
= SCRIPT *noun*[2].

†**scriple** *noun* see SCRUPLE *noun*.

scripophily /skrɪˈpɒfɪli/ *noun.* **L20.**
[from SCRIP *noun*[3] + -O- + -PHILY.]
The collection of old bond and share certificates as a pursuit or hobby; *collect.* articles of this nature.
■ **scripophile** *noun* **L20.**

scrippage /ˈskrɪpɪdʒ/ *noun. rare.* **E17.**
[from SCRIP *noun*[1] after *baggage*.]
Light baggage. Orig. & chiefly in ***scrip and scrippage***, all one's (few) belongings.

📖 SHAKES. *A.Y.L.* Let us make an honourable retreat; though not with bag and baggage, yet with scrip and scrippage.

script /skrɪpt/ *noun*[1]. **LME.**
[Aphet. from Old French *escri(p)t* (mod. *écrit*) from Latin *scriptum* use as noun of neut. pa. pple of *scribere* write. In sense 5a also infl. by MANUSCRIPT. Cf. ESCRIPT.]
1 A written thing; a piece of writing. Now *rare.* **LME.**
2 a Handwriting as distinct from print; handwritten characters as distinct from printed characters. **M19.** ▸**b** TYPOGRAPHY. Any of various typefaces which imitate the appearance of cursive handwriting. Also more fully ***script type***. **M19.** ▸**c** A style of handwriting with the appearance of printed characters, developed as an introductory hand for teaching young children. Also more fully ***script-writing***. **E20.**
3 LAW. An original or principal document. In probate practice, a will, a codicil, or a draft of these; a written record of a will's contents which may be referred to in the event of the original's destruction. **M19.**
4 A system of writing, an alphabet. **L19.**
5 a An author's written copy of a work; a manuscript. *Theatrical slang* (*rare*). **L19.** ▸**b** The text of a film, play, broadcast, etc.; a typescript. **M20.** ▸**c** PSYCHOLOGY. The social role or behaviour appropriate to particular situations that an individual absorbs through cultural influences and asso-

ciation with others. M20. ▸**d** COMPUTING. A formalized description of a commonly occurring situation, intended to assist recognition (usu. by a machine) of descriptions of such a situation in which not all of the details are made explicit. L20. ▸**e** COMPUTING. A program or sequence of instructions intended to be carried out by another program rather than by the computer processor. L20.

6 An examinee's written answer paper or papers. E20.

1 EVELYN This hasty script is to acquaint you that [etc.]. **2a** SLOAN WILSON Written in a bold script. **4** C. SAGAN Some varieties of Cretan script remain completely undecoded. **5b** *Punch* Alfred Bester . . has written everything from TV scripts to recipes. ***prompt script***: see PROMPT *noun* 2.

Comb.: **script girl** a female assistant to the director of a film, television play, etc., who takes details of scenes filmed and performs other administrative duties; **script kiddie** (*slang, derog.*) a person who uses existing computer scripts or codes to hack into computers, lacking the expertise to write his or her own; ***script-writing***: see sense 2c above.

■ **scriptless** *adjective* (of a film, broadcast, etc.) without a script; unscripted: M20.

script /skrɪpt/ *noun*². *slang* (orig. *US*). M20.
[Abbreviation Cf. SCRIP *noun*⁴.]
A prescription, *esp.* one for narcotic drugs.

script /skrɪpt/ *verb trans.* M20.
[from SCRIPT *noun*¹.]
Adapt (a story, novel, etc.) for broadcasting or filming; write a script for (a film etc.).

scripted /ˈskrɪptɪd/ *adjective.* M20.
[from SCRIPT *noun*¹, *verb*: see -ED², -ED¹.]
Of a film, broadcast, etc.: provided with a script; read or spoken from a prepared script as opp. to extempore; adapted from a novel etc.

scripter /ˈskrɪptə/ *noun.* Orig. *US.* M20.
[formed as prec. + -ER¹.]
= SCRIPTWRITER.

scription /ˈskrɪpʃ(ə)n/ *noun.* LME.
[Latin *scriptio(n-)*, from *script-*: see SCRIPTURE, -ION.]
1 A written work; a document; an inscription. Long *rare* exc. *poet.* LME.
2 The action of writing; the writing of a script for a film etc. *rare.* E19.
3 (A style of) handwriting. *rare.* M19.

scriptor /ˈskrɪptə/ *noun*¹. *rare.* M16.
[Latin, from *script-*: see SCRIPTURE, -OR.]
A writer; a scribe.

scriptor /ˈskrɪptə/ *noun*². *obsolete* exc. *Hist.* L17.
[Perh. alt. of SCRUTOIRE after SCRIPT *noun*¹.]
A writing-desk, an escritoire.

scriptoria *noun* pl. of SCRIPTORIUM.

scriptorial /skrɪpˈtɔːrɪəl/ *adjective.* M19.
[from late Latin *scriptorius* SCRIPTORY *adjective* + -AL¹.]
Pertaining to or used for writing.
■ **scriptorially** *adverb* L20.

scriptorium /skrɪpˈtɔːrɪəm/ *noun.* Pl. **-ria** /-rɪə/, **-riums.** L18.
[medieval Latin, from Latin *script-*: see SCRIPTURE, -ORIUM.]
A room set apart for writing; *esp.* one in a monastery where manuscripts are copied.

J. HUTCHINSON A beautiful, round miniscule hand for the text became distinctive characteristics of the St. Martin's scriptorium.

scriptory /ˈskrɪpt(ə)ri/ *adjective & noun. rare.* L15.
[As noun formed as prec. As adjective from Latin *scriptorius*, formed as prec.: see -ORY¹.]
▸ **A** *noun.* A scriptorium. L15.
▸ **B** *adjective.* **1** Pertaining to or used in writing. L17.
2 Expressed in writing, written. E18.

scriptural /ˈskrɪptʃ(ə)r(ə)l/ *adjective.* M17.
[Late Latin *scripturalis*, from Latin *scriptura*: see SCRIPTURE, -AL¹.]
1 Of, based on, or pertaining to the Bible; having the authority of a scripture. M17.
2 Of or pertaining to writing. *rare.* E19.
■ **scripturalism** *noun* close adherence to or dependence on the letter of the Bible M19. **scripturalist** *noun* a person who is well versed in the Bible; an advocate or adherent of scripturalism: E18. **scripturality** *noun* the state or condition of being scriptural M19. **scripturally** *adverb* in accordance with the Bible L17. **scripturalness** *noun* = SCRIPTURALITY L19.

scripturalize /ˈskrɪptʃ(ə)r(ə)lʌɪz/ *verb trans. rare.* Also **-ise.** E19.
[formed as prec. + -IZE.]
Make scriptural; put into writing.

scripture /ˈskrɪptʃə/ *noun.* ME.
[Latin *scriptura*, from *script-* pa. ppl stem of *scribere* write: see -URE.]
1 (Usu. **S-**.) ▸**a** *sing.* & in *pl. The* body of Judaeo-Christian sacred writings, regarded as divinely inspired; *spec.* (*a*) CHRISTIAN CHURCH the Old and New Testaments, the Bible (also ***Holy Scripture***); (*b*) JUDAISM the canonical writings comprising the three divisions of the Law, the Prophets, and the Hagiographa or Writings (also more fully ***Hebrew Scriptures***). Cf. WRIT *noun* 1. ME. ▸**b** A particular passage or text of the Bible. Now *rare.* LME. ▸**c** A thing regarded as surely true. Cf. GOSPEL *noun* 4. L16. ▸**d** *sing.* & in *pl. gen.* Sacred writings or records. L16. ▸**e** Study of the Bible and the Christian religion as a school subject; a lesson in this. E20.
2 The action or art of writing; handwriting, penmanship. Now *rare.* ME.
3 An inscription; a motto, a legend; *gen.* writing, inscribed words. *arch.* LME.
4 A written record or composition; in *pl.*, writings. *arch.* LME. ▸†**b** Written composition. LME–L16.

1a LD MACAULAY The extreme Puritan . . employed, on every occasion, the imagery and style of Scripture. R. NELSON The Perfection and Perspicuity of the holy Scriptures. attrib.: ***scripture account***, ***scripture expression***, ***scripture lesson***, ***scripture story***, ***scripture view***, etc. **b** SIR W. SCOTT I have marked a scripture . . that will be useful to us baith. **c** B. FERGUSSON The Graham Report . . was . . widely circulated as scripture. **d** R. C. ZAEHNER The earliest scripture of the Aryan invaders of India. **2** DISRAELI The handwriting was of that form of scripture which attracts. **3** J. COKE With a scripture over her head, saiyng that Love was lighter then a fether. **4** †**in scripture** in writing; on record.

■ **scriptureless** *adjective* not according to or founded on the Bible M16. **scripturism** *noun* (*rare*) (*a*) reliance on or devotion to the Bible alone; (*b*) a biblical phrase or expression: M19. **scriptured** *adjective* (*rare*) †(*a*) learned or versed in the Bible; †(*b*) warranted by the Bible; (*c*) covered with writing: M16.

scripturient /skrɪpˈtʃʊərɪənt/ *adjective & noun.* Now *rare.* M17.
[Late Latin *scripturient-* pres. ppl stem of *scripturire* desire to write, from Latin *script-*: see SCRIPTURE, -ENT.]
▸ **A** *adjective.* Having a passion for writing or authorship. M17.
▸†**B** *noun.* A person with a passion for writing. Only in M17.
■ †**scripturiency** *noun* a passion or mania for writing M17.

scripturist /ˈskrɪptʃərɪst/ *noun.* E17.
[from SCRIPTURE + -IST.]
1 A person whose religious belief or opinions are based on the Bible alone. Now *rare* or *obsolete.* E17.
2 A person who is learned or versed in the Bible. M17.

scriptwriter /ˈskrɪptrʌɪtə/ *noun.* E20.
[from SCRIPT *noun*¹ + WRITER.]
A person who writes a script for a film, broadcast, etc.

scritch /skrɪtʃ/ *verb & noun.* Now *arch.* & *poet.* ME.
[from imit. base in Old English *scriċċettan*. Cf. SCREAK *verb*, SCREECH *verb*, *noun*¹, SHRITCH.]
▸ **A** *verb intrans.* Utter a loud cry, screech, shriek. ME.
▸ **B** *noun.* A loud cry, a shriek, a screech. E16.
Comb.: **scritch-owl** (*arch.* exc. *US*) a screech owl.

scritch-scratch /ˈskrɪtʃskratʃ/ *noun.* M19.
[Redupl. of SCRATCH *noun*¹.]
Continual scratching.

†**scrivan** *noun.* E16–E18.
[Italian *scrivano* or Portuguese *escrivão* = French *écrivain*: see SCRIVENER.]
A professional writer; a clerk; a notary.

scrive /skrʌɪv/ *verb.* See also SCRIEVE *verb*². ME.
[Origin uncertain: perh. aphet. from DESCRIVE.]
1 †**a** *verb trans.* Describe. ME–M16. ▸**b** *verb intrans.* Write. *obsolete* exc. *Scot.* & *north.* E16.
2 *verb trans.* = SCRIBE *verb* 2. Now chiefly *Scot.* & *north.* exc. in ***scrive-board*** below. E19.
Comb.: **scrive-board** a large platform made of planks on which the lines of a ship to be built are drawn.

scrivello /skrɪˈvɛləʊ/ *noun.* Pl. **-o(e)s.** M18.
[Aphet. from Portuguese *escrevelho* perh. var. of *escaravelho* pin, peg.]
An elephant's tusk weighing less than 20lb or 9.1 kg.

scriven /ˈskrɪv(ə)n/ *verb trans. & intrans.* Now *rare.* L17.
[Back-form. from next.]
Write busily, as a scrivener does. Freq. foll. by *away*, *up*, etc.
■ **scrivening** *noun* the action of the verb; writing, esp. of a routine or arduous kind: E19.

scrivener /ˈskrɪv(ə)nə/ *noun.* ME.
[Aphet. from Old French *escrivein* (mod. *écrivain*) from Proto-Romance from Latin *scriba* SCRIBE *noun*¹: see -ER¹.]
1 A professional writer or scribe; a copyist; a clerk, a secretary. ME.
2 *Hist.* A notary. L15.
3 *Hist.* A person who invested money at interest for clients, and who lent funds to those who wanted to raise money on security. Formerly also ***money scrivener***. E17.

1 *Daily Telegraph* The Lord Chancellor's department . . employs a scrivener to write the document. **3** R. H. TAWNEY The age of Elizabeth saw . . the beginnings of something like deposit banking in the hands of the scriveners.

Phrases: **scrivener's cramp**, **scrivener's palsy** writer's cramp.
■ **scrivenery** *noun* (*a*) the occupation of a scrivener; writing, *esp.* that of a copyist or clerk; (*b*) a room in which scriveners work: M19.

scrobe /skrəʊb/ *noun.* L17.
[Latin *scrobis* trench.]
†**1** A trench. *rare.* Only in L17.
2 ENTOMOLOGY. A groove for the reception or concealment of a limb or other appendage of an insect, *esp.* each of two on either side of the rostrum of a weevil in which the antennae can rest. L19.

scrobicule /ˈskrəʊbɪkjuːl/ *noun.* L19.
[Late Latin *scrobiculus* dim. of *scrobis* trench: see -CULE.]
BOTANY & ZOOLOGY. A small pit or depression; *spec.* a smooth level area around a tubercle in a sea urchin.
■ **scroˈbicular** *adjective* pertaining to or surrounded by scrobicules L19. **scroˈbiculate** *adjective* having many shallow depressions; pitted: E19. **scroˈbiculated** *adjective* = SCROBICULATE M19.

scrod /skrɒd/ *noun. N. Amer.* M19.
[Origin unkn. Cf. ESCROD.]
A young cod weighing less than three pounds, *esp.* one that is split and fried or boiled. Also, a young haddock; a fillet of cod or haddock.

scroddled /ˈskrɒd(ə)ld/ *adjective.* L19.
[Perh. from Low German *schrodel* scrap.]
Of pottery: made of differently coloured scraps of clay to give a marbled or mottled effect.

scrofula /ˈskrɒfjʊlə/ *noun.* Pl. **-las**, **-lae** /-liː/. LME.
[Late Latin *scrofulae* (pl.), medieval Latin *scrofula* swelling of the glands, dim. of *scrofa* breeding sow (supposed to be subject to the disease).]
MEDICINE. Orig. (in *pl.*), tuberculous lymph nodes. Now, tuberculosis of the lymph nodes, esp. in the neck, giving rise to abscesses; *gen.* a constitutional state predisposing a person to tuberculosis, eczema, glandular swellings, etc. Also (*Hist.*) called ***king's evil***. Cf. STRUMA.
■ **scrofulide** *noun* (now *rare*) [French] tuberculosis of the skin M19. **scrofuˈlitic** *adjective* scrofulous M19.

scrofuloderma /ˌskrɒfjʊləˈdəːmə/ *noun.* Pl. **-mata** /-mətə/. Also Anglicized as **-derm.** M19.
[mod. Latin, from prec. + DERMA.]
MEDICINE. Orig., a tuberculous skin lesion. Now, tuberculosis of the skin, in which irregular blue-edged ulcers form.
■ Also **scrofulodermia** *noun* (now *rare*) L19.

scrofulous /ˈskrɒfjʊləs/ *adjective.* LME.
[from SCROFULA + -OUS.]
1 Caused by, resembling, or of the nature of scrofula; affected with scrofula. LME.
2 *fig.* Of a person, literature, etc.: morally corrupt. E18.

scrog /skrɒg/ *noun.* ME.
[Parallel to SCRAG *noun*².]
1 A stunted bush; in *pl.*, brushwood. Chiefly *Scot.* & *north.* ME.
2 HERALDRY. A branch of a tree. *Scot.* L18.
¶ Earliest in place-names.
■ **scrogged** *adjective* stunted E16. **scroggy** *adjective* (*a*) covered with stunted bushes or brushwood; (*b*) (of a tree) stunted: LME.

scroggin /ˈskrɒgɪn/ *noun. Austral.* & *NZ.* M20.
[Origin unkn.]
A mixture of raisins, chocolate, nuts, etc., eaten as a snack esp. by walkers or travellers.

scroll /skrəʊl/ *noun.* LME.
[Alt. of SCROW *noun*¹ after ROLL *noun*¹. Cf. ESCROLL.]
1 A roll of paper or parchment, esp. with writing on it; a document or book in this form. LME.
2 A thing resembling a scroll in shape; a decorative design or carving resembling a partially unrolled scroll of paper or parchment; *spec.* (*a*) ARCHITECTURE a volute on an Ionic, Corinthian, or composite capital; (*b*) NAUTICAL (more fully ***scroll-head***) a curved piece of timber under the bowsprit in place of a figurehead; (*c*) MUSIC the curved head of a bowed stringed instrument in which the tuning-pins are set. LME.
3 a A piece of writing, *esp.* a letter. M16. ▸**b** An itemized list or schedule. M16. ▸**c** A draft or copy of a letter etc. *Scot.* E18.
4 a A long rectangular band of paper bearing a motto or legend. Now chiefly, a representation of this, esp. in a painting. L16. ▸**b** HERALDRY. The representation of a riband (normally with rolled ends) bearing the motto, usu. situated below the shield in an achievement of arms, occas. also above the crest. Also, the motto on this. E17.
5 PHYSICAL GEOGRAPHY. Each of a series of crescent-shaped deposits formed on the inside of a river meander. Cf. ***point bar*** s.v. POINT *noun*¹. E20.
6 COMPUTING. The action or facility of scrolling in order to view new material. L20.

📖 **1** *fig.*: FRANCIS THOMPSON Summoned by some presaging scroll of fate. **Scroll of the Law** = SEFER TORAH. ***VITRUVIAN scroll***. **2** DICKENS Carpets are rolled into great scrolls. *Antique* Note the baroque scrolls of the arm-supports. attrib.: ***scroll back***, ***scroll moulding***, ***scroll-shaped***, etc. **3b** *fig.*: *Daily Telegraph* The latest in a lengthening scroll of sexual scandal. **4a** R. HURD Painters continuing . . to put written scrolls in the mouths of their figures.

Comb.: **scroll bar** COMPUTING a long thin section at the edge of a computer display or window by which material can be scrolled using a mouse; **scroll-bone** = TURBINAL; **scroll-copy** *Scot.* = sense 3c above; **scroll-gall** a malformation consisting in the curling over of a leaf caused by aphids, mites, etc.; ***scroll-head***: see sense 2 above; **scroll-lathe**: adapted to turn spiral and scroll work; **scroll painting** (*a*) a painting on a scroll, chiefly found in oriental art, esp. Japan; (*b*) the practice of painting on scrolls; **scroll salt** a silver or pottery salt cellar decorated with scrolled arms; **scroll saw** a narrow-bladed saw for cutting curved lines in decorative work; **scrollwork** decoration consisting of spiral lines or patterns, esp. as cut by a scroll saw.

■ **scrolly** *adjective* scrolled, curly M19.

scroll /skrəʊl/ *verb*. E17.
[from the noun.]
1 *verb trans.* Write in or on a scroll. *rare*. E17.
2 *verb trans.* Draft, make a rough copy of. Also (*rare*), make a fair copy of, engross. *Scot.* M17.
3 *verb intrans.* Roll or curl up; form a scroll or spiral shape. M19.
4 COMPUTING. **a** *verb trans. & intrans.* Move (displayed text etc.) up, down, or across on a screen or in a window in order to display different parts of it. (Foll. by *down, up, through*, etc.) L20. ▸**b** *verb intrans.* Of displayed text etc.: be moved *up* etc. in a screen or in a window in this way. Of a display: move displayed text etc. upwards in this way. L20.

📖 **3** E. WILSON The walnut frame . . above the mantel would scroll outward . . to form sconces for candles. **4a** *Practical Computing* You can scroll in either direction . . to reach the start or finish of the document. *Your Computer* A programme to scroll part of the screen one byte at a time.

■ **scrollable** *adjective* (COMPUTING) (of text etc. on a screen) able to be scrolled; (of a screen or window) that permits scrolling: L20. **scrolling** *noun* (*a*) *rare* decoration with scrolls; (*b*) COMPUTING the process of scrolling text etc. on a screen: M18.

scrolled /skrəʊld/ *adjective*. E17.
[from SCROLL *noun*, *verb*: see -ED[2], -ED[1].]
1 In the form of or decorated with scrolls; curled. E17.
2 Inscribed with mottoes. *rare*. L19.

scronch /skrɒn(t)ʃ/ *noun*. *US*. E20.
[Origin uncertain: perh. var. of SCRUNCH *noun*.]
A kind of slow dance performed to blues music.

scrooch /skruːtʃ/ *verb*. *colloq.* (orig. & chiefly *US*). M19.
[Dial. var. of SCROUGE *verb*, perh. later reinforced by CROUCH *verb*.]
1 *verb intrans.* Squeeze close; crouch, bend. Freq. foll. by *down*. M19.
2 *verb trans.* Squeeze; screw (the eyes etc.) *up*. E20.

Scrooge /skruːdʒ/ *noun*. M20.
[Ebenezer *Scrooge*, a character in Dickens's *A Christmas Carol*.]
A miserly tight-fisted person; a killjoy.

scroop /skruːp/ *noun*. M19.
[Imit. Cf. next.]
1 A harsh, strident, or scraping noise. Chiefly *dial.* M19.
2 The rustling sound and crisp feel associated esp. with silk and imparted also to other fabrics by special treatment. L19.

scroop /skruːp/ *verb intrans.* Chiefly *dial.* L18.
[Imit. Cf. prec.]
Make a harsh, grating, or scraping sound; grate, creak, squeak.

scrophularia /skrɒfjʊˈlɛːrɪə/ *noun*. Also in Anglicized form †**scrophulary**. LME.
[medieval Latin (sc. *herba*), from *scrophula* SCROFULA.]
= ***figwort*** s.v. FIG *noun*[1]
■ **scrophulariˈaceous** *adjective* of or pertaining to the figwort family Scrophulariaceae M19.

†**scrophulary** *noun* see SCROPHULARIA.

scrotum /ˈskrəʊtəm/ *noun*. Pl. **-tums**, **-ta** /-tə/. L16.
[Latin.]
ANATOMY. The pouch of skin and connective tissue which encloses the testicles and associated structures.
■ **scrotal** *adjective* E19.

scrouge /skruːdʒ, skraʊdʒ/ *verb & noun*. *colloq.* M18.
[Alt. of SCRUZE. Cf. SCROOCH.]
▶ **A** *verb*. Now chiefly *US*.
1 *verb trans.* Cause discomfort to (a person) by coming too close; encroach on (a person's) space; crowd. Also, push or squeeze (something). M18.
2 *verb intrans.* Push, shove. L18.
3 *verb intrans.* Crouch; make one's body smaller or less conspicuous. E20.
4 *verb trans.* Draw tight; screw *up* (the eyes etc.). *rare*. E20.
▶ **B** *noun*. A crush, a squeeze, a crowd. *rare*. M19.
■ **scrouger** *noun* (*US*) an exceptionally large person or thing E19.

scrounge /skraʊn(d)ʒ/ *verb & noun*. Orig. *dial.* E20.
[Prob. alt. of SCRINGE *verb*[1]. Cf. SCUNGE *verb*.]
▶ **A** *verb*. **1** *verb intrans.* Sponge *on* or live at the expense of others. Also foll. by *off*. E20.
2 a *verb intrans.* Seek to obtain something by stealth or at the expense or through generosity of another or others; hunt around. Freq. foll. by *for*. E20. ▸**b** *verb trans.* Obtain (something) by stealth in this way. E20.

📖 **1** R. WESTALL I could go and scrounge off the parents for the rest of the vac. **2a** C. RYAN Forced to scrounge for food, the troopers were living on apples. **b** J. TROLLOPE I'm afraid . . I've come to scrounge a bottle of wine. *Economist* Employers are scrounging technical whizzes from wherever they can find them.

▶ **B** *noun*. **1** The action or an act of scrounging. Freq. in ***on the scrounge***. E20.
2 A person who scrounges. M20.
■ **scrounger** *noun* E20. **scroungy** *adjective* (*colloq.*, orig. & chiefly *US*) (*a*) shabby, dirty; disreputable; (*b*) of poor quality, inferior: M20.

scrow /skrəʊ/ *noun*[1]. ME.
[Aphet. from ESCROW. In sense 4 perh. a different word.]
†**1** = SCROLL *noun* 1. ME–E17. ▸†**b** In *pl.* Writings. E16–M17.
2 In *pl.* Strips of hide used for making glue. Now *Scot. & north.* ME.
3 †**a** A note, a document. LME–M16. ▸**b** A list, an inventory. *obsolete* exc. *Scot.* M16.
4 A state of confusion or agitation; a commotion or fuss. *Scot. & north.* E19.

†**scrow** *noun*[2] var. of SCREW *noun*[2].

scroyle /skrɔɪl/ *noun*. *arch.* L16.
[Origin unkn.]
A scoundrel, a wretch.

scrub /skrʌb/ *noun*[1] *& adjective*. LME.
[Var. of SHRUB *noun*[1].]
▶ **A** *noun*. **I 1** A low stunted tree; a shrub. *obsolete* exc. *dial.*, *Austral.*, & *NZ*. LME.
2 Vegetation consisting chiefly of stunted trees, shrubs, or brushwood; an area of land overgrown with brushwood; *Austral.* & *NZ* (any area of) land thickly or thinly covered with shrubs and stunted trees. E19.

📖 **2** *Emu* The banksia scrubs in and around the Perth district. R. CAMPBELL Disappearing in the grass towards a mass of dense scrub.

▶ **II 3** Orig., (an animal of) a breed of small cattle. Now (*N. Amer.*), any animal of inferior breed or of poor physique or performance. M16.
4 *transf.* **a** A worthless, insignificant, or contemptible person. L16. ▸**b** SPORT. A player belonging to a second or weaker team; a team composed of such players. *US colloq.* L19. ▸**c** = SCRUBBER *noun*[2] 2. *slang*. *derog.* E20.

Phrases: **the Scrubs** Wormwood Scrubs Prison in Greater London.

Comb.: **scrub-bird** either of two small rare terrestrial birds of the Australian family Atrichornithidae, *Atrichornis clamosus* (in full ***noisy scrub-bird***) and *A. rufescens* (in full ***rufous scrub-bird***); **scrub-cutter** (*Austral.* & *NZ*) a person who or machine which clears land of scrub; **scrub-fowl**, **scrub-hen** any of various megapodes of the genera *Megapodius* and *Eulipoa*, esp. *Megapodius freycinet* (more fully ***common scrub-fowl***), found in coastal areas of northern Australia, Indonesia, and Melanesia; **scrub jay** a blue jay with no white markings, *Aphelocoma coerulescens*, occurring in the US and Mexico; **scrub oak** (*a*) *N. Amer.* any of several dwarf oaks, esp. *Quercus ilicifolia*; (*b*) *Austral.* any of several casuarinas; **scrub pine** any of several N. American dwarf pines, esp. *Pinus virginiana*; **scrub-robin** any of various birds of the genera *Drymodes* (of Australia and New Guinea) and *Erythropygia* (of Africa), related to the robin; **scrub tick** *Austral.* any of various ticks that attack humans, esp. *Ixodes holocyclus* and *Haemaphysalis longicornis*; **scrub-tit** a scrub wren, *Sericornis magnus*, found in Tasmania; **scrub turkey** = ***brush-turkey*** s.v. BRUSH *noun*[1]; **scrub typhus** an acute rickettsial fever transmitted to humans by larval mites of the genus *Trombicula*; also called ***mite-borne typhus***, ***mite typhus***, ***tsutsugamushi disease***; **scrub wallaby** = ***brush wallaby*** s.v. BRUSH *noun*[1]; **scrub-wren** any of various small Australian warblers of the genus *Sericornis* (family Acanthizidae).

▶ **B** *attrib.* or as *adjective*. **1** Worthless, insignificant, contemptible. E18.
2 Chiefly *N. Amer.* ▸**a** Of vegetation: stunted, dwarf. M18. ▸**b** Of livestock: of inferior breed or physique. M18.
3 (Of a team or player) not first-class, without regular standing; (of a game) played by scrub teams. *US colloq.* M19.

📖 **2b** B. BROADFOOT The sorriest looking scrub horses you have ever seen.

■ **scrubbed** *adjective* †(*a*) stunted, dwarf; (*b*) (chiefly *Austral.* & *NZ*) covered or overgrown with scrub: L16. **scrubbish** *adjective* (*rare*) scrubby, inferior, contemptible L18.

scrub /skrʌb/ *noun*[2]. E17.
[from SCRUB *verb*.]
1 The action or an act of scrubbing. E17. ▸**b** The action by a tyre of sliding or scraping over the road surface, esp. when cornering. M20. ▸**c** A cancellation or abandonment, esp. of a flying mission. *slang*. M20.
2 A broom or brush with short hard bristles; *spec.* a brush used in stained-glass work to scrape away part of a coat of paint to produce a modelled effect. L17.
3 A person who scrubs; a hard-worked servant, a drudge. E18.
4 The third grade into which fullers' teasels are sorted. M18.
5 An abrasive cosmetic lotion used to cleanse or exfoliate the skin. Freq. as ***body scrub***. L20.

📖 **1** K. TENNANT Rene eyed May's house possessively. 'First thing . . this gets a good scrub'. **b** *News (Portsmouth)* Although . . cornering at speed presents no problem . . there is a noise of tyre scrub.

Comb.: **scrub nurse**: assisting a surgeon by performing some duties with sterilized equipment during an operation; **scrub suit** *US* a garment worn by surgeons and other theatre staff whilst performing or assisting at an operation; **scrub up** a thorough cleansing of the hands and arms with disinfectant before a surgical operation.

scrub /skrʌb/ *verb*. Infl. **-bb-**. ME.
[Prob. from Middle Low German, Middle Dutch *schrobben*, *schrubben*. Cf. SHRUB *verb*.]
▶ **I** *verb trans.* †**1** Curry-comb (a horse). Only in ME.
2 *verb trans.* Scratch; (now *rare* or *obsolete*) rub (a part of one's body) vigorously, esp. so as to dry oneself. L16.
3 Clean by rubbing vigorously (as) esp. with a hard brush. Also foll. by *down*. L16. ▸**b** Treat (a gas or vapour) so as to remove impurities, usu. by bringing it into contact with a liquid; wash *out* or remove (impurities) in such a way. L19. ▸**c** Scrape away (paint) in stained-glass work with a hard brush. L19.
4 Cancel (a plan, order, etc.); eliminate, erase. Also foll. by *out*. *colloq.* E19.
5 *verb trans.* Reprimand severely; punish. *Military slang*. E20.
6 Foll. by *off*: lose or cause the loss of (speed) rapidly when driving. L20.

📖 **2** O. MANNING She sweated a lot and scrubbed her face impatiently with a handkerchief. *Listener* A fresh, scrubbed and shiny picture of Hawick. N. LOWNDES Olga scrubbed the passage with a bar of soap every three weeks. **scrub round** *fig.* (*colloq.*) circumvent, avoid, disregard. **4** L. DEIGHTON Any divergence from what I've told him to do and we'll scrub the whole thing. **6** *Times* Managed to spin it about three times to scrub off some of the speed.

▶ **II** *verb intrans.* **7** Manage with difficulty, barely subsist. Usu. foll. by *along*. *colloq.* M19.
8 Rub a brush vigorously over a surface in cleaning. L19.
9 Wash and disinfect the hands and arms prior to performing or assisting at a surgical operation. Usu. foll. by *up*. E20.
10 Of a rider: rub the arms and legs urgently on a horse's neck and flanks to urge it to move faster. M20.
11 Of a tyre: slide or scrape across the road surface, esp. when cornering. L20.

📖 **8** G. MORTIMER I must scrub and clean for you.

Comb.: **scrub board** *N. Amer.* a washboard; **scrub-brush** *N. Amer.* a scrubbing-brush.
■ **scrubbable** *adjective* able to be cleaned by scrubbing E20. **scrubbery** *noun* (*rare*) drudgery M19.

†**scrubbado** *noun*. M17–E18.
[from SCRUB *verb* + -ADO. Cf. SCABBADO.]
Scabies.

scrubber /ˈskrʌbə/ *noun*[1]. M19.
[from SCRUB *verb* + -ER[1].]
1 A person who or thing which scrubs. M19.
2 *spec.* **a** An apparatus for removing impurities from gas or vapour. M19. ▸**b** A scrubbing-brush. E20.

scrubber /ˈskrʌbə/ *noun*[2]. M19.
[In sense 1 from SCRUB *noun*[1] + -ER[1]; in sense 2 perh. rel. to prec.]
1 *Austral.* & *NZ*. **a** A person or animal that lives in the scrub. M19. ▸**b** *fig.* An inferior animal; an unpleasant or contemptible person; SPORT a player or competitor of low or non-professional standard. *slang*. L19. ▸**c** The grey kangaroo. M20.
2 A sexually promiscuous girl or woman. *slang*. *derog.* M20.

scrubbing /ˈskrʌbɪŋ/ *verbal noun*. E17.
[from SCRUB *verb* + -ING[1].]
The action of SCRUB *verb*; an instance of this.
Comb.: **scrubbing-brush**: with hard bristles for scrubbing floors etc.

scrubble /ˈskrʌb(ə)l/ *verb intrans.* Chiefly *dial.* M19.
[App. var. of SCRABBLE *verb*.]
Scrabble; scratch; scramble.

scrubby /ˈskrʌbi/ *adjective*[1]. L16.
[from SCRUB *noun*[1] + -Y[1].]
1 Of vegetation: stunted, dwarf. L16.
2 Covered with or consisting of scrub or brushwood. L17.
3 Insignificant, inferior, of poor appearance. M18.

📖 **2** G. Gissing A scrubby meadow, grazed . . by broken-down horses. **3** M. Howard The radical . . element—much of it initiating in a scrubby back street of Baltimore.

scrubby /ˈskrʌbi/ *adjective*². **M19.**
[from scrub *verb* + -y¹.]
Rough, stubbly.

📖 N. Sherry His scrubby beard added to his seedy effect.

scruff /skrʌf/ *noun*¹. **LOE.**
[Metathetic alt. of scurf *noun*¹. Cf. screef, shruff *noun*¹.]
1 †**a** = scurf *noun*¹ 1. **LOE–LME.** ▸**b** A scab. Long *rare* or *obsolete* exc. *Scot.* **E18.**
2 = scurf *noun*¹ 2. Now chiefly *Scot.* **E16.**
3 a Worthless or contemptible matter; rubbish. Formerly also *spec.*, counterfeit money. **M16.** ▸**b** An untidy or unkempt person; a contemptible person; *collect.* riff-raff. **M19.**
4 A thin crust or coating. *obsolete* exc. *Scot.* **L16.**
3b ***rough scruff***: see rough *adjective*.

scruff /skrʌf/ *noun*². **L18.**
[Alt. of scuff *noun*².]
The nape of the neck. Freq. in ***scruff of the neck***.

📖 J. Kosinski The man lifted me by the scruff of my neck like a rabbit.

scruff /skrʌf/ *verb*¹ *trans.* **L16.**
[In branch I from scruff *noun*¹. In branch II back-form. from scruffy *adjective*.]
▶ **I 1** Touch slightly, graze; scrape (a surface) off; *fig.* treat superficially, gloss *over*. Orig. *Scot.* & *north.* **L16.**
2 *golf.* Graze (the turf) with the club when striking the ball. **M19.**
3 *painting.* Stroke (oil colour) lightly over a darker tone. **M20.**
▶ **II 4** Foll. by *up*: make (oneself) untidy or scruffy. **L20.**

scruff /skrʌf/ *verb*² *trans. Austral.* **M19.**
[from scruff *noun*².]
1 Seize (a person) by the scruff of the neck; manhandle. **M19.**
2 Seize and hold (a calf) for branding or castration. **L19.**

scruffo /ˈskrʌfəʊ/ *noun. slang.* **M20.**
[from scruff *noun*¹ + -o.]
= scruff *noun*¹ 3b.

scruffy /ˈskrʌfi/ *adjective.* **M17.**
[from scruff *noun*¹ + -y¹.]
1 Scaly, covered with scurf. Now *rare* exc. *Scot.* **M17.**
2 Shabby, dirty; unkempt, untidy. **L19.**
■ **scruffily** *adverb* **L20.** **scruffiness** *noun* **L20.**

scrum /skrʌm/ *noun* & *verb.* **L19.**
[Abbreviation of scrummage. Cf. scrimmage.]
▶ **A** *noun.* **1** *rugby football.* Orig., a disordered struggle during which each team attempted to force the ball and their opponents towards the other's goal. Now, an ordered formation called by the referee to restart play in which the two opposing packs of forwards, arms interlocked and heads down, combine as a single group, whereupon the ball is thrown in between them and the players attempt to kick the ball out to their own team. **L19.**
2 *transf.* & *fig.* A confused noisy crowd, a crush of people; a disorderly or confused mass or arrangement of objects, ideas, etc. **E20.**

📖 **1** ***loose scrum***: see loose *adjective*. ***set scrum***: see set *adjective*. **2** L. Blue The scrum around the departure lounge bar.

▶ **B** *verb intrans.* Infl. **-mm-**.
1 *rugby football.* Form or engage in a scrum. Freq. foll. by *down*. **E20.**
2 *transf.* Jostle, crowd. **E20.**
Comb.: **scrum-cap**: worn to protect the head in a scrum; **scrum-half** (the position of) a half-back who puts the ball into the scrum; **scrum machine**: used to simulate the opposing forwards in a scrum during training sessions.

scrumble /ˈskrʌmb(ə)l/ *verb*¹ *trans. rare.* **E20.**
[Perh. blend of scrape *verb* or scratch *verb* and crumble *verb*.]
Scrape or scratch (something) *out of* or *from*.

scrumble /ˈskrʌmb(ə)l/ *verb*² *trans.* **E20.**
[App. alt. of scumble *verb*.]
Apply (a thin coat of paint) to a surface so as to give a textured appearance or variations in tone. Freq. as ***scrumbled*** *ppl adjective*.

scrummage /ˈskrʌmɪdʒ/ *noun* & *verb.* **E19.**
[Var. of scrimmage. Cf. scrum.]
▶ **A** *noun.* **1** A noisy dispute or tussle; a rough or confused struggle; a scuffle; = scrimmage *noun* 2a. *colloq.* **E19.**
2 *rugby football.* = scrum *noun* 1. In various other sports, a tussle for possession of the ball. **M19.**
2 ***set scrummage***: see set *adjective*.
▶ **B** *verb.* **1** *verb intrans.* = scrimmage *verb* 1. *dial.* **E19.**
2 *verb trans. rugby football.* Put the ball in a scrum; propel or take along in a scrum. **L19.**

scrummy /ˈskrʌmi/ *adjective. colloq.* **E20.**
[from scrum(ptious + -y¹.]
Excellent, marvellous; enjoyable, delicious.

📖 *Harpers & Queen* Scrummy French food in cosy surroundings.

■ **scrumminess** *noun* **L20.**

scrump /skrʌmp/ *noun. dial.* **M19.**
[Perh. rel. to scrimp *adjective* & *adverb*.]
Something withered or dried up; *spec.* a withered or small apple.

scrump /skrʌmp/ *verb trans.* & *intrans. colloq.* (orig. *dial.*). **M19.**
[from the noun.]
Steal (fruit) from orchards or gardens.

📖 A. Sillitoe We . . went through fields, scrumping a few sour apples on our way. P. Barker An orchard where she'd gone scrumping as a child.

scrumple /ˈskrʌmp(ə)l/ *noun* & *verb.* **E16.**
[Alt. of crumple *noun*, *verb*.]
▶ **A** *noun.* A wrinkle, a crease; something crumpled or creased. Long *rare*. **E16.**
▶ **B** *verb trans.* Crush, wrinkle; crumple *up*. **L16.**

scrumptious /ˈskrʌm(p)ʃəs/ *adjective. colloq.* **M19.**
[Origin unkn.]
1 Fastidious, hard to please. *rare. US.* **M19.**
2 Stylish, handsome, impressive (*US*); wonderful, delightful; delicious. **M19.**

📖 **2** G. Clare A country where scrumptious food and luscious drink are free.

■ **scrumptiously** *adverb* **M19.** **scrumptiousness** *noun* **L19.**

scrumpy /ˈskrʌmpi/ *noun. colloq.* (orig. *dial.*) **E20.**
[from scrump *noun* + -y⁶.]
Rough strong cider, esp. as made in the West Country of England.

scrunch /skrʌn(t)ʃ/ *verb* & *noun.* **L18.**
[Prob. imit.: cf. crunch *verb*, *noun*.]
▶ **A** *verb.* **1** *verb trans.* Crunch, bite or eat noisily. **L18.**
2 a *verb trans.* Crush, tread crushingly on; crumple or screw (paper etc.) *up*. **M19.** ▸**b** *verb refl.* Squeeze (oneself) into compact shape. *rare.* **M19.** ▸**c** *verb intrans.* Squeeze oneself into a compact shape; huddle *up* or *together*; cower; crouch *down*. *N. Amer.* **L19.**
3 *verb intrans.* Make a crunching sound. **M19.**

📖 **1** M. Gee There are three leopards . . you'd think they'd be out in seconds and scrunch up the people. **2a** E. Bowen Taking her hand in his, he scrunched the fingers inside her glove together. *Baby* A well-defined face—not a 'scrunched up one'. **c** J. Irving She was slightly taller . . to rest her head against him, she had to scrunch down. **3** B. Moore His footsteps scrunching on the gravel of the yard.

Comb.: **scrunch-dry** *verb trans.* blow-dry (hair) while squeezing or crushing it with the hands, resulting in a softly crinkled or tousled look.
▶ **B** *noun.* **1** A crunching sound. **M19.**
2 An act or an instance of scrunching. **M19.**

📖 **1** G. Durrell The soil had a hard crust . . which the horses' hooves broke with a soft scrunch.

scrunchy /ˈskrʌn(t)ʃi/ *adjective* & *noun.* As noun also **-ie**. **E20.**
[from scrunch *verb* + -y¹.]
▶ **A** *adjective.* Fit for scrunching or being scrunched; making a crunching sound when crushed. **E20.**
▶ **B** *noun.* A circular band of elastic covered in fabric, used for fastening the hair in a pony-tail etc. **L20.**

scrungy /ˈskrʌn(d)ʒi/ *adjective. slang* (chiefly *US*). **L20.**
[Prob. rel. to scroungy, scungy. Cf. also grungy.]
Dirty, grimy; sleazy, shabby; unpleasant.

scrunt /skrʌnt/ *noun. Scot.* **M16.**
[Origin unkn.]
Something stunted or worn out, *esp.* a stump of a tree.

scrunty /ˈskrʌnti/ *adjective.* Orig. *Scot.* & *north.* **E19.**
[from prec. + -y¹.]
Stunted, shrivelled, stumpy.

scruple /ˈskruːp(ə)l/ *noun.* Also (earlier) †**scriple**, †**scrupul(e)**. **LME.**
[French *scrupule* or Latin *scrupulus*, *scripulus* small sharp or pointed stone, smallest division of weight, also fig., dim. of *scrupus* rough or sharp pebble, anxiety.]
▶ **I 1** An apothecaries' weight of 1/24 oz (20 grains). *obsolete* exc. *Hist.* **LME.**
2 *fig.* A very small quantity or amount; a very small part or portion. *arch.* **L16.**
†**3** Each of the units produced by successive division into sixty parts; *spec.* one-sixtieth of a degree of arc, hour, day (a minute of arc, a minute of time, 24 minutes, respectively). **E17–E18.**
†**4** In rabbinical chronology the 1080th part of an hour, equal to 1/18 minute. Only in **18.**
5 = line *noun*² 20. Now *rare* or *obsolete.* **E19.**

📖 **2** E. B. Browning Critics . . will weigh me out, scruple by scruple, their judicial verdicts.

▶ **II 6** A thought or circumstance that causes the mind unease or disquiet; a feeling of doubt or hesitation with regard to the morality or propriety of a course of action; a fine point of conscience, *esp.* one which is regarded as overrefined. **LME.** ▸**b** Regard to the morality or propriety of a course of action; compunction. **M16.**
†**7** A doubt or uncertainty with regard to a factual matter; an intellectual difficulty or objection. **M16–M18.**

📖 **6** L. Gordon The plan to leave Vivienne was foiled . . in Eliot's mind, by his own scruples. **b** M. Bradbury Invest in all their activities with high care and scruple. **7** Defoe Our captain . . raised several scruples about the latitude . . we should keep in such a voyage.

Phrases: **have little or no scruple** have little or no hesitation or compunction (*about*, *in doing*). †**have scruple of** = ***make scruple*** (b) below. **make no scruple to do** have no moral uncertainty or hesitation in doing. **make scruple** (*a*) *arch.* entertain or raise a doubt; hesitate, be reluctant, esp. on conscientious grounds (foll. by *of*, *at*, *to do*); (*b*) (foll. by *of*), hesitate to believe or admit. **without scruple** (*a*) without hesitation or compunction; †(*b*) without question, doubtless.

scruple /ˈskruːp(ə)l/ *verb.* **E17.**
[from prec. or French *scrupuler*.]
†**1** *verb trans.* Have a scruple or scruples about; take exception to or question the propriety of (an action or proposed action); hesitate at (something). **E17–M19.**
†**2** *verb trans.* Doubt, question, hesitate to believe, (a fact etc.); question the validity of. **M17–M19.**
†**3** *verb trans.* Cause (a person) to feel scruples. **M–L17.**
4 *verb intrans.* Be influenced by or feel scruples; hesitate. Chiefly in ***scruple at***. Now *rare.* **M17.**
5 *verb intrans.* Hesitate or be reluctant *to do* something, esp. on conscientious grounds or out of regard for morality or propriety. Chiefly in neg. contexts. **M17.**

📖 **1** Defoe Let no man scruple my honourable mention of this noble enemy. **2** R. Tyler Though I don't scruple your veracity, I have some reasons for believing you were there. **4** H. T. Buckle He scrupled at nothing which could advance its interests. **5** A. Storr Not scrupling to order clothes for which he could not pay.

■ **scrupler** *noun* a person influenced by moral scruples, a person with scruples; *spec.* (*Hist.*) a Scottish divine who objected to taking the Abjuration Oath in 1712: **M17.**

†**scrupul** *noun* see scruple *noun*.

scrupulant /ˈskruːpjʊlənt/ *noun.* **M20.**
[from Latin *scrupulus* scruple *noun* + -ant¹.]
roman catholic church. A person who is overscrupulous in confessing his or her sins; a person who suffers from an excess of conscience.

†**scrupular** *adjective. rare.* **M17–L18.**
[Latin *scrupularis*, from *scrupulus* scruple *noun*: see -ar¹.]
Of, pertaining to, or amounting to a scruple in weight.

†**scrupule** *noun* see scruple *noun*.

scrupulist /ˈskruːpjʊlɪst/ *noun.* **L17.**
[from Latin *scrupulus* scruple *noun* + -ist.]
A person who has moral scruples or raises difficulties.

scrupulosity /skruːpjʊˈlɒsɪti/ *noun.* **E16.**
[Old & mod. French *scrupulosité* or Latin *scrupulositas*, from *scrupulosus*: see next, -ity.]
1 The state or quality of being scrupulous, esp. to excess. **E16.**
2 An instance of this. **M16.**

scrupulous /ˈskruːpjʊləs/ *adjective.* **LME.**
[Old & mod. French *scrupuleux* or Latin *scrupulosus*, from *scrupulus*: see scruple *noun*, -ulous.]
1 Troubled with doubts or questions of conscience; meticulously concerned with matters of morality and propriety; (of a thing, action, etc.), characterized by such doubts or scruples. **LME.** ▸†**b** Prone to hesitation or doubt; cautious in one's actions, decisions, etc; (of an action etc.) characterized by doubt or distrust. **M16–L17.** ▸†**c** Loth or reluctant, through scruples, *to do*; doubtful or suspicious *of*; chary *of* or *in doing*. **E17–M19.**
†**2** Of a thing: causing doubt, raising scruples; meriting scruple or objection. **M16–L17.**
3 Careful to follow the dictates of conscience or propriety, esp. so as to avoid doing wrong. Also foll. by *to do*. **M16.**
4 *gen.* Minutely exact or careful; strictly or overly attentive to details; punctilious. **M16.**
5 Of an action or quality: rigidly directed by the dictates of conscience; characterized by a punctilious concern for what is right. **M18.**

📖 **1** A. C. Benson A religion of scrupulous saints and self-torturing ascetics. **2** Bacon The Iustice of that Cause ought to be Euident; Not Obscure, not Scrupulous. **3** Ld Macaulay His more scrupulous brother ceased to appear in the royal chapel. **4** *New Scientist* Most authorities are scrupulous in installing first-aid boxes and fire-fighting equipment. **5** P. D. James The kind of marital argument, conducted . . with scrupulous fairness, which they both relished.

■ **scrupulously** *adverb* **M16.** **scrupulousness** *noun* **E16.**

scrutable /ˈskruːtəb(ə)l/ *adjective.* L16.
[Prob. from earlier INSCRUTABLE. Cf. late Latin *scrutabilis* searchable.]
That can be understood by scrutiny.

scrutator /skruːˈteɪtə/ *noun.* L16.
[Latin, from *scrutat-* pa. ppl stem of *scrutari*: see SCRUTINY *noun*, -ATOR.]
1 A person who examines or investigates something or someone. L16.
2 A person whose official duty it is to examine or investigate something closely; *spec.* (*a*) (*Hist.*) a university official responsible for examining votes at university elections and announcing the result; (*b*) *gen.* a scrutineer at an election. E17.

scrutineer /skruːtɪˈnɪə/ *noun & verb.* M16.
[from SCRUTINY + -EER.]
▶ **A** *noun.* A person whose duty it is to scrutinize or examine something; *esp.* a person who examines the conduct and result of voting at an election M16.
J. ARCHER Party scrutineers . . often demanding that a particular hundred be rechecked. *Rally Car* After . . the last round . . scrutineers sealed the engines of three leading cars for capacity checks.
▶ **B** *verb trans.* Inspect (a car or boat) in order to ensure compliance with the regulations of motor or motor boat racing. E20.

scrutinize /ˈskruːtɪnʌɪz/ *verb.* Also **-ise**. L17.
[from SCRUTINY + -IZE.]
1 *verb trans.* Subject to a methodical examination; inspect with close attention. L17.
†**2** *verb intrans.* Undertake an inquiry or examination. Usu. foll. by *into*. L17–L18.
1 N. COWARD She takes a small mirror from her handbag and scrutinizes her face in it. D. LEAVITT Another mind . . infinitely more precise and scrutinizing than his own.
■ **scrutiniˈzation** *noun* E20. **scrutinizer** *noun* E18.

scrutinous /ˈskruːtɪnəs/ *adjective.* Now *rare.* L16.
[French †*scrutineux*, from *scrutin* from late Latin *scrutinium* SCRUTINY: see -OUS.]
Closely examining; searching.
■ **scrutinously** *adverb* M17.

scrutiny /ˈskruːtɪni/ *noun & verb.* LME.
[Latin *scrutinium*, from *scrutari* search, examine, (orig.) sort rags, from *scruta* trash, rubbish: see -Y⁴.]
▶ **A** *noun.* **1** Now chiefly ECCLESIASTICAL LAW. The formal taking of individual votes, as a method of electing a person to an official position, or of deciding a question proposed to a deliberative assembly; an instance of this procedure. LME.
2 Investigation, critical inquiry; an instance of this. E17. ▸**b** ECCLESIASTICAL HISTORY. An examination of those about to be baptized. E18. ▸**c** An official examination of the ballot-papers at an election to check their validity and to inspect the accuracy of the counting. E18.
3 The action of looking closely or searchingly at something; a searching gaze. L18.
2 R. G. COLLINGWOOD Under this fresh scrutiny, the old interpretation melted away. *British Medical Journal* The report . . is the last in the current series of scrutinies carried out in the NHS. **3** E. WAUGH He felt himself getting hot and red under their scrutiny. L. GARFIELD The blind man sensed the scrutiny of unseen eyes.
▶†**B** *verb trans.* = SCRUTINIZE. *rare.* M17–M18.

scruto /ˈskruːtəʊ/ *noun.* Pl. **-os**. M19.
[Origin unkn.]
THEATRICAL. A flexible sheet used for rapid scene changes, made of strips of wood hinged together or attached side by side on a canvas backing, on which a subject can be painted and which may be rolled up or down on cue.

scrutoire /skruːˈtwɑː/ *noun.* M17.
[Aphet. from French *escrutoire*, var. of ESCRITOIRE.]
= ESCRITOIRE.

scrutty /ˈskrʌti/ *adjective. colloq. rare.* E20.
[Origin unkn.]
Dirty, scruffy.

scruze /skruːz/ *verb trans. obsolete* exc. *dial.* L16.
[Perh. blend of SCREW *verb* and SQUEEZE *verb*.]
Squeeze.

scry /skrʌɪ/ *noun. obsolete* exc. *dial.* E17.
[App. rel. to SCREEN *noun*¹.]
A kind of sieve.

scry /skrʌɪ/ *verb*¹. Pa. t. & pple **scried** /skrʌɪd/. E16.
[Aphet. from DESCRY *verb*¹.]
1 *verb intrans.* Divine, esp. by crystal-gazing or looking in a mirror or water. E16.
2 *verb trans.* Descry, see, perceive. *obsolete* exc. *dial.* M16.
■ **scryer** *noun* M16.

scry /skrʌɪ/ *verb*² *trans.* Pa. t. & pple **scried** /skrʌɪd/. E17.
[from SCRY *noun*.]
Sieve.

SCSI /ˈskʌzi/ *abbreviation.*
COMPUTING. Small computer systems interface.

scuba /ˈskuːbə, ˈskjuːbə/ *noun & verb.* Also **SCUBA**. M20.
[Acronym, from self-contained underwater breathing apparatus.]
▶ **A** *noun.* Self-contained apparatus to enable a swimmer to breathe under water, comprising tanks of compressed air strapped on the back and feeding air automatically to a mask or mouthpiece; *ellipt.* scuba-diving. M20.
Comb.: **scuba-dive** *verb intrans.* swim under water using scuba apparatus; **scuba-diver** a person who goes scuba-diving; **scuba-diving** swimming under water using scuba apparatus, esp. as a sport.
▶ **B** *verb intrans.* Go scuba-diving. M20.

scud /skʌd/ *noun*¹. E17.
[from SCUD *verb*¹.]
1 The action of scudding, scudding movement; a spell or instance of scudding. E17.
2 a *collect.* Light clouds driven rapidly before the wind. M17. ▸**b** A driving shower of rain or snow; a sudden gust of wind. L17. ▸**c** Wind-blown foam, spray, or snow. M19.
3 (**S-**.) More fully ***Scud missile***. [An arbitrary code-name assigned by NATO.] A type of long-range surface-to-surface guided missile able to be fired from a mobile launcher, orig. developed in the former USSR. M20.

scud /skʌd/ *noun*². M17.
[Origin unkn. Cf. SCUD *verb*².]
†**1** Dirt, refuse. Only in M17.
2 MINING. Extraneous matter in a coal seam. E19.
3 TANNING. Dirt, lime, fat, and fragments of hair, requiring removal from a hide. L19.

scud /skʌd/ *verb*¹. In senses 1, 5 also (*rare*) **skid** /skɪd/. Infl. **-dd-**. M16.
[Perh. alt. of SCUT *noun*³, as if to race like a hare.]
1 *verb intrans.* Run, move, or fly lightly and quickly; dart nimbly; NAUTICAL run before the wind with little or no sail. M16. ▸**b** In *imper.* Go away! Hurry up! E17.
2 *verb trans.* Move, travel, or sail quickly over. Chiefly *poet.* M17.
3 *verb intrans.* Of a cloud, foam, etc.: be driven by the wind. L17.
4 *verb trans.* Slap, beat, spank. *Scot.* E19.
5 *verb trans.* Send (a flat stone) skimming across the surface of water. *Scot.* L19.
1 W. BROWNE The Trout within the weeds did scud. DAY LEWIS He mounts his bicycle . . and goes scudding down the rough drive. **3** W. GOLDING Clouds scudding across a full moon.
■ **scudder** *noun* L19.

scud /skʌd/ *verb*² *trans.* Infl. **-dd-**. L18.
[Prob. from SCUD *noun*².]
1 Clean or scrape with a tool. *dial.* L18.
2 TANNING. Remove scud from (a hide). L19.

scuddick /ˈskʌdɪk/ *noun. slang & dial.* E19.
[Origin unkn.]
An extremely small coin or amount; something very small.

scuddle /ˈskʌd(ə)l/ *verb intrans.* Now *dial.* L16.
[Frequentative of SCUD *verb*¹: see -LE³. Cf. SCUTTLE *verb*¹.]
Run away hastily, scuttle.

scuddy /ˈskʌdi/ *adjective.* L18.
[from SCUD *noun*² + -Y¹.]
Esp. of wine: turbid, full of sediment.
■ **scuddiness** *noun* M19.

scudo /ˈskuːdəʊ/ *noun.* Pl. **scudi** /ˈskuːdi/. M17.
[Italian, from Latin *scutum* shield (whence also ÉCU). Cf. ESCUDO.]
Hist. A coin of silver or occas. gold formerly current in various Italian States.

scuff /skʌf/ *noun*¹. E18.
[from SCUFF *verb*.]
1 A slight glancing blow, a brush with the hand. Also, a scuffle. *Scot.* E18.
2 A rowdy crowd, a rabble; a member of such a crowd, a ruffian. M19.
3 An act or instance of scuffing; a mark or sound made by scraping or scuffing. L19.
4 A type of backless slipper or sandal. Chiefly *US.* E20.
2 rough scuff: see ROUGH *adjective.* **3** G. DURRELL The soft scuff of bare feet on the dusty road. B. LECOMBER A thousand scuffs and scratches in the shabby wood and leather.

scuff /skʌf/ *noun*². L18.
[from Old Norse *skoft* (= Old High German *scuft*, Gothic *skuft*) hair of the head. Cf. SCRUFF *noun*², CUFF *noun*⁴.]
= SCRUFF *noun*².

scuff /skʌf/ *verb.* L16.
[Perh. imit.; perh. rel. to SCURF *verb*, CUFF *verb*². Cf. SKIFF *verb*².]
†**1** *verb trans.* Evade, shirk, (duty). *Scot.* Only in L16.
2 *verb trans.* Graze or brush against, strike with a slight glancing blow; scrape or mark the surface of (a shoe etc.) in this way; wipe off by scuffing. E18. ▸**b** Scrape (the ground etc.) with the feet; throw *up* (dust etc.) by scuffing or shuffling; shuffle, drag, (the feet). L19.
3 *verb intrans.* Walk with dragging feet through dust, leaves, etc., shuffle along. M18.
4 *verb trans.* Buffet, strike, (a person). M19.
5 *verb intrans.* Become marked, worn, or damaged by rubbing or scraping, undergo scuffing. M20.
2 R. CHANDLER The speedboat scuffed the *Montecito*'s ancient sides. N. LOWNDES Sitting on a low nursery chair . . scuffing the heels of his new school shoes. **b** W. GOLDING I . . scuffed my feet into slippers and felt my way out on deck. I. WATSON I venture on to the ice, skating . . and scuffing up the dust of snow. **3** A. DESAI Scuffing through . . litter, he turned into the dark doorway. **5** *Sunday Express* Supple as leather, yet won't scratch, scuff or mark.

scuffer /ˈskʌfə/ *noun*¹. Chiefly *dial.* M19.
[Perh. from SCUFF *noun*² or *verb*: see -ER¹.]
A police officer.

scuffer /ˈskʌfə/ *noun*². *N. Amer.* E20.
[from SCUFF *noun*¹ or *verb* + -ER¹.]
= SCUFF *noun*¹ 4.

scuffing /ˈskʌfɪŋ/ *noun.* L19.
[from SCUFF *verb* + -ING¹.]
The action of SCUFF *verb*; an instance of this; *spec.* (ENGINEERING), the roughening of a metal surface designed to rub against another when the lubrication is inadequate.

scuffle /ˈskʌf(ə)l/ *noun*¹. E17.
[from SCUFFLE *verb*¹.]
1 A short confused struggle at close quarters, a disorderly fight, a tussle. E17.
2 The action of scuffling; confused utterance of speech; shuffling of feet. L19.
1 R. L. STEVENSON There was a sudden scuffle, a sound of blows. *Observer* Scuffles broke out last week between airline staff and passengers.

scuffle /ˈskʌf(ə)l/ *noun*². L18.
[Dutch *schoffel* hoe: see SHOVEL *noun* & *verb*¹, -LE¹.]
1 = SCUFFLER *noun*². L18.
2 A Dutch hoe. *local & US.* L18.

scuffle /ˈskʌf(ə)l/ *verb*¹. L16.
[Prob. from Scandinavian base (cf. Swedish *skuff(a)* push) from Germanic base also of SHUFFLE *verb*, SHOVE *verb*: see -LE³.]
1 *verb intrans.* Engage in a scuffle, struggle confusedly at close quarters *with* or *together*, tussle. L16.
2 *verb trans.* **a** Put on, handle, or move (a thing) in a scrambling or confused manner. Usu. foll. by adverb. L16. ▸**b** Obtain (money) with difficulty, scrape together. Also foll. by *up*. *slang* (chiefly *US*). M20.
3 *verb intrans.* **a** Move or search in hurried confusion. Usu. foll. by adverb or preposition. E18. ▸**b** Struggle *along* or carry *on* hurriedly or haphazardly, muddle *through*; *slang* (chiefly *US*) survive with difficulty, make a bare living by uncongenial or degrading means. L18.
4 *verb intrans.* Move with a shuffling gait, shuffle with the feet. E19.
1 *Independent* Soldiers and . . loyalists scuffling with some of the 15,000 protesters. **3a** P. ANGADI She pulled open a drawer and scuffled about inside it. **b** J. RUNCIMAN Go to school and scuffle on the best way you can.
■ **scuffler** *noun*¹ M17. **scufflingly** *adverb* in a scuffling manner L19.

scuffle /ˈskʌf(ə)l/ *verb*² *trans.* M18.
[from SCUFFLE *noun*².]
Break the surface of or scarify (land) with a scuffler or hoe; hoe.
■ **scuffler** *noun*² a tool for scuffling land, a hoe L18.

scug /skʌg/ *noun*¹ & *verb. Scot. & north.* LME.
[Old Norse *skugge* shadow (Swedish *skugga*, Norwegian *skugge*, Danish *skygge*) = Old English *scu(w)a*, Old High German *scuwo* shade, Gothic *skuggwa* mirror, from Germanic.]
▶ **A** *noun.* Shadow, shade; (a) shelter; *fig.* pretence, outward show. LME.
▶ **B** *verb.* Infl. **-gg-**.
1 *verb trans.* Shade, shelter, protect. E16.
2 *verb intrans.* Take cover or shelter, hide. L18.
3 *verb trans.* Take shelter from. E19.
■ **scuggery** *noun* concealment, secrecy M16.

scug /skʌg/ *noun*². *slang.* E19.
[Origin unkn.]
At Eton College or Harrow School, an undistinguished or unpopular boy, *esp.* one lacking sporting ability.
■ **scuggish**, **scuggy** *adjectives* of the nature of or characteristic of (a scug) E20.

scugnizzo /skuˈɲittso/ *noun.* Pl. ***-zzi*** /-ttsi/. M20.
[Italian dial.]
In Naples, a street urchin. Usu. in *pl.*

sculch /skʌlʃ/ *noun. dial. & US.* M19.
[Alt.]
= CULCH.

sculduddery /skʌlˈdʌd(ə)ri/ *noun. Scot. & US.* E18.
[Origin unkn. Cf. SCULDUGGERY.]
Sexual impropriety; obscenity, indecency.

sculduggery *noun* var. of SKULDUGGERY.

scull /skʌl/ *noun*[1]. ME.
[Origin unkn.]
1 An oar placed over the stern and worked from side to side with a twisting movement to propel a boat. Also, either of a pair of small oars used by a single rower. ME.
2 A small boat propelled with a scull or a pair of sculls; a light racing craft for a single rower. E17.
†**3** A person who sculls, a sculler. *rare*. M17–E18.
4 In *pl.* A race between boats with single pairs of oars. L19.
5 An act of sculling. L19.

†**scull** *noun*[2]. M16–M18.
[Abbreviation.]
A scullion.

scull *noun*[3] var. of SKULL *noun*[2].

scull /skʌl/ *verb*. E17.
[from SCULL *noun*[1]. Cf. earlier SCULLER.]
1 *verb intrans.* Proceed or travel in a boat propelled with a scull or pair of sculls; row with a scull or sculls; (of a boat) admit of being sculled. E17. ▸**b** Skate without lifting the feet from the ice. L19.
2 *verb trans.* Propel (a boat) with a scull or pair of sculls. M17.
3 *verb trans.* Convey (a person) by sculling. E19.

> **1 scull about, scull around** *colloq.* move about aimlessly; (of an object) lie around obstructively. **3** J. K. JEROME Sculling himself along in easy vigorous style.

sculler /ˈskʌlə/ *noun*. M16.
[from (the same root as) prec. + -ER[1].]
1 A person engaged or skilled in propelling a boat with a scull or pair of sculls. M16.
2 A boat propelled by or intended for sculling. M16.

scullery /ˈskʌl(ə)ri/ *noun*. LME.
[Anglo-Norman *squillerie* from Old French *escuelerie*, from *escuelier* maker or seller of dishes, from *escuele* from Proto-Romance from Latin *scutella* salver, waiter, dim. of *scutra* wooden dish or platter: see -ERY.]
1 *Hist.* The department of a household responsible for kitchen dishes, utensils, etc; the room or rooms used by this department. LME.
2 A small kitchen or room attached to a kitchen for the washing of dishes and other dirty household work. M18.

scullion /ˈskʌlɪən/ *noun*. L15.
[Origin unkn.]
A domestic servant of the lowest rank in a household, employed to wash dishes and perform other menial kitchen tasks (*Hist.*); *transf.* *arch.* a despicable person, a menial.

sculp /skʌlp/ *noun*[1]. L17.
[from SCULP *verb*[1].]
†**1** An engraving or woodcut used as an illustration in a book. L17–E18.
2 A piece of sculpture. Now *joc.* & *colloq.* M19.

sculp /skʌlp/ *noun*[2]. *N. Amer. dial.* M18.
[from SCULP *verb*[2].]
A human scalp (*arch.*); a sealskin with the blubber attached.

sculp /skʌlp/ *verb*[1]. Now *joc.* & *colloq.* M16.
[Latin *sculpere* carve.]
†**1** *verb trans.* Carve, engrave, (a design etc.). M16–L17.
†**2** *verb trans.* Cut *out* with an engraving tool. Only in L17.
3 *verb trans.* & *intrans.* Sculpture. L18.

sculp /skʌlp/ *verb*[2] *trans.* *N. Amer. dial.* M18.
[Var. of SCALP *verb*[2].]
Scalp (a person) (*arch.*); skin (a seal).

sculpin /ˈskʌlpɪn/ *noun*. L17.
[Perh. alt. of SCORPENE.]
1 Any of various mainly small spiny fishes with little or no commercial value, now *spec.* of the family Cottidae; any of various fishes of related acanthopterygian families esp. the Arctic family Icelidae (usu. with specifying word). L17.
2 *transf.* A mean worthless person or animal. M19.

sculpt /skʌlpt/ *verb trans.* & *intrans.* M19.
[French *sculpter*, from *sculpteur* SCULPTOR. Later regarded as back-form. from SCULPTOR or SCULPTURE *noun*.]
Sculpture. Freq. as ***sculpted*** *ppl adjective*.

> *Daily Express* He sculpts in almost every material. *Listener* Eucalyptus with smooth sculpted trunks of an exquisite pallor.

†**sculptile** *noun* & *adjective*. ME.
[As noun from late Latin = graven image, as adjective from Latin *sculptilis*, from *sculpt-*: see SCULPTURE *noun*, -ILE.]
▶ **A** *noun.* In *pl.* Graven images. ME–E17.
▶ **B** *adjective.* Sculptured, engraved, graven. E17–E19.

sculptor /ˈskʌlptə/ *noun*. M17.
[Latin, from *sculpt-*: see SCULPTURE *noun*, -OR. Cf. French *sculpteur*.]
1 A person practising the art of sculpture, an artist producing sculptures. M17.
†**2** An engraver. Only in M17.
3 (Usu. **S-**.) (The name of) an inconspicuous constellation of the southern hemisphere, between Grus and Cetus. Also ***the Sculptor***, ***the Sculptor's tools***. M19.
■ **sculptress** *noun* a female sculptor M17.

sculptural /ˈskʌlptʃ(ə)r(ə)l/ *adjective*. E19.
[from next + -AL[1].]
1 Of or pertaining to sculpture. E19.
2 Having the qualities of (a) sculpture; sculptured. M19.

> **2** M. McLUHAN The demand for . . sculptural hairdos. JULIETTE HUXLEY She was solidly sculptural, a little short for perfect beauty.

■ **sculpturally** *adverb* E19.

sculpture /ˈskʌlptʃə/ *noun*. LME.
[Latin *sculptura*, from *sculpt-* pa. ppl stem of *sculpere* var. of *scalpere* SCALP *verb*[1]: see -URE. Cf. SCALPTURE.]
1 The art or process of creating (now usu. large) representational or abstract forms in the round, in relief, or (formerly) in intaglio, by chiselling stone, casting metal, modelling clay or some other plastic substance, carving wood, etc., or, now also, by assembling separate parts; the practice of this art. LME.
2 a The product or this art, that which is sculptured; sculptured forms or designs in general. LME. ▸**b** A work of sculpture; a sculptured form or design. E17.
†**3** A picture or design printed from an engraved plate or block, an engraving; engravings collectively. M17–L18.
4 BOTANY & ZOOLOGY. Indentation of the surface or outline of an animal or plant structure resembling that produced by carving; sculpturing. E19.
5 GEOLOGY. The generation of landforms by the processes of erosion, esp. by wind and water. L19.

> **2a** H. MOORE I had never felt any desire to make relief sculpture. J. F. HENDRY A solo exhibition of her sculpture. **b** *Holiday Which?* A wonderful lifesize horse and rider sculpture in the entrance hall. **4** C. DARWIN The seeds . . differ in shape and sculpture.

Phrases: ***junk sculpture***: see JUNK *noun*[2]. ***mobile sculpture***: see MOBILE *adjective*. ***soft sculpture***: see SOFT *adjective*.

sculpture /ˈskʌlptʃə/ *verb*. M17.
[from the noun.]
1 *verb trans.* & *intrans.* Represent or create (a form) in sculpture, practise sculpture on or with (a medium). Freq. as ***sculptured*** *ppl adjective*. M17.
2 *verb trans.* Decorate with sculpture; mark or form (as) by sculpture, esp. with strong smooth curves. Freq. as ***sculptured*** *ppl adjective*. M17.

> **1** M. GARDINER Antique vases . . on which are sculptured bacchanalian orgies. J. E. HARRISON The snakes sculptured on the top round the hollow cup. **2** D. C. PEATTIE There . . rise minarets of tufa and sculptured talc. *Which Computer?* The keys are sculptured and have a good typing feel.

■ **sculpturer** *noun* (*rare*) M18.

sculpturesque /skʌlptʃəˈrɛsk/ *adjective*. M19.
[from SCULPTURE *noun* + -ESQUE.]
Resembling sculpture, having the qualities of sculpture.
■ **sculpturesquely** *adverb* L19.

sculpturing /ˈskʌlptʃ(ə)rɪŋ/ *noun*. M19.
[from SCULPTURE *verb* + -ING[1].]
1 The action of SCULPTURE *verb*; an act or instance of this; a sculptured marking. M19.
2 BOTANY. The pattern of raised or impressed markings on the surface of a pollen grain, a seed-coat, etc. M20.

scum /skʌm/ *noun* & *verb*. ME.
[Middle Low German, Middle Dutch *schūm* (Dutch *schuim*) = Old High German *scūm* (German *Schaum*: cf. MEERSCHAUM) from Germanic.]
▶ **A** *noun.* †**1** *sing.* & in *pl.* Foam, froth. ME–L17.
2 a A layer of dirt, froth, impurities, or other matter, forming on the surface of a liquid, esp. in boiling or fermentation; a film of algae, refuse, etc., on stagnant water; *gen.* any undesirable surface layer or deposit. LME. ▸†**b** Dross rising to the surface in the purifying of a metal, slag. E16–E19. ▸**c** Semen. *coarse slang* (chiefly *US*). M20.
3 a *collect.* Worthless despicable people; the most contemptible part *of* the population of a place, society, etc. L16. ▸†**b** A group of such people. L16–E19. ▸**c** A worthless despicable person. L16.

> **2** A. RANSOME John let the dirty water and the scum . . on the surface flow away. A. DESAI A ditch in which weeds stood . . in mud and scum. **3a** P. G. WODEHOUSE Don't talk to me about poets! The scum of the earth. **c** W. STYRON Detestable scum that you are . . no more civilized than a sewer rat.

Comb.: **scumbag** *slang* (orig. *US*) (*a*) a condom; (*b*) a worthless despicable person (also as a general term of abuse).
▶ **B** *verb.* Infl. **-mm-**.
1 *verb trans.* Clear scum from the surface of (a liquid), skim; remove as scum, skim *off*. Now also, be or form a scum on. LME. ▸†**b** Travel or search through, scour, (an area). LME–L17.
2 *verb intrans.* Of a liquid: become covered with scum, film *over* with scum, throw up or produce scum. Formerly also, rise to the surface as scum. L15.

> **1** T. PYNCHON The water in the vats . . lay stagnant and scummed over.

■ **scumless** *adjective* L19.

scumber /ˈskʌmbə/ *verb* & *noun*. *obsolete* exc. *dial.* Also **skummer** /ˈskʌmə/. LME.
[App. aphet. from Old French *descombrer* relieve of a load (mod. *décombrer* clear of rubbish): see -ER[5]. Cf. DISCUMBER.]
▶ **A** *verb.* **1** *verb intrans.* Esp. of a dog or fox: defecate. LME.
2 *verb trans.* Void as excrement. L16.
▶ **B** *noun.* Excrement, esp. of a dog or fox. M17.
■ †**scumbering** *noun* a piece of the excrement of a dog or fox E17–E19.

scumble /ˈskʌmb(ə)l/ *verb* & *noun*. L17.
[Perh. frequentative of SCUM *verb*: see -LE[3]. Cf. SCRUMBLE *verb*[2].]
ART. ▶**A** *verb trans.* Apply a thin opaque coat of paint to (a section of a painting) in order to produce a softer or duller effect; apply (paint) thinly to produce such an effect. Also, modify (a drawing) similarly with light shading in pencil, charcoal, etc. L17.
▶ **B** *noun.* A thin opaque coat of paint or layer of shading applied to produce a softened effect; a softened effect produced by scumbling. M19.

scummer /ˈskʌmə/ *noun*. Now *Scot.* ME.
[from SCUM *verb* + -ER[1], in sense 1 after Old French *escumoir* (mod. *écumoire*), in sense 2 after *escumeor* (*écumeur*), both from *escumer* skim, from *escume* SCUM *noun*.]
1 A shallow ladle or sieve for removing scum or floating matter from the surface of a liquid. ME.
†**2** A person scouring the sea, a rover, a pirate. LME–L16.
†**3** A person gathering or removing scum. E–M17.

scumming /ˈskʌmɪŋ/ *noun*. LME.
[from SCUM *verb* + -ING[1].]
†**1** = SCUMMER 1. Only in LME.
2 The action of SCUM *verb*; an instance of this; *sing.* & in *pl.*, matter removed as scum from the surface of a liquid. M16.

scummy /ˈskʌmi/ *adjective*. L16.
[from SCUM *noun* + -Y[1].]
1 Having the nature or appearance of scum; covered or filled with scum. L16.
2 Filthy, dirty, squalid; despicable, disreputable. *colloq.* (orig. *US*). M20.

> **1** B. CHATWIN To miss her footing and almost fall into the scummy brown flood-water. **2** R. DAHL I'd know 'im a mile away, the scummy little bounder. *Times* It was scummy There were holes in the roof and no heat.

■ **scumminess** *noun* L20.

scun /skʊn, skuːn/ *verb intrans.* & *trans.* *Scot.* & *north.* Now *rare* or *obsolete*. Infl. **-nn-**. L18.
[Perh. from Old Norse *skunda* speed, hasten.]
Skim through the air or across the surface of water.
¶ Perh. the source of or rel. to the 1st elem. of SCHOONER *noun*[1].

scunch /skʌn(t)ʃ/ *noun*. *obsolete* exc. *dial.* See also SQUINCH *noun*[1].
[Abbreviation.]
= next.

scuncheon /ˈskʌn(t)ʃ(ə)n/ *noun*. ME.
[Aphet. from Old French *escoinson* (mod. *écoinçon*), from *ex-* EX-[1] + *coin* corner. Cf. SCOINSON.]
ARCHITECTURE. The bevelled inner edge of a window-frame, door-jamb, etc.

scunge /skʌn(d)ʒ/ *noun*. *colloq.* E19.
[Origin uncertain: cf. next.]
1 A sly or vicious person; a scrounger, a sponger. Also as a general term of abuse. Orig. *Scot.* E19.
2 [Cf. GUNGE *noun*[2].] Dirt, filth, mess; *Austral.* & *NZ* a dirty or disagreeable person. M20.
■ **scungy**, **-gey** *adjective* (chiefly *Austral.* & *NZ*) mean, dirty; disreputable, squalid: M20.

scunge /skʌn(d)ʒ/ *verb intrans.* *colloq.* (orig. *Scot.*). M19.
[Origin uncertain: cf. prec., SCROUNGE *verb*.]
Prowl around looking for food etc.; scrounge, sponge.

scungille /skunˈdʒille/ *noun*. Pl. ***-lli*** /-lli/. M20.
[Italian dial. *scunciglio*, prob. alt. of Italian *conchiglia* seashell, shellfish.]
A mollusc, a conch; *esp.* the meat of a mollusc eaten as a delicacy.

scunner /ˈskʌnə/ *verb* & *noun*. *Scot.* & *north.* LME.
[Origin unkn.]
▶ **A** *verb.* **1** *verb intrans.* Orig., shrink back with fear, flinch. Now, be affected with violent disgust, feel sick. LME.
2 *verb trans.* Disgust, sicken. L19.
▶ **B** *noun.* **1** Orig., a loathing disgust. Now also, a grudge, a dislike. Freq. in ***take a scunner at***, ***take a scunner against***, ***take a scunner to***. L15.
2 An annoying person or thing, a nuisance; an object of disgust or loathing. L18.

scuola /ˈskwəʊlə/ *noun.* Pl. ***-le*** /-leɪ/. **M19.**
[Italian = school.]
In Venice, any of the buildings in which the medieval religious confraternities or guilds used to meet, a guildhall; *Hist.* any of these guilds.

scup /skʌp/ *noun.* Pl. same. **M19.**
[from Narragansett *mishcup*, from *mishe* big + *cuppi* close together (because of the shape of the scales).]
A common porgy, *Stenotomus chrysops*, with faint dark vertical bars, occurring off NE American Atlantic coasts.

scupper /ˈskʌpə/ *noun.* **LME.**
[Perh. from Anglo-Norman deriv. of French *escopir* (mod. *écopir*) from Proto-Romance word meaning 'spit', of imit. origin: see -ER[2]. Cf. German *Speigatt* scupper, from *speien* spit + *Gat(t)* hole.]
1 NAUTICAL. An opening in a ship's side on a level with the deck to allow water to run away. Usu. in *pl.* **LME.**
2 A prostitute; *derog.* a woman. *slang.* **M20.**

scupper /ˈskʌpə/ *verb trans.* **L19.**
[Origin uncertain: perh. from prec.]
1 Kill, esp. in an ambush. *Military slang.* **L19.**
2 Defeat, ruin, thwart, put an end to. *colloq.* **E20.**
3 Sink (a ship) deliberately, scuttle. **L20.**

📖 **2** J. ARCHER If they defeat us on certain key clauses they can still scupper the whole bill.

scuppernong /ˈskʌpənɒŋ/ *noun. US.* Also **S-**. **E19.**
[A river in N. Carolina, USA.]
1 (In full ***scuppernong vine***.) A variety of the muscadine, *Vitis rotundifolia*, native to the basin of the Scuppernong River and cultivated; (in full ***scuppernong grape***) the fruit of this vine. **E19.**
2 In full ***scuppernong wine***. Wine made from the scuppernong grape. **E19.**

scuppet /ˈskʌpɪt/ *noun & verb. obsolete* exc. *dial.* See also SKIPPET *noun*[3]. **LME.**
[App. formed as SCOOP *noun* + -ET[1].]
▶ **A** *noun.* A kind of spade used for digging ditches, turning drying hops, etc. **LME.**
▶ **B** *verb trans.* Shovel, scoop. Freq. foll. by *out*, *away*. **L16.**

scur /skəː/ *noun.* **L19.**
[Origin unkn.]
A small horn not rooted in the skull but loosely attached by the skin, found in polled cattle and sheep or their crossbred offspring.
■ **scurred** *adjective* having scurs **M20.**

scurf /skəːf/ *noun*[1].
[Late Old English *sceorf*, (infl. by Old Norse) *scurf*, from base of Old English *sceorfan* gnaw, *sceorfian* cut into shreds. Cf. Middle & mod. High German, Middle & mod. Low German *schorf* scab, scurf. See also SCREEF, SCRUFF *noun*[1].]
†**1** Any condition or disease in people or animals characterized by the production of loose scales or flakes of skin. **LOE–M17.**
2 *collect.* The scales or flakes of epidermis that are continually cast off as fresh skin forms below; *esp.* such scales present in abnormally large numbers, esp. in seborrhoeic conditions of the scalp; dandruff. **LOE.** ▸**b** BOTANY. A scaly covering on a leaf, twig, etc. **M19.**
3 Any incrustation or flaky or scaly deposit on a surface. **LME.** ▸**b** *spec.* A deposit of coke on the inner surface of a gas retort. **L19.**
4 a *collect.* = SCUM *noun* 3a. *rare.* **L17.** ▸**b** A contemptible person; *esp.* a miser, a skinflint. Also *spec.*, an employer paying less than the usual rate of wages; a labourer accepting less than the usual rate. *slang.* **M19.**

📖 **3** P. BARKER Tears . . already dried to a white scurf at the corners of her eyes.

scurf /skəːf/ *noun*[2]. **L15.**
[Perh. identical with prec.]
A sea trout.

scurf /skəːf/ *verb.* **M17.**
[from SCURF *noun*[1].]
1 *verb trans.* Cover with a scurf or incrustation. **M17.**
2 *verb intrans.* Rise *up* in the form of scurf. **M19.**
3 *verb trans.* Remove by scraping, chip off (a deposit etc.). **M19.**
■ **scurfer** *noun* **L19.** **scurfing** *noun* (*a*) (*rare*) the formation of scurf; (*b*) an incrustation, a deposit: **L16.**

scurfy /ˈskəːfi/ *adjective.* **L15.**
[from SCURF *noun*[1] + -Y[1].]
Covered (as) with scurf; suffering from a flaking skin condition; of the nature of or resembling scurf, scaly, flaky.
■ **scurfily** *adverb* **L19.** **scurfiness** *noun* **E16.**

†**scurrier** *noun*[1]. **LME–E17.**
[App. aphet. from Old French *descouvreor* discoverer: see -ER[2]. Cf. SCURRY *verb*.]
A person sent out to reconnoitre, a scout.

scurrier /ˈskʌrɪə/ *noun*[2]. **L19.**
[from SCURRY *verb* + -ER[1].]
A person who or thing which scurries.

scurrile /ˈskʌrɪl/ *adjective. arch.* Also **-il**. **M16.**
[French, or Latin *scurrilis*: see next, -ILE.]
= SCURRILOUS.
■ †**scurrilely** *adverb* **M17–E18.**

scurrility /skəˈrɪlɪti/ *noun.* **E16.**
[French *scurrilité* or Latin *scurrilitas*, from *scurrilis*, from *scurra* buffoon: see -ITY.]
The quality of being scurrilous; gross or obscene abusiveness, coarse humour; an instance of this.

📖 D. M. THOMAS A letter combining lofty scorn with pungent scurrility.

scurrilous /ˈskʌrɪləs/ *adjective.* **L16.**
[from SCURRILE + -OUS.]
Grossly or obscenely abusive, defamatory; given to or expressed with coarse humour; disreputable.

📖 *Times* He described the preface as scurrilous, sour and vindictive.

■ **scurrilously** *adverb* **L16.** **scurrilousness** *noun* **E18.**

scurry /ˈskʌri/ *noun.* Also †**skurry**. **E19.**
[from the verb.]
1 The action or an act of scurrying; a sally, a rush; hurry, haste, bustle. **E19.** ▸**b** A short quick run or race on horseback; *spec.* in showjumping and carriage-driving, a contest in which faults are counted as time penalties. **E19.** ▸**c** A run made by an animal. **M19.**
2 A flurry or whirl of snow, rain, etc. **M19.**

📖 **1** G. HUNTINGTON The usual scurry, shouting of sailors and throwing of ropes. M. GEE She timed her swift scurries downstairs to avoid them.

scurry /ˈskʌri/ *verb.* Also †**skurry**. **L16.**
[Sense 1 app. back-form. from SCURRIER *noun*[1]. Senses 2, 3 app. from HURRY-SCURRY.]
†**1** *verb intrans.* Ride out as a scout. Only in **L16.**
2 *verb intrans.* Move hurriedly or run with short quick steps, freq. furtively or busily; scamper, scuttle. **E19.**
3 *verb trans.* Cause to move in this way. Now *rare.* **M19.**

📖 **2** W. BLACK They scurry away like rabbits when they see her coming. E. ROOSEVELT Everyone scurried around to get ready. *fig.*: A. FRANCE I weathered several major crises, without feeling the need to scurry back to my therapist.

scurvied /ˈskəːvɪd/ *adjective.* **M19.**
[from SCURVY *noun* + -ED[2].]
Affected with scurvy.

scurvily /ˈskəːvɪli/ *adverb. arch.* **L16.**
[from SCURVY *adjective* + -LY[2].]
In a scurvy or contemptible manner.

scurviness /ˈskəːvɪnɪs/ *noun. arch.* **M16.**
[formed as prec. + -NESS.]
The quality or condition of being contemptible or (formerly) scurfy.

scurvy /ˈskəːvi/ *noun.* **M16.**
[from next, partly ellipt. for †*scurvy disease* by assoc. with French *scorbut*, Low German *schorbūk*: see SCORBUTUS.]
1 A disease characterized by general debility, soreness or bleeding of the gums, subcutaneous bleeding, and pain in the limbs, now recognized as due to a deficiency of ascorbic acid (vitamin C) in the diet. Formerly also, any of several conditions having similar symptoms, as purpura. **M16.**
†**2** In *pl.* Attacks of this disease. **L16–M18.**
Comb.: **scurvy-grass** any of various white-flowered cruciferous plants constituting the genus *Cochlearia*, found esp. on sea-coasts; esp. *C. officinalis* (in full ***common scurvy-grass***), whose fleshy leaves were formerly eaten by sailors as an antiscorbutic.
■ **scurvied** *adjective* affected with scurvy **M19.**

scurvy /ˈskəːvi/ *adjective.* **LME.**
[from SCURF *noun*[1] + -Y[1].]
†**1** = SCURFY. **LME–M19.**
2 Worthless, contemptible, paltry; unprincipled, dishonourable, impolite. *arch.* **L16.**
1 †**scurvy disease** = SCURF *noun*[1] 1.

scuse /skjuːz/ *verb trans.* Now *non-standard* & usu. in *imper.* Also **'scuse**. **L15.**
[Aphet.]
= EXCUSE *verb.*

scusi /ˈskuːzi/ *verb intrans.* (*imper.*). *slang.* **E20.**
[Italian, ellipt. for *mi scusi* excuse me, from *scusare* to excuse.]
'Excuse me', 'I beg your pardon'.

scut /skʌt/ *noun*[1]. *dial.* & *slang.* **L19.**
[Origin unkn.]
As a term of contempt: a fool, an objectionable person.

scut /skʌt/ *noun*[2]. *US colloq.* **M20.**
[Origin unkn.: cf. prec.]
More fully ***scut work***. Tedious menial work.

scut /skʌt/ *adjective, noun*[3], & *verb.* **LME.**
[Origin & exact interrelations unkn.]
▶†**A** *adjective.* Short. Only in **ME.**
▶ **B** *noun.* **1** A hare. Long only in HUNTING. **LME.**
2 A short erect tail, *esp.* that of a hare, rabbit, or deer. **M16.**
▶†**C** *verb trans.* Infl. **-tt-**. Cut short, dock. Only in **M16.**

scuta *noun* pl. of SCUTUM.

scutage /ˈskjuːtɪdʒ/ *noun.* **LME.**
[medieval Latin *scutagium* from Latin *scutum* shield after Old French *escuage* ESCUAGE.]
Hist. A tax levied on a feudal landowner's estate. Chiefly *spec.*, money paid in lieu of military service.

scutal /ˈskjuːt(ə)l/ *adjective.* **LME.**
[formed as SCUTUM + -AL[1].]
1 Of, pertaining to, or resembling a shield. Long only in HERALDRY. **LME.**
2 ZOOLOGY. Of or pertaining to a scutum. **M19.**

scutate /ˈskjuːteɪt/ *adjective.* **E19.**
[from SCUTUM: see -ATE[2].]
1 ZOOLOGY. Covered with large flat scales or scutes. **E19.**
2 BOTANY. Buckler-shaped; peltate. **M19.**
■ **scutated** *adjective* (now *rare* or *obsolete*) = SCUTATE 1 **E19.** **scu'tation** *noun* (ZOOLOGY) arrangement of scutes (in reptiles etc.) **M19.**

scutch /skʌtʃ/ *noun*[1]. *dial.* **L17.**
[Var. of SQUITCH *noun*.]
Couch grass, *Elytrigia repens*. Also ***scutch-grass***.

scutch /skʌtʃ/ *noun*[2]. **L18.**
[Old French *escouche* (mod. *écouche*), formed as SCUTCH *verb*[2].]
= SCUTCHER 2.

scutch /skʌtʃ/ *noun*[3]. **L19.**
[from SCUTCH *verb*[3].]
A tool like a two-pronged adze or pick, used in building for dressing stone etc. or cutting bricks.

scutch /skʌtʃ/ *verb*[1] *trans.* Now chiefly *dial.* Also **skutch**. **E17.**
[Prob. imit.]
Strike with a stick or whip, lash.

scutch /skʌtʃ/ *verb*[2] *trans.* Also **skutch**. **L17.**
[Old French *escoucher* dial. var. of *escousser* (mod. *écoucher*) from Proto-Romance, from Latin *excuss-* pa. ppl stem of *excutere*, formed as EX-[1] + *quatere* shake.]
1 TANNING. Remove moss and rough crust from (bark). Long *rare* or *obsolete.* **L17.**
2 Dress (fibrous material, esp. retted flax) by beating. **M18.**
3 Strike the grain from (ears of corn). **M19.**

scutch /skʌtʃ/ *verb*[3] *trans. Scot.* & *US.* **M19.**
[App. var. of SCOTCH *verb*[1]. Cf. SCUTCH *verb*[1], *verb*[2].]
Smooth or trim (a hedge, log, etc.) with a slashing or slicing motion; dress (stone or brick) in building.

scutcheon /ˈskʌtʃ(ə)n/ *noun.* **ME.**
[Aphet. from (the same root as) ESCUTCHEON.]
1 HERALDRY. = ESCUTCHEON 1. **ME.** ▸**b** *fig.* = ESCUTCHEON 3. Chiefly in phrs., esp. ***a blot on one's scutcheon***. **LME.**
†**2** A brooch; a badge. **LME–L16.**
3 a HORTICULTURE. A shield-shaped piece of bark bearing a bud, cut for grafting between the wood and bark of the stock. Now *rare* or *obsolete.* **L16.** ▸**b** ZOOLOGY. A large scale or bony plate, a scute. Now *rare.* **M19.**
4 †**a** The plate of a gunlock. **M17–L18.** ▸**b** An ornamented brass etc. plate round or over a keyhole; a plate for a name or inscription. **E18.** ▸**c** A hatchment. **E18.**
■ **scutcheoned** *adjective* provided or decorated with scutcheons **L18.**

scutcher /ˈskʌtʃə/ *noun.* **M18.**
[from SCUTCH *verb*[2] + -ER[1].]
1 A person scutching flax, corn, etc. **M18.**
2 An implement or apparatus for scutching flax etc.; the part of a threshing machine for striking off the grain from ears of corn. **M18.**

scute /skjuːt/ *noun.* **LME.**
[Latin *scutum* shield. Cf. ÉCU.]
1 = ÉCU. *obsolete* exc. *Hist.* **LME.** ▸**b** Any coin of small value, a small amount. **L16.**
2 A disc, a small patch; *spec.* a small leather patch on a boot or shoe; a metal heel- or toe-plate. Long *dial.* **M17.**
3 ZOOLOGY. A large scale or bony plate forming part of the integument of an animal, as a reptile, an armadillo, various fishes, etc. **M19.**

scutel /ˈskjuːt(ə)l/ *noun.* Now *rare* or *obsolete.* **E19.**
[from SCUTEL(LUM).]
ENTOMOLOGY. = SCUTELLUM.

scutella /skjuːˈtɛlə/ *noun*[1]. Pl. **-llae** /-liː/. **L18.**
[mod. Latin, orig. a use of Latin *scutella* platter, but taken for a dim. of *scutum* shield.]
ZOOLOGY & BOTANY. = SCUTELLUM.

scutella *noun*[2] pl. of SCUTELLUM.

scutellar /skjuːˈtɛlə/ *adjective.* **E19.**
[formed as next + -AR[1].]
Chiefly ENTOMOLOGY. Of, pertaining to, or situated on a scutellum.

scutellate /ˈskjuːtɪleɪt/ *adjective*. L18.
[from SCUTELLUM + -ATE².]
1 *BOTANY*. Shaped like a platter or scutellum, round and flat with a raised rim; (of a lichen) having a scutellum. L18.
2 *ORNITHOLOGY*. Of a bird's foot: covered with scutella. L19.
■ **scutellated** *adjective* = SCUTELLATE E18.

scutellation /skjuːtɪˈleɪʃ(ə)n/ *noun*. L19.
[formed as prec.: see -ATION.]
ZOOLOGY. **1** Scutellate formation (of the feet of birds). L19.
2 Arrangement of scutes or scales (in reptiles etc.), scutation. L19.

scutelliform /skjuːˈtɛlɪfɔːm/ *adjective*. E19.
[from next + -I- + -FORM.]
Having the form of a scutellum; = SCUTELLATE 1.

scutellum /skjuːˈtɛləm/ *noun*. Pl. **-lla** /-lə/. M18.
[mod. Latin, app. intended as a correction of Latin *scutella* SCUTELLA *noun*¹ as if a dim. of *scutum* shield (cf. -ELLA).]
1 *BOTANY*. **a** A round flat apothecium in a lichen, having a raised rim formed from the thallus. M18. ▸**b** A peltate organ in the embryo of a grass, a modified cotyledon. M19.
2 a *ENTOMOLOGY*. The third notal (dorsal) sclerite in each thoracic segment of an insect, posterior to the scutum. E19. ▸**b** *ORNITHOLOGY*. Each of the horny plates which cover the feet of certain birds. M19.

scutiform /ˈskjuːtɪfɔːm/ *adjective*. M17.
[from Latin *scutum* shield + -I- + -FORM.]
Chiefly *ANATOMY*. Shield-shaped.

scutter /ˈskʌtə/ *verb & noun*. Orig. *colloq. & dial.* L18.
[Perh. alt. of SCUTTLE *verb*¹ with substitution of -ER⁵.]
▶ **A** *verb intrans*. Scuttle, scurry. L18.
▶ **B** *noun*. An act or instance of scuttering. E19.

scuttle /ˈskʌt(ə)l/ *noun*¹. Also **skuttle**.
[Late Old English *scutel* from Old Norse *skutill* corresp. to Old Saxon *skutala* = Middle Low German *schötele*, Middle Dutch *schotele* (Dutch *schotel*), Old High German *scuzzila* (German *Schüssel*), all from Latin *scutula* or *scutella* rel. to *scutra* dish, platter: see -LE¹.]
†**1** A dish, a platter. LOE–E18.
2 a A basket for sifting or winnowing corn; a large shovel to cast grain in winnowing. Now *dial.* LME. ▸**b** A large open basket wide at the mouth and narrow at the bottom, used for carrying corn, earth, vegetables, etc. LME. ▸**c** = *COAL-scuttle*. M19.
3 The part of a motor-car body between the bonnet and the windscreen. E20.

scuttle /ˈskʌt(ə)l/ *noun*². Also **skuttle**. L15.
[Perh. from French †*escoutille* (mod. *écoutille*) hatchway from Spanish *escotilla* dim. of *escota* cutting out of cloth, from *escotar* cut out: see -LE².]
1 *NAUTICAL*. A small circular port in a ship's side; the cover or lid of such an opening. L15.
2 An opening in the roof, floor, or wall of a building; the shutter of such an opening, a trapdoor. Now *US*. E18.

scuttle /ˈskʌt(ə)l/ *noun*³. *rare*. M16.
[Alt. of CUTTLE *noun*¹.]
A cuttlefish. Also *scuttle fish*.
Comb.: **scuttle-bone**, **scuttle shell** cuttle-bone.

†**scuttle** *noun*⁴. L16–M18.
[Origin unkn.]
NAUTICAL. A platform at the head of a lower mast, a top.

scuttle /ˈskʌt(ə)l/ *noun*⁵. E17.
[from next.]
The action or an act of scuttling; a hurried gait; precipitate flight or departure.

scuttle /ˈskʌt(ə)l/ *verb*¹ *intrans*. L15.
[Parallel to SCUDDLE.]
Run or move hurriedly with short quick steps, esp. furtively or busily; scurry, scamper; *transf.* flee ignominiously from danger or difficulty, withdraw precipitately.

> D. JACOBSON He scuttled away downstairs like a guilty schoolboy. C. MCCULLOUGH The men in my life all scuttle off into the woodwork. H. CARPENTER Sometimes the live crabs . . would escape from their basket, scuttling under the bed.

■ **scuttler** *noun*¹ a person who scuttles M19.

scuttle /ˈskʌt(ə)l/ *verb*² *trans*. M17.
[from SCUTTLE *noun*².]
1 Sink (a ship) by letting in water, now esp. by opening the seacocks; sink (one's own vessel) deliberately. M17. ▸**b** *fig.* Thwart, spoil, ruin, frustrate, (esp. a plan). L19.
2 Cut a hole in (the deck of a vessel), esp. to salvage the cargo. Now *rare*. L18.

> **1b** *EuroBusiness* The impasse over agriculture now threatens to scuttle the Uruguay Round of negotiations.

■ **scuttler** *noun*² a person who scuttles a ship M19.

scuttlebutt /ˈskʌt(ə)lbʌt/ *noun*. E19.
[Contr. of *SCUTTLED butt*.]
1 A water-butt kept on a ship's deck for drinking from; a drinking-fountain; *fig.* a source of rumour or gossip. E19.
2 Rumour, idle gossip, unfounded report. *colloq.* (orig. *US*). E20.

> **2** R. LUDLUM The scuttlebutt then was that you were responsible for the capture and execution of the killer.

scuttled /ˈskʌt(ə)ld/ *ppl adjective*. M18.
[from SCUTTLE *verb*² + -ED¹.]
NAUTICAL. Having a hole cut in it.
scuttled butt = SCUTTLEBUTT.

scuttleful /ˈskʌt(ə)lfʊl, -f(ə)l/ *noun*. LME.
[from SCUTTLE *noun*¹ + -FUL.]
As much as a scuttle will hold.

scutty /ˈskʌti/ *noun*. *local*. L19.
[Perh. from SCUT *noun*³ + -Y⁶.]
The wren.

scutulum /ˈskjuːtjʊləm/ *noun*. Pl. **-la** /-lə/. L19.
[mod. Latin use of Latin dim. of *scutum* shield.]
1 *MEDICINE*. A shield-shaped crust or disc typical of the scalp disease favus. L19.
2 *ZOOLOGY*. A scutellum. *rare*. E20.

scutum /ˈskjuːtəm/ *noun*. Pl. **-ta** /-tə/. L18.
[Latin = oblong shield.]
1 (Usu. **S-**.) (The name of) a small constellation of the southern hemisphere, lying in the Milky Way between Aquila and Serpens; the Shield. Earliest in *Scutum Sobieski*. L18.
2 *ZOOLOGY*. A shieldlike dermal plate; a scute. L18.
3 *ENTOMOLOGY*. The second notal (dorsal) sclerite in each thoracic segment of an insect. M19.

scuzz /skʌz/ *noun*. *slang* (orig. & chiefly *N. Amer.*). Also **scuz**. M20.
[Prob. abbreviation of DISGUSTING, perh. infl. by *scum* and *fuzz*.]
1 That which is disgusting or sordid, seediness. M20.
2 A disreputable, disgusting, or despicable person; also as a general term of abuse. M20.
Comb.: **scuzzbag**, **scuzzball** = sense 2 above (cf. *scumbag* s.v. SCUM *noun*).

scuzzy /ˈskʌzi/ *adjective*. *slang* (orig. & chiefly *N. Amer.*). M20.
[from prec. + -Y¹.]
Disgusting, disreputable, despicable; seedy, sordid, squalid.

> JULIA PHILLIPS As scuzzy as the music business is, these guys are a little bit scuzzier. JANE OWEN A tall skinny man with lank straggly blond hair and scuzzy black jeans.

■ **scuzziness** *noun* L20.

scybalum /ˈsɪbələm/ *noun*. Pl. **-la** /-lə/. L17.
[Late Latin = dung from Greek *skubalon*.]
MEDICINE. A lump or mass of hardened faeces formed as a result of severe constipation.
■ **scybalous** *adjective* of, pertaining to, or of the nature of, scybala L18.

scye /sʌɪ/ *noun*. Orig. *Scot. & N. Ir. dial.* M19.
[Origin unkn.]
In tailoring and dressmaking: an armhole.

Scylla /ˈsɪlə/ *noun*. E16.
[Latin from Greek *Skulla* a dangerous sea-monster in Greek mythol.]
Either of two dangers or pitfalls such that to avoid one increases the risk from the other. Opp. CHARYBDIS.

> D. M. BAILLIE A middle way, between the Scylla of . . 'historicism' . . and the Charybdis of a merely symbolic Christology.

scypha /ˈsʌɪfə/ *noun*. Pl. **-phae** /-fiː/. M19.
[mod. Latin from Greek *skuphē* var. of *skuphos* large drinking-vessel.]
BOTANY. = SCYPHUS.

scyphate /ˈsʌɪfeɪt/ *adjective*. L19.
[medieval Latin (*nummus*) *scyphatus* cup-shaped (coin), from Latin SCYPHUS: see -ATE².]
NUMISMATICS. Of a coin, esp. one from the late Byzantine Empire: shaped like a shallow bowl, concave.

scyphi *noun* pl. of SCYPHUS.

scyphi- /ˈsʌɪfi, ˈskʌɪfi, ˈskɪfi/ *combining form* of Latin *scyphus* cup: see -I-. Cf. next.
■ **scyphiferous** /sʌɪˈfɪf(ə)rəs/ *adjective* (*BOTANY*) bearing a scyphus L19. **scyphiform** *adjective* (*BOTANY*) resembling a scyphus in shape M19. **scyphistoma** *noun*, pl. **-mae** /-miː/, **-mas**, *ZOOLOGY* the fixed polypoid stage in the life cycle of a scyphozoan, which reproduces asexually by budding or strobilation L19.

scypho- /ˈsʌɪfəʊ, ˈskʌɪfəʊ, ˈskɪfəʊ/ *combining form* of Greek *skuphos* cup: see -O-. Cf. prec.
■ **scyphomeˈdusa** *noun*, pl. **-sae**, **-sas**, the medusoid phase in the life cycle of a scyphozoan L19. **scyphomeˈdusan** *adjective* of or pertaining to a scyphomedusa L19. **scyˈphophorous** /-f(ə)rəs/ *adjective* (*BOTANY*) = SCYPHIFEROUS L19. **scyphostoma** *noun*, pl. **-mae**, **-mas**, *ZOOLOGY* = SCYPHISTOMA L19.

scyphose /ˈsʌɪfəʊs/ *adjective*. L19.
[from SCYPHUS + -OSE¹.]
BOTANY. Having a scyphus or scyphi.

scyphozoan /sʌɪfəˈzəʊən, skʌɪf-, skɪf-/ *noun & adjective*. E20.
[from mod. Latin *Scyphozoa* (see below), from SCYPHO- + Greek *zōa* animals: see -AN.]
▶ **A** *noun*. A jellyfish of the class Scyphozoa. E20.
▶ **B** *adjective*. Of, belonging to, or pertaining to (an animal of) this class. E20.

scyphus /ˈsʌɪfəs/ *noun*. Pl. **-phi** /-fʌɪ/. L18.
[mod. Latin use of Latin *scyphus* from Greek *skuphos* large drinking-vessel.]
BOTANY. In a lichen, a cuplike dilatation of the podetium. Cf. SCYPHA.

†**scytale** *noun*¹. Also **-al**. L16–L18.
[Latin, formed as next.]
(A heraldic representation of) an unidentified or mythical snake having colourful variegated markings.

scytale /ˈsɪtəli/ *noun*². L16.
[Greek *skutalē* staff.]
GREEK HISTORY. A Spartan method of transmitting secret messages by writing on a strip of parchment wound spirally round a cylindrical or tapering staff or rod, the message being legible only when the parchment was wound round an identical staff; a secret dispatch conveyed by this method; a rod used for this.

Scyth /sɪθ/ *noun*. LME.
[Latin *Scytha* from Greek *Skuthēs*.]
1 = SCYTHIAN *noun* 1. LME.
2 = SCYTHIAN *noun* 1b. *rare*. L20.

scythe /sʌɪð/ *noun*. Also (earlier) †**sithe** & other vars.
[Old English *sīþe* = Middle Low German *segede*, *sigde* (Low German *seged*, *seid*, *sichte*), Old Norse *sigðr*, from Germanic, whence also synon. Old Saxon *segisna*, Middle Dutch *seisene* (Dutch *zeis*), Old High German *segansa* (German *Sense*).]
1 A mowing or reaping implement having a long thin curving blade attached at an angle to a long two-handled shaft, swung over the ground with a sweeping motion. OE.
2 *Hist.* A weapon having a long curving blade resembling a scythe. ME.

> **1** *fig.*: SHAKES. *Sonn.* And nothing 'gainst Time's scythe can make defence.

Comb.: **scytheman**, **scythesman** a person using a scythe, a reaper; *spec.* a member of an irregular body of troops, armed with a scythe.
¶ The spelling with *sc-* (first recorded E17) is prob. due to assoc. with SCISSORS.
■ **scytheless** *adjective* E19.

scythe /sʌɪð/ *verb*. L16.
[from the noun.]
1 *verb intrans*. Use a scythe. L16.
2 *verb trans*. Cut or mow (corn etc.) with a scythe; *fig.* cut down or kill swiftly and drastically. L16.
3 *verb intrans*. Move with a sweeping motion as if mowing with a scythe. L19.

> **2** R. P. GRAVES Watching the hay being scythed. H. MCLEAVE The brilliant and original young psychiatrist scythed down so prematurely. **3** *Antiques & Art Monitor* Aerial perspectives of a motorway scything through a city.

■ **scyther** *noun* a person using a scythe, a reaper M19. **scything** *noun* the action of the verb; an instance of this; in *pl.*, scythed grass etc.: M20.

scythed /sʌɪðd/ *adjective*. LME.
[from SCYTHE *noun*, *verb*: see -ED², -ED¹.]
1 Provided with a scythe; *esp.* (*Hist.*, of a chariot) having scythes fastened to a revolving shaft projecting from the axle-trees. LME.
2 Cut down or through (as) with a scythe. M19.

Scythian /ˈsɪðɪən, ˈsɪθ-/ *noun & adjective*. L15.
[from Latin *Scythia* from Greek *Skuthia* from *Skuthēs* Scyth: see -AN.]
▶ **A** *noun*. **1** A native or inhabitant of the large region north and north-east of the Black Sea anciently known as Scythia. L15. ▸**b** An advocate of Scythism. E20.
2 The Iranian language of Scythia. M17.
▶ **B** *adjective*. **1** Of or pertaining to Scythia, its inhabitants, or their language. M17.
†**2** *PHILOLOGY*. Ural-Altaic. M–L19.
Special collocations: **Scythian antelope** = SAIGA. **Scythian lamb** = BAROMETZ.
■ **Scythianism** *noun* = SCYTHISM 2 E20.

Scythic /ˈsɪθɪk/ *adjective*. L16.
[Latin *Scythicus* from Greek *Skuthikos*, from *Skuthēs*: see prec., -IC.]
Scythian.

Scythism /ˈsɪðɪz(ə)m, ˈsɪθ-/ *noun*. E17.
[Late Greek *Skuthismos* from *Skuthēs* Scyth: see -ISM.]
†**1** The class or group of religions to which that of the Scythians belonged. *rare*. E17–E19.
2 [translation of Russian *skifstvo*.] A movement among Russian intellectuals soon after the Revolution of 1917 favouring peasant values associated with eastern Russia over those of western European civilization. E20.

SD *abbreviation*.
1 Sequence date.

2 *Hist.* [German] *Sicherheitsdienst*.
3 South Dakota.
4 STATISTICS. Standard deviation.

S. Dak. *abbreviation.*
South Dakota.

'sdeath /zdɛθ/ *interjection. arch.* E17.
[from 's- + DEATH.]
God's death!: an oath or forcible exclamation.

†sdeign *noun. rare.* Only in L16.
[Italian *sdegno*, formed as next.]
Disdain.
■ **†sdeignful** *adjective* disdainful L16–M18.

†sdeign *verb trans. & intrans.* L16–M17.
[Italian *sdegnare* aphet. from *disdegnare*.]
Disdain.

SDF *abbreviation.*
Social Democratic Federation.

SDI *abbreviation.*
Strategic Defense Initiative.

SDLP *abbreviation.*
Social Democratic and Labour Party.

SDO *abbreviation.*
MILITARY. Subdivisional Officer.

SDP *abbreviation.*
Hist. Social Democratic Party.

SDR *abbreviation.*
ECONOMICS. Special drawing right (from the International Monetary Fund).

SE *abbreviation.*
1 South-East(ern).
2 STATISTICS. Standard error.
3 Stock Exchange.

Se *symbol.*
CHEMISTRY. Selenium.

se /seɪ/ *noun.* L19.
[Chinese *sè*.]
A Chinese twenty-five-stringed plucked musical instrument, being a form of zither.

se- /sə, sɪ/ *prefix* (not productive).
[Repr. Latin *se-* from earlier *se* (also *sed*) preposition & adverb.]
Occurring in words adopted from Latin, with the sense 'without, apart', as *seclude, secure*.

SEA *abbreviation.*
Single European Act.

sea /siː/ *noun.*
[Old English *sǣ* = Old Frisian *sē*, Old Saxon *sēo, sēu*, dative *sēwa*, Old High German *sēo, sē*, dative *sēwe* (Dutch *zee*, German *See*), Old Norse *sær, sjár, sjór*, Gothic *saiws*, from Germanic, of unkn. origin.]

▶ **I 1** The continuous body of salt water that covers the greater part of the earth's surface and surrounds its land masses; any part of this, as opp. to land or fresh water. OE. ▸**b** In *pl.* Different parts or tracts of the ocean, ocean waters. Freq. *poet.* or *rhet.* OE.

2 A part of the general body of salt water, having certain land-limits or washing a particular coast, and usu. having a proper name. OE. ▸**b** ASTRONOMY. = MARE *noun*[3]. M17.

3 A large lake or land-locked sheet of water, whether salt or fresh. *obsolete* exc. in ***inland sea*** s.v. INLAND *adjective* and in proper names. OE.

4 The volume of water in the sea considered with regard to its ebb and flow, the tide. Now *rare*. OE.

5 The state of the sea with regard to the roughness or smoothness of the waves, the presence or absence of swell, etc.; (without specification) a heavy swell, rough water. OE. ▸**b** A large heavy wave. L16. ▸**c** The direction of the waves or swell. M18. ▸**d** Roughness of the sea brought about by wind blowing at the time. Cf. SWELL *noun* 2. E20.

6 A vast or overwhelming quantity or mass (*of*); a large level tract or expanse (*of* some material substance or aggregate of objects). L16.

7 *sing.* & in *pl.* The sea with regard to duration of a voyage, a sea passage. Only in ***long sea(s)***, ***short sea(s)***. M17.

8 PHYSICS. A space filled with particles of a certain kind, *esp.* one in which only the particles near the boundary or surface are significant. M20.

📖 **1** CLARENDON The fleet could have been . . ready for sea. LD MACAULAY Fought battles by sea as well as by land. *Observer* A neat bungalow a stone's throw from the sea. C. FRANCIS The first scent of the sea, . . heavy with a fish-like smell. **b** KEATS Magic casements, opening on the foam Of perilous seas. **2** ***Adriatic Sea, Irish Sea, Red Sea***, etc. **3** ***Caspian Sea, Dead Sea, Sea of Galilee***, etc. **5** LONGFELLOW Some ship in distress, that cannot live In such an angry sea! **b** F. CHICHESTER While I was asleep one sea shot me into the air. **6** J. MARQUAND Her voice . . was lost in that sea of other voices. TOLKIEN Pushing through a sea of bracken. B. MONTGOMERY Rain turned the whole area into a sea of mud.

▶ **II 9** JEWISH ANTIQUITIES. The great brazen laver in the Jewish Temple. LME.

Phrases: **at sea** (*a*) in a ship on the sea; (*b*) (also ***all at sea***) in a state of uncertainty or perplexity, at a loss. ***between the Devil and the deep (blue) sea***: see DEVIL *noun*. **beyond the sea(s)**, **beyond sea(s)** out of the country, in foreign parts, abroad. **by sea** by way of the sea, on or over the sea (as a mode of transit or conveyance), in a ship or ships. ***coast of the sea***: see COAST *noun* 2. ***deep sea***: see DEEP *adjective*. **†full sea** high tide. ***go to sea***: see GO *verb*. ***heave of the sea***: see HEAVE *noun* 1. ***high sea(s)***: see HIGH *adjective, adverb, & noun*. ***inland sea***: see INLAND *adjective*. ***key of the sea***: see KEY *noun*[1]. ***long sea(s)***: see sense 7 above. ***luce of the sea***: see LUCE 2. ***main sea***: see MAIN *adjective*. ***narrow seas***: see NARROW *adjective*. ***ocean sea***: see OCEAN 1. ***old man of the sea***: see OLD MAN *noun phr.* **on the sea**, **on sea** at the sea's edge, on the sea-coast. **over the sea** across or beyond the sea; abroad, overseas. ***Peoples of the Sea***: see PEOPLE *noun*. **put to sea**, **put off to sea**, **put out to sea** leave land or a port in a ship etc. **salt sea** *poet.* seawater. ***seven seas***: see SEVEN *adjective*. ***ship a sea***: see SHIP *verb* 10. ***short sea(s)***: see sense 7 above. **take the sea** *arch.* (*a*) go on board ship, embark; (*b*) put out to sea. ***trough of the sea***: see TROUGH *noun* 5(d). ***use the sea(s)***: see USE *verb*. ***wreck of the sea***: see WRECK *noun*[1] 1.

Attrib. & comb.: In the senses 'of or pertaining to the sea', as ***sea battle, sea foam, sea god, sea swell, sea-wave***; 'undertaken by sea', as ***sea passage***; 'proceeding from the sea', as ***sea fog***; 'living, functioning, or used in, on, or near the sea', as ***sea commander***, (esp. of a marine animal, plant, etc., having a superficial resemblance to the named land or freshwater animal etc.: see below). Special combs., as **sea-acorn** = ACORN ***barnacle***; **sea-adder** a pipefish; **sea air** the fresh, salty air found over or near the sea and now freq. regarded as beneficial or bracing; **sea anchor** a device such as a heavy bag dragged in the water to retard the drifting of a ship; ***sea anemone***: see ANEMONE 2; **sea-angel** = ***monkfish*** (a) s.v. MONK *noun*[1]; **sea-angler** (*a*) = ANGLER 2; (*b*) an angler who fishes in the sea; **sea-angling** angling in the sea; **sea-animal** an animal or creature which lives in the sea; ***sea-ape***: see APE *noun* 4; **sea-arrow** (*a*) a flying squid of the family Ommastrephidae, esp. *Ommastrephes sagittatus*; (*b*) = CHAETOGNATH; ***sea arrow-grass***: see ***arrow-grass*** s.v. ARROW *noun*; **sea-ash** the Hercules' club, *Zanthoxylum clava-herculis*; **sea aster** a wild aster, *Aster tripolium*, found in salt-marshes and on sea-cliffs; **sea bag** (*a*) *US* a sailor's travelling bag or trunk; (*b*) *slang* a heavy artillery shell; **sea bamboo** = ***sea trumpet*** below; **†sea bank** (*a*) the sea-coast, the seashore; (*b*) a dune, a sand-hill; (*c*) an embankment built for protection against the sea, a sea wall; **sea barley** a European wild barley, *Hordeum marinum*, often found on salty ground near the sea; **sea-bass** (*a*) any of various marine fishes of the family Serranidae, esp. *Dicentrarchus labrax* of the NE Atlantic, and (more fully ***black sea-bass***) *Centropristis striata* of the NW Atlantic; (*b*) (more fully ***white sea-bass***) *Atractoscion nobilis* of the family Sciaenidae, found off California; **sea-bat** (*a*) = ***flying gurnard*** s.v. FLYING *ppl adjective*; (*b*) = ***batfish*** s.v. BAT *noun*[3]; (*c*) any of various Indo-Pacific spade-fishes of the genus *Platax*; **sea-bathe** *verb intrans.* bathe in the sea; **sea-bathing** bathing in the sea; **sea beach** = BEACH *noun* 2; **sea-bean** any of various small things found on the coast and used as trinkets etc., *esp.* (*a*) a black pebble; (*b*) a seed of a tropical legume, *Entada gigas*, numbers of which are often washed up on western beaches of the British Isles; (*c*) a gastropod shell of the family Triviidae; (*d*) the operculum of a gastropod of the family Turbinidae; **sea-bear** †(*a*) a sea urchin; (*b*) = ***fur-seal*** s.v. FUR *noun*[1]; **sea-beast** (chiefly *literary*) a beast living in the sea; **sea-beat** *adjective* (*arch.*) = ***sea-beaten*** below; **sea-beaten** *adjective* †(*a*) (of a ship, sailor, etc.) tossed about or beaten by the waves of the sea; (*b*) (of a shore, rock, etc.) lashed by the sea; **seabed** the ground under the sea, the ocean floor; **sea beet** a wild form of beet found on seashores, *Beta vulgaris*, subsp. *maritima*; **sea beggar** *Hist.* a seaman of the small fleet organized by William of Orange in 1572 to combat the Spaniards; **sea belt** a brown seaweed, *Laminaria saccharina*, having an olive ribbon-like frilly-edged frond; **sea bindweed** a bindweed, *Calystegia soldanella*, with pink and white flowers, found esp. on sand-dunes and shingle; **sea bird** a bird frequenting the sea or coast; **sea-biscuit** = ***sand dollar*** s.v. SAND *noun*; **sea-blessing** *Nautical slang* a curse; **sea-blite** either of two maritime plants of the genus *Suaeda*, of the goosefoot family, *S. maritima* (in full ***annual sea-blite***) and *S. vera* (in full ***shrubby sea-blite***), both bearing small green flowers in the axils of fleshy leaves; ***sea blubber***: see BLUBBER *noun* 4; **sea-boat** (*a*) a boat for the sea; (*b*) a boat as coping well or badly etc. with conditions at sea; (*c*) a small manoeuvrable craft sent out from a larger vessel, as in cases of emergency at sea; **sea-born** *adjective* born in or of the sea; produced by, originating in, or rising from the sea; **seaborne** *adjective* conveyed or transported by sea, carried on the sea; **sea-bottle** (the air bladder of) any of several fucoid seaweeds; bladderwrack; **sea-bound** *adjective*[1] [BOUND *adjective*[2]] bound or confined by the sea; **sea-bound** *adjective*[2] [BOUND *adjective*[1]] bound for or on the way to the sea; **sea bream** any of various percoid marine fishes of the family Sparidae, with deep bodies and long dorsal fins; *esp.* (more fully ***red sea bream***) *Pagellus bogaraveo* and (more fully ***black sea bream***) *Spondyliosoma cantharus*, both found in the Mediterranean and NE Atlantic; ***sea breeze***: see BREEZE *noun*[2] 2; **sea breeziness** the quality of being suggestive of sea breezes, spiritedness, airiness; **sea-bristle** a colonial hydroid of the genus *Plumularia*; **sea buckthorn** a thorny shrub of sand-dunes, *Hippophae rhamnoides* (family Elaeagnaceae), with small green flowers and orange berry-like fruits; **sea-bug** a chiton; **sea butterfly** = PTEROPOD; **sea cadet** a trainee in naval affairs; *spec.* (with cap. initials) a member of the Sea Cadet Association, a voluntary youth organization seeking to develop a corps of naval cadets and to provide training and promote education in maritime affairs; **sea-calf** any of various seals or sea lions, *esp.* the common seal *Phoca vitulina*; **sea campion** a campion, *Silene uniflora*, of European coasts, similar to the bladder campion; **sea-canary** *Nautical slang* a cetacean with a whistling call; *spec.* = BELUGA 2; **sea-captain** the captain or commander of a ship, *esp.* the captain of a merchant ship; **sea-cat** (*a*) the nurse hound, *Scyliorhinus stellaris*; (*b*) = CHIMERA 4; (*c*) any of various sea-catfishes; (*d*) *S. Afr.* an octopus; (*e*) (***SeaCat***) (proprietary name for) a large, high-speed catamaran used as a passenger and car ferry; **sea-caterpillar** (*a*) = ***scale-worm*** s.v. SCALE *noun*[3]; (*b*) a chiton; **sea-catfish** (*a*) any of various marine siluroid fishes of the family Ariidae; (*b*) = ***wolf-fish*** s.v. WOLF *noun*; **sea change** a change brought about by the sea; *esp.* (after Shakes. *Temp.* I.ii.403) a notable or unexpected alteration or transformation, a radical change; **sea-chest** (*a*) a sailor's chest or box for storing clothing etc.; (*b*) a pipe closed at one end by a valve, connected to the side of a ship below the water-line and giving access to seawater etc. from inside the vessel; **sea-clam** any of various clams found on the Atlantic coast of N. America, esp. the surf clam; **sea-clerk** the common squid, *Loligo vulgaris*; **sea-cliff** a cliff on the seashore; also (GEOLOGY), an inland cliff on a former shoreline; **sea-cloth** (*a*) THEATRICAL a painted cloth spread over a stage and moved to represent waves; (*b*) cloth used for making sailors' clothing; **sea-coal** *arch.* †(*a*) jet; (*b*) mineral coal as distinguished from charcoal etc.; ***sea-coast***: see COAST *noun* 2; ***sea-cob***: see COB *noun*[2]; **seacock** (*a*) a gurnard; (*b*) *joc.* a bold sailor or sea-rover; (*c*) a valve on a pipe connecting a marine steam boiler with the sea; **sea coconut** *W. Indies* the fruit of a Brazilian palm, *Manicaria saccifera*, found washed up on beaches; **sea-cook** a cook on board ship (esp. in ***son of a sea-cook*** used as a term of abuse); **sea-coot** any of various marine birds resembling the coot, esp. the guillemot; **sea cow** (*a*) = ***STELLER's sea cow***; any sirenian, *esp.* a manatee; †(*b*) the walrus; (*c*) the hippopotamus; **sea-crab** a marine crab; **sea-cradle** a chiton; **seacraft** (*a*) maritime skill, skill in navigation; (*b*) seagoing craft; **sea-crafty** *adjective* (*arch.*, *literary*) skilled in seafaring matters; **sea-crawfish**, **sea-crayfish** any of various large marine decapod crustaceans, esp. the spiny lobster, *Palinurus vulgaris*; **sea-crow** *local* any of various coastal birds that resemble the crow in coloration, voice, or behaviour; **sea crust** the incrustation formed on an iron ship during a sea voyage; **sea cucumber** a holothurian, *esp.* one of the larger, non-burrowing forms; **sea-dace** the bass, *Dicentrarchus labrax*; **sea-daffodil** a bulbous plant of Mediterranean beaches, *Pancratium maritimum* (family Amaryllidaceae), grown for its umbels of large white flowers; **sea-daisy** = ***sea pink*** below; **sea defences** barriers against the sea or tide; **sea devil** (*a*) a devil supposed to inhabit the sea; (*b*) see DEVIL *noun* 5; **sea dingle** *arch.* an abyss or deep in the sea; **sea dragon** (*a*) any of various ugly or bizarre fishes, esp. an Australian pipefish bearing leaflike appendages, a dragonet, or a dragonfish; (*b*) a mythical marine monster resembling a dragon; (*c*) any of various large marine Mesozoic reptiles; **seadrome** an (imagined) offshore airport or floating aerodrome; **sea-duck** any of various sea-frequenting ducks of the tribes Mergini and Somateriini, esp. eiders and scoters; ***Sea*** DYAK; **sea-dyke** (chiefly *dial.*) an embankment against the sea, a sea wall; **sea-eagle** (*a*) any of various fishing eagles of the genus *Haliaeetus*, *esp.* (in full ***white-tailed sea eagle***) *H. albicilla*; ***white-headed sea-eagle***: see WHITE *adjective*; (*b*) the osprey; (*c*) = ***eagle ray*** s.v. EAGLE *noun*; **sea-ear** an abalone or ear-shell, *esp.* the ormer; **sea-eel** any of various marine eels, *esp.* the conger; **sea-egg** a sea urchin; **sea-elephant** (*a*) the elephant seal; †(*b*) the walrus; **sea fan** any of various gorgonian corals that branch in a single flat plane; **seafardinger** *arch.* a seafarer; **seafare** (*a*) food obtained from the sea, seafood; (*b*) (*obsolete* exc. *dial.*) travel by sea, a sea voyage; **sea-farmer** = MARICULTURIST; **sea-farming** = MARICULTURE; **sea-feather** = ***sea-pen*** below; **sea-fern** any of various alcyonarians or colonial hydroids that resemble a fern, *esp.* dried *Sertularia* used for decoration; **sea-fever** longing or desire for the sea or sailing on it; **sea-fight** a naval battle, a fight or engagement between ships at sea; **sea-fingers** = ***dead man's fingers*** (b) s.v. DEAD MAN; **sea-fir** = ***sea hair*** below; **sea-fire** phosphorescence due to marine organisms; **sea-fisher** (*a*) a person who fishes in the sea; †(*b*) an angler-fish; **sea-fisherman** a person who fishes in the sea; **seafishery** (*a*) the business, occupation, or industry of catching fish or other products from the sea; (*b*) a place where marine fish are caught; **sea-fishing** fishing in the sea, catching marine fish; **sea-flood** (long *arch. rare*) the sea, the tide; **sea-floor** the floor of the sea, the seabed; ***sea-floor spreading*** (GEOLOGY), (the hypothesis of) the formation of fresh areas of oceanic crust, occurring through the upwelling of magma at mid-ocean ridges and its subsequent outward movement on either side; **sea-flower** (*a*) a flower growing in or by the sea; (*b*) a sea anemone; (*c*) a tube-dwelling polychaete with a crown of tentacles; **seafood** food obtained from the sea; edible marine fish or shellfish; **sea-fowl** a sea bird; **sea-fox** the thresher or fox shark; ***sea fret***: see FRET *noun*[5]; **sea-frog** = ANGLER 2; **sea front** (*a*) the portion or side of a building etc. on a coast which faces the sea; (*b*) the part of a coastal town etc. directly facing the sea; **sea-gate** (*a*) a gate towards or giving access to the sea; a convenient approach to the sea; a place of access to the sea; (*b*) a gate acting as a barrier against the sea; **sea-gherkin** any of various small holothurians of the genus *Cucumaria*, which inhabit rock crevices; **sea gilliflower** *arch.* = ***sea pink*** below; **sea-girt** *adjective* (*literary*) surrounded by the sea; **Sea Goat** *the* constellation and zodiacal sign Capricorn, = GOAT 4; **seagoing** *noun* going to sea, travelling by sea; **seagoing** *adjective* (*a*) (of a ship etc.) going on the sea, fit for voyages on the open sea; (*b*) able to be used or suitable for use on a seagoing vessel; carried or conducted by sea; (*c*) going to the sea, *esp.* (of a fish) catadromous; (*d*) travelling by sea, seafaring; **sea gooseberry** any of various ovoid ctenophores, esp. of the genus *Pleurobrachia*, bearing two long branched tentacles; **sea-grape** (*a*) a salt-resistant shrub of the knotgrass family, *Coccoloba uvifera*, bearing edible purple fruit in clusters like bunches of grapes, native to coastal regions of tropical America; the fruit of this shrub; (*b*) = SARGASSUM; (*c*) (in *pl.*) the clustered egg-cases of the cuttlefish; **sea grass** any of various grasslike plants growing in or by the sea; *esp.* eel-grass, *Zostera marina*; **sea gypsy** a Bajau; **sea hair** a colonial hydroid of the genus *Sertularia*; ***sea hard-grass***: see ***hard-grass*** s.v. HARD *adjective, adverb, & noun*; **sea hare** any of various sea-slugs of the order Anaspidea, esp. of the genus *Aplysia*, with large anterior tentacles that resemble ears; **sea-hawk** any of various predatory or kleptoparasitic sea birds, *esp.* a skua or a frigate-bird; **sea heath** a small plant of salt-marshes, *Frankenia laevis* (family Frankeniaceae), with small pink flowers and heathlike leaves; **sea-hedgehog** (*a*) a sea urchin; (*b*) = PORCUPINE ***fish***; **sea hen** (*a*) the lumpfish; (*b*) the common guillemot; (*c*) the great skua; **sea-hog** (now *rare*) the porpoise; **sea holly** an eryngium, *Eryngium maritimum*, growing on sandy shores; **sea holm** (now *dial.*) = *sea holly* above; **sea horizon** the line where sky and sea seem to meet; **sea horse** (*a*) (now *rare*) the walrus; (*b*) a mythical horselike marine animal (cf. HIPPOCAMPUS 2); (*c*) any of various small marine fishes of the genus *Hippocampus* and family Syngnathidae, with a slender snout, upright posture, and prehensile tail, and a brood pouch in the male; †(*d*) the hippopotamus; **sea-hound** a dogfish; **sea-insect** (now chiefly *poet.*) any small invertebrate animal of the sea or seashore, *esp.* a crustacean; **sea island** an offshore mooring station where oil tankers can discharge their cargo and from which oil can be pumped ashore; **sea-island** *adjective* designating a fine variety of cotton, *Gossypium barbadense*, distinguished by long silky fibres, orig. grown on islands off the coast of Georgia and S. Carolina in the US; **sea ivory** (*a*) (a piece of) ivory from the tusks or teeth of a marine mammal; (*b*) a pale greyish lichen, *Ramalina siliquosa*, growing on exposed coastal rocks; **seajack** *verb & noun* [after HIJACK] (*a*) *verb trans.* hijack at sea; (*b*) *noun* an act of seajacking; **seajacker** a person who seajacks a ship; **sea-jelly** a jellyfish; **sea jockey** *N. Amer.* (*a*) an adept sailor; (*b*) the sailor of a small craft; **seakale** (*a*) a cruciferous seashore plant, *Crambe maritima*, with white flowers and glaucous wavy-edged leaves; (the blanched shoots of) a cultivated form of this, used as a vegetable; (*b*) *seakale beet*, a form of spinach beet with white stalks and midribs, used as a substitute for seakale (also called *Swiss chard*); **sea-keeping** the ability of a ship, hovercraft, etc., to endure (rough) conditions at sea; **sea-kindliness** the quality of being sea-kindly; **sea-kindly** *adjective* (of a ship) easy to handle at sea; **sea-king** (*a*) the mythological god of the sea; (*b*) any of the piratical Scandinavian chiefs who in the ninth and succeeding centuries ravaged the coasts of Europe; **sea krait** a venomous sea snake of the genus *Laticauda*, occurring in tropical coastal waters of the eastern Indian Ocean and western Pacific; **sea lace** a brown seaweed, *Chorda filum*, with long cordlike fronds; **sea-lake** a land-locked portion of the sea, a lagoon; **sea lamprey** a large marine lamprey, *Petromyzon marinus*; **sea lane** a route at sea designated for use or regularly used by shipping; **sea-lark** *local* any of various small shorebirds, esp. the ringed plover and various sandpipers; **sea lavender** any of various maritime plants constituting the genus *Limonium* (family Plumbaginaceae), with cymes of papery funnel-shaped purple flowers on wiry leafless stems; **sea-lawyer** (*a*) the grey snapper, *Lutjanus griseus*; (*b*) an argumentative sailor who questions orders; *transf.* any argumentative or obstinate person; **sea league** three nautical miles; **sea legs** the ability to keep one's balance and avoid seasickness when at sea; **sea lemon** any of various nudibranch sea-slugs of the family Dorididae, with convex yellowish bodies, esp. of the genus *Archidoris*; **sea-leopard** = LEOPARD *seal*; **sea lettuce** a seaweed, *Ulva lactuca*, with green fronds resembling lettuce leaves; **sea level** the mean level of the surface of the sea, the ordnance datum, used in reckoning altitude and as a barometric standard; **sealift** *noun & verb* (*N. Amer.*) [after *airlift* s.v. AIR *noun*[1]] (*a*) *noun* a large-scale transportation of troops, supplies, etc., by sea; (*b*) *verb trans.* transport (troops, supplies, etc.) by sea; **sea-light** a beacon, lighthouse, etc., to guide ships at sea; **sea-lily** a stalked crinoid; **sealine** (*a*) the coastline, the seaboard; (*b*) the horizon at sea, the line where sea and sky seem to meet; *sea loch*: see LOCH *noun*[1]; **sea lock** a lock at the marine extremity of a ship canal; **Sea Lord** either of two senior naval officers (*First Sea Lord*, *Second Sea Lord*) serving as members of the admiralty board (now of the Ministry of Defence); **sea louse** any of various ectoparasitic marine crustaceans, *esp.* (*a*) an isopod of the family Cymothoidae; (*b*) a copepod of the genus *Lepeophtheirus*; (*c*) a fish louse; *sea-luce*: see LUCE 2; **sea-lungs** (now *rare*) a ctenophore; *sea lungwort*: see LUNGWORT 3b; **sea-maid**, **sea-maiden** *poet.* (*a*) a mermaid; (*b*) a goddess or nymph of the sea; **sea-mall** = GULL *noun*[1]; **sea-mark** (now *literary*) (*a*) the boundary or limit of the flow of the sea, the mark to which the tide rises; (*b*) a conspicuous object distinguishable at sea serving to guide or warn sailors in navigation; **sea marker** a device which can be dropped from an aircraft to produce a distinctive patch on water below it; **sea-mat** a bryozoan, *esp.* one of the family Flustridae; **sea-maw** (chiefly *Scot.*) = GULL *noun*[1]; *seamew*: see MEW *noun*[1]; **sea-mile** a unit of length varying between about 1842 m (2014 yards) at the equator and 1861 m (2035 yards) at the poles (cf. *NAUTICAL mile*); *sea milkwort*: see MILKWORT 2; *sea-monk*: see MONK *noun*[1] 2; **sea monkey** (*a*) *rare* an imaginary animal which is part monkey, part fish; (*b*) a brine-shrimp, *Artemia salina*, often used as food for fish in aquaria; **sea-monster** a monster of the sea; a huge fish, cetacean, etc.; a mythical marine animal of terrifying proportions and shape; **sea-morse** the walrus; **sea moss** a mosslike seaweed; *esp.* = CORALLINE *noun*[1] 1; **sea-moth** any of various small Indo-Pacific fishes of the family Pegasidae, with bony plates covering the body and enlarged horizontal pectoral fins; **seamount** a submarine mountain; **sea mouse** any of various scale-worms of the family Aphroditidae, with broad bodies having a feltlike covering of setae, esp. *Aphrodita aculeata*; **sea myrtle** the groundsel tree, *Baccharis halimifolia*; **sea-needle** the garfish *Belone bellone*; **sea-nettle** any of various jellyfishes, esp. of the genus *Chrysaora*, which are capable of stinging people; **sea-nymph** MYTHOLOGY a nymph supposed to inhabit the sea; **sea oak** any of several brown seaweeds with regularly divided fronds, esp. *Fucus vesiculosus* and *Halidrys siliquosa*; **sea oak coralline** the colonial hydroid *Sertularia pumila*, which grows attached to bladderwrack etc.; **sea-officer** (now *rare*) a naval officer; *sea onion*: see ONION *noun* 1b; **sea-orange** a large globose orange holothurian, *Lophothuria fabricii*; **sea otter** (*a*) a marine otter, *Enhydra lutris*, found along the coasts of the N. Pacific from the Bering Sea to California; (*b*) the thick dark fur of this animal; *sea-owl*: see OWL *noun*; †**sea-ox** a hippopotamus; **sea-palm** a sea-lily with branched arms; *sea-parrot*: see PARROT *noun* 3; **sea-parson** the stargazer; †**sea partridge** the sole; **sea-pen** any of various hydroids of the order Pennatulacea, esp. of the genera *Pennatula* and *Stylatula*, which resemble a feather; **Sea People(s)** = *Peoples of the Sea* s.v. PEOPLE *noun*; **sea-perch** any of various marine percoid fishes of the family Serranidae or the Pacific family Embiotocidae; **sea-pheasant** (*a*) the pintail duck; (*b*) the long-tailed duck; **sea-pie** (*a*) [PIE *noun*[1]] the oystercatcher; (*b*) [PIE *noun*[2]] a dish of (esp. leftover) meat and vegetables boiled together, with a pastry crust; **sea-piece** a picture representing a scene at sea; **sea-pig** (now *rare*) any of various large marine vertebrates believed to resemble a pig, as a porpoise, a dolphin, a dugong, a tuna; **sea-pigeon** *local* any of various marine birds resembling or likened to pigeons, *esp.* a rock dove, kittiwake, or black guillemot; **sea-pike** any of various marine fishes resembling the pike in appearance or behaviour, *esp.* a garfish, hake, or barracuda; **sea-pilot** the oystercatcher; **sea pink** the plant thrift, *Armeria maritima*; **seaplane** an aircraft designed to be able to take off from and land on water, *spec.* one with floats; *sea-poacher*: see POACHER *noun*[1] 2b; **sea poppy** the yellow horned poppy, *Glaucium flavum*; **sea-porcupine** = *PORCUPINE fish*; **seaport** (a town or city with) a harbour or port for seagoing ships; **sea potato** a yellowish-brown European heart urchin, *Echinocardium cordatum*; **sea-power** (*a*) a nation or State having international power or influence in maritime matters; a nation or State with a navy; (*b*) the strength and efficiency of a nation or State for naval warfare; the capacity to fight at sea; **sea price** *Nautical slang* an inflated price; **sea-purple** (*a*) = PURPLE *noun* 4; (*b*) a purple dye obtained from a marine mollusc (cf. PURPLE *noun* 1b); **sea purse** (*a*) the horny egg-case of a skate, ray, or shark; a mermaid's purse; (*b*) a swirl formed by two waves meeting at an angle, making a small whirlpool dangerous to bathers *US.*; **sea purslane** any of several fleshy maritime plants, esp. *Atriplex portulacoides*, a salt-marsh plant of the goosefoot family, and (*US*) *Sesuvium maritimum* (family Aizoaceae), which grows in damp sand; **seaquake** a convulsion or sudden agitation of the sea from a submarine eruption or earthquake; **sea radish** a wild radish, *Raphanus raphanistrum* subsp. *maritimus*, found on seashores, cliffs, etc.; **sea-raven** (*a*) the cormorant; (*b*) a large Atlantic sculpin, *Hemitripterus americanus*, found off N. America; **sea-reed** marram-grass, *Ammophila arenaria*; **sea return(s)** radar reflection from a rough sea, obscuring images of things floating in it or flying close to it; **searobin** *US* a gurnard; **sea rocket** a lilac-flowered European cruciferous plant, *Cakile maritima*, of sandy coasts; **sea room** clear space at sea for a ship to turn or manoeuvre in; **sea-rover** a pirate; a person who roves over the sea; **sea-roving** piracy; roving over the sea; **sea-run** *adjective* designating an anadromous fish which has returned to the sea after spawning; **sea salt** common salt obtained by the evaporation of sea water; **sea-salt** *adjective* (*rare*) salty like the sea; **sea-salted** *adjective* impregnated or seasoned with sea salt; **sea-sand** (*a*) sand of the sea or of the seashore; (*b*) in *pl.*, tracts of sea-sand, sands; **sea sandwort** a sandwort with fleshy leaves, *Honckenya peploides*, found on sandy shores; **sea scorpion** any of various spiny marine fishes; *esp.* either of two Atlantic sciaenids, *Taurulus bubalis* (more fully *long-spined sea scorpion*) and *Myoxocephalus scorpius* (more fully *short-spined sea scorpion*); **Sea Scout** a member of the branch of the Scout Association especially concerned with nautical training; **sea-scurvy** the form of scurvy formerly common on long sea voyages; **sea seiche** PHYSICAL GEOGRAPHY a seiche occurring in the open sea; **sea-serpent** (*a*) (more fully *the great sea-serpent*) a very large serpentine sea creature supposedly seen on occasion; (*b*) (now *rare*) any of various snakelike marine fishes, *esp.* a ribbonfish; (*c*) = *sea-snake* (a) below; **sea-service** service at sea or on the high seas; service in a navy, as opp. to a land army or air force; *sea shanty*: see SHANTY *noun*[2]; **sea shell** the shell of a marine mollusc; **seashore** the coast of the sea, the land lying adjacent to the sea; LAW the ground between high and low water marks; **sea-shrub** a gorgonian; **sea-slater** an isopod of the genus *Ligia*, found abundantly on the shoreline; **sea-slug** (*a*) = *sea cucumber* above; (*b*) any of various shell-less marine gastropods of the subclass Opisthobranchia, *esp.* one of the order Nudibranchia, having external gills; **sea-snail** (*a*) any of various marine gastropods; (*b*) any of various small gelatinous fishes of the family Cyclopteridae, with a ventral sucking disc, esp. *Liparis liparis* of the N. Atlantic; **sea-snake** (*a*) any of various snakes inhabiting coastal waters; *spec.* a proteroglyphous venomous snake of the family Hydrophiidae, often having the rear of the body compressed for swimming; (*b*) = *sea-serpent* (a) above; **sea-snipe** (*a*) any of various sandpipers, esp. the dunlin and the knot; (*b*) = *snipe fish* s.v. SNIPE *noun*; **sea-song** a song such as is sung by sailors, a shanty; **sea-sorrow** *rare* (Shakes.) a catastrophe or cause of trouble at sea; **sea speed** the cruising speed of a ship etc. when at sea; **sea-spider** any of various marine spider-like animals, *esp.* (*a*) a pycnogonid; †(*b*) a spider crab; **sea spurge** a European spurge of sandy coasts, *Euphorbia paralias*, with glaucous fleshy leaves; *sea spurrey*: see SPURREY 2; **sea squirt** an ascidian; **sea-stack** = STACK *noun* 4; **sea-star** †(*a*) a star by which sailors navigate; (*b*) a starfish; *sea starwort*: see STARWORT 1; **sea-state** the degree of turbulence at sea, esp. as measured on a scale of 0 to 9 according to average wave height; **sea-stick** *Hist.* a herring cured at sea; **sea stickleback** the fifteen-spined stickleback, *Spinachia spinachia*; **sea stock** a wild stock, *Matthiola sinuata*, of sandy seashores; **sea-strand** *arch.* the seashore; **sea-sucker** = *clingfish* s.v. CLING *verb*; **sea-swallow** (*a*) = *flying fish* (a) s.v. FLYING *ppl adjective*; (*b*) any of various marine birds resembling swallows, *esp.* a tern; **sea-swine** (*a*) (now *rare*) a porpoise; (*b*) *Scot.* a ballan wrasse; *sea-tangle*: see TANGLE *noun*[1]; **sea-thief** *arch.* a pirate, a sea-rover; **sea thistle** = *sea holly* above; *sea-thong*: see THONG *noun* 2; **sea thrift** = *sea pink* above; **sea tiger** = BARRACUDA; **sea-time** (*a*) time spent at sea in service; (*b*) *Hist.* a way of reckoning time at sea, in which the day begins at noon; **sea-toad** any of various toadlike fishes etc., *esp.* a toadfish; **sea-tortoise** a marine turtle; **sea-town** a town situated on or near the sea, a town with a seaport; **sea train** (*a*) a ship designed to transport railway cars; (*b*) a group of ships carrying supplies or equipment; **sea trial** each of a series of trials to test the performance of a new ship at sea; **sea trout** (*a*) any of various migratory trout, *esp.* a large silvery race of the trout *Salmo trutta*; (*b*) any of various marine fishes that resemble trout, esp. (*US*) a sciaenid of the genus *Cynoscion* and (*Austral.*) the Australian salmon *Arripis trutta*; **sea trumpet** a giant South African kelp, *Ecklonia maxima*; **sea turn** *arch.* a gale or breeze, usu. accompanied by mist etc., from the sea; **sea turtle** (*a*) [TURTLE *noun*[1]] the black guillemot; (*b*) a marine turtle (see TURTLE *noun*[2] 1); **sea-unicorn** the narwhal; **sea urchin** an echinoderm of the class Echinoidea having a rigid rounded or heart-shaped test and numerous mobile spines; **sea-valve** a valve in the bottom or side of a ship below the waterline; **sea-view** (*a*) (now *rare*) a seascape; (*b*) a view or prospect of the sea, or at sea; **sea voyage** a voyage by sea; **sea-voyaging** going on a sea voyage or sea voyages; **sea wall** a wall or embankment made to prevent the encroachment of the sea, or to form a breakwater; **sea-walled** *adjective* (*rare*) surrounded or protected by the sea as a wall of defence; **sea-walling** the building or repairing of sea walls; **sea-ware** [WARE *noun*[1]] seaweed; *esp.* coarse seaweed cast up on the shore and used as manure etc.; **sea-washed** *adjective* washed by the sea, exposed to the tide; *sea-washed turf*, a fine turf from the coast of NW England, used for lawns; **sea wasp** any of various jellyfishes of the order Cubomedusae, having dangerous stings and occurring in Indo-Pacific waters; **seawater** the water of the sea; water taken from the sea; **seaway** (*a*) a way over the sea; the sea as a means of communication; the open sea; (*b*) a man-made or natural channel connecting two tracts of sea; (*c*) *N. Amer.* an inland waterway with passage to the sea, *esp.* one capable of accommodating seagoing vessels; (*d*) a rough sea (chiefly in *in a seaway*); **sea-weary** *adjective* (*rare*) weary with or fatigued by the sea; **sea-wind** a wind from the sea, a sea breeze; **sea-wing** †(*a*) *poet. rare* a wing used in flying over the sea, a means of flight by sea; (*b*) = *wing-shell* (b) s.v. WING *noun*; **sea-wise** *adjective* familiar with the ways of the sea; **sea-wolf** (*a*) = *wolf-fish* s.v. WOLF *noun*; †(*b*) a seal or sea lion; (*c*) *pseudo-arch.* a pirate; a privateer vessel; **seawoman** (*a*) a mermaid; (*b*) a female sailor; a woman working at sea; **sea-worm** any of numerous marine annelids; **sea wormwood** a greyish Eurasian plant of salt-marshes, *Seriphidium maritimum*, allied to mugwort and wormwood; **sea-worn** (*a*) worn or abraded by the sea; (*b*) worn out or wearied by a life on the sea; **sea wrack** seaweed, *esp.* coarse seaweed cast ashore; a particular seaweed of this type.

■ **seamost** *adjective* (*rare*) situated nearest the sea E17.

Seabees /'siːbiːz/ *noun pl.* M20.
[from repr. of initial letters of construction *b*attalion + -S[1].]
(Members of) the construction battalions formed as a volunteer branch of the Civil Engineer Corps of the US Navy in the war of 1939–45.

seaboard /'siːbɔːd/ *noun & adjective.* LME.
[from SEA *noun* + BOARD *noun*.]
▸ **A** *noun.* †**1** A plank to cover up a porthole. Only in LME.
†**2** The seaward side (of a ship etc.). Only after prepositions, as *at*, *on*, *to*. L15–M17.
†**3** The sea as used by ships. Only in *by seaboard*, by sea, on a ship, *on seaboard*, at sea, on board ship. M–L16.
4 The line where land and sea meet, the coastline; the seashore or the land near the sea, esp. considered with reference to its extent or configuration. L18.
▸ **B** *attrib.* or as *adjective*. Situated on the seaboard, bordering on or adjoining the sea. L16.

seaborgium /siː'bɔːgɪəm/ *noun.* L20.
[from Glenn T. Seaborg (1912–99), US nuclear chemist + -IUM.]
A very unstable radioactive chemical element (atomic no. 106), produced artificially. (Symbol Sg.)

sea-cunny /'siːkʌni/ *noun.* Also **-conny** /-kɒni/. E19.
[App. alt. (after SEA) of Persian *sukkānī*, from Arab. *sukkān* rudder.]
Hist. A steersman or quartermaster in a ship manned by Lascars.

sea dog /'siː dɒg/ *noun phr.* M16.
[from SEA + DOG *noun*.]
▸ **I 1** HERALDRY. A doglike animal with fins and scales. M16.
2 The common seal, *Phoca vitulina*. Now *rare*. L16.
3 A dogfish or small shark. *obsolete* exc. *Scot.* E17.
▸ **II 4** A privateer or pirate, esp. of the time of Queen Elizabeth I. L16.
5 An old or experienced sailor. E19.
▸ **III 6** A luminous appearance near the horizon, regarded by sailors as a prognostic of bad weather. E19.

seafarer /'siːfɛːrə/ *noun.* E16.
[from SEA + FARER.]
A traveller by sea; *esp.* a person whose life is spent in voyaging by sea, a sailor.

seafaring /'siːfɛːrɪŋ/ *noun.* L16.
[from SEA + FARE *verb* + -ING[1].]
Travelling by sea; the business or occupation of a sailor.

seafaring /'siːfɛːrɪŋ/ *adjective.* ME.
[from SEA + FARE *verb* + -ING[2].]
Travelling on the sea; following the sea as an occupation, gaining a livelihood at sea.

sea-fish /'siːfɪʃ/ *noun.* Pl. **-es** /-ɪz/, (usu.) same. OE.
[from SEA + FISH *noun*[1].]
A marine fish.

sea-green /siː'griːn, *attrib.* 'siːgriːn/ *adjective & noun.* L16.
[from SEA + GREEN *adjective, noun*.]
(Of) a pale bluish green.

seagull /'siːgʌl/ *noun.* M16.
[from SEA + GULL *noun*[1].]
1 = GULL *noun*[1]. M16.
2 A casual non-union dock labourer. *Austral. & NZ slang.* E20.

seah /ˈsiːə/ *noun*. E17.
[Hebrew *sᵉʼāh*.]
An ancient Hebrew dry measure equal to six times the kab.

seal /siːl/ *noun*[1] & *adjective*. As noun also (*Scot*.) **selch** /sɛlk/.
[Old English *sēol*- inflectional form of *seolh* = Northern Frisian *selich*, Middle Low German *sēl*, Middle Dutch *seel*, *zēle*, Old High German *selah*, Old Norse *selr*, from Germanic, of unkn. origin. Cf. SELKY.]
▶ **A** *noun*. **1** Any of various aquatic carnivorous mammals with limbs developed into flippers for swimming, and an elongated body covered with thick fur, belonging to either of the pinniped families Otariidae and (esp.) Phocidae (lacking external ears). OE.
2 = SEALSKIN *noun* 1. L19.
1 ***common seal***, ***eared seal***, ***elephant seal***, ***grey seal***, ***hooded seal***, ***Ross seal***, etc.
Comb.: **seal calf** a young seal; **seal-fur** the skin of a fur seal used for garments; **seal-hole** a hole in ice kept open by seals for breathing and for getting out of the water; **seal point** (*a*) any of the dark brown markings on the buff fur of one type of Siamese cat; (*b*) a Siamese cat with markings of this colour; **seal rookery** a colony of seals; a place where seals breed.
▶ **B** *attrib*. or as *adjective*. = SEALSKIN *adjective*. E20.

seal /siːl/ *noun*[2]. ME.
[Anglo-Norman *seal*, Old French *seel* (mod. *sceau*) from Latin *sigillum* small picture, statuette, seal, dim. of *signum* SIGN *noun*.]
1 A design, crest, motto, etc., impressed on a piece of wax or other plastic material adhering or attached to a document as evidence of authenticity or attestation; a piece of wax etc. bearing such an impression. ME. ▸†**b** A letter or other document bearing a seal; a promissory note. LME–M17.
2 A piece of wax or some other plastic or adhesive substance (orig. and still freq. one bearing the impression of a signet) fixed on a folded letter or other document, or on a closed door or receptacle, affording security by having to be broken to allow access to the contents. ME.
3 An engraved stamp of metal, gemstone, or other hard material used to make an impression on a seal. Also, a design or inscription engraved on a seal. ME. ▸†**b** (An assembly for the purpose of witnessing) an affixing of the Great Seal to State documents. M17–E18. ▸**c** In *pl*. Ornamental seals and similar trinkets formerly worn as an appendage to a watch-guard. M19.
4 A token or symbol of a covenant; an act, gesture, or event regarded as an authentication or confirmation; a completing and securing addition. ME.
5 Chiefly ECCLESIASTICAL. An obligation to silence, a vow of secrecy. Esp. in ***the seal of confession***, ***the seal of the confessional***. ME.
6 An impressed mark serving as visible evidence of something, as of a claim to possession; *fig*. a mark of ownership. L16. ▸**b** The footprint of an animal, esp. an otter. L17.
7 A device or substance used to prevent the escape of gas etc., close an aperture, or act as a tight (esp. airtight or watertight) fastening, esp. at a place where two surfaces meet. Also, a small quantity of water left in a trap to prevent the escape of foul air from a sewer or drain. M19.

🕮 **7** L. T. C. ROLT Depended . . on this valve maintaining a perfectly air-tight seal. J. S. FOSTER The space . . is filled by some form of weather-proof seal.

Phrases: ***broad seal***: see BROAD *adjective*. ***golden seal***: see GOLDEN *adjective*. **Great Seal** (*a*) the seal used for the authentication of State documents of the highest importance (in Britain in the charge of the Lord Chancellor); †(*b*) the custodian of the Great Seal, the Lord Chancellor or Lord Keeper. ***Hermes seal***: see HERMES 2. ***hermetic seal***: see HERMETIC *adjective* 2. ***Keeper of the Great Seal***: see KEEPER *noun*. ***Keeper of the Privy Seal***: see KEEPER *noun*. ***Lord Keeper of the Great Seal***: see KEEPER *noun*. ***Lord Privy Seal***, ***privy seal***: see PRIVY *adjective*. **set one's seal to**, **set one's seal on**, **set the seal to**, **set the seal on** affix one's seal to, express assent to, authorize (by sealing), confirm. **the seals (of office)** *spec*. those held by the Chancellor or Secretary of State. ***under a flying seal***: see FLYING *adjective*. **under one's seal**, **under seal** in a document attested by one's seal. ***with a flying seal***: see FLYING *adjective*.
Comb.: **seal-ring** a ring for the finger bearing a seal; **seal-stone** a precious stone bearing an engraved device; **seal-top (spoon)** a spoon having a flat design resembling an embossed seal at the end of its handle; †**seal-wax** sealing-wax.

seal /siːl/ *noun*[3]. *obsolete* exc. *dial*. L16.
[Partly from Old Norse *selja*, partly repr. *seal*- inflectional form of Old English (West Saxon) *sealh*, (Anglian) *salh*: see SALLOW *noun*.]
(A) willow.

SEAL /siːl/ *noun*[4]. Also **Seal**. M20.
[Abbreviation of *sea air land* (team).]
A member of an elite force within the US Navy, specializing in guerrilla warfare and counter-insurgency.

seal /siːl/ *verb*[1]. ME.
[Old French *seeler* (mod. *sceller*), from *seel* SEAL *noun*[2].]
▶ **I 1** *verb trans*. Affix a seal to (a document) as evidence of genuineness, or as a mark of authoritative ratification or approval; authenticate or attest solemnly by some comparable act. ME.
2 *verb trans*. Mark by a seal as reserved for a particular destination. Chiefly *fig*., designate or set apart by an inviolable token or pledge. Foll. by *to* a person, *for* a destination or purpose. *arch*. ME.
3 *verb intrans*. Affix a seal to a document. Formerly also, set one's seal *to*, lend one's support or authority *to*. LME. ▸†**b** Become security *for* a person. Also foll. by *under*. E16–M17.
4 *verb trans*. Impress a seal on or stamp officially to indicate correctness or approval; certify with a stamp or seal. Now *rare*. LME.
5 *verb trans*. Conclude or ratify (an agreement, bargain, etc.) by affixing the seals of the parties to the instrument, or by some ceremonial act. L15.
6 *verb trans*. Impose (an obligation, a penalty) *on* a person in a binding manner. *rare*. E17.
7 *verb trans*. Provide authentication, ratification, or confirmation of. M17.
8 *verb trans*. Decide irrevocably (the fate of a person or thing); complete and place beyond dispute or reversal (a victory, defeat, etc.). E19.

🕮 **1** ***signed, sealed, and delivered***. **5** G. F. KENNAN The Treaty . . which sealed Russia's withdrawal from the war. M. KEANE The little drink seemed to seal their easy companionship. **8** A. BROOKNER He seemed to have sealed his fate.

▶ **II 9** *verb trans*. Fasten (a folded letter or other document) with melted wax or some other plastic or adhesive substance so that opening is impossible without breaking the seal; fasten up (a letter, parcel, etc.) with sealing-wax, gum, etc. ME.
10 *verb trans*. Close securely by or as by placing a seal on the opening of; make airtight or watertight with a seal. Also foll. by *up*. ME. ▸**b** SURGERY. Close up (a wound) with a covering that is not removed until healing has taken place. M19. ▸**c** Make (a surface of wood etc.) impervious by the application of a special coating. M20. ▸**d** Prevent access to and egress from (an area or space), esp. as a security measure; close (entrances) for this purpose. Usu. foll. by *off*. M20. ▸**e** Surface (a road) with tarmacadam. Chiefly *Austral*. & *NZ*. M20.
11 *verb trans*. Place in a receptacle secured by a seal; enclose within impenetrable barriers; confine so as to prevent access or egress. Also foll. by *off*, *up*. LME.
12 *verb trans*. Fasten *on* or *down* with or as with wax, cement, or some other adhesive substance. M17.

🕮 **9** C. MCCULLOUGH An envelope . . which she sealed with red wax. **10** SHAKES. *Rom. & Jul.* Searchers of the town Seal'd up the doors, and would not let us forth. K. MANSFIELD Houses were sealed . . behind big wooden shutters. D. LESSING Underground were shelters, sealed against radiation. **c** *Practical Householder* Sand all the table . . and seal with several coats of polyurethane. **d** M. INNES This cellarage had . . been . . sealed off from the studio. A. FRASER Ports had been sealed . . to stop the intelligence reaching the Continent. **11** R. GRAVES To seal it up in a casket.

Phrases: **seal a person's lips** bind or constrain a person to silence or secrecy. ***seal one's testimony with blood***, ***seal one's testimony with one's blood***: see TESTIMONY *noun* 3.
■ **sealable** *adjective* (*a*) able or requiring to be sealed; †(*b*) suitable for use in sealing: L15.

seal /siːl/ *verb*[2] *intrans*. L18.
[from SEAL *noun*[1].]
Hunt seals.

seal *verb*[3] var. of SEEL *verb*[1].

sealant /ˈsiːlənt/ *noun*. M20.
[from SEAL *verb*[1] + -ANT[1].]
A substance designed to seal a surface or container against the passage of a gas or liquid; a material used to fill up cracks.

sealapack *noun* var. of SILLAPAK.

sealed /siːld/ *ppl adjective*. ME.
[from SEAL *verb*[1] + -ED[1].]
That has been sealed; bearing a seal; fastened with a seal.

🕮 SHAKES. *Haml*. A seal'd compact Well ratified by law and heraldry. A. MORICE Five suspects, all together in a sealed room. B. L. C. JOHNSON Roads of a high standard (sealed).

Special collocations & comb.: **sealed-beam** *adjective* designating a motor-vehicle headlamp in which light source, reflector, and lens form a sealed self-contained unit. **sealed book** (*a*) any of the printed copies of the authentic *Book of Common Prayer* of 1662 certified under the Great Seal and deposited as a standard in cathedrals and collegiate churches; (*b*) = ***closed book*** s.v. BOOK *noun*. **sealed orders** written directions on procedure, as to the commander of a vessel concerning the destination of a voyage, not to be opened until a specified time. **sealed source** a pellet of radioactive material in a sealed capsule, used in radiotherapy and radiography. **sealed verdict** a verdict delivered in a sealed packet in the absence of a judge.

sealer /ˈsiːlə/ *noun*[1]. ME.
[from SEAL *verb*[1] + -ER[1].]
1 A person who affixes or stamps a seal on something. In early use also, a maker of seals. ME.
2 A person who or a device or substance which seals receptacles, surfaces, etc. L19.
3 A jar designed to preserve fruit, vegetables, etc. *Canad*. M20.

sealer /ˈsiːlə/ *noun*[2]. M18.
[from SEAL *verb*[2] + -ER[1].]
1 A person who hunts seals. M18.
2 A ship engaged in hunting seals. E19.

sealery /ˈsiːləri/ *noun*. L19.
[from SEAL *noun*[1] + -ERY.]
1 A place where seals are hunted. Also, a place colonized by seals. L19.
2 The occupation of hunting seals. *rare*. L19.

sealike /ˈsiːlʌɪk/ *adjective* & *adverb*. L16.
[from SEA + -LIKE.]
▶ **A** *adjective*. Resembling the sea. L16.
▶ **B** *adverb*. After the manner of the sea. E17.

sealing /ˈsiːlɪŋ/ *noun*. ME.
[from SEAL *verb*[1] + -ING[1].]
1 The action of SEAL *verb*[1]. ME.
2 Material used to seal something; a thing which seals something. M19.
3 An impression on a seal. E20.
Comb.: **sealing-wax** (orig.) beeswax or a composition containing this, (later) a composition consisting of shellac, rosin, and turpentine, and usu. pigment, prepared to receive the impression of seals after softening by heating; ***sealing-wax red***, (of) a bright red colour traditionally used for sealing-wax, vermilion.

sea lion /ˈsiː lʌɪən/ *noun*. E17.
[from SEA + LION *noun*.]
†**1** A lobster. Only in E17.
2 Chiefly HERALDRY. A mythical animal, part lion and part fish. M17.
3 Any of several large-eared seals having broader muzzles and sparser underfur than the fur seals; *esp*. (more fully ***Californian sea lion***) a dark brown seal of the eastern Pacific, *Zalophus californianus*, often trained in captivity. L17.
3 ***northern sea lion***, ***Steller's sea lion***, etc.
■ †**sea lioness** *noun* a female sea lion M–L18.

sealskin /ˈsiːlskɪn/ *noun* & *adjective*. ME.
[from SEAL *noun*[1] + SKIN *noun*.]
▶ **A** *noun*. **1** The skin or prepared fur of a seal, esp. a fur-seal. ME.
2 A garment made of sealskin. M19.
▶ **B** *attrib*. or as *adjective*. Made of sealskin. M18.

Sealyham /ˈsiːlɪəm/ *noun*. L19.
[A village in S. Wales, where the dog was first bred.]
(A dog of) a small stocky breed of wire-haired terrier, having a medium-length largely white coat, drooping ears, a small erect tail, and a square bearded muzzle. Also ***Sealyham terrier***.

seam /siːm/ *noun*[1].
[Old English *sēam* = Old Frisian *sām*, Middle Dutch *sōm* (Dutch *zoom*), Old High German *soum* (German *Saum*), Old Norse *saumr*, from Germanic, from base of SEW *verb*[1].]
▶ **I 1** A junction made by sewing together the edges of two pieces or widths of cloth, leather, etc.; a ridge or furrow in a surface at such a junction. OE. ▸**b** Chiefly *Hist*. An embellished seam; an ornamental strip of material inserted in or laid over a seam. LME. ▸**c** A line (of stitches) down the leg of a stocking, representing or simulating a join. E19.
†**2** ANATOMY. A bone suture. OE–M17.
3 A join, line, groove, furrow, etc., formed by abutting edges, as of planks or the plates of a ship; an indentation or mark resembling such a join; a cleft, a furrow; a scar; a deep wrinkle. OE. ▸†**b** = ***false quarter*** s.v. FALSE *adjective*. E17–M18.
4 GEOLOGY. A thin layer or stratum of ore, coal, etc., between two thicker strata. L16.
5 a A joint uniting the edges of sheet metal, either by folding and pressing them together or by soldering. E19. ▸**b** A superficial linear defect on worked metal, usu. caused by closure of a blow-hole. M19.

🕮 **1** C. STEAD She . . sewed seams by hand with tiny stitches. S. BELLOW Her lips come together like the seams of a badly sewn baseball. R. ILLINGWORTH Grip the ball with the seam upright. **3** W. COWPER Sails ript, seams op'ning wide, and compass lost. K. KESEY A seam runs across his nose . . where somebody laid him a good one in a fight. **4** G. ORWELL Coal lies in thin seams between . . layers of rock.

▶ **II 6** Sewing, needlework. *obsolete* exc. *dial*. LME.
Phrases: **bursting at the seams** *fig*. full to overflowing, crammed, stuffed. **come apart at the seams** *fig*. fall to pieces, collapse emotionally, have a breakdown. ***French seam***: see FRENCH *adjective*. ***round seam***: see ROUND *adjective*. ***thin seam***: see THIN *adjective*, *adverb*, & *noun*.
Comb.: **seam allowance** the amount of material in sewing which is calculated to be taken in by a seam; **seam bowler** CRICKET a medium or fast bowler who uses the seam to make the ball deviate in the air or off the pitch during delivery; **seam bowling** CRICKET the mode of delivery of a seam bowler; **seamfree** *adjective* (of a stocking) seamless; **seam-rent** *adjective* (*obsolete* exc. *dial*.) torn apart at the seams, having torn clothes; **seam-squirrel** *US slang* (chiefly MILITARY) a louse; **seam weld** a

weld obtained by seam welding; **seam welder** a machine for seam welding; **seam welding** welding in which a linear weld is obtained by producing a line of overlapping welds.

seam /siːm/ *noun*². Long *obsolete* exc. *dial.*
[Old English *sēam* = Old High German *soum* (German *Saum*) from West Germanic from medieval Latin *sauma*, *salma* alt. of late Latin *sagma* from Greek = baggage, pack-saddle, from *sattein*, *sag-* to pack, to load. Cf. SUMPTER.]
1 A load carried by a packhorse. In early use also *gen.*, a load, a burden. OE.
2 = ***horse-load*** s.v. HORSE *noun*. ME.
3 A cart-load, esp. as a specific weight. E18.

seam /siːm/ *noun*³. Long *obsolete* exc. *dial.* ME.
[Old French *saim*, later *sain* (mod. only in *saindoux* lard) from Proto-Romance (medieval Latin *sagimen*) alt. of Latin *sagina* fattening, fatness.]
†**1** Fat, grease. ME–L17.
2 Lard. M16.

seam /siːm/ *verb*. L16.
[from SEAM *noun*¹.]
▶ **I 1** *verb trans.* Sew the seam or seams of; sew *on*, *together*, *up* with a seam or seams. L16. ▸†**b** Provide or ornament with an inserted seam. L16–M18.
2 *verb trans.* Mark (a surface) with lines or indentations; furrow; fissure. Chiefly as ***seamed ppl adjective***. L16.
3 *verb trans.* Join (sheets of lead or metal) by means of a seam. E18.
4 CRICKET. **a** *verb intrans.* (Of a pitch) be favourable to seam bowling; (of a ball) deviate while pitching during delivery on account of the seam. M20. ▸**b** *verb trans.* Of a bowler: cause (a ball) to seam. M20.

> 🕮 **2** TENNYSON Seam'd with an ancient swordcut on the cheek. F. NORRIS His . . forehead was seamed with the wrinkles of responsibility. *Scotsman* Seamed with dug-outs . . and pitted with craters. **4b** J. SNOW A damp wicket which helped them seam the ball about.

▶ **II 5** *verb intrans.* Sew. *dial.* M19.
▪ **seaming** *noun* (*a*) the action of the verb; (*b*) a seam, some seams: L15.

seaman /ˈsiːmən/ *noun*. Pl. **-men**.
[Old English *sǣman(n*, formed as SEA + MAN *noun* (with Germanic parallels).]
1 A person whose occupation or business is on the sea; a sailor; now *esp.* a sailor below the rank of officer. Also, with qualifying adjective as *good*, *poor*, etc., a person having the specified type of skill as a sailor. OE.
†**2** A merman. M16–M18.
1 *able seaman*, *foremast seaman*, *leading seaman*, *merchant seaman*, *ordinary seaman*, etc.
▪ **seamanlike** *adjective & adverb* (*a*) *adjective* characteristic of or befitting a (good) seaman; (*b*) *adverb* in a seamanlike manner: M17. **seamanly** *adjective* = SEAMANLIKE *adjective* L18. **seamanship** *noun* the art or practice of managing a ship or boat at sea; the skill of a good seaman: M18.

seamer /ˈsiːmə/ *noun*. OE.
[In branch I from SEAM *noun*¹, in branch II from SEAM *verb*: see -ER¹.]
▶ **I** †**1** A tailor. OE–ME.
▶ **II 2** A person who or machine which sews seams. OE.
3 CRICKET. A seam bowler; a delivery by a seam bowler. M20.

seamless /ˈsiːmlɪs/ *adjective*. LME.
[from SEAM *noun*¹ + -LESS.]
Without a seam or seams; (of a garment) woven without a seam or seams; *fig.* unified, continuous, uninterrupted.

> 🕮 DONNE Christ . . suffered his flesh to be torn, but not his seamless garment. A. MARS-JONES His junior . . administers the paperwork with . . seamless calm. *New Scientist* Modern science is a 'seamless web'. *Vogue* A seamless stretch of . . semi-transparent rayon.

▪ **seamlessly** *adverb* E20.

seamster /ˈsiːmstə/ *noun*. *arch.* Also **sempster** /ˈsɛm(p)stə/. OE.
[from SEAM *noun*¹ + -STER.]
A person who sews; a person whose occupation is sewing, esp. the making and mending of garments; a tailor.
▪ **seamstering**, **sempstering** *noun* (*rare*) the occupation of a seamster E19.

seamstress /ˈsiːmstrɪs/ *noun*. Also **sempstress** /ˈsɛm(p)strɪs/. L16.
[from prec. + -ESS¹.]
A woman who sews; a needlewoman whose occupation is plain sewing.
▪ **seamstress-ship**, **sempstress-ship** *noun* the position, work, or skill of a seamstress E19.

†**seamstry** *noun*. Also **sempstry**. L16–M18.
[from SEAMSTER: see -ERY.]
The occupation or employment of a seamster or seamstress.

†**seamy** *adjective*¹. E16–E17.
[from SEAM *noun*³ + -Y¹.]
Greasy.

seamy /ˈsiːmi/ *adjective*². L16.
[from SEAM *noun*¹ + -Y¹.]
1 Of the nature of or resembling a seam or seams; marked with a seam. L16.
2 Having a seam or seams; characterized by seams; *spec.* having the rough edges of seams visible, *fig.* unpleasant, disreputable, degraded, rough (orig. & chiefly in ***seamy side***). E17.

> 🕮 **1** GEO. ELIOT A one-eyed woman, with a scarred and seamy face. **2** SHAKES. *Oth.* Some such squire he was That turned your wit the seamy side without. E. PAUL The seamy and shiny blue-serge skirt. *Times* Entertaining clients in a seamy hot-spot in Singapore.

▪ **seaminess** *noun* L19.

sean *noun & verb* var. of SEINE.

Seanad /ˈʃanəð, -d/ *noun*. E20.
[Irish *Seanad (Éireann)* senate (of Ireland).]
In full ***Seanad Eireann*** /ˈɛːrən/. The upper house of the Parliament of the Republic of Ireland.

seance /ˈseɪɑːns, -ɒ̃s, -ɒns/ *noun*. Also **séance** /*also* seɑ̃s (*pl. same*)/. L18.
[French *séance*, from Old French *seoir* from Latin *sedere* sit.]
1 ***seance royale*** /rwaˈjal/, a royal audience. L18.
2 A meeting or session of a deliberative or administrative body, esp. of a learned society; a meeting of a discussion group, seminar, etc.; *loosely* (chiefly *US*) any meeting or discussion. E19.
3 *spec.* A meeting for the investigation or exhibition of spiritualistic phenomena; a meeting at which a medium attempts to contact the dead. M19.
4 A sitting for a portrait. Now *rare*. L19.

SEAQ *abbreviation*.
Stock Exchange Automated Quotations (computerized access to share information).

seaquarium /siːˈkwɛːrɪəm/ *noun*. Pl. **-ria** /-rɪə/, **-riums**. M20.
[from SEA + A)QUARIUM.]
An aquarium for large marine animals.

sear /sɪə/ *noun*¹. L19.
[from the verb.]
A mark or impression produced by searing.

sear *noun*², *adjective* see SERE *noun*¹, *adjective*.

sear /sɪə/ *verb*. Also **sere**.
[Old English *sēarian* = Old High German *sōrēn* from Germanic, from base of SERE *adjective*.]
1 *verb intrans.* Dry up, wither away. Now *literary*. OE.
2 *verb trans.* Cause to wither, blight. Now *literary*. LME.
3 *verb trans.* Burn or char (animal tissue) by the application of a hot iron; cauterize (also foll. by *up*); *fig.* (chiefly after 1 *Timothy* 4:2) make incapable of feeling. LME. ▸†**b** Brand, stigmatize. E16–M17.
4 *verb trans. gen.* Burn, scorch; cause a burning sensation in (freq. as ***searing ppl adjective***.). Later also *spec.*, brown (meat) quickly at a high temperature to aid retention of juices in cooking. L16.

> 🕮 **2** A. C. SWINBURNE If no fire of sun . . sear the tender grain. **3** E. A. FREEMAN A long career of . . despotic rule never utterly seared his conscience. H. ALLEN To saw off legs . . , sear stumps with boiling oil. **4** POPE Scorch'd by the sun, or sear'd by heav'nly fire. J. THURBER A fierce liquid . . it seared your throat, burned your stomach. M. RENAULT The naked light . . seared the eyes. T. HILLERMAN Barely conscious of the searing pain.

▪ †**searedness** *noun* the condition of being seared E17–L18. **searing** *noun* (*a*) the action of the verb; (*b*) a seared area or part: LME.

searce /səːs/ *noun & verb*. *obsolete* exc. *dial.* Also **search** /səːtʃ/. LME.
[Old French *saas* (mod. *sas*), ult. from Latin *saeta* bristle.]
▶ **A** *noun*. A sieve, a strainer. LME.
▶ **B** *verb trans.* Sift through a sieve, strain. LME.
▪ **searcer** *noun* = SEARCE *noun* M16.

search /səːtʃ/ *noun*¹. LME.
[Anglo-Norman *serche*, Old French *cerche* (mod. *cherche*), formed as SEARCH *verb*¹, or directly from SEARCH *verb*¹.]
1 The action or an act of searching; (an instance of) examination, investigation, or scrutiny for the purpose of finding someone or something or of finding out something. Foll. by *after*, *for*, †*of*. LME. ▸†**b** An examination of one's conscience, an act of introspection. E16–L17.
2 †**a** An examiner; *spec.* in a Bridgettine convent, each of the sisters entrusted with the supervision of the nuns' behaviour. LME–M17. ▸†**b** A search-party. Only in E17.
†**3** A range to which searching extends. E17–L18.
4 A searching effect (of cold or wind). *rare*. E17.

> 🕮 **1** SIR W. SCOTT Robin . . absconded, and escaped all search. B. JOWETT Our discussion . . has been a search after knowledge. *Science* Without the computer, a visual search through printed lists would have been required. E. BAKER Continued her search and eventually . . found the thin volume. *What Mortgage* Final searches . . made on the title deeds. ***global search***: see GLOBAL 2. **in search of** in quest of, in order to find; occupied in searching for, trying to find. ***LINEAR search***. **make a search**, **make search** search (*for* some lost, concealed, or desired object). ***picture search***: see PICTURE *noun*. **right of search** the right of a ship (esp. a warship) of a belligerent State to stop and search a neutral merchant vessel for prohibited goods. ***tree search***: see TREE *noun*.

Comb.: **search coil** = ***exploring coil*** s.v. EXPLORE 2; **search engine** COMPUTING a program which searches for and identifies specified items in a database or network, esp. the Internet; **searchlight** *noun & verb* (*a*) *noun* a powerful electric light with a concentrated beam that can be turned in any desired direction; the beam of such a light; (*b*) *verb trans.* illuminate with a searchlight; **search-party** a group of people organized to look for a lost person or thing; **search warrant** a warrant authorizing the entering and searching of a building.
▪ **searchful** *adjective* (long *rare*) full of anxious attention; diligent in searching: L16. †**searchless** *adjective* inscrutable, impenetrable, resisting investigation E17–M19.

search *noun*² var. of SEARCE *noun*.

search /səːtʃ/ *verb*¹. ME.
[Anglo-Norman *sercher*, Old French *cerchier* (mod. *chercher*) from late Latin *circare* go round, from Latin *circus* circle.]
▶ **I** *verb trans.* **1** Go about (a country or place) or look through or examine internally (a building, a receptacle, etc.) in order to find, or to ascertain the presence or absence of, some person or thing; explore in quest of some object. ME.
2 Examine (a person) by handling, removal of garments, etc., in order to locate any concealed article. LME.
3 Peruse or read through (a text, computer file, set of archives, etc.) in order to discover whether certain items of information are contained there. LME.
4 a With immaterial obj.: investigate, make oneself thoroughly acquainted with; give rigorous consideration to the motives, thoughts, or feelings of; penetrate the secrets of. Also foll. by *out*. LME. ▸**b** Of an impersonal agency: test, reveal the nature of. L16.
5 Penetrate, reach the weak places of. Formerly also, probe (a wound). LME.
6 Look scrutinizingly at. E19.

> 🕮 *Times* Frogmen . . searched the wreckage and recovered the four bodies. P. B. YUILL They've searched the island twice—helicopters, dogs, the lot. **2** *Times* He was searched and . . found to have 28 bars of gold. B. MALAMUD Stripped . . and searched for the fourth time. **3** BURKE To search the Journals in the period between the . . wars. *Times* A magnetic recording which can be automatically searched and edited. **4a** H. LOUKES Calculated to set the individual searching his own heart. **5** BYRON The ice-wind . . Searching the shivering vassal through his rags. **6** I. MCEWAN Her eyes searched his face for understanding. A. MASON He searched Philip's eyes . . , then looked away.

▶ **II** *verb trans.* **7** Look for or seek diligently, try to find. Usu. foll. by *out*. ME. ▸†**b** Try to find out *what*, *who*, etc. Also foll. by *out*. LME–M17.

> 🕮 **7** *Daily Chronicle* They search out the secret places of past grandeur. R. ARNOLD The hungry sharks . . will cruise searching their prey.

▶ **III** *verb intrans.* **8** Search something or someone; look for or try to find someone or something. (Foll. by *after*, *for*, *into*). ME.
†**9** Devise means (*to do*). ME–M16.

> 🕮 **8** EVELYN Advising the Students to search after true wisdome. CARLYLE Rushing out to search into the root of the matter. SCOTT FITZGERALD If he had searched harder, he might have found her. J. WAIN They both looked about them as if searching for a subject of conversation.

Phrases etc.: **search me** *colloq.* I do not know, do not ask me.
▪ **searchable** *adjective* M16.

search *verb*² var. of SEARCE *verb*.

searcher /ˈsəːtʃə/ *noun*. LME.
[Partly from Anglo-Norman *cerchour*, Old French *cerchere*, *cercheor*, formed as SEARCH *verb*¹; partly from SEARCH *verb*¹ + -ER¹.]
1 *gen.* A person who searches. LME.
2 Chiefly *Hist.* A person whose public function is to search; *spec.* †(*a*) an official appointed by a guild or company to ensure maintenance of its customs, regulations, and standards of work; (*b*) a customs officer appointed to search ships, baggage, or goods for dutiable or contraband articles; (*c*) a person appointed to observe and report on offences against discipline in a religious house, community, etc.; †(*d*) an inspector of markets; †(*e*) a person appointed to examine dead bodies and report on the cause of death; (*f*) a person appointed to search the clothing and person of police detainees. LME.
3 An instrument used in making a search; *spec.* (*a*) a surgical probe or sound; †(*b*) an instrument for testing the

soundness of cannon after discharge; (*c*) MICROSCOPY a low-power objective. LME.

†**4** A penetrating substance. L17–M18.

5 A penetrating or embarrassing question. *colloq.* E20.

1 searcher of hearts, searcher of men's hearts God.

■ **searchership** *noun* (*rare*) the function or office of searcher LME.

searching /ˈsəːtʃɪŋ/ *adjective.* L16.
[from SEARCH *verb*[1] + -ING[2].]
That searches; penetrating; finding out weak points; (of observation or examination) minute, rigorous; (of a look etc.) keenly observant.

■ **searchingly** *adverb* †(*a*) fully, completely; (*b*) in a searching manner: LME. **searchingness** *noun* L17.

seascape /ˈsiːskeɪp/ *noun.* Also †**-skip.** L18.
[from SEA + SCAPE *noun*[3], after *landscape.*]
1 A picture of the sea. L18.
2 A picturesque view or prospect of the sea. E19.
■ **seascapist** *noun* a painter of seascapes L19.

seasick /ˈsiːsɪk/ *adjective.* M16.
[from SEA + SICK *adjective.*]
1 Suffering from seasickness. Chiefly *pred.* M16.
2 Tired or weary of travelling by sea. *rare.* L16.
Comb.: **seasick medicine**, **seasick pill**, **seasick tablet**: taken to counteract seasickness.

seasickness /ˈsiːsɪknɪs/ *noun.* E17.
[from SEA + SICKNESS.]
Nausea or vomiting induced by the motion of a ship at sea.

seaside /ˈsiːsʌɪd, *in sense A.1 also* siːˈsʌɪd/ *noun & adjective.* ME.
[from SEA + SIDE *noun.*]
▸ **A** *noun.* **1** The edge or brink of the sea. Chiefly after prepositions. ME.
2 The sea-coast, esp. as resorted to for health or pleasure. L18.
3 The side towards or facing the sea. M19.

> 🕮 **2** *Times* Motorists . . bound for the seaside or the country.

▸ **B** *attrib.* or as *adjective.* Belonging to, situated at, or taking place at the seaside; characteristic of resorts beside the sea. L18.

> 🕮 M. EDGAR There's a famous seaside place called Blackpool. J. WAINWRIGHT The exaggerated bawdiness of seaside postcards. M. GEE Out for a seaside stroll. **seaside finch** = *seaside sparrow* below. **seaside grape** = *sea-grape* (a) s.v. SEA; **seaside sparrow** a small sparrow, *Ammodramus maritimus*, of the family Emberizidae, found on the Atlantic coast of N. America.

■ **seasider** *noun* (*a*) a frequenter of the seaside; (*b*) a native or inhabitant of a seaside resort: L19.

†**seaskip** *noun* var. of SEASCAPE.

season /ˈsiːz(ə)n/ *noun.* ME.
[Old French *seson* (mod. *saison*) from Latin *satio(n-)* sowing, in Proto-Romance time of sowing, seed-time, from base of *satus* sown. In branch III from the verb.]
▸ **I** A period of the year.
1 Each of a small number of periods into which the year is regarded as divided by the earth's changing position with regard to the sun, and which are marked by varying length of day and night, by particular conditions of weather, temperature, etc.; *spec.* (*a*) each of the four periods (spring, summer, autumn, winter) into which the year is divided by the passage of the sun from equinox to solstice and from solstice to equinox; (*b*) either of the two periods (the rainy and the dry) into which the year is divided in many tropical climates. ME. ▸**b** A period of the year marked by some special festivity, as Christmas and New Year. L18. ▸**c** In reckoning time or age: a year. *arch.* E19.
2 The time of year assigned or regularly devoted to some specific activity; the part of the year during which the greatest or (with appropriate specifying word) least activity in a specific sphere takes place; *the* part of the year devoted to events in fashionable society, esp. in London. ME.
3 The time of year when a plant flourishes, is mature, blooms, bears fruit, etc. ME.
4 The time of year when an animal is in heat, pairs, or breeds. LME.
5 The time of ripeness or maturity; one's prime. Now *rare* or *obsolete.* LME.
6 A period or time of a particular year characterized by specific conditions of weather or assigned or devoted to a specific activity etc. LME. ▸**b** In *pl.* The rains or spells of wet weather of a tropical country. E18. ▸**c** *ellipt.* = *season ticket* below. *colloq.* L19.
†**7** A term or session of a court, university, etc. LME–E19.
8 A period of time astronomically fixed or recurring. Formerly also, a phase of an eclipse. M16.

> 🕮 **1** W. TREVOR The season changed, and . . autumn crept over all England. **2** J. A. FROUDE It was the dead season; but there were a few persons still in London. U. SINCLAIR Jurgis had only about sixty dollars . . , and the slack season was upon them. G. M. TREVELYAN The London season was over by the first week in June. ***breeding season***, ***football season***, ***gooseberry season***, ***growing season***, ***racing season***, ***tourist season***, etc. **6** E. LANGLEY A bad season was predicted for the beans. S. BRETT We were doing a summer season at Torquay.

▸ **II** *gen.* A time.
9 A particular time or period during or (now *rare*) at which something happens; a period defined by some characteristic feature or circumstance. ME.
10 A right time, the proper or appointed time; a fit or favourable occasion, an opportunity. Foll. by *for, to do,* †*to.* ME.

> 🕮 **9** J. K. JEROME The early morning . . is not . . a good season for literary effort. **10** AV *Eccles.* 3:1 To euery thing there is a season, and a time to euery purpose vnder the heauen.

▸ **III** †**11** Seasoning, relish, flavour. L15–M17.
Phrases etc.: **at seasons** (now *rare*) on different or recurring occasions, from time to time. *closed season*, *close season*: see CLOSE *adjective & adverb*. *compliments of the season*: see COMPLIMENT *noun*. **for all seasons** (a man etc.) ready for any situation or contingency, (a man etc.) adaptable to any circumstance. **for a long season**, **for a short season**, etc., for a long, short, etc., time. **for a season** for some time, for a while. *high season*: see HIGH *adjective, adverb, & noun*. **in season** (*a*) at the right and proper time, opportune(ly); in good time *for, to do*; (*b*) (of game etc.) at the best or the permitted time for hunting, shooting, catching, etc; (*c*) (of a plant or animal) in or into a flourishing condition, in the best state for eating, readily available in good condition; (*d*) (of an animal) on heat; (*e*) (of a place) at its time of greatest resort or activity; at the time when most visited or frequented by fashionable society. **in and out of season**, **in season and out of season** at all times, whether usual or appropriate or not. *little season*: see LITTLE *adjective*. *low season*: see LOW *adjective*. OFF-SEASON. *open season*: see OPEN *adjective*. **out of season** (*a*) unseasonably, inopportunely; unseasonable, inopportune; (*b*) not in season for hunting, shooting, catching, eating, etc.; (*c*) not in season for visitors or fashionable society. *silly season*: see SILLY *adjective*. *the festive season*: see FESTIVE 1.
Comb.: **season crack** a longitudinal crack in cold-worked brass or bronze; **season cracking** the occurrence of season cracks; **season ticket** a ticket entitling the holder to any number of journeys, admittances, etc., during a season or specified period, at a reduced rate of payment.
■ **seasonless** *adjective* †(*a*) *rare* lacking flavour, tasteless, insipid; (*b*) having or knowing no change of season: L16.

season /ˈsiːz(ə)n/ *verb.* LME.
[Old French *saisonner*, formed as prec.]
1 *verb trans.* Alter the flavour of (food, a dish) by the addition of some savoury ingredients, as salt, herbs, spices, etc., or (of salt etc.) when added. LME. ▸**b** *verb trans. fig.* Mix or intersperse with something that imparts relish or zest; enhance *with.* E16. ▸†**c** *verb trans.* Improve by admixture; moderate, alleviate, temper. L16–E17. ▸**d** *verb intrans.* Add seasoning. L18.
†**2** *verb trans.* Embalm. LME–L17.
†**3** *verb trans.* Imbue (*with*). M16–L18.
4 *verb trans.* Bring to maturity; make fit for use by prolonged exposure to atmospheric influences, or by gradual subjection to future usual conditions; *spec.* dry and harden (timber) by long keeping. M16.
†**5** *verb trans.* Manure (land). M16–E18.
6 *verb trans.* Fortify (a person) by habit against difficult conditions; familiarize with a certain mode of life or occupation; inure, acclimatize. Chiefly as ***seasoned ppl adjective.*** E17. ▸†**b** Prepare or fit (a person); train. Foll. by *for.* E–M17.
7 *verb intrans.* Become seasoned, mature. L17.

> 🕮 **1** E. REVELEY It's already seasoned which means you don't have to throw a ton of salt on top. **b** R. L. STEVENSON Benefactors who . . season your dinner with good company. **d** L. CHAMBERLAIN Dry the radishes and add them to the dressing . . . Season to taste. **4** G. HERBERT A sweet and vertuous soul Like seasoned timber, never gives. **5** J. DOS PASSOS Lumber laid out to season. *Wine* Pork that has been salted . . and left to season for four . . months. **6** L. URIS This delegation, seasoned by years of frustration. C. RYAN They were seasoned, well-equipped and disciplined.

■ **seasoner** *noun* L16.

seasonable /ˈsiːz(ə)nəb(ə)l/ *adjective.* ME.
[from SEASON *noun, verb* + -ABLE.]
1 Suitable to or usual for the time of year. In early use also, (of weather etc.) favourable. ME.
2 Occurring at the right season, opportune; meeting the needs of the occasion. LME.
■ **seasonableness** *noun* M16. **seasonably** *adverb* LME.

seasonal /ˈsiːz(ə)n(ə)l/ *adjective.* M19.
[from SEASON *noun* + -AL[1].]
Of or pertaining to the seasons of the year, or some other temporal cycle; characteristic of or dependent on a particular season; varying with the season; (of a person) employed or engaged only during a particular season.
seasonal affective disorder MEDICINE a depressive state associated with late autumn and winter and thought to be caused by a lack of sunlight. **seasonal dimorphism** ENTOMOLOGY a variation in the appearance of different broods of an insect according to the time of year.
■ **seasoˈnality** *noun* (*a*) the condition of being dependent on the seasons; the state of recurring at a particular season; (*b*) the degree to which a climate has distinct seasons: M20. **seasonally** *adverb* (*a*) at a certain time of year, at some seasons; (*b*) according to the season: M19.

seasoning /ˈsiːz(ə)nɪŋ/ *noun.* E16.
[from SEASON *verb* + -ING[1].]
1 The action of SEASON *verb*; the process of being seasoned. E16.
2 A substance added to food to season it; a condiment. L16.

seat /siːt/ *noun.* ME.
[Old Norse *sæti* = Old English *gesete*, Middle Dutch *gesæte* (Dutch *gezeet*), Old High German *gasāzi* (German *Gesäss* †seat, buttocks), from Germanic, from base of SIT *verb.* In some uses rendering Latin *sedes.*]
▸ **I 1** Orig., the action of sitting. Later, a sitting, a session, *spec.* a court session. Long *obsolete* exc. *Scot.* ME.
2 A sitting body, a court of justice; *spec.* = ***Court of Session*** s.v. SESSION *noun* 4b. Orig. & chiefly *Scot.* Now *rare* or *obsolete.* E16.
3 A manner of sitting on a horse etc. L16.

> 🕮 **3** E. BAIRD A rider is good because of a secure and balanced seat.

▸ **II 4** The place on which a person is sitting, or usually sits, a place to seat one person at a table, in a theatre, vehicle, etc. ME.
5 A thing designed or used for sitting on, as a chair, bench, stool, sofa, etc.; a piece of furniture for sitting on. ME. ▸**b** The part of a chair, saddle, etc., on which the sitter's weight directly rests; a fitment on a lavatory on which a person may sit. L18.
6 A chair for the holder of some position of authority or dignity, as the throne of a monarch or a bishop, the throne of God or of an angel; *fig.* the authority or dignity symbolized by sitting in a particular chair or throne. ME. ▸**b** *spec.* The throne *of* a particular kingdom. *arch.* L16.
7 The use of, or right to use, a seat (in a church, theatre, vehicle, etc.). E16. ▸**b** *spec.* A right to sit as a member, or the position of being a member, of a deliberative or administrative body, esp. of Parliament or other legislative assembly; a place in the membership of the House of Commons etc. Also, a (parliamentary) constituency. L18. ▸**c** A place in the membership of a stock exchange, orig. and esp. the New York Stock Exchange. E19.
8 The buttocks. E17. ▸**b** The part of a garment, esp. of a pair of trousers, which covers the buttocks. M19.
9 The form of a hare. Now *dial.* M18.

> 🕮 **4** P. MARSHALL A plane to New York . . with a seat for her on it. N. LOWNDES Sasha got up to give the old woman his seat. **5** M. L. KING He boarded a bus and sat in one of the front seats. ***bench seat***, ***booster seat***, ***box-seat***, ***bucket seat***, ***deacon-seat***, ***dicky seat***, ***ejection seat***, ***garden seat***, ***orchestra seat***, ***pillion seat***, etc. **b** B. H. MALKIN Chairs without any seats. *Horse & Rider* A deep seat and a fairly pronounced pommel. **7b** G. BROWN I lost my own seat . . to my Conservative opponent . . by 2,124 votes. JO GRIMOND No Member of Parliament, even in a safe seat, . . can . . ignore his or her constituency. **8** J. HARVEY His father . . sat on the stove, warming his seat. **b** P. CAREY He had . . torn the seat of his knickerbockers.

▸ **III 10** The resting-place of departed souls; a position in this place. Now *arch. & poet.* ME.
11 A place of habitation or settlement. LME. ▸**b** A country mansion, esp. with large grounds. Also ***country seat.*** E17.
12 A city in which a throne, court, or government is established or set up; a capital city or town. Also (now *rare*), a see. LME.
13 The supposed location in the body of a particular faculty, function, disease, sensation, etc., or of the soul. LME.
14 The location or site of something specified. M16.
15 A location as regards environment, climate, etc., or (formerly) orientation. Now *arch. rare.* M16.
†**16** A definite place or position. L16–L18.
†**17** A place prepared for something to be erected or built on it. E–M17.
18 The part of a thing on which it rests or appears to rest; the base. M17.
19 A part or surface of a machine which supports or guides another part. E19.
20 A piece of leather etc. forming the foundation for the heel of a boot or shoe. L19.

> 🕮 **13** F. WELDON The heart, the soul, and the mind—those three majestic seats of female sorrow. **14** A. J. EVANS Many Croats . . were . . leaving for the seat of war. V. WOOLF Leeds as a seat of learning was laughed to scorn. **15** SHAKES. *Macb.* This castle hath a pleasant seat.

Phrases: BACK SEAT. ***by the seat of one's*** PANTS. **hot seat**: see HOT *adjective*. ***in the driver's seat***: see DRIVER 1. **keep one's seat** remain seated, keep from falling from a horse etc. **lose one's seat** fall off a horse etc. ***reserved seats***: see RESERVED 3. ***safe seat***: see SAFE *adjective*. ***seat of the*** SCORNER. **take a seat** sit down in a seat. **take one's seat** sit down in one's allocated or chosen seat; assume one's official position, be formally admitted to Parliament, Congress, etc.

Comb.: **seat belt** a safety belt securing a person in a seat, *spec.* (*a*) one worn in an aircraft, esp. at take-off or landing; (*b*) one worn in a motor vehicle as a protection in an accident or in an emergency stop; **seat-belted** *adjective* wearing a seat belt; **seat-bone** the pelvis, *esp.* the ischium; **seat-mate** *N. Amer.* each of a set of people who share a seat; **seat-mile** one mile travelled by one passenger, *spec.* in travel by air, as a statistical unit.

■ **seatless** *adjective* E19.

seat /siːt/ *verb.* L16.
[from the noun.]

▶ **I 1** *verb refl.* Sit down. L16.

†**2** *verb intrans.* Sit down; (of an animal) lie down; (of a hare) sit in its form. L16–M18.

3 *verb trans.* Cause or enable to sit *in* or *on* a throne, chair of State or office, etc.; establish (a person) in a position of authority or dignity. Formerly also *absol.*, enthrone. Now *rare.* L16.

4 *verb trans.* **a** Place on a seat or seats; cause to sit down; find a seat or seats for. E17. ▸**b** Cause or allow to take a seat in a deliberative assembly. L18. ▸**c** Of a building, room, etc.: afford sitting accommodation for. L19.

5 *verb trans.* In *pass.* Be sitting, be in a sitting posture. E17.

6 *verb trans.* Provide (a building, a room, etc.) with seats, fit seats in. L17.

7 *verb trans.* Fix a seat on (a chair); repair (trousers, a chair) by renewing or mending the seat. M18.

> 📖 **1** A. BRINK Ben seated himself on the easy chair. **3** TENNYSON I find you here but in the second place . . . We will seat you highest. **4a** C. MERIVALE The first object . . was to seat the greatest number of . . people. GEO. ELIOT Dinah . . seated her on the pallet. **b** *Rolling Stone* Despite his election, the . . assembly refused to seat him. **c** *Pall Mall Gazette* Each theatre . . registered . . as capable of seating a specified number. P. S. BUCK We have not chairs enough to seat the guests. **5** J. OSBORNE Jimmy and Cliff are seated in the two armchairs.

▶ **II 8 a** *verb trans.* Place as a resident; settle or establish as colonists. Now *rare.* L16. ▸†**b** *verb refl.* & *intrans.* Take up a permanent residence; settle as colonists. E17–L18. ▸**c** *verb trans.* In *pass.* Have one's (country) seat in a specified place. L17.

9 *verb trans.* Situate, position. Usu. in *pass.*, have its seat, be situated, be located, be established. L16.

10 a *verb trans.* Set or secure in the proper place; fix on a base or support. Now *techn.* E17. ▸**b** *verb intrans.* Be fixed in the proper position; lie, rest, or be fixed *(up)on*. Now *techn.* M17.

†**11** *verb trans.* Found (a city); establish (a plantation). E–M17.

†**12** *verb trans.* Provide with inhabitants, settle with colonists; settle in (a place) as a colonist. Chiefly *N. Amer.* L17–L18.

> 📖 **8c** *Field* Sir John . . is seated at Elmore Court in Gloucestershire. **9** SHAKES. *Merch. V.* They are as sick that surfeit . . as they that starve . . . It is . . happiness . . to be seated in the mean. G. HERBERT A poor man's box conveniently seated, to receive the charity of well-minded people. W. SHENSTONE In thy youthful soul Love's gentle tyrant seats his awful throne. HAZLITT Thoughts passing through the mind and seated on the lips. S. SMILES The disease had become too deeply seated for recovery. T. H. HUXLEY London . . is seated on clay. ***deep-seated***: see DEEP *adverb.*

Seatainer /ˈsiːteɪnə/ *noun. Austral.* M20.
[from SEA + CON)TAINER.]
A container for the transportation of freight by sea.

seater /ˈsiːtə/ *noun.* M17.
[from SEAT *verb, noun* + -ER¹.]
†**1** An established settler. *N. Amer.* M17–E19.
†**2** A person who allocates seats in a meeting-house. *N. Amer.* L17–L19.
3 As 2nd elem. of comb.: (a car, sofa, etc.) having the specified seating capacity, as ***single-seater***, ***two-seater***, etc. E20.

seating /ˈsiːtɪŋ/ *noun.* L16.
[from SEAT *verb* + -ING¹.]
1 The action of SEAT *verb.* L16.
2 Material for upholstering the seats of chairs etc. L18.
3 A part of a structure etc. which rests on another part. E19.
4 MECHANICS. A fitted support for part of a structure or machine. Usu. in *pl.* M19.
5 The seats with which a building etc. is provided; seats collectively, sitting accommodation. L19.

SEATO /ˈsiːtəʊ/ *abbreviation.*
South-East Asia Treaty Organization.

seau /səʊ/ *noun.* Pl. **seaux** /səʊ/. L18.
[French, lit. 'bucket'.]
A ceramic vessel in the shape of a pail or bucket used for cooling wine etc., esp. as part of an 18th-cent. dinner service.

seawant *noun* var. of SEWAN.

seaward /ˈsiːwəd/ *noun, adjective, & adverb.* LME.
[from SEA + -WARD.]
▶ **A** *noun.* The direction or position in which the sea lies. Only in ***to seaward***, ***to the seaward***, towards the sea, in the direction of the sea, in the direction of the open sea, away from the land; ***to the seaward of***, to or at a place nearer the sea (or, at sea, further from the land) than; ***from seaward***, ***from the seaward***. LME.
▶ **B** *adjective.* †**1** Fresh from the sea. *rare.* Only in L15.
2 Going out to sea, going to seaward. E17.
3 Directed or looking towards the sea; facing the sea, or the open sea; situated on the side or section nearest the sea. E18.
4 Of a wind: blowing from the sea. E19.
▶ **C** *adverb.* Towards the sea or the open sea (away from the land). E17.
■ **seawardly** *adjective* accustomed to looking seaward M19. **seawards** *noun* & *adverb* †(*a*) *noun* = SEAWARD *noun* (only in ***to seawards***, ***to the seawards***); (*b*) *adverb* = SEAWARD *adverb*: E16.

seaweed /ˈsiːwiːd/ *noun.* L16.
[from SEA + WEED *noun*¹.]
Any macroscopic marine alga; such plants *en masse* or collectively.
Comb.: **seaweed marquetry**: with a pattern resembling seaweed.
■ **seaweeded** *adjective* covered with seaweed M19. **seaweedy** *adjective* covered with seaweed; characteristic of seaweed: M19.

seaworthy /ˈsiːwəːði/ *adjective.* E19.
[from SEA + -WORTHY.]
Of a ship etc.: in a fit condition to undergo a voyage, and to encounter stormy weather.
■ **seaworthiness** *noun* E19.

seax *noun* see SAX *noun*¹.

sebaceous /sɪˈbeɪʃəs/ *adjective.* E18.
[from Latin *sebaceus*, from *sebum* tallow: see -ACEOUS.]
1 Of the nature of sebum; connected with the secretion of sebum. E18.
2 Of, pertaining to, or resembling tallow or fat; oily, fatty, greasy. *rare.* L18.
3 MEDICINE. Of a cyst or lesion: formed on or associated with a sebaceous gland or glands. L19.
1 ***sebaceous crypt***, ***sebaceous duct***, ***sebaceous follicle***, etc. **sebaceous gland** a small gland of a type distributed over the skin of mammals, esp. associated with hair follicles, which secretes oily matter (sebum) to lubricate the skin and hair.

sebacic /sɪˈbasɪk/ *adjective.* L18.
[formed as prec. + -IC.]
CHEMISTRY. ***sebacic acid***, a saturated fatty acid, $HOOC(CH_2)_8COOH$, obtained by distillation of some oils and used esp. in resins and plasticizers; 1,8-decanedioic acid.

Sebago /sɪˈbeɪgəʊ/ *noun.* L19.
[A lake in Maine, USA.]
Sebago salmon, ***Sebago trout***, a non-migratory freshwater variety of the salmon, *Salmo salar*, native to lakes in eastern N. America.

Sebat /ˈsiːbat/ *noun.* Also **Sh-** /ʃ-/, **Shevat** /ˈʃiːvat/. M16.
[Hebrew *šĕbaṭ*.]
In the Jewish calendar, the fifth month of the civil and eleventh of the religious year, usu. coinciding with parts of January and February.

Sebei /səˈbeɪ/ *noun* & *adjective.* Pl. of noun same. E20.
[Nilo-Cushitic.]
Of or pertaining to, a member of, a people inhabiting parts of eastern Uganda and western Kenya; (of) the Nilotic language of this people. Cf. SAPINY.

sebesten /sɪˈbɛstən/ *noun.* LME.
[medieval Latin from Arab. *sabastān* from Persian *sapistān*, *sagpistān*, from *sag* dog + *pistān* breast, nipple.]
The plumlike fruit of either of two shrubs or small trees of the borage family, *Cordia myxa*, of southern Asia, and *C. sebestena*, of the Caribbean region (also called ***geiger tree***); a preparation of this, used to treat coughs etc. Also, either of these shrubs or trees.

Sebilian /sɪˈbɪlɪən/ *adjective* & *noun.* M20.
[from *Sebil* a village in upper Egypt + -IAN.]
ARCHAEOLOGY. (Designating or pertaining to) a late upper palaeolithic industry of Upper Egypt.

sebkha *noun* var. of SABKHA.

seborrhoea /sɛbəˈriːə/ *noun.* Also ***-rrhea.** L19.
[from SEBUM + -O- + -RRHOEA.]
MEDICINE. A skin condition characterized by overactivity of the sebaceous glands, freq. associated with acne, or occas. with a form of eczema. Cf. STEATORRHOEA.
■ **seborrhoeic** *adjective* of, pertaining to, or affected with seborrhoea L19.

sebotrophic /sɛbə(ʊ)ˈtrəʊfɪk, -ˈtrɒf-/ *adjective.* Also **-tropic** /-trəʊpɪk, -trɒpɪk/. M20.
[from SEBUM + -O- + -TROPHIC, -TROPIC.]
PHYSIOLOGY. Tending to stimulate sebaceous activity.

sebum /ˈsiːbəm/ *noun.* L19.
[mod. Latin use of Latin *sebum* suet, grease, tallow. Cf. SEVUM.]
PHYSIOLOGY. The oily secretion of the sebaceous glands which lubricates and protects the hair and skin.

sebundy /sɪˈbʌndi/ *noun. Anglo-Indian.* Pl. **-ies**, same. L18.
[Urdu *sibandī* from Persian *sih-bandī* three-monthly charge for upkeep of militia member, from *sih* three + *band* bond.]
An irregular soldier chiefly employed in police and revenue duties and on local government service.

SEC *abbreviation. US.*
Securities and Exchange Commission.

sec /sɛk/ *noun*¹. Also **sec.** (point). M18.
[Abbreviation.]
MATH. Secant (of).

sec /sɛk/ *noun*². Also **sec.** (point). L19.
[Abbreviation.]
1 A second (of time). Chiefly *colloq.* L19.
2 *pl.* (As a written form.) Seconds. L19.

sec /sɛk/ *adjective.* ME.
[French from Latin *siccus*.]
Of wine: dry.
extra sec: see EXTRA *adverb.* DEMI-SEC.
¶ Rare between ME and M19.

Sec. *abbreviation.*
Secretary.

SECAM /ˈsiːkam/ *abbreviation.*
French *Séquentiel Couleur à Mémoire*, a colour television system developed in France.

secant /ˈsiːk(ə)nt, ˈsɛk-/ *adjective* & *noun.* L16.
[French *sécant* adjective, *sécante* (sc. *ligne*), from mod. Latin use of Latin *secant-* pres. ppl stem of *secare* to cut: see -ANT¹.]
▶ **A** *adjective.* GEOMETRY. Of a line or surface in relation to another line or surface: cutting, intersecting. *rare.* L16.
▶ **B** *noun.* **1** MATH. One of the fundamental trigonometrical functions (cf. TANGENT *noun* 1, SINE 2): orig., the length of a straight line drawn from the centre of curvature of a circular arc through one end of the arc until it meets the tangent touching the arc at the other end; now, the ratio of this line to the radius; (equivalently, as a function of an angle) the ratio of the hypotenuse of a right-angled triangle to the side adjacent to a given angle (or, if obtuse, its supplement); the reciprocal of a cosine. Abbreviation SEC *noun*¹. L16.
2 GEOMETRY. A line that cuts another; *esp.* a straight line that cuts a curve in two or more parts. L17.

secateur /sɛkəˈtəː, ˈsɛkətəː/ *noun.* M19.
[French *sécateur*, irreg. from Latin *secare* to cut + *-ateur* -ATOR.]
sing. & (usu.) in *pl.* A pair of pruning clippers with crossed blades, for use with one hand. Also ***pair of secateurs***.

Secchi disc /ˈsɛkɪ dɪsk/ *noun phr.* Also **Secchi's disc** /ˈsɛkɪz/, ***Secchi('s) disk.** E20.
[Angelo *Secchi* (1818–78), Italian astronomer.]
An opaque white disc used to gauge the transparency of water by measuring the depth at which the disc ceases to be visible from the surface.

secco /ˈsɛkəʊ/ *noun* & *adjective.* M19.
[Italian from Latin *siccus* dry. In sense A.1 ellipt. for *fresco secco* lit. 'dry fresco'.]
▶ **A** *noun.* Pl. **-os**.
1 The process or technique of painting on dry plaster with colours mixed with water. M19.
2 MUSIC. (A) secco recitative. M20.
▶ **B** *adjective.* MUSIC. Of recitative: plain, lacking or having only sparse instrumental accompaniment. L19.

secede /sɪˈsiːd/ *verb.* E18.
[Latin *secedere*, formed as SE- + *cedere* CEDE.]
†**1** *verb intrans.* Withdraw from society or public view, go into seclusion or retirement. Only in E18.
2 *verb intrans.* Withdraw formally from an alliance, an association, a federal union, or a political or religious organization. (Foll. by *from.*) M18.
3 *verb trans.* Withdraw (a component territory) from a federal union etc.; detach or cede (a piece of land). *rare.* M20.

> 📖 **2** T. JEFFERSON Possibly their colonies might secede from the Union. B. G. M. SUNDKLER Such Independent Bantu Churches as have . . seceded from White Mission Churches chiefly on racial grounds.

■ **seceder** *noun* (*a*) a person who or territory etc. which secedes; (*b*) *spec.* (SCOTTISH ECCLESIASTICAL HISTORY) a member of the Secession Church: M18.

secern /sɪˈsəːn/ *verb.* Now *rare.* E17.
[Latin *secernere*, formed as SE- + *cernere* to separate.]
†**1** PHYSIOLOGY. **a** *verb intrans.* Separate a substance or substances from the blood. Chiefly as ***secerning*** *ppl adjective.* E17–M19. ▸**b** *verb trans.* Separate (a substance) from the blood, esp. (according to former physiological theory) in order to secrete it. M17–M19.
2 *verb trans.* Separate. Latterly *spec.* separate in thought, place in a separate category, distinguish. M17.

▪ **secernment** *noun* the action of secerning something E19.

secernent /sɪˈsəːnənt/ *adjective & noun*. Now *rare* or *obsolete*. E19.
[Latin *secernent-* pres. ppl stem of *secernere*: see prec., -ENT.]
PHYSIOLOGY. ▶**A** *adjective*. Secretory. E19.
▶**B** *noun*. A secretory organ. E19.

secesh /sɪˈsɛʃ/ *noun & adjective*. *US colloq. obsolete* exc. *Hist*. M19.
[Abbreviation of SECESSION.]
▶**A** *noun*. Pl. same.
1 A secessionist. M19.
2 Secession. M19.
▶**B** *adjective*. Secessionist. M19.
▪ **secesher** *noun* a secessionist M19.

secession /sɪˈsɛʃ(ə)n/ *noun*. M16.
[French *sécession* or Latin *secessio(n-)*, from *secess-* pa. ppl stem of *secedere* SECEDE: see -ION.]
1 ROMAN HISTORY. A temporary migration of plebeians to a place outside the city of Rome, to compel patricians to redress their grievances. M16.
†**2 a** The action or an act of withdrawing from public view or going into seclusion or retirement; the condition of having so withdrawn. E17–M19. ▶†**b** (A) removal or separation of a material thing. M17–L18.
3 The action or an act of seceding; *spec.* (also **S-**) (***a***) US HISTORY the seceding of eleven Southern States from the US Union in 1860, which gave rise to the American Civil War; (***b***) SCOTTISH ECCLESIASTICAL HISTORY the seceding of certain ministers from the established Church of Scotland in 1733 to form a separate Church (***the Secession Church***). M17. ▶**b** ART. (Also **S-**.) [translation of German *Sezession*.] A radical movement in art that began in Vienna and was contemporaneous with and related to art nouveau; the style of this movement. Also ***Vienna secession***, ***Viennese secession***. Cf. SEZESSION. L19.
▪ **secessional** *adjective* M19.

secessionism /sɪˈsɛʃ(ə)nɪz(ə)m/ *noun*. L19.
[from prec. + -ISM.]
The principles of those in favour of (a) secession, *spec.* (***a***) US HISTORY of Southern States from the US Union, (***b***) SCOTTISH ECCLESIASTICAL HISTORY of the Secession Church from the established Church of Scotland.

secessionist /sɪˈsɛʃ(ə)nɪst/ *noun & adjective*. M19.
[formed as prec. + -IST.]
▶**A** *noun*. A person who favours (a) secession or who joins in a secession, *spec.* (US HISTORY) of Southern States from the US Union. M19.
▶**B** *attrib.* or as *adjective*. Of or pertaining to secessionists or secessionism. M19.

Sechuana, **Sechwana** *nouns & adjectives* vars. of SETSWANA.

†**seck** *noun*: see SACK *noun*².

Seckel /ˈsɛk(ə)l/ *noun*. Also **Seckle**, **s-**. E19.
[The surname of an early grower.]
In full ***Seckel pear***. A small sweet juicy brownish-red US variety of pear; the tree bearing this fruit.

secko /ˈsɛkəʊ/ *noun*. *Austral. slang*. Pl. **-os**. M20.
[from abbreviation of SEX *noun* + -O.]
A sexual pervert; a sex offender.

†**secle** *noun*. Also **siecle**. LME.
[Old French *secle*, *siecle* (mod. *siècle*) from Latin *saeculum*: see SECULAR.]
1 The secular world. Only in LME.
2 An age, a period. L15–M19.
3 A century. M16–M17.

seclude /sɪˈkluːd/ *verb trans*. LME.
[Latin *secludere*, formed as SE- + *claudere* shut.]
†**1** Shut off, obstruct the access to (a thing). Foll. by *from*. LME–M16.
†**2** Shut or keep out *from*; deny entrance to; debar (*from*); prevent *from doing*. L15–L18. ▶**b** Prohibit (something), preclude. E16–M17. ▶**c** Regard as having no share or playing no part. Foll. by *from*. L16–L17.
†**3** Exclude from consideration, leave out of account. M16–E18.
4 †**a** Banish, expel, (*from*). M16–M18. ▶**b** TEXTUAL CRITICISM. Exclude as spurious. *rare*. L19.
5 Enclose, confine, or shut off so as to prevent access or influence from outside; *spec.* hide or screen from public view; *refl.* live in retirement or solitude. (Foll. by *from*.) L16.
6 Separate, keep apart. Latterly *spec.* select and separate, set aside for use. Now *rare*. E17.

🕮 **5** M. COVARRUBIAS Women . . live restricted and secluded in the palace. E. BOWEN Shrubs inside the paling seclude the place from the street. A. BLOND Harold Robbins secludes himself in a suite in a Manhattan hotel.

▪ **secluded** *adjective* that has been secluded; (of a place) remote, screened from observation or access, seldom visited on account of distance or difficulty of approach: E17. **secludedly** *adverb* M19. **secludedness** *noun* M19. †**secluding** *preposition* apart from, excepting E17–E18.

secluse /sɪˈkluːz/ *adjective*. Now *rare*. L16.
[Latin *seclusus* pa. pple of *secludere* SECLUDE.]
Secluded; withdrawn from view or from society.
▪ Also †**seclused** *adjective*: only in LME.

seclusion /sɪˈkluːʒ(ə)n/ *noun*. E17.
[medieval Latin *seclusio(n-)*, from Latin *seclus-* pa. ppl stem of *secludere* SECLUDE: see -ION.]
1 The action of secluding something or someone. Also, exclusion. Now *rare*. E17.
2 The condition or state of being secluded; retirement, privacy; a period of this. L18.
3 A place in which a person is secluded; a secluded place. L18.

🕮 **1** H. J. LASKI Emphasize its importance to the seclusion of all other factors. **2** E. B. BROWNING After a seclusion of four years and a half from the external air. L. URIS The bride, . . hidden all day, was taken from seclusion. P. ACKROYD Perhaps the tall hedges give this region its air of seclusion and even of secrecy.

▪ **seclusionist** *noun* an advocate of seclusion M19.

seclusive /sɪˈkluːsɪv/ *adjective*. M19.
[from SECLUDE after *include*, *inclusive*, etc.: see -IVE.]
Serving or tending to seclude someone or something; inclined to seclusion. Also (now *rare*), exclusive.
▪ **seclusively** *adverb* L19. **seclusiveness** *noun* E19.

secobarbital /sɛkəʊˈbɑːbɪt(ə)l, -al/ *noun*. Chiefly *US*. M20.
[from SECO(NDARY + BARBITAL.]
PHARMACOLOGY. = QUINALBARBITONE.

secodont /ˈsɛkədɒnt/ *adjective*. L19.
[from Latin *secare* to cut + -ODONT.]
ZOOLOGY. Having or designating teeth with one or more sharp cutting edges.

Seconal /ˈsɛk(ə)nal, -(ə)l/ *noun*. M20.
[from SECON(DARY + AL(YL.]
PHARMACOLOGY. (Proprietary name for) the drug quinalbarbitone; a tablet of this.

second /ˈsɛk(ə)nd/ *noun*¹. LME.
[Old French *seconde* from medieval Latin *secunda* use as noun (sc. *minuta* minute) of fem. of Latin *secundus* SECOND *adjective* (being the result of the second operation of dividing by sixty: cf SECOND *noun*² 6).]
1 A sixtieth part of a minute of angular measurement, ¹⁄₃₆₀₀th part of a degree. Also ***second of arc***. LME.
2 A sixtieth part of a minute of time, ¹⁄₃₆₀₀th of an hour (as an SI unit, defined in terms of the frequency of a spectral transition of caesium-133). (Symbol s.) L16. ▶**b** *loosely*. An extremely short time, an instant. E19.

🕮 **1** ***arc second***: see ARC *noun*. **2b** *Observer* Come in, I'll be down in a second.

Comb.: **second-foot** a unit of the rate of flow of water, equal to one cubic foot per second; **second-hand**, **seconds-hand** a hand or pointer of a timepiece indicating seconds; **second pendulum**, **seconds pendulum** a pendulum of a timepiece vibrating seconds.

second /ˈsɛk(ə)nd/ *adjective*, *noun*², *& adverb* (*ordinal numeral*). ME.
[Old & mod. French *second*, (fem.) *-onde* from Latin *secundus* following, favourable, second, from base of *sequi* follow.]
▶**A** *adjective*. **1** Coming next after the first in time, order, series, succession, position, occurrence, existence, rank, importance, excellence, etc.; that is number two in a series; (represented by 2nd). ME. ▶**b** Next in rank, quality, importance, or degree of any attribute, *to* (a person or thing regarded as first); (in neg. and limiting contexts) inferior (*to*). LME. ▶**c** Qualifying a superl.: only exceeded by one in the specified attribute. LME. ▶**d** In official titles: being the lower of two or the next to the highest of several people having the same title. E18.
2 Having the degree of quality, fineness, etc., next to the best; of the second grade or class. Now chiefly COMMERCE in certain customary collocations. ME.
3 Other, another; additional to that which has already existed, taken place, been mentioned, etc.; (qualifying a proper name) equalling or closely resembling the bearer of the name. ME.

🕮 **1** T. HARDY She was the second Mrs Melbury, the first having died. P. MOYES Henry Heathfield had taken second prize for tomatoes at the County Horticultural Show. J. SIMMS We had thought . . of having a second child. ***second conjugation***, ***second declension***, etc. **b** C. S. LEWIS It ranks second to none except the Bible. P. WARNER As an administrator he was second only to his father. **c** M. C. GERALD The second most widely used class of drugs. **d** C. DEXTER School masters, even experienced second masters, aren't all that highly recompensed. **3** W. FORREST A famous kynge . . Called (in his tyme) the Seconde Salomon. *Guardian* An inexpensive 'second car' for my wife. G. GORDON The playroom served as a second visitors' room when . . more people were staying.

Special collocations, phrases, & comb.: (As ordinal.) Forming compound numerals with multiples of ten, as ***forty-second*** (***42nd***), ***six-thousand-and-second*** (***6002nd***), etc. (As adjective) ***a second opinion***: see OPINION *noun*. **in the second place** as a second consideration, secondly. **second Adam** THEOLOGY Jesus Christ (with ref. to *1 Corinthians* 15:45, 47). **second advent** CHRISTIAN THEOLOGY = ***second coming*** below. ***Second Adventist***: see ADVENTIST. **second ballot** a deciding ballot taken between the candidate who won a previous ballot without securing an absolute majority and the candidate with the next highest number of votes. ***second banana***: see BANANA 3. **second blessing** THEOLOGY an experience of God's grace subsequent to conversion, believed by some Christian groups to be the means of receiving the power to live a sanctified life. **second bottom** (***a***) the last but one position in a ranking etc.; (***b***) *US* the first terrace above the normal flood plain of a stream; (***c***) *Austral.* a second stratum of gold-bearing material found by sinking below the bottom of the first. **second breakfast** a light meal taken late in the morning or early in the afternoon. ***second cause***: see CAUSE *noun*. **second chamber** the upper chamber of a bicameral legislature, usu. chiefly having the function of revising measures prepared and passed by the lower. **second channel** RADIO = IMAGE *noun* 9. ***second childhood***: see CHILDHOOD 1. ***second chop***: see CHOP *noun*³. **second coming** CHRISTIAN THEOLOGY the second advent of Christ on earth. ***second cousin***: see COUSIN *noun*. **second cut** *Austral. & NZ* (the mark of) a blow made to remove badly cut fleece; a piece of short or inferior wool produced by this. †**second day** in the usage of the Society of Friends, Monday. **second degree** *spec.* (***a***) the second most serious category of burn; (***b***) the second most serious category of crime (***principal in the second degree***, an accessory to a crime). **second-degree** *adjective* (***a***) (of a burn) sufficiently severe to cause blistering but not permanent scarring; (***b***) *US* (of murder) next in culpability to first-degree murder, premeditated but with mitigating circumstances. ***Second Empire***: see EMPIRE *noun*. ***second fiddle***: see FIDDLE *noun*. ***second filial generation***: see FILIAL *adjective* 2. **second finger** the finger next to the forefinger, the middle finger. **second floor** the floor or storey of a building two or (*N. Amer.*) one above the ground floor. **second front** *spec.* in the war of 1939–45, a front in Nazi-occupied Europe in addition to the Russian sector of fighting. **second gear** the gear next above the lowest or bottom gear of a motor vehicle, bicycle, etc. **second-generation** *adjective* (of a computer) distinguished by the use of transistors and belonging essentially to the period 1955–60. **second-guess** *verb* (*colloq.*) (***a***) *verb trans.* anticipate, predict, or foresee by guesswork; (***b***) *verb trans. & intrans.* criticize, judge, question, or reconsider by hindsight. **second-guesser** *colloq.* a person who second-guesses; orig., a spectator of baseball who criticizes the playing of a team or the decisions of the umpire, usu. with the benefit of hindsight. ***second honeymoon***: see HONEYMOON *noun*. **second in command** (an officer) holding a position next in rank to the chief commander of an army etc.; (a person) next in authority to the person in charge. ***second intention***. ***Second International***: see INTERNATIONAL *noun* 3. **Second Isaiah** = DEUTERO-ISAIAH. **second language** a language spoken or used in addition to one's native language, a language learned later than one's native language; a foreign language. ***second last***: see LAST *adverb*, *adjective*, *& noun*⁵. ***second law of thermodynamics***. ***second lesson***: see LESSON *noun* 2. ***second lieutenant***. **second line** MILITARY a line behind the front line to support it and make good its losses. **second-line** *adjective* constituting or belonging to a second line, ranking second in ability, value, etc. **second-liner** a member of a second line, a second-line person. **secondman** an assistant driver on a diesel or electric train. **second master** a deputy headmaster. **second messenger** PHYSIOLOGY a substance whose release within a cell is promoted by a hormone and which brings about a response by the cell. **second mortgage** a supplementary or puisne mortgage on the same property as another. **second mourning** *Hist.* = ***half-mourning*** (b) s.v. HALF-. **second name** *spec.* a surname. **second nature** acquired behaviour that has become natural or virtually instinctive (*to*). **second officer** an assistant mate on a merchant ship. ***second pedal***: see PEDAL *noun*¹ 4. ***second person***: see PERSON *noun*. **second position** (***a***) MUSIC the second lowest position of the left hand on the finger-board of a stringed instrument; (***b***) BALLET a disposition of the body in which the turned-out feet are in a straight line separated by the distance of a small step. **second reading** the second of three successive occasions on which a bill is presented to a legislature before it becomes law, in Britain to approve its general principles, in the US to debate committee reports. ***Second Sea Lord***: see SEA. ***second secretary***: see SECRETARY *noun*. **second self** a friend who agrees absolutely with one's tastes and opinions; a person for whose welfare one cares as much as for one's own. **second service** *Hist.* the Eucharist in the Church of England, as following matins. **second sight** the supposed power by which occurrences in the future or things at a distance are perceived as though they were actually present or taking place. **second-sighted** *adjective* having second sight. ***second slip***: see SLIP *noun*³ 11. **second sound** PHYSICS a form of longitudinal wave which has many properties in common with sound and is observed in superfluid helium. **second speed** (the speed attainable in) second gear. **second storey** = ***second floor*** above. **second strike** a retaliatory attack conducted with weapons designed to withstand an initial nuclear attack or first strike. ***second string***: see STRING *noun*. ***second table***: see TABLE *noun*. **second thigh** the gaskin of a horse's leg. **second thoughts** thoughts reversing or altering a previous opinion, conclusion, or determination. **second tooth** each of the teeth that replace the milk teeth in a mammal. **Second War** = ***Second World War*** s.v. WORLD. ***second water***: see WATER *noun*. **second wind** a person's ability to breathe freely during exertion after initial breathlessness; renewed energy to continue an effort. **Second World** (***a***) the developed countries apart from the US and the former USSR; (***b***) the (former) Communist bloc comprising the USSR and some East European countries. ***Second World War***: see WORLD. ***the second sex***: see SEX *noun*.
▶**B** *noun*. **I 1** The second person or thing of a category, series, etc., identified contextually, as day of the month, (following a proper name) person, esp. monarch or pope, of the specified name, base in baseball, etc. ME.
2 HERALDRY. The tincture mentioned second in a blazon. L16.

📖 **1** *Glasgow Herald* Brown squared with a 'birdie' 3 at the second. *Arizona Daily Star* Oakland quarterback Ken Stabler . . played the first quarter and part of the second.

▶ **II 3** *gen.* A person who or thing which is second; another person or thing in addition to the one already mentioned etc. **M16.**

4 *MUSIC.* **a** An interval spanning two consecutive notes in the diatonic scale; a note separated from another by this interval; a chord including two notes a second apart. **L16.** ▸**b** The next to the highest part in a duet, trio, etc. **L18.**

5 In *pl.* Goods of a quality second and inferior to the best; (bread made from) coarse flour. **L16.**

6 A subdivision of a measure or dimension which is itself a subdivision in the same ratio of a greater measure or dimension, as a twelfth of an inch (which is a twelfth of a foot). Cf. SECOND *noun*¹, THIRD *noun* 3. *obsolete* exc. *Hist.* **E17.**

7 A person who is second in command. **E17.**

8 In *pl.* ▸**a** A second helping of food at a meal. *colloq.* **L18.** ▸**b** The second or sweet course of a meal. *colloq.* **M20.**

9 (A person having) a place in the second class of an examination; (a competitor gaining) second place in a race etc. **M19.**

10 The second gear on a motor vehicle or bicycle. **E20.**

11 *MOUNTAINEERING.* The second climber of a team, who follows the leader. **E20.**

📖 **3** J. ERSKINE By seconds in blood, are meant first cousins. R. LOWELL A first tiger cat . . spies on a second. DAY LEWIS The second of my long line of heroes. **8a** A. CARTER Mignon . . helping herself to seconds of bread and milk. ***9 lower second, upper second.***

▶ **III 12** A person who or thing which helps or supports another. Now only *spec.*, a person acting as representative of a principal in a duel, carrying the challenge, arranging locality, and loading weapons, or acting as an attendant to a fighter in a boxing- or wrestling-match etc. **L16.**

▶ **C** *adverb.* **1** Secondly, in the second place; as the second in succession. **LME.**

2 *ellipt.* Travelling second class. **E20.**

■ **secondness** *noun* **L19.**

second /ˈsɛk(ə)nd/ *verb*¹ *trans.* **L16.**

[French *seconder* from Latin *secundare* favour, further, from *secundus* SECOND *adjective.*]

1 Support, back up, assist, encourage. **L16.** ▸**b** Accompany in song. Now *rare.* **L16.**

2 Further the effect of, reinforce, supplement. **L16.**

3 Support (a speaker, proposition, etc.) in a debate or conference; *spec.* formally support or endorse (a mover, candidate, or motion) as a necessary preliminary to further discussion or to the adoption of a motion. **L16.** ▸†**b** Concur with; confirm, corroborate. **L16–M18.**

†**4** Take the place of, substitute for, (a combatant). **L16–E17.**

†**5** Escort, attend, accompany. **E17–L18.**

†**6** Follow up or accompany with a second (different or identical) thing; repeat (an action, esp. a blow). **E17–M19.**

7 Act as second to in a fight or duel. **L19.**

8 *MOUNTAINEERING.* Follow (the leader of a climb) as second climber; be second climber on (a climb). **M20.**

📖 **1** W. STUBBS His efforts were seconded by a somewhat subservient parliament. **2** S. JOHNSON Seconding every fall of rain with a due proportion of sunshine. **3** EVELYN Mr. Seymour made a bold speech against many Elections . . but no one seconded him. E. LONGFORD Sir Edward Knatchbull seconded a motion by Sir Henry Carnell.

second /sɪˈkɒnd/ *verb*² *trans.* **E19.**

[from French *en second* in the second rank (of officers).]

Remove (an officer) temporarily from a regiment or corps, for employment on the staff, or in some other extra-regimental appointment; *gen.* transfer temporarily to another position or employment.

📖 *Listener* British and Indian Army officers seconded for attachment to Japanese military units. H. WILSON The Cabinet Office Unit consists of regular civil servants, mostly seconded from their own departments. A. PRICE A colonel . . seconded to special duty with . . the Ministry of Defence.

seconda donna /sɛˌkɒndə ˈdɒnə/ *noun phr.* Pl. **seconda donnas. L19.**

[Italian = second lady.]

The second-ranking female singer in an opera or opera company.

secondarily /ˈsɛk(ə)nd(ə)rɪli/ *adverb.* **LME.**

[from next + -LY².]

†**1** For the second time; as the second action, event, etc. **LME–E17.**

†**2** Secondly. **LME–M17.**

3 In the second order of importance, not first of all; subordinately. **LME.**

4 As a secondary consequence, indirectly; through an intermediate agency or train of events. **LME.**

secondary /ˈsɛk(ə)nd(ə)ri/ *adjective & noun.* **LME.**

[Latin *secundarius* of the second class or quality, from *secundus* SECOND *adjective*: see -ARY¹. Cf. Old & mod. French *secondaire.*]

▶ **A** *adjective.* **I** *gen.* **1** Not chief or principal; of minor or (*occas.*) second importance; subordinate. **LME.** ▸†**b** Second-best; of the second grade of quality. **LME–E17.** ▸**c** Subsidiary, auxiliary; used only in the second resort. **M18.**

2 Derived from, caused by, based on, or dependent on something else which is primary; not original, derivative. **LME.** ▸**b** Having only a delegated authority; acting under the direction of another, subordinate. **LME.**

3 Of or pertaining to a second period of time or a second stage; subsequent, not primitive. **L15.**

4 Of or pertaining to a second local position. **M18.**

📖 **1** W. J. SEDGEFIELD The vowel that was distinctly pronounced loses under the secondary stress its clear character. ANNE STEVENSON The . . marriage was viable because Aurelia accepted a secondary, wifely role. **c** K. W. GATLAND Instead of landing the entire space-ship, a secondary rocket will descend to the surface.

▶ **II** *spec.* **5** *MEDICINE.* Arising after or in consequence of an earlier symptom, infection, etc.; (esp. of a tumour) arising by metastasis. **E18.**

6 Chiefly *BOTANY.* Of or pertaining to the second order in a series of successive divisions or branchings. **L18.**

7 *BIOLOGY.* Designating sexual characteristics which are not essential to reproduction and typically develop on maturing (in humans, at puberty). **L18.**

8 Of, pertaining to, involved in, or designating education at the level next above primary or elementary education (in Britain usu. for pupils aged between 11 and 16 or 18). **E19.**

9 *GEOLOGY.* Of a second or later formation; *spec.* (**S-**) = MESOZOIC. **E19.**

10 *BIOLOGY.* Belonging to or directly derived from the second stage of development or growth. **M19.**

11 *ELECTRICITY.* **a** (Of current) induced, not supplied directly from a source; of, pertaining to, or carrying the output electrical power in a transformer etc. **M19.** ▸**b** Of a cell or battery: generating electricity by a reversible chemical reaction and therefore able to store applied electrical energy. **L19.**

12 *CHEMISTRY.* (Of an organic compound) having the characteristic functional group located on a saturated carbon atom which is itself bonded to two other carbon atoms; designating, involving, or characterized by such an atom. Also, (of an amide, amine, or ammonium compound) derived from ammonia by replacement of two hydrogen atoms by organic radicals. **M19.**

13 *GEOLOGY.* Of a mineral or rock: formed by the alteration or replacement of the original or primary constituents of a rock. **L19.**

Special collocations & phrases: ***Certificate of Secondary Education, General Certificate of Secondary Education***: see CERTIFICATE *noun* 2. **secondary articulation** *PHONETICS* an additional feature in the pronunciation of a consonant (besides the actual place of articulation), such as palatalization or lip-rounding. **secondary bow** = ***secondary rainbow*** below. **secondary burial** *ARCHAEOLOGY* (*a*) a burial of human remains in a site used for burial at an earlier time; (*b*) burial of human remains some time after death, after decay of the flesh. **secondary cause** a cause which is not the ultimate cause, a cause produced by a primary or first cause. **secondary colour** a colour resulting from the mixture of two primary colours. **secondary constriction** *BIOLOGY* a chromosomal constriction not associated with the centromere. ***secondary*** *COSMIC* ***radiation***. **secondary evidence** *LAW* evidence, esp. documentary evidence, of the existence of unavailable primary evidence. **secondary feather** any of the smaller flight-feathers of a bird's wing, growing from the ulna (forearm). **secondary hardening** *METALLURGY* a further hardening which occurs in some previously hardened steels when they are tempered. **secondary industry** industry that converts the raw materials provided by primary industry into commodities and products for the consumer; manufacturing industry. **secondary interment** *ARCHAEOLOGY* = ***secondary burial*** above. **secondary marriage** †(*a*) concubinage; (*b*) marriage to a secondary wife. **secondary modern** *ellipt.* a secondary modern school. **secondary modern school** *Hist.* a secondary school of a kind offering a general education to children not selected for grammar or technical schools. **secondary oocyte**: that is formed by division of a primary oocyte and gives rise in the second division of meiosis to a mature ovum and a polar body. **secondary picketing** (*a*) picketing of the premises of a firm doing business with an employer engaged in an industrial dispute but not otherwise directly involved; (*b*) picketing of a firm's premises by union members not employed there. ***secondary planet***: see PLANET *noun*¹. **secondary poverty** effective poverty due to waste, inefficiency, or some other drain on resources, rather than to insufficiency of means. **secondary quality** *PHILOSOPHY* (*a*) *Hist.* each of the qualities (hot, cold, wet, dry,) supposedly derived from the four primary qualities recognized by Aristotle; (*b*) a power of physical matter to cause sensations (as colour, smell, taste, etc.) in an observer (cf. ***primary quality*** s.v. PRIMARY *adjective*). ***secondary radar***: see RADAR 1. **secondary rainbow** an additional arch with the colours in the reverse order sometimes seen inside or outside a rainbow, and formed by twofold reflection and twofold refraction. **secondary recovery** the recovery of oil by special techniques from reservoirs which have been substantially depleted. **secondary reinforcement** *PSYCHOLOGY* (reinforcement involving) a stimulus which is not innately reinforcing, but has become so by association with a reinforcing stimulus. **secondary road** a road of a class lower than that of a main road, a minor road. **secondary sector** *ECONOMICS* the sector of the economy concerned with or relating to secondary industry. **secondary smoke** smoke inhaled involuntarily from tobacco being smoked by others. **secondary structure** *BIOCHEMISTRY* the local three-dimensional structure of sheets, helices, etc., assumed by a polynucleotide or polypeptide chain due to non-covalent bonds between neighbouring residues. **secondary succession** *ECOLOGY* a succession established after the disturbance of land previously colonized. ***secondary*** *SYPHILIS*. **secondary teacher** a teacher in a secondary school. **secondary thickening** *BOTANY* (in the stem or root of a woody plant) the increase in girth resulting from the formation of new woody tissue by the cambium. **secondary treatment**: of sewage effluent by biological methods following sedimentation. ***secondary umbel***: see UMBEL 1. **secondary wave** *SEISMOLOGY* an earthquake S wave. **secondary wife**: †(*a*) a woman cohabiting with a man without being his wife, a concubine; (*b*) in some polygamous societies, a wife who has a socially or legally recognized position but not the status or permanent guarantees of the principal wife.

▶ **B** *noun.* **1** A second-ranking official or dignitary; a person subordinate to another; a deputy. Now *rare.* **L16.**

2 A secondary thing, as a secondary quality, school, tumour, etc. **M17.**

3 A secondary planet, a natural satellite. **E18.**

4 *ORNITHOLOGY.* A secondary feather. Usu. in *pl.* **M18.**

5 *ELECTRICITY.* A secondary circuit, coil, etc.; *esp.* the output winding of a transformer. **M19.**

6 *PHYSICS & ASTRONOMY.* A secondary ray or particle, esp. a secondary cosmic ray. **E20.**

7 *GRAMMAR.* = ADJUNCT *noun* 3. **E20.**

8 *AMER. FOOTBALL.* *The* defensive backfield. **M20.**

■ **secondariness** *noun* **L17.**

second-best /sɛk(ə)ndˈbɛst/; *as adjective also* ˈsɛk(ə)ndbɛst/ *adjective, adverb, & noun.* Also **second best. LME.**

[from SECOND *adjective, adverb* + BEST *adjective, noun.*]

▶ **A** *adjective & adverb.* Next in quality to the first; (esp. *attrib.* & as *adverb*) inferior, worse. **LME.**

📖 SHAKES. I give unto my wife my second best bed. J. R. ACKERLEY He was second best, he knew . . that he never could be more to her than that. **come off second-best** be defeated in a contest.

▶ **B** *noun.* A thing inferior to the best; an inferior alternative; a second-best person or thing. **E18.**

📖 B. KOPS Don't settle for second best . . . Marry a girl who shares your interests. C. MACKENZIE Noyall was a second-best to nougat.

second class /sɛk(ə)n(d) ˈklɑːs/; *as adjective also* ˈsɛk(ə)n(d) klɑːs/ *noun phr., adjective, & adverb.* As adjective & adverb also **second-class. E19.**

[from SECOND *adjective* + CLASS *noun.*]

▶ **A** *noun phr.* The second of a ranked series of classes in which things are grouped; the second-best accommodation in a train, boat, aircraft, etc.; mail over which first-class mail is given preference; a compartment of a train etc. offering the second-best accommodation; (a person with) a place in the second highest division of an examination list. **E19.**

▶ **B** *adjective.* Belonging to, achieving, travelling by, etc., the class next to the first; of the second-best quality; inferior in status etc. **M19.**

📖 *Quarterly Review* Six second class cruisers . . have been converted into mine-layers. G. BLACK I drove . . into a second class road that became acutely third class. G. HAMMOND Put a second class stamp on it and it may *never* get there. **second-class citizen** a person deprived of normal civic and legal rights; a person treated socially as inferior.

▶ **C** *adverb.* By second-class accommodation in a train, boat, aircraft, etc.; by second-class mail. **M19.**

seconde /səˈkɔ̃d/ *noun.* **L17.**

[French: see SECOND *adjective.*]

FENCING. †**1** The half of a sword nearest the point. Only in **L17.**

2 The second of eight recognized parrying positions, used to protect the lower outside of the right of the body; a parry in this position. Cf. SACCOON. **E18.**

secondee /sɪkɒnˈdiː/ *noun.* **L20.**

[from SECOND *verb*² + -EE¹.]

A person seconded to a new unit, department, etc.

seconder /ˈsɛk(ə)ndə/ *noun.* **L16.**

[In sense 1 from SECOND *adjective*, in sense 2 from SECOND *verb*¹: see -ER¹.]

1 A person who comes second, a person in the second rank. Long *obsolete* exc. *local*, a second hand on a farm. **L16.**

2 A person who supports or seconds something or someone; *spec.* a person who seconds a motion, candidate, etc. **E17.**

second hand /sɛk(ə)nd ˈhand; *as adjective also* ˈsɛk(ə)ndhand/ *noun phr., adjective, & adverb.* As adjective & adverb also **second-hand**, (now) **secondhand. L15.**

[from SECOND *adjective* + HAND *noun.*]

▶ **A** *noun phr.* **1** ***at second hand***, †***at the second hand***, not directly from the first source; from other than the maker or original vendor (of goods) or the primary source (of information etc.); after previous use or wear by another. L15.

†2 The second person to handle something; an intermediary. M17–E18.

3 A second-hand item, as a book. *colloq.* E20.

▶ **B** *adjective.* **1** Not original, not obtained from the original source; plagiarized, borrowed; imitative, derivative. M17.

2 Not new, having been previously used or worn by another. Also (*attrib.*), dealing in second-hand goods. M17.

> 📖 **1** R. J. FARRER Secondhand impressions are as worthless as secondhand morality. **2** A. LURIE He wore a second-hand Army overcoat he had bought for two dollars. **3** *Country Life* A book very well worth looking out for in second-hand shops. A. WEST What rotten old secondhand stuff. R. RENDELL They ran a mail-order secondhand book business.

▶ **C** *adverb.* Not directly from the first source, at second hand. M19.

> 📖 *Which?* If you're buying secondhand, a diesel-engined version is likely to save you money.

■ **second-handed** *adjective* now *rare* = SECOND HAND *adjective* L17. **second-handedness** *noun* (now *rare*) = SECOND-HANDNESS E20. **second-hander** *noun* (*colloq.*) (*a*) a second-hand commodity; (*b*) a second-hand shop: L19. **second-handness** *noun* the quality or condition of being second hand L19. **second-handiness** *noun* (*rare*) SECOND-HANDNESS M19.

secondi *noun pl.* see SECONDO.

secondly /ˈsɛkəndli/ *adverb & noun.* LME.
[from SECOND *adjective* + -LY².]

▶ **A** *adverb.* †**1** For a second time. LME–M18.

2 As the second point in a topic, argument, etc.; in the second place. LME.

▶ **B** *noun.* A use of the word *secondly*. *rare.* M18.

secondment /sɪˈkɒn(d)m(ə)nt/ *noun.* L19.
[from SECOND *verb*² + -MENT.]

The action of SECOND *verb*²; an instance of this; (a period of) temporary transfer to another position or employment.

> 📖 *Milton Keynes Express* An experienced teacher required . . to cover the secondment of the permanent teacher.

secondo /sɪˈkɒndəʊ/ *noun.* Pl. **-di** /-di/, **-dos.** L18.
[Italian = second.]

MUSIC. The second or lower part in a piano or harpsichord duet; the performer who plays this part.

second-rate /sɛk(ə)n(d)ˈreɪt; *as adjective also* ˈsɛk(ə)n(d)reɪt/ *noun & adjective.* Also (usual form in sense A.1) **second rate.** M17.
[from SECOND *adjective* + RATE *noun*¹.]

▶ **A** *noun.* **1** *Hist.* The second of the rates or classes by which warships were distinguished according to the number of guns they carried. M17.

2 *Hist.* A warship of the second rate. L17.

3 A person or thing of inferior class. Now *rare.* L18.

▶ **B** *adjective.* **1** *Hist.* Of a warship: of the second rate. M17.

2 Of the second class in terms of quality or excellence; not first-rate, of only moderate quality; inferior in quality. M18.

> 📖 **2** O. WILDE The play was second-rate and provincial. A. THIRKELL Not very good books . . but good of a second-rate kind. E. WILSON Greek literature is the real thing and Latin a second-rate imitation. N. BAWDEN 'Luke couldn't make that sort of high grade. He was born second rate.'

■ **second-rateness** *noun* M19. **second-rater** *noun* a second-rate person or thing E19.

secrecy /ˈsiːkrɪsi/ *noun.* LME.
[from SECRET *adjective* + -TY¹ or -Y³, prob. after *private, privacy.*]

1 The quality of being secret or of not revealing secrets; the action, ability, or habit of keeping things secret. LME.

2 A secret; the secret nature or condition of something; in *pl.*, secret matters, mysteries. *arch.* LME.

3 The state or fact of being secret or concealed. M16. ▶†**b** Privacy, seclusion. E–M17.

†**4** The condition of being taken into a person's confidence; intimate acquaintance. L16–L17.

> 📖 **1** F. BURNEY I have Intreated Mrs Selwyn to observe the strictest secrecy. **sworn to secrecy** having promised to keep a secret. **3** LD MACAULAY In spite of all injunctions of secrecy, the news . . had spread fast. **in secrecy** secretly.

secret /ˈsiːkrɪt/ *adjective & noun.* LME.
[Old & mod. French from Latin *secretus* separate, set apart (neut. *secretum* used as noun, a secret), orig. pa. pple of *secernere* SECERN.]

▶ **A** *adjective.* **1** Kept from general knowledge; kept hidden or private from all or all but a few. LME. ▶†**b** Abstruse; beyond unaided human apprehension or intelligence; concerned with mystical or occult matters. L15–L18. ▶**c** Of a place: remote, lonely, secluded; affording privacy or seclusion. Formerly also, (of a person etc.) alone, unobserved. E16. ▶**d** Of a doctrine, ceremony, etc.: kept from the knowledge of the uninitiated. E16. ▶**e** Of a feeling, desire, thought, etc.: not openly admitted to; concealed, disguised. Also, inward, inmost. E16. ▶**f** Of an action, an agreement, negotiations, etc.: carried out or entered into in a clandestine or covert manner. M16. ▶**g** Hidden from sight, unseen; *spec.* (of a door, drawer, passage, etc.) designed to escape observation or detection. M16. ▶**h** Of a person: having a role or position unknown to others. E17. ▶**i** Of a committee, legislative body, etc.: conducted in private; keeping its deliberations unknown to the public. Freq. in ***secret session***. M17.

2 Of a person: fond of preserving secrecy; able to avoid indiscreet disclosures. Formerly also, reserved; reticent in behaviour. LME.

†**3** Of a person: having the position of a confidant; intimate *with*. LME–M17.

> 📖 **1** M. M. KAYE The engagement was . . to be kept secret but . . it leaked out. **b** SHAKES. *Macb.* How now, you secret, black, and midnight hags! **c** A. SILLITOE Glowing light . . made the . . room a secret cave. **e** T. CAPOTE Confessing the true and secret motive. **f** S. LEWIS The secret buying of real-estate options. **g** SHELLEY The men . . drew forth their secret steel, and stabbed each ardent youth. **h** SWIFT Others, who were my secret Enemies. **2** C. G. LELAND It was in the hands of . . persons . . who were all absolutely secret and trustworthy.

Special collocations: **secret agent** a person operating covertly or engaged on secret service; a spy. **secret ballot**: in which votes are cast in secret. **secret dovetail** a joint in which dovetails are used but are not visible on the face of either member. **secret life** a person's private life, *esp.* one involving illicit or covert sexual liaisons. **secret list** a register of research work or developments on sensitive military projects, the details of which may not be disclosed for reasons of national security. †**secret members**, **secret parts** the external sexual organs. **secret police** a police force operating in secret within a society or country for political purposes. **secret service** clandestine or covert work carried out on behalf of a government, and paid for from public funds; a government department or organization concerned with national security and espionage. **secret society** an organization formed to promote some cause by covert methods and whose members are sworn to secrecy about its existence and proceedings. **secret weapon** a weapon, often with decisive capabilities, classified as secret; *fig.* a decisive or powerful person or thing kept in reserve until needed. ***top secret***: see TOP *adjective.*

▶ **B** *noun.* **1** A thing that is unknown or is known only to the initiated or by divine revelation; a mystery; in *pl.*, the hidden workings of God, nature, etc. LME.

2 *ROMAN CATHOLIC CHURCH.* A prayer or prayers said by the minister in a low voice as part of the liturgy after the offertory and before the preface. Cf. SECRETA *noun*¹. LME.

3 A fact, matter, action, etc., which is kept private or is shared only with those concerned; something that cannot be disclosed without a breach of confidence or violation of security. LME.

4 a A method of achieving something which is effective but not generally known; an underlying explanation, reason, etc., for something surprising or extraordinary which is not immediately apparent. LME. ▶†**b** An infallible prescription, a specific remedy. M16–E19.

†**5** A hiding place; a secret place; a place of retreat. M16–M17.

†**6** In *pl.* & (occas.) *sing.* = ***secret parts*** above. M16–M18.

7 *Hist.* A coat of mail concealed under a person's ordinary clothes. M16.

> 📖 **1** J. RUSKIN Those who . . tried to penetrate the secrets of life. **3** D. EDEN She was not so sure that she would divulge her secret even to him. *Japan Times* Its actual effect has been classified as a military secret. **4a** *Listener* The secret of a good bread pudding is adding enough spices.

Phrases: **be in the secret**, **be in on the secret** be one of those to whom something confidential is known or disclosed. **in secret** in private, secretly. **keep a secret** not reveal something told one in confidence. **let a person into the secret** make a person aware of something secret. **make a secret of** conceal, keep to oneself. ***official secrets***: see OFFICIAL *adjective* 4. †**of secret** (*rare*, Shakes.) of a secret character. **open secret** a thing which is ostensibly private or confidential, but which is generally known or requires little effort to discover. ***secret as the grave***: see GRAVE *noun*¹. **the secrets of the heart** the soul's inmost wishes, known only to God.

■ **secretly** *adverb* LME.

†**secret** *verb trans.* L16–M18.
[from the noun Cf. SECRETE *verb*².]

Keep secret, conceal, hide.

secreta /sɪˈkriːtə/ *noun*¹. Pl. ***-tae*** /-tiː/. M18.
[ecclesiastical Latin, use as noun (sc. *oratio* gloss) of fem. of Latin *secretus*: see SECRET *adjective & noun.*]

= SECRET *noun* 2.

secreta /sɪˈkriːtə/ *noun*² *pl. rare.* L19.
[Latin, neut. pl. of pa. pple of *secernere* SECRETE *verb*¹.]

Secreted matter; products of secretion.

secreta *noun*³ pl. of SECRETUM.

secretae *noun* pl. of SECRETA *noun*¹.

secretagogue /sɪˈkriːtəgɒg/ *noun & adjective.* E20.
[from SECRETE *verb*¹ + Greek *agōgos* leading, eliciting.]

PHYSIOLOGY. ▶**A** *noun.* A substance which promotes secretion. E20.

▶ **B** *adjective.* Promoting secretion. E20.

secretaire /sɛkrɪˈtɛː/ *noun.* L18.
[French *secrétaire* formed as SECRETARY *noun.*]

A writing-desk with drawers and pigeon-holes; a bureau.

secretarial /sɛkrəˈtɛːrɪəl/ *adjective.* E19.
[from SECRETARY *noun* + -AL¹.]

1 Of or pertaining to a secretary or secretaries. E19.

2 = SECRETARY *adjective. rare.* M19.

> 📖 M. MAGUIRE She'd left secretarial college bubbling with big job enthusiasm.

†**secretarian** *adjective. rare.* M18–M19.
[formed as SECRETARY *noun* + -AN.]

Secretarial.

secretariat /sɛkrəˈtɛːrɪət/ *noun.* Also **S-.** E19.
[French *secrétariat* from medieval Latin *secretariatus*, formed as SECRETARY *noun*: see -ATE¹.]

The official position of secretary; the place where a secretary works, preserves records, etc. Also, the administrative and executive department of a government or similar organization; such a department's staff or premises.

> 📖 *Political Quarterly* Turnover has been substantial . . but less sweeping than . . in the Secretariat.

secretary /ˈsɛkrɪt(ə)ri/ *noun & adjective.* LME.
[Late Latin *secretarius* confidential officer, use as noun of adjective, from Latin *secretum* SECRET *noun*: see -ARY¹.]

▶ **A** *noun.* †**1** A person entrusted with private or secret matters; a confidant; a person privy *to* a secret. LME–E19.

2 A person whose duty or occupation it is to conduct the correspondence or organize the affairs of another; *spec.* (*a*) a person employed by an individual or a business to assist with correspondence, keep records, make appointments, etc.; (*b*) an official appointed by a society, company board, etc., to conduct its correspondence, keep its records, organize its affairs, etc.; in certain companies, the chief executive. (*c*) a civil servant employed as the principal assistant to a government minister, ambassador, etc. LME.

3 (Freq. **S-.**) In full ***Secretary of State***. A government minister in charge of a particular department of state. Freq. with specifying word, as ***Home Secretary***, ***Foreign Secretary***, etc. LME.

4 *TYPOGRAPHY. ellipt.* Secretary script; secretary type. L16.

5 = ***secretary bird*** (a) below. L18.

6 A writing-desk, a secretaire. Now chiefly *US.* E19.

> 📖 **1** T. LODGE Reueale it she durst not, as daring . . to make none her secretarie. **2** R. MACAULAY I should like a secretary, who would open all my letters and answer them.

Phrases & comb.: **First Secretary** a senior civil servant; a principal Secretary of State, *esp.* the Home Secretary. ***Home Secretary***: see HOME *adjective.* ***honorary secretary***: see HONORARY *adjective.* ***Military Secretary***: see MILITARY *adjective.* ***Patronage Secretary***: see PATRONAGE *noun.* ***Permanent Secretary***, ***Permanent Under-Secretary***: see PERMANENT *adjective.* **private secretary** (*a*) a secretary employed by a minister of state etc. to deal with his or her official correspondence (***Parliamentary Private Secretary***: see PARLIAMENTARY *adjective*); (*b*) a secretary employed by a particular person or working for a particular member of staff in an organization. **Second Secretary** a senior civil servant in the Treasury immediately subordinate to the Permanent Secretary. **secretary bird** (*a*) a long-legged snake-eating African bird, *Sagittarius serpentarius*, having a crest likened to quill pens stuck behind a writer's ear; (*b*) *slang* a young woman employed as a secretary. **Secretary-General** the principal administrator of an organization (as the United Nations). **Secretary of State** (*a*) see sense 3 above; (*b*) *US* the chief government official responsible for foreign affairs. ***Secretary of the Treasury***: see TREASURY 4. ***social secretary***: see SOCIAL *adjective.* **Third Secretary** a senior civil servant in the Treasury immediately subordinate to the Second Secretary.

▶ **B** *adjective. TYPOGRAPHY.* Designating a cursive gothic script used chiefly in legal documents from the 15th to the 17th cents.; designating a kind of black-letter type resembling this. LME.

> 📖 *Library* An italic exhibiting a few secretary features.

■ **secretaryship** *noun* †(*a*) the duties of a secretary; (*b*) the function or office of a secretary: M16.

secretary /ˈsɛkrɪt(ə)ri/ *verb.* E20.
[from the noun.]

1 *verb trans.* Assist (a person) in a secretarial capacity. *rare.* E20.

2 *verb intrans.* Work as a secretary, esp. an office secretary. *colloq.* E20.

secret de Polichinelle /səkrɛ də pɔliʃinɛl/ *noun phr.* M19.
[French = Punchinello's secret: see PUNCHINELLO.]

An apparent secret which is generally known; an open secret.

secrete /sɪˈkriːt/ *verb*[1]. E18.
[Latin *secret-* pa. ppl stem of *secernere* SECERN, partly as back-form. from SECRETION.]
BIOLOGY. **1** *verb trans.* Produce (a substance) by means of secretion. M19.
2 *verb intrans.* Perform the act of secretion. L19.

📖 **1** *Scientific American* The pituitary secretes several complex hormones. R. D. BARNES The underlying epidermis, called the mantle . . , secretes the animals' shell.

secrete /sɪˈkriːt/ *verb*[2] *trans.* M18.
[Alt. after Latin *secretus* SECRET *adjective* of SECRET *verb*.]
1 Conceal or hide (a person or thing, oneself) from view. M18.
2 Remove or transport (a person or thing) secretly, appropriate (goods etc.) secretly. M18.

📖 **1** W. STYRON She had secreted the . . figs in the . . hem of her striped smock. **2** *Private Eye* He wanted to be secreted out of Saudi.

secretin /sɪˈkriːtɪn/ *noun*. E20.
[from SECRETION + -IN[1].]
PHYSIOLOGY. A hormone released into the bloodstream by the duodenum, esp. in response to acidity, to stimulate secretion by the liver and pancreas.

secretion /sɪˈkriːʃ(ə)n/ *noun*. M17.
[French *sécrétion* or Latin *secretio(n-)* separation, from *secret-* pa. ppl stem of *secernere* SECERN: see -ION.]
1 BIOLOGY. The production and release of a specific substance by a cell, gland, or organ into a cavity or vessel or into the surrounding medium. M17.
2 A substance which is or has been secreted. E18.
3 GEOLOGY. The formation of a solid mass by gradual filling of a cavity. *rare*. L19.

📖 **2** *fig.*: POPE Poetry is a natural or morbid Secretion from the Brain.

▪ **secretional**, **secretionary** *adjectives* pertaining to secretion L19.

secretive /ˈsiːkrɪtɪv/ *adjective*. LME.
[In sense 1 from SECRET *adjective* + -IVE. In sense 2 back-form. from next.]
†**1** Secret, hidden. *rare*. Only in LME.
2 Reticent; inclined to secrecy; indicating secretiveness, enigmatic. M19.

📖 **2** ALEXANDER SMITH O'er his dark face . . flitted A secretive smile. K. CLARK So secretive that his friends . . knew nothing about his private life.

▪ **secretively** *adverb* M20.

secretiveness /ˈsiːkrɪtɪvnɪs/ *noun*. E19.
[Formed after French *secrétivité*, from *secret* SECRET *adjective & noun*: see -IVE, -NESS.]
The quality of being secretive; inclination to reticence or secrecy.

secretness /ˈsiːkrɪtnɪs/ *noun*. Now *rare*. LME.
[from SECRET *adjective* + -NESS.]
1 Secrecy; privacy; reticence. LME.
†**2** That which is secret. LME–E17.

secretor /sɪˈkriːtə/ *noun*. M20.
[from SECRETE *verb*[1] + -OR.]
BIOLOGY. A person who or thing which secretes; *spec.* a person who secretes appreciable amounts of blood-group antigens with his or her bodily fluids.

secretory /sɪˈkriːt(ə)ri/ *adjective & noun*. L17.
[formed as prec. + -ORY[1], -ORY[2].]
BIOLOGY. ▶**A** *adjective*. Having the function of secreting; pertaining to or concerned with the process of secretion. L17.
▶**B** *noun*. A secreting vessel or duct. *rare*. M18.

secretum /sɪˈkriːtəm/ *noun*. Pl. ***-ta*** /-tə/. M19.
[Latin = SECRET *noun*. In medieval Latin ellipt. for *sigillum secretum* privy seal.]
Hist. A small private or personal seal.

sect /sɛkt/ *noun*[1]. ME.
[Old & mod. French *secte* or Latin *secta* (used as cognate obj. in *sectam sequi* follow a certain course of conduct, follow a person's guidance) party faction, school of philosophy, from *sect-* pa. ppl stem of *sequi* follow. In sense 2d perh. later infl. by dial. or non-standard pronunc. of *sex*. Cf. SEPT *noun*[1].]
1 a A body of people subscribing to views divergent from those of others within the same religion; a party or faction in a religious body; *spec.* a religious faction or group regarded as heretical or as deviating from orthodox tradition. Formerly also, a system of belief subscribed to by any of the parties or factions into which a religion may be divided; *spec.* a system differing from orthodox tradition, a heresy. ME. ▶†**b** Any of the main religions of the world, as Christianity, Judaism, or Islam; the principles, or the adherents collectively, of any one of these faiths. LME–E18. ▶**c** A separately organized group, existing within a larger religious body, but with its own places of worship; a religious denomination. Also (freq. *derog.*), a body separated from an established Church; a nonconformist Church. L16.
2 †**a** A class or category of people. LME–E17. ▶†**b** A religious order. LME–E19. ▶†**c** The human race. *rare*. LME–L16. ▶**d** Sex. *obsolete* exc. *dial. & non-standard*. LME.
†**3** *gen.* A body of followers or adherents. LME–M17.
4 The system or body of adherents of a particular school of philosophy. LME.
5 *transf.* Orig. (*rare*), way of thinking, frame of mind. Later, a school of thought in politics, science, etc.; (freq. *joc.* or *derog.*) a group of people characterized by an unorthodox or peculiar belief or preference, esp. with regard to social customs etc. L16.

📖 **1a** O. CROMWELL They wyll not discent from the Lutheran sekt. ***the Clapham Sect***: see CLAPHAM 1. **c** R. NIEBUHR Christian sects, such as the Quakers and other small religious communities. **2a** R. GRAFTON Encrease . . the sect and swarme of theues and murderers. **d** H. MAYHEW A lady don't mind taking her bonnet off . . before one of her own sect. **4** L. DURRELL The Cabal was a harmless sect devoted to Hermetic philosophy. ***Ionic sect of philosophy***: see IONIC *adjective* 3. **5** J. REED The Bolsheviki, then a small political sect.

▪ **sectism** *noun* adherence to a sect; sectarian spirit: M19. **sectist** *noun & adjective* (*a*) *noun* (now *rare* or *obsolete*) an adherent or follower of a particular sect; (*b*) *adjective* of or pertaining to a particular sect: E17.

sect /sɛkt/ *noun*[2]. *poet. rare*. E17.
[from Latin *sectum* neut. pa. pple of *secare*: see next.]
A cutting from a plant. Chiefly *fig.*

sect /sɛkt/ *verb trans.* Long *rare*. M17.
[from Latin *sect-*: see -SECT.]
Cut or divide, esp. into equal parts.

sect. *abbreviation*.
Section.

-sect /sɛkt/ *suffix*.
[Latin *sect-* pa. ppl stem of *secare* cut. Cf. prec.]
Forming verbs with the sense 'cut or divide, esp. into a specified number of parts', as ***hemisect***, ***transect***, ***trisect***, etc., and adjectives, chiefly BOTANY, with the sense 'deeply divided in a specified way', as ***palmatisect***, ***pennatisect***.

sectarial /sɛkˈtɛːrɪəl/ *adjective*. E19.
[from SECTARY + -AL[1].]
Pertaining to or characteristic of a sect.

sectarian /sɛkˈtɛːrɪən/ *adjective & noun*. M17.
[Partly from SECTARY + -AN, partly from SECT *noun*[1]: see -ARIAN.]
▶**A** *adjective*. **1** Pertaining to a sectary or sectaries; belonging to a sect regarded as schismatical by a more established or orthodox religious group; *spec.* of or pertaining to the Independents or their party as designated by the Presbyterians during the Commonwealth period. *obsolete* exc. *Hist.* M17.
2 Pertaining to a sect or sects; confined to a particular sect; bigotedly or narrow-mindedly adhering to a particular sect. L18.

📖 **1** H. MOORE To arm the Sectarian Rabbles . . against the orderly Reformed Churches. **2** Y. MENUHIN Not a sectarian venture but an international school.

▶**B** *noun*. **1** Orig., an adherent of the sectarian party during the Commonwealth period. Later, a member of a schismatic sect, a schismatic. Now chiefly *Hist.* M17.
2 An adherent or member of a sect; *rare* a disciple or follower of a particular teacher. E19.
3 A bigoted adherent of a sect; a person with narrow sectarian views or sympathies. E19.

📖 **1** J. L. MOTLEY The Queen . . hated Anabaptists . . and other Sectarians. **3** *Times Lit. Suppl.* McTaggart knew his Hegel as some sectarians know their Bible.

▪ **sectarianism** *noun* adherence to a particular sect or party, esp. in a bigoted or narrow-minded manner M17. **sectarianize** *verb* (*a*) *verb intrans.* act in a sectarian manner; (*b*) *verb trans.* make sectarian; imbue with sectarian tendencies or principles: M19.

sectary /ˈsɛktəri/ *noun & adjective*. M16.
[French *sectaire*, or mod. Latin use in sense 'schismatic' of medieval Latin *sectarius* adherent, partisan from Latin *secta*: see SECT *noun*[1], -ARY[1].]
▶**A** *noun*. **1** A member of a sect; a person who is zealous in the cause of a sect. M16.
2 An adherent of a schismatical or heretical sect. Now chiefly *Hist.* M16.
3 A follower or disciple of a particular leader, school, teacher, etc. Now *rare* or *obsolete* exc. as passing into sense 1. L16.
†**4** A sect. *rare*. M17–M18.

📖 **3** G. HARVEY Fortune hath more sectaries, then Vertue.

▶†**B** *adjective*. Of or pertaining to a sect; sectarian. L16–L18.
▪ **sectarism** *noun* (now *rare*) (*a*) sectarianism; (*b*) a sectarian group or body: M17. †**sectarist** *noun* = SECTARY *noun* 1 E17–M19.

sectator /sɛkˈteɪtə/ *noun*. Now *rare*. M16.
[Latin = follower, from *sectat-* pa. ppl stem of *sectari* frequentative of *sequi* follow: see -ATOR.]
= SECTARY *noun* 3.

sectile /ˈsɛktɪl, -ʌɪl/ *adjective*. E18.
[Latin *sectilis*, from *sect-*: see next. -ILE.]
†**1** ***sectile leek*** [Latin *porrum sectile*], a dwarf or stunted variety of the leek, *Allium porrum*. *rare*. Only in E18.
2 MINERALOGY. Able to be cut by a knife. E19.
▪ **sectility** /sɛkˈtɪlɪti/ *noun* M19.

section /ˈsɛkʃ(ə)n/ *noun*. LME.
[French, or Latin *sectio(n-)*, from *sect-* pa. ppl stem of *secare* cut: see -ION.]
1 *gen.* A part separated or cut off from something; each of the portions into which a thing is cut or divided. LME. ▶**b** A subdivision of a book, newspaper, statute, document, etc. L16. ▶**c** TAXONOMY. A subdivision of a classificatory group, esp. (BOTANY) of a large genus or subgenus. E18. ▶**d** An area of land, a district; *spec.* (*a*) *N. Amer.* an area of one square mile, esp. of undeveloped or agricultural land; (*b*) (chiefly *US*) a district of a town etc. exhibiting particular characteristics and regarded as a discrete or distinct area; (*c*) *Austral. & NZ* an area of undeveloped land; a plot of land suitable for building on; (*d*) in various African countries, an administrative district usu. comprising a town and a number of villages. L18. ▶**e** A distinct subdivision or group forming a separate part of a larger body of people and often characterized by shared political opinions or common aims and interests. M19. ▶**f** MILITARY. Orig., a fourth part of a company or platoon. Now, any of various small tactical fighting units. M19. ▶**g** A portion of a sleeping-car containing two berths. *US*. M19. ▶**h** The smallest administrative subdivision of a railway, usu. a mile or two in length. *US*. L19. ▶**i** Any of a number of component parts of something which can be dismantled or reassembled as required. L19. ▶**j** GEOLOGY. A subdivision of a stratigraphical system. Now *rare* or *obsolete*. L19. ▶**k** Each of two or more trains running on the same schedule and route with a specified interval of time between them. *US*. L19. ▶**l** MUSIC. A group of similar instruments forming part of a band or orchestra; the players of such instruments. L19. ▶**m** A metal bar, *esp.* one with a cross-section that is not simply round, square, or flat. L19. ▶**n** A fare stage on a bus or tram route. *Austral. & NZ*. M20.
2 MATH. †**a** Intersection. LME–M19. ▶†**b** A segment of a circle. L16–E18. ▶**c** The curve of intersection of two surfaces. E18. ▶**d** The cutting of a solid by a plane; (the area of) a plane figure resulting from such a cutting; the figure which would be produced by cutting through a material object in a certain plane. E18. ▶**e** The dividing of a line into parts. E19.
3 The action or an act of cutting or dividing. Now *rare* exc. with ref. to surgery and anatomy. M16. ▶†**b** PROSODY. A caesura. L16–L17. ▶**c** = ***Caesarean section*** s.v. CAESAREAN *adjective* 1. *colloq.* M20.
4 a A representation of an object, as a building, a piece of machinery, the body, etc., as it would appear if cut across along a vertical or horizontal plane. Freq. in ***in section***. M17. ▶**b** GEOLOGY. (An exposed surface showing) the succession of strata in a particular location. M19.
5 TYPOGRAPHY. The sign §, orig. used to introduce the number of a section of a book, document, etc., and now used also as a mark of reference to notes in the margin or at the foot of a page. Also ***section-mark***. E18.
6 A very thin slice of tissue, rock, etc., cut for microscopic examination; *esp.* = ***thin section*** s.v. THIN *adjective, adverb, & noun*. L19.

📖 **1** T. KENEALLY He picked up his axe and began to split the sections of box-tree. **b** A. BLEASDALE He is looking down at the racing section of *The Daily Mirror*. **f** C. RYAN I told one section to open fire and a second . . to rush the bridge. **i** D. PROFUMO Assembling the three sections of his shotgun. **l** *Jazz Journal International* He headed the saxophone section. ***brass section***, ***horn section***, ***string section***, etc. ***rhythm section***: see RHYTHM *noun*. ***2d principal section***: see PRINCIPAL *adjective*. SAGITTAL ***section***. **e** ***golden section***: see GOLDEN *adjective*. **4a** A. GRAY The tunnel was . . circular in section. ***median section***, ***sagittal section***, etc. **6** D. ATTENBOROUGH Cellular structure is preserved so . . you can look at sections . . through the microscope.

Comb.: **Section Eight** *US Military slang* discharge from the army under section eight of army regulations on the grounds of insanity or inability to adjust to army life; **section-eight** *verb trans.* (*US Military slang*) discharge (a person) from the army on grounds of insanity or inability to adjust to army life; **section head** (*a*) the person in charge of a section of an organization; (*b*) the heading of a section in a newspaper or periodical; **section house** *US* a house occupied by the people responsible for maintaining a section of a railway; **section-line** (*a*) the boundary of a section of land (now *US*); (*b*) a line indicating the plane along which a section is (to be) made; ***section-mark***: see sense 5 above; **section sergeant** a police sergeant in charge of a section of a police division.

section /ˈsɛkʃ(ə)n/ *verb*. E19.
[from the noun.]
1 *verb trans.* **a** Divide or cut into sections. E19. ▶**b** Cut through so as to present a section. L19. ▶**c** Foll. by *off*: make (an area, part of a structure, etc.) into a separate section. M20.
2 *verb intrans.* Admit of being cut into sections. E20.

3 *verb trans.* Cause (a person) to be compulsorily committed to a psychiatric hospital in accordance with the relevant section of the Mental Health Act. **L20.**

> 🕮 **1a** C. MACLEOD She . . began to section the grapefruit. **b** *Times* The ramparts of the castle . . have been sectioned. **c** JAYNE PHILLIPS Some girls . . were . . sectioning off each little strand of hair. **3** *Daily Telegraph* A disturbed . . man sectioned under the Mental Health Act.

sectional /ˈsɛkʃ(ə)n(ə)l/ *adjective & noun.* **E19.**
[from SECTION *noun* + -AL[1].]

▶ **A** *adjective.* **1** Pertaining to a section or sections of a country, society, community, etc.; concerned with local or regional interests as opp. to general ones. **E19.**
2 Of or pertaining to a view of the structure of an object in section; of or pertaining to such a section. **E19.**
3 Assembled from or made up of several sections or components. **L19.**
4 Of steel: rolled in the form of sections. **L19.**

> 🕮 **1** H. WILSON Individuals . . destroyed that majority for sectional motives. **2** *Electrician* We are enabled to reproduce photographs and sectional drawings of the . . generator. **3** E. LEONARD A study with a white sectional sofa you could make a square bed out of.

▶ **B** *noun.* A piece of furniture composed of sections which can be used separately, *esp.* one which can be used either as a sofa or as a set of chairs. *N. Amer.* **M20.**
■ **sectionally** *adverb* **M19.**

sectionalise *verb* var. of SECTIONALIZE.

sectionalism /ˈsɛkʃ(ə)n(ə)lɪz(ə)m/ *noun.* **M19.**
[formed as prec. + -ISM.]
Restriction of interest to a narrow sphere, narrowness of outlook; undue concern with local interests or petty distinctions at the expense of general well-being.

> 🕮 P. ZIEGLER Our object should be to break down racial sectionalism.

■ **sectionalist** *noun* an advocate or practitioner of sectionalism **M19.**

sectionalize /ˈsɛkʃ(ə)n(ə)lʌɪz/ *verb trans.* Also **-ise**. **M19.**
[from SECTIONAL *adjective* + -IZE.]
1 Divide into sections. Chiefly as ***sectionalized*** *ppl adjective.* **M19.**
2 Make sectional. **L19.**

> 🕮 **1** *Gramophone* Seen from the . . sectionalized photo . . there are two magnetic gaps. **2** *Nature* Vested interests which will sectionalize its proceedings.

■ **sectionaliˈzation** *noun* **E20.**

sectionary /ˈsɛkʃ(ə)n(ə)ri/ *adjective & noun.* **M18.**
[from SECTION *noun* + -ARY[1].]
▶†**A** *adjective.* **1** Of or pertaining to the sections of a book. *rare.* Only in **M18.**
2 Of or pertaining to a section of a party, country, etc. *rare.* **E–M19.**
▶ **B** *noun.* A member of a section of a party etc.; a partisan. **M19.**

sectionise *verb* var. of SECTIONIZE.

sectionist /ˈsɛkʃ(ə)nɪst/ *noun. rare.* **M19.**
[from SECTION *noun* + -IST.]
†**1** The owner or occupier of a section of undeveloped land. *NZ.* Only in **M19.**
2 A member of a section of a party etc., a partisan. **L19.**

sectionize /ˈsɛkʃ(ə)nʌɪz/ *verb trans.* Also **-ise**. **E19.**
[from SECTION *noun* + -IZE.]
1 Divide into sections or parts. **E19.**
2 Delineate in section. **L19.**
3 Cut sections or thin slices from. **L19.**

†**sective** *adjective. rare.* **M17–M18.**
[Late Latin *sectivus*, from Latin *secare* cut: see -IVE.]
Able to be divided or cut.

sector /ˈsɛktə/ *noun & verb.* **L16.**
[Late Latin techn. use of Latin *sector* cutter, from *sect-*: see SECTION *noun*, -OR.]
▶ **A** *noun.* **1 a** GEOMETRY. A plane figure contained by two radii and an arc of a circle, ellipse, or other curve which they intercept. **L16.** ▸**b** A mathematical instrument consisting of two flat rules hinged together, sometimes attached to a graduated arc, and inscribed with various kinds of scales. **L16.** ▸**c** ASTRONOMY. A telescope turning about the centre of a graduated arc, used to measure large angular distances. **E18.**
2 *gen.* A body, figure, part of a mechanism, etc., having the shape of a geometrical sector; a division, a part; a unit. **E18.** ▸**b** MILITARY. A part or subdivision of an area of military operations, controlled by one commander or headquarters. **E20.** ▸**c** A region or district of a larger geographical area. **M20.** ▸**d** A distinct part or branch of an economy; an area of industry or of economic activity. Freq. with specifying word. **M20.** ▸**e** A route or journey operated non-stop by a commercial airline, often as part of a longer flight schedule. **M20.** ▸**f** COMPUTING. A subdivision of a track on a magnetic drum or disc; the block of data stored on this. **M20.** ▸**g** GRAMMAR. The position in a sentence normally occupied by any one of the basic units into which the sentence may be divided for purposes of analysis. **M20.**

> 🕮 **2c** *Daily Telegraph* Daily oil consumption . . produced from the British sector of the sea. **d** *Media Week* Plans to launch Viva into the same sector of the Market.

Phrases: ***private sector***: see PRIVATE *adjective*. ***public sector***: see PUBLIC *adjective & noun*. **sector of a sphere** a solid generated by the rotation of a radius of a sphere so as to mark out a circle on its surface. ***warm sector***: see WARM *adjective*.
Comb.: **sector analysis** GRAMMAR the analysis of a sentence in terms of the positions occupied by the basic units of which it is composed; **sector-piece** a sector-shaped portion of an object; **sector scan** an instance of sector scanning; (***sector-scan mode***, a mode of operation involving sector scanning); **sector scanning** scanning with radar, sonar, etc., in which the detector rotates to and fro through a fixed angle.

▶ **B** *verb trans.* Divide into sectors; provide with sectors. **L19.**

sectoral /ˈsɛkt(ə)r(ə)l/ *adjective.* **L18.**
[from SECTOR *noun* + -AL[1].]
1 Of or pertaining to a geometrical sector. **L18.**
2 Of or pertaining to an economic or industrial sector. **M20.**
1 sectoral horn a horn antenna having a rectangular cross-section and plane sides flared in one dimension only.

sectored /ˈsɛktəd/ *adjective.* **E20.**
[from SECTOR *noun, verb*: see -ED[2], -ED[1].]
Divided into sectors; *spec.* (of a disc) divided into alternate black and white sectors of equal size.

sectorial /sɛkˈtɔːrɪəl/ *adjective*[1]. **E19.**
[from SECTOR *noun* + -AL[1].]
1 Of or pertaining to the geometrical instrument called a sector. Now *rare.* **E19.**
2 Of or pertaining to a sector of a circle or a sphere. **M19.**
3 BOTANY. Designating a chimera in which tissues of different species or varieties occupy separate sectors of the same stem. **E20.**
■ **sectorially** *adverb* in or into sectors **M20.**

sectorial /sɛkˈtɔːrɪəl/ *adjective*[2]. Now *rare.* **M19.**
[from mod. Latin *sectorius* (from Latin *sector* cutter) + -AL[1].]
Having the function of cutting; *spec.* designating a carnassial tooth.

sectorization /sɛktərʌɪˈzeɪʃ(ə)n/ *noun. rare.* Also **-isation**. **M20.**
[from SECTOR *noun* + -IZATION.]
Division into sectors; administration or operation on the basis of sectors or local divisions.

secular /ˈsɛkjʊlə/ *adjective & noun.* **ME.**
[In branch I from Old French *seculer* (mod. *séculier*) from Latin *saecularis*, from *saeculum* generation, age, in Christian Latin the world (esp. as opp. to the Church); in branch II immed. from Latin *saecularis*: see -AR[1].]
▶ **A** *adjective.* **I 1** ECCLESIASTICAL. Of (a member of) the clergy: not bound by a religious rule; not belonging to or living in seclusion with a monastic or other order. Also, of or pertaining to non-monastic clergy. Opp. ***regular***. **ME.**
2 a Belonging to the world and its affairs as distinguished from the Church and religion; civil, lay; non-religious, non-sacred. **ME.** ▸**b** Not concerned with religious subjects or devoted to the service of religion; *spec.* (***a***) (of a writer, artist, art form, etc.) not sacred; profane; (***b***) (of a school or education) excluding religious instruction; not promoting religious belief. **LME.** ▸†**c** *transf.* Of or belonging to the common or uneducated people. *rare.* **L16–E17.**
3 Caring for this world only (long *rare*); of or belonging to the present or material world as distinguished from the eternal or spiritual world; worldly. **LME.**
4 Pertaining or adhering to the doctrine of secularism; secularist. **M19.**

> 🕮 **1** E. A. FREEMAN A secular, but soon to become a monastic, house. J. K. GALBRAITH A respected secular priesthood . . to rise above questions of religious ethics. **secular abbot** *Hist.* a person not a monk, who had the title and part of the revenues but not the functions of an abbot. ***secular canon***: see CANON *noun*[2] 1. **2a** G. M. TREVELYAN English compromise between the modern secular state and the old religious world. **secular arm** the authority of the civil power as invoked by the Church to punish offenders. **b** C. H. PARRY Secular music had long displayed . . free use of chromaticisms. **3** G. PRIESTLAND A strong vein of secular scepticism. **secular humanism** (orig. & chiefly *US*) liberalism, esp. with regard to the belief that religion should not be taught or practised within a publicly funded education system. **4 secular society** any of a number of associations formed in various English towns from 1852 onwards to promote the spread of secularist opinions.

▶ **II** †**5** Existing in time. Chiefly in ***before the secular worlds***, before the beginning of time. Only in **LME.**
6 Occurring or celebrated once in an age, century, etc. Freq. in ***secular games***, ***secular plays*** below. **M16.**
7 Living or lasting for an age or ages. **E17.**
8 Of process of change: having a period of enormous length, esp. of more than a year or decade; *spec.* in ASTRONOMY, pertaining to or designating slow changes in the orbits or the periods of revolution of the sun or planets. **E19.**
9 ECONOMICS & STATISTICS. Of a fluctuation or trend: occurring or persisting over an indefinitely long period; not periodic or short-term, long-term. **L19.**

> 🕮 **6** GIBBON The philosopher . . might have celebrated his secular festival. **secular games**, **secular plays** in ancient Rome, games continuing three days and three nights and celebrated once in an age or period of 120 years. **7** QUILLER-COUCH A little wood of secular elms. **8 secular equation** any equation of the form $|a_{ij} - b_{ij}\lambda| = 0$ $(i, j = 1, 2, \ldots, n)$, in which the left-hand side is a determinant, now used esp. in quantum mechanics. **9** *Scientific American* The secular trend of workers migrating out of agricultural jobs.

▶ **B** *noun.* **1** ECCLESIASTICAL. A member of the secular clergy. **ME.**
2 A person who is engaged in the affairs of the world as distinct from the Church; a layman. **ME.**

> 🕮 **2** W. S. LANDOR Seculars do not know half the wickedness of the world . . until their pastors . . show it them.

■ **secularly** *adverb* (***a***) as a lay person; in accordance with secular procedure; (***b***) in a worldly or non-spiritual manner; (***c***) ASTRONOMY over a long period of time: **LME.** †**secularness** *noun* (*rare*) secularity, worldliness **M16–M18.**

secularisation *noun*, **secularise** *verb* vars. of SECULARIZATION, SECULARIZE *verb*.

secularism /ˈsɛkjʊlərɪz(ə)m/ *noun.* **M19.**
[from SECULAR *adjective* + -ISM.]
1 The view that religion and religious considerations should be deliberately omitted from temporal affairs; *spec.* (PHILOSOPHY) a system of thought based on the doctrine that morality should be determined solely with regard to the well-being of humankind in the present life, to the exclusion of all considerations drawn from belief in God or in a future existence. **M19.**
2 The view that education, esp. that which is publicly funded, should not promote religious belief or include religious instruction. **L19.**

secularist /ˈsɛkjʊlərɪst/ *noun & adjective.* **E18.**
[from SECULAR *adjective* + -IST.]
▶ **A** *noun.* **1** ECCLESIASTICAL. A member of the secular clergy; a secular. *rare.* **E18.**
2 An adherent or follower of secularism; *spec.* an advocate of purely secular education. **M19.**
▶ **B** *attrib.* or as *adjective.* Of, pertaining to, or characteristic of a secularist or secularism. **L19.**
■ **seculaˈristic** *adjective* = SECULARIST *adjective* **M19.**

secularity /sɛkjʊˈlarɪti/ *noun.* **LME.**
[French *sécularité* or medieval Latin *saecularitas*, from Latin *saecularis* SECULAR: see -ITY.]
†**1** Secular jurisdiction or power. **LME–M16.**
2 a Occupation with secular affairs, esp. on the part of the clergy; secular spirit or behaviour. Also, worldliness, absence of religious principle or feeling. **LME.** ▸**b** Secular or non-sacred character; absence of connection with religion. **L19.**
3 A secular matter; in *pl.*, secular affairs; worldly possessions or pursuits. **E16.**

> 🕮 **2a** ISAAC TAYLOR Pride and secularity have crept upon those to whom mankind . . look up for . . heavenly-mindedness. **3** C. KINGSLEY The morning he spent at the school, or in parish secularities.

secularization /ˌsɛkjʊlərʌɪˈzeɪʃ(ə)n/ *noun.* Also **-isation**. **E18.**
[from next + -ATION.]
1 The conversion of an ecclesiastical or religious institution or its property to civil possession and use; the conversion of an ecclesiastical state or sovereignty to a lay one; an instance of this. **E18.**
2 The giving of a secular or non-sacred character or direction to art, studies, etc.; the placing of morality on a secular basis; the restricting of education to secular subjects. **M19.**

> 🕮 **2** *American Sociological Review* The basic tenet of secularization is that . . material values are replacing the . . spiritual.

secularize /ˈsɛkjʊlərʌɪz/ *verb.* Also **-ise**. **E17.**
[French *séculariser*, from Latin *saecularis* SECULAR: see -IZE.]
1 *verb trans.* Convert from ecclesiastical to civil possession or use; *esp.* place (church property) at the disposal of the secular or civil power. **E17.** ▸**b** Laicize; deprive of clerical character, remove from clerical control. **M19.**
2 *verb trans.* Make (a member of a monastic or other religious order) secular. **L17.**
3 *verb trans.* Dissociate from religious or spiritual concerns, convert to material and temporal purposes; turn (a person etc.) from a religious or spiritual state to worldliness. **E18.**
4 *verb intrans.* Become secular; adopt secular habits. **M19.**

> 1 H. T. BUCKLE It was impious to secularize ecclesiastical property. 3 *Nature* The development of secularized and scientific university education.

■ **secularizer** *noun* L19.

secule /ˈsɛkjuːl/ *noun.* Now *rare.* E20.
[from Latin *saeculum* age.]
GEOLOGY. = MOMENT *noun* 2c.

secund /sɪˈkʌnd/ *adjective.* L18.
[Latin *secundus* SECOND *adjective.*]
BOTANY. Esp. of the flowers in an inflorescence: arranged on or directed towards one side only.
■ **secundly** *adverb* M19.

secundigravida /sɪˌkʌndɪˈɡravɪdə/ *noun.* Also **secunda-.** Pl. **-dae** /-diː/, **-das.** E20.
[mod. Latin, fem. adjective, from Latin *secundus* second + *gravidus* pregnant, after PRIMIGRAVIDA, SECUNDIPARA.]
MEDICINE & ZOOLOGY. A female pregnant for the second time. Cf. MULTIGRAVIDA, PRIMIGRAVIDA.

secundine /ˈsɛkʌndɪn/ *noun.* LME.
[Late Latin *secundinae* fem. pl. (Latin *secundae*), from Latin *secundus* following: see SECOND *adjective*, -INE[1].]
1 *MEDICINE. sing.* & in *pl.* = AFTERBIRTH. Now *rare* or *obsolete.* LME.
†**2** *ENTOMOLOGY.* The inner coat of a cocoon. *rare.* Only in L16.
3 *BOTANY.* The second of the two integuments of an ovule where two are present, orig., the inner one, now, the outer one (which is formed second). Cf. PRIMINE. L17.

secundipara /sɪkʌnˈdɪp(ə)rə/ *noun.* Pl. **-rae** /-riː/, **-ras.** L19.
[mod. Latin, fem. adjective, from Latin *secundus* SECOND *adjective* + *-parus*, from *parere* bring forth. Cf. SECUNDIGRAVIDA.]
MEDICINE & ZOOLOGY. A female giving birth for the second time; a female who has had two pregnancies resulting in viable offspring.

secundogeniture /sɪˌkʌndəʊˈdʒɛnɪtʃə/ *noun.* M19.
[from Latin *secundo* adverbial form of *secundus* SECOND *adjective*, after PRIMOGENITURE.]
The right of succession or inheritance belonging to a second son; property etc. so inherited.

secundum /sɪˈkʌndəm/ *adverb. arch.* M16.
[Latin.]
The Latin for 'according to', occurring in various phrases used in English.
secundum artem /ˈɑːtɛm/ (freq. *joc.*) [lit. 'according to art'] in accordance with the rules of the relevant art or discipline, esp. of medicine. ***secundum idem*** /ˈɪdɛm/ [lit. 'according to the same argument, calculation,' etc.] in the same manner or respect.

secundus /sɪˈkʌndəs/ *adjective.* E19.
[Latin = second.]
= MINOR *adjective* 1b. Cf. PRIMUS *adjective* 2, TERTIUS.

securance /sɪˈkjʊər(ə)ns/ *noun. rare.* M17.
[from SECURE *verb* + -ANCE.]
The action or means of securing something; assurance, security.

secure /sɪˈkjʊə/ *adjective & adverb.* M16.
[Latin *securus*, formed as SE- + *cura* care.]
▶ **A** *adjective.* **I** Feeling no care or apprehension.
1 Untroubled; free from care, apprehension, or anxiety; confident, assured. Also (*arch.*), overconfident, careless. M16. ▸**b** Of a time, place, action, etc.: in or during which a person is free from fear or anxiety. E17.
†**2 a** Free from doubt or distrust; feeling sure or certain. Usu. foll. by *of, that.* L16–L18. ▸**b** Confident in expectation; feeling certain of something in the future. Usu. foll. by *of, to do.* M17–M18.

> 1 LD MACAULAY They were secure where they ought to have been wary. **secure of** *poet.* free from. **b** SHAKES. *Haml.* Upon my secure hour thy uncle stole With juice of cursed hebona in a vial. **2a** W. GODWIN He was secure that his animosity would neither be forgotten nor diminished.

▶ **II** Certain; fully assured; safe.
3 a Protected from or not exposed to danger; justifiably free from anxiety or fear, safe. Freq. foll. by *against, from,* †*of.* L16. ▸**b** Of an action or state: without risk. E17. ▸**c** Of an argument, person, etc.: sound, trustworthy. E18. ▸**d** Fastened so as not to be displaced or to yield under strain; firmly fixed. M19. ▸**e** Of a telephone or telephone line: untapped, protected from being tapped. M20. ▸**f** Sufficiently loyal to be relied on; not a risk to security. M20.
4 *pred.* In safe custody; safely in one's possession or power. Now *rare* or *obsolete.* L16. ▸**b** Of (an area within) a penal or psychiatric institution: designed for the safe confinement of inmates. M20.
5 Of a place: affording protection or safety. E17.
6 Foll. by *of,* †*to do*: free from risk as to the continued or future possession of something; certain to gain or achieve something. M17.
7 That may be counted on to succeed; guaranteed to continue or to be attained. E18.

> **3a** *Spectator* England is rich because she has for . . many years been secure. M. DICKENS Virginia sat . . with Felix, secure in the knowledge that her mother could not join them. **b** B. JOWETT Inaction is secure only . . by the side of activity. **d** A. MACLEAN He laid both hands on one of the bars and tugged firmly. It remained secure. **6** S. HAYWARD The soul . . boldly ventures into eternity, secure of eternal life. **7** F. WELDON Her mid-thirties . . by which time her fame and fortune were secure.

▶ **B** *adverb.* In a carefree or untroubled manner; safely. Chiefly *poet.* L16.

> T. GRAY Against the stream the waves secure he trod.

■ **securely** *adverb* L16. **secureness** *noun* (*rare*) = SECURITY 1, 3 L16.

secure /sɪˈkjʊə/ *verb & noun.* L16.
[from SECURE *adjective.*]
▶ **A** *verb.* **1 a** *verb trans.* & (now *rare*) *refl.* Make or keep (a person, a person's life, oneself, etc.) secure or safe from danger or harm; guard, protect. Now usu. foll. by *from, against.* L16. ▸**b** *verb trans.* Make (a place) safe for transit; protect (a pass etc.) from enemy attack; take defensive measures for the safe execution of (a retreat etc.). E17. ▸**c** *verb intrans.* Guard or take precautions *against* danger etc. M17. ▸†**d** *verb trans.* Take precautions against, prevent, (a danger). Also, prevent (a person) *from* doing something unwise or dangerous. M17–M19.
†**2** *verb trans.* Make (a person) free from care, apprehension, or anxiety (foll. by *of* or *against* some contingency). Also, make (a person) careless or overconfident. *rare.* E–M17.
†**3 a** *verb trans.* & (*rare*) *refl.* Make (a person, oneself) certain *of* a present or future event, *of* an ally, *of* obtaining something, etc. E17–M18. ▸**b** *verb trans.* Assure (a person) *of* a fact. M17–M18.
4 *verb trans.* Make (something) certain or dependable. Now *esp.* ensure (a situation, outcome, result, etc.). M17. ▸**b** Make (a creditor) certain of receiving payment by means of a mortgage, bond, etc. *rare.* L17. ▸**c** Establish (a person) securely *in* a position, state of existence, etc. E18. ▸**d** Make the tenure of (a property, position, privilege, etc.) certain to pass *to* a person. M18. ▸**e** Guarantee (a loan etc.) by the possession of property or other realizable assets. Freq. foll. by *on.* Freq. as ***secured*** *ppl adjective.* E19.
5 *verb trans.* Seize and confine; keep or hold (a person) in custody. Now *rare.* M17.
6 *verb trans.* Fasten or fix firmly. M17. ▸**b** *SURGERY.* Close (a vein or artery) by ligature or otherwise, to prevent loss of blood. M17. ▸**c** *NAUTICAL.* Restore (equipment, engines, a vessel, or crew) to a normal state of readiness after action or drill. *US.* E20.
7 *verb trans.* Succeed in obtaining or achieving; gain possession of. M18.
8 *verb trans. HORTICULTURE.* Ensure the development and flowering of (the main bud of a plant) by removing all side shoots and other unwanted buds. E20.

> **1a** GIBBON He had secured his life by the resignation of the purple. I. WATTS Consult the dictionary . . and thus secure us from mistake. **secure arms** hold a rifle with the muzzle down and the lock under the armpit, so as to guard the weapon from rain. **b** STEELE You, and your Party, fall in to secure my Rear. **d** C. FIENNES Carry . . Carriages on sledges to secure their pitching in the streets. **2** S. PEPYS Holliard . . secures me against ever having the stone again. **4** V. WOOLF Fiction . . in vogue more often misses than secures the thing we seek. **d** SIR W. SCOTT To secure to his heirs a . . slice of his own death-bed . . expenses. **e** *Which?* The loan is secured on your only or main home. **6** B. HINES She secured the waistband with a safety pin. **7** E. WAUGH William and Corker had secured a room together at the Liberty. E. BOWEN Robert . . secured a handsome dowry with the bride.

▶ **B** *noun.* **1** The position in which a rifle is held when it is secured. E19.
2 *NAUTICAL.* A signal sounded on board a ship instructing crew members to stow equipment away, or informing them of release from drill, duty, etc. E20.
■ **securable** *adjective* M19. **securement** *noun* the action or an act of securing a thing or person E17. **securer** *noun* M17.

securiform /sɪˈkjʊərɪfɔːm/ *adjective.* M18.
[from Latin *securis* axe (from *secare* to cut) + -FORM.]
Chiefly *BOTANY & ENTOMOLOGY.* Having the form of an axe or hatchet.

securitize /sɪˈkjʊərɪtʌɪz/ *verb trans.* Also **-ise.** L20.
[from next + -IZE.]
COMMERCE. Convert (an asset, esp. a loan) into securities, usu. for the purpose of raising cash by selling them to other investors.

> *Banker* Assets will be growing more slowly . . as the bank securitizes more of its loans.

■ **securitiˈzation** *noun* L20.

security /sɪˈkjʊərɪti/ *noun.* LME.
[Old & mod. French *sécurité* or Latin *securitas*, formed as SECURE *adjective*: see -ITY.]
▶ **I 1** The condition of being protected from or not exposed to danger; safety; *spec.* the condition of being protected from espionage, attack, or theft. Also, the condition of being kept in safe custody. LME. ▸**b** The provision or exercise of measures to ensure such safety. Also (**S-**), a government department or other organization responsible for ensuring security. M20.
2 Freedom from care, anxiety, or apprehension; a feeling of safety or freedom from danger. Formerly also, overconfidence, carelessness. LME.
3 Freedom from doubt; confidence, assurance. Now chiefly *spec.*, well-founded confidence, certainty. L16.
4 The quality of being securely fixed or attached, stability. *rare.* M19.

> **1** GIBBON The emperor and his court enjoyed . . the security of the . . fortifications. H. T. LANE Before birth the child lay in complete security. **b** C. MCCULLOUGH Security was dealing with another suicide. B. CHATWIN For reasons of Soviet security the locks were unmarked on the map. **2** T. PARKS The mental security of knowing his address was an unassailable secret. **3** C. BRONTË They might count on her with security.

▶ **II 5** Property etc. deposited or pledged by or on behalf of a person as a guarantee of the fulfilment of an obligation (as an appearance in court or the payment of a debt) and liable to forfeit in the event of default. Freq. in ***enter security, enter into security, give security, give in security.*** Cf. SURETY *noun* 1. LME.
6 A thing which protects or makes safe a thing or person; a protection, a guard, a defence. Freq. foll. by *against, from.* L16.
7 A person who stands surety for another. L16.
8 Grounds for regarding something as secure, safe, or certain; an assurance, a guarantee. E17.
9 A document held by a creditor as guarantee of his or her right to payment; a certificate attesting ownership of stock, shares, etc.; the financial asset represented by such a document. Also (*US*), such a document issued to investors to finance a business venture. Usu. in *pl.* L17.
†**10** A means of securing or fixing something in position. L18–M19.

> **5** S. PEPYS Summoned . . to give in security for his good behaviour. *What Mortgage* Your home and . . insurance policy act as security on the loan. **6** H. MARTINEAU A good fire . . was always a perfect security against . . wild beasts. **7** BURKE Croftes offered . . Johnson as one of his securities for the . . contract. **8** LD MACAULAY Goldsmith's character was . . a perfect security that he would never commit . . villany. **9** *Which?* Gilt-edged securities . . pay a fixed amount of income.

Phrases: ***collateral security***: see COLLATERAL *adjective.* **on security of** using as a guarantee. ***senior security***: see SENIOR *adjective.* ***social security***: see SOCIAL *adjective.*
Attrib. & comb.: In the senses 'of or pertaining to the maintenance of security in military, penal, or commercial contexts', as ***security clearance, security fence, security gate, security man, security officer, security rating,*** etc. Special combs., as **securities analyst** (orig. *US*) a person who analyses the value of securities; **securities house** a commercial establishment trading in financial securities; **security analyst** = ***securities analyst*** above; **security blanket** (*a*) an official sanction imposed on information to maintain complete secrecy; (*b*) (orig. *US*) a blanket or other object given to a child to provide comfort or reassurance by its familiarity; **security check** (*a*) a verification of identity or reliability, esp. of the loyalty of an official employee, for the purposes of security; (*b*) a search of a person, building, baggage, etc., for concealed weapons, esp. bombs; (*c*) a phrase incorporated in a communication from a spy as a confirmation of identity or an indication that he or she is not operating under duress; **Security Council** a permanent body of the United Nations, consisting of the major nations as permanent members and other nations in rotation, responsible for the settlement of disputes and the maintenance of world peace and security; **security guard** a person employed to ensure the security of vehicles, buildings, etc.; **security risk** a person, esp. one holding an official position, who constitutes a possible danger to security; a situation endangering security.

secy. *abbreviation.*
Secretary.

sedan /sɪˈdan/ *noun.* M17.
[Perh. alt. of Italian dial. word ult. from Latin *sella*: see SADDLE *noun.*]
1 In full ***sedan chair.*** An enclosed chair for conveying one person, carried on horizontal poles by two porters (one in front and one behind), fashionable in the 17th and 18th cents. Also *transf.*, a litter; a palanquin. Now chiefly *Hist.* M17.
2 More fully ***sedan car.*** An enclosed motor car for four or more people, a saloon. *N. Amer.* E20.
Comb.: **sedan-chair clock, sedan clock** *Hist.* a travelling clock of the kind supposed to have been hung in sedan chairs.

sedanca /sɪˈdaŋkə/ *noun.* Also **S-.** E20.
[from prec. + Count Carlos de *Salamanca*, Spanish nobleman and Rolls-Royce agent.]
An elaborately appointed cabriolet mounted on a Rolls-Royce chassis. Also ***Sedanca de Ville.***

sedate /sɪˈdeɪt/ *adjective.* LME.
[Latin *sedatus* pa. pple of *sedare* settle from *sedere* sit: see -ATE[2].]
†**1** *MEDICINE.* Not sore, not painful. Only in LME.
2 Calm, quiet, composed; cool, sober, collected; tranquil, equable, esp. excessively or tediously so. LME.

†**3** Motionless; smooth and steady in motion. L17–E18.

📖 **2** G. Greene The last mourners seem sedate and sombre. A. Lee Life seemed . . a sedate and ordered affair. **3** I. Newton The river . . she made crooked . . that it might be more sedate.

■ **sedately** *adverb* M17. **sedateness** *noun* M17.

sedate /sɪˈdeɪt/ *verb trans.* M17.
[Latin *sedat-* pa. ppl stem of *sedare*: see prec., -ATE[3].]
†**1** Make calm or quiet; assuage, allay. Only in M17. **2** Make sleepy or quiet by means of drugs; administer a sedative to. M20. ▸**b** *ACUPUNCTURE.* Stimulate (a point or meridian) to produce an decrease of energy; decrease the energy of (a part of the body) in this way. Opp. TONIFY 2b. M20.
■ **sedated** *ppl adjective* (apparently) under the influence of a sedative drug M20.

sedation /sɪˈdeɪʃ(ə)n/ *noun.* M16.
[French *sédation* or Latin *sedatio(n-)*, formed as prec.: see -ATION.]
The action of sedating a person or thing, now usu. with sedative drugs. Also, a state of sleep or quiet (as) produced by sedative drugs.

sedative /ˈsɛdətɪv/ *adjective & noun.* LME.
[Old & mod. French *sédatif*, *-ive* or medieval Latin *sedativus*, formed as prec.: see -IVE.]
▶ **A** *adjective.* That alleviates pain, soothing; now *esp.* pertaining to or designating a sleep-inducing drug administered for its calming effect. Also *transf.*, calming, inducing drowsiness or sleep. LME.
▶ **B** *noun.* A sedative medicine, *esp.* a hypnotic drug. Also *transf. & fig.*, a thing which has a calming effect. LME.

📖 Dickens A late . . breakfast, with the additional sedative of a news-paper. B. Spock He may prescribe a sedative or other relaxing drugs.

se defendendo /ˌsiː diːfɛnˈdɛndəʊ, ˌseɪ deɪ-/ *adverbial phr.* Long *rare.* M16.
[Law Latin.]
LAW. In self-defence, a plea which if established is held to remove legal guilt from a homicide.

sedekah /sɛdeɪˈkɑː/ *noun.* M19.
[Malay from Arab. *ṣadaqa*.]
In Malaysia: alms; a voluntary offering, an act of charity.

sedent /ˈsiːd(ə)nt, ˈseɪ-/ *adjective.* Now *rare.* L17.
[Latin *sedent-*: see SEDENTARY, -ENT.]
Sitting.

sedentarization /ˌsɛd(ə)nt(ə)rʌɪˈzeɪʃ(ə)n/ *noun.* Also **-isation**. M20.
[from SEDENTAR(Y + -IZE: see -ATION.]
The settlement of a nomadic people in a permanent homeland or place of habitation.

sedentary /ˈsɛd(ə)nt(ə)ri/ *adjective & noun.* L16.
[French *sédentaire* or Latin *sedentarius*, from *sedent-* pres. ppl stem of *sedere* sit: see -ARY[1].]
▶ **A** *adjective.* **1 a** Remaining in one place of abode; not migratory; not moving from place to place. Now *rare* in *gen.* sense. L16. ▸†**b** Of an object: continuing in one place, motionless. M17–L18. ▸**c** *ZOOLOGY.* Inhabiting the same region through life; not migratory. Also, confined to one spot, not locomotory, sessile. M19. **2** Of a habit, occupation, etc.: characterized by or requiring much sitting and little physical exercise. E17. **3** Of a person: orig., slothful, inactive; later, accustomed to or spending much time sitting, not in the habit of taking physical exercise. E17. †**4** Deliberate. *rare.* M–L17. **5** *GEOLOGY.* Of a soil or sediment: formed *in situ* without transport of eroded material, residual. L19.

📖 **1a** T. R. Malthus The sedentary labourer is more exposed to . . fortune than he who leads a wandering life. *Daily News* The remedy consists in adding to the sedentary forces. **b** Milton The sedentarie Earth . . without least motion. **2** G. Gordon He led a sedentary nine to five life. I. Colegate The bent shoulders . . associated with sedentary occupations. **3** M. Lane Despite . . hours spent reading . . she was far from being a sedentary child. *absol.*: W. Cowper The sedentary stretch their lazy length. **4** Marvell The cooler blood and sedentary execution of an High Court.

▶ **B** *noun. ZOOLOGY.* A spider which catches prey by means of a web or trap rather than by actively hunting it. *rare.* E19.
■ **sedentarily** *adverb* M19. **sedentariness** *noun* L17.

Seder /ˈseɪdə/ *noun.* M19.
[Hebrew *sēder* order, procedure. Cf. SIDRA.]
A Jewish ritual service and ceremonial dinner for the first night or first two nights of the Passover.

sederunt /sɪˈdɪərənt/ *noun. Scot.* E17.
[Latin = there were sitting (sc. the following persons), use as noun of 3rd person pl. perf. indic. of *sedere* sit.]
1 A sitting of a deliberative or judicial body, esp. an ecclesiastical assembly. Also *gen.* (now *rare*), a (period of) sitting, esp. for discussion or talk. E17. **2** The list of people present at such a sitting. Also in *pl.*, the people named on such a list. E18.
1 Act of Sederunt *SCOTS LAW* an act for regulating the forms of procedure before the Court of Session.

sede vacante /ˌsiːdiː vəˈkantiː, ˌseɪdeɪ/ *adverbial & noun phr.* LME.
[Latin = the seat being vacant.]
ECCLESIASTICAL. ▶**A** *adverbial phr.* During the vacancy of an episcopal see. LME.
▶ **B** *noun phr.* The vacancy of a see or seat. Long *rare.* L16.

sedge /sɛdʒ/ *noun.* Also (*dial.*) **seg** /sɛg/.
[Old English *seċġ* from Germanic, ult. from Indo-European base repr. by Latin *secare* to cut.]
1 Any of various narrow-leaved freq. coarse plants of marshes and watersides; *esp.* one belonging to the family Cyperaceae, *spec.* (more fully ***fen sedge***) a robust plant of fens, *Cladium mariscus*, used for thatching. In *BOTANY*, any plant of the genus *Carex* (family Cyperaceae) which comprises grasslike plants with triangular stems and inconspicuous flowers, the male and female freq. in separate spikes on the same stem. Also, such plants or their stems collectively, an expanse of this plant. Also ***sedge-grass***. OE. ▸**b** An individual plant or stalk of sedge. *rare.* LME. ▸**c** The characteristic greenish- (or reddish-)brown shade of sedge. E20. **2** *ANGLING.* (An artificial fly imitating) an adult or emergent caddis fly. Also more fully ***sedge-fly***. L19.
Comb.: **sedge-bird** = ***sedge-warbler*** below; ***sedge-fly***: see sense 2 above; ***sedge-grass***: see sense 1 above; **sedge reedling** = ***sedge-warbler*** below; **sedge-warbler**, **sedge-wren** a small brown-streaked Old World warbler, *Acrocephalus schoenobaenus*, found esp. around marshes and in reed-beds.
■ **sedged** *adjective* (*a*) *rare* woven with sedge; (*b*) *AGRICULTURE* (of oats) affected with sedging; (*c*) bordered with sedge: E17. **sedging** *noun* (*AGRICULTURE*) a condition in oats characterized by thickening of the stem near the ground E19. **sedgy** *adjective* (*a*) covered or bordered with sedge or sedges; (*b*) having the nature or properties of sedge; (*c*) made of or thatched with sedge: M16.

sedile /sɪˈdʌɪli/ *noun.* Pl. **sedilia** /sɪˈdɪlɪə/. LME.
[Latin = seat, from *sedere* sit.]
†**1** *gen.* A seat. Only in LME. **2** *ECCLESIASTICAL.* Each of a series of usu. canopied and decorated stone seats, usu. three in number, placed on or recessed into the south side of the choir near the altar for use by the clergy. Usu. in *pl.* L18.

sediment /ˈsɛdɪm(ə)nt/ *noun & verb.* M16.
[French *sédiment* or Latin *sedimentum* settling, from *sedere* sit: see -I-, -MENT.]
▶ **A** *noun.* **1** Matter composed of particles that settle to the bottom of a liquid; dregs. M16. **2** *fig.* The worst part, the remnant, the dregs. M17. **3** *spec.* in *GEOLOGY* etc. (A layer of) unconsolidated material composed of particles deposited from a suspension in air, ice, or water, or from solution in water. L17.

📖 **1** P. Carey A claret bottle with half an inch of sediment in it. **3** A. Geikie Ordinary marine sediment . . sand, gravel, silt, and mud.

▶ **B** *verb.* **1** *verb trans.* Deposit as sediment. M19. **2** *verb intrans.* **a** Settle as sediment. E20. ▸**b** Of a liquid: deposit a sediment. M20.
■ **sediˈmentable** *adjective* able to be deposited or obtained as sediment M20. **sediˈmental** *adjective* (*rare*) of the nature of sediment; (of rock) sedimentary: E17.

sedimentary /sɛdɪˈmɛnt(ə)ri/ *adjective & noun.* M19.
[from prec. + -ARY[1].]
▶ **A** *adjective.* **1** Of, pertaining to, or of the nature of (a) sediment. M19. **2** *GEOLOGY.* Pertaining to or formed by the deposition of sediment. M19.
▶ **B** *noun.* A sedimentary formation or deposit. L19.

sedimentation /ˌsɛdɪm(ə)nˈteɪʃ(ə)n/ *noun.* L19.
[formed as prec. + -ATION.]
Deposition of material in the form of a sediment, as a geological process, or in a liquid in a tank, centrifuge, etc.
Comb.: **sedimentation coefficient**, **sedimentation constant** a measure of the size of a microscopic particle, equal to the terminal outward velocity of the particle when centrifuged in a fluid medium divided by the centrifugal force acting on it (expressed in units of time: cf. SVEDBERG); **sedimentation rate** the rate of descent of particles suspended in a fluid; *spec.* in *MEDICINE*, that of red cells in drawn blood; **sedimentation tank**: in which sewage is allowed to stand so that suspended solid matter may settle.

sedimentology /ˌsɛdɪm(ə)nˈtɒlədʒi/ *noun.* M20.
[from SEDIMENT *noun* + -OLOGY.]
The branch of geology that deals with the nature and properties of sediments and sedimentary rocks.
■ **sedimentoˈlogical** *adjective* of or pertaining to sedimentology M20. **sedimentoˈlogically** *adverb* by means of sedimentology; from the point of view of sedimentology: M20. **sedimentologist** *noun* an expert in or student of sedimentology M20.

sedition /sɪˈdɪʃ(ə)n/ *noun.* LME.
[Old & mod. French *sédition* or Latin *seditio(n-)*, from *sed-* SE- + *itio(n-)* going, from *it-* pa. ppl stem of *ire* go: see -ITION.]
†**1** Violent strife between factions; an instance of this. LME–E17. **2** A concerted movement to overthrow an established government; a revolt, a rebellion, a mutiny. Now *rare.* LME. **3** Conduct or language inciting people to rebellion or a breach of public order; agitation against the constituted authority of a State. M16.

📖 **1** Hobbes Thoughts of sedition in one towards another. **2** B. Jowett By reason of inequality, cities are filled with seditions. **3** M. Shadbolt Sedition, they called it. Disloyalty. Agitation against the war. P. B. Clarke Sentenced to two years in prison for sedition.

■ **seditionary** *noun & adjective* (*a*) *noun* = SEDITIONIST; (*b*) *adjective* of, pertaining to, or characterized by sedition, seditious E17. **seditioner** *noun* (*rare*) = SEDITIONIST M16. **seditionist** *noun* a person who practises or incites others to sedition L18.

seditious /sɪˈdɪʃəs/ *adjective.* LME.
[Old & mod. French *séditieux* or Latin *seditiosus*, from *seditio*: see prec., -IOUS.]
1 Given to or guilty of sedition; practising sedition. LME. **2** Of, pertaining to, or of the nature of sedition; tending to provoke sedition. LME.

📖 **1** W. Robertson Reducing to obedience their seditious chieftain. J. O. Dykes An illegal or possibly seditious club. **2** I. D'Israeli To Charles . . the tumultuous acts of the great leaders, appeared seditious. **seditious libel**: maligning the sovereign or the sovereign's family, advocating the violent overthrow of the government, etc.

■ **seditiously** *adverb* LME. †**seditiousness** *noun* L16–M18.

sedoheptulose /siːdəʊˈhɛptjʊləʊz, -s/ *noun.* E20.
[from SEDUM + -O- + HEPT(A- + -ULOSE[2].]
CHEMISTRY. A heptose which is found in the leaves of certain plants of the genus *Sedum* (notably *S. spectabile*), and, as a phosphate, as an intermediate in carbohydrate metabolism in animals.
■ Also †**sedoheptose** *noun* E–M20.

sedra *noun* var. of SIDRA.

seduce /sɪˈdjuːs/ *verb trans.* L15.
[Latin *seducere*, from *se-* SE- + *ducere* lead.]
1 Persuade (a subject, soldier, etc.) to abandon allegiance or duty. L15. **2** Lead (a person) astray in conduct or belief; tempt, entice, or beguile (a person) *to* or *to do* something wrong, foolish, or unintended. L15. **3** Induce (esp. a woman) to abandon chastity; entice into sexual activity. M16. **4** Decoy (*from* or *to* a place), lead astray (*into*). *obsolete* exc. as passing into sense 2. M17. **5** Allure, entice, attract, (chiefly as ***seducing*** *ppl adjective.*). Formerly also, win by charm or attractiveness. *rare.* M18.

📖 **1** H. P. Brougham To seduce the representatives from their duty to their constituents. J. A. Froude He tried to seduce Caesar's garrison, and was put to death for his treachery. **2** Burke We have been seduced, by . . false representations . . into a war. S. Brett He was too old to be seduced by . . childish hope. A. Storr The belief in . . 'spiritualism' which seduced so many scientists. **3** Sir W. Scott She was seduced under promise of marriage. K. Tynan She would have seduced an ex-lover. M. Frayn A homosexual . . allows himself to be seduced by Howard. **5** T. Hardy She seduces casual attention . . she never courts it.

■ **seduˈcee** *noun* (*rare*) a person who is seduced E17. **seducement** *noun* (now *rare* or *obsolete*) (*a*) the action of seducing someone, the fact or condition of being seduced; (*b*) a thing which seduces a person; an insidious temptation: L16. **seducer** *noun* a person who or thing which seduces someone; *esp.* a man who seduces a woman: M16. **seducible** *adjective* able to be seduced E17. **seducing** *ppl adjective* (*a*) that seduces a person; (*b*) (*rare*) alluring, enticing: L16. **seducingly** *adverb* L16. †**seducive** *adjective* (*rare*) (*a*) caused by a misleading influence; (*b*) leading to error: E17–L18.

†**seduct** *verb trans. rare.* L15–L18.
[Latin *seduct-*: see next.]
Seduce.

seduction /sɪˈdʌkʃ(ə)n/ *noun.* LME.
[French *séduction* or Latin *seductio(n-)*, from *seduct-* pa. ppl stem of *seducere* SEDUCE *verb*: see -ION.]
†**1** = SEDITION 1, 2. LME–L15. **2** The action or an act of seducing a person: the fact or process of being seduced. E16. ▸†**b** The condition of being led astray (*lit.* & *fig.*). M16–M17. **3** A thing which seduces a person; something tempting or alluring. M16. **4** Seductiveness, alluring or enticing quality. *rare.* L19.

📖 **2** J. Mackintosh Promises of marriage . . have been employed as means of seduction. P. G. Hamerton An ambitious man will . . withstand the seductions of his senses. *Daily Telegraph* The imaginary seduction of a 16-year-old pupil. **3** W. H. Prescott The seductions most dazzling to youth. **4** R. L. Stevenson The Prince gained the affection of all . . by the seduction of his manner.

■ **seductionist** *noun* (*rare*) a person who practises seduction E19.

seductive /sɪˈdʌktɪv/ *adjective.* M18.
[from prec. after *induction*, *inductive*: see -IVE.]
Tending to seduce a person; alluring, enticing.

> G. H. NAPHEYS The seductive pleasures of opium-eating. P. H. GIBBS Devilish pretty and very seductive.

■ **seductively** *adverb* M19. **seductiveness** *noun* E19.

†**seductor** *noun.* L15–M17.
[Latin, from *seduct-* (see SEDUCTION) + -OR.]
A seducer.

seductress /sɪˈdʌktrɪs/ *noun.* E19.
[from (the same root as) prec.: see -ESS¹.]
A female seducer, a seductive woman.

sedulity /sɪˈdjuːlɪti/ *noun.* M16.
[Latin *sedulitas*, formed as next: see -ITY.]
1 The quality of being sedulous; perseverance, persistence. M16.
†**2** In *pl.* Constant attentions. L17–E18.

sedulous /ˈsɛdjʊləs/ *adjective.* M16.
[from Latin *sedulus* zealous: see -ULOUS.]
Painstaking, persevering, diligent; assiduous, persistent; (of an action etc.) deliberately and consciously continued.

> S. ROSENBERG An assignment that takes up .. his time and requires sedulous coaching.

■ **sedulously** *adverb* L16. **sedulousness** *noun* E17.

sedum /ˈsiːdəm/ *noun.* M16.
[Latin.]
Any of various succulent plants constituting the genus *Sedum* (family Crassulaceae), with fleshy leaves and flat-topped clusters of yellow, white, pink, etc., flowers, including stonecrops.

see /siː/ *noun*¹. ME.
[Anglo-Norman *se(d)*, Old French *sie(d)* from Proto-Romance word repr. Latin *sedes* seat, from *sedere* SIT *verb*.]
†**1** *gen.* A seat, a place where someone sits, (*lit.* & *fig.*); *spec.* (*a*) a royal throne; the rank or authority symbolized by this; (*b*) a person's usual place of abode. ME–L16.
2 ECCLESIASTICAL. **a** The throne of a bishop or archbishop in the principal church of his diocese, a cathedra. Formerly also (*rare*), the church in which this is placed, a cathedral. *arch.* ME. ▸**b** (Usu. **S-**.) The office or jurisdiction of the Pope; the papacy. Freq. with specifying word. ME. ▸**c** The office or jurisdiction of a bishop or archbishop, esp. *of* a particular diocese. Formerly also = DIOCESE 1. LME. ▸†**d** A city regarded as the seat of authority of a bishop or archbishop. M16–M18.
2b *Apostolic See*, *Papal See*, etc. **Holy See**, **See of Rome** the papacy, the papal court.
Comb.: **see-city**, **see-town** a city or town regarded as the principal city or town of a see.

see /siː/ *noun*². *colloq.* M19.
[from SEE *verb*.]
A look, a glance. Chiefly in ***have a see***, ***take a see***.

see /siː/ *verb.* Pa. t. **saw** /sɔː/, (*dial.* & *non-standard*) **seed**; pa. pple **seen** /siːn/. See also SEEN *adjective*.
[Old English *sēon* = Old Frisian *sīa*, Old Saxon, Old High German *sehan* (Dutch *zien*, German *sehen*), Old Norse *séa, sía, siá*, Gothic *saiƕan*, from Germanic strong verb from Indo-European, perh. repr. base also of Latin *sequi* follow. Cf. SIGHT *noun*.]
1 a *verb trans.* Perceive with the eye (an external object, light, colour, movement, etc.). Foll. by simple obj., obj. with compl. OE. ▸**b** *verb intrans.* Perceive an external object, light, colour, movement, etc., with the eye; have the faculty of sight, not be blind. ME. ▸**c** *verb trans.* Become aware of (a visual object) in the mind's eye or in a dream or vision. ME. ▸**d** *verb trans.* Distinguish (a thing) by sight *from* some similar object. LME. ▸**e** *verb trans. transf.* Of radar equipment, a camera, satellite, etc.: detect by means of light or other waves. E20.
2 *verb trans.* Perceive mentally (an idea, quality, etc.), attain to comprehension of, understand, (freq. foll. by obj. clause, esp. indirect interrog.). Also, foresee or forecast (an event, trend, etc.). OE. ▸**b** *verb intrans.* Perceive mentally an idea, quality, etc.; attain to comprehension, understand. Freq. in ***I see***, ***you see*** below. ME. ▸**c** *verb trans.* Have a particular mental view of (a person or thing); understand or appreciate (a question, situation, etc.) in a particular manner. L16. ▸**d** Find (good or attractive qualities) *in* (freq. in interrog. with *what*); recognize (specified characteristics) *in*. M19. ▸**e** Recognize as right or desirable, believe, accept, (freq. foll. by *it*; *colloq.*, orig. *US*); (usu. in neg. & interrog. contexts) envisage as possible or acceptable. M19.
3 *verb trans.* Direct or apply one's sight or mind to (freq. in *imper.* as *interjection*, used to call or direct attention: look!); contemplate, examine, look at, (freq. in obj. clause with *what, how*, etc.). Also, visit (a place); watch (a match, film, etc.) as a spectator. OE. ▸**b** Look at or read (esp. a document). ME. ▸**c** Look at or refer to for specified information. Usu. in *imper.* as a direction in a text etc. E17.
4 *verb trans.* **a** Know by observation or experience; witness; exist at the same time as, be present at; (of a place) be the scene of; (of a period of time) be marked by. Also, be living at (a period); (usu. in neg. contexts) reach (a specified age). OE. ▸**b** Observe, find; come to know in the course of events. Freq. foll. by obj. clause, obj. with compl. LME. ▸**c** Be willing to witness (a person or thing) in a specified situation. Freq. in ***see you damned first*** & similar phrs. below. LME.
5 *verb trans.* Experience; undergo, enjoy, suffer. Now *rare*. OE.
6 a *verb trans.* Perceive or realize the nature of something, esp. by visual signs. Freq. foll. by obj. clause, obj. with compl. ME. ▸**b** *verb trans.* Become aware of (information etc.) by reading. Freq. foll. by *that*. LME. ▸**c** *verb intrans.* Read music. *slang.* M20.
7 *verb trans.* Ascertain by inspection, inquiry, experiment, or consideration, esp. *that* certain specified conditions exist. Freq. *absol.* or with ellipsis of indirect interrog. in ***I'll see***, ***we'll see*** below. ME.
8 *verb trans.* †**a** Keep in view; watch over; take care of. ME–E17. ▸**b** Escort or conduct (a person etc.) to a specified place or in a specified direction. Freq. in ***see off***, ***see out*** below. E17.
9 *verb trans.* Ensure by supervision or vigilance that specified conditions be met. Freq. foll. by obj. clause, obj. & compl. ME.
10 *verb trans.* **a** View or regard as, judge, deem. ME. ▸†**b** In *pass.* Seem, appear. Also, seem good, be approved. LME–L16.
11 *verb trans.* **a** Be in the company of, meet and converse with, visit socially. Also (*colloq.*), meet regularly as a girlfriend or boyfriend. ME. ▸**b** Receive as a visitor; grant an interview to; be at home to. L15. ▸**c** Obtain an interview with, esp. in order to consult. L18.
12 *verb trans.* In gambling, esp. poker, equal (a bet); equal the bet of (another player), esp. to see his or her cards. L16.
13 *verb trans.* MILITARY. Command or dominate (a position). E19.

> **1a** SIR W. SCOTT O'er Roslin .. A wondrous blaze was seen to gleam. G. VIDAL She turned so that he could see all her face. W. BRONK Do you see the light on those green trees? **b** KEATS No ears to hear, or eyes to see. I. MURDOCH He could not see, but knew the way without sight. R. COBB The shop was very dark, so that one could not see in. **c** F. O'CONNOR He saw her in his sleep. **d** MRS H. WOOD I can't see one sort from another; we must have candles. **2** H. JAMES I don't see what you've against her. J. BUCHAN I've my reputation to consider. You see that, don't you? I. MURDOCH I see no point in this .. discussion. **b** *Listener* I believe in having a go, see. P. D. JAMES 'Sir Ronald has engaged me ... ' 'So I see, Miss.' **c** ALDOUS HUXLEY The forest, seen as the hunter or the .. traveller sees it. C. HILL We should see Cromwell's Irish policy as part of his general imperial policy. **d** J. BRYCE Crescentius, in whom modern enthusiasm has seen a patriotic republican. M. FORSTER He was .. boring .. she couldn't see what Celia saw in him. **e** G. B. SHAW The old man never could .. see it. He said the .. profession for me was the bar. R. BANNISTER I could not see myself in the winning place. **3** C. WESLEY See! He lifts his Hands above! THACKERAY My father took me to see a show at Brookgreen Fair. J. D. CARR See here .. Let us get this straight. M. AMIS That film you wanted to see is on. **b** W. CRUISE No man would advance money upon an estate without seeing the title deeds. **c** LD MACAULAY: See Wolley's MS. History, quoted in Lyson's Magna Britannia. **4a** K. H. DIGBY Tartarean years .. when Rome saw five consuls. J. WAIN I know Celia will never see forty again. D. FRASER It was time he saw more of the world. **b** J. A. FROUDE The .. church authorities saw bill after bill hurried .. before the Lords. *absol.*: M. A. VON ARNIM She's bound to be different. You'll see. **c** P. BARKER She wasn't stripping off .. she'd see him in hell first. **5** J. WESLEY Thy Throne; Which shall no Change or Period see. WORDSWORTH They see A happy youth. **6a** S. FOOTE Don't you see I am tired to death? TENNYSON I see thee what thou art. G. VIDAL He looked at his watch and saw .. it was a quarter to seven. **b** HOBBES I could never see in any Author, what a Fundamental Law signifieth. THACKERAY Did you see her death in the paper? **7** SCOTT FITZGERALD What he .. said was: 'Yes .. I'll see'. D. HAMMETT Looking in her compact-mirror to see her mouth had not been smeared. L. DURRELL Feeling his forehead to see if he had a fever. **8a** J. NORDEN He may be on his own Bayly, and see the managing .. of his owne reuenewes. **b** F. WARDEN We saw the ladies into the brougham. J. BUCHAN I'll see you clothed and fed. D. JACOBSON His .. servants will see the princess home. J. JOHNSTON Will you see Captain Rankin to the door? **9** J. PEARSON The landlord .. is interested in seeing that the liquidators discharge their duty. **10** SIR W. SCOTT The dispensation .. the Lord sees meet to send us. CARLYLE The only thing one sees advisable is to bring up soldiers. **11a** M. W. MONTAGU I have been .. to see my Lady Northampton. **b** M. EDGEWORTH My master .. can't see anybody now. **c** B. JOWETT I want him to see a physician about the illness. J. S. WINTER I have to see a lady .. about a sitting. P. CAREY You really should see someone .. To talk about your problems. **12** H. G. WELLS Put the cards down. I'll *see* you.

Phrases: **as far as I can see** to the best of my understanding or belief. **as I see it** in my opinion. **have seen better days** have formerly been better off or in a better condition. **have seen it all before** be thoroughly familiar with a particular situation, be worldly-wise. ***if you see what I mean***: see MEAN *verb*¹. **I'll be seeing you** = *see you* below. **I'll see** I shall await the outcome (freq. indicating an unwillingness to act at once). **I see** I understand (with ref. to an explanation etc.). **let me see** (*a*) let me try to recall to memory, let me consider; (*b*) show me. ***not trust X as far as one can see him or her***: see TRUST *verb*. ***remain to be seen***: see REMAIN *verb*. ***see a hole through a ladder***: see LADDER *noun* 1. **see a man about a dog** *joc.* keep an urgent appointment; *euphem.* go to the lavatory. ***see and serve***: see SERVE *verb*¹. **see a person coming** recognize a person who can be fooled or deceived. ***see a person right***: see RIGHT *adjective*. ***see daylight***: see DAYLIGHT 1. ***see double***: see DOUBLE *adjective* & *adverb*. ***see eye to eye***: see EYE *noun*. ***see far into a millstone***: see MILLSTONE 1. ***see fit***: see FIT *adjective* 3. **see it coming** foresee or anticipate it, be prepared for it, (usu. in neg. contexts). **see life** gain experience of the world. **see little of** be seldom in the company of. **see much of** be often in the company of (usu. in neg. & interrog. contexts). ***see no further than one's nose***: see NOSE *noun*. ***see one's way***: see WAY *noun*. ***see reason***: see REASON *noun*¹. ***see red***: see RED *noun*. ***see service***: see SERVICE *noun*¹. ***see stars***: see STAR *noun*¹. ***see the back of***: see BACK *noun*¹. ***see the colour of a person's money***: see COLOUR *noun*. ***see the ELEPHANT***. ***see the last of a person***: see LAST *noun*⁵ 8. ***see the light***: see LIGHT *noun*. **see the light of day** come into existence (freq. in neg. contexts). ***see the NEW YEAR in***. ***see the world***: see WORLD *noun*. **see things** have hallucinations or false imaginings. ***see through a brick wall***: see WALL *noun*¹. ***see through a ladder***: see LADDER *noun* 1. ***see through the press***: see PRESS *noun*¹. ***see what I mean***: see MEAN *verb*¹. ***see which way the cat jumps***: see CAT *noun*¹. **see you**: an expression on parting (also ***I'll see you***, ***see you later***, etc.). **see you damned first**, **see him damned first**, & vars., refuse categorically and with hostility to do what a person wants. **to see** *spec.* (*a*) (following an adjective) in appearance, to the sight; (*b*) (*pred.* after *be*) visible; remaining to be seen. †**to see to** = *to see* (*a*) above. ***wait and see***: see WAIT *verb*. **we'll see** we shall await the outcome (freq. indicating an unwillingness to act at once). **you see** (*a*) you understand (*b*) you will understand when I explain. ***you see what I mean***: see MEAN *verb*¹. ***you should see***: see SHALL *verb*.

With adverbs in specialized senses: **see off** (*a*) be present at the departure of (a person); (*b*) (esp. of a dog) put to flight, chase off; (*c*) *colloq.* ward off, get the better of; (*d*) ***see off the new ball*** (CRICKET), bat until the shine has been removed from the ball, esp. at the start of an innings. **see out** (*a*) accompany out of a building etc., escort off the premises; (*b*) finish (a project etc.) completely; (*c*) remain awake, alive, etc., until the end of (a specified period); (*d*) last longer than, outlive. **see through** (*a*) support (a person) during a difficult time; (*b*) persist with (a thing) until completion.

With prepositions in specialized senses: **see about** attend to; take account of what can be done with regard to. ***see after***: see AFTER *preposition* 2. **see for** (now *rare* or *obsolete*) look for, try to find. **see into** perceive visually what is below the surface of (*lit.* & *fig.*). **see over** inspect, tour and examine, (esp. a building). **see through** (*a*) penetrate visually; (*b*) not be deceived by, detect the true nature of. **see to** (*a*) attend to; provide for the wants of; (*b*) ***see to it***, ensure (*that*).

Comb.: **see-safe** *adjective* & *adverb* (*a*) *adjective* of or pertaining to a bookseller's order by which the publisher is committed to replacing unsold stock with copies of another title; (*b*) *adverb* in a see-safe manner.

seeable /ˈsiːəb(ə)l/ *adjective.* LME.
[from prec. + -ABLE.]
Able to be seen, visible.
■ **seeableness** *noun* (*rare*) M19. †**seeably** *adverb* (*rare*): only in M16.

Seebeck effect /ˈsiːbɛk ɪˌfɛkt, ˈzeɪbɛk/ *noun phr.* E20.
[from T. J. *Seebeck* (1770–1831), Russian-born German physicist.]
PHYSICS. The thermoelectric phenomenon whereby an electromotive force is generated in a circuit containing junctions between dissimilar metals if these junctions are at different temperatures.

seecatch /ˈsiːkatʃ/ *noun.* Pl. **-tchie** /-tʃi/. L19.
[Russian *sekach*, pl. *sekachi* adult male fur seal, boar (from base meaning 'cut', with ref. to the tusks of a boar).]
A male Alaskan fur-seal (*Callorhinus ursinus*). Usu. in *pl.*

seech *noun* var. of SEEGE.

seed /siːd/ *noun.*
[Old English *sǣd*, Anglian *sēd*, corresp. to Old Frisian *sēd*, Old Saxon *sād* (Dutch *zaad*), Old High German *sāt* (German *Saat*), Old Norse *sáð*, Gothic *-seþs* in *manaseþs*, from Germanic word rel. to base of SOW *verb*¹.]
1 a That which is or may be sown (freq. as obj. of **sow** *verb*¹); the fertilized ovules of a plant or plants, esp. in the form of small roundish bodies or grains dispersed naturally or collected for sowing to produce a new generation of plants. Also (AGRICULTURE & HORTICULTURE) any of various other parts of plants (e.g. tubers, bulbs) by which a new crop may be propagated (freq. *attrib.*, as ***seed potato*** etc.). In *pl.*, varieties or kinds of seed. OE. ▸**b** An individual grain of seed; BOTANY the fertilized ovule of an angiosperm or gymnosperm, composed of a plant embryo, often with a food store, in a protective coat (testa). Also *loosely*, the spore of a lower plant; a small hard fruit resembling a seed. OE. ▸**c** A particle of bran. Usu. in *pl.* Now *dial.* L16. ▸**d** In *pl.* Corn; clover and grasses raised from seed; land sown with this. Chiefly *dial.* L18. ▸**e** = ***birdseed*** s.v. BIRD *noun*. L19.

2 a *fig.* The germ or latent beginning of some growth, development, or consequence. Also, religious or other teaching, viewed esp. with regard to its degree of fruitfulness (with allus. to the parables in *Matthew* 13, *Mark* 4, *Luke* 8). **OE.** ▸**b** A small crystal introduced into a solution or liquid to provide a nucleus for crystal growth, orig. *spec.* of sugar; a nucleus for any kind of growth, condensation, etc. Also ***seed crystal***. **E20.**

3 Offspring, progeny. Now *arch.* & in biblical allusions. **OE.**

4 Semen, sperm. **ME.**

5 *sing.* & in *pl.* The eggs of a silkworm moth. Also, the eggs or young of an oyster or other shellfish, esp. as used as to restock a commercial bed (freq. *attrib.*, as ***seed oyster*** etc.). **E17.**

6 Minute bubbles formed in glass. **M19.**

7 MEDICINE. A small container for radioactive material placed in body tissue in radiotherapy. Freq. as ***RADON seed***. **E20.**

8 SPORT (esp. TENNIS). A player or competitor seeded (at a specified position) in a tournament. Cf. SEED *verb* 7. **M20.**

> 🕮 **1a** J. M. CAMPBELL We plough the fields and scatter The good seed on the land. **b** ANTHONY HUXLEY Gauzy seeds are released to be carried away on the wind. **2a** M. L. KING Evil carries the seed of its own destruction. **b** *Scientific American* Galaxies grew rapidly from the seeds formed in earlier density fluctuations. **3** *Book of Common Prayer* As he promised to our forefathers, Abraham and his seed, for ever. **8** ***number 4 seed, second seed, third seed, top seed***, etc.

Phrases: **go to seed**, †**grow to seed** (*a*) (of a plant) cease flowering as seeds develop; (*b*) *fig.* become habitually unkempt, ineffective, etc.; deteriorate. **in seed** (of a plant) at the stage of growth at which seeds are borne. ***Niger seed***: see NIGER *noun*[2] 2. **run to seed** = ***go to seed*** above. ***sow the seed of***, ***sow the seeds of***: see SOW *verb*[1].

Comb.: **seed ball** a globose, usu. dry or capsular fruit; *esp.* any of the hard swollen fruiting units in the beet plant; **seed bank** a place where seeds of different plant varieties and species are stored as a safeguard against their possible extinction; **seed-bed** (*a*) a piece of ground prepared for sowing seeds; (*b*) *transf.* & *fig.* a place used or favourable for development; **seed-bird** a bird, esp. a wagtail or a seagull, which frequently follows behind ploughs to feed on newly exposed seeds; **seed-box** (*a*) a receptacle for seed, esp. in a grain-drill or machine for sowing seed; (*b*) *US* any plant of the genus *Ludwigia*, of the willowherb family, so called from its cubical pod; **seed bull** a bull kept to serve cows; **seed-cake** a cake flavoured with whole seeds, esp. of caraway; **seed-coat** BOTANY the testa or protective coat of a seed; **seed-corn** (*a*) good-quality grain (*occas.* a grain) of corn for sowing in order to produce a new crop; (*b*) assets or an asset used or reused for future profit or benefit; (*c*) ***seed-corn maggot*** (*US*), the yellowish-white larva of a fly, *Hylemya platura*, which infests the seed of various crops, esp. vegetables, preventing sprouting or weakening the seedlings; the adult fly of this larva; **seed-cotton** cotton in its native state, with the seed not separated; ***seed crystal***: see sense 2b above; **seed dressing** (the use of) a preparation applied to seed to protect it against pests; **seed-eater** a granivorous bird; *spec.* a S. American finch of the genus *Sporophila* or a related genus; **seed fat** a fat obtained from seeds, such as those of the coconut, soya, groundnut, etc.; **seed fern** = PTERIDOSPERM; **seed-field** a field or other place in which seed is sown; **seed-fish** a fish that is ready to spawn; **seed-furrow** *noun* & *verb* (*a*) *noun* (the process of producing) a furrow in which seed is to be sown; (*b*) *verb trans.* plough a seed-furrow into (land); **seed-head** a flower-head in seed; ***seed-lac***: see LAC *noun*[1] 1. **seed-leaf** (*a*) BOTANY a cotyledon; (*b*) a kind of tobacco grown in the northern US (orig. from imported seed) and used chiefly for wrapping cigars; **seed-lip** [var. of LEAP *noun*[2]] a basket in which seed is carried when sowing by hand; **seed metering** automatic control of the numbers of seeds sown or planted by a machine; **seed money** money allocated (esp. from public funds) for the initiation of a project and designed to stimulate its independent economic expansion; **seed orchard** a group of trees cultivated for the production of seed; **seed parent** a plant whose seed is fertilized by pollen from a different plant to produce a hybrid; **seed-pearl** a minute pearl resembling a seed; such pearls collectively; **seed-plant** a spermatophyte; **seed-plot** a seed-bed (now only *transf.* & *fig.*); ***seed potato***: see sense 1a above; ***seed set***: see SET *noun*[1] 8c; **seedsnipe** each of four S. American birds resembling small partridges and constituting the family Thinocoridae, allied to the sandpipers; **seed stitch** EMBROIDERY = SEEDING *noun* (c); **seed-vessel** BOTANY a capsule or other case containing a plant's seeds; **seed year** a year in which a particular tree produces a good crop of seeds. See also SEEDSMAN, SEED-TIME.

■ **seedful** *adjective* (*rare*) full of seed, productive **L16.** **seedless** *adjective* **LME.** **seedlet** *noun* a small seed **M19.** **seedlike** *adjective* resembling (that of) a seed **E18.**

seed /siːd/ *verb.* **LME.**

[from the noun.]

1 *verb trans.* Sow (land, soil, a piece of ground, etc.) with seed. (Foll. by *with*, occas. *to*, a kind of seed or crop.) **LME.** ▸**b** *transf.* & *fig.* Introduce a seed, germ, or latent beginning of something into. **M17.** ▸**c** Introduce a crystal or particle into (a liquid, apparatus, etc.) to induce crystallization; introduce crystals of a substance such as silver iodide or dry ice into (a cloud or storm) to cause rain or other precipitation. **E20.** ▸**d** BIOLOGY. Introduce cultured cells, organisms, etc., into (an area, culture vessel, etc.) to permit propagation. **M20.**

2 *verb trans.* **a** Sow (a kind of seed) on or in soil, the ground, etc. **LME.** ▸**b** *transf.* & *fig.* Introduce or act as a seed, germ, or latent beginning of (something). **E17.** ▸**c** BIOLOGY. Introduce (cultured cells, organisms, etc.) *into* an area or esp. a culture vessel or medium to permit propagation. **M20.**

3 *verb intrans.* **a** Produce seed; run to seed. **LME.** ▸**b** Develop *into* something undesirable. **L19.**

4 *verb intrans.* & *refl.* Sow or scatter seed(s); spread or propagate by means of seeds (*lit.* & *fig.*). **LME.**

†**5** *verb trans.* In *pass.* Run to seed, mature. *rare* (Shakes.). Only in **L16.**

6 *verb trans.* Sprinkle a surface lightly with; decorate (a fabric or garment) with a scattering of small adornments. Long *rare*. **L16.**

7 *verb trans.* SPORT (esp. TENNIS). Assign (each of a chosen number of the better competitors) a position in an ordered list, so that the most highly ranked do not meet until the later stages of an elimination competition; arrange (a draw or event) to this end. Orig. *US*. **L19.**

8 *verb trans.* Remove the seeds from (fruit etc.). **E20.**

> 🕮 **1** F. NORRIS Thirty-three grain drills . . seeding the ten thousand acres of the great ranch. R. FRAME A . . hole in the ground, already seeded with the first quick-growing grasses. **seed down** sow grass or clover seeds, esp. amongst a crop of oats, wheat, etc. **b** *American Poetry Review* The line is seeded with expectation. **3** C. R. MARKHAM The tea plants are now three or four feet high and seeding freely. **4** M. DIBDIN Plants had already seeded in crevices. *fig.*: A. MASON The communities were spreading, seeding into regions beyond the mountains. **7** *Thames Valley Now* The left handed professional . . will be seeded first again this year. **8** L. BLUE Peel and seed the cucumber.

■ †**seedage** *noun* (*rare*) (*a*) sowing of seed; (*b*) production of seed: **E17.** **seeding** *noun* (*a*) the action of the verb; an instance of this; (*b*) *rare* seeds for sowing; (*c*) EMBROIDERY small stitches irregularly placed to fill a large area: **ME.** †**seedness** *noun* the action of sowing, the state of being sown; also = SEED-TIME: **LME–L18.**

seeded /ˈsiːdɪd/ *adjective.* **L16.**

[from SEED *noun*, *verb*: see -ED[1], -ED[2].]

1 Sown with seed. **L16.**

2 Having a seed or seeds (esp. of a specified kind or number); bearing seeds, run to seed, matured. **L16.**

3 HERALDRY. Of a flower: having seeds of a specified tincture. **E17.**

4 Covered with scattered dots or small adornments. **L19.**

5 Of (esp. dried) fruit: having the seeds removed. **E20.**

6 SPORT (esp. TENNIS). (Of a competitor) assigned a position in a list of seeds in an elimination competition; (of a draw or event) arranged in such a manner. Cf. SEED *noun* 8, *verb* 7. **E20.**

seedee *noun* var. of SIDI.

seeder /ˈsiːdə/ *noun.* **OE.**

[from SEED *noun* + -ER[1].]

†**1** A person who sows seed; a sower. **OE–L15.**

2 A device for sowing seed mechanically. **M19.**

3 A machine for removing seeds from fruit etc. **L20.**

seedling /ˈsiːdlɪŋ/ *noun* & *adjective.* **E17.**

[from SEED *noun* + -LING[1].]

▶ **A** *noun.* **1** A small seed (in *fig.* sense). **E17.**

2 A young plant developed from a seed, *esp.* one raised from seed as distinct from a slip, cutting, etc. **M17.**

†**3** The young of an animal hatched from an egg resembling a seed. **E–M18.**

Comb.: **seedling blight** a disease of seedlings, *esp.* a sometimes fatal disease of flax that affects esp. seedlings and is caused by the seedborne fungus *Colletotrichum linicola*; **seedling leaf** BOTANY = ***seed-leaf*** (a) s.v. SEED *noun*.

▶ **B** *attrib.* or as *adjective.* Developed or raised from seed; that is a seedling; *fig.* existing in a rudimentary state. **L17.**

seedman /ˈsiːdmən/ *noun.* Long *rare*. Pl. **-men**. **L16.**

[from SEED *noun* or *verb* + MAN *noun*.]

†**1** = SEEDSMAN 1; *fig.* a seminary priest. **L16–L17.**

2 = SEEDSMAN 2. **M17.**

seedsman /ˈsiːdzmən/ *noun.* Pl. **-men**. **L16.**

[from genit. of SEED *noun* + MAN *noun*.]

1 A sower of seed. **L16.**

2 A dealer in seed. **L17.**

seed-time /ˈsiːdtʌɪm/ *noun.* **LME.**

[from SEED *noun* + TIME *noun*.]

The season in which seed is sown.

> 🕮 AV *Gen.* 8:22 While the earth remaineth, seedtime and harvest . . shall not cease.

seedy *noun* var. of SIDI.

seedy /ˈsiːdi/ *adjective.* **L16.**

[from SEED *noun* + -Y[1] (fig. senses partly with allus. to phr. *go* or *run to seed*).]

1 Full of seed, bearing or containing many seeds. **L16.** ▸**b** Of glass: containing minute bubbles. **M19.**

2 *fig.* Unwell, poorly, esp. as a result of excessive eating or drinking. **E18.**

3 *fig.* Orig., impecunious. Now, having a shabby or squalid appearance, esp. in dress or decor; sordid or disreputable in nature. **E18.**

Special collocations: **seedy toe** a condition of a horse's hoof in which the inner wall becomes soft and crumbly.

■ **seedily** *adverb* **L19.** **seediness** *noun* **M19.**

see-er /ˈsiːə/ *noun. rare.* **E19.**

[from SEE *verb* + -ER[1]. Cf. SEER *noun*[1].]

A person who sees or beholds.

seegar /ˈsiːɡɑː/ *noun. US colloq.* & *dial.* **M20.**

[Repr. a pronunc.]

A cigar.

seege /siːdʒ/ *noun. obsolete* exc. *dial.* Also **seech** /siːtʃ/. **E17.**

[Origin unkn.]

The rush of the waves on the shore; surf.

see-ho /siːˈhəʊ/ *interjection* & *noun.* **L15.**

[Origin uncertain: perh. from SEE *verb* + HO *interjection*[1]. Cf. SA-HA, SOHO *interjection, noun, & verb*.]

(A cry) announcing the first view of the hare in coursing.

seeing /ˈsiːɪŋ/ *noun.* **LME.**

[from SEE *verb* + -ING[1].]

1 The action or process of SEE *verb*. Also (*rare*), an instance of this. **LME.**

2 The faculty of seeing, sight, vision. **LME.**

3 ASTRONOMY. The quality of telescopic observation; the extent to which an image remains steady and sharp (quantified as the apparent angular diameter of a point source). **E20.**

Comb.: **seeing-glass** (now *dial.*) a mirror.

seeing /ˈsiːɪŋ/ *ppl adjective.* **ME.**

[from SEE *verb* + -ING[2].]

That sees; having the faculty of sight.

seeing eye the faculty of seeing; ***Seeing Eye dog*** (US proprietary name for) a guide dog trained to lead the blind.

seeing /ˈsiːɪŋ/ *conjunction.* **E16.**

[Absol. use of pres. pple of SEE *verb*: see -ING[2].]

Considering that; inasmuch as; because, since. Also foll. by *as, that*.

seek /siːk/ *noun.* **L15.**

[from the verb.]

†**1** HUNTING. A series of notes on a horn calling out hounds to begin a chase and encouraging the quarry to run. Chiefly in ***blow a seek***. **L15–E19.**

2 COMPUTING. The movement of a read/write head to a new position on a storage device. Freq. in ***seek-time***, the time taken for this as part of the total access time. **M20.**

seek /siːk/ *verb.* Pa. t. & pple **sought** /sɔːt/.

[Old English *sēcan* (cf. BESEECH *verb*) = Old Frisian *sēka*, *sēza*, Old Saxon *sokian* (Dutch *zoeken*), Old High German *suohhan* (German *suchen*), Old Norse *sœkja*, Gothic *sōkjan*, from Germanic from Indo-European base repr. also by Latin *sagire* perceive by scent.]

▶ **I** *verb trans.* **1** Try to find, look for, (a thing or person of uncertain whereabouts); make a search or inquiry for, attempt to discover, (a thing or person suitable for a purpose etc., an unknown thing); (now *rare*) attempt to find out *if, what, why*, etc. **OE.** ▸**b** Foll. by *out*, †*up*, †*forth*: search for and find; trace, locate, or single out (a person) for companionship, information, etc. **ME.** ▸†**c** In *imper.* As an instruction to a reader: refer to, look up, see. **LME–E19.**

2 Make for, visit, or resort to (a place or person) for health, help, etc. **OE.** ▸**b** CHRISTIAN THEOLOGY. Draw near to (God) in prayer etc. *arch.* **OE.** ▸†**c** Pursue with hostile intention, attack, persecute. **OE–E17.**

3 Try or want to obtain or gain (a thing, esp. something advantageous); try to bring about or effect. **OE.** ▸†**b** Invent, contrive. Also foll. by *out*, *up*. **ME–L16.** ▸†**c** *refl.* Aim at one's own advantage. **LME–M17.** ▸**d** In *pass.* Be in demand because of qualities, value, etc.; be courted as a companion or partner. **L17.**

4 Ask for, demand, request. Foll. by *from*, †*at*, †*of* a person. **OE.**

5 Try or attempt *to do*. Formerly also, endeavour *that*. **OE.**

†**6** Entreat, beseech, (a person *to do*). Foll. by *of* the thing asked for. **ME–E17.**

7 a Search or explore (a place etc.) in order to find something. **ME.** ▸†**b** Try the endurance or worth of, examine, test. Freq. foll. by *out*, *through*. **ME–E17.** ▸†**c** Examine or consult (a book, register, etc.) for information. **L15–M17.**

> 🕮 **1** I. WATTS Men . . who shall seek truth with an unbiassed soul. BARONESS ORCZY We seek him here, we seek him there. D. PARKER She must depend . . on whatever odd jobs she could find, and she must not stop seeking them. A. CROSS Sarah . . stood . . seeking the words to say something. P. ANGADI I have to seek amusements elsewhere. **b** B. PYM When you are lonely . . seek out some other lonely person. M. SEYMOUR He travelled . . , visiting friends, seeking out old acquaintances. **2** TENNYSON A solemn grace Concluded, and we sought the gardens. **3** R. BAGOT She sought consolation in district visiting. J. GALSWORTHY He was not seeking election. **4** SHAKES. *Oth.* I will seek satisfaction of you. H. J. EYSENCK A Jewess whose hand had been sought in marriage. **5** H. MACMILLAN The Committee sought by discussion . . to secure a peaceful settlement.

▶**II** *verb intrans.* **8** Make a search or inquiry; (foll. by *after*, *for*) look for, try to obtain. **OE.** ▸**b** In *imper.* As an instruction to a retriever: go and look for shot game etc. Also foll. by *out.* **M19.**
†**9** Go, move, proceed. **OE–M16.**
10 Go or resort *to* a place; pay a visit or make an appeal *to* (†*on*, †*upon*) a person; have recourse *to* an action etc. *arch.* **ME.**

> 📖 **8** L. STEFFENS It would be absurd to seek for organized reform in St. Louis. *Listener* Beckett . . requires you to seek and not to find.

Phrases: **far to seek**, **much to seek** = *to seek* (a) below. **seek dead** (usu. in *imper.*) = sense 8b above. **seek** GAPE-SEED. ***seek one's fortune***: see FORTUNE *noun*. ***seek repose***: see REPOSE *noun*. **to seek** (*a*) not yet found, lacking, missing; *arch.* wanting or deficient in; (*b*) (now *rare* or *obsolete*) at a loss (*for*), unable to understand or decide.
With prepositions in specialized senses: **seek after** court or desire (a person) as a companion etc.; search for (a thing) on account of qualities, value, etc.; prize (usu. in *pass.*); (see also sense 8 above, ***sought-after*** s.v. SOUGHT *ppl adjective*). †**seek on**, **seek upon** attack, assail.
Comb.: ***hide-and-seek***: see HIDE *verb*[1]; **seek-no-further** a red-streaked variety of winter apple.

seeker /ˈsiːkə/ *noun*. **ME.**
[from prec. + -ER[1].]
1 A person seeking something; a searcher, an explorer, an investigator. Freq. as 2nd elem. of comb. **ME.** ▸**b** ECCLESIASTICAL HISTORY. (**S-**.) A member of a class of sectaries in the 16th and 17th cents. **E17.**
2 An instrument used in seeking or searching; *spec.* (*a*) a slender blunt-tipped probe used in dissection; (*b*) the viewfinder of an astronomical telescope; (*c*) (a device in) a missile which locates its target by detecting emissions of heat, light, radio waves, etc. **M17.**

> 📖 **1** *Blackwood's Magazine* Leonardo was mentally a seeker after truth. M. DAS The promenade . . became crowded with seekers of fresh air. ***office-seeker***, ***pleasure-seeker***, ***truth-seeker***, etc. **2** ***comet-seeker***: see COMET *noun*.

seeking /ˈsiːkɪŋ/ *noun*. **ME.**
[from SEEK *verb* + -ING[1].]
1 The action of SEEK *verb*. **ME.**
†**2** A thing sought. *rare*. **ME–E17.**
1 of one's own seeking, **of one's seeking** (of an honour, quarrel, etc.) sought by oneself.

seeking /ˈsiːkɪŋ/ *ppl adjective*. **L15.**
[formed as prec. + -ING[2].]
That seeks. Freq. as 2nd elem. of comb., as ***heat-seeking***, ***pleasure-seeking***, ***publicity-seeking***, ***self-seeking***, etc.
■ **seekingly** *adverb* (*rare*) in a seeking or enquiring manner, searchingly **E20.**

seel /siːl/ *verb*[1] *trans.* Also **seal**. **L15.**
[Old French *ciller*, *siller* or medieval Latin *ciliare*, from Latin *cilium* eyelid.]
1 FALCONRY etc. Close the eyes of (a hawk etc.) by stitching up the eyelids; stitch *up* (the eyes of a bird). Now *Hist.* **L15.**
2 *transf.* & *fig.* Close (a person's eyes); blind, prevent from seeing or discovering something. *arch.* **L16.**

†**seel** *verb*[2] *intrans.* **E17–M18.**
[Origin unkn.]
NAUTICAL. Of a ship: make a sudden lurch to one side.

seely /ˈsiːli/ *adjective*. Long *obsolete* exc. *dial.*
[Old English (*ge*)*sǣlig* = Old Frisian *sēlich*, Old Saxon *sālig*, Middle Dutch *sālech* (Dutch *zalig*), Old High German *sālig* (German *selig*), from West Germanic base meaning 'luck, happiness'. Cf. SELE, SILLY.]
1 Happy, fortunate, lucky; favoured or blessed by God. **OE.**
2 Pious, holy, good. **ME.**
3 Innocent, harmless; helpless, defenceless; deserving of pity or sympathy. **ME.**
4 Insignificant, trifling, poor; feeble, frail. **ME.**
5 Foolish, simple, silly. **LME.**

seem /siːm/ *noun*. *obsolete* exc. *dial.* (chiefly *Scot.*). **LME.**
[from the verb.]
Seeming, semblance, appearance.

seem /siːm/ *verb*. **ME.**
[Old Norse *sœma* honour (Middle Swedish *befit*), from *sœmr* fitting, seemly.]
†**1 a** *verb trans.* Suit, fit, befit, (a person, place, etc.); be appropriate or suitable *that*, *to do*. Freq. *impers.* with *it*. **ME–E17.** ▸**b** *verb intrans.* Be appropriate, seemly, or fitting. (Foll. by *for*, *to*, *with*.) Usu. *impers.* with *it*. **ME–E17.**
2 *verb intrans.* (In some uses as copular verb.) Appear outwardly or superficially (but not be in reality). Also, give the impression or sensation of being, be perceived as; be apparently, appear so far as can be ascertained; (in weakened sense, freq. in questions) be. Foll. by *to be*, *to do*, *that*, *as if*, *as though*, †*as*. Also *impers.* with *it*. **ME.** ▸**b** Imagine oneself, appear to oneself; *colloq.* do accidentally or for an unspecified or unknown reason (freq. with neg.). Foll. by *to be*, *to do*. **M17.**
†**3** *verb intrans.* Be manifested, come to view, be seen. **ME–L16.**
4 *verb intrans.* Appear to exist or be present. Now *poet.* or *rhet.* exc. as in ***there seems***. **LME.**
†**5** *verb trans.* Think, believe, imagine (*that*, a thing); think fit *to do*. **LME–E17.**

> 📖 **2** F. BROOKE Young women are not the angels they seem to be. M. C. HARRIS It seemed as if earth had . . flowered into a paradise. V. WOOLF A tendency to use the wrong words made her seem . . incompetent. J. STEINBECK The whole body, without seeming to move, had moved. G. MARKSTEIN 'What seems to be the trouble?' asked the operator. A. BROOKNER Romantic heroes always seem to be wandering among ruins. **b** SHELLEY I seem again to share thy smile. I. BAIRD He couldn't seem to get the boy out of his head. I. MURDOCH Oh dear, I seem to have knocked over my water. **4** *Law Times* There seemed a . . consensus of opinion that inventors were a nuisance.

Phrases: **it seems**, **it would seem**, (*arch.*) **it should seem** (in a hesitant, guarded, or ironical statement) it appears to be true or a fact, apparently, (foll. by *that* or parenthetically); see also senses 1, 2 above. **seem good to** *arch.* be the will or decision of, please (a person).
■ **seemer** *noun* a person making a pretence or show **E17.**

seeming /ˈsiːmɪŋ/ *noun*. Now *arch.* or *literary*. **LME.**
[from prec. + -ING[1].]
The fact of seeming or appearing to be someone or something; an instance of this; appearance, look, aspect. Also, external appearance considered as deceptive or as distinguished from reality; (an) illusion, (a) semblance, (a) likeness.

> 📖 GEO. ELIOT That dissidence between inward reality and outward seeming. E. R. EDDISON Light and delicate was his frame and seeming. †**by seeming** = ***in all seeming*** below. †**in a person's seeming** = ***to a person's seeming*** below. **in all seeming**, **in seeming** to all appearance, apparently. †**to a person's seeming** as it seems or appears to a person, in a person's opinion or judgement. ***to outward seeming***: see OUTWARD *adjective* 2.

seeming /ˈsiːmɪŋ/ *adjective*. **ME.**
[formed as prec. + -ING[2].]
†**1** Suitable, appropriate, fitting. **ME–L17.**
2 Apparent but perhaps not real, giving the impression of, having a specified appearance. Also, apparent only, ostensible, professed. Freq. as 1st or 2nd elem. of comb. **ME.**
†**3** Probable, likely. **LME–M17.**

> 📖 **2** J. W. MACKAIL Dreams of some settled and seeming-changeless order. D. H. LAWRENCE Your fair-seeming face covered the . . vice of your true nature. J. BETJEMAN The love between those seeming opposites.

seemingly /ˈsiːmɪŋli/ *adverb*. **LME.**
[from prec. + -LY[2].]
1 Fittingly, becomingly. Now *rare*. **LME.**
2 To external appearance, apparently, so far as can be ascertained. Also, ostensibly, professedly. **L16.**

> 📖 **2** H. JAMES The sight of all the things he wanted to change had seemingly no power to irritate him. *She* Witches . . live seemingly ordinary lives.

seemingness /ˈsiːmɪŋnɪs/ *noun*. **M17.**
[formed as prec. + -NESS.]
The quality or fact of seeming or appearing to be someone or something; pretence; semblance, likeness.

seemless /ˈsiːmlɪs/ *adjective*. Long *arch.* **L16.**
[from SEEM *verb* (assumed to be source of SEEMLY *adjective*) + -LESS.]
Unseemly; shameful; unfitting.

seemlihead /ˈsiːmlɪhɛd/ *noun*. Long *arch.* **LME.**
[from SEEMLY *adjective* + -HEAD.]
The condition of being seemly, seemliness.

seemlily /ˈsiːmlɪli/ *adverb*. Long *non-standard*. **LME.**
[formed as next + -LY[2].]
In a seemly manner; so as to appear seemly or attractive; nobly, elegantly.

seemliness /ˈsiːmlɪnɪs/ *noun*. **LME.**
[from next + -NESS.]
†**1** Pleasing appearance, attractiveness, elegance or nobility of form. **LME–M17.**
2 Propriety, decorum, appropriateness. **M16.**

seemly /ˈsiːmli/ *adjective*. **ME.**
[Old Norse *sœmiligr*, from *sœmr*: see SEEM *verb*, -LY[1].]
1 Pleasing or attractive in appearance; well-formed, noble, fine. *arch.* **ME.**
2 Conforming to propriety or good taste; fitting, decorous, proper. **ME.**
†**3** Suitable *for* or appropriate *to* a person, occasion, etc. **ME–M17.**
†**4** Apparent, seeming. Formerly also, likely. *rare*. **LME–E19.**

> 📖 **1** *Manchester Examiner* A fair and seemly edifice. **2** *Scrutiny* The discreet, self-effacing and seemly behaviour . . of a good undertaker. P. FUSSELL Nor would it be seemly here to dwell on the class significance of religious beliefs.

seemly /ˈsiːmli/ *adverb*. **ME.**
[Old Norse *sœmiliga*, *sœmr*: see -LY[2].]
1 In a pleasing manner; so as to appear pleasing, attractive, or noble. *arch.* **ME.**
2 Fittingly, appropriately; decently, decorously. *arch.* **ME.**
†**3** To a moderate extent, fairly. *rare*. **LME–M17.**
4 Apparently, seemingly. *dial.* **E19.**

seen /siːn/ *adjective*. **ME.**
[pa. pple of SEE *verb*.]
1 That has been seen, able to be seen; visible, open, manifest. Now *rare* exc. opp. ***unseen***. **ME.**
2 (*Well*, *badly*, etc.) informed or versed *in*. *arch.* **E16.**

> 📖 **1** *absol.*: J. R. LOWELL He shall paint the Seen, since the Unseen will not sit to him.

seep /siːp/ *noun*[1]. Also redupl. **seep-seep**. **M20.**
[Imit.: cf. CHEEP, PEEP *verb*[1] & *noun*[3].]
= CHEEP *noun*. Also as *interjection*.

seep /siːp/ *verb* & *noun*[2]. Orig. *dial.* & *US*. **L18.**
[Perh. dial. devel. of Old English *sīpian* SIPE *verb*.]
▶**A** *verb intrans.* Ooze out, trickle gradually, percolate slowly. **L18.**

> 📖 E. WAUGH The rain . . seeped under the front door. P. D. JAMES She felt the dampness seeping through her . . gloves. *fig.*: M. GARDINER The gloom of wartime seeped into every aspect of living.

▶**B** *noun*. **1** Moisture that drips or oozes out. *dial.* **E19.**
2 A small spring; *US* a place where petroleum etc. oozes slowly out of the ground. **E19.**
3 A sip of liquor. *dial.* **L19.**

seepage /ˈsiːpɪdʒ/ *noun*. Orig. *Scot.* & *US*. **E19.**
[from prec. + -AGE.]
The action or an instance of seeping; percolation or oozing of water, fluid, etc.; leakage, esp. into or out of a reservoir or channel. Also, fluid etc. which seeps or oozes out.
Comb.: **seepage lake** a lake that loses water chiefly by seepage into the ground containing it.

seer /sɪə, *in sense 2 also* ˈsiːə/ *noun*[1]. **ME.**
[from SEE *verb* + -ER[1].]
1 A person of supposed supernatural insight, esp. into the future; a person able to see visions, a prophet; *transf.* a predictor of events, trends, etc. **ME.**
2 *gen.* A person who sees. (Foll. by *of* the thing seen.) Cf. SEE-ER. **LME.**
†**3** An overseer, an inspector. **L15–E17.**
■ **seeress** *noun* a female seer **M19.** **seerlike** *adjective* resembling (that of) a seer **M19.** **seership** *noun* the office or function of a seer **L18.**

seer /sɪə/ *noun*[2]. Also **ser**. **E17.**
[Hindi *ser* from Prakrit *satera* from Greek *statēr* hundredweight.]
In the Indian subcontinent, a varying unit of weight of about one kilogram.

seer *noun*[3] var. of SEIR.

seerpaw *noun* var. of SERPAW.

seersucker /ˈsɪəsʌkə/ *noun* & *adjective*. **E18.**
[Alt. of Persian *šīr o šakar* lit. 'milk and sugar', transf. 'striped linen garment'.]
▶**A** *noun*. A thin freq. striped cotton, linen, etc., fabric with a puckered surface; a garment made of seersucker. **E18.**
▶**B** *attrib.* or as *adjective*. Made of seersucker. **M18.**

see-saw /ˈsiːsɔː/ *verb*. Also **seesaw**. **E18.**
[from the noun.]
1 *verb intrans.* Move up and down or backwards and forwards (as) on a see-saw; play see-saw; *fig.* vacillate in policy, emotion, etc., vary or swing rapidly and repeatedly in fortune etc. **E18.**
2 *verb trans.* Cause to move in a see-saw motion. **M18.**

> 📖 **1** GEO. ELIOT She was seesawing on the elder bough. M. GEE A girl who see-sawed between . . wild gaiety and . . total seclusion. *Financial Times* The dollar see-sawed wildly yesterday, first dropping . . and later rising sharply.

see-saw /ˈsiːsɔː/ *interjection*, *noun*, *adjective*, & *adverb*. Also **seesaw**, (as interjection) **see saw**. **M17.**
[Redupl. of SAW *verb*[1], symbolizing alternating movement.]
▶**A** *interjection*. Used as part of a rhythmical refrain, app. orig. by sawyers but now usu. by children, esp. to accompany alternating movements in games. **M17.**

> 📖 *Nursery rhyme*: See saw, Margery Daw.

▶**B** *noun*. **1** An up-and-down or to-and-fro motion. **E18.**
2 *fig.* A situation changing rapidly and repeatedly; a contest in which the advantage repeatedly changes from one side to the other. **E18.** ▸**b** WHIST. = ***cross-ruff*** (a) s.v. CROSS-. **M18.**
3 A plank balanced on a central support, on each end of which people (usu. children) sit and swing up and down by pushing the ground alternately with their feet. **E19.**

1 K. WHITE The delicious see-saw of a post-chaise. 2 A. F. DOUGLAS-HOME There were .. two alternatives .., and there was the usual see-saw of argument. 3 R. DAHL The swings and the see-saws and the high slide.

▶ **C** *adjective & adverb.* Moving or progressing up and down or backwards and forwards like a see-saw (*lit. & fig.*). M18.

Speedway Star The see-saw match eventually turned in their favour.

Phrases: **go see-saw** move with a see-saw motion, vacillate, alternate. **play at see-saw**, **play see-saw** engage in the game or amusement of sitting on a see-saw and swinging up and down.

seesee /ˈsiːsiː/ *noun.* Also **see-see**, **sisi**. M19.
[Imit., from the noise of the wings.]
A small partridge, *Ammoperdix griseogularis*, of SW Asia. Also ***seesee partridge***.

seethe /siːð/ *noun.* E19.
[from the verb.]
Seething or churning of waves etc.; intense commotion or agitation.

seethe /siːð/ *verb.* Pa. t. **seethed**, †**sod**; pa. pple **seethed**, †**sod**, †**sodden**. See also SOD *adjective*, SODDEN *adjective*[1].
[Old English *sēoþan* = Old Frisian *siātha*, Old High German *siodan* (Dutch *zieden*, *sieden*), Old Norse *sjóða*, from Germanic.]
1 *verb trans.* Cook (food etc.) by boiling or stewing, heat in liquid. *arch.* OE. ▸†**b** Digest (food). OE–E17.
2 *verb intrans.* Of a liquid, pot, etc.: be subjected to boiling or stewing; boil, bubble up; *transf.* foam, froth; churn, bubble; be intensely hot. Freq. as ***seething ppl adjective***. ME.
3 *verb trans.* Steep, saturate, or soak in a liquid; reduce or soften by boiling, soaking, etc. Chiefly as ***seethed ppl adjective***. Cf. SODDEN *adjective*[1]. L16.
4 *verb intrans.* (Of a person etc.) be in a state of agitation or turmoil, esp. with (freq. unexpressed) anger; (of a crowd, place, etc.) move or be filled with confused hectic activity. (Foll. by *with*.) Freq. as ***seething ppl adjective***. L16.

2 J. CONRAD The river .. seethed in frothy streaks. *Country Living* Never .. leave cabbage to seethe for long. 4 G. ORWELL A mob of people seethed, shouting and jostling. G. HUNTINGTON Milan station was seething with people. A. STORR She was seething with resentment.

■ †**seether** *noun* a person engaged in boiling food or water; *rare* a utensil for boiling: ME–E18. **seethingly** *adverb* in a seething manner L19.

see-through /ˈsiːθruː/ *adjective & noun.* Also (*informal*, chiefly *commercial*) **-thru**. M20.
[from SEE *verb* + THROUGH *preposition & adverb*.]
▶ **A** *adjective.* That can be seen through, transparent; having spaces allowing the passage of light; (esp. of a garment or fabric) diaphanous, translucent. M20.

B. NORMAN Some slinky girl spy in a see-through night-dress.

▶ **B** *noun.* **1** The quality of allowing the passage of light; the extent to which it is possible to see clearly through something; unimpeded vision. M20.
2 A see-through fabric or garment. M20.

Sefer Torah /ˈseɪfə ˈtɔːrə, -ˈtəʊ-/ *noun.* Also ***Sepher Torah***. Pl. ***Sifrei Torah*** /sɪˈfreɪ/, ***Siphrei Torah***. M17.
[Hebrew *sēper tōrāh* book of (the) Law. Cf. TORAH.]
JUDAISM. A scroll containing the Torah or Pentateuch.

Sefton /ˈsɛft(ə)n/ *noun.* L19.
[from the Earl of *Sefton*.]
Chiefly *Hist.* (In full ***Sefton landau***) a kind of landau or horse-drawn carriage. Also, a kind of curb-bit.

seg /sɛg/ *noun*[1]. *dial.* L15.
[Old Norse *sigg* hard skin.]
A callus, a hard patch of skin, esp. on the hand.

seg /sɛg/ *noun*[2]. *dial.* E17.
[Origin unkn.]
An animal castrated when fully grown.

seg /sɛg/ *noun*[3]. M20.
[Abbreviation of SEGMENT *noun*.]
A metal stud fixed to the toe or heel of a shoe or boot to strengthen or protect it from wear. Freq. in *pl.*

seg /sɛg/ *noun*[4]. M20.
[Abbreviation.]
1 = SEGREGATIONIST *noun*. Cf. OUTSEG. *US colloq.* M20.
2 = SEGREGATION 1(g). *slang* (chiefly *US*). L20.
■ **seggie** *noun* (*US colloq.*) = SEG *noun*[4] 1 M20.

seg *noun*[5] see SEDGE.

segar *noun* var. of CIGAR.

Seger cone /ˈzeɪgə kəʊn/ *noun phr.* Also **s-**. L19.
[from H. A. *Seger* (1839–93), German ceramics technologist.]
Each of a series of small numbered cones or pyramids made of different mixtures of refractory material and flux so that they melt at different specific temperatures, used to indicate the temperature inside a kiln etc.

segholate *adjective & noun* var. of SEGOLATE.

segment /ˈsɛgm(ə)nt/ *noun.* L16.
[Latin *segmentum*, from *secare* cut: see -MENT.]
1 a GEOMETRY. A part of a plane (or solid) figure separated off by an intersecting straight line (or plane); *esp.* (more fully ***segment of a circle***) a plane figure contained by a chord and an arc of a circle. Also *loosely*, an arc of a circle, a sector of a circle. L16. ▸**b** A portion of anything resembling a segment of a circle or sphere. M17.
2 A piece cut or broken off unevenly, a fragment. *rare.* L16.
3 a GEOMETRY. A finite part of a line between two points; a division of a line. E17. ▸**b** ACOUSTICS. Each of the portions into which the length of a vibrating string, wire, etc., is divided by the nodes. M19.
4 BOTANY. Each of the portions into which a leaf or other plant organ is divided by long clefts or incisions. E18.
5 Each of the parts into which a thing is or may be divided; a sharply cut or delineated piece; a division, a section. M18. ▸**b** ANTHROPOLOGY. Any lower level division of a social structure, *esp.* one based on the same principles as higher order units. M20. ▸**c** LINGUISTICS. A unit forming part of a continuum of speech or text; an isolable unit in a phonological or syntactic system. M20. ▸**d** BROADCASTING. A division of the day's broadcasting time, a time slot. Also, a separate broadcast item, esp. within a programme. Orig. *US.* M20. ▸**e** COMPUTING. A functional subdivision of a module. M20.
6 ANATOMY & ZOOLOGY. Each of the series of similar anatomical units of which the body and its appendages are composed in various animals, esp. arthropods and annelids; a somite, a metamere. Also, each of a series of functional or embryological divisions of a vertebrate body or limb, esp. of the spinal column, musculature, or central nervous system. M19.

1a segment of a sphere a solid figure bounded by a portion of the surface of a sphere and an intersecting plane, or two parallel planes. **4** PERIANTH ***segment***. **5** *Times* Every segment of national outlay must be judged. D. PROFUMO He offered the boy two segments of orange.

segment /sɛgˈmɛnt, ˈsɛgm(ə)nt/ *verb.* M19.
[from the noun.]
1 *verb trans.* Divide into segments; subject to or produce by a process of segmentation. M19.
2 *verb intrans.* Become divided into segments; *spec.* (***a***) BIOLOGY undergo a process of segmentation; (***b***) ANTHROPOLOGY (of a lineage group or clan) divide into smaller autonomous branches within a larger social structure. L19.
■ **segmentaˈbility** *noun* ability to be segmented M20. **segˈmentable** *adjective* able to be segmented M20.

segmental /sɛgˈmɛnt(ə)l/ *adjective.* E19.
[from SEGMENT *noun* + -AL[1].]
1 a ARCHITECTURE. Designating or of the form of an arch, the curved part of which forms a shallow arc of a circle, less than a semicircle. E19. ▸**b** Having the form of a segment (or, loosely, of an arc) of a circle. M19.
2 Of, pertaining to, or composed of segments or divisions. M19. ▸**b** LINGUISTICS. Of, pertaining to, or designating the division of speech or (less commonly) text into segments. Freq. in ***segmental phoneme***, a consonant or vowel phoneme, which can occur as one of the units in a sequence of such phonemes. M20.
■ **segmentally** *adverb* L19.

segmentalize /sɛgˈmɛnt(ə)lʌɪz/ *verb trans.* Also **-ise**. M20.
[from prec. + -IZE.]
Divide into segments; *spec.* (LINGUISTICS) represent (a grammatical feature) as a distinct segment of speech or text.
■ **segmentaliˈzation** *noun* division into segments M20. **segmentalizer** *noun* M20.

segmentary /sɛgˈmɛnt(ə)ri/ *adjective.* M19.
[from SEGMENT *noun* + -ARY[1]. Cf. French *segmentaire*.]
1 Of the nature of or resembling a segment or an arc of a circle, segmental. M19.
2 Pertaining to segments or divisions, composed of segments. L19.

segmentation /sɛgm(ə)nˈteɪʃ(ə)n/ *noun.* M17.
[from SEGMENT *verb* + -ATION.]
The action or process of division into segments; the state or manner of being segmented; *spec.* in BIOLOGY, (***a***) cell division by internal partitioning, *esp.* the cleavage of an ovum; (***b***) division into somites or metameric segments.
¶ In isolated use before M19.

segmented /ˈsɛgm(ə)ntɪd, sɛgˈmɛntɪd/ *adjective.* M19.
[from SEGMENT *verb* + -ED[1].]
1 Consisting of or divided into segments; *spec.* (***a***) ZOOLOGY formed of a longitudinal series of similar parts; (***b***) BOTANY (of a leaf) divided into segments or lobes. M19.
2 EMBRYOLOGY. Of a cell, esp. an ovum: divided or split up by segmentation into cells. L19.
3 ARCHAEOLOGY. Of a prehistoric gallery grave: divided into sections or segments; having compartments. E20.

segmenter /sɛgˈmɛntə/ *noun.* E20.
[formed as prec. + -ER[1].]
ZOOLOGY. A fully developed sporozoan schizont ready to divide into a number of merozoites.

sego /ˈsiːgəʊ/ *noun. US.* Pl. **-os**. M19.
[Prob. from Ute.]
A mariposa lily, *Calochortus nuttallii*, with an edible bulb. Also ***sego lily***.

segolate /ˈsɛgələt/ *adjective & noun.* Also **segh-**. M19.
[mod. Latin *seg(h)olatus*, from Hebrew *sĕgōl* a vowel-point (corresp. to English *e*) and its sound.]
HEBREW GRAMMAR. ▶**A** *adjective.* Orig., (of a disyllabic noun) having the vowel *sĕgōl* in both syllables. Now freq. (*gen.*), designating the class of disyllabic nouns having an unaccented short vowel (usu. *sĕgōl*) in the last syllable. M19.
▶ **B** *noun.* A segolate noun. M19.
■ Earlier †**segolated** *adjective*: only in E19.

segoon *noun* var. of SACCOON.

segreant /ˈsɛgrɪənt/ *adjective.* M16.
[Origin uncertain: perh. from French *s'érigeant* lit. 'erecting itself'.]
HERALDRY. Of a griffin: with wings extended; rampant. Usu. *postpositive*.

segregable /ˈsɛgrɪgəb(ə)l/ *adjective.* E20.
[from Latin *segregare* SEGREGATE *verb*: see -ABLE.]
That may be segregated.

segregant /sɛgrɪg(ə)nt/ *adjective & noun.* M17.
[Latin *segregant-* pres. ppl stem of *segregare*: see SEGREGATE *verb*, -ANT[1].]
▶ **A** *adjective.* †**1** Separated, divided. *rare.* Only in M17.
2 GENETICS. Having or designating a genotype derived by segregation, esp. one different from that of either parent. M20.
▶ **B** *noun.* GENETICS. A segregant organism. M20.

segregate /ˈsɛgrɪgət/ *adjective & noun.* LME.
[formed as next: see -ATE[1], -ATE[2].]
▶ **A** *adjective.* **1** Separated, set apart, isolated. Now *rare*. LME.
2 *spec.* in BIOLOGY. Separated (wholly or partially) from the parent or from one another; not aggregated. Also, (of a hybrid) having a phenotype chiefly resembling that of one parent. L18.
▶ **B** *noun.* **1** BOTANY. A species distinguished, freq. on the basis of minute characters, within an aggregate or collective species. L19.
2 METALLURGY. A consituent of an alloy which becomes segregated when the alloy solidifies on cooling. E20.
3 A group, a class, a category. M20.

segregate /ˈsɛgrɪgeɪt/ *verb.* M16.
[Latin *segregat-* pa. ppl stem of *segregare* separate from the flock, formed as SE- + *greg-*, *grex* flock: see -ATE[3].]
1 *verb trans.* Separate (a person, a class of persons, etc.) from the main body or a particular class of people; set apart, isolate; divide or split (people) into groups. M16. ▸**b** Subject (people) to racial segregation; enforce racial segregation in (a community, establishment, etc.); divide or separate on the basis of race. Freq. as ***segregated ppl adjective***. Cf. INTEGRATE *verb* 4. E20.
2 *verb trans.* Set (a thing) aside from other things or from the main body; place in a group apart from the rest; separate out and collect (certain constituents of a mixture). L16.
3 *verb intrans.* Separate from a main body or mass and collect together. M19. ▸**b** GENETICS. Undergo or display segregation of alleles. E20.

1 J. HAYWARD Isolated .. writers, segregated from the world in their ivory towers. M. HOLROYD Pupils .. segregated themselves into two classes: 'gentlemen' and 'cads'. P. KAVANAGH The sexes .. were segregated on opposite sides of the .. aisle. **b** *Time* Negro 'sit-in' demonstrations at segregated lunch counters. E. P. THOMPSON The Irish were .. segregated in their own .. quarters. 3 *Fraser's Magazine* The provinces had segregated into independent principalities.

segregation /sɛgrɪˈgeɪʃ(ə)n/ *noun.* M16.
[Late Latin *segregatio(n-)*, formed as prec.: see -ATION.]
1 The action or an instance of segregating (a person, group, etc.); the state of being segregated; *spec.* †(***a***) separation or schism from a church etc.; (***b***) the separation or isolation of part of a community or group from the main body or from a particular class etc.; (***c***) *rare* dispersal or break-up of a collective unity; (***d***) the separation of a portion or portions of a collective or complex unity from the rest; the isolation of particular constituents of a mixture; (***e***) GENETICS the separation and independent transmission of pairs of homologous alleles, due to the splitting of pairs of homologous chromosomes into separate gametes at meiosis; (***f***) the enforced separation of different racial groups in a country, community, establishment, etc. (cf. INTEGRATION 3); (***g***) (chiefly *US*) the isolation or separate confinement of dangerous or troublesome prisoners. M16.

2 Orig. *spec.*, a schismatic body. Later *gen.*, something segregated. M16.

> 1 *Times* Racial segregation in public schools . . was unconstitutional. T. SHARPE There will be no High Table. All forms of academic segregation will disappear.

segregational /sɛɡrɪˈɡeɪʃ(ə)n(ə)l/ *adjective.* L19.
[from prec. + -AL[1].]
Of, pertaining to, or characterized by segregation.

segregationalist /sɛɡrɪˈɡeɪʃ(ə)n(ə)lɪst/ *adjective & noun.* M20.
[from prec. + -IST.]
= next.

segregationist /sɛɡrɪˈɡeɪʃ(ə)nɪst/ *adjective & noun.* M20.
[from SEGREGATION + -IST. Cf. INTEGRATIONIST.]
▶ **A** *adjective.* Of, pertaining to, or designating a person or policy advocating or supporting political or racial segregation. M20.
▶ **B** *noun.* An adherent or advocate of segregation. M20.

segregative /ˈsɛɡrɪɡeɪtɪv/ *adjective.* L16.
[medieval Latin *segregativus*, formed as SEGREGATE *verb*: see -IVE.]
1 †**a** GRAMMAR & LOGIC. Designating adversative and disjunctive relations or conjunctions; (of a proposition) consisting of members joined by a segregative relation. L16–E17. ▸**b** Having the property of separating the elements or constituent parts of matter. *arch.* L17.
2 Tending to cause separation or disruption. Also, unsociable. L17.

segue /ˈsɛɡweɪ/ *verb & noun.* M20.
[from next.]
▶ **A** *verb intrans.* Pres. pple & verbal noun **segueing**. Of a person or music: move without interruption from one (live or pre-recorded) song or melody to another; *transf.* move smoothly or without interruption to the next matter or stage. Freq. foll. by *into*. M20.

> *Guitar Player* 'Well you needn't' . . segued into 'Foggy Mountain Breakdown'.

▶ **B** *noun.* An uninterrupted transition from one song or melody to another. M20.

segue /ˈsɛɡweɪ/ *adverb.* M18.
[Italian, 3rd person sing. pres. indic. of *seguire* follow.]
MUSIC. A direction: proceed to the next movement without a break; continue with an indicated formula.

seguidilla /seɡiˈdiʎa, sɛɡɪˈdiːljə/ *noun.* Pl. **-as** /-as, -əz/. M18.
[Spanish, from *seguida* following, sequence, from *seguir* follow.]
A Spanish dance in 3/4 or 6/8 time; a piece of music for this dance.

seguiriyas /seɡiˈrias/ *noun.* E20.
[Spanish dial. var. of prec.]
In full ***seguiriyas gitana*** /xiˈtana/ [= Gypsy]. A regional variety of flamenco music; a song or dance accompanying this.

segundo /sɪˈɡʌndəʊ/ *noun.* Pl. **-os**. M19.
[from Juan *Segundo*, author of an 1832 book on bridle bits.]
A kind of bridle bit. Also ***segundo bit***.

Seguridad /sɪˌɡʊərɪˈdad, *foreign* seˌɡuriˈðað/ *noun.* M20.
[Spanish = security.]
The Spanish security service.

Sehna /ˈsɛnə/ *noun & adjective.* Also **sen(n)a**. E20.
[A town (now Sanandaj) in Kurdistan.]
(Designating) a variety of small finely woven Persian rug.
Sehna knot a kind of knot used in weaving some oriental carpets.

Sehnsucht /ˈzeːnzʊxt/ *noun.* M19.
[German.]
Yearning, wistful longing.

†**seiant** *adjective* see SEJANT.

seicentismo /seɪtʃɛnˈtɪzməʊ/ *noun.* Also **S-**. L19.
[Italian, from *seicento* SEICENTO.]
= SEICENTO.

seicentist /seɪˈtʃɛntɪst/ *noun & adjective.* Pl. of noun **-isti** /-ɪsti/. Also **S-**. M19.
[Italian *seicentisti* pl., from *seicento*: see next.]
(Designating) an Italian artist or writer of the seventeenth century.

seicento /seɪˈtʃɛntəʊ/ *noun.* Also **S-**. E20.
[Italian = six hundred.]
The seventeenth century in Italy; the Italian style of art, literature, etc., of this period.
■ **seicentoist** *noun* (*rare*) = SEICENTIST *noun* M19.

seiche /seɪʃ/ *noun.* M19.
[Swiss French, perh. from German *Seiche* sinking (of water).]
PHYSICAL GEOGRAPHY. A short-lived standing oscillation of a lake or other body of water (as a bay or basin of the sea), resembling a tide, caused esp. by abrupt changes in atmospheric conditions or by small earth tremors.
■ **seiching** *noun* the occurrence of a seiche; the motion occurring in a seiche: M20.

seidel /ˈzʌɪd(ə)l/ *noun.* E20.
[German *Seidel*, orig. a liquid measure varying between about a third and a half of a litre.]
A beer mug or glass; the quantity of liquid contained by such a vessel.

Seidlitz /ˈsɛdlɪts, ˈsʌɪdlɪts/ *noun.* L18.
[A village in Bohemia, where there is a spring impregnated with magnesium sulphate and carbonic acid.]
Used *attrib.* to denote substances associated with the spring at Seidlitz (see above) or having its laxative properties.
†**Seidlitz salt** magnesium sulphate. †**Seidlitz water** an artificial laxative of the same composition as the water of the Seidlitz spring. **Seidlitz powder** a laxative consisting of two powders, one of tartaric acid and the other of a mixture of sodium potassium tartrate and sodium bicarbonate, which are mixed in solution and drunk while effervescing.

seif /siːf, seɪf/ *noun.* Also **sif**. E20.
[Arab. *sayf* lit. 'sword'.]
PHYSICAL GEOGRAPHY. A sand-dune in the form of a long narrow ridge parallel to the direction of the prevailing wind. Also ***seif dune***.

Seignette salt /ˈsɛnɛt sɔːlt, sɒlt; seɪˈnjɛt/ *noun phr.* Now *rare* or *obsolete*. Also (earlier) †**Seignette's salt**. M18.
[from name of a 17th-cent. French chemist.]
Sodium potassium tartrate, Rochelle salt.

seigneur /seɪˈnjəː, *foreign* sɛɲœːr (*pl. same*)/ *noun.* Also **S-**. L16.
[Old & mod. French from Latin SENIOR.]
Esp. in France and Canada, a feudal lord, the lord of a manor, (chiefly *Hist.* exc. in the Channel Islands, *spec.* Sark). Now *gen.*, a lord, a person exercising (feudal) authority.

> A. MORICE He still sees himself as the Seigneur of the neighbourhood. ***droit du seigneur***, ***droit de seigneur***, ***droits du seigneur***, ***droits de seigneur***: see DROIT *noun*[1] 1. ***grand seigneur***: see GRAND *adjective*[2].

¶ Cf. SEIGNIOR, SENHOR, SEÑOR, SIGNOR.
■ **ˈseigneuress** *noun* a woman exercising feudal authority; the wife of a seigneur: M19. **seigneurial** *adjective* of or pertaining to a seigneur or lord; lordly, authoritative, feudal: M17.

seigneury /ˈseɪnjəːri/ *noun.* Also ***seigneurie*** /sɛɲœːri (*pl. same*)/. L17.
[French *seigneurie* (Old French *seignorie*) formed as prec.: see -Y[3]. Cf. SEIGNIORY, SIGNORIA, SIGNORY.]
1 *Hist.* Esp. in France and Canada, a landed estate held by feudal tenure, the territory or domain of a seigneur. L17.
2 Esp. in the Channel Islands and Canada, the residence or mansion of a seigneur. L19.

seignior /ˈseɪnjə/ *noun.* ME.
[Anglo-Norman *segnour*, Old French *seignor* (mod. *seigneur*) from Latin SENIOR: see -OR.]
1 = SEIGNEUR. Also (*arch.*) as a form of address. ME.
†**2** Used as a title preceding the name of an Italian or Frenchman. L16–E18.
¶ Cf. SEIGNEUR, SENHOR, SEÑOR, SIGNOR.

seigniorage /ˈseɪnjərɪdʒ/ *noun.* Also **seignorage**. LME.
[Old French *seignorage*, *-eurage* (mod. *-euriage*), from *seignor*: see prec., -AGE.]
1 Profit made by a government by issuing currency; *spec.* the difference or margin between the face value of coins and their production costs; *Hist.* the Crown's right to charge a percentage on bullion brought to a mint for coining; the amount charged. Also (*Hist.*), something claimed by a monarch or feudal lord as a prerogative. LME.
†**2** Lordship, sovereignty. M17–E19.

seigniory /ˈseɪnjəri/ *noun.* Also **seignory**. ME.
[Old French *seignorie*: see SEIGNEURY. Cf. SIGNORIA, SIGNORY.]
Chiefly *Hist.* †**1** Lordship, sovereignty. ME–L17.
2 *spec.* Feudal lordship, sovereign authority. ME. ▸**b** A particular feudal lordship; *spec.* the relation of a lord of a manor to his tenants. LME.
3 The territory or domain of a lord or seigneur. ME.
4 Esp. in Italy, a body of seigniors or (feudal) lords, seigniors collectively. L15.

seignorage *noun* var. of SEIGNIORAGE.

seignoral /ˈseɪnjər(ə)l/ *adjective.* E17.
[App. from SEIGNIOR + -AL[1].]
Hist. = next.

seignorial /seɪˈnjɔːrɪəl/ *adjective.* E19.
[formed as prec. + -IAL.]
Of or pertaining to a seignior or seigniors.

†**seignorize** *verb intrans.* Also **-ise**. M17–L18.
[formed as SEIGNIOR + -IZE.]
Hold sway, act as a lord. Foll. by *in*, *over*.

seignory *noun* var. of SEIGNIORY.

Seilbahn /ˈzaɪlbaːn/ *noun.* M20.
[German, from *Seil* cable, rope + *Bahn* road, way.]
A cable railway, an aerial cableway.

seine /seɪn/ *noun & verb.* Also **sean**.
[Old English *segne* = Old Saxon, Old High German *segina* from West Germanic from Latin *sagena* (whence Old French *saine*, mod. *seine*) from Greek *sagēnē*; reinforced in Middle English from Old French.]
▶ **A** *noun.* A large fishing net having floats at the top and weights at the bottom so as to hang vertically in the water, the ends being drawn together to enclose the fish and the net usu. hauled ashore. OE.
cod seine, ***herring seine***, ***pilchard seine***, etc. ***drag-seine***, ***drift-seine***, etc.
Comb.: **seine-boat** a boat adapted for carrying and throwing out a seine; **seine-net** *noun & verb* (*a*) *noun* a seine; (*b*) *verb intrans.* fish with a seine; **seine-netter** a person or vessel fishing with a seine.
▶ **B** *verb.* **1** *verb intrans.* Fish with a seine. L17.
2 *verb trans.* Catch (fish) with a seine; use a seine in (an area of water). L19.
■ **seiner** *noun* a person or vessel fishing with a seine L16.

se ipse /seɪ ˈɪpseɪ/ *pronoun.* M19.
[Adaptation of Latin *se ipsum*.]
Used emphatically in apposition with a personal noun preceding: himself.

seir /ˈsɪə/ *noun.* Also **seer**. E18.
[Portuguese *serra*, lit. 'saw' from Latin SERRA.]
In full ***seir-fish***. A game-fish of the tropical Indo-Pacific, *Scomberomorus commerson*, of the family Scombridae. Also called ***serra***.

seise *verb* see SEIZE *verb*.

seised *adjective* see SEIZED.

seises /ˈseises/ *noun pl.* M19.
[Spanish, pl. of *seis* six.]
The choristers (formerly six, now usu. ten) in certain Spanish cathedrals, esp. Seville, who perform a ritual dance with castanets before the altar during the octave of Corpus Christi and certain other festivals.

seisin /ˈsiːzɪn/ *noun & verb.* Also **seizin**. ME.
[Anglo-Norman *sesine*, Old French *seisine*, (also mod.) *saisine*, from *saisir* SEIZE *verb*: see -INE[4].]
▶ **A** *noun.* **1** Orig. *gen.*, possession. Now *spec.* in LAW, freehold possession of land or chattels; the action of taking such possession; that which is held thus. ME.
2 SCOTS LAW. = SASINE. ME.
1 ***livery of seisin***: see LIVERY *noun*. ***primer seisin***: see PRIMER *adjective* 1.
▶†**B** *verb.* **1** *verb trans.* = SEIZE *verb* 1. Only in LME.
2 *verb trans.* = SEIZE *verb* 4. LME–M16.
3 *verb intrans.* Seize *upon*. M–L16.

seism /ˈsʌɪz(ə)m/ *noun.* *rare.* L19.
[formed as SEISMIC.]
An earthquake.

seismal /ˈsʌɪzm(ə)l/ *adjective.* *rare.* M19.
[formed as next + -AL[1].]
Seismic.

seismic /ˈsʌɪzmɪk/ *adjective.* M19.
[from Greek *seismos* earthquake (from *seien* to shake) + -IC.]
1 Of, pertaining to, connected with, or produced by an earthquake, earthquakes, or other vibrations of the earth and its crust. Also, pertaining to or involving vibrations of the earth produced artificially by explosions. M19.
2 *fig.* Like an earthquake, earth-shaking, of enormous effect. M20.
Special collocations: **seismic prospecting**: by investigating the propagation in rock of artificially created elastic waves. **seismic reflection** the reflection of elastic waves at boundaries between different rock formations. **seismic refraction** the refraction of elastic waves on passing between formations of rock having different seismic velocities. **seismic sea-wave** = TSUNAMI. **seismic survey** †(*a*) a survey of an area in connection with its liability to earthquakes; (*b*) a survey (for oil and gas) employing seismic methods. **seismic velocity** the velocity of propagation of elastic waves in a particular rock. **seismic wave** an elastic wave in the earth produced by an earthquake or by artificial means.
■ **seismical** *adjective* = SEISMIC M19. **seismically** *adverb* with regard to movements of the earth; by seismic methods: M19. **seismicity** /sʌɪzˈmɪsɪti/ *noun* the frequency per unit area of earthquakes of a particular country E20. **seismics** *noun* seismic exploration techniques, esp. considered collectively M20. **seismism** *noun* seismic phenomena collectively E20.

seismo- /ˈsʌɪzməʊ/ *combining form.*
[from Greek *seismos*: see prec., -O-.]
1 Of or pertaining to earthquakes or other seismic phenomena, as ***seismograph***, ***seismology***, etc.
2 Of or pertaining to shock waves or similar physical phenomena, as ***seismonasty*** etc.
■ **seismoteˈctonic** *adjective* seismic and tectonic; *esp.* of, pertaining to, or designating features of the earth's crust associated with or revealed by earthquakes: E20.

seismocardiography /ˌsʌɪzməʊkɑːdɪˈɒɡrəfi/ *noun.* M20.
[from prec. + CARDIO- + -GRAPHY.]
MEDICINE. The analysis of movements of the chest as a means of studying those of the heart.
■ **seismoˈcardiogram** *noun* a seismocardiographic record M20. **seismocardioˈgraphic** *adjective* M20.

seismograph /ˈsʌɪzmə(ʊ)grɑːf/ *noun & verb.* M19.
[from SEISMO- + -GRAPH.]
▶ **A** *noun.* An instrument for recording earthquakes and other movements of the earth automatically. M19.
▶ **B** *verb trans. & intrans.* Study (a region) by means of seismography or other seismic methods, esp. to locate oil, archaeological remains, etc. M20.
■ **seismogram** *noun* the record produced by a seismograph L19. **seisˈmographer** *noun* a seismologist L19. **seismoˈgraphic**, **seismoˈgraphical** *adjectives* of, pertaining to, or connected with a seismograph; of or pertaining to seismography: M19. **seismoˈgraphically** *adverb* E20. **seisˈmography** *noun* the descriptive science of earthquakes; the use of a seismograph M19.

seismology /sʌɪzˈmɒlədʒi/ *noun.* M19.
[formed as prec. + -LOGY.]
The branch of science that deals with earthquakes and other movements of the earth, their causes and effects, and associated phenomena.
■ **seismoˈlogic** *adjective* = SEISMOLOGICAL E20. **seismoˈlogical** *adjective* of or pertaining to seismology M19. **seismoˈlogically** *adverb* by means of seismology; as regards seismology: L19. **seismologist** *noun* an investigator or student of seismology M19.

seismometer /sʌɪzˈmɒmɪtə/ *noun.* M19.
[from SEISMO- + -METER.]
An instrument for measuring the intensity, direction, and duration of earthquakes; a seismograph.
■ **seismometric** /-ˈmɛtrɪk/ *adjective* of or pertaining to seismometry or a seismometer M19. **seismoˈmetrical** *adjective* = SEISMOMETRIC L19. **seismometry** *noun* the scientific recording and analysis of earthquakes and other movements of the earth, esp. with a seismometer M19.

seismonasty /ˈsʌɪzmə(ʊ)nasti/ *noun.* E20.
[formed as prec. + NASTY *noun*[2].]
BOTANY. A nastic movement made in response to a mechanical shock.
■ **seismoˈnastic** *adjective* E20.

seismosaurus /ˈsʌɪzmə(ʊ)sɔːrəs/ *noun.* L20.
[mod. Latin (see below), from SEISMO- + Greek *sauros* lizard.]
PALAEONTOLOGY. A huge late Jurassic dinosaur of the genus *Seismosaurus*, known from only a few bones and probably the longest animal ever, with a length of 35–45 metres.

seismoscope /ˈsʌɪzməskəʊp/ *noun.* M19.
[from SEISMO- + -SCOPE.]
A simple form of seismometer for detecting the occurrence of an earthquake shock, sometimes also indicating the approximate intensity or direction of the earthquake wave.
■ **seismoscopic** /-ˈskɒpɪk/ *adjective* L19.

Seistan /ˈsiːstɑːn/ *noun.* E20.
[A low-lying region of E. Iran and SW Afghanistan.]
A strong north-westerly wind prevalent in Seistan in the summer months. Also ***Seistan wind***.

seity /ˈsiːɪti/ *noun. rare.* E18.
[medieval Latin *seitas*, from Latin *se* oneself: see -ITY. Cf. HAECCEITY, QUIDDITY.]
That which constitutes the self, selfhood.

Seitz /zʌɪts/ *noun.* E20.
[Name of the inventor.]
Chiefly MEDICINE. Used *attrib.* with ref. to a method of filtration of liquids through a small replaceable disc of compressed asbestos fibres.
Seitz disc, ***Seitz filter***, ***Seitz filtration***, etc.
¶ Proprietary name.

sei whale /ˈseɪ ˈweɪl/ *noun.* E20.
[Norwegian *sejhval*, from *sei* coalfish + *hval* whale.]
A blue-grey rorqual, *Balaenoptera borealis*.

seiza /ˈseɪzə/ *noun.* M20.
[Japanese, from *sei* correct + *za* sitting.]
An upright kneeling position which is the Japanese traditional formal way of sitting and is used in meditation and as part of the preparation in martial arts.

seizable /ˈsiːzəb(ə)l/ *adjective.* LME.
[from SEIZE *verb* + -ABLE.]
Able to be seized; *spec.* (of property) that may lawfully be seized.

seize /siːz/ *noun.* E20.
[from the verb.]
An instance of a machine etc. seizing up or failing to work. Also ***seize-up***.

seize /siːz/ *verb.* In sense 1 usu. **seise**. ME.
[Old French *seizir*, (also mod.) *saisir* from Proto-Gallo-Romance from Frankish Latin *sacire* (in *ad proprium sacire* claim as one's own), from Germanic base meaning 'process, procedure', perh. rel. to base of SET *verb*[1].]
▶ **I** Put in possession.
1 *verb trans.* LAW. Put (a person) in legal possession *of* land or property; establish *in* an office or position. ME.
†**2** *verb trans.* **a** Settle or establish (a person) in a place. LME–M17. ▸**b** Of a predatory animal: fasten (the claws) *on* in attacking. Only in L16.
†**3** *verb trans.* Give possession of, grant, (a thing). Only in LME.
▶ **II** Take possession.
4 *verb trans.* **a** Take possession of (property etc.) forcibly; capture (a place), annex (a country). ME. ▸**b** Take possession of (contraband, assets, documents, etc.) by warrant or legal right; confiscate, impound. L15. ▸**c** Arrest or apprehend (a person); take prisoner. L15.
5 *verb trans.* Take hold of suddenly or forcibly with the hands, claws, etc.; grasp eagerly, clutch, snatch. ME.
6 *verb trans.* **a** Of an idea, emotion, illness, etc.: strike or affect (a person) suddenly, afflict acutely, impress strongly. Freq. in *pass.* (foll. by *with*, *by*). LME. ▸**b** Take advantage of (an opportunity), make use of eagerly or decisively. E17. ▸**c** Comprehend quickly or clearly, grasp with the mind. M19.
7 *verb intrans.* Foll. by *on*, *upon*, †*of*: take hold of forcibly or suddenly; *fig.* exploit another's mistake etc., take eager advantage of; draw attention to, pinpoint. LME. ▸†**b** Of a blow or weapon: penetrate deeply *in*. L16–E17. ▸**c** Grasp or clutch *at*. *rare*. M19.
†**8** *verb trans.* NAUTICAL. Reach, arrive at. L16–M17.
9 *verb trans.* NAUTICAL. Fasten or attach by binding with turns of yarn or rope; *Hist.* (foll. by *up*) bind (a person) by the wrists to the shrouds in preparation for flogging. M17.
10 *verb intrans.* Of a machine, moving part, etc.: become stuck or jammed from undue heat, friction, etc.; fail to operate, break down (*lit.* & *fig.*). Freq. foll. by *up*. L19.

📖 **4a** J. COLVILLE Turkey will not fight Russia if Bessarabia is seized. E. BOWEN The . . idea of seizing freedom by force loomed up again. P. MAILLOUX What she had was eventually seized by the Gestapo. **b** *Times* Officers . . seized 113 'deals' of the cocaine derivative. **5** H. ROTH Aunt Bertha had seized a table knife. W. MARCH Christine seized the little girl and shook her. A. GRAY She seized the pencil from Thaw's fingers. **6a** G. B. SHAW The imagination of the public has . . been strongly seized by the spectacle of . . Tosca. I. MURDOCH I was seized . . by a convulsive desire to laugh. DAY LEWIS A delicious terror seized me. **b** THOMAS HUGHES The latter seized the occasion to propound this question. V. CRONIN In the Far East whenever an opportunity presented itself Catherine seized it. **c** H. T. BUCKLE The reader must firmly seize . . the essential difference between deduction . . and induction. **7** I. COLEGATE Nancy seized on the idea with enthusiasm. A. STORR The pathologically suspicious . . seizes on details which seem to him to confirm his suspicions. **10** D. CAUTE He tries to serve aces, . . then seizes up. *Classic Racer* The oil tank had split and . . the engine seized on the Mountain Mile.

Phrases: **seize hold of** take hold of suddenly and roughly. ***seize the open file***: see FILE *noun*[2].

seized /siːzd/ *adjective.* In sense 1 usu. **seised**. ME.
[from prec. + -ED[1].]
1 Chiefly LAW (foll. by *of*, *in*). In (legal) possession of land etc. Also (*arch.*, foll. by *of*, †*with*) aware or informed of. ME.
2 *gen.* That has been seized, confiscated, or taken. M19.
3 Of a machine etc.: that has jammed or stuck, inoperative. Also foll. by *up*. E20.

📖 **1** *Economist* Leading employers and trade unionists, fully seized of the facts. H. ALLEN The young Irishman seized of his grandfather's estate. **2** CARLYLE The seized cannon are yoked with seized cart-horses. **3** *Classic & Sportscar* The engine is seized but the car was driven to its resting place.

seizer /ˈsiːzə/ *noun.* LME.
[formed as prec. + -ER[1].]
A person who or thing which seizes someone or something; *spec.* †(*a*) a canine tooth; (*b*) *Hist.* a person authorized to arrest people or confiscate goods; (*c*) a dog trained to seize the animal hunted.

seizin *noun & verb* var. of SEISIN.

seizing /ˈsiːzɪŋ/ *noun.* ME.
[formed as prec. + -ING[1].]
1 NAUTICAL. Yarn or cord for seizing or binding something; a length of this. Formerly also, a rope for attaching a boat to a ship. ME.
2 The action of SEIZE *verb*; an instance of this. LME.
1 ***round seizing***: see ROUND *adjective*.

seizing /ˈsiːzɪŋ/ *adjective.* M19.
[from SEIZE *verb* + -ING[2].]
1 That seizes, takes possession, or lays hold of a thing or person. M19.
2 [After French *saisissant*.] That seizes the attention; arresting, powerfully impressive. M19.

†**seizor** *noun.* M16–E18.
[formed as prec. + -OR. Cf. SEIZER.]
LAW. A person authorized to arrest people or confiscate goods.

seizure /ˈsiːʒə/ *noun.* LME.
[from SEIZE *verb* + -URE.]
1 The action or an act of seizing a thing or person; the fact of being seized; (a) confiscation of goods etc. LME. ▸†**b** Grasp, hold; a fastening. L16–E17.
†**2** = SEISIN *noun* 1. L16–M17.
3 A sudden attack of illness; *esp.* a stroke or an epileptic fit. L18.
4 The seizing-up, jamming, or failing of a machine etc.; an instance of this. E20.

sejant /ˈsiːdʒ(ə)nt/ *adjective.* Also (earlier) †**seiant**. L15.
[Alt. of Old French var. of Old & mod. French *séant* pres. pple of *seoir* from Latin *sedere* sit: see -ANT[1].]
HERALDRY. In a sitting posture; *esp.* (of a quadruped) sitting with the forelegs upright. Usu. *postpositive*.

Sejm /seɪm/ *noun.* Also ***Seym***. L19.
[Polish.]
In Poland: a general assembly or diet; a parliament; *spec.* the lower house of the Polish parliament.

sejoin /sɪˈdʒɔɪn/ *verb trans. rare.* M16.
[from SE- + JOIN *verb*, after Latin *sejungere*.]
Separate, disjoin.

séjour /seʒuːr/ *noun.* Pl. pronounced same. M18.
[French, from *séjourner* SOJOURN *verb*.]
1 The action of staying or sojourning in a place. M18.
2 A place of sojourn or residence. M18.

sejugate /ˈsɛdʒʊgeɪt/ *verb trans. rare.* E17.
[Latin *sejugat-* pa. ppl stem of *sejugare*, formed as SE- + *jugare* to join: see -ATE[3].]
Separate, disjoin.

†**sejunct** *adjective. rare.* E17–E20.
[Latin *sejunctus* pa. pple of *sejungere* to separate, formed as SE- + *jungere* to join.]
Separated, separate.

sejunction /sɪˈdʒʌŋkʃ(ə)n/ *noun. rare.* E16.
[Latin *sejunctio(n-)*, from *sejunct-* pa. ppl stem of *sejungere*: see prec., -ION.]
Separation.

sekere /sɛkəˈreɪ/ *noun.* Also **sh-** /ʃ-/. Pl. **-s**, same. E20.
[Yoruba.]
A Yoruba percussion instrument made from a hollow gourd with cowrie shells, beads, etc., attached, which rattle when the instrument is shaken.

sekos /ˈsiːkɒs/ *noun.* Pl. ***-koi*** /-kɔɪ/. E19.
[Greek *sēkos* pen, enclosure.]
A sacred enclosure in an ancient Egyptian temple.

Sekt /zɛkt/ *noun.* E20.
[German.]
A German sparkling white wine; a drink of this.

selachian /sɪˈleɪkɪən/ *noun & adjective.* M19.
[from mod. Latin *Selachii* (see below) or its source *Selache* genus name (from Greek *selakhē* pl. of *selakhos* shark) + -IAN, after French *sélacien*.]
ZOOLOGY. ▶**A** *noun.* Any member of the vertebrate class or subclass Selachii, which comprises sharks, dogfish, rays, skates, and (in some classifications) chimaeras. M19.
▶ **B** *adjective.* Of, pertaining to, or designating (a member of) the Selachii. L19.

seladang /səˈlɑːdaŋ/ *noun.* E19.
[Malay.]
The gaur or Indian bison. Formerly also, the Malayan tapir, *Tapirus indicus*.

selaginella /sɛlədʒɪˈnɛlə, sɪˌladʒɪˈnɛlə/ *noun.* M19.
[mod. Latin, dim. of Latin *selago* clubmoss.]
BOTANY. Any of various chiefly tropical creeping mosslike plants of the genus *Selaginella* (family Selaginellaceae), including the lesser clubmoss *S. selagrinoides*.

Selah /ˈsiːlə, ˈsɛlɑː/ *interjection & noun.* Also **s-**. M16.
[Hebrew *selāh*: see below.]
▶**A** *interjection.* Occurring frequently at the end of a verse in *Psalms* and three times in *Habakkuk*. 3, prob. as a musical or liturgical direction of some kind, perh. indicating a pause or rest or a musical interlude; *transf.* pause, rest, finish. M16.
▶ **B** *noun.* An instance or utterance of the word *Selah*; a pause, a rest, an interlude; a word etc. inserted to avoid a hiatus. E17.

selamlik /sɛˈlɑːmlɪk/ *noun.* M19.
[Turkish *selamlik* lit. 'place of greeting', from *selâm* from Arab. *salām* SALAAM *noun* + *-lik* suitable, intended for.]
1 A room in a Turkish Muslim house set aside for business or the reception of male friends; the part of a Turkish Muslim house reserved for men. M19.
2 *Hist.* The public procession of the Turkish Sultan to a mosque on Friday at noon. L19.

selch *noun* see SEAL *noun*[1].

†**selcouth** *adjective & noun.* OE.
[formed as SELDOM + COUTH *adjective*.]
▶ **A** *adjective.* **1** Unfamiliar, unusual, rare; strange, marvellous, wonderful. OE–E19.
2 Various, different, not of one kind. OE–LME.
▶ **B** *noun.* Something wonderful; a marvel. ME–L15.

†**seld** *adverb & adjective.* LOE.
[formed as next, formed as a positive to the compar. & superl. (*seldor*, *seldost*).]
▶ **A** *adverb.* = SELDOM *adverb.* LOE–M17.
▶ **B** *adjective.* = SELDOM *adjective.* LME–E17.

seldom /ˈsɛldəm/ *adverb & adjective.*
[Old English *seldan* corresp. to Old Frisian *sielden*, Middle Low German, Middle Dutch *selden* (Dutch *zelden*), Old High German *seltan* (German *selten*), Old Norse *sjaldan*, datives from Germanic base repr. also by Old English *seldīc* strange, wonderful, Gothic *sildaleiks* wonderful.]
▶ **A** *adverb.* On few occasions, in few cases or instances, not often; rarely, infrequently. **OE.**

E. B. BROWNING It is seldom perhaps never, that I wish those to love me who do not. J. G. FARRELL An unfamiliar staircase, seldom used, to judge by the spiders' webs. K. LINES Seldom, if ever, had the earth seen so glorious a spectacle. R. COBB He knew how to please and seldom failed to do so.

▶ **B** *adjective.* Rare, infrequent. **L15.**

M. TWAIN The seldomest spectacle on the Mississippi to-day is a wood-pile. *Daily Telegraph* It is a great but seldom pleasure . . to hear a contradiction of the current cant.

■ **†seldomly** *adverb* = SELDOM *adverb* **M16–M19.** **seldomness** *noun* infrequency, rareness **M16.**

seldseen /ˈsɛldsiːn/ *adjective.* Long *arch. rare.*
[Old English *seldsiene* (with Germanic cognates), formed as prec. + *seen* pa. pple of SEE *verb.*]
Seldom to be seen or met with; rare.

sele /siːl/ *noun.* Long *obsolete* exc. *dial.*
[Old English *sǣl*, ult. from West Germanic base also of SEELY, SILLY *adjective.*]
1 Happiness, prosperity, good fortune. **OE.**
2 A favourable time, an opportune moment; the season for something. **OE.**

select /sɪˈlɛkt/ *adjective & noun.* **M16.**
[Latin *selectus* pa. pple of *seligere*: see next.]
▶ **A** *adjective.* **1** Selected, chosen out of a larger number, on account of excellence or suitability; of special value or excellence, choice, superior. **M16.**
2 Careful in selection, selective; exclusive. **M19.**

1 LD MACAULAY To the smaller plot . . only a few select traitors were privy. D. WELCH Li took me upstairs. He said it was quieter and more select. **2** T. IRELAND Tony lived in a 'select' area.

Special collocations & comb.: **select committee** a small parliamentary committee appointed for a special purpose. **selectman** *US* a member of the local government board of a New England town.
▶ **B** *noun.* A selected person or thing. Formerly also, a selected class or group, a selection. **E17.**
■ **selectly** *adverb* (*rare*) **L17.** **selectness** *noun* **E18.**

select /sɪˈlɛkt/ *verb.* **M16.**
[Latin *select-* pa. ppl stem of *seligere*, formed as SE- + *legere* collect, choose.]
1 *verb trans.* Choose or pick out in preference to another or others. Also foll. by *out.* **M16.**
2 *verb intrans.* Choose or pick out something from a number; make a selection. **M19.**

1 A. J. CRONIN Since he gave her free choice she selected *Saint Joan*. A. MACRAE He was playing cricket . . . It was the first time he had been selected.

■ **selectable** *adjective* suitable for selection; able to be selected: **M19.** **selected** *adjective* (*a*) specially chosen, picked out; †(*b*) *rare* choice, select: **L16.** **selecˈtee** *noun* (*US*) a person selected; *spec.* a conscript under the selective service system: **M20.**

selection /sɪˈlɛkʃ(ə)n/ *noun.* **E17.**
[Latin *selectio(n-)*, formed as prec.: see -ION.]
1 The action or an act of selecting something or someone; the fact of being selected. **E17.**
2 A particular choice; a thing or person selected; a number of selected things or persons; a range of things from which one or more may be selected. **E19.**
3 a The action of a breeder in selecting individuals from which to breed, in order to obtain some desired characteristic in the descendants. **M19.** ▸**b** *BIOLOGY.* Any process, artificial or natural, which establishes a particular modification of a kind of organism by favouring in successive generations the reproduction of individuals that have heritable variations from the ancestral form in the direction of that modification; *esp.* = ***natural selection*** s.v. NATURAL *adjective.* **M19.**
4 *AUSTRAL. HISTORY.* More fully ***free selection***. (A scheme enabling) the selection and acquisition of plots of land for small farming, on terms favourable to the buyer; a tract of land so acquired. **M19.**
5 *FORESTRY.* A system of forest management under which there is a continuing selection of individual trees for felling over the whole area, on the basis of their saleability. Usu. *attrib.* (see below). **L19.**
6 A horse or horses or other contestant(s) selected or tipped as likely to win or obtain a place in a race. **E20.**

1 O. DOPPING The selection of cards which fulfill certain conditions. **2** V. S. PRITCHETT She . . bought me a selection of Victor Hugo's poems. A. BROOKNER The elderly pianist . . had now returned with further selections from indeterminate sources. **3b** ***kin selection***: see KIN *noun.* ***natural selection***: see NATURAL *adjective.* ***r selection***: see R, R 5. **5** ***selection felling***, ***selection method***, ***selection system***, etc. **6** ***nap selection***: see NAP *noun*³ 3.

Comb.: **selection pressure** *BIOLOGY* (an agent of) differential mortality or fertility such as tends to make a population adapt genetically; **selection rule** *PHYSICS* any of a number of rules which describe, within certain limits, which particular quantum transitions can occur in an atom, molecule, etc., and which are forbidden.
■ **selectional** *adjective* **M20.** **selectionally** *adverb* **M20.**

selectionism /sɪˈlɛkʃ(ə)nɪz(ə)m/ *noun.* **E20.**
[from prec. + -ISM.]
BIOLOGY. The belief that evolution proceeds chiefly by natural selection; (neo-)Darwinism, as opp. to Lamarckism. Also, the selectionist theory of genetic variation.

selectionist /sɪˈlɛkʃ(ə)nɪst/ *noun & adjective.* **L19.**
[formed as prec. + -IST.]
BIOLOGY. ▶**A** *noun.* A person who believes in or supports the theory of natural selection; *spec.* (*a*) (chiefly *Hist.*) a person who believes that evolution proceeds primarily by natural selection for small variations (opp. ***mutationist***); (***b***) an advocate of the theory that all or most observed genetic variation is maintained by natural selection rather than by random effects (opp. ***neutralist***). **L19.**
▶ **B** *adjective.* Of, pertaining to, or connected with the theory of natural selection; *spec.* of or pertaining to selectionists or selectionism. **M20.**

selective /sɪˈlɛktɪv/ *adjective.* **E17.**
[from SELECT *verb* + -IVE.]
1 Using or involving selection; characterized by selection; careful in making a selection; (of memory etc.) selecting what is convenient; (of a herbicide etc.) affecting only particular species. **E17.**
2 *spec.* in *TELEGRAPHY.* Designating a system by which two or more messages can be transmitted simultaneously without interference; multiplex. Now *rare* or *obsolete.* **E20.**
3 Designating a secondary school or a system of education in which children of supposedly greater intellectual or other abilities are taught separately from others. **E20.**

1 R. CARSON Vegetation management by selective spraying has been adopted. M. SEYMOUR Old men . . grow more selective in their memories.

Special collocations: **selective attention** *PSYCHOLOGY* the capacity for or process of (deliberately) reacting to or noticing certain stimuli and not others. **selective employment tax** *Hist.* a graded or refundable tax on employees, intended to favour selected types of employment. **selective realism** *PHILOSOPHY* a doctrine which maintained that sense-data exist in material objects and that the senses of the perceiver select those which are appropriate to be registered. **selective service** *US HISTORY* a system of military service under which conscripts were selected from a larger number of people required to enrol.
■ **selectively** *adverb* **M17.** **selectiveness** *noun* **M19.** **selectivism** *noun* (belief in) selectivity **M20.** **selectivist** *noun* (*a*) *PHILOSOPHY* an adherent of selective realism; (*b*) a supporter of the principle of selectivity: **M20.**

selectivity /sɪlɛkˈtɪvɪti, ˈsɛl-/ *noun.* **E20.**
[from prec. + -ITY.]
1 *RADIO.* The ability of a receiver to tune separately to signals of adjacent frequencies, measured by the frequency difference between the half-power points of the pass-band of the receiver. **E20.**
2 *gen.* The quality of being selective. **M20.**
3 The principle or belief that State benefits etc. should be distributed selectively. **L20.**

selector /sɪˈlɛktə/ *noun.* **L18.**
[from SELECT *verb* + -OR.]
1 A person who selects. **L18.** ▸**b** *spec.* Any of a number of officials appointed to select a sports team. **E20.**
2 A device for selecting something; *spec.* (*a*) in a gearbox, the part that moves the gearwheels into and out of engagement; (*b*) in a telephone system, a mechanism which automatically establishes electrical connection with one of a group of available contacts according to the number of impulses in the incoming signal; (*c*) in a motor vehicle with automatic transmission, the control by which the driver selects the mode of operation of the transmission. **L19.**
■ **selectorate** *noun* [blend of SELECTOR and ELECTORATE] that section of a political party which has the effective power to choose a representative **M20.** **selectorial** /sɪlɛkˈtɔːrɪəl, sɛl-/ *adjective* of or pertaining to a selector of a sports team. **M20.**

selectron /sɪˈlɛktrɒn/ *noun.* **M20.**
[from SELECT *verb* + -TRON.]
COMPUTING (now *Hist.*). A kind of cathode-ray tube formerly used to store digital information.

selen- /ˈsɛlən/ *combining form.*
[from SELEN(IUM.]
MINERALOGY & CHEMISTRY. Forming names of minerals and other substances containing (or formerly supposed to contain) selenium.
■ **selenˈsulphur** *noun* a native variety of elemental sulphur containing a small proportion of selenium **M19.**

selenate /ˈsɛlɪneɪt/ *noun.* **E19.**
[from SELEN(IUM + -ATE¹.]
CHEMISTRY. A salt or ester of selenic acid.

selendang *noun* var. of SLENDANG.

selenian /sɪˈliːnɪən/ *adjective. rare.* **M17.**
[from Greek *selēnē* moon + -IAN.]
Of or pertaining to the moon, esp. considered as a world.

selenic /sɪˈlɛnɪk/ *adjective*¹. *rare.* **E19.**
[formed as prec. + -IC.]
Of, pertaining to, or derived from the moon.

selenic /sɪˈliːnɪk/ *adjective*². **E19.**
[from SELEN(IUM + -IC.]
CHEMISTRY. Of or containing selenium, esp. in the hexavalent state; ***selenic acid***, a strong hygroscopic corrosive dibasic acid, H_2SeO_4. Cf. SELENIOUS.

selenide /ˈsɛlɪnʌɪd/ *noun.* **M19.**
[from SELEN(IUM + -IDE.]
CHEMISTRY. A compound of selenium with another more electropositive element or a radical.

seleniferous /sɛlɪˈnɪf(ə)rəs/ *adjective.* **E19.**
[formed as prec. + -FEROUS.]
Containing or yielding selenium.

selenious /sɪˈliːnɪəs/ *adjective.* **E19.**
[from SELENI(UM + -OUS.]
CHEMISTRY. Of or containing selenium in the divalent or tetravalent state; ***selenious acid***, a deliquescent solid dibasic acid, H_2SeO_3. Cf. SELENIC *adjective*².

selenite /ˈsɛlɪnʌɪt/ *noun*¹. Orig. in Latin form **†selenites**. **LME.**
[Latin *selenites* from Greek *selēnitēs lithos* lit. 'moonstone' (so called from its lustre, or because it was said to wax and wane with the moon), from *selēnē* moon: see -ITE¹.]
1 *Hist.* A stone variously described by ancient writers, perhaps in part identifiable with the mineral now so called. **LME.**
2 *MINERALOGY.* Gypsum (calcium sulphate), esp. in a crystalline or foliated form having a pearly lustre. Also, a slip or film of this mineral used for the polarization of light. **M17.**
■ **selenitic** /sɛlɪˈnɪtɪk/ *adjective* of, pertaining to, resembling, or containing (solid or dissolved) selenite **M18.**

Selenite /sɪˈliːnʌɪt, ˈsɛlɪnʌɪt/ *noun*². **M17.**
[Greek *selēnitēs*, from *selēnē* moon: see -ITE¹.]
A supposed inhabitant of the moon.

selenite /ˈsɛlɪnʌɪt/ *noun*³. **M19.**
[from SELEN(IUM + -ITE¹.]
CHEMISTRY. A salt of selenious acid.

selenium /sɪˈliːnɪəm/ *noun.* **E19.**
[mod. Latin, from Greek *selēnē* moon + -IUM.]
A non-metallic chemical element, atomic no. 34, closely resembling tellurium, having several allotropic forms, occurring naturally in various metallic sulphide ores, and characterized by a strong photoelectric effect. (Symbol Se.)
Comb.: **selenium cell** a photoconductive or photovoltaic cell containing selenium.

†seleniuret *noun.* **E–M19.**
[from SELENI(UM + -URET.]
CHEMISTRY. = SELENIDE.
■ **†seleniuretted** *adjective* combined with selenium; ***seleniuretted hydrogen***, hydrogen selenide, SeH_2: **E19–M20.**

selenocentric /sɪˌliːnə(ʊ)ˈsɛntrɪk/ *adjective.* **M19.**
[from Greek *selēnē* moon + -O- + -CENTRIC.]
Considered as viewed from the centre of the moon; referring to the moon as centre.

selenodesy /sɛlɪˈnɒdɪsi/ *noun.* **M20.**
[formed as prec., after GEODESY.]
ASTRONOMY. The application of geodesic methods to the investigation of the moon.
■ **selenodetic** /sɪˌliːnə(ʊ)ˈdɛtɪk/ *adjective* **M20.**

selenodont /sɪˈliːnədɒnt/ *adjective & noun.* **L19.**
[formed as prec. + -ODONT.]
▶ **A** *adjective.* Of molar teeth: having crescentic ridges on the crowns. Also, characterized by such teeth. **L19.**
▶ **B** *noun.* A selenodont animal. **L19.**

selenography /sɛlɪˈnɒgrəfi/ *noun.* **M17.**
[from Greek *selēnē* moon + -O- + -GRAPHY.]
1 A description of the moon's surface. Now *rare.* **M17.**
2 The description and delineation of the moon's surface; the descriptive science relating to the moon, lunar geography. **L18.**
■ **selenographer** *noun* a person engaged in selenography **L17.** **selenoˈgraphic** *adjective* of or pertaining to selenography. **L17.** **selenoˈgraphical** *adjective* = SELENOGRAPHIC **M17.**

selenology /sɛlɪˈnɒlədʒi/ *noun.* **E19.**
[formed as prec. + -LOGY.]
The branch of science relating to the moon, esp. (*a*) to its movements and astronomical relations; (*b*) to the formation of its crust, lunar geology.
■ **selenoˈlogical** *adjective* of or pertaining to selenology **M19.** **selenoˈlogically** *adverb* as regards selenology **M19.** **selenologist** *noun* an expert in or student of selenology **L19.**

selenoscope /sɪˈliːnəskəʊp/ *noun. rare.* M17.
[formed as prec. + -SCOPE.]
An instrument for observing the moon.

selenous /ˈsɛlənəs, səˈliːnəs/ *adjective.* E20.
[from SELEN(IUM + -OUS.]
CHEMISTRY. = SELENIOUS.

Seleucian /sɪˈl(j)uːsɪən/ *adjective. rare.* E18.
[from *Seleucus* (see next) + -IAN.]
Hist. = SELEUCID *adjective.*

Seleucid /sɪˈl(j)uːsɪd/ *noun & adjective.* M19.
[Latin *Seleucides* from Greek *Seleukidēs*, from *Seleukos* Seleucus: see below, -ID³.]
▶ **A** *noun.* Pl. **-ids**, **-idae** /-ɪdiː/. A member of the dynasty founded by Seleucus Nicator (a general of Alexander the Great) which reigned over Syria from 312 to 65 BC, and subjugated a great part of Western Asia. M19.
▶ **B** *adjective.* Of or pertaining to this dynasty. E20.

Seleucidan /sɪˈl(j)uːsɪd(ə)n/ *adjective.* E19.
[formed as prec. + -AN.]
= SELEUCID *adjective.*

self /sɛlf/ *pronoun, adjective, & noun.* Pl. **selves** /sɛlvz/, in sense B.7 **selfs**.
[Old English *self* (strong), *selfa* (weak) = Old Frisian *self, selva*, Old Saxon *self, selbo*, Old High German *selb, selbo* (Dutch *zelv, -zelve, -zelfde*, German *selb-, selbe*), Old Norse *sjálfr* (strong), Gothic *silba* (weak), from Germanic base of unkn. origin.]
▶ **A** *pronoun & adjective.* **I** *emphatic.* **1** In apposition to a noun or pronoun: that particular or those particular person(s), animal(s), or thing(s), the person(s) etc. in question; herself, himself, itself, ourselves, yourselves, or themselves. Long *arch.* OE.
†**2** Own, peculiar. OE–M17.
3 (Not appositional.) He or him himself, I or me myself, it itself, she or her herself, we or us ourselves, you yourself, you yourselves, they or them themselves. Now chiefly in commercial use (*spec.* written on a cheque or counterfoil) & *colloq.* OE.

🕮 **2** SHAKES. *Macb.* His fiend-like queen, Who . . by self and violent hands Took off her life. **3** P. G. WODEHOUSE Four of us—Charlotte, self, the old man, and Comrade Butt. G. HEYER He drew a cheque for a hundred pounds to self.

▶ **II** *adjective.* †**4** = SAME *adjective.* OE–M17.
5 a Of a colour: the same throughout, uniform. M16. ▸**b** Of a uniform colour, self-coloured. Also, (of a flower) of the natural wild colour. M19.
†**6** *MINING.* Of a rock etc.: detached, of material different from its surroundings. M18–M19.
7 *ARCHERY.* Of a bow: made all of one piece. E19.
8 Of the trimming of a garment: of the same material as the garment itself. E20.
▶ **B** *noun.* †**1** The same person or thing. OE–M16.
2 a Preceded by a possess. pronoun, forming a comb. or phr. serving as a reflexive or an emphatic personal pronoun (see HERSELF, HIS-SELF, MYSELF, ONESELF, OURSELVES, THEIRSELVES, THYSELF, YOURSELF, etc.). Also qualified by an emphasizing or descriptive adjective. ME. ▸**b** Preceded by a noun in the *possess.*: (the specified noun), herself, himself, itself, themselves. *arch.* ME.
3 a Any of various conflicting personalities conceived of as coexisting within a single person. L16. ▸**b** A person's or thing's individuality or essence at a particular time or in a particular aspect or relation; a person's nature, character, or (occas.) physical constitution or appearance, considered as different at different times. Chiefly with qualifying adjective L17.
4 A person loved as oneself, a counterpart of oneself, an alter ego. *obsolete* exc. in ***second self*** s.v. SECOND *adjective.* E17.
5 True or intrinsic identity; personal identity, ego; a person as the object of introspection or reflexive action. L17.
6 One's personal welfare and interests as an object of concern; concentration on these, selfishness. L17.
7 A self-coloured thing; a flower, animal, garment, etc., of a single colour throughout. Also, a flower of the natural wild colour. M19. ▸**b** *BOTANY.* A plant produced by self-fertilization. E20.
8 *IMMUNOLOGY.* Material regarded by an individual's immune system as a normal component of that individual and so not subject to attack by it. M20.

🕮 **2a** J. CONRAD He . . suddenly beheld his very own self. M. NA GOPALEEN More authentic sources known only to my little self. **b** CARLYLE Were it not better you, your Majesty's self, took the children? **3a** S. BRETT His logical self knew how insubstantial such satisfactions were. A. TYLER When she's in costume it's not she who's going out . . . Her real self is safe at home. **one's better self** the better part of one's nature. **b** P. ACKROYD She seemed quite chatty and more . . her old self. **5** A. J. AYER That which is supposed to survive . . is not the empirical self, but . . the soul. P. TILLICH Aware of the complete loss of self which biological extinction implies. **6** GEO. ELIOT She's better than I am—there's less o' self in her, and pride.

self /sɛlf/ *verb trans.* E20.
[from prec.]
Fertilize with pollen from the same plant; self-fertilize. Usu. in *pass.*

self- /sɛlf/ *combining form.*
[from SELF *pronoun, adjective, & noun.*]
Used with the reflexive sense 'oneself, itself' in various relations, *esp.* (*a*) (objective) 'by or of oneself or itself', freq. *spec.* 'by one's or its own efforts or action, without external agency or help, automatic(ally)'; with nouns as ***self-advocacy***, ***self-caricature***, ***self-correction***, ***self-denigration***, ***self-election***, ***self-enrichment***, ***self-flatterer***, ***self-healing***, ***self-humiliation***, ***self-immolation***, ***self-incrimination***, ***self-inspection***, ***self-production***, ***self-promotion***, ***self-tormentor***, ***self-treatment***, ***self-valuation***, etc.; with adjectives (& their derivs.) as ***self-expressive***, esp. pres. ppl adjectives, as ***self-annihilating***, ***self-exalting***, ***self-fitting***, ***self-incriminating***, ***self-operating***, ***self-programming***, ***self-rewarding***, ***self-tormenting***, ***self-watering***, & pa. ppl adjectives, as ***self-administered***, ***self-built***, ***self-chosen***, ***self-defended***, ***self-destroyed***, ***self-devised***, ***self-evolved***, ***self-indulged***, ***self-originated***, ***self-produced***, etc.; with verb stems forming (esp. attrib.) adjectives, as ***self-feed***, ***self-seal***, etc. (*b*) (adverb) with the sense 'for, in, into, of, on or upon, to or towards, with, etc., oneself or itself', as ***self-dissatisfaction***, ***self-medication***, ***self-mistrust***, etc.
■ **self-aˈbandon** *noun* abandonment of oneself to a passion, impulse, etc. E20. **self-aˈbandoned** *adjective* characterized by self-abandon, profligate L18. **self-aˈbandonment** *noun* = SELF-ABANDON E19. **self-aˈbasement** *noun* abasement or humiliation of oneself, cringing M17. **self-aˈbasing** *adjective* characterized by, involving, or requiring self-abasement M17. **self-ˈabnegating** *adjective* characterized by, involving, or requiring self-abnegation M19. **self-abneˈgation** *noun* abnegation of oneself, one's interests, one's needs, etc. M17. **self-abneˈgatory** *adjective* = SELF-ABNEGATING L19. **self-abˈsorbed** *adjective* absorbed in oneself, one's own feelings, etc. M19. **self-abˈsorption** *noun* (*a*) absorption in one's own emotions, interests, or situation; preoccupation with oneself; (*b*) *PHYSICS* absorption of radiation by the material emitting it: E19. **self-accuˈsation** *noun* (an) accusation of oneself M17. **self-aˈccusatory** *adjective* characterized by, involving, or requiring self-accusation M19. **self-aˈccused** *adjective* accused by oneself L17. **self-aˈccusing** *adjective* accusing oneself, self-accusatory L16. **self-ˈacting** *adjective* (*a*) acting independently, without external influence or control; (*b*) acting automatically, without mechanical intervention: L17. **self-ˈaction** *noun* (*a*) independent action, without external influence or control; (*b*) automatic action, without mechanical intervention: E19. **self-ˈactive** *adjective* = SELF-ACTING M17. **self-acˈtivity** *noun* independent or automatic activity M17. **self-ˈactor** *noun* a self-acting thing, *spec.* a self-acting mule in a spinning-machine M19. **self-actualiˈzation** *noun* (chiefly *PSYCHOLOGY*) realization or fulfilment of one's talents and potentialities, esp. considered as a drive or need present in everyone M20. **self-ˈactualize** *verb* (chiefly *PSYCHOLOGY*) (*a*) *verb intrans.* achieve self-actualization or fulfilment; (*b*) *verb trans.* bring to self-actualization (usu. in *pass.*): L19. **self-aˈddressed** *adjective* addressed to oneself; *spec.* (of an envelope etc.) having one's own address on for return communication M19. **self-adˈhesive** *adjective* (of an envelope, label, etc.) adhesive without being moistened M20. **self-ˈadjoint** *adjective* (*MATH.*) equal to its own adjoint L19. **self-aˈdjusting** *adjective* (of machinery etc.) adjusting itself without intervention M19. **self-aˈdjustment** *noun* adjustment of itself without intervention M19. **self-admiˈration** *noun* admiration of oneself, conceit M17. **self-adˈmired** *adjective* admired by oneself L18. **self-adˈmiring** *adjective* characterized by, involving, or requiring self-admiration; conceited: E17. **self-aduˈlation** *noun* adulation of oneself, excessive self-love L18. **self-adˈvancement** *noun* advancement or promotion of oneself E18. **self-adˈvertisement** *noun* advertisement or promotion of oneself M19. **self-ˈadvertiser** *noun* a person given to self-advertisement L19. **self-ˈadvertising** *noun* advertising or promoting of oneself M18. **self-affirˈmation** *noun* affirmation of oneself; *PSYCHOLOGY* recognition and assertion of the existence of the conscious self: E19. **self-aˈggrandizement** *noun* aggrandizement of oneself, the action or process of enriching oneself or making oneself powerful L18. **self-aˈggrandizing** *adjective* given to or characterized by self-aggrandizement M19. **self-alieˈnation** *noun* alienation of oneself, alienation from one's own feelings or activities E20. **self-aˈligning** *adjective* capable of automatic aligning; (of a bearing etc.) having a degree of flexibility as regards alignment: E20. **self-ˈanalysing** *adjective* analysing oneself, given to self-analysis E20. **self-aˈnalysis** *noun* analysis of one's own character, motives, etc.; psychoanalysis of oneself undertaken by oneself: M19. **self-ˈanalyst** *noun* a person who undertakes self-analysis E20. **self-annihiˈlation** *noun* annihilation or obliteration of self, esp. in mystical contemplation M17. **self-aˈpplauding** *adjective* characterized by, involving, or requiring self-applause M17. **self-aˈpplause** *noun* marked approval or commendation of oneself L17. **self-aˈppointed** *adjective* appointed by oneself; designated so by oneself, without authorization from another: L18. **self-appreciˈation** *noun* high estimation of oneself, conceit E19. **self-approˈbation** *noun* approval of oneself, one's actions, etc.; self-appreciation: M18. **self-aˈpproval** *noun* = SELF-APPROBATION E19. **self-aˈssembly** *noun* (*a*) subsequent assembly of something bought in the form of a kit; usu. *attrib.*, designating items (e.g. furniture) sold in this form; (*b*) *BIOLOGY* the spontaneous formation of a molecular complex or sub-cellular particle, as a ribosome or a virus, in a medium containing the appropriate components: M20. **self-aˈsserting** *adjective* = SELF-ASSERTIVE M19. **self-aˈssertion** *noun* assertion of one's individuality, insistence on one's claims or one's supremacy; aggressive promotion of oneself, one's views, etc.: E19. **self-aˈssertive** *adjective* full of or characterized by self-assertion M19. **self-assertiveness** *noun* the quality or fact of being self-assertive L19. **self-aˈssessment** *noun* assessment or evaluation of oneself, or one's actions or attitudes; an instance of this; *spec.* calculation of one's own taxable liability: M20. **self-aˈssurance** *noun* self-confidence L16. **self-aˈssured** *adjective* self-confident E18. **self-aˈssuredly** *adverb* in a self-confident manner L20. **self-aˈssuredness** *noun* self-assurance M20. **self-aˈware** *adjective* aware or conscious of one's character, feelings, motives, etc. E20. **self-aˈwareness** *noun* the quality, condition, or fact of being self-aware L19. **self-ˈbalancing** *adjective* (*a*) *ACCOUNTANCY* having the debit side equal to the credit side; (*b*) capable of balancing itself automatically; automatically producing balance: L19. **self-beˈgotten** *adjective* produced by oneself or itself, not generated externally L17. **self-ˈbeing** *noun* (*a*) independent existence; †(*b*) a self-existent being: L16. **self-beˈtrayal** *noun* betrayal of oneself; (an) inadvertent revelation of one's true feelings etc.: M19. **self-ˈbetterment** *noun* improvement of oneself, one's character, social position, etc. M20. **self-ˈbias** *noun & verb* (*ELECTRONICS*) (*a*) *noun* bias applied to the grid of a valve by means of a resistor in the cathode circuit or the grid circuit; (*b*) *verb trans.* apply a self-bias to (chiefly as ***self-biased***, ***self-biasing*** *ppl adjectives*): M20. **self-ˈbinder** *noun* a reaping machine with a mechanism for binding corn into sheaves automatically L19. **self-biˈography** *noun* (*rare*) = AUTOBIOGRAPHY L18. **self-ˈblimped** *adjective* (of a cine-camera) fitted with a soundproof cover, insulated from sound by its own housing M20. **self-ˈboasting** *noun* (now *rare*) boasting about oneself L16. **self-ˈborn** *adjective* born of or originating from oneself or itself, not produced externally L16. **self-ˈbred** *adjective* (*rare*) = SELF-BORN L16. **self-ˈcancelling** *adjective* that cancels itself; that negate each other; designed to stop working automatically when no longer required: M20. **self-caˈpacitance** *noun* (*ELECTRICITY*) the inherent capacitance of a circuit or component E20. **self-ˈcare** *noun* taking care of oneself; self-interested behaviour: E20. **self-ˈcatering** *adjective & noun* (*a*) *adjective* designating rented temporary or holiday accommodation where food is provided and prepared by the occupant(s), or a holiday in such accommodation; (*b*) *noun* catering for oneself in rented temporary or holiday accommodation: M20. **self-ˈcensorship** *noun* censorship of oneself, one's thoughts, words, etc. M20. **self-ˈcentring** *adjective* †(*a*) = SELF-CENTRED; (*b*) able to hold an object in a central position without the necessity of tentative adjustments; (*c*) tending to return automatically to a central alignment: L17. **self-certifiˈcation** *noun* provision of a certificate oneself; *spec.* the practice by which an employee declares in writing that an absence from work was due to illness: L20. **self-ˈchanging** *adjective* (*a*) *rare* causing a change in the self; (*b*) (of a gearbox) automatic, preselective: M19. **self-ˈcleaning** *adjective* designed or tending to keep itself clean automatically, (of an oven etc.) cleaning itself when heated L19. **self-ˈcleansing** *adjective* designed or tending to keep itself clean automatically E20. **self-ˈclosing** *adjective* (of a door etc.) closing automatically L19. **self-ˈcocking** *adjective* (of a firearm) cocked by pulling the trigger, not by raising the hammer manually, double-action M19. **self-coˈincidence** *noun* the fact or state of coinciding with the former position following a displacement E20. **self-coˈllected** *adjective* self-possessed, composed, = COLLECTED 1 E18. **self-coˈmmand** *noun* control of one's actions or feelings, self-control M17. **self-coˈmmunion** *noun* communion with oneself, meditation on one's own character, conduct, etc. E19. **self-compatiˈbility** *noun* the state of being self-compatible E20. **self-comˈpatible** *adjective & noun* (a plant or species) able to be fertilized by its own pollen E20. **self-comˈplacence** *noun* (now *rare*) = SELF-COMPLACENCY M18. **self-comˈplacency** *noun* self-satisfaction, complacency L17. **self-comˈplacent** *adjective* self-satisfied, complacent M18. **self-complacential** /-kɒmpləˈsɛnʃ(ə)l/ *adjective* (now *rare*) self-satisfied, complacent E18. **self-conˈceit** *noun* a high or exaggerated opinion of oneself, one's talents, attainments, etc.; self-satisfaction, conceit: L16. **self-conˈceited** *adjective* (now *rare*) full of or marked by self-conceit, having an excessively high opinion of oneself, conceited L16. **self-conˈceitedness** *noun* (now *rare*) = SELF-CONCEIT E17. **self-ˈconcept**, **self-conˈception** *nouns* (*SOCIAL PSYCHOLOGY*) a person's conception or idea of himself or herself M20. **self-conˈcern** *noun* (*a*) a personal interest; (*b*) concern for oneself: L17. **self-conˈcerned** *adjective* concerned for oneself, self-interested M17. **self-condemˈnation** *noun* (*a*) condemnation or blaming of oneself; (*b*) inadvertent revelation of one's own crime, sin, etc.: L17. **self-conˈdemned** *adjective* condemned by one's own action or words, esp. inadvertently E17. **self-conˈdemning** *adjective* condemning oneself, one's way of life, etc., esp. inadvertently L16. **self-condenˈsation** *noun* (*CHEMISTRY*) a condensation reaction between two molecules of the same compound M20. **self-confessed** *adjective* (usu. *attrib.*) so by one's own admission L19. **self-ˈconfidence** *noun* confidence in oneself, one's own powers, judgement, etc. M17. **self-ˈconfident** *adjective* having self-confidence, confident of one's own powers, judgement, etc. E17. **self-ˈconfidently** *adverb* in a self-confident manner M19. **self-conˈfiding** *adjective* (*arch.*) self-confident M17. **self-congratuˈlation** *noun* (a) congratulation of oneself, self-satisfaction E18. **self-conˈgratulatory** *adjective* congratulatory of oneself L19. **self-ˈconquest** *noun* conquest of oneself, one's impulses, etc.; the overcoming of one's worst characteristics: E18. **self-ˈconsequence** *noun* self-importance L18. **self-conˈsistency** *noun* consistency with oneself or itself, constancy of principle etc. L17. **self-conˈsistent** *adjective* (*a*) = CONSISTENT 5, 6; (*b*) *PHYSICS* (of a trial solution of esp. Schrödinger's equation) consistent with its own postulates: L17. **self-conˈsistently** *adverb* in a self-consistent manner M20. **self-ˈconstituted** *adjective* (of a person, group, etc.) assuming a function without authorization or right, self-appointed E19. **self-conˈtempt** *noun* contempt for oneself L16. **self-conˈtemptuous** *adjective* contemptuous of oneself, characterized by or expressive of self-contempt L20. **self-conˈtent** *noun* content with oneself, one's life, achievements, etc., self-satisfaction M17. **self-conˈtented** *adjective* contented with oneself, one's life, achievements, etc., self-satisfied E19. **self-conˈtentedly** *adverb* in a self-contented manner M19. **self-conˈtentedness** *noun* the condition of being self-contented L17. **self-conˈtentment** *noun* contentment with oneself, one's life, achievements, etc., self-satisfaction E19. **self-contraˈdicting** *adjective* contradicting oneself or itself, self-

contradictory M17. **self-contra'diction** *noun* the action or fact of contradicting oneself or itself; internal inconsistency; a statement containing contradictory elements: M17. **self-contra'dictorily** *adverb* in a self-contradictory manner M20. **self-contra'dictory** *adjective* involving self-contradiction, internally inconsistent M17. **self-con'trol** *noun* control of oneself, one's desires, reactions, etc. E18. **self-con'trolled** *adjective* having or showing self-control L19. **self-con'victed** *adjective* convicted by one's own words or action, esp. inadvertently E18. **self-con'viction** *noun* conviction (esp. inadvertent) of oneself by one's own words or action M17. **self-co'rrecting** *adjective* correcting itself without intervention or external assistance M19. **self-cre'ated** *adjective* created, brought into existence, or constituted by oneself or itself L17. **self-cre'ation** *noun* creation of oneself or itself M19. **self-cre'ative** *adjective* capable of self-creation M19. **self-'critical** *adjective* critical of oneself, one's actions, attitudes, etc. M20. **self-'criticism** *noun* (a) criticism of oneself, one's actions, attitudes, etc. M19. **self-culti'vation** *noun* cultivation or development by one's own efforts of one's mind, faculties, manners, etc. L19. **self-'culture** *noun* = SELF-CULTIVATION E19. **self-de'ceit** *noun* self-deception E17. **self-de'ceitful** *adjective* full of or given to self-deception E19. **self-de'ceived** *adjective* deceived by or about oneself, marked by self-deception L17. **self-de'ceiver** *noun* a person who deceives himself or herself E17. **self-de'ceiving** *adjective* deceiving oneself, given to or characterized by self-deception L16. **self-de'ception** *noun* the action or fact of deceiving oneself, esp. about one's true feelings L17. **self-de'ceptive** *adjective* = SELF-DECEIVING L19. **self-de'feating** *adjective* (of an action, attempt, etc.) doomed to failure because of internal inconsistencies, preventing attainment of the end it is designed to bring about E20. **self-de'fensive** *adjective* defensive of oneself; of or pertaining to self-defence, intended as self-defence: E19. **self-defi'nition** *noun* (a) definition of oneself, one's individuality, role in life, etc. M20. **self-de'frosting** *adjective* (of a refrigerator) defrosting automatically M20. **self-de'light** *noun* delight in oneself or one's existence L16. **self-de'liverance** *noun* deliverance of oneself, *spec.* suicide by an incurable patient who finds his or her suffering intolerable L20. **self-de'luded** *adjective* deluded by or about oneself, suffering from self-delusion M18. **self-de'luder** *noun* a person who deludes himself or herself M18. **self-de'luding** *adjective* given to or characterized by self-delusion M17. **self-de'lusion** *noun* the action of deluding oneself; the fact of being deluded about oneself; an instance of this: M17. **self-de'nial** *noun* denial or abnegation of oneself, sacrifice of one's personal desires, self-abnegation M17. **self-de'nied** *adjective* (now *rare*) given to or characterized by self-denial, self-denying L17. **self-de'nier** *noun* a person given to self-denial M17. **self-de'nying** *adjective* given to, characterized by, or involving self-denial (***self-denying ordinance***, a resolution of the Long Parliament (1644) depriving Members of Parliament of military and civil office; *transf.* any course of action by which a person deprives himself or herself of some advantage or benefit) M17. **self-de'nyingly** *adverb* in a self-denying manner M17. **self-de'pendence** *noun* dependence entirely on oneself or itself, independence M18. **self-de'pendent** *adjective* having or characterized by self-dependence L17. **self-'deprecating** *adjective* belittling or disparaging oneself M20. **self-'deprecatingly** *adverb* in a self-deprecating manner E20. **self-depre'cation** *noun* belittlement or disparagement of oneself E20. **self-'deprecatory**, **self-de'preciatory** *adjectives* tending to belittle or disparage oneself M19. **self-de'spair** *noun* despair of oneself L17. **self-de'stroyer** *noun* (*a*) a person who is the cause of his or her own destruction; (*b*) a person who commits suicide: M17. **self-de'stroying** *adjective* destroying oneself or itself, self-destructive M17. **self-de'struction** *noun* (*a*) destruction of oneself or itself; suicide; (*b*) the process or action of self-destructing: L16. **self-de'structive** *adjective* destructive of oneself or itself M17. **self-de'structively** *adverb* in a self-destructive manner M19. **self-de'structiveness** *noun* the quality or state of being self-destructive M18. **self-determi'nation** *noun* (*a*) the capacity to act with free will; (*b*) the action of a people in deciding its own allegiance or form of government; free determination of statehood, postulated as a right: L17. **self-de'termined** *adjective* determined by oneself; having the quality of self-determination: L17. **self-de'termining** *adjective* determining one's own acts; possessing self-determination: M17. **self-de'velopment** *noun* development or cultivation of oneself, one's abilities, etc. E19. **self-de'voted** *adjective* characterized by self-devotion E18. **self-de'votion** *noun* devotion of oneself, one's life, etc., to a person or cause E19. **self-differenti'ation** *noun* differentiation arising from within oneself or itself; *spec.* in BIOLOGY, that of embryonic tissue occurring more or less independently of other parts of the embryo: L19. **self-'diffidence** *noun* diffidence, lack of self-confidence M17. **self-di'ffusion** *noun* diffusion of oneself or itself; *spec.* (CHEMISTRY) migration of constituent atoms or molecules within the bulk of a substance, esp. in a crystalline solid: M19. **self-'discipline** *noun* self-imposed controlled and orderly behaviour; the capacity for this: L18. **self-'disciplined** *adjective* having self-discipline, characterized by self-discipline M20. **self-di'scovery** *noun* acquisition of insight into oneself, one's character, desires, etc. M20. **self-dis'gust** *noun* disgust with oneself E20. **self-di'ssociated** *adjective* that undergoes self-ionization L20. **self-dissoci'ation** *noun* (CHEMISTRY) = SELF-IONIZATION E20. **self-dis'trust** *noun* distrust of oneself, one's abilities etc. L18. **self-'doubt** *noun* (a) doubt about or lack of confidence in oneself, one's abilities, etc. M19. **self-dramati'zation** *noun* dramatization of one's own situation or feelings M20. **self-'drive** *adjective* & *noun* (*a*) *adjective* designating a hired motor vehicle to be driven by the hirer, not by a chauffeur; of or pertaining to the hiring of such vehicles; (*b*) *noun* a self-drive car or van: E20. **self-'driven** *adjective* driven by oneself; (of a motor vehicle) self-drive: L18. **self-'ease** *noun* personal comfort E17. **self-'educated** *adjective* educated by oneself by private study without formal instruction E19. **self-edu'cation** *noun* education of oneself by private study without formal instruction M19. **self-e'ffacement** *noun* the action of effacing oneself, the keeping of oneself out of sight or in the background M19. **self-e'ffacing** *adjective* given to or characterized by self-effacement E20. **self-e'ffacingly** *adverb* in a self-effacing manner E20. **self-e'lected** *adjective* elected by oneself, (of a body) elected by its members E19. **self-e'lection** *noun* election of oneself L18. **self-e'lective** *adjective* having the right to elect oneself; (of a committee etc.) proceeding by co-opting members: L18. **self-em'ployed** *adjective* working for oneself as a freelance or as the owner of a business etc., not employed by an employer M20. **self-em'ployment** *noun* employment of oneself, working for oneself not an employer; the condition or fact of being self-employed: M18. **self-en'closed** *adjective* enclosed within oneself or itself, not communicating freely with others L19. **self-energy** *noun* (PHYSICS) the energy possessed by a particle in isolation from other particles and fields; the energy of interaction of a particle, quasi-particle, or current with its own field: L19. **self-e'steem** *noun* high regard for oneself, good opinion of oneself M17. **self-'estimate** *noun* (an) estimate or valuation of oneself M19. **self-esti'mation** *noun* = SELF-ESTIMATE L18. **self-e'strangement** *noun* estrangement from one's natural self, esp. such as is thought to result from the alienating development of consciousness or from involvement in a complex industrialized culture L19. **self-evalu'ation** *noun* appraisal of one's actions, attitudes, or performance, esp. in relation to an objective standard M20. **self-'evidence** *noun* (*a*) evidence of its own truth; (*b*) the quality or condition of being self-evident: L17. **self-'evidencing** *adjective* providing itself the evidence of its own truth M17. **self-'evident** *adjective* requiring no proof or further explanation; obvious; axiomatic: L17. **self-'evidently** *adverb* in a self-evident manner, obviously L17. **self-evo'lution** *noun* evolution of oneself or itself by inherent power E19. **self-exal'tation** *noun* exaltation of oneself, one's personality, or one's claims L17. **self-exami'nation** *noun* (*a*) examination of one's conduct, motives, etc., esp. as a religious duty; (*b*) examination of one's body for signs of illness etc.: M17. **self-exci'tation** *noun* the characteristic or process of being self-exciting E20. **self-ex'cited** *adjective* self-exciting E20. **self-ex'citing** *adjective* (*a*) ELECTRICITY designating a dynamo-electric machine or analogous system that generates or excites its own magnetic field; (*b*) RADIO designating a unit which both generates and determines the frequency of the transmitted energy; self-oscillating: L19. **self-'executing** *adjective* (LAW) (of a law, legal clause, etc.) not needing legislation etc. for enforcement, automatically applicable M20. **self-'exile** *noun* voluntary exile E19. **self-'exiled** *adjective* voluntarily exiled M18. **self-e'xistence** *noun* existence by virtue of inherent nature independently of any other cause M17. **self-e'xistent** *adjective* having the property of self-existence, existing independently; having a primary or independent existence: L17. **self-ex'perience** *noun* (a) personal trial or experience E17. **self-ex'plained** *adjective* (now *rare*) self-explanatory E18. **self-ex'planatory** *adjective* explaining itself, able to be understood without explanation L19. **self-ex'posure** *noun* exposure of oneself, one's true feelings, etc. M18. **self-ex'pression** *noun* expression of one's feelings, thoughts, etc., esp. in writing, painting, music, or another art L19. **self-'feeder** *noun* (*a*) a furnace, machine, etc., that renews its own fuel or material automatically; (*b*) a device for supplying food to farm animals automatically: L19. **self-'feeding** *adjective* (of a furnace, machine, etc.) replacing its own fuel or material automatically M20. **self-'feeling** *noun* (*a*) *rare* = COENAESTHESIS; (*b*) feeling centred in oneself, egoistical feeling; (*c*) the sense of one's individual identity: M19. **self-'fertile** *adjective* (of a plant or hermaphrodite animal) capable of self-fertilization M19. **self-fertili'zation** *noun* (BOTANY & ZOOLOGY) fertilization by means of pollen or sperm from the same individual M19. **self-'fertilize** *verb* (*a*) *verb trans.* cause (a plant etc.) to undergo self-fertilization (usu. in *pass.*); (*b*) *verb intrans.* undergo self-fertilization: M19. **self-'field** *noun* (PHYSICS) a field intrinsically associated with a charged particle, particle beam, or current, esp. as contrasted with any externally applied field that may be present M20. **self-'finance** *verb trans.* generate enough income from itself to pay for the implementation or continuation of (a project, programme of development, etc.) M20. **self-'financing** *adjective* that finances itself; *spec.* (of a project, programme of development, etc.) that generates enough income to pay for its own implementation or continuation M20. **self-flage'llation** *noun* flagellation of oneself, esp. as a form of religious discipline; *fig.* excessive self-criticism: M19. **self-'flatterer** *noun* a person who flatters or has a flattering conception of himself or herself L17. **self-'flattering** *adjective* flattering to oneself, having a flattering conception of oneself L16. **self-'flattery** *noun* flattery of oneself, the holding of a flattering conception of oneself E17. **self-'fluxing** *adjective* (of iron ore) able to be smelted without the addition of a flux, usu. because of a high proportion of lime L19. **self-for'getful** *adjective* forgetful of one's self or one's own individuality; unselfish: E19. **self-for'getfulness** *noun* the quality or state of being self-forgetful E19. **self-'formed** *adjective* formed or produced by oneself or itself, without extraneous aid L17. **self-ful'filling** *adjective* (of a prophecy or prediction) giving rise to actions which bring about its fulfilment, bound to come true because of the conditions it creates M20. **self-ful'filment** *noun* fulfilment of one's own hopes and ambitions, self-satisfying fulfilment of one's own potential M20. **self-'generating** *adjective* generated by itself or oneself, not externally M19. **self-'given** *adjective* (*rare*) given by oneself or itself, emanating or derived from oneself or itself M18. **self-'giving** *adjective* giving oneself for others, self-sacrificing M19. **self-glorifi'cation** *noun* glorification of oneself, one's abilities, etc., boasting M19. **self-'glorious** *adjective* (long *rare*) given to or characterized by self-glorification L16. **self-'glory** *noun* (now *rare*) self-glorification M17. **self-good** *noun* (now *rare*) personal benefit or advantage E17. **self-'governed** *adjective* (*a*) marked by self-control; (*b*) having self-government; (*c*) acting or living independently: E18. **self-'governing** *adjective* having self-government, autonomous M19. **self-'government** *noun* (*a*) (now *rare*) self-control, self-command; (*b*) administration by a people or State (esp. a former colony) of its own affairs without external direction or interference: L17. **self-gratifi'cation** *noun* gratification or pleasing of oneself L17. **self-gratu'lation** *noun* = SELF-CONGRATULATION E19. **self-'gratulatory** *adjective* = SELF-CONGRATULATORY M19. **self-'gravitating** *adjective* influenced by self-gravitation M20. **self-gravi'tation** *noun* (ASTRONOMY) the gravitational forces acting among the components of a massive body M20. **self-'gravity** *noun* self-gravitation L20. **self-'hate** *noun* = SELF-HATRED M20. **self-'hatred** *noun* hatred of oneself, esp. of one's actual self when contrasted with one's imagined self M19. **self-'heating** *adjective* designed to heat itself automatically; (of food) held in a self-heating container: M20. **self-'help** *noun* the action or condition of providing for or improving oneself without assistance from others; the taking of action on one's own behalf: E19. **self-'helper** *noun* a believer in or practitioner of self-help M19. **self-'homicide** *noun* (now *rare*) self-murder, suicide E17. **self-hunt** *verb intrans.* (orig. *N. Amer.*) (of a dog) hunt independently without human guidance (chiefly as ***self-hunting*** *verbal noun* & *ppl adjective*) M18. **self-hyp'nosis** *noun* self-induced hypnosis, autohypnosis E20. **self-'hypnotism** *noun* hypnotism of oneself, self-hypnosis M19. **self-hypnoti'zation** *noun* hypnotization of oneself L19. **self-'hypnotized** *adjective* hypnotized by oneself, in a state of self-hypnosis E20. **self-i'dentical** *adjective* (PHILOSOPHY) identical with itself L19. **self-identifi'cation** *noun* identification with something outside oneself M20. **self-i'dentity** *noun* (PHILOSOPHY) the identity of a thing with itself M19. **self-'image** *noun* an image or conception of oneself, esp. considered in relation to others M20. **self-im'portance** *noun* the sense of one's (great) importance; conduct arising from this, pompousness: L18. **self-im'portant** *adjective* marked by self-importance; having an exaggerated opinion of one's own importance, pompous: M18. **self-im'portantly** *adverb* in a self-important manner M20. **self-im'posed** *adjective* (of a task, condition, etc.) imposed on one by oneself, not externally L18. **self-im'provable** *adjective* (*rare*) capable of self-improvement L17. **self-im'provement** *noun* improvement of oneself, one's character, etc., by one's own efforts L17. **self-im'proving** *adjective* characterized by or tending towards self-improvement L17. **self-incompati'bility** *noun* the state of being self-incompatible E20. **self-incom'patible** *adjective* & *noun* (a plant or species) unable to be fertilized by its own pollen E20. **self-incon'sistency** *noun* inconsistency in one's thought or action; internal inconsistency: L17. **self-incon'sistent** *adjective* inconsistent in one's thought or action; internally inconsistent: M17. **self-in'duced** *adjective* (*a*) ELECTRICITY produced by self-induction; (*b*) *gen.* induced by oneself or itself: L19. **self-in'ductance** *noun* (ELECTRICITY) (the coefficient of) self-induction; the property by which self-induction is possible: L19. **self-in'duction** *noun* (ELECTRICITY) the production of an induced current in a circuit by means of a variation in the current of that circuit; the coefficient of this: M19. **self-in'ductive** *adjective* (ELECTRICITY) produced by self-induction M19. **self-in'dulgence** *noun* indulgence of one's own inclinations, indulgence of oneself in pleasure, idleness, etc.; (in a work of art etc.) lack of economy and control; a thing in which one indulges oneself: M18. **self-in'dulgent** *adjective* given to self-indulgence, indulging or tending to indulge one's own inclinations; (of a work of art etc.) lacking economy and control: L18. **self-in'dulgently** *adverb* in a self-indulgent manner L19. **self-in'dulging** *adjective* self-indulgent L17. **self-in'flicted** *adjective* inflicted on one by oneself, not externally L18. **self-in'fliction** *noun* infliction of pain, suffering, etc., on oneself, (an) infliction by oneself E19. **self-in'struction** *noun* instruction of oneself, self-education E18. **self-in'surance** *noun* insurance of oneself or one's interests by maintaining a fund to cover possible losses E20. **self-in'sure** *verb intrans.* undertake self-insurance M20. **self-'interest** *noun* (*a*) one's personal profit, benefit, or advantage; regard to or pursuit of this, esp. to the exclusion of regard for others; †(*b*) a private or personal end: M17. **self-'interested** *adjective* characterized or motivated by self-interest M17. **self-'interestedness** *noun* the quality or condition of being self-interested E18. **self-in'vited** *adjective* invited by oneself, not invited to a function etc. that one attends M18. **self-invo'lution** *noun* (*rare*) the condition or fact of being self-involved E19. **self-in'volved** *adjective* wrapped up in oneself or one's own thoughts M19. **self-ioni'zation** *noun* (CHEMISTRY) spontaneous dissociation of a proportion of the molecules of a liquid into separate ions M20. **self-'judgement** *noun* †(*a*) *rare* self-esteem; (*b*) judgement passed on oneself: M17. **self-justifi'cation** *noun* the action of justifying or excusing oneself, one's actions, etc. M17. **self-'justifying** *adjective* (*a*) justifying or excusing oneself, one's actions, etc.; (*b*) TYPOGRAPHY (of a typesetting machine) justifying lines automatically: M18. **self-'killed** *adjective* (now *rare*) killed by one's own hand L16. **self-'knowing** *adjective* knowing oneself, having self-knowledge M17. **self-'knowledge** *noun* knowledge or understanding of oneself, one's character, motives, etc. E17. **self-life** *noun* (*literary*) (*a*) = SELF-EXISTENCE; (*b*) life lived for oneself, life devoted to selfish ends: E17. **self-limi'tation** *noun* (*a*) limitation of oneself, one's nature, etc.; (*b*) MEDICINE the property of being self-limited: E19. **self-'limited** *adjective* (*a*) limited by oneself or itself; (*b*) MEDICINE (of a disease) that runs a definite course, being little modified by treatment: M19. **self-'limiting** *adjective* limiting oneself or itself; *spec.* in MEDICINE, self-limited: M19. **self-'liquidating** *adjective* (COMMERCE) designating or pertaining to credit, a loan, etc., intended to be repaid with money accruing from its investment within a certain period E20. **self-liqui'dation** *noun* (*a*) COMMERCE the action or process of repaying a self-liquidating loan; (*b*) destruction or elimination of oneself by oneself: M20. **self-'liquidator** *noun* (COMMERCE) a self-liquidating premium M20. **self-'loader** *noun* a self-loading firearm etc.; a mechanism for the automatic loading of freight: M20. **self-'loading** *adjective* (of a firearm etc.) loaded automatically or semi-automatically L19. **self-'loathing** *noun* loathing of oneself, self-hatred M18. **self-'locking** *adjective* locking itself, locking automatically L19. **self-'loop** *noun* (MATH. etc.) in a graph or network, a line that returns to the node it leaves M20. **self-'lost** *adjective* (*literary*) lost through one's own action, fault, etc. L16. **self-'love** *noun* love of oneself; in early use usu., self-esteem, vanity; later, regard for one's interests or well-being (chiefly PHILOSOPHY), self-centredness, selfishness: M16. †**self-loved** *adjective* loved by oneself; marked by self-love: L16–E19. **self-'lover** *noun* (long *rare*) a lover of self, a self-centred or selfish person L16. **self-'loving** *adjective* loving or devoted to oneself, self-centred, selfish; characterized by self-love: L16. **self-'luminous** *adjective* possessing in itself the property of emitting light L18. **self-made** *adjective* made by oneself, by one's own action or efforts; of one's own making; successful or rich by one's own efforts: E17. **self-main'taining** *adjective* that maintains or sustains itself or oneself; *spec.* = HOMEOSTATIC: L19.

self-'maintenance *noun* maintenance of itself or oneself **M19.** **self-'management** *noun* management of or by oneself **M19.** **self-'managing** *adjective* managing itself or oneself; (of a school etc.) managed independently, not by the government: **L20.** **self-'mass** *noun* (PHYSICS) the mass of a particle arising relativistically from its self-energy **M20.** **self-'mastery** *noun* mastery of oneself, one's emotions, etc., self-control **M19.** **self-'mockery** *noun* mockery of oneself or itself **M20.** **self-'mocking** *adjective* mocking oneself or itself **M20.** **self-mortifi'cation** *noun* mortification of oneself, subjugation of one's appetites or passions by self-denial or self-discipline **E19.** **self-'motion** *noun* motion produced by one's or its inherent power, not externally; voluntary or spontaneous motion: **E17.** **self-'motivated** *adjective* motivated by oneself; *spec.* motivated by one's own enthusiasm, ambition, etc., to work or act without external pressure: **L20.** **self-moti'vation** *noun* motivation of oneself; motivation to work or act without external pressure: **L20.** **self-'motive** *adjective* (now *rare*) moving by inherent not external power **L17.** **self-'moved** *adjective* moved of itself without external agency **L17.** **self-'movement** *noun* = SELF-MOTION **L19.** **self-'moving** *adjective* moving spontaneously or automatically, capable of self-motion **E17.** **self-'murder** *noun* the action or an act of taking one's own life, suicide **L16.** **self-'murderer** *noun* a person who commits suicide **E17.** **self-muti'lation** *noun* mutilation of oneself, esp. as a symptom of mental disturbance **M19.** **self-neg'lect** *noun* neglect of oneself **E17.** **self-noise** *noun* noise generated directly by a particular object (as a vehicle, microphone, etc.) **M20.** **self-obser'vation** *noun* objective observation of one's own attitudes, reactions, or thought processes **L18.** **self-'opened** *adjective* opened of its own accord, opened automatically **M17.** **self-'opening** *adjective* opening of its own accord, opening automatically **M19.** **self-o'piniated** *adjective* (*rare*) = SELF-OPINIONATED **E17.** **self-o'pinion** *noun* high opinion of oneself, self-esteem; self-conceit, self-opinionatedness: **L16.** **self-o'pinionated** *adjective* (*a*) having an exaggerated opinion of oneself; arrogant; (*b*) obstinate in adhering to one's own opinions, self-willed: **L17.** **self-o'pinionatedness** *noun* the quality of being self-opinionated; arrogance; self-will: **M18.** **self-o'pinionative** *adjective* self-opinionated, characterized by self-opinionatedness **E19.** **self-o'pinioned** *adjective* = SELF-OPINIONATED **E17.** **self-orien'tation** *noun* orientation of one's actions or attitudes towards oneself or by oneself **L19.** **self-'oriented** *adjective* oriented towards or by oneself **M20.** **self-'oscillate** *verb intrans.* display self-oscillation **E20.** **self-'oscillating** *adjective* (capable of) undergoing self-oscillation; self-excited: **M20.** **self-osci'llation** *noun* (ELECTRONICS) the generation of continuous oscillations in a circuit, amplifier, etc., in circumstances of excessive positive feedback **E20.** **self-pa'rodic** *adjective* = *self-parodying* below **M20.** **self-'parody** *noun* (esp. inadvertent) parody of oneself, the way one speaks or writes, etc. **M20.** **self-'parodying** *adjective* parodying oneself, the way one speaks or writes, etc., esp. inadvertently **M20.** **self-parti'ality** *noun* (now *rare*) partiality towards oneself, self-love **E17.** **self-per'petuating** *adjective* perpetuating itself or oneself without external agency or intervention **E19.** **self-perpetu'ation** *noun* perpetuation of itself or oneself without external agency or intervention **M19.** **self-'pity** *noun* pity for oneself, one's own troubles, etc. **E17.** **self-'pitying** *adjective* pitying oneself, one's troubles, etc.; sorry for oneself; given to or expressive of self-pity: **M18.** **self-'pityingly** *adverb* in a self-pitying manner **L19.** **self-'pleased** *adjective* pleased with oneself, complacent **M18.** **self-'poise** *noun* the condition or property of being self-poised **M19.** **self-'poised** *adjective* poised or balanced unaided or without external support **E17.** **self-po'licing** *noun* keeping order or maintaining control without accountability to an external authority **M20.** **self-polli'nation** *noun* (BOTANY) the transfer to a stigma of pollen from stamens within the same flower or another flower on the same plant **L19.** **self-'pollinate** *verb trans.* (BOTANY) cause (a plant, a flower) to undergo self-pollination (usu. in *pass.*) **L19.** **self-'pollinator** *noun* a species which commonly shows self-pollination **M20.** **self-po'llution** *noun* (*arch.*) masturbation **E17.** **self-'portrait** *noun* a portrait of one painted, drawn, written, etc., by oneself **M19.** **self-'portraiture** *noun* (*a*) *rare* a self-portrait; (*b*) the making of self-portraits: **M19.** **self-po'ssessed** *adjective* characterized by self-possession, composed **E19.** **self-po'ssession** *noun* control of one's behaviour or feelings, self-control, composure **M18.** **self-'praise** *noun* praise or commendation of oneself, boasting **M16.** **self-preser'vation** *noun* preservation of one's own life, safety, etc., esp. regarded as a basic instinct of human beings and animals **E17.** **self-pre'servative** *adjective* of or pertaining to self-preservation, aimed at self-preservation **M19.** **self-pre'serving** *adjective* given to or characterized by self-preservation, aimed at self-preservation **M17.** **self-'pride** *noun* pride in oneself, one's achievements, etc.; personal pride: **L16.** **self-pro'claimed** *adjective* (usu. *attrib.*) proclaimed to be so by oneself, without authorization from another **M20.** **self-pro'nouncing** *adjective* (of a word etc.) represented in a phonetic transcription by the letters of the usual spelling **M19.** **self-'propagating** *adjective* (esp. of a plant) able to propagate itself **M19.** **self-pro'pelled** *adjective* (esp. of a motor vehicle etc.) moving or able to move without external propulsion **L19.** **self-pro'pelling** *adjective* = SELF-PROPELLED **M19.** **self-pro'tection** *noun* protection of oneself or itself **M19.** **self-pro'tective** *adjective* functioning or intended as self-protection **L19.** **self-'punishment** *noun* punishment of oneself **L16.** **self-'quenching** *adjective* (PHYSICS) having an intrinsic or internal cause of quenching **M20.** **self-'raised** *adjective* raised by oneself, raised by one's own power; (of a plant) self-sown: **M17.** **self-'raising** *adjective* (of flour) having a raising agent already added **M19.** **self-'rating** *noun* rating of one's own character, feelings, or behaviour; an instance of this: **M20.** **self-reali'zation** *noun* fulfilment by one's own efforts of the possibilities of personal development, esp. regarded as an ethical principle **L19.** **self-re'cording** *adjective* (of a scientific instrument etc.) automatically recording its measurements **M19.** **self-'reference** *noun* reference to oneself or itself, *spec.* (PHILOSOPHY) in certain paradoxes, propositions, or statements **M19.** **self-refe'rential** *adjective* of, pertaining to, or characterized by self-reference **M20.** **self-re'ferral** *noun* referral of oneself to an expert or (esp. medical) specialist for advice or treatment; an instance of this: **L20.** **self-re'ferring** *adjective* referring to oneself or itself, characterized by self-reference **E19.** **self-re'flection** *noun* †(*a*) *rare* a reflection or image of oneself; (*b*) reflection, meditation, or serious thought as to one's character, actions, motives, etc.: **M17.** **self-re'flective** *adjective* given to or characterized by self-reflection **L19.** **self-re'flexive** *adjective* †(*a*) *rare* = SELF-REFLECTIVE; (*b*) characterized by reflexive action on itself; containing a reflection or image of itself: **M17.** **self-re'gard** *noun* (*a*) consideration for oneself, self-interest; selfishness; conceit, vanity; (*b*) self-respect: **L16.** **self-re'garding** *adjective* given to or characterized by self-regard; conceited, vain: **L18.** **self-'registering** *adjective* (of a scientific instrument etc.) automatically registering its measurements **M19.** **self-'regulated** *adjective* regulated from within or automatically, regulated without intervention **M19.** **self-'regulating** *adjective* regulating oneself or itself from within or automatically **M19.** **self-regu'lation** *noun* regulation, control, or direction of one by oneself; regulation from within or without intervention; *spec.* in BIOLOGY = HOMEOSTASIS: **L17.** **self-'regulative** *adjective* characterized by self-regulation **M19.** **self-'regulatory** *adjective* of or pertaining to self-regulation, exercising or characterized by self-regulation **L19.** **self-rein'forcement** *noun* (PSYCHOLOGY) reinforcement or strengthening of one's own response to a stimulus or situation, esp. by praising or rewarding oneself **M20.** **self-re'liance** *noun* reliance on oneself, reliance on one's own powers, resources, etc., independence **M19.** **self-re'liant** *adjective* reliant on oneself, characterized by self-reliance **M19.** **self-re'liantly** *adverb* in a self-reliant manner **M20.** **self-re'lying** *adjective* relying on oneself, self-reliant **E19.** **self-re'newal** *noun* renewal of oneself or itself **M20.** **self-renunci'ation** *noun* renunciation of oneself, one's own desires, etc.; self-sacrifice; unselfishness: **L18.** **self-re'pression** *noun* repression of oneself, one's desires, opinions, etc. **M19.** **self-re'proach** *noun* (a) reproach directed at oneself **M17.** **self-re'proachful** *adjective* full of self-reproach **M19.** **self-reproaching** *adjective* reproaching oneself, self-reproachful **L18.** **self-re'proof** *noun* (a) reproof of oneself **L18.** **self-re'pugnant** *adjective* (now *rare*) self-contradictory **E18.** **self-re'spect** *noun* †(*a*) a private, personal, or selfish end; (*b*) respect for oneself; proper concern for the way one behaves or is treated: **L16.** **self-re'spectful** *adjective* showing self-respect **L19.** **self-re'specting** *adjective* having self-respect **L18.** **self-re'strained** *adjective* characterized by or involving self-restraint **L17.** **self-re'straint** *noun* restraint imposed by oneself on one's actions etc., self-control: **L18.** **self-re'vealed** *adjective* revealed by one's own action, esp. inadvertently **E20.** **self-re'vealing** *adjective* revealing one's character, motives, etc., esp. inadvertently **M19.** **self-reve'lation** *noun* (esp. inadvertent) revelation of one's character, motives, etc. **M19.** **self-re'versal** *noun* (*a*) reversal (of motion) by agency of the mover itself; (*b*) PHYSICS the darkening of the middle of a bright spectral line as a result of radiation emitted by a hot gas being partly reabsorbed as it passes through cooler parts of the gas; (*c*) GEOLOGY the postulated reversal of the magnetization of some rocks by intrinsic means, rather than by reversal of the earth's magnetic field: **L19.** **self-'righting** *adjective* (of a boat) that rights itself after capsizing **M19.** **self-'rising** *adjective* (US) = SELF-RAISING **M19.** **self-'rule** *noun* government of a colony, dependent country, etc., by its own people **L19.** **self-'sacrifice** *noun* sacrifice of oneself; the giving up of one's own interests, happiness, and desires, for the sake of others: **E19.** **self-'sacrificer** *noun* a self-sacrificing person **M17.** **self-sacri'ficial** *adjective* = SELF-SACRIFICING **M19.** **self-'sacrificing** *adjective* sacrificing one's life, interests, happiness, etc., for the sake of others **E19.** **self-satis'faction** *noun* satisfaction with oneself, one's achievements, etc., esp. when excessive or unwarranted; complacency: **M18.** **self-'satisfied** *adjective* satisfied with oneself, one's achievements, etc., esp. excessively or unwarrantedly; characterized by or expressive of self-satisfaction: **M18.** **self-'satisfiedly** *adverb* in a self-satisfied manner **L20.** **self-'satisfying** *adjective* that satisfies oneself, affording self-satisfaction **L17.** **self-'scrutiny** *noun* scrutiny of oneself, one's motives, etc. **E18.** **self-'sealing** *adjective* sealing itself without the usual process or procedure; (of a fuel tank, pneumatic tyre, etc.) automatically able to seal small punctures; (of an envelope) self-adhesive: **L19.** **self-se'cure** *adjective* sure of oneself, one's position, etc., self-confident **L17.** **self-se'curity** *noun* the quality or condition of being self-secure, self-confidence **M18.** **self-'seed** *verb intrans.* = SELF-SOW **M20.** **self-'seeded** *adjective* = SELF-SOWN **M20.** **self-'seeder** *noun* a plant that propagates itself by seed **M20.** **self-'seeker** *noun* a self-seeking person **M17.** **self-'seeking** *noun* & *adjective* (*a*) *noun* the seeking after one's own welfare before that of others, pursuit of selfish ends; (*b*) *adjective* characterized by self-seeking, selfishly pursuing one's own ends: **L16.** **self-se'lected** *adjective* selected by oneself or automatically; about the selection of whom or which there can be no dispute: **E20.** **self-se'lecting** *adjective* selecting oneself or itself, self-selected **L20.** **self-se'lection** *noun* selection by oneself; automatic selection: **M20.** **self-'serve** *adjective* (chiefly *N. Amer.*) = SELF-SERVICE *adjective* **M20.** **self-'serving** *adjective* serving one's own ends before those of others, self-seeking **E19.** **self-'set** *adjective* (of a task etc.) set or imposed on one by oneself **L18.** **self-'shielded** *adjective* (PHYSICS) exhibiting self-shielding **M20.** **self-'shielding** *noun* (PHYSICS) (*a*) shielding of the interior of a body as a result of absorption of external radiation by the outer parts; (*b*) = SELF-ABSORPTION (b): **M20.** **self-shifter** *noun* a car with an automatic gearbox **L20.** **self-'similar** *adjective* similar to itself, having no variety within itself, uniform; *spec.* in MATH. similar to itself at a different time, or to a copy of itself on a different scale: **M19.** **self-simi'larity** *noun* the state or property of being self-similar **M20.** **self-'slaughter** *noun* suicide **E17.** **self-'slaughtered** *adjective* killed by one's own hand **L16.** **self-'slayer** *noun* (*arch.*) a person who commits suicide **L17.** **self-'sow** *verb intrans.* (of a plant) propagate itself by seed **E20.** **self-'sown** *adjective* sown by itself without human or animal agency, grown from seed scattered naturally **E17.** **self-'starter** *noun* (*a*) an electrical device for starting the engine of a motor vehicle without the use of a crank; (*b*) a person who acts on his or her own initiative, an ambitious person who needs no external motivation: **L19.** **self-'starting** *adjective* (*a*) starting automatically or semi-automatically, (of a motor vehicle) fitted with a self-starter; (*b*) able to act on one's own initiative, requiring no external motivation: **M19.** **self-'steering** *noun* (NAUTICAL) the steering or directing of a vessel on a predetermined course by automatic means; apparatus to achieve this: **M20.** **self-'sterile** *adjective* (BOTANY & ZOOLOGY) not self-fertilizing **L19.** **self-ste'rility** *noun* (BOTANY & ZOOLOGY) the condition or fact of being self-sterile **L19.** **self-stimu'lation** *noun* stimulation of oneself or itself for pleasure or excitement; *spec.* masturbation: **M20.** **self-'study** *noun* (*a*) study or contemplation of oneself; (*b*) study by oneself, private study: **L17.** **self-styled** *adjective* (usu. *attrib.*) so styled or described by oneself, without authorization from another; would-be, pretended: **E19.** **self-sub'sistence** *noun* subsistence without dependence on or support from anything external **E17.** **self-sub'sistency** *noun* = SELF-SUBSISTENCE **M17.** **self-sub'sistent** *adjective* subsistent without dependence on or support from anything external, characterized by self-subsistence **M17.** **self-sub'stantial** *adjective* (*rare*) derived from one's own substance **L16.** **self-su'fficing** *adjective* = SELF-SUFFICIENT **L17.** **self-su'ggestion** *noun* = AUTO-SUGGESTION **L19.** **self-su'pport** *noun* support of oneself or itself without external assistance, the fact of being self-supporting **L18.** **self-su'pporting** *adjective* supporting oneself or itself without external assistance; (of a physical object) staying up or standing without the usual support; able to support oneself or itself financially, paying one's or its way: **E19.** **self-su'rrender** *noun* surrender or giving up of oneself to an influence, an emotion, another person, etc. **E18.** **self-su'stained** *adjective* (*a*) sustained by one's own power or efforts; (*b*) *rare* held up without support: **M18.** **self-su'staining** *adjective* sustaining oneself by one's own power or efforts, able to continue without support or external assistance **M19.** **self-'sustenance** *noun* the quality or fact of being self-sustaining **M19.** **self-system** *noun* (PSYCHOLOGY) the organized complex of drives and responses pertaining to (an aspect of) the self; the set of potentialities which develop in an individual's character in response to parental influence: **L19.** **self-tailing** *adjective* (NAUTICAL) (of a winch) designed to maintain constant tension in the rope round it so that it does not slip **L20.** **self-'tapping** *adjective* (of a screw) able to cut its own thread in a hole in metal **M20.** **self-'taught** *adjective* taught by oneself without aid from others, self-educated; (of knowledge, skill, etc.) acquired by one's own unaided efforts: **E18.** **self-'timer** *noun* (PHOTOGRAPHY) a mechanism that introduces a delay between the operation of the shutter release and the opening of the shutter, so that the photographer can photograph himself or herself **M20.** **self-'torment** *noun* the action or an act of tormenting oneself **M17.** **self-'torture** *noun* torture of oneself, the infliction of (esp. mental) pain on oneself **E19.** **self-tran'scendence** *noun* transcendence or surpassing of oneself or one's limitations **L19.** **self-tran'scending** *adjective* transcending or surpassing oneself or one's limitations **L19.** **self-'trust** *noun* trust in oneself, self-confidence **L16.** **self-'twist** *adjective* designating or pertaining to a method of spinning in which yarn is twisted by the lateral movement of a roller **L20.** **self-'violence** *noun* violence against oneself, *spec.* (*euphem.*) suicide **L17.** **self-'winding** *adjective* (of a watch etc.) having an automatic winding apparatus **E19.** **self-'wisdom** *noun* (*arch.*) confidence in or reliance on one's own wisdom **L16.** **self-'wise** *adjective* (*arch.*) confident of or relying on one's own wisdom **M16.** **self-'worth** *noun* intrinsic personal worth; self-esteem: **M20.** **self-'wrought** *adjective* (*literary*) produced or brought about by oneself **L16.**

self-abuse /sɛlfə'bjuːs/ *noun.* **E17.**
[from SELF- + ABUSE *noun.*]
†**1** Self-deception. Only in **E17.**
2 Physical abuse of oneself. Also *spec.*, masturbation. **E18.**
3 Verbal abuse or revilement of oneself. **L18.**

self-black /sɛlf'blak, 'sɛlfblak/ *adjective* & *noun.* Chiefly *north.* **M16.**
[from SELF *adjective* + BLACK *adjective*, *noun.*]
(Of) a uniformly black colour. Also, (of) a naturally black colour.

self-centred /sɛlf'sɛntəd/ *adjective.* Also ***-centered.** **L17.**
[from SELF- + CENTRE *verb* + -ED[1].]
1 Fixed or stationary, as a centre round which other things move. **L17.**
2 Independent of external action or influence. Now usu., selfishly independent, preoccupied with one's own personality or affairs. **M18.**
■ **self-centredly** *adverb* **M20.** **self-centredness** *noun* **L19.**

self-color *noun*, **self-colored** *adjective* see SELF-COLOUR, SELF-COLOURED.

self-colour /'sɛlfkʌlə/ *noun.* Also ***-color.** **M17.**
[from SELF *adjective* + COLOUR *noun.*]
A single uniform colour; a shade of a single colour. Also, the natural colour.

self-coloured /sɛlf'kʌləd/ *adjective.* Also ***-colored.** **E17.**
[formed as prec. + -ED[2].]
Of a single uniform colour; of shades of a single colour. Also, of the natural colour; (of material) undyed; (of a flower) having its colour unchanged by cultivation or hybridization.

self-conscious /sɛlf'kɒnʃəs/ *adjective.* **L17.**
[from SELF- + CONSCIOUS *adjective.*]
1 PHILOSOPHY. Having consciousness of one's identity, one's actions, sensations, etc.; reflectively aware of one's actions. **L17.**
2 Unduly aware of oneself as an object of observation by others; embarrassed, shy. **M19.**
■ **self-consciously** *adverb* **M19.** **self-consciousness** *noun* **L17.**

self-contained /sɛlfkən'teɪnd/ *adjective.* L16.
[from SELF- + CONTAIN *verb* + -ED¹.]
1 Having all that is needed in oneself or itself; independent; (of a person) uncommunicative, reserved or restrained in behaviour. L16.
2 Of living accommodation: having no rooms shared with another household or set of occupants, and usu. having a private entrance. Orig. *Scot.* M18.
3 Of a machine or device: complete in itself. E19.
▪ **self-containedly** *adverb* L19. **self-containedness** *noun* M19. **self-containment** *noun* the condition of being self-contained M19.

self-defence /sɛlfdɪ'fɛns/ *noun.* Also *-**defense**. M17.
[from SELF- + DEFENCE *noun*.]
Defence of oneself, one's rights or position, etc.; aggressive action, speech, etc., intended as defence.

> 🕮 A. KOESTLER One must fight in self-defence. *Argosy* If you force me to shoot, I can plead self-defence. *New Scientist* The Japanese technique of self-defence called Karate. ***the noble art of self-defence, the noble science of self-defence***: see NOBLE *adjective*.

self-destruct /sɛlfdɪ'strʌkt/ *verb & adjective.* Orig. *N. Amer.* M20.
[from SELF- + DESTRUCT *verb*.]
▶**A** *verb intrans.* (Of a spacecraft, bomb, etc.) explode or disintegrate automatically, esp. when pre-set to do so; destroy itself or oneself; ruin one's own life or chances. M20.

> 🕮 D. FRANCIS He's programmed to self-destruct before the end of the season.

▶**B** *attrib. adjective.* Enabling a thing to self-destruct. M20. ***self-destruct button, self-destruct device***, etc.

self-faced /sɛlf'feɪst/ *adjective.* M19.
[from SELF *adjective* + FACED, after *self-coloured*.]
Of stone: retaining its natural face or surface; undressed, unhewn.

selfful /'sɛlf-fʊl, -f(ə)l/ *adjective.* Long *rare.* M17.
[from SELF *noun* + -FUL.]
Self-centred, selfish.
▪ **selffulness** *noun* M17.

self-heal /'sɛlfhiːl/ *noun.* Also **selfheal**. ME.
[from SELF- + HEAL *verb*¹.]
Any of several plants formerly credited with healing properties; esp. *Prunella vulgaris*, a small labiate plant with spikes of purple flowers, common in pastures.

selfhood /'sɛlfhʊd/ *noun.* M17.
[from SELF *noun* + -HOOD, orig. repr. German *Selbheit*.]
1 The quality by virtue of which one is oneself; personal individuality; one's personality. M17.
2 Self-centredness; devotion to self, selfish life or conduct. Now *rare.* M17.

selfish /'sɛlfɪʃ/ *adjective.* M17.
[from SELF *noun* + -ISH¹.]
1 Concerned chiefly with one's own personal advantage or welfare to the exclusion of regard for others, deficient in consideration for others; actuated by or appealing to self-interest. M17.
2 GENETICS. Designating a gene or genetic material considered primarily as tending to replicate itself, any effect on the organism being derivative of this tendency. L20.

> 🕮 **1** E. CALDWELL Very selfish of me—thinking of myself when Annette was in need of help. *Irish Press* An over protective mother whose motives were selfish rather than loving. *Times* The brash and selfish values of a 'get rich quick' society.

▪ **selfishly** *adverb* M18. **selfishness** *noun* M17.

selfism /'sɛlfɪz(ə)m/ *noun.* E19.
[from SELF *noun* + -ISM.]
Concentration on one's own interests; self-centredness, selfishness.

selfist /'sɛlfɪst/ *noun.* M17.
[from SELF *noun* + -IST.]
A self-centred or selfish person.

selfless /'sɛlflɪs/ *adjective.* L18.
[from SELF *noun* + -LESS.]
Having no regard for or thought of oneself or one's own interests; not self-centred; unselfish.

> 🕮 W. SOYINKA He is a dedicated and selfless social reformer. O. SACKS The selfless help and generosity of the patients.

▪ **selflessly** *adverb* E20. **selflessness** *noun* M19.

selfmate /'sɛlfmeɪt/ *noun.* M19.
[from SELF- + MATE *noun*¹.]
CHESS. Checkmate caused by the player who is mated.

selfness /'sɛlfnɪs/ *noun.* L16.
[from SELF *noun* + -NESS.]
1 Self-centredness; egoism; selfishness; self-regard. L16.
2 Individuality, personality, essence. E17.

self-righteous /sɛlf'rʌɪtʃəs/ *adjective.* L17.
[from SELF- + RIGHTEOUS *adjective*.]
Righteous in one's own estimation; excessively conscious of or insistent on one's own righteousness, rectitude, or correctness.
▪ **self-righteously** *adverb* E20. **self-righteousness** *noun* M17.

selfsame /'sɛlfseɪm/ *adjective & noun.* Now *literary.* LME.
[Orig. two words, from SELF *adjective* + SAME *adjective*.]
▶**A** *adjective* (usu. *attrib.*). The very same, the identical. Usu. with *the*. LME.

> 🕮 STEELE The very self-same Action done by different Men. R. W. EMERSON Always selfsame, like the sky. S. HAZZARD Ted wondered . . , and saw Caro smile with the selfsame thought. ***one and the selfsame***: see ONE *adjective, noun, & pronoun*.

▶†**B** *absol.* as *noun*. **1** The selfsame person or thing. LME–M17.
2 In *pl.* Identical things. *rare.* Only in E18.
▪ **selfsameness** *noun* identicalness, identity L16.

self-service /sɛlf'səːvɪs, *as adjective also* 'sɛlfsəːvɪs/ *noun & adjective.* E20.
[from SELF- + SERVICE *noun*¹.]
▶**A** *noun.* **1** A system whereby customers in a shop, restaurant, garage, etc., serve themselves instead of being attended to or waited on by the staff, usu. paying for all purchases at the same checkout desk or counter. E20.
2 An establishment or department operating this system. M20.

> 🕮 **2** J. MANN She had pulled into the motorway café . . and had gone into the self-service.

▶**B** *attrib.* or as *adjective.* Designating a shop, restaurant, garage, etc., operating this system; of or pertaining to self-service. E20.

> 🕮 M. DRABBLE They . . collected themselves a large self-service meal. *Which?* For clothes, some people liked self-service arrangements. B. PYM A small self-service store run by Uganda Asians.

self-sufficiency /sɛlfsə'fɪʃ(ə)nsi/ *noun.* L16.
[from SELF- + SUFFICIENCY.]
The quality or condition of being self-sufficient.

> 🕮 J. NORRIS The . . perfections of the Divinity, . . His self-sufficiency and independency. G. LORD She . . enjoyed the work associated with self-sufficiency. E. FEINSTEIN Her isolation . . gave her the wary self-sufficiency of a natural outsider.

▪ Also **self-sufficience** *noun* (*arch.*) E18.

self-sufficient /sɛlfsə'fɪʃ(ə)nt/ *adjective.* L16.
[from SELF- + SUFFICIENT *adjective*.]
1 Able to supply one's needs oneself, *spec.* (of a person, nation, etc.) self-reliant, self-supporting, independent; able to provide enough of a commodity (as food, oil, etc.) from one's own resources without the need to obtain goods from elsewhere (foll. by *in* the commodity). L16.
2 Content with one's own opinion, confident in one's powers, arrogant. M18.

> 🕮 **1** C. FRANCIS North Sea oil should . . make Britain self-sufficient in energy. S. BELLOW A very self-sufficient person, with a life plan of his own. *absol.*: T. KEN Thou self-originated Deity, . . Thou Self-sufficient, by thy self didst reign.

▪ **self-sufficientness** *noun* (*rare*) = SELF-SUFFICIENCY L19.

selfward /'sɛlfwəd/ *adverb & adjective.* Chiefly *US.* L19.
[from SELF *noun* + -WARD.]
▶**A** *adverb.* Towards or in the direction of oneself. L19.
▶**B** *adjective.* Tending or directed towards oneself. L19.
▪ **selfwards** *adverb* = SELFWARD *adverb* L19.

self-will /sɛlf'wɪl/ *noun.*
[Old English *selfwill* = Middle Low German *sulfwille*, Old High German *selbwillo* (German *Selbstwille*), Old Norse *sjálvili*, from Germanic bases of SELF *pronoun*, WILL *noun*¹.]
†**1** One's own will or desire. OE–LME.
2 Wilful or obstinate persistence in the pursuit of one's own desires or opinions. ME.

self-willed /sɛlf'wɪld/ *adjective.* LME.
[from prec. + -ED².]
Wilful or obstinate in the pursuit of one's own desires or opinions; characterized by self-will.
▪ **selfwilledness** *noun* LME.

selicha /sɪ'liːxə, sɪliː'xɑː/ *noun.* Pl. **-choth** /-xəʊt/. M19.
[Hebrew *sĕlīḥāh* forgiveness, pl. *sĕlīḥōt* penitential prayers.]
A Jewish penitential prayer recited on a fast-day, before Rosh Hashanah, and before and on Yom Kippur. Usu. in *pl.*

†**selictar** *noun.* L17–M19.
[Turkish *silāhtar*, *silihtar* from Persian *silāhdār*, from Arab. *silāḥ* weapon + Persian *-dār* holding, holder.]
In the Ottoman Empire: a sword-bearer.

selion /'sɛljən/ *noun.* Also **sillion** /'sɪljən/. ME.
[Anglo-Norman *seilon* (whence Anglo-Latin *selio*), Old French *seillon* measure of land (mod. *sillon* furrow).]
1 A piece of land comprising a ridge or narrow strip between two furrows formed in dividing an open field. *obsolete* exc. *Hist. & dial.* ME.
2 A furrow turned over by the plough. *poet. rare.* L19.

Seljuk /'sɛldʒuːk/ *noun & adjective.* M19.
[from Turkish *seljūq*, *Selčük*, reputed ancestor of the Seljuk dynasties (see below).]
▶**A** *noun. Hist.* A member of any of the Turkish dynasties of central and western Asia from the 11th to the 13th cents., preceding Ottoman rule; a Turkish subject of any of these dynasties. M19.
▶**B** *adjective.* **1** *Hist.* Of, pertaining to, or designating the Seljuks. M19.
2 Designating a type of Turkish carpet characterized by small geometrical patterns in white, black, indigo, and dark red. M20.

Seljukian /sɛl'dʒuːkɪən/ *adjective & noun.* E17.
[from (the same root as) prec. + -IAN.]
▶**A** *adjective.* = SELJUK *adjective* 1. E17.
▶**B** *noun.* = SELJUK *noun.* M17.

Selkup /sɛl'kuːp/ *noun & adjective.* M20.
[Selkup.]
A member of, of or pertaining to, a Samoyedic people of northern Siberia; (of) the Uralic language of this people.

selky /'sɛlki/ *noun. Scot.* Also **silky** /'sɪlki/. M16.
[from *selch* var. of SEAL *noun*¹ + -Y⁶.]
1 A seal (the animal). *dial.* M16.
2 An imaginary sea creature resembling a seal in the water but able to assume human form on land. M19.

sell /sɛl/ *noun*¹. Now *arch. & dial.* LME.
[Old & mod. French *selle* from Latin *sella* seat, chair, saddle.]
1 Orig., a seat, a low stool. Later (*rare*), a seat of dignity or authority, a site, a location. LME.
2 A saddle. LME.

sell /sɛl/ *noun*². M19.
[from SELL *verb*.]
1 An act of selling; *spec.* an act of betraying a person for money or other reward. *rare.* M19.
2 A contrivance, fiction, etc., by which a person is deceived or disappointed; a planned deception, a hoax. Also, a severe disappointment. *colloq.* M19.
3 A manner of selling esp. by advertising or persuasive salesmanship; the practice or fact of this. Freq. with specifying word. *colloq.* M20.

> 🕮 **2** B. STOKER The whole explanation was simply an elaborate sell. W. S. MAUGHAM It'll be an awful sell if at the end . . you've made a hash of it. **3** ***hard sell, soft sell***, etc.

Comb.: **sell-in** (orig. *US*) the sale of goods to a retail trader, esp. at wholesale prices, prior to public retailing; wholesale selling; **sell-off** STOCK EXCHANGE (chiefly *US*) a sale or disposal of bonds, shares, or commodities, usu. causing a fall in price; **sell-out** (orig. *US*) (*a*) a betrayal, esp. of public to private interest; (*b*) the disposal of a commodity in great demand; *esp.* the selling of all tickets for a play, film, or concert; a completely disposable commodity, *esp.* a play, film, or concert for which all tickets have been sold; **sell-through** (*a*) the quantity of goods bought (wholesale) which have been sold (retail); turnover; (*b*) sale as opp. to rental, esp. of video recordings.

sell /sɛl/ *verb.* Pa. t. & pple **sold** /səʊld/.
[Old English *sellan* = Old Frisian *sella*, Old Saxon *sellian*, Old High German *sellen*, Old Norse *selja* give up, sell, Gothic *saljan* offer sacrifice, from Germanic.]
†**1** *verb trans.* Give; voluntarily hand over (a person or thing) to another; grant (forgiveness etc.). OE–ME.
2 *verb trans.* Betray (a person etc.) esp. for money or other reward. OE.
3 *verb trans.* **a** Make over or dispose of (a thing) to another in exchange for money etc.; *esp.* dispose of (merchandise, possessions, etc.) *to* a buyer *for* or *at* a specified price. Also, be a dealer in or keep a regular stock of (a particular commodity) for sale; (of a publication or recording) attain sales of (a specified number of copies). OE. ▸**b** Cause an increase in the sale of. E18. ▸**c** Advertise or publish the merits of (an idea, commodity, etc.); persuade (a person) to accept or buy. Also, convince (a person) of the worth of something. *colloq.* (orig. *US*). E20.
4 *verb intrans.* **a** Make over or dispose of a thing to another; *esp.* dispose of merchandise, possessions, etc., to a buyer at a specified price. ME. ▸**b** Of a commodity: find a purchaser, be purchased, esp. *for*, *at* a specified price. E17.
5 *verb trans.* **a** Offer dishonourably for money or other consideration, make a matter of corrupt bargaining. ME. ▸**b** Give up or part with (a thing) in exchange *for* another; *esp.* (with allus. to *Genesis* 25:29–34) barter away (something of value) *for* something worthless. ME. ▸†**c** Exact a heavy penalty in return for (an injury). Chiefly with specifying adverbs *dear, dearly.* ME–M16.
6 *verb trans.* Cheat, trick, deceive; disappoint severely. *slang.* E17.

For other words beginning with *self-* see the entry for **self-**

📖 **2** G. J. W. WOLSELEY There were traitors in the Turkish ranks, . . the Turkish Army was more or less sold. **3a** AV *Gen.* 37:28 They . . sold Joseph to the Ishmeelites for twentie *pieces* of silver. A. S. NEILL Stores will sell cheap boots and frozen meat. E. WAUGH His novels sold fifteen thousand copies in their first year. E. O'BRIEN I went to get a stamp to send you a valentine. They didn't sell stamps. **c** *Publishers Weekly* An advertising campaign to sell New York as the printing centre of the world. *Guardian* To sell . . the idea that being a foster mother is a service. **4a** J. CONRAD That scoundrel . . has been coveting the brig for years. Naturally, I would never sell. **b** A. CHRISTIE *The Mystery of the Blue Train* . . sold just as well as my last book. *Times* The painting sold anonymously for £660,000. **5a** SHAKES. *2 Hen. VI* Therefore, when merchant-like I sell revenge, Broke be my sword. W. COWPER When perjury . . Sells oaths by tale, and at the lowest price. **b** SHELLEY Whose applause he sells For the gross blessings of a patriot mob. **6** THOMAS HUGHES I'll bet . . you never see a poacher, and then how sold you will be.

Phrases: ***sell a bill of goods***: see **bill of goods** s.v. BILL *noun*³. ***sell a dummy (to)***, ***sell the dummy (to)***: see DUMMY *noun*. ***sell a person a packet***: see PACKET *noun* 1b. ***sell a person a pup***: see PUP *noun*. **sell-by date**: marked on the packaging of (esp. perishable) food to indicate the latest recommended date of sale. ***sell by the candle***, ***sell by inch of candle***: see CANDLE *noun* 1. ***sell down the river***: see RIVER *noun*¹. ***sell like hot cakes***: see **hot cake** (b) s.v. HOT *adjective*. **sell oneself** (*a*) offer or dispose of one's services for money or other reward, esp. corruptly; be a prostitute; (*b*) promote one's own abilities. **sell one's life dear(ly)** *arch.* do great injury before being killed; make the enemy pay dearly for one's death. **sell one's soul to the Devil**, **sell oneself to the Devil**, etc., make a contract with the Devil exchanging possession of one's soul after death for help in attaining a desired end; *transf.* sacrifice conscience or principle for worldly advantage. ***sell short***: see SHORT *adverb*. ***sell the pass***: see PASS *noun*¹.

With adverbs & prepositions in specialized senses: **sell off** *verb phr. trans.* sell the remainder of (one's stock-in-trade, possessions, etc.) at reduced prices. **sell on** *colloq.* (orig. *US*) make enthusiastic about, convince of the worth of, (freq. in ***be sold on***). **sell out** (*a*) *verb phr. trans.* sell (all or some of one's stock-in-trade, shares in a company, etc.); (*b*) *verb phr. intrans.* sell all one's stock-in-trade, shares in a company, etc.; (*c*) *verb phr. intrans.* (now only MILITARY HISTORY) leave the army by selling one's commission; (*d*) *verb phr. trans.* (*colloq.*, orig. *US*) betray (a person or cause) for money or other reward; (*e*) *verb phr. intrans.* (*colloq.*, orig. *US*) be treacherous or disloyal. **sell up** (*a*) *verb phr. trans.* (now *rare* or *obsolete*) sell (one's business, house, etc.); (*b*) *verb phr. intrans.* sell one's business, house, etc.; (*c*) *verb phr. trans.* sell the goods of (a debtor) for the benefit of a creditor or creditors. **sold out** *colloq.* (chiefly *US*) bankrupt, exhausted, finished.

■ **sellable** *adjective* (*a*) able to be sold, saleable; †(*b*) *rare* (of a person) venal: LME.

sella /ˈsɛlə/ *noun*. L17.
[Latin = seat, saddle.]
ANATOMY & ZOOLOGY. A depression of the sphenoid bone containing the pituitary gland. Also more fully ***sella turcica*** /ˈtəːkɪkə/ [= Turkish].

sellathon /ˈsɛləθɒn/ *noun*. *colloq.* (chiefly *US*). L20.
[from SELL *verb* + -ATHON, after *telethon*.]
1 A prolonged period of selling at reduced prices; an extended sale. L20.
2 A (cable) television programme entirely devoted to advertising a sponsor's products. L20.
3 A marketing convention. L20.

Sellenger's round /ˈsɛlɪndʒəz raʊnd/ *noun phr.* M16.
[from repr. of a pronunc. of *St Leger* + -'S¹ + ROUND *noun*¹.]
A particular country round dance; a piece of music for this dance.

seller /ˈsɛlə/ *noun*. ME.
[from SELL *verb* + -ER¹.]
1 A person who sells. ME.
2 A thing to be sold. *rare*. M19.
3 A commodity that sells in a specified manner (freq. in ***best-seller***). Also (without specifying word), a thing that sells well. L19.
4 A selling race. *colloq.* E20.

📖 **1 seller's market**, **sellers' market** conditions in which goods are scarce and expensive. **3** *Viz* It's an autobiography . . confessions of a T.V. star. Should be a big seller.

sellette /sɛˈlɛt/ *noun*. *rare*. L17.
[French, dim. of *selle*: see SELL *noun*¹.]
Hist. In France and French-speaking countries, a stool for a prisoner under interrogation.

selling /ˈsɛlɪŋ/ *verbal noun*. ME.
[from SELL *verb* + -ING¹.]
The action of SELL *verb* (freq. with specifying word). Also (*rare*), an instance of this.
inertia selling, ***pyramid selling***, etc.
Comb.: **selling plate** = *selling-race* below; **selling plater** a horse entered in a selling plate; *colloq.* an inferior racehorse; **selling price**: at which an article is offered for sale; **selling-race** a horse-race after which the winning horse must be offered for sale at auction at a previously fixed price.

selling /ˈsɛlɪŋ/ *ppl adjective*. L18.
[from SELL *verb* + -ING².]
That sells; *spec.* (*a*) that readily finds a buyer, saleable; (*b*) that helps to effect a sale (freq. in ***selling-point***, an advantageous feature).

Sellotape /ˈsɛlə(ʊ)teɪp/ *noun & verb*. Also **cello-**, **s-**. M20.
[from alt. of CELLULOSE *noun* + -O- + TAPE *noun*.]
▶ **A** *noun*. (Proprietary name for) an adhesive usu. transparent cellulose or plastic tape. M20.
▶ **B** *verb trans.* (Usu. **s-**.) Fasten or fix with Sellotape. M20.

selon les règles /səlɔ̃ le rɛɡl/ *adverbial phr.* E19.
[French.]
According to the rules (of polite society).

Selsdon man /ˈsɛlzdən man/ *noun phr. derog.* Pl. **Selsdon men** /mɛn/. L20.
[from *Selsdon* Park Hotel, Croydon, Surrey (see below) + MAN *noun*.]
Hist. An advocate or adherent of the policies outlined at a conference of Conservative Party leaders held at the Selsdon Park Hotel 30 January–1 February 1970.

selsyn /ˈsɛlsɪn/ *noun*. E20.
[from SEL(F- + SYN(CHRONOUS *adjective*.]
A kind of electric motor resembling a magslip and employed similarly in pairs esp. to transmit and receive information about the position or motion of mechanical equipment. Also ***selsyn motor***.

seltzer /ˈsɛltzə/ *noun*. Also (earlier) †**Seltzers**. M18.
[from alt. of German *Selterser*, from (Nieder)-*Selters* (see below).]
In full ***seltzer water***. An effervescent mineral water from Nieder-Selters near Wiesbaden in Germany. Also, an artificial substitute for this; soda water.

selva /ˈsɛlvə/ *noun*. M19.
[Spanish or Portuguese from Latin *silva* wood.]
PHYSICAL GEOGRAPHY. (A tract of land covered by) dense equatorial forest, esp. in the Amazon basin. Usu. in *pl.*

selvage /ˈsɛlvɪdʒ/ *noun & verb*. Also **-edge**. LME.
[from (alt. of) SELF *adjective* + EDGE *noun* after early mod. Dutch *selfegghe* (now *zelfegge*), Low German *sülfegge*: cf. synon. Dutch *zelfkant* (*kant* border), *zelfeinde* (*einde* end).]
▶ **A** *noun*. **1 a** An edging of a piece of cloth finished so as to prevent unravelling, consisting either of an edge along the warp or a specially woven edging. Also, a border of different material or finish intended to be cut off or hidden. LME. ▸**b** *transf.* A marginal tract, a border, an edge. M17.
2 An ornamental border or edging. Now *rare* or *obsolete*. L15.
3 Chiefly NAUTICAL. = SELVAGEE. E18.
4 a MINING. A thin layer of clay or earthy matter surrounding a vein of ore. M18. ▸**b** GEOLOGY. An alteration zone at the edge of a rock mass. M20.
5 The edge-plate of a lock with an opening for the bolt. L19.
▶ **B** *verb trans.* Form a boundary or edging to. Cf. earlier SELVAGED. L16.
■ **selvaged** *ppl adjective* LME.

selvagee /ˈsɛlvədʒiː/ *noun*. M18.
[App. from SELVAGE *noun* + -EE².]
Chiefly NAUTICAL. An untwisted skein of rope yarn marled together to form a strop.

†**selvatic** *adjective* var. of SYLVATIC.

selve /sɛlv/ *verb trans. & (rare) intrans. literary*. L19.
[from SELF *pronoun* etc.]
(Cause to) become and act as a unique self.

selvedge *noun & verb* var. of SELVAGE.

selves *noun* pl. see SELF *noun*.

SEM *abbreviation*.
1 Scanning electron microscope, microscopy.
2 STATISTICS. Standard error of the mean.

sem /sɛm/ *noun*. L19.
[Egyptian.]
More fully ***sem priest***. In ancient Egypt, an officiating priest who wore a distinctive robe made from a leopard's skin. Cf. SETEM.

sema /ˈsiːmə/ *noun*. Pl. **-mas**, **-mata** /-mətə/. *rare*. M20.
[Greek: see SEME.]
LINGUISTICS. = SEME.

Semainean /səˈmʌɪnɪən/ *adjective*. E20.
[from *Semaine(h* a village in Egypt + -AN.]
ARCHAEOLOGY. Designating or pertaining to the last period of the ancient predynastic culture in Egypt.

Semana Santa /seˌmana ˈsanta/ *noun phr.* E20.
[Spanish.]
In Spain and Spanish-speaking countries, = ***Holy Week*** s.v. HOLY *adjective & noun*.

Semang /səˈmaŋ/ *noun & adjective*. E19.
[Malay.]
▶ **A** *noun*. Pl. **-s**, same. A member of a Negrito people inhabiting the interior of the Malay peninsula. E19.
▶ **B** *adjective*. Of or pertaining to this people. M19.

semanteme /sɪˈmantiːm/ *noun*. E20.
[French *sémantème*, formed as SEMANTIC after *morphème* MORPHEME, *phonème* PHONEME: see -EME.]
LINGUISTICS. A fundamental element expressing an image or idea.

■ **seman'temic** *adjective* M20.

semantic /sɪˈmantɪk/ *adjective*. M17.
[French *sémantique* from Greek *sēmantikos* significant, from *sēmainein* show, signify, from *sēma* sign, mark: see -IC.]
†**1** Relating to signs of the weather. *rare*. Only in M17.
2 Relating to meaning in language; relating to connotations of words. L19.
Special collocations: **semantic aphasia** MEDICINE disturbance in understanding the significance of any but the simplest forms of words or speech caused by certain kinds of lesion in the cerebral cortex. **semantic field** a lexical set of semantically related items. **semantic paradox** LOGIC a paradox arising from ambiguity of meaning in the language of a statement, rather than from its logical reasoning.
■ **semantically** *adverb* in a semantic manner L19. **semantician** /-ˈtɪʃ(ə)n/ *noun* an expert in or student of semantics E20. **semanticism** /-sɪz(ə)m/ *noun* M20. **semanticist** /-sɪst/ *noun* a semantician E20. **semanticity** /-ˈtɪsɪti/ *noun* the quality of being semantic or possessing meaning derived from signs M20. **semanticize** /-sʌɪz/ *verb trans.* make semantic, give meaning to; analyse semantically: M20.

semantico- /sɪˈmantɪkəʊ/ *combining form*. M20.
[from Greek *sēmantikos*: see SEMANTIC, -O-. Cf. SEMO-.]
Forming adjectives and adverbs with the sense 'semantic(ally) and—'.

semantics /sɪˈmantɪks/ *noun pl.* Treated as *sing.* or (now *rare*) *pl.* L19.
[from prec.: see -ICS.]
1 The branch of linguistics that deals with meaning; (the study or analysis of) the relationships between linguistic symbols and their meanings. L19.
2 *transf.* The interpretation of signs in general. M20.

semantron /sɪˈmantrɒn/ *noun*. Also **si-** /siː-/. M19.
[medieval Greek from Greek *sēmantron* sign, mark from *sēma* sign.]
In Orthodox churches esp. in Greece, a wooden or metal bar struck by a mallet used to summon worshippers to service.

semaphore /ˈsɛməfɔː/ *noun & verb*. E19.
[French *sémaphore*, irreg. from Greek *sēma* sign, signal + *-phoros* -PHORE.]
▶ **A** *noun*. **1** A signalling apparatus, consisting of an upright post with a movable arm or arms, lanterns, etc., for use (esp. on railways) by day or night. E19.
2 The method of signalling employed for this apparatus; *spec.* a system for sending messages by holding the arms or two flags in certain positions according to an alphabetic code. Also, a signal sent by means of this system. E20.

📖 **2** *transf.*: R. ANGELL A common semaphore . . is a quick grimace flashed by one man . . to his partner behind his raised glove.

▶ **B** *verb intrans. & trans.* Signal or send (a message etc.) (as) by semaphore. L19.
■ **semaphoric** /-ˈfɒrɪk/ *adjective* E19. **semaphorically** /-ˈfɒrɪk(ə)li/ *adverb* M19. **semaphorist** *noun* (*rare*) L19.

semasiology /sɪˌmeɪzɪˈɒlədʒi/ *noun*. M19.
[German *Semasiologie* from Greek *sēmasia* meaning, from *sēmainein* signify: see SEMANTIC, -OLOGY.]
Semantics.
■ **semasio'logical** *adjective* L19. **semasiologist** *noun* L19.

semata *noun pl.* see SEMA.

sematic /sɪˈmatɪk/ *adjective*. M19.
[from Greek *sēmat-*, *sēma* sign + -IC.]
†**1** Semantic. *rare*. Only in M19.
2 BIOLOGY. Of markings, coloration, etc.: serving as a signal or warning. L19.

sematology /siːməˈtɒlədʒi/ *noun*. M19.
[formed as prec. + -OLOGY.]
1 The theory of the use of signs (esp. words) in relation to thought and knowledge. M19.
2 Semantics. *rare*. L19.
■ **semato'logical** *adjective* (*rare*) L19.

semblable /ˈsɛmbləb(ə)l/ *adjective & noun*. ME.
[Old French, formed as SEMBLE *verb*²: see -ABLE. In mod. use as noun directly from French.]
▶ **A** *adjective*. †**1 a** Like, similar (*to*). ME–M19. ▸**b** Resembling something already mentioned or implied; of such a kind. LME–M17.
†**2** Corresponding, proportional, suitable. E16–E19.
3 Apparent, seeming, not real. *arch.* E17.
▶ **B** *noun*. †**1** Something that is like or similar. LME–E17.
2 With possess.: one's equal, one's counterpart. LME.
¶ As noun not recorded between E17 and E20.
■ **semblably** *adverb* (*rare*) †(*a*) in like manner, similarly; (*b*) *arch.* apparently, seemingly, not genuinely: LME.

semblance /ˈsɛmbləns/ *noun*. ME.
[Old & mod. French, formed as SEMBLE *verb*²: see -ANCE. Superseded SEMBLANT *noun*.]
†**1** The fact of appearing to view; ***in semblance***, visible, to be seen. *rare*. Only in ME.
2 An apparent outward view or impression *of* something not actually there or differing in reality from its perceptible aspect. ME. ▸**b** An apparition or vision *of* a

person etc. **L15.** ▸**c** The bare appearance, the slightest indication, (*of*). Usu. in neg. contexts. **E19.**

3 The appearance or outward aspect of a person or thing; the form or likeness *of* a person or thing, esp. as considered with regard to another similar person or thing. **LME.**

4 A person's bearing or manner. *arch.* **LME.**

5 A person or thing resembling another, a representation or copy *of*. **LME.**

6 The fact or quality of being like something; similarity, resemblance. Also foll. by *to*. **L15.**

†**7** Likelihood, probability. **M16–M17.**

2 M. GORDON I kept up the semblance of a perfectly false cheer. M. LANE The children were united only in preserving before Charles a semblance of harmony. **b** E. FENTON I last the visionary Semblance view'd Of Hercules, a shadowy Form. **c** J. R. GREEN The fall of Strafford had put an end to all semblance of rule. **3** M. ARNOLD The vulgar part of human nature which busies itself with the semblance and doings of . . sovereigns. F. PARKMAN The lake narrowed to the semblance of a tranquil river. **4** POPE Him . . the haughty Suitors greet With semblance fair, but inward deep deceit. **5** J. RUSKIN Constant pleasure from whatever is a type or semblance of divine attributes. **6** J. G. CAMPBELL Recognize in them a semblance to the Fairy tales of the North of Ireland. **7** N. BACON Yet some semblance there is, that it was yet more ancient.

Phrases: **in semblance** now *arch. rare* †(*a*) see sense 1 above; (*b*) in appearance only. **make semblance** (*a*) *arch.* make an appearance or pretence (*of doing, that* etc., *to do*); †(*b*) have or assume a (specified) look or manner. †**show semblance** = ***make semblance*** (b) above.

†**semblant** *noun.* **ME.**

[Old & mod. French, use as noun of pres. pple of *sembler*: see next, -ANT¹. Superseded by SEMBLANCE.]

1 = SEMBLANCE 4. **ME–M17.** ▸**b** The face, the countenance. **ME–L15.**

2 = SEMBLANCE 2, 3. **ME–E17.**

3 = SEMBLANCE 5. **LME–E17.**

Phrases: **make semblant** (*a*) = *make* SEMBLANCE; (*b*) show the least sign of, seem likely *to do* or *to be*, (usu. in neg. contexts).

semblant /ˈsɛmblənt/ *adjective.* Long *rare* or *obsolete.* **LME.**

[Old & mod. French, pres. pple of *sembler*: see SEMBLE *verb*², -ANT¹.]

†**1** Like, similar (foll. by *to*), resembling. **LME–E18.**

2 Seeming, apparent, counterfeit. **M19.**

semblative /ˈsɛmblətɪv/ *adjective. rare.* **E17.**

[from SEMBLE *verb*² + -ATIVE.]

Orig., like, resembling. Later, seeming; simulating the appearance (*of*).

¶ Not recorded between **E17** and **E19.**

semble /ˈsɛmb(ə)l/ *adjective.* Now *poet. rare.* **LME.**

[Old French, from Latin *similis*: see SIMILAR.]

Like, similar.

¶ Revived in **M20.**

semble /ˈsɛmb(ə)l/ *verb*¹. **ME.**

[Aphet. from ASSEMBLE *verb*.]

1 *verb trans.* †**a** = ASSEMBLE *verb* 1. **ME–E17.** ▸**b** *spec.* in ENTOMOLOGY. Of a female moth: cause (male moths) to assemble. *rare.* **L19.**

†**2** *verb intrans.* = ASSEMBLE *verb* 4. **ME–M16.**

†**3** *verb intrans. & trans.* Meet in battle; attack. **ME–E16.**

†**semble** *verb*². **ME.**

[Old & mod. French *sembler* seem from Latin *similare*, *simulare*: see SIMULATE *verb*. Cf. later SEMBLING *verbal noun*².]

1 *verb trans.* Be like, resemble. **ME–E18.**

2 *verb intrans.* Seem, appear. **ME–E16.**

3 *verb trans.* Liken, compare. **LME–M16.**

4 *verb trans.* Simulate, feign; = DISSEMBLE *verb*¹ 1. **M16–M17.**

5 *verb trans.* Represent, picture. **E17–M18.**

semble /ˈsɛmb(ə)l/ *verb*³ *intrans. impers.* **E19.**

[French, 3rd person sing. pres. indic. of *sembler*: see prec.]

LAW. It seems, it appears: introducing in a judgement the incidental statement of an opinion on a point which need not be, or has not been, decided authoritatively.

sembling /ˈsɛmblɪŋ/ *verbal noun*¹. Now *rare.* **ME.**

[from SEMBLE *verb*¹ + -ING¹.]

†**1** *gen.* The action of SEMBLE *verb*¹. *rare.* Only in **ME.**

2 ENTOMOLOGY. The gathering of male and female moths; *spec.* = ASSEMBLING *noun* (b). **M18.**

sembling /ˈsɛmblɪŋ/ *verbal noun*². Long *rare* or *obsolete.* **LME.**

[from SEMBLE *verb*² + -ING¹.]

The action of SEMBLE *verb*²; simulation.

†**sembly** *noun.* **ME.**

[Aphet. from ASSEMBLY.]

1 = ASSEMBLY 2, 2b. **ME–E18.**

2 A hostile encounter, an attack. **LME–M16.**

seme /siːm/ *noun.* Now *rare.* **M19.**

[Greek *sēma* sign, mark. Cf. SEMA.]

LINGUISTICS. A sign. Also, a unit of meaning; *spec.* a sememe.

semé /ˈsɛmi, *foreign* səme/ *adjective.* Also **-ée.** **LME.**

[French, pa. ppl adjective of *semer* to sow. Cf. SEMIS *noun*².]

HERALDRY. Of a field: sprinkled or strewn with numerous representations of a particular charge, powdered. Freq. *postpositive.*

seméed /ˈsɛmiːd/ *adjective.* Now *rare.* **L16.**

[from (the same root as) prec.: see -ED¹.]

HERALDRY. = SEMÉ.

semeiologist, **semeiology** *nouns* vars. of SEMIOLOGIST etc.

semeiosis *noun*, **semeiotic** *adjective & noun* vars. of SEMIOSIS etc.

semelfactive /siːmɛlˈfaktɪv/ *adjective.* **E19.**

[from Latin *semel* once + FACTIVE.]

GRAMMAR. Designating or pertaining to a verbal aspect (in Russian and other Slavonic languages) expressing sudden, completed, and unrepeated action.

semelparous /ˈsɛm(ə)lparəs/ *adjective.* **M20.**

[from Latin *semel* once + -PAROUS.]

BIOLOGY. Of or designating a species or organism which reproduces only once during its lifetime. Cf. ITEROPAROUS.

■ **semelparity** /sɛm(ə)lˈparɪti/ *noun* the state or condition of being semelparous **M20.**

sememe /ˈsiːmiːm, ˈsiːm-/ *noun.* **E20.**

[formed as SEME + -EME.]

LINGUISTICS. A unit of meaning; the unit of meaning carried by a morpheme.

■ **seˈmemic** *adjective* of or pertaining to a sememe **M20.** **seˈmemically** *adverb* **M20.**

semen /ˈsiːmən/ *noun.* **LME.**

[Latin, from base of *serere* SOW *verb*¹.]

The reproductive fluid of male animals, containing spermatozoa in suspension.

Comb.: **semen bank** = ***SPERM bank.***

semence /ˈsiːməns/ *noun. rare.* **L15.**

[French (= Provençal *semensa*, Italian *semenza*) from Latin *sementis* a sowing, from *semen*: see prec., -ENCE.]

†**1** Seed; semen. **L15–L17.**

2 An act of sowing seed etc. **M19.**

semester /sɪˈmɛstə/ *noun.* **E19.**

[German, from Latin *semestris* of six months, from *se-* sex SIX + *mensis* month.]

A period or term of six months; *spec.*, a half-year course or term, esp. in German and US universities and colleges.

■ **semestral**, **semestrial** *adjectives* half-yearly; taking place every six months; lasting for six months: **E18.**

semi /ˈsɛmi/ *noun. colloq.* **E20.**

[Abbreviation: cf. SEMI-.]

1 A semi-detached house. **E20.**

2 A semi-evening dress. Now *rare.* **E20.**

3 A semifinished material, esp. steel. Usu. in *pl.* **M20.**

4 A semi-final. **M20.**

5 A semi-trailer. *N. Amer. & Austral.* **M20.**

6 A semi-submersible offshore drilling platform or barge. **L20.**

7 An official body which is partially but not wholly governmental. Usu. in *pl. Austral.* **L20.**

semi- /ˈsɛmi/ *prefix.*

[Latin (partly through French, Italian, etc.) corresp. to Greek *hēmi-* HEMI-, Sanskrit *sāmi*, from Indo-European base also of SAM-, Old Saxon *sām*, Old High German *sāmi*.]

Used in words adopted (ult.) from Latin and in English words modelled on these, and (almost completely displacing DEMI-) as a freely productive prefix, forming nouns from nouns and adjectives from adjectives and, less commonly, verbs from verbs, with the senses 'half, half-sized', as ***semicircle***, ***semicircular***; 'partly, partially, to some extent', as ***semi-official***, ***semi-detached***; 'imperfectly, incompletely', as ***semi-liquid***; 'occurring or appearing twice in a specified period', as ***semi-annual***.

■ **semi-aˈcoustic** *adjective & noun* (*a*) *adjective* (of a guitar) having a hollow body, typically with f-holes, and one or more electrical pick-ups; (*b*) *noun* a semi-acoustic guitar: **L20.** **semi-ˈanimate** *adjective* half-alive **E19.** **semi-ˈannual** *adjective & noun* (*a*) *adjective* occurring, published, etc., twice a year, half-yearly; (of a plant) living for half a year only; (*b*) *noun* a semi-annual plant: **L18.** **semi-ˈannually** *adverb* every half-year, once in every six months **E19.** **semi-ˈannular** *adjective* of the form of a half-ring **L17.** **semi-anˈtique** *adjective & noun* (*a*) *adjective* (of an oriental rug or carpet) between fifty and one hundred years old (*b*) *noun* a semi-antique oriental rug or carpet: **M20.** **semi-aˈquatic** *adjective* partly aquatic and partly terrestrial; amphibious: **M19.** **semi-ˈarid** *adjective* having slightly more precipitation than an arid climate, coarse grasses and scrub being the characteristic vegetation **L19.** **semi-aˈttached** *adjective* (*rare*) partially or loosely attached; semi-detached: **M19.** **semi-ˈaxis** *noun* half of a diameter of an ellipse etc. **M18.** **semi-Banˈtu** *adjective & noun* (of, designating or pertaining to) a group of languages closely related to Bantu **E20.** **semi-barˈbarian** *noun* a person who is partly a barbarian **L17.** **semi-ˈbarbarism** *noun* the state or condition of being semi-barbarous **L18.** **semi-ˈbarbarous** *adjective* that is partly barbarous **L18.** **semi-ˈbasement** *noun* (ARCHITECTURE) a basement room or rooms sunk only partially below ground level **E20.** **semi-ˈbeam** *noun* (ARCHITECTURE) = CANTILEVER 2 **M19.** **semi-ˈbold** *adjective & noun* (printed in) a weight of typeface between normal and bold **L20.** **semi-ˈbroch** *noun* (ARCHAEOLOGY) a prehistoric hollow-walled fort of the Hebrides and W. Scotland representing a stage of development between the galleried dun and the broch **E20.** **semi-ˈcell** *noun* (BOTANY) either of the two parts of a cell which is constricted in the middle, as in a desmid **L19.** **semi-ˈchemical** *adjective* designating (wood pulp made by) a pulping process in which wood chips are subjected to mild chemical delignification followed by mechanical processing **E20.** **semi-ˈchorus** *noun* (*a*) either of two parts into which the main body of a chorus is divided; a part of a chorus or choir; (*b*) a piece of music etc. to be performed by a semi-chorus: **L18.** **semi-ˈcivilized** *adjective* partially civilized **M19.** **semi-ˈclassical** *adjective* (*a*) *gen.* (esp. in MUSIC) partly classical; (*b*) PHYSICS designating a theory that is intermediate in its assumptions and methods between the classical, or Newtonian, description and that of modern physics, esp. in quantum mechanics and relativity: **M20.** **semi-ˈclosed** *adjective* (MEDICINE) designating a method of administering anaesthetics using a gas supply that is closed from the atmosphere but with gas in excess of the patient's needs being vented off **E20.** **semi-ˈcoke** *noun* a smokeless fuel leaving little ash, made from coal by carbonization at a low temperature (usu. 500–600°C) **E20.** **semi-ˈcoking** *adjective* (of coal) intermediate between coking coal and coal not suitable for making coke **E20.** **semi-ˈcolumn** *noun* (chiefly ARCHITECTURE) half of a column cut longitudinally **E18.** †**semi-commoner** *noun* = DEMY *noun* 2 **L17–E18.** **semi-ˈconscious** *adjective* partially conscious **M19.** **semi-conˈservative** *adjective* (BIOCHEMISTRY) designating or pertaining to (the accepted model of) replication of a nucleic acid in which one complete strand of each double helix is directly derived from the parent molecule **M20.** **semiconˈservatively** *adverb* (BIOCHEMISTRY) by semi-conservative replication **M20.** **semi-conˈvergent** *adjective* (MATH.) designating a series the sum of whose terms converges while the sum of the moduli of its terms diverges **L19.** **semi-ˈcrystalline** *adjective* having a structure consisting of crystals embedded in an amorphous groundmass, or (now usu.) possessing crystalline character in some degree **E19.** **semi-ˈcursive** *adjective & noun* (PALAEOGRAPHY) (of or pertaining to) any of various scripts combining cursive features with elements of a more formal style **E20.** **semiˈcylinder** *noun* half of a cylinder cut longitudinally **M17.** **semicyˈlindric**, **semicyˈlindrical** *adjectives* of the form of a semi-cylinder **M18.** **semi-ˈdeity** *noun* = SEMIGOD **E17.** **semi-deˈponent** *noun & adjective* (GRAMMAR) (of) a Latin verb having active forms in present tenses and passive forms with active sense in perfect tenses **L19.** **semi-ˈdesert** *adjective & noun* (designating) a semi-arid area intermediate between grassland and desert **M19.** **semi-diˈaphanous** *adjective* (now *rare*) partially or not completely transparent **M17.** **semi-diˈrect** *adjective* not completely direct; *spec.* (of lighting) so arranged that most but not all of the light reaches the illuminated area without first being reflected (cf. SEMI-INDIRECT): **E20.** **semi-diˈsplay** *noun* (TYPOGRAPHY) a layout (for an advertisement etc.) intermediate between the run-on and displayed styles **L20.** **semi-diˈsplayed** *adjective* (TYPOGRAPHY) (of an advertisement etc.) set out in semi-display **L20.** **semi-diˈurnal** *adjective* (*a*) ASTRONOMY of, pertaining to, or performed in half the time between the rising and setting of a celestial object; (*b*) (esp. of tides) occurring (roughly) every twelve hours: **L16.** **semi-diˈvine** *adjective* half divine; that is a demigod: **E17.** **semi-docuˈmentary** *adjective & noun* (a film) having a factual basis presented in fictional form **M20.** **semi-dome** *noun* a half-dome, *esp.* one formed by vertical section; a part of a structure more or less resembling a dome: **L18.** **semi-domed** *adjective* having the form of a semi-dome **M19.** **semi-ˈdouble** *adjective* (*a*) (ROMAN CATHOLIC CHURCH, now *Hist.*) (of a feast) ranking in importance between a double and a simple feast; (*b*) (of a flower) intermediate between double and single in having only the outer stamens converted to petals: **L15.** **semi-ˈdouble** *noun* (*a*) (ROMAN CATHOLIC CHURCH, now *Hist.*) a semi-double feast; (*b*) a semi-double flower: **M19.** **semi-eˈllipse** *noun* half of an ellipse bisected by one of its diameters, esp. the transverse **M18.** **semi-eˈlliptical** *adjective* of or pertaining to a semi-ellipse **M18.** **semi-emˈpirical** *adjective* deriving in part from theoretical considerations and in part from the results of experiment **M20.** **semi-emˈpirically** *adverb* in a semi-empirical manner **L20.** **semi-ˈevening** *adjective* (of clothes, esp. a woman's dress) fashionable but not fully formal, suitable for both afternoon and evening wear (chiefly in ***semi-evening dress***) **E20.** **semi-ˈevergreen** *adjective* normally evergreen but shedding some leaves in severe conditions **M20.** **semi-ˈfabricated** *adjective* (of a material) formed into some standard shape for use in the making of finished articles **M20.** **semiˈfabricator** *noun* a manufacturer of semifabricated goods **L20.** **semi-feral** *adjective* half-wild; *esp.* (of an animal) partly feral: **L19.** **semiferine** *adjective* (*rare*) half-wild, semi-feral **M19.** **semi-field** *noun* (MATH.) a set, together with operations answering to addition and multiplication, that has certain specified properties of a field but not all of them **E20.** **semiˈfinal** *noun* a match or round immediately preceding the final **L19.** **semiˈfinalist** *noun* a competitor in a semi-final **L19.** **semi-ˈfinished** *adjective* prepared for the final stage of manufacture **M20.** **semi-ˈfitted** *adjective* (of a garment) shaped to the body but not closely fitted **M20.** **semiflex** *verb trans.* bend (esp. a joint or muscle) into a position halfway between extension and flexure **M19.** **semiˈformal** *adjective & noun* (*a*) *adjective* combining formal and informal elements; (of clothing) neither particularly formal nor casual; (*b*) *noun* (chiefly *US*) an event at which semiformal attire is expected: **L19.** **semi-ˈformed** *adjective* half-formed **E19.** **semi-globe** *noun* half of a globe; a hemisphere or hemispherical form, structure, etc.: **M18.** **semi-ˈglobular** *adjective* of the form of a semi-globe **E18.** **semi-grand** *adjective & noun* (of) a modified form of the grand piano **M20.** **semi-group** *noun* (MATH.) a set together with an associative binary operation under which it is closed **E20.** **semi-hoop** *noun* (*rare*) a semicircular arc or arch **L17.** **semi-indiˈrect** *adjective* (of lighting) so arranged that most but not all of the light reaches the illuminated area indirectly, after reflection or scattering by a surface (cf. SEMI-DIRECT) **E20.** **semi-ˈinfinite** *adjective* (MATH. & PHYSICS) infinite with respect to a particular dimension etc. **E20.** **semi-inˈtensive** *adjective* (AGRICULTURE) of or pertaining to a method of rearing livestock including features of intensive farming **M20.** **semi-ˈinvalid** *noun* a partially disabled or somewhat infirm person M20. **semi-in'variant** *noun* (*a*) MATH. a function of the coefficients of a binary quantic which satisfies only one of two equations satisfied by an invariant function of the coefficients; (*b*) STATISTICS any of a set of functions of a statistical distribution, each expressible as a polynomial in the moments: M19. **semi-'lethal** *adjective & noun* (GENETICS) (of or designating) an allele or chromosomal abnormality which impairs the viability of most of the individuals homozygous for it E20. **semi-'liquid** *adjective & noun* (a substance that is) partly liquid and partly solid; semifluid: L17. **semi-log** *adjective* = SEMI-LOGARITHMIC E20. **semi-loga'rithmic** *adjective* having or designating a scale that is linear in one direction and logarithmic in the other E20. **semi-main** *noun* (*US*) = REPÊCHAGE M20. **semi-'major** *adjective* designating the axis of an ellipse which is half the longest diameter L19. **semi-manufacture** *noun* a product made from raw materials and used in the manufacture of finished goods M20. **semi-ma'ture** *adjective* †(*a*) *rare* half-ripe; (*b*) partially mature: LME. **semi-'minor** *adjective* designating the axis of an ellipse which is half the shortest diameter E20. **semi-'monthly** *adjective & adverb* (*a*) *adjective* occurring, published, etc., twice a month; (*b*) *adverb* twice a month: M19. **semi-'monocoque** *adjective & noun* (designating or based on) an aircraft fuselage etc. having a rigid load-bearing shell together with a framework of longerons or stringers, or a motor vehicle underframe or body combining features of the monocoque and space-frame types E20. **semi-'mute** *adjective & noun* (of) a person who is deaf but has some faculty of speech M19. **semi-noc'turnal** *adjective* (*a*) ASTRONOMY pertaining to, or accomplished in, exactly half a night, semi-diurnal; (*b*) ZOOLOGY partly nocturnal in habits: L16. **semi-'nomad** *adjective & noun* (*a*) *adjective* semi-nomadic; (*b*) *noun* a semi-nomadic person: M20. **semi-no'madic** *adjective* partially nomadic and partially settled; *esp.* designating a social group depending largely on seasonal pasturing: M19. **semi-'nude** *adjective* half-naked M19. **semi-'nudity** *noun* the condition of being semi-nude M19. **semi-o'ccasional** *adjective* (*US*, *rare*) occurring once in a while M19. **semi-o'ccasionally** *adverb* (*US*, *rare*) once in a while M19. **semi-o'fficial** *adjective* partly official; *esp.* (of a communication to a newspaper etc.) made by an official with the stipulation that the source is not revealed: E19. **semi-o'fficially** *adverb* in a semi-official manner M19. **semi-o'pacity** *noun* the condition or quality of being semi-opaque L17. **semi-opal** *noun* [translating German *Halbopal*] an inferior variety of opal with a greater degree of hardness and opacity L18. **semi-o'paque** *adjective* partly opaque; not fully transparent: L17. **semi-'open** *adjective* partially open; *spec.* (MEDICINE) designating a method of administering anaesthetics in which the inspired gas is atmospheric air partially restricted or controlled by some device: E20. **semi-'opera** *noun* (chiefly *Hist.*) a masque or similar entertainment with a substantial proportion of vocal music E18. **semi-'oval** *adjective & noun* (of the form of) half an oval cut longitudinally E18. **semipa'rabola** *noun* (MATH.) (*a*) half of a parabola; (*b*) a curve resembling a parabola, described by an equation of the form $ax^{n-1} = y^n$: M17. **semi-'permanent** *adjective* less than completely permanent L19. **semi-'permanently** *adverb* in a semi-permanent manner M20. **semi-plume** *noun* a feather with a long firm shaft but a downy web L19. **semi-'porcelain** *noun* ware resembling porcelain but having an inferior glaze, finish, etc. L19. **semi-portal** *adjective* of a crane mounted on a frame consisting of a horizontal member supported at one end by an upright E20. **semi'precious** *adjective* (of a mineral stone) able to be cut and polished for use in ornamentation and jewellery but not of sufficient value to rank as a gemstone E20. **semi-'pro** *noun & adjective* (*colloq.*, orig. & chiefly *US*) (pl. of noun **-os**) = SEMI-PROFESSIONAL E20. **semi-pro'fessional** *noun & adjective* (*a*) *noun* a musician, sportsman or -woman, etc., receiving payment for an occupation or activity but not relying on it for a living; (*b*) *adjective* of, pertaining to or designating a semi-professional or semi-professionals; involving or employing semi-professionals: L19. **semi-prole'tariat** *noun* in Marxist theory, the class intermediate between the proletariat and the petty bourgeoisie M20. **semi-'prone** *adjective* lying face downwards with one or both knees flexed to the side; designating this position: L19. **semi-re'tired** *adjective* having partially retired, esp. from occupation or employment L20. **semi-re'tirement** *noun* the state or condition of being semi-retired M20. **semi-'rigid** *adjective & noun* (*a*) *adjective* (of an airship) having a flexible gas container attached to a stiffened keel or framework; *gen.* somewhat rigid; having a certain amount of rigidity; (*b*) *noun* a semi-rigid airship: E20. **semi-ring** *noun* half of a ring; a semi-annular form, object, etc.: M19. **semi-'rotary** *adjective* partly rotary M19. **semi-ro'tatory** *adjective* partly rotatory E19. **semi-'savage** *adjective & noun* (of) a semi-barbarian E19. **Semi-'Saxon** *adjective & noun* (*arch.*) (of, pertaining to or designating) Middle English of the early period, between about 1150 and 1250: M18. **semi-sentence** *noun* (GRAMMAR) a form possessing some but not all of the features of a sentence M20. **semi-'skilled** *adjective* (of work or a worker) having or requiring some skill or special training, but less than that necessary for a skilled task or worker E20. **semi-'skimmed** *adjective* (of milk) from which some cream has been skimmed L20. **semi-smile** *noun* an expression that is not quite a smile M19. **semi-'solid** *adjective* of the consistency of a very thick, stiff fluid or suspension, or a very soft solid; semifluid: M19. **semi'spheroid** *noun* (long *rare* or *obsolete*) a hemispheroid L18. **semisphe'roidal** *adjective* (*rare*) hemispheroidal M17. **semi-'sports** *adjective* (*colloq.*) (*a*) (of clothes) somewhat informal or casual; (*b*) (of a motor car) possessing some of the characteristics of a sports car: E20. **semi-steel** *noun* (now *rare*) a low-carbon cast iron produced by melting mild steel with pig iron M19. **semi-'sterile** *adjective* (BIOLOGY) reduced in fertility by approximately 50 per cent E20. **semi-ste'rility** *noun* the state or condition of being semi-sterile E20. **semi-sub** *noun* = SEMI-SUBMERSIBLE *noun* L20. **semi-sub'mersible** *adjective & noun* (of) an offshore drilling platform or barge with submerged hollow pontoons able to be flooded with water when the vessel is anchored on site in order to provide stability M20. **semi-sweet** *adjective* (of a biscuit etc.) slightly sweetened M20. **semisyn'thetic** *adjective* that is a mixture of synthetic and natural materials, or has been prepared by artificial modification of a natural material; that is a combination of synthetic and natural processes: M20. **semi-'trailer** *noun* a road trailer having wheels at the back but supported at the front by a towing vehicle E20. **semi-trans'parency** *noun* the quality or condition of being semi-transparent; partial transparency: L18. **semi-trans'parent** *adjective* partially or imperfectly transparent L18. **semi-'tropical** *adjective* subtropical M19. **semi-'tropics** *noun pl.* the subtropics E20. **semi-'uncial** *adjective & noun* = *half-uncial* s.v. HALF- M18. **semi-'vitreous** *adjective* partially vitreous L18. **semi-vitrifi'cation** *noun* partial vitrification L18. **semi-'vitrified** *adjective* partially vitrified M18. **semi-'weekly** *adjective & adverb* (*a*) *adjective* occurring, published, etc., twice a week; (*b*) *adverb* twice a week: L18. **semi-works** *noun* (*US*) a manufacturing plant for developing and perfecting a new product or process after testing in a pilot plant and before full-scale production M20.

Semi-Arian /sɛmɪˈɛːrɪən/ *noun & adjective.* E17.
[ecclesiastical Latin *semiarianus*, formed as SEMI- + ARIAN *adjective*[1] & *noun*[1].]
Chiefly *Hist.* ▶**A** *noun.* A person holding views partially in accordance with the heretical Arian doctrine denying that Christ was consubstantial with God. E17.
▶**B** *adjective.* Of or pertaining to Semi-Arians or Semi-Arianism. L18.
■ **Semi-Arianism** *noun* the principles and practices of Semi-Arians E19.

semi-automatic /ˌsɛmɪɔːtəˈmatɪk/ *adjective & noun.* L19.
[from SEMI- + AUTOMATIC.]
▶**A** *adjective.* Partially self-acting; (of a system, device, or machine) not completely automatic; *spec.* (*a*) (of a type of lathe) capable of performing a number of distinct operations on a given work-piece without operator intervention; (*b*) (of a firearm) having a mechanism for continuous loading but not for continuous firing; (*c*) (of a telephone exchange) operating automatically after the required number has been dialled by an operator. L19.
▶**B** *noun.* **1** A semi-automatic lathe. E20.
2 A semi-automatic firearm. M20.

semibreve /ˈsɛmɪbriːv/ *noun.* L15.
[from SEMI- + BREVE, after French †*semibrève*.]
MUSIC. **1** The longest note now in common use, of the value of two minims or four crotchets, and represented by a ring with no stem. L15.
2 The duration of a semibreve. *rare.* E17.

semic /ˈsiːmɪk/ *adjective.* L20.
[from SEME + -IC, after French *sémique*.]
LINGUISTICS. Of or pertaining to a seme.

semicarbazide /sɛmɪˈkɑːbəzʌɪd/ *noun.* L19.
[from SEMI- + CARB- + AZ(O- + -IDE.]
CHEMISTRY. A colourless crystalline basic solid, $NH_2{\cdot}CO{\cdot}NH{\cdot}NH_2$, derived from urea by substitution of a hydrazino group for an amino group, which reacts with carbonyl compounds to form semicarbazones. Also, a derivative of this.

semicarbazone /sɛmɪˈkɑːbəzəʊn/ *noun.* L19.
[from prec. + -ONE.]
CHEMISTRY. Any of a class of (usu. crystalline) compounds of general formula $RR'C{=}N{\cdot}NH{\cdot}CO{\cdot}NH_2$ (where the Rs are alkyl groups), prepared by the condensation of semicarbazide with carbonyl compounds, esp. in order to characterize the parent carbonyl or to protect the carbonyl group in synthesis.

semicha /sɛˈmiːxə/ *noun.* M19.
[Hebrew *sĕmīkah* leaning.]
JUDAISM. The ceremony (orig. a laying-on of hands) by which a rabbi is ordained; the ordination of a rabbi.

semicircle /ˈsɛmɪsəːk(ə)l/ *noun & verb.* E16.
[Latin *semicirculus*, formed as SEMI- + *circulus* CIRCLE *noun*.]
▶**A** *noun.* **1** Half of a circle or of its circumference. E16.
2 A set of objects arranged in, or a formation, structure, etc., in the form of, a half-circle. L16.
3 An instrument in the shape of or marked with a half-circle; *spec.* = GRAPHOMETER. L16.
▶**B** *verb. rare.*
1 *verb trans.* Surround with a semicircle. E19.
2 *verb intrans.* Form a semicircle. M19.
■ **semicircled** *adjective* (chiefly *poet.*) of the form of a semicircle; arranged (as) in a semicircle: L16.

semicircular /sɛmɪˈsəːkjʊlə/ *adjective.* LME.
[Late Latin *semicircularis*, formed as prec. + *-aris* -AR[1].]
Of the form of a semicircle; arranged (as) in a semicircle.
semicircular canal ANATOMY each of the three fluid-filled canals of the internal ear situated at right angles to each other and providing information about orientation to the brain to help maintain balance (usu. in *pl.*).
■ **semicircu'larity** *noun* (*rare*) M19. **semicircularly** *adverb* in a semicircular form; in a semicircle: E17. **semicircularness** *noun* (*rare*) M18.

semicirque /ˈsɛmɪsəːk/ *noun. poet.* L18.
[from SEMI- + CIRQUE.]
A semicircle.

semicolon /sɛmɪˈkəʊlən, -ˈkəʊlɒn/ *noun.* M17.
[from SEMI- + COLON *noun*[2].]
A punctuation mark consisting of a dot placed above a comma (;), indicating a discontinuity of grammatical construction greater than that indicated by a comma but less than that indicated by a full stop.

semiconducting /ˌsɛmɪkənˈdʌktɪŋ/ *adjective.* L18.
[from SEMI- + CONDUCT *verb* + -ING[2].]
PHYSICS. Having the properties of a semiconductor.
■ **semiconductive** *adjective* = SEMICONDUCTING M20. **semiconduction**, **semiconduc'tivity** *nouns* the phenomenon exhibited by a semiconductor; the property of being a semiconductor: M20.

semiconductor /ˌsɛmɪkənˈdʌktə/ *noun.* M19.
[from SEMI- + CONDUCTOR.]
PHYSICS. Orig., any material whose capacity to conduct electricity was intermediate between that of a good conductor (such as most metals) and an insulator. Now *spec.* a solid which is a very poor conductor when pure or at low temperatures, but which is an effective conductor when impure (***extrinsic semiconductor***) or heated (***intrinsic semiconductor***), owing to the narrow gap between permitted energy bands.
Comb.: **semiconductor diode** a diode whose rectifying action depends on the properties of a junction between a semiconductor and either a metal or another type of semiconductor; **semiconductor junction** = JUNCTION *noun* 3b; **semiconductor rectifier** a semiconductor diode, usu. one intended for large currents; **semiconductor triode** a junction transistor having two junctions.

†semicupium *noun.* L16–M19.
[medieval Latin, formed as SEMI- + *cupa* tun.]
A bath in which only one's legs and hips are covered; a hip-bath.

semi-demi- /ˈsɛmɪdɛmi/ *prefix.* As adjective also **semi-demi**. M17.
[from SEMI- + DEMI-.]
Half-half-, quarter-. Freq. *derog.*, insignificant, inadequate. Cf. DEMI-SEMI-.

semidemisemiquaver /ˌsɛmɪdɛmɪˈsɛmɪkweɪvə/ *noun.* E19.
[from SEMI-DEMI- + SEMI- + QUAVER *noun*.]
MUSIC. = HEMIDEMISEMIQUAVER.

semi-det /sɛmɪˈdɛt/ *noun. colloq.* M20.
[Abbreviation of SEMI-DETACHED.]
A semi-detached house.

semi-detached /ˌsɛmɪdɪˈtatʃt/ *adjective & noun.* M19.
[from SEMI- + DETACHED.]
▶**A** *adjective.* **1** Partially detached. M19.
2 *spec.* (Of a house) joined to another by a party-wall on one side only. M19.
▶**B** *noun.* A semi-detached house. E20.
■ **semi-detachment** *noun* (*rare*) M19.

semidiameter /ˌsɛmɪdʌɪˈamɪtə/ *noun.* LME.
[Late Latin, formed as SEMI- + *diametrus* DIAMETER.]
Half of a diameter; *spec.* a radius.

semidine /ˈsɛmɪdiːn/ *noun.* L19.
[German *Semidin*, from *semi-* SEMI- + *Benz)idin* benzidine: see -INE[5].]
CHEMISTRY. Any compound which is either an *ortho*-anilino-derivative, or an *N*-*para*-aminophenyl derivative, of a *para*-substituted aniline (distinguished as ***ortho-semidine*** and ***para-semidine*** respectively). Also ***semidine base***.
Comb.: **semidine reaction**, **semidine transformation** the rearrangement of *para*-substituted hydrazobenzenes in the presence of acid to yield *ortho-* and *para*-semidines.

semifluid /sɛmɪˈfluːɪd/ *noun & adjective.* M18.
[from SEMI- + FLUID.]
▶**A** *noun.* A substance of a consistency between solid and liquid. M18.
▶**B** *adjective.* Of a consistency between solid and liquid. L18.
■ **semiflu'idity** *noun* E19.

semigod /ˈsɛmɪgɒd/ *noun. arch.* LME.
[from SEMI- + GOD *noun*. Cf. DEMIGOD.]
A demigod.

Sémillon /ˈsɛmɪjɒ̃/ *noun.* Also **Se-**. M19.
[French dial., ult. from Latin *semen* seed.]
A white grape of France and other countries; the white wine made from this.

semilunar /sɛmɪˈluːnə/ *adjective & noun.* LME.
[medieval Latin *semilunaris*: see SEMI-, LUNAR *adjective*.]
▶**A** *adjective.* Chiefly ANATOMY, ZOOLOGY, & BOTANY. Shaped like a half-moon or crescent; having one side convex and the other straight or concave; *spec.* designating a bone in the carpus, a cartilage in the knee, a valve in the opening of the aorta or of the pulmonary artery from the heart. LME.
▶**B** *noun.* A semilunar cartilage, valve, etc. L19.
■ **†semilunary** *adjective* = SEMILUNAR *adjective* M17–M18. **semilunate** *adjective* = LUNATE *adjective* M19. **semi-lu'nated** *adjective* having a crescent-shaped indentation E18.

semilune /ˈsɛmɪluːn/ *noun.* M19.
[from SEMI-, after *demilune*.]
A semilunar or crescent-shaped form, structure, etc.; FORTIFICATION = DEMILUNE 1.

semi-metal /ˈsɛmɪmɛt(ə)l/ *noun.* M17.
[from SEMI- + METAL *noun*.]
A material having a partly metallic character in its physical properties (formerly malleability, now esp. electrical conductivity); *spec.* an element (as arsenic, antimony, bismuth) or other substance having properties intermediate between those of metals and those of semiconductors or non-metals; a metalloid.
■ **semi-meˈtallic** *adjective* partly metallic; *spec.* of the nature of a semi-metal M18.

semimicro- /sɛmɪˈmʌɪkrəʊ/ *prefix.* Also as attrib. adjective **semimicro.** M20.
[from SEMI- + MICRO-.]
CHEMISTRY. Designating or pertaining to a scale of quantitative analysis between micro-scale and macro-scale (commonly 0.01–0.1 g).
semimicroanalysis, semimicromethod, etc.

seminal /ˈsɛmɪn(ə)l/ *adjective & noun.* LME.
[Old & mod. French *séminal* or Latin *seminalis*, from *semin-*, *semen* seed: see SEMEN, -AL[1].]
▶ **A** *adjective.* **1** Of, pertaining to, or connected with semen; of the nature of semen. LME.
2 Of or pertaining to the seed, centres of growth, or reproductive elements of living organisms, or those formerly attributed to inorganic substances. Now *rare.* LME.
3 *spec.* Of, pertaining to, connected with, or of the nature of the seed of plants. LME.
4 *fig.* Having the properties of seed; containing the possibility of future development. Also, (of a person, a book, a person's work, etc.) highly original and influential; important, central to the development or understanding of a subject. M17.

1 seminal vesicle ANATOMY either of a pair of glands which secrete many of the components of semen into the vas deferens. **4** *Newsweek* 'Silent Spring' was the seminal text of the modern enviromental movement.

▶†**B** *noun.* **1** A seminal particle; a seed, a germ. M–L17.
2 ANATOMY. A seminal vessel or duct. Only in M18.
■ **seminally** *adverb* in a seminal state or manner; in the form or state of seed; as regards seed (chiefly *fig.*): M17.

seminar /ˈsɛmɪnɑː/ *noun.* L19.
[German, formed as SEMINARY *noun*[1].]
1 A small class at a university etc. for discussion and research; *gen.* a class meeting for systematic study under the direction of a specified person. L19.
2 A conference of specialists. Also, a short intensive course of study on a specified topic. Orig. *US.* M20.

seminarial /sɛmɪˈnɛːrɪəl/ *adjective. rare.* M18.
[formed as next + -AL[1].]
Of or pertaining to a seminary.

seminarian /sɛmɪˈnɛːrɪən/ *noun.* L16.
[formed as next + -AN.]
Orig., a priest trained at a seminary. Later, a student at a seminary or Jesuit school, a seminarist.

seminarist /ˈsɛmɪn(ə)rɪst/ *noun*[1]. L16.
[from SEMINARY *noun*[1] + -IST.]
1 *Hist.* A Roman Catholic priest educated at any of various Continental seminaries, esp. at Douai, founded orig. for English Roman Catholics in exile under Elizabeth I, and training priests for mission work in England in the 16th and 17th cents. Also called ***seminary priest***. L16.
2 a In *pl.* The teaching staff in a seminary. M17. ▸**b** A student in a seminary, esp. one for the training of Roman Catholic priests. M19.

seminarist /ˈsɛmɪn(ə)rɪst/ *noun*[2]. M19.
[from SEMINAR + -IST.]
A member of or participant in a seminar.

seminary /ˈsɛmɪn(ə)ri/ *noun*[1]. LME.
[Latin *seminarium* seed-plot, use as noun of neut. of *seminarius* adjective, from *semin-*, *semen*: see SEMEN, -ARY[1].]
†**1 a** A piece of ground for the sowing, growing, etc. of plants intended for later transplanting; a seed-plot. LME–E19. ▸**b** A place for the breeding of animals, esp. of a specified kind. Also, a specified stock or breed of animal. E–M17.
2 *fig.* **a** A place of origin and early development; a site of development or cultivation, an abundant source. M16. ▸**b** A country, society, etc., favourable to the nurture of certain qualities or to the training of people for a specified role or function. E17.
3 A place of education, now esp. for those intended for a particular profession. L16.
4 A training-college for priests, rabbis, etc.; *Hist.* a Roman Catholic college training priests for mission work in England in the 16th and 17th cents. L16. ▸**b** *Hist.* In full ***seminary priest***. = SEMINARIST *noun*[1] 1. L16.

2a LD MACAULAY The Council chamber at Edinburgh had been . . a seminary of all public and private vices. **b** T. CARTE The north used to be the seminary of Henry's and Margaret's forces, supplying them . . with fresh recruits. **3** W. S. GILBERT Three little maids who, all unwary, Come from a ladies' seminary.

†**seminary** *adjective & noun*[2]. L16.
[Latin *seminarius* pertaining to seed: see prec., -ARY[1].]
▶ **A** *adjective.* = SEMINAL *adjective.* L16–M18.
▶ **B** *noun.* A germ, an embryo, a seminal particle. *spec.* a germ of disease. Only in 17.

seminate /ˈsɛmɪneɪt/ *verb.* Now *rare* or *obsolete.* M16.
[Latin *seminat-* pa. ppl stem of *seminare* sow, from *semin-*, *semen*: see SEMEN, -ATE[3].]
1 *verb trans.* Sow; *fig.* promulgate, disseminate. M16.
2 *verb intrans.* Produce seed. *rare.* L17.

semination /sɛmɪˈneɪʃ(ə)n/ *noun.* Now *arch. rare.* M16.
[Latin *seminatio(n-)*, formed as prec.: see -ATION.]
1 The action or process of SEMINATE *verb*; an instance of this. M16.
2 The production of seed or semen. M17.

seminative /ˈsɛmɪneɪtɪv/ *adjective. rare.* LME.
[formed as prec. + -ATIVE.]
Having the function of or capable of sowing or (*fig.*) propagating or disseminating something.

seminia *noun* pl. of SEMINIUM.

seminiferous /sɛmɪˈnɪf(ə)rəs/ *adjective.* L17.
[from Latin *semin-*, SEMEN + -I- + -FEROUS.]
1 BOTANY. Bearing or producing seed; reproducing by seed (and not vegetatively). L17.
2 ANATOMY. Containing or conveying seminal fluid; bearing or producing semen. M19.
2 seminiferous tubule any of the long convoluted tubules of which the testis is largely composed.

seminium /sɛˈmɪnɪəm/ *noun.* Now *rare* or *obsolete.* Pl. **-nia** /-nɪə/. L17.
[Latin = procreation, also race, stock, breed: see SEMEN, -IUM.]
MEDICINE & BIOLOGY. An embryo, a germ, etc.; *esp.* a germ of disease.

seminivorous /sɛmɪˈnɪv(ə)rəs/ *adjective. rare.* L17.
[formed as next + -I- + -VOROUS.]
Eating or feeding on seeds.

Seminole /ˈsɛmɪnəʊl/ *noun & adjective.* M18.
[Creek *simanó:li* alt. of dial. *simaló:ni* wild, untamed from Amer. Spanish *cimarrón*: see CIMARRON.]
▶ **A** *noun.* Pl. **-s**, same.
1 A member of any of several groupings of N. American Indians comprising Creek Confederacy emigrants to Florida or their descendants in Florida and Oklahoma, esp. the present-day Florida Indians. M18.
2 The Muskogean language of the Seminoles. M19.
▶ **B** *attrib.* or as *adjective.* Of or pertaining to the Seminoles or their language. L18.
Seminole horse a small horse of a feral stock once found in south-eastern N. America and locally domesticated by Indians and others.

seminology /sɛmɪˈnɒlədʒi/ *noun.* M20.
[from Latin *semin-*, SEMEN + -OLOGY.]
The branch of medicine that deals with seminal fluid, esp. in connection with men's fertility.
■ **seminoˈlogical** *adjective* M20.

seminoma /sɛmɪˈnəʊmə/ *noun.* Pl. **-mas**, **-mata** /-mətə/. M20.
[French *séminome*, from Latin *semin-*, SEMEN + *-ome* -OMA.]
MEDICINE. A malignant tumour of the testis, derived from spermatogenic tissue.

semiochemical /ˌsiːmɪə(ʊ)ˈkɛmɪk(ə)l/ *noun.* L20.
[formed as next + CHEMICAL *noun*.]
A chemical that conveys a signal from one organism to another, esp. in such a way as to modify the behaviour of the recipient organism.

semiologist /siːmɪˈɒlədʒɪst, sɛmɪ-/ *noun.* Also **semei-**. M19.
[formed as next + -OLOGIST.]
†**1** An expert in sign language. *rare.* Only in M19.
2 An expert in or student of semiology. L20.

semiology /siːmɪˈɒlədʒi, sɛmɪ-/ *noun.* Also **semei-**. L17.
[from Greek *sēmeion* sign from *sēma* sign, mark: see -OLOGY.]
†**1** Sign language. Cf. later SEMIOLOGIST 1. Only in L17.
2 MEDICINE. Symptomatology. M19.
3 The branch of knowledge that deals with linguistic signs and symbols; semiotics. E20.
■ **semioˈlogical** *adjective* of or pertaining to semiology M19.

semiosis /siːmɪˈəʊsɪs, sɛmɪ-/ *noun.* Also **semei-**. E20.
[Greek *sēmeiosis* (inference from) a sign, from *sēmeion*: see prec., -OSIS.]
The process of signification, esp. in language or literature.

semiotic /siːmɪˈɒtɪk, sɛmɪ-/ *adjective & noun.* Also **semei-**. E17.
[Greek *sēmeiotikos* significance, from *sēmeioun* interpret as a sign, from *sēmeion* (see SEMIOLOGY): see -OTIC, -IC, -ICS.]
▶ **A** *adjective.* **1** MEDICINE. Of or pertaining to symptomatology. E17.
†**2** Symbolic, serving to convey meaning. *rare.* Only in L18.
3 Of or pertaining to semiotics or the production of meanings by sign-systems. E20.
▶ **B** *noun.* **I** In *pl.* (usu. treated as *sing.*).
1 MEDICINE. Symptomatology. L17.
2 The branch of knowledge that deals with the production of meanings by sign-systems in various fields, esp. in language or literature. L19.
▶ **II** *sing.* **3** = sense B.2 above. L19.
■ **semiotical** *adjective* = SEMIOTIC *adjective* 1, 3 L16. **semiotically** *adverb* E20. **semioˈtician** *noun* a semioticist M20. **semioticist** *noun* an expert in or student of semiotics L20.

semi-palmated /ˌsɛmɪpalˈmeɪtɪd/ *adjective.* L18.
[from SEMI- + PALMATED.]
ZOOLOGY. (Having toes etc.) webbed only along part of the length; half-webbed.
semi-palmated sandpiper an American migratory shorebird, *Calidris pusilla*.
■ **semi-ˈpalmate** *adjective* = SEMI-PALMATED E19. **semi-palmation** *noun* the condition of being semi-palmated L19.

semi-ped /ˈsɛmɪpɛd/ *noun. rare.* Also †**-pede**. M17.
[Latin *semiped-*, formed as SEMI- + *ped-*, *pes* foot.]
PROSODY. A metrical unit equal to half a foot.

semi-Pelagian /ˌsɛmɪpɪˈleɪdʒɪən/ *adjective & noun.* L16.
[ecclesiastical Latin *Semipelagianus*, formed as *Semi-* SEMI- + PELAGIAN *adjective*[1] & *noun*[1].]
CHRISTIAN CHURCH. ▶**A** *noun.* A follower of the doctrine, regarded as heretical and ascribed (with questionable justification) to the teachings of John Cassian of Marseilles in the 5th cent AD, that the first steps towards good can be taken by the human will, with a later supervention of the divine grace necessary for salvation. L16.
▶ **B** *adjective.* Of, pertaining to or designating semi-Pelagians or semi-Pelagianism. E17.
■ **semi-Pelagianism** *noun* E17.

semipermeable /sɛmɪˈpəːmɪəb(ə)l/ *adjective.* L19.
[from SEMI- + PERMEABLE *adjective*.]
Of a membrane or other structure: selectively permeable to certain atoms and molecules; *spec.* permeable to molecules of water but not to those of any dissolved substance.
■ **semipermeaˈbility** *noun* the property or condition of being semipermeable E20.

semiquaver /ˈsɛmɪkweɪvə/ *noun.* L16.
[from SEMI- + QUAVER *noun*.]
MUSIC. A note of the value of half a quaver, the sixteenth part of a semibreve, represented by a large dot with a two-hooked stem. Also called ***sixteenth note***.

semiquinone /sɛmɪˈkwɪnəʊn/ *noun.* M20.
[from SEMI- + QUINONE.]
CHEMISTRY. A molecule or ion derived from a quinone and having one of the two oxygen atoms ionized or bonded to a hydrogen atom.

semis /ˈsɛmɪs/ *noun*[1]. M19.
[Latin, app. from reduced form of *semi-* SEMI- + *as* AS noun. Cf. TREMISSIS.]
ROMAN ANTIQUITIES. A Roman coin, orig. equal to half an as, but later reduced to half a solidus.

semis /səmi, səˈmiː/ *noun*[2]. E20.
[French, lit. 'sowing', from *semer* to sow. Cf. SEMÉ.]
A form of decoration used in bookbinding, in which small ornaments are repeated regularly.

semispecies /ˈsɛmɪspiːʃiːz/ *noun.* Pl. same. M20.
[from SEMI- + SPECIES.]
BIOLOGY. A group of interbreeding populations within a species, partly or weakly isolated from the rest, an incipient species. Also, a component group of a superspecies.

Semite /ˈsiːmʌɪt, ˈsɛm-/ *noun.* M19.
[mod. Latin *Semita*, from late Latin from Greek *Sēm* Shem (see below) + -ITE[1].]
A member of any of the peoples supposedly descended from Shem, son of Noah (*Genesis* 10:21–31) including esp. the Jews, Arabs, Assyrians, Babylonians, and Phoenicians.
■ **Semitist** /ˈsɛmɪtɪst/ *noun* an expert in or student of Semitic languages, literature, etc. L19. **Semitization** /ˌsɛmɪtʌɪˈzeɪʃ(ə)n/ *noun* the action of Semitizing someone or something L19. **Semitize** /ˈsɛmɪtʌɪz/ *verb trans.* make Semitic M19.

Semitic /sɪˈmɪtɪk/ *adjective & noun.* E19.
[mod. Latin *Semiticus*, formed as prec. + -ITIC.]
▶ **A** *adjective.* **1** Of, pertaining to the Semites; *spec.* Jewish. E19.
2 Of, pertaining to or designating the language family including esp. Hebrew and Arabic. E19.
▶ **B** *noun.* **1** The Semitic language family. M19.
2 A Semite. *rare.* L19.
3 In *pl.* The branch of knowledge that deals with Semitic language, literature, etc. *US.* L19.
Comb.: **Semitic-Hamitic** *adjective & noun* = SEMITO-HAMITIC.
■ **Semiticize** /-sʌɪz/ *verb trans.* = SEMITIZE M19.

Semitism /ˈsɛmɪtɪz(ə)m/ *noun.* M19.
[from SEMITE + -ISM.]
1 Characteristics or influence attributed to Semitic peoples, esp. the Jews. Chiefly in ***anti-Semitism***. M19.
2 †**a** = SEMITIC *noun* 1. *rare.* Only in M19. ▸**b** A Semitic word or idiom. M19.

For other words beginning with *semi-* see the entry for **semi-**

Semito-Hamitic /ˌsɛmɪtəʊhəˈmɪtɪk/ *adjective & noun.* L19.
[from SEMIT(IC + -O- + HAMITIC.]
= HAMITO-SEMITIC.

semitone /ˈsɛmɪtəʊn/ *noun.* L15.
[Old French *semiton* or medieval Latin *semitonus*, formed as SEMI- + TONE *noun*. Cf. late Latin *semitonium*, Greek *hēmitonion* HEMITONE.]
1 *MUSIC.* An interval approximately equal to half a tone, the smallest interval used in classical European music; a minor second. L15.
2 *ART.* An intermediate tone or tint in a picture; = ***halftone*** (c) s.v. HALF-. L18.
3 A soft or gentle tone of voice; an undertone. E19.
1 ***chromatic semitone***: see CHROMATIC *adjective* 1.
■ **semitonal** *adjective* = SEMITONIC M19. **semitonally** *adverb* L19.

semitonic /sɛmɪˈtɒnɪk/ *adjective.* E18.
[from prec. + -IC.]
MUSIC. Of, pertaining to or consisting of a semitone or semitones; (of a scale) chromatic.
■ **semitonically** *adverb* M19.

†semivocal *noun & adjective. rare.* M16.
[Latin *semivocalis*, formed as SEMI- + VOCAL *adjective*.]
▶ **A** *noun.* A semivowel. Only in M16.
▶ **B** *adjective.* **1** Partially vocal. Only in 17.
2 That is a semivowel. Only in E19.

semivowel /ˈsɛmɪvaʊ(ə)l/ *noun.* M16.
[from SEMI- + VOWEL, after Latin *semivocalis* (see prec.).]
PHONETICS. A speech sound partaking in various ways of the nature of both a vowel and a consonant; now *esp.* a sound which functions as a consonant in that it occurs at the margins of a syllable but which lacks the phonetic characteristics usu. associated with a consonant such as friction and closure, as English /w/, /j/. Also, a letter of the alphabet representing this sound.

semmit /ˈsɛmɪt/ *noun. Scot.* Also **-et**. LME.
[Origin unkn.]
An undershirt, a vest.

semnopithecine /ˌsɛmnəʊpɪˈθiːsʌɪn, -ˈpɪθɪsʌɪn/ *adjective.* L19.
[from mod. Latin *Semnopithecus* (see below) + -INE[1].]
ZOOLOGY. Of, pertaining to, or belonging to the genus *Semnopithecus* or related genera of long-tailed, long-limbed Asian leaf-monkeys.

semo- /ˈsiːməʊ, ˈsɛməʊ/ *combining form* of Greek *sēma* sign, used in *LINGUISTICS*: see -O-. Cf. SEMANTICO-.
■ **semoleˈxemic** *adjective* (of a linguistic rule) governing the conversion of units of meaning into lexical items M20. **semoˈlogical** *adjective* of or pertaining to semology E20. **semoˈlogically** *adverb* in a semological manner, with reference to semology E20. **seˈmology** *noun* semiology, semiotics E20. **semoˈtactic** *adjective* of or pertaining to the ordering of units of meaning M20. **semoˈtactically** *adverb* in a semotactic manner M20.

semolina /sɛməˈliːnə/ *noun.* L18.
[Alt. of Italian *semolino* dim. of *semola* bran, based on Latin *simila* flour. Cf. SIMNEL.]
The hard grains left after the milling of flour, used in puddings etc. and in pasta; a milk pudding made of this (also ***semolina pudding***).

semon /ˈsiːmɒn/ *noun.* M20.
[Irreg. from Greek *sēma*. Cf. -ON.]
LINGUISTICS. In stratificational grammar: a minimal element of meaning; this combining with others to make up a sememe.

semp /sɛmp/ *noun.* M20.
[Origin unkn.]
In Trinidad, a small brightly coloured tanager, *Euphonia violacea*, sometimes kept as a songbird.

semper fidelis /ˌsɛmpə fɪˈdeɪlɪs/ *adjectival phr.* Also (*colloq.*) ***semper fi*** /ˈfʌɪ/. L19.
[Latin.]
Always faithful (the motto of the US Marine Corps).

sempervirent /sɛmpəˈvʌɪr(ə)nt/ *adjective & noun.* M17.
[from Latin *semper* always + *virent-* pres. ppl stem of *virere* be green.]
▶ **A** *adjective.* Evergreen. M17.
▶ **B** *noun.* An evergreen plant. *rare.* M20.

sempervivum /sɛmpəˈvʌɪvəm/ *noun.* Formerly Anglicized as **†sempervive**. L16.
[Latin, neut. of *sempervivus* ever-living.]
Any of various succulent plants constituting the genus *Sempervivum*, of the stonecrop family; *esp.* houseleek, *S. tectorum*.

sempitern /ˈsɛmpɪtəːn/ *adjective. arch.* LME.
[Old French *sempiterne* from Latin *sempiternus*: see next.]
= next.

sempiternal /sɛmpɪˈtəːn(ə)l/ *adjective. poet. & rhet.* LME.
[Old & mod. French *sempiternel* from late Latin *sempiternalis* from Latin *sempiternus*, from *semper* always + *aeternus* eternal: see -AL[1].]
Enduring constantly and continually; everlasting, eternal.
■ **sempiternally** *adverb* L15.

sempiternity /sɛmpɪˈtəːnɪti/ *noun. poet. & rhet.* L16.
[Late Latin *sempiternitas*, from Latin *sempiternus*: see SEMPITERNAL, -ITY.]
Eternal duration, eternity, perpetuity.

†sempiternous *adjective. rare.* M17–E19.
[Old French *sempiterneux* from Latin *sempiternus*: see SEMPITERNAL, -OUS.]
Sempiternal.

Semple /ˈsɛmp(ə)l/ *noun.* M20.
[Lt.-Col. Sir David *Semple* (1856–1937), English bacteriologist.]
MEDICINE. Used *attrib.* and in *possess.* to designate a vaccine against rabies described by Semple, and its preparation and administration.

semplice /ˈsɛmplɪtʃi/ *adverb & adjective.* M18.
[Italian = simple.]
MUSIC. A direction: simply, simple.

sempre /ˈsɛmpreɪ/ *adverb.* E19.
[Italian.]
MUSIC. A direction: always, still, throughout.

sempster *noun* var. of SEAMSTER.

sempstress *noun* var. of SEAMSTRESS.

sempstry *noun* var. of SEAMSTRY.

semsem /ˈsɛmsɛm/ *noun.* M19.
[Arab. *simsim*. Cf. SESAME, SIM-SIM.]
= SESAME 1.

Semtex /ˈsɛmtɛks/ *noun.* Also **s-**. L20.
[Prob. from *Semtín*, a village in the Czech Republic near the place of production + *ex(plosive*.]
A malleable odourless plastic explosive.

semul *noun* var. of SIMOOL.

semuncia /sɪˈmʌnsɪə/ *adjective.* L19.
[from Latin *semuncia* half-ounce, formed as SEMI- + *uncia* OUNCE *noun*[1].]
ROMAN ANTIQUITIES. Of or pertaining to a half-ounce, the twenty-fourth part of an as.

SEN *abbreviation.*
State Enrolled Nurse.

sen /sɛn/ *noun*[1]. Pl. same, **†-i**. E18.
[Japanese.]
A Japanese monetary unit and former coin equal to a hundredth of a yen.

sen /sɛn/ *noun*[2]. Pl. same. M20.
[Repr. CENT *noun*[1] in Indonesia etc.]
In Indonesia, Malaysia, and other Far Eastern countries, a monetary unit equal to one-hundredth of the basic unit.

sen /sɛn/ *preposition, conjunction, & adverb.* Now *rare.* Chiefly *Scot. & north.* ME.
[Contr. of SITHEN. Cf. SIN *adverb, preposition, & conjunction*, SYNE *adverb*, SINCE.]
▶ **A** *preposition.* From, after; subsequent to. ME.
▶ **B** *conjunction.* **1** From or since the time that. ME.
2 Seeing or considering that. ME.
▶ **C** *adverb.* Then, afterwards. Also, ago. *rare.* LME.

Sen. *abbreviation.*
1 Senate. *US.*
2 Senator. *US.*
3 Senior.

†sena *noun*[1] see SENNA *noun*[1].

sena *noun*[2] *& adjective* var. of SEHNA.

senarian /sɪˈnɛːrɪən/ *noun. rare.* E19.
[formed as next + -IAN.]
PROSODY. = next.

senarius /sɪˈnɛːrɪəs/ *noun.* Pl. **-rii** /-riː, -rɪʌɪ/. M16.
[Latin (sc. *versus* line, verse), use as noun of adjective, from *seni* distrib. of *sex* six.]
PROSODY. A (Greek or Latin) verse consisting of six usu. iambic feet; an iambic trimeter. Also ***iambic senarius***.

senary /ˈsiːnəri, ˈsɛn-/ *noun & adjective.* L16.
[formed as prec.: see -Y[3].]
▶†**A** *noun.* **1** The number six; a set or sequence of six things, *esp.* the six days of the creation of the world (as described in Genesis). L16–L17.
2 *PROSODY.* = prec. *rare.* L16–E19.
▶ **B** *adjective.* Of or pertaining to the number six, sixfold. Also, sextal. M17.

senate /ˈsɛnɪt, -ət/ *noun.* Also **S-**. ME.
[Old & mod. French *sénat* from Latin *senatus*, from *senex* old (man): see -ATE[1].]
1 *Hist.* In ancient Rome, the State council of the republican and imperial periods, composed partly of appointed members and partly of serving and former magistrates, sharing legislative power with the popular assemblies, administration with the magistrates, and judicial power with the knights. ME.
2 The governing body or parliament of a nation or State; a legislative body, *esp.* the smaller upper assembly in the US, France, and other countries, in States of the US, etc. LME.
3 A place where a senate meets, a senate house. E17.
4 The governing or deliberative body of certain British universities or US colleges. M18.
Comb.: **senate house** a house or building in which a senate, esp. that of a university or college, meets.

senator /ˈsɛnətə/ *noun.* ME.
[Old & mod. French *sénateur* from Latin *senator* parallel to *senatus* SENATE: see -OR.]
1 *Hist.* A member of the ancient Roman senate. ME.
2 *gen.* A member of a governing body or parliament, *spec.* of the federal senate in the US. LME. ▸**b** *Hist.* In Rome, the civil head of the city government, appointed by the Pope. M19.
3 In full ***Senator of the College of Justice***. In Scotland, a Lord of Session. M16.
■ **senatorship** *noun* the office or position of a senator E17.

senatorial /sɛnəˈtɔːrɪəl/ *adjective.* M18.
[from Latin *senatorius*, from *senator* SENATOR + -AL[1]. Cf. French *sénatorial*.]
1 Of or pertaining to a senator or senators; characteristic of or befitting a senator; consisting of senators; *transf.* dignified, grave. M18.
2 Of a district: entitled to elect a senator. *US.* L18.
3 *Hist.* Of a province under imperial Rome: administered by the senate rather than the emperor. M19.
1 **senatorial order** *Hist.* the highest of the three ranks of citizens in the later Roman republic.
■ **senatorially** *adverb* M18.

senatorian /sɛnəˈtɔːrɪən/ *adjective & noun.* E17.
[formed as prec. + -AN. Cf. Old & mod. French *sénatorien*.]
▶ **A** *adjective.* **1** = SENATORIAL 1. E17.
2 *Hist.* = SENATORIAL 3. *rare.* M19.
▶ **B** *noun.* A partisan of the ancient Roman senate. *rare.* M19.

senatory /ˈsɛnət(ə)ri/ *noun.* E19.
[from SENATOR + -Y[3], perh. after French *sénatorerie*.]
Hist. In France, a landed estate granted to a senator under the consulate and the first empire.

senatress /ˈsɛnətrɪs/ *noun. rare.* M18.
[formed as prec. + -ESS[1]. Cf. Old French *senatresse* wife of a senator.]
A female senator.

senatus /sɛˈnɑːtəs/ *noun.* Also **S-**. M18.
[Latin: see SENATE.]
The governing body or senate of certain universities, esp. in Scotland. Also more fully ***senatus academicus*** /akəˈdɛmɪkəs/ [Latin = academic].

senatus consultum /sɛˌnɑːtuːs kɒnˈsʊltʊm/ *noun phr.* Pl. ***senatus consulta*** /kɒnˈsʊltə/. L17.
[Latin, genit. of *senatus* senate + *consultum* CONSULT *noun*.]
A decree of a senate, *spec.* of the ancient Roman senate.
■ ***senatus consult*** /sɛˌnɑːtəs kənˈsʌlt/ *noun phr.* = SENATUS CONSULTUM L19.

sencion /ˈsɛnʃ(ə)n/ *noun. obsolete* exc. *dial.* Also (*dial.*) **simson** /ˈsɪms(ə)n/. LME.
[Old French *senechion* (mod. *seneçon*) from Latin SENECIO.]
Groundsel, *Senecio vulgaris*.

send /sɛnd/ *noun*[1].
[Old English *sand*, *sond*, from Germanic base of SEND *verb*[1]. In later uses directly from SEND *verb*[1].]
†**1** The action of sending something; a thing which is sent, *spec.* (***a***) God's dispensation or ordinance; (***b***) a message. Chiefly *Scot.* OE–E19.
2 A person or body of people sent on an errand; an embassy; an envoy, a messenger, *spec.* one sent to a bride in advance of the bridegroom; a bridal party. Chiefly *Scot.* OE.
3 An accelerating impulse; impetus. L19.
4 An output socket on an item of electronic audio equipment. L20.

send *noun*[2] var. of SCEND *noun*.

send /sɛnd/ *verb*[1]. Pa. t. & pple **sent** /sɛnt/.
[Old English *sendan* = Old Frisian *senda*, *sēnda*, Old Saxon *sendian*, Old High German *sendan*, *senten* (Dutch *zenden*, German *senden*), Old Norse *senda*, Gothic *sandjan*, from Germanic base also of Old English, Old Saxon *sīþ* SITHE *noun*[1].]
1 *verb trans.* Order, request, or cause (a person) to go to a place or person for a particular purpose or in a specified capacity. OE. ▸**b** Cause, order, or enable (a person) to attend an institution or to follow a course of action; commit (a person) *to* prison. OE. ▸**c** Recommend or advise (a person) to go to a particular place or person; refer (a reader) to an author or authority. LME. ▸**d** Dismiss (a person) with or without force. Usu. foll. by *away*, *off*. M16.
2 *verb trans.* Order or cause (a thing) to be conveyed, transported, or transmitted by an intermediary to a person or place for a particular purpose; *spec.* dispatch (a letter, message, etc.) by post or messenger; transmit (a telecommunications signal). OE. ▸**b** Of a country: export. L16. ▸**c** Serve up (food etc.) from the kitchen (foll.

by *in, up*, or in ***send to table***); cause (food etc.) to be passed to a fellow diner. **M17.**

3 *verb trans.* Of God, fate, etc.: grant, bestow, inflict; cause to happen or be, bring about. Freq. foll. by obj. clause **OE.**

4 *verb intrans.* Dispatch or transmit a message, letter, or messenger. (Foll. by *to, after, to do.*) **OE.** ▸**b** Of a shop: deliver goods ordered. **L19.**

5 *verb trans.* Throw, discharge, direct, (a missile etc.). **OE.** ▸**b** Deliver, strike, (a blow, ball, etc.). **E17.**

6 *verb trans.* Drive, force, impel; cause to move or go, propel. Freq. foll. by *up, down*, ppl adjective. **OE.** ▸**b** Drive or bring (a person) into a specified state or condition, cause to be or become. Foll. by *into, to*, adjective compl. **M19.** ▸**c** Bring (a person) to ecstasy, fill with delight, affect or transport emotionally. *slang* (orig. *US*). **M20.**

7 *verb trans.* Emit, give out, (light, heat, odour, etc.); utter, produce, (sound); cause (a voice, cry, etc.) to carry or travel. Freq. foll. by *off, out, up, forth.* **OE.** ▸**b** Extend or spread out as a branch or offshoot. Freq. foll. by *off, out, forth.* **E18.**

8 *verb trans.* Direct (a look or glance) at a person or thing. Also foll. by *out.* **LME.**

📖 **1** *Century Magazine* He was sent as consul to the Orient. SCOTT FITZGERALD I sent the butler to New York with a letter to Wolfsheim. P. FITZGERALD Frank was sent over to England . . to stay with his relatives. **b** P. MORTIMER I suggest we send the elder children to boarding school. JAN MORRIS Until 1950 Oxford sent three members to Parliament. **c** J. LINGARD Writers who have sent us to the laws of the Christian Emperors. **d** HENRY FIELDING All agreed that he was sent away pennyless . . from the house of his inhuman father. **2** J. CONRAD A boat was sent to take him off. I. MURDOCH The message which Bruno had sent him through Lisa. E. BOWEN He sends his love, of course! *Nature* Pioneer 10 . . sent back more than 300 pictures of Jupiter. L. ELLMANN Daddy . . sent me the money to rent a flat. **c** H. GLASSE Garnish the dish with lemon, and send it to table. **3** SIR W. SCOTT God send my . . people may have no cause to wish their old man back again. J. STEINBECK It was a miracle sent by our Good Saint Francis. **4** M. C. CLARKE He sent to invite her to supper with him. *Radio Times* This is only a receiving station. We can't send. We can only listen. **5b** *Irish Press* He sent across to Jovanovic, who side-footed the ball into the net. **6** R. L. STEVENSON The plunge of our anchor sent up clouds of birds. D. M. THOMAS He took off her bonnet, and sent it, skimming, into a corner. R. BANKS The force of the bullet exploding into his chest sent him flying. *Financial Times* A near-tenfold increase in pre-tax profit . . sent up the share price. **b** W. GOLDING Lack of sleep was what sent people crazy. **c** T. TRYON You got me so darned excited. You really send me. **7** TENNYSON The lost lamb . . Sent out a bitter bleating for its dam. T. HARDY The Duke rode . . on . . the hoofs of his horse sending up a smart sound. **8** J. CONRAD Even his heavy-lidded eyes . . sent out glances of comparative alertness.

Phrases: ***send about his or her*** **BUSINESS**. ***send her down, Hughie! send in an account***: see **ACCOUNT** *noun*. ***send in one's papers***: see **PAPER** *noun*. ***send packing***: see **PACK** *verb*[1]. ***send the hat around***: see **HAT** *noun*. ***send to Coventry***: see **COVENTRY**. ***send to grass***: see **GRASS** *noun*. ***send to table***: see sense 2c above. ***send to the cleaners***: see **CLEANER** *noun*. ***send to the scaffold***: see **SCAFFOLD** *noun* 4. ***send to the wall***: see **WALL** *noun*[1]. **send word (to)** transmit a message (to a person), inform, notify, (foll. by *of, that, to do*).

With adverbs & prepositions in specialized senses: **send abroad** (*arch.* & *poet.*) publish, make known widely; cause to be heard far and wide. **send away** (*a*) *verb phr. trans.* see sense 1d above; (*b*) *verb phr. trans.* dispatch as a messenger; (*c*) *verb phr. intrans.* (foll. by *for*) send an order for a dealer to supply goods by post. **send back** (*a*) *CRICKET* get (a batsman) out, dismiss; (*b*) return (goods, a meal, etc.) to the manufacturer, kitchen, etc., as unsatisfactory. **send down** (*a*) rusticate or expel (an undergraduate) from university, esp. permanently; (*b*) *CRICKET* bowl (a ball or over); (*c*) *slang* sentence or commit (a person) to prison (freq. in *pass.*). **send for** (*a*) summon (a person or thing) by messenger or message, esp. urgently or peremptorily; send (a person) to fetch a thing or person; (*b*) order (goods) by post. **send in** (*a*) cause to go in or be delivered; (*b*) send by post, *spec.* submit (an entry etc.) for a competition etc.; (*c*) *CRICKET* send (a batsman) into the field to bat; nominate (the opposing side) to bat first. **send off** (*a*) *verb phr. trans.* dispatch (a letter, parcel, etc.) by post; (*b*) *verb phr. trans.* attend the departure of (a person) as a sign of friendship, goodwill, etc.; (*c*) *verb phr. trans. SPORT* order (a player) to leave the pitch and take no further part in the game as a punishment; (*d*) *verb phr. intrans.* (foll. by *for*) = ***send away*** (c). **send on** (*a*) dispatch in advance of one's own arrival; (*b*) refer (a person) to a further destination or authority; (*c*) forward (a letter etc.) to a further destination. **send up** (*a*) cause to go up; (*b*) see sense 2c above; (*c*) transmit to a higher authority, *spec.* send (a bill) from the House of Commons to the Lords; (*d*) *US* sentence to imprisonment; (*e*) *colloq.* mock, satirize, esp. by imitating; parody.

Comb.: **send-off** a gathering, demonstration of goodwill, etc., to mark the departure of a person, the start of a project, etc.; **send-up** *colloq.* an act of mocking or teasing; a parody, a satire.

■ **sendable** *adjective* able or suitable to be sent **L15.**

send *verb*[2] var. of **SCEND** *verb.*

Sendai /ˈsɛndʌɪ/ *noun.* **M20.**
[A city in northern Honshu, Japan.]
BIOLOGY & MEDICINE. Used *attrib.* to designate a paramyxovirus which causes disease of the upper respiratory tract in mammals, and is used in the laboratory to produce cell fusion. Chiefly as ***Sendai virus***.

sendal /ˈsɛnd(ə)l/ *noun.* **ME.**
[Old French *cendal*, (also Provençal) *sendal*, ult. from Greek *sindōn* **SINDON**: see **-AL**[1].]
Hist. **1** A thin rich silk material; a covering or garment of this. **ME.**
2 Fine linen, lawn; a piece of this, used esp. as a shroud or as a dressing for wounds etc. **ME.**
■ Also **sendaline** *noun* (now *arch. rare*) **M19.**

sendee /sɛnˈdiː/ *noun.* **E19.**
[formed as next + **-EE**[1].]
A person or party to whom a thing is sent.

sender /ˈsɛndə/ *noun.* **ME.**
[from **SEND** *verb*[1] + **-ER**[1].]
1 A person who or thing which sends something or someone. **ME.**
2a The transmitting instrument of a telephone or telegraphic or short-wave radio apparatus; a transmitter. **L19.** ▸**b** A person signalling or transmitting a message. **E20.**
3 A person who or thing which moves, delights, or affects someone emotionally. Also ***solid sender***. *slang* (orig. & chiefly *US*). **M20.**

📖 **1** S. BEDFORD He wrote Toni a long letter followed by notes . . They were returned to sender. **3** L. ARMSTRONG Life can be . . a drag one minute and a solid sender the next.

Sendero Luminoso /sɛnˌdɛrəʊ luːmɪˈnəʊsəʊ/ *noun phr.* **L20.**
[Spanish, lit. 'shining path'.]
A neo-Maoist Peruvian revolutionary movement and terrorist organization.
■ **Sendeˈrista** *noun & adjective* (*a*) *noun* a member of Sendero Luminoso; (*b*) *adjective* of or pertaining to this organization: **L20.**

sending /ˈsɛndɪŋ/ *noun.* **ME.**
[from **SEND** *verb*[1] + **-ING**[1].]
1 The action of **SEND** *verb*[1]; an instance of this. Also with adverbs, as ***sending off, sending out***, etc. **ME.**
2 A thing sent. **ME.**
3 The transmission of a telecommunication signal. **M19.**
4 [Old Norse, in same sense.] An unpleasant or evil thing, being, or creature supposed to be sent by a wizard to punish or take revenge on a person. **M19.**

sendle /ˈsɛnd(ə)l/ *adverb. Scot.* **LME.**
[Metath. alt. of *selden* var. of **SELDOM**.]
= **SELDOM.**

Sendzimir /ˈsɛn(d)zɪmɪə/ *noun.* **M20.**
[Tadeusz or Thaddeus K. *Sendzimir* (1894–1989), Polish-born US engineer.]
ENGINEERING. Used *attrib.* with ref. to a type of rolling-mill for cold rolling of steel, in which either of two working rolls is supported by two larger rolls, which are themselves backed by three still larger rolls.

sene /ˈsɛni/ *noun.* Pl. same, **-s**. **M20.**
[Samoan from **CENT** *noun*[1].]
A monetary unit of Western Samoa, equal to one-hundredth of a tala.

Seneca /ˈsɛnɪkə/ *noun & adjective.* **M17.**
[Dutch *Sennecca(s)* the upper Iroquois peoples collectively, perh. orig. from Mahican name for the Oneida.]
▶**A** *noun.* Pl. **-s**, same. A member of an Iroquois people, one of the five of the original Iroquois confederation, formerly inhabiting an area south of Lake Ontario; the language of this people. **M17.**
▶**B** *adjective.* Of or pertaining to the Senecas or their language. **E18.**
Seneca grass *US* holy-grass, *Hierochloe borealis*; **Seneca oil** [from Lake *Seneca*, New York State] *Hist.* crude petroleum; ***Seneca snakeroot***: see ***snakeroot*** s.v. **SNAKE** *noun.*

Senecal /ˈsɛnɪk(ə)l/ *adjective & noun.* **E17.**
[from *Seneca* (see below) + **-AL**[1].]
▶**A** *adjective.* Of, pertaining to, or characteristic of the Roman tragedian and Stoic philosopher L. Annaeus Seneca (died AD 65) or his works. **E17.**
▶**B** *noun.* A writer of drama in the Senecan manner; *spec.* a member of a group of early 17th-cent. English playwrights. **E17.**

Senecan /ˈsɛnɪk(ə)n/ *adjective.* **L19.**
[from *Seneca* (see prec.) + **-AN**.]
Of, pertaining to, or characteristic of Seneca (see prec.) or the works written by him or his imitators.
■ **Senecanism** *noun* the style or principles of Seneca or his imitators **M20.**

senecio /səˈniːsɪəʊ, -ʃɪəʊ/ *noun.* Pl. **-os**. **M16.**
[Latin = old man, groundsel, in ref. to the plant's white pappus. Cf. **SENCION**.]
A plant of the large and varied genus *Senecio*, of the composite family, comprising herbaceous herbs and shrubs typically having yellow-rayed flowers, and including groundsels and ragworts.

senectitude /sɪˈnɛktɪtjuːd/ *noun. rare.* **L18.**
[medieval Latin *senectitudo* irreg. from Latin *senectus* old age, from **SENEX**: see **-TUDE**.]
Old age.

senectude /sɪˈnɛktjuːd/ *noun. arch.* **M18.**
[Irreg. from Latin *senectus*: see prec.]
= prec.

senega /ˈsɛnɪɡə/ *noun.* **M18.**
[App. a var. form of **SENECA**.]
(The root of) a N. American milkwort, *Polygala senega*.

Senegalese /sɛnɪɡəˈliːz, -ɡɔːˈl-/ *noun & adjective.* **E20.**
[from *Senegal* (see below) + **-ESE**.]
▶**A** *noun.* Pl. same. A native or inhabitant of Senegal, a country in W. Africa. **E20.**
▶**B** *adjective.* Of or pertaining to Senegal or the Senegalese. **E20.**

Senegambian /sɛnəˈɡambɪən/ *noun & adjective.* **E20.**
[from *Senegambia* (see below) + **-AN**.]
▶**A** *noun.* A native or inhabitant of Senegambia, the region surrounding the Senegal and Gambia rivers in W. Africa; *US slang* (freq. *derog.*) a black person. **E20.**
▶**B** *adjective.* Of or pertaining to Senegambia; *US slang* (freq. *derog.*) black. **E20.**

senes *noun* pl. of **SENEX**.

senesce /sɪˈnɛs/ *verb intrans.* **M17.**
[Latin *senescere*, from *senex* old: see **-ESCE**.]
Grow old, age.

senescence /sɪˈnɛs(ə)ns/ *noun.* **L17.**
[from next: see **-ENCE**.]
The process or condition of growing old or ageing; *BIOLOGY* loss of the power of cell division and growth.

senescent /sɪˈnɛs(ə)nt/ *adjective.* **M17.**
[Latin *senescent-*, pres. ppl stem of *senescere*: see **SENESCE**, **-ENT**.]
Growing old, elderly, ageing.

seneschal /ˈsɛnɪʃ(ə)l/ *noun.* **ME.**
[Old French (mod. *sénéchal*), from medieval Latin *seniscalus*, *siniscalus* from Germanic words meaning 'old' and 'servant' (repr. by Old English *sēcalc*, Gothic *skalks*): see **-AL**[1].]
1 *Hist.* The official responsible for the management of a medieval great house or estate; a steward, a major-domo. **ME.** ▸**b** A cathedral official. **L19.**
2 The governor of a city, county, province, etc.; any of various administrative or judicial officers. Now *Hist.* exc. in Sark, a judge. **ME.**
■ **seneschalship** *noun* (*Hist.*) (*a*) the office or position and functions of a seneschal; †(*b*) = **SENESCHALSY** 1: **L16.**

seneschalsy /ˈsɛnɪʃ(ə)lsi/ *noun.* **LME.**
[Old French *seneschalsie* from medieval Latin *seniscalcia* from *seniscalus* **SENESCHAL**: see **-Y**[3].]
Hist. **1** In France, a territory under the government of a seneschal. **LME.**
2 In France, the administrative seat of a seneschal; the office or position of seneschal. **M17.**

seneschalty /ˈsɛnɪʃ(ə)lti/ *noun.* **L16.**
[from **SENESCHAL** + **-TY**[1].]
Hist. = **SENESCHALSY** 1.

senex /ˈsɛnɛks/ *noun.* Pl. ***senes*** /ˈsɛneɪs/. **L19.**
[Latin = old man.]
In literature (esp. comedy), an old man as a stock figure.

sengi /ˈsɛŋɡi/ *noun.* Also **senghi**. Pl. same. **M20.**
[Kikongo (also *senki*), from French *cinq* five (sous).]
A former monetary unit of the Democratic Republic of Congo (Zaire), equal to one-hundredth of a likuta.

sengreen /ˈsɛŋɡriːn/ *noun.* Now *dial.*
[Old English *singrēne*, use as noun of adjective = evergreen, ult. from Indo-European base *sem-* one, repr. in Latin *semel* once, *semper* always: see **GREEN** *adjective*.]
1 The houseleek, *Sempervivum tectorum*. **OE.**
2 Any of certain other evergreen plants, esp. varieties of stonecrop or saxifrage. **OE.**

senhor /sɛnˈjɔː, *foreign* seˈɲor/ *noun.* **L18.**
[Portuguese from Latin **SENIOR**.]
Used as a title (preceding the surname or other designation) of or as a respectful form of address to a Portuguese or Brazilian man (corresp. to English ***Mr*** or ***sir***); a Portuguese or Brazilian man.
¶ Cf. **SEIGNEUR, SEIGNIOR, SEÑOR, SIGNOR.**

senhora /sɛnˈjɔːrə, *foreign* seˈɲora/ *noun.* **E19.**
[Portuguese, fem. of **SENHOR**.]
Used as a title (preceding the surname or other designation) of or as a respectful form of address to a Portuguese or Brazilian woman, esp. a married one (corresp. to English ***Mrs*** or ***madam***); such a woman.

senhorita /seɲoˈrita, sɛnjəˈriːtə/ *noun.* **L19.**
[Portuguese, dim. of prec.]
Used as a title (preceding the surname or other designation) of or as a respectful form of address to a young esp. unmarried Portuguese or Brazilian woman (corresp. to English ***Miss***); such a woman.

Senhouse /ˈsɛnhaʊs/ *noun.* E20.
[Origin unkn.]
NAUTICAL. In full ***Senhouse slip***. A slip or fastening designed to secure the end of a cable but allow for its disconnection.

senicide /ˈsɛnɪsʌɪd/ *noun. rare.* L19.
[from Latin *senex* old man + -CIDE.]
The killing of the old people of a society, group, etc.

senile /ˈsiːnʌɪl/ *adjective & noun.* M17.
[French *sénile* or Latin *senilis*, from *senex* old (man): see -ILE.]
▶ **A** *adjective.* **1** Now usu. of a disease etc.: of, pertaining to, or characteristic of old age; peculiar to the aged. M17.
2 Having the infirmity, weakness, diseases, etc., of old age, esp. a loss of mental faculties; *spec.* afflicted with senile dementia. M19.
3 *PHYSICAL GEOGRAPHY.* Approaching the end of a cycle of erosion. E20.

> 🕮 **1 senile dementia** a severe form of mental deterioration in old age, characterized by loss of memory and disorientation, and most often due to Alzheimer's disease. **senile plaque** *MEDICINE* a microscopic mass of fragmented and decaying nerve terminals around an amyloid core, numbers of which occur in the cerebral cortex in Alzheimer's disease. **2** P. DALLY Her father had been senile for some years, and an increasing burden on his wife.

▶ **B** *noun.* A senile or aged person. Freq. in *collect. pl.*, *the* class of senile or aged people. M20.

> 🕮 *Times Review of Industry* In past days the senile and the slightly dippy were clapped into institutions.

■ **senilely** *adverb* L19. **senilize** *verb trans. & intrans.* make or become senile E19.

senility /sɪˈnɪlɪti/ *noun.* L18.
[from SENILE *adjective* + -ITY.]
The condition of being senile; mental or physical infirmity due to old age; (now *rare*) old age.

senior /ˈsiːnɪə, ˈsiːnjə/ *adjective & noun.* LME.
[Latin, compar. of *senex* old, rel. to Greek *henos* old (in *henē* last day of the moon), Gothic *sineigs* old, *sinista* elder: see -IOR. Cf. JUNIOR.]
▶ **A** *adjective.* **1** More advanced in age, elder, older, (foll. by *to*); *spec.* (*a*) (after a person's name) that is the elder of two members of a family bearing the same name, esp. a father of the same name as his son; (*b*) (after a simple surname) that is the elder of two pupils of the same surname, usu. brothers, in a public school etc. Now also, advanced in age, old. LME.
2 Of higher standing or rank, of longer service or earlier origin, (foll. by *to*). Now also, of high rank or long service. E16. ▸**b** Of a student at school or college: that has spent longer or a comparatively long time under tuition (foll. by *to*); *spec.* (*N. Amer.*) that is in the final year at a college or school. M17.
3 Suitable or reserved for senior students, staff, members, etc. L18.
4 Most advanced in age or standing, of longest service or earliest origin; *spec.* holding the highest position in an organization (freq. in ***senior partner*** below). M19.

> 🕮 **1** T. HOOK The senior four children re-appeared in the drawing-room. C. M. YONGE 'That is a puzzler, Mohun senior,' said Reginald. JOYCE A gifted man, Mr Bloom said of Mr Dedalus senior. **2** *Club Tennis* Senior lady players . . take very badly to being beaten by up-and-comings. L. DEIGHTON I'm senior in rank and service to you. M. MARRIN The senior management try to mix democratically with . . the production staff. **4** W. FAULKNER He is the senior living ex-freshman of the University of Alabama.

Special collocations & phrases: **senior citizen** (orig. *US*) an elderly person, *esp.* one past the age of retirement. **senior class** *N. Amer.* a class in college or high school made up of students in their final year at that establishment. **senior classic** at Cambridge University, the student achieving the highest place in the first class of the classical tripos. **senior college** *N. Amer.* a college in which the last two years' work for a bachelor's degree is done. **senior combination room** a senior common-room at Cambridge University. **senior common-room** a room for social etc. use by senior members of a college. **senior high (school)** *N. Amer.* a secondary school comprising the three or four highest grades. **senior moralist** at Cambridge University, the student achieving the highest place in the first class of the moral sciences tripos. ***senior nursing officer***: see NURSING *noun*. **senior officer** an officer to whom a junior is responsible. ***senior OPTIME***. **senior partner** the head of a firm of solicitors, doctors, etc. **senior school** a school or part of a school for older children, esp. those of 11 and over. **senior security** *STOCK EXCHANGE* the owner of which has first claim to be repaid by the issuing company (usu. in *pl.*). **senior service** the Royal Navy as opp. to the Army or the Royal Air Force. **senior tutor** a college tutor in charge of the teaching arrangements. **senior wrangler** at Cambridge University, the highest-placed wrangler or student placed in the first class of the mathematical tripos. **senior year** *N. Amer.* the last year of a high school or college course.

▶ **B** *noun.* **1 a** A person of (comparatively) advanced age, high standing, or long service; an old or venerable person; an eminent or responsible person. LME. ▸**b** With *possess.*: one's elder (by a specified amount); one's superior in standing, length of service, etc. LME.
†**2** *ECCLESIASTICAL.* A minister or official of a Church, an elder, a presbyter. LME–L16.
3 a A senior student or pupil; *spec.* (*N. Amer.*) a student in the final year at a college or school. E17. ▸**b** A senior fellow of a college; a member of a college's council or deliberative assembly. Cf. SENIORITY 2. M17.

> 🕮 **1a** *Times* Elastic-sided boots, once deemed proper only to the gravest of seniors. **b** N. WYMER House surgeons, who, unlike their seniors, live in the hospital. M. LANE Mary was five years Edward's senior.

¶ Cf. SEIGNEUR, SEIGNIOR, SENHOR, SEÑOR, SIGNOR, SIRE.

seniority /siːnɪˈɒrɪti/ *noun.* LME.
[medieval Latin *senioritas*, formed as prec.: see -ITY.]
1 The state or quality of being senior; position or priority by reason of greater age, longer service, or higher rank; standing, precedence; age. LME.
2 The body of seniors or senior fellows of a college. L17.

> 🕮 **1** C. THIRLWALL The envoys . . should address the king in the order of seniority. G. SWIFT They don't always promote on seniority alone, they bring people in from outside.

†**seniory** *noun* Only in L16.
[from SENIOR *adjective* + -Y[3].]
1 Seniority. *rare* (Shakes.). Only in L16.
2 *ECCLESIASTICAL.* A body of elders, a presbytery. Only in L16.

seniti /ˈsɛnɪti/ *noun.* Pl. same. M20.
[Tongan, from CENT *noun*[1].]
A monetary unit of Tonga, equal to one-hundredth of a pa'anga.

senium /ˈsiːnɪəm/ *noun.* E20.
[Latin = debility of old age, from *senere* be feeble, from *senex* old.]
MEDICINE. The period of old age. Usu. with *the*.

†**senker** *noun* see SINKER *noun*[2].

senn /sɛn/ *noun. rare.* E19.
[German.]
In the Alps, a herdsman.

senna /ˈsɛnə/ *noun*[1]. Orig. †**sena**. M16.
[medieval Latin *sena* from Arab. *sanā*.]
1 Any of various leguminous plants constituting the genus *Cassia*, chiefly yellow-flowered tropical shrubs including several with laxative properties. Also (with specifying word), any of various plants of other genera having similar properties. M16.
2 A laxative drug derived from species of cassia, esp. from the dried leaflets and pods of *Cassia senna*. L16.

senna *noun*[2] *& adjective* var. of SEHNA.

sennachie /ˈsɛnəxi/ *noun.* Now chiefly *Scot.* Also **shena-** /ʃɛnə-/ & other vars. LME.
[Gaelic *seanachaidh* (= Old Irish *senchaid*), from *sean* old (Old Irish *sen*).]
In Ireland and the Scottish Highlands: a professional recorder and reciter of family or traditional history and genealogy, attached to the household of a clan chieftain or person of noble rank. Now, a teller of traditional Gaelic heroic tales.

sennegrass /ˈsɛnɪɡrɑːs/ *noun.* L19.
[Norwegian *senegras*: cf. Old Norse *sina*, Swedish dial. *sena* withered grass.]
The dried leaves of a sedge, *Carex vesicaria*, used by Lapps as a lining for boots.

sennen *noun* var. of SENNIN.

sennet /ˈsɛnɪt/ *noun*[1]. L16.
[Perh. var. of SIGNET.]
Hist. A call on a trumpet or cornett ordered in the stage directions of an Elizabethan play, apparently as a signal for the ceremonial entrance or exit of a body of actors.

sennet /ˈsɛnɪt/ *noun*[2]. *W. Indies.* Also **sinnet** /ˈsɪnɪt/. L17.
[Perh. from a local language.]
A barracuda.

sennight /ˈsɛnʌɪt/ *noun. arch.*
[Old English *seofon nihta* seven nights: see NIGHT *noun*, SEVEN *adjective*. Cf. FORTNIGHT.]
A period of seven days and nights, a week.
this day sennight, **Sunday sennight**, etc., a week from this day, Sunday, etc.

sennin /ˈsɛnɪn/ *noun.* Also ***-en***. Pl. same. L19.
[Japanese = wizard, sage, recluse, from Chinese *Xi'anren* immortal man.]
In oriental mythology (orig. in TAOISM): an elderly recluse who has achieved immortality through meditation and self-discipline; a human being with supernatural powers, a reclusive mystic or teacher.

sennit /ˈsɛnɪt/ *noun.* M18.
[Var. of SINNET *noun*[1].]
NAUTICAL. **1** = SINNET *noun*[1]. M18.
2 *Hist.* Plaited straw, palm leaves, etc., used for making hats. M19.

senocular /sɪˈnɒkjʊlə/ *adjective. rare.* E18.
[from Latin *seni* six each + *oculi* eyes + -AR[1].]
Having six eyes.

Senoi /sɛˈnɔɪ/ *noun & adjective.* L19.
[Sakai (Temiar) *senoi* man.]
▶ **A** *noun.* Pl. same. A member of a people inhabiting the States of Perak, Kelantan, and Pahang in western Malaysia; the language of this people. L19.
▶ **B** *attrib.* or as *adjective.* Of or pertaining to the Senoi or their language. L19.

señor /sɛnˈjɔː, *foreign* seˈɲor/ *noun.* Pl. **-res** /-rɪz, *foreign* -res/. E17.
[Spanish from Latin SENIOR.]
1 Used as a title (preceding the surname or other designation) of or as a respectful form of address to a Spanish or Spanish-speaking man (corresp. to English ***Mr*** or ***sir***). E17. ▸**b** A Spanish or Spanish-speaking man. M19.
2 *Hist.* In Spain, a feudal lord, a seigneur. M19.
¶ Cf. SEIGNEUR, SEIGNIOR, SENHOR, SIGNOR.

señora /sɛnˈjɔːrə, *foreign* seˈɲora/ *noun.* L16.
[Spanish, fem. of prec.]
Used as a title (preceding the surname or other designation) of or as a respectful form of address to a Spanish or Spanish-speaking woman, esp. a married one (corresp. to English ***Mrs*** or ***madam***; such a woman.

señorita /sɛnjəˈriːtə, *foreign* seɲoˈrita/ *noun.* E19.
[Spanish, dim. of prec.]
1 Used as a title (preceding the surname or other designation) of or as a respectful form of address to a young esp. unmarried Spanish or Spanish-speaking woman (corresp. to English ***Miss***); such a woman. E19.
2 A small labroid fish, *Oxyjulis californica*, of the eastern Pacific. Also ***señorita-fish***. L19.

señorito /seɲoˈrito/ *noun.* Pl. ***-os*** /-ɒs/. E20.
[Spanish, dim. of SEÑOR.]
Used as a title (preceding the surname or other designation) or as a respectful form of address to a young man; a young man, *esp.* (freq. *derog.*) a noble or rich one regarded as leading an ostentatious or frivolous existence.

Senoussi *noun & adjective* var. of SENUSSI.

Senr. *abbreviation.*
Senior.

senryu /ˈsɛnrɪuː/ *noun.* Pl. same. M20.
[Karai *Senryū* (1718–90), Japanese poet.]
A short Japanese poem, similar in form to haiku but more intentionally humorous or satirical in content and usually without seasonal references.

sensa *noun* pl. of SENSUM.

sensal /ˈsɛns(ə)l/ *adjective. rare.* M19.
[from SENSE *noun* + -AL[1].]
PHILOSOPHY. Of or pertaining to sense or meaning or the senses.

sensate /ˈsɛnseɪt, -sət/ *adjective.* LME.
[Late Latin *sensatus* having senses, formed as next: see -ATE[2].]
1 Having senses, capable of sensation. Long *rare* or *obsolete*. LME.
†**2** Of the nature of or involving sensation. L17–E19.
3 Perceived by the senses. M19.
4 *SOCIOLOGY.* Designating a culture which emphasizes or values material needs and desires over spiritual ideals; materialistic. Cf. IDEATIONAL 2. M20.

sensate /sɛnˈseɪt/ *verb.* M17.
[from Latin *sensus* SENSE *noun* + -ATE[3], after next.]
1 *verb trans.* Perceive by sense; have a sensation of. M17.
†**2** *verb intrans.* Have sensation. Only in L17.

sensation /sɛnˈseɪʃ(ə)n/ *noun.* E17.
[medieval Latin *sensatio(n-)*, from Latin *sensus* SENSE *noun*, after late Latin *sensatus* SENSATE *adjective*: see -ATION. Cf. Old & mod. French *sensation*.]
1 The consciousness of perceiving or seeming to perceive some state or condition of one's body or its parts or of the senses; an instance of such consciousness; (a) perception by the senses, (a) physical feeling. Freq. foll. by *of*. E17. ▸**b** The faculty of perceiving by the senses, esp. by physical feeling. L18.
2 A mental feeling, an emotion; the feeling characteristic of a particular circumstance or situation; (a) mental apprehension or awareness. Freq. foll. by *of*. M17.
3 a Strong stimulation, powerful emotion; an instance or feeling of this; *spec.* (a state or display of) intense interest or excitement among a large group of people; the (literary) use of material intended to create such an effect. L18. ▸**b** A person or thing causing such a state of intense interest or excitement. M19.
4 A taste or small quantity of liquor etc. *arch. slang.* M19.

1 SHELLEY Is it only a sweet slumber Stealing o'er sensation? J. HUTCHINSON The sensation of tingling burning pain remaining the same. A. PATON The queer sensations of their bodies as though electricity were passing through them. W. STYRON Food, like everything else within the scope of sensation, was utterly without savor. **2** I. ASIMOV There would scarcely be any sensation of motion once the plane was airborne. G. SWIFT I had the distinct sensation of being watched. P. ACKROYD The sensations which would soon invade him—the loneliness, the self-pity. R. DAHL The sensation of absolute peace and beauty that surrounds you. **3a** H. L. MANSEL Cheap publications which supply sensation for the million in penny . . numbers. E. WAUGH The sensation caused . . by the announcement of her engagement. **b** S. T. FELSTEAD Zozo, the human cannon-ball, was a vast London sensation in the 'eighties.

■ **sensationless** *adjective* without sensation L19.

sensational /sɛnˈseɪʃ(ə)n(ə)l/ *adjective.* M19.
[from prec. + -AL[1].]
1 Of, pertaining to, or dependent on sensation or the senses. M19. ▸**b** *PHILOSOPHY.* Of a theory: regarding sensation as the sole source of knowledge. M19.
2 Causing or intended to cause great interest or excitement among a large group of people; lurid, melodramatic, exaggerated; very striking or remarkable; *colloq.* extremely good or impressive. M19.

1 W. WHEWELL No experience of external things is purely sensational. **2** *Financial Times* Shops and stores generally report buoyant though not sensational, Christmas business. J. HALPERIN This . . deliberately sensational story, touching . . upon murder, abduction, impersonation, illegitimacy. *Hair Flair* Buy a sensational floppy velvet hat and let the wind do its worst.

■ **sensationally** *adverb* in a sensational manner; with respect to sensation or feeling; in a manner causing or intended to cause a sensation: M19.

sensationalise *verb* var. of SENSATIONALIZE.

sensationalism /sɛnˈseɪʃ(ə)n(ə)lɪz(ə)m/ *noun.* M19.
[from SENSATIONAL + -ISM.]
1 *PHILOSOPHY.* The doctrine or theory that knowledge is derived solely from the senses. Cf. EMPIRICISM 2, RATIONALISM 3. M19.
2 Use or exploitation of sensational material or style in journalism, political activism, the arts, etc., to stimulate public interest or excitement; such material. M19.

2 *Philadelphia Inquirer* Network TV . . is dominated by . . voyeuristic pandering, sensationalism, homage to violence.

sensationalist /sɛnˈseɪʃ(ə)n(ə)lɪst/ *noun & adjective.* M19.
[formed as prec. + -IST.]
▸ **A** *noun.* **1** *PHILOSOPHY.* An adherent or student of sensationalism. M19.
2 A person intending to make a sensation; a journalist, artist, etc., making use of sensational material or style to stimulate public interest etc. M19.
▸ **B** *adjective.* Of the nature of or pertaining to sensationalism; intended to cause a sensation. M19.

Courier-Mail (Brisbane) In sensationalist '50s movies when Dracula hypnotises girls to take their clothes off.

■ **sensationaˈlistic** *adjective* pertaining to or of the nature of sensationalism L19.

sensationalize /sɛnˈseɪʃ(ə)n(ə)lʌɪz/ *verb trans.* Also **-ise**. M19.
[formed as prec. + -IZE.]
1 *PHILOSOPHY.* Restrict (a concept) to what is given in sensation. *rare.* M19.
2 Treat or report luridly, exaggerate in a sensational manner. M19.

2 *Daily Telegraph* The film is soberly made with no attempt to sensationalize the material. *Nature* The threat the bees pose to the public has been sensationalized but is, nevertheless, real.

■ **sensationaliˈzation** *noun* M20.

sensationism /sɛnˈseɪʃ(ə)nɪz(ə)m/ *noun.* M19.
[from SENSATION + -ISM.]
1 = SENSATIONALISM 2. M19.
2 *PHILOSOPHY.* = SENSATIONALISM 1. M19.

sensationist /sɛnˈseɪʃ(ə)nɪst/ *noun.* M19.
[formed as prec. + -IST.]
1 = SENSATIONALIST *noun* 2. M19.
2 *PHILOSOPHY.* = SENSATIONALIST *noun* 1. L19.
■ **sensatioˈnistic** *adjective* M20.

sensatory /ˈsɛnsət(ə)ri/ *adjective. rare.* M18.
[from SENSATE *verb* + -ORY[2].]
= SENSORY *adjective.*

sense /sɛns/ *noun.* LME.
[Latin *sensus* faculty or mode of feeling, thought, meaning, from *sens-* pa. ppl stem of *sentire* feel, perceive by the senses. Cf. Old & mod. French *sens.*]
▸ **I** Meaning, signification.
1 The meaning of a word or phrase; any of the various meanings of a word etc., the way a word etc. is to be understood within a particular context; *spec.* (chiefly *Hist.*) any of the various meanings or interpretations able to be derived through exegesis from a biblical word or passage. LME. ▸**b** Such a meaning recorded in a dictionary etc. M18.
†**2** The intended meaning of a speaker or writer. LME–M18.
3 The meaning of words in connected or continuous speech; the substance, import, or gist of a passage, text, etc. L15. ▸**b** The meaning or interpretation of a dream or allegory. Now *rare.* L16.
4 The content or theme of a passage or text. M16. ▸**b** (A passage of) prose to be turned into Latin or Greek verse as an exercise. L17.
5 Satisfactory and intelligible meaning; coherence, intelligibility; speech or writing having this. L16.
6 Wisdom, logic, or reason in a discourse, course of action, etc. E17.
7 Chiefly *MATH.* ▸**a** A direction in which motion takes place. L18. ▸**b** That which distinguishes a pair of objects, vector quantities, etc. which differ only in that each is the reverse or mirror-image of the other. L19.

1 H. CARPENTER Those I believe to be the most intriguing (in both senses of the word). *Guardian* An annual competition . . designed to promote environmental awareness in the widest sense. **b** W. W. SKEAT See the fifth sense of the verb *bield* in Murray's New English Dictionary. **3** E. R. TUFTE Data graphics should draw the viewer's attention to the sense and substance of the data. P. FITZGERALD Even though they don't understand me they might gather the sense of my gestures. **5** M. MARRIN The old-fashioned English habit of not talking sense to women. **6** GEO. ELIOT There's a good deal o' sense in what you say. H. KISSINGER Since Nixon had already made his decision, there was no sense in debating it.

▸ **II** Faculty of perception or sensation.
8 Any of the special bodily faculties, esp. sight, hearing, smell, taste, and touch (***the five senses***), by which humans and animals are able to perceive external objects and stimuli; a similar faculty concerned with internal stimuli esp. relating to balance and motion. Also, an analogous faculty of a hypothetical or undefined kind. E16. ▸†**b** A sensory organ. E16–E17. ▸**c** A sense or faculty indicated by a particular context. Now *rare* or *obsolete.* E17.
9 The senses viewed as a single faculty; the exercise of this faculty, the ability to perceive or feel, sensation. M16.
†**10** Ability to feel pain, irritation, etc., sensitivity. M16–L18.
11 A mental faculty as opp. to a bodily one. M16.
12 a In *pl.* & †*sing.* The mental faculties in a state of sanity; one's reason or wits. M16. ▸**b** In *pl.* & *collect. sing.* The faculties of perception as negated by sleep or unconsciousness. L16. ▸**c** In *pl.* & *collect. sing.* The faculties of sensation as a means of gratifying desire through sensual pleasure. L16.
13 Instinctive or acquired capacity to comprehend or appreciate a (specified) matter, quality, subject, etc.; quick or accurate understanding *of*, awareness *of*, instinct or feel for. E17.
14 Natural soundness of judgement, practical wisdom or intelligence, common sense. L17.
15 *attrib.* or as *adjective. GENETICS.* Relating to or designating a coding sequence of nucleotides, complementary to (and hence capable of binding to) an antisense sequence. Cf. ANTISENSE. L20.

8 M. TIPPETT As a musician my sharpest sense is that of sound. J. GARDNER Nick Blue had a kind of sense . . he'd known . . when the blizzard was coming. Y. MENUHIN He . . sniffed the air, and exclaimed, 'I smell a horse!'—he had the keenest senses. **c** A. RADCLIFFE He perceived the countenance of the knight change . . till his . . form gradually vanished from his astonished sense. **9** E. CAIRD The doctrine that sense is confused thought. **12b** E. PARSONS His senses fled, and he fell extended on the floor. **c** GOLDSMITH Small is the bliss that sense alone bestows, And sensual bliss is all the nation knows. **13** ***dress-sense, money-sense, road-sense***, etc.; ***sense of beauty, sense of colour, sense of duty, sense of fun, sense of honour, sense of humour, sense of rhythm, sense of shame***, etc. **14** J. GALT I thought they had more sense than to secede from Christianity to become Utilitarians. D. MADDEN For Christ's sake have sense You can't lie here . . until you bleed to death. M. FORSTER You have far too much sense to take this personally. **15** ***sense RNA, sense strand***, etc.

▸ **III** Actual perception or feeling.
16 Feeling or perception *of* a thing experienced through the sense of touch, smell, etc. Also, mental awareness or realization *of* a fact, state of affairs, etc. M16. ▸**b** Emotional sensibility or consciousness *of* something; regretful, grateful, or sympathetic appreciation or recognition. E17.
17 An opinion, view, or judgement held or formed by a group of people or (formerly) by an individual (*arch.*); *spec.* the prevailing view *of* a group etc. M16.
18 A more or less vague perception or impression of an object, fact, state of affairs, etc. Foll. by *of, that.* L16.
19 A consciousness or recognition *of* a quality etc. in oneself; awareness *of* one's conduct etc. E17.

16 G. STEIN Then would come strong to him, a sense of the deep sweetness in Melanctha's loving. **b** N. HAWTHORNE No better way of showing our sense of his hospitality . . has occurred to us. **17** BURKE A House of Commons which does not speak the sense of the people. **18** J. GALSWORTHY A sense that a man of his distinction should never have been allowed to . . work. A. J. CRONIN The sense of being buried . . was singularly oppressive. E. TEMPLETON An object left behind by a long-lost friend increases our sense of loss. **19** J. R. LOWELL Giving Eve a due sense of her crime. C. HARE The Chancellor of the Exchequer's sense of his own importance had had time to re-establish itself.

Phrases: **bring a person to his or her senses** cure a person of folly, restore to reality. **come to one's senses** (*a*) regain consciousness; (*b*) become sensible after acting foolishly. COMMON SENSE. ***dress sense***: see DRESS *noun.* **good sense** common sense, practical wisdom. **have the sense** be wise or sensible enough *to do* something. ***horse sense***: see HORSE *noun.* **in a sense**, **in one sense**, **in a — sense** if the statement, situation, etc., is looked at or considered in a particular or specified way. **in no sense** in no way, not at all. †**in one's own sense**, †**in one's sense** in one's opinion, according to one's judgement, (chiefly in ***abound in one's own sense*** s.v. ABOUND 4). **in one's senses** rational, sane. **make sense** be intelligible, logical, or practicable. **make sense of** find or show the meaning of, make comprehensible. **man of sense** a sagacious or sensible man. ***moral sense***: see MORAL *adjective.* **out of one's senses** in or into a state of madness. ***sense of DIRECTION***. ***sixth sense***: see SIXTH *adjective.* ***take leave of one's senses***: see LEAVE *noun*[1]. **take the sense of the meeting** ascertain the prevailing opinion of a group etc. ***the five senses***: see sense 8 above. **under a sense of wrong** feeling wronged.

Comb.: **sense aerial** = ***sense-finder*** below; **sense-content** (***a***) *PHILOSOPHY* = ***sense-datum*** below; (***b***) the sense or meaning contained in an idea or text; **sense-datum** *PHILOSOPHY* an immediate object, usu. non-material, of any of the senses, an element of sensory experience; **sense-experience** experience derived from the senses; **sense-finder** an aerial designed for sense-finding; **sense-finding** in certain radio direction-finders, the operation of determining which of two indicated directions 180 degrees apart is correct; **sense-organ** a bodily organ conveying (esp. external) stimuli to the sensory system.

sense /sɛns/ *verb trans.* M16.
[from the noun.]
1 Perceive (a sensation, object, etc.) by a sense or senses. Formerly also, feel, be conscious of, (an emotion, sensation, inward state, etc.). Now *rare* exc. as passing into sense 4 below. M16.
†**2** Expound the meaning of, explain; take or understand in a particular sense. E17–L18.
3 Understand, comprehend, grasp, (meaning, import, etc.). Chiefly *US & dial.* M19.
4 Be or become vaguely aware of, detect subconsciously or instinctively, intuit. L19.
5 Of a machine, instrument, etc.: detect, observe, measure (a circumstance, entity, etc.). M20.

4 G. VIDAL Jessup was amiable but I sensed a hardness in his tone. M. AMIS No one senses my presence; they walk on by. D. MADDEN Although she could not see . . anyone, she could sense another person there with her.

senseful /ˈsɛnsfʊl, -f(ə)l/ *adjective.* Now *rare.* L16.
[from SENSE *noun* + -FUL.]
1 Full of sense or meaning, coherent, meaningful. L16.
†**2** Intelligent. L16–E18.

sensei /sɛnˈseɪ/ *noun.* L19.
[Japanese, from *sen* previous + *sei* birth.]
In Japan: a teacher, an instructor, freq. of martial or other arts; a professor, a scholar.

senseless /ˈsɛnslɪs/ *adjective.* M16.
[from SENSE *noun* + -LESS.]
1 Of a person etc.: without sensation, physically insentient; in a state of unconsciousness. M16. ▸**b** Of a thing: incapable of sensation or perception. L16.
2 Incapable of feeling, lacking sensitivity or awareness. (Foll. by *of.*) Now *rare* or *obsolete.* M16.
3 Without sense or intelligence, stupid, silly, foolish. Also, without meaning or purpose, meaningless. L16.

1 *Sun* They were stripped and clubbed senseless. **3** D. BREWSTER She would not be so senseless as to accuse such men. S. TERKEL I was in Vietnam. I saw the senseless waste of human beings. P. ROTH His life did not come to a senseless end.

■ **senselessly** *adverb* L17. **senselessness** *noun* L16.

Sen-Sen /ˈsɛnsɛn/ *noun. N. Amer.* E20.
[Prob. fanciful name.]
(Proprietary name for) a breath freshener, freq. used to disguise the smell of drink or cigarettes.

sensibile /sɛnˈsɪbɪleɪ/ *noun.* Pl. ***sensibilia*** /sɛnsɪˈbɪlɪə/. M19.
[Latin, neut. of *sensibilis* SENSIBLE.]
PHILOSOPHY. The kind of thing which, if sensed, is a sense-datum.

sensibilise *verb* var. of SENSIBILIZE.

sensibilité /sɑ̃sibilite/ *noun. rare.* E20.
[French.]
Sensibility.

sensibility /sɛnsɪˈbɪlɪti/ *noun*. LME.
[Late Latin *sensibilitas* from Latin *sensibilis*: partly from SENSIBLE: see SENSIBLE, -ITY. Cf. Old & mod. French *sensibilité*.]
†**1** In *pl.* Emanations from bodies, supposed to be the cause of sensation. Only in LME.
2 Power of sensation or perception; sensitivity to sensory stimuli. LME. ▸**b** *PHILOSOPHY*. Capacity for sensation and emotion as opp. to cognition and will. M19.
†**3** Mental perception, awareness *of* something. LME–M17.
4 a The quality of being quickly or easily affected by emotional or artistic influences; susceptibility or sensitivity *to*, keen awareness *of*. L16. ▸**b** Highly developed sense of emotional or artistic awareness, extreme or excessive sensitivity or sympathy. *arch*. M18.
5 a In *pl.* Emotional capacities or feelings. Formerly also, instincts of liking or aversion. M17. ▸**b** In *pl.* & *sing.* A person's moral, emotional, or aesthetic ideas or standards; sensitive feelings, susceptibilities. M18.
6 Of (part of) a plant, an instrument, etc.: ability to be affected by external influences; sensitiveness, sensitivity. Foll. by *to* (rarely *of*). M17.
7 Emotional consciousness *of* something; grateful, resentful, or sympathetic recognition *of* conduct etc. M18.

> 📖 **4a** P. HALMOS Man's sensibility to his fellow man's needs . . seeks expression in the . . ministrations of the counsellors. **b** W. H. PRESCOTT Monuments of Oriental magnificence . . the admiration of every traveller of sensibility and taste. **5a** GEO. ELIOT The mother's love is at first an absorbing delight, blunting all other sensibilities. **b** R. CHRISTIANSEN The carousing obscenities of the prostitutes offended her sensibilities. *Paragraph* His work is . . totally outrageous to a liberal-humanist sensibility. **7** S. JOHNSON I was . . at Mrs. Montague's, who expressed great sensibility of your loss.

¶ Rare until M18.

sensibilize /ˈsɛnsɪb(ə)lʌɪz/ *verb trans. rare*. Also **-ise**. E20.
[from next + -IZE, after French *sensibiliser*.]
Make sensitive.
■ **sensibilizer** *noun* a thing which makes something sensitive; *PHOTOGRAPHY* = SENSITIZER: E20.

sensible /ˈsɛnsɪb(ə)l/ *adjective* & *noun*. LME.
[Old & mod. French, or Latin *sensibilis*, from *sens-*: see SENSE *noun*, -IBLE.]
▶ **A** *adjective*. **I 1** Perceptible by the senses; *spec.* in *PHILOSOPHY*, able to be apprehended only by the senses rather than by the intellect (opp. INTELLIGIBLE 2). (Foll. by *to*.) LME. ▸†**b** Of or pertaining to the senses or sensation. E17–L18.
2 a Large enough to be perceived or worth considering; appreciable, marked. LME. ▸**b** Easy to perceive, evident, noticeable. L16.
†**3** Easily understood; making a strong impression on the mind, striking, effective. E16–M18.
4 Perceptible by the mind or the inward feelings. L16.
†**5** Acutely felt; markedly painful or pleasurable. (Foll. by *to*.) L16–E19.

> 📖 **1** O. SACKS We have five senses . . that constitute the sensible world for us. *sensible horizon*: see HORIZON *noun* 1. **sensible heat** energy manifest in the form of heat, as opp. to latent heat. **sensible perspiration** sweat as distinguished from the emission of vapour through the pores. **2a** SIR T. BROWNE We could discover no sensible difference in weight. **b** JOHN PHILLIPS The warming influence of the sea air begins to be very sensible in October.

▶ **II 6** Of a bodily part or organ, or (formerly) a living being: having the faculty of sensation. LME.
7 a = SENSITIVE *adjective* 3b. Now *rare*. M16. ▸†**b** = SENSITIVE *adjective* 3a. L17–L18.

> 📖 **6** J. LOCKE It is the Understanding that sets Man above the rest of sensible Beings.

▶ **III 8** Cognizant, conscious, aware. Foll. by *of*, †*to*, *that*. *arch*. LME. ▸**b** Emotionally conscious; having a grateful, resentful, or sympathetic recognition of conduct etc. Foll. by *of*, †*to*, †*for*, *that*. M17.
9 Fully conscious; awake; free from delirium. M18.

> 📖 **8** T. HARDY Towards the end she was sensible of all that was going on. **9** MRS H. WOOD 'He has not many hours to live.' 'I am sorry to hear it, . . Is he sensible?'

▶ **IV 10** Having, showing, or deriving from good sense or practical wisdom; reasonable, judicious. LME. ▸**b** Of clothing, footwear, etc.: practical rather than attractive or fashionable; functional, serviceable. E19.

> 📖 **10** T. HARDY A farm-woman would be the only sensible kind of wife for him. U. BENTLEY I have always . . taken you for a sensible, level-headed young woman. *Green Magazine* It would be . . sensible to subsidise the farmer to make . . part of his land organic. *Country Homes* Quality furniture at sensible prices. **b** L. M. MONTGOMERY Good, sensible, serviceable dresses, without any frills.

▶ **B** *noun*. **1** That which produces sensation or is perceptible; an object of a sense or the senses. L16.
†**2** In a being, the element capable of feeling. *rare* (Milton). Only in M17.
†**3** A being capable of sensation. Only in L17.
4 A person possessing good sense, a judicious person. M18.

sensibleness /ˈsɛnsɪb(ə)lnɪs/ *noun*. LME.
[from SENSIBLE *adjective* + -NESS.]
†**1** The quality or state of being capable of sensation. LME–M18.
†**2** Of speech: intelligibility, clarity. Only in L16.
†**3** Emotional consciousness; grateful or sympathetic awareness; sensibility. Usu. foll. by *of*. E17–E18.
†**4** Perceptibility. M17–L18.
5 The quality of having good sense or sound judgement; practicality, serviceability. L19.

sensiblerie /sɑ̃sibləri/ *noun*. M20.
[French.]
= SENTIMENTALITY 1.

sensibly /ˈsɛnsɪbli/ *adverb*. LME.
[from SENSIBLE *adjective* + -LY[2].]
1 So far as can be perceived, perceptibly, appreciably. LME.
†**2** So as to be easily understood or to impress the mind; clearly, strikingly. LME–L17.
†**3** With self-consciousness, consciously; (of feeling) acutely, intensely. E16–E19.
4 With good sense, judiciously, reasonably; serviceably, practically. M18.

†**sensical** *adjective*. *rare*. L18–M19.
[from SENSE *noun* + -ICAL.]
Sensible.

sensifacient /sɛnsɪˈfeɪʃ(ə)nt/ *adjective*. L19.
[from Latin *sensus* SENSE *noun* + -I- + -FACIENT.]
Producing sensation.

sensiferous /sɛnˈsɪf(ə)rəs/ *adjective*. M17.
[formed as prec. + -I- + -FEROUS.]
Conveying sensation.

sensific /sɛnˈsɪfɪk/ *adjective* & *noun*. Now *rare* or *obsolete*. E19.
[formed as prec. + -FIC.]
▶ **A** *adjective*. Of nerves: sensory. E19.
▶ **B** *noun*. In *pl.* = SIGNIFICS. L19.

sensify /ˈsɛnsɪfʌɪ/ *verb trans. rare*. L17.
[Orig. late Latin *sensificare*; later formed as prec. + -FY.]
Transform (physical changes) into sensation.

sensigenous /sɛnˈsɪdʒɪnəs/ *adjective*. *rare*. L19.
[from SENSE *noun* + -I- + -GENOUS.]
Producing sensation.

sensile /ˈsɛnsɪl, -ʌɪl/ *adjective*. E19.
[Latin *sensilis*, from *sens-*: see SENSE *noun*, -ILE.]
Capable of perception, sentient.

sensillum /sɛnˈsɪləm/ *noun*. Pl. **-lla**. Also **-lla** (pl. **-llae**), **-llium**. E20.
[mod. Latin, neut. noun formed as dim. of Latin *sensus* SENSE *noun*.]
ZOOLOGY. A simple sensory receptor in invertebrates, esp. arthropods, consisting of a modified cell or small group of cells of the cuticle or epidermis, often hair- or rod-shaped.

sensing /ˈsɛnsɪŋ/ *noun*. M17.
[from SENSE *verb* + -ING[1].]
The action of SENSE *verb*; an instance of this; *spec.* (*a*) *US MILITARY* an observation of the point of impact of a shot with respect to the target; (*b*) the action of an automatic device in detecting, observing, or measuring something; (*c*) = ***sense-finding*** s.v. SENSE *noun*.
remote sensing: see REMOTE *adjective*.

sensise *verb* var. of SENSIZE.

sensism /ˈsɛnsɪz(ə)m/ *noun*. *rare*. M19.
[from SENSE *noun* + -ISM.]
1 *PHILOSOPHY*. = SENSATIONALISM 1. M19.
2 = SENSUALITY 2. L19.

sensist /ˈsɛnsɪst/ *noun*. *rare*. L19.
[formed as prec. + -IST.]
PHILOSOPHY. = SENSATIONALIST *noun* 1.

sensitise *verb* var. of SENSITIZE.

sensitive /ˈsɛnsɪtɪv/ *adjective* & *noun*. LME.
[Old & mod. French *sensitif*, *-ive* or medieval Latin *sensitivus*, irreg. from Latin *sens-*: see SENSE *noun*, -IVE.]
▶ **A** *adjective*. **1** Having the function of sensation or sensory perception; connected with or derived from the senses. LME.
2 Having the faculty of sensation. Formerly also, having the faculty of sensation but not reason. L15.
3 a Very susceptible or responsive to emotional, artistic, etc., impressions, possessing delicate or tender feelings, having sensibility; *spec.* (*a*) easily offended or emotionally hurt, touchy; (*b*) naturally perceptive of the feelings etc. of others; tactful, sympathetic, compassionate. Freq. foll. by *to*. E19. ▸**b** Having quick or intense perception or sensation; acutely affected by external stimuli etc.; tender, delicate. Freq. foll. by *to*, *of*. E19. ▸**c** *spec.* Having a temperament receptive to paranormal or occult influences. M19.
4 Of a thing: readily affected by or responsive to external influences (foll. by *to*); *spec.* (*a*) (of photographic paper or other prepared surface, a chemical substance, etc.) susceptible to the influence of light or other radiation; (*b*) (of a measuring instrument etc.) responsive to or recording slight changes of condition etc.; (*c*) (of stock, a market, etc.) liable to fluctuate rapidly in price in response to external factors; (*d*) (of a mathematical, statistical, or physical quantity) appreciably influenced by changes in some other quantity, the choice of method or model, etc. (foll. by *to*). M19. ▸**b** Involved with or likely to affect (esp. national) security; needing careful handling to avoid causing offence, embarrassment, etc., controversial. M20.

> 📖 **3a** J. T. STORY He was never the least bit sensitive to people's finer feelings. K. AMIS He's sensitive about being a bit deaf. G. DALY So sensitive that sunsets . . make him feel faint. P. MAILLOUX Franz's unhappiness . . could have been averted if his father had been . . more sensitive in his treatment of him. **b** DICKENS Madame Defarge being sensitive to cold, was wrapped in fur. P. G. WODEHOUSE Living by his wits had developed in Percy highly sensitive powers of observation. *Which?* Toothpastes for sensitive teeth contain chemicals to desensitise the dentine. **4b** H. KISSINGER The nuclear issue was highly sensitive; we needed to show some understanding for Japanese sensibilities.

Special collocations: ***sensitive brier***: see BRIER *noun*[1]. **sensitive fern** a frost-tender N. American fern, *Onoclea sensibilis*, sometimes cultivated. **sensitive period** *PSYCHOLOGY* a time or stage in a person's development when he or she is more responsive to certain stimuli and quicker to learn particular skills. **sensitive plant** (*a*) a leguminous plant of Brazil, *Mimosa pudica*, whose leaflets fold together when touched; ***false sensitive plant***, a related N. American plant, *Aeschynomene hispida*, having similar properties; (*b*) *fig.* a sensitive, delicate, or easily offended person.

▶ **B** *noun*. †**1** A being or bodily part capable of sensation. LME–E18.
†**2** The faculty of sensation. Only in E17.
3 = ***sensitive plant*** (a) above. E18.
4 a A person sensitive to paranormal or occult influences, a medium. M19. ▸**b** A person very susceptible or responsive to artistic, emotional, etc., impressions; *spec.* an aesthete. L19.
■ **sensitively** *adverb* M17. **sensitiveness** *noun* E19. **sensiˈtivity** *noun* (*a*) the quality or degree of being sensitive or responsive; (*b*) (in *pl.*) a person's sensitive feelings or sensibilities: E19.

sensitize /ˈsɛnsɪtʌɪz/ *verb trans.* Also **-ise**. M19.
[from SENSITIVE *adjective* + -IZE.]
1 *PHOTOGRAPHY*. Make (a film, plate, etc.) sensitive to light. M19.
2 Make (a person) sensitive to art, other people, a particular stimulus, etc. Also foll. by *to*. L19.
3 *PHYSIOLOGY*. Make (a cell, organ, or organism) sensitive *to* some agent or stimulus, esp. by repeated exposure; *esp.* render (the immune system) sensitive *to* the presence of a substance, esp. an allergen; *PSYCHOLOGY* raise the strength of a specific response by repetition of a stimulus that produces it, or by preceding a benign stimulus by a painful one. E20.
■ **sensitiˈzation** *noun* the act or process of sensitizing a thing or person, or of being sensitized L19. **sensitizer** *noun* (*a*) *PHOTOGRAPHY* a substance or preparation used for sensitizing film etc.; †(*b*) *IMMUNOLOGY* an agent which sensitizes the immune system; (*c*) a person who or thing which has a sensitizing effect; *PSYCHOLOGY* a person who reacts by being sensitive to a stimulus (rather than by repressing it): L19.

sensitometer /sɛnsɪˈtɒmɪtə/ *noun*. L19.
[formed as prec. + -OMETER.]
PHOTOGRAPHY. An instrument for ascertaining the degree of sensitiveness of photographic film etc.
■ **sensitoˈmetric** *adjective* of or pertaining to sensitometry L19. **sensitoˈmetrically** *adverb* L19. **sensitometry** *noun* the determination of the degree of sensitiveness of film etc. L19.

sensive /ˈsɛnsɪv/ *adjective*. Now *rare*. M16.
[Old French *sensif*, *-ive* or medieval Latin *sensivus*, from Latin *sens-*: see SENSE *noun*, -IVE.]
Having the function of sensation or sensory perception.
■ **sensiveness** *noun* (*rare*) M19.

sensize /ˈsɛnsʌɪz/ *verb trans. rare*. Also **-ise**. M19.
[from SENSE *verb* + -IZE.]
Perceive by means of the senses.

sensor /ˈsɛnsə/ *noun*. M20.
[from the adjective, or from SENSE *verb* + -OR.]
A device which detects or measures some condition or property and records, indicates, or otherwise responds to the information received.

sensor /ˈsɛnsɔː/ *adjective*. *rare*. M19.
[Irreg. from SENSORY *adjective* after *motor*.]
= SENSORY *adjective*.

sensori- /ˈsɛns(ə)ri/ *combining form* of SENSORY *adjective*: see -I-.
■ **sensorimotor** *adjective* designating or pertaining to a nerve, reflex, activity, etc., that has or involves both sensory and motor

functions or pathways M19. **sensori'neural** *adjective* designating hearing loss that is due to a lesion or disease of the inner ear or the auditory nerve M20.

sensorial /sɛn'sɔːrɪəl/ *adjective.* M18.
[from SENSORIUM + -AL¹.]
1 Of or relating to the sensorium; relating to sensation or sensory impressions. M18.
†**2** Pertaining to the brain as the centre of nervous energy; ***sensorial power***, vital energy supplied from the brain throughout the rest of the nervous system. L18–M19.
■ **sensorially** *adverb* L19.

sensorium /sɛn'sɔːrɪəm/ *noun.* Pl. **-ria** /-rɪə/, **-riums**. M17.
[Late Latin, from Latin *sens-* pa. ppl stem of *sentire* feel: see -ORIUM.]
The seat of sensation in the brain of humans and animals; the percipient centre to which sensory impulses are transmitted by the nerves; the whole sensory apparatus (including the sensory nerves). Formerly also, the brain regarded as centre of consciousness and nervous energy. Also ***common sensorium***.

sensory /'sɛns(ə)ri/ *noun.* E17.
[formed as prec. + -ORY¹.]
†**1** An organ of sense. E17–E18.
2 = SENSORIUM. Also ***common sensory***. Now *rare.* M17.
3 PSYCHOLOGY. A person in whom sensation supposedly dominates over action. Cf. MOTILE *noun. rare.* E20.

sensory /'sɛns(ə)ri/ *adjective.* M18.
[from Latin *sens-* or SENSE *noun* + -ORY².]
Of or pertaining to sensation or the senses; transmitting sensation; transmitted or perceived by the senses.
sensory aphasia MEDICINE: due to cerebral defect or injury affecting the ability to comprehend or integrate incoming acoustic or visual information, rather than to a defect of the mechanism of language production. **sensory deprivation** PSYCHOLOGY the process whereby an organism is (deliberately) deprived of stimulation of one or more sense organs; the state or condition produced by such deprivation.
■ **sensorily** *adverb* E20.

sensual /'sɛnsjʊəl, -ʃʊəl/ *adjective & noun.* LME.
[Late Latin *sensualis*, formed as SENSE *noun*: see -AL¹. Cf. French *sensuel.*]
▶ **A** *adjective.* **1** Of or pertaining to the senses or sensation, sensory; physical, bodily. Now *rare.* LME. ▸**b** Perceptible by the senses. *rare.* E16.
2 Of or depending on the senses only and not the intellect or spirit; appealing to or involving the appetites or desires; carnal, fleshly. Also (*derog.*), lewd, depraved. L15.
3 a Absorbed in material or temporal matters rather than intellectual and spiritual interests; worldly. Now chiefly in ***the average sensual man***. M16. ▸**b** Given or excessively devoted to the pursuit of physical pleasures or the gratification of the senses; *spec.* self-indulgent sexually or with regard to food and drink. Also, indicative of a sensual nature. M16.
†**4** Of a living thing: having the faculty of sensation but not reason. M16–L17.
5 a Of an opinion or idea: materialistic. Now *rare.* M17. ▸**b** PHILOSOPHY. = SENSATIONAL *adjective* 1b. *rare.* M19.

> 🕮 **2** J. O. JUSTAMOND The Monarch was . . soon disgusted of gratifications that were merely sensual. *Modern Painters* The softened, more luscious brushstrokes and warm, sensual colours of these late masterpieces. **3b** R. BAGOT The full mouth, with the sensual lips. INA TAYLOR She was calm and rational but occasionally he glimpsed a powerful sensual spirit.

▶†**B** *noun.* In *pl.*
1 Living things having sensation but not reason. E–M17.
2 The sensual faculties and appetites. M17–E19.
■ **sensually** *adverb* (*a*) in a manner perceptible to the senses; (*b*) with regard to gratification of the senses or to physical pleasure: LME.

sensualise *verb* var. of SENSUALIZE.

sensualism /'sɛnsjʊəlɪz(ə)m, -ʃʊə-/ *noun.* E19.
[from SENSUAL *adjective* + -ISM. Cf. French *sensualisme.*]
1 PHILOSOPHY. = SENSATIONALISM 1. Now *rare* or *obsolete.* E19.
2 (Devotion to) sensual indulgence. E19.
3 Absorption in material interests. L19.

sensualist /'sɛnsjʊəlɪst, -ʃʊə-/ *noun.* M17.
[formed as prec. + -IST. Cf. French *sensualiste.*]
1 A sensual person; a person interested solely in material things; a person devoted to sensual pleasure. M17.
2 PHILOSOPHY. = SENSATIONALIST *noun* 1. Now *rare* or *obsolete.* M19.
■ **sensua'listic** *adjective* pertaining to sensualism in philosophy or art M19.

sensuality /sɛnsjʊ'alɪti, sɛnʃʊ-/ *noun.* ME.
[Old & mod. French *sensualité* from late Latin *sensualitas*, formed as SENSUAL: see -ITY.]
1 The aspect of human nature concerned with the senses as opp. to the intellect or spirit; man's animal nature, esp. as the source of sensual appetites and desires. Now *rare.* ME. ▸†**b** Absorption in material things rather than intellectual or spiritual matters. LME–M16.
2 The pursuit of, or excessive devotion to, physical pleasure or gratification of the senses; sensual self-indulgence. Also (now *rare*), a sensual indulgence or pleasure. LME. ▸**b** *spec.* Sexual activity or excess; lustfulness. LME.

> 🕮 **2** J. S. MILL In its horror of sensuality, it made an idol of asceticism. ANNE STEVENSON Physical sensuality was something she actively enjoyed.

sensualize /'sɛnsjʊəlʌɪz, 'sɛnʃʊə-/ *verb.* Also **-ise**. E17.
[from SENSUAL *adjective* + -IZE.]
1 *verb intrans.* Live sensually. Long *rare* or *obsolete.* E17.
2 *verb trans.* Make sensual, imbue with sensual habits; give a materialistic character to (something spiritual). L17. ▸**b** PHILOSOPHY. Identify with the senses, explain by reference to sensation. Now *rare* or *obsolete.* M19.
■ **sensuali'zation** *noun* (*rare*) L18.

sensuism /'sɛnsjʊɪz(ə)m, 'sɛnʃʊ-/ *noun.* Now *rare* or *obsolete.* E19.
[formed as SENSE *noun* + -ISM.]
PHILOSOPHY. = SENSATIONALISM 1.

sensuist /'sɛnsjʊɪst, 'sɛnʃʊ-/ *noun. rare.* M19.
[formed as prec. + -IST.]
= SENSUALIST *noun* 1.
■ **sensu'istic** *adjective* inclined to sensuous indulgence M19.

sensu lato /sɛnsuː 'lɑːtəʊ/ *adverbial & adjectival phr.* M20.
[Latin.]
Of a scientific etc. term: in the broad sense. Opp. ***sensu stricto***.

sensum /'sɛnsəm/ *noun.* Pl. **sensa** /'sɛnsə/. M19.
[mod. Latin = that which is sensed, neut. pa. pple of Latin *sentire*: see SENSE *noun.*]
PHILOSOPHY. A sense-datum.

sensuous /'sɛnsjʊəs, 'sɛnʃʊəs/ *adjective.* M17.
[from (the same root as) SENSE *noun* + -OUS.]
1 Of or pertaining to the senses or sensation; derived from or affecting the senses. M17. ▸**b** Based on or relating to material objects or beings. Now *rare.* M19.
2 Of, derived from, or affecting the senses aesthetically rather than sensually; readily affected by the senses, keenly responsive to the pleasures of sensation. Also, indicative of a sensuous temperament. L19.

> 🕮 **2** T. HARDY The aesthetic, sensuous, pagan pleasure in natural life and lush womanhood. T. DREISER She beamed upon him in a melting and sensuous way. W. SANSOM With long sensuous strokes he smoothed a patina of paint down the chairlegs. A. WEST Although she was a sensuous woman she had deliberately repressed her sexuality.

¶ App. first used by Milton, to avoid certain associations of the existing word *sensual.*
■ **sensu'osity** *noun* (*rare*) the quality of being sensuous M18. **sensuously** *adverb* E19. **sensuousness** *noun* M19.

Sensurround /'sɛnsəraʊnd/ *noun.* L20.
[Blend of SENSE *noun* and SURROUND *verb.*]
(Proprietary name for) a technique of special effects whereby a cinema audience is apparently surrounded by low-frequency sound generated from the film soundtrack.

sensu stricto /sɛnsuː 'strɪktəʊ/ *adverbial & adjectival phr.* M19.
[Latin = in the restricted sense.]
Of a scientific etc. term: strictly speaking, in the narrow sense. Opp. ***sensu lato***. Cf. STRICTO SENSU.

†**sent** *noun*¹, *verb*¹ see SCENT *noun, verb.*

sent /'sɛnt/ *noun*². M20.
[Respelling of CENT *noun*¹.]
A monetary unit of Estonia, equal to one-hundredth of a kroon.

sent *verb*² *pa. t. & pple* of SEND *verb*¹.

sente /'sɛnti/ *noun.* Pl. **lisente** /lɪ'sɛnti/. L20.
[Sesotho.]
A monetary unit of Lesotho, equal to one-hundredth of a loti.

sentence /'sɛntəns/ *noun.* ME.
[Old & mod. French from Latin *sententia* mental feeling, opinion, philosophical judgement (translating of Greek *doxa* and *gnōmē*), from *sentire* feel: see -ENCE.]
†**1** Way of thinking, opinion, mind. ME–E17.
2 †**a** A decision to excommunicate a person. ME–E16. ▸**b** The declaration in a criminal court of the punishment imposed on a person pleading guilty or found guilty; the punishment imposed. ME. ▸**c** A judgement or decision of a court of law in a civil or criminal case. Now chiefly *techn.* LME.
†**3** The sense, substance, or gist of a passage, book, etc.; *gen.* significance. ME–L16.
4 An opinion expressed by a person on a subject of discussion, *esp.* a disputed biblical passage. Now *rare.* LME.
5 A pithy or memorable saying, a maxim, an aphorism. *obsolete* exc. *Hist.* LME. ▸**b** Aphoristic speech, sententiousness. *obsolete* exc. *poet.* E16.
6 Formerly, an indefinite portion of discourse or writing, a passage. Now *spec.* a short passage of Scripture in liturgical use. LME.
7 A series of words complete in itself as the expression of a thought, containing or implying a subject and predicate, and conveying a statement, question, exclamation, or command, (as *go home!, I go, pardon?, war declared*); *gen.* a piece of writing or speech between two full stops or equivalent pauses. LME. ▸**b** MUSIC. A complete idea, usu. consisting of two or four phrases; a period. L19. ▸**c** LOGIC. A correctly ordered series of signs or symbols expressing a proposition in an artificial or logical language. M20.

> 🕮 **2** *Daily Telegraph* Freed after serving eight months of their two-year sentences. N. GORDIMER The judge pronounced sentence of imprisonment for life. ***death sentence***, ***life sentence***, ***prison sentence***, ***suspended sentence***, etc. ***sentence of death***. *fig.*: C. KINGSLEY Our sentence is to labour from the cradle to the grave. **under sentence of** having been condemned to. **5b** T. S. ELIOT Full of high sentence, but a bit obtuse. **7** N. CHOMSKY Consider the sentence: 'The dog in the corner is hungry.' B. W. ALDISS He had the habit of beginning most sentences with 'Er'. ***complex sentence***: see COMPLEX *adjective*. ***compound sentence***: see COMPOUND *adjective*. INDETERMINATE ***sentence***. ***kernel sentence***: see KERNEL *noun*¹ 6f. ***simple sentence***: see SIMPLE *adjective*.

Comb.: **sentence adverb** GRAMMAR an adverb used to qualify a complete sentence (as *fortunately, hopefully*, etc.); **sentence-word** a word serving as a sentence.
■ **sentencehood** *noun* the condition of constituting a grammatically complete sentence M20.

sentence /'sɛntəns/ *verb.* LME.
[Old & mod. French *sentencier*, formed as prec. Cf. medieval Latin *sententiare* pronounce sentence.]
†**1** *verb intrans.* Pass judgement. LME–E18.
†**2** *verb trans.* Decree or order judicially. Also foll. by *that.* E16–M17.
†**3** *verb trans.* Decide (a dispute etc.) judicially. L16–L17.
†**4** *verb trans.* Pass judgement on, assess, (a person, a thing's merits, etc.). L16–E19.
5 *verb trans.* Pronounce sentence on, declare the sentence of, (a convicted criminal etc.); declare (a person) to be condemned *to* a specified punishment. L16.

> 🕮 **5** *Pall Mall Gazette* You were sentenced for throwing corrosive fluid over your wife. R. P. GRAVES Wilde was convicted and sentenced to two years' hard labour.

■ **sentencer** *noun* L16.

sententia /sɛn'tɛnʃɪə/ *noun.* Pl. ***-iae*** /-ɪiː/. E20.
[Latin: see SENTENCE *noun.*]
A pithy or memorable saying, a maxim, an aphorism, an epigram; a thought, a reflection.

sentential /sɛn'tɛnʃ(ə)l/ *adjective.* L15.
[Late Latin *sententialis*, formed as prec.: see -AL¹.]
†**1** Containing or of the nature of maxims or aphorisms. L15–M17.
†**2** Of the nature of a sentence or judicial decision. E17–E18.
3 Esp. GRAMMAR & LOGIC. Of or pertaining to a verbal sentence; pertaining to sentences or propositions. M17.
3 sentential calculus = PROPOSITIONAL ***calculus***.
■ **sententially** *adverb* (long *rare*) LME.

sententiary /sɛn'tɛnʃ(ə)ri/ *noun.* E17.
[medieval Latin *sententiarius*, formed as SENTENTIA: see -ARY¹.]
Hist. A writer or speaker of maxims or aphorisms. Also, a compiler of or commentator on opinions regarding controversial biblical passages.

sententiosity /sɛnˌtɛnʃɪ'ɒsɪti/ *noun. rare.* M17.
[formed as next + -ITY.]
Sententiousness; a sententious remark.

sententious /sɛn'tɛnʃəs/ *adjective.* LME.
[from Latin *sententiosus*, formed as SENTENCE *noun*: see -OUS.]
†**1** Full of meaning, intelligence, or wisdom. LME–M17.
2 Of language, style, etc.: of the nature of or filled with pointed maxims; aphoristic, pithy; affectedly or pompously formal, turgid. E16.
3 Of a person: given to the use of maxims, having a concise effective style; prone to pompous moralizing or bombastic formality. L16.
†**4** Of a symbol: expressing a sentence rather than a word or phrase. L16–E18.

> 🕮 **2** C. KINGSLEY A long sententious letter, full of Latin quotations. *Pall Mall Gazette* As Harry said in sententious vernacular, 'I wasn't having any.' **3** H. JAMES 'One must be what one is.' Mrs Brook was almost sententious.

■ **sententiously** *adverb* LME. **sententiousness** *noun* M16.

sentience /'sɛnʃ(ə)ns/ *noun.* M19.
[from next + -ENCE.]
The condition or quality of being sentient; consciousness, susceptibility to sensation.
■ Also **sentiency** *noun* M19.

sentient /'sɛnʃ(ə)nt/ *noun & adjective.* E17.
[Latin *sentient-* pres. ppl stem of *sentire* feel: see -ENT.]
▶ **A** *noun.* A person or thing capable of perception by the senses; ***the sentient***, that which has sensation or feeling. E17.

▶ **B** *adjective.* **1** That feels or is capable of feeling; having the power or function of sensation. (Foll. by *of* a thing perceived.) M17.
2 Of organs or tissues: responsive to sensory stimuli. E19.
3 Characterized by the exercise of the senses. E20.
■ **sentiently** *adverb* M19.

sentiment /ˈsɛntɪm(ə)nt/ *noun.* LME.
[Old French *sentement* (mod. *senti-*) from medieval Latin *sentimentum*, from Latin *sentire* feel: see -MENT.]
†**1** Personal experience, one's own feeling. Only in LME.
†**2** Sensation, physical feeling. Later, an awareness gained from vague sensation. LME–E19.
3 *sing.* & in *pl.* The sum of the feelings of a person or group on a particular subject; an opinion, a point of view, an attitude. M17.
4 A mental feeling, an emotion. M17.
5 A thought or view coloured by or based on emotion; an emotional thought expressed in literature or art. Also, the feeling or meaning intended by a passage, as opp. to means of expression; the sense of a statement. E18. ▸**b** A wish, view, etc., expressed as an epigram or proverb, esp. in a toast. L18.
6 Emotional or tender feelings collectively, esp. as an influence; manifestation of or appeal to such feelings; the tendency to be swayed by feeling rather than reason. Now *esp.* mawkish or superficial tenderness or sensitivity, exaggerated or indulgent emotion. M18.

📖 **3** H. MARTINEAU What were his sentiments regarding the meeting? A. TOFFLER In Washington, public sentiment forces a reassessment of missile policy. **4** SIR W. SCOTT A sentiment of bitterness rose in his mind against the government. **5** R. K. NARAYAN Anyone likes to hear flattering sentiments. L. ELLMANN When I told him I loved him, he echoed the sentiment. **6** *Blackwood's Magazine* A man in whose organization sentiment usurps too large a share for practical existence. R. L. STEVENSON As much appearance of sentiment as you would expect from a retired slaver. J. G. COZZENS They resolved, in a passion of generous sentiment, to do something for Ronald's . . young wife.

sentimental /sɛntɪˈmɛnt(ə)l/ *adjective.* M18.
[from prec. + -AL[1].]
1 Of, arising from, or characterized by sentiment; affected by or showing emotion rather than reason. Now *esp.* exaggeratedly or superficially sensitive or emotional, excessively prone to sentiment. M18.
2 Of music, literature, etc.: appealing to sentiment; dealing superficially with emotion, esp. love. M18.

📖 **1** SIR W. SCOTT Dropping a sentimental tear when there was room for . . effective charity. J. GALSWORTHY Fleur was not sentimental, her desires were ever concrete and concentrated. P. D. JAMES Incurably sentimental about wildlife. **sentimental value** value of a thing to a particular person because of its associations rather than its material worth. **2** F. M. FORD Novels of a sentimental type . . in which typewriter girls married Marquises.

■ **sentimentalism** *noun* (*a*) susceptibility to sentiment, tendency to be swayed by emotion rather than reason, proneness to superficial or exaggerated sensitivity; (*b*) a sentimental idea or expression: E19. **sentimentalist** *noun* a person cultivating or affecting sentimentality, a holder of sentimental ideas L18. **sentimentaˈlistic** *adjective* (*rare*) possessing sentimental characteristics, characterized by an exaggerated sentimentality E20. **sentimentless** *adjective* having no sentiment L19.

sentimentalise *verb* var. of SENTIMENTALIZE.

sentimentality /ˌsɛntɪmɛnˈtalɪti/ *noun.* L18.
[from prec. + -ITY.]
1 The quality of being sentimental; exaggerated or superficial sensitivity; sentimental behaviour. L18.
2 In *pl.* Sentimental notions. E19.

sentimentalize /sɛntɪˈmɛnt(ə)lʌɪz/ *verb.* Also **-ise**. M18.
[formed as prec. + -IZE.]
1 *verb intrans.* Indulge in sentimental thoughts or behaviour. M18.
2 *verb trans.* Bring *into* or *out of* a condition by the expression of sentiment. *rare.* L18.
3 *verb trans.* **a** Make sentimental, imbue with sentimental qualities. E19. ▸**b** Turn into an object of sentiment, treat sentimentally. L19.
■ **sentimentaliˈzation** *noun* M19. **sentimentalizer** *noun* M19.

sentimentally /sɛntɪˈmɛnt(ə)li/ *adverb.* L18.
[formed as prec. + -LY[2].]
1 With respect to sentiment. L18.
2 In a sentimental manner. E19.

sentinel /ˈsɛntɪn(ə)l/ *noun.* Also †**cent-**, †**-trinel**, †**-tronel**. L16.
[French *sentinelle* from Italian *sentinella*, of unkn. origin.]
1 A sentry, a lookout, a guard. L16.
†**2** The duty or function of a sentinel. Chiefly in ***keep sentinel***, act as a sentinel or lookout. Cf. SENTRY *noun*[1] 3. L16–E18.
†**3** A military watch-tower for defence of a camp or a city wall. E–M17.
†**4** In full ***private sentinel***. A private soldier. E18–L19.
5 COMPUTING. An item in a list etc. designated as having symbolic significance, esp. as a marker indicating a beginning or end; a tag. M20.

📖 **1** LD MACAULAY The sentinels who paced the ramparts announced that the . . army was in sight. *transf.*: R. BAGOT The grim cliff on which the castle stands sentinel over the North Sea. ***perdu sentinel***: see PERDU *adjective* 1. **stand sentinel** act as a sentinel or lookout.

Comb.: **sentinel pile** MEDICINE a thickening or swelling resembling a haemorrhoid at the lower end of an anal fissure.
■ **sentinelship** *noun* the position or office of sentinel M17.

sentinel /ˈsɛntɪn(ə)l/ *verb trans.* Also †**cent-**. Infl. **-ll-**, ***-l-**. L16.
[from the noun.]
1 Stand guard over, watch as a sentinel. L16.
2 Provide with a sentinel or sentinels. M17.
3 Post or place as a sentinel. E19.

📖 **1** B. J. LOSSING The winding road was . . sentineled by lofty pines.

sentition /sɛnˈtɪʃ(ə)n/ *noun. rare.* M19.
[from Latin *sentire* feel, perceive + -ITION.]
The action of perceiving.

sentoku /ˈsɛntəʊkuː/ *noun.* E20.
[Japanese, abbreviation of *sentokudōki*, from *sentoku* (from Chinese *Hsüan-te*) + *doki* vessel.]
Orig., a Chinese bronze produced during the reign (1426–35) of Emperor Hsüan-te (Pinyin Xuan-de) of the Ming dynasty. Later, a golden-yellow Japanese bronze vessel made after the Chinese fashion; the metal itself.

sentry /ˈsɛntri/ *noun*[1]. Also †**centry**. E17.
[Perh. shortening of †*centrinel*, *-onel* vars. of SENTINEL *noun*, with assim. to -RY.]
†**1** = SENTINEL *noun* 3. E–M17.
2 A soldier stationed to keep watch and prevent unauthorized access to a place; a sentinel, a guard, a lookout. E17.
3 The duty or function of a sentry. Freq. in ***keep sentry***, act as a sentry or lookout. Cf. SENTINEL *noun* 2. M17.

📖 **2** S. RUSHDIE Sentries guard the door with crossed rifles. **stand sentry** act as a sentry or lookout.

Comb.: **sentry-box** a usu. wooden cabin providing shelter for a standing sentry; **sentry-go** [orig. a military order] the duty of pacing up and down as a sentry, a sentry's patrol.

sentry /ˈsɛntri/ *noun*[2]. *obsolete* exc. in comb. L16.
[Contr. of †*sentuary* var. of SANCTUARY, infl. by French *saintuaire*.]
= SANCTUARY.

sentry /ˈsɛntri/ *verb.* E19.
[from SENTRY *noun*[1].]
1 *verb trans.* Guard as a sentry. E19.
2 *verb trans.* Post or place as a sentry. E20.
3 *verb intrans.* Act as a sentry. *rare.* E20.

Senufo /səˈnuːfəʊ/ *noun & adjective.* Pl. same. E20.
[Akan.]
▶ **A** *noun.* A member of a people in the Ivory Coast, Mali, and Burkina Faso in W. Africa; any of the Niger-Congo languages spoken by them. E20.
▶ **B** *attrib.* or as *adjective.* Of or pertaining to the Senufo or their languages. E20.

Senussi /sɛˈnuːsi/ *noun & adjective.* Also **Sanusi**, **Senoussi**. L19.
[from Sīdī Muḥammad ibn ʻAlī as-*Sanūsī* (d. 1859), founder of the fraternity.]
▶ **A** *noun.* Pl. same. A member of a N. African Muslim religious fraternity. L19.
▶ **B** *attrib.* or as *adjective.* Of or pertaining to the Senussi. L19.
■ **Senussia** *noun* the fraternity of the Senussi L19. **Senussian** *noun & adjective* = SENUSSI L19. **Senussiite** *noun & adjective* = SENUSSI E20.

†**senvy** *noun.* ME–M18.
[Old French *seneve* (mod. *sénevé*) from popular Latin enlargement of Latin *sinapi* mustard.]
The mustard plant; mustardseed.

senza /ˈsɛntsa/ *preposition.* E18.
[Italian, prob. from Latin *absentia* absence, with infl. of Latin *sine* without. Cf. SANS *preposition*.]
MUSIC. In directions: without.
senza bassi /ˈbassi/ without the basses. ***senza ritenuto*** /ritɛˈnuːto/ without holding back. ***senza sordini*** /sorˈdiːni/ without mutes or dampers.

sepal /ˈsɛp(ə)l/ *noun.* E19.
[French *sépale*, mod. Latin *sepalum*, from Greek *skepē* covering, after French *pétale* petal.]
BOTANY. Each of the divisions of the calyx of a flower (esp. when separate and not united into a tube), typically green and leaflike.
■ **sepaline** /-lɪn/ *adjective* of or belonging to the sepals M19. **sepalled** *adjective* having sepals, esp. of a specified number or kind E19. **sepalody** *noun* an abnormal condition in which the petals of a flower are transformed into sepals M19. **sepaloid** *adjective* of the nature of or resembling a sepal M19.

separable /ˈsɛp(ə)rəb(ə)l/ *adjective.* LME.
[French *séparable* or Latin *separabilis*, from *separare*: see SEPARATE *verb*, -ABLE.]
1 Able to be separated. LME. ▸**b** GRAMMAR. Of a prefix, or a verb in respect of a prefix: written as a separate word in some collocations. L18.
†**2** Capable of separating. *rare* (Shakes.). Only in L16.

📖 **1** I. MCEWAN Space and time were not separable categories but aspects of one another.

■ **separaˈbility** *noun* M17. **separableness** *noun* M17. **separably** *adverb* E17.

separate /ˈsɛp(ə)rət/ *adjective & noun.* LME.
[Latin *separatus* pa. pple of *separare*: see next, -ATE[2].]
▶ **A** *adjective* (orig. *pa. pple*).
†**1** Separated. LME–L17.
2 a Solitary, secluded. Now *rare.* E17. ▸**b** Detached, set apart, (*from* something); not incorporated or joined. M17.
3 a Existing or regarded as a unit by itself. L17. ▸**b** Belonging or exclusive to an individual person or thing, not shared. L17.

📖 **2b** R. RENDELL Spacious bathroom and separate W.C. ELLIS PETERS Not even the tower would be visible as separate from the dark rock from which it rose. **3a** W. EMPSON A musical chord is a direct sensation, but not therefore unanalysable into its separate notes. F. FORSYTH Three separate harbours, one for freighters, one for yachts . . and one for fishing vessels. **b** C. STORR In the cottage we have separate rooms.

Phrases & special collocations: **go *separate* ways**: see WAY *noun*. **separate but equal** *US* racially segregated but ensuring equal opportunities to all races. **separate development** (chiefly *S. Afr.*) the allocation of separate areas of land to different racial groups as a means of securing racial segregation. ***separate maintenance***: see MAINTENANCE 6b. **separate school** *Canad.* a school receiving pupils from a particular racial or religious group. ***under separate cover***: see COVER *noun*[1].
▶ **B** *noun.* †**1** A person who withdraws from the Church; a separatist. E–M17.
2 A period of solitary prison confinement. Now *rare.* M19.
3 An offprint; = SEPARATUM. Chiefly *US*. L19.
4 GEOLOGY & SOIL SCIENCE. Any of the fractions into which a soil or similar material can be separated according to particle size, mineral composition, etc. E20.
5 In *pl.* Garments suitable for wearing in various combinations to form different outfits. M20.
6 AUDIO. A self-contained, free-standing component of a sound-reproduction system. Usu. in *pl.* L20.

📖 **5** *Times* Casual sweatshirts . . and sporty separates. **6** *attrib.*: *Which?* A £400 separates system made up from amplifier, speakers and CD.

■ **separately** *adverb* LME. **separateness** *noun* M17.

separate /ˈsɛpəreɪt/ *verb.* LME.
[Latin *separat-* pa. ppl stem of *separare*, formed as SE- + *parare* make ready: see -ATE[3].]
▶ **I** *verb trans.* **1 a** Put apart, disunite, part, (two or more persons or things, or one *from* another); detach, disconnect, treat as distinct, (one thing); make a division between (two things). Also, divide into component parts. LME. ▸**b** Discharge (a person) from the armed forces, the police, etc.; dismiss from employment. *US*. M19.
2 Cause (a married couple) to cease living together, esp. by judicial separation. L15.
3 a Remove or extract (a substance) from another with which it is combined or mixed, esp. by a technical process. L15. ▸†**b** Of a gland: secrete. Of a material substance: give off or emit from itself. L17–E19.
4 a Put on one side or segregate for a special purpose; devote *to*. Chiefly in biblical use. E16. ▸†**b** Exclude, prohibit. *rare.* L16–M17.
5 Prevent union, contact, or connection between; part by occupying an intervening space. M16.
6 Divide into two or more parts. *rare.* L16.

📖 **1a** R. MACAULAY I'm sorry you two will be separated. *Quilting Today* To make the hair, separate the yarn into strands. *refl.*: P. MAILLOUX In becoming a writer he has separated himself from ordinary life. ***separate the men from the boys***: see MAN *noun*. ***separate the sheep from the goats***: see GOAT *noun*. ***separate the wheat from the chaff***: see CHAFF *noun*[1]. **4a** H. PRIDEAUX Whoever of the ancient Patriarchs first separated a Tenth. **5** L. DURRELL I found myself separated from that forgotten evening by centuries. M. MCCARTHY The dinette, which was separated from the kitchen by a . . folding door.

▶ **II** *verb intrans.* †**7** Cause a rift *between*. *rare.* M16–M17.
8 a Leave the company or society of another or others, withdraw; part *from*; secede from a Church. M16. ▸**b** Of two or more people: leave each other's company, disperse; (of a married couple) cease to live together as man and wife. L17.
9 a Of a thing: draw away (*from* something else); become disconnected or detached; become divided *into*. M17. ▸**b** Of a substance: become physically distinct from the material containing it, *spec.* form a precipitate; (also

foll. by *out*). Of a liquid: change from being homogeneous to consisting of two or more layers of different composition. M19.

> 8b G. W. TARGET The pair . . separated at the bottom of the stairs. b B. BAINBRIDGE Her parents didn't know anybody who had even separated, let alone divorced. 9a *John Bull* The roof of the nave has separated . . from the wall. *Omni* The fingers themselves separate into even smaller fingers. b G. FOWNES The salt separates in minute crystals. *Guardian* Single cream will separate during long slow cooking.

With adverbs in specialized senses: **separate off** treat as distinct. **separate out** make separate, isolate; extract; (see also sense 9b above).

separated /ˈsɛpəreɪtɪd/ *ppl adjective & noun*. M16.
[from prec. + -ED[1].]
▶ **A** *ppl adjective*. Put apart, isolated, disconnected; *MATH.* (of two or more sets) each having no point in common with the closure of the other. M16.
▶ **B** *noun*. Either of a married couple who have ceased to live together, esp. after a result of judicial separation (usu. in *pl.*). Also, *the* class of separated people collectively. E18.

separation /sɛpəˈreɪʃ(ə)n/ *noun*. LME.
[Old & mod. French *séparation* from Latin *separatio(n-)*, formed as SEPARATE *verb* + -ATION.]
▶ **I 1** The action or an act of separating something; the state of being separated. LME.
2 The action or an act of withdrawing oneself or leaving the company of others; secession. LME.
†**3** *ALCHEMY.* A process of analysis, extraction, etc. L15–E18.
4 *ASTROLOGY.* The apparent moving apart in the sky of two planets etc. Now *rare* or *obsolete*. L16.
5 *LAW.* An arrangement whereby a couple remain married but cease to live together, either by mutual consent or following a judicial decree granted at the suit of one of them. Also more fully ***judicial separation***, ***legal separation***. E17.
6 *MEDICINE.* The detachment of tissue, esp. dead tissue, from the body. Now *rare* or *obsolete*. E17.
7 Discharge from the armed forces, the police, etc.; resignation or dismissal from employment. *US.* L18.

> 1 H. JAMES As if they had been old friends meeting after a separation. *Times* The separation of the lunar module . . from the command service module. †**make separation** make a severance or division. **separation of powers** *POLITICS* the vesting of the legislative, executive, and judiciary powers of government in separate bodies. 2 J. A. FROUDE The first . . movement towards a separation from Rome.

▶ **II** A separated thing.
†**8** A Christian denomination or sect of dissenters from a Church, esp. the Church of England; the body of Protestant nonconformists collectively. L16–E18.
9 A separated portion, a part, a division. *rare*. L16.
▶ **III** A thing that separates.
10 The place or point where two or more objects separate or are divided from one another; a divergence, a line of division. E17.
11 A thing that constitutes a division or partition; an intervening space or break; a cause of separating. *rare*. E18.

> 10 W. CHAMBERS We come now to the separation of the Maas and Waal branches of the river.

▶ **IV** *techn.* **12** *PHOTOGRAPHY & PRINTING.* Each of a set of three or more monochrome reproductions of a coloured picture, each in a different colour, which reproduce the full colour of the original when combined; the process of obtaining such a set. E20.
13 *PHYSICS & AERONAUTICS.* The generation of a turbulent boundary layer between the surface of a body and a moving fluid, or between two fluids moving at different speeds. E20.
14 Distinction or difference between the signals carried by the two channels of a stereophonic system; a measure of this. M20.

Comb.: **separation anxiety** *PSYCHOLOGY* anxiety provoked in a child by (the threat of) separation from its mother or familiar surroundings; **separation-order** *LAW* an order of court for the judicial separation of a married couple.

■ **separationism** *noun* advocacy of separation, or of a theory of separation L19. **separationist** *noun & adjective* (*a*) *noun* an advocate of political separation; (*b*) *adjective* of or pertaining to political separation: M19.

separatist /ˈsɛp(ə)rətɪst/ *noun & adjective*. Also **S-**. E17.
[from SEPARATE *adjective, noun* + -IST.]
▶ **A** *noun*. **1** An advocate of ecclesiastical separation; a member of a Christian denomination or sect separated from a Church; *spec.* (*Hist.*) a member of a denomination or sect separated from the Church of England, *esp.* an Independent. Also *gen.*, a schismatic, a sectarian. E17.
2 A person who keeps himself or herself apart from others on the ground of superior piety. E17.
3 An advocate of political separation; a supporter of political independence or autonomy for a region, group, etc. L19.
4 A critic who ascribes the *Iliad* and the *Odyssey* or any sections of them to separate authors. Cf. SEPARATOR 1. E20.

> 3 *Times* Threats by Basque separatists to mount a . . bombing campaign.

▶ **B** *attrib.* or as *adjective*. Of, pertaining to, or characteristic of separatists or their views. M19.

> *Times Lit. Suppl.* The . . Sicilian separatist bandit Salvatore Giuliano.

■ **separatism** *noun* the principles and practices of separatists E17. **separaˈtistic** *adjective* of, pertaining to, or of the nature of separatism M19. †**separatistical** *adjective* = SEPARATISTIC: only in E17.

separative /ˈsɛp(ə)rətɪv/ *adjective*. L16.
[French *séparatif* or late Latin *separativus*, formed as SEPARATE *verb* + -IVE.]
1 Tending to separate or to cause separation. L16.
2 *GRAMMAR.* (Of the genitive case) expressing separation, departure, removal, etc.; (of a conjunction) alternative, disjunctive. M19.

separator /ˈsɛpəreɪtə/ *noun*. E17.
[Partly from ecclesiastical Latin = schismatic, formed as SEPARATE *verb*, partly from SEPARATE *verb* + -OR.]
1 A person who or thing which separates; *spec.* †(*a*) an ecclesiastical separatist; (*b*) a critic who ascribes the *Iliad* and the *Odyssey* to different authors, = SEPARATIST *noun* 4. E17.
†**2** In *pl.* The four lateral incisor teeth of a horse, on either side of the central incisors. E18–E19.
3 An instrument or appliance for a process of separation, e.g. of grain from chaff, cream from milk, threads from each other, etc. M19. ▸**b** A partition; a plate interposed between compartments, as in a voltaic cell, a beehive, etc. L19.

†**separatory** *noun*. LME–M19.
[medieval Latin *separatorium*, from Latin as SEPARATE *verb*: see -ORY[1].]
A thing which separates something from something else, esp. (*a*) a surgical instrument for this purpose; (*b*) a vessel for separating liquids of different densities.

separatory /ˈsɛpəreɪt(ə)ri/ *adjective*. E18.
[from SEPARATE *verb* + -ORY[2].]
Having the function of separating.

separatrix /sɛpəˈreɪtrɪks/ *noun*. Pl. **-trices** /-trɪsiːz/. M17.
[Late Latin, fem. of SEPARATOR: see -TRIX.]
†**1** The mark (orig. a capital L, later capital I), formerly used in place of the decimal point. Also, the line separating the numerator and denominator of a fraction. M17–L18.
2 A slanting stroke used in proof correction to mark and separate alterations. L19.
3 *PHYSICS.* A boundary between adjacent regions, esp. regions having differing configurations of magnetic lines of force. E20.

separatum /sɛpəˈreɪtʌm/ *noun*. Pl. **-ta** /-tə/. L19.
[Latin, use as noun of neut. sing. of *separatus* pa. pple of *separare* SEPARATE *verb*.]
An offprint; = SEPARATE *noun* 3.

separist /ˈsɛp(ə)rɪst/ *noun & adjective*. *rare*. E17.
[from French *séparer* from Latin *separare* SEPARATE *verb*: see -IST.]
= SEPARATIST *noun & adjective*.

sepetir /sɛpəˈtɪə/ *noun*. E20.
[Malay.]
Any of several leguminous trees of SE Asia belonging to the genera *Pseudosindora* and *Sindora*; the lightweight hardwood of these trees.

Sephadex /ˈsɛfədɛks/ *noun*. M20.
[Origin unkn.]
CHEMISTRY. (Proprietary name for) a preparation of dextran gel used for the separation and purification of chemicals on the basis of molecular size. Cf. SEPHAROSE.

Sephardi /sɪˈfɑːdi/ *noun & adjective*. M19.
[mod. Hebrew, from *sĕpāraḏ*, a country mentioned in *Obadiah* 20 and taken to be Spain.]
▶ **A** *noun*. Pl. **-dim** /-dɪm/. A Jew of Spanish or Portuguese descent. Later also, a Jew from a Middle Eastern country. Cf. ASHKENAZI. M19.
▶ **B** *attrib.* or as *adjective*. = SEPHARDIC *adjective*. E20.
■ **Sephardic** *adjective* of or pertaining to the Sephardim M19.

Sepharose /ˈsɛfərəʊz/ *noun*. M20.
[Origin unkn.]
CHEMISTRY. (Proprietary name for) a preparation of agarose used for similar purposes to Sephadex.

Sepher Torah *noun phr.* var. of SEFER TORAH.

sephira /ˈsɛfɪrɑː/ *noun*. Pl. **-roth** /-rəʊθ/. M16.
[Hebrew *sĕpīrāh* (pl. *sĕpīrōt*), from *sāpar* to number.]
In the philosophy of the Jewish cabbala, each of the ten hypostatized attributes or emanations surrounding the Infinite, by means of which the Infinite enters into relation with the finite. Usu. in *pl.*
■ **sephirothic** /-ˈrɒθɪk/, **-rotic** /-ˈrɒtɪk/ *adjective* L19.

sepia /ˈsiːpɪə/ *noun & adjective*. LME.
[Latin from Greek *sēpia* cuttlefish. In sense 2 (as French *sépia*) prob. immed. from Italian *seppia*.]
▶ **A** *noun*. **1** A cuttlefish. Now chiefly as mod. Latin genus name. LME.
2 a A rich brown pigment prepared from the black secretion of the cuttlefish, used in monochrome drawing and watercolour painting; the dark reddish-brown colour of this pigment. Also, a brown tint used in photography. E19. ▸**b** The black secretion itself. L19.
3 *ellipt.* A sepia photograph or drawing. M19.

> 2a F. BUNSEN Her outlines are in pen and sepia.

▶ **B** *adjective*. **1** Of the colour of sepia; drawn or tinted in sepia. E19.
2 *euphem.* Of a person: black. *US.* M20.

> 1 *Liverpool Echo* An old sepia photograph of the Emblematic.

Sepik /ˈsiːpɪk/ *noun & adjective*. M20.
[A river and district in Papua New Guinea.]
▶ **A** *noun*. Pl. same. A member of a people of NW Papua New Guinea; the language of this people. M20.
▶ **B** *attrib.* or as *adjective*. Of or pertaining to the Sepik or their language. M20.

sepiment /ˈsɛpɪm(ə)nt/ *noun*. Now *rare* or *obsolete*. M17.
[Latin, from *sepire* to hedge, from *sepes* hedge: see -MENT.]
1 A hedge, a fence. M17.
†**2** *transf.* & *fig.* A thing that encloses or protects. M–L17.

sepiolite /ˈsiːpɪəlʌɪt/ *noun*. M19.
[German *Sepiolith*, from Greek *sēpion* SEPIUM (with allus. to the similarity of texture): see -LITE.]
GEOLOGY. = MEERSCHAUM 1.

sepiostaire /siːpɪəˈstɛː/ *noun*. Now *rare* or *obsolete*. M18.
[French *sépiostaire*, from Greek *sēpia* cuttlefish + *ostoun* bone + French *-aire* -ARY[1].]
ZOOLOGY. = ***cuttle-bone*** s.v. CUTTLE *noun*[1].

sepium /ˈsiːpɪəm/ *noun*. Now *rare*. M18.
[mod. Latin from Greek *sēpion*.]
ZOOLOGY. = ***cuttle-bone*** s.v. CUTTLE *noun*[1].

sepoy /ˈsiːpɔɪ/ *noun*. E18.
[Persian & Urdu *sipāhī* horseman, soldier, from *sipāh* army.]
Hist. A native of the Indian subcontinent employed as a soldier under European, esp. British, military discipline.
Comb.: ***Sepoy Mutiny***: see MUTINY *noun* 2.

seppuku /sɛˈpuːkuː/ *noun*. L19.
[Japanese, from *setsu* to cut + *fuku* abdomen.]
= HARA-KIRI.

seps /sɛps/ *noun*. M16.
[Latin from Greek *sēps*, from base of *sēpein* make rotten.]
1 A very venomous serpent whose bite is described by classical writers as causing putrefaction. Now *Hist.* M16.
2 A European skink of the genus *Chalcides* (formerly *Seps*) with a snakelike body and very short or non-existent legs. Now *rare*. E19.

sepsis /ˈsɛpsɪs/ *noun*. L19.
[Greek *sēpsis*, from *sēpein* make rotten.]
MEDICINE. The state of being septic; blood-poisoning or destruction of tissue by pathogenic micro-organisms or their toxins, esp. through infection of a wound.
PUERPERAL ***sepsis***.

sept /sɛpt/ *noun*[1]. M16.
[Latin SEPTUM.]
1 An enclosure; an area marked off for a special purpose. M16.
2 *ARCHITECTURE.* A dividing screen, railing, etc. E19.

sept /sɛpt/ *noun*[2]. E16.
[Prob. alt. of SECT *noun*[1]: cf. Anglo-Latin *septus* and medieval Latin *septa*, repr. Old French *sette*, Italian *setta* sect.]
1 A division of a nation or tribe; a clan, *esp.* a Scottish or Irish one. E16.
2 *transf.* A category, esp. of people. E17.

sept- *prefix* see SEPTI-.

Sept. *abbreviation*.
September.

septa *noun* pl. of SEPTUM.

septage /ˈsɛptɪdʒ/ *noun*. *N. Amer.* L20.
[from SEPTIC + -AGE, after *sewage*.]
Waste, esp. excremental matter, contained in or removed from a septic tank.

septagon /ˈsɛptəg(ə)n/ *adjective*. *rare*. M18.
[Late Latin *septagonus*, from Latin *septem* seven + Greek *-gōnos* -GON.]
Heptagonal.

septal /ˈsɛpt(ə)l/ *adjective*[1]. M19.
[from SEPT *noun*[1] + -AL[1].]
1 Pertaining to or consisting of a septum or septa; constituting a septum. M19.
2 *ECOLOGY.* Growing in hedges. M19.
3 *ARCHAEOLOGY.* Of a stone or slab: forming a barrier between compartments in a burial chamber. E20.

septal /ˈsɛpt(ə)l/ *adjective*[2]. **L19.**
[from SEPT *noun*[2] + -AL[1].]
Of or pertaining to a sept or clan.

septangular /sɛpˈtaŋgjʊlə/ *adjective.* **M17.**
[from SEPTI- + ANGULAR, after *triangular* etc.]
Having seven angles, heptagonal.

septanose /ˈsɛptənəʊz, -s/ *noun.* **M20.**
[from SEPTI- after *furanose* etc.: see -OSE[2].]
CHEMISTRY. A sugar with a molecular structure containing a seven-membered ring.
■ **septanoside** /sɛpˈtanəsʌɪd/ *noun* a glycoside in the form of a septanose **M20.**

septarium /sɛpˈtɛːrɪəm/ *noun.* Pl. **-ria** /-rɪə/. **L18.**
[mod. Latin, from Latin SEPTUM: see -ARIUM.]
GEOLOGY. A nodule of argillaceous limestone, ironstone, etc., having radial cracks near the centre filled with another mineral, formerly much used for cement.
■ **septarian** *adjective* of the form or nature of a septarium or septaria **M19.**

septate /ˈsɛpteɪt/ *adjective.* **M19.**
[from SEPTUM + -ATE[2], after *dentate*, *foliate*, etc.]
Containing or divided by a septum or septa; partitioned.
■ **sepˈtated** *adjective* = SEPTATE **L19.** **sepˈtation** *noun* division by a septum or septa **M19.**

septcentenary /sɛp(t)sɛnˈtiːn(ə)ri, -ˈtɛn-, sɛptˈsɛntɪn-/ *noun.* **E20.**
[from SEPTI- + CENTENARY, after *bicentenary* etc.]
(A celebration of) a seven-hundredth anniversary.

septectomy /sɛpˈtɛktəmi/ *noun.* **M20.**
[from SEPTUM + -ECTOMY.]
1 Surgical resection of the nasal septum; an instance of this. *rare.* **M20.**
2 Surgical resection of the atrial septum; an instance of this. Also called ***septostomy.*** **L20.**

septem- /ˈsɛptɛm/ *combining form.*
[Latin *septem* seven.]
Forming chiefly adjectives with the sense 'having seven, sevenfold'.
■ **septemdeˈcenary** *adjective* occurring once in 17 years **M19.** **septemfid** *adjective* (BOTANY) divided into seven parts by deep clefts or notches **M19.** **septemfoil** *noun* = SEPTFOIL 2 **M19.** **septemˈfoliate** *adjective* (BOTANY) having seven leaflets **M19.**

September /sɛpˈtɛmbə/ *noun.* **LOE.**
[(French *septembre* from) Latin *September*, from *septem* seven: orig. the seventh month of the Roman year. The origin of *-ber* is unkn. (cf. *December* etc.).]
The ninth month of the year in the Gregorian calendar. Also *fig.*, with allusion to September's position at the beginning of autumn in the northern hemisphere.
Comb.: **September massacres** *Hist.* a mass killing of political prisoners during the French Revolution in Paris on 2–6 September 1792.

septembrise *verb* var. of SEPTEMBRIZE.

Septembriser *noun* var. of SEPTEMBRIZER.

Septembrist /sɛpˈtɛmbrɪst/ *noun.* **E19.**
[from prec. + -IST.]
Hist. **1** = SEPTEMBRIZER. **E19.**
2 In Portugal, a supporter of the successful insurrection of September 1836 in favour of the restoration of the 1822 constitution. **M19.**

septembrize /ˈsɛptɛmbrʌɪz/ *verb trans. & intrans. obsolete* exc. *Hist.* Also **-ise.** **L18.**
[French *septembriser*, from *septembre* SEPTEMBER: see -IZE.]
Assassinate (a person or persons) like the Septembrizers.

Septembrizer /ˈsɛptɛmbrʌɪzə/ *noun.* Also **-iser.** **L18.**
[French *septembriseur*, formed as prec. + -IZER.]
1 *Hist.* A person who took part in or advocated the September massacres in Paris in 1792. **L18.**
2 A person who shoots partridges in September. Now *rare* or *obsolete.* **E19.**

septemvir /sɛpˈtɛmvə/ *noun.* Pl. **-viri** /-vɪrʌɪ/. **M18.**
[Latin, sing. of *septemviri*, from *septem* seven + *viri* men.]
Each of a body of seven men associated in an official function.

septemvirate /sɛpˈtɛmvɪrət/ *noun.* **M17.**
[Latin *septemviratus* formed as prec. + -ATE[1].]
1 The position or office of septemvir; government by septemviri. Long *rare.* **M17.**
2 A group or set of seven men. **L18.**

septemviri *noun* pl. of SEPTEMVIR.

septenar /ˈsɛptɪnɑː/ *noun.* **E20.**
[formed as next.]
PROSODY. = next.

septenarius /sɛptɪˈnɛːrɪəs/ *noun.* Pl. **-arii** /-ˈɛːrɪʌɪ/. **E19.**
[Latin, from *septeni* distrib. of *septem* seven.]
PROSODY. A line of seven feet, *esp.* a trochaic or iambic catalectic tetrameter.

septenary /ˈsɛptɪn(ə)ri, -ˈtiːn(ə)ri/ *noun & adjective.* **LME.**
[formed as prec.: see -ARY[1].]
▶ **A** *noun.* **1** A group or set of seven. **LME.**
2 A period of seven years. **L16.**
†**3** The number seven. **M–L17.**
4 MUSIC. The seven notes of the diatonic scale. **M17.**
5 PROSODY. = SEPTENARIUS. **L19.**
▶ **B** *adjective.* **1** Of or pertaining to the number seven; forming a group of seven. **LME.** ▶**b** Pertaining to or designating a sevenfold division of a period of time. **M17.**
1 †**septenary number** the number seven.

septenate /ˈsɛptɪnət/ *adjective.* **E19.**
[from Latin *septeni* seven each + -ATE[2].]
BOTANY. Of a leaf: having seven lobes or leaflets.

septennary /sɛpˈtɛn(ə)ri/ *adjective.* **M17.**
[from Latin *septennis*, from *septem* seven + *annus* year: see -ARY[1].]
Septennial.

septennate /sɛpˈtɛnət/ *noun.* **L19.**
[French *septennat*, formed as prec.: see -ATE[1].]
1 A period of seven years during which an official position is held. **L19.**
2 *Hist.* Any of several successive periods of seven years, beginning in 1874, during which the strength of the German army was to remain fixed. **L19.**

septennial /sɛpˈtɛnɪəl/ *adjective.* **M17.**
[from Latin SEPTENNIUM + -AL[1].]
1 Lasting seven years. **M17.**
2 Occurring every seven years. **M17.**
■ **septennially** *adverb* every seven years **L18.**

septennium /sɛpˈtɛnɪəm/ *noun.* Pl. **-nnia** /-nɪə/, **-nniums.** **M19.**
[Late Latin (for classical Latin *septuennium*), from Latin *septem* seven + *annus* year: see -IUM.]
A period of seven years.

Septentrion /sɛpˈtɛntrɪən/ *noun & adjective.* Now *arch. rare.* Pl. **-ones** /-əʊniːz/, **-ons.** **LME.**
[Latin *septentrio(n-)*, sing. of *septentriones* (orig. *septem triones*) the seven stars of the Great Bear, from *septem* seven + *triones* pl. of *trio* plough-ox. Cf. TRIONES.]
▶ **A** *noun.* **1** *sing.* & (usu.) in *pl. The* constellation of the Great Bear (the Plough) or the Little Bear. **LME.**
†**2** The north; the northern region of the earth or the heavens. **LME–M17.**
3 A northerner. **E17.**
▶ **B** *adjective.* Northern. **M17.**
■ **septentriˈonic** *adjective* (*rare*) **M19.** †**septentrionical** *adjective*: only in **M17.**

septentrional /sɛpˈtɛntrɪən(ə)l/ *adjective & noun.* Now *arch. rare.* **LME.**
[Latin *septentrionalis*, formed as prec.: see -AL[1].]
▶ **A** *adjective.* Belonging to the north, northern; pertaining to northern countries. **LME.**
▶†**B** *noun.* = SEPTENTRION *noun* 2. Only in **LME.**

septet /sɛpˈtɛt/ *noun.* Also **-ette.** **E19.**
[German *Septett*, from Latin *septem* seven: see -ET[1], -ETTE.]
1 MUSIC. A composition for seven voices or instruments. **E19.**
2 A group of seven persons or things; *esp.* (MUSIC) a group of seven singers or instrumentalists. **L19.**

septfoil /ˈsɛtfɔɪl/ *noun.* **L16.**
[Late Latin *septifolium*, after CINQUEFOIL, TREFOIL.]
1 The plant tormentil, *Potentilla erecta.* Now *rare.* **L16.**
2 ARCHITECTURE. An ornamental design of seven cusps, usu. found inscribed in an arch. **M19.**

septi- /ˈsɛpti/ *combining form.* Also (chiefly before a vowel) **sept-.**
[from Latin *septem* seven: see -I-.]
Forming chiefly adjectives with the sense 'having seven, sevenfold'.
■ **septichord** *adjective* (of an instrument) seven-stringed **E18.** **septiˈlateral** *adjective* seven-sided **M17.** **septipartite** *adjective* divided into seven parts **E19.** **septiˈvalent** *adjective* (CHEMISTRY) = HEPTAVALENT **L19.**

septic /ˈsɛptɪk/ *adjective & noun.* **E17.**
[Latin *septicus* from Greek *sēptikos*, from *sēpein* make rotten: see -IC.]
▶ **A** *adjective.* **1** Of, pertaining to, or characterized by the destruction of tissue by pathogenic micro-organisms or their toxins; affected by sepsis; putrefying. **E17.**
2 *transf.* Unpleasant, nasty, rotten. *slang.* **E20.**
📖 **2** T. MALLON The author was . . septic with resentment.
Special collocations: **septic tank** a tank (associated either with a sewage works or with a residence not connected to a sewer) in which the solid content of sewage is allowed to settle and accumulate and is purified by the action of anaerobic bacteria.
▶ **B** *noun.* †**1** A septic or putrefactive substance. **E17–L18.**
2 *ellipt.* A septic tank. *Austral. colloq.* **M20.**
■ **septicity** /sɛpˈtɪsɪti/ *noun* the quality or condition of being septic **E19.**

septicaemia /sɛptɪˈsiːmɪə/ *noun.* Also ***-cem-.** **M19.**
[formed as SEPTIC + -AEMIA.]
Blood-poisoning caused by the multiplication of pathogenic bacteria in the bloodstream.
■ **septicaemic** *adjective* **L19.**

†**septical** *adjective.* **M17–E19.**
[formed as SEPTIC: see -ICAL.]
= SEPTIC *adjective.*

septicemia *noun* see SEPTICAEMIA.

septicidal /sɛptɪˈsʌɪd(ə)l/ *adjective.* **E19.**
[from SEPTUM + -I- + Latin *caedere*, *-cid-* to cut (cf. -CIDE) + -AL[1].]
BOTANY. (Of the dehiscence of a fruit) occurring along the septa separating the carpels; (of a carpel of a fruit) that undergoes such dehiscence. Cf. LOCULICIDAL.
■ **septicidally** *adverb* **M19.**

septier /sɛtje/ *noun. obsolete* exc. *Hist.* **E16.**
[French, earlier *sestier*, from Latin *sextarius*, from *sextus* sixth.]
A former French unit of capacity equal to about 150 litres (approx. four bushels); a unit of land area equal to about 0.4 hectare (approx. one acre).

septiferous /sɛpˈtɪf(ə)rəs/ *adjective.* **E19.**
[from SEPTUM + -I- + -FEROUS.]
BOTANY & ZOOLOGY. Having a septum or septa.

septiform /ˈsɛptɪfɔːm/ *adjective*[1]. **L15.**
[Old French *septiforme* or Latin *septiformis*, formed as SEPTI-: see -FORM.]
Sevenfold.

septiform /ˈsɛptɪfɔːm/ *adjective*[2]. **E19.**
[mod. Latin *septiformis* or French *septiforme*, formed as SEPTUM: see -FORM.]
Of the form or nature of a septum.

septifragal /sɛpˈtɪfrəg(ə)l/ *adjective.* **E19.**
[from SEPTUM + -I- + Latin *frag-* base of *frangere* to break + -AL[1].]
BOTANY. Of the dehiscence of a fruit: in which the septa separate from the valves.
■ **septifragally** *adverb* **L19.**

septillion /sɛpˈtɪljən/ *noun.* **L17.**
[French, formed as SEPTI- after *million*, *billion*, etc.]
The seventh power of a million (10^{42}); (orig. *US*) the eighth power of a thousand (10^{24}).

septimal /ˈsɛptɪm(ə)l/ *adjective.* **M19.**
[from Latin *septimus* seventh + -AL[1], after *decimal*.]
Of the number 7; MUSIC pertaining to a seventh.

septime /ˈsɛptɪm/ *noun.* **M18.**
[Latin *septimus* ordinal of *septem* seven.]
1 MUSIC. An octave. Also, a seventh. *rare.* **M18.**
2 FENCING. The seventh of eight recognized parrying positions, defending the lower inside of the body, with the sword-hand to the left in supination and the tip of the blade pointing at the opponent's knee; a thrust in this position. **L19.**

septimole /ˈsɛptɪməʊl/ *noun.* **M19.**
[Arbitrary formation from SEPTI-.]
MUSIC. = SEPTUPLET 1.

Septinsular /sɛpˈtɪnsjʊlə/ *adjective & noun.* **E19.**
[from SEPTI- + Latin *insula* island + -AR[1].]
Hist. ▶**A** *adjective.* Designating or pertaining to the Ionian Islands. **E19.**
▶ **B** *noun.* A native or inhabitant of the Ionian Islands. **L19.**

†**septleva** *noun.* **E–M18.**
[Contr. of French *sept-et-le-va* = seven and the first stake.]
In the card-game of basset, a bid to leave a won stake in place and bet it on the turn of another card of the same rank for a sevenfold win.

†**septon** *noun.* **L18–M19.**
[Greek *sēpton* neut. of *sēptos* verbal adjective from *sēpein* make rotten.]
MEDICINE. Nitrogen (formerly regarded as the agent in putrefaction).

septoria /sɛpˈtɔːrɪə/ *noun.* **L19.**
[mod. Latin *Septoria* (see below), from Latin SEPTUM.]
Any of numerous parasitic fungi constituting the genus *Septoria*, which includes forms having spores borne in dark pycnidia; a leaf spot disease caused by such a fungus.

septostomy /sɛpˈtɒstəmi/ *noun.* **M20.**
[from SEPTUM + -O- + -STOMY.]
MEDICINE. Surgical creation of a hole through a septum, esp. that between the atria of the heart; an instance of this.
■ Also **septotomy** *noun* **M20.**

septuagenarian /ˌsɛptjʊədʒɪˈnɛːrɪən/ *adjective & noun.* **E18.**
[from Latin *septuagenarius*, from *septuageni* distrib. of *septuaginta* seventy: see -ARIAN.]
▶ **A** *adjective.* **1** Pertaining to the number seventy. *rare.* **E18.**
2 Between 70 and 79 years of age; of or pertaining to a septuagenarian or septuagenarians. **L18.**
▶ **B** *noun.* A person between 70 and 79 years of age. **E19.**

septuagenary /ˌsɛptjʊəˈdʒiːn(ə)ri/ *adjective & noun.* Now *rare.* E17.
[formed as prec.: see -ARY[1].]
▶ **A** *adjective.* = SEPTUAGENARIAN *adjective* 2. E17.
▶ **B** *noun.* = SEPTUAGENARIAN *noun.* E19.

Septuagesima /ˌsɛptjʊəˈdʒɛsɪmə/ *noun.* LME.
[Latin *septuagesima* (sc. *dies*) fem. of *septuagesimus* seventieth, from *septuaginta* seventy.]
ECCLESIASTICAL. **1** In full ***Septuagesima Sunday***. The third Sunday before Lent. LME.
†**2** The seventy days beginning with the third Sunday before Lent and ending with the Saturday after Easter. LME–L15.
■ †**septuagesimal** *adjective* (*rare*) of or pertaining to Septuagesima Sunday; of or pertaining to the number seventy: M17–L18.

Septuagint /ˈsɛptjʊədʒɪnt/ *noun.* M16.
[Latin *septuaginta* seventy.]
†**1** *sing.* & in *pl.* The translators of the Old Testament into Greek (see sense 2). M16–L17.
2 The most influential Greek version of the Old Testament, differing from the Hebrew version in containing the books known as the Apocrypha, and formerly believed to have been made by seventy-two translators. (Symbol LXX.) M17.
3 A group of seventy. M19.
■ **Septuaˈgintal** *adjective* M18.

†**septuary** *adjective. rare.* E17–E18.
[Irreg. from Latin *septem* seven + -ARY[1], by assoc. with *septuaginta* SEPTUAGINT.]
1 Consisting of seven; septenary. Only in E17.
2 Of seven days. Only in E18.

septum /ˈsɛptəm/ *noun.* Pl. **septa** /-tə/. M17.
[Latin (also *saeptum*), from *sepire*, *saepire* enclose, from *sepes*, *saepes* hedge.]
1 *gen.* A partition; a dividing wall, layer, membrane, etc., esp. in a living organism. Formerly also, a communion rail. M17.
2 *spec.* in ANATOMY. A thin layer of tissue forming a partition in a cavity, organ, etc.; *esp.* (**a**) the partition between the nostrils; (**b**) each of the muscular membranes separating the chambers of the heart. L17.
3 GEOLOGY. A thin sheet of material filling a crack, esp. in a septarian nodule. E18.
4 ELECTRONICS. A metal plate placed transversely across a waveguide and attached to the walls by conducting joints. M20.

septuor /ˈsɛptjʊɔː/ *noun.* M19.
[French, from Latin *septem* seven. Cf. SEXTUOR.]
= SEPTET 1.

septuple /ˈsɛptjʊp(ə)l, sɛpˈtjuːp(ə)l/ *verb, noun, & adjective.* E17.
[from late Latin *septuplus*, from Latin *septem* seven, after *quadruplus* QUADRUPLE *noun & adjective*.]
▶ **A** *verb trans.* Multiply by seven. E17.
▶ **B** *noun.* A sevenfold number or amount. L17.
▶ **C** *adjective.* Consisting of seven parts or things; seven times as many or as much, sevenfold; MUSIC (of time) having seven beats in a bar. M19.

septuplet /ˈsɛptjʊplɛt/ *noun.* L19.
[formed as prec. + -ET[1], after *triplet*, etc.]
1 MUSIC. A group of seven notes to be played in the time of four or six. L19.
2 Each of seven children born at one birth. L19.

sepulcher *noun & verb* see SEPULCHRE.

sepulchral /sɪˈpʌlkr(ə)l/ *adjective.* E17.
[French *sépulchral* or Latin *sepulchralis*, from *sepulc(h)rum*: see SEPULCHRE, -AL[1].]
1 Of or pertaining to burial or funeral rites and customs; of or pertaining to a sepulchre; serving as a sepulchre, forming part of a sepulchre. E17.
2 Resembling or appropriate to a sepulchre; dismal, gloomy, melancholy. E18.

> 🕮 **1** T. GRAY A sepulchral marble at the villa Giustiniani. **2** K. AMIS Trying to sound serious and yet not sepulchral.

■ **sepulchrally** *adverb* E19.

Sepulchran /sɪˈpʌlkrən/ *adjective.* M19.
[from next + -AN.]
CHRISTIAN CHURCH. Of or pertaining to the Sepulchrine order.

sepulchre /ˈsɛp(ə)lkə/ *noun & verb.* Also ***-cher**. ME.
[Old & mod. French *sépulchre* from Latin *sepulc(h)rum*, from *sepult-* pa. ppl stem of *sepelire* bury.]
▶ **A** *noun.* **1** A tomb, a burial place, *esp.* one cut into rock or built in stone, a burial vault or cave. ME.
2 ANTIQUITIES. A permanent or temporary structure in a church for receiving the reserved sacrament on Maundy Thursday or Good Friday. LME.
3 = SEPULTURE *noun* 1. *rare.* LME.

> 🕮 **1** J. DAVIES On Pilgrimage to Mecca, to Mahomet's Sepulchre. *fig.*: SHELLEY I will . . make his youth The sepulchre of hope. **the Holy Sepulchre** (**a**) the tomb in which the body of Jesus was laid after being taken down from the Cross; the church in Jerusalem erected over the traditional site of this; (**b**) ***Knight of the Holy Sepulchre*** (*Hist.*), a member of a secular confraternity, later a religious order, composed of those knighted during the Crusades, esp. at the Holy Sepulchre itself. **whited sepulchre** *fig.* (with ref. to *Matthew* 23:27) a hypocrite, an ostensibly virtuous or pleasant person who is inwardly corrupt.

▶ **B** *verb trans.* **1** Place in or as in a sepulchre; bury. L16.
2 Receive (a person, a person's body) as in a sepulchre, serve as a tomb for. E17.

> 🕮 **1** J. A. BAKER It will be sepulchred in the ice. **2** BYRON When ocean shrouds and sepulchres our dead.

Sepulchrine /sɪˈpʌlkrʌɪn/ *noun & adjective.* M18.
[from SEPULCHRE *noun* + -INE[3].]
CHRISTIAN CHURCH. (A member) of the religious order of Canonesses Regular of the Holy Sepulchre. Cf. SEPULCHRAN.

sepulture /ˈsɛp(ə)ltʃə/ *noun & verb.* ME.
[Old & mod. French *sépulture* from Latin *sepultura*, from *sepult-*: see SEPULCHRE, -URE.]
▶ **A** *noun.* **1** Interment; (a) burial. Chiefly *literary.* ME.
2 A sepulchre. *arch.* LME.
†**3** = SEPULCHRE *noun* 2. LME–M16.
▶ **B** *verb trans.* Bury, inter. L15.
■ **seˈpultural** *adjective* L18.

sepurture /ˈsɛpətjə/ *adjective. rare.* L17.
[Origin unkn.]
HERALDRY. Of wings: endorsed.

seq. *abbreviation.* Also (pl.) **seqq.**
Latin *sequens*, *sequentes*, *-tia* the following page(s) etc. (see ET ***sequens*** etc.).

sequacious /sɪˈkweɪʃəs/ *adjective.* M17.
[from Latin *sequac-* *sequax*, from *sequi* follow: see -ACIOUS.]
1 Of a person: inclined to follow another, esp. in a servile or unthinking manner; lacking independence or originality of thought. *arch.* M17.
†**2** Of a thing: easily moulded; ductile, pliable, flexible. M17–M18.
3 Of musical notes or metrical feet: following one another with consistent and ordered regularity. *rare.* L18.
4 Of reasoning, thought, etc.: logical, coherent. E19.

> 🕮 **4** N. FRYE Socrates . . orders his discussion in a sequacious argument.

■ **sequaciously** *adverb* L19. **sequaciousness** *noun* M17.

sequacity /sɪˈkwasɪti/ *noun.* E17.
[Late Latin *sequacitas*, formed as prec.: see -ACITY.]
The condition or quality of being sequacious.

sequel /ˈsiːkw(ə)l/ *noun & verb.* LME.
[Old & mod. French *séquelle* or Latin *sequel(l)a*, from *sequi* follow: see -EL[2].]
▶ **A** *noun.* †**1** A body of followers or adherents, a following; *rare* a follower, an adherent. Also (FEUDAL LAW), the children, household, etc., of a villein. LME. ▸**b** SCOTS LAW. In *pl.* Small quantities of meal (or money in lieu) given in payment by the tenants of a mill to the miller's assistants. *obsolete* exc. *Hist.* E17.
2 Descendants collectively, posterity; successors in inheritance. Long *rare.* LME.
3 A thing which follows as a result of an event or course of action; a direct consequence. Now *rare* or *obsolete* exc. as passing into sense 4. LME. ▸†**b** The outcome of a process of logical reasoning; an inference. M16–M17. ▸**c** MEDICINE. = SEQUELA 1. L19.
4 What happened or will happen afterwards; the ensuing course of affairs, a subsequent train of events; an outcome, an upshot. E16. ▸†**b** The remaining period of a longer period of time. L16–E17. ▸**c** An age or period as following and influenced by an earlier one. M19.
5 The ensuing or remaining part of a narrative, discourse, etc.; *esp.* a book, film, etc., that, although complete in itself, takes up and develops the story of a preceding one. E16.
†**6** Sequence, order of succession; a number of things in succession, a series. L16–L18.

> 🕮 **3** J. A. FROUDE Every phenomenon . . was the sequel of a natural cause. **b** R. LOVELACE 'Tis a false sequel . . to suppose That, 'cause it is now ill, 'twill ere be so. **4** *Guardian* We did get about 2,000 votes more than we expected. It was the sequel that was bizarre. *Independent* This fairy-tale debut has had an increasingly unhappy sequel. **in the sequel** as things developed subsequently. **5** G. K. WOLFE Arthur C. Clarke's *2010: Odyssey Two* . . is . . a sequel to his *2001: A Space Odyssey*.

▶ **B** *verb trans.* Infl. **-ll-**, ***-l-**. Follow; constitute a sequel for (a book, story, film, etc.). *rare.* LME.

sequela /sɪˈkwiːlə/ *noun.* Pl. **-lae** /-liː/. L18.
[Latin: see prec.]
1 MEDICINE. A disease or condition occurring as the result of a previous disease or accident. Usu. in *pl.* L18.
2 A consequence, a result. L19.

> 🕮 **2** A. STORR Congestion . . seems to be an inevitable sequela of urbanization.

sequenator /ˈsiːkw(ə)neɪtə/ *noun.* M20.
[Irreg. from SEQUENCE *verb* + -ATOR.]
BIOCHEMISTRY. = SEQUENCER *noun*[2] 2.

sequence /ˈsiːkw(ə)ns/ *noun & verb.* LME.
[Late Latin *sequentia*, from Latin *sequent-* pres. ppl stem of *sequi* follow: see -ENCE.]
▶ **A** *noun.* **1** ECCLESIASTICAL. A liturgical chant or hymn recited or sung after the Alleluia and before the Gospel in the Eucharist. Also called ***prose***. LME.
2 The action or condition of following or succeeding; the following of one thing after another; an instance of this. L16.
3 The order in which things succeed one another. L16.
4 A continuous series of things, a succession; a set of related things arranged in a certain order. L16. ▸**b** MUSIC. The repetition of a phrase or melody at a higher or lower pitch. M18. ▸**c** MATH. An ordered set of quantities, *esp.* an infinite one. L19. ▸**d** A passage in a film consisting of several shots dealing with a single event or theme. E20.
5 CARDS. A group of three or more cards, usu. of the same suit, with consecutive values; a run. L16.
6 a A logical consequence. Formerly also, an inference, a conclusion. E17. ▸**b** A subsequent event; a result. M19.
7 The fact of following as a consequence or necessary result; continuity, consecutiveness. E19.

> 🕮 **2** A. P. STANLEY Works . . arranged in chronological sequence. **3a** R. RENDELL The sequence of events from the time he left Olson until he ran from the car park. **4** J. MOYNAHAN The poem-sequence *Look! We Have Come Through!* J. S. FOSTER An orderly sequence of operations. M. MEYER He took on a sequence of mistresses. **sequence of tenses** GRAMMAR the manner in which the tense of a subordinate verb in a sentence is determined by the tense of the principal verb according to certain rules. **6** J. YEATS Maritime commerce was the natural sequence to that along . . rivers. **7** H. ADAMS The windows of Chartres have no sequence. V. S. PRITCHETT His memory is going, his ideas . . lack sequence.

Phrases: **in sequence** one after another. ***main sequence***: see MAIN *adjective*.
Comb.: **sequence book** ECCLESIASTICAL HISTORY = SEQUENTIARY; **sequence dancing** a type of ballroom dancing in which all the couples perform the same steps and movements simultaneously; **sequence date** ARCHAEOLOGY a relative chronological date based upon comparison of series of objects from an archaeological site or sites; **sequence shot** a complete scene of a film photographed in a single shot; **sequence space** MATH. a space whose points are sequences.
▶ **B** *verb trans.* **1** Arrange in a definite order. M20.
2 Ascertain the sequence of monomers in (a polypeptide etc.). L20.

> 🕮 **1** *Camera Weekly* The selection and sequencing of images.

sequencer /ˈsiːkw(ə)nsə/ *noun*[1]. L15.
[Old French *sequencier* formed as SEQUENTIARY.]
ECCLESIASTICAL HISTORY. = SEQUENTIARY.

sequencer /ˈsiːkw(ə)nsə/ *noun*[2]. M20.
[from SEQUENCE *noun* + -ER[1].]
1 An apparatus for performing or initiating operations in the correct sequence; *spec.* one forming part of the control system of a computer. M20. ▸**b** MUSIC. A programmable electronic device that can store chosen sequences of musical notes, chords, rhythms, etc., for reproduction as desired. L20.
2 BIOCHEMISTRY. An apparatus for determining the sequence of monomers in a biological polymer. L20.

sequency /ˈsiːkw(ə)nsi/ *noun.* M17.
[formed as SEQUENCE *noun* + -ENCY.]
= SEQUENCE *noun* 7.

sequent /ˈsiːkw(ə)nt/ *adjective & noun.* M16.
[Old French, or Latin *sequent-*: see SEQUENCE *noun*, -ENT.]
▶ **A** *adjective.* **1** †**a** That one is about to say or mention; *the following.* M16–E19. ▸**b** That follows in time or order; subsequent. Now *rare.* E17.
2 Following one another in a series, successive; forming a continuous series, consecutive. L16.
3 That follows as a necessary result or logical conclusion. (Foll. by *to*, *on*.) E17.

> 🕮 **1b** R. A. PROCTOR From his sequent remarks it appears . . he had . . imperfect information. **2** SHAKES. *Oth.* The galleys have sent a dozen sequent messengers. **3** *Zoologist* The inferences drawn are not sequent on the premises.

▶ **B** *noun.* †**1** A follower, an attendant. *rare* (Shakes.). Only in L16.
†**2** An item in a sequence, esp. of playing-cards. E17–M18.
3 A thing which follows in order. M19.
4 A natural result, a necessary consequence; the consequent of an antecedent. M19.
■ **sequently** *adverb* E20.

sequential /sɪˈkwɛnʃ(ə)l/ *adjective*. E19.
[from (the same root as) SEQUENCE *noun* + -AL¹, after *consequence*, *consequential*.]
1 a MEDICINE. Following as a secondary condition; occurring as a sequel to a previous disease. E19. ▸**b** Following as a sequel *to*; (of two or more things) successive. M19. ▸**c** Resultant, consequent. L19.
2 Characterized by the regular sequence of its parts; occurring in a particular order; (esp. COMPUTING) performed or used in sequence. M19.

📖 **1c** *Howard Journal* The neglect of sequential effects has obscured . . some phenomena. **2** I. MCEWAN Different kinds of time, not simply the linear, sequential time of common sense.

Special collocations: **sequential circuit** ELECTRONICS a logic circuit whose output depends on the order or timing of the inputs. **sequential induction** BIOCHEMISTRY the formation in sequence of a group of related enzymes, consequent upon the induction of the first enzyme of the series. **sequential scanning** the usual method of scanning a television image, in which each line is traversed in the same direction with a rapid blanked fly-back after each.
■ **sequentially** *adverb* M17. **sequentiality** /-ʃɪˈalɪti/ *noun* L19.

sequentiary /sɪˈkwɛnʃ(ə)ri/ *noun*. E16.
[Late Latin *sequentiarius*, formed as SEQUENCE *noun*: see -ARY¹.]
ECCLESIASTICAL HISTORY. A book containing sequences (SEQUENCE *noun* 1).

†**sequester** *noun*. M16.
[Old & mod. French *séquestre* from medieval Latin *sequestrum* sequestration, thing sequestrated, from *sequester*: see next.]
1 An office or court to which goods seized by an act of sequestration were taken. Only in M16.
2 Seclusion, isolation. *rare* (Shakes.). Only in E17.
3 MEDICINE. = SEQUESTRUM. *rare*. Only in M19.

sequester /sɪˈkwɛstə/ *verb*. LME.
[Old & mod. French *séquestrer* or late Latin *sequestrare* place in safe keeping, from *sequester* trustee.]
†**1** *verb trans.* **a** Separate and reject; eliminate; exclude; dismiss from consideration. LME–M17. ▸**b** Orig., remove from membership of the Church, excommunicate. Later, remove from a public or official position. (Foll. by *from*.) LME–E19.
2 *verb trans.* **a** Separate from general access, isolate; make secluded; keep apart from society. (Foll. by *from*.) Now chiefly *US* and as ***sequestered*** *ppl adjective*. LME. ▸†**b** Set apart for a religious purpose, consecrate. M16–L17.
3 *verb trans.* LAW. ▸**a** = SEQUESTRATE *verb* 2b. LME. ▸†**b** = SEQUESTRATE *verb* 2c. E–M17. ▸**c** Sequestrate the property or benefice of (a person, esp. (ECCLESIASTICAL HISTORY) a minister). M17.
4 *verb trans.* Confiscate, take forcible possession of, (goods, an estate, etc.). E16.
†**5** *verb intrans.* Withdraw into seclusion, keep oneself apart. E17–M19.
6 *verb trans.* CHEMISTRY. Form a stable complex, esp. a chelate, with (an ion) so as to make it unreactive or remove it from solution; form a stable complex with (a biochemical molecule). M20.

📖 **1b** D. HUME Strafford was sequestered from parliament. **2** A. COHEN Drawing-rooms sequestered from the public's gaze. *refl.*: *Time* She sequestered herself in her house . . to study. **4** *Times Lit. Suppl.* A banker . . whose family and fortune were sequestered by the Nazis.

■ **sequesterment** *noun* (*rare*) a private, secluded condition or situation L18. †**sequestrable** *adjective* (*rare*) able to be sequestered, liable to sequestration M17–E19. †**sequestree** *noun* (*rare*) = SEQUESTRATOR E17–M19.

sequestra *noun* pl. of SEQUESTRUM.

sequestrant /sɪˈkwɛstr(ə)nt/ *noun & adjective*. M20.
[Late Latin *sequestrant-* pres. ppl stem of *sequestrare* SEQUESTER *verb*: see -ANT¹.]
CHEMISTRY. (That acts as) a sequestering agent.

†**sequestrate** *adjective*. L15.
[formed as next: see -ATE².]
1 Separated, cut off, (*from*). L15–M17.
2 Secluded. M17–E19.

sequestrate /sɪˈkwɛstreɪt, ˈsiːkwɛs-/ *verb*. LME.
[Late Latin *sequestrat-* pa. ppl stem of *sequestrare* SEQUESTER *verb*: see -ATE³.]
1 *verb trans.* = SEQUESTER *verb* 2a. Now *rare*. LME.
2 *verb trans.* LAW. ▸†**a** = SEQUESTER *verb* 3c. M16–M17. ▸**b** Temporarily remove (property etc.) from the possession of its owner, esp. until a court order is complied with or creditors' claims are satisfied; ECCLESIASTICAL apply (the income of a benefice) to clearing an incumbent's debts or to accumulating funds for the next incumbent. E17. ▸†**c** Remove (disputed property) from the possession of contending parties in a suit, until a third party has been referred to as arbitrator. M17–M18. ▸**d** Orig., place (a person's lands, property, etc.) under a judicial trustee so that the income may be used for the benefit of creditors, usu. while ownership is the subject of a legal action. Now, place (the property of a bankrupt) in the hands of a trustee for division among the creditors; make (a person) bankrupt. *Scot.* E18.
3 *verb trans.* = SEQUESTER *verb* 4. M17.
†**4** *verb intrans.* Perform an act of sequestration. *rare*. L18–E19.
5 PHYSIOLOGY. Make (a biochemical compound) metabolically unavailable without destroying it; effectively remove from the body's circulation. M20.

sequestration /siːkwɛˈstreɪʃ(ə)n/ *noun*. LME.
[Old & mod. French *séquestration* or late Latin *sequestratio(n-)*, formed as prec.: see -ATION.]
1 a The action or an act of isolating or banishing someone; *spec.* (ECCLESIASTICAL), removal from membership of the Church, excommunication. Now *rare*. LME. ▸†**b** Consecration. *rare*. M–L17.
2 LAW. **a** The action or process of sequestrating property. LME. ▸**b** A court order for the administration of the estate of a deceased person whose executors have renounced probate. Also, a writ giving authority for the seizure of a person's property. L16.
3 A sequestered state; seclusion, isolation. M16.
4 Confiscation, seizure. M17.
5 CHEMISTRY. The process or state of being sequestered. M20.

📖 **3** SHAKES. *Hen. V* Sequestration from open haunts and popularity.

sequestrator /ˈsiːkwɛstreɪtə/ *noun*. M17.
[Anglo-Latin = collector, receiver, formed as SEQUESTRATE *verb* + -OR.]
LAW. A person who sequestrates something; *esp.* one with judicial authority for sequestrating property or funds.

Sequestrene /sɪˈkwɛstriːn/ *noun*. M20.
[from SEQUESTR(ATION + -ENE.]
(Proprietary name for) a preparation of EDTA (ethylenediamine tetra-acetic acid) or its salts used as a sequestering agent; *spec.* one containing sequestered iron for use on iron-deficient soils.

sequestrum /sɪˈkwɛstrəm/ *noun*. Pl. **-stra** /-strə/. M19.
[medieval Latin: see SEQUESTER *noun*.]
MEDICINE. A piece of dead bone in a sheath of live bone, formed by necrosis and occurring esp. in cases of osteomyelitis. Also, a portion of skin separated by disease from the surrounding parts.
■ **sequestral** *adjective* L19. **sequestrectomy** /-ˈstrɛktəmi/ *noun* (an instance of) surgical removal of a sequestrum or sequestra M20.

sequin /ˈsiːkwɪn/ *noun & verb*. In sense A.1 also (earlier) **chequeen** /tʃɪˈkiːn/, †**chequin**. L16.
[French from Italian *zecchino*, from *zecca* mint, from Arab. *sikka* a die for coining, a coin. Cf. ZECCHIN.]
▶ **A** *noun*. **1** *Hist.* Any of various Italian and Turkish gold coins. L16.
2 A small shiny usu. circular piece of material for attaching to garments as a decoration. L19.

📖 **2** L. LOCHHEAD Sewing sequins On your carnival costume.

▶ **B** *verb trans.* Infl. **-n(n)-**. Decorate with sequins. Chiefly as ***sequinned*** *ppl adjective*. L19.

📖 *fig.*: E. SITWELL The sea, metallic-bright And sequined with the noisy light.

sequitur /ˈsɛkwɪtə/ *noun*. M19.
[Latin = it follows.]
An inference or conclusion which follows logically from the premisses; a logical deduction, a logical remark. Cf. earlier NON SEQUITUR.

📖 *Daily Telegraph* Food-writer . . and (not necessarily a *sequitur*) enthusiastic food eater.

sequoia /sɪˈkwɔɪə/ *noun*. M19.
[mod. Latin (see below), from *Sequoya* (Cherokee *Si:kwa:yi*) (c 1770–1843), a Cherokee Indian, inventor of the Cherokee syllabary.]
Either of two giant Californian coniferous trees, the redwood, *Sequoia sempervirens*, and (more fully ***giant sequoia***) the related wellingtonia, *Sequoiadendron giganteum*.

ser *noun* var. of SEER *noun*².

sera *noun* pl. of SERUM.

serab /sɛˈrɑːb/ *noun*. E19.
[Arab. (whence also Persian) *sarāb*.]
A mirage.

sérac /ˈsɛrak, səˈrak/ *noun*. M19.
[Swiss French *sérac*, orig. the name of a compact white cheese, prob. from Latin *serum* whey.]
A pinnacle or ridge of ice on the surface of a glacier where crevasses intersect.

seraglio /sɛˈrɑːlɪəʊ, sɪ-/ *noun*. Pl. **-os**. L16.
[Italian *serraglio*, formed as next with assim. to Italian *serraglio* cage (from medieval Latin *serraculum* dim. of Latin *sera* bolt).]
1 A harem, *esp.* one in a palace. L16. ▸**b** The women of a harem. M17. ▸†**c** *gen.* An enclosure; a place of confinement. M–L17.
2 *Hist.* A Turkish palace, *esp.* that of the Sultan in Istanbul. L16.
†**3 a** = SERAI *noun*¹ 1. E–M17. ▸**b** A store, a warehouse. E17–E18.
†**4** (A barracks for) a corps of Turkish soldiers. E–M17.

serai /səˈrʌɪ/ *noun*¹. E17.
[Turkish *saray* palace, mansion from Persian: cf. prec.]
1 In various SW Asian countries: a building for the accommodation of travellers, a caravanserai. E17.
2 *Hist.* = SERAGLIO 2. E17.

serai *noun*² see SURAI.

serail /səˈreɪl/ *noun*. Now *rare* or *obsolete*. L16.
[French *sérail* formed as SERAGLIO.]
1 = SERAGLIO 1. L16.
†**2** = SERAGLIO 2. L16–L18.

seral /ˈsɪər(ə)l/ *adjective*. E20.
[from SERE *noun*² + -AL¹.]
ECOLOGY. Of or pertaining to a sere; being a member of a sere other than its climax.

seralbumin /sɪəˈralbjʊmɪn/ *noun*. Also **-en** /-ɛn/. M19.
[from SER(UM + ALBUMEN.]
BIOCHEMISTRY. The albumin of blood serum.

serang /səˈraŋ/ *noun*. Orig. *Anglo-Indian*. Also **sar-**. L18.
[Persian & Urdu *sar-hang* commander, from *sar* head + *hang* authority.]
1 A headman among Lascars, *esp.* a boatswain. L18.
2 More fully ***head serang***. A person in authority, a person in charge. *Austral. slang*. E20.

serape /sɛˈrɑːpeɪ, *foreign* seˈrape/ *noun*. Also **sa-** /sa-/, **za-** /za-/. E19.
[Mexican Spanish.]
A shawl or blanket worn as a cloak by Spanish-Americans.

seraph /ˈsɛrəf/ *noun*. Pl. **SERAPHIM**, **seraphs**. OE.
[Back-form. from SERAPHIM after *cherubim*, *cherub*.]
1 In Christian theology, a member of the first and highest order of the ninefold celestial hierarchy, ranking directly above the cherubim, and gifted with love and associated with light, ardour, and purity (usu. in *pl.*). Also, a conventional representation of such a being, esp. as a human face or figure with six wings (cf. *Isaiah* 6:2). OE.
2 *transf.* A person distinguished for seraphic qualities. M19.
¶ As *seraph* or *seraphs*, rare before M17.

seraphic /səˈrafɪk/ *adjective & noun*. M17.
[medieval Latin *seraphicus*, formed as next: see -IC.]
▶ **A** *adjective*. Of or pertaining to the seraphim; resembling (that of) a seraph, esp. in beauty, purity, serene bliss, or fervent devotion; beatific, angelic. M17.
the Seraphic Doctor: St Bonaventura; in Spain freq., St Teresa of Avila. **the Seraphic Father**: St Francis of Assisi.
▶ **B** *noun*. †**1** A Franciscan friar; *transf.* a zealot. M–L17.
2 In *pl.* Rapturous moods or discourses. Now *rare* or *obsolete*. E18.
■ †**seraphical** *adjective* = SERAPHIC *adjective* M16–M18. **seˈraphically** *adverb* L17. **seraphicness** *noun* (*rare*) E18.

seraphim /ˈsɛrəfɪm/ *noun*. Also (*arch.*) **-phin** /-fɪn/. OE.
[Late Latin *seraphim*, *-in* (= Greek *seraphim*, *-pheim*) from Hebrew *śərāpīm*.]
▶ **I** *pl.* **1** Pl. of SERAPH. OE.
▶ **II** *sing.* Pl. same, (now *rare*) **-s**.
2 = SERAPH 1. LME.
3 a A fossil eurypterid, *esp.* one of the genus *Pterygotus*. Now *rare* or *obsolete*. M19. ▸**b** Either of two geometrid moths, *Lobophora halterata* and (in full ***small seraphim***) *Pterapherapteryx sexalisata*, which appear to have an extra wing-lobe. Also ***seraphim moth***. M19.

seraphin /ˈsɛrəfɪn/ *noun*¹. *obsolete* exc. *Hist.* L16.
[Portuguese *xerafim*, *xarafim*, from Arab. *šarīfī*, orig. a gold coin.]
A silver coin formerly in use in India.

seraphin *noun*² see SERAPHIM.

seraphine /ˈsɛrəfiːn/ *noun*. M19.
[from SERAPH + -INE⁴.]
MUSIC (now chiefly *Hist.*). A kind of small reed organ or harmonium.

†**serapias** *noun*. L16–L18.
[Latin, from *Serapis*, an Egyptian god.]
(The dried medicinal roots of) any of various orchids.

seraskier /sɛrəˈskɪə/ *noun*. L17.
[Turkish *serasker*, *sar-* from Persian *sar'askar*, from *sar* head + Arab. *'askar* army from Latin *exercitus*.]
Hist. The commander-in-chief and minister of war of the Ottoman Empire.

Serax /ˈsɛraks/ *noun*. M20.
[Origin unkn.]
PHARMACOLOGY. The drug oxazepam.
¶ Proprietary name in the US and Canada.

seraya /sɛˈrʌɪə/ *noun*. **L19.**
[Malay.]
(The timber of) any of various SE Asian forest trees of the genus *Shorea* (more fully ***red seraya***) and *Parashorea* (more fully ***white seraya***), both of the family Dipterocarpaceae.

Serb /səːb/ *noun & adjective*. **E19.**
[Serbo-Croat *Srb*.]
▶ **A** *noun*. †**1** = SORB *noun*[2] 1. Only in **E19.**
2 A native of Serbia, a person of Serbian descent. **M19.**
3 The Serbo-Croat dialect used by Serbs. **L19.**
▶ **B** *adjective*. Serbian. **L19.**
📖 *Economist* Winning control of Serb enclaves in Croatia is one task.

Serbian /ˈsəːbɪən/ *noun & adjective*. **M19.**
[from prec. + -IAN.]
▶ **A** *noun*. **1** = SERB *noun* 2. **M19.**
2 The language of the Serbs, a form of Serbo-Croat written in the Cyrillic alphabet. **M19.**
▶ **B** *adjective*. Of, pertaining to, or belonging to Serbia, one of the Balkan States, or its inhabitants or their language. **L19.**
¶ Cf. SERVIAN *noun & adjective*[1].

Serbo- /ˈsəːbəʊ/ *combining form* of SERB, SERBIAN: see -O-.
■ **Serbo-ˈCroat** *adjective & noun* (designating or pertaining to) a S. Slavonic language spoken in Serbia, Croatia, and other Balkan States, and having two main forms, Serbian and Croatian **E20.** **Serbo-Croˈatian** *adjective & noun* = SERBO-CROAT **L19.**

Serbonian /səːˈbəʊnɪən/ *adjective*. *literary*. **M17.**
[from Greek *Serbōnis* (*limnē*) a marshy region in Lower Egypt: see -IAN.]
Serbonian bog, a great marsh which swallows up everything; chiefly *fig.* with allus. to Milton.
📖 MILTON A gulf profound as that Serbonian Bog . . where Armies whole have sunk.

SERC *abbreviation*.
Science and Engineering Research Council.

Sercial /ˈsəːsɪəl/ *noun*. Also **s-**. **E19.**
[Portuguese.]
A particular variety of wine-making grape grown esp. in Madeira; (a drink of) dry light Madeira made from this.

serdab /səːˈdɑːb/ *noun*. **M19.**
[Arab. *sirdāb* cellar, underground vault or directly from Persian *sardāb* grotto, cellar for ice, from *sard* cold + *āb* water.]
1 In the Middle East: a cellar, an underground chamber. **M19.**
2 EGYPTOLOGY. A secret passage or chamber in an ancient tomb. **L19.**

sere /sɪə/ *noun*[1]. In sense 1 also **sear**. **M16.**
[Old & mod. French *serre* †grasp, †lock, †bolt, talon, from *serrer* grasp, hold fast, from Proto-Romance var. of late Latin *serare* to bar, bolt, from *sera* bar for a door.]
1 A catch of a gunlock which engages with the notches of the tumbler in order to keep the hammer at full or half cock, and which is released by pressure on the trigger. **M16.**
2 A claw, a talon. Long *arch.* **E17.**

sere /sɪə/ *noun*[2]. **E20.**
[from Latin *serere* join in a series.]
ECOLOGY. A series of plant (or occas., animal) communities, each naturally succeeding the previous one. Also as 2nd elem. of comb.
hydrosere, ***lithosere***, etc.

†**sere** *noun*[3] var. of CERE *noun*.

sere /sɪə/ *adjective*. Now *poet.* or *literary*. Also **sear**.
[Old English *sēar* = Middle Low German *sōr* (Low German *soor*, Dutch *zoor*) from Germanic (of the Low German area, but cf. Old High German *sōrēn* become dry).]
1 Dried up, withered (esp. from old age). **OE.**
2 Of fabric: thin, worn. *obsolete* exc. *dial.* **E16.**
📖 **1** SHAKES. *Macb.* My way of life Is fall'n into the sear, the yellow leaf. *absol.*: T. HARDY What earthly woman . . would care for a belated friendship with him now in the sere.

sere *verb* var. of SEAR *verb*.

serein /sərɛ̃/ *noun*. **L19.**
[Old & mod. French from Proto-Gallo-Romance, from Latin *serum* evening, use as noun of *serus* late.]
METEOROLOGY. A fine rain (apparently) falling from a cloudless sky. Cf. SERENE *noun*[1].

†**serena** *noun* see SERENE *noun*[1].

serenade /sɛrəˈneɪd/ *noun & verb*. **M17.**
[French *sérénade* from Italian SERENATA.]
▶ **A** *noun*. **1** A piece of music sung or played in the open air, esp. by a lover at night under the window of his beloved. **M17.**
2 MUSIC. Orig., a piece of music suitable or specially composed for performance in the open air. Now usu., a suite of diverse pieces for an instrumental ensemble, with or without voices. Also = SERENATA 1. **E18.**
▶ **B** *verb*. **1** *verb intrans.* Perform a serenade. **M17.**
2 *verb trans.* Entertain with a serenade. **L17.**
📖 **2** J. BARTH We were serenaded by banjo and fiddle. *Scots Magazine* She serenaded the company after dinner.
■ **serenader** *noun* **L17.**

serenata /sɛrəˈnɑːtə/ *noun*. **M18.**
[Italian, from *sereno* SERENE *adjective*, infl. by *sera* evening.]
MUSIC. **1** A kind of elaborate cantata with a pastoral or mythological theme, composed esp. during the 17th and 18th cents. for performance at court or on special occasions. **M18.**
2 = SERENADE *noun* 2. **L19.**

serendipitous /sɛr(ə)nˈdɪpɪtəs/ *adjective*. **M20.**
[from next: see -OUS.]
1 Of people: having a supposed talent for making happy and unexpected discoveries by accident. **M20.**
2 Of an event, discovery, meeting, etc.: occurring by (esp. fortunate) chance; fortuitous. **M20.**
■ **serendipitously** *adverb* **M20.**

serendipity /sɛr(ə)nˈdɪpɪti/ *noun*. **M18.**
[from *Serendip*, *-dib*, said to be a former name of Sri Lanka + -ITY; formed by Horace Walpole after the title of a fairy tale, *Three Princes of Sarendip*, the heroes of which 'were always making discoveries, by accidents and sagacity, of things they were not in quest of'.]
(A supposed talent for) the making of happy and unexpected discoveries by accident or when looking for something else; such a discovery. Also *loosely*, good luck, good fortune.
¶ Rare before **20.**
■ **serendipitist** *noun* (*rare*) a serendipitous person **M20.**

†**serene** *noun*[1]. Also (*rare*) **serena**. **L16–E18.**
[formed as SEREIN: cf. Italian *serena*.]
A dew or mist, formerly regarded as an unhealthy fall of moisture, appearing after sunset in hot countries. Cf. SEREIN.

serene /sɪˈriːn, sə-/ *adjective & noun*[2]. **LME.**
[Latin *serenus* clear, fair, calm (of weather etc.).]
▶ **A** *adjective*. **1** Of the weather, the air, the sky: clear, fine, and calm (without cloud or rain or wind). **LME.**
2 An honorific epithet given to a reigning prince (formerly esp. of Germany), member of a royal house, etc.; *joc.* of or pertaining to a person so designated. Now only in ***Serene Highness*** below. Cf. SERENITY 1. **E16.**
3 (Of a place, a period of time, a person's demeanour, etc.) calm, tranquil, untroubled, unperturbed; *poet.* (of light) clear and pure; expressive or suggestive of tranquillity. **M17.**
📖 **2 Serene Highness** (with possess. adjective, as ***Her Serene Highness*** etc.) a title used in addressing or referring to members of some European royal families. **3** POPE The moon, serene in glory, mounts the sky. J. RUSKIN The magnificent and serene constructions of the early Gothic. HENRY MILLER His face beaming with a quiet serene joy.

Phrases: **all serene** *slang* all's well; all right. **drop serene** [translating mod. Latin ***gutta serena*** S.V. GUTTA *noun*[1]] (*rare*, only with allusion to Milton) = AMAUROSIS.
▶ **B** *noun*. Chiefly *poet.* (now *rare*).
†**1** A condition of fine quiet weather. **M17–L18.**
2 An expanse of clear sky or calm sea. **M18.**
3 Serenity, tranquillity (of mind, conditions, etc.). **M18.**
4 Calm brightness, quiet radiance. **E19.**
■ **serenely** *adverb* **E17.** **sereneness** *noun* **E17.**

serene /sɪˈriːn, sə-/ *verb trans.* Now *rare* or *obsolete*. **E17.**
[Latin *serenare*, formed as prec.]
1 Make (esp. the sky, the air) clear, bright, and calm. **E17.**
2 Make (a person) calm and tranquil; make (a person's expression) calm, unruffled, or cheerful. **M17.**

serenise *verb* var. of SERENIZE.

Serenissima /sereˈnissima, sɛrəˈnɪsɪmə/ *noun*. **E20.**
[Italian, fem. of *serenissimo* most serene.]
La Serenissima /la/, ***The Serenissima***, Venice; the former Venetian Republic.

serenity /sɪˈrɛnɪti/ *noun*. **LME.**
[Old & mod. French *sérénité* or Latin *serenitas*, formed as SERENE *adjective & noun*[2]: see -ITY.]
1 An honorific title given to some reigning princes and other dignitaries. **LME.**
2 Clear, fair and calm weather; clearness and stillness of air and sky. **LME.**
3 Contented tranquillity of mind, temper, countenance, etc.; inner calm; tranquillity or peacefulness of conditions etc. **L16.**

serenize /ˈsɛrɪnʌɪz, sɪˈriːnʌɪz/ *verb trans. rare*. Also **-ise**. **L16.**
[from SERENE *adjective* + -IZE.]
Make serene.

sereno /sɛˈreɪnəʊ, *foreign* seˈreno/ *noun*. Pl. **-os** /-əʊz, *foreign* -os/. **L19.**
[Spanish.]
In Spain and Spanish-speaking parts of America, a night-watchman.

Seres /ˈsɪəriːz/ *noun pl. obsolete* exc. *Hist.* **ME.**
[Latin from Greek *Sēres* (whence *sericum* SILK).]
The inhabitants of the Far Eastern countries from which silk reached Europe overland during ancient times; the Chinese and Tibetans.

serf /səːf/ *noun*. **L15.**
[Old & mod. French from Latin *servus* slave.]
†**1** A slave. Only in **L15.**
2 Chiefly *Hist.* A person in a condition of servitude or modified slavery, in which the powers of the master are more or less limited by law or custom; *spec.* a labourer not allowed to leave the land on which he works, a villein. **E17.**
■ **serfage** *noun* (**a**) serfdom; (**b**) serfs collectively: **L18.** **serfdom** *noun* the state or condition of a serf, bondage **M19.** **serfhood** *noun* (*rare*) = SERFAGE (b) **M19.** **serfish** *adjective* characteristic of a serf; of or having the (debasing) qualities of the servile condition: **L19.** **serfishness** *noun* (*rare*) **E20.** **serfship** *noun* serfdom **M19.**

serge /səːdʒ/ *noun & adjective*. Also (earlier) †**sarge**. **LME.**
[Old French *sarge* (mod. *serge*) from Proto-Romance var. of Latin *serica* (sc. *lana* wool) fem. of *sericus*: see SILK.]
▶ **A** *noun*. **1** A durable woollen fabric. Now usu. *spec.*, a hard-wearing twilled woollen or worsted fabric, used mainly for clothing. **LME.**
2 A garment, curtain, etc., made of serge. **LME.**
3 A twilled fabric of silk, cotton, etc. **M19.**
📖 **1** B. MASON Sergeant Robinson arrives, buttoned to the neck in official serge. **3** ***serge denim***: see DENIM.
▶ **B** *adjective*. Made of serge. **E17.**

sergeancy /ˈsɑːdʒ(ə)nsi/ *noun*. Also **serje-**, **-antcy**. **ME.**
[Orig. from Anglo-Norman *seargeancie* var. of *sergeantie* SERJEANTY; later from SERGEANT + -CY.]
†**1** The body of sergeants in a county; sergeants collectively. Only in **ME.**
†**2** A district governed by a sergeant. Only in **LME.**
†**3** *Hist.* = SERJEANTY 2. **E–M17.**
4 The rank or office of sergeant or serjeant; the commission of sergeant in the army. **M17.**

sergeant /ˈsɑːdʒ(ə)nt/ *noun*. Also **serje-** (see note below), (esp. in titles) **S-**. **ME.**
[Old French *sergent*, *serjent* (mod. *sergent*) from Latin *servient-* pres. ppl stem of *servire* SERVE *verb*[1]: see -ENT.]
†**1** A serving-man, an attendant, a servant. **ME–L16.**
†**2** A common soldier. **ME–L15.**
†**3** A tenant by military service below the rank of knight; *esp.* one attending a knight in the field. Only in **ME.**
4 An officer whose duty is to enforce the judgements of a tribunal or the commands of a person in authority, arrest offenders, or summon people to appear before a court. Long *obsolete* exc. *Hist.* **ME.**
5 (Now **-j-**.) LAW (now *Hist.*). More fully ***serjeant-at-law***, pl. ***serjeants-at-law***. A member of the highest rank of barristers (abolished in 1880) from which common-law judges were formerly chosen. **ME.**
6 The head, or an officer, of a specified department of the royal household. Usu. used preceding a designation of office. **LME.**
7 Any of various officials of a court, guild, city, etc., with ceremonial duties. **LME.**
8 MILITARY. An army officer. In mod. use, a non-commissioned army, air force, or marines officer usu. ranking below warrant officer (or lieutenant) and above corporal. Also used preceding a designation of office. **M16.**
9 (Now **-g-**.) A police officer, of higher rank than a constable, ranking next below an inspector in Britain and next below a captain in the US. **M19.**
6 ***sergeant-painter***, ***sergeant-surgeon***, ***sergeant-trumpet***, etc. **8** ***sergeant bugler***, ***sergeant cook***, ***sergeant drummer***, ***sergeant-pilot***, etc.
Phrases & comb.: ***Common Sergeant***: see COMMON *adjective*. ***Dashing White Sergeant***: see DASHING *ppl adjective*. FIRST ***sergeant***. **King's Serjeant**, **Queen's Serjeant** *Hist.* an honorary title given to certain serjeants-at-law, orig. supposed to have the duty of pleading in the courts on behalf of the Crown. ***orderly sergeant***: see ORDERLY *adjective*. **sergeant-at-arms**, pl. **sergeants-at-arms**, orig., an armed officer in the service of a lord, *spec.* each of a body of men of knightly rank, originally 24 in number, required to attend the monarch personally, to arrest traitors and other offenders; now, an officer of the House of Lords, House of Commons, or Lord Chamberlain's Office whose duty includes maintaining order and security; an officer with similar duties elsewhere, as in the US Senate and House of Representatives. ***sergeant-at-law***: see sense 5 above. **sergeant-at-mace**, pl. **sergeants-at-mace**, a legal officer of lesser rank who carries a mace as a badge of office. **Sergeant Baker** *Austral.* a brightly coloured fish, *Aulopus purpurissatus*, of southern Australian coasts. **sergeant-fish** any of various fishes having marks like the stripes on the sleeve of a sergeant's uniform, esp. the cobia, *Rachycentron canadum*. †**sergeant of arms**, pl. **sergeants of arms**, = sense 6 above. †**sergeant of law**, pl. **sergeants of law**, = sense 5 above. †**sergeant of the coif**, pl. **sergeants of the coif**, = sense 5 above. ***top sergeant***: see TOP *adjective*.
¶ The spelling *serjeant* is now usu. restricted to legal and ceremonial offices, exc. in historical and in certain official contexts.
■ **sergeantship** *noun* the rank or office of sergeant or serjeant **LME.**

sergeantcy *noun* var. of SERGEANCY.

sergeant-major /sɑːdʒ(ə)ntˈmeɪdʒə/ *noun & verb.* Also (now *rare*) **serje-**. L16.
[from SERGEANT + MAJOR *adjective*.]
▶ **A** *noun.* †**1** *MILITARY.* **a** A field officer, one in each regiment, who ranked below a lieutenant colonel, corresponding partly to major, partly to adjutant, in modern usage. L16–E18. ▸†**b** A general officer, corresponding to the modern major-general. Also ***sergeant-major major***, ***sergeant-major general***. L16–M17.
2 *MILITARY.* A non-commissioned officer of the highest rank. Also (in full ***regimental sergeant-major***), a warrant officer assisting the adjutant of a regiment or battalion; (in full ***company sergeant-major***), the senior warrant officer of a company. E19.
3 A distinctively striped damselfish, *Abudefduf saxatilis*, of warm seas worldwide. L19.
4 More fully ***sergeant-major's tea***, ***sergeant-major's coffee***. Strong sweet tea or (*US*) coffee with milk; tea with rum. Also ***sergeant-major's***. *Military slang.* E20.
▶ **B** *verb trans. & intrans.* Speak (to) or shout (at) in a brusque, stentorian, or commanding manner. M20.
■ **sergeant-majorish**, **sergeant-majorly** *adjectives* characteristic of or resembling a sergeant-major E20. **sergeant-majorship** *noun* the rank or office of sergeant-major L19.

†**sergeantry** *noun.* Also **serje-**. LME.
[Old French *sergenterie* (Anglo-Latin *sergenteria* etc.) formed as SERGEANT: see -ERY.]
1 = SERJEANTY 1. LME–M19.
2 The rank or office of sergeant or serjeant. LME–M17.

sergeanty *noun* var. of SERJEANTY.

serging /ˈsəːdʒɪŋ/ *noun.* E20.
[from SERGE *noun* + -ING[1].]
A method of overcasting used to prevent fabric fraying at the edge; stitching of this kind.
■ **serger** *noun* a sewing machine used for serging E20.

Seri /ˈsɛri, ˈsɛːri/ *noun & adjective.* Also (earlier) †**Ceres**, †**Ceris**, (pl. of noun same). E19.
[Amer. Indian.]
▶ **A** *noun.* Pl. same, **-s**.
1 A member of a N. American Indian people of Tiburón Island and the adjacent region of NW Mexico. E19.
2 The Hokan language of this people. E20.
▶ **B** *attrib.* or as *adjective.* Of or pertaining to the Seri or their language. E19.
■ **Serian** *noun* = SERI *noun* 2 E20.

serial /ˈsɪərɪəl/ *adjective & noun.* M19.
[from SERIES + -AL[1], perh. after French *sérial*. Cf. medieval Latin *serialis* continuous.]
▶ **A** *adjective.* **1** Belonging to, forming part of, or consisting of a series; taking place or occurring in a regular succession. M19. ▸**b** *COMPUTING.* Performed or used in sequence, sequential; *esp.* (of a device) involving the transfer of data as a single sequence of bits. Opp. ***parallel***. M20.
2 *spec.* Published in successive instalments (as in a periodical or newspaper); broadcast in episodes at regular intervals. M19.
3 *SCIENCE.* Esp. of parts of an organism: arranged in a straight line or in longitudinal succession. M19.
4 *BIOLOGY.* Involving or produced by the propagation of a micro-organism or of tissue by means of a series of cultures, each grown from material derived from the previous one. E20.
5 *EDUCATION & PSYCHOLOGY.* Pertaining to or designating the learning of words, numbers, etc., as a series so that the items can be recalled in their original order. E20.
6 *GRAMMAR.* Designating a construction consisting of a series of words, esp. verbs. M20.
7 *MUSIC.* Designating or involving a method of composition based on a fixed sequence of tones (also occas. durations, volumes, etc.), esp. the twelve tones of the chromatic scale. Cf. DODECAPHONIC *adjective*, SERIES *noun* 18. M20.
8 *attrib.* Of a criminal: repeatedly committing the same offence (and typically following a characteristic, predictable behaviour pattern). Of crime: committed by such a person. Freq. in ***serial killer*** below. M20. ▸**b** Of a person or his or her actions: repeatedly or habitually following the same behaviour pattern. Often *derog.* M20.

> 📖 **8** *Entertainment Weekly* A criminal psychiatrist . . is snared in a web of deceit with a handsome stranger . . and a serial rapist. *Icon Thoughtstyle* We profiled a white male because serial homicides are rarely interracial. **b** S. MACLEOD The institution known as serial marriage (marriage, divorce, remarriage). *Guardian* A serial espouser of every reactionary cause.

▶ **B** *noun.* **1** **a** A serial or periodical publication; *esp.* a novel or story published in serial form. M19. ▸**b** A radio or television programme, esp. a play, broadcast in episodes; a film shown in episodes. E20.
2 A military unit or group of units organized under a single commander for troop movements or for drill; any squad, esp. of police officers, formed for a special purpose. Orig. *US.* M20.
Special collocations & comb.: **serial homology** *BIOLOGY* the relationship of structural similarity between parts or organs which form a series, as leaves, vertebrae, etc. **serial killer** a person who murders repeatedly with no apparent motive. **serial monogamy** (participation in) a series of successive, often short-lived monogamous relationships. **serial number** a number assigned to a person, item, etc., indicating position in a series; *spec.* a number printed on a banknote or manufactured article by which it can be individually identified. **serial port** *COMPUTING* a connector by which a device that sends data one bit at a time may be connected to a computer. **serial rights** rights attaching to the publication of a story in serial form. **serial section** *MEDICINE & BIOLOGY* each of a series of sections through tissue made in successive parallel planes. **serial-section** *verb trans.* (*MEDICINE & BIOLOGY*) cut in serial sections. **serial symmetry** *BIOLOGY* occurrence of homologous parts in successive parts of the body; *MEDICINE* occurrence of a condition affecting such parts (e.g. the knee and the elbow) simultaneously. **serial temperatures**: taken at different successive depths between the bottom and the surface of water.
■ **seriality** /-ˈalɪti/ *noun* serial arrangement, serial nature M19. **serially** *adverb* in (a) series, in serial form or arrangement M19.

serialise *verb* var. of SERIALIZE.

serialism /ˈsɪərɪəlɪz(ə)m/ *noun.* E20.
[from SERIAL *adjective* + -ISM.]
1 A theory of the serial nature of time developed by J. W. Dunne (1875–1949) to account for the phenomenon of precognition, esp. in dreams. E20.
2 *MUSIC.* The practice or principles of serial composition. M20.

serialist /ˈsɪərɪəlɪst/ *noun & adjective.* M19.
[formed as prec. + -IST.]
▶ **A** *noun.* **1** A writer of serials. M19.
2 A person who holds views that accord with a serial theory; *spec.* an advocate or practitioner of serial learning. M20.
3 *MUSIC.* A composer or advocate of serial music. M20.
▶ **B** *attrib.* or as *adjective.* Of or pertaining to serialism or serialists; characterized by serialism. M20.

serialize /ˈsɪərɪəlʌɪz/ *verb trans.* Also **-ise**. M19.
[from SERIAL *adjective* + -IZE.]
1 Arrange in a series. M19.
2 Publish in serial form; broadcast serially; publish the work of (an author) in serial form. L19.
3 *MUSIC.* Incorporate into a serial technique of composition. M20.
■ **serializable** *adjective* able to be arranged in a series; suitable for publishing or broadcasting in serial form: L20. **seriali'zation** *noun* (*a*) the act or process of serializing something; (*b*) a serial version of a story etc.: M19.

seriate /ˈsɪərɪət/ *adjective.* M19.
[from SERIES + -ATE[2].]
Chiefly *ZOOLOGY & BOTANY.* Arranged or occurring in one or more series or rows.
■ **seriated** *adjective* = SERIATE *adjective* L19. **seriately** *adverb* in a seriate manner, in series M19.

seriate /ˈsɪərɪeɪt/ *verb trans.* M20.
[Back-form. from SERIATION: see -ATE[3].]
Arrange (items) in a sequence according to prescribed criteria.

seriatim /sɪərɪˈeɪtɪm/ *adverb & adjective.* L15.
[medieval Latin, formed as SERIES + *-atim* after Latin *gradatim*, *literatim*.]
▶ **A** *adverb.* One after another, one by one in succession. L15.
▶ **B** *adjective.* Following one after the other. *rare.* L19.

seriation /sɪərɪˈeɪʃ(ə)n/ *noun.* M17.
[from SERIES + -ATION.]
Succession in series; formation of or into a series or ordered sequence; *esp.* in *ARCHAEOLOGY*, the action or result of arranging items in a sequence according to prescribed criteria.

sericeous /sɪˈrɪʃɪəs/ *adjective.* L18.
[from Latin *sericus* silken, of the Seres: see -EOUS. Cf. medieval Latin *sericeus* silken.]
ZOOLOGY & BOTANY. Silky, covered with silky down.

sericiculture /ˈsɛrɪsɪˌkʌltʃə/ *noun.* L19.
[French: see SERICULTURE.]
= SERICULTURE.
■ **serici'cultural** *adjective* = SERICULTURAL E20. **serici'culturist** *noun* = SERICULTURIST L19.

sericin /ˈsɛrɪsɪn/ *noun.* M19.
[from Latin *sericum* silk + -IN[1].]
BIOCHEMISTRY. A gelatinous soluble protein that is a minor constituent of silk.

sericite /ˈsɛrɪsʌɪt/ *noun.* M19.
[formed as prec. + -ITE[1].]
MINERALOGY. A fibrous or scaly variety of muscovite.
■ **sericitic** /sɛrɪˈsɪtɪk/ *adjective* containing or of the nature of sericite E19. **sericiti'zation** *noun* conversion into or replacement by sericite L19. **sericitized** *adjective* converted into (a form containing) sericite M20.

sericon /ˈsɛrɪkɒn/ *noun.* Long *obsolete* exc. *Hist.* E17.
[medieval Latin, of unkn. origin.]
ALCHEMY. An unidentified substance involved in the transmutation of metals.

sericulture /ˈsɛrɪkʌltʃə/ *noun.* M19.
[Abbreviation of French *sériciculture*, from late Latin *sericum* SILK + French *culture* CULTURE *noun*.]
The production of raw silk; the rearing of silkworms for this purpose.
■ **seri'cultural** *adjective* of, pertaining to, or engaged in sericulture M19. **sericulturist** *noun* a person engaged in sericulture, a silk-grower M19.

seriema /sɛrɪˈiːmə/ *noun.* Also **cariama** /karɪˈɑːmə/, **ça-** /sa-/. M19.
[mod. Latin *seriema*, *cariama* from Tupi *siriema*, *sariama*, *çariama*, explained as 'crested'.]
Either of two large long-legged and long-necked S. American birds, the red-legged *Cariama cristata* (also called ***crested screamer***) and the black-legged *Chunga burmeisteri*, which together constitute the gruiform family Cariamidae.

series /ˈsɪəriːz/ *noun & adjective.* E17.
[Latin = row, chain, series, from *serere* join, connect.]
▶ **A** *noun.* Pl. same, †**serieses**.
▶ **I** *gen.* **1** A number or set of material things of one kind ranged in a line, either contiguously or at more or less regular intervals; a continued spatial succession of similar objects. E17.
2 **a** A number of things of one kind (freq. immaterial, as events, actions, conditions, periods of time) following one another in time or in logical order. E17. ▸**b** A number of people who successively hold the same office or have some characteristic in common. Formerly also, a succession of persons in descent, a family line. E17.
†**3** **a** Order of succession; sequence. E17–L18. ▸**b** The connected sequence (*of* discourse, writing, thought). M17–E18.
†**4** **a** A succession, sequence, or continued course (*of* action, time, life, etc.). M17–L19. ▸**b** A continued state or spell. M–L18.
5 A set of objects of the same kind which differ progressively in size or some other respect, or have a recognized order of enumeration or a constant relation between successive members. Also, a number of magnitudes, degrees of an attribute, etc., which can be formed into a progressive order or sequence. L18.

> 📖 **1** H. JAMES A row of small red-brick houses, showing a series of homely, domestic-looking backs. **2** J. B. PRIESTLEY The astonishing series of events that had taken him to Rawsley. **b** DAY LEWIS A series of Irish nursemaids of whom I remember nothing. **3a** S. JOHNSON The series of his works I am not able to deduce. **4a** R. L. STEVENSON The hours . . marked out from each other only by the series of our own affairs. **b** J. SMEATON A series of unsettled weather. **5** C. DARWIN These differences blend into each other by an insensible series.

▶ **II** *spec.* **6** *MATH.* A set of terms in ordered succession (finite or infinite in number), the value of each being determined by a specific relation to adjacent terms; a progression; the sum of such a set. L17.
7 **a** A set of coins, medals, etc., belonging to a particular period, locality, or government. Also, a set of postage stamps, banknotes, etc., of a particular issue. L17. ▸**b** A set or class of aircraft, vehicles, machines, etc., developed over a period and sharing many features of design or assembly. M20.
8 **a** A set of written compositions having certain features in common, published successively or intended to be read in sequence; a succession of volumes or fascicles (of a periodical, occasional publication, etc.) forming a separately numbered set. Also, a succession of books having some similarity of subject or purpose, issued by a publisher in a common form and usu. with an overall title. E18. ▸**b** A set of radio or television programmes concerned with the same theme or having the same cast of characters and broadcast in sequence. M20.
9 *GEOLOGY.* **a** Orig., a set of successive, usu. conformable, deposits or formations, esp. having certain common fossil or mineral features. Now *spec.* a major subdivision of a stratigraphical system, composed of a number of stages and corresponding to an epoch in time; the rocks deposited during a specific epoch. E19. ▸**b** A group of (usu. igneous) rocks having similar petrographic characteristics. M19.
10 **a** *CHEMISTRY.* A group of elements, compounds, or radicals having similar or progressively varying properties or structures; a set of elements, compounds, or radicals arranged in order of magnitude of some property. M19. ▸**b** = ***radioactive series*** s.v. RADIOACTIVE *adjective*. E20.
11 *BIOLOGY.* Orig., a group of similar, esp. structurally related, organisms. Now usu., a subgeneric taxonomic category ranked below a section; a group of species of this rank. M19.

12 A set of alloys or minerals having the same chemical composition except for the relative proportions of two elements that can replace one another. **M19.**

13 *SPORT.* A number of games played between two teams; *esp.* (*a*) *BASEBALL* a set of games played on successive days between two league teams; *spec.* = ***World Series*** s.v. **WORLD** *noun*; (*b*) (*CRICKET & RUGBY FOOTBALL* etc.) a set of test matches between two sides during a single tour. **M19.**

14 *ELECTRICITY.* A number of components each connected with the preceding, so as to form a single circuit, link, or path between two points. Chiefly in ***in series*** below. **L19.**

15 a *PHILOLOGY.* In full ***ablaut series***. A set of sounds which are mutually related by ablaut. **L19.** ▸**b** *PHONOLOGY.* A group of sounds produced in a similar manner but having a different point of articulation. **M20.**

16 *PHYSICS.* A set of lines in a spectrum whose frequencies are mathematically related, esp. corresponding to a set of transitions to or from a particular lower electronic orbital. Also ***spectral series***. **L19.**

17 More fully ***soil series***. A group of soils similar in origin, profile, and other characteristics, but varying in the texture of the surface horizon. **E20.**

18 *MUSIC.* An arrangement of notes of the chromatic scale (usu. all twelve) used as the basis for a piece of serial music; = ***tone-row*** s.v. **TONE** *noun*. **M20.**

19 *ECCLESIASTICAL.* With specifying number: each of three experimental alternative forms of service used in the Church of England between 1965 and 1980. **M20.**

📖 **6** ***arithmetical series, Fibonacci series, Fourier series, geometrical series, harmonic series, power series***, etc. **7b** *Motor Trend* Mercedes' pricey 200- and 300-series wagons. **8** G. K. WOLFE Individual stories in a series may range from short story to novel length. M. BERGMANN The paper was the first of a series written by both Freud and Abraham. **9a** ***Karoo series, Moine series***, etc. **10a** ***actinide series, electrochemical series, lanthanide series, lyotropic series, transition series***, etc. **12** C. S. HURLBUT The plagioclase feldspars . . form a complete solid-solution series from pure albite . . to pure anorthite. **16** ***Balmer series, Lyman series***, etc.

Phrases: **in series** (*a*) *adjectival phr.* (of two or more wires, components, etc.) connected each to the next in a line or sequence so as to form a single path between two points; (*b*) *adverbial phr.* so as to be in series; while in series; (foll. by *with*). ***reversion of a series, reversion of series***: see **REVERSION** 6b.

▸ **B** *attrib.* or as *adjective*. Chiefly *ELECTRICITY.* Arranged or connected in series; pertaining to or involving connection in series; *spec.* = ***series-wound*** below. **L19.**

Comb.: **series-parallel** *adjective* (*ELECTRICITY*) involving combinations of series and parallel connections; *esp.* designating or involving electric traction motors which work in series on starting and switch to parallel working when a certain speed is reached; **series-wound** *adjective* (of an electric generator or motor) having the coils on the field magnets wound so as to be in series with the outer circuit.

serif /ˈsɛrɪf/ *noun.* Also (*arch.*) **ceriph**. **M19.**
[Origin uncertain: perh. from Dutch *schreef* dash, line, from Germanic.]
TYPOGRAPHY & CALLIGRAPHY. A usu. fine cross-stroke at the end of a principal stroke of a letter. Cf. **SANS SERIF**.
square serif: see **SQUARE** *adjective*.
■ **serifed, seriffed** *adjective* having serifs **M20.**

serigala /səˈriːɡələ/ *noun.* **E20.**
[Malay from Sanskrit *sṛgāla* jackal.]
= **DHOLE**.

serigraph /ˈsɛrɪɡrɑːf/ *noun.* **L19.**
[Irreg. from Latin *sericum* silk + **-GRAPH**.]
1 An instrument for testing the uniformity of raw silk. *rare.* **L19.**
2 *ART.* An original print produced by serigraphy. **M20.**

serigraphy /sɛˈrɪɡrəfi/ *noun.* Orig. *US.* **M20.**
[formed as prec.: see **-GRAPHY**.]
ART. Silk-screen printing, esp. of original designs.
■ **serigrapher** *noun* **M20. serigraphic** /-ˈɡrafɪk/ *adjective* **M20.**

serin /ˈsɛrɪn/ *noun.* **M16.**
[French = canary, of unkn. origin.]
Orig., a canary. Now, any bird of the same genus, *Serinus*, *esp.* (more fully ***serin finch***) *Serinus serinus*, a small yellow finch of western and central Europe.

serine /ˈsɪəriːn, ˈsɛr-/ *noun.* **L19.**
[German *Serin*, from Latin *sericum* silk + *-in* **-INE**[5].]
BIOCHEMISTRY. A hydrophilic amino acid, $CH_2OH{\cdot}CHNH_2{\cdot}COOH$, which occurs in proteins; 2-amino-3-hydroxypropanoic acid.

serinette /sɛrɪˈnɛt/ *noun. rare.* **M19.**
[French, formed as **SERIN** *noun* + **-ETTE**.]
A small barrel organ used for teaching singing birds.

seringa /səˈrɪŋɡə/ *noun.* **M18.**
[French from Portuguese from Latin **SYRINGA**.]
1 = **SYRINGA**. **M18.**
2 In Brazil, the rubber tree, *Hevea brasiliensis*. **M19.**

seringueiro /serĩˈɡeru/ *noun.* Pl. **-os**. **M19.**
[Portuguese, from *seringa*: see prec.]
In Brazil, a person employed to gather natural rubber.

serio- /ˈsɪərɪəʊ/ *combining form.*
[from **SERIOUS**: see **-O-**.]
Partly serious and partly —.
■ **serio-ˈcomedy** *noun* a serio-comic work or performance **L19. serio-ˈcomic** *adjective & noun* (*a*) *adjective* partly serious and partly comic; (of an actor, performance, etc.) presenting a comic plot, situation, etc., in a serious manner; (*b*) *noun* a serio-comic actor, vocalist, etc.: **L18. serio-ˈcomical** *adjective* = **SERIO-COMIC** *adjective* **M18. serio-ˈcomically** *adverb* in a serio-comic fashion **L19.**

seriosity /sɪərɪˈɒsɪti/ *noun.* **M17.**
[Late Latin *seriositas*, from *seriosus* **SERIOUS**: see **-ITY**. In sense 2 after *jocosity*.]
1 Seriousness. **M17.**
2 A serious saying, a piece of seriousness. **L19.**

serious /ˈsɪərɪəs/ *adjective.* **LME.**
[Old & mod. French *sérieux* or late Latin *seriosus*, from Latin *serius* (used only of things in classical times): see **-OUS**.]
1 Of persons, actions, etc.: having, involving, expressing, or arising from earnest purpose or thought; grave, solemn, sober, or sedate in disposition or intention; responsible, not reckless or careless; sincere, not joking; not trifling or superficial. **LME.** ▸†**b** Firmly resolved on a purpose, intent. **M16–L17.**
2 Requiring earnest consideration or application; performed with earnestness. **M16.**
3 Important, grave; having (potentially) important, esp. undesired, consequences; giving cause for concern; of significant degree or amount, worthy of consideration; *colloq.* (of a price or value) high. **L16.**
4 Of grave or solemn aspect or appearance. **E17.**
5 Dealing with or concerning grave or factual matters; (of drama, actors, etc.) not jocular or comic; (of music, literature, etc.) not intended simply to amuse, please, or entertain (freq. opp. ***light*** or ***popular***). **E18.**
6 Earnestly religious. Now *rare.* **L18.**

📖 **1** F. A. KEMBLE I really entertain serious thoughts of learning how to use a gun. D. H. LAWRENCE Quite a serious flirtation with a man who played a flute. G. GREENE The generation now reaching middle-age has been a peculiarly serious one. **2** C. LAMB I have played at serious whist with Mr. Liston. *Manchester Examiner* Perhaps more serious reading would . . dethrone the eternal novel. **3** H. JAMES He wondered if she had been in serious want of food. E. V. KNOX I expect it's a serious offence to allow a pet panther to . . bite the public. L. URIS Kitty had been . . reassured that Karen's condition was not serious. *Indy* Chunky trainers are the new fashion . . but . . the prices are pretty serious! **4** M. O. W. OLIPHANT His dress seemly and serious. E. HEMINGWAY Lieutenant Berrendo . . came riding up, his thin face serious and grave. **5** *Times Lit. Suppl.* Sensational elements began to infiltrate . . into the work of serious novelists.

■ **seriousness** *noun* **L15.**

seriously /ˈsɪərɪəsli/ *adverb.* **LME.**
[from prec. + **-LY**[2].]
1 In a serious manner; with earnest thought or application; with serious intent; in earnest, not lightly or superficially. Also (introducing a sentence), to speak sincerely, not trivially or facetiously. **LME.**
2 To a serious degree or extent. **M18.**
3 Very, really, substantially (as intensifier). *colloq.* **L20.**

📖 **1** G. VIDAL Do you seriously believe a man can predict the future? A. BROOKNER He ate seriously, his eyes cast down. **2** W. S. BURROUGHS Those so seriously wounded they could not live. **3** *Sunday Times* You have to be seriously rich to shop at . . London's leading antique dealer.

Phrases: **take seriously** be serious in one's dealings with or attitude towards; regard as serious.

serir /səˈrɪə/ *noun.* Pl. same, **-s**. **L19.**
[Arab. = dry.]
PHYSICAL GEOGRAPHY. In Libya and Egypt, a flat area of desert strewn with rounded pebbles and boulders. Cf. **REG** *noun*[1].

serishtadar *noun* var. of **SHERISTADAR**.

serjeancy *noun* var. of **SERGEANCY**.

serjeant, serjeantcy *nouns* etc., see **SERGEANT** etc.

serjeanty /ˈsɑːdʒ(ə)nti/ *noun.* Also **serge-**. **ME.**
[Old French *serjantie, sergantie* (Anglo-Latin *serjantia* etc.), formed as **SERGEANT**: see **-Y**[3].]
†**1** Sergeants collectively. Only in **ME.**
2 *Hist.* A form of feudal tenure conditional on rendering some specified personal service to the monarch. **LME.**
2 grand serjeanty: obliging the tenant to some important (esp. military) service. **petty serjeanty**: obliging the tenant to a minor or ceremonial service.

sermon /ˈsəːmən/ *noun.* **ME.**
[Anglo-Norman *sermun*, Old & mod. French *sermon*, from Latin *sermo(n-)* talk, discourse.]
†**1** Speech, talk, discourse. **ME–L16.** ▸**b** A speech, a discourse; in *pl.*, words, talk. **ME–M16.** ▸**c** [Latin *sermones*.] In *pl.* The satires of Horace. **M16–L17.**
2 A discourse conveying religious instruction or exhortation, *esp.* one delivered orally in a Christian act of worship and based on a text of Scripture. **ME.** ▸**b** (Without article.) A sermon, a church service. Chiefly in ***after sermon*** etc. below. Now only *Scot.* **LME.**
3 *transf.* & *fig.* **a** A discourse on a serious subject containing (esp. moral) instruction or exhortation. Also, a long or tedious admonitory lecture, reproof, or harangue. **L16.** ▸**b** A thing that affords instruction or example; a moral reflection suggested by a natural object etc. **E17.**

📖 **2** *Daily News* Bp. Barry preached a special sermon at St. George's Chapel. **Sermon on the Mount** the discourse in *Matthew* 5–7 in which teachings of Jesus are presented. **b after sermon** after church. **at sermon** at church. **hear sermon** listen to a sermon. **3a** K. AMIS A straightforward Vernean sermon on the dangers of scientific progress.

■ **sermonˈeer** *noun* (*rare*) a sermonizer **M17. sermoˈnesque, sermonish** *adjectives* = **SERMONIC M19. sermonoid** *noun* (*rare*) a thing of the nature of a sermon **M19. sermoˈnology** *noun* sermonizing; sermons collectively: **M19.**

sermon /ˈsəːmən/ *verb.* Now *rare.* **ME.**
[Anglo-Norman *sarmuner*, Old French †*sermo(u)ner* (mod. *sermonner*), formed as prec.]
1 *verb trans.* Preach to or at (a person). **ME.**
2 *verb intrans.* †**a** Preach (*of* a thing). Only in **ME.** ▸**b** Preach *at* a person. **E19.**
†**3** *verb intrans.* Speak (*of* a thing). **ME–E17.**
†**4** *verb trans.* Speak of, utter, declare. **LME–L16.**

sermoner /ˈsəːmənə/ *noun. rare.* **ME.**
[from **SERMON** *noun, verb* + **-ER**[1].]
A preacher of sermons.

sermonette /səːməˈnɛt/ *noun.* **E19.**
[from **SERMON** *noun* + **-ETTE**.]
A short sermon; a brief discourse or digression on moral or religious matters.

sermonic /səːˈmɒnɪk/ *adjective.* Freq. *depreciative.* **M18.**
[formed as prec. + **-IC**.]
Of the form or nature of a sermon; resembling (that of) a sermon.
■ **sermonical** *adjective* = **SERMONIC L18. sermonically** *adverb* after the fashion of a sermon **M19.**

sermonise *verb* var. of **SERMONIZE**.

sermonist /ˈsəːmənɪst/ *noun.* **M17.**
[from **SERMON** *noun, verb* + **-IST**.]
A preacher, a sermonizer.

sermonize /ˈsəːmənʌɪz/ *verb.* Chiefly *joc.* or *depreciative.* Also **-ise**. **M17.**
[formed as prec. + **-IZE**.]
1 *verb intrans.* Deliver or compose a sermon. **M17.** ▸**b** Give serious advice or earnest exhortation; = **PREACH** *verb* 1b. **M18.**
2 *verb trans.* Bring into some condition by preaching. **M18.**
3 *verb trans.* Preach a sermon to; talk seriously or earnestly to, admonish, lecture. **E19.**

📖 **1** A. JESSOPP Like a young curate sermonising. **b** *Science* I have sermonized on the sin of irrelevance. **2** W. S. LANDOR Which of us shall . . sermonize the other fast asleep. **3** B. ASKWITH Harriet did her best to sermonize . . her sister.

■ **sermonizer** *noun* **M17.**

†**sermountain** *noun.* **LME–M18.**
[Old French *sermontain, sermontayne*, from medieval Latin *siler montanum* lit. 'mountain withy'.]
An umbelliferous plant of the mountains of southern Europe, *Laserpitium siler*.

Sernyl /ˈsəːnɪl/ *noun.* **M20.**
[Origin unkn.]
PHARMACOLOGY. (Proprietary name for) the drug phencyclidine.

sero- /ˈsɪərəʊ/ *combining form.*
[from **SERUM**: see **-O-**.]
MEDICINE & BIOLOGY. **1** Of or pertaining to serum.
2 Pertaining to, consisting of, or involving serum and—.
3 Characterized by serous effusion or infiltration, or involving a serous membrane. *rare.*
■ **seroaggglutiˈnation** *noun* agglutination of cultured cells of a micro-organism by an antiserum, showing the serological identity of the micro-organism with the one that gave rise to the antiserum **E20. seroconˈversion** *noun* a change from a seronegative to a seropositive state **M20. seroconˈvert** *verb intrans.* undergo seroconversion **M20. serodiagˈnosis** *noun* diagnosis by serological means **L19. serodiagˈnostic** *adjective* of or pertaining to serodiagnosis **L19. serodifferentiˈation** *noun* differentiation between micro-organisms by serological means **M20. seroepidemioˈlogic** *adjective* (chiefly *US*) = **SEROEPIDEMIOLOGICAL M20. seroepidemioˈlogical** *adjective* of, pertaining to, or involving seroepidemiology **M20. seroepidemiˈology** *noun* the branch of science that deals with the prevalence and distribution of a pathogen in a population, as investigated by serological means **M20. seroˈfibrinous** *adjective* consisting of fibrin-rich serum **E20. serogroup** *noun & verb* (*a*) *noun* a group of serotypes with similar but distinguishable serological reactions; (*b*) *verb trans.* assign to a particular serogroup: **M20. sero-iˈmmunity** *noun* immunity conferred by the administration of antiserum **E20. seroˈnegative** *adjective* showing or characterized by the absence of a specific serological reaction **M20. seroˈpositive** *adjective* showing or characterized by the presence of a specific serological reaction

M20. **seroposi'tivity** *noun* the degree to which something is seropositive M20. **sero'prevalence** *noun* the prevalence of a pathogen in a population as measured serologically L20. **sero'purulent** *adjective* of or characterized by sero-pus M19. **sero-pus** *noun* a mixture of serum and pus L19. **sero-san'guineous** *adjective* consisting of blood and serum M19. **serotaxo'nomic** *adjective* of, pertaining to, or involving serotaxonomy M20. **serota'xonomy** *noun* the investigation of taxonomic relationships by means of the serological cross-reactions between proteins from different organisms M20. **serothera'peutic** *adjective* of or pertaining to serotherapy E20. **sero'therapy** *noun* treatment (of disease or infection) with serum L19. **serovar** *noun* = SEROTYPE *noun* L20.

serology /sɪə'rɒlədʒi/ *noun.* E20.
[from SERO- + -LOGY.]
The branch of medicine and biology that deals with blood serum, esp. the immune responses induced in it by pathogens and other antigens. Also, the serological characteristics *of* a disease or individual.
■ **sero'logic** *adjective* = SEROLOGICAL E20. **sero'logical** *adjective* of, pertaining to, or involving serology; pertaining to, detectable or distinguishable by a specific serum immune response: E20. **sero'logically** *adverb* E20. **serologist** *noun* E20.

seron /'sɪərən/ *noun.* Also **ceroon**, **seroon**, /sɪ'ru:n/. M16.
[Spanish = hamper, crate (from *sera* large basket), partly through French *serron*.]
A bale or package (esp. of tropical plant products) bound with hide.

serosa /sɪ'rəʊsə/ *noun.* Pl. **-sae** /-si:/, **-sas**. L19.
[from mod. Latin *membrana serosa* serous membrane.]
ANATOMY & MEDICINE. A serous membrane; the tissue of serous membranes.
■ **serosal** *adjective* M20. **sero'sitis** *noun* inflammation of a serous membrane L19.

serosity /sɪ'rɒsɪti/ *noun.* Now *rare* or *obsolete.* LME.
[medieval Latin *serositas*, from *serosus*: see SEROUS, -ITY.]
1 The condition of being serous. LME.
2 Watery fluid in an animal body; serum. E17.

serotinal /sɪ'rəʊtɪn(ə)l/ *adjective.* L19.
[from Latin *serotinus*: see SEROTINE *adjective & noun*[2].]
Produced or occurring late in the season or the year; autumnal.

serotine /'sɛrətʌɪn, -tɪn/ *noun*[1]. L18.
[French *sérotine* from fem. of Latin *serotinus*: see next.]
Any of several small brown bats of the genus *Eptesicus*, *esp.* the chestnut-coloured *E. serotinus* of Eurasia and N. Africa. Also ***serotine bat***.

serotine /'sɛrətʌɪn/ *adjective & noun*[2]. L16.
[Latin *serotinus* belated, late-flowering, (in late Latin) of the evening, from *sero* adverb of *serus* late: see -INE[1].]
▶ **A** *adjective.* Occurring or developing late in the day, year, or season; autumnal; (of a plant) late-flowering. L16.
▶ **B** *noun.* A late-flowering plant. M17.

serotinous /sɪ'rɒtɪnəs/ *adjective.* M17.
[formed as prec. + -OUS.]
1 = SEROTINE *adjective.* M17.
2 BOTANY. Of a cone: remaining unopened for a long time after maturing; *spec.* releasing seed only after burning. L19.
■ **serotiny** *noun* M20.

serotonin /sɛrə'təʊnɪn/ *noun.* M20.
[from SERO- + TONIC *adjective* + -IN[1].]
BIOCHEMISTRY. A compound present in blood serum, which acts as a neurotransmitter and is involved in vasoconstriction, anaphylactic shock, and the regulation of circadian cycles; 5-hydroxytryptamine, $C_{10}H_{12}N_2O$.
■ **seroto'nergic**, **serotoni'nergic** *adjectives* releasing or involving serotonin as a neurotransmitter M20.

serotype /'sɪərə(ʊ)tʌɪp/ *noun & verb.* M20.
[from SERO- + -TYPE.]
MICROBIOLOGY. ▶**A** *noun.* A serologically distinguishable strain of a micro-organism. M20.
▶ **B** *verb trans.* Assign to a particular serotype. M20.
■ **serotypic** /-'tɪpɪk/ *adjective* of or pertaining to serotypes M20.

serous /'sɪərəs/ *adjective.* LME.
[French *séreux* or medieval Latin *serosus*, formed as SERUM: see -OUS.]
ANATOMY & MEDICINE. **1** Of, pertaining to, or of the nature of serum; consisting of or containing serum. LME. ▶**b** Of a disorder: characterized by the presence of serum. L18.
2 Secreting or moistened with serum. Chiefly in ***serous membrane*** below. M18.
2 serous membrane a smooth transparent membrane such as the peritoneum which lines a cavity of the body in a double layer lubricated by fluid; also called *serosa*.

serow /'sɛrəʊ/ *noun.* Pl. **-s**, same. M19.
[Prob. from Lepcha *sā-ro*.]
Either of two stocky goat-antelopes with long ears, short horns, and thick coats, *Capricornis sumatrensis* of mountain regions from Kashmir to Sumatra and eastern China, and *C. crispus* of Japan and Taiwan. Formerly also (by confusion), the goral.

Serpasil /'sə:pəsɪl/ *noun.* M20.
[from RE)SERP(INE + arbitrary elems.]
PHARMACOLOGY. (Proprietary name for) reserpine.

serpaw /'sɪəpɔ:/ *noun.* Also **seer-**. L17.
[Persian, Urdu *sar-ā-pā* lit. 'head to foot'.]
Hist. In India etc.: a robe or garment presented as a *khilat* or gift of honour by a monarch or person of rank.

Serpens /'sə:pɛnz/ *noun.* M17.
[Latin *serpens*: see next.]
Orig. †***Serpens Ophiuchi***. (The name of) a constellation in two parts either side of Ophiuchus on the celestial equator; the Serpent.

serpent /'sə:p(ə)nt/ *noun & adjective.* ME.
[Old & mod. French from Latin *serpent-*, *-ens* use as noun of pres. pple of *serpere* creep, rel. to Greek *herpein*: see -ENT.]
▶ **A** *noun.* **1 a** A scaly limbless reptile, usu. characterized by sinuous slithering movement, hissing, and freq. a venomous bite; a snake. Also, a mythical creature resembling a snake; a dragon. Freq. *rhet.* or *poet.*, with allus. to the proverbial attributes of guile, treachery, or malignancy. ME. ▶†**b** A creeping thing; an animal regarded as venomous or noxious. LME–L17. ▶**c** A marine animal resembling a snake; a sea-serpent. E17. ▶**d** = ***serpent-green*** below. L19.
2 (Freq. **S-**.) *The* Devil, Satan (as tempter: *Genesis* 3:1–5, *Revelation* 12:9). ME. ▶**b** A treacherous, deceitful, or malicious person. L16.
3 A representation of a serpent, esp. as a symbol or an ornament (sometimes with its tail in its mouth as a symbol of eternity). LME.
4 (Usu. **S-**.) Orig., *the* constellation Hydra. Now, *the* constellation Serpens. M16.
5 A firework which burns with a serpentine motion or flame. M17.
6 MUSIC. An archaic bass wind instrument of leather-covered wood, about 8 feet long and formed in three U-shaped turns, with a cup-shaped mouthpiece and few keys. Also, an organ-stop of similar tone. M18.
7 A thing resembling a serpent, esp. in being long and twisted or sinuous; *esp.* a tress of hair of this kind, dangling or plaited in a loop. E19.
8 *Hist.* = SERPENTINE *noun* 2. M19.

> **1a *plumed serpent***: see PLUMED 1. ***spectacled serpent***: see SPECTACLED 2. **b** EVELYN Mr. Charlton's collection of spiders, birds, scorpions, and other serpents. **2** H. WADDELL Open are the woods again That the Serpent lost for men. **3** AV *Num.* 21:9 And Moses made a serpent of brasse, and put it upon a pole. **5 *Pharaoh's serpent***: see PHARAOH *noun*[1].

▶ **B** *attrib.* or as *adjective.* Resembling (that of) a serpent, serpent-like, serpentine. L16.

> BYRON Thy cold breast and serpent smile.

Comb.: **Serpent-bearer** = OPHIUCHUS; **serpent eagle** any of several birds of prey of the genus *Spilornis* and related genera, of central Africa and SE Asia; also called ***harrier-eagle***; **serpent-green** *adjective & noun* (of) a shade of pale green; **serpent-star** a brittle-star; **serpent-stone** †(*a*) a fossil ammonite; (*b*) *arch.* an artificial stone or bead supposed to be a remedy for the poison of serpents (cf. SERPENTINE *noun* 3); (*c*) *arch.* = BEZOAR 2; **serpent-wand** the caduceus.
■ **serpen'tiferous** *adjective* (*rare*) (*a*) bearing or containing a serpent; (*b*) having many serpents: M18. **serpentiform** /-'pɛnt-/ *adjective* having the form of (that of) a serpent, serpentine L18. **serpent-like** *adjective & adverb* (*a*) *adjective* resembling a serpent, serpentine; (*b*) *adverb* in a serpentine manner: L16. **serpently** *adverb* in the manner of a serpent, serpent-like LME.

serpent /'sə:p(ə)nt/ *verb intrans.* Now *rare.* E17.
[Old & mod. French *serpenter*, formed as prec.]
Move like a serpent; follow a tortuous course, wind. Cf. SNAKE *verb*[1].

serpentaria /sə:p(ə)n'tɛ:rɪə/ *noun*[1]. E19.
[medieval Latin (sc. *planta* plant), fem. of *serpentarius* SERPENTARIUS.]
= SERPENTARY 2.

serpentaria *noun*[2] see next.

serpentarium /sə:p(ə)n'tɛ:rɪəm/ *noun.* Chiefly *US.* Pl. **-ria** /-rɪə/, **-riums**. L19.
[from SERPENT *noun* + -ARIUM.]
A building or enclosure in which snakes (and other reptiles) are kept for public display or observation; a snake-house, a reptiliary.

Serpentarius /sə:p(ə)n'tɛ:rɪəs/ *noun. obsolete* exc. *Hist.* M16.
[mod. Latin, use as noun of medieval Latin *serpentarius*, from Latin *serpent-* SERPENT *noun* + *-arius* -ARY[1].]
ASTRONOMY. = OPHIUCHUS.

serpentary /'sə:p(ə)nt(ə)ri/ *noun.* LME.
[medieval Latin *serpentaria* (sc. *planta* or *retorta*) fem. of *serpentarius*: see prec.]
1 Orig., dragon arum, *Dracunculus vulgaris*. Now, Virginian snakeroot, *Aristolochia serpentaria*; (more fully ***serpentary root***) the root of this plant, reputed to cure snakebite. LME.
†**2** CHEMISTRY. A kind of retort or still. Cf. SERPENTINE *noun* 4. LME–E17.

serpenticide /sə:'pɛntɪsʌɪd/ *noun.* E19.
[from SERPENT *noun* + -I- + -CIDE.]
1 A killer of serpents. E19.
2 The killing of serpents. L19.
■ **serpenti'cidal** *adjective* E19.

serpenticone /sə:'pɛntɪkəʊn/ *noun & adjective.* E20.
[from SERPENT *noun* + -I- + CONE *noun.*]
PALAEONTOLOGY. (Designating) an ammonoid with slender whorls which scarcely overlap, so that the shell resembles a coiled snake.

serpentile /'sə:p(ə)ntʌɪl/ *adjective. rare.* L18.
[from SERPENT *noun* + -ILE.]
= SERPENTINE *adjective.*

serpentin /'sə:p(ə)ntɪn, *foreign* sɛrpɑ̃tɛ̃/ *noun.* Now *rare.* L19.
[French: see SERPENTINE *adjective.*]
A long coloured paper ribbon unrolled and thrown into the air at times of rejoicing.

serpentine /'sə:p(ə)ntʌɪn/ *noun.* LME.
[medieval Latin *serpentina*, *-tinum* uses as noun of fem. and neut. of late Latin *serpentinus*: see next.]
1 Any of various plants reputed to contain an antidote to the poison of serpents, such as dragonwort and fenugreek. *obsolete* exc. *Hist.* LME.
2 A kind of cannon, used esp. in the 15th and 16th cents. as a ship's gun. *obsolete* exc. *Hist.* LME.
3 Orig., any of various semiprecious stones with markings resembling snake skin, reputed to have magical powers. Now, any of a group of common rock-forming minerals, freq. a dull green with veins or spots, formed by alteration of magnesium-rich silicates. Also (more fully ***serpentine rock***), a rock consisting largely of such minerals. LME. ▶**b** An object, esp. a bowl, made of serpentine. *rare.* L15.
4 [French *serpentin*.] A coiled pipe inside a distilling or cooling apparatus. E16.
†**5** A malicious act; a wily, cunning person. E–M16.
6 The matchlock of a harquebus. *obsolete* exc. *Hist.* L16.
†**7** = SERPIGO. M17–E18.
8 a A winding curve or line. M19. ▶**b** A lake or canal of a winding shape; *spec.* (***the Serpentine***) the one constructed in Hyde Park, London, in 1730. M19. ▶**c** HORSEMANSHIP. A riding exercise consisting of a series of half-circles alternately to right and left. M19.
Comb.: **serpentine asbestos** chrysotile; **serpentine jade** a translucent ornamental variety of serpentine resembling soft jade; **serpentine marble** a dark greenish stone resembling marble, consisting mainly of massive serpentine; also called ***verd antique***; **serpentine superphosphate** *NZ* a mixture of superphosphate and crushed serpentinite, used as a fertilizer; †**serpentine powder** finely ground gunpowder for use in a serpentine.
■ **serpentinic** /-'tɪnɪk/ *adjective* (GEOLOGY) of, pertaining to, or containing serpentine L19.

serpentine /'sə:p(ə)ntʌɪn/ *adjective.* LME.
[Old & mod. French *serpentin*, from late Latin *serpentinus*, from Latin *serpent-* SERPENT *noun*: see -INE[1].]
1 Of or pertaining to a serpent or serpents; resembling (that of) a serpent. LME. ▶**b** Designating a form of verse in which the lines begin and end with the same word. *rare.* E17.
2 Deceitful, treacherous; wily, cunning, subtle. LME.
3 Following a winding course resembling that of a serpent in motion; forming a succession of curves; tortuous, sinuous. E17.
Special collocations & comb.: **serpentine front** a multiply-bowed front on a piece of furniture. **serpentine-fronted** *adjective* having a serpentine front. **serpentine stone** *arch.* = SERPENTINE *noun* 3.
■ **serpentinely** *adverb* in a serpentine manner; by a serpentine path: M17.

serpentine /'sə:p(ə)ntʌɪn/ *verb.* L18.
[from prec.]
1 *verb intrans.* Move in a serpentine manner; pursue a serpentine path; wind. L18.
2 *verb trans.* Cause to take a serpentine direction. Also, move or affect by serpentine motion. L18.

serpentinise *verb* var. of SERPENTINIZE.

serpentinite /'sə:p(ə)ntɪnʌɪt/ *noun.* M20.
[from SERPENTINE *noun* + -ITE[1].]
GEOLOGY. A rock consisting largely of serpentine or related minerals.
■ **serpentinitic** /-'nɪtɪk/ *adjective* L20.

serpentinize /'sə:p(ə)ntɪnʌɪz/ *verb.* Also **-ise**. L18.
[from SERPENTINE *noun, adjective* + -IZE.]
1 *verb intrans.* = SERPENTINE *verb* 1. *rare.* L18.
2 *verb trans.* GEOLOGY. Convert into serpentine. L19.
■ **serpentini'zation** *noun* (GEOLOGY) L19.

serpentinous /'sə:p(ə)ntʌɪnəs/ *adjective.* M19.
[from SERPENTINE *noun, adjective* + -OUS.]
1 GEOLOGY. Of the nature of or consisting of serpentine. M19.
2 Serpentine, winding. L19.

serpentize /ˈsəːp(ə)ntʌɪz/ *verb*. Now *rare*. Also **-ise**. **E17**.
[from SERPENT *noun* + -IZE.]
1 *verb intrans.* = SERPENTINE *verb* 1. **E17**.
2 *verb trans.* Cause to take a serpentine shape, motion, or course. **M18**.

serpentry /ˈsəːp(ə)ntri/ *noun*. **E19**.
[from SERPENT *noun* + -RY.]
1 Serpents or serpentine creatures collectively. **E19**.
2 A serpentarium. *rare*. **M19**.

serpigines *noun pl.* see SERPIGO.

serpiginous /səːˈpɪdʒɪnəs/ *adjective*. **LME**.
[from medieval Latin *serpiginosus*, from *serpigin-*, SERPIGO: see -OUS. Mod. sense by assoc. with SERPENTINE *adjective* etc.]
MEDICINE. Orig., of the nature of a creeping skin eruption. Now usu. (of a skin lesion or eruption), having a wavy or indented margin.
■ **serpiginously** *adverb* **L19**.

serpigo /səːˈpʌɪgəʊ/ *noun*. Now *rare* or *obsolete*. Pl. **serpigines** /səːˈpɪdʒɪniːz/, **serpigoes**. **LME**.
[medieval Latin, from Latin *serpere* creep.]
MEDICINE. A creeping or spreading skin eruption; *spec.* ringworm.

serpolet /ˈsəːpəlɛt/ *noun*. **L17**.
[French from Provençal, dim. of Old French *serpol* from Latin *serpullum*, Greek *herpullon* (from Latin *serpere*, Greek *herpein* creep): see -ET[1].]
Wild thyme, *Thymus praecox*. Now only in ***serpolet oil***, a medicinal oil extracted from this plant.

SERPS /səːps/ *abbreviation*.
State earnings-related pension scheme.

serpula /ˈsəːpjʊlə/ *noun*. Pl. **-lae** /-liː/. **M18**.
[mod. Latin *Serpula* (see below) from late Latin *serpula* small serpent.]
ZOOLOGY. A serpulid, *esp.* one of the genus *Serpula*.

serpulid /ˈsəːpjʊlɪd/ *noun & adjective*. **L19**.
[from prec. + -ID[3].]
ZOOLOGY. ▶**A** *noun*. A member of the polychaete family Serpulidae of small marine worms, which live in twisted calcareous tubes, often in colonies, and have retractable tentacles for filter-feeding and possess the respiratory pigment chlorocruorin. **L19**.
▶**B** *adjective*. Of, pertaining to, or designating this family. **M20**.

†**serr** *verb trans.* **M16–M18**.
[French *serrer*, Italian *serrare* close up the ranks, ult. from Latin *serare*: see SERRY.]
Press close *together*, form into a serried company. Chiefly *refl.* & in *pass.*

serra /ˈsɛrə/ *noun*[1]. Pl. **serrae** /ˈsɛriː/, (in sense 1c) **serras**. **LME**.
[Latin = saw, sawfish.]
1 a A kind of dragon or sea-monster. *obsolete* exc. *Hist.* **LME**. ▸**b** A sawfish. **M19**. ▸**c** Any of various fishes with serrated fins or markings; *esp.* = SEIR. **L19**.
2 A serrated organ, structure, or edge; in *pl.*, the teeth of a serrated edge. **E19**.

serra /ˈsɛrə/ *noun*[2]. **M19**.
[Portuguese formed as prec. Cf. SIERRA.]
In Portuguese-speaking regions, a ridge of mountains or hills.

serradilla /sɛrəˈdɪlə/ *noun*. **M19**.
[Portuguese, dim. of *serrado* serrated.]
A Mediterranean clover, *Ornithopus sativa*, grown as fodder.

serrae *noun pl.* see SERRA *noun*[1].

serran /ˈsɛrən/ *noun*. Now *rare*. **E19**.
[mod. Latin *Serranus*: see next.]
A serranid fish.

serranid /səˈranɪd, ˈsɛrə-/ *noun & adjective*. **M20**.
[mod. Latin *Serranidae* (see below), from *Serranus* genus name, formed as SERRA *noun*[1]: see -ID[3].]
▶**A** *noun*. A member of the widespread family Serranidae of mainly large, heavy-bodied, predatory fishes, including sea-bass, groupers, and jewfish. **M20**.
▶**B** *adjective*. Of, pertaining to, or designating this family. **M20**.
■ Also **serranoid** *noun & adjective* **L19**.

Serrano /sɛˈrɑːnəʊ/ *noun & adjective*. Pl. of noun same, **-os**. **M19**.
[Spanish = highlander.]
1 A member of, of or pertaining to, a N. American Indian people of southern California. **M19**.
2 (Of) the Uto-Aztecan language of this people. **L19**.

serrate /ˈsɛreɪt/ *adjective*. **M17**.
[Latin *serratus*, formed as SERRA *noun*[1]: see -ATE[2].]
Chiefly BOTANY & ZOOLOGY. Serrated; *spec.* (of a leaf etc.) having small, forwardly-directed teeth.

serrate /sɪˈreɪt/ *verb*. **LME**.
[Late Latin *serrat-* pa. ppl stem of *serrare*, formed as SERRA *noun*[1]: see -ATE[3].]
†**1** *verb trans. & intrans.* Perform an amputation (on), saw (off). **LME–L16**.
2 *verb trans.* Make serrated or saw-toothed; give a serrated edge or form. **M18**.

serrated /sɪˈreɪtɪd/ *adjective*. **E18**.
[formed as SERRATE *adjective* + -ED[1].]
Having or designating an edge formed of a row of small sharp notches or projections like the teeth of a saw.
***serrated* TUSSOCK *grass*.**

serratic /sɪˈratɪk/ *adjective*. *rare*. **LME**.
[formed as SERRATE *adjective* + -IC.]
MEDICINE. Resembling or suggesting the motion of a saw or the sound of sawing. Formerly also = SERRATED.

†**serratile** *adjective*. **LME–E18**.
[medieval Latin *serratilis*, formed as prec.: see -ILE.]
= prec.

serration /sɪˈreɪʃ(ə)n/ *noun*. **E18**.
[from SERRATE *verb* + -ION.]
†**1** SURGERY. The operation of sawing. *rare* (only in Dicts.). Only in **E18**.
2 The condition of being serrated; an instance of this; in *pl.*, the teeth of a serrated edge or surface. **M19**.

serrature /ˈsɛrətʃə/ *noun*. **M16**.
[Late Latin *serratura*, from *serratus* SERRATE *adjective*: see -URE.]
= SERRATION 2.

serratus /sɪˈreɪtəs/ *noun*. **L19**.
[Latin: see SERRATE *adjective*.]
ANATOMY. Any of several muscles having a serrated border where they are attached to the ribs; *esp.* (in full ***serratus anterior***) a flat muscle attached to the upper ribs and acting to pull the shoulder-blade forward.

serré /sɛre/ *adjective*. **M19**.
[French: see SERRY.]
Tightly compact; *fig.* constricted by grief or emotion.

serrefile /ˈsɛrəfʌɪl/ *noun*. **L18**.
[French, from *serrer* close together + *file* FILE *noun*[2].]
MILITARY. Each of the line of supernumerary and non-commissioned officers placed in the rear of a squadron or troop (esp. of cavalry).

serrefine /ˈsɛːfʌɪn, *foreign* sɛrfin (*pl. same*)/ *noun*. **L19**.
[French = fine clamp.]
SURGERY. A small clamp or spring forceps used esp. to close a blood-vessel.

serried /ˈsɛrɪd/ *adjective*. **M17**.
[Either from SERRY + -ED[1], or repr. a disyllabic pa. pple of SERR.]
1 (Of ranks of soldiers etc.) pressed close together, shoulder to shoulder; *gen.* arranged in close-packed rows or lines. **M19**.
2 Of argument, etc.: closely reasoned, compact in expression. *rare*. **L19**.

> 🕮 **1** R. GODDEN Those back-to-back, serried houses of the Midlands. D. BOGARDE Tables carrying a wide assortment of glasses in serried ranks.

serrulate /ˈsɛrjʊleɪt/ *adjective*. **L18**.
[mod. Latin *serrulatus*, from Latin *serrulus* dim. of *serra* saw: see -ULE, -ATE[2].]
BOTANY & ZOOLOGY. Minutely serrated; having small serrations.
■ Also **serrulated** *adjective* **L18**.

serrulation /sɛrjʊˈleɪʃ(ə)n/ *noun*. **E19**.
[from prec.: see -ATION.]
The condition of being serrulated; a minute serration.

serry /ˈsɛri/ *verb*. **L16**.
[Prob. from Old & mod. French *serré* pa. pple of *serrer* press close, from Proto-Romance var. of Latin *-serare* (in compounds), from *sera* lock, bolt. Cf. SERRIED.]
1 *verb intrans.* Press close *together* in ranks; stand or move in close or serried order. **L16**.
2 *verb trans.* Cause to stand in close order, close up (ranks). **M17**.

sertão /ˈsɛːtɑ̃ːʊ/ *noun*. Pl. **-os** /-ʊʃ/. **E19**.
[Portuguese.]
GEOGRAPHY. An arid barren region of Brazil characterized by caatinga; *spec.* such an area in the interior of NE Brazil. Also more widely, the remote interior of Brazil.
■ **sertanista** /sɛːtəˈniːstə/ *noun* a person active in the sertão or knowledgeable about the sertão and its inhabitants **M20**.

Sertoli /səːˈtəʊli/ *noun*. **L19**.
[Enrico *Sertoli* (1842–1910), Italian histologist.]
ANATOMY. Used *attrib.*, with *of*, and in *possess.* to designate a type of somatic cell found in the walls of the seminiferous tubules.

serum /ˈsɪərəm/ *noun*. Pl. **sera** /ˈsɪərə/, **serums**. **L17**.
[Latin = whey, watery fluid.]
1 Watery fluid, as a normal or pathological constituent of animal tissues; *spec.* the yellowish protein-rich liquid which separates from coagulated blood. **L17**.
2 MEDICINE. The blood serum of an animal used as a therapeutic or diagnostic agent. **L19**.
Comb.: **serum agglutination** the agglutination of antigens by components of serum; **serum broth** BACTERIOLOGY a broth (culture medium) containing added serum; **serum disease** = ***serum sickness*** below; **serum hepatitis** a viral form of hepatitis transmitted through infected blood products, causing fever, debility, and jaundice. **serum reaction** = ***serum sickness*** below; **serum sickness** anaphylactic reaction to injected foreign serum.

servage /ˈsəːvɪdʒ/ *noun*. **ME**.
[Old & mod. French, from *serf* SERF: see -AGE.]
†**1** Servitude, slavery. **ME–L16**.
†**2** Feudal homage, allegiance. **ME–M16**.
†**3** A service, or its equivalent in money or kind, due from a serf to a superior lord. **ME–M16**.
4 Serfage, serfdom. *rare*. **M19**.

serval /ˈsəːv(ə)l/ *noun*. **L18**.
[mod. Latin or French, from Portuguese (*lobo*) *cerval* lynx, lit. 'deerlike wolf', from *cervo* deer from Latin *cervus*.]
Orig., any of several Asiatic and American wild cats or lynxes. Now *spec.* a medium-sized carnivore of the cat family, *Felis serval*, found in Africa south of the Sahara and having a tawny coat with black spots and stripes, a short tail, and large ears; the bush-cat. Also ***serval cat***.

servaline /ˈsəːv(ə)lʌɪn/ *adjective & noun*. **L19**.
[from prec. + -ING[1].]
ZOOLOGY. ▶**A** *adjective*. ***servaline cat***, a serval in a dark speckled colour phase, once considered a separate species. **L19**.
▶**B** *noun*. A servaline cat. **L20**.

servant /ˈsəːv(ə)nt/ *noun & verb*. **ME**.
[Old French (mod. *servante*) use as noun of pres. pple of *servir* SERVE *verb*[1]: see -ANT[1].]
▶**A** *noun*. **1** A personal or domestic attendant; a person employed in a house to perform various household duties according to the orders and requirements of his or her employer. Freq. with specifying word. **ME**.
2 a *gen.* A person who has undertaken to perform various duties for and to carry out the orders of an individual or corporate employer, usu. in return for wages or a salary. **ME**. ▸†**b** An armed retainer (freq. in ***servant of arms***). Also, an officer of a household with a specified area of responsibility. **ME–M16**. ▸**c** A member of a company of actors (esp. in the 16th and 17th cents.) enjoying the patronage of a specified person. Now *Hist.* exc. in ***Her Majesty's servants***, ***His Majesty's servants*** below. **M16**. ▸**d** A State official; a person professionally committed to serving the interests of the State, the monarch, etc. Chiefly with specifying word or phr. **L16**.
3 *transf.* †**a** A person owing service to a feudal overlord, a vassal. **ME–E16**. ▸**b** A devoted follower *of* God, a god, etc. **ME**. ▸†**c** A lover, esp. of a woman; a devoted admirer. **LME–M18**.
4 A person in a state of servitude; *spec.* a slave. *obsolete* exc. in biblical translations & US HISTORY. **ME**.

> 🕮 **1** M. MEYER We had . . servants: a cook, . . kitchenmaid and chauffeur. ***domestic servant***, ***household servant***, etc. **2a** R. CHURCH A servant of the Midland Railway, he settled in London. *fig.*: *Daily News* The Empire was the best servant that mankind had ever had.

Phrases: ***civil servant***: see CIVIL *adjective*. **Her Majesty's servants**, **His Majesty's servants** *joc.* the theatrical profession. PUBLIC **servant**. **servant of servants** a person subjected to the most degrading servitude or slavery. ***servant's hall***: see HALL *noun*. ***your humble servant***: see HUMBLE *adjective*[1]. ***your obedient servant***: see ***your obedient*** s.v. OBEDIENT *adjective* 1. ***your obliged servant***: see OBLIGE *verb* 7. **your servant** *arch.*: a formula (freq. *iron.*) expr. (*a*) resigned acceptance of another's opinion, statement, etc.; (*b*) a greeting or farewell.
▶†**B** *verb trans.* **1** Put in subjection *to*. *rare* (Shakes.). Only in **E17**.
2 Foll. by *it*: behave as a servant. *rare*. Only in **M17**.
■ **servantdom** *noun* (*rare*) the world of servants; servants collectively: **L19**. **servantless** *adjective* **M17**. **servantry** *noun* (*rare*) servants collectively **M19**. **servantship** *noun* the state or condition of being a servant **L16**.

servante /sɛrvɑ̃ːt/ *noun*. Pl. pronounced same. **L19**.
[French = side-table.]
An extra table or concealed shelf used in conjuring tricks.

†**serve** *noun*[1].
[Old English *syrfe*, ult. from Latin *sorbus*. See also SERVICE *noun*[2].]
1 = SERVICE *noun*[2]. **OE–LME**.
2 The fruit of the service-tree. *rare*. Only in **E17**.

serve /səːv/ *noun*[2]. **LME**.
[from SERVE *verb*[1].]
†**1** Service, adoration. *rare*. Only in **LME**.
2 TENNIS & BADMINTON etc. The action or an act of serving; the manner or quality of serving; a person's turn to serve

the ball; a game in which a particular player serves; = **SERVICE** *noun*[1] 29. **L17.**
3 A serving or helping of food. *colloq.* (chiefly *Austral.*). **E20.**
4 A reprimand. Chiefly in ***give a person a serve***, criticize or reprimand a person sharply. *Austral. slang.* **M20.**

📖 **2** MARTIN WALKER It was a nice serve, flat and low. ***hold one's serve***, ***hold serve***: see **HOLD** *verb.*

serve /sɜːv/ *verb*[1]. **ME.**
[Old & mod. French *servir* or Latin *servire*, from *servus* slave.]
▶ **I 1** *verb intrans.* Be a servant, esp. a personal or domestic one. Formerly also, be or work as a slave (chiefly in biblical translations). **ME.**
2 *verb trans.* Be a servant to; *esp.* be employed in the personal or domestic service of. **ME.** ▸**b** Attend or wait on (a person) in the manner of a personal or domestic servant; minister to. **ME.** ▸**c** Work for (an individual or corporate employer) in return for wages or a salary; be an employee of. **M19.**
3 a *verb trans.* (orig. with dat. obj.). Be committed to the worship of (God or a god), *spec.* as a priest. **ME.** ▸†**b** *verb trans.* Worship (God or a god) with religious rites; offer praise and prayer to. **ME–E18.** ▸†**c** *verb intrans.* Officiate as a priest, hold a service. **ME–L17.**
4 CHRISTIAN CHURCH. **a** *verb trans.* Assist (a priest) as a server; act as a server at (the Eucharist). **ME.** ▸**b** *verb intrans.* Act as a server at the Eucharist. Also foll. by *at*. **LME.**
5 *verb trans.* & †*intrans.* with *to*. Give obedience and service to (God, a god, a ruler, etc.). **ME.** ▸**b** *verb trans.* Be the lover or devoted admirer of (esp. a woman). Now *rare* or *obsolete*. **LME.**
†**6** *verb trans.* **a** Obey (a person's will); execute (a command etc.). **ME–E19.** ▸**b** Gratify (a desire); satisfy (a need). **LME–L18.**
7 *verb trans.* Go through an allotted period or term of (service, training, a prison sentence, etc.). Freq. in ***serve one's time***, ***serve time***, below. Also foll. by *out*. **ME.**
8 *verb trans.* **a** Perform the duties of (an official position, esp. an ecclesiastical one). Also, complete the full period of tenure of (an official position). **LME.** ▸**b** Assist at or take part in (a function); perform official duties in the service of (an institution, esp. an ecclesiastical one). **L15.**
9 *verb intrans.* Perform official duties, hold an official position. **LME.**
10 *verb trans.* Be a member of the armed forces of (a State, ruler, commander, etc.); fight for. **E16.**
11 *verb intrans.* Be a member of the armed forces; fight for a State, ruler, commander, etc. **E16.**
12 *verb trans.* Do a service for (a person, the community, etc.); work for (a cause). **M17.**

📖 **1** S. T. WARNER He had been carried off . . to serve as a slave. **2** SHAKES. *All's Well* A gentleman that serves the Count. *fig.*: W. GOLDING One must break a rule, an oath, to serve a higher truth. **b** TENNYSON The good House . . Endures not that her guest should serve himself. **c** GLADSTONE All the civilians who had ever served the Company. **5** DISRAELI Serving a master for whose service he felt no zeal. **7** THACKERAY Having served his full time in India. C. EASTON She served a three-year prison sentence. **8a** G. CHALMERS A Vicarage was established for serving the Cure. **b** K. H. DIGBY His monasteries were served by priests from without. **9** A. TOFFLER Citizens are expected to serve on juries where needed. **10** R. BURN Forced to serve the king in his fleet. **11** D. FRASER He had served . . almost entirely as a Gunner. **12** T. BENN Leaders . . represent those whom they serve.

▶ **II** †**13** *verb trans.* & *intrans.* Be subordinate or subsidiary to or *to*. **ME–M17.**
14 *verb trans.* **a** Be useful or advantageous to; meet the requirements of; be serviceable for. Freq. foll. by *as*, *for*. **ME.** ▸**b** Esp. of a bodily organ: fulfil a prescribed function for; contribute to the functioning of. **ME.** ▸†**c** Be used in common by (a number of people). **LME–L18.**
15 a *verb intrans.* Have a definite use or function, fulfil a need, bring about or contribute to a desired result. Also foll. by †*of*, *as*, *for*, *to*, *to do*. **ME.** ▸†**b** *verb intrans.* Be usable or available *for*. **E16–E17.** ▸**c** *verb trans.* Help to fulfil (an end, a purpose, etc.); contribute to, tend to promote. **M16.**
16 *verb intrans.* & (*arch.*) *trans.* Be opportune, convenient, or favourable (to, *to do*); afford occasion or opportunity (to a person). **LME.** ▸**b** *verb intrans.* & †*trans. spec.* Of the wind, tide, etc.: be favourable for (a voyage etc.). **LME.**
†**17** *verb trans.* Of the conscience etc.: prompt, encourage, or (usu. in neg. contexts) permit (a person) *to do*. **LME–L16.**
18 *verb trans.* & *intrans.* Avail, suffice. Freq. in neg. contexts. Also foll. by *to do*, *for*. **LME.** ▸†**b** *verb trans.* Be sufficient for, provide what is requisite for. **M16–E18.**
†**19** *verb intrans.* Be valid, hold good; be available *for*; pass inspection. **LME–E18.**
20 *verb trans.* Of clothes etc.: suit, fit. *obsolete* exc. *Scot.* **M16.**
21 *verb trans.* & (*rare*) *intrans.* Of the memory: assist or prompt (a person); prove reliable to (a person). **M17.**

📖 **14a** G. GREENE He had risen quickly by the very quality which had served him so ill at the Bar. **15a** M. L. KING Instead of stopping the movement, the opposition's tactics had only served to give it greater momentum. S. BRETT The girl in the . . cupboard which served as reception. **c** *Scotsman* A desire to serve the interests of trade unionists. **16** SHAKES. *3 Hen. VI* If fortune serve me, I'll requite this kindness. SIR W. SCOTT Large boughs . . had been left on the ground till time served to make them into . . billets. H. SPENCER The sportsman, narrating his feats when opportunity serves. **17** SHAKES. *Merch. V.* My conscience will serve me to run from this . . master. **18** THOMAS HUGHES Nothing would serve him but that we . . turn off for Hungerford at once. M. BRAGG A peck served where a bushel had been needed before. **21** MRS H. WOOD I did tell you so . . if my memory serves me right.

▶ **III 22** *verb trans.* Wait on (a person) at table; set food or drink before (a person), help (a person) to food or drink. Also (now *rare*), feed (an animal). Freq. foll. by *with*. **ME.**
23 *verb intrans.* Wait at table; offer or hand food or drink to guests. **ME.** ▸**b** *verb trans.* Set food on (a table), spread (a table) *with* food. Now *rare*. **LME.**
24 *verb trans.* **a** Set (food or drink) on the table or before a person; offer (food or drink, esp. an accompanying portion) to a person; present (food) in a specified manner or *with* another food item; bring in or dish up (a meal or course). Also foll. by *up*. **ME.** ▸**b** Hand out, distribute. Freq. foll. by *out*. **L17.**
25 *verb trans.* Supply or provide (a person, a place, etc.) *with* goods or services. Also foll. by †*of*, *with*. **ME.** ▸†**b** Supply, provide, (a commodity); yield a supply of. **L16–L17.**
26 a *verb trans.* Attend to (a customer) in a shop etc.; supply (a customer) *with* goods. **LME.** ▸**b** *verb intrans.* Attend to customers in a shop etc. **E19.**
27 *verb refl.* & †*intrans.* Make use *of*; avail oneself *of*. *arch.* **LME.**
28 *verb trans.* Assist (a worker) by handing him or her materials; supply *with* material for work. *obsolete* exc. *dial.* **LME.**
29 *verb trans.* Give alms to (a beggar). *Scot.* & *dial.* **M18.**
30 *verb trans.* Make (a person) satisfied or content *with* food etc. Also, give (a person) a glut *of*, weary (a person) *of*. *Scot.* **M18.**

📖 **22** J. RATHBONE Mr Curtis . . served us tea in dainty cups. **24** P. P. READ Lunch was served on the terrace. E. DAVID Serve it with small roast potatoes and a green salad. *fig.*: A. BROOKNER Her mouth down-drooping . . at what fate had served up to her. **b** J. RABAN She served out portions of . . stew. **25** A. GRAY A reservoir to serve the new housing scheme. *Caravan Magazine* Le Bugue is served by the French railway system. **26b** R. WARNER The bar, behind which Bess was serving, to order myself a drink. R. CAMPBELL His grown-up sons . . served at the counter inside. **27** W. WARBURTON You may serve yourself of the following hints.

▶ **IV** *transf.* & *fig.* **31** *verb trans.* Treat or behave towards (a person etc.) in a specified manner. **ME.**
32 *verb trans.* Attack (a hostile force etc.) *with* a weapon. Long *rare* or *obsolete*. **LME.**
33 *verb trans.* Play (a trick) on. Also, do (a person) a good or bad turn. **L16.**

📖 **31** F. MARRYAT If I served you as you deserve, I should . . put my bullet into you.

▶ **V 34** *verb trans.* Of a male (esp. a stud) animal: copulate with (a female). **ME.**
35 *verb trans.* LAW. ▸**a** Deliver (a writ or other legal document) to a person in the legally required manner. Freq. foll. by *on*. **LME.** ▸**b** Declare (a person) heir to an estate, formerly by an inquest or retour, later by petition to a sheriff. Now chiefly in ***serve heir to***. *Scot.* **E16.** ▸**c** Deliver a writ or other legal document to (a person) in a legally formal manner. Usu. foll. by *with*. **L16.**
36 a *verb intrans.* Orig. in REAL TENNIS, act as an assistant or marker for the players, *spec.* by putting the ball in play. Later, in TENNIS & BADMINTON etc., start or resume play by striking the ball into the opposite court. Also foll. by *out*. **M16.** ▸**b** *verb trans.* Orig. in REAL TENNIS, stop (the ball) before the second bounce. Later in TENNIS & BADMINTON etc. put (the ball) in play. **E17.** ▸**c** *verb trans.* Hit or throw the ball to (one's opponent). *rare*. **M17.**
37 *verb trans.* **a** FALCONRY. Drive out the quarry into the view of (a hawk). **L16.** ▸**b** COURSING. Of a dog: gain an advantage for (itself) or give an advantage to (another dog) by keeping or losing its place when turning a hare. **L16.**
38 *verb trans.* Wrap (a rope, bandage) round an object; *spec.* (NAUTICAL) bind (a rope etc.) with thin cord, esp. to prevent it from rotting or unravelling. **L16.**
39 *verb trans.* MILITARY. Operate, keep (a gun, battery, etc.) firing. **E18.**

📖 **34** *Greyhound Star* He was . . exported to Australia where he has now served over 100 bitches. **36a** *Age (Melbourne)* I've never served so well in such a big tournament.

Phrases, & with adverbs in specialized senses: **be served**, **be well served**, **be poorly served**, etc., receive (good, bad, etc.) service. †**see and serve** (*rare*, Shakes.) have experience of military service. ***serve and sue***: see **SUE**. ***serve a person in some***, ***serve a person in no stead***: see **STEAD** *noun*. **serve a person right** treat a person, esp. a wrongdoer as he or she deserves; be the deserved punishment or misfortune of a person; freq. in ***it serves you right***, ***serves him right***, etc., expr. satisfaction when a person's foolishness, wrongdoing, etc., is justly rewarded or punished. ***serve a writ on***: see **WRIT** *noun* 2. **serve one's country** fight for one's country; work or offer one's services for the greater public good. **serve one's turn**, **serve the turn** fulfil a function; meet a need; be adequate. **serve one's time** hold office, undertake a term of service, training, etc., for a certain period. **serve out** (*a*) (chiefly NAUTICAL) mete out or administer (corporal punishment); (*b*) *arch. colloq.* take revenge on (a person) *for* something; (see also senses 7, 24b, 36a above). **serve the purpose of** take the place of; be used as. †**serve the time** [Latin *tempori servire*] shape one's conduct in conformity to the views that happen to be in favour at the time (cf. *time-server*, *time-serving*, etc. s.v. **TIME** *noun*). ***serve the turn***: see ***serve one's turn*** above. ***serve the stead of***: see **STEAD** *noun*. **serve time** undergo imprisonment. **serve up** offer for acceptance; present; (see also sense 24a above). ***serve with the same sauce***: see **SAUCE** *noun*. **what serves it?** *arch.* what is the use of it?

Comb.: **serve-and-volley** *adjective* (of a tennis player etc.) designating a style of play in which the server moves close to the net after serving ready to play an attacking volley shot off the service return; **serve-yourself** *adjective* (of a shop, restaurant, buffet, etc.): in which the customer helps himself or herself to goods, food, etc.

■ **servable** *adjective* (*rare*) able to be served, fit to be served **M19.**

†**serve** *verb*[2]. Chiefly *Scot.* & *north*. **ME.**
[Perh. aphet. from Old French *deservir* **DESERVE**.]
1 *verb trans.* = **DESERVE** *verb* 1, 2. **ME–E18.**
2 *verb intrans.* = **DESERVE** *verb* 3. **ME–L16.**

serventism /sɜːˈventɪz(ə)m/ *noun*. *rare*. **M19.**
[from Italian *servente* (in **CAVALIERE SERVENTE**) + **-ISM**.]
The practice of attending a married woman as a male companion or lover.

server /ˈsɜːvə/ *noun*. **LME.**
[from **SERVE** *verb*[1] + **-ER**[1].]
1 A person who serves or attends to the requirements of another; *spec.* (*a*) a person who waits at table; †(*b*) an artisan's assistant; (*c*) *arch.* a worshipper, a person who serves God or a god; (*d*) ECCLESIASTICAL a person assisting the celebrant at a service, esp. the Eucharist. **LME.**
2 TENNIS & BADMINTON etc. A player who serves the ball etc. to start or resume play. **L16.**
3 A thing which serves or supplies something; a thing which is used for serving; *spec.* †(*a*) *rare* a conduit or pipe for conveying water; (*b*) (chiefly *Scot.*) a salver, a serving tray; (*c*) in *pl.*, a spoon and fork for serving food, esp. salad. **E17.** ▸**b** COMPUTING. A program which manages shared access to a centralized resource or service in a network; a (usu. dedicated) device on which such a program is run; *esp.* = ***file server*** s.v. **FILE** *noun*[2]. **L20.**

servery /ˈsɜːv(ə)ri/ *noun*. **L19.**
[from **SERVE** *verb*[1] + **-ERY**.]
A room from which meals etc. are served and in which kitchen utensils are kept. Also, a serving-hatch.

Servetian /sɜːˈviːʃ(ə)n/ *adjective* & *noun*. **M17.**
[from *Servetus* (see below) + **-IAN**.]
ECCLESIASTICAL HISTORY. ▶**A** *adjective*. Of or pertaining to Michael Servetus (Miguel Servede) (1511–53), a Spanish heresiarch of semi-pantheistic beliefs. *rare*. **M17.**
▶**B** *noun*. A follower or adherent of Servetus or his beliefs. **M17.**
■ **Servetist** *noun* (now *rare* or *obsolete*) = **SERVETIAN** *noun* **E17.**

Servian /ˈsɜːvɪən/ *noun* & *adjective*[1]. *arch.* **M16.**
[from mod. Latin *Servia* Serbia + **-AN**.]
▶ **A** *noun*. **1** A Serbian; = **SERB** *noun* 2. **M16.**
2 = **SERBIAN** *noun* 2. **E19.**
▶ **B** *adjective*. = **SERBIAN** *adjective*. **L17.**

Servian /ˈsɜːvɪən/ *adjective*[2]. **M19.**
[Latin *Servianus*, from *Servius* (see below): see **-AN**.]
ROMAN HISTORY. Of or pertaining to Servius Tullius (fl. 573–534 BC), the semi-legendary sixth king of Rome, said to have organized the citizens into classes according to wealth, and to have encircled the city with a wall, of which extensive remains still exist.

service /ˈsɜːvɪs/ *noun*[1] & *verb*. **OE.**
[Old French *servise*, (also mod.) *service* or Latin *servitium* slavery, from *servus* slave: see **-ICE**[1].]
▶ **A** *noun*. **I** ECCLESIASTICAL. **1 a** A form of liturgy prescribed for public worship, or for a particular occasion. Freq. with specifying word. **OE.** ▸†**b** *spec.* A non-Eucharistic form of liturgy prescribed for daily use, the divine office. **ME–L16.**
2 Religious devotion; the serving of God or a god by obedience, piety, and charitable works. *arch.* **ME.**
3 Worship; *esp.* public worship conducted according to a prescribed form. Now *rare* or *obsolete* exc. in ***divine service***. **ME.**
4 A ceremony of public worship according to a prescribed form of liturgy. **LME.**
5 In full ***service-book***. A book containing the authorized forms of worship of a Church. **L16.**

6 A musical setting of the sung portions of the liturgy, *esp.* a setting of the canticles at matins and evensong. L17.

> 📖 **1a** ***burial service, communion service, marriage service***, etc. **3** R. HOOKER Solemne duties of publique seruice. **4** G. SWIFT I was asked to attend a memorial service at St Bride's. ANNE STEVENSON The service took place in the . . nineteenth-century church.

▶**II 7** The condition, status, or occupation of being a servant or employee, esp. (foll. by *of* or with possess.) of a specified person or organization. ME. ▸†**b** *transf.* The condition of being in love; the condition of being a devoted admirer, esp. of a woman. LME–E17.

8 The condition of a public servant, esp. a soldier or sailor, in the employment of a ruler or the State. ME.

9 A position as a servant in the employment of an individual person or household; (long *dial.*) the place of such employment. LME.

10 a A branch of public employment, *esp.* a Crown department or organization employing officials working for the State. Freq. with specifying word. L17. ▸**b** ***the service***, the army, navy, etc., considered as a sphere of duty or as a profession. Now only in *pl.*, the armed forces. E18.

> 📖 **7** DICKENS That's the very housemaid . . . She went into Fanny's service when we were first married. C. H. HERFORD Grumshall . . goes to take service with . . a well-reputed Naples merchant. **9** TENNYSON It will be hard . . to find Another service such as this. **10a** ***customs service, diplomatic service, Civil Service, probation service***, etc.

▶**III 11** Performance of the duties of a servant; work undertaken according to the instructions of an individual or organization; a period of employment with an individual or organization. ME. ▸†**b** An act or instance of serving; a duty undertaken for a superior. ME–E17.

†**12** Reward for work or duties undertaken; wages, payment. ME–M16.

13 †**a** Feudal allegiance; homage. ME–L16. ▸**b** *Hist.* A duty, as a payment, an amount of forced labour, etc., which a tenant was bound to render periodically to a feudal lord. ME.

14 The duty of a soldier, sailor, etc.; the performance of this duty; *esp.* actual participation in warfare, = ***active service*** s.v. ACTIVE *adjective* 5. ME. ▸**b** A military or naval operation or engagement in which a soldier or a regiment takes part. Usu. in *pl.* Now *rare*. L16. ▸†**c** A manner of participating in warfare, as mounted, on foot, etc.; a branch or arm of the army categorized in this way. E17–M18.

15 The devotion of a lover; professed love. *arch.* LME.

16 Employment by the Crown or State in an official capacity; the duties or work of public servants. LME.

17 Respect, regard. Chiefly in phrs. Now *rare* or *obsolete*. E17.

> 📖 **11** R. J. MANN Her share of the service is the parlour and pantry work. J. MORTIMER Forty years' service in the accounts department. **14** H. ACTON Called up for military service. **b** CLARENDON Forces entered the town after a very warm service . . many . . being killed. **15** SPENSER He wooed her . . With humble seruice.

▶**IV 18** Provision of a facility to meet the needs or for the use *of* a person or thing. ME.

†**19** A person's interest or advantage. LME–M18.

20 Assistance or benefit provided to someone by a person or thing; the work which an animal or thing is made to do or the use to which it is put. LME.

21 a An act of helping or benefiting another; an instance of beneficial, useful, or friendly action. M16. ▸**b** The action of serving, helping, or benefiting another; behaviour conducive to the welfare or advantage of another. Chiefly in ***do service***, ***render service***. L16. ▸**c** *collect. pl.* Friendly or professional assistance. M19.

22 Serviceableness, usefulness. Now *rare*. exc. in ***be of service*** below. L17.

> 📖 **18** GIBBON The baths . . were open, at stated hours, for the indiscriminate service of the . . people. **19** A. TUCKER A reasonable prospect of promoting her service. **20** A. HIGGINS A disorganised game of football, their coats doing service as goalposts. **21a** LD MACAULAY Whether the murder . . would really be a service to the . . cause. **b** *Guardian* The Howard Association is doing good service by its persistent watchfulness in . . the treatment of crime. **c** F. WELDON We're going to be dependent on your good services.

▶**V 23** The action of waiting at table or serving a meal, food, etc.; the action of serving a customer in a shop etc.; the manner in which this is done. ME. ▸**b** That which is served up or placed on the table for a meal; the food set before a person; a portion of food; a course of a meal. Also, a particular kind of food. Now *rare*. ME. ▸**c** The serving of a meal at one of a number of separate sittings, esp. on a train, ship, etc. E20.

24 A set of cups, dishes, plates, etc., used for serving meals. Freq. with specifying word. Also (*rare*), a set of serving vessels for an altar; a toilet set. M17.

25 An application *of* something. *rare*. M17.

26 a In full ***service-pipe***. A pipe used to supply gas or water from a main to individual users in houses, businesses, etc. E19. ▸**b** The provision or system of supplying necessary utilities, such as gas, water, or electricity, to the public; the apparatus of pipes, wiring, etc., by which this is done. Usu. in *pl.* L19.

27 a The organized system of providing labour, equipment, etc., to meet a public need such as health or communications; a regular public transport provision operating over a specified route. M19. ▸**b** Expert advice or assistance given by a manufacturer or dealer to a customer after the sale of goods; the provision of the necessary installation, maintenance, or repair work to ensure the efficient running of a machine etc.; a periodic routine inspection and maintenance of a motor vehicle etc. E20. ▸**c** The supply of programmes by a broadcasting organization, esp. on a specific wavelength. E20. ▸**d** ECONOMICS, in *pl.* The sector of the economy that supplies the needs of the consumer but produces no tangible goods, as banking or tourism. M20. ▸**e** In *pl.* The provision of petrol, refreshments, etc., for motorists at specific sites close to or beside a motorway or other major road; the group of buildings providing such facilities. M20.

> 📖 **23** *Holiday Which?* Service can be inefficient, but . . you'll usually get what you want. **24** ***dinner-service, tea-service***, etc. **26b** R. V. JONES The architect . . had omitted all services except electric light, and water for the lavatories. **27a** *Holiday Which?* The Swansea-Cork Car Ferries service takes about 10 hr. **b** *Western Morning News* Backed by our . . skilled after-sales service. *Practical Caravan* Although it . . does not replace a full service, an examination report could save you . . money.

▶**VI 28** LAW. **a** The action or an act of formally serving a writ or other legal document on a person. LME. ▸**b** The procedure for transmitting heritable property to an heir. Usu. in ***general service***, ***special service***, below. *Scot. obsolete* exc. *Hist.* L16.

29 TENNIS & BADMINTON etc. The action or an act of serving the ball; the manner or quality of serving; a person's turn to serve; (in full ***service game***) a game in which a particular player serves; = SERVE *noun*² 2. E17.

30 NAUTICAL. Thin cord used as a binding round rope etc. to prevent rotting or unravelling. E18.

31 The action by a male animal of copulating with a female animal. E19.

> 📖 **29** *Times* A glorious backhand cross-court pass off second service.

Phrases: ***accept service of a writ***: see ACCEPT *verb* 3. ***active service***: see ACTIVE *adjective* 5. ***answering service***: see ANSWER *verb* 12. **armed services** the army, navy, and air force. **at a person's service** ready to assist or serve a person. **be of service** be available to assist; be useful. ***British Service warm***: see WARM *noun* 3. ***divine service***: see DIVINE *adjective* 3. **do a person service** (now chiefly *poet.*) serve or attend on a person. **for services rendered** in recognition of or as a recompense for a person's having performed a beneficial act for another. **general service** SCOTS LAW a procedure used to determine generally who is heir. **give my service to** (now *rare* or *obsolete*) give my regards to, remember me respectfully to. ***hold one's service***, ***hold service***: see HOLD *verb*. ***Home Service***: see HOME *adjective*. **in service** (*a*) employed as a servant; (*b*) in or available for use. ***long service***: see LONG *adjective*¹. ***merchant service***: see MERCHANT *adjective*. ***military service***: see MILITARY *adjective*. **my service to you** (now *rare* or *obsolete*): a toast said when drinking to a person. ***national service***: see NATIONAL *adjective*. **On Her Majesty's Service**, **On His Majesty's Service**: a formula (esp. as printed on an envelope) indicating that a letter is of an official nature. **out of service** out of order; not available for use. ***press into service***: see PRESS *verb*² 2. ***private service***: see PRIVATE *adjective*. ***public service***: see PUBLIC *adjective & noun*. ***second service***: see SECOND *adjective*. ***secret service***: see SECRET *adjective*. **see service** (of a soldier) have experience of warfare, be involved in fighting; (of a thing) be much used or worn. ***SELECTIVE service***. ***senior service***: see SENIOR *adjective*. ***short service***: see SHORT *adjective*. ***silver service***: see SILVER *noun & adjective*. ***social service***: see SOCIAL *adjective*. **special service** SCOTS LAW a procedure used to determine the heir to a specific estate. **take service** enlist under a military commander, join a fighting force. **take service with** *arch.* become a servant to.

Comb.: **service alley** a minor road or passage giving access to the back of a row of houses; **service area** (*a*) a space adjoining a house in which dustbins etc. are situated; (*b*) an area beside a major road providing petrol, refreshments, etc.; (*c*) the geographical area within which transmissions can be satisfactorily received from a particular broadcasting station; ***service-book***: see sense 5 above; **service bureau** COMPUTING an organization providing services such as scanning, pre-press, and colour printing; **service bus** (*a*) a bus operating regular public services, as opp. to a special works bus, school bus, etc.; (*b*) *Austral. & NZ* = ***service car*** below; **service car** *Austral. & NZ* a motor coach; **service ceiling** AERONAUTICS the maximum height at which an aircraft can sustain steady level flight; **service charge** an additional sum, usu. calculated as a percentage of a bill, charged for service, esp. in a hotel or restaurant; **service club** *N. Amer.* an association of business or professional people having the aims of promoting community welfare and goodwill; **service contract** (*a*) a contract of employment; (*b*) a business agreement between contractor and customer, usu. guaranteeing the maintenance and servicing of equipment over a specified period; **service court** (TENNIS & BADMINTON etc.) a division of the court into which the ball must be served in order to start or resume play; **service dress** ordinary military etc. uniform; **service engineer**: engaged on the maintenance and servicing of machinery or equipment; **service flat**: in which domestic service and sometimes meals are provided for a tenant at a charge included in the rent; **service industry**: engaged in the provision of services rather than the manufacture of goods; **service line**: (TENNIS & BADMINTON etc.) marking the limit of the area into which the ball must be served; **serviceman** (*a*) a man serving or who formerly served in the armed forces; (*b*) a man providing the repair and maintenance of equipment or machinery; (***national serviceman***: see NATIONAL *adjective*); **service mark** (orig. *US*) a legally registered name or designation, used as a trade mark is for goods to distinguish an organization's services from those of its competitors; **service measure**, **service metre** PROSODY a 14-syllable line equivalent to a couplet of common metre; **service module** ASTRONAUTICS a separable section of a spacecraft containing the main engine and other supporting equipment; ***service-pipe***: see sense 26a above; **service plate** *US* a large ornate plate which marks a place at table and which serves as an under plate during the first courses of a meal; **service-program** COMPUTING a program which performs routine tasks in support of other functions, a utility routine; **service provider** COMPUTING a company which provides its subscribers with access to the Internet; **service record** the record of service of a soldier, employee, etc.; **service reservoir** a (usu. small) reservoir filled from an impounding reservoir at times of low demand to supplement the supply to the local area at times of high demand; **service road** a minor road parallel to a main road, giving access to houses, shops, etc.; **service routine** COMPUTING = ***service program*** above; **service station** an establishment beside a road selling fuel etc. to motorists and often able to carry out maintenance for vehicles; **servicewoman** a woman serving or who formerly served in the armed forces.

▶**B** *verb trans.* **1** Be of service to; serve; provide with a service. L19.

2 Perform maintenance or repair work on (a motor vehicle etc.). Orig. *US*. E20.

3 Pay interest on (a debt). M20.

4 (Of a male animal) copulate with (a female animal); *coarse slang* (of a man) have sexual intercourse with (a woman). M20.

5 Supply (a person) with a commodity etc.; process. M20.

> 📖 **1** *Sunday Times* Chain stores . . need to be serviced twice weekly by giant container lorries. **3** *Investors Chronicle* Income will be used to service loan interest. **5** *Daily Telegraph* Building societies have been without funds to service all the mortgages required.

■ **serviceless** *adjective* †(*a*) *rare* lacking work; without reward or pay; (*b*) without usefulness, useless: LME. **servicer** *noun* a person who services or maintains something; a person providing a service: L20.

service /ˈsəːvɪs/ *noun*². M16.

[Orig. pl. SERVE *noun*¹.]

1 A southern European tree, *Sorbus domestica*, related to and resembling the mountain ash, which is sometimes cultivated for its small pear-shaped or round fruit, eaten when overripe. Also ***service tree***. M16. ▸**b** More fully ***wild service (tree)***. A related small Eurasian tree, *Sorbus torminalis*, with triangularly lobed leaves and bitter fruit. M16.

†**2** The fruit of *Sorbus domestica*. M16–L18.

Comb.: **service-berry** †(*a*) = sense 2 above; (*b*) *N. Amer.* (the fruit of) the Juneberry, *Amelanchier*; ***service tree***: see sense 1 above.

serviceable /ˈsəːvɪsəb(ə)l/ *adjective*. ME.

[Old French *servisable*, from *service*: see SERVICE *noun*¹, -ABLE.]

1 Ready to do service; willing to be of service or assistance. ME. ▸†**b** Of an action or state: involving or expressing readiness to serve. L16–E18. ▸†**c** Subservient. *rare*. E17–M19.

†**2** Of food: suitable for serving. *rare*. Only in LME.

3 a Of a thing: able to be used for an appropriate purpose; capable of performing a certain function or withstanding adverse conditions. Also, suitable for ordinary use, functional rather than decorative. LME. ▸**b** Of a person: useful. M17.

> 📖 **1** R. L. STEVENSON The storekeeper . . one of the most serviceable of men. **3a** J. HIGGINS His Arabic was not as good as his English, but serviceable. K. MOORE She would have chosen the plainer . . more serviceable shelves. **b** GEO. ELIOT Johnson was a most serviceable subordinate.

■ **servicea'bility** *noun* (*a*) readiness for service; usefulness; (*b*) the capacity of a machine to be maintained or repaired: M19. **serviceableness** *noun* (*a*) (now *rare*) readiness to assist or serve, helpfulness; (*b*) usefulness: M16. **serviceably** *adverb* †(*a*) obediently; (*b*) usefully: M16.

servient /ˈsəːvɪənt/ *adjective*. M16.

[Latin *servient-* pres. ppl stem of *servire* SERVE *verb*¹: see -ENT.]

1 LAW. Designating (a tenement of) land whose owner is subject to an easement or servitude favouring the owner of a dominant land or tenement. M16.

2 Subordinate, subject to authority or rule. Formerly also, serving. Now *rare*. E17.

serviette /səːvɪˈɛt/ *noun*. L15.

[Old & mod. French = towel, napkin, from *servir* SERVE *verb*¹: see -ETTE.]

A table-napkin, now *esp.* a paper one.

servile /ˈsəːvʌɪl/ *adjective & noun.* LME.
[Latin *servilis*, from *servus* slave: see -ILE.]
▶ **A** *adjective.* **1** Of, pertaining to, or suitable for a slave or slaves. Freq. *derog.* LME. ▸**†b** Of, pertaining to, or suitable for the working class; engaged in menial employment or manual labour. LME–E18. ▸**c** That is a slave, living in servitude. M16.
2 Characteristic of or resembling a slave; slavish, fawning; lacking all independence in thought or action; abjectly submissive or deferential (*to*). E16.
3 Of a people, State, etc.: politically enslaved; subject to despotic or oppressive rule or to foreign control. Formerly also *fig.*, subject to the control or influence of something else; not free. Usu. foll. by *to*. Now *rare*. M16.
4 Of imitation, esp. in the arts, a translation, etc.: unintelligently or slavishly adhering to the model or original. E17.
5 PHILOLOGY. **a** Of a particle: expressing grammatical relations; auxiliary. Now *rare*. M17. ▸**b** SEMITIC GRAMMAR. Of a letter: not belonging to the root of the word in which it occurs; serving to express a derivative or inflectional element. Also, designating those letters of the alphabet which represent sounds that may be used in derivation or inflection. Opp. ***radical***. M17. ▸**c** Of a letter: not sounded but serving to indicate that a preceding vowel should be lengthened. *rare*. E18.

🕮 **1** C. THIRLWALL Demetrius was of very low, if not . . servile origin. **servile work** ROMAN CATHOLIC CHURCH heavy manual labour which is forbidden on Sundays and certain Church festivals. **c** W. STUBBS The peasant population . . had been servile before the Conquest. **2** E. WILSON Acting merely as a servile tool of others. P. D. JAMES He was meticulous in his attitude to senior officers, respectful without being servile.

▶ **B** *noun.* **1** PHILOLOGY. **a** A servile particle. *rare*. M17. ▸**b** SEMITIC GRAMMAR. A servile letter. M18.
2 A servile person; *Hist.* a 19th-cent. Spanish royalist. Also, a servant. E19.
■ **servilely** *adverb* M16. **servileness** *noun* (*rare*) servility L17. **†servilize** *verb trans.* (*rare*) make servile E17–M18.

servilism /ˈsəːvɪlɪz(ə)m/ *noun. rare.* M19.
[from SERVILE *adjective* + -ISM.]
1 Systematic servility. M19.
2 A social system based on the existence of slaves. *US* (now *Hist.*). L19.

servility /səːˈvɪlɪti/ *noun.* L16.
[from SERVILE *adjective* + -ITY.]
†1 The quality or status of being a slave; the condition of being in servitude. L16–M17.
2 Servile disposition or behaviour; *esp.* abject submissiveness or deferentiality, lack of independence in thought or action. L16.

serving /ˈsəːvɪŋ/ *noun.* ME.
[from SERVE *verb*[1] + -ING[1].]
1 a The action of SERVE *verb*[1]; an instance of this. Also foll. by adverb. ME. ▸**†b** The part or character served by a disguise. *rare* (Shakes.). Only in E17. ▸**c** A helping; a quantity of food served to one person. Also (*Scot.*), as much as satisfies a person. M18.
2 NAUTICAL. The material used for serving or binding a rope etc. E17.
1a attrib.: ***serving dish***, ***serving hatch***, ***serving spoon***, etc.
Comb.: **serving cart** *N. Amer.* a small trolley from which food and drink may be served.

serving /ˈsəːvɪŋ/ *ppl adjective.* ME.
[from SERVE *verb*[1] + -ING[2].]
1 That serves or does service to another; performing the duties of a servant. ME.
2 Of a member of the armed forces etc.: on service. M16.
1 serving-man *arch.* a male servant or attendant. **serving-woman** *arch.* a female servant or attendant.

Servite /ˈsəːvʌɪt/ *noun & adjective.* M16.
[medieval Latin *Servitae* (pl.) from Latin *servus* servant (in *Servi Beatae Mariae* the formal title of the order): see -ITE[1].]
▶ **A** *noun.* A friar or nun of the religious order of the Servants of Blessed Mary, founded in 1233. M16.
▶ **B** *adjective.* Of or belonging to the order of the Servants of Blessed Mary. M18.

servitor /ˈsəːvɪtə/ *noun.* ME.
[Old French (mod. *serviteur*) from late Latin, from Latin *servit-* pa. ppl stem of *servire* SERVE *verb*[1]: see -OR.]
1 A (male) personal or domestic attendant, a servant. Formerly *esp.*, a person who waits at table. *arch.* ME. ▸**b** Any person in a subordinate post or employment; *spec.* †(***a***) an apprentice; †(***b***) a lawyer's clerk; (***c***) an assistant janitor or attendant at Edinburgh University. *Scot.* L15. ▸**c** A squire, a page. Long *rare*. E16. ▸**d** A devoted admirer, a lover. Long *rare*. E16. ▸**e** An official or semi-official title of certain officers of the royal household, municipal bodies, etc. M16.
2 A person on military service; a soldier; *spec.* a person to whom lands were assigned in Ulster in the reign of James I, in return for military or civil service in Ireland. *obsolete* exc. *Hist.* M16.
3 In certain colleges of Oxford University, an undergraduate performing menial duties for fellows in return for free board, lodging, and attendance at lectures. *obsolete* exc. *Hist.* M17.
■ **serviˈtorial** *adjective* (*rare*) M19. **servitorship** *noun* L18.

servitress /ˈsəːvɪtrɪs/ *noun. arch.* M19.
[from SERVITOR + -ESS[1].]
= next.

servitrix /ˈsəːvɪtrɪks/ *noun.* Chiefly *Scot.* Now *rare*. Pl. **-trices** /-trɪsiːz/, **-trixes**. M16.
[medieval Latin, fem of Latin SERVITOR: see -TRIX.]
A female servant or assistant.

servitude /ˈsəːvɪtjuːd/ *noun.* LME.
[Old French from Latin *servitudo*, from *servus* slave: see -TUDE.]
1 The condition of being a slave or a serf; absence of personal freedom. Now *esp.*, a state of subjection entailing enforced rigorous or excessive labour. Also, a state of slavery or serfdom. LME. ▸**b** The condition of being politically enslaved; subjection to foreign control or to despotic or oppressive rule. L15. ▸**c** *transf.* & *fig.* A condition resembling slavery; a state of being dominated by something in a degrading or abject manner. L15. ▸**†d** Slaves or servants collectively. *rare* (Milton). Only in M17.
†2 Feudal subjection; vassalage, subordination. L15–M17. ▸**b** Feudal homage or service. L15–E19.
3 CIVIL & SCOTS LAW. A subjection of property either to a definite person other than its owner (***personal servitude***) or to the (adjacent) property of another owner for the benefit of the dominant property (***predial servitude***). L16.
4 The condition of being a servant, esp. a domestic one. Now *rare* or *obsolete*. M17.
5 Apprenticeship. Now *rare* or *obsolete*. L18.
6 Compulsory hard labour as a punishment for criminals. Chiefly in ***penal servitude*** s.v. PENAL *adjective* 1c. L18.
7 A person's (period of) armed service, esp. in the Navy. *rare*. E19.

servo /ˈsəːvəʊ/ *noun & verb.* L19.
[French *servo-moteur* servomotor, from Latin *servus* slave + *-o-* -O- + French *moteur* MOTOR *noun*.]
▶ **A** *noun.* Pl. **-os**.
1 In full ***servomotor***. Orig., an auxiliary motor used to direct the rudders of a torpedo or the reversing gear of a large marine engine. Now *gen.*, any device used as the motive element in a servomechanism. L19.
2 In full ***servomechanism***. A powered mechanism which produces controlled motion at a high energy or power level in response to an input motion of lower energy; *esp.* one in which feedback is employed to make the control automatic, generally comprising a measuring device, a servo-amplifier, and a servomotor; *transf.* & *fig.* a non-mechanical (esp. physiological) system characterized by self-regulating feedback. E20.
Comb.: **servo-amplifier** the part of a servomechanism that responds to a small error signal and delivers a corresponding large signal to the servomotor; **servo brake** (***a***) a vehicle brake whose application is assisted by the momentum of the vehicle; (***b***) a brake operated by a servomechanism; **servo control** †(***a***) an aircraft control using a servo tab; (***b***) a servomechanism; (***c***) the use of a servomechanism to assist with the control of a system; the action or practice of controlling a system by means of a servomechanism; **servo-control** *verb trans.* control by means of a servomechanism; **servo flap** AERONAUTICS = *servo tab* below; **servohydraulic** *adjective* both servo-controlled and hydraulic; **servomechanical** *adjective* of or pertaining to a servomechanism; ***servomechanism***: see sense 2 above; ***servomotor***: see sense 1 above; **servo system** a servomechanism; **servo tab** AERONAUTICS a tab, operated directly by the pilot, which gives rise to aerodynamic forces that assist in moving the main flap.
▶ **B** *verb trans.* Control or operate by a servomechanism. L20.

Servo- /ˈsəːvəʊ/ *combining form. arch.* L19.
[from SERVIAN *adjective*[1] + -O-.]
= SERBO-.

servus /ˈzɛrvʊs/ *interjection.* L19.
[German from Latin = servant.]
In Austria and southern Germany, used as an informal greeting or farewell.

sesame /ˈsɛsəmi/ *noun.* LME.
[Latin *sesamum*, *sisa-*, *sesama*, *-ima* from Greek *sēsamon*, *sēsamē*, of oriental origin (cf. Arab. *simsim*). In sense 2 with allus. to the magic words used to open the door of a robbers' cave in the *Arabian Nights' Entertainments* (see OPEN SESAME).]
1 An African plant, *Sesamum orientale* (family Pedaliaceae), widely grown in the tropics, producing seeds used as food and yielding an edible oil; *collect.* the seeds of this plant. LME.
2 A magic password; a thing which acts like magic in achieving or acquiring what would otherwise be unobtainable; = OPEN SESAME. L18.

🕮 **2** *attrib.*: G. GREENE The sesame phrase: 'A friend of Harry Lime's.'

sesamoid /ˈsɛsəmɔɪd/ *adjective & noun.* L17.
[from prec. + -OID, perh. after Greek *sēsamoeidēs*.]
▶ **A** *adjective.* Shaped like a sesame-seed; ANATOMY designating certain small nodular bones formed in tendons passing over an angular structure, such as the kneecap and the navicular bone. L17.
▶ **B** *noun.* A sesamoid bone. M19.

sesamum /ˈsɛsəməm/ *noun.* Also **†sesamus**. M16.
[Latin from Greek *sēsamon*.]
= SESAME 1.

sesban /ˈsɛsban/ *noun.* M19.
[French †*sesban*, ult. from Arab. *saysabān* from Persian *sīsabān*.]
Any plant of the leguminous genus *Sesbania*; esp. *S. bispinosa* and *S. sesban*, valuable sources of fibre.

sescuple /ˈsɛskjʊp(ə)l/ *adjective.* Now *rare*. L17.
[Latin *sescuplus*, *-plex* var. of *sesquiplus*, *-plex*, from *sesqui-* SESQUI- + *-plus*, *-plex* -FOLD.]
= SESQUIALTER *adjective*.

seseli /ˈsɛsɪli/ *noun.* M16.
[Latin *seseli(s)* from Greek. Cf. CICELY.]
Any of various umbelliferous plants constituting the genus *Seseli* or formerly included in it.

sesh /sɛʃ/ *noun. colloq.* (orig. *Military slang*). M20.
[Abbreviation.]
A session or bout, esp. of drinking.

Sesotho /sɛˈsuːtuː/ *noun & adjective.* M19.
[Sesotho, from *se-* prefix + SOTHO.]
(Of) the South Eastern Bantu language of the Basotho.

sesqui- /ˈsɛskwi/ *prefix.*
[Latin, formed as SEMI- + *-que* and.]
Used in words adopted from Latin and in English words modelled on these in senses (***a***) designating, denoting, or involving a ratio of an integer to the next lower integer, as ***sesquialtera***, ***sesquitertia***, ***sesquiquarta*** (5:4 or 1¼:1), ***sesquioctave*** (9:8 or 1⅛:1), etc., or occas. a similar integral ratio (no longer productive); (***b***) designating, denoting, or involving multiplication by one and a half, as ***sesquicentenary*** etc.; (***c***) CHEMISTRY denoting combination in a compound of three equivalents of a named radical or element to two others, as ***sesquioxide*** etc.

sesquialter /sɛskwɪˈaltə/ *adjective.* Now *rare*. L16.
[Latin, formed as SESQUI- + *alter* second.]
Designating or involving a proportion of or equivalent to 1½ to 1 (= 3:2); in such a proportion *to*; that is a multiple by 1½ *of*.
■ Also **sesquialteral** *adjective* E17. **sesquialterate** *adjective* E17.

sesquialtera /sɛskwɪˈalt(ə)rə/ *adjective & noun.* LME.
[Latin, fem. (sc. *ratio*) of SESQUIALTER.]
▶ **A** *adjective.* **1** MUSIC. Designating the ratio 3:2 in mensurable music; designating an interval of a fifth. LME.
▶ **B** *noun.* **1** The ratio 3:2 in mensurable music; an interval of a fifth. LME.
2 A mixture stop in an organ, usu. consisting of two ranks of narrow-scaled open flue pipes. L17.

sesquicentenary /ˌsɛskwɪsɛnˈtiːn(ə)ri, -ˈtɛn-, sɛskwɪˈsɛntɪn-/ *noun.* M20.
[from SESQUI- + CENTENARY.]
(A celebration of) a one-hundred-and-fiftieth anniversary.

sesquicentennial /ˌsɛskwɪsɛnˈtɛnɪəl/ *adjective & noun.* Orig. *US*. L19.
[from SESQUI- + CENTENNIAL.]
▶ **A** *adjective.* Of or pertaining to a hundred-and-fiftieth anniversary. L19.
▶ **B** *noun.* = SESQUICENTENARY. L19.

sesquioxide /sɛskwɪˈɒksʌɪd/ *noun.* M19.
[from SESQUI- + OXIDE.]
CHEMISTRY. An oxide containing three equivalents of oxygen to two of another element or radical.
■ **sesquioxiˈdation** *noun* M19. **sesquioˈxidic** *adjective* E20.

sesquipedalian /ˌsɛskwɪpɪˈdeɪlɪən/ *noun & adjective.* E17.
[from Latin *sesquipedalis*, from SESQUI- + *ped-*, *pes* foot + *-alis* -AL[1]: see -IAN.]
▶ **A** *noun.* **†1** A person or thing a foot and a half high or long. E–M17
2 A polysyllabic word. M19.
▶ **B** *adjective.* **1** Of a word etc.: polysyllabic, lengthy. M17.
2 Characterized by long words; tending to be lengthy or ponderous in speech. M19.
■ **seˈsquipedal** *adjective & noun* = SESQUIPEDALIAN E17. **sesquipedalianism** *noun* M19. **sesquipedality** /-pɪˈdalɪti/ *noun* M18.

sesquiplane /ˈsɛskwɪpleɪn/ *noun.* E20.
[French *sesquiplan*, from *sesqui-* SESQUI- + *plan* PLANE *noun*[3].]
Hist. A biplane having one wing (usu. the lower) with not more than half the surface area of the other.

sesquiterpene /sɛskwɪˈtəːpiːn/ *noun.* L19.
[from SESQUI- + TERPENE.]
CHEMISTRY. Any terpene with the formula $C_{15}H_{24}$; a simple derivative of such a compound.
■ **sesquiterpenoid** *noun & adjective* (designating or pertaining to) a sesquiterpene M20.

sesquitertia /sɛskwɪˈtəːʃə/ *adjective.* LME.
[Latin, fem. (sc. *ratio*) of *sesquitertius*, from SESQUI- + *tertius* third.]
Designating a ratio of 1⅓ to 1, i.e. 4 to 3; *spec.* (*a*) designating a musical interval of a perfect fourth; (*b*) designating a rhythm of three notes against four.
■ Also †**sesquitertial** *adjective* E17–E19. **sesquitertian** *adjective* (*rare*) E17.

sess /sɛs/ *noun*¹ & *interjection. obsolete* exc. *dial.* E17.
[Origin unkn.]
(A call) commanding a dog to attack, approach for food, etc.

†**sess** *noun*², *verb* vars. of CESS *noun*¹, *verb*¹.

sess *noun*³ var. of CESS *noun*².

†**sessa** *interjection. rare* (Shakes.). L16–E17.
[Perh. var. of SA SA or from French *cessez* cease!]
Let it (him, her, etc.) go!

sessile /ˈsɛsʌɪl, ˈsɛsɪl/ *adjective.* E18.
[Latin *sessilis*, from *sess-* pa. ppl stem of *sedere* SIT *verb*: see -ILE.]
1 BOTANY, ZOOLOGY, & MEDICINE. Attached directly to a surface; having no stalk, neck, etc. Also, (of a plant) having stalkless fruit. E18.
2 Chiefly BIOLOGY. Sedentary, living fixed to one spot; immobile, fixed. M19.
3 CRYSTALLOGRAPHY. Of a dislocation in a crystal: unable to migrate through the lattice; fixed. M20.

🕮 **1 sessile oak** the durmast oak, *Quercus petraea*, which has stalkless acorns **2** M. WEBB People remained in a sessile state over tea for a long time. *Nature* The more important sessile components of the coral reef ecosystem . . corals and sponges.

■ **sessility** /-ˈsɪlɪti/ *noun* (chiefly BIOLOGY) sessile character or condition E20.

session /ˈsɛʃ(ə)n/ *noun & verb.* LME.
[Old & mod. French, or from Latin *sessio(n-)*, from *sess-* pa. ppl stem of *sedere* SIT *verb*: see -ION.]
▸ **A** *noun.* **1** †**a** A place for sitting. *rare.* Only in LME. ▸**b** The action or an act of sitting; the state of being seated; occupation of a seat in an assembly; CHRISTIAN THEOLOGY the enthronement of Christ at the right hand of God after the Ascension. Now *rare.* M16.
2 a The meeting of a legislative or deliberative body to conduct its business; a single continuous meeting for this purpose. LME. ▸**b** A continuous series of meetings of a legislative or deliberative body, held daily or at short intervals; the period during which such meetings continue to be held; *spec.* the period between the opening of Parliament and its prorogation. M16.
3 a *sing.* & in *pl.* (usu. treated as *sing.*). A judicial inquiry. Long *arch.* LME. ▸**b** In *pl.* (treated as *sing.* or *pl.*) & (*rare*) sing. The periodical court sittings of justices of the peace or of a stipendiary magistrate. Now chiefly with specifying word. LME.
4 SCOTS LAW. **a** *Hist.* A court of justice consisting of the Chancellor and others selected by the king from his council and sitting three times a year to judge cases previously brought before the king and his council, superseded by the Court of Session. L15. ▸**b** More fully (& now only) ***Court of Session***. The supreme civil court of Scotland, established in 1532 to encompass the powers and jurisdiction of the earlier session and the King's council. M16.
5 The lowest court in a Presbyterian Church, composed of the minister and elders of the congregation of a parish. Orig. *Scot.* L16.
6 The period of the academic year during which teaching takes place. Also, the period of a day during which classes are held at a school etc. or papers given at a conference etc. Orig. *Scot.* E18.
7 A period of time set aside for or spent in pursuing a particular activity; *spec.* (*a*) a business period on a stock exchange or another financial or commodity market; (*b*) a period of time devoted to the performance or recording of music; = ***jam session*** s.v. JAM *noun*⁴; (*c*) *colloq.* a period of heavy or sustained drinking; (*d*) *colloq.* (chiefly *Austral.* & *NZ*) a disturbance, an argument. E20.

🕮 **1b** F. KILVERT Wooden . . chairs polished smooth by the friction of continual sessions. **3a** SHAKES. *Wint. T.* Summon a session, that we may arraign Our most disloyal lady. **7** R. K. NARAYAN She . . began a practice session which went on for . . hours. *Times* Sterling enjoyed another good session.

Phrases etc.: ***Court of session***: see sense 4b above. **great session(s)**, **grand session(s)** *Hist.* a court of justice formerly held half-yearly in each of the counties of Wales, presided over by itinerant judges forming a distinct body from the judges of assize in England. **in session** assembled for or proceeding with business; in conference; not on vacation. **kirk-session** = sense 5 above. **petty sessions** *Hist.* a court held by two or more justices of the peace or a stipendiary magistrate, for the summary trial of minor offences within a particular district (now replaced by a magistrates' court). ***plenary session***: see PLENARY *adjective* 2b. **sessions of the peace** = sense 3b above. **special sessions** a regular court held by two or more justices of the peace for the exercise of a distinct branch of their authority, such as the granting or renewal of licences to sell alcoholic drinks.

Comb.: **session clerk** a chief lay official in the session of a Presbyterian Church; **session man** = *session musician* below; **session musician**: hired to play for a recording session.
▸ **B** *verb trans.* Bring (a person) before the session of a church. *Scot. rare.* E18.
■ **sessional** *adjective* of or pertaining to a session or sessions E18. **sessionally** *adverb* E18. **sessionary** *adjective* (*rare*) (*a*) = SESSIONAL; (*b*) during which business is transacted: E18. **sessioˈneer** *noun* a session musician M20. **sessioner** *noun* †(*a*) *Scot.* a member of the Court of Session; †(*b*) a member of a session of a Presbyterian Church; (*c*) *colloq.* a session musician: L16.

†**sessment** *noun.* M16–M18.
[Aphet.]
= ASSESSMENT.

†**sessor** *noun.* LME–E18.
[Aphet.]
= ASSESSOR.

sester /ˈsɛstə/ *noun. obsolete* exc. *Hist.* OE.
[Anglo-Norman = Old French *sestier* from Latin *sextarium* SEXTARY. In Old English from Latin.]
†**1** A container for liquid; a jar, a pitcher, a vat. OE–ME.
2 A liquid measure for beer, wine, etc. OE.
3 A dry measure for grain etc. OE.

sesterce /ˈsɛstəːs/ *noun.* Pl. **sesterces** /ˈsɛstəsɪz/. Also **sestertius** /sɛˈstəːtʃəs/, pl. **-tii** /-ʃɪɪ/. L16.
[Latin *sestertius* (sc. *nummus* coin) that is two and a half, from *semis* half + *tertius* third: see SEMI-, cf. SESQUI-.]
An ancient Roman silver or bronze coin and monetary unit, equal to a quarter of a denarius.

sestertium /sɛˈstəːʃɪ(ə)m/ *noun.* Pl. **-tia** /-ʃɪə/. M16.
[Latin, prob. use as neut. sing. of genit. pl. of *sestertius* SESTERCE (with ellipsis of *mille* a thousand).]
ROMAN HISTORY. An amount of a thousand sesterces.

sestertius *noun* var. of SESTERCE.

sestet /sɛsˈtɛt/ *noun.* Also **sestette**, **sestetto** /sɛsˈtɛtəʊ/ (pl. **-os**). E19.
[Italian *sestetto*, from *sesto* from Latin *sextus* a sixth + *-etto* -ET¹. Cf. SEXTET.]
1 MUSIC. A composition for six voices or instruments. E19.
2 The last six lines of a sonnet following the octet. M19.

sestetto *noun* var. of SESTET.

sestiere /sestiˈɛːre/ *noun.* Pl. ***-ri*** /-ri/. L16.
[Italian, from Latin *sextarius* the sixth part of a measure.]
In Italy, each of six districts or areas of a city. Cf. QUARTIERE.

sestina /sɛˈstiːnə/ *noun.* M19.
[Italian, from *sesto*: see SESTET. Cf. next.]
A form of rhymed or unrhymed poem of six stanzas of six lines and a concluding triplet in which the same six words at the line-ends occur in each stanza in six different sequences, apart from the final triplet, in which each line contains two of these words, one at the middle and one at the end. Cf. SEXTAIN.

sestine /sɛˈstiːn/ *noun.* Long *rare.* L16.
[French †*sestine* from Italian SESTINA. Cf. SEXTINE.]
= prec.

seston /ˈsɛstən/ *noun.* E20.
[German from Greek *sēston* neut. of *sēstos* that which is filtered, from *sēthein* strain, filter: cf. PLANKTON.]
BIOLOGY & OCEANOGRAPHY. (The living organisms present in) fine particulate matter suspended in water. Cf. TRIPTON.
■ **seˈstonic** *adjective* of, pertaining to, or consisting of seston M20.

set /sɛt/ *noun*¹. Also (now chiefly in senses 16, 23, 24, 32, 33) **sett**. See also SATE *noun.* OE.
[from SET *verb*¹. Old English use after Old Norse *sólarsetr*, *-seta* sunset (not recorded again in sense 1 until LME). See also next, SETT *noun*¹.]
▸ **I** The action of setting; the condition of being set.
1 The action of setting (of the sun, the moon, a star, etc.); the apparent descent of a celestial object towards the horizon at the close of its diurnal period; the time of this. Now *poet.* exc. in SUNSET. OE.
†**2** A hostile encounter, an attack. Only in ME.
3 Letting, leasing; a let, a lease. Chiefly *Scot.* LME.
4 More emphatically ***dead set***. ▸**a** The condition of being stopped or checked; a check; a standstill; a serious setback. E17. ▸**b** An abrupt stop made by an animal pointing in the direction of prey; the position taken up by a dog in pointing game. E18.
5 More emphatically ***dead set***. A determined attempt or onslaught; a firm action or movement; *spec.* a determined attempt to gain a person's attention or affections. E18.
6 The action of hardening, solidifying, or coagulating; the condition of being set. M19.
7 A hostile attitude or feeling, a grudge. Chiefly in ***have a set on***, ***take a set on***. *Austral.* & *NZ colloq.* M19.

🕮 **1 set of day** (*a*) the time at which the sun sets; (*b*) the west. **5** THACKERAY A girl . . who made a dead set at me. A. MAYHEW A direct set upon Phil was made by the satirical young rogues. *Observer* Almost every member of the British Press made a dead set for the hosiery counter. **6 initial set** a condition attained by cement when it begins to stiffen, but before hardening commences. ***permanent set***: see PERMANENT *adjective*.

▸ **II** A thing which is set.
8 a A cutting or young plant used for bedding out or grafting. LME. ▸**b** (More fully ***potato set***) a (portion of a) small potato tuber used in the propagation of new plants. Also = ***onion set*** s.v. ONION *noun.* M18. ▸**c** (More fully ***fruit set***, ***seed set***) the development of fruit or seed following fertilization. Also, the rudimentary fruit formed. L19.
†**9** The stake put down at dice etc. M16–E17.
†**10** A game at dice or cards; a match, a contest. L16–L17.
11 In real tennis (also **sett**) & (lawn) tennis, a group of at least six games counting as a unit towards the match for the side that wins six first, usually with a margin of at least two. Also in darts, volleyball, & other games, a similar group of games counting as a unit. L16.
12 Each of the pleats of a ruff; the arrangement of a ruff in pleats. Long *rare.* L16.
13 The finishing coat of plaster on a wall. E19.
14 a A net set across a river etc., esp. to catch eels. E19. ▸**b** A trap, a snare; a series of traps. *N. Amer.* E20.
15 = ***set scene*** s.v. SET *adjective.* Also, the setting, stage furniture, or other properties used on stage in a theatre or to create a scene in filming; the place or area in which a play is performed or filming takes place. M19.
16 (Usu. **sett.**) A squared paving-stone, esp. of granite. M19.

🕮 **11 *game, set, and match***: see GAME *noun.* **15** P. G. WODEHOUSE She was supposed to be on the set, made up, at six on the following a.m. R. BOLT When the curtain rises, the set is in darkness but for a single spot. A. ROAD Studio time is costly . . so the sets have all been erected in great haste.

▸ **III** The manner or position in which a thing is set.
†**17** The way in which something is set down in writing. *rare.* Only in M16.
18 Tendency, inclination; determination (of the mind, character, action, etc.) in a certain direction; settled direction, fixed habit. Also, a predisposition or expectation influencing response. M16.
19 The way in which an article of dress is arranged or hangs; the way in which a ship's sails are set. L16.
20 The build of a person. Now *Scot.* & *dial.* E17.
21 CAMPANOLOGY. The inverted position of a bell when it is set. L17.
22 The direction in which a current flows or a wind blows; the action of water etc. in taking a particular direction. E18.
23 (Usu. **sett.**) Each of the squares in the pattern of a tartan; the pattern of a tartan. E18.
24 (Usu. **sett.**) The adjustment of the reeds of a loom necessary for the making of a fabric of a particular texture; the make of a fabric as determined by this. L18.
25 A form resulting from strain or pressure or a process of solidification etc.; a warp, bend, or displacement caused by continued pressure or a fixed position. E19.
26 The inclination or dip of the arm of an axle-tree; the elevation of a gun. M19.
27 The slight lateral deflection in opposite directions of the alternate teeth of a saw; the amount of this deflection. M19.
28 A position or attitude (either occasional or habitual) given to a limb or other part of the body. M19.
29 TYPOGRAPHY. The amount of spacing in type controlling the distance between letters; the width of a piece of type or a character. L19.
30 An action or result of setting the hair. M20.

🕮 **18** A. LURIE He's got this set against social psychology. ***mental set***: see MENTAL *adjective*¹. **28** S. BELLOW It was evident from the set of her arms that she did not wish to be pushed. J. FOWLES His face has a sort of natural 'hurt' set. **30** B. BAINBRIDGE The hairdresser . . had sworn her set would last a week.

▸ **IV** A place where something is set.
31 A place where stationary fishing nets are fixed. M18.
32 (Usu. **sett.**) The earth or burrow of a badger. L19.
▸ **V 33** (Usu. **sett.**) A tool or device used for setting; *esp.* a heavy punch or chisel for use on metal or stone. M18.
Comb.: **set point** *noun*¹ the state of a set when one side or player needs only one point to win the set; this point.

set /sɛt/ *noun*². Also †**sett**. LME.
[Old French *sette* from Latin *secta* SECT *noun*¹, infl. by & merging with SET *noun*¹. In branch II perh. partly due to Middle Low German *gesette*.]
▸ **I** Of people.
†**1** A religious body, a sect. LME–M16.

2 A number, company, or group *of* people associated by community of status, habits, occupations, or interests; a social group, esp. of a select or exclusive character. LME.
3 The number of couples required to perform a country dance or square dance. E18.
4 A subdivision of pupils or students for instruction on a particular subject, freq. constituted according to ability. L18.
5 A (regular) meeting of a gang or group in a particular urban locality, *esp.* a party; the place where such a group meets. *US colloq.* M20.

📖 **2** SIR W. SCOTT A set of smugglers, gipsies, and other desperadoes. C. CONNOLLY He moved in a fast set of hard-smoking and hard-swearing cronies. M. BRADBURY All the girls . . in her set round the village are buying Miele dishwashers. ***Bloomsbury set***, ***jet set***, ***smart set***, etc.

▶ **II** Of things.
6 A complete collection of the individual pieces or items belonging together, as composing a suite of furniture, a service of china, a clothing outfit, etc.; a collection of instruments, tools, or machines customarily used together in a particular operation; a complete apparatus employed for some specific purpose. LME. ▸**b** A piece of electrical or electronic apparatus, as a telephone, a telegraph receiver or transmitter, a radio or television receiver, etc. L19.
7 a A number *of* musical instruments arranged to play together. Now only, a suite of bells to be rung together. M16. ▸**b** An assemblage of pipes constituting bagpipes or (formerly) an organ. L18.
†**8** A string of beads. M16–M17.
9 A collection of volumes by one author, dealing with one subject, belonging to one department of literature, or issued in a series; a complete series of the parts of a periodical publication. Also, a series of prints by the same engraver. L16.
10 A number of things connected in temporal or spatial succession or by natural production or formation. E17.
11 The complement of teeth which a person or animal has; a pair of plates holding artificial teeth. L17.
12 A team of (usu. six) horses. Now *rare* or *obsolete*. L17.
13 A number of things grouped together according to a system of classification or conceived as forming a whole. L17.
14 A series of buildings or apartments associated in use; *esp.* a suite of apartments let as lodgings. E18.
15 The series of movements or figures that make up a square dance or country dance, esp. the quadrille. E18.
16 MATH. & LOGIC. An assemblage or collection of (real or notional) entities which either satisfy specified conditions or else are specified individually. M19.
17 A number of pieces of jazz or popular music performed in sequence by a musician or group. M20.
18 A fixed number of repetitions of a particular body-building exercise, performed as a unit. M20.

📖 **6** SAKI A liqueur glass, one out of a set of seven that would be impossible to match. R. LARDNER A 'set' of jewelry consisting of an opal brooch, a bracelet of opals . . , and an opal ring. A. BLEASDALE A complete and matching set of pyjamas, top and bottom. ***chess set***, ***duchesse set***, ***giving-set***, ***pumpset***, ***starter set***, ***twin set***, etc. ***break a set***: see BREAK *verb*. **b** B. VINE If you want television . . why don't you buy a set of your own? ***handset*** etc. **7b** ***set of bagpipes***. **9** LD MACAULAY All the Edinburgh Reviews are being bound, so that we shall have a complete set up to the forthcoming number. L. HELLMAN There were no books other than a set of Prescott. **10** SIR W. SCOTT A new set of words to the old tune. **13** GOLDSMITH An exact plan . . of Nature's operations in this minute set of creatures. M. EDGEWORTH The set of notions which he had acquired from his education. ***a set of steps***: see STEP *noun*[1] 9b. **14** C. P. SNOW The room was cosier . . than in most college sets. **15** ***running set***: see RUNNING *adjective*. **16** ***empty set***: containing no elements. ***universal set***: see UNIVERSAL *adjective*.

Comb.: **set theory** the branch of mathematics that deals with sets without regard to the nature of the elements of which they are composed; an axiomatization which allows of the discussion of sets; **set-theoretic**, **set-theoretical** *adjectives* of or pertaining to set theory; **set-theoretically** *adverb* by means of or as regards set theory; **set-top box** a box-shaped signal decoder for viewing cable or satellite television or giving television access to the Internet, or for converting a digital television signal to analogue for viewing on a conventional set.

set *noun*[3] var. of SETT *noun*[1].

set /sɛt/ *adjective*. LOE.
[pa. pple of SET *verb*[1].]
1 *gen.* That has been set; that has set. Also foll. by adverb. LOE.
2 Appointed or prescribed beforehand; determined in advance; (of a phrase, form of expression, etc.) having conventional or predetermined wording, formulaic; (of a book, text, etc.) prescribed to be read or studied as part of a course or for an examination. Also, definite, not subject to uncertainty or alteration. LOE.
3 With prefixed adverb. Having a specified position, location, arrangement, conformation, build, adjustment, disposition, pitch, etc. ME.
4 Formal, ceremonious, regular; carefully prearranged; *spec.* (of a speech, passage, etc.) elaborate, carefully composed and usu. self-contained. E16.
†**5** Of a plant or tree: planted, not self-sown or growing wild; (occas.) that has been set by hand, not sown broadcast. M16–L18.
6 Unvarying, unmoving, immovable, persistent; fixed, rigid. E17.
7 Of the teeth: clenched. E19.
8 Of a meal or menu in a hotel etc.: consisting of a limited number of dishes or items of food at a fixed price. E20.

📖 **1** B. H. MALKIN A well-designed set out table! G. PRIESTLAND Those believers . . who will not . . deal with a set-apart ministry. **2** E. BANCROFT The Indians have no set time of eating. A. HELPS There always will be a set amount of wrongdoing. DICKENS It had no set beginning. **3** ***in good set terms*** [after Shakes. *A.Y.L.*] with outspoken severity, roundly. ***deep-set***, ***thickset***, ***well-set***, etc. **4** LD MACAULAY He was no speaker of set speeches. J. K. JEROME Not a set meal . . but a series of snacks. ***of a set purpose***: see PURPOSE *noun*. **6** F. NORRIS He assumed a set smile of amiability which never left his face the whole evening. J. FOWLES Too complicated for set ideas. **8** J. PATTINSON If you have the set lunch, it comes cheaper.

Special collocations: †**set battle** a pitched battle. **set copper** a form of metallic copper containing about 6 per cent of cuprous oxide, produced by oxidation during refining. **set net** a fishing net fastened across a stream or channel, into which fish are driven. **set play** SPORT a prearranged manoeuvre carried out from a restart by the team who have the advantage. **set point** *noun*[2] the value of a physical quantity that an automatic controller or regulator is set to maintain. **set scene** THEATRICAL scenery built up of more or less solid material. **set scrum**, **set scrummage** RUGBY FOOTBALL an organized scrum ordered by the referee during the course of play. **set shot** BASKETBALL a shot at the basket made from a still position. **set square** (*a*) a plate of wood, metal, plastic, etc., in the form of a right-angled triangle, used as a guide for drawing lines at a fixed angle, usu. 30° or 60°, or 45°; (*b*) a form of T-square with an additional arm turning on a pivot, for drawing lines at fixed angles to the head; (*c*) a joiner's square. **set stocking** AGRICULTURE the grazing of animals, esp. sheep, in the same pasture for a considerable period.
¶ For *pred.* uses see SET *verb*[1].

set /sɛt/ *verb*[1]. Infl. **-tt-**. Pa. t. & pple **set**.
[Old English *settan* = Old Frisian *setta*, Old Saxon *settian* (Dutch *zetten*), Old High German *sezzan* (German *setzen*), Old Norse *setja*, Gothic *satjan*, from Germanic causative from base of SIT *verb*. Cf. SEIZE *verb*.]
▶ **I** Seat; sit.
1 *verb trans.* Place in a sitting posture; cause to occupy a seat; seat. Chiefly with specification of place, passing into other senses. OE. ▸**b** Put (a hen bird) to sit on eggs. LME.
2 Also foll. by *down*: ▸**a** *verb refl.* Seat oneself, take a seat, sit down. Now chiefly *Scot.* ME. ▸**b** *verb trans.* In *pass.* Be seated. ME. ▸**c** *verb intrans.* Sit, be seated. Now chiefly *Scot. & N. Amer. dial.* ME.
3 *verb intrans.* **a** Remain, continue, lie; weigh *(up)on*. Now chiefly *US & dial.* LME. ▸**b** Have a certain set or hang; sit (well or ill, tightly or loosely, etc.). E19.
4 *verb trans.* Become, befit, suit. Chiefly *Scot.* L15.
5 *verb trans.* Sit on (a horse etc.) in riding. *rare.* M17.

📖 **1** S. JOHNSON Who setting us upon Camels, conducted us to Mazna. *Proverb*: Set a beggar on horseback, and he'll ride to the Devil. **2c** E. WELTY A perfect lady—just set in her seat and stared. **4** J. M. BARRIE Do you think this bonnet sets me?

▶ **II** Sink, descend.
†**6** *verb intrans.* Subside, abate. OE–ME.
7 *verb intrans.* Of the sun or other celestial object: go down; make an apparent descent towards and below the horizon. ME. ▸**b** Of the day: come to its close. *poet.* E17. ▸**c** *fig.* Decline, wane. E17.
†**8** *verb intrans.* NAUTICAL. Fall with a heavy sea. Only in ***heave and set***. E16–L17.

📖 **7** A. F. LOEWENSTEIN The almost round moon was setting. P. L. FERMOR The sun had set and left the river a pale zinc colour.

▶ **III** Put (more or less permanently) in a definite place.
†**9** *verb trans.* Place on or as on a foundation; build, erect. OE–L15.
10 *verb trans.* & (now *rare*) *intrans.* Put (a young plant, a cutting, etc.) in the ground to grow. Also, plant (a seed) individually (and not broadcast). OE.
11 †**a** *verb trans.* Put down as a deposit or security. OE–M17. ▸**b** *verb trans.* & *intrans.* Put (a sum of money) down as a stake; stake, wager. Now chiefly *Austral.* L15. ▸**c** *verb intrans.* DOMINOES. Play first. M19.
12 *verb trans.* Put or place, cause to be, lie, rest, or stand, in a locality specified by an adverbial expression; (foll. by *to*) place against, apply (one thing) to another. OE. ▸**b** In *pass.* Be situated, lie (in a certain locality); be placed (at a certain height, interval, etc.); have a certain position or arrangement by nature. OE. ▸**c** Represent (a story, play, scene, etc.) as happening in a certain place or at a certain time. E20.
13 *verb trans.* Put down in writing or in print; put down or enter in a catalogue, account, etc.; mention or discuss in a text; record. Now only foll. by *down*. ME.
14 *verb trans. spec.* Put (an ornament, fitting, piece of furniture, etc.) in a place allotted or adapted to receive it; fit, fix. Passing into branch VI. ME.
15 *verb trans.* GEOMETRY etc. Lay or mark off (a line of a definite length). E17.

📖 **12** LD BERNERS He sette his horne to his mouthe and blewe it. J. W. BURGON His birth . . and his parentage have been fully set before the public. C. KERNAHAN The worst of reasons . . inexperienced writers put forward for setting pen to paper. W. J. LOCKE The wondrous dish was set before them. A. SILLITOE He folded the mat and set it at the back of the niche. D. STOREY Wooden chairs were set against a wall. **b** S. BELLOW My eyes are set high in the face. **c** G. GREENE The novels were now set in Cumberland. **14** E. L. DOCTOROW She was putting on a hat and setting it in place with hatpins.

▶ **IV** Place or cause to be in a certain position (other than simply local).
16 *verb trans.* Place in a state, condition, relation, connection, sphere, position, or posture specified by an adverbial or complementary adjectival expression. OE.
†**17** *verb trans.* Give, bestow, assign (a name). OE–M17.
†**18** *verb trans.* Add (one thing) *to* another; apply or allot (money) *to*; apply (a remedy) *to*. OE–L16.
19 *verb trans.* †**a** Lay as a burden or trial *(up)on*; impose or inflict (a penalty, tax, etc.) *(up)on*. OE–M18. ▸**b** Place as a distinguishing mark, token, or imprint *(up)on*. Now *rhet.* OE. ▸**c** Lay or spread as a surface or coating *(up)on*. Now chiefly *fig.*, put (a favourable or specious appearance) *(up)on* a thing. M16. ▸**d** Fix (a certain price or value) *(up)on* a thing. Now chiefly in ***set a price on a person's head*** s.v. PRICE *noun*. M16. ▸**e** Stake the welfare or existence of (something) *(up)on*; in *pass.*, be dependent for its destiny *(up)on*. L16.
20 *verb trans.* Foll. by *against*: put (one thing) in the balance against another; enter on the opposite side to (a previous entry) in an account etc.; reckon as a counterpoise or compensation for. Formerly also (foll. by *by*, *to*), compare (one thing) to another. L16.

📖 **16** THACKERAY She had set her mind on the Major. T. F. TOUT The death of the old king set them free. H. GREEN Your suggestions as to how this scheme can best be set in motion. C. RAYNER There is only one way to set your mind at rest. J. RATHBONE He caught the bottle I had toppled and set it upright. P. BARKER Charging around a messy house and setting it all to rights. A. COHEN He had yet to set his business on a solid basis. **19c** SHAKES. *Haml.* We'll . . set a double varnish on the fame The Frenchman gave you. **20** I. FLEMING A tax-loss to set against more profitable enterprises elsewhere.

▶ **V** Appoint, institute, establish.
21 *verb trans.* Post or station (a person) in a certain place to perform certain duties. Formerly also, give an official appointment to. Passing into sense 54a. OE.
22 *verb trans.* Place in a position of superiority or control *over* another (e.g. as a ruler, protector, guard). OE.
23 *verb trans.* Determine, decide, establish, appoint, (now esp. a boundary, a limit, a pace). Formerly also, lay down (a law), prescribe (a form or order). OE.
24 *verb trans. spec.* Fix or appoint (a time) for the transaction of an affair or as the termination of a period. Also, fix or allow a time for. OE.
25 *verb trans.* Present (an example or pattern) for others to follow; exhibit as a type or model; initiate, introduce (a fashion). ME. ▸†**b** Start (a hymn etc.) for others to take up. LME–M18.
26 *verb trans.* Present or impose as work to be done or a matter to be dealt with; allot (a task). ME. ▸**b** *spec.* Present (a question or set of questions) for solving or answering; prescribe (a text) for an examination or a course of study. E18.
27 *verb trans.* Let on lease, lease, let. Now *local*. ME.
28 *verb trans.* Fix the amount of (a fine or other payment), fix or put down *at* a certain figure. LME.

📖 **21** SIR W. SCOTT How came he to leave the Castle after the watch was set? **22** M. J. GUEST He promoted the French clergy, and set them over the English. **23** S. PEPYS When our rules are once set . . no Governor should . . alter them. SMOLLETT Ambitious fellows, who set no bounds to their desires. *Daily Express* He . . raced out . . to set the fastest lap of the race. **24** HENRY MORE God had set his time wherein these afflictions . . should end. E. LEONARD My family and his wanted to set the date. **25** E. BLYTON There might be a chance for the wretched boy if he were . . set a good example. Q. CRISP Their wealth has given teenagers . . the power to set fashions. D. ROWE He saw his father as setting the standards which he had to attain. **26** F. MARRYAT I shall not set him anything to do. J. SNOW Ray was able to declare, setting Australia 416 to win.

▶ **VI** Fix or arrange in a required position or manner.
29 *verb trans.* Spread out (a net) to catch animals; lay (a trap). OE.

30 *verb trans.* Put (a thing) in place or in a certain position; fix up in the proper or required manner. OE. ▸**b** Put in operation, set going. L15.

31 *verb trans.* Fix (a stone or gem) in a surface or framework of metal or (formerly) on a garment, as an ornament. Also, fashion (a design or pattern) *in* precious stones. ME. ▸**b** *transf.* & *fig.* Place or insert (a thing) *in* a certain setting or framework. Formerly also *spec.*, frame (a picture). M16.

32 *verb trans.* Put (a sail) up in position to catch the wind; (of a ship) carry (so much canvas) with the sails set. ME.

33 *verb trans.* Regulate or adjust *by* a standard; *esp.* adjust (a clock etc.) to tell the right time. LME.

34 *verb trans. techn.* Put in a particular place as part of a manufacturing etc. process; put into an oven or furnace to bake or harden; put (milk) in a vessel for the addition of rennet in cheese-making; add yeast to (flour). L15.

35 *verb trans.* CAMPANOLOGY. Pull on (a bell) until it stands still in an inverted position, either balanced or held by the stay and the slider. L17.

36 *verb trans.* COMPUTING. Cause (a binary storage unit) to enter a prescribed state, *spec.* that representing the numeral 1. M20.

📖 **29** G. SWIFT He would always set his eel traps at night. **31** F. FORSYTH He had had Cartier of London cut and set the stones. **32** *Practical Boat Owner* With a beam of 8 ft. she sets 164 sq. ft. of sail. *Boards* The sail . . is virtually impossible to set any other way than full.

▸ **VII** Put in a certain order, give a planned or required arrangement, shape, or form to.

†**37** *verb trans.* Compose, write, (a treatise or book); translate. OE–E17.

†**38** *verb trans.* Array (an army) for battle. ME–E17.

39 *verb trans.* †**a** Adjust (one's clothing, the hair). ME–E18. ▸**b** Arrange and fix (the hair) when damp so that it dries in the desired style. E20.

40 *verb trans.* Make (a table) ready for a meal, spread (a table) *with* food etc.; lay out (a meal) ready for eating, put out ready for use at a meal. LME.

41 a *verb trans.* Put (a broken or dislocated bone, limb, etc.) into a position allowing healing and the restoration of the normal condition; deal with (a fracture or dislocation) in this way. LME. ▸**b** *verb intrans.* Of a bone etc.: be restored to the normal condition after fracture or dislocation. L16.

42 *verb trans.* Put an edge on (a cutting instrument, esp. a razor). LME.

†**43** *verb trans.* Tune (an instrument). L15–L16.

44 *verb trans.* Provide (words) with music for singing (more fully ***set to music***); write (a musical composition) *for* certain voices or instruments. E16.

45 *verb trans.* PRINTING & TYPOGRAPHY. Arrange (characters) by hand or machine, or electronically, in the order to be reproduced in print, compose; arrange the type or type images for (a book etc.), put (a book etc.) into print. M16.

†**46** *verb trans.* Pleat (a ruff); arrange the pleats of (a gown). M16–E17.

47 *verb trans.* Adjust (the teeth of a saw) by deflection alternately in opposite directions so as to produce a cut of the required width; adjust the teeth of (a saw) in this way; adjust (the blade of a plane) in relation to the sole in order to vary the depth of cut. L17.

48 *verb trans.* Fix the pattern, weave, or texture of (a fabric). L17.

49 *verb trans.* THEATRICAL. Construct (a scene) on the stage; arrange (an item of scenery) in a particular way on the stage; arrange scenery on (a stage). L18.

50 *verb trans.* Give the required adjustment, alignment, or shape to; arrange (an insect specimen, an insect's wings, etc.) so as to dry in a suitable position; dispose suitably for use or action; make (a mechanical contrivance, an instrument, etc.) ready for operation; adjust (an alarm, an alarm clock) to sound at a certain time. M19.

📖 **39b** N. FREELING Ash-blonde hair cut fairly short and set every week. **40** S. DELANEY I'll set the cups and we'll have a celebration. M. GARDINER The bare refectory table was set for lunch with well-polished silver and engraved glass. **41a** R. CHURCH The arm was never set properly, and this . . caused the muscles of the hand to wither. A. MOOREHEAD He set a young man's broken arm. **b** *Field* Dogs' bones soon set. **44** V. BRITTAIN He was setting to music . . a poem called 'L'Envoi'. **45** V. CRONIN No printer would touch the book, and Radischev had to set the 453 pages himself. **50** S. BELLOW He had forgotten to set the alarm and he woke up late. *Which?* You have to go back . . at the end of the pre-wash to set the main programme.

▸ **VIII** (Cause to) take a particular direction.

51 *verb trans.* Take (a journey), direct (one's course). Long only NAUTICAL, fix the direction of (a ship's course). OE.

52 *verb intrans.* **a** Proceed in a specified direction; begin to move, start off, put out. Without adverb (phr.) now only *Scot.* OE. ▸**b** (Of a current, wind, etc.) take or have a specified direction or course; *fig.* tend in a specified direction. LME.

53 *verb trans.* **a** Cause to go into a certain place or from one place to another; convey, transport. Now *rare.* ME. ▸**b** Of a current, wind, etc.: cause to move, carry along in a specified direction. LME. ▸**c** Accompany or escort (a person) for part or all of the way. Chiefly *Scot.* & *north.* M18.

54 a *verb trans.* Put (a person) *to* a piece of work or a task, *to doing*; instruct or cause (a person) *to do*; start (a person or thing) *doing, on doing,* (*arch.*) *a-doing,* (*up*)*on* a piece of work or a task. ME. ▸**b** *verb trans.* Direct (one's mind, intention, or will) *to* the consideration or performance of something, *to do*; fix (one's mind etc.) (*up*)*on* a piece of work or a task. ME. ▸**c** *verb refl.* & *intrans.* Start *to do, doing,* (*arch.*) *a-doing*; apply oneself *to doing, to do, to* a piece of work or a task. LME. ▸**d** *verb trans.* Cause (a person, oneself) to be busy *about.* E17.

55 a *verb trans.* Place in a position of hostility or opposition; cause to be hostile or antagonistic (foll. by *against,* †*at,* †*to*); pit *against*; *refl.* & in *pass.* be hostile or antagonistic. ME. ▸**b** *verb intrans.* Make an attack. Only foll. by preposition (see below). ME. ▸**c** *verb trans.* Incite (esp. a dog or other animal) to make an attack or go in pursuit. Usu. foll. by *at, on.* LME.

56 *verb trans.* Direct or point (one's face, foot, etc.) *to, towards, for* a place; put (a person) on the way leading to a destination. LME.

57 *verb intrans.* & *trans.* Propel (a boat or other craft) with a pole; punt. M16.

📖 **52b** M. ARNOLD As the vast tide Of the bright rocking Ocean sets to shore. *Practical Boat Owner* A fair tide can be carried well past Lands End before the stream sets to the north. **54a** J. KEBLE Is this not a thought to set us on praying? THACKERAY Those cards set people sadly a-quarrelling. M. PATTISON This rude shock . . set Usher upon a more careful examination. R. CHURCH We had been set to learn a passage from . . Paul's Epistles by heart. E. BLISHEN I set the class to work. E. BIRNEY Turvey was set to peeling potatoes in the . . kitchen. E. BOWEN He set the screen-wiper going. D. CECIL They admired his conversation most for its power to set them thinking. **b** M. J. GUEST He set his mind to govern his people well. J. W. KRUTCH Confident of his ability to *do* whatever he sets his mind upon. S. DELANEY I can do anything when I set my mind to it. **c** T. BEDDOES A young man . . reached a book from a shelf . . and set to read. E. WILSON Taine set himself to master politics and economics. I. MURDOCH I set myself to wondering what I ought to do next. **d** A. HELPS It set me . . about thinking of Cicero's *De Senectute.* **55a** SHAKES. *Tr. & Cr.* Will you set your wit to a fool's? G. GISSING She gets more and more set against me. A. LIVINGSTONE He too had . . done his share of slandering, trying to set her against Rée. K. ISHIGURO There were some powerful forces set against us then. **c** CONAN DOYLE They set dogs on us as though we were rats. **56** BUNYAN Turning thee from the way in which I had set thee. J. GALSWORTHY Lawrence . . set his fine nose towards the east wind.

▸ **IX** Place mentally; suppose, estimate.

†**58** *verb trans.* Posit, assume, suppose. ME–E18.

59 *verb trans.* Place mentally or conceptually in a certain category or on a certain point on a scale. ME.

60 *verb trans.* Fix the value or price of (a thing) *at* so much; estimate the amount of *at* so much; assess (a person) *at* so much. Now *arch.* & *literary* exc. *US.* ME.

61 *verb trans.* with adverbial obj. Have (a certain estimate) of a person or thing: in idiomatic phrs. expr. high or low regard, great or little esteem. Foll. by *by,* (*up*)*on.* Now *arch.* & *dial.* exc. in phrs. LME.

📖 **58** BUNYAN Set the case that there be two men who make a covenant. **59** POPE And justly set the Gem above the Flow'r. **60** SHAKES. *Haml.* I do not set my life at a pin's fee. LD MACAULAY Setting so wealthy a man at so low a rate. ***set at naught*** etc. **61** R. GRENEWEY The souldyers . . set nought by all military discipline. SIR W. SCOTT A fool . . to set light by that which Heaven has so often preserved. S. JUDD How hard it is to help setting a good deal by one's children.

▸ **X** Put or come into a settled or rigid position or state.

62 *verb trans.* In *pass.* Be resolved or determined (*to do,* (occas.) *that*). Now usu., be likely *to do,* be poised or about *to do*; also, be destined or heading *for.* ME.

63 *verb trans.* In *pass.* Have one's mind or will fixed (*up*)*on.* LME. ▸†**b** Be *well* etc. disposed. LME–E18. ▸**c** PSYCHOLOGY. Be predisposed *towards, to do.* M20.

64 *verb trans.* DYEING. ▸**a** Prepare (woad) for dyeing. Now *rare.* LME. ▸**b** Make (a colour) fast or permanent. E17.

65 a *verb trans.* Give a fixed or settled expression to (the eyes, the face, etc.); give a fixed or rigid position to (a part of the body, etc.). Usu. in *pass.*, have or assume a fixed look or expression; have or assume a rigid attitude or state; *spec.* (of an athlete) be poised to start a race, *gen.* be prepared for action, be ready (*to do, for*). M16. ▸**b** *verb trans.* Press (the teeth, lips) together into a rigid position; clench (the teeth), compress (the lips, mouth). E17. ▸**c** *verb intrans.* (Of the teeth) clench *against* each other (now *rare*); (of the face etc.) have or assume a fixed or settled expression. E17. ▸**d** *verb intrans.* Become bent or twisted as a result of strain. L18.

66 *verb trans.* Puzzle, nonplus, baffle; tax the resources of. Now *Scot.* & *north.* L16.

67 *verb intrans.* DANCING. Take up a position and perform a number of steps with one's face to one's partner or to the dancer on one's right or left. Foll. by *to.* M17.

68 a *verb trans.* Cause (a fruit or vegetable) to form by the process of fertilization; cause (a flower) to develop into fruit. L17. ▸**b** *verb intrans.* (Of a flower) form into a fruit or vegetable following fertilization; (of a fruit or vegetable) develop from a fertilized flower. Also, (of a tree) develop fruit. E18.

69 *verb trans.* Put a finishing coat of plaster on (a wall etc.). L17.

70 *verb trans.* & *intrans.* (Cause to) become firm, hard, or rigid in consistency; curdle, coagulate. M18. ▸**b** *verb intrans.* Of cream: collect and settle on the top of the milk. M19.

71 *verb trans.* In *pass.* Get stuck. Chiefly *dial.* M18.

72 a *verb trans.* Settle, establish; *spec.* (**a**) establish (a flock or stock) by breeding from particular sheep; (**b**) CRICKET, in *pass.*, become accustomed to the bowling; (**c**) settle the growth of (a plant) at the desired rate etc. L18. ▸**b** *verb intrans.* Of a period of time or weather: become settled. L18.

📖 **62** P. SIDNEY My hart is already set . . to lead a virgins life to my death. *Daily Telegraph* Electricity prices are set to go up again. J. O'FAOLAIN The woman in the next seat was set to chat. **63** D. H. LAWRENCE When she had once set upon anything . . the family failed before her. L. M. MONTGOMERY It's pretty rough not to let her go to the picnic when she's so set on it. **65a** N. BLAKE Get set! Go! That was the starting-pistol you heard. S. BELLOW Wearing a seersucker suit . . made him feel set for the holiday. R. K. NARAYAN I never gave the signal until I satisfied myself that everything was set. P. BAILEY The girl our Gerald was all set to marry when he got home from Flanders. V. S. PRITCHETT He stared at her rudely and she set her chin. R. INGALLS His face went set in an expression she recognized. D. PROFUMO 'Ready?' asked Benson . . . 'All set?' **c** M. DRABBLE Her features never set into a civil parade of attention. **70** N. LOWNDES A half-empty bucket of cement had set hard.

▸ **XI** Senses which appear to have arisen by reversal of construction or by an ellipsis.

†**73** *verb trans.* People or garrison *with.* OE–ME.

74 *verb trans.* Plant (ground) *with* 'sets' or young trees. Also, in *pass.*, be overgrown *with.* ME.

75 *verb trans.* In *pass.* Be ornamented, inlaid, or encrusted *with*; be studded, dotted, lined, etc., *with.* LME.

76 *verb trans.* Beset, besiege. Long only *fig.* (in *pass.*), in ***hard set***, in difficulties, hard put to it (*to do*). LME.

77 *verb trans.* & *intrans.* Of a hunting dog: mark the position of (game) by stopping, adopting a rigid attitude, and pointing the muzzle towards it. Cf. earlier SETTER *noun*[1] 3. E17.

78 *verb trans.* NAUTICAL. Take the bearings of (an object). E17.

79 *verb trans.* Mark down as prey, fix on as a victim; watch for the purpose of apprehending or robbing. Cf. earlier SETTER *noun*[1] 1b. *slang.* L17.

📖 **75** EVELYN Whose belt was set with pearle. ADDISON How thick the City was set with Churches.

Phrases: (A selection of cross-refs. only is included: see esp. other nouns.) **be set fair** (of the weather) be fine and likely to continue so; be in a favourable position (*for*). **be set round**, (*arch.*) **be set about with** be surrounded or encircled by, have a circle of. ***hard set***: see sense 76 above. **set a copy to** *arch.* give (a person) a specimen of work to copy. **set a fire** *US* kindle or start a fire. **set a lot by** attach great value or significance to. ***set an edge on, set an edge upon***: see EDGE *noun.* ***set a person at his or her ease***: see EASE *noun.* ***set a person's teeth on edge***: see EDGE *noun.* ***set a price on the head of***: see PRICE *noun* 3. **set a stitch** *arch.* sew. ***set at ease***: see EASE *noun.* ***set at naught***: see NAUGHT *pronoun* & *noun* 1. ***set at nought***: see NOUGHT *pronoun* & *noun* 1. ***set at rest***: see REST *noun*[1]. ***set by the ears***: see EAR *noun*[1]. ***set by the heels***: see HEEL *noun*[1]. ***set eyes on***: see EYE *noun.* ***set fire to***: see FIRE *noun.* ***set foot in, set foot on***: see FOOT *noun.* **set free** release from captivity or restraint. **set in hand** †(**a**) take in hand, undertake; (**b**) put out to be done, put in train. **set little by** consider to be of little value or significance. ***set measures to***: see MEASURE *noun.* **set much by** = *set a lot by* above. †**set naught by** have no esteem or regard for. ***set one's cap at***: see CAP *noun*[1]. ***set one's eyes at flow***: see FLOW *noun*[1]. ***set one's face against***: see FACE *noun.* ***set one's face like a flint***: see FLINT *noun* 3. ***set one's face to, set one's face towards***: see FACE *noun.* ***set one's hand to***: see HAND *noun.* **set one's heart on, set one's hopes on** have a strong desire for, look forward to eagerly, want wholeheartedly. ***set one's seal to, set one's seal on***: see SEAL *noun*[2]. ***set one's sights on***: see SIGHT *noun.* ***set one's teeth***: see TOOTH *noun.* ***set on fire***: see FIRE *noun.* ***set right***: see RIGHT *adjective.* **set sail** (**a**) hoist sails; (**b**) start on a sea voyage. ***set store by, set store on***: see STORE *noun.* ***set the pace***: see PACE *noun*[1]. ***set the record straight***: see RECORD *noun.* ***set the seal to, set the seal on***: see SEAL *noun*[2]. **set the scene** *fig.* describe the location or context of events; give preliminary or background information. **set the stage** *fig.* prepare the way or conditions (*for* an event etc.). ***set to music***: see sense 44 above. **set well with** be acceptable or pleasing to, be popular with.

With prepositions in specialized senses: **set about** — (**a**) begin working at, take steps towards, begin *doing, to do*; (**b**) *colloq.* start beating or hitting. **set against** — †(**a**) make an attack on, be hostile to; (**b**) compensate for, balance; (**c**) move in a direction opposed to; (see also sense 65c above). **set at** — assail, attack. **set by** — (now *arch. & dial.*) [by substitution of *not* for *naught* in ***set naught by*** above] (with neg.) have no esteem or regard for; (without neg.) esteem or value highly, think or make much of. **set on** — attack violently, assail suddenly. **set upon** — (*a*) = ***set on*** above; (*b*) = ***set about*** above.

With adverbs in specialized senses: **set about** (chiefly *north.*) circulate, spread about (a statement, report, etc.). **set abroach** *arch.* (*a*) broach (a cask, liquor); (*b*) set going, give currency or publicity to. **set abroad** †(*a*) spread abroad, spread wide; (*b*) publish; circulate (a report etc.); put in train. **set afloat** *arch.* (*a*) launch, float (*lit. & fig.*); (*b*) bring to the surface of a liquid; *fig.* set in motion, stir up, make active. **set apart** †(*a*) lay aside, put on one side; dismiss from consideration; put out of one's mind; (*b*) separate out for a special purpose; devote to some use. **set aside** †(*a*) discontinue the performance or practice of; (*b*) dismiss from consideration; ***setting aside***, excluding, not counting, except for, apart from; (*c*) reject as of no value, cogency, or pertinence; overrule; (*d*) discard or reject from use or service, in favour of another; (*e*) (chiefly LAW) annul, quash, make void, vacate; (*f*) separate out for a particular purpose or for future use; (*g*) remove (land) from agricultural production for fallow, forestry, or other use. **set back** (*a*) hinder or reverse the progress of, give a check to; *colloq.* cost (a person) a specified sum of money; take aback, disconcert; (*b*) put (a clock, the hands or digits of a clock) to an earlier time. **set by** †(*a*) put on one side, lay aside, (*lit. & fig.*); reject, dismiss; (*b*) lay up or lay by for future use. **set down** (*a*) place so as to rest on a surface; put down, as on the ground; cause or allow to alight from a vehicle; (of a vehicle) stop and allow (a person) to alight; land (an aircraft); (*b*) put down in writing; put on paper; put down or enter in a catalogue, account, etc.; record, relate; (*c*) attribute *to*; †(*d*) lay down (a principle), prescribe (a regulation etc.); (*e*) regard *as*, take *for*, consider to be; †(*f*) reckon *that*; †(*g*) encamp *before* (a town) for a siege; (*h*) depose from office; quell; lower (a person's pride etc.); take down, snub; †(*i*) slacken (the strings or pegs of a musical instrument); (see also sense 2 above). **set forth** †(*a*) direct or send forward, set on the way; send out for military or naval service; equip or fit out for a voyage or expedition; †(*b*) provide; allot or set apart for a purpose; (*c*) promulgate, publish; issue (a regulation, proclamation, etc.); (*d*) give an account of, esp. in order, distinctly, or in detail; expound, relate, narrate, state, describe; (*e*) (now *rare*) adorn, decorate; †(*f*) help to progress; advance, promote; praise, commend; †(*g*) exhibit, display; (*h*) begin a journey; set out *on* a journey, *against* an enemy, *in* pursuit, etc. **set forward** (*a*) carry, send, or thrust forward; put (a clock, the hands or digits of a clock) to a later time; (*b*) help to progress; advance, promote; (*c*) put forward, promulgate; advance (an opinion); (*d*) go forward, set out, start. **set in** †(*a*) join a fight; intervene in a dispute; (*b*) (*obsolete* exc. *dial.*) start to work, settle down (*to, to do*); (*c*) (of weather, a condition, etc.) begin (and seem likely to continue), become prevalent, become established; (*d*) (of a current or wind) flow or blow towards the shore; (*e*) insert (a sleeve etc.) into a garment. **set off** (*a*) give a start to; start off, initiate, stimulate; send off *into* a fit of laughter etc; (*b*) cause to go off or explode, let off, detonate (a bomb etc.); (*c*) assign to a particular purpose; (*d*) mark or measure off (a certain distance) on a surface; separate from the surrounding context, mark off; (*e*) set in relief, make prominent or conspicuous by contrast; show to advantage, enhance, embellish; (*f*) *arch.* give a flattering description of, commend, praise; (*g*) take into account by way of compensation; put in the balance (*against*); *spec.* in LAW, allow or recognize as a counter-claim; counterbalance, compensate; (*h*) start on a journey or course; start *to do*; (*i*) PRINTING (of ink, a freshly printed sheet or page) accidentally mark or transfer an impression on to the next sheet or page. **set on** †(*a*) instigate, promote; (*b*) cause or urge (an animal, esp. a dog) to attack; incite or urge on (a person) *to do*; †(*c*) advance, send forward; set in motion, set going; start (a person) doing something; (*d*) go forward, advance. **set out** †(*a*) equip or fit out for a voyage or expedition; send out for military or naval service; †(*b*) give currency or vogue to; promulgate; †(*c*) exhibit on the stage or in public; put into print, publish; †(*d*) declare, proclaim; express, denote; (*e*) display (wares) for sale; †(*f*) display to advantage, put forward to attract attention, make attractive, embellish, adorn; set in relief, set off by contrast etc.; †(*g*) praise, commend, extol; †(*h*) put out at interest; let or lease out; †(*i*) put (a child) out to nurse; send to board with a teacher or at a school; †(*j*) set apart *for* certain treatment; put aside or reserve, *spec.* as a tithe; (*k*) put down in writing or in print in explicit or detailed form; describe or enumerate exhaustively or in detail; (*l*) delimit, define, mark out; portion out (land) into lots; plan, lay out (a town, road, garden, etc.); lay out (ground) *with* plants; (*m*) arrange or put out for a meal or other purpose; place at suitable intervals or with an appropriate amount of display; (*n*) begin or start on a journey or course; start on one's way, esp. on a journey undertaken with some deliberation or of an important or arduous nature; (foll. by *to do*) begin with the object of doing; begin or start off *with* or *by doing*. **set over** †(*a*) convey to the other side of a stretch of water; (*b*) *arch.* make over, transfer; (*c*) *US Criminals' slang* kill, murder. **set to** †(*a*) affix (one's seal or signature); †(*b*) *rare* set (a broken limb); = sense 41a above; (*c*) put (cocks) beak to beak to fight; (*d*) make a beginning, get to work, esp. seriously or energetically; begin fighting or competing (*with*). **set up** (*a*) *lit.* place in a high or lofty position; raise to an elevated situation; †(*b*) hoist (a sail or flag); (*c*) begin uttering (vocal sound), raise (a cry); †(*d*) put up for sale or auction; (*e*) *arch.* give notice of, advertise; †(*f*) throw into relief, make brilliant, heighten the lustre of; (*g*) place in an exalted, eminent, or superior position; raise to power or authority; appoint to or nominate for a position; (*h*) make elated, proud, or vain (usu. in *pass.*); †(*i*) speak highly of, extol, praise; (*j*) place in an erect position; set or stand upright; erect; (*k*) *US* offer or supply (drink etc.) to customers, esp. on the house; treat to; (*l*) = sense 45 above; (*m*) assemble and erect (a machine etc.); make ready for operation or for a particular operation; make necessary interconnections and initial settings in (a computer); (*n*) ***well set up***, (of a person) well-built, sturdy; (*o*) (now *rare*) bring into use or vogue; establish a course or series of; cause (a certain condition, esp. a disease) to arise (usu. in *pass.*); (*p*) establish (a state of things, a custom, a form of government, a society, etc.); organize and start up (a business etc.); institute; begin the use or practice of; make preparations or arrangements for (a meeting etc.); contrive, plot (a move, trick, etc.); (***set up house***: see HOUSE *noun*[1]; ***set up shop***: see SHOP *noun*); (*q*) provide (a person) with means or resources; place in a position of prosperity or in the way of retrieving one's fortune; establish or start (a person) in a business or profession; establish or present (oneself) *as*; (*r*) bring (a person) to a position from which he or she may be knocked down, make vulnerable to a punch etc.; *fig.* (*slang*) lead on in order to fool, cheat, or incriminate, 'frame'; (*s*) restore, repair, make good; now only *spec.*, bring to a proper state of health and strength, restore to health; †(*t*) put away for future use, store away; put (a horse etc.) up in a stable; (*u*) cause hostility or opposition in (a person, *against*); bring to bay; (*v*) propose or put forward (a claim, a defence, a case in law, a theory, plan, etc.); (*w*) start in business or on a career, begin the exercise of a trade or profession; (foll. by *for*) put oneself forward as being, lay claim to or to being; lay claim or pretend *to be*; †(*x*) put up *at* an inn or other lodging.

Comb.: **set-aside** (*a*) *US* a thing set aside for a special purpose; (*b*) the action of setting something, *spec.* land, aside for a special purpose (freq. *attrib.*); **set-in** the beginning of a period of time, a spell of weather, etc.; **set-on** the way in which a thing is set on; **set-screw** a screw, usu. threaded the full length of the shank, that enables two contiguous parts to be brought into and held in their correct relative position.

set /sɛt/ *verb*[2] *trans. & intrans.* Infl. **-tt-**. M20.
[from SET *noun*[2].]
Group (pupils or students) into sets for instruction on a particular subject.

seta /ˈsiːtə/ *noun.* Pl. **-tae** /-tiː/. L18.
[Latin *seta*, *saeta* bristle.]
1 BOTANY. A stiff hair, a bristle. Also, in bryophytes, the stalk which supports the capsule. L18.
2 ZOOLOGY. A bristle; an appendage resembling a bristle (esp. in an invertebrate). E19.

setaceous /sɪˈteɪʃəs/ *adjective.* M17.
[from mod. Latin *setaceus*, from Latin SETA: see -ACEOUS.]
1 Having the form or character of a bristle; *esp.* (ANATOMY, ZOOLOGY, & BOTANY) of the nature of or shaped like a seta or setae. M17.
2 Having or covered with setae or bristles; *joc.* bristly, unshaven. L18.
■ **setaceously** *adverb* E19.

setal /ˈsiːt(ə)l/ *adjective.* L19.
[from SETA + -AL[1].]
Of or pertaining to setae.

setaria /sɪˈtɛːrɪə/ *noun.* M20.
[mod. Latin (see below), formed as SETA: see -ARY[1].]
Any of the grasses constituting the genus *Setaria*, which have spikelets arranged in spikelike panicles; *esp.* one of those grown for fodder in tropical countries. Also called ***bristle-grass***.

setback /ˈsɛtbak/ *noun.* L17.
[from ***set back*** s.v. SET *verb*[1].]
1 A check to progress, a slowing or reversal of forward movement, a relapse. L17.
2 ARCHITECTURE. A plain flat offset in a wall. M19.
3 The action or an act of setting something back, *spec.* (*N. Amer.*) a building from the edge of a roadway or higher storeys of a skyscraper from the line of lower storeys; the area formed by such setting back. M19.

set-down /ˈsɛtdaʊn/ *noun.* E18.
[from ***set down*** s.v. SET *verb*[1].]
1 a A lift in a passing vehicle. Now *rare*. E18. ▸**b** (The distance covered by) a single drive in a cab. Now *rare*. M18.
2 An unexpected and humiliating rebuff. Also, a severe scolding. L18.
3 A sit-down meal. *US slang*. E19.
4 The action or an instance of landing in or from an aircraft. M20.

setem /ˈsɛtɛm/ *noun.* M20.
[Egyptian *stm*.]
EGYPTOLOGY. = SEM.

se-tenant /sətənɑ̃/ *adjective.* E20.
[French, lit. 'holding together'.]
PHILATELY. Of postage stamps, esp. of different denominations or designs: joined together as when printed.

setfast /ˈsɛtfɑːst/ *noun.* E18.
[from SET *verb*[1] or *adjective* + FAST *adverb*.]
A hardened saddle-gall on a horse; = SIT-FAST *noun* 1.

seth /seɪt/ *noun.* M18.
[Hindi *seth* from Sanskrit *śreṣṭha* best, chief.]
In the Indian subcontinent, a prominent Hindu merchant or banker.

Sethian /ˈsɛθɪən/ *noun.* E18.
[ecclesiastical Latin *Sethiani* pl., from *Seth* son of Adam and ancestor of Noah (in *Genesis*): see -IAN.]
A member of a Gnostic sect of the 2nd cent. AD, holding Seth in great veneration, and believing that Jesus was Seth revived.

Sethite /ˈsɛθʌɪt/ *noun & adjective.* M17.
[from *Seth* (see prec.) + -ITE[1].]
▶ **A** *noun*. **1** A descendant of Seth. M17.
2 = SETHIAN. M18.
▶ **B** *adjective*. Of or pertaining to Seth, descended from Seth. L18.

SETI /ˈsɛti/ *abbreviation.*
ASTRONOMY. Search for extraterrestrial intelligence.

setiferous /sɪˈtɪf(ə)rəs/ *adjective.* E19.
[from SETA + -I- + -FEROUS.]
Chiefly ZOOLOGY & ENTOMOLOGY. Having setae or bristles.

setiform /ˈsiːtɪfɔːm/ *adjective.* E19.
[formed as prec. + -I- + -FORM.]
ZOOLOGY & BOTANY. Having the form of a seta or bristle; bristle-shaped.

setigerous /sɪˈtɪdʒ(ə)rəs/ *adjective.* M17.
[formed as prec. + -GEROUS.]
Chiefly ZOOLOGY & BOTANY. Having setae or bristles.

Setine /ˈsɛtɪn/ *noun.* L17.
[Latin *Setinum*, from *Setia*: see below, -INE[4].]
Hist. Wine from the ancient Latin city of Setia.

†**setling** *noun.* LME–E18.
[from SET *noun*[1] + -LING[1].]
A slip taken from a tree and planted.

setness /ˈsɛtnɪs/ *noun.* M17.
[from SET *adjective* + -NESS.]
The quality, state, or character of being set; an instance of this.

Seto /ˈsɛtɔː/ *adjective & noun.* L19.
[A city north-east of Nagoya in Japan.]
(Designating) Japanese pottery and porcelain produced from the kilns established in Seto in the 13th cent.

set-off /ˈsɛtɒf/ *noun.* E17.
[from ***set off*** s.v. SET *verb*[1]. Cf. OFFSET *noun*.]
1 A thing used to set off something; an adornment, a decoration, an ornament. E17.
2 a ARCHITECTURE. A reduction in the thickness of a wall, buttress, etc. Also, a sloping or flat projection or ledge formed by this, = OFFSET *noun* 5. E18. ▸**b** A similar reduction or shoulder in a metal bar etc. M19.
3 An act of setting off on a journey, course, etc.; a start. M18.
4 An act of setting off one item of an account against another; an item or amount (to be) set off against another in the settlement of accounts; a counter-claim or a counterbalancing debt, pleaded by the defendant in an action to recover money due; *gen.* a taking into account of something as a counterbalance or partial compensation for something else; a counterbalancing or compensating circumstance or consideration. Cf. OFFSET *noun* 6. M18.
5 PRINTING. **a** The (unwanted) transference of ink from one sheet or page to another. M19. ▸**b** An impression transferred. M19.

> 📖 **3** E. H. COLERIDGE Keble's sermon . . was the start or set-off of the Catholic Revival. **4** T. JEFFERSON Something is required from you as a set off against the sin of your retirement.

seton /ˈsiːt(ə)n/ *noun & verb.* LME.
[medieval Latin *seto(n)-*, app. from Latin *seta* bristle, (in medieval Latin also) silk.]
SURGERY (now chiefly *Hist.*).
▶ **A** *noun*. **1** A thread, piece of tape, etc., drawn through a fold of skin to maintain an opening for discharges, or drawn through a sinus or cavity to keep it from healing up. LME.
2 The opening thus formed. L16.
▶ **B** *verb intrans.* Apply a seton. *rare*. M16.

setose /ˈsiːtəʊs/ *adjective.* M17.
[Latin *setosus*, formed as SETA: see -OSE[1].]
ANATOMY, ZOOLOGY, & BOTANY. Covered with bristles or setae, bristly. Also, of a bristly nature.

set-out /ˈsɛtaʊt/ *noun.* Chiefly *colloq. & dial.* Now *rare*. E19.
[from ***set out*** s.v. SET *verb*[1].]
1 A display; *spec.* (*a*) a display or set of plate, china, etc.; (*b*) a spread of food; (*c*) a carriage with its horses, harness, etc.; (*d*) a show, a public performance, an entertainment for a number of people, a party. E19.
2 An outfit; a set of equipment; a person's costume or get-up. M19.
3 A commotion, a disturbance. M19.
4 A beginning, a start. M19.

set piece /sɛt ˈpiːs/ *noun phr. & adjective.* Also (esp. as adjective) **set-piece**. M19.
[from SET *adjective* + PIECE *noun*.]
▶ **A** *noun phr.* **1** A formal composition in art or literature; *spec.* a more or less self-contained passage or section of a literary work. M19.
2 THEATRICAL. A piece of scenery representing a single feature such as a tree, a gate, etc. M19.

3 An arrangement of fireworks composing a picture or design. **L19.**
4 An organized movement, action, or manoeuvre; *spec.* in team ball games, a (usu. rehearsed) movement or feature of the game by which the ball is returned to play, as at a scrummage or a free kick. **M20.**

> 1 M. DIBDIN Iovino's speech had been a brilliant set piece. *Times Lit. Suppl.* The novel is really a series of set-pieces.

▶**B** *attrib.* or as *adjective.* Having the attributes of a set piece; formally or elaborately planned or composed. **M20.**

> P. ZIEGLER Jutland had been the last great set-piece battle. B. BEAUMONT Some of the backs . . demanding quicker ball from the set-piece play.

Setswana /sɛt'swɑːnə/ *noun & adjective.* Also **Sechuana**, **-wana**, /sɛtʃʊ'ɑːnə, sɛ'tʃwɑːnə/. **E19.**
[from Setswana *se-* lang. prefix + TSWANA.]
(Of) the Bantu language of the Batswana.

sett /sɛt/ *noun*[1]. Also **set**. **L17.**
[Perh. a use of SET *noun*[1], perh. from Middle Low German *set(te)* ordinance, law.]
SCOTTISH HISTORY. The constitution or form of government of a burgh, fixed by charter.

sett *noun*[2] see SET *noun*[1].

†**sett** *noun*[3] var. of SET *noun*[2].

settable /'sɛtəb(ə)l/ *adjective.* **M17.**
[from SET *verb*[1] + -ABLE.]
Able to be set.

settecento /sɛtɪ'tʃɛntəʊ/ *noun.* **E20.**
[Italian = seven hundred.]
The eighteenth century in Italy; the style of Italian art, architecture, music, etc., of this period.

settee /sə'tiː/ *noun*[1]. **L16.**
[Italian *saettia*, perh. from *saetta* arrow from Latin *sagitta*.]
Hist. A lateen-rigged sailing vessel with a long sharp prow and two or three masts, used in the Mediterranean.

settee /sɛ'tiː/ *noun*[2]. **E18.**
[Perh. fanciful alt. of SETTLE *noun*[1]: see -EE[2].]
A (usu. upholstered) seat for two or more people, with a back and (usu.) arms.

setter /'sɛtə/ *noun*[1]. **LME.**
[from SET *verb*[1] + -ER[1].]
1 *gen.* A person who sets something. Also ***setter-on***, ***setter-out***, ***setter-to***, ***setter-up***, etc. **LME.** ▶**b** *spec.* A confederate of sharpers or swindlers, employed as a decoy. Also, a person employed by robbers or murderers to spy on intended victims; a police spy or informer. *arch. slang.* **L16.**
2 An instrument, tool, or machine used in setting. **E16.**
3 A dog trained to set or point at game; *spec.* (a dog of) any of several breeds of large silky-haired gun dog (usu. with specifying word: see below). **L16.**

> 1 R. C. TRENCH A Redeemer . . a setter free of man . . from alien powers which held him in bondage. *Evening Standard* Setter-out required . . experienced in setting-out shops fronts and interiors. *New Statesman* Mr Holloway is severe on other people's abuses of English—particularly the setters of examination questions. H. BRAUN The scaffold, where the 'setters' laid the stones sent up to them. *Arab Times* With more skilled setters setting up business . . there is a market for loose stones. M. COREN He was a gifted setter of scenes, letting his imagination take control of his pen. ***bone-setter***, ***pace-setter***, ***pin-setter***, ***typesetter***, etc. **2** ***typesetter***, etc. **3** ***English setter***, ***Gordon setter***, ***Irish setter***, ***Laverack setter***, ***red setter***, etc.

setter *noun*[2] var. of SAETER.

setterwort /'sɛtəwəːt/ *noun.* **M16.**
[Middle Low German *siterwort*, from unkn. 1st elem. + *wort* WORT *noun*[1].]
Either of two hellebores, stinking hellebore, *Helleborus foetidus*, or green hellebore, *H. viridis*.

setting /'sɛtɪŋ/ *noun.* **ME.**
[from SET *verb*[1] + -ING[1].]
▶**I** Corresp. to transitive uses of SET *verb*[1].
1 The action of SET *verb*[1] *trans.* Also, the fact of being set. Also ***setting-out***, ***setting-up***, etc. **ME.** ▶**b** *spec.* The action of a setter in indicating game; the sport of hunting game with a setter. **E17.**
2 The manner or position in which something is set, fixed, or placed; the way in which or level at which a machine or device is set to operate. **LME.** ▶**b** The manner in which a stone or gem is set or mounted; the frame or bed in which a gem etc. is set. **E19.** ▶**c** CROQUET. Any of the different arrangements of the hoops and pegs on the ground. **M19.** ▶**d** A person's or thing's immediate environment or surroundings; a place or time in or at which a story, play, scene, etc., is represented as happening; the scenery or staging of a play. **M19.** ▶**e** The manner in which a poem or form of words is set to music; a piece of music composed for a particular poem or form of words. **L19.**
3 A lease. *Scot. & dial.* **LME.**
4 The finishing coat of plaster on a wall etc. **E19.**
5 A clutch (of eggs). **E20.**
6 More fully ***place-setting***. A set of cutlery, crockery, glasses, etc., required to set a place for one person at a table. **M20.**

> 1 BACON A Tree, at the first Setting, should not be Shaken, vntill it hath taken Root. G. GORER The setting of household tasks as a punishment. *Globe & Mail (Toronto)* Chauffeurs are requested not to leave their cars when setting down or picking up. M. M. KAYE The . . setting of broken bones without the help of anaesthetics. **2** *Homes & Gardens* A thermometer and control dial so you are able to alter the setting. **b** B. VINE The dark green stone . . embedded in a setting of densely woven gold strands. **d** A. HIGGINS The Bavarian lakes had been the setting for his own early amours. H. MOORE The figure I carved . . has found a perfect setting in the grounds of Dartington Hall. H. SEGAL The analysis of a child . . needs a proper psychoanalytical setting, away from its home and family. **e** F. J. CROWEST Settings for the Canticles by modern Church writers.

▶**II** Corresp. to intransitive uses of SET *verb*[1].
7 The sinking of a celestial object towards and below the horizon; the direction in which this occurs. Also, the fall of night or darkness. **ME.**
8 The flowing of a current in a particular direction; the direction of flow. **L16.**
9 The process or fact of becoming set, hard, or stiff; solidification, coagulation. **L18.**

> 7 *fig.*: LONGFELLOW The setting of a great hope is like the setting of the sun.

Comb.: **setting coat** a finishing coat of fine plastering; **setting-dog** *arch.* = SETTER *noun*[1] 3; **setting lotion** (a) lotion applied to the hair to assist the process of setting; **setting-pole** (chiefly *N. Amer.*) a pole used for punting a boat, esp. on mudbanks; **setting-stick** (*a*) (now *dial.*) a stick used for making holes for setting plants; (*b*) a printer's composing-stick; **setting stuff** fine plaster from which a setting coat is made; **setting-up** *adjective* designating or pertaining to a gymnastic exercise used to improve posture etc.

setting /'sɛtɪŋ/ *adjective.* **M16.**
[from SET *verb*[1] + -ING[2].]
1 That sets something or someone. **M16.**
2 Becoming, suitable, graceful. *obsolete* exc. *Scot.* **M16.**
3 That sets; in the process of setting. **L16.**

settle /'sɛt(ə)l/ *noun*[1].
[Old English *setl* corresp. to Middle Low German, Middle Dutch *setel*, Old High German *sezzal* (German *Sessel*), Gothic *sitls*, from Germanic, rel. to Latin *sella* seat.]
1 A sitting place; something to sit on; a chair, a bench, a stool. Long *arch. rare* in *gen.* sense. **OE.**
2 *spec.* A long bench, usually with arms and a high back and a locker or box under the seat. **M16.**
3 A ledge, a raised platform. *dial. & techn.* **E17.**
Comb.: **settle bed** a settle adapted for alternative use as a seat or bed.

settle /'sɛt(ə)l/ *noun*[2]. *rare. obsolete* exc. *Scot.* **M17.**
[from the verb.]
The action of settling; the fact of being settled; settlement.

settle /'sɛt(ə)l/ *verb.* **OE.**
[from SETTLE *noun*[1].]
▶**I** †**1** *verb trans.* Seat; put in a seat or place of rest; cause to sit down. **OE–L17.**
2 *verb trans.* Place (material things) in order, or in a convenient or desired position; adjust (one's clothing etc.). **E16.**
3 *verb trans.* Place (a person) in an attitude of repose, so as to be undisturbed for a time; make comfortable. **E16.** ▶**b** *verb refl. & intrans.* Dispose oneself comfortably, adjust one's position on a chair etc. with the intention of remaining seated. **M16.**
4 *verb trans.* In *pass. & refl.* Have taken up one's abode; be installed in a residence, have completed one's arrangements for residing. **M16.**
5 *verb trans.* Fix or establish permanently (one's abode, residence, etc.). **M16.**
†**6** *verb trans.* Fix, implant (*in* a person's heart, mind, etc.); set firmly on a foundation. **M16–E18.**
7 *verb trans.* Cause to take up residence in a place; *esp.* establish (a body of people) as residents in a town or country; introduce as colonists. **L16.** ▶**b** *Hist.* Assign to (a person) a legal domicile in a particular parish. Usu. in *pass.* **L16.** ▶**c** Sentence (a person) to imprisonment, put in prison. *US slang.* **L19.**
†**8** *verb trans.* Establish or set up (an institution, a business, etc.) in a particular town or country. **L16–L18.**
9 *verb trans.* Provide (a place) with inhabitants or settlers; establish a colony in. **L17.**

> 2 A. TROLLOPE When you're settling the room after breakfast. J. AGEE With great care . . settled it into the breastpocket of his shirt. A. UTTLEY Mrs. Garland settled her bonnet. **3** I. MCEWAN Caroline was settling Mary in one of the . . wooden chairs. **b** E. WAUGH They settled themselves in easy chairs and drank brandy. A. CARTER He settled back among the cushions. **4** W. BINGLEY You, I presume, are by this time comfortably settled in your new residence. J. H. NEWMAN A tribe of them . . settled themselves between the high Tartar land and the sea of Aral. **5** SIR W. SCOTT The town at which I had settled my temporary establishment. **7** EVELYN I went . . to settle physitians, chirurgeons, . . marshals and other officers in all the Sea Ports. **9** K. WEATHERLY When this country is closely settled . . the red kangaroos will die out.

▶**II** †**10** *verb intrans.* Take a seat, sit down; (of the sun) set. **OE–LME.**
11 *verb intrans.* Take up a position of rest after flying or floating; alight *on*; come down and remain. **ME.**
12 *verb intrans.* Come to rest after moving about; become fixed *in* or *on*; (of pain or disease) establish itself *in* or *on* a definite part of the body. **L16.**
13 *verb intrans.* Stop moving about and adopt a fixed abode; establish a permanent residence, make one's permanent home, become domiciled. Also foll. by *down.* **E17.** ▶**b** *spec.* Of a group of people: begin to live permanently in a foreign country; establish a colony. **L17.**
14 *verb intrans.* HUNTING. Of hounds: keep steadily to the scent. Foll. by *to*, *upon.* **L18.**
15 *verb intrans.* Foll. by *in*: ▶**a** Dispose oneself comfortably for remaining indoors. **M19.** ▶**b** Become established in a new home; become accustomed to a new home or to new surroundings. **E20.**

> 11 M. MUGGERIDGE Explosions whose dust has never had time to settle before others have erupted. C. MILNE A flock of starlings rise from a field . . and then settle again a hundred yards away. E. FIGES A large amber butterfly . . settled on a poppy. **13** J. BARTH The Macks settled just outside Baltimore to live. **15a** E. H. YATES The inhabitants . . had pulled their blinds down and settled in for the night.

▶**III 16** *verb intrans.* Sink down gradually (as) by its own weight; subside; (of a ship) sink gradually. **ME.** ▶†**b** *fig.* Sink deeply *into* (the mind, the heart). **ME–L16.**
17 a *verb intrans.* Subside into a solid mass; become consolidated (as) by its own weight. **M16.** ▶**b** *verb trans.* Cause to subside into a solid mass; consolidate, compact. **E17.**
18 *verb trans.* NAUTICAL. Diminish the height of, reduce to a lower level (a deck, a topsail). **E17.**

> 16 B. B. SCHOFIELD The *Navarino* was struck by two torpedoes . . and at once started to settle. **17a** C. WESTON The familiar night sounds of the old house settling.

▶**IV 19** *verb intrans.* Of a liquid: become still after agitation or fermentation, so that suspended particles or impurities are separated as scum or sediment. **LME.** ▶**b** *verb trans.* Cause (liquor) to deposit dregs or work off impurities; clarify. *rare.* **L16.**
20 *verb intrans.* Of suspended particles or impurities in a liquid: come to rest after agitation or disturbance; collect as scum or sediment by gravitation. Now chiefly (with mixture of sense 16), sink to the bottom as sediment. **LME.** ▶**b** Of food or a meal: be digested. **M20.**
21 *verb trans.* Quiet, tranquillize, compose, remedy the disordered state of (the nerves, the stomach, etc.); allay (passion). **M16.**
22 *verb intrans.* Become calm or composed, subside, calm down; come to a quiet or orderly state after excitement or restless activity. Also foll. by *down.* **L16.**
23 *verb trans.* Quiet with a blow; knock down dead or unconscious, stun. **E17.**
24 *verb intrans.* Come to an end of a series of changes or fluctuations and assume a definite form or condition. Also foll. by *down*, (of weather) *in.* **L17.**

> 20b L. P. HARTLEY We've given our tea time to settle. **21** BUNYAN Hoping that sleep might settle his brains . . they got him to bed. A. TROLLOPE Cold pudding is good to settle a man's love. T. MORRISON You need to have some babies. It'll settle you. **22** SIR W. SCOTT Better let her mind settle a little. R. P. JHABVALA After cooking my meal, I settle down cross-legged on the floor. D. PROFUMO It was a long time before he could settle again into sleep. **24** BARONESS ORCZY The wind had changed, and was settling down to a comfortable north-westerly breeze. A. S. NEILL To see the world before they settle down to university work. P. MAILLOUX Finished his article . . and then settled back into his office routine.

▶**V 25** *verb trans.* Ensure the stability or permanence of (a condition of things, a quality, power, etc.). **LME.**
26 *verb trans.* Make steadfast or constant, end the irresolution of. **LME.**
27 *verb refl. & intrans.* Fix one's attention *(up)on* an object; make up one's mind *to do*; dispose or set oneself steadily *to* some employment. Now usu. with mixture of sense 21, compose oneself after excitement or restlessness and apply oneself quietly to work. Freq. foll. by *down.* **M16.**
28 *verb trans.* Secure or confirm (a person) *in* a position of authority or an office; install permanently, establish *in* an office or way of life; provide a secure future for (a

dependant etc., oneself) through marriage. **M16.** ▸**b** In Presbyterian Churches: appoint (a minister) to the charge of a parish. (Foll. by *over*.) Chiefly *Scot. & US.* **E18.**

29 *verb trans.* Subject to permanent regulations, set permanently in order, place on a permanent footing; bring into a permanent form. **L16.**

30 *verb trans.* Secure by decree, ordinance, enactment, or a deed of settlement. Foll. by *to, on,* or *upon* (a person). **E17.**

31 *verb intrans.* Adopt a regular or secure style of life, esp. with a partner in marriage. Also foll. by *down.* **E18.**

📖 **25** TENNYSON 'Tis hard to settle order once again. **26** DEFOE William settled my mind to more prudent steps. **27** HOR. WALPOLE The Opposition, like schoolboys, don't know how to settle to their books again after the holidays. H. MARTINEAU I settle myself down to my pursuits. **28** T. HOOK The prudent gentlewoman . . wishes to settle her daughter. C. KINGSLEY A practice large enough to enable him to settle two sons well in his own profession. **30** W. BLACKSTONE It became usual . . to settle by express deed some special estate to the use of the husband and his wife. J. RATHBONE He settled a sum of money on . . Teresa. *Accountancy* Mrs Kalms settled shares on discretionary trusts for the benefit of her daughter. **31** M. T. SADLER Their very object in leaving their native countries is to settle in life. A. C. CLARKE It seemed a pity that he had never married and settled down.

▸**VI 32** *verb intrans.* Arrange matters in dispute, come to terms or agreement *with* a person. **E16.**

33 a *verb trans.* Appoint or fix definitely beforehand, decide or agree on (a time, place, plan of action, price, conditions, etc., *to do*). **L16.** ▸**b** *verb intrans.* Come to a decision or agreement; decide *(up)on* a plan of action, an object of choice; (foll. by *for*) decide or agree on, content oneself with. **M19.**

34 *verb trans.* Decide, come to a fixed conclusion on (a question, a matter of doubt or discussion); bring to an end (a dispute) by agreement or intervention; put beyond dispute, establish (a principle or fact). **M17.**

35 a *verb trans.* Close (an account) by a money payment; pay (an account, a bill, etc.). **L17.** ▸**b** *verb intrans.* Settle accounts by payment. Usu. foll. by *with.* **L18.**

📖 **33** S. E. FERRIER These matters being settled, Miss Pratt . . accepted the arm of her companion. E. B. BROWNING It was settled that I should pay her a visit. E. M. FORSTER We can settle how much you can give Charles. N. MOSLEY They must finally have settled to go to their room. **b** J. GARDAM My mum . . settled on marrying Bell. *Times* Workers settle for single figure rises. L. CODY He conjured up beef . . while she settled for chicken. JANET MORGAN The house on which they eventually settled, after a year or so of looking. **34** W. GERHARDIE Violent disputes which he was called upon to settle. F. FITZGERALD The conflict could not be settled except by unconditional surrender. C. HILL The question of power in England had been finally settled. W. ABISH We might give it a try . . . 'Have you eaten there?' 'No'. 'Then, that settles it.' **35** P. SCOTT If you find things more expensive than I've put down . . I'll settle the balance during the week.

Phrases: ***settle a person's hash***: see HASH *noun*[1]. **settle one's affairs, settle one's estate** arrange for the disposal of one's property, the payment of one's debts, etc., esp. with a view to one's death, removal to a distance, or retirement. ***settle on the lees, settle upon the lees***: see LEES. ***wait until the dust settles***: see DUST *noun*.

■ **settleable** *adjective* (*a*) *rare* able to be settled; (*b*) having the property of settling or sinking to the bottom of a liquid: **M19.**

settled /ˈsɛt(ə)ld/ *adjective.* **M16.**
[from prec. + -ED[1].]

1 That has been settled; that has settled; fixed, established, unchanging. **M16.**

2 Of a person's expression or bearing: indicating a settled purpose, mind, or character. **L16.**

3 Of weather: calm and fine. **E18.**

📖 **1** BURKE Settled governments have not the bold resources of new experimental systems. E. GASKELL It was not . . a settled thing that Mrs Fitz-Adam was to be visited. J. RUSKIN I wish this were a settled question in London markets. E. F. BENSON You have no settled object in life. A. MOOREHEAD They were passing through settled districts. *Times* 26 of the 427 women who had come down from Oxford that year were without a settled job. **3** S. MIDDLETON The weather was . . less settled, with cloud about.

■ **settledness** *noun* (now *rare*) **L16.**

settlement /ˈsɛt(ə)lm(ə)nt/ *noun.* **E17.**
[from SETTLE *verb* + -MENT.]

▸**I 1** The action of settling and clarifying after agitation or fermentation; an instance of this. **E17.**

2 The action of depositing a sediment; an instance of this; a deposit, a sediment. *obsolete* exc. *dial.* **L17.**

3 The action of sinking down or subsiding; subsidence; an instance of this. **L18.**

4 The process of becoming calm or tranquil. **M19.**

📖 **3** L. T. C. ROLT The bridges would not be affected by any settlement of the approach embankments.

▸**II 5** The action of fixing something in a secure or steady position; the state of being so fixed; a fixed or steady position. **M17.**

6 Establishment of a person in life, in marriage, or in an office or employment. **M17.** ▸**b** In Presbyterian Churches: the appointing or installing of a minister in a parish. Chiefly *Scot. & US.* **E18.**

7 *Hist.* Legal residence or establishment in a particular parish, entitling a person to relief from the poor rates; the right to relief acquired by such residence. **M17.**

8 The action of settling in a fixed or comfortable place or position, in a permanent home, etc.; the state of being so settled; an instance of this. **L17.**

9 The action of settling as colonists or newcomers; the action of peopling or colonizing a new country, the establishment of a colony; an instance of this. **E19.**

▸**III 10** The action or process of regulating or putting something on a permanent footing; the action of establishing security or tranquillity; the state of being settled and established; a settled arrangement, an established order of things. Also, determination or decision of a question, dispute, etc.; the establishing of a fact; an instance of this; an agreement. **M17.**

11 *LAW.* The action of settling property on or (*Scot.*) bequeathing property to a person or persons; *esp.* the settling for life on a beneficiary of income from property administered by trustees; the particular terms of such an arrangement; the deed or instrument by which such an arrangement is effected. Also *spec.*, = ***marriage settlement*** s.v. MARRIAGE *noun.* **L17.** ▸**b** An amount settled on a person. **E19.**

12 The settling or payment of an account; the action of satisfying a claim or demand; the action of coming to terms (*with* a person). **E18.**

📖 **10** J. R. LOWELL An affair of taste, which does not admit of any authoritative settlement. A. BULLOCK Germany's defeat in 1918 . . and the peace settlement which followed were not decisive. **11** J. DIDION Betty . . had received the . . house as part of the settlement from her first husband. **Act of Settlement** *Hist.*: by which the succession to the British Crown was settled on Princess Sophia of Hanover and her descendants. ***protector of the settlement***: see PROTECTOR 3. ***STRICT settlement.***

▸**IV 13** A community settled in a new country; a colonized tract of country; a colony, esp. in an early stage. Also, a small village or collection of houses, esp. in a remote or outlying district. **L17.** ▸**b** *Hist.* The huts forming the living quarters of the slaves on a plantation. **E19.**

14 *Hist.* An establishment in a poor part of a large city lived in by people engaged or interested in social work or reform. **L19.**

📖 **13** A. TOFFLER Outside Khartoum . . former nomads have created a . . ring of settlements. ***Straits Settlements***: see STRAIT *noun*[1].

Comb.: **settlement day** = *SETTLING day*; **settlement house** *US* an institution in an inner-city area, usu. sponsored by a church or college, providing educational, recreational, and other social services to the community.

settler /ˈsɛtlə/ *noun.* **L16.**
[from SETTLE *verb* + -ER[1].]

1 *gen.* A person who or thing which settles something. **L16.**

2 A person who settles in a new country or place; an early colonist. Orig. *N. Amer.* **M17.**

3 A pan or vat into which a liquor is run off to settle or deposit a sediment. **L17.**

4 A final (esp. alcoholic) drink, a nightcap. *arch. colloq.* **M18.**

5 A thing that settles an encounter or argument; a crushing or finishing blow, shot, speech, etc. *arch. colloq.* **E19.**

6 A clerk in a betting shop who calculates the winnings. **M20.**

2 settler's clock *Austral.* the kookaburra. **settler's matches** *Austral.* the loose strips of bark on some eucalypts, used for kindling. **settler's twine** *Austral.* a fibre plant of the arum family, *Gymnostachys anceps*, used for cord.

■ **settlerdom** *noun* settlers collectively, the world of settlers **M19.**

settling /ˈsɛtlɪŋ/ *noun.* **OE.**
[from SETTLE *verb* + -ING[1].]

†**1** A sitting down. Also, the setting of the sun. Only in **OE.**

2 *gen.* The action of SETTLE *verb*; an instance of this. Also foll. by *down, in, up,* etc. **LME.**

3 *sing.* & (usu.) in *pl.* Sediment, lees, dregs. **L16.**

📖 **2** W. R. BURNETT Scrupulous about settling her bill on the dot. *Times* A subterranean movement caused mainly by the settling of strata disturbed by mining activity. *Wireless World* Free air travel will be provided . . and a 'settling in' allowance will also be paid on arrival. A. BROOKNER Women seemed more restless these days, less attracted by the prospect of settling down.

Comb.: **settling day** a day appointed for settling accounts; *spec.* the fortnightly pay-day on the Stock Exchange; **settling time** *ENGINEERING* the time taken for a measuring or control instrument to get within a certain distance of a new equilibrium value without subsequently deviating from it by that amount.

settlor /ˈsɛtlə/ *noun.* **E19.**
[from SETTLE *verb* + -OR.]

LAW. A person who makes a settlement of property, *esp.* the creator of a trust.

set-to /ˈsɛt-tuː/ *noun. colloq.* Pl. **set-tos.** **M18.**
[from ***set to*** s.v. SET *verb*[1].]

The action or an act of setting to; a renewed attack or bout in boxing; a bout, a round, a match, a sporting encounter; *gen.* a fight, a contest. Also, an argument, a heated debate.

setule /ˈsiːtjuːl, ˈsɛtjuːl/ *noun.* **E19.**
[mod. Latin *setula* dim. of Latin SETA: see -ULE.]

ZOOLOGY & BOTANY. A small seta or bristle.

■ **setulose** *adjective* covered with setules **E19.**

set-up /ˈsɛtʌp/ *noun.* **M19.**
[from ***set up*** s.v. SET *verb*[1].]

1 An object set up or upright, an upright; *spec.* a stand or display at a carnival etc. **M19.**

2 The way in which something is organized, arranged, or constituted; an organization, an arrangement, a system, a situation; a layout; *spec.* (***a***) *US* a style of personal bearing or carriage; (***b***) (*BILLIARDS & SNOOKER* etc.) a position of the balls from which it is easy to score; (***c***) a team, *esp.* a sports team. **L19.** ▸**b** The difference between the maximum and minimum heights of a water surface tilted by wind action. **M20.**

3 A boxer who can be easily defeated by a particular opponent (and chosen on these grounds); *gen.* an opponent who is easy to defeat; a thing easily overcome, dealt with, or accomplished. *colloq.* (chiefly *US*). **E20.**

4 A glass along with ice, soda, etc., required for mixing a drink, served in unlicensed premises where customers can supply their own spirits. *US colloq.* **M20.**

5 A place-setting at a restaurant. *US colloq.* **M20.**

6 A scheme or trick whereby an innocent person is caused to incriminate himself or herself or a criminal is caught red-handed. *colloq.* (orig. *US*). **M20.**

📖 **2** *Times* At the time of the battle of Marathon the Athenians had . . a rather inefficient command set-up. P. ARROWSMITH The whole economic set-up has to be changed. B. PYM I'd . . get to know the general set-up, what was involved and all that. T. BARR Every new camera position or change in photographic composition is called a 'set-up'. C. MCCULLOUGH The best computer setup in the world. *Cricketer International* The first time for years that we have had top Test players in our set-up.

setwall /ˈsɛtw(ə)l/ *noun.* **ME.**
[Anglo-Norman *zedewale*, Old French *citoual* from medieval Latin *zedoale* (cf. Anglo-Latin *zituale, cytowalla*) var. of *zedoarium* ZEDOARY.]

†**1** (The root of) the zedoary, *Curcuma zedoaria.* **ME–M17.**

2 (The root of) any of several kinds of valerian, esp. garden valerian, *Valeriana phu*, and wild valerian, *V. officinalis*. Also, red valerian, *Centranthus ruber.* **M16.**

sev /seɪv/ *noun.* **L20.**
[Hindi.]

In Indian cookery: a snack consisting of long, thin strands of gram flour, deep-fried and spiced.

sève /sɛv/ *noun.* **M18.**
[French = sap.]

The quality and flavour appropriate to a specified wine; liveliness, savour.

seven /ˈsɛv(ə)n/ *adjective & noun (cardinal numeral).*
[Old English *seofon* = Old Frisian *soven* etc., Old Saxon *sibun*, Old High German *sibun* (Dutch *zeven*, German *sieben*), Old Norse *sjau*, Gothic *sibun*, from Germanic from Indo-European, whence also Latin *septem*, Greek *hepta*, Old Church Slavonic *sedmĭ*, Sanskrit *sapta*.]

▸**A** *adjective.* One more than six (a cardinal numeral represented by 7 in arabic numerals, vii, VII in roman). **OE.**

📖 G. GORDON For a whole week, for seven days. G. SWIFT I was a good husband for seven years to Anna. *Jerusalem Post* The Soviets put seven airborne divisions on alert. **seven champions** *arch.* the patron saints of England, Scotland, Wales, Ireland, France, Spain, and Italy (SS George, Andrew, David, Patrick, Denis, James, and Antony respectively). **seven days** *arch.* a week. **seven deadly sins** those entailing damnation (traditionally pride, covetousness, lust, envy, gluttony, anger, and sloth). ***Seven Last Words***: see WORD *noun*. **Seven Sages** the seven wise Greeks of the 6th cent. listed in Plato (Bias, Chilon, Cleobulus, Periander, Pittacus, Solon, and Thales), to each of whom a moral saying is attributed. **seven seas** the world's seas; *spec.* the Arctic, Antarctic, N. and S. Pacific, N. and S. Atlantic, and Indian Oceans. **Seven Sisters** (***a***) the Pleiades; (***b***) *SCOTTISH HISTORY* seven similar cannon used by the Scots at the battle of Flodden; (***c***) in the Indian subcontinent, a babbler, *Turdoides striatus*; = SAT-BHAI; (***d***) the seven international oil companies (Exxon, Mobil, Gulf, Standard Oil of California, Texaco, British Petroleum, and Royal Dutch Shell) held to dominate the production and marketing of petroleum; (***e***) seven long-established US colleges founded for women (Barnard, Bryn Mawr, Mount Holyoke, Radcliffe, Smith, Vassar, and Wellesley) regarded as having high academic and social prestige; (***f***) ***Seven Sisters' rose, Seven Sister rose***, a climbing rose, a variety of *Rosa* *multiflora*, producing densely clustered heads of white, cream, or pinkish flowers. **Seven Sleepers** the seven young Christian noblemen of Ephesus said to have hidden in a cave during the Decian persecution, fallen asleep there, and awoken 187 years later. **seven stars** (now chiefly *literary*) seven stars forming a group; *spec.* (*a*) the Pleiades; (*b*) Ursa Major. ***seven wonders of the world***: see WONDER *noun*. ***Seven Words***: see WORD *noun*. ***the City of the Seven Hills***: see CITY 2. ***the seven heavenly bodies***: see BODY *noun*.

▸**B** *noun*. **1** Seven persons or things identified contextually, as parts or divisions, years of age, points, runs, etc., in a game, chances (in giving odds), minutes, inches, shillings (now *Hist.*), pence, etc. **OE**.

2 One more than six as an abstract number; the symbol(s) or figure(s) representing this (7 in arabic numerals, vii, VII in roman). **OE**.

3 The time of day seven hours after midnight or midday (on a clock, watch, etc., indicated by the numeral seven displayed or pointed to). Also ***seven o'clock***. **LME**.

4 The seventh of a set or series with numbered members, the one designated seven, (usu. ***number seven***, or with specification, as ***book seven***, ***chapter seven***, etc.); a size etc. denoted by seven, a shoe, glove, garment, etc., of such a size, (also ***size seven***). **E16**.

5 A set of seven; a thing having a set of seven as an essential or distinguishing feature; *spec.* (*a*) a playing-card marked with seven pips or spots; (*b*) PROSODY a line of seven syllables; (*c*) in *pl.*, rugby football matches with seven players on each side. **L16**.

📖 **1** *Oxford Times* 23 attempts . . of which seven were successful. **3** P. FITZGERALD At a quarter to seven the telephone rang. **4** M. DUGGAN Mum with a shoehorn wedging nines into sevens. ***on cloud seven***: see CLOUD *noun*. **5** A. CHRISTIE Miss Ramsbotham continued with her patience . . . 'Red seven on black eight.' ***at sixes and sevens***: see SIX *noun* 4.

Comb.: Forming compound cardinal numerals with multiples of ten from twenty to ninety, as ***thirty-seven***, (*arch.*) ***seven-and-thirty***, etc., and (*arch.*) their corresponding ordinals, as ***seven-and-thirtieth*** etc., and with multiples of a hundred, as ***207*** (read ***two hundred and seven***, US also ***two hundred seven***), etc. With nouns + -ER[1] forming nouns with the sense 'something (identified contextually) being of or having seven —s', as ***seven-seater*** etc. Special combs., as **seven-bore** a shotgun with calibre seven; **seven-day** *adjective* consisting of or extending over seven days or a week; ***seven-day disease*** (*arch.*), a form of tetanus; **seven-eyes** the lamprey (in allusion to its gill-openings); **seven-hilled** *adjective* having or standing on seven hills; *spec.* designating the city of Rome; **seven-hilly** *adjective* (*rare*) = ***seven-hilled*** above; **seven-league** *adjective* measuring or covering seven leagues; chiefly in ***seven-league boots***, boots (in the fairy story of Hop o' my Thumb) enabling the wearer to go seven leagues at each stride; **sevenpence** seven pence, esp. of the old British currency before decimalization; **sevenpenny** *adjective* worth or costing sevenpence; **sevenscore** *arch.* one hundred and forty; **seven-sleeper** [with allus. to *Seven Sleepers* above or to seven months of hibernation] an animal which hibernates, *esp.* a dormouse; **seven-up** (*a*) *US* a variant of the card-game all fours played for seven points; (*b*) (orig. *N. Amer.*; with cap. initial(s)) proprietary name for a lemon-lime carbonated soft drink. See also SEVEN YEAR.

■ **sevener** *noun* (*a*) (**S-**) a member of a Shiite sect acknowledging seven as opp. to twelve Imams or religious leaders (opp. ***Twelver***); (*b*) (*Austral. colloq.*, now *Hist.*) a person sentenced to seven years' imprisonment: **M19**. **sevenfold** *adjective & adverb* (*a*) *adjective* seven times as great or as numerous; having seven parts, divisions, elements, or units; *poet.* seven in number; (*b*) *adverb* to seven times the number or quantity: **OE**. **sevenfolded** *adjective* (*arch.*) = SEVENFOLD *adjective* **L16**. **sevensome** *noun & adjective* (long *rare* or *obsolete*) (*a*) *noun* seven in all, a group of seven; (*b*) *adjective* consisting of seven: **E18**.

seven /ˈsɛv(ə)n/ *verb intrans. US slang.* **M20**.
[from SEVEN *noun*.]
Foll. by *out*: make a losing throw of seven in the game of craps.

seventeen /sɛv(ə)nˈtiːn, ˈsɛv(ə)ntiːn/ *adjective & noun (cardinal numeral)*.
[Old English *seofontiene* = Old Frisian *soventene*, Old High German, (German *siebzehn*), Old Norse *sjautján*, from Germanic base of SEVEN *adjective & noun*, -TEEN.]

▸**A** *adjective*. One more than sixteen (a cardinal numeral represented by 17 in arabic numerals, xvii, XVII in roman). **OE**.

📖 J. MORLEY A Lyons silk weaver, working . . for over seventeen hours a day.

▸**B** *noun*. **1** Seventeen persons or things identified contextually, as years of age, points, runs, etc. in a game, chances (in giving odds), minutes, shillings (now *Hist.*), pence, etc. **ME**.

2 One more than sixteen as an abstract number; the symbols or figures representing this (17 in arabic numerals, xvii, XVII in roman). **LME**.

3 The seventeenth of a set or series with numbered members, the one designated seventeen, (usu. ***number seventeen***, or with specification, as ***book seventeen***, ***chapter seventeen***, etc.); a size etc. denoted by seventeen, a garment etc. of such a size, (also ***size seventeen***). **E16**.

4 A set of seventeen; a thing having a set of seventeen as an essential or distinguishing feature. **L20**.

📖 **1** J. L. MOTLEY Of the tenders and zabras, seventeen were lost. *Westminster Gazette* Seventeen are filled with four-cylinder engines. ***sweet seventeen***: see SWEET *adjective & adverb*.

Comb.: Forming compound cardinal numerals with multiples of a hundred, as ***517*** (read ***five hundred and seventeen***, US also ***five hundred seventeen***), etc. In dates used for one thousand seven hundred, as ***1715*** (read ***seventeen fifteen***), ***seventeen-nineties***, etc. With nouns + -ER[1] forming nouns with the sense 'something (identified contextually) being of or having seventeen —s', as ***seventeen-tonner***, ***seventeen-wheeler***, etc. Special combs., as **seventeen-hunder linen** *Scot.* linen in the weaving of which 1700 threads go to the warp; **seventeen-year cicada**, **seventeen-year locust** an American cicada, *Magicicada septendecim*, whose nymphs emerge in large numbers periodically in a 17-year (or, in the south, a 13-year) cycle (cf. ***THIRTEEN-year cicada***).

seventeenth /sɛv(ə)nˈtiːnθ, ˈsɛv(ə)ntiːnθ/ *adjective & noun (ordinal numeral)*.
[Old English *seofontēoþa*, repl. in Middle English by forms from SEVENTEEN + -TH[2].]

▸**A** *adjective*. Next in order after the sixteenth, that is number seventeen in a series, (represented by 17th). **OE**.

📖 J. L. LOW On the seventeenth green at St. Andrews. **seventeenth part** *arch.* = sense B.3 below.

▸**B** *noun*. **1** The seventeenth person or thing of a category, series, etc., identified contextually, as day of the month, (following a proper name) person, esp. monarch or pope, of the specified name, etc. **OE**.

2 MUSIC. An interval embracing seventeen notes on the diatonic scale; a note a seventeenth above another given note; a chord of two notes a seventeenth apart. **L16**.

3 Each of seventeen equal parts into which something is or may be divided, a fraction which when multiplied by seventeen gives one, (= ***seventeenth part*** above). **E18**.

📖 **1** R. M. WILSON On the seventeenth of February . . I was . . working behind the bar.

Comb.: Forming compound ordinal numerals with multiples of a hundred, as ***five-hundred-and-seventeenth*** (***517th***) etc.

■ **seventeenthly** *adverb* in the seventeenth place **E17**.

seventh /ˈsɛv(ə)nθ/ *adjective & noun (ordinal numeral)*.
[Old English *seofoþa*, repl. in Middle English by forms from SEVEN *adjective & noun* + -TH[2].]

▸**A** *adjective*. Next in order after the sixth, that is number seven in a series, (represented by 7th). **OE**.

📖 AV *Gen.* 2:2 And on the seuenth day God ended his worke. E. M. THOMPSON Their conquest of Egypt in the seventh century. ***Seventh-day Adventist***: see ADVENTIST. ***seventh heaven***: see HEAVEN *noun*. **seventh part** *arch.* = sense B.2 below. **seventh wave** the wave regarded as the biggest in an increasing swell of the sea; *fig.* a culminating act or experience.

▸**B** *noun*. **1** The seventh person or thing of a category, series, etc., identified contextually, as day of the month, (following a proper name) person, esp. monarch or pope, of the specified name, etc. **OE**.

2 Each of seven equal parts into which something is or may be divided, a fraction which when multiplied by seven gives one, (= ***seventh part*** above). **M16**.

3 MUSIC. An interval embracing seven consecutive notes in the diatonic scale; a note a seventh above another given note; a chord of two notes a seventh apart, or based around the seventh of a note. **L16**.

📖 **1** J. R. GREEN The accession of Henry the Seventh ended . . the Civil Wars. F. FORSYTH Quinn poured another beer, their seventh. **2** *New Scientist* The shaking is one-third to one-seventh of what it is on the surface. **3** ***diminished seventh***, ***dominant seventh***, etc.

Comb.: Forming compound ordinal numerals with multiples of ten, as ***forty-seventh*** (***47th***), ***five-thousand-and-seventh*** (***5007th***), etc.

■ **seventhly** *adverb* in the seventh place **LME**.

seventieth /ˈsɛv(ə)ntɪɪθ/ *adjective & noun*. **ME**.
[from SEVENTY + -TH[2].]

▸**A** *adjective*. Next in order after the sixty-ninth, that is number seventy in a series, (represented by 70th). **ME**.

▸**B** *noun*. **1** The seventieth person or thing of a category, series, etc., identified contextually. **E17**.

2 Each of seventy equal parts into which something is or may be divided, a fraction which when multiplied by seventy gives one. **L20**.

Comb.: Forming compound ordinal numerals with multiples of a hundred, as ***one-hundred-and-seventieth*** (***170th***) etc., and (*arch.*) with numerals below ten, as ***three-and-seventieth*** etc.

seventy /ˈsɛv(ə)nti/ *adjective & noun (cardinal numeral)*.
[Old English *hundseofontig*, from *hund* of uncertain origin + *seofon* SEVEN *adjective & noun* + *-tig* -TY[2]. 1st elem. lost early in Middle English (cf. EIGHTY).]

▸**A** *adjective*. Seven times ten (a cardinal numeral represented by 70 in arabic numerals, lxx, LXX in roman). **OE**.

▸**B** *noun*. **1** Seven times ten as an abstract number; the symbols or figures representing this (70 in arabic numerals, lxx, LXX in roman). **ME**.

2 Seventy persons or things identified contextually, as years of age, points, runs, etc., in a game, chances (in giving odds), etc. **LME**.

3 The seventieth of a set or series with numbered members, the one designated seventy, (usu. ***number seventy***, or with specification, as ***chapter seventy***, ***verse seventy***, etc.); a size etc. denoted by seventy (also ***size seventy***). **E16**.

4 A set of seventy; a thing having a set of seventy as an essential or distinguishing feature. **L16**.

5 In *pl.* The numbers from 70 to 79 inclusive, esp. denoting years of a century or units of a scale of temperature; *one's* years of life between the ages of 70 and 79. **M19**.

Comb.: Forming compound numerals (cardinal or ordinal) with numerals below ten, as ***seventy-nine*** (***79***), ***seventy-first*** (***71st***), etc., and (cardinals) with multiples of a hundred, as ***470*** (read ***four hundred and seventy***, US also ***four hundred seventy***), etc. Special combs., as **seventy-eight** *Hist.* a gramophone record designed to be played at the (formerly standard) speed of seventy-eight revolutions per minute; **seventy-five** (*a*) ARCHERY (now *Hist.*) a bow requiring a drawing-power of 75 lb (approx. 34 kg); (*b*) *Hist.* a gun of 75 mm calibre, esp. as used in the French and US armies; **seventy-four** (*a*) (now *Hist.*) a warship carrying seventy-four guns; (*b*) *S. Afr.* an edible sparid fish, *Polysteganus undulosus*, silver with black barred markings; **seventy-seven**: ***Group of Seventy-Seven***, the developing countries of the world.

■ **seventyfold** *adjective & adverb* (*a*) *adjective* seventy times as great or as numerous, having seventy parts, divisions, elements, or units; (*b*) *adverb* to seventy times the number or quantity: **LME**. **seventyish** *adjective* about seventy (in age, measurements, etc.) **L20**.

seven year /ˈsɛv(ə)n jɪə/ *adjectival phr.* Also **seven-years'** /sɛv(ə)nˈjɪəz/. **L16**.
[from SEVEN *adjective & noun* + YEAR *noun*[1].]
Consisting of or lasting for seven years; having a period of seven years.

seven year itch *colloq.* (orig. *US*) (*a*) a form of scabies alleged to last for or recur after seven years; (*b*) (chiefly *joc.*) a supposed tendency to infidelity after seven years of marriage. **seven-year apple**, **seven-years apple** a shrub of Central America, *Casasia clusiaefolia*, of the madder family; the fruit of this shrub, supposed to require seven years to ripen. **seven-year-vine** *W. Indies* a morning glory, *Ipomoea tuberosa*, with seven-lobed leaves. **the Seven Years War**, **the Seven Years' War** the third Silesian war of 1756–63 in which Austria, France, Russia, Saxony, and Sweden were allied against Frederick II of Prussia.

sever /ˈsɛvə/ *verb*. **ME**.
[Anglo-Norman *severer*, Old French *sevrer* (mod. 'wean') from Proto-Romance from Latin *separare* SEPARATE *verb*.]

▸**I** *verb intrans*. **1** Part, separate, be separated (*from*). **ME**. ▸**b** Be or become separated into parts. **LME**. ▸**c** Of the lips etc.: move apart, open. **L18**.

2 LAW. **a** Of two or more defendants: plead independently. Freq. in ***sever in their challenges***. **E17**. ▸**b** Of joint tenants: divide their jointure. **L19**.

3 Make a separation or division *between*. Long *arch. rare.* **E17**.

📖 **1** R. BURNS Ae fond kiss, and then we sever. T. JEFFERSON Should we sever from each other . . no foreign power will ally with us. **b** G. CHAPMAN The soul departed . . , The body . . Can not consist but seuer and dissolue. **c** M. R. MITFORD The deaf man . . Saw her lips sever. **3** AV *Exod.* 9:4 And the Lord shall seuer betweene the cattel of Israel, and the cattell of Egypt.

▸**II** *verb trans*. **4** Put or set apart; part or separate, esp. by putting in different places; dissociate, disunite. Also foll. by *from*. **LME**. ▸**b** Cause (the lips etc.) to move apart or open. **LME**. ▸†**c** Set apart for a special purpose (chiefly in biblical translations). Also foll. by *out*. **LME–E18**. ▸†**d** Deprive *of*; hinder *from*; free *from*. **E16–E17**. ▸†**e** = SEPARATE *verb* 3a. **E17–L18**.

5 Separate in thought or idea; distinguish, treat as distinct; mark off *from*. **LME**.

6 Keep distinct or apart by an intervening space, barrier, etc.; (of a space, barrier, etc.) intervene between. **LME**.

7 Divide (a thing) into two or more parts; cut up *into* (now *rare* or *obsolete* exc. as in sense 8 below). Formerly also, divide according to kind or quality, sort. **LME**.

8 Divide by cutting, slicing, etc., esp. suddenly or forcibly; cut through; *fig.* put an end to, break off, (a link or connection). **LME**. ▸**b** Break up, scatter, or disperse (an assembly, group, etc.). Now *rare*. **LME**.

9 Detach or remove (*from*) by cutting, slicing, etc., esp. suddenly and forcibly; cut off. **LME**.

10 LAW. **a** Divide (a joint estate) into independent parts. **M16**. ▸**b** Remove (crops, minerals, fixtures, etc.) from land, a building, etc. **E17**. ▸**c** Separate and remove by a nonsuit (a plaintiff in a joint action). **E17**. ▸**d** Cause (two or more defendants) to plead independently. **M17**.

▭ **4** BACON The chaffe may and ought to be seuered from the corne in the Eare. W. S. CHURCHILL The Dutch and English . . have seldom been severed in the . . course of European events. **b** TENNYSON Her lips are sever'd as to speak. **c** AV *Ezek.* 39:14 And they shall seuer out men of continual emploiment. **d** B. GOOGE Weeding . . seuereth the Corne from all anoyances. **5** MILTON To know Both spirituall powre & civill, what each meanes, What severs each. *Expositor* He severs his own position most definitely from that of Sabbatier. **6** AV *Exod.* 8:22 I will seuer . . the lande of Goshen . . that no swarmes of flies shall be there. WORDSWORTH Immense The space that severed us! **7** M. HANMER He sheweth this heresie . . to have been severed into sundry sects. **8** A. WILSON A vein in his neck was severed and he bled to death. W. S. CHURCHILL King William was able to sever diplomatic relations with France. **b** SPENSER Let the flitting aire my vaine words sever. **9** M. PUZO Severed from its body, the black silky head . . was stuck fast in a thick cake of blood.

■ **severa'bility** *noun* the property of being severable; *esp.* (*US LAW*) the property of a contract, bill, etc., of having clauses or parts that can be treated independently as regards validity: L19. **severable** *adjective* †(*a*) distinct, separate; (*b*) able to be severed: LME. **seve'ration** *noun* (*rare*) separation, severance M17. **severer** *noun* (*rare*) a person who severs or separates something M17.

several /ˈsɛv(ə)r(ə)l/ *adjective, noun, adverb, & pronoun.* LME.
[Anglo-Norman (whence Anglo-Latin *severalis*) from Anglo-Latin *separalis*, from Latin *separ* SEPARATE *adjective* (sense B.3 perh. another word from SEVER *verb*): see -AL[1].]
► **A** *adjective.* **I** †**1** Of a person or thing: having a position, existence, or status apart; distinct or different *from*; distinctive, particular. LME–M18.
2 More than two but not many; *LAW* more than one. Formerly also, (of two or more persons or things) individually separate; different; various, sundry. LME.
3 Constituting an individual member of a specified class. *arch.* M16.
†**4** Consisting of different elements or parts; of diverse origin or composition. Chiefly *poet.* L16–L17.

▭ **1** R. WHITLOCK Keeping the Delivery of others Opinions and my own severall. DRYDEN The Reeve, the Miller, and the Cook, are several Men. **2** SHAKES. *Jul. Caes.* I will . . In several hands . . throw, As if they came from several citizens, Writings. J. CONRAD Several times that night he woke up. DAY LEWIS For several summers between 1908 and 1914. **3** SHAKES. *Two Gent.* I'll kiss each several paper for amends. R. G. COLLINGWOOD To create or renew a bond . . between the host and each several guest. **4** SPENSER A heavy load he bare Of nightly stelths, and pillage severall.

► **II 5** Chiefly *LAW.* Private; privately owned or occupied. *obsolete* exc. in ***several fishery*** below. LME.
6 Belonging, attributed, or assigned distributively to specified individuals; different for each respectively. *arch.* LME.
7 *LAW.* Applied or regarded separately, not joint; pertaining individually to each of a number of tenants, parties, etc.; (of an obligation) enforceable against each of the parties individually. M16.

▭ **5** P. STUBBES The commons . . are inclosed, made seueral. **several fishery** fishing rights derived through or on account of ownership of land. **6** MILTON Each fetter'd Ghost slips to his severall grave. B. JOWETT The Acharnians . . guarded their several districts. **7** ***joint and several***: see JOINT *adjective* 3. **several tenancy** ownership of land by one person absolutely, not jointly or in common with another.

► **B** *noun.* **1** (A piece of) land in private ownership or over which a person has a particular right, esp. enclosed pasture-land as opp. to common land. *obsolete* exc. *dial.* & in place-names. LME. ►†**b** *gen.* Private property, a private possession. M16–M17.
2 †**a** An individual point, quality, etc.; a particular, a detail. Usu. in *pl.* L16–E18. ►**b** In *pl.* Orig., individual persons or things. Later (*Scot., Anglo-Irish, & US*), several persons or things. E17.
†**3** A partition, a boundary. L16–M17.
Phrases: **in several** †(*a*) (of land, esp. enclosed pasture-land) in private ownership, not common; (*b*) (now *rare*) separately, individually; †(*c*) *rare* divided into separate portions.
►†**C** *adverb.* = SEVERALLY *adverb.* M16–L18.
► **D** *pronoun.* More than two but not many of or *of* a specified group. L17.

▭ HOR. WALPOLE Several of the court who ingratiated themselves by offerings of pictures.

■ **severalfold** *adjective & adverb* (*a*) *adjective* several times as great or as numerous; having several parts, divisions, elements, or units; (*b*) *adverb* to several times the number or quantity: M18. **severalize** *verb trans.* (*rare*) separate or distinguish (*from*) M17.

†**several** *verb trans. rare.* Infl. **-ll-**. L15.
[from prec.]
1 Enclose (a piece of land, esp. pasture-land) as private property; deprive of the status of common land. L15–L18.
2 Divide or break up into separate parts or branches. L16–M17.

severality /sɛvəˈralɪti/ *noun. rare.* M16.
[Alt. of SEVERALTY by substitution of -ITY.]
1 An individual or particular point, matter, feature, etc. Usu. in *pl.* M16.
†**2** = SEVERALTY 1. Only in M17.
in severality = ***in severalty*** (b) s.v. SEVERALTY.

severally /ˈsɛv(ə)r(ə)li/ *adverb.* LME.
[from SEVERAL *adjective* + -LY[2].]
1 Separately, individually; each successively or in turn; *LAW* pertaining to or involving several persons individually, not jointly. LME.
2 Apart from others or from the rest; not together or in a company. *arch.* LME.
3 Respectively. L16.
†**4** Differently, variously. E–M17.

▭ **1** T. HARDY There emerged from the shade severally five men of different ages and gaits. E. F. BENSON Brayton . . had sacked them severally, after conviction. **2** M. HANMER They assembled together, severally men, and severally women. R. L. STEVENSON A great variety of oaks stood, now severally, now in a becoming grove. **3** C. WORDSWORTH The parts which I and they have severally taken are openly justified. **4** W. CHILLINGWORTH How severally Satan plants his Engines for the subversion of the Church.

severalth /ˈsɛv(ə)r(ə)lθ/ *adjective. US dial.* E20.
[from SEVERAL *adjective* + -TH[2].]
That is an indefinite number in a series.

severalty /ˈsɛv(ə)r(ə)lti/ *noun.* LME.
[Anglo-Norman *severalte*, *-aute* (whence Anglo-Latin *separalitas*), formed as SEVERAL *adjective* + -TY[1]. Cf. SEVERALITY.]
1 The condition of being separate or distinct; separateness, distinctness. LME.
2 a The tenure of land held by an individual absolutely, not jointly or in common with another; the condition of land so held. Orig. in ***in severalty*** (a) below. LME. ►**b** A piece of land held in severalty. L16.
†**3** = SEVERALITY 1. M16–M17.
Phrases: **in severalty** (*a*) *LAW* (of land) held by an individual absolutely, not jointly or in common with another; held as private enclosed property (cf. ***in common*** (c) s.v. COMMON *noun*); (*b*) separately, apart from others, particularly; (*c*) in or into several divisions or parts.

Severan /ˈsɛvərən/ *adjective.* E20.
[from Latin cognomen *Severus* (◐ see below) + -AN.]
Of, pertaining to, or characteristic of the Roman Emperor (Lucius) Septimius Severus (reigned AD 193–211) or the period of rule of the dynasty established by him (AD 193–235).

severance /ˈsɛv(ə)r(ə)ns/ *noun.* LME.
[Anglo-Norman *severance*, Old French *sevrance*, from *severer*, *sevrer*: see SEVER, -ANCE.]
1 The action or fact of severing; the state of being severed; an instance of this; (a) separation. Formerly also, a distinction or difference *between*. LME.
2 *LAW.* **a** The division of a joint estate into independent parts; the ending by this means of a joint tenancy. M16. ►**b** The removal of crops, minerals, fixtures, etc. from land, a building, etc. E17. ►**c** The separation and removal by a nonsuit of a plaintiff of two or more in a joint action. Also, the entering of independent pleas by two or more defendants. E17.
3 Discharge from contractual employment. Also *ellipt.* = ***severance pay*** below. M20.
Comb.: **severance pay** money paid to an employee on the early termination of a contract.

severe /sɪˈvɪə/ *adjective & adverb.* M16.
[Old & mod. French *sévère* or Latin *severus*.]
► **A** *adjective.* **I 1** Rigorous, strict, or harsh in attitude, manner, or treatment; unsparing; not inclined to or indicative of indulgence or leniency. Also foll. by *to*, *with*. M16.
2 Involving strict and rigorous treatment; executed or carried out with rigour; imposing rigorous conditions, stringent. M16.
3 Unsparing in judgement, criticism, or reproof; strongly condemnatory (freq. foll. by *on*). M16.

▭ **1** SIR W. SCOTT Charles of Burgundy deserved the character of a just though severe prince. A. WILSON The small twinkling glance . . always charmed, coming out of a face so severe in repose. I. MURDOCH Don't be so severe with me . . , I'm under an awful strain. **2** DEFOE Everyone was forbid to . . converse with him, on severe Penalties. SHELLEY To pursue this monstrous crime By the severest forms of law. **3** LD MACAULAY Nor . . will the severest of our readers blame us. B. HARTE He was arrested . . and discharged with a severe reprimand.

► **II 4** Strict in matters of conduct or behaviour; austere; not inclined to laxity or self-indulgence. Cf. earlier SEVERITY 1. M16.
5 Conforming to an exacting standard of mental effort; rigidly exact or accurate; serious, not light; not avoiding the intellectually arduous or difficult. E17.
6 Unadorned, austerely simple or plain; not florid or exuberant; sober, restrained. M17.

▭ **4** S. LEE Emily affected severe economy in her travelling expences. J. A. FROUDE A Roman matron of the strictest and severest type. **5** HAZLITT A day spent in . . elegant relaxation from severer studies. DE QUINCEY Under the continual restraint of severe good sense. **6** F. NORRIS Dressed in black, the cut and fashion of the gown severe, almost monastic. U. HOLDEN Her study was severe, with just a desk and a cupboard for her files.

► **III 7** Disagreeably intense, unpleasantly extreme; (esp. of bad weather, illness, injury, etc.) causing hardship, pain, or suffering by its degree of extremity. M17.
8 Hard to sustain or endure; making great demands on one's powers or resources; arduous; (of terrain etc.) negotiable only with exertion or skill. L18.
9 Very big or powerful; hard to beat. *colloq.* (chiefly *N. Amer.*). E19.

▭ **7** R. C. HUTCHINSON The pain in her back had become severe. W. S. CHURCHILL Hopton's losses were so severe that he took refuge in Devizes. **8** J. TYNDALL The ice was subjected to a still severer test. *Guardian* A broad expanse of smooth sheer rock classed as 'very severe'. **9** T. E. WHITE The determination to have a severe nap before night.

► **B** *adverb.* Severely. Now *rare* or *obsolete.* L16.
¶ In sense A.4 SEVERITY (L15) is earlier than SEVERE *adjective.* In all other corresponding senses, SEVERITY is of the same date or later than SEVERE *adjective.*
■ **severely** *adverb* in a severe manner; ***leave severely alone***, ***let severely alone***, avoid deliberately; pursue a deliberate policy of ignoring or isolating: M16. **severeness** *noun* (long *rare* or *obsolete*) severity L16. **severish** *adjective* (*rare*) somewhat severe E19.

Severian /sɪˈvɪərɪən/ *noun & adjective.* LME.
[Latin *Severiani* (pl.), from (in sense A.1) *Severus* supposed founder of the sect or *severus* SEVERE *adjective*, (in sense A.2) *Severus* (see below): see -AN, -IAN.]
ECCLESIASTICAL HISTORY. ►**A** *noun.* **1** A member of an austere 2nd-cent. Encratite or Gnostic sect. Usu. in *pl.* LME.
2 A follower or adherent of Severus, the early 5th-cent. Monophysite patriarch of Antioch. Usu. in *pl.* L17.
► **B** *attrib.* or as *adjective.* Of or pertaining to the Severians or their beliefs. *rare.* E18.

†**Severite** *noun.* E17–E18.
[from *Severus*: see prec., -ITE[1].]
= SEVERIAN *noun.*

severity /sɪˈvɛrɪti/ *noun.* L15.
[Old & mod. French *sévérité* or Latin *severitas*, formed as SEVERE *adjective*: see -ITY.]
1 The fact or condition of being severe; severe behaviour, speech, etc.; extreme strictness or harshness; rigorous exactitude. L15.
2 An instance of this; a severe action, speech, etc.; a harsh rebuke. Freq. in *pl.* M16.

▭ **1** M. SCHORER The excessive intellectual severity of one style is the counterpart of the excessive lyric relaxation of the other. K. LINES Zeus punished Prometheus with terrible severity. A. STORR A disorder which ranges in severity from mild compulsions . . to . . total disablement. **2** J. VENEER Sharp rebukes and legal severities. G. F. RUXTON The severities of a prolonged winter . . had robbed his bones of fat.

¶ See note s.v. SEVERE *adjective & adverb.*

severy /ˈsɛvəri/ *noun.* LME.
[Old French *civoire* ciborium.]
ARCHITECTURE. A space or compartment in a vaulted roof. Formerly also, a section of scaffolding.

seviche /sɛˈviːtʃeɪ/ *noun.* Also **c-**. M20.
[S. Amer. Spanish *seviche*, *cebiche*.]
A S. American dish of marinaded raw fish or seafood, usu. garnished and served as a starter.

sévigné /seviɲe/ *noun.* Also **se-**. Pl. pronounced same. E19.
[Prob. from Mme de *Sévigné* (1626–96), French letter-writer.]
Hist. A kind of bandeau, esp. for the hair; a jewel or ornament for decorating a head-dress.

Sevillan /sɛˈvɪlən/ *adjective & noun.* L19.
[from (the same root as) SEVILLE + -AN. Cf. SEVILLIAN.]
► **A** *adjective.* Sevillian. L19.
► **B** *noun.* A Sevillian. E20.

Sevillana /sɛvɪˈljɑːnə/ *noun. rare.* L19.
[Spanish.]
A female Sevillian. Also, a variant of the Spanish dance the *seguidilla*, originating in Seville.

Sevillano /sɛvɪˈljɑːnəʊ/ *noun.* Pl. **-os**. L19.
[Spanish.]
A male Sevillian.

Seville /səˈvɪl, ˈsɛvɪl/ *noun.* LME.
[Anglicized from Spanish *Sevilla* a city and province in Andalusia.]
†**1** ***Seville oil***, olive oil produced in Seville. LME–E17.
2 ***Seville orange***, a bitter variety of orange, chiefly used to make marmalade and liqueurs. Also, the tree, *Citrus aurantium*, which bears this fruit, and whose flowers yield neroli oil. L16.

Sevillian /səˈvɪlɪən/ *noun & adjective.* M19.
[from (the same root as) prec.: see -IAN. Cf. SEVILLAN.]
► **A** *noun.* A native or inhabitant of Seville. M19.
► **B** *adjective.* Of or pertaining to Seville or the Sevillians. M19.

Sevin /ˈsɛvɪn/ *noun.* **M20.**
[Origin unkn.]
(Proprietary name for) a preparation of 1-naphthyl-N-methylcarbamate, used as an insecticide.

Sèvres /ˈseɪvrə, *foreign* sɛːvr/ *noun.* **M18.**
[*Sèvres* in France (see below).]
In full ***Sèvres china***, ***Sèvres porcelain***, etc. A kind of fine porcelain, esp. with elaborate decoration, made at Sèvres, now a suburb of Paris, from the 18th cent.

sevruga /sɛvˈruːɡə/ *noun.* **L16.**
[Russian *sevryuga*.]
(Caviar from) the sturgeon *Acipenser stellatus*, of the Caspian and Black Seas.

sevum /ˈsiːvəm/ *noun.* Now *rare* or *obsolete*. **LME.**
[Latin *sevum*, *sebum*. Cf. **SEBUM**.]
Suet, esp. as used by pharmacists in ointments etc.

sew /suː, sjuː/ *noun.* Long *obsolete* exc. *dial.* **L15.**
[Old French, aphet. from *essever*: see **SEW** *verb*[2].]
A sewer, a drain.

sew /səʊ/ *verb*[1]. Pa. t. **sewed** /səʊd/; pa. pple **sewed**, **sewn** /səʊn/.
[Old English *siwan*, *siowan* = Old Frisian *sia*, Old High German *siuwen*, Old Norse *sýja*, Gothic *siujan*, from Germanic, from Indo-European base repr. also by Latin *suere*, Greek (*kas-*)*suein*.]
1 *verb trans. & intrans.* Fasten, attach, or join (pieces of cloth, leather, etc.) by the insertion of a thread drawn repeatedly through a series of punctures made with a threaded needle or with an awl. **OE.** ▸**b** *verb trans.* Fasten, attach, or fix *on, in, to, round*, etc., by sewing. **OE.** ▸**c** *verb trans.* Make (a garment etc.) by sewing. **ME.** ▸**d** *verb trans.* Fasten together the edges of (esp. a wound) by sewing; = ***sew up*** (a) below. Now *rare*. **E16.** ▸**e** *verb trans.* **BOOKBINDING.** Fasten together the folded sheets of (a book) by passing a thread or wire backwards and forwards through their spine folds in order to attach them to the bands or tapes. Cf. **STITCH** *verb*[1] 4. **M17.**
2 *verb trans.* Enclose *in*, put *into* a cover or receptacle secured by sewing; = ***sew up*** (b) below. **ME.**

> **1** C. ACHEBE She could sew and bake. ***sew pillows under a person's elbows***: see **PILLOW** *noun*. **sew up** (*a*) join or fasten together the edges of (an orifice, wound, tear, etc.) by sewing, close in this way; (*b*) enclose securely *in* a cover or receptacle; (*c*) *arch. slang* tire out, exhaust; confound; outwit, cheat, swindle; make hopelessly drunk; (*d*) *colloq.* (orig. *US*) bring to a desired conclusion or condition; complete satisfactorily; *spec.* ensure the favourable outcome of (a game or match); (freq. in ***all sewn up***, ***all sewed up***); (*e*) *colloq.* enclose, seal off. **b** L. LOCHHEAD Sewing sequins On your carnival costume. **c** T. HOOD Sewing at once, with a double thread, A Shroud as well as a Shirt. D. KYLE The women sew mini-dresses. **2** DICKENS Nell had still the piece of gold sewn in her dress. *City Limits* She had to be sewn into those sequinned ballgowns.

Comb.: **sew-on** *adjective* (intended to be) attached by sewing; **sew-round** *adjective & noun* (*a*) *adjective* designating a method of sewing the upper of a shoe directly to the sole; (*b*) *noun* a shoe made by this method.

sew /suː, sjuː/ *verb*[2]. **E16.**
[Aphet. from Old French *essewer*, *essever* drain off (whence medieval Latin *sewar*e) from Proto-Romance, from Latin **EX-**[1] + *aqua* water. Cf. **SEWER** *noun*[1].]
1 *verb trans.* Drain, draw off the water from. Formerly also, draw off (water). Now *dial.* **E16.**
2 *verb intrans.* (Of a liquid) ooze out, exude; (of a containing vessel) allow liquid to ooze out or exude. Now *dial.* **M16.**
3 *verb intrans.* **NAUTICAL.** Of a ship: be grounded, be high and dry; have the water-line a specified height above the water. **L16.**

sewable /ˈsuːəb(ə)l, ˈsjuː-/ *adjective*[1]. *rare*. **M19.**
[from **SEW** *verb*[2] + **-ABLE**.]
Able to be drained.

sewable /ˈsəʊəb(ə)l/ *adjective*[2]. **L20.**
[from **SEW** *verb*[1] + **-ABLE**.]
Able to be sewn.
■ **sewaˈbility** *noun* **M20.**

sewage /ˈsuːɪdʒ, ˈsjuː-/ *noun & verb.* **M19.**
[Formed after **SEWER** *noun*[1] by substitution of suffix: see **-AGE**.]
▸**A** *noun.* **1** Waste, esp. excremental, matter conveyed in sewers. **M19.**
2 = **SEWERAGE** 1, 2. *rare*. **M19.**
Comb.: **sewage farm** (*a*) *rare* a farm on which sewage irrigation is practised; (*b*) a place where sewage is treated, esp. to produce manure; **sewage grass** grass grown on land fertilized by sewage; **sewage irrigation** the system of irrigating esp. agricultural land with liquid sewage for disposal; **sewage lagoon** *N. Amer.* = **LAGOON** *noun* 4.
▸**B** *verb trans. rare.*
1 Irrigate or fertilize with sewage. **M19.**
2 = **SEWER** *verb* 2. (Earlier in **SEWAGING** 1.) **L19.**
■ **sewaged** *adjective* (*a*) fertilized or irrigated with sewage; (*b*) *rare* contaminated with sewage: **M19.**

sewaging /ˈsuːɪdʒɪŋ, ˈsjuː-/ *verbal noun. rare*. **E17.**
[formed as prec.: see **-ING**[1].]
1 The action of draining by means of sewers. **E17.**
2 The action of irrigating or fertilizing with sewage. **L19.**
¶ Not recorded between **E17** and **L19**.

sewan /ˈsiːwɒn/ *noun. obsolete* exc. *Hist.* Also **seawant** /ˈsiːwɒnt/. **E17.**
[Algonquian. Cf. Narragansett *siwân* unstrung beads.]
Wampum.

sewed /səʊd/ *ppl adjective.* **L16.**
[pa. pple of **SEW** *verb*[1]: see **-ED**[1]. Cf. **SEWN** *ppl adjective*.]
= **SEWN** *ppl adjective*.

Sewee /ˈsiːwiː/ *adjective & noun.* **L17.**
[N. Amer. Indian.]
▸**A** *adjective.* Designating or pertaining to a N. American Indian people of the S. Carolina coast, generally regarded as being of Sioux origin. **L17.**
†**Sewee bean** = **SIEVA BEAN**.
▸**B** *noun.* Pl. **-s**, same. A member of this people. **M19.**

sewee bean *noun phr.* see **SIEVA BEAN**.

sewellel /sɪˈwɛləl/ *noun.* **E19.**
[Chinook Jargon *šwalál* robe of mountain beaver skin.]
= ***MOUNTAIN beaver***.

sewen *noun* var. of **SEWIN**.

sewer /ˈsuːə, ˈsjuː-/ *noun*[1]. **ME.**
[Anglo-Norman *sever(e)*, Old Northern French *se(u)wiere* channel for carrying off overflow from a fish-pond (whence medieval Latin *seweria*) from Proto-Romance, from base also of **SEW** *verb*[2].]
1 A watercourse built to drain marshy land and carry off surface water into a river or the sea. Also ***water-sewer***. **ME.**
2 A channel or conduit, now usually covered and underground, built to carry off and discharge drainage water and sewage. **E17.**
3 *ellipt.* = ***commissioner of sewers*** below. *obsolete* exc. *Hist.* **E17.**
Phrases: **commission of sewers** *Hist.* (*a*) a royal commission constituting specified people; a temporary court with authority for the repair and maintenance of sewers (sense 1 above), bridges, streams, and other coastal defences of a district liable to flooding; such people collectively; (*b*) a body of municipal officers responsible for the control of sewers (sense 2 above) in the City of London. **commissioner of sewers** *Hist.* a member of a commission of sewers. **common sewer** a drain through which most of the sewage of a town passes, a main drain collecting and discharging the contents of auxiliary drains. **law of sewers** a local law relating to embankment and draining. ***storm sewer***: see **STORM** *noun*.
Comb.: **sewer-air**, **sewer-gas** atmospheric air mixed with gas formed by the decomposition of sewage; **sewer-rat** a rat which lives in sewers and drains, *esp.* the brown rat, *Rattus norvegicus*.
■ **sewerless** *adjective* not provided with sewers, without sewers **M19**. **sewery** *adjective* (*rare*) of, pertaining to, or resembling a sewer or sewers; (of a smell) unpleasant, offensive: **M19.**

sewer /ˈsjuːə/ *noun*[2]. *obsolete* exc. *Hist.* **ME.**
[Aphet. from Anglo-Norman *asseour*, from Old & mod. French *asseoir* place a seat for from Latin *assidere*, formed as **AD-** + *sedere* sit: see **-ER**[2].]
An attendant at a meal responsible for supervising the arrangement of the table, the seating of the guests, and the tasting and serving of the dishes.

sewer /ˈsəʊə/ *noun*[3]. **LME.**
[from **SEW** *verb*[1] + **-ER**[1].]
A person who sews.

sewer /ˈsuːə, ˈsjuː-/ *verb trans.* **M16.**
[from **SEWER** *noun*[1].]
†**1** Drain. Only in **M16.**
2 Provide (a town, road, etc.) with a system of sewers. Chiefly as ***sewering*** *verbal noun*. **M19.**
¶ Not recorded between **M16** and **M19**.

sewerage /ˈsuːərɪdʒ, ˈsjuː-/ *noun.* **M19.**
[formed as prec. + **-AGE**.]
1 Drainage by sewers; a system of draining by sewers. **M19.**
2 Sewers collectively; the system of sewers belonging to a particular locality. **M19.**
3 = **SEWAGE** *noun* 1. **M19.**

sewin /ˈsjuːɪn/ *noun.* Also **-en**. **M16.**
[Origin unkn.: cf. **SUANT** *noun*.]
In Wales, a sea trout.

sewing /ˈsəʊɪŋ/ *noun.* **ME.**
[from **SEW** *verb*[1] + **-ING**[1].]
1 The action of **SEW** *verb*[1]. Freq. prefixed with specifying word. **ME.**
2 Sewn work or material; work or material to be sewn. **LME.**
3 In *pl.* Thread or silk for sewing. **M19.**

> **1** *Nature* The speed of expert hand-sewing, thirty stitches per minute. *Country Life* The sewing together of different materials for ornamentation. ***plain sewing***: see **PLAIN** *adjective*[1] *& adverb*. **2** J. HATTON Mrs. Grey looked up from her sewing.

Attrib. & comb.: In the sense 'suitable for or used in sewing', as ***sewing cotton***, ***sewing-room***, etc. Special combs., as **sewing-machine** a machine for sewing or stitching, esp. in dressmaking etc.

sewn /səʊn/ *ppl adjective.* **M19.**
[pa. pple of **SEW** *verb*[1]: see **-N**, **-EN**[6]. Cf. **SEWED**.]
That has been sewn; fastened, attached, joined together, or made by sewing. Freq. prefixed with specifying word.
hand-sewn, ***machine-sewn***, etc.
Comb.: **sewn-in**, **sewn-on** *adjectives* that has been sewn in or on.

sewn *verb pa. pple*: see **SEW** *verb*[1].

sewster /ˈsəʊstə/ *noun.* Long *obsolete* exc. *Scot.* **LME.**
[from **SEW** *verb*[1] + **-STER**.]
A seamstress.

sex /sɛks/ *noun & adjective.* **LME.**
[Old & mod. French *sexe* or Latin *sexus*.]
▸**A** *noun.* **1** Either of the two main divisions (male and female) into which many organisms are placed on the basis of their reproductive functions or capacities; *collect.* (treated as *sing.* or *pl.*) the males or females of a particular species, esp. the human race. **LME.** ▸**b** ***the sex***, the female sex, women collectively. *arch.* **L16.**
2 The quality or fact of belonging to a particular sex; possession or membership of a sex. **E16.**
†**3** [By confusion.] A sect. **L16–E18.**
4 The difference between male and female, esp. in humans. Now *spec.* the sum of the physiological and behavioural characteristics distinguishing members of either sex; (manifestations or consequences of) sexual instincts, desires, etc. Cf. **GENDER** *noun* 3b. **M17.** ▸**b** Physical contact between individuals involving sexual stimulation of the genitals, sexual intercourse; *spec.* copulation, coitus. Freq. in ***have sex (with)***. *colloq.* **E20.** ▸**c** *euphem.* Genitals; a penis; a vagina. **M20.**

> **1** P. G. WODEHOUSE You are a pearl . . , the queen of your sex. M. HADFIELD The flowers are in catkins, the sexes nearly always on different trees. *Which?* Equal pension rights for both sexes. **2** SMOLLETT As for me, my sex protects me. M. ELPHINSTONE When persons of different sexes walk together, the woman . . follows the man. *Health Promotion* Greater mortality of people with no sick days was independent of age, sex, . . and health habits. *Nature* The dandelion . . probably lost sex only recently. **4** W. CARTWRIGHT My Soul's as Male as yours; there's no Sex in the mind. M. FRAYN Pornography, marriage, . . tenderness, striptease . . were all 'sex'. G. DALY Rose . . knew little about sex. **b** *Woman's Own* Trends . . that make sex before marriage . . easy.

Phrases: ***safe sex***: see **SAFE** *adjective*. **sex and shopping** a genre of popular novels concerning wealthy and glamorous characters typically indulging in frequent sexual relationships and extravagant spending. ***softer sex***, ***soft sex***: see **SOFT** *adjective*. **the fair sex**, **the fairer sex**, **the gentle sex**, **the gentler sex** the female sex, women collectively. ***the opposite sex***: see **OPPOSITE** *adjective* 3b. ***the rougher sex***: see **ROUGH** *adjective*. **the second sex** the female sex, women collectively. **the sterner sex** the male sex, men collectively. **the third sex** homosexuals collectively. **the weaker sex** = ***the fairer sex*** above.
Comb.: **sex act** the act of sexual intercourse; **sex appeal** sexual attractiveness; **sex attractant** a substance produced by one sex of a species that attracts members of the opposite sex; a synthetic substance with the same property; **sex-blind** *adjective* not discriminating between the sexes; **sex bomb** *colloq.* = **sexpot** below; **sex cell** a reproductive cell, with either male or female function; a sperm cell, an egg cell; **sex change** a change of sex; *spec.* an apparent change of sex brought about by surgical means, treatment with hormones, etc.; **sex chromatin** (the material of) a Barr body; **sex chromosome** each of the chromosomes (normally two in number) in a cell's chromosomal complement, the particular combination of which (as XX or XY) determines an individual's sex; **sex crime** a crime involving sexual assault or having a sexual motive; a sexual act regarded as a crime; **sex criminal** a person committing a sex crime; **sex determination** the biological mechanism that determines the sex of an individual; **sex discrimination** = ***SEXUAL discrimination***; **sex drive** the urge to seek satisfaction of sexual needs; **sex factor** (*a*) a chromosome or gene which determines sex; (*b*) a bacterial plasmid which can promote the transfer of genetic material from its ('male') host to another ('female') bacterium in which recombination then takes place; **sex hormone** any of the (natural or synthetic) hormones that affect sexual development or behaviour, esp. those produced by the gonads; **sex industry** the commercial trade in sex and sexually stimulating materials, including prostitution, pornography, etc.; **sex instinct** the behaviour and feelings associated with sexual reproduction considered as an instinct for the survival of the species; **sex kitten** *colloq.* a young woman who provocatively asserts or exploits her sex appeal; **sex life** a person's sexual activities and relationships collectively; **sex-limited** *adjective* †(*a*) = ***sex-linked*** (a) below; (*b*) designating or having a genetic character or a phenotype capable of occurring only in individuals of one sex; (*c*) = ***sex-linked*** (b) below; **sex-linkage** the state or condition of being sex-linked; **sex-linked** *adjective* (*a*) designating or determined by a gene that is carried on a sex chromosome; (*b*) occurring only or characteristically in one sex; **sex maniac** *colloq.* a person obsessed with sex or needing excessive sexual gratification; **sex object** a person regarded mainly in terms of sexual attractiveness or as providing sexual gratification; **sex offence** a breach of law involving sexual assault or having a sexual motive; **sex-offender** a person guilty of a sex offence; **sexpot** *colloq.* a person, esp. a woman, who is very sexually attractive or active; **sex-**

reversal adoption of a form or role characteristic of the opposite sex; **sex role** = *SEXUAL role*; **sex shop** a shop selling sex magazines, sex aids, etc.; **sex-starved** *adjective* deprived of or lacking sexual gratification; **sex surrogate** a person employed as a sexual partner for a person undergoing therapy for sexual problems; **sex symbol** (*a*) a person, esp. an actor, musician, etc., widely noted for sex appeal and glamour; (*b*) a symbol with a sexual signification; **sex therapist** a practitioner of sex therapy; **sex therapy** therapy dealing with a person's psychological impediments to sexual intercourse or with other sexual problems; **sex tourism** the organization of holidays with the purpose of taking advantage of the lack of restrictions imposed on sexual activity and prostitution by some countries; **sex-typed** *adjective* (SOCIOLOGY & PSYCHOLOGY) typified as being characteristic of either the male or the female sex; **sex typing** SOCIOLOGY & PSYCHOLOGY stereotyping people according to the characteristics or behaviour considered typical of their sex; **sex worker** a worker in the sex industry.

► **B** *attrib.* or as *adjective.* Of or pertaining to sex or sexual activity; arising from a difference or consciousness of sex. L19.

sex aid, *sex antagonism*, *sex education*, *sex film*, *sex partner*, *sex urge*, *sex war*, etc.

¶ *Sex* when used attributively is now freq. synonymous with *sexual*.

sex /sɛks/ *verb.* L19.
[from the noun.]
1 *verb trans.* Determine the sex of (a person or animal) by anatomical etc. examination, label as male or female; divide into the two sexes. L19.
2 *verb trans.* Foll. by *up*: give a sexual flavour to, increase the sexual content of; arouse sexually (usu. in *pass.*). *slang.* M20.
3 *verb intrans.* Have sexual intercourse. *slang.* M20.
■ **sexer** *noun* M20.

sex- /sɛks/ *combining form.* Before a consonant also **sexa-** /ˈsɛksə/, **sexi-** /ˈsɛksi/.
[Latin *sex* six (+ euphonic *-a-*, *-i-*).]
Sixfold, having six.
■ **sexa'decimal** *adjective* = HEXADECIMAL *adjective* L19. †**sexangle** *noun* (*rare*) a hexagon M17–L18. **se'xangular** *adjective* having six angles, hexagonal E17. **sexa'valent** *adjective* = HEXAVALENT E20. **sex'digitism** *noun* the condition of having six fingers or toes on one or more hands or feet L18. **sexfid** *adjective* (BOTANY) divided into six parts by deep clefts or notches M18. **sexi'valent** *adjective* = HEXAVALENT L19. **sex'valent** *adjective* (now *rare*) = HEXAVALENT M19.

sexagenae *noun pl.* see SEXAGENE.

sexagenarian /ˌsɛksədʒɪˈnɛːrɪən/ *noun & adjective.* M18.
[formed as next: see -ARIAN, -IAN.]
► **A** *noun.* A person between 60 and 69 years of age. M18.
► **B** *adjective.* Of between 60 and 69 years of age; of, pertaining to, or characteristic of a sexagenarian or sexagenarians. M19.
■ **sexagenarianism** *noun* the state or fact of being in one's sixties L19.

sexagenary /sɛkˈsadʒɪn(ə)ri/ *adjective & noun.* L16.
[Latin *sexagenarius*, from *sexageni* distrib. of *sexaginta* sixty: see -ARY[1].]
► **A** *adjective.* **1** MATH. = SEXAGESIMAL *adjective.* Now *rare* or *obsolete.* L16.
2 = SEXAGENARIAN *adjective.* M17.
► **B** *noun.* †**1** MATH. = SEXAGESIMAL *noun.* M17–E18.
2 = SEXAGENARIAN *noun.* Now *rare* or *obsolete.* E19.

†**sexagene** *noun.* Pl. **-genae**, **-genes**. L16–M18.
[mod. Latin *sexagena* fem. sing. from Latin *sexageni*: see prec.]
MATH. A quantity or number multiplied by (a power of) sixty; an arc of sixty degrees. Cf. SEXAGESM.

Sexagesima /sɛksəˈdʒɛsɪmə/ *noun.* LME.
[ecclesiastical Latin, fem. (sc. *dies*) of Latin *sexagesimus* sixtieth, from *sexaginta* sixty, prob. named by analogy with *Quinquagesima*, *Quadragesima*.]
ECCLESIASTICAL. The second Sunday before Lent (also more fully ***Sexagesima Sunday***). Formerly also, the week beginning with this day and ending on Quinquagesima.

sexagesimal /sɛksəˈdʒɛsɪm(ə)l/ *adjective & noun.* L17.
[from Latin *sexagesimus* sixtieth + -AL[1].]
► **A** *adjective.* Proceeding by sixties; *esp.* designating or pertaining to a system of numerical notation or measurement using sixty as a base or based on division into sixty equal parts (as seconds and minutes). L17.
sexagesimal fraction a fraction whose denominator is 60 or a power of 60.
► **B** *noun.* In *pl.* (The system of) sexagesimal fractions. L17.
■ **sexagesimally** *adverb* into sixtieths L19.

†**sexagesm** *noun.* L16–M18.
[from mod. Latin *sexagesima* (sc. *pars*) sixtieth part: see SEXAGESIMA.]
MATH. A sexagesimal fraction; the sixtieth part of a degree, a minute. Cf. SEXAGENE.

sexagon /ˈsɛksəg(ə)n/ *noun. rare.* E17.
[Blend of SEX- and HEXAGON.]
= HEXAGON.
■ **sexagonal** /sɛkˈsagən(ə)l/ *adjective* = HEXAGONAL M18.

sexational /sɛkˈseɪʃ(ə)n(ə)l/ *adjective. slang* (orig. *US*). Also **sexs-**. E20.
[Blend of SEX *noun* and SENSATIONAL.]
Sexually sensational.
■ **se'xationalism** *noun* exploitation of sexually sensational material E20.

sexcapade /ˈsɛkskəpeɪd/ *noun. slang.* M20.
[Blend of SEX *noun* + ESCAPADE.]
A sexual escapade.

sexcentenary /sɛk(s)sɛnˈtiːn(ə)ri, -ˈtɛn-, sɛk(s)ˈsɛntɪn-/ *adjective & noun.* L18.
[In sense A.1 from Latin *sexcenteni* 600 each; in sense A.2 and B. from SEX- + CENTENARY.]
► **A** *adjective.* **1** Pertaining to the number 600. L18.
2 Of or pertaining to a period of six hundred years or a sexcentenary; occurring every six hundred years. M19.
► **B** *noun.* (A celebration of) a six-hundredth anniversary. L19.

sexduction /sɛksˈdʌkʃ(ə)n/ *noun.* M20.
[Blend of SEX *noun* and TRANSDUCTION.]
MICROBIOLOGY. The transfer of part of a bacterial genome from one bacterium to another by a sex factor.

sexed /sɛkst/ *adjective.* L16.
[from SEX *noun* + -ED[2].]
1 Pertaining to or possessing a specified sex or sexes. L16.
2 Of an animal or plant: having a sex, not neuter or asexual. L19.
3 Having sexual desires or needs of a specified nature or intensity. L19.

🕮 **3** *Times Lit. Suppl.* He . . marries . . a highly sexed waitress.
HYPER-SEXED, OVERSEXED, UNDERSEXED.

sexenary /sɛkˈsiːn(ə)ri/ *adjective. rare.* E19.
[from Latin *sex* six, after *septenary*.]
= SENARY *adjective.*

sexennial /sɛkˈsɛnɪəl/ *adjective.* M17.
[from Latin *sexennis* or *sexennium* + -AL[1].]
Lasting for six years, occurring every six years.
■ **sexennially** *adverb* M19.

sexennium /sɛkˈsɛnɪəm/ *noun.* Pl. **-iums**, **-ia** /-ɪə/. M20.
[Latin, formed as SEX- + *annus* year.]
A period of six years.

sexercise /ˈsɛksəsʌɪz/ *noun. slang* (orig. *US*). M20.
[Blend of SEX *noun* and EXERCISE *noun.*]
Sexual activity perceived as exercise. Also, (an) exercise designed to enhance sexual attractiveness or improve sexual performance.

sexfoil /ˈsɛksfɔɪl/ *noun & adjective.* L17.
[from SEX- after *cinquefoil*, *trefoil*, etc.: see FOIL *noun*[1].]
► **A** *noun.* ARCHITECTURE & HERALDRY. An ornamental figure having six lobes or petals radiating from a common centre. L17.
► **B** *adjective.* Having six foliations. M19.
■ Also **sexfoiled** *adjective* M19.

sexful /ˈsɛksfʊl, -f(ə)l/ *adjective. rare.* L19.
[from SEX *noun* + -FUL.]
Conveying sexual emotions; sexy.

sexhood /ˈsɛkshʊd/ *noun.* M19.
[formed as prec. + -HOOD.]
The quality or condition of belonging to one or other sex.

sexi- *combining form* see SEX-.

sexism /ˈsɛksɪz(ə)m/ *noun.* M20.
[from SEX *noun* + -ISM, after *racism*.]
(Behaviour, language, etc., reflecting) the assumption that one sex, esp. the female, is inferior to the other; prejudice or discrimination, esp. against women, on the grounds of sex; insistence on (esp. a woman's) conformity to a sexually stereotyped social role.

🕮 *Publishers Weekly* The Women's . . panel . . on 'sexism' in children's books. R. RENDELL With the sexism of the stand-up comic . . Burden interrupted him: 'Women drivers!'

sexist /ˈsɛksɪst/ *noun & adjective.* M20.
[formed as prec. + -IST, after *racist*.]
► **A** *noun.* A person advocating, practising, or conforming to sexism. M20.

🕮 *New Yorker* He was . . disagreeable and a gross sexist.

► **B** *adjective.* Of, pertaining to, or characteristic of sexism or sexists. M20.

🕮 J. IRVING The sexist notion that women are . . the acceptable prey of predatory males.

sexless /ˈsɛkslɪs/ *adjective.* L16.
[formed as next + -LESS.]
1 Without sex or its characteristics, asexual; lacking sexual desire or attractiveness. L16.
2 BIOLOGY. = NEUTER *adjective* 4. E19.

🕮 **1** D. ROWE Many men . . see women only as sex objects or as sexless good women.

■ **sexlessly** *adverb* M19. **sexlessness** *noun* L19.

sexology /sɛkˈsɒlədʒi/ *noun.* Orig. *US.* E20.
[from SEX *noun* + -OLOGY.]
The branch of science that deals with sexual life and relationships, esp. in human beings.
■ **sexo'logical** *adjective* E20. **sexologist** *noun* E20.

sexpartite /sɛksˈpɑːtʌɪt/ *adjective.* M18.
[from SEX- + PARTITE, after *bipartite*, *tripartite*, etc.]
Divided into or consisting of six parts.

sexpert /ˈsɛkspəːt/ *noun. slang* (orig. *US*). E20.
[Blend of SEX *noun* and EXPERT *noun.*]
An expert in sexual matters.

sexploitation /sɛksplɔɪˈteɪʃ(ə)n/ *noun.* M20.
[Blend of SEX *noun* and EXPLOITATION.]
The exploitation of sex, esp. commercially as in films.
■ **sex'ploit** *verb trans.* [back-form.] exploit sexually L20. **sex'ploitative** *adjective* sexually exploitative L20. **sex'ploiter** *noun* M20.

sexsational *adjective* var. of SEXATIONAL.

sext /sɛkst/ *noun.* In sense 2 also **S-**. LME.
[In sense 1 from Latin *sexta* (sc. *hora* hour) fem. of *sextus* sixth (cf. PRIME *noun*[1]). In sense 2 from Latin *sextus* (sc. *liber* book). In sense 3 from Latin *sexta* (sc. *pars* part).]
1 ECCLESIASTICAL. The fourth of the daytime canonical hours of prayer, appointed orig. for the sixth hour of the day (about noon); the office appointed for this hour. LME.
2 ECCLESIASTICAL. The sixth book added to the decretals by Pope Boniface VIII. M17.
3 MUSIC. **a** An interval of a sixth. L19. ▸**b** An organ-stop of two ranks of pipes having an interval of a sixth between them. L19.

sextain /ˈsɛksteɪn/ *noun. rare.* M17.
[Prob. alt. of French †*sestine* after *quatrain*, *sixain*. Cf. SESTINE.]
= SESTINA.

sextal /ˈsɛkst(ə)l/ *adjective.* M20.
[from Latin *sextus* sixth + -AL[1].]
Pertaining to or designating a system of numerical notation in which the base is 6 rather than 10. Cf. SENARY *adjective.*

sextan /ˈsɛkst(ə)n/ *adjective.* M17.
[medieval Latin *sextana* (sc. *febris*). Cf. QUARTAN, QUINTAN.]
MEDICINE. Designating a fever recurring every fifth (by inclusive reckoning every sixth) day.

sextans /ˈsɛkst(ə)nz/ *noun.* L16.
[Latin: see next.]
†**1** See SEXTANT. L16.
2 (**S-**.) (The name of) an inconspicuous constellation lying on the celestial equator between Leo and Hydra; the Sextant. L18.

sextant /ˈsɛkst(ə)nt/ *noun.* Also (earlier) †**-ans**, pl. **-antes**. See also SEXTANS. L16.
[Latin *sextant-*, *sextans* sixth part, from *sextus* sixth: see -ANT[1]. Cf. OCTANT, QUADRANT *noun*[1].]
†**1** The sixth part of a circle. L16–M18.
†**2** ROMAN HISTORY. The sixth part of an as. Only in 17.
3 An instrument consisting of a graduated arc equal to a sixth part of a circle and a sighting mechanism, used for measuring angular distances between objects and esp. for taking altitudes in astronomy and navigation. E17.
4 (**S-**.) *The* constellation Sextans. L18.

sextary /ˈsɛkstəri/ *noun. obsolete* exc. *Hist.* LME.
[Latin *sextarius*, from *sextus* sixth: see -ARY[1].]
An ancient Roman liquid measure containing the sixth part of a congius; any of various later liquid measures. Also, a dry measure containing the sixteenth part of a modius.
■ Also **sextar** *noun* (*rare*) M16.

sextern /ˈsɛkstəːn/ *noun.* L19.
[medieval Latin *sexternum* from Latin *sex* six.]
A quire consisting of six sheets.

sextet /sɛksˈtɛt/ *noun.* Also **-ette**. M19.
[Alt. of SESTET after Latin *sex* six: see -ET[1].]
1 MUSIC. A composition for six voices or instruments. M19.
2 A stanza of six lines. M19.
3 A group of six persons or things; *esp.* (MUSIC) a group of six singers or instrumentalists. L19.

sextic /ˈsɛkstɪk/ *adjective & noun.* M19.
[from Latin *sextus* sixth + -IC.]
MATH. ► **A** *adjective.* Of the sixth degree or order. M19.
► **B** *noun.* A quantic or function of the sixth degree; a curve or surface of the sixth order. L19.

sextile /ˈsɛkstʌɪl, -ɪl/ *adjective, noun, & verb.* LME.
[Latin *sextilis*, from *sextus* sixth: see -ILE. Cf. *quartile*, *quintile*, etc.]
ASTROLOGY. ► **A** *adjective & noun.* (Designating) the aspect of two planets which are one-sixth of a circle (60 degrees) apart in the sky. LME.
► **B** *verb trans.* Be in or come into a sextile aspect with. L20.

sextillion /sɛks'tɪljən/ *noun.* L17.
[French, from Latin *sex* six, after *million, billion*, etc.]
Orig. (esp. in the UK), the sixth power of a million (10^{36}). Now usu. (orig. *US*), the seventh power of a thousand (10^{21}).
■ **sextillionth** *adjective & noun* L19.

sextine /'sɛkstiːn/ *noun. rare.* L16.
[French, from Portuguese *sextina*, Italian SESTINA: see -INE[4].]
= SESTINA.

sexto /'sɛkstəʊ/ *noun. rare.* Pl. **-os**. M19.
[Latin, abl. of *sextus* sixth. Cf. OCTAVO, QUARTO.]
A size of book or paper in which each leaf is one-sixth of a standard printing-sheet; a book or leaf of this size.

sextodecimo /sɛkstəʊ'dɛsɪməʊ/ *noun.* Pl. **-os**. L17.
[Latin *sexto decimo* abl. of *sextus decimus* sixteenth.]
A size of book or paper in which each leaf is one-sixteenth of a standard printing-sheet; a book or leaf of this size.

sextole /'sɛkstəʊl/ *noun.* M19.
[German *Sextole*, arbitrarily from Latin *sextus* sixth.]
MUSIC. A group of six notes of equal length to be played in the time of four.
■ Also **sextolet** *noun* L19.

sexton /'sɛkst(ə)n/ *noun.* ME.
[Anglo-Norman, Old French *segerstein, secrestein* from medieval Latin *sacristanus* SACRISTAN.]
A person responsible for looking after a church, its contents, and the churchyard, freq. acting as bell-ringer and gravedigger.
Comb.: **sexton beetle** any of various black or red and black carrion-beetles of the genus *Nicrophorus*, a burying beetle.
■ **sextoness** *noun* a female sexton LME. **sextonship** *noun* the office or position of a sexton E16.

sextry /'sɛkstri/ *noun.* LME.
[Perh. from prec. after *vestry*, or alt. of Old French *sacrestie* (mod. *sacristie*) from medieval Latin *sacristia*: see -Y[3].]
†**1** A sacristy. LME–L17.
2 The residence of a sacristan. L16.

sextula /'sɛkstjʊlə/ *noun.* Pl. **-lae** /-liː/. M17.
[Latin, from *sexta* (sc. *pars* part) fem. of *sextus* sixth + *-ula* -ULE.]
ROMAN HISTORY. A sixth part of a Roman ounce.

sextumvirate /sɛks'tʌmvɪrət/ *noun. rare.* E18.
[from Latin *sex* six after *triumvirate*: see -ATE[1].]
A group of six people.

sextuor /'sɛkstjʊɔː/ *noun.* E19.
[French, from Latin *sex* six after *quatuor* quartet. Cf. SEPTUOR.]
MUSIC. = SEXTET 1.

sextuple /'sɛkstjʊp(ə)l, sɛks'tjuːp(ə)l/ *adjective, noun, & verb.* E17.
[medieval Latin *sextuplus* irreg. from Latin *sex* six, after medieval Latin *quintuplus* quintuple.]
▶**A** *adjective.* Consisting of six parts or things; six times as many or as much, sixfold; MUSIC (of a rhythm or time) having six beats in a bar. E17.
▶**B** *noun.* A sixfold number or amount. M17.
▶**C** *verb.* **1** *verb trans.* Multiply by six; make six times as large, numerous, etc. M17.
2 *verb intrans.* Increase sixfold. M19.

sextuplet /'sɛkstjʊplɪt, -'tjuːplɪt/ *noun.* M19.
[from SEXTUPLE *adjective* after *triplet*: see -ET[1].]
1 MUSIC. = SEXTOLE. M19.
2 Each of six children born at one birth. L19.

📖 **2** *Times* The sextuplets, two girls and four boys, were born . . prematurely.

sextuplex /'sɛkstjʊplɛks/ *adjective.* M17.
[medieval Latin, irreg. from Latin *sex* six after Latin QUADRUPLEX *adjective.*]
1 Sixfold. M17.
2 TELEGRAPHY. Designating a system etc. allowing six messages to be transmitted simultaneously by the same wire. L19.

sextuplicate /sɛks'tjuːplɪkət/ *adjective & noun.* M17.
[medieval Latin *sextuplicat-* pa. ppl stem of *sextuplicare*, from *sextuplic-, -plex*: see prec., -ATE[2].]
▶†**A** *adjective.* Sixfold. *rare.* Only in M17.
▶**B** *noun.* A sixth of six things exactly alike, a sixth copy. Chiefly in ***in sextuplicate*** below. M20.
in sextuplicate in sixfold quantity, in six identical copies.

sextuplication /sɛks,tjuːplɪ'keɪʃ(ə)n/ *noun. rare.* L17.
[medieval Latin *sextuplicatio(n-)*, formed as prec.: see -ATION.]
Multiplication by six.

sextupole /'sɛkstjʊpəʊl/ *adjective & noun.* M20.
[from Latin *sextus* sixth, after *quadrupole*: see POLE *noun*[2].]
PHYSICS. (A device) having six magnetic (or electric) poles, three of each polarity.

sexual /'sɛksjʊəl, -ʃʊəl/ *adjective.* M17.
[Late Latin *sexualis*, from Latin *sexus* SEX *noun*: see -UAL.]
1 Pertaining to or arising from the possession of a particular sex; relating to the sexes or to social relations between them. M17.
2 Pertaining to or involving physical intercourse, as in reproduction; deriving from or relating to desire for sex or for carnal pleasure. L18.
3 Characteristic of or peculiar to one sex or the other. E19.
4 a Of an animal or plant: having a sex, separated into two sexes; having sexual organs, producing offspring by means of sexual union. Opp. ***asexual***. M19. ▶**b** Of reproduction: taking place by means of physical union between (cells of) the two sexes. Opp. ***asexual*** or ***agamic***. L19.

📖 **1** A. LURIE The blurring of . . sexual differences. ***sexual equality, sexual stereotype***, etc. **2** M. WARNER The prelapsarian state of Eve, before sexual knowledge corrupted her. T. BEATTIE She had never had any trouble in reaching a sexual climax. M. AMIS They were fond of each other at first but then the relationship became purely sexual. L. ELLMANN I'm here to talk through any sexual . . problems. ***sexual act, sexual activity, sexual assault, sexual attraction, sexual morality, sexual orgasm, sexual orientation, sexual partner, sexual preference, sexual prowess***, etc.

Special collocations: **sexual cell** a male or female reproductive cell; a sperm cell, an egg cell. **sexual dimorphism** distinct variation in form or appearance between the sexes of a species in addition to the sexual organs themselves. **sexual discrimination** discrimination in employment etc. against a person, esp. a woman, on grounds of sex. **sexual harassment** harassment, esp. of a woman, in a workplace etc. involving the making of unwanted sexual advances, obscene remarks, etc. **sexual intercourse** physical contact between individuals involving sexual stimulation of the genitals; *spec.* the insertion of a man's erect penis into a woman's vagina, followed by rhythmic movement and usu. ejaculation of semen; copulation, coitus. **sexual interference** *euphem.* sexual assault or molestation. ***sexual inversion***: see INVERSION 9. **sexual organ** a reproductive organ in an animal or plant (freq. in *pl.*). **sexual politics** the principles determining the relationship of the sexes, relations between the sexes regarded in terms of power. **sexual revolution** the liberalization of established social and moral attitudes to sex. **sexual role** the culturally determined role or behaviour learned by a person as appropriate to his or her sex. **sexual selection** natural selection arising through preference by one sex for certain characteristics in individuals of the other sex. **sexual system** *Hist.* the Linnaean classification of plants, in which plants are grouped according to the number of stamens and pistils per flower.
¶ See note s.v. SEX *noun & adjective.*
■ **sexualism** *noun* (now *rare* or *obsolete*) sexuality as a principle of action or thought M19.

sexualise *verb* var. of SEXUALIZE.

sexuality /sɛksjʊ'alɪti, sɛkʃʊ-/ *noun.* L18.
[from prec. + -ITY.]
1 The quality of being sexual or having a sex, possession of a particular sex. L18.
2 Recognition of or preoccupation with what is sexual. M19.
3 Possession of sexual powers, capacity for sexual feelings; sexual feelings, desires, etc., collectively; the expression of these. Also, sexual orientation or preference. L19.

📖 **1** ***relative sexuality***: see RELATIVE *adjective.* **3** *Ms.* Lesbian sexuality . . and the lesbian lifestyle. P. D. JAMES He was unhappy, muddled, uncertain about . . his sexuality. A. STEVENS Sexuality is concerned as much with pleasure . . as with procreation.

sexualize /'sɛksjʊəlʌɪz, 'sɛkʃʊ-/ *verb trans.* Also **-ise**. M19.
[formed as prec. + -IZE.]
Make sexual; attribute sex or a sexual role to.
■ **sexuali'zation** *noun* the action or process of sexualizing a person etc.; the state of being sexualized; adaptation to a sexual role: L19.

sexually /'sɛksjʊəli, 'sɛkʃʊ-/ *adverb.* M17.
[from SEXUAL + -LY[2].]
In a sexual manner; by means of sexual intercourse. Also, with respect to sex.

📖 *Listener* To be sexually attractive was one thing, but to become a sexual fetish was another. A. TAYLOR AIDS is mainly a sexually transmitted disease.

sexuparous /sɛk'sjuːp(ə)rəs/ *adjective.* L19.
[mod. Latin *sexuparus*, from Latin *sexus* SEX *noun*: see -PAROUS.]
BIOLOGY. Esp. of an asexual generation of insects: producing sexual offspring.
■ **sexupara** *noun*, pl. **-rae** /-riː/, in some aphids, a member of a parthenogenetically-produced generation which gives birth to sexual males or females L19.

sexy /'sɛksi/ *adjective.* E20.
[from SEX *noun* + -Y[1].]
1 Concerned with or engrossed in sex; sexually aroused. E20.
2 Sexually attractive or provocative, sexually exciting. Now also (*fig.*), exciting, appealing, esp. financially or popularly. E20.

📖 **1** *Parents* Extra . . energy and happiness make some women feel especially sexy in pregnancy. **2** J. DIDION You looked so sexy in your white pants. *Globe & Mail (Toronto)* Nuclear disarmament is one of the eighties' sexy issues.

■ **sexily** *adverb* M20. **sexiness** *noun* E20.

sey /seɪ/ *noun.* Now *rare* or *obsolete.* L17.
[Var. of SAITHE: cf. Norwegian *sei*, Danish *sej*.]
= SAITHE. Also ***sey-fish, sey-pollack***.

seyal /seɪ'jɑːl/ *noun.* Also **sayall**. M19.
[Arab. *sayāl*.]
An acacia of East and NE Africa, *Acacia seyal*.

Seychellois /seɪʃɛl'wɑː/ *noun & adjective.* Pl. same. Fem. **-oise** /-'wɑːz/, pl. **-oises** /-'wɑːz/. L19.
[French.]
▶**A** *noun.* A native or inhabitant of the Seychelles, a group of islands in the Indian Ocean. L19.
▶**B** *adjective.* Of or pertaining to the Seychelles or their inhabitants. M20.

Seyfert /'seɪfəːt/ *noun.* M20.
[Carl K. *Seyfert* (1911–60), US astronomer.]
ASTRONOMY. Used *attrib.* or *absol.* with ref. to a class of galaxies characterized by bright compact cores that show strong infrared emission.

Seym *noun* var. of SEJM.

seymouriamorph /siː'mɔːrɪəmɔːf/ *noun.* M20.
[mod. Latin *Seymouriamorpha* (see below), from *Seymouria* genus name (from *Seymour* a town in Texas + -IA[1]): see -MORPH.]
PALAEONTOLOGY. A fossil tetrapod belonging to the suborder Seymouriamorpha, including forms considered to be transitional between amphibians and reptiles.

sez /sɛz/ *verb trans. & intrans. colloq.* M19.
[Repr. a pronunc.]
Says, say, said. Freq. in ***sez you*** (see SAY *verb*[1]).

Sézary /'seɪzəri/ *noun.* M20.
[Albert *Sézary* (1880–1956), French dermatologist.]
MEDICINE. Used *attrib.* and in *possess.*, esp. in ***Sézary's syndrome, Sézary syndrome***, to designate a type of cutaneous lymphoma with symptoms including exfoliative dermatitis with intense itching and the presence of abnormally large cells in the blood.

Sezession /zetsɛsɪ'oːn/ *noun.* Pl. ***-en*** /-ən/. E20.
[German.]
ART. = SECESSION 3b.
■ ***Sezessio'nist*** *noun* an artist belonging to the *Sezession* M20. ***Sezessionsstil*** /-ʃtiːl/ *noun* the style of the *Sezession* L20.

SF *abbreviation*[1].
1 San Francisco.
2 Science fiction.

sf *abbreviation*[2].
MUSIC. Sforzando.

SFA *abbreviation.*
Scottish Football Association.

sferics /'sfɛrɪks/ *noun pl.* Also **spherics**. M20.
[Contr. of *atmospherics*: see ATMOSPHERIC *noun* 2.]
Atmospherics; the branch of science that deals with these, esp. for the radiolocation of electrical storms.
■ **sferic** *adjective* of or pertaining to sferics M20.

†**'sfoot** *interjection.* E–M17.
[Contr. of *God's foot*.]
Expr. asseveration.

sforzando /sfɔː'tsandəʊ/ *adjective, adverb, & noun.* E19.
[Italian, pres. pple of *sforzare* use force.]
MUSIC. ▶**A** *adjective & adverb.* A direction: with special emphasis or sudden loudness. Abbreviation ***sf., sfz.*** E19.
▶**B** *noun.* Pl. **-di** /-di/, **-dos**. A note or group of notes specially emphasized; an increase in emphasis and loudness. M19.

sforzato /sfɔː'tsɑːtəʊ/ *adjective, adverb, & noun.* Pl. of noun **-ti** /-ti/, **-tos**. E19.
[Italian, pa. pple of *sforzare*: see prec.]
MUSIC. = prec.

sfumato /sfu'maːto, sfʊ'mɑːtəʊ/ *adjective & noun.* M19.
[Italian, pa. pple of *sfumare* shade off, from *s-* EX-[1] + *fumare* to smoke.]
PAINTING. ▶**A** *adjective.* Painted with or using indistinct outlines, depicting hazy forms. M19.
▶**B** *noun.* The technique of softening outlines and allowing tones and colours to shade gradually into one another; an indistinct outline or hazy form produced in this way. E20.

SFX *abbreviation.*
[*FX* repr. a pronunc. of *effects*.]
Special effects.

sfz *abbreviation.*
MUSIC. Sforzando.

SG *abbreviation.*
1 Senior grade. *US.*
2 LAW. Solicitor-General.
3 Specific gravity.

Sg *symbol.*
CHEMISTRY. Seaborgium.

sgd. *abbreviation.*
Signed.

SGML *abbreviation.*
COMPUTING. Standard Generalized Mark-up Language, an international standard for encoding electronic texts with tags describing layout, structure, syntax, etc., and enabling the text to be used for analysis or displayed in any desired format.

sgraffiato /zgraffiˈaːto/ *noun.* Pl. **-ti** /-ti/. M19.
[Italian, pa. pple of *sgraffiare*: see next.]
= next.

sgraffito /sgraˈfiːtəʊ/ *noun.* Pl. **-ti** /-ti/. M18.
[Italian, from *sgraffiare* scratch away: *s-* repr. Latin *ex* EX-¹. Cf. later GRAFFITO.]
A form of decoration or design made by scratching through wet plaster on a wall or through slip on pottery to reveal a different colour below.

Sgt. *abbreviation.*
Sergeant.

sh.
A consonantal digraph, pronounced /ʃ/, introduced in Middle English, at first used for Old English words in *sc-* and in adoptions of Old French words in *s-*, *ss-*. Since L15 it has been the established notation for /ʃ/ in all words except those which are spelt unphonetically on etymological grounds (as ***machine***, ***schedule***, ***Asia***, derivs. in ***-tion***, etc.).

sh /ʃ/ *interjection & verb.* Also redupl. **sh-sh**, **shhh**, & other vars. M19.
[Imit. Cf. HUSH *verb²*, *interjection.*]
▶ **A** *interjection.* **1** = HUSH *interjection.* M19.
2 Expr. a low faint rustling or swishing sound. L19.
▶ **B** *verb.* Infl. **sh'd**, **sh-ed**, etc.
1 *verb trans.* (Attempt to) make silent or tranquil with an utterance of 'sh!'. L19.
2 *verb intrans.* Become quiet in response to an utterance of 'sh!'. E20.

sh. *abbreviation.*
Hist. Shilling(s).

shab /ʃab/ *noun.*
[Old English *sćeabb* = Old Norse base also of SCAB *noun.*]
1 = SCAB *noun* 1, 2a, 3. Now only (*dial.*), a cutaneous disease in sheep. OE.
2 A contemptible or worthless person. *slang.* Now *rare* or *obsolete.* M17.

shab /ʃab/ *verb. slang & dial.* Now *rare* or *obsolete.* Infl. **-bb-**. L17.
[Origin uncertain: sense perh. rel. to SHAB *noun* 2.]
1 *verb trans.* Foll. by *off*: ▸**a** Get (a person) out of the way, get rid of. L17. ▸**b** Put (a person) off *with* something inferior or unsatisfactory. Cf. FOB *verb¹* 2a. M19.
2 *verb intrans.* Slink *away*, sneak *off*. L17.

Shabak /ʃaˈbak/ *noun.* L20.
[mod. Hebrew, acronym, from *šērūt biṭṭāḥōn kĕlālī* general security service. Cf. SHIN BET.]
The division of the Israeli security service concerned with counter-espionage and internal security.

†**shabaroon** *noun. slang.* Also **-bb-**, **shabroon**. L17–M19.
[Prob. from SHAB *noun* or SHABBY *adjective* after *picaroon*.]
A disreputable person, *spec.* an unkempt one.

shabash /ˈʃaːbaːʃ/ *interjection. Indian subcontinent.* M19.
[Urdu, Persian *šābāš*, from *šād* joyful + *bāš* imper. of *būdan* to be.]
Well done!

†**shabbaroon** *noun* var. of SHABAROON.

Shabbat /ʃaˈbat/ *noun.* M19.
[Hebrew *šabbāṯ*. Cf. SHABBOS.]
Among Sephardic Jews and in Israel; the Sabbath. Freq. in ***Shabbat shalom***, peaceful Sabbath.

shabbed /ʃabd/ *adjective. obsolete* exc. *dial.* LOE.
[from SHAB *noun* + -ED².]
1 Afflicted with scab or scabs, scabbed. LOE.
2 Shabby. L17.

shabbify /ˈʃabɪfʌɪ/ *verb trans.* M19.
[from SHABBY *adjective* + -FY.]
Make shabby.

shabble *noun* var. of SHABLE.

Shabbos /ˈʃabəs/ *noun.* Pl. ***-bosim*** /-bəsɪm/. M19.
[Yiddish from Hebrew *šabbāṯ* SABBATH. Cf. SHABBAT.]
Among Ashkenazic Jews, the Sabbath.
Comb.: ***Shabbos-goy*** = *Sabbath goy* s.v. SABBATH.

shabby /ˈʃabi/ *adjective.* M17.
[from SHAB *noun* + -Y¹.]
1 In bad repair or condition; faded and worn, dingy, dilapidated; seedy, mean; (of a person) dressed in old or worn clothes, unkempt, scruffy. M17. ▸**b** *transf.* Of poor quality or appearance. E19.
2 Of a person, action, etc.: contemptibly mean, ungenerous, or dishonourable; discreditable, ungracious. L17.
3 †**a** Dirty, muddy. *rare.* Only in E18. ▸**b** Of weather: wet, drizzly, damp. Chiefly *dial.* M19.
4 (Of a person) unwell, indisposed; (of the pulse) weak. *colloq. & dial.* L18.
5 Afflicted with scab or scabs, scabby. *dial.* E19.

📖 **1** W. J. BATE His clothes, already shabby, became rags. M. MUGGERIDGE Leningrad seemed a battered, shabby place . . in sore need of renovation. **2** V. S. PRITCHETT It was shabby of him to . . claim the credit.

Comb.: **shabby-genteel** *adjective* attempting to look genteel and keep up appearances in spite of shabbiness.
¶ Sense 5 was app. the original meaning though not recorded earlier.
■ **shabbily** *adverb* M18. **shabbiness** *noun* E18. **shabbyish** *adjective* somewhat shabby M19.

shabby /ˈʃabi/ *verb.* L19.
[from the adjective.]
1 *verb intrans.* Act shabbily or discreditably. *rare.* L19.
2 *verb trans. & intrans.* Make or become shabby. E20.

shable /ˈʃab(ə)l/ *noun. Scot.* Also **shabble**. M17.
[Italian *sciab(o)la* or Hungarian *szablya*, Polish *szabla*, parallel to Dutch *sabel*, German *Säbel*: see SABRE *noun¹*.]
A curved sword, a sabre.

shabrack /ˈʃabrak/ *noun.* Also **shabracque**. E19.
[German *Schabracke*, French *schabraque*, of east European origin (Turkish *çaprak*).]
Hist. A cavalry saddle-cloth used in European armies.

shab-rag /ˈʃabrag/ *adjective & noun. dial. & slang.* M18.
[from SHAB *noun* + RAG *noun¹*.]
▶ **A** *adjective.* Shabby, scruffy, dilapidated. M18.
▶ **B** *noun.* A scruffy disreputable person. E19.

†**shabroon** *noun* var. of SHABAROON.

shabti /ˈʃabti/ *noun.* Pl. **-tiu** /-tɪuː/, **-tis**. M19.
[Egyptian *šbty*.]
EGYPTOLOGY. = USHABTI. Cf. SHAWABTI.

shabu-shabu /ˈʃabuːˈʃabuː/ *noun.* L20.
[Japanese.]
A Japanese dish of pieces of thinly sliced beef or pork cooked quickly with vegetables in boiling water and then dipped in sauce.

shack /ʃak/ *noun¹.* Now *dial.* ME.
[Dial. var. of SHAKE *noun.*]
1 Grain fallen from the ear and available for the feeding of pigs, poultry, etc., after harvest; fallen beechmast, acorns, etc., used thus. Cf. SHAG *noun³* 2, SHAKE *noun.* ME.
2 The right or custom of letting pigs etc. into the stubble after harvest; land or stubble used thus. Freq. in ***at shack***, ***to shack***. E17.
3 An animal or animals at shack. M19.

shack /ʃak/ *noun².* *dial. & US.* L17.
[Perh. short for *shack-rag* obsolete var. of ***shake-rag*** s.v. SHAKE *verb.*]
An idle disreputable person.

shack /ʃak/ *noun³.* L19.
[Perh. shortened from Mexican Spanish *jacal*, Aztec *xacatli* wooden hut, more closely repr. by SHACKLE *noun²*.]
1 A roughly built cabin or hut, esp. of logs, metal sheeting, etc.; a shanty. L19.
2 A house; a small shop. *slang* (chiefly *US*). E20.
3 = ***radio shack*** s.v. RADIO *noun. slang* (orig. *US*). E20.

📖 **1** W. S. MAUGHAM The house was . . just a wooden shack of one room.

shack /ʃak/ *noun⁴.* *US.* L19.
[Origin uncertain: perh. rel. to SHACK *noun¹*.]
1 Bait, as refuse fish etc., picked up at sea. L19.
2 A catch of marine fish made up of cheaper varieties, as cod etc.; such fish collectively. E20.

shack /ʃak/ *noun⁵.* *US.* L19.
[Prob. rel. to SHACK *noun²*, *verb²*.]
A slow trot.

shack /ʃak/ *noun⁶.* *N. Amer. slang.* L19.
[Origin unkn.]
The brakeman or guard on a train.

shack /ʃak/ *verb¹.* *dial.* L17.
[from SHACK *noun¹*.]
1 *verb intrans.* Of a pig etc.: roam about feeding on stubble. L17.
2 *verb trans.* Turn (a pig etc.) out into a stubble field; feed on (stubble). E19.

shack /ʃak/ *verb² intrans.* *dial.* L18.
[from or cogn. with SHACK *noun²*.]
1 Idle away one's time; loaf *about*. L18.
2 Move with a slow ambling gait, go at a slow trot. *US.* M19.

shack /ʃak/ *verb³.* *slang* (orig. *N. Amer.*). L19.
[from SHACK *noun³*.]
1 *verb intrans.* Live in a shack. L19.
2 a *verb trans.* Foll. by *up*: provide (esp. a lover) with accommodation or lodging; in *pass.*, lodge, cohabit, (*with* a lover). E20. ▸**b** *verb intrans.* Obtain temporary accommodation or shelter; cohabit, esp. as lovers, set up house *with*. Usu. foll. by *up*. M20.

📖 **2a** D. LODGE Philip . . is shacked up with Melanie at that address.

Comb.: **shack-job**, **shack-up** (an instance of) cohabitation; a partner in cohabitation, a lover.

shack *verb⁴* see SHAKE *verb.*

shackage /ˈʃakɪdʒ/ *noun.* L19.
[from SHACK *noun¹* + -AGE.]
The turning of pigs etc. out into stubble to eat fallen grain.

shackbolt /ˈʃakbəʊlt/ *noun.* E17.
[Perh. shortened from *shackle-bolt*: see next.]
HERALDRY. A charge representing a shackle or fetter; a fetterlock.

shacked *verb* see SHAKE *verb.*

shackle /ˈʃak(ə)l/ *noun¹.*
[Old English *sć(e)acul* corresp. to Low German *shäkel* link of a chain, shackle, hobble, Dutch *schakel*, Old Norse *skǫkull* wagon-pole, from Germanic base repr. also by Old English *sćeac*, Low German *schake*: see -LE¹.]
1 A chain or ring enclosing the ankle or wrist, a manacle, a fetter; *spec.* either of a pair connected together by a chain fastened to the floor, wall, etc. Freq. in *pl.* OE. ▸**b** An ornament, as an armlet or anklet, resembling a shackle. *rare.* LME.
2 *fig.* A restraint on freedom of action etc., a restriction, an impediment. Usu. in *pl.* ME.
3 A usu. metal loop or link, freq. U-shaped, closed by a bolt or bar and used to connect chains, couple vehicles, etc. ME.
4 A chain, rope, etc., used for tethering cows; a hobble for a horse. Now *dial.* LME.
5 In full ***shackle-bone***. The wrist; *rare* the ankle. *Scot. & dial.* L16.
6 TELEGRAPHY. A form of insulator used in overhead lines for supporting the wire where a sharp angle occurs. M19.
7 NAUTICAL. A length of cable usu. measuring 12½ or 15 fathoms. L19.

📖 **2** N. BAWDEN Free . . from the shackles of childhood.

Comb.: **shackle-bolt** a bolt for closing a shackle; HERALDRY a charge representing this. **shackle-bone** (*Scot. & dial.*) (*a*) see sense 5 above; (*b*) the knuckle-bone of a pig etc.

shackle /ˈʃak(ə)l/ *noun².* *Scot. & US.* M19.
[Prob. formed as SHACK *noun³*: see -LE¹.]
= SHACK *noun³*.

shackle /ˈʃak(ə)l/ *verb¹.* LME.
[from SHACKLE *noun¹*.]
1 *verb trans.* Put a shackle or shackles on, fetter, (a person). LME.
2 *verb trans. fig.* Limit, tie down, restrict, restrain. Freq. in *pass.* (foll. by *to*). M16.
3 a *verb trans.* Join, couple, or fix with a shackle. M19. ▸**b** *verb intrans.* Admit of being joined or coupled with a shackle. M19.

📖 **2** J. TROLLOPE I'm sick of being shackled to a man who doesn't give a damn.

shackle /ˈʃak(ə)l/ *verb².* *dial.* L17.
[Frequentative of SHAKE *verb.*]
1 *verb trans.* Flatten down (standing corn); litter, disorder, scatter about. Also, send (pigs etc.) to feed in stubble. Cf. SHACK *verb¹*. L17.
2 *verb intrans.* Idle or loaf *about*, shirk work. Cf. SHACK *verb²*. E19.

shackles /ˈʃak(ə)lz/ *noun pl.* (treated as *sing.* or *pl.*). *dial. & slang.* L19.
[Prob. from ***shackle-bone*** s.v. SHACKLE *noun¹*.]
Broth, soup, stew.

shackling /ˈʃaklɪŋ/ *adjective.* L18.
[from SHACKLE *verb²* + -ING². In sense 2 perh. infl. by *ramshackle*.]
1 Loafing, dissipated, idle. *dial.* L18.
2 Rickety, ramshackle. *US.* L18.

shackly /ˈʃakli/ *adjective. US & dial.* M19.
[from SHACKLE *noun²* or *verb²* + -Y¹.]
Shaky, rickety, ramshackle.

shacky /ˈʃaki/ *adjective. colloq.* E20.
[from SHACK *noun³* + -Y¹.]
Resembling a shack, dilapidated, ramshackle.

shad /ʃad/ *noun & verb.*
[Late Old English *sćeadd*, of unkn. origin.]
▶ **A** *noun.* Pl. **-s**, same. Any of various migratory clupeoid fishes resembling herring, of the genus *Alosa* or related genera, esp. the American *A. sapidissima*. Also (*rare*) as a term of abuse. LOE.
ALLIS *shad*. TWAITE *shad*.
Comb.: **shad-bellied** *adjective* (*a*) (of a coat) having curved front edges sloping down to the tail; (*b*) (of a person) having an abnormally thin or flat belly; **shad-belly** *US* a man's shad-bellied coat, formerly associated with the Society of Friends; a Friend; **shadberry** *N. Amer.* (the fruit of) the shadbush; **shadblow**, **shadbush** *N. Amer.* [so called because it flowers when shad appear in rivers] a Juneberry, esp. *Amelanchier canadensis*; **shad-fly** ANGLING an insect which appears when shad are running; **shad-trout** the weakfish.
▶ **B** *verb intrans.* Infl. **-dd-**. Fish for shad. *rare.* M19.

Shadai *noun* var. of SHADDAI.

shadchan /ˈʃadxən/ *noun*. Also **-khan**, **schad-**, & other vars. Pl. **-chen** /-xən/, **-chanim** /-xənɪm/. **M19.**
[Yiddish *shadkhn* from Hebrew *šaddĕkān*, from *šiddēk* negotiate. Cf. SHIDDUCH.]
A Jewish professional matchmaker or marriage broker.

shadda /ˈʃada/ *noun*. Also **-ah**. **L19.**
[Arab. *šadda* strengthening.]
GRAMMAR. In Arabic, a sign marked above a consonant to indicate that it is doubled.

Shaddai /ˈʃadaɪ/ *noun*. Also ***Shadai***. **E17.**
[Hebrew, of uncertain meaning: in English versions of the Bible usu. translated 'Almighty'.]
JUDAISM. In the Bible, one of the names of God.

shaddock /ˈʃadək/ *noun*. **L17.**
[Captain *Shaddock*, who brought the seed to Barbados.]
A citrus fruit, resembling but larger than a grapefruit; the tree bearing this fruit, *Citrus maxima*, believed to be a parent of the grapefruit. Also called ***pomelo***, ***pompelmous***, ***pompoleon***.

shaddup /ʃʌˈdʌp/ *verb intrans. (imper.). colloq.* **M20.**
[Repr. a pronunc. Cf. SHUDDUP, SHURRUP.]
Shut up! Be quiet!

shade /ʃeɪd/ *noun*.
[Old English *sc̄e (e)adu* fem., *scead* neut. (oblique cases repr. by SHADOW *noun*).]
▶ **I 1** Partial or comparative darkness (and usu. coolness), esp. as caused by shelter from direct light or heat. Also, a thing, as foliage etc., providing such sheltered darkness. Freq. with *the*. **OE.** ▸**b** In *pl.* The darkness of night, the growing darkness of evening. Chiefly *poet.* **L16.** ▸**c** *fig.* Comparative obscurity or inferiority. Chiefly in ***be in the shade***, ***cast into the shade***, ***put into the shade***, ***throw into the shade***. **M17.** ▸**d** *transf.* A fleeting look of displeasure, a cloud on a person's face or expression. **E19.**
2 *sing. & collect. pl.* A place sheltered from the sun, *spec.* a piece of ground overshadowed by trees. Now *rare.* **OE.** ▸**b** A secluded spot or corner. Usu. in *pl.* Now *poet.* or *rhet.* **E17.** ▸**c** A meadow or piece of ground open to the breeze. *dial.* **E19.** ▸**d** In *pl.* (treated as *sing.* or *pl.*). An underground or sheltered public house or bar. Now *rare.* **E19.**
3 a A screen excluding or moderating light or giving shelter from draughts, heat, or cold; *US* a window-blind. **E17.** ▸**b** A woman's lace headscarf. *obsolete* exc. *dial.* **E18.** ▸**c** A dome-shaped cover of glass to protect ornaments from dust or damage. **E18.** ▸**d** A usu. translucent cover for a lamp, used to soften or direct the light; a lampshade. **L18.** ▸**e** A patch or visor for shielding the eyes from strong light, an eye-shade; the peak of a cap. Also in *pl.* (*colloq.*, orig. *US*), sunglasses. **E19.** ▸**f** In scientific apparatus, a shutter etc. for intercepting light falling on or through an object. **M19.**
4 Comparative darkness as represented pictorially; dark colour or a darker part or parts in a painting or drawing; *transf. & fig.* a quieter passage in music, less dramatic part of a story, etc., providing necessary artistic contrast. Freq. in ***light and shade***. **M17.** ▸**b** *ENTOMOLOGY*. An ill-defined patch of darker colour on the wing of a moth. **M19.**
5 a A colour's degree of darkness or depth; any of the varieties, esp. in terms of darkness or depth, within one colour; *gen.* a colour, a tint. **L17.** ▸**b** *transf. & fig.* A slightly differing degree or variety of a quality, opinion, meaning, etc. **M18.** ▸**c** A small quantity or addition of a quality, substance, etc.; a tinge, a touch. **L18.**

📖 **1** E. BLUNDEN They . . Toiled in the sun, lolled in the shade. A. RANSOME It was pleasant to come into the shade of the woods. C. STEAD It was a hundred degrees in the shade. B. VINE The sun had moved enough to leave . . the garden in shade. ***shine and shade***: see SHINE *noun*. **b** J. FORBES The shades of evening . . descend. **c** *Edinburgh Review* Volumes that have cast . . into the shade all contemporary prose. **2** J. KITTO The climate is . . exceedingly hot . . ; a shade is not easily found. **3a** J. AGEE We can be seen, Hannah realised; for the shades were up. **e** E. FAIRWEATHER He resembles a . . bandit, with his . . moustache and shades. **4** W. GILPIN The whole is in dark shade, except three figures on the foreground. L. STEPHEN The forcible light and shade of Rembrandt. W. E. GOSSE The light and shade that make biography amusing. **5a** M. MITCHELL All shades of red hair were represented. U. HOLDEN Her clothes . . were a pale greyish shade. **b** R. GODDEN Dear honest Brighton, . . welcoming . . all shades of life. *Resurgence* Opposition from all shades of opinion. **c** J. TYNDALL Unwilling to accept an observation . . with a shade of doubt attached. **a shade** *adverb* somewhat, rather; by a small amount, to a slight degree.

▶ **II 6 a** = SHADOW *noun* 1. Now *poet. & dial.* **OE.** ▸**b** *fig.* = SHADOW *noun* 3a. Now *poet.* or *rhet.* **ME.**
7 A ghost, a spectre, a phantom; a disembodied spirit, an inhabitant of Hades. Also in *pl.*, *the* world of spirits, Hades. **LME.**
8 = SILHOUETTE *noun* 1. Now chiefly *Hist.* **M18.**

📖 **7** CLIVE JAMES Speer . . insulted the shades of innocent millions. **shade of** (*joc.*, now *rare*): invoking the spirit of a deceased person as likely to be horrified or amazed by a current event etc. **shades of**: (*a*) = ***shade of*** above; (*b*) suggesting reminiscence of or (esp. unfavourable) comparison with a person, event, etc., in the past.

Comb.: **shade-bearing** *adjective* = ***shade-tolerant*** below; **shade card** a card illustrating the range of colours in which merchandise is supplied; **shade deck** an upper deck of a passenger vessel, covered at the top but open at the side, forming a sheltered promenade; **shade maximum** the highest temperature recorded in a single day by a thermometer placed in the shade; **shade-reading** the indication of a thermometer protected from direct influence of the sun's rays; **shade-tolerant** *adjective* able to grow without adverse effect in the shade of taller plants; **shade tree**: planted to give shade.
■ **shadeless** *adjective* **E17.** **shadelessness** *noun* **L19.**

shade /ʃeɪd/ *verb*[1]. **LME.**
[from the noun.]
1 *verb trans.* Screen from (esp. the sun's) light or heat; *spec.* shield (the eyes or face) from glare with the hand etc.; place in the shade. **LME.** ▸**b** Cover, moderate, or exclude the light of (a lamp etc.). **E19.**
2 *verb trans.* Conceal from view, hide partially, veil; disguise. **E16.**
3 *verb trans.* **a** Cover with shadow, darken. **L16.** ▸**b** Represent shade or shadow on (a drawing, painting, etc.), esp. with a darker colour or with closely spaced dots or parallel lines; colour or embellish thus. Also foll. by *in*. **E18.** ▸**c** Colour (fabric etc.) with gradually merging shades. **M19.**
4 *verb trans.* Represent roughly, symbolize; sketch *out*. *rare.* **L16.**
5 *verb trans.* Put into the shade, eclipse; defeat, surpass, or win narrowly. **M18.** ▸**b** Exceed (a particular age, weight, etc.) narrowly. *colloq.* (orig. *US*). **M20.**
6 *verb trans. & intrans.* **a** Change or (cause to) pass by imperceptible degrees. Foll. by *into*, *to*, *away*, *off*. **E19.** ▸**b** Make or undergo a slight or gradual reduction in (price, value, etc.). **L19.**

📖 **1** V. WOOLF Great trees now shaded . . the road. W. CATHER An old Panama hat . . shaded his eyes. **b** I. MURDOCH He put a newspaper over the lamp to shade the light. **3b** T. SEATON I have not shaded the leaf to show any depth of the carving. **5** *Sydney Morning Herald* University slightly shade Gordon in points scored. **6a** *New Quarterly (Canada)* Afternoon shades into evening V. GLENDINNING A rose-red wash shading to grey-pink.

■ **shader** *noun* (*rare*) **E18.**

shade *verb*[2] see SHED *verb*[1].

shaded /ˈʃeɪdɪd/ *ppl adjective*. **L16.**
[from SHADE *verb*[1] + -ED[1].]
That has been shaded; *spec.* (*a*) (of a lamp etc.) covered with a shade (of a specified colour etc.); (*b*) marked with gradually merging colours; edged or variegated *with* a darker colour.

shadi /ˈʃɑːdiː/ *noun*. **L19.**
[Urdu, Persian *šādī*.]
In the Indian subcontinent: a wedding, a marriage.

shadine /ʃaˈdiːn/ *noun*. **L18.**
[Blend of SHAD *noun* and SARDINE *noun*[2].]
The menhaden, preserved in oil like a sardine.

shading /ˈʃeɪdɪŋ/ *noun*. **E17.**
[from SHADE *verb*[1] + -ING[1].]
The action of SHADE *verb*[1]; an instance of this; *spec.* (*a*) closely spaced dots or parallel lines, a wash of darker colour, etc., used to represent shade or shadow in a drawing, picture, etc.; the graduation of tones from light to dark to create a sense of depth; (*b*) a minute variation or difference in colour, quality, meaning, etc.; (*c*) *MUSIC* etc. the imparting of light and shade; a subtle stress or emphasis; (*d*) a spurious variation in brightness over parts of a televised image.

📖 DICKENS The words emblazoned in . . gilt letters and dark shading. *Westminster Gazette* A map of the United States, with prohibition States . . indicated by shading. P. GRIFFITHS Debussy was a master of delicate orchestral shadings.

shadkhan *noun* var. of SHADCHAN.

shadoof /ʃəˈduːf/ *noun*. Also **shaduf**. **M19.**
[Egyptian Arab. *šādūf*.]
A device consisting of a pivoted rod or pole with a bucket at one end and a counterbalancing weight at the other, used esp. in Egypt for raising water.

shadow /ˈʃadəʊ/ *noun & adjective*.
[Old English *scead(u)we* oblique forms of *sceadu* SHADE *noun*, corresp. to Old Saxon *scado* (Dutch *schaduw*), Old High German *scato* (German *Schatte*, later *Schatten*), Gothic *skadus*, from Germanic from Indo-European. Cf. Greek *skotos* darkness.]
▶ **A** *noun*. **I 1** A dark figure projected or cast on a surface by a body intercepting rays of light (esp. from the sun), showing the approximate form of the body and freq. regarded as an appendage. **OE.** ▸**b** A dark area in a (positive) radiograph (appearing as a light area in a negative). **E20.**
2 A reflected image, a reflection. Now *rare.* **ME.**
3 a An unreal or insubstantial thing or person, an illusory image. Freq. contrasted with ***substance***. **ME.** ▸**b** A prefiguration, a foreshadowing; a foreboding, a threat (*of*). **LME.** ▸**c** A weak or attenuated remnant of or *of* a thing or person. **M16.** ▸**d** A very small amount or portion, the slightest trace (*of*). **L16.** ▸**e** An imitation, a copy; a counterpart; *spec.* the Opposition counterpart of a Cabinet Minister, a member of the Shadow Cabinet. **L17.**
4 = SHADE *noun* 7. **ME.**
5 a Orig., a parasite, a hanger-on. Now, an inseparable companion or attendant. **L16.** ▸**b** A person who follows and watches another; *spec.* (*a*) a bodyguard; (*b*) a detective, a spy; (*c*) a person accompanying another at his or her place of work in order to gain experience or understanding of a job. **M19.** ▸**c** *FOOTBALL* etc. A player closely marking a specific opponent. **L20.**

📖 **1** E. CASWALL As a shadow life is fleeting. T. S. ELIOT Your shadow at morning striding behind you Or . . at evening rising to meet you. M. KLINE The shadow of the earth on the moon, seen in lunar eclipses. W. BOYD The late afternoon sun cast long shadows. **3a** HENRY MORE This life . . is but a shadow. S. WYNTER Queen Victoria bestowed a freedom . . more shadow than substance. **b** D. JUDD It is under this shadow of the possibility of global death that we all live. **c** *Grimsby Evening Telegraph* He was wearing himself to a shadow touring the country. *Daily Express* He had not eaten for a month and was a shadow of his former self. **d** J. BRAINE I'd . . known, without a shadow of a doubt . . the guilt was mine.

▶ **II 6** Partial or comparative darkness, esp. as caused by a body intercepting light. Freq. in *pl.*, patches or areas of shade or darkness; *fig.* obscurity. **ME.** ▸**b** In *pl.* The darkness of night, the growing darkness of evening. Chiefly *poet.* **LME.** ▸**c** *fig.* Gloom, unhappiness. Also, something marring or threatening a prospect, friendship, reputation, etc. **M19.** ▸**d** *JUNGIAN PSYCHOLOGY*. The dark aspect of personality formed by fears and unpleasant emotions rejected by the conscious self but persisting in the personal unconscious; an archetype in which this aspect is concentrated. **E20.**
7 a Protection from the sun; *the* shade; *fig.* protection, shelter. Now *rare.* **ME.** ▸†**b** A shady place. **E16–L17.**
8 Comparative darkness as represented pictorially; dark colour or a darker part or parts in a painting or drawing. **L15.** ▸**b** Eye-shadow. **M20.**
9 a A sunshade, a parasol, an umbrella. Now *rare.* **L15.** ▸**b** (A shading peak or projection on) a woman's hat or bonnet. Now *rare.* **L16.**
10 *THEATRICAL*. A penthouse or roof over the stage. *obsolete* exc. *Hist.* **E17.**

📖 **6** *Times* Norwich . . deserved to win, yet . . are left behind in the shadows. J. HIGGINS A place of shadows, the only illumination coming from . . candles. P. ACKROYD The forest acted as a canopy, and we were continually in shadow. **c** A. PRICE The only shadow on Mr Ratcliffe's good fortune is the recent death of his cousin.

Phrases: **afraid of one's own shadow** unreasonably timid or nervous. *FIVE o'clock shadow*. **in the shadow of**, **under the shadow of** (*a*) close to, very near; (*b*) under the influence or power of; (*c*) dominated or eclipsed by the personality of. **may your shadow never grow less!**: wishing a person happiness and prosperity (freq. as a toast). **the valley of the shadow of death**, **the shadow of death** (with ref. to *Psalms* 23:4) (a place or period of) intense gloom or peril. ***under the shadow of***: see ***in the shadow of*** above.
Comb.: **shadow box** a case with a protective transparent front for the display of a painting, jewel, etc.; **shadow-box** *verb intrans. & trans.* box against (an imaginary opponent) as a form of training; **shadow-cast** *verb trans.* enhance (a microscopic image) by shadow-casting, subject (a microscopic specimen) to shadow-casting; **shadow-casting** *ppl adjective & verbal noun* (*a*) *adjective* that casts a shadow or shadows; (*b*) *noun* the casting of a shadow or shadows; *spec.* a technique for enhancing an electron-microscope image by projecting a beam of small particles or atoms (usu. of a heavy metal) on to the sample at a shallow angle, to form a deposit giving the appearance of shadows cast by sideways illumination; **shadowland** a place in shadow; an indeterminate borderland between other places, states, etc.; an abode of ghosts, spirits, etc.; **shadow mask** *TELEVISION* a perforated metal screen situated directly behind the phosphor screen in certain types of colour television tube, having a pattern of precisely located holes through which the electron beams pass so as to strike the correct dots on the phosphor screen (freq. *attrib.*, as ***shadow-mask tube***); **shadow picture** †(*a*) an X-ray photograph; (*b*) a picture formed by a shadow (usu. of a person's hand or hands) thrown upon a screen etc.; **shadow play** (*a*) a play in which the actors appear as shadows cast on a screen placed between the stage and the auditorium; (*b*) a puppet play of the shadow theatre; **shadow price** *ECONOMICS* the estimated price of a good or service for which no market price exists; **shadow puppet** a puppet used in a shadow play; **shadow quilting**: in which a transparent fabric is quilted on to a pieced or more elaborate background; **shadow-stitch** a criss-cross embroidery stitch used on sheer materials for filling in spaces, worked on the reverse side so as to show through in a shadowy way with an outline resembling a backstitch; **shadow stripe** a faint stripe usu. of a similar colour to that of the background, produced by use of yarn of different directions of twist; a cloth or garment having such striping; **shadow-striped** *adjective* having shadow stripes; **shadow test** *OPHTHALMOLOGY* a method of examining an

eye, esp. with regard to its refractive properties, by deflecting light out on to the retina with a small mirror; **shadow theatre** a form of puppetry in which flat figures are passed between a strong light and a translucent screen, the audience watching on the other side of the screen; a place where such puppet shows are performed; **shadow work** embroidery done in shadow-stitch.

▶**B** *attrib.* or as *adjective*. **1** Designating a member or members of a political party in opposition holding responsibilities parallel to those of a counterpart or counterparts in government. **E20.**

2 Designating or pertaining to a factory etc. built or instituted to provide extra or specialized output in an emergency, esp. in the war of 1939–45. **M20.**

1 *shadow cabinet, shadow minister*, etc.

■ **shadower** *noun* **M16. shadowish** *adjective* (long *rare*) characterized by shadow, resembling a shadow; insubstantial, fleeting, figurative: **M16.**

shadow /ˈʃadəʊ/ *verb*.

[Old English *sčeadwian*, from *sčeadu* **SHADOW** *noun*.]

1 *verb trans.* Shelter or protect as with covering wings. Formerly also, screen or shield from attack etc., put under patronage. Now usu. foll. by *over*. *obsolete* exc. *poet.* **OE.**

2 *verb trans.* Protect or shelter from the sun; shade. Now *rare* or *obsolete*. **LME.**

3 a *verb trans.* Cast a shadow on; cover, darken, or obscure (as) with a shadow. **LME.** ▶**b** *verb intrans.* Cast a shadow. Now *rare*. **LME.** ▶**c** *verb intrans.* Grow dark or gloomy. Now *rare*. **L19.**

†**4** *verb trans.* Intercept or dim the light of (the sun etc.). **LME–M17.**

†**5** *verb trans.* Hide or conceal from knowledge. **LME–E17.**

6 *verb trans.* Represent, symbolize; illustrate roughly, outline, sketch out. Now freq. foll. by *out*, *forth*. **L16.**

†**7** *verb trans.* Portray, paint the likeness of; draw, paint, (a picture). **L16–M17.**

†**8** *verb trans.* Depict shadow in or on; shade or tint with pencil, colour, etc. **L16–E19.**

9 a *verb trans.* Follow and watch (a person etc.), now esp. secretly, in order to provide protection or gain information. **E17.** ▶**b** *verb trans. & intrans.* Repeat (another's words) with the minimum of delay, as a treatment for stuttering in speech therapy. **M20.** ▶**c** *verb trans. & intrans.* Of a politician: act as a shadow to (a parliamentary minister etc.). **M20.** ▶**d** *verb trans.* Accompany (a person) at his or her place of work as a shadow. **L20.**

10 *verb intrans.* Shade *to* or *into* a certain colour. Formerly also, be tinged *with* a darker colour; agree in colour *with*; border or verge *on* in colour. **M17.**

11 *verb trans.* MICROSCOPY. Subject (a specimen) to the process of shadow-casting. **M20.**

📖 **3a** SOUTHEY Dark battalions . . Shadowing the distant plain. W. BOYD Her face was shadowed by a wide straw hat. **9a** M. HOLROYD She would arrange for him to be shadowed by a private detective.

■ **shadowing** *noun* the action of the verb; an instance of this; *spec.* (*a*) a shadow, shadows cast; (*b*) the placing or distribution of shadow; shading in a drawing or picture: **OE.**

shadowgraph /ˈʃadəʊgrɑːf/ *noun*. **L19.**

[from **SHADOW** *noun* + **-GRAPH**.]

1 A picture formed by a shadow (usu. of a hand or hands) cast on a lighted screen or surface; an exhibition or producer of such pictures. **L19.**

2 An image or photograph taken by means of X-rays, a radiograph. **L19.**

3 An image formed by light which has passed through a fluid and been refracted differently by regions of different density (used esp. in studying fluid flow). **E20.**

■ **shadowˈgraphic** *adjective* pertaining to shadowgraphs **L19. shadowgraphist** *noun* a producer of shadowgraphs **L19. shadowgraphy** *noun* the production of shadowgraphs **L19.**

shadowless /ˈʃadəʊlɪs/ *adjective*. **M17.**

[from **SHADOW** *noun* + **-LESS**.]

1 Casting no shadow. **M17.** ▶**b** Of a lamp etc.: so constructed as to cast no shadow. **M19.**

2 Having no shadows on the surface; unsheltered from the sun; (of light, the sky, etc.) unclouded. **E19.**

■ **shadowlessness** *noun* **L19.**

shadowly /ˈʃadəʊli/ *adverb*. *rare*. **M19.**

[formed as prec. + **-LY**².]

In the manner of a shadow, obscurely.

shadowy /ˈʃadəʊi/ *adjective*. **LME.**

[from **SHADOW** *noun* + **-Y**¹.]

1 a Insubstantial, transitory, fleeting; unreal, imaginary. **LME.** ▶**b** Spectral, ghostly. **L17.** ▶**c** Faintly perceptible, indistinct, vague; of uncertain identity or nature, mysterious. **L18.**

2 a Full of shadows, enveloped in or obscured by shadow; shaded from the sun. **LME.** ▶†**b** Screened from observation; remote, inaccessible. **M16–E17.**

3 Casting a shadow, providing shade. **E17.**

📖 **1a** *Blackwood's Magazine* The shadowy . . evanescence of the regal office. **b** T. MOORE Yon shadowy bark hath been to that wreck. **c** D. H. LAWRENCE Watching the shadowy fish slide through the gloom of the mill-pond. *Observer* A shadowy, unchartered collection of terrorists. **2a** T. HARDY From the shadowy archway came a shining lantern. **3** SOUTHEY Yon tree . . Forms with its shadowy boughs a cool retreat.

■ **shadowily** *adverb* **M19. shadowiness** *noun* **L17.**

shaduf *noun* var. of **SHADOOF**.

shady /ˈʃeɪdi/ *adjective*. **L16.**

[from **SHADE** *noun* + **-Y**¹.]

1 Providing shade. **L16.**

2 Shaded, protected by shade. **L16.** ▶†**b** Inhabiting or favouring shade or seclusion. **L16–E18.**

3 Opaque; not luminous, dark. Now *poet.* **E17.**

†**4** Faintly perceptible, indefinite, shadowy. **E17–E18.**

5 Of questionable merit or prospects of success; uncertain, unreliable. Also, of doubtful honesty or legality, disreputable. **M19.**

📖 **2** C. HARKNESS Sun-drenched terraces and shady alcoves. **5** P. H. GIBBS A shady customer with a bad reputation in . . business. G. DALY He made a good profit from . . shady deals . . without Ned's knowledge.

■ **shadily** *adverb* in a shady, esp. a questionable or disreputable, manner **M19. shadiness** *noun* **E17.**

SHAEF /ʃeɪf/ *abbreviation*.

Hist. Supreme Headquarters of the Allied Expeditionary Force (which invaded occupied Europe in 1944–5).

†**Shaffee** *noun* var. of **SHAFII**.

Shafii /ˈʃafiː/ *noun*. Also **Shāfiʿī**, †**Shaffee**. **E17.**

[Arab. *Šāfiʿī* (see below).]

A follower of the school of Sunni Muslim law founded by the jurist Muḥammad ibn Idrīs ash-Shāfiʿī (767–820).

shaft /ʃɑːft/ *noun*.

[Old English *sčæft*, *sčeaft* = Old Frisian *sceft*, Old Saxon, Old High German *scaft*, (Dutch *schaft*, German *Schaft*), Old Norse *skaft*, from Germanic, perh. rel. to Latin *scapus* shaft, Greek *skapton* staff, *skēptron* **SCEPTRE** *noun*. In branch II corresp. to Middle Low German (whence Middle & mod. High German) *schacht*.]

▶**I 1** The long slender rod forming the body of a lance, spear, arrow, harpoon, etc. **OE.**

2 A spear, a lance (*arch.*); an arrow, esp. for a longbow. **OE.** ▶**b** *loosely*. A missile. *rhet.* **L18.**

3 A pole, a flagstaff. Now *rare*. **OE.** ▶**b** ARCHITECTURE. A slender column. **M19.** ▶**c** An obelisk or column erected as a memorial. *US*. **M19.**

4 A columnar or straight portion of something, a stem, as (*a*) (now *rare*) the stem or trunk of a tree; (*b*) the top of a chimney protruding above a roof etc.; (*c*) ARCHITECTURE the body of a column or pillar between the base and the capital; (*d*) the long straight handle of a tool etc.; (*e*) the shank of an anchor; (*f*) the stem of a pipe; (*g*) the upright part of a cross, *esp.* the part between the limbs and the base; (*h*) the central main stem of a feather; (*i*) the part of a hair between the root and the point; (*j*) ANATOMY the middle portion of a long bone. **LME.**

5 A beam or ray of light etc.; a streak or bolt of lightning. **LME.**

6 *fig.* A quality or action which pierces or hurts (like an arrow etc.); a remark etc. intended to hurt or provoke. Also, a sudden brilliant remark. **L16.**

7 Either of a pair of poles or long bars between which a horse etc. is harnessed to a vehicle. **E17.**

8 A long cylindrical rotating rod for the transmission of motive power in a machine. **L17.**

9 The penis. *slang*. **L18.**

10 (Either of) a pair of long laths between which the heddles are stretched in a loom. **M19.**

11 A human leg. *US slang*. **M20.**

12 An act or instance of unfair or harsh treatment; rejection. Chiefly in ***give the shaft***, ***get the shaft***. *slang* (chiefly *N. Amer.*). **M20.**

📖 **6** J. WAIN Your shaft seems to have gone home . . . Our friend doesn't quite know how to answer. T. WOGAN Some . . polished shaft, such as 'Ere! 'ow much are the bookies payin' you . . ?' **8** ***countershaft***, ***crankshaft***, ***drive shaft***, ***mill-shaft***, ***propeller shaft***, ***screw shaft***, etc.

▶**II 13** A long, narrow, vertical or slightly inclined well-like excavation or hole giving access to underground workings in a mine; a vertical space or passageway in a building, for a lift, ventilation, etc. **LME.**

13 ***air-shaft***, ***escape shaft***, ***lift shaft***, ***upcast shaft***, etc.

Comb.: **shaft-alley** NAUTICAL the area of a ship's propeller; *attrib.* designating or pertaining to unofficial or unreliable information, attributed to gossip in the shaft-alley; **shaft-drive** *adjective* (of a bicycle) having the power transmitted from the pedals to the wheel by means of shafts inside the frame, instead of by a chain; **shaft grave** ARCHAEOLOGY a prehistoric grave with a vertical shaft (found esp. in Mycenae dating from the 16th cent. BC); **shaft-hole** ARCHAEOLOGY the hole in an axe-head or similar implement for the insertion of the haft or handle; **shaft-horse** a horse put between the shafts to pull a vehicle (cf. ***trace-horse*** s.v. **TRACE** *noun*²); a cart-horse; **shaft horsepower** brake horsepower, *esp.* power delivered to a propeller shaft or the shaft of a turbine; **shaft pillar** MINING a body of coal or rock unworked in order to provide support for an adjacent shaft; **shaftsman** a man employed in sinking mine shafts; **shaft-tailed whydah**, **shaft-tailed widow bird** a dark-coloured African weaver-bird, *Vidua regia*, having long tail feathers with bare shafts; **shaft turbine** a gas turbine aero-engine which delivers power through a shaft.

■ **shaftless** *adjective* **E19.**

shaft /ʃɑːft/ *verb*. **LME.**

[from the noun.]

▶**I** *verb intrans.* **1** Of the sun: send out shafts of light. *rare*. **LME.**

▶**II** *verb trans.* **2** Fit (an arrowhead, a weapon or tool) with a shaft. **LME.**

3 Propel (a barge etc.) with a pole. **M19.**

4 Treat unfairly or harshly; cheat, deceive; take advantage of; slight, reject. *slang* (chiefly *N. Amer.*). **M20.**

5 Of a man: copulate with. *coarse slang*. **L20.**

shafted /ˈʃɑːftɪd/ *adjective*. **L16.**

[from **SHAFT** *noun* + **-ED**².]

1 HERALDRY. Of a spear, arrow, etc.: having the shaft of a specified tincture. **L16.**

2 Having a shaft or handle. Chiefly as 2nd elem. of comb. **M17.**

3 ARCHITECTURE. Ornamented with or resting on shafts. **E19.**

4 ORNITHOLOGY. As 2nd elem. of comb.: having the shafts of the feathers of a specified colour, character, or number. **E19.**

shafter /ˈʃɑːftə/ *noun*. **M19.**

[from **SHAFT** *noun* + **-ER**¹.]

= ***shaft-horse*** s.v. **SHAFT** *noun*.

Shaftesburian /ʃɑːftsˈbjʊəriən/ *adjective*. Also **-burean**. **M18.**

[from *Shaftesbury* (see below) + **-AN**.]

Of or pertaining to the moral philosophy or literary style of Anthony Ashley Cooper, third Earl of Shaftesbury (1671–1713).

shafting /ˈʃɑːftɪŋ/ *noun*. **E19.**

[from **SHAFT** *noun* + **-ING**¹.]

▶**I 1** A system of connected shafts for transmitting motion. Also, material from which to cut lengths of shafts. **E19.**

2 Shafts or ornamental columns collectively. **M19.**

▶**II 3** The shafts of a mine collectively. **L19.**

shaftment /ˈʃɑːf(t)m(ə)nt/ *noun*¹. *obsolete* exc. *dial.*

[Old English *sčeaftmund*, formed as **SHAFT** *noun* + *mund* hand, hand-breadth.]

The distance from the end of the extended thumb to the opposite side of the hand, about 15 cm or 6 inches. Cf. **FISTMELE**.

shaftment /ˈʃɑːf(t)m(ə)nt/ *noun*². *rare*. **M17.**

[from **SHAFT** *noun* + **-MENT**.]

†**1** An arrow. Only in **M17.**

2 The feathered part of an arrow. **E19.**

shafty /ˈʃɑːfti/ *adjective*. **L19.**

[from **SHAFT** *noun* + **-Y**¹.]

Of wool: having long and strong fibres.

shag /ʃag/ *noun*¹ *& adjective*.

[Late Old English *sčeacga* rel. to Old Norse *skegg* beard, from Germanic. Rel. to **SHAW** *noun*¹.]

▶**A** *noun*. **1** Rough matted hair, wool, etc.; a mass of this. **LOE.** ▶**b** A (tangled) mass of shrubs, trees, foliage, etc. **M19.**

2 Cloth having a velvet nap on one side; *esp.* cloth having a long and coarse nap. **L16.**

3 The nap of cloth, esp. when long and coarse. **M17.**

4 In early use, a rug or mat of shaggy material. Now *spec.* (*ellipt.*), a shag carpet or rug; shag pile. Formerly also, a garment of shaggy material. **M17.**

5 *fig.* Uncouthness, roughness, brutality of manner. Now *rare*. **L18.**

6 A strong tobacco cut into shreds. **E19.**

▶**B** *attrib.* or as *adjective*. **1** Having shaggy hair. Now *rare*. **L16.**

2 Of hair, a mane, etc.: long and rough, shaggy. Now *rare*. **L16.**

3 Made of the cloth shag. **E17.**

4 Of tobacco: of a strong kind cut in shreds. **L18.**

5 (Of a carpet, rug, etc.) having a long rough pile; (of a pile) long and rough. **M20.**

Comb.: **shag-haired** *adjective* (*arch.*) having shaggy hair.

shag /ʃag/ *noun*². **M16.**

[Perh. a use of prec. with ref. to the 'shaggy' crest.]

A greenish-black cormorant of European and N. African coasts, *Phalacrocorax aristotelis*, which in the breeding season has a crest of long curly plumes. Also (esp. *NZ*), any of various other cormorants (usu. with specifying word).

like a shag on a rock *Austral. colloq.* in an isolated or exposed position.

shag /ʃag/ *noun*[3]. **L16.**
[from **SHAG** *verb*[1] (& so perh. repr. two words). Cf. **SHAG** *noun*[4].]
▶ **I** †**1** A shake. Only in **L16.**
2 The refuse of barley, corn, oats, etc. Cf. **SHACK** *noun*[1] 1. *Scot. & dial.* **E19.**
▶ **II 3** An act of copulation. *coarse slang.* **M20.**

shag /ʃag/ *noun*[4]. **M20.**
[Prob. from **SHAG** *verb*[1] or *verb*[2].]
A dance popular esp. in the US in the 1930s and 1940s, and characterized by vigorous hopping from one foot to the other.

shag /ʃag/ *verb*[1]. Infl. **-gg-**. **LME.**
[Origin unkn.: cf. **SHOG** *verb*. Branch II perh. a different word.]
▶ **I 1** *verb trans.* Toss about, shake. Long *obsolete* exc. *dial. rare.* **LME.**
†**2** *verb intrans.* Shake, waggle; vacillate. **LME–L16.**
▶ **II 3** *verb trans. & intrans.* Copulate (with). *coarse slang.* **L18.**
■ **shagger** *noun coarse slang* a person who copulates **L20.**

shag /ʃag/ *verb*[2]. Infl. **-gg-**. **L16.**
[from **SHAG** *noun*[1].]
1 *verb intrans.* Be shaggy; hang down in a shaggy manner. **L16.**
2 *verb trans.* Make rough or shaggy, give a shaggy appearance to (earth, a hillside, a rock, etc.). (Foll. by *with*.) Usu. in *pass.* **E17.**

🕮 **1** R. B. PARKER His mustache . . shagged over his upper lip. **2** MILTON Caverns shag'd with horrid shades. W. D. HOWELLS Woods . . shagged the hills with a stunted . . growth.

shag /ʃag/ *verb*[3]. Infl. **-gg-**. **M19.**
[Origin unkn. Perh. two words.]
1 *verb intrans.* Go, make off; wander aimlessly. Freq. foll. by adverb. *slang.* **M19.**
2 a *verb trans.* Chase; retrieve; *spec.* in **BASEBALL**, go for or catch (fly balls), esp. in a practice session. *US colloq.* **E20.** ▸**b** *verb intrans.* **BASEBALL.** Catch or retrieve balls in a batting-practice session. **E20.**

🕮 **1** W. H. CANAWAY We'd been shagging around over these mountains for four days. **2a** J. T. FARRELL Demons . . would come . . until his old man . . shagged them away. F. ASTAIRE Three hundred golf balls and five men shagging them. *New Yorker* I stayed to watch practice, and shagged balls for a while.

shag /ʃag/ *verb*[4] *intrans.* Infl. **-gg-**. **M20.**
[from **SHAG** *noun*[4].]
Dance the shag.

shaganappi /ʃagəˈnapi/ *noun & adjective. N. Amer.* **M18.**
[Ojibwa.]
▶ **A** *noun.* Thread, cord, or thong made from rawhide, rawhide cut into strips; a strip of rawhide. Also, a rough pony. **M18.**
▶ **B** *adjective.* Made of a strip or strips of rawhide; *fig.* tough, rough; cheap, inferior, makeshift. **E19.**

shag-bag /ˈʃagbag/ *noun & adjective. arch. colloq.* **L17.**
[Alt. of **SHAG-RAG**.]
▶ **A** *noun.* A shabby or worthless person. **L17.**
▶ **B** *adjective.* Shabby and worthless; poor in quality. **L19.**

shagbark /ˈʃagbɑːk/ *noun.* **L17.**
[from **SHAG** *adjective* + **BARK** *noun*[2].]
1 A W. Indian leguminous tree, *Pithecellobium alexandri.* **L17.**
2 A N. American hickory, *Carya ovata*, with shaggy bark which peels in strips; the wood or nut of this tree. Also ***shagbark hickory***, ***shagbark walnut***. **M18.**

shagetz *noun* var. of **SHEGETZ**.

shagged /ʃagd/ *adjective*[1]. Now *rare.* **OE.**
[from **SHAG** *noun*[1] + **-ED**[2].]
1 Esp. of an animal: having or covered with shaggy hair; rough-coated. **OE.** ▸**b** Of a hillside etc.: covered with scrub, trees, or some rough or shaggy growth. **L18.**
2 Jagged; having a rough uneven surface. **L16.** ▸†**b** Of a cloth, a garment: having a rough or long nap. **M–L17.**
3 Of hair etc.: long and rough; shaggy. **L16.**

shagged /ʃagd/ *adjective*[2]. *slang.* **M20.**
[Perh. from **SHAG** *verb*[1] + **-ED**[1].]
Weary, exhausted. Also foll. by *out*.

shaggery /ˈʃag(ə)ri/ *noun. NZ.* **L19.**
[from **SHAG** *noun*[2] + **-ERY**.]
A breeding colony of shags.

shaggy /ˈʃagi/ *adjective.* **L16.**
[from **SHAG** *noun*[1] + **-Y**[1].]
1 Covered with or having long coarse or bushy hair; (of a person) unkempt. **L16.**
2 Of the earth, a hillside, etc.: covered with a rough tangled growth. **L16.**
3 (Of cloth) having a long and coarse nap; rough in texture; having a rough surface. **M17.**
4 Of hair etc.: rough, coarse and abundant, tangled. **M17.** ▸**b** Of a wood, trees, etc.: resembling a rough growth of hair, dense and tangled. **L18.**

Special collocations & comb.: **shaggy cap** = *shaggy ink-cap* below. **shaggy-dog story** a lengthy tediously detailed story, more amusing to the teller than the audience, or amusing only by its inconsequentiality or pointlessness. **shaggy ink-cap** a tall rough-surfaced mushroom, *Coprinus comatus*, edible when young but black and deliquescent when mature. **shaggy parasol** a non-poisonous mushroom, *Lepiota rhacodes*, with a rough scaly upper surface.
■ **shaggily** *adverb* **M19.** **shagginess** *noun* **L18.**

shagitz *noun* var. of **SHEGETZ**.

shag-rag /ˈʃagrag/ *adjective & noun.* Now *arch. & dial.* **L16.**
[Rhyming alt. of *shake-rag* s.v. **SHAKE** *verb*.]
▶ **A** *adjective.* Of a person: ragged, rascally; shaggy, unkempt. **L16.**
▶ **B** *noun.* A ragged, disreputable person; a low rascally fellow. **E17.**

shagreen /ʃəˈgriːn/ *noun & adjective.* **L17.**
[Var. of **CHAGRIN** *noun*.]
▶ **A** *noun.* **1** A kind of untanned leather with a rough granular surface, frequently dyed green; an imitation of this. **L17.**
2 The skin of various sharks, rays, etc., which is covered with close-set pointed scales (denticles) forming a hard rough surface, esp. as used for polishing etc. **L19.**
▶ **B** *attrib.* or as *adjective.* Made of shagreen. **E18.**
■ **shagreened** *adjective* (*a*) having a roughened surface or appearance like shagreen; (*b*) covered with shagreen: **E18.**

shagroon /ʃəˈgruːn/ *noun. NZ slang. obsolete* exc. *Hist.* **M19.**
[Perh. from Irish *seachrán* wandering.]
An early settler in Canterbury, New Zealand, from a place other than Britain, *esp.* one from Australia.

shah /ʃɑː/ *noun.* Also **S-**. **M16.**
[Persian *šāh* from Old Persian *xšāyaθiya* king.]
Hist. (A title of) the monarch of Iran (Persia).
■ **Shahanshah** /ʃɑːənˈʃɑː/ *noun* [Persian *šāhanšāh* king of kings] (a title of) the Shah of Iran (Persia) **E19.** **shahbanu** /ˈʃɑːbɑːnuː/ *noun* [Persian *bānū* lady] (the title of) the wife of the Shah of Iran (Persia) **E20.** **shahdom** *noun* the position, dignity, or territory of a shah **L19.** **shahzadah** /ʃɑːˈzɑːdə/ *noun* [Persian *zāda* son] the son of a shah **M17.**

shahada /ʃaˈhɑːdɑ/ *noun.* **L19.**
[Arab. *šahāda* testimony, evidence.]
The Muslim profession of faith, *Lā ilāha illā (A)llāh, Muḥammadun rasūl Allāh* ('there is no God but Allah, [and] Muhammad is the messenger of Allah').

Shahaptan *noun & adjective* var. of **SAHAPTIN**.

shahbandar /ʃɑːˈbʌndə/ *noun.* Also **S-**. **L16.**
[Persian *šāhbandar* lit. 'king of the port'.]
Hist. (The title of) an officer at a SE Asian port responsible for dealing with foreign trade and ships. Also, (the title of) any of various other officers with wider responsibilities, *spec.* each of three chief local officials who administered Sarawak under the Sultan of Brunei.

shaheed *noun* var. of **SHAHID**.

shaheen /ʃɑːˈhiːn/ *noun.* **M19.**
[Urdu, Persian *šāhīn* lit. 'royal (bird)', from *šāh* **SHAH**.]
In NW India and adjoining regions, a peregrine falcon.

shahi /ˈʃɑːiː/ *noun.* **M16.**
[Persian *šāhī* royal, formed as **SHAH**.]
Hist. Orig., a small silver Persian coin of relatively low value. Later, a more valuable copper Persian coin.

shahid /ʃəˈhiːd/ *noun.* Also **-eed**. **L19.**
[Arab. *šahīd* witness, martyr.]
A Muslim martyr.

shahnai /ˈʃɑːnʌɪ/ *noun.* Also ***shan-***, ***sheh-*** /ˈʃeɪ-/. **E20.**
[Urdu *šahnāī* from Persian *šāhnāy* lit. 'large flute'.]
A wind instrument of the oboe class resembling a shawm, from the Indian subcontinent.

shahtoosh /ʃɑːˈtuːʃ/ *noun.* Also (earlier) **shah tush**. **M19.**
[Panjabi *śāhtūś*, ult. from Persian *šāh* king + Panjabi *tūś*, Kashmiri *tośa* fine shawl-stuff.]
High-quality wool from the neck-hair of the Himalayan ibex; a material woven from this.

shaikh, **Shaikha** *nouns* vars. of **SHEIKH**, **SHEIKHA**.

shail /ʃeɪl/ *verb intrans.* Long *obsolete* exc. *dial.* **LME.**
[Perh. rel. to Old English *sceolh* oblique. Cf. **SHAUCHLE**.]
Stumble, walk or move in a shuffling, shambling manner.

Shaitan /ʃeɪˈtɑːn/ *noun.* **M17.**
[Arab. *šayṭān* from Hebrew *śāṭān* **SATAN**.]
In the Middle and Far East: the Devil, Satan; an evil spirit; *transf.* an evilly disposed, vicious, or cunning person or animal. Also, a dust-storm.

shakable *adjective* var. of **SHAKEABLE**.

shake /ʃeɪk/ *noun.* **ME.**
[from the verb.]
▶ **I** Action.
1 A sudden movement; a rush; an onrush; a (specified) rate of motion. Long *obsolete* exc. *dial. rare.* **ME.**
2 An act of shaking someone or something; an instance of being shaken; a stroke, blow, or other event which shakes someone or something (*lit. & fig.*). **M16.** ▸**b** The small amount of time taken to shake something; a short period of time, a moment. Chiefly in adverbial phrs. *colloq.* **E19.** ▸**c** *spec.* (orig. **NAUTICAL**). An act of shaking a sleeper to rouse him or her; a morning call. **M20.**
3 The shock of an earthquake; an earthquake. Now chiefly *US & NZ.* **E17.**
4 A shivering or trembling of the body or limbs; a state of tremor; an attack of a shaking disease characterized by this. **E17.**
5 Irregular vibratory or tremulous movement; irregular lateral movement; an instance of this. **M17.**
6 **MUSIC.** A trill. Also, an example or use of vibrato. **M17.**
7 A tremor in the voice. **M19.**
8 A shaking movement in a dance; a jerk. **M20.**
9 A party, *esp.* a rent party. *US slang.* **M20.**

🕮 **2** C. LAMB It seemed to have given a shake to memory, calling up notice after notice. R. BAGOT Jim . . gave her hand a very British shake. B. VINE A refusal . . indicated by a smiling shake of the head. A. TYLER He gave his shoulders a slight shake. **b** M. TWAIN Spos'n he can't fix that leg just in three shakes of a sheep's tail? E. NESBIT Wait a shake, and I'll undo the . . gate. J. WAIN In two shakes he'd solved the problem. **5** G. S. NARES The sail will come in without a shake. L. DEIGHTON A slow motion movie would be less subject to camera shake.

▶ **II** Result (cf. **SHACK** *noun*[1]).
10 A natural cleft or fissure produced during growth or formation of timber, rock, etc. **M17.**
11 In *pl.* Pieces of split timber, a kind of shingles. Also (*rare*), the staves of a cask or barrel taken to pieces (cf. **SHOOK** *adjective* 1b, *noun*). Chiefly *N. Amer.* **L18.**
12 A drink produced by shaking ingredients; *spec.* a milk shake. Earliest in ***milk shake*** s.v. **MILK** *noun.* **L19.**

Phrases: **a fair shake** *N. Amer. slang* a fair deal. **give a person the shake** (chiefly *US*) cold-shoulder, rebuff, evade, escape, (a person). **no great shakes** *colloq.* nothing extraordinary in ability or importance. **the Shake** a dance popular in the 1960s characterized by shaking movements. **the shakes** *colloq.* (*a*) nervous agitation caused by fear or horror; (*b*) a disease characterized by a trembling of the muscles and limbs, *esp.* delirium tremens.
Comb.: **shake dancer** *slang* a female dancer who shakes her (usu. wholly or partially bared) breasts to music; **shake hole** a swallow-hole; **shake wave** **SEISMOLOGY** an S wave.

shake /ʃeɪk/ *verb.* Pa. t. **shook** /ʃʊk/, (now *dial.*) **shaked**; pa. pple **shaken** /ˈʃeɪk(ə)n/, (now *dial. & non-standard*) **shook**. Also (*dial.*) **shack** /ʃak/, pa. t. & pple **shacked**.
[Old English *sċ(e)acan* = Old Saxon *skakan*, Old Norse *skaka*, from Germanic.]
▶†**I 1** *verb intrans.* Go, pass, move, journey; flee, depart. *poet.* **OE–E16.**
▶ **II 2** *verb intrans.* Of a thing having more or less freedom of movement: move irregularly and quickly to and fro, up and down, or from side to side; quiver, quake, vibrate, waver; flutter. **OE.**
3 *verb intrans.* Of a thing normally stable or still: vibrate irregularly, tremble, as the result of impact or disturbance; totter, lose stability, become weakened. **ME.**
4 *verb intrans.* Of a person, a person's body, limbs, etc.: quake or tremble with physical infirmity or disease; quiver with emotion; shiver with cold, quake with fear. **ME.** ▸**b** *spec.* Be convulsed with laughter. **E18.**

🕮 **2** TENNYSON The long light shakes across the lakes. C. S. CALVERLEY The . . pine-forests which shake In the wind. **3** SIR W. SCOTT The postern gate shakes, . . it crashes. B. VINE The . . express . . roared past and the whole station shook. **4** W. MAXWELL He is deathly pale and his hands shake. R. ROBINSON I found myself shaking with fear.

▶ **III 5** *verb trans.* Brandish or flourish threateningly (a weapon etc.). Also, flourish, wave (something) ostentatiously or in triumph. **OE.**
6 *verb trans.* Cause to move irregularly and quickly to and fro, up and down, or from side to side; cause to flutter or quiver; agitate. **OE.** ▸**b** *refl.* Of a person or animal: give a shake to his, her, or its body; *fig.* bestir oneself, arouse oneself to activity. **LME.** ▸**c** Wave (the hand) in farewell. **M16.**
7 *verb trans.* Cause to change from a normal state of stability or stillness into a state of quaking, quivering, or vibrating; cause (a structure) to totter; impair the stability of, weaken, (*lit. & fig.*); change the mind of, alter the resolve of. **OE.**
8 *verb trans.* Grasp or seize and move (a person) roughly to and fro; rouse or startle from sleep or inactivity. **ME.**
9 *verb trans.* (Of physical infirmity, emotion, etc.) cause (a person etc.) to quiver or tremble; agitate, convulse; move or stir the feelings of, disturb, upset; *colloq.* upset the composure or complacency of. **LME.**
10 *verb trans.* Send in a specified direction or bring to a specified condition by shaking or by an effort or shock; distribute with a shake, scatter, sprinkle; dislodge or eject *from* by shaking; move *from* a position or opinion etc. **LME.** ▸†**b** *verb trans.* Bring down, scatter (fruit, blossom, corn, etc.) by shaking. Also, turn out (a fox) from a bag. **M16–E19.** ▸**c** *verb trans.* Cast (dice) usu. with a preliminary shake. **L16.** ▸**d** *verb intrans.* Of fruit, blossom,

corn, etc.: fall, scatter. Now *dial.* **E18.** ▸**e** *verb trans.* Steal. *slang* (chiefly *Austral.*). **E19.** ▸**f** Get rid of, give up (a habit etc.), abandon; evade; shake off (an illness, feeling, etc.). **L19.**

11 *verb trans.* Rob (a person). Foll. by *of*, †*out of*. Now only *Austral. slang.* **LME.**

12 a *verb trans.* Split, crack, (timber). Chiefly as ***shaken*** *ppl adjective.* **E16.** ▸**b** *verb intrans.* Of timber: split, crack. **L17.**

13 a *verb intrans.* MUSIC. Execute a trill; perform, play, or sing with vibrato. **E17.** ▸**b** *verb trans.* Give vibrato to (the voice); accompany or execute with a trill or vibrato. **M17.**

14 *verb intrans.* Shake hands. **L19.**

5 SHAKES. *All's Well* Home, where I will never come Whilst I can shake my sword. C. HARE Shaking his fist under the historian's nose. **6** MILTON The Tawnie Lion . . Rampant shakes his Brinded main. *House & Garden* Shake one measure of . . rum with the juice of half a lime. **b** E. WELTY He shook himself in the sun like a dog. **7** G. GREENE A sonic boom . . shook the old glass of the . . window. R. LARDNER When he once makes up his mind to a thing, there's nothing in the world can shake him. J. TROLLOPE Nothing shakes people's faith so badly. **8** SIR W. SCOTT Though he shake thee . . roughly . . to awake thee. J. CONRAD As if I could have done her some violence—shaken her, beaten her. **9** P. HEMINGWAY Memory of his loss shook him with sobs. D. C. PEATTIE I was . . shaken with impotent hatred. V. CRONIN Madame . . appeared extremely shaken by her stormy interview. **10** E. BOWEN She . . shook the dust out of her motor veil. J. POTTS He couldn't shake her loose—she hung on to his arm. R. TRAVERS Edmunds tried hard to shake the doctor from his opinion. H. NORMAN Maybe this time will shake some sense into him. **f** D. BLOODWORTH Most habits are difficult to shake. *New Yorker* I never really shook the reputation. E. SEGAL That damn flu, he could not seem to shake it. **14** M. SHADBOLT 'I don't want to argue. Can we shake?' He offered his hand.

Phrases: **be shook on** *Austral. & NZ slang* have an infatuation for; be keen on, be impressed by, admire. **more than you can shake a stick at** & vars. (*colloq.*) more than one can count, a considerable amount or number. ***shake a leg***, ***shake a loose leg***: see LEG *noun*. **shake a person's hand** shake hands with a person. **shake by the hand** shake hands with (a person). ***shake free of***: see ***shake oneself free of*** below. **shake hands** (of two persons) shake hands with each other. **shake hands with** (of one person) clasp one of the hands of (another) in one of one's own as a greeting, or farewell, as a sign of friendship or goodwill, confirmation of a promise, bargain, etc., as a sign of reconciliation or the absence of ill feeling. **shake in one's shoes** tremble with fear. **shake one's elbow** *arch.* gamble with dice. **shaken baby syndrome** MEDICINE a sometimes fatal condition observed in infants who have been violently shaken or jolted, characterized esp. by intracranial injury and retinal haemorrhages. **shake (oneself) free of** disengage oneself from by shaking or by an effort. ***shake one's finger at***: see FINGER *noun*. **shake one's head** turn the head slightly to one side and the other to express refusal, disapproval, dissent, or doubt, or in sorrow or scorn. ***shake one's sides***: see SIDE *noun*. ***shake the dust off one's feet***: see DUST *noun*. ***shake the midriff***: see MIDRIFF 1. ***shake the plum-tree***: see PLUM *noun*. ***shake your shambles***: see SHAMBLE *noun*[2] 1.

With adverbs in specialized senses: **shake down** (*a*) cause to totter and fall, bring down by shaking; (*b*) cause to settle or subside by shaking; (*c*) settle down, accommodate to circumstances, a condition, position, etc. (foll. by *into*); (*d*) *colloq.* find temporary accommodation, esp. for sleeping; sleep on a makeshift bed, esp. on a floor; (*e*) *slang* (chiefly *N. Amer.*) extort money from, blackmail or otherwise pressurize (a person) *for* (occas. *of*) money, etc.; (*f*) *slang* (chiefly *US*) (esp. of police) search (a person or place). **shake off** cast off or remove with a shake or an effort (*lit. & fig.*); get rid of (a person); draw away from (another competitor) in a race. **shake out** (*a*) cast out or remove with a shake or an effort (*lit. & fig.*); (*b*) cast out the contents of; empty by shaking; (*c*) unfasten or unfurl and let out with a shake; straighten out by shaking (something crumpled or folded); (*d*) remove or get rid of by means of a shake-out, *esp.* shed (personnel) as a result of reorganization. **shake together** shake so as to mix or bring closer together. **shake up** †(*a*) lift up with a shake, rattle (a chain); †(*b*) berate soundly, abuse violently; harass, afflict; (*c*) shake together for the purpose of combining or mixing; shake (a liquid) so as to stir up sediment; (*d*) loosen or restore to shape by shaking; (*e*) rouse up with or as with a shake; rouse from lethargy, apathy, etc.; (*f*) upset the feelings of, agitate, confuse.

Comb.: **shake-bag** (*obsolete* exc. *dial.*) (*a*) a gamecock brought to fight in a bag and unseen until the fight begins; a large gamecock; (*b*) a rogue, a scoundrel; **shakefork** (*a*) (*obsolete* exc. *dial.*) a fork with two tines or prongs used by threshers to shake and remove straw from the grain; a pitchfork; (*b*) HERALDRY a pall with limbs cut short and pointed; **shake-hands** an act of shaking hands with another person; **shake-rag** *noun & adjective* (*arch.*) (*a*) *noun* a ragged disreputable person; (*b*) *adjective* beggarly.

shakeable /ˈʃeɪkəb(ə)l/ *adjective.* Also **shakable**. **M19.**
[from prec. + -ABLE.]
Able to be shaken.

shake-down /ˈʃeɪkdaʊn/ *noun & adjective.* **E18.**
[from ***shake down*** s.v. SHAKE *verb*.]
▸**A** *noun.* **1** A bed made on straw loosely disposed upon the floor or ground; any makeshift bed, *esp.* one made up on the floor. **E18.**
2 An act of shaking something down. **L19.**
3 A forced contribution; (an instance of) extortion. *slang* (chiefly *US*). **E20.**
4 A search of a person or a place. *slang* (chiefly *US*). **E20.**
5 A period or process of adjustment or change. **M20.**
▸**B** *attrib.* or as *adjective.* Designating a cruise, flight, etc., designed to test a new craft and its equipment and to train its crew. **E20.**

shaken *verb pa. pple*: see SHAKE *verb.*

shake-out /ˈʃeɪkaʊt/ *noun.* **L19.**
[from ***shake out*** s.v. SHAKE *verb*.]
1 STOCK EXCHANGE. A crisis in which the weaker speculators are driven out of the market. Also, a sudden fall in prices, a sudden general disposal of particular stocks, etc. **L19.**
2 An upheaval or reorganization, *esp.* one involving contraction, streamlining, shedding of personnel, closure of some businesses, etc. **M20.**

shaker /ˈʃeɪkə/ *noun & adjective.* **LME.**
[from SHAKE *verb* + -ER[1].]
▸**A** *noun.* **1** *gen.* A person who or thing which shakes something or someone. **LME.**
2 *gen.* A person who or thing which shakes. Formerly also, a boaster, a swaggerer. **LME.**
†**3** In *pl.* Thin vibrating plates of metal as a trimming for clothes. *Scot.* **E16–E17.**
4 (**S-**.) ▸†**a** A member of a religious sect characterized by devotional exercises accompanied by shaking or convulsions. **M–L17.** ▸**b** A member of an American religious sect (named from its religious dances) living simply and in celibacy in mixed communities of men and women. **L18.**
5 A fantail pigeon. More fully ***shaker pigeon***. **M17.**
6 An implement, machine, etc., used for shaking or agitating something. **L18.** ▸**b** *spec.* A container in which cocktails or other mixed drinks are blended by shaking. **M19.**
7 A caster for salt, sugar, etc. Chiefly *N. Amer.* **E20.**
8 A simple percussion instrument that is shaken. **M20.**
1 mover and shaker (chiefly *N. Amer.*) a person who influences events, a person who gets things done.
▸**B** *attrib.* or as *adjective.* (**S-**.) Of an artefact: produced by or of a type produced by Shakers. **E19.**
■ **Shakeress** *noun* a female Shaker **M19.** **shakerful** *noun* the contents of a (cocktail) shaker, as much as a shaker will hold **M20.** **Shakerism** *noun* the principles and practices of the Shakers **E19.**

Shakespeare /ˈʃeɪkspɪə/ *noun.* Also (now *rare*) **Shakspere**. **E19.**
[See next.]
1 A person comparable to Shakespeare, esp. as being pre-eminent in a particular sphere. **E19.**
2 ***Shakespeare collar***, (*a*) = ***polo collar*** (a) s.v. POLO *noun*[1]; (*b*) a turnover collar with downward projecting points. **M19.**

Shakespearian /ʃeɪkˈspɪərɪən/ *adjective & noun.* Also **-ean**, (now *rare*) **Shaksper-**. **M18.**
[from *Shakespeare* (see below) + -IAN.]
▸**A** *adjective.* Of, pertaining to, or characteristic of the English playwright and poet William Shakespeare (1564–1616) or his works. Also = STRATFORDIAN *adjective.* **M18.**
▸**B** *noun.* An expert in or student of the works of Shakespeare; a Shakespearian scholar; an imitator of Shakespeare. Also, a person who believes that Shakespeare did write the plays generally attributed to him, = STRATFORDIAN *noun* 2. **M19.**
■ **Shakespeariˈana** *noun pl.* [-ANA] publications or other items concerning or associated with Shakespeare **E18.** **Shakespearianism** *noun* (*a*) a form of expression peculiar to or imitated from Shakespeare; (*b*) the imitation of Shakespeare, Shakespeare's influence on literature or drama: **E19.** **Shakespearianly** *adverb* in a Shakespearian manner **M19.**

shake-up /ˈʃeɪkʌp/ *noun.* **M19.**
[from ***shake up*** s.v. SHAKE *verb*.]
An act of shaking something or someone up; an instance of being shaken up; an upheaval, a drastic reorganization.

shakey *adjective* var. of SHAKY.

shakily /ˈʃeɪkɪli/ *adverb.* **M19.**
[from SHAKY *adjective* + -LY[2].]
In a shaky manner, unsteadily.

shakiness /ˈʃeɪkɪnɪs/ *noun.* **M19.**
[from SHAKY *adjective* + -NESS.]
The condition of being shaky, unsteadiness.

shaking /ˈʃeɪkɪŋ/ *noun.* **LME.**
[from SHAKE *verb* + -ING[1].]
1 The action of SHAKE *verb*; an instance of this. Also foll. by *down*, *up*, etc. **LME.**
2 That which is shaken off, out, down, etc. (also foll. by *down*, *off*, *out*). Now usu. in *pl.*, discarded things, sweepings, remainders, refuse. Now chiefly *Scot.* **LME.**
3 A disease of various animals characterized by tremor and loss of balance. Freq. in *pl.* Now *rare* or *obsolete.* **M17.**

shaking /ˈʃeɪkɪŋ/ *adjective.* **ME.**
[from SHAKE *verb* + -ING[2].]
1 That shakes. **ME.**
2 Of a disease: characterized by tremor of the head or limbs. **E16.**
1 Shaking Quaker (now *rare*) a Shaker. **2 shaking palsy** (*obsolete* exc. *Hist.*) Parkinson's disease.

shako /ˈʃeɪkəʊ, ˈʃakəʊ/ *noun.* Also (now *rare*) **chaco**. Pl. **-os**. **E19.**
[French *schako* from Hungarian *csákó* prob. from German *Zacken* peak, point, spike.]
A cylindrical military hat with a peak and a plume or pompon.

Shakspere *noun*, **Shaksperian** *adjective & noun* see SHAKESPEARE etc.

Shakti *noun* var. of SAKTI.

shaku /ˈʃakuː/ *noun.* Pl. same. **E18.**
[Japanese.]
1 A Japanese measure of length, approximately a third of a metre or a foot. **E18.**
2 A flat narrow board of wood or horn on which a Japanese court noble formerly would note memoranda, later carried as a mark of honour in the presence of the emperor, by the emperor himself, or by a Shinto priest. **L19.**

shakudo /ˈʃakuːdəʊ/ *noun & adjective.* **M19.**
[Japanese, from *shaku* red + *dō* copper.]
(Made of) a Japanese alloy of copper and gold.

shakuhachi /ʃakuːˈhaːtʃi/ *noun.* **L19.**
[Japanese, from SHAKU + *hachi* eight (tenths).]
An end-blown Japanese flute, made of bamboo.

shaky /ˈʃeɪki/ *adjective.* Also **shakey**. **E18.**
[from SHAKE *noun* or *verb* + -Y[1].]
1 Of timber: split, cracked. **E18.**
2 Given to shaking or vibrating; liable to break down or give way; unsound; unsteady; (of ground) not firm or solid. **M19.**
3 a Of a person, a person's body, limb, etc.: trembling with age, disease, nervousness, etc.; very weak. **M19.** ▸**b** Of writing: tremulous. **M19.**
4 Characterized by or causing shaking or jolting. **M19.**
5 Unreliable, insecure, liable to fail or be upset; uncertain, not to be depended on. **M19.**

2 J. TYNDALL The bridge was . . frail and shaky. R. BANKS Pop's shaky old red truck. **the Shaky Isles** *Austral. & NZ colloq.* New Zealand (from the frequency of earthquakes). **3a** A. TYLER I felt short of breath and shaky. M. ATWOOD Cordelia . . produces a cigarette. Her hand, lighting it, is shaky. **5** M. MUGGERIDGE A letter . . with no punctuation, and shaky spelling. A. THWAITE Gosse . . was often shaky on dates. E. FEINSTEIN The finances of the family were extremely shaky.

shale /ʃeɪl/ *noun*[1] *& verb.* Long *obsolete* exc. *dial.*
[Old English *scealu*: see SCALE *noun*[1]. Partly as if var. of SCALE *noun*[3]. Cf. next, SHELL *noun*.]
▸**A** *noun.* †**1** A dish; a cup, a goblet. **OE–ME.**
†**2** A weighing-scale. Only in **OE.**
†**3** A shell, a husk; the pod of peas or beans, etc. **OE–L18.**
4 A scale (of a fish, of metal, of a scaly disease, etc.). **LME.**
5 A mesh of a net. **E17.**
6 (A mass of) loose rock or soil in a mine or quarry. *dial.* **L18.**
▸**B** *verb.* **1** *verb trans.* Free from the shell or husk; remove, take *off* (the shell or husk) from a nut, bean, fruit, etc. **LME.**
2 *verb intrans.* Of grain, seed, etc.: drop out. **M17.**

shale /ʃeɪl/ *noun*[2]. **M18.**
[Prob. from German *Schale* (not used in this sense, but cf. *Schalstein* laminated limestone, *Schalgebirge* mountain system of thin strata) corresp. to Old English SHALE *noun*[1].]
Soft finely stratified rock which splits easily into fragile laminae, consisting of consolidated mud or clay; a variety of this.
bituminous shale, ***oil shale***, ***paper shale***, etc.
Comb.: **shale oil** oil obtained by distillation of bituminous shale; **shale shaker** a vibrating screen used in oil and gas drilling to remove drill cuttings from the circulating drilling mud that is passed through it.

†**shaler** *noun* see SHEILA.

shaley *adjective* var. of SHALY.

shalgram /ˈʃaːlgraːm/ *noun.* Also (earlier) **sal-**. **L18.**
[Hindi *śālgrām* formed as SALAGRAMA.]
HINDUISM. An ammonite or other fossil, sacred to Vishnu.

shall /ʃal/ *noun.* **M16.**
[from the verb.]
An utterance or use of the word shall; an instance of what is expressed by the auxiliary verb shall, a command, a promise, a determination.

shall /ʃal, *unstressed* ʃ(ə)l/ *verb.* Pres.: 1, 2, 3 sing. & pl. **shall**; 2 sing. (*arch.*) **shalt** /ʃalt/. Pa.: 1, 2, 3 sing. & pl. **should** /ʃʊd, *unstressed* ʃəd/; 2 sing. (*arch.*) **shouldst** /ʃʊdst/. Neg.: **shall not**, (*informal*) **shan't** /ʃaːnt/; **should not**, (*informal*) **shouldn't** /ˈʃʊd(ə)nt/. No other parts used.
[Old English *sceal* (pl. *sculon*) pres., *sceolde* pa. = Old Frisian *skel*, Old Saxon *skal*, Old High German *scal* (Dutch *zal*, German *soll*), Old Norse, Gothic *skal*, from Germanic preterite-present verb orig. meaning 'owe', from Indo-European.]

▶†**I** As full verb.

1 *verb trans.* = OWE *verb* 4. OE–LME.

▶ **II** The present tense *shall* as auxiliary verb. Foll. by inf. without *to* or *ellipt.*

†**2** Ought to as the right or suitable thing. OE–M16.

†**3** Must of necessity, have to. OE–LME. ▸**b** Must as a necessary condition, will have to, is to. LME–E17.

†**4** Be going to, be about to. OE–E17.

5 Must according to a command or instruction. In the 3rd person (chiefly in statutes, regulations, etc.), in the 2nd person (chiefly *biblical*), equivalent to an imper. OE.

6 In the 2nd and 3rd persons: expr. the speaker's determination to bring about (or, with neg., prevent) some action, event, or state of things in the future, or (occas.) to refrain from hindering what is otherwise certain to take place, or is intended by another person. OE.

7 In special interrog. uses related to senses 5 and 6: in the 1st person, where the expected answer is a command or direction, advice or permission, or a resolve on the speaker's own part; in the 2nd and 3rd persons, where the expected answer is a decision on the part of the speaker or of some person other than the subject. OE.

8 Forming (with present infinitive) the future, and (with perfect infinitive) the future perfect tense; in more or less definite contexts. Latterly esp. in the 1st person, *will* being more usual and less formal in the 2nd (exc. in categorical questions) and 3rd persons (in informal and unemphatic contexts *'ll* is now more usual than either); in hypothetical, relative, temporal, and final clauses used for all persons (though in final clauses where no ambiguity results *should* is now preferred, and in other contexts the present tense is commonly used for the future, and the perfect for the future perfect). OE. ▸**b** *ellipt.* Shall go. *arch.* OE.

🕮 **5** AV *Exod.* 20:13 Thou shalt not kill. **6** THACKERAY Others, whose names . . shan't . . be mentioned here. E. O'NEILL I give you my word of honour . . , you shall be paid tomorrow. **7** C. KINGSLEY Where shall we stow the mare? C. FRY Shall I knock him down? J. BRAINE Where shall we go this afternoon anyway? J. I. M. STEWART How long shall you be staying here? **8** SHAKES. *Jul. Caes.* Now do I prophesy—A curse shall light upon the limbs of men. G. CRABBE A man so learn'd you shall but seldom see. SOUTHEY I trust in God your labour shall not be in vain. LD MACAULAY Mr. Mill recommends that all males of mature age . . shall have votes. M. ARNOLD It may well happen that a man who lives and thrives under a monarchy shall yet theoretically disapprove the principle of monarchy. TENNYSON If you shall fail to understand, What England is . . On you will come the curse of all the land. A. AUSTIN When War's loud shuttle shall have woven peace. F. H. STODDARD Mankind demands that it shall show conformity. J. S. HUXLEY Those bodies which taken together appear to determine the characteristics of the offspring, . . whether it shall be tall or short, fair or dark. M. BEERBOHM One name I must and shall name. O. JESPERSEN In this book I shall use the word 'philology' in its continental sense. F. H. BURNETT You propose to suggest that she shall marry *you*? F. STARK I am afraid I shall not be well enough . . after all. A. DE SEVERSKY Either we shall continue to divide our national potential three ways . . , or we shall concentrate it. A. E. DUNCAN-JONES In order that he shall be said to make a moral judgement, his attitude must be 'universalisable'. L. P. HARTLEY I didn't expect you to proclaim it on the housetops, and I shan't either. J. GARDNER I shall personally arrange for you to be back pounding the beat.

▶ **III** The past form *should* as auxiliary verb with temporal function. Foll. by inf. without *to* or (in sense 11) *ellipt.*

†**9** Had to of necessity, was bound to. OE–LME.

†**10** Was to, was going to, was about to. OE–E17.

11 As past tense corresp. to *shall* in senses 5, 6, 8. OE.

12 In indirect reported speech, implying that the speaker does not commit himself or herself to the truth of the statement. *obsolete* exc. *dial.* OE.

13 In indirect questions relating to a past matter of fact. (Present usage prefers a past tense or, when the notion of uncertainty is emphasized, *might* or *could*.) *arch.* ME.

14 In questions introduced by *who, whom, what*, and followed by *but*: expr. the unexpectedness of some past occurrence. E17.

🕮 **11** THACKERAY Old Osborne thought she would be a great match, too, for his son. He should leave the army; he should go into Parliament. T. L. PEACOCK He had wished that the doctor should inquire into the cause of his trouble. C. THIRLWALL You had reason to expect that I should have returned the enclosed papers before now. H. JAMES If he should not come she should be annoyed, and if he should come she should be furious. *Observer* He felt it to be essential that he should maintain a proud and haughty demeanour. R. MACAULAY He did not want to go upstairs till Pamela should be asleep. **13** J. KEBLE Some . . may have wondered what this 'present distress' should mean. **14** R. GIBBINGS On the 23rd of March 1889 who should be born in Cork but myself?

▶ **IV** The past form *should* as auxiliary verb with modal function. Foll. by inf. without *to* or *ellipt.*

15 In statements of duty, obligation, or propriety (orig., as applicable to hypothetical conditions not regarded as real), and in statements of expectation, likelihood, prediction, etc.: ought to. OE.

16 In special interrog. uses. ▸**a** In questions introduced by *why* (or equivalent word), implying the speaker's inability to conceive any reason or justification for something actual or contemplated, or any ground for believing something to be fact. OE. ▸**b** In questions introduced by *how*, implying that the speaker regards something as impossible or inadmissible. ME.

17 In the apodosis of a hypothetical proposition (expressed or implied), indicating that the supposition, and therefore its consequence, is unreal. Latterly esp. in the 1st person, *would* being more usual and less formal in the 2nd (exc. in categorical questions) and 3rd persons, exc. where *should* could be interpreted as sense 15. OE.

18 In a hypothetical clause expressing a rejected supposition: were to; (formerly) were obliged to, must, were about to. ME.

19 In a noun-clause (as obj. or subj., usu. introduced by *that*). ▸**a** Dependent on expressions of will, desire, command, advice, request. ME. ▸**b** In expressions of surprise or its absence, or approval or disapproval. ME. ▸**c** In a clause (now almost always with *lest*) expressing the object of fear or precaution. LME. ▸**d** In statements relating to the necessity, justice, propriety, etc., of something contemplated as future, or as an abstract supposition. E16. ▸**e** In a clause dependent on a sentence (negative, interrogative, or hypothetical) expressing possibility, probability, or expectation. E17.

20 In a hypothetical clause relating to the future, indicating that the supposition, though entertained as possible, is viewed as less likely or less welcome than some alternative. L17.

🕮 **15** R. B. CATTELL These books vary more in thickness than they do in height—as books on a tidy shelf should. A. WESKER Oh, grow up, Ronnie. You should know that by now. E. F. SCHUMACHER Proved oil reserves should be enough for forty years. *iron.*: V. WELBURN Don't try to digest everything at once. Hell, I should talk. **16a** *Punch* Why should there be separate magazines for men and women at all? **17** BOSWELL Shall you not like to see Dublin, Sir? E. A. FREEMAN I should like to have stayed longer at Noyon. M. HASTINGS A blonde bombshell I should call her. **18** TENNYSON And no flower, not The sun himself, should he be changed to one, Could shine away the darkness of that gap. **19a** L. OLIPHANT I found it to contain a request . . that I should repair . . to the Horse Guards. A. KOESTLER I could wish that everyone who talks of mass psychology should experience a year of prison. J. I. M. STEWART All I want is that all these people should blow. **b** E. FITZGERALD Alas, that Spring should vanish with the Rose! That Youth's sweet-scented manuscript should close. **c** G. F. NEWMAN An individualist to be watched unless he should develop into too much of a lone wolf. *Sunday Times* Venting anxiety lest advertising should threaten his position. **d** TENNYSON It is time . . That old hysterical mock-disease should die. **e** C. THIRLWALL It is quite impossible that I should not at least have looked into it enough to remember having seen it.

Phrases: **as who should say** as much as to say. **I should think**, **I should suppose**, etc. (*a*) I am inclined to think, suppose, etc.; (*b*) *colloq.* as a strong affirmation in reply to a tentative suggestion. **should be** (*a*) ought according to appearances to be, presumably is; ***no better than one should be***: see BETTER *adjective*; (*b*) ought according to expectation to be, presumably will be. **you should hear**, **you should see** *colloq.* I wish you could hear or see, if only you could hear or see.

¶ Cf. WILL *verb*[1].

shallon /ˈʃalən/ *noun.* Also **shallun**. E19.
[App. rel. to SALAL.]
(The fruit of) the salal, *Gaultheria shallon*.

shalloon /ʃəˈluːn/ *noun & adjective.* M17.
[French *chalon*, formed as CHALON.]
(Made of) a twilled worsted material chiefly used for linings.

shallop /ˈʃaləp/ *noun.* Also **chaloupe** /ʃəˈluːp/, †**shalloop**. L16.
[French *chaloupe* from Dutch *sloep* SLOOP *noun*[1].]
1 *Hist.* A large heavy boat fitted with one or more masts and carrying fore-and-aft or lug sails and sometimes furnished with guns. L16.
2 A boat for use in shallow waters, a dinghy. L16.

shallot /ʃəˈlɒt/ *noun.* Also (now *rare*) **shalot**. M17.
[Aphet. formed as ESCHALOT.]
1 A small perennial variety of onion which forms clumps of small separate bulbs of similar size (formerly confused with *Allium ascalonicum*, an onion of the Near East); a bulb of this plant, esp. as used in cooking. M17.
2 The metal reed in some kinds of organ-pipes. E18.

shallow /ˈʃaləʊ/ *adjective, noun, & adverb.* LME.
[Obscurely rel. to SHOAL *adjective*.]
▶ **A** *adjective.* **1** Having little extension downward from the top, not deep. LME. ▸**b** Of the soil of agricultural land: forming only a thin stratum over rock. M18.
2 Extending only a short distance inward from the surface or edge. M16.
3 Having or showing little knowledge, learning, or insight; lacking emotional or intellectual depth; superficial, trivial. L16.
4 Of respiration: slight, not drawing much air in or out. L19.

🕮 **1** K. MANSFIELD A wide, shallow tray full of pots. R. P. JHABVALA The spring was so shallow . . I could touch . . its bed. M. MARRIN I walked up the shallow steps. **b** *fig.*: N. HERMAN Love was . . taking root despite my shallow, stony soil. **2** J. STEINBECK He looked into the shallow caves. S. J. PERELMAN The closets were too shallow for her evening gowns. **3** N. COWARD Very pretty, I suppose, in . . a shallow way. M. GARDINER She felt shallow . . in face of his amazing authenticity. **4** I. D. YALOM He began to breathe rapidly, taking short . . shallow breaths.

▶ **B** *noun.* **1** A shallow part of the sea, a lake, or river. Freq. in *pl.*, shallow water; a shallow place. L16.
2 A flat basket used by costermongers and street-hawkers. Also, a costermonger's cart. M19.

🕮 **1** T. KENEALLY No shallows; the river cut a clean bank. *fig.*: SIR W. SCOTT She sounded every deep and shallow of her daughter's soul.

▶ **C** *adverb.* To or at a slight depth. M17.

Special collocations & comb.: †**shallow-brained** *adjective* = *shallow-pated* below. **shallow end** the shallower end of a swimming pool. **shallow-fry** *verb trans.* & *intrans.* fry (food) in fat or oil which does not cover it completely. **shallow-pate** *arch.* a person having no depth of intellect or understanding. **shallow-pated** *adjective* (*arch.*) having no depth of intellect or understanding.
■ **shallowly** *adverb* L16. **shallowness** *noun* M16.

shallow /ˈʃaləʊ/ *verb.* E16.
[from the adjective.]
1 *verb trans.* Make shallow or shallower. E16.
2 *verb intrans.* Become shallow or shallower. L18.

shallun *noun* var. of SHALLON.

shalom /ʃəˈlɒm, *foreign* ʃaˈlɔm/ *interjection & noun.* L19.
[Hebrew *šālōm* peace.]
In Jewish society, used as a salutation at meeting or parting; an utterance of 'shalom'.
SHABBAT ***shalom***. ***shalom aleichem*** /aˈlexɛm/ *interjection* [Hebrew *'ălēḵem*] peace be upon you.

shalot *noun* see SHALLOT.

shalt *verb* see SHALL *verb*.

shalwar /ˈʃʌlvɑː/ *noun.* Also **-var**, **sal-**. E19.
[Persian & Urdu *šalwār*.]
sing. & in *pl.* Loose trousers worn in some South Asian countries and by some Muslims elsewhere, *esp.* those worn by women together with a kameez.
Comb.: **shalwar-kameez** a woman's outfit consisting of matching shalwar and kameez.

shaly /ˈʃeɪli/ *adjective.* Also **shaley**. L17.
[from SHALE *noun*[2] + -Y[1].]
Composed of or having a resemblance to shale.

sham /ʃam/ *noun*[1] *& adjective.* L17.
[Perh. north. var. of SHAME *noun*, *verb*. Cf. SHIM-SHAM.]
▶ **A** *noun.* †**1 a** A trick, a hoax; something contrived to delude or disappoint expectation. L17–E19. ▸**b** Trickery, hoaxing. L17–E18.
2 a A thing that is intended to be mistaken for something else, or that is not what it is pretended or appears to be; a deliberate imitation of a genuine or more costly article or substance, a counterfeit; a person who pretends or who is falsely represented to be what he or she is not. E18. ▸**b** Imposture, pretence. M19.
3 †**a** A false shirt-front; a false sleeve. Only in 18. ▸**b** = ***pillow-sham*** s.v. PILLOW *noun*. L19. ▸**c** A decorative strip of linen put under the bedclothes at the head of a bed and turned over, so as to simulate a folded-back sheet. *US*. L19.

🕮 **1a** DEFOE He . . seem'd to laugh that she should . . put such a Sham upon him. **2a** G. SANTAYANA The . . round tower is a sham, all hollow inside. R. GODDEN If I felt a sham in my white . . dress and veil nobody knew it. **b** N. KING People can see through sham.

▶ **B** *adjective.* **1** Pretended, feigned; made in deliberate imitation of a genuine or more costly article or substance; counterfeit. L17.
2 Of a person: pretending or falsely represented to be what he or she is not. L17.

🕮 **1** R. FRY No one was . . taken in by sham suede gloves. J. CHANCELLOR Borrowing from foreigners to maintain what seems to me a sham prosperity. ***sham fight***: see FIGHT *noun*. **2** DICKENS His foot upon the breast of their sham deliverer.

Special collocations & comb.: **sham-operate** *verb trans.* (BIOLOGY) perform a sham operation on (freq. as ***sham-operated*** *ppl adjective*). **sham operation** BIOLOGY an operation consisting simply of the making and closing of an incision, performed on animals of an experimental control group so that the incidental effects of the operation can be compared with those of a true operation.

sham /ʃam/ *noun*[2]. *slang.* M19.
[Abbreviation.]
Champagne. Cf. SHAMPOO *noun* 2.

sham /ʃam/ *verb*. Infl. **-mm-**. L17.
[from (the same root as) SHAM *noun*¹.]
1 *verb trans.* Trick, hoax; delude with false pretences. *obsolete* exc. *dial.* L17. ▸†**b** Bring (a person) into or out of a specified state, deprive (a person) of something, by trickery or deception. L17–M18. ▸†**c** Put or fob off (a person) with something deceptive or worthless. Also foll. by *off*. L17–M18.
†**2** *verb trans.* Attempt to pass off (something) on a person, attempt to pass off something on (a person), by deceit. Usu. foll. by *upon*. L17–M18.
†**3** *verb intrans.* Practise deception or deceit. Only in L17.
4 *verb trans.* Be or produce a deceptive imitation of; pretend to be; simulate the appearance of, (a specified state, action, etc.). L17.
5 *verb intrans.* Make false pretences; pretend; feign. Freq. with adjectival compl. L18.

1c G. LAVINGTON You have . . shammed us off with Counterfeit Coin. **4** W. GERHARDIE They would . . suspect him of shamming poverty. ***sham Abraham***: see ABRAHAM *noun* 2. **5** F. KING He . . lay totally still . . shamming dead.

■ **shammer** *noun* †(*a*) *rare* a person who tricks or hoaxes someone; (*b*) a person who simulates illness, death, etc.: L17

shama /ˈʃɑːmə/ *noun*¹. L19.
[Bengali *sāmā*, Hindi *sāmā* from Sanskrit *śyāmāka*.]
= ***jungle-rice*** s.v. JUNGLE *noun*. Also ***shama millet***.

shama /ˈʃɑːmə/ *noun*². M19.
[Hindi *śāma* from Sanskrit *śyāmā*.]
A long-tailed thrush, *Copsychus malabaricus*, usu. having black and white plumage with a rufous belly, native to forests in the Indian subcontinent and Andaman Islands, and introduced in Hawaii.

shamal /ʃəˈmɑːl/ *noun*. L17.
[Arab. *šamāl* north, north wind.]
A strong north-westerly wind blowing across the Persian Gulf.

shaman /ˈʃamən/ *noun & adjective*. L17.
[German *Schamane*, Russian *shaman* from Tungus *šaman*.]
▸ **A** *noun*. A priest among certain peoples of northern Asia, regarded as one with healing and magical powers who can influence the spirits who bring about good and evil; a healer among N. American Indians, regarded as possessing magical powers. Now also, a person regarded as having powers of spiritual guidance and healing through direct access to and influence in the spirit world. L17.
▸ **B** *attrib.* or as *adjective*. Of or pertaining to a shaman or shamanism. L18.
■ **shamaness** *noun* a female shaman M20. **shaˈmanic** *adjective* of or pertaining to a shaman or shamans; characteristic of shamanism: L19.

shamanism /ˈʃamənɪz(ə)m/ *noun*. L18.
[from prec. + -ISM.]
The traditional religion of certain peoples of northern Asia, according to which good and evil are believed to be brought about by spirits who can be influenced only by shamans; any system of religion, esp. among N. American Indians, in which shamans are recognized. Also, the beliefs and practices associated with a shaman.
■ **shamanist** *noun & adjective* (*a*) *noun* an adherent or practitioner of shamanism; (*b*) *adjective* = SHAMANISTIC: M19. **shamanistic** /-ˈnɪstɪk/ *adjective* of or pertaining to shamanism or shamanists E20. **shamanize** *verb* (*a*) *verb intrans.* perform the rituals, chants, etc., proper to a shaman; (*b*) *verb trans.* imbue with shamanist beliefs: E20.

shamash /ˈʃamaʃ/ *noun*. Pl. **-im** /-ɪm/. M17.
[Yiddish *shames*, Hebrew *šammaš* attendant, from *šimmēš* to serve.]
1 An official in a synagogue whose duties are similar to those of a sexton or caretaker. M17.
2 An extra candle used for lighting the candles at the festival of Hanukkah. M20.

shamateur /ˈʃamətə, -tjʊə/ *noun & adjective*. *derog.* L19.
[from SHAM *adjective* + AM)ATEUR *noun*.]
▸ **A** *noun*. A sportsman or sportswoman who makes money from sporting performances and appearances while officially retaining amateur status. L19.
▸ **B** *attrib.* or as *adjective*. Of or pertaining to shamateurs or shamateurism. M20.
■ **shamateurism** *noun* the characteristic practice of a shamateur E20.

shamba /ˈʃambə/ *noun*. L19.
[Kiswahili.]
In E. Africa, a cultivated plot of ground. Also, a farm, a plantation.

shamble /ˈʃamb(ə)l/ *noun*¹ & *verb*¹.
[Old English *sc(e)amul* = Old Saxon (*fōt*)*skamel*, Old High German (*fuoz*)*scamil* footstool (also Middle Dutch, Middle High German *schamel*, *schemel*, German *Schemel*), from West Germanic from Latin *scamellum* dim. of *scamnum* bench.]
▸ **A** *noun*. †**1** A stool, a footstool. Chiefly *fig.* OE–L15.
2 †**a** A table or counter for displaying goods for sale, counting money, etc. OE–ME. ▸**b** *spec.* A table or stall for the sale of meat. Usu. in *pl.* *obsolete* exc. *dial.* ME.
3 In *pl.* (treated as *sing.* or *pl.*) & †*sing.* A place, esp. a row of covered stalls, for the sale of meat or fish; a meat-market. Also *gen.*, a market, a row of shops, etc. Now chiefly in street-names and place-names. LME.
4 In *pl.* (treated as *sing.*) & (occas.) *sing.* A slaughterhouse, an abattoir. M16.
5 *transf.* & *fig.* **a** A place of carnage, a scene of wholesale slaughter. Usu. in *pl.* L16. ▸**b** In *pl.* (treated as *sing.*). A scene of disorder or devastation; a muddle, a mess. *colloq.* (orig. *US*). E20.
6 MINING. Any of a series of ledges or platforms in a mine on to which ore may be successively shovelled for raising it to the surface in convenient stages. L17.
7 In *pl.* A wooden frame used to harness a horse to a cart. Also more fully ***shamble stave***. *dial.* L17.

5a COLERIDGE His iron heart endured To make of Lyons one vast human shambles. **b** C. P. SNOW The room might be a shamble, but his desk had to be in order. P. MAILLOUX Their marriage was soon a shambles.

▸ **B** *verb trans. rare.*
1 Cut up or slaughter as in a slaughterhouse or shambles. L16.
2 Wreck, devastate, make a shambles of. Chiefly as ***shambled*** *ppl adjective*. *US*. M20.

shamble /ˈʃamb(ə)l/ *adjective*. *rare*. E17.
[Perh. orig. from SHAMBLE *noun*¹ (from a supposed or perceived resemblance between straddling legs and the trestles of a meat-vendor's table; cf. West Frisian *skammels* pl. of *skammel* board on trestles).]
Esp. of the legs: ungainly, awkward; misshapen.

shamble /ˈʃamb(ə)l/ *verb*² & *noun*². L16.
[Prob. from SHAMBLE *adjective*. Cf. SCAMBLE.]
▸ **A** *verb*. **1** *verb intrans.* Walk or move along with an awkward or shuffling gait. L16.
2 *verb trans.* Make (one's way) or move (one's feet) shamblingly. M19.

1 M. FRAYN Goldwasser . . watched Nobbs shamble back to his office.

▸ **B** *noun*. †**1** A leg. Only in ***shake your shambles***, go away, be off with you. *slang*. Only in L17.
2 A shambling gait. E19.
■ **shambling** *ppl adjective* (*a*) characterized by an awkward, ungainly gait or motion; (*b*) *transf.* & *fig.* rambling, disorganized, clumsy: L17. **shamblingly** *adverb* L19.

shambly /ˈʃambli/ *adjective*. *colloq.* M20.
[from SHAMBLE *noun*¹, *verb*² + -Y¹.]
That shambles, shambling; awkward, ungainly; ramshackle, rickety.

shambok *noun & verb* var. of SJAMBOK.

shambolic /ʃamˈbɒlɪk/ *adjective*. *colloq.* L20.
[from SHAMBLE *noun*¹ 5b, perh. after *symbolic*.]
Chaotic, disorderly; inept, mismanaged.

Observer Bring order to its shambolic economy. *Daily Telegraph* The Government's handling of the ban . . has been little short of shambolic.

shambrier /ˈʃambrɪə/ *noun*. *rare*. M17.
[French *chambrière* a long whip.]
HORSEMANSHIP. A short whip with a wide flap used in manège by an assistant on foot.

sham-damn /ˈʃamdam/ *adjective*. *rare*. M19.
[from SHAM *noun*¹ + DAMN *verb*.]
(Of scrap-iron) of an inferior kind, as used in the manufacture of gun barrels; (of a firearm) of inferior quality, shoddy.

shame /ʃeɪm/ *noun*.
[Old English *sc(e)amu* = Old Frisian *skame*, *skome*, Old Saxon, Old High German *skama* (Dutch *schaam-* in comb., German *Scham*), Old Norse *skǫmm*, from Germanic.]
1 a The feeling of humiliation or distress arising from the consciousness of something dishonourable or ridiculous in one's own or another's behaviour or circumstances, or from a situation offensive to one's own or another's sense of propriety or decency. OE. ▸**b** A feeling of this kind. *rare*. M19.
2 a Disgrace, loss of esteem or reputation; an instance of this. OE. ▸†**b** Infliction of disgrace or injury; expression of reproach in language or behaviour. Freq. in ***do a person shame*** below. ME–E17. ▸**c** *spec.* A woman's loss of chastity or a violation of her honour. Now chiefly in ***child of shame***, a child born to an unmarried woman. *arch.* ME.
3 a Without article: a fact or circumstance bringing disgrace or dishonour; the cause of reproach, disappointment, or regret. Chiefly *pred.* Long *arch.* OE. ▸**b** An instance of this; a matter for (extreme) reproach or regret. Freq. in ***a great shame***, ***what a shame!***, ***it's a shame***, etc. Now *colloq.* LME. ▸**c** A person who or thing which is a cause or source of disgrace; *colloq.* something regarded as shockingly ugly, indecent, or badly made. L16.
4 The genitals. Long *arch. rare*. OE.
5 As *interjection*. Expr. shock, reproach, disgust, etc. (freq. in ***for shame*** below); *S. Afr.* expr. sympathy or pleasure. ME.
†**6** Disgracefulness or wickedness in conduct or behaviour. ME–L17.
7 Regard for propriety or decency, esp. as imposing a restraint on behaviour; modesty, shyness. Formerly also, an instance of this. ME.

1a R. PARK A tear splashed on the table, and . . made Carrie burn with shame. **2a** *New York Review of Books* The journalist . . exposing the griefs and shames of others. **3a** SIR W. SCOTT It were shame to our profession were we to suffer it. **b** E. JOLLEY Many people . . thought it . . a shame he was not married. **7** OED I am not surprised at his request; he is quite without shame.

Phrases: **cry shame on**, **cry shame upon** express vigorous disapproval of. **dead to shame** *arch.* no longer capable of feeling shame, grown hardened to shame. †**do a person shame** inflict disgrace or injury on a person, reproach a person. **for shame** (*a*) *arch.* because one feels shame; in order to avoid shame; (*b*) a reproof to a person for not feeling or showing shame (cf. sense 5 above). **have shame** (*obsolete* exc. *poet.*) be ashamed, feel ashamed. †**in shame of** (*rare*, Shakes.) in order to put to shame. **put to shame** (*a*) bring into disgrace, bring disgrace on, esp. publicly; (*b*) outshine by virtue of superior qualities or a more praiseworthy action. **shame on you!** you should be ashamed. **take shame on oneself**, **take shame to oneself** accept blame or disgrace as merited; acknowledge that one is at fault. **think shame** (*arch.* exc. *Scot.*) be ashamed. **to one's shame** so as to cause one shame, in a way that brings one discredit. **what a shame!** how unfortunate! what a pity! **without shame** shamelessly.
Comb.: **shame culture** ANTHROPOLOGY a culture in which conformity of behaviour is maintained through the individual's fear of being shamed.
■ **shameworthy** *adjective* (*rare*) of which one ought to be ashamed E19.

shame /ʃeɪm/ *verb*.
[Old English *sc(e)amian* (corresp. immed. to Old Saxon *skamon*, Old High German *skamōn* and rel. to Old High German *skamēn*, Gothic *skaman* and Middle High German *schemen* (German *schämen*), Old Norse *skemma*), formed as prec.]
▸ **I 1** *verb intrans.* Feel shame; become or be ashamed. Foll. by *of*, *at*, *to do* (now *rare*), *that*. Now *arch.* & *dial.* OE. ▸†**b** *verb refl.* Be ashamed *of*. ME–E19.
2 *verb trans.* Make ashamed, fill with shame, cause to feel shame. In earliest use (long *rare*) *impers.* (usu. with *it*). Foll. by *to do*, *that*. OE.
3 *verb trans.* Bring disgrace on; disgrace, dishonour, esp. publicly. ME.
4 *verb trans.* Cause to feel or appear inferior in comparison, outshine by virtue of superior qualities or a more praiseworthy action, put to shame. LME.
5 *verb trans.* With adverb or adverbial phr.: ▸**a** Force (a person) to leave or retreat from a place or position through shame. *arch.* L16. ▸**b** Force or coerce (a person) to enter or leave a state, or to embark on or abandon a course of action, through shame. Freq. foll. by *into*, *out of*. L17.

1 C. BURY A folly I shamed to confess. **b** SIR W. SCOTT 'Rise . . and shame thee of thy petition', said the King. **2** C. THUBRON She . . shames me for underestimating her. **3** W. COWPER He . . prostitutes and shames His noble office. **4** W. SHENSTONE Her blushing cheeks that sham'd the purple morn. **5a** SHAKES. *1 Hen. IV* I have power to shame him hence. **b** R. BUSH Friends . . shamed him into following the life of art.

▸ **II 6** *verb trans.* Feel shame with regard to (a person or thing); dread or avoid through shame. *arch.* ME.
■ **shamedly** /ˈʃeɪmɪdli/ *adverb* (*rare*) in a shamed manner L19. **shamer** *noun* (*rare*) a person who or thing which brings shame to someone or something E17.

shameface /ˈʃeɪmfeɪs/ *noun*. *rare*. M17.
[from SHAME *noun* + FACE *noun*, after next.]
A bashful expression or appearance.

shamefaced /ʃeɪmˈfeɪst, ˈʃeɪm-/ *adjective*. M16.
[Alt. of next by assim. to FACE *noun*: see -ED².]
1 Modest; bashful, shy. M16.
2 Showing shame, abashed. L19.

1 J. MORLEY He felt shamefaced as a schoolboy before the great world. **2** D. MADDEN James came home, shamefaced at his lack of success.

■ **shamefacedly** /-feɪstli, -feɪsɪdli/ *adverb* E17. **shamefacedness** /-feɪsɪdnɪs/ *noun* M16.

shamefast /ˈʃeɪmfɑːst/ *adjective*. *arch.* OE.
[from SHAME *noun* + FAST *adjective*.]
1 Bashful, modest; characterized by or indicating modesty or bashfulness; shy. OE.
†**2** = SHAMEFACED 2. ME–M17.
†**3** Of or pertaining to the genitals. LME–M16.
■ **shamefastly** *adverb* LME. **shamefastness** *noun* (*a*) modesty, decency; bashfulness, shyness; †(*b*) a feeling of shame, ashamedness: ME.

shameful /ˈʃeɪmfʊl, -f(ə)l/ *adjective*. OE.
[from SHAME *noun* + -FUL.]
1 Modest, shamefaced. *obsolete* exc. *Scot.* OE.
2 That causes or ought to cause shame or humiliation; disgraceful, scandalous. ME.
3 Having a feeling or appearance of shame, full of shame, ashamed. Now *rare*. LME.
†**4** Of or pertaining to the genitals. Chiefly in ***shameful parts***, the genitals. LME–L17.
†**5** Of language: abusive, reproachful. Only in 16.
📖 **2** *Times* We . . consider it especially shameful that . . Pope Pius XII should be wrongly portrayed. C. EASTON Psychiatric treatment was considered a shameful secret.
■ **shamefully** *adverb* ME. **shamefulness** *noun* ME.

shameless /ˈʃeɪmlɪs/ *adjective & adverb*. OE.
[from SHAME *noun* + -LESS.]
▶ **A** *adjective*. **1** Lacking a sense of shame, devoid of feelings of modesty; characterized by or indicating absence of shame; impudent, brazen. OE.
†**2** Suffering no shame, free from disgrace. Only in ME.
📖 **1** J. R. GREEN A shameless sale of peerages. S. T. WARNER She has always been shameless about reading letters not meant for her.
▶ **B** *adverb*. In an immodest or impudent manner; shamelessly. *rare*. LME.
■ **shamelessly** *adverb* OE. **shamelessness** *noun* (*a*) the quality of lacking shame or modesty; impudence; (*b*) *rare* freedom from shame, uninhibitedness: M16.

shamiana /ʃamɪˈɑːnə, ʃɑːm-/ *noun*. Also **-myana**. E17.
[Persian & Urdu *šāmiyāna*.]
In the Indian subcontinent and some Middle Eastern countries: a kind of richly embroidered, esp. Persian, fabric, usu. of wool with silk embroidery (freq. in *pl.*); a canopy or awning made from this.

shamisen *noun* var. of SAMISEN.

shamma /ˈʃamə/ *noun*. M19.
[Amharic.]
In Ethiopia, a long loose robe resembling a toga, worn by both men and women.

Shammar /ˈʃamɑː/ *noun & adjective*. E20.
[Arab. *šammar*.]
▶ **A** *noun*. Pl. same. A member of a Bedouin people originating in the Nafud desert of Saudi Arabia. E20.
▶ **B** *attrib.* or as *adjective*. Of or pertaining to this people. E20.

shammel /ˈʃam(ə)l/ *noun & verb*. L18.
[Dial. form of SHAMBLE *noun*[1].]
MINING. ▶ **A** *noun*. = SHAMBLE *noun*[1] 6. L18.
▶ **B** *verb intrans*. Infl. **-l(l)-**. Work a mine by the use of a series of shammels. L18.

shammock /ˈʃamək/ *noun & verb*. Chiefly *dial.* E18.
[Origin unkn. Cf. SHAMBLE *verb*[2].]
▶ **A** *noun*. A lazy, slovenly person; a starved, miserable-looking person or animal. E18.
▶ **B** *verb intrans*. Walk with a shambling, awkward, or unsteady gait; slouch; dawdle; idle about. Earliest & chiefly as ***shammocking*** *ppl adjective*. E18.

shammy *noun, adjective, & verb*, **shamoy** *noun & adjective* see CHAMOIS.

shampoo /ʃamˈpuː/ *verb & noun*. M18.
[Hindi *cāṁpo* imper. of *cāṁpnā* press, knead.]
▶ **A 1** *verb trans*. Massage (a person, a person's body), esp. as a part of the process of a Turkish bath. Now *arch. rare.* M18.
2 *verb trans*. Clean with an application of shampoo or soap and water; apply shampoo or soap and water to; shampoo the hair of. M19. ▸**b** *verb intrans*. Shampoo the hair. L20.
📖 **2** E. BOWEN She had had . . her hair shampooed and re-set. P. D. JAMES The dull brown hair with the clinging specks of scurf which daily shampooing seemed only to exacerbate. **b** *Glasgow Herald* Conditioning treatment is used before you shampoo.
▶ **B** *noun*. **1** A cleansing preparation for the hair, usu. in liquid or cream form, to be rubbed into the scalp or worked into the hair; a similar cleansing agent to be applied to upholstery, carpets, etc., or to the paintwork of a car or other vehicle; the action or an act of shampooing. M18.
2 [alt. of CHAMPAGNE.] Champagne. Cf. SHAM *noun*[2]. *slang.* M20.
📖 **1** A. CHRISTIE Is it a shampoo and set, or are you having a tint? ***dry shampoo***: see DRY *adjective*.
■ **shampooer** *noun* (*a*) a person who shampoos something; (*b*) a machine for applying shampoo to a carpet: E19.

shamrock /ˈʃamrɒk/ *noun*. L16.
[Irish *seamróg* (= Gaelic *seamrag*), dim. of *seamar* clover.]
A plant with trifoliate leaves, said to have been used by St Patrick to illustrate the doctrine of the Trinity, and hence adopted as the national emblem of Ireland; a spray or leaf of this plant.
drown the shamrock *colloq.* drink, or go drinking on St Patrick's day.
Comb.: **shamrock organization** a tripartite employment structure within a company consisting of a core of essential executives and workers, backed up by a system of outside subcontractors and part-time employees.
¶ The 'shamrock' of the legend has been conjecturally identified with many different plants, esp. white clover, *Trifolium repens*, black medick, *Medicago lupulina*, and (now most commonly) the lesser yellow trefoil, *Trifolium minus*, which is the plant favoured as an emblem on St Patrick's Day.

shamus /ˈʃeɪməs/ *noun*. *US slang.* E20.
[Origin uncertain; perh. from SHAMASH or the Irish male forename *Séamus*.]
A police officer; a private detective.

shamyana *noun* var. of SHAMIANA.

shan /ʃan/ *noun*[1]. E18.
[Origin unkn.]
= SHANNY.

Shan /ʃɑːn/ *noun*[2] & *adjective*[1]. E19.
[Burmese.]
▶ **A** *noun*. Pl. same, **-s**. A member of a group of Thai peoples, inhabiting parts of Myanmar (Burma), south China, and Indo-China. Also, the Sino-Tibetan language of these peoples. E19.
▶ **B** *attrib.* or as *adjective*. Of or pertaining to the Shan or their language. E19.

shan /ʃan/ *adjective*[2]. *Scot. & north.* E18.
[Origin unkn.]
Pitiful, silly; poor, mean, shabby.

shanachie *noun* var. of SENNACHIE.

shanai *noun* var. of SHAHNAI.

Shandean /ˈʃandɪən, ʃanˈdiːən/ *adjective & noun*. M18.
[from (*Tristram*) *Shandy* (see below) + -EAN. Cf. SHANDY *adjective*.]
▶ **A** *adjective*. Of, pertaining to, or characteristic of the novel *Tristram Shandy* (1759–67), by Laurence Sterne, or the Shandy family there portrayed. M18.
📖 W. GOLDING A Shandian outrage . . a novel with a preface, a wandering middle and no end.
▶ **B** *noun*. A Shandean person. *rare*. M19.
■ **Shandyism**, **Shandeism** *noun* the style, spirit, or philosophy of the novel *Tristram Shandy* M18.

shandry /ˈʃandri/ *noun*. *dial.* E19.
[Perh. abbreviation of next.]
A light cart or open trap on springs. Also ***shandry cart***.

shandrydan /ˈʃandrɪdan/ *noun*. L18.
[Origin unkn.]
A kind of chaise with a hood (chiefly *Hist.*). Later (*joc.*), any rickety or old-fashioned vehicle.

shandy /ˈʃandi/ *noun*. L19.
[Abbreviation of SHANDYGAFF.]
A drink composed of a mixture of beer with ginger beer or lemonade.

shandy /ˈʃandi/ *adjective*. *dial.* L17.
[Origin unkn.]
Wild, boisterous. Also, empty-headed, half-crazy.

shandygaff /ˈʃandɪgaf/ *noun*. M19.
[Origin unkn. Cf. SHANDY *noun*.]
= SHANDY *noun*.

Shang /ʃaŋ/ *noun*[1] & *adjective*. M17.
[Chinese *Shāng*.]
(Designating or pertaining to) a dynasty ruling in China from the 16th to the 12th cent. BC.
¶ Also called *Yin*.

shang /ʃaŋ/ *noun*[2]. L19.
[Chinese *shǎng*.]
In China, a unit of area varying locally but equal to 15 *mou* in the north-east, and 3 or 5 *mou* in the north-west.

Shangaan /ʃaŋˈgɑːn/ *noun & adjective*. Also **-gana** /-gɑːnə/. L19.
[Bantu.]
▶ **A** *noun*. Pl. same, **-s**, **Machangana** /matʃaŋˈgɑːnə/.
1 A member of a Bantu-speaking people of southern Mozambique and adjacent parts of S. Africa (also called ***Tsonga***). Also, a member of either of two Shona peoples of Zimbabwe. L19.
2 The Bantu language of the Shangaan of southern Mozambique and S. Africa, Tsonga; the Bantu languages of the Shangaan of Zimbabwe. M20.
▶ **B** *attrib.* or as *adjective*. Of or pertaining to these peoples or their languages. E20.

†**shangan** *noun*. *Scot.* L18–E19.
[Gaelic *seangan*, perh. from *seang* slender, narrow.]
A cleft stick for putting on a dog's tail, esp. to control or frighten the animal. Cf. SHANGY *noun*.

Shangana *noun & adjective* var. of SHANGAAN.

shanghai /ʃaŋˈhʌɪ/ *noun*. In sense 2 also **shangeye**. M19.
[*Shanghai*, one of the chief seaports in China.]
1 (A bird of) a breed of large domestic fowl with long legs and feathered shanks, said to originate from Shanghai. Now *rare*. M19.
2 A catapult. *Austral. & NZ.* M19.
3 A variation of the game of darts, in which players accumulate points by aiming for the single, double, and treble of each number in succession, players failing to score on certain numbers or during any round being eliminated. Also, a winning shot or score of a single, double, and treble of a number. M20.

shanghai /ʃaŋˈhʌɪ/ *verb trans*. L19.
[formed as prec. In sense 1a from the former practice of forcibly crewing ships bound for the Orient.]
1 a Force (a person), esp. by underhand or unscrupulous means, to join a ship which is lacking a full crew. *Nautical slang* (orig. *US*). L19. ▸**b** *transf.* Transfer (a person) forcibly, abduct; coerce (a person) into doing something. *colloq.* (orig. *US Military slang*). E20. ▸**c** Eliminate (a darts player) from a game of shanghai. M20.
2 Shoot with a catapult. *Austral. & NZ.* L19.
📖 **1b** M. MARRIN I didn't . . intend to work on children's programmes but I was shanghaied.

Shanghailander /ʃaŋˈhʌɪləndə/ *noun*. E20.
[formed as SHANGHAI *noun* after *highlander*, *islander*, etc.]
A native or inhabitant of Shanghai.

Shanghainese /ʃaŋhʌɪˈniːz/ *noun & adjective*. M20.
[formed as prec. + *-n-* + -ESE, after *Chinese* etc.]
▶ **A** *noun*. Pl. same. The Chinese dialect of the Wu group spoken in Shanghai; a native or inhabitant of Shanghai. M20.
▶ **B** *attrib.* or as *adjective*. Of or pertaining to the Chinese dialect of Shanghai; of or pertaining to Shanghai, its inhabitants, their cuisine, etc. L20.

Shango /ˈʃaŋgəʊ/ *noun*. M20.
[Yoruba, the god of thunder.]
1 A religious cult originating in W. Nigeria and now chiefly practised in parts of the Caribbean. M20.
2 A spirit dance associated with this cult. M20.

Shangri-La /ʃaŋgrɪˈlɑː/ *noun*. M20.
[A Tibetan utopia set in a hidden valley in the novel *Lost Horizon* (1933) by James Hilton.]
An earthly paradise, a place of retreat from the worries of modern civilization.

shangy /ˈʃaŋi/ *noun*. *Scot. & north.* E19.
[Perh. alt. of SHANGAN.]
1 A shackle; in *pl.*, handcuffs. E19.
2 = SHANGAN. E19.

shank /ʃaŋk/ *noun*.
[Old English *sċeanca*, Low German *schanke*, Flemish *schank*, from West Germanic, rel. to Middle Low German *schenke*, Dutch *schenk* leg bone, Low German, Middle & mod. High German *Schenkel* thigh.]
1 a The part of the leg which extends from the knee to the ankle; the tibia or shin-bone. Also (now *joc.*) the leg as a whole (usu. in *pl.*). OE. ▸**b** The lower part of the foreleg of some animals; *spec.* the part of a horse's foreleg between the knee and the fetlock, corresponding to the metacarpus. Also, the tarsus of a bird; the tibia or fourth joint of the leg of an insect. OE. ▸**c** Part of an animal's leg as a cut of meat. E19.
2 A downward spur or projection of a hill; a narrow ridge which joins a hill summit to the plain. *Scot. & north.* ME.
3 In *pl.* Locks of soft or shiny hair obtained from the legs of goats, sheep, etc., dressed and used for trimming garments. *obsolete* exc. *dial.* LME.
4 The straight part, stem, or shaft of a tool, implement, etc., as (*a*) the straight part of a nail, pin, or fish-hook; the blank part of a screw; (*b*) the stem of a glass, anchor, key, spoon, tobacco-pipe, etc.; (*c*) the shaft of a tool, oar, golf club, etc., connecting the handle to the operational end; the cylindrical part of a bit by which it is held in a drill. L15. ▸**b** The stem of a plant; the stalk or pedicel of a flower, fruit, etc. Formerly (*Scot.*), the trunk of a tree. Cf. REDSHANK 3. E16. ▸†**c** The tunnel of a chimney. E16–E18. ▸**d** TYPOGRAPHY. The body of a type, the section between the shoulder and the foot. L17. ▸**e** The shaft of a pit, mine, well, etc. *Scot.* L18. ▸**f** The narrow middle section of the sole of a shoe etc. L19. ▸**g** A straight piece of metal tubing which can be fitted to a brass instrument to change its pitch. Cf. CROOK *noun* 9. L19.
5 A (knitted) stocking, the leg of a stocking (*Scot.*); in *pl.* (*US*), leggings. E16.
6 †**a** Either of the legs of a pair of compasses. Also, either of the sides or legs of a triangle (cf. LEG *noun* 13a). L16–L17. ▸**b** ARCHITECTURE. In *pl.* The plane spaces between the grooves of a Doric triglyph. E19. ▸**c** Either of the parts of a pair of scissors between the handle and the pivot. M19.
7 A part or appendage by which something is attached; a projecting lug or stud enabling an object to be held, or providing a bearing or point of attachment; *esp.* a wire loop attached to the back of a button. L17. ▸**b** The band of a ring as opp. to the setting or gemstone. L17.
8 a *ellipt.* = ***shank-painter*** s.v. PAINTER *noun*[2] 1. E18. ▸**b** A clay-lined ladle with a long handle used in a foundry to

carry molten metal from the furnace to the mould. M19. ▸**c** In full ***shank-net***. A trawl-net used in shrimping. L19. ▸**d** A line of pots attached to a rope, used to catch crabs, whelks, etc. M20.

9 The latter end or last part of something: the remainder. Chiefly in ***shank of the evening***, twilight, dusk. Now *dial. & US.* E19.

10 *GOLF.* An act of striking the ball with the heel of the club. M20.

1a Shanks's mare, **Shanks' mare**, **Shanks's pony**, **Shanks' pony** one's own legs as a means of conveyance.

Comb.: **shank-bone** the tibia (usu. of an animal); ***shank-net***: see sense 8c above; ***shank-painter***: see PAINTER *noun*² 1; †**shank-pillion** (*rare*, Spenser) a pommel.

shank /ʃaŋk/ *verb.* E18.

[from prec.]

1 *verb trans.* Sink or bore (a shaft). *Scot.* E18.

2 a *verb intrans. & trans.* (with *it*). Walk, travel on foot. *Scot. & dial.* L18. ▸**b** *verb trans. & refl.* Cause to walk off, march (a person) off; take oneself *away*. Freq. foll. by *off*. *Scot.* E19.

3 *verb intrans.* Knit stockings. *Scot.* E19.

4 *verb intrans.* Of a plant or fruit: decay at the stem or stalk; be affected with shanking. Usu. foll. by *off*. M19.

5 *verb trans. GOLF.* Strike (the ball) with the heel of the club. E20.

shanked /ʃaŋkt/ *adjective.* L16.

[from SHANK *noun, verb*: see -ED², -ED¹.]

1 Provided with or having a shank or shanks. L16.

2 *BOTANY.* Of a plant or fruit: affected with shanking. L19.

shanker /ˈʃaŋkə/ *noun.* E17.

[from SHANK *noun, verb*: see -ER¹.]

†**1** A shank-bone. *rare.* Only in E17.

2 A person who knits stockings. *Scot.* M17.

3 A person who makes the shanks of nails, buttons, etc. L19.

4 A person who sinks or bores shafts for a mine, pit, well, etc. *Scot.* L19.

shanking /ˈʃaŋkɪŋ/ *noun.* L17.

[from SHANK *noun, verb*: see -ING¹.]

1 Orig., the process of making a shank for a tobacco-pipe. Later, the action or process of SHANK *verb*, an instance of this. L17.

2 *BOTANY.* Any of several diseases resulting in the darkening and shrivelling of a plant or fruit from the base of a stem or stalk. M19.

¶ Rare before 19.

Shannon /ˈʃanən/ *noun.* M20.

[C. E. *Shannon* (1916–2001), US mathematician.]

Used *attrib.* and in *possess.* to designate various concepts arising from Shannon's work in information theory.

Shannon's theorem, **Shannon's second theorem**, **Shannon's capacity theorem** a theorem regarding the ability of a noisy channel to carry information with no more than an arbitrarily small frequency of errors.

shanny /ˈʃani/ *noun.* M19.

[Origin unkn. Cf. SHAN *noun*¹.]

A European blenny, *Blennius pholis*, of the intertidal zone. Also (with specifying word), any of several N. American pricklebacks.

shant /ʃant/ *noun. slang.* M19.

[Origin unkn.]

A quart, a mug; such a vessel and its contents; *gen.* a drink, *esp.* an alcoholic one.

shan't /ʃɑːnt/ *noun. colloq.* M19.

[from *shan't*: see SHALL *verb*.]

An utterance of 'shan't'; a refusal to do something.

shan't *verb* see SHALL *verb*.

shanti /ˈʃɑːnti/ *interjection & noun.* L19.

[Sanskrit *śānti* peace, tranquillity.]

HINDUISM. (A prayer for) peace; peace be with you (usu. repeated three times at the end of an Upanishad for the peace of the soul).

shantung /ʃanˈtʌŋ/ *noun & adjective.* L19.

[*Shantung* a province of NE China where the silk was originally manufactured.]

(Made of) a soft undressed Chinese silk (formerly undyed, now available in any colour).

shanty /ˈʃanti/ *noun*¹ *& verb.* E19.

[Perh. from Canad. French *chantier* a lumberjack's log cabin or logging camp.]

▸ **A** *noun.* **1 a** A temporary, poor, or roughly built dwelling; a cabin, a hut. Chiefly *N. Amer.* E19. ▸**b** A lumberjack's log cabin; a logging camp. Chiefly *N. Amer.* E19.

2 A public house, *esp.* an illicit or unlicensed one. *Austral. & NZ.* M19.

> 🕮 **1a** R. CAMPBELL One tin shanty of a so-called 'Hotel'.

Comb.: **shanty Irish** *adjective & noun* (*US, derog.*) (**a**) *adjective* of or belonging to people of Irish descent in poor circumstances; (**b**) *noun* shanty Irish people collectively; **shantyman** (chiefly *N. Amer.*) a lumberjack; **shanty town** a poor or depressed area of a city or town, consisting of shanties.

▸ **B** *verb intrans.* **1** Live in a shanty or temporary log hut. Chiefly *N. Amer.* E19.

2 Drink frequently or habitually at a shanty or public house. *Austral.* L19.

shanty /ˈʃanti/ *noun*². Also **ch-** /tʃ-/. M19.

[Prob. repr. French *chantez* imper. of *chanter* sing.]

A song, usu. with a pronounced rhythm and consisting of an alternating solo and chorus, orig. sung by sailors whilst hauling ropes etc. Also ***sea shanty***.

shanty /ˈʃanti/ *adjective. obsolete* exc. *dial.* L17.

[from French *gentil*: see GENTEEL, JAUNTY *adjective*.]

Showy, smart.

Shaoshing /ʃaʊˈʃɪŋ/ *noun & adjective.* M20.

[*Shaoxing*, a town in the Zhejiang province of China.]

(Designating) a rice wine produced in Shaoxing.

shapable /ˈʃeɪpəb(ə)l/ *adjective.* Also **shapeable**. M17.

[from SHAPE *noun, verb* + -ABLE.]

1 Able to be shaped, plastic. M17.

2 Well-formed, characterized by shapeliness. *rare.* E18.

shape /ʃeɪp/ *noun*¹.

[Old English *ġesċeap* corresp. to Old Saxon *giskapu* (pl.) creatures, Old Norse *skap* condition, (pl.) fate, from Germanic base. In later senses directly from the verb.]

▸ **I 1** †**a** Creation, the created universe; something created, a creature. OE–LME. ▸**b** An imaginary or ghostly form; a phantom. Now *rare.* L16. ▸**c** A person or thing seen indistinctly or uncertainly. M19.

2 a External form or contour; the total effect produced by the outline of an object, geometrical figure, etc.; a configuration; a particular instance of this. OE. ▸**b** An impressed mark, a representation; a picture, an image. *obsolete* exc. *dial.* LME.

3 a The outward appearance of a human or animal body; a person's figure; the visible form characteristic of or assumed by a particular person or thing. OE. ▸†**b** Excellence of form; beauty. LME–M16.

†**4** The make or cut of a garment. Only in ME.

†**5** The manner in which a thing is fashioned or made; arrangement of parts; form, order, and arrangement of words. ME–L17.

6 Assumed appearance, guise, disguise. L16.

7 A posture or attitude in equestrianism, dancing, etc. *obsolete* exc. *Scot.* L16.

8 Orig., a part or character in a play; the appropriate make-up and costume for a particular part. Later, a stage outfit or costume. E17.

9 Any of the various forms, ways, or diversities of appearance, structure, etc., in which a thing may exist or present itself. Freq. in ***in any shape or form***, ***in no shape or form*** below. M17.

10 Definite, regular, or proper form; orderly arrangement. Freq. in ***take shape***, ***put into shape*** etc. below. M17.

11 a A mould for forming jelly, blancmange, etc., into a decorative shape; a jelly, blancmange, etc., shaped in a mould. M18. ▸**b** A portion of material cut or moulded to a particular shape; *spec.* a piece of rolled or drawn metal of uniform cross-section, esp. other than round, oval, square, rectangular, or hexagonal; a section. M19. ▸**c** The body of a bonnet, hat, etc., previous to trimming. L19. ▸**d** In *pl.* In gambling: dice with certain faces which have been bevelled so that they are more likely to fall in a particular way. *US slang.* E20. ▸**e** *BRIDGE.* The distribution of suits in a hand of cards. M20.

12 Condition; state of health, repair, or fitness. Freq. with specifying word. Orig. *US.* M19.

> 🕮 **1c** J. G. WHITTIER He hears quick footsteps—a shape flits by. **2a** J. TROLLOPE Martin was . . using his hands to make a box shape in the air. *Japan Times* The . . explosive . . can be molded into any shape. **3a** TENNYSON Temper'd with the tears Of angels to the perfect shape of man. **6** MILTON The . . Serpent in whose shape Man I deceav'd. **9** R. L. STEVENSON One question in modern . . politics . . appears in many shapes. **10** R. W. CHURCH He . . beat out his thoughts into shape in talking. **12** P. DALLY Her mother was in no better shape, with . . neuralgia. *International Business Week* Telecommunications systems of Eastern Europe are in bad shape.

▸†**II 13** What is decreed or destined. OE–LME.

▸ **III 14** The sexual organs, now *spec.* of a female. Long *dial.* OE.

Phrases: **in all shapes and sizes** in a great variety of forms. **in any shape or form** in any manner, at all. **in no shape or form** in no manner, not at all. **in the shape of** (**a**) represented by, embodied in the person of; (**b**) in the way of, of the nature of; (**c**) in the form of, existing or presenting itself as. **keep in shape** (**a**) preserve from change of form; (**b**) (of a person) stay fit and in good physical condition. ***lick into shape***: see LICK *verb*. **out of shape** (**a**) deformed, bent; changed from its proper shape; (**b**) (of a person) unfit; in poor physical condition. **put into shape** give a definite or orderly form to; arrange in an orderly manner. **shape of things to come** the way in which future events etc. will develop; *the* form the future will take. **take shape** acquire, or be given, a definite or ordered form. ***whip into shape***: see WHIP *verb*.

Comb.: **shape-changer** a being capable by supernatural or magical means of assuming different forms or embodiments; **shape-changing** *adjective & noun* (**a**) *adjective* (of a being with supernatural or magical powers) capable of assuming different forms or embodiments; (**b**) *noun* the supernatural or magical ability to assume different forms or embodiments; **shape elastic** *adjective* (*PHYSICS*) pertaining to or designating a component of the scattering cross-section of an atomic nucleus that is regarded as independent of the formation of a compound nucleus; **shape factor** *PHYSICS* an algebraic factor in the expression predicting the profile of a spectral line; **shape memory** a property exhibited by certain alloys of recovering their initial shape when they are heated after having been plastically deformed (also called *marmem*); **shape-note** (chiefly *US*) any of a series of notes having heads of different shapes, used to represent the degrees of a scale; **shape-shifter** (chiefly in mythology and science fiction) a person or being with the ability to change their physical form at will.

■ **shapeful** *adjective* (*arch.*) shapely E17.

SHAPE /ʃeɪp/ *noun*². M20.

[Acronym, from Supreme Headquarters Allied Powers in Europe.]

An organization established in 1951 by the NATO Council embodying a structure of command for the defence of western Europe.

shape /ʃeɪp/ *verb.* Pa. t. & pple **shaped** /ʃeɪpt/, (*arch.*) **shapen** /ˈʃeɪp(ə)n/.

[Old English *sċeppan* (pa. t. *sċōp*, pa. pple *sċapen*) corresp. to Old Frisian *skeppa*, Gothic *gaskapjan* create. In early Middle English a new formation on the pa. pple. Cf. SCOOP *noun*.]

▸ **I 1** *verb trans.* Create; later (of God, or nature personified), form, fashion. Long *arch. rare.* OE. ▸**b** Be naturally suited for or likely to do something. Only as pa. pple. LME–E16.

2 *verb trans.* Fashion, mould, or carve in a definite shape; form *out of*. OE. ▸**b** Frame, produce, (a sound, a mental image, a person's opinion, etc.). ME.

3 *verb trans.* In *pass.* Have a certain shape. OE.

4 *verb trans.* Cut out (cloth), make (a garment). *obsolete* exc. *Scot.* ME.

5 *verb trans.* Fashion an image of, depict, portray. *obsolete* exc. in ***shape forth*** below. ME.

†**6** *verb trans.* Cause, bring about. ME–M19.

†**7** *verb trans.* Transform or turn *into*, *to*; cause to assume an uncharacteristic shape or appearance. ME–M17.

8 a *verb trans.* Give a definite structure to; put into a certain form, embody in words; *refl.* assume a definite form or structure; develop from a disorganized state or form *into* a more coherent one. ME. ▸**b** *verb intrans.* Assume a definite or coherent shape; develop. Freq. foll. by *up*. M19.

9 *verb trans.* Adapt to a particular shape; make (a thing) fit the shape of. Freq. foll. by *to*. LME.

10 *verb trans.* Give a direction and character to (one's life, conduct, etc.). E19.

> 🕮 **1** AV *Ps.* 51:5 I was shapen in iniquitie. **2** J. HAWKES Men shaping stone into rectangular forms. **b** B. BETTELHEIM Early experiences . . shaping our views of the world. **3** R. L. Fox Egyptian society . . was as rigidly shaped as . . its pyramids. **7** T. GAGE From a rich . . Merchant did it shape him to a Courtier. **8a** M. LEITCH Trying to shape his features into an expression of . . anger. **b** R. MACAULAY They would . . want to know . . how our football teams were shaping. **9** S. KINNS The sarcophagus is slightly shaped to the body. **10** L. NKOSI Opportunities for shaping my own . . destiny.

▸ **II** †**11** *verb trans.* Of God, fate, fortune, etc.: destine, decree. OE–M16.

†**12** *verb trans.* Give (a name) to a person or thing. OE–M16.

†**13** *verb trans.* Deliver (a judgement); condemn (a person) to punishment. Only in ME.

▸ **III 14** *verb trans.* Take measures for, contrive, endeavour to bring about. Freq. foll. by *to do*. *obsolete* exc. *Scot. & north.* OE.

15 *verb trans.* Direct the course of, direct (one's way) to; send (a person) away. *obsolete* exc. *Scot. & dial.* ME.

16 *verb trans.* Direct, address (speech). *obsolete* exc. in ***shape an answer*** below. ME.

†**17** *verb intrans.* **a** Turn out, take a course; bear in a certain direction. ME–M18. ▸**b** Be conducive, tend. *rare* (Shakes.). Only in E17.

18 *verb trans.* Devise (a plan, a solution). LME.

†**19** *verb refl.* Set oneself, prepare. Foll. by *to do*, *for*. LME–L16.

20 *verb intrans.* Show promise; give signs of future progress or development. Orig. *Scot.* M18.

21 *verb intrans.* **a** Of a boxer: adopt a fighting stance. Freq. foll. by *out*, *up*. M19. ▸**b** In *CRICKET* (of a batsman), adopt the correct stance for receiving a particular kind of delivery from the bowler; in *GOLF*, adopt the correct stance to play a shot. L19.

> 🕮 **20** *Times* Bishah shaped like a certain future winner. **21b** *Times* Caught at leg-slip as he shaped to glance.

Phrases: **shape an answer** *arch.* answer a person's questioning etc.; form or prepare a reply to a person. **shape forth** *arch.* picture, describe; give an outline of. **shape one's course** *NAUTICAL* steer *for*, *to* a place; *transf. & fig.* go or direct oneself in a particular direction; plan a course of action. **shape out** mould or form by giving shape to material. **shape up** (chiefly *colloq.*) meet a required standard; show one's capabilities; reach a good physical condition; ***shape up well***, be promising; ***shape up or ship out*** (*slang*, orig. *US MILITARY*) achieve a satisfactory performance or face the threat of transference or dismissal (freq. in *imper.*); see also senses 8b, 21a above.

shapeable *adjective* var. of SHAPABLE.

shaped /ʃeɪpt/ *adjective*. M16.
[from SHAPE *noun*, *verb*: see -ED^{2}, -ED^{1}.]
1 That has been shaped; formed, fashioned, etc. M16.
2 Having a shape of a specified kind. Freq. as 2nd elem. of comb. L16.
1 shaped charge an explosive charge having a cavity which causes the blast to be concentrated into a small area. **2 *heart-shaped***, ***kidney-shaped***, ***lyre-shaped***, ***oyster-shaped***, ***S-shaped***, ***U-shaped***, etc.

shapeless /ˈʃeɪplɪs/ *adjective*. ME.
[from SHAPE *noun*^{1} + -LESS.]
1 Lacking shape or form; having no definite shape. ME.
2 Lacking in beauty or elegance of form, unshapely. LME.
3 Without guidance or direction, aimless. *rare*. L16.
■ **shapelessness** *noun* L16.

shapely /ˈʃeɪpli/ *adjective*. LME.
[from SHAPE *noun*^{1} + -LY^{1}.]
†**1** Fit, likely, suitable. Only in LME.
2 Of attractive or elegant shape; well-formed, well-proportioned. LME. ▸**b** Having definite form. *rare*. E19.

> 📖 **2** K. VONNEGUT She was also much shapelier than my mother, who let herself become quite heavy.

■ **shapeliness** *noun* LME.

shapen /ˈʃeɪp(ə)n/ *ppl adjective*. *arch*. ME.
[pa. pple of SHAPE *verb*: see -EN^{6}.]
1 Having a shape of a specified kind. *obsolete* exc. in ***well-shapen*** below. ME.
2 Provided with a definite shape; fashioned, shaped. L15.
1 well-shapen well-formed, shapely.

shapen /ˈʃeɪp(ə)n/ *verb*^{1} *trans*. *rare*. M16.
[from SHAPE *noun*^{1} + -EN^{5}. Cf. earlier MISSHAPEN *verb*.]
Shape, impart a shape to.

shapen *verb*^{2} *pa. t. & pple*: see SHAPE *verb*.

shaper /ˈʃeɪpə/ *noun*. ME.
[from SHAPE *verb* + -ER^{1}.]
1 God; the creator or maker of the universe. Long *rare*. ME.
2 A person who or thing which makes something to a required shape or form; a person who forms or fashions something. ME.
3 A poet. Now *arch*. *rare*. E19.
4 *ELECTRONICS*. A device which modifies an input to produce an output having a specific waveform. M20.

> 📖 **2** B. BETTELHEIM Freud . . was the shaper of modern man's thought about man.

shape-up /ˈʃeɪpʌp/ *noun*. *US*. M20.
[from ***shape up*** s.v. SHAPE *verb*.]
1 The action or an act of shaping up. M20.
2 Chiefly *Hist*. A system of hiring dock workers for the day or half-day by arbitrary selection from a gathering of men on site. M20.

> 📖 **1** *attrib.*: *Time* As the Central Intelligence Agency became mired in inefficiency, Schlesinger was tapped for the shape-up operation.

shaping /ˈʃeɪpɪŋ/ *noun*. ME.
[from SHAPE *verb* + -ING^{1}.]
1 The action of SHAPE *verb*; an instance of this; *spec*. (***a***) *ELECTRONICS* the process of modifying the waveform of an electrical signal; (***b***) *RADAR* modification of a radar beam to obtain a desired spatial configuration. ME.
2 A shaped, fashioned, or created thing; a creature, a form, a shape; a figment of the imagination. ME.
3 In *pl*. Offcuts of material. *Scot*. E19.
Comb.: **shaping knife** (*obsolete* exc. *Hist.*) a shoemakers' knife used for cutting blocks of wood to fit the shape of the foot.

shapka /ˈʃapkə/ *noun*. E20.
[Russian = hat.]
A brimless Russian hat of fur or sheepskin.

shapoo /ˈʃɑːpuː/ *noun*. M19.
[Tibetan *sha-pho* wild sheep.]
In Tibet and Ladakh, the urial, *Ovis vignei*.

sharara /ʃʌˈrɑːrə/ *noun*. L20.
[Urdu.]
A pair of loose pleated trousers worn by women from the Indian subcontinent, typically with a kameez and dupatta.

Shararat *noun & adjective* var. of SHERARAT.

sharashka /ʃaˈraʃkə/ *noun*. *Hist*. M20.
[Russian.]
In the USSR, a prison camp for scientists and other specialists in which prisoners were engaged in specialist scientific research rather than manual labour.

sharav /ʃaˈrav/ *noun*. M20.
[Hebrew *šārāḇ* parching heat.]
A hot desert wind occurring in the Middle East in March, April, and May; = KHAMSIN.

Sharawaggi /ʃarəˈwadʒi/ *noun*. L17.
[Origin unkn.]
Variety, asymmetry or irregularity of an aesthetically pleasing nature, esp. with regard to landscape gardening and architecture.
¶ Not recorded between L18 and M20.

shard /ʃɑːd/ *noun*^{1} & *verb*. Also **sherd** /ʃəːd/.
[Old English *sceard* corresp. to Old Frisian *skerd* cut, notch, Middle Low German *skart* crack, chink, Middle Dutch *scarde*, *schart* flaw, fragment (Dutch *schaard*), Middle & mod. High German *scharte*, Old Norse *skarðr* notch, gap, from Germanic base also cf. SHEAR *verb*. Cf. SCARTH *noun*^{1}.]
▶**A** *noun*. **I 1** A gap in an enclosure, esp. in a hedge or bank. Also (*rare*), a notch in the blade of a tool. Now *dial*. OE. ▸†**b** An intervening stretch of water. *rare* (Spenser). Only in L16.
▶**II 2 a** A piece of broken pottery etc.; *spec*. = POTSHERD. OE. ▸**b** *transf. & fig*. A fragment, esp. of something brittle; a sliver; *Scot*. a worn or decayed remnant of something. M16.
†**3** A scale of a reptile. *rare*. Only in LME.

> 📖 **2b** U. LE GUIN Shards of splintered bone stuck out like toothpicks. J. UPDIKE Their . . shattered name, a shard of grandeur.

▶**B** *verb*. *rare*.
1 *verb trans. & intrans*. Break or become broken into fragments or slivers. L16.
2 *verb trans*. Notch the blade of (a tool). *dial*. M18.

shard /ʃɑːd/ *noun*^{2}. M16.
[App. alt. of SHARN. Sense 2 perh. rel. to SHARD *noun*^{1}.]
1 Cow-dung; a patch of this. Now *arch. & dial*. M16.
2 An elytron or wing-case of a beetle. *dial. & literary*. E19.
Comb.: **shard-beetle** *arch*. a dor-beetle; **shard-born** *adjective* (*arch.*) (of a beetle) hatched or found in dung; ***shard-born beetle***, a dor-beetle; **shard-borne** *adjective* (*arch.*) carried or supported on elytra or wings.
¶ Sense 2 may be repr. earlier in *shard-born(e)*, *sharded*, and *shards* in Shakes., the interpretation of which is disputed.
■ **sharded** *adjective* (*rare*) (***a***) (of a beetle) living in dung; (***b***) having elytra or wings: E17.

shard *noun*^{3} var. of CHARD.

Shardana /ʃɑːˈdɑːnə/ *noun pl*. Also **Sherden** /ˈʃəːd(ə)n/. L19.
[Egyptian *Šrdn*.]
One of the Peoples of the Sea, tentatively identified with the later Sardinians, who fought against the Egyptians in the 13th cent. BC and afterwards served them as mercenaries.

share /ʃɛː/ *noun*^{1}.
[Old English *scær*, *scear* corresp. to Old Frisian *sker*, Middle Low German *schar(e*, Old High German *scar*, *scaro* (German *Schar*), from West Germanic, from base also of SHEAR *verb*. Cf. next.]
1 = PLOUGHSHARE. OE.
2 A similar blade on a seed-drill, or other agricultural implement. M18.
Comb.: **share-beam** *Hist*. the wooden beam carrying the share in a plough of an early type.

share /ʃɛː/ *noun*^{2}.
[Old English *scearu* corresp. to Old Saxon *scara* feudal service, troop, Middle Low German *schare* troop, share, Old High German *scara* troop, share of forced labour (Dutch *schare*, German *Schar* troop, multitude), Old Norse *skari*, from Germanic, from base also of SHEAR *verb*. Cf. prec.]
▶**I** †**1** The action or an act of cutting or shearing. Only in OE.
†**2** The fork of the human body; the pubic region, the groin. Long only in ***share-bone*** = PUBIS 1. *arch*. OE.
▶**II 3** A division, a section; a part, a piece, a portion, esp. of land; any of several parts into which something is or may be divided. (Earliest as 2nd elem. of comb.) Long *obsolete* exc. *dial*. OE. ▸†**b** A piece cut out or shorn away. *rare*. L16–E18.
4 a A part or portion which a person receives from or contributes to a jointly owned or larger amount. Formerly also *spec*., a duty levied on fishing boats; a portion of booty or prize-money received by a ship's crew. LME. ▸**b** A part or portion which a person is entitled to have; a person's allotted amount, due, or full measure of a quality, condition, or common experience. M17.
5 A part taken *in* something. Chiefly in ***have a share in***, ***take a share in*** below. L16.
6 *COMMERCE*. Part-proprietorship of property held by joint owners; *esp*. any of the equal parts into which a company's capital is divided entitling the shareholder to a proportion of the company's profits. E17.

> 📖 **4a** M. WESLEY I have brought . . your share of money for the things you gave . . for my stall. *Maclean's Magazine* What share the republic would assume of the Soviet Union's . . budget deficit. **b** SIR W. SCOTT That . . agility of which he possessed an uncommon share. L. M. MONTGOMERY We can't get through this world without our share of trouble. **5** LD MACAULAY Having borne a principal share in the emancipation of the press. **6** attrib.: ***share capital***, ***share certificate***, ***share index***, ***share price***, etc.

Phrases: ***deferred share***: see DEFER *verb*^{1} 2. **fall to one's share** (***a***) be assigned as one's portion; (***b***) fall to one's lot. **for my share** (now *rare*) = ***for my part*** s.v. PART *noun*. **go shares with** enjoy a part *in*, participate *in*, contribute towards (a possession, an enterprise, etc.) with another or others. **have a share in** have a part in, participate in. **on shares** (chiefly *US*) a system whereby two or more people participate in the risks and profits of a venture (chiefly in ***go on shares (with)***, ***work on shares***). ***ordinary share***: see ORDINARY *adjective* 5b. *PREFERENCE* ***share***. **share and share alike** with equal amounts, each having an equal portion. **take a share in** take a part in, participate in. ***the lion's share***: see LION *noun*.
Comb.: ***share-bone***: see sense 2 above; **share economy** a system of economic organization in which employees receive a share of their company's profits as a regular element of their pay (cf. ***wage economy*** s.v. WAGE *noun*); **share-farmer** (chiefly *Austral.*) a tenant farmer receiving an agreed portion of the farm's profits from the landowner in exchange for cultivating the land; **share-farming** (chiefly *Austral.*) the system of tenant farmers receiving an agreed portion of farm profits from landowners in exchange for cultivating the land; **shareman** *N. Amer*. a fisherman who shares in the profits of a fishing voyage with the shipowner in lieu of wages; **share-milker** *NZ* a person who works on a dairy farm in return for an agreed portion of the farm's profits; **share-milking** *NZ* the system of workers on a dairy farm providing their labour in return for an agreed portion of the farm's profits; **share option** a benefit given by a company to an employee, in the form of an option to buy shares in the company at a discount or at a stated fixed price; **share premium** *FINANCE* the amount by which the income received by a company for a stock issue exceeds the face value of the stock; **share-pusher** *colloq*. a person who attempts to sell shares to the public by advertisement instead of via the stock market; **share-pushing** the practice of selling shares to the public by advertisement instead of via the stock market; the selling of shares at what may be an inflated price; **share shop** a place (usu. within a bank or department store) in which members of the public can receive investment advice, or buy and sell shares without needing to conduct such transactions via a stockbroker; **sharesman** = ***shareman*** above; **share tenant** *US* a tenant farmer providing his or her own equipment etc. and paying a fixed percentage of the crop value as rent (cf. SHARECROPPER).

†**share** *verb*^{1} *trans*. M16–M18.
[Var. of SHEAR *verb*.]
Cut into parts; cut off. Also with adverb or adverbial phr.
¶ An E16 use of *share* in Skelton may represent this or SHARE *verb*^{2}.

share /ʃɛː/ *verb*^{2}. L16.
[from SHARE *noun*^{2}.]
1 *verb trans*. **a** Divide and distribute in portions amongst a number of recipients; divide up between oneself and another or others; (of a number of people) take or have portions of (a thing), divide up (something) amongst themselves. Now usu. foll. by *out*. L16. ▸**b** Give to (a person) as a due share. Also foll. by *out*. *arch*. L16. ▸**c** Give away part of. Freq. foll. by *with*. L16. ▸**d** Divide *into* parts or sections. *rare*. L16.
2 *verb trans*. **a** Receive, possess, use, or occupy jointly with others. Formerly also (*poet.*), receive or possess (an allotted portion). L16. ▸**b** *CHEMISTRY*. Of an atom, orbital, etc.: hold (one or more electrons) in common with another atom or orbital, so as to form a covalent bond. Freq. as ***shared*** *ppl adjective*. E20.
3 *verb trans*. Participate in (an activity, opinion, feeling, etc.); experience in common with others; possess (a quality) in common with others. L16.
4 *verb intrans*. Have a share; participate *in*; (*rare*) participate *with* (a person) *in* something. L16. ▸†**b** Be equal with. *rare* (Shakes.). Only in E17.
5 *verb trans*. Give another or others a share in or of (something). Also foll. by *with*. M17.
6 *verb intrans. & trans*. *spec*. Of a member of the Oxford Group Movement: confess (one's sins) openly; declare or relate (one's spiritual experiences) to others in a group. Also foll. by *with*. M20.

> 📖 **1a** *Household Words* Part of this money shall be shared among us. R. P. GRAVES Edward . . had failed to share out . . £1,000 which Thomas had left to be divided. **c** C. BEATON When you give a dog a bone he does not . . share it. **2a** E. SEGAL If we were . . in Boston we could share an apartment. *Listener* First-time users will get . . injections through shared needles. **3** F. WELDON Boys and girls . . shared lessons. D. M. THOMAS We . . shared a sense of the ridiculous. **4** L. STEFFENS Foreign corporations came into the city to share in its despoliation. **5** D. HALBERSTAM General Otis was not a man to share power.

Phrases: **share and share (alike)** make an equal division; have or receive an equal share. **shared ownership** a system by which the occupier of a dwelling buys a proportion of the property, and pays rent on the remainder, typically to a local authority or housing association. †**share from** *rare* (Shakes.) gain at the expense of.

Comb.: **share-out** the action or an act of distributing in shares; that which is distributed; a portion or share of profits, interest, etc.; **shareware** COMPUTING software available free of charge, and often distributed informally for evaluation, after which a fee is requested for continued use.

¶ See note s.v. SHARE *verb*[1].

▪ **sharea'bility** *noun* ability to be shared M20. **shareable** *adjective* able to be shared E20. **sharedness** *noun* the quality or fact of being shared; the quality or fact of experiencing or using in common: M20.

sharecrop /ˈʃɛːkrɒp/ *noun & verb*. Chiefly *US*. E20.
[from SHARE *noun*[2] + CROP *verb*.]
▶ **A** *noun*. A crop grown by a sharecropper. E20.
▶ **B** *verb*. Infl. **-pp-**.
1 *verb intrans*. Be a sharecropper. M20.
2 *verb trans*. Grow (a crop) according to a sharecropping system. M20.

sharecropper /ˈʃɛːkrɒpə/ *noun*. Chiefly *US*. E20.
[formed as prec. + -ER[1].]
A tenant farmer paying a large percentage of the crop value as rent after being provided with all his or her equipment etc. by a landowner.

shareef *noun* var. of SHARIF.

shareholder /ˈʃɛːhəʊldə/ *noun*. L18.
[from SHARE *noun*[2] + HOLDER *noun*[1].]
A person who owns or holds a share or shares in a company, or other jointly owned property.
▪ **shareholding** *noun* the possession of shares; in *pl*., the shares held by a person in various undertakings: E20.

sharer /ˈʃɛːrə/ *noun*. L16.
[from SHARE *verb*[2] + -ER[1].]
†**1** A shareholder, a person who owns a share or shares in a joint concern; *spec*. a member of a company of actors who paid the expenses, received the profits, and hired other members of the company. L16–E19.
2 A person who shares something or *in* something. E17.

Sharia /ʃəˈriːə/ *noun*. Also **-iah**. M19.
[Arab. *šarīʿa*.]
The Islamic code of religious law, based on the teachings of the Koran and the traditional sayings of Muhammad.

sharif /ʃəˈriːf/ *noun*. Also **shareef**, **shereef**, **sherif**. L16.
[Arab. *šarīf* noble, high-born.]
1 A descendant of Muhammad through his daughter Fatima. L16.
2 (Freq. **S-**.) (The title of) any of various Arab rulers, magistrates, or religious leaders; *spec*. (*a*) the ruler of Morocco; (*b*) the governor of Mecca. E17.
▪ **sharifate** *noun* the office of sharif E20. **sharifial** *adjective* = SHARIFIAN *adjective* E20. **sharifian** *adjective & noun* (*a*) *adjective* of, pertaining to, or designating a sharif; (*b*) *noun* a supporter of a sharif, *spec*. of the Sharif of Mecca: L19.

sharifa /ʃəˈriːfə/ *noun*. Also **shereefa**, **sherifa**, **S-**. E20.
[Arab. *šarīfa* fem. of *šarīf* SHARIF.]
The wife of a Moroccan sharif.

shark /ʃɑːk/ *noun*. LME.
[Origin uncertain. Sense 2 perh. from German *Schurke* worthless rogue. Cf. SHIRK *noun*.]
1 A member of a large superorder of marine cartilaginous fishes (selachians) typically having a long streamlined body, many pointed teeth, five to seven gill slits, rough scaly skin, and freq. a prominent dorsal fin; *esp*. a large voracious fish of this kind. Freq. with specifying word. LME.
2 A person who unscrupulously exploits or swindles others, esp. through financial dealing, property letting, gambling, card-games, etc. *colloq*. L16. ▸†**b** A pickpocket. *slang*. Only in 18. ▸**c** A customs officer; a lawyer. Also (*Hist*.) in *pl*., the press-gang. *Nautical slang*. L18. ▸**d** A highly intelligent or able student; an expert at a specified subject. Now *rare*. *US slang*. L19.
3 ENTOMOLOGY. Any of various noctuid moths of the genus *Cucullia* (usu. with specifying word). E19.

📖 **1** ***basking shark***, ***blue shark***, ***carpet shark***, ***Greenland shark***, ***hammerhead shark***, ***mackerel shark***, ***nurse shark***, ***tiger shark***, ***white shark***, etc. **2** *Today* The fear is that residents . . will . . succumb to the methods these sharks use. ***land-shark***, ***loan-shark***, ***pool-shark***, etc. **3** ***MULLEIN shark***.

Comb.: **shark-bait** *Austral. slang* a lone swimmer well out from shore; **shark-louse** an ectoparasitic crustacean infesting sharks; **shark-moth** = sense 3 above; **shark-ray** (*a*) an angelfish (genus *Squatina*); (*b*) a guitar-fish (family Rhinobatidae); **sharkskin** *noun & adjective* (*a*) *noun* the skin of a shark, used for making shagreen, for polishing, etc.; a smooth slightly lustrous fabric; (*b*) *adjective* made of sharkskin; **shark's teeth** *attrib. adjective* designating a primitive weapon edged with sharks' teeth; **shark-sucker** (*a*) a remora, *esp*. one that attaches itself to sharks; (*b*) = ***shark-louse*** above; **shark's tooth**, **shark-tooth** *noun & adjective* (*a*) *noun* the tooth of a shark; (*b*) *attrib. adjective* of or resembling the tooth of a shark; **shark-toothed** *adjective* full of (ornaments etc. resembling) sharks' teeth.

shark /ʃɑːk/ *verb*. L16.
[from the noun.]
1 *verb intrans*. †**a** Foll. by *on*, *upon*: swindle, exploit; live off, sponge on. L16. ▸**b** Live by swindling or exploitation, practise fraud, act as a shark or cheat. E17.
2 *verb trans*. **a** Foll. by *up*: collect (a body of people etc.) hastily and arbitrarily. *arch*. E17. ▸**b** Steal or obtain by underhand or cheating means. Freq. foll. by *away*, *from*. *arch*. E17.
3 *verb intrans*. Sneak *off* or *out* from duty, danger, etc. Cf. SHIRK *verb*. *dial*. E19.
4 *verb intrans*. Fish for sharks. Chiefly as ***sharking*** *verbal noun*. M19.

sharka /ˈʃɑːkə/ *noun*. M20.
[from Bulgarian *sharka na slivite* pox of plums.]
= ***plum pox*** s.v. PLUM *noun*.

sharker /ˈʃɑːkə/ *noun*. L16.
[Sense 1 from SHARK *verb*, sense 2 partly from SHARK *noun*: see -ER[1].]
†**1** A swindler, a cheat. L16–L17.
2 A person fishing for sharks. L19.

sharkish /ˈʃɑːkɪʃ/ *adjective*. M19.
[from SHARK *noun* + -ISH[1].]
Of the nature of, resembling, or characteristic of a shark.

sharky /ˈʃɑːki/ *adjective*. M19.
[from SHARK *noun* + -Y[1].]
Infested with or inhabited by sharks.

sharm *verb* var. of CHIRM *verb*.

sharn /ʃɑːn/ *noun*. *Scot. & dial*.
[Old English *scearn* neut. corresp. to Old Frisian *skern*, Middle Low German *scharn*, Old Norse (Swedish, Danish) *skarn*, from Germanic. Cf. SHARD *noun*[2].]
Dung, esp. of cattle.
Comb.: **sharn-bud**, **sharn-bug** a beetle, *esp*. a dung-beetle.
▪ **sharny** *adjective* covered or smeared with dung L17.

sharp /ʃɑːp/ *noun*. ME.
[from SHARP *adjective*.]
1 A sharp weapon; *spec*. (*a*) a small sword, as formerly carried by civilians; (*b*) a rapier used for duelling as opp. to a blunt weapon or one with a button affixed. Now *arch*. *rare*. ME.
2 A sharp edge, *spec*. of a sword or the hand. Now *rare* or *obsolete*. ME.
3 MUSIC. A note raised a semitone above the natural pitch; a sign (♯) indicating this raising. L16.
4 The termination of anything pointed. *rare*. M17.
5 **a** = SHARPER. *colloq*. L18. ▸**b** An expert, a connoisseur. *colloq*. M19.
6 In *pl*. The finer particles of the husk and the coarser flour particles of wheat etc., separated from the bran and the fine flour during milling. E19.
7 A needle, *spec*. a long sharply pointed one used for general sewing; MEDICINE a sharply pointed instrument. Usu. in *pl*. M19. ▸**b** A sharp piece of diamond used to mark out an intended cut in another diamond; a tool resembling a pencil holding such a diamond. E20.
8 A second-hand car in excellent condition. *N. Amer. slang*. M20.

1 †***at sharp(s)***, †***at the sharp(s)*** with unblunted swords, in earnest. **3** ***double sharp***: see DOUBLE *adjective & adverb*. ***sharps and flats***: see FLAT *noun*[1].

sharp /ʃɑːp/ *adjective & adverb*.
[Old English *sc(e)arp* = Old Frisian *skarp*, *skerp*, Old Saxon *skarp* (Dutch *scherp*), Old High German *skarf*, *scarpf* (German *scharf*), Old Norse *skarpr*, from Germanic.]
▶ **A** *adjective*. **1** Able to cut or pierce easily, having a keen edge or point. Opp. ***blunt***. OE. ▸†**b** Prickly. OE–E17. ▸**c** Of sand, gravel, etc.: composed of grains having sharp points; hard, angular, gritty. E17.
†**2** Rough, rugged. OE–L16.
3 Acute or penetrating in intellect or perception; quick-witted, clever. Of a remark etc.: pointed, apt, witty. OE. ▸**b** (Of the eyes or ears) acute, keen; (of observation or an observer) vigilant, alert. OE. ▸**c** Practical, business-like. Freq. *derog*., quick to take advantage of others; artful, unscrupulous, dishonest. L17.
4 †**a** Eager for battle. OE–L15. ▸**b** Of conflict or (formerly) feelings: intense, fierce, ardent. LME. ▸**c** (Of a storm, shower, etc.) heavy, violent; (of weather) cuttingly cold, biting; (of frost) severe, hard. LME. ▸**d** Quick, active, energetic; vigorous, lively, brisk; (of a stream) (now *rare*) rapid. LME. ▸**e** Hungry, eager for food. (Orig. in FALCONRY.) L15. ▸**f** (Of public transport) ahead of schedule, early; (of a timetable etc.) tight, demanding. *colloq*. M20.
5 **a** Of words, temper, a person, etc.: harsh, cutting, peremptory; indicating anger or rebuke, irascible; acrimonious. OE. ▸**b** (Of a pain, feeling, etc.) acute, intense; (of an experience) intensely painful. OE. ▸**c** Of a punishment, judge, etc.: severe, merciless. ME. ▸†**d** Of a way of life: austere. ME–E17.
6 Acid, sour, or bitterly pungent in taste or smell; tart. OE. ▸†**b** Of water: hard; hot, scalding. *rare*. M17–M18.
7 Tapering to a (relatively) fine point or edge, pointed, peaked. ME. ▸**b** Of an angle: acute. Of a turn, rise, fall, etc.: involving sudden change of direction; abrupt, steep, angular. M16. ▸**c** NAUTICAL. Of a vessel: having a narrow and wedge-shaped bottom. E18. ▸**d** Of the face or features: emaciated, peaked, thin. M19.
8 Of sound: penetrating, shrill, high-pitched; PHONETICS (*rare*) designating a high-front vowel or an unvoiced consonant. LME
9 MUSIC. Relatively high in pitch; *esp*. (of a note, singer, or instrument) above the desired or true pitch; (of a key) having a sharp or sharps in the signature. L16.
10 Distinct in outline or detail; well-defined, clear-cut, with strongly marked contrast; (of a lens) producing a sharp image. L17. ▸**b** SCIENCE. Of a phenomenon, condition, or state, esp. resonance: having or occurring over a narrow range of values of everything; capable of graphical representation by a curve showing a sharp peak; clearly defined. E20.
11 **a** Excellent, fine; well-equipped, impressive. *slang* (orig. *US*). M20. ▸**b** Of clothes or their wearer: stylish, neatly fashionable, smart. *colloq*. M20.

📖 **1** C. BOUTELL A straight flat wide blade, that is pointed and very sharp at either edge. R. WEST Sharp thorns on those roses. **3** F. DHONDY She was sharp, you couldn't lie to her. **b** L. M. MONTGOMERY Mrs. Rachel was keeping a sharp eye on everything that passed. B. TRAPIDO Jonathan, who had sharp ears, heard his name immediately. **d** L. DEIGHTON I listen to what these sharp estate agents tell me and I believe it—that's my trouble. **4c** J. TROLLOPE A little sharp frosty bite to the air. **d** E. DUNPHY We are not playing well . . . We are not sharp. G. GORDON The girl . . gave him a sharp, almost karate, chop across his shoulder blades. **5a** R. LINDNER Ma . . nagging, critical, sharp in her words and tone. R. DAVIES He was sharp about mistakes and demanded more and more. **b** OED A sharp pain, followed by a dull ache. **c** L. R. BANKS Giving young offenders a short sharp shock. **6** I. MCEWAN The sharp smell of strong coffee and cigar smoke. **7** B. P. POORE Long, flat-bottomed boats, sharp at both ends, called 'gondolas'. **b** D. H. LAWRENCE Land . . bounded on the east by the sharp dip of the brook course. *Times* Macarthys Pharmaceuticals . . turned in a sharp jump in profits. **8** E. BOWEN It was twelve noon: sharp and deep Sunday chimes broke from two belfries. **9** **A sharp**, **C sharp**, **D sharp**, etc., (a note) a semitone higher than A, C, D, etc.; a key, string, fret, etc., producing such a note in a musical instrument. **10** *Observer* No sharp dividing line between sanity and insanity. J. KOSINSKI The picture was so sharp . . I could almost count the straws in the thatched roofs. **11** W. ASH When Jacques turned up, he was looking pretty sharp . . in the sort of dark suit which . . looks expensive.

Phrases: ***better than a poke in the eye with a sharp stick***: see POKE *noun*[4] 1. ***sharp as a needle*** very sharp; *fig*. extremely quick-witted. ***the sharp edge of one's tongue***: see EDGE *noun*.
▶ **B** *adverb*. **1** In a sharp manner, sharply; MUSIC above the true pitch; *colloq*. smartly, stylishly. OE. ▸**b** Abruptly, suddenly; at a sharp angle. M19. ▸**c** Punctually, precisely at the time specified. Usu. *postpositive*. M19.
2 NAUTICAL. As near fore and aft as possible, trimmed as near as possible to the wind. M17.

📖 **1** M. ARNOLD Loud howls the wind, sharp patters the rain. D. SHANNON He was dressed real sharp, a gray suit, not just sports clothes. ***look sharp***: see LOOK *verb*. **b** J. CARLYLE The horse . . turns sharp round. **c** M. MEYER To meet at eight sharp, since Bergman was insistent on punctuality.

Special collocations & comb.: **sharpbill** a stocky bird, *Oxyruncus cristatus* (sole member of the family Oxyruncidae), having a sharp conical bill and speckled plumage with an olive back and red crest, and found in humid forest canopy in Central and S. America. **sharp cedar** an evergreen tree with sharp needles, *Juniperus oxycedrus*, which yields oil of cade. **sharp end** *colloq*. (*a*) the bows of a ship; (*b*) the centre of activity or decision-making, the front line. **sharp-eyed** *adjective* having good sight; observant. **sharp eyespot** a fungal disease of cereals similar to eyespot but characterized by more clearly defined markings. **sharp practice** hard bargaining; dishonest or barely honest dealings. **sharp rush** a sand-dune rush, *Juncus acutus*, with rigid sharply pointed leaves. **sharp-set** *adjective* very hungry; *transf*. very keen *on* or eager *for*. **sharpshin** (*a*) US HISTORY each of the pieces of a small coin cut into pieces to provide smaller change (later as a type of little value); (*b*) the sharp-shinned hawk. **sharp-shinned** *adjective* having slender legs or shanks; ***sharp-shinned hawk***, a common hawk, *Accipiter striatus*, of N. American woodland. **sharp-shod** *adjective* (chiefly *N. Amer*.) (of a horse) having caulked shoes, rough-shod. **sharp-sighted** *adjective* having keen sight; *fig*. perceptive, intelligent. **sharp-tail** *N. Amer*. the sharp-tailed grouse. **sharp-tailed** *adjective* having a tapering tail or pointed tail feathers; ***sharp-tailed grouse***, a grouse of N. American prairies, *Tympanuchus phasianellus*. **sharp-tongued** *adjective* harsh or cutting in speech, abrasive. **sharp-witted** *adjective* perceptive, intelligent.

sharp /ʃɑːp/ *verb*.
[Old English *scerpan* from Germanic. In Middle English prob. a new formation on the adjective.]
1 *verb trans*. = SHARPEN 1. Now *arch. & dial*. OE.
†**2** *verb trans*. = SHARPEN 2. OE–M17. ▸**b** = SHARPEN 2b. LME–M16.
†**3** *verb intrans*. = SHARPEN 4. ME–M16.
4 *verb trans*. MUSIC. = SHARPEN 5. Now chiefly *US*. M17.

5 a *verb trans. & intrans.* Cheat, swindle, or trick (a person), esp. at cards. *colloq.* L17. ▸**b** *verb trans.* Obtain by swindling, steal. *colloq.* L17.
6 *verb trans.* Shoe (a horse) so as to be roughshod. Cf. SHARPEN 6. Now *Scot.* M19.
7 *verb intrans.* Dress *up*, dress smartly. *US colloq.* M20.

Shar Pei /ʃɑː ˈpeɪ/ *noun.* L20.
[Chinese *shā pí* lit. 'sand skin'.]
(An animal of) a compact squarely built breed of dog of Chinese origin, with a characteristic wrinkly skin and short bristly coat of a fawn, cream, black, or red colour.

sharpen /ˈʃɑːp(ə)n/ *verb.* LME.
[from SHARP *adjective* + -EN⁵.]
1 *verb trans.* Put a sharp or sharper edge or point on; whet, point. LME.
2 *verb trans.* Intensify, make keener or more acute; make more stringent or severe; aggravate. Freq. foll. by *up.* LME. ▸**b** Give an acid flavour or quality to, make sour or bitter. Freq. foll. by *up.* L17. ▸**c** Make (the features) sharp or thin. Freq. foll. by *up.* M19. ▸**d** *refl.* Improve one's appearance, smarten oneself *up. colloq.* M20.
3 *verb trans.* Make eager for conflict, goad *on.* Now *dial.* L15.
4 *verb intrans.* Become sharp; taper to a point, grow thin; grow more acute or shrill. Freq. foll. by *up.* E17.
5 *verb trans.* MUSIC. Raise the pitch of a note sung or played. E19.
6 *verb trans.* = SHARP *verb* 6. Now *Scot.* L19.

> 🕮 **1** A. HIGGINS Sharpening the curved blade with professional sweeps of the whetstone. **sharpen one's pencil** prepare to work, revise or improve one's work. **2** W. BLACKSTONE It was found necessary to sharpen and strengthen these laws. E. WEETON The keen mountain air had sharpened our appetites. B. PYM The drinks . . seemed to have sharpened her perceptions. K. ISHIGURO Maths sharpens children's minds. **4** F. KING For the first time her tone sharpened to exasperation.

■ **sharpener** *noun* M17.

sharper /ˈʃɑːpə/ *noun.* M16.
[from SHARP *verb* + -ER¹.]
1 A person who or thing which sharpens something, a sharpener. Now *rare.* M16.
2 A person who (habitually) cheats, swindles, or tricks another, esp. in card-games. L17.

sharpie /ˈʃɑːpi/ *noun.* Also **-y.** M19.
[App. from SHARP *adjective* + -IE.]
1 A sharp-prowed flat-bottomed sailing boat used esp. in fishing. *US.* M19.
2 = SHARPER 2. *colloq.* (orig. *US*). M20.
3 A young person adopting certain extreme or provocative styles of hair, dress, etc., resembling those of a skinhead. *Austral. colloq.* M20.
4 A thing, esp. a car, that is smart or in good condition. *N. Amer. colloq.* L20.

sharpish /ˈʃɑːpɪʃ/ *adjective & adverb.* L16.
[from SHARP *adjective* + -ISH¹.]
▸ **A** *adjective.* Fairly sharp. L16.
▸ **B** *adverb.* Fairly sharply, quickly, or punctually. Also, as quickly or punctually as possible. *colloq.* L19.

> 🕮 A. CARTER Let's be off, sharpish, or else we'll be accessories to the fact.

sharpling /ˈʃɑːplɪŋ/ *noun.* Now *dial.* LME.
[from SHARP *adjective* + -LING¹.]
†**1** A kind of nail. LME–M16.
2 A stickleback. M16.

sharply /ˈʃɑːpli/ *adverb.* OE.
[from SHARP *adjective* + -LY².]
In a sharp manner.

> 🕮 G. GREENE A piece of brick . . struck him sharply on the cheek. *Times* Oil exploration . . has increased sharply during the past few months. J. KOSINSKI A car suddenly pulled in front . . and the chauffeur braked sharply. B. LOPEZ Sharply differing explanations of why all these animals died out.

sharpness /ˈʃɑːpnɪs/ *noun.* OE.
[from SHARP *adjective* + -NESS.]
The quality or state of being sharp; an instance of this.

> 🕮 GOLDSMITH Those . . whom I formerly rebuked with such sharpness. C. MCCULLOUGH Colonial axes had only one blade, honed to hair-splitting sharpness.

Sharps /ʃɑːps/ *noun. US.* Also **Sharps', s-.** M19.
[See below.]
Any of various firearms invented and made by the American gunsmith Christian Sharps (1811–74), *esp.* a kind of breech-loading single-shot rifle. Also ***Sharps rifle.***

sharpshooter /ˈʃɑːpʃuːtə/ *noun.* E19.
[from SHARP *adjective* + SHOOTER.]
1 A person skilled in shooting accurately, an expert marksman. E19. ▸**b** MILITARY. A rifleman of a particular grade. *US.* L19.
2 †**a** CRICKET. = SHOOTER 6. Only in M19. ▸**b** SPORT. A player having particularly accurate aim. Chiefly *N. Amer.* E20. ▸**c** = SHARP *noun* 5b. *US colloq.* M20.
3 Any of several N. American leafhoppers which are vectors of viral disease in grapevines. E20.

> 🕮 **1** *Time* Helicopters and sharpshooters positioned on rooftops kept constant watch.

■ **sharpshooting** *noun* accurate shooting E19. **sharpshooting** *adjective* shooting accurately M19.

sharpster /ˈʃɑːpstə/ *noun. colloq.* (chiefly *US*). M20.
[from SHARP *noun* + -STER.]
1 = SHARPER 2. M20.
2 A smart or stylish dresser. M20.

sharpy *noun* var. of SHARPIE.

sharrer /ˈʃarə/ *noun. colloq.* M20.
[Repr. an abbreviated pronunc.]
= CHARABANC.
■ Also **sharry** *noun* E20.

†**shash** *noun* see SASH *noun*¹.

shashlik /ˈʃaʃlɪk/ *noun.* E20.
[Russian *shashlyk* from Crimean Turkish *şişlik* from *şiş* skewer. Cf. SHISH KEBAB.]
An eastern European and Asian kebab of mutton and garnishings, freq. served on a skewer.

Shasta /ˈʃastə/ *noun & adjective.* M19.
[Origin uncertain: perh. ult. from a place-name.]
▸ **A** *noun.* Pl. same, **-s.** A member of a N. American Indian people of the highlands of northern California; the language of the Hokan group spoken by this people. M19.
▸ **B** *attrib.* or as *adjective.* Of or pertaining to the Shasta or their language. M19.
Shasta daisy a plant of the composite family, a cultivar or hybrid of the Pyrenean *Leucanthemum maximum*, grown for its large flowers resembling ox-eye daisies.
■ **Shastan** *adjective & noun* (**a**) *adjective* designating a linguistic grouping of the Shasta and certain other peoples; (**b**) *noun* this linguistic group; a Shasta Indian: E20.

Shastra /ˈʃɑːstrə/ *noun.* Also **Sa-, s-.** M17.
[Sanskrit *śāstra.*]
Any of the sacred writings of the Hindus (freq. in *pl.*). Also, a body of teaching, a science; a treatise.
■ **Shastraic** /ʃɑːˈstreɪɪk/ *adjective* of or pertaining to a shastra or the Shastras M20.

shastri /ˈʃɑːstriː/ *noun.* Also **sa-.** M17.
[Sanskrit *śāstrī*, formed as prec.]
A scholar or teacher of the Shastras.

shat *verb pa. t. & pple*: see SHIT *verb.*

shatter /ˈʃatə/ *noun.* M17.
[from the verb.]
1 In *pl.* Pieces into which a thing is broken or torn; fragments, tatters. Chiefly in ***break into shatters, break to shatters, be in shatters.*** *obsolete* exc. *dial.* M17.
2 A shattered state of nerves. *rare.* L18.
3 A scattered or shed thing; a crop; a shower of rain. Cf. SCATTER *noun* 2. *dial.* L19.

shatter /ˈʃatə/ *verb.* ME.
[Perh. of imit. origin, with frequentative ending: cf. *batter, hatter,* etc.: see -ER⁵. Cf. SCATTER *verb.*]
1 *verb trans.* Scatter, disperse, throw about in all directions. *obsolete* exc. *dial.* ME.
2 *verb intrans.* Clatter, rattle. *rare.* ME.
3 *verb trans.* Break in pieces by a sudden blow or concussion, smash into fragments. LME. ▸**b** Damage severely or destroy by battery or violent concussion. E16. ▸**c** *fig.* Ruin, put an end to, utterly destroy, (something immaterial). L17. ▸**d** Wreck the health of; exhaust, wear out; greatly upset or discompose. Freq. as ***shattered*** *ppl adjective.* L18. ▸**e** Cause (earth) to crumble. *dial.* L19.
4 *verb intrans.* Become broken suddenly or violently into fragments, fly into pieces. M16. ▸**b** Of earth: fall or crumble in pieces. *dial.* M18.
5 *verb intrans.* Become scattered or dispersed, be strewn about; (of grain etc.) drop from the husk. *obsolete* exc. *dial.* L16.

> 🕮 **3** A. HIGGINS An unidentified object, evading her nervous grasp, fell, and was shattered to bits in the grate. M. ATWOOD Thin bubbles of ice form across those puddles overnight; we shatter them with the heels of our boots. **b** W. CATHER One ball . . had shattered the carotid artery. **c** L. LOCHHEAD The lady Whose high heels shattered the silence. **d** F. BURNEY Her shattered nerves could not bear the interview. G. MEREDITH The little baby fell sick and died . . . This quite shattered us. *Listener* I was absolutely shattered. G. DALY He felt shattered and guilty, for he knew that he bore a share of responsibility for Fanny's death. **4** *Which?* When ordinary glass shatters it breaks into long, very sharp pieces.

Comb.: **shatter belt** GEOLOGY a belt of fractured or brecciated rock formed as a result of faulting; **shatter-brain** (*arch.*) = *scatterbrain* s.v. SCATTER *verb*; **shatter-brained** *adjective* (*arch.*) = *scatterbrained* s.v. SCATTER *verb*; **shatter cone** GEOLOGY a fluted conical structure produced in rock by intense mechanical shock, esp. by that associated with meteoritic impact; **shatter crack** METALLURGY a fine internal crack, esp. in a steel rail; **shatter-pate** (*arch.*) = *shatter-brain* above; **shatter-pated** *adjective* (*arch.*) = *shatter-brained* above; **shatterproof** *adjective* (esp. of glass in a vehicle) proof against shattering.
■ **shatterer** *noun* M19.

shattering /ˈʃat(ə)rɪŋ/ *noun.* E17.
[from prec. + -ING¹.]
The action of SHATTER *verb*; an instance of this; a shattered piece or fragment.

> 🕮 *Athenaeum* The sudden shattering of his belief in a miraculous apparition.

shattering /ˈʃat(ə)rɪŋ/ *adjective.* M16.
[formed as prec. + -ING².]
That shatters; that breaks or is broken suddenly or forcibly; very shocking, upsetting, or astounding.

> 🕮 B. MONTGOMERY A shattering blow to Allied morale. A. HALEY Grief and mourning with the shattering news of the assassination of President Lincoln.

■ **shatteringly** *adverb* E19.

shattery /ˈʃat(ə)ri/ *adjective.* E18.
[formed as prec. + -Y¹.]
1 Of rock or soil: apt to break in pieces or crumble, friable. E18.
2 Scatterbrained, silly. *dial.* E19.
3 Of furniture etc.: loose, rickety. *dial.* E19.
■ **shatteryness** *noun* M19.

shauchle /ˈʃɑːx(ə)l, ˈʃɔː-/ *verb. Scot.* E18.
[Origin unkn. Cf. SHAIL.]
1 *verb intrans.* Shuffle the feet, move in a shuffling way. E18.
2 *verb trans.* Put out of shape, distort, (esp. shoes). Freq. as ***shauchled*** *ppl adjective.* M18.
■ **shauchliness** *noun* unsteadiness L19. **shauchly** *adjective* rickety, shaky, unsteady in gait M19.

shaughraun /ˈʃɑːxrɑː, ʃɑːxˈrɑːn/ *noun. Anglo-Irish & Canad. dial.* M19.
[Irish *seachrán* a wandering, a straying, an error.]
1 ***go a shaughraun***, go wrong. M19.
2 A wandering person, a vagrant. Also, an itinerant state. L19.

shauri /ˈʃaʊriː/ *noun.* Pl. ***-i(e)s.*** E20.
[Kiswahili, from Arab. *šūrā* consultation, deliberation, counsel.]
In E. Africa: counsel, debate; a problem.

shave /ʃeɪv/ *noun*¹.
[Old English *sćeafa* = Middle Dutch *schave* (Dutch *schaaf*), Old High German *scaba* (German *Schabe*), Old Norse *skafa*, from Germanic base also of SHAVE *verb.*]
Any of various tools or knives for scraping or shaving wood etc.
draw-shave, spokeshave, etc.

shave /ʃeɪv/ *noun*². E17.
[from the verb.]
1 A thing shaved off; a shaving, a paring, a thin slice. E17.
2 An unauthenticated report. *Military slang.* E19.
3 The action or an act of shaving the face etc.; the process of being shaved. M19.
4 A slight or grazing touch; a close approach without touching; a narrow miss or escape. Freq. in ***close shave, narrow shave, near shave.*** M19.
5 An act or instance of swindling or extortion, a swindle. *colloq.* M19.
6 An exorbitant premium on a bill of exchange. *US slang.* M19.

> 🕮 **3** P. FITZGERALD Having a shave at one of the many barbers. ***wet shave***: see WET *adjective.* **4** C. A. DAVIS I did not . . get . . wet when the bridge fell, though it was a close shave.

shave /ʃeɪv/ *verb.* Pa. t. **shaved**; pa. pple **shaved, shaven** /ˈʃeɪv(ə)n/.
[Old English *sć(e)afan* = Old High German *scaban* (Dutch *schaven*, German *schaben*), Old Norse *skafa*, Gothic *skaban*, from Germanic.]
1 *verb trans.* **a** Scrape away the surface of with a sharp tool, smooth or shape (wood etc.) by paring very thin strips or slices from. OE. ▸**b** Remove by scraping or paring, cut off in thin slices or shavings. Also foll. by *off.* LME.
2 *verb trans. & intrans.* Remove (hair or bristles) smoothly from the face etc. (as) with a razor (also foll. by *off, away*); remove hair or bristles thus from the face etc. of (a person etc.), make (a bodily part) smooth and hairless, in this way. ME.
3 *verb trans.* Strip (a person) of money or possessions by fraud, extortion, etc.; fleece, swindle. Now *colloq.* LME. ▸†**b** Steal. *slang.* L16–E18. ▸**c** Charge an exorbitant premium on (a note of exchange). *US slang.* M19.
4 a *verb trans.* Touch lightly in passing, graze; pass close to without touching, miss narrowly. E16. ▸**b** *verb intrans.* Get *through* narrowly, scrape *through.* M19.
5 *verb trans.* **a** Cut off cleanly or closely. Also foll. by *off.* L16. ▸**b** Cut off (grass etc.) short, crop. M18.

6 *verb trans.* **a** Cut down in amount, reduce slightly. Orig. *US*. L19. ▸**b** Take (a small amount) away *from* or *off*. M20.

📖 2 B. MALAMUD He was not permitted to shave, and his beard was growing long. R. P. JHABVALA He had shaved his head completely. P. SAYER The tedious business of . . shaving me with the electric razor. *Daily Star* Kev accepts a dare to shave off his whiskers. **4a** *Field* An attempt . . which just shaved the bar. J. M. BARRIE Three hansoms shaved him by an inch. **6a** P. G. WODEHOUSE In the hope of making him shave his price a bit.

Comb.: **shavecoat** a man's casual garment resembling a dressing-gown; **shavegrass** = ***rough horsetail*** s.v. ROUGH *adjective*; **shavehook** a plumbers' tool used for scraping metal preparatory to soldering; **shavetail** *slang* (orig. *US MILITARY*) (*a*) an untrained pack animal, identified by a shaven tail; (*b*) *fig.* a newly commissioned officer, *spec.* a second lieutenant; *gen.* an inexperienced person.

shaved /ʃeɪvd/ *ppl adjective.* L17.
[pa. pple of SHAVE *verb.* Cf. SHAVEN *ppl adjective.*]
That has been shaved, having been shaved; cut off in very thin slices, cut into shavings; trimmed or polished by shaving.

📖 R. BOLDREWOOD Men . . with . . close-shaved faces, cropped heads, and prison-clothes. J. P. PHILIPS The martini shaker in its bed of shaved ice. **half-shaved** *US slang* partly intoxicated.

shaveling /ˈʃeɪvlɪŋ/ *noun & adjective. arch.* E16.
[formed as prec. + -LING[1].]
▸ **A** *noun.* **1** A monk, friar, or priest, orig. a tonsured one. E16. ▸**b** *gen.* A person with shaven head. *rare.* E17.
2 A youth, a young lad. *rare.* M19.
▸ **B** *adjective.* **1** Of, pertaining to, or characteristic of a tonsured cleric. L16.
2 Shaven, having the hair cut off. E17.

shaven /ˈʃeɪv(ə)n/ *ppl adjective.* ME.
[pa. pple of SHAVE *verb.* Cf. SHAVED.]
Esp. of the chin, the head: that has been shaved (freq. in ***clean-shaven***). Of a lawn etc.: closely cut.
shaven latten: see LATTEN *noun.*

shaven *verb pa. pple*: see SHAVE *verb.*

shaver /ˈʃeɪvə/ *noun.* LME.
[from SHAVE *verb* + -ER[1].]
1 A person who shaves. LME.
2 A shaving instrument or tool. Now *esp.*, a small electrical appliance with a set of blades working against a perforated guard, an electric razor. M16.
3 Orig. (now *dial.*), a fellow, a chap; a humorous person, a joker. Now *colloq.*, a youth, a child, a young lad, (freq. in ***young shaver***, ***little shaver***). L16.
4 = ***shavecoat*** s.v. SHAVE *verb. colloq.* E20.
Comb.: **shaver point**, **shaver socket** a power point for an electric shaver.

Shavian /ˈʃeɪvɪən/ *adjective & noun.* E20.
[from *Shavius* Latinized form of the surname *Shaw* (see below): see -IAN. Cf. SNOVIAN.]
▸ **A** *adjective.* Pertaining to, characteristic of, or resembling the Irish-born dramatist and critic George Bernard Shaw (1856–1950), or his works or opinions. E20.
▸ **B** *noun.* An admirer or follower of George Bernard Shaw. E20.
■ **Shaviˈana** *noun pl.* [-ANA] objects or texts relating to George Bernard Shaw E20. **Shavianism** *noun* the collective characteristics or tenets, or a characteristic saying, of George Bernard Shaw E20.

shavie /ˈʃeɪvi/ *noun. Scot.* M18.
[from SHAVE *noun*[2] + -IE.]
A trick.

shaving /ˈʃeɪvɪŋ/ *noun.* ME.
[from SHAVE *verb* + -ING[1].]
1 The action of shaving something, esp. the face; an instance of this. ME.
2 A very thin strip or slice shaved or scraped from the surface of something, esp. wood, with a sharp tool. Usu. in *pl.* LME.

📖 1 DICKENS The operation of shaving, dressing, and coffee-imbibing was soon performed. **2** A. C. AMOR An Oxford carpenter's shop with . . wood shavings on the floor.

Attrib. & comb.: In the sense 'used in shaving the face', as ***shaving foam***, ***shaving mirror***, ***shaving mug***, ***shaving soap***, ***shaving water***, etc. Special combs., as **shaving brush** a small brush used to apply lather to the face before shaving; **shaving cream** creamy soap, now freq. in an aerosol, applied to the face to assist shaving; **shaving horse** a workbench for a person to sit astride while smoothing or shaving wood etc.; **shaving stick** a cylindrical stick of shaving soap.

Shavuoth /ʃəˈvuːəs, ʃɑːvʊˈɒt/ *noun.* Also **She-**, /ʃə-/ **-uot**. L19.
[Hebrew *šāḇūʻōṯ* pl. of *šāḇūaʻ* week, with ref. to the weeks between Passover and Pentecost.]
= PENTECOST 1.

shaw /ʃɔː/ *noun*[1]. Now *arch. & dial.*
[Old English *sceaga* corresp. to Old Frisian *skage* farthest edge of cultivated land, Old Norse *skagi* promontory, from Germanic, rel. to SHAG *noun*[1].]
1 A thicket, a small wood, a grove. Also, ***shaw of wood***, ***greenwood shaw***. OE.
2 *spec.* A strip of trees or bushes forming the border of a field. L16.

shaw /ʃɔː/ *noun*[2] *& verb.* Chiefly *Scot.* E19.
[Origin uncertain: perh. var. of SHOW *noun*[1].]
▸ **A** *noun.* In *pl. & sing.* The stalks and leaves of certain plants, esp. potatoes and turnips. E19.
▸ **B** *verb trans.* Cut off the tops of (potatoes, turnips, etc.). L19.

shawabti /ʃəˈwabti/ *noun.* Pl. **-tiu** /-tɪuː/, **-tis**. E20.
[Egyptian *šwꜣbt(y)*, prob. from *šwꜣb* persea wood, perhaps the original material.]
EGYPTOLOGY. = USHABTI. Cf. SHABTI.

†**Shawanee** *noun & adjective* var. of SHAWNEE.

shawl /ʃɔːl/ *noun & verb.* E17.
[Persian & Urdu *šāl*.]
▸ **A** *noun.* **1** A usu. square or rectangular piece of woven, knitted, or crocheted material, freq. fringed, esp. as worn folded into a triangle around a woman's head or shoulders or wrapped around a baby. E17.
2 A prostitute. *Anglo-Irish slang.* E20.
Comb.: **shawl collar** a rolled collar extending down the front of a garment without lapel notches.
▸ **B** *verb trans.* Cover or wrap (as) with a shawl, put a shawl on. Freq. as ***shawled*** *ppl adjective.* E19.
■ **shawling** *noun* (*a*) the action of covering with or wearing a shawl; (*b*) the material of a shawl: E19. **shawlless** /-l-l-/ *adjective* M19.

shawlie /ˈʃɔːli/ *noun. colloq.* (chiefly *Scot.*, *Anglo-Irish*, *& north.*). E20.
[from SHAWL *noun* + -IE.]
A working-class woman (associated with) wearing a shawl over her head.

shawm /ʃɔːm/ *noun & verb.* ME.
[Old French *chalemel* (mod. *chalumeau*), *chalemeaus* (pl.), *chalemie*, ult. from Latin *calamus* reed from Greek *kalamos*.]
▸ **A** *noun.* A medieval and Renaissance wind instrument resembling an oboe, having a double reed and a loud penetrating tone. ME.
▸ **B** *verb intrans.* Play on a shawm. *rare.* L15.
■ †**shawmer** *noun* = SHAWMIST: only in E16. **shawmist** *noun* a player of a shawm M20.

Shawnee /ʃɔːˈniː/ *noun & adjective.* Also †**Shawa-**, †**-nese**. L17.
[Delaware *ša:wano:w.*]
▸ **A** *noun.* Pl. same, **-s**. A member of an Algonquian people formerly resident in the eastern US and now chiefly in Oklahoma; the language of this people. L17.
▸ **B** *attrib.* or as *adjective.* Of or pertaining to the Shawnee or their language. L17.
Shawnee salad the Virginia water-leaf, *Hydrophyllum virginianum*.

shay /ʃeɪ/ *noun*[1]. Also **ch-** /tʃ-/. E18.
[Back-form. from CHAISE taken as a plural.]
Chiefly *Hist.* = CHAISE 1.

Shay /ʃeɪ/ *noun*[2]. *N. Amer.* L19.
[from Ephraim *Shay* (1839–1916), Amer. engineer.]
A geared steam-powered locomotive designed for hauling timber.

shaykh *noun* var. of SHEIKH.

shay-shay *noun* var. of SHEY-SHEY.

shazam /ʃəˈzam/ *interjection.* M20.
[Invented word.]
Used by conjurors to introduce an extraordinary deed, story, or transformation.

📖 *Film Monthly* Two . . Sixties chaps . . return to New York 20 years later to find—shazam!!—their hippy friends transformed into yuppies.

shchi /ʃtʃiː/ *noun.* E19.
[Russian.]
A Russian cabbage soup.

she /ʃiː, *unstressed* ʃɪ/ *pers. pronoun, 3 sing. fem. subjective (nom.), adjective, & noun.* ME.
[Prob. phonet. devel. of Old English *hīo*, *hēo* HOO *pronoun* fem. of HE *pronoun*.]
▸ **A** *pronoun.* **1** The female person or animal, or the person or animal of unknown or unspecified sex, previously mentioned or implied or easily identified. ME.
2 The thing personified or conventionally treated as female (as a cat, a ship, the moon, the Church) or (in early use) the thing grammatically feminine, previously mentioned or implied or easily identified. ME. ▸**b** It; the state of affairs. Freq. in ***she's jake***, ***she's right***. *Austral. & NZ colloq.* ME.
3 The or any female person *who* (or *that*); (with prepositional phr., now *arch.* or *literary*) the female person *of*, *with*, etc. ME.
†**4** ***she & she***, ***she & he***, etc., this and that, the one and the other, both. LME–M16.
5 a Objective: her. *literary* or *colloq.* Now *rare.* M16. ▸**b** Possessive: her. *Black English* (chiefly *W. Indies*). L19.

📖 1 DRYDEN He first, and close behind him followed she. J. STEINBECK She has masses sung for her father. P. KAVANAGH So like her brothers was she. **2** COLERIDGE The moving Moon went up the sky . . : Softly she was going up. R. KIPLING The Liner she's a lady by the paint upon 'er face. **3** T. HARDY Anne Garland, she who could make apples seem like peaches. *Times* Suzanne Vega, she of the porcelain features and plaintive lyrics.

▸ **B** *adjective.* (Usu. hyphenated with following noun.) Female. Now chiefly of animals. ME.
she-devil a malicious or spiteful woman. **she-male** (*a*) *US colloq. & dial.* a female; (*b*) *slang* a (passive) male homosexual or transvestite. ***she-wolf*** etc.
▸ **C** *noun.* **1** The female; a female. LME.
2 *spec.* A female person, a woman, a girl. LME.

📖 1 BACON He-lions are Hirsute . . ; the She's are smooth like Cats. R. TATE 'What's the trouble with him?' . . 'It's a she. Broken wing.' **2** SHAKES. *Sonn.* I think my love as rare As any she belied with false compare. *British Medical Journal* It was always suspected . . that he was a she.

¶ Other suggested etymologies include derivation from Old English *sēo*, *sīo* fem. adjective (see THE), or from hypothesized forms in West Germanic.

s/he *pers. pronoun.* L20.
He or she (used in writing as an abbreviation).

shea /ʃiː, ˈʃiːə/ *noun.* L18.
[Mande *si*, *se*, *sye*.]
A nut-bearing tree of tropical Africa, *Vitellaria paradoxa* (family Sapotaceae).
Comb.: **shea butter** an edible fatty substance obtained from the kernels of the nuts of the shea, used locally in lamps etc. and elsewhere in the manufacture of chocolate etc.

sheading /ˈʃiːdɪŋ/ *noun.* L16.
[Var. of SHEDDING *noun*[1].]
Each of the six administrative subdivisions of the Isle of Man.

sheaf /ʃiːf/ *noun.* Pl. **sheaves** /ʃiːvz/.
[Old English *scēaf* = Old Saxon *skōf* (Dutch *schoof*), Old High German *scoub* sheaf, bundle, or wisp of straw (German *Schaub*), Old Norse *skauf* fox's brush, from Germanic, from base also of SHOVE *verb*.]
1 A large bundle of the stalks and ears of wheat or other grain, laid lengthways and tied together after reaping. Also, a bundle of the stalks or blooms of other plants resembling this. OE. ▸**b** A cluster of flowers, leaves, etc., growing together. *rare.* M19.
†**2** A measure of quantity of iron, steel, or glass. ME–L16.
3 A bundle or quiverful of 24 arrows. Also, a container for arrows; a quiver; *transf.* (long *rare*) a sheath. ME.
4 Esp. *HERALDRY.* A charge representing a sheaf of reeds, arrows, etc. L15.
5 *gen.* **a** A cluster or bundle of objects of one kind, esp. laid lengthways and tied up together; a quantity of sheets of paper etc. placed together in a batch. E18. ▸**b** In *pl.* A large number, mass, or quantity, very many *of*. M19.
6 a *PHYSICS & MATH.* A bundle of rays, lines, etc., all passing through a given point. M19. ▸**b** *MATH.* A topological space each point of which is associated with a structure having all the properties of an abelian group (e.g. a vector space or a ring) in such a way that there is an isomorphism between the structures on neighbouring points. M20.

📖 1 L. M. MONTGOMERY A sheaf of white narcissi in her hands. D. H. LAWRENCE Sheaves lay on the ground where the reapers had left them. **b** *Garden* The plant shown bore quite a sheaf of large blooms. **5a** S. KAUFFMANN Chester had already picked up a sheaf of papers. **b** G. B. SHAW Female murderers get sheaves of offers of marriage.

Comb.: **sheaf catalogue** a library catalogue recorded on sheets of paper in a loose-leaf binder; **sheaf oats** *US* (now *rare*): bound in sheaves.
■ **sheafy** *adjective* consisting of or resembling a sheaf or sheaves E18.

sheaf /ʃiːf/ *verb trans.* E16.
[from the noun Cf. SHEAVE *verb*[1].]
1 Tie or make into a sheaf or sheaves. Also foll. by *up*. E16.
2 Provide with a sheaf or sheaves. *rare.* M17.

shealing *noun* var. of SHIELING.

shear /ʃɪə/ *noun*[1].
[Old English *scērero* pl., *scēara* pl. of *scēar* fem. corresp. to Middle Low German *schēre*, Middle Dutch *scāre*, *scēre* (Dutch *schaar*), Old High German *skar*, pl. *skari* (whence German *Schere*), Old Norse *skæri* pl., from Germanic base of SHEAR *verb*. In branch II directly from SHEAR *verb*. Cf. SHEER *noun*[2].]
▸ **I 1 a** In *pl.* (treated as †*sing.* or *pl.*) & †*sing.* Orig. (now *Scot. & dial.*), scissors. Later *spec.*, any of various large clipping or cutting instruments operating (manually or mechanically) by the simultaneous action of two blades on opposite sides of the material to be cut, used esp. in tailoring, gardening, and sheep-shearing. OE. ▸**b** The weapon used by Atropos, one of the three Fates in Greek mythology, for severing the thread of life. Chiefly *literary.* L16. ▸**c** Either of the blades of a pair of shears. L18.
2 A knife; a scythe. Long *rare* or *obsolete.* LME.
†**3** In *pl.* Something resembling a pair of shears in function or shape; *spec.* a crustacean's claws. E16–E18.

4 In *pl.* (treated as *sing.* or *pl.*) A lifting apparatus for heavy gear, consisting of a hoisting tackle supported by two or more poles held in a sloping position by guys and fastened together at the top, and with their lower ends separated as a base and secured, used esp. on board ship and in dockyards and mines. **E17.**

5 In *pl.* (treated as *sing.*) Any of several small noctuid moths with grey and white markings, esp. *Hada nana*. Usu. with specifying word. **M19.**

> **1a** T. OKEY The ends . . are now cut off by the shears. P. D. JAMES Seed trays, pruning shears, a trowel and small fork. ***pinking shears***: see **PINKING** *noun*[1]. **b** MILTON Comes the blind Fury with th'abhorred shears, And slits the thin spun life.

▶ **II 6** The action or an act of shearing, esp. sheep; the result of this, *esp.* the quantity of wool shorn from a sheep at one time, a fleece. (Freq. with a preceding number indicating the number of times a sheep has been shorn as a statement of its age.) Now chiefly *Scot. & dial.* **OE.**

7 a *PHYSICS & MECHANICS.* A kind of strain consisting in a movement of planes within a body that are parallel to a particular plane, in a direction parallel to that plane, their displacement being proportional to their distances from that plane. Also, the stress caused in a body which undergoes such strain. **M19.** ▸**b** *GEOMETRY.* The transformation produced in a plane figure by motion in which all the points of the figure describe paths parallel to a fixed axis and proportional in length to their distance from it. **L19.**

8 *GEOLOGY.* Transverse compression on a mass of rock, resulting in alteration of structure or breach of continuity. **L19.**

Comb.: **shear board** *Hist.* a padded board over which cloth was stretched for cropping with shears; **shear centre** the point in the plane of a section of a structural member through which a shear force can be applied without producing torsion; **shear flow**: which is accompanied by or occurs under the influence of a shearing force; **shear force**: produced by a shearing stress; **shear-head** the upper part of a lifting apparatus for heavy gear (sense 4 above); †**shear-hook** *NAUTICAL* a sickle-shaped hook intended to destroy the enemy's rigging; ***shear-hulk***: see **SHEER-HULK**; **shear-legs** a device consisting of three poles of wood or iron bolted together at their upper ends and extended below, carrying tackle for raising heavy weights for machinery (cf. sense 4 above); **shear mark** a mark on a hide or fleece made when clipping an animal; **shear plane** *GEOLOGY* a boundary surface between bodies of rock or ice which have experienced relative motion parallel to the surface; **shear steel** blister steel improved in quality by reheating and rolling pieces together; **shear strength** = ***SHEARING strength***; **shear stress** = ***SHEARING stress***; **shear-thickening** *noun & adjective* (the property of) becoming more viscous when subjected to shear; **shear wave** an elastic wave in a solid which vibrates transversely to the direction of propagation; an S-wave.

¶ Rare in branch II before **E17.**

shear /ʃɪə/ *noun*[2]. **E19.**

[Origin unkn.]

The bar, or either of the two parallel bars, forming the bed of a lathe.

shear /ʃɪə/ *verb.* Pa. t. **sheared**, (*arch.* exc. *Austral. & NZ*) **shore** /ʃɔː/, pa. pple **sheared**, **shorn** /ʃɔːn/.

[Old English *scéran* = Old Frisian *skera*, Old Saxon (*bi*)*sceran* (Dutch *scheren*), Old High German *sceran* (German *scheren*), Old Norse *skera*, from Germanic base meaning 'cut, divide, shear, shave'.]

1 *verb trans.* Orig. (*arch.*), cut with a sword or other sharp weapon (*asunder, in pieces, in two*, etc.). Later, cut with shears etc. **OE.** ▸**b** *verb intrans.* Cut *through* (as) with a weapon. **ME.** ▸†**c** *verb trans. & intrans.* Carve (meat) at table. Only in **ME.** ▸†**d** *verb trans.* Cut up or chop (meat etc.) finely, mince. **LME–E18.** ▸†**e** Make (a hole, a wound) by cutting. **LME–E17.** ▸†**f** *verb trans.* Rend, tear. **LME–E16.** ▸†**g** *verb trans. & intrans.* Gnaw or bite through or *through* with the teeth. **M16–M17.**

2 *verb trans.* Remove (the hair or beard) with a sharp instrument; shave (the head or face); cut (the hair) close or short; cut or shave the hair or beard of (a person). *rare.* **OE.** ▸**b** Tonsure (a person), qualify as a monk by tonsuring (freq. in ***be shorn a monk***). Long *arch.* **OE.**

3 *verb trans.* Cut the fleece from (a sheep etc.); cut off (the fleece) from a sheep etc. **OE.** ▸†**b** *verb intrans.* Of a sheep etc.: be shorn. Only in **L16.** ▸**c** *verb trans.* Of a sheep etc.: produce (a fleece) by being shorn. **M19.** ▸**d** *verb trans.* Own or keep (sheep). *Austral. & NZ.* **M20.**

4 *verb trans.* Remove (a part) from a body by cutting with a sharp instrument. Freq. foll. by *off, out, away*. **ME.**

5 *verb trans.* Cut off (nap) from cloth as superfluous; remove superfluous nap from (cloth) by cutting. **ME.**

6 a *verb trans.* Cut down or reap (grain, crops, etc.), esp. with a sickle. Now *Scot. & dial.* **ME.** ▸**b** *verb intrans.* Cut down or reap grain, crops, etc.; use a sickle. Now *Scot. & dial.* **ME.** ▸**c** *verb trans.* Orig., cut off (a branch). Later, clip, cut, or trim (a bush, lawn, etc.). *arch.* **ME.**

7 *verb trans.* Pierce and penetrate (air, water, etc.); make one's way through (air, water, etc.). Formerly also, make (one's way) through air, water, etc. **ME.**

8 *verb trans.* Deprive *of* a part or feature (as) by cutting. Usu. in *pass.* **M18.**

9 *verb trans. PHYSICS, MECHANICS, & GEOLOGY* etc. Subject to a shearing stress; distort or fracture by shear. **M19.**

> **1** W. J. M. RANKINE Blades long enough to shear a plate at one cut. W. MORRIS I sheared the hawser of my ship. **b** LYTTON His own cimeter shore through the cuirass. *Sun (Baltimore)* The plane sheared down through the . . trees of the mountainside. **d** J. MAY Flox . . which they can sheare as small as dust. **2** E. B. BROWNING They have shorn their bright curls off. A. KOESTLER Two peasants were having their heads shorn. **3** P. L. FERMOR The ewes . . were already shorn. **4** CARLYLE The guillotine-axe, which sheers away thy . . head. **7** SPENSER And through the brackish waues their passage sheare. D. C. PEATTIE The long wings of . . nighthawks shear the gloom. **8** E. A. POE I am shorn of my strength. *Times* The opening of Parliament . . was shorn of all . . spectacle.

Comb.: **shear-grass** (now *dial.*) any of several kinds of grass or sedge with sharp-edged leaves, esp. great fen sedge, *Cladium mariscus*.

■ **shearer** *noun* (*a*) a person who shears something, esp. a sheep; †(*b*) an incisor; (*c*) a thing which shears metal etc.: **ME.**

sheared /ʃɪəd/ *ppl adjective.* **E17.**

[from **SHEAR** *noun*[1], *verb*: see -**ED**[2], -**ED**[1].]

1 That has undergone shearing; shorn. Formerly also, (of a coin) clipped. **E17.** ▸**b** Of dressed fur, piled fabric, etc.: trimmed to a close and even finish. **M20.**

2 Subjected to shear; strained or distorted by shearing stress. **M20.**

shearing /ˈʃɪərɪŋ/ *noun.* **ME.**

[from **SHEAR** *verb* + -**ING**[1].]

1 The action of **SHEAR** *verb*; an instance of this. **ME.**

2 A thing cut off with shears or some other sharp implement. Usu. in *pl.* **M16.**

3 A sheep after the first shearing, a shearling. *dial.* **M17.**

4 *MINING.* The action of making vertical side-cuts in a seam of coal. **L19.**

Comb.: **shearing strain** (*MECHANICS* etc.) a strain of the nature of a shear; **shearing strength** (*MECHANICS* etc.) power of resistance to shearing; **shearing stress** (*MECHANICS* etc.) a stress tending to produce or to resist a shear.

shearling /ˈʃɪəlɪŋ/ *noun.* **LME.**

[from **SHEAR** *verb* + -**LING**[1].]

1 A sheep that has been shorn once. **LME.**

2 A fleece or wool from such a sheep; *spec.* (chiefly *US*) the woollen lining or body of a coat etc. **L15.**

shearman /ˈʃɪəmən/ *noun.* Pl. **-men. ME.**

[from **SHEAR** *verb* + **MAN** *noun.*]

A person who shears something; *esp.* (now *Hist.*) a person who shears woollen cloth.

shearwater /ˈʃɪəwɔːtə/ *noun.* **M17.**

[from **SHEAR** *verb* + **WATER** *noun.*]

1 Any of a number of sea birds of the family Procellariidae, related to petrels, which habitually skim low over the open sea with wings outstretched. **M17.**

2 The black skimmer, *Rhynchops nigra*. *US.* **L18.**

1 ***Manx shearwater***. ***sooty shearwater***: see **SOOTY** *adjective.*

sheat /ʃiːt/ *noun.* Long *dial.* **M16.**

[Rel. to **SHOAT**: ult. origin unkn.]

A pig under a year old.

sheat-fish /ˈʃiːtfɪʃ/ *noun.* Now *rare.* Also (earlier) **sheath-** /ˈʃiːθ-/. Pl. **-es**, (usu.) same. **L16.**

[from (alt. of) next + **FISH** *noun*[1], prob. after German *Scheide(n)*.]

A catfish; orig. & *spec.* the large European catfish or wels, *Silurus glanis*.

sheath /ʃiːθ/ *noun*[1]. Pl. **sheaths** /ʃiːðz, ʃiːθz/.

[Old English *scǣð*, *scēaþ* = Old Saxon *skēþia* (Dutch *scheede, schee*), Old High German *sceida* (German *Scheide*), Old Norse *skeiðir* (pl.) scabbard, from Germanic, prob. from base also of **SHED** *verb*[1], **SHIDE**.]

1 A close-fitting case or covering for the blade esp. of a sword, dagger, etc., when not in use. Cf. **SCABBARD** *noun*[1] 1. **OE.** ▸**b** A case or covering with a similar function or purpose; *spec.* (*Scot. & dial.*) = **KNITTING** ***sheath***. **OE.**

2 A natural structure acting as a case or covering; *spec.* (*a*) the tubular fold of skin in various animals into which the penis is retracted; (*b*) *BOTANY* a tubular or enrolled structure surrounding an organ or part; esp. (in a grass) the lower part of the leaf, embracing the stem; also, the spathe enclosing certain types of flower-bud; (*c*) *ZOOLOGY* a tubular part or structure which contains or surrounds another; (*d*) the fold of skin into which the claws of a cat etc. are or may be retracted; (*e*) *ANATOMY* the connective tissue forming a close covering and binding for a part or organ; (*f*) *arch.* the wing-case of a beetle; (*g*) *BOTANY* a surrounding layer of cellular tissue; *esp.* = ***bundle-sheath*** s.v. **BUNDLE** *noun.* **M16.**

3 A contraceptive made of thin rubber worn on the penis; a condom. **M19.**

4 a A thin-walled, hollow part of a device or mechanism which surrounds another part; formerly *esp.*, the anode of a thermionic valve. **L19.** ▸**b** *PHYSICS.* A region of charged particles or plasma surrounding an object. **E20.**

5 A long close-fitting dress or skirt, esp. with a slit or pleat on one side. Also ***sheath dress***, ***sheath skirt***, etc. **E20.**

> **1** M. MOORCOCK He pulled one of his long daggers from its red velvet sheath. **2** GOLDSMITH Their claws . . thrust forth from their sheath when they seize their prey. ***medullary sheath***: see **MEDULLARY** 1b. ***MESTOME sheath***. **5** S. PLATH I stood quietly . . in my black sheath and . . stole.

Comb.: **sheathbill** any of several sea birds of islands in the southern oceans, forming the genus *Chionis* and family Chionidae, resembling pigeons and having a horny case around the base of the bill; **sheath cell** *ANATOMY* a Schwann cell; ***sheath dress***: see sense 5 above; ***sheath-fish***: see **SHEAT-FISH**; **sheath knife** a short knife carried in a sheath; ***sheath skirt***: see sense 5 above.

■ **sheathless** *adjective* (*a*) *arch.* not in a sheath; (of a sword, dagger, etc.) unsheathed; (*b*) not provided with a sheath, having no sheath: **E18.**

sheath /ʃiːθ/ *noun*[2]. *obsolete* exc. *dial.* **LME.**

[Prob. var. of **SHETH**.]

In a kind of plough formerly in use, the bar connecting the beam and sole in front.

sheathe /ʃiːð/ *verb trans.* Also (*arch.*) **sheath** /ʃiːθ/. **LME.**

[from **SHEATH** *noun*[1].]

†**1** Provide (a sword, dagger, etc.) with a sheath. **LME–L16.**

2 Replace (a drawn sword, dagger, etc.) in a sheath or scabbard, esp. as signalling an end to hostilities. Also foll. by †*up*. **LME.** ▸**b** Of a cat etc.: retract or draw in (the claws). **L17.**

3 a Cover from view. Long *rare* or *obsolete.* **L16.** ▸**b** Cover or encase in something, esp. a protective coating. Freq. foll. by *in, with*. **E17.** ▸†**c** Foll. by *up*: envelop so as to confine or obstruct. *rare.* **M17–M18.**

4 *BOTANY & ZOOLOGY.* Surround with a sheath or covering. Freq. as ***sheathing*** *ppl adjective.* **M17.**

5 †**a** *MEDICINE.* Mitigate the acridity or pungency of (a drug) by the use of an emollient vehicle. **M18–E19.** ▸**b** *gen.* Mitigate the painfulness of. *rare.* **E19.**

> **2** W. STYRON Did Saul and Gideon . . long to sheath their swords and turn their backs upon the strife? *transf.*: DRYDEN 'Tis in my breast she sheaths her Dagger now. **3a** SHAKES. *Lucr.* Her eyes, like marigolds, had sheath'd their light. **b** P. H. HUNTER The exterior of the dome is sheathed with . . copper. V. NABOKOV Her . . tight-fitting tailored dress sheathing in pearl-grey her young body.

sheathed /ʃiːθd, ʃiːðd/ *adjective.* **L16.**

[from **SHEATH** *noun*[1], **SHEATHE**: see -**ED**[2], -**ED**[1].]

Having or provided with a sheath; that has been sheathed; able to be sheathed.

sheather /ˈʃiːθə/ *noun*[1]. Long *obsolete* exc. *Hist.* **ME.**

[from **SHEATH** *noun*[1] + -**ER**[1].]

A maker of sheaths for swords, daggers, etc.

sheather /ˈʃiːðə/ *noun*[2]. Long *rare* or *obsolete.* **M18.**

[from **SHEATHE** + -**ER**[1].]

A person who or thing which sheathes something.

sheathing /ˈʃiːðɪŋ/ *noun.* **L15.**

[from **SHEATHE** + -**ING**[1].]

1 The action of **SHEATHE** *verb. rare.* **L15.** ▸**b** *spec.* The action of putting a protective layer on to the underwater surface of a ship. Formerly also, the method or manner of doing this. **E17.**

2 A protective layer, esp. of thin copper plates, put on to the underwater surface of a wooden ship, usu. to prevent boring by marine life. Also, a wooden covering to prevent corrosion of the underwater surface of an iron ship. **L16.** ▸**b** *gen.* A protective or ornamental case or covering. **M19.**

sheave /ʃiːv/ *noun*[1]. **ME.**

[Corresp. to Old Frisian *skīve*, Old Saxon *scība*, Middle & mod. Low German, Middle Dutch *schīve* (Dutch *schijf*), Old High German *scība* (German *Scheibe*), from Germanic base meaning 'disc, wheel, pulley, slice of bread', etc.: prob. already in Old English. Cf. **SHIVE** *noun*[1], **SHIVER** *noun*[2].]

1 A grooved wheel in a pulley-block etc. for a cord to run on. Also, a grooved wheel capable of running on a rail or bar. **ME.**

2 = **SHIVE** *noun*[1] 1. Long *obsolete* exc. *Scot. & dial.* **LME.**

sheave /ʃiːv/ *noun*[2]. **M16.**

[Var. of **SHIVE** *noun*[2].]

1 = **SHIVE** *noun*[2] 1. Long *dial.* **M16.**

2 = **SHIVE** *noun*[2] 2. Now *rare* or *obsolete.* **L19.**

sheave /ʃiːv/ *verb*[1] *trans.* **L16.**

[from *sheave(s* pl. of **SHEAF** *noun.* Cf. **SHEAF** *verb.*]

Tie or make into a sheaf or sheaves.

sheave /ʃiːv/ *verb*[2] *intrans.* Also (earlier) †**shieve**. **E17.**

[Perh. a var. of **SHOVE** *verb.*]

Back a boat, work the oars backwards.

sheaved /ʃiːvd/ *ppl adjective.* **L16.**

[from (the same root as) **SHEAVE** *verb*[1]: see -**ED**[2], -**ED**[1].]

1 That has been sheaved. **L16.**

†**2** Made of straw. *rare* (Shakes.). Only in **L16.**

3 Of a glass: having a flared top resembling a sheaf of corn etc. in shape. *rare.* **M19.**

sheaves *noun* pl. of **SHEAF** *noun.*

shebang /ʃɪˈbaŋ/ *noun. N. Amer. slang.* **M19.**
[Origin unkn.]
1 A hut, a shed; one's dwelling, quarters. **M19.** ▸**b** A disreputable drinking establishment. **E20.**
2 A thing, a matter, an affair (freq. in ***the whole shebang***). **M19.**

Shebat *noun* var. of **SEBAT.**

shebeen /ʃɪˈbiːn/ *noun.* Orig. *Anglo-Irish.* **L18.**
[Irish *síbín*, of unkn. origin: see **-EEN**².]
An unlicensed house or shop selling alcoholic liquor; a disreputable public house.
Comb.: **shebeen queen** *S. Afr.* a woman who runs a shebeen.
■ **shebeener** *noun* a person who keeps a shebeen **L19.**

Shechinah *noun* var. of **SHEKINAH.**

shechita /ʃɛˈxiːtɑ/ *noun.* **L19.**
[Hebrew *šəḥīṭāh*, from *šāḥaṭ* to slaughter.]
The method of slaughtering animals that fulfils the requirements of Jewish law.

shed /ʃɛd/ *noun*¹.
[Old English *(ge)scēad* alt. of *(ge)scēād* from base of **SHED** *verb*¹. Cf. Old High German *sceitil* division, German *Scheitel* parting of the hair.]
†**1 a** Distinction, discrimination, separation of one thing from another. **OE–E18.** ▸**b** The faculty of discerning or distinguishing things. **OE–ME.**
2 a The dividing line of combed hair along the top of the head; the top of the head, the crown. *obsolete* exc. *dial.* **ME.** ▸**b** A parting made in a sheep's wool in order to apply grease etc. to the skin. **E16.**
3 A piece cut or broken off, a slice, a fragment. *obsolete* exc. *Scot. & north.* **LME.**
4 a An area of land, esp. as distinguished from an adjoining section; *Hist.* a measure of land larger than a ridge (**RIDGE** *noun*¹ 4a). *obsolete* exc. *Scot.* **L15.** ▸**b** A ridge of high ground dividing two valleys or tracts of lower country; a divide. Cf. earlier **WATERSHED** 1. **M19.**
5 The opening made between the threads of the warp in a loom allowing the passage of the shuttle. **L18.**
Comb.: **shed-rod**, **shed-stick** a device by which the shed (sense 5 above) is made between the threads of the warp in a loom.

shed /ʃɛd/ *noun*². Also (*obsolete* exc. *dial.*) **shud** /ʃʌd/. **L15.**
[App. var. of **SHADE** *noun.*]
1 A single-storey esp. wooden structure, erected separately or as a lean-to, and serving for storage, shelter for animals etc., or use as a workshop. Freq. prefixed by specifying word. **L15.** ▸**b** A large roofed structure with one side open, for the storage and maintenance of locomotives etc. **M19.** ▸**c** An open-sided building for sheep-shearing, wool-baling, and cattle-milking. *Austral. & NZ.* (Earliest in ***woolshed*** s.v. **WOOL** *noun.*) **M19.**
2 A hut, a cottage, a poor dwelling. Also, something giving shelter or protection; the hiding place, lair, or nest of an animal. Chiefly *poet.* (now *rare*). **E17.**
3 †**a** A lid. Only in **E17.** ▸**b** A covering in a telegraph-line insulator in the form of an inverted cup. **M19.**
4 *PHYSICS.* A unit of area equal to 10^{-24} barn (10^{-52} sq. metre) (cf. **BARN** *noun*¹ 4). *rare.* **M20.**
1 ***cart-shed***, ***cowshed***, ***tool-shed***, ***woodshed***, etc. **c** ***ring the shed***: see **RING** *verb*².
Comb.: **shedhand** *Austral. & NZ* an unskilled assistant in a shearing shed; **shedload** *colloq.* a large amount or number (freq. a euphemism for *shitload*); **shed master** a person in charge of a locomotive shed (sense 1b above) for the storage and maintenance of locomotives; **shed roof** a roof with only one slope as in a lean-to; **shed-roofed** *adjective* having a shed-roof structure; **shed-room** *US* a structure attached to a house and serving as a room.
¶ Recorded in **ME** in place-names and surnames.

shed /ʃɛd/ *noun*³. *rare.* **M17.**
[from next.]
Something that is or has been shed.

shed /ʃɛd/ *verb*¹. Also (*Scot.*) **shade** /ʃeɪd/. Pa. t. & pple **shed**, (now *arch. rare*) **shedded**. Infl. **-dd-**.
[Old English *sc(e)ādan* corresp. to Old Frisian *skēda*, *skētha* (weak), Old Saxon *skēdan*, *skēthan* (Dutch *scheiden*), Old High German *sceidan* (German *scheiden*), Gothic *skaidan*, from Germanic. Cf. **SHEATH** *noun*¹, **SHIDE.**]
1 a *verb trans.* Separate, divide (one selected group, esp. of cattle, sheep, etc.) *from* another. Now *Scot. & dial.* **OE.** ▸†**b** *verb intrans.* Separate, divide; part company (*with*); depart. **OE–M17.**
2 †**a** *verb trans.* Scatter, sprinkle; *spec.* sow (seed). **OE–L18.** ▸†**b** *verb trans.* Disperse; rout, put to flight. **ME–M17.** ▸**c** *verb trans.* Throw off, repel, (water, light, etc.). Now chiefly *dial.* **LME.** ▸†**d** *verb refl. & intrans.* Be dispersed, scatter. **LME–M17.**
3 *verb trans.* **a** Part, make a parting in (the hair, an animal's fur, etc.). Now *Scot. & dial.* **ME.** ▸**b** Make a shed (**SHED** *noun*¹ 5) in (the warp-threads in a loom). **M19.**
4 *verb trans.* Spill (liquid), drop (crumbs etc.). *obsolete* exc. *dial.* **ME.**
5 a *verb trans.* Pour, pour out, pour forth (water etc.). Also foll. by *out*. Long *arch. rare.* **ME.** ▸**b** *verb trans.* Emit, discharge, lay, (spawn, eggs, etc.). **LME.** ▸†**c** *verb refl.* Of a river etc.: flow *into*, *over*. **M16–M17.**
6 *verb trans.* Cause (blood) to flow by cutting or wounding a person. Freq. (*literary*) in ***shed the blood of***, kill, esp. violently. **ME.**
7 a *verb trans.* Allow (tears) to flow or fall; ***shed tears***, cry, weep; *literary* cause (rain etc.) to fall. **ME.** ▸†**b** *verb intrans.* Of rain, snow, etc.: fall. **ME–E17.**
8 *verb trans.* Throw (light) *on* something (freq. in ***shed light on***); diffuse, radiate, (sound, heat, etc.); impart (influence etc.). **ME.**
9 *verb trans. & intrans.* Cast off or lose by a natural process, cause to fall off; *spec.* (of an animal) slough (a skin), lose (hair), etc.; (of a plant or tree) drop (leaves). **LME.** ▸**b** *verb intrans.* Of hair, leaves, etc.: be cast off or lost by a natural process, fall off. **E16.** ▸**c** *verb trans.* Take off (clothes); divest oneself of. **M19.** ▸**d** *verb trans.* Of a share: fall in price by (a specified amount). *colloq.* **M20.** ▸**e** *verb trans.* Of an organization, company, etc.: divest itself or dispose of (excess employees or jobs), esp. by dismissal or redundancy. *colloq.* **L20.**
†**10** *verb trans.* **a** Cut in two, divide (a thing) with a sword, dagger, etc. **LME–L15.** ▸**b** Make one's way through or cleave (air, water, etc.). **L15–L16.**
11 *verb intrans.* Slope. Long *dial. rare.* **M16.**

> 🕮 **1a** P. HOLLAND Of the captives there were some . . who were shed apart from the rest. **2a** WYCLIF *Gen.* 38:9 He . . shede the seed into the erthe. **d** SPENSER Sike prayse is smoke, that sheddeth in the skye. **3a** A. RODGER Let me shed your shining hair. **4** J. TRUSLER A bag of tea . . was burst, and a good deal . . shed. **5a** G. SANDYS Banefull poyson; which she sheads Into her bones. W. C. BRYANT A fountain sheds Dark waters streaming down a precipice. **b** *Times* Salmon . . ready to shed their eggs. **c** T. RISDON The riveret Sid shedding itself into the sea. **6** AV *Gen.* 9:6 Whoso sheddeth mans blood, by man shall his blood be shed. **7** J. WILSON When evening sheds her dew. A. SCHLEE Ellie continued to shed . . tears down a motionless face. **8** T. MOORE The harp that once . . The soul of music shed. CARLYLE The waving of it shed terror through the souls of men. I. MURDOCH Lamps . . shed a soft radiance. **9** *Country Companion* Their antlers . . are . . shed in early summer. *transf.*: A. CARTER She shed hairpins like the White Queen. **b** K. DIGBY The haire of women with childe, is apt to shedde. **c** J. WAIN My clothes were on the floor. How eagerly . . I had shed them. **d** *Estates Gazette* Cardiff Property shed 5p to 28op.

■ **sheddable** *adjective* (*rare*) **L16.**

shed /ʃɛd/ *verb*² *trans.* Infl. **-dd-**. **M16.**
[from **SHED** *noun*².]
†**1** Roof over. *rare.* Only in **M16.**
2 Place (sheep etc.) in a shed. Also foll. by *up*. *NZ colloq.* **M19.**

shedder /ˈʃɛdə/ *noun.* **LME.**
[from **SHED** *verb*¹ + **-ER**¹.]
1 A person who or thing which sheds something. **LME.**
2 *spec.* **a** A female salmon or similar fish after spawning. **L16.** ▸**b** A crab in the process of casting its shell. **L19.**

shedding /ˈʃɛdɪŋ/ *noun*¹. **ME.**
[from **SHED** *verb*¹ + **-ING**¹.]
1 The action of **SHED** *verb*¹; an instance of this. **ME.**
2 That which is shed, *esp.* something cast off or lost by a natural process. Usu. in *pl.* **E19.**
3 *ELECTRICITY.* = ***load-shedding*** s.v. **LOAD** *noun.* **M20.**

shedding /ˈʃɛdɪŋ/ *noun*². **M19.**
[from **SHED** *noun*² + **-ING**¹.]
Sheds collectively; a collection of sheds.

Sheehan's syndrome /ˈʃiːənz ˌsɪndrəʊm/ *noun phr.* **M20.**
[H. L. *Sheehan* (1900–88), Brit. pathologist.]
MEDICINE. Amenorrhoea and infertility caused by necrosis of the anterior pituitary gland after severe postpartum haemorrhage (cf. **SIMMONDS' DISEASE**).

sheel /ʃiːl/ *verb trans.* Now *Scot. & dial.* Also (earlier) **shill.** **LME.**
[Rel. to **SHALE** *noun*¹.]
Shell; take off the husk or outer covering of.
■ **sheeling** *noun* (***a***) the action of the verb; (***b***) grain removed from the husk; the husks of oats, wheat, etc., collectively: **LME.**

sheela /ˈʃiːlə/ *noun.* **L19.**
[Abbreviation.]
= next.

Sheela-na-gig /ˈʃiːlənəˌɡɪɡ/ *noun.* **M19.**
[Irish *Síle na gcíoch* Julia of the breasts.]
A medieval carved nude female figure, esp. shown with hands emphasizing the genitals and legs wide apart, found on churches or castles in Britain and Ireland.

sheen /ʃiːn/ *noun*¹. **ME.**
[from **SHEEN** *adjective*, assumed to be rel. to **SHINE** *verb.*]
†**1** A beautiful person, esp. a woman. **ME–M16.**
2 The pupil of the eye. *Scot.* Now *rare* or *obsolete.* **L15.**
3 Radiance, brightness; a gloss or lustre on a surface. **E17.** ▸**b** Magnificent or bright attire. *arch.* **E19.**
4 A very thin film or slick of oil, esp. on water. **L20.**

> 🕮 **3** A. S. SWAN Her hair . . had a sheen like gold upon it. I. FLEMING The silver sheen of the moon on the quiet sea. **b** BYRON In costly sheen and gaudy cloak array'd.

■ **sheenless** *adjective* (*rare*) without sheen **L19.**

sheen /ʃiːn/ *noun*². *slang.* **M19.**
[Origin unkn.]
Base coin, bad money.

sheen /ʃiːn/ *noun*³. *US slang.* **M20.**
[Prob. alt. of **MA)CHINE** *noun.*]
A car; an automobile.

sheen /ʃiːn/ *adjective & adverb.* Now *poet.*
[Old English *scēne*, *sciene* = Old Frisian *skēne*, Old Saxon, Old High German *scōni* (Dutch *schoon*, German *schön*), Gothic *skauns*, from Germanic base also of **SHOW** *verb.*]
▶ **A** *adjective.* **1** Beautiful, attractive. Formerly also, noble, illustrious; pure. **OE.**
2 Bright, shining, resplendent; (of the day, the sky, etc.) clear. **OE.** ▸†**b** Bright-coloured. **ME–E19.**

> 🕮 **1** SPENSER Her daintie corse so faire and sheene. J. A. SYMONDS Narcissus will I twine, and lilies sheen. **2** SIR W. SCOTT His vest of changeful satin sheen. LONGFELLOW Shadows dark and sunlight sheen. **b** J. FLORIO A . . rich garment . . of a sheene and garish colour.

▶ **B** *adverb.* Brightly, resplendently. Long *rare.* **ME.**
■ **sheenly** *adverb* (*rare*) **LME.**

sheen /ʃiːn/ *verb.* **ME.**
[from prec.]
1 *verb intrans.* **a** = **SHINE** *verb. lit. & fig.* Now only *Scot. & dial.* **ME.** ▸**b** Cast a gleam, glisten. *poet.* **E19.**
2 *verb trans.* Cast a sheen on. *rare.* **E20.**

sheened /ʃiːnd/ *adjective.* **E20.**
[from **SHEEN** *noun*¹, *verb* + **-ED**², **-ED**¹.]
Having a sheen, shining. Freq. foll. by *with*.

sheeny /ˈʃiːni/ *noun. slang. offensive* **E19.**
[Origin unkn.]
A Jew.

sheeny /ˈʃiːni/ *adjective.* **E17.**
[from **SHEEN** *noun*¹ + **-Y**¹.]
Having a sheen, glossy, lustrous.

sheep /ʃiːp/ *noun.* Pl. same.
[Old English (Anglian) *scēp*, (West Saxon) *scǣp*, *scēap* = Old Frisian *skēp*, Old Saxon *scāp* (Dutch *schaap*), Old High German *scāf* (German *Schaf*), from West Germanic. No cognates outside West Germanic are known.]
1 a A medium-sized, freq. horned, gregarious grazing ruminant animal, *Ovis aries*, the numerous varieties of which are widely domesticated for their woolly fleece, meat, skin, milk, etc. **OE.** ▸**b** Any of various grazing mammals of the genus *Ovis* and related genera, closely allied to goats, as the mouflon, the American bighorn, etc. Usu. with specifying word. **E17.**
2 The domestic sheep as a symbol of a righteous person (freq. with ref. to *Matthew* 25:32–33); *collect. pl.* God's chosen people, the Church, esp. with ref. to Christ as the Good Shepherd (*John* 10:1–16); (usu. in *pl.*) a person receiving or requiring spiritual direction or sustenance, a member of a congregation, a parishioner. Cf. **GOAT** 3. **OE.**
3 A person likened to a sheep in being defenceless, inoffensive, liable to stray, etc.; *esp.* a stupid, timid, or poor-spirited person. **M16.**
4 Leather made from the hide or skin of a sheep. Now *rare.* **E18.**
1 ***Cheviot sheep***, ***Dartmoor sheep***, ***Herdwick sheep***, ***Jacob sheep***, ***Kerry Hill sheep***, ***Leicester sheep***, ***Soay sheep***, ***Suffolk sheep***, etc. **b** ***Barbary sheep***, ***Rocky Mountain sheep***, ***wild sheep***, etc.
Phrases: ***black sheep***: see **BLACK** *adjective.* **count sheep** count imaginary sheep jumping over an obstacle one by one as a soporific. ***make sheep's eyes at***: see **EYE** *noun.* ***pack sheep***: see **PACK** *noun* 3b. ***placer sheep***: see **PLACER** *noun*³ 2. ***scabby sheep***: see **SCABBY.** ***separate the sheep from the goats***: see **GOAT.** ***vegetable sheep***: see **VEGETABLE** *adjective.* ***wolf in sheep's clothing***: see **WOLF** *noun.*
Comb.: **sheep-back** = **ROCHE MOUTONNÉE**; **sheep-bell** a bell which is or may be hung on a sheep's neck (cf. ***bell-wether*** s.v. **BELL** *noun*¹); **sheepberry** (the edible fruit of) a N. American viburnum, *Viburnum lentago*; **sheep-biter** (long *rare* or *obsolete*) (***a***) a dog that bites or worries sheep; †(***b***) a malicious or censorious person; a shifty, sneaking, or thievish person; †(***c***) a person who consumes mutton in great quantities; †(***d***) a sexually promiscuous man, a lecher; †**sheep-biting** *ppl adjective* that is a sheep-biter; **sheep blowfly** a large greenish blowfly of the genus *Lucilia*, esp. *L. coprina*, the larva of which is a pest of sheep in Australia; **sheep-bot**, **sheep botfly** the botfly *Oestrus ovis*, the larvae of which parasitize the nasal passages of sheep; **sheep-bug** a mite of the genus *Argas*, which infests sheep; **sheep-bush** *Austral.* the wilga tree, *Geijera parviflora*, sometimes eaten by sheep in times of scarcity; **sheep-camp** (***a***) *N. Amer.* a camp for sheep-herders; (***b***) *Austral. & NZ* an assembly place for sheep (cf. **CAMP** *noun*² 2b); (***c***) *S. Afr.* a fenced-in enclosure for sheep (cf. **CAMP** *noun*² 6); **sheep-crook** (now *rare* or *obsolete*) a shepherd's crook; **sheep-dip** (***a***) a liquid preparation in which sheep are dipped to kill vermin on them; (***b***) a place where this is done; a vat or tank for this purpose; **sheep-dipping** the action or practice of dipping sheep to kill vermin on them; **sheep-fly** (***a***) = ***sheep-tick*** (***a***) below; (***b***) a sheep blowfly, *Lucilia sericata*; **sheep-herder** *US* a

person who herds sheep in large numbers in unfenced country; **sheep-hook** (now *rare*) a shepherd's crook; **sheep-house** (now *rare*) a covered enclosure for sheep, a sheepcote; ***sheep-ked***: see KED *noun*[1]; **sheepkill** = *sheep laurel* below; **sheep laurel** a N. American evergreen shrub of the heath family, *Kalmia angustifolia*, reputedly very poisonous to stock; **sheepman** †(*a*) a shepherd; (*b*) (orig. *N. Amer.*) a breeder or owner of sheep; **sheep-mark** (*a*) a mark on a sheep, esp. an earmark, indicating ownership; †(*b*) *rare* a tool for marking sheep to indicate ownership; **sheep-master** a sheep-owner; **sheepmeat** meat obtained from sheep; mutton and lamb (chiefly in commercial use); **sheep-money** = *sheep-silver* below; **sheepnose** a variety of cider apple with small fruit; **sheep-nose-bot**, **sheep nostril fly** = *sheep bot* above; **sheep-pen** a pen in which to keep sheep; **sheep pox** an infectious virus disease of sheep characterized by fever and skin lesions; **sheep-rack** a rack from which sheep feed; **sheep-ree** a permanent sheepfold; **sheep-rot** (*a*) disease in sheep caused by the presence of liver flukes; (*b*) *dial.* any of several plants supposed to cause disease in sheep, esp. marsh pennywort, *Hydrocotyle vulgaris*; **sheep-run** (orig. *Austral.*) an extensive sheepwalk; **sheep's bane** marsh pennywort, *Hydrocotyle vulgaris*; **sheep's-bit** a plant of sandy banks, *Jasione montana*, of the bellflower family, with flowers like those of scabious; also called ***sheep's scabious***; ***sheep scab***: see SCAB *noun* 2a; **sheep's eye** an amorous glance (usu. in *pl.*, chiefly in ***make sheep's eyes at*** s.v. EYE *noun*); **sheep's fescue** a small wiry fescue, *Festuca ovina*, characteristic of hill grassland; **sheep's foot** (*a*) the foot of a sheep; †(*b*) a kind of claw-hammer; (*c*) ***sheep's foot roller***, a tamping roller consisting of a steel drum studded with projecting feet; †**sheep's gut(s)** catgut; **sheep-shagger** (*coarse slang, offensive*) a member of a Scottish regiment of the British army; *gen.* a man from a hilly or rural region, a rustic; **sheep-shear** *verb* (*rare*) (*a*) *verb intrans.* shear sheep; †(*b*) *verb trans.* cheat or swindle (a person); **sheep-shearer** (*a*) a person who or machine which shears sheep; †(*b*) *rare* a cheater, a swindler; **sheep-shearing** (*a*) the action or practice of shearing sheep; (*b*) the time or occasion of the festival (now rarely held) celebrating this; †(*c*) *rare* cheating, swindling; **sheep-shears** shears for sheep-shearing; **sheep's heart** (*a*) the heart of a sheep; (*b*) *arch.* a timid person, a coward; **sheep-sick** *adjective* (of land) that has been overgrazed by sheep; **sheep-silver** *Hist.* a tax on sheep kept by a tenant; †**sheep's leather** leather made from the hide or skin of a sheep; **sheep-sleight** (now *dial.*) (the right of) pasturage for a sheep or sheep; **sheep-smearing** the smearing of sheep with tar to kill vermin; a kind of tar used for this purpose; ***sheep sorrel***: see SORREL *noun*[1]; **sheep's scabious** = *sheep's-bit* above; ***sheep's sorrel***: see SORREL *noun*[1]; **sheep's tongue** the tongue of a sheep, esp. as used for food; **sheep-tick** (*a*) any of numerous ticks of the genus *Ixodes*, parasitic on sheep and other domesticated animals; (*b*) *loosely* an adult sheep-ked; **sheepwalk** (*a*) a tract of grassland used for pasturing sheep; (*b*) = TERRACETTE; **sheep-wash** (*a*) the washing of sheep before shearing; the place where this is done; (*b*) a preparation used in washing sheep, sheep-dip; **sheepwash** *verb trans. & intrans.* wash (sheep) before shearing.

■ **sheeplike** *adjective* (freq. *derog.*) resembling (that of) a sheep L16. **sheepling** *noun* (now *arch. rare*) a young or small sheep M17. **sheepy** *adjective* (*rare*) (*a*) of, pertaining to, or resembling (a) sheep; (*b*) full of sheep: LME.

sheep /ʃiːp/ *verb trans. local.* E19.
[from the noun.]
Pasture sheep on (land).

sheepcot /ˈʃiːpkɒt/ *noun.* LME.
[from SHEEP *noun* + COT *noun*[1].]
= next.

sheepcote /ˈʃiːpkəʊt/ *noun.* LME.
[formed as prec. + COTE *noun*[1].]
A light building or enclosure for sheltering or confining sheep.

sheepdog /ˈʃiːpdɒg/ *noun & verb.* L18.
[from SHEEP *noun* + DOG *noun.*]
▶ **A** *noun.* A dog trained to guard and herd sheep; *spec.* (a dog of) any of several breeds suitable or originally bred for this, as a collie, an Old English sheepdog, etc. Also *fig.*, a chaperon, a guide. L18.
Old English sheepdog, ***Pyrenean sheepdog***, ***Shetland sheepdog***, etc.
Comb.: **sheepdog trials** a contest or competition in which sheepdogs are assessed on their performance in various tests of their ability to control sheep under the direction of a shepherd.
▶ **B** *verb trans.* Infl. **-gg-**. Act as a chaperon or guide to. L20.

sheepfold /ˈʃiːpfəʊld/ *noun.* LME.
[formed as prec. + FOLD *noun*[1].]
A pen or enclosure for sheep. Formerly also (*rare*), the sheep enclosed in this.

sheepish /ˈʃiːpɪʃ/ *adjective.* ME.
[from SHEEP *noun* + -ISH[1].]
1 Of or pertaining to sheep; ovine; resembling a sheep or sheep. Now *rare.* ME.
2 †**a** Meek, innocent; simple, silly. ME–L17. ▸**b** Excessively submissive, fearful, or cowardly; poor-spirited. *obsolete* exc. as passing into sense 3. E16.
3 Bashful, shy, reticent; diffident, feeling or showing embarrassment. L17.

> 🕮 **1** A. STAFFORD How to excell in sheepish surgery. **2b** ADDISON If the former was too furious, this was too sheepish, for his Part. **3** J. HARVEY The plater . . hung his head, he was sheepish at being singled out. J. D. SUTHERLAND Having made a fool of myself . . I would dwell on what had happened . . and feel sheepish.

■ **sheepishly** *adverb* in a sheepish manner E16. **sheepishness** *noun* L16.

sheep-o /ˈʃiːpəʊ/ *interjection & noun. Austral. & NZ.* Pl. of noun **-os**. Also **-oh**. E20.
[formed as prec. + -O.]
▶ **A** *interjection.* A shearer's call: get a sheep to shear. E20.
▶ **B** *noun.* = ***penner-up*** s.v. PENNER *noun*[3] 1. E20.

sheepshank /ˈʃiːpʃaŋk/ *noun & verb.* E17.
[formed as next + SHANK *noun.*]
▶ **A** *noun.* **1** NAUTICAL. A knot used to shorten a rope's length temporarily without cutting it or unfastening the ends. E17.
2 The shank or leg of a sheep. *rare.* L17.
3 An unimportant person or thing. Usu. in neg. contexts. *Scot.* L18.
▶ **B** *verb trans.* Shorten (a rope's length) with a sheepshank. M18.

sheep's head /ʃiːps ˈhɛd/ *noun phr.* In senses 2, 3 also **sheepshead**. M16.
[from SHEEP *noun* + -'S[1] + HEAD *noun.*]
1 The head of a sheep, esp. as food. M16.
2 a A fool, a simpleton. *arch.* M16. ▸**b** CARDS. A simple early form of skat. L19.
3 A large food fish, *Archosargus probatocephalus*, of N. American coasts. Also, any of several similar N. American fishes, as the freshwater drumfish, *Aplodinatus grunniens*. Also ***sheepshead fish***. M17.

sheepskin /ˈʃiːpskɪn/ *noun & adjective.* ME.
[formed as prec. + SKIN *noun.*]
▶ **A** *noun.* **1 a** The skin or hide of a sheep with the wool on, esp. as dressed and used for clothing. ME. ▸**b** A coat made of this. E20.
2 a The skin or hide of a sheep without the wool, dressed and prepared for parchment, for use in bookbinding, etc. ME. ▸**b** A parchment diploma received on taking a degree; the holder of such a diploma. *N. Amer. slang.* E19.
▶ **B** *attrib.* or as *adjective.* Made or consisting of sheepskin. E17.
■ **sheepskinned** *adjective* dressed in sheepskin E17.

sheer /ʃɪə/ *noun*[1]. L17.
[from SHEER *verb*[1].]
NAUTICAL. **1** An abrupt divergence or deviation of a ship from the line of its course. L17.
2 The angle given to or taken by a ship relative to its cable when lying to an anchor. Freq. in ***break her sheer***, (of a ship) be forced by change of wind or current out of the original angle of sheer. L18.

sheer /ʃɪə/ *noun*[2]. L17.
[Prob. from SHEAR *noun*[1].]
NAUTICAL. **1** The upward curvature or rise of the deck or bulwarks of a ship towards the bow and the stern; the curve of the upper line of a ship as shown in vertical section. Freq. with specifying word. L17.
2 In full ***sheer-strake***. The uppermost strake of the side planking or plating of a ship. M19.
1 great sheer a sheer with a small radius of curvature. **little sheer** a hardly noticeable rise at the bow and stern.
Comb.: **sheer-line** the line of elevation of a ship's deck; **sheer-plan** the longitudinal elevation of a ship made by a vertical plane passing through the keel; **sheer-pole** a horizontal steel rod at the base of the shrouds supporting a ship's mast to prevent turns when they are set up; **sheer-rail** a moulding running in a continuous line around the top deck of a ship; ***sheer-strake***: see sense 2 above.

sheer /ʃɪə/ *noun*[3]. Orig. *US.* M20.
[from next.]
A very thin, fine, or diaphanous fabric.

> 🕮 *Lancashire Life* A new range of Swiss sheers and prints with louvred blinds to match.

sheer /ʃɪə/ *adjective & adverb.* ME.
[Prob. alt. of SHIRE *adjective.*]
▶ **A** *adjective.* †**1** Exempt, free from obligation; acquitted, blameless. Only in ME.
2 Esp. of water; clear, pure; translucent. Now *arch. & dial.* M16.
3 Of a fabric etc.: very thin, fine, diaphanous. M16.
4 a Of a substance: unmixed or unaccompanied with other matter; *esp.* (of alcohol) undiluted; taken unaccompanied by food. L16. ▸**b** Of an immaterial thing: taken or existing by itself, alone. Now *rare* or *obsolete.* E17.
5 No more or less than; unmitigated, unqualified; absolute, pure. L16.
6 Thin, insubstantial; lean. Long *rare* or *obsolete.* M17.
7 Of a descent or ascent, a cliff, etc.: perpendicular, very steep; having an uninterrupted rise or fall. E19.

> 🕮 **3** *Sun (Baltimore)* sheer nylons with contrast or self-color seams. **5** J. MOYNAHAN His tension mounts, and the last quarter hour before they meet is sheer torture. I. MURDOCH The sheer fact of their opposition stirred and wounded his conscience. **7** RIDER HAGGARD The precipice, which to our left was quite sheer.

▶ **B** *adverb.* **1** Completely, absolutely; directly. L16.
2 Perpendicularly, very steeply; straight up or down. E19.

> 🕮 **1** W. SOMERVILLE Cautious he crept, and with His crooked Bill Cut sheer the frail Support. **2** M. BRADBURY The ship's side fell sheer to the . . black water.

■ **sheerly** *adverb* LME. **sheerness** *noun* (*rare*) LME.

sheer /ʃɪə/ *verb*[1]. E17.
[Perh. from Middle & mod. Low German (whence German) *scheren* = SHEAR *verb.*]
NAUTICAL. **1** *verb intrans.* Of a ship: turn aside, alter direction, deviate from the line of its course, either deliberately, or abruptly due to a current, change of wind, etc. Freq. foll. by *off, away, round.* E17. ▸**b** *transf. & fig.* Change one's course; take a new direction; go away, esp. from something feared or unpleasant. Freq. foll. by *off, away.* E18.
2 *verb trans.* Cause (a ship) to deviate from the line of its course; direct (a ship) obliquely towards a given point. Also foll. by *off.* M17.

> 🕮 **1** *Lifeboat* In the heavy seas . . she sheered around and rolled heavily. **b** I. MURDOCH Gerard . . sheered off the subject which was evidently secret.

sheer /ʃɪə/ *verb*[2] *trans. rare.* E18.
[from SHEER *noun*[2].]
Give (a ship) a particular sheer or rise.

sheer /ʃɪə/ *verb*[3] *intrans. rare.* M19.
[from SHEER *adjective.*]
Of a cliff etc.: rise or descend perpendicularly or very steeply.

sheered /ʃɪəd/ *adjective.* M18.
[from SHEER *noun*[2] + -ED[2].]
NAUTICAL. Of a ship: built with a (particular kind of) sheer. Freq. with specifying word.
round-sheered, ***straight-sheered***, etc.

sheer-hulk /ˈʃɪəhʌlk/ *noun.* Also **shear-hulk**. M18.
[from SHEAR *noun*[1] + HULK *noun*[2].]
The hulk of a disused ship fitted with shears for hoisting purposes. Also, a ship specially built and fitted with shears.

Sheer Thursday /ʃɪə ˈθəːzdeɪ/ *noun phr. obsolete* exc. *Hist.* ME.
[from SHEER *adjective* + THURSDAY.]
Maundy Thursday.

sheesh /ʃiːʃ/ *interjection.* L20.
[Prob. alt. of JEEZ.]
Expr. disbelief or exasperation.

> 🕮 C. BERESFORD-HOWE Haven't heard from him since? Sheesh. Aren't men the pits.

sheet /ʃiːt/ *noun*[1].
[Old English (Anglian) *scēte*, (West Saxon) *sciete* weak grade corresp. to *scēat* (see next), from Germanic base also of SHOOT *verb*, SHOT *noun*[1], of which one of the senses was 'to project'.]
1 A broad piece of linen, cotton, or other fabric, for covering, wrapping, protecting against damage, cold, etc. Formerly also, a napkin, a cloth, a towel. Now freq. with specifying word. OE.
2 A burial shroud, a winding-sheet. *arch.* OE.
3 A large rectangular piece of cotton or other fabric, used esp. in a pair as inner bedclothes immediately above and below the person. ME.
4 A broad flat expanse or stretch of water, ice, vegetation, tissue, sediment, etc., forming a relatively thin continuous covering or layer. Freq. foll. by *of.* LME.
5 a A complete piece of paper of the size in which it was made or sold, esp. for writing, printing, etc. E16. ▸**b** A set of postage stamps, paper money, etc., printed on a single piece of paper and perforated for later separation. L18. ▸**c** An American dollar bill; a pound note; the amount of a dollar or a pound sterling. *slang.* M20. ▸**d** = ***rap sheet*** s.v. RAP *noun*[1]. *US slang.* M20.
†**6** A sail. Chiefly *poet.* E16–E18.
7 a In printing and bookbinding, a piece of paper printed and folded so as to form pages of a required size. Also, a quantity of printed matter equal to that contained on such a piece of paper. L16. ▸**b** In *pl.* Pages or leaves of a book. Freq. in ***these sheets***, ***the following sheets***, the book now in front of the reader. Now *rare.* L16. ▸†**c** A pamphlet. L17–E18. ▸**d** A newspaper, *esp.* a disreputable or mass-circulation one. M18.
8 A continuous extent of lightning, rain, cloud, etc., manifesting itself as falling or moving in a certain direction. Freq. foll. by *of.* E17. ▸**b** In an organ, the current of air directed through the wind-way against the upper lip of a pipe. L19.
9 a A relatively thin broad piece of a malleable, ductile, or pliable material, esp. iron, steel, rubber, etc. Freq. foll. by *of.* L17. ▸**b** A metal tray used for baking cakes etc. M18.
10 GEOMETRY. A portion of a surface within which a continuous line can be drawn between any two points without leaving the surface. E19.

> 1 *dust-sheet*, *fly-sheet*, *groundsheet*, etc. 4 D. LEAVITT A thin sheet of ice covered much of the sidewalk. 5a S. RADLEY She . . put a fresh sheet of paper in the typewriter. ***balance sheet***, ***score-sheet***, ***time sheet***, etc. 7d P. FITZGERALD I am being asked to read . . . instead of my *Daily Mail*, this revolutionary sheet. ***free sheet***. 8 R. DAHL The rainy seasons came and the water poured down in solid sheets. 9a M. DIBDIN The property . . was fenced off by sheets of corrugated iron.

Phrases: **between the sheets** *colloq.* (*a*) in bed; (*b*) having sexual intercourse. ***clean sheet***: see CLEAN *adjective*. **in sheets** (of a book) printed and folded but not bound. SMOKED ***sheet***. ***tympan sheet***: see TYMPAN 3. **stand in a sheet** *arch.* stand in public view wrapped in a sheet as a form of penance, esp. for adultery.

Attrib. & comb.: In the senses 'rolled out in a sheet (esp. of metal)', as ***sheet iron***, ***sheet steel***, etc.; 'pertaining to the manufacture of sheet metal', as ***sheet-mill***, ***sheet-worker***, etc.; 'printed on a single sheet', as ***sheet-almanac*** etc. Special combs., as **sheet erosion** the erosion of soil by rainwater acting more or less uniformly over a wide area; **sheet-fed** *adjective* (PRINTING) (of a press, copier, etc.) using paper in the form of cut sheets as opp. to reels; **sheet feeder** COMPUTING a device for feeding paper into a printer a sheet at a time; **sheet film** PHOTOGRAPHY a flat piece of film cut to size before it is loaded into a camera; **sheet-flood** a temporary spreading of a layer of running water over a large area following sudden heavy rain; **sheet-flow** PHYSICAL GEOGRAPHY a flow that covers a wide expanse of a surface instead of being confined in a channel; **sheet glass** (*a*) (a vessel made of) crown glass; (*b*) flat glass made by a vertical drawing process; **sheet ice**: formed in a thin, smooth layer on water; **sheet lightning**: which illuminates a wide area equally at once; **sheet metal**: formed into thin sheets by rolling, hammering, etc.; **sheet music**: published in cut or folded sheets, not bound; **sheet-pile** *noun & verb* (*a*) *noun* a flat pile driven vertically into the ground to prevent the material of a foundation from spreading; (*b*) *verb trans.* protect with sheet-piles; **sheet-piling** a continuous wall of sheet-piles; **Sheetrock** (proprietary name for) a plasterboard made of gypsum between heavy paper; **sheet-wash** sheet erosion, (erosion caused by) a sheet-flood.

■ **sheetful** *noun* as much or as many as a sheet (esp. a sheet of paper) will hold E16. **sheetless** *adjective* M18. **sheetlet** *noun* a small sheet, *esp.* a small unseparated set of postage stamps M20. **sheetlike** *adjective* resembling a sheet or sheets M19. **sheety** *adjective* (esp. of a stretch of water) spreading in a broad sheet M18.

sheet /ʃiːt/ *noun*[2].

[Old English *scēat* (esp. in branch I), *scēata* (esp. in branch II), corresp. to Middle & mod. Low German *schōte*, Old High German *scōza* skirt, Old Norse *skauti* kerchief, from Germanic. Cf. prec.]

▶ **I** †**1** A garment; a cloth, a napkin. Only in OE.

▶ **II** †**2** A corner, an angle; a lower corner of a sail. Only in OE.

3 NAUTICAL. A rope or chain attached to the lower corner of a sail for securing the sail or altering its direction relative to the wind. ME.

4 NAUTICAL. In *pl.* The (boarded) fore and aft sections of an open boat. Cf. FORESHEET 2, STERNSHEET 1, 3. M17.

3 †**betwixt a pair of sheets** (of a ship) sailing right before the wind. **flowing sheet**: slackened to allow free movement in the wind. **three sheets to the wind** very drunk. ***jib-sheet***: see JIB *noun*[1]. ***mainsheet***: see MAIN *adjective*.

Comb.: **sheet bend** a knot used for temporarily fastening one rope through the loop of another; **sheet-block** a block or pulley through which a sheet runs.

sheet /ʃiːt/ *verb*[1]. E17.

[from SHEET *noun*[1].]

1 *verb trans.* Wrap or fold (as) in a sheet or protective covering. E17.

2 *verb trans.* Form into sheets; spread a sheet or layer of a substance on (a surface); cover (a surface) with a sheet of snow, ice, etc. Also foll. by *with*. E17.

3 *verb trans.* Provide or cover (a bed) with sheets. Now chiefly *US*. E18.

4 *verb intrans.* Spread or flow in a sheet; (of rain) fall in sheets (freq. foll. by *down*). M19.

> 1 J. P. KENNEDY The pale moon that now sheeted with its light her whole figure. P. WAYRE Our Land Rover . . was sheeted and lashed to the fore-deck. 4 W. MCILVANNEY The river . . stretching tight as a skin and sheeting over a three-foot drop.

sheet /ʃiːt/ *verb*[2] *trans.* L18.

[from SHEET *noun*[2].]

sheet home: (*a*) NAUTICAL extend (esp. a square sail) by hauling on the sheets so that the sail is set as flat as possible; (*b*) *colloq.* (chiefly *Austral.* & *US*) fix the responsibility for; cause to realize, bring home to.

sheet anchor /ˈʃiːt aŋkə/ *noun phr.* Also **sheet-anchor**. L15.

[Origin uncertain: perh. rel. to SHOT *noun*[2], later infl. by SHEET *noun*[2].]

1 NAUTICAL. A second anchor, formerly always the largest of a ship's anchors, for use in an emergency. L15.

2 *fig.* A person or thing on which one relies as a last resort; an ultimate source of security. E16.

> 2 M. BARING: C . . . found himself isolated in a crowd . . without the sheet-anchor of Burstall.

sheet cable /ˈʃiːt keɪb(ə)l/ *noun phr.* E17.

[formed as prec. + CABLE *noun*.]

NAUTICAL. The cable attached to the sheet anchor.

sheeted /ˈʃiːtɪd/ *adjective*. E17.

[from SHEET *noun*[1], *verb*[1]; see -ED[2], -ED[1].]

1 (Of the dead, a ghost) wrapped in a sheet or burial shroud (*arch.*); wrapped or covered in a sheet or sheets for protection against damage, cold, etc. E17.

2 Of rain, snow, etc.: in the form of a sheet; spread out in a thin layer. L18.

3 Of cattle: having a broad band of white round the body. M19.

4 GEOLOGY. Of rock (esp. granite) or a rock formation: divided into thin laminae; *esp.* designating a zone of highly fissured rock associated with a fault, the fissures often being occupied by veins of minerals. E20.

> 2 F. B. YOUNG A wood where sheeted bluebells lay like pools reflecting the . . sky.

sheeting /ˈʃiːtɪŋ/ *noun*. E18.

[from SHEET *noun*[1] + -ING[1].]

1 Fabric for making bedlinen. E18.

2 a A protective lining or cladding of timber or metal. L18. ▶**b** A layer of soil, stones, etc. L19.

3 The action or an act of making sheet metal; the action of covering something with sheets or laying something in sheets. L18.

4 GEOLOGY. The occurrence or development of closely spaced, approximately parallel fractures or joints in rock. Freq. *attrib.* L19.

Sheffer's stroke /ˈʃɛfəz strəʊk/ *noun phr.* M20.

[H. M. *Sheffer* (1883–1964), US philosopher.]

LOGIC. The symbol |; the logical function of non-conjunction (and sometimes non-disjunction) that this represents.

Sheffield /ˈʃɛfiːld/ *noun*. LME.

[A manufacturing city in S. Yorkshire, England. In sense 2 from Henry North Holroyd, 3rd Earl of *Sheffield* (1832–1909).]

1 Used *attrib.* to designate cutlery made in, or manufacturing processes etc. associated with, Sheffield. LME.

2 In full ***Sheffield Shield***. A trophy presented by the 3rd Earl of Sheffield in 1892 and contested annually by Australian State cricket teams. E20.

1 Sheffield plate (*a*) silverware made in Sheffield; (*b*) (wares made of) copper coated with silver by rolling and edging with silver film and ribbon, made esp. in Sheffield between 1760 and 1840.

shegetz /ˈʃeɪɡɪts/ *noun*. Orig. & chiefly *US* (usu. *derog.*). Also **shagetz**, **shagitz**. Pl. **shkotsim** /ˈʃkɔːtsɪm/. E20.

[Yiddish *sheygets*, *sheyhets* from Hebrew *sheqes* detested thing. Cf. SHIKSA.]

Among Jewish people, a Gentile boy; a Jewish boy not observing traditional Jewish behaviour.

shehecheyanu /ʃɛ,hɛxɛˈjaːnuː/ *noun*. L19.

[Hebrew *še-heheyānū* lit. 'let us live'.]

A Jewish benediction pronounced on the evening of a principal holy day and on new occasions of thanksgiving.

shehnai *noun* var. of SHAHNAI.

Sheika *noun* var. of SHEIKHA.

sheikh /ʃeɪk, ʃiːk/ *noun*. Also **shaikh**, **shaykh**, **sheik**. L16.

[Ult. from Arab. *šayk* sheikh, old man, elder, from *šāka* be or grow old. In sense 1b from *The Sheik*, a novel by E. M. Hull (1919) and a film (1921) starring Rudolph Valentino.]

1 a (Also **S-**.) Orig., an Eastern governor, prince, or king. Later *esp.*, a chief or head of an Arab family, people, or village. Also, a title of respect. L16. ▶**b** A strong, romantic, or dashing male lover. E20.

2 A leader of a Muslim religious order or community; a great religious doctor or preacher; now *esp.*, a saint with a localized cult. L16.

3 In the Indian subcontinent, a Hindu convert to Islam. L19.

2 Sheikh-ul-Islam the supreme Muslim authority in matters relating to religion and sacred law; in Turkey, the mufti.

■ **sheikhdom** *noun* the status or position of a sheikh; the territory ruled by a sheikh: M19. **sheikhly** *adjective* pertaining to or characteristic of a sheikh E20.

Sheikha /ˈʃeɪkə/ *noun*. Also **s-**, **Shaikha**, **Sheika**. M19.

[Arab. *šayka*.]

An Arab lady of good family; the (chief) wife of a sheikh. Also, a title of respect.

sheila /ˈʃiːlə/ *noun*. *Austral.* & *NZ colloq.* Orig. †**shaler**. M19.

[Origin uncertain: later assim. to female forename *Sheila*.]

A girl, a young woman; a girlfriend.

> M. SHADBOLT Ned said he wasn't married yet . . . 'Still looking for the right sheila?'

sheitel /ˈʃeɪt(ə)l/ *noun*. L19.

[Yiddish *sheytl* from Middle High German *scheitel* crown of the head.]

Among orthodox Ashkenazic Jews: a wig worn by a married woman.

shekel /ˈʃɛk(ə)l/ *noun*. M16.

[Hebrew *šeqel*, from *šāqal* weigh.]

1 *Hist.* A unit of weight and silver coin used in ancient Israel and the Middle East, equal to one-sixtieth of a mina. Cf. SICLE. M16.

2 In *pl.* Money; wealth, riches. Freq. in ***rake in the shekels***, make a large amount of money rapidly. *colloq.* L19.

3 The basic monetary unit of Israel, equal to 100 agorot. L20.

shekere *noun* var. of SEKERE.

Shekinah /ʃɪˈkʌɪnə/ *noun*. Also **Shechinah**. M17.

[Late Hebrew *šěḵīnāh*, from *šāḵan* rest, dwell.]

CHRISTIAN CHURCH. God's divine presence, esp. in the temple of Solomon; *transf.* a radiant light symbolizing God's presence.

sheld /ʃɛld/ *adjective*. *dial.* E16.

[Rel. to Middle Dutch *schillede* variegated, from *schillen* (mod. Dutch *verschillen* differ) diversify.]

Particoloured, pied, piebald.

sheld-duck *noun* var. of SHELDUCK.

sheldrake /ˈʃɛldreɪk/ *noun*. Pl. same, **-s**. Also (now *rare* or *obsolete*) **shiel-** /ˈʃiːl-/. ME.

[Prob. from prec. + DRAKE *noun*[2]; var. form assim. to SHIELD *noun*[1], app. with ref. to the knob on the bill of a breeding male.]

= next.

shelduck /ˈʃɛldʌk/ *noun*. Pl. same, **-s**. Also **sheld-duck**, (earlier) †**shell-duck**. E18.

[from prec. with substitution of *-duck* (DUCK *noun*[1]) for *-drake*.]

Any of various large gooselike ducks of the tribe Tadornini, esp. of the Old World genus *Tadorna*, as the common *T. tadorna* of shores and brackish inland waters in Eurasia and N. Africa. Also occas., any of various other ducks with variegated plumage, as the canvas-back.

ruddy shelduck: see RUDDY *adjective*[1].

■ **sheldgoose** *noun* a shelduck; *esp.* any of the larger members of the tribe Tadornini native to Africa and S. America, as the Egyptian goose: E20.

shelf /ʃɛlf/ *noun*[1]. Pl. **shelves** /ʃɛlvz/. ME.

[Middle & mod. Low German *schelf* shelf, set of shelves, rel. to Old English *scylfe* partition, compartment, *scylf* crag, pinnacle.]

▶ **I 1** A thin flat piece of wood or other rigid material, projecting horizontally from a wall, or as part of a bookcase, cabinet, etc., used to hold books, ornaments, commodities, etc.; a flat-topped recess in a wall etc. used for holding or displaying objects. ME. ▶**b** An object or objects placed on a shelf; the contents of a shelf. M18.

†**2** A cupboard, a cabinet. ME–L16.

3 a PRINTING. In a wooden hand-press, a flat wooden bar divided in two which clasps the hose and causes it to come down perpendicularly. Also called ***till***. *obsolete* exc. *Hist.* E18. ▶**b** A timber bolted on to the inner side of the frame of a wooden ship to support the deck-beams. M19.

4 A police informer. *Austral. slang.* E20.

> 1 B. CHATWIN A narrow room, made narrower by . . plate-glass shelves . . crammed with porcelain. **off the shelf** (of goods etc.) supplied ready-made; available from existing stock. **on the shelf** (*a*) put aside, deferred; no longer active or of use; (*b*) (of a woman) past the age at which she might expect to be married. ***hanging shelf***: see HANGING *adjective*. ***open shelf***: see OPEN *adjective*.

▶ **II 5** A ledge, projecting layer, or terrace of land, rock, etc. LME.

6 MINING & GEOLOGY. Bedrock. L17.

> 5 C. KILIAN The Shelf extended to the horizon; a vast plain of ice. ***continental shelf***: see CONTINENTAL *adjective*.

Comb.: **shelf appeal** the attractiveness to a customer of packaged goods displayed in a shop; **shelf back** *US* the spine of a book; **shelf-catalogue** a short-title catalogue of the books in a library arranged according to their location on the shelves and consequently according to their class or subject; **shelf cod**: found in inshore waters above the continental shelf; **shelf company** COMMERCE a public company, without assets but constituted as a legal corporation, which is kept on the shelf until ready to be used as a listing vehicle for an existing private company; **shelf ice** [translating German *Schelfeis*] ice which forms a thick level layer on water (usu. the sea) but is attached to land; **shelf-life** (*a*) the length of time that a commodity may be stored without becoming unfit for use or consumption; (*b*) (esp. of a book) the period of time during which an item is considered as saleable; **shelf-list** = ***shelf-catalogue*** above; **shelf-mark** *noun & verb* (*a*) *noun* a notation on a book, and listed in a catalogue, specifying the book's location in a library, a press-mark; (*b*) *verb trans.* give a shelf-mark to; **shelf paper**: used for lining shelves; **shelf-room** available space on a shelf; **shelf sea** an expanse of sea overlying continental shelf.

¶ First recorded as a place-name.

■ **shelfful** *noun* as much or as many as a shelf will hold L19. **shelflike** *adjective* resembling (that of) a shelf M19. **shelfy** *adjective*[1] having ledges or terraces of rock etc. M18.

shelf /ʃɛlf/ *noun*[2]. Now *rare*. Pl. **shelves** /ʃɛlvz/. M16.

[Prob. alt. by assoc. with prec. of †*shelp*, repr. Old English *scylp* sharp rock, of unkn. origin. Cf. SHELVE *noun*[1].]

A sandbank in the sea or a river making the water shallow and hazardous to shipping. Also, a submerged ledge of rock.

¶ Very common until *c* 1750.

■ **shelfy** *adjective*[2] having many sandbanks lying near the surface of the water **L16.**

shelf /ʃɛlf/ *verb trans.* **E19.**

[from SHELF *noun*[1].]

1 = SHELVE *verb*[2] 4. **E19.**

2 Inform on. Cf. SHELF *noun*[1] 4. *Austral. slang*. **M20.**

shell /ʃɛl/ *noun & adjective.*

[Old English *sćell*, (West Saxon) *sćiell* = Middle & mod. Low German, Middle Dutch *schelle, schille*, Dutch *schel, schil* pod, rind, scale, shell, Old Norse *skel* sea shell, Gothic *skalja* tile, from Germanic. Cf. SCALE *noun*[3], SHALE *noun*[1], *noun*[2].]

▶ **A** *noun*. **I 1** The hard protective outer covering secreted by a soft-bodied invertebrate animal; *esp.* that of a marine mollusc, freq. spiral, conical, or in two curved pieces, and made largely of calcium salts; the material of this. Freq. with specifying word, passing into sense 8. **OE.** ▸**b** *spec.* The hard coiled covering of a snail, into which its body can be withdrawn for extra protection. **LME.**

2 The thin hard brittle calcareous outer layer of a bird's egg; eggshell. Also, a similar outer protective layer around the eggs of other animals. **OE.**

3 The hard outer case embracing a seed or the kernel of a nut. **ME.**

4 A sea shell or a receptacle resembling one used for a specific purpose; *spec.* †(*a*) a drinking-vessel; †(*b*) *Scot.* a target; †(*c*) (in *pl.*) shells used as a medium of exchange; (*d*) *Hist.* a mussel-shell containing artist's pigment to be mixed with a medium before use; †(*e*) *poet.* a conch shell blown by a Triton. **ME.**

5 a The husk or outer covering of a fruit, *esp.* the pod of a legume. **LME.** ▸**b** The empty case of a citrus fruit. **E20.**

6 A potsherd; *spec.* a potsherd or tile used for voting by the ancient Greeks to decide the temporary banishment of a citizen in the custom of ostracism. **LME.**

7 a The hard external covering of a tortoise or turtle; the horny material of which this is composed, tortoiseshell. **M16.** ▸†**b** A lyre (with ref. to the legend that the first lyre was a tortoise shell stringed). *poet.* **M18–E19.**

8 With specifying word: a mollusc or other shelled invertebrate (of a specified kind). **M18.**

9 In various animals, a hard external covering, as the armour of an armadillo, the wing-case of an insect, the cast skin of a pupa, etc. **L18.**

1 ***cockle-shell, mussel-shell, oyster-shell***, etc. **8** ***acorn shell, lamp-shell, razor-shell***, etc.

▶ **II** †**10** A scale of a fish, reptile, etc. *rare*. **OE–M17.**

11 A flattened fragment, a scale, a lamina (of stone, bone, etc.). Long *rare*. **ME.**

†**12** In *pl.* Scurf. **LME–E16.**

13 In *pl.* ▸**a** Fragments. *obsolete* exc. *Scot.* **M16.** ▸**b** Burnt limestone before it is slaked. Chiefly *Scot.* **M16.**

14 *Hist.* Any of the thin metal plates composing scale-armour. **L16.**

15 A thin metal plate worn as an epaulette. *rare*. **M19.**

▶ **III 16** †**a** The bowl of a chalice. Only in **M16.** ▸**b** A scale of a balance. *Scot.* **L16.**

17 a *gen.* Any hollow spherical, hemispherical, or dome-shaped object. **L16.** ▸**b** A thin body bounded by two closely spaced curved surfaces, *esp.* a thin curved sheet used as a structural member. **L19.** ▸**c** A saucer-shaped structure designed to accommodate a band or orchestra. *US*. **E20.**

18 The semicircular guard of a sword, often elaborately worked. **L17.**

19 The apsidal end of the schoolroom at Westminster School, so called from its resemblance in shape to a conch shell. Hence, the form (intermediate between the fifth and sixth) which originally occupied this part of Westminster School. Also *transf.*, an intermediate form in any of several public schools. **M18.**

20 A tool, artefact, etc., having (an effective part with) a thin concave form. **E19.**

21 The outer ear; the concha or pinna. **M19.**

22 A light narrow racing-boat. **M19.**

23 PHYSICS. (A set of electrons forming) each of a number of concentric structures or sets of orbitals around the nucleus of an atom (also ***electron shell***). Also, (a set of nucleons forming) a corresponding structure within a nucleus. **E20.**

24 COMPUTING. A program in some operating systems, such as Unix, which translates commands keyed by a user into ones understood by the operating system. Also ***shell program***. **L20.**

📖 **17a** B. TAYLOR The whole vast shell of the firmament. ***c band shell, music shell***, etc. **23** ***K-shell, L-shell***, etc. ***valence shell***: see VALENCE *noun*[1].

▶ **IV 25 a** A covering of earth, stone, etc. Now *rare*. **M17.** ▸**b** The earth's crust. Now *rare* or *obsolete*. **E18.**

26 a A hollow case of metal or paper used as a container for explosives, fireworks, cartridges, etc.; *US* a cartridge. **M17.** ▸**b** An explosive projectile or bomb for use in a cannon, large gun, or mortar. **M17.**

27 a The walls or external structure of a building, ship, etc., *esp.* an unfinished or gutted one. **M17.** ▸**b** A roughly made wooden building without decoration or furniture. *US*. **M19.** ▸**c** MUSIC. The cylindrical or hemispherical frame of a drum which supports the skin or head. **L19.**

28 The external part, outward appearance, or containing framework of something immaterial. **M17.**

29 Any of various objects forming or resembling an outer case, as (*a*) NAUTICAL the outer part or body of a block inside which the sheave revolves and to which the hook or shackle is attached; (*b*) *US* a (usu. sleeveless) overblouse or light all-weather jacket; (*c*) the metal body of a vehicle; (*d*) a roughly made or temporary wooden coffin; an inner coffin of lead etc.; (*e*) a pastry case, *esp.* an unfilled or hollow one for a tart, flan, etc.; (*f*) the more or less rigid (freq. plastic) outer casing of any manufactured object. **M18.**

30 a A mere semblance; a hollow or empty form. **L18.** ▸**b** In full ***shell company***. A company which is quoted on a stock exchange, although no longer trading, and which is made the subject of a takeover bid. **M20.**

31 COMPUTING. A program that requires the addition of data relevant to a particular application in order to function. **L20.**

📖 **26b** A. MACLEAN Armour piercing shells . . designed to go through two inches of steel plate . . before they explode. **27a** A. S. BYATT The Castle . . was now a stone shell encircling mown humps and hillocks. **28** CONAN DOYLE There were some whose piety was a shell for their ambition. **30a** *Times* The marriage was . . at an end, and had become a shell.

Phrases: **come out of one's shell** become more outgoing, sociable, or communicative. **creep into one's shell, draw into one's shell, withdraw into one's shell** avoid social contact; become reserved, shy, or uncommunicative. **in the shell** (*a*) (of shellfish) served for food with the shell on; (*b*) (of an egg, a bird, etc.) unhatched; *fig.* in embryo, not yet fully developed. **out of one's shell** having emerged into life; having experience of the world and its ways (usu. in neg. contexts). ***staircase shell***: see STAIRCASE *noun* 2. ***withdraw into one's shell***: see ***creep into one's shell*** above. ***yellow shell***: see YELLOW *adjective*.

▶ **B** *attrib.* or as *adjective*. **1** Of an animal, fruit, etc.: having a shell. Now *rare* exc. in SHELLFISH. **LME.**

2 Of a geological formation, (a deposit of) sand, gravel, etc.: consisting wholly or largely of (sea) shells (esp. in a fragmented or powdered state). **L16.**

3 Consisting of or made from a shell or shells; decorated with shells; *US* (of a road) having a bed or layer of shells. **E17.**

4 Of the shape or colour of a shell; (of material etc.) having a pattern of shells. **L18.**

5 Of an implement: hollow; having a concave part. **E19.**

6 Of or pertaining to an explosive shell or shells. **E20.**

7 Of or pertaining to transactions in a shell company (sense 30b above). **M20.**

📖 **3** B. HARTE A shell workbox. **6** S. HILL They . . dropped down into a shell hole.

Comb. & special collocations: **shell-back** (*a*) *joc.* a sailor, *esp.* a hardened or experienced one; (*b*) a marine turtle; **shellbark (hickory)** any of several N. American hickories with bark which peels off in patches, esp. *Carya laciniosa*; **shell beach** a beach composed wholly or predominantly of sea shells; **shell bean** any of various types of bean, the seeds of which are cooked and eaten rather than the pods; **shell-bird** *Canad.* the red-breasted merganser, *Mergus serrator*; **shell-bit** a gouge-shaped boring bit; **shell-briar** *adjective* designating a type of tobacco-pipe with a rough, dark-stained stem and bowl; **shell cocoa** the husks of cocoa beans or the drink made from these; **shell concrete** BUILDING concrete used in shell construction; **shell construction** BUILDING the use of thin curved sheets (shells) to roof areas having wide spans; **shellcracker** *US* = ***red-ear (sunfish)*** s.v. RED *adjective*; ***shell-duck***: see SHELDUCK; **shell egg** a hen's egg sold or bought in the shell as opp. to dried; **shell-flower** an ornamental labiate plant of Asia Minor, *Moluccella laevis*, having small white flowers surrounded by a large inflated calyx; **shell-game** *US* a sleight-of-hand game or trick in which a small object is concealed under a walnut shell etc., with bystanders encouraged to place bets or to guess as to which shell the object is under (cf. THIMBLERIG *noun*); **shell-gland** ZOOLOGY a gland which secretes the shell of a mollusc, a bird's egg, etc.; **shell-gold** *Hist.* powdered gold for painting etc., kept in a mussel-shell ready for mixing with a medium before use; **shell-gritted** *adjective* (ARCHAEOLOGY) denoting pottery made of a paste mixed with fragments of shell; **shell-heap** a mound of domestic waste consisting mainly of shells, common at prehistoric sites; *spec.* (*Hist.*) such a mound accumulated by aborigines who subsisted on shellfish; **shell ice** *Canad.* thin, brittle ice; cat-ice; **shell-jacket** an army officer's tight-fitting undress jacket, reaching to the waist; **shell-lime** lime of a fine quality produced by burning sea shells; **shell midden** = ***shell-heap*** above; **shell-money** shells used as a medium of exchange, e.g. wampum; **shell-mould** a mould made by shell-moulding; **shell-moulding** FOUNDING a method of making moulds and cores in which a shell of resin-bonded sand is formed in parts around a heated metal pattern, the parts being joined together after removal of the pattern; **shell-mound** = ***shell-heap*** above; **shell parrakeet, shell parrot** = BUDGERIGAR; **shell-pink** a delicate pale pink; **shell-plate** one of the plates forming the outer shell of a ship, boiler, etc.; ***shell program***: see sense A.24 above; **shellproof** *adjective* able to resist attack by explosive shells; **shell rock** *N. Amer.* hard rock consisting largely of compacted sea shells; **shell roof** a roof consisting of a shell (sense 17b above); **shell-sand**: consisting largely of fragmented or powdered shells; **shell-shock** *noun & verb* (*a*) *noun* a nervous breakdown or other psychological disturbance resulting from bombardment or prolonged exposure to conditions of active warfare (also *transf.*); (*b*) *verb trans.* affect (as) with shell-shock; **shell-shocked** *adjective* suffering from shell-shock; **shell-silver** *Hist.* silver for painting etc. in the same form as shell-gold; **shell-snail** †(*a*) a retiring or shy person; (*b*) a snail with a shell; **shell steak** a steak cut from the short loin; **shell-stitch** any of various knitting or sewing stitches producing shell-like patterns; **shell suit** a usu. brightly coloured tracksuit with a soft lining and a weatherproof nylon outer 'shell', used for leisurewear; **shell transformer** = ***shell-type transformer*** below; **shell top** a short sleeveless top, typically having button fastenings down the back and a simple shape with a high neckline; **shell-type** *noun & adjective* (designating) something having or resembling a shell in any sense; ***shell-type transformer***, a transformer having its windings wholly or largely enclosed within the metal core; **shell-work** ornamentation consisting of a decorative arrangement of shells cemented on to wood etc.

■ **shell-less** /-l-l-/ *adjective* **L18.** **shell-like** /-l-l-/ *adjective & noun* (*a*) *adjective* resembling (that of) a shell; (*b*) *noun* (*colloq.*) a person's ear (esp. in ***a word in your shell-like***): **L17.**

shell /ʃɛl/ *verb.* **M16.**

[from prec. Cf. SHALE *verb*.]

1 *verb trans.* Remove (a nut etc.) from its shell, husk, etc.; remove the shell, husk, etc., of. Cf. UNSHELL. **M16.** ▸**b** *verb intrans.* Of grain, a seed, etc.: be separated or removed from its shell, husk, etc. **E19.** ▸**c** MEDICINE. Extrude, expel, (a growth). **L19.** ▸**d** *verb trans.* Of a child, a young animal: shed or lose (the milk teeth). *Scot. & dial.* **L19.**

2 *verb trans.* **a** Enclose (as) in a shell; encase. **M17.** ▸**b** Provide or cover with a shell or a layer of shells. **L19.**

3 *verb intrans.* Come away or fall off as a shell or outer layer; peel off in thin pieces or scales. Usu. foll. by *off.* **L17.**

4 *verb trans.* Bombard (an enemy position etc.) with shells; drive (a person) *out of* a place by shelling. **E19.**

5 *verb trans. & intrans.* Foll. by *out*: pay (money), hand over (a required sum). *colloq.* **E19.**

6 *verb trans.* BASEBALL. Score heavily against (an opposing pitcher or team). Freq. in *pass.* Cf. SHELLAC *verb* 2. **M20.**

📖 **1** DICKENS Shelling peas into a dish. E. B. TYLOR The women who shell almonds. **2a** N. WHITING His body shelled in a Satten skin Of azure dye. **5** *Scootering* They'd only have to shell out . . £1.00 to buy you another.

Comb.: **shell-out** a game of snooker etc. played by three or more people in which the same balls are used as in the game pyramids and a stake is paid by the other players each time a player pockets a ball.

■ **sheller** *noun* a person who or machine which shells peas, molluscs, corn, etc. **L17.**

shellac /ʃəˈlak/ *noun & verb.* **M17.**

[from SHELL *noun* + LAC *noun*[1], translating French *laque en écailles* lac in thin plates.]

▶ **A** *noun.* **1** Lac melted into thin plates and used for making varnish, later used esp. in the manufacture of gramophone records. **M17.**

2 A gramophone record made of shellac. **M20.**

📖 **1** *attrib.*: S. ELDRED-GRIGG Afternoon tea on a shellac tray.

▶ **B** *verb trans.* Orig. & chiefly *N. Amer.* Infl. **-ck-**.

1 Coat or varnish (as) with shellac. **L19.**

2 Beat, thrash soundly; defeat thoroughly. *slang*. **M20.**

📖 **2** R. COOVER The Knicks shellacked Mel Trench's Cels, and hung on to their two-game lead.

■ **shellacked** *ppl adjective* (*a*) coated or varnished (as) with shellac; (*b*) *US slang* intoxicated: **L19.**

shellacking /ʃəˈlakɪŋ/ *noun.* Chiefly *N. Amer.*. **L19.**

[from prec.]

1 A coating of shellac. **L19.**

2 A beating, a sound thrashing; a thorough defeat. *slang*. **M20.**

shelled /ʃɛld/ *adjective.* **LME.**

[from SHELL *noun, verb*: see -ED[2], -ED[1].]

1 Of an animal, a fruit, etc.: having a shell or shells (of a specified kind). **LME.**

2 That has been separated from its shell; from which the shell has been removed. **L17.**

3 Of a beach: covered with shells. **L19.**

4 Of explosives etc.: contained in a shell or shells. **E20.**

2 shelled corn *US* maize removed from the cob.

Shelleyan /ˈʃɛliən/ *adjective & noun.* **M19.**

[from Percy Bysshe *Shelley* (1792–1822) + -AN.]

▶ **A** *adjective.* Of, pertaining to, or characteristic of Shelley or his poetry, or the ideas expressed in his works. **M19.**

▶ **B** *noun.* A student or admirer of Shelley or his poetry. **L19.**

■ **Shelleyˈana** *noun pl.* writings etc. connected with Shelley **L19.** **Shelleyism** *noun* thought or action characteristic of Shelley **E19.** **Shelleyite** *noun* = SHELLEYAN *noun* **L19.**

shellfish /ˈʃɛlfɪʃ/ *noun.* Pl. **-es** /-ɪz/, (usu.) same.
[Old English *scilfisc* = Old Norse *skelfiskr*.]
Any aquatic invertebrate animal whose outer covering is a shell, usu. a mollusc (as an oyster, a winkle, a mussel, etc.) or a crustacean (as a crab, a prawn, a shrimp, etc.), esp. one regarded as edible.

shelling /ˈʃɛlɪŋ/ *noun.* L16.
[from SHELL *verb* + -ING¹.]
1 a In *pl.* Husks, chaff. L16. ▸**b** Grain etc. from which the husk has been removed. E18.
2 The action of SHELL *verb*; *spec.* (*a*) removal of the shell of peas, nuts, etc.; (*b*) covering or spreading with (a layer of) shells; (*c*) the firing of explosive shells, bombardment with shells. E18.
3 The collecting of sea shells. M19.

†shellpad *noun.* M16–L18.
[from SHELL *noun* + PAD *noun*¹, after Middle & mod. Low German *shildpadde*, Middle Dutch *schiltpadde* (Dutch *schildpad*) lit. 'shield-toad'.]
A tortoise.

shelly /ˈʃɛli/ *adjective.* M16.
[from SHELL *noun* + -Y¹.]
1 Having many shells, esp. sea shells; (of a geological formation) consisting wholly or mainly of shells. M16.
2 Of the nature of a shell; forming a covering resembling a shell; shell-like. L16. ▸**b** Of a thin, bony, and lanky build. M19.
3 Of an animal: having a shell. L16.
4 Formed from a shell, esp. a sea shell; consisting of sea shells or shell fish. E18.
Comb.: **shelly-coat** *Scot.* (*a*) a water-spirit wearing sea shells which make a clattering noise; (*b*) a sheriff's officer or bailiff (so named from the buttons and badges of office on his coat).

shelt /ʃɛlt/ *noun. Scot.* L18.
[Abbreviation of SHELTIE.]
A Sheltie, a Shetland pony.

Shelta /ˈʃɛltə/ *noun & adjective.* L19.
[Origin unkn.]
(Of) an ancient cryptic language used by tinkers, gypsies, etc., composed partly of Irish or Gaelic words, mostly disguised by inversion or by arbitrary alteration of initial consonants.

shelter /ˈʃɛltə/ *noun.* L16.
[Origin uncertain: perh. alt. of SHELTRON.]
1 a A structure giving protection from rain, wind, or sun; anything serving as a shield or a place of refuge from the weather. L16. ▸**b** A thing giving a refuge from danger, attack, or observation; a place of safety; a structure giving protection from air raids, nuclear fallout, etc., usu. underground. E17. ▸**c** Protection from the weather; a line of trees, a wall, etc., providing such protection. E17. ▸**d** A covering to protect an object from damage. L17. ▸**e** A place providing accommodation or refuge for the homeless, the oppressed, etc. L19. ▸**f** An animal sanctuary. *N. Amer.* L20. ▸**g** = ***tax shelter*** s.v. TAX *noun.* L20.
2 The state of being in a sheltered or protected condition or location; security from harm or attack. Freq. in ***find shelter in***, ***take shelter in***, ***find shelter under***, ***take shelter under***. L16.

> 🕮 **1a** A. P. HERBERT A covered shelter . . to which the mothers and children could retire on showery . . evenings. *fig.*: T. T. LYNCH The storms of the law may drive men to the shelter of the gospel. **b** ***Anderson shelter***, ***Morrison shelter***. attrib.: ***shelter life***, ***shelter warden***, etc. **c** J. C. LOUDON The trees . . produce . . shelter and shade. **e** A. MUNRO Denise runs a Women's Centre . . . She gets beaten women into shelters. **2** G. SAYER A most generous person, who gave shelter to many. *fig.*: LD MACAULAY The tribunals ought to be sacred places of refuge, where . . the innocent . . may find shelter.

Comb.: **shelter-belt** a narrow strip of trees planted as a windbreak to protect crops etc.; **shelterdeck** *noun & adjective* (NAUTICAL) (*a*) *noun* a light deck above the main deck of a passenger craft more or less closed at the sides but open at the ends; (*b*) *adjective* designating or pertaining to a deck of this type; **shelter foot** (now *Hist.*) a painful swollen foot or leg caused by sleeping in a sitting position esp. in an air-raid shelter; **shelter half** MILITARY half of a shelter tent; **shelter leg** = ***shelter foot*** above; **shelter magazine** a periodical concerned with home improvements, interior decoration, etc.; **shelter tent** MILITARY a small ridged tent; a dog-tent; **shelter tree** any tree grown to provide shelter; **shelter wood** mature trees left standing to provide shelter in which saplings can grow.
¶ Recorded earlier in ME as a place-name.
■ **shelterage** *noun* (*rare*) a place of shelter M17. **shelterless** *adjective* (*a*) without a shelter or covering; unprotected from the elements; (*b*) that provides no shelter: E18. **sheltery** *adjective* (*rare*) providing shelter E18.

shelter /ˈʃɛltə/ *verb.* L16.
[from the noun.]
1 *verb trans.* Be or provide a shelter for; protect from the weather, danger, attack, etc.; conceal; be a place of safety or refuge for. L16. ▸**b** Protect (invested income) from taxation; invest (money) with this purpose. M20.
2 *verb intrans.* & *refl.* Take shelter (*from*); find refuge from danger, attack, etc.; find protection or safety. L16.

> 🕮 **1** W. CRUISE The vendor . . made use of the act for sheltering fraud. *Times* A . . centre that shelters battered women. R. FRASER No trees then sheltered the building. **2** SIR W. SCOTT Sheltering myself behind the Prelate's authority. F. SPALDING Rows of figures sheltering from air-raids on the underground platforms.

■ **shelterer** *noun* a person who takes shelter, esp. from an air raid; a person who gives shelter to another: E18.

Sheltie /ˈʃɛlti/ *noun.* Orig. *Scot.* Also **Shelty**. E16.
[Prob. repr. Orkney pronunc. of Old Norse *Hjalti* Shetlander.]
1 A Shetlander. Chiefly *joc.* E16.
2 A Shetland pony; now, any small pony. Also more fully †***Shelty horse***. E17.
3 A Shetland sheepdog. E20.

sheltron /ˈʃɛltrɒn/ *noun.* Long *obsolete* exc. *Hist.*
[Old English *scieldtruma*, from *scield* SHIELD *noun*¹ + *truma* troop.]
A close, compact formation of troops; a phalanx.

Shelty *noun* var. of SHELTIE.

shelve /ʃɛlv/ *noun*¹. Now *arch. rare.* L16.
[A new sing. evolved from *shelves* pl. of SHELF *noun*².]
= SHELF *noun*².
Comb.: †**shelveflat** a level sandbank, a shoal.

shelve /ʃɛlv/ *noun*². Now *arch. rare.* E18.
[from SHELVE *verb*².]
A ledge or overhang of rock.

shelve /ʃɛlv/ *verb*¹. LME.
[Origin uncertain: perh. from SHELF *noun*¹.]
1 *verb intrans.* Of ground, a surface, etc.: slope gradually. Usu. foll. by *away*, *down*, etc. LME.
2 *verb trans.* Tilt or tip up (a cart) for unloading. *Scot. & dial.* L16.
†**3** *verb intrans.* Have an inclined position. M17–M18.

> 🕮 **1** J. RULE Mountains shelving down . . to the edge of the desert.

■ **shelver** *noun*¹ a person employed to tilt and unload carts L16.

shelve /ʃɛlv/ *verb*². L16.
[from *shelves* pl. of SHELF *noun*¹.]
†**1** *verb intrans.* Project like a shelf, overhang. *rare* (Shakes.). Only in L16.
2 *verb trans.* Provide or fit (a room, cupboard, etc.) with shelves. L16.
3 *verb trans.* Place (esp. books) on a shelf or shelves. E17.
4 *verb trans.* Remove (a person) from active or useful service; put aside, defer consideration of, (a question, a plan, etc.); abandon. E19.

> 🕮 **2** L. I. WILDER One whole long wall was shelved. **3** M. L. KING Books . . shelved neatly in his library. **4** A. KENNY Problems which his predecessors had shelved. *Sounds* Costello's legal battle with Warner Brothers is unexpectedly shelved.

■ **shelver** *noun*² a person who shelves something; *esp.* (orig. & chiefly *US*) a person who shelves books in a library: L19.

shelves *noun* pl. of SHELF *noun*¹, *noun*².

shelving /ˈʃɛlvɪŋ/ *noun*¹. L16.
[from SHELVE *verb*¹ + -ING¹.]
1 The action of SHELVE *verb*¹ 2. *Scot. & dial.* L16.
2 The fact or condition of sloping; the degree of sloping; a sloping surface. L17.

shelving /ˈʃɛlvɪŋ/ *noun*². E17.
[from SHELVE *verb*² + -ING¹.]
1 A detachable side-rail for a waggon or cart. Usu. in *pl.* Chiefly *Scot. & dial.* E17.
2 The action of SHELVE *verb*². M17.
3 A set of shelves; shelves collectively; material for making shelves. E19.

shelvy /ˈʃɛlvi/ *adjective*¹. L16.
[from SHELVE *noun*¹ + -Y¹.]
Of a shore: having shelves or dangerous sandbanks.

shelvy /ˈʃɛlvi/ *adjective*². *rare.* E19.
[from SHELVE *noun*² + -Y¹.]
Projecting like a shelf; overhanging.

Shema /ˈʃeɪmə, *foreign* ʃɛˈma/ *noun.* E18.
[Hebrew *šĕma'* imper. of *šāma'* hear.]
The first word of *Deuteronomy* 6:4: the section of the liturgy consisting of three passages of the Pentateuch (*Deuteronomy* 6:4–9, 11:13–21, *Numbers* 15:37–41) repeated twice daily and used as a Jewish statement of faith.

Shemite /ˈʃɛmʌɪt/ *noun & adjective.* M17.
[from *Shem* Noah's eldest son (cf. *Genesis* 6:10) + -ITE¹.]
▸**A** *noun.* A Semite. M17.
▸**B** *adjective.* Of or pertaining to the Semites. L18.
■ **Shemitic** *adjective & noun* = SEMITIC *adjective & noun* E19.

shemozzle /ʃɪˈmɒz(ə)l/ *noun & verb. slang.* Also **schemozzle**. L19.
[Yiddish, prob. formed as SCHLIMAZEL.]
▸**A** *noun.* A muddle, a complicated situation; a quarrel, a brawl, a mêlée. L19.

> 🕮 *New Zealand Listener* His lyrics . . all rolled together into one lumpy, verbose shemozzle.

▸**B** *verb intrans.* Make one's escape, leave hastily. E20.

shen /ʃɛn/ *noun.* Pl. same. M19.
[Chinese *shén*.]
In Chinese philosophy, a god, a person of supernatural power; the spirit of a dead person.

shenachie *noun* var. of SENNACHIE.

shenanigan /ʃɪˈnanɪɡ(ə)n/ *noun. colloq.* (orig. *US*). M19.
[Origin unkn.]
Skulduggery, dubious conduct; teasing, nonsense; a trick, a prank, an instance of high-spirited behaviour. Usu. in *pl.*

> 🕮 *Mail on Sunday* Merciless shenanigans by the staff to get the new editor sacked.

†shench *noun.* OE–LME.
[Old English *scenc*, from Germanic.]
A drink, a draught; a cupful.
¶ Repr. in 2nd elem. of NUNCHEON.

shend /ʃɛnd/ *verb.* Now *arch. & dial.* Pa. t. & pple **shent** /ʃɛnt/.
[Old English *scendan* put to shame, ruin, discomfit = Old Low German *scendian* (Dutch *schenden*), Old High German *scentan* (German *schänden*) from West Germanic base also of SHAME *verb*.]
1 *verb trans.* Put to shame or confusion; confound, disgrace. OE. ▸†**b** Outshine; put to shame by superiority. *rare* (Spenser). Only in L16.
2 *verb trans.* Blame, reproach; scold; in *pass.*, be punished. OE.
3 *verb trans.* Destroy, ruin, bring to destruction. Also, injure, damage, spoil. OE. ▸**b** Disfigure; corrupt; defile. Long *obsolete* exc. *poet.* OE. ▸**c** Overcome with fatigue; bewilder, stupefy. LME.
†**4** *verb trans.* Defeat in battle, in a dispute, etc. OE–E19.
†**5** *verb intrans.* Become ruined or spoilt; suffer shame or disgrace. LME–M16.

> 🕮 **1** SPENSER The famous name of knighthood fowly shend. **2** BROWNING Masters being lauded and sciolists shent. **3c** *Outlook* I stood utterly shent and powerless.

■ **shending** *verbal noun* the action of the verb; confusion, disgrace: ME.

sheng /ʃʌŋ/ *noun*¹. Pl. same. L18.
[Chinese *shēng*.]
MUSIC. A Chinese form of mouth-organ consisting of a rigid wind chest and a set of reed pipes.

sheng /ʃʌŋ/ *noun*². Pl. same. L19.
[Chinese *shēng*.]
The principal male character in a Chinese opera.

shent *verb pa. t. & pple* of SHEND.

shenzi /ˈʃɛnzi/ *noun.* Chiefly *derog.* E20.
[Kiswahili.]
In E. Africa, an uncivilized African; a barbarian, a person outside one's cultural group.

she-oak /ˈʃiːəʊk/ *noun. Austral.* Also **sheoak**. L18.
[from SHE + OAK. Cf. *he-oak* s.v. HE *pronoun, noun, & adjective*.]
1 Any of various trees constituting the genus *Casuarina* (family Casuarinaceae), esp. *C. stricta* (more fully ***drooping she-oak***) and *C. littoralis* (more fully ***black she-oak***). L18.
†**2** Australian-brewed beer. *slang.* M19–M20.
Comb.: **she-oak net** a safety net on a ship's gangway to prevent (esp. drunken) sailors from falling into the water.

sheogue /ˈʃiːɒɡ/ *noun.* M19.
[Irish *sióg* fairy.]
In Ireland, a fairy.

Sheol /ˈʃiːəʊl, ˈʃiːɒl/ *noun.* L16.
[Hebrew *šĕʼōl*.]
The Hebrew abode of the dead or departed spirits, conceived as a subterranean region clothed in thick darkness, return from which is impossible. Now also (*joc. & colloq.*, freq. **s-**), hell.

> 🕮 B. CRONIN Them big bugs are the meanest thing this side Sheol.

shep /ʃɛp/ *noun. obsolete* exc. *dial.* LME.
[Abbreviation.]
A shepherd.

shepherd /ˈʃɛpəd/ *noun.* OE.
[from SHEEP *noun* + HERD *noun*².]
1 a A person employed to guard, tend, and herd sheep, esp. at pasture; a member of a pastoral people herding and usually owning sheep etc. OE. ▸**b** In pastoral literature etc., an idealized or romanticized shepherd; a rustic lover. Formerly also, a writer of pastoral poetry, a fellow-poet in the pastoral tradition. *poet.* L16. ▸**c** ***the Shepherds*** [= French *les Pastoureaux*], those who took part in the French peasant uprisings of 1251 ff. and 1320. M18.
2 *fig.* A person, esp. a member of the clergy, who watches over, guides, or cares for a group of people; a

spiritual guardian, a pastor. Also, (in biblical use) God in relation to Israel or the Church; Jesus Christ (esp. with ref. to *John* 10:12). ME.
†**3** More fully ***shepherd-spider***. A harvestman (arachnid). *rare*. E17–M19.
4 A shepherd king of Ancient Egypt. E19.
5 *Hist.* A person who takes token occupation of a gold-mining claim to retain legal rights over it; a person employed to do this. *Austral.* M19.
6 = ***German shepherd (dog)*** s.v. GERMAN *noun*[1] & *adjective*[1]. M20.

📖 **1b** MILTON Nymphs and Shepherds dance no more. **2** CARLYLE The shepherd of the people has .. been put to bed in .. Versailles. F. E. GRETTON Then the shepherd read, .. explaining a portion of Scripture. **the Good Shepherd** Jesus Christ.

Comb.: **shepherd dog** a dog used to control and guard sheep; a sheepdog; (*German shepherd dog*: see GERMAN *noun*[1] & *adjective*[1]); **shepherd moon** = *shepherd satellite* below; **shepherd plaid** = *shepherd's plaid* below; **shepherd satellite** ASTRONOMY a small moon which orbits close to a planetary ring (esp. of Saturn), and whose gravitational field confines the ring within a narrow band; **shepherd's calendar** a calendar containing weather lore etc. for shepherds (app. proverbially regarded as an unreliable source of information); **shepherd's check** = *shepherd's plaid* below; **shepherd's club** the great mullein, *Verbascum thapsus*; **shepherd's cress** a dwarf cruciferous plant of sandy heaths, *Teesdalia nudicaulis*; **shepherd's crook** (having the shape of) a staff with a large hook at one end used by shepherds; **shepherd's dog** = *shepherd dog* above; †**shepherd's hour** [translating French *l'heure du berger*] the lover's opportunity; **shepherd's needle** a formerly common umbelliferous cornfield weed, *Scandix pecten-veneris*, whose fruit ends in a long needle-like beak; †**shepherd-spider** = sense 3 above; **shepherd's pie** a baked dish consisting mainly of minced meat covered with a layer of mashed potato; **shepherd's pipe** MUSIC a small oboe or musette; **shepherd's plaid** (of) a small black and white check pattern; (made of) woollen cloth with this pattern; **shepherd's purse** (*a*) a common cruciferous weed, *Capsella bursa-pastoris*, with small white flowers and pouch-shaped siliculae; (*b*) *dial.* a fossil sea urchin found in chalk; **shepherd's staff** the small teasel, *Dipsacus pilosus*; **shepherd's weather-glass** the scarlet pimpernel, *Anagallis arvensis*.

■ †**shepherdish** *adjective* pertaining to or like a shepherd or shepherds; pastoral: L16–E19. **shepherdless** *adjective* without a shepherd or shepherds; unprotected; without a guide: M17. **shepherdry** *noun* (*rare*) †(*a*) the practice or occupation of a shepherd; (*b*) the affairs of the Order of Ancient Shepherds, a friendly society: L16. **shepherdship** *noun* (*rare*) the post or position of a shepherd M16. †**shepherdy** *noun* (*rare*) the profession, practice, or occupation of a shepherd; shepherdry: E17–E18.

shepherd /ˈʃɛpəd/ *verb*. E18.
[from the noun.]
1 *verb intrans.* Be a shepherd; work as a shepherd. E18.
2 *verb trans.* Guard, tend, and herd (sheep) as a shepherd. Also (*rare*), keep or breed (sheep). L18.
3 *verb trans.* Watch over, guide, protect, or care for (a person, a group of people) as a shepherd. E19.
4 *verb trans.* & *intrans.* *Hist.* Watch over or guard (a gold-mining claim) by working on it superficially so as to retain legal rights. *Austral.* & *NZ*. M19.
5 *verb trans.* Follow closely and watchfully; guide in a certain direction; drive or direct (a crowd etc.) like sheep. Also (*Austral. slang*), follow (a person) with the aim of cheating. L19.

📖 **1** *Kendal Mercury* Two farmers .. were out shepherding, when they were overtaken by an awful storm. **3** A. PATON Into the room, shepherded by an older girl, came his little nephew. **5** C. HILL He was shepherded south-west to Worcester.

■ **shepherded** *ppl adjective* protected, guarded L19.

shepherdess /ˈʃɛpədɪs, ʃɛpəˈdɛs/ *noun*. ME.
[from SHEPHERD *noun* + -ESS[1].]
A female shepherd; a woman or girl who guards, tends, and herds sheep. Also in pastoral literature etc., an idealized or romanticized shepherdess; a rustic maiden.

📖 DICKENS The dress of a china shepherdess: so dainty in its colours.

shepherdize /ˈʃɛpədʌɪz/ *verb. rare.* Also **-ise**. M17.
[formed as prec. + -IZE.]
1 *verb intrans.* Act the part of the shepherd or shepherdess; pretend to lead the pastoral life. M17.
2 *verb trans.* Tend or guide as a shepherd. L19.

shepherd king /ˈʃɛpəd kɪŋ/ *noun phr.* L16.
[In sense 1 translating Greek *basileis poimenes*, rendering Egyptian *heqa khoswe*: see HYKSOS. In sense 2 from SHEPHERD *noun* + KING *noun*.]
1 In *pl.* = HYKSOS *noun*. L16.
2 *gen.* A king who is a shepherd. M18.

shepherdly /ˈʃɛpədli/ *adjective*. Now *rare*. M16.
[from SHEPHERD *noun* + -LY[1].]
1 Pertaining to or befitting a shepherd; characteristic of a shepherd. Formerly also, that is a shepherd. M16.
†**2** Pastoral, rural, rustic. L16–M18.

📖 **2** HOR. WALPOLE I hate the country: I am past the shepherdly age of groves and streams.

shepstare /ˈʃɛpstə/ *noun. north.* Also **-ster** & other vars. M16.
[from SHEEP *noun* + STARE *noun*[1].]
A starling.

shepster /ˈʃɛpstə/ *noun*[1]. *obsolete* exc. *dial.* ME.
[Fem. agent-noun of Old English *scēppan* SHAPE *verb*.]
A female cutter-out of material; a dressmaker.

shepster *noun*[2] var. of SHEPSTARE.

Sherarat /ʃɛrəˈrɑːt/ *noun* & *adjective*. Also **Shara-** /ʃarə-/. M19.
[Arab. *Šarārāt*.]
▶**A** *noun.* Pl. same. A member of a nomadic people of northern Saudi Arabia. Usu. in *pl.* M19.
▶**B** *attrib.* or as *adjective*. Of, pertaining to, or designating the Sherarat. L19.

sherardize /ˈʃɛrədʌɪz/ *verb trans.* Also **-ise**. E20.
[from *Sherard* O. Cowper-Coles (1867–1936), English chemist + -IZE.]
METALLURGY. Coat (iron or steel articles) with zinc by heating in contact with zinc dust at a temperature below the melting point of zinc. Freq. as ***sherardized*** *ppl adjective*, ***sherardizing*** *verbal noun*.

Sherari /ʃɛˈrɑːri/ *noun* & *adjective*. Also **-ary**. L19.
[Arab. *Šarārī*.]
▶**A** *noun.* Pl. **-s**, same. A member of the Sherarat. Also, a dromedary bred by the Sherarat. L19.
▶**B** *adjective.* Of, pertaining to, or designating the Sherarat. L19.

Sheraton /ˈʃɛrət(ə)n/ *adjective* & *noun*. L19.
[Thomas *Sheraton* (1751–1806), English furniture-maker and designer.]
▶**A** *adjective.* Of, designating, or characteristic of a simple, delicate, and graceful style of furniture developed in England towards the end of the 18th cent. L19.
▶**B** *noun.* (A piece of) Sheraton furniture. E20.

sherbet /ˈʃəːbət/ *noun*. E17.
[Turkish *şerbet*, Persian *šerbet* from Arab. *šarba(t)* draught, drink, from *šariba* to drink. Cf. SHRAB, SHRUB *noun*[2], SYRUP.]
1 A cooling drink made of sweetened and diluted fruit juice, drunk esp. in Arab countries. Now also, an effervescing drink made of sherbet powder (see sense 2 below). E17.
2 A flavoured sweet powder containing bicarbonate of soda, tartaric acid, etc., eaten as a confection or used to make an effervescing drink. Also more fully ***sherbet powder***. M19.
3 a A water-ice. *N. Amer.* L19. ▶**b** (A glass of) alcoholic liquor, esp. (*spec.* in *Austral.*) beer. *slang*. L19.
Comb.: **sherbet dab** a confection consisting of a bag of sherbet with a small lollipop for dipping into the sherbet; **sherbet fountain** a confection consisting of a bag of sherbet with a liquorice straw through which it is sucked up; *sherbet powder*: see sense 2 above.

Sherbro /ˈʃəːbrəʊ/ *noun* & *adjective*. M19.
[Sherbro.]
▶**A** *noun.* Pl. same. A member of a people of the south coast of Sierra Leone; the Niger-Congo language of this people. M19.
▶**B** *attrib.* or as *adjective*. Of or pertaining to the Sherbro or their language. M20.

sherd *noun* & *verb* var. of SHARD *noun*[1] & *verb*.

Sherden *noun pl.* var. of SHARDANA.

shereef, **shereefa** *nouns* vars. of SHARIF, SHARIFA.

Sheridanesque /ˌʃɛrɪdəˈnɛsk/ *adjective*. M20.
[from *Sheridan* (see below) + -ESQUE.]
Of, pertaining to, or characteristic of the English playwright Richard Sheridan (1751–1816) or his works.
■ **Sheridaniˈana** *noun pl.* [-IANA] things, esp. anecdotes, connected with Sheridan E19.

sherif, **sherifa** *nouns* vars. of SHARIF, SHARIFA.

sheriff /ˈʃɛrɪf/ *noun*. Also †**shrieve**.
[Old English *scīrġerēfa*, from *scīr* SHIRE *noun* + *ġerēfa* REEVE *noun*[1].]
1 In England, Wales, and formerly Scotland and Ireland, the chief executive officer of the Crown in a shire or county, responsible (now mainly nominally) for keeping the peace, administering justice, overseeing elections, etc. (also ***high sheriff***); an honorary officer elected annually in some English towns. In Scotland, the chief judge of a county or district (also ***sheriff principal***, (*Hist.*) ***sheriff-depute***); a judge hearing cases in the first instance (formerly ***sheriff substitute***). OE. ▶†**b** A foreign official with analogous duties; a governor of a district or city. ME–E19.
2 In the US, an elected officer in a county, responsible for keeping the peace, administering justice, etc. M17.

📖 **2** B. BETTELHEIM The gunfighter—symbolises man's potential to become either .. outlaw or .. sheriff.

Comb. & phrases: ***high sheriff***: see sense 1 above. ***sheriff clerk***: see ***sheriff's clerk*** below; ***sheriff court***: see ***sheriff's court*** below; ***sheriff-depute***: see sense 1 above; ***sheriff officer***: see ***sheriff's officer*** below; ***sheriff principal***: see sense 1 above; **sheriff's clerk**, **sheriff clerk** *Scot.* the clerk of a sheriff court; **sheriff's court**, **sheriff court** *Scot.* a county court; **sheriff's officer**, **sheriff officer** = BAILIFF 2; **sheriff's sale** *N. Amer.* a public sale, conducted by a sheriff, of property seized to satisfy a judgement; ***sheriff substitute***: see sense 1 above.
■ **sheriffdom** *noun* (*a*) *Scot.* a district or territory under the jurisdiction of a sheriff; (*b*) the office or post of sheriff; (*c*) *joc.* the world of sheriffs, sheriffs collectively: LME. †**sheriffess** *noun* (*rare*) a female holder of a hereditary sheriff's office M17–E19. **sheriffing** *noun* (*rare*) the holding of the office of sheriff; the discharge of its duties: L17. **sheriffry** *noun* (*rare*) = SHRIEVALTY E17. **sheriffship** *noun* the office or post of sheriff L15.

sheriffalty /ˈʃɛrɪf(ə)lti/ *noun*. E16.
[from prec. + -AL[1] + -TY[1], after *royalty* etc.]
= SHRIEVALTY.

sheriffwick /ˈʃɛrɪfwɪk/ *noun*. LME.
[formed as prec. + -WICK.]
1 The office or post of sheriff. LME.
2 A district under the jurisdiction of a sheriff. LME.

sherifi /ʃəˈriːfi/ *noun*. E17.
[Arab. *šarīfī* formed as SHARIF. Cf. SERAPHIN *noun*[1].]
Hist. A gold coin formerly current in the Near East.

sheristadar /ʃɛˌrɪstəˈdɑː/ *noun*. Also **serishta-** /sɛˌrɪʃtə-/. L18.
[Urdu, from Persian *sarišta* register, registry + *-dār* holding, holder.]
In the Indian subcontinent, the head clerk or registrar of a court of justice.

Sherlock /ˈʃəːlɒk/ *noun* & *verb*. E20.
[from *Sherlock* Holmes: see next.]
= next.
■ **Sherlockian** *noun* & *adjective* (*a*) *noun* a Sherlock; (*b*) *adjective* = HOLMESIAN: E20. **Sherlockiˈana** *noun pl.* [-ANA] things connected with Sherlock Holmes, writings about Sherlock Holmes M20.

Sherlock Holmes /ʃəːlɒk ˈhəʊmz/ *noun* & *verb*. L19.
[The amateur detective hero of the stories of Arthur Conan Doyle (1859–1930). Cf. HOLMESIAN.]
▶**A** *noun.* An investigator of mysteries, *esp.* a remarkably astute one; a private detective; a very perceptive person. L19.
▶**B** *verb.* **1** *verb trans.* Make deductions about, assess, deduce. E20.
2 *verb intrans.* Engage in detective work, make investigations. E20.
■ **Sherlock ˈHolmesian** *adjective* = SHERLOCKIAN *adjective* M20.

Sherman /ˈʃəːmən/ *noun*. M20.
[W. T. *Sherman* (1820–91), US general.]
In full ***Sherman tank***, ***General Sherman tank***. An American type of medium tank, much used during the war of 1939–45.

Sherpa /ˈʃəːpə/ *noun* & *adjective*. M19.
[Tibetan *sharpa* inhabitant of an eastern country.]
▶**A** *noun.* Pl. **-s**, same.
1 A member of a Tibetan people inhabiting the southern slopes of the Himalayas on the borders of Nepal and Tibet, noted for their skill in mountaineering. Also, the Tibetan dialect of this people. M19.
2 *transf.* & *fig.* A (mountain) guide or porter; an official making the preparations for a summit conference. M20.
▶**B** *attrib.* or as *adjective*. Of, pertaining to, or designating the Sherpas or their language. E20.

sherris /ˈʃɛrɪs/ *noun. arch.* L16.
[Repr. old pronunc. of *Xeres* (now Jerez de la Frontera) in Andalusia, Spain, the original place of production. Cf. XERES.]
= SHERRY *noun* 1. Also ***sherris sack***, ***sherris wine***, etc.

sherry /ˈʃɛri/ *noun*. L16.
[Alt. of prec. interpreted as pl. or with loss of final *-s* in *sherris sack*.]
1 A fortified white wine orig. from S. Spain, drunk esp. as an appetizer. Also, a drink or glass of sherry. L16.
2 A glass used for sherry. E20.

📖 **1** E. NORTH The vicar .. offered them sherry (sweet, medium or dry).

Attrib. & comb.: Designating food or drink containing sherry, as ***sherry cobbler***, ***sherry negus***, ***sherry trifle***, etc. Special combs., as **sherry glass** a small wineglass (as) used for sherry; **sherry party** a party, esp. before lunch or dinner, at which sherry is the principal drink served; **sherry wine** = sense 1 above.

sherry /ˈʃɛri/ *verb*[1] *intrans. slang* & *dial.* L18.
[Perh. a var. of SHEER *verb*[1].]
Scurry, run away; retreat hastily. Also foll. by *off*.

sherry /ˈʃɛri/ *verb*[2] *trans.* E20.
[from SHERRY *noun*.]
1 Supply with sherry, give sherry to. *rare*. E20.
2 Add sherry to. Chiefly as ***sherried*** *ppl adjective*. L20.

sherryvallies /ʃɛrɪˈvalɪz/ *noun pl. US. obsolete* exc. *Hist.* L18.
[Prob. immed. from Polish *szarawary* corresp. to Russian *sharovary* wide trousers, Greek *sarabara* rendering Aramaic *sarbālā*, Arab. *sirbāl* cloak, mantle, app. ult. from Persian *sirwāl*. Cf. late Latin *sarabara*, *saraballa*.]
Loose riding breeches of leather or thick cloth buttoned or laced on the outside of each leg.

sherut /ʃɛr'ruːt/ *noun*. **M20.**
[Hebrew *šērūt* lit. 'service'.]
In Israel, a large taxi shared by several passengers.

sherwani /ʃəː'wɑːni/ *noun*. **E20.**
[Urdu, Persian *širwānī* of or from Shirvan, a town in NE Persia.]
In the Indian subcontinent, a man's knee-length coat buttoning to the neck.

sheshbesh /'ʃɛʃbɛʃ/ *noun*. **L20.**
[Turkish *şeşbeş*, from Persian *šaš* six + Turkish *beş* five.]
A variety of backgammon played in the Middle East.

sheth /ʃɛθ/ *noun*. *dial. & techn.* **LME.**
[Cogn. with Western Flemish *schet(te)* rail, bar.]
1 A group of furrows, mine workings, etc., crossing each other at right angles. **LME.**
2 A bar, a lath, *esp.* one of a number fixed together to form a framework. **L15.**

Shetland /'ʃɛtlənd/ *adjective & noun*. **L18.**
[A group of islands NE of the mainland of Scotland. Cf. ZETLANDIC.]
▶ **A** *adjective*. **1** Designating things coming from or associated with Shetland. **L18.**
2 Designating a fine loosely twisted wool from Shetland sheep; made of this wool. **L18.**
1 Shetland lace a black or white bobbin lace made of Shetland wool. **Shetland pony** (an animal of) a small hardy rough-coated breed of pony. **Shetland sheep** (an animal of) a hardy short-tailed breed of sheep native to Shetland and bred esp. for its fine wool. **Shetland sheepdog** (an animal of) a small breed of dog similar to the collie.
▶ **B** *ellipt.* as *noun*. **1** A Shetland pony, sheep, or sheepdog. **L18.**
2 A Shetland sweater or shawl. **L19.**
■ **Shetlander** *noun* (*a*) a native or inhabitant of the Shetland Islands; (*b*) a Shetland pony: **E19. Shet'landic** *adjective* of or pertaining to Shetland **L19.**

sheugh /ʃuːx/ *noun & verb*. *Scot. & north.* **E16.**
[Var. of SOUGH *noun*[2].]
▶ **A** *noun*. **1** A ditch; a trench, a drain, a furrow. **E16.**
2 A furrow for the temporary reception of plants. **E19.**
▶ **B** *verb trans*. **1** Plough, make furrows in; dig *up*. **E16.**
2 a Lay (a plant) temporarily in the earth in order to maintain freshness. **E18.** ▸**b** *transf.* Cover slightly, bury. **M18.**

sheva /ʃə'vɑː/ *noun*. Also **shewa**. **L16.**
[Hebrew *šəwā'* app. arbitrary alt. of *šāw'* emptiness, vanity, spelt in German books *Schwa*, whence SCHWA.]
1 HEBREW GRAMMAR. The sign ꞉ placed under a consonant to express the absence of a following vowel sound, having in certain positions no sound (***quiescent sheva***) but in others sounding as a schwa /ə/ (***movable sheva***); the sound of movable sheva. **L16.**
2 PHONETICS. = SCHWA. **E19.**

Shevat *noun* var. of SEBAT.

shevelled /'ʃɛv(ə)ld/ *ppl adjective*. Now *arch. rare*. **E17.**
[Aphet.]
Dishevelled.

Shevuoth *noun* var. of SHAVUOTH.

†**shew** *noun* var. of SHOW *noun*[1].

shew *verb* see SHOW *verb*.

shewa *noun* var. of SHEVA.

†**shewage** *noun*. *rare*. **E16–E19.**
[Etymologizing alt.]
= SCAVAGE *noun*.

shewbread /'ʃəʊbrɛd/ *noun*. **M16.**
[from †*shew* var. of SHOW *noun*[1] + BREAD *noun*[1], after German *Schaubrot* repr. Hebrew *leḥem pānīm* lit. 'bread of the face (of God)', Greek *artoi enōpioi*, late Latin (Vulgate) *panes propositionis*.]
JEWISH ANTIQUITIES. Twelve loaves placed every Sabbath beside the altar in the Jewish Temple and eaten by the priests at the end of the week.

shewel /'ʃʊəl/ *noun*. *obsolete* exc. *dial.* **ME.**
[Cogn. with Middle Low German *schūwelse* (= German *Scheusal*), from verb appearing as Old High German *sciuhen* (German *scheuen*) scare. Cf. SHY *adjective*.]
A scarecrow. Also (HUNTING), something set up to keep a deer from entering a place or going in a particular direction.
■ **shewelling** *noun* the action of setting up shewels **L16.**

shewt *noun* var. of SHOOT *noun*[2].

shey-shey /'ʃeɪʃeɪ/ *noun*. Also **shay-shay**. **E20.**
[Prob. from French *chassé*. Cf. SASHAY *noun*.]
In the W. Indies: a rhythmic shuffling dance usu. performed by women to jazz music.

SHF *abbreviation*.
RADIO. Superhigh frequency.

shhh *interjection & verb* var. of SH *interjection & verb*.

Shia /'ʃiːə/ *noun & adjective*. Also **-ah**. **E17.**
[Arab. *šī'a* faction, party (sc. of Ali: see below).]
▶ **A** *noun*. Pl. same, **-s**. The minority religious group of Muslims, differing from the Sunni in their understanding of the Sunna and in their acceptance of the claim of Ali, Muhammad's son-in-law and the fourth caliph, to be the first true successor of the Prophet. Also, a member of this group, a Shiite. **E17.**
▶ **B** *attrib.* or as *adjective*. Of, pertaining to, or designating the Shia or their religion. **L17.**

shiatsu /ʃɪ'atsuː/ *noun*. **M20.**
[Japanese, lit. 'finger pressure'.]
A kind of therapy of Japanese origin, in which pressure is applied with the thumbs and palms to certain points of the body.

Shibayama /ʃiːbə'jɑːmə/ *adjective & noun*. **E20.**
[Name of a Japanese family of carvers.]
(Designating) a distinctive style of carving and inlay using shell, pearl, stone, etc.; (work) in this style.

shibboleth /'ʃɪbəlɛθ/ *noun*. **M17.**
[Hebrew *šibbōlet* ear of corn, stream in flood, used as a test of nationality for the difficulty for foreigners of pronouncing /ʃ/ (*Judges* 12:4–6).]
1 A word used as a test for detecting people from another district or country by their pronunciation; a word or sound very difficult for foreigners to pronounce correctly. **M17.** ▸**b** A peculiarity of pronunciation or accent indicative of a person's origin; the distinctive mode of speech of a profession, class, etc. **M17.** ▸**c** A custom, habit, style of dressing, etc., distinguishing a particular class or group of people. **E19.**
2 A long-standing formula, idea, phrase, etc., held (esp. unreflectingly) by or associated with a group, class, etc.; a catchword, a slogan; a taboo. Also, a received wisdom; a truism, a platitude. **M17.**

📖 **2** A. GUINNESS Middle-class shibboleths about not wearing the collar of your cricket shirt outside your blazer.

shibui /'ʃɪbui/ *adjective & noun*. Also **shibu** /'ʃɪbʊ/. **M20.**
[Japanese = astringent, from *shibu* an astringent substance.]
▶ **A** *adjective*. Tasteful in a quiet, profound, or unostentatious way. **M20.**
▶ **B** *noun*. Tastefulness, refinement; appreciation of elegant simplicity. **M20.**

shibuichi /ʃɪbʊ'ɪtʃi/ *noun & adjective*. **L19.**
[Japanese, from *shi* four + *bu* part(s) + *ichi* one.]
(Of) an alloy consisting of three parts of copper to one of silver and having a silver-grey patina, extensively used in Japanese metalwork.

shice /ʃʌɪs/ *noun & adjective*. *slang*. Now *rare*. **M19.**
[German *Scheiss* excrement. Cf. next.]
▶ **A** *noun*. Nothing; something worthless, *spec.* counterfeit money. **M19.**
▶ **B** *adjective*. Worthless, counterfeit, spurious. **L19.**

shicer /'ʃʌɪsə/ *noun*. Now *Austral.* **M19.**
[German *Scheisser* defecator, contemptible person: see -ER[1]. Cf. SHYSTER.]
1 A worthless or contemptible thing or person; a failure. Also, a swindler, a defaulter, a cheat. *slang.* **M19.**
2 An unproductive claim or mine. *Austral.* **M19.**

shicker /'ʃɪkə/ *adjective, noun, & verb*. *slang* (chiefly *Austral. & NZ*). Also **-kk-**. **L19.**
[Yiddish *shiker* from Hebrew *šikkōr*, from *šākar* be drunk. Cf. SHICKERY.]
▶ **A** *adjective*. Drunk, intoxicated. **L19.**
▶ **B** *noun*. **1** A drunk. **E20.**
2 Alcoholic liquor. Esp in ***on the shicker***. **E20.**
▶ **C** *verb intrans*. Consume alcoholic liquor, get drunk. **E20.**
■ **shick** *adjective & noun* = SHICKER *adjective, noun* **E20. shickered** *adjective* drunk, intoxicated **E20.**

shickery /'ʃɪk(ə)ri/ *adverb & adjective*. *slang*. Now *rare* or *obsolete*. **M19.**
[Origin unkn. Cf. SHICKER *adjective & noun*.]
▶ **A** *adverb*. Shabbily, badly. **M19.**
▶ **B** *adjective*. Shabby, rickety, shaky. Also, drunk. **M19.**

shickster /'ʃɪkstə/ *noun*. *slang*. Now *rare* or *obsolete*. **M19.**
[from SHIKSA: see -STER.]
A Gentile woman or girl; a promiscuous woman.

shidduch /'ʃɪdəx/ *noun*. **L19.**
[Yiddish, from Hebrew *šiddūḵ* negotiation, esp. of an arranged marriage. Cf. SHADCHAN.]
An arranged marriage, a (good) match.

shide /ʃʌɪd/ *noun*. *obsolete* exc. *dial.*
[Old English *scīd* = Old Frisian *skīd*, Old High German *scīt* (German *Scheit*), Old Norse *skíð*, from Germanic. Cf. SHEATH *noun*[1], SHED *verb*[1], SKI *noun & adjective*, SKID *noun*.]
A piece of wood split off from timber; a plank, a beam. Also, a measure of timber, equal to half a cubic foot.

shiel /ʃiːl/ *noun*. *Scot. & north.* Also **shield**. **ME.**
[Origin unkn. Cf. SCALE *noun*[2].]
1 = SHIELING 2. **ME.**
2 A small house, a cottage. **ME.**
†**3** = SHIELING 1. **M16–M19.**

shield /ʃiːld/ *noun*[1].
[Old English *sceld*, *sċield* = Old Frisian *skeld*, Old Saxon, Old High German *scild* (Dutch, German *Schild*), Old Norse *skjǫldr*, Gothic *skildus*, from Germanic word prob. meaning 'board' from base meaning 'divide, separate'.]
▶ **I 1** A piece of metal, wooden, hard plastic, etc., armour having a circular, oblong, or (esp.) characteristic flat-topped heart shape and strapped on the arm or held in the hand as a protection from blows and missiles. **OE.**
2 HERALDRY. A stylized representation of a shield on which a coat of arms is depicted; a representation of this, a coat of arms. **ME.** ▸**b** A shield-shaped trophy offered as a prize in a sporting etc. competition; such a competition. **M19.** ▸**c** A police officer's shield-shaped badge of office. *US.* **E20.**
†**3** [translating Old French *escu*.] = ÉCU. *rare*. **LME–L16.**
4 a HORTICULTURE. A shield-shaped piece of bark bearing a bud, for grafting between the wood and bark of a stock. **L16.** ▸**b** BOTANY. The apothecium of a lichen. Now *rare*. **L18.**
5 A shield-shaped ornamental or functional plate or surface. **M17.** ▸**b** A (breed of) fancy pigeon having shield-shaped wing markings. **M19.**
6 (Usu. **S-**.) *The* constellation Scutum. Earliest in ***Sobieski's shield***. **L18.**
7 PHYSICAL GEOGRAPHY. **a** A large seismically stable mass of Archaean basement rock having the form of a flat or gently convex peneplained platform and usu. forming the nucleus of a continent. Freq. with cap. initial in proper names, as ***Baltic Shield***, ***Canadian Shield***. Cf. CRATON, KRATOGEN. **E20.** ▸**b** The dome of a shield volcano. **M20.**

📖 **1** W. MORRIS Every man had ready to his hand Sharp spear, and painted shield. *Sunday Mirror* Half-bricks pound against shaking Perspex shields. **2** C. BOUTELL The well-known Shield of Piers de Gaveston . . vert, six eaglets or. **b** M. SPARK Every house must go all out for the Shield. **5** J. RUSKIN The shield of stone which . . occupied the head of early windows.

▶ **II** A thing serving as a protection or shelter.
8 *gen.* A thing or person serving as a protection against attack, danger, exposure, etc. **ME.**
9 The thick tough skin on the sides and flanks of a boar. Also (in full ***shield of brawn***), an article of food consisting of chopped boar's meat moulded inside a piece of this tough skin and cooked. Cf. BRAWN *noun* 2. Now *rare*. **ME.**
10 A protective screen or cover; *spec.* (*a*) one used to guard machinery or machine operators; (*b*) a machine or structure used in tunnelling, orig. to protect digging workers from roof falls or leaks and now also to bore through soft ground; (*c*) = ***dress-shield*** s.v. DRESS *noun*; (*d*) PHYSICS an electrically conducting cover of a device or apparatus intended to protect it from external electric or magnetic fields, or to reduce or eliminate interference radiated by the device or apparatus itself; (*e*) PHYSICS a mass of material, usu. lead or concrete, intended to absorb neutrons and other ionizing radiation emitted by a reactor or accelerator; (*f*) ZOOLOGY a protective plate on an animal, e.g. the carapace of a turtle or crustacean, the pronotum of an insect; a large scale or scute, esp. on the head of a snake or the carapace of a turtle. **E18.**

📖 **8** R. W. EMERSON No dignity or wealth is a shield from its assault. D. CECIL She hid her true self behind the shield of an aloof formality. *Daily Telegraph* His . . hill-tribe force form the . . only credible shield against the North Vietnamese.

Phrases: ***gum-shield***: see GUM *noun*[1]. ***heat shield***: see HEAT *noun*. ***Laurentian Shield***: see LAURENTIAN *adjective*[1]. **the other side of the shield** = ***the reverse of the shield*** s.v. REVERSE *noun*. ***the reverse of the shield***: see REVERSE *noun*. **two sides of a shield** two ways of looking at something, two sides to a question.
Comb.: **shield arm** the left arm; **shield-back** *adjective* (of a chair) having a shield-shaped back; **shield-bearer** *Hist.* an attendant who carried a warrior's shield; **shield-board** (*obsolete* exc. *dial.*) = ***mould-board*** s.v. MOULD *noun*[1]; **shield-bud** = sense 4a above; **shield-budding** BOTANY the operation of grafting a shield; **shieldbug** ENTOMOLOGY any of various broad flat hemipteran bugs, esp. pentatomids, with a shield-shaped pronotum and scutellum; also called ***stink-bug***; **shield cartilage** (*a*) ANATOMY = THYROID *noun* 1; (*b*) ZOOLOGY any of several protective cartilages in the cranium of a cyclostome; **shield fern** any of various ferns constituting the genus *Polystichum*, esp. *P. aculeatum* and *P. setiferum*, with shield-shaped indusia and sharp pinnules; **shield-maid**, **shield-maiden**, **shieldmay** *arch.* a female warrior, an Amazon; a Valkyrie; **shield-money** = SCUTAGE; **shield-nose snake**, **shield snake** a venomous southern African elapid snake, *Aspidelaps scutatus*, with a large shieldlike scute on the snout; **shieldtail** = ***shield-tailed snake*** below; **shield-tailed snake** any of various blind burrowing snakes of the family Uropeltidae, found in southern India and Sri Lanka, with a flat disc of enlarged scutes on the upper surface of the tail; **shield volcano** a volcano having the form of a very broad dome with gently sloping sides, characteristic of the eruption of basic lavas of low viscosity.
■ **shieldless** *adjective* **LME. shieldlike** *adjective* resembling a shield in shape **M16.**

shield *noun*[2] var. of SHIEL.

shield /ʃiːld/ *verb trans.*
[Old English *scildan*, from SHIELD *noun*[1]. Cf. German *schilden*, Old Norse *skjalda* provide with a shield.]
1 Protect, shelter, or screen (as) with a shield from attack, danger, exposure, etc., or from blame or judicial punishment; cover or hide with a shield. OE. ▸**b** *ELECTRICITY.* = SCREEN *verb* 1e. Foll. by *from*, *against*. E20.
†**2** Arm with a shield. ME–M17.
†**3 a** Prevent, forbid. Chiefly in ***God shield (that)***. ME–L17. ▸**b** Ward off, keep away. Also foll. by *off*. ME–E19.

🕮 **1** R. MACAULAY He suspects that Jane did it . . He's trying to shield her. M. FRAYN Shielding his eyes against the . . sun. P. ACKROYD My mother did her best to shield me from the world.

■ **shielder** *noun* LME.

shielded /ˈʃiːldɪd/ *adjective.* OE.
[from SHIELD *noun*[1], *verb*: see -ED[2], -ED[1].]
1 Carrying a shield; protected with or by a shield; *ZOOLOGY* having a hard shieldlike carapace or scute. M17.
2 Provided or hung with shields. E19.

shielding /ˈʃiːldɪŋ/ *noun.* L16.
[from SHIELD *verb* + -ING[1].]
1 The action of SHIELD *verb*; an instance of this. L16.
2 *PHYSICS.* Material which protects or shields against electric and magnetic fields or against radiation; a shield which does this. M20.

shieldrake *noun* var. of SHELDRAKE.

shieling /ˈʃiːlɪŋ/ *noun. Scot.* Also **sheal-**. M16.
[from SHIEL + -ING[1]. Cf. SCALE *noun*[2].]
1 A piece of summer pasture for cattle or sheep. Cf. SHIEL 3. M16.
2 A roughly constructed building or shelter, orig. as used by a shepherd; a shack, a hut. Cf. SHIEL 1. L16.

†**shieve** *verb* see SHEAVE *verb*[2].

shift /ʃɪft/ *noun.* ME.
[from the verb.]
†**1** A movement to do something, a beginning. Only in ME.
†**2** A share, a portion assigned on division. LME–E17.
3 An expedient, an ingenious device, a stratagem; (*obsolete* exc. *dial.*) an available means of achieving an end (freq. in ***(have) no other shift***). E16. ▸**b** Ingenuity, initiative, resourcefulness. Cf. SHIFTLESS. *rare.* M16. ▸†**c** Means of living, livelihood. Freq. in ***honest shift***. *Scot.* L16–L18.
4 *spec.* **a** A fraudulent or deceiving device or expedient, a trick, a subterfuge. M16. ▸**b** An expedient necessitated by circumstances, a forced measure. M17.
†**5** A set or succession of things of the same kind. M16–E17.
6 a (A) change of clothing. Now *arch.* & *dial.* M16. ▸**b** A change of wind. L16.
7 a *Hist.* A woman's loose-fitting undergarment, orig. worn also by men; a slip, a chemise. L16. ▸**b** A woman's loose, straight, unwaisted dress. M20.
8 Each of the successive crops in a course of rotation; a field used for such crops. *obsolete* exc. *Scot.* E18.
9 A relay or change of workers or (formerly) horses. Now *spec.*, a group of people working for a specific period of time, usu. one equivalent to a day's work; a period worked by such a group of people. E18.
10 *MUSIC.* A change of hand position on the finger-board of a violin etc. L18.
11 The action or an instance of shifting; a transfer, a transition; (a) change, a move; *dial.* a change of residence or employment; *BRIDGE* a change of suit in bidding or (*US*) playing. E19. ▸**b** *PHYSICS.* A displacement of a spectral line from the expected position or from some reference position; a change of an energy level in an atom, molecule, etc. L19. ▸**c** A systematic change in pronunciation as a language evolves. L19. ▸**d** *AMER. FOOTBALL.* A change of position made immediately before a snap by two or more players of the team in possession of the ball. E20. ▸**e** *CHEMISTRY.* A migration of an atom or group, or of electrons, from one point in a molecule to another, or occas. between molecules, in a chemical reaction. M20. ▸**f** *COMPUTING.* The movement of the digits of a word in a register one or more places to left or right, equivalent to multiplying or dividing the corresponding number by a power of whatever number is the base. M20.
12 The correct arrangement of joints in brickwork, plates in shipbuilding, etc. E19.
13 *MINING.* A slight fault or dislocation in a seam or stratum. E19.
14 a The mechanism for or an act of changing the action of a piano etc. keyboard with the soft pedal. L19. ▸**b** A motor vehicle's gear lever or transmission system; a change of gear. Cf. ***gear-shift*** s.v. GEAR *noun*. *N. Amer.* E20.
15 a In full ***shift key***. A key on a typewriter etc. keyboard for switching between upper and lower case etc. L19. ▸**b** A switch between cases, fonts, etc., on a typewriter or printer. Also, a set of characters indicated by a particular shift code. E20. ▸**c** *COMPUTING & TELEGRAPHY.* In full ***shift character***, ***shift code***. A character or code that causes subsequent characters to be produced in a different font, case, or coding scheme. M20.

🕮 **3** BOSW. SMITH The thousand shifts and devices of which Hannibal was a master. **4b** J. G. HOLLAND That pride . . that resorts to desperate shifts rather than incur an obligation. **9** *Listener* A thousand men working in three shifts round the clock. ***graveyard shift***, ***night shift***, ***split shift***, ***twilight shift***, etc. attrib.: ***shift system***, ***shift work***, ***shift worker***, etc. **11** T. BENN The Labour Party exists to bring about a shift in the balance of power and wealth. H. KOHUT Psychoanalysis needed a decisive shift in emphasis. R. HOLT A shift towards a more casual . . style of life. **c** ***consonant shift***, ***vowel shift***, etc. **14b** J. OSBORNE A 1956 Chevrolet . . car complete with automatic shift.

Phrases: ***blue shift***: see BLUE *adjective*. **chemical shift** in nuclear magnetic resonance or Mössbauer spectroscopy, the position of a resonance in the spectrum measured relative to some standard signal, the separation being characteristic of the chemical environment of the resonating nucleus. ***drive to one's shifts***: see ***put to one's shifts*** below. **get a shift on** *colloq.* = ***get a move on*** s.v. MOVE *noun*. **make a shift**, **make shift** (*a*) (now *dial.*) make efforts, try all means; (*b*) be successful; (*c*) succeed with difficulty, contrive or manage with effort *to do* something; (*d*) get by, manage somehow, be content, put up (*with*). **put to one's shifts**, **drive to one's shifts** *arch.* drive to desperate measures. ***red shift***: see RED *adjective*. ***risky shift***: see RISKY 1. **sound shift** = sense 11c above.

Comb.: ***shift character***, ***shift code***: see sense 15c above; **shift dress** = sense 7b above; ***shift key***: see sense 15a above; **shift-lever** *N. Amer.* a gear lever; **shift lock** a device for holding the shift key of a typewriter etc. continuously depressed; **shift register** *COMPUTING* a register specifically intended for subjecting data to a shift (sense 11f above); **shift-round** *colloq.* an exchange or reallocation of positions; **shift-stick** *colloq.* a gear lever; **shift-terminator** *COMPUTING* a character introduced into a string of text to cancel the effect of a preceding shift code; **shift valve** a valve moving to produce automatic gear-changes in a motor vehicle.

shift /ʃɪft/ *verb.*
[Old English *sċiftan* = Old Frisian *skifta*, Middle Low German *schiften*, *schichten* (German *schichten*), Old Norse *skipta* divide, separate, change, from Germanic base repr. also in Old Norse *skipa* arrange, assign. Cf. SKIFT *verb*[1].]
▸ **I** †**1** *verb trans.* Arrange, assign, place in order. OE–LME.
2 *verb trans.* Apportion, distribute, divide. Long *obsolete* exc. *dial.* OE.
†**3** *verb intrans.* Deal, bargain, (*with*); make provision *for*. ME–M16.
4 *verb intrans.* **a** Make a living, survive; succeed; manage, fare, (*well*, *badly*, etc.). Now *Scot.* & *dial.* M16. ▸**b** Contrive or manage as best one can; get by, make do. (Foll. by *with*, *without*.) L17.
5 *verb intrans.* Be evasive or indirect; live by or practise fraud, cheat. *arch.* L16.
▸ **II 6 a** *verb trans.* Change (a thing), replace (a thing) by another of a similar kind. ME. ▸**b** *verb intrans.* Undergo change, be transformed. E17. ▸**c** *verb trans.* & *intrans.* Change or exchange (places) (*with*). Now *Scot.* & *dial.* E18.
7 *verb trans.* **a** Change (one's own or another's clothing), dress in fresh clothing. Now *Scot.* & *dial.* LME. ▸**b** *verb intrans.* & *refl.* Change one's clothing. Now *Scot.* & *dial.* M16.
8 a *verb trans.* Change (a scene); change the scene of. L16. ▸**b** *verb intrans.* Of a scene: change. (Foll. by *to*.) E19.

🕮 **6a** T. HUTCHINSON How many times did . . the clergy . . change or shift their opinions? **b** B. TAYLOR Let Proteus shift in ocean From shape to shape. **8a** *City Limits* Visconti shifts the action from California to . . Ferrara.

▸ **III 9 a** *verb trans.* Transfer from one place to another (*lit.* & *fig.*); change the position of, esp. slightly, with difficulty, or to remove an obstruction. LME. ▸**b** *verb intrans.* Move, change position, esp. slightly, heavily, or to remove an obstruction (*lit.* & *fig.*). L16. ▸**c** *verb trans.* & *intrans.* Change (gear) in a motor vehicle. Chiefly *N. Amer.* E20. ▸**d** *verb trans.* *COMPUTING.* Move (data) to the right or left in a register. M20.
10 *verb trans.* & *intrans.* Alter, change, (one's place of residence, location, etc.); move (house). Now chiefly *Austral.* & *NZ.* M16.
†**11** *verb trans.* **a** Pass, get through, (a period of time). Also, put off, defer. Chiefly *Scot.* M16–M18. ▸**b** Avoid, elude, escape. L16–E19. ▸**c** Quit, leave, (a place). *rare.* M17–E19.
12 *verb intrans.* Move away, withdraw, depart, esp. unobserved. Now only foll. by *away*. L16.
13 *verb trans.* **a** Dispose of, get rid of, remove, (an unwanted person or thing); *colloq.* (of a horse) throw (a rider); *euphem.* kill, murder. E17. ▸**b** Consume (food or drink) hastily or in bulk; spend (money). *colloq.* L19. ▸**c** Sell (goods), esp. quickly, in large quantities, or dishonestly. *colloq.* L20.
14 a *verb intrans.* Of the wind: change direction. (Foll. by *to*.) M17. ▸**b** *verb trans.* Alter the direction of (esp. the wind). L17.
15 a *verb intrans.* *NAUTICAL.* Of cargo or ballast: move from the proper position, so as to disturb the equilibrium of the vessel. L18. ▸**b** *verb trans.* Of a ship etc.: undergo displacement of (cargo or ballast). M19.
16 *verb intrans.* & *refl.* Move, travel, esp. quickly; hurry. *colloq.* E20.

🕮 **9a** E. LANGLEY Go and shift our things to the house we rented. D. ABSE The driver shifted some packages from the front seat. W. S. CHURCHILL Responsibility for this deed she shifted . . on to the shoulders of her . . advisers. J. WAIN Huge articulated lorries . . shifting hundreds of tons of goods. **b** J. GARDNER A strange sensation: as if the floor were moving, shifting gently. R. FRAME Penelope shifted uneasily in her chair. A. TAYLOR In a hospice the concept of care shifts from quantity to quality of life. **c** M. GORDON Clare shifted into second gear. **13a** *Harpers & Queen* Advice on how to shift stains without bleach. **b** H. WYNDHAM Lord, but he can shift his liquor! **c** *New Musical Express* Fleetwood Mac . . cracked the American market . . shifting over three million copies of their album. **16** M. KENYON You'll have time for a bite at Murphy's if you shift.

Phrases, & with adverbs in specialized senses: **shift for oneself** provide for one's own safety, interests, etc., rely on one's own efforts. **shift off** †(*a*) remove (a garment); (*b*) relieve oneself of (a responsibility etc.); evade (an argument, duty, etc.); (*c*) *arch.* fob (a person) off with an excuse etc. ***shift one's ground***: see GROUND *noun*.

shifta /ˈʃɪftə/ *noun.* Also **S-**. Pl. same, **-s**. M20.
[Somali *shúfto* bandit from Amharic.]
A Somali bandit or guerrilla, operating mainly in northern Kenya.

shiftable /ˈʃɪftəb(ə)l/ *adjective.* M18.
[from SHIFT *verb* + -ABLE.]
1 Able to be shifted, movable. M18.
2 Capable of shifting or moving independently. M19.
■ **shiftaˈbility** *noun* M20.

shiften /ˈʃɪftən/ *verb trans. obsolete* exc. *dial.* M16.
[formed as prec. + -EN[5].]
Move (a thing) from one place to another. Also, change (one's clothes).
■ **shiftening** *noun* a change of clothes L17.

shifter /ˈʃɪftə/ *noun.* M16.
[from SHIFT *verb*, *noun* + -ER[1].]
1 A dishonest or evasive person; a trickster, a cheat. *obsolete* exc. *dial.* M16.
2 A person who shifts something, *spec.* a theatrical scene. L16.
3 *NAUTICAL.* A cook's assistant. *obsolete* exc. *Hist.* E18.
4 *MINING.* A person preparing the working areas of a mine for the next shift of miners. M19.
5 *MECHANICS.* **a** A device used for shifting, *esp.* a clutch serving to transfer a belt from one pulley to another. M19. ▸**b** The gear-change mechanism or control in a motor vehicle. *N. Amer.* E20.
6 *LINGUISTICS.* A word whose referent can only be understood from context. E20.

shiftful /ˈʃɪftfʊl, -f(ə)l/ *adjective. rare.* E17.
[from SHIFT *noun* + -FUL.]
Full of shifts, devices, or tricks.
■ **shiftfulness** *noun* M19.

shifting /ˈʃɪftɪŋ/ *noun.* ME.
[from SHIFT *verb* + -ING[1].]
†**1** A division of the Jewish priesthood. Only in ME.
2 The action of SHIFT *verb*; an instance of this, a shift; (a) movement, (a) change; a trick, a device. LME.

shifting /ˈʃɪftɪŋ/ *adjective.* L15.
[formed as prec. + -ING[2].]
1 That shifts or changes position or direction; changeable in character. L15.
2 That uses shifts, tricks, or subterfuge; cunning; dishonest; shifty. L16.

🕮 **1** SIR W. SCOTT A whole parish was swallowed up by the shifting sands. W. MCILVANNEY His sons were supposed to grow up decent among the shifting values that surrounded them. **shifting agriculture** = ***shifting cultivation*** below. **shifting centre** = METACENTRE. **shifting cultivation** any of several forms of agriculture in which an area of ground is cleared of vegetation and cultivated for a (usu. small) number of years and then abandoned for a new area. **shifting keyboard** a type of piano etc. keyboard moved by the soft pedal. **shifting pedal** the soft pedal of a piano etc. **shifting spanner** an adjustable spanner.

■ **shiftingly** *adverb* L16. **shiftingness** *noun* M19.

shiftless /ˈʃɪftlɪs/ *adjective.* M16.
[from SHIFT *noun* + -LESS.]
†**1** Helpless; lacking cunning or artifice. M16–L17.
2 Lacking resourcefulness, initiative, or ambition; lazy, inefficient, incompetent; (of an action) ineffective, futile. L16.
3 Lacking a shift or shirt. *rare.* L17.

🕮 **2** J. CAREW He was shiftless, a good-for-nothing.

■ **shiftlessly** *adverb* M19. **shiftlessness** *noun* L17.

shifty /ˈʃɪfti/ *adjective.* L16.
[formed as prec. + -Y[1].]
1 Full of shifts or expedients; resourceful, capable. L16.
2 Not straightforward; evasive, furtive; cunning; insincere; dishonest, deceitful. M19.
3 Changeable, variable, inconstant; wavering. *rare.* L19.
4 Changing or shifting in position. L19.

2 S. R. CROCKETT A red, foxy-featured man, with mean and shifty eyes. J. BARNES Leslie behaved as if he suspected things might be his fault . . he looked a little shifty.

■ **shiftily** *adverb* L19. **shiftiness** *noun* M19.

Shiga /ˈʃiːɡə/ *noun*. E20.
[Kiyoshi *Shiga* (1870–1957), Japanese bacteriologist.]
BACTERIOLOGY. Used *attrib.* and in *possess.* to designate the Gram-negative bacillus *Shigella dysenteriae* serotype 1, which causes dysentery, and the toxin produced by it.

shigella /ʃɪˈɡɛlə/ *noun*. Pl. **-llae** /-liː/, **-llas**. M20.
[mod. Latin *Shigella* (see below), from prec. + -ELLA.]
BACTERIOLOGY. **1** Any of various Gram-negative, rod-shaped bacteria of the genus *Shigella* (family Enterobacteriaceae), which includes several intestinal pathogens. M20.
2 In full ***Shigella dysentery***. = SHIGELLOSIS. M20.
■ **shigeˈllosis** *noun*, pl. **-lloses** /-ˈləʊsiːz/, infection with, or a disease caused by, shigellae M20.

Shihan /ˈʃɪhan/ *noun*. M20.
[Japanese, from *shi* master, teacher + *han* exemplary.]
JUDO. An honorific title: master, teacher.

†**Shiho** *noun & adjective* see SAHO.

shih-tzu /ʃiːˈtsuː/ *noun*. E20.
[Chinese *shīzigǒu*, (Wade-Giles *shih-tzŭ kou*) shih-tzu, pug-dog, Pekingese, from *shizi* lion + *gǒu* dog.]
(An animal of) a small long-coated short-legged breed of dog originating in China, with long ears and a tail curling over the back.

Shiism /ˈʃiːɪz(ə)m/ *noun*. Also **Shi'ism**. L19.
[from SHIA or SHIITE + -ISM.]
The doctrines or principles of the Shia branch of Islam.

shiitake /ʃɪˈtɑːkeɪ, ʃɪ-/ *noun*. L19.
[Japanese, from *shii* a kind of oak + *take* mushroom.]
An edible agaric (mushroom), *Lentinus edodes*, cultivated in Japan and China on logs of various oaks and allied trees. Also ***shiitake mushroom***.

Shiite /ˈʃiːʌɪt/ *noun & adjective*. Also **Shi'ite**. E18.
[from SHIA + -ITE¹.]
▶ **A** *noun*. An adherent of the Shia branch of Islam. E18.
▶ **B** *attrib.* or as *adjective*. Of, pertaining to, or designating the Shiites or their religion. E19.

shikar /ʃɪˈkɑː/ *noun & verb*. *Indian subcontinent*. E17.
[Persian & Urdu *šikār*.]
▶ **A** *noun*. Hunting, shooting; game. E17.
on shikar on a hunting expedition, out hunting.
▶ **B** *verb*. Infl. **-rr-**.
1 *verb intrans.* Hunt animals for sport. L19.
2 *verb trans.* Hunt (an animal). L19.

shikara /ʃɪˈkɑːrɑː/ *noun*. L19.
[Kashmiri from Persian *šikārī* of hunting, formed as prec.]
A long swift boat used in Kashmir.

shikari /ʃɪˈkɑːriː/ *noun*. E19.
[Urdu from Persian *šikārī*: see prec.]
In the Indian subcontinent: a hunter; an expert guide or tracker.

shikasta /ʃɪˈkastə/ *noun*. L18.
[Persian, lit. 'broken'.]
A late cursive Persian script.

shikhara /ˈʃɪkhərə/ *noun*. Also **si-**. E19.
[Sanskrit *śikhara* peak, spire.]
A pyramidal tower on a Hindu temple, sometimes having convexly curved sides.

shikho /ˈʃɪkəʊ/ *noun & verb intrans.* Also **shiko**. Pl. of noun **-os**. M19.
[Burmese.]
(Assume) the posture of prostration with joined hands and bowed head traditionally adopted by Burmese in the presence of a superior or before an object of reverence or worship.

shikimi /ʃɪˈkiːmi/ *noun*. E18.
[Japanese, from *(a)shiki* harmful + *mi* fruits.]
A small evergreen tree of Japan and Korea, *Illicium anisatum* (family Illiciaceae), which has aromatic leaves used in Buddhist funeral rites. Also called ***Japanese anise***.

shikimic /ʃɪˈkɪmɪk/ *adjective*. L19.
[from prec. + -IC.]
BIOCHEMISTRY. Pertaining to or designating a cyclic acid, $C_6H_6(OH)_3(COOH)$, formed in many bacteria and higher plants as an intermediate in the synthesis of phenylalanine, tyrosine, etc.

New Scientist A chemical route unique to plants and microbes called the shikimic pathway.

■ **shikimate** *noun* a salt or ester of shikimic acid L19.

shikker *adjective, noun, & verb* var. of SHICKER.

shiko *noun & verb* var. of SHIKHO.

shikra /ˈʃɪkrə/ *noun*. M19.
[Persian & Urdu *šikara(h)*.]
A small hawk, *Accipiter badius*, that resembles a small stocky sparrowhawk and occurs in Africa and central and southern Asia.

shiksa /ˈʃɪksə/ *noun & adjective*. *derog.* Also **-se(h)**. L19.
[Yiddish *shikse* from Hebrew *šiqṣāh* from *šeqeṣ* detested thing + *-āh* fem. suffix Cf. SHICKSTER.]
▶ **A** *noun*. A Gentile girl or woman; a Jewish girl or woman not observing traditional Jewish behaviour. L19.
▶ **B** *attrib.* or as *adjective*. Of a girl or woman: Gentile. M20.

Shilha /ˈʃɪlhə/ *noun & adjective*. Also **-h**, **Shluh** /ʃluː/. E18.
[Berber.]
▶ **A** *noun*. Pl. same, **-s**. A member of a Berber people of southern Morocco; the language of this people. E18.
▶ **B** *attrib.* or as *adjective*. Of or pertaining to the Shilha or their language. M19.

shill /ʃɪl/ *noun*. *slang* (chiefly *N. Amer.*). E20.
[Perh. abbreviation of SHILLABER.]
A decoy, an accomplice, *esp.* one posing as an enthusiastic or successful customer to encourage buyers, gamblers, etc.; *transf.* an adherent of a party, point of view, etc., posing as a disinterested advocate.

shill /ʃɪl/ *adjective & adverb*. Long *obsolete* exc. *dial.* ME.
[App. repr. Old English word corresp. to Middle High German *schel(le)* sonorous, quick, luminous, early mod. Dutch *schelle* (now *schel*) shrill, Old Norse *skjallr* sonorous, from Germanic.]
▶ **A** *adjective*. Sonorous, resonant; shrill. ME.
▶ **B** *adverb*. Sonorously, resonantly; shrilly. ME.

shill /ʃɪl/ *verb*¹. Now *dial.*
[Old English *scylian* rel. to Old Norse *skilja*: see SKILL *verb*.]
1 *verb trans.* Separate, divide, set apart. OE.
2 a *verb trans.* Curdle (milk). L17. ▸**b** *verb intrans.* Of milk: curdle. L19.

shill /ʃɪl/ *verb*² *intrans.* Long *obsolete* exc. *dial.* ME.
[Prob. repr. Old English word corresp. to Old High German *scellan* resound (German *schellen*), Old Norse *skjalla* rattle, from Germanic.]
Resound; sound loudly.

shill /ʃɪl/ *verb*³. *slang* (chiefly *N. Amer.*). E20.
[from SHILL *noun*.]
1 *verb intrans.* Act as a 'shill' or accomplice. E20.
2 *verb trans.* Entice (a person) as a 'shill'; act as a 'shill' for (a gambling game etc.). L20.

shill *verb*⁴ see SHEEL.

shillaber /ˈʃɪləbə/ *noun*. *slang* (chiefly *N. Amer.*). E20.
[Origin unkn.]
= SHILL *noun*.

shillelagh /ʃɪˈleɪlə, -li/ *noun*. L18.
[*Shillelagh*, a town in Co. Wicklow, Ireland.]
In Ireland, a thick stick or cudgel, esp. of blackthorn or oak.

shillibeer /ˈʃɪlɪbɪə/ *noun*. *colloq.* (now *Hist.*). M19.
[George *Shillibeer* (1797–1866), English coach proprietor.]
A horse-drawn omnibus. Also, a horse-drawn vehicle combining a mourning coach and a hearse.

shilling /ˈʃɪlɪŋ/ *noun*.
[Old English *scilling* = Old Frisian, Old Saxon, Old High German *scilling* (Middle Dutch, Dutch *schelling*, German *Schilling*), Old Norse *skillingr*, Gothic *skilliggs*, from Germanic. Cf. SCHELLING, SCHILLING *noun*¹, SKILLING *noun*².]
▶ **I 1 a** *Hist.* A monetary unit and cupro-nickel (formerly silver) coin of the old English (later British) currency before decimalization, equal to twelve old pence (five new pence) or one-twentieth of a pound (abbreviation **s**, (formerly) **sh.**, repr. **/-**); *colloq.* five new pence, a five pence coin. OE. ▸**b** *Hist.* A former monetary unit and coin of equal or similar value in Scotland and Ireland. LME ▸**c** A monetary unit and coin of Kenya, Uganda, Tanzania, and of Somalia, equal to 100 cents. E20.
2 Orig. (in biblical translations), a silver coin, a piece of silver. Later (now *rare* or *obsolete*), any of various foreign coins resembling a British shilling in size, appearance, or value. OE.

1a WELLINGTON Not . . one shilling more than the expenses really incurred. **c** *Times* 100 Uganda shillings usually bring no more than 20 Kenya shillings.

▶ **II** †**3** [After Latin *solidus*.] A unit of weight equal to one-twentieth of a pound. Also (*Scot.*), the weight of twelve silver pennies. OE–L16.
Phrases: ***cut off with a shilling***: see CUT *verb*. **King's shilling**, **Queen's shilling** the shilling formerly given to a recruit when enlisting in the army during the reign of a king or queen respectively; chiefly in ***take the King's shilling***, ***take the Queen's shilling***, enlist as a soldier. ***MEXICAN shilling***. ***ninepence in the shilling***, ***no more than ninepence in the shilling***: see NINE. ***pounds, shillings, and pence***: see POUND *noun*¹. ***Queen's shilling***: see ***King's shilling*** above. ***shovelboard shilling***: see SHOVELBOARD 2b. **take the shilling** = ***take the King's shilling***, ***take the Queen's shilling*** above.
Comb.: **shilling dreadful** *arch.* a cheap and sensational short novel; **shilling-mark** TYPOGRAPHY (*Hist.*) = SOLIDUS 2; **shilling shocker** *arch.* = ***shilling dreadful*** above; **shillingsworth** (chiefly *Hist.*) an amount or quantity able to be bought for a shilling or a specified number of shillings.
■ **shillingless** *adjective* L18.

shilloo /ʃɪˈluː/ *noun*. *Anglo-Irish*. M19.
[Imit.]
A loud shouting or outcry.
■ Also **shillooing** *noun* M19.

Shilluk /ʃɪˈluːk/ *noun & adjective*. L18.
[Shilluk.]
▶ **A** *noun*. Pl. same, **-s**. A member of a Sudanese people living mainly on the west bank of the Nile; the Nilotic language of this people. L18.
▶ **B** *attrib.* or as *adjective*. Of or pertaining to the Shilluk or their language. E20.

shilly-shally /ˈʃɪlɪʃali/ *verb intrans.* L18.
[from next.]
Hesitate to act or choose, be irresolute or undecided, vacillate.

L. CODY She would have to stop shilly-shallying and come to some decision.

■ **shilly-shallyer**, **shilly-shallier** *noun* M19.

shilly-shally /ˈʃɪlɪʃali/ *adverb, adjective, & noun*. E18.
[Orig. *shill I, shall I*, redupl. of *shall I*. Cf. DILLY-DALLY, WISHY-WASHY.]
▶ **A** *adverb*. ***stand shilly-shally***, ***go shilly-shally***, = SHILLY-SHALLY *verb*. Now *rare*. E18.
▶ **B** *adjective*. Vacillating, irresolute, undecided. M18.
▶ **C** *noun*. **1** Vacillation, indecision. M18.
2 A vacillating or irresolute person. *rare*. M19.
1 stand at shilly-shally *rare* = SHILLY-SHALLY *verb*.

shilpit /ˈʃɪlpɪt/ *adjective*. *Scot.* E19.
[Origin unkn.]
1 Of a person or animal: pale and sickly-looking, feeble, puny. E19.
2 Of liquor: insipid, weak, thin. E19.
■ †**shilpitness** *noun*: only in M17. **shilpy** *adjective* = SHILPIT E19.

shim /ʃɪm/ *noun*¹. *dial.* M17.
[Repr. Old English *scīma* shadow, gloom, from Germanic base also of SHINE *verb*.]
1 A streak of white on a horse's face, a blaze. M17.
2 A faint or transient appearance, a glimpse. L18.

shim /ʃɪm/ *noun*² *& verb*. E18.
[Origin unkn.]
▶ **A** *noun*. **1** A piece of iron attached to an agricultural implement for scraping the surface of the soil. *local*. E18.
2 In full ***shim-plough***. A kind of horse-hoe or shallow plough for hoeing up weeds between rows of crops. *local*. M18.
3 A thin slip, wedge, or washer inserted in a space in machinery etc. to make parts fit or align. M19. ▸**b** = LOID *noun*. *Criminals' slang* (chiefly *US*). M20.
4 An imperfect shingle or stave of irregular thickness. *US*. L19.
▶ **B** *verb*. Infl. **-mm-**.
1 *verb trans. & intrans.* Hoe (crops) with a shim-plough. *local*. L18.
2 *verb trans.* Wedge or fill up with a shim. Also foll. by *out*. L19. ▸**b** = LOID *verb*. *Criminals' slang* (chiefly *US*). L20.
■ **shimming** *noun* (*a*) the action of the verb; (*b*) a shim; shims collectively: L18.

shim /ʃɪm/ *noun*³. *slang. derog.* L20.
[from SHE + HIM.]
A transvestite; a transsexual. Also, an effeminate or passive homosexual man.

shimada /ʃɪˈmɑːdə/ *noun & adjective*. E20.
[A town in Honshu, central Japan.]
(Designating) a formal hairstyle traditionally worn by young unmarried women in Japan, in which the hair is drawn into a plait and fastened at the top of the head.

shime-waza /ˈʃiːmeɪwazə/ *noun*. M20.
[Japanese, from *shimeru* tighten, constrict + *waza* technique.]
JUDO. The art of strangulation; a stranglehold.

shimiyana /ʃɪmjɑːnə/ *noun*. *S. Afr.* Also **-yane**. L19.
[Zulu *isishimeyana*.]
An intoxicating home-brewed drink made from treacle or sugar and water.

shimmer /ˈʃɪmə/ *verb & noun*.
[Late Old English *scymrian* = Middle & mod. Low German, Middle & mod. Dutch *schēmeren* be shaded or shadowy, glimmer, glitter, German *schimmern*, from Germanic base also of SHINE *verb*: see -ER⁵. See also SKIMMER *verb*.]
▶ **A** *verb intrans.* **1** Shine with a tremulous or flickering light; gleam faintly and waveringly, glimmer. Formerly also, shine brightly, glisten. LOE.
2 Move effortlessly; glide, drift. E20.

1 J. A. SYMONDS Distant islands shimmering in sun-litten haze. H. STURGIS A sinuous young lady, clad in a sheath of some glittering, shimmering blackness. A. HIGGINS What shimmers on the ceiling? Sunlight in dancing waves.

▶ **B** *noun*. A shimmering light or glow; a subdued tremulous light. E19.

M. E. BRADDON The first shimmer of the moonlight was silvery on the water. W. BOYD The soft light set shimmers glowing in her thick auburn hair.

■ **shimmeringly** *adverb* in a shimmering manner M20.

shimmery /ˈʃɪm(ə)ri/ *adjective*. L19.
[from SHIMMER *verb* + -Y[1]. Cf. German *schimmerig*, West Frisian *skimerich*.]
Giving out a shimmering light, glimmering.

J. DOS PASSOS We can look way down into the cold rainy shimmery water.

■ **shimmeriness** *noun* E20.

shimmy /ˈʃɪmi/ *noun*[1]. Chiefly *dial.* & *US*. M19.
[Alt. of CHEMISE.]
A simple undergarment, a shirt, a chemise.

shimmy /ˈʃɪmi/ *noun*[2] & *verb*. E20.
[Origin unkn.]
▶ **A** *noun*. **1** A kind of lively ragtime dance involving much shaking of the body; *gen.* a shake or sway of the body. Freq. in ***shake a shimmy***. Orig. *US*. E20.
2 Oscillation or vibration of the wheels etc. of a motor vehicle or aircraft; an instance of this. E20.

1 B. MALAMUD Annamaria . . did a fast shimmy to rhythmic handclapping.

Comb.: **shimmy damper** a device fitted to motor vehicles etc. to prevent or reduce shimmy; **shimmy-foxtrot**, **shimmy shake** = sense 1 above.

▶ **B** *verb*. **1 a** *verb intrans.* Dance the shimmy; move as in a shimmy, shake or sway the body. E20. ▸**b** *verb trans.* Dance (the shimmy); shake (part of the body) as in a shimmy. E20.
2 *verb intrans.* Of a wheel, vehicle, etc.: shake or vibrate abnormally. E20.
3 *verb intrans.* [Infl. by SHIMMER *verb*.] Move effortlessly, glide, drift. E20.

shim-sham /ˈʃɪmʃam/ *noun*[1] & *adjective*. *obsolete* exc. *dial.* E18.
[Redupl. of SHAM *noun*[1] & *adjective*.]
= FLIMFLAM *noun & adjective*.

shin /ʃɪn/ *noun*[1] & *verb*.
[Old English *scinu* = Middle & mod. Low German, Middle Dutch *schēne* (Dutch *scheen*), Old High German *scina* shin, needle (German *Schiene* thin plate, *Schienbein* shin-bone), prob. ult. from Germanic word meaning 'thin or narrow piece'.]
▶ **A** *noun*. **1 a** The front part of the human leg between the knee and the ankle; the front or sharp edge of the tibia. Also (occas.), an analogous part of the leg of an animal. OE. ▸**b** A cut of beef from the lower foreleg. M18.
2 [After German *Schiene*.] An iron plate or band. M18.
3 A ridge of a hill. *Scot.* E19.

1 V. S. PRITCHETT She said I was a nasty, common little boy, so I kicked her on the shins.

Phrases: **break shins** *arch. slang* borrow money.
Comb.: **shin-bone** the tibia; **shin-cracker** *Austral.* a hard white brittle siliceous claystone which overlies deposits of opal; **shin-guard** = *shin-pad* below; **shin-leaf** *N. Amer.* a wintergreen of the genus *Pyrola*, esp. *P. elliptica*; **shin-oak** *US* any of several dwarf oaks which form thick scrub; **shin-pad** a protective pad for the shins, worn when playing football etc.; **shin-plaster** (*a*) *Hist.* (orig. *US*) a square piece of paper saturated with vinegar etc., used as a plaster for sore legs; (*b*) *US & Austral. slang* a banknote, *esp.* one of a low denomination, or which has depreciated in value; a promissory note issued by an individual, as a storekeeper etc.; (*c*) *Canad. slang* (now *Hist.*) a twenty-five cent bill; **shin-splints** (treated as *sing.* or *pl.*) acute pain in the shin and lower leg caused by prolonged running esp. on hard surfaces; **shin-tangle** *Canad.* dense undergrowth.

▶ **B** *verb*. Infl. **-nn-**.
1 *verb intrans.* Orig. NAUTICAL. Climb *up*, *down*, etc., (something) by clasping it with the arms and legs and hauling oneself up without the help of steps etc. E19. ▸**b** *verb trans.* Climb up (something). L19.
2 *verb trans.* Injure (a person) on the shins, esp. by kicking. E19.
3 *verb intrans.* & *trans.* with *it*. Move quickly; run around. *US colloq.* M19.
4 *verb intrans.* Borrow money. *US slang*. M19.

1 MOLLIE HARRIS The girls could shin up a tree as quickly as any boy. *Daily Express* Others shinned down pipes to escape. **3** J. C. ATKINSON Didn't I shin it along the bridge, pretty speedily!

■ **shinning** *verbal noun* the action of the verb; an instance of this: M19.

Shin /ʃiːn/ *noun*[2] & *adjective*[1]. L19.
[Shina *Šīn*.]
▶ **A** *noun*. Pl. **-s**, same. A member of a Dard people inhabiting northern Kashmir. L19.
▶ **B** *adjective*. Of or pertaining to this people. L19.

Shin /ʃiːn/ *noun*[3] & *adjective*[2]. L19.
[Japanese, abbreviation of SHINSHU.]
(Designating or pertaining to) a major Japanese Buddhist sect teaching salvation by faith in the Buddha Amida and emphasizing morality rather than orthodoxy.

Shina /ˈʃiːnɑː/ *adjective & noun*. M19.
[Shina *sinā bāṣ* Shina language.]
(Designating or pertaining to) the Dard language of the Shin of northern Kashmir.

Shin Bet /ʃɪn ˈbɛt/ *noun phr.* Also **Shinbet**, **Shin Beth**. M20.
[mod. Hebrew, from *šīn* + *bēt*, the initial letters of *šērūt biṭṭāhōn kĕlālī* (general) security service. Cf. SHABAK.]
The principal security service of Israel, concerned primarily with counter-espionage.

attrib.: L. DEIGHTON Samantha was a Shinbet agent after him for war crimes.

shinbin /ˈʃɪnbɪn/ *noun*. *rare*. L18.
[Burmese *shin-byin*, from *shin* put together side by side + *pyin* plank.]
A thick plank split from a green tree.

shindig /ˈʃɪndɪg/ *noun*[1]. *colloq.* M19.
[Origin uncertain: perh. from SHIN *noun*[1] + DIG *noun*[1], but infl. by SHINDY in later senses.]
†**1** A blow on the shins. *US*. Only in M19.
2 A (country) dance; a party, a lively noisy gathering. Orig. *US*. L19.
3 = SHINDY 2. M20.

2 P. BAILEY Wine left over from our New Year shindig. **3** *World Soccer* Apart from the shindig over the penalty shootout . . squabbling also continued between clubs.

shindle /ˈʃɪnd(ə)l/ *noun*. L16.
[Var. of SHINGLE *noun*[1]. Cf. German *Schindel*.]
1 A wooden roofing-tile. L16.
2 In full ***shindle-stone***. Thin stone from which slates are cut. M17.

shindy /ˈʃɪndi/ *noun*. *colloq.* E19.
[Perh. alt. of SHINTY. Cf. SHINE *noun*.]
1 = SHINDIG 2. E19.
2 A brawl, a commotion, a quarrel. E19.
3 = SHINTY 1. *dial.* M19.

2 V. WOOLF A Colonial insulted the House of Windsor, which led to words, broken beer glasses, and a general shindy. **kick up a shindy** make a commotion; pick a quarrel.

shine /ʃʌɪn/ *noun*. LME.
[from SHINE *verb*. In branch II perh. also rel. to SHINDY.]
▶ **I 1** Brightness or radiance emanating from a light or a source of illumination. LME. ▸†**b** A beam or ray of light; a halo. L16–M17.
2 *fig.* **a** Glory, splendour. M16. ▸**b** A splendid display, an impressive show. E19.
3 (A) lustre or sheen of light reflected from metal, water, a polished surface, etc.; a shiny patch on the surface of a painting etc. L16. ▸**b** The pupil of the eye. *dial.* E18. ▸**c** The action or an act of polishing esp. shoes. Chiefly *US*. L19.
4 a Sunshine, fine weather (freq. in ***rain or shine***, ***come rain or shine*** s.v. RAIN *noun*[1]). Also, moonlight. E17. ▸**b** = MOONSHINE *noun* 3. *colloq.* M20.
5 A black person. *US slang. derog.* & *racially offensive*. E20.

1a T. HARDY The shine from her window . . had lighted the pole. **2a** BROWNING To bask . . in shine which kings and queens . . shed. **b** CARLYLE To celebrate the nuptials with due shine and demonstration. **3** S. RADLEY Her hair had lost its shine. T. BERGER He had himself put that shine on the parquet with real wax.

▶ **II 6** A party, a social or festive gathering. *Scot. & dial.* E19.
7 In *pl.* Tricks, capers. *US colloq.* E19.
8 = SHINDY 2. *colloq.* M19.

6 J. CARLYLE Two tea-shines went off with éclat. **8** R. ADAMS The moment he smelt . . an intruder he would start barking and kicking up a shine.

Phrases: ***come rain or shine***: see RAIN *noun*[1]. ***cut a shine***, ***cut up shines***: see CUT *verb*. ***rain or shine***: see RAIN *noun*[1]. **shine and shade** light and dark; sunshine and shadow. **take a shine to** *colloq.* (orig. *US*) take a fancy to; develop a liking for. **take the shine out of** (*a*) spoil the brilliance or newness of; (*b*) outshine, throw into the shade by surpassing.
■ **shineless** *adjective* without brightness, dull L19.

†**shine** *adjective*. *poet.* L16–E17.
[Alt. of SHEEN *adjective* by assim. to SHINE *verb*.]
Shining, bright.

SPENSER Champions all in armour shine, Assembled were in field.

shine /ʃʌɪn/ *verb*. Pa. t. & pple **shone** /ʃɒn/, (now esp. in sense 8) **shined**.
[Old English *scīnan* = Old Frisian *skīna*, Old Saxon *skīnan*, Old High German *scīnan* (Dutch *schijnen*, German *scheinen*), Old Norse *skína*, Gothic *skeinan*, from Germanic.]
1 *verb intrans.* **a** Of the sun, a source of illumination, etc.: shed beams of bright light; give out light *through*; be radiant. Also foll. by *forth*, *over*, *out*. OE. ▸**b** Of the day: be sunny or bright; dawn. Chiefly *poet.* LME. ▸**c** *impers.* in ***it shines***, ***it is shining***, etc., it is sunny. LME.
2 *verb intrans.* Of metal, water, etc.: be lustrous or bright; gleam or glitter with reflected light. Also foll. by *with*. OE.
3 *verb intrans.* Be brilliant or rich in colour, attire, etc.; be glowing with splendour or beauty. Now *rare*. OE.
4 *verb intrans.* Of a person: be conspicuously excellent or brilliant in some respect; excel. OE.
5 *verb intrans.* Of a quality, attribute, etc.: stand out conspicuously or clearly; be evident or visible. ME.
6 *verb trans.* Shed light on, illuminate. Long *rare* or *obsolete*. LME.
7 *verb trans.* **a** Cause (light) to shine, emit (rays). L16. ▸**b** HUNTING. Direct a light on to (the eyes of an animal); locate the position of (an animal) in this way. Cf. LAMPING *noun*. *US*. M19. ▸**c** Cause (a lamp, torch, etc.) to shine; direct the light of (a lamp, torch, etc.). Freq. foll. by *on*, *on to*, *towards*. L19.
8 *verb trans.* Put a polish on or give a shine to (shoes etc.). E17.

1a I. MURDOCH The light from the candlesticks shone upon her golden head. **2** E. WELTY The water shone like steel. **3** T. KENDALL In all thy body bewty shines. **4** B. BAINBRIDGE Ashburner wished he had shone a little more at the luncheon. M. COREN It was only later that he began to shine as a scholar. **5** C. BRONTË What fun shone in his eyes as he recalled some of her fine speeches! **7c** G. GREENE I shone my torch to show that I was there. *Scientific American* To see the objects in a furnace . . one must shine light in from an external source. **8** M. FRENCH They . . sold newspapers, shined shoes, ran errands.

Phrases, & with adverbs in specialized senses: ***make hay while the sun shines***: see HAY *noun*[1]. ***rise and shine***: see RISE *verb*. **shine away** *rare* drive away by shining a light at. **shine down** *rare* surpass in brilliance. **shine through** be clearly evident. **shine upon** *arch.* (of heaven, fortune, etc.) look favourably on, be favourable to. **shine up to** *US* seek to ingratiate oneself with.

shiner /ˈʃʌɪnə/ *noun*. LME.
[from SHINE *verb* + -ER[1].]
1 A thing that shines, glitters, or reflects light. LME. ▸**b** In *pl.* Money, *esp.* sovereigns or guineas. Also (occas.) *sing.*, a silver or gold coin. *arch. slang*. M18. ▸**c** A mirror; *spec.* one used to cheat at cards. *arch. slang*. E19. ▸**d** A jewel. Usu. in *pl.* *slang*. L19. ▸**e** A black eye. *colloq.* E20. ▸**f** PAPER-MAKING. A glistening particle of a mineral impurity on the surface of finished paper. E20.
2 Any of various small silvery fishes, as a dace, a young mackerel; *esp.* (usu. with specifying word) any of the N. American minnows of the genus *Notropis*. L18.
3 a A person who shines at or excels in something; a star. E19. ▸**b** A person who shines or polishes something; *esp.* (*a*) a person who polishes shoes; (*b*) *slang* a window-cleaner. E20.

1 F. MAHONY A small twinkling shiner . . in the wide canopy of heaven. **e** S. BELLOW A person . . is liable to come home with a shiner or bloody nose. **3b** *New Yorker* Like all shoe shiners, these people are great philosophers.

shingle /ˈʃɪŋg(ə)l/ *noun*[1]. ME.
[App. from Latin *scindula*, earlier *scandula* a split piece of wood, after Greek *skhidax*, *skhindalmos*.]
1 A thin rectangular tile, esp. of wood, used as a roofing material or for cladding walls etc. Also, such tiles collectively. ME.
2 *gen.* A piece of board. ME.
3 A small signboard, *esp.* a signboard or nameplate of a lawyer, doctor, etc. *N. Amer.* M19.
4 Shingled hair; a shingled hairstyle. Also, the action or an act of shingling hair. E20.

1 HARPER LEE Rain-rotted shingles drooped over the eaves of the veranda. **a shingle short** *colloq.* (chiefly *Austral.*) of low intelligence, not very bright, stupid. **3 hang out one's shingle**, **set up one's shingle** begin to practise a profession. **4** C. BEATON With her hair snipped in a short shingle.

Attrib. & comb.: In the senses 'consisting of, covered or built with, shingles', as ***shingle house***, ***shingle roof***, etc., 'used in making shingles', as ***shingle machine***, ***shingle saw***, etc. Special combs., as **shingleback (lizard)** a slow-moving heavily built Australian lizard, *Trachydosaurus rugosus*, with scales resembling those of pine cones; **shingle cap** a cap-shaped hairnet for keeping a shingled hairstyle in place; **shingle-nail** a nail used in building to secure shingles; **shingle-oak** an oak of the US, *Quercus imbricaria*, used to make shingles.
■ **shingly** *adjective*[1] covered with shingles or tiles M19.

shingle /ˈʃɪŋg(ə)l/ *noun*[2]. LME.
[Origin unkn.]
1 *sing.* & in *pl.* Small rounded stones; loose waterworn pebbles, esp. as accumulated on a seashore; *Austral. & NZ* loose angular stones on a mountainside. LME.
2 A beach or other stretch of land covered with loose rounded pebbles. E16.

1 E. NORTH From . . the shore came the sound of fine shingle being pulled out and dropped back. attrib.: ***shingle bank***, ***shingle beach***, etc.

Comb.: **shingle slide**, **shingle-slip** *Austral. & NZ* mountainside covered with shingle.

■ **shingly** *adjective*[2] consisting of or covered with shingle; of the nature of shingle: L17.

shingle /ˈʃɪŋɡ(ə)l/ *verb*[1] *trans.* M16.
[from SHINGLE *noun*[1].]
1 Roof (a building), clad (a wall etc.), with shingles. M16.
2 a Cut (hair) so as to create an effect of overlapping shingles. Also (*US*), cut (hair) so that it tapers from the back of the head to the nape of the neck. M19. ▸**b** Cover like a shingled roof. *US*. M19.

shingle /ˈʃɪŋɡ(ə)l/ *verb*[2] *trans.* Now *rare*. L17.
[French *cingler* from German *zängeln*, from *Zange* tongs, pincers.]
METALLURGY. Hammer or squeeze (puddled wrought iron).

shingled /ˈʃɪŋɡ(ə)ld/ *adjective*. ME.
[from SHINGLE *noun*[1], *verb*[1]: see -ED[2], -ED[1].]
1 Covered or tiled with shingles. ME.
2 Overlapping like tiles or shingles. L19.
3 (Of hair) cut in a shingle; (of a person) having the hair so cut. L19.

shingler /ˈʃɪŋɡlə/ *noun*[1]. ME.
[from SHINGLE *noun*[1] or *verb*[1]: see -ER[1].]
1 A person who shingles houses etc. Also (*US*), a person who or machine which cuts and prepares shingles. ME.
2 A woman with shingled hair. *rare*. E20.

shingler /ˈʃɪŋɡlə/ *noun*[2]. Now *rare*. M19.
[from SHINGLE *verb*[2] + -ER[1].]
METALLURGY. A person who or machine which shingles puddled iron.

shingles /ˈʃɪŋɡ(ə)lz/ *noun pl.*, also used as *sing.* LME.
[Repr. medieval Latin *cingulus* var. of *cingulum* girdle, translating Greek *zōnē*, *zōstēr*.]
1 A disease caused by a herpes virus and characterized by a rash of minute blisters on the skin, often in a band across the body above an affected nerve, and accompanied by localized pain; herpes zoster. LME.
2 A similar disease in horses. Now *rare* or *obsolete*. M17.

Shingon /ˈʃɪŋɡɒn/ *noun & adjective*. E18.
[Japanese = true word, mantra, from *shin* true + *gon* word.]
(Designating or pertaining to) a Japanese Buddhist sect founded in the 9th cent. and devoted to esoteric Buddhism.

shining /ˈʃʌɪnɪŋ/ *adjective*. OE.
[from SHINE *verb* + -ING[2].]
1 That shines; lustrous, gleaming; radiant. Also, of rich or brilliant appearance, colour, attire, etc. OE. ▸**b** BOTANY & MINERALOGY. Having a smooth even polished surface. E17.
2 Conspicuously excellent, distinguished, brilliant. Now *rare* exc. in ***shining example***. OE.

> 📖 **1** A. SILLITOE Dust covered his shining toe-caps. **2** E. E. SMITH To her Moffatt's work seemed a shining example of the . . movement.

Special collocations & phrases: **improve the shining hour** [after Isaac Watts *Divine Songs*] make good use of time; make the most of one's time. **shining armour** (freq. *iron.*) willingness or preparedness to devote oneself nobly to a good cause (***knight in shining armour***: see KNIGHT *noun*). **shining cuckoo** the golden-bronze cuckoo, *Chalcites lucidus*, of New Zealand and other Pacific islands. **shining light** [after *John* 5:35] a person conspicuously excellent in some respect. **shining path** [translating Spanish *sendero luminoso*] = SENDERO LUMINOSO.
■ **shiningly** *adverb* LME. **shiningness** *noun* E18.

Shinkansen /ˈʃiːnkɑːnsɛn/ *noun*. Pl. same. M20.
[Japanese, from *shin* new + *kansen* (railway) main line.]
In Japan, a railway system carrying high-speed passenger trains; a train operating on such a system; *transf.* a similar train or system elsewhere.

shinner /ˈʃɪnə/ *noun*[1]. L16.
[from SHIN *noun*[1] & *verb* + -ER[1].]
†**1** A stocking. *rare*. Only in L16.
2 A blow or kick on the shin. *dial.* M19.
3 A person who borrows money. *US slang*. M19.
4 A person who moves around quickly; an active person. *US colloq.* M19.

Shinner /ˈʃɪnə/ *noun*[2]. *colloq.* E20.
[Abbreviation.]
A Sinn Feiner.

shinnery /ˈʃɪn(ə)ri/ *noun*. *US*. E20.
[from SHIN *noun*[1] + -ERY.]
An area of scrub in which shin-oak predominates.

shinny /ˈʃɪni/ *noun*[1]. Now chiefly *N. Amer.* L17.
[Var.]
= SHINTY 1.

shinny /ˈʃɪni/ *noun*[2]. *Southern US*. M20.
[Alt. of SHINE *noun*: see -Y[6].]
= MOONSHINE *noun* 3.

shinny /ˈʃɪni/ *verb*. *N. Amer. colloq.* L19.
[from SHIN *noun*[1] + -Y[6].]
1 *verb intrans.* Shin *up* or *down* a tree etc. L19.
2 *verb trans.* Make (one's way) thus. M20.

Shinola /ʃʌɪˈnəʊlə/ *noun*. *US*. E20.
[from SHINE *noun*, *verb* + -OLA.]
(US proprietary name for) a brand of boot polish; *euphem.* = SHIT *noun* 3.
not know shit from Shinola *coarse slang* be ignorant or innocent. **neither shit nor Shinola** *coarse slang* neither one thing nor the other.

Shinshu /ˈʃɪnʃuː/ *noun & adjective*. *rare*. E18.
[Japanese, from *shin* true, genuine, authentic + *shū* sect.]
= SHIN *noun*[3] & *adjective*[2].

Shinto /ˈʃɪntəʊ/ *noun & adjective*. E18.
[Japanese, *shin* gods + *tō* way.]
▶**A** *noun*. Pl. (*rare*) -**os**.
1 A religious system incorporating the worship of ancestors, nature-spirits and other divinities, and (until 1945) a belief in the divinity of the Japanese emperor, until 1945 the State religion of Japan. E18.
2 = SHINTOIST. *rare*. E19.
▶**B** *attrib.* or as *adjective*. Of, pertaining to, or designating Shinto. E18.
■ **Shintoism** *noun* = SHINTO 1 M19. **Shintoist** *noun* an adherent of Shinto E18. **Shintoistic** *adjective* of, pertaining to, or characteristic of Shinto L19.

shinty /ˈʃɪnti/ *noun*. See also SHINNY *noun*[1]. M18.
[App. from the cries used in the game, *shin ye*, *shin you*, *shin t'ye*, of unkn. origin.]
1 A game originating in Scotland and similar to hockey, played with a light wooden ball and narrow sticks curved at one end, but with taller goalposts. Also, a stick, a ball, used in this game. M18.
2 = SHINDY 2. *rare*. M19.

Shinwari /ʃɪnˈwɑːri/ *noun*. Pl. -**s**, same. L19.
[Local name.]
A member of a nomadic people inhabiting areas of Afghanistan around the Khyber Pass.

shiny /ˈʃʌɪni/ *adjective*, *adverb*, & *noun*. L16.
[from SHINE *noun* + -Y[1].]
▶**A** *adjective*. **1** Full of light or brightness; luminous; having a bright, polished, or glistening surface. Also (of a garment, esp. the seat of trousers etc), having the nap worn off. L16.
2 *fig.* Beaming, radiant. Also, outstanding; conspicuously or apparently excellent. L19.

> 📖 **1** F. KING The boy wheeled the shiny new bicycle from the shed. **2** *Publishers Weekly* A shiny Ph.D in English literature.

▶**B** *adverb*. Shinily; in a bright manner. *rare*. L16.
▶**C** *noun*. A shiny or bright object; esp. ***the shiny*** (*slang*), money. *rare*. M19.
■ **shinily** *adverb* L19. **shininess** *noun* L19.

ship /ʃɪp/ *noun*.
[Old English *scip* = Old Frisian, Old Saxon *skip* (Dutch *schip*), Old High German *skif*, *schif*, (German *Schiff*), Old Norse, Gothic *skip*, from Germanic. Cf. SKIFF *noun*[1], SKIPPER *noun*[2] & *verb*[1].]
1 A large seagoing vessel propelled by sail or engine (cf. BOAT *noun*); *spec.* a sailing vessel with a bowsprit and three, four, or five square-rigged masts. Freq. with specifying word. OE. ▸**b** *fig.* In full ***ship of State***, ***ship of the State***. The State and its affairs regarded as being subject to adverse or changing circumstances, as a ship is to the weather. L17. ▸**c** A boat; *esp.* (ROWING) an eight-oared racing-boat. *colloq.* L19.
2 A ship's crew. ME.
†**3** An amount of goods shipped, a shipful. LME–L16.
4 A thing resembling a ship in form or appearance; *spec.* †(*a*) a noble coined under Edward III, which bore the image of a ship; (*b*) *Hist.* an incense boat; a vessel used in saltmaking into which the brine runs from the pits. LME.
5 A thing resembling a ship in function, esp. in its (perceived) ability to be navigated; *spec.* †(*a*) Noah's ark; (*b*) a balloon; (*c*) *US* an aircraft; (*d*) a spaceship. LME.
6 (Usu. **S-**.) *The* constellation Argo. Also ***the Ship Argo***. L16.

> 📖 **1** M. KRAMER The . . majority of European wines are sent . . by ship. ***battleship***, ***flagship***, ***hospital-ship***, ***long ship***, ***merchant ship***, ***post ship***, ***slave ship***, ***steamship***, ***tall ship***, ***troop-ship***, ***warship***, etc. ***abandon ship***: see ABANDON *verb* 4. ***break ship***: see BREAK *verb*. ***burn one's ships***: see BURN *verb* 8. ***capital ship***: see CAPITAL *adjective* & *noun*[2]. ***great ship***: see GREAT *adjective*. ***happy ship***: see HAPPY *adjective*. **in the same ship** = ***in the same boat*** s.v. BOAT *noun* 1. ***jump ship***: see JUMP *verb*. **king's ship** *Hist.* (*a*) any of the fleet of ships provided and maintained out of the royal revenue; a ship of the Royal Navy; (*b*) a warship equipped at the public expense (opp. ***privateer***). ***old ship***: see OLD *adjective*. **ship in a bottle** a model ship inside a bottle, the neck of which is smaller than the ship. **ship of fools** [after *The shyp of folys of the worlde* (1509) translation of German work *Das Narrenschiff* (1494)] a ship whose passengers represent various types of vice, folly, or human failings; *fig.* the world, humankind. ***ship of the line***: see LINE *noun*[2]. **ship-of-war** (now *rare*) a warship, a man-of-war. †**ship-royal** a ship of the Royal Navy. **ships that pass in the night** *fig.* people whose contact or acquaintance is necessarily fleeting or transitory. ***take ship***: see TAKE *verb*. **tight ship**, **taut ship** (*a*) a ship in which ropes etc. are tight; a strictly run ship; (*b*) *transf.* & *fig.* a disciplined or well-run organization, state of affairs, etc. (freq. in ***run a tight ship***). **when a person's ship comes home**, **when a person's ship comes in** when a person comes into an expected fortune; when a person becomes successful. **5 ship of the desert** the camel.

Comb.: ***ship biscuit***: see ***ship's biscuit*** below; **shipborne** *adjective* carried by ship; **ship-boy** *Hist.* a boy serving on board ship; **ship-breaker** a person who buys old ships to break them up for sale; a company engaged in this business; **ship-breaking** †(*a*) shipwreck; (*b*) the occupation of a ship-breaker; (*c*) the action of breaking into a ship with intent to rob etc.; **ship-broken** *adjective* (chiefly *Scot.*, long *rare*) shipwrecked; destitute through shipwreck; **ship-broker** an agent handling a ship's business when it is in port, and who also may be engaged in buying, selling, or insuring ships; **ship-brokerage**, **ship-broking** the action or trade of a ship-broker; **ship burial** ARCHAEOLOGY burial in a wooden ship under a mound, a Scandinavian and Anglo-Saxon custom for the bodies of those particularly honoured; **ship-canal** a canal large enough to allow ocean-going ships to travel to inland ports, or to travel between one stretch of ocean and another; ***ship carpenter***: see ***ship's carpenter*** below; ***ship chandler***: see ***ship's chandler*** below; **ship-craft** (*a*) the art of navigation; (*b*) the art of ship-construction; ***ship decanter***: see ***ship's decanter*** below; **ship-fever** typhus (as formerly occurring esp. on crowded ships); **ship-keeper** a person who takes care of a ship when the crew is absent from it; **ship-ladder** a ladder used to board or leave a ship; **shiplap** *noun* & *verb* (*a*) *noun* a form of joint in carpentry made by halving (HALVE *verb* 4); *collect.* boards interlocked by rabbets, used esp. for cladding; (*b*) *verb trans.* fit (boards) together in this way; **ship-lapped** *adjective* (*a*) having a cladding of shiplap; (*b*) (of boards etc.) interlocked by rabbets; **ship-letter** *Hist.* a letter carried by a private vessel rather than the regular mail-boat; **shipload** as many or as much as a ship can carry; **shipmate** a fellow-member of a ship's crew; *colloq.* an acquaintance, a friend; ***be shipmates with*** (*fig.*, *colloq.*), be acquainted with, have knowledge of; **shipowner** a person owning, or having a share in, a ship or ships; **ship plane** an aeroplane specially adapted to operate from an aircraft carrier; **ship-rat** a rat found on board ship, usu. the black rat *Rattus rattus*; **ship-rigged** *adjective* (of a sailing ship) square-rigged; **ship's articles** the terms according to which seamen take service on a ship; **ship's biscuit**, **ship biscuit** *Hist.* a very hard coarse kind of biscuit kept and eaten on board ship; ***ship's boat***: see BOAT *noun* 1; **ship's-carpenter**, **ship-carpenter** a carpenter employed in the building or repairing of ships; **ship's chandler**, **ship chandler** a retailer specializing in the supply of provisions, equipment, etc., for ships and boats; **ship's company** a ship's crew; ***ship's corporal***: see CORPORAL *noun*[2] 2; **ship's decanter**, **ship decanter** a decanter with a base of greater width than the shoulder; ***ship's husband***: see HUSBAND *noun* 3; **shipside** (*a*) the outside of a ship's hull; (*b*) the dock adjacent to a moored ship; **ship's papers** documents establishing ownership, nationality, details of cargo, etc., which a ship is required to carry by law; **ship's store**, **ship store** (*a*) *US* a shop on board ship; (*b*) in *pl.*, provisions and supplies for use on board ship; **ship's time**, **ship time** the local mean time of the meridian where the ship is; **ship's writer** a ship's petty officer responsible for record-keeping and other clerical duties; **ship-timber** timber suitable for shipbuilding; ***ship time***: see ***ship's time*** above; †**ship-tire** (*rare*, Shakes.) a head-dress shaped like a ship or having a shiplike ornament; **ship-to-air** *adjective* (of a missile) fired from a ship at an aerial target; **ship-to-ship** *adjective* from one ship to another; **ship-to-shore** *adjective* & *noun* (*a*) *adjective* from a ship to land; (*b*) *noun* a radio-telephone operating in this manner; **shipway** (*a*) a slope on which a ship is built and down which it slides to be launched; (*b*) a ship-canal; **ship-work** work at a ship or on board ship; shipbuilding; **shipworm** any of various bivalve molluscs of the family Teredinidae, esp. *Teredo navalis*, which have greatly elongated bodies and bore tunnels in wooden ships, piers, and other submerged wood; **shipwright** a shipbuilder; a ship's carpenter.
■ **shipful** *noun* as much or as many as a ship will hold ME. **shipless** *adjective* (*a*) (of a sea, harbour, etc.) devoid of ships, unoccupied by ships; (*b*) lacking or deprived of one's ship or ships: E18. **shiplike** *adjective* resembling (that of) a ship L16. **shippy** *adjective* (*rare*) †(*a*) suitable for ships; (*b*) characteristic of a ship or ships: M17.

ship /ʃɪp/ *verb*. Infl. **-pp-**.
[Late Old English *scipian*, from prec.]
1 *verb trans.* In *pass.* Be provided with a ship or ships. Long *obsolete* exc. as UNSHIPPED. LOE.
†**2** *verb trans.* Equip or launch (a vessel). LOE–E16.
3 *verb intrans.* & (*arch.*) *refl.* Go on board a ship, embark. LOE.
4 a *verb trans.* Put or take (passengers, cargo, etc.) on board a ship, cause to embark. ME. ▸**b** *verb trans.* Send or transport by ship; *fig.* send packing, get rid of. Also foll. by *off*. LME. ▸**c** *verb trans.* Transport (goods) by rail or other means. *N. Amer.* M19. ▸**d** *verb intrans.* Of perishable, fragile, or delicate goods: be transportable by ship without spoiling or damage. M19.
†**5** *verb trans.* In *pass.* Of a person: have gone on board ship, have embarked. ME–E18.
6 *verb intrans.* Travel by ship *to* or *from* a place. Freq. foll. by *from*, *over*, *to*, etc. Now chiefly *US*. ME.
7 *verb trans.* Put (an object) in its correct position in readiness to function; *spec.* fix (an oar) in its rowlock, in readiness to row. Orig. & chiefly NAUTICAL. E17.
8 *verb trans.* **a** Take or draw (an object) into the ship or boat to which it belongs. M17. ▸**b** Lift (an oar) out of its rowlock, and lay inside the boat. E18.

9 a *verb trans.* Engage (a person) to serve on a ship. **M17.** ▸**b** *verb intrans.* Of a sailor: take service on a ship. **E19.**
10 *verb trans.* Of a vessel: take in (water) over the side; be awash with (water) by waves breaking over it. Freq. in ***ship a sea*** below. **L17.**
11 Put on (clothing etc.); shoulder (a load). Now *rare* exc. in ***ship a stripe*** below. **E19.**

📖 **1** SHAKES. *Oth.* Is he well shipp'd? His bark is stoutly timber'd. **3** *Spectator* People wishing to get from London to New York . . ship at Liverpool. **4a** SIR W. SCOTT A quantity of game which was shipped awhile ago at Inverness . . never reached him. **b** *Times* Goods shipped in the mail vessels. **c** H. KISSINGER To ship oil thousands of miles overland without pipelines would be a formidable undertaking. **6** H. JAMES You regularly make me wish . . I had shipped back to American City. **ship out** *N. Amer. slang* (orig. MILITARY) depart, be transported (***shape up or ship out***: see SHAPE *verb*.); **ship over** *US Military slang* re-enlist, volunteer for a tour of duty. **7** J. COULTER Mast and sail are . . never shipped until required. **8a** W. W. JACOBS The gangway was shipped, and . . the *Curlew* drifted slowly away from the quay. **b** J. LE CARRÉ The old man had shipped his oars and let the dinghy drift. **10** C. JACKSON It seemed certain the . . motor-boat would ship water . . and they would be swamped. **ship a sea** be flooded by a wave. **11** E. J. TRELAWNY He . . took off his white jacket, and shipped a blue one. **ship a stripe** *colloq.* gain promotion in the navy or air force.

■ **shippable** *adjective* †(*a*) *rare* navigable; (*b*) able to be shipped: **L15. shippage** *noun* (*rare*) shipping, shipment **E17.**

-ship /ʃɪp/ *suffix.*
[Old English *-scipe*, *-scype*, from Germanic base also of SHAPE *verb*.]
1 Forming nouns from nouns denoting (*a*) status, official position, or rank, as ***ambassadorship***, ***chaplainship***, ***citizenship***, ***headship***, ***professorship***, etc.; (*b*) a tenure of an official post, as ***chairmanship***, ***fellowship***, etc., the emoluments etc. pertaining to such a post, as ***postmastership***, ***scholarship***, etc.; (*c*) (with possess. pronoun) a title or a humorous form of address, as ***his Deanship***, ***their hagships***, ***her ladyship***, etc.
2 Forming nouns from nouns or (now *rare*) from adjectives, denoting a quality, state, or condition, as ***companionship***, ***friendship***, ***hardship***, ***relationship***, etc.
3 Forming nouns from nouns denoting skill or expertise in a certain capacity, as ***craftsmanship***, ***entrepreneurship***, ***horsewomanship***, etc.
4 Forming nouns from nouns denoting the collective members of a group, as ***guildship***, ***membership***, ***monkship***, ***township***, etc.
5 Forming nouns from nouns denoting a state of life, occupation, or behaviour, as ***courtship***, ***husbandship***, etc. Now *rare*.

shipboard /ˈʃɪpbɔːd/ *noun & adjective.* **ME.**
[from SHIP *noun* + BOARD *noun*.]
▶ **A** *noun.* **1** The side of a ship. Chiefly in phrs. below. Long *rare* or *obsolete*. **ME.**
†**2** A plank of a ship. **ME–M16.**
1 from shipboard off a ship. **on shipboard** on board a ship. †**over shipboard**, †**over the shipboard** overboard. **to shipboard** on a ship. †**within shipboard** on board a ship.
▶ **B** *attrib.* or as *adjective.* Used or occurring on board a ship. **M19.**

📖 F. BALDWIN A shipboard romance will do a lot for his ego.

shipbuilder /ˈʃɪpbɪldə/ *noun.* **L17.**
[from SHIP *noun* + BUILDER.]
A person or company whose occupation or business is the design and construction of ships; a naval architect.
■ **shipbuilding** *verbal noun* the business or art of constructing ships; naval architecture: **E18.**

shipentine /ˈʃɪp(ə)ntiːn/ *noun. rare.* **L19.**
[from SHIP *noun* after *barquentine*.]
A four-masted vessel with three square-rigged masts (like a ship), plus an additional fore-and-aft rigged mast.

Shipibo /ʃɪˈpiːbəʊ/ *noun & adjective.* Also **Sipibo.** **E19.**
[Panoan, lit. 'little monkey people'.]
▶ **A** *noun.* Pl. same, **-s.** A member of a S. American Indian people inhabiting the upper Ucayali River region in the Andes mountains of Peru; the Panoan language of this people. **E19.**
▶ **B** *attrib.* or as *adjective.* Of or pertaining to the Shipibo or their language. **L19.**

shipman /ˈʃɪpmən/ *noun. arch.* Pl. **-men.** **OE.**
[from SHIP *noun* + MAN *noun*.]
1 A seaman, a sailor. **OE.**
2 A master mariner; the master of a ship; a skipper. Also, a pilot. **LME.**
Comb.: †**shipman's card** *rare* (Shakes.) (*a*) the mariner's compass; (*b*) a map of the sea.

shipmaster /ˈʃɪpmɑːstə/ *noun.* **LME.**
[from SHIP *noun* + MASTER *noun*[1].]
1 The master, captain, or commander of a ship. Formerly also, a pilot, a steersman. **LME.**
2 A person owning and in command of a ship. **M16.**

shipmen *noun* pl. of SHIPMAN.

shipment /ˈʃɪpm(ə)nt/ *noun.* **L18.**
[from SHIP *verb* + -MENT.]
1 An amount of goods shipped or transported; a consignment. **L18.**
2 The action or an act of shipping or transporting goods etc. **E19.**

📖 **1** M. KRAMER Shipments of Portuguese wines. **2** SLOAN WILSON A burned-out tank . . left there to await shipment back to Germany.

ship-money /ˈʃɪpmʌni/ *noun. Hist.* **M17.**
[from SHIP *noun* + MONEY *noun*.]
In England, a tax formerly levied in wartime on ports and maritime towns, cities, and counties (later also, inland counties) to provide ships for the monarch's service, abolished in 1640.

shipo *noun & adjective* var. of SHIPPO.

shippen *noun* var. of SHIPPON.

shipper /ˈʃɪpə/ *noun.* **LOE.**
[from SHIP *noun* + -ER[1].]
†**1** A seaman, a sailor. **LOE–E18.**
†**2** A ship's skipper. **L15–M17.**
3 a A person who or company which transports or receives goods by ship. **M18.** ▸**b** A person who or company which transports or receives goods by land or air. Orig. *US.* **M19.** ▸**c** A commodity which is shipped or is suitable for shipping. *rare.* **L19.**
4 MECHANICS. A device for shifting a belt from one pulley to another. **M19.**

shipping /ˈʃɪpɪŋ/ *noun.* **ME.**
[from SHIP *verb* + -ING[1].]
1 (Without article.) A ship or ships for the use or accommodation of a person or thing; accommodation on board ship, provision of a ship or ships. Formerly also (in *pl.*), ships. *arch.* **ME.**
†**2 a** Navigation. **LME–L17.** ▸**b** A voyage, a sailing. **L15–L17.**
3 The action or an act of shipping or transporting goods. **LME.**
4 Ships collectively, esp. of a particular country, frequenting a particular port, or used for a particular purpose. **L16.**

📖 **1** SIR W. SCOTT I will . . seize on shipping, and embark for Flanders. †**put to shipping** put on board. **take shipping** embark; go abroad. **3** G. ANSON A licence for the shipping of his stores. attrib.: ***shipping clerk***, ***shipping company***, ***shipping line***, etc. **4** *Practical Boat Owner* These things are strictly out-of-bounds to all shipping. ***LLOYD'S Register of Shipping***.

Comb.: **shipping-agent** a licensed agent transacting a ship's business, as insurance, documentation, etc., for the owner; **shipping-articles** = *ship's articles* s.v. SHIP *noun*; **shipping-bill** a manifest of goods shipped; **shipping fever** VETERINARY MEDICINE (orig. *US*) any of several diseases typically contracted by cattle while being shipped from place to place, *esp.* one caused by bacteria of the genus *Pasteurella*; **shipping-master** an official superintending the signing of ship's articles, paying off of seamen, etc.; **shipping-note** a document containing particulars of goods for shipment made out by the sender and handed to the carrier; **shipping-office** the office of a shipping-master or a shipping-agent; **shipping ore** ore suitable for being shipped; **shipping tobacco** tobacco grown for export.

shippo /ˈʃiːpəʊ/ *noun & adjective.* Also **shipo.** **L19.**
[Japanese *shippō* seven precious things, from *shichi* seven + *hō* jewel.]
(Made of) Japanese cloisonné-enamel ware.

shippon /ˈʃɪp(ə)n/ *noun.* Now *dial.* Also **shippen.**
[Old English *scypen* fem., from Germanic, repr. also Middle Low German *schoppen*, *schuppen* (German *Schuppen*) shed: see -EN[2]. Cf. SHOP *noun*.]
A cattle-shed, a cow-house.

shippound /ˈʃɪppaʊnd/ *noun.* **LME.**
[Middle Low German *schippunt*, Middle Dutch *schippond*, from Germanic base of SHIP *noun*, POUND *noun*[1].]
Hist. A unit of weight used in the Baltic trade, varying from 300 to 400 pounds, and equivalent to 20 lispounds.

ship-repair /ˈʃɪprɪpɛː/ *noun.* **M20.**
[from SHIP *noun* + REPAIR *noun*[2].]
The business or craft of restoring a ship to a sound condition.
■ **ship-repairer** *noun* a company engaged in the business of repairing ships **L20. ship-repairing** *noun* **M20.**

shipshape /ˈʃɪpʃeɪp/ *adjective & adverb.* Orig. NAUTICAL. **M17.**
[from SHIP *noun* + SHAPEN *ppl adjective* (later reduced to *shape*).]
▶ **A** *adjective.* Arranged properly, as things on board ship should be; trim, orderly. **M17.**
shipshape and BRISTOL fashion.
▶ **B** *adverb.* In a seamanlike manner, in good order. **M18.**

shipton moth /ˈʃɪpt(ə)n mɒθ/ *noun phr.* **M19.**
[from Mother *Shipton*, a renowned 16th-cent. seer.]
= ***Mother Shipton*** s.v. MOTHER *noun*[1].

shipwreck /ˈʃɪprɛk/ *noun, adjective, & verb.* **LOE.**
[from SHIP *noun* + WRECK *noun*[1].]
▶ **A** *noun.* **1** The remains of a wrecked ship, wreckage. **LOE.**
2 Destruction or loss of a ship by its being sunk or broken up by the violence of the sea, or by its foundering or striking a rock etc., as experienced by those on board; an instance of this. **LME.**
3 *fig.* Destruction, total loss or ruin, esp. of a person's hopes, dreams, fortune, etc. **E16.**

📖 **1** *fig.*: MILTON Gentlemen indeed; . . the spawn and shiprack of Taverns and Dicing Houses. **2** SWIFT Having . . narrowly escaped shipwreck in his passage from Normandy. **3** F. W. FARRAR Agrippina was . . maddened by the shipwreck of her ambition. **make shipwreck of** *arch.* (*a*) suffer the loss of; (*b*) bring to destruction or total ruin.

▶ **B** *adjective.* Having suffered (a) shipwreck; shipwrecked. *rare.* **L16.**
▶ **C** *verb.* **1** *verb trans.* **a** Cause (a person, a ship) to suffer shipwreck. Also (*rare*), cause the loss of (goods) by shipwreck. Freq. as ***shipwrecked*** *ppl adjective.* **L16.** ▸**b** *fig.* Destroy or cause the loss of (a person's hopes, dreams, fortunes, etc.); bring to ruin. **L16.**
2 *verb intrans.* Suffer shipwreck. **E17.**

📖 **1a** LD MACAULAY Precious effects from shipwrecked vessels. *Smithsonian* The first Westerners to invade the Maya world were Spanish conquistadores, shipwrecked off the Yucatán coast. **b** B. JOWETT The next definition . . is shipwrecked on a refined distinction between the state and the act. **2** *fig.*: SIR W. SCOTT Your fortunes shall not shipwreck upon the same coast.

shipyard /ˈʃɪpjɑːd/ *noun.* **L17.**
[from SHIP *noun* + YARD *noun*[1].]
A large enclosed area adjoining the sea or a major river, in which ships are built or repaired.
Comb.: **shipyard eye** an epidemic form of viral keratoconjunctivitis.

shiralee /ˈʃɪrəliː/ *noun. Austral. slang.* **L19.**
[Origin unkn.]
A tramp's swag or bundle of personal belongings.

Shiraz /ˈʃɪəraz, ʃɪˈraz/ *noun.* **M17.**
[See sense 1. In sense 3, app. alt. of French *syrah* (*scyras*, *sirrah*) infl. by the belief that the vine was brought from Iran by the Crusaders.]
▶ **I** *attrib.* **1** Used to designate things made in or associated with Shiraz, a city in SW Iran; *spec.* (*a*) (now *rare*) a red or white wine made in the Shiraz district; (*b*) a kind of soft woollen rug or carpet, often having richly-coloured geometrical designs. **M17.**
2 Used to designate (the vine bearing) a black grape used in wine-making and grown orig. in the Rhône valley of France, or the red wine made from these grapes. **M19.**
▶ **II** *ellipt.* **3** The Shiraz vine or grape; (a drink of) red wine made from Shiraz grapes. **M19.**
4 A Shiraz rug or carpet. **E20.**

Shirburnian /ʃəːˈbəːnɪən/ *noun & adjective.* **M19.**
[from pseudo-Latin *Shirburnia*, based on the medieval forms (e.g. *Scireburne*) of *Sherborne* a town in Dorset and a public school situated there + -AN.]
▶ **A** *noun.* A pupil or former pupil of Sherborne School. **M19.**
▶ **B** *attrib.* or as *adjective.* Of or pertaining to Sherborne School or its pupils or former pupils. **L19.**

shire /ˈʃʌɪə, as 2nd elem. ʃə/ *noun & verb.*
[Old English *scīr* = Old High German *scīra*. Cf. Anglo-Latin *schira* (*scir-*), *shira* shire.]
▶ **A** *noun.* †**1** Care, official charge; administrative office or position, as of a steward, bishop, governor, etc. Only in **OE.**
†**2** A province or district under the rule of a governor; the see of a bishop, the province of an archbishop; *gen.* a country, a region, a district. **OE–E19.**
3 a *spec.* Orig. (*Hist.*), in Anglo-Saxon times, an administrative district consisting of a number of smaller districts (*hundreds* or *wapentakes*), ruled jointly by an alderman and a sheriff who presided over a shire-moot or judicial assembly; under Norman rule, an English administrative division, equivalent to a county. Now *gen.*, a county in Great Britain, esp. in England, and formerly also in Ireland. Freq. as 2nd elem. in names of counties, as *Berkshire*, *Derbyshire*, etc. **OE.** ▸**b** The inhabitants of a shire collectively. **OE.** ▸†**c** A shire-court. **ME–E16.** ▸†**d** An English city or town with the status or powers of a county. Cf. COUNTY *noun*[1] 3. **LME–L15.** ▸**e** A rural administrative district, often with its own elected council. *Austral.* **M19.**
4 ***the Shires***: ▸**a** The parts of England extending north-east from Hampshire and Devon; the midland counties of England; *gen.* those English counties with names ending or formerly ending in *-shire*. Also, the shire counties. **L18.** ▸**b** The foxhunting district of England, chiefly comprising Leicestershire and Northamptonshire. **M19.**
5 A shire horse. **L19.**
Comb.: **shire-bishop** *Hist.* the bishop of a shire; **shire county** a non-metropolitan county of the UK, as instituted by the local government reorganization of 1974; †**shire-court** = COUNTY

noun[1] 1; **shire-ground** *Hist.* land divided into shires; a tract of land subject to the control of the authorities of a shire; **shire-hall** *Hist.* a building where the county quarter sessions, assizes, etc., were held (cf. ***county hall*** s.v. COUNTY *noun*[1]); **shire horse** a heavy powerful breed of draught horse with long hair on the fetlocks, originally bred chiefly in the midland counties of England; **shire-house** *Hist.* = ***shire hall*** above; **shire-jury** *Hist.* the members of a shire-court; **shireman** (***a***) LAW (now *Hist.*) in Anglo-Saxon England, a sheriff; a bailiff; a steward; (***b***) (*obsolete* exc. *dial.*) a native or inhabitant of the Shires; **shiremoot** *Hist.* in Anglo-Saxon times, the judicial assembly of a shire; **shire-oak** *Hist.* an oak tree marking the boundary of a shire or a meeting place for a shire-court; **shire-reeve** *Hist.* a sheriff, an administrative officer of a shire; **shire-stone** *Hist.* a stone marking the boundary of a shire; **shire-town** (***a***) the chief town of a shire, a county town; (***b***) *US* = ***county seat*** s.v. COUNTY *noun*[1].

▶ **B** *verb trans.* Divide (a country) into shires. E19.

shire /ˈʃʌɪə/ *adjective. obsolete* exc. *dial.*

[Old English *scīr* = Old Frisian *skīre*, Old Saxon *skīr(i)*, Old Norse *skírr*, Gothic *skeirs*, from Germanic base also of SHINE *verb*. Cf. SHEER *adjective & adverb*.]

†**1** Bright, shining; *fig.* illustrious, noble. OE–L15.
†**2** Of water etc.: clear, translucent. OE–L18.
†**3** Of a substance: pure, unmixed. OE–LME.
†**4** Morally or spiritually clean; blameless. Only in ME.
5 Unmitigated, unqualified; absolute; (with neg.) mere. ME.
6 Thin; insubstantial; sparse, scanty; (of beer) low in alcohol, weak. LME.

shirk /ʃəːk/ *noun.* M17.

[Perh. from German *Schurke* scoundrel. In senses 2, 3 from the verb.]

1 A person who unscrupulously exploits or swindles others, = SHARK *noun* 2. *obsolete* exc. *dial.* M17.
2 A person who shirks his or her duty, work, etc. E19.
3 An act or the practice of shirking. *rare.* M19.

shirk /ʃəːk/ *verb.* M17.

[Rel. to prec.]

1 a *verb intrans.* Practise fraud or trickery, esp. instead of working for a living; prey or sponge on others. M17. ▸†**b** *verb trans.* Obtain by trickery or by sponging. Also foll. by *up*. M–L17. ▸**c** *verb intrans.* Shift or fend *for* oneself. *US.* M19.
2 *verb intrans.* Go or move evasively or slyly; slink, sneak. Freq. foll. by *away*, *out*, etc. Now *rare*. L17. ▸†**b** Withdraw or draw *back* through lack of courage *from* one's word, commitment, etc. L18–E19.
3 *verb trans.* Evade (a person); avoid meeting, dodge. Now *rare*. L18.
4 a *verb trans.* Evade or endeavour to get out of (a duty, responsibility, work, etc.). L18. ▸**b** *verb trans.* Shift (responsibility etc.) *on to* or *on* another person. Also foll. by *off*. *US.* M19. ▸**c** *verb intrans.* Practise evasion of work, one's duties, responsibilities, etc. M19.

> 📖 **2** THACKERAY His comrades had been obliged to shirk on board at night, to escape from their wives. **3** H. MAYHEW Us sailor chaps . . shirks the Custom-house lubbers. **4a** G. DALY She could not shirk the unpleasant task. **c** J. G. HOLLAND The disposition to shirk seems . . constitutional with the human race.

■ **shirker** *noun* L18.

shirl /ʃəːl/ *verb trans.* Now *dial.* L17.

[App. an extended form of SHEAR *verb*: see -LE[3].]

Trim with shears; *spec.* cut the new fleece of (a lamb).

shirl /ʃəːl/ *adverb & adjective. obsolete* exc. *dial.* ME.

[Metath. alt. of SHRILL *adjective*.]

▶†**A** *adverb.* Shrilly. ME–L16.
▶ **B** *adjective.* Shrill. LME.

Shirley poppy /ˈʃəːlɪ ˈpɒpi/ *noun phr.* L19.

[*Shirley*, a district of Croydon, Surrey.]

A garden variety of poppy bearing single or double flowers, usu. red, pink, or white, developed by William Wilks (1843–1923), vicar of Shirley, from the corn poppy, *Papaver rhoeas*.

Shirley Temple /ʃəːlɪ ˈtɛmp(ə)l/ *noun.* M20.

[Amer. child film star (b. 1928).]

A non-alcoholic drink, usu. consisting of ginger ale and grenadine, served so as to resemble a cocktail.

Shirodkar /ʃɪˈrɒdkɑː/ *noun.* M20.

[V. N. *Shirodkar* (1900–71), Indian obstetrician.]

Used ***attrib.*** with ref to a method of treating cervical incompetence during pregnancy, involving the use of a distinctive suture round the entrance to the cervix.

shirr /ʃəː/ *noun.* Orig. *US.* M19.

[Origin unkn.]

1 Elastic webbing; elastic thread used in the composition of such webbing. M19.
2 Two or more gathered rows of esp. elastic threads forming a decorative trimming for a garment etc. L19.

shirr /ʃəː/ *verb trans.* Orig. *US.* L19.

[App. back-form. from next.]

1 Gather (material) by means of parallel threads. L19.
2 Bake (eggs without the shells) in individual dishes or in a single shallow dish. Chiefly as ***shirred ppl adjective***. L19.

shirred /ʃəːd/ *adjective.* Orig. *US.* M19.

[from SHIRR *noun* + -ED[2].]

1 Of material: having elastic threads woven into the texture. M19.
2 Gathered; decorated with shirr. M19.

> 📖 **2** *fig.*: P. V. WHITE A brisk day: the harbour waters slightly shirred, newspaper . . flapping in gutters.

shirt /ʃəːt/ *noun & verb.*

[Old English *sċyrte* corresp. to Middle & mod. Low German *schört(e)*, *schorte*, Middle Dutch *schorte* (Dutch *schort*, German *Schürze* apron), Old Norse *skyrta* shirt (whence SKIRT *noun*), from Germanic base also of SHORT *adjective, noun, & adverb*.]

▶**A** *noun.* **1** A garment for the upper body, made of cotton, linen, flannel, or other washable material, and formerly worn by both sexes next to the skin as an undergarment. Now *esp.* (***a***) a man's or boy's upper garment with sleeves, usu. having a collar and fastening down the front with buttons, worn under a jacket or sweater; (***b***) a similar garment worn by a woman or girl, a blouse; (***c***) (usu. with specifying word) an upper garment designed to be put on over the head, without fastenings, or full fastenings, freq. of stretchable material, and usu. worn as casual wear or for sports. OE. ▸**b** A long loose garment resembling a shirt; *spec.* = ***nightshirt*** s.v. NIGHT *noun.* M16. ▸†**c** *fig.* A type of something nearest to a person, a person's thoughts, heart, etc. M16–M17. ▸**d** A shirt of a specified colour worn as the emblem or uniform of a political party or movement; *transf.* a person wearing such a shirt. M19.
2 *transf.* An inner casing, covering, or lining. OE.

> 📖 **1** B. W. ALDISS He wore a striped light jacket . . a white shirt and a pair of blue trousers. ***Hawaiian shirt***, ***Oxford shirt***, ***ruffle shirt***, ***sweatshirt***, ***T-shirt***, etc. *attrib.*: ***shirt-collar***, ***shirt cuff***, ***shirtpocket***, etc. **d** ***blackshirt***, ***redshirt***, etc.

Phrases: **bloody shirt** (***a***) a bloodstained shirt exhibited as a symbol of murder or outrage; (***b***) *fig.* something likely to provoke outrage. BOILED ***shirt***. **get a person's shirt out** *colloq.* cause (a person) to lose his or her temper. ***habit-shirt***: see HABIT *noun*. ***hair shirt***: see HAIR *noun*. **in one's shirt** *arch.* in one's night attire; without one's outer garments. **keep one's shirt on** *colloq.* (orig. *US*) keep one's temper, remain calm. **lose one's shirt** *colloq.* lose all one's possessions. NESSUS ***shirt***. **not a shirt to one's back** no goods or possessions. †**not tell one's shirt** keep a matter strictly secret. **put one's shirt on** *colloq.* bet all one has on; be certain of. ***read one's shirt***: see READ *verb*. **shirt of hair** *arch.* = ***hair shirt*** s.v. HAIR *noun*. **shirt of mail** = ***coat of mail*** s.v. COAT *noun* 1. ***shirt of Nessus***. STUFFED ***shirt***. **the shirt off one's back** *colloq.* one's last remaining possessions.

Comb.: **shirt-blouse** a woman's or girl's blouse; **shirt-button** (***a***) a small button, esp. of mother-of-pearl, pierced with thread holes, used as a fastening for shirts; (***b***) in *pl.*, the greater stitchwort, *Stellaria holostea*; **shirt-cutter** a person who cuts out shirts as a trade; **shirt-dress** = ***shirtwaister*** below; **shirt-frill** *Hist.* a frill worn on the front and wrist-bands of a shirt; **shirt front** *noun & adjective* (***a***) *noun* the breast of a shirt, esp. of a stiffened evening shirt; a dicky; *transf.* a white patch on an animal's chest; (***b***) *adjective* (*colloq.*) (of a cricket pitch) very smooth and even; **shirt-jac** *W. Indies* = ***shirt-jacket*** below; **shirt-jacket** (chiefly *US*) a loose-fitting linen jacket; a garment resembling a shirt but worn as a jacket; **shirtlifter** *slang* (orig. *Austral.*), *derog.* a male homosexual; **shirtmaker** (*US* proprietary name for) a shirtwaister; **shirt-pin** an ornamental pin used to fasten a shirt at the throat; **shirt stud** a stud for fastening a shirt; **shirt-tail** *noun & adjective* (***a***) *noun* the lower curved part of a shirt below the waist; (***b***) *adjective* (*N. Amer.*) designating something small and insignificant or a remote relationship; **shirt-waist** (orig. *US*) (***a***) a shirt-blouse; †(***b***) a similar article of male clothing; **shirt-waist dress**, **shirtwaister** (orig. *US*) a dress with a bodice buttoning at the front like a shirt.

▶ **B** *verb trans.* Clothe (as) with a shirt. LME.

■ **shirtless** *adjective* E17.

shirting /ˈʃəːtɪŋ/ *noun.* E17.

[from SHIRT *noun* + -ING[1].]

Any of several types of material for making shirts; *spec.* a kind of hard-wearing cotton suitable for shirts and other garments.

Oxford shirting: see OXFORD *adjective*.

shirtsleeve /ˈʃəːtsliːv/ *noun & adjective.* Also **shirt-sleeve**. M16.

[from SHIRT *noun* + SLEEVE *noun*.]

▶**A** *noun.* The sleeve of a shirt. Usu. in *pl.* Freq. in ***in shirtsleeves***, ***in one's shirtsleeves***, wearing a shirt without a jacket etc., informally dressed. M16.
▶**B** ***attrib.*** or as ***adjective***. That is in shirtsleeves; *fig.* hard-working, workmanlike, informal. M19.

shirtsleeve diplomacy informal or unsophisticated management of political affairs. **shirtsleeve order** MILITARY the wearing of uniform without a jacket.

shirty /ˈʃəːti/ *adjective.* M19.

[from SHIRT *noun* + -Y[1].]

1 Annoyed; bad-tempered. (Cf. ***keep one's shirt on*** s.v. SHIRT *noun*.) *colloq.* M19.
2 Resembling or modelled on a shirt. M20.

> 📖 **1** A. N. WILSON His mother had taken it the wrong way and been rather shirty. **2** *Vogue* Jersey suit in . . red with a shirty top.

■ **shirtily** *adverb* L20. **shirtiness** *noun* L19.

Shirvan /ʃəːˈvɑːn/ *noun & adjective.* L19.

[An area of Azerbaijan in SW Asia.]

(Designating) a short-napped rug or carpet made in Shirvan and similar to those of Dagestan.

shish /ʃɪʃ/ *noun*[1], *interjection, & verb.* L19.

[Imit.]

▶ **A** *noun.* A prolonged or reiterated hissing sound. L19.
▶ **B** *interjection.* Expr. disapproval. Also, shush! E20.
▶ **C** *verb intrans.* Say 'shish'; make a hissing noise. E20.

shish /ʃɪʃ/ *noun*[2]. L20.

[from SHISH KEBAB.]

PHYSICAL CHEMISTRY. The central rod or ribbon of a shish kebab polymer structure (see SHISH KEBAB 2).

shisha /ˈʃiːʃə/ *noun.* M20.

[Urdu *šīša(h)*, Persian *šīša* glass, mirror.]

Used ***attrib.*** to designate mirror-work and items connected with it.

shisha embroidery, ***shisha stitch***, ***shisha work***, etc.

shisham /ˈʃɪʃəm/ *noun.* M19.

[Persian & Urdu *šīšam* ult. from Sanskrit *śiṃśapā*.]

The sissoo tree, *Dalbergia sissoo*.

shishi /ˈʃiʃi/ *noun.* L20.

[Japanese.]

A lion as a decorative motif on Japanese porcelain.

shish kebab /ʃɪʃ kɪˈbab/ *noun.* Also **sheesh kebab** /ʃiːʃ/. E20.

[Turkish *şiş kebab*, from *şiş* skewer + KEBAB roast meat. Cf. SHASHLIK.]

1 A dish consisting of pieces of marinated meat (usu. lamb) and vegetables grilled and served on skewers. E20.
2 PHYSICAL CHEMISTRY. A fibrous crystalline structure formed in some flowing or agitated polymer solutions, consisting of many platelike crystallites growing outwards from a long ribbon or rod. M20.

shit /ʃɪt/ *noun.* Now *coarse slang.* Also (now *joc.*, *euphem.*, & *dial.*) **shite** /ʃʌɪt/.

[Old English *scitte*, from Germanic base of next. Rel. to Middle Low German *schite* dung, Middle Dutch *schitte* excrement.]

1 ***the shits***, †***the shit***. Diarrhoea, orig. esp. in cattle, now of people. (Not recorded between LME and 20.) OE.
2 A contemptible, obnoxious, or worthless person. Cf. TURD 2. E16.
3 Faeces, dung. L16. ▸**b** An act of defecation. E20.
4 *transf.* & *fig.* **a** In neg. contexts: anything. Chiefly in ***not give a shit*** below. E20. ▸**b** Rubbish; nonsense; something worthless or not to be believed. Cf. BULL *noun*[4] 3. M20. ▸**c** Misfortune, unpleasantness. Chiefly in ***be in the shit*** below. M20. ▸**d** An intoxicating drug; *spec.* (***a***) cannabis; (***b***) heroin; (***c***) cocaine. M20. ▸**e** Personal belongings; stuff. L20.

> 📖 **2** S. CONRAN You were quite right to divorce Robert. He was my idea of a prize shit. **3** P. P. READ The dog shit on the pavement. **4a** R. RAYNER Auden, it seemed to me, didn't know shit. **b** E. SEGAL He treated you like shit.

Phrases: **beat the shit out of**, **kick the shit out of**, **knock the shit out of** thrash or beat (a person) severely. **be in the shit** be in trouble or a difficult or unpleasant situation. **full of shit** rubbishy; worthless; not to be believed or trusted. **get one's shit together** *US* organize oneself, manage one's affairs. ***kick the shit out of***, ***knock the shit out of***: see ***beat the shit out of*** above. ***neither shit nor Shinola***: see SHINOLA. **no shit!**: expr. astonishment, disbelief, derision, etc. **not give a shit** not care at all. ***not know shit from Shinola***: see SHINOLA. **scare the shit out of** give (a person) a severe shock, frighten. **shit-for-brains** (chiefly *N. Amer.*) a stupid person. **shit happens** bad things often happen unavoidably. ***the shits***, †***the shit***: see sense 1 above. ***tough shit***: see TOUGH *adjective*. **up shit creek** in an unpleasant situation, in an awkward predicament. **when the shit hits the fan** at a moment of crisis; when the disastrous consequences become known.

Comb.: **shitcan** *verb trans.* throw away, discard; reject as worthless; **shit-eating** *adjective* despicable; smug, self-satisfied; **shit-face** (a term of abuse for) an obnoxious person; **shit-faced** *adjective* extremely drunk; **shithead** (a term of abuse for) an obnoxious person; **shit-hole** (***a***) the anus; (***b***) *fig.* an extremely unpleasant place; **shit-hot** *adjective* very good, excellent; **shit-house** *noun & adjective* (***a***) *noun* a lavatory; a disgusting or contemptible thing; (***b***) *adjective* disgusting, contemptible; **shit-kicker** *US* an unsophisticated or oafish person, *esp.* one from a rural area; **shit-list** *US* a list of those who one dislikes or plans to harm etc.; a blacklist; **shitload** a large amount or number; **shit-scared** *adjective* extremely frightened; **shit-stirrer** a person who takes pleasure in causing trouble or discord; **shitwork** work considered esp. by feminists to be menial or routine, *esp.* housework.

shit /ʃɪt/ *verb.* Now *coarse slang.* Pa. t. & pple **shitted**, **shit**, **shat** /ʃat/; pa. pple also (now *rare* or *obsolete*) **shitten** /ˈʃɪt(ə)n/; pres. pple & verbal noun **shitting**. Also (now *dial.*) **shite** /ʃʌɪt/. ME.

[Corresp. to Middle Low German *schīten* (Dutch *schijten*) Old High German *scīzan* (Middle High German *schīzen*, German *scheissen*), Old Norse *skíta*, from Germanic: prob. already in Old English (cf. *bescītan* daub with excrement).]

1 *verb intrans.* Expel faeces from the body. ME.
2 *verb trans.* Cause (faeces) to be expelled from the body; expel as faeces. ME.

3 *verb trans.* Soil (one's clothes, oneself) with faeces; *refl.* be very frightened. L19. ▸**b** Tease; attempt to deceive or mislead. Cf. ***bullshit*** s.v. BULL *noun*[1]. M20.

> 📖 **2** *fig.*: T. L. SMITH The planes . . had shit a neat stream of . . orange bricks. **3** *Spare Rib* I was shitting myself before I came, looking for all kinds of excuses. **b** T. O'BRIEN Don't let him shit you . . . That whole thing last night was a fake.

Phrases: **shit a brick**, **shit bricks** (*a*) be extremely scared; (*b*) *interjection* expr. surprise or amazement. **shit on** humiliate, cause to feel inferior, reprimand (usu. in *pass.*). **shit or get off the pot** take action or make a decision one way or another, or else give another the opportunity to do so.

▪ **shitten** *adjective* (now *rare* or *obsolete*) = SHITTY ME. **shitter** *noun* (*a*) a person who or thing which shits; (*b*) a privy, a lavatory; a lavatory pan: L16.

shit /ʃɪt/ *interjection. coarse slang.* Also (chiefly *dial.*) **shite** /ʃʌɪt/. E20.
[from SHIT *noun*, *verb*.]
Expr. annoyance, astonishment, dismissiveness, etc., or interjected with little or no meaning.

> 📖 D. LODGE The sound . . of a bottle . . shattering . . also a cry of 'Shit!' P. CAVE 'Aw, shit It was nothing,' she muttered, writing the matter off casually.

shite *noun*, *verb*, *interjection* see SHIT *noun*, *verb*, *interjection*.

shite-hawk /ˈʃʌɪthɔːk/ *noun.* M20.
[from *shite* var. of SHIT *noun* + HAWK *noun*[1].]
1 In India, the Egyptian vulture, *Neophron percnopterus*. Orig. *Military slang*. M20.
2 *transf.* = SHIT *noun* 2. *coarse slang*. M20.

shitepoke /ˈʃʌɪtpəʊk/ *noun. US.* L18.
[from *shite* var. of SHIT *noun*, *verb* (from the birds' habit of defecating when disturbed).]
1 The small green heron of N. America, *Butorides virescens*. Also, the black-crowned night heron, *Nycticorax nycticorax*; the bittern, *Botaurus lentiginosus*. L18.
2 *transf.* = SHIT *noun* 2. *coarse slang*. E20.

shitless /ˈʃɪtlɪs/ *adjective. coarse slang.* M20.
[from SHIT *noun* + -LESS.]
Extremely frightened; senseless with fear or physical distress. Freq. in ***scared shitless***.

†**shittah tree** *noun phr. rare.* Only in E17.
[Hebrew *šiṭṭāh* from Egyptian *šnd.t*.]
In the Authorized Version of the Bible: a kind of acacia, perhaps *Acacia seyal*, from which shittim wood was obtained.

shittim /ˈʃɪtɪm/ *noun.* LME.
[Hebrew *šiṭṭīm*, pl. of *šiṭṭāh* SHITTAH TREE.]
A kind of acacia wood. Also, an acacia tree. Cf. prec.
Comb.: **shittim wood** (*a*) acacia wood; (*b*) *US* (the wood of) several freq. thorny shrubs, esp. *Bumelia lanuginosa* (family Sapotaceae).

†**shittle** *adjective.* See also SHUTTLE *adjective*. LME.
[Origin uncertain: prob. ult. from Germanic base of SHOOT *verb*.]
1 Inconstant, wavering; fickle. LME–M17.
2 Of a thing: unstable. Only in E17.

shitty /ˈʃɪti/ *adjective. coarse slang.* E20.
[from SHIT *noun* + -Y[1].]
1 Disgusting; contemptible; awful. E20.
2 Soiled or covered with faeces. E20.

> 📖 **1** I. MURDOCH Yes, our shitty parents let us down. *Guardian* You keep asking shitty questions that are irrelevant.

▪ **shittiness** *noun* L20.

shiur /ˈʃiːʊə/ *noun.* Pl. **-rim** /-rɪm/. M20.
[Hebrew *šī'ūr* measure, portion.]
JUDAISM. A Talmudic study-session, usually led by a rabbi.

shiv *verb* & *noun* var. of CHIV.

shiva /ˈʃɪvə/ *noun*[1]. Also **shivah**. L19.
[Hebrew *šiḇ'āh* seven.]
JUDAISM. A period of seven days' formal mourning for the dead, beginning immediately after the funeral. Freq. in ***sit shiva***, observe this period.

Shiva *noun*[2] var. of SIVA.

shivah *noun* var. of SHIVA *noun*[1].

shivaree /ʃɪvəˈriː/ *noun* & *verb.* Chiefly *US*. Pa. t. & pple **-reed**. M19.
[Alt.]
= CHARIVARI *noun* & *verb*.

shive /ʃʌɪv/ *noun*[1]. Chiefly *dial.* ME.
[Parallel form of SHEAVE *noun*[1]. Cf. next, SKIVE *verb*[1] & *noun*[2].]
1 A slice, esp. of bread. ME.
†**2** = SHEAVE *noun*[1] 1. ME–E16.
3 A piece of split wood, a piece of firewood. *obsolete* exc. *dial.* M17.
4 A thin flat cork for stopping a wide aperture; a circular wooden bung or plug hammered into a cask when the cask has been filled. M19.

shive /ʃɪv, ʃʌɪv/ *noun*[2]. See also SHEAVE *noun*[2]. LME.
[Corresp. to Western Flemish *schif*, Middle Dutch *scheve* (Dutch *scheef*), German *Schebe*, from Germanic base meaning 'to split', whence also SHIVER *noun*[1]: prob. already in Old English. Cf. prec., SHOVE *noun*[2].]
1 A particle of chaff; a splinter; a piece of thread or fluff on the surface of cloth etc.; in *pl.*, the refuse of hemp or flax. Long *obsolete* exc. *dial.* LME.
2 PAPER-MAKING. A dark particle in finished paper resulting from incomplete digestion of impurities in the raw material; such particles collectively. E20.
▪ **shivey** *adjective* (*rare*) full of shives L19.

shive *noun*[3] & *verb* var. of CHIVE *noun*[3] & *verb*.

shiveau /ʃɪˈvəʊ/ *noun. dial.* Now *rare* or *obsolete*. L18.
[Origin unkn.]
= SHIVOO.

shiver /ˈʃɪvə/ *noun*[1]. ME.
[Corresp. to Old High German *scivaro* splinter (German *Schiefer* slate, for *Schieferstein*) from Germanic base also of SHIVE *noun*[2]: prob. already in Old English.]
1 A fragment, a chip; a splinter, a sliver, esp. of shattered glass. Usu. in *pl.* ME. ▸**b** *spec.* A flake or splinter of stone, *esp.* one broken off during stone-dressing. Now *Scot.* & *dial.* E17.
†**2** A loose fibre or filament in undressed hemp. Cf. SHIVE *noun*[2] 1. LME–L18.
3 A slaty or schistose kind of stone. E18.
1 break in shivers, **break into shivers**, **burst in shivers**, **burst into shivers**, etc., shatter, break into fragments. **in shivers** broken, in small fragments.

shiver /ˈʃɪvə/ *noun*[2]. ME.
[Alt. of SHIVE *noun*[1], SHEAVE *noun*[1].]
1 = SHIVE *noun*[1] 1. *obsolete* exc. *dial.* ME.
2 A pulley. Cf. SHEAVE *noun*[1] 1. Now *rare*. L15.

shiver /ˈʃɪvə/ *noun*[3]. E18.
[from SHIVER *verb*[2].]
An act of shivering; *sing.* & in *pl.*, a momentary quivering or trembling, esp. from cold or fear.

> 📖 G. GREENE He sat . . close to the steam radiator . . but sometimes he couldn't help a shiver. *fig.*: *EuroBusiness* A shiver went through the boardrooms . . when the group unveiled plans to increase its debt. **the shivers** *colloq.* a fit of shivering.

▪ **shiversome** *adjective* causing shivers M20.

shiver /ˈʃɪvə/ *verb*[1]. ME.
[from SHIVER *noun*[1].]
1 *verb trans.* & *intrans.* Break into small fragments or splinters; shatter. ME.
2 *verb intrans.* Of stone: split along the natural line of cleavage. *rare*. E18.

> 📖 **1 shiver my timbers**: a mock oath attributed to sailors. **2** J. A. FROUDE His statue fell, and shivered on the stones.

▪ **shiverer** *noun*[1] (*rare*) a person who breaks something into small pieces M19.

shiver /ˈʃɪvə/ *verb*[2]. ME.
[Origin uncertain: perh. alt. of CHAVEL *verb* by substitution of -ER[5].]
1 *verb intrans.* Tremble, quiver, shudder, esp. with cold or fear. ME.
2 *verb trans.* Give a sensation of coldness to, cause to shiver. ME. ▸**b** Give out or emit with a trembling motion. Chiefly *poet.* L17.
3 NAUTICAL. **a** *verb intrans.* Of a sail: flutter or shake when a vessel is brought so close to the wind that the wind spills out of the sail. M18. ▸**b** *verb trans.* Cause (a sail) to flutter or shake in the wind, bring (a sail) edge-on to the wind. M18.

> 📖 **1** A. MACLEAN She was shivering violently, her face blue-tinged with the extreme cold. **2a** *fig.*: H. E. BATES The thump of presses shivered the crockery on the table.

▪ **shiverer** *noun*[2] (*a*) a person who trembles or shakes; (*b*) *dial.* a horse afflicted by shivering (SHIVERING *noun*[2] 2): L19. **shiveringly** *adverb* in a shivering manner E19.

shivering /ˈʃɪv(ə)rɪŋ/ *noun*[1]. LME.
[from SHIVER *verb*[1] + -ING[1].]
1 The action of SHIVER *verb*[1]; an instance of this. LME.
2 POTTERY. Peeling and splitting of the glaze. E20.

shivering /ˈʃɪv(ə)rɪŋ/ *noun*[2]. LME.
[from SHIVER *verb*[2] + -ING[1].]
1 The action of SHIVER *verb*[2]; an instance of this. LME.
2 VETERINARY MEDICINE. A condition of horses in which certain muscles, esp. those in the hindquarters, undergo rapid spasms. M19.

shivery /ˈʃɪv(ə)ri/ *adjective*[1]. LME.
[from SHIVER *noun*[1] + -Y[1].]
Apt to splinter or flake; splintery; brittle, flaky.

shivery /ˈʃɪv(ə)ri/ *adjective*[2]. M18.
[from SHIVER *verb*[2] + -Y[1].]
1 Characterized by a quivering motion. M18.
2 Inclined to shiver. M19.
3 Causing a shivering feeling, esp. from cold or fear. M19.

> 📖 **2** F. MARRYAT I'm all wet and shivery.

shivoo /ʃɪˈvuː/ *noun. Austral. colloq.* M19.
[Var. of SHIVEAU.]
A boisterous celebration, a party. Also, a disturbance, a row.

Shiv Sena /ʃɪv ˈseɪnə/ *noun.* M20.
[Sanskrit *śiva* SIVA + *sena* army.]
A Hindu nationalist organization centred in Maharashtra.

shkotsim *noun* pl. of SHEGETZ.

shlimazel, **shlimazle** *nouns* vars. of SCHLIMAZEL.

shlub /ʃlʌb/ *noun. US slang.* Also **sch-**. M20.
[Yiddish, perh. from Polish *żłób* blockhead.]
A worthless person, an oaf.

Shluh *noun* & *adjective* var. of SHILHA.

shlump *noun* var. of SCHLUMP.

SHM *abbreviation.*
PHYSICS. Simple harmonic motion.

shmatte /ˈʃmatə/ *noun. US colloq.* Also **sch-**. L20.
[Yiddish *schmatte*, from Polish *szmata* rag.]
A rag; a garment, *esp.* a ragged one.

shmear /ʃmɪə/ *noun. N. Amer. colloq.* Also **sch-**, **-eer**. M20.
[Yiddish *schmirn* flatter, grease, smear: cf. German *schmieren* SMEAR *verb*.]
Bribery, corruption, flattery.
the whole shmear everything (possible or available), every aspect of the situation.

shmegegge, **shmegeggy** *nouns* vars. of SCHMEGEGGE.

shmendrik, **schmendrick** *nouns* vars. of SCHMENDRIK.

shmoo /ʃmuː/ *noun. N. Amer.* M20.
[Invented word (see below).]
A fictitious animal invented by the US cartoonist Al Capp in 1948, represented as small, round, and ready to fulfil immediately any material need; a model or toy version of this.

SHO *abbreviation.*
Senior House Officer.

sho /ʃəʊ/ *noun*[1]. Pl. **-os**. L19.
[Japanese *shō*.]
A small Japanese hand-held mouth-organ of seventeen vertical bamboo pipes.

sho /ʃɔː/ *noun*[2]. Pl. same. E20.
[Tibetan.]
Hist. A former Tibetan monetary unit, equal to one-hundredth of a sang; a coin of this value.

sho /ʃɔː/ *adverb. Black English.* Also **sho'**. L19.
[Repr. a pronunc.]
= SURE *adverb*.
▪ **sholy** *adverb* = SURELY *adverb* E20.

shoad /ʃəʊd/ *noun. local.* Also **shode**. E17.
[Prob. ult. from SHED *verb*[1].]
MINING. Any of a number of loose fragments of tin, lead, or copper ore mixed with earth, lying on or near the surface and indicating the proximity of a lode. Usu. in *pl.*
▪ **shoading** *noun* the action or process of searching for shoads L18.

Shoah /ˈʃəʊə/ *noun.* M20.
[mod. Hebrew *šō'āh*, lit. 'catastrophe'.]
In Jewish use: *the* holocaust.

shoal /ʃəʊl/ *noun*[1]. ME.
[from SHOAL *adjective*.]
An area of shallow water; a submerged sandbank, *esp.* one that is visible at low water; *fig.* a hidden danger or difficulty (usu. in *pl.*).

> 📖 *Yachting World* Running aground is the result of . . a mistake in assessing the depth of water over a shoal. *London Review of Books* The real shoals ahead lie in policy and in SDP/Liberal relations.

Comb.: **shoal-mark** a buoy or other mark set to indicate a shoal.

shoal /ʃəʊl/ *noun*[2]. L16.
[Prob. from Middle Low German, Middle Dutch *schōle*: see SCHOOL *noun*[2]. Cf. next.]
1 A large number of fish, whales, etc. swimming together, = SCHOOL *noun*[2] 1. L16.
†**2** A flock of birds. L16–E19.
3 A large number of people or things; a multitude, a crowd. L16.

> 📖 **3** R. MACAULAY They would flee to Great Britain in shoals, from the fearful atrocities of their government.

†**shoal** *noun*[3]. M17–M18.
[Dutch *schol* = Middle Low German *scholle*, *schulle* clod, sod, Old High German *scolla* (fem.), *scollo* (masc.) (Middle High German, German *Scholle*) clod, mass of ice, perh. ult. from base also of SCHOOL *noun*[2], SHOAL *noun*[2].]
A mass of floating ice; an iceberg, a floe.

shoal /ʃəʊl/ *adjective & adverb.* Now *arch., Scot., & N. Amer. dial.*
[Old English *sc(e)ald*, from Germanic base also of SHALLOW *adjective*.]
▶ **A** *adjective.* Of water etc.: not deep; shallow. OE.
▶†**B** *adverb.* To or at a slight depth. ME–E19.
¶ In Old English only in place-names.
■ **shoalness** *noun* M16.

shoal /ʃəʊl/ *verb*[1] *trans.* Long *obsolete* exc. *dial. rare.* L16.
[Origin unkn.]
†**1** Separate. Freq. foll. by *out.* L16–M17.
2 Divide into classes or groups. E19.

shoal /ʃəʊl/ *verb*[2]. L16.
[from SHOAL *adjective*.]
1 *verb intrans.* Of water etc.: become shallower. Also foll. by *out.* L16. ▸**b** *verb trans.* Cause (water etc.) to become shallower. *rare.* M19.
2 *verb trans.* & (*rare*) *intrans.* NAUTICAL. Of a ship etc.: move into a shallower area of (water). E17.
3 *verb intrans.* Slant, slope; taper. Also foll. by *away. rare.* E17.
†**4** *verb trans.* Drive (a plough) less deeply in the soil. Only in L17.
5 *verb intrans.* Drive a hunted otter into shallow water. Now *rare* or *obsolete.* L19.
■ **shoaling** *noun* (*a*) a place where water becomes shallower; (*b*) the process of becoming shallower; an instance of this; (*c*) *Scot. rare* the action of spearing fish, esp. salmon, in shallow water: L16.

shoal /ʃəʊl/ *verb*[3] *intrans.* E17.
[from SHOAL *noun*[2].]
1 Of fish, whales, etc.: collect or swim together in a shoal or shoals. E17.
2 Throng together, form a crowd or multitude. Also foll. by *together, in, up.* E17.

shoaly /ˈʃəʊli/ *adjective.* E17.
[from SHOAL *noun*[1] + -Y[1].]
Full of shoals or shallows.
■ **shoaliness** *noun* (*rare*) L17.

shoat /ʃəʊt/ *noun.* Now *Scot., dial., & US.* LME.
[Origin uncertain: cf. Western Flemish *schote(ling)* a pig under one year old.]
1 A young pig, *esp.* one newly weaned. LME.
2 *transf.* An idle worthless person. E19.

shoch /ʃɒk, -x/ *noun & verb. Anglo-Irish.* M19.
[Irish *seach, sloch* a turn at something, a go, *seach tobac* a draw at a pipe.]
▶ **A** *noun.* A draw at a tobacco-pipe, a smoke. M19.
▶ **B** *verb intrans.* Draw at a tobacco-pipe, smoke. L19.

shochet /ˈʃɒkɛt, -x-/ *noun.* Pl. **-im** /-ɪm/. L19.
[Hebrew *šōḥēṭ* pres. pple of *šāḥaṭ* to slaughter.]
A person officially certified as competent to kill cattle and poultry in the manner prescribed by Jewish law.

shochu /ˈʃəʊtʃuː/ *noun.* M20.
[Japanese *shōchū*.]
A rough Japanese spirit distilled from various ingredients, including sake dregs.

shock /ʃɒk/ *noun*[1]. ME.
[Anglo-Latin *socca, scoka*, either repr. unrecorded Old English word or from Middle & mod. Low German, Middle & mod. Dutch *schok*, Old Saxon *scok* shock of corn, group of 60 units = Middle High German *schoc* heap, three score (German *Schock* three score), ult. origin unkn. Cf. SHOCK *noun*[3], *noun*[4].]
1 A group of usu. twelve sheaves placed upright and supporting each other to allow the drying and ripening of the grain. Cf. STOOK *noun*[1] 1. ME.
2 A crowd of people; a heap, bunch, or bundle of things. Long *rare.* LME.

shock /ʃɒk/ *noun*[2]. M16.
[French *choc*, from *choquer* SHOCK *verb*[2].]
1 An encounter between two charging hostile forces, jousters, etc. *arch.* M16.
2 a A sudden and violent blow, impact, or collision; a disturbance of equilibrium or oscillation resulting from this; a sudden large application of energy (cf. ***thermal shock*** s.v. THERMAL *adjective*). Also, a shock wave. E17. ▸**b** *spec.* A sudden violent shake or tremor of the earth's surface as part of an earthquake. L17.
3 A sudden disturbance in stability, esp. as causing fluctuations in or permanent damage to an organization, monetary system, etc. M17.
4 a A sudden and disturbing effect on the mind or feelings, esp. as causing depression or distress; a start of surprise, excitement, etc. Also, an occurrence, discovery, etc., occasioning such an effect. E18. ▸**b** A feeling of being shocked (SHOCK *verb*[2] 4); a pained sense of something offensive to decency or morality. L19.
5 = ***electric shock*** s.v. ELECTRIC *adjective*. M18.
6 a A paralytic seizure or stroke. Chiefly *Scot. & US dial.* L18. ▸**b** A sudden debilitating effect produced by severe injury, blood loss, violent emotion, etc.; the state of nervous exhaustion resulting from emotional trauma; *spec.* the condition associated with circulatory collapse and sudden drop in blood pressure, characterized esp. by cold sweaty pallid skin and a weak rapid pulse. E19. ▸**c** = ***shell-shock*** s.v. SHELL *noun & adjective*. E20.
7 *ellipt.* = ***shock absorber*** below. Chiefly *N. Amer.* M20.

🕮 **1** SOUTHEY Anon the hosts met in the shock of battle. **2a** TENNYSON With twelve great shocks of sound, the shameless noon Was clash'd. ***osmotic shock.*** **b** *World Archaeology* Major earthquakes . . are not common, but minor shocks are fairly frequent. **3** A. RADCLIFFE It gave a severe shock to his constitution. H. MARTINEAU The shock given to commercial credit. ***culture shock***: see CULTURE *noun*. ***future shock***: see FUTURE *adjective & noun*. **4** F. BURNEY When Cecilia was a little recovered from the shock of the first interview. J. FIELD I do not remember what I saw but only the shock of delight in just looking. **b** G. O. TREVELYAN The concession of Catholic Emancipation gave a moral shock to the Tory party. **6b** ***anaphylactic shock, insulin shock, spinal shock***, etc. **delayed shock**: occurring some time after the event causing it. ***toxic shock syndrome***: see TOXIC *adjective*.

Comb.: **shock-absorbent** *adjective* functioning as a shock absorber; **shock absorber** a device on a motor vehicle etc. serving to absorb mechanical shock and to damp vibration; *fig.* a person who or thing which reduces or mitigates the worst effects of a new and unpleasant occurrence or experience; **shock-absorbing** *adjective* = *shock-absorbent* above; **shock-brigade** a body of esp. voluntary workers in the former USSR engaged in a particularly arduous task; **shock cone** AERONAUTICS a nose cone or other conical fairing serving to streamline an aircraft for supersonic flight; **shock cord** heavy elasticated cord designed to absorb or resist mechanical shock; a length of this; **shock excitation** the excitation of natural oscillations in a system (esp. electronic) by a sudden external input of energy; **shock-excited** *adjective* (of a natural oscillation) that has been subjected to shock excitation; **shock-horror** *adjective* (*colloq.*) causing great public outrage, esp. as represented by sensationalized or indignant press coverage; **shock jock** *colloq.* a presenter on a talk-radio show who expresses opinions in a deliberately offensive or provocative way; **shock-mount** *noun & verb* (*a*) *noun* a mounting designed to absorb or resist mechanical shock; (*b*) *verb trans.* attach by means of a shock-mount; **shock-mounting** (*a*) the action or an act of attaching something by means of a shock-mount; (*b*) a shock-mount; **shockproof** *adjective* resistant to the effects of (esp. physical) shock; **shockproofing** the process of making something shockproof; **shock stall** AERONAUTICS loss of lift produced by air resistance in an aircraft approaching the speed of sound; **shock strut** a strut containing a shock absorber in the landing gear of an aircraft; **shock tactics** (*a*) MILITARY tactics in which a massed cavalry charge (chiefly *Hist.*) or the advance of armoured units forms a principal part; (*b*) sudden and violent or extreme action, esp. in pursuit of a particular aim; **shock test** a test in which an object is subjected to mechanical shock; **shock-testing** the action of subjecting an object to a shock test; **shock therapy, shock treatment** MEDICINE & PSYCHIATRY treatment by means of convulsions artificially induced by anaphylactic or electric shock or by drugs; *spec.* electro-convulsive therapy; **shock troops** [translating German *Stosstruppen*] forces of selected and specially armed soldiers trained for assault; **shock tube** an apparatus for producing shock waves by making a gas at high pressure expand suddenly into a low-pressure tube or cavity; **shock wave** a transient disturbance that travels through a fluid as a narrow region in which there is a large abrupt change in pressure etc., *esp.* one created by an object moving faster than sound or by an explosion; any pressure wave of large amplitude; **shock-worker** a member of a shock-brigade.

shock /ʃɒk/ *noun*[3]. *obsolete* exc. *Hist.* L16.
[German *Schock*, Dutch *schok*: prob. a specialized use of *Schock, schok* SHOCK *noun*[1].]
A lot of sixty pieces, esp. of articles of merchandise originally imported from abroad.

shock /ʃɒk/ *noun*[4] *& adjective.* M17.
[Origin uncertain: perh. rel. to SHOUGH or fig. use of SHOCK *noun*[1].]
▶ **A** *noun.* †**1** A shock dog. M17–E19.
2 A shaggy and unkempt mass of hair. E19.
▶ **B** *adjective.* **1** Designating (an animal of) a breed of dog having long shaggy hair, *spec.* a poodle. *obsolete* exc. *Hist.* M17.
2 *gen.* Having unkempt or shaggy hair; (of hair) unkempt, shaggy. L17.
Comb. & special collocations: **shock-head** a shaggy and unkempt head of hair; **shock-headed** *adjective* having a shock-head; ***shock-headed Peter*** [translation: see STRUWWELPETER], a person with long thick unkempt hair.

shock /ʃɒk/ *verb*[1]. LME.
[from SHOCK *noun*[1]. Cf. Anglo-Latin *soccare*.]
1 *verb trans.* Arrange (sheaves) in a shock. Also foll. by *up.* LME.
†**2** *verb refl. & intrans.* Crowd together. LME–E17.

shock /ʃɒk/ *verb*[2]. M16.
[French *choquer* = Spanish *chocar*, of unkn. origin.]
1 *verb trans.* †**a** Throw (troops) into confusion by a charge; damage or weaken physically by impact or collision; destroy the stability of. M16–L18. ▸**b** Subject to or transform by mechanical shock. M20.
2 *verb intrans.* Esp. of hostile forces: come into violent contact, collide, clash. Also foll. by *together. arch.* L16.
†**3** *verb trans.* Assail with a sudden and violent attack, charge (an enemy force etc.). E17–M18.
4 a *verb trans.* Orig., wound the feelings of, offend, displease. Later, affect with a painful feeling of intense aversion or disapproval; scandalize, horrify; outrage, disgust; startle. M17. ▸**b** *verb intrans.* Cause shock. E19. ▸**c** *verb intrans.* Experience shock. M20.
5 *verb trans.* Impart a physical shock to (a person or a part of the body); cause (a person) to suffer a physical shock; give (a person or animal) an electric shock. Chiefly as ***shocked*** *ppl adjective.* M18.

🕮 **1** DEFOE That Sea that shock'd the Vessel, was a Forerunner of a greater. **2** GOLDSMITH Two mountains shocked against each other, approaching and retiring with the most dreadful noise. TENNYSON If New and Old, disastrous feud, Must ever shock, like armed foes. **4a** W. CONGREVE Thy stubborn temper shocks me. G. DURRELL Jacob . . was shock beyond belief at the disgusting inquisitiveness of the villagers. J. ELLIOTT Then something she was saying shocked him into wavering attention. M. GARDINER Austin shocked his parishioners by sunbathing nude. **b** R. HEILBRONER A problem so well known it has almost lost its power to shock. **c** N. CLAD She liked to say things to shock Clarence, partly because he shocked so easily.

■ **shockaˈbility** *noun* ability to be shocked; the quality of being shockable: E20. **shockable** *adjective* able to be shocked, easily shocked L19. **shockableness** *noun* (*rare*) M20. **shockedly** /ˈʃɒkɪdli, ˈʃɒkt-/ *adverb* (*rare*) E20. **shockedness** /ˈʃɒkɪdnɪs, ˈʃɒkt-/ *noun* (*rare*) L19.

shocker /ˈʃɒkə/ *noun*[1]. L18.
[from SHOCK *verb*[1] + -ER[1].]
A person who shocks sheaves.

shocker /ˈʃɒkə/ *noun*[2]. E19.
[from SHOCK *verb*[2] + -ER[1].]
1 A person who or thing which shocks; *spec.* (*a*) *arch.* an unpleasantly sensational novel etc., a thriller; (*b*) a strikingly bad or disagreeable person or thing. E19.
2 A shock absorber. *colloq.* M20.

🕮 **1** *Horse & Hound* Lucky Sovereign ran a shocker, either unable or unwilling to give his true running. *Chicago* The jury found the guy guilty on only one count. A real shocker.

shocking /ˈʃɒkɪŋ/ *adjective & adverb.* E18.
[from SHOCK *verb*[2] + -ING[2].]
▶ **A** *adjective.* **1** That shocks; *esp.* causing indignation or disgust. E18.
2 Very bad, execrable. M18.

🕮 **1** R. L. STEVENSON It was shocking, in that house of mourning, to hear him singing . . his ugly old sea-song. A. E. STEVENSON That the government of a free democracy should seek deliberately to manipulate the news . . is indeed shocking. **shocking pink** *noun & adjective* (of) a vivid garish shade of pink. **2** TOLKIEN He had . . a shocking cold. For three days he sneezed and coughed. A. MCCOWEN In shocking Urdu, I would play the burra sahib.

▶ **B** *adverb.* Shockingly. *colloq.* M19.
■ **shockingly** *adverb* in a shocking manner, to a shocking degree; *colloq.* very, extremely: M18. **shockingness** *noun* M18.

Shockley /ˈʃɒkli/ *noun.* M20.
[William Bradford *Shockley* (1910–89), US physicist.]
Used *attrib.* to designate concepts and devices invented by Shockley.
Shockley diode a semiconductor diode consisting of four regions of alternate conductivity types (*n* and *p*), with the anode and the cathode connected to the end ones. **Shockley partial (dislocation)** a partial dislocation in which the lattice displacement lies in the fault plane, so that the dislocation is capable of gliding.

shod /ʃɒd/ *ppl adjective.* ME.
[pa. pple of SHOE *verb*.]
1 Wearing shoes, esp. of a specified kind. Chiefly as 2nd elem. of comb. ME.
2 a Of a weapon, tool, etc.: provided with a shoe of metal; tipped, edged, or sheathed with metal. ME. ▸**b** Orig., (of a cartwheel) provided with tyres; (of a cart) having wheels provided with tyres. Later, (of a motor vehicle) having tyres of a specified kind (chiefly as 2nd elem. of comb., as ***well shod***). L15.
1 ***neatly shod, dry-shod***, etc.
¶ Earlier in UNSHOD.

shod *verb pa. t. & pple* of SHOE *verb.*

shoddy /ˈʃɒdi/ *noun & adjective.* M19.
[Origin unkn.]
▶ **A** *noun.* **1** Shredded fibre of old woollen cloth; inferior cloth made partly from this. M19.
2 *transf. & fig.* Worthless material having the appearance of superior quality; anything of poorer quality than is asserted or appears. M19.
3 Any of the smaller stones at a quarry (usu. in *pl.*). Also, inferior coal. *dial. rare.* L19.
4 Reclaimed rubber. Now *rare.* L19.
Comb.: **shoddy dropper** *Austral. & NZ slang* a pedlar of cheap or falsely described clothing; a hawker; **shoddy-hole** a place in which rubbish is deposited, a dust-hole.
▶ **B** *adjective.* **1** Of a person: claiming an unjustified superiority, esp. in social station or influence. Now *rare.* M19.
2 Of a thing: worthless, having the appearance of superior quality; of poorer quality than is asserted or appears; trashy, shabby; poorly made. Also, pertaining to or dealing in goods of this kind. M19.

📖 **2** R. MACAULAY I, . . think bad, shallow shoddy work . . damnable. R. OWEN Russians seeking routine health care face indifferent medical staff and shoddy facilities.

■ **shoddily** *adverb* L19. **shoddiness** *noun* L19. **shoddyism** *noun* (*rare*) shoddy principles and practices; pretentious and inferior quality: M19. **shoddyite** *noun* (*rare*) a person characterized by shoddyism M19.

shode *noun* var. of SHOAD.

shoder /ˈʃəʊdə/ *noun*. M18.
[French *chaud(e)ret*.]
A packet of gold-beater's skin in which separated leaves of gold are placed for beating out before a final beating in the mould (MOULD *noun*[3] 6).

shoe /ʃuː/ *noun*. Pl. **shoes** /ʃuːz/, (now *dial., arch., & poet.*) **shoon** /ʃuːn/.
[Old English *scō(h)* = Old Frisian, Old Saxon *scōh* (Dutch *schoen*), Old High German *scuoh* (German *Schuh*), Old Norse *skór*, Gothic *skōhs*, from Germanic. No cognates outside Germanic are known.]
▶ **I 1** An outer foot-covering of leather, plastic, fabric, etc., having a fairly stiff sole; *spec.* such a foot-covering not extending above the ankle (as opp. to a boot). OE.
2 A band of iron etc. shaped to the hard part of the hoof of an animal, esp. a horse, and secured by nails to the underside to prevent wear or injury; = HORSESHOE 1. ME.
1 *court shoe*, *Cromwell shoe*, *elevator shoe*, *gaiter shoe*, *Oxford shoe*, *piked shoe*, etc.
▶ **II** A thing resembling a shoe in shape, position, or function;
†**3** The iron cutting edge fitted to a wooden spade or shovel. LME
4 A metal rim, ferrule, or casing, esp. of a sledge runner. L15.
5 *Hist.* An ingot of silver etc. formerly used as currency in the Far East and China. E18.
6 A piece of iron etc. serving to brake the wheel of a vehicle, a drag; *esp.* = ***brake shoe*** s.v. BRAKE *noun*[7]. M19.
7 A socket for a bolt, pin, etc.; a block, plate, cap, etc., serving as a socket or support for or to prevent slippage or sinking of the foot of a pole, ladder, etc. M19.
8 A block attached to an electric vehicle, esp. a tramcar, which slides along a conductor-wire or rail and collects the current for propulsion. L19
9 A box from which cards are dealt at baccarat etc., esp. as used in casinos. E20
10 A mounting on a camera for the temporary attachment of an accessory. M20.
Phrases: **another pair of shoes** quite a different matter or state of things. **be in another person's shoes** be in another person's situation, difficulty, etc. (usu. in neg. contexts). ***clouted shoe***: see CLOUT *verb* 2. ***CO-RESPONDENT's shoes***. **dead men's shoes** property, a position, etc., coveted by a prospective successor but available only on a person's death. ***die in one's shoes***, ***die with one's shoes on***: see DIE *verb*[1]. ***give a person his or her running shoes***: see RUNNING *noun*. ***goody two-shoes***: see TWO. †**high shoes** boots extending only to the ankle. **hot shoe** a socket on a camera incorporating electrical contacts for a flash etc. ***KURDAITCHA shoe***. ***lick a person's shoes***: see LICK *verb*. ***lunette-shoe***: see LUNETTE 1. ***patten-shoe***: see PATTEN *noun*. ***shake in one's shoes***: see SHAKE *verb*. **shoes and stockings** *dial.* bird's-foot trefoil, *Lotus corniculatus*. **step into the shoes of** occupy the position vacated by (a person). **the shoe fits** *N. Amer.* = ***the cap fits*** s.v. CAP *noun*[1]. **the shoe is on the other foot** = ***the boot is on the other foot*** s.v. BOOT *noun*[2]. **where the shoe pinches** where one's difficulty or trouble is.
Comb.: **shoebill (stork)**, **shoe-billed stork** = ***whale-headed stork*** s.v. WHALE *noun*; **shoeblack** a person who cleans the shoes of passers-by for payment; ***shoe-black plant***, the Chinese hibiscus (cf. ***shoe-flower*** below); **shoebox** (*a*) a box for packing a pair of shoes; (*b*) *transf.* a very small or cramped building or room; **shoe-brush** a brush for cleaning and polishing shoes; **shoe buckle** a buckle worn as a fastening or an ornament on a shoe; **shoe-deep** *adjective* (*US*) (of snow etc.) deep enough to cover a person's shoes; **shoe-flower** *Anglo-Indian* the flower of the Chinese hibiscus, *Hibiscus rosa-sinensis*, used to shine shoes; **shoehorn** *noun & verb* (*a*) *noun* a curved instrument of horn, metal, etc., for easing the heel into a shoe; (*b*) *verb trans.* force *on* or *into* by means of an instrument or tool; *fig.* manoeuvre or compress *into*, *in*, or *on to* an inadequate space; **shoelace** a cord or leather strip for lacing shoes; **shoe-last** (*a*) a wooden, metal, etc., model of the foot, on which a shoemaker shapes shoes; (*b*) ARCHAEOLOGY a form of axe or wedge of polished stone, flat on one side and curved on the other, characteristic of early neolithic communities in central Europe; **shoe-leather** leather for the manufacture of shoes; the leather of which one's shoes are made, esp. when worn through by walking; **shoe-piece** (*a*) NAUTICAL a plank; the base of a spar; (*b*) a piece of wood at the back of a chair, supporting the splat; **shoeshine** (orig. & chiefly *N. Amer.*) a polish given to shoes, esp. by a shoeshiner; **shoeshiner** a person who polishes shoes for money; **shoesmith** *arch.* a shoeing-smith; **shoe-tie** *arch.* a shoelace; **shoe-tree** a shaped block for keeping a shoe in shape when not worn; **shoe-valve** a valve at the foot of a pump-stock, or at the bottom of a reservoir.
■ **shoeless** *adjective* not having or wearing shoes E17. **shoelessness** *noun* (*rare*) M19.

shoe /ʃuː/ *adjective*. *US slang*. M20.
[Origin unkn.]
Of dress, behaviour, etc.: of, pertaining to, or characteristic of an exclusive educational establishment.

shoe /ʃuː/ *verb trans*. Pa. t. & pple **shod** /ʃɒd/, (*rare*) **shoed** /ʃuːd/; pres. pple **shoeing**.
[Old English *scōg(e)an* = Middle Low German *schoi(g)en* (Dutch *schoeien*), Old High German *scuohōn* (German *schuhen*), Old Norse *skúa*, from Germanic.]
1 Put shoes on (a person, oneself, the feet); protect (the feet) with shoes; provide (a person, oneself) with footwear of a specified kind. Usu. in *pass*. OE.
2 a Provide (a horse or other animal) with a shoe or shoes. ME. ▸**b** Provide (a motor vehicle) with tyres of a specified type or quality. E20.
3 Protect (the point, edge or face of an object, esp. a wooden one) with a metal plate, rim, ferrule, or casing. ME.
4 *transf.* Cover or protect as with a shoe or shoes. ME.
■ **shoer** *noun* (*a*) (long *rare* or *obsolete*) a shoemaker; (*b*) a person who shoes esp. a horse etc.: OE. **shoey** /ˈʃuːi/ *noun* (*Military slang*) a shoeing-smith in a cavalry regiment E20.

shoed /ʃuːd/ *adjective*. E17.
[from SHOE *noun*, *verb*: see -ED[2], -ED[1].]
Provided or protected with a shoe or shoes; shod.

shoeing /ˈʃuːɪŋ/ *noun*. ME.
[from SHOE *verb* + -ING[1].]
1 a Shoes collectively. ME. ▸**b** The protective casing or covering with which a thing is shod. E19.
2 The action of SHOE *verb*; *esp.* the action of providing a horse or other animal with a shoe or shoes. LME.
Comb.: **shoeing-horn** *arch.* a shoehorn; **shoeing-smith** a smith who shoes horses.

shoemaker /ˈʃuːmeɪkə/ *noun*. LME.
[from SHOE *noun* + MAKER *noun*.]
1 A person whose occupation is the making of boots and shoes. LME.
2 Any of various fishes, as the rainbow runner, *Elagatis pinnulata*. M19.
1 ***shoemaker's end***: see END *noun* 7a.
■ **shoemaking** *noun* the making of boots and shoes as an occupation E17.

shoepack /ˈʃuːpak/ *noun*. *N. Amer.* M18.
[Delaware (Unami) *seppock*, *sippack* shoes from *čipahko* moccasins, with later assim. to SHOE *noun*, PACK *noun*.]
Orig. (now *local*), a moccasin with an extra sole. Later, a commercially manufactured oiled leather boot, esp. with a rubber sole. Cf. PAC *noun*[1].

shoestring /ˈʃuːstrɪŋ/ *noun & adjective*. E17.
[from SHOE *noun* + STRING *noun*.]
▶ **A** *noun*. **1** A shoelace. *arch. rare*. E17.
2 A small or inadequate amount of money; a very small amount of capital; a small margin. E20.
3 = ***shoestring potato*** below. M20.

📖 **1** SMOLLETT She is not worthy to tie her majesty's shoestrings. **2** *Atlantic Monthly* Every business man who has made a big success . . started on a shoestring.

▶ **B** *attrib.* or as *adjective*. Barely adequate, precarious. E17.

📖 R. C. A. WHITE The Council operates on a shoestring budget . . and is supported by a staff of only 13 people.

Comb. & special collocations: **shoestring catch** BASEBALL a running catch made close to the ground; **shoestring fungus** = ***honey-fungus*** s.v. HONEY *noun*; **shoestring potato** *N. Amer.* a julienne potato; **shoestring root rot**, **shoestring rot** the tree disease caused by honey-fungus; **shoestring tie** a very narrow necktie.

shofar /ˈʃəʊfə/ *noun*. Pl. **-froth** /-frəʊt/. M19.
[Hebrew *šōpār*, pl. *šōpārōt*.]
A ram's-horn trumpet used in Jewish religious services and in biblical times as a war-trumpet.

shoful /ˈʃəʊfʊl, -f(ə)l/ *noun*. *arch. slang*. E19.
[Yiddish *schofel* worthless stuff, rubbish, from use as noun of German *schofel* base, mean, worthless from Hebrew *šāpēl*. In sense 2 perh. a different word.]
1 Counterfeit money. E19.
2 A hansom cab. M19.

shog /ʃɒg/ *noun*. Orig. & chiefly *Scot.* L16.
[from SHOG *verb*.]
†**1** A shaking condition. *rare*. L16–L17.
2 A shake, a jerk. E17.
3 A bumpy jerking gait, a jog. Cf. SHOG *verb* 3. L19.
■ **shoggy** *adjective* shaky, insecure M19.

shog /ʃɒg/ *verb*. Now chiefly *Scot. arch. & dial.* Infl. **-gg-**. LME.
[Prob. rel. to Middle Low German, Middle High German *schocken* swing, sway, expr. a swaying jolting movement. Cf. JOG *verb*, SHAG *verb*[1].]
1 *verb trans.* **a** Shake or roll (a heavy body) from side to side; rock (a cradle); shake, agitate (liquid or its containing vessel); jolt, jar. Also (*rare*), shake *off* (a load). LME. ▸†**b** Shake (a person) violently; jog esp. so as to attract attention. LME–M17. ▸†**c** *fig.* Upset, discompose; irritate, annoy. M17–E18.
2 *verb intrans.* Jerk, jolt; shake to and fro, rock. Formerly also, be shaky or insecurely fixed, get shaken *out*. LME.
3 *verb intrans.* **a** Walk, ride, or move, esp. bumpily or jerkily; jog along. Freq. foll. by *on*. LME. ▸**b** Foll. by *off*: go away, begone. L16.

shoggle /ˈʃɒg(ə)l/ *verb*. Now chiefly *Scot. & dial.* Also **shoogle**, **shuggle** /ˈʃʊg(ə)l/. L16.
[Frequentative of SHOG *verb*: see -LE[3].]
1 *verb trans.* Shake, cause to move; shake *off*. L16.
2 *verb intrans.* Shake; swing about, dangle; shake or settle *down*. E18.
3 *verb intrans.* Walk unsteadily. E19.

shogi /ˈʃəʊgi/ *noun*. M19.
[Japanese *shōgi*.]
A Japanese board game resembling chess.

shogun /ˈʃəʊgʊn/ *noun*. E17.
[Japanese *shōgun*, from Chinese *jiāng jūn* general.]
Hist. Any of a succession of hereditary commanders-in-chief of the Japanese army, before 1868 the virtual rulers of Japan. Cf. TYCOON.
■ **shogunal** *adjective* of or pertaining to a shogun or the shogunate L19. **shogunate** *noun* the office, position, or dignity of a shogun; the period of a shogun's rule: L19.

†**Shoho** *noun & adjective* see SAHO.

shoji /ˈʃəʊdʒi/ *noun*. Pl. same. L19.
[Japanese *shōji*.]
In Japan, a sliding outer or inner door made of a latticed screen covered usu. with white paper. Also ***shoji screen***.

shola *noun & adjective* var. of SOLA *noun*[1] & *adjective*[1].

sholt /ʃəʊlt/ *noun*. Long *obsolete* exc. *dial. rare*. L16.
[Origin unkn.]
A dog; *spec.* a cur.

shomer /ˈʃəʊmə/ *noun*. Pl. **-rim** /-rɪm/. E20.
[Hebrew *šōmēr* watchman.]
1 A watchman, a guard, now esp. in Israel. E20.
2 An inspector who verifies that food is prepared in accordance with Jewish religious laws. E20.

Shona /ˈʃəʊnə/ *noun & adjective*. M20.
[Bantu. Cf. MASHONA.]
▶ **A** *noun*. Pl. **-s**, same. A member of any of several related Bantu-speaking peoples inhabiting Mashonaland in Zimbabwe and parts of Zambia and Mozambique; the group of closely related languages of these peoples. M20.
▶ **B** *attrib.* or as *adjective*. Of or pertaining to the Shona or their languages. M20.

shonda /ˈʃɒndə/ *noun*. *colloq.* (chiefly *US*). M20.
[Yiddish *shande* from Middle High German *schande*.]
A disgrace.

shone *verb pa. t. & pple*: see SHINE *verb*.

shoneen /ˈʃəʊniːn/ *noun & adjective*. *Anglo-Irish* (*derog.*). M19.
[Irish *seóinín*, from *Seón* JOHN + *-ín* -EEN[2].]
▶ **A** *noun*. A person favouring English rather than Irish standards and attitudes in cultural life, sport, etc. M19.
▶ **B** *attrib.* or as *adjective*. Of, pertaining to, or characteristic of such a person. E20
■ **shoneenism** *noun* the principles or practices of a shoneen E20.

shonicker /ˈʃɒnɪkə/ *noun*. *US slang*. *offensive*. E20.
[Origin unkn. Cf. SHONK *noun*[1].]
A Jew.

shonk /ʃɒŋk/ *noun*[1]. *slang*. *offensive*. M20.
[Alt. of SHONICKER.]
A Jew.

shonk /ʃɒŋk/ *noun*[2]. *Austral. slang*. L20.
[Back-form.]
= SHONKY *noun*.

shonkinite /ˈʃɒŋkɪnʌɪt/ *noun*. L19.
[from *Shonkin* N. Amer. Indian name for the Highwood Mountains, Montana + -ITE[1].]
GEOLOGY. A dark granular form of syenite consisting largely of augite and orthoclase.
■ **shonki'nitic** *adjective* having the character or consisting of shonkinite E20.

shonky /ˈʃɒŋki/ *adjective & noun*. *Austral. slang*. L20.
[Perh. from SHONK *noun*[1] + -Y[1].]
▶ **A** *adjective*. Unreliable, dishonest. L20.
▶ **B** *noun*. A person engaged in irregular or illegal business activities. L20.

shoo /ʃuː/ *interjection & verb*. LME.
[Natural exclam. Cf. HOOSH *interjection & verb*.]
▶ **A** *interjection*. Frightening or driving away birds, animals, etc. LME.
▶ **B** *verb*. **1** *verb trans.* **a** Frighten or drive away (birds, animals, etc.) by an utterance of 'shoo!' Also foll. by *away*, *from*, *off*, *out* (*of*). E17. ▸**b** Drive or urge (a person, animal, etc.) in a desired direction. E20.
2 *verb intrans.* Utter 'shoo!' in order to frighten or drive away birds, animals, etc. Also foll. by *at*. M18.
3 *verb intrans.* Be frightened or driven away (as) by an utterance of 'shoo!' M19.

4 *verb trans.* Foll. by *in*: allow (a racehorse) to win easily. *US slang.* E20.
Comb.: **shoo-in** *N. Amer.* (*a*) (the winner of) a horse-race for which the result has been fraudulently arranged; (*b*) a certain or easy winner; a certainty, something easy or sure to succeed.

shood /ʃuːd/ *noun.* Long *dial.* Also **shude**. E17.
[Prob. cogn. with Middle Low German *schode*, Middle High German *schōte* (German *Schote*) husk, pod of peas or beans.]
Orig., the refuse of hemp or flax. Later, the husk of oats after threshing. Usu. in *pl.*

shoofly /ˈʃuːflʌɪ/ *noun.* Orig. & chiefly *US.* Also **shoo-fly**. L19.
[from SHOO-FLY *interjection.*]
†**1** A device or structure intended to afford protection from flies. Only in L19.
2 A police officer, usu. in plain clothes, detailed to watch and report on other police officers. *slang.* L19.
3 A rocking-horse in which the seat is placed between two rockers representing the animal. Also ***shoofly rocker***. L19.
4 A temporary railway track constructed for use while the main track is obstructed or under repair. Also, a temporary road. E20.
5 PRINTING. In some flat-bed presses, a set of narrow strips which lift the edge of the sheet off the cylinder ready for delivery. Also ***shoofly finger***. E20.
6 In needlework, a traditional patchwork design. M20.
Comb.: **shoofly pie** a rich tart made of molasses baked in a pastry case with a crumble topping; **shoofly plant** a Peruvian plant of the nightshade family, *Nicandra physalodes*, with pale blue flowers and a calyx which enlarges in fruit, reputed to repel flies.

shoo-fly /ˈʃuːflʌɪ/ *interjection. US* (now *rare* or *obsolete*). M19.
[from SHOO *interjection* + FLY *noun*¹, *verb.*]
Expr. annoyance.

shoogle *verb* var. of SHOGGLE.

shoogly /ˈʃuːɡli/ *adjective. Scot.* ME.
[from prec. + -Y³.]
Unsteady, wobbly.

J. TORRINGTON A pencil stub with a shoogly lead.

shook /ʃʊk/ *noun.* Now chiefly *US.* L18.
[Origin uncertain: perh. from SHOOK *adjective.*]
A set of staves and headings for a cask, ready for fitting together. Cf. earlier SHOOK *adjective* 1b.

shook /ʃʊk/ *adjective.* L17.
[pa. pple of SHAKE *verb.*]
1 Shaken. *arch.* L17. ▸**b** Of a cask: having or consisting of a set of staves and headings made to be readily fitted together. Cf. SHAKE *noun* 11, SHOOK *noun. US. rare.* M18.
2 Emotionally or physically disturbed, discomposed, upset. Chiefly *pred.* Usu. foll. by *up. colloq.* L19.
3 Foll. by *on*: be keen on or enthusiastic about. *Austral. & NZ colloq.* L19.

1 FRANCIS THOMPSON Reversing the shook banners of their song. **2** *Wilderness Odyssey* Gil never appeared . . nervous, or shook up.

shook *verb pa. t. & pple*: see SHAKE *verb.*

shool /ʃuːl/ *verb intrans.* Chiefly *dial. & slang.* M18.
[Origin unkn.]
Beg; go about begging; sponge.

shooldarry /ʃuːlˈdari/ *noun. Indian subcontinent. rare.* E19.
[Urdu *chholdārī*, ult. origin unkn.; perh. rel. to Urdu *jhūl*, *jull* horse-cloth from Arab. *jul.*]
A small ridge tent with a steep sloping roof and very low side-walls.

†**Shooli** *noun & adjective* var. of ACHOLI.

shoon *noun pl.* see SHOE *noun.*

shoot /ʃuːt/ *noun*¹. LME.
[from SHOOT *verb.* Cf. earlier SHOTE. Cf. also SHUTE *noun*¹, *noun*².]
1 †**a** Weapons for shooting, esp. firearms, collectively. *rare.* Only in LME. ▸**b** An act of shooting; a discharge of arrows, bullets, etc. *arch.* M16. ▸†**c** Range, distance, or reach of a shot; shooting distance. M16–E18. ▸**d** A game-shooting expedition, esp. in a specified area; a shooting party; the result of a shooting expedition. Also, the right to shoot game in a specified area; a specified area in which game may be shot. M19. ▸**e** A shooting match or contest; a round of shots in such a contest. L19. ▸**f** The action of shooting a film. E20. ▸**g** MILITARY. An act of bombardment; *esp.* an exercise in which anti-aircraft drill is practised. M20.
2 a A young branch or sucker springing from the main stock of a tree, plant, etc. LME. ▸**b** Orig., the rising of sap in a plant etc. Later, (the amount of) new growth produced by a plant over a specified period; the action or process of sprouting or growing. L16. ▸**c** *fig.* An offshoot, a scion. E17.
3 a A movement of an object (as if) shooting or being shot in a particular direction; the space or distance covered by such movement or by propulsion. L16. ▸**b** *fig.* A surge; a sudden advance. Now *rare.* M18. ▸**c** A sharp short twinge of pain. M18. ▸**d** A breaking and falling away or down of ice, soil, etc.; a landslip. E19.
4 a A heavy and sudden rush of water down a steep channel; a place in a river where this occurs, a rapid. E17. ▸**b** A channel built to convey water by gravity, esp. to drive a water-wheel. Also, any man-made channel. E18.
5 WEAVING. A single movement or throw of the shuttle between the threads of the warp; the length of thread thus placed. Also, the weft. E18.
6 A crossbar connecting the beam and sole in front in a former kind of plough; = SHEATH *noun*². *dial.* M18.
7 A sloping channel or conduit down which coal, ore, wheat, etc., may be conveyed to a lower level. Also, a slope for shooting rubbish down, a tip. M19. ▸**b** A narrow passageway between enclosures for cattle or sheep. Chiefly *US & Austral.* L19.
8 MINING. A large somewhat regular body or mass of ore in a vein, usually elongated and vertical or inclined in position. M19.

1b R. L. STEVENSON Many a rogue would give his . . ears to have a shoot at . . us! **d** W. W. HUNTER Their return . . was celebrated by a . . shoot in the jungle. *Country Life* Most shoots have finished their season with a . . fair partridge stock. **e** *Target Gun* A Springfield rocket bayonet for the H.B.S.A. fixed bayonet shoot. **f** *Broadcast* Had you crewed in . . television productions and . . found yourself part of a commercial shoot? *Direction* The ad . . is the product of a two-day live action shoot. **2a** *Garden News* Side shoots root better than main . . shoots. **b** *Boston Herald* The shoot of Spring grass is . . unusually late. **c** LONGFELLOW Monsieur d'Argentville was a shoot from a wealthy family. **3a** *Times* Both [yachts] had a long shoot up in the eye of the wind. **b** S. JOHNSON His sudden shoot of success. **c** J. HUTCHINSON Shoots of pain . . like those of an electric discharge. **4a** SIR W. SCOTT A single shoot carried a considerable stream over the . . rock.

Phrases: **LAMMAS shoot**. **leading shoot**: see LEADING *adjective*. ***rough shoot***: see ROUGH *adjective*. **the whole shoot** *colloq.* the whole lot, everything. ***tiller shoot***: see TILLER *noun*³ 2.

shoot /ʃuːt/ *noun*². *obsolete* exc. *dial.* Also **shewt**, **shute**. L16.
[App. a special use of prec.]
Diarrhoea in cattle.

shoot /ʃuːt/ *verb.* Pa. t. & pple **shot** /ʃɒt/, pa. pple (*arch.*) **shotten** /ˈʃɒt(ə)n/.
[Old English *scēotan* (pa. t. *scēat*, *scuton*, pa. pple *scoten*, cf. SHOTTEN *ppl adjective*) = Old Frisian *skiata*, Old Saxon *skietan*, Old High German *sciozzan* (Dutch *schieten*, German *schiessen*), Old Norse *skjóta*, from Germanic base also of Old English *scēat*, *scīete* (see SHEET *noun*¹, *noun*²), *scot* SHOT *noun*¹, *scotian* shoot with arrows, *scyttan* SHUT *verb.* Cf. SCOUT *noun*¹, *noun*², SHOUT *noun*².]
▸ **I 1** *verb intrans.* Be caused to go or pass suddenly and swiftly through space; rush, be involuntarily precipitated. Also foll. by *up*, *down*, *forward*, etc. OE. ▸**b** Of a meteor etc.: move swiftly across the sky. Now chiefly in ***shooting star***. ME. ▸†**c** Of tears, blood, etc.: issue suddenly, spurt. LME–L15. ▸**d** *fig.* Of a thought etc.: pass suddenly *into*, *across*, etc., the mind. M16. ▸**e** Of a wall, cliff, etc.: fall precipitately. Now chiefly *Scot.* L16. ▸**f** (Of light etc.) be emitted in rays, dart (foll. by *out*, *up*); (of a glance) be darted, esp. in a particular direction. L17. ▸**g** NAUTICAL. Of ballast: become displaced, shift. L17. ▸**h** Of a ball: move with accelerated speed after striking something; *spec.* in CRICKET (of a bowled ball) move rapidly along the ground after pitching. E19.
2 *verb intrans.* Come or go swiftly and vigorously; precipitate oneself, rush, dart. Also foll. by *off*, *out*. OE. ▸**b** Of a ship etc.: move swiftly in a certain direction, esp. to a desired position. LME. ▸**c** Slide *down* a slope at full speed. *rare.* M18. ▸**d** Depart, go away. Freq. in *imper. colloq.* L19.
3 *verb intrans.* (Of a pain) be felt with a sudden piercing sensation (freq. foll. by *through*). Also, (of a part of the body etc.) have a number of such pains. OE.
4 *verb intrans.* Project, abruptly jut *out*; extend in a particular direction; tower *up*. OE.
5 *verb intrans.* **a** Of a bud, shoot, etc.: appear, sprout, grow (*up*). Also (now *rare*), (of teeth, hair, etc.) develop. LME. ▸**b** Of a plant etc.: put forth buds, shoots, etc.; germinate. M16.
6 *verb intrans.* Grow rapidly; advance, esp. quickly, to maturity; (of a price etc.) rise sharply. Now only foll. by *up* etc. M16. ▸†**b** *verb trans.* Cause to grow rapidly or advance, esp. quickly, to maturity. Usu. in *pass.* M16–L19.
7 *verb trans.* Pass rapidly through, over, or under; *spec.* (*a*) (of a boat etc.) pass quickly under (a bridge) or down (rapids or falls); (*b*) (of a motor vehicle etc.) pass (traffic lights at red). M16. ▸**b** NAUTICAL. Successfully negotiate (a dangerous strait, passage, gulf, etc.). E17. ▸**c** RACING. Swiftly overtake (a competitor). M19.
8 *verb intrans. & trans.* Form (crystals), crystallize. Now *rare* or *obsolete.* E17.

1 CONAN DOYLE The . . creature stumbled, and the rider came . . near to shooting over its head. M. MITCHELL Torrents of sparks shot to the sky and descended slowly. E. J. HOWARD Her hands shot upwards with a convulsive gesture. **b** SOUTHEY Gone like . . A star that shoots and falls. **d** LEIGH HUNT It shot across me . . that I was doing the very thing I described. **2** I. FLEMING The . . MG two-seater shot down the slope. I. MURDOCH Danby darted to the . . gate and shot through it. D. ATTENBOROUGH Highly accomplished flyers, shooting over the . . pond in a blur of gauzy wings. **b** M. ARNOLD 'Tis . . the boat, shooting round by the trees! **3** G. HERBERT Preachers make His head to shoot and ake. POPE Pain, That . . shoots thro' ev'ry Vein. **4** T. BURNET The Promontories and Capes shoot into the Sea. M. REID Mountains, whose tops shot heavenwards in fantastic forms. **5a** J. MOXON The Bough . . shoots out of the Trunk of a Tree. W. E. SHUCKARD A . . quantity of . . mustard plant shot up. **b** W. KING The Cypress . . when cut down, never shoots again. R. JEFFERIES Furze and fern soon shoot again, yet animal life is not so quickly repaired. **6** R. HUGHES Emily grew . . a lot . . suddenly shot up, as children will. *Listener* Sales of vodka . . shot up by 25 per cent. **b** SPENSER Well shot in yeares he seem'd. **7** F. MORYSON Having shot two . . small bridges . . we came to the Village. P. PEARCE He had been taken in a . . canoe to shoot rapids. **c** *Field* Cannon . . managed, after a fine specimen of riding . . to shoot Fordham by a head.

▸ **II 9 a** *verb trans.* Throw suddenly or violently. Formerly also, throw or pull *down*, overthrow. Also foll. by *out*, *down*, etc. *obsolete* exc. as passing into sense 19. OE. ▸**b** *verb trans.* Empty out (grain, earth, etc.) by overturning or tilting a receptacle; let (rubbish, a load, etc.) fall or slide from a container, lorry, etc.; send (goods, debris, etc.) down a chute. Also, empty (a receptacle) by overturning or tilting. Freq. foll. by *down*, *out*. LME. ▸**c** *verb refl.* Throw or precipitate *oneself*. Now *rare.* L16. ▸**d** *verb trans.* Cause (rain etc.) to run *from* or *off* a surface without absorption. L16. ▸**e** *verb trans.* Separate (esp. poor quality animals) from a herd or flock. Orig. & chiefly *Scot.* M18. ▸**f** *verb trans.* Put hurriedly and carelessly. Also, dispatch (a thing) rapidly. M19. ▸**g** *verb trans.* Discard, get rid of. *slang* (orig. *US*). L19.
10 *verb trans.* Push or slide (a bar or bolt) to fasten or unfasten a door etc. Also, force (a lock). OE.
11 *verb trans.* Utter (a word, sound, etc.). Freq. foll. by *out*, *forth*. Now only as passing into sense 19d below. ME. ▸**b** Emit swiftly and strongly (a ray of light, heat, etc.). LME.
12 *verb trans.* **a** Thrust (one's hand, a weapon, etc.) *into*, *out*, *forth*, *up*, etc. ME. ▸**b** Cause one's lips, tongue, etc., to stick *out*, esp. in mockery or derision. M16.
13 *verb trans.* Orig., ***shoot in***, fix firmly to (usu. in *pass.*). Later, cause to project or protrude, esp. in a particular direction. Long *rare.* ME.
14 *verb trans.* **a** Launch (a ship etc.); drop (an anchor); lower and place in position (a ring-net or drift-net). Also, allow (line) to run out through the hand at the forward motion of a fishing-rod in casting. LME. ▸**b** Cause (a ship etc.) to move forward suddenly or swiftly, esp. *to* a required position. LME.
15 *verb trans.* & (*rare*) *intrans.* Of an animal: eject (matter) from the body. Now only *spec.* (of a fish) discharge (spawn). LME. ▸**b** *verb intrans. & trans.* Of a man: ejaculate (semen) on achieving orgasm. *slang.* L19.
16 *verb trans.* **a** Of a plant: put forth (buds, shoots, etc.) (freq. foll. by *forth*, *out*). Also (*rare*), (of an organism etc.) develop (a process). E16. ▸**b** Cause to grow or spring *up*. *rare.* E17.
17 *verb trans.* **a** Weave (a fabric, esp. silk) with warp-threads of one colour and weft-threads of another so as to show different colours at different angles; variegate (an expanse of colour) by interspersing streaks or flecks of another colour. Chiefly as SHOT *ppl adjective.* M16. ▸**b** In weaving, pass (the shuttle, the weft) between the threads of the warp. E17.
18 *verb trans.* Orig. (now *dial.*), send out or dispatch (a person). Later (*colloq.*), convey or transfer (a person) with speed. M16.

9b *Law Times* Bales were shot from the top to the bottom floors by means of . . inclined planes. **c** ADDISON The Gulf thro' which . . Alecto shoots her self into Hell. **f** H. MARTINEAU He . . shot his instrument into its case. **10** J. GARDNER The door's open. Close it and shoot the bolt. **11** DICKENS Shooting out whatever she had to say in . . one breath. **b** SIR W. SCOTT His keen eyes . . shot forth . . a quick and vivid ray. **12a** GOLDSMITH They . . shoot forth their arms in every direction. **b** A. C. SWINBURNE At my Lord the Jews shot out their tongues. **16** S. PATRICK Rosemary and Sweet-Brier . . which shoot flowers, and dart forth Musk. **b** J. CLARE The Power . . Who rules the year, and shoots the spindling grain.

▸ **III 19 a** *verb trans.* Discharge (an arrow, bullet, etc.) from a bow, gun, etc. Also foll. by *at*. OE. ▸†**b** *verb trans.* Throw (a spear etc.). OE–L16. ▸**c** *verb trans.* Discharge (a bow, gun, etc.). Also foll. by *off*. LME. ▸**d** *verb trans.* Send out, discharge, or propel swiftly or violently; *esp.* direct (a glance, question, etc.) suddenly and sharply in a specified direction. E17. ▸**e** *verb intrans.* & (*rare*) *trans.* Proceed or go ahead with (a speech, question, etc.) in a rapid or energetic manner. Freq. in *imper.* **E20.**

20 *verb intrans.* Discharge an arrow, bullet, etc. from a bow, gun, etc. **OE.** ▸**b** Engage in archery, rifle-practice, etc., as a sport or contest. **ME.** ▸**c** Of a bow, gun, etc.: discharge an arrow, bullet, etc., esp. over a certain distance or in a specified manner; be discharged, fire. **L16.**

21 *verb trans.* **a** Propel (a marble, pellet, etc.) with the thumb and forefinger, esp. in play. Also *N. Amer.*, throw (a die or dice); play at (dice). *colloq.* **E19.** ▸**b** Play a game of (craps, pool, etc.). *N. Amer. colloq.* **E20.**

22 *SPORT.* **a** *verb trans.* Kick, hit, or drive (the ball etc.) at a goal. Also, score (a goal), take a shot at (a goal). **L19.** ▸**b** *verb intrans.* Kick, hit, or drive the ball etc. at a goal. Also foll. by *at*. **L19.** ▸**c** *verb trans. GOLF.* Make (a specified score) for a round or hole. Orig. *US.* **E20.**

23 *verb trans.* & (*rare*) *intrans.* Photograph or film (a scene, action, person, etc.); use (a film) to take a photograph or film. **L19.**

24 *verb trans. & intrans.* Inject (oneself or another) esp. with an addictive drug; inject oneself or another with (esp. an addictive drug). Freq. foll. by *up*. *slang* (orig. *US*). **E20.**

25 *verb intrans. BRIDGE.* In a tournament, play deliberately to win by achieving a particular outcome through abnormal play. **M20.**

📖 **19a** DAY LEWIS I shot an arrow which whizzed over his head. **c** HARPER LEE I haven't shot a gun in thirty years. **d** EVELYN A porcupine . . that shoots its quills. J. GLASSCO He shot a swift look at . . me that was frightening in its intensity. **20c** *Guns & Weapons* These pistols apparently shot very well. **21b** M. MOORCOCK Leon . . preferred . . shooting pool with his mates. **22a** F. HEWITT The best play is to shoot the puck at the boards. **b** *New York Times* Ross shot . . from the centre of the rink. **c** *Saturday Evening Post* They shot a twelve-under-par score. **23** G. GREENE To synchronise pictures with music . . he found it necessary to shoot 600,000 feet of film. A. ROAD The scene has to be shot three times. **24** R. INGALLS Heard of a doctor who didn't . . shoot you full of drugs? J. DIDION What I don't do is shoot heroin.

▸**IV 26** *verb trans.* Wound or kill (a person etc.) with an arrow, bullet, etc., from a bow, gun, etc. Freq. foll. by *with*. **OE.** ▸**b** Injure or kill by witchcraft or magic. (*obsolete* exc. in ***elf-shoot*** s.v. ELF *noun*[1]). *rare.* **OE.**

27 a *verb intrans.* Hunt game etc. with a gun (formerly a bow etc.), esp. as a sport. **ME.** ▸**b** *verb trans.* Go over (an estate, covert, etc.) hunting game with a gun, esp. as a sport. **M19.** ▸**c** *verb intrans.* Go *over* an estate, covert, etc., hunting game with a gun, esp. as a sport. **L19.**

28 *verb trans.* Blow up (rocks etc.) by explosion, blast. Also *esp.*, detonate an explosive charge in (an oil-well etc.) in order to increase the flow of oil or gas. **M19.**

📖 **26** D. HUME Tromp . . was shot through the heart with a musket ball. THACKERAY The colonel . . went and shot pheasants. *Daily Mirror* Gunmen . . shot dead a . . government official. **27a** J. W. CROKER Peel and I were to have gone . . to shoot at Sudbourne. **b** N. MITCHISON Tom and her brother were out shooting Ardfeochan. **c** *Times* During his stay the Belvoir covers were shot over.

▸**V 29** Splice (a rope); mend (a bar); weld (metal). *obsolete* exc. *dial.* **L15.**

30 *verb trans.* †**a** Avoid, escape. *Scot.* **M16–L17.** ▸**b** In *pass.* Be rid *of*. *colloq.* (orig. *dial.*). **E19.**

31 *CARPENTRY.* Plane (the edge of a board) accurately, esp. using a shooting-board. **M17.**

Phrases, & with adverbs & prepositions in specialized senses: **I'll be shot if** — *colloq.* I certainly do not —, I will not —. **shoot ahead** come quickly to the front of other competitors etc.; be carried forward by momentum. ***shoot a line***: see LINE *noun*[2]. ***shoot a profile***: see PROFILE *noun*. **shoot at** (*a*) *arch.* aim at; †(*b*) have reference to. **shoot away**, **shoot off** remove or detach from by shooting; destroy or break off by a shot. **shoot back** *colloq.* riposte, retort. ***shoot craps***: see CRAPS 1. **shoot down** (*a*) kill (a person) by a shot, esp. with merciless cruelty or determination; (*b*) (more fully ***shoot down in flames***) bring down (an aircraft etc.) by shooting; *fig.* overwhelm (a person) in argument, destroy (an argument or theory). **shoot flying** shoot birds on the wing, esp. as a sport. **shoot from the hip** *colloq.* react suddenly or without careful consideration of one's words or actions. **shoot it out** *colloq.* settle a dispute by shooting, engage in a decisive gun-battle. ***shoot off***: see ***shoot away*** above. ***shoot off one's mouth***: see ***shoot one's mouth off*** below. **shoot one's cuffs** pull one's shirt-cuffs out to project beyond the cuffs of one's coat or jacket. **shoot oneself in the foot** *colloq.* inadvertently make a situation worse for oneself. **shoot one's mouth off**, **shoot off one's mouth** *colloq.* talk too much or indiscreetly; boast, brag. ***shoot one's wad***: see WAD *noun*[1] 3b. **shoot out** destroy or make useless by shooting with a bullet etc.; *spec.* puncture (a tyre), extinguish (a lamp) in this way. **shoot the breeze** *N. Amer. colloq.* chat, talk idly. **shoot the cat** *arch. slang* vomit. **shoot the chute(s)** *US* = ***chute the chute(s)*** s.v. CHUTE *verb* 2. ***shoot the moon***: see MOON *noun*[1]. ***shoot the sun***: see SUN *noun*[1]. **shoot the works** *US slang* do everything necessary; tell the truth, reveal all. **shoot through** (*a*) (*verb trans.*) pierce (a person etc.) with a shot; (*b*) (*verb intrans.*) *Austral. & NZ slang* depart, escape, abscond. **shoot to kill** shoot at a person etc. intending to kill him or her. **shoot up** (*a*) terrorize (a district) by indiscriminate shooting; (*b*) see sense 6 above; (*c*) see sense 24 above.

Comb.: **shoot-'em-up** *slang* (orig. *US*) a fast-moving story or film, esp. a Western, of which gunplay is a dominant feature; **shoot-off** the subsequent competition between tied contestants in a shooting-match; **shoot-out** *colloq.* (orig. *US*) (*a*) a decisive gun-battle; a gunfight, *fig.* an intense and decisive contest; (*b*) *FOOTBALL* a tie-breaker, *esp.* one which is decided by each side taking a specified number of penalty shots; **shoot-the-chute** = ***chute-the-chutes*** s.v. CHUTE *noun*[1] & *verb*; **shoot-up** *colloq.* a furious exchange of shooting, a gun-battle, a shoot-out.

▪ **shootable** *adjective* able to be shot; suitable for shooting: **M19.** **shootee** *noun* a person shot (at) **M19.** **shootist** *noun* (*US colloq.*) a person who shoots; *esp.* a marksman: **M19.**

shoot /ʃuːt/ *interjection. N. Amer. slang.* **M20.**
[Euphem. alt. of SHIT *interjection*, perh. also infl. by imper. of SHOOT *verb*.]
Expr. disgust, anger, annoyance, etc.

shooter /ˈʃuːtə/ *noun.* **ME.**
[from SHOOT *verb* + -ER[1].]
▸**I 1** A person who shoots; *spec.* †(*a*) an archer; (*b*) a person who shoots game for sport. **ME.** ▸†**b** Usu. **S-**. = ARCHER 2. **LME–E17.**

2 *SPORT.* A player who shoots or whose duty is to shoot a goal in basketball, football, netball, etc. **E20.** ▸**b** A person who throws a die, dice, or marble (cf. ***crapshooter*** s.v. CRAPS). **E20.**

▸**II 3** A board placed between the cheeses in a press. Long *obsolete* exc. *dial.* **L16.**

4 A plant that shoots. Freq. with specifying word. **M18.**

5 A gun or other device for shooting. Freq. as 2nd elem. of comb. **E19.**

6 *CRICKET.* A bowled ball which moves rapidly along the ground after pitching. **M19.**

7 A black morning coat. *School slang.* Now *rare* or *obsolete.* **L19.**

8 A marble used for shooting; a taw. Orig. & chiefly *US.* **L19.**

9 A measure or drink of spirits, *esp.* one intended to be drunk in a single gulp. *N. Amer. slang.* **L20.**

5 ***peashooter***, ***six-shooter***, etc.

shooting /ˈʃuːtɪŋ/ *noun.* **ME.**
[formed as prec. + -ING[1].]
1 The action or practice of SHOOT *verb*. Also, an instance of this. **ME.** ▸**b** The right to shoot game over a particular estate, covert, etc. Also, an estate, covert, etc., over which a person has the right to shoot game. **M19.** ▸**c** An incident in which a person is shot with a firearm. **L19.**

2 The feeling of a sudden pain; a sudden piercing pain. **E16.**

3 A shoot of a plant etc.; such shoots collectively. **M17.**

Comb.: **shooting board** *CARPENTRY* a board with a step-shaped profile used to guide the motion of a plane relative to a workpiece to ensure accurate planing; **shooting box** a small house or lodge for use during the shooting season; ***shooting brake***: see BRAKE *noun*[6] 5; **shooting-gallery** (*a*) a long room or fairground booth used for shooting at targets with rifles etc.; (*b*) *N. Amer. slang* a place where addictive drugs may be illicitly obtained and injected; **shooting-glove** *ARCHERY* a glove worn to protect the hand in drawing a bow; **shooting-ground** a district or place where shooting is carried on; *spec.* = sense 1b above; **shooting-iron** (chiefly *US colloq.*) a firearm, *esp.* a revolver; **shooting-lodge** a lodge for use during the shooting season; **shooting match** a competition testing skill in shooting; ***the whole shooting match*** (*colloq.*), everything; **shooting-range** a ground with butts for rifle-practice; **shooting season** the time of year assigned to the shooting of game; **shooting-stick** (*a*) *PRINTING* a piece of hard wood or metal to be struck by a mallet to tighten or loosen the quoins in a forme; (*b*) a walking-stick with a handle consisting of a foldable seat; **shooting war** hostilities involving armed conflict.

shooting /ˈʃuːtɪŋ/ *adjective.* **OE.**
[from SHOOT *verb* + -ING[2].]
That shoots; *spec.* (*a*) (of a pain) sudden and piercing; (*b*) moving swiftly, darting; growing quickly.

shooting star (*a*) a meteor; (*b*) *US* the American cowslip, *Dodecatheon meadia* and allied species.

shop /ʃɒp/ *noun.* **ME.**
[Aphet. from Anglo-Norman, Old French *eschoppe* (mod. *échoppe*) lean-to booth, cobbler's stall from Middle Low German *schoppe* corresp. to Old English *sc(e)oppa* rendering late Latin (Vulgate) *gazophylacium* treasury (of the temple), Old High German *scopf* porch, vestibule (German *Schopf* porch, lean-to, cart-shed, barn), rel. to Old English *scypen* SHIPPON.]
1 A house or building where goods are made or prepared for sale and sold. **ME.**

2 A building, room, or other establishment used for the retail sale of merchandise or services. Also, the contents of a shop, the merchandise itself. Also as *interjection*, used to summon a shop assistant. **LME.** ▸**b** An act of shopping for purchases. *colloq.* **M20.**

3 a A building or room equipped and used for a particular craft or manufacturing industry; a workshop, freq. as opp. to an office. Now also (*spec.*), a room or department in a factory where a particular stage of production is carried out. **LME.** ▸†**b** *fig.* A place, bodily organ, etc., where something is produced or where some process is carried out. **M16–M18.** ▸**c** In glass-manufacturing, a team of workers. **L19.** ▸**d** A school-room equipped for teaching skills for use in a workshop; this study as a classroom discipline. Chiefly *N. Amer.* **E20.** ▸**e** A group of trade union members within a particular place of employment. Cf. ***CLOSED shop***. **M20.**

4 a A prison. *slang.* Long *rare* or *obsolete.* **L17.** ▸**b** The mouth. *obsolete* exc. *dial.* **M18.**

5 a A place of business, an office; the place where one works. **L18.** ▸**b** An engagement, a position of employment. *slang* (esp. *THEATRICAL*). **L19.**

6 (Discussion of) matters pertaining to one's trade or profession; business. Chiefly in ***talk shop*** s.v. TALK *verb*. **E19.**

7 *STOCK EXCHANGE.* The inside influences affecting or controlling a company by the exercise of special knowledge. Also, the South African gold market. **L19.**

📖 **2** S. J. PERELMAN Souvenir shops whose mementoes surpass anything I have seen . . for sheer vapidity. **b** D. SIMPSON On Thursday she goes into Sturrenden for the weekly shop. **3a** *Empire* I do some woodworking in my shop. **6** B. CASTLE We annoyed everyone by talking interesting shop . . instead of engaging in small talk.

Phrases: **all over the shop** *colloq.* (*a*) everywhere, in all directions; (*b*) wildly, erratically; in a state of disorder or confusion. ***CLOSED shop***. **come to the right shop**, **come to the wrong shop** apply to the right, wrong, person in order to obtain something. ***jerry-shop***: see JERRY *noun*[1] 2. **keep shop** own and work in a shop; work as a shopkeeper. **live over the shop** live on the premises where one works. ***malt shop***: see MALT *noun*[1] & *adjective*. ***mind the shop***: see MIND *verb*. ***multiple shop***: see MULTIPLE *adjective*. ***open shop***: see OPEN *adjective*. **set up shop** start or enter a business. ***shut up shop***: see SHUT *verb*. **smell of the shop** (of a person's action, remark, etc.) indicate (unduly) the spirit characteristic of the person's profession (*spec.* that of shopkeeper). ***talk shop***: see TALK *verb*. **the Shop** *slang* (*a*) *Hist.* the Royal Military Academy, Woolwich; (*b*) *Austral.* Melbourne University.

Comb.: **shop assistant** a person who serves customers in a retail shop; **shop-board** *arch.* (*a*) a counter on which business is transacted or goods are displayed for sale; (*b*) a table or raised platform on which a tailor sits when sewing; **shop-book** a shopkeeper's or mechanic's account-book; **shop-boy** a young male shop assistant; **shop-breaker** a burglar who breaks into a shop; **shop class** *N. Amer.* a class in which workshop skills are taught (cf. sense 3d above); **shop committee** *US*: elected by factory etc. workers to represent them in dealings with management; **shopcraft** *N. Amer.* an association of railway employees working in repair shops etc.; **shop-finish** the professional finish of an article produced in a commercial workshop; **shop-fitter** a person whose job is shop-fitting; **shop-fitting** (*a*) (in *pl.*) counters, shelves, etc., with which a shop is equipped; (*b*) the action or process of fitting out a shop with these; **shop floor** the part of a workshop or factory where production as opp. to administrative work is carried out; *transf.* the workers in this area as opp. to management; **shop-gaze** *verb intrans.* window-shop; **shop-girl** a female shop assistant; **shop-house** in SE Asia, a shop opening on to the pavement and also used as the owner's residence; **shoplift** *verb intrans. & trans.* [back-form. from *shoplifting*] steal (goods) from a shop while pretending to be a customer; **shoplifter** a person who steals goods from a shop while pretending to be a customer; **shoplifting** the action of stealing goods from a shop while pretending to be a customer; **shopman** (*a*) a male owner of or assistant in a shop; (*b*) a man employed in a railway workshop; **shop-soiled** *adjective* dirty, damaged, or faded by display for sale in a shop; *fig.* tarnished, no longer fresh; **shop steward** a person elected by union members in a factory etc. to represent them in dealings with management; **shop-talk** = sense 6 above; **shopwalker** an attendant who supervises assistants and directs customers in a department of a large shop; **shop window** (*a*) a window of a shop, in which goods are displayed for sale; *transf. & fig.* an opportunity to display talents or skills; †(*b*) ***open one's shop window***, ***open shop window***, begin business; ***shut one's shop window***, ***shut shop window***, close business; **shop-within-a-shop** (pl. **shops-within-shops**) a shop which functions independently within the premises of a larger store, usu. dealing in the goods of one manufacturer; **shopwoman** a female owner of or assistant in a shop; **shop-worn** *adjective* = ***shop-soiled*** above.

¶ Perh. Old English in place-name.

▪ **shopful** *noun* as much or as many as a shop will hold **M17.** **shopless** *adjective* **L19.** **shoplet** *noun* (*rare*) a little shop **L19.** **shoppie** *noun* (*Scot.*) a little shop **L19.** **shoppish** *adjective* (*rare*) (*a*) characteristic of a person or persons connected with a shop; (*b*) = SHOPPY *adjective* 1: **E19.** **shoppishness** *noun* (*rare*) professionalism **L19.**

shop /ʃɒp/ *verb.* Infl. **-pp-**. **M16.**
[from the noun.]
1 *verb trans.* **a** Shut up (a person), imprison; now *esp.* inform on, get (a person) into trouble. Also foll. by *up*. Now *slang* or *dial.* **M16.** ▸**b** Dismiss (a person) from a position or post. *slang. rare.* **M19.**

2 *verb trans.* Deliver (goods) to a shop; display for sale in a shop. Now *rare.* **L17.**

3 a *verb intrans.* Go to a shop or shops to buy or view goods. **M18.** ▸**b** *verb intrans.* Foll. by *around*: go to different shops to compare prices before making a purchase; buy goods at different shops according to which offers the best price. **E20.** ▸**c** *verb trans.* Go shopping at (a store); examine goods on sale in (a shop). *N. Amer.* **M20.**

4 *verb trans.* Give (a person) a job or situation. Now *rare.* **E19.**

📖 **1a** *Daily Mirror* A MUGGER was jailed . . after being shopped by his mother. **3a** ANNE STEVENSON Dido shopped for groceries. **b** *Which?* It's worth shopping around since prices can vary. *transf.*: *Home Finder* Home buyers . . shop around to get the best value loan.

shopaholic /ʃɒpəˈhɒlɪk/ *noun. colloq.* L20.
[from SHOP *noun, verb* + -AHOLIC.]
A compulsive shopper.

Shope /ʃəʊp/ *noun.* M20.
[Richard Edwin *Shope* (1902–66), US physician.]
VETERINARY MEDICINE. Used **attrib.** to designate a transmissible papilloma of rabbits described by Shope, and the DNA virus which causes it.

shopkeeper /ˈʃɒpkiːpə/ *noun.* M16.
[from SHOP *noun* + KEEPER *noun.*]
1 The owner and manager of a shop. M16.
2 An article that has remained long in a shop unsold. *arch. slang.* M17.
1 a nation of shopkeepers *derog.* a nation whose chief interest and concern lies in commerce; usu. *spec.* England, the English.
■ **shopkeeperish** *adjective* (*rare*) having the nature of a shopkeeper M19. **shopkeeperism** *noun* (*rare*) the characteristics of shopkeepers as a class M19. **shopkeeping** *adjective & noun* (*a*) *adjective* having the characteristics of a shopkeeper; pertaining to a shopkeeper's business; (*b*) *noun* the business of a shopkeeper: E17.

shopocracy /ʃɒˈpɒkrəsi/ *noun.* Now *rare.* M19.
[from SHOP *noun* + -O- + -CRACY.]
Shopkeepers as a class aspiring to social importance; a wealthy or influential body of shopkeepers.
■ ˈ**shopocrat** *noun & adjective* (a member) of the shopocracy M19.

shoppe /ʃɒp, ˈʃɒpi/ *noun. pseudo-arch.* E20.
[Alt. of SHOP *noun.* Cf. OLDE, YE *demonstr. adjective.*]
A shop having (usu. spurious) old-fashioned charm or quaintness.

shopper /ˈʃɒpə/ *noun.* M19.
[from SHOP *verb* + -ER[1].]
1 a A person who goes to a shop or shops to buy or view goods. M19. ▸**b** An advertising sheet or newspaper. M20. ▸**c** A shopping bag or trolley. M20. ▸**d** A small-wheeled bicycle with a basket, suitable for use while shopping. L20.
2 An informer. *slang.* E20.

shopping /ˈʃɒpɪŋ/ *noun.* M18.
[from SHOP *verb* + -ING[1].]
1 a The action of SHOP *verb* 3a, b. M18. ▸**b** = SHOP *noun* 2b. *colloq.* M20.
2 Goods that have been bought at a shop or shops. M20.
Attrib. & comb.: In the sense 'for the purpose of or pertaining to shopping', as ***shopping arcade***, ***shopping expedition***, ***shopping precinct***, ***shopping spree***, etc. Special combs., as **shopping-bag**: used to hold goods purchased; ***shopping-bag lady*** (*US*), a homeless woman carrying her possessions in shopping-bags; **shopping cart** (orig. *N. Amer.*) = ***shopping trolley*** (b) below; **shopping centre** an area or complex of shops; **shopping list** (*a*) a list of purchases to be made or shops to be visited; (*b*) a list of items to be considered or acted on; *spec.* a list of weaponry sought for purchase, esp. by a country; ***shopping mall***: see MALL *noun* 3b; **shopping tray** an open wire receptacle for shopping designed to fit over the chassis of a pram; **shopping trolley** (*a*) a shopping-bag set on a wheeled frame; (*b*) a large wire basket on wheels provided for the use of supermarket customers.

shoppy /ˈʃɒpi/ *noun. slang.* E20.
[from SHOP *noun* + -Y[6].]
A shop assistant.

shoppy /ˈʃɒpi/ *adjective.* M19.
[from SHOP *noun* + -Y[1].]
1 Of the nature of professional concerns or business conversation. M19.
2 Characterized by having a number of shops; forming a centre for business. M19.
3 Belonging to retail trade. M19.
■ **shoppiness** *noun* (*rare*) M19.

shor /ʃɔː/ *noun.* L19.
[Persian *šor.*]
In Turkestan, an elongated saline depression in desert sand.

shoran /ˈʃɔːran, ˈʃɒran/ *noun.* Orig. *US.* M20.
[from *short-range navigation.*]
A secondary radar navigation system in which an aircraft or ship determines its precise position by interrogating two widely-spaced ground stations. Cf. LORAN.

shore /ʃɔː/ *noun*[1]. ME.
[Middle Low German, Middle Dutch *schōre*, perh. from base of SHEAR *verb.*]
1 a The land bordering on the sea or a large lake or river; a coast, a bank; (*sing.* & in *pl.*) a country bounded by a coast. ME. ▸**b** LAW & PHYSICAL GEOGRAPHY. Land lying between ordinary high and low water marks. E17.
2 Part of a seashore built up as a landing-place; a quay, a wharf. *Scot.* E16.

> **1a** R. MACAULAY The . . Black Sea and its steep forested shores. *Dance* The man . . brought Balanchine to our shores. *fig.*: SHAKES. *Hen. V* The tide of pomp That beats upon the high shore of this world. **in shore** on the water near or nearer to the shore. **on shore** on the shore, ashore, on land.

Comb.: **shore-based** *adjective* operating from a base on shore; **shorebird** a bird which frequents the shore; *spec.* (chiefly *N. Amer.*) a wader; **shore-boat** a small boat plying near the shore, or between the shore and large vessels further out; **shore break** SURFING the part of the sea where the waves break close to the beach; **shorebug** any of various heteropteran bugs of the family Saldidae, which occur on the margins of fresh and brackish water, *esp.* one of the common European species *Saldula saltatoria*; **shore crab** any of various crabs of the genus *Carcinus*, which frequent rocky seashores, *esp.* one of the common European species *C. maenas*, the adults of which are blackish-green in colour; **shore dinner** *US* consisting mainly of seafood; **shoreface** PHYSICAL GEOGRAPHY a narrow sloping coastal zone below low-water mark, within which the seabed is affected by wave action; **shore-fish** a fish which occurs close to the shore; **shore fly** any of various small black flies of the family Ephydridae, which occur near water and in marshy places; **shore-going** *noun & adjective* going or living on shore (opp. ***seagoing***); **shore-gun**: for shore-shooting; **shore-gunner**, **shore-gunning** = ***shore-shooter***, ***-shooting*** below; **shore-hopper** = ***sand-hopper*** s.v. SAND *noun*; **shore lark** a brown and white lark, *Eremophila alpestris*, which has two black tufts on the head, and is of worldwide distribution; also called ***horned lark***; **shore leave** (*a*) leave of absence granted to a sailor to go on shore; (*b*) a period of time spent ashore by a sailor; **shoreline** (*a*) the line where shore and water meet; (*b*) = ***shore-rope*** below; **shoreman** (*a*) a man living on a seashore; (*b*) a man employed on shore by a fishery; **shore party** a group of people going ashore from a ship; **shore patrol** *US* a naval police organization responsible for the conduct of sailors on land; **shore patrolman** *US* a member of the shore patrol; **shore platform** a horizontal or gently sloping platform cut in a cliff by wave action; **shore-rope**: connecting a net with the shore; **shore seine**: used near the shore; **shore-shooter** a person who shoots birds on the shore; **shore-shooting** the sport of shooting birds on the shore; **shoreside** *noun, adjective, & adverb* (*a*) *noun & adjective* (on) the edge of a shore; (*b*) *adverb* to the shore, towards land; **shoresman** = ***shoreman*** (b) above; **shore station** a base on land used for shore-whaling; **shoreweed** a small plantain, *Littorella uniflora*, growing on the shores of lakes and ponds or submerged in shallow water at the edge; **shore-whaling**: near the shore in open boats; *spec.* = ***bay whaling*** s.v. BAY *noun*[3]; **shore zone** PHYSICAL GEOGRAPHY the zone affected by wave action; *spec.* = SHORE *noun*[1] 1b.
■ **shoreless** *adjective* having no shore; *spec.* (of a sea etc.) boundless: E17. **shoreward** *adverb & adjective* [orig. *to* (*the*) *shoreward*] (situated or directed) towards the shore L16. **shorewards** *noun & adverb* (in) the direction of the shore; shoreward: M18.

shore /ʃɔː/ *noun*[2]. ME.
[Middle Low German, Middle Dutch *schōre* (Dutch *schoor*) prop, stay.]
A piece of timber or iron set obliquely against the side of an unsafe building, a ship undergoing repair, etc., as a support; a prop, a strut, a stake, a post.

shore /ʃɔː/ *noun*[3]. L16.
[Prob. from SHORE *noun*[1].]
= SEWER *noun*[1] 2. Orig. in ***common shore***, no-man's-land at the waterside where filth was deposited for the tide to wash away.

Shore /ʃɔː/ *noun*[4]. E20.
[Albert F. *Shore* (fl. 1907–18), US manufacturer.]
METALLURGY. Used **attrib.** with ref. to the scleroscope and to a scale of relative hardness associated with the use of this instrument.

shore /ʃɔː/ *adjective & adverb. non-standard* (esp. *US dial.*). L19.
[Repr. a pronunc.]
= SURE *adjective & adverb.*

shore /ʃɔː/ *verb*[1]. ME.
[Middle & mod. Low German, Middle & mod. Dutch *schōren*, from *schōre* SHORE *noun*[2].]
1 *verb trans.* Prop *up*, support with a prop. ME.
†**2** *verb intrans.* Lean, slope, shelve. E16–E17.
†**3** *verb trans.* Foll. by *up*: raise (the eyes). *rare.* L16–E17.

> **1** P. SAYER Shoring up the . . cliff in front of our cottage. *fig.*: S. WEINTRAUB Stockman offered advice to shore up her confidence.

■ **shorer** *noun* a prop, a shore (*lit.* & *fig.*) LME. **shoring** *noun* (*a*) the action of propping up or supporting something; (*b*) shores or props used to support a building, vessel, etc.: L15.

shore /ʃɔː/ *verb*[2] *trans. Scot. & north.* LME.
[Origin unkn.]
1 Threaten (*to do*), scold. LME.
2 Offer. L18.

shore /ʃɔː/ *verb*[3]. L16.
[from SHORE *noun*[1].]
1 a *verb intrans.* Go ashore; (of a vessel) run aground. L16. ▸**b** *verb trans.* Put ashore; land (passengers or goods); beach, run aground (a vessel). E17.
2 †**a** *verb trans.* Pass by the side of. Only in L16. ▸**b** *verb intrans.* Sail along a coast. *rare.* M17.
3 *verb trans.* Border as a shore, be the shore of. M19.

shore *verb*[4] see SHEAR *verb.*

†**shorling** *noun.* ME.
[from SHOR(N + -LING[1].]
1 (Wool from) the skin of a sheep that has been recently shorn. ME–L17. ▸**b** A shorn sheep. *rare.* Only in M18.
2 A tonsured person. Only in M16.

shorn /ʃɔːn/ *ppl adjective.* LOE.
[pa. pple of SHEAR *verb.*]
1 Shaven, tonsured. LOE.
2 (Of corn) cut with a sickle; (of grass, a field) cut close. LME.
3 Of a sheep etc.: having undergone shearing. E16.
4 Chopped up. Formerly also, carved. *Scot.* M16.
5 Diminished; deprived *of.* M19.
3 shorn lamb the dressed wool of a young sheep used in garment-making.

short /ʃɔːt/ *adjective, noun, & adverb.*
[Old English *sċeort* = Old High German *scurz* from Germanic: cf. SHIRT *noun*, SKIRT *noun.*]
▶ **A** *adjective.* **I** With ref. to spatial measurement.
1 Having small longitudinal extent; small in measurement from end to end. OE. ▸**b** Of action, vision, etc.: acting at or extending to a small distance; *fig.* (of a mental power etc.) restricted in range. LME. ▸**c** *fig.* In biblical and derived uses: (of a person's authority) having a limited range of power; inadequate. Long *arch.* M16. ▸**d** (Of distance) not great; (of a journey) extending over a small distance. L16. ▸**e** Foll. by *in*: having a specified part (too) short. E19.
2 Of a person: low in stature, not tall. OE.
3 Of the sea: having small waves; choppy. L17.

> **1** JAN MORRIS The cathedral . . is the shortest in England (155 feet long). C. PRIEST I don't like your hair as short as that. P. FITZGERALD When the little one sat down . . her legs were . . too short to reach the ground. **c** AV *Num.* 11:23 And the Lord said unto Moses, Is the Lords hand waxed short? **d** J. F. LEHMANN She was going for a short walk. **e** THACKERAY My coat was . . high in the waist and short in the sleeves. **3** *Lifeboat* The . . trip was uncomfortable with short steep seas.

▶ **II** With ref. to serial extent or duration.
4 a Of a period of time, or a process, state, or action: having little extent in duration; not lasting a long time, brief, short-lived. OE. ▸**b** Of a person's memory: not retaining the recollection of events for a long period. ME.
5 Of a series, succession, a speech, a sentence, a word, a literary work, etc.: having a small extent from beginning to end; soon finished. OE.
6 PHONETICS & PROSODY. Of a vowel, in mod. use also of a consonant or syllable: having the lesser of two recognized contrastive durations. Also (PROSODY) (of a vowel or syllable) unstressed. OE.
7 a (Of a point in time) early, soon, near at hand; COMMERCE (of a bill of exchange) maturing at an early date. Chiefly in ***short date*** below, and in legal phr. ***a short day***. ME. ▸**b** Of notice: given not long beforehand. E19.
†**8** Quick, speedy, prompt. ME–L18.
9 Brief in a rude, angry, or stern manner; curt, sharp, impatient (foll. by *with* a person). LME.
10 (Of breathing) coming in hurried gasps, impeded; (of a cough) abrupt, dry, fast; (of a pulse) quick. LME.
11 Of a style of language, later also of a writer or speaker: concise, brief. L15.
12 Of an alcoholic drink, esp. spirits: undiluted. *colloq.* E19.

> **4a** N. FARAH Too many things had taken place in such a short time. J. HIGGINS Are you ready? Time's getting short. A. MACRAE At the vet's there was a short wait. **5** D. H. LAWRENCE She read the short letter quickly. R. QUIRK Very short words like *cat*. **9** T. WOGAN That audience had a short way with comedians. J. ELLIOT Rainbird, whose temper was short after a sleepless night.

▶ **III** Not reaching to some standard.
13 a Not attaining some standard or amount; scarce, inadequate in quantity; unfairly deficient. LME. ▸**b** Designating a period of time, a number, a weight, or a quantity smaller than the usual period etc. of that name. Also, felt as unusually or excessively short in duration or small in quantity. E18.
14 Of a throw, a missile, etc.: travelling too short a distance, not reaching the mark. M16.
15 Not fully attaining or amounting to (some condition or degree); not equalling, inferior to, less than. Freq. with adverb or adverbial phr. expressing the extent of the deficiency. Usu. foll. by *of.* M16.
16 a Defaulting in payments. Formerly also, inefficient, defective. L16. ▸**b** Having an insufficient supply (*of* money, food, etc.); lacking (something necessary), deficient. Now also foll. by *on.* L17. ▸**c** STOCK EXCHANGE. Having sold as yet unacquired stock which the seller hopes can be bought at a lower price before the time fixed for delivery; pertaining to such stock. Also foll. by *of.* *US.* M19. ▸**d** Of a race-horse: not on top form. *US colloq.* M20.

> **13** J. BETJEMAN When sugar was short and the world was fighting. **b** *International Combat Arms* Warfare . . is vastly more dangerous . . than it was only a few short years ago. **15** G. DURRELL Nothing short of a . . catastrophe would shake them. R. GITTINGS A fortnight short of his twenty-first birthday. J. TROLLOPE He regarded her with something little short of loathing. **16b** R. MACAULAY I was getting pretty

short, and had only twenty pounds left. G. NAYLOR Willie's a little . . short on cash.

▶ **IV** Brittle.

17 a Of pastry, meat, etc.: crumbly, easily crumbled. LME. ▸**b** Of clay, metal, etc.: brittle, fragile, friable. E17.

18 Of a liquid: not viscous. *rare*. E17.

Phrases: **at short intervals** at times separated by brief intervals. ***at short range***: see RANGE *noun*[1]. **cut a long story short** be brief or concise (freq. in ***to cut a long story short***, to be brief, in short). ***draw the short straw***: see ***draw straws*** (b) s.v. STRAW *noun*. **get by the short and curlies, get by the short hairs** *slang* gain complete control of (a person). **have by the short and curlies, have by the short hairs** *slang* be in complete control of (a person). ***in short order***: see ORDER *noun*. ***in short supply***: see SUPPLY *noun* 8. ***long short story***: see LONG *adjective*[1]. †**make short** cut one's speech short. **make short work of** deal with, dispose of, or consume quickly. ***run short***: see RUN *verb*. **short and sweet** brief and pleasant; *iron.* unusually brief and severe or decisive. ***short back and sides***: see BACK *noun*[1]. **short for** an abbreviation for. **the short answer is** is used to introduce a straightforward or immediate response or solution. **the short robe** *fig. (arch.)* swordsmen, those who (are accustomed to) bear arms (cf. ***the long robe*** s.v. LONG *adjective*[1]). ***thick as two short planks***: see THICK *adjective*.

Special collocations & comb.: **short-arc** *adjective* (of a discharge lamp) that has a short gap between the electrodes. **short-arm** *adjective & noun* (*a*) (a punch) delivered with the arm not fully extended; (*b*) *slang* (orig. & chiefly MILITARY) (designating) an inspection of the penis for venereal disease or other infection. **short-arse** *slang* a person of small stature; a worthless person. **short-arsed** *adjective* (*slang*) of small stature; worthless. **short-ass** *US slang* = ***short-arse*** above. **short-assed** *adjective* (*US slang*) = ***short-arsed*** above. **short ball** CRICKET a ball which pitches short of a length. **short ballot** *US* a ballot in which only the main offices are elected, the minor offices being filled by appointment; a form for such a ballot. **short bill** COMMERCE a bill having fewer than ten days to run. **short-breathed** *adjective* short of breath, suffering difficulty in breathing. **short cards** *US* any of various card-games played for money. **short chain** *adjective* (CHEMISTRY) a relatively small number of atoms (usu. of carbon) linked together in a line (freq. *attrib.* with hyphen). **short change** insufficient money given as change. **short-change** *verb trans.* (orig. *US*) rob or cheat by giving insufficient change; *fig.* cheat, deceive. **short cloth** a kind of cotton cloth or calico manufactured in short pieces. **short clothes** *arch.* garments used to clothe a baby when long clothes are no longer used. **short-coat** *noun & verb* (*arch.*) (*a*) *noun* a person wearing a short coat; (*b*) *verb trans.* dress (a baby) in short clothes. **short-coating** *collect.* (*arch.*) the various articles required when a baby is short-coated. ***short commons***: see COMMONS 5. **short con** *US slang* a small-scale confidence racket. **short corner** HOCKEY a penalty hit taken from a spot on the goal-line up to within ten yards of the goalposts. **short covering** STOCK EXCHANGE the buying in of stock or goods to cover a short sale (see sense 16c above). **short cross** †(*a*) PRINTING in a handpress, a bar dividing a chase the shortest way; (*b*) NUMISMATICS a cross of which the arms extend only to the inner circle on a coin. **short date** an early date for the maturing of a bill etc. **short-dated** *adjective* †(*a*) lasting a short time; (*b*) due for early payment or redemption. **short-day** *adjective* (*a*) having a short working day; (*b*) (of a plant) needing days with less than a certain maximum length of daylight to induce flowering. **short delivery** COMMERCE delivery of goods less in quantity than agreed on or invoiced. ***short division***: see DIVISION *noun* 5. **short dog** *slang* cheap wine. **short drink** a strong alcoholic drink, esp. spirits, served in small measures. **short dung** = ***short manure*** below. **short-eared owl** a light-coloured day-flying owl flecked with brown or black, *Asio flammeus*, which has very short ear-tufts and is of almost worldwide distribution. **short-eat** in Sri Lanka, a snack. **short end** (*a*) (in *pl.*) odds and ends; (*b*) a remnant of cloth; (*c*) *N. Amer. colloq.* the inferior part (*of* something), the losing end, a bad deal; (*d*) COMMERCE that part of a stock market which deals in short-term stocks. ***Shorter Catechism***: see CATECHISM *noun* 2. **short field** BASEBALL that part of the field in which the short stop plays. **short fielder** BASEBALL a short stop. **short focus** PHOTOGRAPHY a focal point that is near to the lens; ***short-focus lens***, (*a*) a wide-angle lens; (*b*) a close-up lens. **short fuse** *colloq.* a quick temper. **short-fused** *adjective* (*colloq.*) quick-tempered. **short game** GOLF play at the approach to and on the green. **short gown** *arch.* a dress with a very short skirt. **short grain** a condition of the fibres in wood which gives rise to brittleness. **short-grained** *adjective* (of wood) having a short fibre rendering it liable to snap easily; (of rice) having a relatively short grain. **short-grass** *adjective* (of a prairie etc.) characterized by certain short drought-resistant grasses. **short-hair** (an animal of) a breed of short-haired cat. **short-haired** *adjective* having short hair; of a kind or breed characterized by short hair; ***short-haired terrier***: see TERRIER *noun*[1] 1a. **short-hairs** *slang* (*a*) *US* a branch of the Democratic Party in the Western States who show discontent with the administration; (*b*) pubic hair. **short-haul** *adjective* designating or pertaining to travel, transport of goods, or any effort made, over a short distance. **short head** (*a*) a person who has a skull of less than average length; *spec.* in ANTHROPOLOGY a brachycephalic person; (*b*) RACING a distance less than the length of a horse's head. **short-head** *verb trans.* beat by a short head. **short-headed** *adjective* having a short head; brachycephalic. **short-headedness** the quality or state of being short-headed. **shorthorn** (*a*) (an animal of) a breed of dairy cattle having short horns, orig. bred in County Durham and formerly widely distributed in Britain etc. (also more fully ***Durham shorthorn***); (*b*) a small round variety of carrot; (*c*) *US slang* a new arrival, a greenhorn. **short-horned** *adjective* having short horns. **short horse** *US* = ***quarter-horse*** s.v. QUARTER *noun*. **short hour** an hour indicated by one of the smaller number of strokes on a clock etc. ***short hundredweight***: see HUNDREDWEIGHT. ***short leet***: see LEET *noun*[2]. ***short leg***: see LEG *noun*. **short list** a list of selected names, esp. of candidates for a post, from which a final selection is made. **short-list** *verb trans.* put on a short list. **short manure** manure containing brittle straw in an advanced state of decay. **short mark** a mark ˘ placed over a vowel letter to indicate short quantity. **short measure** (*a*) less than the stipulated or expected amount; (*b*) MUSIC an arrangement of the keyboard of a spinet in which advantage is taken of the short octave. **short metre** a hymn stanza of four lines of which the first, second, and fourth are of six syllables and the third of eight. **short notice** an insufficient amount of warning time. **short octave** MUSIC a lower octave of some early keyboard instruments in which some of the intermediate keys are omitted. **short odds** nearly equal stakes or chances in betting. **short order** *N. Amer.* an order for food to be prepared and served up quickly; a dish so served. ***Short Parliament***: see PARLIAMENT *noun*. **short-period** *adjective* lasting for a brief period of time; recurring at short intervals. **short prescription** LAW a prescription established by a short period of use. **short price** a low price; low odds in betting. **short-punt** *verb intrans.* (RUGBY FOOTBALL) punt the ball a short distance. **short-range** *adjective* having a short range; of or pertaining to a short period of future time. **short rib** any of the lower ribs which do not attach to the sternum; a piece of meat containing one or more of such ribs. **short run** (*a*) CRICKET a run not properly completed by the batsman; (*b*) ***in the short run***, over a brief period of time, in the short term; (*c*) a short period of continuous presentation (of a play, a broadcast programme, etc.); (*d*) a class or line of goods produced in limited quantity. **short-run** *adjective* taken or considered in the short run; short-term. **short score** MUSIC a reduced version of a full score on usu. two staves. ***short sea(s)***: see SEA *noun* 7. **short service** military service limited to a prescribed short period. **short-sheet** *verb trans.* (*colloq.*) make an apple-pie bed for (someone); play a trick on (someone); **short shorts** *US* very short trousers.; briefs. ***short shrift***: see SHRIFT *noun*. **short sight** the defect of sight by which only near objects are seen distinctly; myopia. **short-sighted** *adjective* (*a*) lacking in foresight or in extent of intellectual outlook; (*b*) having short sight; unable to distinguish objects clearly at a distance; myopic. **short-sightedly** *adverb* in a short-sighted manner. **short-sightedness** the condition of being short-sighted. †**short-six** *Hist.* (*a*) (in pl.) short candles, six of which went to the pound; (*b*) *US* a kind of cigar. **short sleeve** a sleeve which does not extend below the elbow. **short-sleeved** *adjective* having short sleeves. †**short slip** CRICKET = ***first slip*** s.v. SLIP *noun*[3] 11. **short-snorter** *US Military slang* a list of signatures written on a string of bills of money. **short-spined** *adjective* having short spines; ***short-spined sea scorpion***: see SEA *noun*. **short square (leg)** CRICKET a square leg standing close in to the wicket. **short-staffed** *adjective* having insufficient staff, understaffed. **short-stage** *noun & adjective* (*Hist.*) (a coach travelling) with short distances between stopping places. **short staple** *adjective & noun* (designating) cotton having a short fibre. **shortstop** (*a*) CRICKET = ***first slip*** s.v. SLIP *noun*[3] 11; (*b*) BASEBALL (the position of) a fielder defending the infield area who stands between second and third base. **short story** a story with a fully developed theme but shorter than a novel; ***short short story***, a very short story. **Short Street** *colloq.* an imaginary street where people in financial difficulty are supposed to live. **short subject** (chiefly *US*) a short film, typically one shown before the screening of a feature film. **short suit** CARDS a suit of which a player has few cards; *fig.* one's weak point. **short-suited** *adjective* having a short suit. **short sweetening** *US* cane or maple sugar. **short sword** *Hist.* a sword with a short blade. **short temper** self-control soon or easily lost. **short tempered** *adjective* quick to lose one's temper. **short tennis**: played on a small court with a small racket and a soft ball. **short time** (*a*) the condition of working less than the regular number of hours per day or of days per week (freq. *attrib.*); (*b*) *slang* a brief visit to a prostitute; a brief stay in a hotel for sexual purposes. **short-timer** (*a*) *Hist.* a child who is allowed to attend school for less than the full number of hours daily; (*b*) *US Military slang* a person nearing the end of his or her period of military service; (*c*) *slang* a person serving a short prison sentence; (*d*) *slang* a person who makes a brief stay in a hotel for sexual purposes; a person who visits a prostitute. **short title** an abbreviated form of a title of a book etc. **short-toed** *adjective* having short toes; ***short-toed eagle***, an Old World eagle, *Circaetus gallicus*, which has prominent white underparts and feeds largely on snakes etc.; ***short-toed lark***, any of several small pale Old World larks of the genera *Calandrella* and *Spizocorys*, esp. *C. cinerea*, which occurs throughout southern Europe, Asia, and Africa. ***short ton***: see TON *noun*[1] 4. **short-tongued** *adjective* having a short tongue; (now *dial.*) inarticulate, stammering, lisping; taciturn. **short trousers**: reaching only to the knee (esp. as worn by young boys). **short view** a consideration or regard for the present only, not the future. **short waist** (*a*) a high or shallow waist of a dress; (*b*) a short upper body. **short-waisted** *adjective* having a short waist. **shortwall** *noun & adjective* (MINING) (pertaining to or involving) a short coalface. **short wave** (*a*) a wave of relatively short wave-length; *spec.* in RADIO a radio wave with a wavelength of less than about 100 metres (a frequency of three to 30 megahertz); radio communication or broadcasting employing such waves (usu. *attrib.*, freq. with hyphen); (*b*) *attrib.* (with hyphen) MEDICINE designating diathermy which uses electrical frequencies within the short-wave radio range. **short weight** weight less than it is alleged to be. **short-weight** *verb trans.* (*US*) give less than the alleged weight to. ***short whist***: see WHIST *noun*[2]. **shortwing** any of several small S. Asian songbirds of the thrush family and esp. of the genus *Brachypteryx*, with long legs, short wings and tail, and dark brown or blue plumage. **short-wool** (*a*) wool having a short staple or fibre; (*b*) a sheep of a breed with short wool. **short-woolled** *adjective* (of a sheep) having short wool.

▶ **B** *noun*. **I** *absol.* **1 a** ***in short***, briefly, concisely; to sum up. Earliest in †***in short and plain***. LME. ▸**b** ***for short***, as an abbreviation. M19.

2 *The* total, *the* result, *the* upshot (*of*). Now chiefly in ***the long and the short of it*** s.v. LONG *noun* 2. L16.

📖 **1a** M. WHEELER Our brief . . visit . . was, in short, not without incident. **b** *Times Lit. Suppl.* A 'cumulative sum' chart, or 'cusum' chart for short.

▶ **II** As count noun.

3 a A short note in music; a short syllable or vowel; a mark indicating that a vowel or (formerly) a note is short. L16. ▸**b** = ***short drink*** above. *colloq.* E19. ▸**c** A contraction or abbreviation of a name or phrase. L19. ▸**d** A dot in Morse code; a short buzz etc. sounded as a signal. L19. ▸**e** ELECTRICITY. = SHORT CIRCUIT *noun phr.* E20. ▸**f** A short story, film, etc. E20. ▸**g** A streetcar; a car. *US slang*. E20. ▸**h** MILITARY. A shot that falls short of its target. E20.

4 In *pl.* ▸**a** A mixture of bran and coarse flour. M18. ▸**b** Cuttings of tobacco. M19.

5 In *pl.* & (*US*) *sing.* ▸**a** Trousers reaching only to the knees or higher; *US* underpants. E19. ▸**b** Short clothes for a baby. *arch.* M19.

6 In *pl.* Short whist. Now *rare*. E19.

7 Anything that is short or lacking. M19.

8 STOCK EXCHANGE. **a** A person who sells as yet unbought stock, in expectation of a drop in price before having to buy it. M19. ▸**b** In *pl.* Short-dated stocks. M20.

9 BASEBALL. = ***shortstop*** (b) above. M19.

3a ***longs and shorts***: see LONG *noun*.

▶ **C** *adverb*. **1** In a concise manner of speaking; briefly, curtly. Now *rare*. LME.

2 Rigidly confined, under strict discipline; closely, tightly. *obsolete* exc. in ***hold short***, ***ride short*** below. LME.

3 a For (only) a brief while. LME. ▸†**b** In a brief space of time, soon. M16–M17.

4 To a short distance or extent; with short length, steps, etc. LME.

5 On the nearer side of a point specified or aimed at; (foll. by *of*) distant from, not as far as. LME.

6 Abruptly, suddenly. M16.

📖 **5** J. POYER Terrain this rough was unusual short of the mountains. **6** *Horse & Hound* Camille turned very short into the combination.

Phrases: **be caught short** *colloq.* urgently need to urinate or defecate. **break short (off)**, **snap short (off)** break straight across. **breathe short** take short breaths. **bring up short** check abruptly, take by surprise. **come short** †(*a*) arrive too late; (*b*) be imperfect or inadequate, fail to reach a standard; (foll. by *of*) be less than; ***come short home***: see HOME *adverb*. **cut short** put a sudden end to; stop abruptly in a course of action, interrupt. **falling short** a failure in attainment, a deficiency. ***fall short***: see FALL *verb*. **go short** (*a*) not have enough (freq. foll. by *of*); (*b*) (of a horse) take short strides, esp. as a symptom of lameness. **hold short**, **ride short** hold or ride (a horse) with a tight rein. **pull up short** = ***bring up short*** above. ***ride short***: see ***hold short*** above. **sell short** (*a*) sell stock, a commodity, or goods which one does not own at the time, in the hope of buying at a lower price before the delivery time; (*b*) undervalue, belittle (freq. *refl.*). **short of** (*a*) less than; without going so far as, except; (see also sense 5 above); (*b*) *colloq.* (in ***a brick short of a load***, ***two sandwiches short of a picnic***, and similar phrs.) (of a person) not completely rational or sensible, mildly deranged. ***snap short (off)***: see ***break short*** above. **stop short at**, **stop short of** not go the length of (some extreme action). ***strike short***: see STRIKE *verb*. **take short** (*a*) take by surprise; *colloq.* (in *pass.*) = ***be caught short*** above; (*b*) interrupt with a reply (freq. foll. by *up*). **walk short** = ***go short*** (b) above.

Comb.: **short-acting** *adjective* (PHARMACOLOGY) (of a drug) relatively transient in effect; **short-pitched** *adjective* (CRICKET) (of a ball) pitching relatively near the bowler. **short-running** *adjective* (*a*) (of a hound or hare) running with short strides, slow in pace; (*b*) making short runs; **short-set** *adjective* (*rare*) of short build, stocky; **short-spoken** *adjective* abrupt or curt in speech.

■ **shortish** *adjective* somewhat short E19.

short /ʃɔːt/ *verb*[1].

[Old English *sc(e)ortian*, formed as prec.]

†**1** *verb intrans.* Grow short or shorter. OE–E16.

2 *verb trans.* Make short or shorter; shorten. Long *rare*. ME.

3 *verb trans.* Make (the time etc.) appear short by amusement etc.; *refl.* amuse oneself. Long *obsolete* exc. *Scot.* LME.

†**4** *verb trans.* Make of no effect. *rare* (Shakes.). Only in E17.

†**5** *verb intrans.* Come short in one's reckoning. *rare*. Only in M17.

6 *verb trans.* Give short measure to; cheat (a person) out of something. *US colloq.* M20.

7 *verb trans.* STOCK EXCHANGE. Sell (stock, a commodity, etc.) short (cf. ***sell short*** (a) s.v. SHORT *adverb*). M20.

short /ʃɔːt/ *verb*[2] *trans. & intrans.* E20.

[Abbreviation.]

= SHORT-CIRCUIT *verb* 1. Also foll. by *out*.

shortage /ˈʃɔːtɪdʒ/ *noun*. Orig. *US*. M19.

[from SHORT *noun* + -AGE.]

Deficiency in quantity; an amount lacking.

📖 *Woman* With the staff shortage I sometimes have to take charge. *Modern Maturity* There's no shortage of guidebooks about Paris.

shortall /ˈʃɔːtɔːl/ *noun*. *US*. M20.

[from SHORT *adjective* + OVER)ALL *noun*.]

A child's one-piece suit with short sleeves and short trouser legs. Freq. in *pl.*

shortbread /ˈʃɔːtbrɛd/ *noun*. **E18**.
[from SHORT *adjective* + BREAD *noun*[1].]
A rich crumbly biscuit made from flour, sugar, and a large proportion of butter.

shortcake /ˈʃɔːtkeɪk/ *noun*. **L16**.
[from SHORT *adjective* + CAKE *noun*.]
Shortbread; a cake made of layers of shortbread or short pastry filled with fruit and cream.

short-circuit /ʃɔːtˈsəːkɪt/ *verb*. **M19**.
[from prec.]
1 *ELECTRICITY*. **a** *verb trans.* Connect by a short circuit; establish a short circuit in (an electric system). **M19**. ▸**b** *verb trans.* Of a conducting body: act as a short circuit for (a current). **L19**. ▸**c** *verb intrans.* Of electrical apparatus: fail or cease working as a result of a short circuit occurring in it. **E20**.
2 *verb trans. fig.* Interrupt, cut short; bypass or avoid by taking a more direct route or course of action. **L19**.

> **2** *Trout & Salmon* A replacement was sent direct . . to my home, thus short-circuiting the dealer.

short circuit /ʃɔːt ˈsəːkɪt/ *noun phr*. **M19**.
[from SHORT *adjective* + CIRCUIT *noun*.]
ELECTRICITY. A circuit made through a small resistance, *esp.* one that acts as a shunt to a circuit of comparatively large resistance.

shortcoming /ˈʃɔːtkʌmɪŋ/ *noun & adjective*. **L15**.
[from *come short* S.V. SHORT *adverb*.]
▸ **A** *noun*. Failure to reach a standard or amount or to fulfil a duty; a defect, a deficiency. Usu. in *pl.* **L15**.

> K. CROSSLEY-HOLLAND There's no-one so perfect that he has no shortcomings. M. MEYER He was so embarrassed by the play's shortcomings that he left before the end.

▸ **B** *adjective*. Defective. *rare*. **L19**.
■ **short-comer** *noun* (*rare*) a person who fails to fulfil a duty **M19**.

shortcrust /ˈʃɔːtkrʌst/ *noun*. **M18**.
[from SHORT *adjective* + CRUST *noun*.]
In full ***shortcrust pastry***. A type of crumbly pastry made with flour and fat.

short-cut /ˈʃɔːtkʌt/ *verb*. Infl. **-tt-**. Pa. t. & pple **-cut**. **E20**.
[from SHORT CUT *noun*[1].]
1 *verb trans.* **a** Overtake by taking a short cut. **E20**. ▸**b** Travel by a short cut. **M20**.
2 *verb intrans. & trans.* (with *it*). Take a short cut. **E20**.

short cut /ʃɔːt ˈkʌt, ˈʃɔːt kʌt/ *noun*[1]. Also **short-cut**. **M16**.
[from SHORT *adjective* + CUT *noun*[2].]
†**1** A short passage or journey. **M16–L17**.
2 A route between two places which shortens the distance travelled; *fig.* a quick way of accomplishing something. **L16**.

> **2** N. SHUTE He made for the Western Highway by a short cut through suburban roads. *Listener* Attempts . . to find short cuts to the process of manufacturing H-bombs.

short cut /ʃɔːt ˈkʌt, ˈʃɔːt kʌt/ *adjective & noun*[2]. Also **short-cut**. **L16**.
[from SHORT *adverb* + CUT *ppl adjective*.]
▸ **A** *adjective*. Cut to a short length. **L16**.
▸ **B** *noun*. **1** A kind of tobacco. **L18**.
2 A ham that is cut short or round. **E20**.

shorten /ˈʃɔːt(ə)n/ *verb*. **ME**.
[from SHORT *adjective* + -EN[5].]
1 *verb trans.* Make shorter, diminish the length or duration of; abridge, contract, curtail. **ME**. ▸**b** Make (time, a journey, etc.) appear shorter by conversation or amusement. **L16**. ▸**c** Diminish in working length; *spec.* hold (a weapon etc.) nearer to the middle so as to deliver a more effective blow or thrust. **L16**. ▸**d** *PHONETICS & PROSODY*. Diminish the duration or stress of (a vowel or syllable). **L16**. ▸†**e** Diminish in number or quantity. **L16–E17**. ▸**f** *HORTICULTURE*. Cut back in pruning. **E18**. ▸**g** Clip (coinage). *rare*. **M19**.
2 *verb intrans.* Grow shorter; diminish in length or duration. Orig. *spec.* of breathing: become shorter or more difficult. **ME**. ▸**b** *verb trans. & intrans.* Of gambling odds, prices: become or make lower; decrease. **L19**.
3 *verb trans.* †**a** Hold in check, restrain. **L16–E18**. ▸†**b** Render (an intention) ineffectual. *rare* (Shakes.). Only in **E17**. ▸**c** Keep from the attainment *of*. *rare*. **M19**.
†**4** *verb trans.* Cause to go short, supply insufficiently. Foll. by *of*, *in*. **L16–E17**.
5 *verb trans.* Make crumbly or friable. **M18**.
6 *verb trans.* Begin to dress (a baby) in short clothes. *arch.* **L19**.
7 *verb intrans.* Esp. of a horse: shorten the stride. Also foll. by *up*. **L20**.

> **1** J. GALSWORTHY He was going to shorten the proposed two months into six weeks. J. RHYS I've had my fur coat shortened. S. TERKEL Driving a cab tends to shorten your life span. **2** *Amateur Gardening* Natural light is important as the days shorten. M. WARNER Talia felt her steps shorten.

Phrases: **shorten in** *NAUTICAL* heave in (an anchor cable) so that a shorter length remains overboard. ***shorten one's grip***: see GRIP *noun*[1]. ***shorten one's stride***: see STRIDE *noun* 1a. **shorten sail(s)** *NAUTICAL* take in some of the sails of a vessel in order to slacken speed. **shorten the arm of**, **shorten the hand of** (in biblical and derived uses) limit the power of.
■ **shortened** *adjective* made shorter, short **L16**. **shortener** *noun* **M16**.

shortening /ˈʃɔːt(ə)nɪŋ/ *noun*. **L15**.
[from prec. + -ING[1].]
1 The action of SHORTEN *verb*; an instance of this. **L15**.
2 Fat or oil used for making pastry, esp. shortcrust pastry. **L18**.

shortfall /ˈʃɔːtfɔːl/ *noun*. **L19**.
[from *fall short* S.V. FALL *verb*.]
A shortage, a deficit below what was expected; a decline, a shortcoming; a loss.

> H. EVANS £2 million was lost in production shortfalls. *New York Times* The shortfall in tax revenue might require budget cuts.

shorthand /ˈʃɔːthand/ *noun, adjective, & verb*. **M17**.
[from SHORT *adjective* + HAND *noun*.]
▸ **A** *noun*. **1** A method of rapid writing by means of abbreviations or symbols, used esp. for taking dictation; stenography. **M17**.
2 Any abbreviated or symbolic mode of expression. **L17**.

> **1** *Pitman's Shorthand*: see PITMAN *noun*[2]. **2** *Spectator* A 'lunchbag' is New York's . . shorthand for a paper-pushing, culture-bashing executive.

▸ **B** *adjective*. Designating a person who uses shorthand; of the nature of shorthand. **M17**.
shorthand typist: who takes dictation in shorthand and then prepares a typed transcription of the text.
▸ **C** *verb trans. & intrans.* Transcribe (text) in shorthand. **M18**.
■ **shorthander** *noun* a writer of shorthand, a stenographer **M18**.

short-handed /ʃɔːtˈhandɪd/ *adjective*. **E17**.
[from SHORT *adjective* + HANDED.]
†**1** Niggardly, mean; inefficient, ineffective. **E–M17**.
2 Lacking workers; undermanned, understaffed. **L18**. ▸**b** *ICE HOCKEY*. Having fewer players on the ice than the opposing team because a penalty has been imposed; (of a goal) scored while a team is short-handed. **M20**.
■ **shorthandedness** *noun* (*rare*) **L19**.

shorthold /ˈʃɔːthəʊld/ *noun & adjective*. **L20**.
[from SHORT *adjective* + HOLD *noun*[1], after *freehold*, *leasehold*, etc.]
(Of or pertaining to) a type of lease or system of tenure in which the tenant agrees to rent a property for a fixed short term and the landlord retains the right to recover the property at the end of the term.

shortia /ˈʃɔːtɪə/ *noun*. **L19**.
[mod. Latin (see below), from Charles W. *Short* (1794–1863), US botanist + -IA[1].]
Any of several small stemless alpine plants constituting the genus *Shortia* (family Diapensiaceae), native to N. Carolina and temperate Asia, with glossy leaves and white, pink, or blue flowers.

shortie *noun & adjective* var. of SHORTY.

short-lived /ʃɔːtˈlɪvd/ *adjective*. **L16**.
[Orig. from SHORT *adjective* + *live* infl. form of LIFE *noun* + -ED[1], later also taken as from SHORT *adverb* + *lived* pa. pple of LIVE *verb*.]
1 Having a short life or existence. **L16**.
2 Lasting only a short time; brief, ephemeral. **L16**. ▸**b** Of a radioisotope or sub-atomic particle: having a relatively short half-life. **E20**.
■ **shortlivedness** *noun* brief duration **E19**.

shortly /ˈʃɔːtli/ *adverb*. **OE**.
[from SHORT *adjective* + -LY[2].]
1 Briefly, concisely, in few words. Formerly also (in full ***shortly to say***), in short. **OE**. ▸**b** Abruptly, curtly, sharply. **E19**.
2 In a short time; not long after; soon. Formerly also, speedily, quickly. **OE**.
3 At a short time *after* or *before*. **M16**.
4 In a limited space or compass. *rare*. **M16**.
5 For a short time. *rare*. **E19**.
6 At a short distance. *rare*. **E20**.

> **1b** D. H. LAWRENCE He laughed shortly, and went on. **2** I. MURDOCH Maisie . . was shortly going to return to America. **3** J. F. HENDRY He left for Italy shortly after their meeting.

shortness /ˈʃɔːtnɪs/ *noun*. **OE**.
[from SHORT *adjective* + -NESS.]
1 The quality or fact of being short in duration, linear extent, etc.; brevity. Opp. ***length***. **OE**. ▸†**b** Brevity or conciseness in speech or writing. **LME–L16**. ▸†**c** A short period of time. **L16–L17**.
2 Defective range or extent of vision or memory. **M17**.
†**3** Defectiveness, imperfection; in *pl.* defects, shortcomings. **M17–M18**.
4 The condition of being short of something; deficiency, lack (of money, food, etc.); scarcity. **M17**.
5 The quality of being short in texture or substance; friability, brittleness. **M17**.
Phrases: **for shortness** (now *rare*) for the sake of brevity, to save time or distance. **shortness of breath** difficulty in breathing, breathlessness.

short-term /ʃɔːt ˈtəːm/ *adjective & adverb*. **E20**.
[from SHORT *adjective* + TERM *noun*.]
▸ **A** *adjective*. Lasting for or pertaining to a relatively short period of time; maturing or becoming effective after a short period. **E20**.
▸ **B** *adverb*. Over or at the end of a short period of time. **M20**.
■ **short-ˈtermer** *noun* a person engaged in an activity for a short time only; *spec.* a person serving a short prison sentence: **M20**. **short-ˈtermism** *noun* concentration on short-term investments, projects, etc., for immediate profit at the expense of long-term security or investment **L20**. **short-ˈtermist** *noun & adjective* (*a*) *noun* an advocate or adherent of short-termism; (*b*) *adjective* of or pertaining to short-termism: **L20**.

shortwards /ˈʃɔːtwədz/ *adverb*. **L20**.
[from SHORT *adjective* + -WARDS.]
PHYSICS. Towards shorter wavelengths; on the short-wavelength side *of*.
■ Also **shortward** *adverb* **L20**.

short-winded /ʃɔːtˈwɪndɪd/ *adjective*. **LME**.
[from SHORT *adjective* + WINDED *adjective*[1].]
1 Liable to difficulty in breathing; soon becoming out of breath with any exertion. **LME**.
2 *transf. & fig.* Incapable of sustained effort; not given to or displaying longwindedness of expression. **L16**.
■ **short-windedness** *noun* **E17**.

shorty /ˈʃɔːti/ *noun & adjective*. *colloq.* Also (esp. in senses A.1, B.) **shortie**. **L19**.
[from SHORT *adjective* + -Y[6], -IE.]
▸ **A** *noun*. **1** (A piece of) shortbread. *Scot.* **L19**.
2 (A nickname for) a person of short stature. **L19**.
3 A drink of spirits; a short drink. Orig. *US*. **M20**.
4 A short story, article, film, etc. **M20**.
5 A short article of clothing; *spec.* (in *pl.*) shorts. **M20**.
▸ **B** *adjective*. Designating products which are shorter than the norm. **M20**.

> P. CORNWALL On the floor at the foot of the bed was a pair of shorty pyjamas.

shosagoto /ʃɒsəˈgəʊtəʊ/ *noun*. Pl. same. **E20**.
[Japanese, from *shosa* acting, conduct + *koto* matter, affair.]
In Japanese kabuki theatre: a dance play, a mime performed to music.

shosha /ˈʃəʊʃə/ *noun*. Pl. same. **L20**.
[Japanese *shōsha* business firm, from *shō* mercantile + *sha* society, company.]
= SOGO SHOSHA.

Shoshone /ʃə(ʊ)ˈʃəʊniː/ *noun & adjective*. **E19**.
[Origin unkn.]
▸ **A** *noun*. Pl. same, **-s**.
1 A member of a N. American Indian people of Wyoming, Idaho, Nevada, and neighbouring States. **E19**.
2 The Uto-Aztecan language of this people. **M19**.
▸ **B** *attrib.* or as *adjective*. Of or pertaining to the Shoshone or their language. **E19**.

Shoshonean /ʃə(ʊ)ˈʃəʊnɪən/ *adjective & noun*. **L19**.
[from prec. + -AN.]
(Of or pertaining to) a branch of the Uto-Aztecan languages including Shoshone. Also, designating or pertaining to (any of) the peoples speaking a Shoshonean language.

shoshonite /ʃəˈʃəʊnʌɪt/ *noun*. **L19**.
[from the *Shoshone* River, Wyoming (cf. SHOSHONE) + -ITE[1].]
GEOLOGY. A variable basaltic rock containing olivine, augite, and labradorite, with potassium feldspar etc.
■ **shoshonitic** /ʃəʊʃəˈnɪtɪk/ *adjective* resembling or consisting of shoshonite **M20**.

shot /ʃɒt/ *noun*[1].
[Old English *sc(e)ot*, *gesc(e)ot* = Old Frisian *skot*, Old Saxon *sīlscot* ballista, Middle Low German *(ge)scot*, Old High German *scoz*, *giscoz* (German *Schoss*, *Geschoss*), Old Norse *skot* (see SCOT *noun*[2]), from Germanic base of SHOOT *verb*.]
▸ **I 1 a** An act of shooting, an instance of firing a gun, cannon, etc. **OE**. ▸**b** The action of shooting with a bow, gun, etc.; the discharge of arrows, bullets, etc.; discharged arrows, bullets, etc., collectively. *arch.* **LME**. ▸**c** *MINING*. An explosion of a blasting charge. **E19**. ▸**d** A photograph; a film sequence photographed continuously by a single camera; the action or process of photographing such a sequence. **L19**. ▸**e** An injection of a drug, vaccine, etc; a specified measure of a drug, vaccine, etc., for injection. *colloq.* (orig. *US*). **E20**. ▸**f** The action or an act of launching a rocket. Chiefly in ***moon-shot***, ***space shot***, etc. **M20**.
2 a A rapid movement or motion. Formerly also, a rush, an onset. *rare*. **OE**. ▸**b** A sudden sharp pain; *dial.* a

sudden attack of an illness. *rare*. LME. ▸†**c** A rush of water. *rare*. LME–L17. ▸**d** A sheet of ice. *obsolete* exc. *dial. rare*. M17.

3 The range, reach, or distance to or at which a thing will carry or be effective. ME.

4 a A place where a fishing net is lowered. *Scot.* Now *rare*. LME. ▸**b** The action or an act of lowering and pulling in a fishing net; a catch of fish made with a fishing net. M19.

5 A discharge from the body, a flux, an issue. Now chiefly *Scot.* LME.

†**6** A result of shooting; *spec.* (**a**) an injury caused by magic or witchcraft (cf. SHOOT *verb* 26b); (**b**) a gunshot wound. Only in L16.

7 a An attempt to hit a target with a missile, esp. a bullet fired from a gun. M17. ▸**b** *fig.* A remark aimed at a person. M19.

8 a An attempt, a try. Also, a random guess. M18. ▸**b** A thing with a chance of success (freq. with specified odds). *colloq.* E20. ▸**c** A single occasion of doing or obtaining something; a turn, a go. *colloq.* (orig. *US*). M20.

9 a CURLING. A delivery of a stone at the tee; a point scored for this. L18. ▸**b** A stroke, kick, etc., in a game using a ball or shuttlecock; (FOOTBALL & HOCKEY etc.) an attempt to drive the ball etc. into goal. M19. ▸**c** In a bumping-race (esp. at Oxford and Cambridge Universities), an attempt to overtake and touch the boat in front. M19. ▸**d** A successful stroke, kick, etc., made by a player in a game using a ball or shuttlecock. Freq. as *interjection* in ***good shot!*** E20.

10 In weaving, a passage of the shuttle across the web. Also (*dial.*), a thread of each colour or kind of yarn. L18.

📖 **1a** DEFOE Several regiments . . never . . fired a shot. SIR W. SCOTT They heard a shot. **b** R. GRAFTON The shot of the Englishmen was long and fierce. **d** I. MCEWAN Shots of Henry . . posing in costume. **e** SLOAN WILSON Someone had given him a shot of morphine. A. LURIE Did you get your allergy shots this week? **3** M. MAGUIRE The camera pulled back as she dashed into shot. **7a** *Field* Seeing a large buck . . I . . prepared to have a long shot at him. P. V. WHITE As the . . hawk flew . . Turner did take a shot at it, but missed. **b** A. STORR Brabantio's parting shot to Othello is 'Look to her, Moor.' **8a** D. L. SAYERS We might have a shot at looking for it. L. P. HARTLEY Wondering how she knew that he was married, or whether it was just a shot. **b** *New Yorker* Proud Birdie, a . . 4–1 shot in the betting, was next to last. **c** W. KENNEDY Francis turned up in Albany . . to register for the Democrats at five dollars a shot.

▶ **II 11** †**a** *collect. sing.* & in *pl.* Missiles, esp. arrows, (to be) discharged from a bow, catapult, or other weapon. Also *sing.* (*rare*), such a missile. OE–M17. ▸**b** *collect. sing.* Missiles, esp. balls or bullets as opp. to shells, (to be) discharged from a gun or cannon by an explosive. Formerly also (*sing.*), such a missile. Freq. with specifying word. LME. ▸**c** A cannon-ball; (treated as *sing.* or *pl.*) cannon-balls. *obsolete* exc. *Hist.* E17. ▸**d** A heavy ball resembling a cannon-ball, (to be) propelled over a long distance as an event in field athletics (freq. in ***putting the shot***); the sporting event in which this is thrown. L19.

†**12** A bolt or bar which is pushed or slid to fasten a door etc. LME–L16.

13 †**a** A charge of powder etc. for a gun. E–M18. ▸**b** *collect. sing.* & in *pl.* Small lead pellets used in quantity in a single charge or cartridge in a shotgun. Also *sing.*, a small lead pellet of this kind. Freq. with specifying word. L18.

14 A charge of powder for a blasting operation in a mine, esp. a coalmine; the bored hole in which such a charge is placed. M19.

📖 **11a** S. BUTLER The Law of Arms doth bar The use of venom'd shot. **b** TENNYSON Storm'd at with shot and shell. ***grape-shot*** etc. **13b** *Target Gun* No criticism could be levelled at the shot in the cartridges. ***bird shot, duck-shot***, etc.

▶ **III 15** †**a** A festival, a feast to which each guest contributed a share. Also, a fixed levy or contribution from each member of a group for a specified purpose. ME–E17. ▸**b** A sum of money owed or due, esp. at a public house or for entertainment, a reckoning; a person's share of such a sum. Now *colloq.* LME. ▸**c** Orig., a supply or amount of drink. Later *spec.* (*colloq.*), a drink of spirits. L17.

📖 **15b** J. R. ACKERLEY 'Another drink? It's my turn.' Millie always paid her shot. **c** *Logophile* I . . took out the bottle of Cutty Sark, and I poured myself a shot.

▶ **IV** †**16** *collect. sing.* & in *pl.* Weapons for shooting; firearms. Also *sing.* (*rare*), a weapon for shooting, a cannon, a musket. LME–E18.

†**17** *collect. sing.* & in *pl.* Soldiers armed with weapons for shooting, esp. firearms. Also *sing.* (*rare*), a soldier armed with a firearm. L16–E18.

18 A person who shoots, esp. in a specified manner. Freq. with specifying word. L18.

▶ **V 19** A division of land. Chiefly *Scot.* L15.

20 = *shot-window* below. *Scot.* Now *rare* or *obsolete*. E16.

21 *Hist.* A corpse illegally exhumed for dissection. E19.

22 A compartment in the stern of a boat used in Shetland. E19.

23 A proposition, a suggestion. Only in ***that's the shot!, the shot!*** below. *Austral. colloq.* M20.

Phrases: **a shot in the arm** *colloq.* (orig. *US*) (**a**) a much-needed stimulus or encouragement; (**b**) an alcoholic drink. ***a shot in one's locker, a shot in the locker***: see LOCKER *noun*. ***big shot***: see BIG *adjective*. **call one's shot** (orig. *US*) (**a**) (BILLIARDS & SNOOKER etc.) say which ball one intends for which pocket; (**b**) *fig.* ***call one's shots***, predict one's course of action. **call the shots** *colloq.* (orig. *US*) make the decisions; be in control; take the initiative. ***Indian shot***: see INDIAN *adjective*. **like a shot** *colloq.* at once, rapidly; without hesitation, willingly. ***long shot***: see LONG *adjective*[1]. ***loose shot***: see LOOSE *adjective*. **make a shot (at)** guess (at). ***mug shot***: see MUG *noun*[3]. ***noddy-shot***: see NODDY *noun*[4]. ***passing shot***: see PASSING *adjective*. ***powder and shot***: see POWDER *noun*[1]. ***shot across the bows***: see BOW *noun*[3] 1. ***shot in the dark***: see DARK *noun*[1] 1. **small shot** (**a**) small lead pellets (sense 13b above), as opp. to bullets; †(**b**) musket bullets as opp. to cannon-balls; (**c**) soldiers armed with small arms as opp. to artillerymen. **that's the shot!, the shot!** *Austral. colloq.* (that is) a good idea. ***wood shot***: see WOOD *noun*[1] 7c. ***zoom shot***: see ZOOM *noun* 2a.

Comb.: **shot alloy** an alloy used for making lead shot, which consists of lead with around 0.9 per cent arsenic; **shot-bag** (chiefly *US*) a bag for carrying shot; a shot-pouch; **shot-blast** *noun & verb* (**a**) *noun* a high-speed stream of steel particles employed in shot-blasting; (**b**) *verb trans.* subject to shot-blasting; **shot-blaster** a person employed in shot-blasting; **shot-blasting** the cleaning of metal etc. by the impact of a high-speed stream of steel particles; **shot-borer** = PINHOLE *borer*; **shot-bush** *US* either of two aralias, the angelica tree, *Aralia spinosa*, and the wild sarsaparilla, *A. nudicaulis*; **shot-drill** *Hist.* a form of military punishment involving drilling while carrying a cannon-ball; **shot effect** a fluctuation in the magnitude of the anode current in thermionic valves etc. due to the random character of electron emission; **shot-firer** (**a**) a person who fires a blasting-charge in a mine etc.; (**b**) an electrical device for detonating a blasting-charge; **shot-firing** the action of detonating a blasting-charge; **shot-free** *adjective* (now *rare*) †(**a**) safe from shot, shotproof; (**b**) scot-free; **shot-glass** *N. Amer.* a small glass in which a drink of spirits is served; **shot gold** (orig. *US*) gold occurring in the form of small spheres like lead shot; ***shot-group***: see GROUP *noun* 1d; **shot line** = ***shot rope*** below; **shotmaker** *US* a person who plays (esp. successful or attacking) strokes in golf, tennis, etc.; **shotmaking** *US* the playing of (esp. successful or attacking) strokes in golf, tennis, etc.; **shotman** (*rare*) (**a**) a person who shoots with a firearm; (**b**) MINING a person employed to place the blasting-charge in a shot-hole; **shot-mark** (*rare*) †(**a**) a mark to aim or shoot at; (**b**) a mark made by a shot; **shot-metal** = ***shot alloy*** above; **shot noise** = ***shot effect*** above; **shot-peen** *verb trans.* subject (a metal part) to shot-peening; **shot-peened** *ppl adjective* (of a metal part) that has been subjected to shot-peening; **shot-peening** the use of a stream of hard metal particles directed against a metal part to harden and strengthen its surface; **shot-pouch** a usu. leather pouch or bag, for carrying shot; **shot-put** the action or an act of shot-putting; this activity as a sporting event; **shot-putter** a person who practises shot-putting; **shot-putting** the action of propelling a heavy ball resembling a cannon-ball a long distance as an event in field athletics; **shot rope** a weighted rope hung over the side of a boat to guide the descent and ascent of a diver; **shot-tower** *Hist.* a tower in which shot was made from molten lead poured through sieves at the top and falling into water at the bottom; **shot-window** (now only *Scot.*) a vertically-hinged window, a casement; a shutter with a few panes of glass at the top.

■ **shotty** *adjective* (**a**) resembling lead shot; hard and round; (**b**) *spec.* (of gold) in the form of small roundish lumps: M19.

†**shot** *noun*[2]. ME–M18.

[Perh. a use of prec.]

NAUTICAL. Two cables spliced together.

shot /ʃɒt/ *ppl adjective*. LME.

[pa. pple of SHOOT *verb*. Cf. SHOTTEN *ppl adjective*.]

1 *gen.* That has shot; that has been shot. LME.

2 (Of a fabric, esp. silk) woven so as to show different colours at different angles; (of a colour etc.) resembling the effect of such a fabric, changeable, interspersed with a different colour. M18.

3 Of a person etc.: wounded or killed by an arrow, bullet, etc., from a bow, gun, etc. M19.

4 Drunk. *slang* (chiefly *US, Austral.*, & *NZ*). M19.

5 Of a person: exhausted. Of a thing: worn out, ruined, used up. *slang* (chiefly *N. Amer.*). M20.

shot /ʃɒt/ *verb*[1]. Infl. **-tt-**. ME.

[from SHOT *noun*[1].]

†**1** *verb intrans.* Participate or consort *with*. Only in ME.

2 *verb trans.* Load (a firearm) with shot. L17.

3 *verb trans.* Weight by attaching a shot or shots. M19.

■ **shotting** *verbal noun* the action of weighting something with shot; *esp.* (ANGLING) the weighting of the line with shot: L19.

shot *verb*[2] *pa. t. & pple* of SHOOT *verb*.

shotcrete /ˈʃɒtkriːt/ *noun*. M20.

[from SHOT *ppl adjective* + CON)CRETE *adjective & noun*.]

BUILDING. = GUNITE.

†**shote** *noun*. ME–L16.

[Rel. to or var. of SHOOT *noun*[1], SHOT *noun*[1].]

The action or an act of shooting; a missile discharged by shooting.

¶ Earlier than corresponding senses of SHOOT *noun*[1], SHOT *noun*[1].

shotgun /ˈʃɒtɡʌn/ *noun, adjective, & verb*. Orig. *US*. E19.

[from SHOT *noun*[1] + GUN *noun*.]

▶ **A** *noun*. **1** A smooth-bore gun for firing small shot at short range, a fowling-piece. E19.

2 *ellipt.* A shotgun house or other building; a shotgun formation. *US*. M20.

1 ***ride shotgun***: see RIDE *verb*.

▶ **B** *attrib.* or as *adjective*. **1** Of, pertaining to, or resembling a shotgun. L19. ▸**b** *spec.* Designating a house or other building with rooms on either side of a long central hallway. *US*. M20.

2 *fig.* Made or done hastily or under pressure of necessity. M20.

Special collocations & comb.: **shotgun formation** AMER. FOOTBALL an offensive formation to facilitate passing in which the quarterback is positioned some yards behind the centre and the other backs are stationed to act as pass receivers or blockers. **shotgun marriage** = ***shotgun wedding*** below; **shotgun microphone** a highly directional microphone with a long barrel to be directed towards a distant source of sound; **shotgun wedding** *colloq.* (orig. *US*) an enforced or hurried wedding esp. because of the bride's pregnancy.

▶ **C** *verb trans.* Infl. **-nn-**.

1 Shoot with a shotgun. *colloq.* (orig. & chiefly *US*). L19.

2 Force as if with a shotgun; bring about forcibly. *colloq.* (orig. & chiefly *US*). M20.

shot-hole /ˈʃɒthəʊl/ *noun*. M18.

[from SHOT *noun*[1] + HOLE *noun*[1].]

1 A hole made by the passage of a shot. M18.

2 A small hole in a fortified wall for shooting through. *arch.* E19.

3 MINING. A hole bored in rock for the insertion of a blasting-charge. L19.

4 A small round hole made in a leaf by a fungus or bacterium, esp. in a fruit tree following an attack of leaf-spot; (more fully ***shot-hole disease***) the disease in which this occurs. L19. ▸**b** A small hole made in wood by a boring insect. E20.

Comb.: **shot-hole borer** = PINHOLE *borer*; ***shot-hole disease***: see sense 4 above; **shot-hole fungus** a fungus which causes shot-hole disease.

Shotokan /ʃə(ʊ)ˈtəʊkan/ *noun*. Also **Shoto-kan**. M20.

[Japanese, from *shō* right, true + *to* way + *kan* mansion.]

One of the five main styles of karate, and now the most widely practised in the UK and a number of other countries. Usu. *attrib.*

shott /ʃɒt/ *noun*. Also **chott**. L19.

[Arab. *šaṭṭ* shore, strand; (in N. Africa) salt lake; (in Iraq) waterway, river.]

A shallow brackish lake or marsh esp. in Algeria and southern Tunisia, usu. dry in summer and covered with saline deposits. Cf. SABKHA.

shotted /ˈʃɒtɪd/ *adjective*. L18.

[from SHOT *noun*[1], *verb*[1]: see -ED[2], -ED[1].]

1 Of metal: formed into small particles by being poured when molten into cold water. L18.

2 Loaded with shot or ball as well as powder. E19.

3 Having a shot or shots attached; *spec.* weighted with shot. M19.

shotten /ˈʃɒt(ə)n/ *ppl adjective*. ME.

[pa. pple (now arch.) of SHOOT *verb*. Cf. SHOT *ppl adjective*.]

1 = SHOT *ppl adjective* 1. Long *rare* or *obsolete* exc. in ***nook-shotten*** s.v. NOOK *noun* and ***shoulder-shotten*** s.v. SHOULDER *noun*. ME.

2 Of a fish, esp. a herring: that has spawned. Also *fig.*, (of a person etc.) weak, wretched (*rare*). LME.

3 Blood-shot. *arch. rare*. LME.

4 Of milk: sour, curdled. *dial.* M17.

2 shotten herring *fig.* (*arch.*) a weakened or dispirited person, a person destitute of strength or resources.

shotten *verb pa. pple*: see SHOOT *verb*.

†**shough** *noun*. L16–L17.

[Origin uncertain: perh. same word as SHOCK *noun*[4] & *adjective*.]

(An animal of) a breed of lap-dog said to originate in Iceland.

📖 SHAKES. *Macb.* Spaniels, curs, Shoughs.

should /ʃʊd/ *noun*. LME.

[from past of SHALL *verb*.]

An utterance or use of the word should; what should be.

should *verb* etc., see SHALL *verb*.

should-be /ˈʃʊdbiː/ *noun & adjective*. L18.

[from past of SHALL *verb* + BE: cf. *would-be*.]

What or that should be.

shoulder /ˈʃəʊldə/ *noun*.

[Old English *sc̄uldor* corresp. to Old Frisian *skuldere*, Middle Low German *schuldere*, Middle & mod. Dutch *schouder*, Old High German *scult(e)r(r)a* (German *Schulter*) from West Germanic, of unkn. origin.]

1 a In the human body, the upper joint of either arm with its integuments and the portion of the trunk between this and the base of the neck; *esp.* the curved upper surface of this; in *pl.*, the upper part of the back and arms. In quadrupeds, the upper part of the forelimb and the adjacent part of the back. Also, the shoulder-joint, the pectoral girdle. OE. ▸**b** The upper part of the wing of a bird or insect, adjoining the point of articulation; the humerus of the wing-case or thorax. M18.

▸**c** *sing.* & *in pl.* The front part of the body of a fish, adjoining the head. **E19.**

2 A person's shoulder regarded as having the function of carrying heavy weights, providing strength, or bearing hardship. Freq. in *pl.* **OE.**

3 The foreleg area of a sheep, pig, etc., cut as a joint of meat for food. **ME.**

4 a That part of a garment which covers a person's shoulder. **ME.** ▸**b** An arched piece of wood or other rigid material placed under the shoulders of a garment that is to be hung up. **L19.**

5 (A part of) something resembling a human shoulder in shape, position, or function; a sudden inward curvature in the outline of something; *spec.* (*a*) a point at which a steep slope descends from a plateau or highland area; (*b*) a projection which serves as a support for a structure; (*c*) the flat surface of printing type from which the raised character projects; (*d*) (in *pl.*) the broadest part of a bunch of grapes; (*e*) in surfing, the unbroken part of a wave at the side; (*f*) a poorly resolved subsidiary maximum in a graph otherwise having a fairly uniform or smoothly varying slope. **LME.**

6 With specifying word: any of several noctuid moths which have a distinctively coloured streak at the base of the leading edge of the forewing. Also more fully ***shoulder moth***. **L19.**

7 The edge of a road; *spec.* = ***hard shoulder*** s.v. **HARD** *adjective, adverb, & noun.* **M20.**

📖 **1a** F. KING Kirsti called out over her shoulder. S. ROSENBERG Asta . . threw an arm around my shoulders, and guided me to a seat. *Men's Health* That supposed male ideal—the V-shaped torso, broad shoulders and slim waist. **2** THACKERAY All the debts are put upon my shoulders. TENNYSON Make broad thy shoulders to receive my weight. J. O. HOBBES Few men . . can bear authority if they haven't been born with the shoulders for it. **5** L. G. GIBBON She could see across the brae's shoulder the red light of Kinraddie House. D. A. THOMAS Cape Ortegal, the north-west shoulder of Spain. **6** ***flame shoulder, tawny shoulder.*** **7** D. LEAVITT Her hands shook and the car veered onto the shoulder.

Phrases: **an old head on young shoulders** a young person as staid or experienced as an elderly one (freq. in ***have an old head on young shoulders, put an old head on young shoulders***). **a shoulder to cry on** a sympathetic and consoling listener to a person's troubles. ***cold shoulder***: see **COLD** *adjective.* **cry on a person's shoulder** pour out one's troubles to a person. **from the shoulder** = ***straight from the shoulder*** below. ***have a chip on one's shoulder***: see **CHIP** *noun.* **HEAD AND SHOULDERS.** ***natural shoulder***: see **NATURAL** *adjective.* **open the shoulders** give free play to the muscles of the shoulders in making a stroke. ***over the left shoulder***: see **LEFT** *adjective.* **put one's shoulder to the wheel** set to work or to a task vigorously. ***rub shoulders***: see **RUB** *verb.* **set one's shoulder to the wheel** = ***put one's shoulder to the wheel*** above. **shoulder to shoulder** side by side, (of soldiers) in close formation; *fig.* with united effort, with mutual cooperation and support. **straight from the shoulder** (of a blow) with the fist brought to the shoulder and then swiftly sent forward; (of a pulling movement) with the arm kept straight. **weep on a person's shoulder** = ***cry on a person's shoulder*** above.

Comb.: **shoulder-bag** a bag with a shoulder-strap that can be carried suspended from the shoulder; **shoulder-belt** a strap passing over one shoulder and under the opposite arm, a bandolier; **shoulder-blade** either of the two flat triangular bones lying over the ribs in the upper part of the back and articulated with the humerus; **shoulder board** either of the two stiffened pieces of material worn at the shoulders of military uniform and bearing the insignia of rank; **shoulder-bone** (now *rare*) = ***shoulder-blade*** above; **shoulder charge** *noun & verb* (*a*) *noun* a charge in which the shoulder is directed at the target; (*b*) *verb trans.* charge at with the shoulder first; †**shoulder-clapper** (*rare*, Shakes.) an officer undertaking the arrest of an offender, a bailiff; **shoulder flash** a shoulder patch or tab (see below); ***shoulder-girdle***: see **GIRDLE** *noun*[1] 4a; **shoulder-height** *adverb* = ***shoulder-high*** *adverb* below; **shoulder-high** *adjective & adverb* up to or as high as the shoulders; **shoulder-holster** a gun holster worn in the armpit suspended from a shoulder-strap; **shoulder-in** HORSEMANSHIP a movement in which a rider bends a horse evenly round inside leg from head to tail, with the animal's legs crossing and the head bent away from the direction of movement; **shoulder-joint** the joint of the shoulder; the articulation by which the humerus of the upper arm or forelimb is connected with the trunk; **shoulder-knot** (*a*) a knot of ribbon, metal, lace, etc., worn on the shoulder often as part of a ceremonial dress; *spec.* = **AGLET** 2b; (*b*) any of several noctuid moths which have a dark streak at the base of the forewing; **shoulder-lappet** ENTOMOLOGY (*a*) = **PATAGIUM** 1; (*b*) = **TEGULA** 1; **shoulder-length** *adjective* (of hair etc.) reaching down to the shoulders; **shoulder line** (*a*) a line drawn on the shoulder of an object; (*b*) the line of a woman's garment over the shoulders; **shoulder loop** *US* the shoulder-strap of an army, air-force, or marine officer; **shoulder mark** *US* the shoulder-strap of a naval officer; **shoulder moth** = sense 6 above; **shoulder-note** PRINTING a note inserted at the top of the side margin of a page; **shoulder-of-mutton** *adjective* resembling a shoulder of mutton, esp. in shape; ***shoulder-of-mutton fist*** (*arch.*), a large heavy fleshy fist; ***shoulder-of-mutton sail***, a triangular sail attached to a mast; **shoulder-pad**: sewn into a garment to make the shoulders appear larger; **shoulder patch**: attached to the shoulder of a garment and bearing an emblem or insignia; **shoulder period** a travel period between peak and off-peak seasons; **shoulder-piece** (*a*) *Hist.* a piece of armour covering the shoulder; (*b*) a piece or pieces of material composing the shoulders of a garment; (*c*) the piece forming the shoulder of a tool etc.; **shoulder plane** CARPENTRY a plane with a narrow mouth and a low-pitched cutter, used on end grain; **shoulder pod** a support for a camera that rests against the shoulder; **shoulder season** = ***shoulder period*** above; **shoulder-shotten** *adjective* (*arch.*) (of an animal) having a strained or dislocated shoulder; **shoulder stand** a gymnastic movement in which the body and legs are held up in the air and supported on the shoulders; **shoulder-strap** (*a*) either of two short straps which go over the shoulders, connecting and supporting the front and back parts of a garment; (*b*) each of the narrow straps fastened on the shoulders of a military tunic; *esp.* an ornamental strap distinguishing the corps and grade of an officer; (*c*) a strap to go over one shoulder as a support for a bag etc. to which it is connected; **shoulder stripe** a geometrid moth, *Anticlea badiata*, which has a dark stripe across the base of the forewing; **shoulder tab** either of the two pieces of material worn at the shoulders of military or other uniform and bearing insignia of rank; **shoulder-tuft** = ***shoulder-lappet*** above; **shoulder wing** a monoplane wing mounted high on the fuselage but not in the highest position.

■ **shoulderless** *adjective* (esp. of a garment) without a shoulder or shoulders **E20.**

shoulder /ˈʃəʊldə/ *verb.* **ME.**

[from the noun.]

1 *verb trans.* **a** Push against with the shoulder; (of a crowd) push shoulder against shoulder; push aside with the shoulder; hustle, jostle. Now usu. with adverb or prepositon phr. **ME.** ▸**b** Rub shoulders with, mix with. *rare.* **M19.**

2 a *verb intrans.* Push with the shoulder; use the shoulders in a struggle etc. (Foll. by *against, at.*) **LME.** ▸**b** *verb intrans. & trans.* Make (one's way) by pushing with the shoulders. W. adverbial or prepositional phr. **L16.**

3 *verb trans.* Provide or fit (a thing) with a shoulder; cut a shoulder or shoulders on. Also foll. by *down, up.* **LME.**

4 *verb trans.* Of soldiers: drive back (an opposing force); manoeuvre, turn. **L16.**

†**5 a** *verb trans.* Put (soldiers etc.) shoulder to shoulder in close rank. Also foll. by *up.* **L16–E17.** ▸**b** *verb intrans.* Stand shoulder to shoulder. **E17–L18.**

6 *verb trans.* Place, support, or carry on the shoulder or shoulders; *spec.* (of a racehorse) carry (a specified weight) on the back. Also (*fig.*), take on (a burden, responsibility, etc.). **L16.**

7 *verb trans.* MILITARY. Place (a weapon etc.) on the shoulder. **L16.**

8 *verb intrans.* Of a hill, structure, etc.: form a shoulder, project as or spread out into a shoulder. Also foll. by *out, up.* **E17.**

9 *verb trans.* **a** Of a coach-driver etc.: take up (passengers) on one's own account without consulting the proprietor. *arch. slang.* **E19.** ▸**b** Embezzle (another's money). *arch. slang.* **M19.**

📖 **1a** M. KEANE Andrew got between them, almost shouldering Nicandra out of his way. *transf.*: COLERIDGE Walls of rock . . shouldering back the billows. *fig.*: *Literary Review* Roy . . was shouldered . . into a ménage that persisted over four years. **2b** M. DUGGAN Harry watched a few people shouldering through the rain. *fig.*: Q. BELL Shouldering his way through the horrors of a British public school. **6** B. CHATWIN The bearers had shouldered the coffin and were advancing. F. KAPLAN Used to shouldering the burdens of leadership. N. HERMAN Mary had shouldered the role as her mother's deputy. **8** C. D. SIMAK Great humps of rock that shouldered out of the contour of the land.

Phrases: **shoulder arms** (*a*) hold one's rifle in a nearly vertical position, the barrel resting against the shoulder and the butt in the hollow of the hand (freq. in *imper.*); (*b*) CRICKET hold the bat over one's shoulder to let the ball pass without attempting a stroke.

■ **shouldering** *noun* (*a*) the action of the verb; (*b*) a thing which projects or supports as a shoulder: **LME.**

shouldered /ˈʃəʊldəd/ *adjective.* **ME.**

[from **SHOULDER** *noun, verb*: see **-ED**[2], **-ED**[1].]

†**1** Scaly. Only in **ME.**

2 Having shoulders; provided or fitted with shoulders, esp. of a specified kind. Chiefly as 2nd elem. of comb., as ***broad-shouldered, round-shouldered***, etc. **LME.**

3 Having a shoulder or projection; made with a shoulder or shoulders. **L17.**

4 Placed and carried at, on, or over the shoulder. **M18.**

3 shouldered arch ARCHITECTURE a form of head for an opening somewhat resembling the outline of a person's shoulders and part of the neck.

†**shoupiltin** *noun. Shetland.* **E18–L19.**

[from Old Norse *sjór* sea + *piltr* boy.]

A Triton; a water-spirit or demon.

shouse /ʃaʊs/ *noun. Austral. slang.* **M20.**

[Contr. of ***shit-house*** (a) s.v. **SHIT** *noun.*]

A privy, a lavatory.

shout /ʃaʊt/ *noun*[1]. *obsolete* exc. *dial.* **ME.**

[Prob. from Middle Dutch *schûte*: cf. **SCHUIT**, **SCOUT** *noun*[2].]

A flat-bottomed boat.

shout /ʃaʊt/ *noun*[2] & *verb.* **LME.**

[Perh. rel. to **SHOOT** *verb*: cf. Old Norse *skúta, skúti* a taunt (see **SCOUT** *verb*[2]).]

▶ **A** *noun.* **1 a** A loud cry expressing joy, pain, etc., or to attract attention at a distance; *transf.* any loud noise which attracts attention. **LME.** ▸**b** Among black Americans, a form of dancing accompanied by loud singing of religious origin; a song of the type sung during such a performance. *US.* **M19.**

2 Orig., a call to a waiter to refill the glasses of a group. Now, one's turn to buy a round of drinks. *colloq.* **M19.**

📖 **2** P. BARKER Audrey picked up her empty glass and said, 'My shout'.

Phrases: **in with a shout** *colloq.* having a chance.

Comb.: **shout-up** *colloq.* a noisy argument.

▶ **B** *verb.* **1** *verb intrans.* Utter a loud call or cry expressive of joy, pain, etc., or to attract attention, incite to action, etc.; *rare* (of a place or thing) resound with shouts, make a loud noise. **LME.** ▸**b** *verb trans.* Bring into a specified state by shouting. **L19.**

2 *verb trans.* Utter with a loud voice (also foll. by *out*); *dial.* proclaim the marriage banns of. **LME.**

3 *verb intrans.* Foll. by *at*, †*on*: attack verbally with angry shouts, insult or scold loudly. **LME.** ▸**b** *verb trans.* Foll. by *down*: reduce to silence by shouts of disapproval or derision. **E20.**

4 *verb trans.* Shout at with derision or welcome; insult or acclaim loudly. Now *rare* or *obsolete* exc. *Scot.* **LME.**

5 *verb trans.* Call; summon or urge by shouting. (Foll. by *in, on, out, up.*) *dial.* **L18.**

6 *verb intrans. & trans.* Buy a round of (drinks); treat (a person or group) *to* or to something. *Austral. & NZ colloq.* **M19.**

7 a *verb intrans.* Be unmistakably significant or relevant; speak to the point. *US slang.* **L19.** ▸**b** *verb trans.* Indicate plainly. **M20.**

📖 **1** SWIFT I called and shouted with the utmost strength of my voice. **b** *refl.*: H. S. MERRIMAN He waved his silk hat and shouted himself hoarse. **2** T. HARDY Mr. Swancourt shouted out a welcome to Knight. C. S. FORESTER 'I'll thank you, sir!' shouted Edrington with lungs of brass. R. K. NARAYAN I could hear my classmates shouting their lessons in unison. **3** G. DALY He flew into a rage, shouting and cursing at Gabriel. **b** V. S. PRITCHETT He was . . despot in the family, shouting his wife down. **6** G. LORD I'll shout everyone a hamburger in Coolbarah. **7b** CLIVE JAMES In purple-starred gold letters as high as itself the car shouts a single word—MITCH.

Phrases: ***shout the odds***: see **ODDS** *noun pl.* **within shouting distance** = ***within hailing distance*** s.v. **DISTANCE** *noun.*

Comb.: **shouting match** a loud altercation.

■ **shouting** *ppl adjective* (*a*) that shouts; (*b*) *US* designating a religious (esp. Methodist) sect whose worship is characterized by shouting: **E17.** **shoutingly** *adverb* vociferously **E19.**

shouter /ˈʃaʊtə/ *noun.* **L17.**

[from **SHOUT** *verb* + **-ER**[1].]

1 a A person who shouts or cries out loudly; a person expressing loud acclaim or welcome. **L17.** ▸**b** A person who loudly supports a particular political candidate. *US* (now *rare* or *obsolete*). **L19.**

2 (**S-**.) ▸**a** *Hist.* A member of a Methodist sect found in the north of Ireland in the 18th cent. whose religious worship was characterized by leaping and shouting. **E19.** ▸**b** A member of a Baptist sect in the W. Indies influenced by African religious practices. **M20.**

3 A person who buys a round of drinks etc. *Austral. & NZ colloq.* **M19.**

4 A person who participates in a shout (see **SHOUT** *noun*[2] 1b); a gospel-singer; a blues-singer. *US.* **M19.**

shove /ʃʌv/ *noun*[1]. **LME.**

[from the verb.]

1 An act of shoving; a forcible or rough thrust or push. **LME.** ▸**b** *fig.* An impulse given to make a person or thing act more quickly; an exertion of influence to help a person; a hint. **E18.**

†**2** An onset, an attack. **LME–L15.**

3 A forward movement of packed and piled ice in a thawing river. *Canad.* **M19.**

4 ***the shove***, dismissal from employment. *slang.* **L19.**

📖 **1** J. WYNDHAM A slight shove on his chest sent him staggering back. **b** R. RENDELL He must . . avoid pushing witnesses. Guide them, yes, but not give them enthusiastic shoves.

shove /ʃʌv/ *noun*[2]. **L17.**

[App. alt. of **SHIVE** *noun*[2], perh. assim. to prec.]

The woody core of flax or hemp; in *pl.* fragments of the stems of flax or hemp broken off when beating.

shove /ʃʌv/ *verb.*

[Old English *scūfan* = Old Frisian *skūva*, Middle Low German, Middle Dutch *schūven* (Dutch *schuiven*), Old High German *scioban* (German *schieben*), Gothic *afskiuban* push away, from Germanic. Cf. **SCUFFLE** *verb*[1], **SHUFFLE** *verb.*]

1 *verb trans.* **a** Thrust away with violence; throw (into prison etc.). *arch.* **OE.** ▸†**b** Thrust (a weapon etc.) *into, through*, etc. **ME–L16.** ▸†**c** Reject, banish; dismiss from an office or position, a society, etc. **ME–M17.**

2 a *verb trans. & intrans.* Launch (a boat) by pushing at the stern; push (one's vessel) away from the bank. Freq. foll.

by *off*. OE. ▸**b** *verb intrans.* Of a person: leave, go away; move. Usu. foll. by *off*. *colloq.* M19.

3 *verb intrans.* Push vigorously, apply force against an object in order to move it. Also foll. by *at*. OE.

4 *verb intrans.* **a** Push one's way forward or onward; move forcefully. Now *esp.* push about roughly in a crowd, make one's way by jostling or elbowing. OE. ▸†**b** Make an attack with violence; charge. ME–L15. ▸**c** Protrude, project. *rare.* M19.

5 *verb trans.* Move or force (a person, heavy object, etc.) by pushing hard or roughly; drive, propel or impel with vigour. (Foll. by *into*, *out of*, *over*, etc.) ME. ▸**b** Throw *down* with a push. ME.

6 *verb trans.* **a** Force into or out of a situation; oblige or compel (a person) to adopt a course of action etc.; impose (a thing) forcibly (formerly also surreptitiously) on a person LME. ▸**b** Move or slide (something) along a surface etc. Foll. by *away*, *down*, *up*, etc. M17. ▸**c** Put casually or hastily in a particular place; thrust *aside* or *away*. Also, write (*down*) quickly or without much thought. *colloq.* E19.

7 *verb trans.* Push (a person) roughly with one's body or elbows; knock against, jostle. M16.

8 *verb intrans.* Of river-ice: move forward so as to become more compact. Cf. SHOVE *noun*[1] 3. *Canad.* M19.

9 *verb trans.* (usu. with *it*). Leave; desist from (a course of action). Usu. in *imper. slang.* M20.

> 🕮 **2b** *Best of Buster Monthly* Oi! You two! Shove off! Fishing's not allowed here! **3** C. PRIEST I shoved at the door with my shoulder; it moved slightly. **4a** M. FRAYN 'Jolly good,' he cried, shoving past dowdy departmental wives like a rugby forward. A. LURIE I was appalled by . . all those people pushing and shoving. **5** G. SWIFT The guards pulled me on to my feet and I was shoved along the corridor. R. J. CONLEY Colvert shoved the door all the way . . to the wall to be sure that no-one was . . behind it. **6a** J. MOYNAHAN The owners are being shoved out of their places by . . the industrial masses. C. LASCH This dogma enabled the teacher . . to shove them into more courses in manual training. **b** J. AGEE Jimmy shoved a stick under the snake and flipped him. **c** J. WAINWRIGHT He shoved his left hand into the pocket of his trousers. ALAN BENNETT Shove the kettle on. *What Diet & Lifestyle* To have maximum appeal, you just shove the word 'natural' onto the container.

Phrases: ***shove one's oar in***: see OAR *noun*. **shove the queer** *arch. slang* pass counterfeit money. ***when push comes to shove***: see PUSH *verb*.

Comb.: †**shoveboard** = SHOVELBOARD; **shove-groat** (*obsolete* exc. *Hist.*) = SHOVELBOARD; **shove-halfpenny**, **-ha'penny** a game similar to shovelboard, played with coins etc. on a table; **shove-net** a fishing net with a broad mouth expanded by means of a frame, worked by pushing along a river-bed or through shallow seawater.

shovel /ˈʃʌv(ə)l/ *noun & verb*[1].

[Old English *scofl* corresp. to Middle & mod. Low German *schuffel*, Middle Dutch *schof(f)el* (Dutch *schoffel*) shovel, hoe (parallel forms with long vowel include Old High German *scūvala* (German *Schaufel*)), from Germanic base of SHOVE *verb*: see -EL[1].]

▸ **A** *noun.* **1** A spadelike tool, consisting of a broad blade, esp. with the sides curved upwards, attached to a handle and used for moving quantities of earth, coal, etc. OE. ▸**b** A shovelful. L19.

2 = ***shovel hat*** below. M19.

3 A person using a shovel. M19.

4 MILITARY. A device fitted to a field-gun to act as a brake to lessen the recoil. L19.

> 🕮 **1** P. FITZGERALD Sergei . . snatched up a shovel . . and scooped out a heap of red-hot charcoal. ***call a spade a bloody shovel***: see SPADE *noun*[1]. **shovel and broom** *rhyming slang* (chiefly *US*) a room. ***fire-shovel***: see FIRE *noun*.

Comb.: **shovel hat** a black felt hat with a low round crown and a broad brim turned up at the sides, worn esp. by some clergymen; **shovel-hatted** *adjective* wearing a shovel hat; *transf.* of or pertaining to the ideas of a wearer of a shovel hat; **shovelhead**, **shovelhead shark** = ***bonnethead*** s.v. BONNET *noun*; **shovel-man** a labourer who uses a shovel; **shovelnose**, **shovelnose ray**, **shovelnose shark** any of various bottom-dwelling fishes of the family Rhinobatidae, esp. of the genera *Rhinobatos* and *Rhynchobatus*, which are intermediate between sharks and skates; also called ***guitar-fish***, ***sand shark***; **shovelnose sturgeon** a freshwater sturgeon, *Scaphirhynchus platorynchus*, which has a broad flattened snout and is found in the Mississippi river system of N. America; **shovel pass** AMER. FOOTBALL an under-arm forward or lateral pass made with a shovelling movement of the arms; **shovel-penny** = SHOVELBOARD; **shovel-plough** an implement for clearing cornland of weeds; **shovel-stirrup**: having a broad rest for the foot and extending behind the heel.

▸ **B** *verb.* Infl. **-ll-**, ***-l-**.

1 *verb trans.* Take up and remove with a shovel; *transf.* shift or clear as rubbish. Foll. by *away*, *off*, *out*, etc. LME.

2 *verb trans.* Excavate, dig up (earth etc.), dig (a hole etc.) with a shovel. Later also, turn *over* with a shovel. L15.

3 *verb intrans.* Intrude. *obsolete* exc. *dial.* M16.

4 *verb trans.* **a** Throw or pile (earth, coal, etc.) *into*, *on*, etc., with or as with a shovel; *colloq.* load or move (esp. food) in large quantities or roughly. E17. ▸**b** Gather *up* in quantities as with a shovel. L17.

5 *verb intrans.* Use a shovel. L17.

> 🕮 **1** S. SMILES The labourers were at work shovelling away the snow. **4** N. FARAH They shovelled earth on to the grave. P. FARMER He ate, shovelling his food up into his mouth in huge forkfuls.

■ **shovelful** *noun* the amount contained in a shovel; as much as a shovel will hold: M16. **shovelling** *noun* (*a*) the action of the verb; (*b*) a thing which is shovelled up (usu. in *pl.*): LME.

shovel /ˈʃʌv(ə)l/ *verb*[2] *intrans.* Long *rare.* Infl. **-ll-**, ***-l-**. LME.

[App. frequentative of SHOVE *verb*. Cf. SHUFFLE *verb*.]

Move while dragging the feet; walk languidly or lazily.

shovelard /ˈʃʌv(ə)lɑːd/ *noun.* Long *rare* or *obsolete* exc. *dial.* LME.

[from SHOVEL *noun* + -ARD, perh. after MALLARD.]

A spoonbill.

shovelboard /ˈʃʌv(ə)lbɔːd/ *noun.* Also **shuffle-** /ˈʃʌf(ə)l-/. M16.

[Alt. of earlier †*shoveboard*.]

1 A game, now played esp. on a ship's deck, by pushing coins or discs with the hand or with the shaped end of a long-handled implement over a surface marked with lines or squares. M16.

2 †**a** More fully ***shovelboard shilling***. A shilling used in the original game of shovelboard. L16–E17. ▸**b** A table on which shovelboard is played. Also ***shovelboard table***. Now *rare.* E17.

shoveler /ˈʃʌv(ə)lə/ *noun*[1]. Also **-veller**. LME.

[Alt. of SHOVELARD.]

†**1** A spoonbill. LME–L18.

2 Any of several dabbling ducks of the genus *Anas* which have broad and long spatulate bills; *esp.* (more fully ***common shoveler***, ***northern shoveler***) *A. clypeata*, which occurs throughout Eurasia and N. America. Also ***shoveler duck***. L17.

shoveler *noun*[2] see next.

shoveller /ˈʃʌv(ə)lə/ *noun*[1]. Also ***-veler**. LME.

[from SHOVEL *verb*[1] + -ER[1].]

A person who works with a shovel.

shoveller *noun*[2] var. of SHOVELER *noun*[1].

shover /ˈʃʌvə/ *noun*[1]. E16.

[from SHOVE *verb* + -ER[1].]

1 A person who or thing which shoves. E16.

2 A person who passes counterfeit money. *arch. slang.* M19.

shover /ˈʃʌvə/ *noun*[2]. *joc.* E20.

[Alt.]

= CHAUFFEUR *noun* 2.

show /ʃəʊ/ *noun*[1]. Also †**shew**. ME.

[from the verb.]

▸ **I 1** The action or an act of exhibiting or presenting something; (a) display. Now *rare* exc. in phrs. below. ME. ▸**b** *spec.* A demonstration or display of military strength or of intention to take severe measures. Chiefly in ***make a show***. M16.

2 a A deceptive, unreal, or illusory appearance of some quality, feeling, activity, etc.; a feigned or misleading display; simulation, pretence. Also, a half-hearted or inadequate attempt or offer. E16. ▸**b** A genuine appearance or display *of* some quality, feeling, activity, etc. L16. ▸**c** Ostentatious display. Earliest in ***of show*** below. L16.

3 a *gen.* External appearance; the visual aspect of a person or thing. Now *rhet.* or *poet.* M16. ▸**b** A specified appearance; *spec.* a fine or striking appearance, an imposing display. Chiefly in ***make a show***, ***make a fine show***, ***make a good show***, etc. L16. ▸**c** An opportunity for achieving or displaying something; a chance, a possibility. Freq. in ***give a show***, ***have a show***. Now *US*, *Austral.*, *& NZ.* L16.

4 a An indication, sign, or trace *of* something. Now only in neg. contexts. M16. ▸**b** An appearance or prospect of something to come. *obsolete* exc. *dial.* M17. ▸**c** An indication of the presence of metal in a mine, oil in a well, etc. Also (*Austral.*), a mine. *US & Austral.* M18.

> 🕮 **2a** L. GRANT-ADAMSON Once they left the hotel his show of concern for her was dropped. CLIVE JAMES His co-pilot made a great show of understanding the map. **b** S. BELLOW Iva, with a show of temper unusual for her, banged on the wall. M. EDWARDES A partial walkout at Longbridge with some show of support from other factories. **3b** B. PYM The dahlias round the mausoleum made quite a show. **c** A. D. RICHARDSON As long as there is any show for us, we shall fight you. **4a** SIR W. SCOTT No show or sign of greeting passed between the Earls.

▸ **II 5** A large display of objects for public viewing; *esp.* a temporary exhibition of a collection of pictures, objects, animals, etc., arranged for public inspection or purchase, or for a competition. L15. ▸**b** A display *of* objects casually brought or found together. *rare.* L17.

6 A person or thing exhibited or displayed as an object of interest; *transf.* a person whose unusual appearance attracts attention, curiosity, or mockery. M16. ▸†**b** A thing presented or exhibited as a specimen or sample. L16–M17.

7 a A large spectacle organized as an entertainment; a pageant, a procession, a ceremony. M16. ▸**b** An exhibition or entertainment featuring strange objects, wild animals, dancers, acrobats, etc., often held at a fair with a small charge for admission. Also, a booth or building where such a show is held. M18. ▸**c** Any public display or entertainment; *spec.* (*a*) a dramatic (esp. musical) performance in a theatre; (*b*) a showing of a film in a cinema. M19. ▸**d** A light entertainment programme on television or radio; *gen.* (*N. Amer.*) any broadcast. M20.

8 *gen.* A sight, a spectacle. Usu. with specifying word. L16.

9 A vision, an apparition. Long *rare* or *obsolete.* E17.

10 A matter, an affair, a concern. Also, a body or collection of people. *colloq.* L18.

11 A battle, a raid; a war. *Military slang.* L19.

> 🕮 **5** *Lancashire Life* Others who have his pictures include Lord Rhodes . . who has opened shows for him. ***cat show***, ***dog show***, ***flower show***, etc. **6** G. CRABBE That marble arch, our sextons's favourite show. **7b** R. DAVIES A Fat Lady . . is almost a necessity for a show like Wanless's. ***Punch-and-Judy show***, ***puppet-show***, etc. **c** S. BOOTH Hours before the show, kids were crowding outside. K. VONNEGUT He never . . took her on trips or to a show. **d** A. ROAD *Doctor Who* is a show with a reputation for encouraging young writers. **8** WORDSWORTH That one upright twig . . Studded with apples, a beautiful show! **10** *Banker* A central book-entry clearing system to keep the whole show in order.

▸ **III** *techn.* **12** MEDICINE. A discharge of blood-tinged mucus from the vagina as a forerunner of labour or menstruation. M18.

13 MINING. A lambent blue flame appearing above the ordinary flame of a candle or lamp when methane is present. Now *rare* or *obsolete.* M19.

14 HORSE-RACING. The third place in a race. Freq. *attrib. N. Amer.* E20.

Phrases: **all over the show** *colloq.* = ***all over the shop*** s.v. SHOP *noun*. **a show of hands** an indication of opinion etc. among a group of people by the raising of hands. **bad show!**, **poor show!**: expr. dismay or disapproval. **big show** *Military slang* a major battle campaign. **for show** for the sake of (mere) appearance or display. **get the show on the road** *colloq.* get started, begin an undertaking. **give the show away**, **give the whole show away** reveal the inadequacies or the truth of a matter. **good show!** expr. pleasure or approval. **have a show of** (long *arch.*) have the appearance of. **in show** in appearance; ostensibly, seemingly. ***Lord Mayor's Show***: see LORD *noun*. **make a show** assume a deceptive appearance; pretend; (see also senses 1b, 3b above). **make a show of** (*a*) make a half-hearted attempt at (doing something); (*b*) exhibit for public viewing; *esp.* expose to public mockery or contempt. †**of show** suitable for display; fine, splendid. **on show** being exhibited; on view. ***passing show***: see PASSING *adjective*. ***poor show!***: see ***bad show!*** above. **put on a good show** give a good account of oneself; do well. **put on a poor show** give a poor account of oneself; do poorly. **put on a show**, **put up a show** present a good appearance concealing the reality; put a good or brave face on something. **put up a good show** = ***put on a good show*** above. **put up a poor show** = ***put on a poor show*** above. **run one's own show** *colloq.* be independent. ***run the show***: see RUN *verb*. ***steal the show***: see STEAL *verb*. ***stop the show***: see STOP *verb*. **the show must go on** things must carry on as planned despite difficulty etc.

Comb.: **show band** a jazz band which performs with verve and theatrical extravagance; a band which plays cover versions of popular songs; **showbiz** *colloq.* = ***show business*** below; **showbizzy** *adjective* (*colloq.*) characteristic of show business; **showboat** *US* a river steamer on which theatrical performances are given; *colloq.* a show-off; **showboater** *US* an actor on or manager of a showboat; **showboating** *US* the activity of giving theatrical performances on a showboat; **show-box** a box in which objects of curiosity are exhibited; *esp.* a box containing a peep-show; **show business** the entertainment industry, esp. theatrical light entertainment; **show-card**: used for advertising; **showcase** *noun & verb* (*a*) *noun* a glass case for exhibiting delicate or valuable articles in a shop, museum, etc.; *fig.* a place or medium for presenting something (esp. attractively) to general attention; (*b*) *verb trans.* display in or as in a showcase; **show flat**: decorated and furnished for exhibition as an advertisement to prospective buyers; **showfolk** = ***show-people*** below; **showgirl** (*a*) an actress who sings and dances in a musical, variety show, etc., *esp.* one selected more for looks than ability; (*b*) a model, a mannequin; **show-glass** a glass case for exhibiting valuable or delicate objects; **show home** = ***show house*** (d) below; **show house** †(*a*) a shop or other building in which wares are displayed; (*b*) a house noted for its architectural beauty, splendid furniture, etc., *esp.* one open to the public for viewing at certain times; (*c*) a building used for staging theatrical performances; a travelling theatre; (*d*) a house decorated and furnished for exhibition as an advertisement to prospective buyers, usu. on a new estate; **showjump** *verb intrans.* [back-form.] compete in showjumping competitions; **showjumper** a horse or rider competing in showjumping competitions; **showjumping** the sport of riding a horse over a prepared course of fences and other obstacles, with penalty points for errors; **show-people**: connected with the presentation or performance of a show; **show-piece** (*a*) an item presented for exhibition or display; (*b*) an outstanding example or specimen; **show-place** †(*a*) a place for public shows or spectacles, a theatre; (*b*) a mansion, estate, etc., which is regularly open to the public for viewing; a place much visited for its beauty, antiquities, etc.; **showreel** *Hist.* a short television or cinema programme or film; **showroom** (*a*) a room in a factory, office building, etc., used for the display of goods or merchandise; (*b*) (usu. in *pl.*) the rooms in a large mansion which are regularly open to the public for viewing; **show-stopper** in a show, a performer, song, or item receiving prolonged applause;

fig. anything which draws great attention and admiration; **show-stopping** *adjective* receiving prolonged applause or admiration; **show trial** a judicial trial accompanied by great publicity; *spec.* a prejudged trial of political dissidents, esp. by a communist government; **show tune** a popular tune from a light musical entertainment; **show-window** a shop window in which goods are displayed; **show-woman** a woman who runs a show or who is employed to display goods etc.; a female guide; **show wood** the exposed wood of the frame of an upholstered chair.

■ **showance** *noun* (*rare*) display, appearance L19. †**showish** *adjective* = SHOWY L17–M18.

show /ʃəʊ/ *noun*². *Scot. & dial.* M18.
[Var.]
= SHOVE *noun*².

show /ʃəʊ/ *verb*. Pa. pple **shown** /ʃəʊn/, **showed** /ʃəʊd/. Also (*arch.*) **shew**, pa. pple **shewn**, **shewed**.
[Old English *scēawian* = Old Frisian *skawia*, *skowia*, *schoia*, Old Saxon *skawon* (Dutch *schouwen*), Old High German *scouwōn* (German *schauen*), from West Germanic weak verb meaning 'see, look'.]

▸ **I** †**1** *verb trans.* Look at, gaze on; inspect, consider; reconnoitre (land etc.); read or find (in a book). OE–ME.

▸ **II** Make known by statement or argument.

†**2** *verb trans.* Award or assign (*to* a person) in a legal or formal manner; fix or appoint authoritatively; decree (*that*). In later use *Scot.* OE–M16.

3 *verb trans.* **a** Point out, reveal; make clear or explain (*that*, *what*, etc.). Orig. also, confess (one's sins). ME. ▸**b** Teach (a person); instruct in a skill or course of action by example. (Foll. by *how*, †*to*.) M16.

4 *verb trans.* **a** Communicate, announce, tell, (a fact, story, etc.); describe, give an account of. (Foll. by †*that*.) *arch.* ME. ▸**b** Now chiefly LAW. State, allege, plead, (a cause, reason, etc.). ME. ▸†**c** Tell or inform (a person) *of* something. ME–L16. ▸**d** Set out or allege in a legal document. LME.

5 *verb trans.* Prove or demonstrate (a fact or statement) by argument, experiment, etc.; prove (a person or thing) to be something. Also foll. by *that*. ME.

6 *verb trans.* Of a thing: be proof or an indication of. Also foll. by *that*, *to be*. ME.

> 🕮 **3a** A. LIVINGSTONE Nietzsche could praise intelligence while showing the ambiguity of all its achievements. ANTHONY SMITH Innumerable . . memories have been shown as wrong when confronted with the facts. P. FITZGERALD The books showed that the . . business would have to be wound down. **b** D. PROFUMO He showed the boy how to operate the hand-line. **6** J. CONRAD A businesslike air about him . . showed he had been on such service before.

▸ **III** Cause or allow to be seen.

7 a *verb trans.* Present or display (an object) in order that it may be looked at; expose to view; exhibit (*to* a person). Also foll. by double obj. ME. ▸**b** *verb refl.* Present oneself (*to* a person or persons) to be looked at; appear, become visible; allow oneself to be seen. ME. ▸**c** *verb trans.* Display in a specified condition or with a specified appearance. ME. ▸**d** *verb trans.* Exhibit (a sign); work (a miracle). *arch.* ME. ▸**e** *verb trans.* Hold up or place (a light) where it can be seen as a signal etc. LME. ▸**f** *verb trans.* Hang out or unfurl (a banner, ensign, etc.). Also foll. by †*out*. LME. ▸**g** *verb trans.* Exhibit (a spectacle, interesting object, etc.) for the amusement of the public; make a show of. Also, perform (a play, trick, etc.) for (a person). L15. ▸**h** *verb trans.* Exhibit (a picture, animal, etc.) in a show or competition. M19. ▸**i** *verb trans.* Display or present (a film, television programme, slide, etc.) on a screen for public viewing. E20. ▸**j** *verb intrans.* Of an artist, fashion designer, etc.: hold an exhibition of one's work. E20.

8 *verb trans.* Produce or submit for inspection (something in one's possession); *spec.* (**a**) produce (a legal document etc.) for official inspection; (**b**) exhibit (something) as proof of possession; (**c**) *fig.* present or demonstrate (an achievement, historical record, etc.). ME.

†**9** *verb trans.* Bring or put forward for some purpose or use. ME–M17.

†**10** *verb trans.* Perform openly (a deed, feat, etc.); demonstrate (something declared or proposed) to be carried out. ME–M18.

11 *verb trans.* **a** Enable (a person) to discover or identify (a place or object) by pointing to it or taking him or her to a place where it can be seen; point out or indicate the parts or features of (a town, building, etc.) *to* (a person). ME. ▸**b** Guide or lead (a person) *to*, *into*, *over*, or *through* a place, house, etc. LME. ▸**c** With double obj.: let (a person) read or examine (a book etc.); bring to (a person's) notice. L17.

12 *verb trans.* **a** Of a plant, season, etc.: display, cause to appear (fruit, flowers, etc.). ME. ▸**b** Of the moon, sun, stars, etc.: display or shine (light). LME. ▸**c** Of an animal or plant: exhibit (colour, beauty, etc.). M17.

13 *verb trans.* Allow (esp. a part of the body) to be seen; reveal, expose (a feature, mark, etc.); serve to exhibit or indicate. ME. ▸†**b** Wear or display (an expression, look, etc.) of a specified sort. LME–L16. ▸**c** Of a list, instrument, etc.: be found on inspection to indicate. M19.

14 *verb trans.* Display deliberately or ostentatiously in order to gain attention or admiration. E16.

15 *verb trans.* Represent in art, sculpture, or film. M17.

> 🕮 **7a** G. M. FRASER She smiled back timidly, showing rather pretty teeth. **g** C. P. SNOW I'm just showing your mother some tricks. **h** R. BERTHOUD Some Moores were shown at the Musée des Beaux Arts. **i** L. SPALDING Mr. Ray Jerome Baker . . is going to show a travel film. W. MCILVANNEY The television was showing some kind of afternoon chat-show. **8** *Raritan* Employers came under pressure to show a profit. **11a** S. LEACOCK He took me about his place, to show it to me. *fig.*: E. G. WHITE Show me a man's books . . and I will show you the man himself. **b** J. DICKEY A fellow in white showed us into the ward where Lewis was. E. NORTH 'This is a very fine room,' said Campbell on being shown into the study. **13** N. FREELING A white blouse will show the blood. G. GREENE A tall . . figure in an out-dated skirt which showed to advantage her fine ankles. **c** I. WALLACE His watch . . showed sixteen minutes after five o'clock. **14** *refl.*: M. KEANE I had meant to . . pivot about and show myself from every side to papa. **15** K. CLARK There is a marginal drawing by Holbein, showing Erasmus at his desk. D. PIPER All Surrey's portraits show him as courtier and aristocrat.

▸ **IV** Exhibit or manifest by outward signs.

16 *verb trans.* Display, indicate, or allow to be seen (some inward quality, condition, sign, etc.) by outward appearance or behaviour; *refl.* exemplify a specified quality or character, exhibit oneself *to be*. Also foll. by *that*. ME. ▸**b** *refl.* Of a quality, condition, etc.: manifest itself, become evident. ME.

17 *verb trans.* **a** Demonstrate (kindness, rudeness, etc.) *to* or *towards* a person by one's actions or behaviour; accord or grant (favour, honour, etc.). Also with double obj. ME. ▸†**b** Set or be (an example). ME–L15.

†**18** *verb trans.* Exert or wield (power, strength, etc.) (*on*, *against*). LME–L16.

> 🕮 **16** J. CONRAD Mr. Verloc showed himself the most generous of lodgers. D. HAMMETT I grunted to show scepticism. G. VIDAL Those who show particular aptitude for therapy are assigned clinical work. *Observer* He showed signs . . of physical and mental degeneration. **17a** L. STEFFENS No more mercy was shown Democrats than Republicans. O. MANNING Mrs. Mackie had never shown friendliness to Ellie. *American Speech* A country that once showed me the greatest respect as a . . scholar. P. KAVANAGH The men . . would show their gratitude by working harder.

▸ **V 19** *verb intrans.* **a** With compl.: look, seem, appear. Also foll. by *like*. ME. ▸**b** Present a specified appearance; make a (good, bad, etc.) show or display. LME. ▸†**c** Appear or seem (*as if*, *to do*, etc.); claim or pretend *to be*. LME–E18.

20 *verb intrans.* **a** Be or become visible or apparent; make an appearance; *colloq.* (of a woman) manifest visible signs of pregnancy. LME. ▸**b** Of a thing: be seen *through*, *under*, etc., something that partly covers or conceals it (see also ***show through*** below). Also, be visible as a fault or defect. M19. ▸**c** Of an oil well: give an indication of the presence of oil. E20.

21 *verb intrans.* **a** Appear in public, make a display in public; *colloq.* make an appearance at a gathering, arrive, turn up. E17. ▸**b** BOXING. Enter the ring as a combatant. E19. ▸**c** COMMERCE. Of a commodity: appear or be prominent in the market. E20. ▸**d** HORSE-RACING. Finish third or in the first three in a race. *N. Amer.* E20.

22 *verb intrans.* Of a film or play: be presented at a cinema, theatre, etc. M20.

> 🕮 **19a** J. GARDNER With the veil lifted up her face showed angular and grim. **b** B. WEBB Lloyd George showed at his best in his lack of self-consciousness. **20a** J. STEINBECK Actual alarm showed in the nurses' eyes. D. HEWETT Shirl was . . four months gone and just starting to show. I. MURDOCH Its bright surface showed against the dark material of her dress. *Vogue* When you look after your skin every day—it shows. **b** A. S. NEILL The plaster of the ceiling came down . . and the lathes are still showing. J. MOORE Small ruffians . . had . . bottoms showing through ragged trousers. **21a** E. BIRNEY I stood hoping for a taxi to show. *Tennis World* A good field . . showed for the Dow Chemical Classic. **22** F. WYNDHAM A good picture, too. If it's . . showing anywhere near you . . take my advice and go.

Phrases etc.: ***go to show***: see GO *verb*. **have nothing to show for**, **have something to show for** be able to exhibit nothing, something, as a result of (one's efforts etc.). **I'll show you**, **that'll show him**, etc. expr. defiance: I'll teach you a lesson, that will teach him a lesson, etc. ***show a clean pair of heels***: see CLEAN *adjective*. ***show a leg***: see LEG *noun*. ***show a person the door***. ***show a person the ropes***: see ROPE *noun*¹. ***show a thing or two***: see THING *noun*¹. ***show fight***: see FIGHT *noun*. **show one's cards** display one's cards face upwards; *fig.* disclose one's plans. ***show one's colours***: see COLOUR *noun*. **show one's face** allow oneself to be seen, make an appearance. **show one's hand** = ***show one's card*** above. **show one's head** = ***show one's face*** above. ***show one's mettle***: see METTLE *noun*. ***show one's teeth***: see TOOTH *noun*. ***show one's colours***, ***show one's true colours***: see COLOUR *noun*. ***show*** SEMBLANCE. ***show sport***: see SPORT *noun*. ***show temper***: see TEMPER *noun*. **show the cloven foot**, **show the cloven hoof** betray something devilish or sinister in one's character or motives. ***show the flag***: see FLAG *noun*⁴. **show the way** guide in the required direction by leading or giving instructions. ***show the white feather***: see FEATHER *noun*. **show willing** display readiness to help etc. **your slip is showing** *fig.* you are unwittingly exposing a fault.

With adverbs & prepositions in specialized senses: **show for** †(**a**) claim to be, have, or do; (**b**) *dial.* be a sign of, suggest, portend. **show forth** *arch.* exhibit; expound. **show in** bring (a person) into a house or room. **show off** (**a**) display ostentatiously or to advantage; (**b**) act or talk for show; make a deliberate or pretentious display of one's abilities or accomplishments. **show out** (**a**) take (a person) to the exit; turn out of doors; (**b**) become visible; *fig.* exhibit one's true character; (**c**) BRIDGE show that one has no more cards of a particular suit. **show round** show (a person) over a place, show the sights to. **show through** be visible although supposedly concealed; (of feelings etc.) be revealed inadvertently; see also sense 20b above. **show up** (**a**) lead or take (a person) upstairs; (**b**) hand in (work) for inspection by a teacher or examiner; (**c**) disgrace or discredit by exposure; show (a person) to be an impostor; expose (a person's fault, misdeed, etc.); (**d**) be conspicuous or clearly visible; (**e**) *colloq.* put in an appearance, be present, turn up; (**f**) *colloq.* embarrass, humiliate.

Comb.: **show-and-tell** (orig. *N. Amer.*) a method used in teaching young children, by which they are encouraged to bring objects to school and describe them to their classmates; freq. *attrib.*; **show-cause** *adjective* (LAW) requiring a party to produce a satisfactory explanation of a failure to comply with a court order etc.; **show-me** *adjective* (*US*) believing nothing until it is demonstrated, very sceptical; **show-through** PRINTING the fact of print on one side of a sheet of paper being visible from the other side; **show-up** (**a**) the action of exposing someone to ridicule; an exposé; (**b**) *US slang* a police identification parade.

■ **showable** *adjective* †(**a**) demonstrative, able to prove; (**b**) demonstrable, provable; (**c**) that can be shown or presented for viewing: LME.

Showa /ˈʃəʊwə/ *noun*. E20.
[Japanese, from *shō* clear, bright + *wa* harmony, concord.]
The traditionally auspicious name or title given to the period of rule of the Japanese emperor Hirohito (1926–89).

showdown /ˈʃəʊdaʊn/ *noun*. L19.
[from SHOW *verb* + DOWN *adverb*.]

1 CARDS. An act of players laying down their cards face up, esp. in poker. L19.

2 An open disclosure of plans etc.; a declaration or trial of strength; a final test or confrontation, a decisive situation. E20.

> 🕮 **2** *Campaign* Stoessl . . left after a showdown with Channel 4 chief executive Michael Grade.

Comb.: **showdown inspection** *US* MILITARY a surprise inspection of kit; **showdown poker** CARDS a form of poker in which all the players stake an ante, receive five cards, and have a showdown without a draw.

shower /ˈʃaʊə/ *noun*¹ & *verb*.
[Old English *scūr* = Old Frisian *skūr* fit of illness, Old Saxon *skūr* (Middle Dutch *schuur*, Dutch *schoer*), Old High German *scūr* (German *Schauer*), Old Norse *skúr*, Gothic *skūra* storm, from Germanic.]

▸ **A** *noun*. **1** A usu. light fall of rain, hail, sleet, or snow, of short duration. Also with specifying word. OE. ▸**b** A copious downfall of anything coming or supposed to come from the sky. (Foll. by *of*.) LME. ▸**c** A dust-storm. Freq. qualified by a place-name, as ***Darling shower***. *Austral.* L19.

2 a A copious fall or flight of solid objects, as stones, bullets, etc. OE. ▸**b** A copious fall or discharge of water or other liquid in drops; *poet.* an outpouring of grief, sorrow, etc. LME. ▸**c** A device for producing a shower of small slow-burning stars from a rocket (firework). M19.

3 A copious or liberal supply of gifts, praise, etc. ME.

4 †**a** A conflict, a battle, an assault. ME–M17. ▸**b** An attack of pain, a pang; *spec.* (in *pl.*) labour pains. *obsolete* exc. *Scot.* ME.

5 A bath or cubicle in which a person stands under a spray of water; the apparatus used for this; an act of bathing in a shower. Also more fully ***shower-bath***. L18.

6 A number of gifts brought by guests to a party esp. to celebrate a wedding or birth. Now also, a party given for this purpose, *spec.* by a bride-to-be. *N. Amer.*, *Austral.*, & *NZ*. E20.

7 PHYSICS. A number of high-energy particles appearing together; *spec.* a group generated in the atmosphere by cosmic radiation. M20.

8 A worthless or contemptible person or group; a pitiful collection. *slang*. M20.

9 A light decorated cloth covering cups etc. on a tray or table. *Austral.* & *NZ*. M20.

> 🕮 **1** V. WOOLF There had been a shower of rain. **I didn't come down in the last shower** (chiefly *Austral.*) I am not inexperienced, I am not easily fooled. **b** ***METEOR shower***. **2a** R. FRAME A tree shook down a shower of pine needles. **b** SHELLEY Rosalind . . wept A shower of burning tears, which fell upon His face. *fig.*: R. S. HAWKER What showers of gold the sunbeams rain! **3** J. W. BURGON Hawkins's election . . was the signal for a shower of . . letters of hearty congratulation. **5** ***have a shower***, ***take a shower***, ***cold shower***, ***hot shower***, etc. **6** ***kitchen shower***, ***linen shower***, ***wedding shower***, etc. **8** *Observer* Some of the people who go out with the hounds these days are a shower. *Sunday Express* What a hopeless shower most of these oloroso and amontillados were.

Comb.: **shower-bath**: see sense 5 above; **shower-bouquet** a large bouquet from which many smaller bouquets hang; **shower box** *NZ* = *shower cubicle* below; **shower-cap**: worn to keep the hair dry when having a shower or bath; **shower-cloud** a cumulonimbus cloud; **shower cubicle**: containing a shower; **shower curtain** a waterproof curtain separating a shower from the rest of the room; **shower head** a rose or nozzle from which the water sprays out in a shower; **showerproof** *adjective, verb, & noun* (*a*) *adjective & verb trans.* (make) resistant to light rain; (*b*) *noun* a showerproof garment, *esp.* a raincoat; **shower-room**: housing one or more showers; **shower stall** *N. Amer.* = *shower cubicle* above; **shower tree** = CASSIA 2; **shower unit** (the main apparatus of) a shower.

▶ **B** *verb*. **1** *verb intrans.* Rain in a shower or showers. Usu. *impers.* in *it showers*, *it is showering*, etc. LME.

2 *verb intrans.* Descend in a shower or showers, or as a shower of rain; pour copiously. Formerly also, attack. Also foll. by *down*. LME.

3 *verb trans.* Pour down or discharge (solid objects, tears, etc.) in a shower or showers; send *down* or pour out copiously. L16.

4 *verb trans.* Water with or as with a shower; *transf.* cover or strew *with*. M17.

5 *verb intrans.* Have a shower. M20.

> 🕮 **2** *fig.*: N. ANNAN Honours began to shower upon him. **3** J. G. COZZENS The cigarette flew ten feet and showered sparks on the floor. *absol.*: SHAKES. *Rom. & Jul.* What, still in tears? Evermore show'ring? *fig.*: N. MOSLEY The children . . showered love on their mother. **4** *fig.*: J. FRAME Her life had been showered with entitlements of wealth.

■ **showerer** *noun* (*rare*) a person who showers gifts etc. copiously L19. **showerless** *adjective* (*rare*) M18.

shower /ˈʃəʊə/ *noun*[2].

[Old English *scēawere* scout, watchman, from *scēawian* SHOW *verb*. Later from SHOW *verb* + -ER[1].]

†**1** A person who looks out, observes, or inspects; an observer; a scout, a spy. OE–ME.

†**2** A mirror. OE–LME.

3 A person who shows, points out, or exhibits something. ME.

†**4** A thing which shows something, an indicator; an indicative symptom of a disease. LME–M17.

5 An animal that makes a (good or bad) display of its qualities, esp. at a show. L19.

showery /ˈʃaʊəri/ *adjective*. L16.

[from SHOWER *noun*[1] + -Y[1].]

1 Raining or falling in showers; characterized by frequent showers of rain. L16.

2 Pertaining to, produced by, or resembling a shower or showers. M17.

3 Of a cloud, wind, constellation, etc.: causing, bringing, or associated with showers. L17.

■ **showeriness** *noun* (*rare*) M19.

showing /ˈʃəʊɪŋ/ *noun*. OE.

[from SHOW *verb* + -ING[1].]

1 The action of SHOW *verb*; the fact of being shown; an instance of this. Also foll. by *off*, *up*. OE. ▸**b** The projection of a film on to a screen; a presentation or broadcasting of a film or television programme, a show. M20. ▸**c** A public exhibition of the work of an artist or fashion designer; an art or fashion show. M20.

2 LAW (now *Hist.*). A duty or toll payable in the Anglo-Saxon period for the right to display goods for sale. OE.

3 Outward appearance. ME.

4 a A thing that is shown or that appears, a manifestation, a revelation; a sign; a vision. *obsolete* exc. *Hist.* ME. ▸**b** = SHOW *noun*[1] 4c. E20.

5 The presentation of a case; evidence. Freq. in ***on one's own showing***. M19.

6 A statement or presentation of figures, accounts, etc. Chiefly *US*. M19.

7 An appearance, display, or performance of a specified kind. L19.

> 🕮 **1** *Belfast Telegraph* Alsatian Dog, championship quality, excellent results in showing. *South African Panorama* The showing of the comet . . depends on the . . positions of the sun, earth and comet. **b** F. WELDON Going to the pictures, for the first showing every Sunday evening. **7** B. MONTGOMERY He made a very poor showing in Parliament during the debate.

showman /ˈʃəʊmən/ *noun*. Pl. **-men**. M18.

[from SHOW *noun*[1] + MAN *noun*.]

1 A person who exhibits a show; the proprietor or manager of a show or circus. M18.

2 A person who performs with a display of style or panache; a person skilled in publicity or self-promotion. L18.

■ **showmanship** *noun* the art of being a showman; skill in presentation, publicity, etc.: M19.

shown *verb pa. pple* of SHOW *verb*.

show-off /ˈʃəʊɒf/ *noun & adjective*. L18.

[from *show off* s.v. SHOW *verb*.]

▶ **A** *noun*. **1** A display or exposure of something. L18.

2 An imposing or specious display; an opportunity for display. Also, showiness. M19.

3 A person given to showing off. (Now the predominant sense.) E20.

▶ **B** *attrib.* or as *adjective*. Given to display; ostentatious, showy. E19.

■ **show-offish**, **show-offy** *adjectives* ostentatious, showy M20.

showy /ˈʃəʊi/ *adjective*. E18.

[from SHOW *noun*[1] + -Y[1].]

1 Presenting an imposing or striking appearance; gaudy, ostentatious, esp. excessively so. E18.

2 Of a person, quality, etc.: brilliant, striking, effective. E18.

> 🕮 **1** *Horse & Hound* Magnificent looking showy Thoroughbred mare. M. FRENCH Rather showy clothes: lots of sequins and chiffon.

■ **showily** *adverb* L18. **showiness** *noun* E19.

shox /ʃɒks/ *noun pl. informal*. L20.

[Repr. pronunc. of *shocks*.]

Shock absorbers.

shoyu /ˈʃəʊjuː/ *noun*. E18.

[Japanese *shōyu*: see SOY. Cf. SOYA.]

= SOY 1. Also ***shoyu sauce***.

s.h.p *abbreviation*.

Shaft horsepower.

Shqip /ʃkjɪp/ *noun & adjective*. Also **Shqyp**. M20.

[Albanian.]

(An) Albanian.

■ **Shqipetar** /ˈʃkjɪpətɑː/ *noun* the Albanian language M19.

shrab /ʃrɑːb/ *noun*. M17.

[Persian & Urdu from Arab. *šarāb*: see SYRUP. Cf. SHERBET, SHRUB *noun*[2].]

A drink prepared from wine or spirits.

shradh /ˈʃrɑːd/ *noun*. Also **s(h)raddha** /ˈʃrɑːdə/. L18.

[Sanskrit *śrāddha*, from *śraddhā* faith, trust.]

A Hindu ceremony to honour and make offerings to a deceased relative.

shrag /ʃrag/ *noun & verb*. ME.

[Parallel to SCRAG *noun*[2].]

▶ **A** *noun*. †**1** A rag, a tatter. *rare*. Only in ME.

2 A twig; a lopped branch. *dial.* M16.

▶ **B** *verb trans.* Infl. **-gg-**. Lop, trim, prune. *obsolete* exc. *dial.* ME.

■ **shragging** *noun* (*obsolete* exc. *dial.*) trimmings from a tree etc. LME.

shram /ʃram/ *verb trans. dial.* Infl. **-mm-**. L18.

[Parallel to SCRAM *verb*[1].]

Numb or shrink with cold. Chiefly as ***shrammed*** *ppl adjective*.

shrank *verb pa. t.* of SHRINK *verb*.

shrap /ʃrap/ *noun. colloq.* E20.

[Abbreviation.]

= SHRAPNEL 1, 3.

shrape /ʃreɪp/ *noun. obsolete* exc. *dial.* M16.

[Parallel to SCRAPE *noun*[2].]

A bait of chaff or seed laid for birds.

†**shrape** *verb* var. of SCRAPE *verb*.

shrapnel /ˈʃrapn(ə)l/ *noun*. E19.

[General Henry *Shrapnel* (1761–1842), Brit. soldier, the inventor.]

1 A shell containing bullets or pieces of metal timed to explode before impact. E19.

2 Small change. *Austral. & NZ slang*. E20.

3 Fragments thrown out by an exploded shell or bomb. M20.

shrdlu /ˈʃəːdluː/ *noun*. M20.

[Sequence of letters on the second column of keys on a Linotype machine used as a temporary marker and sometimes printed by mistake: see ETAOIN.]

In full ***shrdlu etaoin***. An absurd or unintelligible sequence of type. Cf. ETAOIN.

†**shreadings** *noun pl.* M17–M19.

[from alt. of SHREDDING + -S[1].]

CARPENTRY. Strips of timber used in furring.

shred /ʃrɛd/ *noun*.

[Late Old English *scrēad(e)*, corresp. to Old Frisian *skrēd* hair-cutting, clipping of coin, Old Saxon *skrōd*, Middle Low German *schrōt*, *schrāt* cut-off piece, Old High German *scrōt* (German *Schrot*), from West Germanic word rel. to base of SHROUD *noun*[1].]

1 A fragment, a broken piece of something; *spec.* (*rare*) a shard of pottery. Now *rare* exc. as passing into senses below. LOE.

2 A finely cut strip of some material, esp. paper, (the peel of) a fruit or vegetable, etc. Usu. in *pl.* (foll. by *of*.) LOE.

3 A cut or torn scrap of fabric, esp. from or for use in clothing; a thread of (esp. worn) fabric; in *pl.*, ragged clothing, clothing worn to threads. ME. ▸†**b** A tailor. *slang*. L16–L17. ▸**c** *transf.* A thin line *of* cloud etc. *poet.* M19.

4 *fig.* A small or paltry thing; the least amount or remnant *of* something. LME.

> 🕮 **2** THACKERAY Three shreds of celery in a glass. **3** R. L. STEVENSON A . . skeleton lay, with a few shreds of clothing. A. J. CRONIN He picked a shred of lint from his sleeve. B. ENGLAND Tattered slacks were now reduced to shreds. **4** S. MIDDLETON Anyone with a shred of taste would have been horrified. S. BRETT A shred of evidence to support our . . unlikely thesis.

Phrases: **in shreds** in small pieces; *fig.* destroyed, ruined. **of shreds (and patches)** made up of rags or scraps, patched together (with allus. to Shakes. *Haml.* III iv). **tear to shreds** tear into small pieces; *fig.* destroy, demolish.

■ **shreddy** *adjective* consisting of or resembling shreds; ragged: M19.

shred /ʃrɛd/ *verb*. Infl. **-dd-**. Pa. t. & pple **shredded**, (*arch.*) **shred**.

[Late Old English *scrēadian*, formed as prec. Cf. SCREED *verb*.]

1 *verb trans.* Trim, strip, prune; lop or cut off. Freq. foll. by *off*. Now *arch. & dial.* LOE.

2 *verb trans.* Cut or divide into small pieces. Formerly *esp.* hack to pieces. Now *rare*. ME.

3 *verb trans.* Cut or tear into shreds or thin strips; reduce to shreds or torn scraps; *spec.* (*a*) chop (food) finely; (*b*) reduce (a document) to unreadable strips by passing through a shredder, esp. for security reasons. ME. ▸**b** *fig.* Defeat overwhelmingly, trounce. *slang* (chiefly *US*). M20.

4 *verb trans.* Cut or divide in two; sever; part. Chiefly *poet.* Now *rare*. M16.

5 *verb intrans. & trans. transf.* Thin out, esp. into fine lines; disperse, scatter. Also foll. by *away*, *out*. M17.

> 🕮 **3** F. FORSYTH Simply to shred the file . . was not possible. M. MARRIN A large . . dish piled with finely shredded cabbage. **shredded wheat** wheat grain cut into long shreds and formed into biscuits as a breakfast cereal. **b** *New York Times* The Celtics shredded the Los Angeles Lakers. **4** SPENSER When ye shred with fatall knife His line. **5** TOLKIEN They saw the clouds breaking and shredding. B. BOVA He . . watched the plane taxi . . its whirling propeller shredding the fog.

Comb.: **shred-pie** *Hist.* a mince-pie.

■ **shredder** *noun* a person who or thing which shreds something; *spec.* a machine for reducing documents to unreadable strips, esp. for security reasons: L16. **shredding** *noun* (*a*) the action of the verb; (*b*) (now *rare*) a fragment, a shred; †(*c*) (in *pl.* & *collect. sing.*) tree trimmings: LOE.

shrew /ʃruː/ *noun*[1].

[Old English *scrēawa*, *scrǣwa* rel. to Old High German *scrawazz* dwarf, Middle High German *schrawaz*, *schrat*, *schröuwel* devil, Old Norse *skrǫggr* fox, Icelandic *skröggur* old man, Norwegian *skrogg* wolf, *skrugg* dwarf, Swedish dial. *skrugge* devil, *skragga*.]

1 Any of numerous small mammals of the insectivore family Soricidae (esp. of the genera *Sorex* and *Crocidura*), superficially resembling mice but having a long sharp snout, small eyes, and carnivorous habits, formerly believed to be injurious to humans. OE.

2 With specifying word: any of various mammals of other insectivore families or other orders that resemble shrews. M19.

2 ***elephant shrew***, ***otter shrew***, ***tree shrew***, etc.

Comb.: **shrew-ash** (*obsolete* exc. *dial.*) an ash tree whose branches were formerly believed to cure shrew-stroke; **shrew-hedgehog** a moon rat, *Hylomys sinensis*, of forests in SE Asia; **shrew-mole** any of various moles found in eastern Asia and N. America; **shrew-run** (*obsolete* exc. *dial.*) = ***shrew-struck*** below; **shrew-stroke** (*obsolete* exc. *dial.*) paralysis formerly believed to result from being run across by a shrew; **shrew-struck** (*obsolete* exc. *dial.*) affected with shrew-stroke; **shrew-tenrec** any of various tenrecs of the genus *Microgale*.

■ **shrewlike** *adjective* resembling (that of) a shrew L19.

shrew /ʃruː/ *noun*[2] *& adjective*. ME.

[Either formed as prec. with the sense of 'malevolent person or thing', or transf. use of prec.]

▶ **A** *noun*. **1** A malevolent or mischievous person; a villain, a rascal. Also as a term of abuse. Long *arch. rare*. ME.

†**2** An evil or troublesome act, circumstance, or other thing. ME–E17.

3 A scolding or bad-tempered person, esp. (and now only) a woman. ME.

> 🕮 **1** R. L. STEVENSON Our poor shrew of a parson. **3** W. IRVING A wife, who seemed to be a shrew, and to have the upper hand.

▶†**B** *adjective*. Shrewish. ME–M17

■ **shrewish** *adjective* †(*a*) evil, malevolent; (*b*) characteristic of or having the disposition of a shrew or bad-tempered person, sharp, scolding: LME. **shrewishly** *adverb* E17. **shrewishness** *noun* L16. **shrewly** *adverb* (now *rare*) = SHREWDLY E16.

shrew /ʃruː/ *verb trans. rare*. ME.

[App. from prec. Cf. BESHREW.]

1 In imprecations: curse, (a person etc.). Chiefly in ***I shrew***. Long *arch.* ME.

†**2** Scold, rail at. L17–L19.

shrewd /ʃruːd/ *adjective & noun*. ME.

[Partly from SHREW *noun*[2], partly from SHREW *verb*: see -ED[2], -ED[1].]

▶ **A** *adjective*. **1** Of a person or (formerly) a thing: evil in nature or character; having an evil or bad influence; vile. Formerly also, mischievous, naughty. Long *obsolete* exc.

dial. ME. ▸†**b** (Of an animal or thing) dangerous; vicious; (of a weapon) deadly. LME–M17.

†**2 a** Characterized or accompanied by evil or misfortune; having harmful or dangerous consequences. ME–E19. ▸**b** Indicating or portending ill; ominous; unfavourable. LME–M18.

3 As an intensifier: serious, extreme. Now *rare* or *obsolete*. LME.

4 In bad (esp. physical) condition or order; poor, unsatisfactory. Long *arch. rare*. LME.

†**5** Of a person, speech, etc.: harsh, abusive; shrewish. LME–M17.

6 Of a blow, wound, or (formerly) fighting: severe, hard. *arch.* L15.

7 Of a person, action, observation, etc.: orig., cunning, artful, (chiefly *derog.*); later, characterized by or displaying astuteness or sagacity, sharply perceptive, clever and judicious. E16.

8 Sharp to the senses; (of wind etc.) piercing, keen. *arch.* E17.

> 🕮 **2a** T. MIDDLETON A shrewd business, and a dangerous. **b** DONNE If our own heart . . condemne us, this is shrewd evidence. **3** SIR W. SCOTT That is a shrewd loss. **4** A. C. SWINBURNE As a fresh odour from a bleak, shrewd soil. **7** TENNYSON I find you a shrewd bargainer. H. GARLAND A stream of shrewd comment on Western writers. R. WEST He made a shrewd guess. **8** R. L. STEVENSON A shrewd tang of . . salt.

Comb.: **shrewd-head** *Austral. & NZ slang* a shrewd or cunning person.

▶ **B** *noun. rare.*

1 A shrewd or cunning person. M19.

2 Shrewdness, sagacity. L20.

■ **shrewdie** *noun* (*colloq.*, chiefly *Austral. & NZ*) a shrewd or cunning person E20. **shrewdish** *adjective* somewhat or fairly shrewd E19. **shrewdly** *adverb* ME. **shrewdness** *noun* ME.

shrewmouse /ˈʃruːmaʊs/ *noun. arch.* Pl. **-mice** /-mʌɪs/. L16.
[from SHREW *noun*[1] + MOUSE *noun*.]
= SHREW *noun*[1] 1.

Shrewsbury /ˈʃrəʊzb(ə)ri, ˈʃruːz-/ *noun.* L16.
[A town in Shropshire, England.]

1 ***by Shrewsbury clock*** [with allus. to Shakes. *1 Hen. IV*], (of a specified length of time) exactly, precisely. Freq. *iron.* L16.

2 ***Shrewsbury cake***, a flat round biscuit-like cake. E18.

Shri /ʃriː/ *noun.* Also **Sri**. L18.
[Sanskrit *Śrī* beauty, fortune, used as an honorific title.]
In the Indian subcontinent, a title of respect preceding the name of a deity or distinguished person, or the title of a sacred book. Now also, the Indian equivalent of ***Mr***.

> 🕮 E. M. FORSTER Infinite love took upon itself the form of Shri Krishna. S. RUSHDIE My cousin, Shri Ramram Seth, is a great seer.

shriek /ʃriːk/ *noun.* L16.
[from next.]

1 A high-pitched piercing cry or utterance, esp. expr. terror, pain, or excitement; a loud high-pitched laugh. L16. ▸**b** A loud high-pitched jarring sound. L16. ▸**c** The high-pitched cry of a bird or animal. M18.

2 *fig.* An emphatic exclamation of protest or alarm. M19.

3 More fully ***shriek-mark***. An exclamation mark. *colloq.* M19.

> 🕮 **1** SIAN EVANS Her voice rose to a shriek. P. ANGADI 'Darling!' There was a shriek from Mum as she charged into the hall. **b** E. BIRNEY The sudden shriek of chalk on a blackboard. **2** C. KINGSLEY Biographers . . break into virtuous shrieks of 'flattery', 'meanness', . . and so forth. **3** *Independent* Ha!! Ha!!!, as Wolfe . . might say, never mean with the shriek-mark.

shriek /ʃriːk/ *verb.* L15.
[Parallel to SCREAK *verb*. Cf. SHRIKE *verb*, SKRIKE *verb*, SQUEAK *verb*.]

1 *verb intrans.* Emit a shriek or shrieks. L15.

2 *verb trans.* Utter or express with a shriek or shrieks; cause to emit a shriek. L16.

3 *verb trans.* Bring into a specified condition by shrieking. M17.

4 *verb trans. & intrans. fig.* Provide a clear or emphatic indication of or *of* a particular condition, attribute, etc. E20.

> 🕮 **1** SHAKES. *Ven. & Ad.* The owl, night's herald, shrieks.V. WOOLF A giant voice had shrieked . . in its agony. G. GREENE A police siren came shrieking through the dark. **shriek with laughter** laugh uncontrollably. **2** *Punch* 'My God!' shrieked the broker. 'Charles has . . done it!' **shriek out** say in high-pitched piercing tones. **3** *National Observer (US)* Liberals shrieked themselves hoarse with . . horror. **4** E. AMBLER That hat . . shrieks English to high Heaven.

Comb.: **shriek-owl** (now *rare*) the barn owl.

■ **shrieker** *noun* a person who shrieks, esp. habitually E18. **shrieking** *verbal noun* the action of the verb; an instance of this: E17. **shrieking** *ppl adjective* (**a**) that shrieks; (**b**) *fig.* emphatic, glaring; *esp.* (of a colour) excessively bright, lurid: L16.

shrieky /ˈʃriːki/ *adjective.* M19.
[from SHRIEK *noun* or *verb* + -Y[1].]
Given to or characterized by shrieking; *fig.* hysterical.

shrieval /ˈʃriːv(ə)l/ *adjective.* L17.
[from *shrieve* obsolete var. of SHERIFF + -AL[1].]
Of or pertaining to a sheriff.

shrievalty /ˈʃriːv(ə)lti/ *noun.* E16.
[formed as prec. + *-alty* repr. Old French *-alté* (mod. *-auté*): see -TY[1].]
The office or position of sheriff; a sheriff's jurisdiction or term of office. Cf. SHERIFFRY, SHERIFFALTY.

†**shrieve** *noun* var. of SHERIFF.

shrift /ʃrɪft/ *noun & verb.*
[Old English *scrift* corresp. to Old Frisian *skrift*, Middle & mod. Dutch *schrift*, Old High German *scrift* (German *Schrift*), Old Norse *skript*, *skrift*, formed as SHRIVE.]

▶ **A** *noun.* †**1** Penance imposed after confession. OE–LME.

†**2** A confessor. OE–M17.

3 Absolution, esp. as implied in the imposition of penance. *arch.* OE.

4 (A) confession to a priest; *transf.* (an) admission, (a) revelation. (Foll. by *of*.) *arch.* ME.

Phrases: **short shrift** (**a**) *arch.* little time allowed for making confession before execution or punishment; (**b**) *transf.* curt treatment; ***give short shrift to***, treat curtly. **go to shrift** *arch.* go to confession, seek absolution.

Comb.: **shrift-district** *Hist.* = ***shrift-shire*** below; **shrift-father** *arch.* a confessor; **shrift-shire** *Hist.* a district to which a priest ministered.

▶ **B** *verb trans.* = SHRIVE 2. *arch. rare.* E17.

shright /ʃrʌɪt/ *noun. arch.* M16.
[Rel. to SKRIKE *verb*.]
Shrieking; a shriek.

shrike /ʃrʌɪk/ *noun*[1]. *obsolete* exc. *dial.* LME.
[from SHRIKE *verb*.]
A shriek, a shrill sound.

shrike /ʃrʌɪk/ *noun*[2]. M16.
[Origin uncertain: perh. rel. to Old English *scrīc* thrush, Middle Low German *schrīk* corncrake, Swedish *skrika* jay. Cf. SCREECH *noun*[1], SHRIEK *noun*.]

1 Any of numerous passerine birds of the family Laniidae, having a strong hooked beak and preying on small animals, some of which they may impale on thorns etc. Also called ***butcher-bird***. M16.

2 With specifying word: any of various birds of other families which resemble shrikes. M19.

1 ***bush-shrike***, ***loggerhead shrike***, ***red-backed shrike***, etc. **2** ***cuckoo-shrike***, ***swallow-shrike***, ***vanga shrike*** etc.

Comb.: **shrike babbler** any of several Asian babblers of the genera *Pteruthius* and *Gampsorhynchus*; **shrike-thrush** any of several Australasian thickheads of the genus *Colluricincla*; **shrike-tit** either of two Australasian thickheads of the genus *Eulacestoma*; **shrike tyrant** any of several S. American tyrant flycatchers of the genus *Agriornis*; **shrike vireo** each of three Central and S. American vireos of the genus *Vireolanius*.

shrike /ʃrʌɪk/ *verb intrans. obsolete* exc. *dial.* ME.
[Parallel to SKRIKE *verb*, perh. from base of Old English *scrīċċettan*. Cf. SHRIEK *verb*.]
Make a shrill sound, shriek.

shrikhand /ˈʃriːkand/ *noun.* M20.
[Sanskrit *śrīkhaṇḍa* sandalwood.]
An Indian sweet dish made from curd, sugar, almonds, and spices.

shrill /ʃrɪl/ *verb & noun.* ME.
[Rel. to next, ult. from Germanic: cf. Old English *scrallettan*, Dutch *schrallen*, Icelandic *skrölta*.]

▶ **A** *verb.* **1** *verb intrans.* Sound shrilly; make a shrill noise; speak or cry with a shrill voice. ME.

2 *verb trans.* Emit or express in a shrill tone; utter with a shrill voice. Also foll. by *out*. L16.

> 🕮 **1** M. M. ATWATER A myriad flying and crawling things shrilled happily. *Church Times* London is full of faulty . . burglar alarms shrilling away. **2** C. MACKENZIE 'What?' Jockey shrilled like a questing falcon. W. SOYINKA The drill-major shrilled his orders.

▶ **B** *noun.* A shrill sound or cry. L16.

> 🕮 B. HINES The shrill of the whistle immediately obliterated every other sound.

shrill /ʃrɪl/ *adverb & adjective.* ME.
[Rel. to prec., ult. from Germanic: cf. Low German *schrell*, German *schrill*, SHIRL *adjective & adverb*.]

▶ **A** *adverb.* Shrilly. *arch.* ME.

▶ **B** *adjective.* **1** Of a voice or sound: high-pitched and piercing. LME. ▸**b** *transf.* Keen or sharp to the senses; *esp.* (of a colour) bright, glaring. E17.

2 a Emitting or producing a high-pitched piercing sound; *transf.* (esp. of a protester) unreasoning, hysterical. LME. ▸**b** Characterized or accompanied by sharp high-pitched sounds; *transf.* (of an emotion etc.) expressed in an unrestrained or hysterical tone. E18.

> 🕮 **1** ALDOUS HUXLEY Boys and girls were running with shrill yells over the lawns. W. CATHER Birds and insects . . began to make . . shrill noises. **b** M. SCHAPIRO The color of the Impressionists had appeared . . shrill and loud. **2a** TOLKIEN The wind came shrill among the rocks. I. MURDOCH Keep your voice down, you are getting quite shrill. **b** DICKENS The night was black and shrill. G. GREENE His shrill rage has . . lack of dignity.

■ **shrillish** *adjective* somewhat shrill L16. **shrillness** *noun* L16. **shrilly** *adjective* (*poet.*) = SHRILL *adjective* L16. **shrilly** *adverb* LME.

shrim /ʃrɪm/ *verb trans. & intrans.* Long *obsolete* exc. *dial.* Infl. **-mm-**.
[Old English *scrimman*.]
Shrink, shrivel. Chiefly as ***shrimmed*** *ppl adjective*.

shrimp /ʃrɪmp/ *noun & adjective.* ME.
[Obscurely rel. to Middle Low German *schrempen* contract, wrinkle, *schrimpen* wrinkle the nose, *schrumpen* wrinkle, fold (whence German *schrumpfen*), Middle High German *schrimpfen* contract, Old Norse *skreppa* slip away. Cf. SCRIMP *adjective & adverb*.]

▶ **A** *noun.* Pl. same, **-s**.

1 Any of numerous small, chiefly marine decapod crustaceans closely related to prawns, having slender long-tailed bodies and one pair of pincers; esp. *Crangon vulgaris* (also ***common shrimp***), which occurs in sand on the coasts of Europe and is a common article of food. ME. ▸**b** With specifying word: any of various crustaceans of other orders which resemble shrimps. M19.

2 *fig.* A diminutive or puny person or thing. *derog.* LME.

3 The colour of a cooked shrimp, a bright pink. L19.

> 🕮 **1b** ***brine shrimp***, ***mantis shrimp***, ***opossum shrimp***, etc. **2** J. O'FAOLAIN They . . had grown and developed, while I was still a shrimp. **a shrimp of a** — a diminutive or puny —.

▶ **B** *attrib.* or as *adjective.* **1** Of or pertaining to shrimp; consisting of or containing shrimp. M18.

2 Of the colour of a cooked shrimp; bright pink. E20.

Special collocations & comb.: **shrimp-boat**: that fishes for shrimp. ***shrimp cocktail***: see COCKTAIL 4. **shrimp cracker** a light crisp made from rice or tapioca flour and shrimp flavouring which puffs up when deep-fried, eaten esp. with Chinese food (usu. in *pl.*). **shrimp-pink** (of) the bright pink colour of a cooked shrimp. **shrimp plant** a Mexican shrub, *Justicia brandegeana* (family Acanthaceae), popular as a house-plant, which bears small white flowers hidden in clusters of pinkish-brown bracts.

■ **shrimper** *noun* (**a**) a fisher for shrimp; (**b**) a shrimp-boat: M19. **shrimpish** *adjective* diminutive, puny, insignificant M16. **shrimplet** *noun* a little shrimp L17. **shrimplike** *adjective* resembling (that of) a shrimp E19. **shrimpy** *adjective* resembling a shrimp; having many shrimps: M19.

shrimp /ʃrɪmp/ *verb intrans.* M19.
[from prec.]
Fish for shrimp.

shrimped /ʃrɪmpt/ *adjective.* Now *dial.* M17.
[Parallel to *scrimped* ppl adjective of SCRIMP *verb*.]
Shrivelled, withered.

shrine /ʃrʌɪn/ *noun & adjective.*
[Old English *scrīn* = Old Frisian *skrīn*, Middle Low German *schrīn*, Middle Dutch *schrīne* (Dutch *schrijn*), Old High German *scrīni* (German *Schrein*), Old Norse *skrín*, from Germanic from Latin *scrinium* case or chest for books or papers.]

▶ **A** *noun.* †**1** *gen.* A box, a cabinet, a chest. OE–M17.

2 A reliquary, *esp.* one encased in a decorated structure resembling a tomb. Also, the part of a church or other building in which this stands. OE. ▸**b** *transf.* A receptacle for any sacred object; a niche for sacred images. E16.

3 Orig., a coffin. Later, an elaborate tomb or monument. LME.

4 *fig.* Something enclosing or protecting a prized or honoured person, thing, quality, etc. Chiefly *poet.* LME.

†**5** A revered person. *rare* (Shakes.). L16–E17.

6 A place of worship or devotion to a saint or deity; a temple, a church. E17.

> 🕮 **2** SHAKES. *2 Hen. VI* A blind man at Saint Albans shrine . . hath receiv'd his sight. J. AGEE He put down . . both knees before the desolate shrine. **b** H. ALLEN She . . brought the figure in its little shrine to him. **3** SIR W. SCOTT This peculiar shrine of the Whig martyrs . . much honoured by their descendants. **4** A. O'SHAUGHNESSY The heart was a shrine For that memory to dwell in divine. **6** V. BRITTAIN The place has become for me a shrine, the object of a pilgrimage. M. FITZHERBERT Aubrey was determined to visit the Shi'ite shrine of Kerbela during the time of Muharram.

▶ **B** *adjective.* **1** Of or pertaining to a shrine or shrines. L16.

2 *spec.* (**S-**). Of or pertaining to the Shriners. *N. Amer.* M20.

■ **shrined** *adjective* (*rare*) containing or contained in a shrine L16.

shrine /ʃrʌɪn/ *verb trans.* ME.
[from prec.]

1 = ENSHRINE. *arch.* ME.

†**2** Canonize. *rare.* LME–L19.

Shriner /ˈʃrʌɪnə/ *noun. N. Amer.* L19.
[formed as prec. + -ER[1].]
A member of the Order of Nobles of the Mystic Shrine, a charitable society founded in the US in 1872.

shrink /ʃrɪŋk/ *noun*. LME.
[from next.]
†**1** In *pl*. Wrinkles of skin. *rare*. Only in LME.
2 The action or an act of shrinking; shrinkage. L16.
3 A psychiatrist. Cf. ***head-shrinker*** (b) s.v. HEAD *noun & adjective*. *slang*. M20.

3 A. F. LOEWENSTEIN 'Vat seems to be the problem?' the shrink was saying.

shrink /ʃrɪŋk/ *verb*. Pa. t. **shrank** /ʃraŋk/; (now *non-standard*) **shrunk** /ʃrʌŋk/; pa. pple **shrunk** /ʃrʌŋk/, **shrunken** /ˈʃrʌŋk(ə)n/. See also SHRUNK, SHRUNKEN *ppl adjectives*.
[Old English *scrincan* corresp. to Swedish *skrynka* wrinkle (Old Swedish *skrunkin* shrivelled, wrinkled), Norwegian *skrekka*, *skrøkka*.]
▶**I** *verb intrans*. **1** Wrinkle or shrivel permanently through old age, disease, etc.; wither *away*. Formerly also *fig*. (*rare*), pine away. Now chiefly as SHRUNKEN. OE.
2 Contract or diminish physically, esp. through contact with heat, cold, or wet; *spec*. (***a***) draw in or curl up the body in pain or discomfort; (***b***) (of a textile) contract when wetted. Also foll. by *into, to, up*. OE. ▶**b** Diminish in scope or significance. Also foll. by *into, to*. LME.
3 Draw back or recoil physically in fear or disgust; flinch, wince, cower. Also foll. by *at, back, from*. ME. ▶**b** *fig*. Refuse or be reluctant to act, esp. from fear, dislike, or disgust; recoil *at* or *from* an action, thought, etc. LME. ▶†**c** Shiver, shudder. Only as ***shrinking*** *ppl adjective*. *rare* (Shakes.). Only in E17.
4 Withdraw to a position of safety or shelter; draw inwards for protection. Also foll. by *in, into*. LME.
5 Withdraw from a position secretly or furtively; slip or slink away. Also foll. by *away, back, from*. LME. ▶†**b** Withdraw one's support or allegiance; abandon one's duty. Also foll. by *away, from*. M–L16. ▶†**c** Of the wind: blow fitfully. E17–E18.

2 R. L. STEVENSON Our western gable, where the boards had shrunk and separated. E. BOWEN Her cotton frock . . had shrunk in the wash. F. NORRIS The shadows of these trees had shrunk . . contracting close about the trunks. **b** G. GREENE Wormold's cheque shrank to insignificance in his fingers. *Fortune* Years of expansion have shrunk the number of unemployed from . . 12 million . . to 6.3 million. **3** E. WAUGH Any who have heard that sound will shrink at the recollection of it. J. AGEE Richard shrank as small against the wall as he could. R. SILVERBERG Shrinking back from him as though . . afraid she'd catch a disease. **b** D. L. SAYERS A course of deception from which her conscience shrank appalled. F. KING My father shrank from hurting feelings with a complaint. **4** A. RADCLIFFE I shrink into my cell again for terror of the sound. **5** B. BETTELHEIM Children who . . try to shrink away when confronted with danger.

▶**II** *verb trans*. **6** Cause to contract or diminish physically, esp. by applying heat, cold, or wet; cause to wrinkle or shrivel; *spec*. (***a***) draw in or curl up (the body, oneself), esp. in pain or discomfort; (***b***) cause (a textile) to contract by wetting, esp. during manufacture to prevent further shrinkage. LME. ▶**b** Fit (a piece of machinery etc.) tightly *on* or *on to* another by expanding it with heat and then cooling it rapidly after positioning. M19.
7 †**a** Draw back or retract (a hand, claw, etc.). Also foll. by *back, in*. LME–E18. ▶**b** Draw (the head) aside or down in shame or reticence. Now *rare*. L15.
†**8** Shun, avoid. E16–L17.
9 Reduce in number, extent, scope, or significance. Also foll. by *into, to*. E17.

6 C. LAMB Death does not shrink up his human victim at this rate. F. T. BUCKLAND A human head . . by some process . . shrunk to about the size of a large orange. **9** CARLYLE Logical cobwebbery shrinks itself together.

Phrases: †**shrink up one's shoulders** shrug one's shoulders; *fig*. (foll. by *at*) regard with dislike or indifference. **shrinking violet** a person who is shy or modest, esp. exaggeratedly so. **shrink into oneself** become withdrawn. **shrunk in the wash** *fig*. damaged, depreciated in value.
Comb.: **shrink film** = *shrink-wrap* (a) below; **shrink fit** = SHRINKAGE *fit*; **shrink-resistant** *adjective* (of a textile etc.) resistant to shrinkage when wet etc. **shrink-ring** a metal ring that has been shrunk on; a ring designed to bear the strain of expansion and shrinkage; **shrink-wrap** *noun & verb* (***a***) *noun* thin usu. transparent plastic film wrapped around and then shrunk tightly on to an article as packaging; (***b***) *verb trans*. enclose in shrink-wrap.
■ **shrinkable** *adjective* able to be shrunk; liable to shrink: L19. **shrinkaˈbility** *noun* M20. **shrinker** *noun* (***a***) a person who shrinks or recoils from a duty, danger, etc.; (***b***) a person employed in shrinking materials, esp. textiles; (***c***) *slang* a psychiatrist: M16. **shrinkingly** *adverb* in a shrinking manner, *esp*. in a manner suggesting reluctance, dislike, shyness, etc. E19.

shrinkage /ˈʃrɪŋkɪdʒ/ *noun*. E19.
[from prec. + -AGE.]
1 The action or fact of shrinking; *esp*. reduction in size or volume due to contraction caused by heat, cold, or wet. E19.
2 The amount or degree of shrinking. M19.
3 (A) reduction in a company's budget or profits due to wastage, theft, etc. M20.

3 *attrib*.: *Observer* Businessmen who come into catering from outside find kitchen 'shrinkage' allowances breathtaking.

Comb.: **shrinkage cavity** METALLURGY a cavity in metal caused by shrinkage or cooling; **shrinkage crack** GEOLOGY a crack in mud or rock due to shrinkage or drying out; **shrinkage fit**: made by shrinking one cylindrical piece of machinery on to another.

shrip /ʃrɪp/ *verb trans*. Now chiefly *dial*. Infl. **-pp-**. E17.
[App. from Germanic base of SCRAPE *verb*.]
Clip, prune, trim. Also foll. by *off*.

shritch /ʃrɪtʃ/ *verb & noun*. Long *obsolete* exc. *dial*. ME.
[Parallel to SCRITCH *verb*.]
▶**A** *verb intrans*. Shriek, screech. ME.
▶**B** *noun*. A screech, a shriek. LME–M17.

shrive /ʃraɪv/ *verb*. *arch*. Pa. t. **shrove** /ʃrəʊv/; pa. pple **shriven** /ˈʃrɪv(ə)n/.
[Old English *scrīfan* impose as a penance = Old Frisian *skrīva* write, impose penance, Old Saxon *skrīban*, Old High German *scrīban* write, prescribe (Dutch *schrijven*, German *schreiben* write, spell); from Germanic from Latin *scribere* write.]
1 *verb intrans*. Of a priest: act as a confessor; hear a confession or confessions. OE.
2 *verb trans*. Hear the confession of; prescribe penance for; give absolution to; absolve *from* or *of* a sin. Freq. in *pass*. OE. ▶**b** *transf*. Relieve *of* a burden; remove (a burden). Chiefly *poet*. E17.
3 a *verb refl. & intrans*. Confess one's sins, go to confession. ME. ▶†**b** *verb trans*. Orig., confess (one's sins). Later *transf*., (*poet*.), reveal, disclose. ME–E19.

2 J. BETJEMAN God shrive me from this morning lust For supple farm girls. C. THUBRON Zealots were encouraged to scrutinize, shrive and denounce each other. **b** R. BRIDGES A . . tomb: Such as to look on shrives The heart of half its care. **3b** KEATS I cannot live Another night, and not my passion shrive.

■ **shriven** *ppl adjective* confessed, absolved M19. **shriver** *noun* a confessor ME.

shrivel /ˈʃrɪv(ə)l/ *noun*. *rare*. M16.
[from next.]
Orig. (in *pl*.), wrinkles of skin. Later, a shrivelled or shrunken thing.

shrivel /ˈʃrɪv(ə)l/ *verb*. Infl. **-ll-**, ***-l-**. M16.
[Perh. from Old Norse: cf. Swedish dial. *skryvla* wrinkle. See also SWIVEL *verb*².]
1 *verb trans*. Cause to contract or shrink by wrinkling or curling, esp. from lack of moisture. Freq. foll. by *up*. M16. ▶**b** *fig*. Cause to lose will, desire, or momentum; make ineffectual or insignificant. M17.
2 *verb intrans*. Contract or shrink by wrinkling or curling, esp. from lack of moisture. Also foll. by *up, away*. L16. ▶**b** *fig*. Lose will, desire, or momentum; become ineffectual or insignificant. L17.

1 T. HOOK The lamb was shrivelled up to a cinder. H. B. STOWE That fearful collapse shrivels the most healthy countenance . . to the shrunken . . image of decrepit old age. **b** L. LOCHHEAD My sharp tongue will shrivel any man. **2** K. VONNEGUT You'll shrivel up like a raisin. **b** *New Musical Express* It makes most of the present Radio One playlist shrivel into insignificance. P. ANGADI Mary's conviction shrivelled at once.

■ **shrivelled** *ppl adjective* (***a***) contracted or shrunk into wrinkles, esp. from lack of moisture; (***b***) (of a person) having wrinkled skin, shrunken with age; (***c***) *fig*. diminished adversely, constricted: M16.

shriven *verb pa. pple* of SHRIVE.

shroff /ʃrɒf/ *noun & verb*. E17.
[formed as SARAF.]
▶**A** *noun*. In the Indian subcontinent, a banker, a money-changer; in the Far East, an expert employed to detect counterfeit or base coin. E17.
▶**B** *verb trans. & intrans*. Examine (coin) in order to separate the genuine from the counterfeit or base. M18.
■ **shroffage** *noun* the commission charged for shroffing coin E17.

Shropshire /ˈʃrɒpʃə/ *noun*. L16.
[A county in central England.]
Used *attrib*. to designate things from or associated with Shropshire; *esp*. (***a***) (an animal of) an old breed of horned sheep native to Shropshire; (***b***) (an animal of) a modern breed of black-faced hornless sheep.

shroud /ʃraʊd/ *noun*¹.
[Late Old English *scrūd* corresp. to Old Norse *skrúð(i)* fittings, gear, fabric, etc., from Germanic base meaning 'cut', rel. to West Germanic base of SHRED *noun*.]
▶**I** †**1** A garment; an article of clothing; *sing*. & in *pl*. (one's) clothes. LOE–M17. ▶**b** *gen*. Clothing. LOE–ME.
2 †**a** A place providing (esp. temporary) shelter. LME–M17. ▶**b** The branches of a tree, considered as providing shade (cf. SHROUD *noun*³). Formerly also *transf*., shadow, shade, protection. Now *rare* or *obsolete*. L16.
3 In *pl*. (treated as *sing*. or (*rare*) *pl*.). A crypt, a vault, *esp*. the one in St Paul's Cathedral. *obsolete* exc. *Hist*. M16.
4 A covering; a screen, a veil, a disguise. M16.
5 A sheet or sheetlike garment in which a corpse is wrapped for burial etc. L16.

4 C. KINGSLEY A grey shroud of rain. **5** W. H. PRESCOTT His remains, rolled in their bloody shroud.

▶**II** *techn*. **6** Either of the two annular plates at the sides of a water-wheel, forming the ends of the buckets. Formerly also, a protective part on the horizontal sails of a windmill. LME.
7 A rim or flange cast on the ends of the teeth of a gear-wheel. L18.
8 ENGINEERING. A circular band attached to the circumference of the rotor of a turbine; a flange on the tip of a turbine rotor blade interlocking with adjacent blades so as to form a continuous band. E20.
9 A temporary covering for part of a spacecraft, *esp*. one which protects and streamlines the payload of a rocket during launching. M20.
10 A dome-shaped metal covering on a tap, from which the spindle or handle emerges. M20.
Comb.: **shroud-brass** a memorial brass in which the deceased is represented in a shroud.
■ **shroudless** *adjective* M18. **shroudlike** *adjective* L17. **shroudy** *adjective* (*rare*) providing shelter M17.

shroud /ʃraʊd/ *noun*². LME.
[Prob. a specialized use of prec.]
1 NAUTICAL. In *pl*. & (occas.) *sing*. A set of ropes, usu. in pairs, forming part of the standing rigging of a ship and supporting the mast or topmast. Freq. with specifying word. LME. ▶**b** Any such rope. M18.
2 In full ***shroud line***. Any of the straps joining the canopy of a parachute to the harness. Usu. in *pl*. E20.
Comb.: **shroud hawser** NAUTICAL a shroud-laid rope; **shroud-knot** NAUTICAL a knot used in repairing a parted shroud; **shroud-laid** *adjective* NAUTICAL (of a rope) having four strands laid right-handed on a core; ***shroud line***: see sense 2 above.
■ **shroudage** *noun* (*poet*.) the shrouds of a ship L19.

shroud /ʃraʊd/ *noun*³. *obsolete* exc. *dial*. L15.
[Formally identical with SHROUD *noun*¹, but in sense derived from Germanic base of SHROUD *noun*¹.]
sing. & in *pl*. Branches or twigs cut off a tree; loppings. Also (*sing*.), a branch.

shroud /ʃraʊd/ *verb*¹. ME.
[from SHROUD *noun*¹.]
†**1** *verb trans*. Clothe. Only in ME. ▶**b** *transf*. Adorn, deck. ME–E16.
2 *verb trans*. Cover so as to protect; screen from injury or attack; shelter. Formerly also *refl*., seek protection, take shelter. *arch*. exc. as passing into sense 4 below. ME. ▶**b** *verb intrans*. Seek or take shelter. *arch*. L16.
†**3** *verb trans. & intrans*. Hide or be hidden in a secret place. LME–M17.
4 *verb trans*. Hide from view; cover or envelop so as to conceal; obscure, screen, disguise, (*lit*. & *fig*.). LME.
5 *verb trans*. Put a shroud on (a corpse); *transf*. bury. L16.
6 *verb trans*. *techn*. Provide with a shroud or shrouds. M17.

2 SIR W. SCOTT Scotland's king who shrouds my sire. F. W. FARRAR The joyous birds, shrouded in cheerful shade. **4** S. O'FAOLÁIN The woods . . were . . shrouded in haze. V. BRITTAIN The . . darkness of a June evening shrouded the quiet garden. T. BENN The decision-making of multinationals . . is shrouded in . . secrecy.

■ **shrouder** *noun* (*rare*) L16. **shrouding** *noun* †(***a***) clothing; (***b***) the action of the verb; (***c***) the shrouds of a water-wheel: ME.

shroud /ʃraʊd/ *verb*² *trans*. *local*. LME.
[from SHROUD *noun*³.]
Lop (a tree or its branches).

Shrove /ʃrəʊv/ *noun*. *obsolete* exc. *dial*. L16.
[Abbreviation.]
Shrovetide.

shrove /ʃrəʊv/ *verb*¹ *intrans*. *obsolete* exc. *dial*. M16.
[formed as SHROVE-.]
Take part in festivities at Shrovetide; make merry. Chiefly as ***shroving*** *verbal noun*.

shrove *verb*² *pa. t*. of SHRIVE.

Shrove- /ʃrəʊv/ *combining form*. Also as attrib. adjective **Shrove**. LME.
[Irreg. from *shrove* pa. t. of SHRIVE.]
Designating days of the beginning of the week preceding the start of Lent, when it was formerly customary to be shriven and to take part in festivities.
Shrove Monday (now *rare* or *obsolete*) the Monday before Shrove Tuesday. †**Shrove Sunday** Quinquagesima. **Shrovetide** the period comprising Quinquagesima and the following Monday and Tuesday. **Shrove Tuesday** the Tuesday before Ash Wednesday; also called ***pancake day***.

shrub /ʃrʌb/ *noun*¹. See also SCRUB *noun*¹ & *adjective*
[Old English *scrubb*, *scrybb* shrubbery, underwood, app. rel. to Northern Frisian *skrobb* broom, brushwood, Western Flemish *schrobbe* climbing wild pea or vetch, Norwegian *skrubba* dwarf cornel, Danish dial. *skrub* brushwood.]
1 A woody plant smaller than a tree; *spec*. in BOTANY, a perennial plant having several woody stems rising from the base. Cf. TREE *noun* 1. OE.

†**2** A twig, a sprig. **LME–M17.**
†**3** = **SCRUB** *noun*[1] 4a. **M16–L17.**
Comb.: **shrub mallow** the garden hibiscus, *Hibiscus syriacus*; **shrub oak** = ***scrub oak*** s.v. **SCRUB** *noun*[1]; **shrub rose** any of various non-climbing garden roses, esp. old-fashioned varieties and species roses; **shrub trefoil** (*a*) the tree-medick, *Medicago arborea*; (*b*) *N. Amer.* = ***hop tree*** s.v. **HOP** *noun*[1].
¶ Not recorded between **OE** and **LME**.
■ **shrubbage** *noun* = **SHRUBBERY** 2 **E18. shrubless** *adjective* **E19. shrublet** *noun* a small shrub **L19. shrublike** *adjective* resembling (that of) a shrub **L18.**

shrub /ʃrʌb/ *noun*[2]. **E18.**
[Arab. *šurb*, *šarāb*: see **SYRUP**. Cf. **SHERBET**, **SHRAB**.]
1 A drink made of sweetened fruit juice and spirits, esp. rum. **E18.**
2 A cordial made from raspberry juice, vinegar, and sugar. *US.* **M19.**

shrub /ʃrʌb/ *verb*. Infl. **-bb-**. **ME.**
[Partly parallel to **SCRUB** *verb*; partly from **SHRUB** *noun*[1].]
†**1** *verb trans.* = **SCRUB** *verb* 1. Only in **ME.**
†**2** *verb intrans.* Scratch the body; fidget. **ME–L16.** ▸**b** *verb trans.* Scratch. Only in **M17.**
3 *verb trans.* Orig., dig up (a bush). Later (now *US dial.*), rid (ground) of bushes. **M16.**
†**4** *verb trans.* Lop (a tree or its branches). **L16–L17.**
†**5** *verb trans.* Cudgel. **L16–E18.**
6 *verb trans.* In *pass.* Be planted with shrubs. **L19.**

shrubbed /ʃrʌbd/ *adjective*. **M16.**
[from **SHRUB** *noun*[1], *verb*: see **-ED**[2], **-ED**[1].]
†**1** Stunted; shrubby. **M16–L17.**
2 Planted with shrubs. **L19.**

shrubbery /ˈʃrʌb(ə)ri/ *noun*. **M18.**
[from **SHRUB** *noun*[1] + **-ERY**.]
1 An area planted with shrubs. **M18.**
2 Vegetation consisting of shrubs; shrubs collectively. **L18.**

shrubby /ˈʃrʌbi/ *adjective*. **M16.**
[from **SHRUB** *noun*[1] + **-Y**[1].]
1 Of the nature of or consisting of shrubs. **M16.**
2 Having the habit, growth, or size of a shrub; like (that of) a shrub; *spec.* having several perennial woody stems rising from the base (freq. in specific names of plants). **L16.**
3 Covered, planted, or overgrown with shrubs. **L16.**
2 ***shrubby cinquefoil***, ***shrubby St John's wort***, ***shrubby sea-blite***, etc.
■ **shrubbiness** *noun* (*rare*) **E18.**

shruff /ʃrʌf/ *noun*[1]. *obsolete* exc. *dial.* **LME.**
[Parallel to **SCRUFF** *noun*[1].]
Refuse wood or other material, used esp. for burning as fuel.

†**shruff** *noun*[2]. **M16–E19.**
[Perh. from German *Schroff* fragment of mineral.]
Old brass or copper.

shrug /ʃrʌg/ *verb & noun*. **LME.**
[Origin unkn.]
▶ **A** *verb*. Infl. **-gg-**.
†**1** *verb intrans. & refl.* Move the body from side to side; fidget. **LME–M17.**
2 *verb intrans.* Shiver; shudder. Now *rare* or *obsolete*. **LME.** ▸†**b** Shrink away, cower. **L16–L17.**
3 *verb intrans.* Raise and contract the shoulders slightly and momentarily, esp. as an expression of disdain, indifference, ignorance, etc. **LME.**
4 *verb trans.* Raise and contract (the shoulders) in this way. **M16.** ▸**b** Express by shrugging. **L19.**
5 *verb refl. & intrans.* **a** Draw oneself together, curl oneself up. Now *rare* or *obsolete*. **E17.** ▸**b** Get *into* a coat etc. with a shrugging movement. **M20.**
6 *verb trans.* Pull or tug *up*. *US.* **E19.**

> 📖 **3** J. T. STORY Ask anybody a question and they shrug. R. SILVERBERG Are you telling us just to shrug and give up? **4** D. LESSING The only thing to do is to shrug your shoulders and forgive everyone. G. JOSIPOVICI When I ask . . why he shrugs his shoulders.

With adverbs in specialized senses: **shrug aside** = ***shrug off*** (b) below. **shrug off** (*a*) take off (a coat etc.) with a shrugging movement; (*b*) *fig.* dismiss or reject as unimportant etc. (as) by shrugging. **shrug on** put on (a coat etc.) with a shrugging movement.
▶ **B** *noun*. **1** An act of shrugging the shoulders. **L16.** ▸**b** A woman's short close-fitting jacket. Also ***shrug jacket***. **M20.**
†**2** A tug, a pull; a shake (of the hand). **E17–M18.**

> 📖 **1** H. J. EYSENCK Infringement of the social code which most people would dismiss with a shrug of the shoulders. R. FRAME The question was answered by a shrug.

■ **shruggingly** *adverb* with a shrug **L16.**

shrunk /ʃrʌŋk/ *ppl adjective*. **M16.**
[pa. pple of **SHRINK** *verb*. Cf. next.]
= **SHRUNKEN** *ppl adjective*. Now usu. *pred.*

shrunk *verb pa. pple* of **SHRINK** *verb*.

shrunken /ˈʃrʌŋk(ə)n/ *ppl adjective*. **OE.**
[pa. pple of **SHRINK** *verb*. Cf. prec.]
That has shrunk or been shrunk; contracted or reduced in size; (of a person, bodily part, etc.) withered or shrivelled through old age, disease, etc.

shrunken *verb pa. pple* of **SHRINK** *verb*.

shtetl /ˈʃtɛt(ə)l, ˈʃteɪt(ə)l/ *noun*. Pl. ***-lach*** /-lɑːx/, ***-ls***. **M20.**
[Yiddish = little town, from German *Stadt* town.]
Hist. A small Jewish town or village in eastern Europe.

shtibl /ˈʃtiːb(ə)l/ *noun*. Also ***shtiebel***. Pl. ***-lach*** /-lɑːx/. **E20.**
[Yiddish, dim. of *shtub* room, house. Cf. German dial. *Stüberl* small room.]
A small synagogue.

shtick /ʃtɪk/ *noun*. *slang* (chiefly *N. Amer.*). Also **shtik**. **M20.**
[Yiddish, from German *Stück* piece, play.]
1 A (comedian's) stage routine; a joke; *transf.* a patter, a gimmick. **M20.**
2 A particular area of activity or interest. **M20.**

shtik *noun* var. of **SHTICK**.

Shtokavian /ʃtɒˈkɑːvɪən, -ˈkeɪvɪən/ *noun & adjective*. Also **Što-**. **M20.**
[Serbo-Croat *štokavski* adjective (from the use of *što* for 'what?'): see **-IAN**.]
▶ **A** *noun*. A widely spoken dialect of Serbo-Croat on which the literary forms of the language are based. **M20.**
▶ **B** *attrib.* or as *adjective*. Of, pertaining to, or designating this dialect. **M20.**

shtook /ʃtʊk/ *noun*. *slang*. Also **shtuck**, **sch-**. **M20.**
[Origin unkn.]
Trouble. Only in ***in shtook***, ***in dead shtook***, ***out of shtook***, ***out of dead shtook***.

shtoom /ʃtʊm/ *adjective & verb*. *slang*. Also **s(h)tumm** /ʃtʌm/, **sch-**. **M20.**
[Yiddish from German *stumm*.]
▶ **A** *adjective*. Silent, mute. Chiefly in ***keep shtoom***, ***stay shtoom***, refrain from disclosing information etc. **M20.**
▶ **B** *verb intrans.* Become silent, shut *up*. **M20.**

shtreimel, ***shtreiml***, ***shtreimlach*** *nouns* see **STREIML**.

shtuck *noun* var. of **SHTOOK**.

shtumm *adjective & verb* var. of **SHTOOM**.

shtup /ʃtʊp/ *verb*. *slang*. Infl. **-pp-**. **M20.**
[Yiddish, perh. from German dial. *stupfen* nudge, jog.]
1 *verb trans.* Push. **M20.**
2 *verb trans. & intrans.* Have sexual intercourse (with). **M20.**

shuba /ˈʃuːbə/ *noun*. Now *Hist.* Also Anglicized as **shooba**, **shub(e)** /ʃuːb/. **L16.**
[Russian.]
A fur gown or greatcoat as traditionally worn in parts of Russia.

shubunkin /ʃəːˈbʌŋkɪn, ʃuː-/ *noun*. **E20.**
[Japanese, from *shu* vermilion + *bun* portion + *kin* gold.]
(A fish of) an ornamental breed of goldfish that is multicoloured with black spots and red patches and has elongated fins and tail.

shuck /ʃʌk/ *noun*[1].
[Old English *scucca*, perh. from Germanic base of **SHY** *adjective*.]
†**1** A devil, a fiend. **OE–ME.**
2 A ghost in the form of a large usu. black dog. *dial.* **M19.**

shuck /ʃʌk/ *noun*[2] *& verb*. Chiefly *US*. **L17.**
[Origin unkn.]
▶ **A** *noun*. **1** A husk, a pod, a shell; *esp.* the husk of an ear of maize. **L17.** ▸**b** The shell of an oyster or a clam. **M19.** ▸**c** The integument of some insect pupae or larvae. **M19.**
2 a A worthless thing. Also, a mean or contemptible person. *colloq.* **M19.** ▸**b** Nonsense; (a) sham. *colloq.* **M20.**
3 In *pl.* As *interjection*. Expr. contempt or regret, or self-deprecation in response to praise. *colloq.* **M19.**

> 📖 **1 light a shuck** *slang* leave in a hurry. **3** C. E. MULFORD 'Thank you for getting it . .' 'Oh, shucks; that was nothing,' he laughed awkwardly.

▶ **B** *verb*. **1** *verb trans.* Remove the shucks from (maize etc.); shell. **M18.**
2 *transf. verb trans.* Remove, throw or strip *off*; get rid of, abandon. *colloq.* **M19.** ▸**b** *verb intrans.* Slip *out of* one's clothes. **M19.**
3 *verb trans. & intrans.* Deceive or fool (someone). *slang.* **M20.**

> 📖 **1** C. LLOYD I really enjoy shucking peas. **2** *Listener* Miners' sons . . don't easily shuck off the legacy of . . struggle. F. RAPHAEL Stephen shucked his shoes. **b** M. MACHLIN Larry opened the door, shucked out of his cords and shirt.

■ **shucker** *noun* a person who shucks oysters or clams **L19.**

shudder /ˈʃʌdə/ *verb & noun*. **ME.**
[Middle Low German *schōderen*, Middle Dutch *schūderen*, frequentative from Germanic word meaning 'shake' repr. also in Old Frisian *schedda*, Old Saxon *skuddian*, Old High German *scutten* (German *schütten*): see **-ER**[5].]
▶ **A** *verb*. **1** *verb intrans.* Have a convulsive tremor of the body caused by fear, abhorrence, cold, etc.; shiver or tremble violently. (Foll. by *at*.) **ME.** ▸**b** Foll. by *to do*: feel repugnance or horror in doing. **M18.**
2 *verb trans.* Cause to shudder. *rare. poet.* **M17.**
3 *verb intrans.* Vibrate; quiver. **M19.**

> 📖 **1** J. UGLOW She . . shuddered at the thought of perpetual domesticity. D. PROFUMO James's mind seethed with the idea of maggots . . and he shuddered. **b** A. PRICE What he'll make of you I shudder to think! **2** D. WALCOTT Hurtling cavalry shuddering the shore. **3** G. VIDAL The . . sky shuddered with heat. S. J. PERELMAN The plane slid . . down the asphalt . . and shuddered to a stop.

▶ **B** *noun*. **1** An act of shuddering; a convulsive tremor of the body. **E17.**
2 A vibratory movement; a quiver. **M19.**

> 📖 **1** E. BLISHEN Bing was sitting next to me, and I felt his horror as a positive shudder. **give a person the shudders** *colloq.* make him or her shudder. **2** D. H. LAWRENCE Devil dancers . . dancing to the shudder of drums.

■ **shuddering** *verbal noun* the action of the verb; an instance of this: **LME. shuddering** *ppl adjective* (*a*) that shudders; (*b*) characterized or accompanied by shuddering: **L16. shudderingly** *adverb* **L16. shuddersome** *adjective* causing a shudder **L19. shuddery** *adjective* characterized by or causing shuddering **M19.**

shuddup /ʃʌˈdʌp/ *verb intrans.* (*imper.*). *non-standard*. **M20.**
[Repr. a pronunc. Cf. **SHADDUP**, **SHURRUP**.]
Shut up! Be quiet!

shude *noun* var. of **SHOOD**.

shuffle /ˈʃʌf(ə)l/ *noun*. **E17.**
[from the verb.]
1 An evasive trick; subterfuge; sharp practice. **E17.**
2 The action or an act of shuffling or moving with a slow dragging, scraping, or sliding motion; a gait characterized by such movement. **M17.** ▸**b** *spec.* A dragging or scraping step in dancing; a dance performed with such steps; a piece of music for such a dance. **E19.**
3 An act of shuffling playing-cards. **M17.** ▸**b** A change of relative positions; a rearrangement, esp. of ministerial posts within a government or Cabinet. Cf. **RESHUFFLE** *noun*. **L17.**
4 An exchange or alternation of arguments, expedients, etc. *rare*. **M17.**

> 📖 **2** K. WATERHOUSE He crossed the floor . . with an old man's shuffle. J. M. COETZEE I . . hear the shuffle of your footsteps. **b** ***double-shuffle***: see **DOUBLE** *adjective & adverb*. **3** ***riffle-shuffle***: see **RIFFLE** *noun* 2. **3b** G. BROWN If . . Gordon Walker had . . remained Foreign Secretary, there would have been no shuffle. J. BARNES A neurotic shuffle between repression and anarchy. **lost in the shuffle** *N. Amer.* overlooked or missed in the multitude.

shuffle /ˈʃʌf(ə)l/ *verb*. **M16.**
[from or cogn. with Low German *schuffeln* walk clumsily or with dragging feet, ult. from Germanic base also of **SHOVE** *verb*, **SCUFFLE** *verb*[1]: see **-LE**[3]. Cf. **SHOVEL** *verb*[2].]
1 *verb trans.* Insert or extract in a deceitful, surreptitious, or haphazard manner, smuggle *in*, *into*, or *out of*. *arch.* **M16.** ▸†**b** Remove or take away with haste or secrecy. (Foll. by *away*.) **L16–M18.**
2 *verb intrans. & refl.* Get oneself *in*, *into*, or *out of* a position or condition, by fortuitous or underhand means. **M16.** ▸†**b** *verb intrans.* Scramble (*for*). Only in **E17.** ▸**c** *verb intrans.* Foll. by *through*: perform hurriedly or perfunctorily. **M17.**
3 *verb trans.* Move (a thing) with a dragging, sliding, or clumsy motion. Usu. foll. by *around*, *back*, *on*, *off*. **M16.** ▸**b** *verb intrans.* Fumble. **E19.** ▸**c** *verb intrans.* Get *into* a garment clumsily. **M19.**
4 *verb trans. & intrans.* Rearrange (the cards in a pack, dominoes, etc.), esp. by sliding them over each other quickly, so as to prevent the players from knowing the order in which the cards etc. lie. **L16.** ▸**b** *verb trans.* Produce or put *in* (a card) in such rearranging. Chiefly *fig.* **L16.** ▸**c** *verb trans. gen.* Rearrange; shift from one place to another; put together in one indiscriminate mass, intermingle, confuse. **L16.**
5 *verb intrans.* Walk without lifting the feet off the ground; move with a slow dragging, scraping, or sliding motion. **L16.** ▸**b** *verb trans.* Move (the feet) along the ground without lifting them. **L16.** ▸**c** *verb trans. & intrans.* Dance (a shuffle). **E19.** ▸**d** *verb intrans.* Move restlessly; fidget. **L19.**
6 *verb intrans.* Act in a shifting or evasive manner; equivocate; prevaricate; hedge. **L16.** ▸†**b** *verb trans.* Treat in an equivocal manner. **M17–E18.**
7 Foll. by *off*: ▸**a** *verb trans.* Escape, evade, shirk. **E17.** ▸†**b** *verb trans.* Palm (a person) off *with*. **M–L17.** ▸**c** *verb trans.* Palm (a thing) off *on* or *upon*. **L17.** ▸**d** *verb intrans.* [With allus. to Shakes. *Haml.* III.i.67.] Die. *joc.* or *colloq.* **E20.**

📖 **1** W. ROBERTSON He had shuffled in this letter among other papers. M. ARNOLD They had been shuffled into their places by . . accident. **2** A. HELPS To shuffle awkwardly out of wealth and dignities. **3** A. TROLLOPE She could only shuffle her letter back into her pocket. R. P. JHABVALA Indian sandals . . I can shuffle off and leave on the thresholds. L. ELLMANN He started to shuffle books and papers around. **4** HOR. WALPOLE Astonished at seeing the Count shuffle with the faces of the cards upwards. J. STEINBECK George shuffled the cards noisily. **c** B. PYM He shuffled the papers on his desk. **5** B. BAINBRIDGE The aged crew . . shuffled to the rails. P. LIVELY Shuffling around on his crutches. J. RABAN The traffic shuffled forward . . fifty yards and locked again. **b** D. JACOBSON We shuffle our feet, we exchange glances.

Comb.: **shuffle beat** = *shuffle rhythm* below; **shuffle rhythm** a slow strongly syncopated rhythm; **shufflewing** *dial.* the dunnock.

■ **shuffler** *noun* E17. **shuffling** *ppl adjective* (*a*) that shuffles; (*b*) (of a gait) consisting of or characterized by shuffling; (*c*) (of a person, action, etc.) evasive, shifty: L16. **shufflingly** *adverb* M17. **shuffly** *adjective* characterized by shuffling; inclined to shuffle: E20.

shuffleboard *noun* var. of SHOVELBOARD.

shufti /ˈʃʊfti/ *noun. slang* (orig. MILITARY). Also **shufty**. M20.
[from the verb.]
A look, a glance. Esp. in ***take a shufti***, ***have a shufti***.

shufti /ˈʃʊfti/ *verb intrans. slang* (chiefly MILITARY). Now *rare*. Also **shufty**. M20.
[from colloq. Arab. *šuftī* have you seen?, from *šāfa* see.]
Look; glance. Usu. in *imper.*

shufty *noun, verb* vars. of SHUFTI *noun, verb*.

shuggle *verb* var. of SHOGGLE.

shugo /ˈʃuːɡəʊ/ *noun*. Pl. same. L19.
[Japanese.]
Hist. In the Japanese feudal system, a military governor.

shuka /ˈʃuːkə/ *noun*. M19.
[Kiswahili from colloq. Arab. *šukka* piece, (oblong) piece of fabric.]
A garment resembling a shawl, traditionally worn in E. Africa.

shul /ʃuːl/ *noun*. L19.
[Yiddish from German *Schule* school.]
A synagogue.

shun /ʃʌn/ *verb*. Infl. **-nn-**.
[Old English *scūnian*, of unkn. origin. Cf. SHUNT *verb*.]
†**1** *verb trans.* Abhor, loathe. OE–ME.
†**2** *verb trans.* **a** Seek safety by concealment or flight from (an enemy, pursuer, etc.). OE–M17. ▸**b** Evade (a blow or missile). L16–M17.
†**3** *verb intrans.* **a** Shrink with fear; be afraid. OE–LME. ▸**b** Shrink back physically; move *aside* or *away from*; refrain *from*. ME–L16.
4 *verb trans.* Avoid (now *spec.* persistently or habitually) from repugnance, fear, or caution; keep away from. ME.
5 *verb trans.* Escape (a threatened evil, an unwelcome task). Formerly also, prevent the occurrence of, guard against. Now *rare* or *obsolete*. ME.
6 *verb trans.* Screen, hide. Now *dial.* E17.
7 *verb trans.* Shove, push. Cf. SHUNT *verb* 2. *dial.* L17.

📖 **4** B. BETTELHEIM English authors . . shun ambiguities. P. AUSTER He preferred to remain indoors, shunned bright light. O. SACKS He . . became unpopular . . and found himself shunned.

Comb.: **shunpike** *noun & verb* (*US*) (*a*) *noun* a minor road taken to avoid toll roads; (*b*) *verb intrans.* drive along minor roads to avoid tolls or to travel at a leisurely pace.

■ **shunless** *adjective* (*rare*) that cannot be shunned or avoided E17. **shunnable** *adjective* L16. **shunner** *noun* E19.

'shun /ʃʌn/ *interjection*. L19.
[Abbreviation (repr. a pronunc.).]
MILITARY. A command to troops etc. to stand to attention. Cf. ATTENTION 4.

shunga /ˈʃuːŋɡɑː/ *noun*. Pl. same. M20.
[Japanese, from *shun* spring + *ga* picture.]
An example of Japanese erotic art.

shunt /ʃʌnt/ *noun*. LME.
[from the verb.]
†**1** A sudden start or jerk. *rare*. Only in LME.
2 The action or an act of shunting a train etc. on to a siding. M19. ▸**b** A motor accident, *esp.* a collision of a number of vehicles travelling one close behind the other. *slang*. M20.
3 a ELECTRICITY. A component connected in parallel; *esp.* a low-value resistor connected in parallel with an instrument, in order to reduce the current passing through it. M19. ▸**b** MEDICINE. A natural or artificial route connecting two vessels, whereby blood is diverted from one to the other; the passage of blood along such a route. Also, the surgical construction of such a route. E20. ▸**c** BIOCHEMISTRY. An alternative metabolic pathway; *spec.* (in full ***hexose monophosphate shunt***) the pentose phosphate cycle. M20.
4 A railway point. M19.
5 A method of rifling cannon so that the projectile undergoes a lateral change of position in the process of loading. Freq. *attrib.* M19.

Comb.: **shunt circuit**: ELECTRICITY containing or acting as a shunt (sense 3a above); **shunt line** a railway siding; **shunt machine**, **shunt motor** ELECTRICITY a d.c. motor in which the field and armature windings are connected in parallel with respect to the supply; **shunt-wound** *adjective* (ELECTRICITY) having a shunt circuit wound in parallel with the main circuit.

shunt /ʃʌnt/ *verb*. ME.
[Origin uncertain: perh. from SHUN.]
†**1** *verb intrans.* Move suddenly aside; start, shy. ME–L18. ▸†**b** *verb trans.* Evade (a blow etc.). Only in LME.
2 *verb trans.* Push, shove. Cf. SHUN 7. Chiefly *dial.* E18.
3 *verb trans.* Move (a train or a part of it) from the main line to a siding or from one line of rails to another, esp. by pushing; *fig.* push aside or out of the way. M19. ▸**b** *verb intrans.* (Of a train) be moved in this way; *fig.* move out of the way. M19.
4 *verb trans.* **a** ELECTRICITY. Divert (a portion of an electric current) by means of a shunt (SHUNT *noun* 3a); divert current from (an instrument). L19. ▸**b** MEDICINE. Pass (blood) through a shunt (SHUNT *noun* 3b). E20.

📖 **3** P. THEROUX Our train was shunted back and forth. S. MIDDLETON They were . . shunted off to eat in another room. **b** R. CAMPBELL The train had to shunt . . on to different lines.

■ **shunter** *noun* (*a*) a railway worker employed in shunting rolling-stock; (*b*) a small locomotive used for shunting rolling-stock: M19.

shura /ˈʃʊərə/ *noun*. M20.
[Arab. *šūrā* consultation.]
The Islamic principle of (rule by) consultation; an Islamic consultative council.

shuriken /ˈʃʊərɪkɛn/ *noun*. L20.
[Japanese *shuri-ken* lit. 'dagger in the hand', from *shu* hand + *ri* inside + *ken* sword, blade.]
A missile in the form of a star with projecting blades or points, used in some martial arts.

shurrup /ʃʊˈrʊp/ *verb intrans. (imper.). non-standard*. L19.
[Repr. a pronunc. Cf. SHADDUP, SHUDDUP.]
Shut up! Be quiet!

shush /ʃʊʃ, ʃʌʃ/ *verb & noun*. E20.
[Imit., repr. repetition of SH *interjection*. Cf. HUSH *verb*¹, *noun*¹.]
▶ **A** *verb*. **1** *verb trans. & intrans.* Call or reduce (a person) to silence esp. by uttering 'sh!'. E20.
2 *verb intrans.* Become or remain silent. Usu. in *imper.* E20.
3 *verb intrans.* Make or move with a soft rustling or swishing sound. L20.

📖 **1** A. CARTER A child . . began to cry; some woman shushed it. J. HERRIOT I did a bit of shushing and . . the babel died down. T. MORRISON Gideon held up one hand to shush her. **2** J. B. PRIESTLEY Requested by . . his colleagues to 'shush'. **3** L. GILLEN The trees shushing softly . . in the breeze. DENNIS POTTER The automatic door shushed open.

▶ **B** *noun*. An utterance of 'sh!'; *transf.* silence. *colloq.* M20.

📖 H. ROSENTHAL Changing one's position . . met with loud shushes from one's neighbours.

Shuswap /ˈʃʊswɒp/ *noun & adjective*. M19.
[Shuswap.]
▶ **A** *noun*. Pl. **-s**, same. A member of a Salish people inhabiting southern British Columbia; the language of this people. M19.
▶ **B** *attrib.* or as *adjective*. Of or pertaining to the Shuswap or their language. E20.

shut /ʃʌt/ *noun*. LME.
[from the verb.]
1 a A bar, a bolt. *obsolete* exc. *dial.* LME. ▸**b** A window shutter. *obsolete* exc. *dial.* E17. ▸**c** A small hinged or sliding door or plate. Formerly also, a valve. *obsolete* exc. *dial.* M17.
†**2** An enclosure, esp. for fish. E–M17.
3 The action, time, or place of shutting; *esp.* (*poet.*) the close (of day). M17.
4 A join; a splice; a weld. E18.
5 A riddance. Chiefly in ***a good shut***. *dial.* M19.

Comb.: **shut-knife** *dial.* a clasp-knife.

shut /ʃʌt/ *verb*. Infl. **-tt-**. Pa. t. & pple **shut**.
[Old English *scyttan* = Old Frisian *sketta*, Middle & mod. Low German, Middle & mod. Dutch *schutten* shut up, obstruct, from West Germanic verb rel. to Germanic base of SHOOT *verb*.]
†**1** *verb trans.* Put (a bar, bolt, etc.) in position so as to fasten a door etc. Cf. SHOOT *verb* 10. OE–M17.
†**2** *verb trans.* Fasten (a door, chest, etc.) with a lock or bar. ME–E19.
3 *verb trans.* Move (a door, window, lid, etc.) into position so as to cover or block an opening. Also (now *rare*) foll. by *up*. ME. ▸**b** *verb trans.* Block, obstruct, or prevent access through (an opening). Also foll. by *up*. Now *rare*. LME. ▸**c** *verb intrans.* Of a door etc.: move so as to cover or block an opening; admit of being closed. LME.
4 *verb trans. & intrans.* Close by folding up or bringing together of parts, esp. those forming an outward covering. Also foll. by *up*. ME.
5 *verb trans.* Prevent entry to or exit from (a place or building) by closing the doors or openings; *spec.* close (a shop or business) for trade. Also foll. by *up*. See also ***shut up*** (c), (d) below. ME. ▸**b** *verb intrans.* Of a place, building, etc., *spec.* a shop: become closed in this way. E19.
6 *verb trans.* Enclose, secure, or confine (a person or thing) *in* or *within* a place, building, etc., by closing a door or opening; *fig.* enclose with a barrier, hem in. ME. ▸**b** *verb trans.* Catch (a finger, garment, etc.) *in* a door etc. by closing it. L19.
†**7** *verb trans.* Bar or exclude (a person) *from* an action, possession, etc. LME–M19.
8 *verb trans.* Relieve (a person) *of* a burden. *obsolete* exc. in ***be shut of***, ***get shut of*** below. L15. ▸**b** Spend or waste (money). *dial.* L18.
9 *verb trans.* Weld. Cf. SHOOT *verb* 29. L15.

📖 **3** W. CATHER He shut the gate . . with a slam. I. ASIMOV Daneel closed the door . ., sliding it shut carefully. P. CAREY He . . shut the door on her. **b** E. A. FREEMAN Not a road was shut against him. **c** J. F. HENDRY The roll-top desk would not shut properly. **4** D. HAMMETT She opened her mouth as if to speak, shut it, opened it again. W. GOLDING He shut the exercise book. A. SCHLEE She shut her eyes, the better to concentrate. **5** C. E. PASCOE Bank-Holiday with the shops . . shut. **b** J. TROLLOPE There's the sherry money-sprint, will you or the shops will shut. **6** D. H. LAWRENCE A valley . . shut in beyond access. G. GREENE They were all shut together in a . . shed.

Phrases: **be shut of**, **get shut of** *dial.* & *colloq.* get rid of. ***keep one's mouth shut***: see MOUTH *noun*. ***keep one's trap shut***: see TRAP *noun*¹. ***shut a person's mouth***: see MOUTH *noun*. **shut it!** *slang* be quiet! ***shut one's eyes against***, ***shut one's eyes to***: see EYE *noun*. ***shut one's heart to***: see HEART *noun*. ***shut one's mind (to)***: see MIND *noun*¹. ***shut one's mouth***: see MOUTH *noun*. ***shut one's pan***: see PAN *noun*¹. ***shut the stable door when the horse has bolted***: see STABLE *noun*¹. ***shut your trap!***: see TRAP *noun*¹. ***with one's eyes shut***: see EYE *noun*.

With adverbs in specialized senses: **shut down** (*a*) push or pull (a sash-window etc.) down into a closed position; (*b*) *fig.* come down like a lid; (*c*) stop (a machine, nuclear reactor, factory, etc.) from operating; (*d*) (of a factory etc.) stop operating. **shut in** (*a*) (now *rare*) = ***draw in*** (c) s.v. DRAW *verb*; (*b*) *rare* become cut off from view; (*c*) stop drawing oil or gas from (a well); (see also sense 6 above). **shut off** (*a*) stop the flow of (water, gas, etc.) by shutting a valve; (*b*) (chiefly *US*) stop the operation of, turn off; *fig.* restrict, hinder; (*c*) cut off or separate *from*; (*d*) *US* cease talking or writing. **shut out** (*a*) exclude (a person, light, etc.) from a place; exclude (a person) from a situation; prevent (a possibility etc.); block (esp. a painful memory) from the mind; (*b*) screen (a landscape etc.) from view; (*c*) SPORT (chiefly *N. Amer.*) prevent (the opposing team) from scoring. **shut to** (*a*) shut (a door); *spec.* move (a door) into a position so as to be almost shut; (*b*) (of a door) move into such a position. **shut up** (*a*) put (a thing) away in a closed container etc.; (*b*) imprison; confine to a room etc. by shutting a door; (chiefly MILITARY) confine to a place by cutting off a means of escape; in *pass.*, be closeted with; (*c*) close all the doors and windows of, bolt and bar, (a house etc.); AGRICULTURE (now *rare*) close (a field) to pasture, in preparation for a hay crop; (*d*) ***shut up shop***, close a shop or business for trade; cease trading permanently; (*e*) close (a box etc.) securely, decisively, or permanently; †(*f*) conclude or bring to an end (a discourse, period of time, etc.); (*g*) *arch.* (of a discourse, period of time, etc.) come to an end; (*h*) *colloq.* reduce to silence by rebuke etc.; (*i*) *colloq.* stop talking (freq. in *imper.*); (see also senses 3, 5 above).

Comb.: **shut-down** (*a*) the closure of a factory etc.; (*b*) (the time of) the cessation of broadcasting for the day on a particular radio or television station; (*c*) the cessation of operation of a machine, nuclear reactor, etc.; **shut-eye** *colloq.* sleep; **shut-off** *noun & adjective* (*a*) *noun* the action or an act of shutting off something; a thing which shuts off something, a tap, a valve; (*b*) *adjective* that is shut off; **shut-up** *adjective* that has been or can be shut up. See also SHUT-IN, SHUT-OUT.

shute /ʃuːt/ *noun*¹. E18.
[Var. of SHOOT *noun*¹.]
WEAVING. **1** The weft. E18.
2 Tram silk. M19.

shute /ʃuːt/ *noun*². *dial.* L18.
[Partly var. of SHOOT *noun*¹; partly var. of CHUTE *noun*¹.]
1 A channel for conveying water, esp. to a lower level; a gutter; a sloping channel for conveying coal, grain, etc., to a lower level; a chute. L18.
2 A sudden flood in a river. M19.
3 = CHUTE *noun*¹ 3. M20.
¶ Recorded earlier in ME as a place-name.

shute *noun*³ var. of SHOOT *noun*².

shut-in /ˈʃʌtɪn/ *adjective & noun*. M19.
[from *shut in* s.v. SHUT *verb*.]
▶ **A** *adjective*. **1** That is shut in; *spec.* (of a person) confined by physical or mental disability. M19.
2 (Of capacity in an oil or gas well) available but unused; of or pertaining to such capacity. M20.
▶ **B** *noun*. **1** A shut-in person. E20.
2 A state or period of an oil or gas well being shut in. M20.

shuto /ˈʃuːtəʊ/ *noun.* M20.
[Japanese, from *shu* hand + *tō* sword.]
A movement of the hand in the manner of a sword in judo, karate, etc.

shut-out /ˈʃʌtaʊt/ *adjective & noun.* M19.
[from *shut out* s.v. SHUT *verb.*]
▶ **A** *adjective.* **1** That is shut out or excluded. M19.
2 BRIDGE. Of a bid: pre-emptive or otherwise intended to discourage the opposition from bidding. E20.
3 SPORT. Designating or pertaining to a game in which one's opponents do not score. Chiefly *N. Amer.* M20.
▶ **B** *noun.* **1** SPORT. A shut-out game or innings. Chiefly *N. Amer.* L19.
2 BRIDGE. A shut-out bid. M20.

shuttance /ˈʃʌt(ə)ns/ *noun. dial.* E19.
[from SHUT *verb* + -ANCE.]
Riddance.

shutter /ˈʃʌtə/ *noun & verb.* M16.
[from SHUT *verb* + -ER[1].]
▶ **A** *noun.* **1** *gen.* A person who or thing which shuts. Also foll. by adverb. M16.
2 *spec.* **a** THEATRICAL. Either of a pair of movable flats run in from opposite wings to meet in the middle of the stage. Now chiefly *Hist.* M17. ▸**b** Either of a pair or set of movable (esp. wooden) panels fixed to the outside or the inside of a window for security or privacy or to shut out the light. Also, a structure of slats on rollers serving the same purpose. L17. ▸**c** A hinged folding cover for protecting a picture in a frame from light, dust, etc. L17. ▸**d** In *pl.* The louvre-boards forming one or more sides of the swell-box of an organ, used for controlling the sound level. L19. ▸**e** A lid or sliding cover for obscuring the light of a lamp. E20. ▸**f** A device for regulating the supply of cooling air to the radiator of an internal-combustion engine, esp. a tractor. E20. ▸**g** = FORM *noun* 15. M20.
3 PHOTOGRAPHY. A device in a camera which opens and closes to regulate the duration of an exposure. M19.

📖 **2b** P. MARSHALL Closed shutters . . barring the noon heat. E. LONGFORD Shopkeepers put up their shutters. **put up the shutters** (*a*) cease business for the day; (*b*) cease business permanently. ***storm shutter***: see STORM *noun.* ***Venetian shutter***: see VENETIAN *adjective.* **3** C. ISHERWOOD I am a camera with its shutter open. ***between-lens shutter***, ***leaf shutter***, ***rotary shutter***, etc.

Comb.: **shutter-blind** a blind with louvres to allow air to circulate; **shutter-bug** *slang* an enthusiastic photographer; **shutter-dam**: having gates which are opened and closed by hydraulic pressure obtained by water driven through pipes by a turbine; **shutter release** the button on a camera that is pressed to cause the shutter to open; **shutter speed** the nominal time for which a shutter is open at a given setting; **shutter weir** a movable weir with gates pivoted about a horizontal axis at or towards the bottom and held nearly vertical until released.

▶ **B** *verb trans.* **1** Close with a shutter; *refl.* shut oneself *in* or *off* (as) with shutters. E19.
2 Provide with shutters. Only as ***shuttered*** *ppl adjective.* M19.

📖 **1** A. MASON The window had been shuttered. **2** T. N. TALFOURD Green-shuttered white 'Pensions'.

■ **shuttering** *noun* (*a*) the action of the verb; (*b*) material for making shutters; (*c*) = FORM *noun* 15b: M19. **shutterless** *adjective* E19.

shutting /ˈʃʌtɪŋ/ *noun.* LME.
[from SHUT *verb* + -ING[1].]
1 The action of SHUT *verb.* LME.
2 A thing which shuts something, a bar, a shutter. Also, a place where two things come together. LME.
Comb.: **shutting joint**, **shutting post**, **shutting stile**: against which a door, gate, or window closes.

shuttle /ˈʃʌt(ə)l/ *noun*[1].
[Old English *scyt(t)el* corresp. to Old Norse *skutill* harpoon, bolt, from Germanic base also of SHOOT *verb*, SHUT *verb*: see -LE[1].]
▶ **I** †**1** A dart, an arrow, a missile. Only in OE.
2 A bobbin with two pointed ends used in weaving for carrying the thread of the weft across between the threads of the warp. ME. ▸**b** A similar thread-carrying device used in knotting, tatting, and embroidery. M18. ▸**c** A device in a sewing-machine which carries the lower thread through the loop of the upper one to make a stitch; a sewing-machine bobbin. M19.
3 †**a** The game of battledore and shuttlecock. Only in LME. ▸**b** A shuttlecock. Now only in BADMINTON. L16.
4 More fully ***shuttle shell***. (The shell of) any of several spindle-shaped marine gastropod molluscs, esp. *Volva volva* of the Indo-Pacific, which has both ends extended into long narrow projections. M18.
5 A train, bus, aircraft, etc., travelling back and forth over a short route at frequent intervals. L19. ▸**b** In full ***space shuttle***. A rocket-launched spacecraft for repeated use, able to land like an aircraft. M20. ▸**c** A journey in a series made in the course of shuttle diplomacy (see below). L20.
▶ **II 6** A bolt; a bar. Long only *spec.* (*dial.*), any of the bars of a gate. OE.

Comb.: **shuttle armature** ELECTRICITY a former type of armature having a single coil wound on an elongated iron bobbin; **shuttle bombing**: carried out by planes taking off from one base and landing at another; **shuttle car** a vehicle for making frequent short journeys, *spec.* for underground coal-haulage; **shuttle diplomacy** diplomatic negotiations conducted by a mediator travelling between disputing parties; **shuttle-race** the ledge or track on a loom along which the shuttle passes; **shuttle service** a train, bus, etc., service operating back and forth over a short route at frequent intervals; ***shuttle shell***: see sense 4 above; **shuttle-wound armature** ELECTRICITY = ***shuttle armature*** above.
■ **shuttleless** /-l-l-/ *adjective* (of a machine) adapted to work without a shuttle L19.

shuttle /ˈʃʌt(ə)l/ *noun*[2]. LME.
[from SHUT *verb* + -LE[1].]
A floodgate for regulating the supply of water in a mill-stream; a similar gate in a drain.

shuttle /ˈʃʌt(ə)l/ *noun*[3]. *Scot. & dial.* M16.
[Origin uncertain: perh. from SHUT *verb* + -LE[1].]
A small drawer, esp. in a chest, for storing small articles.

shuttle /ˈʃʌt(ə)l/ *adjective. obsolete* exc. *dial.* M16.
[Var. of SHITTLE.]
Inconstant, wavering; fickle.

shuttle /ˈʃʌt(ə)l/ *verb.* M16.
[from SHUTTLE *noun*[1].]
1 *verb trans.* **a** Move (a thing) quickly back and forth like a shuttle. *obsolete* exc. *dial.* M16. ▸**b** Transport back and forth, *spec.* in a vehicle or craft operating a shuttle service. M20.
2 *verb intrans.* Move back and forth like a shuttle. Also, travel back and forth or in one direction using a shuttle service. E19.
3 *verb intrans.* Weave. *Scot.* M19.

📖 **1b** B. GUEST Perdita was . . shuttled back and forth from Kenwin to London. **2** G. HUNTINGTON The little steamboat . . shuttled back and forth across the lake.

■ **shuttler** *noun* (*a*) *rare* a weaver; (*b*) a person who habitually travels back and forth between destinations, esp. by air: L19. **shuttling** *noun* (*a*) the action of the verb; (*b*) a thing used like a weaver's shuttle: L19.

shuttlecock /ˈʃʌt(ə)lkɒk/ *noun, adjective, & verb.* E16.
[from SHUTTLE *noun*[1] + COCK *noun*[1].]
▶ **A** *noun.* **1** A small piece of cork, rubber, etc., fitted with a ring of feathers, or a similar object made of plastic and rubber, hit backwards and forwards by players in the games of badminton and battledore and shuttlecock. E16.
2 The game of battledore and shuttlecock (see BATTLEDORE 3). L16.
▶ **B** *adjective.* Light, fickle; tossed back and forth (chiefly *fig.*). M16.
▶ **C** *verb.* **1** *verb trans.* Throw or send backwards and forwards. L17.
2 *verb intrans.* Move backwards and forwards. L18.

shwa *noun* var. of SCHWA.

shy /ʃʌɪ/ *adjective.*
[Old English *scēoh* = Middle High German *schiech* (German *scheu* (new formation)) from Germanic base also of Old High German *sciuhen* (German *scheuen* shun, *scheuchen* scare). Cf. ESCHEW, SHEWEL, SHUCK *noun*[1].]
1 †**a** Of a horse: easily frightened or startled. OE–M17. ▸**b** (Of a horse) unmanageable; *transf.* (of a person) flighty, skittish. *dial.* L18.
2 Reluctant to approach or encounter a particular person or thing, strangers, etc., due to timidity, caution, or distrust; *spec.* (of an animal or bird) timid towards humans. Also foll. by *of.* E17. ▸**b** As 2nd elem. of comb.: frightened of or averse to. L19.
3 Reluctant to undertake or averse to a particular course of action; chary, unwilling. Foll. by *about, at, of, to (do)*, etc. E17. ▸**b** Foll. by *of*: unwilling to accept (a theory) or consider (a subject). Long *rare* or *obsolete.* M17.
4 a Of a thing, action, etc.: characterized by or done with reserve or self-effacement; timid, cautious. M17. ▸**b** Avoiding self-assertion, self-effacing or bashful in company; reserved. L17. ▸**c** *transf.* Of a place etc.: secluded. E19.
5 Dubious, suspect; *esp.* of questionable character, disreputable. *slang.* E19.
6 a Of a plant etc.: not prolific. E19. ▸**b** Short (of), lacking; (of time) before. Foll. by *of, on. colloq.* L19.

📖 **2** J. BUCHAN The blighter is as shy as a wood-nymph. R. CAMPBELL Kruger National Park, where the animals have ceased to be shy. ***fight shy of***: see FIGHT *verb.* **3** O. WISTER He was always very shy of demonstration. P. CAREY It was his opinion—and he was not shy of expressing it. **4a** G. GREENE He made a tentative shy sketch of a wave towards Scobie. **b** H. JAMES He was still shy—he laughed . . faintly and vaguely, at nothing. M. KEANE Men he knew, but had been too shy to make friends with. **5** C. J. CHERRYH The shy side of legal . . . Doing trading on the side, without customs looking on. **6b** *Times* Britoil dipped . . yesterday—just 2p shy of the year's low. M. CHABON Six months shy of my thirteenth birthday.

■ **shyish** *adjective* M18. **shyly** *adverb* E18. **shyness** *noun* M17.

shy /ʃʌɪ/ *verb*[1] & *noun*[1]. M17.
[from SHY *adjective.*]
▶ **A** *verb.* **1** *verb intrans.* Take (esp. sudden) fright at or aversion to a person or thing; start; recoil, shrink. Freq. foll. by *at.* M17. ▸**b** Of a horse: start back or aside suddenly in fright. Freq. foll. by *at.* L18.
2 *verb intrans.* Slip away as a means of evasion; evade, avoid, or shun a person or thing. Foll. by *away (from), off.* L18. ▸**b** *verb trans.* Evade; shun, avoid. E19.
3 *verb trans.* Make timid or shy; frighten *off.* M19.

📖 **1** H. JAMES She had seemed to want to take her in, then she had shied at her. E. GLYN That . . oblivion from which . . thoughts unconsciously shy. **b** J. L. WATEN The mare shied at a passing motor-car. **2** A. ROBERTSON Elsie was shying off from Alec. D. H. LAWRENCE The natives shied off as if he had offered . . poisoned robes. W. STYRON He knows when to open up a subject, when to shy away from it. **b** A. GRAY I shy or refuse such applications. **3** M. FORSTER They were both shying off each other like startled deer.

▶ **B** *noun.* A sudden start aside by a horse in fright. L18.
■ **shyer** *noun* a horse which shies E19.

shy /ʃʌɪ/ *verb*[2] & *noun*[2]. Chiefly *colloq.* L18.
[Origin unkn.]
▶ **A** *verb.* **1** *verb trans. & intrans.* Throw or fling (a missile) carelessly or casually, esp. at or *at* a particular target. L18.
2 *verb trans. fig.* Produce, deliver, or discard carelessly or casually. E19.

📖 **1** THACKERAY Shying at the sticks better than any man in the army. P. MATTHIESSEN Shying quick stones to keep the beasts in line. **2** SIR W. SCOTT I cannot keep up with the world without shying a letter now and then.

▶ **B** *noun.* **1** A quick or casual throw, esp. *at* a particular target. L18. ▸**b** A point scored in the Eton College wall game. M19.
2 *fig.* **a** An attempt, a try. E19. ▸**b** A sarcastic usu. verbal attack. M19.

📖 **1** DICKENS Jack-in-the-box—three shies a penny. ***COCONUT shy***. **2a** C. GIBBON Have a shy at putting the case . . to me. **b** THACKERAY You are always having a shy at Lady Ann and her relations.

Shylock /ˈʃʌɪlɒk/ *noun & verb. slang.* Also **s-**. L18.
[A character in Shakespeare's *Merch. V.*]
▶ **A** *noun.* A moneylender, *esp.* an extortionate or hard-hearted one. Also (*derog. & racially offensive*), a Jew. L18.
▶ **B** *verb trans.* Force (a person) to repay a debt, esp. with exorbitant interest. M20.
■ **Shy'lockian** *adjective* (of a commercial transaction etc.) having extortionate terms L19.

shypoo /ˈʃʌɪpuː, ʃʌɪˈpuː/ *noun. Austral. slang.* L19.
[Origin unkn.]
(A public house selling) inferior liquor.

shyster /ˈʃʌɪstə/ *noun & adjective. colloq.* M19.
[Origin uncertain: perh. rel. to German *Scheisser* worthless person, from *Scheisse* excrement. Cf. SHICER.]
▶ **A** *noun.* **1** A person, orig. and esp. a lawyer, who uses unprofessional or unscrupulous methods in business. Chiefly *N. Amer.* M19.
2 = SHICER. *Austral.* M20.

📖 **1** DOUGLAS STUART The let-down of finding . . Charlie . . was just a trickster, a shyster.

▶ **B** *adjective.* **1** Practising, characterized by, or involving unprofessional or unscrupulous business methods, esp. in law. Chiefly *N. Amer.* M19.
2 Of a mine: unproductive. *Austral.* E20.

📖 **1** J. WAINWRIGHT The bastards are guilty and, all . . shyster evidence to the contrary, they *stay* guilty. *Literary Review* A shyster lawyer, defending drug dealers and taking payment in cocaine.

■ **shystering** *noun & adjective* (chiefly *N. Amer.*) (practising or characteristic of) unprofessional or unscrupulous business methods, esp. in law M19. **shysterism** *noun* (chiefly *N. Amer.*) unprofessional or unscrupulous business methods, esp. in law E20.

SI *abbreviation.*
1 (Order of) the Star of India.
2 French *Système International (d'unités)* International System of Units.

Si *symbol.*
CHEMISTRY. Silicon.

si /siː/ *noun.* E18.
[from the initial letters of Latin *Sancte Iohannes* (St John): see UT.]
MUSIC. = TE *noun*[1].

siafu /sɪˈɑːfuː/ *noun.* M20.
[Kiswahili.]
= ***safari ant*** s.v. SAFARI *noun.*

sial /ˈsʌɪəl/ *noun.* E20.
[from SI(LICON + AL(UMINIUM.]
GEOLOGY. The layer of the earth's crust represented by the continental masses, composed of rocks rich in silica and

alumina; the material of which this is composed. Cf. SIMA.

sial- *combining form* see SIALO-.

sialagogue /ˈsʌɪələɡɒɡ/ *noun & adjective.* Also **sialo-**. L18.
[from Greek *sialon* saliva + *agōgos* leading, eliciting.]
MEDICINE. ▶**A** *noun.* A drug which induces a flow of saliva. L18.
▶ **B** *adjective.* Inducing a flow of saliva. M19.

sialectasis /sʌɪəˈlɛktəsɪs/ *noun.* Pl. **-ases** /-əsiːz/. M20.
[from SIALO- + Greek *ektasis* dilatation.]
MEDICINE. Dilatation of the ducts of the salivary glands, esp. the parotids.

sialic /sʌɪˈalɪk/ *adjective*¹. E20.
[from SIAL + -IC.]
GEOLOGY. Of or pertaining to the continental crust or the material of which it is made.

sialic /ˈsʌɪəlɪk/ *adjective*². M20.
[from Greek *sialon* saliva + -IC.]
BIOCHEMISTRY. ***sialic acid***, any acyl or related derivative of a neuraminic acid.
■ **sialidase** /sʌɪˈalɪ-/ *noun* = NEURAMINIDASE M20.

siallite /ˈsʌɪəlʌɪt/ *noun.* M20.
[formed as SIAL + -ITE¹.]
GEOLOGY. Weathered rock that is largely composed of aluminosilicate clay minerals and is highly leached of alkalis.
■ **siaˈllitic** *adjective* M20.

sialo- /ˈsʌɪələʊ/ *combining form.* Before a vowel also **sial-**.
[from Greek *sialon* saliva: see -O-.]
1 MEDICINE. Saliva.
2 BIOCHEMISTRY. Forming nouns denoting compounds containing sialic acid residues.
■ **sialoadeˈnitis**, **sialadenitis** *noun* inflammation of a salivary gland M19. **sialoglycoˈprotein** *noun* a glycoprotein in which sialic acid residues form a major constituent of the side-chains M20. **sialogram** *noun* an X-ray photograph made by sialography M20. **sialoˈgraphic** *adjective* of or pertaining to sialography M20. **siaˈlography** *noun* radiography of the ducts of a salivary gland after they have been injected with a radio-opaque fluid M20. **sialolith** *noun* a calculus in a salivary gland M19. **sialoliˈthiasis** *noun*, pl. **-ases** /-əsiːz/, the presence of a sialolith M19. **sialomucin** /-ˈmjuːsɪn/ *noun* a mucin containing sialic acid residues in its molecule M20. **sialoˈrrhoea** /-ˈrɪə/ *noun* excessive flow of saliva M19.

sialogogue *noun & adjective* var. of SIALAGOGUE.

sialon /ˈsʌɪəlɒn/ *noun.* L20.
[from *Si*, *Al*, *O*, *N*, chem. symbols for silicon, aluminium, oxygen, and nitrogen.]
CHEMISTRY. Any of a large class of refractory materials which have crystal structures similar to those of silica and the silicates but contain aluminium and nitrogen in addition to silicon and oxygen.

siamang /ˈsʌɪəmaŋ, ˈsiːə-/ *noun.* E19.
[Malay.]
The largest of the gibbons, *Hylobates syndactylus*, having long black hair and found in Sumatra and the Malay peninsula.

Siamese /sʌɪəˈmiːz/ *adjective, noun, & verb.* L17.
[from *Siam* (see below) + -ESE.]
▶ **A** *adjective.* **1** Of or pertaining to Siam (now Thailand), a country in SE Asia, its inhabitants, or their language. L17.
2 United as (if) Siamese twins (see below); *spec.* (of a mechanical connection etc.) converting the power or pressure from two outlets into one. M19.

> 📖 **2** E. BOWEN In step, in Siamese closeness, they paced. N. J. BERRILL Siamese conditions meant death of mother and offspring.

Special collocations: **Siamese cat** (an animal of) a breed of cat, orig. from Thailand, usu. with a light body, cream-coloured short hair, a narrow brown head and blue eyes. **Siamese fighter**, **Siamese fighting fish** a tropical freshwater fish, *Betta splendens* (family Anabantidae), native to Malaysia and Thailand, the male of which is highly aggressive. **Siamese twin** [after famous twins, Chang and Eng (1811–74), who were congenitally united near the waist] (*a*) in *pl.*, a pair of conjoined twins, *transf.* & *fig.* any closely associated pair; (*b*) either of a pair of such twins.
▶ **B** *noun.* Pl. same.
1 A native or inhabitant of Siam (now Thailand). L17.
2 The language of Siam; Thai. M18.
3 = ***Siamese cat*** above. L19.
4 A Siamese connection (see sense A.2 above). E20.
▶ **C** *verb trans.* Unite as (if) Siamese twins; *spec.* join in a Siamese connection. Chiefly as ***Siamesed*** *ppl adjective.* M19.

> 📖 B. KNOX The Jaguar . . had twin carburetters plus a siamesed exhaust.

SIB *abbreviation.*
Securities and Investment Board.

sib /sɪb/ *noun*¹. Now *rare* or *obsolete* exc. *Scot.*
[Old English *sibb* = Old Frisian *sibbe*, Old Saxon, Old High German *sibbia* (Middle & mod. High German *sippe*), Old Norse *sifjar* (pl.) kinship, Gothic *sibja*, rel. to SIB *adjective & noun*³.]
†**1** Peace, amity, concord. OE–ME.
2 Kinship, relationship. OE.

sib /sɪb/ *noun*². *colloq.* M20.
[Abbreviation.]
= SIBILANT *noun* 2.

sib /sɪb/ *adjective & noun*³.
[Old English *sib(b)* = Old Frisian *sibbe*, Middle Dutch *sib(b)e*, Old High German *sibbi*, *sippi*, Old Norse pl. fem. *sifjar*, Gothic *sibjis*, of unkn. origin. Cf. SIB *noun*¹.]
▶ **A** *adjective.* **1** Related by birth or descent (*to*), akin (*to*) (*arch.* exc. *Scot.*); *spec.* (of canaries) related by birth or descent. OE. ▶**b** *transf.* Allied or similar (*to*). *arch.* exc. *Scot.* ME.
2 Having a right or claim *to* a thing, esp. by birth. *Scot.* E18.

> 📖 **1** R. KIPLING I'm all o'er-sib to Adam's breed.

▶ **B** *noun.* **1** A blood relation; blood relations collectively, kin. OE. ▶**b** ANTHROPOLOGY. (A member of) a lineal or cognatic kinship group, orig. and esp. among Germanic peoples. L19.
2 Chiefly GENETICS. A sibling, a brother or sister; = SIBLING 2. E20.
■ **sibbed** *adjective* (long *obsolete* exc. *dial.*) = SIB *adjective* 1 L15. **sibness** *noun* (long *obsolete* exc. *Scot.*) relationship, kinship ME. **sibred** *noun* (*a*) (now *Scot.*) blood relationship, blood relations; (*b*) *dial.* marriage banns: OE. **sibship** *noun* (*a*) ANTHROPOLOGY the state or fact of belonging to a sib or to the same sib; (*b*) BIOLOGY & MEDICINE a group comprising all the offspring born to a particular pair of parents: E20.

Sibbald's rorqual /ˈsɪb(ə)ldz ˈrɔːkw(ə)l/ *noun phr.* L19.
[from Sir Robert *Sibbald* (1641–1722), Scot. naturalist.]
The blue whale.

†**sibber-sauce** *noun* see SIPPER-SAUCE.

Sibelian /sɪˈbeɪlɪən/ *adjective & noun.* M20.
[from *Sibelius* (see below) + -IAN.]
▶ **A** *adjective.* Of, pertaining to, or characteristic of the Finnish composer Jean Sibelius (1865–1957) or his music. M20.
▶ **B** *noun.* An admirer or adherent of Sibelius; an interpreter of Sibelius' works. L20.

Siberia /sʌɪˈbɪərɪə/ *noun.* M19.
[See SIBERIAN *adjective.*]
An extremely cold, inhospitable, or remote place; a place of exile, banishment, or imprisonment.

> 📖 C. PLUMB The seas shall not seem vast Siberias of Time. J. LE CARRÉ Guillam departed for the siberias of Brixton.

Siberian /sʌɪˈbɪərɪən/ *adjective & noun.* E18.
[from *Siberia* (see below) + -AN.]
▶ **A** *adjective.* Of, pertaining to, or characteristic of Siberia, the northernmost part of Russia between the Urals and the Pacific; *esp.* (of weather) fiercely or bitterly cold. E18.
Special collocations: **Siberian crab** a crab tree, *Malus baccata*, with white flowers and small edible red fruit, native to eastern Asia and planted elsewhere, esp. as a street tree. **Siberian crane** = ***Siberian white crane*** below. **Siberian husky** (an animal of) a hardy breed of husky, orig. from Siberia, with stocky body and blue eyes. **Siberian ibex** a large ibex of a race found in the mountains of central Asia, with long horns, a long beard, and a dark stripe down the back. **Siberian jay** a jay, *Perisoreus infaustus*, of Scandinavia and northern Asia, having a mainly dull brown plumage with reddish wings, rump, and tail. **Siberian mammoth** = ***woolly mammoth*** s.v. WOOLLY *adjective.* **Siberian pea-tree** an ornamental shrub, *Caragana arborescens*, with spine-tipped dark green leaves and yellow flowers like those of the pea. **Siberian purslane** = ***pink purslane*** s.v. PINK *adjective*². ***Siberian rubythroat***: see ***rubythroat*** (a) s.v. RUBY. **Siberian tiger** a very large tiger of an endangered race occurring in SE Siberia and NE China, having a long thick coat. **Siberian tit** a tit, *Parus cinctus*, of Scandinavia, northern Asia, and north-western N. America, having dusky brown upperparts and whitish cheeks and breast. **Siberian wallflower** an orange-flowered hybrid garden plant, *Erysimum* × *marshallii*, related to the wallflower. **Siberian weasel** = KOLINSKY. **Siberian white crane** a large endangered crane, *Grus leucogeranus*, now found in two small populations in northern Siberia, having white plumage and a red face and legs.
▶ **B** *noun.* **1** A native or inhabitant of Siberia. E18.
2 = ***Siberian husky*** above. E20.

sibia /ˈsɪbɪə/ *noun.* E20.
[Nepalese *sibya*.]
Any of several S. Asian babblers of the genera *Heterophasia* and *Crocias*, typically having a blackish or greyish head and a long tail.

sibilant /ˈsɪbɪlənt/ *adjective & noun.* M17.
[Latin *sibilant-* pres. ppl stem of *sibilare* hiss, whistle: see -ANT¹.]
▶ **A** *adjective.* **1** Characterized or accompanied by a hissing sound; *spec.* (PHONETICS) designating a fricative produced by the formation of a groove with the sides of the tongue in contact with the roof of the mouth, as English /s/, /z/. M17. ▶**b** MEDICINE. Of stethoscopic sounds: characterized by an abnormal whistling or hissing. M19.
2 Emitting a hissing or whistling sound. E19.
▶ **B** *noun.* **1** PHONETICS. A sibilant speech sound or letter. L18.
2 A rumour started and spread deliberately for propaganda or selling purposes. M20.
■ **sibilance** *noun* (*a*) the fact or quality of being sibilant; a hissing sound; (*b*) an undue prominence of sibilants or hissing, esp. due to interference in reproduced sound: E19. **sibilantly** *adverb* L19.

sibilate /ˈsɪbɪleɪt/ *verb.* M17.
[Latin *sibilat-* pa. ppl stem of *sibilare*: see prec., -ATE³.]
1 *verb intrans.* Hiss; make a hissing sound. M17.
2 *verb trans.* **a** Pronounce or utter with a hissing sound. M19. ▶**b** Hiss at (a person), esp. as a sign of disapproval. M19.
■ **sibiˈlation** *noun* (*a*) the action or an act of sibilating, esp. as a sign of disapproval; (*b*) a hissing or whistling sound: L15. **sibilator** *noun* (*rare*) a person who hisses or whistles LME. **sibilatory** *adjective* characterized, accompanied, or expressed by hissing M19.

sibilous /ˈsɪbɪləs/ *adjective.* M18.
[from Latin *sibilus*, from *sibilare* (see prec.) + -OUS.]
Hissing, sibilant.

Sibiriak /sɪˈbɪrɪak/ *noun.* E20.
[Russian *Sibiryak* Siberian.]
A Siberian descendant of European Russian settlers.

siblicide /ˈsɪblɪsʌɪd/ *noun.* L20.
[from next + -CIDE.]
ORNITHOLOGY. The action by a young bird of killing a sibling or fellow nestling.

sibling /ˈsɪblɪŋ/ *noun.* OE.
[from SIB *adjective & noun*³ + -LING¹.]
†**1** A relative. OE–LME.
2 Each of two or more offspring of the same parent or parents. E20.
Comb.: **sibling rivalry**: arising from jealousy between siblings; **sibling species** BIOLOGY each of a pair or group of reproductively isolated species whose members are morphologically very similar; cf. ***twin species***.
■ **siblingship** *noun* = SIBSHIP (a) M20.

sibyl /ˈsɪbɪl/ *noun.* In sense 1 also in Latin form (long *rare*) **sybylla** /sɪˈbɪlə/, pl. **-llae** /-liː/. ME.
[Old French *Sibile* (mod. *Sibylle*), or medieval Latin *Sibilla*, from Latin *Sibylla*, *-ulla* from Greek *Sibulla*.]
1 (Usu. **S-**.) Any of various women in classical antiquity supposed to utter the oracles and prophecies of a god. ME.
2 *transf.* A prophetess; a fortune-teller. M16.
■ **siˈbyllic** *adjective* (chiefly *poet.*) = SIBYLLINE *adjective* 1, 2a M19. **sibyllism** *noun* prophecy, soothsaying M19. **Sibyllist** *noun* an early Christian believer in the authenticity of the Sibylline oracles E17. **sibyˈllistic** *adjective* (*rare*) = SIBYLLINE *adjective* 1, 2a L18.

sibylline /ˈsɪbɪlʌɪn/ *adjective & noun.* Also **S-**. L16.
[Latin *Sibillinus*, from *Sibylla*: see prec., -INE¹.]
▶ **A** *adjective.* **1** Of or pertaining to a sibyl or the sibyls. L16.
2 *transf.* **a** Resembling or characteristic of a sibyl; oracular; occult, mysterious. E19. ▶**b** Excessive, exorbitant (with allus. to the Sibylline books: see below). M19.

> 📖 **2a** E. BOWEN For all her sibylline grandeur, Georgina remained an aunt. P. ACKROYD His Sibylline whisper would change to a louder note. **b** J. R. LOWELL To set a Sibylline value on their verses in proportion as they were unsalable.

Special collocations: **Sibylline books**: containing the prophecies of the Cumaean Sibyl, three of which she supposedly sold to Tarquinus Superbus, king of ancient Rome, at the price of the original nine. **Sibylline oracles** ECCLESIASTICAL HISTORY a collection imitating the Sibylline books, probably written by early Christian or Jewish authors.
▶ **B** *noun.* In *pl.* The Sibylline books or oracles. L19.

sic /sɪk/ *adjective & pronoun. Scot. & north.* LME.
[Reduced form.]
= SUCH *adjective & pronoun.*

sic *verb* var. of SICK *verb*².

sic /sɪk/ *adverb & noun.* L19.
[Latin = so, thus.]
▶ **A** *adverb.* Used or spelt as written. Used parenthetically after a quoted word etc. to call attention to an anomalous or erroneous form or prevent the supposition of misquotation. L19.

> 📖 *New Scientist* A brilliant, bold, hair-brained (sic) . . undertaking.

▶ **B** *noun.* An instance of using 'sic'. M20.

Sican /ˈsɪkən/ *noun.* L19.
[Latin *Sicanus*.]
= SICANIAN *noun.*

Sicanian /sɪˈkeɪnɪən/ *noun & adjective.* E17.
[Latin *Sicanius*, from *Sicani* pl. of *Sicanus* SICAN, from Greek *Sikanoi*.]
▶ **A** *noun.* A member of an ancient people inhabiting west central Sicily at the time of Greek colonization in the 8th and 7th cents. BC. E17.
▶ **B** *adjective.* **1** Sicilian. *poet. rare.* M17.
2 ARCHAEOLOGY. Designating or pertaining to the neolithic period in Sicily. E20.
3 Of or pertaining to the Sicanians. E20.

sicarius /sɪˈkɛːrɪəs/ *noun. obsolete* exc. *Hist.* Pl. **-rii** /-rɪiː/. Orig. †**-rien**. LME.
[Latin, from *sica* curved dagger.]
An assassin using a dagger as a weapon; *spec.* a member of a sect of assassins active during the zealot disturbances in Palestine in the 1st cent. AD.

sicca /ˈsɪkə/ *noun*[1]. E17.
[Urdu, Persian *sikka(h)* from Arab. *sikkat*: see SEQUIN.]
Hist. In full ***sicca rupee***. In the Indian subcontinent: orig., a newly coined rupee, having a higher value than one worn by use; later, a rupee coined under the government of Bengal from 1793, and current until 1836.

sicca /ˈsɪkə/ *noun*[2]. M20.
[Ellipt. for mod. Latin *keratoconjunctivitis sicca*.]
MEDICINE. The reduction or absence of lachrymation, with consequent dryness and inflammation of the conjunctiva, characteristic of Sjögren's syndrome.
Comb.: **sicca syndrome** the occurrence of sicca in the absence of rheumatoid arthritis.

siccan /ˈsɪkən/ *adjective. Scot. & north.* E16.
[from SIC *adjective* + KIN *noun*.]
Such, suchlike.

siccative /ˈsɪkətɪv/ *adjective & noun.* LME.
[Late Latin *siccativus*, from *siccare* to dry: see -ATIVE.]
▶ **A** *adjective.* Capable of absorbing moisture; drying. LME.
▶ **B** *noun.* A drying agent; now *esp.* one used in painting or pottery. LME.
¶ As noun not recorded between LME and E19.

†**siccity** *noun.* LME–M19.
[Latin *siccitas*, from *siccus* dry: see -ITY.]
Dryness.

sice /sʌɪs/ *noun.* Also **size** /sʌɪz/. LME.
[Old French *sis* (mod. *six*) from Latin *sex* six.]
1 The six on a die; a throw of six at dice; *fig.* good luck. *arch.* LME.
†**2** Sixpence. *slang.* M17–M19.
Comb.: **sice ace** *arch.* a throw of six and one at dice (so ***sice cinque***, ***sice quatre***, etc.); **sice-point** *arch.* in backgammon, the sixth point from the inner end of each table.

Sicel /ˈsɪs(ə)l, ˈsɪk(ə)l/ *noun & adjective.* M19.
[Greek *Sikelos*, from *Sikelik*: see next.]
▶ **A** *noun.* **1** A member of an ancient people inhabiting eastern Sicily at the time of Greek colonization in the 8th and 7th cents. BC. M19.
2 The language of this people. M20.
▶ **B** *attrib.* or as *adjective.* Of or pertaining to the Sicels or their language. L19.

Siceliot /sɪˈsɛlɪɒt, -ˈkɛlɪɒt/ *noun & adjective.* M19.
[Greek *Sikeliōtēs*, from *Sikelik* Sicily: see -OT[2].]
▶ **A** *noun.* Any of the ancient Greek colonizers who arrived in Sicily in the 8th and 7th cents. BC. M19.
▶ **B** *adjective.* Of, pertaining to, or designating the Siceliots. M19.

sic et non /ˈsɪk ɛt ˈnɒn/ *noun phr.* E20.
[Latin, lit. 'yes and no', a work by Abelard (see below).]
THEOLOGY. A method of argument used by Peter Abelard, 12th-cent. French theologian and philosopher, and later Scholastics, in which contradictory passages of scripture are presented without commentary in order to stimulate readers to resolve the contradictions themselves. Freq. *attrib.*

sich *adjective* see SUCH *demonstr. adjective & pronoun.*

Sicherheitsdienst /ˈzɪçərhaɪtsdiːnst/ *noun.* M20.
[German, from *Sicherheit* security + *dienst* service.]
Hist. The security branch of the Nazi Schutzstaffel (SS), set up in 1931–2. Abbreviation ***SD***.

Sichuan *adjective* var. of SZECHUAN.

Sicilian /sɪˈsɪlɪən/ *noun & adjective.* E16.
[from Latin *Sicilia* Sicily + -AN.]
▶ **A** *noun.* **1** A native or inhabitant of Sicily, an island off the tip of SW Italy. E16.
2 Orig. (*poet.*), = SICEL *noun* 2. Now, the dialect of modern Italian spoken in Sicily. E19.
▶ **B** *adjective.* **1** Of, pertaining to, or characteristic of Sicily or its inhabitants. L16.
2 Of or pertaining to the Italian dialect of Sicily. M19.
Special collocations: **Sicilian defence** CHESS a defence with many variations replying to the king's pawn opening with a two-square move of the queen's bishop's pawn. **Sicilian Vespers** *Hist.* the general massacre of French settlers in Sicily in 1282, signalled by the toll to vespers on Easter Monday.

siciliana /sitʃiˈljana, sɪˌtʃɪlɪˈɑːnə/ *noun.* Pl. ***-ne*** /-ne, -ni/. Also ***-no*** /-no, -nəʊ/, pl. ***-nos*** /-nəʊz/, ***-ni*** /-ni/. E18.
[Italian, fem. of *Siciliano* Sicilian.]
MUSIC. A piece of music for a Sicilian peasant dance, resembling a slow jig; *transf.* a composition in 6/8 or 12/8 time, freq. in a minor key and evoking a pastoral mood.

sicilienne /sɪˌsɪlɪˈɛn/ *noun.* L19.
[French, fem. of *sicilien* Sicilian.]
1 A fine poplin of silk and wool. L19.
2 MUSIC. = SICILIANA. L19.

sick /sɪk/ *adjective & noun.*
[Old English *sēoc* = Old Frisian *siāk*, Old Saxon *siok*, Old High German *sioh* (Dutch *ziek*, German *siech*), Old Norse *sjúkr*, Gothic *siuks*, from Germanic: ult. origin unkn.]
▶ **A** *adjective.* **I 1** Affected by illness; unwell, ailing. Also foll. by †*of*, *with*. OE. ▸**b** Of a part of the body: not in a healthy state. Now *rare*. ME. ▸**c** Craving or suffering withdrawal from an addictive drug. *slang* (chiefly *US*). M20.
2 Having an inclination to vomit; vomiting. E17.

> 1 T. DREISER You two'll get sick . . , if you don't get more rest. P. ROAZEN When she was sick . . he wanted her to get the best doctor. *fig.*: J. CAREW This whole continent is sick with race hatred. **2** A. SILLITOE Falling downstairs and being sick over people. D. PROFUMO After a few minutes in the car he felt sick.

▶ **II** †**3** Spiritually or morally unsound; corrupt. OE–M18.
4 a Deeply affected by a strong emotion; *spec.* (***a***) sorrowful; (***b***) pining or longing (*for*); (***c***) envious (†*of*); (***d***) *colloq.* mortified, chagrined. OE. ▸**b** Full of repugnance or loathing; deeply disgusted. Chiefly in ***make a person sick***. Now *colloq.* M16.
5 Bored or weary through surfeit of a person or thing. Usu. foll. by *of*. Now *colloq.* L16.

> **4a** TENNYSON This girl, for whom your heart is sick. D. LODGE They're sick as hell because of the raves he gets in the *Course Bulletin*. ***homesick***: see HOME *noun*. **b** P. BARKER You make me sick, you and your bloody mother. **5** J. TROLLOPE I'm sick of being shackled to a man.

▶ **III 6** Mentally ill or disordered; perverted. ME. ▸**b** Of humour, a joke, etc.: referring to something taboo or extremely unpleasant; in very bad taste, perverse. *colloq.* M20.
7 Characterized or accompanied by illness or nausea. LME.
8 Not in perfect or normal condition; spoiled, corrupted. LME. ▸**b** Of a bird's feathers: moulting. Long *rare*. L16. ▸**c** Of a ship: needing repair of a specified kind. Usu. in *comb.*, as ***paint-sick*** etc. E17. ▸**d** STOCK EXCHANGE. Of a market etc.: slow, dull. L19.
9 Of a sickly colour; pale, wan. L16.
10 Of or pertaining to those who are ill; *esp.* set aside for or occupied by those who are ill. E19.

> **6** A. C. CLARKE They must have been . . sick people . . to take a morbid delight in collecting such material. **7** J. F. LEHMANN A slightly sick feeling in the pit of their stomachs. **8** A. PATON The soil is sick, almost beyond healing. **9** M. SINCLAIR Robin's pale, blank face had a sick look. **10** ***sick cookery***, ***sick nurse***, etc. ***sick-berth***, ***sickroom***, etc.

▶ **IV 11** Excellent. *slang.* L20.

> **11** *Snowboard UK* The skating was sick and . . everyone was stoked on it.

Phrases: **get sick** *N. Amer. colloq.* (***a***) = ***take sick*** below; (***b***) vomit. **go sick** report oneself as ill to an employer etc. **look sick** *colloq.* be unimpressive or embarrassed. ***make a person sick***: see sense 4b above. **sick and tired of** fed up of, wearied of. **sick as a dog**, (*joc.*) **sick as a parrot**, etc. extremely ill or sick; thoroughly disgusted or fed up. **sick at the stomach** = sense 2 above. **sick man (of X)** (a ruler of) a country etc. which is politically or economically unsound, esp. in comparison with its neighbours (of the region specified). **sick man of Europe** *Hist.* (the Sultan of) Turkey in the late 19th cent. **sick to death of** extremely wearied by or fed up with. **sick to the stomach** = sense 2 above. **take sick** *colloq.* be taken ill. **worried sick** ill with worrying, extremely worried. **worry oneself sick** worry excessively, make oneself ill with worrying.
Comb. & special collocations: **sick-bag**: provided in an aircraft, ship, etc., as a receptacle for vomit; **sickbay** (***a***) part of a ship used as a hospital; (***b***) any room etc. for sick people; **sickbed** (***a***) an invalid's bed; (***b***) the state or condition of being an invalid; **sick-benefit** = ***SICKNESS benefit***; **sick building syndrome** a condition affecting office workers, typically including headaches and respiratory problems, attributed to stressful factors in the working environment such as poor ventilation; **sick-call** (***a***) MILITARY a summons for those reporting sick to assemble for treatment; (***b***) a visit by a doctor to a sick person; **sick-flag** a yellow flag indicating disease on a ship or at a quarantine station etc.; **sick headache** a migraine headache with vomiting; *fig.* a useless or unhelpful thing; **sick-in** *US* group industrial action by taking unwarranted sick-leave; **sick-leave** leave of absence from work etc. granted because of sickness; **sick-list**: of employees, competitors, etc. absent through sickness; **sick-making** *adjective* (*colloq.*) sickening; **sick note**: given to an employer, teacher, etc. as a record of absence due to illness; **sickout** (chiefly *US*) = ***sick-in*** above; **sick parade** MILITARY an inspection of those who are ill; the people on sick parade; **sick pay**: given to an employee on sick-leave.
▶ **B** *noun.* **1** A sick or ill person (now *dial.*); *collect. pl.*, *the* class of sick or ill people. OE.
2 Orig., a disease, an illness. Later, a fit of nausea. OE.
3 Vomit. *colloq.* M20.

> **1** *Renewal* Jesus told his followers to . . heal the sick. **3** B. EMECHETA He would . . look at the food . . as if he was being forced to eat sick.

Phrases: **give a person the sick** *colloq.* nauseate or disgust a person. **on the sick** *colloq.* receiving sick-benefit. ***the sacrament of the sick***: see SACRAMENT *noun*.
■ **sickie** *noun* (***a***) *colloq.* a period of sick-leave, *esp.* one taken without sufficient medical reason; (***b***) *N. Amer. slang* a mentally ill or perverted person: M20. **sickish** *adjective* (***a***) somewhat ill or sick; (***b***) somewhat nauseating or sickening: L16. **sickishly** *adverb* M19. **sickishness** *noun* E18. **sickless** *adjective* (now *rare*) free from sickness or ill health M16. **sickling** *noun* (*rare*) a sickly person M19. **sicknik** *noun* (*US slang*) (***a***) a mentally ill person; (***b***) a person indulging in sick humour: M20. **sicko** *noun*, pl. **-os**, *N. Amer. slang* = SICKIE (b) L20.

sick /sɪk/ *verb*[1]. OE.
[from SICK *adjective*.]
†**1** *verb intrans.* = SICKEN 1. OE–L16.
2 *verb trans.* = SICKEN 2. Now *rare* or *obsolete*. ME.
3 *verb trans. & intrans.* Vomit. Usu. foll. by *up*. E20.

> **3** P. LEACH His infant misdeeds like the time he . . sicked up in the bus. J. LE CARRÉ He'd given her . . pills but she'd sicked them up.

sick /sɪk/ *verb*[2] *trans.* Also **sic**. M19.
[Dial. var. of SEEK *verb*.]
1 Of a dog: set on, attack. Freq. in *imper.* M19.
2 Foll. by *at*, *on*: incite (a person) to attack another; set (an animal) on another animal or person. M19. ▸**b** *fig.* Foll. by *on*: set (a person) to work on a task; set (a person) to follow, pursue, etc., another. E20.

> **1** P. G. WODEHOUSE 'Sic 'em, Tulip,' he said. **2** W. FAULKNER They couldn't run him away if they was to sick them bloodhounds on him. **b** R. STOUT Who had sicked the cops on Laidlaw. R. THOMAS Penry works for me. If you need something done . . I'll sic him on it.

sicken /ˈsɪk(ə)n/ *verb.* ME.
[from SICK *adjective* + -EN[5].]
1 *verb intrans.* Become affected with illness; fall ill or sick (*with*). ME. ▸**b** Begin to pine or yearn; long eagerly *to do*. E19. ▸**c** Of a thing: grow pale or weak; fade. M19. ▸**d** Foll. by *for*: show or feel symptoms of a particular illness. L19.
2 *verb trans.* Affect with illness; make ill or sick; *transf.* weaken. E17.
3 a *verb intrans.* Foll. by *at*, *with*: feel nausea, loathing, or disgust. E17. ▸**b** *verb trans.* Affect with nausea, loathing, or disgust. E19.
4 *verb intrans. & trans.* (Cause to) grow weary or tired *of* a person or thing. L18.

> **1** E. WAUGH Laura sickened with 'flu. C. HARMAN William the chow began to sicken and fail. **c** P. WYLIE His brilliant eyes had sickened. **d** F. MONTGOMERY I was sickening for the mumps. **2** J. BUCHAN His fetid breath sickened me. **3a** E. JOHNSON He sickens at the cruelty of mass murder. **b** A. S. NEILL The brick squalor that stretches for miles sickened me. **4** SIR W. SCOTT I . . learned enough . . to give Jekyl a hint that sickened him of his commission. O. W. HOLMES Men sicken of their houses until at last they quit them.

■ **sickener** *noun* a nauseating or disgusting thing or experience E19. **sickening** *adjective* (***a***) falling ill or sick; (***b***) causing or liable to cause sickness or nausea; loathsome, disgusting; (***c***) *colloq.* very annoying: E18. **sickeningly** *adverb* M19.

sicker /ˈsɪkə/ *adjective & adverb.* Now *Scot. & north.*
[Old English *sicor* = Old Frisian, Old Saxon *sīkor* (Middle Dutch *seker*, Dutch *zeker*), Old High German *sihhur* (German *sicher*), from early West Germanic, from late form of Latin *securus* SECURE *adjective*.]
▶ **A** *adjective.* **I 1** Free from danger or harm; secure, safe. OE.
2 Dependable, reliable; trustworthy. OE.
3 Firmly grounded or supported; solid, unshakable. ME. ▸**b** Securely fastened or held. LME. ▸**c** Prudent or cautious, esp. in financial matters; wary. M17.
4 Effective, telling; (of a blow) severe; *transf.* harsh, rigorous. ME.
5 Indubitable; absolutely certain. LME.

> **3** R. BURNS Setting my staff wi' a' my skill, To keep me sicker. **5** SIR W. SCOTT 'Do you leave such a matter to doubt?' said Kirkpatrick, 'I will make sicker'.

▶ **II 6** Confident or certain of some object or prospect. Usu. foll. by *of*. Now *rare* or *obsolete*. ME.
7 Confident of a fact or assertion; assured, convinced. Usu. foll. by *of*, *in*, *on*, *that*, etc. ME.
▶ **B** *adverb.* †**1** In safety, safely. Only in ME.
2 Without doubt; confidently; assuredly; as a certainty or fact. ME.
3 Effectively, tellingly. ME.
4 Securely; firmly, solidly. L16.
■ **sickerly** *adverb* LOE.

sicker /ˈsɪkə/ *verb*[1]. *obsolete* exc. *Scot.* ME.
[from the adjective.]
†**1** *verb trans.* Assure (a person) of safety. Only in ME.
†**2** *verb trans.* Make a pledge or surety to; confirm by pledge or surety. Only in ME.
†**3** *verb trans.* Assure (a person) of a fact. Only in ME.
4 *verb trans.* Secure; make certain of; make fast. E18.

sicker /ˈsɪkə/ *verb*² *intrans. rare.* Long *dial.*
[Old English *sicerian* = Low German *sikeren*, German *sickern* (dial. *sikern*).]
Of water: trickle; leak.

sickerness /ˈsɪkənɪs/ *noun. obsolete* exc. *Scot.* LOE.
[from SICKER *adjective* + -NESS.]
†**1 a** Certainty *of* a future prospect or possession. LOE–E16. ▸**b** Confidence or assurance of a fact. ME–M16.
†**2** (A sense of) security from danger or harm. ME–L16.
†**3** A means or source of security; *spec.* security for a treaty or contract, a bond, a pledge. ME–M16.
4 Harshness. L19.
5 Prudence, wariness. E20.

Sickertian /sɪˈkəːtɪən/ *adjective.* M20.
[from *Sickert* (see below) + -IAN.]
Of, pertaining to, or characteristic of the work of the English painter W. R. Sickert (1860–1942).

sickle /ˈsɪk(ə)l/ *noun & verb.*
[Old English *sicol*, *sicel* = Middle Low German, Middle Dutch *sekele*, *sikele* (Dutch *sikkel*), Old High German *sichila* (German *Sichel*), from var. of Latin *secula* (cf. Italian *segolo* pruning-hook), from *secare* cut.]
▸ **A** *noun.* **1** A short-handled farming implement with a crescent-shaped usu. serrated blade, used for cutting grain, lopping and trimming. OE.
2 A thing resembling a sickle in shape; *spec.* (**a**) *poet.* the crescent moon; (**b**) (**S-**.) a conspicuous group of stars in the constellation Leo. LME.

📖 **1** J. BRONOWSKI That sawing motion of the sickle that reapers have used for . . ten thousand years. ***hammer and sickle***: see HAMMER *noun.* **2** LONGFELLOW The blue Salernian bay With its sickle of white sand.

Comb.: **sickle-bill** any of various birds with long narrow curved bills; *spec.* either of two hummingbirds of the genus *Eutoxeres*; **sickle-feather** each of the long middle feathers on the tail of a cock; **sickle hock** an unusually bent hock, considered a defect in horses, cattle, etc., but desirable in a running hound; **sickle medick** a medick with sickle-shaped pods, *Medicago falcata*, allied to lucerne but with yellow flowers; **sicklepod** a N. American leguminous plant, *Cassia tora*, with long sickle-shaped pods; **sickle scaler** an instrument with a curved blade for removing scale from teeth.

▸ **B** *verb.* **1 a** *verb intrans.* Cut grain with a sickle; reap. Chiefly as ***sickling*** *verbal noun*. Now *rare*. OE. ▸**b** *verb trans.* Cut with a sickle. E20.
2 MEDICINE. **a** *verb intrans.* Of red blood cells: become crescent- or sickle-shaped. Of blood: develop cells of this shape. E20. ▸**b** *verb trans.* Cause to sickle. L20.
■ **sickled** *adjective* (**a**) *rare* cut with a sickle; (**b**) MEDICINE (of a red blood cell) sickle-shaped: M18. **sickler** *noun* (**a**) a person who uses a sickle; (**b**) MEDICINE a person with sickle-cell anaemia or with sickle-cell trait: M17.

sickle-cell /ˈsɪk(ə)lsɛl/ *noun.* E20.
[from SICKLE *noun* + CELL *noun*¹.]
MEDICINE. Any of the crescent-shaped red blood cells found in the blood of people with sickle-cell anaemia.
Comb.: **sickle-cell anaemia**, **sickle-cell disease** a frequently fatal form of anaemia, characterized by the presence of red blood cells that are rich in sickle-cell haemoglobin and sickle readily; **sickle-cell gene** an autosomal gene which when heterozygous produces the sickle-cell trait and when homozygous sickle-cell anaemia, common in tropical Africa; **sickle-cell haemoglobin** an abnormal haemoglobin which tends to produce a characteristic crescent shape in red blood cells containing it; **sickle-cell trait** a relatively harmless condition, characterized by the presence of red blood cells containing some sickle-cell haemoglobin and conferring some resistance to malaria.

sicklemia /sɪk(ə)lˈiːmɪə/ *noun.* M20.
[Contr. of *sickle(-cell anae)mia*.]
MEDICINE. Sickle-cell anaemia; sickle-cell trait.
■ **sicklemic** *adjective* M20.

sickly /ˈsɪkli/ *adjective & verb.* LME.
[Prob. after Old Norse *sjukligr*: see SICK *adjective*, -LY¹.]
▸ **A** *adjective.* **1** Affected by sickness or ill health, esp. habitually; (apt to be) ill; weak. LME. ▸**b** Of light or colour: faint, pale, weak. L17.
2 Caused by, suggesting, or characterized by sickness or ill health; unhealthy. LME. ▸†**b** Of or pertaining to sickness or the sick. E17–E19.
3 Causing sickness or ill health; (esp. of taste, colour, smell, etc.) inducing nausea. Also, (of a place, climate, etc.) conducive to sickness. L15. ▸**b** Sentimental, mawkish. M18.

📖 **1** S. RUSHDIE That girl is so sickly from too much soft living. E. SEGAL We don't retouch our pictures to make patients look more sickly. **2** V. WOOLF My pursed lips, my sickly pallor. J. WAIN I gave him a sickly grin. **3** G. BERKELEY In the late sickly season of the year. A. S. BYATT Paving-stone steaks and sickly chocolate-sauced pears. **b** P. MORTIMER I was writing sickly little verses modelled on Flower Fairies of the Spring.

▸ **B** *verb.* Chiefly *literary.*
1 *verb trans.* In *pass.* Foll. by *over*, (*arch.*) *o'er*: be suffused with a sickly colour or shade. E17.
2 *verb trans.* & (*rare*) *intrans.* Make or become sickly or pale. M18.

📖 **1** SHAKES. *Haml.* The native hue of resolution Is sicklied o'er with the pale cast of thought. **2** G. MEREDITH The . . lustre of the maid sicklied the poor widow.

¶ Sense B.1 used chiefly with allus. to Shakes.
■ **sicklied** *adjective* made sickly or mawkish M19. **sicklily** *adverb* E18. **sickliness** *noun* M16.

sickly /ˈsɪkli/ *adverb.* LME.
[from SICK *adjective* + -LY².]
In a sick manner; unhealthily; weakly, feebly.

📖 J. STEINBECK The dazed man stared sickly at Casy.

sickness /ˈsɪknɪs/ *noun.* OE.
[from SICK *adjective* + -NESS.]
1 The state or condition of being sick or ill; illness, ill health; *transf.* & *fig.* the imperfect, weak, or corrupt condition *of* something. OE.
2 An instance of ill health; a (specified) disease or illness. OE. ▸**b** = BRAXY *noun* 1. L18.
3 An attack of nausea or vomiting. E17.
4 *fig.* Utter disgust with or weariness *of* something. L18.

📖 **1** H. KUSHNER Is good health . . normal . . and sickness an aberration? V. S. PRITCHETT Chekhov is the doctor examining the moral sickness of industrial life. ***bed of sickness***: see BED *noun.* **2** J. FRAME Giving up her life to a sickness that behaved like a predator. ***falling sickness***: see FALLING *ppl adjective.* ***sleeping sickness***: see SLEEPING *verbal noun.* ***SLEEPY sickness***. ***walking sickness***: see WALKING *ppl adjective.* **3** *Practical Health* The headache of meningitis . . comes on rapidly, with sickness. **4** C. LAMB The spirit . . tired to sickness of the . . world.

Comb.: **sickness benefit** in Britain, benefit paid by the State for sickness interrupting paid employment.

sicle /ˈsɪk(ə)l/ *noun.* Long *obsolete* exc. *Hist.* ME.
[Old French from late Latin *siclus* from Greek *siklos*, *siglos*, formed as SHEKEL.]
= SHEKEL 1.

sic-like /ˈsɪklʌɪk/ *adjective, pronoun, & adverb. Scot. & north.* LME.
[from SIC *adjective* + -LIKE.]
▸ **A** *adjective.* = SUCHLIKE *adjective.* LME.
▸ **B** *pronoun.* = SUCHLIKE *pronoun.* L15.
▸ **C** *adverb.* In such a manner; similarly. L15.

sicsac *noun* var. of ZICZAC.

sicula /ˈsɪkjʊlə/ *noun.* Pl. **-lae** /-liː/. L19.
[Latin, dim. of *sica* curved dagger: see -ULE.]
PALAEONTOLOGY. A small conical or dagger-shaped structure secreted by the initial zooid of a colony of graptolites.

Siculan /ˈsɪkjʊlən/ *adjective & noun.* E20.
[from Latin *Siculus* Sicilian, formed as SICEL + -AN.]
ARCHAEOLOGY. ▸**A** *adjective.* Designating or pertaining to (a culture of) the Chalcolithic, Bronze, and Iron Ages in Sicily. E20.
▸ **B** *noun.* A person of this culture. E20.

Siculo- /ˈsɪkjʊləʊ/ *combining form.* M18.
[formed as prec. + -O-.]
Forming adjective and noun combs. with the sense 'Sicilian (and)', as ***Siculo-American***, ***Siculo-Arabic***, etc.

Sicyonian /sɪkɪˈəʊnɪən/ *noun & adjective.* M17.
[Latin *Sicyonius*, from *Sicyon* from Greek *Sikuōn*: see -IAN.]
▸ **A** *noun.* A native or inhabitant of Sicyon, an ancient Greek city in the northern Peloponnese. M17.
▸ **B** *adjective.* Of or pertaining to Sicyon. L19.

sida /ˈsʌɪdə/ *noun.* E19.
[mod. Latin (see below), from Greek *sidē* pomegranate tree, water lily.]
Any of various plants constituting the genus *Sida*, of the mallow family, native to tropical or subtropical countries.
Comb.: **sida-weed** *Austral.* Paddy's lucerne, *Sida rhombifolia*.

sidalcea /sɪˈdalsɪə/ *noun.* L19.
[mod. Latin genus name (see below), from blend of *sida* + *Alcea*, related genera.]
Any of various plants of western N. America constituting the genus *Sidalcea*, of the mallow family with palmately divided leaves and long racemes of usu. pink or white flowers; *esp.* any of the garden forms or hybrids of this genus grown for ornament.

Sidamo /sɪˈdɑːməʊ/ *noun & adjective.* Also **-ma** /-mə/. M19.
[African name.]
▸ **A** *noun.* Pl. same. A member of a group of Cushitic-speaking peoples in SW Ethiopia; the language of these peoples. M19.
▸ **B** *attrib.* or as *adjective.* Designating or pertaining to these peoples. E20.

Sidcot /ˈsɪdkɒt/ *noun.* E20.
[*Sidney Cotton* (see below).]
A warm one-piece flying suit designed by the Australian-born aviator Sidney Cotton (1894–1969), worn in older aircraft. Also more fully ***Sidcot flying suit***, ***Sidcot suit***.

sidder *adjective* var. of SIDDOW.

siddha /ˈsɪdhə/ *noun.* M19.
[Sanskrit.]
In Indian religions: a person who has attained perfection, a saint, a semi-divine being; *spec.* in Jainism, a perfected bodyless being freed from the cycle of rebirths.

siddhi /ˈsɪdhi/ *noun.* L19.
[Sanskrit.]
sing. & in *pl.* In Indian religions: supernatural or magical powers acquired by meditation etc.

Siddonian /sɪˈdəʊnɪən/ *adjective.* L18.
[from *Siddon(s* (see below) + -IAN.]
In the style of, or typical of, the acting of the English tragic actress Mrs Sarah Siddons (1755–1831).

siddow /ˈsɪdəʊ/ *adjective.* Now *dial.* Also **sidder** /ˈsɪdə/. E17.
[Origin unkn.]
Esp. of vegetables: soft, tender.

siddown /sɪˈdaʊn/ *verb intrans.* (*imper.*). *non-standard.* M20.
[Repr. a pronunc.]
Sit down!

Siddur /ˈsɪdʊə/ *noun.* Also **Sidur**. Pl. **-rim** /-rɪm/. M19.
[Hebrew *siddūr* lit. 'order'.]
A Jewish prayer book containing prayers and other information relevant to the daily liturgy. Cf. MACHZOR.

side /sʌɪd/ *noun.*
[Old English *sīde* = Old Frisian, Old Saxon *sīde*, Old High German *sīta* (Dutch *zijde*, *zij*, German *Seite*), Old Norse *síða*, from Germanic noun prob. from an adjective meaning 'extending lengthways, long, deep, low' (cf. SIDE *adjective*). Rel. to Old English *sīþ* late.]
▸ **I 1** Either of the two surfaces or parts of the human trunk between the left or right shoulder and the corresponding hip; the analogous part of an animal's body. OE. ▸**b** Either of the lateral halves of the body of a butchered animal, or an animal prepared for the table. ME.
2 A position or place closely adjacent to a person or thing. Only in phrs. & as 2nd elem. of comb. OE.

📖 **1** B. KEATON A miniature comedian . . making the ladies hold their sides. *Premiere* She swivels around, . . stroking her sides with her hands. **b** N. FREELING A whole side of smoked salmon already sliced. **2** M. L. KING I left the courtroom with my wife at my side. L. ELLMANN One doll lay with her head to the side.

▸ **II 3** Each of the two (or more) longer, usually vertical, surfaces of an object that are contrasted with the ends or the top and bottom; either of the two receding surfaces of an object that are contrasted with the front and back; a part of the surface of a round object having a particular aspect. OE. ▸**b** Each of the straight lines or flat surfaces that form or bound a figure or object. LME. ▸†**c** MATH. A number raised to a power, a root. Also, the number of terms taken when an arithmetical progression is summed, in relation to the sum. M17–M19.
4 The part of the hull of a boat extending from stem to stern between the gunwale and the water-line. OE.
5 The slope of a hill or bank, esp. one extending for a considerable distance. ME. ▸**b** The outskirts of a wood, town, etc. Now *rare* or *obsolete.* ME.
6 The bank or shore of a river, lake, sea, etc.; the land or district bordering this. ME.
7 Either of the two surfaces of a thin object. LME. ▸**b** Either of the two surfaces of a sheet of paper; an amount of writing sufficient to occupy a side; THEATRICAL a page of typescript containing the words of a particular character together with the cue words. M16. ▸**c** Either of the two faces of a gramophone record; each of two or more tracks on the same length of tape; *slang* a recording. M20. ▸**d** Each of two or more available television channels. Freq. in ***the other side***. *colloq.* L20.
8 Any of several aspects or views of a question, character, etc. LME.
9 A more or less vertical surface that encloses or bounds a space or hollow. L15.
10 TANNING. Either of the two pieces produced by cutting an animal's hide along the back. M18.

📖 **3** *Lancet* Catheters should be inserted from the side of the nose. B. VINE His room was . . on the side of the house that overlooked the meadow. **5** GOLDSMITH It is . . overlooked by tremendous mountains; their sides covered with snow. **6** A. A. MILNE Eeyore . . stood by the side of the stream. **7b** *Bookman* Some forty-seven pages, printed on one side only. **c** *Jazz Journal International*: Marshmallow came from a memorable series of sides made for Prestige. **d** *My Guy Monthly* You want . . *Top of the Pops* but your little brother's demanding the other side. **8** M. LASKI You can't help seeing the funny side. M. FRAYN This display of determination is a new side to your character. **9** J. JOHNSTON He blew into his cocoa and watched the rings expand . . to the sides of the mug.

▸ **III 11** A place or direction relative to a particular person, thing, or point; a point of the compass (freq. with specifying word). OE.
12 Either of two directions to either hand of an object, place, or imaginary line; the position implied in this; the space lying to either hand of, or in any direction from, a specified object, place, etc.; a part of a place or thing

lying in one or other direction from a centre line; a part near the edge and away from the middle of an area. Also with ellipsis of *of* in ***this side***, ***that side***, ***the other side***. **OE.**

13 A portion of a building allocated to a particular category of person or a particular purpose; a division of a school devoted to a particular class of studies (cf. ***modern side*** s.v. **MODERN** *adjective*). **ME.** ▸†**b** Either of two parts of a choir singing antiphonally. **LME–L16.** ▸**c** In Cambridge University, the body of students under the supervision of a particular tutor in a college. **M19.**

14 The line or limit to which something extends in opposite directions. **ME.**

15 A region, a district; the inhabitants of a region. Now *rare* exc. in adjectival & adverbial phrs. with preceding place-name, and as 2nd elem. of comb. **LME.**

16 *MATH.* Either of two quantities or expressions stated to be equal by an equation and separated by an equals sign. **E18.**

17 *ellipt.* A side dish, an entrée. *rare.* **M19.**

18 A spinning motion given to a ball in billiards, snooker, etc., by striking it to the left or right of centre. **L19.**

🕮 **11** W. GASS He would see them from all sides, observe from every angle. *Holiday Which?* The eastern side of Chianti is the hilliest. **12** MILTON Before the Gates there sat On either side a formidable shape. K. H. DIGBY The men . . on one side of the church and the women on the other. BROWNING That's all we may expect of man, this side The grave. E. PEACOCK She was on the less enviable side of fifty. J. WAIN He wanted a table at the side of the room. **14** TENNYSON The mirror crack'd from side to side. **15** E. M. FORSTER Jolly good poems, I'm getting published Bombay side. B. GRANGER A childhood on the streets of Chicago's South Side.

▸ **IV 19 a** The action, attitude, etc., of one person or a set of people in relation to another or others. **ME.** ▸**b** Either of two alternative views of a matter. **L16.**

20 The position or interests of one person, party, etc., in contrast to that of an opposing one. Chiefly in ***on one's side***, ***take sides***, ***take the side of***. **ME.**

21 Either of two sets of opponents in war, politics, games, etc. **ME.**

22 Kinship or descent through father or mother. **ME.**

🕮 **19a** THACKERAY He was, on his side too, very anxious to see Mrs Osborne. **b** *Scotsman* Three Ministers . . gave a Press conference . . to put their side of the case. **20** G. DALY In a fight he was a terrific man to have on your side. **21** T. HOOD Which side had won the cricket match. **22** DAY LEWIS I am of Anglo-Irish stock on both sides of my family.

▸ **V** [Perh. a different word.]

23 Pretentiousness, conceit. *slang.* **L19.**

🕮 **23** I. COLEGATE Not that he ever had any side, . . even when he was a very important man.

Phrases: ***a thorn in one's side***, ***a thorn in the side***: see **THORN** *noun* 1b. ***blind side***: see **BLIND** *adjective*. **burst one's sides**, **shake one's sides**, **split one's sides** laugh violently. **by the side of** (*a*) close to; (*b*) compared with. *ERR* ***on the right side***. *ERR* ***on the side of***. **from side to side** (*a*) across the whole width, right across; (*b*) alternately in each direction from a central line. ***have the laugh on one's side***: see **LAUGH** *noun*. ***Jack of both sides***: see **JACK** *noun*[1]. ***laugh on the other side of one's face***, ***laugh on the other side of one's mouth***, ***laugh on the wrong side of one's face***, ***laugh on the wrong side of one's mouth***: see **LAUGH** *verb*. ***lean to one side***: see **LEAN** *verb*. ***lee side***: see **LEE** *noun*[1] *& adjective*. ***leg side***: see **LEG** *noun* 4. **let the side down** fail one's colleagues, esp. by frustrating their efforts or embarrassing them. ***look on the bright side***: see **BRIGHT** *adjective* 1b. ***no side***: see **NO** *adjective*. **on one side** (*a*) not in the central or dominant position; (*b*) = **ASIDE** *adverb* 1, 3, 4. ***on the right side (of)***: see **RIGHT** *adjective*. **on the — side** tending towards being —, somewhat — (***on the safe side***: see **SAFE** *adjective*). **on the side** (*a*) *N. Amer.* served separately from the main dish; (*b*) in addition; surreptitiously, without acknowledgement; illicitly; outside marriage; (*c*) in addition to one's regular or ordinary occupation; as a subsidiary source of income (sometimes with implication of irregularity). **on the side of the angels** in favour of a spiritual interpretation of human nature; on the side of right despite the risk of unpopularity. ***on the windy side of***: see **WINDY** *adjective*[1]. ***on the wrong side (of)***: see **WRONG** *adjective & adverb*. **on this side (of)** †(*a*) short of, lacking; (*b*) before (a specified date). **on this side of the grave**, **on this side the grave** in this life. ***pipe the side***: see **PIPE** *verb*[1]. ***prompt side***: see **PROMPT** *noun*. ***right side***: see **RIGHT** *adjective*. ***shake one's sides***: see ***burst one's sides*** above. ***short back and sides***: see **BACK** *noun*[1]. **side by side** close together and abreast of each other; *spec.* (of people) standing thus, esp. for mutual support. ***spindle side***: see **SPINDLE** *noun & adjective*. ***split one's sides***: see ***burst one's sides*** above. ***SUNNY side***. **take sides** support one cause, person, etc., against another or others. ***the other side***: see **OTHER** *adjective*. ***the other side of the coin***: see **COIN** *noun* 3. **the other side of the hill** those aspects of a situation which are unknown at present; the latter part of life; *MILITARY* the enemy position or activities. ***the other side of the shield***: see **SHIELD** *noun*[1]. ***the rough side of one's tongue***: see **ROUGH** *adjective*. ***the wrong side of the tracks***: see **TRACK** *noun*. **turn sides to middle** cut (a worn sheet) down the middle and resew with the two halves interchanged, so that what were the sides become the middle and the sheet's useful life is extended. ***two sides of a shield***: see **SHIELD** *noun*[1]. ***weak side***: see **WEAK** *adjective*.

Attrib. & comb.: In the senses 'situated at or towards the side, fixed or placed at the side', as ***side-aisle***, ***side-gate***, ***side-rail***, ***side-window***, etc.; 'growing out to the side', as ***side-branch***; 'occurring in or affecting the side of the body', as ***side-stitch***; 'directed or tending sideways', as ***side-blow***, ***side-kick***, ***side-thrust***, etc.; 'spoken aside or in an undertone', as ***side-remark***, ***sidetalk***, etc.; 'subsidiary, incidental', as ***side-result***. Special combs., as **sideband** *TELECOMMUNICATIONS* a band of frequencies above or below a carrier frequency, within which lie the frequencies produced by modulation of the carrier; **side-bar** (*a*) *LAW* (now *Hist.*) a former bar in the Outer Parliament House, Edinburgh, and in Westminster Hall, London; (*b*) a lateral bar, a longitudinal side-piece, as in a saddle, carriage, etc.; (*c*) ***side-bar whiskers*** (*US dial.*), a man's sideboards; (*d*) *US* a short, usu. boxed, article in a newspaper placed alongside a main article and containing additional or explanatory material; (*e*) (chiefly *US*) a secondary, additional, or incidental thing; a side-issue; (*f*) *US LAW* a discussion between the lawyers in a case and the judge out of earshot of the jury; **side bend** an exercise movement in which a person bends the upper half of the body to one side while standing (usu. in *pl.*); **side-bet** a bet made with another player, esp. at cards, in addition to one's principal bet or one's bet with the house; a bet that does not form part of the game being played; **side-bone** (*a*) the part of the pelvis on either side of a bird or fowl which is easily separated from the backbone in carving; (*b*) a bird's scapula or shoulder-blade; **side-box** (the occupants of) a box at the side of a theatre; **side boy** *NAUTICAL* a boy or man who looks after the man-ropes and attends people coming on board or leaving a ship; **sideburn** [from **BURNSIDE**] = **SIDEBOARD** 4 (usu. in *pl.*); **sideburned** *adjective* having sideburns; **side-by-side** *adjective & noun* (designating) a double-barrelled shotgun with barrels mounted side by side; **side-chain** †(*a*) a chain at the side of a vehicle; (*b*) *CHEMISTRY* a group of atoms attached to the principal part of a molecule; **side chair** an upright wooden chair without arms; **side-chapel**: in the aisle or at the side of a church; **side-coat** (*a*) (now *dial.*) a long coat, a greatcoat; †(*b*) in *pl.*, long clothes worn by children; **side-comb** a comb used to secure a woman's hair, esp. at the side of the head; **side cut** (*a*) *OIL INDUSTRY* = ***side stream*** (b) below; (*b*) a curve in the side of a ski; **side dish** a dish served as an accessory to a main course; a dish or plate of the kind used for this purpose; **side-door** a door in the side of a building, garden, vehicle, etc.; a door subsidiary to a main door; ***by a side-door*** (*fig.*), indirectly; **side drift** *MINING* a horizontal tunnel leading off a main passage; **side-drum** a small double-headed drum used in military bands, orchestras, and jazz ensembles (orig. hung at the drummer's side); **side entry** (*a*) an entrance at the side; an area outside the side-door of a house; (*b*) *BRIDGE* a card providing access to a hand in a suit other than trumps; **side-face** (a view or representation of) a person's face in profile; **side-foot** *verb trans.* (*AMER. FOOTBALL*) kick with the inside of the foot; **side frequency** *TELECOMMUNICATIONS* a particular frequency in a sideband, in the case of amplitude modulation equal to the carrier frequency plus or minus a particular modulating frequency; **side gallery** either of the two galleries along the side of the debating chamber of the House of Commons, divided to seat Members and others; **side-glance** a glance directed sideways; *fig.* an indirect or passing reference; **sideguard** a protective panel along the side of a lorry, below the body; **side-head**, **side-heading** a newspaper heading run in at the beginning of a paragraph or placed adjacent to it; **sidehill** (now *US*) a hillside; **side-hold** *MOUNTAINEERING* a hold in which the rock is gripped from the side; **side-horse** = ***pommel horse*** s.v. **POMMEL** *noun*; **side-issue** a subsidiary issue or matter; a point that distracts attention from what is important; **side-ladder** *NAUTICAL* allowing access to and from a boat etc. alongside; **side lamp** a lamp at the side of a guard's van of a train; a sidelight of a motor vehicle; **side-land** a strip of land along the side of a ploughed field; **side lever** (*a*) either of two beams on the sides of some forms of steam engine, which transmit motion from the cross-head of the pistons to the connecting rods; (*b*) a lever at the side of a rifle for recocking it; **side-loader** a fork-lift truck in which the fork is at the side of the vehicle; **side lobe** a lobe in the response or radiation pattern of a radio aerial other than the central, or main, lobe; **side-lock** a lock of hair at the side of the head; **side-look** an oblique look, a side-glance; **side-looking** *adjective* looking sideways; (of radar and sonar) sending a beam sideways and downwards, usu. from an aircraft for the mapping of relief; **side meat** *US* salt pork or bacon, usu. cut from the side of the pig; **side mill** *ENGINEERING* (*a*) a circular milling cutter with teeth on its face, so that it cuts in the direction of its axis of rotation; (*b*) a cylindrical cutter used with its axis parallel to the surface of the workpiece, so that the cutting action occurs along its length; **side-necked turtle** any of various freshwater turtles of the families Pelomedusidae and Chelidae, mainly of the southern hemisphere, having a long neck curved round to the side for protection; **side-note** a note made or placed at the side of a page; **side-of-the-mouth** *adjective* delivered in a rough drawling manner; forcefully demotic; **side order** a side dish; **side-partner** *US colloq.* a close associate at work; a colleague; **side-piece** a piece fixed or attached at one side; **side play** *MECHANICS* freedom of movement from side to side; **side-pocket** in the side of a garment, esp. a jacket or coat; **side pond**, **side pound** a pond alongside a canal lock such that water can flow between them when the lock is operated; **side-post** (*a*) a doorpost (chiefly in biblical allusions); (*b*) a post supporting a roof away from the centre-line; **side reaction** a subsidiary chemical reaction taking place in a system at the same time as a more important reaction; **side road** (*a*) a minor or subsidiary road; a road leading from or to a main road; (*b*) *spec.* (*Canad.*) in Ontario, a road along the side boundary of a concession; **side-rope** (*a*) (*obsolete* exc. *Scot.*) a trace for a horse; (*b*) a rope for climbing up a ship's side; **side salad** a salad served as a side dish; **side-scan**, **side-scanning** *adjectives* (of sonar and radar) sending a beam sideways (from a ship) or sideways and downwards (from an aircraft); **side scraper** *ARCHAEOLOGY* a prehistoric flint implement, usu. made on a broad flake by retouching one of the sides to give a blunt edge useful for scraping tasks; **side-screen** †(*a*) in landscape painting, a secondary feature set on both sides of the principal to show perspective; (*b*) a side-curtain of an open motor vehicle; **side-seat** a seat facing or placed at the side of a vehicle; **side-shoot**: growing out from the side of a stem; **side-split** *Canad.* a split-level house with fewer storeys on one side than the other; **side-splitter** a very funny story, farce, etc.; **side-splitting** *adjective* causing violent laughter, extremely funny; **side-splittingly** *adverb* in a side-splitting way; **side-stick** *PRINTING* (*obsolete* exc. *Hist.*) the longer of a pair of wedge-shaped sticks with one side slanting, used in locking up a forme; **side-stream** (*a*) a tributary stream, a subsidiary current; ***side-stream smoke***, smoke that passes from a cigarette into the surrounding air, not into the smoker; (*b*) *OIL INDUSTRY* a fraction drawn off at an intermediate tray in a distillation column; **side-street** a minor or subsidiary street; **side-stroke** (*a*) a swimming stroke in which the swimmer lies on his or her side; (*b*) a stroke towards or from the side; *fig.* an incidental action; **side suit** *CARDS* a suit other than trumps; a long suit in bridge; **side-sway** a rolling or swaying motion from side to side in a moving vehicle or a building; **side-table**: placed next to the wall of a room or at the side of a larger table; **side-taking** the taking of one side in a dispute etc.; **side tone** the reproduction of the user's own voice in a telephone receiver; a sound so reproduced; a signal reaching a radiotelephone from itself; **side trip** a detour, a deviation, an excursion aside from the main journey, esp. for sightseeing; **side valve** *MECHANICS* a valve that is mounted alongside the cylinder in an internal-combustion engine and opens into a sideways extension of the combustion chamber; **side-view** a view obtained or taken from the side; a profile; ***side-view mirror***, a mirror at the side of a motor vehicle to give the driver a view behind and to one side of it; **side-wheel** *adjective* designating a steamer with paddle-wheels at the sides; **side wheeler** (*a*) a side-wheel steamer; (*b*) *BASEBALL* (*rare*) a side-arm or left-handed pitcher; (*c*) *US* a pacing horse with a rolling gait; **side-wing** (*a*) *THEATRICAL* = **WING** *noun* 9c; (*b*) *slang* (in *pl.*) sideburns; **side-whiskers**: growing on a man's cheeks.

side /sʌɪd/ *adjective & adverb*[2]. Now *Scot. & north.*

[Old English *sīþ* = Middle Dutch *sīde*, *zīde*, Old Norse *síðr*.]

▸ **A** *adjective.* †**1** Large, ample, spacious, extensive. **OE–LME.** ▸**b** Far-off, distant; going far. *rare.* Only in **LME.**

2 Extending lengthways; long. Chiefly in ***wide and side***. **OE.** ▸†**b** Of a roof: high, steep. **LME–L18.**

3 Of (part of) a garment: reaching or hanging far down on the person; long. Also (*rare*), narrow, clinging. **OE.**

4 Haughty, proud. **E16.** ▸**b** Severe or hard *on* a person. *Scot.* **E19.**

▸ **B** *adverb.* †**1** To a great distance or length; far. Chiefly in ***wide and side***. **OE–E17.**

2 Towards or on the ground; in a long trailing manner. **ME.**

side /sʌɪd/ *verb.* **LME.**

[from **SIDE** *noun*.]

†**1** *verb trans.* Cut or carve (an animal) into sides. **LME–E16.**

†**2** *verb trans.* Have on the side referred to. *rare* (Spenser). Only in **L16.**

†**3** *verb trans.* Support, countenance, (a person or party). **L16–E17.**

4 *verb intrans.* & (*rare*) *refl.* Take a side in a conflict, dispute, or debate. Usu. foll. by *with*. **L16.**

†**5** *verb trans.* Assign to either of two sides or parties. **L16–E17.**

6 *verb trans.* Walk or stand by the side of; *fig.* (now *rare*) rival, equal, match. **E17.**

7 *verb intrans.* Move or turn sideways. *rare.* **M17.**

8 *verb trans.* Provide (a structure) with sides. Cf. earlier **SIDING** *noun* 1. *rare.* **L17.**

9 *verb trans.* Make of certain dimensions on the side; square the sides of (timber). **L18.**

10 *verb trans.* Put in order, arrange; clear or tidy *up*. *dial.* **E19.** ▸**b** Put aside, remove; clear *away*. **M19.**

11 *verb trans.* *NAUTICAL.* Draw (a rope) *over* or *out*. **M19.**

🕮 **4** A. ALVAREZ He found himself siding with Charles . . against this troublesome, offended woman. **6** L. GRIBBLE The man from the embassy . . was sided by a pair of companions with shoulder holsters.

side /sʌɪd/ *adverb*[2]. Now *rare.* **LME.**

[from **SIDE** *noun* by ellipsis of preposition.]

By, from, or to the side. Only in comb. with pples. ***side-flowing***, ***side-hanging***, etc.

side-arm /ˈsʌɪdɑːm/ *adjective & adverb.* **E20.**

[from **SIDE** *noun* + **ARM** *noun*[1].]

▸ **A** *adjective.* Esp. *BASEBALL.* Performed, delivered with, or employing a swing of the arm extended sideways. **E20.**

▸ **B** *adverb.* In a side-arm manner. **M20.**

side-arms /ˈsʌɪdɑːmz/ *noun pl.* **L17.**

[from **SIDE** *noun* + **ARM** *noun*[2] + **-S**[1].]

MILITARY. **1** Weapons worn at the side, such as sword, dagger, or pistol. **L17.**

2 Instruments carried for use in loading a gun. **E19.**

sideboard /ˈsʌɪdbɔːd/ *noun.* **LME.**

[from **SIDE** *noun* + **BOARD** *noun*.]

1 a A table placed towards the side of a room, *esp.* one for taking meals at. Now *rare.* **LME.** ▸**b** A piece of dining-room furniture for holding dishes, cutlery, table linen, etc., *esp.* one with a flat top, cupboards, and drawers. **L17.**

2 A board forming the side, or a part of the side, of a structure; *spec.* an additional and removable board at the side of a cart or lorry. **LME.**

3 In *pl.* A stand-up collar. *arch. slang.* **M19.**

4 Hair grown as a whisker at the side of a man's face (sometimes continuing on to his cheek). Usu. in *pl. colloq.* L19.

side-car /ˈsʌɪdkɑː/ *noun & verb.* L19.
[from SIDE *noun* + CAR.]
▶ **A** *noun.* **1** *Hist.* A conveyance in which the seats face to the sides; a jaunting car. L19.
2 A small low vehicle designed to be attached to the nearside of a motorcycle to carry one or more passengers. E20.
3 A cocktail made of brandy and lemon juice with a dash of orange liqueur. E20.
▶ **B** *verb intrans.* Infl. **-rr-**. Travel in or with a motorcycle side-car. Chiefly as ***side-carring*** *verbal noun.* E20.
■ **sidecarist** *noun* a person who drives or travels in a motorcycle and side-car combination E20.

sided /ˈsʌɪdɪd/ *adjective.* LME.
[from SIDE *noun, verb*: see -ED², -ED¹.]
1 Having sides; provided with a side or sides. Freq. as 2nd elem. of comb. LME.
2 NAUTICAL. Of a timber: having a (specified) dimension in the direction contrary to that of the moulding. L18. ▸**b** Of timber: dressed on one or more sides. M19.
1 ***double-sided, four-sided, open-sided, steep-sided***, etc.
■ **sidedness** *noun* (**a**) the property of having a specified number or kind of sides; (**b**) lack of symmetry in a superficially symmetrical thing: E20.

side-effect /ˈsʌɪdɪfɛkt/ *noun.* L19.
[from SIDE *noun* + EFFECT *noun*.]
A subsidiary consequence of an action, occurrence, or state of affairs; an unintended secondary result; *spec.* (MEDICINE) an effect (usu. for the worse) of a drug other than that for which it is administered.

sidekick /ˈsʌɪdkɪk/ *noun. colloq.* E20.
[Back-form. from next].
1 A companion, a close associate, a friend, a colleague; *spec.* an accomplice, a partner in crime; a subordinate member of a pair or group. E20.
2 A side-pocket. *US Criminals' slang.* E20.
3 An incidental criticism; a passing or indirect attack. M20.

side-kicker /ˈsʌɪdkɪkə/ *noun. slang* (orig. *US*). Now *rare.* E20.
[from SIDE *noun* + KICKER.]
= SIDEKICK 1.

sideless /ˈsʌɪdlɪs/ *adjective.* E19.
[from SIDE *noun* + -LESS.]
Having no sides; open at the sides.

side-light /ˈsʌɪdlʌɪt/ *noun.* E17.
[from SIDE *noun* + LIGHT *noun*.]
1 Light coming from the side. E17. ▸**b** (A piece of) incidental information on a subject. M19.
2 a A window in the side of a building, ship, etc.; an opening in the side of a lamp. E19. ▸**b** A pane or light in the side of a large window; a window by the side of a door or other window. M19.
3 The red port or green starboard light on a ship under way at night. L19.
4 A small light on either side of the front of a motor vehicle to indicate its presence in poor light. E20.

🕮 **1b** J. BRODSKY The importance of this book goes . . beyond the sidelights it casts on the poet's own progress.

sideline /ˈsʌɪdlʌɪn/ *noun & verb.* M18.
[from SIDE *noun* + LINE *noun*².]
▶ **A** *noun.* **1** A line extending along or towards one side of a thing or space; *spec.* in SPORT, a line marking the edge of the playing area at the side, a touch-line; the area immediately outside this (usu. in *pl.*). M18.
2 a = ***side road*** (b) s.v. SIDE *noun. Canad.* M19. ▸**b** A railway or tramway line extending away from the main line. L19.
3 A line for tying together the fore and hind leg on one side of an animal. *rare.* M19.
4 A job in addition to one's main occupation; an auxiliary line of goods or trade. L19.

🕮 **1 on the sidelines, from the sidelines** *fig.* in, from, a situation removed from the main action; without direct involvement. **4** MALCOLM X Smuggling to prisoners was the guards' sideline.

▶ **B** *verb.* **1** *verb trans.* Secure (an animal) with a sideline. M19.
2 *verb trans.* Esp. of an injury: cause or compel (a player) to remain out of a game or a team. Usu. in *pass.* M20. ▸**b** Remove from the centre of activity or attention; place in an inferior position. L20.
3 *verb intrans.* Engage *in* as a subsidiary occupation or sport. M20.
4 *verb trans.* Mark (a passage of text) for special attention or treatment by a line in the margin. M20.

🕮 **2** *Rugby World & Post* Falmouth player Dave Stone was in the visiting party, but an injury sidelined him. **b** *Times* The opposition refused to countenance such a sidelining of the national parliament.

sideling /ˈsʌɪdlɪŋ/ *noun.* Now *dial.* ME.
[from SIDE *noun* + -LING¹.]
†**1** A piece of land lying by the side of a larger portion or by a stream. ME–E18.
2 A slope, *esp.* one along the side of which a track or road runs. E19.

sideling /ˈsʌɪdlɪŋ/ *adverb & adjective.* ME.
[from SIDE *noun* + -LING².]
▶ **A** *adverb.* **1** = SIDELONG *adverb* 1. Now *rare.* ME.
†**2 a** To or on one side of something. *rare.* M16–L18. ▸†**b** With an inclination to one side. E17–E18.
†**3** On a side-saddle; facing to the side. Only in 17.
▶ **B** *adjective.* †**1** Situated towards or at the side(s). LME–M16.
2 Directed or moving sideways; oblique, sidelong. *arch.* E17.
3 Sloping, steep. Now chiefly *dial.* E17.

sidelings /ˈsʌɪdlɪŋz/ *adverb.* Now *dial.* ME.
[from SIDE *noun* + -LINGS.]
1 = SIDELONG *adverb* 1. Also, indirectly, with indirect speech; with a side-glance. ME.
†**2** = SIDELING *adverb* 2a. LME–E17.
3 Side by side; abreast. M16.
4 = SIDELING *adverb* 3. E19.

sidelong /ˈsʌɪdlɒŋ/ *adverb, adjective, & preposition.* LME.
[Alt. of SIDELING *adverb*: see -LONG.]
▶ **A** *adverb.* **1** Towards the side; sideways, obliquely. LME.
2 To the side *of*; side by side; presenting the side *to* something. M17.
3 On the side; with the side to the ground. M17.

🕮 **1** W. HORWOOD Watching her sidelong as she greeted some new young male. **2** N. HAWTHORNE Seated within the shop, sidelong to the window.

▶ **B** *adjective.* **1** In a slanting direction; in a sloping position; (of ground) sloping; lying on the side. L16.
2 Directed to one side, oblique; glancing, moving, or extending sideways. E17.
3 Indirect; not straightforward or open. M17.

🕮 **2** B. CHATWIN She risked a sidelong glance.

▶ **C** *preposition.* By or along the side of. *rare.* E16.

sideman /ˈsʌɪdmən/ *noun.* Pl. **-men**. L16.
[from SIDE *noun* + MAN *noun*.]
†**1** = SIDESMAN 1. L16–L17.
2 A supporting musician in a jazz or dance band. Orig. *US.* M20.

side-on /*as adjective* ˈsʌɪdɒn, *as adverb* sʌɪdˈɒn/ *adjective & adverb.* E20.
[from SIDE *noun* + ON *adverb*.]
▶ **A** *adverb.* With a side directed towards a point of reference; from the side. E20.
▶ **B** *adjective.* Directed from or towards a side; (of a collision) involving the meeting of a side of a vehicle with an object. E20.

sider /ˈsʌɪdə/ *noun.* M19.
[from SIDE *noun* + -ER¹.]
A person who or thing which lives or is situated on a side specified by a preceding word; *spec.* (esp. *Austral.*) a native or inhabitant of a specified district.

sideral /ˈsʌɪd(ə)r(ə)l, ˈsɪd-/ *adjective.* L16.
[Latin *sideralis*, from *sider-*: see SIDEREAL, -AL¹.]
1 = SIDEREAL 1. L16.
2 Coming from or caused by the stars. E17.

sideration /sʌɪdəˈreɪʃ(ə)n/ *noun.* Now *rare* or *obsolete.* E17.
[Latin *sideratio(n-)*, from *siderat-* pa. ppl stem of *siderari* be planet-struck, from *sider-*: see SIDEREAL, -ATION.]
1 The blasting of a plant, esp. due to excessive heat. E17.
2 Sudden paralysis; necrosis of a part of the body. E17.
3 Erysipelas of the face or scalp. E19.

sidereal /sʌɪˈdɪərɪəl/ *adjective.* M17.
[from Latin *sidereus*, from *sider-*, *sidus* star: see -AL¹.]
1 Of or pertaining to the stars. M17.
†**2** Starlike, lustrous, bright. *rare.* Only in M17.
3 Of (a period of) time: determined or measured with reference to the apparent motion of the stars. Of planetary or lunar motion: relative to the stars. L17.
4 Concerned with the stars. M19.

🕮 **3** J. F. W. HERSCHEL The sidereal periods of the planets may be obtained . . by observing their passages. **sidereal clock**: showing sidereal time. **sidereal day** the interval between successive meridional transits of a star or esp. of the first point of Aries at a place, about four minutes shorter than a solar day. **sidereal month** the time it takes the moon to orbit once around the earth, measured with respect to the stars (approx. 27¼ days). **sidereal year** a year longer than the solar year by 20 minutes 23 seconds because of precession.

■ **sidereally** *adverb* E19.

siderean /sʌɪˈdɪərɪən/ *adjective. rare.* M17.
[formed as prec. + -AN.]
= SIDEREAL 1.

siderite /ˈsʌɪdərʌɪt/ *noun.* Also (earlier) †**-ites**. M16.
[In early use from French *sidérite* or Latin *siderites*, *-itis* from Greek *sidēritēs*, *-itis*, from *sidēros* iron; later directly from Greek *sidēros* + -ITE¹.]
MINERALOGY. **1** An iron-coloured stone supposed to cause discord. Long *obsolete* exc. *Hist.* M16.
†**2** = LODESTONE 1. L16–L17.
3 Orig., any of various minerals. Now *spec.* (**a**) native ferrous carbonate, a mineral that is a source of iron and occurs in sedimentary rocks and ore veins as translucent, usu. brown crystals of the trigonal system; (**b**) a blue variety of quartz. L18.
4 A meteorite consisting mainly of iron and nickel. L19.
■ **sideritic** /sʌɪdəˈrɪtɪk/ *adjective* (*rare*) of the nature of siderite L18.

†**siderites** *noun* see SIDERITE *noun.*

sidero- /ˈsɪdərəʊ, ˈsʌɪ-/ *combining form*¹.
[from Greek *sidēros* iron: see -O-.]
Of, pertaining to, or involving iron.
■ **sideroblast** *noun* (MEDICINE) a normoblast containing a granule of ferritin M20. **sideroˈblastic** *adjective* (MEDICINE) of, pertaining to, or (esp. of anaemia) characterized by the presence of sideroblasts M20. **siderochrome** *noun* (BIOCHEMISTRY) any of various compounds involved in the transport of iron in micro-organisms M20. **siderocyte** *noun* (MEDICINE) an erythrocyte containing a granule of non-haemoglobin iron M20. **sideroˈcytic** *adjective* (MEDICINE) of, pertaining to, or characterized by the presence of siderocytes M20. **siderodromoˈphobia** *noun* [Greek *dromos* running] irrational fear of rail travel L19. **siderograph** *noun* (*Hist.*) an engraving produced by siderography L19. **sideroˈgraphic** *adjective* (*Hist.*) pertaining to siderography E19. **sideˈrography** *noun* (*Hist.*) a method of engraving on steel introduced for banknotes E20. **sideroˈpenia** *noun* (MEDICINE) an abnormally low concentration of iron in the blood M20. **sideroˈpenic** *adjective* (MEDICINE) of or characterized by sideropenia M20. **siderophile** *adjective & noun* (GEOLOGY & CHEMISTRY) (designating) an element which commonly occurs in a metallic phase rather than combined as a silicate or sulphide, and is supposed to have become concentrated in the earth's core E20. **sideroˈphilin** *noun* = TRANSFERRIN M20. **siderophore** *noun* (BIOLOGY & MEDICINE) an agent which binds and transports iron in micro-organisms L20. **siderosome** *noun* (MEDICINE) a particle of non-haemoglobin iron in a cell L20.

sidero- /ˈsʌɪdərəʊ, ˈsɪd-/ *combining form*².
[from Latin *sider-*, *sidus* star + -O-.]
Of, pertaining to, or involving the stars.
■ **siderostat** *noun* an astronomical instrument by which a celestial object may be kept within the same part of the field of view of a telescope M19. **sideroˈstatic** *adjective* designating or pertaining to a siderostat L19.

siderolite /ˈsɪd(ə)rəlʌɪt, ˈsʌɪ-/ *noun.* M19.
[from SIDERO-¹ + -LITE.]
A meteorite composed of iron (and nickel) and stone in similar proportions.

siderosis /sɪdəˈrəʊsɪs, sʌɪ-/ *noun.* Pl. **-roses** /-ˈrəʊsiːz/. L19.
[from SIDERO-¹ + -OSIS.] MEDICINE.
1 The accumulation in body tissues of iron-containing material; *spec.* the deposition of iron dust in the lungs. L19.
2 Discoloration of the lens of the eye by an embedded particle of iron. L19.
■ **siderotic** /-ˈrɒt-/ *adjective* formed from or rich in insoluble iron compounds derived from the breakdown of haemoglobin; of or pertaining to siderosis: M20.

siderurgy /ˈsɪdərəːdʒi/ *noun.* L19.
[Greek *sidērourgia*, from *sidēros* iron + *ergon* work: see -Y³.]
The metallurgy of iron and steel.
■ **sideˈrurgical** *adjective* L19.

ˈsides /sʌɪdz/ *preposition & adverb.* Long *dial.* & *colloq.* Also **sides**. L16.
[Aphet.]
Besides.
¶ Rare before 19.

side-saddle /ˈsʌɪdsad(ə)l/ *noun, verb, & adverb.* L15.
[from SIDE *noun* + SADDLE *noun*.]
▶ **A** *noun.* A saddle for a rider sitting with both feet on one side of a horse, now usu. with supports for the knees of the rider, who sits facing forward with the right knee raised. L15.
side-saddle flower any of several N. American pitcher-plants of the genus *Sarracenia*.
▶ **B** *verb trans.* Equip (a horse) with a side-saddle. L18.
▶ **C** *adverb.* On a side-saddle. L19.

sideshow /ˈsʌɪdʃəʊ/ *noun.* M19.
[from SIDE *noun* + SHOW *noun*¹.]
1 A show which is subsidiary to a larger one; a minor attraction in an exhibition or entertainment. M19.
2 A minor incident or issue, a subordinate matter or affair. M19.

side-slip /ˈsʌɪdslɪp/ *noun & verb.* M17.
[from SIDE *noun* + SLIP *noun*³.]
▶ **A** *noun.* **1** A slope, a rise. *rare.* M17.
2 An illegitimate child. *rare.* L19.
3 a The action or fact of slipping sideways, esp. on the part of a bicycle or motor vehicle; an instance of this. L19. ▸**b** AERONAUTICS. A sideways movement of an aircraft in flight, esp. downwards towards the centre of curvature

of a turn; a manoeuvre in which this is deliberately produced. E20. ▸**c** *SKIING & SURFING*. The action of travelling at an angle down a slope or wave. E20.
▶**B** *verb*. Infl. **-pp-**.
1 *verb intrans.* Slip sideways. L19.
2 *AERONAUTICS*. **a** *verb intrans.* Of an aeroplane: move sideways, esp. towards the centre of curvature while turning. E20. ▸**b** *verb trans.* Cause to side-slip. E20.
3 *verb intrans. SKIING & SURFING*. Travel downwards at an angle. E20.
4 a *verb intrans.* Move elusively or adroitly. E20. ▸**b** *verb trans.* Elude, give the slip. M20.

sidesman /ˈsʌɪdzmən/ *noun*. Pl. **-men**. M17.
[Alt. of SIDEMAN.]
1 A person elected as an assistant to the churchwardens of a parish or church; a person whose duties include taking the collection during a church service and giving assistance to members of the congregation. M17.
2 An assistant to a municipal or civil officer. *local*. M19.

sidestep /ˈsʌɪdstɛp/ *noun & verb*. L18.
[from SIDE *noun* or *adverb*² + STEP *noun*¹.]
▶**A** *noun*. A step to one side; *spec.* (*RUGBY FOOTBALL*), one made while running with the ball, in order to avoid a tackle. L18.
▶**B** *verb*. Infl. **-pp-**.
1 *verb intrans.* Step to one side; *fig.* practise evasion, prevaricate. E20. ▸**b** *SKIING*. Climb or descend by lifting alternate skis at an angle to the slope. E20.
2 *verb trans.* Evade; *spec.* (*RUGBY FOOTBALL*) evade (a tackle or opponent) by sidestepping. E20.
3 *verb trans.* Cause to move sideways; transfer to the side. M20.
■ **sidestepper** *noun* E20.

side-swipe /ˈsʌɪdswʌɪp/ *verb & noun*. E20.
[from SIDE *noun* + SWIPE *verb*.]
▶**A** *verb trans.* Strike a glancing blow on or with the side, esp. the side of a motor vehicle. Chiefly *N. Amer.* E20.
▶**B** *noun*. **1** A glancing blow from or on the side, esp. of a motor vehicle. Chiefly *N. Amer.* E20.
2 A passing jibe or verbal attack; an indirect rebuke or criticism. E20.

📖 **2** *City Limits* Poliakoff takes some effective side-swipes at the bureaucratic mind.

■ **sideswiper** *noun* M20.

sidetrack /ˈsʌɪdtrak/ *noun & verb*. Orig. *US*. M19.
[from SIDE *noun* + TRACK *noun*.]
▶**A** *noun*. **1** A railway siding. M19.
2 A minor path or track. L19.
▶**B** *verb*. **1** *verb trans. & intrans.* Run or shunt (a train) into a siding. L19.
2 *verb trans.* Distract (a person) from the subject in hand; divert (a thing) from its intended purpose or aim. L19.

📖 **2** S. TERKEL The mail had been sidetracked. We had no idea what was happenin' in the world outside. M. BISHOP Lab work had sidetracked him and he had never managed to get to bed.

sidewalk /ˈsʌɪdwɔːk/ *noun*. L16.
[from SIDE *noun* + WALK *noun*.]
†**1 a** A stroll, a walk around. *rare*. Only in L16. ▸**b** A walk or path running parallel to a main one. *rare*. Only in M17.
2 A pedestrian path along the side of a street or road; a pavement. Now *N. Amer.* M18.
Comb.: **sidewalk superintendent** *joc.* (*US*) an onlooker who watches and gives unsolicited advice at building sites, road repairs, etc.

side-wall /ˈsʌɪdwɔːl/ *noun*. LME.
[from SIDE *noun* + WALL *noun*¹.]
1 A wall forming the side of a structure, room, or enclosure; *spec.* one forming a side of a squash court. LME.
2 The side of a vehicle's tyre, usu. untreaded and freq. distinctively marked or coloured; (in full ***side-wall tyre***) a tyre with distinctive side-walls. E20.
3 A surface at either side of a hovercraft that projects downwards underneath it and helps to contain the air-cushion. M20.

sideward /ˈsʌɪdwəd/ *adverb & adjective*. LME.
[from SIDE *noun* + -WARD.]
▶**A** *adverb*. Towards one side or the other. LME.
▶**B** *adjective*. Directed, moving, or tending towards one side. M19.

sidewards /ˈsʌɪdwədz/ *adverb*. L15.
[from SIDE *noun* + -WARDS.]
1 = SIDEWARD *adverb*. L15.
2 In a position on one side; by the side. (Foll. by *of*, *from*.) E18.

sideway /ˈsʌɪdweɪ/ *noun*. LME.
[from SIDE *noun* + WAY *noun*.]
1 A path or way diverging from or to the side of a main road; a byway. LME.
2 A footpath at the side of a road; a footway. Cf. SIDEWALK 2. Now *US*. M18.

sideway /ˈsʌɪdweɪ/ *adverb & adjective*. E17.
[from SIDE *noun* + -WAY.]
▶**A** *adverb*. = SIDEWAYS *adverb*. E17.
▶**B** *adjective*. = SIDEWAYS *adjective* 1. L18.

sideways /ˈsʌɪdweɪz/ *adverb & adjective*. L16.
[from SIDE *noun* + -WAYS.]
▶**A** *adverb*. **1** From one side. L16.
2 So as to present the side instead of the face, front, or end; with one side facing forward; facing to the side. L16.
3 Towards one side; obliquely. E17.
4 So as to incline to one side. M17.
5 At one side (*of* a place). *rare*. E18.
6 By an indirect way; indirectly. *rare*. E18.
7 As intensifier: thoroughly, to the limits of one's tolerance. *colloq.* M20.

📖 **2** DAY LEWIS Keyes, sitting sideways, his legs dangling over a wheel. **sideways on** from the side; side-on. **3** M. AMIS I glanced sideways at Fielding Goodney. ***knock sideways***: see KNOCK *verb*. ***look sideways***: see LOOK *verb*. **4** J. CONRAD His knees up and his head drooping sideways. **7** *Times* Broadstairs bored him sideways.

▶**B** *adjective*. **1** Directed or moving towards or from one side; oblique, indirect. M19.
2 Unconventional, unorthodox; unusual. L20.

📖 **1** R. P. JHABVALA She gave me a sideways glance. **2** *Sun* Jasper Carrott takes his final sideways look at recent events.

side-wind /ˈsʌɪdwɪnd/ *noun & adjective*. LME.
[from SIDE *noun* + WIND *noun*¹.]
▶**A** *noun*. **1** A wind blowing from the side or on to the side of a vehicle etc. LME.
2 *fig.* An indirect means, method, or manner. Chiefly in ***by a side-wind***. *arch.* M17.
▶**B** *attrib.* or as *adjective*. Indirect, oblique; illegitimate. *rare*. L17.

sidewinder /ˈsʌɪdwɪndə/ *noun*¹. *N. Amer. & dial.* M19.
[from SIDE *noun* + WINDER *noun*³.]
A blow delivered from or on the side.

sidewinder /ˈsʌɪdwʌɪndə/ *noun*². *US*. L19.
[from SIDE *noun* + WIND *verb*¹ + -ER¹.]
Any of several small rattlesnakes that move with a side-to-side motion, esp. *Crotalus cerastes*, a desert rattlesnake of N. America.
■ **sidewind** *verb intrans.* [back-form.] move like a sidewinder E20.

side-wipe /ˈsʌɪdwʌɪp/ *noun*. M18.
[from SIDE *noun* + WIPE *noun*.]
1 An indirect rebuke, censure, or hint. *dial.* M18.
2 = SIDEWINDER *noun*¹. *dial. & US*. M19.
■ Also **side-wiper** *noun* (*dial. & US*) L19.

sidewise /ˈsʌɪdwʌɪz/ *adverb & adjective*. L16.
[from SIDE *noun* + -WISE.]
▶**A** *adverb*. **1** = SIDEWAYS *adverb* 3. L16.
2 = SIDEWAYS *adverb* 2. E17.
3 On or from the side. E17.
▶**B** *adjective*. = SIDEWAYS *adjective* 1. M19.

Sidhe /ʃiː/ *noun pl.* L18.
[from Irish *aos sidhe* people of the fairy mound, from *sídhe* fairies.]
IRISH MYTHOLOGY. The hills of the fairies; fairyland, faerie. Also, the fairy folk, esp. as the mythical gods of ancient Ireland.

sidi /ˈsiːdiː/ *noun*. *arch.* Also **seedee**, **seedy**. E17.
[Urdu *saiyidī*, *sīdī* from Persian *saiyidī* from colloq. Arab. *sīdī* for literary Arab. *sayyidī* my lord, formed as SAYYID.]
Orig., (a title of respect given in the west of the Indian subcontinent to) an African Muslim holding a high position under any of the kings of the Deccan. Later, a black African (latterly chiefly in ***sidi-boy***).

siding /ˈsʌɪdɪŋ/ *noun*. LME.
[from SIDE *verb* + -ING¹.]
▶**I** The action or an act of SIDE *verb*.
†**1** The provision or replacement of the sides of something. Only in LME.
2 The action or an act of taking sides in a conflict, dispute, or debate; party spirit, partisanship, factiousness. Also, a faction. E17.
3 The action of moving or turning sideways. M17.
4 The action of siding timber. *N. Amer.* L19.
▶**II** An object.
5 †**a** A side of something. Only in E17. ▸**b** Cladding for the outside of a building; (a piece of) weatherboarding. Chiefly *N. Amer.* E19. ▸**c** = SIDELING *noun* 2. *Austral. & NZ*. L19.
6 *NAUTICAL*. The breadth of a deck beam of a ship. L18.
7 a A short length of railway track connected to an adjacent through line (often at one end only) for storing and shunting rolling-stock and for enabling trains on the same line to pass each other; a similar line on a tramway. E19. ▸**b** A passing-place in a canal. M19.

sidle /ˈsʌɪd(ə)l/ *verb & noun*. L17.
[Back-form. from SIDELING, SIDELONG *adverbs* after verbs in -LE³.]
▶**A** *verb*. **1** *verb intrans.* Move or go sideways or obliquely; *esp.* walk in a furtive, unobtrusive, or timid manner. L17. ▸**b** Chiefly *MOUNTAINEERING*. Make one's way in a transverse direction along an incline, traverse. *NZ*. M20.
2 *verb intrans.* Saunter, lounge about. *dial.* L18.
3 *verb trans.* Move, turn, or direct sideways or obliquely. L18.

📖 **1** E. BLISHEN He would sidle up to your desk and lean on it. K. WATERHOUSE I muttered: 'Excuse me,' and sidled out of their way. **3** G. GREENE Getting nearer to Rowe, sidling his body to the chair's edge.

▶**B** *noun*. An act of sidling; a sideways or oblique movement. M19.

Sidneian /ˈsɪdnɪən, sɪdˈniːən/ *adjective*. Also **Sidneyan**. E17.
[from *Sidney* (see below) + -IAN.]
Of, pertaining to, or characteristic of the English statesman, soldier, and man of letters Sir Philip Sidney (1554–86), or his work.
¶ Not recorded between M17 and M20.

Sidonian /sʌɪˈdəʊnɪən/ *noun & adjective*. M16.
[from Latin *Sidonius* from Greek *Sidōnios*, from *Sidōn* Sidon: see -IAN.]
▶**A** *noun*. A native or inhabitant of Sidon (Saida), a port in Lebanon that in ancient times was a famous Phoenician city. M16.
▶**B** *adjective*. Of or pertaining to Sidon. L16.

sidra /ˈsɪdrə/ *noun*. Also **se-**, **-ah**, **S-**. Pl. **-ra(h)s**, **-rot(h)** /-rəʊt/. E20.
[Yiddish, ult. from Aramaic *sedre*. Cf. SEDER.]
In Jewish liturgy, a section of the Torah read at a Sabbath morning synagogue service. Cf. PARASHAH.

SIDS *abbreviation*.
Sudden infant death syndrome.

Sidur *noun* var. of SIDDUR.

sidy /ˈsʌɪdi/ *adjective*. *colloq.* L19.
[from SIDE *noun* + -Y¹.]
Pretentious, conceited.

Siebel /ˈsiːb(ə)l/ *noun*. M20.
[*Siebel* Flugzeugwerke, German aircraft manufacturing company.]
Hist. In full ***Siebel ferry***. A German troop and freight landing-craft used in the war of 1939–45.

†**siecle** *noun* var. of SECLE.

siege /siːdʒ/ *noun & verb*. ME.
[Old French *sege* (mod. *siège*), formed as ASSIEGE.]
▶**A** *noun*. **I 1** †**a** A chair, a seat, *esp.* one used by a person of rank or distinction. ME–E17. ▸**b** A bench; now *esp.* a mason's workbench. Chiefly *Scot.* M16.
2 †**a** An ecclesiastical see. ME–L16. ▸†**b** A person's place of residence; a station, a position; a royal or imperial seat. LME–M17. ▸†**c** The place in which something is set, or on which a ship lies. *rare*. LME–E16. ▸**d** Orig. a heron's position while watching for prey. Later, a group of herons. LME.
†**3 a** A privy, a lavatory. LME–M16. ▸**b** (An act of) defecation; faeces. LME–E18.
†**4** The anus; the rectum. M16–L17.
1a the Siege Perilous the vacant seat at King Arthur's Round Table, occupied with impunity only by the Knight destined to achieve the Grail.
▶**II 5** The action or an act of surrounding a town, building, etc., with a hostile (esp. military) force in order to cut off all outside communication and supplies and so facilitate capture. Also, the period during which this action lasts. ME. ▸**b** *transf.* A prolonged and determined attack; *US* a long period of illness or difficulty. E17.

📖 **5** J. A. MICHENER Capturing the well outside the wall and mounting siege until the internal cisterns were empty. N. MONSARRAT Bringing food and weapons to an island under siege. **b** DRYDEN Love stood the siege, and would not yield his breast. R. CHANDLER She is weakened by a long siege of bronchitis. *Reader's Digest* The three-pin, British electric plug is under siege from its two-pin cousin, the Europlug.

Phrases: ***lay siege to***: see LAY *verb*¹. **raise the siege of** abandon or cause the abandonment of an attempt to take (a place) by siege.
Comb.: **siege economy**: in which import controls are imposed and the export of capital is curtailed; **siege gun** *Hist.* a heavy gun used to lay siege to a town etc.; **siege mentality** a defensive or paranoid attitude based on an assumption of hostility in others; **siege-piece** *Hist.* An imperfectly made coin struck and issued during a siege; **siege-train** artillery and other equipment for a siege, together with troops and transport vehicles.
▶**B** *verb trans.* Besiege, lay siege to. ME.
■ **sieger** *noun* (now *rare* or *obsolete*) a person who takes part in a siege LME.

Siegfried Line /ˈsiːgfriːd lʌɪn/ *noun phr.* M20.
[translating German *Siegfriedlinie*, from *Siegfried* hero of the Middle High German epic poem the *Nibelungenlied* and Wagner's *Ring* cycle.]
Hist. The line of defence constructed along Germany's western frontier before the war of 1939–45. Also, the line

of fortifications occupied by the Germans in France during the war of 1914–18.

Sieg Heil /ziːk ˈhʌɪl/ *noun phr. & interjection.* **M20.**
[German, lit. 'Hail victory'.]
(An exclamation of) a victory salute used esp. at a political rally orig. during the Nazi regime in Germany.

Siemens /ˈsiːmənz, ˈziːməns/ *noun.* In sense 2b usu. **s-**. **M19.**
[The name of four German-born brothers, Ernst Werner (1816–92), Karl Wilhelm (or Charles William) (1823–83), Friedrich (1826–1904), and Karl (1829–1906) (von) *Siemens*.]
1 Used *attrib.* and in *possess.* to denote processes or devices discovered, invented, or developed by one or more of the Siemens brothers, esp. for the electrical and steel industries. **M19.**
2 †**a** A unit of electrical resistance, formerly used esp. in Germany, slightly smaller than the ohm. **M–L19.** ▸**b** (Usu. **s-**.) The SI unit of electrical conductance, equal to the mho. (Symbol S.) **M20.**
1 Siemens furnace an open-hearth furnace. **Siemens-Martin process** [P. B. E. *Martin* (1824–1915), French engineer] the process of melting pig iron and scrap steel together in a Siemens furnace, usu. in alkaline conditions. **Siemens process** a process similar to the Siemens-Martin process, but usu. carried out in acidic conditions. **Siemens producer** a form of gas producer developed by the Siemens brothers.

Siena *noun* see **SIENNA**.

Sienese /sɪəˈniːz, sʌɪə-/ *noun & adjective.* **M18.**
[formed as next + **-ESE**.]
▶ **A** *noun.* Pl. same.
1 A native or inhabitant of Siena in western Italy. **M18.**
2 (A painting by) an artist of the Italian school of painting developed at Siena during the 14th and 15th cents. **L19.**
▶ **B** *adjective.* Of or pertaining to Siena; *spec.* of or designating the Sienese school of painting. **E19.**

sienna /sɪˈɛnə/ *noun.* Also (in sense 2) **Siena**. **L18.**
[from *Siena*, a city and province in Tuscany, western Italy.]
1 A ferruginous earth used as a pigment in oil and watercolour painting; the colour of this pigment, a yellowish or (when roasted) rich reddish brown. Also more fully ***Terra Sienna***. **L18.**
2 ***Sienna marble***, a reddish mottled stone obtained from the area around Siena. **L18.**
1 *BURNT sienna. raw sienna*: see **RAW** *adjective.*

sierozem /ˈsɪərə(ʊ)zɛm/ *noun.* **M20.**
[Russian *serozëm*, from *seryĭ* grey + Slavonic base *zem-* (cf. Russian *zemlya*) earth, soil.]
SOIL SCIENCE. A soil, usu. calcareous and humus-poor, characterized by a brownish-grey surface horizon grading into harder, carbonate-rich lower layers, and developed typically under mixed shrub vegetation in arid climates.

Sierpinski /ʃɪəˈpɪnski/ *noun.* **M20.**
[Wacław *Sierpiński* (1882–1969), Polish mathematician.]
MATH. Used *attrib.* to designate certain complex curves constructed iteratively in the interior of a square or triangle.
Sierpinski gasket, **Sierpinski triangle** a fractal based on a triangle with four equal triangles inscribed in it, the central triangle being removed and each of the other three treated as the original was, and so on, creating an infinite regression in a finite space.

sierra /sɪˈɛrə, sɪˈɛːrə/ *noun.* Pl. **-s**, (in sense 3, also) same. **M16.**
[Spanish, from Latin *serra* saw. Cf. **SERRA** *noun*².]
1 A long mountain range rising in jagged peaks, esp. in Spain and Latin America. **M16.**
2 *ASTRONOMY.* = **CHROMOSPHERE**. Now *rare* or *obsolete.* **M19.**
3 = **CERO**. **L19.**
■ **sierran** *adjective* of or pertaining to a sierra or sierras **L19.**

Sierra Leone /sɪˌɛrə lɪˈəʊn/ *noun phr.* **M19.**
[A republic in W. Africa.]
Used *attrib.* to designate things found in or associated with Sierra Leone.
Sierra Leone peach: see **PEACH** *noun*¹ 2(a).
■ **Sierra Leonean** *noun & adjective* (**a**) *noun* a native or inhabitant of Sierra Leone; (**b**) *adjective* of or pertaining to Sierra Leone: **E20.** **Sierra Leonian** *noun & adjective* = **SIERRA LEONEAN** **L18.**

sies *interjection* var. of **SIS** *interjection.*

siesta /sɪˈɛstə/ *noun & verb.* **M17.**
[Spanish, from Latin *sexta* (*hora*) sixth hour of the day.]
▶ **A** *noun.* An afternoon rest or nap; *esp.* one taken during the hottest hours of the day in a hot country. **M17.**
📖 E. MANNIN The afternoon was too hot for anything but siesta. F. KING Mechanics were . . drifting back to . . work from their siestas.
▶ **B** *verb intrans.* Take a siesta. **M19.**

sieur /sjəː/ *noun*¹. *arch.* **L18.**
[French Cf. **MONSIEUR**.]
Used as a respectful title or form of address to a French or French-speaking man.

sieur /sjœːr/ *noun*². *S. Afr.* **E19.**
[S. African Dutch, from Dutch *sinjeur* (Afrikaans *seur*) lord, master, ult. rel. and assim. to prec.]
A polite or respectful form of address to a man.

sieva bean /ˈsiːvə biːn/ *noun phr.* **M19.**
[Prob. alt. of ***sewee bean*** s.v. **SEWEE** *adjective.*]
An American bean-plant, *Phaseolus lunatus*, allied to the Lima bean; the edible seed of this bean.

sieve /sɪv/ *noun & verb.*
[Old English *sife* = Middle Low German, Middle Dutch *seve* (Dutch *zeef*), Old High German *sib, sip* (German *Sieb*), from West Germanic.]
▶ **A** *noun.* **1** A utensil consisting of a meshed or perforated surface enclosed in a frame, used to separate the coarser from the finer particles of a loose material, to strain solids from a liquid, or to reduce a soft solid to a pulp or purée; *esp.* a kitchen utensil so used formed of a fine rounded metal or plastic mesh in a circular frame with a handle. **OE.** ▸**b** *fig.* A selective or purifying process or sytem. **E17.** ▸**c** *fig.* A person or thing unable to retain something; *esp.* a person who cannot keep a secret. **E17.**
2 (A vessel used as) a measure for grain, fruit, etc. **LME.**
3 *MATH.* **a** In full ***sieve of Eratosthenes*** [Greek writer of the 3rd cent. BC]. A method of finding the prime numbers in a (usu. consecutive) list of numbers by deleting in turn all the multiples of all possible prime factors. **E19.** ▸**b** A method of estimating or finding upper and lower limits for the number of primes, or of numbers not having factors within a stated set, that fall within a stated interval. **L19.**
📖 **1** B. FUSSELL Push pulp through a sieve and discard the seeds. **c** *New Age* People could . . stop living in sieves, fix up the buildings. R. LUDLUM Not much to . . lock up these days. The White House is a sieve. **head like a sieve** *colloq.* a memory that retains little.
Comb.: **sieve analysis**: of the sizes of particles in a powdered or granular material made by passing it through sieves of increasing fineness; **sieve cell** *BOTANY* a primitive type of sieve element, characteristic of gymnosperms and lower cryptogams, having uniformly narrow pores; **sieve element** *BOTANY* an elongated conducting cell in the phloem, in which the primary wall is perforated by pores; **sieve map** a map on which the distribution of a number of features is depicted by means of transparent overlays; **sieve plate** *BOTANY* an area of relatively large pores found in the end walls of sieve tube elements; **sieve tube** *BOTANY* a series of sieve tube elements placed end to end to form a continuous tube; ***sieve tube element*** a type of sieve element having a sieve plate, characteristic of angiosperms.
▶ **B** *verb.* **1** *verb trans.* Pass (as) through a sieve; sift, strain; *fig.* submit to a selective or screening process. **L15.** ▸**b** Foll. by *out*: remove or separate (as) by passing through a sieve. Chiefly as ***sieved ppl adjective.*** **M19.**
2 *verb intrans.* Pass material through a sieve; *fig.* submit material to a selective or screening process. Also, (of material) pass (as) through a sieve. Freq. foll. by *through.* **M19.**
📖 **1** C. CONRAN If there are any coarse fibres in the purée, sieve it. A. TYLER They sieved the news . . and passed it on. **b** W. SOYINKA He continued to stare . . , probing with a million antennae, sieving out distracting atmospherics. **2** H. MELVILLE That man should be a thing for immortal souls to sieve through!
■ **sieveful** *noun* as much or as many as a sieve can hold **ME.** **sievelike** *adjective* perforated like a sieve; *fig.* unable to retain information, heat, etc.: **L16.** **siever** *noun* (**a**) (now *rare* or *obsolete*) a sieve-maker; (**b**) a person who uses a sieve: **ME.**

Sievers' law /ˈsiːvəz lɔː, *foreign* ˈziːfərs/ *noun phr.* **M20.**
[Eduard *Sievers* (1850–1932), German philologist.]
PHILOLOGY. A rule stating that in Indo-European, (post-consonantal) unaccented *i* and *u* before a vowel were consonantal after a short syllable and vocalic after a long syllable. Also ***Sievers–Edgerton law.***

sievert /ˈsiːvət/ *noun.* **M20.**
[R. M. *Sievert*, 20th-cent. Swedish radiologist.]
An SI unit of dose equivalent of ionizing radiation, defined as that which delivers one joule of energy per kilogram of recipient mass, and equal to 100 rem. Formerly also, a unit of gamma-ray roughly equal to 8.4 roentgens. (Symbol Sv.)

sif *noun* var. of **SEIF**.

sifaka /sɪˈfakə/ *noun.* **M19.**
[Malagasy.]
Each of three arboreal lemurs of Madagascar, of the genus *Propithecus* (family Indriidae) having silky fur varying in colour from white to blackish brown, and a long tail.

siffle /ˈsɪf(ə)l/ *verb intrans. rare.* **LME.**
[Old French *sifler* (mod. *siffler*) from Latin *siflare* var. of *sibilare* **SIBILATE**.]
Whistle; hiss.

siffleur /siːˈfləː/ *noun.* Fem. (sense 2) **-ffleuse** /-ˈfləːz/. **E18.**
[French, from *siffler* (see prec.) + *-eur* **-OR**.]
1 Any of various animals that make a whistling noise; *esp.* the hoary marmot *Marmota caligata*, or the flesh of this used as food. *Canad.* **E18.**
2 A person who entertains professionally by whistling. **E19.**

Sifrei Torah *noun phr.* pl. of **SEFER TORAH**.

sift /sɪft/ *verb & noun.*
[Old English *siftan* = Middle Low German, Middle Dutch *siften, sichten* (Dutch *ziften*), from West Germanic base also of **SIEVE** *noun.*]
▶ **A** *verb.* **1** *verb trans.* Pass through a sieve, esp. in order to separate coarser from finer particles; strain, filter. **OE.**
2 *verb trans. fig.* Orig., subject (a person) to a test or trial. Later also, subject to close questioning. **ME.** ▸**b** Examine closely, scrutinize, esp. as part of a selection process; search through. Also foll. by *out.* **M16.**
3 *verb trans.* Separate or remove (as) by passing through a sieve; *fig.* identify or discover by close inquiry. Usu. foll. by *from, out.* **LME.**
4 *verb intrans.* Use a sieve; (chiefly *fig.*) make a close inquiry or examination; scrutinize evidence, material, etc., esp. as part of a selection process. (Foll. by *into, through.*) **M16.**
5 *verb intrans.* Pass or fall lightly (as) through a sieve. Usu. foll. by *down, on, through*, etc. **L16.**
6 *verb trans.* Let fall through a sieve; sprinkle or disperse lightly (as) from a sieve. Freq. foll. by *over.* **M17.**
📖 **1** D. M. THOMAS Crushers sifted the ashes for any gold that had escaped the prospectors. M. ATWOOD Mother makes the batter . . sifting the flour. **2** HOR. WALPOLE I sifted Dr Pringle . . but he would not give me a positive answer. **b** B. BETTELHEIM I have been sifting the ideas presented here. L. GRANT-ADAMSON Holly pocketed the letter . . and sifted the pile for others. **3** E. M. FORSTER I did try to sift the thing. Mr. Eager would never come to the point. E. WAUGH Time to sift out the genuine requests from the spurious. **4** J. HERBERT Sifting through with a finger he found . . 10p. *Harper's Magazine* We need reviewers to sift through the great volume of material. **5** E. BOWEN Soot, dislodged by the rain, sifted sharply on to the . . grate. **6** W. GOLDING The trees sifted chilly sunlight over their naked bodies.
▶ **B** *noun. rare.*
†**1** A sieve. **L15–M17.**
2 The action or an act of sifting; the fact of being sifted. **E19.**
3 Sifted material. **L19.**
■ **siftage** *noun* (*rare*) sifted material **L19.** **sifter** *noun* (**a**) a person who sifts; (**b**) a sieve, *esp.* a fine sieve for dusting flour, sugar, etc. on to a surface: **L16.** **sifting** *noun* (**a**) the action of the verb; (**b**) in *pl.*, material removed or separated by sieving: **LME.**

SIG *abbreviation.*
COMPUTING. Special interest group.

sig /sɪg/ *noun*¹. **LME.**
[Origin unkn. Cf. Middle Dutch *seike, seie*, Middle Low German *seyche*.]
1 Urine, esp. as used in fulling cloth. Long *dial.* **LME.**
2 A solution applied to leather before staining. Now *rare* or *obsolete.* **L19.**

sig /sɪg/ *noun*². **M19.**
[Abbreviation.]
PRINTING. = **SIGNATURE** *noun* 5a.

Sig. *abbreviation.*
Signor.

Sig. /sɪg/ *verb imper.* **L19.**
[Abbreviation of Latin *signa* (lit. 'label it') imper. sing., or *signetur* (lit. 'let it be labelled') 3rd person sing. pres. subjunct. pass., of *signare* **SIGN** *verb.*]
MEDICINE. As an instruction to a pharmacist on a prescription: mark (medication etc.) with the following directions for use.

Sigalert /ˈsɪgələːt/ *noun.* Chiefly *US.* **M20.**
[from Loyd Sigmon (b. 1909), US broadcaster + **ALERT** *noun.*]
1 (US proprietary name for) a system of broadcasting an audible emergency signal or bulletin (now esp. warning of traffic congestion), using special radio receivers kept on standby for this purpose. **M20.**
2 (Also **s-**.) A message broadcast on the radio giving warning of traffic congestion; a traffic jam. **L20.**

Sigatoka /sɪŋgəˈtəʊkə/ *noun.* Also **Sing-**. **E20.**
[A district in Fiji.]
In full ***Sigatoka disease***. A disease of banana plants caused by the fungus *Cercospora musae*, characterized by elongated spots on the leaves, which then rot completely.

sigh /sʌɪ/ *noun.* **LME.**
[from the verb.]
1 A long deep and audible exhalation expressive of sadness, weariness, longing, etc. **LME.**
2 *transf.* A sound resembling this; *esp.* one made by the wind. **E19.**
📖 **1** R. KIPLING The last sentence . . ended with a sigh as of faintness. G. GREENE With a sigh of relief, Myatt found himself alone.

sigh /sʌɪ/ *verb.* **ME.**
[Prob. back-form. from pa. t. of Middle English form of Old English *sīcan*, of unkn. origin. Cf. **SIKE** *verb*, **SITHE** *verb*¹.]
1 *verb intrans.* Emit a sigh. **ME.**

2 *verb intrans. transf.* Express sadness, weariness, longing, etc., (as) with a sigh. Foll. by *for, over*, etc. ME.
3 *verb trans.* Lament with sighing. *poet. rare.* L15.
4 *verb trans.* Utter or express with a sigh. Also foll. by *forth* (*arch.*), *out.* M16.
5 *verb trans.* **a** Spend or while away (time) by sighing. Usu. foll. by *away, out. poet. rare.* L16. ▸**b** Bring into a specified state or condition by sighing. E17.

📖 **1** W. CATHER He sighed when he saw . . he was . . next to her at the dinner table. H. BASCOM The coconut trees . . sigh in the wind. **2** F. MARRYAT He sighed for the time when the King's cause should be again triumphant. L. BLUE I have decided to stop sighing over British Rail and am going to enjoy it instead. **3** M. PRIOR Ages to come . . Shall . . sigh her Fate. **4** C. MACLEOD 'That's the way it's been all day long', Helen sighed. G. GREENE Sighing a shrill breath of exhaustion. **5a** MILTON Wearied I am with sighing out my days. **b** SIR W. SCOTT The gale had sigh'd itself to rest.

■ **sigher** *noun* E17. **sighful** *adjective* (*poet.*) sorrowful, sad E17. **sighfully** *adverb* E20. **sighing** *verbal noun* the action of the verb; an instance of this, a sigh: ME. **sighing** *ppl adjective* (*a*) accompanied by or expressed with a sigh; (*b*) that sighs: LME. **sighingly** *adverb* LME.

sight /sʌɪt/ *noun.*
[Old English *sihþ*, more usu. *ġesihþ* corresp. to Old Saxon *gisicht*, Middle Low German *sichte*, Middle Dutch *sicht* (Dutch *zicht*), Old High German, Middle High German (*ge*)*sicht* (German *Gesicht*) sight, vision, face, appearance, from West Germanic, ult. rel. to SEE *verb*.]
► **I 1** A thing seen, *esp.* one that is striking or remarkable; a spectacle. Formerly also (*spec.*), a vision, an apparition. OE. ▸**b** In *pl.* The noteworthy features of a particular town, area, etc. L16. ▸**c** A person or thing having a repulsive, ridiculous, or dishevelled appearance. *colloq.* M19.
†**2** Aspect, appearance. ME–L17.
3 A show, a display, (*of*); *transf.* a considerable number or amount (*of*). Now *colloq.* & *Scot.* LME. ▸**b** In adverbial phrs.: to a considerable degree or extent. *colloq.* M19.

📖 **1** F. SPALDING Palmers Green was still . . rural and a . . car a very rare sight. **b** *Holiday Which?* The best of the sights are at the other end of the island. **c** W. FAULKNER 'Ain't he a sight now,' Snopes cackled. T. MORRISON I'll try to get myself together. I know I look a sight. **3** S. COOLIDGE What a sight of washing those children made. **b** F. FORSYTH Shannon . . still in bed but feeling a sight better. J. ELLIOTT Wearing . . a sight too much make-up.

► **II 4** The faculty or power of seeing with the eyes; eyesight. ME. ▸**b** *fig.* Mental or spiritual vision *spec.* (***the sight***) second sight, clairvoyance (chiefly *Scot.*). ME.
5 The visual perception or apprehension of a person or thing; a view *of* something; a look, a glimpse. Formerly also (*fig.*), an insight *into* a matter. ME. ▸**b** POKER. A show of hands; *esp.* one called for by a player unable to equal another's bet. *US.* E19. ▸**c** An observation or measurement taken with an optical device. Cf. sense 10. M19. ▸**d** A sale of packets of uncut diamonds. M20.
6 The action of seeing or looking. Chiefly in ***by sight*** below. ME. ▸**b** (A) close examination or scrutiny; (a) supervision. Now *rare* exc. *Scot.* LME.
7 a The range or extent of a person's vision. Chiefly in ***in sight, out of one's sight.*** ME. ▸**b** Opinion, judgement; regard. Now chiefly in ***in one's sight.*** ME. ▸†**c** Foll. by *in*: knowledge, skill, insight. M16–E17.
8 A range of space within which a particular person or thing can be seen. Chiefly in ***out of sight (of), within sight (of).*** M16. ▸**b** A station on a river-bank for observing salmon. *Scot.* L18.

📖 **4** DAY LEWIS Aged voters who, . . through failing sight . . confused C.S. with C.D. Lewis on their voting papers. P. FITZGERALD He . . took off his spectacles, changing from a creature of sight to one of faith. **b** E. H. CLEMENTS The factor stared . . 'Why Kilmorrin, you have the sight!' **5** H. JAMES Waymarsh had not . . come down, and our friend . . went forth without a sight of him. J. HERRIOT I could see into the pen and the sight was rewarding. **7a** A. TYLER She was . . quick to . . order you out of her sight. *fig.*: *Banker* Punters preferred to go for capital gain . . out of sight of the tax authorities. **8** H. KISSINGER I . . chatted . . with Le Duc Tho within sight of photographers.

► **III 9** The pupil of the eye. Now *Scot.* & *dial.* LME. ▸†**b** A visor. E16–M17. ▸**c** In *pl.* Spectacles. Now *dial.* E17.
10 a A device on an optical (esp. surveying) instrument to guide the eye. M16. ▸**b** *sing.* & in *pl.* A (freq. telescopic) device on a gun etc. to aid precise aiming. L16. ▸**c** BILLIARDS. Any of the nails placed around the frame of the table as markers in some forms of the game. M19.

📖 **10b** *Guns Illustrated* The Target Model has . . adjustable sights.

Phrases: ***a damn sight***: see DAMN *adjective & adverb*. ***a sight fit for the gods, a sight for the gods***: see GOD *noun*. **at first sight** at the first view or impression of a person or thing (***love at first sight***: see LOVE *noun*). **at sight** as soon as a person or thing has been seen. **by sight** by visual recognition; ***know by sight***, recognize without having close acquaintance. **catch sight of** begin to see or be aware of. **in one's sights** visible through one's gun sights; *fig.* within one's expectations or ambitions. **in sight** visible; *fig.* near at hand, approaching. **line of sight** a straight line (sight-line) along which an observer has unobstructed vision, or (*transf.*) along which radio waves, etc. may be transmitted directly (freq. *attrib.*, with hyphens). ***long sight***: see LONG *adjective*[1]. **lose sight of** cease to see or be aware of; cease to know the whereabouts of. **lower one's sights** lessen one's ambitions. ***night sight***: see NIGHT *noun*. **on sight** = ***at sight*** above. OUT OF SIGHT. ***out of one's sight***: see sense 7a above. PISGAH ***sight***. **put out of sight** hide, ignore. **raise one's sights** increase one's expectations or ambitions. ***second sight***: see SECOND *adjective*. **set one's sights on** aim at, have as an ambition. ***short sight***: see SHORT *adjective*. **sight for sore eyes** a welcome person or thing, *esp.* a welcome visitor. **sight unseen** (of a purchase etc.) made without previous inspection. **take a sight at** *arch. slang* gesture with thumb to nose and little finger extended as a sign of derision. **take sights** *slang* (chiefly *Criminals'*) observe, watch closely. ***telescopic sight***: see TELESCOPIC 1. **upon sight** = ***at sight*** above. **within sight** = ***in sight*** above.

Comb.: **sight bar**: forming part of a gun-sight; **sight bill** *US* a bill of exchange payable on presentation; **sight-board** = ***sight-screen*** below; **sight cheque** *US* a cheque payable on presentation; **sight deposit** a bank deposit that can be withdrawn immediately without notice or penalty; **sight distance** an unobstructed view of the course of a road etc. from any point along it; **sight draft** *US* = ***sight cheque*** above; **sight feed** a supply line for lubricant or fuel incorporating a sight-glass; **sight gag** *colloq.* a visual joke; **sight-glass** a glass tube or window through which the level of liquid in a reservoir, supply line, etc. can be checked visually; **sight-holder** [proprietary name] a diamond merchant entitled to buy diamonds at a sight; **sight-hole** a hole to see through, esp. in a surveying or other optical instrument; **sighthound** any of the group of hounds originally bred to hunt independently from humans, e.g. greyhounds and whippets; **sight liability** an obligation to pay money on presentation of a cheque or bill of exchange; **sight-line** (*a*) a line representing the horizon in a perspective drawing; (*b*) a hypothetical line from a person's eye to an object seen; *esp.* one extending from the eye of a theatre spectator to the edge of the stage; **sight-player** a person able to play music at sight; **sight-read** *verb intrans. & trans.* read and perform (music) at sight; **sight-reader** a person able to sight-read; **sight record** ORNITHOLOGY: of the sighting as opp. to the capture of a bird; ***sight-screen***: see SCREEN *noun*[1] 3e; **sightsee** *verb intrans. & trans.* [back-form.] go sightseeing (in); **sightseeing** the action or occupation of seeing sights or places of interest in a particular area; **sightseer** a person who goes sightseeing; **sight-setter** a member of a gun-crew on a warship responsible for keeping the gun-sight at the correct elevation; **sight-sing** *verb intrans. & trans.* sing (music) at sight (chiefly as ***sight-singing*** *verbal noun*); **sightsman** (now *rare*) (*a*) a local guide; (*b*) = ***sight-reader*** above; **sight tube** a transparent tube for displaying the level of liquid in a tank or cistern.

■ **sighted** *adjective* (*a*) having sight, *esp.* of a specified kind (freq. as 2nd elem. of comb., as ***long-sighted, short-sighted***, etc.); (*b*) capable of seeing (as opp. to blind); (*c*) (of a gun etc.) provided with a sight or sights: M16. **sightful** *adjective* †(*a*) = SIGHTLY *adjective* 1a, 2; (*b*) (now *literary*) having sight, sighted: LME. **sightworthy** *adjective* worth seeing or visiting E17. **sighty** *adjective* (now *dial.*) †(*a*) = SIGHTLY *adjective* 1, 2; (*b*) perceptive, clever: LME.

sight /sʌɪt/ *verb.* M16.
[from the noun.]
1 a *verb trans.* View; examine, scrutinize. Chiefly *Scot.* M16. ▸**b** *verb trans. & intrans.* Take a detailed visual measurement (of), esp. with a sight; take aim (at) with a gun sight. M16.
2 *verb trans.* Catch sight of; come within sight of, esp. for the first time. Also, note the presence of, observe. E17.
3 *verb trans.* **a** Aim (a gun etc.) with sights. E20. ▸**b** Foll. by *in*: adjust the sights of (a gun etc.). *N. Amer.* M20.

📖 **1b** G. GREENE He . . reloaded with a sharp, feathered pellet, sighted quickly . . and fired. M. SCHAPIRO Linear perspective was . . a quality of the landscape . . he was sighting. T. MO He sights down the line of his extended pencil. **sighting shot** an experimental shot used as a guide for adjusting the sights of a gun etc.; *fig.* an initial proposal or enquiry. **2** V. WOOLF The Scilly Isles had been sighted by Timmy Durrant. W. MARCH At the party Christine sighted Reginald at once.

■ **sightable** *adjective* (*rare*) able to be sighted (earlier in UNSIGHTABLE) L19. **sighter** *noun* †(*a*) *Scot.* an inspector; (*b*) = ***sighting shot*** s.v. SIGHT *verb*: E18. **sighting** *noun* †(*a*) *rare* a method of cheating at dice; (*b*) the action of the verb; an instance of this: M18.

sightless /ˈsʌɪtlɪs/ *adjective.* ME.
[from SIGHT *noun* + -LESS.]
1 Blind; *transf.* unseeing, unobservant. ME.
2 Invisible, unseen; out of sight. *literary.* L16.
†**3** Unsightly. *poet.* L16–M17.

📖 **1** LYTTON His sightless and gore-dropping sockets. A. MILLER His eyes are sightless, inward-looking. **2** SIR W. SCOTT Their tears . . as they fall, sink sightless. TENNYSON Drown'd in yonder . . blue, the lark becomes a sightless song. **3** SHAKES. *John* Full of unpleasing blots, and sightless stains.

■ **sightlessly** *adverb* M19. **sightlessness** *noun* M19.

sightly /ˈsʌɪtli/ *adjective & adverb.* LME.
[from SIGHT *noun* + -LY[1], -LY[2].]
► **A** *adjective.* **1** †**a** Visible; conspicuous. LME–L16. ▸**b** Of a place: open to view; commanding a wide prospect. *US.* LME.
2 Pleasing to look at; handsome, beautiful. LME.
► **B** *adverb.* †**1** Visibly. *rare.* Only in LME.
2 Handsomely, finely. Long *rare.* L16.
■ **sightliness** *noun* M16.

sigil /ˈsɪdʒɪl/ *noun.* LME.
[formed as SIGILLUM.]
1 Orig., a sign, a mark. Later *spec.*, a seal, a signet. *arch.* LME.
2 An occult symbol. M17.

📖 **2** *Prediction* Each talisman consists of eight sigils . . set around . . an eight-pointed star.

■ **sigillary** *adjective* of or pertaining to a sigil or sigils M17.

sigilla *noun* pl. of SIGILLUM.

sigillaria /sɪdʒɪˈlɛːrɪə/ *noun.* M19.
[mod. Latin, formed as SIGILLUM + *-aria* -ARY[1].]
PALAEONTOLOGY. A large treelike fossil lycopod, marked with rows of scars resembling the impressions of a seal, found esp. in Carboniferous coal deposits. Now chiefly as mod. Latin genus name.
■ **sigillarian** *adjective & noun* (pertaining to or designating) a fossil lycopod of the genus *Sigillaria* or a related genus L19.

sigillata /sɪdʒɪˈleɪtə, sɪgɪˈlɑːtə/ *noun.* E20.
[Latin = sealed: see TERRA SIGILLATA.]
ARCHAEOLOGY. = TERRA SIGILLATA 3.

sigillate /ˈsɪdʒɪlət/ *adjective.* L15.
[Late Latin *sigillatus*, formed as next: see -ATE[2].]
Orig., impressed with a seal. Later *spec.*, (of pottery) decorated with impressed marks.

sigillate /ˈsɪdʒɪleɪt/ *verb trans.* Now *rare.* LME.
[Late Latin *sigillat-* pa. ppl stem of *sigillare* in medieval Latin senses, from SIGILLUM: see -ATE[3].]
Seal (up); impress with a seal or stamp.
■ **sigilˈlation** *noun* (*a*) the action or an act of sealing something; the fact of being sealed; (*b*) the impression of a seal; LME.

sigillography /sɪdʒɪˈlɒgrəfi/ *noun.* L19.
[from SIGILL(UM + -O- + -GRAPHY.]
The branch of knowledge that deals with historical seals.
■ **sigillographer** *noun* L19.

sigillum /sɪˈdʒɪləm/ *noun.* Pl. ***-lla*** /-lə/. M17.
[Late Latin = sign, trace, impress, (in medieval Latin) seal (classical Latin *sigilla* pl. little images, seal), dim. of Latin *signum* SIGN *noun*.]
†**1** In *pl.* Small human images. *rare.* Only in M17.
2 ROMAN CATHOLIC CHURCH. The seal of confession. E20.
3 A sign, a symbol; an abbreviation. M20.

SIGINT /ˈsɪgɪnt/ *noun.* Also **Sigint.** M20.
[Abbreviation.]
= ***signals intelligence*** s.v. SIGNAL *noun*.

sigla *noun* pl. of SIGLUM.

siglos /ˈsɪglɒs/ *noun.* Pl. ***-li*** /-li/, ***-loi*** /-lɔɪ/. E20.
[Greek.]
Hist. A silver coin of ancient Persia.

siglum /sɪgləm/ *noun.* Pl. **-la** /-lə/. E18.
[Late Latin *sigla* pl., perh. for *singula* neut. pl. of *singulus* SINGLE *adjective*.]
A letter (esp. an initial) or other symbol used as an abbreviation for a word, proper name, etc., in a printed text; BIBLIOGRAPHY such a letter or symbol used to designate a particular version of a literary text.

sigma /ˈsɪgmə/ *noun.* LME.
[Latin from Greek.]
1 The eighteenth letter (Σ, σ, or, when final, ς), of the Greek alphabet represented in English by *S, s*, its uncial form having the shape of English *C*. LME.
2 PHYSICS & CHEMISTRY. **a** Used *attrib.* to designate an electron, orbital, molecular state, etc., possessing zero angular momentum about an internuclear axis; ***sigma-bond, σ-bond***, a bond formed by a σ-orbital. Freq. written σ with ref. to one electron or orbital, Σ with ref. to a molecule as a whole. E20. ▸**b** PARTICLE PHYSICS. Used (usu. *attrib.*), to denote each of a triplet of hyperons (and their antiparticles) having an average mass of about 1190 MeV (2340 times that of the electron), a spin of ½, zero hypercharge, and unit isospin, which on decaying usu. produce a nucleon and a pion (if charged) or a lambda particle and a photon (if neutral). Freq. written Σ. M20.
3 BIOCHEMISTRY. In full ***sigma factor***. A component of RNA polymerase which determines where transcription begins. L20.
4 STATISTICS. A (unit of) standard deviation. L20.
■ **sigmate** *adjective* having the form of a sigma or *s* L19. **sigmate** *verb trans.* add a sigma or *s* to (a word, stem, etc.) M19. **sigmatic** /-ˈmatɪk/ *adjective* (of a word etc.) characterized by the addition of sigma or *s* to the stem L19. **sigmatism** *noun* (*a*) (an instance of) the marked use or repetition of *s*; (*b*) defective articulation of sibilants: L19. **sigmatropic** /-ˈtrəʊpɪk, -ˈtrɒpɪk/ *adjective* (CHEMISTRY) involving the movement of a sigma-bond to a new pair of atoms within a molecule M20.

sigmoid /ˈsɪgmɔɪd/ *adjective & noun.* L17.
[Greek *sigmoeidēs*, formed as prec. + -OID.]
► **A** *adjective.* **1** Chiefly ANATOMY. Having the shape of the uncial sigma C; crescent-shaped, semicircular. L17.
2 Having a double curve like the letter S; MATH. designating or described by a curve or graph having a steep central portion which flattens out at top and bottom. L18.

1 *sigmoid cavity*, *sigmoid notch*, *sigmoid valve*, etc. **2 sigmoid colon**, **sigmoid flexure** ANATOMY the terminal portion of the descending colon, leading to the rectum.

▶ **B** *noun*. **1** ANATOMY. The sigmoid colon. L19.

2 A sigmoid curve. L19.

■ **sigmoiˈdectomy** *noun* (an instance of) surgical removal of the sigmoid flexure E20. **sigmoiˈdicity** *noun* the extent to which a curve is sigmoid (S-shaped) M20.

sigmoidal /sɪɡˈmɔɪd(ə)l/ *adjective*. M17.
[formed as prec. + -AL[1].]
= SIGMOID *adjective*.

sigmoidally /sɪɡˈmɔɪd(ə)li/ *adverb*. M19.
[from SIGMOID, SIGMOIDAL: see -ALLY.]
In a sigmoid(al) manner; so as to describe a sigmoid curve.

sigmoidoscope /sɪɡˈmɔɪdəskəʊp/ *noun*. E20.
[from SIGMOID *noun* + -O- + -SCOPE.]
MEDICINE. A tubular (now usu. fibre-optic) instrument for examining the colon and rectum through the anus.

■ **sigmoidoˈscopic** *adjective* performed or ascertained by means of a sigmoidoscope E20. **sigmoidoˈscopically** *adverb* as regards (the results of) sigmoidoscopy M20. **sigmoiˈdoscopy** *noun* examination by means of a sigmoidoscope E20.

sign /sʌɪn/ *noun*. ME.
[Old & mod. French *signe* from Latin *signum* mark, token.]

▶ **I 1** A gesture, esp. with the hand or head, used to convey information, give an order or request, etc.; *spec.* any of the gestures comprising a system of sign language. Also, an agreed gesture used as a password. ME. ▸**b** A signal. E17. ▸**c** Sign language; *spec.* (**S-**) = ***American Sign Language*** s.v. AMERICAN *adjective*. L20.

2 *gen.* A mark, symbol, or device used to represent something or distinguish the object on which it is put. ME. ▸†**b** A mark of attestation or ownership written or stamped on a document etc. LME–E17. ▸**c** A conventional symbol used in music, algebra, etc., in place of a word or words. M16. ▸**d** MATH. That aspect of a quantity which consists in being either positive or negative. E19. ▸**e** Chiefly LINGUISTICS. A basic element of communication, either linguistic (a written or spoken word) or non-linguistic (an image, article of clothing, etc.), consisting of two indivisible elements the relation between which is arbitrary (*signifiant* and *signifié*), and which derives its meaning only from its relationship to other signs within the same sign-system. Cf. SIGNIFIANT, SIGNIFIÉ. M20.

3 An identifying banner or standard (long *obsolete* exc. *poet.*). Formerly also, a badge, an insignia. LME.

4 A board or other device outside a shop, hotel, etc., to distinguish its name or identify its function; *gen.* any publicly displayed board or advice giving information or directions. LME.

†**5** An image; an effigy. LME–L16.

> **1** J. GARDNER He didn't answer, made . . a confused sign with his head. **b** SHAKES. *Jul. Caes.* Mark Antony, shall we give sign of battle? **2** I. FLEMING There was a sign tattooed in red on the skin. **c** *Personal Software* When entering the program replace . . '£' signs with '≠' signs. **4** SIR W. SCOTT An appointment to meet . . at the sign of the Griffin. T. MCGUANE Then the intersection of A1A and the sign to Key West. E. JONG As soon as the seat-belt sign goes off . . I glance around nervously. ***signpost*** etc.

▶ **II 6** An indication or suggestion *of* a present state, fact, quality, etc.; evidence; a trace, a vestige, (freq. with neg.). Freq. foll. by *of*, *that*. ME. ▸**b** The trail or trace of a wild animal. *US*. L17. ▸**c** MEDICINE. An objective indication of disease, as opp. to a subjective one (cf. SYMPTOM 1). Freq. with prefixed name of a person who associated an indication with a particular disease, as ***Hoffman's sign***, etc. M19.

7 a An indication or suggestion of a future state or occurrence; an omen, a portent. ME. ▸**b** A miracle as evidence of supernatural power or authority. ME.

8 Each of the twelve equal parts into which the zodiac is divided; = ***sign of the*** ZODIAC. ME. ▸†**b** A constellation. *rare*. LME–E17.

> **6** B. WEBB The P. M. has shown signs, throughout the contest, of neurosis. *New York Review of Books* Signs that the British . . have become more reconciled to . . the European Community. J. JOHNSTON There was no sign of life at the hut. **7a** A. UTTLEY Tom . . scanned the sky and read the weather signs. M. TIPPETT It is a hopeful sign. **b** A. MASON God gave many signs . . by healing, and the casting-out of demons. **8** W. TREVOR Born beneath Gemini, the sign of passion.

Phrases: ***high sign***: see HIGH *adjective*, *adverb*, & *noun*. **in sign of**, **in sign that** as a token or indication of or that. **make no sign** seem unconscious; not protest. ***minus sign***: see MINUS *noun* 1. **outward visible sign** THEOLOGY the sacrament as the outward symbol of inner grace etc. ***plus sign***: see PLUS *noun* 1. ***sign of the cross***: see CROSS *noun* 4. **sign of the times** an indication or typical example of current trends. ***sign of the*** ZODIAC.

Comb.: **sign bit** COMPUTING a sign digit located in a sequence of binary digits; **signboard** (*a*) a board displaying the sign of a shop, inn, or other business; (*b*) (chiefly *US*) a board on a guide-post displaying a sign to direct travellers etc; **sign digit** COMPUTING a digit, located in a sequence of digits, whose value depends on the algebraic sign of the number represented; **sign language** a system of communication by visual gesture, used esp. by the deaf; **sign-painter** a person employed to paint signs for shops etc.; **sign stimulus** BIOLOGY the component or characteristic of an external stimulus which is effective in initiating a particular innate behavioural response in an animal perceiving it, regardless of the presence or absence of the remainder of the stimulus; **sign-vehicle** SOCIOLOGY an object, letter, etc., that acts as a sign or symbol; **sign-writer** = ***sign-painter*** above.

■ **signage** *noun* (*N. Amer.*) signs collectively, *esp.* commercial or public display signs L20. **signed** *adjective*[1] (MATH.) having a (plus or minus) sign; esp. in ***signed number***, a positive or negative integer: L19. **signless** *adjective* (*a*) without a sign, having no sign; (*b*) making no sign; (*c*) MATH. of a quantity: having no sign of direction; having no distinction of positive or negative; L17.

sign /sʌɪn/ *verb*. ME.
[Old & mod. French *signer* from Latin *signare*, from *signum* SIGN *noun*.]

▶ **I 1** *verb trans.* CHRISTIAN CHURCH. Consecrate or protect with or *with* the sign of the cross; *refl.* cross oneself. ME. ▸**b** Make the sign of (the cross). *literary*. E19.

2 *verb trans.* Mark with a sign; place a distinguishing mark or symbol on; BIBLIOGRAPHY (in *pass.*) have as a signature or signatures. ME.

3 *verb trans.* Add one's signature or (formerly) seal to (a document etc.) as authorization or affirmation; confirm the authenticity of (a work of art) by adding one's signature. Also, engage (a person) for employment with a contract. ME. ▸**b** *verb trans.* Write or inscribe (one's name) as a signature; use a specified form of signature on (a document etc.); *refl.* designate oneself by a specified signature. E19.

4 *verb intrans.* Add one's signature to a document etc. as authorization or affirmation (also foll. by *to*); authorize or acknowledge receipt of something by this action (foll. by *for*). Also, be engaged by agreeing a written contract *with*. E17.

> **1** J. AGEE He signed himself carefully with the Cross. **2** R. B. MCKERROW A page referred to as 3K2 would . . be actually signed KKK2. **3** M. AYRTON Each etching was . . numbered and signed in pencil. *Isis* Signing the Pistols was another watershed for Branson. A. TYLER Her lawyer sent him . . papers to sign. **b** A. RANSOME Roger . . signed his name in the place the porter showed him. J. T. STORY It was signed: 'Yours sincerely—Charmian Moss.' J. BARNES 'Your faithful rat' she signs herself. **4** R. ANGELL He signed with the Rangers for a hundred-thousand-dollar bonus.

▶ **II 5** *verb trans.* & (*rare*) *intrans.* Give an indication or sign (of). Formerly also, bode. Now *rare*. ME.

6 a *verb intrans.* Make a sign or signs with the hand etc.; gesture; *spec.* express oneself in sign language. E18. ▸**b** *verb trans.* Convey or communicate by a sign or signs; *spec.* express in a sign language. Freq. foll. by *that*, *to do*. E18.

> **5** SHAKES. *Ant. & Cl.* Music i' th' air . . It signs well, does it not? **6a** *Scientific American* His hearing cousin learned to sign with her deaf father. T. C. BOYLE The TV roared . . and Konrad stood . . signing at the screen. **b** I. COMPTON-BURNETT Nance stopped . . but Alison signed to her to continue. *Oxford Times* The . . Deaf Association Choir . . 'signed' the hymns.

With adverbs in specialized senses: **sign away** convey (one's right, property, etc.) by signing a deed etc. **sign in** (*a*) record one's arrival at a hotel, club, etc., by signing a register; (*b*) authorize the admittance or record the entrance of (a person or thing) into a building by signing a register etc. **sign off** (*a*) end work, a letter, broadcast, etc., esp. by writing or announcing one's name; (*b*) end a period of employment, contract, etc.; (*c*) end the employment or contract of (a person); (*d*) stop registering to receive unemployment benefit; (*e*) withdraw one's attention, fall silent; (*f*) BRIDGE indicate by a conventional bid that one is ending the bidding. **sign off on** *US colloq.* assent or give one's approval to (something). **sign on** (*a*) begin work, a broadcast, etc., esp. by writing or announcing one's name; (*b*) register to obtain unemployment benefit; (*c*) = ***sign up*** (b) below. **sign out** (*a*) record one's departure from a hotel, club, etc., by signing a register; (*b*) authorize the release or record the departure of (a person or thing) from a building by signing a register, etc. **sign over** = ***sign away*** above. **sign up** (*a*) enrol or enlist (*for*); (*b*) sign or have sign a contract for employment.

Comb.: **sign-in** (*a*) the action of signing in, esp. at a hotel or club; (*b*) a register used for this; **sign-off** the action of signing off; *esp.* the (announcement of) the end of a broadcast transmission; **sign-on** the action of signing on; *esp.* the start of a broadcast transmission; **sign-out** (*a*) the action of signing out; (*b*) the signature of a person who has signed out; **sign-up** (*a*) the action of signing up or the state of having signed up; (*b*) a person who has signed up for employment etc.

■ **signable** *adjective* E19. **signed** *adjective*[2] (*a*) having a signature or signatures; (*b*) MUSIC (*rare*) placed or given as a signature: M17. **sigˈnee** *noun* a person who has signed a contract, register, etc. M20. **signer** *noun* (*a*) a signatory; (*b*) (usu. **S-**) *spec.* (*US*) any of the signatories to the Declaration of Independence; (*c*) a person who communicates by sign language: E17.

signa *noun* pl. of SIGNUM.

†**signacle** *noun*. LME.
[Old French *si(g)nacle* from late Latin *signaculum* dim. of *signum* SIGN *noun*.]
1 An identifying mark, a symbol. LME–M17.
2 A gesture. LME–L15.
3 A small amount, a trace. *Scot.* M–L18.

signal /ˈsɪɡn(ə)l/ *noun*. LME.
[Old & mod. French, alt. of earlier *seignal* from Proto-Romance, medieval Latin *signale* use as noun of late Latin *signalis*, from Latin *signum* SIGN *noun*: see -AL[1].]

†**1** A distinguishing mark; a badge, a symbol. LME–E17.

2 A sign or indication of a fact or quality, a future occurrence, etc. Also foll. by *of*, *that*. LME.

3 A sound or gesture intended as a sign to convey warning, direction, or information; BRIDGE a play or bid intended to convey information about a defender's hand to his or her partner. Also foll. by *that*, *to do*. L16. ▸**b** A visible or audible device used to make such a sign; *spec.* (*a*) a traffic light; (*b*) a light or semaphore on a railway controlling the movement of trains. L17. ▸**c** A modulation of an electric current, electromagnetic wave, etc., by means of which information is conveyed from one place to another; the current or wave itself, esp. regarded as conveying information by its presence about its source. Also = ***signal strength*** below. M19.

4 A usu. prearranged sign, freq. given at a distance, acting as the prompt for a particular action, esp. a military manoeuvre; *fig.* an immediate occasion or cause of movement, action, etc. Also foll. by *for*, *that*, *to do*. L16.

> **2** E. CALDWELL Her sobs . . became more subdued . . a signal to Dan that she would soon relent. *Times* Sterling M3 . . had given misleading signals. **3** R. L. STEVENSON If any one of you . . make a signal of any description, that man's dead. K. A. PORTER The tolling of the midnight bell is a signal. **b** G. GREENE Ida . . broke her way across the Strand; she couldn't . . wait for the signals. *Independent* A driver stopped his train to report a faulty signal. **4** G. K. CHESTERTON Await Captain Bruce's signal to advance. A. J. TOYNBEE The kindling of a light . . gave the signal for . . bombardment.

Phrases: **signal of distress** an appeal for help, esp. from a ship by firing guns. ***yeoman of signals***: see YEOMAN 2.

Comb.: **signal-book**: containing a list of agreed naval and military signals; **signal-box** a building beside a railway track from which signals are controlled; **signal-caller** AMER. FOOTBALL a player who signals the next move or formation to other team members; **signal generator** ELECTRONICS an instrument that can generate modulated or unmodulated electrical waveforms of known amplitude and frequency, used in adjusting and testing electronic apparatus; **signal intelligence** = ***signals intelligence*** below; **signalman** (*a*) a person employed to make or transmit signals, esp. in the army or navy; (*b*) an employee attending to the signals on a railway line; **signal-noise ratio** = ***signal-to-noise ratio*** below; **signal plate** TELEVISION in some types of camera tube, a plate electrode whose capacitance relative to the adjacent photoelectric surface is used to provide the picture signal; **signal red** bright red, vermilion; **signals intelligence**: derived from the monitoring, interception, and interpretation of radio signals etc.; **signal strength** the amplitude or power of a signal, esp. of a broadcast signal as it reaches a given location or is received by a given aerial; **signal-to-noise ratio** the ratio of the strength of a signal carrying information to that of unwanted interference (in ELECTRICITY freq. expressed in decibels); **signal-tower** *US* = ***signal-box*** above.

signal /ˈsɪɡn(ə)l/ *adjective*. E17.
[French *signalé*, †*segnalé* from Italian *segnalato* pa. pple of *segnalare* make illustrious, from *segnale* SIGNAL *noun*.]
1 Constituting or serving as a sign; formerly *esp.* distinctive, characteristic. Now *rare*. E17.
2 Striking, remarkable; notable, noteworthy. E17.

> **2** JOHN FOSTER Signal villains of every class. K. TYNAN To have done this at all would be a signal achievement.

■ **signally** *adverb* M17.

signal /ˈsɪɡn(ə)l/ *verb*. Infl. **-ll-**, ***-l-**. E19.
[from the noun.]

1 *verb trans.* Give a signal or signals to; summon or direct by signal. Freq. foll. by *that*, *to do*. E19.

2 *verb trans.* **a** Be a sign or signal of; indicate (a fact, quality, future occurrence, etc.) clearly. M19. ▸**b** Communicate or make known by a signal or signals. L19.

3 *verb intrans.* Give a signal or signals; communicate by signal. Also foll. by *for*, *to*, etc. M19.

4 *verb trans.* Operate the signals on (a railway); provide (a railway) with signals. L19.

> **1** P. G. WODEHOUSE Seeing him enter the room . . she signalled him to approach. B. MALAMUD Threw open the door and signalled the escort captain. **2a** P. BARKER The sound of men's boots signalled the first shift. B. MOORE She came . . bowing in a manner that signalled she knew who he was. **b** G. SWIFT Impossible to tell . . from their movement what emotion was being signalled. R. RENDELL The kind of driver to signal his intention to turn a hundred yards before the turning. **3** P. MORTIMER With his free hand, Conway signalled to her. A. TYLER Ira signaled and made a U-turn. V. GLENDINNING 'I intend to marry you', said Harry, signalling for the bill.

■ **signaller** *noun* (*a*) a person who signals, *esp.* a signalman; (*b*) a device used for signalling: M19.

signalisation *noun* var. of SIGNALIZATION.

signalise *verb* var. of SIGNALIZE.

signality /sɪɡˈnalɪti/ *noun*. Now *rare*. M17.
[from SIGNAL *noun* or *adjective* + -ITY.]
†**1** Signification; significance. M–L17.
2 Notability, distinction. M17.

signalization /sɪɡn(ə)lʌɪˈzeɪʃ(ə)n/ *noun. rare.* Also **-isation**. E20.
[from SIGNAL *noun* + -IZATION.]
PSYCHOLOGY. The process whereby a signal comes to elicit the same response as the original stimulus, according to the behaviouristic model of conditioned reflexes.

signalize /ˈsɪɡn(ə)lʌɪz/ *verb.* Also **-ise**. E17.
[from SIGNAL *adjective* + -IZE.]
1 *verb trans.* Make remarkable or noteworthy; distinguish. E17. ▸**b** Make known or display in a striking manner. E18.
2 *verb trans.* Be a feature of; characterize. L17.
3 *verb trans.* Point out, draw attention to. E18.
4 *verb trans. & intrans.* Give a signal or signals (to); communicate (with) by means of a signal or signals. E19.
5 *verb trans.* = SIGNAL *verb* 2a, b. L19.
6 *verb trans.* Provide with traffic signals. *US & Austral.* M20.

🕮 **1** H. S. SALT A . . little flower, with not much except its rarity to signalize it. **2** C. PEBODY Cheers . . signalised the success of the Minister's speech. **3** W. S. CHURCHILL This expression *rex Anglorum* is . . signalised by historians as a milestone in our history. **5** W. DEEPING Putting-up of the shutters had signalized a voluntary bankruptcy. F. TOMLIN A letter . . signalized . . arrangements for the next meeting.

signans /ˈsɪɡnanz/ *noun.* M20.
[Latin, pres. pple of *signare* SIGN *verb*.]
LINGUISTICS. = SIGNIFIANT. Opp. SIGNATUM.

signa panthea *noun phr.* pl. of SIGNUM PANTHEUM.

signary /ˈsɪɡnəri/ *noun. rare.* E20.
[from Latin *signum* sign + -ARY[1], after *syllabary*.]
An arrangement of signs; the syllabic or alphabetic symbols of a particular language.

signatary /ˈsɪɡnət(ə)ri/ *noun.* Now *rare.* M19.
[French *signataire*.]
= SIGNATORY *noun*.

signate /ˈsɪɡnət/ *adjective.* M17.
[Latin *signatus*, pa. pple of *signare* SIGN *verb*.]
Marked or distinguished in some way.

signation /sɪɡˈneɪʃ(ə)n/ *noun.* Now *rare.* E17.
[Late Latin *signatio(n-)* signing (of the cross), from Latin *signare* SIGN *verb*: see -ATION.]
The action of making the sign of the cross or marking something with a seal.

signator /sɪɡˈneɪtə/ *noun. rare.* M17.
[Latin *signator*, from *signare* SIGN *verb*.]
= SIGNATORY *noun*.

signatory /ˈsɪɡnət(ə)ri/ *adjective & noun.* M17.
[Latin *signatorius*, formed as prec.: see -ORY[2].]
▶ **A** *adjective.* †**1** Esp. of a ring: used in sealing documents. Only in M17.
2 Of a person or State: having signed a particular document, esp. a treaty. L19.
▶ **B** *noun.* A person who or State which has signed a particular document, esp. a treaty etc. M19.

🕮 H. MACMILLAN Considerable support among the six countries, signatories to the Treaty of Rome. R. BERTHOUD He was the sole signatory of a long . . letter to the *Yorkshire Post*.

signatum /sɪɡˈnɑːtəm/ *noun.* M20.
[Latin, neut. sing. pa. pple of *signare* SIGN *verb*.]
LINGUISTICS. = SIGNIFIÉ. Opp. SIGNANS.

signature /ˈsɪɡnətʃə/ *noun & verb.* M16.
[medieval Latin *signatura* sign manual (in late Latin a marking on sheep), from Latin *signare* SIGN *verb*.]
▶ **A** *noun.* **1** *SCOTS LAW.* A document prepared by a writer to the signet, outlining and specifying the provenance of a royal grant, charter, etc. *obsolete* exc. *Hist.* M16.
2 A person's name, initials, or distinctive mark, used in signing a letter, document, etc. L16. ▸**b** The action of (authenticating a document by) signing one's name, initials, or distinctive mark. E17.
3 A distinguishing mark; *spec.* (now *Hist.*) the form, colouring, markings, etc., of a plant or animal, regarded as resembling or symbolizing the organ or disease for which it is effective. E17. ▸**b** A stamp, an impression. M17. ▸**c** Any typical physical or behavioural characteristic, pattern, or response, by which an object, substance, etc. may be identified. Also, a distinctive identifying feature incorporated into the work of an artist, designer, musician, etc. M20. ▸**d** In full ***signature tune***. A particular tune associated with and used esp. to introduce a particular performer or programme on television or radio. M20.
4 An image; a figure; an imitative mark. Now *rare* or *obsolete.* M17.
5 *PRINTING.* **a** A letter, figure, or combination of letters or figures, placed at the foot of one or more pages of each sheet of a book to show their order for binding. Abbreviation ***sig.*** M17. ▸**b** A folded sheet, as distinguished by such a letter, figure, etc. E18.
6 *MUSIC.* A sign or set of signs at the beginning of a piece or passage of music, indicating its key or time. See ***key signature*** s.v. KEY *noun*[1] & *adjective*, ***time signature*** s.v. TIME *noun.* E19.
7 Directions for the use of a medication etc. given to a patient as part of a prescription. Chiefly *US.* M19.

🕮 **2** G. GISSING At the end of her letters came a signature . . 'Miriam Baske'. **b** *Independent* Once that treaty, due for signature . . was in place. **3c** P. BROOK The signature of the Brecht theatre, the white half-curtain. *Nature* Geochemical signatures indicate that heterotrophic bacteria were present in Proterozoic communities. *Aircraft Illustrated* Reduction of an aircraft's radar signature is now a paramount feature of military aircraft.

▶ **B** *verb trans.* †**1** Indicate symbolically; mark out, designate. M17–M18.
2 Put a signature on; *esp.* sign (a document), authenticate or confirm by one's signature. L19.

🕮 **2** *India Today* Accords did get signatured.

■ **signatureless** *adjective* M19. **signaturist** *noun* (*rare*, now *Hist.*) a person who subscribes to the theory of signatures in plants etc. M17.

signet /ˈsɪɡnɪt/ *noun & verb.* LME.
[Old & mod. French, dim. of *signe*, or medieval Latin *signetum*, dim. of *signum* seal: see SIGN *noun*, -ET[1].]
▶ **A** *noun.* **1** A small seal, usu. set in a finger-ring, used with or instead of a signature to authenticate a (formal or official) document etc. LME. ▸**b** *spec.* The small royal seal used orig. by English and Scottish sovereigns for private and some official purposes, and later in Scotland as the seal of the Court of Session. Now *Hist.* LME.
2 The stamp or impression of a seal, esp. a signet. LME. ▸**b** *fig.* An identifying or authenticating mark, sign, stamp, etc. M17.
†**3** A signal. Cf. SENNET *noun*[1]. *rare.* L16–L17.
1b ***Writer to the Signet***: see WRITER.
▶ **B** *verb trans. Scot.* Stamp with a signet. L15.

signet-ring /ˈsɪɡnɪtrɪŋ/ *noun.* L17.
[from SIGNET *noun* + RING *noun*[1].]
1 A finger-ring containing a signet. L17.
2 *MEDICINE.* A cell or parasitic protozoan resembling a signet-ring. Usu. *attrib.* E20.

signifer /ˈsɪɡnɪfə/ *noun.* Now *rare.* LME.
[Latin, from *signum* SIGN *noun*: see -FER.]
†**1** The zodiac. LME–E17.
2 A standard-bearer, a leader. LME.

signifiant /siɲifjɑ̃/ *noun.* Pl. pronounced same. M20.
[French, pres. pple of *signifier* signify.]
Chiefly *LINGUISTICS.* A physical medium (as a sound, symbol, image, etc.) expressing meaning, as distinct from the meaning expressed; the element of a sign perceived by the senses. Cf. SIGN *noun* 2e, SIGNIFIER 2. Opp. SIGNIFIÉ.

signific /sɪɡˈnɪfɪk/ *noun.* E20.
[from SIGNIFIC(ANT.)]
LINGUISTICS. = RADICAL *noun* 1b.

significacio /sɪɡˌnɪfɪˈkɑːsɪəʊ/ *noun.* Also **-tio** /-tɪəʊ/. Pl. **-ones** /-əʊniːz/. M20.
[medieval Latin from Latin *significatio(n-)*: see SIGNIFICATION.]
A parallel or second meaning not directly stated in a text; the deeper or implied meaning of an allegory, emblem, symbol, etc.

significance /sɪɡˈnɪfɪk(ə)ns/ *noun.* LME.
[Old French, or Latin *significantia*, from *significant-* SIGNIFICANT: see -ANCE.]
1 (Implied or unstated) meaning. Usu. foll. by *of.* LME.
2 Importance; consequence. E18.
3 *STATISTICS.* The level at or extent to which a result is statistically significant. Freq. *attrib.* L19.

🕮 **1** J. MARQUAND The significance of what was happening was . . clearer to me than . . to her. A. N. WILSON We hardly need to dwell on the psychological significance of the wardrobe in the . . story. **2** D. H. LAWRENCE He had lost his significance, he scarcely mattered in her world. E. SEGAL The case . . today has significance far beyond . . this courtroom.
3 ***level of significance***: see LEVEL *noun* 4d. **significance test**: for calculating the significance of a result.

significancy /sɪɡˈnɪfɪk(ə)nsi/ *noun.* L16.
[formed as prec.: see -ANCY.]
1 The quality of being very expressive; expressiveness. L16.
2 a Meaning, significance. Also foll. by *of.* E17. ▸**b** The quality of being significant or having meaning. M17.
3 Importance, consequence. L17.

significans /sɪɡˈnɪfɪkanz/ *noun.* M20.
[Latin, pres. pple of *significare* SIGNIFY.]
Chiefly *LINGUISTICS.* = SIGNIFIANT. Opp. SIGNIFICATUM.

significant /sɪɡˈnɪfɪk(ə)nt/ *adjective & noun.* L16.
[Latin *significant-* pres. ppl stem of *significare* SIGNIFY: see -ANT[1].]
▶ **A** *adjective.* **1** Having or conveying a meaning. Also foll. by *of.* L16. ▸**b** Expressive; suggesting or implying deeper or unstated meaning. Also foll. by *of.* L16. ▸**c** *MATH.* Conveying information about the value of a quantity; esp. in ***significant digit***, ***significant figure***, a digit which has its precise numerical meaning in the number containing it, and is not a zero used simply to fill a vacant place at the beginning or end. L17.
2 Important, notable; consequential. M18.
3 *STATISTICS.* Of an observed or calculated result: having a low probability of occurrence if the null hypothesis is true. L19.

🕮 **1** A. J. AYER Without changing a significant sentence into a piece of nonsense. **b** J. B. PRIESTLEY I do not know . . anything more moving and more significant than that old patched boat. O. MANNING She gave a grim, significant nod. **2** F. WELDON Men's lives were without importance and . . only the lives of women were significant. P. DALLY He failed to make significant economies and live within his means. **3 statistically significant** significant at some conventionally chosen level, freq. five per cent.

Special collocations: ***significant digit***, ***significant figure***: see sense 1c above. **significant form** a hypothetical aesthetic and formal quality of great art, considered more significant than subject-matter. **significant other** a person who greatly affects or influences one's thoughts, feelings, or actions; *spec.* a spouse or committed lover.
▶ **B** *noun.* A thing which expresses or conveys meaning; a sign, a symbol. L16.
■ **significantly** *adverb* L16.

significate /sɪɡˈnɪfɪkət/ *noun.* LME.
[Late Latin *significatum*, use as noun of neut. pa. pple of Latin *significare* SIGNIFY: see -ATE[1].]
That which is signified or symbolized.

significatio *noun* var. of SIGNIFICACIO.

signification /ˌsɪɡnɪfɪˈkeɪʃ(ə)n/ *noun.* ME.
[Old & mod. French from Latin *significatio(n-)*, from *significat-*, pa. ppl stem of *significare* SIGNIFY: see -ATION.]
1 The fact, property, or process of having or expressing meaning. ME.
2 A thing, event, action, etc., which signifies, symbolizes, or expresses something. Now *rare.* LME. ▸**b** An indication of an idea, emotion, etc.; an intimation of a future event, *spec.* legal notification. LME. ▸†**c** An indication or trace of (the presence of) a physical thing. M16–E17.
3 That which is signified by something; implication or meaning, esp. of a word or phrase. Freq. foll. by *of.* LME. ▸**b** Importance, consequence, significance. Now *rare* or *dial.* M16.

🕮 **1** R. ALTER Which details to . . connect with each other as patterns of signification. **2b** C. MIDDLETON Caesar . . could never draw from the people any public signification of their favour. **3** R. L. STEVENSON Set phrases, each with a special signification.

■ **significational** *adjective* M20.

significative /sɪɡˈnɪfɪkətɪv/ *adjective & noun.* LME.
[Old & mod. French *significatif*, *-ive*, or late Latin *significativus*, formed as prec.: see -IVE.]
▶ **A** *adjective.* **1** Signifying; having or expressing (esp. implied or unstated) meaning. LME. ▸**b** Very significant or expressive. L17.
2 Serving as a sign or indication *of.* M17.
▶ **B** *noun.* A thing (esp. a word) which signifies or indicates something; a sign, a symbol. E17.
■ †**significatively** *adverb* LME–M17. **significativeness** *noun* M17.

significator /ˈsɪɡnɪfɪkeɪtə/ *noun.* L16.
[Late Latin, from *significare* SIGNIFY: see -OR.]
1 *ASTROLOGY.* The planet by which the querent or the quesited is specially signified. L16.
2 That which signifies or indicates something. *rare.* M17.
■ **significatrix** *noun* (*rare*) = SIGNIFICATOR 1 M17.

significatory /sɪɡˈnɪfɪkət(ə)ri/ *adjective.* L16.
[Late Latin *significatorius* (in medieval Latin *litteræ significatoriæ*), formed as prec.: see -ORY[2].]
Signifying; intimating.

significatum /sɪɡˌnɪfɪˈkɑːtəm/ *noun.* M19.
[Latin, neut. sing. pa. pple of *significare* SIGNIFY.]
Chiefly *LINGUISTICS.* That which is signified or denoted; *spec.* = SIGNIFIÉ. Opp. SIGNIFICANS.

significavit /sɪɡˌnɪfɪˈkeɪvɪt/ *noun.* ME.
[Latin, 3rd person sing. perf. indic. of *significare* SIGNIFY.]
ECCLESIASTICAL LAW. A form of writ (*spec.* one formerly issued by Chancery for the arrest of an excommunicated person) used in ecclesiastical cases; the bishop's certificate granting or supporting such a writ.

significs /sɪɡˈnɪfɪks/ *noun.* Now *rare.* L19.
[from SIGNIFIC(ANCE, after *economics*, *politics*, etc. Cf. -ICS.]
The branch of knowledge that deals with significance or (implied or unexpressed) meaning.

signifié /siɲifje/ *noun.* Pl. pronounced same. M20.
[French, pa. pple of *signifier* signify.]
Chiefly *LINGUISTICS.* A meaning or idea, as distinct from its expression in a physical medium (as a sound, symbol, image, etc.); the semantic element of a sign. Cf. SIGN *noun* 2e, SIGNIFIED *noun*. Opp. SIGNIFIANT.

signified /ˈsɪɡnɪfʌɪd/ *ppl adjective & noun.* M17.
[from SIGNIFY + -ED[1].]
▶ **A** *ppl adjective.* Indicated. M17.
▶ **B** *absol.* as *noun.* That which is signified; (chiefly LINGUISTICS) = SIGNIFIÉ (opp. SIGNIFIER 2). M20.

signifier /ˈsɪɡnɪfʌɪə/ *noun.* M16.
[from SIGNIFY + -ER[1].]
1 A person who or thing which signifies something; a significator. M16.
2 LINGUISTICS. = SIGNIFIANT. Opp. SIGNIFIED *noun.* M20.
3 A person who boasts or makes insulting remarks etc., esp. in competitive exaggeration. *US slang.* M20.

signify /ˈsɪɡnɪfʌɪ/ *verb.* ME.
[Old & mod. French *signifier* from Latin *significare*, from *signum* SIGN *noun*: see -FY.]
1 *verb trans.* Be a sign or symbol of; mean; (of a thing) represent; (of a word etc.) denote. ME. ▸**b** *verb trans. & (rare) intrans.* Foreshow (a future event, condition, etc.). Now *rare.* LME.
2 *verb trans.* Make known, indicate, announce, declare, (an idea, fact, etc.). Freq. foll. by *to.* ME. ▸†**b** Notify or inform (a person). E16–L17.
†**3** *verb trans.* Compare or liken *to* something. *rare.* LME–L15.
4 *verb intrans.* Be of importance or consequence; have significance or meaning; avail, matter. Freq. foll. by adverb. E17.
5 *verb intrans.* Boast or brag; make insulting remarks etc., esp. in competitive exaggeration. *US slang.* M20.

> 🕮 **1** B. BAINBRIDGE Madness by no means signifies an utter want of design. E. SEGAL The . . dean lowered his head, perhaps to signify that he was deep in thought. A. S. BYATT The candles are lit to signify the new world, the new year, the new life. **2** LD MACAULAY Refused to comply with the . . wish of his people signified to him by his Parliament. L. NAMIER An anonymous letter . . signifying the day the parliament would meet. **4** H. JAMES I don't care who you may be . . it signifies very little today. A. P. HERBERT Don't worry, Fred. It don't signify.

■ **signiˈfiable** *adjective (rare)* able to be signified M19.

signing /ˈsʌɪnɪŋ/ *noun.* LME.
[from SIGN *verb* + -ING[1].]
†**1** A sign, a symbol, an indication. Only in LME.
2 The action or an act of writing one's signature, esp. on a document etc.; authorization or affirmation by signature. Also foll. by adverb. E17. ▸**b** A person who has signed a contract, esp. to join a professional sports team, record company, etc. L20.
3 a CHRISTIAN CHURCH. The action or an act of making the sign of the cross. L18. ▸**b** The action of making signs with the hand, *spec.* in sign language. M20.
4 The action or process of providing a place, street, etc., with signs; the design and arrangement of public signs. M20.

signing /ˈsʌɪnɪŋ/ *ppl adjective.* E19.
[from SIGN *verb* + -ING[2].]
That signs or is entitled to sign, esp. an official document, record, etc.

†**signior, signiora, signiory** *nouns* vars. of SIGNOR etc.

sign-manual /ˈsʌɪn manjʊ(ə)l/ *noun.* LME.
[Anglo-Latin *signum manuale* (earlier *signum manus*): see SIGN *noun*, MANUAL *adjective.*]
1 An autograph signature (esp. that of the sovereign) authenticating a document. LME.
2 A sign made with the hand or hands. *rare.* M19.

signor /ˈsiːnjɔː/ *noun.* Also †**signior**. Pl. **-ri** /-ri/. L16.
[Italian, reduced form of SIGNORE from Latin *senior*(-): see SENIOR.]
1 Used as a title (preceding the surname or other designation) of or as a respectful form of address to an Italian or Italian-speaking man (corresp. to English *Mr* or *sir*). L16. ▸**b** An Italian man, esp. a singer. L18.
2 A man of distinction, rank, or authority; a gentleman or nobleman. L16.
¶ Cf. SEIGNEUR, SEIGNIOR, SENHOR, SEÑOR.

signora /siːnˈjɔːrə/ *noun.* Also †**signiora**. M17.
[Italian, fem. of SIGNORE.]
Used as a title (preceding the surname or other designation) of or as a respectful form of address to an Italian or Italian-speaking (esp. married) woman (corresp. to English *Mrs* or *madam*). Also, an Italian (esp. married) woman.

signore /siːnˈjɔːreɪ/ *noun.* L16.
[Italian: see SIGNOR.]
= SIGNOR.

signori *noun* pl. of SIGNOR.

signoria /siːnjəˈriːə/ *noun.* M16.
[Italian, formed as SIGNOR. Cf. SEIGNEURY, SEIGNIORY, SIGNORY.]
Hist. The governing body of any of various medieval Italian republics, esp. Venice.

signorina /siːnjəˈriːnə/ *noun.* E19.
[Italian, dim. of SIGNORA.]
Used as a title (used preceding the surname or other designation) of or as a respectful form of address to a young (esp. unmarried) Italian or Italian-speaking woman (corresp. to English *Miss*). Also, a young (esp. unmarried) Italian woman.

signory /ˈsiːnjəri/ *noun.* Also †**signiory**. LME.
[Orig. from Old French *signerie, -norie*, etc., vars. of *seignorie* SEIGNEURY; later infl. by Italian SIGNORIA. Cf. SEIGNIORY.]
1 Lordship, domination, rule. LME. ▸**b** Appearance, expression, bearing, etc., suggesting authority or supremacy. *rare.* L16.
2 A domain, a territory. M16.
3 *Hist.* A governing body, esp. of any of various medieval Italian republics, esp. Venice. M16.
■ **siˈgnorial** *adjective* of or pertaining to a signory L19. †**signority** *noun (rare)* lordship, government E16–L18.

signpost /ˈsʌɪnpəʊst/ *noun & verb.* Also **sign-post**. E17.
[from SIGN *noun* + POST *noun*[1].]
▶ **A** *noun.* **1** A post supporting a sign. E17.
2 A post bearing a sign or signs indicating the direction (and occas. distance) to a place or places; *fig.* a guide, an indicator. M19.

> 🕮 **2** J. C. POWYS The words 'To Northwold' upon a newly whitewashed signpost. A. SINCLAIR The Beatles, with their lyrics being treated as signposts of modern thought.

▶ **B** *verb trans.* Provide with a signpost or signposts; guide, direct, or indicate (as) with a signpost. L19.

> 🕮 S. NAIPAUL No specific destination had ever been signposted. *Community Librarian* They hope . . eventually to signpost all libraries in eight major languages.

■ **signpostless** *adjective* M20.

signum /ˈsɪɡnəm/ *noun.* Pl. ***signa*** /ˈsɪɡnə/. M19.
[Latin: see SIGN *noun.*]
A mark, a sign.
¶ Earlier in SIGNUM PANTHEUM.

signum pantheum /sɪɡnəm panˈθiːəm/ *noun phr.* Pl. ***signa panthea*** /sɪɡnə panˈθiːə/. E18.
[Latin = divine statue, from *signum* statue + *pantheus* from Greek *pantheios* dedicated to all the gods (formed as PAN- + *theios* divine). Cf. PANTHEUM.]
CLASSICAL ANTIQUITIES. A statue combining the figures, symbols, or attributes of several gods.

sigri /ˈsɪɡriː/ *noun.* M20.
[Panjabi *sagṛī.*]
In the Indian subcontinent: a fire or stove used for cooking.

sijo /ˈsiːdʒəʊ/ *noun.* Pl. **-os**. L19.
[Korean.]
1 A type of Korean vocal music. *rare.* L19.
2 A Korean lyric poem usu. consisting of twenty-four syllables divided into three lines. M20.

sika /ˈsiːkə/ *noun*[1]. L19.
[Japanese = deer.]
More fully ***sika deer***. A deer, *Cervus nippon*, native to Japan and SE Asia and widely naturalized elsewhere, that is related to the red deer but smaller and with white spots. Also called ***Japanese deer***.

sika /ˈʃɪkɑː, s-/ *noun*[2]. L20.
[Bengali *sikā* from Sanskrit *śikya* sling.]
In the Indian subcontinent: a rope net for suspending pots etc.

sike /sʌɪk/ *noun*[1]. *Scot. & north.* Also **syke**. ME.
[Repr. Old English *sīc* SITCH: cf. Old Norse *sík* and DYKE *noun*[1], DITCH *noun.*]
1 A small stream or rill, *esp.* one flowing through flat or marshy ground and often dry in summer; a ditch or channel through which this flows. ME. ▸**b** A gully; a hollow. M19.
2 A stretch of meadow, a field. *rare.* LME.

sike /sʌɪk/ *noun*[2]. Long *obsolete* exc. *dial.* ME.
[Rel. to next.]
1 A sigh. ME.
†**2** Sighing. Only in ME.

sike /sʌɪk/ *verb intrans.* Also †**syke**. ME.
[Repr. Old English *sīcan* SIGH *verb.*]
1 Sigh. Long *obsolete* exc. *dial.* ME.
2 Sob, cry. *dial.* M19.

siket /ˈsɪkət/ *noun.* Long *obsolete* exc. *dial.* ME.
[from SIKE *noun*[1] + -ET[1].]
A small watercourse.

Sikh /siːk/ *noun & adjective.* L18.
[Panjabi, Hindi, from Sanskrit *śiṣya* disciple.]
▶ **A** *noun.* A member of a monotheistic religion founded in the Punjab by Guru Nanak in the early 16th cent. and combining Hindu and Islamic elements. L18.
▶ **B** *attrib.* or as *adjective.* Of or pertaining to the Sikhs or Sikhism. M19.
■ **Sikhism** *noun* the beliefs and principles of the Sikhs M19.

sikhara *noun* var. of SHIKHARA.

Sikkimese /sɪkɪˈmiːz/ *adjective & noun.* M19.
[from *Sikkim* (see below) + -ESE.]
▶ **A** *adjective.* Of or pertaining to Sikkim, a country in the eastern Himalayas (now part of India). M19.
▶ **B** *noun.* Pl. same. A native or inhabitant of Sikkim. M20.

Siksika /ˈsɪksɪkə/ *noun pl.* M19.
[Blackfoot, from *siksi-* black + *-ka* foot.]
The northernmost of the three peoples which constitute the Blackfoot confederacy of N. American Indians. Also, the Blackfeet.

silage /ˈsʌɪlɪdʒ/ *noun & verb.* L19.
[Alt. of ENSILAGE, after SILO.]
▶ **A** *noun.* Green fodder preserved by pressure in a silo or (occas.) a stack. Also, storage in a silo. L19.
Comb.: **silage cutter** (*a*) a stationary machine for chopping green fodder into short lengths for silage and lifting it into a silo; (*b*) = *silage harvester* below; **silage harvester** a harvester which chops a crop into short lengths for silage as it travels and lifts it into another vehicle.
▶ **B** *verb trans.* Store in a silo; turn into or preserve as silage. L19.

silajit /sɪˈlɑːdʒɪt, ˈsɪlədʒɪt/ *noun.* E19.
[Sanskrit *śilājit, śilājatu*, from *śilā* rock + *jatu* bitumen.]
In the Indian subcontinent: any of various solid or viscous substances found on rock and used in traditional Indian medicine.

silane /ˈsʌɪleɪn/ *noun.* E20.
[formed as SIL(ICON + -ANE.]
CHEMISTRY. Any of a large class of hydrides of silicon analogous to the alkanes; *spec.* silicon tetrahydride, SiH_4, a colourless gas with strong reducing properties which is spontaneously flammable in air.

silanize /ˈsʌɪlənʌɪz/ *verb trans.* Also **-ise**. M20.
[from prec. + -IZE.]
Treat (silica-based material) with reagents which make the surface more inert by converting reactive groups to organosilicon groups.
■ **silaniˈzation** *noun* M20.

Silastic /sɪˈlastɪk/ *noun.* Also **s-**. M20.
[from SI(LICON + E)LASTIC *adjective & noun.*]
CHEMISTRY. (Proprietary name for) silicone rubber.

Silat /sɪˈlat/ *noun.* E20.
[Malay.]
The Malay art of self-defence, practised as a martial art or accompanied by drums as a ceremonial display or dance.

Silbo /ˈsɪlbəʊ/ *noun.* M20.
[Spanish = a whistle, whistling.]
A form of Spanish articulated in whistles, used on Gomera in the Canary Islands for long-distance communication. Also ***Silbo Gomero*** /ɡɒˈmɛːrəʊ/ [of Gomera].
■ **silbador** /sɪlbəˈdɔː/ *noun*, pl. **-dores** /-ˈdɔːriz/, **-dors**, a person who uses Silbo M20.

silcrete /ˈsɪlkriːt/ *noun.* E20.
[from SIL(ICA + CON)CRETE *noun.*]
PETROGRAPHY. A quartzite formed of sand grains or pebbles cemented together by silica; a siliceous duricrust.

sild /sɪld/ *noun.* E20.
[Danish, Norwegian = herring.]
A small immature herring, *esp.* one caught in northern European seas.

sildenafil /sɪlˈdɛnəfɪl/ *noun.* L20.
[Invented word.]
PHARMACOLOGY. A sulphur-containing piperazine derivative, $C_{22}H_{30}N_6O_4S$, that acts as a selective enzyme inhibitor, increasing the diameter of blood vessels (esp. in the penis), and is given to enhance erectile function.
¶ A proprietary name for this drug is VIAGRA.

sile /sʌɪl/ *verb*[1] *intrans.* Long *obsolete* exc. *north.* LME.
[Prob. of Scandinavian origin.]
1 Pass, move; glide. Chiefly with prepositions or adverbs. LME.
2 Fall, sink. Usu. foll. by *down.* LME. ▸**b** Faint *away. dial.* L18.
3 †**a** Of tears etc.: flow. LME–L19. ▸**b** Of rain: pour (*down*). *dial.* E18.

sile /sʌɪl/ *verb*[2] *trans.* Now *dial.* LME.
[Of Scandinavian origin: cf. Middle Swedish *siila, sila*, Swedish *sila*, Norwegian *sile.*]
Pass (esp. milk) through a sieve, strain.

silen /ˈsʌɪlən/ *noun.* Also **S-**. L16.
[formed as SILENUS.]
GREEK MYTHOLOGY. = SILENUS.

silence /ˈsʌɪləns/ *noun & verb.* ME.
[Old & mod. French = Latin *silentium*, formed as SILENT *adjective & noun*: see -ENCE.]
▶ **A** *noun.* **1** Absence of sound; complete quietness. ME.
2 The fact of abstaining from speech (altogether, or on a particular subject); a state or condition resulting from

this; muteness, taciturnity. ME. ▸**b** The renunciation of speech as a religious discipline or vow, esp. of the Trappists; a set period during which the members of a religious community renounce speech. LME. ▸**c** As *imper.* Be silent, make no noise. L16. ▸**d** A period of silence observed in memory of a particular deceased person or group of people. E20.

3 Omission of mention or discussion of a particular subject. E16.

4 *allus.* Oblivion; the state or condition of not being spoken of; *spec.* death. E16.

5 *MUSIC.* A rest. M18.

6 Lack of flavour (in distilled spirit) or scent (in a perfume, flower, spice, etc.). L19.

> 🕮 **1** *Defense Update International* Attacking units can maintain sonar silence, possibly throughout the attack. R. FRAME Her father's death still made a terrible silence in the house. **2** S. PLATH We didn't speak, but sat . . in a close, sisterly silence. W. F. BUCKLEY Rufus was pensive. One of his silences ensued. *Proverb:* Silence gives consent. **3** A. TAYLOR A society . . condemning us . . to suffer in silence. **4** T. HARDY She had . . gone down into silence like her ancestors and shut her . . eyes for ever.

Phrases: **break one's silence**, **break silence** begin to speak, esp. on a subject previously avoided. ***conspiracy of silence***: see CONSPIRACY 1. ***deafening silence***: see DEAFEN 1. **keep silence** abstain from speaking, esp. on a particular subject. **put to silence** (*a*) = ***reduce to silence*** below; (*b*) prevent from speaking; †(*c*) put to death. **reduce to silence** refute or defeat in argument. ***tower of silence***: see TOWER *noun*[1].

▸ **B** *verb.* **1** *verb intrans.* Cease speaking; become silent or still. *rare.* M16.

2 *verb trans.* **a** Prohibit or prevent (a person) from speaking, esp. to prevent the free expression of opinion; *spec.* (*Hist.*) forbid (a dissenting minister of religion) to preach or hold services. Also = ***reduce to silence*** above. L16. ▸**b** Cause (a person) to stop speaking or (an animal or thing) from making its natural sound; make silent. E17. ▸**c** Repress (a thought, emotion, expression, etc.); suppress (a sound). M17.

†**3** *verb trans.* Leave unmentioned or undiscussed; omit. E–M17.

4 *verb trans. MILITARY.* Force (a gun, battery, etc.) to cease firing; disable by superior fire. M18.

> 🕮 **2a** A. WEST Every voice that did not . . echo that of the party was being silenced. **b** SIR W. SCOTT The mountain eagle . . Silenced the warblers of the brake. *Christian Science Monitor* This mill and another nearby . . were silenced by the onset of recession in the construction industry. **c** GIBBON The complaints of the people could no longer be silenced.

■ **silenced** *ppl adjective* made silent; *spec.* (of a gun) fitted with a silencer: E17. **silencer** *noun* (*a*) a person who or thing which silences something; (*b*) a conclusive argument etc.; (*c*) a device for reducing the noise made by a vehicle's exhaust system, a firearm, etc.: E17.

silene /sʌɪˈliːni/ *noun.* L18.
[mod. Latin (see below), from Latin SILENUS.]
Any of numerous plants constituting the genus *Silene*, of the pink family, which have chiefly pink or white flowers and a tubular or campanulate calyx. Also called ***campion***, ***catchfly***.

sileni *noun* pl. of SILENUS.

silent /ˈsʌɪlənt/ *adjective & noun.* L15.
[Latin *silent-* pres. ppl stem of *silere* be silent: see -ENT.]
▸ **A** *adjective.* **1** Refraining from speech; speechless, mute; (of an animal) not making its natural sound. Also, reserved, taciturn. L15. ▸**b** *fig.* Of a quality, emotion, etc.: not manifesting itself. E17.

2 Characterized or marked by absence of speech; done, experienced, etc., without speaking. L16. ▸**b** Of a letter: not pronounced though present in the spelling of a word. E17. ▸**c** Unmentioned; unrecorded. *rare.* E17. ▸**d** Of a cinema film: without a synchronized soundtrack. Also, of or pertaining to such a film or films. E20.

3 Characterized or marked by the absence of sound; making or emitting no sound; (of machinery etc.) operating with little or no noise. L16.

4 Of a speaker, writer, book, etc.: omitting mention or discussion of a particular subject; offering no account or record. Freq. foll. by *as to*, *on*, etc. E17.

5 Inactive, quiescent; *spec.* †(*a*) (of the moon) not shining; (*b*) (of distilled spirit) unflavoured; (*c*) (of a perfume, flower, spice, etc.) lacking scent; (*d*) *MEDICINE* producing no detectable signs or symptoms. M17.

> 🕮 **1** G. GREENE He could . . work better when she talked than when she was silent. W. MARCH Reginald was silent until they passed out of earshot; then he talked once more. **2** A. C. CLARKE A silent communion between them which they did not wish to break with words. G. GORDON I'd rather you said it . . than . . boil with silent rage. **3** DAY LEWIS This part of the garden . . was always silent. *New York Review of Books* The effects of the slump in the silent shipyards of Merseyside. **4** E. A. FREEMAN As to the other shire . . history is equally silent. **5** *British Medical Journal* Our results show a silent peripheral neuropathy . . concomitant with the HIV infection.

Phrases & special collocations: **as silent as the grave** (of a place) extremely quiet; (of a person) secretive, discreet. **silent cop** *Austral. slang* a small, usu. hemispherical, concrete marker set in the centre of a road or crossroads to direct the flow of traffic. **silent dog whistle**, **silent whistle** a high-frequency whistle producing a note audible to a dog but not (usually) to a person. **silent heat** *VETERINARY MEDICINE* ovulation occurring without discernible signs of oestrus. **silent majority** those people holding, but rarely expressing or asserting, moderate opinions. **silent partner** *N. Amer.* = ***sleeping partner*** s.v. SLEEPING *ppl adjective*. ***silent whistle***: see ***silent dog whistle*** above. **strong silent type** a person (esp. a man) who controls or conceals emotion.

▸ **B** *noun.* †**1** The time of silence. *rare* (Shakes.). Only in L16.

2 A device for stopping a clock from striking or an alarm from sounding. M19.

3 A silent film. E20.

■ **silentish** *adjective* (*rare*) M18. **silently** *adverb* L16. **silentness** *noun* the fact or condition of silence; an instance of this: E17.

silential /sʌɪˈlɛnʃ(ə)l/ *adjective. rare.* E18.
[from SILENT after *confident*, *confidential* etc.]
Accompanied by or associated with silence.

silentiary /sʌɪˈlɛnʃ(ə)ri/ *noun.* E17.
[Latin *silentiarius* (orig.) a trusted or confidential domestic servant, (later) a privy counsellor of the Roman Empire, from *silentium* SILENCE *noun*: see -ARY[1].]
1 A person who observes or advises silence, esp. as a religious discipline. E17.

2 An official of the Byzantine court whose duty orig. was to maintain silence and order, but who freq. acted as a confidential adviser or agent (now *Hist.*); any official whose duty is to maintain silence and order. L17

silentious /sʌɪˈlɛnʃəs/ *adjective.* E19.
[from SILENT + -IOUS: cf. late Latin *silentiosus*.]
Given to silence.

silenus /sʌɪˈliːnəs/ *noun.* Also **S-**. Pl. **-ni** /-nʌɪ/. E17.
[Latin *Silenus* from Greek *Seilēnos* foster-father of Bacchus and leader of the satyrs.]
GREEK MYTHOLOGY. A wood-god, a satyr, *esp.* one represented as a bearded old man with the tail and legs of a horse. Cf. SILEN.

■ **Silenic** *adjective* resembling Silenus or (one of) the Sileni E19.

Silesia /sʌɪˈliːzjə, -ʒə/ *adjective & noun.* L17.
[Latinized form of *Schlesien*, German name of the region (see next).]
1 (Designating) a fine twilled linen or cotton cloth for dress linings etc. L17.

†**2** (Designating) a variety of cabbage lettuce. M–L18.

Silesian /sʌɪˈliːzjən, -ʒ(ə)n/ *noun & adjective.* M16.
[from prec. + -AN.]
▸ **A** *noun.* A native or inhabitant of Silesia, a region now chiefly in SW Poland. M16.
▸ **B** *adjective.* Of, pertaining to, originating in, or associated with Silesia. M17.

Silesian stem a shouldered stem of a goblet, candlestick, etc., supposedly named in honour of George I for whom it was designed.

silex /ˈsʌɪlɛks/ *noun.* L16.
[Latin = flint.]
Flint; quartz.

silhouette /sɪlʊˈɛt/ *noun & verb.* L18.
[French, from Étienne de *Silhouette* (1709–67), French author and politician.]
▸ **A** *noun.* **1** A portrait obtained by tracing the outline of a profile, head, or figure, esp. by means of its shadow, and filling in the whole with black or cutting the shape out of black paper; a figure or picture drawn or printed in solid black. L18. ▸**b** *fig.* A brief verbal description of a person etc. E19.

2 a An object seen as a dark outline against a lighter background; a dark shadow of something. M19. ▸**b** The contour or outline of a garment or a person's body. E20.

> 🕮 **2a** J. G. WHITTIER The cat's dark silhouette on the wall. RIDER HAGGARD I saw the black silhouette of the old Zulu raise its arm in mute salute. **in silhouette** [French *en silhouette*] in outline, in profile.

▸ **B** *verb.* **1** *verb trans.* Represent in silhouette, throw up the outline of. Usu. in *pass.* (foll. by *against*, *on*). L19.

2 *verb intrans.* Show up as a silhouette. L19.

■ **silhouettist** *noun* a maker of silhouettes M19.

silica /ˈsɪlɪkə/ *noun.* E19.
[from Latin *silic-*, SILEX after *alumina* etc.]
A hard mineral substance, silicon dioxide, occurring in many rocks, soils, and sands as crystals, esp. of quartz or cristobalite, or amorphous, as in flint, opal, and obsidian, and also as a structural material of living organisms.

VITREOUS silica.

Comb.: **silica glass** = *QUARTZ glass*; **silica gel** hydrated silica in a hard granular hygroscopic form which is used as an adsorbent and desiccant.

silicate /ˈsɪlɪkeɪt, -kət/ *noun.* E19.
[from prec. + -ATE[1].]
A salt or ester of a silicic acid; any of the compounds regarded as formed from silica and other oxides, which include many rock-forming minerals and have a characteristic structure based on metal cations and SiO_4 tetrahedra.

silicated /ˈsɪlɪkeɪtɪd/ *adjective.* E19.
[formed as SILICA + -ATE[3] + -ED[1].]
Combined with silica; *GEOLOGY* that has undergone silication.

silication /sɪlɪˈkeɪʃ(ə)n/ *noun.* M19.
[from SILICA, SILICATE: see -ATION.]
GEOLOGY. Conversion into or replacement with silica or a silicate.

siliceous /sɪˈlɪʃəs/ *adjective.* M17.
[from Latin *siliceus*, formed as SILICA: see -OUS.]
Containing or consisting of silica.

silicic /sɪˈlɪsɪk/ *adjective.* E19.
[from SILICA + -IC.]
CHEMISTRY. Pertaining to, consisting of, or formed from silicon or silica.

> 🕮 *Journal of Petrology* Less silicic melts (such as dacites). **silicic acid** an oxyacid of silicon; *esp.* a weakly acidic colloidal hydrated form of silica made by acidifying solutions of alkali metal silicates.

siliciclastic /sɪˌlɪsɪˈklastɪk/ *adjective.* M20.
[from SILICA + -I- + CLASTIC.]
GEOLOGY. Designating or pertaining to clastic rocks which are not carbonates (and usu. are silicates).

silicicolous /sɪlɪˈsɪk(ə)ləs/ *adjective.* E20.
[formed as prec. + -COLOUS.]
BOTANY. Growing best on siliceous (sandy or acidic) soil, calcifuge.

■ Also ˈ**silicicole** *adjective* M20.

silicide /ˈsɪlɪsʌɪd/ *noun.* M19.
[from SILICON + -IDE.]
CHEMISTRY. A binary compound of silicon with a metallic or other element of lower or comparable electronegativity.

siliciferous /sɪlɪˈsɪf(ə)rəs/ *adjective.* L18.
[formed as SILICA + -I- + -FEROUS.]
Containing or yielding silica.

silicification /sɪˌlɪsɪfɪˈkeɪʃ(ə)n/ *noun.* M19.
[from SILICIFY + -FICATION.]
GEOLOGY & PALAEONTOLOGY. Conversion into or replacement by silica or a silicate.

silicify /sɪˈlɪsɪfʌɪ/ *verb.* E19.
[from SILICA + -FY.]
1 *verb trans.* Convert into or impregnate with silica. E19.

2 *verb intrans.* Undergo silicification. *rare.* E19.

silicious /sɪˈlɪʃəs/ *adjective.* E18.
[formed as SILICA + -IOUS.]
= SILICEOUS.

†**silicium** *noun.* E19–E20.
[formed as prec. + -IUM.]
CHEMISTRY. Silicon.

†**siliciuret** *noun.* E–M19.
[formed as prec. + -URET.]
CHEMISTRY. = SILICIDE.

■ †**siliciuretted** *adjective* combined with silicon: only in M19.

silicle *noun* see SILICULA.

silico- /ˈsɪlɪkəʊ/ *combining form.*
[from SILICA or SILICON: see -O-.]
Of, connected with, or containing silicon or silica, as ***silico-alkaline***, ***silico-aluminous*** *adjectives*, ***silicocarnotite***, ***silicofluoride*** *nouns*, etc.

silicoflagellate /ˌsɪlɪkəʊˈfladʒ(ə)leɪt/ *noun.* E20.
[from prec. + FLAGELLATE *noun*.]
BIOLOGY. A marine flagellate of the order Silicoflagellida, distinguished by a siliceous skeleton and radiating spines.

silicon /ˈsɪlɪk(ə)n/ *noun.* E19.
[from Latin *silic-*, SILEX (after earlier SILICIUM) + *-on* after *boron*, *carbon*.]
▸ **I 1** A chemical element, atomic no. 14, that is a metalloid occurring abundantly in the earth's crust in oxides and silicates, and is used in electronic components for its semiconducting properties. (Symbol Si.) E19.

▸ **II 2** See SILICONE.

Comb.: **silicon carbide** a hard crystalline compound of silicon and carbon, SiC, used as an abrasive and refractory; also called ***carborundum***; ***silicon chip***: see CHIP *noun* 10; **silicon iron**, **silicon steel** cast iron, steel, containing a relatively high proportion of silicon, which increases magnetic permeability and resistance to corrosion and heat; **Silicon Valley** an area with a high concentration of electronics industries; orig. and *spec.* the Santa Clara valley, south-east of San Francisco; **silicon wafer** *ELECTRONICS* a wafer of silicon bearing an integrated circuit; a large silicon chip.

silicone /ˈsɪlɪkəʊn/ *noun & verb.* In sense A.1 also †**-on**. **M19.**
[from SILICIUM + -ONE.]
▶ **A** *noun.* CHEMISTRY.
1 A yellow solid obtained by the action of concentrated hydrochloric acid on calcium silicide. *obsolete exc. Hist.* **M19.**
2 Orig., a supposed organic compound of silicon analogous to a ketone, containing an :Si=O group. Now, any of a class of synthetic organosilicon polymers based on chains or networks of alternating silicon and oxygen atoms, used as electrical insulators, waterproofing agents, rubbers, and resins. **E20.**
▶ **B** *verb trans.* Coat, impregnate, or otherwise treat with a silicone or silicone-based material. **M20.**

siliconize /ˈsɪlɪk(ə)nʌɪz/ *verb trans.* Also **-ise**. **L19.**
[from SILICON, SILICONE + -IZE.]
1 Cause to combine with silicon or one of its compounds; *esp.* impregnate the surface of (a metal) with a protective coating of silicon. **L19.**
2 = SILICONE *verb*. Chiefly as ***siliconized*** *ppl adjective.* **M20.**
■ **siliconiˈzation** *noun* **E20.**

silicosis /sɪlɪˈkəʊsɪs/ *noun.* Pl. **-coses** /-ˈkəʊsiːz/. **L19.**
[from SILICA + -OSIS.]
MEDICINE. Fibrosis of the lung induced by inhaling fine particles of silica.
■ **silicotic** /-ˈkɒtɪk/ *adjective* of or affected by silicosis **E20.**

silicula /sɪˈlɪkjʊlə/ *noun.* Pl. **-lae** /-liː, -lʌɪ/, **-las**. Also Anglicized as **silicle** /ˈsɪlɪk(ə)l/, (*rare*) **silicule** /ˈsɪlɪkjuːl/. **M18.**
[mod. Latin, dim. of next: see -ULE.]
BOTANY. A short seed-pod; *spec.* (in the family Cruciferae) a fruit resembling a siliqua but as broad as or broader than it is long. Cf. SILIQUA 2.
■ **siliculose** *adjective* bearing siliculae **M18.**

siliqua /ˈsɪlɪkwə/ *noun.* Pl. **-quae** /-kwiː, -kwʌɪ/, **-quas**. Also (in senses 1, 2) Anglicized as **silique** /sɪˈliːk/. **LME.**
[Latin = pod.]
†**1** The carob tree, *Ceratonia siliqua*. Only in **LME.**
2 BOTANY. A long seed-pod; *spec.* (in the family Cruciferae) a dry dehiscent fruit, longer than it is broad, consisting of two loculi separated by a false septum. Cf. prec. **E18.**
3 A Roman silver coin of the 4th and 5th cents. AD, worth 1/24 solidus. **L19.**
■ **siˈliquiform** *adjective* (BOTANY) having the form of a siliqua **E19.** **siliquose** *adjective* (BOTANY) bearing pods or siliquas; having the form of a siliquae: **L17.** **siliquous** *adjective* (now *rare*) BOTANY = SILIQUOSE **M17.**

silk /sɪlk/ *noun, adjective, & verb.*
[Old English *sioloc, seol(e)c*, corresp. to Old Norse *silki*, Russian *shëlk*, Lithuanian †*zìlkaĩ*, Old Prussian *silkas* (genit.), from or cogn. with late Latin *sericum* neut. of Latin *sericus* from Greek *sērikos* rel. to Latin *Seres*, Greek *Sēres* SERES.]
▶ **A** *noun.* **1** A fine strong soft lustrous protein fibre produced by various invertebrates, esp. by the caterpillars of certain moths and by many spiders; *spec.* that produced by silkworms and used to make thread for textiles. **OE.** ▶**b** This fibre in the form of thread or twist for sewing. **L15.** ▶**c** A silken thread. *rare.* **L17.**
2 Cloth or fabric made from this fibre. **OE.** ▶**b** A particular kind of silk cloth or fabric. **M16.**
3 A garment made of silk; *esp.* (***a***) a woman's silk dress; (***b***) a silk-covered hat; (***c***) a silk stocking. Freq. in *pl.* **E16.** ▶**b** LAW. A King's or Queen's Counsel (with ref. to the right to wear a silk gown); such lawyers collectively. **E19.** ▶**c** *sing.* & (now usu.) in *pl.* A jockey's cap and jacket carrying an employer's or horse-owner's colours. **L19.**
4 (Each of) the long silklike filiform styles of the female flower of maize. Chiefly *N. Amer.* **M18.**
5 A silky lustre in rubies and sapphires due to microscopic crystal inclusions (usu. considered a defect). **L19.**
6 A parachute. Chiefly in ***hit the silk*** below. *US Air Force slang.* **M20.**

> 📖 **1** *Science* Spiders . . spin silk for egg sacs, for drag lines . . and for aerial webs. **2** C. ISHERWOOD You'd expect an important film man to wear silk next to his skin. **3** W. COWPER As she sweeps him with her whistling silks. **c** *New Yorker* In his first appearance in silks since the accident, he won.

Phrases: ***artificial silk***: see ARTIFICIAL *adjective* 2. **corn silk** = sense 4 above. **hit the silk** (*US Air Force slang*) bale out of an aircraft by parachute. **in silk** (chiefly *N. Amer.*) (of maize) at the stage when the silk is prominent. ***Jap silk***: see JAP *adjective*. ***Japanese silk***: see JAPANESE *adjective*. ***Persian silk***: see PERSIAN *adjective*. **receive silk, take silk** be appointed King's or Queen's Counsel. ***Thai silk***: see THAI *adjective*. ***waste silk***: see WASTE *noun & adjective*. ***wild silk***: see WILD *adjective* etc.
▶ **B** *attrib.* or as *adjective.* **1** Made of silk, silken; (of a fabric) containing or resembling silk. **ME.**
2 Of a person: clad in silk. *rare.* **E17.**
3 Resembling silk in lustre or shine; silky; (of paint) giving a finish of this kind. **E17.**

> 📖 **1** *Proverb*: You can't make a silk purse out of a sow's ear.

Comb. & special collocations: **silkbark** a small evergreen tree of southern Africa, *Maytenus acuminata* (family Celastraceae); **silk cotton** the silky fibre surrounding the seeds of various tropical trees of the family Bombycaceae, used as a packing and stuffing material etc.; ***silk-cotton tree***, a tree which produces such fibre, *esp.* (***a***) the kapok, *Ceiba pentandra*, (***b***) (in full ***Indian silk-cotton tree***) *Bombax ceiba*; **silk-fowl** a breed of fowl with a silky plumage; **silk-gland** a gland secreting the substance which hardens in air to form silk; **silk grass** any of various fibre-yielding bromeliads (esp. *Bromelia magdalenae*), agaves, and yuccas of the southern US, Central America, etc.; the fibre obtained from these plants; **silk hat** a tall cylindrical hat covered with silk plush; **silk moth** any of various large moths whose larvae spin silk cocoons, esp. of the families Saturniidae and Bombycidae, *spec.* the moth *Bombyx mori* (cf. ***SILKWORM moth***); **silk road, silk route** (freq. with cap. initials) a trade route from China through India to Europe, used in ancient times by traders in silk; **silk screen** a screen of fine mesh (orig. silk) for use in screen printing (usu. *attrib.*); a print made by the silk screen process; **silk-screen** *verb trans.* print, decorate, or reproduce by the silk screen process; **silk snapper** *W. Indies* any of several Caribbean fishes of the snapper family, Lutjanidae; **silk stocking** a stocking made of silk (usu. in *pl.*); a wearer of silk stockings, a wealthy person; **silk-stockinged** *adjective* clad in silk stockings; **silk-tail** a waxwing; **silk-tassel (bush)** = GARRYA; **silk-throwing** the process of converting raw silk into silk yarn or thread; **silk-tree** a pink-flowered leguminous tree of eastern Asia, *Albizia julibrissin*, resembling a mimosa and widely naturalized; **silk waste** silk fibres left after the reeling of silk yarn, or obtained from damaged cocoons; **silkweed** any of various N. American milkweeds (genus *Asclepias*). See also SILKWORM.
▶ **C** *verb.* **1** *verb trans.* Remove the silk from (maize). *N. Amer.* **M19.**
2 *verb intrans.* Of maize: produce the silk. *N. Amer.* **L19.**
■ **silked** *adjective* clothed in or covered with silk; *spec.* (of a book, its pages, etc.) strengthened by silking: **M19.** **silker** *noun* a person who works in or with silk **L19.** **silking** *verbal noun* (***a***) the attachment of a piece of silk or other fine material to a sheet of paper to strengthen or preserve it; (***b***) development of the silk in maize: **M20.** **silklike** *adjective* resembling (that of) silk **L17.**

silkaline *noun* var. of SILKOLINE.

silken /ˈsɪlk(ə)n/ *adjective & verb.* **OE.**
[from SILK *noun* + -EN⁴.]
▶ **A** *adjective.* **1** Made or consisting of silk. **OE.** ▶**b** *fig.* Of bonds, ties, etc.: strong but not burdensome. **L17.**
2 Silky, silklike; soft; glossy, shining, lustrous. **E16.**
3 Soft, smooth, gentle. **L16.**
4 Of words, persons, etc.: elegant; ingratiating, flattering. **L16.**
5 Clad in silk; effeminate, luxurious. **L16.**
6 Producing or containing silk; *transf.* associated with silk. **E17.**

> 📖 **1** GIBBON Silken robes . . embroidered with gold. **2** F. T. PALGRAVE All day . . in silence The silken butterflies glide. **3** D. C. PEATTIE With a soundless silken uncurling of their petals. **4** P. DE VRIES The silken guile of which he was capable. **5** R. MANT The silken sons of luxury and pride. **6** KEATS Spiced dainties . . From silken Samarcand.

▶ **B** *verb trans.* Give a silky lustre to. Also, dress in silk. *rare.* **M18.**
■ **silkenly** *adverb* **M19.**

silkie /ˈsɪlki/ *noun.* **L19.**
[from SILK *noun* + -IE.]
A small chicken of a variety characterized by long soft plumage.

silkily /ˈsɪlkɪli/ *adverb.* **E19.**
[from SILKY *adjective* + -LY².]
In a silky manner; *esp.* smoothly, quietly.

silkoline /ˈsɪlkəliːn/ *noun.* Also **-olene**, **-aline**. **L19.**
[from SILK *noun*, app. after *crinoline*.]
A soft cotton fabric with a smooth finish resembling that of silk.

silkworm /ˈsɪlkwəːm/ *noun.* **OE.**
[from SILK *noun* + WORM *noun*.]
1 The caterpillar of the moth *Bombyx mori* (family Bombycidae), orig. a native of N. China, which lives on mulberry leaves and is bred for the cocoon of silk which it spins before pupating; any caterpillar whose cocoons are of commercial value. **OE.**
2 A person who wears silk clothes. *derog. rare.* **E17.**
Comb.: **silkworm disease** = PÉBRINE; **silkworm gut** a fine strong thread made of the drawn-out glands of the silkworm, used esp. for surgical sutures; **silkworm moth** a silk moth, *esp.* one (such as *Bombyx mori*) used for commercial silk production.

silky *noun*¹ var. of SELKY.

silky /ˈsɪlki/ *adjective & noun*². **LME.**
[from SILK *noun* + -Y¹.]
▶ **A** *adjective.* **1** Made or consisting of silk; silken. **LME.**
2 Having a material quality resembling that of silk, such as a delicate softness, a lustre, or a smooth texture. **M17.**
3 a Of speech, manners, etc.: smooth, ingratiating, insinuating. **L18.** ▶**b** Of a person, or a machine, mechanism, etc.: quiet or smooth in manner or action. **E19.**
4 BOTANY. Covered with soft fine close-set hairs having a silklike gloss; sericeous. **L18.**
5 ZOOLOGY. Having silklike hair, plumage, wings, etc. **L18.**
4 silky oak any of several tall Australian trees of the family Proteaceae, esp. *Grevillea robusta* and *Cardwellia sublimis*; the silky-textured timber, similar to oak, of these trees. **5 silky flycatcher** any of several long-tailed gregarious insectivorous birds related to waxwings, of the genus *Ptilogonys* and related genera, e.g. the phainopepla.
▶ **B** *noun.* A spirit said to haunt houses in the form of a woman in a silk dress. *local.* **E19.**
■ **silkiness** *noun* **M18.**

sill /sɪl/ *noun*¹ *& verb.* Also (*rare*) **cill**.
[Old English *syll*, *sylle* = Middle Low German *sul(le*, Middle Dutch *sulle* rel. to Middle Low German, Middle Dutch *sille*, Old Norse *svill*, *syll*, Old High German *swelli*, *swella* (German *Schwelle* threshold). In sense 4a perh. var. of THILL *noun*².]
▶ **A** *noun.* **1** A strong horizontal beam forming a base or foundation, esp. in the wooden frame of a house. Formerly also, any large beam or piece of squared timber. Cf. GROUNDSEL *noun*² 1. **OE.** ▶**b** Each of the lower horizontal members of the frame of a cart, railway car, or motor vehicle. **L19.**
2 a A horizontal piece of wood or stone forming the bottom part of a window-opening. Also ***window-sill***. **LME.** ▶**b** A horizontal beam forming the top or bottom of a ship's port; the lower edge of an embrasure etc. **E19.**
3 a The threshold of a door or gateway; the bottom timber or lowest part of a door-frame, a door-sill. Cf. GROUNDSEL *noun*² 2. **L16.** ▶**b** A horizontal structure across the bottom of the entrance to a dock or to a lock in a canal. **L18.** ▶**c** GEOLOGY. A high ridge on the seabed that effectively separates the water on each side. **M20.**
4 a A kind of clay found in coal measures. **L18.** ▶**b** MINING & GEOLOGY. Orig., a bed or stratum of (esp. igneous) rock. Now *spec.* a sheet of intrusive igneous rock parallel to the surrounding strata. **L18.**
5 The foot or lower part of a title-page or title. **M19.**
▶ **B** *verb trans.* Provide with a sill. *rare.* **M16.**

sill *noun*² see THILL *noun*¹.

sillabub *noun* var. of SYLLABUB.

silladar /ˈsɪlədɑː/ *noun. Anglo-Indian obsolete exc. Hist.* Also (*sing. & pl.*) **-dari** /-ˈdɑːri/. **E19.**
[Urdu *silāhdār*, Persian *silahdār* armour-bearer, from Arab. *silāh* arms, armour + Persian *-dār* holding, holder.]
An irregular cavalryman who provided his own horse and arms.

sillapak /ˈsiːləpak/ *noun.* Also **sealapack**. **M20.**
[Inupiaq *silapak*.]
A white outer garment worn by Eskimo hunters.

sillar /siːˈljɑː/ *noun.* **M20.**
[Spanish.]
GEOLOGY. An ignimbrite or volcanic tuff that has not become indurated by welding.

siller *noun & adjective* see SILVER *noun & adjective*.

sillikin /ˈsɪlɪkɪn/ *noun. slang.* Now *rare* or *obsolete*. **M19.**
[from SILLY *adjective* + -KIN.]
A simpleton, a naive or silly person.

sillily /ˈsɪlɪli/ *adverb.* **L16.**
[from SILLY *adjective* + -LY².]
†**1** Poorly, badly. *rare.* **L16–E17.**
2 In a foolish, absurd, or senseless manner. **E17.**

sillimanite /ˈsɪlɪmənʌɪt/ *noun.* **M19.**
[from Benjamin *Silliman* (1779–1864), US chemist + -ITE¹.]
MINERALOGY. An orthorhombic aluminium silicate usu. occurring as fibrous masses and as a constituent of schists and gneisses.

silliness /ˈsɪlɪnɪs/ *noun.* **E17.**
[from SILLY *adjective* + -NESS.]
1 The quality of being silly; foolishness, senselessness. **E17.** ▶**b** A silly thing, act, etc. **M18.**
2 Mental weakness. **E19.**

sillion *noun* var. of SELION.

sillock /ˈsɪlək/ *noun.* Chiefly *Scot.* **M17.**
[Norn *sillek* rel. to Old Norse *silungr* small salmon, trout.]
A young coalfish (saithe) in its first year.

silly /ˈsɪli/ *adjective, adverb, noun, & verb.* **LME.**
[Alt. of SEELY.]
▶ **A** *adjective.* **1 a** Deserving of pity, compassion, or sympathy. Cf. POOR *adjective* 4. *obsolete exc. dial.* **LME.** ▶**b** Esp. of a woman, child, or animal: helpless, defenceless. Long *rare* exc. as a conventional (poetic) epithet of sheep. **E16.**
2 Weak, feeble; insignificant, trifling. *obsolete exc. Scot.* **M16.** ▶**b** Sickly, ailing. *Scot. & north.* Now *rare.* **L16.** ▶†**c** Scanty, meagre. **L16–M18.**
†**3 a** (Of a person) unsophisticated, rustic, ignorant; (of a thing) plain, simple, homely. **M16–L18.** ▶**b** Of humble rank; lowly. **M16–M17.**
4 Of very low intelligence, having a mental handicap. Orig. *Scot.* **L16.**
5 Displaying a lack of judgement or common sense; fatuous, foolish, senseless, empty-headed. **L16.** ▶**b** Associated with foolishness; absurd, ridiculous, contemptible. **L16.** ▶**c** CRICKET. Very close to the batsman. Chiefly in ***silly mid-on***, ***silly mid-off***, ***silly point***. **L19.**
6 Stunned, stupefied, dazed (as) by a blow. Esp. in ***knock silly***, ***knocked silly***. **L19.**

📖 **1b** SHAKES. *Two Gent.* Do no outrages On silly women or poor passengers. W. COWPER His silly sheep, what wonder if they stray? **5** N. COWARD It's so silly to get cross at criticism. **b** T. HEGGEN He looked pretty silly . . with his nose sticking out from the bandages. N. FREELING Janine was snuffling in a silly little hanky. *Listener* Beware street-market tapes at silly prices.

Phrases: ***play silly buggers***: see BUGGER *noun*[1] 3.

Special collocations: **silly ass** a foolish or stupid person; *spec.* an amiable upper-class idiot. **silly billy** a foolish or feeble person. **silly house** *slang* a mental hospital. **Silly Putty** (proprietary name for) a mouldable silicone-based substance with remarkable properties of stretching, shattering, and bouncing sharply when appropriately handled, sold chiefly as a plaything. **silly season** the months of August and September, when newspapers make up for the lack of serious news with articles on trivial topics; *transf.* a period dominated by the trivial or absurd.

▶ **B** *adverb.* = SILLILY *adverb* 2. Now *dial.* or *colloq.* **E18.**

▶ **C** *noun.* A silly or foolish person. *colloq.* **M19.**

📖 J. GRENFELL I am a big silly, aren't I?

▶ **D** *verb.* Chiefly *dial.*

1 *verb trans.* Stupefy, stun, daze. **M19.**

2 *verb intrans.* Act foolishly; fool *about*. **L19.**

■ **sillyism** *noun* a silly expression or utterance **E18.**

silly-how /ˈsɪlɪhaʊ/ *noun.* Now *Scot.* & *north.* **L16.**
[from SEELY + *how* HOO *noun*[1].]
A child's caul.

silo /ˈsʌɪləʊ/ *noun & verb.* **M19.**
[Spanish from Latin *sirus* from Greek *siros*.]

▶ **A** *noun.* Pl. **-os**.

1 A pit or underground chamber used for storing grain, roots, etc.; *spec.* one in which green crops are compressed and preserved for fodder as silage. Also, a cylindrical tower or other structure built above ground for the same purpose. **M19.** ▸**b** = SILAGE. *rare.* **L19.**

2 *transf.* A large bin used for storing loose materials etc. **E20.**

3 An underground structure in which a guided missile is stored and from which it may be fired. **M20.**

Comb.: **silo buster** *slang* a missile which can destroy an enemy missile in its silo.

▶ **B** *verb trans.* Put (green crops) into a silo; turn into silage. Also, keep (a missile) in a silo. *rare.* **L19.**

siloxane /sɪˈlɒkseɪn/ *noun.* **E20.**
[from SIL(ICON + OX(YGEN + -ANE.]
CHEMISTRY. Any compound having a molecular structure based on a chain of alternate silicon and oxygen atoms.

Silozi /sɪˈləʊzi/ *noun & adjective.* **M20.**
[Silozi, from *si-* prefix + LOZI.]
(Of) the Bantu language of the Malozi.

silphium /ˈsɪlfɪəm/ *noun.* **M18.**
[Latin from Greek *silphion*.]

1 A Mediterranean plant of classical times (perhaps thapsia) yielding the gum resin laser; the gum resin itself. *obsolete* exc. *Hist.* **M18.**

2 = ***rosinweed*** s.v. ROSIN *noun. US.* **L18.**

silt /sɪlt/ *noun.* **LME.**
[Prob. orig. denoting a salty deposit, and so perh. from a Scandinavian word repr. by Norwegian, Danish *sylt*, Norwegian and Swedish dial. *sylta* salt-marsh, sea-beach, corresp. to Old Low German *sulta* (Low German *sulte*, *sülte*; Dutch *zult*), Old High German *sulza* (German *Sülze*) salt-marsh, salt-pan, brine, from Germanic base also of SALT *noun*[1].]

1 Fine sand, clay, or other soil carried by moving or running water and deposited as a sediment on the bottom or on a shore or flood plain. **LME.** ▸**b** A bed or layer of this. Usu. in *pl.* **L19.** ▸**c** *spec.* in SOIL SCIENCE. (Material consisting of) particles whose sizes fall within a specified range (typically 0.002–0.06 mm) between those of sand and clay; soil having a specified proportion of such particles. **L19.**

2 In full ***silt-snapper***. = ***silk snapper*** s.v. SILK *noun. W. Indies.* **M19.**

Comb.: ***silt-snapper***: see sense 3 above; **siltstone** GEOLOGY a fine-grained sandstone whose particles are of the size of silt (sense 1c).

■ **silty** *adjective* consisting of, resembling, or containing silt **M17.**

silt /sɪlt/ *verb.* **M17.**
[from the noun.]

1 *verb trans.* **a** Fill or block by gradual accumulation of silt. Usu. foll. by *up*. **M17.** ▸**b** Cover *up* or *over* with silt. Usu. in *pass.* **M19.**

2 *verb intrans.* Become filled or blocked with silt. Usu. foll. by *up*. **L18.**

3 *verb intrans.* Flow or drift like silt; settle or be deposited like silt; *transf.* pass gradually. **M19.**

📖 **1a** C. LYELL The deposits . . have silted up some of our estuaries. **2** R. DAHL The little harbour . . has silted up so the . . ships can no longer use it. **3** *fig.*: D. H. LAWRENCE Into the shadow-white chamber silts the white Flux of another dawn.

■ **siltage** *noun* (*rare*) silt, silted material **L19.** **sil'tation** *noun* **M20.**

silumin /ˈsɪljʊmɪn/ *noun.* **E20.**
[from SIL(ICON + AL)UMIN(IUM.]
METALLURGY. Any of a series of casting alloys of aluminium containing about 9 to 13 per cent silicon.

silure /ˈsʌɪljʊə/ *noun.* **E19.**
[Anglicization.]
= SILURUS.

silurian /sɪˈljʊərɪən/ *noun*[1]. *rare.* **M19.**
[from SILURUS + -IAN.]
ZOOLOGY. = SILUROID *noun.*

Silurian /sɪˈljʊərɪən, sʌɪ-/ *adjective & noun*[2]. In senses A.3, B.2 also **s-**. **E18.**
[from Latin *Silures* (= sense 1 below) + -IAN.]

▶ **A** *adjective.* **1** Of or belonging to an ancient British tribe of SE Wales, or the region they inhabited. **E18.**

2 GEOLOGY. Designating or pertaining to the third period of the Palaeozoic era, following the Ordovician (which it was originally regarded as including) and preceding the Devonian, in which corals and eurypterids flourished and fish and land plants diversified. **M19.** ▸**b** *loosely.* Belonging to the remote past; primitive, prehistoric. **L19.**

3 Pertaining to or designating paper or stationery with a mottled appearance, esp. of a mainly blue-grey colour. **L19.**

▶ **B** *noun.* **1** GEOLOGY. The Silurian period; the system of rocks dating from this time. **M19.**

2 Silurian paper or stationery. **M20.**

silurid /sɪˈljʊərɪd/ *adjective & noun.* **L19.**
[from SILURUS + -ID[3].]
ZOOLOGY. ▶**A** *adjective.* Of, pertaining to, or designating the Eurasian family Siluridae of freshwater catfish. **L19.**

▶ **B** *noun.* A catfish of this family. **L19.**

siluroid /sɪˈljʊərɔɪd/ *adjective & noun.* **M19.**
[from next + -OID.]
ZOOLOGY. ▶**A** *adjective.* Of, pertaining to, or belonging to the suborder Siluroidea, which includes several families of catfish. **M19.**

▶ **B** *noun.* A siluroid fish, a catfish. **M19.**

silurus /sɪˈljʊərəs/ *noun.* Pl. **-ri** /-rʌɪ/. **E17.**
[Latin from Greek *silouros*.]
ZOOLOGY. A catfish of the genus *Silurus*, *esp.* the very large European catfish *S. glanis* (also called ***sheat-fish***, ***wels***).

silva *noun*, **silvan** *noun & adjective*, **silvatic** *adjective* vars. of SYLVA etc.

silver /ˈsɪlvə/ *noun & adjective.* Also (*Scot.*) **siller** /ˈsɪlə/.
[Old English *siolfor*, *seolfor* = Old Frisian *sel(o)ver*, Old Saxon *silubar*, *silobar*, Old High German *sil(a)bar*, *silbir* (Dutch *zilver*, German *Silber*), Old Norse *silfr*, Gothic *silubr*, from Germanic, rel. indeterminately to various Balto-Slavonic forms, all perh. ult. of oriental origin.]

▶ **A** *noun.* **1** A precious metal which is characterized by its lustrous white colour and great malleability and ductility, and is a chemical element of the transition series, atomic no. 47 (symbol Ag). Also (with defining word), any of various substances containing, resembling, or imitating, this. **OE.** ▸†**b** *transf.* Quicksilver, mercury. *rare.* **L15–E17.** ▸**c** = ***silver medal*** below. **M20.**

2 Silver as a valuable possession or medium of exchange; coin(s) made of silver or, later, cupro-nickel; (chiefly *Scot.*) money in general. **OE.**

3 Silver used to ornament textiles; thread or wire wholly or partly made of silver. **OE.**

4 *collect.* Articles made of silver; *spec.* vessels or implements, esp. cutlery, made of silver; *transf.* household cutlery of any material. **ME.**

5 HERALDRY. = ARGENT 3. **LME.**

6 A very pale grey colour. **L15.**

7 Any of various animals having silvery colouring or markings. **L18.**

8 A salt or compound of silver; a mixture, stain, etc., containing a silver salt. **L19.**

📖 **1** ***Britannia silver***, ***German silver***, ***mock silver***, ***native silver***, *red silver*, ***shell silver***, ***sterling silver***, etc. **2** J. BUCHAN You're a merchant . . . Are you here to make siller? J. K. JEROME George . . paid the man four-and-six in silver. **4** R. DAHL The . . . shining silver, the three wineglasses to each person. **6** E. WAUGH An enormous limousine of dove-grey and silver. *Chicago Tribune* Shimmering silvers, and rich plum purples.

▶ **B** *adjective.* **1** Made wholly or chiefly of silver. **OE.**

2 Coloured like silver; *spec.* (of hair) grey, white. **LME.**

3 Of a sound: having a clear gentle resonance; melodious. **E16.**

4 †**a** Of a payment, charge, etc.: made or levied in silver. *Scot.* & *US.* **L16–L18.** ▸**b** Advocating the adoption of silver as a currency or standard. *obsolete* exc. *Hist.* **L19.**

📖 **1** A. S. BYATT Breakfast was . . in silver dishes. **2** J. CONRAD His long silver locks stirred in the breeze. G. VIDAL The silver scales of fresh-caught fish. **3** F. MARRYAT He recalled . . her silver voice.

Phrases (of noun & adjective): ***born with a silver spoon in one's mouth***: see SPOON *noun.* ***cloth of silver***: see CLOTH *noun* 4. **dark red silver ore** = PYRARGYRITE. **light red silver ore** = PROUSTITE. ***litharge of silver***: see LITHARGE *noun* 1. ***on a silver platter***: see PLATTER 1. ***plate of silver***: see PLATE *noun* 18. ***piece of silver***: see PIECE *noun.* ***worth its weight in silver***, ***worth one's weight in silver***: see WEIGHT *noun.*

Special collocations & comb.: **silver age** a period regarded as inferior to a golden age; *spec.* (**a**) the period of Latin literature between the death of Augustus (AD 14) and *c* 150; (**b**) the period of Russian literature and art in the early 20th cent. **silver amalgam** a naturally occurring amalgam of silver and mercury. **silverback** a mature male mountain gorilla, distinguished by an area of white or silvery hair across the back. **silver band** a brass band playing silver-coloured instruments. **silver bath** PHOTOGRAPHY a solution of silver nitrate for the sensitizing of plates and printing paper; a dish to contain this. **silver beech** an evergreen beech, *Nothofagus menziesii*, native to New Zealand, with greyish-white bark; the timber of this tree. **silver beet** *Austral.* & *NZ* = ***seakale beet*** s.v. SEA *noun.* **silver-bell (tree)** = HALESIA. **silverberry** a silvery-leaved N. American oleaster, *Elaeagnus commutata*. **silverbill** either of two African and southern Asian waxbills of the genus *Lonchura*, *esp.* (more fully ***common silverbill***) *L. malabarica*. ***silver birch***: see BIRCH *noun* 1. **silverbird** a flycatcher, *Melaenornis semipartitus*, of NE Africa. **silver blond**, **silver blonde** *adjective* (of hair) of a very pale, silvery colour, esp. as the result of bleaching. **silver bream** (**a**) (see BREAM *noun* 1); (**b**) *Austral.* any of several sea breams. ***silver bridge***: see BRIDGE *noun*[1]. **silver bullet** (**a**) a bullet made of silver, supposedly the only weapon that could kill a werewolf; (**b**) (chiefly *N. Amer.*) a simple and seemingly magical solution to a complicated problem. **silver-bush** = ***Jupiter's beard*** (a) JUPITER 1. **silver certificate** US HISTORY a certificate or note certifying that silver to the amount stated on the face of the certificate has been deposited and is redeemable. **silver cord** (**a**) [*Ecclesiastes* 12:6] an imaginary cord whose loosening allows life to depart; (**b**) a symbol of excessive devotion between mother and child. **silver disc** a framed silver-coloured disc awarded to a recording artist or group for sales of a recording exceeding some figure (lower than those required for a gold disc), e.g. 250,000 for a single in the UK. **silver doctor** an artificial fishing-fly with a body of tinsel. ***silver-eared mesia***: see MESIA. **silver eel** (**a**) the young of eels of the genus *Anguilla* before the adult coloration is developed; (**b**) *US* = ***CUTLASS-fish***. **silver-eye** a white-eye, *esp.* one of an Australasian species of *Zosterops*. ***silver FIR***. **silverfish** (**a**) any of various silver-coloured fishes, *esp.* the tarpon; (**b**) a silvery bristletail, esp. *Lepisma saccharina*, found commonly in houses. **silver foil** (**a**) silver beaten into a thin sheet, slightly thicker than silver leaf; (**b**) thin metal (usu. aluminium) foil for wrapping confectionery etc. **silver-fork** *adjective* designating a school of novelists (orig. one of *c* 1830) or a style of novel distinguished by an affectation of gentility. **silver fox** (**a**) a N. American variety of the red fox with black silver-tipped hairs; the fur of this animal, esp. as a garment; (**b**) *S. Afr.* = ***Cape fox*** s.v. CAPE *noun*[1]. **silver gilt** (**a**) gilded silver; (**b**) an imitation gilding of silver leaf with yellow lacquer. **silver-glance** MINERALOGY = ARGENTITE. **silver grain** the glistening bands formed by the medullary rays when a plant stem is cut longitudinally. **silver-grey** *adjective & noun* (of) a pale grey colour. **silver jubilee** the twenty-fifth anniversary of a monarch's accession etc. ***silver key***: see KEY *noun*[1]. **silver king** = TARPON. ***silver lace***: see LACE *noun* 5. **silver Latin** literary Latin of the silver age. **silver-lead** a lead ore, usu. galena, containing silver. **silver leaf** (**a**) silver beaten into a wafer-thin sheet, thinner than silver foil; (**b**) any of several trees having silvery leaves, e.g. white poplar, *Populus alba*; (**c**) a disease of ornamental and fruit trees, esp. plum-trees, caused by the fungus *Stereum purpureum*, usu. indicated by silvery discoloration of the leaves and often fatal to affected branches. **silver-line(s)** any of several moths of the geometrid genus *Petrophora* or the noctuid genera *Bena* and *Pseudoips*, characterized by two or three whitish lines on the forewing. **silver lining** a consolation or hopeful feature in misfortune. ***silver mail***: see MAIL *noun*[1] 2. **silver maple** a maple of eastern N. America, *Acer saccharinum*, with leaves that are silvery underneath. **silver medal** a silver-coloured medal awarded for a second place in a contest, esp. the modern Olympic Games. **silver nitrate** a colourless solid, $AgNO_3$, that is used in photographic emulsions, as an antiseptic, etc. **Silver Office** *Hist.* an office formerly attached to the Court of Common Pleas. ***silver ORFE***. **silver paper** (**a**) a fine white tissue-paper; (**b**) paper covered with silver foil; (**c**) = ***silver foil*** (b). **silver perch** = MADEMOISELLE 4. **silver pheasant** a SE Asian grassland pheasant, *Lophura nycthemera*, the male of which has silvery-grey back, wings, and tail. **silver plate** (**a**) a thin flat piece of silver; (**b**) vessels or utensils made of or plated with silver or an alloy of silver; the material of which these are made. **silver plating** (**a**) the application of silver plate, the making of silver plate; (**b**) a coating of silver plate. **silver-point** (**a**) the art of drawing with a silver-pointed stylus on specially prepared paper; a drawing made in this way; (**b**) (usu. ***silver point***) the freezing point of silver under normal atmospheric pressure (about 962°C), as a thermometric fixed point. **silver-pointed** *adjective* coloured or tinged like a silver-point drawing. **silver poplar** *N. Amer.* the white poplar, *Populus alba*. **silver print** (now *rare*) a photograph produced by silver-printing. **silver-printing** (now *rare*) the process of producing a photograph on paper sensitized with a silver salt. ***silver quandong***: see QUANDONG 1b. **silver ring** HORSE-RACING an enclosure at a racecourse where smaller bets are laid. **silver salmon** = COHO. **silver sand** a fine pure white sand used in gardening. **silver screen** (**a**) a film projection screen with a highly reflective silver-coloured surface; (**b**) *the* cinema industry; motion pictures collectively. **silver service** a style of serving food in which an empty plate is placed before a diner and the different items of food are served separately on to it. **silverside** (**a**) the upper side of a round of beef from the outside of the leg; (**b**) *sing.* & in *pl.* any of various small mainly marine fishes of the family Atherinidae, which have an intense silvery line along each side (also called ***sand-smelt***, ***atherine***). **silver solder** a brazing alloy containing silver. **silver spoon** *fig.* a sign of future prosperity. ***silver standard***: see STANDARD *noun.* **Silver Star (medal)** a decoration awarded to members of the US Army and Navy for gallantry. **Silver State** *US* the State of Nevada. **Silver Stick** (the bearer of) a silver-tipped rod borne on State occasions by a particular officer of the Life Guards or their successors the

Household Cavalry Regiment. **silver string** *MUSIC*: covered with silver wire. **silver-studded blue** a European lycaenid butterfly, *Plebejus argus*, found esp. on sandy heathland. **silversword** a Hawaiian plant of the composite family, *Argyroxiphium sandwicense*, bearing long narrow leaves with silvery hairs and clusters of purplish flowers. ***silver sycamore***: see SYCAMORE 3b. **silver tabby** a tabby cat of silver-grey with darker stripes. **silver table** (*a*) a table made of or plated with silver; (*b*) a table used for the display of silverware, freq. with raised edges and a glass lid. **silvertail** *noun & adjective* (*Austral. & NZ slang*) (a person who is) socially prominent; (a person) displaying social aspirations. ***silver* TERAGLIN**. ***silver thatch***: see THATCH *noun* 2b. **silver thaw** the formation of a glassy coating of ice caused by rain freezing on impact or the refreezing of thawed ice. **silver-tip** a mature grizzly bear, with white-tipped hairs. **silver tongue** a gift of eloquence or persuasiveness. **silver-tongued** *adjective* sweet-spoken; eloquent, persuasive. **silver-tree** a South African tree with light silvery green leaves, *Leucadendron argenteum* (family Proteaceae). **silver trout** *N. Amer.* (*a*) any of several silver-coloured trout, *esp.* a variety of cutthroat trout, *Salmo clarki*, or rainbow trout, *S. gairdneri*; (*b*) = KOKANEE. **silverware** articles, esp. tableware, made of silver or an alloy of silver, or a metal coated with silver. **silver-washed fritillary** a large European woodland fritillary (butterfly), *Argynnis paphia*, with silvery bands across the underside of the hindwing. **silver wattle** a wattle, *Acacia dealbata*, with silvery-grey leaves, and small fragrant yellow flowers used in bouquets etc.; also called ***mimosa***. **silver wedding** the twenty-fifth anniversary of a wedding. **silverweed** a stoloniferous potentilla of roadsides etc., *Potentilla anserina*, with silvery leaves. **silver-white** *adjective & noun* (*a*) *adjective* of a silvery whiteness; (*b*) *noun* a silvery-white thing; *spec.* white lead used as a pigment. **silver-work** silverware. **silver Y** either of two noctuid moths, *Autographa gamma* and *Syngrapha interrogationis*, having a white Y-shaped mark on the forewing.

■ **silverish** *adjective* (*rare*) silvery M16. **silverize** *verb trans.* (*rare*) = SILVER *verb* 1, 2 E17. **silverless** *adjective* having no money ME. **silverlike** *adjective* resembling silver in colour or substance L17. **silverly** *adverb* (*poet.*) (*a*) with a silvery appearance or colour; (*b*) with a silvery sound: L16.

silver /ˈsɪlvə/ *verb.* ME.
[from the noun.]
1 *verb trans.* Cover or plate with silver. Freq. foll. by *over*. ME. ▸**b** Provide (glass) with a coating to make it reflective. M17.
2 *verb trans.* Make (esp. hair) silver in colour; give a silvery lustre to. LME.
3 *verb intrans.* Become silver in colour; flow with a silvery gleam. *poet.* M18.

📖 **1** G. W. FRANCIS Copper may be silvered over. **b** A. CARTER Glass walls . . silvered on the outside, so the whole room was a perfect mirror. **2** DISRAELI Thought, not time, had partially silvered . . his raven hair. R. RENDELL The frost . . would silver all the little grass verges. **3** J. CLARE The river silver'd down the plains.

■ **silverer** *noun* a person who silvers something; *esp.* a person who practises silver plating as an occupation: L16. **silvering** *noun* (*a*) the action of the verb; (*b*) silver plating: E18.

silverballi /sɪlvəˈbali/ *noun.* M19.
[Alt. of Arawak *siruaballi*.]
Any of several Guyanese trees of the genus *Nectandra*, of the laurel family, yielding a hard heavy timber; the wood of these trees.

Silverblu /ˈsɪlvəbluː/ *noun.* M20.
[from SILVER *adjective* + BLU(E *adjective*.]
A variety of mink distinguished by silvery fur; the fur of this mink.

silveriness /ˈsɪlv(ə)rɪnɪs/ *noun.* M19.
[from SILVERY + -NESS.]
The quality or character of being silvery.

silverite /ˈsɪlvərʌɪt/ *noun.* L19.
[from SILVER *noun* + -ITE[1].]
US HISTORY. An advocate of a silver monetary standard.

silverling /ˈsɪlvəlɪŋ/ *noun.* *arch.* E16.
[German *Silberling*.]
A shekel.

silvern /ˈsɪlv(ə)n/ *adjective.* Now *poet. & arch.* OE.
[from SILVER *noun & adjective* + -EN[4].]
1 = SILVER *adjective* 1. OE.
2 = SILVER *adjective* 2. LME.

silversmith /ˈsɪlvəsmɪθ/ *noun.* OE.
[from SILVER *noun* + SMITH *noun*.]
A worker in silver; a person who makes silverware.
■ **silversmithing** *noun* the art or practice of making silverware M20.

silvery /ˈsɪlv(ə)ri/ *adjective.* LME.
[from SILVER *noun* + -Y[1].]
1 Of the colour or brilliance of silver; *spec.* (of hair) white and lustrous. LME.
2 Having a clear gentle ringing sound; melodious. E17.

📖 **1** M. DIBDIN The roofs . . all silvery in the moonlight. **2** C. KINGSLEY In his ears one silvery voice was ringing.

Special collocations: **silvery arches** a Eurasian noctuid moth, *Polia hepatica*, which has silvery-grey forewings with brown and grey markings. **silvery gibbon** a silvery-grey gibbon, *Hylobates moloch*, occurring on Java; also called ***moloch gibbon***. **silvery marmoset** a Brazilian marmoset, *Callithrix penicillata*, with a mottled grey body, black face, and ringed tail. **silvery pout** a small gadid marine fish, *Gadiculus argenteus*, occurring in deeper waters off NW Europe and in the Mediterranean.

silvester, **silvestrian** *adjectives* vars. of SYLVESTER *adjective*, SYLVESTRIAN *adjective*[1].

silvex /ˈsɪlvɛks/ *noun.* M20.
[formed as next + arbitrary elem. *-ex*.]
A hormone weedkiller that is also effective against some woody plants.

silvi- /ˈsɪlvi/ *combining form.*
[from Latin *silva* a wood, woodland: see -I-.]
Of or pertaining to trees.
■ **silviˈchemical** *noun* a chemical obtained from part of a tree M20. **ˈsilvicide** *noun* a substance that kills trees M20.

silvics /ˈsɪlvɪks/ *noun.* Chiefly *US.* E20.
[formed as prec. + -ICS.]
The branch of forestry that deals with the growth and life of forest trees.
■ **silvical** *adjective* E20.

silviculture /ˈsɪlvɪkʌltʃə/ *noun.* Also **sylvi-**. L19.
[French *sylviculture*, *silvi-*, formed as SYLVA + French *culture* cultivation.]
The cultivation of woods or forests; the growing and tending of trees as a branch of forestry.
■ **silviˈcultural** *adjective* L19. **silviˈculturalist** *noun* (*rare*) = SILVICULTURIST L20. **silviˈculturist** *noun* a person engaged or skilled in silviculture L19.

silyl /ˈsʌɪlʌɪl, -lɪl/ *noun.* E20.
[from SIL(ANE + -YL.]
CHEMISTRY. The monovalent group or radical $\cdot SiH_3$; a substituted derivative of this, *esp.* one in which alkyl groups replace the hydrogen atoms. Usu. in *comb.*
■ **silyˈlation** *noun* a reaction or process in which a substance is converted into a form having silyl substituents M20. **silylate** *verb trans.* subject to silylation M20.

sim /sɪm/ *noun*[1]. *colloq.* L20.
[Abbreviation of SIMULATION.]
A video game that simulates an activity such as flying an aircraft or playing a sport.

SIM /sɪm/ *noun*[2]. L20.
[Abbreviation of *subscriber identification module*.]
In full ***SIM card***. A smartcard inside a mobile phone, carrying an identification number unique to the owner, storing personal data, and preventing operation if removed.

sima /ˈsʌɪmə/ *noun.* E20.
[from SI(LICA + MA(GNESIUM.]
GEOLOGY. The basal layer of the earth's crust, composed of rocks rich in silica and magnesia, which underlies the continental masses and forms the crust under the oceans; the material of which this is composed. Cf. SIAL.
■ **siˈmatic** *adjective* M20.

simantron *noun* var. of SEMANTRON.

simar /sɪˈmɑː/ *noun.* Also **cymar**. M17.
[French *simarre* from Italian *cimarra*, *zimarra*: cf. CHIMERE.]
1 A loose robe for women; *esp.* a chemise. M17.
2 = CHIMERE. M19.

simarouba /sɪməˈruːbə/ *noun.* Also **-ruba**. M18.
[French *simarouba*, Portuguese *simaruba* from Galibi *simaruppa*.]
1 Any of several tropical American trees of the former genus *Simarouba*, now included in the genus *Quassia* (family Simaroubaceae); esp. *Quassia amara* of Suriname. M18.
2 = ***Suriname*** QUASSIA. L18.

simazine /ˈsɪməziːn, ˈsʌɪ-/ *noun.* M20.
[from SYM(METRIC *adjective* + TRI)AZINE.]
A pre-emergence herbicide used esp. against broad-leaved weeds and grass among crops.

simba /ˈsɪmbə/ *noun.* Chiefly *E. Afr.* E20.
[Kiswahili.]
A lion; *fig.* a warrior.

simchah /ˈsɪmtʃə, -xə/ *noun.* M20.
[Hebrew *śimḥāh* rejoicing.]
A Jewish private party or celebration.

Simchat Torah /ˈsɪmtʃət ˈtɔːrə, ˈtəʊ-, ˈsɪmxət/ *noun.* L19.
[Hebrew *śimḥat tōrā*, from *śimḥat* construct case of *śimḥāh* SIMCHAH + TORAH.]
JUDAISM. The final day of the festival of Succoth, on which the annual cycle of the reading of the Torah is completed and begun anew.

Simeonite /ˈsɪmɪənʌɪt/ *noun & adjective.* E19.
[from *Simeon* (see below) + -ITE[1].]
(Designating) a follower or adherent of the Revd Charles Simeon (1759–1836), a leader of the Evangelical revival in the Church of England, or his doctrines.

simetite /ˈsɪmətʌɪt, ˈsiːm-/ *noun.* L19.
[from *Simeto*, a river in Sicily + -ITE[1].]
MINERALOGY. A variety of reddish or golden amber found in Sicily.

simi /ˈsɪmi/ *noun.* M20.
[Kiswahili *sime*.]
In E. Africa, a large two-edged knife.

simian /ˈsɪmɪən/ *adjective & noun.* E17.
[from Latin *simia* ape, perh. from *simus* from Greek *simos* snub-nosed, flat-nosed: see -AN.]
▶ **A** *adjective.* **1** Characteristic of apes; apelike. E17.
2 Of or pertaining to apes; consisting of apes. M19.

📖 **1** BETTY SMITH Her face almost simian with its wide mouth and flat thick nostrils. P. MATTHIESSEN I am almost on all fours . . and this simian stance shifts the weight forward. **2** *New Scientist* The relationship between the simian immunodeficiency viruses (SIVs) and the human viruses (HIVs).

▶ **B** *noun.* An ape, a monkey. L19.
■ **simial** *adjective* (now *rare*) = SIMIAN *adjective* E19.

similar /ˈsɪmɪlə/ *adjective & noun.* L16.
[French *similaire* or medieval Latin *similaris*, from Latin *similis* like: see -AR[1].]
▶ **A** *adjective.* †**1** Chiefly *ANATOMY.* Of the same substance or structure throughout; homogeneous. L16–E18.
2 Having a resemblance or likeness; of the same nature or kind. (Foll. by *to*, †*with*.) L16.
3 *spec.* in *MATH.* **a** Of two geometrical figures etc.: containing the same angles, having the same shape or proportions (though of different sizes). E18. ▸**b** Of two square matrices: such that one is equal to the other premultiplied by some matrix and postmultiplied by the inverse of the same matrix. E20.

📖 **2** H. JAMES Pictures, tapestries, enamels, porcelains, and similar gewgaws. S. J. PERELMAN A mechanism similar to a jukebox. M. FRAYN We come from similar backgrounds . . . We were at the same university. **similar motion** *MUSIC*: in which the voice parts move in the same direction.

▶ **B** *noun.* A person or thing similar to another; a counterpart (*of*). M17.
■ **similarize** *verb trans.* (*rare*) compare, liken E19. **similarly** *adverb* M18.

similarity /sɪmɪˈlarɪti/ *noun.* M17.
[from prec. + -ITY or from French *similarité*.]
1 The state or fact of being similar; resemblance. M17.
2 A point of resemblance. M19.

similative /ˈsɪmɪlətɪv/ *adjective & noun.* L19.
[from Latin *similis* like, SIMILAR + -ATIVE.]
GRAMMAR. ▶**A** *adjective.* Denoting or expressing similarity or likeness. L19.
▶ **B** *noun.* A similative word, case, etc. E20.

simile /ˈsɪmɪli/ *noun & verb.* LME.
[Latin, neut. of *similis* like, SIMILAR.]
▶ **A** *noun.* **1** A figure of speech involving the comparison of one thing with another of a different kind, as an illustration or ornament. LME.
†**2** Resemblance, similarity. Only in 17.
▶ **B** *verb trans.* Pres. pple & verbal noun **simileing**. Express by a simile. *rare.* E18.

simili- /ˈsɪmɪli/ *combining form.* *rare.* L19.
[from Latin *similis* like, SIMILAR: see -I-.]
Mock, imitation, as ***simili-diamond***, ***simili-gold***, etc.

similise *verb* var. of SIMILIZE.

similitude /sɪˈmɪlɪtjuːd/ *noun.* LME.
[Old & mod. French, or Latin *similitudo*, from *similis*: see SIMILAR, -TUDE.]
1 A person or thing resembling another; a counterpart or equal (*of*). *arch.* LME.
2 A likeness, an image. LME.
3 †**a** A sign, a symbol. LME–M16. ▸**b** A comparison drawn between two things; the expression of such comparison. Formerly also, a simile. LME. ▸†**c** A parable; an allegory. LME–L17.
4 The quality or state of being similar; similarity. Now *rare.* LME. ▸†**b** Likelihood, probability. LME–M16.

📖 **2** MILTON Man in our own image, Man in our similitude.

similize /ˈsɪmɪlʌɪz/ *verb.* Now *rare.* Also **-ise**. E17.
[from Latin *similis* like, or English SIMILE: see -IZE.]
1 *verb trans.* Imitate, copy. *rare.* E17.
†**2** *verb trans.* Compare, liken. Foll. by *to*, *with*. E–M17.
3 a *verb trans.* Symbolize; describe in similes. M17. ▸**b** *verb intrans.* Use a simile. L17.

simillimum /sɪˈmɪlɪməm/ *noun.* M19.
[Latin, neut. of *simillimus* superl. of *similis* like, SIMILAR.]
HOMOEOPATHY. A remedy which given in minute doses would produce in a healthy person symptoms most like those of the person to be treated.

similor /ˈsɪmɪlɔː/ *noun.* L18.
[French, from Latin *similis* like + French *or* gold.]
A very yellow kind of brass used in making cheap jewellery.

simious /ˈsɪmɪəs/ *adjective.* Now *rare.* E19.
[formed as SIMIAN: see -OUS.]
= SIMIAN *adjective.*

simkin /ˈsɪmkɪn/ *noun*[1]. *rare.* L17.
[Dim. of *Sim* pet-form of male forename *Simon*: see -KIN.]
A fool; a simpleton.

simkin /ˈsɪmkɪn/ *noun*[2]. *Anglo-Indian.* Also **simp-** /ˈsɪm(p)-/. **M19.**
[Repr. an Urdu pronunc.]
Champagne.

simlin /ˈsɪmlɪn/ *noun.* Also (earlier) **cymling** /ˈsɪmlɪŋ/. **L18.**
[Alt. of SIMNEL.]
1 The plant custard marrow. Cf. SIMNEL 3. *US.* **L18.**
2 = SIMNEL 2. *dial.* **M19.**

SIMM *abbreviation.*
COMPUTING. Single in-line memory module.

Simmental /ˈsɪm(ə)ntɑːl/ *noun.* **M20.**
[A valley in central Switzerland.]
(An animal of) a breed of large red and white cattle farmed for both milk and meat.

simmer /ˈsɪmə/ *verb & noun.* **M17.**
[Alt. of SIMPER *verb*[1].]
▶ **A** *verb.* **1** *verb intrans.* Of liquid: be at a heat just below boiling point; boil or bubble gently by reason of its temperature. Also predicated of the containing vessel or of any substance in the heated liquid (for cooking etc.). **M17.** ▸**b** *verb trans.* Keep in a heated condition just below boiling point; cause to simmer. **E19.**
2 *fig.* **a** Of a feeling etc.: be on the verge of developing; be in a state of subdued activity. **M18.** ▸**b** Of a person: be in a state of suppressed anger or excitement. **M19.**

📖 **1** A. GUINNESS Hot water simmered over a methylated spirits burner. H. NORMAN She brought it . . to a boil, then let it simmer. **b** J. GRIGSON When sauce is smooth, simmer it . . uncovered. **2a** M. RICHLER The fight that had been simmering for years. **b** D. L. SAYERS Wimsey was still simmering inwardly from this encounter. **simmer down** calm down from an angry or excited state.

▶ **B** *noun.* A simmering condition. **E19.**

📖 *Guardian* Bring back to a simmer, and cook gently.

■ **simmering** *verbal noun* the action of the verb; an instance of this: **E18.**

Simmerstat /ˈsɪməstat/ *noun.* Also **s-**. **M20.**
[from SIMMER *verb* + THERMO)STAT.]
(Proprietary name for) a thermostatic control for regulating the temperature of a hotplate on an electric cooker etc.

simmon /ˈsɪmən/ *noun & verb.* Now *dial.* **LME.**
[Alt.]
▶ **A** *noun.* Cement. **LME.**
▶ **B** *verb trans.* Cement. **M16.**

'simmon /ˈsɪmən/ *noun. US colloq.* **L18.**
[Abbreviation.]
A persimmon. Freq. *attrib.*

Simmonds' disease /ˈsɪmən(d)z dɪˌziːz/ *noun phr.* Also **Simmonds's disease** /ˈsɪmən(d)zɪz/. **E20.**
[Morris *Simmonds* (1855–1925), German pathologist.]
MEDICINE. Loss of pituitary function as a result of destruction of the anterior pituitary, resulting in gonadal, adrenocortical, and thyroid insufficiency; *esp.* the chronic form (cf. SHEEHAN'S SYNDROME).

simnel /ˈsɪmn(ə)l/ *noun.* **ME.**
[Old French *simenel* (mod. dial. *simnel*), ult. from Latin *simila*, *similago* or Greek *semidalis* fine flour. Cf. SEMOLINA.]
1 A kind of bread made with fine flour and cooked by boiling or baking. *obsolete* exc. *Hist. & dial.* **ME.**
2 More fully ***simnel cake***. A rich fruit cake with a marzipan layer on top and sometimes one inside, usually eaten at Easter or during Lent. **M17.**
3 = SIMLIN 1. *US.* **M17.**

simo chart /ˈsʌɪməʊ tʃɑːt/ *noun phr.* **E20.**
[Acronym, from *si*multaneous *mo*tion-cycle.]
A chart representing the bodily movements of a worker in relation to a time scale.

simoleon /sɪˈməʊlɪɒn/ *noun. US slang.* **L19.**
[Perh. after NAPOLEON *noun* 1.]
A dollar.

simoniac /sɪˈməʊnɪak/ *noun & adjective.* **ME.**
[Old & mod. French *simoniaque* or medieval Latin *simoniacus*, from late Latin *simonia*: see SIMONY, -AC.]
▶ **A** *noun.* A person who practises simony. **ME.**
▶ **B** *adjective.* = SIMONIACAL 1, 2. **LME.**

simoniacal /sʌɪməˈnʌɪək(ə)l/ *adjective.* **M16.**
[from prec. + -AL[1].]
1 Of the nature of or involving simony. **M16.**
2 Of a person: guilty of or practising simony. **M16.**
†**3** Tainted by simony. **L16–M17.**

simoniacally /sʌɪməˈnʌɪək(ə)li/ *adverb.* **E17.**
[from (the same root as) prec.: see -ICALLY.]
In a simoniacal manner.

Simonian /sʌɪˈməʊnɪən/ *noun & adjective.* Now *rare.* **E17.**
[medieval Latin *simonianus* simoniac, from *Simon*: see below, -IAN.]
Hist. ▶**A** *noun.* A member of an early Gnostic sect named after Simon Magus, 1st-cent. Samaritan sorcerer. Cf. SIMONY. **E17.**
▶ **B** *adjective.* Pertaining to or characteristic of this sect. **L19.**
■ **Simonianism** *noun* the doctrine of the Simonians **L19.**

simonious /sɪˈməʊnɪəs/ *adjective.* Now *rare* or *obsolete.* **E17.**
[from SIMONY + -OUS.]
= SIMONIACAL.

simonise *verb* var. of SIMONIZE.

simonist /ˈsʌɪmənɪst, ˈsɪm-/ *noun.* **M16.**
[from SIMONY + -IST.]
A person who practises or upholds simony.

Simonite /ˈsʌɪmənʌɪt/ *noun & adjective.* **M20.**
[from *Simon* (see below) + -ITE[1].]
Hist. ▶**A** *noun.* A supporter of the Liberal politician Sir John Simon (1873–1954); *spec.* a member of the Liberal National Party which seceded in 1931 from the official Liberal Party led by Sir Herbert Samuel (see SAMUELITE). **M20.**
▶ **B** *adjective.* Of or pertaining to Simon or his supporters. **M20.**

simonize /ˈsʌɪmənʌɪz/ *verb trans.* Chiefly *US.* Also **-ise**. **M20.**
[from *Simoniz* proprietary name: see -IZE.]
Polish using Simoniz car polish.

Simon Pure /sʌɪmən ˈpjʊə/ *noun & adjective. colloq.* **L18.**
[A character in Centlivre's *A Bold Stroke for a Wife* (1717), who is impersonated by another character during part of the play.]
▶ **A** *noun.* ***the Simon Pure***, ***the real Simon Pure***, the real or genuine person or thing. **L18.**

📖 W. C. PRIME Show us the real mummy, the Simon Pure.

▶ **B** *adjective.* (With hyphen.) Real, genuine. Also, pure, unadulterated; honest. **M19.**

📖 W. A. PERCY Mistaken my unwilling preparations for battle for simon-pure heroism.

Simon Says /sʌɪmən ˈsɛz/ *noun phr.* **M19.**
[from male forename *Simon* + SAY *verb*[1].]
A children's game in which players must obey the leader's instructions if (and only if) they are prefaced with the words 'Simon says'.

simony /ˈsʌɪməni, ˈsɪm-/ *noun.* **ME.**
[Old & mod. French *simonie* from late Latin *simonia*, from *Simon* Magus: see -Y[3].]
1 The buying or selling of ecclesiastical privileges, e.g. pardons or benefices. **ME.**
†**2** The money paid for such privileges. *rare.* **L16–E18.**

simool /ˈsɪmʊl, ˈʃɪm-/ *noun.* Also **simul**, **semul** /ˈsɛmʊl/. **M19.**
[Bengali, Hindi, etc. *simul*.]
The Indian silk-cotton tree, *Bombax ceiba*.

simoom /sɪˈmuːm/ *noun.* Also **-moon** /-ˈmuːn/. **L18.**
[Arab. *samūm*, from *samma* to poison.]
A hot dry dust-laden wind blowing at intervals in the African and Asian (esp. Arabian) deserts.

simp /sɪmp/ *noun. colloq.* (now chiefly *US*). **E20.**
[Abbreviation.]
A simpleton, a fool.

simpatico /sɪmˈpatiko, sɪmˈpatɪkəʊ/ *adjective.* Also (fem.) ***-ca*** /-ka, -kə/. **M19.**
[Spanish *simpático*, from *simpatía*, or Italian *simpatico*, from *simpatia*, both formed as SYMPATHY.]
Pleasing, likeable; congenial.

simper /ˈsɪmpə/ *noun.* **L16.**
[from SIMPER *verb*[2].]
An affectedly coquettish, coy, or bashful smile.

simper /ˈsɪmpə/ *verb*[1] *intrans. obsolete* exc. *dial.* **L15.**
[Perh. imit.: see -ER[5].]
Simmer.

simper /ˈsɪmpə/ *verb*[2]. **M16.**
[Origin uncertain: cf. Danish, Norwegian, and Swedish dial. *semper*, *simper*, German *zimper*, *zimpfer* elegant, delicate. Cf. next.]
1 *verb intrans.* & †*trans.* (with *it*). Smile in an affectedly coquettish, coy, or bashful manner. **M16.**
†**2** *verb intrans.* Glimmer, twinkle. *rare.* **E–M17.**
3 *verb trans.* Say with or express by a simper. **E19.**
4 *verb intrans.* Whimper. *dial.* **M19.**

📖 **1** S. MIDDLETON Girls simpered over their tips, thanking him with blushes. **3** C. MERIVALE 'Friends everywhere!' simpered the fool.

■ **simperer** *noun* **M18.** **simpering** *ppl adjective* (**a**) that simpers; (**b**) accompanied by simpering; affected: **L16.** **simperingly** *adverb* **L16.**

†**simper-de-cocket** *noun.* **E16–E18.**
[Fanciful formation, from prec. + COCKET *adjective.*]
An affected coquettish air; a person with such an air, a flirt.

simpkin *noun* var. of SIMKIN *noun*[2].

simple /ˈsɪmp(ə)l/ *adjective, noun, & adverb.* **ME.**
[Old & mod. French from Latin *simplus*.]
▶ **A** *adjective.* **1** Free from duplicity or guile; honest, open, ingenuous. **ME.**
2 Free from pride or ostentation; unpretentious. **ME.**
3 Not complicated or elaborate; characterized by a lack of grandeur or luxury; plain, unadorned. **ME.** ▸**b** Of a person: unsophisticated, unspoiled. **L18.**
4 Of a person: of low rank or status; mean, common, humble. **ME.** ▸**b** Of a titular rank: ordinary; not further distinguished. **ME.**
†**5** Poor, wretched, pitiful. **ME–L15.**
6 Small, insignificant, slight; of little account or value. Now *arch. & dial.* **ME.**
7 a Deficient in knowledge through lack of learning; uneducated; inexperienced. **ME.** ▸**b** Deficient in ordinary sense or intelligence; foolish, stupid; mentally handicapped. **LME.**
8 a With nothing added; unqualified; neither more nor less than; mere, pure. **ME.** ▸**b** *MEDICINE.* Of wounds, diseases, etc.: unaccompanied by complications. **LME.** ▸**c** *LAW.* Not qualified or restricted by further facts or circumstances; *spec.* (of a contract) made not under seal but orally or in writing. **M16.**
9 Composed of a single substance, ingredient, or element; not composite or complex in structure; *BOTANY* (of a leaf or stem) not divided or branched; *GRAMMAR* (of a tense) formed without an auxiliary; *OPTICS* (of a lens, microscope, etc.) consisting of a single lens or component. **LME.** ▸**b** *MATH.* Designating a group that has no proper normal subgroup, and an algebra or ring that has no proper ideal. **L19.**
10 Presenting little or no difficulty; easily done or understood. **M16.**

📖 **1** R. RENDELL The happy man's simple, unclouded smile. Q. BELL She was . . simple with the simplicity of a child. **2** TENNYSON Some of the simple great ones. **3** H. L. MENCKEN He purged his style of ornament and it became almost baldly simple. J. WYNDHAM It's . . Jane's economies and simple-living that's built up the savings. M. SCHAPIRO Simple as it looks, the painting is deeply contrived. A. BURGESS She wore straight simple dresses. **b** SHELLEY Pastoral people . . , Simple and spirited. **4** R. BURNS There's wealth and ease for gentlemen, And semple folk maun fecht and fen'. **6** SHAKES. *Hen. VIII* I am a simple woman, much too weak T'oppose your cunning. **7a** SHAKES. *Two Gent.* I'll show my mind According to my shallow simple skill. W. COWPER All the simple and unlettered poor, Admire his learning. G. GREENE She is very ignorant, very simple. **b** B. CHATWIN She sang . . incoherent songs and was thought to be simple. **8a** T. HARDY Suffering under an agitation more than that of simple fatigue. A. SILLITOE Grow out of lying by the simple process of growing up. **10** I. MURDOCH It was all so absurdly simple. J. OSBORNE The most simple, everyday actions. *Which?* Children learn by repeating simple exercises.

Phrases: ***pure and simple***: see PURE *adjective.* **Simple Simon** [a character in a nursery rhyme] a foolish person. ***tout simple***: see TOUT *adverb.*

Special collocations: **simple eye** an eye of an arthropod with only one lens; also called ***ocellus***. **simple family** *ANTHROPOLOGY*: consisting of a father and mother and their children. **simple feast** *ECCLESIASTICAL HISTORY* any of the lower ranking feasts. **simple fracture** a fracture of the bone only, without damage to surrounding tissues and no break in the overlying skin. ***simple harmonic motion***: see ***harmonic motion*** s.v. HARMONIC *adjective.* **simple-hearted** *adjective* ingenuous, honest; unsophisticated, unspoiled. **simple-heartedness** the quality of being simple-hearted. ***simple interest***: see INTEREST *noun.* **simple interval** *MUSIC*: of one octave or less. ***simple machine***: see MACHINE *noun* 4b. **simple majority** a majority in which the highest number of votes cast for any one person etc. exceeds the second highest number, while not constituting an absolute majority. ***simple pendulum***: see PENDULUM *noun.* ***simple*** PISTIL. ***simple reproduction***: see REPRODUCTION 1f. **simple sentence** *GRAMMAR*: with a single subject and predicate. **simple structure** *STATISTICS* a model in which numerous variables, showing various degrees of correlation, have their variances assigned to a smaller number of factors so that no one factor affects all the variables. **simple time** *MUSIC*: with two, three, or four beats in a bar. **simple vow** *ECCLESIASTICAL* a dispensable vow taken by a member of a religious order.

▶ **B** *absol.* as *noun.* **1 a** A person of humble or low rank (usu. in *pl.*); such people collectively. **LME.** ▸**b** A person who is uneducated, unsophisticated, or unsuspecting; such people collectively. **L15.** ▸**c** In *pl.* Foolish behaviour; foolishness. *obsolete* exc. *dial.* **M17.**
2 a A single uncompounded thing; *esp.* one serving as an ingredient in a mixture. Now *rare.* **LME.** ▸**b** *spec.* = SIMPLEX *noun* 1. Now *rare.* **LME.** ▸**c** *LOGIC.* A simple proposition or idea. **M17.**
3 Orig., a medicine made from only one constituent, esp. from one plant. Now (*arch.*), a plant used for medicinal purposes. Usu. in *pl.* **M16.**
4 *WEAVING.* In a draw-loom, each of a set of weighted lines pulled by the draw-boy. **M18.**
▶ **C** *adverb.* Simply. *poet.* **L16.**

simple /ˈsɪmp(ə)l/ *verb intrans. arch.* M17.
[from SIMPLE *noun*.]
Seek for or gather medicinal plants.
■ **simpler** *noun* a person who gathers medicinal plants L16.

simple-minded /sɪmp(ə)lˈmʌɪndɪd/ *adjective.* M18.
[from SIMPLE *adjective* + MINDED.]
Ingenuous, unsophisticated, unspoiled; deficient in knowledge; foolish, stupid.

📖 DAY LEWIS Such people, easy-going, simple-minded, affectionate. J. MORTIMER A remarkably simple-minded view of the Christian religion.

■ **simple-mindedly** *adverb* M20. **simple-mindedness** *noun* M19.

simpleness /ˈsɪmp(ə)lnɪs/ *noun.* LME.
[from SIMPLE *adjective* + -NESS.]
The quality or state of being simple.

simplesse /ˈsɪmplɛs/ *noun. arch.* ME.
[Old & mod. French, formed as SIMPLE *adjective, noun, & adverb*: see -ESS[2].]
Simpleness.

simpleton /ˈsɪmp(ə)lt(ə)n/ *noun.* M17.
[from SIMPLE *adjective* + -TON, as in many surnames derived from place-names.]
A foolish or gullible person; a mentally handicapped person.

simplex /ˈsɪmplɛks/ *adjective & noun.* L16.
[Latin = single, var. of *simplus* SIMPLE *adjective* with 2nd elem. as in *duplex*, *multiplex*, etc.]
▶ **A** *adjective.* **1** Composed of or characterized by a single part or structure. L16.
2 TELECOMMUNICATIONS & COMPUTING. Designating a system, circuit, etc., along which signals can be sent in only one direction at a time. L19.
3 GENETICS. Of a polyploid individual: having the dominant allele of a particular gene represented once. E20.
▶ **B** *noun.* **1** A word without an affix; a simple uncompounded word. L19.
2 GEOMETRY. The figure, in any given number of dimensions, that is bounded by the least possible number of hyperplanes (e.g. the simplex in two dimensions is a triangle). E20.
3 LINGUISTICS. = KERNEL *noun*[1] 6f. M20.
Comb.: **simplex method** MATH. a method of maximizing a linear function of several variables under several constraints on other linear functions; ***simplex tableau***: see TABLEAU 2b.

simplex munditiis /ˌsɪmplɛks mʊnˈdɪtiːs/ *noun & adjectival phr.* M18.
[Latin, lit. 'simple in your adornments'.]
▶ **A** *noun phr.* Beauty without adornment or ostentation. M18.
▶ **B** *adjectival phr.* Unostentatiously beautiful. L19.

simplicial /sɪmˈplɪʃ(ə)l/ *adjective.* E20.
[from Latin as next + -IAL.]
GEOMETRY. Designating or pertaining to a simplex.

simplicist /ˈsɪmplɪsɪst/ *noun & adjective.* L16.
[from Latin *simplic-*, SIMPLEX + -IST.]
▶ **A** *noun.* †**1** A simplist. *rare.* L16–E17.
2 A person who simplifies something. *rare.* E20.
▶ **B** *adjective.* Characterized by simplicity; simplistic. M20.
■ **simpliˈcistic** *adjective* characterized by excessive simplicity M20.

simpliciter /sɪmˈplɪsɪtə/ *adverb.* LME.
[Latin, formed as prec.]
Chiefly SCOTS LAW. Simply; without qualification; unconditionally.

simplicity /sɪmˈplɪsɪti/ *noun.* LME.
[Old & mod. French *simplicité* or Latin *simplicitas*, *-tat-*, formed as SIMPLICIST: see -ITY.]
1 The quality or state of being simple. LME.
2 An instance of this. L16.
3 A simple person. *rare.* L16.

simplification /ˌsɪmplɪfɪˈkeɪʃ(ə)n/ *noun.* L17.
[French, formed as next: see -ATION.]
1 The action or an act of simplifying something; the result of this. L17.
2 LOGIC. A principle of inference, that the joint assertion of two propositions implies the assertion of the first. E20.
■ **simplificatory** *adjective* that simplifies something M20.

simplify /ˈsɪmplɪfʌɪ/ *verb.* M17.
[French *simplifier* from medieval Latin *simplificare*, from Latin *simplus*: see SIMPLE *adjective, noun, & adverb*, -FY.]
†**1** *verb trans.* Make into a single form or structure; unify. *rare.* M–L17.
2 a *verb trans.* Make simple or less complex or elaborate; make easy or more understandable. M18. ▸**b** *verb intrans.* Become (more) simple. M20.
■ **simplifier** *noun* E19.

simplism /ˈsɪmplɪz(ə)m/ *noun.* L19.
[from SIMPLE *adjective* + -ISM.]
†**1** Affected simplicity of literary style. *rare.* Only in L19.
2 A tendency to oversimplify; an oversimplification. M20.

simplist /ˈsɪmplɪst/ *noun*[1]. *arch.* L16.
[from SIMPLE *noun* + -IST.]
A person who studies medicinal plants.

simplist /ˈsɪmplɪst/ *noun*[2] *& adjective.* Also ***simpliste*** /sɛ̃plist (*pl. same*)/. E20.
[French *simpliste*, formed as SIMPLE *adjective* + -IST.]
▶ **A** *noun.* A person who adopts an oversimplified or one-sided view of something. E20.
▶ **B** *adjective.* That oversimplifies; one-sided; plain in style. E20.

simplistic /sɪmˈplɪstɪk/ *adjective.* M19.
[from SIMPLE *adjective* + -ISTIC.]
1 Of or pertaining to a simplist or simples. *rare.* M19.
2 Of the nature of or characterized by extreme, excessive, or misleading simplicity. L19.

📖 **2** *Health Promotion* Gross averages of alcohol consumption are simplistic and have little use.

■ **simplistically** *adverb* M20.

simply /ˈsɪmpli/ *adverb.* ME.
[from SIMPLE *adjective* + -LY[2].]
1 In an honest or ingenuous manner; without guile; openly. ME.
2 a Plainly; without luxury; in a simple unelaborate style; without complication. Formerly also, humbly. ME. ▸**b** So as to be readily understood, clearly. LME. ▸**c** LOGIC. By which the quantity of the proposition remains unchanged in a conversion. Opp. PER ACCIDENS 2. L16.
3 a Without addition or qualification; merely, only. ME. ▸**b** Without exception; without doubt, absolutely. Freq. as an intensive. L16.
†**4** Poorly, wretchedly; indifferently; inadequately. ME–M18.
5 In a foolish or stupid manner; without ordinary intelligence or sense. Formerly also, ignorantly. M16.

📖 **1** J. RUSKIN Beautifully and simply, as a child ought to dance. **2a** S. BEDFORD He lives very simply. *Punch* The story develops as simply as one could imagine. **b** H. JAMES The great views, to put it simply, would be too much for her. **3a** J. B. PRIESTLEY The woman had not been unfriendly but simply absent-minded. J. M. COETZEE Ready to believe he was simply a vagrant. *Good Housekeeping* Simply add water . . simmer and serve. **b** I. MURDOCH You simply haven't the faintest idea. E. FIGES Make a house under the . . table and vanish for simply ages.

Phrases: **simply connected** MATH. (of a surface or other continuous set of points) connected in such a way that every closed curve lying within it forms the boundary of some surface lying within it.

Simpson's rule /ˈsɪmps(ə)nz ruːl/ *noun phr.* L19.
[Thomas *Simpson* (1710–61), English mathematician.]
MATH. An arithmetical rule for estimating the area under a curve where the values of an odd number of ordinates, including those at each end, are known.

simpulum /ˈsɪmpjʊləm/ *noun.* Pl. **-la** /-lə/. M18.
[Latin.]
ROMAN ANTIQUITIES. A small ladle used in libations.

simpy /ˈsɪmpi/ *adjective. US colloq.* M20.
[Perh. from SIMP + -Y[1].]
Foolish, simple-minded.

sim-sim /ˈsɪmsɪm/ *noun.* E20.
[Arab. *simsim*. Cf. SEMSEM, SESAME.]
= SESAME.

simson *noun* see SENCION.

simul /ˈsɪm(ə)l/ *noun*[1]. M20.
[from SIMUL(TANEOUS).]
A display in which a player plays a number of games of chess simultaneously against different opponents.

simul *noun*[2] var. of SIMOOL.

simulacre /ˈsɪmjʊleɪkə/ *noun. arch.* LME.
[Old & mod. French, or its source Latin SIMULACRUM.]
1 An image of a god etc. as an object of worship; an idol, an effigy. LME.
2 A material or mental representation of a person or thing. LME.
■ **simuˈlacral** *adjective* (*rare*) resembling an image L19.

simulacrum /sɪmjʊˈleɪkrəm/ *noun.* Pl. **-crums**, **-cra** /-krə/. L16.
[Latin, from *simulare* SIMULATE *verb*. Cf. prec.]
1 A material image or representation of a person or thing, *esp.* a god. L16.
2 A thing having the appearance but not the substance or proper qualities of something; a deceptive imitation or substitute; a pretence. E19.

📖 **1** R. SCRUTON Removed her as she died, leaving this waxy simulacrum in her place. **2** L. STRACHEY He was a mere simulacrum of his former self. M. SCAMMELL Life reverted to a simulacrum of what it had been.

simuland /ˈsɪmjʊland/ *noun.* M20.
[from Latin *simulandum* neut. gerundive of *simulare* simulate: see -AND.]
That which is simulated by a mathematical or computer model.

simulant /ˈsɪmjʊlənt/ *noun & adjective.* M18.
[Latin *simulant-* pres. ppl stem of *simulare* SIMULATE *verb*: see -ANT[1].]
▶ **A** *noun.* A person who or thing which simulates something else. M18.

📖 *Nature* Yttrium aluminium garnet . . and cubic zirconia are . . used as diamond simulants.

▶ **B** *adjective.* Simulating; presenting the appearance *of* something else. E19.

simular /ˈsɪmjʊlə/ *noun & adjective.* Now *rare.* E16.
[Irreg. from Latin *simulare* + -AR[1], perh. after SIMILAR *adjective*.]
▶ **A** *noun.* A person who or thing which simulates something. (Foll. by *of*.) E16.
▶ **B** *adjective.* Simulated, pretended, feigned. E17.

simulate /ˈsɪmjʊlət/ *adjective. arch.* LME.
[Latin *simulatus* pa. pple of *simulare*: see next, -ATE[2].]
Simulated, pretended, feigned.

simulate /ˈsɪmjʊleɪt/ *verb.* M17.
[Latin *simulat-* pa. ppl stem of *simulare*, from *similis* like: see -ATE[3].]
▶ **I** *verb trans.* **1** Assume the appearance or signs of (a feeling etc.); feign; pretend, pretend to be; imitate. M17.
2 Present a strong resemblance to (a thing). M17.
3 Imitate the conditions of (a situation or process), esp. for the purpose of training etc.; *spec.* produce a computer model of (a process). M20.

📖 **1a** B. MOORE That painful posture . . which simulates the outstretched arms of the crucified Christ. J. A. MICHENER She lay there simulating a corpse. R. RENDELL It was impossible . . to force a smile, to simulate pleasure. **b** M. COOKE Flowering plants which . . simulate cryptograms. **c** M. DIBDIN A complicated electronic box of tricks that switched on and off at random to simulate occupancy.

▶ **II** *verb intrans.* **4** Pretend, feign. *rare.* E19.
■ **simulated** *ppl adjective* (**a**) that simulates something; (**b**) (of a material etc.) manufactured in imitation of some other (esp. more expensive) material: E17.

simulation /sɪmjʊˈleɪʃ(ə)n/ *noun.* ME.
[Old & mod. French, or Latin *simulatio(n-)*, formed as prec.: see -ATION.]
1 The action or an act of simulating something; COMPUTING a model produced by this means. ME.
2 PHILOLOGY. The development of an altered form of a word by association with another word wrongly taken to be its source. *rare.* L19.

📖 **1** T. COLLINS A ghastly simulation of cheerfulness. *Which Micro?* Exact simulation of Britain's top golf courses.

simulative /ˈsɪmjʊlətɪv/ *adjective.* L15.
[from SIMULATE *adjective, verb* + -IVE.]
Characterized by simulation or pretence.
■ **simulatively** *adverb* E19.

simulator /ˈsɪmjʊleɪtə/ *noun.* M19.
[from SIMULATE *verb* + -OR.]
1 A person who or thing which simulates something. M19.
2 *spec.* **a** An apparatus designed to simulate the operations of a more complex system (e.g. a vehicle), esp. for training purposes. M20. ▸**b** COMPUTING. In full ***simulator program***. A program enabling a computer to execute programs written for a different computer. M20.

simulcast /ˈsɪm(ə)lkɑːst/ *verb & noun.* M20.
[from SIMUL(TANEOUS + BROAD)CAST *verb, noun*.]
▶ **A** *verb trans.* Pa. t. & pple **-cast**. Broadcast (a programme) simultaneously on radio and television, or on two or more channels. M20.
▶ **B** *noun.* A programme broadcast in this way. M20.

simulfix /ˈsɪm(ə)lfɪks/ *noun.* M20.
[from Latin *simul* at the same time + AF)FIX *noun*.]
PHONETICS. = SUPERFIX.
■ **simulfiˈxation** *noun* the action of affixing a simulfix M20.

simulium /sɪˈmjuːlɪəm/ *noun.* E20.
[mod. Latin *Simulium* (see below), from Latin *simulare* imitate + -IUM.]
Any of various small dark gnatlike flies of the family Simuliidae, esp. of the genus *Simulium*, which are serious pests in some areas because of their bloodsucking habits, and may be the vector of certain diseases. Also called ***blackfly***, ***buffalo gnat***.

simultanagnosia /ˌsɪm(ə)ltanag'nəʊsɪə/ *noun.* M20.
[from German *simultan* simultaneous + Greek *agnōsia* ignorance (cf. AGNOSIA).]
PSYCHOLOGY. The loss or absence of the ability to perceive elements (such as the details of a picture) as components of a whole.

Simultaneism /sɪm(ə)l'teɪnɪɪz(ə)m, -nɪz(ə)m/ *noun.* Also in French form ***Simultanéisme*** /simyltaneism/. E20.
[French *Simultanéisme*.]
1 = ORPHISM 2. E20.
2 A movement in modern French poetry aiming at the effect of simultaneity of images and sounds. M20.
▪ **simultaneist** *noun & adjective* (*a*) *noun* a practitioner of Simultaneism; (*b*) *adjective* characteristic of Simultaneism: E20.

simultaneous /sɪm(ə)l'teɪnɪəs/ *adjective.* M17.
[from medieval Latin *simultaneus*, prob. after late Latin *momentaneus*: see -OUS.]
1 Occurring, operating, or existing at the same time. M17.
2 Of a chess display or exhibition: involving a number of games played against a number of opponents at the same time by one player. M19.

> 📖 **1** D. M. THOMAS The simultaneous translations into five languages. *Japan Times* Amenities . . designed for simultaneous use by the disabled and non-disabled.

Special collocations: **simultaneous contrast** ART the effect of mutual modification of two contiguous areas of colour. **simultaneous equation** MATH. two or more equations all of which are satisfied by the same set of values of the variables.
▪ **simultaneity** /-tə'niːɪti, -tə'neɪɪti/ *noun* the quality or fact of being simultaneous; *spec.* (ART) the simultaneous representation of several aspects of the same object: M17. **simultaneously** *adverb* L17. **simultaneousness** *noun* L18.

simurg /sɪ'məːg/ *noun.* Also **simurgh**. L18.
[Persian *sīmurġ*, from Pahlavi *sēn* eagle + *murġ* bird.]
IRANIAN MYTHOLOGY. A giant bird believed to have the power of speech and reasoning and to be of great age.

sin /sɪn/ *noun*[1].
[Old English *syn(n)* rel. to Indo-European forms with dental, as Old French *sende*, Old Saxon *sundea*, Old High German *sunt(e)a*, *sund(e)a* (German *Sünde*), Old Norse *synd*, prob. cogn. with Latin *sons*, *sont-* guilty.]
1 Transgression of divine law; action or behaviour constituting this; the condition or state resulting from such transgression. OE.
2 An act constituting transgression of divine law; a violation of a religious or moral principle. OE. ▸**b** *transf.* An offence against a principle or standard. L18.
3 A pity; a shame. Now only *Scot. dial.* ME.

> 📖 **1** DRYDEN 'Tis sin to misemploy an hour. B. TARKINGTON They could not spend money . . without a sense of sin. **2** R. FRAME He managed to resist the too easy sin of vanity. M. FRAYN Tortured by the consciousness of having committed every sin. **b** *Nursing Times* Overspending is not always a sin.

Phrases: ***actual sin***: see ACTUAL *adjective* 1. **as sin** *colloq.* very (after an adjective with unfavourable meaning, as *ugly*, *miserable*). ***besetting sin***: see BESET *verb* 2. **live in sin** *colloq.* (of an unmarried couple) live together as man and wife, cohabit. ***original sin***: see ORIGINAL *adjective*. ***seven deadly sins***: see SEVEN *adjective*. ***sin of commission***: see COMMISSION *noun*. ***sin of omission***: see OMISSION 1. ***sins of the flesh***: see FLESH *noun*.
Comb.: **sin bin** *slang* (*a*) = PENALTY **box**; (*b*) a place where young offenders are sent for detention, punishment, or rehabilitation; a prison; **sin-bin** *verb trans.* (*slang*) send to a 'sin bin'; **sin bosun** *Nautical slang* a ship's chaplain; **sin-flood** *arch.* the Deluge; **sin-offering** [prob. after German *Sündopfer* translating Hebrew *ḥaṭṭā't*, from *ḥāṭā'* to sin] in the older Jewish religion, an offering made as an atonement for sin; **sin-shifter** *slang* a clergyman; **sin tax** *colloq.* a tax on a thing considered undesirable, such as alcohol, tobacco, or gambling.
▪ **sinward** *adverb* [orig. *to sinward*] towards or in the direction of sin LME.

sin /sʌɪn/ *noun*[2]. M18.
[Abbreviation.]
MATH. Sine (of).

sin /sɪn/ *verb.* Infl. **-nn-**.
[Old English *syngian*, from Germanic; later from the noun.]
1 *verb intrans.* Commit a sin. OE. ▸**b** *spec.* Fornicate or commit adultery *with*. ME. ▸**c** Offend *against* a principle or standard. E18.
2 *verb trans.* Commit (a sin). ME.
3 *verb trans.* **a** Bring (oneself) *into* a state by sinning. M17. ▸**b** Drive *away* by sinning. L17.

> 📖 **1** T. F. POWYS He believed that men had souls, that men sinned. **2 sin one's mercies** be ungrateful for one's good fortune.

▪ **sinnable** *adjective* (*rare*) capable of sinning L16.

sin /sɪn/ *adverb, preposition, & conjunction.* Now *Scot. & north.* ME.
[Contr. of SITHEN; later interpreted as abbreviation of SINCE. Cf. SEN *preposition, conjunction, & adverb*, SYNE *adverb*.]
▸ **A** *adverb.* †**1** = SINCE *adverb* 1. ME–E16.
2 = SINCE *adverb* 2. LME.
3 = SINCE *adverb* 3. LME.
▸ **B** *preposition.* = SINCE *preposition*. ME.
▸ **C** *conjunction.* = SINCE *conjunction*. ME.

Sinaean /sʌɪ'niːən/ *adjective. rare.* M17.
[Irreg. from late Latin *Sinae* from Greek *Sinai*, from Arab. *ṣīn*, name for the Chinese empire: see -AN.]
Chinese.

Sinaitic /sʌɪneɪ'ɪtɪk/ *adjective.* L18.
[from *Sinai* (see below) + -ITIC.]
Of or pertaining to Mount Sinai or the Sinai peninsula, in Egypt.
▪ Also **Sinaic** *adjective* M18.

Sinanthropus /sɪ'nanθrəpəs/ *noun.* E20.
[mod. Latin former genus name, from SINO-[1] + Greek *anthrōpos* man.]
= ***PEKING man***.
▪ **Sinanthropic** /-'θrɒp-/ *adjective* M20. **Sinanthropoid** *adjective* resembling Sinanthropus M20.

sinapine /'sɪnəpiːn/ *noun.* Also †**-in**. M19.
[from Latin *sinapis* mustard + -INE[5].]
CHEMISTRY. An alkaloid, $C_{16}H_{25}NO_6$, which occurs in the seeds of black mustard.
▪ **sinapic** *adjective*: ***sinapic acid***, an aromatic carboxylic acid, $C_{11}H_{12}O_5$, derived from sinapine M19. **sinapyl** /-pʌɪl, -pɪl/ *noun* the radical $C_{10}H_{11}O_3{\cdot}CH_2{\cdot}$ derived from sinapic acid E20

sinapism /'sɪnəpɪz(ə)m/ *noun.* Now *rare.* L16.
[French *sinapisme* or late Latin *sinapismus* from Greek *sinapismos* use of a mustard plaster (*sinapisma*), from *sinapi* mustard, of Egyptian origin; see -ISM.]
MEDICINE. A mustard plaster.

since /sɪns/ *adverb, conjunction, preposition, & adjective.* LME.
[Contr. of SITHENCE, or from SIN *adverb* + -S[3] (cf. HENCE for the *-ce* spelling).]
▸ **A** *adverb.* †**1** Then; immediately afterwards. LME–M16.
2 a From that time until now or until the time being considered. Freq. preceded by *ever*. LME. ▸**b** At some or any time between that time and now or that time and the time being considered. M16.
3 Ago; before now. Preceded by a specified interval of time or *long*. L15.

> 📖 **2a** I. COLEGATE He had been elected to Parliament in 1934 and had been there ever since. M. KEANE A mammoth range . . installed in . . 1897 . . had devoured coal with voracious greed ever since. **b** G. GREENE Smashed last week, and I haven't been into town since. *Daily Mirror* Scotland Yard have since taken out a warrant for his arrest. **3** A. CARTER The tribe had long since abandoned this pursuit. *Country Walking* The time, a hundred years since, when foxes were imported.

▸ **B** *conjunction.* **I** From the time that.
1 During or in the time subsequent to that when. LME.
2 With preceding interval of time specified: from the time in the past when. Also (*arch.*), that. M16.
3 Up to the present time or the time being considered from the time in the past when. Freq. with *ever*. M16. ▸†**b** With verbs of recollection: the time when; when. L16–L17.

> 📖 **1** J. SIMMS Since we came to Paris I have started again. R. COBB He seemed to have put on . . weight since I had last seen him. **2** J. CONRAD It was . . years since I had seen the sun set over that land. W. GOLDING It is a long time since God had Wiltshire to himself. **3** A. BROOKNER She has known him so long—since she was a child. *Punch* Since he moved . . he has been doing even better. **b** SHAKES. *Wint. T.* Remember since you ow'd no more to time Than I do now.

▸ **II 4** Because, seeing that. Formerly also foll. by *that*. LME.

> 📖 **4** ELLIS PETERS Cadfael did not . . ask, since he was about to be told.

▸ **C** *preposition.* During or throughout the period between (a specified time or event in the past) and the present time or the time being considered; at some time subsequent to or after. E16.

> 📖 J. CONRAD Unchanged since the days of his boyhood. E. WAUGH She had been hard at it since . . seven. D. ABSE The first time I had seen him since the funeral.

▸ **D** *adjective.* That has been since; former, past. *rare.* L16.

> 📖 J. A. FROUDE My since experience of Sunday evenings.

sincere /sɪn'sɪə/ *adjective.* M16.
[Latin *sincerus* clean, pure, sound.]
1 Not falsified; true; correct. Now *rare.* M16.
2 Pure, free from any foreign element or ingredient; *spec.* unadulterated. Now *rare.* M16. ▸**b** Devoid *of* something. *rare.* M18.
3 Of a quality or feeling: not feigned or pretended; real; genuine. M16.
4 Of a person, action, etc.: characterized by the absence of pretence or hypocrisy; honest, straightforward. M16.

> 📖 **1** G. S. FABER When sincere Christianity was propounded in . . its native lustre. R. WILLIAMS Some sincere editions of the Bible. **2** M. HALE Their enjoyments are sincere, unallayed with fears. BROWNING Wood is cheap And wine sincere outside the city gate. **3** LD MACAULAY A sincere anxiety for the prosperity . . of his excellent friend. **4** *Observer* The greatest horrors . . are committed by people who are totally sincere. A. TYLER I want to offer my sincere condolences.

▪ **sincereness** *noun* M16.

sincerely /sɪn'sɪəli/ *adverb.* M16.
[from prec. + -LY[2].]
†**1** Without falsification; correctly. M16–E17.
2 Without pretence or hypocrisy; honestly; straightforwardly. M16.
†**3** Purely, absolutely; completely, wholly. L16–L17.

> 📖 **2** A. C. AMOR All of them . . sincerely loved the young man, despite his cowardice. **Yours sincerely**: a customary formula for closing a letter, esp. an informal one.

sincerity /sɪn'sɛrɪti/ *noun.* LME.
[Latin *sinceritas*, formed as SINCERE: see -ITY.]
1 Freedom from pretence or hypocrisy; honesty; straightforwardness; genuineness. LME. ▸**b** In *pl.* Sincere feelings or actions. M19.
†**2** Freedom from falsification or adulteration; purity, correctness. M16–M17.

sinciput /'sɪnsɪpʌt/ *noun.* L16.
[Latin, from *semi* half + *caput* head.]
Chiefly ANATOMY. The anterior and upper part of the head or skull, *esp.* the brows and forehead.
▪ **sincipital** /sɪn'sɪpɪt(ə)l/ *adjective* M17.

sind /sʌɪnd/ *verb & noun. Scot. & north.* Also **syne** /sʌɪn/. LME.
[Origin unkn.]
▸ **A** *verb trans.* Rinse, wash out. Also foll. by *down*, *out*. LME.
▸ **B** *noun.* A rinsing; a quick swill or wash. Also, a drink. E16.
▪ **sinding** *noun* (*a*) the action of the verb; (*b*) in *pl.*, the liquid used for rinsing: E19.

sindaco /'sindako, 'sɪndəkəʊ/ *noun.* Pl. ***-chi*** /-ki/, ***-cos***. E20.
[Italian.]
In Italy: a mayor.

Sindbis /'sɪndbɪs/ *adjective & noun.* M20.
[A village in Egypt.]
BIOLOGY & MEDICINE. (Designating or pertaining to) an insect-borne togavirus used esp. in genetic research.

Sindebele /sɪndə'biːli, -'beɪli/ *noun & adjective.* Also **Isinde-** /ˌɪsɪndə-/. E20.
[Bantu, from *isi-* prefix + NDEBELE.]
(Of) the Bantu language of the Indebele.

Sindhi /'sɪndi/ *noun & adjective.* Also **-di**. E19.
[Persian & Urdu *sindī* from *Sind*. (see below) from Sanskrit *sindhu* river, spec. the Indus or surrounding area.]
▸ **A** *noun.* **1** A native or inhabitant of Sind, a province in SE Pakistan through which the Indus passes. E19.
2 The Indo-Aryan (Indic) language of Sind, used also in western India. M19.
▸ **B** *attrib.* or as *adjective.* Of or pertaining to Sind, the Sindhis, or their language. M19.
▪ Also **Sindhian** *noun & adjective* M19.

sindicato /sindi'kato/ *noun.* Pl. **-os** /-ɔs/. M20.
[Spanish = syndicate, trade union.]
In Spain and Spanish-speaking countries: a trade union.

sindon /'sɪndən/ *noun & adjective.* ME.
[Latin from Greek *sindōn*, prob. of oriental origin.]
▸ **A** *noun.* **1** A fine thin fabric of linen, cotton, or silk. *obsolete* exc. *Hist.* ME.
2 A piece of this fabric used as a cover or wrapper, esp. a shroud. Now chiefly *spec.* the shroud in which the body of Jesus was wrapped. L15.
▸†**B** *adjective.* Made of sindon. L15–L17.

sindonology /sɪndə'nɒlədʒi/ *noun.* M20.
[from prec. + -OLOGY.]
The branch of knowledge that deals with the Turin Shroud, thought by some to be the shroud in which the body of Jesus was wrapped.
▪ **sindono'logical** *adjective* M20. **sindonologist** *noun* M20.

sine /sʌɪn/ *noun.* L16.
[Latin *sinus* curve, bay, fold of a toga, used in medieval Latin as translation of Arab. *jayb* bosom, pocket, sine.]
†**1** A gulf, a bay. Cf. SINUS 3. *rare.* Only in L16.
2 MATH. One of the three fundamental trigonometric functions (cf. SECANT *noun* 1, TANGENT *noun* 1): orig., the length of a straight line drawn from one end of a circular arc parallel to the tangent at the other end, and terminated by the radius to that end; now, the ratio of this line to the radius; (equivalently, as a function of an angle) the ratio of the side of a right-angled triangle opposite a given angle to the hypotenuse. Abbreviation SIN *noun*[2]. L16.
2 hyperbolic sine a hyperbolic function defined by $y = \frac{1}{2}(e^x - e^{-x})$; abbreviation ***sinh***. ***LOGARITHMIC sine***.

Comb.: **sine bar** MECHANICS a device used to set out or measure angles accurately, in which one end of a bar of known length is raised on gauge blocks; **sine tone** a pure tone; **sine wave** a periodic oscillation of pure and simple form in which the displacement at any point is proportional to the sine of the phase angle at that point; a wave or curve resembling (a segment of) this in form.

sinecure /ˈsʌɪnɪkjʊə, ˈsɪn-/ *noun & adjective.* M17.
[Latin (*beneficium*) *sine cura*, from *beneficium* benefice + *sine* without + *cura* abl. sing. of *cura* care.]
▶ **A** *noun.* **1** An ecclesiastical benefice without cure of souls. M17.
2 A position or office requiring little or no work, *esp.* one yielding profit or honour. L17.
📖 **2** H. CARPENTER Found a sinecure as companion to the son of a wealthy family.
▶ **B** *adjective.* **1** Of the nature of a sinecure; involving little or no work. M18.
2 Holding a sinecure. E19.
■ **sinecurism** *noun* the practice of holding or permitting sinecures; the prevalence of sinecures: E19. **sinecurist** *noun* a person who has or seeks a sinecure E19.

sine die /sʌɪnɪ ˈdʌɪiː, sɪneɪ ˈdiːeɪ/ *adverbial phr.* E17.
[Latin = without day, from *sine* without + *die* abl. sing. of *dies* day.]
With ref. to adjourned business etc.: without any day being appointed for resumption; indefinitely.

sine qua non /ˌsʌɪnɪ kweɪ ˈnɒn, ˌsɪneɪ kwɑː ˈnəʊn/ *adjectival & noun phr.* Also in Latin pl. form ***sine quibus non*** /ˌsʌɪnɪ kwiːbəs ˈnɒn, ˌsɪneɪ kwiːbəs ˈnəʊn/, (chiefly SCOTS LAW) Latin masc. form ***sine quo non*** /ˌsʌɪnɪ kwəʊ ˈnɒn, ˌsɪneɪ kwəʊ ˈnəʊn/. E17.
[Latin (*causa*) *sine qua non* lit. '(cause) without which not', from *sine* without + *qua* abl. sing. fem. of *qui* which + *non* not.]
▶ **A** *adjectival phr.* Indispensable, absolutely essential. Also *postpositive.* E17.
📖 DE QUINCEY Publication is a *sine qua non* condition for the generation of literature.
▶ **B** *noun phr.* **1** An indispensable person or thing; *esp.* an essential condition or element. E17.
2 SCOTS LAW. (***sine quo non.***) A curator, a trustee. *arch.* L17.
📖 **1** E. CRANKSHAW Obedience was all, the *sine qua non* of order. *Antiquaries Journal* Detailed section drawings . . are surely the *sine qua non* of a modern archaeological report.

Sinetic /sɪˈnɛtɪk/ *adjective.* L19.
[Alt. of SINITIC.]
Chinese.

sinew /ˈsɪnjuː/ *noun & verb.*
[Old English *sin(e)we*, *sionwe*, *seonew-* oblique forms of *sinu*, *seonu* = Old Frisian *sini*, *sin(e)*, Middle & mod. Low German, Middle Dutch, Middle High German *sene* (Dutch *zeen*, German *Sehne*), Old Norse *sin*, from Germanic (whence also Old Saxon, Old High German *senawa*).]
▶ **A** *noun.* **1** ANATOMY. A tendon. OE. ▸**b** A tendon used for binding or tying something. ME. ▸**c** The strong fibrous tissue of which tendons consist. E19.
†**2** A nerve. LME–E17.
3 *sing.* & (usu.) in *pl.* **a** Strength, force. LME. ▸**b** The mainstay or chief supporting force *of* a thing. M16.
📖 **3** W. WOLLASTON Gives sinews to an inference, and makes it just. *Times* The political sinew to keep the Opposition off-balance. **b the sinews of war** money.
▶ **B** *verb trans.* **1** Tie together or cover over (as) with sinews. *rare.* L16.
2 Strengthen as by sinews. *poet.* E17.
■ **sinewed** *adjective* (*a*) having sinews of a specified kind; (*b*) strengthened with sinews; strong, powerful: L16. **sinewless** *adjective* M16. **sinewous** *adjective* sinewy L15.

sinewy /ˈsɪnjuːi/ *adjective.* LME.
[from SINEW *noun* + -Y¹.]
1 Having (many) sinews; having strong or prominent sinews. LME.
2 Having the strength characteristic of sinews. L16.
3 Of the nature of sinews; tough, stringy. L16.
†**4** Strung with sinews. *rare.* L16–M17.
📖 **1** N. MONSARRAT The small body was sinewy and compact, . . rippling with muscle. S. BEDFORD A slight, sinewy elderly woman. **2** *Time* This reflective and sinewy biography.

sinfonia /sɪnfəˈniːə, sɪnˈfəʊnɪə/ *noun.* L18.
[Italian: see SYMPHONY.]
MUSIC. **1** In baroque music, an orchestral piece used as an introduction to an opera, cantata, or suite; an overture. Also (*rare*), a symphony. L18.
2 (**S-**.) (The title of) a small symphony orchestra. L20.
1 sinfonia concertante /sɪnfəˌniːə kɒntʃəˈtanti/ a symphonic work exhibiting characteristics of the concerto.

sinfonietta /sɪnfəʊnɪˈɛtə/ *noun.* E20.
[Italian, dim. of SINFONIA.]
MUSIC. **1** A short or simple symphony. E20.
2 (**S-**.) = SINFONIA 2. E20.

sinful /ˈsɪnfʊl, -f(ə)l/ *adjective & noun.* OE.
[from SIN *noun*¹ + -FUL.]
▶ **A** *adjective.* **1** Of a person: committing a sin, esp. habitually; wicked. OE.
2 Of an act, practice, etc.: involving or characterized by sin. ME. ▸**b** Highly reprehensible. Also, excessive in manner or extent. *colloq.* M19.
📖 **1** W. COWPER What is man? Sinful and weak, . . a wretch. **2** *Punch* At a time when novels were thought of as practically sinful. **b** P. G. WODEHOUSE The money that boy makes is sinful.
▶ **B** *absol.* as *noun.* **1** Sinful people collectively. Usu. with *the.* OE.
†**2** A sinful person. OE–LME.
■ **sinfully** *adverb* ME. **sinfulness** *noun* OE.

sing /sɪŋ/ *noun.* M19.
[from the verb.]
1 An act or spell of singing; *US* a meeting for amateur singing. M19.
2 The sound made by a bullet or other projectile in its flight. L19.

sing /sɪŋ/ *verb*¹. Pa. t. **sang** /saŋ/, (*arch. & non-standard*) **sung** /sʌŋ/. Pa. pple **sung**.
[Old English *singan* = Old Frisian *siunga*, *sionga*, Old Saxon, Old High German *singan* (Dutch *zingen*, German *singen*), Old Norse *syngva*, Gothic *siggwan*, from Germanic. Cf. SONG.]
▶ **I** *verb intrans.* **1** Produce sounds in succession with musical modulations of the voice; utter words in this way, esp. to a set tune; *spec.* do this in a skilled manner. OE. ▸**b** Of words: admit of being sung; be usually sung. E18.
2 Tell *of* in song or verse. OE. ▸**b** Compose poetry. M17.
3 a Of an animal, esp. a bird: make a characteristic call or melodious sound. OE. ▸**b** (Of a thing) make a ringing, whistling, humming, etc., sound; *spec.* (of a weapon) make a ringing sound by reason of rapid motion through the air. OE.
†**4** Chant or intone in the performance of divine service. ME–L16.
5 Cry or shout out, esp. with pain. Also foll. by *out.* LME.
6 Turn informer; confess. *slang.* E17.
7 Of the ears: be affected with a buzzing sound; ring. E17.
📖 **1** R. L. STEVENSON Every one who is happy desires to sing. I. MURDOCH He began to sing in his . . ringing bass. C. THUBRON A choir sang reedily from the chancel. **3a** *Scientific American* The male cricket sings by scraping his wings. D. PROFUMO Somewhere . . the noise of larks singing. **b** B. ENGLAND Bullets sang off the rocks . . above and beside him. G. MOFFAT The kettle started to sing. C. CONRAN Butter is . . heated until . . you can no longer hear it singing. **5** A. RANSOME Keep your eyes skinned and sing out the moment you see anything. **6** R. HIMMEL She's singing like a canary. She turned up at headquarters . . and said she had some information on a killing.
▶ **II** *verb trans.* **8** Utter (words, a song, tune, note, etc.) with musical modulations of the voice. Also with adverbs OE.
9 a Recount or celebrate in song or verse. OE. ▸**b** Proclaim; announce clearly or distinctly; shout *out.* E17.
10 Chant or intone (a lesson, mass, etc.). OE.
11 Bring into a specified state or accompany to a specified place by or with singing; *spec.* usher (the new or old year) *in* or *out* with singing. L15. ▸**b** Move or drive by or with singing. Foll. by *away*, *out of*, etc. E17. ▸**c** Of an Australian Aborigine: endow (an object) with magical properties by singing; bring a magical (esp. malign) influence to bear on (a person or thing) by singing. L19.
📖 **8** E. SHANKS Sing a song to cheer him up. G. VIDAL In a low voice he sang an Irish ballad. **9a** W. JONES He sung the woes of artless swains. **b** THACKERAY The watchman sang the hours when she was asleep. **11** J. CLARE The blackbird sang the sun to bed. DICKENS In my childhood I . . had never been sung to sleep.
Phrases, & with adverbs in specialized senses: **all-singing, all-dancing** *adjective* (*colloq.*) equipped with an impressive or extravagant array of features or functions. **hear a bird sing** *arch.* receive private or secret information. **sing a different tune** assume a different manner of speech or behaviour. **sing along** sing in accompaniment to a song or piece of music. **sing another song** = ***sing a different tune*** above. **sing for one's supper** *fig.* provide a service in order to earn a benefit. **sing from the same hymn sheet** present a united front in public by appearing to agree with one another. ***sing one's nunc dimittis***: see NUNC DIMITTIS 1. ***sing small***: see SMALL *adverb*. ***sing the praises of***: see PRAISE *noun*. **sing the same song** tell the same tale.
Comb.: **sing-along** *noun & adjective* (*a*) *noun* a (simple) song to which one can sing along in accompaniment; a meeting for amateur singing, an impromptu concert, an occasion of community singing; (*b*) *adjective* (of a song) to which one can sing along in accompaniment; of or characterized by a simple, cheerful style. **sing-in** a musical performance in which the audience participates in the singing.
■ **singable** *adjective* able to be sung; suitable for singing: ME. **singaˈbility** *noun* L19. **singableness** *noun* M19.

sing /sɪŋ/ *verb*² *trans. Scot. & north.* E16.
[North. var.]
Singe.

sing. *abbreviation.*
Singular.

Singaporean /sɪŋəˈpɔːrɪən, sɪŋɡ-/ *adjective & noun.* L19.
[from *Singapore* (see below) + -AN.]
▶ **A** *adjective.* Of or pertaining to Singapore, a city and island-republic in SE Asia. L19.
▶ **B** *noun.* A native or inhabitant of Singapore. L19.

Singapore sling /sɪŋəˌpɔː ˈslɪŋ, sɪŋɡ-/ *noun phr.* M20.
[from *Singapore* (see prec.) + SLING *noun*³.]
A cocktail with a base of gin and cherry brandy. Also ***Singapore gin sling***.

singara *noun* var. of SINGHARA.

singe /sɪn(d)ʒ/ *noun.* M17.
[from the verb.]
The action of singeing; a slight surface burn, a scorch.

singe /sɪn(d)ʒ/ *verb trans.* Pres. pple **singeing**.
[Old English *senċġan*, chiefly as *besenċġan* = Old Frisian *senga*, *sendza*, Old Saxon *bisengian* (Dutch *zengen*), Middle & mod. High German *sengen*, from West Germanic. Cf. SWINGE *verb*².]
1 Burn superficially or lightly; *spec.* (***a***) burn the bristles or down off (the carcass of a pig or fowl) preparatory to cooking; (***b***) burn off the ends of (the hair) in hairdressing; (***c***) burn off the superfluous fibres of (a woven fabric) preparatory to printing etc. OE. ▸†**b** Consume with fire; cauterize (a wound). LME–E17.
2 Foll. by *off*: remove by singeing. L16.
📖 **1** C. SAGAN It is very hot: You singe your eyebrows if you get too close. V. GLENDINNING A moth, singed by a candle-flame, falls. **singed cat** *US* a thing which proves to be better than its appearance suggests. **2** SHAKES. *Com. Err.* The doctor, Whose beard they have sing'd off with brands of fire.

singer /ˈsɪŋə/ *noun*¹. ME.
[from SING *verb*¹ + -ER¹.]
1 A person who sings; *spec.* a trained or professional vocalist; *slang* an informer. ME. ▸**b** A bird which sings, a songbird. LME.
2 A poet. M16.
Phrases: ***playback singer***: see PLAYBACK 2. ***sweet singer***: see SWEET *adjective & adverb*.
Comb.: **singer's node**, **singer's nodule** MEDICINE a small pale swelling on a vocal cord; **singer-songwriter** a person who sings and writes songs, esp. professionally.

singer /ˈsɪn(d)ʒə/ *noun*². L19.
[from SINGE *verb* + -ER¹]
A person who or thing which singes something.

singerie /sɛ̃ʒri/ *noun.* Pl. pronounced same. E20.
[French, from *singe* monkey.]
A painting depicting monkeys in human roles and attitudes; a piece of porcelain decorated with such paintings; work done in this style.

Singh /sɪŋ/ *noun.* E17.
[Panjabi *siṅgh* lion from Sanskrit *siṃha* lion.]
(A respectful title for) a member of a military caste of northern India; (a surname adopted by) a male Sikh initiated into the Khalsa.

singhara /sɪŋˈhɑːrə/ *noun.* Also **-gara** /-ˈɡɑːrə/. M19.
[Hindi *sighāṛā* from Sanskrit *śṛṅgāṭa*.]
A water chestnut, *Trapa bispinosa*, of the Indian subcontinent; the edible nut produced by this plant (also ***singhara-nut***).

singing /ˈsɪŋɪŋ/ *verbal noun.* ME.
[from SING *verb*¹ + -ING¹.]
1 The action of SING *verb*¹; an instance of this, *spec.* (*N. Amer.*) a gathering for collective singing. ME.
2 A ringing, whistling, humming, etc., esp. in the ears. L15.
3 TELEPHONY. A continuous audible oscillation in a telephone circuit, resulting from excessive positive feedback. E20.
Comb.: **singing game** a traditional children's game in which associated actions accompany singing; **singing point** TELEPHONY the maximum gain that a telephone repeater can have without being liable to self-oscillation in the circuit.

singing /ˈsɪŋɪŋ/ *ppl adjective.* ME.
[from SING *verb*¹ + -ING².]
1 That sings. ME. ▸**b** *spec.* Professionally employed in singing; engaged or hired to sing. E16.
2 Of the nature of singing; ringing. LME.
Special collocations: **singing arc** ELECTRICITY a d.c. arc across which is connected a tuned circuit, causing the arc to oscillate and emit a sound at the frequency of the tuned circuit. **singing bird** *arch.* a songbird. ***singing hinny***: see HINNY *noun*². **singing man** *arch.*: engaged to sing in an ecclesiastical choir. **singing sand** desert or beach sand that emits a singing sound when disturbed (also called ***sounding sand***). **singing tree** *W. Indies* a naturalized leguminous tree, *Albizia lebbeck* (the kokko), the pods of which make a singing sound when stirred by the wind.
■ **singingly** *adverb* LME.

single /ˈsɪŋɡ(ə)l/ *noun*. ME.
[from the adjective.]
1 An unmarried person. Freq. in *pl*. ME.
2 a Either of the middle or outer claws on the foot of a bird of prey. *arch*. L15. ▸**b** The tail of a deer. L16.
3 A handful, esp. of gleaned corn. *Scot. & north*. E16.
4 An individual person or thing as opp. to a pair or group. M17.
5 *spec*. **a** CAMPANOLOGY. A kind of change affecting two bells. L17. ▸**b** A single as opp. to a double flower. L18. ▸**c** A single-stranded silk thread or woollen yarn. M19. ▸**d** SPORT. A play which scores a single point; *spec*. (*a*) CRICKET a hit for one run; (*b*) BASEBALL a one-base hit. M19. ▸**e** In *pl*. A game, esp. tennis-match, played with one person on each side. L19. ▸**f** A one-way ticket for a journey; a ticket for a single seat at the theatre, cinema, etc. L19. ▸**g** *Hist*. A locomotive engine with a single pair of driving-wheels. E20. ▸**h** A solo performer on stage. *US*. E20. ▸**i** A single bedroom, esp. in a hotel. M20. ▸**j** A one-dollar bill (*US*). Also (chiefly *Hist*.), a one-pound note. *colloq*. M20. ▸**k** A record with one piece of music on each side; a piece of music released in this form. M20. ▸**l** (A motorcycle or car with) a single cylinder engine. M20.

> 🕮 **1** M. GORDON 'Refer to me as a bachelorette.' 'I think the term is swinging single now.' D. LEAVITT She lived in a condominium complex for singles. **4** *Coarse Fishing* Several twenties are present along with some doubles and a . . number of singles. **5d** *Toronto Star* Raines hit a two-out single in the fifth. *Cricketer* He contributed only a single to Gypsies's score of 104 for nine. **e** *Time Out* Wimbledon 1977 . . . Fourth day; Ladies' Singles. **f** *Punch* 'Single to Liverpool Street,' I said. **h** O. KEEPNEWS He's played . . in big bands, small combinations, and as a single. **i** E. PACE The hotel could provide two singles with a bath. **j** H. FAST He . . took out a wad of bills, peeling off two fives and two singles. **k** *Sky Magazine* The video featuring the hit singles.

Comb.: **singles bar** a bar catering for single people seeking company.
¶ In sense 1 rare before M20.

single /ˈsɪŋɡ(ə)l/ *adjective & adverb*. ME.
[Old French *single*, *sengle*, from Latin *singulus*, from *sim-* as in *simplus* SIMPLE *adjective*.]
▸**A** *adjective*. **I 1** *pred*. Unaccompanied or unaided by others; alone, solitary. ME.
2 Individual, isolated; not one of a group. LME. ▸**b** Of or pertaining to an individual person. Chiefly with possess. pronoun. L16.
3 Regarded separately; distinct from each other or others in a group. LME.
4 One only; one and no more; (with neg.) even one. LME.
5 Undivided, united. Formerly also, complete, absolute. L16.
6 Sole, only, one; mere. M17.
7 Unique, singular. Now *rare*. M17.

> 🕮 **1** WORDSWORTH Behold her, single in the field, yon solitary Highland lass. D. H. LAWRENCE She was quite single and by herself, deriving from nobody. **2** G. GREENE The schoolboys had swarmed round a single able-seaman. **b** SIR W. SCOTT By his single and unassisted talents. **3** A. EDEN Every single chocolate in the box had been nibbled. **4** I. MURDOCH He drank it in a single draught. M. ROBERTS She tries not to hear a single word he says. **5** ISAIAH BERLIN European liberalism wears the appearance of a single coherent movement. **6** *New Yorker* The single biggest travel buy to anywhere, ever. D. WILLIAMS The single day of the week when Lucy . . went up to town.

▸**II 8** Unmarried. ME.
†**9** Scantily or simply dressed. Only in ME.
†**10** (Of cloth etc.) of one thickness of material; (of a garment) unlined. LME–L17.
11 Consisting of only one part, feature, etc.; not double or multiple. LME. ▸**b** Of a flower: having only one whorl or set of petals. Cf. DOUBLE *adjective* 1c. M16. ▸**c** For the use of one person. M19.
†**12 a** Simple; plain; without qualification or addition. LME–M18. ▸**b** Slight, poor, trivial. LME–M17.
13 Honest, sincere; without duplicity or guile. *arch*. E16.

> 🕮 **8** S. JOHNSON They that have grown old in a single state. P. ROTH A . . good-looking, young Jewish lawyer (and single! a match for somebody's daughter). **11c** C. DEXTER Yes, they had a single room with private bath. **13** T. JEFFERSON To those whose views are single and direct.

▸**B** *adverb*. Singly, alone; one by one. *arch*. ME.

> 🕮 ADDISON My Dear, Misfortunes never come Single. E. WEETON You say Mrs. W. had the offer of a horse. Did she, then, ride single?

Phrases: ***at a single heat***: see HEAT *noun*. **with a single eye** *arch*. sincerely, honestly, guilelessly (with allus. to *Luke* 11:34).
Special collocations & comb.: ***single acrostic***: see ACROSTIC *noun* 1. **single-acting** *adjective* acting in one way or direction; *spec*. (of an engine) having pressure applied to only one side of the piston. **single-action** *adjective* acting once or in one way; *spec*. (of a gun) needing to be cocked by hand before it can be fired. **single beer** *arch*. = ***small beer*** s.v. BEER *noun*[1] 1. ***single*** BLESSEDNESS. **single-blind** *adjective & noun* (designating) a test etc. in which information that may lead to biased results is concealed from either tester or subject. **single bond** CHEMISTRY a covalent bond in which one pair of electrons is shared between two atoms. **single-breasted** *adjective* (of a jacket etc.) having only one set of buttons and buttonholes, not overlapping at the front. **single carriageway** a road intended for vehicular traffic with only one lane in each direction and no dividing strip between traffic in opposite directions. **single-cell protein**: derived from a culture of single-celled organisms. ***single combat***: see COMBAT *noun* 1. **single-copy** BIOCHEMISTRY (of a gene or genetic sequence) present in a genome in only one copy. **single cream** thin cream with a relatively low fat-content. **single currency** a currency used by all the members of an economic federation; *spec*. = ***single European currency*** below; **single cut** *adjective* (of a file) with grooves cut in one direction only. **single-decker** *noun & adjective* (designating) a thing, esp. a bus, with one deck or layer. **single digging** (in gardening) digging in which only the topsoil is turned over, to the depth of one spit. **single-electrode** CHEMISTRY an electrode or half-cell considered in isolation (usu. *attrib*.). **single-ended** *adjective* (ELECTRONICS) (of a device) designed for use with unbalanced signals and therefore having one input and one output terminal connected to earth. **single entry** a method of bookkeeping in which each transaction is entered in one account only. **single European currency** the currency (the euro) which replaced the national currencies of twelve member states of the EU in 2002. **single European market** a single market between countries of the EU. **single-eyed** *adjective* (*arch*.) (*a*) one-eyed; (*b*) *fig*. sincere, honest, straightforward. **single file** *noun & adverb* (*a*) *noun* a line of people or things arranged one behind another; (*b*) *adverb* in a single file. **single-file** *verb intrans*. move in a single file. **single-foot** *noun & verb* (*US*) (*a*) *noun* a horse's fast walking pace with one foot on the ground at a time; (*b*) *verb intrans*. (of a horse) go at this pace. **single Gloucester (cheese)** a cheese of the same composition but smaller than double Gloucester (see DOUBLE *adjective*). **Single Grave** ARCHAEOLOGY (designating) a culture characterized by individual burial, stone battle-axes, and corded-ware pottery, appearing in N Germany and Scandinavia in the later neolithic period. **single-hand** *adjective & adverb* = ***single-handed*** below. **single-handed** *adjective & adverb* (*a*) alone, unaided, unassisted; (*b*) (used or done) with one hand only. **single-handedly** *adverb* in a single-handed manner. **single-hander** (*a*) a person who sails a boat or yacht single-handed; (*b*) a boat etc. that can be sailed single-handed. **single harness** harness for a draught animal working alone. **single-hearted** *adjective* (*arch*.) straightforward, honest, sincere. **single-horse** *adjective* (of a vehicle) one-horse. **single-lens reflex** (designating) a reflex camera in which a single lens serves the film and the image in the viewfinder. **single-line** *adjective* (*a*) (esp. of traffic) consisting of or having only a single line; (*b*) allowing movement of traffic etc. in one direction at a time. **single malt (whisky)** (a) malt whisky unblended with any other malt. **single market** an association of countries between which movement of goods and currencies largely occurs without tariffs and other restrictions; *spec*. = ***single European market*** above. **single-minded** *adjective* (*a*) sincere, honest, straightforward; ingenuous; (*b*) having a single aim or purpose. **single-mindedly** *adverb* in a single-minded manner. **single-mindedness** the quality or fact of being single-minded. **single parent** a person bringing up a child or children without a partner. ***single*** OXER. ***single*** PNEUMONIA. **single reed** a wind instrument reed with one blade. **single-reef** *verb trans*. (NAUTICAL) reduce the spread of (a sail) by one reef. **single-seater** a vehicle with one seat. **single-soled** *adjective* (*a*) (of a boot or shoe) having a single layer in the sole; (*b*) *fig*. (of a person) poor, mean, insignificant. **single-source** *verb intrans*. give a franchise to a single supplier for a particular product. **single spacing**: with no line left empty between successive lines, esp. in typewritten text. **single standard** (*a*) monometallism; (*b*) (the application of) a single set of principles etc. applied to all people or situations. **single-start** ENGINEERING designating a screw-thread or worm gear that has one continuous thread along its entire length. **single-step** *verb intrans*. (COMPUTING) run a program one step or instruction at a time, esp. for debugging. **single-stick** (one-handed fencing with) a basket-hilted stick of about sword's length. **single-stranded** *adjective* (BIOCHEMISTRY) (of a nucleic acid) consisting of only one continuous sequence of nucleotides. **single suckling** *noun & adjective* (designating) a system of dairy farming in which each cow suckles only her own calf. **single-tasking** COMPUTING the performance of operations or functions sequentially. **single tax** ECONOMICS a tax on land value as the sole source of public revenue. **single-tax** *adjective* (ECONOMICS) based on or advocating a single tax. **single-taxer** ECONOMICS an advocate of a single-tax system. ***single team***: see TEAM *noun* 5a. **single track** (*a*) a single pair of railway lines or tramlines; (*b*) a recorded strip on magnetic tape with no other alongside it. **single-track** *adjective* (*a*) of or pertaining to a single-track; (*b*) = ***one-track*** s.v. ONE *adjective, noun, & pronoun*. **singletree** *US & Austral*. = ***swingletree*** (b) s.v. SWINGLE *noun*[1]. **single-tuned** *adjective* (ELECTRONICS) having one tuned circuit between two active devices. **single-valued** *adjective* (MATH.) having a unique value for each value of its argument(s); that maps to one and only one point, number, etc. **single-vision** *adjective* (OPHTHALMOLOGY) (of spectacles) of which each lens is a single optical element, not bifocal, etc. **single-wicket** CRICKET a form of play with only one wicket and batsman at a time. **single-wide** *US* a single self-contained mobile home. **single-wire** *adjective* designating an electrical wiring system in which current is carried by one wire, the return being provided by the chassis or frame of the apparatus or installation or the earth.
■ **singlehood** *noun* the state of being single or unmarried M19.

single /ˈsɪŋɡ(ə)l/ *verb*. L16.
[from the adjective.]
1 *verb trans*. Separate or part from each other. Now *rare* exc. as in sense b. L16. ▸**b** *verb trans*. Thin out (seedlings, saplings, etc.). Also foll. by *off*, *out*. M18.
2 *verb trans*. Separate from a group; take aside or apart; isolate. Now usu. foll. by *out*. L16.
3 *verb trans*. Select from a group as worthy of special attention, praise, persecution, etc.; choose or identify *as*; mark out or destine *for* or *to do*. Now usu. foll. by *out* (*from*). L16.
4 *verb intrans*. Go singly; separate from others. Also foll. by *off*, *out*. Now *rare* exc. *dial*. E17.
5 *verb trans*. Make single, reduce to one; now *esp*., reduce (a railway track) to a single line. E19. ▸**b** NAUTICAL. Foll. by *up*: cast off all (moorings) except one. E20.
6 BASEBALL. **a** *verb intrans*. Hit a single. E20. ▸**b** *verb trans*. Enable (another player) to advance by hitting a single. L20.

> 🕮 **2** N. M. GUNN His early sheep knowledge came back to him as he began to single out the ewe. S. PLATH When I talk to a group of people I always have to single one out and talk to him. **3** N. FARAH My brother was singled out for this singular honour from all those who died. R. GODDEN Ian had singled me out when I was eleven. H. S. STREAN Why is he singling you out and making you suffer? G. DALY Lizzie's work was singled out . . as worthy of special attention. **5** *Railway Magazine* On the Bradford to Keighley side, the track has been singled. **6a** *New York Times* Devon White singled twice, doubled and hit a home run.

■ **singling** *noun* (*a*) the action of the verb; (*b*) DISTILLING (in *pl*.) the first spirits drawn off: E17.

singleness /ˈsɪŋɡ(ə)lnɪs/ *noun*. E16.
[from SINGLE *adjective* + -NESS.]
1 Sincerity, honesty, straightforwardness; guilelessness. Also foll. by *of*. E16.
2 The state or condition of being unmarried. M16. ▸**b** Solitude, isolation. *rare*. E19.
3 The fact of being one in number or kind; oneness; now *esp*. unity or concentration *of* purpose, mind, etc. L16.

> 🕮 **1** DISRAELI With artlessness . . and a degree of earnest singleness. **2** H. JAMES She appeared to have accepted the idea of eternal singleness. **3** L. GORDON The multiplicity of Eliot's roles conceals an extraordinary singleness of mind. S. J. LEONARDI She . . with her singleness of purpose, first penetrates Wimsey's disguise.

single-o /ˈsɪŋɡ(ə)ləʊ/ *noun, adjective, & adverb*. *US slang*. E20.
[from SINGLE *adjective* + -O.]
▸**A** *noun*. Pl. **-o(e)s**.
1 In gambling, the number one. *rare*. E20.
2 A crime committed without an accomplice; a criminal who works alone. M20.
▸**B** *adjective*. (Of a criminal) working without an accomplice; (of a crime) committed without an accomplice. M20.
▸**C** *adverb*. Alone; without an accomplice. M20.

singlet /ˈsɪŋlɪt/ *noun*. M18.
[from SINGLE *adjective* + -ET[1], after DOUBLET.]
1 Orig., a man's woollen garment resembling a doublet but unlined. Now, a close-fitting usu. sleeveless garment worn under or instead of a shirt; a vest. M18.
2 a PHYSICS & CHEMISTRY. A single line or peak in a spectrum, not part of a multiplet; an atomic or molecular energy level or state characterized by zero spin (giving a single value for a particular quantum number); a molecular state in which all electron spins are paired. Freq. *attrib*. E20. ▸**b** PARTICLE PHYSICS. A single subatomic particle considered as a multiplet. M20.

singleton /ˈsɪŋɡ(ə)lt(ə)n/ *noun & adjective*. L19.
[from SINGLE *adjective* + -TON. Cf. SIMPLETON.]
▸**A** *noun*. **1** *gen*. A single person or thing. L19.
2 In bridge etc., the only card of a suit in a hand. L19.
3 BIBLIOGRAPHY. A single leaf not part of a conjugate pair. M20.
4 a A child or animal of a single as opp. to a multiple birth. M20. ▸**b** An only child; an unmarried person. M20.
5 LINGUISTICS. A word unrelated to others in a language. M20.

> 🕮 **1** S. MIDDLETON It had stood at the back of an ugly china cabinet . . a singleton. **4a** *Contact* Twin children were six months behind singletons in speech development. **4b** HELEN FIELDING Head is full of moony fantasies about . . being trendy Smug Married instead of sheepish Singleton.

▸**B** *adjective*. Of, pertaining to, or designating a singleton. L19.

> 🕮 *Bridge Magazine* Flint held a singleton King of clubs. *Nursing Times* Usually a singleton conception, but . . rarely . . accompanied by a normal twin.

singlo /ˈsɪŋləʊ/ *noun*. L17.
[from *Sung-lo* (see below).]
A kind of green China tea, orig. obtained from the Sung-lo hills in southern Gan-hwuy (Anhui) province.

singly /ˈsɪŋɡli/ *adverb*. ME.
[from SINGLE *adjective* + -LY[2].]
1 As a single person or thing; separately; independently. ME. ▸**b** Unaided, single-handed. E17.
†**2 a** Simply; without addition. *rare*. LME–L16. ▸**b** Solely, only; merely. M17–L18.

†**3** Sincerely, honestly, truly. E16–M17.

1 M. MITCHELL Men began straggling in, singly and in groups. **b** SHAKES. *Tr. & Cr.* He must fight singly to-morrow with Hector.

singsing /ˈsɪŋsɪŋ/ *noun.* L19.
[Tok Pisin, ult. repr. redupl. of SING *verb*¹.]
In Papua New Guinea, a festival marked by dancing, singing, and various ceremonies, and culminating in a feast.

sing-sing /ˈsɪŋsɪŋ/ *noun.* M19.
[Malinke *si-nsing* antelope.]
A form of water-buck found in western and central Africa. Also ***sing-sing water-buck***, ***sing-sing antelope***.

singsong /ˈsɪŋsɒŋ/ *noun, adjective, & verb.* Also **sing-song**. E17.
[from SING *verb*¹ + SONG *noun*¹.]
► **A** *noun.* **1** (A piece of) verse with a monotonous or jingling songlike rhythm. E17. ▸**b** (A) tone of voice resembling this, marked by a monotonous rise and fall. E19.
2 An informal amateur concert; now *esp.* an informal gathering for or session of group singing. M18.

1b V. S. PRITCHETT She spoke in a flat . . voice and not in the singsong of this part of the country. **2** P. CARTER Mr Gannon brought out his accordion and we had a singsong.

► **B** *adjective.* **1** Of a person: enjoying or given to producing singsong. L17.
2 Resembling (a) singsong; characterized by a jingling or monotonous rhythm. M18.

2 A. DESAI Recited . . in a voice that grew increasingly sing-song. A. GHOSH Their dialect . . was a nasal sing-song Bengali.

Comb.: **singsong girl** in China, a girl performing singing and dancing as entertainment; *euphem.* a prostitute; **singsong theory** (chiefly *joc.*) the hypothesis that language evolved from primitive singing.
► **C** *verb.* **1** *verb trans.* †**a** Force *out of* by means of singing. *rare.* Only in E18. ▸**b** Utter or express in a monotonous or singsong rhythm. M19.
2 *verb intrans.* Sing, write, speak, etc., in a singsong manner. M19.

1b J. T. FARRELL She dragged out monotonous singsonged syllables. RUTH WOLFF 'You can't catch me. You can't catch me,' he singsonged. **2** J. T. FARRELL The bystanders . . sing-songing simultaneously.

■ **singsongy** *adjective* = SINGSONG *adjective* 2 L19.

singspiel /ˈzɪŋʃpiːl/ *noun.* Pl. **-e** /-ə/. L19.
[German, from *singen* sing + *Spiel* play.]
MUSIC. A dramatic performance alternating between song and dialogue, popular esp. in late eighteenth-cent. Germany; (a) comic opera.

singular /ˈsɪŋɡjʊlə/ *adjective, noun, & adverb.* ME.
[Old French *singuler* (mod. *-ier*) from Latin *singularis*, from *singulus* SINGLE *adjective*.]
► **A** *adjective.* **I 1** Orig. *spec.* in early biblical translations, (of an animal) living and feeding alone. Later, alone; apart from others; solitary. Long *rare* or *obsolete.* ME.
2 Separate, individual, single. Now only in ***all and singular***, every one of. *arch.* ME.
†**3** Of or pertaining to an individual; personal, private. Also, peculiar *to* a person or group; special. *rare.* ME–E18.
4 One only; particular, specific; exclusive, sole; unique. LME.
5 a GRAMMAR. Of the form or class of a noun, verb, etc.: denoting no more than one. Opp. PLURAL *adjective* 1. LME. ▸**b** LOGIC. Of a proposition etc.: applicable only to a single object. M16. ▸**c** MATH. Having some generally or locally unique property; (of a point) that is a singularity; (of a solution of a differential equation) that cannot be obtained directly from the general solution, *esp.* that represents the envelope of all the curves represented by the general solution. M19.
6 †**a** Of a person: holding no office or special position; private. LME–L16. ▸**b** SCOTS LAW. ***singular successor***, a person who acquires heritable property by a single title, esp. a purchase, rather than inheritance. M17.

5a K. AMIS The treatment of *media* as a singular noun . . is spreading.

► **II 7** Above or beyond the average; especially good or great; excellent, rare. Formerly also *spec.*, (of medicine) particularly beneficial (freq. foll. by *against, for*). ME. ▸†**b** Of a person: eminent, distinguished. L15–L17.
†**8** Superior to all others; pre-eminent. LME–M17.
9 Remarkable or extraordinary in some respect; not conforming to the general or the norm; strange, eccentric, peculiar. Also foll. by *in*. LME.

7 DEFOE To our singular satisfaction we found the water . . ran . . eastward. G. GORDON The singular advantage that . . no-one in the restaurant could observe you. **9** G. GREENE It would indeed be singular if the religious sense were absent. A. CROSS I thought I'd heard that singular name Umphelby before.

Special collocations: †**singular combat** = *single combat* s.v. COMBAT *noun* 1. ***singular successor***: see sense 6b above.
► **B** *noun.* **1** GRAMMAR. The singular number; a singular word or form. Opp. PLURAL *noun* 1. LME.
2 A single person; an individual; a single thing, *esp.* a single point or detail. Now *rare.* LME.
†**3** = SANGLIER. *rare.* L15–L17.

1 N. PODHORETZ I refer to them from now on in the singular . . as The Boss.

► **C** *adverb.* Singularly. Now *non-standard.* M16.
■ **singularly** *adverb* ME. **singularness** *noun* (now *rare*) = SINGULARITY 1 M16.

singulare tantum /sɪŋɡjʊˌlɑːreɪ ˈtantəm/ *noun phr.* Pl. ***-laria tantum*** /-ˌlɑːrɪə/. M20.
[Latin, lit. 'singular only'.]
GRAMMAR. A word having only a singular form; *esp.* a non-count noun.

singularise *verb* var. of SINGULARIZE.

singularism /ˈsɪŋɡjʊlərɪz(ə)m/ *noun.* Now *rare.* L19.
[from SINGULAR + -ISM.]
PHILOSOPHY. A theory or system of thought recognizing a single ultimate principle, being, force, etc.; monism.

singularist /ˈsɪŋɡjʊlərɪst/ *noun.* L16.
[from SINGULAR + -IST.]
†**1** A person differing from others or from the norm; an individualist. L16–L17.
2 ECCLESIASTICAL. A holder of a single benefice. *rare.* L18.

singularity /sɪŋɡjʊˈlarɪti/ *noun.* ME.
[Old & mod. French *singularité* from late Latin *singularitas*, from Latin *singularis* SINGULAR: see -ITY.]
1 The quality, state, or fact of being singular; now *esp.*, the quality or fact of being remarkable or peculiar in some respect; eccentricity, strangeness. Also foll. by *of*. ME. ▸**b** An exceptional or unusual trait or feature; a peculiarity. Freq. foll. by *of*. L16.
†**2** A single or separate thing; a unit. LME–E18.
3 MATH. A point at which a function is not differentiable (i.e. takes an infinite value), though differentiable in the neighbourhood of the point. L19. ▸**b** ASTRONOMY. A region in space–time at which matter is infinitely dense. M20.

1 R. CHURCH He showed some singularity by knocking the ceiling out of his wife's parlour. V. S. PRITCHETT Among the married she felt her singularity. **b** G. GISSING A strong illustration of one of the singularities of his character.

singularize /ˈsɪŋɡjʊlərʌɪz/ *verb trans.* Also **-ise**. L16.
[from SINGULAR *adjective* + -IZE.]
Make singular; distinguish, individualize.
■ **singulariˈzation** *noun* L19.

singulary /ˈsɪŋɡjʊləri/ *adjective.* Now *rare.* M20.
[from Latin *singularis* SINGULAR: see -ARY².]
LOGIC. Involving just one element.

singulative /ˈsɪŋɡjʊlətɪv/ *noun.* M20.
[French *singulatif*, formed as SINGULAR: see -ATIVE.]
LINGUISTICS. An affix denoting a singular form.

singult /ˈsɪŋɡʌlt/ *noun.* In sense 2 also in Latin form **singultus** /sɪŋˈɡʌltəs/. L16.
[Latin *singultus*.]
1 A gasping breath; a sob. *arch.* L16.
2 MEDICINE. Hiccups, hiccuping. M17.

1 SIR W. SCOTT It was to cost you these tears and singults.

singultient /sɪŋˈɡʌlʃ(ə)nt/ *adjective. arch. rare.* M17.
[Latin *singult-* pres. ppl stem of *singultire* sob, formed as SINGULT: see -ENT.]
Sobbing.

singultus *noun* see SINGULT.

sinh /ʃʌɪn, sɪntʃ, sʌɪˈneɪtʃ/ *noun.* L19.
[from SIN(E *noun* + *h* (for *hyperbolic*).]
MATH. Hyperbolic sine (of).

Sinhala /sɪnˈhɑːlə/ *adjective & noun.* E20.
[formed as next.]
► **A** *adjective.* = SINHALESE *adjective.* E20.
► **B** *noun.* = SINHALESE *noun* 2. M20.

Sinhalese /sɪnhəˈliːz, sɪnə-/ *adjective & noun.* Also **Singhalese** /sɪŋhəˈliːz, sɪŋɡə-/. L18.
[Portuguese *Singhalez*, from Sanskrit *Siṁhala* var. of *Siṁhala* Sri Lanka from *siṁha* (see SINGH): see -ESE. Cf. earlier CINGALESE.]
► **A** *adjective.* Of or pertaining to Sri Lanka; *esp.* of or pertaining to a people of northern Indian origin now forming the majority of the population of Sri Lanka, or their language. L18.
► **B** *noun.* Pl. same.
1 A member of the Sinhalese people. E19.
2 The Indo-Aryan language of the Sinhalese. E19.

Sinic /ˈsɪnɪk/ *adjective. rare.* M17.
[medieval Latin *Sinicus*, formed as SINAEAN: see -IC.]
Chinese.

sinical /ˈsɪnɪk(ə)l/ *adjective.* Now *rare* or *obsolete.* L16.
[from SINE *noun* + -ICAL.]
MATH. Of or relating to a sine or sines; using or based on sines.

sinicize /ˈsɪnɪsʌɪz/ *verb trans.* Also **-ise**. L19.
[from SINIC + -IZE.]
Make Chinese in character.
■ **siniciˈzation** *noun* L19.

Sinico- /ˈsɪnɪkəʊ/ *combining form.* Now *rare.*
[formed as SINIC *adjective*.]
= SINO-¹.

sinify /ˈsɪnɪfʌɪ/ *verb trans.* E20.
[from late Latin *Sini-* combining form of *Sinae* (see SINAEAN) + -FY.]
= SINICIZE.
■ **sinifiˈcation** *noun* = SINICIZATION E20.

sinigrin /ˈsɪnɪɡrɪn, sɪˈnɪɡrɪn/ *noun.* L19.
[Irreg. from Latin *sinapis* mustard + *nigra* black + -IN¹.]
CHEMISTRY. A sulphur-containing glycosidic salt obtained from black mustard; potassium myronate.

sinister /ˈsɪnɪstə/ *adjective.* LME.
[Old & mod. French *sinistre* or Latin *sinister* left, left-hand.]
► **I 1** †**a** Prejudiced against a person or thing; adverse, unfavourable; malicious. LME–L18. ▸**b** Harmful or prejudicial *to*. Now *rare.* E18.
2 Dishonest or suggestive of dishonesty; underhand; shady. LME.
3 Corrupt, evil, wicked; base. L15. ▸†**b** Erring; erroneous; heretical. E16–M17.
4 Portending or suggestive of misfortune or disaster; ill-omened; inauspicious. Also, attended by misfortune or disaster; unlucky, unfortunate. L16.
5 Suggestive of evil or malice. L18.

1b N. HAWTHORNE Sinister to the intellect, and sinister to the heart. **2** *Listener* The record of his sinister 'missing years' was . . available for all. **3** P. D. JAMES An alien and sinister power ruled the night. **4** M. HOCKING The doctor did not seem to suspect anything sinister. **5** R. RENDELL Something sinister about the place . . the way you never saw anyone else, heard no sound.

► **II 6** Of or on the left-hand side of a person or thing. *arch.* L15. ▸**b** HERALDRY. Of or on the left-hand side of a shield etc. (i.e. to an observer's right). Opp. DEXTER. M16.
7 In a left-hand direction; anti-clockwise. *rare.* E17.
7b ***bar sinister***: see BAR *noun*¹ 5. ***baton sinister***: see BATON *noun* 3. ***bend sinister***, ***sinister bend***: see BEND *noun*² 2.
■ **sinisterly** *adverb* LME. **sinisterness** *noun* M17.

sinisterity /sɪnɪˈstɛrɪti/ *noun.* Now *rare* or *obsolete.* E17.
[Late Latin *sinisteritas*, from Latin SINISTER: see -ITY.]
1 Lack of dexterity; clumsiness. E17.
†**2** Sinister character or quality. M17–M18.
3 Left-handedness. L19.

sinistral /ˈsɪnɪstr(ə)l/ *adjective & noun.* LME.
[from SINISTER + -AL¹.]
► **A** *adjective.* **I** †**1** Attended by misfortune or disaster, unlucky, unfortunate. *rare.* Only in LME.
†**2** = SINISTER 1. M–L16.
► **II 3** Situated on the left-hand side; of or pertaining to the left hand or left-hand side. E19.
4 CONCHOLOGY. Of a spiral shell: having the whorls ascending from right to left (of the observer); reversed, left-handed. M19.
5 Of a person: (predominantly) left-handed. E20.
6 GEOLOGY. Of, pertaining to, or designating a strike-slip fault in which the motion of the block on the further side of the fault from an observer is towards the left. M20.
► **B** *noun.* A (predominantly) left-handed person. E20.
¶ Opp. DEXTRAL.
■ **siniˈstrality** *noun* the state or quality of being sinistral; *esp.* left-handedness: M19. **sinistrally** *adverb* (**a**) *rare* adversely, falsely; †(**b**) in a sinistral direction, to the left: M16.

sinistro- /ˈsɪnɪstrəʊ/ *combining form.*
[formed as SINISTER: see -O-.]
Chiefly ANATOMY. Of, on, towards, or pertaining to the left (side), as ***sinistro-cerebral***.

sinistrorse /ˈsɪnɪstrɔːs/ *adjective.* M19.
[Latin *sinistrorsus*, from SINISTER.]
Turned or spiralling upwards towards the left.
■ Also **siniˈstrorsal** *adjective* (now *rare*) E19.

sinistrous /ˈsɪnɪstrəs/ *adjective.* Now *rare.* M16.
[from SINISTER + -OUS.]
†**1** = SINISTER 3b. M16–M17.
†**2** = SINISTER 1. L16–M18.
3 = SINISTER 4. L16.
†**4** = SINISTER 2. E17–E18.
†**5** = SINISTER 5. M–L17.
■ **sinistrously** *adverb* LME.

Sinitic /sɪˈnɪtɪk/ *adjective*. L19.
[formed as SINAEAN + -ITIC.]
Designating a Chinese group of Sino-Tibetan languages, including Chinese, Thai, and Tibetan.

sink /sɪŋk/ *noun*. ME.
[from the verb.]
► I 1 A fixed basin made of stone, metal, etc., with a pipe; *esp.* such a basin with a water supply. ME. ▸b A pool or pit in the ground for collecting waste water or sewage; a cesspool. Now *rare*. LME. ▸c A conduit or drain for carrying away dirty water or sewage; a sewer. Now *rare*. L15.
2 *fig.* A place where vice, corruption, or social deprivation is rampant. Also foll. by *of*. E16. ▸†b A mass of unpleasant matter; the most worthless part *of* a place etc., the dregs. L16–M18. ▸c A place where things are lost. *rare*. M17.
3 *transf.* A receptacle of foul or waste matter. L16.
1 ***everything but the kitchen sink***: see KITCHEN *sink*.
► II †4 a The well of a lamp. Only in LME. ▸b The well of a ship. E17–E18.
5 MINING. A mine shaft, *esp.* one dug as a preliminary to a full-sized shaft. L16.
6 a A flat low-lying area where water collects and forms a marsh or pool, or disappears by percolation or evaporation. L16. ▸b A swallow-hole. Chiefly *US*. L18.
7 PHYSICS. A place where, or a process by which, energy or some specific component leaves a system; a device that acts as a sink. Opp. SOURCE *noun* 5b. M19.
Comb.: **sinkhole** (*a*) a hole or hollow into which foul matter runs or is thrown; (*b*) a swallow-hole.
■ **sinkful** *noun* as much or as many as will fill a (kitchen) sink M20.

sink /sɪŋk/ *verb*. Pa. t. **sank** /saŋk/, **sunk** /sʌŋk/. Pa. pple **sunk**, (*arch.*) **sunken** /ˈsʌŋkən/. See also SUNK, SUNKEN *adjectives*.
[Old English *sincan* = Old Frisian *sinka*, Old Saxon, Old High German *sinkan*, Middle Low German, Middle Dutch *sinken* (Dutch *zinken*, German *sinken*), Old Norse *sǫkkva*, Gothic *sigqan*, from Germanic strong verb of unkn. origin.]
► I *verb intrans.* 1 Go or penetrate below the surface of something, esp. liquid; become submerged; *spec.* (esp. of a ship) go to the bottom of the sea etc. OE. ▸b Be received *into* the yielding surface of something; (of a weapon, the teeth, a blow) penetrate *into* or *through*. ME. ▸†c Descend into hell. Usu. foll. by *into*. ME–M16. ▸d Recede or be depressed *into* something. *rare* exc. as SUNKEN *adjective* 2. M16.
2 Fall or go slowly downwards; descend to a lower level. Freq. foll. by *down*. OE. ▸b Of the sun or moon: disappear below the horizon; pass out of sight. E16. ▸c Of ground: reach a lower level as a result of subsidence; slope downwards; dip. M16. ▸d Excavate a well, mine shaft, etc.; bore a hole. M19. ▸e Of the eye: glance or look downwards. M19.
3 a Of a river etc.: fall to a lower level, go down. OE. ▸b Of a flame or fire: burn less strongly; die down. E17.
4 Fall gradually down through fatigue etc.; droop; slump; collapse, give way; *spec.* drop down slowly or easily into a lying or sitting position. ME.
5 Of a liquid: penetrate a substance, soak through. Foll. by *in*, *into*, *through*, etc. ME. ▸†b Of paper: cause ink to spread on application. L16–L18. ▸c Of an oil-painting: develop dull spots on the surface where the pigments have sunk into the ground. Also foll. by *in*. M20.
6 Penetrate into the mind, heart, etc.; be comprehended. Usu. foll. by *in*, *into*. ME. ▸b Weigh *on* mentally, burden. *rare*. M18. ▸c Of darkness etc.: descend *on* or *upon* a person or place. E19.
7 Be absorbed or plunged deeply *in* thought etc. Chiefly as ***be sunk in***. ME.
8 Fall or pass gradually *into* or *from* a state or condition. Also foll. by *to*. ME.
9 a Give way *under* or *beneath* misfortune, affliction, etc.; be weighed down or crushed. L16. ▸b Become depressed or dejected; lose vitality; *spec.* (of a person) approach death. E17.
10 Decline in the scale of fortune, prosperity, or (esp.) estimation; descend to a lower level or type, degenerate. L16. ▸b Use profane language, swear. (Cf. sense 15 below.) Now *arch.* & *dial.* M17.
11 Diminish, decrease; *spec.* (of a sound) lower in volume, become less audible. M17.

1 R. BRADBURY They leaped into the canal water, and he let himself sink down and down to the bottom. M. FRAYN It rolled . . off the raft and sank without hesitation to the bottom of the tank. L. HELLMAN I sank into the mud. *fig.*: *Times* The film . . sank virtually without trace. b G. F. SIMS Letting his feet sink deep into the . . carpet. R. FRAME She let her head sink into the pillow. 2 M. ARNOLD He lets his lax right hand . . Sink upon his mighty knees. J. A. MICHENER The oxen were lured into the water, and slowly the wagons sank, sank, sank until it looked as if they must go under. b J. TYNDALL The sun sank behind the neighbouring peaks. 3b R. C. HUTCHINSON The fire, unattended, had sunk to whispering ashes. 4 D. CUSACK Gwyn sinks back in her chair with a gesture of despair. R. P. JHABVALA She sank to her knees . . and covered her face. 6 W. S. MAUGHAM He needed a little time to let a notion sink into his mind. *Daily Express* It hasn't really sunk in yet that . . the children are ours. 7 WALKER PERCY Northern Virginia . . , where he sat sunk in thought on old battlegrounds. 8 G. ORWELL He sank . . into deep sleep. W. S. CHURCHILL Berwick sank . . to the minor seaport which exists today. E. BLISHEN I sank into a . . gloomy silence. 9a SHAKES. *Rom. & Jul.* Under love's heavy burden do I sink. b C. HARE His heart sank to see . . another visitor in the pantry. G. M. FRASER Dusk came down, my spirits sank with it. C. HARMAN Frank was sinking fast (and died within twelve hours). 10 LD MACAULAY The Whigs . . had lately sunk in the opinion both of the King and of the nation. R. LAWLER How low I'd sunk, . . covered in stinkin' paint.

► II *verb trans.* 12 Cause (a thing) to go or penetrate below the surface of something, esp. liquid; submerge; *spec.* send (a ship) to the bottom of the sea etc. Also, cause to be received *into* the yielding surface of something; cause (a weapon, the teeth, a blow) to penetrate *into* or *through*. ME.
13 Cause (a thing) to fall or descend to a lower level. ME. ▸b Lower the level of (ground, a river, etc.). Now *rare*. E17. ▸c NAUTICAL. Lose sight of (an object on the horizon) by sailing away. M18. ▸d HUNTING. Move down (a slope). M19. ▸e In GOLF, hole a ball from (a putt); hole (a ball) by putting. In BILLIARDS & SNOOKER etc., pot (a ball). In BASKETBALL, score a goal or basket from (a shot). E20. ▸f Consume (an alcoholic drink), esp. rapidly. *colloq.* M20.
14 Excavate (a well, mine shaft, etc.) by digging vertically downwards; bore. LME. ▸b Cut or carve (a shape) into a surface; form (a cavity etc.) by cutting or by heavy pressure; *spec.* engrave (a die), inlay (a design). (Earlier in SINKER *noun*[1].) M17. ▸c Insert into a thing by hollowing, cutting, etc. E19.
15 Reduce to ruin; overwhelm; destroy; defeat. Also (*arch.*) used in oaths. L16.
16 Lower in estimation. E17. ▸b Debase, degrade. E18.
17 Cause (a person, the mind, spirits, etc.) to become depressed or dejected. M17. ▸b Reduce or exhaust the strength of (a person). Now *rare*. E18.
18 Reduce the inflexibility of (a bow). *rare*. M17.
19 a Reduce in amount or value. Now *rare*. L17. ▸b Lower the volume of (the voice), make less audible. M18.
20 a Cease to use; give up; conceal; *spec.* avoid mentioning. Now *rare*. E18. ▸b Deduct (the offal) when reckoning the weight of a carcass. Now *rare*. L18. ▸c Set aside; overlook; forget. M19.
21 Appropriate (money) for one's own use. Now *rare*. E18.
22 Invest; *esp.* invest unprofitably, lose (money) in investment. E18. ▸b Pay up (a debt). E18.

12 B. CRUMP One of the dogs sank his teeth into a tender part. N. MONSARRAT Two Italian battleships had been sunk. G. NAYLOR Luther . . sank his head back into his leather recliner. 13f *Superbike* Stay long enough to sink a . . cold beer. 14 J. GATHORNE-HARDY Into its rich . . seams deep shafts have been sunk. *Daily Telegraph* The labour involved in . . sinking lakes and planting woods. c S. HEANEY I sink my crowbar in a chink . . under the masonry. *Practical Householder* Enlarge . . each hole to allow the screwhead to be sunk . . below the surface. 15 N. MARSH Sink me if I don't believe she knows. 16 J. AUSTEN It has sunk him in my opinion. 19b CONAN DOYLE He had a trick . . of suddenly sinking his voice to a whisper. 20c A. MASON Religious and political fanatics . . sank their . . differences and joined forces. 22 P. KAVANAGH The unfortunate Roscommon farmer who sank his life's savings in it.

Phrases: **sink or swim** fail or succeed with no external help or intervention; *adverbial phr.* regardless of whether the outcome is success or failure. **sink the wind** HUNTING move downwind of a person or animal; *spec.* (of a fox) pass below the line of scent.
¶ Formerly (now only in sense 7) the perfect tenses were freq. formed with *be* rather than *have*.
■ **sinkable** *adjective* able to be sunk (earlier in UNSINKABLE) M19. **sinkage** *noun* (*a*) the action of sinking, subsidence; an instance of this; (*b*) a surface that has been sunk as ornamentation: L19. **sinky** *adjective* (*rare*) (of sand or soil) yielding E19.

sinkeh /ˈsɪŋkeɪ/ *noun*. L19.
[Malay *singke(h)* or directly from Chinese dial. *sinkheh*, from *sin* new + *kheh* visitor.]
In Malaysia, a person, esp. a labourer, recently arrived from China.

sinker /ˈsɪŋkə/ *noun*[1]. E16.
[from SINK *verb* + -ER[1].]
► I 1 A person who engraves figures or designs on dice. Chiefly *Scot.* E16.
2 A person who causes something to sink; *rare* a person who sinks. M17.
3 A person who excavates a well, mine shaft, etc. E18.
► II 4 A thing which causes something to sink, a heavy object used as a weight. Now chiefly *spec.*, a weight used to sink a fishing-line, sounding-line, etc., in water. M16. ▸b *spec.* A device for depressing a lever in a knitting-machine. Usu. with specifying word. L18. ▸c A base coin; *US* a dollar. *slang*. M19. ▸d A doughy cake, *esp.* a doughnut. *slang*. Now *rare*. L19.
5 A sink, a cesspool, a sewer. Now *dial.* E17.
6 A sunken or partly submerged log. *N. Amer.* L19.
7 BASEBALL. A ball which drops markedly after being pitched or hit. Also ***sinker-ball***. M20.
8 A very short board designed for experienced windsurfers sailing in high winds. L20.
Phrases: ***hook, line, and sinker***: see HOOK *noun*.
■ **sinkerless** *adjective* (of a fishing-line) having no sinker L19.

sinker /ˈsɪŋkə/ *noun*[2]. Orig. †**senker**. M19.
[German *Senker* process, shoot, assim. to SINKER *noun*[1].]
BOTANY. A process of the root system of a mistletoe that grows radially into the tissues of the stem of the host.

sinking /ˈsɪŋkɪŋ/ *noun*. LME.
[from SINK *verb* + -ING[1].]
1 The action of SINK *verb*; an instance of this. LME.
2 A depression, a recess, a worked hollow. E18.
3 A dull spot on the surface of an oil-painting caused by the absorption of the pigments by the ground. E20.
Comb.: **sinking feeling** a bodily sensation caused by hunger or apprehension; **sinking fund** a fund formed by periodically setting aside money to accumulate at interest, for the gradual repayment of a debt.

sinking /ˈsɪŋkɪŋ/ *ppl adjective*. M16.
[from SINK *verb* + -ING[2].]
That sinks; (of ground) soft, yielding (*rare*).
sinking sand *rare* a quicksand.

sinless /ˈsɪnlɪs/ *adjective*. OE.
[from SIN *noun*[1] + -LESS.]
Free from sin.
■ **sinlessness** *noun* M17. **sinlessly** *adverb* L17.

sinner /ˈsɪnə/ *noun* & *verb*. ME.
[from SIN *verb* + -ER[1].]
► A *noun*. 1 A person who sins. ME.
2 A reprobate; an offender against any rule or custom. *joc.* E19.

1 P. CAREY Rejoicing in the Lord's house when . . one sinner returned to the fold. R. MACNEIL Sinners . . in hope of purchasing redemption.

► B *verb trans.* with *it*. Act as a sinner. M18.
■ **sinneress** *noun* (*rare*) a female sinner ME. **sinnership** *noun* the condition of being a sinner M18.

sinnet /ˈsɪnɪt/ *noun*[1]. E17.
[Origin unkn. Cf. SENNIT.]
NAUTICAL. Braided cordage made in flat, round, or square form from 3 to 9 cords.

sinnet *noun*[2] var. of SENNET *noun*[2].

Sinn Fein /ʃɪn ˈfeɪn/ *noun phr.* E20.
[Irish *sinn féin* lit. 'we ourselves'. Cf. SHINNER *noun*[2].]
An Irish political movement and party founded in 1905, orig. aiming at the independence of Ireland and a revival of Irish culture, now seeking a united republican Ireland and linked to the IRA.
■ **Sinn Feiner** *noun* a member or adherent of Sinn Fein E20.

sinningia /sɪˈnɪŋgɪə/ *noun*. E19.
[mod. Latin (see below), from Wilhelm *Sinning* (1794–1874), German botanist + -IA[1].]
Any of various tropical American plants constituting the genus *Sinningia* (family Gesneriaceae), with velvety-hairy trumpet-shaped flowers; esp. *S. speciosa*, the parent of many varieties commonly known as gloxinias.

Sino- /ˈsʌɪnəʊ, ˈsɪnəʊ/ *combining form*[1].
[from Greek *Sinai*, Latin *Sinae* the Chinese: see -O-.]
Forming nouns and adjectives with the senses 'Chinese, of China'; 'Chinese and —', as ***Sino-American***, ***Sino-British***, ***Sino-Soviet***.
■ **Sinoˈlogical** *adjective* of or pertaining to Sinology L19. **Sinˈologist** *noun* an expert in or student of Sinology E19. **Sinologue** *noun* (now *rare*) = SINOLOGIST M19. **Siˈnology** *noun* the branch of knowledge that deals with the history, language, and culture of China L19. **Sinophile** *noun* & *adjective* (a person who is) friendly towards China or fond of China and things Chinese E20. **Sinoˈphilia** *noun* friendliness towards China; excessive fondness for China and things Chinese: L20. **Sinophobe** *noun* & *adjective* (a person who is) affected with Sinophobia E20. **Sinoˈphobia** *noun* dread or dislike of China and things Chinese M20. **Sino-Tiˈbetan** *noun* a language family comprising the Chinese, Tibeto-Burman, and (according to some scholars) the Tai languages E20.

sino- /ˈsʌɪnəʊ/ *combining form*[2].
[from SINUS: see -O-.]
MEDICINE. Forming nouns and adjectives with the sense 'of or petaining to a sinus'.
■ **sino-ˈatrial**, **sino-auˈricular** *adjectives* of, pertaining to, or designating a small node or body of tissue in the wall of the right atrium of the heart that acts as a pacemaker by producing a contractile signal at regular intervals E20. **sinogram** *noun* an X-ray photograph of a sinus into which a contrast medium has been introduced M20. **siˈnography** *noun* the radiographic examination of sinuses M20.

Sinon /ˈsʌɪnən/ *noun*. *arch.* L16.
[The Greek who induced the Trojans to bring the wooden horse into Troy.]
A person who deceives with false information; a betrayer.

†**sinonimia** *noun* see SYNONYMY.

†**sinoper** *noun*. LME.
[Old French *sinopre* var. of SINOPLE.]
1 A red colour. LME–L17.
2 A kind of red earth used as a pigment; sinopia; *spec.* cinnabar. LME–E18.

sinopia /sɪˈnəʊpɪə/ *noun*. Pl. **-pie** /-pɪeɪ/. M19.
[Italian.]
1 A red pigment containing sinopite or similar-coloured minerals. M19.
2 *transf.* A preliminary rough sketch for a fresco, covered by the final work. M20.

Sinopic /sɪˈnɒpɪk/ *adjective*. M18.
[Latin *Sinopicus* from Greek *Sinōpikos*, from *Sinōpē*, a Greek colony in Paphlagonia: see -IC.]
Of, pertaining to, or obtained from (the area round) Sinope.

sinopie *noun* pl. of SINOPIA.

sinopis /sɪˈnəʊpɪs/ *noun*. M19.
[Latin: see SINOPLE.]
= SINOPIA 1.

sinople /ˈsɪnəp(ə)l/ *noun & adjective*. ME.
[Old & mod. French *sinople* from Latin *sinopis* (sc. *terra* earth) from Greek. *Sinōpis*, from *Sinōpē* Sinope: see SINOPIC. Cf. SINOPER.]
▶ **A** *noun*. †**1** = SINOPER 2. ME–L17.
†**2** = SINOPER 1. LME–M16.
3 The colour green; *spec.* (HERALDRY) the tincture vert, in French blazon. *obsolete* exc. *Hist.* LME.
4 MINERALOGY. A variety of ferruginous quartz. Now *rare* or *obsolete*. L18.
▶ **B** *adjective*. Of a green colour; *spec.* (HERALDRY) vert, in French blazon. *obsolete* exc. *Hist.* L16.

SINS *abbreviation*.
Ship's inertial navigation system.

sinsemilla /sɪnsəˈmɪlə/ *noun*. L20.
[Amer. Spanish, lit. 'without seed'.]
A seedless form of the cannabis plant, *Cannabis sativa* subsp. *indica*, having a particularly high narcotic content; the drug obtained from this plant.

sinsyne /sɪnˈsʌɪn/ *adverb*. *Scot. & north.* M16.
[from SIN *preposition* + SYNE *adverb*.]
Since then, from that time.

sinter /ˈsɪntə/ *noun*. L18.
[German = CINDER *noun*.]
1 A hard incrustation or deposit formed on rocks etc. by precipitation from mineral waters; *spec.* = GEYSERITE. L18.
2 Material which has been subjected to sintering; *spec.* iron ore prepared for smelting by sintering the powdered material, usu. together with coke etc.; the solid waste from smelting or refining. E20.

sinter /ˈsɪntə/ *verb*. L19.
[from the noun.]
1 *verb intrans.* Of powder or particulate material: coalesce into a solid or porous mass under the influence of heat or pressure without liquefaction, esp. after compression in a shaped die. L19.
2 *verb trans.* Cause to coalesce in this way. E20.
2 sintered carbide a very hard material manufactured by sintering a pulverized mixture of cobalt or nickel and carbides of metals such as tungsten and tantalum, used in the cutting parts of tools. **sintered glass** a porous form of glass made by sintering glass powder, used esp. in chemical filtration apparatus.

sintok /ˈsɪntɒk/ *noun*. Also **-toc**. M19.
[Malay.]
A Malayan tree, *Cinnamomum sintok*, related to cinnamon; the aromatic bark of this tree.

Sintu /ˈsɪntuː/ *adjective & noun*. *S. Afr.* L20.
[from (*i*)*si-* language or culture + *-ntu* person, elems. common to several Bantu langs.]
W. ref. to language: = BANTU.
¶ Introduced in order to avoid the offensive connotations of BANTU.

sinuate /ˈsɪnjʊət/ *adjective*. L17.
[Latin *sinuatus* pa. pple of *sinuare* bend, wind, curve, formed as SINUS: see -ATE².]
BOTANY & ZOOLOGY. Having a wavy margin, with alternate rounded sinuses and lobes; sinuose.
▪ **sinuately** *adverb* M19.

sinuate /ˈsɪnjʊeɪt/ *verb intrans.* M19.
[Latin *sinuat-* pa. ppl stem of *sinuare*: see prec., -ATE³.]
Follow a winding course.

sinuated /ˈsɪnjʊeɪtɪd/ *ppl adjective*. L16.
[formed as prec. + -ED¹.]
†**1** Having a sinus or hollow. Only in L16.
2 BOTANY & ZOOLOGY. = SINUATE *adjective*. Now *rare*. E18.
3 That follows a winding course. *rare*. M19.

sinuation /sɪnjʊˈeɪʃ(ə)n/ *noun*. M17.
[Late Latin *sinuatio(n-)*, from Latin *sinuat-* pa. ppl stem of *sinuare*: see SINUATE *adjective*, -ATION.]
†**1** The action of following a winding course. *rare*. Only in M17.
2 A winding in and out; a sinuosity. L17.

sinuatrial /sʌɪnjʊˈeɪtrɪəl/ *adjective*. M20.
[from Latin *sinu-* stem of SINUS + ATRIAL *adjective*.]
ANATOMY. = SINO-ATRIAL.

sinumbra /sɪˈnʌmbrə/ *noun*. *obsolete* exc. *Hist.* M19.
[from Latin *sine umbra* without a shadow.]
In full ***sinumbra lamp***. A type of oil lamp designed to cast very little shadow when lit.

sinuose /ˈsɪnjʊəʊs/ *adjective*. E19.
[Latin *sinuosus*, formed as SINUS: see -OSE¹.]
BOTANY & ZOOLOGY. = SINUATE *adjective*
▪ **sinuosely** *adverb* L19.

sinuosity /sɪnjʊˈɒsɪti/ *noun*. L16.
[French *sinuosité* or medieval Latin *sinuositas*, formed as prec.: see -ITY.]
1 The state or quality of being sinuous. L16.
2 A curve or bend, *esp.* in a river or road. E18.
3 *fig.* A complexity, an intricacy. Usu. in *pl.* E19.

sinuous /ˈsɪnjʊəs/ *adjective*. L16.
[French *sinueux* or formed as SINUS: see -OUS.]
1 Characterized by many curves; undulating; curving. L16. ▸**b** *transf.* Complex, intricate. M19. ▸**c** *fig.* Not straightforward or direct; dishonest, crooked. M19.
2 Supple, lithe, agile. L19.

📖 **1** T. C. WOLFE A sinuous road . . curved up along the hill-side. W. HENRY A sinuous, stomping . . line of growling, drink-crazed warriors. **2** ANNE STEVENSON She found Richard's slender sinuous body . . attractive.

▪ **sinuously** *adverb* M19. **sinuousness** *noun* L17.

sinus /ˈsʌɪnəs/ *noun*. LME.
[Latin = curve, bend, bay, etc.]
1 MEDICINE. An infected tract leading from a deep-seated infection and discharging pus to the surface. Formerly also, a fistula. LME.
2 a A curvature, a flexure, a bend; a curved recess. Now *rare*. E17. ▸**b** BOTANY. Any of a series of small rounded depressions on the margin of a leaf etc. M18.
3 A bay, a creek. Now only (ASTRONOMY) in proper names of surface features of the moon, planets, etc. M17.
4 ANATOMY. **a** Any of various irregular venous or lymphatic cavities, reservoirs, or dilated vessels. L17. ▸**b** A cavity within a bone or other tissue, esp. within the bones of the face or skull, connecting with the nasal cavities. Freq. in *pl.* E18.
†**5** A cavity or hole in the earth. L17–L18.
Comb.: **sinus gland** ZOOLOGY a neurohaemal organ in the eye-stalk or head of a crustacean in which are stored various hormones concerned with growth, reproduction, and metabolism; **sinus rhythm** the normal rhythm of the heart, proceeding from the sino-atrial node; **sinus venosus** ZOOLOGY the first chamber of the heart in fish, amphibians, and reptiles, emptying into the right atrium.
▪ **sinuˈsitis** *noun* (MEDICINE) inflammation of a sinus, esp. a paranasal sinus L19.

sinusoid /ˈsʌɪnəsɔɪd/ *noun*. E19.
[from SINUS + -OID.]
1 MATH. A curve having the form of a sine wave. E19.
2 An irregular capillary-sized blood-vessel, without the continuous endothelial lining of capillaries. E20.
▪ **sinuˈsoidal** *adjective* resembling, pursuing, or flowing in the wavelike course of a sinusoid; having the form of a sinusoid; varying periodically (with time, distance, etc.) as a sine varies with an angle: L19. **sinuˈsoidally** *adverb* L19.

sion /ˈsʌɪən/ *noun*¹. *rare*. OE.
[Latin from Greek.]
A kind of aquatic plant with hot-tasting leaves. Cf. LAVER *noun*¹ 1.

Sion *noun*² var. of ZION.

Siouan /ˈsuːən/ *noun & adjective*. L19.
[from SIOU(X + -AN.]
▶ **A** *noun*. **1** = SIOUX *noun* 1. L19.
2 A N. American Indian language family including Sioux, Crow, and Omaha. E20.
▶ **B** *adjective*. Of or pertaining to this language family or the speakers of (any of) its languages. E20.

†**sioun** *noun* see SCION.

Sioux /suː/ *noun & adjective*. E18.
[N. Amer. French *Nadouessioux* from Ojibwa (Ottawa dial.) *nātowēssiwak*, with French pl. ending *-x* replacing Ojibwa pl. ending *-ak*.]
▶ **A** *noun*. Pl. same /suː, suːz/.
1 Orig., a member of any of the N. American Indian peoples speaking a Siouan language. Now usu. *spec.*, a member of a Siouan people inhabiting the upper Mississippi and Missouri river valleys (also called ***Dakota***). E18.
2 Orig., the Siouan language family. Now usu. *spec.*, the language of the (present-day) Sioux (also called ***Dakota***). L18.
▶ **B** *attrib.* or as *adjective*. Of or pertaining to the Sioux or their language. Also (now *rare*), Siouan. E18.

sip /sɪp/ *noun*. L15.
[from the verb.]
1 An act of sipping; a small mouthful *of* liquid taken by sipping. L15.
2 *fig.* A brief experience *of* something. E18.

📖 **1** J. DOS PASSOS Eleanor lifted her teacup and drank several little sips. R. P. GRAVES The children joined him . . for a sip of wine after dinner. N. GORDIMER She tasted the lemon juice and took swallows in sips because it was very hot.

sip /sɪp/ *verb trans. & intrans.* Infl. **-pp-**. LME.
[Prob. symbolic modification of SUP *verb*¹ to express less vigorous action.]
1 Take small mouthfuls of (a liquid); drink (a liquid) slowly or with care. LME. ▸**b** *fig.* Experience (something) briefly. E17.
2 Take nectar from (a flower) in small quantities. Chiefly *poet.* L17.

📖 **1** C. S. FORESTER They had to sip slowly, as the liquid was steaming hot. K. VONNEGUT You sit in a café for hours sipping coffee. D. PROFUMO She sipped some claret.

▪ **sipper** *noun* (*a*) a person who sips; a drinker (*of* some liquid); (*b*) in *pl.* (*Nautical slang*), a sip of rum, esp. from another's tot, as a reward or in celebration: L16. **sipping** *noun* the action of the verb; an instance of this, a sip: LME. **sippingly** *adverb* by or in sips E19.

sipe /sʌɪp/ *noun*. OE.
[Rel. to next.]
1 Chiefly *Scot. & US*. ▸**a** The action of percolating or oozing through; a liquid which percolates or oozes through. OE. ▸**b** A small spring or pool of water. E19.
2 A groove or channel in the tread of a tyre to improve its grip. M20.
▪ **sipage** *noun* leakage or oozing of water E19.

sipe /sʌɪp/ *verb*. Chiefly *Scot., north., & US*.
[Old English *sīpian* corresp. to Old Frisian *sīpa*, Middle Low German *sīpen*, of unkn. origin. Cf. SEEP *verb*.]
1 *verb intrans.* Of water or other liquid: percolate or ooze through; drip, trickle slowly. OE.
2 *verb trans.* Cause to drip or ooze. L19.
▪ **siping** *noun* (*a*) the action of the verb; an instance of this; (*b*) water or other liquid that has oozed through: E16.

sipeera /sɪˈpɪərə/ *noun*. M18.
[Guyanese name.]
The greenheart tree, *Ocotea rodiaei* of northern S. America (also ***sipeera tree***); the bark of this tree.

Siphnian /ˈsɪfnɪən/ *noun & adjective*. E18.
[from Greek *Siphnios* + -AN.]
▶ **A** *noun*. A native or inhabitant of the Greek Cycladic island of Siphnos. E18.
▶ **B** *adjective*. Of, pertaining to, or characteristic of Siphnos or the Siphnians. L19.

siphon /ˈsʌɪf(ə)n/ *noun*. Also **sy-**. LME.
[French, or Latin *sipho(n-)* from Greek *siphōn* pipe, tube.]
†**1** A tube, a hose. Only in LME.
2 A pipe or tube used for conveying liquid from one level to a lower level, using the liquid pressure differential to force a column of the liquid up to a higher level before it falls to the outlet. LME. ▸**b** *transf.* A closed channel through which liquid passes on the principle of the siphon. M18. ▸**c** In full ***siphon-bottle***. A bottle containing carbonated water which is forced out through a spout by the pressure of the gas. L19.
3 ZOOLOGY. A tubular organ (other than a blood-vessel) that conveys fluid in certain aquatic invertebrates etc.; *esp.* one in a mollusc through which water is drawn in or expelled. E19.
▪ **siphoˈnaceous** *adjective* (BOTANY) = SIPHONEOUS E20. **siphonage** *noun* the action of drawing off liquid by means of a siphon M19. **siphonal** *adjective* (chiefly ZOOLOGY) having the form or character of a siphon; of or pertaining to a siphon: E19. **siphonate** *adjective* (ZOOLOGY) provided with, or characterized by having, a siphon L19. **siphoneous** /sʌɪˈfəʊnɪəs/ *adjective* (BOTANY) (of an alga) having a tubular thallus without septa M19. **siphonic** /sʌɪˈfɒnɪk/ *adjective* of or pertaining to a siphon; working by means of, or on the principle of, a siphon: M19.

siphon /ˈsʌɪf(ə)n/ *verb trans.* Also **sy-**. M19.
[from the noun.]
1 Draw off or convey (liquid etc.) by means of a siphon. Foll. by adverb or preposition. M19. ▸**b** Empty (as if) by means of a siphon. L19.
2 *fig.* Draw off as if by means of a siphon; divert or set aside (esp. funds etc.). Freq. foll. by *off*. M20.

📖 **1** A. C. CLARKE Siphoning fuel out of the hydrojet's tank. SHELLEY SMITH Edmund . . siphoned . . soda into his glass. **2** P. CAREY Sergei has been cheating me . . . He has been siphoning funds. B. CHATWIN He siphoned off . . money to pay for . . another object. *Business* Other airlines . . siphon . . traffic away from the U.K. hubs.

▪ **siphoner** *noun* a person who siphons off liquid etc. M20.

siphonapteran /sʌɪfəˈnapt(ə)r(ə)n/ *noun & adjective*. M19.
[from mod. Latin order name *Siphonaptera* (see below), from Greek *siphōn* SIPHON *noun* + *apteros* wingless: see -AN.]
ENTOMOLOGY. ▶ **A** *noun*. An insect belonging to the order Siphonaptera, which comprises the fleas. M19.
▶ **B** *adjective*. = SIPHONAPTEROUS. M20.

■ **siphonapterous** *adjective* of or pertaining to the Siphonaptera L19.

siphonaxanthin *noun* var. of SIPHONOXANTHIN.

siphonein /ˈsʌɪf(ə)niːn/ *noun.* M20.
[from SIPHONO- + -*ein*, perh. after LUTEIN.]
BIOCHEMISTRY. An ester of siphonoxanthin present in certain green algae.

siphono- /ˈsʌɪf(ə)nəʊ/ *combining form* of Greek *siphōn* siphon: see -O-. Before a vowel also **siphon-**.
■ **sipho'nogamy** *noun* (*BOTANY*) fertilization by means of a pollen-tube E20. **siphonoglyph** *noun* a ciliated groove in the pharynx of sea anemones L19. **sipho'nophoran** *noun & adjective* (*a*) *noun* = SIPHONOPHORE; (*b*) *adjective* of or pertaining to the order Siphonophora, which comprises colonial pelagic hydrozoans with both polyps and medusae and a float, including the Portuguese man-of-war: L19. **siphonophore** *noun* an animal or colony of this order M19. **siphonostele** *noun* (*BOTANY*) a stele consisting of a core of pith surrounded by concentric layers of xylem and phloem E20. **siphono'stelic** /-ˈstiːlɪk/ *adjective* (*BOTANY*) pertaining to or of the nature of a siphonstele L19. **siphono'zooid** *noun* a modified polyp without tentacles, serving to maintain water circulation in some soft corals L19.

siphonous /ˈsʌɪf(ə)nəs/ *adjective.* M20.
[from SIPHON *noun* + -OUS.]
BOTANY. = SIPHONEOUS.

siphonoxanthin /ˌsʌɪf(ə)nəˈzanθɪn, sʌɪˌfɒnə-/ *noun.* Also **siphona-**. M20.
[from SIPHONO- + XANTHIN.]
BIOCHEMISTRY. A xanthophyll pigment, $C_{40}H_{56}O_4$, present in certain green algae.

Siphrei Torah *noun phr. pl.* see SEFER TORAH.

siphuncle /ˈsʌɪfʌŋk(ə)l/ *noun.* Also (earlier) in Latin form **siphunculus** /sʌɪˈfʌŋkjʊləs/, pl. **-li** /-lʌɪ, -liː/. M18.
[Latin *siphunculus* small tube, dim. of *sipho* SIPHON *noun*: see -UNCLE.]
1 *ZOOLOGY.* A calcareous tube containing living tissue, running through all the shell-chambers in cephalopods such as nautiloids and ammonites. M18.
2 *ENTOMOLOGY.* A cornicle. Formerly also, a suctorial proboscis. E19.
■ **si'phuncular** *adjective* of or pertaining to a siphuncle, acting or serving as a siphuncle M19. **si'phunculate** *adjective* possessing a siphuncle; *spec.* in *ENTOMOLOGY*, of or pertaining to sucking lice of the order Siphunculata: L19. **si'phunculated** *adjective* possessing a siphuncle E19.

Sipibo *noun & adjective* var. of SHIPIBO.

sipid /ˈsɪpɪd/ *adjective. rare.* E17.
[Back-form. from INSIPID.]
†**1** = SAPID 1. E–M17.
2 = SAPID 2. E20.

sipper-sauce /ˈsɪpəsɔːs/ *noun.* Long *obsolete* exc. *dial.* Orig. †**sibber-**. M16.
[Perh. from Latin *cibarius* of food (see -ER²) + SAUCE *noun*.]
A sauce, a relish; *fig.* a concoction.

sippet /ˈsɪpɪt/ *noun.* M16.
[Irreg. dim. of SOP *noun*¹: see -ET¹.]
1 A small piece of (esp. toasted or fried) bread, usually served in soup or used for dipping into gravy etc. M16.
2 *transf.* A fragment. E17.

sipple /ˈsɪp(ə)l/ *verb.* M16.
[from SIP *verb* + -LE³.]
1 *verb trans.* Drink slowly or with small sips. M16.
2 *verb intrans.* Sip a drink in a leisurely manner. E17.

sipunculid /sʌɪˈpʌŋkjʊlɪd/ *noun & adjective.* L19.
[mod. Latin *Sipunculidae* (see below), from *Sipunculus* genus name from Latin *sipunculus* var. of *siphunculus*: see SIPHUNCLE, -ID³.]
ZOOLOGY. ▶**A** *noun.* Any member of the family Sipunculidae or phylum Sipuncula (formerly Sipunculoidea) of unsegmented burrowing marine worms, which have an anterior retractable proboscis or introvert; a peanut worm. L19.
▶**B** *adjective.* Of, pertaining to, or designating this family or phylum. M20.
■ **sipunculan** *noun & adjective* = SIPUNCULID L20. **sipunculoid** *noun & adjective* = SIPUNCULID M19.

si quis /sʌɪ ˈkwɪs/ *noun.* L16.
[Latin *si quis* (sc. *invenerit*) if anyone (shall have found etc.).]
A public notice or bill requesting information etc.; later *spec.* (*ECCLESIASTICAL*) a notice announcing that a candidate seeks ordination and asking if there is any known impediment.

sir /səː/ *noun & verb.* ME.
[Reduced form of SIRE *noun.* See also SIRRAH *noun*¹. Cf. STIR *noun*².]
▶**A** *noun.* **1** Used as a form of respectful or polite address or mode of reference, orig. by a servant to his or her master, or by any person addressing a man of rank; later used more widely to address or refer to a man of any rank or position, *spec.* by a sales assistant to or of a male customer, by children to or of a male teacher, or (more fully ***dear sir***) at the beginning of a letter to a man. Cf. *madam, miss.* ME. ▸**b** Used as a form of respectful or polite address or mode of reference to a woman: madam. Now *dial.* L16.
2 As a title: used preceding a man's forename, *spec.* (*a*) as the distinctive honorific title for a knight or baronet; †(*b*) as an honorific for an ordinary priest, esp. one who had not graduated in a university. ME. ▸**b** Used preceding a man's designation of rank or office or (formerly) playfully or derisively preceding any noun personified as a man. Formerly also, used preceding a man's surname as a title for a Bachelor of Arts in some Universities. *arch.* ME.
3 A man usually addressed as 'sir'. LME. ▸**b** A priest. Now *dial.* L16.

> **1** R. KIPLING Please, sir, what am I to do about prep? DAY LEWIS A porter crooned soothingly, 'Time enough, sir, time enough.' *Times* 'Would sir like a shampoo?' ***no sir***: see NO *adverb*³ *& interjection*. **2a** R. KIPLING Sir Huon . . setting off from Tintagel Castle. *Times* Mr. (later Sir) Robert Menzies. **Sir Garnet** [Sir *Garnet* Wolseley (1833–1913), leader of several successful military expeditions] (*a*) *arch. slang* (in full ***all Sir Garnet***) highly satisfactory, all right; (*b*) a variety of the card-game nap. **b** TENNYSON It is not meet, Sir King, to leave thee thus. **3** P. GORE-BOOTH Becoming a 'Sir' is one of the tools of the trade.

▶**B** *verb trans.* Infl. **-rr-**. Address as 'sir'. Also foll. by *up.* L16.

> A. BURGESS It was pleasant to be sirred by the company commander.

■ **sirship** *noun* (*a*) the position of a man addressed or referred to as 'sir'; (*b*) (with possess. adjective, as ***your sirship*** etc.) a mock title of respect given to a man in authority: L19.

Sir. *abbreviation.*
In biblical references: Sirach (Apocrypha).

siratro /sɪˈratrəʊ/ *noun.* M20.
[Acronym, from the Commonwealth Scientific and Industrial Research Organization + *atro*(*purpureum* specific epithet of the parent plant.]
A legume grown in pastures in Australia, developed from Mexican strains of the tropical *Macroptilium atropurpureum*.

sirdar *noun* var. of SARDAR.

sire /sʌɪə/ *noun & verb.* ME.
[Old & mod. French from Proto-Romance alt. of Latin SENIOR. Cf. SIR, SIRRAH *noun*¹.]
▶**A** *noun.* **1** Used as a polite form of address to a male superior or equal, now *esp.* a king. *arch.* ME.
†**2 a** = SIR *noun* 2. ME–L15. ▸**b** = SIR *noun* 2b. ME–L15.
3 A ruler; a lord, a sovereign. Formerly also, a ruler *of* a specified place. Now *rare* or *obsolete.* ME.
4 A (human) father; a forefather. Now *poet. & arch.* ME.
5 A person usually addressed as 'sire', a man of rank or importance; an elderly man; *gen.* a man, a fellow. *arch.* LME.
6 A male parent of a quadruped; *esp.* a stallion kept for breeding. Correl. to ***dam***. E16.
▶**B** *verb trans.* Esp. of a stallion: procreate; become the sire of. E17.

> E. BIRNEY His father . . at the age of seventy . . sired two boys and a girl. *Horse & Hound* The great stallion . . had sired . . Derby winners.

■ **sireless** *adjective* fatherless L16. **sireship** *noun* fatherhood M19.

siredon /sʌɪˈriːdən/ *noun.* Now *rare.* M19.
[Late Latin from Greek *Seirēdōn* late form of *Seirēn* SIREN.]
An axolotl.

siree /sɪˈriː/ *noun. US colloq.* Also **sirree**. E19.
[from alt. of SIRRAH *noun*¹ or SIR + emphat. suffix.]
Sir. Chiefly as *interjection*.
no siree no indeed, certainly not. **yes siree** yes indeed, certainly.

sireen /sʌɪˈriːn/ *noun. colloq.* (chiefly *US*). E20.
[Repr. a pronunc.]
= SIREN *noun.*

siren /ˈsʌɪr(ə)n/ *noun, adjective, & verb.* ME.
[Old French *sereine, sirene* (mod. *sirène*) from late Latin *Sirena* fem. form of Latin *Siren* (to which the English word was finally assim.) from Greek *Seirēn*.]
▶**A** *noun.* †**1** An imaginary type of snake. ME–E16.
2 *GREEK MYTHOLOGY.* Any of several women or winged creatures, half-woman half-bird, whose singing was supposed to lure unwary sailors to destruction on the rocks. Formerly also, a mermaid. LME.
3 *fig.* A person who sings sweetly; a dangerously fascinating woman, a temptress; anything tempting or alluring. L16.
4 *ZOOLOGY.* Any of three eel-like aquatic N. American amphibians of the family Sirenidae, with external gills, no hindlimbs, and tiny forelimbs, esp. *Siren lacertina* (more fully ***greater siren***). L18.
5 a An acoustical instrument for producing musical tones and used in numbering the vibrations in any note. E19. ▸**b** A device for making a loud prolonged or ululating sound as a signal or warning, esp. by revolving a perforated disc over a jet of compressed air or steam. L19.

> **3** E. JOHNSON An artful siren entrapping him. B. NEIL Quite a little siren, aren't you? **5b** L. DEIGHTON Flashing . . lights and sirens as . . police cars mounted the pavement. M. GARDINER The air-raid sirens sounded.

Comb.: **siren suit** a one-piece garment for the whole body, easily put on or taken off, orig. for use in air-raid shelters.
▶**B** *adjective.* Alluring, irresistibly tempting. M16.

> O. SACKS They called . . with Siren voices, they enticed her. D. LESSING Mark . . was attentive to the radiant Charlie, listening to the siren song.

▶**C** *verb.* **1** *verb trans.* Allure, entice. *rare.* L17.
2 *verb intrans.* Make signals with a siren; (of a police car etc.) proceed with siren blaring. L19.
■ **sirenic** /sʌɪˈrɛnɪk/ *adjective* (*rare*) = SIRENICAL E18. **si'renical** *adjective* (now *rare*) melodious; fascinating, alluring: L16.

sirename *noun & verb* see SURNAME.

sirenian /sʌɪˈriːnɪən/ *noun & adjective.* L19.
[from mod. Latin *Sirenia* (see below), from Latin SIREN + -IA²: see -IAN.]
ZOOLOGY. ▶**A** *noun.* Any of various aquatic herbivorous mammals of the order Sirenia, with stocky streamlined bodies, forelimbs modified as flippers, and no hindlimbs; a dugong or sea cow, a manatee. L19.
▶**B** *adjective.* Of, belonging to, or characteristic of this order. L19.

sirenin /ˈsʌɪrənɪn/ *noun.* M20.
[from SIREN + -IN¹.]
BIOCHEMISTRY. A hormone, secreted by female gametes of fungi of the genus *Allomyces*, which attracts male gametes of the same group.

sirex /ˈsʌɪrɛks/ *noun.* Also **S-**. L19.
[mod. Latin *Sirex* (see below) from Greek *seiren* siren, a solitary bee or wasp + -*ex*.]
ENTOMOLOGY. More fully ***sirex wasp***, ***sirex wood wasp***. Any of various woodwasps or horntails now or formerly included in the genus *Sirex*, whose larvae burrow into the trunks of trees.

Sirian /ˈsɪrɪən/ *adjective.* L16.
[from Latin *Sirius* of a star name from Greek *Seirios*: see -AN.]
ASTRONOMY. **1** Of or belonging to the star Sirius. L16.
2 Having a spectrum like that of Sirius. L19.

siriasis /sɪˈrʌɪəsɪs/ *noun.* Pl. **-ases** /-əsiːz/. E17.
[Latin from Greek *seiriasis*, from *seirian* be hot and scorching: see -IASIS.]
MEDICINE. Sunstroke, esp. in children.

sirih /ˈsɪəri/ *noun.* L18.
[Malay.]
The betel pepper, *Piper betle*.

siris /ˈsɪrɪs/ *noun.* L19.
[Hindi from Sanskrit *śirīṣa*.]
Any of several tropical leguminous trees, esp. the kokko, *Albizia lebbeck*, of tropical Asia, and (more fully ***red siris***) the related *A. toona* of Australia.

sirkar *noun* var. of SARKAR.

sirloin /ˈsəːlɔɪn/ *noun.* LME.
[Old French (mod. *surlonge*), formed as SUR- + *longe*: see LOIN.]
The upper and choicer part of a loin of beef.

†**sirly** *adverb & adjective* var. of SURLY.

sirmark /ˈsəːmɑːk/ *noun.* M17.
[Perh. from SUR- + MARK *noun*¹.]
SHIPBUILDING. Any of several marks made on a mould to indicate where the respective bevellings are to be applied to the frame-timbers of a vessel.

siroc /ˈsʌɪrɒk, sɪˈrɒk/ *noun.* L18.
[French †*siroc*(*h*, formed as next.]
= SIROCCO *noun* 1.

sirocco /sɪˈrɒkəʊ/ *noun & verb.* Also **sci-**. E17.
[Italian *scirocco* ult. from Hispano-Arab. *šalūk*, *šu-*, *-k* south-east wind, perh. of Romance origin. Cf. prec.]
▶**A** *noun.* Pl. **-os**.
1 A hot, oppressive, and often dusty or rainy wind which blows from the north coast of Africa over the Mediterranean and parts of southern Europe; *gen.* any hot southerly wind. Also ***sirocco wind***. E17.
2 *fig.* A blighting influence; a fiery storm. M19.
3 A machine or oven for drying hops or tea leaves by means of a hot, moist current of air. Also more fully ***sirocco drying-machine***, ***sirocco oven***. L19.
▶**B** *verb intrans. & trans.* Blow (about) like a sirocco. *rare.* E20.

sirop /siro/ *noun.* Pl. pronounced same. L19.
[French: see SYRUP *noun*.]
(A drink made from) a syrupy preparation of sweetened fruit-juice.

sirrah /ˈsɪrə/ *noun*[1]. *arch.* E16.
[Prob. repr. form of SIRE *noun* with last syll. finally assim. to AH *interjection*. See also SIR. Cf. SORRY *noun*[1].]
Sir. Chiefly as a form of address to a man or boy (formerly also to a woman), expressing contempt, reprimand, or authoritativeness.

Sirrah *noun*[2] var. of SYRAH.

sirree *noun* var. of SIREE.

sir-reverence /səːˈrɛv(ə)r(ə)ns/ *noun. obsolete* exc. *dial.* L16.
[from alt. of SA(VE *preposition* (after SIR) + REVERENCE *noun*.]
†**1** Apology; respect; an instance of this. Also as *interjection*, with apologies, with all respect. L16–L17.
2 (A piece of) human excrement. L16.
1 sir-reverence of with all respect for, with apologies to.

sirtaki /səːˈtaki/ *noun.* L20.
[mod.Greek, from Greek *surtos* SYRTOS + *-aki* dim. suffix.]
A Greek folk-dance in which dancers form a line or chain.

sirup *noun & verb* see SYRUP.

sirvente /sirvɑ̃ːt/ *noun.* Pl. pronounced same. E19.
[French, from Provençal *sirventes*, the final *s* of which was mistaken for a pl. ending; of unkn. origin.]
Hist. A (usu. satirical) poem or lay recited by a medieval troubadour.

Siryenian /səːˈjiːnɪən/ *noun & adjective.* M19.
[mod. Latin *Syriaenus*, formed as ZYRIAN: see -IAN.]
= KOMI.

SIS *abbreviation.*
Secret Intelligence Service.

sis /sɪs/ *noun. colloq.* Also **siss**. M17.
[Abbreviation.]
= SISTER *noun*.

sis /siːs, sɪs/ *interjection. S. Afr.* Also **sies**. M19.
[Afrikaans *sies*, perh. from Nama *si* or *tsi*.]
Expr. disgust or disappointment.

sisal /ˈsʌɪs(ə)l/ *noun.* M19.
[A port in Yucatan.]
Fibre from the leaves of any of several Mexican agaves, esp. *Agave sisalana*, used for cordage, matting, etc.; any of the plants producing this fibre.
sisal hemp, sisal plant, etc.

sis-boom-bah /sɪsbuːmˈbɑː/ *interjection & noun. US.* E20.
[Imit., repr. the sound of a sky-rocket followed by an exclamation of delight.]
(An exclamation) expr. support or encouragement, esp. to a college team.

siscowet /ˈsɪskəʊɛt/ *noun.* M19.
[Ojibwa, lit. 'cooks itself'.]
A N. American lake trout, *Salvelinus namaycush*, of a variety found in Lake Superior.

sisel *noun* var. of ZIZEL.

siserary /sɪsəˈrɛːri/ *noun.* Now *dial.* Also **sisserara** /sɪsəˈrɛːrə/ & other vars. L15.
[Pop. alt. of CERTIORARI.]
†**1** LAW. A writ of certiorari. L15–M18.
2 A loud clanging noise. M18.
3 A severe rebuke or scolding; a sharp blow; a tirade. L18.
Phrases: **with a siserary** with a vengeance; suddenly, promptly.

sisi *noun* var. of SEESEE.

siskin /ˈsɪskɪn/ *noun.* M16.
[Middle Dutch *siseken*, early Flemish *sijsken* (Dutch *sijsje*), dim. based on Middle Low German *sīsek*, *czītze*, Middle High German *zīsec*, *zīse* (German *Zeisig*), of Slavonic origin (cf. Russian *chizh*).]
Any of various small streaked yellowish-green finches of the genus *Carduelis*, esp. *C. spinus* of northern Eurasia and (*N. Amer.*, more fully ***pine siskin***) *C. pinus* of N. American pinewoods.

siss *noun*[1] var. of SIS *noun*.

siss /sɪs/ *verb & noun*[2]. Now *dial.* & *US.* ME.
[Middle Dutch *cissen*, Dutch, Low German *sissen*, of imit. origin.]
▶ **A** *verb intrans.* Hiss. ME.
▶ **B** *noun.* A hissing sound. L19.

sisserara *noun* var. of SISERARY.

sissonne /ˈsiːsɒn, *foreign* sisɔn (*pl. same*)/ *noun.* E18.
[French.]
BALLET. A jump in the air from fifth position, landing on one foot with the other leg extended.

sissoo /ˈsɪsuː/ *noun.* E19.
[Panjabi *sissū*, Hindi *sīso*, from Sanskrit *śiṃśapā*.]
An Indian leguminous timber tree, *Dalbergia sissoo*; the valuable wood of this tree. Also called ***shisham***.

†**sissors** *noun pl.* var. of SCISSORS.

sissy /ˈsɪsi/ *noun & adjective. colloq.* Also **cissy**. M19.
[from SIS *noun* + -Y[6]. Cf. PRISSY.]
▶ **A** *noun.* **1** A sister. M19.
2 An effeminate person; a coward. L19.

> 📖 **2** *Look In* Garfield, you sissy, I can't believe you're afraid of a little spider.

Comb.: **sissy bar** a metal loop rising from behind the seat of a bicycle or motorcycle.
▶ **B** *adjective.* Effeminate; cowardly. L19.
■ **sissifiˈcation** *noun* effeminacy M20. **sissified** *adjective* effeminate E20. **sissiness** *noun* effeminacy; cowardice: E20. **sissyish** *adjective* somewhat effeminate or cowardly L19.

sist /sɪst/ *noun.* L17.
[from the verb.]
SCOTS LAW. A suspension of a court proceeding; an injunction.

sist /sɪst/ *verb trans. Scot.* M17.
[Latin *sistere* cause to stand.]
1 Suspend (a proceeding etc.), esp. by judicial decree. M17.
2 †**a** Present (oneself) before a court. *rare.* M17–E18.
▸**b** Cause or order to appear *before* a court; summon, cite. E18.

sister /ˈsɪstə/ *noun & adjective.*
[Old English *sweoster*, *swuster*, *swyster*, *suster* = Old Frisian *swester*, *suster*, *sister*, Old Saxon *swestar*, Middle Low German, Middle Dutch *suster* (Dutch *zuster*), Old High German *swester* (German *Schwester*), Gothic *swistar*, from Germanic from Indo-European, repr. in Latin *soror*.]
▶ **A** *noun.* **1** A female related to one or more others (male or female) by having the same parents or by having one parent in common. OE.
2 Also used preceding a name and as a form of address or reference. ▸**a** A woman who is a close friend; a female fellow citizen or creature; a female of the same race, colour, class, profession, etc., a fellow female member of a trade union; a female associate or equal, a fellow feminist. OE. ▸**b** A female member of a religious order, society, or sect; *spec.* a nun. Also (*gen.*), a female fellow Christian. LME. ▸**c** A usu. senior female nurse, *esp.* one in charge of a hospital ward. M19. ▸**d** A (male) fellow homosexual. *slang* (orig. *US*). M20.
3 Used as a form of address to a woman. Now *colloq.* ME.
4 An identical, similar, or related thing; a counterpart. ME. ▸**b** Either of the cheeks of a cider-press. E19.

> 📖 **1** J. CHEEVER We are four children; there is my sister Diana and the three men. ***adoptive sister, foster sister, full sister, half-sister, stepsister***, etc. **2a** *Ramparts* Our sisters in Vietnam have taught us many lessons. **b** SIR W. SCOTT Sister Clare.., As yet a novice unprofess'd. *Catholic Herald* The Hospice.. is.. under the management of the Irish Sisters of Mercy. *Evangelical Times* Countless missionary sisters.. who faithfully serve the church. **c** C. AIRD Sister Casualty.. would ring down to the police station. *Nursing* Sister accompanying the consultant on the ward round. **4** F. O'CONNOR 'Give me one...' she said, holding out the money... 'A buck fifty, sister,' he said. **5** P. G. HAMERTON Inspiration decidedly the sister of daily labor. B. NEIL Ben's house.. seemed to stand alone, separate from its terraced sisters.

Phrases: ***full sister***: see FULL *adjective*. ***lay sister***: see LAY *adjective*. ***Seven Sisters***: see SEVEN *adjective*. **sister german**: having the same parents. ***Sister of Mercy***: see MERCY *noun*. ***sisters under the skin***: see SKIN *noun*. **sister uterine**: having the same mother only. **the three sisters**, **the sisters** MYTHOLOGY the three goddesses of destiny, the fates. **uterine sister** = ***sister uterine*** above. ***weak sister***: see WEAK *adjective*. ***weird sisters***: see WEIRD *adjective*.
▶ **B** *adjective.* That is a sister; belonging to the same group, of the same type or origin, fellow. M17.
Special collocations & comb.: **sister-block** NAUTICAL: with two sheaves, one below the other. **sister cell** BIOLOGY either of two cells produced by the division of an existing cell. **sister chromatid** BIOLOGY either of a pair of identical chromatids held together at the centromere. **Sister Dora** [from Dorothy ('*Dora*') Pattison (1832–78), a famous nurse] *Hist.* a nurse's cap tied under the chin. **sister-hook** NAUTICAL either of two hooks fitting together to make a ring. **sister-in-law**, pl. **sisters-in-law**, (*a*) the sister of one's husband or wife; (*b*) the wife of one's brother(-in-law). **sister keelson** NAUTICAL either of two additional strengthening keelsons along the bottom of a ship. **sister nucleus** BIOLOGY (*a*) either of two nuclei produced by the division of an existing nucleus; (*b*) either of two nuclei which fuse together in an autogamous unicellular organism. **sister ship**: built to the same design as another. **sisters thread** *Hist.* bleached thread. **sister tutor** a nursing sister who teaches trainee nurses. **sister-wife**: who is the sister of her husband.
■ **sisterless** *adjective* M19. **sisterlike** *adverb & adjective* like or resembling (that of) a sister L16. **sistership** *noun* (a) sisterhood M19.

sister /ˈsɪstə/ *verb trans.* E17.
[from the noun.]
Be a sister to; make a sister of; treat or address as a sister.
■ **sistering** *ppl adjective* (now *rare*) being a sister; having a sisterly relationship: L16.

sisterhood /ˈsɪstəhʊd/ *noun.* LME.
[from SISTER *noun* + -HOOD.]
1 The quality or state of being a sister; the relation of a sister; sisterly companionship or alliance. LME.
2 a A society of sisters; *esp.* a community of women living a life devoted to religion or charitable work. L16. ▸**b** *transf.* A group of women having some common aim, characteristic, or calling. E17.

> 📖 **1** *Independent* The 12 women.. have become as close as sisters, but sisterhood was not their aim. **2a** G. BATTISCOMBE She.. announced her intention of joining the Anglican sisterhood of All Saints. **b** OUIDA Lady Dolly and her sisterhood were audacious but cowardly. *fig.*: R. POLLOK A little orb... With her fair sisterhood of planets seven.

sisterly /ˈsɪstəli/ *adjective.* L16.
[formed as prec. + -LY[1].]
1 Of or pertaining to a sister; characteristic of or befitting a sister. L16.
2 Of or pertaining to a sisterhood. L19.
■ **sisterliness** *noun* the quality of being sisterly, sisterly feeling L19.

sisterly /ˈsɪstəli/ *adverb.* E17.
[formed as prec. + -LY[2].]
In the manner or spirit of a sister.

Sistine /ˈsɪstiːn, -tʌɪn/ *adjective & noun.* L18.
[from Italian *sistino* of Sixtus (see below): see -INE[1]. Cf. SIXTINE.]
▶ **A** *adjective.* Pertaining to Pope Sixtus IV (1471–84) or the chapel built by him; *gen.* pertaining to any of the Popes called Sixtus. L18.
Sistine Chapel a chapel in the Vatican at Rome, built for Sixtus IV and decorated with frescoes by Michelangelo and other painters.
▶ **B** *noun ellipt.* *The* Sistine Chapel. L19.

sistrum /ˈsɪstrəm/ *noun.* Pl. **-tra** /-trə/, **-trums**. LME.
[Latin from Greek *seistron*, from *seiein* shake.]
EARLY MUSIC. A musical instrument of ancient Egyptian origin, consisting of a metal frame with transverse metal rods which rattled when the instrument was shaken.

sisymbrium /sɪˈsɪmbrɪəm/ *noun.* M16.
[mod. Latin (see below), from Greek *sisumbrion* watercress.]
A plant of the cruciferous genus *Sisymbrium*, which comprises yellow-flowered, siliquose, often weedy plants including hedge-mustard and London rocket, and formerly included watercress.

Sisyphean /sɪsɪˈfiːən/ *adjective.* Also (earlier) **-phian**. L16.
[Latin *Sisypheius* from Greek *Sisupheios*, from *Sisuphos* Sisyphus: see below, -EAN, -IAN.]
Of or pertaining to Sisyphus, in Greek mythology a king of Corinth whose punishment in Hades was to push uphill a stone which rolled down again as soon as he reached the top; resembling the fruitless toil of Sisyphus; endless and ineffective.

> 📖 *American Speech* The more such chores are postponed, the more Sisyphean the task becomes.

Sisyphism /ˈsɪsɪfɪz(ə)m/ *noun.* M19.
[from *Sisyphus*: see prec., -ISM.]
Unceasing and fruitless labour like that of Sisyphus, esp. as a characteristic of modern industrial conditions.

sisyrinchium /sɪsɪˈrɪŋkɪəm/ *noun.* L18.
[mod. Latin (see below), from Greek *sisurinkhion* a plant resembling iris.]
A plant of the largely American genus *Sisyrinchium* of the iris family, the members of which have linear leaves and clusters of small flowers, usu. blue, yellow, or white; *esp.* blue-eyed grass.

sit /sɪt/ *noun*[1]. M18.
[from the verb.]
1 A sinking of the surface of a wall etc.; a subsidence. M18.
2 a The manner in which an article of clothing etc. fits a person. L18. ▸**b** A manner of sitting. E19. ▸**c** Inherent character or tendency. *rare.* M19.
3 A period of sitting. M19.
4 The bottom, the buttocks. *rare.* E20.

sit /sɪt/ *noun*[2]. *colloq.* M19.
[Abbreviation.]
= SITUATION *noun* 7. Now esp. in ***sits vac***, situations vacant.

sit /sɪt/ *noun*[3]. Also **sitt**. M20.
[Abbreviation.]
A sitting-room.

sit /sɪt/ *verb.* Pa. t. & pple **sat** /sat/; pa. pple also (*obsolete* exc. *Scot.*) **sitten** /ˈsɪt(ə)n/.
[Old English *sittan* = Old Frisian *sitta*, Old Saxon *sittian*, Old High German *sizzen* (Dutch *zitten*, German *sitzen*), Old Norse *sitja* from Germanic (Gothic *sitan*) from Indo-European base repr. also by Latin *sedere*, Greek *hezesthai*.]
▶ **I** *verb intrans.* **1 a** Of a person: be in a position in which the body is supported on the buttocks, usu. with the torso upright and thighs horizontal; be seated. (Foll. by *at, back, on, up*, etc.) OE. ▸**b** Adopt such a position; take a seat, seat oneself. (Foll. by *down, on*, etc.) OE. ▸**c** Sit down in a public place as a form of protest; take part in a sit-in. M20. ▸**d** Babysit. M20.
2 a Have a seat in or be a member of a council, assembly, jury, etc.; *spec.* preside as a judge. (Foll. by *for* a parliamentary constituency, *in* an assembly, *on* a council, jury, the judicial bench, etc.) OE. ▸**b** Occupy an episcopal see or the papal see. LME.

3 Be, continue, or remain in a certain situation or condition. (Formerly foll. by *in*.) **OE.**

4 a Live, dwell, or remain in a place. **OE.** ▸**b** Occupy or rent a house etc.; be a tenant. Freq. foll. by *at* a specified rent. Cf. ***sitting tenant*** s.v. **SITTING** *ppl adjective* 4. **L16.**

5 a Of a bird: perch, roost, rest; *spec.* rest on an egg for the purpose of incubation. **OE.** ▸**b** Of an animal: rest with the hind legs bent and the rear part of the body close to the ground. **ME.**

6 Support oneself *(up)on* one's knees; kneel. *obsolete* exc. *dial.* **OE.**

7 a Of a thing or place: be located, be situated; rest, lie. (Foll. by *on*.) **OE.** ▸**b** Of the wind: blow from a particular direction, be in a particular quarter. **L16.** ▸**c** Set; stick; settle down. *rare.* **E17.** ▸**d** Remain untouched or unused. **L20.**

8 †**a** Be suitable, fitting, or proper. (Foll. by *for, to*.) **ME–L16.** ▸**b** Esp. of clothing: fit (well, badly, etc.); suit a person. (Foll. by *on, to*, etc.) **LME.**

9 Of a court or other assembly: hold a session; carry out business. **LME.**

10 a Pose in a sitting position to be photographed or to have one's portrait painted; serve as a model. Also foll. by *for* one's portrait, *to* a painter etc. **M16.** ▸**b** Present oneself *for* an examination, test, etc.; be a candidate. **M19.**

> 📖 **1a** P. FITZGERALD Volodya . . was sitting on a wooden chair. I. MURDOCH Gildas . . was sitting at the piano. **b** W. CATHER Niel dropped on the turf and sat with his back against a tree trunk. P. P. READ When . . they sat down to eat . . his appetite had left him. **2a** JAN MORRIS Dr. Jenkins . . once claimed to be sitting on 50 . . committees at the same time. **3** S. JOHNSON That he can sit secure in the enjoyment of inheritance. **4b** SHAKES. *Merry W.* I sit at ten pounds a week. **7a** J. STEINBECK Pacific Grove and Monterey sit side by side on a hill. R. DAHL A small . . white wooden vessel which sat far too low in the water. M. BRETT £5000 of cash sitting in the bank. **d** *New York Times* Two choices: Let the place sit, or fix it up like a Hollywood home. **8b** *Catch* Dress the model to make sure the clothes sit well. *fig.*: SIR W. SCOTT Her little air of precision sits so well upon her. **9** C. PRIEST A panel of international judges was appointed to sit annually. **10a** G. DALY Both parents sat for their son, to save the expense of professional models. **b** I. MURDOCH Sit for a Cambridge College entrance examination in chemistry.

▸**II** *verb trans.* **11** Make (a person) sit *down, up*, etc.; *refl.* seat (oneself). **OE.** ▸**b** Make (a bird) sit on an egg for the purpose of incubation. *rare.* **L19.**

†**12** Ignore, pay no attention to (a command, call, etc.). *Scot. & north.* **ME–M19.**

†**13** Affect (a person) in a specified way; distress, vex, grieve. **ME–M16.**

14 Esp. of clothing: fit, suit (a person). Now *rare.* **LME.**

15 Resist; endure, put up with. Now *rare.* **LME.**

16 a Ride, sit on (a horse, bicycle, etc.). **M16.** ▸**b** Of a bird: sit on (an egg) for the purpose of incubation. **E17.** ▸**c** Sit in (a boat) moving one's body to adjust its balance. **M19.**

†**17** Place; set *down. rare.* **M16–E19.**

18 a = ***sit out*** (b) below. **L18.** ▸**b** Keep (a person) company; sit with. *rare.* **E19.** ▸**c** Babysit (a child). **M20.** ▸**d** Present oneself for or take (an examination, test, etc.); be a candidate for. **M20.**

> 📖 **11** *Jerusalem Post* My father sat us down. **14** *fig.*: J. J. AUBERTIN With a proud confidence, which sat him well. **16a** E. BAIRD The rider must be taught . . to sit the horse well. **b** *Country Life* The blackbird had been robbed of her eggs after sitting them for a week. **18d** *Motor Cycle News* Riders have to sit a stringent test before being allowed on the road.

Phrases, & with adverbs & prepositions in specialized senses: **sit about, sit around** be idle; lounge. **sit at a person's heart** *arch.* affect a person deeply. **sit at the feet of** be the disciple or pupil of. ***sit at the stern***: see **STERN** *noun*[2]. **sit back** be inactive, relax; (see also sense 1a above). **sit down** (*a*) settle, take up residence in a place; *fig.* settle down; (*b*) encamp *before* a town etc. in order to besiege it; (*c*) put up *with*, be content *with*; (*d*) get down to business; (*e*) ***sit down to***, seat oneself and begin (a game, meal, etc.); (see also senses 1b, 11, 17 above). **sit heavy on** (*a*) *arch.* press or weigh heavily *on*; (*b*) ***sit heavy on the stomach***, take a long time to be digested. **sit in** (*a*) be present at an event; take part in or observe a game etc. (also foll. by *at, on* the event etc.); (*b*) play or sing with a band or orchestra of which one is not a regular member; (*c*) occupy a building as a demonstration of protest; (*d*) take someone else's place, be a substitute *for*; (see also senses 2a, 3 above. ***sit in JUDGEMENT***. ***sit loose***: see **LOOSE** *adverb*. ***sit mum***: see **MUM** *adjective & adverb*. **sit on** (*a*) *colloq.* squash, rebuke, snub; (*b*) hold back, keep to oneself, delay action on; (*c*) suppress, silence; (*d*) wait for (a person or thing) to change or develop; observe, trail; (*e*) ***sit on the throne***, reign; (*f*) ***sit on one's hands***, refuse to applaud; be inactive; (*g*) ***sit on the splice***: see **SPLICE** *noun* 1b;(see also senses 1a, b, 2a, 6, 7, 8b above). **sit out** (*a*) *verb phr. trans. & intrans.* take no part in (a dance, etc.); (*b*) *verb phr. trans.* endure, stay until the end of; (*c*) *verb phr. trans.* stay longer than (another) on a visit, outstay. **sit over** be occupied with or linger over while sitting; *spec.* pore over (a book). ***sit pillion***: see **PILLION** *noun*. ***sit shiva***: see **SHIVA** *noun*[1]. ***sit tall***: see **TALL** *adverb*. **sit through** endure while sitting; stay until the end of. ***sit tight***: see **TIGHT** *adverb*. ***sitting next to Nelly***: see **NELLY** *noun*[2] 4. ***sitting pretty***: see **PRETTY** *adverb*. **sit under** listen to, attend the lessons or sermons of (a teacher, minister, etc.). **sit up** (*a*) rise from a lying to a sitting position; (*b*) sit with the torso firmly upright; (*c*) put off going to bed; wait up (*for*), stay up (*with*); (*d*) be startled; ***sit up and take notice***, become suddenly interested; (see also senses 1a, 11 above). **sit upon** (*a*) *arch.* = ***sit on*** above; (*b*) ***sit upon a person's skirts***: see **SKIRT** *noun* 1. **sit with** (*a*) *arch.* be in harmony with, suit. (*b*) be received (well, badly, etc.) by; (see also sense 6 above).

Comb.: **sit-me-down** *colloq.* the buttocks; **sit-up** *noun & adjective* (*a*) *noun* an exercise in which the upper half of the body is raised from a supine position to a sitting one; (*b*) *adjective* at, against, or in which one sits up; **sit-upon** *colloq.* (*a*) *arch.* (in *pl.*) trousers; (*b*) the buttocks.

sitar /ˈsɪtɑː, sɪˈtɑː/ *noun.* **M19.**
[Persian & Urdu *sitār*, from *sih* three + *tār* string.]
A stringed Indian musical instrument, resembling a lute, with a long neck and (usu.) seven principal strings which the player plucks.
■ **sitarist** *noun* a person who plays the sitar **M20.**

sitatunga /sɪtəˈtʌŋɡə/ *noun.* Also **situ-** /sɪtʊ-/ Pl. same, **-s. L19.**
[Kiswahili.]
A medium-sized brown or greyish antelope, *Tragelaphus spekii*, found in swamps and reed-beds of E. and central Africa, with elongated splayed hoofs that enable it to walk on marshy ground, and spiral horns in the male. Also called ***marshbuck***.

sitch /sɪtʃ/ *noun.* Now *dial.*
[Old English *sīc* = Old Norse *sík* (Icelandic *síki*, Norwegian *sik(e)*, Danish *sig*), from Germanic. See also **SIKE** *noun*[1].]
= **SIKE** *noun*[1].

sitcom /ˈsɪtkɒm/ *noun.* Also **sit-com. M20.**
[Abbreviation.]
A situation comedy.

sit-down /ˈsɪtdaʊn/ *noun & adjective.* **L18.**
[from **SIT** *verb* + **DOWN** *adverb*, in senses 2 & 3 directly from the adjective.]
▸**A** *noun.* **1** An act of sitting down, esp. as an opportunity to relax. **L18.**
2 A (free) sit-down meal. *N. Amer. slang.* **E20.**
3 A sit-down strike or demonstration. **M20.**
▸**B** *adjective.* **1** (Of a meal) eaten sitting at a table; (of a restaurant, party, etc.) at which people sit down. **M19.**
2 (Of a strike, demonstration, etc.) in which people sit down and refuse to leave a workplace, public building, etc.; (of a person) participating in such a strike or demonstration. **M20.**
■ **sit-downer** *noun* a participant in a sit-down strike or demonstration **M20.**

site /sʌɪt/ *noun.* **LME.**
[Anglo-Norman, or Latin *situs* local position, perh. from *sit-* pa. ppl stem of *sinere* leave, allow to remain.]
†**1 a** The place occupied by something; (a) position. **LME–E18.** ▸**b** Attitude, posture (of the body etc.). **E17–E18.**
2 a The position of a town, building, etc., esp. with reference to the surrounding district or locality; (a) location, (a) setting. **LME.** ▸**b** *SCIENCE.* A position or location in or on a molecule, gene, etc., esp. one where a specific activity takes place. **M20.**
3 a The ground on which a building, town, etc., has been or is to be built; a plot or plots of land intended for building purposes. Also more widely, any area set apart for a specified purpose; a place where some activity is or has been conducted. **LME.** ▸**b** *transf.* The seat *of* an industry etc.; the scene *of* a condition or event. **M17.** ▸**c** *ARCHAEOLOGY.* A place containing the remains of former human habitation; an excavation. **E20.**
4 *BUILDING.* A framework of timber forming the foundation of a piece of scaffolding. **E20.**
5 A job, a situation. *US Nautical slang.* **M20.**
6 *COMPUTING.* = ***website*** s.v. **WEB** *noun.* **L20.**

> 📖 **2a** H. MARTINEAU The loss of health caused by the pestilential site of a dwelling. R. GODDEN A soap factory in London—now the site of the Festival Hall. **3a** A. J. P. TAYLOR The use . . of the rockets was delayed . . by bombing their launching sites. *Freight Distribution* Many of BP's 2,000 filling stations have shops on their sites. ***building site, caravan site, picnic site***, etc. **b** W. C. WILLIAMS A fellow caught at the site of a recent crime.

Phrases: **off site** *adverb & adjective* (*a*) *adverb* away from or not on or at a particular site; (*b*) *adjective* occurring or situated off site. **on site** *adverb & adjective* (*a*) *adverb* on or at a particular site; (*b*) *adjective* occurring or situated on site. **Site of Special Scientific Interest** an area of land designated and protected as being of special scientific interest in terms of flora, fauna, or geology; abbreviation ***SSSI***. ***substitutional site***: see **SUBSTITUTIONAL** 2b.

Comb.: **site assembly**: of building components on the site; **site value** the amount for which a site may be sold.

site /sʌɪt/ *verb trans.* **L16.**
[from the noun, or back-form. from next.]
Locate, place (a building etc.).

sited /ˈsʌɪtɪd/ *ppl adjective.* **LME.**
[from **SITE** *noun* + **-ED**[2], or Latin *situs* placed, situated (in later use also directly from the verb) + see **-ED**[1].]
Of a building, town, etc.: having a certain site or position; situated, located.

sitella *noun* var. of **SITTELLA.**

sit-fast /ˈsɪtfɑːst/ *noun & adjective.* Also **sitfast. E17.**
[from **SIT** *verb* + **FAST** *adverb*.]
▸**A** *noun.* **1** *FARRIERY.* A hard excrescence tending to ulceration, produced on the back of a horse by the pressure or chafing of a saddle, or by the presence of a warble. **E17.** ▸**b** A hard substance in a wound which prevents healing. *dial.* **E19.**
2 Any of several weeds with tenacious roots, esp. creeping buttercup, *Ranunculus repens*, and rest-harrow, *Ononis repens*. *Scot.* **M18.**
▸**B** *adjective.* **1** Of a stone: firmly embedded in the ground. *Scot.* **E19.**
2 *gen.* Fixed, firm. **E19.**

sith /sɪθ/ *adverb, conjunction, & preposition.* Long *arch. & dial.* **OE.**
[Reduced form of **SITHEN**. Cf. **SEN** *preposition, conjunction, & adverb*, **SYNE** *adverb*.]
▸†**A** *adverb.* **1** Then, thereupon; afterwards. **OE–E16.**
2 = **SITHEN** *adverb* 2. **ME–E17.**
3 At some time or at any time since that time. **ME–M16.**
4 Ago; before now. **LME–M16.**
▸**B** *conjunction.* †**1** = **SITHEN** *conjunction* 1. **OE–L16.**
2 Seeing that; since. Formerly foll. by *that*. **ME.**
▸†**C** *preposition.* Continuously or at some time since (a specified time). **ME–L16.**
¶ Not recorded between **L17** and **E19.**

†**sithe** *noun*[1].
[Old English *sīþ* = Old Saxon *sīþ*, Old High German *sind, sint*, Old Norse *sinn*, Gothic *sinþs* journey, from Germanic base also of **SEND** *verb*[1].]
1 A journey, a path, a course. **OE–LME.**
2 A time; an occasion. **OE–M17.**

sithe /sʌɪð/ *noun*[2]. *rare.* **L16.**
[Alt. of *cive*, **CHIVE** *noun*[2].]
A chive. Usu. in *pl.*

sithe /sʌɪð/ *verb*[1] *intrans. obsolete* exc. *dial.* **ME.**
[Var. of **SIGH** *verb*.]
Sigh.

sithe /sʌɪð/ *verb*[2] *trans. obsolete* exc. *Scot. & dial.* **LME.**
[Prob. var. of **SIEVE** *verb*.]
Strain; pass through a sieve.

sithen /ˈsɪθ(ə)n/ *adverb, conjunction, & preposition.* Long *arch. & dial.*
[Old English *siþþon, -an*, ult. from Germanic. Cf. **SEN** *preposition, conjunction, & adverb*, **SITH**.]
▸**A** *adverb.* †**1** = **SITH** *adverb* 1. **OE–LME.**
2 Continuously, ever since or from that time. **OE.**
†**3** = **SITH** *adverb* 3. **OE–M17.**
†**4** = **SITH** *adverb* 4. **LME–L15.**
▸**B** *conjunction.* **1** From or since the time that. **OE.**
2 = **SITH** *conjunction* 2. **ME.**
▸†**C** *preposition.* = **SITH** *preposition.* **OE–E17.**

sithence /ˈsɪθ(ə)ns/ *adverb, conjunction, & preposition.* Long *arch.* **ME.**
[from prec. + **-S**[1]. Cf. **SINCE**.]
▸**A** *adverb.* †**1** = **SITH** *adverb* 1. **ME–M18.**
2 = **SITHEN** *adverb* 2. **ME.**
†**3** = **SITH** *adverb* 3. **E16–M17.**
†**4** = **SITH** *adverb* 4. **M16–M17.**
▸**B** *conjunction.* †**1** = **SITHEN** *conjunction* 1. **LME–E17.**
2 = **SITH** *conjunction* 2. **LME.**
▸**C** *preposition.* = **SITH** *preposition.* **L15.**

sitient /ˈsɪtɪənt/ *adjective. rare.* **M17.**
[Latin *sitient-* pres. ppl stem of *sitire* thirst: see **-ENT**.]
Thirsty; greedy.

sit-in /ˈsɪtɪn/ *adjective & noun.* **M20.**
[from ***sit in*** s.v. **SIT** *verb*: cf. **-IN**[2].]
▸**A** *adjective.* Of or pertaining to a strike, demonstration, etc., in which people occupy a workplace, public building, etc. **M20.**
▸**B** *noun.* (A participant in) a sit-in strike or demonstration. **M20.**
■ **sit-inner** *noun* a participant in a sit-in **M20.**

sitio- /ˈsɪtɪəʊ/ *combining form.* **M19.**
[from Greek *sition* food made from grain, bread: see **-O-**.]
= **SITO-**.

Sitka /ˈsɪtkə/ *noun & adjective.* **E19.**
[See sense A.1 below.]
▸**A** *noun.* Pl. **-s**, same.
1 A member of a group of Tlingit formerly living principally in Sitka, a town in Alaska. Also, the Tlingit dialect of this people. **E19.**
2 *ellipt.* = ***Sitka spruce*** below. **E20.**
▸**B** *attrib.* or as *adjective.* Of or pertaining to the Sitkas or their dialect. **E19.**
Sitka cypress the Nootka cypress, *Chamaecyparis nootkatensis.* **Sitka spruce** a spruce of western N. America, *Picea sitchensis*, grown for timber; the wood of this tree.

sitkamer /ˈsɪtkamər/ *noun. S. Afr.* **E20.**
[Afrikaans, from Dutch *sit* sitting + *kamer* room.]
A sitting-room, a lounge.

sito- /ˈsʌɪtəʊ/ *combining form.*
[from Greek *sitos* food made from grain, bread: see -O-.]
Of or pertaining to food.
■ **siˈtology** *noun* dietetics M19. **sitoˈmania** *noun* †(*a*) sitophobia; (*b*) excessive hunger or craving for food: M19. **sitoˈphobia** *noun* repugnance or aversion to food M19.

sitosterol /sʌɪˈtɒstərɒl/ *noun.* L19.
[formed as prec. + STEROL.]
BIOCHEMISTRY. Any of several similar sterols of the formula $C_{29}H_{50}O$, widely distributed in plants; *spec.* (more fully **β-*sitosterol***) a white waxy solid obtained from soya beans.

sitrep /ˈsɪtrɛp/ *noun.* M20.
[Abbreviation.]
MILITARY. = ***situation report*** s.v. SITUATION.

sitringee *noun* see SATRANJI.

sitt *noun* var. of SIT *noun*[3].

sittella /sɪˈtɛlə/ *noun. Austral.* Also **sitella**. M19.
[mod. Latin *Sittella* former genus name, dim. of *sitta*, Greek *sittē* nuthatch.]
Each of three small Australasian birds of the genera *Neositta* and *Daphoenositta* resembling nuthatches, esp. (more fully ***varied sittella***) *N. chrysoptera* of Australia.

sitten *verb* pa. pple: see SIT *verb.*

sitter /ˈsɪtə/ *noun*[1]. ME.
[from SIT *verb* + -ER[1].]
1 *gen.* A person who sits or occupies a seat. Also foll. by adverb. ME. ▸**b** A passenger in a rowing boat. M17. ▸**c** A person who has a sitting with a medium. E20. ▸**d** A person employed to sit in a bar and induce customers to buy drinks. *US slang.* M20. ▸**e** A babysitter. Also, a person who looks after a house, pet, etc., while the owners are away. M20. ▸**f** A participant in a sit-in. M20.
2 *spec.* †**a** A person who sits on a horse or other animal; a rider. ME–E17. ▸**b** A person who sits as a model for an artist or photographer. M17.
3 A bird, *esp.* a domestic hen, which sits on eggs for the purpose of incubation. E17.
4 Anything easy or bound to succeed; an easy catch, shot, etc.; a certainty. L19.
Comb.: **sitter-in**, pl. **sitters-in**, (*a*) a babysitter; (*b*) a participant in a sit-in; (*c*) a person who sits in with a band.

sitter /ˈsɪtə/ *noun*[2]. *slang.* E20.
[from SIT *verb* + -ER[6].]
A sitting-room.

sitting /ˈsɪtɪŋ/ *noun.* ME.
[from SIT *verb* + -ING[1].]
1 a The action of SIT *verb*; the fact of being seated; an instance of this. Also foll. by adverb. ME. ▸**b** Position, posture. *rare.* E18.
2 a Deliberation on judicial affairs; a meeting of a legislative body, a court session; a period during which a court sits. ME. ▸**b** *Hist.* A fair for the hiring of servants, a statute. Usu. in *pl. north.* M17. ▸**c** A meeting of members of the Society of Friends for family worship. M19.
3 a The action of a bird sitting on and hatching eggs; incubation. LME. ▸**b** A number of eggs on which a bird sits for the purpose of incubation; a clutch. M19.
4 A thing or place on or in which one sits; a seat. Later *esp.*, a seat for one person in a church. LME.
5 A period of remaining seated; *spec.* a period of sitting as a model for an artist or photographer. L16. ▸**b** A seance. L19. ▸**c** Any of a series of sessions in which a meal is served in a restaurant etc. M20.

> 📖 **4** SYD. SMITH The people who had sittings in the great pew. **5** *Artist* A portrait . . might take . . 10 or 12 sittings of a couple of hours. **at a sitting**, **at one sitting** in one period of continuous activity, in one go. **c** *attrib.*: *Holiday Which?* A first sitting dinner at 6.45 p.m.

Comb.: **sitting-room** (*a*) a room used for sitting in, a living-room; (*b*) a section of a poultry-house in which hens hatch eggs; (*c*) space available for sitting.

sitting /ˈsɪtɪŋ/ *ppl adjective.* ME.
[from SIT *verb* + -ING[2].]
†**1** Of a garment: fitting *well* or closely to the body. *rare.* ME–L15.
†**2** Becoming, befitting; suitable, appropriate. LME–L16.
3 (Of a person or animal) that sits, seated; *spec.* (of a bird) that sits on eggs for the purpose of incubation. E17. ▸†**b** BOTANY. Sessile. L18–M19. ▸**c** Of a target: stationary, easily hit. Also (*fig.*), extremely easy or vulnerable, impossible to miss. M19.
4 Of a person: currently holding a specified position or office. E18.
3c ***sitting duck***: see DUCK *noun*[1]. **4 sitting member** a Member of Parliament holding a seat in the House of Commons at the time referred to. **sitting tenant** a tenant already occupying a property.

situal /ˈsɪtjʊəl/ *adjective. rare.* L17.
[medieval Latin *situalis*, from *situs* SITE *noun.*]
Positional.

situate /ˈsɪtjʊeɪt/ *verb.* Pa. t. & pple **-ated**, (*arch.* exc. LAW) **-ate** /-ət/. LME.
[medieval Latin *situat-* pa. ppl stem of *situare*, from Latin *situs* SITE *noun*: see -ATE[3].]
1 *verb trans.* Place, locate; *fig.* put in a context. Usu. in *pass.* LME. ▸**b** Subject to certain circumstances; place in a certain situation. E18.
†**2** *verb intrans.* Have or take up a certain position. L16–E17.

> 📖 **1a** J. K. JEROME A . . little town, situate among lakes and woods. I. MURDOCH The . . works were situated on the other side. **b** CONAN DOYLE I was so situated that I could not come earlier.

situation /sɪtjʊˈeɪʃ(ə)n/ *noun.* LME.
[Old & mod. French, or medieval Latin *situatio(n-)*, from *situat-*: see prec., -ATION.]
1 The place or position of a thing in relation to its surroundings. LME.
2 The place occupied by a thing; a site. Now *rare.* M16.
3 A place, a locality. E17.
4 The condition or state of a thing; *spec.* a particular physical condition, *esp.* pregnancy. *arch.* E18.
5 The position in life held or occupied by a person; *gen.* a set of circumstances, a state of affairs. E18.
6 A critical point or complication in a drama. M18.
7 A position of employment, a job. E19.
8 HORSE-RACING. Any of the first three places in a race. L19.

> 📖 **1** SIR W. SCOTT Educated in a remote situation. P. CUNNINGHAM The situation of the music room is . . at the side of the stage. **5** B. MONTGOMERY The food situation became difficult and the whole B.E.F. was put on half-rations. A. TOFFLER If each situation were wholly novel, . . our ability to cope would be hopelessly crippled. P. MAILLOUX The familiar Kafka protagonist . . in the familiar Kafkan situation.

Comb. & phrases: ***save the situation***: see SAVE *verb*; **situation comedy** a comedy series for television or radio in which the humour derives largely from the particular conjunction of characters and circumstances; **situation ethics**, **situation morality** PHILOSOPHY the belief in flexibility in the application of moral laws according to individual circumstances; **situation report**: on the current progress of a military operation etc.; **situation room**, **situations room** a room in a military or political headquarters set aside for reporting on the current state of any action or operation; **situations vacant**, **situations wanted** (a newspaper column or page) advertising jobs to be filled or sought.
■ **situational** *adjective* E20. **situationalism** *noun* = SITUATIONISM 2 L20. **situationalist** *adjective* of or pertaining to situation ethics L20. **situationally** *adverb* with respect to situation M20. **situationer** *noun* (*Journalists' slang*) an article constituting a general report on a situation M20.

situationism /sɪtjuˈeɪʃ(ə)nɪz(ə)m/ *noun.* M20.
[from SITUATION + -ISM.]
1 The theory or doctrine that the views and behaviour of a person are determined by (*spec.* a false representation of) the surrounding circumstances rather than by personal attributes or qualities. M20.
2 Adherence to situation ethics. M20.
■ **situationist** *adjective & noun* (*a*) *adjective* of or pertaining to situationism; (*b*) *noun* an adherent of situationism: M20.

situla /ˈsɪtjʊlə/ *noun.* Pl. **-lae** /-liː/, **-las**. L19.
[Latin = bucket.]
ARCHAEOLOGY. A vessel resembling a bucket in shape.
■ **situlate** /ˈsɪtjʊlət/, **siˈtuliform** *adjectives* having the form of a situla M20.

situs /ˈsʌɪtəs/ *noun.* E18.
[Latin: see SITE *noun.*]
1 Situation, position. *rare.* E18.
2 LAW. **a** The place to which for purposes of legal jurisdiction or taxation a property belongs. Chiefly *US.* E19. ▸**b** A work-site, *esp.* (in full ***common situs***) one occupied by two or more employers. *US.* M20.

situs inversus /sʌɪtəs ɪnˈvəːsəs, siːtəs/ *noun phr.* L19.
[Latin, in full *situs inversus viscerum* inverted disposition of the internal organs.]
MEDICINE. The condition in which the organs of the body are transposed through the sagittal plane (so that the heart lies on the right side etc.).

situtunga *noun* var. of SITATUNGA.

Sitwellian /sɪtˈwɛlɪən/ *adjective & noun.* E20.
[from the surname *Sitwell* (see below) + -IAN.]
▶ **A** *adjective.* Of, pertaining to, or characteristic of the English writers Edith Sitwell (1887–1964), and her brothers Osbert (1892–1969) and Sacheverell (1897–1988). E20.
▶ **B** *noun.* An admirer of the Sitwells. E20.
■ **Sitwellism** *noun* style or behaviour characteristic of the Sitwells E20.

sitz bath /ˈsɪtsbɑːθ/ *noun phr.* Also **sitz-bath**. M19.
[Partial translation of German *Sitzbad*, from *sitzen* sit + *Bad* bath.]
A hip-bath.

Sitzfleisch /ˈzɪtsflaɪʃ/ *noun.* E20.
[German, from *sitzen* sit + *Fleisch* flesh.]
The ability to persist in or endure an activity.

Sitz im Leben /ˈzɪts ɪm leːbən/ *noun phr.* M20.
[German, lit. 'place in life'.]
THEOLOGY. In biblical criticism, the determining circumstances in which a tradition developed.

sitzkrieg /ˈsɪtskriːg/ *noun.* M20.
[After BLITZKRIEG, German *sitzen* sit.]
(A part of) a war marked by a (relative) absence of active hostilities.

sitzmark /ˈsɪtsmɑːk/ *noun.* M20.
[from German *sitzen* sit + MARK *noun*[1].]
An impression made by a skier falling backwards in the snow.

SIV *abbreviation.*
MEDICINE. Simian immunodeficiency virus.

Siva /ˈsiːvə, ˈʃiːvə/ *noun.* Also **Sh-** /ʃ-/. L18.
[Sanskrit *Śiva* lit. 'the auspicious one'.]
One of the three major Hindu deities to whom are attributed the powers of reproduction and dissolution, regarded by his worshippers as the supreme being; a representation of Siva.
■ **Sivaism** *noun* the worship of Siva M19. **Sivaite** *noun & adjective* (*a*) *noun* a person who worships Siva; (*b*) *adjective* of or pertaining to Sivaism: L19. **Sivite** *noun & adjective* = SIVAITE E19.

Sivan /ˈsiːvɑːn/ *noun.* LME.
[Hebrew *sīwān*.]
In the Jewish calendar, the ninth month of the civil and third of the religious year, usu. coinciding with parts of May and June.

sivatherium /sɪvəˈθɪərɪəm/ *noun.* Also Anglicized as **sivathere** /ˈsɪvəθɪə/. M19.
[mod. Latin *Sivatherium* genus name, from SIVA + Greek *thērion* wild animal.]
PALAEONTOLOGY. A very large fossil giraffid, found in the Pleistocene of northern India and Africa, resembling a giant antelope with two pairs of horns, the hinder pair being large and branched.

sivvens /ˈsɪv(ə)nz/ *noun. Scot. obsolete* exc. *Hist.* M18.
[Local Gaelic *suibhean* raspberry.]
Venereal disease, characterized by a chancre resembling a raspberry.

Siwash /ˈsʌɪwɒʃ/ *noun, adjective, & verb. N. Amer.* M19.
[Chinook Jargon, from (Canad.) French *sauvage*.]
▶ **A** *noun.* **1** A N. American Indian, *spec.* of the north Pacific coast. *derog.* M19.
2 Chinook Jargon. E20.
▶ **B** *adjective.* Of or pertaining to N. American Indians. *derog.* M19.
Siwash camp an open camp with no tent. **Siwash duck** a scoter, *esp.* the surf scoter. **Siwash sweater** a thick sweater decorated with symbols from Indian mythology.
▶ **C** *verb intrans.* (**s-**.) Camp without a tent. E20.

six /sɪks/ *adjective & noun* (*cardinal numeral*).
[Old English *si(e)x*, *syx*, *se(o)x* = Old Frisian *sex*, Old Saxon, Old High German *sehs* (Dutch *zes*, German *sechs*), Old Norse *sex*, Gothic *saihs*, from Germanic from Indo-European, whence also Latin *sex*, Greek *hex*. Cf. ZAC.]
▶ **A** *adjective.* One more than five (a cardinal numeral represented by 6 in arabic numerals, vi, VI in roman). OE.

> 📖 *Scientific American* The accumulation . . will probably be a six-hundreth of the amount built up thus far. F. FORSYTH Six million of his fellow Jews who died in the holocaust. R. RAYNER Six lanes of traffic nose-to-bumper. G. DALY By sixteen Millais had shot up over six feet. **six feet under** *colloq.* dead and buried; in the grave. **the Six Counties** the counties of Northern Ireland (cf. ***twenty-six Counties*** s.v. TWENTY *adjective*). **the Six Dynasties** the Chinese dynasties belonging to the period 220–589; this period of Chinese history.

▶ **B** *noun.* **1** Six persons or things identified contextually, as parts or divisions, years of age, points, runs, etc., in a game, chances (in giving odds), minutes, inches, shillings (now *Hist.*), pence, horses in hand, etc. OE.
2 One more than five as an abstract number; the symbol(s) or figure(s) representing this (6 in arabic numerals, vi, VI in roman). OE.
3 The time of day six hours after midnight or midday (on a clock, watch, etc., indicated by the numeral six displayed or pointed to). Also ***six o'clock***. LME. ▸**b** The position directly behind one (with ref. to the position of six on a clock-face). Freq. with *possess. Military slang.* L20.
4 A set of six; a thing having a set of six as an essential or distinguishing feature; *spec.* (*a*) a playing-card, domino, or side of a die marked with six spots or pips; (*b*) a line or verse with six syllables; (*c*) a group of six Brownies or Cub Scouts; (*d*) an engine or motor vehicle with six cylinders; (*e*) CRICKET a hit scoring six runs, made by striking the ball over the boundary without bouncing. LME.
5 The sixth of a set or series with numbered members, the one designated six, (usu. ***number six***, or with specification, as ***book six***, ***chapter six***, etc.); a size etc. denoted by six, a shoe, glove, garment, etc. of such a size, (also ***size six***). E16.

6 Each of a set of six; *spec.* (*a*) a large plant-pot of which six are formed from one cast of clay; (*b*) a candle of which six constitute a pound in weight. E19.

📖 **1** G. GREENE A wife and a boy of six. *Scientific American* Of the 10 who die before that, six do not survive the first month. ***deep six, deep-six***: see DEEP *adjective*. ***one in six***: see ONE *adjective, noun, & pronoun*. **six and half a dozen, six of one and half a dozen of the other** a situation of little or no difference between two alternatives. ***six of the best***: see BEST *adjective, noun, & adverb*. **the Six** *Hist.* the group of countries which were the original members of the European Community from 1958. **3** P. FITZGERALD I'll have dinner at six, as usual. ***six o'clock swill***: see SWILL *noun*. **b** T. C. MCQUEEN They come at you in groups. Check your six. **4 at sixes and sevens** in confusion, disorder, or disagreement. **hit for six, knock for six** (*a*) CRICKET hit (the ball or bowler) for six runs; (*b*) *fig.* give a severe blow, surprise, etc., to, defeat in an argument etc.

Comb.: Forming compound cardinal numerals with multiples of ten from twenty to ninety, as ***thirty-six***, (*arch.*) ***six-and-thirty***, etc., and (*arch.*) their corresponding ordinals, as ***six-and-thirtieth*** etc., and with multiples of a hundred, as ***206*** (read ***two hundred and six***, US also ***two hundred six***), etc. With nouns + -ER[1] forming nouns with the sense 'something (identified contextually) being of or having six —', as ***six-seater***, ***six-wheeler***, etc. Special combs., as **six by six** *slang* (orig. US MILITARY) a six-wheeled truck with six-wheel drive; **Six Clerk** *Hist.* any of the six official clerks formerly connected with the Court of Chancery; **Six Day War**, **Six Days War** *Hist.* the Arab-Israeli war that lasted from 5 to 10 June 1967; **six-eight** *adjective & noun* (MUSIC) (designating) time or rhythm with six quavers in a bar; **six-four** *adjective & noun* (MUSIC) (designating) time or rhythm with six crotchets in a bar; **six-gun** *N. Amer.* = ***six-shooter*** below; **sixpence** six pence, esp. of the old British currency before decimalization; *Hist.* a silver (subsequently cupro-nickel) coin worth six old pence; **sixpenny** *adjective* (*a*) worth or costing sixpence; *fig.* (*arch.*) inferior, paltry; (*b*) ***sixpenny nail*** [orig. costing sixpence per hundred], a nail approx. 2 inches long; **six-pounder** a gun throwing a shot that weighs six pounds; **six-rowed barley** a commonly cultivated barley, *Hordeum vulgare*, usually having six longitudinal rows of fertile spikelets in each spike; **sixscore** *adjective & noun* (*arch.*) one hundred and twenty; **six-shooter** a revolver with six chambers; **six-two** *adjective & noun* (MUSIC) (designating) time or rhythm with six minims in a bar.

■ **sixer** *noun* (*a*) the leader of a Brownie or Cub Scout six; (*b*) SPORT a hit, kick, etc., scoring six; *esp.* (CRICKET) a hit for six runs; (*c*) *slang* a prison sentence of six months' imprisonment or hard labour: M19. **sixfold** *adjective & adverb* (*a*) *adjective* six times as great or as numerous; having six parts, divisions, elements or units; (*b*) *adverb* to six times the number or quantity: OE. **sixmo** *noun* = SEXTO E19.

sixain /ˈsɪkseɪn/ *noun*. L16.
[French, from *six* six + *-ain* -AN.]
A set or series of six lines of verse.

sixfoil /ˈsɪksfɔɪl/ *noun*. M19.
[from SIX *adjective* + FOIL *noun*[1], after *cinquefoil* etc.]
ARCHITECTURE & HERALDRY. = SEXFOIL *noun*.

six-pack /ˈsɪkspak/ *noun*. M20.
[from SIX + PACK *noun*.]
1 A package containing six units, esp. six cans of beer. M20.
2 A set of well-developed abdominal muscles; a lean, muscular midriff. *colloq.* L20.
1 Joe Six-pack *US colloq.* (a nickname for) a hypothetical average blue-collar man.

sixsome /ˈsɪks(ə)m/ *adverb, pronoun, noun, & adjective*. OE.
[from SIX + -SOME[2].]
▶†**A** *adverb*. As one of six. Only in OE.
▶**B** *pronoun & noun*. Formerly, six in all. Now, a group of six. LME.
▶**C** *attrib.* or as *adjective*. For six; *esp.* (of a dance) performed by six people together. E19.

sixte /sɪkst/ *noun*. L19.
[French = sixth.]
FENCING. The sixth of eight recognized parrying positions, used to protect the upper right-hand side of the body; a thrust in this position.

sixteen /sɪksˈtiːn, ˈsɪkstiːn/ *adjective & noun* (*cardinal numeral*).
[Old English *s(i)extiene*, *syx-*, *sex-* = Old Frisian *sextine*, Old Saxon *se(h)stein* (Dutch *zestien*), Old High German *seh(s)zēn* (German *sechszehn*), Old Norse *sextán*, from Germanic base of SIX, -TEEN. Aphet. to STEEN *adjective*.]
▶**A** *adjective*. **1** One more than fifteen (a cardinal numeral represented by 16 in arabic numerals, xvi, XVI in roman). OE.
†**2** = SIXTEENTH *adjective*. LME–L17.

📖 **1** J. TROLLOPE The office was a single room about sixteen feet square.

▶**B** *noun*. **1** One more than fifteen as an abstract number; the symbols or figures representing this (16 in arabic numerals, xvi, XVI in roman). OE.
2 Sixteen persons or things identified contextually, as years of age, chances (in giving odds), minutes, shillings (now *Hist.*), pence, etc. ME.
3 The sixteenth of a set or series with numbered members, the one designated sixteen, (usu. ***number sixteen***, or with specification, as ***book sixteen***, ***chapter sixteen***, etc.); a size etc. denoted by sixteen, a garment etc. of such a size, (also ***size sixteen***). E16.
4 A set of sixteen; a thing having a set of sixteen as an essential or distinguishing feature; *spec.* (*a*) in *pl.*, sixteen leaves to the sheet in a printed book, sextodecimo; (*b*) an engine or motor vehicle with sixteen cylinders. E17.
5 Each of a set of sixteen; *spec.* a medium-sized plant-pot of which sixteen are formed from one cast of clay. E19.

📖 **2** *New Yorker* The Phillies . . put sixteen on the board in their first two turns at bat. *Health Guardian* Menstruation . . starts during puberty, usually between the ages of ten and sixteen. ***sweet sixteen***: see SWEET *adjective & adverb*.

Comb.: Forming compound cardinal numerals with multiples of a hundred, as ***516*** (read ***five hundred and sixteen***, US also ***five hundred sixteen***), etc. In dates used for one thousand six hundred, as ***1612*** (read ***sixteen twelve***), ***sixteen-nineties***, etc. With nouns + -ER[1] forming nouns with the sense 'something (identified contextually) being of or having sixteen —s', as ***sixteen-tonner***, ***sixteen-wheeler***, etc. Special combs., as **sixteen millimetre (film)** a cine film which is sixteen millimetres wide; **sixteen pounder** a gun throwing a shot that weighs sixteen pounds.

■ **sixteenmo** *noun* = SEXTODECIMO M19. **sixteensome** *noun & adjective* (*a*) *noun* a group of sixteen people; (*b*) *adjective* for sixteen; *esp.* (of a dance) performed by sixteen people together: E20.

sixteenth /sɪksˈtiːnθ, ˈsɪkstiːnθ/ *adjective & noun* (*ordinal numeral*).
[Old English *s(i)extēoþa* etc., repl. in Middle English by forms from SIXTEEN + -TH[2]. Cf. Old Frisian *sextinda*, *-tenda*, *-tiensta*, Old Norse *sextándi*. Aphet. to STEENTH.]
▶**A** *adjective*. Next in order after the fifteenth, that is number sixteen in a series, (represented by 16th). OE.

📖 M. HOCKING A rambling sixteenth century house. **sixteenth note** MUSIC (chiefly *N. Amer.*) a semiquaver. **sixteenth part** *arch.* = sense B.2 below.

▶**B** *noun*. **1** The sixteenth person or thing of a category, series, etc., identified contextually, as day of the month, (following a proper name) person, esp. monarch or pope, of the specified name, etc. OE.
2 Each of sixteen equal parts into which something is or may be divided, a fraction which when multiplied by sixteen gives one, (= ***sixteenth part*** above). E17.
3 MUSIC. A semiquaver, a sixteenth note. Also, an interval of two octaves and a second. L19.
Comb.: Forming compound ordinal numerals with multiples of a hundred, as ***three-hundred-and-sixteenth*** (***316th***) etc.
■ **sixteenthly** *adverb* in the sixteenth place M17.

sixth /sɪksθ/ *adjective & noun* (*ordinal numeral*).
[Old English *si(e)xta* etc., repl. in 16 by forms from SIX + -TH[2].]
▶**A** *adjective*. Next in order after the fifth, that is number six in a series, (represented by 6th). OE.

📖 *Classic CD* Prokofiev's sixth opera . . did not receive its first production until 1929. **sixth form**: in a secondary school for pupils over sixteen; ***sixth-form college***, a college for pupils over sixteen. **sixth former** a pupil in the sixth form. **sixth part** *arch.* = sense B.3 below. **sixth sense** a supposed faculty giving intuitive or extrasensory knowledge; such knowledge.

▶**B** *noun*. **1** The sixth person or thing of a category, series etc., identified contextually, as a day of the month, (following a proper name) person, esp. monarch or pope, of the specified name, etc. OE.
2 MUSIC. An interval embracing six consecutive notes in the diatonic scale; a note a sixth above another given note; a chord including two notes a sixth apart, or based around the sixth of a note. LME.
3 Each of six equal parts into which something is or may be divided, a fraction which when multiplied by six gives one, (= ***sixth part*** above). M16.

📖 **1** I. HAY The Head . . probably takes the sixth for an hour or two a day. **3** *Listener* To surrender voluntarily a sixth of their land for distribution to the poor.

Comb.: Forming compound ordinal numerals with multiples of ten, as ***forty-sixth*** (***46th***), ***five-thousand-and-sixth*** (***5006th***), etc.
■ **sixthly** *adverb* in the sixth place LME.

sixtieth /ˈsɪkstɪɪθ/ *adjective & noun* (*ordinal numeral*).
[Old English *si(e)xteogoþa*, repl. in Middle English by forms from SIXTY + -TH[2].]
▶**A** *adjective*. Next in order after the fifty-ninth, that is number sixty in a series, (represented by 60th). OE.
▶**B** *noun*. **1** The sixtieth person or thing of a category, series, etc. identified contextually. OE.
2 Each of sixty equal parts into which something is or may be divided, a fraction which when multiplied by sixty gives one. E19.
Comb.: Forming compound ordinal numerals with multiples of a hundred, as ***five-hundred-and-sixtieth*** (560th) etc., and (*arch.*) with numerals below ten, as ***three-and-sixtieth*** etc.

Sixtine /ˈsɪkstiːn, -tʌɪn/ *adjective*. M19.
[mod. Latin *Sixtinus*, from *Sixtus*, papal name: see -INE[1].]
= SISTINE *adjective*.

sixty /ˈsɪksti/ *adjective & noun* (*cardinal numeral*).
[Old English *s(i)extiġ*, from SIX + -TY[2].]
▶**A** *adjective*. Six times ten (a cardinal numeral represented by 60 in arabic numerals, lx, LX in roman). OE.
▶**B** *noun*. **1** Sixty persons or things identified contextually, as years of age, points, runs, etc., in a game, chances (in giving odds), etc. OE.
2 Six times ten as an abstract number; the symbols or figures representing this (60 in arabic numerals, lx, LX in roman). ME.
3 The sixtieth of a set or series with numbered members, the one designated sixty, (usu. ***number sixty***, or with specification, as ***chapter sixty***, ***verse sixty***, etc.); a size etc. denoted by sixty (also ***size sixty***). E16.
4 Each of a set of sixty; *spec.* a small plant-pot of which sixty are formed from one cast of clay. E19.
5 In *pl.* The numbers from 60 to 69 inclusive, esp. denoting years of a century or units of a scale of temperature; *one's* years of life between the ages of 60 and 69. L19.

📖 **2 like sixty** *slang* at a great rate. **5** *attrib.*: *Blitz* Sixties liberalism does not hold up well in the conservatism of the Eighties.

Comb.: Forming compound numerals (cardinal or ordinal) with numerals below ten, as ***sixty-seven*** (***67***), ***sixty-third*** (***63rd***), etc., and (cardinals) with multiples of a hundred, as ***460*** (read ***four hundred and sixty***, US also ***four hundred sixty***), etc. Special combs., as **sixty-four dollar question**, **sixty-four hundred dollar question**, **sixty-four thousand dollar question** [from the top prize in a broadcast quiz show] *the* crucial issue, a difficult question, a dilemma; **sixty-six** a card-game in which a point is scored for first reaching 66 card points; **sixty-nine** [from the position of the couple] sexual activity between two people involving mutual oral stimulation of the genitals; a position enabling this (cf. SOIXANTE-NEUF); **sixty per cent** *arch. colloq.* a usurer; **sixty-fourmo** a size of book or page in which each leaf is one sixty-fourth that of a standard printing-sheet; a book or page of this size.
■ **sixtyfold** *adjective & adverb* (*a*) *adjective* sixty times as great or as numerous; having sixty parts, divisions, elements, or units; (*b*) *adverb* to sixty times the number or quantity: OE. **sixtyish** *adjective* about sixty (in age, measurements, etc.) M20.

sizable *adjective* var. of SIZEABLE.

sizar /ˈsʌɪzə/ *noun*. L16.
[from SIZE *noun*[1] + -AR[3].]
In Cambridge University and at Trinity College, Dublin, an undergraduate receiving an allowance from the college to enable him or her to study, and formerly required to perform certain menial duties.
■ **sizarship** *noun* L18.

size /sʌɪz/ *noun*[1]. ME.
[Old French (also *sise*) aphet. from *assise* ASSIZE, or aphet. from the English word.]
▶**I 1** = ASSIZE *noun* 3, 5. Formerly also (*Scot.*), a jury. Now *dial.* ME.
†**2** An ordinance fixing the amount of a payment or tax. ME–L18.
†**3** A (proper) manner or method; a custom; a standard. ME–L16.
†**4** = ASSIZE *noun* 2b. L15–L17.
†**5** A quantity or portion *of* bread, beer, etc.; *spec.* (*Univ. slang*) a particular quantity of bread, beer, etc. M16–E19.
▶**II 6** The relative bigness or extent of a thing or person; the dimensions of a thing or person; *spec.* large dimensions, magnitude. ME. ▸**b** Suitable or normal dimensions. *rare* exc. in ***cut down to size*** (*colloq.*), expose the limitations of a person's importance, knowledge, etc. M19. ▸**c** Consistency of a liquid mixture. M19.
7 Any of the (usu. numbered) classes into which things (esp. garments) otherwise similar are divided according to size; a person's size as corresponding to such a numbered class. L16.

📖 **6** E. SIMON Stop bullying me . . . Choose someone your own size. E. YOUNG-BRUEHL At five feet three inches she was not formidable in size. G. DALY Gabriel poured himself into decorating his new home, an enormous undertaking because of its size. **7** A. BLEASDALE A pair of trousers several . . sizes too big for him. D. LEAVITT His feet looked about size thirteen.

Phrases: CRITICAL ***size***. ***in all shapes and sizes***: see SHAPE *noun*[1]. **of a size** having the same size or dimensions. **of some size** quite large. **the size of** as big as (***that's about the size of it***, ***that's the size of it***, that is what it amounts to, that is a true account of the matter). **try for size**, **try on for size** test (a thing) to determine whether it fits (*lit.* & *fig.*). **what size?** how big?
Comb.: **size-bone** NAUTICAL a whalebone measuring six feet or above; **size distribution** the way in which size varies among members of a population of particles; **size-stick** a shoemaker's measure for determining the length and width of a person's foot.
■ **sizeless** *adjective* L19.

size /sʌɪz/ *noun*[2]. ME.
[Perh. identical with prec.]
Any of various sticky gelatinous or liquid solutions used to seal a surface before gilding, painting, etc., or to stiffen textiles.

size *noun*[3] var. of SICE.

size /sʌɪz/ *verb*¹. LME.
[In early use aphet. from ASSIZE *verb*; later from SIZE *noun*¹.]
†**1** *verb trans.* = ASSIZE *verb* 4. LME–L18.
2 *verb trans. & intrans.* Enter (food, drink, etc., taken) in the buttery or kitchen books; record (a meal etc.) as a debt to be paid. *Univ. slang.* Now *rare* or *obsolete*. L16.
3 *verb trans.* Make of or adjust to a certain size. E17. ▸**b** Plough new ridges in (a field). *dial.* E18.
4 *verb trans.* Classify or arrange according to size. M17. ▸**b** Single (plants). *rare.* M17.
5 *verb intrans.* **a** Be equal or match *with*. Also foll. by *up*. *rare.* M17. ▸**b** Increase in size. M17. ▸**c** Foll. by *up*: develop; amount (*to*); reach the required standard. Chiefly *US*. L19.
6 *verb trans.* Foll. by *up*, (rare) *down*: estimate the size of; *colloq.* assess, appraise, form an opinion of. L19.

3 *Scientific American* The book was sized to fit into a briefcase. **5c** *Daily Telegraph* The contest is sizing up to be one of the closest races in years. **6** SLOAN WILSON It took Everett only about a minute to size Tom up as a 'possibility'. G. DALY She was also busy sizing up this curious, handsome young man.

■ **sizer** *noun*¹ a device for determining the size of articles, or for separating them according to size L17. **sizing** *noun*¹ (*a*) the action of the verb; (*b*) *Univ. slang* (now *rare* or *obsolete*) a portion, a size: L16.

size /sʌɪz/ *verb*² *trans.* M17.
[from SIZE *noun*². Cf. earlier OVERSIZE *verb*².]
Cover, prepare, or stiffen with size.
■ **sizer** *noun*² M19. **sizing** *noun*² (*a*) the action of the verb; (*b*) size; the materials for making this: M17.

sizeable /ˈsʌɪzəb(ə)l/ *adjective.* Also **sizable**. E17.
[from SIZE *verb*¹ + -ABLE.]
Large; fairly large; substantial.

M. SPARK Milly's .. back garden .. was good and sizeable for a London house.

■ **sizeably** *adverb* E20.

sized /sʌɪzd/ *adjective.* L16.
[from SIZE *noun*¹, *verb*¹: see -ED², -ED¹.]
1 Having a specified or specific (relative) size. L16.
2 Matched in size. *rare.* E18.
3 Of a fair or standard size. *arch.* M18.

1 J. BOWYER The storage tank is sized to hold enough heat for a day. ***different-sized***, ***fair-sized***, ***large-sized***, etc.

sizeism /ˈsʌɪzɪz(ə)m/ *noun.* L20.
[from SIZE *noun*¹ + -ISM.]
Prejudice or discrimination against a person or persons on the basis of physical size.
■ **sizeist** *adjective & noun* L20.

sizy /ˈsʌɪzi/ *adjective.* Now *rare* or *obsolete*. L17.
[from SIZE *noun*² + -Y¹.]
Resembling size, esp. in consistency; glutinous.
■ **siziness** *noun* E18.

sizz /sɪz/ *verb.* Chiefly *dial.* & *US*. L17.
[Imit.]
†**1** *verb trans.* Burn, brand. Only in L17.
2 *verb intrans.* Hiss; sizzle. L18.

sizzle /ˈsɪz(ə)l/ *verb & noun.* E17.
[Imit.]
▶ **A** *verb.* **1** *verb trans.* Fry or burn so as to produce a hissing sound. E17.
2 *verb intrans.* Make a hissing sound, esp. in the process of being fried or roasted; *fig.* be very hot, be salacious or risqué. E19.

2 R. FRAME A gas fire sizzles in the grate. *Sun* Britain carried on sizzling yesterday as the heatwave scorched up to .. 90 degrees.

▶ **B** *noun.* A hissing sound, *esp.* one produced by something being fried or roasted; *fig.* intense heat or excitement. E19.

S. RADLEY The sizzle of cooking and appetizing smells.

Comb.: **sizzle cymbal** a cymbal having several small rivets set loosely through it to make a sizzling sound when the cymbal is struck.
■ **sizzler** *noun* (*colloq.*) (*a*) a very hot day, season, etc.; (*b*) a salacious thing; (*c*) a thing characterized by great speed, activity, etc.: E20. **sizzling** *adjective & adverb* (*a*) *adjective* that sizzles; *fig.* intensely hot or exciting, salacious, risqué; (*b*) *adverb* (*colloq.*) ***sizzling hot***, very hot: M19. **sizzlingly** *adverb* so as to sizzle; *colloq.* intensely, extremely: M20.

SJ *abbreviation.*
Society of Jesus.

SJAA *abbreviation.*
St John Ambulance Association.

SJAB *abbreviation.*
St John Ambulance Brigade.

sjambok /ˈʃambɒk/ *noun & verb.* *S. Afr.* Also **sam-**, **sham-**. L18.
[Afrikaans, from Malay *sambuk*, *chambuk* from Persian & Urdu *chābuk* horsewhip.]
▶ **A** *noun.* A heavy whip made of rhinoceros or hippopotamus hide. L18.
▶ **B** *verb trans.* Infl. **-kk-**, **-k-**. Strike or flog with a sjambok. L19.
■ **sjambokker** *noun* M20.

SJC *abbreviation. US.*
Supreme Judicial Court.

Sjögren /ˈʃəːgrən/ *noun.* M20.
[H. S. C. *Sjögren* (1899–1986), Swedish physician.]
MEDICINE. ***Sjögren's disease***, ***Sjögren's syndrome***, a condition characterized by wasting of the salivary and lacrimal glands and by autoimmune antibodies in the blood.

SK *abbreviation.*
Saskatchewan (in official postal use).

ska /skɑː/ *noun.* M20.
[Origin uncertain: perh. imit.]
A style of popular music originating in Jamaica, with a fast tempo and accentuated offbeat; a song or dance set to this music. Cf. REGGAE, ROCKSTEADY, SKANK *noun*¹.

skaal *noun & interjection* var. of SKOL *noun & interjection*.

skaapsteker /ˈskɑːpsteɪkə/ *noun.* E19.
[Afrikaans, from Dutch *schaap* sheep + *steker* stinger.]
Either of two venomous but rarely dangerous southern African colubrid grass snakes of the genus *Psammophylax*, *P. rhombeatus* (more fully ***spotted skaapsteker***) and *P. tritaeniatus* (more fully ***striped skaapsteker***).

skaff *noun* var. of SCAFF *noun*¹.

skag *noun* var. of SCAG *noun*.

skail /skeɪl/ *verb. Scot. & north.* ME.
[Origin unkn.]
1 *verb trans. & intrans.* Spread, disperse, break up, scatter. ME. ▸**b** *verb trans.* Rake out, clear with a poker. *north.* L18.
2 *verb trans.* Break up (an assembly, school, etc.) by dismissal. Formerly also, disband (an army). ME.
3 *verb trans.* Put (an army etc.) to flight, rout. LME. ▸†**b** Raise (a siege). LME–L16.
4 *verb trans.* Pour out, shed, spill. E16.

skaith *noun, verb* see SCATHE *noun, verb*.

skald /skɔːld, skald/ *noun.* Also **scald**. M18.
[Old Norse *skáld*, of unkn. origin.]
Hist. An (itinerant or court) oral poet, a bard, orig. and esp. in ancient Scandinavia.
■ **skaldic** *adjective* of or pertaining to the skalds or their poetry L18.

skance /skans/ *adjective. rare.* M19.
[Aphet. from ASKANCE *adverb*¹, *adjective*, & *verb*.]
Of a look, glance, etc.: oblique, sidelong.

skandalon /ˈskandəlɒn/ *noun.* Also **sc-**. M20.
[Greek.]
THEOLOGY. A stumbling-block; a cause of offence; a scandal.

skank /skaŋk/ *noun*¹ *& verb.* L20.
[Origin unkn.]
▶ **A** *noun.* A steady-paced dance performed to reggae music, characterized by rhythmically bending forward, raising the knees, and extending the hands palms-downwards; (a piece of) reggae music suitable for such dancing. L20.
▶ **B** *verb.* **1** *verb intrans.* Play reggae music or dance in this style. Chiefly as ***skanking*** *verbal noun & ppl adjective*. Cf. REGGAE, ROCKSTEADY, SKA. L20.
2 *verb trans.* Swindle or deceive (a person). Also, obtain (something) by deception or theft. *slang.* L20.

skank /skaŋk/ *noun*². *slang* (orig. *US Black English*). L20.
[Origin unkn.]
A person perceived to be extremely sleazy or unpleasant; a sexually promiscuous person, esp. a woman.
■ **skanky** *adjective* unattractive, dirty; revolting, offensive L20.

skarn /skɑːn/ *noun.* Also **scarn**. E20.
[Swedish = dung, filth from Old Norse.]
PETROGRAPHY. Orig., silicate gangue of certain Archaean iron ore or sulphide deposits. Now, any lime-bearing siliceous rock produced by contact metamorphism of limestone or dolomite with the introduction of new elements.

skat /skɑːt/ *noun.* M19.
[German from Italian *scarto* (= French *écart*) cards laid aside, from *scartare* discard. Cf. ÉCARTÉ.]
A three-handed card-game with bidding for contract, originating in Germany; *collect.* the two cards dealt to the table in this game.

skate /skeɪt/ *noun*¹. ME.
[Old Norse *skata*.]
Any of various rays of the family Rajidae, with a roughly diamond-shaped body and a long thin tail; *spec.* (*a*) the large *Raja batis*, which is common in the NE Atlantic and much used as food; (*b*) *colloq.* = THORNBACK 1. Also, the flesh of any of these fishes as food. Cf. THORNBACK 1, 1b.
little skate, ***thornback skate***, etc.
Comb.: **skate-barrow** the egg-case of a skate; **skate-leech**, **skate-sucker** a large leech, *Pontobdella muricata*, which infests skates and rays.

skate /skeɪt/ *noun*² *& verb.* See also SKETCH *verb*² & *noun*². M17.
[Dutch *schaats* (taken as pl.) from Middle Dutch *schaetse* from Old Northern French *eschasse* (mod. *échasse*) stilt.]
▶ **A** *noun.* **1** Either of a pair of steel blades curved upward at the toe and fixed or attached to boots, for gliding over ice; a boot with such a blade permanently attached (also ***ice-skate***). Also, a roller-skate. Usu. in *pl.* M17. ▸**b** A ski. Usu. in *pl.* L17. ▸**c** The runner of a sledge. *US.* L18. ▸**d** A set of tackle for fishing for halibut etc., used chiefly on the Pacific coast of N. America. *N. Amer.* L19. ▸**e** *transf.* A board, plate, or runner, freq. with wheels on the underside, for placing under a heavy or unwieldy object to facilitate its movement. E20.
2 An act or period of skating; any of various manoeuvres in figure-skating. M19.
1 **get one's skates on** *colloq.* hurry up (freq. as *imper.*).
Comb.: **skate key**: for tightening roller-skates; **skatepark** a park or rink for skateboarding; **skate-sail**: for fixing to a skater's back so that the wind may carry him or her along.
▶ **B** *verb.* **1** *verb intrans.* Glide over ice on skates, esp. for transportation, exercise, or amusement. Also foll. by *on*, *over*. Also ***ice-skate***. L17. ▸**b** *transf.* Slide or glide along; move lightly and quickly. L18. ▸**c** *fig.* Foll. by *over* or *round*: Pass over hurriedly or avoid mentioning a fact, subject, etc. M19. ▸**d** Leave quickly. *colloq.* E20. ▸**e** Avoid work or duty, shirk. *US slang.* M20.
2 *verb trans.* Knock (a person) *down* in skating (*rare*); compete in (a skating match or race). L18. ▸**b** Cause (a thing) to glide over a smooth surface. L19.
1 ***free skating***: see FREE *adjective*. **skate on thin ice** *colloq.* behave rashly, risk danger, esp. in dealing with a subject requiring tactful treatment. **skating-rink** = RINK *noun* 3.
■ **skateable** *adjective* able to be skated on or over L19. **skater** *noun* (*a*) a person who skates; (*b*) a skateboarder: E18. **skatist** *noun* (*rare*) an enthusiastic skater L19.

skate /skeɪt/ *noun*³. Chiefly *US*. L19.
[Origin unkn.]
1 A worn-out decrepit horse. *slang.* L19.
2 A mean, contemptible, or dishonest person. Esp. in ***cheapskate***. *colloq.* L19. ▸**b** ***labour skate***, a trade-union official. *US slang.* M20.

skateboard /ˈskeɪtbɔːd/ *noun & verb.* M20.
[from SKATE *noun*² + BOARD *noun*.]
▶ **A** *noun.* A short narrow board mounted on roller-skate wheels, on which the rider stands and coasts along, propelled by occasional pushes of one foot against the ground. M20.
▶ **B** *verb intrans.* Ride on a skateboard; perform stunts etc. on a skateboard. M20.
■ **skateboarder** *noun* M20.

skatole /ˈskatəʊl/ *noun.* Also †**-ol**. L19.
[from Greek *skatos*, genit. of *skōr* dung + -OLE².]
CHEMISTRY. A fetid substance, 3-methylindole, C_9H_9N, present in faeces and in secretions of civets, and used in perfumery.

skaz /skaz/ *noun.* E20.
[Russian.]
First-person narrative in which the author assumes a persona.

skean /skiːn/ *noun.* Also **skene**. LME.
[Irish, Gaelic *sgian*. Cf. Welsh *ysgien*.]
1 A (long) Gaelic knife or dagger, formerly used in Ireland and Scotland. Now *Hist.* LME.
2 **a** ***skean-occle*** /-ˈɒk(ə)l/ [Gaelic *achlais* armpit], a Gaelic knife or dagger for carrying concealed in the sleeve near the armpit. Now *Hist.* E18. ▸**b** ***skean-dhu*** /-ˈduː/ [Gaelic *dubh* black], an ornamental dagger, freq. worn thrust into the stocking, now only as part of Highland costume. E19.

sked /skɛd/ *noun & verb. colloq.* (chiefly *US*). E20.
[Abbreviation.]
▶ **A** *noun.* A schedule. Also, a scheduled event, *esp.* a scheduled flight, concert appearance, etc. E20.
▶ **B** *verb trans.* Infl. **-dd-**. Schedule. E20.

skedaddle /skɪˈdad(ə)l/ *verb & noun. colloq.* M19.
[Origin unkn. Cf. SKIDOO.]
▶ **A** *verb.* **1** *verb intrans.* Depart quickly, run away; *spec.* (of a regiment, troop of soldiers, etc.) retreat hurriedly, suddenly, or in a disorderly manner. Also, (of an animal) run off, stampede. M19.
2 *verb trans.* Spill, spatter, scatter, (milk etc.). *dial.* M19.

1 R. DAVIES He'd grabbed up all his plans, and skedaddled but that didn't bother me. J. TORRINGTON The grey moggie .. had skedaddled via the door and could be heard pelting to safety along the lobby carpet.

▶ **B** *noun.* (A) hurried or sudden retreat, departure, or flight. L19.
■ **skedaddler** *noun* M19.

Skeeball /ˈskiːbɔːl/ *noun.* Also **Skee-Ball**, **s-**. E20.
[from SKI *noun & verb* + BALL *noun*¹.]
An indoor game in which a ball is rolled down an alley and over a bump etc. into a target.
¶ Proprietary name in the US.

skeel /skiːl/ *noun*. Now *dial*. ME.
[Old Norse *skjóla* pail, bucket.]
A wooden bucket or tub, usu. with a handle or handles formed by staves rising above the rim, used chiefly for holding milk or water.
■ **skeelful** *noun* as much as a skeel will hold L16.

skeeler /ˈskiːlə/ *noun*. M20.
[Perh. from SKI *noun* + ROL)LER *noun*¹.]
Either of a pair of skates with a central line of wheels in place of a blade. Usu. in *pl*.
■ **skeeling** *noun* skating on skeelers M20.

skeer /skɪə/ *verb trans*. Now *dial*. M17.
[Origin uncertain: cf. SKIRR.]
= SKIRR *verb* 3.

skeet /skiːt/ *noun*¹ & *verb*. LME.
[Origin unkn.]
▶ **A** *noun*. A long-handled scoop or shovel. Later *spec*. (NAUTICAL), such a scoop used for wetting a ship's planks or rigging. LME.
▶ **B** *verb trans*. NAUTICAL. Throw (water) over rigging etc. with a skeet; wet (rigging) in this way. L19.

skeet /skiːt/ *noun*². E20.
[App. pseudo-arch. alt. of SHOOT *verb*.]
A form of sports shooting in which clay targets are thrown at a variety of angles in a semicircular range to simulate birds in flight. Also (usu. *attrib*.), a clay pigeon.
■ **skeeting** *noun* skeet shooting E20.

skeeter /ˈskiːtə/ *noun*¹. *dial*. & *colloq*. (chiefly *N. Amer*. & *Austral*.). M19.
[Aphet.]
A mosquito, a gnat.

skeeter /ˈskiːtə/ *noun*². E20.
[from SKEET *noun*² + -ER¹.]
A person who participates in skeet; a skeet shooter.

skeeter *verb* var. of SKITTER *verb*².

skeezicks /ˈskiːzɪks/ *noun*. *N. Amer. slang*. Now chiefly *joc*. M19.
[Fanciful.]
A rascal, a rogue.

skeg /skɛɡ/ *noun*¹. ME.
[Old Norse *skegg* beard; in sense 2 perh. from Dutch *scheg(ge)* from Old Norse *skegg*.]
1 An inferior variety of bearded oat. ME.
2 *a* NAUTICAL. A small slanting segment of the keel of a vessel, which connects and braces the keel and sternpost. E17. ▸**b** SURFING. The fin of a surfboard. M20.

skeg /skɛɡ/ *noun*². Now *dial*. E17.
[Origin unkn.: cf. SCAD *noun*¹.]
(The fruit of) any of several kinds of wild plum, esp. the bullace, *Prunus insititia*, and sloe, *P. spinosa*.

skeg /skɛɡ/ *noun*³. *rare*. Now *dial*. E17.
[Origin unkn.]
The broken stump of a branch. Also, a tear in cloth, *esp*. one made by such a stump.

skegger /ˈskɛɡə/ *noun*. M17.
[Origin unkn.]
A young salmon, a samlet; salmon fry.

skeigh /skiːx/ *adjective* & *adverb*. *Scot*. E16.
[Rel. to Old English *scēoh* SHY *adjective*: cf. Middle High German *schiuhe*, *schiech*-, German *scheuch*.]
▶ **A** *adjective*. (Of a horse) skittish, spirited; (of a person, esp. a woman) shy, coy, disdainful, proud. E16.
▶ **B** *adverb*. Proudly, disdainfully. L18.

skein /skeɪn/ *noun*¹ & *verb*. ME.
[Aphet. from Old French *escaigne* (mod. dial. *écagne*), of unkn. origin.]
▶ **A** *noun*. **1** A length of thread or yarn, loosely coiled and knotted (esp. into a figure of eight). ME. ▸**b** *fig*. A tangle, a confusion. E17.
2 *transf*. A small cluster or arrangement resembling a skein. L17. ▸**b** A flight of wildfowl, esp. geese or swans. M19.

> 📖 **1** J. MORIER Fifty skanes of silk were spun in one day. **b** SIR W. SCOTT The unwinding of the perilous skein of . . politics. **2b** D. ATTENBOROUGH Long skeins of them keep a . . purposeful course across the . . sky.

▶ **B** *verb trans*. Make into skeins; mark with a pattern resembling a skein. L18.
■ **skeiner** *noun* E20.

skein /skeɪn/ *noun*². M19.
[Dutch *scheen*: see SHIN *noun*¹.]
1 A prepared strip of willow used in fine basket-work. M19.
2 A metal head or cap for protecting the spindle of a wooden axle. *US*. M19.

skelder /ˈskɛldə/ *verb*. *arch. slang*. L16.
[Origin unkn.]
1 *verb intrans*. Beg; live by begging, esp. claiming to be a (wounded) ex-serviceman. L16.
2 *verb trans*. Cheat, swindle, defraud, (a person); obtain (money) by cheating. L16.

skelet /ˈskɛlət/ *noun*. *obsolete* exc. *dial*. M16.
[French †*squelete*, *sc*-, *sk*- (now *squelette*) or Greek *skeletos*, -*on*: see SKELETON.]
A skeleton.

skeletal /ˈskɛlɪt(ə)l/ *adjective*. M19.
[from SKELETON *noun* + -AL¹.]
1 Of or pertaining to, forming or formed by, a skeleton. M19.
2 Resembling or suggesting a skeleton owing to paucity of flesh; emaciated; skinny. M20.
3 Having or consisting of only a framework or outline; bare, meagre. M20.

> 📖 **1** B. LOPEZ Pieces of bone, representing the skeletal debris of . . musk oxen. **2** D. JUDD How skeletal his limbs are. **3** *Atlantic* Skeletal dories lie beached . . in the tidal mud.

Special collocations: **skeletal muscle**: attached to part of a skeleton and usu. under voluntary control; striated muscle. **skeletal soil** = LITHOSOL.
■ **skeletally** *adverb* M20.

skeletogenous /skɛlɪˈtɒdʒɪnəs/ *adjective*. L19
[from next + -GENOUS.]
EMBRYOLOGY. Producing or helping to form skeletal or bony structures.

skeleton /ˈskɛlɪt(ə)n/ *noun* & *verb*. L16.
[mod. Latin from Greek, use as noun of neut. of *skeletos* dried up, from *skellein* dry up.]
▶ **A** *noun*. **1** The hard internal or external framework of bones, cartilage, shell, woody fibre, etc., supporting or containing the body of an animal or plant. Also, the dried bones of a human being or other animal fastened together in the same relative positions as in life. L16. ▸**b** *Hist*. A member of a skeleton army (see below). L19.
2 *transf*. A bare or meagre thing; *spec*. a very thin, lean, or emaciated person or animal. E17.
3 The supporting framework, esp. *of* an object, structure, etc.; the minimum or essential parts of a thing. Also, the remains of a disused or ruined thing. Freq. foll. by *of*. E17. ▸**b** The minimum or essential personnel representing or performing duties of a greatly reduced military regiment, ship's crew, etc. E19. ▸**c** CHEMISTRY. The basic atomic framework of a molecule, disregarding substituents (and sometimes also side-chains). E20.
4 *fig*. An outline, sketch, or plan of basic features or elements, esp. *of* an idea, institution, etc. M17.
5 *ellipt*. = ***skeleton in the closet***, ***skeleton in the cupboard*** below. M19.
6 PRINTING. In full ***skeleton forme***. The chase, quoins, furniture, and reusable segments of type (as running titles, borders, etc.) of a forme. L19.
7 A light sparsely structured bobsleigh or toboggan. E20.

> 📖 **1** D. HAMMETT You can't tell whether a man was thin . . by his skeleton. **2** W. GOLDING He was a . . skeleton, held together by skin. **3** D. HAMMETT An office building . . was being put up—just the skeleton. F. O'CONNOR It was . . a shell . . the skeleton of a house. **4** V. NABOKOV Deprived of . . purpose, the skeleton of her day . . collapsed.

Phrases: FAMILY ***skeleton***. ***living skeleton***: see LIVING *adjective*. **skeleton at the feast** something that spoils one's pleasure; an intrusive worry, grief, etc. **skeleton in the closet**, **skeleton in the cupboard** a secret source of discredit, pain, or shame.
Attrib. & *comb*.: In the senses 'part of, forming, or formed by, a skeleton or skeletons', as ***skeleton form***, ***skeleton hand***, ***skeleton horse***, etc.; 'having or consisting of a framework or outline', as ***skeleton building***, ***skeleton map***, ***skeleton plot***, etc.; 'having or consisting of the minimum or essential elements, features, members, etc.', as ***skeleton crew***, ***skeleton service***, ***skeleton staff***, etc. Special combs., as **skeleton army** *Hist*. a group of people attempting to disrupt the activities of the Salvation Army or Church Army; **skeleton brass** a memorial brass depicting a skeleton; **skeleton clock**: in which the internal mechanism is visible; ***skeleton forme***: see sense 6 above; **skeleton key**: designed to fit many locks by having the inner edge of the bit hollowed or filed away; **skeleton suit** *Hist*.: with narrow-legged high-waisted ankle-length trousers which buttoned on to a short jacket, worn by young boys in the late 18th and early 19th cents; **skeleton weed** *Austral*. a naturalized weed, *Chondrilla juncea*, of the composite family, native to the Mediterranean region.
▶ **B** *verb trans*. **1** Outline; mark the outline of. M19.
2 Construct a framework or outline for. L19.
3 Make into or reduce to a skeleton. L19.
■ **skeleˈtonian** *adjective* (*rare*) skeletal E19. **skeleˈtonic** *adjective* skeletal L19. **skeletonless** *adjective* L19. **skeletony** *adjective* resembling a skeleton M19.

skeletonize /ˈskɛlɪt(ə)nʌɪz/ *verb*. Also **-ise**. M17.
[from SKELETON *noun* + -IZE.]
1 *verb trans*. Make into or reduce to a skeleton; *fig*. reduce to an outline, sketch, or plan; identify the basic features or elements of. M17.
2 *verb trans*. Outline, sketch, plan, (an idea etc.). M19.
3 *verb intrans*. Become a skeleton. M19.
■ **skeletoniˈzation** *noun* L18. **skeletonized** *adjective* (*a*) reduced to a skeleton; (*b*) outlined, sketched, planned; (*c*) having (developed) a skeleton: M19.

skelf /skɛlf/ *noun*. *Scot*. & *north*. LME.
[Prob. from (the same root as) SHELF *noun*¹.]
1 A shelf. LME.
2 A splinter, a sharp fragment of wood etc. E17.
3 A small or slight person; one who is a nuisance. *colloq*. E20.

skell /skɛl/ *noun*. *US slang*. L20.
[Origin uncertain; perh. abbreviation of SKELETON *noun*.]
Esp. in New York, a homeless person, a derelict, *spec*. one living in the subway system.

skelloch /ˈskɛlək, -x/ *noun*¹. *Scot*. L17.
[Obscurely rel. to KEDLOCK.]
Wild mustard, *Sinapis arvensis*.

skelloch /ˈskɛlək, -x/ *noun*² & *verb*. *Scot*. E19.
[Prob. imit.]
(Make or emit) a shrill cry, scream, or shriek.

skellum *noun* & *adjective* var. of SKELM.

skelly /ˈskɛli/ *noun*. M18.
[Perh. from Middle English form of SHELL *noun* + -*y*.]
1 A form of the freshwater houting, *Coregonus lavaretus*, occurring in the English Lake District. Cf. GWYNIAD, POWAN. M18.
2 Any of several fishes of the carp family, *esp*. the chub and the dace. *north*. M18.

skelly /ˈskɛli/ *verb intrans*. *Scot*. & *north*. L18.
[from Old Norse verb, from *skjálgr* wry, oblique.]
Squint.

skelm /skɛl(ə)m/ *noun* & *adjective*. Also **skellum**. E17.
[Dutch *schelm* from German *Schelm* rascal. Cf. earlier SCHELM.]
▶ **A** *noun*. **1** A rascal, a scoundrel, a villain. *arch*. exc. *S. Afr*. E17.
2 A spirited, bad-tempered, or dangerous animal. *S. Afr*. E19.
▶ **B** *attrib*. or as *adjective*. (Of a person) rascally, villainous; untrustworthy; wily, cunning; (of an animal) bad-tempered, dangerous. Now *S. Afr*. L17.

skelp /skɛlp/ *noun*¹. Chiefly *Scot*. & *north*. LME.
[Rel. to SKELP *verb*.]
A blow, esp. with an open hand; a slap, a smack; the noise made by this.

skelp /skɛlp/ *noun*². E19.
[Origin unkn.]
A long narrow strip of iron or steel, out of which a gun barrel is made; iron or steel in the form of long narrow strips, used in making pipes, gun barrels, etc.

skelp /skɛlp/ *verb*. Chiefly *Scot*. & *north*. LME.
[Prob. imit.]
1 *verb trans*. Strike; slap, smack. Later *spec*. spank. LME. ▸**b** Drive or rout with blows. E19.
2 *verb intrans*. & *trans*. (with *it*). Skip, walk, or run quickly; hurry. E18.
3 *verb trans*. Kick violently. E19.
■ **skelper** *noun* (*a*) a person who slaps or smacks someone; (*b*) a specially large person or thing: L18. **skelping** *adjective* (*a*) that skelps; (*b*) large, lusty: E17.

skelpie-limmer /ˈskɛlpɪˌlɪmə/ *noun*. *Scot*. L18.
[Perh. from SKELP *verb* + LIMMER *noun*¹.]
A hussy, a promiscuous woman.

skelt /skɛlt/ *verb intrans*. *obsolete* exc. *Scot*. ME.
[Origin unkn.]
Hasten; work hard; be diligent.

skelter /ˈskɛltə/ *verb intrans*. M19.
[from HELTER-)SKELTER.]
Hurry, rush, scurry.

Skeltonic /skɛlˈtɒnɪk/ *adjective* & *noun*. M19.
[from John *Skelton* (c 1460–1529), English poet + -IC.]
▶ **A** *adjective*. Pertaining to, characteristic of, or imitating the poetry of Skelton; (of verse, metre, etc.) consisting of short irregular lines with frequent running on of the same rhyme. M19.
▶ **B** *noun*. A Skeltonic line, verse, poem, etc. Usu. in *pl*. E20.
■ Also **Skeltonian** *adjective* M19.

Skeltonical /skɛlˈtɒnɪk(ə)l/ *adjective*. L16.
[from *Skelton* (see prec.) + -ICAL.]
= SKELTONIC *adjective*.

skelvy /skɛlvi/ *adjective*. *Scot*. *rare*. L18.
[from SKELF + -Y¹.]
Having many shelves or ledges.

Skene /skiːn/ *noun*¹. L19.
[Alexander Johnston Chalmers *Skene* (1838–1900), Scottish-born Amer. gynaecologist.]
ANATOMY. Used in *possess*. to designate two small blind ducts which open into the female urethra, and the glands which they drain.

skene /ˈskiːni/ *noun*². L19.
[Greek *skēnē* hut, tent. Cf. SCENE.]
THEATRICAL. In ancient Greek theatre, a three-dimensional structure forming part of the stage or set and able to be

decorated according to the current play's theme. Cf. SCENE 5.

skene *noun*³ var. of SKEAN.

skeo /skjəʊ/ *noun. Scot. dial.* Pl. **-os**. E17.
[Norwegian *skjå* shed.]
A small dry-stone building, used for drying fish and meat in.

skep /skɛp/ *noun & verb.* Also **skip**. See also SKIP *noun*²
[Late Old English *sceppe* from Old Norse *skeppa* basket, bushel. Rel. to Old Saxon *scepil*, Old High German *sceffil* (German *Scheffel*).]
▶ **A** *noun.* **I 1** A basket, hamper, tub, etc., of locally varying size, form, and use; *transf.* the quantity *of* grain, malt, charcoal, etc., contained in this. LOE.
2 A (straw or wicker) beehive. L15.
▶ **II** See SKIP *noun*² II.
▶ **B** *verb trans.* Infl. **-pp-**. Cause (bees) to enter a skep. Chiefly *Scot.* E19.
■ **skepful** *noun* M16.

skepsel /ˈskɛps(ə)l/ *noun. S. Afr. colloq.* M19.
[Afrikaans *skepsel*, Dutch *schepsel* creature, from *scheppen* create.]
A creature, a villain, a rascal. Freq. used (*derog.* & considered *offensive*) in addressing a black person.

skeptic *noun & adjective*, **skeptical** *adjective*, etc., see SCEPTIC etc.

skerm /skəːm, ˈskɛr(ə)m/ *noun. S. Afr.* Also **scherm**. M19.
[Afrikaans from Dutch *scherm* = German *Schirm* screen, protection.]
A screen or barrier made of brushwood etc., for protecting troops, concealing a game hunter, or penning cattle. Also, a temporary dwelling made of brushwood etc., used by nomads.

skerrick /ˈskɛrɪk/ *noun.* Orig. *dial.* Now chiefly *Austral. & NZ colloq.* E19.
[Origin unkn.]
A small amount; a fragment; the slightest bit. Formerly also (*dial.*), a halfpenny. Usu. in neg. contexts.

skerry /ˈskɛri/ *noun*¹. Now *rare* or *obsolete.* M16.
[Origin unkn.]
A small (usu. two-man) boat, esp. for crossing fen-land.

skerry /ˈskɛri/ *noun*². E17.
[Orkney dial., from Old Norse *sker* (whence Gaelic *sgeir*). Cf. SCAR *noun*¹.]
A reef or rocky island covered by the sea at high tide or in stormy weather. Freq. in place-names.

skerry /ˈskɛri/ *adjective & noun*³. L18.
[Origin unkn.]
▶ **A** *adjective.* Of the nature of shale; shaly, slaty. L18.
▶ **B** *noun.* Shaly earth or stone. M19.

sketch /skɛtʃ/ *noun*¹ & *verb*¹. M17.
[Dutch *schets* or German *Skizze* from Italian *schizzo*, from *schizzare* make a sketch from Proto-Romance, from Latin *schedius* from Greek *skhedios* done extempore.]
▶ **A** *noun.* **1** A rough drawing, giving outlines or minimum, essential, or prominent features, esp. made as the basis of a more detailed picture; a rough draught or design. Later also, a drawing or painting of a slight or unpretentious nature. M17.
2 A brief account, description, or narrative, giving minimum, essential, or prominent facts, incidents, etc.; a brief tale, essay, or study (freq. in *pl.* as a title). M17. ▸**b** A general plan or outline, conveying the main idea or features of something. L17.
3 A very short play or performance in a show or revue, usu. comic and limited to one scene, freq. with music, singing, or dancing. L18.
4 MUSIC. **a** A short evocative or descriptive piece, usu. of a single movement. M19. ▸**b** A preliminary study made for a larger composition. L19.
5 A small quantity; a drop. *slang.* M19.
6 A comical or amusing person or thing. *colloq.* E20.

> 🕮 **1** J. HILTON The sketch was . . a miniature in coloured inks. J. ROSENBERG A quick pen sketch of this portrait. H. NORMAN He did a pencil sketch first, then painted. **2** DAY LEWIS Short stories and sketches she had written for parish magazines. P. F. BOLLER I have . . written a sketch of each President to accompany . . anecdotes.

Phrases: ***thumbnail sketch***: see THUMBNAIL *noun* 2.
▶ **B** *verb.* **1** *verb trans. & intrans.* Draw the outline or the minimum, essential, or prominent features (of), esp. as the basis of a more detailed picture; make a sketch or rough draft (of). Also foll. by *in, out, over.* L17.
2 *verb trans.* Describe or narrate briefly or generally; give the minimum, essential, or prominent facts, incidents, etc., of; outline. Also foll. by *out.* L17.

> 🕮 **1** C. S. FORESTER Randall sketched hasty diagrams. A. GRAY He began to sketch . . a steep mountain on the cover of a book. A. COHEN That first sitting . . he sketched in charcoal. **2** R. L. STEVENSON Should the scheme he had . . sketched prove feasible. B. CASTLE Up at 6am to sketch out my . . speech.

Comb.: **sketch-block** = ***sketch-book*** (a) below; **sketch-book** (*a*) a book or pad of drawing-paper for making sketches in or on; (*b*) (usu. as a title) a book containing narrative or descriptive essays, studies, etc.; (*c*) a notebook containing preliminary pictorial, verbal, or musical sketches or studies. **sketch-map** a roughly drawn map with few details.
■ **sketchaˈbility** *noun* the quality of being sketchable M19. **sketchable** *adjective* suitable for being sketched M19. **sketching** *noun* (*a*) the action of the verb; (*b*) a sketch: E19. **sketchist** *noun* (*rare*) a writer of literary sketches M19.

sketch /skɛtʃ/ *verb*² & *noun*². *Scot.* L18.
[Var. of SKATE *noun*² & *verb*.]
▶ **A** *verb intrans.* = SKATE *verb* 1. L18.
▶ **B** *noun.* **1** A skate. E19.
2 An act or period of skating. L19.

sketcher /ˈskɛtʃə/ *noun*¹. *Scot.* M18.
[from SKETCH *verb*² & *noun*² + -ER¹.]
1 A skate. M18.
2 A skater. L18.

sketcher /ˈskɛtʃə/ *noun*². E19.
[from SKETCH *verb*¹ + -ER¹.]
1 A person who makes or composes sketches. E19.
2 A tool for sketching. L19.

sketchy /ˈskɛtʃi/ *adjective.* E19.
[from SKETCH *noun*¹ + -Y¹.]
1 Giving only a slight or rough outline of the minimum, essential, or prominent features, facts, etc. E19.
2 Of a picture etc.: resembling or of the nature of a sketch; consisting or composed of outline without much detail. E19.
3 Insubstantial or imperfect, esp. through haste. *colloq.* L19.

> 🕮 **1** *Construction News* Details of the expansion are sketchy. **2** E. H. GOMBRICH The picture looks sketchy and unfinished. **3** S. CHITTY Her education . . was so sketchy as to be almost invisible.

■ **sketchily** *adverb* E19. **sketchiness** *noun* M19.

skete /skiːt/ *noun.* M19.
[mod. Greek *skētos* from Greek *askētēs* monk, hermit.]
An association of hermits belonging to the Greek Orthodox Church.

skeuomorph /ˈskjuːə(ʊ)mɔːf/ *noun.* L19.
[Greek *skeuos* vessel, implement + *morphē* form.]
ARCHAEOLOGY. **1** An ornamental design on an artefact resulting from the nature of the material used or the method of working it. L19.
2 An object or feature copying the design of a similar artefact in another material. M20.
■ **skeuoˈmorphic** *adjective* L19.

Skevington /ˈskɛvɪŋt(ə)n/ *noun.* M16.
[Leonard *Skevington*, Lieutenant of the Tower in the reign of Henry VIII, who invented the instrument.]
Skevington's daughter, (earlier †***Skevington's gyves***, †***Skevington's irons***), an instrument of torture which so compressed the body as to force blood from the nose and ears. Also called ***Scavenger's daughter***.

skew /skjuː/ *noun*¹. ME.
[Old French *escu* (mod. *écu*) from Latin *scutum* shield.]
1 †**a** A stone suitable to form part of the sloping head or coping of a gable, rising slightly above the roof; *collect.* a line of these. ME–M17. ▸**b** The line of coping on a gable. Chiefly *Scot.* L18.
2 A slate used in forming the gutter of a roof. *rare.* L19.

†**skew** *noun*². *slang.* M16–M18.
[Origin unkn.]
A cup; a wooden dish.

skew /skjuː/ *noun*³. E17.
[from SKEW *adjective* or *verb*¹.]
1 A sideways glance. *rare.* E17.
2 A deviation from the straight line; a slant; an angle, esp. at which a bridge spans a road or river; a sideward movement; *fig.* an error, a mistake. L17.
3 MINING. A piece of rock lying in an irregular slanting position and liable to fall. L18.
4 STATISTICS. The condition of being skewed, skewness. L20.

> 🕮 **2** N. BAKER My glasses . . would revert to their normal slight skew in five minutes. **on the skew, on a skew** askew.

■ **skewed** *adjective* (*a*) set obliquely, askew; (*b*) distorted, shifted in emphasis or character; (*c*) biased; (*d*) STATISTICS = SKEW *adjective* 3; (*e*) (of a sample, data, etc.) not representative: E17. **skewness** *noun* L19. **skewy** *adjective* (*colloq.*) somewhat askew or twisted M19.

skew /skjuː/ *adjective & adverb.* E17.
[from SKEW *verb*¹ or aphet. from ASKEW.]
▶ **A** *adjective.* **1** Oblique in direction or position; slanting; turned to one side. E17.
2 MATH. Neither parallel nor intersecting; not lying in the same plane. M19.
3 STATISTICS. Of a statistical distribution: not symmetrical about its mean. L19.

> 🕮 **1** A. FUGARD The toes were crooked, the nails skew.

Special collocations & comb.: **skew arch**, **skew bridge** an arch or bridge whose line of arch is not at right angles to the abutment. **skew chisel**: with an oblique edge. **skew field** MATH. a ring whose non-zero elements form a group with respect to multiplication; a set which satisfies the axioms for a field except that multiplication is not commutative. **skew gear**: consisting of two cog-wheels having non-parallel, non-intersecting axes. **skew-symmetric** *adjective* (MATH.) (of a matrix etc.) having all the elements of the principal diagonal equal to zero, and each of the remaining elements equal to the negative of the element in the corresponding position on the other side of the diagonal; *gen.* designating an array of any dimension having an analogous equivalence between its elements. **skew-symmetry** the property of being skew-symmetric. **skew system** MATH. = ***skew field*** above.
▶ **B** *adverb.* Obliquely, askew. *rare.* E18.

skew /skjuː/ *verb*¹. LME.
[Aphet. from Old Northern French *eskiu(w)er*, *eskuer* var. of Old French *eschiver* ESCHEW.]
1 *verb intrans.* Take an oblique course or direction; move obliquely; turn aside; twist. Formerly also, escape, slip away. LME. ▸**b** Esp. of a horse: shy, swerve. E17.
2 *verb intrans.* Look *at* or *on* sideways, esp. slyly, suspiciously, or slightingly; contemplate or reflect (*up*)*on*. L16.
3 *verb trans.* Cut (a thing) *off* with or at an angle; set (a thing) *into* or *back* obliquely or diagonally. E17.
4 *verb trans.* Throw, hurl, fling. *dial.* E19.
5 *verb trans.* Depict or represent unfairly; distort, bias. L19.
6 *verb trans.* STATISTICS. Make skew (SKEW *adjective* 3). E20.

> 🕮 **1** D. PROFUMO Mrs Walker skewed around on her seat. **5** B. FUSSELL In the desert, time gets skewed. *English World-Wide* This impression is . . skewed by the data that survive.

■ **skewing** *noun* (*a*) the action of the verb; (*b*) bias, distortion: E17.

skew /skjuː/ *verb*² *intrans. & trans.* L17.
[Origin unkn.]
Brush (loose gold or silver particles) from metalwork.

skew-back /ˈskjuːbak/ *noun.* E18.
[from SKEW *noun*³ or *verb*¹ + BACK *adverb*.]
ARCHITECTURE. The line of an arch; the sloping face of an abutment on which an end of an arch rests; a stone, brickwork, or metal plating supporting the foot of an arch.

skewbald /ˈskjuːbɔːld/ *adjective & noun.* M17.
[from next after *piebald*.]
▶ **A** *adjective.* Of an animal, esp. a horse: marked with irregular patches of white and some shade of brown or red. M17.
▶ **B** *noun.* A skewbald animal, esp. a horse. M19.

†**skewed** *adjective*¹. LME–L18.
[Perh. from Old French *escu* (mod. *écu*) shield from Latin *scutum* (cf. Latin *scutulatus* as the colour of a horse. Cf. prec., SKEW *noun*¹.]
Skewbald.

skewed /skjuːd/ *adjective*². E17.
[from SKEW *noun*³, *verb*¹: see -ED², -ED¹.]
1 Set obliquely or askew. E17.
2 Distorted, shifted in emphasis or character. M20.
3 a STATISTICS. = SKEW *adjective* 3. M20. ▸**b** Of a sample or data: not representative, biased. L20.

skewer /ˈskjuːə/ *noun & verb.* LME.
[Origin uncertain; rel. to SKIVER *noun*¹, SKUETT.]
▶ **A** *noun.* **1** A long wooden or metal pin, esp. for holding meat etc. together while cooking. LME. ▸**b** A metal pin for fastening clothing or securing hair. L18.
2 A sharp weapon, as a sword, spear, arrow, etc. M19.
Comb.: **skewer tree**, **skewer wood** the spindle tree, *Euonymus europaea*; the wood of this, used for making skewers.
▶ **B** *verb trans.* **1** Fasten (meat etc.) with or on a skewer. Also foll. by *together, up, upon.* E18. ▸**b** Fix or fasten to or into (as) with a skewer. Foll. by *in, into, to, down, up.* L18.
2 Pierce or run through with a sword etc. M19. ▸**b** Fix or thrust (*into* or *through*) like a skewer. M19.

> 🕮 **1** W. STYRON Bent nails upon which we skewered crickets. **b** J. BUCHAN A long knife through his heart . . skewered him to the floor.

skewgee /skjuːˈdʒiː/ *adjective. colloq.* (chiefly *N. Amer.*). L19.
[from SKEW *adjective* + *-gee*, after *agee* var. of AJEE. Cf. next.]
Askew, crooked; mixed-up, confused.

skew-whiff /skjuːˈwɪf/ *adjective & adverb. colloq.* Also **-wiff**. M18.
[from SKEW *adjective & adverb* + WHIFF *noun*¹ or *verb*¹. Cf. prec.]
Askew, awry, to one side; crooked(ly), confused(ly).

skey /skeɪ/ *noun. S. Afr.* M19.
[Afrikaans *skei*, Dutch *schei* tie-piece.]
Either of a pair of wooden pegs which pass through either end of an ox-yoke and are fixed to the neckstraps.

ski /skiː/ *noun & adjective.* M18.
[Norwegian (also *skji*, *sjii*, *skid*), from Old Norse *skíð* billet of cleft wood, snowshoe = Old English *scīd* SHIDE.]
▶ **A** *noun.* Pl. **-s**, (now *rare*) same.

1 Either of two long narrow pieces of wood etc., usu. pointed and turned up at the front, fastened under the foot for travelling over snow, esp. downhill. Usu. in *pl.* M18. ▸**b** A launching site or ramp for flying bombs. Freq. *attrib.* M20.
2 Each of two or three runners forming part of the landing gear of an aircraft etc. designed to land on snow or ice. E20.
3 A water-ski. M20.
▶ **B** *attrib.* or as *adjective.* Of or pertaining to skis or skiing; *esp.* (of a garment etc.) for wear when skiing. M19.
Comb. & special collocations: **ski-boat** (*a*) *S. Afr.* a boat resembling a raft with two outboard motors, used esp. for offshore fishing; (*b*) a small powerboat used for towing water-skiers; **ski-bob** *noun & verb* (*a*) a vehicle resembling a bicycle with skis instead of wheels; (*b*) *verb intrans.* ride a ski-bob; **ski-bobber** a person who ski-bobs; **ski-flying** a form of ski jumping from a higher slope so that the skier jumps further; **ski-jump** (*a*) an artificial structure consisting of a steep ramp levelling off at the end and built on a natural slope, used in ski-jumping; (*b*) a jump made from this; **ski-jumper** a person who takes part in ski-jumping; **ski-jumping** the sport of jumping off a ski-jump, with marks awarded for style and distance covered by the jump; **ski-lift** a lift for carrying skiers up a slope, consisting of seats hung from an overhead cable; **ski-mask** a protective, usu. knitted, covering for the head and face, with holes for the eyes, nose, and mouth; **skimobile** *N. Amer.* (*a*) a vehicle for travelling over snow, with tracks at the back and steerable skis in front; a snowmobile; (*b*) (now *rare*) a ski-lift; **ski pants** (*a*) trousers worn for skiing; (*b*) women's trousers imitating a style of these, made of stretchy fabric with tapering legs and an elastic stirrup under each foot; **ski-plane** an aeroplane having its undercarriage fitted with skis for landing on snow or ice; **ski pole** = *ski stick* below; **ski run** a slope prepared for skiing; **ski stick** either of two long sticks held by a skier to assist in balancing, propulsion, or braking; **ski touring** a form of skiing in which people travel across mountainous terrain, both skiing downhill and climbing using skins; **ski tow** (*a*) a type of ski-lift, consisting of an endless moving rope or of bars or seats suspended from an overhead cable; (*b*) a tow rope for water-skiers; **ski-wax**: applied to the undersides of skis to improve performance.

ski /skiː/ *verb.* L19.
[from the noun.]
1 *verb intrans.* Travel on skis. Also ***snow-ski***. L19. ▸**b** Water-ski. M20.
2 *verb trans.* Travel over (a slope etc.) on skis; travel on skis at (a place), esp. as a sport. L20.

🕮 **1** M. MEYER We skied . . in the extreme north of Sweden. *Japan Times* Jean-Louis Etienne, the first man to ski alone to the North pole.

■ **skiable** *adjective* (of a slope, snow, etc.) able to be skied on M20.

skiagram /ˈskʌɪəgram/ *noun.* Also **skio-**. E19.
[formed as next + -GRAM.]
1 A picture or figure consisting of the outline of an object filled in with black; a silhouette. *rare.* E19.
2 = SKIAGRAPH *noun.* Now *rare* or *obsolete.* L19.

skiagraph /ˈskʌɪəgrɑːf/ *noun & verb.* Now *rare* or *Hist.* Also **skio-**. L19.
[from Greek *skia* shadow + -GRAPH. Cf. SCIAGRAPH.]
▶ **A** *noun.* An X-ray photograph. Cf. SCIAGRAPH 2. L19.
▶ **B** *verb trans.* Photograph by means of X-rays. L19.
■ **skiaˈgraphic** *adjective* of or pertaining to X-ray photography L19.

skiagrapher /skʌɪˈagrəfə/ *noun. rare.* Also **skiographer** /skʌɪˈɒgrəfə/. E20.
[from SKIAGRAPHY: see -GRAPHER. Cf. SCIAGRAPHER.]
1 A radiographer. E20.
2 A person who practises skiagraphy. M20.

skiagraphy /skʌɪˈagrəfi/ *noun.* Also **skiography** /skʌɪˈɒgrəfi/. M19.
[from Greek *skiagraphia*: see SCIAGRAPHY, -GRAPHY.]
1 The technique of drawing or painting skiagrams. *rare.* M19.
2 Radiography. L19.

skiamachy *noun* var. of SCIAMACHY.

skiapod *noun* var. of SCIAPOD.

skiascopy /skʌɪˈaskəpi/ *noun.* L19.
[from Greek *skia* shadow + -SCOPY.]
MEDICINE. Retinoscopy.
■ **skiascope** /ˈskʌɪə-/ *noun* a retinoscope L19. **skiascopic** /skʌɪəˈskɒpɪk/ *adjective* retinoscopic L19. **skiaˈscopically** *adverb* M20.

Skiatron /ˈskʌɪətrɒn/ *noun.* M20.
[formed as prec. + -TRON.]
ELECTRONICS (now *Hist.*). More fully ***Skiatron tube***. (Proprietary name for) a type of cathode-ray tube in which the electron beam produces a dark trace.

skibbet /ˈskɪbɪt/ *noun.* Now *dial.* LME.
[Origin unkn. Cf. SKIPPET *noun*[1].]
A small box or compartment.

skice /ˈskʌɪs/ *verb intrans.* Now *Scot. & dial.* L16.
[Origin unkn.]
Move or get away quickly; skip or frisk about.

skid /skɪd/ *noun.* E17.
[Origin uncertain: in form and sense resembling Old Norse *skíð* (see SHIDE, SKI *noun & adjective*).]
1 A supporting beam or plank; *spec.* (*NAUTICAL*) any of a number of beams or supports holding a vessel under construction or repair in position. E17.
2 A plank or roller on which a heavy object may be placed to facilitate moving. E18. ▸**b** *spec.* Each of a number of peeled and partially sunk timbers forming a road along which logs are hauled. *N. Amer.* E19. ▸**c** A runner attached to the underside of an aircraft for use when landing. E20.
3 *NAUTICAL.* A wooden fender on a ship. M18.
4 A braking device; *esp.* a wooden or metal shoe used to prevent a wheel from revolving or as a drag. Cf. earlier SKID *verb*[1] 1. M18.
5 [from the verb.] An act of skidding or sliding sideways. E20. ▸**b** *AERONAUTICS.* A sideways movement of an aircraft, esp. away from the centre of curvature of a turn. E20.
2 hit the skids *colloq.* enter a rapid decline or deterioration. **on the skids** *colloq.* about to be defeated or discarded; in a steadily worsening state. **put the skids under** *colloq.* cause or hasten the downfall or failure of.
Comb.: **skid beam** a horizontal supporting beam; **skid-lid** *slang* a crash-helmet; **skid mark** a mark made on the road by the tyre of a skidding vehicle (usu. in *pl.*); **skid-mounted** *adjective* mounted on runners; **skid-pan** (*a*) a slippery road surface prepared to enable drivers to practise control of skidding; (*b*) a braking device; **skid road** *N. Amer.* (*a*) a road formed of skids along which logs are hauled; (*b*) orig., a downtown area frequented by loggers; now *gen.* = *skid row* below; **skid row** (chiefly *N. Amer.*) [alt. of *skid road* above] a run-down part of a town frequented by vagrants, alcoholics, etc.; **skidsteer (loader)** a small, highly manoeuvrable wheeled or tracked vehicle with a large bucket or fork at the front end, used in construction and farming; **skidway** *N. Amer.* (*a*) a road formed from logs, planks, etc.; (*b*) a platform (usu. inclined) for piling logs before transportation or sawing.
■ **skidded** *adjective* provided with a skid or skids M20.

skid /skɪd/ *verb*[1]. Infl. **-dd-**. L17.
[from the noun.]
1 *verb trans.* Apply or fasten a skid or brake to (a wheel); lock or check (a wheel) in this way. L17.
2 *verb intrans.* (Of a wheel or a vehicle or its driver etc.) slip or slide after sudden braking, turning, etc.; slip or slide obliquely or sideways on a slippery or loose surface; *gen.* slip, slide. M19. ▸**b** *AERONAUTICS.* Of an aircraft: move sideways, esp. away from the centre of curvature while turning. E20. ▸**c** *fig.* Fail; err; decline rapidly. *colloq.* (chiefly *N. Amer.*). E20.
3 *verb trans.* Move on or along skids; pile (logs) on a skidway. L19.
4 *verb trans.* Cause (a vehicle etc.) to skid; turn (a corner etc.) with a sideways sliding movement. E20.

🕮 **2** V. CANNING The car moved off, the wheels skidding a little in the mud. G. TINDALL He skidded to a stop. A. TAYLOR A car skidded on an icy road and hit a child. **c** *Boxing Scene* From the day his boxing skills fled, Louis' life skidded into hard times. *Wall Street Journal* U.K. retail sales skidded 1.5% in January. **3** *Scientific American* When the tower framework is completed, it will be skidded onto a long barge.

■ **skidder** *noun* (*N. Amer.*) a person who or machine which hauls logs along skids to a skidway L19. **skidding** *noun* (*a*) the action of the verb; (*b*) timber used as a support or to facilitate movement: M19. **skiddy** *adjective* (of a surface etc.) liable to cause skidding, slippery, loose E20.

skid *verb*[2] see SCUD *verb*[1].

Skiddaw slate /ˌskɪdɔː ˈsleɪt/ *noun phr.* M19.
[from a mountain in the English Lake District.]
GEOLOGY. (Any of) a thick group of slates, flags, and mudstones that outcrops in the northern part of the Lake District.

Skidoo /skɪˈduː/ *noun & verb*[1]. Also (esp. as verb) **s-**. M20.
[Arbitrary formation from SKI *noun* or *verb.*]
▶ **A** *noun.* (Proprietary name for) a motorized toboggan. M20.
▶ **B** *verb intrans.* Ride on a motorized toboggan. M20.

skidoo /skɪˈduː/ *verb*[2] *intrans. N. Amer. slang.* Also **-dd-**. E20.
[Perh. from SKEDADDLE *verb.*]
Go away; depart hurriedly. Usu. in *imper.* Also (*arch.*) in ***twenty-three skidoo!***

skied /skʌɪd/ *adjective.* M18.
[from SKY *noun, verb*: see -ED[2], -ED[1].]
1 Seeming to touch the sky; lofty. *rare.* M18.
2 Having a sky of a specified kind. M19.
3 *CRICKET.* (Of a ball) that has been skied or hit high in the air; (of a stroke or catch) resulting in or from this. M19.

skied *verb pa. t. & pple* of SKY *verb.*

skier /ˈskiːə/ *noun.* L19.
[from SKI *verb* + -ER[1].]
A person who skis.

skiff /skɪf/ *noun*[1]. Also (*US dial.*) **skift** /skɪft/. L15.
[French *esquif* from Italian *schifo*, prob. ult. from Old High German *schif* SHIP *noun.*]
A small light boat; *spec.* (*a*) one adapted for rowing and sailing and attached to a ship for purposes of communication, transport, etc.; (*b*) a small light rowing- or sculling-boat for a single rower.

skiff /skɪf/ *noun*[2]. Chiefly *Scot.* Also (chiefly *N. Amer.*) **skift** /skɪft/. E19.
[from SKIFF *verb*[2].]
A slight gust of wind; a light or fleeting shower of rain or snow. (Foll. by *of.*)

skiff /skɪf/ *verb*[1]. E17.
[from SKIFF *noun*[1].]
1 *verb trans.* †**a** Cross (a river) in a skiff. *rare.* Only in E17. ▸**b** Row or transport in a skiff. M19.
2 *verb intrans.* Row or scull in a skiff. M19.

skiff /skɪf/ *verb*[2]. *Scot.* E18.
[Perh. alt. of SKIFT *verb*[2] or SCUFF *verb.*]
1 *verb intrans.* Move lightly and quickly, esp. so as barely to touch a surface. Also, rain or snow slightly. E18.
2 *verb trans.* Touch lightly in passing over; brush. E19.

skiffle /ˈskɪf(ə)l/ *noun & verb.* E20.
[Origin unkn.]
▶ **A** *noun.* **1** Orig. (*US*), a style of jazz derived from blues, ragtime, and folk music and played on standard and improvised instruments. Now, a style of popular music in which the vocal part is supported by a rhythmic accompaniment of guitars and other standard and improvised (esp. percussion) instruments; a song written in this style. E20.
2 = ***rent party*** s.v. RENT *noun*[1]. *US Black slang.* M20.
▶ **B** *verb intrans.* Play skiffle. M20.
■ **skiffler** *noun* M20.

skift *noun*[1] see SKIFF *noun*[1].

skift *noun*[2] see SKIFF *noun*[2].

skift /skɪft/ *verb*[1]. *obsolete* exc. *dial.* ME.
[Old Norse *skipta* (Middle Swedish *skipta*, Swedish *skifta*, Norwegian *skipte*) = Old English *sciftan* SHIFT *verb.*]
1 a *verb trans.* Shift, change, move, (a thing). ME. ▸**b** *verb intrans.* Change, move; change position. LME.
†**2 a** *verb trans.* Arrange, devise, cause to occur. Only in ME. ▸**b** *verb intrans.* Ordain; act. ME–E16.
†**3** *verb trans.* Divide, distribute. Only in LME.

skift /skɪft/ *verb*[2] *intrans. Scot.* L16.
[Perh. specialized use of prec. Cf. SKIFF *verb*[2].]
Move lightly and quickly; skim, glide.

ski-joring /ˈskiːdʒɔːrɪŋ, ʃiːˈjəːrɪŋ/ *noun.* E20.
[Norwegian *skikjøring*, from *ski* SKI *noun* + *kjøring* driving.]
A winter sport in which a skier is towed by a horse or vehicle.
■ **ski-jorer** *noun* M20.

skil /skɪl/ *noun.* Pl. **-s**, (usu.) same. L19.
[Haida *sqil.*]
A large marine fish, *Erilepis zonifer* (family Anoplopomatidae), found throughout the N. Pacific, with a dark green or blue back. Also ***skilfish***.

skilful /ˈskɪlfʊl, -f(ə)l/ *adjective.* Also ***skill-**. ME.
[from SKILL *noun* + -FUL.]
†**1** Endowed with reason, rational. Also, following reason. Only in ME.
†**2** Reasonable, just, proper. ME–E16.
3 Having practical ability or skill; expert, clever. (Foll. by *at*, *in*, (*arch.*) *to.*) ME. ▸†**b** Having a good knowledge *of* a subject. L16–M17.
4 Displaying or requiring skill. L16.

🕮 **3** B. JOWETT Trained and exercised under a skilful master. **4** K. CLARK The tenth century produces work as splendid and as technically skilful . . as any other age.

■ **skilfully** *adverb* ME. **skilfulness** *noun* LME.

skill /skɪl/ *noun.* LOE.
[Old Norse *skil* rel. to *skila* (see next) and Middle Low German *schēle*, Middle & mod. Dutch *geschil*, *verschil* difference.]
1 Knowledge (*of*). *arch.* LOE.
2 Ability to do something (esp. manual or physical) well; proficiency, expertness, dexterity; an ability to do something, acquired through practice or learning (freq. in *pl.*). (Foll. by *at*, *in*, (*arch.*) *of*, *to do.*) ME. ▸†**b** An art, a science. L16–M17.
†**3 a** Reason as a mental faculty. ME–L15. ▸**b** Reasonableness; discrimination; discretion; justice. ME–M16.
†**4** That which is reasonable, right, or just. Only in ME.
†**5** (A) cause, (a) reason. ME–M17. ▸**b** An explanatory statement; a reasoned argument. Only in ME.

🕮 **2** *Listener* To teach children skills like reading. K. TYNAN An actor . . whose skill in playing upstarts is unrivalled. E. NORTH Without any particular skill at sport. A. TAYLOR The principal skill a good counsellor needs to acquire is . . active listening.

Phrases: †**can skill** [in later use *skill* prob. regarded as a verb (cf. SKILL *verb* 3b)] have knowledge (foll. by *of*, *in*, *to do*).
■ **skilled** *adjective* (*a*) (of a person) having or showing skill or practical ability; highly trained or experienced, esp. in a particular accomplishment; (*b*) (of work) requiring skill or special training: M16. **skill-less**, (*arch.*) **skilless** /-l-l-/ *adjective* (*a*) lacking skill; (*b*) (of work) showing a lack of skill: ME.

skill /skɪl/ *verb*. ME.
[Old Norse *skila* give reason for, expound, decide, *skilja* divide, distinguish, decide, rel. to prec. and Middle Low German, Middle Dutch *schillen*, *schēlen* differ, make a difference.]
†**1** *verb intrans.* Separate *from*. Only in ME. ▸**b** *verb trans.* Separate. Only in ME.
2 *verb intrans.* †**a** Cause a thing to differ or be distinct. Only in ME. ▸**b** In neg. & interrog. contexts: make a difference, be of importance, matter. *arch.* LME. ▸**c** Avail, help. *arch.* E16.
3 *verb trans.* Understand; determine. Now *dial.* L15. ▸†**b** *verb intrans.* = ***can skill*** s.v. SKILL *noun*. M16–M19.
4 *verb trans.* Teach. *rare*. E19.

skillet /ˈskɪlɪt/ *noun*. ME.
[Prob. from Old French *escuelete* dim. of *escuele* (mod. *écuelle*) platter, from popular Latin from Latin *scutella* SCUTTLE *noun*[1]: see -ET[1].]
Orig., a small metal cooking-pot with a long handle and usu. three or four feet. Now chiefly (*N. Amer.*), a frying-pan.

skillful *adjective* see SKILFUL.

skilligalee /ˌskɪlɪɡəˈliː/ *noun*. *arch. slang*. E19.
[Fanciful formation.]
= SKILLY *noun* 1.

skilling /ˈskɪlɪŋ/ *noun*[1]. Chiefly *dial.* & *Austral.* LME.
[Origin unkn. See also SKILLION.]
A shed, an outhouse; *esp.* a lean-to.

skilling /ˈskɪlɪŋ/ *noun*[2]. L17.
[In sense 1 from Dutch *schelling*; in sense 2 from Danish, Swedish, or Norwegian *skilling*. Cf. SCHILLING *noun*[1], SHILLING.]
†**1** = SCHELLING. L17–E18.
2 *Hist.* A small copper coin and monetary unit formerly in use in Scandinavia. L18.

skillion /ˈskɪljən/ *noun*. *Austral.* & *NZ*. E19.
[Alt. of SKILLING *noun*[1].]
A lean-to serving as a shed or small room; *spec.* one attached to a shearing-shed as a shelter for sheep waiting to be shorn.
Comb.: **skillion roof**: pitched only one way.

skilly /ˈskɪli/ *noun*. M19.
[Abbreviation of SKILLIGALEE.]
1 A thin gruel or soup, usu. made from oatmeal and flavoured with meat. Chiefly *Hist.* M19.
2 An insipid drink; tea, coffee. Chiefly *Nautical slang*. E20.

skilly /ˈskɪli/ *adjective*. Long *obsolete* exc. *Scot.* & *north*. LME.
[from SKILL *noun* + -Y[1].]
Skilled, skilful.

skim /skɪm/ *adjective*. *rare*. L18.
[from ***skim milk*** s.v. SKIM *verb* & *noun*.]
(Of milk) skimmed; (of cheese) made of skimmed milk.

skim /skɪm/ *verb* & *noun*. ME.
[Back-form. from SKIMMER *noun*, or from Old French *escumer* (mod. *écumer*), from *escume* scum.]
▶ **A** *verb*. Infl. **-mm-**.
▶ **I 1** *verb trans.* Remove scum or floating matter from the surface of (a liquid); *spec.* take off cream from the surface of (milk). ME. ▸**b** Plough (land) very lightly. L18.
2 *verb trans.* Remove or collect (scum, cream, etc.) from the surface of a liquid. Freq. foll. by *off*. M17. ▸**b** *verb trans.* & *intrans.* Conceal or divert (some of one's income) to avoid paying tax. *US slang*. M20.
3 a *verb trans.* Cover with a thin layer. *rare*. M17. ▸**b** *verb intrans.* Put on a thin layer. *rare*. M19.
4 *verb trans.* Throw lightly *over* or *upon* the surface of a thing. *rare*. L18.

> 1 G. BERKELEY The clear water, having been first carefully skimmed. 2 J. KOSINSKI Mitka . . skimmed the fat off the soup. b *New Yorker* Suspicions about whether Kohl had been skimming from the take for years.

▶ **II** †**5** *verb trans.* = SCUM *verb* 1b. ME–E16.
6 a *verb intrans.* Go or move lightly and rapidly over or on a surface or through the air. L16. ▸**b** *verb trans.* Cause (esp. a flat object) to glide through the air; *spec.* throw (a flat stone etc.) across a surface so that it bounces at intervals. E17. ▸**c** *verb trans.* Keep touching lightly or nearly touching (a surface) in passing over. L17.
7 *verb trans.* & *intrans.* (with *over*, *through*). Deal with or treat (a subject) superficially; *esp.* read or look over cursorily, gather rapidly the salient facts in (a book etc.). L16.
8 *verb trans.* Fraudulently copy the details of (a credit or debit card) with a card swipe or other device. L20.

> 6a P. PEARCE Seagulls . . wheeled and skimmed far away overhead. R. DAHL We skimmed across the sound. b J. SNOW To develop skills like . . skimming stones across a pond. S. BELLOW She opened the window . . and skimmed his paperback into Park Avenue. c E. L. DOCTOROW Gulls skimmed the breakers. D. LEAVITT He and Walter are in a balloon, skimming the land. 7 W. J. BATE He could repeat by memory a page he had lightly skimmed. C. P. SNOW He had skimmed through the weekend journals.

▶ **B** *noun*. **1** †**a** = SCUM *noun* 2. ME–M18. ▸**b** A thin layer *of* ice. *N. Amer.* E19. ▸**c** The fraction of latex which is poor in rubber and is separated by centrifugation in the manufacture of rubber. E20.
2 A metal plate fitted to the coulter of a plough for paring off the surface of the ground. L18.
3 The action or an act of skimming or moving lightly. M19.
4 *ellipt.* Skimmed milk. L19.

> 3 D. BOGGIS One urgent hungry skim through the photocopied papers.

Comb.: **skim-board** a type of surfboard used for riding shallow water; **skim-coulter**: fitted with a metal plate to pare off the surface of the ground and turn it into the furrow; **skim milk** milk with the cream skimmed off; skimmed milk; **skim-plough**: fitted with a skim-coulter.
■ **skimming** *noun* (*a*) the action of the verb; (*b*) (usu. in *pl.*) that which is removed or collected by skimming: LME. **skimmingly** *adverb* in a skimming manner; lightly, superficially: M19.

skimble-skamble /ˈskɪmb(ə)lskamb(ə)l/ *adjective*, *noun*, & *adverb*. L16.
[Redupl. of SCAMBLE *verb*, with vowel variation in 1st elem.]
▶ **A** *adjective*. Confused, nonsensical. L16.
▶ **B** *noun*. Confused or worthless talk or writing. E17.
▶ **C** *adverb*. Confusedly; in a muddle. L18.

skimmed /skɪmd/ *ppl adjective*. M16.
[from SKIM *verb* + -ED[1].]
1 That has been skimmed. M16.
2 Of cheese: made from skimmed milk. L19.
1 skimmed milk milk from which the cream has been skimmed; skim milk.

skimmer /ˈskɪmə/ *noun*. ME.
[Old French *escumoir* (mod. *écumoire*), from *escumer* (see SKIM *verb* & *noun*); later from SKIM *verb*: see -ER[1].]
1 A utensil or device used for skimming liquids; *esp.* a shallow, usu. perforated, utensil. ME. ▸**b** (The shell of) any of several clams, *esp.* the surf clam, formerly used for skimming milk. *US*. L19.
2 A person who skims. E17.
3 ORNITHOLOGY. Any of three birds of the genus *Rynchops* (family Rynchopidae), resembling terns, which have an extended and laterally flattened lower bill, and feed by flying low over water with the tip of the lower bill immersed. L18.
4 Orig. (*US*), a plough for shallow ploughing. Now, a type of skim-coulter. E19.
5 A vessel which skims over water; *spec.* a hydroplane, hydrofoil, hovercraft, or similar vessel that has little or no displacement at speed. M19.
6 A flat hat; *esp.* a broad-brimmed straw boater. Formerly also more fully ***skimmer hat***. M19.
7 Esp. CRICKET. A ball that travels with a low trajectory. M19.
8 A metal hook for trundling a child's iron hoop. Now chiefly *Hist.* L19.
9 A sheath dress fitting closely to the body. Chiefly *US*. M20.
Comb.: **skimmer-cake**: made from leftovers and cooked in a shallow dish; ***skimmer hat***: see sense 6 above.

skimmer /ˈskɪmə/ *verb intrans.* Chiefly *dial.* LME.
[North. var. of SHIMMER.]
1 Shimmer, glitter. LME.
2 Flutter, move rapidly. E19.

skimmia /ˈskɪmɪə/ *noun*. M19.
[mod. Latin (see below), from Japanese SHIKIMI (in full *miyama shikimi* deep-mountain shikimi).]
Any of various evergreen shrubs constituting the genus *Skimmia*, of the rue family, native to the Himalayas, China, and Japan, with starry white flowers and red berries.

skimmington /ˈskɪmɪŋtən/ *noun*. E17.
[Perh. from *skimming-ladle*, used in the procession as an instrument to thrash with: see -TON.]
Hist. A ludicrous procession made through a village, intended to bring ridicule on and make an example of a nagging wife or unfaithful husband. Formerly also, the man or woman playing the part of the husband or wife in such a procession; a nagging wife, an unfaithful husband.
ride skimmington, **ride the skimmington** hold such a procession.

skimp /skɪmp/ *adjective*, *noun*, & *verb*. L18.
[Origin uncertain: cf. SCRIMP *verb*, SCAMP *verb*[2].]
▶ **A** *adjective*. Scanty; skimpy. L18.
▶ **B** *noun*. A small or scanty thing; *esp.* a skimpy garment. *colloq.* M19.
▶ **C** *verb*. **1** *verb trans.* Restrict in supplies, stint. L19.
2 *verb trans.* Use a meagre or insufficient amount of. L19.
3 *verb intrans.* Economize (*on*); be parsimonious; save. L19.

> 1 M. MEYER Never the man to skimp a job, he went through every poem. 2 C. P. SNOW She skimped my father's food and her own . . for several weeks. 3 *Nature* British manufacturing industry . . is still skimping on development. A. S. BYATT Ashamed of the way we live—skimping and saving.

■ **skimped** *adjective* scanty; meagre, mean: M19. **skimping** *adjective* skimpy; that skimps: L18.

skimpy /ˈskɪmpi/ *adjective*. M19.
[from SKIMP *adjective* + -Y[1].]
Scanty, meagre; not sufficient; lacking the proper size.

> M. ATWOOD Skimpy skirts . . designed for a woman a lot skinnier than I am. *Minnesota Monthly* The lunch serving—just four lonely ravioli—seemed skimpy.

■ **skimpily** *adverb* M19. **skimpiness** *noun* L19.

skin /skɪn/ *noun*. LOE.
[Old Norse *skinn* rel. to Middle Low German (Dutch) *schinden* flay, peel, Old High German *scinden* (German *schinden*).]
▶ **I 1** The integument of an animal removed from the body, *esp.* one (intended to be) dressed or tanned (with or without the hair); *spec.* that of a small animal, as a sheep, calf, etc. (cf. HIDE *noun*[1]); a pelt. LOE. ▸**b** This used as material for clothing etc. Usu. with specifying word. ME. ▸**c** A strip of sealskin or other material attached to the underside of a ski to prevent slipping backwards during climbing. Usu. in *pl.* E20.
2 (A part of) a skin of a sheep, calf, etc., specially prepared for writing or painting on. LOE. ▸**b** A dollar. *US slang*. M20.
3 A container made from the skin of a sheep, goat, etc., used for holding liquids. M16. ▸**b** A purse, a wallet. *slang*. L18. ▸**c** Chiefly JAZZ. A drum-head; *slang* a drum. Usu. in *pl.* E20.

> 1 S. HOOD They must have built their huts of skins or wattle. b *calfskin*, *pigskin*, *sheepskin*, etc.

▶ **II 4** The continuous flexible covering of an animal body; the various layers, tissues, etc., of which this is composed, the epidermis; *spec.* a person's skin with respect to colour or (esp. on the face) condition. LOE. ▸**b** The skin of the palm of the hand. Freq. in ***give skin***, ***give some skin***, shake or slap hands (with). *US Black slang*. M20.
5 An outer layer or covering; *spec.* (*a*) the peel of certain fruits and vegetables; (*b*) the outermost layer of a pearl; (*c*) the facing of a wall. ME. ▸**b** A film resembling skin on the surface of a liquid. L15. ▸**c** A duplicating stencil. M20.
6 A membrane covering an organ or other internal part of an animal body. Now *rare* or *obsolete*. LME.
7 The inner or outer planking or plating covering the ribs of a vessel; the plating covering the frame of any craft or vehicle. M18. ▸**b** NAUTICAL. The part of a sail that is outside when furled. M19.
8 a Orig., an objectionable person. Now *gen.* (chiefly *Anglo-Irish*), a person (of a specified kind). E19. ▸**b** A horse, a mule. *slang*. E20. ▸**c** = SKINHEAD 2a. *slang*. L20.
9 A card-game in which each player has one card which he or she bets will not be the first to be matched by a card dealt from the pack. *US*. E20.
10 COMPUTING. A customized graphic user interface for an application or operating system. L20.

> 4 W. DEEPING She had one of those ivory skins that are proof against sunburn or worry. L. LOCHHEAD Two toothprints On the skin of your shoulder. I. MURDOCH She looked healthy and strong . . her skin glowing. 5 B. FUSSELL Boil the potatoes in their skins . . about 10 minutes. *Do-It-Yourself* Highlight the natural features rather than hiding them under a thick paint skin. *attrib.*: *Practical Householder* For single skin walls you may need to saw the vent shorter.

Phrases: ***be ready to leap out of one's skin***: see LEAP *verb*. **be skin and bone** be very thin or emaciated. **by the skin of one's teeth**, **with the skin of one's teeth** by a very narrow margin, barely. **change one's skin** undergo an impossible change of character etc. **get under a person's skin** *colloq.* (*a*) annoy or interest a person intensely; (*b*) empathize with or understand a person. ***give skin***, ***give some skin***: see sense 4b above. ***goldbeater's skin***: see ***gold-beater*** s.v. GOLD *noun*[1] & *adjective*. **have a thick skin**, **have a thin skin** be insensitive, sensitive, to criticism etc. **in one's skin** naked. ***jump out of one's skin***: see JUMP *verb*. ***leap out of one's skin***: see LEAP *verb*. **no skin off one's nose** *colloq.* a matter of indifference or even benefit to one. ***save one's skin***, ***save one's own skin***: see SAVE *verb*. **skin and blister** *rhyming slang* sister. **the Skins** *Military slang* (now *Hist.*) [alt. of *Inniskilling*] the 5th Royal Inniskilling Dragoon Guards. ***soaked to the skin***: see SOAK *verb* 4. STRESSED ***skin***. **under the skin** in reality, as opp. to superficial appearances. ***vagabond's skin***: see VAGABOND *noun* 1. **wet to the skin**: see WET *adjective*. **with a whole skin** unwounded. ***with the skin of one's teeth***: see ***by the skin of one's teeth*** above.
Comb.: **skin-beater** *slang* (chiefly JAZZ) a drummer; **skin beetle** *US* any of various beetles of the families Trogidae and Dermestidae, which feed on carrion, dry skins, etc.; **skin cream** an emollient for the skin esp. of the face; **skin-deep** *adjective* & *adverb* (*a*) *adjective* (of a wound, an impression, etc.) superficial, slight; (*b*) *adverb* superficially, slightly; **skin depth** ELECTRICITY the distance from the surface of a conductor at which an electromagnetic wave of a given frequency is attenuated by a factor of $1/e$ (approx. 0.3679); **skin-dive** *verb intrans.* go skin-diving; **skin-diver** a

person who goes skin-diving; **skin-diving** swimming under water without a diving suit, usu. in deep water with an aqualung and flippers; **skin-dried** *adjective* (of a mould) subjected to skin-drying; **skin-drying** drying of the surface of a greensand mould before casting; **skin effect** *ELECTRICITY* the tendency of an alternating current of high frequency to flow through the outer layers only of a conductor, resulting in an increase in effective resistance; **skin flap** *SURGERY* a flap of living skin attached to the body by one edge, used to close a wound after amputation or in plastic surgery; **skin-flick** *slang* a pornographic film; **skinfold** *MEDICINE* a fold of skin and underlying fat formed by pinching, the thickness of which is a measure of nutritional status; ***skinfold calliper(s)***, a pair of callipers for measuring the thickness of a skinfold; **skin-food** a preparation for improving the skin esp. of the face; **skin friction** the friction between a solid object and a fluid or gas that it moves through; *esp.* that between the surface of an aircraft etc. and the air; **skin game** *slang* (*a*) *US* a gambling game rigged to swindle the players; a swindle, a dishonest operation; (*b*) the pornography trade; **skin graft** (*a*) (an instance of) a surgical operation involving the transplantation of living skin to a new site or to a different individual; (*b*) a piece of skin so transplanted; **skin-grafting** the surgical process of transplanting living skin; **skin house** *slang* (*a*) a gambling establishment; (*b*) an establishment providing pornographic entertainment; **skin magazine** *colloq.* a pornographic magazine; **skinman** a dresser of or dealer in skins; **skin pass** *METALLURGY* a final cold-rolling given to heat-treated strip steel, bringing it to final thickness and surface finish; **skin-pop** *verb intrans.* (*slang*, chiefly *US*) inject a drug subcutaneously; **skin potential** *PHYSIOLOGY* the electrical potential between different points on the skin, esp. as exhibited in the galvanic skin response; **skin resistance** †(*a*) = ***skin friction*** above; †(*b*) the resistance of the skin of an electrical conductor; (*c*) *PHYSIOLOGY* the electrical resistance of the skin of an organism; **skin-search** *noun* & *verb* (*slang*) = ***strip-search*** s.v. STRIP *verb*[1]; **skin test** *noun* & *verb* (*a*) *noun* a test to determine whether an immune reaction is elicited when a substance is applied to or injected into the skin; (*b*) *verb trans.* perform a skin-test on; **skin-tight** *adjective* (of a garment) very close-fitting; **skin tonic** a cosmetic astringent for the skin esp. of the face; **skin trade** (*a*) (now *rare*) trade in animal skins; (*b*) *slang* = ***skin game*** (b) above; **skin worm** the Guinea worm.

■ **skinless** *adjective* ME. **skinlike** resembling (that of) skin *adjective* L18.

skin /skɪn/ *verb*. Infl. **-nn-**. Pa. t. & pple **skinned**, (*US colloq.*) **skun** /skʌn/. ME.

[from the noun.]

▶ **I 1** *verb trans.* Remove or strip the skin from; peel, flay. ME. ▸**b** Rub or scrape the skin from, bark. M19. ▸**c** Keep (one's eyes) open. Cf. ***keep an eye skinned***, ***keep one's eye(s) skinned*** s.v. EYE *noun*. *US colloq.* M19. ▸**d** *fig.* Beat or overcome completely. *slang*. M19.

2 *verb trans.* Strip or pull *off* (a skin etc.). M17.

3 *verb intrans.* Shed or cast the skin. *rare*. L18.

4 *verb trans.* Deprive (a person) of or *of* all money, *spec.* at a card-game; fleece, swindle. *slang*. E19. ▸**b** Exhaust of stock by excessive fishing, mining, etc. M19.

5 *verb intrans.* Abscond, make off, (also (*US*) foll. by *out*); slip *through*. *N. Amer. slang*. L19.

📖 **1** J. A. MICHENER An expert in skinning beaver. **b** A. HOPKINS He had stripped a bolt and skinned his knuckles. **c** F. BLAKE Skinning his eyes for the main chance. **2** G. GREENE She skinned the rest of the meringue off the pudding. **4** W. KENNEDY I ain't no dummy, and I know when I'm bein' skinned.

▶ **II 6** *verb trans.* Cover with skin; cause skin to grow on; heal in this way; *fig.* cover superficially. Also foll. by *over*. M16.

7 *verb trans.* Clothe, attire. *rare*. L16.

8 *verb intrans.* Form (new) skin; become covered with skin; heal *over* in this way. L16.

📖 **6** COLERIDGE Short Peace shall skin the wounds of causeless War. **8** RIDER HAGGARD The hole in his skull skinned over.

▶ **III 9** *verb trans.* & *intrans.* Inject (a drug) subcutaneously. *slang* (chiefly *US*). M20.

Phrases: **skin a flint** go to extreme lengths to save or gain something. **skin the cat** *US* pull one's body over a bar by hanging from it by the hands and passing the feet and legs between the arms.

■ **skinning** *verbal noun* the action of the verb; an instance of this: LME.

skinch /skɪn(t)ʃ/ *verb intrans. dial.* L19.

[Origin unkn.]

In children's games: encroach; cheat; call a truce.

skinflint /ˈskɪnflɪnt/ *noun* & *adjective*. L17.

[from ***skin a flint*** s.v. SKIN *verb*.]

▶ **A** *noun*. A miserly person. L17.

▶ **B** *attrib.* or as *adjective*. Miserly. L17.

■ **skinflinty** *adjective* miserly M19.

skinful /ˈskɪnfʊl, -f(ə)l/ *noun*. M17.

[from SKIN *noun* + -FUL.]

1 The quantity contained within the skin. *rare*. M17.

2 As much alcoholic liquor as will make one drunk. *colloq.* L18.

3 As much as will fill a skin container. E19.

skinhead /ˈskɪnhɛd/ *noun*. M20.

[from SKIN *noun* + HEAD *noun*.]

1 (A person with) a bald head. *colloq.* M20.

2 a A person, esp. a youth, characterized by closely cropped hair and heavy boots and frequently part of an aggressive gang. M20. ▸**b** A recruit in the Marines. *US*. M20.

skink /skɪŋk/ *noun*[1]. L16.

[French †*scinc* (now *scinque*) or Latin *scincus*, from Greek *skigkos*.]

ZOOLOGY. Orig., a small N. African lizard, *Scincus officinalis*, formerly used in medicine. Now, any of numerous lizards of the family Scincidae, which have smooth elongated bodies, small heads, and limbs that are small or entirely absent.

skink /skɪŋk/ *noun*[2]. L16.

[Prob. from Middle Low German, German *Schinke* ham.]

A kind of Scottish soup made esp. with shin of beef or smoked haddock.

skink /skɪŋk/ *noun*[3]. Now *rare*. E17.

[In sense 1 from early mod. Dutch or Low German *schenke*; in sense 2 from the verb.]

1 A tapster, a waiter. E17.

2 Poor-quality liquor. *Scot.* E19.

skink /skɪŋk/ *verb trans.* & *intrans.* Now *arch.* & *dial.* LME.

[Middle Low German, Middle Dutch *schenken* rel. to Old Frisian *skenka*, Old Saxon *skenkian*, Old High German *skenken* (German *schenken*), corresp. to Old English *scencan*.]

1 Pour out or draw (liquor); offer or serve (drink etc.). LME.

†**2** Fill (a cup) with liquor. Only in 16.

■ **skinker** *noun* (*a*) a person who draws or serves liquor, a tapster; (*b*) a jug: L16. **skinking** *adjective* (*a*) that skinks; (*b*) *Scot.* thin, watery: L16.

skinkle /ˈskɪŋk(ə)l/ *verb intrans. Scot.* M18.

[Perh. frequentative from Old Norse *skína* shine: see -LE[3].]

Glitter, sparkle.

skinned /skɪnd/ *adjective*. LME.

[from SKIN *noun*, *verb*: see -ED[2], -ED[1].]

1 Having a skin, *esp.* of a specified kind. LME.

2 That has been skinned. M17. ▸**b** = SKINT. *colloq.* M20.

2 ***keep an eye skinned***, ***keep one's eye(s) skinned***: see EYE *noun*.

skinner /ˈskɪnə/ *noun*[1]. ME.

[from SKIN *noun*, *verb* + -ER[1].]

1 A person who prepares skins for selling; a person who sells skins, a furrier. ME.

2 A person who skins animals. L17. ▸**b** *US HISTORY*. Any of a group of marauders who committed depredations on the neutral ground between the British and American lines during the War of Independence. L18.

3 A person who deprives another of money. Now *esp.* (*Austral. slang*) a racing result very profitable to the bookmakers. M19.

4 A driver of a team of horses or mules. Now also, a lorry driver. *N. Amer.* L19.

Phrases: **be a skinner** *NZ colloq.* have run out (of money etc.); be broke; be used up. ***Jimmy Skinner***: see JIMMY *noun*[2].

■ **skinnery** *noun* a place where skins are prepared for selling; the working premises of a skinner: L15.

Skinner /ˈskɪnə/ *noun*[2]. M20.

[B. F. *Skinner* (1904–1990), US psychologist.]

Used *attrib.* to designate theories or methods concerned with conditioning human or animal behaviour associated with Skinner.

Skinner box a box in which an animal is isolated, equipped with a bar, switch, etc. that the animal learns to use to obtain a reward or to escape punishment.

■ **Skiˈnnerian** *adjective* & *noun* (*a*) *adjective* of or pertaining to Skinner's behaviourist theories or methods; (*b*) *noun* a follower or adherent of Skinner: M20. **Skinnerism** *noun* Skinnerian behaviourism M20.

skinny /ˈskɪni/ *adjective*, *noun*, & *verb*. LME.

[from SKIN *noun* + -Y[1].]

▶ **A** *adjective*. **1** Of, pertaining to, or with respect to the skin; affecting the skin. *rare*. LME.

2 Consisting of or resembling skin. L16.

3 Thin, emaciated. E17.

4 Mean, miserly. Chiefly *dial.* M19.

5 Of clothing: tight-fitting. L20.

📖 **3** D. H. LAWRENCE Her thin, skinny wrist seemed hardly capable of carrying the bottle. A. ALVAREZ She no longer looked delicate; she looked skinny.

Comb.: **skinny-dip** *verb* & *noun colloq.* (chiefly *N. Amer.*) (*a*) *verb intrans.* swim naked (chiefly as ***skinny-dipping*** *verbal noun*); (*b*) *noun* a naked swim; **skinnymalink**, **skinnymalinks**, **skinnymalinky** *Scot.* & *dial.* (a name for) a thin person or animal; **skinny-rib** *adjective* (of a sweater etc.) fitting tightly.

▶ **B** *noun*. **1** A skinny person. M20.

2 Information. *slang* (chiefly *US*). M20.

▶ **C** *verb intrans.* Become skinny. Usu. foll. by *down*. *colloq.* M20.

■ **skinniness** *noun* E18.

skint /skɪnt/ *adjective*. *colloq.* E20.

[Var. of SKINNED.]

Without money, penniless.

skintle /ˈskɪnt(ə)l/ *verb trans.* L19.

[Perh. from SQUINT *adjective* + -LE[3].]

Separate and reset (half-dried bricks) at angles to each other, so as to complete the drying.

skiogram *noun* var. of SKIAGRAM.

skiograph *noun* & *verb* var. of SKIAGRAPH.

skiomachy *noun* var. of SCIAMACHY.

skip /skɪp/ *noun*[1]. LME.

[from SKIP *verb*[1]. In sense 3 prob. abbreviation of ***skip-kennel*** s.v. SKIP *verb*[1].]

1 A skipping movement or action; a light jump or spring. LME. ▸**b** An act or instance of absconding; a flit. *colloq.* (chiefly *N. Amer.*). M20.

2 An act or instance of skipping or passing over an intervening stage, intervening material, etc.; an omission; a break, a gap. M17. ▸**b** *MUSIC*. A passing from one note to another at a greater interval than one degree. M18. ▸**c** Unimportant material which may be skipped in a book etc. M19. ▸**d** *POKER*. = ***skip straight*** s.v. SKIP *verb*[1]. L19. ▸**e** *RADIO*. The poor reception or non-reception of signals from a particular station between the points at which direct signals become undetectable and the point at which signals can be received by reflection in the upper atmosphere. Also, this silent region (more fully ***skip zone***); radio signals received from beyond it. E20. ▸**f** In automatic data processing, the action of a machine (e.g. a punch) in passing over material not requiring its functioning; a computer instruction or routine specifying such action. M20.

3 Orig., a footman, a manservant. Now *spec.* at Trinity College, Dublin, a college servant. L17.

4 A person who absconds, esp. to avoid paying a debt; a defaulter. *N. Amer. colloq.* E20.

📖 **1** A. UTTLEY They walked . . , Susan in the middle, giving a little skip to keep up with them. P. H. JOHNSON A buoyant stride that was almost a skip. ***hop, skip, and jump***: see HOP *noun*[2]. **2** E. K. KANE A twelve hours' skip in their polar reckonings. S. C. HALL A long skip between 1789 and 1807. **c** R. MACAULAY There is some skip in the book, but I like it nearly all.

skip /skɪp/ *noun*[2]. Also **skep**. See also SKEP. LME.

[Var. of SKEP.]

▶ **I 1** See SKEP. LME.

▶ **II 2** A bucket, cage, or vehicle for lowering and raising materials or workers in a mine or quarry. Now also, a large transportable container for builders' refuse etc. E19.

skip /skɪp/ *noun*[3]. Orig. *Scot.* E19.

[Abbreviation of SKIPPER *noun*[2].]

The director or captain of a side at curling, bowls, etc. Also *gen.*, a commanding officer; a manager, a boss.

skip /skɪp/ *noun*[4]. M19.

[from SKIP *verb*[2].]

= SKIPPING *noun*[2].

skip /skɪp/ *noun*[5]. Orig. *Scot.* L19.

[Origin unkn.]

The peak of a cap.

skip /skɪp/ *verb*[1]. Infl. **-pp-**. ME.

[Prob. of Scandinavian origin.]

▶ **I** *verb intrans.* **1** Spring or jump lightly off the ground or *over* an obstacle; (of a person or animal) gambol, caper, frisk; *spec.* jump repeatedly with both or alternate feet in order to clear a skipping-rope. ME.

2 Spring or move along lightly, esp. by taking two steps or hops with each foot in turn. Freq. foll. by adverb or preposition. ME. ▸**b** Move hurriedly; depart quickly (*for*); abscond, disappear. Freq. foll. by *off*, *out*. Now *colloq.* ME.

3 Pass quickly from one point, subject, occupation, etc., to another, omitting or giving superficial treatment to intervening material; *esp.* do this in reading. Also foll. by *from*, *over*, *through*, *to*. LME.

📖 **1** N. GORDIMER Gina had run off to skip with Nyiko, who had an old dressing-gown cord for a rope. *Winning* Heading . . into the finishing straight . . his back wheel skipped over a bump. **2** BEVERLEY CLEARY Instead of running or skipping, she trudged. C. EASTON She had skipped down the hall . . so lightheartedly. **3** *Glasgow Herald* An official statement appeared to skip lightly over the subject of oil prices. G. SWIFT Marian once skipped half-heartedly through Dad's book.

▶ **II** *verb trans.* **4** Pass over quickly or omit (intervening material, a stage or item in a series, etc.), esp. in reading; leave out of consideration or account. E16. ▸**b** Pass by without touching or affecting. L16. ▸**c** Forgo, abstain from; not attend or participate in. M20.

5 Cause to skip; *esp.* cause (a stone etc.) to skim or bounce over a surface. L17.

6 Spring or jump lightly over; (of a railway train) go off (a track). M18. ▸**b** Absent oneself from (work, school, etc.). E19. ▸**c** Depart quickly from; leave hurriedly. *colloq.* (chiefly *N. Amer.*). L19.

> 📖 **4** HARPER LEE When Jem came to a word he didn't know, he skipped it. *USA Today* Should we ask the school to let him skip a grade? **b** STEVIE SMITH Greatness skips a generation. **c** J. BLUME I wish I could skip the whole school year. H. KUSHNER Skipping meals to raise money for the hungry. **5** JAYNE PHILLIPS The dirt . . was . . dry, and puffed like smoke when Riley skipped stones across it. **6** SWIFT Tom could move with lordly grace, Dick nimbly skip the gutter. **b** J. D. SALINGER If I let you skip school this afternoon . . , will you cut out the crazy stuff? **c** U. SINCLAIR The offending gambler . . had skipped the town.

Phrases: ***hop, skip, and jump***: see HOP *verb*[1]. **skip bail** *slang* = ***jump bail*** s.v. BAIL *noun*[1]. **skip it** *slang* (*a*) abandon a topic etc.; (*b*) abscond, disappear. **skip rope** *N. Amer.* play or exercise with a skipping-rope.

Comb.: **skip-bombing**: in which an aerial bomb is released from a low altitude causing it to skim or bounce along the surface of water or land towards the target; †**skip-kennel** a footman, a lackey; **skip-read** *verb trans. & intrans.* read (a book) while skipping the less important passages; **skip-rope** *N. Amer.* = ***skipping-rope*** s.v. SKIPPING *verbal noun*[1]; **skip straight** POKER a sequence consisting of cards of alternate ranks.

■ **skippable** *adjective* able to be skipped or passed over in reading, consideration, etc. E19. **skipped** *ppl adjective* that has been skipped; CHEMISTRY (of a compound) containing a chain in which two double bonds are separated by two intervening single bonds: E20. **skippy** *adjective* characterized by skipping or jumping L19.

skip /skɪp/ *verb*[2] *trans.* Infl. **-pp-**. E19.
[Dutch *scheppen* ladle, bale, draw (water).]
In sugar manufacture, transfer (sugar) from one vessel to another.

skip /skɪp/ *verb*[3] *trans.* Orig. *Scot.* Infl. **-pp-**. E20.
[from SKIP *noun*[3].]
Be the skip of (a side) at curling, bowls, etc.; captain, manage.

skipjack /ˈskɪpdʒak/ *noun & adjective.* M16.
[from SKIP *verb*[1] + JACK *noun*[1].]
▶ **A** *noun.* **1** A foolish conceited person; a fop, a dandy. Now *arch. & dial.* M16.
2 A horse-dealer's boy. Now *rare* or *obsolete.* M16.
3 Any of various fishes which have a habit of leaping out of the water, as the blue fish, *Pomatomus saltatrix*, of tropical and subtropical seas. Freq. *attrib.*, esp. in ***skipjack tuna***, a small tropical bonito or striped tuna, *Katsuwonus pelamis*, much used as food. E18.
4 (A toy made of) the wishbone of a bird. L18.
5 A click-beetle. Also ***skipjack beetle***. E19.
6 A kind of sailing boat used off the east coast of the US. *US.* L19.
▶ **B** *adjective.* **1** Trifling, petty; foppish. Now *arch. & dial.* L16.
2 Skipping, nimble, sprightly. Now *dial.* E17.

skipper /ˈskɪpə/ *noun*[1]. ME.
[from SKIP *verb*[1] + -ER[1].]
1 A person who or thing which skips; *esp.* a person who omits passages in reading. ME.
2 Any of various jumping insects, as a click-beetle, a cheese-maggot, or (formerly) a locust; *spec.* a small mothlike butterfly of the family Hesperiidae, a hesperiid. M18.
3 Any of several fishes, *esp.* the saury pike, *Scomberesox saurus.* L19.

2 Arctic skipper *N. Amer.* = ***chequered skipper*** below. ***cheese skipper***: see CHEESE *noun*[1]. **chequered skipper** a holarctic hesperiid butterfly, *Carterocephalus palaemon*, with a pattern of orange or yellow spots on dark brown. LULWORTH SKIPPER. **3** ***mud-skipper***: see MUD *noun*[1]. ***rock-skipper***: see ROCK *noun*[1].

■ **skippery** *adjective* (*dial.* & *US*) (of meat or cheese) full of maggots E19.

skipper /ˈskɪpə/ *noun*[2] *& verb*[1]. LME.
[Middle Low German, Middle Dutch *schipper*, from *schip* SHIP *noun*: see -ER[1].]
▶ **A** *noun.* **1** The captain or master of a ship, esp. of a small trading or fishing vessel. Now also, the captain of an aircraft. LME.
2 The captain or director of a sports side. M19.
3 A commanding officer in the army or airforce. *Military slang.* E20. ▸**b** A police captain or sergeant. *slang* (chiefly *US*). E20. ▸**c** The leader of a Scout troop, esp. in the Sea Scouts. E20.

> 📖 **1** P. M. M. KEMP The Skipper wondered if you'd like to go forward to the flight deck. T. MCGUANE James Davis . . was skipper of the shrimper *Marquesa*. **2** *Scottish Daily Express* Hearts . . include skipper Jim Brown in the squad.

▶ **B** *verb trans.* Act as skipper or captain of. L19.

> 📖 *Rugby World & Post* Still skippering Eastleigh . . Clive . . is confident his side will have a successful league season.

■ **skippership** *noun* the office, rank, or authority of a skipper E19.

skipper /ˈskɪpə/ *noun*[3] *& verb*[2]. *slang.* M16.
[Origin uncertain: perh. from Cornish *skyber* or Welsh *ysgubor* barn.]
▶ **A** *noun.* **1** A place for sleeping rough. Formerly *spec.* a barn or shed used for this purpose. M16.
2 A person who sleeps rough; a vagrant. E20.
3 An act of sleeping rough. Chiefly in ***do a skipper***, sleep rough. M20.

> 📖 **1** *St Martin's Review* He burnt his leg after falling on the fire in his skipper. **2** *Daily Telegraph* I'd seen a group of skippers on the river bank without particularly noticing them.

▶ **B** *verb intrans. & trans.* (with *it*). Sleep rough. M19.

skipper /ˈskɪpə/ *noun*[4]. L17.
[Dutch *schepper* scoop, ladle, formed as SKIP *verb*[2].]
A ladle or scoop used in sugar manufacture.

skippet /ˈskɪpɪt/ *noun*[1]. LME.
[Origin uncertain: perh. rel. to SKIBBET.]
A small round wooden container for documents or seals.

skippet /ˈskɪpɪt/ *noun*[2]. *rare.* Long *obsolete* exc. *dial.* LME.
[from SKIP *noun*[2] + -ET[1].]
A basket.

skippet /ˈskɪpɪt/ *noun*[3]. Now *dial.* M18.
[Var. of SCUPPET.]
A long-handled ladle or scoop.

skipping /ˈskɪpɪŋ/ *verbal noun*[1]. LME.
[from SKIP *verb*[1] + -ING[1].]
The action of SKIP *verb*[1]

Comb.: **skipping-rope** a length of rope, freq. with a handle at either end, revolved over the head and under the feet while jumping as a game or exercise.

skipping /ˈskɪpɪŋ/ *noun*[2]. E19.
[from SKIP *verb*[2] + -ING[1].]
A quantity of sugar transferred between vessels in manufacture.

skipping /ˈskɪpɪŋ/ *ppl adjective.* M16.
[from SKIP *verb*[1] + -ING[2].]
1 That skips or jumps. M16.
2 Characterized by skips or jumps. L16.
■ **skippingly** *adverb* L16.

skipple /ˈskɪp(ə)l/ *noun. US.* Now *rare* or *obsolete.* M17.
[Dutch *schepel* bushel.]
In the eastern US, a dry measure equal to three pecks.

skire /skɪə/ *adjective, verb, & adverb.* ME.
[Old Norse *skír* (Norwegian & Middle Swedish *skir*) = Old English *scīr* SHIRE *adjective.*]
▶ **A** *adjective.* **1** Of water, colour, etc.: pure, clear; bright. Long *Scot. rare.* ME.
2 Thorough, absolute. *Scot.* E18.

Special collocations: **Skire Thursday** *Scot. & north.* the Thursday before Easter, Maundy Thursday.

▶ **B** *verb.* †**1** *verb refl.* Cleanse or purify oneself. *rare.* Only in ME.
2 *verb intrans.* Shine brightly; glitter, be gaudy. Chiefly in ***skiring ppl adjective.***, gleaming, garish, gaudy. *Scot.* E18.
▶ **C** *adverb.* Quite; thoroughly, absolutely. *Scot.* L16.

skirl /skəːl/ *verb*[1] *& noun.* Orig. *Scot. & north.* LME.
[Prob. of Scandinavian origin (cf. Norwegian dial. *skrylla*), ult. imit. Cf. SCREEL.]
▶ **A** *verb.* **1** *verb intrans.* **a** Cry out shrilly, shriek. LME. ▸**b** Emit a loud shrill sound; *esp.* (of bagpipes) produce a characteristic shrill sound. M17.
2 *verb trans.* Sing or utter in a loud shrill tone; play (a piece of music) on the bagpipes. L18.
3 *verb intrans. & trans.* Produce a characteristic shrill sound with (bagpipes). E19.

> 📖 **1a** J. M. BARRIE The women-folk fair skirled wi' fear. **b** R. BURNS He screw'd the pipes and gart them skirl. **3** C. MCCULLOUGH The pipers skirled . . and the serious dancing began.

▶ **B** *noun.* **1** A shrill cry, a shriek. E16.
2 A shrill sound, *esp.* that characteristic of bagpipes. M19.

> 📖 **2** L. G. GIBBON You'd hear the skirl of the blades ring down the Howe for mile on mile. G. M. BROWN Skop the piper . . had to sit in a corner . . making skirls and rants.

skirl /skəːl/ *verb*[2] *intrans.* M19.
[Origin unkn.]
Sweep; whirl.

> 📖 K. M. PEYTON The wind soughed . . skirling in the flowers and the Mothers' Union banners.

skirlie /ˈskəːli/ *noun. Scot.* E20.
[from SKIRL *noun* + -IE.]
A dish of oatmeal, and onions, and seasoning fried together in fat.

skirmish /ˈskəːmɪʃ/ *noun.* See also SCRIMISH. LME.
[Partly from Old French *escar(a)muche* (mod. *escarmouche*) from Italian *scaramuccia*, of unkn. origin; partly formed as next.]
1 A bout of irregular or unpremeditated fighting, esp. between small or detached parts of opposing armies or fleets. Formerly also, the method of fighting by such an encounter. LME.
2 *transf.* A brief struggle or contest, an encounter; *esp.* a short argument or contest of wit. M16. ▸**b** A slight display *of* something. Long *rare* or *obsolete.* M17.

> 📖 **1** C. RYAN In the fierce skirmish that followed . . two soldiers were killed. **2** *Golf Monthly* The skirmishes she had had with the lady members . . had been nothing out of the ordinary.

skirmish /ˈskəːmɪʃ/ *verb.* ME.
[Old French *eskermiss-*, *eskirmiss-*, lengthened stem of *eskermir*, *eskirmir* (mod. *escrimer* fence), from Frankish verb meaning 'defend': see -ISH[2].]
1 *verb intrans.* Engage in a skirmish or skirmishes. Freq. foll. by *with.* ME.
†**2** *verb intrans.* Make a threatening display *with* a weapon. LME–M18.
†**3** *verb trans.* Engage in or attack with a skirmish or skirmishes. L15–L17.
4 *verb intrans.* Search or scout around for something. Usu. foll. by *after, around, for. colloq.* (chiefly *US*). M19.

> 📖 **1** D. A. THOMAS A squadron skirmished with units of the Italian battle fleet. **4** M. TWAIN He goes through the camp-meetings and skirmishes for raw converts.

■ **skirmisher** *noun* (*a*) a person, esp. a soldier, who takes part in a skirmish; (*b*) *fig.* something sent out in advance: ME. **skirmishing** *verbal noun* the action of the verb; an instance of this: LME. **skirmishingly** *adverb* in a skirmishing manner M19.

skirp /skəːp/ *verb.* ME.
[Old Norse *skirpa* spit.]
†**1 a** *verb intrans.* Behave with contempt; hiss *at* a person contemptuously. ME–E18. ▸**b** *verb trans.* Mock, deride. *rare.* Only in LME.
2 *verb trans. & intrans.* Splash; spatter. *Scot.* M19.

skirr /skəː/ *verb & noun.* See also SQUIRR. M16.
[Origin uncertain: perh. rel. to SCOUR *verb*[2].]
▶ **A** *verb.* **1** *verb intrans.* Move with great speed or impetus, esp. causing or producing a whirring sound. Formerly also, run away hastily, flee. Usu. foll. by adverb or preposition. M16.
2 *verb trans.* = SCOUR *verb*[2] 2a, b. E17.
3 *verb trans.* Throw with a skimming or flicking motion. Now *rare.* M17.

> 📖 **1** S. BELLOW In a helicopter . . I was skirring around New York. D. PROFUMO Five dark birds rose skirring away.

▶ **B** *noun.* A whirring or rasping sound. M19.

skirret /ˈskɪrɪt/ *noun*[1]. Orig. †**skirwhit(e)**. ME.
[Perh. from SKIRE *adjective* + WHITE *adjective.*]
An umbelliferous plant, *Sium sisarum*, formerly cultivated in Europe for its edible tubers; the root of this plant, eaten like salsify. Also ***skirret-root***.

skirret /ˈskɪrɪt/ *noun*[2]. E19.
[Origin unkn.]
An instrument with revolving centre-pin and attached line, used to mark out an area of land etc.

skirt /skəːt/ *noun.* ME.
[Old Norse *skyrta* = Old English *scyrte* SHIRT *noun.* Cf. Low German *schört* woman's gown, SHORT *adjective, noun, & adverb.*]
▶ **I 1** The lower part of a dress, gown, robe, etc., extending down from the waist or bodice; now *esp.* a separate woman's outer garment hanging from the waist. Also (in *pl.*), several of these worn together in layers. ME. ▸**b** The tail or lower portion of a coat. Usu. in *pl.* L16. ▸**c** An underskirt, a petticoat. M19.
2 A woman, *esp.* one regarded as an object of sexual desire; women collectively viewed in this way (freq. in ***bit of skirt***). *slang* (usu. considered *offensive*). M16.

> 📖 **1** DAY LEWIS The high-waisted skirt of her costume touches the ground. N. GORDIMER A blanket hitched round her waist in place of a skirt. *fig.*: M. ROBINSON Britain cannot sidestep . . its errors, nor can Europe pull back its skirts from the mess. ***divided skirt***, ***grass skirt***, ***miniskirt***, ***pencil skirt***, etc. **b** E. HEMINGWAY Pulling the belt of his raincoat tight . . and the skirts well down, he stepped out. **2** J. R. ACKERLEY What are you sticking out your eyes at? A skirt, I suppose.

▶ **II 3 a** A small flap on a saddle covering the stirrup bars. LME. ▸**b** = LEECH *noun*[3]. E17.
4 *sing.* & in *pl.* The lower or outer part of some structure or object; a base, a rim, an edging; *spec.* (*a*) the lower part of a parachute canopy; (*b*) a flared rim around a rocket nozzle. M16. ▸**b** A surface concealing or protecting the wheels or underside of a vehicle or aircraft. E20. ▸**c** The lower part of the surface of a piston. E20. ▸**d** A flexible surface projecting underneath a hovercraft to contain or divide the air-cushion. M20.
5 a The diaphragm and other membranes of an animal used as food. Also, a cut of meat from the lower flank of an animal. E18. ▸**b** In *pl.* = SKIRTING 2C. M19. ▸**c** In *pl.* Trimmings from an animal carcass. L19.

> 📖 **4** *Amateur Photographer* The . . magnifier . . has a translucent skirt for film or print viewing. *New Scientist* A strengthening of the aft skirt, the conical base of the rocket. **b** T. MCGUANE The car. Its . . bubble skirts . . declared it to be Nichol Dance's.

▶ **III 6** *sing.* & (usu.) in *pl.* An outlying part or area; a border, a boundary; a verge. Usu. foll. by *of.* LME. ▸**b** In *pl.* The outer parts or fringes of a body of people. M16.
7 *sing.* & in *pl.* A tract of land or wooded area forming a border or edge. L16.

8 In *pl.* & (*rare*) *sing.* The beginning or end *of* a period of time. *poet.* **E17.**
9 The lower sloping portions of a peak or rise on a graph, esp. of one representing electrical resonance. **M20.**

📖 **6** TOLKIEN A track led to the skirts of the wood. *Village Voice* The monster residence . . would carry some kind of restaurant in its skirts. **b** E. BLUNDEN I . . was listlessly standing on the skirts of the meeting. **7** *New Yorker* The seawall rises to the skirts of palms that stand . . behind it. **8** J. GALT It was then the skirt of the afternoon.

Phrases: **bit of skirt**: see BIT *noun*[2] 6. **hide behind a person's skirts** use a person as a means of protection. **sit upon a person's skirts** (now *rare* or *obsolete*) punish or deal severely with a person.

Comb.: **skirt-board** (*a*) = SKIRTING 2b; (*b*) an ironing-board for skirts; **skirt-chase** *verb intrans.* (*slang*) pursue women amorously; **skirt-chaser** *slang* a person who pursues women amorously; **skirt-dance** a form of ballet accompanied by graceful manipulation of a full skirt; **skirt-dancer** a person who performs a skirt dance; **skirt-dancing** = *skirt-dance* above; **skirt duty** *slang* (*a*) acting so as to attract men; (*b*) keeping company with women, regarded as an obligation or duty; **skirt-land** land having skirt soil; **skirt patrol** *slang* a search for a female partner; **skirt soil** a loam composed of a mixture of peat and clay, sand, or silt.

■ **skirted** *adjective* (*a*) having or wearing a skirt or skirts; (*b*) having a skirt or border of a specified kind: **L16. skirtless** *adjective* **E19. skirtlike** *adjective* resembling (that of) a skirt **M19. skirty** *noun* (*colloq.*) a skirt; an underskirt: **E20.**

skirt /skəːt/ *verb.* **E17.**
[from the noun.]
▶ **I** *verb trans.* **1** Lie alongside of; bound, border, edge. **E17.**
2 Surround, edge, or border *with* something. **M17.**
3 a Search the outskirts of. *rare.* **E18.** ▸**b** Go along, round, or past the edge of; go around as opp. to over or through; *fig.* avoid mention or consideration of. **M18.**
4 a Plough (land) in strips leaving untilled earth between. *dial.* **L18.** ▸**b** Trim (a hedgerow); trim the skirtings from (a fleece). *dial.* & *Austral.* **M19.**

📖 **1** G. SWIFT The road skirts the garden wall. *fig.*: R. W. EMERSON So is man's narrow path By strength and terror skirted. **3b** J. WAIN I led the way along the path . . skirting rocks and clumps of gorse. J. M. COETZEE He skirted the town and joined the road . . into the Swartberg. B. NEIL They talked lightly, skirting all subjects that might hurt.

▶ **II** *verb intrans.* **5** Foll. by *about, along, (a)round*: go or lie along or round an edge, side, or border; *fig.* avoid mention or consideration of an issue etc. Also, move or linger *on* the outskirts of something. **E17.** ▸**b** Of a hunting dog: stray from the pack. **L18.**

📖 **5** J. E. TENNENT As the path ascends it skirts round scarped acclivities. R. D. BLACKMORE I set off up the valley, skirting along one side of it. A. LIVELY It never does to say anything direct. You gotta skirt around it.

■ **skirter** *noun* (*a*) a hunting dog which strays from the pack; (*b*) a horse-rider who goes round rather than over an obstacle; (*c*) *Austral.* a person who trims fleeces: **L18.**

skirting /ˈskəːtɪŋ/ *noun.* **L17.**
[from SKIRT *verb* + -ING[1].]
†**1** Light or superficial treatment of something. *rare.* Only in **L17.**
2 a *gen.* A border, an edge, a margin. **M18.** ▸**b** In full ***skirting-board***. A narrow usu. wooden board or edging placed vertically along the base of an interior wall next to the floor. **M18.** ▸**c** *sing.* & in *pl.* The trimmings from a fleece. *Austral.* **L19.** ▸**d** A ground-level screen surrounding the wheels of a mobile home. *N. Amer.* **M20.**
3 The action of skirting or ploughing land in alternate strips. *dial.* **L18.**
4 a *sing.* & in *pl.* The skirt of a garment. *rare.* **E19.** ▸**b** Material suitable for making a skirt or skirts. **M19.**
Comb.: **skirting radiator**: positioned along a wall at the level of the skirting.

†**skirwhit(e)** *noun* see SKIRRET *noun*[1].

skish /skɪʃ/ *noun. US.* **M20.**
[Perh. from SK(EET *noun*[2] or SK(ILL *noun* + F)ISH *noun*[1].]
A game using fishing tackle to cast on dry land.

skit /skɪt/ *noun*[1]. **ME.**
[Old Norse *skitr* excrement, *skíta* defecate (see SKITE *verb*[1]), Norwegian *skit* dirt, filth, Norwegian & Icelandic *skita* diarrhoea.]
†**1** Dirt, trash. *rare.* Only in **ME.**
2 Diarrhoea in animals, esp. sheep. Now *Scot.* & *dial.* **LME.**

skit /skɪt/ *noun*[2]. **L16.**
[Rel. to SKIT *verb*[2]. Cf. SQUIT *noun*[1].]
1 A vain or frivolous woman. Chiefly *Scot.* Now *rare* or *obsolete.* **L16.**
2 A satirical comment or attack. Usu. foll. by *at, upon.* **E18.** ▸**b** A usu. short piece of light satire or burlesque, freq. as part of a dramatic performance. Also foll. by *on.* **E19.** ▸**c** A trick; a hoax. Now *Scot.* & *dial.* **M19.**
3 A light stroke, a flick. *rare.* **L18.**
4 A light shower *of* rain, snow, etc. Now chiefly *Scot.* **M19.**

📖 **2** W. H. PYNE No more of your skits at my right noble country. **b** A. S. NEILL A Shakespearian skit as, for example, Julius Caesar with an American gangster setting. *Japan Times* The Drifters perform in three comical skits on 'power'. **3** R. W. EMERSON In the city, where money follows the skit of a pen.

skit /skɪt/ *noun*[3]. *colloq.* **E20.**
[Origin unkn.]
sing. & in *pl.* Foll. by *of*: a large number, quantity, or amount.

skit /skɪt/ *verb*[1] *intrans.* Chiefly *Scot.*. Infl. **-tt-**. **LME.**
[Rel. to SKIT *noun*[1].]
Defecate.

skit /skɪt/ *verb*[2]. Now *rare.* Infl. **-tt-**. **E17.**
[Perh. ult. from Old Norse alt. of stem of *skjóta* SHOOT *verb.* Cf. SKITE *verb*[2].]
1 *verb intrans.* Move lightly and rapidly (away); flit. **E17.**
2 a *verb trans.* Comment indirectly on (*dial.*); satirize or ridicule in a skit. **L18.** ▸**b** *verb intrans.* Foll. by *at*: make a satirical comment or attack on a person or thing. **E19.**

skite /skʌɪt/ *noun.* **M18.**
[Rel. to SKITE *verb*[2].]
1 A sharp glancing stroke or blow; an oblique punch or slap. *Scot.* & *north.* **M18.**
2 A trick; a hoax. *Scot.* **L18.**
3 An objectionable person. *Scot.* & *north.* **L18.**
4 a Boasting, boastfulness; ostentation; conceit. *Austral.* & *NZ colloq.* **M19.** ▸**b** A boaster; a conceited person. *Austral.* & *NZ colloq.* **E20.**
5 A jollification, a spree, a binge. Freq. in ***on the skite***. Chiefly *Scot.* **M19.**

skite /skʌɪt/ *verb*[1]. *Scot.* & *dial.* **LME.**
[Old Norse *skíta* (Norwegian *skite*, Swedish *skita*, Danish *skide*), or Middle Low German *schîten*, Middle Dutch *schijten* SHIT *verb.* Cf. SKIT *noun*[1].]
Defecate; have diarrhoea.

skite /skʌɪt/ *verb*[2] *intrans.* **E18.**
[Perh. from Old Norse *skýt-* stem of *skjóta* SHOOT *verb.* Cf. SKIT *verb*[2], SKITE *noun.*]
1 Move quickly and forcefully, esp. in an oblique direction; glance or ricochet *off* a surface. *Scot.* & *dial.* **E18.**
2 Slip or slide suddenly, esp. on a slippery surface. *Scot.* & *dial.* **M19.**
3 Brag, boast. *Austral.* & *NZ colloq.* **M19.**
■ **skiter** *noun* (*Scot.*, & *Austral.* & *NZ colloq.*) (a term of abuse for) an objectionable or esp. conceited person **L19.**

skitter /ˈskɪtə/ *verb*[1] & *noun*[1]. **ME.**
[Frequentative of SKITE *verb*[1].]
▶ **A** *verb intrans.* Have diarrhoea. *Scot.* & *dial.* **ME.**
▶ **B** *noun.* Thin excrement (*Scot.*); ***the skitters***, diarrhoea (*Scot.*, *dial.*, & *slang*). **E16.**

skitter /ˈskɪtə/ *verb*[2] & *noun*[2]. **M19.**
[App. frequentative of SKITE *verb*[2].]
▶ **A** *verb.* **1** *verb intrans.* Move lightly and rapidly; hurry; scamper. Usu. foll. by adverb. **M19.** ▸**b** Skip or skim across a surface. Usu. foll. by *across, along*, etc. Orig. *dial.* **M19.**
2 *verb trans.* & *intrans.* ANGLING. Draw (bait) jerkily across the surface of the water. Chiefly *US.* **L19.**
3 *verb trans.* Move, pass, throw, etc., jerkily, rapidly, or with a skimming motion. **E20.**

📖 **1** A. TYLER His grandmother skittered around him. T. O'BRIEN Her eyes skittered from object to object. **b** M. PUZO Tired of the glittering red dice skittering across green felt. **3** M. J. BOSSE Edgar Gear . . skittered his hand through his hair.

▶ **B** *noun.* (A sound caused by) a skittering movement or action. **E20.**

📖 P. BARKER The skitter of a stone over the pavement as children played hopscotch.

skittery /ˈskɪt(ə)ri/ *adjective.* **E20.**
[from prec. + -Y[1].]
1 Trifling. *rare.* **E20.**
2 Skittish, restless. **M20.**
3 Producing or developing speckles in dyeing. **M20.**

📖 **2** A. TYLER Then he changed the subject. (He had a rather skittery mind.)

■ **skitteriness** *noun* **M20.**

skittish /ˈskɪtɪʃ/ *adjective.* **LME.**
[Origin uncertain: perh. formed as SKIT *verb*[2] + -ISH[1].]
1 a Characterized by levity; excessively light; frivolous. **LME.** ▸**b** Spirited, lively; playful. **L16.**
2 (Of an animal, esp. a horse) inclined to shy or be restive; *transf.* (of a person) nervous or shy (*of*), fidgety. **E16.**
3 Fickle, changeable; tricky, difficult to deal with. **L16.**

📖 **1a** S. RICHARDSON If you think you can part with her for her skittish tricks. **b** E. BOWEN She was skittish . . though . . playfulness did not ill become her. **2** W. CATHER Signa is apt to be skittish at mealtime, when the men are about, and to spill the coffee. J. A. MICHENER Sometimes a horse would become skittish and move sideways for a distance. **3** *Times* An extremely skittish . . market over the short term.

■ **skittishly** *adverb* **L16. skittishness** *noun* **E17.**

skittle /ˈskɪt(ə)l/ *noun* & *verb.* **M17.**
[Perh. rel. to SKIT *verb*[2] (cf. Swedish, Danish, *skyttel* shuttle, marble, gate-bar), but cf. earlier KITTLES.]
▶ **A** *noun.* **1** In *pl.* (treated as *sing.*) ▸**a** A game played with usu. nine wooden pins set in a square angled towards the player or in a row at the end of an alley, to be bowled down with wooden balls or a wooden disc in as few attempts as possible. Now also (more fully ***table skittles***), a similar game played with pins set up on a board and knocked down by swinging a suspended ball. **M17.** ▸**b** Nonsense; rubbish. Also as *interjection. colloq.* **M19.** ▸**c** Chess played without serious intent. *colloq.* **M19.**
2 Any of the pins used to play skittles. **L17.**
Phrases & comb.: **all beer and skittles** all enjoyment or amusement (usu. in neg. contexts). **skittle-alley** (a building containing) an alley for playing skittles. **skittle-pot** a skittle-shaped crucible used esp. in glass-making. ***table skittles***: see sense 1 above.
▶ **B** *verb.* **1** *verb intrans.* Play skittles. *rare.* **M19.**
2 *verb trans.* Knock down or aside; CRICKET bowl out (a side) in rapid succession, defeat or dismiss easily (also foll. by *out*). **L19.**

📖 **2** R. H. MORRIESON With those shoulders I could . . skittle them right, left and centre. *Sun* He skittled Sri Lanka in a Test match . . 4½ years ago.

■ **skittler** *noun* a player of skittles; *colloq.* a person who plays chess without serious intent: **M19.**

skive /skʌɪv/ *noun*[1]. **E19.**
[Dutch *schijf*, Middle Dutch *schîve*: see SHIVE *noun*[1].]
A rotating wheel for grinding or polishing gems (esp. diamonds).

skive /skʌɪv/ *verb*[1] & *noun*[2]. **E19.**
[Old Norse *skífa*; rel. to SHIVE *noun*[1].]
▶ **A** *verb trans.* Cut (esp. leather or rubber) into strips; shave, pare, trim, (also foll. by *off*). **E19.**

📖 W. MAYNE Adam skived off a shaving of grey wood.

▶ **B** *noun.* = SKIVER *noun*[2] 1. *rare.* **L19.**
■ **skiving** *noun* (*a*) = SKIVER *noun*[2] 1; (*b*) the action or an act of paring leather etc.: **E19.**

skive /skʌɪv/ *verb*[2] & *noun*[3]. *colloq.* **E20.**
[Perh. from French *esquiver* dodge, slink away.]
▶ **A** *verb intrans.* Evade a duty or fatigue (MILITARY); shirk; absent oneself in order to avoid an unpleasant task, or from work, school, etc., (freq. foll. by *off*). **E20.**

📖 P. LIVELY Don't skive off for a drink with some crony when the Reading Room shuts. *Scottish Daily Express* Those who skive off work for the day.

▶ **B** *noun.* The action or an act of shirking; an undemanding task or course of action; an easy option. **M20.**

skiver /ˈskɪvə/ *noun*[1] & *verb*[1]. Chiefly *Scot.* & *dial.* See also SKEWER *noun* & *verb.* **M17.**
[Origin unkn.]
▶ **A** *noun.* = SKEWER *noun* 1. **M17.**
▶ **B** *verb trans.* = SKEWER *verb* 1, 2. **E19.**

skiver /ˈskʌɪvə/ *noun*[2] & *verb*[2]. **E19.**
[from SKIVE *verb*[1] + -ER[1].]
▶ **A** *noun.* **1** (A piece of) thin dressed leather pared from the grain side of a sheepskin. **E19.**
2 A person who or thing which skives or pares leather. **E19.**
▶ **B** *verb trans.* = SKIVE *verb*[1]. *rare.* **L19.**

skiver /ˈskʌɪvə/ *noun*[3]. *colloq.* **M20.**
[from SKIVE *verb*[2] + -ER[1].]
A person who avoids work, school, etc.; a shirker; a truant.

skivie /ˈskʌɪvi/ *adjective. Scot.* **E19.**
[Origin uncertain: cf. Old Norse *skeifr*, Norwegian dial. *skeiv* oblique, askew.]
Mentally deranged.

skivvy /ˈskɪvi/ *noun*[1] & *verb. colloq.* (chiefly *derog.*). **E20.**
[Origin unkn.]
▶ **A** *noun.* A female domestic servant; *transf.* a person whose job is regarded as menial or poorly-paid. **E20.**
▶ **B** *verb intrans.* Work as a skivvy. **M20.**

📖 A. CARTER The house in which she skivvied was stuck in . . the country.

skivvy /ˈskɪvi/ *noun*[2]. *colloq.* **M20.**
[Origin unkn.]
1 a An undershirt, a vest. Also ***skivvy shirt***. *N. Amer.* **M20.** ▸**b** In *pl.* Underwear comprising vest and underpants. *N. Amer.* **M20.**
2 A thin high-necked pullover. *Austral.* & *US.* **M20.**

sklent /sklɛnt/ *verb & noun.* LME.
[Var. of SLENT *verb*[1], *noun*[1].]
▶ **A** *verb. Scot. & north.*
1 *verb intrans.* Move sideways or obliquely; slope, slant; give a sideways glance. LME. ▸**b** *fig.* Deviate morally; prevaricate; lie. M16.
2 *verb trans.* Aim or direct obliquely. L18.
▶ **B** *noun. Scot.* Orig., a slanting cut. Later, a sideways movement or glance; a slant, a slope. L16.

Skoda /ˈskəʊdə/ *adjective.* E20.
[Emil von *Škoda* (1839–1900), Czech engineer and industrialist.]
Designating (the operation of) any of the machine-guns produced by Skoda's factories.

skoff /skɒf/ *noun. S. Afr.* L18.
[Afrikaans *skof* from Dutch *schoft*: see SCOFF *noun*[2].]
A stage of a journey; a period of travel between outspans. Also, a period of work, a shift.

skokiaan /ˈskɒkɪɑːn/ *noun. S. Afr.* E20.
[Afrikaans, perh. ult. of Zulu origin.]
A strong home-brewed alcoholic liquor fermented with yeast.

Skokomish /skəˈkəʊmɪʃ/ *noun & adjective.* M19.
[Twana, lit. 'river people'.]
▶ **A** *noun.* Pl. same.
1 A member of a Salish people inhabiting the area around Puget Sound in NW Washington. M19.
2 The Salish language of this people. E20.
▶ **B** *attrib.* or as *adjective.* Of or pertaining to the Skokomish or their language. M19.

skol /skəʊl, skɒl/ *noun & interjection.* Also **skaal**; orig. (*Scot.*) †**skole**. E17.
[Danish & Norwegian *skål*, Swedish *skål*, repr. Old Norse *skál* bowl.]
(A drinking toast) wishing good health.

skol /skəʊl, skɒl/ *verb.* Infl. **-l(l)-**. L16.
[formed as prec.]
1 *verb intrans.* Drink a health or healths (*to*); drink deeply. Orig. *Scot.* L16.
2 *verb trans.* Drink the health of. M20.

†**skole** *noun & interjection* see SKOL *noun & interjection*.

skolly /ˈskɒli/ *noun. S. Afr.* M20.
[Afrikaans, prob. from Dutch *schoelje* rogue.]
A Coloured street ruffian or gangster. Also more fully †***skolly boy***. Cf. TSOTSI.

skoob /skuːb/ *noun & adjective. rare.* Pl. of noun same. M20.
[Reversal of *books*.]
(Of or pertaining to) a pile of books destroyed in protest against the undue veneration of the printed word.

skookum /ˈskuːkəm/ *noun & adjective. N. Amer.* M19.
[Chinook Jargon.]
▶ **A** *noun.* Esp. among north-west N. American Indians, an evil spirit. Now *rare* or *obsolete*. M19.
▶ **B** *adjective.* Strong, brave; fine, splendid. Now *colloq.* M19.
Special collocations: **skookum chuck** *colloq.* a fast-moving body of water, rapids. **skookum house** *slang* a jail.

skoosh /skuːʃ/ *verb & noun. Scot.* Also **sc-**. L19.
[Imit.]
▶ **A** *verb.* **1** *verb intrans.* Of a liquid: gush, spurt, squirt. L19. ▸**b** *verb trans.* Squirt or spray (a liquid); splash with liquid. L20.
2 *verb intrans.* Move rapidly with a swishing sound. E20. ▸**b** Leave rapidly, make oneself scarce. M20.
📖 **1** C. DOLAN The water skooshed out fast and hot.
▶ **B** *noun.* **1** A drink; esp. a carbonated soft one. M20.
2 (A spurt or gush of) any liquid. L20.
3 Something easily accomplished; an easy victory. L20.
📖 **3** M. MUNRO The drivin test wis a skoosh.

skoptophilia *noun* var. of SCOPOPHILIA.

Skoptsi /ˈskɒp(t)si/ *noun pl.* M19.
[Russian, pl. of *skopets* eunuch.]
ECCLESIASTICAL HISTORY. The members of a Russian ascetic sect practising self-castration.
■ **Skoptsism** *noun* the practice and principles of the Skoptsi E20.

skort /skɔːt/ *noun. N. Amer.* L20.
[Blend of SKIRT and *short(s* (s.v. SHORT *noun*).]
A pair of shorts with full legs and a central flap at the front (and sometimes the back) to give the appearance of a skirt.

skosh /skəʊʃ/ *noun. US slang.* M20.
[Japanese *sukoshi*.]
A small amount, a little. Freq. *adverbial* in ***a skosh***, somewhat, slightly.

skothending /ˈskɒthɛndɪŋ/ *noun.* M19.
[Old Norse, from *skot* shot, shooting + *hending* a catching.]
PROSODY. Esp. in skaldic verse: rhyme formed with the same consonant or consonant cluster preceded by differing vowels; half-rhyme.

skotophil *adjective* var. of SCOTOPHIL.

Skraeling /ˈskreɪlɪŋ/ *noun.* M18.
[Old Norse *Skrælingr(j)ar* (pl.).]
Hist. A member of a people prob. of Eskimo origin, inhabiting Greenland at the time of early Norse settlement. Also, any of the inhabitants of Vinland (sometimes identified with the NE coast of N. America) as described by early Norse colonists.

Skraup /skraʊp/ *noun.* L19.
[Zdenko Hans *Skraup* (1850–1910), Bohemian chemist.]
CHEMISTRY. Used *attrib.* and in *possess.* to denote a reaction in which a quinoline is made by heating a primary aromatic amine with glycerol, sulphuric acid, and an oxidizing agent.
Skraup method, ***Skraup reaction***, ***Skraup synthesis***, ***Skraup's method***, ***Skraup's reaction***, ***Skraup's synthesis***.

skreek /skriːk/ *noun. Scot.* Also **screak**, **skreigh** /skriːx/ L18.
[Var. of CREEK *noun*[2]; later forms infl. by SKREIGH *noun*[1].]
Daybreak, dawn. Only in ***skreek of day***, ***skreek of morning***, etc.

skreel *verb & noun* var. of SCREEL.

†**skreen** *verb* var. of SCREEN *verb*.

skreigh *noun*[2] var. of SKREEK.

skreigh /skriːx/ *verb & noun*[1]. *Scot.* E16.
[Alt. of SCREAK.]
▶ **A** *verb.* **1** *verb intrans.* Screech, shriek. E16.
2 *verb trans.* Utter in a screeching tone. L18.
▶ **B** *noun.* A screech, a shriek. M16.

skrik /skrɪk/ *noun. S. Afr. colloq.* L19.
[Afrikaans from Dutch *schrik*.]
A sudden fright, a start; a shock.

skrike /skrʌɪk/ *noun & verb.* Now *dial.* ME.
[Prob. of Scandinavian origin: cf. Norwegian *skrike*, Danish *skrige*. See also SCREAK. Cf. SHRIEK *verb*, SHRIKE *verb*.]
▶ **A** *noun.* A shrill cry; a shriek, a screech. ME.
▶ **B** *verb intrans.* **1** Shriek, screech. ME.
2 Weep, cry. E20.

skrimshander, **skrimshandy** *verbs & nouns* see SCRIMSHANDER.

skrimshank *verb & noun* var. of SCRIMSHANK.

skrimshaw *verb & noun* var. of SCRIMSHAW.

skua /ˈskjuːə/ *noun.* L17.
[mod. Latin from Faeroese *skúvur* (mod. *skugvur*) from Old Norse *skúfr* (app. imit., assim. to *skúfr* tassel).]
Any of several large predatory sea birds of the genera *Stercorarius* and *Catharacta*, typically having brown or brown and white plumage, breeding in polar or cold regions, and with a habit of robbing other sea birds of food.
Arctic skua a common Arctic-breeding skua, *Stercorarius parasiticus*. **great skua** a large skua, *Stercorarius* (or *Catharacta*) *skua*, which breeds in subarctic and cold temperate regions. **long-tailed skua** an Arctic-breeding skua, *Stercorarius longicaudus*, having elongated central tail feathers. ***POMARINE skua***. ***POMATORHINE skua***. ***Richardson's skua***: see RICHARDSON *noun*[1].

skuett /ˈskjuːɪt/ *noun. obsolete* exc. *Hist.* E18.
[App. rel. to SKEWER *noun*.]
A dish consisting of pieces of meat and bacon grilled on a skewer.

skulduggery /skʌlˈdʌɡ(ə)ri/ *noun.* Orig. *US.* Also **scul-**, **skull-**. M19.
[Alt. of SCULDUDDERY.]
Underhand or unscrupulous behaviour; trickery.

skulk /skʌlk/ *verb & noun.* ME.
[Of Scandinavian origin: cf. Norwegian *skulke* lurk, lie watching, Swedish *skolka*, Danish *skulke* shirk, play truant.]
▶ **A** *verb.* **1** *verb intrans.* Move stealthily or sneakily so as to escape notice. Usu. foll. by *about*, *along*, *away*, etc. ME.
2 *verb intrans.* Conceal oneself, keep out of sight, esp. with a sinister or cowardly motive; lurk; hide; ORNITHOLOGY (of a bird) habitually stay under the cover of reeds or grasses. ME. ▸**b** Shirk duty; malinger. L18.
3 *verb trans.* Shun or avoid in a sinister or cowardly manner. Now *rare*. E17.
📖 **1** K. A. PORTER David had . . followed her and Freytag about, skulking along very like a private detective. M. IGNATIEFF He skulked around the . . house, seeking entry. **2** J. LE CARRÉ Don't skulk outside the door like a spy. J. C. OATES The bright-eyed beast, skulking in the corners, watching. **b** W. BESANT Not one who will skulk, or suffer his crew to skulk.
▶ **B** *noun.* **1** = SKULKER. ME.
2 A group of people or creatures characterized by skulking; *spec.* a company of foxes. LME.
3 The action or an act of skulking. M19.
■ **skulker** *noun* a person or creature which skulks; a shirker: ME.

skull /skʌl/ *noun*[1]. ME.
[Origin unkn. Cf. Old Norse *skoltr* (Norwegian *skolt*, *skult*, Swedish *skult*, dial. *skulle*).]
1 The bone framework or skeleton of the head, esp. that part enclosing the brain, in people and other vertebrate animals; the cranium. ME. ▸**b** The head as the centre of thought or intellect. E16. ▸**c** Orig., the head of an Oxford college. Now *gen.* (chiefly *US & Austral.*), a chief, a head, an expert. *slang.* E18. ▸**d** A representation of a human skull, esp. as a symbol of death or mortality. E19.
2 The crown of the head; the pate. LME.
†**3** = SKULLCAP 1b. E16–L17.
4 METALLURGY. (A crust of) partially cooled molten metal, esp. steel. L18.
📖 **1** R. FRAME He had fallen badly, tripped backwards . . . And split his skull. **b** R. S. THOMAS Stray thoughts pass Over the floor of my wide skull. J. O'FAOLAIN Couldn't get it through their skulls that now the outsiders were their own people. **c** G. JOHNSTON All the brass-hats and the skulls down at the Barracks. **2** M. DIBDIN His reddish hair was cropped close to the skull.
Phrases: **a skull** *slang* per person. **bored out of one's skull** *slang* beside oneself with boredom, bored stiff. **out of one's skull** *slang* out of one's mind, crazy. **skull and crossbones** a representation of a bare skull above two crossed thigh-bones symbolizing death, esp. on a pirate's flag.
Comb.: **skull-buster** *US slang* a taxing problem or course of action; **skull-busting** *adjective* (*US slang*) strong, powerful; **skull-fish** WHALING a whalebone whale above two years of age; **skull session** *US slang* a discussion, a conference.
■ **skulled** *adjective* having a (specified kind of) skull L19. **skullery** *noun* (*rare*) (a place containing) a collection of skulls E19. **skull-less** /-l-l-/ *adjective* L19.

skull /skʌl/ *noun*[2]. *Scot.* and (formerly) *north.* Also **scull**. E16.
[Origin unkn.]
A large round shallow basket made of a strong material (esp. wire), used to carry farm produce, fish, etc.

skull /skʌl/ *verb.* M20.
[from SKULL *noun*[1].]
1 *verb trans.* Strike (a person) on the head. *slang* (chiefly *US*). M20.
2 *verb intrans. & trans.* (foll. by *up*). METALLURGY. Of molten metal: solidify to form a skull or crust (in). M20.
📖 **1** A. BERGMAN My waking came in drugged stages . . . I had been skulled. RODDY DOYLE She had the teapot now . . . For a second I thought she was going to skull me with it.

skullcap /ˈskʌlkap/ *noun.* L17.
[from SKULL *noun*[1] + CAP *noun*[1].]
1 A small close-fitting peakless cap, usu. of a soft material, as silk or velvet. L17. ▸**b** A protective helmet resembling this; now *esp.* one worn in horse-riding. E19.
2 Any of various labiate plants constituting the genus *Scutellaria*, in which the calyx is closed and helmet-shaped after flowering; esp. *S. galericulata*, a plant of riversides etc., with small violet-blue flowers. L17.
3 The dome of the skull; (the bone covering) the top of the head. M19.
■ **skullcapped** *adjective* L20.

skullduggery *noun* var. of SKULDUGGERY.

skun *verb pa. t. & pa. pple*: see SKIN *verb*.

skunk /skʌŋk/ *noun.* M17.
[Cognate of Western Abnaki *segᵒgw*.]
1 Any of several American animals of the subfamily Mephitinae in the weasel family, having black and white striped or streaked fur and a bushy tail, and able to spray a foul-smelling liquid from the anal glands when threatened; *esp.* the common N. American striped skunk, *Mephitis mephitis*. M17. ▸**b** The fur of the skunk. M19.
2 A mean or contemptible person. *colloq.* E19. ▸**b** A worthless or corrupt thing, idea, etc. *colloq.* E20. ▸**c** An unidentified surface craft. *US Military slang.* M20.
3 An extremely potent variety of marijuana made from hybrid plants grown esp. under artificial conditions, having a pungent smell when smoked. *slang.* L20.
📖 **2** N. WEST I'm through with that skunk, I tell you. **b** D. H. LAWRENCE That superior stuff is just holy skunk.
Comb.: **skunk bear** = WOLVERINE; **skunk-bird**, **skunk-blackbird** *US* the male bobolink in black and white breeding plumage; **skunk cabbage** any of several foul-smelling N. American plants, esp. *Symplocarpus foetidus* and *Lysichiton americanus*, both of the arum family; **skunk currant** a foul-smelling N. American wild currant, *Ribes glandulosum*; **skunk porpoise** *US* the Atlantic white-sided dolphin, *Lagenorhynchus acutus*; **skunkweed** (*a*) = ***skunk cabbage*** above; (*b*) = sense 3 above; **skunk works** *US colloq.* a specialized division, laboratory, etc., producing experimental designs or ideas for a larger company or institution.
■ **skunkdom** *noun* (*a*) the fact or condition of being a skunk; (*b*) the domain of skunks, skunks collectively: M19. **skunkish** *adjective* resembling a skunk; mean, contemptible: M19. **skunky** *adjective* characteristic of or resembling a skunk; unpleasant; foul-smelling: L19.

skunk /skʌŋk/ *verb. slang* (orig. & chiefly *N. Amer.*). **M19.**
[from the noun.]
1 a *verb intrans.* Fail. *rare.* **M19.** ▸**b** *verb trans.* Defeat, get the better of, esp. by a large margin. Freq. in *pass.* **M19.**
2 *verb trans.* **a** Fail to pay (a bill, a creditor, etc.). **M19.** ▸**b** Cheat (*out of*). **L19.**

📖 **1b** D. DELMAN She'll skunk Nell Duncan today, and win. *Field & Stream* The uninformed angler will spend day after day getting skunked. **2b** ELIZABETH FENWICK I'm beginning to think we skunked you over the price.

Skupština /ˈskuːpʃtiːnə/ *noun.* **M19.**
[Serbo-Croat, from *skupa* together, *skupiti* assemble.]
Hist. The federal assembly of Yugoslavia; (earlier) the national assembly of Serbia and Montenegro.

†**skurry** *noun, verb* vars. of SCURRY *noun, verb.*

skutch *verb* var. of SCUTCH *verb*[1], *verb*[2].

skutterudite /ˈskʊt(ə)rədʌɪt/ *noun.* **M19.**
[from *Skutterud* (now Skotterud) a village in SE Norway + -ITE[1].]
MINERALOGY. Cobalt arsenide occurring as grey cubic crystals with a metallic lustre, commonly containing other elements, esp. nickel, iron, bismuth, and sulphur.

skuttle *noun* var. of SCUTTLE *noun*[1], *noun*[2].

sky /skʌɪ/ *noun.* **ME.**
[Old Norse *ský* cloud, rel. to Old English *scēo*, Old Saxon *scio* and (more remotely) Old English *scūwa*, Old High German *scuwo*, Old Norse *skuggi* shade, shadow, Gothic *skuggwa* mirror.]
†**1** A cloud; in *pl.*, *the* clouds. **ME–M16.**
2 a *sing.* & (chiefly *poet.*) in *pl.* The region of the atmosphere and outer space seen from the earth. **ME.** ▸**b** Heaven, esp. as regarded as having power or influence over mortals; the firmament. *poet.* **L16.**
3 *sing.* & in *pl.* The part of the sky visible in a particular place or on a particular day; the condition of this, the climate. **E16.**
4 = SKY-BLUE *noun* 1. **M17.**
5 A pictorial representation of sky. **M18.**
6 = SKY-ROCKET *noun* 2. *slang.* **L19.**

📖 **2a** DRYDEN Night, when Stars adorn the Skies. HUGH THOMAS In winter one could see little of the sky. **b** W. COWPER Thou that hast . . dared despise Alike the wrath and mercy of the skies. **3** A. NORMA Sing a mournful song and low Beneath Jamaican skies. P. MATTHIESSEN We . . wonder how long fair skies will hold. J. C. OATES It's a white November sky. **6** T. HAWKINS I have nearly £300 in my sky so it's unlikely to be a problem.

Phrases: ***out of a clear sky***: see CLEAR *adjective*. ***pie in the sky***: see PIE *noun*[2] 4a. ***spy in the sky***: see SPY *noun*. **the great — in the sky** God regarded as the supreme exponent of a particular art or profession; a type of paradise especially suited to a particular person or group. **the sky is the limit** there is no apparent limit. **to the skies, to the sky** very highly; enthusiastically, extravagantly. **under the open sky** out of doors.

Comb.: **sky bear** *N. Amer. slang* (an officer in) a police helicopter; **sky border** THEATRICAL a strip of cloth painted to represent sky concealing the top of the stage; **skybox** *N. Amer.* a luxurious enclosed seating area high up in a sports arena; **sky burial** a Tibetan funeral ritual involving the exposure of a dismembered corpse to sacred vultures; **skycap** *N. Amer.* a porter at an airport; **sky-clad** *adjective* (*slang*) (esp. of a witch) nude; **sky cloth** THEATRICAL a backcloth painted or coloured to represent the sky; **sky-colour** *noun & adjective* sky-blue, azure; **sky-coloured** *adjective* sky-blue, azure; **skydive** *verb intrans.* [back-form.] perform acrobatic manoeuvres under free fall with a parachute; **skydiver** a person who skydives; **skydiving** the performance of acrobatic manoeuvres under free fall with a parachute; **sky-farmer** *derog.* (*obsolete* exc. *Hist.*) in Ireland, a tenant-farmer; **sky fighter** (the pilot of) an aeroplane engaged in aerial combat; **sky filter** PHOTOGRAPHY a usu. yellow filter designed to improve the rendering of a bright sky; **sky-flower** a shrub of Central and S. America, *Duranta erecta*, of the verbena family, with clusters of lilac flowers and yellow berries; also called ***pigeon-berry***; **sky-god**, **sky-goddess**: supposed to inhabit or preside over the sky; **sky-high** *adverb & adjective* (as if) reaching the sky; very high; ***blow sky-high*** (*fig.*), refute utterly; **sky-hook** (*a*) an imaginary or fanciful device for suspension in or attachment to the sky; (*b*) a launching device for aircraft, satellites, etc.; (*c*) MOUNTAINEERING a small flattened hook with an eye for attaching a rope etc. fixed temporarily into a rock-face; (*d*) BASKETBALL a high-arcing throw, a lob; **skyhoot** *verb intrans.* (*joc.*) = SCOOT *verb*[1] 1a; **skyjack** *verb & noun* (*a*) *verb trans.* hijack (an aeroplane); (*b*) *noun* a hijack of an aeroplane; **skyjacker** a hijacker of an aeroplane; **skyjam** *colloq.* a congestion in air traffic; **skyline** (*a*) (a representation of) the visible horizon; (*b*) the outline or silhouette of buildings, hills, etc., defined against the sky; (*c*) FORESTRY an overhead cable for transporting logs; (*d*) a line printed above the name on the first page of a newspaper etc. **skylined** *adjective* visible or silhouetted on the skyline; **skylounge** *US* a vehicle lifted by helicopter conveying passengers from a city terminal to an airport; **skyman** *slang* a paratrooper; **sky-marker** MILITARY a parachute flare used to mark a target; **sky marshal** *US* a plain-clothes armed guard on an aeroplane employed to counter hijacking; **sky-parlour** *colloq.* (now *rare*) an attic, a garret; **sky-path** a route through the sky, an airway; **sky pilot** *slang* a member of the clergy; **sky-ride** *US* a monorail etc. for conveying passengers at a considerable height above ground; **skysail** /ˈskʌɪseɪl, -s(ə)l/ NAUTICAL a light sail set above the royal; **skyscape** (*a*) a view of the sky; (*b*) a picture etc. chiefly representing the sky; **sky-scraping** *adjective* extremely high or tall; **sky screen** an array of photocells used to record or detect the travel of an aircraft, projectile, etc.; **sky shade** PHOTOGRAPHY (*a*) a shield or lens hood that prevents direct sunlight from entering a lens; (*b*) a graduated filter; **sky-ship** a large aircraft or spacecraft; **sky-shouting** the announcement of advertisements, propaganda, etc., from an aircraft by loudspeaker; **sky-sign** (*a*) *poet.* a divine portent; (*b*) an advertisement etc. placed on the roof of a building to stand out against the sky; (*c*) a message formed by sky-writing; **sky-surfing** *US* hang-gliding; **skytrain** *US* a convoy of several gliders towed in a line for transporting freight etc.; **sky-walk** = ***skyway*** (c) below; **skywatch** the process or activity of watching the sky for aircraft etc.; **sky wave** a radio wave reflected back towards the earth's surface by the ionosphere; **skyway** (chiefly *US*) (*a*) = AIRWAY 2; (*b*) an overhead motorway; (*c*) a covered overhead walkway between buildings; **sky-write** *verb trans. & intrans.* [back-form.] trace (a legible message, esp. an advertisement) in the sky by means of an aeroplane's smoke trails; **sky-writing** (the action of making) legible smoke trails traced in the sky by an aeroplane, esp. for advertising purposes.

■ **skyey** *adjective* (*a*) of or pertaining to the sky; emanating from the sky or heaven; (*b*) of the colour of the sky, azure: **E17.** **skyful** *noun* as much or as many as the sky can hold **M17.** **skyish** *adjective* (*a*) approaching the sky, sky-high; (*b*) resembling the sky: **E17.** **skyless** *adjective* without visible sky; dark, cloudy: **M19.** **skylike** *adjective* resembling the sky in colour or shape **L16.**

sky /skʌɪ/ *verb.* Pa. t. & pple **skied** /skʌɪd/. **E19.**
[from the noun.]
1 *verb trans.* Throw or toss into the air; *spec.* (CRICKET & BASEBALL) hit (a ball) high into the air. *colloq.* **E19.** ▸**b** Raise the price of (an auctioned item) by high bidding; raise (bidding) by a considerable amount. *slang.* **L19.**
2 *verb trans.* Position high up; *spec.* hang (a picture etc.) high on a wall, esp. at an exhibition. *slang.* **M19.**
3 *verb intrans.* Travel rapidly; leave quickly. Now *slang.* **M19.**

📖 **1** *Times* He skied the ball to the height of the . . Tower. **sky the wipe** *Austral. slang* = ***throw in the sponge*** s.v. SPONGE *noun*[1] 1. **2** G. DALY His picture would be skied . . to the . . top of the room.

■ **skyer** *noun* (*colloq.*) a high-flying hit at cricket or baseball **M19.**

skybald /ˈskʌɪbɔːld/ *noun. Scot. & north.* **M16.**
[Origin unkn.]
A worthless person or thing; a wretch. Also, a lean or worn-out person or animal.

sky-blue /skʌɪˈbluː/ *adjective & noun.* **E18.**
[from SKY *noun* + BLUE *adjective, noun.*]
▶ **A** *adjective.* Of the blue colour of a clear sky; azure. **E18.**
▶ **B** *noun.* **1** The blue colour of a clear sky; azure. **M18.**
2 †**a** Gin. *slang.* **M–L18.** ▸**b** Thin or watery milk. **L18.** ▸†**c** Barley broth. *Nautical slang.* **L19–E20.**
Comb.: **sky-blue-pink** *noun & adjective* (of) an imaginary colour.

Skye /skʌɪ/ *noun.* **M19.**
[The largest island of the Inner Hebrides, NW Scotland (Gaelic Eilean *Sgiathanach*, lit. 'winged island').]
In full ***Skye terrier***. A small long-haired breed of dog with long body and short legs.

skylark /ˈskʌɪlɑːk/ *noun & verb.* **L17.**
[from SKY *noun* + LARK *noun*[1].]
▶ **A** *noun.* **1** Either of two Eurasian larks of the genus *Alauda*, well known for their high, hovering song flight, *esp.* the common *A. arvensis*. **L17.**
2 Any of several esp. American birds that resemble the Eurasian skylarks. *US.* **L19.**
▶ **B** *verb intrans. & trans.* (with *it*). *colloq.* (orig. NAUTICAL). Play tricks or practical jokes; indulge in horseplay; frolic. **L17.**
■ **skylarker** *noun* **M19.**

skylight /ˈskʌɪlʌɪt/ *noun & verb.* **L17.**
[from SKY *noun* + LIGHT *noun.*]
▶ **A** *noun.* **1** Light emanating from the sky. **L17.** ▸**b** PHOTOGRAPHY. In full ***skylight filter***. An almost colourless lens filter used to counter excessive blueness from skylight. **M20.**
2 A window set in the plane of a roof or ceiling. **L17.**

📖 **2** S. BECKETT Too cold to open the skylight in the garret. J. GLASSCO The moon shining through the skylight.

▶ **B** *verb trans.* Provide with a skylight or skylights. *rare.* **M19.**
■ **skylighted** *adjective* provided with or lit by a skylight or skylights **M19.** **skylit** *adjective* illuminated by the sky; *esp.* = SKYLIGHTED: **L19.**

Skylon /ˈskʌɪlɒn/ *noun.* Also **s-**. **M20.**
[from SKY *noun*, after *pylon*.]
ARCHITECTURE. A spire resembling a spindle in shape, orig. & esp. in the South Bank exhibition in London at the Festival of Britain in 1951.

skyphos /ˈskʌɪfɒs/ *noun.* Pl. **-phoi** /-fɔɪ/. **M19.**
[Greek *skuphos*.]
GREEK ANTIQUITIES. A large drinking-cup with two handles not extending above the rim.

skyr /skɪə/ *noun.* **M19.**
[Icelandic.]
A dish consisting of curdled milk.

skyrmion /ˈskəːmɪɒn/ *noun.* **L20.**
[from A. H. R. *Skyrme* (1922–87), Brit. physicist + *-i-* + -ON.]
PARTICLE PHYSICS. A chiral soliton.

sky-rocket /ˈskʌɪrɒkɪt/ *noun & verb.* Also **skyrocket**. **L17.**
[from SKY *noun* + ROCKET *noun*[3], *verb.*]
▶ **A** *noun.* **1** A rocket exploding high in the air. **L17.** ▸**b** *transf.* An enthusiastic cheer. *US slang.* **M19.**
2 A pocket. *rhyming slang.* **L19.**
▶ **B** *verb.* **1** *verb trans.* CRICKET. = SKY *verb* 1. *colloq. rare.* **M19.**
2 *verb intrans.* Rise very steeply and rapidly; *esp.* (of a price or prices) increase dramatically. **L19.**
3 *verb trans.* Propel rapidly forward or upward; increase sharply. **E20.**

📖 **2** A. E. STEVENSON The cost of adequate medical care has skyrocketed out of the reach of millions of Americans. *Isis* Sales rose steadily and then . . skyrocketed. **3** *National Observer (US)* A disease that skyrocketed my chances of dying.

■ **sky-rockety** *adjective* resembling a sky-rocket; rising or increasing sharply: **L19.**

skyscraper /ˈskʌɪskreɪpə/ *noun.* **L18.**
[from SKY *noun* + SCRAPER.]
1 NAUTICAL. = ***skysail*** s.v. SKY *noun.* **L18.**
2 A very tall person or thing; *esp.* a tall building of many storeys. **E19.**
3 CRICKET & BASEBALL. A ball hit high in the air. *slang.* **M19.**
■ **sky-scrapered** *adjective* in the form of a skyscraper; having many skyscrapers: **M20.**

skytale *noun* var. of SCYTALE *noun*[2].

skyward /ˈskʌɪwəd/ *adverb & adjective.* As adverb also **-wards** /-wədz/. **L16.**
[from SKY *noun* + -WARD.]
▶ **A** *adverb.* Towards the sky. **L16.**
▶ **B** *adjective.* Moving or directed towards the sky. **M19.**

slab /slab/ *noun*[1]. **ME.**
[Origin unkn. Cf. SLOB *noun*[2].]
1 A flat comparatively thick and usu. square or rectangular piece of solid material, esp. stone. Also *transf.*, a large bulky person or thing; a considerable amount *of* something. **ME.** ▸**b** *spec.* in METALLURGY. A piece of metal of this form, produced from an ingot for subsequent rolling into sheet or plate. **M19.** ▸**c** MOUNTAINEERING. A large smooth body of rock lying at a (usu. sharp) angle to the horizontal. **E20.** ▸**d** A thick slice of cake, bread, meat, etc.; a large flat block of chocolate. Also *spec.*, = ***slab-cake*** below. **E20.** ▸**e** A rectangular block of precast reinforced concrete used in building. **E20.** ▸**f** A high-rise building with uniform features. **M20.** ▸**g** STATISTICS. Any of the bands in a system of fiscal or other stratification. **M20.**
2 a A rough plank of timber with one side bark. **L16.** ▸**b** A coarse thick plank cut with an axe. *Austral. & NZ.* **E19.**
3 a A flat heavy tabletop or counter, esp. of wood or marble. Also, a thick heavy chopping-board. **M18.** ▸**b** An artist's block or palette for grinding, mixing, or distributing colours. **M19.** ▸**c** A flat piece of stone etc. forming a hearth. **L19.** ▸**d** A mortuary table. **E20.**

📖 **1** P. D. JAMES The floor was of ancient stone slabs. R. RENDELL Her rich relatives kept dying and leaving her slabs of wealth. **c** B. PYM Unrequited love caused me to . . eat halfpound slabs of . . chocolate. **e** *Listener* Other high-rise slabs for offices and flats. **3a** INA TAYLOR A fishmonger's who displayed an appetizing selection of eels wriggling on the slab. P. D. JAMES Alice made short pastry: sieving the flour on to a marble slab.

Comb.: **slab avalanche**: formed by a sheet of snow breaking cleanly along a fracture line; **slab bacon** unsliced bacon; **slab-cake**: baked in a large broad rectangular tin; **slab-hut** *Austral. & NZ* a hut built of coarse wooden planks; **slab-sided** *adjective* having sides made of or resembling slabs; **slab-stone**: having the form of a slab.
■ **slabbing** *noun* slabs collectively **L19.** **slabby** *noun* (*NZ colloq.*) a person working with slabs of timber **E20.** **slabby** *adjective*[1] formed of or resembling slabs **M19.**

slab /slab/ *noun*[2]. **E17.**
[Prob. of Scandinavian origin (cf. Old Danish *slab* mud, Icelandic, Norwegian, Swedish *slabb* wet filth). Cf. SLOB *noun*[1] & *verb.*]
1 A muddy place; a puddle. Now *dial.* **E17.**
2 Slimy material; ooze, sludge. Now *rare.* **E17.**
■ **slabby** *adjective*[2] (*a*) (now *dial.*) miry, muddy, slushy; (*b*) (of a liquid) thick, viscous: **M16.**

slab /slab/ *noun*[3]. Orig. *NZ.* **M20.**
[Origin unkn.]
ANGLING. A weak or exhausted game-fish, *esp.* a diseased trout; a kelt.

slab /slab/ *adjective.* Now *dial. & literary.* **E17.**
[Rel. to SLAB *noun*[2].]
Thick, viscous. Chiefly in ***thick and slab*** (after Shakes.).

📖 SHAKES. *Macb.* Make the gruel thick and slab.

slab /slab/ *verb*[1]. Now *Scot.* Infl. **-bb-**. **M16.**
[Middle Dutch *slabben* lap, slobber food (Dutch *opslabben* gobble up).]
Eat or drink (*up*) hastily or messily.

slab /slab/ *verb*[2] *trans.* Infl. **-bb-**. E18.
[from SLAB *noun*[1].]
1 Dress (timber) by removing the outer slabs. E18.
2 Form into a slab or slabs. M19.
3 Attach a slab or slabs to; lay or support with slabs. M19.
4 Of a path etc.: traverse (a slope) horizontally or at a slight angle. *US.* L19.

slabber /ˈslabə/ *noun*[1]. E18.
[Rel. to SLABBER *verb*. Cf. SLOBBER *noun*.]
1 Slaver, saliva; a lap, a slobber. *obsolete* exc. *Scot.* E18.
2 Senseless talk; drivel. *obsolete* exc. *Scot.* M19.
3 Soft mud; slop, slush. *Scot.* L19.

slabber /ˈslabə/ *noun*[2]. L19.
[from SLAB *verb*[2] + -ER[1].]
1 A saw for slabbing or dressing timber. L19.
2 A person who cuts or forms material into slabs. E20.

slabber /ˈslabə/ *verb*. Now *Scot. & dial.* M16.
[Rel. to SLAB *noun*[2]: see -ER[5]. Cf. SLAB *verb*[1], SLAVER *verb*, SLOBBER *verb*.]
1 *verb trans.* Wet or stain with saliva; dribble on. M16.
2 *verb trans.* Wet or splash dirtily. L16.
3 *verb trans. & intrans.* Eat, drink, etc., hastily or messily. L16.
4 *verb intrans.* Slaver; dribble at the mouth. M17.
5 *verb intrans.* Work messily or carelessly. *Scot.* M19.
Comb.: **slabber-sauce** (*obsolete* exc. *Hist.*) a thinnish mixture of palm oil, flour, and water.
■ †**slabberer** *noun* E17–M18.

slabbery /ˈslab(ə)ri/ *adjective*. Now *Scot. & dial.* E17.
[from SLABBER *noun*[1] or *verb* + -Y[1].]
Sloppy, slushy.

slabline /ˈslablʌɪn/ *noun*. M17.
[Prob. from Dutch *slaplijn*, from *slap* slack.]
NAUTICAL. A rope used to truss up the foot of a lower sail to allow the helmsman a clear forward view.

slack /slak/ *noun*[1]. ME.
[Old Norse *slakki*.]
1 A small shallow dell or valley; a hole, dip, or depression in the ground. Now *Scot. & north.* ME. ▸**b** A hollow in sandbanks or mud-flats, *esp.* one containing water; a damp depression among sand-dunes. LME.
2 A boggy hollow; a morass. Now *Scot. & north.* E17.

slack /slak/ *noun*[2]. LME.
[Prob. of Low Dutch origin: cf. Low German *slakk*, Dutch *slak*, German *Schlacke* dross.]
Coal of an inferior quality or size.
nutty slack: see NUTTY *adjective* 1.

slack /slak/ *noun*[3]. M16.
[from SLACK *adjective* or *verb*. Cf. SLATCH.]
†**1** The passing *of* time. *rare.* Only in M16.
2 a A period of comparative inactivity, esp. in trade; an abatement, a lull. M17. ▸**b** A lessening of a speed limit, esp. on a railway line. L19. ▸**c** In critical path analysis, the length of time by which a particular event can be delayed without delaying the completion of the overall objective. M20.
3 a A cessation in the strong flow of a current or of the tide, esp. at high or low water. M18. ▸**b** A stretch of comparatively still water in a river or the sea. E19.
4 The slack or unstrained part of a rope, sail, etc.; *transf.* a space between vehicles or railway carriages in a line. L18. ▸**b** A loose part *of* a garment; *spec.* the seat of a pair of trousers. *colloq.* M19.
5 In *pl.* Trousers; *esp.* full-length loosely cut trousers for informal wear. E19.
6 Impertinence, cheek. *dial. & US colloq.* E19.
7 PROSODY. An unstressed syllable. L19.
8 A prostitute. *slang.* M20.

> 🕮 **3b** *Coarse Fishing* In the 'slacks' two members of the Yale team . . had caught a gudgeon. **4** K. KESEY He . . heaved harder on the pole . . and reeled the slack. **b** W. DE LA MARE She gripped him by the slack of his coat. **5** H. WILLIAMSON He wore . . breeches; other subalterns had changed into slacks.

Phrases: **cut a person some slack**, **give a person some slack** *N. Amer. slang* show a person understanding or restraint, give a person a chance. **hold on the slack** *arch. slang* skulk, be lazy. **take up the slack** use up a surplus, make up a deficiency; avoid an undesirable lull.
Comb.: **slack adjuster** an automatic device on a vehicle which compensates for variations caused by brake wear; **slack suit** *US* informal wear comprising a pair of slacks with matching jacket or shirt; **slack variable** MATH. a variable which expresses the difference between the two sides of an inequality.

slack /slak/ *adjective & adverb*.
[Old English *slæc* = Old Saxon, Middle & mod. Dutch *slak*, Old High German *slah*, Old Norse *slakr*, from Germanic, cogn. with Latin *laxus* LAX *adjective & adverb*. See also SLAKE *adjective*. Cf. SLOCK *verb*[1].]
▶**A** *adjective*. **I 1** Of a person: inclined to be lazy or negligent; remiss. Also foll. by *in*, *to do*. OE.
2 (Of an action etc.) characterized by laziness or negligence; (of pace) slow, unhurried. OE.
3 Comparatively weak or slow in operation; dull, sluggish. LME. ▸**b** Esp. of heat or the wind: not strong, gentle, moderate. Also, (of tide) neither ebbing nor flowing. L15.
4 a Of work, trade, etc.: not brisk or busy. L15. ▸**b** Of a period of time: characterized by inactivity; quiet. E19.

> 🕮 **1** SIR W. SCOTT The . . armourer was not . . slack in keeping the appointment. C. MACKENZIE To smarten up my men. They're getting terribly slack. **2** DICKENS The slack pace of the horse. J. CONRAD Lolled against the rails in such a slack, improper fashion. **3** R. C. HUTCHINSON Slack from want of sleep, my brain groped feebly. **b** A. DILLARD He could row it in while the tide was still slack.
> **4a** A. BROOKNER Business was . . very slack at this time of year. **b** J. SUTHERLAND Fiction was . . associated . . with leisure and slack moments.

▶**II 5** Not drawn or held tautly; (of skin, muscle, etc.) not firm or tight; relaxed, loose. ME. ▸**b** Of the hand: having a loose grip. M17. ▸**c** PHONETICS. = LAX *adjective* 5c. E20.
6 Soft or loose in texture; *esp.* (of dough) wet, pliable. LME.

> 🕮 **5** TENNYSON Now with slack rein . . Now with dug spur . . he rode. S. MIDDLETON Her belly was . . slack . . not recovered from her last child-bearing.

Comb. & special collocations: **slack hand** lack of control in riding or governing; **slack-jaw** *arch.* tiresome or impertinent talk; **slack rein** = *slack hand* above; **slack-rope** a loosely stretched rope on which an acrobat performs (opp. TIGHTROPE); **slack water** = SLACK *noun*[3] 3; **slack-water navigation**: using locks or dams on a river.
▶**B** *adverb*. In a slack manner; loosely; insufficiently, imperfectly. LME.
Comb.: **slack-twisted** *adjective* (of a rope) not tightly twisted; *fig.* (of a person) lazy, idle.
■ **slackly** *adverb* OE. **slackness** *noun* (**a**) the state or quality of being slack, *esp.* lack of diligence or effort; (**b**) the slack part *of* something; (**c**) NAUTICAL the condition of a ship's bow falling off from the wind: OE.

slack /slak/ *verb*. E16.
[from the adjective. In some senses superseding earlier SLAKE *verb*[1].]
▶**I** *verb trans.* **1** Cease to pursue vigorously or energetically; allow to fall off or decline. E16.
2 Neglect or be remiss in (one's duty etc.); leave undone. M16. ▸†**b** Fail to take advantage of (an opportunity etc.); lose or waste (time). M16–M17.
3 Lessen the tension of; slacken, loosen, (esp. a rope). Also foll. by *back*, *off*, etc. M16. ▸**b** = SLAKE *verb*[1] 11. E18.
4 Reduce the force or intensity of; *esp.* slake (one's thirst). L16.
5 Make neglectful or remiss. Now *rare.* L16.
6 Delay, retard; slow down (one's pace etc.). Now *rare.* L16.

> 🕮 **1 slack one's hand(s)** (now *rare*) reduce one's efforts or activity. **3** SIR W. SCOTT Tak the gentleman's horse . . and slack his girths. **4** *Steam Railway News* The 'Junction Hotel' . . often slacked the thirst of crews.

▶**II** *verb intrans.* **7** Be idle; fail to exert oneself. Also foll. by *about*. Now *colloq.* M16. ▸**b** Neglect or be backward *to do* something. Now *rare.* M16.
8 Become less energetic or diligent; apply less force or effort to something. Also foll. by *off*, *up*. M16.
9 Diminish in strength, speed, or intensity; moderate, abate. Also foll. by *off*. L16. ▸**b** Of trade etc.: be less brisk, fall off. E17.
10 Become slack or loose. L16. ▸**b** = SLAKE *verb*[1] 4. E18.

> 🕮 **7** J. HILTON We . . can't slack about here doing nothing. M. SHADBOLT Find the boy slacking because his boss was out. **8** J. DICKEY Pull like hell . . then slack off; don't hit a constant speed. JILLY COOPER Work to keep sin at bay, feel guilty if you slack. **9** D. A. DYE The rain had slacked a bit.

Comb.: **Slack-ma-girdle** a variety of cider apple.
■ **slacker** *noun* (**a**) (now *dial.*) a gate in a river lock; (**b**) *colloq.* a person who avoids work, military service, etc.; a shirker: L18. **slackster** *noun* (*rare*, *slang*) = SLACKER (b) E20.

slacken /ˈslak(ə)n/ *verb*. L16.
[from SLACK *adjective* + -EN[5].]
▶**I** *verb trans.* **1** Slow down; delay, retard; lessen (one's pace etc.). L16.
2 Make slack or less tense; relax, loosen; *transf.* make less strict or severe. Also foll. by *off*. E17.
3 Reduce in strength or intensity; cause or allow to fall off or decline. M17.

> 🕮 **1** J. BUCHAN Then came a bit of thick wood where I slackened speed. **2** A. BURGESS Siegmund's violin lies mute, the bow slackened. **3** M. DAS Ravi sat sunk in the stacks of moth-eaten documents without slackening his vigilance.

▶**II** *verb intrans.* **4** Become remiss or negligent; grow less energetic or enthusiastic. M17.
5 Diminish in strength or intensity; abate. Also foll. by *off*. M17. ▸**b** Of trade etc.: become less brisk. Also foll. by *off*. M18.
6 Reduce in speed, slow down; become less frequent or regular. Also foll. by *off*. L17.
7 Become slack or loose; relax; *spec.* (of lime) become slaked. E18.

> 🕮 **4** E. BOWEN People who had no more slackened in fair weather than . . in foul. A. S. BYATT Whoever slackens and tires . . is mercilessly cuffed. **5** A. MCCOWEN With the passing years the intensity of the relationship slackened. M. DIBDIN The storm showed no sign of slackening. **6** V. WOOLF The speed of the . . traffic slackened. R. SUTCLIFF Our afternoon treks had slackened off. **7** H. CAINE Her clenched hands slackened away from his neck.

■ **slackener** *noun* M19.

slade /sleɪd/ *noun*[1].
[Old English *slæd* = Old Saxon *slada*, Low German *slade*, Icelandic *slǫður*, Danish, Norwegian *slad(e*: the present form derives from Old English oblique cases.]
An open area of grassland or marsh, esp. between banks or woods; a valley; a glade, a dell.

slade /sleɪd/ *noun*[2]. Chiefly *Scot. & dial.* L15.
[Var. of SLEAD or SLED *noun*.]
A sledge.

slade /sleɪd/ *noun*[3]. M19.
[Perh. rel. to SLIDE *verb*.]
The heel of a plough.

slade *verb pa. t.*: see SLIDE *verb*.

slag /slag/ *noun*. M16.
[Middle Low German *slagge*, perh. from *slagen* strike, with ref. to fragments resulting from hammering.]
1 (A piece of) stony material composed of waste matter or dross separated from metals during smelting or refining; scoria, clinker; any similar product resulting from the fusion etc. of other substances. M16.
2 GEOLOGY. (A lump of) scoriaceous lava. L18.
3 a A worthless or objectionable person; *spec.* (**a**) a petty criminal; (**b**) a promiscuous woman, a prostitute. *slang. derog.* L18. ▸**b** Worthless matter; rubbish, nonsense. *colloq.* M20.

> 🕮 **1** *basic slag*: see BASIC *adjective* 2. **3a** *She* Pressure for early intercourse was heavy, yet boys called girls who 'did it' slags.

Comb.: **slag-glass** variously coloured glass made with a proportion of slag, manufactured esp. in the US in the 19th cent.; **slag-heap** a hill of refuse from a mine etc.; **slag-hearth** (*obsolete* exc. *Hist.*) a furnace for resmelting slag from lead-smelting; **slag-lead** (*obsolete* exc. *Hist.*): obtained by resmelting partly fused ore; **slag notch** a hole in a smelting-furnace for letting out slag; **slag-wool** a fibrous form of blast-furnace slag that resembles asbestos and is used as an insulator etc.
■ **slaggy** *adjective* (**a**) of, pertaining to, or resembling slag; (**b**) *slang derog.* objectionable, offensive; (of a woman) promiscuous, coarse: L17. **slagless** *adjective* (of metal) free from slag E20.

slag /slag/ *adjective*. Now *Scot.* LME.
[Prob. of Scandinavian origin: cf. Old Norwegian *slag* wet, dampness, Old Norse *slagna* flow over.]
Wet, moist; muddy.

slag /slag/ *verb*. Infl. **-gg-**. L19.
[from SLAG *noun*.]
1 *verb trans.* Separate slag from; convert into slag, scorify. L19.
2 *verb intrans.* Form slag; cohere into a mass resembling slag. L19.
3 *verb trans.* Denigrate; criticize, insult. Freq. foll. by *off*. *slang.* L20.

> 🕮 **3** *Times* Fell into the . . trap of slagging off social workers. D. BOLGER A grey underworld . . where people slagged Shay for . . having a job.

slagger /ˈslagə/ *verb intrans.* Now *dial.* E17.
[Origin unkn.]
Walk slowly; loiter, lag.

slaik /sleɪk/ *verb & noun*. *Scot. & north.* Also **slake**. LME.
[Old Norse *sleikja*.]
▶**A** *verb intrans. & trans.* Lick or smear (a surface); slobber (over). LME.
▶**B** *noun*. A lick; a smear, a daub. E18.

slain /sleɪn/ *ppl adjective & noun*. ME.
[pa. pple of SLAY *verb*[1].]
▶**A** *ppl adjective*. **1** Killed, slaughtered. *arch.* ME.
2 Of grain: blighted. *dial.* M17.
▶**B** *absol.* as *noun*. A person who has been killed; ***the slain***, those who have been killed, esp. in battle. *arch.* ME.
letter of slains SCOTS LAW (now *Hist.*) a letter subscribed by the relatives of a person who had been killed, acknowledging receipt of compensation etc. and asking the Crown to pardon the killer.

slainte /ˈslɑːntʃə/ *interjection*. E19.
[Gaelic *slàinte* (*mhór*) = '(good) health'.]
Expr. good wishes, esp. before drinking.

slaister /ˈsleɪstə/ *verb & noun*. *Scot. & north.* M18.
[Origin unkn.]
▶**A** *verb*. **1** *verb intrans.* Eat or work messily or sloppily. M18.
2 *verb trans.* Make messy or sloppy; splash, bespatter. L18.
▶**B** *noun*. A dirty or sloppy mess. L18.

slake /sleɪk/ *noun*¹. Now *rare* or *obsolete*. ME.
[from SLAKE *verb*¹.]
The action or an act of slackening or lessening; abatement; respite.

slake /sleɪk/ *noun*². *Scot. & north.* L15.
[Rel. to SLAWK, SLOKE *noun*¹.]
= SLAWK.

†**slake** *noun*³. E17–M19.
[Origin unkn.]
A flake.

slake /sleɪk/ *noun*⁴. Chiefly *north.* M18.
[Origin unkn.]
1 Mud, slime. M18.
2 A muddy piece of ground; a mud-flat. E19.
■ **slaky** *adjective* muddy M19.

†**slake** *adjective*. ME–L18.
[Var. of SLACK *adjective*.]
= SLACK *adjective*.
slake water = *slack water* s.v. SLACK *adjective*.

slake /sleɪk/ *verb*¹.
[Old English *slacian*, formed as SLACK *adjective*; corresp. to Middle & mod. Dutch *slaken* relax, diminish. Largely superseded by SLACK *verb*.]
▶ **I** *verb intrans.* †**1** Decline in one's efforts or enthusiasm; become less energetic or eager. Also foll. by *of*. OE–L16.
†**2** Become loose, slacken. OE–L16.
3 Diminish in force, intensity, or number; fall off; abate, subside; (of fire) burn less strongly. *arch.* ME.
4 Of lime: become hydrated to produce calcium hydroxide. M18.

📖 **3** T. H. WHITE I . . feel daily that thy love beginneth to slake.

▶ **II** *verb trans.* †**5** Slacken; lessen the tension of. ME–L16.
†**6** Reduce in number or size. ME–E17.
7 Make less oppressive or painful; mitigate, assuage. Formerly also, relieve (a person) *from* or *of* pain etc. Now *rare.* ME.
8 Reduce the force or intensity of; moderate; *esp.* cause (fire) to burn less strongly. Now *rare.* ME.
9 Quench (one's thirst); *fig.* appease or satisfy (desire, revenge, etc.). ME.
10 Moisten, wet, soak; *esp.* cool or refresh by this action. LME.
11 Hydrate (lime) to produce calcium hydroxide. M17.

📖 **9** CLIVE JAMES The back of her, . . that was the angle from which he preferred to slake his . . desires. P. CAREY It was hot and her thirst could not be slaked. **10** L. STEPHEN I reached a . . patch of snow, and managed to slake my parched lips.

■ **slaked** *ppl adjective* that has been slaked; *slaked lime*, calcium hydroxide that has been made by hydrating lime (see LIME *noun*¹ 3): LME. **slakeless** *adjective* (chiefly *literary*) unquenchable, insatiable L16.

slake *verb*² & *noun* var. of SLAIK *verb & noun*.

slalom /ˈslɑːləm/ *noun & verb*. E20.
[Norwegian *slalåm*, from *sla* sloping + *låm* track.]
▶ **A** *noun*. **1** A downhill ski race on a zigzag course marked by artificial obstacles, usu. flags, and descended singly by each competitor in turn. E20.
2 A similar obstacle race for canoeists, waterskiers, skateboarders, etc. M20.

📖 **1** *attrib.*: *Ski* The fastest line through a slalom course . . depends on the terrain. **giant slalom** a long distance slalom. **2** *attrib.*: *Oxford Mail* Slalom canoeist Bob Doman . . won the bronze medal.

▶ **B** *verb intrans.* Perform or compete in a slalom; make frequent sharp turns (as) in a slalom. M20.
■ **slalomer** *noun* L20. **slalomist** *noun* M20.

slam /slam/ *noun*¹. E17.
[Origin unkn.]
†**1** The card-game ruff or trump. Only in 17.
2 CARDS. The winning of every trick in a game. M17.
Phrases: **grand slam** (*a*) the winning of 13 tricks in a game of bridge; (*b*) the winning of all of a series of (sports) matches, competitions, championships, etc.; (*c*) BASEBALL a home run hit when all three bases are occupied by a runner, thus achieving 4 runs; (*d*) a complete success; (*e*) an attack in force. **little slam**, **small slam** the winning of 12 tricks in a game of bridge.

slam /slam/ *noun*². L17.
[Rel. to SLAM *verb*².]
1 A violent impact or blow. L17. ▸**b** BASEBALL. A powerful, usu. long-distance, hit. M20.
2 A violent shutting of a door etc.; a noise made (as) by this, a loud bang. E19.
3 An insult. *US slang.* L19.
4 (Usu. with *the*.) Prison. Cf. SLAMMER *noun* 3. *slang* (chiefly *N. Amer.*). M20.
5 In full ***poetry slam***. An informal poetry contest in which competitors recite their entries and are judged by members of the audience, the winner being elected after several elimination rounds. Chiefly *N. Amer.* L20.

📖 **2** G. STEIN She went into the house, giving the door a shattering slam. B. MOORE Pulled the heavy front door shut with a slam like a gunshot. **4** *Which Video?* He is a racketeer just out of the slam.

Comb.: **slam-dancer** a participant in slam-dancing; **slam-dancing** a form of dancing to rock music in which the dancers deliberately collide with one another; **slamdunk** BASKETBALL a play in which a player jumps and thrusts the ball forcefully down into the basket.

†**slam** *verb*¹ *trans. & intrans. rare.* Infl. **-mm-**. M17–L18.
[Euphem. substitute for DAMN *verb*.]
= DAMN *verb*.

slam /slam/ *verb*² & *adverb*. L17.
[Prob. of Scandinavian origin. Cf. Old Norse *slam(b)ra*, Swedish *slämma*, Norwegian *slemma*.]
▶ **A** *verb*. Infl. **-mm-**.
1 *verb trans.* Hit or slap violently or with great force. Chiefly *dial. & US.* L17.
2 *verb trans.* **a** Shut (a door, window, lid, etc.) forcefully and loudly. Also foll. by *down, to, up*. L18. ▸**b** *verb trans.* Push, thrust, etc., put *down*, forcefully and loudly. L19. ▸**c** *verb trans. & intrans.* Put or come into action, or some state or condition, suddenly and forcefully. Also foll. by *into, on*, etc. M20. ▸**d** *verb trans.* SPORT. Score (a goal etc.) forcefully; accumulate (a large score) quickly. *colloq.* M20.
3 *verb intrans.* Of a door, window, lid, etc.: shut, or strike against anything, forcefully and loudly. Also foll. by *down, into, to*, etc. E19.
4 a *verb intrans.* Be severely critical or insulting. *US slang.* L19. ▸**b** *verb trans.* Criticize severely. Now also, refute or contradict forcefully. *colloq.* (orig. *US*). E20.
5 *verb intrans.* Move violently or loudly; crash; NAUTICAL (of a boat) crash into (the trough of) a wave; plunge or pitch. Foll. by *around, through*, etc. L20.
6 *verb trans.* Switch (a customer) from one telephone service provider to another without permission, on the basis of a dishonestly acquired signature. Freq. as ***slamming*** *verbal noun*. *US.* L20.

📖 **1** F. O'CONNOR A terrible bristly claw slammed the side of his face. **2a** V. GLENDINNING Charlotte slammed the back door. **b** R. RENDELL She slammed the phone down. **c** W. M. RAINE The car slammed to a halt. **d** T. TRYON Abernathy slammed three homers. **3** DICKENS Big doors slam and resound when anybody comes in. *New Yorker* The punch lines slam into our brains. **4b** J. IRVING A long, cocky letter . . slamming Franz Grillparzer. *Courier-Mail (Brisbane)* Card artists slam claims of deception. **5** T. C. BOYLE Eduardo, . . slammed into the kitchen with a drawn face.

▶ **B** *adverb*. With a slam or heavy blow; suddenly and violently. E18.

📖 G. B. SHAW They're coming slam into the greenhouse.

slam /slam/ *verb*³ *trans.* Infl. **-mm-**. M18.
[from SLAM *noun*¹.]
CARDS. Beat by winning a slam; trump; *transf.* defeat completely.

slambang /slamˈbaŋ/ *adjective, adverb, & verb*. Also **slam-bang**. E19.
[from SLAM *verb*² + BANG *verb*¹.]
▶ **A** *adjective*. **1** Noisy; violent. E19.
2 Exciting, impressive; vigorous, energetic. *colloq.* M20.

📖 **2** *Philadelphia Inquirer* Slambang Action, Two Marvelous Stars . . The Best Cop Movie.

▶ **B** *adverb*. With a slam; loudly and violently. M19.

📖 D. BAGLEY I walked slambang into this character.

▶ **C** *verb intrans. & trans.* Slam or bang. M19.

slammakin /ˈslaməkɪn/ *noun & adjective*. Chiefly *dial.* Also **slammerkin**. M18.
[Origin unkn. Cf. SLUMMOCK *noun*.]
▶ **A** *noun*. †**1** A loose gown or dress. M18.
2 An untidy or dirty girl or woman, a sloven. M18.
▶ **B** *adjective*. Untidy, slovenly. L18.

slammer /ˈslamə/ *noun*. L19.
[from SLAM *verb*² + -ER¹.]
1 A person who slams (a door etc.). L19.
2 A violent gust (of wind). L19.
3 (Usu. with *the*.) Prison. Cf. SLAM *noun*² 4. *slang* (orig. *US*). M20.
4 A strong drink of (neat) alcohol, esp. tequila. Chiefly *US.* L20.
5 A slam-dancer. L20.

slammerkin *noun & adjective* var. of SLAMMAKIN.

slammock *noun* var. of SLUMMOCK.

slamp /slamp/ *noun*. Long *dial.* E17.
[Origin unkn.]
A blow, a thump, a slap.

slander /ˈslɑːndə/ *noun*. Orig. †**scl-**. ME.
[Aphet. from Anglo-Norman *esclaundre*, Old French *esclandre*, alt. of *escandle* SCANDAL *noun*.]
1 (The utterance or spreading of) a false or malicious statement about a person, intended to injure or defame; *spec.* (LAW) a false and defamatory oral statement; the act or offence of making such a statement. Cf. LIBEL *noun* 5. ME.
†**2** Discredit, disgrace, or shame, esp. incurred by transgression of moral law; disrepute, opprobrium. ME–L17. ▸**b** A source of shame or dishonour; a discreditable act or person. LME–L16.
†**3** A cause of moral lapse or fall. ME–L16.

📖 **1** R. RENDELL Vile slanders had been repeated . . during that phone conversation about Robin's black eye. *attrib.*: DENNIS POTTER The . . slander actions which I shall . . bring against some of my former acquaintances.

slander /ˈslɑːndə/ *verb*. Orig. †**scl-**. ME.
[Old French *esclaundrer*, from *esclandre*: see prec.]
†**1** *verb trans.* Cause to lapse or fall spiritually or morally. ME–M16. ▸**b** Bring into discredit, disgrace, or disrepute. LME–E17.
2 *verb trans.* Defame; utter or spread slander about; *spec.* (LAW) speak slander against. ME. ▸†**b** Accuse (a person) *of*; charge or reproach (a person) *with*. LME–E17. ▸**c** *verb intrans.* Spread or utter slanders. LME.
†**3** *verb trans.* Misrepresent or vilify (a thing). LME–E17.
†**4** *verb trans.* Make widely known. *rare.* LME–L15.

📖 **2** S. NAIPAUL The cleverly orchestrated plot designed to slander and besmirch their memory.

■ **slanderer** *noun* ME.

slanderous /ˈslɑːnd(ə)rəs/ *adjective*. Orig. †**scl-**. LME.
[Old French *esclandreux*, from *esclandre* SLANDER *noun*: see -OUS.]
†**1 a** Having a bad reputation; discreditable, disgraceful, shameful. LME–L16. ▸**b** Causing shame or disgrace *to* a person. *rare.* Only in L16. ▸**c** Giving cause or occasion for slander. *rare* (Shakes.). Only in E17.
2 Of a person etc.: given to slandering. LME.
3 Of a statement, language, etc.: of the nature of, characterized by, or containing slander; calumnious, defamatory. LME.

📖 **2** J. A. FROUDE His supposed offences were slanderous expressions used against the king. **3** T. ARNOLD Narrow-minded in the last degree, fierce and slanderous.

■ **slanderously** *adverb* (*a*) in a slanderous manner; with slander; unjustly, falsely; †(*b*) scandalously, shamefully: LME. **slanderousness** *noun* L16.

slane /sleɪn, slɑːn/ *noun*. *Anglo-Irish.* Also **slean**. M18.
[Irish *sleán, sleaghán*.]
In Ireland, a long-handled spade with a wing at one or both sides of the blade, used for cutting peat or turf.

slang /slaŋ/ *noun*¹. M18.
[Origin unkn.]
1 Language that is regarded as very informal or much below standard educated level. M18. ▸**b** The special vocabulary and usage of a particular period, profession, social group, etc. Freq. with specifying word. E19. ▸**c** *transf.* Abuse, impertinence. Cf. SLANG *verb* 3. Now *rare.* E19.
2 A licence, esp. for a street-trader. *arch. slang.* E19.
3 A travelling show; a performance. *arch. slang.* M19.

📖 **1** M. MEYER He wanted me to be . . less colloquial, and was always rebuking me for using slang. **b** JAN MORRIS 'Brain Basil' is Oxford schoolboy slang for a clever boy.

■ **slangish** *adjective* somewhat slangy E19. **slangishly** *adverb* E19. **slangism** *noun* a slang expression M19. **slangster** *noun* a person who uses slang E19. **slanguage** *noun* (*joc. & colloq.*) slangy speech; a form of slang: L19.

slang /slaŋ/ *noun*². *arch. slang.* E19.
[App. from Dutch = snake, serpent.]
A chain, esp. a watch-chain; in *pl.*, fetters, leg-irons.

slang *noun*³ see SLING *noun*².

slang /slaŋ/ *adjective*. M18.
[Rel. to SLANG *noun*¹.]
1 Of language etc.: of the character of, belonging to, or expressed in, slang. M18.
2 Of a person: given to using slang. Now *rare.* E19. ▸**b** Rakish, impertinent. Now *rare.* E19. ▸**c** Of dress: loud, extravagant; flashy, obtrusive. Now *rare* or *obsolete*. E19.

📖 **1** M. ATWOOD *Bog* is a slang word for toilet, and . . you know the toilet will be a . . smelly one.

slang /slaŋ/ *verb*. L18.
[from SLANG *noun*¹, *adjective*.]
1 *verb intrans.* Exhibit or sell at a fair, market, etc. *slang.* Now *rare* or *obsolete*. L18.
2 *verb trans. & intrans.* Defraud, cheat. *slang.* Now *rare.* E19.
3 *verb intrans. & trans.* Use abusive or vulgar language (to); abuse or scold (a person etc.). *colloq.* E19.

📖 **3** A. C. BOULT My mother once heard her slanging an unfortunate maid. **slanging-match** a prolonged exchange of insults.

slangwhang /ˈslaŋwaŋ/ *verb trans. & intrans. colloq.* (chiefly *US*). E19.
[from SLANG *noun*¹ + WHANG *verb*¹.]
Use abusive or violent language (to).
■ **slangwhanger** *noun* E19.

slangy /ˈslaŋi/ *adjective.* M19.
[from SLANG *noun*[1] + -Y[1].]
1 Of a person: given to using slang. M19.
2 Flashy, pretentious; loud, extravagant. Now *rare.* M19.
3 Of language etc.: pertaining to or of the character of slang. M19.
■ **slangily** *adverb* M19. **slanginess** *noun* M19.

slank /slaŋk/ *adjective.* Now *Scot. & north.* M17.
[Prob. from Dutch or Low German (Middle Dutch, Middle High German *slanc*, German *schlank*) = thin, slender.]
Of a person, a person's hair, etc.: lank, thin.

slant /slɑːnt/ *noun*[1]. LME.
[Var. of SLENT *noun*[1].]
1 The slope or inclination of or *of* a thing, esp. a hill or piece of ground; a sloping stretch of ground; an inclined plane or surface. Cf. SLENT *noun* 1. LME. ▸**b** A short oblique line or surface. E18. ▸**c** An oblique beam or ray of or *of* light. M19. ▸**d** MICROBIOLOGY. A sloping surface of culture medium, prepared by letting it solidify in a sloping test-tube. L19. ▸**e** TYPOGRAPHY. A character, appearing as an oblique stroke leaning to the right, used to indicate line endings, the start and finish of the phonetic representation of a linguistic element, etc.: a solidus. Cf. ***slant-line*** s.v. SLANT *adverb & adjective.* M20.
2 An oblique course or movement; *spec.* (AMER. FOOTBALL) a play in which the ball or ball-carrier enters or leaves the scrimmage line obliquely or diagonally. E18.
3 A sly insult or piece of sarcasm. Cf. SLENT *noun*[1] 2. *dial. & US.* E19.
4 An occasion, chance, or opportunity (for a journey). *slang.* Now *rare.* M19.
5 A receptacle with a sloping bottom, for storing paint-brushes to keep them moist. L19.
6 A way of regarding a thing, a point of view; an interpretation; a bias. E20. ▸**b** A glance, a look. *US colloq.* E20.
7 A slant-eyed (*spec.* oriental) person. Cf. ***slant-eye(s)*** s.v. SLANT *adverb & adjective. US slang. derog. & racially offensive.* M20.

> 🕮 **1** M. TWAIN The slant of a ladder that leans against a house. C. J. CHERRYH He walked down the slant past the guard. **on a slant**, **on the slant** aslant. **c** C. MCCULLERS The sun made long, yellow slants through the window. **6** *Bird Watching* To have your eyes opened to a new slant on things, a fresh outlook. *Marketing* Organisations with an environmental slant.

slant /slɑːnt/ *noun*[2]. E19.
[Var. of SLENT *noun*[2].]
NAUTICAL. A slight breeze; a spell (*of* wind etc.).

slant /slɑːnt/ *verb.* E16.
[Var. of SLENT *verb*[1], prob. infl. by ASLANT *adverb.*]
1 *verb intrans.* Strike obliquely *on*, *upon*, or *against*. Now *rare.* E16.
2 *verb intrans.* Lie or move in an oblique position or direction; slope; deviate from a straight line or course. L17. ▸**b** *fig.* Incline or be inclined *towards* a particular thing, position, etc. M19.
3 *verb trans.* Cause to deviate from a straight line; cause to slope. E19. ▸**b** Present (information etc.) from a particular perspective, esp. in an unduly biased way. M20.

> 🕮 **2** DICKENS We went along Cheapside, and slanted off to Little Britain. M. WARNER Her shadow slanted across the familiar brilliance out of doors. **3** F. BURNEY I turned suddenly from my walk . . to slant my steps close to where he sat. **b** D. ACHESON Arrange the material so as to avoid . . attempts to slant it towards a particular conclusion.

■ **slanting** *noun* (*a*) the action of the verb; (*b*) (long *rare* or *obsolete*) perspective, bias: E17. **slanting** *adjective & adverb* (*a*) *adjective* that slants; situated or directed obliquely; (*b*) *adverb* in a slanting direction; slantingly: E16. **slantingly** *adverb* aslant, obliquely; indirectly: L16. **slantingways** *adverb* (*rare*) slantwise L19.

slant /slɑːnt/ *adverb & adjective.* L15.
[Aphet. from ASLANT.]
► **A** *adverb.* In a slanting, sloping, or oblique manner or direction; aslant. L15.
► **B** *adjective.* **1** Of wind etc.: coming from the side; moving obliquely. E17.
2 Having an oblique position or direction; inclined from the perpendicular or horizontal. L18. ▸**b** Of direction: oblique. L18.
Special collocations & comb.: **slant-eyed** *adjective* having slanting eyes. **slant-eye(s)** *slang* (*derog. & racially offensive*) a slant-eyed (*spec.* oriental) person. **slant height** the height of a cone from the vertex to the periphery of the base. **slant-line** = SLANT *noun*[1] 1e.
■ **slantly** *adverb* slantingly, obliquely E18. **slanty** *adjective* slanting E20.

slanter *noun & adjective* see SCHLENTER.

slantindicular /slɑːntɪnˈdɪkjʊlə/ *adjective & adverb. joc. & colloq.* (orig. & chiefly *US*). M19.
[from SLANTING *adjective & adverb* after *perpendicular.*]
► **A** *adjective.* Slanting, oblique. M19.
► **B** *adverb.* = SLANTINDICULARLY. M19.
■ **slantindicularly** *adverb* slantingly, obliquely; indirectly: M19.

slantways /ˈslɑːntweɪz/ *adverb.* E19.
[from SLANT *adjective* + -WAYS. Cf. SLAUNCHWAYS.]
= next.

slantwise /ˈslɑːntwʌɪz/ *adverb & adjective.* L16.
[from SLANT *adjective* + -WISE. Cf. SLAUNCHWISE.]
► **A** *adverb.* In a slanting direction or position; slantingly, obliquely. L16.
► **B** *adjective.* Slanting, oblique. M19.

slap /slap/ *noun*[1]. *Scot.* LME.
[Middle Dutch, Middle Low German *slop*, of unkn. origin.]
1 An opening or gap in a wall, hedge, etc. LME. ▸**b** An opening left in a salmon-cruive from Saturday evening to Monday morning, to allow the fish to pass; the period during which such an opening is left. Freq. in ***Saturday slap***, ***Saturday's slap***. LME. ▸**c** A narrow mountain pass. E18.
2 *transf.* A gap *in* or in the ranks of a body of troops. LME.

slap /slap/ *noun*[2]. M17.
[Rel. to SLAP *verb*[1]. Cf. Low German *slapp.*]
1 A smart blow, *esp.* one given with the palm of the hand or a flat object; a smack; the sound made by this. M17. ▸**b** MECHANICS. = ***piston slap*** s.v. PISTON *noun.* M20. ▸**c** The percussive sound made when the strings of a double-bass or bass guitar strike the finger-board in slap-bass playing; the slap-bass technique. Cf. SLAP *verb*[1] 1d. M20.
2 *transf.* **a** A reprimand or reproof; a rebuff. Freq. in ***a slap in the face***, ***a slap on the wrist***. M18. ▸**b** An attempt *at* something. *arch. colloq.* M19. ▸**c** A dash, a rush. *rare.* E20.
3 Theatrical make-up, greasepaint; *transf.* any make-up, esp. when applied thickly or carelessly. *slang.* (orig. THEATRICAL). M19.

> 🕮 **1** TOLKIEN He pushed his way through the tangled twigs with many a slap in the eye. P. MARSHALL He heard the dry slap of her feet behind him. P. ACKROYD Martha gave him a playful slap on the hand. **slap and tickle** light-hearted amorous activity. **slap on the back** congratulations. **2a** *Guardian* Industry will regard action to tighten price control . . as a slap in the face. **3** A. WILSON Vin's guests came in costume with plenty of slap.

slap /slap/ *verb*[1]. Infl. **-pp-**. LME.
[Prob. imit.]
1 *verb trans.* Strike smartly, esp. with the palm of the hand or with a flat object; smack. LME. ▸**b** Drive or knock *back*, *down*, etc., with a slap or slaps; *colloq.* (foll. by *down*), reprimand. E19. ▸**c** SPORT. Strike (the ball or puck) with a sharp slap; score (a run etc.) in this way. *N. Amer.* E20. ▸**d** In jazz and popular music, play (a double-bass or bass guitar) by pulling and releasing the strings sharply against the finger-board. Cf. SLAP *noun*[2] 1c. M20.
2 *verb trans.* Strike (one's hand etc.) *against* or *on* something with a slap; put or throw *down*, *on*, etc., (as) with a slap; put *together*, place or lay *down*, *on*, etc. hastily, carelessly, or forcefully. L17. ▸**b** Apply or daub (a substance, esp. make-up or paint) thickly or carelessly. Freq. foll. by *on*. *colloq.* E20. ▸**c** Punish *with* a fine, sentence, etc. *N. Amer.* M20.
3 *verb trans.* Slam (a door etc.). Also foll. by *to*. E18. ▸**b** *verb intrans.* Of a door etc.: slam. *rare.* L18.
4 *verb intrans.* Move or walk quickly. Chiefly *dial.* E19.
5 *verb intrans.* Beat or strike *on* or *against* something with the sound of a slap. M19.

> 🕮 **1** A. SETON Her palm itched to slap the smug sallow face. R. DAHL He would slap me on the back and shout, 'We'll sell it by the million!' D. PROFUMO The men started shaking with laughter, slapping their knees. **b** V. NABOKOV You will . . slap down such rumormongers as contend that the book is pornographic. **2** J. G. FARRELL He soaked the garments and slapped them rhythmically against the . . slabs. C. MCCULLOUGH Fee slapped the contents of the butter churn onto the table. P. BARKER She got it out of the oven and slapped it down in front of him. *Golf Illustrated* PGA Tour men . . had £12 on-the-spot fines slapped on them. B. VINE An imposing Palladian façade slapped on to something . . older. **5** B. ENGLAND Little waves slapping softly against the side of the boat. J. DIDION The only sound was the film slapping against the projector.

Phrases: **slap a person's wrist** give a person a mild rebuke or reprimand. **slap on the back** congratulate.
Comb.: **slap-bass** *noun & adjective* (*a*) *noun* a style of playing double-bass or bass guitar by pulling and releasing the strings sharply against the finger-board, in jazz or popular music; (*b*) *attrib. adjective* of or pertaining to this style of playing; **slaphead** (*slang, derog.*) a bald or balding man; **slapjack** (*a*) *N. Amer.* a pancake cooked on a griddle (cf. FLAPJACK 1); (*b*) a card-game in which a player gains by being the first to slap a jack when played; **slap shot** ICE HOCKEY a shot made with a sharp slapping movement of the stick; **slap-tongue** *verb intrans.* produce a staccato effect in playing the saxophone by striking the tongue against the reed (chiefly as ***slap-tonguing*** *verbal noun*).
■ **slapper** *noun* (*a*) *dial.* a large object; a large strapping person; (*b*) a person who or thing which slaps something; (*c*) (*slang, derog.*) a promiscuous or vulgar woman: L18. **slapping** *verbal noun* the action of the verb; an instance of this: M17. **slapping** *adjective* (*a*) that slaps; (*b*) (of a pace etc.) rapid, rattling; (*c*) (chiefly *dial.*) unusually large or powerful; strapping: E19.

slap /slap/ *verb*[2] *trans. Scot.* Infl. **-pp-**. E16.
[from SLAP *noun*[1].]
Make gaps or openings in (a wall etc.).

slap /slap/ *verb*[3] *trans.* Now *dial.* Infl. **-pp-**. E17.
[Low German *slappen*, German *schlappen.*]
Lap *up*.

slap /slap/ *adverb.* Chiefly *colloq.* L17.
[Imit. Cf. Low German *slapp.*]
With the suddenness, effectiveness, or direct aim of a slap or smart blow; quickly, suddenly; directly, precisely; straight.

> 🕮 M. DICKENS He . . ran slap into a rozzer. R. H. MORRIESON The bottle was slap in the middle of the table.

Comb.: **slap-bang** *adverb, adjective, & noun* (*colloq.*) (*a*) *adverb* suddenly; violently; headlong; without due consideration; directly, precisely; (*b*) *adjective* characterized by carelessness or haste; ***slap-bang shop*** (*arch.*), a rough eating-house; (*c*) *noun* (*arch.*) a slap-bang shop. **slap-dab** *adverb* (*N. Amer. dial. & colloq.*) slap-bang.

slapdash /ˈslapdaʃ/ *adverb, noun, adjective, & verb.* L17.
[from SLAP *adverb* + DASH *adverb.*]
► **A** *adverb.* Hastily, suddenly; *esp.* hastily and without much care; haphazardly. L17.

> 🕮 CARLYLE Record of the tour, written slapdash after my return.

► **B** *noun.* **1** Roughcast. *arch.* L18.
2 Carelessness or lack of finish in style or workmanship; work done in this style. *arch.* E19.
► **C** *adjective.* Characterized by or done with haste and esp. lack of care; haphazard. L18.

> 🕮 A. S. DALE Characteristically slapdash scholarship . . made this book full of misquotations. D. ATHILL As an editor . . he was slapdash about detail. J. WEBSTER Lulu had cooked one of her slapdash but exotic stews.

► **D** *verb intrans.* Work, do, etc., in a slapdash manner. E19.

> 🕮 E. TAYLOR The children slap-dashed through the last of their homework.

■ **slapdashery** *noun* (*rare*) slapdash work; slapdash character: L19. **slapdashness** *noun* (*rare*) E20.

slap-happy /ˈslaphapi/ *adjective. colloq.* M20.
[from SLAP *noun*[2] + HAPPY *adjective.*]
1 Dazed; punch-drunk. M20.
2 Carefree; cheerfully casual; thoughtless. M20.
■ **slap-ˈhappily** *adverb* M20. **slap-ˈhappiness** *noun* M20.

slapstick /ˈslapstɪk/ *noun & adjective.* L19.
[from SLAP *verb*[1] + STICK *noun*[1].]
► **A** *noun.* **1** A device consisting of two flexible pieces of wood joined together at one end, designed to produce a loud slapping noise, used as a percussion instrument or in pantomime etc. to simulate the dealing of a severe blow. L19.
2 Boisterous knockabout comedy. E20.

> 🕮 **2** *Stage* Scores of jokes, visual gags and slapstick.

► **B** *adjective.* Designating, involved in, or reminiscent of boisterous knockabout comedy. E20.

> 🕮 R. L. WOLFF The . . tone of the book is highly satirical, with strong overtones of slapstick farce. G. ADAIR He walked like a slapstick clown, crazily flinging his knees out.

slap-up /ˈslapʌp/ *adjective. colloq.* E19.
[from SLAP *verb*[1] or *adverb* + UP *adverb*[2].]
Excellent; first-rate; *esp.* (of a meal) lavish, superb.

slash /slaʃ/ *noun*[1]. L16.
[from the verb. Cf. SLISH.]
1 A sweeping cutting stroke made with a knife, sword, whip, etc.; the sound made by this. L16. ▸**b** CRICKET. A violent attacking stroke played with a sharp swing of the bat. E20. ▸**c** A severe or drastic reduction. M20.
2 A long narrow cut or wound; a gash. L16.
3 A vertical or oblique slit made in a garment in order to show a contrasting lining, piece of fabric, etc. E17.
4 Debris resulting from the felling or destruction of trees; an open tract in a forest, *esp.* one strewn with such debris. *N. Amer.* E19.
5 TYPOGRAPHY. A character appearing as a line sloping to the right; an oblique, a solidus. M20.

> 🕮 **1** SIR W. SCOTT The slashes, stabs and pistol-balls . . were flying in various directions. E. SEGAL A voice like the slash of a stiletto. **c** *Guardian Weekly* A 50 per cent slash in the army's budget. **2** CONAN DOYLE Bleeding from a slash across the forehead.

Comb.: **slash fiction** [from the use of a slash to link names, orig. in *Kirk/Spock* or *K/S*, with ref. to characters in the US science-fiction series *Star Trek*], a genre of fiction, chiefly published in fanzines, in which any of various male pairings from the popular media is portrayed as having a homosexual relationship; **slash pocket**: set in a garment with a slit for the opening.

slash /slaʃ/ *noun*[2]. E17.
[Origin uncertain: perh. same word as prec.]
†**1** A drink. *rare.* E17–L18.
2 A large splash of liquid. *Scot.* M19.
3 An act of urinating. *slang.* M20.

slash /slaʃ/ *noun*[3]. *US*. **M17**.
[Origin uncertain: cf. **FLASH** *noun*[1].]
Swampy ground; a swamp.
Comb.: **slash-pine** a pine growing in a slash or low-lying coastal region, esp. *Pinus caribaea*, of Central America and the W. Indies; the wood of this tree.

slash /slaʃ/ *verb*. **LME**.
[Prob. imit. (cf. **FLASH** *verb*), or aphet. from Old French *esclachier* break, rel. to *esclater* (mod. *éclater*) (see **SLAT** *verb*[3]).]
1 *verb trans.* Cut or wound with a sweeping stroke of a knife, sword, etc.; make a long narrow cut or cuts in; cut *off* with such a stroke. **LME**. ▸**b** Clear (land) of vegetation; cut down (trees or undergrowth). Also foll. by *down*. Chiefly *N. Amer.* **E19**. ▸**c** Reduce (esp. a price) drastically. **E20**.
2 *verb intrans.* Deliver or aim a sweeping cutting stroke or strokes, esp. at random (freq. foll. by *at*); make gashes or wounds. **M16**. ▸**b** *CRICKET*. Play a violent attacking stroke. **E20**.
3 *verb trans.* **a** Cut or lash with a whip. **E17**. ▸**b** Crack (a whip). **M17**.
4 *verb trans.* Rebuke or criticize severely. **M17**.
5 *verb trans.* Cut vertical or oblique slits in (a garment) to show a contrasting lining etc.; insert a contrasting piece of fabric in; ornament *with* a contrasting colour or fabric in this way. Chiefly as **SLASHED** *adjective*. **L17**.

> 🕮 **1** A. J. TOYNBEE A man armed with a . . machete slashes a track . . through the undergrowth. P. THEROUX The thieves . . slashed open your suitcase. P. MAILLOUX Weiss . . killed himself by slashing his wrists. **c** *Daily Mirror* Labour held their seat in yesterday's . . by-election. But their majority was slashed. *Stage* The Tower Hamlets Council had decided to slash its grant to the arts. **2** M. TWAIN In the fights . . these lads hacked and slashed with the same tremendous spirit. M. SINCLAIR Slashing at nothing with her racquet. **4** G. S. HAIGHT Believing that it was Lewes who had slashed the book, Mrs. Phillipson attacks the 'Westminster Reviewer'. **5** J. BUCHAN A doublet of purple velvet slashed with yellow satin.

Comb.: **slash-and-burn** *adjective & noun* (*a*) *adjective* designating a system of cultivation in which vegetation is cut down, allowed to dry, and then burned off before crops are planted; (*b*) *noun* this system; **slash-burning** = *slash-and-burn* (b) above; **slash-hook** = **SLASHER** 2b.
■ **slashed** *adjective* (*a*) (esp. of a part of a garment) having slits to show a contrasting lining etc.; (*b*) *BOTANY* deeply cut; laciniate; (*c*) *CRICKET* played with or resulting from a slash: **M17**. **slashy** *adjective* (*rare*) of a slashing nature; sharp: **M19**.

slasher /ˈslaʃə/ *noun*. **M16**.
[from **SLASH** *verb* + **-ER**[1].]
1 A person who slashes; *colloq.* a fighter; a bully. **M16**.
2 A sword or similar weapon. **E19**. ▸**b** A billhook. **M19**. ▸**c** A form of circular saw with several blades, used to cut logs into predetermined lengths. **L19**.
3 A severe criticism. *rare*. **M19**.
4 A high-speed machine for sizing yarn. **M19**.
5 In full ***slasher film***, ***slasher movie***. A film depicting a series of violent murders or assaults by an attacker armed with a knife etc. **L20**.

slashing /ˈslaʃɪŋ/ *noun*. **L16**.
[from **SLASH** *verb* + **-ING**[1].]
1 The action of **SLASH** *verb*. **L16**.
2 = **SLASH** *noun*[1] 4. **M19**.
3 A contrasting insert in a garment. **M19**.
4 The sizing of yarn using a slasher. **L19**.

slashing /ˈslaʃɪŋ/ *adjective*. **L16**.
[from **SLASH** *verb* + **-ING**[2].]
1 That slashes (*lit.* & *fig.*); cutting; severely critical; incisively sarcastic. **L16**.
2 Esp. of a horse: spirited; dashing. **E19**.
3 Very large or fine; splendid. *colloq.* (now chiefly *Austral.*). **M19**.
■ **slashingly** *adverb* **M17**.

slat /slat/ *noun*[1]. **LME**.
[Aphet. from Old French *esclat* (mod. *éclat*) splinter, piece broken off, from *esclater*: see **SLAT** *verb*[3]. Cf. **SLATE** *noun*.]
1 (A) slate, esp. as used for roofing. Now *dial.* **LME**.
2 A slate used for writing on. *obsolete* exc. *dial.* **LME**.
3 A thin narrow strip of wood, plastic, metal, etc., esp. as fixed together in a series to form a fence or blind. **M18**. ▸**b** In *pl.* The ribs; the buttocks. *slang* (chiefly *US*). **L19**. ▸**c** The part of an aeroplane wing forward of a slot near the leading edge or able to be moved forward to create such a slot and so provide additional lift. Cf. **SLOT** *noun*[2] 2d. **M20**.
4 *BASKET-MAKING*. The framework of a basket. **M19**.

> 🕮 **3** V. WOOLF The sun coming through the slats of the blinds striped the white walls. S. PLATH The paper . . wedged . . between the slats of the park bench.

Comb.: **slat-back** *adjective & noun* (chiefly *US*) (a chair) having a back constructed of several horizontal bars; **slat fence** *US* a fence made of slats.

slat /slat/ *noun*[2]. **E17**.
[from **SLAT** *verb*[1].]
1 A slap, a sharp blow. Now *dial.* **E17**.
2 A sudden gust or blast *of* wind. Now *rare*. **M19**.

slat /slat/ *noun*[3]. **L19**.
[Perh. from Irish.]
A salmon after spawning, a kelt.

slat /slat/ *verb*[1]. Now chiefly *dial.* Infl. **-tt-**. **ME**.
[Origin unkn.]
1 *verb trans.* Cast, dash, or hurl violently; splash, spatter, (liquid etc.). **ME**.
2 *verb trans.* Strike, beat; knock *out*. **L16**.
3 *verb intrans.* Of rain etc.: splash, spatter; beat *against*. *dial.* **M19**.
4 *verb intrans.* Esp. of a sail: flap or slap violently. **M19**.

slat /slat/ *verb*[2] *trans.* Now *dial.* Infl. **-tt-**. **L15**.
[from **SLAT** *noun*[1].]
Cover with slates.

slat /slat/ *verb*[3] *intrans. & trans.* Long *dial.* Infl. **-tt-**. **E17**.
[Old French *esclater* (mod. *éclater*) split, splinter, shatter, from Proto-Romance. Cf. **SLASH** *verb*, **SLAT** *noun*[1].]
Split.

slatch /slatʃ/ *noun*. Now *rare*. **E17**.
[Var. of **SLACK** *noun*[3].]
1 A small seam or pocket of coal. *dial.* **E17**.
2 *NAUTICAL*. †**a** The slack of a rope or cable lying over a ship's side. Only in **E17**. ▸**b** A brief respite or interval; a short period or spell (*of* a particular kind of weather etc.). **E17**.

slate /sleɪt/ *noun & adjective*. Also (long *obsolete* exc. *Scot.* & *north.*) **scl-**, **skl-**. **ME**.
[Old French *esclate* fem. corresp. to masc. *esclat* **SLAT** *noun*[1].]
▶ **A** *noun*. **1** A fine-grained metamorphosed sedimentary rock, typically dark grey, blue, or green in colour, characterized by splitting readily into smooth parallel-sided flat plates, and used for making roofing-tiles etc. **ME**. ▸**b** Any of several other rocks that split readily into plates, some of which are also used for making roofing-tiles. Usu. with specifying word. **L17**. ▸**c** A bluish-grey colour like that of slate. **E19**.
2 A thin piece of slate; *spec.* a usu. rectangular piece used as a roofing-tile. **LME**. ▸**b** A similar roofing-tile of some other material. **L19**.
3 A flat piece of slate used for writing on, usu. framed in wood. **LME**. ▸**b** A record made concerning or against a person, esp. of debt or credit. **M19**. ▸**c** A list of nominees for election or appointment to an official, esp. political, post; the candidates so nominated; a group of candidates or (occas.) electors sharing a set of political views. Orig. & chiefly *N. Amer.* **M19**. ▸**d** *CINEMATOGRAPHY*. A board showing the number etc. of the shot which is held in front of the camera at the beginning and end of each spell of shooting so as to identify it subsequently; a single spell of shooting. **M20**.
4 [from **SLATE** *verb*[1].] A severe criticism, a slating. *colloq.* **L19**.
Phrases: ***clean slate***: see **CLEAN** *adjective*. **have a slate loose**, **have a slate off** *colloq.* be very foolish or slightly mad. **on the slate** on credit. **SKIDDAW SLATE**. **STONESFIELD SLATE**. **wipe the slate clean** forgive or cancel a record of past offences, debts, etc.; (allow to) make a fresh start.
Comb.: **slate-black**, **slate-blue** a shade of black or blue occurring in slate; **slate club** *Hist.* a cooperative society having accounts nominally kept on a slate; **slate colour** = sense 1c above; **slate-coloured** *adjective* of a slate colour; **slate-grey** *noun & adjective* (of) a shade of grey occurring in slate; **slate-pencil** a small rod of soft slate used for writing on slate; **slate-stone** (a single piece of) slate or stone resembling slate; **slate-writer** a practitioner of slate-writing; **slate-writing** in spiritualism, writing on a slate performed allegedly without physical contact between the medium and the writing instrument.
▶ **B** *attrib.* or as *adjective*. Made of, resembling, or having the colour of slate. **L16**.
■ **slateful** *noun* (*rare*) as much or as many as can be written on a slate **M19**.

slate /sleɪt/ *verb*[1]. **L15**.
[from the noun.]
1 *verb trans.* Cover or roof with slates. Freq. as ***slated*** *ppl adjective*. **L15**.
2 *verb trans.* Write down (a name etc.) on a slate, mark down or book (a person etc.) *for* or *to do* something; *spec.* propose or nominate (a candidate or candidates) for political etc. office. Also, plan, propose, schedule, (an event etc.). Chiefly *N. Amer.* **E19**.
3 *verb trans.* Beat or thrash severely; inflict heavy punishment on (an enemy). *slang*. **E19**.
4 *verb trans.* Reprimand, scold; criticize (esp. a book, author, etc.) severely, review unfavourably. *colloq.* **M19**.
5 *verb intrans. & trans.* *CINEMATOGRAPHY*. Identify (a shot) with the aid of a slate. **M20**.

> 🕮 **2** *Computerworld* The unit is slated for shipment in June. *Financial Weekly* Up to 60,000 . . workers are slated to lose their jobs. **4** P. ARROWSMITH The police were slated in the Press.

slate /sleɪt/ *verb*[2] *trans.* *Scot.* & *north.* **LME**.
[from Old Norse word corresp. to Old English *slǣtan*: see **SLEAT**.]
Set (a dog) *on*, *at*, or *against* a person etc.; hunt, bait, or drive (an animal etc.) with dogs.

slater /ˈsleɪtə/ *noun*. **LME**.
[from **SLATE** *noun* or *verb*[1] + **-ER**[1].]
1 A person engaged or employed in laying slates on a roof etc. **LME**.
2 A woodlouse. *Scot., Austral., & NZ*. **L17**.
2 *SEA-**slater***.

Slater determinant /ˈsleɪtə dɪˌtəːmɪnənt/ *noun phr.* **M20**.
[John Clarke *Slater* (1900–76), US physicist.]
PHYSICS. A determinant which expresses the total wave function of an atom and is totally anti-symmetric with respect to an interchange of electrons, the elements being single-electron wave functions.

slath /slaθ/ *noun*. **L19**.
[Origin unkn.]
= **SLAT** *noun*[1] 4.

slather /ˈslaðə/ *verb & noun*. Chiefly *dial.* & *N. Amer.* **E19**.
[Origin unkn. Cf. **SLATTER** *verb*[2].]
▶ **A** *verb*. **1** *verb intrans.* Slip, slide; move in a sliding or trailing manner. **E19**.
2 *verb trans.* **a** Use in large quantities, squander; spread or smear (a substance etc.) thickly. Also spill, scatter. **M19**. ▸**b** Spread or cover (a surface etc.) thickly *with* a substance etc. **M20**.
3 *verb trans.* Thrash, defeat thoroughly; castigate. *slang*. **E20**.

> 🕮 **2a** B. MOORE Watching the man greedily slather mustard on his sausages. **b** M. GORDON She scooped out . . hot wax and slathered their legs with it.

▶ **B** *noun*. **1** In *pl.* or (occas.) *sing.* A large amount, lots. *US colloq.* **M19**.
2 A spread or smeared thing; mud, a muddy state. *Scot. & north.* **L19**.
Phrases: **open slather** *Austral. & NZ colloq.* freedom to operate without interference, a free-for-all.

slating /ˈsleɪtɪŋ/ *noun*. **LME**.
[from **SLATE** *verb*[1] + **-ING**[1].]
1 The action of **SLATE** *verb*[1]. **LME**.
2 The slates covering a roof etc. **E19**.
3 **a** A severe punishment or beating. *slang*. **M19**. ▸**b** A severe reprimand; severe criticism, an unfavourable review. *colloq.* **L19**.
4 A kind of wash for blackboards; the action of covering a blackboard with such a wash. **L19**.

> 🕮 **3b** A. WEST She wrote a slating of my father's novel . . in which she took issue with his ideas about women.

slating /ˈsleɪtɪŋ/ *adjective*. **L19**.
[formed as prec. + **-ING**[2].]
Severely critical or condemnatory.

slatish /ˈsleɪtɪʃ/ *adjective*. **M19**.
[from **SLATE** *noun*.]
Somewhat resembling the colour of slate.

slatted /ˈslatɪd/ *adjective*. **L19**.
[from **SLAT** *noun*[1] + **-ED**[2].]
Consisting of or having slats.

> 🕮 M. FORSTER Watching the . . sun make patterns through the slatted . . blind.

slatter /ˈslatə/ *noun*. Now *dial.* **ME**.
[formed as prec. + **-ER**[1].]
1 = **SLATER** 1. **ME**.
†**2** = **SLATER** 2. Only in **M18**.

slatter /ˈslatə/ *verb*[1] *intrans.* Now *rare*. **M17**.
[Imit.]
Clatter.

slatter /ˈslatə/ *verb*[2] *trans.* Chiefly *dial.* **L17**.
[Prob. frequentative of **SLAT** *verb*[1]: see **-ER**[5]. Cf. **SLATHER** *verb & noun*.]
Spill, scatter, slop, (a substance etc.), esp. carelessly.
■ **slattering** *adjective* careless, slovenly **L17**.

slattern /ˈslat(ə)n/ *noun, adjective, & verb*. **M17**.
[Origin uncertain: rel. to prec.]
▶ **A** *noun*. An untidy and slovenly woman or girl. **M17**.

> 🕮 W. S. MAUGHAM She was a terrible slattern. Her house was always in a mess.

▶ **B** *adjective*. Slovenly, untidy, slatternly. **L17**.
▶ **C** *verb*. **1** *verb trans.* Fritter or throw *away* (time, opportunity, etc.) by carelessness or slovenliness. **M18**. ▸**b** Foll. by *over*: accomplish (work etc.) in a slovenly manner. *rare*. **E19**.
2 *verb intrans.* Act as a slattern. *rare*. **M19**.
■ **slatternish** *adjective* somewhat slatternly **M19**.

slatternly /ˈslatənli/ *adjective & adverb*. **L17**.
[from **SLATTERN** *noun* + **-LY**[1], **-LY**[2].]
▶ **A** *adjective*. Of the nature of, appropriate to, or characteristic of a slattern; slovenly, untidy. **L17**.
▶ **B** *adverb*. In a slatternly way. **M18**.
■ **slatternliness** *noun* **E19**.

slatterness /ˈslat(ə)nnɪs/ *noun*. Now *rare*. **M18**.
[from **SLATTERN** *adjective* + **-NESS**.]
Slatternliness.

slatting /ˈslatɪŋ/ *noun. rare.* M16.
[from SLAT *verb*² + -ING¹.]
= SLATING *noun* 1, 2.

†slatty *adjective.* M17–M18.
[from SLAT *noun*¹ + -Y¹.]
Slaty.

slaty /ˈsleɪti/ *adjective.* E16.
[from SLATE *noun* + -Y¹.]
Composed of slate; of the nature or characteristic of slate; resembling slate in colour, texture, flavour, etc.
■ **slatiness** *noun* (*rare*) L19.

slaughter /ˈslɔːtə/ *noun & verb.* ME.
[Old Norse *slátr* butcher's meat, rel. to SLAY *verb*¹.]
▶ **A** *noun.* **1** The killing of cattle, sheep, or other animals for food etc. ME.
2 The killing of a person, esp. in a brutal or ruthless manner; (a) murder, (a) homicide. ME.
3 The killing of many people etc. at once or continuously, as in war; massacre, carnage; an instance of this. ME. ▸**b** A crushing defeat in sport. Cf. MASSACRE *noun* 1b. *slang.* M20.

📖 **1** *Cook's Magazine* Two weeks before slaughter, the chicken is penned up and fed corn. *Daily Telegraph* Following their . . leaders like lambs to the slaughter. **2** SHAKES. *Cymb.* Against self-slaughter There is a prohibition. **3** R. BLACKMORE Vultures . . To the red fields of slaughter shall repair. D. JUDD The mass slaughter of the First World War. *transf.*: *Rand Daily Mail* The slaughter on our roads.

Comb.: **slaughterhouse** (*a*) a place or building for the slaughter of animals for food; a scene of carnage; (*b*) *slang* a cheap brothel; **slaughterman** (*a*) a person engaged or employed in the slaughter of animals; a butcher; (*b*) a murderer, an executioner.
▶ **B** *verb trans.* **1** Kill (cattle, sheep, or other animals) for food etc. M16.
2 Kill or murder (a person), esp. brutally or ruthlessly. L16.
3 Kill large numbers of (people etc.) at once or continuously, massacre. L16. ▸**b** Defeat heavily or completely. Also, criticize heavily, demolish by argument. *slang.* E20.

📖 **1** J. CARY The beasts had been slaughtered for meat. **2** W. S. CHURCHILL Catholic victims had been slaughtered on false . . evidence. **3** *Economist* The . . guerrillas . . slaughtered 60 unarmed Iraqi soldiers. **b** C. E. MERRIAM He was . . slaughtered . . in the primaries of 1915.

■ **slaughterable** *adjective* able or fit to be slaughtered E20. **slaughterdom** *noun* (*rare*) slaughter, massacre; slaughtered condition: L16. **slaughterer** *noun* a person who slaughters a thing or person, *esp.* an animal; a butcher: L16. **slaughtering** *noun* (*a*) the action of the verb; (*b*) *rare* an instance of this: L16. **slaughtering** *adjective* (*a*) that slaughters; (*b*) *rare* (of a price) lower than is profitable: L16. **slaughteringly** *adverb* M19.

slaughterous /ˈslɔːt(ə)rəs/ *adjective.* L16.
[formed as prec. + -OUS.]
Murderous, destructive.
■ **slaughterously** *adverb* M19.

slaughtery /ˈslɔːt(ə)ri/ *noun.* Now *rare.* E17.
[formed as prec. after *butchery*.]
1 Slaughter. E17.
2 A slaughterhouse. M17.

slaunchways /ˈslɔːn(t)ʃweɪz/ *adverb & adjective. US dial. & colloq.* E20.
[Alt. of SLANTWAYS.]
Sideways, slanting(ly), oblique(ly); out of true.

slaunchwise /ˈslɔːn(t)ʃwʌɪz/ *adverb & adjective. US dial. & colloq.* E20.
[Alt. of SLANTWISE.]
= prec.

Slav /slɑːv/ *noun & adjective.* Also **†Sclav**, **†Slave**. LME.
[In earliest use from medieval Latin *Sclavus* corresp. to medieval Greek *Sklabos*; later after medieval Latin *Slavus*, French *Slave*, German *Slave*, *Slawe*. Cf. SLAVE *noun*¹ & *adjective*¹.]
▶ **A** *noun.* **1** A member of a large group of peoples inhabiting central and eastern Europe and speaking Slavonic languages. LME.
2 = SLAVONIC *noun.* E20.
▶ **B** *adjective.* Of, pertaining to, or characteristic of the Slavs; Slavic, Slavonic. L19.
■ **Slavdom** *noun* Slavonic people generally, Slavs collectively L19.

slava /ˈslɑːvə/ *noun.* E20.
[Serbo-Croat, lit. 'honour, renown'.]
Among Orthodox Serbs, a festival of a family saint.

slave /sleɪv/ *noun*¹ & *adjective*¹. ME.
[Aphet. from Old & mod. French *esclave* use as noun of fem. of *esclaf* = medieval Latin *sclavus*, *sclava* captive, identical with the ethnic name *Sclavus* SLAV, the Slavonic peoples having been reduced to a servile state by conquest during the 9th cent.]
▶ **A** *noun.* **I 1** A person who is the property of another or others and is bound to absolute obedience, a human chattel; a servant, worker, or subject completely without freedom and rights. ME. ▸**b** A wretch, a knave. *arch.* M16.
2 a A person submitting in a servile way to the authority or will of another or others; a submissive or devoted servant. E16. ▸**b** A person completely under the domination *of* or subject *to* a specified influence. M16. ▸**c** A person working very hard, esp. without appropriate reward or appreciation; a drudge. L18.
3 ENTOMOLOGY. An ant captured by, and made to work for, ants of another species. E19.
4 a NAUTICAL. = *slave jib* below. M20. ▸**b** A slave device (see sense B.3 below). Opp. ***master***. M20.

📖 **1** P. DALLY The Barretts had a reputation for treating their slaves better than most. R. MALAN A rich man, owner of a score of slaves, twice that many horses. ***galley-slave***, ***wage-slave***, etc. **Slave of the Lamp** [from the story of Aladdin in the *Arabian Nights' Entertainments*] a performer of swift miracles; a person under an inescapable obligation. ***white slave***: see WHITE *adjective*. **2a** R. GILPIN Mark Anthony . . became a slave to Cleopatra and . . dallied himself into his ruin. **b** A. HELPS The serf to custom points his finger at the slave to fashion. J. K. JEROME We are but the . . sorriest slaves of our stomach. K. ATKINSON Auntie Babs is also a slave to housework.

▶ **II 5** (**S-**.) Pl. same, **-s**. [translating Cree *awahkān*.] A member of a group of Athapaskan peoples of northern Alberta; the language of these peoples. E19.
▶ **B** *attrib.* or as *adjective.* **I 1** Of or pertaining to a slave or slaves; characteristic or of the nature of a slave; servile. L16.
2 Designating a subsidiary device; *esp.* one which is controlled by, or which follows accurately the movements of, another device. Opp. ***master***. E20.

📖 **1** L. NAMIER Slave troubles were endemic to the West Indies. *Country Living* He dreams of soaking like some Roman Emperor with slave girls to fold his toga.

▶ **II 3** (**S-**.) Of or pertaining to the Slave or their language. L18.
Comb. & special collocations: **slave ant** = sense A.4 above; **slave bangle** (orig. *US*) orig., a slave's identity bracelet worn on the wrist or ankle; now, a woman's bangle of metal, glass, bone, etc., worn usu. above the elbow; **slave-born** *adjective* born in slavery, born of slave parents; **slave bracelet** (orig. *US*) = ***slave bangle*** above; **Slave Coast** *Hist.* a part of the west coast of Africa from which slaves were exported; **slave-drive** *verb* (*a*) *verb intrans.* exploit slave labour; (*b*) *verb trans. & intrans.* demand excessively hard work (from); **slave-driver** (orig. *US*) an overseer of slaves at work; *transf.* a person who works others very hard; **slave-fork** *Hist.* a forked piece of wood etc. secured around a slave's neck to prevent escape; **slave jib** NAUTICAL a working jib, almost permanently set; **slave labour** forced labour, work under conditions of slavery; labour provided by slaves; **slave-maker** ENTOMOLOGY any of various ants that use ants of a different species as slaves, *esp.* the European *Formica sanguinea*; **slave market** (*a*) a market for the buying and selling of slaves; (*b*) *N. Amer. slang* an employment exchange; **slave ship** *Hist.* a ship transporting slaves, esp. from Africa; **Slave State** *Hist.* any of the Southern States of the US, in which slavery was legal before the Civil War; **slave-trade** *Hist.* the procuring, transportation, and sale of humans, esp. black Africans, as slaves; **slave-trader** *Hist.* a person engaged in the slave-trade; **slave worker** a forced labourer; *spec.* (in the 1939–45 war) a person, esp. a foreigner deported to Germany, made to labour by the German Nazi regime.
■ **slavedom** *noun* the condition of a slave, slaves collectively; slavery: M16. **slaveless** *adjective* M19.

†Slave *noun*² & *adjective*² var. of SLAV.

slave /sleɪv/ *verb.* M16.
[from SLAVE *noun*¹.]
1 *verb trans.* **a** Reduce to the condition of a slave, enslave. (Foll. by *to* a person, nation, etc.) Now *rare.* M16. ▸**b** Subject (a device) to control or regulation by another device. Foll. by *to* the controlling device. M20.
2 *verb trans.* Treat as a slave, employ in hard or servile labour. L17.
3 a *verb intrans.* Toil or work very hard. Freq. foll. by *at*, *away*, *over*. E18. ▸**b** *verb trans.* Foll. by *out*, *away*: wear out or consume by severe toil. E19.
4 *Hist.* **a** *verb trans.* Load (a ship) with slaves. *rare.* E18. ▸**b** *verb intrans.* Traffic in slaves. *rare.* E18.

📖 **3a** B. HOLIDAY Mom . . slaving away as somebody's maid. G. DALY Spending half a year slaving over his mural. **b** E. SEGAL I slave my guts out . . to put bread in their mouths.

slaveocracy *noun* var. of SLAVOCRACY.

slaver /ˈslavə, ˈsleɪvə/ *noun*¹. ME.
[Rel. to SLAVER *verb*.]
1 Saliva running from the mouth, now esp. of an animal. ME.
2 *fig.* Drivel, nonsense. Also, excessive flattery. E19.

slaver /ˈsleɪvə/ *noun*². Chiefly *Hist.* E19.
[from SLAVE *noun*¹ + -ER¹.]
1 A ship used in the slave-trade. E19.
2 A person dealing in or owning slaves. M19.

slaver /ˈslavə, ˈsleɪvə/ *verb.* ME.
[Ult. imit., prob. immed. from Low Dutch: see -ER⁵. Cf. SLABBER *verb*, SLOBBER *verb*.]
1 *verb intrans.* Now esp. of an animal: let saliva run from the mouth, slobber, dribble. ME. ▸**b** *fig.* Talk nonsense, drivel; indulge in sycophantic flattery; show excessive desire or eagerness. Freq. foll. by *over*, *for*, *to do*. M18.
2 *verb intrans.* Run or trickle as or like slaver. L16.
3 *verb trans.* Wet with saliva, slobber over. L16. ▸**b** *fig.* Flatter sycophantically; show excessive desire for. L18.
4 *verb trans.* Utter in a slavering fashion. Also foll. by *out*. L16.

📖 **1** A. CARTER A . . black dog . . felled me to the ground and slavered at my throat. **b** H. CAINE His uncle . . had snubbed and then slavered over him. P. FUSSELL He's middle-class and slavering to be upper.

■ **slaverer** *noun* E17. **slavering** *noun* (*a*) the action of the verb; (*b*) (in *pl.*) saliva; *fig.* nonsense: ME. **slavering** *adjective* that slavers; *spec.* very eager or lustful: L16. **slaveringly** *adverb* M18.

slavery /ˈsleɪv(ə)ri/ *noun.* M16.
[from SLAVE *noun*¹ + -ERY.]
1 Severe toil, exhausting labour, drudgery. M16.
2 The condition or fact of being a slave, servitude; onerous subjugation; (now *rare*) an instance of this. L16. ▸**b** Subjection to or domination by a specified influence. (Foll. by *to*.) L16.
3 The practice or institution of keeping slaves, the existence of slaves as a class. E18.

📖 **1** *Daily News* Such people . . ought never to keep servants, but do their own slavery. **2** L. HELLMAN An old, very black lady who had been born into slavery. W. T. WATTS-DUNTON The famous elegy . . furnishes a striking proof of the poet's slavery to Augustanism. **3** M. LOWRY A country of slavery, where human beings were sold like cattle. *Interview* China abolished slavery on March 10, 1910. ***white slavery***: see WHITE *adjective*.

slavery /ˈslav(ə)ri, ˈsleɪv(ə)ri/ *adjective.* LME.
[from SLAVER *noun*¹ + -Y¹.]
Resembling or covered with slaver; characterized by slaver, given to slavering.

slavey /ˈsleɪvi/ *noun. colloq.* E19.
[from SLAVE *noun*¹ + -Y⁶.]
1 A male servant or attendant. E19.
2 A maidservant, *esp.* a hard-worked one. E19.

Slavian /ˈslɑːvɪən/ *adjective. rare.* M19.
[from SLAV *noun* + -IAN.]
= SLAVONIC *adjective*.

Slavic /ˈslɑːvɪk/ *adjective & noun.* Also **†Scl-**. E19.
[formed as prec. + -IC.]
= SLAVONIC.
■ **Slavicist** /-sɪst/ *noun* = SLAVIST *noun*² M20. **Slavicize** /-sʌɪz/ *verb trans.* make Slavic L19.

Slavification /slɑːvɪfɪˈkeɪʃ(ə)n/ *noun. rare.* L19.
[from SLAV + -I- + -FICATION.]
The action or process of making something Slavonic.

Slavise *verb* var. of SLAVIZE.

slavish /ˈsleɪvɪʃ/ *adjective*¹. M16.
[from SLAVE *noun*¹ + -ISH¹.]
1 Of, pertaining to, or characteristic of a slave; appropriate to or resembling a slave; servile, submissive. M16. ▸**b** Base, ignoble. L16. ▸**c** Involving hard toil, laborious. E19.
2 Of, pertaining to, or characteristic of slavery. L16.
3 Minutely imitative, showing no attempt at originality or development. M18.

📖 **1** W. LITHGOW Twelve thousand Christians delivered from their slavish bondage. SARA MAITLAND The slavish devotion that Phoebe lavished on the child. **3** H. P. BROUGHAM There was no slavish adherence to the old law. P. BARRY Slavish copyists of the English dockyard system.

■ **slavishly** *adverb* M16. **slavishness** *noun* E17.

Slavish /ˈslɑːvɪʃ/ *adjective*² & *noun.* M19.
[from SLAV *noun* + -ISH¹.]
= SLAVONIC.

Slavism /ˈslɑːvɪz(ə)m/ *noun.* L19.
[formed as prec. + -ISM.]
Slavonic qualities or character.

slavist /ˈsleɪvɪst/ *noun*¹. *rare.* M19.
[from SLAVE *noun*¹ + -IST.]
An advocate or supporter of slavery; *spec.* (*Hist.*) a member of the pro-slavery party in the US.
■ Also **slavite** *noun* (*US*) M19.

Slavist /ˈslɑːvɪst/ *noun*². *rare.* M19.
[from SLAV *noun* + -IST.]
An expert in or student of Slavonic languages and literature, a Slavonic scholar.

Slavistic /sləˈvɪstɪk/ *noun. rare.* L19.
[formed as prec. + -ISTIC.]
Slavonic research. In *pl.*, Slav linguistic studies.

Slavize /ˈslɑːvʌɪz/ *verb trans. rare.* Also **-ise**. L19.
[from SLAV *noun* + -IZE.]
Make Slavonic, Slavicize.

Slavo- /ˈslɑːvəʊ/ *combining form.*
[from SLAV + -O-.]
Forming adjective & noun combs., with the meaning 'Slav (and)' as ***Slavo-Germanic***, ***Slavophobic***, etc.
■ **Slavophil(e)** *noun & adjective* (a person who is) friendly towards Slavs or fond of things Slavonic L19. **Slavoˈphilism** *noun* admiration or support for Slavs or things Slavonic L19.

slavocracy /sleɪˈvɒkrəsi/ *noun.* Now *rare.* Also **slaveocracy.** M19.
[from SLAVE *noun*[1]: see -CRACY.]
The domination of slave-owners; slave-owners collectively as a dominant or powerful class, esp. in the US before the Civil War.
■ **ˈslavocrat** *noun* a member of the slavocracy M19.

Slavon /ˈslɑːvɒn/ *noun & adjective.* Now *rare* or *obsolete.* Also †**Scl-.** M16.
[French *Esclavon* = Italian *Schiavone* from medieval Latin *S(c)lavonius*, formed as next.]
▶ **A** *noun.* **1** A Slav. M16.
2 = SLAVONIC *noun.* Long *rare.* M17.
▶ **B** *adjective.* Slavonic. M16.

Slavonian /sləˈvəʊnɪən/ *noun & adjective.* Also †**Scl-.** M16.
[from medieval Latin *S(c)lavonia* the country of the Slavs, from *S(c)lavus* SLAV: see -IAN.]
▶ **A** *noun.* **1** = SLAVONIC *noun.* M16.
2 A person of Slavonic origin, a Slav. L16.
▶ **B** *adjective.* **1** = SLAVONIC *adjective.* L16.
2 Of or pertaining to Slavonic countries. E19.
2 Slavonian grebe a holarctic grebe, *Podiceps auritus*, which in the breeding plumage has golden ear-tufts.
■ **Slavonianize** *verb trans.* (*rare*) Slavize L19.

Slavonic /sləˈvɒnɪk/ *adjective & noun.* Also †**Scl-.** E17.
[medieval Latin *S(c)lavonicus*, formed as prec.: see -IC.]
▶ **A** *adjective.* Of, pertaining to, or designating the branch of Indo-European languages including Russian, Polish, and Czech and spoken through much of central and eastern Europe; pertaining to, characteristic of, or designating the Slavs; Slavic, Slavonian. E17.
▶ **B** *noun.* The Slavonic languages collectively; a Slavonic language. M17.
Balto-Slavonic, ***East Slavonic***, ***South Slavonic***, etc. **Church Slavonic**, **Old Church Slavonic** the earliest written Slavonic language, into which the Bible was translated in the 9th cent. and which survives as a liturgical language in certain Orthodox Churches.
■ **Slavonicize** *verb trans.* (*rare*) Slavize L19.

Slavonise *verb* var. of SLAVONIZE.

Slavonism /ˈslɑːv(ə)nɪz(ə)m/ *noun. rare.* M19.
[from SLAVON(IC + -ISM.]
= SLAVISM.

Slavonize /ˈslɑːv(ə)nʌɪz/ *verb trans.* Also †**Scl-**; **-ise.** M19.
[from SLAVON(IC + -IZE.]
Make Slavonic, Slavize.
■ **Slavoniˈzation** *noun* L19.

slaw /slɔː/ *noun. N. Amer.* L18.
[Dutch *sla* syncopated form of *salade* SALAD.]
Coleslaw.

slawk /slɔːk/ *noun. Scot. & north.* LME.
[Prob. from Irish *slabhac*, *sleabhac*: cf. SLAKE *noun*[2], SLOKE *noun*[1].]
1 Any of several edible seaweeds, including sea lettuce, *Ulva lactuca*, and laver, *Porphyra umbicalis.* LME.
2 Slimy alga in streams etc. E19.

slay *noun* var. of SLEY *noun.*

slay /sleɪ/ *verb*[1]. Pa. t. **slew** /sluː/, (*non-standard*) **slayed**; pa. pple **slain** /sleɪn/.
[Old English *slēan* = Old Frisian *slā*, Old Saxon, Old High German *slahan* (Dutch *slaan*, German *schlagen*), Old Norse *slá*, Gothic *slahan*, from Germanic. Cf. SLAUGHTER.]
†**1 a** *verb trans.* Strike, beat. OE–ME. ▸**b** *verb intrans.* Strike a blow or blows (freq. foll. by *on*); knock. OE–LME. ▸**c** *verb trans.* Strike (a spark, fire) from flint etc. OE–E16. ▸**d** *verb trans.* Throw, cast; bring *down* heavily. OE–LME.
2 *verb trans.* Kill, esp. in a brutal or violent manner; murder, slaughter. Now *literary*, *arch.*, or *joc.* exc. *N. Amer.* OE. ▸**b** Kill in an accident etc. *obsolete* exc. *dial.* OE. ▸**c** Slaughter (an animal) for food etc. *arch.* exc. *N. Amer.* OE. ▸†**d** Destroy (an animal) as vermin. ME–L16. ▸†**e** Put to death as a criminal, execute. ME–M17.
3 *verb intrans.* Cause (esp. violent) death, commit murder. Now *literary* or *arch.* exc. *N. Amer.* OE.
†**4** *verb trans.* THEOLOGY. Bring to spiritual death; destroy (the soul) by sinning. ME–E17.
5 *verb trans.* Destroy, extinguish, put an end to, (esp. something bad). *arch.* ME.
6 a *verb trans.* Blight (vegetation). Long *obsolete* exc. *Scot.* ME–L16. ▸**b** *verb intrans.* Of grain: become affected by smut, blight, etc. Now *dial.* M17.
†**7** *verb trans.* Overcome with affliction or distress. LME–M16.
8 *verb trans.* Overcome with delight or love; impress or amuse greatly, convulse with laughter. *colloq.* L16.

🕮 **2** A. S. NEILL Henceforward . . the wasp that enters this room is to be slain. W. S. CHURCHILL They thirsted to . . slay their foes. *Billings (Montana) Gazette* She was found slain with a hatchet. SARA MAITLAND George, the Christian saint who slew the dragon. **3** P. A. ROLLINS Inhuman brutes who would slay for personal gain. **5** *Pall Mall Gazette* In the very act of slaying the Bill. **8** R. CHANDLER A hoodlum with sentiment . . . That slays me. D. FRANCIS 'Oh God, Dolly, you slay me,' said Chico, laughing warmly. *Guardian Weekly* 'Who could meet Margaret . . without being completely slain by her personality and intellectual brilliance?'

■ **slayable** *adjective* (*literary* or *arch.*, *rare*) able to be (justly) slain L19. **slayer** *noun* (chiefly *arch.* or *joc.* exc. *N. Amer.*) LME. **slaying** *noun* (chiefly *arch.* or *joc.* exc. *N. Amer.*) the action of the verb; an instance of this; (a) killing, (a) murder, (a) homicide: LME.

slay *verb*[2] var. of SLEY *verb.*

SLBM *abbreviation.*
Submarine-launched ballistic missile.

SLCM *abbreviation.*
Submarine-launched cruise missile.

SLD *abbreviation.*
Hist. Social and Liberal Democrats.

SLE *abbreviation.*
MEDICINE. Systemic lupus erythematosus.

slead /sliːd/ *noun.* Now *dial.* LME.
[Middle Dutch or Middle Low German *slēde* (Dutch *slede*, *slee*) = Old Norse *sleði* (Norwegian *slede*, Danish *slæde*), Old High German *slito*, *slita* (Middle High German *slite*), from weak grade of base of SLIDE *verb.* Cf. SLADE *noun*[2].]
= SLED *noun.*

sleak /sliːk/ *verb.* Now *dial. rare.* LME.
[Var. of SLECK.]
1 *verb trans.* Quench, extinguish, assuage. LME.
2 *verb trans.* Slake (lime). LME.

slean *noun* var. of SLANE.

sleat /sliːt/ *verb trans. obsolete* exc. *north.*
[Old English *slǣtan*, from stem of *slītan* SLITE *verb.*]
†**1** Bait (an animal) with dogs. OE–ME.
2 Incite, set on, (a dog etc.). ME.

sleave /sliːv/ *noun.* L16.
[from the verb.]
1 A slender filament of silk obtained by separating a thicker thread; silk in the form of such filaments, floss-silk. *obsolete* exc. (*fig.*) in echoes of Shakes. L16.
2 A tangle; a tangled string. *dial.* L19.

🕮 **1** SHAKES. *Macb.* Sleep that knits up the ravell'd sleave of care.

sleave /sliːv/ *verb trans.* Now *dial.* L16.
[Rel. to Old English causative verb (evidenced in *tōslǣfan*) from stem rel. to SLIVE *verb*[1].]
1 Divide (silk) by separation into filaments. L16.
2 Cleave, split, tear apart. *dial.* E19.
Comb.: †**sleave-silk** silk thread that can be separated into smaller filaments for use in embroidery etc.

sleaze /sliːz/ *noun. slang.* M20.
[Back-form. from SLEAZY.]
1 Squalid or sleazy material or conditions. M20.
2 A sleazy person; *spec.* a slut. L20.

🕮 **1** *Sunday Express* Soho, . . known as London's square mile of sleaze. **2** *Time* Red nail polish—I look like a sleaze.

Comb.: **sleazebag**, **sleazeball** *slang* (orig. *US*) a sordid, despicable person, *esp.* one considered morally reprehensible.

sleaze /sliːz/ *verb intrans.* Also **sleeze.** L18.
[Prob. formed as prec.]
1 Of loosely or badly woven cloth: separate, come apart. *dial.* (now *rare*). L18.
2 Move in a sleazy fashion. *slang.* M20.

sleazo /ˈsliːzəʊ/ *adjective & noun. US slang.* Pl. of noun **-os.** L20.
[from SLEAZE *noun* or SLEAZY + -O.]
(Something) sleazy, esp. pornographic.

sleazoid /ˈsliːzɔɪd/ *adjective & noun. slang* (chiefly *US*). L20.
[from SLEAZ(E *noun* + -OID.]
(A person who is) sleazy, sordid, or despicable.

🕮 *Premiere* Ridley Scott's bleak vision of the future as a giant, sleazoid Times Square . . is the best dystopia yet. *Washington Post* How refreshing—a martial arts movie that isn't about murderous sleazoids . . or giant nuclear-powered turtles.

sleazy /ˈsliːzi/ *adjective.* Also **sleezy.** M17.
[Origin unkn.]
1 Rough with projecting fibres. *rare.* M17.
2 (Of a fabric) thin or flimsy in texture; *fig.* slight, unsubstantial. M17.
3 Dilapidated, slatternly, squalid; disreputable in character; cheap and inferior. *colloq.* M20.

🕮 **3** *Listener* A gigolo in a sleazy night club. B. W. ALDISS Some sleezy and probably malevolent god.

■ **sleazily** *adverb* M20. **sleaziness** *noun* E18.

sleck /slɛk/ *verb trans.* Now *dial.* ME.
[North. form repr. Old English *sleccan*, from *slæc* SLACK *adjective.*]
1 Extinguish (a fire); assuage (thirst etc.). ME.
2 Cool by means of water etc.; slake (lime). LME.
■ Also **slecken** *verb trans.* (now *dial.*) ME.

sled /slɛd/ *noun.* Now chiefly *dial.* & *N. Amer.* ME.
[Middle Low German *sledde* corresp. to Middle High German *slitte* (German *Schlitten*) and rel. to Middle Low German, Middle Dutch *slēde*, Dutch *slede*, *slee* (see SLEIGH *noun*[1]), Old High German *slito*, Old Norse *sleði*, from base also of SLIDE *verb*: see SLEDGE *noun*[2]. Cf. SLADE *noun*[2].]
1 = SLEDGE *noun*[2] 1. ME. ▸**b** Any of various devices made to be towed along the seabed. M20.
2 More fully ***rocket sled***. A rocket-propelled vehicle running on rails, used to subject things to controlled high acceleration and deceleration. M20.

sled /slɛd/ *verb.* Chiefly *N. Amer.* Infl. **-dd-.** E18.
[from the noun.]
1 *verb trans.* Convey on a sled or sleds. E18.
2 *verb intrans.* Travel in a sledge. E18.
■ **sledder** *noun* a person who or horse which conveys things on a sled M17. **sledding** *verbal noun* (*a*) conveyance by sled; (*b*) *fig.* (easy, hard, etc.) progress in any sphere of action: LME.

sledded /ˈslɛdɪd/ *adjective. rare.* E17.
[from SLED *noun* + -ED[2].]
Mounted on or made like a sled.

sledge /slɛdʒ/ *noun*[1].
[Old English *sleċġ* = Middle & mod. Dutch *slegge*, Old Norse *sleggja*, from Germanic base meaning 'to strike': cf. SLAY *verb*[1].]
A large heavy hammer usually wielded with both hands; *esp.* a sledgehammer.

sledge /slɛdʒ/ *noun*[2]. L16.
[Middle Dutch *sleedse* (Dutch dial. *sleeds*) rel. to *slēde* SLED *noun.*]
1 A low vehicle mounted on runners for transporting heavy loads, *esp.* one (freq. drawn by horses or dogs) for conveying passengers or loads over snow or ice. Also, a toboggan. Cf. SLED *noun*, SLEIGH *noun*[1]. L16.
2 In rope-making: a heavy travelling structure to which the rope-yarns are attached at one end. L18.
1 *old sledge*: see OLD *adjective.*
Comb.: **sledge-meter** a device towed behind a sledge to measure the distance travelled.

sledge /slɛdʒ/ *verb*[1]. M17.
[from SLEDGE *noun*[1].]
1 *verb intrans.* Use a sledgehammer. *rare.* M17.
2 *verb trans.* Break or drive in (a thing) with a sledgehammer. E19.
3 *verb trans. & intrans.* SPORT (esp. CRICKET). Heap insults on (an opposing player) with the object of breaking his or her concentration. Chiefly as ***sledging*** *verbal noun. slang* (orig. *Austral.*). L20.

sledge /slɛdʒ/ *verb*[2]. E18.
[from SLEDGE *noun*[2].]
1 *verb intrans. & trans.* (with *it*). Travel on a sledge. E18.
2 *verb trans.* Carry on a sledge. M19.

sledgehammer /ˈslɛdʒhamə/ *noun, adjective, & verb.* L15.
[from SLEDGE *noun*[1] + HAMMER *noun.*]
▶ **A** *noun.* A large heavy hammer used for breaking rocks, forging iron, etc. L15.
take a sledgehammer to crack a nut, **use a sledgehammer to crack a nut** use disproportionately drastic measures to deal with a simple problem.
▶ **B** *adjective.* Resembling a sledgehammer; (of a blow) heavy and powerful; (of wit etc.) ponderous, heavy-handed. M19.

🕮 *New Yorker* Broadway comedy, with its . . sledgehammer laugh lines.

▶ **C** *verb trans.* Strike or work at (as) with a sledgehammer. M19.

sledger /ˈslɛdʒə/ *noun.* M17.
[from SLEDGE *noun*[2] + -ER[1].]
A person who drives or draws a sledge.

sleech /sliːtʃ/ *noun. dial.* L16.
[App. a later form of SLITCH.]
Mud deposited by the sea or a river; soil composed of this.
■ **sleechy** *adjective* slimy, muddy L18.

sleek /sliːk/ *adjective & adverb.* L16.
[Later var. of SLICK *adjective & adverb.*]
▶ **A** *adjective.* **1** (Of an animal etc.) having smooth glossy hair or fur, esp. as a sign of good condition or careful attention; (of hair etc.) in this condition. L16.
2 Of a surface or object: perfectly smooth or polished. L16. ▸**b** Of the sea or sky: unruffled, tranquil. *rare.* E17.
3 Ingratiating, suave, plausible. L16.
4 Of a person: smooth-skinned, esp. through being in good condition; having the appearance of being well-fed and comfortable. M17.

🕮 **2** M. KEANE Lal's sleek expensive car. **4** J. TROLLOPE He was wearing a dinner jacket and looked very sleek.

▶ **B** *adverb.* In a smooth or sleek manner. E17.
■ **sleeken** *verb trans.* make smooth and glossy E17. **sleekly** *adverb* M18. **sleekness** *noun* E17.

sleek /sliːk/ *verb trans.* LME.
[Later var. of SLICK *verb*.]
1 Make sleek or smooth by rubbing or polishing. LME. ▸**b** Reduce (water etc.) to a smooth unruffled appearance. E16.
2 a Make (the skin, hair, etc.) smooth and glossy. E16. ▸**b** Draw (a comb) through hair with a smoothing effect. M20.
3 *fig.* Make sleek, polished, or comfortable; free from agitation, disturbance, etc. E17. ▸**b** Make (one's appearance or speech) friendly or flattering. Cf. SLEEKED (a) below. E17.

📖 **3** SHAKES. *Macb.* Sleek o'er your rugged looks. **b** MILTON The perswasive Rhetoric That sleek't his tongue.

■ **sleeked**, (*Scot.*) **sleekit** *adjective* (**a**) *Scot.* flattering, plausible; sly, cunning; (**b**) having a glossy skin, surface, etc.: LME. **sleeker** *noun* a person who sleeks anything; an implement used for sleeking leather, cloth, etc.: E17.

sleekstone /ˈsliːkstəʊn/ *noun. obsolete* exc. *dial.* LME.
[from SLEEK *verb* + STONE *noun*: cf. SLICKSTONE.]
A smooth stone used for smoothing and polishing things.

sleeky /ˈsliːki/ *adjective.* L16.
[from SLEEK *adjective* + -Y¹.]
1 = SLEEKED (a). L16.
2 Sleek, glossy. E18.

sleep /sliːp/ *noun.*
[Old English *slēp*, *slǣp* = Old Frisian *slēp*, Old Saxon *slāp* (Dutch *slaap*), Old High German *slāf* (German *Schlaf*), Gothic *slēps*, from Germanic noun corresp. to the verb forming the source of Old English *slǣpan*, Old Saxon *slāpan*, etc.: see the verb.]
1 The naturally recurring (esp. nightly) condition of repose and inactivity assumed by people and most higher animals, in which consciousness, response to external stimuli, and voluntary muscular action are largely suspended. Also, the inert condition of a hibernating animal. OE. ▸**b** The effects or signs of sleep; *spec.* a gummy secretion in the corners of the eyes after sleep. Freq. in ***rub the sleep out of one's eyes*** & similar phrs. M19.
2 a Usu. with specifying word or phr.: the repose of death. Freq. in ***the last sleep***. OE. ▸**b** A state of inactivity or sluggishness. OE. ▸**c** BOTANY. A condition assumed by many plants, esp. at night, marked by the closing of petals or folding of leaves. M18. ▸**d** Complete absence of noise or bustle; silence. E19.
3 a A period or spell of sleep. ME. ▸**b** Among N. American Indians, in measuring distances: the interval of time between one night's rest and the next, a day. L17. ▸**c** A (short) prison term. *slang* (orig. *US*). L19.

📖 **1** I. MURDOCH You look tired, are you getting enough sleep? **2a** A. MASON The dead were raised from their sleep. **b** *American Poetry Review* Poets . . suffering through the sleep of the critical audience. **d** WORDSWORTH The sleep that is among the lonely hills. **3a** P. ANGADI After lunch Sam fell into a deep sleep.

Phrases: ***a wink of sleep***: see WINK *noun*¹. BEAUTY ***sleep***. ***get off to sleep***: see OFF *adverb*. **go to sleep** fall asleep; (of a limb) become numb as a result of prolonged pressure. **in one's sleep** while sleeping (**could do it in one's sleep**, could do it without any effort). **lay to sleep** = ***put to sleep*** (b) below. **lose sleep over a thing** lie awake worrying about a thing (usu. in neg. context). **put to sleep** (**a**) kill (a pet animal) painlessly; (**b**) *fig.* silence, make inactive, (a feeling). **the sleep of the just** a deep untroubled sleep. ***twilight sleep***: see TWILIGHT *noun & adjective*. ***walk in one's sleep***: see WALK *verb*¹.
Comb.: **sleep-learning** the (alleged) process of learning through exposure to radio broadcasts, tape-recordings, etc., while asleep; **sleep mode** ELECTRONICS a power-saving mode of operation in which (parts of) devices are switched off until needed; **sleep movement** BOTANY a nyctinastic movement of a part of a plant, esp. a flower or leaf; **sleep paralysis** a temporary inability to move immediately on waking; **sleep-shorts** shorts as an item of nightwear; **sleep sofa** *US* a sofa which converts into a bed; **sleep-talker** a person who speaks in his or her sleep; **sleep-talking** the action of speaking in one's sleep; **sleep-teaching** by means of sleep-learning; **sleep-waker** a mesmerized or hypnotized person; **sleep-waking** a mesmeric or hypnotic state.

sleep /sliːp/ *verb.* Pa. t. & pple **slept** /slɛpt/.
[Old English *slēpan*, *slǣpan* = Old Frisian *slepa*, Old Saxon *slāpan* (Dutch *slapen*), Old High German *slāfan* (German *schlafen*), Gothic *slepan*: see prec.]
▸ **I** *verb intrans.* **1** Be in a state of sleep; (occas.) fall asleep. Also, stay the night in a specified place. OE. ▸**b** Have sexual intercourse *with*, *together*. OE. ▸**c** Postpone decision *on* a matter until the following day. E16.
2 Be at peace in death; lie buried. OE.
3 a Of a limb: be numb, esp. as the result of pressure. Cf. ***go to sleep*** s.v. SLEEP *noun*. OE. ▸**b** Of a top: spin so fast as to seem motionless. E16. ▸**c** Of a plant: have its flowers or leaves folded together in sleep (SLEEP *noun* 2c). L18.
4 a Remain dormant, inactive, or quiescent; act as a sleeping partner or sleeper (SLEEPER 7b). OE. ▸**b** Remain calm, still, or motionless. L16.
5 Be remiss or idle; live thoughtlessly. LME.

📖 **1** G. GISSING He . . went to bed, but did not sleep for a long time. W. F. HARVEY I slept . . at this . . inn at Chedsholme. H. CARPENTER Gertrude would sleep late, rising at noon. **b** J. OSBORNE We never slept together before we were married. **2** J. W. BURGON He sleeps . . in Holywell cemetery. **4a** LD MACAULAY The question, having slept during eighteen years, was suddenly revived. J. BUCHAN Her anxiety would never sleep till she saw me again. A. S. NEILL Repressed feelings are not dead; they are only sleeping. **b** R. BROOKE Cool gardened homes slept in the sun.

▸ **II** *verb trans.* **6** Continue for a period of time in (sleep); experience (sleep) of a specified kind. Freq. in ***sleep the sleep of the just*** s.v. SLEEP *noun*. OE.
†**7** Neglect, put off decision on, (a matter); disregard, pay no attention to. L15–L18.
8 a Foll. by *off*, †*out*: dispel the effects of (esp. eating or drinking) by sleeping. L15. ▸**b** Foll. by *away*: lose, waste, or get rid of by sleeping. M16. ▸**c** *refl.* with compl. Make oneself *sober* etc. by sleeping. M16.
9 Pass (time) in sleep. Also foll. by *out*, *away*. M16.
10 Cause to sleep or fall asleep. E19.
11 Provide with sleeping accommodation. M19.

📖 **8a** THACKERAY In the morning, after he had slept his wine off, he was very gay. S. RADLEY He got . . stoned on cannabis last night, and was sleeping it off this morning. **9** W. HORWOOD Hulver and Bracken had slept their first night in the clearing. **11** *Spectator* Some hotels were sleeping . . five guests to a room.

With adverbs in specialized senses, & phrases: **sleep around** *colloq.* engage in sexual intercourse casually with many different partners. **sleep a wink** enjoy a brief moment of sleep (usu. with neg.). **sleep in** (**a**) sleep on the premises where one is employed; (**b**) lie in, sleep late; (orig. *Scot.*) oversleep. **sleep like a log**, **sleep like a top** sleep very soundly. **sleep on** continue sleeping, sleep late. **sleep out** (**a**) sleep in the open air; (**b**) sleep away from the premises where one is employed. **sleep over** (chiefly *N. Amer.*) spend the night at a place other than one's own residence. ***sleep rough***: see ROUGH *adverb*. ***sleep sound***: see SOUND *adverb* 2. **sleep through** (esp. of a baby) sleep uninterruptedly through a period of time, usu. the night. **sleep tight** (as a formula when parting at night) sleep well! **sleep up** catch up on one's sleep. **sleep with one eye open** sleep very lightly.
Comb.: **sleep-away** *adjective* (*US*) (esp. of a camp) at which one sleeps away from home; **sleep-over** *noun & adjective* (chiefly *N. Amer.*) (**a**) *noun* an occasion of spending the night away from home; (**b**) *adjective* (involving) spending the night away from home.

sleeper /ˈsliːpə/ *noun.* ME.
[from prec. + -ER¹.]
▸ **I 1** A person who sleeps (esp. well, badly, etc.) or remains asleep; a person who spends much time in sleep. ME.
2 A thing in a dormant or dead state; *esp.* a bet or tip which remains unclaimed. E17.
3 ZOOLOGY. **a** Any of numerous perciform fishes of the worldwide family Gobiidae characterized by separated pelvic fins (cf. GOBY). M17. ▸**b** A dormouse. Now chiefly *dial.* L17.
4 a A vehicle with sleeping facilities; *esp.* a train made up of or including sleeping-cars. Also, a railway sleeping-car. Freq. *attrib.* L19. ▸**b** A sofa or chair which converts into a bed. *US*. L20.
5 A thing which turns out an unexpected success; *esp.* a book or film which proves popular without much expenditure or promotion. Also, an antique etc. whose true value is not recognized. Orig. *US*. L19.
6 a An unbranded calf which has had a notch cut in its ear. *US*. L19. ▸**b** An earring worn in a pierced ear to keep the hole from closing. L19. ▸**c** A sleeping-suit for a baby or a small child. Also in *pl.* Orig. *N. Amer.* E20. ▸**d** A sleeping-pill. *slang.* M20.
7 a A sleeping partner. E20. ▸**b** A spy etc. who remains dormant for a long period before being activated; *loosely* any undercover agent. Also ***sleeper agent***. M20.
▸ **II** *techn.* **8** Any strong usu. horizontal beam or timber; *spec.* (**a**) one supporting a wall, floor, or other structure; (**b**) NAUTICAL one connecting a transom to the after timbers of a ship; (**c**) one carrying the transverse planks of a wooden bridge. E17. ▸**b** A piece of timber or other material forming a transverse (formerly longitudinal) support for the rails of a railway or (*Hist.*) tramway. L18.
Comb.: ***sleeper agent***: see sense 7b above; **sleeper seat** a reclining seat on which one can sleep during a journey; **sleeper shark** a shark of the genus *Somniosus*; esp. = ***GREENLAND shark***; **sleeper wall** BUILDING a low wall built under a ground floor to support joists where there is no basement.
■ **sleepered** *adjective* (of a rail, floor, etc.) having sleepers L19.

Sleeperette /sliːpərˈɛt/ *noun.* M20.
[from prec. + -ETTE.]
(Proprietary name for) a kind of reclining seat or sleeper seat.

sleepery /ˈsliːp(ə)ri/ *adjective. Scot. & north.* Now *rare*. E16.
[Prob. Middle Low German *sleperich*, *slaperich*, or Middle Dutch *slaperich* (Dutch *slaperig*) = Old High German *slāfarag* (Middle High German *slaefric*, German *schläfrig*).]
†**1** Inducing sleep; characterized by a tendency to sleep. E–M16.
2 Of a person: somnolent, sleepy. M16.

sleepful /ˈsliːpfʊl, -f(ə)l/ *adjective.* LME.
[from SLEEP *noun* + -FUL.]
1 Somnolent, sleepy. *rare.* LME.
2 Marked by sleep; restful through sleep. E19.
■ **sleepfulness** *noun* sleepiness E19.

sleep-in /ˈsliːpɪn/ *noun & adjective.* M20.
[Partly from ***sleep in*** s.v. SLEEP *verb*. Sense A.1 from SLEEP *verb* + -IN².]
▸ **A** *noun.* **1** A form of protest in which the participants sleep overnight in premises which they have occupied. M20.
2 A period or act of lying in bed in a morning after one's usual time for getting up. L20.
▸ **B** *adjective.* Sleeping on the premises where one works; (of a place) in which one can stay the night, residential. M20.

sleeping /ˈsliːpɪŋ/ *verbal noun.* ME.
[from SLEEP *verb* + -ING¹.]
The action of SLEEP *verb*.
Comb.: **sleeping-bag** a lined or padded bag to sleep in when camping etc.; **sleeping-car**, **sleeping-carriage** a railway coach provided with beds or berths; **sleeping-draught** a drink to induce sleep; **sleeping-pill**: for inducing sleep; **sleeping-potion** *arch.* = ***sleeping-draught*** above; **sleeping sickness** (**a**) a tropical African disease caused by the protozoans *Trypanosoma gambiense* and *T. rhodesiense*, which are transmitted by tsetse-flies, and proliferate in the blood-vessels, ultimately affecting the central nervous system and leading to lethargy and death; trypanosomiasis; (**b**) (now *rare*) = ***SLEEPY sickness*** (b); **sleeping-suit** a one-piece night-garment worn esp. by children.

sleeping /ˈsliːpɪŋ/ *ppl adjective.* ME.
[from SLEEP *verb* + -ING².]
1 That sleeps or is asleep; pertaining to a person who is asleep. ME.
†**2** Inducing sleep; soporific. *rare.* LME–L16.
3 Numb; devoid of sensation. M16.
4 Inactive, quiescent. M16.
5 Quiet, silent; motionless. L18.
Special collocations & phrases: ***let sleeping dogs lie***: see DOG *noun*. **sleeping beauty** [with allus. to the heroine of a fairy tale who slept for 100 years until woken by the kiss of a prince] an unconscious or inactive person or thing. **sleeping giant** a dormant or inactive force. **sleeping lizard** (chiefly *Austral.*) any of various lizards, esp. the stump-tailed skink, *Trachydosaurus rugosus*. **sleeping partner** a partner in a business who takes no part in the actual work. ***sleeping policeman***: see POLICEMAN 2b. **sleeping princess** = ***sleeping beauty*** above. ***wake a sleeping wolf***: see WOLF *noun*.
■ **sleepingly** *adverb* †(**a**) when asleep; (**b**) sleepily: LME.

sleepless /ˈsliːplɪs/ *adjective.* LME.
[from SLEEP *noun* + -LESS.]
1 Unable to sleep, esp. through insomnia; (of night etc.) marked by lack of sleep. LME.
2 Continually active or operative; unceasing in motion. L18.

📖 **2** J. CONRAD The traffic . . went on . . upon the sleepless river.

■ **sleeplessly** *adverb* M19. **sleeplessness** *noun* the state of being sleepless; *esp.* inability to sleep, insomnia: M17.

sleep-out /ˈsliːpaʊt/ *noun & adjective.* E20.
[from ***sleep out*** s.v. SLEEP *verb*. Sense A.2 partly after -IN².]
▸ **A** *noun.* **1** A veranda, porch, or outbuilding providing sleeping accommodation. *Austral. & NZ*. E20.
2 An act of sleeping outdoors, esp. as a protest against homelessness. M20.
▸ **B** *adjective.* Sleeping away from the premises where one works. M20.

sleepwalk /ˈsliːpwɔːk/ *verb intrans.* L18.
[from SLEEP *noun* + WALK *verb*¹.]
Walk or perform other actions in one's sleep as though awake. Orig. & chiefly as ***sleepwalking*** *verbal noun & ppl adjective*.
■ **sleepwalker** *noun* a person who walks while asleep, a somnambulist M18.

sleepy /ˈsliːpi/ *adjective.* ME.
[from SLEEP *noun* + -Y¹.]
1 Ready to fall asleep; drowsy, somnolent. ME. ▸**b** Given to sleep; lethargic. LME. ▸**c** *fig.* Dormant, inactive. L16. ▸**d** (Of a pear etc.) about to become rotten; (of cream) that will not churn to butter in the proper time. L18.
2 Characterized by, appropriate to, or suggestive of sleep or repose. ME. ▸**b** Of a disease or morbid state: marked by an inordinate desire for sleep. E17. ▸**c** Of a place: marked by (excessive) tranquillity or lack of bustle. M19.
3 Inducing sleep; soporific. Now *rare*. LME.

📖 **2c** M. E. BRADDON The quiet streets . . of that sleepy Belgian city. **3** DRYDEN Sleepy Poppies harmful Harvests yield.

Special collocations & comb.: **sleepy-head** a sleepy or lethargic person. **sleepy-headed** *adjective* sleepy, lethargic. **Sleepy Hollow**, **sleepy hollow** (**a**) [with allus. to Washington Irving's story *The Legend of Sleepy Hollow*] (a nickname for) a place marked by torpor or a soporific atmosphere; (**b**) (also ***sleepy-hollow chair***) a type of comfortable deep-upholstered armchair. **sleepy lizard** (chiefly *Austral.*) = ***sleeping lizard*** s.v. SLEEPING *ppl adjective*.

sleepy sickness †(*a*) = *sleeping sickness* (a) s.v. SLEEPING *verbal noun*; (*b*) encephalitis lethargica, an often fatal disease pandemic between 1916 and 1928, characterized by disturbance of the sleep cycle (often with daytime sleepiness and nocturnal wakefulness) and symptoms resembling Parkinsonism, owing to brain damage; (*c*) a form of toxaemia caused in pregnant ewes by imbalance between the degree of nourishment and the stage of pregnancy, and characterized by somnolence and neuromuscular disturbance. **sleepy-time** *N. Amer. (nursery & colloq.)* bedtime.
■ **sleepily** *adverb* E17. **sleepiness** *noun* L16.

sleet /sliːt/ *noun & verb.* ME.
[Prob. repr. Old English form rel. to Middle Low German *slōten* (pl.) hail, Middle High German *slōȥe*, *slōȥ* (German *Schlosse*) hail(stone), from Germanic.]
▶ **A** *noun.* **1** Snow which has been partially thawed as it falls; a mixture of snow and rain falling together. ME. ▸**b** A storm or shower of sleet. *rare.* M18.
2 A thin coating of ice formed by sleet or rain freezing on contact with a cold surface. *US.* M19.
▶ **B** *verb intrans.* **1** *impers.* in ***it sleets***, ***it is sleeting***, etc., sleet falls, sleet is falling, etc. ME.
2 Fall as, or like, sleet. L16.

📖 **1** *New Yorker* It was dark and cold and it had begun to sleet. **2** H. WYNDHAM A sleeting drizzle beat against the panes.

sleety /ˈsliːti/ *adjective.* E18.
[from prec. + -Y[1].]
1 a Of a storm, wind, etc.: laden with or accompanied by sleet. E18. ▸**b** Resembling or suggestive of sleet. E19.
2 Of weather or time: characterized by sleet. E19.

sleeve /sliːv/ *noun.*
[Old English (Anglian) *slēfe*, (West Saxon) *slīefe*, and *slief*, *slȳf*, corresp. to East Frisian *slēwe*, Northern Frisian *slev*, *slīv* sleeve, ult. rel. to Middle Dutch *sloove*, *sloof* covering.]
1 That part of a garment which wholly or partially covers the arm. In early use freq., and still occas., a separate item of clothing wearable with any, or (now usu.) a particular, garment for the upper body. Also (*Hist.*), such an item of clothing worn as a favour or borne as a heraldic charge (cf. MAUNCH). OE. ▸**b** A piece of armour for covering and protecting the arm. *obsolete* exc. *Hist.* LME. ▸**c** *Hist.* A university gown with sleeves, usu. worn by someone of a certain status; the wearer of such a gown. M18.
2 a [After French *La Manche* lit. 'the sleeve'.] The English Channel. *joc.* Now *rare* or *obsolete.* L16. ▸**b** A channel, a strait. Long *rare.* E17.
†**3** MILITARY. A body *of* troops on the flanks of an army, battalion, etc.; a wing, a flank. L16–E17.
4 *techn.* **a** A protective or connecting tube fitting over or enclosing a rod, spindle, etc. M19. ▸**b** ELECTRICITY. A metal cylinder fitted round the full length of the core of an electromagnetic relay to modify the speeds of opening and closing. Cf. SLUG *noun*[2] 7a. E20. ▸**c** AERONAUTICS. = DROGUE *noun* 3, 4. M20.
5 A close-fitting protective cover or case, esp. for a gramophone record. M20.

📖 **1** TENNYSON He wore . . upon his helm A sleeve of scarlet. A. UTTLEY He had only one arm, and his empty sleeve was pinned . . to his coat. ***bell-sleeve***, ***cap sleeve***, ***hanging sleeve***, ***long sleeve***, ***mandarin sleeve***, etc. **5** *Which?* Having your negatives . . in sleeves makes them easier to store. *Sounds* They've designed the sleeve for his new single.

Phrases: ***a card up one's sleeve***: see CARD *noun*[2] 1. ***an ace up one's sleeve***: see ACE *noun.* **a sleeve across the windpipe** an assault; *fig.* a severe blow, a major setback. HIPPOCRATES' SLEEVE. **hold by the sleeve**, **pull by the sleeve**, etc., take by the arm in order to detain, attract attention, etc. **laugh in one's sleeve**, **laugh up one's sleeve** be secretly or inwardly amused. *poke sleeve*: see POKE *noun*[1] 3. ***pull by the sleeve***: see ***hold by the sleeve*** above. **put the sleeve on** (*a*) beg or borrow money from; (*b*) arrest; cause to be arrested. **roll up one's sleeves** prepare to work or fight. **up one's sleeve** concealed but ready for use, in reserve. ***wear one's heart on one's sleeve***: see HEART *noun.*

Comb.: **sleeve bearing**: in which an axle or shaft turns in a lubricated sleeve; **sleeve-board** a small ironing-board on which sleeves may be ironed; **sleeve-button** a button for fastening the wristband or cuff of a garment; **sleeve-cap** *US* the topmost part of a sleeve; **sleeve-coupling** a tube for connecting shafts or pipes; **sleeve dog** a very small Chinese or Japanese dog, *esp.* = ***sleeve Pekingese*** below; **sleeve-fish** (now *rare* or *obsolete*) a squid; **sleeve-garter** an elasticated band worn round the upper arm over a shirtsleeve to regulate its length; **sleeve gun** *US* a miniature gun which can be concealed in the clothing; †**sleeve-hand** the wristband or cuff of a sleeve; **sleeve link** a cuff-link; **sleeve-note** (usu. in *pl.*): giving descriptive information about a gramophone record, printed on the sleeve; **sleeve-nut** a long nut with right-hand and left-hand threads for drawing together pipes or shafts conversely threaded; **sleeve Pekingese** a Pekingese under six pounds in weight; **sleeve-valve** a valve in some internal-combustion engines, consisting of a hollow cylindrical sleeve sliding between the cylinder and piston to control the inlet and exhaust ports.
■ **sleevelet** *noun* a small or detachable sleeve L19.

sleeve /sliːv/ *verb.* Now *rare* exc. as SLEEVED *ppl adjective.* LME.
[from the noun.]
1 *verb trans.* **a** Fit (a garment) with a sleeve or sleeves. LME. ▸**b** Cover (the arm etc.) *with* a sleeve. L19.
†**2** MILITARY. **a** *verb trans.* Provide (a body of troops) with a wing or wings. L16–E17. ▸**b** *verb intrans.* Draw or line *up* on the wings. L16–M17.
3 *verb trans. techn.* ▸**a** Fix *on* or connect by means of a sleeve. L19. ▸**b** Reduce in size (the bore of a firearm or engine) by fitting metal shafts etc. inside the barrel or cylinder. L20.
4 *verb trans.* Provide with or enclose in a protective cover. L20.
■ **sleeving** *noun* (*a*) the action of the verb; (*b*) a tubular covering for a cylindrical object, *esp.* one of insulating material for an electric cable; material for this: L15.

sleeved /sliːvd/ *ppl adjective.* L15.
[from SLEEVE *verb* or *noun*: see -ED[1], -ED[2].]
1 Fitted or provided with sleeves; having sleeves of a certain kind. Freq. as 2nd elem. of comb. L15.
2 Fitted or covered with a sleeve or sleeves (SLEEVE *noun* 4, 5). E20.

📖 **1** R. ADAMS Her sleeved dress was of yellow cotton. ***long-sleeved***, ***short-sleeved***, etc.

sleeveen /ˈsliːviːn, sliːˈviːn/ *noun. Anglo-Irish & Canad. dial.* M19.
[Irish *slighbhín*, *slíbhín* sly person, trickster.]
An untrustworthy or cunning person.

sleeveless /ˈsliːvlɪs/ *adjective.* OE.
[from SLEEVE *noun* + -LESS.]
1 Of a garment: having no sleeves; made without sleeves. OE.
2 †**a** Of a word, tale, answer, etc.: futile, trivial, unsatisfactory. LME–L17. ▸**b** Of an errand: pointless. Now *rare.* M16. ▸**c** *gen.* Petty, frivolous; unprofitable; shiftless. *arch. & dial.* M16.
■ **sleevelessness** *noun* L18.

sleever /ˈsliːvə/ *noun. dial., Austral., & NZ.* L19.
[from SLEEVE *noun* + -ER[1].]
A tall glass; a drink contained in such a glass. Cf. ***long-sleever*** s.v. LONG *adjective*[1].

sleeze *verb* var. of SLEAZE *verb.*

sleezy *adjective* var. of SLEAZY.

†**slei** *adverb* see SLY *adverb.*

†**sleided** *adjective. rare* (Shakes.). L16–E17.
[Irreg. var. of pa. pple of SLEAVE *verb.*]
Of silk: separated into filaments.

sleigh /sleɪ/ *noun*[1] *& verb.* Orig. *N. Amer.* E18.
[Dutch *slee*: see SLED *noun.*]
▶ **A** *noun.* **1** A sledge, *esp.* one for riding on. E18.
2 MILITARY. A wheelless carriage for a heavy gun or cannon. L18.
Comb.: **sleigh bed** *N. Amer.* a bed resembling a sleigh, with outward curving head- and footboards; a French bed; **sleigh-bell** any of several small bells attached to a sleigh or to the harness of a horse etc. drawing a sleigh, or joined in a row attached to a handle and shaken as a percussion instrument.
▶ **B** *verb intrans. & trans.* (with *it*). Travel or ride in a sleigh. Freq. as ***sleighing*** *verbal noun.* E18.
■ **sleigher** *noun* a person who rides in or drives a sleigh M19.

sleigh *noun*[2] var. of SLEY *noun.*

sleigh-ride /ˈsleɪrʌɪd/ *noun & verb.* Also **sleigh ride.** L18.
[from SLEIGH *noun*[1] + RIDE *noun.*]
▶ **A** *noun.* **1** A ride in a sleigh. L18.
2 The action of taking a narcotic drug, usu. cocaine; the euphoria resulting from this. Chiefly in ***take a sleigh-ride***, ***go on a sleigh-ride***, etc. *US slang.* E20.
3 An implausible or false story; a hoax, a deception. Chiefly in ***take for a sleigh-ride***, mislead. *US slang.* M20.
▶ **B** *verb intrans.* Pa. t. **-rode**/-rəʊd/, pa. pple **-ridden** /-rɪd(ə)n/.
1 Ride in a sleigh. E19.
2 Take a narcotic drug. *US slang.* E20.
■ **sleigh-rider** *noun* L19.

sleight /slʌɪt/ *noun & adjective.* ME.
[Old Norse *slægð* (Old Swedish *slögdh*, Swedish *slöjd* SLOYD), from *slægr* SLY *adjective*: see -T[2].]
▶ **A** *noun.* **1** Cunning; deceitful dealing or policy; artifice, trickery. Now *rare* or *obsolete.* ME.
2 Skill, manual dexterity. (Foll. by *in*, *at.*) Now *rare.* ME. ▸**b** Adroitness, smartness, nimbleness *of* mind, body, etc. In later use influenced by SLEIGHT OF HAND. LME.
3 The precise art or method, the knack *of* (doing) something. Now *dial.* ME. ▸**b** *spec.* Skill in jugglery or conjuring; sleight of hand. M17.
4 A cunning trick; an artful device or design; an artifice, a ruse, a wile. Now *rare.* ME. ▸**b** A feat of jugglery or legerdemain; a trick or action performed with great dexterity, esp. so as to deceive the eye. L16. ▸†**c** A design, a pattern. *rare* (Spenser). Only in L16.

📖 **2b** A. S. BYATT By some sleight of perception he was looking out at once from the four field-corners. *Times* He is foolish to suppose that he can solve his difficulties by sleight of words.

▶†**B** *adjective.* **1** Artful, crafty, wily. ME–L16.
2 Skilful, clever; dexterous. E16–M17.
■ †**sleightly** *adverb* (*a*) cunningly, craftily; (*b*) skilfully, dexterously: ME–E17. **sleighty** *adjective* (now *rare*) (*a*) having or using sleight or craft; (*b*) characterized by sleight or dexterity; crafty, subtle: LME.

sleight of hand /slʌɪt əv ˈhand/ *noun phr.* Also **sleight-of-hand.** Pl. **sleights of hand.** LME.
[from prec. + OF *preposition* + HAND *noun.*]
1 Manual dexterity or skill, esp. in conjuring or fencing. LME.
2 A display of dexterity, *esp.* a conjuring trick. E17.

slendang /ˈslɛndaŋ/ *noun.* Also **selen-** /ˈsɛlɛn-/. L19.
[Javanese *slēndang*, Indonesian *selēndang.*]
In Indonesia, a long scarf or stole worn by women.

slender /ˈslɛndə/ *adjective.* LME.
[Origin unkn.]
1 a Of a person, a person's body, an animal, etc.: not stout or fleshy; gracefully slim. LME. ▸**b** Of a thing: small in breadth in proportion to length; long and thin. E16.
2 Lacking thickness or solidity in proportion to extent of surface; slight or slim in size or structure. LME. ▸**b** Of a thin or poor consistency; lacking body. Long *rare.* E16. ▸**c** PHONETICS. Of a vowel: narrow, close. M18.
3 †**a** Lacking in strength or energy. LME–M17. ▸**b** Weak, not robust. L15.
4 Relatively small or scanty; slight, insignificant, inadequate. LME.
5 a Small or limited in amount, number, range, etc. M16. ▸**b** Of small extent, size, or capacity. E17.
6 (Of an argument etc.) inconclusive, unconvincing; (of a claim etc.) having little foundation or justification. M16.

📖 **1a** H. KANE Nora was slender and graceful in a . . jump suit. **b** *Listener* Cables slung between . . slender steel masts. **2** H. E. MANNING I dedicated to you a very slender book. **4** LD MACAULAY A young man of slender abilities. B. JOWETT Their only hope, however slender, was in victory. C. RYAN Depending . . on one slender channel of communication. **5a** J. IRVING The slender handful of . . professional seamen. **b** T. HOOD A slender space will serve . . , For I am small and thin. **6** H. MACMILLAN Trying to draw the most profound deductions from the most slender evidence.

Comb. & special collocations: **slender-billed** *adjective* having a slender bill; ***slender-billed curlew***, an endangered pale slim curlew, *Numenius tenuirostris*, now breeding in only two small areas of Siberia; ***slender-billed gull***, a small to medium-sized gull, *Larus genei*, with a long bill and pink-flushed underside, occurring from the Mediterranean to central Asia; **slender-bodied** *adjective* having a slender body; ***slender*** LORIS; **slender mongoose** a solitary African mongoose, *Herpestes sanguineus*, inhabiting savannah south of the Sahara.
■ **slenderly** *adverb* LME. **slenderness** *noun* slender quality; ***slenderness ratio*** (ENGINEERING), the ratio of the effective length of a column or pillar to its least radius of gyration (formerly, to its least diameter): LME.

slender /ˈslɛndə/ *verb trans. & intrans.* M16.
[from prec.]
Attenuate; make or become thin or slender.

slenderize /ˈslɛndərʌɪz/ *verb.* Also **-ise.** E20.
[formed as prec. + -IZE.]
1 *verb intrans.* Make oneself slender, slim. E20.
2 *verb trans. & intrans.* Make (a person or thing) slender, make (the figure) appear slender. E20.

📖 **2** *Detroit Free Press* A slenderizing lunch of cottage cheese.

slent /slɛnt/ *noun*[1]. Now *dial.* See also SLANT *noun*[1]. ME.
[Of Scandinavian origin (cf. Norwegian *slent* side-slip, Swedish *slänt* slope, slant): rel. to SLENT *verb*[1].]
1 A slope, a declivity; = SLANT *noun*[1] 1. ME.
†**2** A sly hit, a piece of sarcasm; = SLANT *noun*[1] 3. L15–E17.

slent /slɛnt/ *noun*[2]. Long *rare* or *obsolete.* LME.
[Of Scandinavian origin (cf. Norwegian *slett*, Old Norse *sletta* dash, splash). See also SLANT *noun*[2].]
†**1** A splash or sprinkling of water. *rare.* Only in LME.
2 = SLANT *noun*[2]. L16.

slent /slɛnt/ *verb*[1] *intrans.* Now *dial.* ME.
[Of Scandinavian origin (cf. Norwegian *slenta*, Old Danish *slente*, Middle & mod. Swedish *slinta*). Cf. SLANT *verb*, SLENT *noun*[1].]
1 Slip, fall, or glide obliquely; strike or lie aslant. ME.
2 Make sly hits or gibes. M16.

slent /slɛnt/ *verb*[2] *trans.* Now *dial.* L16.
[Origin unkn.]
Split, cleave; tear.

slept *verb pa. t. & pple* of SLEEP *verb.*

sleugh *noun* var. of SLEW *noun*[1].

sleuth /sluːθ/ *noun*[1] *& verb.* ME.
[Old Norse *slóð* track, trail. Cf. SLOT *noun*[3].]
▶ **A** *noun.* †**1** The track or trail of a person or animal; a definite track or path. ME–L15.
2 In full ***sleuth-dog***. A bloodhound, a sleuth-hound. Now *rare.* E19.
3 A detective. L19.
▶ **B** *verb.* **1** *verb trans.* Track (a person); investigate. Also foll. by *out.* E20.

2 *verb intrans.* Act as a detective; conduct an investigation. Also foll. by *around*. E20.
Comb.: **sleuth-dog**: see sense A.2 above; **sleuth-hound** (orig. *Scot. & north.*) (*a*) a bloodhound; (*b*) *colloq.* an investigator, a tracker, a detective.

†**sleuth** *noun*² var. of SLOTH *noun*.

†**sleve** *verb trans.* OE–L19.
[Old English *slefan*. Cf. SLIVE *verb*².]
Cause to slip (*in, on, over*, etc.).

slew /sluː/ *noun*¹. Also **sleugh**, **slue**. E18.
[Alt. of SLOUGH *noun*¹.]
1 A marshy or reedy pool, pond, inlet, etc. *N. Amer.* E18.
2 *gen.* An expanse or mass of water. *rare*. E20.

slew /sluː/ *noun*². Also **slue**. M19.
[from SLEW *verb*¹.]
The action of turning, or causing to turn, without change of place; a turn, a twist; the position to which a thing has been turned.
Comb.: **slew rate** = *slewing rate* s.v. SLEWING 2.

slew /sluː/ *noun*³. *colloq.* Chiefly *N. Amer.* M19.
[Irish *slua(gh)* crowd, multitude.]
A very large number or quantity *of*.

> 🕮 C. HOPE Dragged . . across the ground in a slew of pebbles. *City Limits* The new crop of . . stars are . . picking up a slew of awards.

slew /sluː/ *noun*⁴. E20.
[Origin uncertain: perh. from SLEW *noun*².]
BASKET-MAKING. A filling made of two or more strands worked together.

slew /sluː/ *verb*¹. Also **slue**. M18.
[Origin unkn.]
1 *verb trans.* Orig. NAUTICAL. Turn (a thing) round or *round* on its own axis, or without moving it from its place; *loosely* swing round. M18. ▸**b** Intoxicate. Chiefly as ***slewed*** *ppl adjective*. E19. ▸**c** Beat, outwit, trick. *Austral. & NZ*. L19.
2 *verb intrans.* Turn about; swing *round* or *over*; *esp.* (of a motor vehicle etc.) skid or slide uncontrollably (*across* or *round*). E19.
3 *verb intrans.* Of a control mechanism or electronic device: undergo slewing (SLEWING 2). M20.

> 🕮 **1** G. A. BIRMINGHAM A great sea lifts her stern and slews it round. J. REED Detached the cannon and slewed it around until it aimed . . at our backs. W. SOYINKA Ofeyi slewed his eyes sharply back to Iriyise. **b** D. LODGE I was somewhat slewed . . and kept calling him Sparrow. **2** M. BRADBURY The car slewed across the road and angled round again. A. MACLEAN The *San Andreas* is . . slewing rapidly to port.

Comb.: **slew-foot** *noun & adjective* (*US slang*) (designating) a person who walks with turned-out feet or who is clumsy; **slew-rope** NAUTICAL a rope used in slewing something.

slew /sluː/ *verb*² *intrans.* E20.
[from SLEW *noun*⁴.]
BASKET-MAKING. Form a filling by working two or more strands together.

slew *verb*³ *pa. t.*: see SLAY *verb*¹.

slewing /ˈsluːɪŋ/ *verbal noun*. L19.
[from SLEW *verb*¹ + -ING¹.]
1 *gen.* The action of SLEW *verb*¹. L19.
2 The response of a control mechanism or electronic device to a sudden large increase in input, esp. one that causes the device to respond at its maximum rate (***slewing rate***, ***slewing speed***). Usu. *attrib.* M20.

sley /sleɪ/ *noun*. Also **slay**, **sleigh**.
[Old English *slege* = Old Saxon *slegi*, from base of SLAY *verb*¹.]
= REED *noun*¹ 7a.

sley /sleɪ/ *verb trans.* Also **slay**. E17.
[from the noun.]
Set (a warp). Earliest & chiefly as ***sleying*** *verbal noun*.
■ **sleyer** *noun* L19.

slice /slʌɪs/ *noun*¹. ME.
[Aphet. from Old French *esclice* (mod. *éclisse*) small piece of wood etc., from *esclicier*: see SLICE *verb*¹.]
▶ **I** †**1** A fragment, a chip, a splinter. ME–L16.
2 a A thin, flat, broad piece or wedge cut off or out esp. from bread, meat, or cake. L15. ▸**b** GEOLOGY. A relatively thin, broad mass of rock situated between two approximately parallel thrust faults, esp. when these make a small angle with the horizontal. Also ***thrust slice***. E20. ▸**c** ELECTRONICS. A small thin slab of semiconducting material on which circuit elements have been formed. M20.
3 *transf.* A portion, a share, a piece. M16.

> 🕮 **2a** HARPER LEE She cut from the big cake and gave the slice to Jem. J. HERRIOT I bit into the first slice of bread. A. DAVIES Whiskey and hot water, with the lemon slice and cloves. **3** W. S. MAUGHAM Five years is a big slice out of a man's life. *Music Week* His debut . . single . . is a smooth slice of hard funk. **slice of life** a realistic and detailed representation of everyday life (freq. *attrib.*). ***slice of the cake***: see CAKE *noun*.

▶ **II 4** A usu. broad flattish instrument or implement; *spec.* (*a*) a cooking utensil with a broad flat blade used esp. for serving fish, cake, etc.; (*b*) a kind of fire-shovel; (*c*) an instrument for clearing the bars of a furnace; (*d*) a wide flat plate or tray used for standing something on. LME.
4 ***cake-slice***, ***fish-slice***, etc.

slice /slʌɪs/ *noun*². E17.
[from next.]
†**1** A sharp cut, a slash. *rare*. Only in E17.
2 A slicing stroke in golf, tennis, etc. L19.

> 🕮 **2** *Daily Telegraph* A series of brilliant passing shots and gentle slices.

slice /slʌɪs/ *verb*¹. L15.
[Old French *esclicier* splinter, shatter from Frankish *slītjan* (= Old High German *slīzan*, German *schleissen*, Old English *slītan*: see SLIT *verb*).]
1 *verb trans. & intrans.* **a** Cut (esp. an item of food) into slices; cut (*into* or *through*) with a sharp instrument. L15. ▸**b** *fig.* Penetrate or cut through as with something sharp; move quickly and effortlessly through or *through*. L15.
2 *verb trans.* **a** Cut *out* or *off* in the form of a slice or slices; remove with a clean cut. M16. ▸**b** Remove by means of a slice. L17.
3 *verb intrans.* Cut cleanly or easily; admit of being cut. E17.
4 *verb trans. & intrans.* In GOLF, strike (a ball) so as to cause deviation away from the striker. Also in other sports (esp. TENNIS), make a sharp stroke across (a ball) so that the ball travels forward at an angle. L19.

> 🕮 **1a** E. DAVID Leave the meat to cool . . then slice it into strips. L. CHAMBERLAIN Slice the tomatoes thinly. **b** W. H. RUSSELL Our sharp bow sliced the blue depths. J. STEINBECK Afternoon sun sliced in through the cracks of the barn walls. *Cycling Weekly* Curren sliced through the 14 riders spreadeagled between him and Dunne. **2a** V. GLENDINNING He had sliced the wing of a yellow Fiat. **3** T. HERBERT An Indian sword which slices easily. ARTEMAS WARD Goat's milk cheese . . firm enough to slice well.

■ **sliceable** *adjective* L20. **slicer** *noun* a person who or thing which slices (freq. in *comb.*) M16.

†**slice** *verb*² *intrans.* L15–E18.
[Old French *esclisser* squirt, splash.]
FALCONRY. Of a bird: mute with projectile force.

sliced /slʌɪst/ *ppl adjective*. L16.
[from SLICE *verb*¹ + -ED¹.]
1 a That has been cut into slices; cut cleanly. L16. ▸**b** Of food: sold already cut into slices. M20.
2 Of a ball: played with a slice. L19.
1b the best thing since sliced bread, **the greatest thing since sliced bread** *colloq.* the most wonderful thing to happen, be discovered, etc.

slick /slɪk/ *noun*¹. E17.
[from SLICK *adjective* or *verb*.]
†**1** A cosmetic, an unguent. Only in E17.
†**2** CARDS. The smoothing of playing-cards before play begins. L17–E18.
3 A smooth patch on the surface of water, usu. caused by some oily or greasy substance; *spec.* a floating mass of oil. M19.
4 A wild unbranded horse, cow, or other range animal; a maverick. *US*. L19.
5 A glossy magazine. *US*. M20.
6 A smooth tyre used on a racing vehicle. M20.
7 A small helicopter with runners instead of wheels. M20.
8 A clever or smart person; a cheat, a swindler, a slickster. *US slang*. M20.

> 🕮 **3** H. INNES The slick now stretched in a . . greasy layer right across the bay. ***oil slick***: see OIL *noun*.

Comb.: **slick-licker** *Canad. colloq.* an apparatus for removing an oil slick.
■ **slickster** *noun* (*US slang*) a swindler M20.

slick /slɪk/ *noun*². *rare*. L17.
[from German SCHLICH.]
MINING. = SCHLICH.

slick /slɪk/ *adjective & adverb*. ME.
[Repr. Old English word (evidenced in *nīgslicod* newly polished, glossy) rel. to Old Norse *slíkr* smooth, Icelandic *slíkja*, Norwegian *slikja* be or make smooth. Cf. SLEEK *adjective & adverb*.]
▶ **A** *adjective*. **1** (Of skin, hair, etc.) smooth, glossy, sleek; (of a surface) slippery. ME.
2 a Of an animal etc.: sleek in hair or skin; plump; well-conditioned. Now *rare*. LME. ▸**b** Of a range animal: unbranded, wild. *US*. M20.
3 Smooth; specious, plausible. Cf. sense 4 below. L16.
4 Of a person: adroit, deft, smart; skilful in action or execution. Also, glibly clever or assured. E19.
5 Of a thing, action, etc.: first-class, excellent; neat, smart, efficient, attractive (freq. superficially or pretentiously so); smooth-running. M19.

> 🕮 **1** J. CARROLL He could barely hold on . . because his hands were so slick with perspiration. M. HUGHES Beneath the sparse cover of grass . . the ground was slick. **4** A. CHRISTIE You're a pretty slick guesser. R. BANKS He was . . a slick left fielder for the local softball team. **5** A. E. STEVENSON I have no slick formula . . to cure our problems. *Independent* Slick television advertisements . . screened . . before the election.

Special collocations & comb.: **slick ear** *US* = SLICK *noun*¹ 4. **slick magazine** a magazine printed on slick paper. **slick paper** *US* a glossy paper used esp. for printing popular magazines.
▶ **B** *adverb*. **1** Smartly, cleverly; easily; quickly. ME.
2 Completely; right, clean. E19.
■ **slicken** *verb trans.* (*rare*) make smooth or polished E17. **slickly** *adverb* (*a*) *rare* sleekly, smoothly; (*b*) cleverly, deftly: L16. **slickness** *noun* (*a*) *rare* smoothness; (*b*) (freq. *derog.*) dexterity, cleverness: M17.

slick /slɪk/ *verb*. ME.
[Prob. from Old English: see prec. Cf. SLEEK *verb*.]
1 a *verb trans.* Make smooth or glossy; polish. ME. ▸**b** *verb trans. transf.* Make elegant or fine. (Foll. by *off, up*.) ME. ▸**c** *verb trans.* Remove by smoothing or polishing. Foll. by *away, out*. M17. ▸**d** *verb intrans.* Smarten or tidy oneself *up*. *US*. M19.
2 *verb trans.* Make (the skin, hair, etc.) sleek or glossy, esp. by some special treatment; (foll. by *back, down*) pull back or flatten as part of this process. ME.

> 🕮 **1a** *Daily Telegraph* The streets had been slicked by hours of rain. **2** J. BLUME His hair is short and slicked down. A. LEE I had slicked my hair back into a bun.

slickens /ˈslɪkɪnz/ *noun*. *US*. L19.
[Perh. from SLICK *noun*².]
Finely pulverized waste or washings from a hydraulic mine.

slickenside /ˈslɪk(ə)nsʌɪd/ *noun*. M18.
[from dial. var. of SLICK *adjective* + SIDE *noun*.]
1 MINERALOGY. A specular variety of galena found in Derbyshire. Now *rare* or *obsolete*. M18.
2 GEOLOGY. A polished and freq. striated surface that results from friction along a fault or bedding plane. E19.
■ **slickensided** *adjective* (GEOLOGY) (of a rock surface) polished or striated by friction L19.

slicker /ˈslɪkə/ *noun & verb*. M19.
[from SLICK *adjective* or *verb* + -ER¹.]
▶ **A** *noun*. **1** A tool for scraping or smoothing leather. M19.
2 A raincoat of a smooth and usu. brightly coloured material. Also ***rain slicker***. Chiefly *N. Amer.* L19.
3 = CITY ***slicker***. Chiefly *N. Amer.* E20.
4 = ***silverfish*** (b) s.v. SILVER *noun & adjective*. *US*. E20.
▶ **B** *verb trans.* Cheat, swindle. M20.
■ **slickered** *adjective* (*US*) wearing a slicker L20.

slickstone /ˈslɪkstəʊn/ *noun*. Now *rare*. ME.
[from SLICK *verb* + STONE *noun*.]
= SLEEKSTONE.

slid /slɪd/ *noun*. Now *rare*. L15.
[Prob. rel. to SLED *noun*, SLIDE *verb*.]
A device by which something may be slid along the ground; a sled, a sledge; a runner, a roller.

slid *verb pa. t. & pple*: see SLIDE *verb*.

'slid /slɪd/ *interjection*. *arch.* L16.
[Contr. of *God's lid* (= eyelid): see GOD *noun* 5(h).]
An oath, expr. asseveration or adjuration.

slidable /ˈslʌɪdəb(ə)l/ *adjective*. Also **slideable**. M17.
[from SLIDE *verb* + -ABLE.]
†**1** Liable to slide or alter. *rare*. Only in M17.
2 That may be slid. L19.
■ **slidably** *adverb* E20.

slidden *verb pa. pple*: see SLIDE *verb*.

slidder /ˈslɪdə/ *noun*. Long *obsolete* exc. *Scot. & dial.* ME.
[Cf. SLIDDER *adjective*, *verb*.]
A trench or hollow running down a hill; a steep slope.

slidder /ˈslɪdə/ *adjective*. *obsolete* exc. *dial.*
[Old English *slidor*, from *slid-* weak grade of *slīdan* SLIDE *verb*. Cf. SLITHER *adjective*.]
1 Slippery. OE. ▸†**b** *fig.* Uncertain, unstable, changeable. L15–L16.
†**2** Of a smooth or slippery nature; *fig.* treacherous. ME–L17.
†**3** Inclined to slip or fall. *rare*. LME–L15.

slidder /ˈslɪdə/ *verb*. Now *Scot. & dial.*
[Old English *slid(e)rian* = Middle Low German, Middle Dutch *slid(d)eren*, German dial. *schlittern* frequentative (see -ER⁵) of *slid-*: see prec. Cf. SLITHER *verb*.]
1 *verb intrans.* Slide, slip. OE.
2 *verb trans.* Make slippery or smooth. LME.

sliddery /ˈslɪd(ə)ri/ *adjective*. Now *Scot. & dial.* ME.
[from prec. + -Y¹. Cf. SLITHERY.]
1 Slippery; on which one may readily slip. ME. ▸**b** *fig.* Uncertain, unstable, changeable. LME.
2 Of a smooth or slippery nature; *fig.* sly, treacherous. ME.
3 Inclined or prone to slip. *rare*. LME.

slide /slʌɪd/ *noun*. L16.
[from the verb.]
▶ **I 1** The action or fact of sliding; an instance of this. L16. ▸**b** *MUSIC*. A kind of grace in which two or more notes are used in approaching the main note. Also, portamento. L18. ▸**c** *fig*. A rapid decline; a downturn. Chiefly in ***on the slide***. L19. ▸**d** *BASEBALL*. A sliding approach made to a base along the ground. L19. ▸**e** *SURFING*. A ride across the face of a wave; a wave suitable for this. M20.
2 A landslip, an avalanche; a place where this has happened; material which has so fallen. M17.
3 *MINING*. (A vein of clay etc. marking) a fault in a lode. L18.
▶ **II 4** A sliding part of a mechanism or firearm; a device which slides or may be slid; *spec*. (on a brass wind instrument) a sliding part used to alter the length of the tube. E17.
5 A sledge; a runner on which something is mounted. L17. ▸**b** *ROWING*. A sliding seat. L19.
6 A tongueless buckle or ring used as a fastener, clasp, or brooch; *spec*. (in full ***hair-slide***) a clip, usu. ornamental, for keeping the hair in place. L18.
7 A thing (to be) slid into place; *spec*. (*a*) a transparent picture prepared for use in a projector, magic lantern, stereoscope, etc.; a photographic transparency; (*b*) (more fully ***microscope slide***) a slip of glass etc. on which an object is mounted or placed for examination with a microscope. E19.
8 *ellipt*. A slide guitar. M20.
▶ **III 9** A smooth surface, esp. of ice, for sliding on or formed by being slid on; a slippery place. L17. ▸**b** The track formed where an otter habitually enters the water. M19.
10 An inclined plane for the transit of timber etc. Also, a chute made to assist the passage of logs downstream. *N. Amer*. M19.
11 A bed, track, groove, etc., on or in which something may slide. M19.
12 A structure with a smooth sloping surface down which children or others may slide at a playground, in a garden, etc. L19.

slide /slʌɪd/ *verb*. Pa. t. **slid** /slɪd/, (*Scot. & north*.) **slade** /sleɪd/. Pa. pple **slid** /slɪd/, (*rare*) **slided**, **slidden** /ˈslɪd(ə)n/.
[Old English *slīdan* (= Low German *slīden*, Middle High German *slīten*) rel. to *slidor* slippery and cogn. with SLED *noun*, SLEDGE *noun*², etc.]
▶ **I** *verb intrans*. **1** Move from one point to another with a smooth and continuous movement; move along a smooth surface whilst in continuous contact with it through the same part; *spec*. glide over ice on one or both feet without skates. OE. ▸**b** Of a stream, liquid, etc.: flow. Now *rare*. LME. ▸**c** *BASEBALL*. Perform a slide (sense 1d). L19. ▸**d** *SURFING*. Ride across the face of a wave. M20.
2 Slip, lose one's foothold; escape through being slippery, hard to hold, or not being grasped; *fig*. lapse morally, go wrong, err. OE.
3 Move, go, or proceed unnoticed, quietly, or stealthily; steal, creep, or slink (*away, into, out of*, etc.); (of a reptile etc.) slither (now *rare*). ME. ▸**b** Go away, make off. *colloq*. (orig. *US*). M19.
4 With adverb or adverbial phr.: pass easily, gradually, or imperceptibly; change or be transformed smoothly. ME. ▸†**b** Fall *asleep, aslumber*, etc. ME–E16. ▸**c** Take its own course; decline through neglect. Chiefly in ***let slide***. LME.

> 🕮 **1** S. JOHNSON I had been sliding in Christ-Church meadow. J. HAWKES At night I see meteors slide across the sky. SCOTT FITZGERALD The ebony panels of one wall had slid aside on a sort of track. C. ISHERWOOD He lets the paper slide to the floor. **2** J. WESLEY Lead me in all thy righteous Ways, Nor suffer me to slide. TENNYSON The snake of gold slid from her hair. D. WELCH My foot slid on something slimy. P. MAILLOUX Franz could get to the top only . . after repeatedly sliding back. **3** S. RICHARDSON He slid away . . as soon as I open'd my Door. LYTTON Steele slid into a seat near my own. **4** HENRY FIELDING How happily must my old age slide away. E. A. FREEMAN It was an easy step for the patron to slide into the beneficiary. J. MORTIMER So the year 1969 slid into history. **c** *New Yorker* His replacement . . found the going rough and let the matter slide.

▶ **II** *verb trans*. **5** Cause to move with a smooth, gliding motion; push over a level surface; slip (a thing) dexterously or unobtrusively *in* or *into*. E17.
6 Cross or descend (a surface etc.) with a smooth, gliding motion. Now *poet*. E17.

> 🕮 **5** R. KIPLING He dropped into a camp-chair . . and slid off his boots. G. VIDAL He slid the window open. M. DUFFY The sergeant slid pencil and paper across the table. E. WELTY He . . slid the key into his pocket.

slide- /slʌɪd/ *combining form*. M16.
[Repr. SLIDE *verb* or *noun*.]
In combs. in various relations with the senses 'that slides', 'along which something slides', 'that has or relates to a slide', etc. Often not hyphenated.
slide-bar either of two bars attached to a steam locomotive's cylinder, between which the piston cross-head slides. **slide copier**, **slide duplicator** *PHOTOGRAPHY* an optical device attached to the front of camera lens for rephotographing a transparency. **slide fastener** (chiefly *US*) a zip-fastener. **slide guitar**: played with a glissando effect produced by moving an object along the strings. **slide projector**: for displaying photographic slides. **slide-rest** an adjustable appliance for holding tools on a lathe. **slide-rock** talus rock. **slide-rule** a ruler having two parts, one of which slides along the other; (now only) a ruler which has a sliding (central) strip and is graduated logarithmically for making rapid calculations by appropriate movement of the sliding strip. **slide trombone**, **slide trumpet**, etc.: having slides for adjusting the pitch. **slide-valve** a valve having a sliding plate for opening and closing an orifice. **slideway** a groove, surface, etc., along which something is meant to slide. **slide-wire** *ELECTRICITY* a resistance wire along which a contact slides in a Wheatstone bridge etc.

slideable *adjective* var. of SLIDABLE.

slider /ˈslʌɪdə/ *noun*. M16.
[from SLIDE *verb* + -ER¹.]
1 A person or thing which slides. Formerly also, a skater. M16.
2 A beam or plank on which something heavy may be slid. L16.
†**3** *MINING*. A horizontal timber for supporting a shaft. M17–E19. ▸**b** A sliding part or device in some mechanical apparatus. L17. ▸†**c** A sliding ring, loop, etc., used to fasten clothing, the hair, etc. L17–E19. ▸†**d** A device for holding and inserting in a microscope a plate with the specimen to be studied. E18–M19. ▸**e** A stand or holder for a bottle or decanter, intended to be slid along the table. M18. ▸†**f** A lantern-slide. L18–M19. ▸**g** A sliding electrical contact serving to control the output etc. of a piece of equipment. L19.
4 Any of various N. American freshwater turtles of the genus *Pseudemys*. Cf. COOTER *noun*¹. L19.
5 Ice-cream served as a sandwich between two wafers. *colloq*. E20.
6 *BASEBALL*. A fast pitch that deviates from its original path. M20.

†**'slidikins** *interjection*. L17–M18.
[from 'SLID + -I- + -KINS.]
God's dear eyelids!: an oath.

sliding /ˈslʌɪdɪŋ/ *ppl adjective*. OE.
[from SLIDE *verb* + -ING².]
1 That slides; that moves or operates by sliding; gliding, flowing; *fig*. (*arch*.) fleeting, inconstant. OE. ▸**b** Of a knot: made so as to slip along a cord, running. L16. ▸**c** Of a door, panel, etc.: that is opened or shut by sliding. E18.
2 Slippery; steeply sloping. *rare*. ME.
3 Accompanied by a sliding movement. L18.
Special collocations: **sliding contact** a connection in an electric circuit that can be slid along a length of resistance wire. **sliding hernia** (*MEDICINE*) a hernia of an organ which is normally partly outside the peritoneum. **sliding keel** a centreboard. **sliding rule** (now *rare*) a slide-rule. **sliding scale** †(*a*) a slide-rule; (*b*) a scale of fees, taxes, wages, etc., that varies as a whole in accordance with variation in some standard. **sliding seat** a seat in an outrigger which moves backwards and forwards with the action of the rower.
■ **slidingly** *adverb* M17.

slied *verb pa. t. & pple* of SLY *verb*.

'slife /slʌɪf/ *interjection*. Now *rare* or *obsolete*. M17.
[Abbreviation.]
God's life!: an oath.

slift /slɪft/ *noun*. *dial*. Also (earlier) †**sliff**. E19.
[Origin unkn.]
The fleshy part of a leg of beef.

slifter /ˈslɪftə/ *noun*. *obsolete* exc. *dial*. E17.
[Rel. to SLIVE *verb*¹.]
A cleft, a crack, a crevice.

slifting /ˈslɪftɪŋ/ *noun*. L20.
[from S(ENTENCE *noun* + LIFTING *noun*.]
LINGUISTICS. In transformational grammar, a rule or transformation which promotes material from an embedded sentence following a cognitive verb to a main sentence.

slight /slʌɪt/ *noun*. M16.
[from SLIGHT *adjective*, *verb*.]
†**1** A very small amount or weight; a small matter, a trifle. M16–M18.
2 a Marked indifference or disregard, supercilious treatment. Now *rare*. E18. ▸**b** An instance of slighting or being slighted; a marked display of disregard, a failure to show due respect. E18.

> 🕮 **2b** J. CAREY She has to put up with constant slights and humiliations. B. UNSWORTH He had demeaned me, imposed a slight on me.

slight /slʌɪt/ *adjective & adverb*. ME.
[Old Norse *sléttr* level, smooth, soft = Old Frisian *sliuht*, Old Saxon *sliht*, Middle Low German, Middle Dutch *slecht*, *slicht* simple, defective (Dutch *slecht* bad, *slechts* merely), Old High German *sleht* level (German *schlecht* bad, *schlicht* simple), Gothic *slaihts* level, from Germanic.]
▶ **A** *adjective*. **1** Smooth; glossy; sleek. *obsolete* exc. *dial*. ME.
2 Small and slender; frail-looking; insubstantial, flimsy; thin in texture. ME.
3 Small in amount, quantity, degree, etc.; scanty; barely perceptible. Also, unimportant, trifling. ME. ▸†**b** Of low status; humble in position. LME–L17.
4 Half-hearted, lacking spirit. Formerly also, slighting, contemptuous. *rare*. M17.

> 🕮 **2** F. SPALDING Whereas Stevie remained slight in build, Molly . . had grown thickset. *Plays International* The character-list virtually tells the story of this slight play. †**slight falcon** = ***falcon-gentle*** s.v. FALCON 1. **3** DRYDEN Slight is the Subject, but the Praise not small. THACKERAY He never had had the slightest liking for her. E. BOWEN His knowledge of French is slight. N. FARAH The family's economy couldn't afford the slightest waste. A. SILLITOE The uniform fitted, except for a slight pressure at the shoulders. I. MURDOCH She spoke . . with a slight accent, an Edinburgh accent. **make slight of** *arch*. treat as of little importance.

▶ **B** *adverb*. Slightly. Now *arch. & poet*. L16.
■ **slightish** *adjective* somewhat slight M18. **slightness** *noun* L16.

slight /slʌɪt/ *verb trans*. ME.
[Sense 1a from Old Norse *slétta*, from *sléttr* (see the adjective); sense 1b from Dutch *slechten*, Low German *slichten*; sense 2 from the adjective.]
1 †**a** Make smooth or level. ME–E17. ▸**b** *Hist*. Raze to the ground, make (a fortification) militarily useless by complete or partial demolition. M17.
2 Treat with indifference or disrespect; pay little or no attention to; disregard, ignore. Formerly also, pass *off* or *over* as unimportant or negligible. L16. ▸†**b** Throw contemptuously. *rare* (Shakes.). Only in L16.

> 🕮 **1b** *Country Life* Parliament gave orders that Corfe [Castle] should be slighted. **2** R. W. EMERSON He delighted in . . men of science, . . but the men of letters he slighted. G. DALY She . . refused no one, so that no partner felt slighted or rejected.

■ **slighter** *noun* a person who slights or disdains something or someone M17. **slightingly** *adverb* contemptuously, disdainfully; with little regard or respect: M17.

slighten /ˈslʌɪt(ə)n/ *verb trans*. *rare*. E17.
[from SLIGHT *adjective* or *verb* + -EN⁵.]
1 = SLIGHT *verb* 2. E17.
2 Level, raze. *Scot*. E20.
3 Make smaller or more slight. M20.

slightly /ˈslʌɪtli/ *adverb*. E16.
[from SLIGHT *adjective* + -LY².]
1 Slimly, slenderly; flimsily, unsubstantially. E16.
2 Carelessly; lightly; half-heartedly, indifferently. M16.
3 With little respect or ceremony; slightingly. Now *rare*. M16.
4 In a slight or small degree; to a slight extent; hardly perceptibly. L16.

slighty /ˈslʌɪti/ *adjective*. *obsolete* exc. *dial*. E17.
[from SLIGHT *adjective* + -Y¹.]
†**1** Negligent, careless; lacking in thoroughness. Only in 17.
2 Slighting, contemptuous. M17.
3 Slight, unimportant, trivial. Also, insubstantial, slender, weak. M17.

slily *adverb* var. of SLYLY.

slim /slɪm/ *noun*. M16.
[Sense 1, 3 formed as the adjective; sense 2 from the verb.]
†**1** A (lanky and) lazy or worthless person. Latterly *dial*. M16–M19.
2 A course of slimming, a diet. L20.
3 (Usu. **S-**.) In central Africa: Aids (so-called from the severe weight loss associated with the disease). Also more fully ***Slim disease***. L20.

> 🕮 **2** *Navy News* Skilliter went on a sponsored slim and lost 3st.

¶ In sense 1 recorded earlier than the adjective and repr. a pejorative sense found in Dutch and German but little developed in English.

slim /slɪm/ *adjective*. Compar. & superl. **-mm-**. M17.
[Low German, Dutch, repr. Middle Low German *slim(m)*, Middle Dutch *slim(p)*, slanting, cross, bad = Middle High German *slimp*, *-b* slanting, oblique, German *schlimm* grievous, bad, from Germanic.]
1 Slender, (gracefully) thin; of small girth or thickness, long and narrow; *esp*. (of a person) not fat or overweight. M17. ▸**b** Small, slight; insubstantial, insufficient; meagre. L17. ▸**c** Of a garment: cut on slender lines, designed to give an appearance of slimness. L19. ▸**d** (Of goods etc.) low in price, economical; (of an organization) trimmed down to an economical level. L20.
2 Sly, cunning, crafty, wily; malicious. *dial. & colloq*. (esp. *S. Afr*.). M17.
3 In poor health, delicate, not robust. *US*. E19.

> 🕮 **1** I. MURDOCH Gracie was a great eater, but remained slim. **slim cake** a plain cake of a kind made in Ireland. **slim jim** (*colloq*.) a very slim person or thing; *spec*. (*a*) (in *pl*.) long narrow trousers; (*b*) a long thin tie (freq. *attrib*.). **slim volume** a book, usu. of verse, by a little-known author. **b** G. R. TURNER Chances of promotion were slim. **d** *Birmingham Post* A slimmer public service was inevitable.

■ **slimly** *adverb* (*a*) *rare* cunningly, artfully; (*b*) slenderly, thinly, sparsely; so as to give an appearance of slimness: L17. **slimness** *noun* E18.

slim /slɪm/ *verb*. Infl. **-mm-**. E19.
[from the adjective.]
1 *verb trans.* Skimp (work). Also, idle *away* (time). *dial.* E19.
2 *verb trans.* Make slim or slender; *fig.* reduce in size or extent. Freq. foll. by *down*. M19.
3 *verb intrans.* (Try to) reduce one's weight by dieting, exercise, etc.; become slim. Also foll. by *down*. Freq. as ***slimming*** *verbal noun*. M20.

> 🕮 **2** *Observer* Tate & Lyle has slimmed its labour force. **3** *Punch* The hostess ate hardly any. She is slimming. *fig.*: *International Business Week* Another bid to slim down and generate profits.

■ **slimmer** *noun* a person who practises slimming; ***slimmers' disease***, ***slimmer's disease***, anorexia nervosa: L20. **slimming** *ppl adjective* conducive to slimness, producing an appearance of slimness E20.

slime /slʌɪm/ *noun*.
[Old English *slīm* = Old Frisian, Middle Low German, Middle Dutch, Middle High German *slīm* (Dutch *slijm*, German *Schleim* phlegm, slime, mucus), Old Norse *slím*, from Germanic word rel. to Latin *limus* mud, slime, Greek *limnē* marsh.]
1 Thick slippery mud; soft glutinous matter, esp. when noxious or unpleasant; mucus or a similar viscous secretion. OE. ▸**b** *spec.* Natural bitumen. M16. ▸**c** MINING. Powdered ore in the form of mud. M18. ▸**d** Insoluble matter deposited at the anode in the electrolytic refining of copper etc. Also ***anode slime***. E20.
2 *fig.* (The material of) the human body, considered as sinful or base; something morally filthy or disgusting. Also (*slang*), an obnoxious person. ME.

> 🕮 **1** S. WEYMAN The clinging slime and the reek of the marsh. R. FRAME Snails trailed their silver slime. **2** SPENSER Th'eternall Lord in fleshly slime Enwombed was. HAZLITT Varnished over with the slime of servility.

Comb.: **slime bacterium** = MYXOBACTERIUM; **slime-ball** *slang* a repulsive or despicable person; **slime-eel** a hagfish; **slime-flux** a slimy excretion from diseased trees, the result of fungal or bacterial attacks; **slime mould** any spore-bearing micro-organism that secretes slime; *spec.* a myxomycete.

slime /slʌɪm/ *verb*. LME.
[from the noun.]
1 *verb trans.* Smear or cover with slime. LME.
2 *verb trans.* Clear of slime by scraping. E18.
3 *verb trans.* & *intrans.* Make (one's way) by crawling or stealthily. M19.

> 🕮 **1** O. MANNING The cells slimed with damp. E. BOWEN Seaweed slimed some exposed rocks. **3** *fig.*: A. CROSS A few girl students . . slimed all over him.

slimline /ˈslɪmlʌɪn/ *adjective*. M20.
[from SLIM *adjective* + LINE *noun*[2].]
Slim, narrow; of slender design; *fig.* stripped of unnecessary elaboration, meagre.

slimnastics /slɪmˈnastɪks/ *noun*. *N. Amer.* M20.
[Blend of *slimming* (verbal noun from SLIM *verb*) and *gymnastics*.]
Gymnastic exercise intended to promote slimming.

slimsy /ˈslɪmzi, -si/ *adjective*. *US colloq.* Also **slimpsy** /ˈslɪm(p)si/. M19.
[from SLIM *adjective* + -SY.]
Flimsy, frail.

slimy /ˈslʌɪmi/ *adjective*. LME.
[from SLIME *noun* + -Y[1].]
1 Of the nature or consistency of slime; viscous (and noxious or unpleasant). LME.
2 Covered or smeared with slime; full of slime. LME.
3 *fig.* Morally objectionable, base, vile; now *colloq.*, deceitfully meek or flattering, dishonest. L16.

> 🕮 **1** V. WOOLF The shell broke and something slimy oozed from the crack. **2** M. MEYER We ate under-fried eggs . . . all slimy. **3** G. B. SHAW The slimy little liar! I. WATSON To violate an oath . . is a pretty slimy thing.

■ **slimily** *adverb* E17. **sliminess** *noun* E16.

sline /slʌɪn/ *noun*. E19.
[Origin unkn.]
MINING. A vertical joint parallel to the face in a coal seam.

sling /slɪŋ/ *noun*[1]. ME.
[Prob. from Low Dutch (cf. Middle Low German *slinge*, German *Schlinge* noose, snare, arm-sling), of symbolic origin. Branch III from the verb.]
▸**I 1** A simple weapon for throwing stones etc., consisting essentially of a loop of leather or other material in which the missile is whirled and then let fly. ME. ▸**b** *Hist.* A ballista or similar device for hurling rocks etc. Now *rare*. M16.

> 🕮 **1** *fig.*: SHAKES. *Haml.* The slings and arrows of outrageous fortune.

▸**II 2** A strap, belt, rope, etc., in the form of a loop, in which an object may be raised, lowered, or suspended, or (later) in which a baby may be carried. ME. ▸**b** *spec.* A strap attached to a rifle etc. enabling it to be carried slung over the shoulder. E18. ▸**c** A band of material formed into a loop and suspended from the neck so as to support an injured arm. E18. ▸**d** A short length of rope used to provide additional support for the body in abseiling etc. E20.
3 NAUTICAL. A rope by which the middle of a yard is suspended from the mast; in *pl.*, the middle part of a yard. E17.

> 🕮 **2** *Times* With . . sling, earthmover and helicopter the . . forest is planted. **c** ***have one's ass in a sling*** (*US slang*) be in trouble. ***wear one's arm in a sling***: see WEAR *verb*[1].

▸**III 4** The action or an act of slinging; a fling, a throw. M16.
5 A gratuity; a bribe. *Austral.* M20.
Comb.: **sling-back** *noun* & *adjective* (*a*) (designating) a woman's shoe with an open back, held on by a strap across the heel; (*b*) (designating) a chair with a fabric seat suspended from a rigid frame; **sling-bag**: with a long strap which may be hung from the shoulder; **sling-cart** MILITARY a two-wheeled cart for carrying a cannon; **sling chair** *US* a sling-back chair; **sling pump** *N. Amer.* a sling-back shoe; **slingsman** *Hist.* a soldier armed with a sling; **sling-stone** a stone or pebble (suitable to be) cast by a sling.

†**sling** *noun*[2]. Also (earlier, chiefly *Scot.*) **slang**. E16–M18.
[Middle Dutch, Middle Low German *slange* (Dutch *slang*, German *Schlange*) serpent, cannon, etc.; perh. infl. by prec.]
A cannon; a serpentine; a culverin.

sling /slɪŋ/ *noun*[3]. M18.
[Origin unkn.]
1 A sweetened and flavoured drink of spirits (esp. gin) and water. Orig. *N. Amer.* M18.
2 In sugar refining, the juice of the sugar cane. E19.
1 ***gin sling***: see GIN *noun*[2]. SINGAPORE SLING.

sling /slɪŋ/ *verb*. Pa. t. & pple **slung** /slʌŋ/. ME.
[from SLING *noun*[1] or (branch I) Old Norse *slyngva*.]
▸**I 1** *verb trans.* Cast (a stone etc.) by means of a sling. ME.
2 *verb trans. gen.* Throw or fling in some direction or to some point, esp. with a whirling action. Now *colloq.* ME. ▸**b** Hand or give out, dispense, distribute; utter, say, speak; (also foll. by *in*) give up, abandon. *colloq.* LME.
3 *verb intrans.* Move as if thrown by a sling; fling oneself. ME. ▸**b** Advance with long or swinging strides. Chiefly *Scot., north., & Austral.* E19.
4 *verb intrans.* Pay a bribe or gratuity. *Austral.* M20.

> 🕮 **1** *absol.*: C. READE The besieged slung at the tower. **2** J. DICKEY I took the gun . . and slung it . . over the river. W. MARSHALL He was so . . stupid we slung him out. R. CARVER She slings the shirt over the line. **b** H. ALLEN Don't leave me stranded, . . I can't sling the lingo. K. TENNANT We both slung in our jobs . . and went. **3** J. CLARE Thou corner-chair, In which I've oft slung back.

▸**II 5** *verb trans.* Place in or secure with a sling or slings; raise, lower, or suspend using a sling or slings. E16. ▸**b** NAUTICAL. Secure (a yard) to the mast with chains or lashings. E17.
6 *verb trans.* Hang, attach, or carry (as) in a sling; allow to hang loosely; *esp.* carry loosely about one's person. Also, suspend by attachment at two or more points; *esp.* put up (a hammock). Freq. as ***slung*** *ppl adjective*. L17.

> 🕮 **5** CONAN DOYLE Horse after horse was slung . . up from the barges. **6** S. BECKETT A tray of flowers slung from her neck by a strap. P. BROOK A wire had to be slung from wall to wall. J. LE CARRÉ With a . . satchel slung across his little chest. E. WELTY His belt slung low about his hips.

Phrases: ***sling mud***: see MUD *noun*[1]. **sling off** *Austral.* & *NZ colloq.* jeer (*at*). ***sling one's hammock***: see HAMMOCK *noun*[1] 1. ***sling one's hook***: see HOOK *noun*. ***sling the bat***: see BAT *noun*[5]. ***sling the hatchet***: see HATCHET *noun* 1.

slinge /slɪn(d)ʒ/ *verb intrans. dial.* & *Canad.* M18.
[Origin unkn.]
Slink, skulk; lounge, loaf *about*; play truant.

slinger /ˈslɪŋə/ *noun*. ME.
[from SLING *verb* + -ER[1].]
1 A person who throws missiles using a sling; *Hist.* a soldier armed with a sling; *gen.* (*colloq.*) a person who slings something. ME.
2 A worker who uses a sling for lifting. L19.
3 Bread soaked in tea. Usu. in *pl. slang* (chiefly *Services*'). L19.

slingshot /ˈslɪŋʃɒt/ *noun* & *verb*. Orig. *US*. M19.
[from SLING *verb* + SHOT *noun*[1].]
▸**A** *noun*. **1** A catapult. M19.
2 A shot (as) from a catapult. M20. ▸**b** ASTRONAUTICS. The use of the gravitational pull of a celestial body to accelerate and change the course of a spacecraft. Freq. *attrib.* L20.
▸**B** *verb intrans.* Infl. **-tt-**. Move as if from a slingshot; *esp.* (of a vehicle) accelerate rapidly. *colloq.* M20.

slink /slɪŋk/ *adjective* & *noun*. E17.
[from the verb.]
▸**A** *adjective*. **1** (Of hide, meat, etc.) from a premature or abortive animal, inferior; (of an animal) premature or abortive; (of a butcher) dealing in slink meat. E17.
2 Lank, lean, ill-conditioned. *dial.* L17.
▸**B** *noun*. **1** An abortive or premature calf or other animal. Chiefly *dial.* M17.
2 The skin or flesh of a premature calf or other animal; a piece of this. M18.
3 A small, weak or immature animal, *esp.* a thin salmon in poor condition. *N. Amer. dial.* L18.
4 A person who slinks; a sneak, a coward. *colloq.* E19.
5 A slinking movement or walk. M19.

slink /slɪŋk/ *verb*. Pa. t. & pa. pple **slunk** /slʌŋk/.
[Old English *slincan*, corresp. to Middle & mod. Low German *slinken* subside.]
1 *verb intrans.* Orig. (in Old English), crawl, creep. Now, move in a stealthy, guilty, or sneaking manner. (Foll. by *away*, *by*, *off*, etc.) OE.
2 *verb trans.* Move or turn stealthily or quietly. *rare*. E17.
3 *verb trans.* Of an animal: bear (young) prematurely or abortively. M17.

> 🕮 **1** SIR W. SCOTT He slunk from college by . . secret paths. D. DU MAURIER A cat that slinks by night, its belly to the ground. I. MURDOCH I must tell her I'm going . . , I can't just slink away. **2** J. GALSWORTHY Slinking her eyes round at the Countess.

■ **slinker** *noun* (*a*) *rare* an animal which slinks its young; (*b*) a person who slinks about; a shirker, a sneak: E19. **slinkingly** *adverb* in a slinking manner, stealthily, furtively M19.

slinky /ˈslɪŋki/ *adjective* & *noun*. E20.
[from prec. + -Y[1], -Y[6].]
▸**A** *adjective*. (Orig. esp. of a woman) gracefully or alluringly slender, sinuous in movement, lithe; (of a garment) close-fitting and flowing. Also, stealthy, furtive, dishonest. *colloq.* E20.

> 🕮 *Glasgow Herald* A slinky gown of flat crepe. A. TYLER Walking that slinky way he has.

▸**B** *noun*. (**S-**.) (Proprietary name for) a toy consisting of a flexible helical spring which can be made to somersault down steps. M20.
■ **slinkily** *adverb* M20. **slinkiness** *noun* L19.

slip /slɪp/ *noun*[1].
[Old English *slipa*, *slyppe*: cf. Norwegian *slip(a)* slime on fish. Cf. SLOP *noun*[2].]
†**1** A soft semi-liquid mass, slime; mud. OE–L15.
2 Curdled milk. Now *rare* or *obsolete*. LME.
3 A creamy mixture of clay and water used in pottery-making, esp. for decorating earthenware. M17.
Comb.: **slip casting** the manufacture of ceramics by allowing slip to solidify in a porous mould; **slip-ware** pottery decorated with slip.
¶ The 2nd elem. of COWSLIP, OXLIP.
■ **slipped** *adjective* painted or ornamented with slip E20.

slip /slɪp/ *noun*[2]. LME.
[Prob. from Middle Low German, Middle Dutch *slippe* (Dutch *slip*) cut, slit, strip.]
†**1** A cut, a slit. *rare*. LME–L17.
2 The edge, skirt, or flap of a garment etc.; a border. *rare*. LME. ▸**b** A light underwaistcoat with the edge showing as a border. M20.
3 a A cutting taken from a plant for grafting or planting. L15. ▸**b** *fig.* A scion, a descendant; an offshoot, an outgrowth. L16.
4 A spoon-handle with the top cut off obliquely; a spoon with a handle of this style fashionable in the 16th cent. Now chiefly in ***slip-top***. E16.
5 A long, relatively thin and narrow piece or strip of or *of* a material. M16. ▸**b** *spec.* A small piece of or *of* paper, esp. for writing on. L17. ▸†**c** A newspaper printed in the form of a long slip of paper. L17–E18. ▸**d** A printer's proof (usu. unpaged) on a long piece of paper; a galley proof. E19. ▸**e** A memorandum summarizing the terms of an insurance, before a policy is drawn up. E19.
6 A strip *of* land, ground, etc. L16.
7 A quantity *of* yarn etc. *obsolete* exc. *dial.* L16.
8 A young person of either sex, *esp.* one of small or slender build; also, a thin person of any age. Freq. foll. by *of*, esp. in ***slip of a girl***. L16. ▸**b** A young store-pig. Also foll. by *of*. *dial.*, *Austral.*, & *NZ*. M19 ▸**c** A sole (fish) of intermediate size. L19.
9 An elongated or slender specimen *of* something. M18.
10 A narrow elongated window, passage, etc.; *spec.* (in *pl.*) the sides of the gallery of a theatre. (Cf. SLIP *noun*[3] 5.) M18.

> 🕮 **3a** L. M. MONTGOMERY I took a slip of the . . Scotch rosebud his mother brought out from Scotland. **b** G. CRABBE He talk'd of bastard slips, and cursed his bed. CARLYLE Some small slip of heathendom. **5** F. RUTLEY A glass slip is now placed on the hot plate. M. M. KAYE He broke the little slip of mother-of-pearl in two. **b** M. DAS A rubber-stamped . . slip served as a ticket. U. HOLDEN It was decided to draw lots from slips of paper. ***pink slip***: see PINK *adjective*[2]. **6** *Landscape* A slip of derelict railway land sandwiched between traffic . . and trains. **8** BROWNING He was puny, an under-sized slip. J. GALSWORTHY A poor thin slip of a shop-girl. **9** T. HOOK A neat sanded slip of a coffee-room.

slip /slɪp/ *noun*³. LME.
[from SLIP *verb*¹.]
▶ **I 1** A man-made slope of stone etc. on which boats are landed. Later also (chiefly *US*), a small dock or individual berth for a boat. LME. ▶**b** An inclined structure sloping down to the water, on which ships are built and repaired. Also ***building-slip***. Also in *pl.* M18.
2 A stairway; a narrow descending roadway or passage; a defile. *local.* L15.

📖 **1** C. MILNE I stand on the ferry slip looking across the river.

▶ **II 3 a** A leash which enables an animal to be released quickly. L16. ▶**b** A noose; a loop; a loose cord. Now *esp.* in BOOKBINDING, the end of a cord which is frayed before being attached to the boards. L17. ▶**c** NAUTICAL. A rope with a shackle or other fastening for quick release. L19.
4 a A child's pinafore or frock. Long *obsolete* exc. *dial.* L17. ▶**b** A loose-fitting garment for women or girls. Now *spec.*, an underskirt or petticoat worn from the waist or the shoulders and having no sleeves. M18. ▶**c** More fully ***pillowslip***. A pillowcase. E19. ▶**d** A case or holder for carrying a gun. Also ***gun slip***. L20.
5 In *pl.* The side of a theatrical stage, where the actors stand before entering. Cf. SLIP *noun*² 10. L18.
3c *SENHOUSE slip*. **4b** *your slip is showing*: see SHOW *verb*.
▶ **III 6** An act of evading or escaping. Chiefly in ***give someone the slip*** below. L16.
7 An act or process of slipping, sliding, or falling down; *ellipt.* a landslip. L16. ▶**b** GEOLOGY. A slight fault or dislocation. Also (now usu.), the extent of relative displacement of adjacent points on either side of a fault plane. L18. ▶**c** (The extent of) deviation of an object from its expected path through a fluid; *spec.* (*a*) the difference between the pitch of a propeller and the distance moved through the ambient medium in one revolution; (*b*) sideways movement of an aircraft in flight, esp. downwards towards the centre of curvature of a turn (cf. SIDE-SLIP *noun* 3b). M19. ▶**d** (The extent of) relative movement of a solid object or surface and a solid surface with which it is in contact; *spec.* (*a*) a reduction in the movement of a pulley etc. due to slipping of the belt, rope, chain, etc.; (*b*) relative movement of the plates of a clutch when they are in contact; (*c*) movement of a layer of ions over another in a stressed crystal. L19. ▶**e** The proportion by which the speed of an electric motor falls short of the speed of rotation of the magnetic flux inside it. L19. ▶**f** A delay in the completion of a task; the length of time by which something is behind schedule. M20.
8 A mistake, an oversight, *esp.* an accidental or slight error; a moral lapse. L16.
9 The action of releasing a dog to pursue a deer, hare, etc. E17.
10 An abortion. *obsolete* exc. *Scot. rare.* M17.
11 CRICKET. A close fielder (freq. one of a number) stationed behind the batsman usu. on the off side; a position which is or could be occupied by such a fielder, between wicket-keeper and gully (often in *pl.*). See also ***leg slip*** s.v. LEG *noun*. E19.

📖 **6 give someone the slip** evade or escape from someone, slip away from someone unperceived. **7** DEFOE By . . some Slip of my Foot . . I fell down. O. S. NOCK The tendency of the engine . . to go into a heavy slip which resulted in buckled side rods. *Proverb*: There's many a slip 'twixt cup and lip. **8 slip of the pen** an accidental written mistake. **slip of the tongue** an accidental spoken mistake. **11** *Times* He varied his lustier blows with deft glances through the slips. attrib.: ***slip-catch***, ***slip-fielder***, etc. **first slip**, **second slip**, **third slip**, etc.: nearest to, next nearest to, further from, the wicket-keeper.

†**slip** *noun*⁴. L16–M17.
[Perh. a use of SLIP *noun*², *noun*³.]
A counterfeit coin.

slip /slɪp/ *verb*¹. Infl. **-pp-**. ME.
[Prob. from Middle Low German, Dutch *slippen* = Middle High German *slipfen*, from Germanic base of SLIPPER *adjective*. Sense 11 from SLIP *noun*³.]
▶ **I** *verb intrans.* **1** With adverbs & prepositions: pass or go lightly, quietly, smoothly, or easily; move quickly and softly, without attracting notice; glide, steal; pass gradually, inadvertently, or imperceptibly; (of time) go by rapidly or unnoticed. ME. ▶**b** Get *out of* or *into* a garment etc. in an easy or hurried manner; slide *in* or *into* a socket etc. Also, admit of being taken *off* or put *on* by sliding. E16.
2 Escape, get away. Usu. (with adverbs & prepositions), escape restraint or capture by being slippery, hard to hold, or not being grasped.; freq. *fig.*; (of speech etc.) escape from (a person, the lips, etc.); (of news etc.) leak *out*. ME.
3 Slide inadvertently on a smooth or slippery surface, esp. for a short distance; lose one's footing; fail to hold or stick. ME. ▶**b** AERONAUTICS. Side-slip. E20.
4 Fall into error; make a careless or casual mistake. Now freq. foll. by *up* (*colloq.*). ME. ▶**b** Fall away from a standard in behaviour, achievement, etc.; deteriorate, lapse; decline in value etc.; (of a task) fall behind schedule. *colloq.* E20.
5 Of bark: peel off. *rare.* L18.

📖 **1** TENNYSON The silent water slipping from the hills. T. HARDY I came downstairs without any noise and slipped out. H. JAMES How had their time together slipped along so smoothly . . ? R. DAHL Our little vessel slipped between two . . islands. J. M. COETZEE Making barely a splash, I slipped overboard. J. DISKI He was slipping into madness. S. ROSENBERG Summer had slipped into autumn. **b** H. GLASSE Boil your beans so that the skin will slip off. R. JAFFE She slipped into her dress. R. CARVER She'd slipped out of her underthings. **2** W. ROBERTSON Elizabeth did not suffer such a favourable opportunity to slip. I. GURNEY Memory, let all slip save what is sweet. W. S. MAUGHAM The words slipped out . . independent of her will. A. CARTER The glasses slip from her fingers and smash. **3** J. TYNDALL The snow . . frequently slips and rolls down in avalanches. W. J. M. RANKINE The . . force which prevents the . . wheels from slipping on the rails. A. GRAY His foot slipped and he fell. M. GEE The cool silky stuff of his shirt slipping over his skin. **4** SHAKES. *Meas. for M.* I am sorry one so . . wise . . Should slip so grossly. B. BETTELHEIM Sooner or later I would slip up. **b** E. FERRARS He'd been slipping lately, drinking too much. *European Investor* The . . shares slipped 2 per cent. R. BELBEN Father lived to eighty-four, his mind slipped towards the end.

▶ **II** *verb trans.* **6** With adverbs & prepositions: cause to move lightly, quietly, smoothly, or easily; insert, transfer, or place stealthily, casually, or with a sliding motion; take or pull (a garment etc.) easily or hastily *on* or *off*. ME. ▶**b** Give quietly, slyly, or clandestinely. M19.
7 Let go, allow to escape; loosen one's hold or grasp of; release (an animal) from a leash or slip. ME. ▶**b** Allow to escape one's lips, utter inadvertently. L16. ▶**c** NAUTICAL. Allow (an anchor-cable etc.) to run out, freq. with a buoy attached, when leaving an anchorage in haste; disengage (an anchor) in this way. M17. ▶**d** Of an animal: produce (young) prematurely, give birth to by miscarriage. M17. ▶**e** KNITTING. Move (a stitch) to the other needle without knitting the stitch. M19. ▶**f** Detach (a carriage) from a moving train, in order to allow passengers to get out at a certain station (cf. ***slip-carriage*** s.v. SLIP-). M19.
8 Allow (an occasion, opportunity, etc.) to pass by; fail to take advantage of (an opportunity). Formerly also, waste (time). Now *rare.* LME. ▶**b** Pass over, fail to mention or consider; neglect to do; skip, miss. L16. ▶†**c** Fail in keeping (a prescribed time). E17–E18.
9 Elude or evade, esp. in a stealthy manner, escape from; give the slip to; outdistance; escape from the grasp of, get loose from. E16. ▶**b** Escape from (one's memory); elude (one's notice, knowledge, etc.). M17. ▶**c** Pass or escape inadvertently from (the pen, tongue, etc.). M18. ▶**d** BOXING. Avoid (a punch) by moving quickly aside. E20.
10 Cause to slide or lose hold; *esp.* undo (a knot) in this way. Also, suffer an accidental sliding of (one's foot etc.). E17. ▶**b** Dislocate (a joint). E18.
11 Place (a boat) on a slip for inspection, repair, etc. M20.

📖 **6** F. BURNEY I was obliged to slip on my morning gown. W. CATHER She slipped her hand through his arm. C. ISHERWOOD The left hand is . . on the wheel; the right slips the gearshift . . into high. R. INGALLS She told him the answers to all his questions and slipped in all her own. A. DESAI Clumsily slipped off the . . pink ribbon that held together the cards. G. SWIFT Ray . . slipped a halter over the pony's neck. **b** CARLYLE The Custom-house people . . were pacified by slipping them a ducat. S. BRILL At . . lunch . . he slipped Provenzano $1,500. A. DAVIES For these small favours he slips me a case of port now and then. **7** TENNYSON Our falcon . . Who lost the hern we slipt her at. **b** GOLDSMITH They . . mortified us . . by slipping out an oath. **c** R. H. DANA We made sail, slipped our cable. *absol.*: J. SMEATON The Weston . . was . . ordered to slip and make her best port. **8** DEFOE Advantages slipt in war are never recovered. **9** J. VANBRUGH He sees me; 'tis too late to slip him. CARLYLE Rascality has slipped its muzzle. C. J. TOLLEY We were allowed to slip our guards and go . . in the pine woods. *Observer* In racing parlance, Weinstock has slipped his rivals. **b** G. GREENE It slipped Wormold's memory that his nephew was . . past seventeen. P. BARKER She had promised to collect them: it had slipped her mind till now. **10** SHAKES. *Tr. & Cr.* The bonds of heaven are slipp'd, dissolv'd, and loos'd. **b** J. GAY May . . my mare slip her shoulder . . if I ever forsake thee!

Phrases: ***let slip***: see LET *verb*¹. ***let slip through one's fingers***: see FINGER *noun*. **slip a disc** sustain a slipped disc. **slip in the clutch**, **slip the clutch** release the clutch of a vehicle etc. slightly or momentarily. **slip into** *slang* assail with blows, attack. **slip one's cable**, (now *rare*) **slip one's wind** *fig.* die. ***slipped disc***: see DISC *noun*. **slip something over on** *colloq.* take advantage of by trickery, hoodwink, outwit. ***slip the clutch***: see **slip in the clutch** above. ***slip the painter***: see PAINTER *noun*² 2. **slip through the net** *fig.* evade detection or apprehension; escape someone's vigilance; be overlooked.

slip /slɪp/ *verb*² *trans.* Infl. **-pp-**. L15.
[Middle & mod. Low German, Middle Dutch *slippen* cut, incise, cleave, etc.]
† **1** Cut (a spoon-handle) obliquely at the end. L15–E17.
2 Part (a slip or cutting) from a stock, stalk, etc., esp. for the purpose of propagation. Freq. foll. by *off*, *from*. L15. ▶**b** HERALDRY. As ***slipped*** *ppl adjective*: designating a flower etc. represented with its stem. E17.

slip /slɪp/ *verb*³ *trans.* Infl. **-pp-**. L19.
[from SLIP *noun*².]
Note or enter on a slip or slips (of paper etc.).

slip- /slɪp/ *combining form*. E16.
[from SLIP *verb*¹ or *noun*³.]
In combs. in various relations with the senses 'that slips', 'that can be readily slipped in, on, off, etc.', 'that involves a slip or slipping'. Often not hyphenated.
slip-carriage (chiefly *Hist.*) a railway carriage (to be) detached from a moving train in order to coast under its own momentum to a station where the rest of the train does not stop. **slip-case** a close-fitting case for a book or books, allowing the spine(s) to remain visible. **slip-cased** *adjective* contained in a slip-case. **slip-coach** (chiefly *Hist.*) = ***slip-carriage*** above. **slip-coat (cheese)** (now *rare* or *obsolete*) a kind of soft cream cheese. **slip-cover** (*a*) *N. Amer.* = ***loose cover*** s.v. LOOSE *adjective*; (*b*) a calico etc. cover for furniture out of use; (*c*) a dust-jacket or a slip-case for a book. **slip edition** a special (usu. local) edition of a newspaper, carrying extra news items. **slip face** the steepest face of a sand-dune, down which sand slips. **slip-form** *noun & verb* ENGINEERING (*a*) *noun* an open-ended mould in which a long uniform structure can be cast by filling the mould with concrete and continually moving and refilling it as the concrete sets; (*b*) *verb trans.* cast using this technique. **slip-hook** NAUTICAL a hinged hook with the tongue held in place by a link to allow a quick release. **slip-horn** a slide-trombone. **slip-in** *adjective* that allows a person or thing to slip in or be slipped in easily or readily. **slip joint** a joint in a pipe, one section of which can move telescopically within another, allowing longitudinal expansion and contraction. **slip-knot** (*a*) a knot which can be readily slipped or untied; (*b*) a knot made to slip along the cord round which it is made, a running knot. **slip-noose** a noose which tightens and slackens by means of a slip-knot. **slip-on** *noun & adjective* (a garment etc., now *esp.* a shoe) that may be slipped on and off readily. **slipover** *adjective & noun* (*a*) *adjective* (of a garment) made to be slipped on over the head; (*b*) *noun* a pullover, usu. with a V-neck and no sleeves. **slip-plane** CRYSTALLOGRAPHY = ***glide-plane*** (a) s.v. GLIDE *verb*. **slip-rail** (chiefly *Austral.*) a fence-rail which can be easily removed so as to leave an opening. **slip ratio** the ratio of the slip of a propeller to the pitch. **slip ring** ELECTRICAL ENGINEERING a ring of conducting material which is attached to and rotates with a shaft, so that electric current may be transferred to a stationary circuit through a fixed brush pressing against the ring. **slip-road** a short (usu. one-way) road giving access to or exit from a motorway etc. **slip-rope** NAUTICAL a rope that can be easily slipped; *spec.* one with both ends on board so that casting loose either end releases it. **slip sheet** PRINTING a sheet of paper interleaving newly printed sheets to prevent set-off or smudging. **slip-shoe** (*obsolete* exc. *dial.*) a light or loose shoe, a slipper. **slip-stitch** (*a*) a loose stitch joining layers of fabric, not visible externally; (*b*) in knitting, a stitch moved to the other needle without being knitted. **slipstone** a shaped oilstone used for sharpening gouges. **slip-string** (*obsolete* exc. *dial.*) a person who deserves to be hanged; a rogue, a rascal. **slip-up** *colloq.* an act or instance of slipping up; a failure, a mistake, a blunder. **slipway** a sloping way leading down into the water for launching ships; a building- or landing-slip.

slipe /slʌɪp/ *noun*¹. *Scot. & north.* LME.
[App. from Low German *slīpe* var. of *slēpe* = Middle High German *sleife* (German *Schleife*) sledge, train, loop, knot, etc., rel. to Low German *slīpen* whet, *slēpen* drag.]
1 A sledge for carrying loads. LME.
2 The mould-board of a plough. Now *rare.* E17.

slipe /slʌɪp/ *noun*². *obsolete* exc. *dial.* M16.
[Prob. alt. of SLIP *noun*². Cf. SLYPE *noun*¹.]
A long narrow piece or strip, esp. of ground.

slipe /slʌɪp/ *noun*³. M19.
[from the verb.]
A certain quality of skin-wool (also in *pl.*); *Austral. & NZ* wool chemically removed from sheepskin (also ***slipe wool***).

slipe /slʌɪp/ *verb trans.* *obsolete* exc. *dial.* LME.
[Origin unkn. Cf. SLYPE *verb & noun*².]
Strip, peel, skin. Also foll. by *off*.

slippage /ˈslɪpɪdʒ/ *noun*. M19.
[from SLIP *verb*¹ + -AGE.]
1 The action or an instance of slipping or subsiding; the amount or extent of this. M19.
2 The difference between expected and actual output of a mechanical system. E20.
3 Falling away from a standard; delay; decline in value, popularity, etc.; the extent of this. E20.

📖 **3** *Guardian* Living standards could be eroded by a continued slippage of sterling. M. LEE There were signs of mental slippage.

slipper /ˈslɪpə/ *noun*. LME.
[from SLIP *verb*¹ + -ER¹.]
1 A light loose comfortable shoe, usu. of soft material, for indoor wear. Also, a light slip-on shoe for dancing etc. LME. ▶**b** A temporary shoe for a horse. E20.
2 HERALDRY. A support for a spindle or fusil. *obsolete* exc. *Hist.* E17.
3 A person who or thing which slips. M17. ▶**b** A person appointed to slip the hounds in coursing etc. E19.
4 A skid used to brake a vehicle travelling downhill. E19.
5 MECHANICS. A sliding part of a mechanism; *spec.* a guide block attached to a piston rod or cross-head so as to slide

with the rod against a fixed plate and prevent bending of the rod. L19.

6 *CRICKET.* A person who fields in the slips. *colloq. rare.* E20.

Phrases: BEDROOM ***slipper***. ***carpet slipper***: see CARPET *noun*. ***Devonshire slipper***: see DEVONSHIRE *noun* 1. ***glass slipper***: see GLASS *noun & adjective*. ***Grecian slipper***: see GRECIAN *adjective*. ***hunt the slipper***: see HUNT *verb*. ***lady's slipper (orchid)***: see LADY *noun & adjective*. **take a slipper to**, **take one's slipper to** punish (a child etc.) by beating with a slipper. ***Turkish slipper***: see TURKISH *adjective*.

Comb.: **slipper animalcule** *arch.* a paramecium; **slipper bath** a bath shaped somewhat like a slipper, with a covered end; **slipper chair** *US* a low-seated, freq. upholstered chair with a high back; **slipper flower** = CALCEOLARIA; **slipper limpet** any of various marine gastropods of the genus *Crepidula*, resembling limpets; **slipper-orchid** = ***lady's slipper (orchid)*** s.v. LADY *noun & adjective*; **slipper plant** a Central American shrub of the spurge family, *Pedilanthus tithymaloides*; **slipper satin** a semi-glossy satin used for making slippers, furnishings, etc.; **slipper shell** (the shell of) a slipper limpet; **slipper sock** a slipper and sock combined.

■ **slippered** *adjective* wearing a slipper or slippers; characterized by or associated with the wearing of slippers: E17.

slipper /ˈslɪpə/ *adjective. obsolete* exc. *dial.*
[Old English *slipor* = Middle Low German *slipper*, from Germanic.]
1 = SLIPPERY *adjective* 1, 4. OE.
2 Orig., morally repugnant, detestable. Later = SLIPPERY *adjective* 3. OE.
3 Voluble; given to talk. M19.

slipper /ˈslɪpə/ *verb.* L17.
[from the noun.]
1 *verb trans.* Beat or strike with a slipper. L17.
2 *verb intrans.* Walk or shuffle along in slippers. L19.
■ **slippering** *verbal noun* a beating with a slipper M19.

slipperette /slɪpəˈrɛt/ *noun.* Also (US proprietary name) **S-**. M20.
[from SLIPPER *noun* + -ETTE.]
A soft slipper or similar foot-covering; *esp.* a disposable slipper of a kind distributed to airline passengers.

slippery /ˈslɪp(ə)ri/ *adjective.* L15.
[from SLIPPER *adjective* + -Y[1], perh. after Luther's *schlipfferig* (Middle High German *slipferig*).]
1 Difficult to stand on, grip, or hold because of smoothness, wetness, or sliminess of surface; on which slipping is easy or likely; slipping readily from any hold or grasp; of a soft oily or greasy consistency. L15. ▸†**b** (Of the bowels) loose, open; (of food) laxative. M16–M18.
2 Of the tongue: talking too freely. *rare.* E16.
3 Unstable, uncertain, insecure; that cannot be relied on; fickle, untrustworthy, insincere, shifty, deceitful. M16.
4 Liable or prone to slip; readily giving way. Also, (of the memory) forgetful. Now *rare* or *obsolete.* M16.
5 Able to slip away or escape easily; difficult to catch or hold, elusive. L16.
6 Licentious, unchaste; of doubtful morality. Now *rare.* L16.
7 Designed to reduce air resistance; streamlined. *colloq.* L20.

> **1** V. WOOLF Guillemots whose feathers are slippery with oil. G. GREENE The road was slippery after the rain. K. AMIS He.. picked up a slippery fried egg. **3** C. COTTON Th' slippery Trick he meant to play her. W. BAGEHOT Families owning.. a slippery allegiance to a single head. J. K. JEROME Such a slippery customer as King John.

Special collocations: **slippery dip** *Austral.* a children's playground slide. **slippery elm** the N. American red elm, *Ulmus rubra*; (more fully ***slippery elm bark***) the mucilaginous inner bark of this tree, used medicinally as a demulcent etc. **slippery hitch** *NAUTICAL* a knot made fast by catching part of the rope beneath the bight, released by pulling on the free end. **slippery pole** = ***GREASY pole***. **slippery slope** *fig.* a course leading to disaster or destruction.
■ **slipperily** *adverb* E17. **slipperiness** *noun* E16.

slipping /ˈslɪpɪŋ/ *noun.* LME.
[from SLIP *noun*[2] + -ING[1].]
†**1** A thin strip. Only in LME.
2 A skein or hank of yarn. Now *rare* or *obsolete.* M16.
3 The action of taking slips from a plant; a cutting of a plant, a slip. M16.

slippy /ˈslɪpi/ *adjective*[1]. M16.
[from SLIP *verb*[1] + -Y[1].]
1 = SLIPPERY. M16.
2 Nimble, spry; sharp, quick; alert. *colloq.* M19.
2 look slippy look sharp, make haste.
■ **slippiness** *noun* L18.

slippy /ˈslɪpi/ *adjective*[2]. *rare.* L19.
[from SLIP *noun*[2] + -Y[1].]
Slim, slender.

slipshod /ˈslɪpʃɒd/ *adjective.* L16.
[from SLIP *verb*[1] + SHOD *ppl adjective.*]
1 Orig., wearing slippers or loose shoes. Now, wearing shabby or down-at-heel shoes. L16. ▸**b** (Of shoes) loose and untidy, shabby, down-at-heel; *gen.* shabby, unkempt. L17.
2 *fig.* Slovenly, careless, esp. in working or in handling ideas or words; unsystematic; poorly arranged. E19.

> **2** B. BETTELHEIM Slipshod translations deprive his words of.. the subtle sensory tones. *Guardian* Disclosures of.. official mendacity and slipshod workmanship.

■ **slipshoddiness** *noun* = SLIPSHODNESS M19. **slipshodness** *noun* slipshod condition, poor workmanship, carelessness L19.

slip-slap /ˈslɪpslap/ *noun & verb. rare.* M17.
[Redupl. of SLAP *noun*[2] with vowel variation.]
▶ **A** *noun.* †**1** A slipper. Only in M17.
2 A flapping sound. L19.
▶ **B** *verb intrans.* Infl. **-pp-**.
†**1** Slap repeatedly in rapid succession. Only in E18.
2 Move with a slapping sound. E20.

slip-slop /ˈslɪpslɒp/ *noun, adjective, verb, & adverb. colloq.* L17.
[Redupl. of SLOP *noun*[2] with vowel variation. In sense A.2 etc. with allus. to Mrs *Slipslop*, a character in Fielding's novel *Joseph Andrews* (1742).]
▶ **A** *noun.* **1** A sloppy substance used as a food, drink, or medicine. *arch.* L17.
2 A blunder in the use of words, *esp.* (a) malapropism. Also, a person given to making such blunders. Now *rare* or *obsolete.* L18.
3 Trifling talk or writing; nonsense, twaddle. E19.
4 A floppy item of footwear; a flip-flop (sandal). Chiefly *S. Afr.* M19.
▶ **B** *adjective.* †**1** Characterized by or given to blundering in the use or forms of words. M18–E19.
2 Having no substance or solidity; sloppy, feeble, trifling. E19.
▶ **C** *verb intrans.* Infl. **-pp-**.
†**1** Misuse words, utter a malapropism. *rare.* Only in L18.
†**2** Drink a sloppy liquid. *rare.* Only in M19.
3 Move about in a sloppy manner or with a flapping sound. L19.
▶ **D** *adverb.* With a flapping or slopping sound. L19.

slipstream /ˈslɪpstriːm/ *noun & verb.* E20.
[from SLIP *noun*[3] + STREAM *noun.*]
▶ **A** *noun.* **1** The current of air or water driven back by a revolving propeller; any localized current associated with an object, esp. a moving vehicle etc. E20.
2 *fig.* An assisting force considered to draw something along with or behind something else. M20.
▶ **B** *verb trans.* Travel in the slipstream of, follow closely behind; use a slipstream to assist in overtaking (a vehicle). Chiefly as ***slipstreaming*** *verbal noun.* M20.

slish /slɪʃ/ *noun. rare.* L16.
[Jingling alt. of SLASH *noun*[1].]
A slit.

slit /slɪt/ *noun.* LOE.
[formed as the verb.]
1 A (usu. long and straight) narrow cut, incision, or opening. LOE.
2 *spec.* **a** A long narrow opening in a wall; a window of this form. E17. ▸**b** The vulva. *coarse slang.* M17. ▸**c** A narrow, usu. straight aperture in an optical instrument through which a beam of light can pass. M19. ▸**d** A short connecting passage in a mine. M19.

> **1** B. STEWART The thermometer is inserted through a.. slit in a.. piece of india-rubber. M. CONEY Her eyes narrowed to fierce slits as she squinted against the.. sun.

Comb.: **slit drum** a primitive percussion instrument made out of a hollowed log with a longitudinal slit; **slit-eyed** *adjective* having long narrow eyes; **slit fricative** *PHONETICS*: produced by expelling the breath through a narrow aperture; **slit gong** = ***slit drum*** above; **slit lamp** *OPHTHALMOLOGY* a lamp which emits a narrow but intense beam of light, used for examining the interior of the eye; **slit-limpet** a limpet of the family Fissurellidae, having a slit running up from one edge of the shell; **slit-planting** (chiefly *FORESTRY*) a mode of planting in which a slit is made in the ground with a spade and the tree etc. inserted; **slit-pocket** a pocket with a vertical opening giving access to the pocket or to a garment beneath; **slit sampler** a device having a slit through which air is drawn to analyse its bacterial content; **slit spirant** *PHONETICS*: produced by expelling the breath through a narrow aperture; **slit trench** a narrow trench made to accommodate and protect a soldier or weapon in battle.
■ **slitless** *adjective* L19. **slitted** *adjective* having a slit or slits; shaped like a slit: E20.

slit /slɪt/ *adjective.* LME.
[from the verb.]
1 That has been slit. LME.
2 Naturally divided or cloven. Now *rare* or *obsolete.* E17.

slit /slɪt/ *verb trans.* Infl. **-tt-**. Pa. t. **slit**; pa. pple **slit**, (*rare*) **slitted** /ˈslɪtɪd/. ME.
[Rel. to Old English *slītan* SLITE *verb.*]
1 Cut into or *open* with a sharp instrument or weapon; make a slit in (something); cut or tear, esp. lengthwise; divide, sever. ME.
2 Cut into strips or thin pieces; *spec.* cut (iron) into rods. E16.
3 Form (the eyes) into slits, esp. for protection, as a sign of distrust, or in order to concentrate one's gaze. M20.

> **1** A. TROLLOPE Slit the picture from the top to the bottom. J. CLAVELL Blackthorne slit the hare's belly and neatly turned out the.. entrails. G. GREENE Did they expect him to pull out a razor blade and slit open a vein? **3** D. MADDEN Slitting his eyes against the smoke.

Comb.: **slitting-mill** a mill or machine by which iron bars or plates are slit into nail-rods etc.

slitch /slɪtʃ/ *noun. obsolete* exc. *dial.* LME.
[Origin unkn.]
= SLEECH.

slite /slʌɪt/ *noun. obsolete* exc. *dial.* E17.
[from the verb.]
Impairment through use; wear and tear.

slite /slʌɪt/ *verb trans. obsolete* exc. *dial.*
[Old English *slītan* = Old Frisian *slīta*, Old Saxon *slītan*, Old High German *slīzan* (Dutch *slijten*, German *schleissen*), Old Norse *slíta*, from Germanic base.]
1 Slit, split; cut or rip up; tear, rend. Formerly also, bite. OE.
2 Impair by wear; wear out. *rare.* OE.
†**3** Whet, sharpen. *Scot.* M18–E19.

slithe /slʌɪð/ *verb intrans.* Long *rare.* ME.
[App. alt. of SLIDE *verb*, after *slither* or under Scandinavian influence.]
Slip, slide.

slither /ˈslɪðə/ *noun.* E19.
[from the adjective or the verb.]
1 In *pl.* Loose stones on a hillside, esp. forming a scree. *Scot.* E19.
2 An instance of slithering. M19.
3 A smooth slippery mass; a sliver. E20.

> **3** *Good Motoring* It came, in a glass, with cube sugar.. and slithers of lemon.

slither /ˈslɪðə/ *adjective.* Long *rare* (now *dial.*). ME.
[Alt. of SLIDDER *adjective.*]
Slippery.

slither /ˈslɪðə/ *verb.* ME.
[Alt. of SLIDDER *verb.*]
1 *verb intrans.* Slip, slide, esp. *down* a loose or broken slope or with a clattering noise. ME. ▸**b** *verb trans.* Make or cause to slide. M19.
2 *verb intrans.* Move along with an irregular slipping motion; (of a reptile) creep, crawl, glide. M19.

> **1** D. H. LAWRENCE He slithered down a sheer snow slope. **2** J. KOSINSKI The snake slithered among the leaves sinuously. D. M. THOMAS I slithered through a blizzard up a hill.

slithery /ˈslɪð(ə)ri/ *adjective.* Orig. *dial.* L18.
[Alt. of SLIDDERY.]
Slippery.

slithy /ˈslʌɪði/ *adjective.* M19.
[Invented by Lewis Carroll: app. blend of SLIMY and LITHE *adjective.*]
Smooth and active.

slitter /ˈslɪtə/ *noun.* E17.
[from SLIT *verb* + -ER[1].]
A person who or thing which slits something.

slitty /ˈslɪti/ *adjective.* E20.
[from SLIT *noun* + -Y[1].]
Of the eyes: long and narrow.
Comb.: **slitty-eyed** *adjective* = ***slit-eyed*** s.v. SLIT *noun.*

slive /slʌɪv/ *noun.* L16.
[from next.]
1 A piece cut off; a slice. *obsolete* exc. *dial.* L16.
†**2** A cut, a stroke. *rare.* L16–M18.

slive /slʌɪv/ *verb*[1] *trans. obsolete* exc. *dial.* ME.
[Prob. rel. to Old English verb evidenced in pa. t. *tōslāf*: cf. SLEAVE *verb.*]
1 Cleave, split, divide. ME.
2 Take *off* or remove by cutting or slicing. LME.
■ **sliving** *noun* (*a*) the action of the verb; a slash; (*b*) a slip, a cutting; a shoot or branch cut off: LME.

slive /slʌɪv/ *verb*[2]. *obsolete* exc. *dial.* Pa. t. **-ed**, **slove** /sləʊv/; pa. pple **-ed**, **sliven** /ˈslɪv(ə)n/. LME.
[Alt. of SLEVE.]
1 *verb trans.* Cause to slip; slip or put *on* (a garment), esp. hastily or carelessly. LME.
2 *verb intrans.* **a** Slide; slip. *rare.* LME. ▸**b** Slip *off* or away; hang *about*, loiter. E18.
■ **sliving** *adjective* slow-moving, dilatory; sneaking: M17.

sliver /ˈslɪvə, ˈslʌɪ-/ *noun & verb.* LME.
[from SLIVE *verb*[1].]
▶ **A** *noun.* **1** A piece of wood, metal, etc., esp. a long thin one, cut, split, or sliced off; a thin shoot or slip; a splinter, a thin slice. LME. ▸**b** A side of a small fish sliced off for use as bait. *US.* M19.
2 A continuous strip or band of loose untwisted textile fibres after carding, ready for drawing, roving, etc. E18.
3 A slashing cut or stroke. E19.

📖 **1** E. DAVID Cut the peeled garlic clove into little slivers. A. LIVELY Cleaning the dirt from under his fingernails with a sliver of wood. *Daily Express* Windows were shattered and slivers of glass embedded in walls. *fig.*: J. CARROLL People . . traded slivers of information as if they were coins.

▸ **B** *verb*. **1** *verb trans.* Separate or remove as a sliver; cut, split, or tear into slivers. LME. ▸**b** *verb intrans.* Split (off). L19.
2 *verb trans.* Convert (textile fibres) into slivers. L18.

slivovitz /ˈslɪvəvɪts/ *noun*. Also **-ic**. L19.
[Serbo-Croat *šljivovica* from *šljiva* plum.]
A plum brandy made chiefly in Romania, Serbia, and neighbouring States.

slize /slʌɪz/ *verb intrans.* Long *obsolete* exc. *dial.* LME.
[Origin unkn.]
Look askance.

Sloane /sləʊn/ *noun & adjective*. L20.
[Ellipt.]
= SLOANE RANGER.
■ Also **Sloanie** *noun & adjective* L20.

Sloane Ranger /sləʊn ˈreɪndʒə/ *noun & adjectival phr.* L20.
[A play on *Sloane* Square, London, and *Lone Ranger*, a fictitious cowboy hero.]
▸ **A** *noun phr.* A fashionable and conventional upper-class young woman (occas., a man), esp. living in London. L20.
▸ **B** *adjectival phr.* Of, pertaining to, or characteristic of a Sloane Ranger or Sloane Rangers. L20.

slob /slɒb/ *noun*¹ & *verb*. L18.
[Irish *slab* from SLAB *noun*², perh. partly also from SLOBBER *noun*.]
▸ **A** *noun*. **1 a** Mud, *esp.* soft mud on the seashore; (a stretch of) muddy land; = OOZE *noun*² 1. Chiefly *Anglo-Irish*. L18. ▸**b** In full ***slob ice***. Densely packed sludgy ice, esp. sea ice. Chiefly *Canad.* M19.
2 ANGLING. A large soft worm, used for bait. E19.
3 A stupid careless person, a coarse or fat person. *colloq.* M19.

📖 **1a** R. PAYNE-GALLWEY When the birds gather on an island of slob . . at about half-tide. P. WAYRE The slob itself consists of . . acres of reclaimed marshland. **3** A. CAVANAUGH 'I'm a slob,' Shirley said. 'I'm not an intellectual.' *Chicago Sun* Those tasteless slobs who make crude and rude remarks to ladies. *Private Eye* The slob began to throw his considerable weight around.

Comb.: ***slob ice***: see sense 1b above; **slob-land** (a stretch of) muddy ground, esp. alluvial land reclaimed from the water; **slob trout** a trout which migrates only to the estuary of a river, not out to the open sea.
▸ **B** *verb trans.* Infl. **-bb-**. Spill or dribble (*out*). L19.
■ **slobbish** *adjective* (*colloq.*) behaving like a slob, having the qualities of a slob, loutish, slovenly L20. **slobby** *adjective* (*a*) muddy; (*b*) sloppy, sentimental; (*c*) = SLOBBISH: M19.

slob /slɒb/ *noun*². *rare*. M18.
[Alt. of SLAB *noun*¹.]
A slab of timber.

slobber /ˈslɒbə/ *noun*. LME.
[Rel. to the verb. Cf. SLABBER *noun*¹, SLUBBER *noun*.]
1 Mud, slime; sleety rain; a sloppy mess or mixture. LME.
2 Saliva running from the mouth; slaver. M18.

slobber /ˈslɒbə/ *adjective*. *rare*. M19.
[from prec. or next.]
1 Clumsy, awkward. M19.
2 Wet, slobbery. L19.

slobber /ˈslɒbə/ *verb*. LME.
[Prob. from Middle Dutch *slobberen* walk through mud, feed noisily: cf. SLABBER *verb*, SLUBBER *verb*.]
▸ **I** *verb intrans.* **1 a** Dribble from the mouth while eating; slaver. LME. ▸**b** *fig.* Be too attentive or overaffectionate towards a person; be excessively sentimental or enthusiastic about a thing. Freq. foll. by *over*. E19. ▸**c** Blubber, cry. *dial.* L19.

📖 **1b** W. OWEN He received me like a lover . . . He quite slobbered over me.

▸ **II** *verb trans.* **2** Execute (a job etc.) in a careless or slovenly way. Usu. foll. by *over*. L17.
3 a Wet in a dirty or disagreeable manner; dribble over (a thing). E18. ▸**b** Make wet with kissing. E18.
4 Utter thickly and indistinctly. M19.
Comb.: **slobber-chops** a person who slobbers while eating.
■ **slobberer** *noun* M18.

slobberhannes /ˈslɒbəhanɪs/ *noun*. L19.
[Perh. rel. to Dutch dial. *slabberjan* the name of a game, and Dutch *Hannes* Jack.]
A card-game for four people played with only high-ranking cards, in which the object is to avoid winning certain tricks and the queen of clubs.

slobbery /ˈslɒb(ə)ri/ *adjective*. LME.
[from SLOBBER *noun* or *verb*.]
1 Characterized by slobber or slobbering; unpleasantly wet, slimy, or dirty. LME.
2 Slovenly, careless. M19.

slock /slɒk/ *verb*¹. *obsolete* exc. *Scot.* LME.
[Old Norse *slokinn* pa. pple of *slǫkkva* to be extinguished, from base also of *slakr* SLACK *adjective*.]
1 *verb intrans.* Slacken, cease; *spec.* (of fire, light, thirst, etc.) be quenched. LME.
2 *verb trans.* Extinguish, quench, (fire, thirst, etc.). LME. ▸**b** Slake (lime). M17.

slock /slɒk/ *verb*² *trans. obsolete* exc. *dial.* LME.
[Perh. from Anglo-Norman *esloquer* or Old French *eslochier* move, shake, stir.]
Entice (away); draw, lead, or lure *away*. Also (*dial.*), pilfer.

†**slockster** *noun*. E17.
[from SLOCK *verb*² + -STER.]
1 A person who lures away another's servant. E17–E18.
2 A pilferer. *dial.* Only in L18.

sloe /sləʊ/ *noun*.
[Old English *slā(h)* = Middle Low German, Middle Dutch *slē*, *sleuuwe* (Low German *slē*, *slī*, Dutch *slee*), Old High German *slēha*, *slēwa* (German *Schlehe*), from Germanic base prob. rel. to Latin *livere* be blue, Slavonic base repr. by Russian *sliva* plum.]
1 The fruit of the blackthorn, *Prunus spinosa*, a small globose blue-black drupe with a sharp sour taste. OE. ▸†**b** A very little; the least possible amount. Usu. in neg. contexts. Only in ME.
2 The blackthorn, *Prunus spinosa*. M18.
Comb.: **sloe-eyed** *adjective* (*a*) having eyes of the colour of the sloe, dark-eyed; (*b*) slant-eyed; **sloe-gin** a liqueur of sloes steeped in gin; **sloe-thorn**, **sloe tree** = sense 2 above.

sloff /slɒf/ *verb intrans. rare*. Long *obsolete* exc. *dial.* LME.
[Imit.]
Eat greedily or messily.

slog /slɒg/ *noun*. *colloq.* M19.
[from the verb.]
1 A vigorous blow; spec. in CRICKET, an unrestrained attacking stroke. M19.
2 (A spell of) hard steady work. L19.

📖 **1** H. W. BLEACKLEY Sixey made a mighty slog, but failed to strike the ball. **2** J. WAIN Hours of hard slog, pulling yourself up the ladder rung by rung. R. HARRIES Work, or lack of work . . involves some sheer drudgery, much plain slog.

slog /slɒg/ *verb*. *colloq.* Infl. **-gg-**. E19.
[Origin unkn.: cf. SLUG *verb*³.]
1 *verb trans.* **a** Hit or strike hard; drive with blows; *fig.* attack violently. E19. ▸**b** CRICKET. Score (runs) by unrestrained aggressive hitting. L19.
2 *verb intrans.* **a** Deal heavy blows; work hard (*at* or *through* something), toil *on* or *away*. M19. ▸**b** CRICKET. Make an unrestrained attacking stroke. M19.
3 *verb intrans.* Walk heavily or doggedly. L19.

📖 **2a** M. LAVIN He'd have to slog at this thing till he got it right. B. CHATWIN He and his brother had slogged at one another with bare fists. R. DAHL All that . . morning . . slogging away cleaning Carleton's study. **3** E. SEGAL He slogged home through the gray slush and staggered up the steps.

Phrases: ***slog one's guts out***: see GUT *noun*.

slogan /ˈsləʊg(ə)n/ *noun*. E16.
[Gaelic *sluagh-ghairm*, from *sluagh* host + *gairm* cry, shout. Cf. SLUGHORN.]
1 A war cry, a battle-cry; *spec.* a Scottish Highland war cry usu. consisting of a personal surname. E16.
2 The distinctive watchword, motto, cry, etc., of a person or group; a short memorable phrase used esp. in advertising or political campaigning, etc. E18.

📖 **2** F. FITZGERALD Soldiers and civil servants marched with the dock workers shouting anti-government . . slogans. M. L. KING Black power has proved to be a slogan without a program.

■ **sloganed** *adjective* having or marked with a slogan M20. **slogaˈneer** *noun & verb* (orig. *US*) (*a*) *noun* a person who devises or who uses slogans; (*b*) *verb intrans.* express oneself in (esp. political) slogans: E20. **sloganize** *verb trans. & intrans.* (*a*) *verb trans.* make (something) the subject of a slogan, express in a slogan or slogans; (*b*) *verb intrans.* compose or utter slogans: E20.

slogger /ˈslɒgə/ *noun*. *colloq.* E19.
[from SLOG *verb* + -ER¹.]
1 A person who delivers heavy blows; *spec.* a cricketer who slogs. E19. ▸**b** A person who works hard, esp. in a ponderous or uninspired manner. E20.
2 A heavy weight on a string; *esp.* a piece of metal, stone, etc., fastened to a strap or thong and used as a weapon. *Criminals' slang*. L19.

slogger /ˈslɒgə/ *verb intrans.* Orig. & chiefly *dial.* E19.
[Origin unkn.]
Dawdle, loiter; go about untidily. Chiefly as ***sloggering*** *ppl adjective*.

sloid /slɔɪd/ *noun*. Also **slojd**, **sloyd**. L19.
[Swedish *slöjd* from Old Norse *slægð* SLEIGHT *noun*.]
A system of instruction in elementary woodwork, orig. developed and taught in Sweden.

sloka /ˈʃləʊkə/ *noun*. Also **sloke** /ʃləʊk/. L18.
[Sanskrit *śloka* noise, praise, stanza.]
A couplet of Sanskrit verse, *esp.* one in which each line contains sixteen syllables.

sloke /sləʊk/ *noun*¹. Chiefly *Anglo-Irish*. L18.
[Var. of SLAWK. Cf. SLAKE *noun*².]
= SLAWK.

sloke *noun*² var. of SLOKA.

slomo /ˈsləʊməʊ/ *noun*. *colloq.* (chiefly *US*). Also **slo-mo**. L20.
[Abbreviation of ***slow motion*** s.v. SLOW *adjective*.]
CINEMATOGRAPHY. Slow motion; slow motion replay or a facility for producing this.

slonk /slɒŋk/ *verb trans. rare*. L15.
[Perh. rel. to Dutch *slokken* swallow, or to German dial. *Schlunk*, *Schlonk* gullet, gorge, abyss.]
Swallow greedily.

sloom /sluːm/ *noun & verb*. Now *Scot. & north*.
[Old English *slūma*, from Germanic. Cf. SLUMBER *verb*.]
▸ **A** *noun*. A gentle sleep or slumber; a light doze. OE.
▸ **B** *verb intrans.* Slumber; doze. ME.

sloop /sluːp/ *noun*¹. E17.
[Dutch *sloep*, †*sloepe* (whence also French *chaloupe* SHALLOP), of unkn. origin.]
1 A small one-masted fore-and-aft rigged vessel with mainsail and jib. E17.
†**2** A large open boat; a longboat. M17–E18.
3 *Hist.* A small sailing warship carrying guns on the upper deck only (more fully ***sloop-of-war***). Also, one of the smaller classes of anti-submarine convoy escort vessels in the war of 1939–45. L17.
Comb.: ***sloop-of-war***: see sense 3 above; **sloop-rigged** *adjective* rigged like a sloop.

sloop /sluːp/ *noun*². *Canad.* L19.
[Origin unkn.]
A sledge used for hauling logs etc.

sloosh /sluːʃ/ *noun & verb*. *colloq.* E20.
[Imit.]
▸ **A** *noun*. A pouring of water or other liquid; a noise (as) of heavily splashing or rushing water. E20.
▸ **B** *verb*. **1** *verb trans.* Wash with a copious supply of water; pour water or other liquid copiously over; pour (water etc.) with a rush. E20.
2 *verb intrans.* Make a heavy splashing or rushing noise; flow or pour with a rush. E20.

sloot *noun* var. of SLUIT.

sloothering /ˈsluːð(ə)rɪŋ/ *noun*. *Anglo-Irish*. L19.
[Perh. from alt. of Irish *lúdar* fawning, flattery + -ING¹.]
Cajolery, wheedling; an instance of this.

sloothering /ˈsluːð(ə)rɪŋ/ *adjective*. *Anglo-Irish*. E20.
[formed as prec. + -ING².]
Cajoling, wheedling.

slop /slɒp/ *noun*¹. ME.
[from 2nd elem. of OVERSLOP.]
†**1** A bag, *spec.* a magic bag for stealing milk from cows. *rare*. Only in ME.
2 A loose outer garment, as a jacket, cassock, gown, smock, overall, etc. LME.
3 In *pl.* & †*sing.*, wide baggy breeches or hose, commonly worn in the 16th and early 17th cents.; baggy trousers, esp. as worn by sailors. Formerly also (*sing.*), either leg of such a garment. *arch.* L15.
4 In *pl.* (exc. in comb.). Clothes and bedding supplied to sailors from a ship's stores; ready-made or cheap clothing. M17.
Comb.: **slop-clothing** (now *arch.* or *Hist.*) cheap or ready-made clothing; **slopseller** (now *arch.* or *Hist.*) a dealer in ready-made or cheap clothing; **slop-shop** (now *arch.* or *Hist.*): where ready-made or cheap clothing is sold; **slop-work** (*a*) (the making of) slop-clothing; (*b*) cheap shoddy work; **slop-worker** a person who does slop-work.

slop /slɒp/ *noun*² & *verb*. LME.
[Prob. repr. 2nd elem. of Old English *cūsloppe* COWSLIP. Cf. SLIP *noun*¹, SLIP-SLOP.]
▸ **A** *noun*. **1** †**a** A muddy place; a mudhole. Only in LME. ▸**b** A splash of mud or slush (*rare*). Also, liquid mud; slush. M18.
2 a Liquid or semi-liquid food, esp. regarded as being weak or unappetizing. Usu. in *pl.* M17. ▸**b** Beer. Usu. in *pl.* *US & Austral. slang*. E20.
3 a An act of spilling or splashing liquid; a quantity of liquid spilled or splashed. E18. ▸**b** NAUTICAL. A choppy sea. M20.
4 Waste (esp. household) liquid; *spec.* (*a*) the dregs of tea, coffee, etc.; (*b*) dirty water left after washing or cleaning; (*c*) the contents of a chamber-pot, faeces and urine; (*d*) *US dial. & colloq.* liquid kitchen refuse used as pig-food, swill. Usu. in *pl.* E19.
5 *fig.* **a** Sentimentality; sentimental language. *colloq.* (orig. *US*). M19. ▸**b** Nonsense, rubbish; insolence. M20.

6 A dance during which partners stand facing one another, swinging their arms like pendulums across their bodies. **M20.**

> 📖 **2a** A. GRAY After the slops of the invalid ward you will appreciate stronger meat. **4** G. BLOOMFIELD The slops had never been emptied, so the rooms were anything but odoriferous. R. JAFFE The slop you had to scrape into those huge disgusting garbage pails. **a** M. TWAIN Writing that slop about balmy breezes and fragrant flowers.

Comb.: **slop-basin**: for the dregs of tea, coffee, etc., esp. as forming part of a teaset; **slop-bucket**: for removing bedroom or kitchen slops; **slop-moulding** a moulding process in which the mould is dipped in water before receiving the clay; **slop-pail** = ***slop-bucket*** above.

▶ **B** *verb.* Infl. **-pp-**.

1 a *verb trans.* Spill or splash (liquid). **M16.** ▸**b** *verb intrans. & trans.* Empty *out* the contents of (a chamber-pot). **M20.**

2 *verb trans.* Lap *up* greedily or noisily; gobble *up*. *obsolete* exc. *dial.* **L16.**

3 *verb trans.* Make wet with spilled liquid. **E18.**

4 *verb intrans.* **a** Prepare or drink any weak liquid. Now *rare* or *obsolete*. **M18.** ▸**b** Foll. by *up*: become intoxicated. *US slang.* **L19.**

5 *verb intrans.* **a** Walk or travel through or *through* a wet or muddy place. **M19.** ▸**b** Wander (*about* or *around*) in an aimless or slovenly manner; mess *about*. *colloq.* **E20.**

6 *verb intrans.* Run, flow, or spill *over* (*lit. & fig.*). **M19.**

7 *verb intrans.* Feed (pigs or cattle) with slops. *US dial. & colloq.* **M19.**

> 📖 **1a** A. ALVAREZ His cup hit the saucer . . slopping coffee on the table. *transf.*: J. K. JEROME You get fooling about with the boat, and slop me overboard. **b** *Times* They queue at communal lavatories to slop out their pots. A. GARVE Prisoners rise at 6:30 a.m. Slop out. Clean their cells. **5b** M. GORDON Slopping around the house in her slippers. **6** N. HAWTHORNE A great deal of the wine slopped over. *Publishers Weekly* Sidey's prose portrait is affectionate and admiring without slopping over into pure fudge.

Comb.: **slop-over** *US* an act or instance of slopping over (*lit. & fig.*).

■ **sloppage** *noun* (*rare*) slops collectively; the action of slopping: **L19.** **slopped** *adjective* soiled or marked with slops, sloppy **E19.**

slop /slɒp/ *noun*[3]. *slang.* **M19.**
[Modification of *ecilop* back slang for *police*.]
A police officer. Usu. in *pl.*

slope /sləʊp/ *noun*[1]. **E17.**
[Aphet. from ASLOPE.]

1 A stretch of rising or falling ground; *spec.* a place for skiing on the side of a hill or mountain. **E17.** ▸**b** (A thing having) an inclined surface; *spec.* (*a*) a man-made bank; (*b*) MINING an inclined roadway; (*c*) a desk with a sloping top. **E18.**

2 Upward or downward inclination; (an amount or degree of) deviation from the horizontal or perpendicular. Also, an inclined position or direction; a position in a line neither parallel nor perpendicular to level ground or to a given line; *spec.* (MILITARY) *the* position in which a rifle is held against the shoulder. **E17.** ▸**b** The tangent of the angle between a line and the horizontal; the gradient of a graph at any point; the value of the first differential of a quantity, esp. with respect to distance. **L19.**

3 ELECTRONICS. The mutual conductance of a valve (numerically equal to the gradient of one of the characteristic curves of the valve). **M20.**

4 An oriental; *spec.* a Vietnamese person. *US slang (derog. & racially offensive).* **M20.**

5 A quantity defined as a rate of change or derivative instead of as a ratio. Usu. *attrib.* in ***slope resistance***. **M20.**

> 📖 **1** P. V. PRICE Vineyards on a slope . . are generally superior to those on a plain. J. FARRIS Clothing for the slopes and for après-ski. V. GLENDINNING Running down the grassy slope. ***continental slope***: see CONTINENTAL *adjective*. ***Pacific slope***: see PACIFIC *adjective*. ***slippery slope***.

Comb.: **slope circuit** ELECTRONICS = ***slope filter*** below; **slope current** (*a*) an air current produced when wind is deflected upwards by a hill; (*b*) an ocean current that arises when the surface of the sea slopes as a result of wind action; **slope detection** ELECTRONICS the detection of a frequency-modulated signal by means of a slope filter followed by a detector for amplitude-modulated signals; **slope filter** ELECTRONICS a filter whose response increases or decreases more or less uniformly over the frequency range in which it is used; **slopehead** (*US slang (derog. & racially offensive)*) = sense 4 above; **slope wash** PHYSICAL GEOGRAPHY the downhill movement of soil or rock under the action of gravity assisted by running water not confined to a channel.

slope /sləʊp/ *noun*[2]. *colloq.* **M19.**
[from SLOPE *verb*[2].]
An act of running off or slinking away. Esp. in ***do a slope***.

slope /sləʊp/ *verb*[1]. **L16.**
[from (the same root as) SLOPE *noun*[1].]

1 *verb intrans.* Move in an oblique direction; lie or tend obliquely, esp. downwards; have or follow a slope, slant. **L16.**

2 *verb trans.* Bring into or put in a sloping or slanting position; *spec.* place or hold (a weapon) in a sloping position, esp. against the shoulder. Also, direct downwards or obliquely. **E17.**

3 *verb trans.* Cut, form, or make with a slope or slant. **E17.**

> 📖 **1** V. WOOLF A shaft of light . . sloped from roof to floor. A. N. WILSON A road which sloped, surprisingly steeply, downwards. **2** C. MACKENZIE Through the . . windows . . the sun sloped quivering ladders of golden light. **slope arms** MILITARY place one's rifle in a sloping position against one's shoulder.

■ **sloping** *noun* the fact of being or forming a slope; degree of slope; a sloping surface: **E17.** **sloping** *adjective & adverb* (*a*) *adjective* that slopes; (*b*) *adverb* in a sloping manner, slopeways: **E17.** **slopingly** *adverb* slopeways **M17.**

slope /sləʊp/ *verb*[2]. *colloq.* **E19.**
[Origin uncertain: in sense 2 perh. rel. to LOPE *verb*.]

1 *verb trans.* Cheat, trick, or defraud (a person); evade. *dial.* **E19.**

2 *verb intrans.* Make off or *off*; sneak *off*, depart, esp. surreptitiously to avoid work, trouble, etc. Also, move (*off*, *in*, etc.) in a leisurely manner; amble. **M19.**

> 📖 **2** P. LIVELY You can slope off . . and leave me. A. MACRAE When you get tired of your responsibilities you can slope off.

slope /sləʊp/ *adverb & adjective.* Now *poet.* **LME.**
[formed as SLOPE *noun*[1].]

▶ **A** *adverb.* In a sloping or slanting manner or position. **LME.**

▶ **B** *adjective.* Sloping, slanting. **L15.**

sloped /sləʊpt/ *adjective.* **L17.**
[from SLOPE *noun*[1], *verb*[1]: see -ED[2], -ED[1].]
Formed with a slope; cut, raised, or placed in a sloping position; that has been sloped.

sloper /ˈsləʊpə/ *noun. US colloq.* **L19.**
[from SLOPE *noun*[1] + -ER[1].]
A native or inhabitant of the Pacific slope of the United States.

slopeways /ˈsləʊpweɪz/ *adverb.* **L17.**
[from SLOPE *noun*[1] or *adjective* + -WAYS.]
In a sloping manner or position.
■ Also †**slopewise** *adverb* **L15–L18.**

slopey /ˈsləʊpi/ *noun. US slang (derog. & racially offensive).* **M20.**
[from SLOPE *noun*[1] or *verb*[1] + -Y[6].]
An oriental person; *spec.* a Chinese person.

sloppery /ˈslɒp(ə)ri/ *noun.* **M19.**
[from SLOP *noun*[2] + -ERY.]
Sloppy matter.

slopping /ˈslɒpɪŋ/ *noun.* **L18.**
[from SLOP *verb* + -ING[1].]
The action of SLOP *verb*.
Comb.: **slopping-out** the action of emptying the contents of a chamber-pot; **slopping-up** *N. Amer. slang* a drinking-bout.

sloppy /ˈslɒpi/ *adjective.* **E18.**
[from SLOP *noun*[2] + -Y[1].]

1 Of the ground etc.: very wet and splashy; covered with water or thin mud. **E18.**

2 Of snow, food, etc.: semi-liquid; unpleasantly watery. **L18.**

3 a Of work, writing, character, etc.: weak; imprecise, careless, superficial; untidy, slovenly. **E19.** ▸**b** Maudlin, sentimental. *colloq.* **L19.**

4 Of a garment: loose, slack, ill-fitting. **E19.**

5 a Splashed with liquid; covered with slops; messy. **M19.** ▸**b** Of the sea: choppy. *colloq.* **L20.**

> 📖 **3a** A. LURIE Emmy dropped her skirt, stockings, and shoes in a heap . . . She had become very sloppy. S. BRILL Shannon . . had cleaned up the sloppy record keeping. **5a** T. WILLIAMS The table is sloppy with remains of breakfast.

Special collocations: **sloppy joe** *colloq.* (*a*) a long loose-fitting sweater; (*b*) *N. Amer.* a hamburger in which the minced-beef filling is made into a kind of meat sauce; (*c*) a slovenly person.

■ **sloppily** *adverb* **L19.** **sloppiness** *noun* **E18.**

slopy /ˈsləʊpi/ *adjective.* **M18.**
[from SLOPE *noun*[1] or *verb*[1] + -Y[1].]
Sloping.

slosh /slɒʃ/ *noun & verb.* **E19.**
[Var. of SLUSH *noun*[1].]

▶ **A** *noun.* **1** Slush, sludge. **E19.**

2 Watery or unappetizing food or drink. **E19.** ▸**b** Weak insubstantial work, writing, etc. **L19.**

3 A quantity of liquid. Now also, a splash of liquid; the sound of splashing liquid. **L19.**

4 A heavy blow. *slang.* **M20.**

5 A game played on a billiard-table, in which each player tries to pocket six coloured balls in a certain order, using the white cue-ball. **M20.**

> 📖 **3** N. FREELING He poured a big slosh of whisky.

▶ **B** *verb.* **1** *verb intrans.* Splash (about); flounder (around); move with a splashing sound. Freq. with adverb (phr.). **M19.**

2 *verb intrans.* Move *around* aimlessly; hang *about*; loaf *around*. *US colloq.* **M19.**

3 *verb trans.* **a** Pour (liquid, esp. clumsily): splash, throw, or swallow (liquid) carelessly. Usu. with adverb (phr.). *colloq.* **L19.** ▸**b** Pour or throw liquid on (a person or thing). *colloq.* **E20.**

4 *verb trans.* Hit, esp. heavily; strike; crush, defeat. *colloq.* **L19.**

> 📖 **1** J. D. ASTLEY I then slipped . . and sloshed down into Balaclava. T. O'BRIEN Canteens bouncing . . water sloshing, we stepped . . through the night. B. BREYTENBACH They slosh through pools of stagnant water. *fig.*: A. LURIE Clouds like . . soapy washing slosh across the sky. **3a** L. DEIGHTON He laughed . . and sloshed down some beer. I. WALLACE Abrahams . . sloshed some Scotch over ice for himself. J. LYMINGTON She sloshed out porridge into plates. K. AMIS He . . started to slosh handfuls of water on to his face.

■ **sloshed** *adjective* (*slang*) drunk, tipsy **M20.** **sloshing** *noun* the action of the verb, an instance of this; the sound made by a moving liquid striking a solid object: **L19.**

sloshy /ˈslɒʃi/ *adjective.* **L18.**
[from SLOSH *noun* + -Y[1].]
Slushy; sloppy, sentimental.
■ **sloshiness** *noun* **L19.**

slot /slɒt/ *noun*[1]. Chiefly *Scot. & north.* **ME.**
[Middle & mod. Low German, Middle & mod. Dutch = Old High German *sloz* (German *Schloss* door-bolt, lock, castle), from West Germanic, whence also Old Saxon *slutil*, Old High German *sluzzil* (German *Schlüssel*) key, Old Frisian *slūta*, Middle Low German, Middle Dutch *slūten* (Dutch *sluiten*), Old High German *sliozan* (German *schliessen*) close, lock. Cf. SLOTE.]

1 A bar or bolt used to secure a door, window, etc.; a bolt forming part of the mechanism of a lock. Now *Scot. & dial.* **ME.**

2 A metal rod; a flat wooden bar, *esp.* one forming a crosspiece. **LME.** ▸**b** *spec.* Any of the crossbars connecting the main bars of a harrow. **L18.**

slot /slɒt/ *noun*[2]. **LME.**
[Old French *esclot*, ult. origin unkn.]

1 The hollow depression running down the middle of the chest. Now *Scot. rare.* **LME.**

2 *gen.* An elongated narrow depression, channel, or groove into which something fits. Also more fully ***slot hole***. **L15.** ▸**b** A slit or opening in a machine for a coin etc. to be inserted; *slang* a slot-machine. **L19.** ▸**c** The middle of the semicircular or horseshoe-shaped desk at which a newspaper's subeditors work. *US slang.* **E20.** ▸**d** AERONAUTICS. A linear gap in an aerofoil parallel to its leading edge, allowing the passage of air from the lower to the upper surface. **E20.** ▸**e** The vulva. *coarse slang.* **M20.** ▸**f** A (usu. marked-out) parking space. Chiefly *N. Amer.* **M20.** ▸**g** A prison cell. *Austral. slang.* **M20.** ▸**h** In motor rallying, a turning or other opening, *esp.* one marked out for the driver to take. *colloq.* **M20.** ▸**i** ICE HOCKEY. An unmarked area in front of the goal affording the best position for an attacking player to make a successful shot at goal. **M20.** ▸**j** COMPUTING. An elongated, more or less rectangular socket; *spec.* = ***EXPANSION slot***. **L20.**

3 A crevasse. *Austral. & NZ.* **M20.**

4 A position in a series, hierarchy, system, etc.; a position to be filled; *spec.* an allotted place in a broadcasting schedule. **M20.** ▸**b** LINGUISTICS. A grammatical position in a sentence etc. which can be filled by any of a particular category of items. **M20.**

> 📖 **2b** *San Francisco Chronicle* Depositing a nickel in a slot to release the handle. E. LEONARD I lost sixty dollars, playing the slots. **4** P. GOODMAN A . . caste system in which everyone has a slot. P. LARKIN This poetry slot on the radio, 'Time for Verse'. *International Business Week* Access to . . crucial landing slots at Japanese airports.

Comb.: **slot aerial**, **slot antenna** an aerial in the form of one or more slots in a metal surface; **slot-back** AMER. FOOTBALL (the position of) a back who stands behind a gap in the forward line; **slot car** a miniature racing car, powered by electricity, which travels in a slot in a track; ***slot hole***: see sense 2 above; **slot-machine**: operated by inserting a coin in a slot, *esp.* such a machine for selling small articles or for gambling; **slot man** *US slang* a news editor; **slot-meter**: operated by inserting a coin in a slot; **slot racer** = ***slot car*** above; **slot-racing** racing by slot cars; **slot radiator** = ***slot aerial*** above; **slot seam** a clothing seam reinforced underneath; **slot television** a coin-operated television; **slot wedge** ELECTRICAL ENGINEERING a strip of material that holds the winding of an armature in place; **slot winding** ELECTRICAL ENGINEERING an armature winding in which the conductors are laid in slots or grooves in the core; **slot-wound** *adjective* (ELECTRICAL ENGINEERING) having the conductors of an armature winding laid in this manner.

slot /slɒt/ *noun*[3]. **L16.**
[Old French *esclot* horse's hoof-print, prob. from Old Norse *slōð* track: see SLEUTH *noun*[1] & *verb*.]

1 The track or trail of an animal, esp. a deer; a footmark. **L16.**

2 A deer's foot. **L19.**

Comb.: **slot-hound** a sleuth-hound.

slot /slɒt/ *verb*¹. Infl. **-tt-**. LME.
[from SLOT *noun*².]
†**1** *verb trans.* Pierce through a slot. Only in LME.
2 *verb trans.* Cut a slot or slots in. Also foll. by *out*. M18.
3 *verb trans.* Put (a coin) in a slot-machine. L19.
4 *verb trans.* Thread (material etc.) *with* ribbon. Usu. in *pass.* E20.
5 a *verb intrans.* Fit *in* or *into* a position, space, etc.; take up a position in an allotted space or slot. E20. ▸**b** *verb trans.* Fit (something) *in* or *into* a position, space, or slot. M20.
6 *verb trans.* FOOTBALL. Kick (the ball, a pass) accurately through a narrow space, esp. *in* or *into* the goal; score (a goal) in this way. L20.
7 Kill or injure (a person) by shooting. *Military slang.* L20.

5a *Autopart* Mears took the lead . . with . . Sullivan slotting into second. **b** B. HINES Bicycles . . with their front wheels slotted into concrete blocks. **6** *absol.*: *Times* Maradona slotted home to give his side . . a 2–1 win.

slot /slɒt/ *verb*² *trans.* Now *Scot. & dial.* Infl. **-tt-**. M16.
[from SLOT *noun*¹ 1.]
Bolt, lock (a door, window, etc.); secure (a lock) by means of a bolt.

slot /slɒt/ *verb*³ *trans.* Infl. **-tt-**. L16.
[from SLOT *noun*³.]
Follow the track of (a deer etc.); trace, trail.

slote /sləʊt/ *noun.* Now *rare.* LME.
[Var. of SLOT *noun*¹.]
†**1** = SLOT *noun*¹ 1. LME–E18.
2 A bar; a crossbar. L15.
3 A trapdoor in a theatre stage. M19.

sloth /sləʊθ/ *noun.* Also †**sleuth**. OE.
[from SLOW *adjective* + -TH¹.]
1 Inactivity, reluctance to exert oneself; sluggishness, laziness. OE.
2 Slowness; tardiness. LME.
3 A company *of* bears. LME.
4 Any of several arboreal edentate mammals of the families Bradypodidae and Megalonychidae, of tropical Central and S. America, having long limbs and hooked claws for hanging upside down from branches of trees, and renowned for their slowness of movement. Formerly also, any of various unrelated animals that move slowly. E17.

1 A. GUINNESS There was a brief period . . during which I got up in the early hours . . but my habitual sloth soon prevailed. **4** *ground sloth*, *three-toed sloth*, *ursine sloth*, etc.

Comb.: **sloth bear** a small to medium-sized bear, *Melursus ursinus*, found in the lowland forests of Sri Lanka and eastern India, with a shaggy blackish coat and long curved claws; **sloth-monkey** = *slow loris*.
■ **slothful** *adjective* (of a person) inactive, lazy, sluggish; (of a habit etc.) characterized by laziness or inaction: LME. **slothfully** *adverb* E16. **slothfulness** *noun* E16.

sloth /sləʊθ/ *verb.* Now *rare.* LME.
[from the noun.]
1 *verb trans.* Allow to slip through slothfulness or delay; neglect. Long *obsolete* exc. *Scot.* LME.
2 *verb intrans.* Be or become lazy. LME.

slotted /ˈslɒtɪd/ *ppl adjective.* M19.
[from SLOT *noun*², *verb*¹: see -ED², -ED¹.]
1 Having a slot or slots. M19.
2 Threaded through a hole or slot. M20.
Special collocations: **slotted armature** ELECTRICAL ENGINEERING an armature having slots or grooves to contain the conductors; a slot-wound armature. **slotted line** a length of coaxial cable or waveguide having a slot running lengthwise in its outer conductor to receive a probe for investigating standing waves. **slotted spoon** a large spoon with slots for straining food.

slotter /ˈslɒtə/ *noun.* L19.
[from SLOT *verb*¹ + -ER¹.]
A person who or thing which makes slots.

slotter /ˈslɒtə/ *verb.* ME.
[Origin unkn.]
1 *verb trans.* Make messy or dirty. Also, splash about, spill. *obsolete* exc. *dial.* ME.
2 *verb intrans.* Be slothful or slovenly. *Scot.* Long *rare.* E16.

slouch /slaʊtʃ/ *noun & adjective.* E16.
[Origin unkn. In later sense, partly from the verb.]
▸ **A** *noun.* **1 a** A lazy, slovenly, or ungainly person; a lout, a clown. E16. ▸**b** A poor, indifferent, or inefficient person or thing. *colloq.* (orig. *US*). L18.
2 An awkward stooping position or movement; a walk characterized by this. E18.
3 *ellipt.* = *slouch hat* below. E18.
4 A downward bend or droop of a hat-brim etc. M19.

1b *Guitar Player* Orbison was no slouch as a guitarist.

▸ **B** *adjective.* **1** Drooping or hanging loosely; slouching, slouched. Now *rare* exc. in *slouch hat* below. L17.
2 Clownish, loutish; slovenly. M19.
Special collocations & comb.: **slouch-eared** *adjective* (now *rare* or *obsolete*) having loose hanging ears. **slouch hat** a soft hat with a wide flexible brim, esp. turned or pulled down.

slouch /slaʊtʃ/ *verb.* M18.
[Back-form. from SLOUCHING or directly from the noun.]
1 *verb intrans.* Move, stand, or sit with a stooping ungainly posture; droop the head and shoulders. M18. ▸**b** Hang down, droop; *esp.* (of a hat) be turned or pulled down. E19.
2 *verb trans.* Pull down the brim of (a hat) over one's face. M18.
3 *verb trans. rare.* ▸**a** Make (one's way) in a slouching manner. M19. ▸**b** Stoop or bend (the shoulders). M19. ▸**c** Make (a bow) with a slouch or stoop. L19.

1 B. RUBENS She . . slouched wearily up the stairs.

■ **sloucher** *noun* a person who slouches; *spec.* in HORSE-RACING, a jockey who intentionally rides slowly in the early stages of a race: L19.

slouched /slaʊtʃt/ *ppl adjective.* L18.
[from prec. + -ED¹.]
1 *slouched hat*, = *slouch hat* s.v. SLOUCH *noun & adjective*. L18.
2 In a slouching position or posture. M19.

slouching /ˈslaʊtʃɪŋ/ *adjective.* E17.
[from SLOUCH *noun & adjective* (in later senses partly from the verb) + -ING².]
1 Hanging down, drooping; *spec.* (of a hat) having a brim which hangs over the face. E17.
2 Having an awkward stooping posture or gait; walking or sitting with a slouch; characterized by a stooping posture or gait. M17.
■ **slouchingly** *adverb* M19.

slouchy /ˈslaʊtʃi/ *adjective.* L17.
[from SLOUCH *noun*, *verb* + -Y¹.]
Slouching; slovenly, untidy.
■ **slouchily** *adverb* L19. **slouchiness** *noun* L19.

slough /slaʊ, *in sense 4* sluː/ *noun*¹. OE.
[Origin unkn. Cf. SLEW *noun*¹.]
1 a A piece of soft miry ground, a swamp; *esp.* a hole in the ground filled with wet mud. OE. ▸**b** Soft mud etc. of which a slough is composed. Long *rare* or *obsolete.* ME.
2 A state of degradation, depression, etc., into which a person sinks. ME.
†**3** A ditch, a drain; a rut. M16–L17.
4 A slew, a body of stagnant water. Also, a side channel of a river. *N. Amer.* M17.

1a J. IRVING The driveway was a slough of mud. **2** P. ANGADI He cringed into . . a slough of self-hate. *Slough of Despond*: see DESPOND *noun*.

Comb.: **slough grass** *N. Amer.* any of several coarse grasses of sloughs or watery depressions, *esp.* species of the genus *Muhlenbergia*.
■ **sloughy** *adjective*¹ of the nature of slough or soft mud; miry, muddy: LME.

slough /slʌf/ *noun*². Also ***sluff**. ME.
[Perh. rel. to Low German *sluwe*, *slu* husk, peel, shell.]
1 A skin or membrane covering (some part of) the body. Later *gen.*, any enclosing or covering layer; a sheath. Now *rare* or *obsolete.* ME. ▸**b** The outer skin or husk of a fruit. *Scot. & dial.* M17.
2 The outer skin cast off by a snake. Formerly also, the skin of a snake etc. ME. ▸**b** The skin of a caterpillar or other immature insect, cast during metamorphosis. L17. ▸**c** Clothing. E19.
3 MEDICINE. A layer or mass of dead tissue formed on the surface of a wound etc.; a scab. E16.
4 A feature, habit, etc., which is cast off or abandoned. L16.
■ **sloughy** *adjective*² (*a*) *rare* consisting of slough or cast skin; (*b*) MEDICINE of the nature of a slough; characterized by the presence of a slough or sloughs: L15.

slough /slaʊ/ *noun*³. *obsolete* exc. *Scot. & dial.* E18.
[Corresp. to Norwegian *slo*, Icelandic *sló*.]
The core of an animal's horn.

slough /slʌf/ *noun*⁴. M19.
[App. from SLOUGH *verb*¹.]
The collapse of soil or rock down a bank or into a hole; a fissure filled with rock, a fault.

slough /slʌf/ *verb*¹. Also ***sluff**. E18.
[from SLOUGH *noun*².]
1 *verb intrans.* Of skin, tissue, etc.: come *away*, drop *off*, be shed as a slough. E18.
2 a *verb trans.* MEDICINE. Remove or cast *off* as a slough; eat *away* by the formation of a slough or sloughs. M18. ▸**b** *verb trans. & intrans.* Of a snake etc.: cast *off* or shed (the skin) as a slough. M19.
3 *verb trans.* Discard, give up, get rid of. Also foll. by *off*. M19.
4 *verb intrans.* Of soil, rock, etc.: fall *away* or slide *down* into a hole or depression. L19.

1a *Practitioner* The whole of the skin of the . . thigh . . sloughed. *fig.*: C. IRWIN The years sloughed away, . . generations lived . . and died. **3** JO GRIMOND Responsibility . . could not be sloughed off.

slough /slaʊ/ *verb*² *trans.* M19.
[from SLOUGH *noun*¹.]
1 In *pass.* Be swallowed (*up*) or stuck in a swamp. M19.
2 Imprison; lock *up*. Usu. in *pass. slang.* M19.

sloughi *noun* var. of SALUKI.

slougi *noun* var. of SALUKI.

Slovak /ˈsləʊvak/ *noun & adjective.* E19.
[Slovak, Czech, Russian, from Slavonic base also of SLOVENE.]
▸ **A** *noun.* A member of a Slavonic people inhabiting Slovakia in central Europe, formerly part of Hungary and later of Czechoslovakia, now an independent republic; the language of this people. E19.
▸ **B** *attrib.* or as *adjective.* Of or pertaining to Slovakia, its people, or their language. L19.
■ **Sloˈvakian** *adjective & noun* = SLOVAK E19. **Sloˈvakish** *adjective & noun* (*a*) *adjective* = SLOVAK *adjective*; †(*b*) *noun* the Slovak language: M19.

slove *verb pa. t.*: see SLIVE *verb*².

sloven /ˈslʌv(ə)n/ *noun & adjective.* L15.
[Perh. based on Flemish *sloef* dirty, squalid, Dutch *slof* negligent.]
▸ **A** *noun.* †**1** A person of low character or manners; a knave, a rascal. L15–L17.
†**2** A person of slothful habits; a lazy, idle fellow. Only in 16.
3 A person who is negligent in personal appearance or cleanliness; an untidy or dirty person. M16.
4 A careless or slipshod worker. L18.
5 A low wagon. Also *sloven-wagon*. *Canad.* L19.
6 FORESTRY. The splintered part of the stump left when a tree is felled. M20.
▸ **B** *adjective.* Slovenly. Also (*US*), uncultivated, untrained. E19.
■ **slovenlike** *adjective & adverb* (*rare*) = SLOVENLY *adjective*, *adverb* E19. †**slovenness** *noun* slovenliness M17–L18. **slovenry** *noun* (now *rare*) slovenliness, carelessness, negligence M16.

sloven /ˈslʌv(ə)n/ *verb*¹. *rare.* M16.
[from the noun.]
†**1** *verb intrans.* Be slothful or indolent. Only in M16.
†**2** *verb refl.* Dress in a slovenly or untidy manner. Only in L16.
3 *verb trans.* Treat or do in a slovenly or careless manner. E19.

sloven *verb*² *pa. pple*: see SLIVE *verb*¹.

Slovene /ˈsləʊviːn, sləʊˈviːn/ *noun & adjective.* L19.
[German *Slowene* from Slovene *Sloven(ec)* a Slovene from Slavonic base also of SLOVAK, perh. ult. from stem of *slovo* word, *sloviti* speak.]
▸ **A** *noun.* A member of a Slavonic people inhabiting Slovenia in south-east central Europe, formerly part of Austria and later of Yugoslavia; a native or inhabitant of Slovenia. Also, the language of the Slovenes, closely related to Serbo-Croat. L19.
▸ **B** *adjective.* Of or pertaining to Slovenia, its people, or their language. E20.
■ **Sloˈvenian** *noun & adjective* = SLOVENE M19. **Sloˈvenish** *noun & adjective* (now *rare*) (*a*) *noun* the Slovene language; (*b*) *adjective* of or pertaining to the Slovenes or their language: L19.

slovenly /ˈslʌv(ə)nli/ *adjective.* E16.
[from SLOVEN *noun* + -LY¹.]
†**1** Low, base; lewd. *rare.* Only in 16.
2 Of a person, the appearance, habits, etc.: untidy, dirty; careless, negligent. M16.
3 Of an action, style, etc.: characterized by a lack of care or precision; unmethodical. E17.
■ **slovenliness** *noun* the quality or state of being slovenly; an instance of this: E17.

slovenly /ˈslʌv(ə)nli/ *adverb.* L16.
[from SLOVEN *noun* + -LY².]
In a careless, negligent, or untidy manner.

Slovincian /sləˈvɪnsɪən/ *noun.* L19.
[French *Slovince*, German *Slowinze* from Kashubian *Słovinsći*: see -IAN.]
Hist. An extinct form of Kashubian.

slow /sləʊ/ *noun.* OE.
[from SLOW *adjective & adverb*.]
1 A slow person; a sluggard. OE.
2 a A slow-paced horse. E19. ▸**b** A slow train. M20. ▸**c** A slow tune in pop music. M20.
3 CRICKET. **a** A slowly bowled ball. *rare.* M19. ▸**b** A slow bowler. *rare.* L19.
4 In *pl.* ▸**a** = *milk-sickness* s.v. MILK *noun & adjective*. *US.* M19. ▸**b** An imaginary disease or ailment accounting for slowness. Usu. with *the*. M19.

slow /sləʊ/ *adjective & adverb.*
[Old English *slāw* = Old Frisian *slēwich*, West Frisian *sleau*, Old Saxon *slēu*, Middle Dutch *sleeuw*, *slee*, Old High German *slēo* (German dial. *schleh*), Old Norse *slær*, *sljár*, *sljór*, from Germanic from Indo-European.]
▸ **A** *adjective.* **1** Of a person, the mind, etc.: not quick to understand, learn, think, etc.; obtuse, dull. OE.
2 a Naturally disinclined to exert oneself; inactive, sluggish, lacking in vigour. OE. ▸**b** Of a tool etc.: having a dull edge, blunt. Now *dial.* LME.

3 Not quick, prompt, or willing to do something; not readily affected; unsusceptible. (Foll. by *in*, *of*, *to do*.) ME. ▸**b** Inattentive *to* something. Long *rare*. M17.

4 a Displaying a lack of speed or energy in an activity, process, etc.; taking or requiring a comparatively long time to do something; tardy, dilatory. ME. ▸**b** Of a period of time: taking a long time to pass. M16.

5 a Of a thing, action, etc.: lasting or occurring over a long time; not rapid in operation or effect, gradual. ME. ▸**b** Of the pulse: below the average rate. E18. ▸**c** Of trade, business, etc.: slack, unproductive. L19. ▸**d** PHOTOGRAPHY. (Of film etc.) requiring a long exposure; (of a lens) having a small aperture; (of a shutter) providing a long exposure time. L19. ▸**e** MEDICINE. (Of a disease) caused by a virus etc. that multiplies slowly in the host and has an incubation period of months or years. M20.

6 a (Of a fire) burning gently; (of heat) gentle. LME. ▸**b** Of an oven: of such a temperature that food cooks slowly. M18.

7 Moving in a sluggish manner; taking a comparatively long time to cover a distance; having a relatively low speed. LME.

8 a Of pace, movement, etc.: leisurely; not quick or hurried. Also *spec.* (of a ballroom dance), with steps at walking-pace. LME. ▸**b** Suitable for or productive of slow movement; *spec.* (of a lane or track) intended for traffic travelling at low speed. M19.

9 Of a clock or watch: indicating a time earlier than the true time. L17.

10 a Behind the times; out of fashion; not smart or up-to-date. E19. ▸**b** Dull, tedious, tiresome; lifeless, insipid. M19.

> 📖 **1** SCOTT FITZGERALD I must be slow, for only then did I realize that Stahr was . . Smith. **3** SIR W. SCOTT Maiden's ears must be slow in receiving a gentleman's language. DAY LEWIS Slow to grow up—reluctant . . to leave . . childhood. **b** MILTON To prayer . . and obedience due . . Mine eare shall not be slow. **4a** A. THWAITE A slow worker, spending a long time on one poem. ***be slow off the mark***: see MARK *noun*[1]. **5a** D. H. LAWRENCE The slow, smouldering patience of American opposition. D. W. GOODWIN Alcoholism has been called 'slow suicide'. **7** M. MARRIN I arrived . . on a slow train. *absol.*: SHAKES. *Macb.* The valued file Distinguishes the swift, the slow, the subtle. **10** M. FRANKLIN The boys . . drifted outback . . . They found it too slow at home.

▸**B** *adverb.* Slowly; at a slow rate or pace. Now chiefly in comb., as ***slow-acting***, ***slow-burning***, ***slow-going***, ***slow-moving***, etc. LME.

> 📖 G. GREENE He . . said to the driver, 'Go as slow as you can.' ***go slow***: see GO *verb*. **take it slow** *colloq.* be careful.

Special collocations & comb.: **slow back** a direction to a golfer when the club is swung back from the ball in making a stroke. **slow bell** *N. Amer.*: signalling to a ship to proceed slowly. **slow bowler** CRICKET: employing slow bowling. **slow bowling** CRICKET: in which the ball travels at a low speed. ***slow burn***: see BURN *noun*[2] 1. **slowcoach** a person who acts or moves slowly; a slow or idle person. **slow-drag** *noun & verb* (**a**) *noun* a slow blues rhythm; a dance or piece of music in this rhythm; (**b**) *verb intrans.* dance to such a rhythm. **slow-foot**, **slow-footed** *adjectives* that walks or goes slowly; slow-moving, slow-paced. **slow handclap** *noun & verb* (**a**) *noun* a round of slow rhythmic applause expressing disapproval; (**b**) *verb trans. & intrans.* give such applause (to). **slow-hound** a sleuth-hound. ***slow loris***. ***slow march***: see MARCH *noun*[3] 6. **slow match** a match or wick which burns very slowly without a flame. **slow motion** motion of slower speed than normal; the technique of making a film or video recording so that actions and movements appear to be slower than in real life. **slow neutron** NUCLEAR PHYSICS a neutron with little kinetic energy, esp. as a result of being slowed down by a moderator. **slow pass** BRIDGE: made after a long wait to indicate that the player was considering an alternative action. **slowpoke** *colloq.* (chiefly *N. Amer.*) = ***slowcoach*** above. **slow puncture**: from which the air escapes gradually. **slow reactor**: in which fission is produced primarily by moderated neutrons; a thermal reactor. **slow-scan** *adjective* (TELEVISION) scanning at a much slower rate than usual, so that the resulting signal has a much smaller bandwidth and can be transmitted more cheaply. **slow time** a rate of marching in which only 75 paces, of 30 inches each, are taken in a minute. **slow-twitch** *adjective* (of a muscle fibre) that contracts slowly, providing endurance rather than strength. **slow virus**: which multiplies slowly in the host and has an incubation period of months or years. **slow wheel** a potter's wheel turned at a slow speed. **slow-witted** *adjective* slow to understand, learn, etc.; unintelligent. **slow-worm** [Old English *wyrm* snake: see WORM *noun*] a legless lizard, *Anguis fragilis* (family Anguidae), found in most of Europe and adjoining areas, with a smooth-scaled snakelike body.

■ **slowish** *adjective* somewhat slow or dull E19.

slow /sləʊ/ *verb*. ME.

[from the adjective; not continuous with Old English *slāwian* (see FORSLOW).]

▸**I** *verb intrans.* †**1** Be slow to do something. Only in ME.

2 Slacken in rate or speed; move more slowly. Also foll. by *down*, *up*. L16.

3 Become less active or vigorous. Usu. foll. by *down*. L19.

> 📖 **2** J. M. COETZEE My breathing slowed and I grew calmer. J. UPDIKE Traffic . . slowed to a honking . . crawl. **3** G. DALY He had to slow down and take better care of himself.

▸**II** *verb trans.* †**4** Lose (time) by delay. Only in E16.

5 a Delay, check, retard; reduce the rate or speed of, ease. Also foll. by *down*. M16. ▸**b** Cause (a vehicle) gradually to slacken in speed. Also foll. by *down*, *up*. M19.

> 📖 **5a** E. BOWEN She slowed down her running steps to a walk. E. YOUNG-BRUEHL Anna Freud's circuitous methods seemed to slow the development of child analysis.

Comb.: **slow-down** the action of slowing down; *spec.* (**a**) an industrial go-slow; (**b**) a decline in productivity or demand; **slow-up** an act of slowing a train etc.

■ **slower** *noun* that which checks or impedes; a retarding influence: E17.

slow-belly /ˈsləʊbɛli/ *noun*. *arch.* E17.

[from SLOW *adjective* + BELLY *noun*, after Greek *gasteres argai* lit. 'slothful bellies' (with ref. to Tindale *Titus* 1:12).]

A lazy or indolent person; a sluggard. Usu. in *pl.*

slowly /ˈsləʊli/ *adverb*. OE.

[from SLOW *adjective* + -LY[2].]

†**1** In a remiss or negligent manner; sluggishly; slackly. OE–M16.

2 Not quickly or hastily; at a slow pace. ME.

> 📖 **2** J. M. COETZEE He was slowly overtaken by a cart. J. MARSH His feelings for her grew slowly.

slowness /ˈsləʊnɪs/ *noun*. ME.

[from SLOW *adjective* + -NESS.]

†**1** Sloth, indolence, sluggishness. ME–M18.

2 The quality of being slow in action or progress. LME.

3 The quality of being slow in motion. LME. ▸**b** A soft or heavy condition of ground which is productive of slow movement. L19.

4 a Dullness of intellect or comprehension; lack of acuteness or readiness. L15. ▸**b** Lack of animation; dullness, tediousness. L19.

sloyd *noun* var. of SLOID.

SLP *abbreviation*.

Scottish Labour Party.

SLR *abbreviation*.

1 Self-loading rifle.

2 Single-lens reflex (camera).

slub /slʌb/ *noun*[1]. Now chiefly *Scot. & dial.* L16.

[Perh. from Middle Dutch *slubbe* in same sense.]

Thick wet mud, mire; ooze.

■ **slubby** *adjective* muddy; sticky, slippery: L16.

slub /slʌb/ *noun*[2] & *adjective*. E19.

[Origin unkn.]

▸**A** *noun*. **1** A lump on a thread. E19.

2 A yarn containing lumps or thickened parts at intervals; a fabric woven from such a yarn. M20.

▸**B** *adjective*. Of a yarn, fabric, etc.: having an irregular appearance caused by uneven thickness. E20.

■ **slubbed** *adjective* (of a fabric) containing slubs M20.

slub /slʌb/ *noun*[3]. M19.

[from SLUB *verb*[2].]

(A thread of) wool or cotton twisted in preparation for spinning.

slub /slʌb/ *verb*[1] *trans. dial.* Infl. **-bb-**. E19.

[from SLUB *noun*[1].]

Cover with mud.

slub /slʌb/ *verb*[2] *trans.* Infl. **-bb-**. M19.

[Origin unkn.]

Draw out and twist (wool or cotton) in preparation for spinning.

slubber /ˈslʌbə/ *noun*. M19.

[from SLUB *verb*[2] + -ER[1].]

A person who operates a machine for slubbing wool or cotton; a machine for slubbing wool or cotton.

slubber /ˈslʌbə/ *verb*. Now chiefly *dial.* M16.

[Prob. var. of SLOBBER *verb*.]

1 *verb trans.* Stain, smear; *fig.* sully. M16.

2 *verb trans.* Do, make, deal with, etc., in a hurried or careless manner. Also foll. by *over*, *through*, *up*. M16.

3 *verb trans.* Foll. by *over*: cover, conceal; *fig.* gloss over. M17.

4 *verb trans. & intrans.* Gobble (food) noisily. Also foll. by *up*. M17.

5 *verb intrans.* Be clumsy or messy; slobber. E19.

■ **slubbery** *adjective* untidy; slovenly: L19.

slubberdegullion /ˌslʌbədɪˈɡʌljən/ *noun*. *arch.* E17.

[from prec. with fanciful ending.]

A slobbering or dirty fellow; a sloven.

slubbing /ˈslʌbɪŋ/ *noun*. L18.

[from SLUB *verb*[2] + -ING[1].]

1 A process of drawing and twisting by which cotton is prepared for spinning. L18.

2 Any of the threads obtained by this process; *collect.* wool or cotton which has been slubbed. L18.

slud /slʌd/ *noun*. L18.

[Origin uncertain: perh. rel. to Low German *sleuder* lather, German dial. *Schluder* slush, mud, or a blend of SLUDGE *noun* + MUD *noun*[1].]

1 Mud. *dial.* L18.

2 *spec.* in GEOLOGY. Soil or similar material made susceptible to solifluction, esp. by saturation with water from underlying permafrost. Cf. SLUDGE *verb* 6. M20.

sludge /slʌdʒ/ *noun & adjective*. E17.

[Origin uncertain. Cf. SLUSH *noun*[1], SLUTCH.]

▸**A** *noun*. **1 a** Mud, mire, or ooze on the surface of the ground, in the bed of a river, etc. E17. ▸**b** NAUTICAL. Ice imperfectly formed, or broken up into minute pieces. E19. ▸**c** The colour of mud, a dull greenish-brown. M20.

2 a Any muddy or slimy matter or deposit; a thick suspension of fine particles or gel in a liquid, esp. one formed as waste in any of various industrial and mechanical processes. E18. ▸**b** Finely crushed or cut rock mixed with water, produced in rock drilling or during the extraction of metals. M18. ▸**c** A loose sediment formed in a boiler or other vessel in which water is habitually heated. M19. ▸**d** A precipitate in a sewage tank. L19. ▸**e** A dark viscous liquid or semi-solid mass deposited when a petroleum distillate is mixed with strong sulphuric acid during refining. Also ***sludge acid***, ***acid sludge***. L19. ▸**f** A deposit of fine insoluble particles formed at the anode during electrolysis; anode slime. E20. ▸**g** A thick semi-solid deposit formed in oil when it is heated, exposed to air, or mixed with another kind of oil. E20. ▸**h** MEDICINE. (A quantity of) blood which has undergone sludging (cf. SLUDGING *noun* 4). M20.

3 *fig.* An amorphous or undifferentiated mass. E20.

> 📖 **1a** B. ENGLAND The shallow sludge of water and mud. **3** *Times* Each instrument is reduced to a sludge of pentatonically tinted Mantovani.

▸**B** *attrib.* or as *adjective*. Of the colour of mud, dull greenish-brown. E17.

■ **sludgy** *adjective* (**a**) muddy, miry; (**b**) consisting of newly formed particles of ice; (**c**) of the colour of mud, dull greenish-brown; (**d**) dull and confused, tedious: L18.

sludge /slʌdʒ/ *verb*. M18.

[from the noun.]

▸**I 1** *verb trans.* Convert into sludge. M18.

2 *verb trans.* Clear of sludge or mud. M19.

3 *verb trans.* Fill the crevices of (an embankment) with liquid mud. *rare*. L19.

4 *verb intrans.* Form or deposit sludge. M20.

▸**II 5** *verb intrans.* Trudge, tramp; labour. E20.

6 *verb intrans.* Move slowly by solifluction. M20.

■ **sludger** *noun* an appliance for removing sludge from a borehole, or for boring in quicksand M19.

sludging /ˈslʌdʒɪŋ/ *noun*. M19.

[from SLUDGE *noun* or *verb* + -ING[1].]

1 The action of filling up crevices in dried clay with mud; the mud so used. M19.

2 The formation of sludge, esp. in oil. E20.

3 = SOLIFLUCTION. M20.

4 MEDICINE. The aggregation of blood cells into jelly-like masses which impede the circulation. M20.

slue *noun*[1], *noun*[2], *verb* vars. of SLEW *noun*[1], *noun*[2], *verb*[1].

sluff *noun*, *verb* see SLOUGH *noun*[2], *verb*[1].

slug /slʌɡ/ *noun*[1]. LME.

[Rel. to SLUG *verb*[1]: cf. Norwegian dial. *slugg* large heavy body, *sluggje* heavy slow person. See also next.]

1 Orig., slothfulness personified. Later, a slow, lazy fellow; a sluggard. LME.

†**2** A slow sailing vessel. M16–M18.

3 An animal, vehicle, etc., of a slow-moving or sluggish character. E17.

4 a Any of numerous slow-moving slime-producing gastropod molluscs in which the shell is rudimentary or entirely absent. E18. ▸**b** = ***sea-slug*** (b) s.v. SEA. M19. ▸**c** MYCOLOGY. = GREX. M20.

5 Any of various insect larvae, esp. those of certain sawflies, resembling a slug. Also ***slug-worm***. L18.

6 A contemptible person; a fat person. M20.

Comb.: **slug pellet**: of bait containing a poison to kill slugs; **slug-snail** (now *rare* or *obsolete*) = sense 4a above.

■ **sluggy** *adjective*[1] (*rare*) having many slugs L19.

slug /slʌɡ/ *noun*[2]. E17.

[Perh. same word as prec.]

1 A piece of lead etc. for firing from a gun; a bullet. E17.

2 a A drink of spirits etc.; a dram. M18. ▸**b** A compact moving mass of liquid or semi-liquid material. M20.

3 The stunted horn of an animal (more fully ***slug-horn***). Also, the core of an animal's horn. E19.

4 a A heavy, usu. rounded, piece of crude metal; a nugget (of gold). M19. ▸**b** *gen.* A thick piece or lump of some material; a (usu. large) portion or amount. M19.

5 *US*. **a** A heavy gold piece privately coined in California in 1849 and subsequently prohibited. M19. ▸**b** A dollar; a counterfeit coin; a token. *slang*. L19.

6 a PRINTING. (A strip of type-metal containing) a line of characters produced by a Linotype machine. L19. ▸**b** JOURNALISM. An identifying title accompanying a news story in draft and galleys. Also ***slug-line***. E20.

7 a *ELECTRICITY.* A metal cylinder fitted round the end of the core of an electromagnetic relay to modify the speeds of opening and closing. Cf. SLEEVE *noun* 4b. **E20.** ▸**b** *ELECTRICITY.* An adjustable magnetic core used to vary the inductance of a coil containing it. Chiefly in ***slug tuning***. **M20.** ▸**c** *NUCLEAR PHYSICS.* A rod or bar of nuclear fuel. **M20.**
8 *ENGINEERING.* A unit of mass equal to 32.1740 lb (approx. 14.594 kg), being the mass of a body which accelerates at one foot per second per second when acted on by one pound force. Now *rare* or *Hist.* **E20.**

> 🕮 **1** *Listener* The pain of heavy .45 slugs ripping into my flesh. **2a** W. BOYD He poured a slug of brandy into his coffee. **4b** G. BENFORD He chewed on a hemp slug. *Times* The management . . disposed of a large slug of its assets.

Comb.: ***slug-horn***: see sense 3 above; ***slug-line***: see sense 6b above; **slug-setting** *PRINTING* a method of setting an entire line of type on a single slug.

slug /slʌg/ *noun*³. Now *dial.* & *N. Amer.* **M19.**
[from SLUG *verb*³.]
A hard blow; a beating.
Comb.: **slug-fest** *N. Amer. slang* a hard-hitting contest, *spec.* in boxing and baseball; **slug-nutty** *adjective* (*US slang*) punch-drunk.

slug /slʌg/ *verb*¹. Now *rare.* Infl. **-gg-**. **LME.**
[Prob. of Scandinavian origin: cf. Swedish dial. *slogga* be sluggish, *sluggjen* slow, backward. Cf. SLUG *noun*¹.]
1 *verb intrans.* Be lazy, slow, or inactive; lie idly. **LME.**
2 *verb intrans.* Move slowly; loiter. **M16.**
3 *verb trans.* Pass (time) in inactivity or idleness. Also foll. by *out*. **M16.**
4 *verb trans.* Relax, slacken; make sluggish. **E17.**
5 *verb trans.* Hinder, delay. **E17.**
■ **sluggy** *adjective*² (now *rare* or *obsolete*) sluggish, indolent **ME.**

slug /slʌg/ *verb*². Infl. **-gg-**. **M19.**
[from SLUG *noun*².]
1 *verb trans.* Load (a gun) with slugs. **M19.**
2 *verb trans.* & *intrans.* Drink in deep draughts; swig. **M19.**
3 *verb trans.* *JOURNALISM.* Mark with a slug-line; give as a title or heading. **E20.**

> 🕮 **2** *Washington Post* Players wearily slumped in their chairs and slugged water.

slug /slʌg/ *verb*³. Chiefly *dial.* & *N. Amer.* Infl. **-gg-**. **M19.**
[Parallel to SLOG *verb*.]
1 *verb trans.* **a** Hit hard, strike violently. **M19.** ▸**b** Treat roughly, exploit; *Austral. slang* charge excessively. Also, churn or force *out*. **E20.**
2 *verb intrans.* Slog (*along*, *away*). **M20.**

> 🕮 **1a** I. SHAW He . . slugged the ball as though he were disposing of enemies. **b** *Sun (Melbourne)* Government is reaping enormous benefit . . and the motorist gets slugged.

Phrases: **slug it out** fight it out; stick it out.

slugabed /ˈslʌgəbɛd/ *noun*. *arch.* **L16.**
[from SLUG *verb*¹ + ABED.]
A lazy person who lies late in bed.

sluggard /ˈslʌgəd/ *noun* & *adjective*. **ME.**
[from SLUG *verb*¹ + -ARD.]
▸ **A** *noun*. **1** A person who is habitually lazy or sluggish; a person disinclined to work. **ME.**
†**2** A sloth (the animal). *rare.* **M17–L18.**
▸ **B** *adjective*. Lazy, sluggish, slothful. **E16.**
■ **sluggardize** *verb trans.* & *intrans.* (*rare*) make or be lazy **L16.** **sluggardness**, **sluggardry** *nouns* (now *rare*) laziness **LME.**

sluggardly /ˈslʌgədli/ *adjective*. **M19.**
[from prec. + -LY¹.]
Lazy, slothful; sluggish.

> 🕮 *Financial Times* Fast movements . . always had some life even under the most sluggardly conductors.

■ **sluggardliness** *noun* **L20.**

slugged /slʌgd/ *adjective*¹. Now *rare.* **LME.**
[from SLUG *noun*¹, *verb*¹: see -ED², -ED¹.]
Sluggish.

slugged /slʌgd/ *adjective*². **E20.**
[from SLUG *noun*² + -ED².]
Having a slug or slugs.

slugger /ˈslʌgə/ *noun*. **L19.**
[from SLUG *verb*³ + -ER¹.]
1 A person who hits hard in boxing, baseball, etc.: a slogger. Orig. & chiefly *N. Amer.* **L19.**
2 Usu. in *pl.* Side whiskers worn from the ear to the chin. *US slang.* **L19.**
3 A flat-surfaced knob or projection on a roll for crushing ore. **E20.**

sluggish /ˈslʌgɪʃ/ *adjective*. **LME.**
[from SLUG *noun*¹, *verb*¹: see -ISH¹.]
1 Of a person: inclined to be slow or slothful; lazy, inactive. **LME.** ▸**b** Of an animal: habitually slow-moving or inactive. **M19.**
2 Of the mind, disposition, etc.: characterized by lack of vigour or alertness; dull, slow. **LME.**
3 a Of a condition etc.: characterized by inaction or laziness. **M16.** ▸**b** [translating Russian *vyalotekushchiĭ*] Designating an alleged type of schizophrenia ascribed to political or religious dissidents confined in state psychiatric hospitals in the former USSR. **L20.**
4 Moving slowly or tardily; (of motion etc.) slow. **E17.**
5 Of a thing: not readily moved or stirred, slow to act, respond, or make progress. **M17.** ▸**b** *MEDICINE.* Slow in responding to treatment. **L19.**
■ **sluggishly** *adverb* **LME.** **sluggishness** *noun* **LME.**

slughorn /ˈslʌghɔːn/ *noun*. Now *arch.* & *poet.* **L16.**
[Var. of SLOGAN *noun*, sense 2 perh. by a misunderstanding.]
†**1** = SLOGAN *noun* 1. **L16–M19.**
2 A trumpet. **M18.**

sluice /sluːs/ *noun*. **ME.**
[Old French *escluse* (mod. *écluse*) from Proto-Gallo-Romance use as noun (sc. *aqua* water) of fem. pa. pple of Latin *excludere* EXCLUDE.]
1 a A structure on a river, canal, etc., with an adjustable gate or gates by which the volume or flow of water is controlled; a gate in such a structure. Also, the body of water so controlled. **ME.** ▸**b** A paddle or slide in a gate or barrier by which water is held back. **E17.** ▸**c** Any device by which a flow of water is regulated; a valve, pipe, etc., by which water may be let in or run off. **E17.**
2 A channel, a drain, *esp.* one carrying off overflow or surplus water. **M16.**
†**3** A gap, an opening; a gash, a wound. **M17–M18.**
4 In gold-mining, a man-made channel or trough fitted with grooves into which a current of water is directed in order to separate gold from auriferous ore. *US* & *Austral.* **M19.**

> 🕮 **1a** D. H. LAWRENCE Open the sluice that let out the water.

Comb.: **sluice-box** *US* & *Austral.* a trough in a gold-miner's sluice; **sluice-fork** used to break up lumps of gravel in a gold-miner's sluice-box; **sluice-gate** the gate of a sluice able to be opened or shut to control the flow of water; the upper gate of a lock; **sluice-head** a supply of water sufficient for flushing out a sluice; **sluice-way** a channel or waterway controlled by means of a sluice or sluices.
■ **sluicy** *adjective* (chiefly *poet.*) (*a*) (of rain etc.) pouring as if from a sluice, streaming; (*b*) *rare* resembling a sluice: **L17.**

sluice /sluːs/ *verb*. **L16.**
[from the noun.]
1 *verb trans.* Let out (water) from a place by the opening of a sluice; draw off (water) by the opening of a sluice. Foll. by *from*, *off*, *out*. **L16.**
2 *verb trans.* Draw off or let out water from (a river, lake, etc.) by means of a sluice or sluices. Also foll. by *in*, *into*. **L16.**
3 *transf.* & *fig.* **a** *verb intrans.* Flow or rush (*down* or *out*) as if through a sluice. **L16.** ▸**b** *verb trans.* Throw or pour (something) as if through a sluice. **E17.**
4 *verb trans.* Throw or pour water over; rinse or flush with water. Also, fill with water. **M18.** ▸**b** Wash (auriferous ore) in a gold-miner's sluice. Also foll. by *out*. *US* & *Austral.* **M19.**
5 Float (logs) down a sluice-way. **L19.**

> 🕮 **3a** G. ORWELL He . . let the rain sluice down on his bare body. **b** M. KRAMER Wealthy outsiders . . sluiced enormous sums into vineyards. **4** W. S. MAUGHAM Naked coolies . . sluicing themselves with boiling water. A. COHEN Sanitation trucks . . routinely sluicing the streets, cleaning up. **sluice one's gob** *slang* drink heartily.

■ **sluicer** *noun* (*a*) *US* & *Austral.* a gold-miner who uses a sluice; (*b*) a person in charge of a sluice on a waterway: **M19.**

sluit /ˈsluːɪt/ *noun*. *S. Afr.* Also **sloot** /sluːt/. **E19.**
[Afrikaans *sloot* ditch = Low German *sloot*, Old Frisian *slât* (West Frisian *sleat*).]
A ditch, a gully, *esp.* one formed by heavy rain or made for irrigation purposes.

slum /slʌm/ *noun*¹. **E19.**
[Origin unkn. Cf. SLURB.]
▸ **I 1** A room. *slang.* Long *rare* or *obsolete.* **E19.**
2 An overcrowded district of a town or city, having squalid housing conditions and inhabited by very poor people; a street situated in such a district (freq. in *pl.*). Also *transf.*, a house materially unfit for human habitation. **E19.**

> 🕮 **2** D. HOGAN Men come from the slums of Dublin to the middle classes. ***attrib.***: R. ALTER An ugly, distended slum building.

▸ **II 3** Nonsensical talk or writing. Also, Gypsy jargon or cant. *slang.* Long *rare* or *obsolete.* **E19.**
4 *N. Amer.* **a** Cheap or imitation jewellery. *Criminals' slang.* **E20.** ▸**b** Cheap prizes at a fair, carnival, etc. **E20.**
Comb.: **slum clearance** the demolition of slums, usu. accompanied by the rehousing of the inhabitants; **slumland** the slums of a town or city; **slum landlord**: who lets slum property to tenants; **slumlord** *US* = ***slum landlord*** above.
■ **slumdom** *noun* (the inhabitants of) slums collectively; the condition or character of these: **L19.** **slumism** *noun* the existence of slums; deprivation associated with life in the slums: **M20.** **slumless** *adjective* containing no slums **E20.**

slum /slʌm/ *noun*². *US.* **M19.**
[Perh. from German *Schlamm* or infl. by next.]
MINING. = SLUDGE *noun* 2b. Freq. in *pl.*

slum /slʊm/ *noun*³. *slang.* **M19.**
[App. abbreviation Cf. prec.]
= SLUMGULLION *noun* 4.
Comb.: **slum burner** an army cook; **slum gun** a field-kitchen.

slum /slʌm/ *verb*. Infl. **-mm-**. **M19.**
[from SLUM *noun*¹.]
1 *verb trans.* & *intrans.* Do (work) hurriedly and carelessly. **M19.** ▸**b** *spec.* Shear (a sheep) in a careless manner. *Austral.* **M20.**
2 *verb intrans.* & *trans.* (with *it*). ▸**a** Visit slums for charitable purposes or out of curiosity. **L19.** ▸**b** Accept temporarily a lower standard of living, travel, etc., than usual; put up with squalid or uncomfortable conditions. **E20.**

> 🕮 **2a** M. GEE For you it's fun to go slumming with me. But your real life's back there. **b** W. MCILVANNEY 'Beers? For ladies of your obvious sophistication?' 'We're slumming to-day.'

slumber /ˈslʌmbə/ *noun*. **ME.**
[Alt. of SLOOM *noun* or directly from the verb.]
1 a *sing.* & in *pl.* Sleep, rest; a state of sleep. Chiefly *poet.* & *literary.* **ME.** ▸**b** A (usu. short) period of sleep. **LME.**
2 *fig.* A state of rest or inactivity. **M16.**

> 🕮 **1a** J. BUCHAN He wakened me from my slumbers. H. CARPENTER Crept back . . and fell into an alcoholic slumber. **2** A. BROOKNER A street sunk in the slumber of mid-afternoon.

Comb.: **slumber cap** a light close-fitting cap worn in bed to keep the hair tidy; **slumbercoach** *US* a railway car with cheap private sleeping accommodation; **slumberland** *joc.* sleep; **slumber net** a slumber cap made of net; **slumber party** *N. Amer.*: for youngsters (esp. girls) who stay and sleep overnight; **slumber room** *US*: in which a corpse is laid out by an undertaker until the funeral; **slumberwear** nightclothes.
■ **slumberful** *adjective* (*rare*) marked by slumber **M19.** **slumberless** *adjective* (*rare*) sleepless **E19.** **slumbersome** *adjective* slumberous, sleepy **L19.** **slumbery** *adjective* (now *rare* or *obsolete*) sleepy; of the nature of sleep: **LME.**

slumber /ˈslʌmbə/ *verb*. **ME.**
[Alt. of SLOOM *verb*, or corresp. to Middle Low German, Middle Dutch *slūmen*, Middle Low German *slummen*, with parallel forms in Middle Low German, Middle Dutch *slūmeren* (Dutch *sluimeren*), Middle High German *slumeren*, German *schlummern*. For the intrusive *b* cf. *ember*.]
1 *verb intrans.* Sleep, doze. Also (*fig.*), lie at rest in death. **ME.**
2 *verb intrans.* Be inactive or negligent; remain sunk *in* sin, sloth, etc.; be tardy *in* doing something. **ME.**
†**3** *verb trans.* Cause to sleep; make inactive, deaden. **M16–M17.**
4 *verb intrans.* Be dormant, inoperative, or still. **L16.**
5 *verb trans.* Spend or waste (time) sleeping. (Foll. by *away*, *out*.) **M18.**

> 🕮 **4** W. JAMES Any given day . . there are energies slumbering in him.

■ **slumberer** *noun* a person who sleeps or is asleep; an indolent person: **LME.** **slumbering** *verbal noun* the state or fact of being asleep; an instance of this: **ME.**

†**slumbered** *adjective*. *rare* (Spenser). Only in **L16.**
[from SLUMBER *noun*, *verb*: see -ED², -ED¹.]
Wrapt in slumber; unconscious.

slumberous /ˈslʌmb(ə)rəs/ *adjective*. Also **slumbrous** /-brəs/. **L15.**
[from SLUMBER *noun* + -OUS.]
1 Sleepy, drowsy, lethargic. **L15.** ▸**b** Of the eyes or eyelids: heavy with sleep. **E19.**
2 Inducing sleep; soporific. **M17.**
3 Moving very slightly or slowly; calm, still, peaceful. **M18.**
4 Characterized by or suggestive of sleep. **E19.**
5 Characterized by inactivity or sluggishness. **E19.** ▸**b** Of a place: quiet, sleepy, tranquil. **M19.**
■ **slumberously** *adverb* **E19.** **slumberousness** *noun* **M19.**

slumgullion /slʌmˈgʌljən/ *noun*. *N. Amer. slang.* **M19.**
[Prob. fanciful formation. Cf. SLUM *noun*³.]
1 A muddy deposit in a mining sluice. **M19.**
2 A beverage. **L19.**
3 Offal from fish; *spec.* the refuse from whale blubber. **L19.**
4 A watery stew of meat and vegetables. **E20.**

slumgum /ˈslʌmgʌm/ *noun*. *US.* **L19.**
[from SLUM *noun*² + GUM *noun*².]
The residual wax and impurities that remain when the honey and most of the wax are extracted from honeycombs.

slummer /ˈslʌmə/ *noun*. **L19.**
[from SLUM *noun*¹, *verb*: see -ER¹.]
1 A person who visits slums, esp. for charitable purposes. **L19.**
2 An inhabitant of a slum area. **L19.**

slummie *noun* var. of SLUMMY *noun*.

slummock /ˈslʌmək/ *noun & verb.* Chiefly *dial. & colloq.* Also **slammock** /ˈslamək/. M19.
[Origin unkn. Cf. SLAMMAKIN.]
▶ **A** *noun.* A dirty, untidy, or slovenly person; a slut. M19.
▶ **B** *verb.* **1** *verb trans.* Eat up greedily. M19.
2 *verb intrans.* Move, speak, or behave awkwardly or clumsily. L19.

2 G. B. SHAW The country isn't governed: it just slummocks along anyhow.

▪ **slummocker** *noun* an awkward or careless person E20. **slummockiness** *noun* the condition of being slovenly M20. **slummocky** *adjective* slovenly, untidy M19.

slummy /ˈslʌmi/ *noun. colloq.* Also **slummie**. M20.
[from SLUM *noun*[1] + -Y[6].]
A slum-dweller.

slummy /ˈslʌmi/ *adjective.* M19.
[from SLUM *noun*[1] + -Y[1].]
1 Given to frequenting slums; pertaining to slums. M19.
2 Of the nature of a slum; (of a town or city) possessing slums. L19.
3 Slovenly, careless. L19.
▪ **slumminess** *noun* L19.

slump /slʌmp/ *noun*[1]. *Scot.* L17.
[Low German = heap, mass, quantity (= Dutch *slomp*, Frisian *slompe*).]
A large quantity or number. Chiefly in ***by slump, by the slump, by a slump, in slump, in the slump, in a slump***, as a whole, collectively, at a rough estimate.
Comb.: **slump sum** a lump sum.

slump /slʌmp/ *noun*[2]. *dial.* E19.
[Perh. rel. to SLUMP *verb*[1].]
A marsh, a swamp; a muddy or boggy place.

slump /slʌmp/ *noun*[3]. M19.
[from SLUMP *verb*[1].]
▶ **I 1** A slumping movement or fall; a reduction in activity, performance, commitment, etc.; a period of decline or depression. M19.
2 *spec.* **a** ECONOMICS. A sharp or sudden decline in economic activity, usu. accompanied by widespread unemployment; a collapse in the prices of goods, shares, etc. L19. ▸**b** PHYSICAL GEOGRAPHY. A landslide in which a mass of soil, sediment, etc., slides down a short distance, usu. with slight backward rotation along a concave surface of separation from the parent mass; movement of this kind; a mass of material that has so fallen. E20. ▸**c** ENGINEERING. The height through which the top of a mass of fresh concrete sinks when the mould containing it is removed, as in the slump test. E20.

1 J. IRVING He finally broke out of his writing slump with a . . competitive surge. *First Base* How much further ahead would the Tigers be if their star pitchers . . weren't in a slump? **2a** *Property Weekly (Oxon.)* The surge of repossessions that has sent the house market into its worst slump this century.

▶ **II 3** A dessert consisting of stewed fruit with a biscuit or dough topping. *US* (chiefly *local*). M19.
4 A slovenly person, a slob. Chiefly *dial.* E20.
Comb.: **slump test** ENGINEERING a test of the consistency of fresh concrete in which the slump is measured following the removal of a mould of specified size and shape (usu. a truncated cone).

slump /slʌmp/ *verb*[1]. L17.
[Prob. imit.; perh. rel. to Norwegian *slumpe* to fall.]
▶ **I** *verb intrans.* **1** Fall or sink *in* or *into* a bog, swamp, etc.; fall *in* water with a dull splashing sound. L17.
2 Fall, esp. suddenly, heavily or clumsily, collapse; subside, slouch, lean; *spec.* in PHYSICAL GEOGRAPHY (of soil, sediment, etc.) fall in a slump. M19
3 Move or walk in a clumsy or laborious manner. M19.

2 H. ROTH Exhausted, he slumped back against the edge of the stair. A. HALEY She slumped toward the ground, young, strong arms . . supporting her. L. AUCHINCLOSS I found him slumped over his great black Italian table-desk. A. GUINNESS A fist landed unexpectedly on my jaw and I slumped to the carpet.

▶ **II** *verb trans.* **4** Slam (*down*). *rare.* M19.

slump /slʌmp/ *verb*[2] *trans.* Chiefly *Scot.* E19.
[from SLUMP *noun*[1].]
Lump *together*; deal with or regard as a single whole.

slumper /ˈslʌmpə/ *verb intrans. rare.* E19.
[Prob. imit. (cf. SLUMP *verb*[1]): see -ER[5].]
Flounder *through* or *along* a muddy track, lane, etc.

slumpflation /slʌmpˈfleɪʃ(ə)n/ *noun.* L20.
[Blend of SLUMP *noun*[3] and INFLATION. Cf. STAGFLATION.]
(A state of) economic depression in which decreasing output and employment in industry are accompanied by increasing inflation.

slumpy /ˈslʌmpi/ *adjective.* Orig. *dial.* E19.
[from SLUMP *noun*[2].]
Marshy, swampy, muddy, boggy.

slung *verb pa. t. & pple* of SLING *verb.*

slung-shot /ˈslʌŋʃɒt/ *noun. US.* M19.
[from *slung* pa. pple of SLING *verb* + SHOT *noun*[1].]
A hard object, as shot, piece of metal, or stone, fastened to a strap or thong, and used as a weapon.

slunk *verb pa. t. & pple* of SLINK *verb.*

slup /slʌp/ *verb trans.* Infl. **-pp-**. L16.
[Perh. rel. to SLOP *verb* or German dial. *schluppen* suck.]
Sup, swallow.

slur /sləː/ *noun*[1]. *obsolete* exc. *dial.* ME.
[Origin unkn.]
Thin or fluid mud. Cf. SLURRY *noun.*

slur /sləː/ *noun*[2]. L16.
[from SLUR *verb*[1].]
†**1** A gliding movement in dancing. L16–L17.
†**2** An illegal method of throwing a die. Cf. SLUR *verb*[1] 1. M–L17.
3 A sliding piece of mechanism in a knitting-machine, serving to depress the sinkers. Also ***slur-cock***. L18.

slur /sləː/ *noun*[3]. E17.
[from SLUR *verb*[2].]
1 An insult, a disparaging remark; an imputation of wrongdoing; an aspersion; a stigma. E17.
2 MUSIC. A curved line over or under two or more notes which are to be sung to one syllable or played or sung legato. M17.
3 PRINTING. A blurred or smudged impression; image distortion caused during the printing process, an instance of this. L18.
4 The action or an instance of slurring in pronunciation, singing, writing, etc. M19.

1 J. D. SUTHERLAND Extremely angry at . . a serious slur on his professional integrity. **cast a slur on**, **put a slur on**, **throw a slur on** cast an aspersion on, slander, (also foll. by *upon*).

slur /sləː/ *verb*[1]. Infl. **-rr-**. L16.
[Perh. rel. to Low German *slurren* shuffle, Middle & mod. Low German *slūren*, Middle Dutch *sloren*, Dutch *sleuren* drag, trail.]
▶ **I** *verb trans.* †**1** Slip or slide (a die) out of the box so that it does not roll. L16–E18.
†**2** *verb trans.* Cheat, trick, (a person). M17–M18.
▶ **II** *verb intrans.* **3** Slide (about). Now also, drag, move heavily. E17.

3 P. BARKER In the street outside there were sounds, voices, heavy boots slurring over cobbles.

slur /sləː/ *verb*[2]. Infl. **-rr-**. E17.
[from SLUR *noun*[1].]
1 *verb trans.* Smear, stain, smirch. *obsolete* exc. *dial.* E17. ▸**b** Esp. in PRINTING. Smudge, blur. L17.
2 *verb trans.* Disparage, cast a slur on, (a person, a person's character, etc.). Now chiefly *US.* M17.
3 *verb trans.* Pass over or conceal (a fact, fault, etc.); gloss *over*, minimize. M17.
4 a *verb trans.* MUSIC. Sing, play, or mark (notes) with a slur. M18. ▸**b** *verb trans. & intrans.* Speak or write (words) indistinctly so that sounds or letters run into one another. L19.

1b *fig.*: J. M. ROBERTSON Lax imagination slurs and confuses the lineaments of living character. **2** G. F. NEWMAN Try and slur the integrity of the police . . to secure an acquittal. **3** C. KINGSLEY Biographers have slurred a few facts. **4b** N. BAWDEN Since I no longer get drunk . . it offends me to hear voices slurring.

▪ **slurred** *adjective* (*a*) that has been slurred; (*b*) (of speech, pronunciation, etc.) indistinct: M18.

slurb /sləːb/ *noun. derog.* (orig. *US*). M20.
[Prob. blend of SLUM *noun*[1] and SUBURB.]
(An area of) unplanned suburban development. Also (in *pl.*), *the* suburbs.

slurbow /ˈsləːbəʊ/ *noun.* Long *obsolete* exc. *Hist.* L16.
[from unidentified 1st elem. + BOW *noun*[1].]
A type of crossbow used esp. for firing incendiary arrows.

slurp /sləːp/ *verb & noun.* M17.
[Dutch *slurpen*.]
▶ **A** *verb.* **1** *verb trans.* Drink or eat greedily or noisily. Freq. foll. by *down*. M17.
2 *verb intrans.* Make a sucking noise in drinking or eating. E20.
▶ **B** *noun.* A slurping sip or lick; the noise of slurping. Also as *interjection.* M20.
▪ **slurper** *noun* L20.

slurry /ˈslʌri/ *noun.* LME.
[Rel. to SLUR *noun*[1].]
Thin semi-liquid mud or cement. Now also, any semi-liquid mixture of a pulverized solid or fine particles with a liquid (usu. water); *spec.* (*a*) a residue of water and fine particles of coal left at pit-head washing plants; (*b*) farmyard manure in fluid form.
Comb.: **slurry seal** a tarlike mixture with the consistency of slurry, used for preserving road surfaces.

slurry /ˈsləːri/ *adjective.* M20.
[from SLUR *noun*[3], *verb*[2] + -Y[1].]
Esp. of speech: blurred, indistinct.
▪ **slurrily** *adverb* M20.

slurry /ˈslʌri/ *verb trans.* Long *obsolete* exc. *dial.* LME.
[Perh. rel. to prec.]
Dirty, soil, smear, daub, (*lit. & fig.*).

slush /slʌʃ/ *noun*[1]. See also SLOSH *noun.* M17.
[Prob. imit. Cf. SLUDGE *noun.*]
1 a Partially melted snow or ice. M17. ▸**b** Watery mud or mire. L18.
2 a The fats, grease, etc., obtained from boiling meat. Orig. *Nautical slang.* M18. ▸**b** Food, esp. of a watery consistency. *slang.* M20.
3 A slovenly or dirty person; a slut. Also, a drudge. *dial.* E19.
4 Nonsense, drivel; sentimental rubbish. Also as *interjection. colloq.* M19.
5 Counterfeit paper money. *slang.* E20.
Comb.: **slush-cast** *verb t & intrans.* make (a thing) by slush casting; **slush casting** a method of making hollow castings by pouring molten metal into a mould and then out again after a layer of metal has solidified on the inner surface of the mould; a casting produced thus; **slush fund** (*a*) (orig. *Nautical slang*) money collected from the sale of slush, for buying luxuries for the crew; (*b*) *colloq.* a reserve fund, *esp.* one used for purposes of bribery or illicit political activities; **slush-lamp**, **slush light**: consisting of a vessel containing fat with a wick inserted; **slush-money** *colloq.* (orig. *US*): paid out of a slush fund; **slush mould**: for use in slush moulding; **slush moulding** a process identical to slush casting but carried out with plastic or latex; **slush pit**: for catching mud or other refuse from oil-drilling; **slush pump** (*a*) a pump circulating mud through a rotary oil-drilling column; (*b*) *US slang* a trombone.

slush /slʌʃ/ *noun*[2]. L19.
[Imit., or from next.]
A heavy splashing sound.

slush /slʌʃ/ *verb.* Orig. *Scot.* E18.
[Partly from SLUSH *noun*[1]; partly imit.]
▶ **I** *verb intrans.* **1** Splash, squelch, or wade, esp. through muddy water, snow, etc. E18.
2 Rush (*down*) with a splashing sound. L19.

1 C. PHILLIPS The cars slushed past throwing up . . melted ice and water. **2** E. BIRNEY The snow slushed down from the hill farms.

▶ **II** *verb trans.* **3** Splash or soak with slush or mud. E19.
4 NAUTICAL. Grease (a mast) with slush obtained from boiling meat. E19.
5 Wash by dashing on water, esp. copiously; dash (water) *over*. Chiefly *dial.* M19.
6 Fill *up* or cover by dashing on mortar and cement. Chiefly as ***slushed*** *ppl adjective.* L19.

slusher /ˈslʌʃə/ *noun.* L19.
[from prec.]
1 A cook's assistant, esp. on a sheep-station. *Austral. & NZ.* L19.
2 MINING. A mechanical device for loading or packing broken material by drawing a bucket to and fro through a pile of the material, using ropes wound round a drum at each end of its length of travel. E20.

slushie *noun* var. of SLUSHY *noun.*

slushing /ˈslʌʃɪŋ/ *verbal noun.* M19.
[from SLUSH *verb* or *noun*[1] + -ING[1].]
The action of SLUSH *verb*; *spec.* (MINING) the action or process of moving or scraping broken ore into a dump or on to a wagon or chute.

slushing /ˈslʌʃɪŋ/ *adjective.* M19.
[from SLUSH *verb* or *noun*[1] + -ING[2].]
1 *gen.* That slushes or splashes. M19.
2 Pertaining to or designating a viscous oil or grease for protecting bright metal surfaces on which paint or other fixed coatings cannot be used. E20.

slushy /ˈslʌʃi/ *noun.* Also **slushie**. M19.
[from SLUSH *noun*[1] or *verb* + -Y[6].]
Orig., (a nickname for) a ship's cook. Also (*gen.*), any cook; an unskilled kitchen or domestic help; = SLUSHER 1.

slushy /ˈslʌʃi/ *adjective.* L18.
[from SLUSH *noun*[1] + -Y[1].]
1 Having much slush, consisting of or having the character of slush. L18.
2 Weak, washy; *fig.* sloppy, insipid, trivial. M19.

2 J. T. HEWLETT Something stronger and better than water or slushy tea. *Times* Steeped in a sloppy and slushy sentimentalism.

▪ **slushily** *adverb* M20. **slushiness** *noun* M19.

slut /slʌt/ *noun & verb.* ME.
[Origin unkn.]
▶ **A** *noun.* **1** A woman of slovenly habits or appearance. ME. ▸**b** A kitchen maid; a drudge. *rare.* ME.
2 A sexually promiscuous woman. ME.
3 A makeshift candle, *esp.* one made from a piece of rag dipped in lard or fat. E17.

4 A female dog. E19.
Comb.: **slut's wool** fluff, dust, etc., left to accumulate under beds etc. through slovenly cleaning.
▶†**B** *verb.* Infl. **-tt-**.
1 *verb trans.* Make sluttish. E17–M17.
2 *verb intrans.* Act as a drudge; behave like a slut. Also foll. by *about*. E19.
■ **sluttery** *noun* (now *rare*) (*a*) sluttishness, dirtiness, untidiness; (*b*) an untidy room, a workroom: L16. **slutty** *adjective* dirty, slovenly LME.

slutch /slʌtʃ/ *noun. obsolete* exc. *dial.* M17.
[Prob. imit.: cf. SLUDGE *noun*, SLUSH *noun*¹.]
Mud, mire, slush.
■ **slutchy** *adjective* muddy, slushy E18.

sluttish /ˈslʌtɪʃ/ *adjective.* LME.
[from SLUT *noun* + -ISH¹.]
1 Of a woman (formerly also of a man): dirty and untidy in dress and habits, esp. to a repulsive degree. LME.
2 Of a thing: dirty, grimy; untidy. Now *arch. rare.* M16.
3 Of behaviour, manners, etc.: characteristic or typical of a slut; low, immoral, lewd. M16.
■ **sluttishly** *adverb* in a sluttish manner; untidily, dirtily; carelessly: L15. **sluttishness** *noun* L15.

sly /slʌɪ/ *adjective, adverb, & noun.* ME.
[Old Norse *slœgr* clever, cunning, orig. 'able to strike', from *slóg-* pa. ppl stem of *slá* strike. Cf. SLEIGHT.]
▶ **A** *adjective.* **1** Of a person: skilful, clever, dexterous; possessing practical skill, wisdom, or ability. Formerly foll. by *in*, *of*, *to do*. *obsolete* exc. *Scot. & north.* ME.
2 Of an object, material, a work, etc.: characterized by or displaying skill or ingenuity; cleverly or finely made. Long *obsolete* exc. *Scot.* ME.
3 Characterized by, displaying, or indicating artifice, craft, or cunning; guileful, wily; deceitful, disingenuous, hypocritical. ME.
4 Characterized by or practising secrecy or stealth; done etc. in secret. LME. ▶**b** Esp. of liquor: illicit. Chiefly *Austral. & NZ slang.* E19.
5 Playfully mischievous, ironical; roguish; waggish. M18.

> 📖 **3** G. CRABBE A sly old fish, too cunning for the hook. N. FREELING He struck me always as a sly nasty fellow, . . always on the make. **4** J. BARLOW With . . the sly watch-word whisper'd from the tongue. DISRAELI Rigby had a sly pension. **5** S. J. PERELMAN Sightseers wandered through the garden poking sly fun at our vegetables.

▶ **B** *adverb.* = SLYLY. Now *Scot. & poet.* ME.
▶ **C** *noun.* **1** *The* class of sly persons. Formerly also *sing.*, a sly person. ME.
2 ***on the sly***, secretly, covertly, without publicity; in a covert or clandestine manner. E19.
Comb. & special collocations: **slyboots** *colloq.* (freq. *joc.*) a sly person, *esp.* one who does things on the sly; **sly dog** a sly person, *esp.* one who is discreet about mistakes or pleasures.
■ **slyish** *adjective* E19. **slyness** *noun* ME.

sly /slʌɪ/ *verb intrans. Scot. & US.* Pa. t. & pple **slied** /slʌɪd/. E19.
[from prec.]
Move or go stealthily; slink.

slyly /ˈslʌɪli/ *adverb.* Also **slily**. ME.
[from SLY *adjective* + -LY².]
In a sly manner.

> 📖 Z. N. HURSTON Lucy and John sniggered together slyly. *L.A. Style* Adlon's slyly sardonic send-up of American financial kite-flying.

slype /slʌɪp/ *noun*¹. M19.
[Perh. var. of SLIPE *noun*².]
ARCHITECTURE. A covered way or passage, *esp.* one leading from the cloisters and running between the transept and chapter house of a cathedral or monastic church.

slype /slʌɪp/ *verb & noun*². E20.
[Prob. var. of SLIPE *verb*.]
BASKET-MAKING. ▶**A** *verb trans.* Cut away one side of (a rod or cane) with a long slanting cut, so that it comes to a point. E20.
▶ **B** *noun.* A slyping cut. E20.

SM *abbreviation.*
1 Also **S/M**. Sado-masochism.
2 Sergeant-Major.
3 THEATRICAL. Stage-manager.

Sm *symbol.*
CHEMISTRY. Samarium.

smack /smak/ *noun*¹.
[Old English *smæc* = Old Frisian *smek*, Middle Low German, Middle Dutch *smak* (Dutch *smaak*), Old High German *gismac* (German *Geschmack*), from Germanic. Cf. SMATCH *noun*.]
▶**I 1** A taste, a flavour; the characteristic taste *of* something. OE.
†**2** Scent, smell. OE–M16.
3 A trace or suggestion *of* something specified; a very small amount *of* something; *fig.* a barely discernible quality. M16. ▶†**b** A superficial knowledge; a smattering. M16–L18.

> 📖 **3** R. DAVIES A look that is neither domestic nor professional, but has a smack of both.

▶†**II 4 a** The sense of taste. Only in ME. ▶**b** Delight, enjoyment, relish. ME–E17.

smack /smak/ *noun*². L16.
[Rel. to SMACK *verb*²: cf. Middle Dutch *smack*, Low German *smacke*, German dial. *Schmacke*.]
1 A sharp sound made by parting the lips quickly, as in relish or anticipation; a loud kiss. L16.
2 (A loud sharp sound made by) a blow delivered with the flat of the hand or something having a flat surface; a slap. M18. ▶**b** *spec.* A hard hit with a cricket-bat. L19.
3 The crack *of* a whip, lash, etc. L18.

> 📖 **1** SHAKES. *Tam. Shr.* He . . kiss'd her lips with such a clamorous smack That . . all the church did echo. G. KEILLOR He hugs women and gives them a good smack on the lips. **2** R. L. STEVENSON The clean flat smack of the parental hand in chastisement. J. BETJEMAN The smack of breakers upon windy rocks.

Phrases: **a smack in the eye**, **a smack in the face** *colloq.* a sharp rebuff; a setback. **have a smack at** *colloq.* make an attempt at or attack on.

smack /smak/ *noun*³. E17.
[Low German, Dutch *smacke* (mod. *smak*), of unkn. origin.]
A single-masted fore-and-aft rigged sailing vessel, usu. employed for coasting or fishing.

smack /smak/ *noun*⁴. *slang* (orig. *US*). M20.
[Prob. alt. of SCHMECK.]
A hard drug, *esp.* heroin.

smack /smak/ *verb*¹. ME.
[from SMACK *noun*¹, superseding SMATCH *verb*.]
1 *verb trans.* Perceive by tasting. Now *rare* or *obsolete.* ME.
2 *verb intrans.* **a** Of food or drink: have a (specified) taste or flavour; taste or smell *of* something. ME. ▶**b** *fig.* Suggest the presence or effects *of* something; be reminiscent *of*. L16.

> 📖 **2a** J. TYNDALL Tea . . smacked strongly of tannin. **b** G. S. LAYARD It was part of his nature to love everything that smacked of antiquity. R. HEILBRONER This general line of arguments smacks of the worst kind of reactionary ideology.

smack /smak/ *verb*² *& adverb.* M16.
[Middle Low German, Middle Dutch *smacken* (Low German, Dutch *smakken*), of imit. origin: cf. German *schmatzen* eat or kiss noisily.]
▶ **A** *verb.* **I** *verb trans.* **1** Separate (the lips) so as to produce a sharp sound, esp. in relish or anticipation; *fig.* express relish or delight in this way. M16. ▶**b** Kiss noisily or loudly. *obsolete* exc. *Scot.* L16. ▶**c** [perh. infl. by prec.] Taste (wine or liquor) with keen relish or satisfaction. E19.
2 Crack (a whip etc.). L17.
3 Bring, put, or throw (*down* or *together*) with a smack or slap. E19.
4 Strike (a person, part of the body, etc.) with the open hand or something having a flat surface; slap. M19. ▶**b** *spec.* Hit (a ball etc.) hard or smartly, as with a cricket-bat, golf club, etc. L19.

> 📖 **1** DISRAELI He smacked his lips after dashing off his glass. **3** G. MEREDITH He smacked his hands together. D. C. PEATTIE Lake Michigan shouldering up its ice and stones to smack them on the beach. **4** G. B. SHAW If I catch you doing that again I will . . smack your behind. R. P. WARREN Mr Munn . . smacked the man solidly across the mouth. **b** *Golf* Hogan smacked a 2-iron four feet from the cup.

▶ **II** *verb intrans.* **5** Smack the lips. M16.
6 Crack a whip etc. E19.
7 Make or give out a sharp smacking sound; move, hit, etc., with a smack. L19.

> 📖 **7** Z. TOMIN The bogs . . smacked and bubbled under every footstep.

Comb.: **smack-bottom** *nursery & colloq.* a smack on the buttocks given as punishment.
▶ **B** *adverb.* **1** With a smack; suddenly, violently. L18.
2 Completely, entirely; directly. E19.

> 📖 **1** T. HEGGEN Rounding a corner . . he ran smack into Captain Morton. P. H. NEWBY One man, whose parachute failed to open, fell smack into the water. **2** *Church Times* Facts cut smack across the argument. A. TYLER We started walking . . smack down the middle of the road.

Comb.: **smack-dab** *adverb* (*colloq.*, orig. *US*) exactly, directly, with a smack; **smack-smooth** *adjective & adverb* (*colloq.*) (*a*) *adjective* (*obsolete* exc. *dial.*) perfectly smooth, level, or even; (*b*) *adverb* so as to leave a smooth or level surface.
■ **smacking** *verbal noun* the action of the verb; an instance of this: E17.

smacker /ˈsmakə/ *noun.* E17.
[from SMACK *verb*² + -ER¹.]
1 A person who or thing which gives a smack. E17.
2 A resounding smack; *spec.* a loud kiss. L18.
3 A coin or note of money; a dollar; a pound. *slang* (orig. *N. Amer.*). E20.
■ Also **smacke'roo** *noun* (*slang*, orig. & chiefly *N. Amer.*) M20.

smackering /ˈsmak(ə)rɪŋ/ *noun.* Long *rare.* L16.
[Perh. alt. of SMATTERING *noun* infl. by SMACK *noun*¹.]
†**1** A slight or superficial knowledge *in* or *of* a subject; a smattering. L16–M17.
2 An inclination *towards* or hankering *after* or *for* a person or thing. L16.

smacking /ˈsmakɪŋ/ *adjective.* L16.
[from SMACK *verb*² + -ING².]
1 That smacks. L16.
2 Of a breeze: blowing strongly or vigorously. E19.
3 Unusually large or fine. Now *colloq. & dial.* L19.

smacksman /ˈsmaksmən/ *noun.* Pl. **-men**. L19.
[from SMACK *noun*³ + -'S¹ + MAN *noun*.]
An owner or crewman of a smack.

smahan /ˈsmahən, -han/ *noun. Anglo-Irish.* E20.
[Irish *smeathán*.]
A drop (to drink); a taste, a nip.

smaik /smeɪk/ *noun. Scot. arch.* LME.
[Perh. from Middle Dutch, Middle Low German *smēker*, *smeiker*, from *smēken*, *smeiken* flatter.]
A rascal, a rogue.

Smalcaldic /smalˈkaldɪk/ *adjective.* M17.
[mod. Latin *Smalcaldicus* from *Smalcaldica*, from German *Schmalkalden* (see below): see -IC.]
Hist. Belonging or pertaining to Schmalkalden, a town in Thuringia in central Germany, *spec.* designating or pertaining to an alliance of Protestant States formed there in 1534.
■ Also **Smalcaldian** *adjective* L17.

small /smɔːl/ *adjective, adverb, & noun.*
[Old English *smæl* = Old Frisian *smel*, Old Saxon, Old High German *smal* (Dutch *smal*, German *schmal*), Old Norse *smalr*, Gothic *smals*, from Germanic.]
▶ **A** *adjective.* **I 1 a** Of relatively little girth or circumference in comparison with length; slender, thin. Now *dial.* exc. of the waist. OE. ▶†**b** Of a person etc.: slim, graceful. ME–L16.
2 Having little breadth or width in proportion to length; narrow. Now *rare.* OE.

> 📖 **1a** T. MOORE Like an hour-glass, exceedingly small in the waist.

▶ **II 3 a** Not large; of limited or restricted size, esp. in comparison with others of the same kind. OE. ▶**b** (Of a child etc.) not fully grown or developed; young; (of a sibling) younger. Later also, (of a family) consisting of young children. ME. ▶**c** Of a letter: lower case, of a lesser size than and often different form from a capital letter; *spec.* (of the initial letter of a word) not capitalized, indicating that the word is a general or less serious variety of the thing denoted. L17.
4 Little in amount, quantity, or number; not great. ME. ▶**b** Of low numerical value; *spec.* (of money) of little size and low value; consisting of coins of low denomination. ME.
5 Not much; hardly any. LME.
6 Of time, distance, etc.: short, brief. LME.
7 Below or less than the usual standard. M16.

> 📖 **3a** J. CONRAD The broad river . . had been swollen . . carrying small drift-wood. A. C. CLARKE A small man, his head barely reaching the level of Franklin's shoulders. S. RADLEY A felt hat . . a little too small for his large head. G. VIDAL A small, airless, icy room in the harem of the winter palace. **b** I. MURDOCH The brothers . . now small children, now growing towards manhood. **c** *Times* A newspaper . . serious, lively, and radical with a small r. **4** DRYDEN A small but faithful Band Of Worthies. GOLDSMITH They consider the loss of them as but a small misfortune. T. HARDY Rewarded the old woman as far as her small means afforded. **b** R. L. STEVENSON Four pounds . . in . . notes, and the balance in small silver. **5** D. H. LAWRENCE Lettie . . paid small attention to my eloquence. C. S. LEWIS I could put up with . . monotony far more patiently than even the smallest disturbance.

▶ **III 8** Consisting of fine or minute particles, drops, etc.; not coarse. OE.
9 Of cloth, yarn, a garment, etc.: fine in texture or structure. *obsolete* exc. *dial.* OE.
10 Of little power or strength; *spec.* (*a*) (of a sound) low; (*b*) (of alcohol content) weak; (*c*) (of the wind) gentle. ME. ▶**b** PHONETICS. Of a vowel: narrow, close. L16.

> 📖 **10** R. BROUGHTON 'Thank you,' she says, in a small voice. ALDOUS HUXLEY Even the smallest of *vins ordinaires* are very drinkable.

▶ **IV 11 a** Of a person: low in rank or position; of minor or little importance, authority, or influence; common, ordinary. Now *rare.* ME. ▶**b** That is (such) to a small or limited extent, degree, etc. Now *rare.* E16. ▶**c** Having little land, capital, etc.; dealing, doing business, etc., on a minor or limited scale. M18.
12 Of a thing etc.: of little or minor consequence or importance; trifling, trivial, unimportant. ME.
13 Not prominent or notable; humble, modest; unpretentious. LME.

14 Base, low; petty, mean, ungenerous. **E19.**

📖 **11a** D. M. MULOCK A very great lady, and Hilary . . felt an exceedingly small person beside her. **c** J. B. PRIESTLEY Small family businesses, in which the employer is well acquainted with all his workpeople. *Daily Telegraph* The small investor barred from securing premium rates from a clearing bank. *Independent* Nicholson has been in small publishing for 20 years. **12** W. A. WALLACE 'Well, don't let us split on a small point of detail,' he began. **14** *Spectator* Trickery, not statesmanship; and . . small trickery too.

Phrases: ***a small matter***: see MATTER *noun*. **feel small** feel mean or humiliated. **in a small way** unambitiously, on a small scale. **in the smallest** *rare* in the least. **look small** appear mean or humiliated. ***no small***: see NO *adjective*. **small is beautiful**: expr. the notion that something small-scale is better than a large-scale equivalent. **small profits and quick returns** the policy of a cheap shop etc. which relies on low prices and a large turnover. ***small thanks to***: see THANK *noun*. ***thankful for small mercies***: see THANKFUL 1. ***the small screen***: see SCREEN *noun*[1] 7.

▶ **B** *adverb*. **1** Into small pieces. **OE.**

2 Quietly, gently; in a small or low voice. **ME.**

†**3** To a small extent or degree; not much; slightly. **LME–M17.**

4 On a small scale, to a small size. **M17.**

5 *NAUTICAL*. Close to the wind. **M19.**

Phrases: **sing small** *colloq.* adopt a humble tone or manner; be less assertive, back down; say nothing.

▶ **C** *noun*. **1 a** *collect.* People or animals of small size or stature. Now only with *the*. **ME.** ▸**b** A child. **E20.**

2 *collect.* People of inferior rank or ability. **ME.**

3 A small quantity or amount; a little piece, a morsel. *obsolete* exc. *Scot.* **ME.**

4 a ***the small***, something trifling, petty, or unimportant. **ME.** ▸**b** ***the smalls*** (*THEATRICAL*), small towns, often with poor theatrical facilities, as theatrical venues. **L19.**

†**5** Little, not much. **LME–M17.**

6 The slenderest or narrowest part *of* something, as the leg or (esp.) the back. **LME.**

7 In *pl.* Items of small size; *spec.* (***a***) small articles of laundry or clothing, *esp.* underwear; (***b***) small (varieties of) coal; (***c***) relatively lightweight parcels or consignments; (***d***) small advertisements. **M19.**

8 *Hist.* In *pl.* = RESPONSION 3. **M19.**

📖 **6** A. DAVIES A skimpy . . vest that only came as far as the small of her back.

Phrases: †**by small and small** little by little; gradually, slowly. **in small** on a small scale; (of a painting etc.) in miniature. ***the small***: see sense C.4a above. ***the smalls***: see sense C.4b above.

Special collocations & comb. (of adjective & adverb): **small ad**, **small advertisement** a small simple advertisement in a newspaper, usu. in a separate section for that purpose and inserted by an individual. **small-arm** *adjective* using or provided with small arms. **small arms** portable firearms, as rifles, pistols, light machine-guns, etc. ***small beer***: see BEER *noun*[1] 1. **small-bore** *adjective* (of a firearm) having a narrow bore, in international and Olympic shooting usu. .22 inch calibre (5.6 mm bore). **small-bourgeois** = PETIT BOURGEOIS (usu. *attrib.*). ***small bower***: see BOWER *noun*[3]. ***small CALORIE***. **small cap**, **small capital** a capital letter of virtually the same size as lower case letters in the same font and designed to harmonize with them. **small-cell** *adjective* (*MEDICINE*) (of a tumour) composed of small cells, esp. of uncertain origin. ***small change***: see CHANGE *noun* 3. ***small circle***: see CIRCLE *noun*. **small-claims court** a local tribunal in which claims for small amounts can be heard and decided quickly and cheaply without legal representation. **small clause** *LINGUISTICS* a clause which contains neither a finite verb nor the infinitive marker 'to', for example *him groan* in *I heard him groan*. **small-clothes** (now *rare*) breeches; knee-breeches. **small coal** †(***a***) charcoal; (***b***) coal of small size. **small craft** *NAUTICAL* small boats and fishing vessels collectively. ***small debt***: see DEBT *noun*. ***small deer***: see DEER *noun* 1. **small end** in a piston engine, the end of a connecting rod nearer to the piston. **smallest room** *colloq.* the lavatory in a building (cf. ***small room*** below). **small-for-dates** *adjective* (of a newborn baby) small in size in relation to the time since its conception. ***small fortune***: see FORTUNE *noun*. **small forward** *BASKETBALL* a versatile forward who is effective outside the key as well as near the net. **small fruit** = ***soft fruit*** s.v. SOFT *adjective*. ***small fry***: see FRY *noun*[1] 4. **smallgoods** *Austral.* small meat products, as sausages, bacon, etc. **small gut(s)** the small intestine. **smallholder** a person who owns or works a smallholding. **smallholding** (***a***) a holding smaller than a normal farm; (***b***) the practice or occupation of working a smallholding. **small hours** *the* early hours of the morning after midnight. ***small intestine***: see INTESTINE *noun*. ***small MERCY***. **small-minded** *adjective* of narrow outlook and rigid opinions, lacking vision and generosity. **small-mindedly** *adverb* in a small-minded manner. **small-mindedness** the state of being small-minded. **small-mouth (bass)** a small-mouthed bass. **small-mouthed** *adjective* having a small mouth; ***small-mouthed bass***, a N. American freshwater bass, *Micropterus dolomieui*, introduced elsewhere as a game-fish. ***small MUNSTERLANDER***. ***small pastern***: see PASTERN 2c. **small-pipe(s)** a Northumbrian bellows-filled bagpipe. ***small potatoes***: see POTATO *noun*. **small print** printed matter in small type, *esp.* such matter as part of a document or contract containing detailed information or conditions relating to the main text. **small reed** any of several reedlike grasses constituting the genus *Calamagrostis*, of damp woods and marshes. **small room** *colloq.* a lavatory (cf. ***smallest room*** above). **small sail** *NAUTICAL* any of various main- and topsails in a vessel. **small-scale** *adjective* operating or executed on a small scale; drawn to a small scale; relating to small numbers, of small size or extent. ***small seraphim***: see SERAPHIM 3b. ***small shot***: see SHOT *noun*[1]. ***small slam***: see SLAM *noun*[1]. ***small-still (whisky)***: see STILL *noun*[2] 1. **small stores** *NAUTICAL* (***a***) small items for personal use on a sea voyage; (***b***) *US* (a shop selling) articles of regulation clothing. **small-sword** a light tapering thrusting-sword, used esp. (*Hist.*) for duelling. **small-talk** *noun & verb* (***a***) *noun* light social conversation; chit-chat; (***b***) *verb intrans.* engage in small-talk. **small-time** *noun & adjective* (*slang*) (***a***) *noun* the lower ranks of a (usu. theatrical) profession; (***b***) *adjective* operating on a small scale, second-rate, unimportant, insignificant. **small-timer** a small-time operator, an insignificant person. ***small TORTOISESHELL***. **small-town** *adjective* of, pertaining to, or characteristic of a small town; unsophisticated, provincial. **small-townish** *adjective* = ***small-town*** above. **small type** = ***small print*** above. **smallwares** haberdashery. ***small wonder***: see WONDER *noun*. **small world**: expr. surprise etc. at a coincidental or unexpected meeting (esp. in ***it's a small world***). **small-yield** *adjective* = ***low-yield*** *adjective* s.v. LOW *adjective*.

small /smɔːl/ *verb trans. & intrans. rare*. **LME.**
[from SMALL *adjective*.]
Make or become small.

smallage /ˈsmɔːlɪdʒ/ *noun*. **ME.**
[from SMALL *adjective* + ACHE *noun*[2]. Cf. SMELLAGE.]
Any of several varieties of celery or parsley; *esp.* wild celery, *Apium graveolens*.

smallish /ˈsmɔːlɪʃ/ *adjective*. **LME.**
[from SMALL *adjective* + -ISH[1].]
Somewhat small; rather little.

smallness /ˈsmɔːlnɪs/ *noun*. **LME.**
[from SMALL *adjective* + -NESS.]
†**1** Slimness; slenderness. **LME–M18.**
2 The fact, quality, or state of being small. **LME.**
3 Meanness, pettiness. **E19.**

†**small-pock** *noun sing.* For pl. see next. **LME–E19.**
[from SMALL *adjective* + POCK *noun*.]
Each of the pustules which appear on the skin in smallpox; the disease itself.

smallpox /ˈsmɔːlpɒks/ *noun & verb*. Also (earlier) †**-pocks**. **E16.**
[Alt. of pl. of prec.: cf. POX *noun*.]
▶ **A** *noun*. An acute and sometimes fatal contagious viral disease (now eradicated by vaccination) characterized by fever and a scarring rash of spots which develop into vesicles and then pustules; also called ***variola***. Formerly also *pl.*, the pustules characteristic of this disease. **E16.**
▶ **B** *verb trans.* Affect or infect with smallpox; *fig.* cover with little spots or pock-marks. Freq. as ***smallpoxed*** *ppl adjective*. **L18.**

smally /ˈsmɔːli/ *adverb*. Now *rare*. **ME.**
[from SMALL *adjective* + -LY[2].]
1 In or into small or minute pieces, fragments, etc.; finely, minutely. **ME.**
2 Sparsely, scantily. **E16.**
3 Not much, very little. **E16.**
4 In small form or compass; slenderly. **E17.**
5 Of a sound: with low volume. **M20.**
¶ Long rare or obsolete in senses 1-3.

smalt /smɔːlt, smɒlt/ *noun & adjective*. **M16.**
[French, from Italian *smalto* (cf. SMALTO) from Germanic, rel. to SMELT *verb*[1]. Cf. SMALTS.]
▶ **A** *noun*. **1** A kind of glass, usually coloured deep blue with cobalt oxide, finely pulverized after cooling for use as a pigment, esp. in glazes. **M16.**
2 A piece of coloured glass. **M19.**
3 A deep blue colour like that of smalt. **L19.**
Comb.: **smalt-blue** *adjective* powder blue.
▶ **B** *adjective*. Of the colour of smalt; deep blue. **L19.**

smalti *noun* pl. of SMALTO.

smaltine /ˈsmɔːltʌɪn, ˈsmɒl-/ *noun*. Now *rare*. **M19.**
[from SMALT + -INE[5].]
MINERALOGY. = next.

smaltite /ˈsmɔːltʌɪt, ˈsmɒl-/ *noun*. **M19.**
[from (the same root as) prec. + -ITE[1].]
MINERALOGY. Any of several cobalt arsenide minerals; now *spec.* an arsenic-deficient variety of skutterudite. Also called ***speiss-cobalt***.

smalto /ˈsmalto/ *noun*. Pl. **-ti** /-ti/. **E18.**
[Italian: see SMALT.]
Coloured glass or enamel used in mosaics etc.; a small piece of this.

smalts /smɔːlts, smɒlts/ *noun*. **E17.**
[App. the pl. of SMALT taken as sing.]
= SMALT *noun* 1.

smaragd /ˈsmaragd/ *noun*. Now *rare*. **ME.**
[Old French *smaragde* or directly from Latin SMARAGDUS.]
A bright green precious stone; an emerald.

smaragdine /sməˈragdɪn, -ʌɪn/ *noun & adjective*. **LME.**
[Latin *smaragdinus* of emerald from Greek *smaragdinos*, from *smaragdos* SMARAGDUS: see -INE[2].]
▶ **A** *noun*. = prec. Long *rare*. **LME.**
▶ **B** *adjective*. Of, belonging to, or consisting of a smaragd; resembling that of a smaragd; of an emerald green. **LME.**

smaragdite /sməˈragdʌɪt/ *noun*. **E19.**
[formed as next + -ITE[1].]
MINERALOGY. A brilliant grass-green or emerald-green variety of amphibole or hornblende.

smaragdus /sməˈragdəs/ *noun*. Now *rare*. **LME.**
[Latin from Greek *smaragdos* var. of *maragdos* from Hebrew *bāreqeṯ* emerald, from *bāraq* flash, sparkle.]
= SMARAGD.

smarm /smɑːm/ *verb & noun*. *colloq.* **M19.**
[Origin unkn.]
▶ **A** *verb*. **1** *verb trans.* **a** Smear, bedaub. Orig. & chiefly *dial.* **M19.** ▸**b** Make smooth with cream, oil, etc.; smooth or slick (hair etc.) *down*. **E20.**
2 a *verb intrans.* Behave in a fulsomely flattering or toadying manner, suck *up to* a person. Also foll. by *about*, *over*. **E20.** ▸**b** *verb trans.* Flatter fulsomely, toady; utter in a fulsomely flattering or toadying manner. **E20.**

📖 **1b** E. BOWEN He spat into a hand and smarmed a side of his hair back. **2b** G. BARKER 'I would like to pay a tribute to the Foreign Secretary,' he smarmed out dangerously.

▶ **B** *noun*. An unctuous manner; fulsome flattery or toadying. **M20.**

smarmy /ˈsmɑːmi/ *adjective*. *colloq.* **E20.**
[from prec. + -Y[1].]
1 Smooth and sleek. **E20.**
2 Ingratiating, obsequious; smug, unctuous. **E20.**
■ **smarmily** *adverb* **M20.** **smarminess** *noun* **M20.**

smart /smɑːt/ *noun*. **ME.**
[In branch I app. from base of SMART *adjective*, rel. to Middle Low German, Middle Dutch *smerte*, *smarte*, Old High German *smerza*, *smerzo* (German *Schmerz*); in branch II directly from SMART *adjective*.]
▶ **I 1** (An instance of) sharp physical pain, esp. caused by a blow, sting, or wound. **ME.**
2 Sharp mental pain or suffering; an instance of this, a pang. **ME.**
3 *ellipt.* = ***smart-money*** below. **E19.**

📖 **1** W. C. BRYANT Patroclus . . applied a root . . to assuage the smart.

▶ **II 4** A person who affects smartness in dress, manners, or talk. Now *Hist.* **E18.**
5 *The* quality of smartness in talk or writing. **M19.**
6 Chiefly ***right smart***. A fair quantity, a reasonable number. *US colloq.* **M19.**
7 *sing.* & (usu.) in *pl.* Intelligence, acumen, nous. *N. Amer. slang*. **L20.**

📖 **6** W. FAULKNER There is a right smart of folks in Jefferson I don't know. **7** *New Yorker* Beep Jennings . . lacked the smarts to close a loan properly. ***street smarts***: see STREET *noun*.

Comb.: **smart-money** (***a***) money paid to sailors, soldiers, workmen, etc., as compensation for injuries received while on duty or at work; (***b***) money paid to obtain the discharge of a recruit who has enlisted in the army; **smartweed** (chiefly *dial.* & *US*) any of various kinds of persicaria; *esp.* water-pepper, *Persicaria hydropiper*, with peppery-tasting leaves.

smart /smɑːt/ *adjective & adverb*. **LOE.**
[Rel. to SMART *verb*: not repr. in the cognate langs. Cf. SMART *noun*.]
▶ **A** *adjective*. **I 1** Of a weapon, blow, etc.: causing sharp pain. (Foll. by *on*.) *obsolete* exc. as merging into sense 4 below. **LOE.**
†**2** Of pain, sorrow, etc.: sharp, keen, severe. **ME–L17.**
3 Of words etc.: severe, critical. Now *rare*. **ME.**
4 Vigorous, forceful; (of pace) briskly maintained. **ME.**
5 Sharply outlined. *rare*. **M18.**
6 Considerable in amount, extent, etc. Chiefly *dial.* & *N. Amer.* **L18.**

📖 **1** JOSEPH HALL Thy hand hath been smart and heavy upon me. **3** SWIFT A smart word or two upon my littleness. **4** G. MEREDITH The . . twang of a musical instrument that has had a smart blow. G. ORWELL The van moved . . at a smart trot. **6** *Times* Leading Equities . . had firmed up to score smart gains.

▶ **II 7** Pert, forward, impudent. Now chiefly *N. Amer.*, esp. in ***be smart***, ***get smart***. **ME.**
8 Of a person: quick, active; prompt. **ME.** ▸**b** Healthy, well. Now *dial.* & *US*. **L18.**
9 Clever, adept; *esp.* clever in looking after one's interests, astute. Now chiefly *N. Amer.* **E17.** ▸**b** Of a device: capable of independent and seemingly intelligent action; *spec.* (of a powered missile, bomb, etc.) guided to a target by an optical system. **L20.**
10 a Alert and brisk. **E17.** ▸**b** Well-groomed, appearing neat and stylish. Also, bright and fresh in appearance, in good repair. **E18.**
11 Clever in talk or argument; quick-witted; (of a remark) pointed, witty. **M17.**
12 Fashionable, sophisticated; *esp.* of or belonging to fashionable society. Freq. in ***smart set*** below. **E18.**

📖 **7** J. WAINWRIGHT Don't get smart with me. **8** F. MARRYAT Heave ahead, my lads, and be smart. **9** K. TENNANT How smart he was dishing everybody. **b** R. MACNEIL We turn increasingly to computers and smart typewriters. **10a** W. COWPER He.. sighs for the smart comrades he has left. C. KINGSLEY To a tight smart Viking's son. **b** D. G. MITCHELL Bound in smart red leather. **11** S. JOHNSON He mistakes the questions, that he may return a smart answer. **12** J. AUSTEN I.. preferred the church.. but that was not smart enough. JILLY COOPER Sotheby's or.. smart art galleries.

Phrases: ***as smart as paint***: see PAINT *noun*.

▶ **B** *adverb*. = SMARTLY. ME.

Special collocations & comb.: **smartcard** (orig. *US*) a plastic card with a built-in microprocessor; *esp.* a credit or other bank card providing instant transfer of funds, etc. **smart money** *US* money invested or bet by people with expert or inside knowledge; *transf.* knowledgeable people collectively. **smart-mouth** *verb trans.* (*US colloq.*) give a cheeky retort to. **smart quotes** COMPUTING quotation marks which, although all keyed the same, are automatically interpreted and set as opening or closing marks (inverted or raised commas) rather than vertical lines. **smart set** fashionable people considered as a group.

▪ **smarten** *verb trans. & intrans.* make or become smart, spruce, lively, etc. (usu. foll. by *up*) E19. **smartish** *adjective & adverb* (*a*) *adjective* somewhat smart; pretty considerable in amount, degree, etc; (*b*) *adverb* somewhat smartly: M18. **smartly** *adverb* ME. **smartness** *noun* ME.

smart /smɑːt/ *verb*.

[Old English *smeortan* = Middle Dutch *smerten*, (also mod.) *smarten*, Old High German *smerzan* (German *schmerzen*), based on West Germanic base perh. rel. to Latin *mordere* to bite, Greek *smerdnos*, *smerdaleos* terrible.]

1 *verb intrans.* Of a wound etc.: be acutely painful. OE.

2 *verb trans.* Cause sharp physical or mental pain to. ME.

3 *verb intrans.* Feel sharp physical or mental pain; suffer severely *from* a person, *for* an offence, etc. ME.

📖 **1** DICKENS This.. rankled and smarted in her.. breast, like a poisoned arrow. **2** D. HEWETT The sour taste.. smarted his throat. **3** M. MITCHELL Her hands.. smarted intolerably from burns. R. SUTCLIFF Peat-smoke.. made his eyes smart. E. JOHNSON The pupil-boarders were constantly smarting from his ferocity.

▪ **smarting** *ppl adjective* that smarts, that feels or causes sharp physical or mental pain M16. **smartingly** *adverb* M16.

smart alec /ˈsmɑːt alɪk/ *noun & adjective*. *colloq.* (orig. *US*). Also **smart aleck**, **smart alick**. M19.

[from SMART *adjective* + *Alec* dim. of male first name *Alexander*.]

(A person) displaying ostentatious or smug cleverness.

▪ **smart-aleckism** *noun* = SMART-ALECKRY M20. **smart-aleckry** *noun* behaviour characteristic of a smart alec E20. **smart-alecky** *adjective* characteristic of a smart alec E20.

smart-arse /ˈsmɑːtɑːs, -as/ *noun & adjective*. *slang*. Also ***-ass**. M20.

[from SMART *adjective* + ARSE *noun*.]

= SMART ALEC.

▪ **smart-arsed** *adjective* = SMART-ALECKY M20.

smarty /ˈsmɑːti/ *noun & adjective*. Orig. *US*. Also (chiefly as noun) **smartie**. M19.

[from SMART *adjective* + -Y[6], -IE.]

▶ **A** *noun*. A would-be smart, witty, or fashionable person, a know-all, a smart alec. M19.

▶ **B** *adjective*. Characteristic of or resembling a smarty; smart-alecky. L19.

Comb.: **smarty-boots**, (orig. *US*) **smarty-pants** *colloq.* a smugly clever person, a smart alec.

smash /smaʃ/ *noun*[1]. E18.

[from SMASH *verb*[1].]

1 A violent blow with the fist etc. E18. ▸**b** TENNIS & BADMINTON etc. A hard fast overarm volley. L19.

2 A shattered or broken condition. Chiefly in ***break to smash***, ***go to smash***, etc. M18.

3 A severe or extensive crushing or breaking of something; a violent collision or impact; the loud sound of this. E19.

4 a A sudden overwhelming collapse of a bank, business, etc.; a crash; a series of commercial failures. M19. ▸**b** A crushing defeat. L19.

5 a A drink of spirits (esp. brandy) with ice, water, sugar, and mint. Chiefly *US*. M19. ▸**b** Any alcoholic drink, *esp.* wine. *N. Amer. slang*. M20.

6 An extremely popular film, person, song, etc.; a hit. Also ***smash hit***. E20.

7 A wild or rowdy party. *N. Amer. slang*. M20.

📖 **1** *Boxing* Clay took command.. with.. quick smashes to the face. **3** S. ELDRED-GRIGG Jimmie.. died in a motorbike smash. **6** *New Yorker*: '*Rambo II*'.. is the runaway box-office smash of the summer.

smash /smaʃ/ *noun*[2]. *Criminals' slang*. L18.

[Origin unkn.]

1 Counterfeit coin. L18.

2 Loose change (esp. as distinguished from paper money). E19.

smash /smaʃ/ *verb*[1] & *adverb*. L17.

[Prob. imit., repr. a blend of *smack*, *smite*, etc., with *bash*, *mash*, etc.]

▶ **A** *verb*. **I** *verb trans.* †**1** Kick (a person) downstairs. *rare*. Only in L17.

2 Break (a thing) in pieces, esp. as the result of a blow or impact; shatter. L18.

3 Drive or fling forcibly and violently *down*, *against*, etc.; cause (a thing) to strike against something with force and violence (freq. foll. by *on*, *against*); cause (a moving vehicle to collide with a stationary object or another moving vehicle (foll. by *into*). Also, batter (*in*, *out*, etc.); break (one's way) violently *in*, *out*, etc.; hit violently with the fist etc. E19. ▸**b** TENNIS & BADMINTON etc. Strike (the ball) with a hard fast overarm volley. L19.

4 Defeat overwhelmingly; crush, destroy. E19.

5 Make bankrupt, cause to fail financially. *colloq.* M19.

📖 **2** CONAN DOYLE His second bust.. had been smashed to atoms. *Financial Times* Prisoners smashed the china pans. **3** D. MARECHERA The landlady.. smashed the rolling pin on his great head. A. RICH The swell smashed her against the reef. **4** A. F. DOUGLAS-HOME A win.. for the Conservative Party could.. have smashed the Socialists. *City Limits* The attempt to smash the drugs ring.

▶ **II** *verb intrans.* **6** Move rapidly and violently, esp. with shattering effect, *over*, *through*, etc.; strike against something with force and violence (freq. foll. by *on*, *against*); (of a moving vehicle) collide with a stationary object or another moving vehicle (foll. by *into*). M19.

7 Go bankrupt, fail financially. *colloq.* M19.

8 Break in pieces, esp. as the result of a blow or impact, shatter. L19.

📖 **6** H. B. STOWE Picking up the silver dollar, he sent it smashing through the window-pane. P. MARSHALL Repeatedly she sent her fist smashing out. A. TYLER A Pepsi truck.. smashed into her left front fender. **8** CONAN DOYLE The glass smashed into a thousand pieces.

With adverbs in specialized senses: **smash up** break or destroy thoroughly and systematically (*lit. & fig.*).

Comb.: **smash-and-grab** *adjective & noun* (*a*) *adjective* (of a raid) in which a thief smashes a shop window and grabs the goods displayed there; (*b*) *noun* a smash-and-grab raid; **smash-mouth** *adjective* (N. AMER. SPORT) (of a style of play) aggressive and confrontational.

▶ **B** *adverb*. With a smash or smashing sound. E19.

play smash *dial. & US colloq.* come to grief.

▪ **smashed** *ppl adjective* (*a*) that has been smashed, shattered, etc.; (*b*) *slang* (orig. *US*) completely under the influence of alcohol or drugs: E19.

smash /smaʃ/ *verb*[2] *trans. Criminals' slang*. E19.

[from SMASH *noun*[2].]

Pass (counterfeit money).

smasher /ˈsmaʃə/ *noun*[1]. L18.

[from SMASH *verb*[1] + -ER[1].]

1 An unusually large or excellent thing; an outstandingly attractive person. *slang*. L18.

2 A heavy blow or fall; *fig.* a severe or crushing reply, review, etc. *colloq.* E19.

3 A person who or thing which smashes something; *spec.* a bookbinder's machine for compressing book blocks between iron plates. E19.

smasher /ˈsmaʃə/ *noun*[2]. *Criminals' slang*. L18.

[from SMASH *verb*[2] + -ER[1].]

A person who passes counterfeit money.

smasheroo /smaʃəˈruː/ *noun*. *slang* (orig. & chiefly *N. Amer.*). M20.

[from SMASH *noun*[1] or SMASHER *noun*[1]: see -EROO.]

A smash hit.

smashery /ˈsmaʃ(ə)ri/ *noun*. M19.

[from SMASH *verb*[1] + -ERY.]

An act of smashing something; a state of smashing or being smashed.

smashing /ˈsmaʃɪŋ/ *adjective*. M19.

[from SMASH *verb*[1] + -ING[2].]

That smashes; *colloq.* outstandingly pleasant, good, handsome, etc.

📖 M. LASKI Martin, what a smashing idea. L. CODY He's a smashing man and I love going out with him.

▪ **smashingly** *adverb* L19.

smash-up /ˈsmaʃʌp/ *noun*. Also **smashup**. M19.

[from ***smash up*** s.v. SMASH *verb*[1].]

A complete smash; *spec.* (chiefly *N. Amer.*) a collision, esp. of road or rail vehicles.

smatch /smatʃ/ *noun*. ME.

[App. alt. of SMACK *noun*[1], infl. by SMATCH *verb*.]

1 Taste, flavour. ME. ▸**b** A mere taste. *rare*. LME.

2 A slight indication or suggestion *of* a quality, etc.; a slight touch *of* illness, pain, etc. E16.

3 A slight knowledge, a smattering, *of* something. L16.

†**smatch** *verb*.

[Old English *smæccan* = Old Frisian *smekka*, *smetsa* (West Frisian *smeitsje*), Middle Low German, Low German *smecken*, Old High German *smecchen* (German *schmecken*), from SMACK *noun*[1]. Superseded by SMACK *verb*[1].]

1 a *verb intrans.* Have a specified taste or flavour, smack *of*. OE–E17. ▸**b** *verb trans.* Smack of. LME–L16.

2 *verb trans.* Taste, perceive the taste of; = SMACK *verb*[1] 1. Only in ME.

smatter /ˈsmatə/ *noun*. M17.

[from the verb.]

Superficial knowledge; a smattering.

smatter /ˈsmatə/ *verb*. ME.

[Origin unkn.]

1 *verb trans.* †**a** Make dirty; pollute. ME–E17. ▸**b** Splash, splatter. *US*. L19.

2 *verb intrans.* Talk foolishly or superficially; chatter. (Foll. by *of*.) Now *Scot.* LME.

3 *verb intrans.* & †*refl.* Have slight or superficial knowledge of a subject; dabble. (Foll. by *of*, *in*, *at*.) L15.

4 *verb trans.* **a** Speak (a language) without proper knowledge or proficiency. E17. ▸**b** Dabble in (a subject); study superficially. *rare*. L19.

📖 **1b** D. RICHARDS A long grey coat, smattered with mud. **2** C. LAMB A.. chemist.. who smatters of literature and is immeasurably unlettered. **3** J. P. MAHAFFY More lucrative to smatter through.. these things than to learn the great subjects. **4a** T. E. LAWRENCE A science fatally easy.. to smatter, but too difficult.. to master.

▪ **smatterer** *noun* a person who smatters; *spec.* a person who has only superficial knowledge of a matter, a dabbler (*in*): E16.

smattering /ˈsmat(ə)rɪŋ/ *noun*. M16.

[from SMATTER *verb* + -ING[1]. Cf. SMACKERING.]

1 A slight or superficial knowledge of a subject. (Freq. foll. by *in*, *of*.) M16. ▸**b** A sparse collection, a sprinkling; a small amount. E20.

2 The action of speaking or studying in a superficial manner. *rare*. M17.

📖 **1** S. KAUFFMANN I have a smattering of piano and violin, but I can't really play them. G. S. HAIGHT He picked up smatterings of mathematics, a little French, and less Latin. **b** T. TRYON A fine silvery mist.. began to fall, refracting the smattering of pallid moonlight.

smattering /ˈsmat(ə)rɪŋ/ *adjective*. L15.

[from SMATTER *verb* + -ING[2]. Sense 1 may be a different word.]

†**1** Ready for kissing; attractive. *rare*. Only in L15.

2 (Of knowledge) slight, superficial; (of a person) having imperfect knowledge. L16.

▪ **smatteringly** *adverb* M19.

smay /smeɪ/ *verb intrans.* Now *dial.* M17.

[Aphet. for DISMAY *verb*.]

Show faintness of heart; flinch.

smaze /smeɪz/ *noun*. M20.

[Blend of SMOKE *noun* and HAZE *noun*.]

A mixture of smoke and haze.

SME *abbreviation*.

Small to medium-sized enterprise, a company with no more than 500 employees.

smear /smɪə/ *noun*.

[Old English *smeoru* = Old Frisian *smere*, Old High German *smero* (Dutch *smeer*, German *Schmer*), Old Norse *smjǫr*, Gothic *smairþr*, from Germanic; cogn. with Greek *muron* ointment, *smuris* EMERY.]

†**1** Fat, grease; ointment. OE–M17.

2 A greasy or dirty mark or smudge; a thin layer of a substance smeared on something. E17. ▸**b** Chiefly MEDICINE. A small quantity of a substance smeared on a slide for microscopic examination, *esp.* a sample of human or other tissue obtained without surgery; *spec.* (more fully ***cervical smear***) a specimen of tissue from the cervix of the womb, examined to ascertain whether cancer or precancerous changes are present; ***ellipt.*** a smear test (see below). E20.

3 a An ointment for killing vermin etc. on sheep. E19. ▸**b** POTTERY. A mixture used for glazing. L19.

4 JAZZ. A short glissando; a slurring effect produced by a brass instrument, esp. a trombone. E20.

5 A slanderous story, *esp.* one circulated to discredit a public figure; stories of this nature. *colloq.* M20.

📖 **2** D. HOGAN A smear of red lipstick on her lips. N. LOWNDES The floor was wet and his feet left smears. **5** A. POWELL Laying his.. reputation open to smear and boycott. *Tribune* Some of the more outrageous smears and falsehoods.

Comb.: **smear campaign** a plan to discredit a public figure by means of slanderous stories; **smear glaze** = sense 3b above; **smear test** a test for cancer of the cervix of the womb made by means of a smear; the process of obtaining or of examining such a smear.

smear /smɪə/ *verb trans.*

[Old English *smeirwan* corresp. to Middle Low German *smeren*, Old High German *smirwen* (German *schmieren*), Old Norse *smyrva*, *smyrja*, from Germanic.]

1 Coat thickly or mark with a greasy, sticky, or staining substance (usu. foll. by *with*). Formerly *spec.*, anoint (a person) with oil as part of a religious ceremony. OE.

2 Spread a thick layer of (a greasy or sticky substance) *on* something. ME. ▸**b** Rub *out* or *off* with a smear or smudge; blot; smudge or obscure the outline of (writing,

artwork, etc.); rub or draw *across, over*, etc., something so as to smudge or dirty it. **M19.**
3 *spec.* **a** Rub (a sheep) with a mixture of tar and grease to prevent disease or to kill vermin. **LME.** ▸**b** Glaze (pottery) by a process of evaporation. **M19.**
4 (Attempt to) discredit (a public figure, a person's reputation) by slanderous stories; defame the character of; slander. **E20.**
5 Kill; destroy by bombing. *slang.* **M20.**

> 🕮 **1** J. MASEFIELD His dungarees were smeared with paraffin. J. L. WATEN Bread thickly smeared with treacle. A. TOFFLER Soot smeared our faces. **2** J. M. COETZEE He . . smears ointment on the hundred little stabs. I. MURDOCH He smeared some butter onto a fragment of a loaf with his fingers. **b** W. GOLDING One delver relaxed and smeared a hand over his sweaty face. **4** *Here & Now* Red-baiters . . try to smear the UN as a Communist-dominated organisation.

▪ **smeared** *ppl adjective* that has been smeared; ***smeared out*** (SCIENCE), distributed or averaged out over a volume of space or a period of time: **M16.** **smearer** *noun* **M17.** **smearing** *noun* (*a*) the action of the verb; (*b*) a layer of ointment, paint, etc., smeared on: **OE.**

smear-case /ˈsmɪəkeɪs/ *noun. US.* **E19.**
[formed as SCHMIERKÄSE.]
Cottage cheese.

smear-dab /ˈsmɪədab/ *noun.* **M18.**
[Perh. from SMEAR *noun* or *verb*, from its slimy skin: see DAB *noun*[2].]
The lemon-sole, *Microstomus kitt.*

smeary /ˈsmɪəri/ *adjective.* **E16.**
[from SMEAR *noun* or *verb* + -Y[1].]
1 Showing smears or dirty marks; smudged. **E16.**
2 Tending to leave a greasy or dirty mark; greasy, sticky. **L16.**

> 🕮 **1** J. WYNDHAM A smeary, tear-stained face. *New Yorker* Patches of smeary, expressionistic brushwork.

▪ **smeariness** *noun* **M19.**

smectic /ˈsmɛktɪk/ *adjective & noun.* **L17.**
[Latin *smecticus* from Greek *smēktikos*, from *smēkhein* rub, cleanse (cf. SMEGMA): see -IC.]
▸ **A** *adjective.* **1** Cleansing, detergent. *rare.* **L17.**
2 PHYSICAL CHEMISTRY. Designating or pertaining to a mesophase or liquid crystal in which the molecules all have the same orientation and are arranged in well-defined planes. Opp. ***nematic.*** **E20.**
▸ **B** *noun.* A smectic substance. **L20.**

smectis /ˈsmɛktɪs/ *noun. obsolete* exc. *Hist.* **E18.**
[Greek *smēktis* fuller's earth.]
= SMECTITE 1.

smectite /ˈsmɛktʌɪt/ *noun.* **E19.**
[from prec. + -ITE[1].]
MINERALOGY. **1** Fuller's earth. *obsolete* exc. *Hist.* **E19.**
2 A montmorillonoid. **M20.**

Smectymnuan /smɛkˈtɪmnjʊən/ *noun & adjective.* **M17.**
[from *Smectymnuus* (see below), pen-name formed from the initials of the five authors + -AN.]
Hist. ▸**A** *noun.* Each of the five Presbyterian divines who in 1641 published an attack on episcopacy under the collective pen-name Smectymnuus. Also, a person who accepted their views. **M17.**
▸ **B** *adjective.* Of, pertaining to, or characteristic of the Smectymnuans. **L17.**

smeddum /ˈsmɛdəm/ *noun.* See also SMIDDUM.
[Old English *smed(e)ma*, of unkn. origin. Cf. SMITHAM.]
1 A fine powder, *esp.* fine flour or malt. *obsolete* exc. *Hist.* **OE.** ▸**b** MINING. = SMITHAM 2. **M18.**
2 Spirit, go; mental or physical vigour. *Scot.* **L18.**

smeech /smiːtʃ/ *noun & verb. obsolete* exc. *dial.*
[Old English *smēc*, from *smēocan* SMEEK *verb.* See also next.]
▸ **A** *noun.* Smoke; thick vapour; fumes. **OE.**
▸ **B** *verb.* †**1** *verb trans.* Blacken with smoke. *rare.* Only in **E17.**
2 *verb intrans.* Emit smoke or vapour. **M19.**
3 *verb trans.* Perfume, scent. **L19.**

smeek /smiːk/ *noun. obsolete* exc. *Scot.* **ME.**
[North. var. of prec. Cf. next.]
Smoke; thick vapour; fumes.

smeek /smiːk/ *verb. obsolete* exc. *Scot.*
[Old English *smēocan* = Middle Dutch *smieken*, German dial. *smiechen*, rel. by ablaut to Old English *smocian* SMOKE *verb.* Cf. prec., SMEECH, SMOKE *noun & adjective.*]
1 *verb intrans.* Emit smoke or vapour. **OE.**
2 *verb trans.* Apply smoke or fumes to, esp. in order to cleanse or dry; suffocate (bees) or drive out (an animal) by means of smoke. **OE.**

smeeth /smiːθ, -ð/ *adjective & verb. obsolete* exc. *dial.*
[Old English *smǣþe*, *smēþe* rel. by ablaut to SMOOTH *adjective.* Cf. SMOOTH *verb.*]
▸ **A** *adjective.* Smooth. **OE.**
▸ **B** *verb trans.* Make smooth. **OE.**

▪ **smeethly** *adverb* **ME.** **smeethness** *noun* **LOE.**

smegma /ˈsmɛɡmə/ *noun.* **E19.**
[Latin from Greek *smēgma* soap, from *smēkhein* rub, cleanse.]
A sebaceous secretion, *esp.* that found under the foreskin.

smell /smɛl/ *noun.* **ME.**
[from the verb.]
1 The property of things by which they are perceptible by the sensation they produce in the nose; an odour, a scent; a stench. **ME.**
2 The faculty of perceiving things by this property. Now chiefly in ***sense of smell.*** **ME.**
3 A trace or suggestion of something; the quality by which something is sensed or suspected. Also, the special or subtle character of an object, event, etc. **L15.**
4 An act of inhaling to detect an odour or scent; a sniff. **M16.**

> 🕮 **1** I. FLEMING Lorrydrivers brought in a smell of sweat and petrol. *Which?* An in-house bakery wafts . . irresistible fresh bread smells around. **3** J. CONRAD There is a smell of treachery about this. *New Yorker* These endeavours do not have the smell of success about them.

▪ **smell-less** /-l-l-/ *adjective* (*a*) giving out no smell, scentless; (*b*) having no sense of smell: **E17.**

smell /smɛl/ *verb.* Pa. t. & pple **smelt** /smɛlt/, **smelled.** **ME.**
[Origin unkn.: prob. already in Old English but not recorded and no cognates known.]
▸ **I** *verb trans.* **1 a** Perceive by means of the sense of smell; perceive (an odour or scent). **ME.** ▸**b** Inhale the smell of; sniff at; examine in this way. **M19.**
2 *fig.* Perceive as if by smell; detect, discern; suspect. **LME.**
3 a Search or find *out* by or as if by smell; distinguish (one thing *from* another) in this way. **M16.** ▸**b** Find or make (one's way) by sense of smell. *rare.* **E17.**
4 Have or emit a smell of. Now *rare.* **L16.**
5 Cause to smell; fill or affect with an (offensive) odour. Usu. foll. by *out. colloq.* **L19.**

> 🕮 **1a** J. G. COZZENS I could smell spirits on his breath. *Japan Times* We can . . smell the warm fragrance of Taiwanese spices flowing from the kitchen. **b** G. VIDAL She smelled the . . flower; a strong odour of cigar smoke spoiled the scent. **2** I. FLEMING Like all really good crooks although he couldn't see it, he smelt the trap. *Far Eastern Economic Review* Officials . . smell trouble from a public growing angry with corruption. ***smell a rat***: see RAT *noun*[1]. ***smell the ground***: see GROUND *noun.* **3a** T. F. POWYS A fox . . being smelt out by the hounds. *Cycling Weekly* Media people . . smelling out the best stories. **b** SHAKES. *Lear* Thrust him out . . and let him smell His way to Dover. **4** THACKERAY There's . . crumbs on your cheek, and you smell sherry. **5** JONATHAN ROSS A dead body smelling out the house.

▸ **II** *verb intrans.* **6** Have or use a sense of smell; (be able to) perceive an odour or odours; (foll. by *at*, (now *rare*) *of, to*) inhale the smell of something. **ME.**
7 a Emit or give off an odour; have a specified smell or scent. Also foll. by *of.* **ME.** ▸**b** *spec.* Give out an offensive odour; stink. **LME.**
8 *fig.* **a** Have an air of a particular quality; exhibit a suggestion *of*, be redolent *of.* **LME.** ▸**b** *spec.* Have an air of dishonesty or fraud; give rise to suspicion. **M20.**

> 🕮 **6** C. READE She smelt at her salts, and soon recovered. *Daily Telegraph* Greenfly smell with specialised sensors . . on their antennae. **7a** J. STEINBECK The earth smelled dry and good. G. GREENE He smelt strongly of rum. K. GIBBONS Her house . . smelled like a Christmas tree. **b** K. M. PEYTON This coat *smells*! . . I should have taken it to the cleaner's. **8a** *Receiver* A players' committee was in charge and it didn't smell right . . so I resigned. *New Statesman* The public pillorying of Higgs and Wyatt smells strongly of messenger bashing. **smell of oil** = ***smell of the candle*** below. ***smell of roses***: see ROSE *noun.* **smell of the candle**, **smell of the lamp** show signs of laborious study and effort. ***smell of the shop***: see SHOP *noun.* **b** G. GREENE Percival's conversation with you . . I simply can't believe it . . it smells to heaven.

▪ **smellable** *adjective* able to be smelt **LME.**

smellage /ˈsmɛlɪdʒ/ *noun. US.* **M19.**
[Alt. of SMALLAGE.]
The herb lovage, *Levisticum officinale.*

smeller /ˈsmɛlə/ *noun.* **LME.**
[from SMELL *verb* + -ER[1].]
1 a A person who perceives something by sense of smell; a person who smells something (out). **LME.** ▸**b** A person who emits an (offensive) odour; a stinker. *rare.* **E17.**
2 A feeler; a slender tactile organ, hair, etc.; *esp.* a whisker of a cat. **M17.**
3 *slang.* **a** The nose; in *pl.*, the nostrils. **L17.** ▸**b** A blow on the nose. **E19.** ▸**c** Anything exceptionally violent or severe; *spec.* a heavy fall. **L19.**

smell-feast /ˈsmɛlfiːst/ *noun. arch.* **E16.**
[from SMELL *noun* or *verb* + FEAST *noun.*]
A person who searches out and comes uninvited to a feast, party, etc.; a sponger.

smellfungus /smɛlˈfʌŋɡəs/ *noun. literary & joc.* Pl. **-guses, -gi** /-dʒi, -dʒʌɪ, -gi, -gʌɪ/. **E19.**
[Sterne's name for Smollett, with ref. to the carping tone of Smollett's *Travels through France and Italy* (1766).]
A discontented person; a grumbler, a fault-finder.

smellie /ˈsmɛli/ *noun.* **E20.**
[from SMELL *verb* + -IE. Cf. MOVIE.]
A film in which smell is synchronized with the picture. Usu. in *pl.*

smelling /ˈsmɛlɪŋ/ *noun.* **ME.**
[from SMELL *verb* + -ING[1].]
1 The sense of smell. **ME.**
2 The action or fact of smelling or giving off a smell. **LME.**
Comb.: **smelling-bottle** a small bottle containing smelling-salts; **smelling-salts** ammonium carbonate mixed with scent, sniffed as a restorative in cases of faintness or headache.

smelly /ˈsmɛli/ *adjective.* **LME.**
[from SMELL *noun* + -Y[1].]
1 Orig., having an odour. Later *spec.*, having a strong or unpleasant smell; stinking. **LME.**
2 Suspicious. *rare.* **E20.**
▪ **smelliness** *noun* **L19.**

smelt /smɛlt/ *noun.*
[Old English *smelt*, *smylt* (Anglo-Latin *smeltus*, *smyltus*), obscurely rel. to various European fish names. Cf. SMOLT.]
1 A small slender silvery migratory fish, *Osmerus eperlanus*, of European coasts and rivers, having a characteristic odour and caught for food. Also called ***sparling.*** **OE.**
2 A smolt. *north.* **M17.**
3 Any of various small fishes of northern waters, esp. sand-smelts; *spec.* any of the family Osmeridae, related to salmons, as *Osmerus mordax* (in full ***rainbow smelt***) and *O. dentex* (in full ***Asiatic smelt***), of coastal and fresh waters in N. America and Asia. **L18.**

smelt /smɛlt/ *verb*[1] *trans.* **M16.**
[Middle Low German, Middle Dutch *smelten* = Old High German *smelzan* (German *schmelzen*) weak trans. verb corresp. to strong intrans. from var. of base of MELT *verb.* Cf. SMALT.]
Fuse or melt (ore etc.) in order to extract the metal; obtain (metal) by this process.
▪ **smeltery** *noun* a place where ores are smelted, a smelting works **E19.**

smelt *verb*[2] *pa. t. & pple* of SMELL *verb.*

smelter /ˈsmɛltə/ *noun*[1]. **LME.**
[from SMELT *verb*[1] + -ER[1].]
1 A person engaged in smelting; an owner of a smelting works. **LME.**
2 A smelting works; a smeltery. Chiefly *US.* **L19.**

smelter /ˈsmɛltə/ *noun*[2]. *rare.* **M19.**
[from SMELT *noun* + -ER[1].]
A person who fishes for smelts; a smelt-catcher.

SMERSH /sməːʃ/ *noun.* Also **Smersh.** **M20.**
[Russian abbreviation of *smert' shpionam* lit. 'death to spies'.]
In the former USSR, a counter-espionage organization, originating during the war of 1939–45, responsible for maintaining security within the armed forces and intelligence services.

smetana /ˈsmɛtənə/ *noun.* **E20.**
[Russian, from *smetat'* sweep together, collect.]
Sour cream. Freq. in ***smetana sauce.***

smeuse /smjuːs, smjuːz/ *noun & verb.* Chiefly *dial.* **E19.**
[Alt. of MEUSE.]
▸ **A** *noun.* A hole in a hedge, wall, etc. **E19.**
▸ **B** *verb intrans.* Go through a smeuse. **M19.**

smew /smjuː/ *noun.* **L17.**
[Obscurely rel. to Dutch *smient*, †*smeente*, Low German *smēnt* wigeon, German *Schmeiente*, *Schmi-*, *Schmü-* small wild duck (from *Ente* duck).]
A medium-sized Eurasian saw-billed duck, *Mergus albellus*, having grey and white plumage with the head red-brown and white, or in the breeding male, black and white. Also called ***white merganser.***
red-headed smew: see RED *adjective.*

†**smicker** *adjective.* **OE–M17.**
[Old English *smicer*: cf. Old High German *smehhar*, *smechar* (Middle High German *smecker*) elegant, delicate.]
Beautiful, handsome, elegant.

smicket /ˈsmɪkɪt/ *noun.* Now *dial.* **L17.**
[App. dim. of SMOCK *noun*: see -ET[1].]
A woman's or girl's smock or chemise.

smiddum /ˈsmɪdəm/ *noun.* **E19.**
[Var. of SMEDDUM.]
MINING. = SMITHAM 2.

smidge /smɪdʒ/ *noun. colloq.* Orig. & chiefly *N. Amer.* **E20.**
[Origin uncertain: perh. from SMITCH. Cf. next, TAD, TIDGE.]
A tiny amount.

S. KING He had bought the land a little smidge at a time.

smidgen /ˈsmɪdʒɪn/ *noun. colloq.* Orig. *N. Amer.* Also **-dgin**, **-dgeon**. M19.
[Origin uncertain: perh. from SMITCH. Cf. prec.]
A tiny amount; a very small person or thing.

Blactress He'll speak English with a smidgen of French and Italian. *Listener* A smidgin of *foie gras* about the size of a bee's knee.

smift /smɪft/ *noun.* M19.
[Origin unkn.]
MINING. A fuse or slow match used in blasting.

smig /smɪg/ *noun.* L19.
[Origin unkn.]
collect. Very young fry of the herring and other fishes, having thin transparent scaleless bodies, before their development into whitebait. Also ***smig bait***, ***smig herring***.

smilacina /smʌɪləˈsʌɪnə/ *noun.* E19.
[mod. Latin (see below), from Latin *smilac-*, SMILAX + -INA[2].]
Any of various ornamental plants constituting the genus *Smilacina*, of the lily family, with broad stem-leaves and terminal clusters of small white flowers, native to N. America and temperate Asia. Also called ***false Solomon's seal***.

smilax /ˈsmʌɪlaks/ *noun.* L16.
[Latin from Greek = bindweed, smilax.]
1 Any of various spiny climbing monocotyledonous plants constituting the genus *Smilax* (family Smilacaceae); esp. *S. aspera*, of the Mediterranean region, and the Central American *S. ornata* and *S. regelii*, both sources of sarsaparilla. L16.
2 A South African asparagus, *Asparagus asparagoides*, much used by flower arrangers. L19.

smile /smʌɪl/ *noun.* ME.
[from the verb.]
1 An act of smiling; a facial expression of pleasure, amusement, affection, or scepticism, or a forced imitation of these, characterized by an upturning of the corners of the mouth. ME.
2 A drink, esp. of whisky. *colloq.* Orig. *US.* M19.

1 E. O'NEILL A smile of affectionate admiration. *Japan Times* A smile creases his . . face. *fig.*: TENNYSON Fortune, turn thy wheel with smile or frown. **all smiles** smiling broadly, beaming. ***force a smile***: see FORCE *verb*[1]. ***wan smile***: see WAN *adjective*[1].

■ **smileful** *adjective* full of smiles; smiling: E17. **smilet** *noun* (*rare*) a brief or slight smile L16.

smile /smʌɪl/ *verb.* ME.
[Perh. of Scandinavian origin (cf. Swedish *smila*, Danish *smile*); parallel to Old High German (in pres. pple *smilenter*), Middle High German *smielen*, from base also of SMIRK *verb*.]
▶ **I** *verb intrans.* **1 a** Of a person: assume an expression of pleasure, amusement, affection, or scepticism, or a forced imitation of these, by turning up the corners of the mouth. ME. ▸**b** Of the eyes: express pleasure, amusement, or affection. M18.
2 a Look *at*, *on*, or *upon* with a smile or pleasant expression. Also foll. by adverbs. LME. ▸**b** Regard with favour, approval, or encouragement. Foll. by *on*, *upon*. Chiefly *fig.* LME.
3 Of a physical feature etc.: have or present a pleasing aspect. *poet.* LME.
4 Of wine, beer, etc.: be pleasantly smooth; sparkle. Long *rare* or *obsolete*. LME.
5 Have a drink. *US slang.* M19.

1a *Times* Miss Rewis's victory gave her plenty to smile about. U. HOLDEN She went on admiring her hair, smiling to herself. *fig.*: SHAKES. *Two Gent.* Inward joy enforc'd my heart to smile! ***come up smiling***: see COME *verb*. **I should smile** *colloq.*: expr. ridicule at an idea. **2a** E. O'NEILL She smiles down at Jim, her face softening. I. MURDOCH He smiled at Ludens in a polite and friendly manner. **b** BOSW. SMITH Circumstances . . seemed to smile on the project.

▶ **II** *verb trans.* **6** Bring into a specified state or position by smiling; *esp.* get rid of or drive *away* by smiling. L16.
†**7** Treat with contempt; deride, laugh at. *rare* (Shakes.). Only in E17.
8 a Indicate or express by smiling; grant with a smile; say while smiling. M17. ▸**b** Give (a smile). M19.

8a W. SOYINKA He could afford to smile his benediction on the orchestra. **b** W. TREVOR Her mother smiled a slanting smile.

■ **smileable** *adjective* (*rare*) at which one may smile M19. **smiler** *noun* LME.

smileless /ˈsmʌɪl-lɪs/ *adjective.* E18.
[from SMILE *noun* + -LESS.]
1 Of a person, expression, etc.: not smiling; grave, severe. E18. ▸**b** Of speech: uttered without a smile. E19.
2 *fig.* Devoid of brightness or cheerfulness; dark, dull. M19.
■ **smilelessly** *adverb* M19.

Smilesian /ˈsmʌɪlzɪən/ *adjective.* L19.
[from Samuel *Smiles* (1812–1904), author of *Self-Help* (1859) and other works on self-improvement by personal effort and initiative: see -IAN.]
Of, pertaining to, or characteristic of Smiles or his theories or writings.

smiley /ˈsmʌɪli/ *adjective & noun.* M19.
[from SMILE *noun* + -Y[1].]
▶ **A** *adjective.* **1** Inclined to smile; smiling, cheerful. M19.
2 Caused by or causing a smile. L20.
▶ **B** *noun.* In full ***smiley face***. A simple representation of a smiling face, *spec.* (***a***) a cartoon drawing on a round yellow background; (***b***) (COMPUTING) an emoticon formed by the characters :-) and used to indicate that the writer is pleased or joking. L20.

smiling /ˈsmʌɪlɪŋ/ *ppl adjective.* LME.
[from SMILE *verb* + -ING[2].]
1 That smiles; having a smile on the face. LME.
2 Of a physical feature etc.: looking bright or cheerful; pleasant, attractive. *poet.* E18.
3 Characterized by smiles or a cheerful manner; accompanied by a smile. E19.
■ **smilingly** *adverb* in a smiling manner; pleasantly, cheerfully: LME. **smilingness** *noun* (*rare*) a smiling condition or expression E19.

S-mine /ˈɛsmʌɪn/ *noun.* M20.
[Abbreviation of German *Schützenmine* lit. 'infantryman mine'.]
A German anti-personnel mine used in the war of 1939–45.

smir *noun & verb* var. of SMUR.

smirch /sməːtʃ/ *noun.* L17.
[from the verb.]
1 A dirty mark, a smudge. Also, that which smears or stains something. L17.
2 A moral stain or flaw; a fault, a defect. M19.
■ **smirchless** *adverb & adjective* (*rare*) without (leaving) a smirch or stain M19.

smirch /sməːtʃ/ *verb trans.* L15.
[Prob. symbolic: cf. *smite*, *smudge*, *smut*, etc.]
1 Make dirty; soil, stain, discolour. Also foll. by *with*. L15.
2 Cast discredit on (a person, his or her honour, etc.); bring into ill-repute; taint, tarnish. E19.

1 R. C. HUTCHINSON Faces . . pallid and smirched with blood. **2** P. H. GIBBS Fleet Street is no place for you . . Your lovely innocence will be smirched.

■ **smircher** *noun* (*rare*) L19.

†**smiris** *noun.* E17–E19.
[Greek *smiris*, *smuris*.]
= EMERY *noun* 1.

smirk /sməːk/ *noun.* M16.
[from the verb.]
An affected, conceited, or silly smile; a simper; a smug look.

Daily Mirror You can wipe that self-satisfied smirk off your chops.

smirk /sməːk/ *adjective.* Now chiefly *dial.* E16.
[App. from the verb, but perh. partly suggested by SMICKER *adjective*.]
Neat, trim, smart in dress or appearance; pleasant. Also (*US*), smug.

smirk /sməːk/ *verb intrans.*
[Old English *sme(a)rcian*, from base repr. by Old English *smerian* laugh at, *bismerian* scorn, *gālsmǣre* given to frivolous laughter, Old High German *smierōn* (German †*schmieren*) smile. Cf. SMILE *verb*.]
Orig., smile. Later *spec.*, smile in an affected, smug, or silly manner; simper. (Foll. by *at*, *on*, *upon*.)
■ **smirker** *noun* M18. **smirkingly** *adverb* in a smirking manner; with a smirk: M16.

smirkish /ˈsməːkɪʃ/ *adjective. rare.* L17.
[from SMIRK *noun* or *adjective* + -ISH[1].]
Smiling, pleasant; somewhat smirky or simpering.

smirky /ˈsməːki/ *adjective.* E18.
[from SMIRK *noun* or *adjective* + -Y[1].]
Smiling smugly; simpering; of the nature of a smirk. Also (*Scot. & US*) smart, neat.
■ **smirkily** *adverb* L20.

smirr *noun & verb* var. of SMUR.

smit /smɪt/ *noun*[1]. Long *Scot. & north.*
[Old English *smitte* = Middle Dutch, Middle & mod. Low German *smitte* (whence Danish *smitte*, Swedish *smitta*), Middle High German *smitze* (German *Schmitze*) spot, stain, smear. Cf. SMIT *verb*[1].]
†**1** A stain, a blemish; *fig.* a moral taint, defilement. OE–M16.
2 a A soft reddish earth or ore, used esp. for marking sheep. Now *rare* or *obsolete*. E18. ▸**b** A mark of ownership put on a sheep. E19.
3 A particle of soot; a smut, a black spot. E19.
4 Infection; contagion. E19.

smit /smɪt/ *noun*[2]. *obsolete* exc. *dial.* LME.
[Rel. to SMITE *verb*.]
A blow, a stroke; the sound of this.

smit /smɪt/ *verb*[1] *trans.* Long *Scot. & north.* Infl. **-tt-**.
[Old English *smittian* (from weak grade of *smītan* SMITE *verb*) = Middle Dutch, Middle Low German *smitten* (whence Danish, Norwegian *smitte*, Swedish *smitta*), Old High German *(pi)smizzan* (Middle High German *smitzen*, German *schmitzen*). Cf. SMIT *noun*[1].]
1 Stain, mark; colour, tinge. OE. ▸**b** *fig.* Taint, sully; bring into disgrace. LME. ▸**c** Mark (a sheep) with reddish earth or ruddle. E19.
2 Of a contagious disease etc.: infect, affect by contagion. (Foll. by *with*.) OE.

smit *verb*[2] *pa. t. & pple*: see SMITE *verb*.

smitch /smɪtʃ/ *noun. Scot. & N. Amer.* M19.
[Origin unkn. Cf. SMIDGE, SMIDGEN.]
A particle; a bit, a tiny amount.

smite /smʌɪt/ *noun.* ME.
[from the verb.]
1 A forceful stroke, a heavy blow; the sound of this. ME.
2 †**a** A slight indication or intimation *of* something. *rare.* Only in M17. ▸**b** A tiny amount; a particle. *US & dial.* M19.

smite /smʌɪt/ *verb.* Now chiefly *arch.* or *poet.* Pa. t. **smote** /sməʊt/, †**smit**; pa. pple **smitten** /ˈsmɪt(ə)n/, (*arch.*) **smit**, †**smote**.
[Old English *smītan* smear, pollute = Old Frisian *smīta*, Old Saxon *bismītan*, Middle Low German, Middle Dutch *smīten* (Dutch *smijten*), Old High German *smīzan* smear (German *schmeissen* throw, fling), Gothic *(bi)smeitan*, *(ga)smeitan* smear, from Germanic. Prob. ult. symbolic: cf. *smirch*, *smudge*, *smut*, etc.]
▶ **I** *verb trans.* †**1** Pollute, blemish. Only in OE.
†**2** Smear (a substance) *on* something. Only in OE.
3 Strike with the hand, a weapon, etc.; hit, beat. Also (chiefly in biblical use), strike down, kill, slay, destroy; afflict, punish. LOE. ▸**b** Touch or strike (a harp etc.) so as to produce sound. Now *poet.* LME.
4 Strike or deliver (a blow, stroke, etc.). ME. ▸†**b** Fight (a battle). ME–M17.
5 Cut *off* with a slashing blow; cut, chop, or break *in* pieces etc. Long *rare* or *obsolete*. ME.
6 Knock or force *away*, *back*, *down*, etc. with a blow or stroke; drive, hammer, or strike (a thing) with force *against*, *into*, *on*, etc., something else; strike or clap *together*. ME. ▸†**b** Produce (fire) by striking a stone etc. against another. ME–L17.
7 Bring into a certain condition by or as by striking. *rare.* ME.
8 a Of hail, lightning, fire, etc.: strike and injure; destroy. ME. ▸**b** (Of wind etc.) beat or dash against; (of sunlight etc.) beat or shine strongly on. LME.
9 Of a disease, disaster, etc.: attack, affect severely. Freq. in *pass.* ME.
10 a Impress or strike suddenly or strongly *with* some feeling or thought. Later also, impress favourably. Usu. in *pass.* ME. ▸**b** Inspire or inflame with love; enamour. Usu. in *pass.* M17.
11 Disquiet, affect painfully; distress, perturb. LME.

3 R. KIPLING The other Sahib . . smote the stabber with a short gun. G. B. SHAW By rights I should smite you dead with my scimitar. E. BOWEN The tram-driver . . smiting his bell. ***smite hip and thigh***: see HIP *noun*[1] 1. ***smite under the* FIFTH *rib***. **5** AV *Eccles.* 36:10 Smite in sunder the heads of the . . heathen. **6** TENNYSON He smote his palms together. E. A. FREEMAN The last hopes of the House of Godwine had been smitten to the ground. **8b** W. HARRIS The sun smote me as I descended the steps. **9** E. LONGFORD Three months later . . he was smitten again, first with giddiness . . and soon afterwards with another seizure. M. HOCKING Were the village to be smitten by plague, he would stay. J. COX *Corn* is a high-risk crop . . Smut can smite it.
10a L. M. MONTGOMERY Anne had been smitten with delighted admiration when she first saw that brooch.
b M. RICHLER After a turbulent six years of marriage . . she was still smitten with him. **11** J. LONDON His haggard face smote her to the heart. T. HARDY His heart smote him at the thought.

▶ **II** *verb intrans.* **12** Deliver a blow or blows; strike. (Foll. by *at*, *on*, *upon*.) ME. ▸**b** Strike with a hammer in doing smith-work. Now *spec.*, strike with a sledge. LME. ▸**c** Of a clock: strike, chime. Long *rare.* LME.
13 †**a** Come *together* in conflict. ME–L16. ▸**b** Knock *together* with force; strike or dash *on* or *against* something. Long *rare* or *obsolete*. ME.
14 a Penetrate with force *in*, *into*, or *through* something. ME. ▸**b** Give pain *to* one's heart; cause distress. *rare.* LME. ▸**c** Occur suddenly to one. Foll. by *in*, *upon*. *rare.* LME.

12 W. DE LA MARE He smote upon the door . . a second time. **13a** SPENSER With hideous horror both together smite.

■ **smiter** *noun* (***a***) *arch.* a person who smites; (***b***) (now *rare* or *obsolete*) a variety of the domestic pigeon with a habit of loudly clapping its wings in flight: ME. **smiting** *noun* the action of the verb; an instance of this: ME.

smith /smɪθ/ *noun.*
[Old English *smiþ* = Old Frisian *smith*, Middle Dutch *smit*, (also mod.) *smid*, Old High German *smid* (German *Schmied*, †*Schmid*), Old Norse *smiðr*, from Germanic (repr. also in Gothic *aizasmiþa* coppersmith).]
A person who works in iron or other metals; *esp.* a blacksmith. Also, a skilled worker in other arts or crafts. Freq. as 2nd elem. of comb.

Jo GRIMOND A smith in leather apron hammered out red-hot horse-shoes. ***blacksmith, goldsmith, locksmith, silversmith, wordsmith***, etc.

Comb.: **smithcraft** the work, craft, or art of a smith; **smith's coal** fine coal, slack; **smith shop** a smith's workshop, a smithy; **smith's work**, **smith work** work done by or the occupation of a smith, smithery.

smith /smɪθ/ *verb.*
[Old English *smiþian* (= Old Saxon, Old High German *smiþōn*, Old Norse *smiþa*, Gothic *gasmiþōn*), from the noun.]
1 *verb trans.* Make or fashion (a weapon, iron implement, etc.) by forging; forge. **OE.** ▸**b** Treat by forging, heat and hammer; hammer or beat (a blade etc.) on an anvil. **LME.**
2 *verb intrans.* Work at a forge; practise the occupation of a smith. **ME.**
■ **smither** *noun* (*rare*) a smith **LME.**

smitham /ˈsmɪð(ə)m/ *noun.* **E17.**
[Alt. of SMEDDUM.]
1 The finest particles or dust of ground malt. Now *dial.* **E17.**
2 MINING. The finest part of lead ore, usu. obtained by sieving and grinding. Cf. SMIDDUM. **M17.**

Smith & Wesson /smɪθ (ə)nd ˈwɛs(ə)n/ *noun phr.* **M19.**
[Horace *Smith* (1808–93) and Daniel B. *Wesson* (1825–1906), founders of a US firm of gunsmiths.]
(Proprietary name for) a type of firearm, *esp.* a type of cartridge revolver.

smithereen /smɪðəˈriːn/ *verb trans.* **E20.**
[from next.]
Smash or blow up into tiny fragments.

smithereens /smɪðəˈriːnz/ *noun pl.* **E19.**
[Prob. from Irish *smidirín*: see -EEN[2], -S[1].]
Tiny fragments. Chiefly in ***to smithereens***, ***into smithereens***, after verbs like *blow*, *kick*, *smash*, etc.
■ Also **smithers** *noun pl.* (*colloq.*) **M19.**

smithery /ˈsmɪθ(ə)ri/ *noun.* **E17.**
[from SMITH *noun* + -ERY.]
1 The occupation, work, or craft of a smith. **E17.**
2 The forge or workshop of a smith; a smithy. **M18.**

Smithfield /ˈsmɪθfiːld/ *noun*[1]. *rare.* **M17.**
[A locality in London, long the site of a cattle- or meat-market.]
A cattle-market, a meat-market.
Comb.: **Smithfield bargain** a sharp bargain, in which the buyer may be deceived; *transf.* a marriage of usu. financial convenience.

Smithfield /ˈsmɪθfiːld/ *noun*[2]. *US.* **L19.**
[*Smithfield*, a town in Virginia, USA.]
Smithfield ham, a type of cured ham.

Smithian /ˈsmɪθɪən/ *adjective.* **L19.**
[from Adam *Smith* (see below) + -IAN.]
Of, pertaining to, or advocating the principles of Adam Smith (1723–90), Scottish philosopher and economist.

smithiantha /smɪθɪˈanθə/ *noun.* **M20.**
[mod. Latin (see below), from Mathilda *Smith* (1854–1926), Brit. botanical artist + Greek *anthos* flower.]
Any of several Mexican plants constituting the genus *Smithiantha* (family Gesneriaceae), with cordate variegated leaves and red, yellow, or orange bell-shaped flowers, grown as house-plants.

smithier /ˈsmɪðɪə/ *noun. arch. rare.* **LME.**
[from SMITH *verb* + -IER; later from SMITHY *verb* + -ER[1].]
A smith.

Smithsonian /smɪθˈsəʊnɪən/ *adjective.* **E19.**
[from *Smithson* (see below) + -IAN.]
Of or pertaining to James L. M. Smithson (1765–1829), British chemist and mineralogist; *spec.* of, pertaining to, or designating the institution endowed by Smithson and founded in 1846 in Washington DC as a museum and centre of learning.

smithsonite /ˈsmɪθs(ə)nʌɪt/ *noun.* **M19.**
[from *Smithson* (see prec.) + -ITE[1].]
MINERALOGY. Orig., zinc silicate (hemimorphite). Now, zinc carbonate, an ore of zinc crystallizing in the rhombohedral system and occurring as yellowish, greyish, or greenish masses esp. associated with limestone. Cf. CALAMINE.

Smith Square /smɪθ ˈskwɛː/ *noun phr.* **M20.**
[A square in Westminster, London, location of the headquarters of the Labour Party between 1928 and 1980 and of the Conservative Party since 1958.]
The leadership of the Conservative Party. Also occas., leadership of both the Conservative and Labour parties.

Economist An honest message from Smith Square . . is that domestic rates are a much less onerous tax than people think.

Smith–Trager *noun* var. of TRAGER–SMITH.

smithy /ˈsmɪði/ *noun & verb.*
[Old English *smiþþe*, *smiððe* corresp. to Old Norse *smiðja*, Old Frisian *smithe*, Middle Low German *smede*, Middle Dutch *smisse* (Dutch *smidse*), Old High German *smidda*, *smitte* (German *Schmiede*). Replaced in Middle English by forms from Old Norse.]
▸ **A** *noun.* **1** A blacksmith's workshop; a forge. **OE.** ▸**b** A blacksmith. *US.* **M19.**
2 Smithcraft; smithery. *rare.* **E19.**
▸ **B** *verb.* **1** *verb trans.* = SMITH *verb* 1. **ME.**
2 *verb intrans.* = SMITH *verb* 2. **M18.**

smitten *verb pa. pple* of SMITE *verb.*

smock /smɒk/ *noun.*
[Old English *smoc* = Old High German *smoccho*, Old Norse *smokkr* (perh. from Old English); rel. to Middle High German *gesmuc* (German *Schmuck* ornament); prob. rel. to Old English *smūgan* creep, Middle High German *smiegen*, Old Norse *smjúga* creep into, put on a garment, Old English *æsmogu* snake skin, *smygel(ls)* burrow. Cf. SMICKET.]
1 A woman's loose-fitting undergarment resembling a shirt and worn next to the skin; a shift, a chemise. Now *arch. & dial.* **OE.** ▸†**b** A woman, *esp.* a promiscuous one. Usu. *attrib.* **L16–E18.**
2 a *Hist.* = SMOCK-FROCK 1. **M19.** ▸**b** A woman's or child's (now, girl's) loose dress or blouse resembling a smock-frock in having the upper part closely gathered in smocking. **E20.** ▸**c** Any loose overgarment or overall, esp. as worn by artists etc. to protect the clothes. **M20.**
Comb.: **smock-face** (now *rare*) (a person having) a pale and smooth or effeminate face; **smock-faced** *adjective* (now *rare*) having a pale smooth face; effeminate-looking; **smock-mill** a windmill with a revolving top; **smock-race** *Hist.* a race run by women or girls with a smock as a prize.
■ **smockless** *adjective* (*rare*) **LME.**

smock /smɒk/ *verb.* **E17.**
[from the noun.]
†**1** *verb trans.* Make effeminate or womanish. Only in **E17.**
†**2** *verb intrans.* Consort with women. *rare.* **E–M18.**
3 *verb trans.* Dress in a smock. **M19.**
4 *verb trans.* NEEDLEWORK. Adorn (material, a garment) with smocking. **L19.**
■ **smocker** *noun* †(*a*) a person who consorts with women; (*b*) a person who smocks garments or material: **E18.**

smock-frock /ˈsmɒkfrɒk/ *noun.* **L18.**
[from SMOCK *noun* + FROCK *noun.*]
Hist. **1** A loose outer garment resembling a shirt and reaching to the knees or below, with the upper part closely gathered in smocking, formerly worn by a field-labourer or workman. **L18.**
2 A wearer of such a garment. **M19.**
¶ Earlier as simply *frock.*

smocking /ˈsmɒkɪŋ/ *noun.* **L19.**
[from SMOCK *verb* + -ING[1].]
NEEDLEWORK. Ornamentation of a garment produced by gathering a section of material into tight pleats which are held in place by parallel lines of stitches in an ornamental (esp. honeycomb) pattern.

U. HOLDEN A green frock with smocking across the yoke.

smog /smɒg/ *noun & verb.* **E20.**
[Blend of SMOKE *noun* and FOG *noun*[2].]
▸ **A** *noun.* **1** Fog intensified by smoke. **E20.**
2 *fig.* A state or condition of obscurity or confusion; something obscure or confusing. **M20.**
1 PHOTOCHEMICAL *smog.*
▸ **B** *verb trans.* Infl. **-gg-**. Cover or obscure with smog. Foll. by *out*, *up*. *N. Amer. colloq.* **M20.**
■ **smogless** *adjective* **M20.**

smoggy /ˈsmɒgi/ *adjective.* **E20.**
[from SMOG + -Y[1].]
Characterized by the presence of smog.
■ **smoggily** *adverb* **M20.**

smokable /ˈsməʊkəb(ə)l/ *adjective & noun.* Also **smokeable**. **E19.**
[from SMOKE *verb* + -ABLE.]
▸ **A** *adjective.* **1** Able to be ridiculed. Cf. SMOKE *verb* 8. *arch. rare.* **E19.**
2 That may be smoked; fit or suitable for smoking. **M19.**
▸ **B** *noun.* A thing which may be smoked. Usu. in *pl.* **M19.**

smoke /sməʊk/ *noun & adjective.*
[Old English *smoca*, from Germanic weak grade of base repr. by Old English *smēocan* SMEEK *verb*, (with different grade) Old English *smēoc*, Middle Dutch *smoock* (Dutch *smook*), Middle & mod. Low German *smōk*, Middle High German *smouch* (German *Schmauch*). Cf. next.]
▸ **A** *noun.* **1** The visible suspension of carbon and other particles in air, given off by a burning or smouldering substance. **OE.** ▸**b** A colour like that of smoke; a brownish or bluish shade of grey. **L19.**
2 a A volume, cloud, or column of smoke; *spec.* (*US & Austral.*) such a column etc. serving as a signal, sign of an encampment, etc. Also, a particular kind of smoke. **LME.** ▸**b** The smoke rising from a hearth or fireplace; *transf.* a hearth, a fireplace, a house. Now *rare.* **L16.** ▸†**c** = SMUDGE *noun*[1] 2. *N. Amer.* **L17–M19.**
3 a Fume or vapour caused by the action of heat on moisture. Now *rare.* **LME.** ▸**b** A mist, a fog, a miasma. **M17.**
4 a A superficial or insubstantial thing. **M16.** ▸**b** A clouding or obscuring medium or influence; *spec.* false information intended as a distraction. **M16.**
5 a A substance for smoking; *spec.* (*a*) (now *rare*) tobacco; (*b*) opium; (*c*) marijuana. **E17.** ▸**b** A cigar; a cigarette. **L19.**
6 [from the verb.] An act or spell of smoking tobacco etc. **M19.**
7 a In full ***Cape smoke***. A cheap kind of brandy. *S. Afr. obsolete* exc. *Hist.* **M19** ▸**b** Cheap whiskey; an alcoholic concoction used as a whiskey substitute. *N. Amer.* **E20.**
8 (An animal of) a breed of Persian cat of a deep cinder-colour, with a white undercoat (also ***smoke Persian***); (an animal of) a short-haired breed of cat with similar colouring. **L19.**
9 A black person. *US slang* (*derog. & racially offensive*). **E20.**

1 J. BALDWIN Smoke rose out of the chimney, melting into the . . air. E. J. HOWARD Ann lit a cigarette, and blew the smoke away from Saki's face. L. SPALDING Fires burned all day, adding thick smoke to our . . crowded air. **2a** R. W. EMERSON On eastern hills I see their smokes. BROWNING They level: a volley, a smoke. J. KEROUAC Mexico City . . spewing city smokes. **4a** B. JOWETT The ambitious man will think . . knowledge without honour all smoke and nonsense. **b** F. W. FARRAR The lurid smoke of sectarian hate. **5b** J. R. ACKERLEY He misses his smokes . . . I always take a packet when I go. **6** JOYCE Ideal spot to have a quiet smoke.

Phrases: ***Cape smoke***: see sense 7a above. **end in smoke**, **vanish into smoke** *arch.* come to nothing, be unrealized. †**from the smoke into the smother** (*rare*, Shakes.) from one evil to an even worse one. **go up in smoke** *colloq.* (*a*) be consumed by fire; be destroyed completely; (*b*) lose one's temper; (*c*) (of a plan etc.) come to nothing. **have a smoke** smoke a cigarette, pipe, etc. **in smoke**, **into smoke** (*slang*, chiefly *Austral.*) in(to) hiding. **like smoke** very quickly, rapidly. ***no smoke without fire***: see FIRE *noun.* ***side-stream smoke***: see ***side-stream*** (a) s.v. SIDE *noun.* **smoke and mirrors** *N. Amer.* the obscuring or embellishing of the truth of a situation with misleading or irrelevant information. **take a smoke** = ***have a smoke*** above. **the Smoke**, **the big Smoke**, **the great Smoke** *colloq.* London; (chiefly *Austral.*) any large city or town. ***vanish into smoke***: see ***end in smoke*** above. **watch someone's smoke** (*slang*, chiefly *US*) watch someone go, observe someone's actions.

Comb.: **smoke alarm** a device that automatically detects and gives a warning of the presence of smoke; **smoke-ball** (*a*) a puff-ball; (*b*) a projectile filled with material which emits dense smoke on ignition, used to conceal military operations etc.; **smoke-black** a form of lampblack obtained by the combustion of resinous materials; **smoke-boat** *Nautical slang* a steamer; **smoke bomb**: that produces a smokescreen on exploding; **smoke-box** a chamber in a steam engine or boiler between the flues and the funnel or chimney stack; **smoke bush** = ***smoke plant*** below; **smoke candle** an oil-based smoke-producing munition; **smoke canister** a canister whose contents can be ignited to produce smoke, used as a signal; **smoke concert** *NZ* a concert at which smoking is allowed; **smoke detector** a device that automatically detects the presence of smoke; **smoke dry** *verb trans.* dry or cure (meat, fish, etc.) by exposure to smoke (usu. as ***smoke-dried*** *ppl adjective*); **smoke-farthing** *Hist.* (*a*) a Whitsuntide offering made by the householders of a diocese to the cathedral church; (*b*) a hearth-tax; **smoke goggles**: that protect the eyes against smoke; **smoke grenade**: that emits a cloud of smoke on impact; **smoke-head** (*a*) the head of a column of smoke; (*b*) NAUTICAL a funnel; **smoke helmet**: enabling the wearer to see and breathe while in smoke; **smoke-hole** the vent or outside opening of a flue; a hole in a roof through which the smoke of a fire can escape; **smoke-house** (*a*) (chiefly *N. Amer.*) a house or room for curing meat, fish, etc., by exposure to smoke; (*b*) a room in a tannery, heated by smouldering spent tan, where hides are unhaired; **smoke-jack** (*a*) *Hist.* an apparatus set in a chimney for turning a roasting-spit, moved by the air current passing up the chimney; (*b*) a flue in the roof of a locomotive engine; **smoke-jumper** *N. Amer.* a fire-fighter who arrives by parachute to extinguish a forest fire; **smoke-jumping** *N. Amer.* jumping by parachute from an aircraft, in order to extinguish a forest fire; **smoke-meter** an instrument for measuring the density or composition of smoke; ***smoke Persian***: see sense 8 above; **smoke plant** any of several plants of the genus *Cotinus* (family Anacardiaceae) having a feathery inflorescence suggestive of smoke; esp. *C. coggygria*, a Mediterranean shrub allied to sumac, with similar uses in tanning (also called ***Venetian sumac***); **smoke point** (*a*) the lowest temperature at which an oil or fat gives off smoke; (*b*) the height of the tallest flame with which a particular sample of kerosene or fuel oil will burn without giving off smoke; **smoke-pole** *slang* a firearm; **smoke pot** a container holding burning material to keep off insects etc.; **smoke respirator**: enabling the wearer to breathe while in smoke; **smoke-ring** smoke from a cigarette etc. exhaled in the shape of a ring; **smoke rocket**: that emits smoke; **smoke shell**: that emits dense smoke after firing; **smoke-shop** (now *N. Amer.*) †(*a*) a tobacconist's shop with a smoking-room; (*b*) a tobacconist's shop, a newsagent's shop; (*c*) a place where people gather to smoke and talk; (*d*) a bar, *esp.* one selling cheap liquor; **smoke-signal** a column of smoke used as a signal; **smoke-stick** *slang* = ***smoke-pole*** above; **smoke-stone** cairngorm; **smoke-tree** (*a*) = ***smoke plant*** above; (*b*) an allied N. American shrub, *Cotinus obovatus*; **smoke tunnel** a form of wind tunnel using smoke filaments to make the airflow visible; **smoke-wagon** *US slang* a firearm.

▶ **B** *adjective.* Of the colour of smoke; brownish- or bluish-grey. **L19.**

■ **smokish** *adjective* (now *rare*) resembling smoke; somewhat smoky: **L15.**

smoke /sməʊk/ *verb.*
[Old English *smocian*, from *smoca* SMOKE *noun*; corresp. (with different grade) to Middle & mod. Dutch, Middle & mod. Low German *smoken*, Low German *smöken*, German *schmauchen, schmäuchen*. Cf. prec., SMEEK *verb*.]

▶ **I 1** *verb intrans.* **a** Emit smoke. **OE.** ▶**b** (Of an oil-lamp etc.) burn badly with the emission of smoke; (of a chimney or fire) discharge smoke into a room; (of a room) become filled with smoke. **M17.**

2 *verb intrans.* **a** Emit visible vapour, dust, spray, etc.; *esp.* emit steam. Now *poet.* **LME.** ▶**b** Rise, spread, or move like smoke. Also foll. by *along.* **L16.** ▶**c** Move or travel *along* rapidly. **L17.** ▶**d** Depart; slope *off. Austral. slang.* **L19.**

3 *verb intrans.* Smart, suffer severely. *arch.* **M16.**

📖 **1a** J. CONRAD An indolent volcano which smoked faintly. *fig.*: DE QUINCEY Ireland was . . smoking with the embers of rebellion. **2a** C. CAUSLEY Although the month was May, my breath On the morning smoked. **b** J. CLARE Thin clouds smoke along the sky.

▶ **II 4** *verb trans.* **a** Expose to smoke, *spec.* in order to (*a*) cleanse, purify, or fumigate, (*b*) suffocate or stupefy. **OE.** ▶**b** Darken or discolour by exposure to smoke. **E17.** ▶**c** Dry or cure (meat, fish, etc.) by exposure to smoke. **M18.**

5 *verb trans.* Drive *out* or *away* by means of smoke; *fig.* force or bring *out* into the open. **L16.**

6 a *verb trans.* Get an inkling of, suspect, (a plot, design, etc.). *arch.* **E17.** ▶**b** *verb intrans.* Have an inkling or idea; understand. *arch.* **L17.**

7 *verb trans.* †**a** Urge on at high speed. *rare.* Only in **M17.** ▶**b** Cause (a tyre) to smoulder from sudden friction with the road surface. *colloq.* **L20.**

8 *verb trans.* Make fun of; ridicule, torment. *arch.* **L17.**

9 *verb trans.* Observe, note. *arch.* **E18.**

10 *verb trans.* Shoot with a firearm. *US slang.* **E20.**

📖 **4c** J. W. BODDAM-WHETHAM The fish are smoked over a fire. T. MCGUANE Edward gave the secretaries duck he smoked himself. **5** *Listener* We were using a food guide, . . determined to smoke out tasty food. P. WARNER The garrison tried to smoke them out by lighting a fire at the entrance.

▶ **III 11 a** *verb intrans.* Inhale and exhale the smoke of tobacco, or some other substance, from a pipe, cigar, or cigarette; do this habitually. **E17.** ▶**b** *verb trans.* Use (tobacco, a cigarette, etc.) in this way. **L17.** ▶**c** *verb intrans.* Of a pipe: draw. **E19.**

12 *verb trans.* Wear *out*, waste (*away*), bring *into* a specified condition, by smoking tobacco etc. **E17.**

📖 **11a** G. GREENE He smoked while he talked, never taking the cigarette from his mouth. *New Yorker* He neither drinks nor smokes. ***smoke like a chimney***: see CHIMNEY *noun* 4. **b** W. IRVING Smoking his pipe in the . . evening sunshine. *Times* Three boys have been expelled . . for smoking cannabis resin.

smokeable *adjective & noun* var. of SMOKABLE.

smoked /sməʊkt/ *ppl adjective.* **E17.**
[from SMOKE *verb* + -ED[1].]

1 Of meat, fish, etc.: dried, cured, or tainted by exposure to smoke, or *loosely* by a process that produces a similar effect. **E17.**

2 Esp. of glass: darkened by exposure to smoke. **M18.**

3 Of the colour of smoke. Cf. SMOKE *adjective.* **E19.**

1a ***smoked chicken, smoked ham, smoked mackerel***, etc. **smoked sheet** a form of raw rubber that is preserved for transportation by drying the coagulated latex in a smoky atmosphere.

smoke-ho *noun* var. of SMOKO.

smokeless /ˈsməʊklɪs/ *adjective.* **L16.**
[from SMOKE *noun* + -LESS.]

Emitting or producing no smoke; free from or clear of smoke.

smokeless zone a district in which only smokeless fuel may be used for fires etc.

■ **smokelessly** *adverb* **L19.** **smokelessness** *noun* **L19.**

smoker /ˈsməʊkə/ *noun.* **L16.**
[from SMOKE *verb* + -ER[1].]

1 A person who cures food by means of smoke. **L16.**

2 A person who habitually smokes tobacco etc. **E17.**

3 A thing which emits smoke; *spec.* †(*a*) a vessel used to conceal hostile operations by discharging volumes of smoke; †(*b*) a smoky chimney, locomotive, etc.; (*c*) a device for stupefying bees; (*d*) *colloq.* a motor vehicle or engine that emits excessive exhaust fumes. **L17.** ▶**b** *OCEANOGRAPHY.* A hydrothermal vent from which water and mineral particles issue; a cylindrical or other structure formed by mineral deposition around such a vent. **L20.**

4 a (A section of) a railway carriage in which smoking is permitted. **L19.** ▶**b** A concert, cabaret, or other entertainment (orig. *spec.* at which smoking was permitted). **L19.** ▶**c** An informal social gathering of men. Chiefly *US.* **L19.**

📖 **2** M. C. GERALD The . . greater incidence of lung cancer among cigarette smokers. A. N. WILSON He was a heavy smoker—sixty cigarettes a day. ***passive smoker***: see PASSIVE *adjective.*

Comb.: **smoker's cough** a severe cough caused by smoking; **smoker's heart**, **smoker's throat** a diseased condition of the heart or throat caused by smoking.

smoke-room /ˈsməʊkruːm/ *noun.* **L19.**
[from SMOKE *noun* or *verb* + ROOM *noun*[1].]

A smoking-room.

smokery /ˈsməʊkəri/ *noun.* **M17.**
[from SMOKE *noun* or *verb* + -ERY.]

A place where something is subjected to the effects of smoke. Long only *spec.*, a place where meat, fish, etc., are cured by exposure to smoke.

smokescreen /ˈsməʊkskriːn/ *noun & verb.* **E20.**
[from SMOKE *noun* + SCREEN *noun*[1].]

▶ **A** *noun.* **1** A cloud of smoke, *spec.* one diffused to conceal esp. military or naval operations or a stretch of land or sea. **E20.**

2 *fig.* Something designed to conceal or mislead; a deliberate distraction or diversion. **E20.**

📖 **2** L. KENNEDY Condon was ready with a smoke-screen of verbiage. *City Limits* The grammar school issue has dominated everything, but it's a smokescreen.

▶ **B** *verb trans.* Deceive or conceal by a smokescreen. **E20.**

📖 I. S. BLACK You made a balls of it . . . Nothing is going to smoke-screen that. H. H. TAN Don't think you can smoke-screen me with all that literary crap.

smokestack /ˈsməʊkstak/ *noun.* **M19.**
[from SMOKE *noun* + STACK *noun.*]

1 The funnel of a steamer. **M19.**

2 A chimney, esp. of a locomotive or factory. **M19.**

Comb.: **smokestack industry** a heavy manufacturing industry, typically coal-powered and associated with high pollution levels and outmoded technology.

smokey *adjective & noun* see SMOKY.

smokie *adjective & noun* see SMOKY.

smoking /ˈsməʊkɪŋ/ *noun.* **M16.**
[from SMOKE *verb* + -ING[1].]

1 The action of SMOKE *verb*; *spec.* the action of inhaling and exhaling smoke from a cigarette, cigar, etc. **M16.**

2 A train compartment, section of a restaurant, etc., in which smoking is allowed. Usu. *attrib.* **M16.**

3 In full ***smoking-jacket***. A jacket of velvet or other rich cloth, usu. trimmed with braid, formerly worn by men when smoking. Also, a dinner jacket. **L19.**

1 ***passive smoking***: see PASSIVE *adjective.*

Comb.: **smoking concert**: at which smoking is allowed; ***smoking jacket***: see sense 3 above; **smoking point**, **smoking temperature** = ***smoke point*** (a) s.v. SMOKE *noun*; **smoking-room** a room in a house, hotel, club, etc., set aside for smoking in; **smoking stand** an ashtray on a low pedestal.

smoking /ˈsməʊkɪŋ/ *ppl adjective.* **LME.**
[from SMOKE *verb* + -ING[2].]

1 That smokes. **LME.**

2 (Freq. **smokin'**.) Lively and exciting; skilful; 'hot'. *slang.* **L20.**

📖 **1 smoking gun, smoking pistol** *fig.* (chiefly *US*) a piece of incontrovertible incriminating evidence. **2** *Relix* The boys [a rock group] respond with a smokin' first set.

smoko /ˈsməʊkəʊ/ *noun. Austral. & NZ colloq.* Also **smoke-ho**. Pl. **-os** **M19.**
[from SMOKE *noun* 6 + -O.]

1 A stoppage of work for a rest and a smoke; a tea break; a cup of tea or snack taken at work. **M19.**

2 = ***smoke concert*** s.v. SMOKE *noun.* **E20.**

smoky /ˈsməʊki/ *adjective & noun.* Also (esp. in sense B.2) **smokey**, (esp. in senses B.1, 2) **smokie**. **ME.**
[from SMOKE *noun* + -Y[1].]

▶ **A** *adjective.* **1** Emitting smoke in considerable volume. **ME.**

2 Of vapour, mist, etc.: resembling smoke. **LME.**

3 Full of or obscured by smoke. **LME.** ▶**b** Blackened by smoke. **M16.** ▶**c** Foggy, misty. Now *rare. US.* **M18.**

4 *fig.* Obscure, insubstantial, mysterious. **LME.**

5 Tasting or smelling of smoke. Also, having the taste or flavour of smoked food. **M16.** ▶**b** *fig.* Of a sound: smooth, low, sultry. **M20.**

6 Of the colour of smoke. **M16.**

7 Steaming; rising in fine spray. **L16.**

8 Addicted to or associated with the smoking of tobacco etc. *arch.* **L16.**

†**9** Quick to suspect or take note of something; shrewd, suspicious. **L17–L18.**

📖 **1** *St James's Gazette* The noisiest and smokiest fireworks procurable. **3** U. HOLDEN The kitchen, smoky . . with burning fat. **5** E. DAVID The smoky wines of Pouilly-sur-Loire. **b** G. LEES The smoky autumnal trombone of Lawrence Brown.

Special collocations: **Smokey Bear** *slang* (chiefly *US*) [a character in US fire-prevention advertising] (*a*) a type of wide-brimmed hat; (*b*) = sense B.2 below. **smoky quartz** a greyish-brown to nearly black semiprecious variety of quartz (cf. ***cairngorm***).

▶ **B** *noun.* Pl. **smokeys**, **smokies**.

1 A smoked haddock. Chiefly *Scot.* **L19.**

2 A police officer; *collect.* the police. *slang* (chiefly *US & Austral.*). **L20.**

📖 **1** *Sunday Telegraph* The . . Arbroath smokie, which gets its colour from the . . smoke when the fish is cured. **2** *Courier-Mail (Brisbane)* Lorry drivers . . warn: 'Smokey down the line'.

■ **smokily** *adverb* **E17.** **smokiness** *noun* **L16.**

smolt /sməʊlt/ *noun.* Orig. *Scot. & north.* **LME.**
[Origin uncertain: cf. SMELT *noun.*]

1 A young salmon in the stage after the parr, when it becomes silvery in appearance and migrates to the sea. **LME.**

2 *transf.* A small person or thing. **E19.**

smon /smɒn/ *noun.* Also **SMON**. **L20.**
[Acronym, from subacute *myelo-optico-neuropathy*.]

MEDICINE. A disease of the nervous system characterized by recurrent motor, sensory, and visual symptoms, freq. including numbness of the legs, and sometimes associated with the use of clioquinol or related drugs.

smooch /smuːtʃ/ *noun. colloq.* **M20.**
[from SMOOCH *verb*[3]. Cf. SMOUCH *noun*[1].]

A kiss; a spell of kissing and caressing. Also, (a spell of) slow close dancing; (music suitable for) a dance of this nature.

smooch /smuːtʃ/ *verb*[1] *trans.* Now *US.* **M17.**
[Cf. SMUTCH *verb.*]

Sully, dirty.

smooch /smuːtʃ/ *verb*[2] *intrans. dial. & colloq.* **E20.**
[App. alt. of MOOCH *verb.*]

Sneak, creep; wander or prowl *(a)round.*

smooch /smuːtʃ/ *verb*[3] *intrans. colloq.* **M20.**
[Var. of SMOUCH *verb*[1].]

Engage in a smooch; kiss, esp. while dancing to slow music.

■ **smoocher** *noun* (*a*) a person who engages in a smooch; (*b*) a song or piece of music suitable for slow close dancing: **M20.**

smoochy /ˈsmuːtʃi/ *adjective. colloq.* **M20.**
[from SMOOCH *verb*[3] or *noun* + -Y[1].]

Amorous, sexy; *spec.* (of music) suitable to accompany slow close dancing.

📖 *Debbie* Smoochy music . . to get him in the mood for romance.

■ **smoochily** *adverb* **L20.** **smoochiness** *noun* **L20.**

smoodge /smuːdʒ/ *verb intrans. Austral. & NZ colloq.* Also **smooge**. **L19.**
[Prob. alt. of SMOUCH *verb*[1].]

Act in an ingratiating or fawning manner; display affection, behave amorously.

■ **smoodger** *noun* a flatterer, a sycophant **L19.**

smoor /smʊə/ *verb & noun. Scot. & north.* **LME.**
[Perh. from Middle Dutch or Middle Low German *smōren* (Dutch *smoren*, Low German *smoren, smören*, German *schmoren*), corresp. to Old English *smorian* SMORE *verb.*]

▶ **A** *verb.* **1** *verb intrans.* Be suffocated. **LME.**

2 *verb trans.* Smother, suffocate; *fig.* conceal, suppress. **L15.**

▶ **B** *noun.* A stifling or suffocating atmosphere. **L19.**

smoot *verb* var. of SMOUT.

smooth /smuːð/ *noun.* **LME.**
[from the adjective Sense 3 from the verb.]

1 The smooth part or surface *of* something; smoothness; level ground, calm water; *fig.* the agreeable or pleasant part or aspect of something (freq. contrasted with ***rough***). **LME.**

2 a A level space or area. *local.* **LME.** ▶**b** *NAUTICAL.* A stretch of comparatively calm water in a rough sea. **M19.**

3 An act of smoothing something. **M19.**

4 A file etc. for smoothing a surface; a smoother. **L19.**

📖 **1** AV *Gen.* 27 She put the skinnes of the kids . . vpon the smooth of his necke. MILTON On smooth the Seale and bended Dolphins play.

smooth /smuːð/ *adjective & adverb.*
[Old English *smōþ*, prob. from Germanic but no known cognates. See also SMEETH *adjective.*]

▶ **A** *adjective.* **1** Having a surface free from projections, indentations, irregularities, or inequalities; presenting no roughness or unevenness to the touch or sight. **OE.** ▶**b** *MATH.* Of a graph, function, distribution, etc.: having no breaks, discontinuities, or irregularities; *esp.*

differentiable. M19. ▸**c** Designating the side of a tennis, squash, etc., racket opposite to the rough side (ROUGH *adjective* 1d), esp. used as a call when the racket is spun to decide the right to serve first or to choose ends. L19. ▸**d** BACTERIOLOGY. Of a bacterial phenotype: characterized by regular, smooth-looking colonies, and by cells having polysaccharide capsules. E20.

2 Free from hairs or bristles. LME.

3 Of ground, a route, etc.: not rugged, rough, or broken; level; free from obstructions; easy to traverse. LME.

4 Of water, the sea, etc.: not broken or turbulent; calm, not rough; running or flowing evenly or calmly. Also, (of a passage, voyage, etc.) accompanied by or undertaken in calm conditions. LME.

5 Of wind or weather: not rough or stormy; agreeable, pleasant. Now *rare*. LME.

6 a Having a uniform or even consistency, free from lumps. LME. ▸**b** Of alcoholic liquor: soft or pleasing to the taste, not astringent. M18.

7 Affable or polite of manner or speech; seemingly amiable or friendly; using specious or attractive language; plausible, bland, insinuating, flattering. LME. ▸**b** Superior, excellent, clever; stylish, suave, chic. *colloq.* L19.

8 Having an easy flow or correct rhythm, running smoothly; pleasantly modulated; (of sound) not harsh or grating. Also, having an easy polished style. L16.

9 Smoothing, producing smoothness. *rare*. L16.

10 Free from disturbance or excitement, untroubled; uninterrupted, unobstructed; not jerky. L18.

> 📖 **1** TENNYSON Brows as pale and smooth As . . deathless marble. B. BAINBRIDGE Not the slightest . . blemish disfigured the smooth surface. **2** COVERDALE *Gen.* 27:11 My brother Esau is rough, and I am smooth. **3** B. JOWETT The road to wickedness is smooth. **4 in smooth water** *fig.* having passed obstacles or difficulties. **6a** E. ACTON Mash to a smooth paste three pounds of . . potatoes. **7** J. TRAPP I . . with smooth Words Persuaded him t'intrust me with his Letter. W. COWPER That man, when smoothest he appears, Is most to be suspected. G. J. WHYTE-MELVILLE She is not to be won by a smooth tongue. **b** P. G. WODEHOUSE Smooth work, Uncle Percy . . . There can't be many fellows about with brains like yours. M. DICKENS Smooth characters with fast cars. **8** WORDSWORTH Smooth verse, inspired by no unlettered Muse. *Which?* Engine smooth and willing, pulling well even in . . fourth gear. **10** CARLYLE Consider too whether he had smooth times. I. MCEWAN When she opened the door . . it was a smooth, co-ordinated action.

▸ **B** *adverb*. Smoothly. LME.

> 📖 SHAKES. *Mids. N. D.* The course of true love never did run smooth. J. MASEFIELD The . . smooth-running . . typewriting machine.

Special collocations & comb.: **smooth blenny** the shanny, *Blennius pholis*. †**smooth-boots** (a name for) a flatterer, a slyly ingratiating or persuasive person. **smooth-bore** a cannon or gun with a smooth or unrifled barrel. ***smooth breathing***: see BREATHING 5. **smooth-faced** *adjective* having a smooth face or surface; clean-shaven, beardless; *fig.* having a bland, ingratiating, or plausible manner. **smooth flounder** a flounder, *Liopsetta putnami*, inhabiting muddy estuaries and inshore waters of the N. American Atlantic coast. ***smooth-haired terrier***: see TERRIER *noun*[1] 1a. **smooth-head** any of various deep-sea fishes constituting the family Alepocephalidae, resembling a herring with a larger body and dark-coloured skin. **smooth hound** any of various small shallow-water sharks of the genus *Mustelus*, spec. *M. asterias* and *M. mustelus* of European waters. **smooth muscle** ANATOMY unstriated muscle capable of sustained slow contraction and generally not under voluntary control, forming part of the walls of the alimentary canal, blood-vessels, etc. **smooth newt** the common European newt, *Triturus vulgaris*. **smooth snake** a usu. greyish non-venomous Eurasian colubrid snake, *Coronella austriaca*, occurring in small numbers in S. England. **smooth-spoken** *adjective* smooth-tongued, soft-spoken. ***smooth tare***: see TARE *noun*[1] 2a. **smooth-talk** *verb trans.* (*colloq.*) address or persuade with bland specious language; win (one's way) by this means. ***smooth tingle***: see TINGLE *noun*[2]. **smooth-tongued** *adjective* smooth or plausible in speech; (insincerely) using fair or flattering words; specious, persuasive.

■ **smoothish** *adjective* somewhat smooth L17. **smoothly** *adverb* LME. **smoothness** *noun* LME.

smooth /smuːð/ *verb*. Also **smoothe**. ME.
[from the adjective Cf. SMEETH *verb*.]

1 *verb trans.* Make (more) smooth, even, or level; remove or reduce the roughness, irregularity, inequality, or unevenness of; give a smooth or glossy surface to; make (a way) easy or plain; free from obstruction, difficulty, or impediment; make (the brow etc.) free from wrinkles, lines, frowns, etc.; give a calm or placid expression to; make more plausible or specious; make smooth to the ear, soften; refine, polish; make (the mind etc.) more tranquil, soothe. ME. ▸**b** Iron (linen etc.). *obsolete* exc. *dial.* E17. ▸**c** Cause (feathers, hair, etc.) to lie smooth and even. M17. ▸**d** PHONOLOGY. Reduce (a diphthong) to a simple vowel. Chiefly as ***smoothing verbal noun***. L19. ▸**e** MATH. Transform or modify (a graph, distribution, function, etc.) so as to make it smooth; lessen irregularities or fluctuations in (an output or other entity that can be represented by a graph etc.). L19.

†**2** *verb trans.* Use smooth, flattering, or complimentary language to. LME–E18.

3 *verb trans.* Remove, reduce, or get rid of (an irregularity, projection, wrinkle, inequality, roughness, etc.); diminish or clear away (an obstruction or difficulty); assuage, allay; hush up, gloss over. Also foll. by *over*, *out*. L16.

4 *verb intrans.* Become smooth, calm, or tranquil. M19.

> 📖 **1** SHAKES. *Rich. III* Grim-visag'd Warre, hath smooth'd his wrinkled Front. MILTON Harmonie Divine So smooths her charming tones. TENNYSON Hesperus . . Smoothing the wearied mind. J. H. BLUNT His . . work was to smooth the way for Cardinal Pole's return. J. STEINBECK He smoothed out his crushed hat. J. BETJEMAN Unrelenting tide . . smoothed the strata of the steep hillside. K. A. PORTER She . . smoothed the . . rumpled sheet. **smoothing-iron** *Hist.* a flat-iron. **smoothing-plane** a small fine-set plane for finishing wood. **c** A. BROOKNER He . . smoothed her hair back from her forehead. ***smooth a person's ruffled feathers***: see FEATHER *noun*. **2** *absol.*: SHAKES. *Rich. III* Smile in men's faces, smooth, deceive. **3** W. BLACK Minor inconveniences were soon smoothed over. N. CHOMSKY New Deal measures had smoothed many of the rough edges of the great depression. I. MURDOCH He smoothed the frown from his face. *Daily Telegraph* The Americans will . . smooth out fluctuations in the exchange rate. N. FARAH She smoothed his wrinkles with her . . palm.

■ **smoothable** *adjective* M17. **smoother** *noun* E17. **smoothingly** *adverb* in a smoothing manner, so as to smooth matters M19.

smoothen /ˈsmuːð(ə)n/ *verb*. M17.
[from SMOOTH *adjective* + -EN[5].]

1 *verb trans.* = SMOOTH *verb* 1,3. M17.

2 *verb intrans.* = SMOOTH *verb* 4. L19.

smoothie /ˈsmuːði/ *noun & adjective*. *colloq.* Also **-y**. E20.
[from SMOOTH *adjective* + -IE.]

▸ **A** *noun*. **1** A person who is smooth; *esp.* a suave or stylish man; a slick but shallow or insincere man. E20.

2 A smooth thick drink of fresh fruit puréed with milk, yoghurt, or ice-cream. L20.

> 📖 **1** C. RICE This poetic-looking smoothie makes a thing out of marrying women with money. H. JENKINS The international art-market . . . is a racket . . operated by cultivated smoothies.

▸ **B** *adjective*. = SMOOTH *adjective* 7. M20.

smørbrød /ˈsməːbrəːd/ *noun*. M20.
[Norwegian, from *smøre* butter + *brød* bread: cf. SMØRREBRØD.]

In Norway: an open sandwich; food consisting of open sandwiches.

smore /smɔː/ *verb & noun*. Now *Scot. & north*.
[Old English *smorian* corresp. to Middle & mod. Low German, Middle & mod. Dutch *smoren*, of unkn. origin. Cf. SMOOR, SMOTHER *noun*, *verb*.]

▸ **A** *verb*. **1** *verb trans.* Suffocate, smother; *fig.* suppress, keep down. OE.

2 *verb intrans.* Choke, be suffocated. LME.

3 *verb intrans.* Smoulder. *rare*. LME.

▸ **B** *noun*. A stifling or dense atmosphere heavy with smoke, mist, rain, snow, etc. LME.

smorgasbord /ˈsmɔːɡəsbɔːd/ *noun*. L19.
[Swedish *smörgåsbord*, from *smörgås* (slice of) bread and butter (from *smör* butter, *gås* goose, lump of butter) + *bord* board, table.]

1 Open sandwiches served with delicacies as hors d'oeuvres or a buffet, orig. and esp. in Scandinavia. L19.

2 *fig.* A medley, a miscellany, a variety. M20.

smørrebrød /ˈsməːrəbrəːd, -ð/ *noun*. E20.
[Danish, from *smør* butter + *brød* bread: cf. SMØRBRØD.]

In Denmark: an open sandwich; food consisting of open sandwiches.

smorzando /smɔːˈtsandəʊ/ *adverb, adjective, & noun*. E19.
[Italian, pres. pple of *smorzare* extinguish.]

MUSIC. ▸**A** *adverb & adjective*. A direction: dying away. E19.

▸ **B** *noun*. Pl. **-dos**, **-di** /-di/. A smorzando passage. E19.

smote *verb pa. t. & pple*: see SMITE *verb*.

smother /ˈsmʌðə/ *noun & verb*. ME.
[from Old English base of *smorian* SMORE *verb*.]

▸ **A** *noun*. **1** Dense, suffocating, or stifling smoke. Also, a smouldering state or condition, a smouldering fire. ME.

2 Dense or suffocating dust, fog, etc., filling the air; a surging mass (*of* water etc.). L17.

3 a RUGBY FOOTBALL. A high tackle in which a player smothers an opponent. Also ***smother-tackle***. E20. ▸**b** An incident in which sheep are suffocated by others falling on top of them. *NZ*. M20.

> 📖 **2** R. H. DANA We . . brought the boat to in a smother of foam. R. L. STEVENSON The muffle and smother of these fallen clouds.

▸ **B** *verb*. **I** *verb trans.* **1** Suffocate, stifle; kill by stopping the breath of or excluding air from. ME. ▸**b** *fig.* Defeat rapidly or utterly. Chiefly *US*. L19.

2 Deaden or extinguish (fire etc.) by covering so as to exclude the air; cause to smoulder. L16. ▸**b** Cook in a covered vessel. E18.

3 a Cover up so as to conceal or cause to be forgotten; suppress all mention of, hush up. Freq. foll. by *up*. L16. ▸**b** Repress or refrain from displaying (feeling, etc.) by self-control. L16.

4 Cover up so as to prevent from having free play or development; suppress or check in this way; make (words etc.) indistinct or inaudible. L16. ▸**b** SPORT. Stop the motion of (the ball, a shot, etc.); RUGBY FOOTBALL tackle with a powerful embrace of the body and arms, preventing the release of the ball. M19.

5 Cover densely or thickly with something; *fig.* overwhelm with kisses, kindness, etc. (Foll. by *in*, *with*.) L16.

> 📖 **1** DEFOE The House . . fell in upon them, and they were smothered. H. NORMAN He hugs me like he's going to smother me. **2b** J. WOODFORDE Rabbits smothered with onions. **3a** R. L. STEVENSON He's as anxious as you and I to smother things up. **b** L. GRANT-ADAMSON Oliver smothered another yawn. **4** SHAKES. *Macb.* Function is smother'd in surmise. A. MACRAE All this always doing things *together* . . I'm so smothered by him. *Wonder Woman* Babiri's cries are smothered beneath the deafening roar of a city gone mad. **5** H. JAMES Its clustered chimneys, its windows smothered in creepers. A. C. AMOR Smothered in his mother's love from infancy.

▸ **II** *verb intrans.* **6** Be suffocated or stifled; be prevented from breathing freely. E16.

7 Of a fire: die down through lack of air, smoulder, burn slowly. *obsolete* exc. *dial.* M16.

Comb. & phrases: ***from the smoke into the smother***: see SMOKE *noun*. **smother crop** a crop grown to suppress weeds. **smothered mate** CHESS: in which the king, having no vacant square to move to, is checkmated by a knight. **smother-fly** *dial.* an aphid, a blackfly infesting plants. **smother-kiln**: in which pottery in the process of firing is blackened by smoke. ***smother-tackle***: see sense A.3a above.

■ **smotherable** *adjective* (earlier in UNSMOTHERABLE) E19. **smotheˈration** *noun* (*colloq.*) the action of smothering; the state or condition of being smothered; suffocation: E19. **smotherer** *noun* M17. **smotheringly** *adverb* so as to smother someone or something L18. **smothery** *adjective* tending to smother a person or thing; stifling: E17.

smouch /smaʊtʃ/ *noun*[1]. *obsolete* exc. *dial.* L16.
[Imit. Cf. SMOOCH *noun*.]

A kiss.

†**smouch** *noun*[2]. *slang*. M18–M19.
[Alt. of SMOUSE *noun*. Cf. SMOUCH *verb*[2].]

A Jew.

smouch /smaʊtʃ/ *noun*[3]. *slang*. *obsolete* exc. *Hist.* L18.
[Origin unkn.]

Dried leaves of ash etc. used to adulterate tea.

smouch /smaʊtʃ/ *verb*[1] *intrans. & trans.* *obsolete* exc. *dial.* L16.
[Imit. Cf. German dial. *schmutzen*. Cf. SMOOCH *verb*[3], SMOODGE.]

Kiss.

smouch /smaʊtʃ/ *verb*[2] *trans.* *slang*. Chiefly *US*. E19.
[Perh. rel. to SMOUCH *noun*[2].]

Acquire dishonestly; pilfer.

smoulder /ˈsməʊldə/ *verb & noun*. Also ***smolder**. LME.
[Origin uncertain: obscurely rel. to Low German *smöln*, Middle Dutch *smölen* (Dutch *smeulen*), Flemish *smoel* sultry.]

▸ **A** *verb*. **1** *verb trans.* Smother, suffocate. Long *obsolete* exc. *dial.* LME.

2 *verb intrans.* Burn slowly with smoke but without flame. LME. ▸**b** *fig.* Exist or continue in a suppressed or concealed state; (of emotions etc.) burn internally or invisibly; (of a person) show or feel silent or suppressed anger, resentment, etc. E19.

> 📖 **2** *fig.*: E. F. BENSON Little bits of reflected sky, in which the starlight smouldered. **b** L. STRACHEY Opposition to the whole scheme, which had long been smouldering . . suddenly burst forth. J. P. HENNESSY His resentment at . . his mother's long desertion smouldered on. A. C. CLARKE Brant was still smouldering slightly from the major's reprimand.

▸ **B** *noun*. **1** Smoky vapour; smoke from smouldering or slow combustion. LME.

2 A slow-burning fire; smouldering ashes. M16.

¶ From E17 rare exc. as *smouldering ppl adjective* until revived by Sir Walter Scott and others in E19.

■ **smoulderingly** *adverb* with smouldering L19. †**smouldery** *adjective* suffocating, stifling L16–M17.

smouse /smaʊz/ *noun*. In sense 2 also **smous** /smaʊs/. E18.
[Dutch, corresp. to German *Schmus* talk, patter from Yiddish *schmuess*, Hebrew *šĕmūʿōt* tales, news.]

1 A Jew. *slang*. Now *rare* or *obsolete*. E18.

2 An itinerant trader. *S. Afr.* (chiefly *Hist.*). M19.

smouse /smaʊz/ *verb trans. & intrans.* *rare*. L18.
[German *schmausen* (Low German *smûsen*).]

Feast (on).

smout /smuːt/ *verb intrans.* *arch. slang*. Also **smoot**. L17.
[Origin unkn.]

PRINTING. Do casual work in a printing-house where one is not regularly employed.

SMP *abbreviation*.

Statutory maternity pay.

SMPTE *abbreviation.*
Society of Television and Motion Picture Engineers (used to denote a time coding system for synchronizing video and audio tapes).

SMS *abbreviation.*
Short Message (or Messaging) Service, a system that enables mobile phone users to send and receive text messages.

smudge /smʌdʒ/ *noun*[1]. Chiefly *N. Amer.* **M18.**
[from SMUDGE *verb*[2].]
1 (A) dense or suffocating smoke. **M18.**
2 A smoky fire lit as a means of keeping off insects, protecting plants against frost, etc. **E19.**
Comb.: **smudge-fire** = sense 2 above; **smudge-pot** a container holding burning material to act as a smudge.

smudge /smʌdʒ/ *noun*[2]. **L18.**
[from SMUDGE *verb*[1].]
1 A dirty mark or stain, such as is caused by trying to rub out a previous mark; a smear of dirt; a blurred mark, a blot. **L18.**
2 a The scum of paint. Now *rare.* **E19.** ▸**b** Very small coal, slack. *local.* **L19.**
3 A smeary condition; the result of smudging. **M19.**
4 (A photograph taken by) a street or press photographer. *slang.* **M20.**

📖 **1** V. WOOLF There was a green smudge on her pinafore. *fig.*: T. HARDY The smudge which Tess had set upon that nobility.

smudge /smʌdʒ/ *verb*[1]. **LME.**
[Prob. symbolic: cf. *smirch, smut*, etc.]
1 *verb trans.* Mark with a smudge or smudges; soil, stain. **LME.** ▸**b** *fig.* Defile, sully, disgrace. **E17.**
2 *verb trans.* Make a smudge of; rub out, paint on, etc., in a smearing or daubing manner; blur or smear the lines of. **M19.**
3 *verb intrans.* Make or leave a smudge; become smeared or blurred. **E20.**

📖 **1** A. RANSOME Eyes sore from smoke . . and faces smudged with charcoal. P. CAREY This was a boy . . whose school books would be smudged and blotted. **b** *Guardian Weekly* Those who opposed my attacks . . found it much easier . . to try to smudge my own character. **2** M. ATWOOD Her eyeshadow was smudged. *fig.*: A. N. WILSON Details of his disgrace . . had been smudged by the passage of time.

■ **smudger** *noun* (**a**) a person who smudges; (**b**) *slang* a street or press photographer: **L19.**

smudge /smʌdʒ/ *verb*[2]. **L16.**
[Origin unkn. Cf. SMUDGE *noun*[1].]
†**1** *verb trans.* Cure (herring) by smoking. Only in **L16.**
2 *verb intrans.* Smoulder. *dial.* **E19.**
3 *verb trans.* Orig. *N. Amer.* ▸**a** Fill with smoke from a smudge; cause (a fire) to smoke; drive (insects) *away* by smoke. Now *rare.* **M19.** ▸**b** Among N. American Indians, smoke (pottery) in order to produce a black shiny finish. **M20.** ▸**c** Burn sage, cedar, or other fragrant materials in (a room, house, etc.), as part of a N. American Indian or New Age purification ritual. Usu. as ***smudging*** *verbal noun.* **L20.**

smudgeless /ˈsmʌdʒlɪs/ *adjective.* **E20.**
[from SMUDGE *noun*[2], *verb*[1] + -LESS.]
That will not smudge or smear; not having a smudge, clean.

smudgy /ˈsmʌdʒi/ *adjective*[1]. **M19.**
[from SMUDGE *noun*[2] or *verb*[1] + -Y[1].]
1 Marked with smudges; grimy, dirty; likely to produce smudges. **M19.**
2 Smeared, blurred, indistinct. **M19.**
■ **smudgily** *adverb* **M19.** **smudginess** *noun* **M19.**

smudgy /ˈsmʌdʒi/ *adjective*[2]. **M19.**
[from SMUDGE *noun*[1] or *verb*[2] + -Y[1].]
1 Stifling, stuffy; foggy. *dial.* **M19.**
2 Giving out much smoke; smoky. Chiefly *N. Amer.* **L19.**

†**smug** *noun*[1]. **E17–E18.**
[Origin unkn.]
A blacksmith.

smug /smʌg/ *noun*[2]. **L19.**
[from the adjective.]
1 A hard-working student, a swot. *Univ. slang.* Now *rare.* **L19.**
2 A smug or self-satisfied person. **L19.**

smug /smʌg/ *adjective.* Compar. & superl. **-gg-**. **M16.**
[Low German *smuk* pretty. For final *g* cf. SAG *verb.*]
Orig., trim, neat, spruce, smart, tidy; (esp. of the face) smooth, sleek. Now, having a self-satisfied, conceited, complacent, or consciously respectable air; indicative of or characterized by complacency or self-satisfaction.

📖 SHAKES. *1 Hen. IV* The smug and silver Trent shall run. W. COWPER Sleek their heads And smug their countenances. C. KINGSLEY Addressing the audience . . in the most smug and self-satisfied tone. E. TAYLOR She wore the smug expression of an expert being watched by the unskilled.

■ **smuggery** *noun* (*rare*) smugness, self-satisfaction; an instance of smug behaviour: **E20.** **smuggish** *adjective* (*rare*) somewhat smug **M18.** **smugly** *adverb* **L16.** **smugness** *noun* **M17.**

smug /smʌg/ *verb*[1] *trans.* Infl. **-gg-**. **L16.**
[from the adjective Sense 2 perh. a different word: cf. SMUGGLE *verb*[2].]
1 Smarten up (oneself, one's appearance, etc.), make neat or spruce. Usu. foll. by *up.* Now *rare.* **L16.**
2 *verb intrans.* Caress, fondle. *dial. rare.* **E19.**

smug /smʌg/ *verb*[2] *trans. slang.* Infl. **-gg-**. **E19.**
[Origin unkn.]
Steal, filch, run away with.

smuggle /ˈsmʌg(ə)l/ *verb*[1] *trans.* **L17.**
[Low German *smukkelen, smuggelen*, Dutch *smokkelen*, of unkn. origin.]
1 Convey (goods) clandestinely into or out of a country etc., esp. in order to avoid payment of customs duties or in contravention of legal prohibition; import or export illegally. **L17.**
2 Obtain, convey, remove, etc., stealthily or secretly. **M18.**

📖 **1** I. MURDOCH The . . cognac which I always smuggle had been taken from me by the Customs. M. FRAYN Their manuscripts are smuggled out of the country and published in the West. *absol.*: J. R. MCCULLOCH The temptation to smuggle was diminished. **2** P. WARNER Soldiers were smuggled into the castle under a load of hay. G. SWIFT I thrust it inside my shirt and smuggle it up to my bedroom.

■ **smugglable** *adjective* **E19.**

smuggle /ˈsmʌg(ə)l/ *verb*[2] *trans. obsolete* exc. *dial.* **L17.**
[Origin unkn. Cf. SNUGGLE *verb.*]
Cuddle, fondle, caress.

smuggler /ˈsmʌglə/ *noun.* **M17.**
[Low German *smukkeler, smugg(e)ler*, formed as SMUGGLE *verb*[1]: see -ER[1].]
1 A person who smuggles commodities; *esp.* a person who makes a trade or practice of smuggling. **M17.**
2 A ship or boat employed in smuggling. **L18.**

smur /smɜː/ *noun & verb. Scot. & dial.* Also **-rr**, **smir(r)**. **E19.**
[Origin unkn.]
▶ **A** *noun.* Fine rain, drizzle; a drizzle *of* rain etc. **E19.**
▶ **B** *verb intrans.* Infl. **-rr-**. Drizzle. **E19.**

smush /smʌʃ/ *noun & verb.* **E19.**
[Alt. of MUSH *noun*[1], *verb*[1].]
▶ **A** *noun.* **1** Soft pulp, mush; a messy pulp. *dial.* **E19.**
2 The mouth; = MUSH *noun*[1] 3. *slang. rare.* **M20.**
▶ **B** *verb trans.* Mash, crush. *colloq. & dial.* **E19.**

smut /smʌt/ *noun.* **M17.**
[from the verb.]
1 A black mark or stain; a smudge. **M17.**
2 Any of several fungal plant diseases characterized by the formation of black powdery spores, esp. in place of the grain in cereals; (more fully ***smut fungus***) any of the basidiomycetous fungi causing such a disease, constituting the order Ustilaginales. **M17.**
3 (A particle of) soot or sooty material. **L17.** ▸**b** *ANGLING.* A tiny fly eaten by fish. **E19.**
4 Lascivious or obscene language, writing, events, or pictures. **L17.**
5 Soft earthy coal. Now *local.* **L17.**

📖 **1** HENRY MORE There is not the least smutt of Antichristianism in Episcopacy. **2** ***loose smut***: see LOOSE *adjective.* ***STINKING smut.*** **3** D. WELCH Large, velvety smuts . . blew down from the chimney. **4** GOLDSMITH The gentlemen talked smut, the ladies . . were angry. *Country Life* The manager . . sat . . in the back row of stalls, to make sure that no smut crept into the acts.

Comb.: **smut-ball** a grain of cereal affected by smut or bunt; a cohesive body of smut; ***smut fungus***: see sense 2 above; **smut-grass** *US* a W. Indian grass, *Sporobolus poiretii*, introduced in the southern US, the spikelets of which are frequently infested with smut; **smut-hound** *colloq.* a person who seeks to censor or suppress smut in literature etc. **smut-mill** a machine for removing smut from grain.

smut /smʌt/ *verb.* Infl. **-tt-**. **LME.**
[Symbolic: cf. *smirch, smite, smudge, smutch*, etc. Cogn. with Low German *smutt*, Middle High German *smutz, smutzen* (German *Schmutz, schmutzen*).]
1 *verb trans.* Stain with some fault or imperfection; defile, corrupt. Also, introduce smut into, make obscene. **LME.**
2 *verb trans.* Mark with a black or dirty substance; blacken, smudge. **L16.**
3 *verb trans.* Affect (grain) with smut. Chiefly as ***smutted*** *ppl adjective.* **E17.** ▸**b** *verb intrans.* Of grain: be affected by smut. **M17.** ▸**c** *verb trans.* Remove smut from (grain). Chiefly as ***smutting*** *verbal noun.* **M19.**
4 *verb intrans. ANGLING.* Of fish: rise at or feed on smuts (SMUT *noun* 3b). **L19.**
■ **smutter** *noun* **E17.**

smutch /smʌtʃ/ *noun & verb.* **M16.**
[Rel. to SMUDGE *noun*[2], *verb*[1]. Cf. SMOOCH *verb*[1], SMUT *verb.*]
▶ **A** *noun.* **1** A black or dirty mark; a stain; a smudge; *fig.* a moral stain. **M16.** ▸**b** A slight mark or indication; a trace; a slight or light touch. **L18.**
2 Soot, grime, dirt. **L18.**
▶ **B** *verb trans.* Blacken, make dirty, smudge; *fig.* defile, corrupt. **L16.**
■ **smutchy** *adjective* **L16.**

smutty /ˈsmʌti/ *adjective.* **L16.**
[from SMUT *noun* + -Y[1].]
1 Of grain: affected by smut. **L16.**
2 Soiled with, full of, or characterized by smut or soot; dirty; blackened. **M17.**
3 Of the colour of smut or soot; dusky; dark. **M17.**
4 Indecent, lascivious, obscene. **M17.**

📖 **4** E. WAUGH A . . chatty journalist telling him smutty stories. A. S. DALE The smutty language and habits of the typical schoolboy.

■ **smuttily** *adverb* **L17.** **smuttiness** *noun* **M17.**

Smyrna /ˈsmɜːnə/ *noun.* **M18.**
[A port in Turkey, now called Izmir.]
Used ***attrib.*** to designate things produced at or exported through Smyrna (Izmir), esp. Turkish carpets.
■ **Smyrnaean** /smɜːˈniːən/ *noun & adjective* (**a**) *noun* a native or inhabitant of (ancient) Smyrna; (**b**) *adjective* of or pertaining to Smyrna (Izmir): **L16.**

Smyrniote /ˈsmɜːnɪət/ *noun & adjective.* Also **-ot**. **L17.**
[from prec. + -OTE, -OT[2].]
▶ **A** *noun.* A native or inhabitant of Smyrna (Izmir) in Turkey. **L17.**
▶ **B** *adjective.* Smyrnaean. **M19.**

smythite /ˈsmʌɪðʌɪt/ *noun.* **M20.**
[from Charles H. *Smyth* (1866–1937), US geologist + -ITE[1].]
MINERALOGY. A trigonal sulphide of iron and nickel, usu. occurring as bronze-coloured strongly magnetic crystals with a metallic lustre.

Sn *symbol.*
[Latin *stannum.*]
CHEMISTRY. Tin.

snab *noun & adjective* see SNOB *noun*[1] *& adjective.*

snack /snak/ *noun.* **LME.**
[Middle Dutch *snac(k)* rel. to *snacken*: see the verb. Cf. SNOOK *noun*[1].]
1 A snap, a bite, esp. of a dog. Also, a snappish remark. *obsolete* exc. *dial.* **LME.**
2 A share, a portion, a part. Now chiefly in ***go snacks***, have a share or shares (*in*), divide the profits. *colloq.* **L17.**
3 Orig. (now *rare*), a sip of drink, a bite or morsel of food. Now, a light, casual, or hurried meal; a small quantity of food eaten or intended to be eaten between meals. **L17.**
4 A thing that is easy to accomplish. *Austral. slang.* **M20.**

📖 **3** C. KINGSLEY And take his snack of brandy for digestion. P. SCOTT Cook had remembered to prepare Mrs Bhoolabhoy's midnight snack. *Times* PepsiCo is also expected to introduce large boxes containing assorted bags of snacks. ***snack food***, ***snack lunch***, ***snack meal***, etc.

Comb.: **snack bar** a bar, counter, or simple restaurant serving snacks.
■ **snackery** *noun* a snack bar **M20.**

snack /snak/ *verb.* **ME.**
[Middle Dutch *snacken* var. of *snappen* SNAP *verb.* Cf. SNATCH *verb.*]
1 *verb intrans.* Bite or snap (*at*). Also, make or exchange snappish remarks. Chiefly *Scot. & north.* **ME.** ▸**b** *verb trans.* Foll. by *up*: snap up, seize on. *Scot.* **L19.**
2 *verb trans.* Share, divide. Now *rare* or *obsolete.* **L17.**
3 *verb intrans.* Eat a snack; (foll. by *on*) eat (an item of food) as a snack. **E19.**

📖 **3** P. DRISCOLL The stalls were tiny places . . crowded with Chinese snacking on noodles. *Country Homes* She has never been one for snacking without a plate and napkin.

snackette /snaˈkɛt/ *noun. colloq.* **L20.**
[from SNACK *noun* + -ETTE.]
1 A snack bar; *W. Indies* (the earliest use) a small shop selling snacks, cigarettes, etc. **L20.**
2 A tiny snack; a small item of food. **L20.**

snaffle /ˈsnaf(ə)l/ *noun.* **M16.**
[Prob. from Low Dutch (cf. Old Frisian *snavel* mouth, Middle & mod. Low German, Middle & mod. Dutch *snavel*, corresp. to Old High German *snabul* (German *Schnabel*) beak, spout, nose): see -LE[1].]
A simple bridle-bit without a curb and usu. with a single rein; *fig.* (*arch.*) a light curb, a mild restraint.
Comb.: **snaffle-bit** a snaffle; **snaffle-bridle** a bridle with a snaffle; **snaffle-mouth**: of a horse which can be managed with a snaffle alone.

snaffle /ˈsnaf(ə)l/ *verb*[1] *trans.* **M16.**
[from the noun In sense 2 perh. a different word. Cf. SNAVEL.]
1 Put a snaffle on (a horse), restrain or guide with a snaffle; *fig.* (*arch.*) curb lightly. **M16.**
2 Steal; appropriate; seize. *colloq.* **E18.**
3 Arrest. *slang.* **M19.**

snaffle /'snaf(ə)l/ *verb*[2] *intrans. & trans. obsolete* exc. *dial.* L16.
[Imit. Cf. SNUFFLE *verb*.]
Speak or say through the nose; snuffle.

snafu /'snafu:/ *adjective, noun, & verb. slang* (orig. *US* MILITARY). M20.
[Acronym, from situation normal: all fouled (or fucked) up.]
▶ **A** *pred. adjective.* In the usual or expected state of utter confusion; chaotic, muddled. M20.
▶ **B** *noun.* Utter confusion or chaos; a confused state, a muddle; a mistake. M20.
▶ **C** *verb.* **1** *verb trans.* Mess up, play havoc with. M20.
2 *verb intrans.* Go wrong. L20.

snag /snag/ *noun*[1]. L16.
[Prob. of Scandinavian origin: cf. Old Norse *snaghyrndr* sharp-pointed (axe), Norwegian dial. *snag(e)* sharp point, spike, Old Norse (Icelandic) *snagi* peg. See also SNUG *noun*[1].]
1 A sharp, angular, or jagged projection. L16. ▸**b** A short tine or branch of an antler. L16. ▸**c** A broken stump of a tooth; a large or unshapely tooth. E17.
2 A short stump (left) standing out from a tree-trunk or branch; *N. Amer.* a standing dead tree. L16. ▸**b** A tree-trunk or branch embedded under water, forming an obstruction to navigation etc. Orig. *US*. E19.
3 (Now the predominant sense.) An unexpected or hidden obstacle or drawback. Also, a disadvantage, a hitch; a defect. E19.
4 A rent or tear such as is made by a sharp projection. M19.

> 🕮 **1c** P. S. BUCK Her teeth were yellow snags loose in her jaws. **3** P. G. WODEHOUSE At this point the scenario struck another snag. B. EMECHETA The only snag was that on Monday mornings she seldom got very hot water. L. GRANT-ADAMSON His plan, concocted in the night, did have snags. It might fail.

Comb.: **snag-tooth** a snaggle-tooth.

snag /snag/ *noun*[2]. Long *obsolete* exc. *dial.* L16.
[Origin unkn.]
A sloe.

snag /snag/ *noun*[3]. *Austral. colloq.* M20.
[Origin unkn.]
A sausage.

snag /snag/ *verb*[1] *intrans. obsolete* exc. *dial.* Infl. **-gg-**. M16.
[Origin unkn.]
Carp, sneer, nag. Also foll. by *at*.

snag /snag/ *verb*[2]. Infl. **-gg-**. L18.
[from SNAG *noun*[1]. Cf. next.]
1 *verb trans.* Cut (a tree, bush, etc.) roughly so as to leave snags. L18.
2 *verb trans.* Catch, damage, pierce, or tear on a snag or projection. Freq. in *pass.* E19. ▸**b** *verb intrans.* Strike a snag, get caught *on* a projection or obstacle. M19.
3 *verb trans.* Obstruct, hinder, impede, inconvenience. Also foll. by *up*. M19.
4 *verb trans.* Clear (a river etc.) of snags. L19.
5 *verb trans.* **a** Catch, get hold of, grab, steal, pick up, acquire. *colloq.* L19. ▸**b** ANGLING. Catch (fish), *spec.* with a bare hook; catch illicitly or improperly. *N. Amer.* M20.

> 🕮 **2** CECIL ROBERTS I started to haul my line in, but found I was snagged. J. DIDION She had snagged her stocking on the lock of her . . case. **b** W. FAULKNER Cant you never crawl through here without snagging on that nail. P. THEROUX They can't throw them [nets] in there—they'd snag on the trees. **3** *Guardian* No place to work and insufficient funds . . had snagged her. COLIN BURKE He was going to do whatever he could to snag things up. **5a** E. SEGAL The fond hope of snagging a real Harvard husband.

snagged /'snagd/ *adjective.* M17.
[from SNAG *noun*[1], *verb*[2]: see -ED[2], -ED[1].]
1 Having projecting points or jagged protuberances; jagged, ragged. M17.
2 Caught or impaled on a snag or projection; obstructed, blocked. M19.

snagger /'snagə/ *noun.* M19.
[from SNAG *verb*[2] + -ER[1].]
1 A kind of billhook. *dial.* Now *rare* or *obsolete.* M19.
2 A slow or inexpert sheep-shearer. *Austral. slang.* L19.
3 A person who snags fish; a person who fishes illicitly. *N. Amer.* M20.

snaggle /'snag(ə)l/ *noun.* E19.
[from SNAG *noun*[1] + -LE[1].]
1 In full ***snaggle-tooth***. An irregular or projecting tooth; a person with such teeth. E19.
2 A tangle; a knotted or projecting mass. E20.
Comb.: ***snaggle-tooth***: see sense 1 above; **snaggle-toothed** *adjective* having snaggle-teeth.
▪ **snaggled** *adjective* (*US*) (*a*) (esp. of a tooth) irregular, projecting; (*b*) knotty, intricate: L19. **snaggly** *adjective* (chiefly *dial.* & *colloq.*) irregular, tangled, ragged L18.

snaggy /'snagi/ *adjective*[1]. L16.
[from SNAG *noun*[1] + -Y[1].]
1 Having sharp protuberances; jagged; knotty. L16.
2 Having many underwater snags. E19.

snaggy /'snagi/ *adjective*[2]. *Scot. & dial.* L18.
[from SNAG *verb*[1] + -Y[1].]
Bad-tempered, peevish, snappish, cross.

snail /sneɪl/ *noun.*
[Old English *snæg(e)l*, *sneg(e)l* = Old Saxon *snegil*, Middle Low German *sneil*, Old High German *snegil* (Low German *snagel*), Old Norse *snigill*, from base rel. to Middle Low German *snigge*, Old High German *snecko* (German *Schnecke*): see -LE[1].]
1 Any of numerous terrestrial or freshwater gastropod molluscs having a well-developed spiral or whorled shell capable of housing the whole body; such an animal regarded as the type of very slow motion. Also, *loosely* or with specifying word, any of various animals related to or likened to any of these molluscs; *dial.* a slug. OE. ▸**b** A slow or indolent person; a sluggard. L16.
2 A structure or (*spec.* military) formation resembling a snail-shell. Now *spec.*, a flat spirally curved toothed disc in the striking mechanism of a clock. LME.
3 In *pl.* Any of several medicks, esp. the southern European *Medicago scutellata*, which have spirally coiled seed-pods resembling a snail's shell; the pods of such a plant. E17.

> 🕮 **1** ***dew-snail***, ***garden snail***, ***glass-snail***, ***mud-snail***, ***pond-snail***, etc. SEA-***snail***. **b** *Dialect Notes* We'll have to wait for Edith. She's such a snail.

Comb.: **snail-creeping** the carving of channels in the surfaces of wooden beams to allow circulation of air; **snail darter** a small percoid freshwater fish, *Percina tanasi*, found in some US rivers (cf. DARTER 5); **snail-fever** schistosomiasis; **snailfish** = SEA-***snail*** (b); **snail-flower** a S. American leguminous plant, *Vigna caracalla*, whose flowers have a spirally coiled keel; **snail-horn** (*obsolete* exc. *dial.*) (*a*) a snail-shell; a snail; (*b*) an animal with short curled horns; **snail mail** *colloq.* (mail sent using) the ordinary postal system, as opposed to electronic mail; **snail-paced** *adjective* very slow, sluggish; slothful, slow-moving; **snail's gallop** *arch.* = ***snail's pace*** below; **snail-slow** *adjective & adverb* as slow(ly) as a snail; very slow(ly) or sluggish(ly); **snail's pace** a very slow rate of progress or motion.
▪ **snailery** *noun* a place where edible snails are bred or reared E18.

snail /sneɪl/ *verb.* M16.
[from the noun.]
†**1** *verb intrans.* Of soldiers: form into a protective ring. Only in M16.
2 a *verb intrans. & trans.* with *it*. Move, walk, or travel lazily or sluggishly; proceed very slowly. L16. ▸**b** *verb trans.* Make (one's way) very slowly. M20.
3 *verb trans.* Make or construct after the spiral form of a snail-shell. L16.
4 *verb trans.* Clear of or keep free from snails. *rare.* M17.

> 🕮 **2a** A. ADAMS We snailed on westward at our leisurely gait. **b** M. FRANKLIN Two bullock drays were snailing their way from the Port.

snailish /'sneɪlɪʃ/ *adjective.* L16.
[from SNAIL *noun* + -ISH[1].]
Somewhat like (that of) a snail; slow, sluggish.
▪ **snailishly** *adverb* E19. **snailishness** *noun* E20.

snail-like /'sneɪl-lʌɪk/ *adjective & adverb.* E17.
[from SNAIL *noun* + -LIKE.]
▶ **A** *adjective.* **1** Like a snail in appearance, habits, etc. E17.
2 Very slow or sluggish; tardy. M17.
▶ **B** *adverb.* Like a snail; very slowly or sluggishly; tardily. E19.

'Snails /sneɪlz/ *interjection.* Long *arch.* L16.
[Abbreviation.]
God's nails!: an oath.

snaily /'sneɪli/ *adjective.* L16.
[from SNAIL *noun* + -Y[1].]
1 Snail-like. L16.
2 Infested with snails; covered with the slime of snails. L19.
3 (Of a horn) slightly curled like a snail-shell; (of an animal) having such horns. *Austral.* L19.

snaith *noun* var. of SNATH.

snake /sneɪk/ *noun & adjective.*
[Old English *snaca* = Middle Low German *snake*, Old Norse *snákr*, *snókr*.]
▶ **A** *noun.* **1** Any of numerous reptiles constituting the suborder Ophidia, characterized by elongated cylindrical limbless bodies, tapering tails, and smooth scaly skins, and including many kinds whose bite is venomous. Also *loosely*, a limbless lizard (as a slow-worm) or amphibian. OE. ▸**b** A representation, image, or figure of a snake. L16. ▸**c** In *pl.* As *interjection*, expr. surprise, indignation, etc. Also in ***great snakes!***, ***snakes alive!***, etc. Now *rare.* M19.
2 *fig.* A treacherous or deceitful person or thing, a secret enemy, a lurking danger, (freq. in ***snake in the grass***). Also, a despicable or contemptible person. L16.
3 A thing resembling a snake in appearance, movement, etc.; a long sinuous or twisting thing; *spec.* †(*a*) a long tail attached to a wig; (*b*) the long flexible tube of a hookah; (*c*) (also ***plumber's snake***) a long flexible wire for clearing obstacles in piping. L17. ▸**b** ECONOMICS. *The* system of interconnected exchange rates of the currencies of member states of the European Community. *colloq.* L20.
4 (**S-**.) A Snake Indian (see below). E19.

> 🕮 **1** ***black-snake***, ***brown snake***, ***carpet-snake***, ***corn snake***, ***diamond snake***, ***grass snake***, ***king-snake***, ***night snake***, ***rattlesnake***, ***smooth snake***, ***spectacled snake***, ***whip snake***, etc. **1b snakes and ladders** (*a*) a board game in which counters are moved by dice-throws along a board on which snakes and ladders are depicted, a counter that lands on the head of a snake being moved back to the tail, while one that lands at the foot of a ladder advances to the top; (*b*) *fig.* an unpredictable sequence of successes and setbacks (freq. *attrib.*). **2** A. C. GUNTER Do you remember a little toadying snake who used to be at school with us? *Observer* For many, he is the snake in the trades union grass, a traitor to the movement. **poor snake** *arch.* a poor, needy, or humble person, a drudge. **3** RIDER HAGGARD The long black snake of men winding . . across the plain. A. THWAITE The water itself An uneven grey-blue snake.

Comb.: **snakebark (maple)** any of several maples, esp. *Acer pennsylvanicum* of eastern N. America and *A. davidii* of eastern Asia, distinguished by having their bark streaked with white; **snake bird** (*a*) an anhinga, esp. *A. anhinga* of tropical and subtropical America; (*b*) *dial.* the wryneck; **snake-bit**, **snake-bitten** *adjectives* (*a*) bitten by a snake; (*b*) *US slang* unlucky, doomed to misfortune; **Snakeboard** (proprietary name for) a form of skateboard consisting of two footplates joined by a bar, allowing for greater speed and manoeuvrability than a standard skateboard; **snake charmer** a person who appears to hypnotize and make snakes move by playing music and moving rhythmically, esp. in Asia; **snake dance** a dance in which the performers handle live snakes, imitate the motions of snakes, or form a line which moves in a zigzag fashion; *spec.* a ritual dance of the N. American Hopi Indians involving the handling of live rattlesnakes; **snake-doctor** (*a*) a person who treats snake-bites; (*b*) *US* (the larva of) a dragonfly; **snake eyes** *N. Amer. slang* (*a*) tapioca; (*b*) a throw of two ones with a pair of dice; *fig.* bad luck; **snake feeder** *US* = ***snake-doctor*** (b) above; **snake-fence** *N. Amer.*: made of roughly split rails or poles laid in a zigzag fashion; **snakefish** any of various fishes with slender elongated bodies; *spec.* (*a*) the cutlass-fish, *Trichiurus lepturus*; (*b*) a lizardfish, *Trachinocephalus myops*, found in warm seas worldwide; **snake fly** any insect of the neuropteran family Raphidiidae, having an elongated thorax resembling a long neck; **snake-gourd** a tropical gourd, *Trichosanthes cucumerina*, with long narrow snake-shaped edible fruit; **snake-head** (*a*) a representation of or an object resembling the head of a snake; (*b*) *US* the plant turtle-head, *Chelone glabra*; (*c*) *US* (*obsolete* exc. *Hist.*) the bent end of a rail projecting above the level of a railway track; (*d*) any of various African and Asian freshwater fishes of the family Channidae and esp. of the genus *Ophicephalus*; (*e*) [translating Chinese *shetou*] a member of a Chinese criminal network engaged in smuggling illegal immigrants to the West; **snake hips** (*a*) very narrow hips; (*b*) a jazz dance in which the hips are gyrated; **snake house** a building at a zoo etc. in which snakes are kept; **snake juice** *slang* (chiefly *Austral.*) whisky or other alcoholic liquor, esp. of local or home manufacture; **snake lizard** a snakelike lizard; *spec.* any of numerous nocturnal legless lizards native to Australia and New Guinea; **snake mackerel** = ESCOLAR; **snake oil** *colloq.* a quack remedy or panacea; **snake pipefish** = OCEAN ***pipefish***; **snake-pit** (*a*) a pit containing poisonous snakes; (*b*) *fig.* a scene of vicious behaviour or ruthless competition; **snake plant** mother-in-law's tongue, *Sansevieria trifasciata*; **snakeroot** (*a*) (a medicinal preparation made from) the root of any of various N. American plants used as an antidote to snake-bites; any of these plants, *esp.* a milkwort, *Polygala senega* (more fully ***Seneca snakeroot***), a bugbane, *Cimicifuga racemosa* (more fully ***black snakeroot***), and a birthwort, *Aristolochia serpentaria* (more fully ***Virginia snakeroot***); any of these plants; (*b*) any of several plants thought to resemble a snake in shape, esp. rauwolfia, *Rauvolfia serpentina*; **snake's head** (*a*) a fritillary, *Fritillaria meleagris* (see FRITILLARY *noun* 1(a)) (also ***snake's head fritillary***, ***snake's head lily***); (*b*) *US* (*obsolete* exc. *Hist.*) = ***snake-head*** (c) above; (*c*) ***snake's-head iris***, a Mediterranean iris, *Hermodactylus tuberosa*, with solitary purple and green flowers; **snakeskin** *noun & adjective* (*a*) *noun* the skin of a snake, esp. when used as leather; (*b*) *adjective* made of snakeskin; **snakesman** *slang* (*obsolete* exc. *Hist.*) a child used by thieves to wriggle into a building etc. through a narrow passage and then open the door; **snake-stone** (*a*) (*obsolete* exc. *dial.*) a fossil ammonite; (*b*) = ***serpent-stone*** (b) s.v. SERPENT *noun & adjective*; (*c*) *dial.* = ***adder-stone*** s.v. ADDER *noun*[1]; **snake story** a tall tale, *spec.* one about a snake of great length or size; **snakeweed** (*a*) the plant bistort, *Polygonum bistorta*; (*b*) *US* = ***snakeroot*** (a) above; **snakewood** (*a*) the wood of any of several trees, shrubs, etc., used as an antidote to snake-bites; any of these trees, esp. *Strychnos minor* (family Loganiaceae) of India and Sri Lanka; (*b*) (the mottled wood of) a S. American timber tree, *Brosimum rubescens*, of the mulberry family.
▶ **B** *adjective.* (**S-**.) Designating or pertaining to a group of Shoshonean peoples of Oregon and adjacent regions. L18.
▪ **snakelike** *adjective* resembling (that of) a snake; long and slender; sinuous: E17. **snakeology**, **snakology** /-'kɒl-/ *noun* (*rare*) the branch of science that deals with snakes E19. **snakeship** *noun* (*rare*) (with possess. adjective, as ***his snakeship*** etc.) a mock title of respect given to a snake M19. **snakewise** *adverb* in the manner of a snake; with snakelike movement: L19.

snake /sneɪk/ *verb*[1]. L16.
[from the noun.]
1 *verb intrans.* Wind, twist, or curve in a snakelike manner; follow a twisting or winding course. L16. ▸**b** Move in a stealthy manner; creep, crawl. M19. ▸**c** Of a

vehicle, boat, etc.: follow a zigzag course because of lateral oscillation. Chiefly as ***snaking verbal noun***. M20.

2 *verb trans.* **a** Twist or wind into the form of a snake; NAUTICAL wind a smaller rope around (a larger one). M17. ▶**b** Move or stretch out (the head, a limb, etc.) after the manner of a snake. L19. ▶**c** Make (one's way) in a sinuous or creeping manner. L19.

3 *verb trans.* Drag or pull forcibly; *esp.* haul a log along the ground lengthwise by means of chains or ropes. Chiefly *US*. E19.

1 G. ORWELL Unpruned vines were snaking across the ground. *Bicycle Action* A gravel track . . snaked to and fro along the side of the mountain. **c** *Times* The boat had snaked all over the place at high speeds. *Caravan Magazine* To counteract snaking . . take your foot off the accelerator. **2b** M. DORRIS I smiled and snaked my arms around his waist. **c** J. DISKI The river . . snaked its way through the dense forest. **3** *fig.*: *Scribner's Magazine* He never studied, and had to be snaked through by tutors.

snake /sneɪk/ *verb*². *dial.* & *US*. L17.
[Prob. from Old Norse *snaka*; cf. German dial. *schnaken* creep.]
1 *verb intrans.* Skulk, sneak; prowl. L17.
2 *verb trans.* Get or obtain furtively or surreptitiously; steal, pilfer. Also, cheat (a person). M19.

snakey *adjective* var. of SNAKY.

snakish /ˈsneɪkɪʃ/ *adjective*. M16.
[from SNAKE *noun* + -ISH¹.]
Snakelike; of the nature or characteristic of a snake. Chiefly *fig.*, venomous, treacherous, deceitful.
■ **snakishly** *adverb* M20. **snakishness** *noun* E20.

snaky /ˈsneɪki/ *adjective*. Also **-key**. M16.
[from SNAKE *noun* + -Y¹.]
1 Of hair (*spec.* that of the Furies): formed or composed of snakes. M16.
2 **a** Entwined with snakes. L16. ▶**b** Infested with snakes. M19.
3 Of the nature or characteristic of a snake. Chiefly *fig.*, venomous, deceitful, treacherous. L16. ▶**b** Angry, irritable; savage. *Austral.* & *NZ slang*. L19.
4 Resembling the form of a snake; long and winding or twisting; sinuous, tortuous. L16.
■ **snakily** *adverb* in a snaky or snakelike manner, sinuously L19. **snakiness** *noun* M19.

snallygaster /ˈsnalɪɡɑːstə/ *noun*. *US dial.* M20.
[German *schnelle Geister* lit. 'quick spirits'. Cf. SNOLLYGOSTER.]
A mythical monster supposedly found in Maryland.

snap /snap/ *noun*. L15.
[Rel. to SNAP *verb*: partly imit., but cf. also Low German, Dutch *snap*.]
▶**I 1** A quick or sudden closing of the jaws or teeth in biting, or of scissors etc. in cutting, usu. accompanied by a short sharp sound; a bite or cut made in this way. L15.
2 **a** A sudden short sharp sound or report. E17. ▶**b** An act of snapping or breaking suddenly; a break, a fracture. M18.
3 **a** A small crisp cake or biscuit. Orig. *Scot.* E17. ▶**b** = ***snap-bean*** s.v. SNAP-. *US*. L18.
4 An implement, a device; *spec.* (*a*) an implement for pulling out a tooth; (*b*) a tool for rounding the head of a rivet; (*c*) a strip in a cracker which makes a bang when the cracker is pulled. E17.
5 A fastening that snaps shut, *spec.* a press-stud; a thing with such a fastening, *spec.* in *pl.* (*slang*), handcuffs. M18.

2a D. BAGLEY Julie heard . . the snap of metal as he slipped off the safety-catch. A. S. BYATT Maud closed *The Great Ventriloquist* with a snap. **3a** ***brandy-snap***: see BRANDY *noun*. ***ginger-snap***: see GINGER *noun* & *adjective*¹. **5** A. LURIE A blue western-cut shirt with pearl snaps.

▶**II 6** **a** A share; something worth having; a chance. M16. ▶**b** THEATRICAL. A short run or engagement. L19. ▶**c** An easy task, a soft option. *N. Amer. slang*. L19.
7 A small piece or portion; a scrap, a morsel. *obsolete* exc. *dial.* E17. ▶**b** A light quick meal; a snack. Now chiefly *dial.* M17.
8 **a** A sudden snatch or catch at something; a short quick movement. M17. ▶**b** An informal faro game. M19. ▶**c** A party game in which one player chases another round a ring formed by the rest of the players. *US*. M19. ▶**d** A card-game in which 'snap' is called when two matching cards are exposed. L19. ▶**e** AMER. FOOTBALL. A backward pass; = SNAP-BACK 1b. E20.
9 A curt sharp speech or manner of speaking; an angry dispute. M17.
10 More fully ***cold snap***. A sudden brief spell of cold weather. M18.
11 ***Scotch snap***, a musical rhythm in which a short note precedes a long one, characteristic of many traditional Scottish melodies. L18.
12 **a** = SNAPSHOT *noun* 1a, b. M19. ▶**b** = SNAPSHOT *noun* 2. L19.
13 Alertness, energy, vigour, liveliness, zest. M19.

6c M. FRENCH The classroom will be a snap after this. **7b** B. HINES Jud's snap was . . on the table, wrapped up in a cut bread wrapper. **9** GOLDSMITH I was at once contradicted with a snap. **10** *Which Motorcaravan* A late cold snap in April had me using the gas convector fire. **12b** G. SWIFT I remember Harry taking photos of me. Just holiday snaps.

▶**III** †**14** A person who cheats or deceives someone; a swindler. *slang*. L16–L17.
15 A lad, a chap, a fellow. M17.
16 A trick, a deception. *US*. M19.
Phrases: ***cold snap***: see sense 10 above. **in a snap** in a moment, immediately. **not care a snap** not care at all. ***Scotch snap***: see sense 11 above. **snap, crackle, and pop**, **snap, crackle, pop** [an advertiser's catchphrase repr. the sound produced when milk is added to a particular brand of breakfast cereal] vigour, energy.

snap /snap/ *adjective*. Orig. *Scot.* M18.
[from SNAP *noun*, *verb*. Cf. Middle Danish *snap* quick, smart.]
Quick; smart; done or taken on the spur of the moment or without warning, sudden.

N. SHUTE This isn't any snap decision on my part. *Times* The Government should hold a snap general election.

snap /snap/ *verb*. Infl. **-pp-**. L15.
[Prob. from Middle & mod. Low German, Middle & mod. Dutch *snappen* seize (= Middle High German *snappen*, German *schnappen*), but partly also imit.: cf. SNAP *noun*, SNIP *verb*.]
▶**I 1** *verb intrans.* Esp. of an animal: make a quick or sudden audible bite at something; feed on something in this way. (Foll. by *at*, *on*.) L15. ▶**b** *verb trans.* Close (the jaws, mouth, etc.) suddenly or with a snap. L16. ▶**c** *verb intrans.* Of jaws etc.: close suddenly or with a snap. L19.
2 *verb trans.* **a** Catch or seize quickly, suddenly, or unexpectedly. Usu. foll. by *up*. L15. ▶**b** Snatch or take quickly for one's own use. Also foll. by *away*, *up*. E17. ▶**c** Secure, obtain, or accept quickly or readily; *spec.* secure (a partner) in marriage or some other long term relationship. Usu. foll. by *up*. L18. ▶**d** Make (a decision), pass (legislation), etc., without due consideration or discussion. L19. ▶**e** AMER. FOOTBALL. Put (the ball) into play on the ground by a quick backward movement. L19.
3 *verb trans.* Bite *off* sharply and quickly. L16.
4 **a** *verb intrans.* Utter sharp or cutting words; speak or reply irritably or abruptly. Usu. foll. by *at*. L16. ▶**b** *verb trans.* Utter or say sharply or irritably. Also foll. by *out*. L17.
5 *verb trans.* Interrupt, esp. with an abrupt or sharp remark (usu. foll. by *up*); cut *short* abruptly or irritably; snub. Now *rare*. M17.
6 *verb intrans.* Snatch or catch quickly *at* a thing. L17.
7 *verb trans.* Cause to make or emit a short sharp sound, as a crack or click; (with adverb compl.) open, close, put off or on, etc., with such a sound. Also, fire (a gun). L17.
8 *verb intrans.* Of a thing: make or emit a short sharp sound, as a crack or click; (with adverb compl.) open, close, fit in, come off, etc., with such a sound. L17.
9 **a** *verb trans.* Wink or blink (the eyes) quickly in anger or excitement. M19. ▶**b** *verb intrans.* Of the eyes: blink quickly and angrily; sparkle with anger or excitement. L19.
10 **a** *verb trans.* & *intrans.* Take a snapshot (of). L19. ▶**b** *verb trans.* Take as a snapshot. L19.

1 W. IRVING Dogs . . snapping at the heels of the terrified friar. **b** *Field* He snapped his beak with a noise like pistol shots. **2a** *Observer* Owen snapped up the rebound for City's third goal. **c** G. MEREDITH All my first editions have been snapped up. G. PRIESTLAND She was a remarkable beauty . . and was snapped up by Sir Richard Cooper. **3** GOLDSMITH The shark . . snapped off his leg. **snap a person's head off**, **snap a person's nose off** = ***bite a person's head off*** s.v. BITE *verb*. **4a** A. TYLER Babies were crying and mothers were snapping at children. **b** T. DREISER 'That's not so!' she snapped, angrily and bitterly. **5** W. RAYMOND To snap a body off short who had any . . favour to ask. **6** R. DAHL The wind howled around him and snapped at his coat. **7** J. GALSWORTHY Firmly snapping the door to, she crossed the corridor. J. BUCHAN Lights were not lit . . . I snapped the switch. E. BOWEN She . . snapped the bag shut. D. PROFUMO He snapped forward the bolt on his rifle. **snap one's fingers at** (*a*) make a sharp noise by bending the last joint of the finger against the ball of the thumb and suddenly releasing it, esp. in time to music; (*b*) show contempt or disregard (for) (usu. foll. by *at*). **8** J. AGEE She stood up and her joints snapped. G. F. NEWMAN The door swung to and snapped shut. L. ERDRICH The wood burns too hot and the sticks are snapping. **9b** M. ALLINGHAM Mrs Austin was breathing heavily, her eyes snapping with excitement. **10a** *Which?* We asked them to snap away with each of three cameras for a week. M. BINCHY Prints of the romantic twosomes that he would snap. **b** M. PUZO A photographer jumped out to snap pictures of the bleeding Don Corleone.

▶**II 11** *verb intrans.* **a** Break suddenly, usu. with a sharp sound; give way or come apart suddenly from strain or tension. E17. ▶**b** Be broken *off* with a sharp sound. E19.
12 *verb trans.* **a** Break (something) suddenly and cleanly; cause to part or give way; *spec.* (*N. Amer.*) in SPORT, break (a tie), interrupt or change the course of (a performance pattern). L17. ▶**b** Break *off* with a sharp sound. E19.
13 **a** *verb intrans.* Quickly change one's behaviour or position; revert *back* to a former better position; throw oneself *into* an activity; pull oneself suddenly *out of* a mood, behaviour pattern, etc. *colloq.* E20. ▶**b** *verb trans.* Get or pull (a person) *out of* a mood, behaviour pattern, etc. M20.

11a A. CARTER She looked as if she might snap in two. N. BAKER My left shoelace had snapped. *fig.*: L. NIVEN Under pressure something could snap in her mind. ***snap short (off)***: see SHORT *adverb*. **12a** *Washington Post* Lawson's goal . . of the third period snapped a 4-4 tie. **b** K. VONNEGUT I deliberately snapped the point off the pencil. **13a** K. TENNANT Time we were getting a move on . . . Snap into it, Joe. J. POYER He snapped awake as if from a trance. I. MCEWAN Charles's fantasies . . seemed merely silly, something he should snap out of. **b** G. PRIESTLAND One activity . . snapped me out of my gloom.

■ **snappable** *adjective* that may be snapped or broken M19.

snap /snap/ *adverb*. L16.
[from SNAP *verb*.]
With or as with the sound of a snap; quickly, smartly. Freq. in ***go snap***.

snap /snap/ *interjection*. L19.
[from SNAP *noun*.]
Called out in the card-game snap on noticing two matching cards; *transf.* called out on noticing any two (esp. unexpectedly) similar things.

snap- /snap/ *combining form*. L17.
[Repr. SNAP *noun*, *verb*.]
In combs. in various senses, as 'that snaps', 'that opens, closes, etc., with a snap.'
snap-action *adjective* (*a*) designating a gun whose hinged barrel is secured by a spring catch; (*b*) designating a switch or relay that makes and breaks contact rapidly, independently of the speed of the activating mechanism. **snap-bean** *US* a bean grown for its pods which are broken into pieces and cooked, as a French bean or a runner bean; a pod of such a bean. **snap-beetle** = ***click-beetle*** s.v. CLICK *noun*¹. **snap-bolt** a bolt which locks automatically when a door or window closes. **snap-brim** *adjective* & *noun* (*a*) *adjective* (of a hat) having a brim which may be turned up and down at opposite sides; (*b*) *noun* a hat with such a brim. **snap-brimmed** *adjective* = ***snap-brim*** (a) above. **snap-fastener** a press-stud. **snap gauge** MECHANICS a form of caliper gauge used to check the precise size of a component. **snap head** (a tool used to shape) a round head on a rivet, bolt, etc. **snap-hook** (*a*) ANGLING a device consisting of several connected hooks; (*b*) a hook etc. with a spring allowing the entrance but barring the escape of a cord, link, etc.; a karabiner. **snap-in** *adjective* that is attached or secured with a snap. **snap-link** = ***snap-hook*** (b) above. **snap-lock** = ***snap-bolt*** above. **snap-off** *adjective* that is removed with a snap. **snap-on** *adjective* that is attached or secured with a snap. **snap-ring** = ***snap-hook*** (b) above. **snap roll** AERONAUTICS a manoeuvre in which an aircraft in level flight makes a single quick revolution about its longitudinal axis. **snap-sound** MEDICINE a snapping sound heard in auscultation of the heart. **snap switch** a snap-action switch. **snapweed** any of the balsams (genus *Impatiens*), so called from their explosively dehiscent capsules.

snap-back /ˈsnapbak/ *noun*. L19.
[from SNAP- + BACK *adverb*.]
1 AMER. FOOTBALL. **a** A centre player. Now *rare* or *obsolete*. L19. ▶**b** A backward pass from the centre, or a handing backwards of the ball from the centre, which puts the ball in play to begin a scrimmage. E20.
2 **a** A recovery of an earlier position or circumstances. M20. ▶**b** A reaction, a retaliation. M20.
3 BOXING. A swift backward movement to evade a blow. M20.

snapdragon /ˈsnapdraɡ(ə)n/ *noun*. L16.
[from SNAP- + DRAGON *noun*.]
1 The garden antirrhinum, *Antirrhinum majus*, so called from its personate corolla (thought to resemble a dragon's mouth). Also (usu. with specifying word), any of several allied plants with similar flowers which were formarly included in the genus *Antirrhinum*; *esp.* (*a*) (more fully ***wild snapdragon***, ***yellow snapdragon***) toadflax, *Linaria vulgaris*; (*b*) (more fully ***lesser snapdragon***) weasel's snout, *Misopates orontium*. L16.
2 A figure or representation of a dragon, *esp.* one with a mouth that opens and shuts, used in public processions. *obsolete* exc. *Hist.* L16.
3 A game in which raisins are snatched from burning brandy etc. and eaten while alight; a bowl or quantity of the liquor etc. used in this game. Cf. FLAP-DRAGON *noun*. *obsolete* exc. *Hist.* E18.

snape /sneɪp/ *noun*. *rare*. M17.
[Rel. to SNAPE *verb*².]
A bevel.

snape /sneɪp/ *verb*¹ *trans.* Now *dial.* ME.
[Old Norse *sneypa* outrage, dishonour, disgrace. Cf. Icelandic *sneypa* chide, snub, Norwegian *snøypa* withdraw, draw in, etc., Middle & mod. Swedish *snöpa* castrate. See also SNEAP *verb*.]
1 Rebuke or snub sharply or severely; check or restrain (a child); call off (a dog). ME.
2 Check or stop (growth); blight or nip the growth of (a plant etc.). M17.

snape /sneɪp/ *verb*². L18.
[Perh. from prec. Cf. SNEAP *verb*, SNAPE *noun*.]
1 *verb trans.* Cause to taper; *spec.* in SHIPBUILDING, bevel the end of. L18.
2 *verb intrans.* Taper (*off*). L18.

snaphance /ˈsnaphɑːns/ *noun.* Also **snaphaunce**. M16.
[Repr. Dutch, Flemish *snaphaan*, from *snappen* SNAP *verb* + *haan* cock, in sense either 'snapping or vicious cock' or 'cock-stealer'.]
Hist. †**1** An armed robber or marauder; a highwayman; a thief. M16–E17.
2 An early form of flintlock used in muskets and pistols; the hammer of this. L16.
3 A musket, gun, etc., fitted with a flintlock of this kind, used in the 16th and 17th cents. L16.

snapper /ˈsnapə/ *noun*¹. M16.
[from SNAP *verb* + -ER¹. Cf. SCHNAPPER.]
1 An accomplice. *slang.* Long *rare.* M16.
2 a A thing that makes a snapping sound; *spec.* (*a*) *rare* a pistol; (*b*) in *pl.* (now *rare* or *obsolete*) castanets; (*c*) *US* a cracker on the end of a whiplash; *fig.* a sharp or caustic remark. L16. ▸**b** A punch-line. *US.* M19. ▸**c** In *pl.* Teeth; a set of false teeth. *slang.* E20. ▸**d** A device with closing jaws for taking samples from the seabed. E20.
3 A person who snaps *up* or seizes on a thing quickly. E17. ▸**b** AMER. FOOTBALL. More fully ***snapper-back***. = SNAP-BACK 1a. L19.
4 A snappish person; a person who speaks or answers sharply or irritably. M17.
5 a Any of various large marine food fishes of the family Lutjanidae, freq. reddish in colour and with a triangular head-profile. Also, any of various fishes of other families; *esp.* (*a*) *US* the bluefish, *Pomatomus saltatrix*; (*b*) *Austral.* an important food fish, *Chrysophrys auratus*, of the family Sparidae. L17. ▸**b** = ***snapping turtle*** s.v. SNAPPING *ppl adjective.* L18.
6 a A casual or (*joc.*) professional photographer. E20. ▸**b** A ticket inspector. *slang.* M20.

📖 **2e** P. G. WODEHOUSE You shrink from entrusting the snappers to a strange dentist. **5a** ***grey snapper, red snapper, silk snapper***, etc. **6a** *Observer* Freelance photographer Chris Cole . . was standing in for another snapper.

Comb.: ***snapper-back***: see sense 3b above; **snapper ending** *US* = sense 2b above; **snapper fish** = sense 5a above; **snapper grab**, **snapper sampler** = sense 2d above.

snapper /ˈsnapə/ *noun*². *Scot.* M16.
[from next.]
A stumble, a trip; *fig.* a lapse in conduct, a fault, an error; a difficulty.

snapper /ˈsnapə/ *verb*¹ *intrans.* Chiefly & now only *Scot.* & *north.* ME.
[App. frequentative from stem corresp. to dial. German *schnappen* to stumble, limp, rel. to Middle High German *snaben*, Middle Low German *snaven*, whence Middle Danish *snave*, Middle Swedish *snava*, Swedish *snafva*, Norwegian *snåve* to stumble: see -ER⁵.]
Stumble, trip; *fig.* make a slip in action or conduct, fall into error.

snapping /ˈsnapɪŋ/ *verbal noun.* L16.
[from SNAP *verb* + -ING¹.]
The action of SNAP *verb*; an instance of this.
Comb.: **snapping-point** = BREAKING-*point*.

snapping /ˈsnapɪŋ/ *ppl adjective.* M17.
[from SNAP *verb* + -ING².]
1 Sharp, curt; peevish. M17.
2 That snaps. M17.
3 Violent, severe, extreme. Now *rare.* M19.
3 snapping shrimp any of various shrimps of the family Alpheidae, having one greatly enlarged pincer which is used to make a snapping noise. **snapping turtle** either of two large aggressive Central and N. American freshwater turtles of the family Chelydridae, having large heads and long tails, *Chelydra serpentina* (more fully ***common snapping turtle, Florida snapping turtle***), and *Macroclemys temminckii* (more fully ***alligator snapping turtle***).
■ **snappingly** *adverb* M16.

snappish /ˈsnapɪʃ/ *adjective.* M16.
[from SNAP *verb* + -ISH¹.]
1 Characterized by sharpness or curtness of speech; peevish, ill-natured. M16.
2 Of words, language, etc.: sharp, curt, peevish, ungracious. M16.
3 Of a dog etc.: inclined to snap. L17.
4 Breaking with a snap; brittle. M19.
■ **snappishly** *adverb* M16. **snappishness** *noun* L16.

snappy /ˈsnapi/ *adjective.* E19.
[from SNAP *verb* + -Y¹.]
1 Keen, shrewd; hard-bargaining. *Scot.* E19.
2 = SNAPPISH *adjective* 1, 2. M19.
3 = SNAPPISH *adjective* 4. L19.
4 Of the nature of or emitting a snap or crack. L19.
5 a Bright, brisk, full of zest; (of language etc.) to the point, cleverly concise. L19. ▸**b** Neat and elegant; smart, natty. L19. ▸**c** Of weather: cold, crisp, frosty. *N. Amer. colloq.* E20.
6 Quick, sudden; jerky. L19.

📖 **2** M. DIBDIN Douglas was in a foul mood, tense and snappy. **5a** J. W. KRUTCH His attention has to be caught by a snappy title, a striking picture. **b** J. O'HARA English wasn't what you would call a snappy dresser, but he was always neat. *Detroit Free Press* Strap on our high-spirited sandal in five snappy colours. **6 make it snappy** *colloq.* be quick about it, hurry.

■ **snappily** *adverb* (*a*) snappishly; (*b*) smartly, nattily; deftly: L19. **snappiness** *noun* M20.

snaps /snaps/ *noun.* M19.
[Dutch, Danish, Swedish.]
= SCHNAPPS.

snapsack /ˈsnapsak/ *noun.* Now *dial.* M17.
[Low German *snappsack* (German *Schnappsack*), from *snappen* SNAP *verb* + *sack* SACK *noun*¹.]
A knapsack.

snap-shooting /ˈsnapʃuːtɪŋ/ *noun.* L19.
[from SNAP- + SHOOTING *noun.*]
The action of making a snapshot; *spec.* (*a*) the firing of a quick or hurried shot at a target, esp. without deliberate aim; (*b*) the taking of a casual photograph, esp. with a small camera.
■ **snap-shooter** *noun* (*a*) a person who fires snap-shots; (*b*) a person who takes, or a camera for taking, snapshots: L19.

snapshot /ˈsnapʃɒt/ *noun & verb.* E19.
[from SNAP- + SHOT *noun*¹.]
▶ **A** *noun.* **1 a** A quick or hurried shot fired without deliberate aim, esp. at a rising bird or quickly moving animal. E19. ▸**b** A person who fires such shots. M19.
2 A casual photograph, *esp.* one taken with a small camera. L19. ▸**b** COMPUTING. A record of the contents of the storage locations in a computer at a given time. M20.
3 SPORT. A quick shot at goal. M20.

📖 **2** S. BEDFORD She showed me snapshots of herself lying in a gondola. *fig.*: *Business* The results of the poll are not a forecast, they are a snapshot in time. *attrib.*: *Professional Photographer* Designers use cameras to record details, often in snapshot style.

▶ **B** *verb intrans. & trans.* Infl. **-tt-**. Take a snapshot (of) with a camera. L19.

📖 W. DE MORGAN No interesting girls . . whom he could have snap-shotted . . as models.

■ **snapshotter** *noun* a person who takes snapshots L19.

†**snar** *verb intrans.* Infl. **-rr-**. M–L16.
[Corresp. to Middle & mod. Low German *snarren* = Middle High German *snarren* (German *schnarren*, Swedish *snarra*, Danish *snærre*) rattle, whirl, snarl, prob. ult. imit.]
Of a dog etc.: snarl, growl.

snare /snɛː/ *noun.*
[Late Old English *sneare* from Old Norse *snara* = Old Saxon *snari* (Dutch *snaar*) string, Old High German *snarahha* snare; rel. to (and in sense 2 prob. from) Middle Low German, Middle Dutch *snare* harp-string, Old High German *snerhan* bind, knot, Old Norse *snara* wind, twist.]
1 A trap for catching small wild animals or birds, usu. with a noose of wire or cord in which a foot or the head may be secured. Also (*transf.*), a device to tempt out an enemy or opponent to danger, capture, defeat, etc. LOE. ▸**b** *fig.* A trial, a temptation, a trap. ME. ▸**c** SURGERY. An instrument that uses a wire loop for removing polyps, small tumours, etc. L19.
2 a Any of the gut, rawhide, or wire strings which are stretched across the lower head of a side-drum to produce a rattling sound. L17. ▸**b** In full ***snare-drum***. A drum fitted with snares. L19.

📖 **1** G. MEDLEY Several Snares, made of Horse-Hairs . . are hung between the Branches. **b** A. MASON Trapped . . by the . . snares of false hopes. **2b** *New Yorker* An astonishing series of accents on the snare drum.

■ **snareless** *adjective* (*rare*) free from snares, without a snare E19.

snare /snɛː/ *verb trans.* LME.
[from prec.]
1 a Trap (a small wild animal or bird) in a snare; catch by entangling. LME. ▸**b** *fig.* Entangle, entrap; lure with a snare. LME.
2 SURGERY. Catch in a wire loop, esp. in order to remove; cut off with a snare. L19.

📖 **1b** G. DALY Mothers dreamed of snaring him for their daughters.

■ **snarer** *noun* a person who sets snares or traps L16.

snarf /snɑːf/ *verb trans. US slang.* M20.
[Perh. imit.]
Eat or drink quickly or greedily; wolf, gobble. Also foll. by *down*, *up*.

snark /snɑːk/ *noun.* L19.
[Nonsense word invented by Lewis Carroll in *The Hunting of the Snark* (1876).]
A fabulous animal. Also (*transf.*), an elusive truth or goal.

snark /snɑːk/ *verb. dial.* M19.
[Corresp. to Middle & mod. Low German *snarken*, Middle High German *snarchen* (German *schnarchen*), ult. imit. See also SNORK *verb.*]
1 *verb intrans.* Snore; snort. M19.
2 *verb intrans. & trans.* Find fault (with), nag. L19.

snarky /ˈsnɑːki/ *adjective. colloq.* E20.
[from prec. + -Y¹.]
Irritable, short-tempered.
■ **snarkily** *adverb* M20.**snarkiness** *noun* M20. **snarkish** *adjective* (*rare*) M20.

snarl /snɑːl/ *noun*¹. LME.
[from SNARE *noun* or *verb*: see -LE¹. Cf. SNARL *verb*¹.]
1 A snare, a trap; a noose. *obsolete* exc. *dial.* LME.
2 a A tangle, a knot, as in the hair. E17. ▸**b** *fig.* A muddle, a state of confusion; a mistake. Also (*colloq.*), a confused hold-up, a traffic jam. Freq. ***snarl-up***. M17.
3 A swarm, a large number. *US.* L18.
4 A knot in wood. *dial.* L19.

📖 **2b** S. CONRAN She . . straightened out the inevitable snarls in arrangements. *Oxford Mail* Frustrated drivers, nose to tail in the daily snarl-up.

snarl /snɑːl/ *noun*². E17.
[from SNARL *verb*².]
An act of snarling; a display of the teeth accompanied by an angry sound.

snarl /snɑːl/ *verb*¹. LME.
[Rel. to SNARL *noun*¹.]
1 *verb trans.* Catch in a snare or noose; entangle with a cord, rope, etc. Now *dial.* LME. ▸**b** *fig.* Ensnare, entrap. LME.
2 *verb trans.* **a** Tangle; twist together confusedly; make a tangle of. Now chiefly *dial.* & *US.* LME. ▸**b** *fig.* Complicate; muddle; throw into confusion. Also, hamper the smooth running of. Now usu. foll. by *up.* M17.
3 *verb intrans.* Become twisted, entangled, or confused; form or get into tangles or knots. Also foll. by *up.* E17.

📖 **2a** W. H. PRESCOTT Complicated roots snarled into formidable coils under the water. **b** W. J. BATE The . . human desire for security . . can so easily become snarled by panic. T. SHARPE Wilt . . was snarled up in a traffic jam. *New Yorker* A number of bills . . have been snarled in committee. **3** *New Scientist* If the tape snarls, all data are lost. *fig.*: G. F. NEWMAN Traffic snarled . . along Brompton Road at a snail's pace.

snarl /snɑːl/ *verb*². L16.
[Extension of SNAR: see -LE³.]
1 *verb intrans.* Of a dog or other animal: make an angry sound with bared teeth. L16.
2 *verb intrans.* Of a person: quarrel; grumble or criticize viciously; show strong resentment or ill feeling (*against* or *at*). L16.
3 *verb trans.* Utter in a harsh, rude, or ill-tempered manner. L17.

📖 **1** *Independent* Their own private island, with . . guards and snarling mastiffs. **2** A. HOLLINGHURST I snarled at him to shut up. **3** R. DAVIES 'Don't be daft . .', Ivor snarled, surly from lack of sleep.

■ **snarler** *noun*¹ (*a*) a person who snarls or grumbles; an ill-tempered person; (*b*) a dog etc. given to snarling: M17. **snarling** *ppl adjective* (*a*) that snarls; (*b*) of the nature of or accompanied by snarling; (*c*) having or producing the sound of a snarl: L16. **snarlingly** *adverb* M19.

snarl /snɑːl/ *verb*³ *trans.* L17.
[Perh. from SNARL *noun*¹.]
Raise or force *up* (metal) into bosses or projections with a snarling iron; adorn in this way.
Comb.: **snarling iron**, **snarling tool** a sharp tool struck with a hammer to produce bosses etc. in metal.
■ **snarler** *noun*² (a person who works with) a snarling iron M19.

snarlish /ˈsnɑːlɪʃ/ *adjective.* E19.
[from SNARL *noun*² or *verb*² + -ISH¹.]
Somewhat snarly or ill-tempered.

snarly /ˈsnɑːli/ *adjective*¹. Now *dial.* M17.
[from SNARL *noun*¹ or *verb*¹ + -Y¹.]
1 Tangled, ravelled. M17.
2 Full of snarls or knots. L18.

snarly /ˈsnɑːli/ *adjective*². L18.
[from SNARL *noun*² or *verb*² + -Y¹.]
Inclined to snarl; irritable, ill-tempered.

snash /snaʃ/ *noun & verb. Scot. & north.* L18.
[Prob. imit.]
▶ **A** *noun.* Abuse, impertinence, insolence. L18.
▶ **B** *verb intrans.* Use abusive or impertinent language. E19.

snaste /sneɪst/ *noun. obsolete* exc. *dial.* L16.
[Origin unkn.]
(The burning or burnt part of) a candle-wick.

snatch /snatʃ/ *noun.* ME.
[from the verb. Cf. SNECK *noun*¹.]
†**1** A trap, a snare, an entanglement. ME–M17.
2 A short spell *of* time, sleep, activity, etc. M16.

3 A small amount or portion; a brief piece, a fragment, esp. of a melody, conversation, etc. L16.
4 a A hasty catch or grasp; a sudden grab or snap *at* something. L16. ▸**b** A check, a hesitancy. *rare.* E17. ▸**c** A sudden twitch or jerk. Also, jerkiness in the running of a motor vehicle. E19.
5 A light hasty meal; a snack. L16.
6 a A hasty copulation; *derog.* a woman or women regarded as suitable for this. *slang.* L16. ▸**b** The female external genitals. *dial. & slang.* E20.
†**7** A quibble; a captious argument. Only in 17.
8 NAUTICAL. = ***snatch-block*** s.v. SNATCH *verb.* M19.
9 a A quick unexpected robbery; an act of stealing something, esp. by grabbing it. M19. ▸**b** A kidnapping. *colloq.* (orig. *US*). M20.
10 WEIGHTLIFTING. A lift in which the weight is raised in one movement from the floor to above the head with the arms straight. E20.

📖 **2** M. O. W. OLIPHANT Snatches of momentary sleep . . had fallen upon her. J. L. WATEN A snatch of sun and then spits of rain. **3** M. AYRTON I sing the same couplet, or snatch, over and over again. V. S. PRITCHETT Snatches of Italian . . picked up from waiters in Italy. J. UPDIKE He scribbled down snatches of conversation and descriptions of landscape. **4c** *Times* Players get the 'snatches' when the all-important cue action disintegrates. **6a** M. HOWARD Clever women whom he openly called snatch.

Phrases: **by snatches**, **in snatches** hurriedly, by fits and starts; intermittently.

snatch /snatʃ/ *verb.* ME.
[Obscurely rel. to SNACK *verb* and SNECK *noun*¹, implying a base repr. by Middle & mod. Dutch *snakken* gasp, perh. orig. open the jaws suddenly: cf. SNAP *verb.*]
1 *verb intrans.* **a** Suddenly snap or bite (*at* something). ME. ▸**b** Suddenly catch at a thing, in order to secure hold or possession of it. Usu. foll. by *at.* M16.
2 *verb trans.* Seize or take hold of suddenly, quickly, or unexpectedly. Also foll. by *up.* M16.
3 *verb trans.* Seize, catch, or take suddenly *away, from, off,* or *out of.* L16.
4 *verb trans.* Remove suddenly and quickly from sight or life. Usu. foll. by *away, from.* L16.
5 *verb trans.* Save or rescue *from* or *out of* danger etc., by prompt or vigorous action. E17.
6 *verb trans.* **a** Steal (a wallet, handbag, etc.), esp. by grabbing suddenly. M18. ▸**b** Kidnap. *colloq.* (orig. *US*). M20.
7 *verb trans.* NAUTICAL. Place (a rope or line) in a snatch-block. M18.
8 *verb trans.* Partake hurriedly or with difficulty of (food, sleep, etc.). E19.
9 *verb intrans.* Of a mechanism or its control in a motor vehicle, aircraft, etc.: run jerkily or roughly. M20.

📖 **1b** R. FRAME I . . snatched at the handbrake. *fig.*: J. F. HENDRY He snatched at Frau Faehndrich's invitation to stay at her villa. **2** K. MANSFIELD He snatched his bowler hat . . and swung down the garden path. K. AMIS He . . turned off the water and snatched up the towel. *fig.*: G. GREENE I must snatch a moment away from these harpies. **snatch it**, **snatch one's time** *Austral. slang* resign, leave a job and take the wages due. **3** E. A. FREEMAN A new English host was coming to snatch the victory from the conquerors. J. GALSWORTHY The young man, snatching off his hat, passed on. G. KEILLOR Mrs. Meiers snatched him out of his seat. **4** G. BERKELEY Several who are snatched away by untimely death. C. BOWEN Clouds snatch from the Teucrians' sight Sunlight and sky. **5** *Evening Post (Nottingham)* A 'brave and heroic' . . housewife today snatched three small children from a blazing house. **6a** A. PATON Boys snatched a bag . . from an old white woman. **b** *News of the World* Plotting to have the youngster snatched from school. **8** D. CECIL They snatched some breakfast . . in the glimmering dawn light.

Comb.: **snatch-back** the action of taking something back, esp. suddenly and forcibly; **snatch-block** NAUTICAL a block with a hinged opening to receive the bight of a rope; **snatch crop**: grown for quick returns without regard to the future productivity of the soil; **snatch squad** MILITARY a group of soldiers detailed to seize troublemakers in a crowd.
■ **snatchable** *adjective* L19. **snatcher** *noun* a person who or thing which snatches; *esp.* a thief, a robber, (*colloq.*) a kidnapper: L16.

snatchy /ˈsnatʃi/ *adjective.* M19.
[from SNATCH *noun* or *verb* + -Y¹.]
Consisting of or characterized by snatches; irregular, spasmodic.

snath /snaθ/ *noun.* Chiefly *dial. & US.* Also **snaith** /sneɪθ/, **sneath** /sniːθ/. L16.
[Var. of SNEAD.]
The shaft of a scythe.

snatter /ˈsnatə/ *verb intrans. rare* (long *obsolete* exc. *Scot.*). M17.
[Dutch *snateren* or Low German *snat(t)ern* (German *schnattern*, Swedish *snattra*), of imit. origin.]
Chatter.

snavel /ˈsnav(ə)l/ *verb trans. slang & dial.* (now chiefly *Austral.*). Infl. **-ll-**. Also **snav(v)le**. L18.
[Perh. var. of SNAFFLE *verb*¹.]
Steal, take; catch, grab.

snax /snaks/ *noun pl. informal* (chiefly *commercial*). M20.
[Respelling.]
Snacks.

snazzy /ˈsnazi/ *adjective. colloq.* M20.
[Origin unkn.]
Attractive; stylish; smart, flashy.
■ **snazzily** *adverb* L20. **snazziness** *noun* M20.

SNCF *abbreviation.*
French *Société Nationale des Chemins de fer Français*, the French State railway authority.

snead /sniːd/ *noun. obsolete* exc. *dial.* Also **sned** /snɛd/. See also SNATH.
[Late Old English *snǣd*, of unkn. origin.]
The shaft of a scythe.

sneak /sniːk/ *verb, noun, & adjective.* L16.
[Perh. rel. to SNIKE: cf. earlier SNEAKISHLY.]
▶ **A** *verb.* Pa. t. & pple **sneaked**, (chiefly *US*) **snuck** /snʌk/.
▶ **I** *verb intrans.* **1** Move or go stealthily; creep or steal furtively; slink. Freq. with adverb (phr.). L16. ▸**b** Make off quietly. *US colloq.* L19.
2 Cringe or be servile *to* (a person). M17.
3 Tell tales, turn informer. *School slang.* L19.

📖 **1** F. ASTAIRE I decided to sneak off to Paris for a few days without letting anyone know. R. MACDONALD We sneaked down the trail into the canyon. The man didn't see us. *East (Tokyo)* A burglar snuck in through the window. J. MAY I still can't figure how anything that big could have snuck up on me unawares. **3** D. WELCH Sneaking to one of the masters about a big boy's misdemeanour.

▶ **II** *verb trans.* **4** Move, place, or convey (a person or thing) stealthily. With adverb (or adverbial phr.). M17.
5 Steal or make off with (a thing) stealthily or unobserved; take or partake of surreptitiously. L19.

📖 **4** B. BAINBRIDGE She wondered if she could sneak him upstairs without Freda knowing. **5** J. K. JEROME Somebody must have sneaked it, and run off with it. R. FRAME The specimens . . are excellent (I sneaked a look one morning).

▶ **B** *noun.* **1** A mean-spirited cowardly person; a person who acts in a shifty or underhand manner. Also *spec.*, an informer, a tell-tale. M17.
2 The action or an act of sneaking; a stealthy movement, a furtive expedition or departure, orig. *spec.* for the purpose of committing theft; a theft committed in this way. L17. ▸**b** A furtive thief; a person who enters a place furtively to commit theft. L18.
3 CRICKET. A daisy-cutter. M19.
4 = SNEAKER 4. *slang.* M19.
5 *ellipt.* A sneak preview. *US colloq.* M20.
6 AMER. FOOTBALL. = ***quarterback sneak*** s.v. QUARTERBACK *noun.* L20.
Phrases: **on the sneak**, **upon the sneak** on the sly, by stealth.
▶ **C** *attrib.* or as *adjective.* Acting or done by stealth, deceit, or surprise; unexpected. L17.
Comb. & special collocations: **sneak-boat** *US* a boat which can readily move or approach unobserved, *esp.* a sneak-box; **sneak-box** *US* a small flat shallow boat masked with brush or weeds, used in wildfowl shooting; †**sneak-cup** (*rare*, Shakes.) = ***sneak-up*** below; **sneak-current** TELEPHONY a current slightly in excess of normal due to leakage but insufficient to blow a fuse; **sneak-guest**: who makes public the events of private social gatherings; **sneak-hunting** hunting from an unobserved approach; **sneak preview** (orig. *US*) (*a*) a screening of a film before public release to test audience reaction; (*b*) an unofficial preview; **sneak-preview** *verb trans.* (orig. *US*) have or show a sneak preview of (a film etc.); **sneaksman** *slang* a petty thief, a sneak-thief; **sneak-thief** a thief who steals without breaking in; a pickpocket; **sneak-thievery** the occupation of a sneak-thief; **sneak-up** a mean, servile, or cringing person; a sneak.

sneaker /ˈsniːkə/ *noun.* L16.
[from SNEAK *verb* + -ER¹.]
1 A person or animal that sneaks; a sneak. L16.
2 †**a** A small bowl (*of* punch). L17–L18. ▸**b** A glass *of* brandy. E19.
3 CRICKET. = SNEAK *noun* 3. M19.
4 A soft-soled canvas etc. shoe, a plimsoll, a training shoe. Chiefly *N. Amer.* L19.

📖 **4** P. P. READ Dressed in jeans, sneakers and an orange T-shirt.

■ **sneakered** *adjective* (chiefly *N. Amer.*) wearing sneakers M20.

sneaking /ˈsniːkɪŋ/ *adjective.* L16.
[from SNEAK *verb* + -ING².]
1 That sneaks; *esp.* that moves, walks, or acts furtively. L16.
2 Characterized by or suggestive of sneaking; contemptible. L16.
†**3** Niggardly; mean in character, appearance, etc.; contemptibly poor or small. L17–L18.
4 Of a feeling etc.: unavowed, undisclosed; persistent, nagging. M18.
■ **sneakingly** *adverb* L16. **sneakingness** *noun* (*rare*) M17.

sneakish /ˈsniːkɪʃ/ *adjective.* L16.
[Prob. rel. to SNEAK. Cf. next.]
†**1** Farcical, ludicrous. Only in L16.
2 Somewhat sneaky. M19.

sneakishly /ˈsniːkɪʃli/ *adverb. rare.* M16.
[Prob. rel. to SNEAK. Cf. prec.]
Meanly, despicably; sneakily.

sneaksby /ˈsniːksbi/ *noun.* Long *rare.* L16.
[from SNEAK + -BY.]
A mean-spirited person, a sneak.

sneaky /ˈsniːki/ *adjective & noun.* M19.
[from SNEAK *noun* + -Y¹.]
▶ **A** *adjective.* **1** Of a person: like or resembling a sneak; mean, sneaking. M19.
2 Characterized by sneaking. M19.
Special collocations: ***sneaky pete***: see PETE 3.
▶ **B** *noun.* A small concealed microphone or other device for surveillance or espionage. L20.
■ **sneakily** *adverb* M20. **sneakiness** *noun* M19.

sneap /sniːp/ *noun. arch.* L16.
[from next.]
A snub; a rebuke, a reproof.

sneap /sniːp/ *verb.* Now *arch. & dial.* L16.
[Later form of SNAPE *verb*¹.]
1 *verb trans. & intrans.* Of cold, wind, etc.: nip, bite. Chiefly as ***sneaped***, ***sneaping*** *ppl adjectives.* L16.
2 *verb trans.* Check; snub, reprove, chide. E17.

sneath *noun* var. of SNATH.

sneb /snɛb/ *verb trans. obsolete* exc. *dial.* Infl. **-bb-**. LME.
[Var. of SNIB *verb*¹.]
Reprimand, reprove; snub.

sneck /snɛk/ *noun*¹ & *verb*¹. Chiefly *Scot. & north.* ME.
[Obscurely rel. to SNATCH *noun*: cf. SNATCH *verb.*]
▶ **A** *noun.* **1** The latch of a door or gate; the lever which raises the bar of a latch. ME.
2 A small stone inserted into a gap between larger stones in a rubble wall. Usu. in *pl.* E19.
Comb.: **sneck-band** a piece of string fastened to a latch and passed through a hole to the outside of a door.
▶ **B** *verb.* **1** *verb trans.* Latch (a door or gate); close or fasten with a sneck. LME. ▸**b** *verb intrans.* Of a door or gate: latch, shut. L19.
2 *verb trans.* Fill in (a gap in a rubble wall) with lime or tightly packed small stones. L18.
■ **snecked** *adjective* (of a wall) built of squared stones of irregular sizes L19.

sneck /snɛk/ *noun*². M19.
[Imit.]
A sharp clicking sound.

sneck /snɛk/ *verb*² *trans. obsolete* exc. *dial.* E17.
[Origin unkn.]
Snatch; take or seize quickly.

†**sneck** *verb*³ var. of SNICK *verb*¹.

sneck-drawer /ˈsnɛkdrɔː(r)ə/ *noun. obsolete* exc. *Scot. & north.* LME.
[from SNECK *noun*¹ + DRAWER. Cf. DRAWLATCH *noun.*]
A person who draws or lifts a sneck or latch (in order to enter stealthily); a crafty, flattering, or sly person.
■ **sneck-draw** *noun* = SNECK-DRAWER L19. **sneck-drawing** *adjective* guileful, artful, crafty L18.

snecket /ˈsnɛkɪt/ *noun. obsolete* exc. *dial.* E17.
[Dim. of SNECK *noun*¹.]
= SNECK *noun*¹ 1. Also *transf.*, a noose, a halter.

sned *noun* var. of SNEAD.

sned /snɛd/ *verb trans.* Infl. **-dd-**.
[Old English *snǣdan* rel. to *sniþan* cut.]
1 a Cut or lop off (a branch). Also foll. by *off.* Long *Scot. & north.* OE. ▸**b** Prune, remove the branches of, (a tree). L16.
2 Cut; form by cutting. *Scot. & north.* L18.
■ **snedder** *noun* (chiefly *Scot. & north.*) L16.

sneer /snɪə/ *verb & noun.* LME.
[Perh. alt. of Old English *fnǣran* to snort (cf. Northern Frisian *sneere* to scorn).]
▶ **A** *verb.* **I** *verb intrans.* **1** Smile scornfully or contemptuously; speak or write in a manner suggesting or expressing contempt or disparagement. Freq. foll. by *at.* LME.
2 Of a horse: snort. Earlier as SNEERING. *obsolete* exc. *dial.* M16.

📖 **1** M. HOCKING Money is not to be sneered at . . . I often wish I had a little more. M. FORSTER She hates the Summer Exhibition, sneers . . at my pleasure in it.

▶ **II** *verb trans.* **3** Speak or write of (a person or thing) with scorn, contempt, or disparagement; deride, mock. *obsolete* exc. *dial.* LME.
4 Utter sneeringly. L17.
5 Drive or force (a person, quality, etc.) by sneers or scorn. Foll. by adverb (phr.). M18.

📖 **4** TENNYSON 'A ship of fools,' he sneer'd. **5** A. J. WILSON The world has not sneered it . . entirely out of existence. G. R. TURNER Bastard Kovacs tried to sneer down my success.

▶ **B** *noun.* **1** A snort, esp. of a horse. Chiefly *Scot.* Now *rare* or *obsolete.* LME.

2 An act of sneering; a derisive, contemptuous, or scornful look or remark. E18. ▸**b** Sneering, scorn. L18.

📖 **2** V. SACKVILLE-WEST He . . despised mankind so much that he seldom spoke without a sneer. G. S. HAIGHT Huxley's sneer that he was a mere 'book-scientist' stung . . sharply.

▪ **sneerer** *noun* a person who sneers E18. **sneerful** *adjective* given to sneering, scornful M18. **sneery** *adjective* of a sneering or scornful character L19.

sneering /ˈsnɪərɪŋ/ *adjective.* E16.
[from SNEER *verb* + -ING².]
1 That sneers. E16.
2 Of the nature of or characterized by a sneer; scornful, contemptuous, disparaging. L17.
▪ **sneeringly** *adverb* in a sneering manner; with a sneer: E18.

sneeshing /ˈsniːʃɪŋ/ *noun. Scot., Anglo-Irish, & north.* M17.
[App. alt. of SNEEZING.]
1 Snuff. M17.
2 A pinch of snuff; *fig.* (usu. in neg. contexts) something of very little value. L17.

sneeze /sniːz/ *verb & noun.*
[Old English *fnēosan* = *fnese*; of imit. origin. Alt. in Middle English as *fn-* became unfamiliar. Cf. NEEZE.]
▸ **A** *verb.* **1** *verb intrans.* Expel air suddenly through the nose and mouth by an involuntary convulsive or spasmodic action caused by irritation of the nostrils. OE.
2 *verb trans.* **a** Expel by sneezing. L17. ▸**b** Utter with a sneeze. Foll. by *out.* M19.
3 *verb intrans.* Regard as of little value, note, or importance; despise, disregard, underrate. Foll. by *at.* Usu. in neg. contexts. *colloq.* E19.

📖 **1** V. WOOLF The seeds and dust from the sacks made them sneeze. **3** C. O. SKINNER The actual figure was not to be sneezed at.

▸ **B** *noun.* **1** A powder etc. for inducing sneezing; snuff. *obsolete* exc. *north.* M17.
2 (The sound of) an act of sneezing. M17.
Comb.: **sneeze gas**: for incapacitating people by causing them to sneeze when it is inhaled or absorbed through the skin; **sneezeweed** *N. Amer.* any of several yellow-rayed plants of the genus *Helenium*, of the composite family, esp. *H. autumnale*; **sneezewood** a South African tree, *Ptaeroxylon obliquum* (family Ptaeroxylaceae), the sawdust of which causes violent sneezing; the wood of this tree; **sneezewort** a kind of yarrow, *Achillea ptarmica*, the powdered leaves of which are said to cause sneezing.
▪ **sneezy** *adjective* (*a*) (of a person) inclined to sneeze; (*b*) (of a thing) causing one to sneeze, dusty: M19.

sneezer /ˈsniːzə/ *noun.* M17.
[from prec.]
1 A person who sneezes. M17.
2 a A snuffbox. *slang.* E18. ▸**b** The nose; a handkerchief. *slang.* E19. ▸**c** A dram or drink, *esp.* a stiff one. *dial.* or *slang.* E19. ▸**d** Something exceptionally good, strong, violent, etc., in some respect. *dial.* or *slang.* E19.

📖 **2d** F. FRANCIS What a fine breeze . . ! A regular sneezer.

sneezing /ˈsniːzɪŋ/ *noun.* LME.
[from SNEEZE *verb* + -ING¹.]
1 The action of SNEEZE *verb*; an instance of this. LME.
†**2** Snuff. M17–E18.
Comb.: **sneezing gas** = SNEEZE *gas*.

sneg /snɛɡ/ *noun. rare.* Long *obsolete* exc. *dial.* ME.
[Perh. from Middle Low German *snigge* (cf. German *Schnecke*).]
A snail.

snekkja /ˈsnɛkjə/ *noun.* Pl. **-jur** /-jʊə/. M19.
[Old Norse (Icelandic).]
Hist. An ancient Icelandic or Scandinavian long ship.

snell /snɛl/ *noun & verb. US.* M19.
[Origin unkn.]
▸ **A** *noun.* A short line of gut or horsehair by which a fish-hook is attached to a longer line. M19.
▸ **B** *verb trans.* Tie or fasten (a hook) to a line. L19.

snell /snɛl/ *adjective & adverb.* Long *Scot. & north.*
[Old English *snel(l)* = Old Saxon, Old High German *snel* (German *schnell*) swift, active, quick, Old Norse *snjallr*.]
▸ **A** *adjective.* **1** Quick in movement or action, nimble; prompt, smart, clever, keen-witted, sharp. Formerly also, good. OE.
2 Of an action, words, weather, etc.: harsh, sharp, severe. Also (of a blow, rebuff, etc.) grievous, heavy, painful. ME.
3 Shrill, clear-sounding. E18.
▸ **B** *adverb.* Quickly, promptly; harshly; keenly. ME.
▪ **snelly** *adverb* OE.

Snellen /ˈsnɛlən/ *noun.* M19.
[Hermann *Snellen* (1834–1908), Dutch ophthalmologist.]
OPHTHALMOLOGY. Used *attrib.* and in *possess.* to designate (*a*) a scale of typefaces of different sizes used on test cards for ophthalmic patients, who are asked to read out as many lines as they can; the letters, test cards, etc., associated with this scale; (*b*) a fraction which expresses a patient's visual acuity as the actual reading distance over the rated distance of the smallest Snellen letters read.

Snell's law /ˈsnɛlz lɔː/ *noun phr.* L19.
[from Willebrord Van Roijen *Snell* (1591–1626), Dutch astronomer and mathematician.]
OPTICS. The law which states that for a ray of light passing from one uniform medium to another the sines of the angles of incidence and refraction are always in the same ratio.

snelskrif /ˈsnɛlskrɪf/ *noun. S. Afr.* M20.
[Afrikaans, from *snel* rapid + *skrif* writing.]
A system of shorthand for Afrikaans.

snew /sn(j)uː/ *verb intrans.* Long *obsolete* exc. *dial.*
[Old English *snīwan* = Middle Low German *snīghen*, Middle Dutch *snī(w)en*, Old High German *snīwan* (German *schneien*, from West Germanic word rel. to SNOW *noun*¹. Cf. SNOW *verb*.]
Snow.

SNG *abbreviation.*
Simulated, substitute, or synthetic natural gas.

snib /snɪb/ *noun*¹. *obsolete* exc. *Scot.* ME.
[from SNIB *verb*¹.]
A sharp rebuke, a snub.

†**snib** *noun*². *slang.* E17–E19.
[Origin unkn.]
A petty thief.

snib /snɪb/ *noun*³. Orig. *Scot. & Anglo-Irish.* E19.
[Perh. from Low German *snibbe* (German *Schnippe*), *snib* (Swedish *snibb*) beak, beaklike point.]
A lock, catch, or fastening for a door, window, etc.

snib /snɪb/ *verb*¹ *trans. obsolete* exc. *Scot. & dial.* Infl. **-bb-**. ME.
[Middle Danish *snibbe*, Middle Swedish *snybba*: see SNUB *verb*¹. See also SNEB.]
Reprimand, rebuke; check sharply or by some repressive action.

snib /snɪb/ *verb*² *trans.* Orig. *Scot.* Infl. **-bb-**. E19.
[Rel. to SNIB *noun*³.]
Fasten, lock, or bolt (a door etc.) with a snib; shut *in*, catch.

snibble /ˈsnɪb(ə)l/ *noun.* Orig. & chiefly *Scot.* E19.
[Perh. rel. to SNIB *noun*³.]
†**1** A wooden knob at the end of a rope or tether, fitting into a loop to make it fast. *rare.* Only in E19.
2 MINING. A small bar serving as a brake for a truck on an inclined road. L19.

snick /snɪk/ *noun*¹. *slang & dial.* E18.
[Origin unkn.]
A share. Usu. in *pl.*

snick /snɪk/ *noun*². L18.
[from SNICK *verb*².]
1 A small cut; a nick, a notch. L18.
2 CRICKET. A slight deflection of the ball by (esp. the edge of) the bat. M19.

snick /snɪk/ *noun*³. L19.
[from SNICK *verb*³.]
A sharp noise; a click.

snick /snɪk/ *verb*¹ *intrans. (imper.). obsolete* exc. *dial.* Also †**sneck**. L16.
[Origin unkn.]
snick up, ***go snick up***, go to hell, go away, get lost.

snick /snɪk/ *verb*² *trans.* L17.
[Prob. suggested by *snick* in SNICK OR SNEE.]
1 Cut or snip (*off*, *out*); cut a small notch or make a small incision in (a thing). L17.
2 a Strike or hit sharply. L19. ▸**b** CRICKET. Deflect (the ball) with the edge of the bat. L19.

snick /snɪk/ *verb*³. E19.
[Imit.]
1 *verb trans.* **a** Cause to click or sound sharply. E19. ▸**b** Turn (*on*, *off*, etc.) with a clicking noise. E20.
2 *verb intrans.* **a** Make a sharp clicking noise. L19. ▸**b** Move with a click. M20.

📖 **2b** C. D. SIMAK The lock snicked back and the door came open.

†**snick-a-snee** *noun.* In sense 1 also **snick and snee**. L17.
[Alt. of SNICK OR SNEE *noun phr.*]
1 = SNICKERSNEE *noun* 1. L17–M19.
2 = SNICKERSNEE *noun* 2. M18–M19.

snicker /ˈsnɪkə/ *verb & noun.* See also SNIGGER *verb*¹ & *noun*¹. L17.
[Imit. Cf. SNITTER.]
▸ **A** *verb intrans.* **1** Give a half-suppressed or smothered laugh; snigger. L17.
2 Of a horse: neigh, whinny. E19.
▸ **B** *noun.* A smothered laugh; a snigger. Also, a whinny, a neigh. M19.
▪ **snickeringly** *adverb* in a snickering manner, with a snicker L19.

snicker-snack /ˈsnɪkəsnak/ *adverb.* L19.
[Imit.]
With a snipping or clicking sound.

📖 P. WAY The little man next door was chopping his hedge. The shears were going snicker-snack.

snickersnee /ˈsnɪkəsniː/ *verb & noun. arch.* L17.
[Alt. of SNICK OR SNEE.]
▸†**A** *verb intrans.* = SNICK OR SNEE *verb phr.* L17–L18.
▸ **B** **1** Combat with knives adapted for cut and thrust. E18.
2 A large knife; a knife adapted for cut and thrust. L18.

snicket /ˈsnɪkɪt/ *noun.* Chiefly *north.* L19.
[Origin unkn.]
A narrow passage between houses, an alleyway.

snickle /ˈsnɪk(ə)l/ *verb & noun. obsolete* exc. *dial.* E17.
[Origin unkn.]
▸ **A** *verb trans.* Catch with a noose; snare. E17.
▸ **B** *noun.* A snare; a noose. L17.

†**snick or snee** *verb & noun phr.* As verb also (earlier) **stick or snee**. E17.
[from Dutch *steken* (German *stechen*) thrust, stick, & *snee* dial. var. of *snij(d)en* (German *schneiden*) cut, with later assim. of initial *st-* to the *sn-* of *snee*.]
▸ **A** *verb phr. intrans.* Cut or thrust in fighting with a knife; use a knife in this manner; fight with knives, use a knife as a weapon. E17–E18.
▸ **B** *noun phr.* = SNICKERSNEE *noun* 1. L17–E18.

snick-snarl /ˈsnɪksnɑːl/ *noun. obsolete* exc. *dial.* M17.
[from unkn. 1st elem. + SNARL *noun*¹.]
A tangle, a knot, a twist.

snick-up /ˈsnɪkʌp/ *noun.* Long *obsolete* exc. *dial.* L17.
[Imit.]
A sneeze, a sneezing-fit.

sniddy *adjective* var. of SNIDEY.

snide /snʌɪd/ *adjective & noun.* M19.
[Origin unkn.]
▸ **A** *adjective.* **1** Counterfeit, bogus. Also, inferior, worthless. *slang.* M19.
2 Of a person: cunning, devious; (chiefly *US*) mean, underhand. L19.
3 Insinuating, sneering, slyly derogatory. M20.

📖 **3** *Listener* Hostility from the fielders, with snide comments from the corner of the mouth.

▸ **B** *noun.* **1 a** Counterfeit jewellery or coin. *slang.* L19. ▸**b** A stolen pearl. *Austral. slang.* M20.
2 A snide or contemptible person; a swindler, a cheat, a liar. L19.
3 Hypocrisy; malicious gossip; a snide remark. E20.
▪ **snidely** *adverb* M20. **snideness** *noun* M20. **snidery** *noun* = SNIDE *noun* 3 M20.

Snider /ˈsnʌɪdə/ *noun.* M19.
[Amer. inventor Jacob *Snider* (d. 1866).]
MILITARY HISTORY. In full ***Snider rifle***. A form of breech-loading rifle.

snidey /ˈsnʌɪdi/ *adjective. colloq.* Also **sniddy** /ˈsnɪdi/, **snidy**. L19.
[from SNIDE *adjective* + -Y¹.]
Bad, contemptible; snide, derogatory.

snidge /snɪdʒ/ *noun. obsolete* exc. *north.* M16.
[Var. of SNUDGE *noun*.]
A greedy or miserly person.

snidy *adjective* var. of SNIDEY.

sniff /snɪf/ *verb & noun.* ME.
[Imit.]
▸ **A** *verb.* **1** *verb intrans.* Inhale through the nose with a short or sharp audible inhalation, esp. to clear the nose, detect a smell, or express contempt, disdain, etc. ME. ▸**b** *spec.* Inhale cocaine, the fumes of glue, etc., through the nostrils. E20.
2 *verb trans.* Inhale, take *up*, or draw *in* (air, a smell, cocaine, etc.) through the nostrils. L18.
3 *verb trans.* Smell (a thing); *fig.* perceive as if by smell, smell *out*, discover, suspect, (a plot etc.). M19.
4 *verb trans.* Say with a scornful sniff, say disdainfully. M19.

📖 **1** P. ROAZEN He . . frequently sniffed to see whether he could breathe properly. R. PILCHER She stopped crying and started sniffing instead. J. TROLLOPE The room smelt of man and dog . . . Martin sniffed. **sniff at** (*a*) try the smell of; show interest in; (*b*) show contempt for or discontentment with. **2** L. DURRELL The encouraging smell of food which we sniff appreciatively. **3** HARPER LEE I sniffed it and it smelled all right. M. HOLROYD He began to sniff some of the power that his personality could exert. *Fortune* The dollar may stay down . . but that's just when long-term speculators sniff opportunity. **sniff the wind** test the atmosphere, take soundings. **4** *Gay News* One gay sniffed: 'It's like a hairdresser's convention in there.'

▸ **B** *noun.* **1** (The sound of) an act of sniffing; an amount of air, cocaine, etc., inhaled in this act. M18. ▸**b** A smell, a scent; sniffing distance. M19. ▸c *fig.* A hint, an intimation. M20.

2 A domino game in which the first double played has special significance; *the* first double played. Orig. *US.* E20.

1 J. O'KEEFFE Rain over.. I'll take a sniff of the open air too. H. DRUMMOND The creature.. gives vent to a tremendous sniff, as if he had.. caught a severe cold. W. S. MAUGHAM The doctor's wife gave a little sniff of contempt. b DICKENS He was brought at length within sniff of the sea. R. H. MORRIESON A sniff of dark smoke from the railway station in the air.

▪ **sniffable** *adjective* L20. **sniffing** *verbal noun* the action of the verb; an instance of this: L16. **sniffingly** *adverb* with a sniff (esp. of scorn or contempt) L19. **sniffish** *adjective* somewhat sniffy M20.

sniffer /ˈsnɪfə/ *noun.* M19.
[from SNIFF *verb* + -ER¹.]
1 A person who sniffs; *spec.* a person who sniffs cocaine, the fumes of glue, etc. (freq. in ***glue-sniffer***). M19.
2 The nose. *slang.* M19.
3 a Any device for detecting gas, radiation, etc. *colloq.* M20. ▸b More fully ***sniffer dog***. A dog trained to detect specific odours, esp. those of drugs or explosives. *colloq.* M20.

sniffle /ˈsnɪf(ə)l/ *verb & noun.* M17.
[Imit.: cf. SNIVEL *verb.*]
▸ **A** *verb intrans.* 1 Snivel or snuffle slightly or repeatedly. Earliest as ***sniffling*** *verbal noun & ppl adjective.* M17.
2 *transf.* Of a breeze: blow smartly or briskly. Earlier in SNIFFLER (a). L19.
▸ **B** *noun.* 1 *sing.* & in *pl.* A cold in the head causing a running nose and sniffling. E19.
2 An act of sniffling; a slight snivel or snuffle. L19.
▪ **sniffler** *noun* (*a*) a smart or brisk breeze or wind; (*b*) a person who sniffles: M18. **sniffly** *adjective* that sniffles, characterized by sniffling M19.

sniffy /ˈsnɪfi/ *adjective. colloq.* L19.
[from SNIFF *verb* + -Y¹.]
Inclined to sniff; scornful, contemptuous, disdainful; ill-tempered.
▪ **sniffily** *adverb* E20. **sniffiness** *noun* E20.

snift /snɪft/ *verb intrans. obsolete* exc. *dial.* E18.
[Perh. from Middle Swedish *snypta* or Middle Danish *snyfte*, of imit. origin.]
Sniff; puff, snort, blow. Earlier as SNIFTING.
Comb.: **snifting valve** = ***snifter-valve*** s.v. SNIFTER *noun.*
▪ **snifting** *verbal noun* the action of the verb; *spec.* the action of releasing air, gas, or vapour from a container: LME.

snifter /ˈsnɪftə/ *verb & noun.* ME.
[Imit.: cf. prec.]
▸ **A** *verb intrans.* Sniff, snivel, snuffle. *rare.* ME.
▸ **B** *noun.* 1 A strong or rough breeze or wind; a strong blast, as of wind, sleet, etc. Chiefly *Scot. & north.* M18.
2 In *pl.* A bad cold in the head; the nasal congestion caused by this. *Scot.* E19.
3 A sniff. Chiefly *Scot. & north.* E19.
4 A usu. small quantity of alcoholic liquor, a nip. *colloq.* M19. ▸b A glass with a wide body narrowing towards the top, used esp. for brandy. Chiefly *N. Amer.* M20.
5 a A cocaine addict. *US slang.* E20. ▸b A small quantity of cocaine inhaled through the nose. *slang* (chiefly *US*). M20.
6 A portable radio direction-finder. *US slang.* M20.
Comb.: **snifter-valve**: to control the passage of air in and out of a steam engine.

snifty /ˈsnɪfti/ *adjective. slang* (chiefly *US*). L19.
[from SNIFT + -Y¹.]
Haughty, disdainful.

snig /snɪɡ/ *noun.* L15.
[Origin unkn.]
A young or small eel; = GRIG *noun*¹ 2.

snig /snɪɡ/ *verb trans.* Now chiefly *Austral. & NZ.* Infl. **-gg-**. L18.
[Origin unkn.]
Drag (a heavy load, esp. timber) by means of ropes and chains.
Comb.: **snigging chain**: used for moving logs.

snigger /ˈsnɪɡə/ *verb*¹ *& noun*¹. E18.
[Later var. of SNICKER. Cf. SNITTER.]
▸ **A** *verb.* 1 *verb intrans.* Give a half-suppressed or secretive laugh. E18.
2 *verb trans.* Utter with a snigger. M19.
▸ **B** *noun.* An act of sniggering. E19.
▪ **sniggerer** *noun* M19. **sniggering** *adjective* (*a*) of the nature of or characterized by a snigger or sniggers; (*b*) that sniggers: L18. **sniggeringly** *adverb* L19. **sniggery** *adjective* characterized by sniggering; prone to or liable to cause sniggering; immature, childish: prurient: M20.

snigger /ˈsnɪɡə/ *verb*² *& noun*². *local.* L19.
[Perh. rel. to SNIGGLE *verb*¹.]
▸ **A** *verb trans.* Catch (salmon) by means of weighted hooks. L19.
▸ **B** *noun.* A kind of grapple used by salmon-poachers. E20.

†**'sniggers** *interjection.* M17–M19.
[Origin unkn.: for 's- cf. 'SLID, 'SLIDIKINS, etc.]
Expr. asseveration. indignation, etc.

sniggle /ˈsnɪɡ(ə)l/ *verb*¹ *& noun*¹. M17.
[from SNIG *noun* + -LE³.]
▸ **A** *verb.* 1 a *verb intrans.* Fish *for* eels by means of a baited hook or needle thrust into their burrows. M17. ▸b *verb trans.* Fish for, catch, or pull out (an eel or eels) in this way. M19.
2 *verb trans.* Catch (a fish) by striking a hook into it. M19.
▸ **B** *noun.* A baited hook or needle used in sniggling for eels. M19.
▪ **sniggler** *noun*¹ M19.

sniggle /ˈsnɪɡ(ə)l/ *verb*² *& noun*². E19.
[Imit.]
▸ **A** *verb intrans.* Snigger, snicker. E19.
▸ **B** *noun.* A snigger, a snicker. M19.

sniggle /ˈsnɪɡ(ə)l/ *verb*³. *dial.* or *colloq.* M19.
[Origin unkn.]
1 *verb intrans.* a In a game of marbles, shuffle the hand forward unfairly. M19. ▸b Wriggle, crawl, creep stealthily. L19.
2 *verb trans.* Sneak (a thing) *in.* L19.
▪ **sniggler** *noun*² a person who plays unfairly or incorrectly M19.

†**snike** *verb intrans.* OE–ME.
[Old English *snīcan*, prob. rel. to Old Norse *sníkja* to sneak. Cf. SNEAK.]
Of a reptile: creep, crawl.

snip /snɪp/ *noun.* M16.
[from the verb, or from Low German *snip*, *snippe* (German dial. *Schnipf*, *Schnipp*) small piece, Dutch, Frisian *snip* snappish woman.]
▸ **I** 1 A small piece cut off or out of cloth etc.; a shred. M16.
2 A white or light patch on a horse, esp. on the nose or mouth. M16.
3 a A small amount or portion, a little bit. L16. ▸b An insignificant or contemptible person. Later also, a young, slight, or diminutive person. E17.

3a *Smash Hits* He's just a snip more sophisticated.. than before. b H. WOUK Heavens! If that little snip hasn't come up in the world.

▸ **II** 4 a A small cut or incision; *dial.* a small hole or crack. L16. ▸b POTTERY. A small projection on the lip of a vessel, the place for which is prepared by cutting a notch. M19.
5 (A name for) a tailor. *colloq.* L16.
6 a An act of snipping with scissors etc. L17. ▸b A nip, a pinch, a bite. M18.
7 In *pl.* ▸a Hand shears, *esp.* those for cutting metal. M19. ▸b Handcuffs. *slang.* L19.
8 a A thing easily obtained or achieved; a sure thing, a certainty. *colloq.* L19. ▸b A bargain, a good buy. *colloq.* E20. ▸c A piece of good fortune. *colloq.* M20.

6a A. MACLEAN With eight.. snips eight.. telephone wires fell to the ground. 8a *Tool World* This.. durable planer.. makes planing even the toughest materials a snip. b *Blue Jeans* For only £9.99 it's a complete snip.

Phrases: **a snip of a** — an extremely agreeable —. **go snips** (now *dial.*) go shares, divide the profits, (*with*).

snip /snɪp/ *verb & interjection.* Infl. **-pp-**. L16.
[Low German, Dutch *snippen* (cf. German dial. *schnippen*), of imit. origin: cf. SNAP *verb.*]
▸ **A** *verb.* **I** *verb trans.* 1 Take quickly or suddenly; snatch. Long *obsolete* exc. *Canad. dial.* L16.
2 Cut (cloth, a hole, etc.) using scissors etc., esp. with small quick strokes. (Foll. by *away*, *off*, *out*). L16.
3 Snub, check, repress. Now *dial.* E17.
4 CRICKET. Hit (the ball) lightly; snick. *rare.* L19.

2 *Which?* Snip out the coupons.. to send off for the offer. *Confident Cooking* Snip the fat.. to prevent curling.

▸ **II** *verb intrans.* 5 Make a cut or cuts using scissors etc., esp. with small quick strokes. L17.
▸ **B** *interjection.* Repr. the sound or action of snipping. M17.

C. MCCULLOUGH He began to cut..—snip! snip!—until all the long curls were.. on the floor.

▪ **snipped** *ppl adjective* (*a*) BOTANY irregularly notched or serrated; (*b*) that has been subjected to snipping; jagged, irregularly cut: L16.

snipe /snʌɪp/ *noun.* Pl. **-s**, (in sense 1 now usu.) same. ME.
[Prob. of Scandinavian origin (cf. Old Norse (Icelandic) *mýrisnípa*, Norwegian *myr-*, *strand-snípa*), obscurely rel. to Middle & mod. Low German, Middle Dutch *snippe* (Dutch *snip*), *sneppe*, and Old High German *snepfa* (German *Schnepfe*). Cf. SNITE *noun.*]
1 Any of various wading birds of the genus *Gallinago* and related genera (family Scolopacidae), which have a long straight bill and frequent marshy places; the flesh of any of these as food; *esp.* (more fully ***common snipe***) *G. gallinago*, found throughout the northern Holarctic. Formerly also (with specifying word), any of several other waders of the same family. ME.
2 As a term of abuse: a contemptible or worthless person. Cf. GUTTERSNIPE. E17.
3 a In *pl.* Scissors. *slang* (now *rare*). E19. ▸b The stub of a cigar or cigarette. *US slang.* L19. ▸c Any of a group of workers, esp. on board ship. *US slang.* E20. ▸d A sloping surface or bevel cut on the fore end of a log to ease dragging. M20.
4 (Also S-.) A class of sloop-rigged racing yacht; a yacht of this class. M20.
5 An instance of sniping; a long-range shot or attack from a sharpshooter. M20.
Comb.: **snipe bill** (*a*) a narrow moulding-plane with a sharp arris, used for forming or cutting quirks; (*b*) ZOOLOGY an Indo-Pacific gastropod, *Haustellum haustellum*, which has a thick shell with a very long siphonal canal; this shell; **snipe eel** any of various long, slender, mainly deep-sea fishes of the family Nemichthyidae, with long thin jaws and fragile bodies, esp. *Nemichthys scolopaceus* of the N. Atlantic; **snipe fish** any of various marine fishes of the genus *Macrorhamphosus* (family Macrorhamphosidae), which have a deep compressed body and a long snout, esp. *M. scolopax* of the Atlantic; **snipe fly** any of various long-legged slender-bodied flies of the family Rhagionidae, esp. the large *Rhagio scolopacea*; **snipe's-head**, **snipe-shell** = ***snipe bill*** (b) above.

snipe /snʌɪp/ *verb.* L18.
[from the noun.]
1 a *verb trans.* Shoot or fire at (people, targets, etc.) one at a time, usu. from cover and at long range; wound or kill in this manner. L18. ▸b *verb intrans.* Fire shots in this manner. Also foll. by *at*, *away.* M19.
2 *verb intrans.* Shoot snipe. Chiefly as ***sniping*** *verbal noun.* M19.
3 *verb intrans.* Express persistent criticism; make a sly critical attack or attacks, carp. Usu. foll. by *at.* L19.
4 *verb trans.* Cut a snipe or bevel on (a log) to ease dragging. L19.
5 *verb trans. & intrans.* Pilfer, steal; pick up; *spec.* prospect for (gold). *slang* (chiefly *N. Amer.*). L19.

1a C. C. TRENCH The patrol moving out.. was heavily sniped and had to return. 3 J. VIORST William used to snipe at Henry's much admired.. literary style.

sniper /ˈsnʌɪpə/ *noun.* E19.
[from prec. + -ER¹.]
1 A person who snipes or shoots from cover; a sharp-shooter. E19.
2 A snipe-shooter. M19.
3 A gold prospector. *US.* E20.
4 A person who cuts a snipe on a log. E20.
5 A non-union worker. *Austral. slang.* M20.

sniperscope /ˈsnʌɪpəskəʊp/ *noun.* E20.
[from prec. + -SCOPE.]
†1 A rifle sight incorporating a periscope, which can be aimed by a soldier under cover. Only in E20.
2 A telescopic rifle sight, *esp.* one incorporating an image intensifier so that it can be aimed in the dark. M20.

snipey *adjective* var. of SNIPY.

snipocracy /snɪˈpɒkrəsi/ *noun. joc. rare.* M19.
[from SNIP *noun*: see -CRACY.]
The tailoring profession.

snipper /ˈsnɪpə/ *noun.* L16.
[from SNIP *verb* + -ER¹.]
1 An instrument for snipping or clipping; in *pl.*, scissors. L16.
2 A person who snips material, clips hair, etc.; a tailor; a hairdresser. E17.

snipper-snapper /ˈsnɪpəsnapə/ *noun.* Now *dial.* L16.
[Fanciful: from SNIP-SNAP *verb*, WHIPPERSNAPPER.]
A young insignificant or conceited fellow.

snippet /ˈsnɪpɪt/ *noun.* M17.
[from SNIP *verb* + -ET².]
1 A small piece of material etc. cut off; a fragment or scrap of information etc. M17.
2 *spec.* A short passage from a piece of writing, a conversation, etc.; a cutting. M19.

1 W. DE LA MARE A silver snippet of moon hung low. S. MIDDLETON Fisher was only too willing to hand round.. opinions or snippets of knowledge. P. P. READ Going off.. to look at snippets and samples for wallpaper.. and loose covers. 2 N. SHERRY Sending Vivien a snippet from *The Times*.

▪ **snippetiness** *noun* the condition of being snippety L19. **snippety** *adjective* of the nature of or suggestive of a snippet or snippets; composed of snippets or scraps: M19.

snipping /ˈsnɪpɪŋ/ *noun.* L16.
[from SNIP *verb* + -ING¹.]
1 The action of SNIP *verb*; cutting, clipping. L16.
2 A piece snipped or cut off; a clipping, a cutting. Usu. in *pl.* E17.

snippy /ˈsnɪpi/ *adjective.* E18.
[from SNIP *verb* + -Y¹.]
1 Mean, stingy; covetous. *dial.* E18.
2 Fault-finding, snappish, sharp; supercilious. *colloq.* M19.

■ **snippily** *adverb* L20. **snippiness** *noun* M20.

snip-snap /ˈsnɪpsnap/ *noun & adjective.* L16.
[from SNIP *noun* + SNAP *noun*: imit.]
▶ **A** *noun.* **1** The action or sound of snipping or clipping with scissors etc.; an instance of this. L16.
2 Smart use of words; sharp repartee. L16.
▶ **B** *adjective.* †**1** Making a snipping sound; acting by snipping or clipping. Only in 17.
2 Of the nature of sharp repartee. L17.
3 Given to sharp repartee. Also, snappish, quarrelsome, irritable. *rare.* L18.

snip-snap /ˈsnɪpsnap/ *verb & adverb.* L16.
[from the noun.]
▶ **A** *verb intrans.* Infl. **-pp-**.
1 Indulge in smart repartee; speak in a snappy manner. L16.
2 Snip; clip with a snipping sound. *rare.* E20.
▶ **B** *adverb.* With a snipping or snapping sound. L16.

snip-snap-snorum /snɪpsnapˈsnɔːrəm/ *noun.* Also **-snorem**. M18.
[Low German *snipp-snapp-snorum*, of fanciful coinage.]
A card-game played esp. by children, in which players on turning up cards matching those held call in turn 'snip', 'snap', and 'snorum'.

snipy /ˈsnʌɪpi/ *adjective.* Also **-pey**. E19.
[from SNIPE *noun* + -Y¹.]
1 Having a long pointed nose or muzzle suggestive of a snipe's bill; *gen.* resembling a snipe. E19.
2 Frequented by snipe. E20.
■ **snipiness** *noun* M20.

snirt /snəːt/ *verb & noun.* Chiefly *Scot. & north.* E18.
[Imit.: cf. SNITTER, SNURT.]
▶ **A** *verb intrans.* Laugh in a suppressed manner; snigger. E18.
▶ **B** *noun.* A suppressed laugh; a snigger. L18.

snirtle /ˈsnəːt(ə)l/ *verb intrans. Scot. & north.* L18.
[from prec. + -LE³.]
= SNIRT *verb.*

snit /snɪt/ *noun. N. Amer. slang.* M20.
[Origin unkn.]
A state of agitation; a fit of rage; a bad temper, a sulk. Chiefly in ***in a snit***.
■ **snitty** *adjective* bad-tempered, sulky L20.

snitch /snɪtʃ/ *noun & verb. slang.* L17.
[Origin unkn.]
▶ **A** *noun.* †**1** A fillip (on the nose). Only in L17.
2 The nose. L17.
3 An informer; a person who turns King's or Queen's evidence. L18.
Phrases: **get a snitch on**, **have a snitch on** *NZ slang* have a grudge against, dislike.
▶ **B** *verb.* **1** *verb intrans.* Inform *on* a person; reveal information (*to* someone). M18.
2 *verb trans.* Take surreptitiously, steal. E20.

> 🕮 **1** B. SCHULBERG I felt a little guilty about snitching on my neighbor. **2** W. WHARTON I've snitched a . . magazine from . . the foyer.

■ **snitcher** *noun* a person who snitches; an informer: M18.

snite /snʌɪt/ *noun.* Now *dial.*
[Old English *snīte.*]
1 = SNIPE *noun* 1. OE.
2 = SNIPE *noun* 2. *obsolete* exc. *Scot.* M17.

snite /snʌɪt/ *verb.* Now *Scot. & dial.*
[Old English *snȳtan* = Middle & mod. Low German *snüten*, Old High German *snūzen* (German *schneuzen* snuff a candle, blow the nose), Old Norse *snýta*. Cf. SNOT *noun*, SNOUT *noun*¹.]
1 *verb trans.* Snuff (a candle). OE.
2 a *verb intrans.* Clean or wipe one's nose; remove mucus. OE. ▸**b** *verb trans.* Remove by wiping. OE.
3 *verb trans.* Clean or clear (the nose) of mucus, esp. with the thumb and finger; blow (one's nose). Also (*fig.*), tweak, pull. ME.

snitter /ˈsnɪtə/ *verb & noun. Scot. & north.* E19.
[Rel. to SNICKER, SNIGGER *verb*¹ & *noun*¹, SNIRT, TITTER *verb*¹.]
▶ **A** *verb intrans.* Laugh in a suppressed or nervous manner (*at*). E19.
▶ **B** *noun.* A suppressed or nervous laugh. E19.

snittle /ˈsnɪt(ə)l/ *noun. obsolete* exc. *dial.* E17.
[Origin unkn.]
A loop with a running knot; a noose; a slip-knot.

snivel /ˈsnɪv(ə)l/ *noun.* ME.
[from the verb.]
1 Mucus collected in, or running from, the nose. ME. ▸**b** In *pl.* & *sing.* The accumulation of mucus in the nose. E17.
2 A slight sniff indicating suppressed crying. M19. ▸**b** A pretence of crying; hypocritical expression of feeling. L19.

snivel /ˈsnɪv(ə)l/ *verb.* Infl. **-ll-**, *-**l-**. LOE.
[Repr. Old English verb. implied in late Old English *snyflung* mucus of the nose, from synon. *snofl*. Cf. Low German, Dutch *snuffelen* smell out, *snuiven* sniff, Swedish *snövla*, Norwegian *snuvla*, Danish *snøvle*, †*snevle*, SNIFFLE *verb*, SNUFFLE *verb*, -LE³.]
1 *verb intrans.* Emit mucus from the nose; run from the nose. Also, draw up mucus audibly, snuffle. LOE.
2 *verb trans.* **a** Affect in some way by whining or snivelling; address in a snivelling manner. *rare.* M17. ▸**b** Utter with a sniffing sound; shed (tears) snufflingly. Also foll. by *out*. L18.
3 *verb intrans.* Make a snuffling sound indicative of crying; be in, or affect, a tearful state. L17.

> 🕮 **1** R. MACAULAY Wipe your nose and don't snivel. **3** B. CHATWIN She cried at mealtimes. She kept snivelling into a lace handkerchief.

■ **sniveller** *noun* L15.

†**snivelled** *adjective.* Also **-eled**. M16–M18.
[from SNIVEL *noun*, *verb*: see -ED², -ED¹.]
Soiled or dirty with nasal mucus.

snivelling /ˈsnɪv(ə)lɪŋ/ *adjective.* Also ***-eling**. ME.
[from SNIVEL *verb* + -ING².]
1 (Of the nose) containing or emitting mucus; (of a person) given to snivelling or snuffling. ME.
2 Sounding through the nose. *rare.* LME.
3 In or affecting a tearful state; mean-spirited, weak. M17.
■ **snivellingly** *adverb* M20.

snob /snɒb/ *noun*¹ *& adjective.* Also (*Scot.*) **snab** /snab/. L18.
[Origin unkn.]
▶ **A** *noun.* **1 a** A shoemaker, a cobbler; a cobbler's apprentice. *dial.* or *colloq.* L18. ▸**b** = COBBLER 1b. *Austral. & NZ colloq.* E20.
2 *Hist.* A person who was not a university member; a townsman as opp. to a student. *Cambridge Univ. slang.* L18.
3 a A person belonging to the ordinary or lower classes of society. *arch.* M19. ▸**b** A person of low breeding or poor taste; a vulgar person. *arch.* M19.
4 Orig., a person seeking to imitate or associate with those of superior rank or wealth. Now usu., a person with an exaggerated respect for social position, who looks down on those of lower rank; a person who despises people considered inferior in (usu. specified) attainments or tastes. M19.

> 🕮 **4** L. MACNEICE Spiritually bankrupt Intellectual snobs. M. GARDINER She was a bit of a snob: she had . . enjoyed being presented at court. *Sunday Times* He was not a snob . . . His friends came from all walks of life. INVERTED ***snob***.

Comb.: **snob appeal** attractiveness to snobs; **snob-screen** a frosted glass screen with hinged panels instead of fixed glass, common in Victorian public houses above the bar; **snob value**: as a commodity prized by snobs or as an indication of superiority.
▶ **B** *adjective.* Fashionable, snobbish, pretentious. M20.
■ **snobbess** *noun* (*rare*) a female snob M19. **snobbily** *adverb* snobbishly M19. **snobbiness** *noun* snobbishness M19. **snobbism** *noun* snobbishness; an instance or manifestation of this: M19. **snobby** *adjective* snobbish M19. **snobdom** *noun* snobs collectively M19. **snobling** *noun* (*rare*) a little, young, or petty snob M19. **snoˈbographer** *noun* (*rare*) a writer on or describer of snobs M19. **snoˈbography** *noun* (*rare*) writing on or description of snobs M19.

snob /snɒb/ *noun*². L19.
[Origin unkn.]
Hist. In full ***snob-cricket***. Cricket played with a soft ball and a thick stick instead of a bat.

snob /snɒb/ *verb intrans. obsolete* exc. *dial.* Infl. **-bb-**. See also SNUB *verb*². ME.
[Imit.]
Sob.

snobbery /ˈsnɒb(ə)ri/ *noun.* M19.
[from SNOB *noun*¹ + -ERY.]
1 The class of snobs, snobs collectively. M19.
2 The character or quality of being a snob; snobbishness. Also, an instance of this; a snobbish trait. M19.

> 🕮 **2** S. J. LEONARDI Loyalty to Somerville takes the form of snobbery toward . . other women's colleges. INVERTED ***snobbery***.

snobbing /ˈsnɒbɪŋ/ *verbal noun. rare.* M19.
[from SNOB *noun*¹ + -ING¹.]
Cobbling, shoemaking.

snobbish /ˈsnɒbɪʃ/ *adjective.* M19.
[from SNOB *noun*¹ + -ISH¹.]
1 Of behaviour etc.: pertaining to or characteristic of a snob. M19.
2 Of a person: having the character of a snob. M19.
■ **snobbishly** *adverb* M19. **snobbishness** *noun* M19.

snobisme /snobism/ *noun.* Pl. pronounced same. E20.
[French.]
= SNOBBISM.

snobocracy /snɒˈbɒkrəsi/ *noun.* M19.
[from SNOB *noun*¹: see -CRACY.]
The class of snobs regarded as having some power or influence.
■ **snoboˈcratic** *adjective* (*rare*) M20.

SNOBOL /ˈsnəʊbɒl/ *noun.* M20.
[Acronym, from string-oriented symbolic language, after COBOL.]
COMPUTING. A high-level programming language used chiefly in literary research and symbolic computation.

Sno-cat /ˈsnəʊkat/ *noun.* M20.
[from *sno*, respelling of SNOW *noun*¹, + CAT(ERPILLAR. Cf. SNOWCAT.]
(US proprietary name for) a snowmobile.

snock /snɒk/ *noun. dial.* E19.
[Prob. imit.]
A knock; a blow.

snockered /ˈsnɒkəd/ *adjective. N. Amer. slang.* See also SCHNOCKERED. M20.
[Perh. alt. of *snookered*.]
Drunk, intoxicated.

snod /snɒd/ *adjective & verb. Scot. & north.* L15.
[Origin unkn.]
▶ **A** *adjective.* **1** Smooth, sleek; even. L15.
2 Neat, tidy, trim, smart. L17.
3 Comfortable, snug, cosy. L17.
▶ **B** *verb trans.* Infl. **-dd-**. Make smooth, trim, or neat; tidy, put in order. Also foll. by *up*. L16.

> 🕮 SIR W. SCOTT I . . am snodding up the drive of the old farm house.

■ **snodly** *adverb* E18.

snodger /ˈsnɒdʒə/ *adjective & noun. Austral. & NZ slang.* E20.
[Origin uncertain: cf. SNOD *adjective*, SNOG *adjective*.]
(Something) excellent or first-rate.

snoek /snuːk, snʊk/ *noun & verb.* Chiefly *S. Afr.* Pl. same. L18.
[Dutch = pike: see SNOOK *noun*¹.]
▶ **A** *noun.* = BARRACOUTA 2. L18.
▶ **B** *verb intrans.* Fish for snoek. E20.

snoff /snɒf/ *noun.* Now chiefly *Hist.* M19.
[Var. of SNUFF *noun*¹.]
MINING. A candle-end or other combustible substance used in blasting to light a fuse.

snog /snɒg/ *adjective. Scot. & north.* E16.
[App. from Old Norse *snǫggr* smooth, short-haired.]
Smooth, sleek; neat, tidy.

snog /ˈsnɒg/ *verb & noun. slang.* M20.
[Origin unkn.]
▶ **A** *verb.* Infl. **-gg-**.
1 *verb intrans.* Engage in kissing and cuddling (*with*). Freq. as ***snogging*** *verbal noun.* M20.
2 *verb trans.* Engage in kissing and cuddling with. M20.

> 🕮 **1** *Independent* An Israeli couple . . snog energetically, oblivious of his presence.

▶ **B** *noun.* A period of snogging. M20.

> 🕮 J. MORTIMER Gary and Tina were interrupted in the middle of a snog.

■ **snogger** *noun* M20.

Snohomish /snəʊˈhəʊmɪʃ/ *adjective & noun.* M19.
[Salish *snuhumš*.]
▶ **A** *adjective.* Of, pertaining to, or designating a Salish people of western Washington State or their language. M19.
▶ **B** *noun.* Pl. same.
1 A member of this people. E20.
2 The language of this people. M20.

snoke /snəʊk/ *verb intrans.* Chiefly *Scot. & north.* LME.
[Prob. of Scandinavian origin: cf. Norwegian dial. *snōka* to snuff or smell.]
Snuff, smell; sniff (*at*); poke about with the nose. Also (*fig.*), sneak about, keep watch *over*.

snollygoster /ˈsnɒlɪgɒstə/ *noun. US dial. & slang.* M19.
[Perh. alt. of SNALLYGASTER.]
A shrewd unprincipled person; *esp.* a politician of this nature.

snood /snuːd/ *noun & verb.*
[Old English *snōd*, of unkn. origin.]
▶ **A** *noun.* **1** Orig., a band or ribbon for the hair. Later, a hairband worn by young unmarried women in Scotland and northern England. Now, an ornamental pouchlike hairnet, worn to hold hair at the back of the head; a ring of woollen etc. material worn as a hood. OE.
2 a In sea-fishing: any of a number of short lines, each with a baited hook, attached at regular distances along the main line. L17. ▸**b** In angling, a fine line attaching the hook to the rod line. E19.
▶ **B** *verb trans.* **1** Tie *up*, fasten *back*, or secure (the hair) with a snood. E18.
2 In angling, attach (a hook) to a snood. M19.

■ **snooded** *ppl adjective* (of hair) tied with a snood; (of a person) wearing a snood: **M18**. **snooding** *noun* material used for fishing-snoods **E19**.

snoodle /ˈsnuːd(ə)l/ *verb intrans. dial.* (chiefly *north.*) or *nursery*. Now *rare*. **L19**.
[Origin unkn.]
Snuggle, nestle.

snook /snuːk/ *noun*[1]. **L17**.
[Dutch *snoek* pike from Middle & mod. Low German *snōk*, prob. rel. to the base of **SNACK** *noun*. Cf. **SNOEK**.]
Any of various fishes, esp. Caribbean food fishes of the family Centropomidae, spec. *Centropomus undecimalis*.

snook /snuːk/ *noun*[2]. **L18**.
[Origin unkn.]
A gesture of contempt made with one thumb on the nose and fingers spread out. Chiefly in ***cock a snook***, make this gesture (*at* a person); *fig.* express contempt or rebelliousness (foll. by *at* for a person, establishment, etc.).

📖 N. SHERRY Cocking a snook at convention, challenging accepted principles.

Comb.: **snook-cocking** *verbal noun & adjective* (the action of) cocking a snook at a person etc.

snooker /ˈsnuːkə/ *noun*[1]. *slang*. **L19**.
[Origin unkn.]
Hist. A newly joined cadet at the Royal Military Academy, Woolwich.

snooker /ˈsnuːkə/ *noun*[2] & *verb*. **L19**.
[Origin unkn.]
▶ **A** *noun*. **1** A game played with one white, 15 red, and 6 coloured balls on a billiard table, in which two players use a cue to strike the white ball with the aim of pocketing the other balls in a set order. Formerly also ***snooker's pool***. **L19**.
2 A position in snooker in which a player is unable to make a direct shot at any permitted ball; a shot which puts one's opponent in this position. **E20**.
▶ **B** *verb trans*. **1** Subject (oneself or another player) to the position of a snooker. **L19**.
2 Place in an impossible situation; defeat, thwart. Chiefly as ***snookered*** *ppl adjective*. **E20**.

📖 **1** *Pot Black* Hendry led . . but then snookered himself. **2** W. BOYD Balked, frustrated, all his good intentions . . snookered.

Snooks /snuːks/ *noun*. **M19**.
[Origin unkn.]
(A nickname for) a hypothetical person in a particular case. Cf. ***Joe Bloggs*** s.v. **JOE** *noun*[2].

snool /snul/ *noun & verb*. *Scot. & north*. **E18**.
[Origin unkn.]
▶ **A** *noun*. An abject, cowardly, or mean-spirited person. **E18**.
▶ **B** *verb*. **1** *verb trans*. Keep in subjection; snub. **E18**.
2 *verb intrans*. Submit meekly; cringe. **L18**.

snoop /snuːp/ *verb & noun*. *colloq*. (orig. *US*). **M19**.
[Dutch *snoepen* eat on the sly.]
▶ **A** *verb*. **1** *verb intrans. & trans*. Steal; orig. *spec*. steal and eat (food) in a clandestine manner. Now *rare*. **M19**.
2 *verb intrans*. **a** Go *about* or *around* in a sly or prying manner; look *round* or investigate something surreptitiously. **M19**. ▸**b** Pry *into* another's private affairs; nose; also spy *on*. **E20**.

📖 **2a** W. C. WILLIAMS The press began snooping around. **b** P. BOOTH Those Secret Service people . . snooping into everything.

▶ **B** *noun*. **1** = **SNOOPER** *noun* 1. **L19**.
2 An act of snooping or prying; a surreptitious investigation. **E20**.

📖 **2** B. W. ALDISS I had a snoop round the churchyard.

■ **snoopery** *noun* the activity of snooping or prying; surreptitious investigation: **M20**.

snooper /ˈsnuːpə/ *noun*. *colloq*. (orig. *US*). **L19**.
[from prec. + **-ER**[1].]
1 A person who pries or spies; *spec*. a person making an official investigation, a detective. **L19**.
2 A thief. *rare*. **E20**.

snooperscope /ˈsnuːpəskəʊp/ *noun*. **M20**.
[from prec. + **-SCOPE**.]
An infrared image intensifier; *esp*. (*sing*. & in *pl*.) a pair of such devices worn on the head to provide binocular vision in the dark.

snoopy /ˈsnuːpi/ *adjective*. *colloq*. (orig. *US*). **L19**.
[from **SNOOP** *verb* + **-Y**[1].]
Inquisitive, excessively curious or prying.
■ **snoopiness** *noun* **M20**.

snoose /snuːs, snuːz/ *noun*. *N. Amer. dial*. **E20**.
[Danish, Norwegian, Swedish *snus* snuff.]
A variety of snuff, esp. as taken (usu. orally) by loggers.

snoot /snuːt/ *noun*. **M19**.
[Dial. var. of **SNOUT** *noun*[1]. Sense 4 prob. back-form. from **SNOOTY**.]
1 A person's nose. *dial. & colloq*. **M19**.
2 The nose of an aircraft, car, etc. **M20**.
3 A tubular or conical attachment used to produce a narrow beam from a spotlight. **M20**.
4 A snooty person; snootiness. *colloq*. **M20**.

snoot /snuːt/ *verb*. *US*. **L19**.
[from the noun.]
1 *verb intrans*. Nose around. *dial. rare*. **L19**.
2 *verb trans*. Snub; treat with disdain. *colloq*. **E20**.

📖 **2** E. FERBER In Texas the cotton rich always snooted the cattle rich.

snootful /ˈsnuːtfʊl, -f(ə)l/ *noun*. *colloq*. **E20**.
[from **SNOOT** *noun* + **-FUL**.]
As much (alcohol etc.) as one can take; a quantity of alcohol, *esp*. one sufficient to induce drunkenness.

snooty /ˈsnuːti/ *adjective*. **E20**.
[from **SNOOT** *noun* + **-Y**[1].]
Supercilious, haughty, conceited; snobbish.

📖 B. CASTLE A rather snooty cleric . . greeted me when we arrived late. *Face* We are not snooty about who comes in with us.

■ **snootily** *adverb* **M20**. **snootiness** *noun* **M20**.

snoove /snuːv/ *verb*. *Scot*. **E16**.
[Middle Swedish *snoa*, Swedish *sno*, Danish *snoe* = Old Norse (Icelandic) *snúa* (Faeroese *snúgva*, Norwegian *snu*).]
1 *verb trans. & intrans*. Twirl, (cause to) turn. **E16**.
2 *verb intrans*. Move or advance steadily; glide. **E18**.

📖 **2** R. BURNS Just thy step a wee thing hastet, Thou snoov't awa.

snooze /snuːz/ *noun & verb*. *colloq*. **L18**.
[Origin unkn.]
▶ **A** *noun*. **1** A short sleep; a nap, a doze. **L18**.
2 A bed. *slang*. **E19**.
▶ **B** *verb intrans*. Take a snooze, sleep, doze. **L18**.
Comb.: **snooze alarm**: on a bedside clock which may be set to repeat after a short interval, allowing the sleeper a further nap; **snooze button**: which sets the snooze alarm on a clock.
■ **snooziness** *noun* the state of being snoozy **L19**. **snoozy** *adjective* drowsy, sleepy **L19**.

snoozer /ˈsnuːzə/ *noun*. **M19**.
[from **SNOOZE** *verb* + **-ER**[1].]
†**1** A thief who steals from the building in which he or she is staying. *slang*. **M–L19**.
2 A person who snoozes. *colloq*. **L19**. ▸**b** A fellow, a chap. *slang*. **L19**.

snoozle /ˈsnuːz(ə)l/ *verb*. *colloq. & dial*. **M19**.
[Cf. **SNOOZE** *verb*, **NUZZLE** *verb*[1].]
1 *verb intrans*. Of an animal: nestle and sleep; nuzzle. **M19**.
2 *verb trans. & intrans*. Esp. of a dog: poke (the nose) affectionately *around* or *into*. **M19**.

Snopes /ˈsnəʊps/ *noun*. Pl. same. **M20**.
[The surname of a series of vicious characters in the fiction of William Faulkner (1897–1962), US novelist.]
An unscrupulous or heartless person.

snore /snɔː/ *noun*. **ME**.
[formed as the verb.]
†**1** A snort; snorting. *rare*. **ME–E16**.
2 A disease or illness which causes snuffling; in *pl*., *the* snivels. *rare*. **L16**.
3 An act of snoring; a snorting sound made in breathing during sleep. **E17**.
4 A sound resembling that of a snore; a loud roaring or droning noise. **E18**.

snore /snɔː/ *verb*. **LME**.
[from imit. base repr. by Middle & mod. Low German, Middle & mod. Dutch *snorken* (whence dial. *snork*): cf. **SNORT** *verb*[2].]
1 *verb intrans*. **a** Of an animal, esp. a horse: snort. Now *Scot. & dial*. **LME**. ▸**b** Of wind etc.: make a roaring or droning noise. *Scot., north., & US*. **E19**. ▸**c** Of a ship etc.: move or cut *through* the water with a roaring sound; travel quickly. Chiefly *Scot*. **M19**.
2 *verb intrans*. Make snorting or grunting sounds in breathing while asleep, due to vibration of the soft palate; *joc. & colloq*. sleep, esp. heavily. **LME**.
3 *verb trans*. Foll. by *away*, *out*: get rid of or pass (time etc.) in snoring. **L16**. ▸**b** Bring into a certain state by snoring. *rare*. **L18**.
4 *verb trans*. Utter with a (sound resembling a) snore. **L18**.

📖 **2** G. GREENE His mouth was open . . and he snored irregularly. **3** N. FARAH The inhabitants of the city snored away their dreams. **4** *Daily News* People seemed to snore prayer; they were so sleepy.

Comb.: **snore-hole** MINING: through which water to be raised from a well etc. enters the bottom of the pump; **snore-off** *colloq*. (chiefly *Austral. & NZ*) a sleep or nap, esp. after drinking; **snore-piece** MINING the lowest part of a pump, with holes for letting in water from the bottom of a well etc.

■ **snoreless** *adjective* (of sleep) unaccompanied by snoring **M19**. **snorer** *noun* (*a*) a person who snores; (*b*) *slang* the nose; (*c*) *colloq*. a stiff breeze: **LME**.

snoring /ˈsnɔːrɪŋ/ *ppl adjective*. **L16**.
[from **SNORE** *verb* + **-ING**[2].]
1 That snores. **L16**.
2 Of a breeze: strong, stiff. *colloq*. **E19**.
3 Having the characteristic sound of a snore; loud and harsh. **M19**.
■ **snoringly** *adverb* **E19**.

snork /snɔːk/ *noun*. **E19**.
[from the verb.]
1 A snort, a grunt; a noisy sniff. *Scot. & dial*. **E19**.
2 A young pig; a piglet. *dial*. **L19**.
3 A baby. *Austral. & NZ slang*. **M20**.

snork /snɔːk/ *verb intrans*. Now *Scot. & dial*. **M16**.
[Prob. from Middle & mod. Dutch or Middle & mod. Low German *snorken* (whence Danish *snorke*) var. of *snarken* **SNARK** *verb*.]
1 Snore. **M16**.
2 Esp. of a horse or pig: snort, grunt; breathe noisily. **E19**.
■ **snorker** *noun* (*rare*) = **SNORK** *noun* 2 **L19**.

snorkel /ˈsnɔːk(ə)l/ *noun & verb*. Also (esp. in sense A.1) **schnor-** /ʃnɔː-/. **M20**.
[German *Schnorchel*.]
▶ **A** *noun*. **1** (Also **S-**.) An extendible device on a submarine containing tubes used to draw in air for the engines and for ventilation, and to expel engine exhaust, while the vessel is submerged at periscope depth. Cf. **SNORT** *noun*[2]. **M20**.
2 A short breathing-tube used by underwater swimmers. **M20**.
3 (Also **S-**.) (Proprietary name for) a type of hydraulically elevated platform used for fighting fires in tall buildings. **M20**.
▶ **B** *verb intrans*. Infl. **-ll-**, ***-l-**. Use a snorkel; swim under water using a snorkel. **M20**.
■ **snorkeller** *noun* a person who snorkels **M20**.

snort /snɔːt/ *noun*[1]. **E17**.
[from **SNORT** *verb*[2].]
†**1** A snore. *rare*. Only in **E17**.
2 An act of snorting; a loud sound made by the sudden forcing of breath out through the nose, often as an expression of contempt, indignation, or incredulity. **E19**.
3 a An alcoholic drink; a measure of spirits. *colloq*. **L19**. ▸**b** A dose of cocaine or heroin in powder form, taken by inhalation; an instance of taking this. *slang*. **M20**.

📖 **2** H. KELLER The indulgent snort of my pony, as we . . put the bit in his mouth. N. ANNAN He would say little (though he timed his snorts admirably). **3a** F. FORSYTH 'Fancy a snort?' 'Bit early,' protested Preston.

snort /snɔːt/ *noun*[2] & *verb*[1]. *Nautical slang* (now *Hist*.). **M20**.
[Anglicized from German *Schnorchel* **SNORKEL**, after prec.]
▶ **A** *noun*. = **SNORKEL** *noun* 1. **M20**.
▶ **B** *verb intrans*. Travel under water using a snorkel. **M20**.

snort /snɔːt/ *verb*[2]. **LME**.
[Ult. imit.: cf. **SNORE** *verb*, **SNURT**.]
†**1** *verb trans*. Turn *up* (one's nose) in scorn. Only in **LME**.
†**2** *verb intrans*. Snore; sleep heavily. **LME–L17**.
3 *verb intrans*. Of a horse etc.: make a loud sound by suddenly forcing breath out through the nostrils, esp. when excited or frightened. **LME**.
4 *verb intrans*. Of a vehicle etc.: emit a sound resembling a snort; move with such a sound. **L16**.
5 *verb trans*. **a** Utter with a snort; give *out* or drive *away* by snorting. **M17**. ▸**b** Eject through the nostrils with a snort. Also foll. by *out*. **E19**.
6 *verb intrans*. **a** Express contempt, indignation, incredulity, etc., by making a snorting sound. **E19**. ▸**b** Laugh loudly or roughly. **E19**.
7 *verb trans*. Inhale (cocaine, heroin, etc.) through the nostrils. *slang*. **M20**.

📖 **4** *Sunday Express* Container lorries snort past. **5a** M. KINGTON 'A likely story!' she would snort. **6b** JULIA HAMILTON Baillie snorted with laughter.

■ **snorty** *adjective* (*a*) characterized by or given to snorting; (*b*) *colloq*. ill-tempered, disagreeable: **L16**.

snorter /ˈsnɔːtə/ *noun*[1]. **E17**.
[from prec. + **-ER**[1].]
1 A person who or thing which snorts; (*dial. & colloq*.) a pig. **E17**.
2 a (A blow on) the nose. *slang*. **E19**. ▸**b** A dashing lively man. *US slang*. **M19**. ▸**c** A thing exceptional in size, strength, severity, etc.; *spec*. a strong wind, a gale. *colloq*. **M19**.

📖 **2c** *Harper's Magazine* It was blowing a snorter. R. H. MORRIESON There was another snorter of a frost.

snorter /ˈsnɔːtə/ *noun*[2]. **M18**.
[Var. of **SNOTTER** *noun*[2].]
NAUTICAL. = **SNOTTER** *noun*[2].

snorting /ˈsnɔːtɪŋ/ *ppl adjective*. L16.
[from SNORT *verb*[2] + -ING[2].]
1 That snorts; of the nature of or resembling a snort. L16.
2 Of weather or wind: severe, rough, violent. *colloq.* E19.
3 Exceptional in size, strength, etc. *colloq. rare.* E20.
■ **snortingly** *adverb* (*rare*) in a snorting manner; with a snort: M19.

snortle /ˈsnɔːt(ə)l/ *verb intrans. obsolete* exc. *dial.* L16.
[from SNORT *verb*[2] + -LE[3].]
Snort.

snot /snɒt/ *noun*. LME.
[Prob. from Middle & mod. Low German, Middle Dutch *snotte*, Dutch *snot*, corresp. to Old English *ġesnot*, Old Frisian *snotta*, Middle High German *snuz* (German dial. *Schnutz*), from Germanic: cf. SNITE *verb*, SNOUT *noun*[1].]
1 The snuff or burnt wick of a candle. Now *Scot.* & *north.* LME.
2 Nasal mucus. Now *slang*. LME.
3 A worthless or contemptible person. *slang*. E19.

📖 **2** A. HALEY Breathe through nostrils . . plugged with snot. **3** S. O'FAOLÁIN He cursed me for a city snot.

Comb.: **snotnose** *slang* a childish, conceited, or contemptible person; **snot-nosed** *adjective* (*slang*) childish, conceited, contemptible; **snot-rag** *slang* (**a**) a pocket handkerchief; (**b**) a contemptible person.

snot /snɒt/ *verb*. Now *Scot.* & *north.* Infl. **-tt-**. LME.
[from the noun.]
1 *verb trans.* Snuff (a candle). LME.
2 *verb trans.* Blow or clear (the nose). L15.
3 *verb intrans.* Sniff, snivel; snort. M17.

snotter /ˈsnɒtə/ *noun*[1]. *Scot.* & *north.* L17.
[from SNOT *noun*. Cf. Middle Dutch *snoter*, Middle Low German *snotter* (German dial. *Schnotter*, *Schnodder*).]
= SNOT *noun* 2. Also (*fig.*), something of little or no value or importance.

snotter /ˈsnɒtə/ *noun*[2]. M18.
[Origin unkn.: cf. SNORTER *noun*[2].]
NAUTICAL. **1** A fitting which holds the heel of a sprit close to the mast. M18.
2 A length of rope with an eye spliced in each end. M20.

snotter /ˈsnɒtə/ *verb intrans. Scot.* & *north.* E18.
[Prob. rel. to SNOTTER *noun*[1].]
1 Breathe heavily; snore, snort. E18.
2 Snivel, cry noisily. L18.

snotty /ˈsnɒti/ *noun. Nautical slang.* E20.
[Perh. a specific application of next.]
A midshipman.

snotty /ˈsnɒti/ *adjective*. Now *slang*. L16.
[from SNOT *noun* + -Y[1].]
1 a (Esp. of a person's nose) full of or running with mucus; (of a person) having a nose full of mucus. L16. ▸**b** Consisting of or resembling mucus; viscous, slimy. Long *rare* or *obsolete*. M17.
2 a Dirty, mean, contemptible. L17. ▸**b** Angry, short-tempered; impudent; conceited. Now *esp.*, supercilious, snooty. *slang*. L19.

📖 **2a** L. CODY 'Snotty cow,' Alf replied, when she was . . out of earshot. **b** *Listener* Viennese are, in the matter of opera, . . exceedingly snotty.

Comb.: **snotty-nose** (**a**) a person with a snotty nose; (**b**) a dirty, mean, or contemptible person; **snotty-nosed** *adjective* (**a**) having a snotty nose; (**b**) dirty, mean, contemptible.
■ **snottily** *adverb* M19. **snottiness** *noun* M16.

snouch /snaʊtʃ/ *verb trans.* Now *rare* or *obsolete*. M18.
[Origin unkn.]
Snub; treat scornfully.

snous /snaʊs/ *noun*. M20.
[Danish or Swedish *snus* snuff.]
Powdered tobacco, snuff, esp. as taken orally.

snout /snaʊt/ *noun*[1]. ME.
[Middle Low German, Middle Dutch *snūt(e* (Dutch *snuit*), whence Middle Swedish *snuta*, Danish *snude*, German *Schnauze*, ult. from Germanic word repr. also by SNITE *verb*, SNOT *noun*. Cf. SNOOT *noun*.]
1 a The trunk of an elephant. ME. ▸**b** The projecting part of an animal's face including the nose and mouth; the rostrum of a weevil. Formerly also, a bird's beak. ME.
2 A person's nose, esp. when large or badly shaped. Formerly also, the face. Chiefly *joc.* or *derog.* ME.
3 The end of a ship's prow; the beak of a vessel. LME.
4 A structure, projecting point of land, etc., resembling a snout; a nozzle. LME. ▸**b** The steep terminal part of a glacier. M19.
5 Any of various noctuid moths that have long palps projecting in front of the head; esp. *Hypena proboscidalis*. Also *snout-moth*. E19.
6 A police informer. *slang*. E20.

📖 **1b** P. THEROUX Pigs . . stick their snouts into the coconuts. **4** D. HEWETT Black snouts of factory chimneys. J. CARROLL The snout of a German Luger . . pressing against the flesh.

Phrases: **have a snout on** *Austral. slang* dislike or bear ill will towards.
Comb.: **snout-beetle** a weevil; **snout-face** *slang* a contemptible person; *snout-moth*: see sense 5 above.
■ **snouted** *adjective* having a snout (of a specified kind); shaped like a snout: LME. **snoutish** *adjective* L19. **snoutless** *adjective* (*rare*) M19. **snouty** *adjective* resembling a snout or muzzle; having a prominent snout: L17.

snout /snaʊt/ *noun*[2]. *slang*. L19.
[Origin unkn.]
1 Tobacco. L19.
2 A cigarette. M20.

snout /snaʊt/ *verb*. M18.
[from SNOUT *noun*[1].]
†**1** *verb trans.* Finish (a costume) *off* by putting on a snout. *rare*. Only in M18.
2 *verb intrans.* Search with the snout; root around. M19.
3 *verb trans.* Dislike, bear ill will towards; treat with disfavour, rebuff. Chiefly as ***snouted*** *ppl adjective. Austral. slang*. E20.
4 *verb intrans.* Act as a police informer. *slang*. E20.

📖 **2** D. DAVIE The wild boar . . snouts in the bracken.

Snovian /ˈsnəʊvɪən/ *adjective*. M20.
[from Charles Percy *Snow* (1905–80), English writer + -IAN, after *Shavian*.]
Of or pertaining to the writings or ideas of C. P. Snow.
■ **Snovianism** *noun* (*rare*) the beliefs or theories of C. P. Snow M20.

snow /snəʊ/ *noun*[1]. Also (*Scot.* & *north.*) **snaw**.
[Old English *snāw* = Old Frisian *snē*, Old Saxon, Old High German *snēo* (Dutch *sneeuw*, German *Schnee*), Old Norse *snær*, *snjár*, *snjór*, Gothic *snaiws*, from Germanic; rel. to Latin *niv-*, *nix*, Greek *nipha* (accus.). Cf. SNEW.]
▸ **I 1** The frozen moisture of the atmosphere, composed of minute hexagonal ice crystals and usu. aggregated in feathery white flakes; the fall of such flakes. Also, a layer formed by such flakes on the ground. OE. ▸**b** The pure white colour of snow; whiteness. Chiefly *poet.* OE.
2 a A fall of snow; a snowstorm. OE. ▸**b** A period of time consisting of one winter. Also, a year. Chiefly *poet.* or (freq. *joc.*) in representations of N. American Indian speech. L18.
3 a A mass or expanse of snow. Usu. in *pl.* LME. ▸**b** In *pl.* The regions of perpetual snow; the Arctic regions. *rare*. M19.
4 = *snow tyre* below. *N. Amer.* M20.

📖 **1** SHELLEY Some, whose white hair shone Like mountain snow. ANNE STEVENSON Distant moors . . covered by pure untroubled snow. **b** SIR W. SCOTT Daughters . . with . . fair hair, and bosoms of snow. **2a** H. NORMAN The first snows each autumn. **b** R. WIEBE It was the most successful raid they had had for many snows. **3a** R. FISK Along the . . frontier from the sea to the snows of Hermon.

▸ **II** A thing resembling snow.
5 Any of various substances having the colour or appearance of snow; *spec.* (**a**) a dessert resembling snow in appearance, made with whipped egg-white; (**b**) CHEMISTRY any of various solids, esp. frozen gases, that resemble snow; *esp.* solid carbon dioxide; (**c**) *slang* (orig. *US*) cocaine, heroin. L16.
6 a White hair. Chiefly *poet.* E17. ▸**b** White blossom. Also, spray, foam. M19.
7 a Clean linen. *slang* (now *rare*). E19. ▸**b** (Silver) money. *slang*. E20.
8 Spots that appear as a flickering mass on a television or radar screen, caused by interference or poor signal reception. M20.

📖 **5** L. CODY You can get a fair stretch for dealing snow. **7a** *Household Words* Lifting snow from some railings, where it was hanging to dry.

Phrases etc.: ***old snow***: see OLD *adjective*. ***red snow***: see RED *adjective*. **snow-in-summer** any of several white-tomentose summer-flowering plants grown for ornament, esp. *Cerastium tomentosum*, a southern European plant of the pink family, and *Helichrysum rosmarinifolium*, an Australian everlasting. **snow-on-the-mountain** (**a**) *US* an annual spurge, *Euphorbia marginata*, with white-bordered bracts; (**b**) *dial.* any of several low white-flowered cruciferous garden plants, esp. *Arabis caucasica* and sweet alyssum, *Lobularia maritima*.
Attrib. & comb.: In the sense 'consisting of or covered in snow', as ***snow-bank***, ***snowcap***, ***snow-cloud***, etc.; 'used in connection with snow', as ***snow buggy***, ***snow fence***, ***snow goggles***, ***snow tractor***, etc. Special combs., as **snow bear** a brown bear of a race found in the Kashmir area; **snowbell** any of various plants with white bell-shaped flowers; *spec.* an Asian storax tree, *Styrax japonica*, bearing clusters of fragrant white hanging flowers at midsummer; **snow-belt** *US* a region subject to heavy snowfalls; **snowberry** any of various shrubs bearing white berries or similar fruit; *esp.* (**a**) a N. American shrub, *Symphoricarpos albus*, commonly grown in shrubberies; (**b**) ***creeping snowberry***, a trailing N. American shrub of the heath family, *Gaultheria hispidula*, of woods and bogs; **snow-blink** a white reflection in the sky of lying snow; **snowblower** a machine that clears snow from a road etc. by blowing it to the side; **snow-break** (**a**) the breaking of trees or branches by the weight of snow; an area over which this has occurred; (**b**) a strip of trees or fencing serving as a protection against snow; **snow-broth** melted snow; **snow bunny** *N. Amer. slang* an inexperienced (esp. female) skier; **snow bunting** a holarctic bunting, *Plectrophenax nivalis*, the male of which has predominantly white plumage, breeding in rocky areas on mountains or near Arctic coasts; **snow-camel** the Bactrian camel; **snow cannon** a machine which makes artificial snow and blows it on to ski slopes; **snowcap** (**a**) the top of a mountain when covered with snow; (**b**) a white-crowned hummingbird, *Microchera albocoronata*, native to Central America; **snowcapped** *adjective* (esp. of a mountain) topped with snow; **snow chains**: fitted around a vehicle's tyres to give extra grip in snow; **snow-clad** *adjective* covered with snow; **snowcock** any of several large partridges of the genus *Tetraogallus*, found at high altitudes from Iran to western China; **snow-cold** *adjective* as cold as snow; **snow-cone** *US* a paper cup of crushed ice flavoured with fruit syrup; **snow course** a line along which the depth of snow is periodically measured at fixed points; **snow crab** either of two edible spider crabs, (**a**) *Chionoecetes opilio*, found off eastern Canadian coasts, (**b**) a giant white deep-sea species found off northern Australia; **snow-craft** skill in moving over or dealing with snow in mountaineering; **snow-creep** the gradual movement of snow down a slope; **snow cruiser** *N. Amer.* a motor vehicle designed to travel over snow; *spec.* (with cap. initials) (Canadian proprietary name for) a motorized toboggan; **snow devil** a column of snow whirled round by the wind; **snowdrift** a bank of snow heaped up by the action of the wind; **snow-dropper** *slang* a person who steals clothes from washing-lines, *esp.* a man who steals women's underwear; **snow-dropping** *slang* the action of stealing clothes from washing-lines; **snow-eater** METEOROLOGY [translating German *Schneefresser*] a warm wind, esp. a Chinook, that causes rapid melting of snow; **snowfall** a fall of snow; a quantity of snow falling at a certain time or place; **snowfield** an expanse of snow; **snow finch** any of several Eurasian montane sparrows of the genus *Montifringilla*, esp. *M. nivalis*, which has a grey head, black throat, and mainly white wings, and is found from the Pyrenees to western China; **snow flea** (**a**) any of several vestigial-winged scorpion flies of the family Boreidae, resembling ants and found on moss in boreal regions, esp. *Boreus hyemalis* of Eurasia; (**b**) any of several small dark springtails that swarm on snow, esp. *Isotoma saltans* of the Alps and *Hypogastrura nivicola* of N. America; **snow-fleck** the snow bunting (cf. SNOWFLAKE 2); **snow-fly**, **snow-gnat** any of several insects found frequently on snow; *esp.* a wingless cranefly of the genus *Chionea*; **snow goose** a N. American goose, *Anser caerulescens*, which has all-white plumage with black primaries and breeds near Arctic coasts; **snow grain** METEOROLOGY a small opaque precipitated ice particle, usu. flattened and less than 1 mm in diameter, that does not bounce on a hard surface (cf. ***snow pellet*** below); **snow-grass** any of several coarse upland grasses; *esp.* (*NZ*) *Danthonia raoulii* (see DANTHONIA); **snow-grouse** the ptarmigan; **snow gum** a eucalyptus, *Eucalyptus niphophila*, with white bark and glaucous leaves, native to high regions of New South Wales, Australia; **snow gun** = ***snow cannon*** above; **snow-hole**: in snow used as a temporary shelter; **snow-ice** opaque white ice formed from melted snow; **snow-insect** = ***snow-fly*** above; **snow job** *slang* (orig. *US*) an attempt at flattery, deception, or persuasion; **snow-job** *verb trans. slang* (orig. *US*) attempt to flatter, deceive, or persuade (someone); **snow leopard** a large endangered member of the cat family, *Panthera uncia*, which has a greyish-white coat with dark markings and is found in the mountains of central Asia; also called ***ounce***; **snow lily** a dog's tooth violet, *Erythronium grandiflorum*, of alpine regions in western N. America; **snowline** the level above which snow never completely disappears; **snow machine** *N. Amer.* a motor vehicle designed to travel over snow; **snow-maker** (a person who uses) a device for the artificial production of a snow-like precipitate for ski slopes etc.; **snow-making** the production of a snowlike precipitate; **snow-melt** the melting of fallen snow; water that results from this; **snow mould** (a crop disease caused by) any of several fungi that develop under snow, spec. *Fusarium nivale*; **snow-mouse** (**a**) = ***snow vole*** below; (**b**) *N. Amer.* the American arctic lemming, *Dicrostonyx groenlandicus*; **snow owl** *US* the snowy owl; **snowpack** *US* lying snow that is compressed and hardened by its own weight; **snow panther** = ***snow leopard*** above; **snow partridge** (**a**) a partridge, *Lerwa lerwa*, which has barred black and white plumage and bright red bill and legs, and is found in the Himalayan region; (**b**) = ***snowcock*** above; **snow pea** the mange-tout pea; **snow pellet** METEOROLOGY an opaque precipitated ice particle, usu. a few millimetres in diameter, that will bounce on a hard surface; a soft hailstone; (cf. ***snow grain*** above); **snow petrel** an all-white petrel, *Pagodroma nivea*, found in the Antarctic; **snow pheasant** = ***snowcock*** above; **snow pigeon** a brown and white pigeon, *Columba leuconota*, found in China and the Himalayas; **snow plane** *N. Amer.* a snowmobile mounted on skis and propelled by an engine-driven propeller; **snow plant** (**a**) an alga, *Chlamydomonas nivalis*, which is a cause of red snow; (**b**) a blood-red saprophytic plant, *Sarcodes sanguinea* (family Monotropaceae), of forests in the Sierra Nevada; ***snow powder***: see POWDER *noun*[1] 1d; **Snow Queen** [from a character in a Hans Christian Andersen fairy tale] a cold-hearted woman; **snow roller** a cylinder of snow formed by the wind rolling it along; **snowscape**, **snow scene** (a picture of) a landscape covered with snow; **snow scorpion fly** *N. Amer.* = ***snow flea*** (a) above; **snow-ski** *verb intrans.* = SKI *verb* 1; **snow-sleep** sleepiness induced by walking in snow; **snow-slip** an avalanche; **snow-snake(s)** a N. American Indian game played by hurling a straight wooden rod along an icy or snowy surface; the rod used in this game; **snow sparrow** any of various small birds; *esp.* (*N. Amer.*) a junco; **snow-sports**: which take place on snow, *spec.* skiing; **snowstorm** (**a**) a storm accompanied by a heavy fall of snow; (**b**) a transparent dome or globe containing a representation of a scene and loose silvery or metallic particles suspended in liquid, which, when shaken, creates the appearance of a snowstorm; (**c**) an appearance of dense snow (SNOW *noun*[1] 8) on a television or radar screen; **snowsure** *adjective* (of a ski resort or slope) likely to have enough snow to ski on during

the season; **snow-tyre**: having a tread which gives extra traction on snow or ice; **snow vole** a vole, *Microtus nivalis*, found at high altitudes from the Pyrenees to Iran; **snow-water**: derived from melted snow; **snow-white** *adjective & noun* white (as snow), pure white; **snow wolf** a wolf that lives in snowy regions; the (imitation) fur of this animal; **snow worm** any of various small worms frequenting or living in snow; *esp.* = ***ice-worm*** s.v. ICE *noun*; **snow-wreath** a snowdrift.

■ **snowless** *adjective* E19. **snowlike** *adjective & adverb* resembling or after the manner of snow M17.

snow /snəʊ/ *noun*[2]. L17.
[Dutch *snauw, snaauw*, or Low German *snau* (whence Danish, Swedish *snau*, German *Schnau(e)*, French *senau*), of unkn. origin.]
A small sailing vessel resembling a brig, having a main and fore mast and a supplementary trysail mast close behind the mainmast.

snow /snəʊ/ *verb.* Also (*Scot. & north.*) **snaw** ME.
[from SNOW *noun*[1], repl. Old English *snīwan* SNEW.]
1 *verb intrans. impers.* in ***it snows***, ***it is snowing***, etc.: snow falls, snow is falling, etc. ME.
2 *verb intrans.* Fall as or like snow. LME.
3 *verb trans.* Let fall as snow; send down like snow; shower down. LME.
4 *verb trans.* Cover with or as with snow. LME.
5 *verb trans.* Cause (hair etc.) to turn white. *poet. & literary.* L16.
6 *verb trans.* **a** Block, obstruct, or imprison with snow. Chiefly as ***snowed*** *ppl adjective.* Foll. by *in*, *up*. E19. ▸**b** Drive *out* or take *away* by means of snow. M19. ▸**c** Foll. by *under*: bury in snow; *fig.* overpower or overwhelm (*with* work etc.). Usu. in *pass.* L19.
7 *verb trans.* Drug, dope. Chiefly as ***snowed*** *ppl adjective. US slang.* E20.
8 Deceive with words; kid, dupe. *slang* (chiefly *US*). M20.

> 🕮 **3** M. TWAIN A sweep of . . air . . snowing the flaky ashes broadcast about the fire. *fig.*: R. CAMPBELL And a / fine aeroplane was snowing propaganda. **6a** *Daily Telegraph* I was snowed up for four days. *Truckin' Life* Winter weather means many . . snowed-in mountain passes. **c** D. JUDD He's been snowed under with . . urgent cases. **8** N. FREELING Don't snow me with any sob-sister business.

snowball /ˈsnəʊbɔːl/ *noun & verb.* ME.
[from SNOW *noun*[1] + BALL *noun*[1].]
▶ **A** *noun.* **1** A ball of snow pressed together, esp. used for throwing in play. ME. ▸**b** A scheme, organization, etc., which grows or increases rapidly like a snowball rolled on snow. E17. ▸**c** In bingo etc.: a cash prize which accumulates through successive games. M20.
2 a A cake or dish intended to resemble a ball of snow in appearance. M18. ▸**b** A cocktail usu. containing advocaat and lemonade. M20. ▸**c** An ice-cream; a confection made of crushed ice covered in syrup. *US & W. Indies.* M20.
3 A black person. *slang. joc.* or *derog.* L18.
4 Any of various plants bearing rounded clusters of white flowers etc.; *esp.* (more fully ***snowball bush***, ***snowball tree***) a cultivated form of the guelder rose, *Viburnum opulus* var. *roseum*, bearing round-topped cymes consisting entirely of large sterile flowers. L18.

> 🕮 **1 not a snowball's chance (in hell)** *colloq.* no chance at all. **b** *Arab Times* It could result in a snowball of Arab investment in Shepway.

▶ **B** *verb.* **1** *verb intrans.* Form balls or masses of snow. Now *rare* or *obsolete.* L17.
2 *verb trans.* **a** Throw a snowball at (a person); pelt with snowballs. M19. ▸**b** *verb intrans.* Throw snowballs. M19.
3 *verb intrans. & trans.* (Cause to) grow or increase rapidly like a snowball rolled on snow. E20.

> 🕮 **3** *New York Times* A single assault case had snowballed into at least 26 different incidents.

snowbird /ˈsnəʊbəːd/ *noun.* L17.
[from SNOW *noun*[1] + BIRD *noun.*]
1 Any of several small finchlike birds, *esp.* the snow bunting, snow finch, and junco. L17.
2 A person who sniffs cocaine; *gen.* a drug addict. *US slang.* E20.
3 a A person who enlists in the army for a job in winter. *US slang* (now *rare*). E20. ▸**b** A northerner who moves to a warmer southern State in the winter. *N. Amer. slang.* E20.
4 A person who likes snow; a winter sports enthusiast. *colloq.* E20.

snow-blind /ˈsnəʊblʌɪnd/ *adjective.* M18.
[from SNOW *noun*[1] + BLIND *adjective.*]
Temporarily blinded or having vision made defective by the glare of light reflected by large expanses of snow.
■ **snow-blinded** *adjective* = SNOW-BLIND M19. **snow-blindness** *noun* M18.

snowboard /ˈsnəʊbɔːd/ *noun.* L20.
[from SNOW *noun*[1] + BOARD *noun.*]
A wide ski resembling a large skateboard without wheels, used for sliding downhill on snow.
■ **snowboarder** *noun* a person who rides on a snowboard L20. **snowboarding** *noun* the activity of riding on a snowboard L20.

snowcat /ˈsnəʊkat/ *noun.* M20.
[Respelling of SNO-CAT.]
A tracked vehicle for travelling over snow.

Snowcem /ˈsnəʊsɛm/ *noun.* M20.
[from SNOW *noun*[1] + CEM(ENT *noun.*]
(Proprietary name for) a cement-based paint used for covering external walls.
■ **Snowcemmed** *adjective* painted with Snowcem M20.

Snowdonian /snəʊˈdəʊnɪən/ *adjective.* E19.
[from *Snowdon* (see below) + -IAN.]
Of or pertaining to Snowdon, the highest mountain in Wales; located at or near Snowdon.

Snowdon lily /ˈsnəʊd(ə)n ˈlɪli/ *noun phr.* L20.
[*Snowdon* (see prec.).]
A lloydia, *Lloydia serotina*, confined in Britain to the Snowdon range. Also called ***mountain spiderwort***.

snowdrop /ˈsnəʊdrɒp/ *noun.* M17.
[SNOW *noun*[1] + DROP *noun.* Cf. German *Schneetropfen.*]
1 An early-flowering bulbous plant, *Galanthus nivalis* (family Amaryllidaceae), having a single drooping pure white flower; a flowering stem of this plant. M17.
2 A military police officer, orig. in the US. *slang.* M20.
Comb.: **snowdrop tree** any of several trees with pendulous white flowers; *esp.* (***a***) the fringe-tree, *Chionanthus virginicus*; (***b***) = HALESIA.

snowflake /ˈsnəʊfleɪk/ *noun.* M18.
[from SNOW *noun*[1] + FLAKE *noun*[2].]
1 Any of the small feathery aggregations of crystals in which snow falls. M18.
2 The snow bunting. Cf. ***snow-fleck*** s.v. SNOW *noun*[1]. L18.
3 Any of several bulbous plants constituting the genus *Leucojum* (family Amaryllidaceae), resembling snowdrops but more robust and with larger, green-tipped flowers; esp. *L. vernum* (more fully ***spring snowflake***) and *L. aestivum* (more fully ***summer snowflake***), both cultivated. L18.
4 = HAIRLINE 5. *US.* E20.
Comb.: **snowflake curve** MATH. a mathematically conceived curve whose sixfold symmetry resembles that of a snow crystal, of interest because its infinite length bounds a finite area.

snowman /ˈsnəʊman/ *noun.* Pl. **-men**. E19.
[from SNOW *noun*[1] + MAN *noun.*]
1 A mass of snow made into a shape resembling a human figure. E19.
2 a ARCHAEOLOGY. A technique of clay-modelling; a figurine so produced. Usu. *attrib.* E20. ▸**b** A pottery figure with a thick white glaze. Usu. *attrib.* M20.
3 A person who deceives someone with words. *US slang.* M20.
4 = YETI. Cf. ***Abominable Snowman*** s.v. ABOMINABLE *adjective* 1. M20.

snowmobile /ˈsnəʊməbiːl/ *noun.* M20.
[from SNOW *noun*[1] + AUTO)MOBILE.]
A motor vehicle designed for travelling over snow; *spec.* a small light passenger vehicle fitted with runners at the front and a traction chain at the rear.
■ **snowmobiler** *noun* a person who drives or rides on a snowmobile M20. **snowmobiling** *noun* the action or sport of using a snowmobile M20.

snowplough /ˈsnəʊplaʊ/ *noun & verb.* Also ***-plow**. L18.
[from SNOW *noun*[1] + PLOUGH *noun.*]
▶ **A** *noun.* **1** An implement or machine for clearing away snow from a road, railway track, etc. L18.
2 SKIING. An act of turning the front points of the skis inwards to slow down. E20.
▶ **B** *verb intrans.* Execute a snowplough in skiing. E20.

snowshoe /ˈsnəʊʃuː/ *noun & verb.* M17.
[from SNOW *noun*[1] + SHOE *noun.*]
▶ **A** *noun.* **1** A kind of footwear for walking on snow without sinking in; *esp.* either of a pair of racket-shaped frames strung with a network of narrow strips of leather etc., attached to the shoes or boots. M17.
2 Either of a pair of skis. M19.
Comb.: **snowshoe hare**, **snowshoe rabbit** a N. American hare, *Lepus americanus*, which has large furry hind feet and an entirely white coat in winter.
▶ **B** *verb intrans.* Pres. pple & verbal noun **-shoeing**. Travel on snowshoes or skis. L19.
■ **snowshoed** *adjective* wearing snowshoes L19. **snowshoer** *noun* a person who uses snowshoes M19.

snowy /ˈsnəʊi/ *adjective & noun.* OE.
[from SNOW *noun*[1] + -Y[1].]
▶ **A** *adjective.* **1** (Of weather) characterized by snow; (of a period of time) during which snow falls; (of a place) in which snow is frequent. OE.
2 a Consisting or made of snow. ME. ▸**b** Covered with snow; having much snow. M16.
3 Of or resembling the pure white colour of snow; snow-white. Also ***snowy white***. LME.
4 Of the picture on a television screen: affected with snow (SNOW *noun*[1] 8). M20.
Special collocations: **snowy egret**, **snowy heron** an American egret, *Egretta thula*, with all-white plumage. **snowy** MESPILUS. **snowy owl** a large holarctic day-flying owl, *Nyctea scandiaca*, which has predominantly white plumage and breeds mainly in the Arctic tundra. **snowy petrel** = ***snow petrel*** s.v. SNOW *noun*[1]. **snowy plover** *N. Amer.* = ***Kentish plover*** s.v. KENTISH *adjective.*
▶ **B** *noun.* **1** Linen. *slang* (now *rare*). L19.
2 *ellipt.* The snowy owl. E20.
■ **snowily** *adverb* in a snowy manner; with or through snow; as snow: M19. **snowiness** *noun* the condition of being snowy; whiteness: E18. **snowyish** *adjective* (*rare*) somewhat snowy E19.

snozzle /ˈsnɒz(ə)l/ *noun. slang* (orig. *US*). M20.
[Alt. of SCHNOZZLE.]
The nose.

SNP *abbreviation.*
Scottish National Party.

Snr. *abbreviation.*
Senior.

SNU /snjuː/ *abbreviation.*
ASTRONOMY. Solar neutrino unit.

snub /snʌb/ *noun & adjective.* M16.
[from SNUB *verb*[1].]
▶ **A** *noun.* **I 1** An act or instance of snubbing someone; a remark or action intended to rebuff or humiliate a person, a rebuff. M16. ▸**b** In *pl.* As *interjection*, expr. indifference or contempt. *slang.* M20.
2 †**a** A check, a hindrance. L16–L17. ▸**b** A sudden check given to a rope etc. in running out; a post or stake enabling this to be done. *US.* L19.
3 A projecting snag, a stub. *rare.* L16.

> 🕮 **1** L. KENNEDY The slightest snub . . brought on a sense of hurt. **b** E. WAUGH I have had it straight from a real artist, and snubs to her. **3** W. DE LA MARE Not so much as . . a snub of soap.

▶ **II 4** A snub nose. M19.
5 GEOMETRY. A snub polyhedron or polytope. M20.
6 A snub-nosed handgun. *US slang.* L20.
▶ **B** *adjective.* **1** Short and blunt in shape. Orig. and esp. in ***snub nose*** below. E18.
2 Snub-nosed. L19.
3 GEOMETRY. Designating any of certain symmetrical polyhedra and polytopes having additional faces and hence more nearly spherical shape compared with the corresponding regular polyhedron etc. M20.

> 🕮 **2** V. WOOLF What a little bank clerk, snub, common, he's grown. **3** ***snub cube***, ***snub dodecahedron***, etc.

Comb. & special collocations: **snub nose** (***a***) a short and turned-up nose; (***b***) (***snubnose***) *US slang* a snub-nosed handgun; **snub-nosed** *adjective* (***a***) having a snub nose; (***b***) stumpy; short and broad at the front; (of a handgun) small and short-barrelled.

snub /snʌb/ *verb*[1]. Infl. **-bb-**. ME.
[Old Norse *snubba* (cf. Swedish dial. *snubba*, Danish, Norwegian dial. *snubbe* cut short), rel. to Middle Swedish *snybba*, Middle Danish *snibbe*: see SNIB *verb*[1].]
1 *verb trans.* Orig., reprove or rebuke cuttingly. Now, rebuff or humiliate with sharp words or a marked lack of cordiality etc.; deliberately spurn, ignore, or offend. ME.
2 *verb trans.* †**a** Restrain (a thing); prevent from having free course or development. L16–L17. ▸**b** Check or stop (a rope etc.) suddenly while it is running out; stop or bring *up* (a boat, horse, etc.) sharply, esp. by passing a rope round a post; fasten or tie (*up*). *US* exc. NAUTICAL. M19.
3 *verb trans.* Check the growth of; shorten; cut or break *off* the end of. Now *rare.* E17. ▸**b** Make snub-nosed or snub. L18.
4 *verb intrans.* Press bluntly (*against*). *rare.* M19.

> 🕮 **1** L. A. FIEDLER Faulkner is snubbed and the comic books are banned. R. FRAME I was being cut by her, snubbed. *Canoeist* I apologise to anyone who feels snubbed by not being invited.

■ **snubbing** *noun* (***a***) the action of the verb; an instance of this; (***b***) ENGINEERING the action of reducing or suppressing oscillation; damping: E17. **snubbingly** *adverb* in a snubbing manner M19.

snub /snʌb/ *verb*[2] *intrans. rare.* Now *dial. & US.* Infl. **-bb-**. E17.
[Var. of SNOB *verb.*]
Sob.

snubber /ˈsnʌbə/ *noun.* M19.
[from SNUB *verb*[1] + -ER[1].]
1 A person who administers a snub or snubs. M19.
2 A person who snubs a rope, boat, etc.; a device for snubbing a rope etc. *US.* M19.
3 A device for damping or checking vibrations; *spec.* (***a***) ENGINEERING a simple kind of shock absorber; (***b***) ELECTRONICS a circuit intended to suppress voltage spikes. E20.

snubbish /ˈsnʌbɪʃ/ *adjective.* E19.
[from SNUB *adjective* or *verb*[1] + -ISH[1].]
1 Somewhat snub. E19.
2 Inclined to snub people. M19.
■ **snubbishly** *adverb* M19. **snubbishness** *noun* M19.

snubby /ˈsnʌbi/ *adjective & noun.* M18.
[from SNUB *noun & adjective* or *verb*[1]: see -Y[1].]
▶ **A** *adjective.* **1** Knotty. *obsolete* exc. *dial. rare.* M18.
2 Somewhat snub; short, stumpy. E19.

3 Inclined to snub people; repressing with snubs. M19.
▶ **B** *noun.* A snub-nosed handgun. *US slang.* L20.
■ **snubbiness** *noun* E19.

snuck *verb pa. t. & pple*: see SNEAK *verb*.

snudge /snʌdʒ/ *noun & verb*[1]. Long *obsolete* exc. *dial.* See also SNIDGE. M16.
[Perh. from Low Dutch.]
▶ **A** *noun.* A miser, a skinflint. M16.
▶ **B** *verb intrans.* †**1** Be miserly or stingy. M16–E18.
2 Walk in a stooping or pensive attitude. L17.

snudge /snʌdʒ/ *verb*[2] *intrans.* Long *obsolete* exc. *dial.* M17.
[Perh. rel. to SNUG *verb*.]
Remain snug and quiet; nestle.

snuff /snʌf/ *noun*[1]. See also SNOFF. LME.
[Origin unkn. Sense 2 may be assoc. with SNUFF *noun*[2].]
1 The charred part of the wick of a candle or lamp. LME. ▶**b** *fig.* A feeble or dying light. Also, something insignificant or ephemeral. *arch.* L16. ▶**c** The nozzle of a lamp, holding the wick. Now *rare* or *obsolete*. E17.
2 A fit of indignation; a huff, a rage; umbrage, offence. Now *Scot.* M16.
†**3** A portion of a drink left at the bottom of a cup. L16–M18.

📖 **1** A. TROLLOPE She was going out like the snuff of a candle. **b** W. S. GILBERT You don't care the snuff of a candle. **2** S. PEPYS They go up in snuffe to bed without taking . . leave of them. R. L. STEVENSON Dinnae fly up in the snuff at me.

Comb.: **snuff-dish** a dish to hold the snuff of candles or lamps.
■ **snuffless** *adjective* leaving no snuff L19.

snuff /snʌf/ *noun*[2]. M16.
[from SNUFF *verb*[2].]
1 The action or an act of snuffing, esp. as an expression of contempt or disdain. M16.
2 Smell, odour, scent; an inhalation or sniff *of* something. M18.

snuff /snʌf/ *noun*[3] *& adjective.* L17.
[Dutch *snuf*, prob. abbreviation of *snuftabak* (cf. Low German *snuv-*, German *Schnupftabak*), from Middle Dutch *snuffen* SNUFF *verb*[2].]
▶ **A** *noun.* **1** A preparation of powdered tobacco taken by inhalation through the nostrils or occas. orally. L17. ▶**b** A medicinal powder taken by sniffing. *rare.* M19. ▶**c** The dark yellowish-brown colour of snuff. L20.
2 A pinch of snuff; an inhalation of snuff; a pinch or very small quantity *of* something. Chiefly *Scot.* L17.
Phrases: **up to snuff** *slang* knowing, sharp, not easily deceived; up to the required standard, up to scratch.
Comb.: **snuffbox** (*a*) a box for holding snuff, usu. one small enough to be carried in the pocket; (*b*) *arch. slang* the nose; (*c*) ***snuffbox gourd*** = ***snuff-gourd*** below; **snuff-brown** *adjective & noun* dark yellowish brown; **snuff-coloured** *adjective* snuff-brown; **snuff-dipping** the practice of chewing snuff; **snuff-gourd** a small dried bottle-gourd used to hold snuff etc.; **snuffman** a dealer in snuff; **snuff-mill** (*a*) *Scot.* a snuffbox; (*b*) a mill for grinding tobacco into snuff.
▶ **B** *adjective.* Snuff-coloured; dark yellowish brown. M20.

snuff /snʌf/ *verb*[1]. LME.
[from SNUFF *noun*[1].]
1 *verb trans.* Remove or cut off the snuff from (a candle, wick, etc.). LME. ▶†**b** *fig.* Make clearer; purge. L16–E18.
2 *verb trans.* Extinguish, put out; cause to go out or disappear; wipe out; terminate (life). Usu. foll. by *out*. L17.
3 *verb trans.* (with *it*) & *intrans.* Die. *slang.* M19.
4 *verb trans.* Kill, murder. Usu. foll. by *out*. *slang.* M20.

📖 **2** DICKENS Yellow specks . . rapidly snuffed out. T. PYNCHON He . . without wetting his fingers snuffs the candle. R. BERTHOUD The great war had snuffed out the spirit of adventure. **3** P. INCHBALD If the old codger were to snuff it . . was there a will? **4** T. GIFFORD We should have snuffed this little shit.

Comb.: **snuff film**, **snuff movie** *slang* a pornographic film in which an actual murder takes place.
■ **snuffing** *noun* (*a*) the action of the verb; (*b*) the burnt part of a wick which is removed with snuffers etc.: (usu. in *pl.*): LME.

snuff /snʌf/ *verb*[2]. LME.
[Middle Dutch *snuffen* snuffle.]
▶ **I** *verb intrans.* **1** Draw air into the nostrils or clear one's nose by inhalation; sniff (*at*). LME.
†**2** Express scorn, disdain, or contempt by sniffing (*at*). M16–E19.
3 Take snuff. L17.
▶ **II** *verb trans.* **4** Inhale. Freq. foll. by *in*, *up*. E16.
5 Detect, perceive, or anticipate by inhaling the odour of. L17.
6 Smell at, examine by smelling. M19.

📖 **4** V. WOOLF 'The air's . . delicious.' She snuffed it like a racehorse.

■ **snuffingly** *adverb* in a snuffing manner L16.

snuffer /ˈsnʌfə/ *noun*[1]. LME.
[from SNUFF *verb*[1] + -ER[1].]
More fully ***candle-snuffer***.
1 In *pl.* or as ***pair of snuffers***: an implement resembling a pair of scissors, used to trim the wick of or extinguish a candle etc. Also in *sing.*, a small hollow cone with a handle used to extinguish a candle. LME.
2 *Hist.* A person who snuffed and otherwise attended to candles, esp. in a theatre. E17.

snuffer /ˈsnʌfə/ *noun*[2]. E17.
[from SNUFF *verb*[2] + -ER[1].]
1 A person who snuffs something or who sniffs disdainfully. E17.
†**2** In *pl.* The nostrils. *slang & dial.* M17–E19.
3 A porpoise. *US local.* E19.
4 A person who takes snuff. L19.

snuffle /ˈsnʌf(ə)l/ *noun.* M17.
[from the verb.]
†**1** The surge of the sea. Only in M17.
2 The action or an act of snuffling. M18.
3 In *pl. & sing.* A partial blockage of the nose, e.g. through a cold, causing snuffling; *spec.* in MEDICINE (now *rare*), a nasal discharge characteristic of congenital syphilis in infants. L18.
4 A nasal tone in the voice. E19.

snuffle /ˈsnʌf(ə)l/ *verb.* L16.
[Prob. from Low German, Dutch *snuffelen*, from imit. base repr. also by SNUFF *verb*[2], Old English *snoffa* nausea, *snofl* catarrh: see -LE[3]. Cf. SNAFFLE *verb*[2], SNIVEL *verb*.]
▶ **I** *verb intrans.* **1** Draw air into the nostrils in order to smell something; sniff or smell *at*. Formerly also, show dislike or disdain by sniffing. L16.
2 Draw up air or mucus through the nostrils audibly or noisily; breathe noisily (as) through a partially blocked nose. L16.
3 Speak through the nose, have a nasal twang, formerly esp. as a sign of hypocrisy or insincerity. L16.
4 Of the wind: blow in fitful gusts. Now *rare.* M17.
▶ **II** *verb trans.* **5** Inhale; clear (the nose etc.) by sniffing; search out or examine by sniffing. L16.
6 Say or voice in a nasal tone. Also foll. by *out*. M17.
■ **snuffler** *noun* a person who snuffles M17. **snuffling** *ppl adjective* (*a*) that snuffles; characterized by sniffing or noisy inhalation through the nose; (*b*) speaking or uttered through the nose; *arch.* hypocritical, sanctimonious: L16. **snufflingly** *adverb* E17.

snuffly /ˈsnʌfli/ *adverb & adjective.* E19.
[from SNUFFLE *noun* or *verb* + -Y[1].]
▶†**A** *adverb.* With snuffling. *rare.* Only in E19.
▶ **B** *adjective.* Characterized by snuffling; suffering from snuffles. L19.
■ **snuffliness** *noun* M19.

snuffy /ˈsnʌfi/ *adjective*[1]. L17.
[from SNUFF *noun*[1] or *verb*[2] + -Y[1].]
1 Annoyed, displeased; irritable; ready to take offence; supercilious, contemptuous. L17.
2 Of an animal: excitable, spirited, wild. M20.
■ **snuffiness** *noun*[1] E19.

snuffy /ˈsnʌfi/ *adjective*[2]. M18.
[from SNUFF *noun*[3] + -Y[1].]
1 a Soiled or discoloured with snuff. M18. ▶**b** Given to taking snuff; bearing marks of this habit. L18.
2 Like snuff in colour or substance. L18.
3 Tipsy, drunk. *slang* (now *rare*). E19.
■ **snuffiness** *noun*[2] L19.

snug /snʌg/ *noun*[1]. M17.
[Perh. var. of SNAG *noun*[1].]
1 A rugged projection; a hard knob or knot. *rare. obsolete* exc. *dial.* M17.
2 A projection or ridge cast on a plate, bolt, etc., in order to keep something in position, prevent rotation, etc. M19.

snug /snʌg/ *noun*[2]. M18.
[from the adjective.]
1 *absol.* Snug existence or surroundings; that which is snug. M18.
2 A small comfortable room or parlour in an inn or public-house. Also, a compartment in the taproom of an inn. M19.

snug /snʌg/ *adjective & adverb.* Compar. & superl. **-gg-**. L16.
[Prob. from Low Dutch: cf. Low German *snügger*, *snögger* slender, smooth, dainty, smart, Dutch *snuggher*, *snoggher* slender, slim, active (mod. *snugger* lively, sprightly).]
▶ **A** *adjective.* **1 a** NAUTICAL. Of (part of) a ship: properly prepared for or protected from bad weather; shipshape, compact. L16. ▶**b** *gen.* Neat, trim. *obsolete* exc. *dial.* E18. ▶**c** Close-fitting; tight. M19.
2 In a state of ease, comfort, or quiet enjoyment; well placed or arranged; *esp.* cosily protected from the weather or cold. M17.
3 a In concealment or hiding; out of sight or observation. Chiefly in ***lie snug***. L17. ▶**b** Private, secret. Chiefly in ***keep snug***, keep quiet about (something). *obsolete* exc. *dial.* E–M18.
4 Marked or characterized by ease or comfort; conducive to ease and comfort; (of a place, building, etc.) comfortable and warm, cosy, *esp.* combining comfort with neatness and compactness. E18. ▶**b** Moderately well-to-do; comfortably off. Chiefly *Anglo-Irish.* E19. ▶**c** Fairly large or substantial. *arch. colloq.* M19.

📖 **1a** M. KINGSLEY We let go the anchor, make all snug and go ashore. **c** J. F. FIXX Running shoes should be a bit snugger than street shoes. **2** SOUTHEY The Painter is snug in his bed. T. HOOK You might sit as snug as a bug in a rug. J. C. POWYS They were like birds in a nest, warm and snug against each other. **3a** G. BORROW Lying snug in cave by day. **4** HAZLITT A few hundreds a year are something snug and comfortable. THACKERAY He liked snug dinners. J. HAWKES The snug villages of the Anglo-Saxons. A. SILLITOE Safe . . in the warm snug kitchen. **c** THACKERAY Having a snug legacy from Miss Crawley.

▶ **B** *adverb.* Snugly. L17.
■ **snuggish** *adjective* somewhat snug; rather comfortable: E19. **snugly** *adverb* E17. **snugness** *noun* M18.

snug /snʌg/ *verb.* Infl. **-gg-**. L16.
[Origin uncertain; later from or assoc. with the adjective.]
1 *verb intrans.* Lie or nestle closely or comfortably, esp. in bed; snuggle; settle down, make oneself snug or comfortable, (usu. foll. by *down*). *colloq. & dial.* L16.
2 *verb trans.* Place or put (*away*) snugly; make snug, comfortable, cosy, or safe (freq. foll. by *down*, *up*). *colloq.* M18. ▶**b** NAUTICAL. Make (a ship etc.) snug or trim, esp. by lashing or stowing movables, reducing sails, lowering topmasts, etc., in preparation for bad weather; furl (a sail). Freq. foll. by *down*. L19.

📖 **1** T. L. SMITH Folding bipod which snugs under the barrel when not in use. C. J. CHERRYH Alison . . snugged down more comfortably in . . bed and drifted off again. **2** W. C. RUSSELL I snugged her in rugs. S. JUDD She had no sister to nestle with her, and snug her up. A. PRICE There had to be a copy snugged away in the KGB files. **2b** *Guardian* When all was snugged down the cabin boy was left at the helm. *transf.*: R. KIPLING I don't know how one snugs down an aeroplane.

snuggery /ˈsnʌg(ə)ri/ *noun.* E19.
[from SNUG *adjective* + -ERY.]
1 A cosy or comfortable room, esp. a small one, into which a person may retire for seclusion or quiet; a den; *spec.* the snug of an inn or public-house. E19.
2 A snug, comfortable, or cosy dwelling; a snug place or situation. M19.
3 A snug company or party. *rare.* M19.

📖 **2** A. TROLLOPE The comfortable arcana of ecclesiastical snuggeries.

snuggle /ˈsnʌg(ə)l/ *verb & noun.* L17.
[from SNUG *adjective* + -LE[3]. Cf. SMUGGLE *verb*[2].]
▶ **A** *verb.* **1** *verb intrans.* Of a person, esp. a child: lie snug or close for warmth or comfort, settle down or curl up cosily or comfortably; press close to a person, esp. as a mark of affection; nestle. Freq. foll. by *up*, *down*. L17. ▶**b** Of a building etc.: lie in a sheltered or snug situation. M19.
2 *verb trans.* Clasp or draw to oneself closely or affectionately; hug, cuddle; settle or nestle (oneself) snugly or comfortably; wrap (*up*) *in* a warm garment etc. Also, push, place, or, fit snugly, closely, or affectionately. L18.

📖 **1** T. H. WHITE He snuggled down between the roots of the tree. E. CALDWELL If I feel . . lonely . . I can snuggle up close to Mr. Truelove. P. ABRAHAMS Sarah snuggled deeper under the . . bedclothing. **b** H. MARRYAT Under these bastions snuggle small wood tenements. **2** K. AMIS The . . violinist was snuggling his instrument in under his chin. D. LODGE It makes one think of being snuggled up in a blanket. M. PIERCY Tracy was snuggling Sheba under her chin. A. DAVIES She snuggled her face into my neck.

▶ **B** *noun.* The action of snuggling. Also, a group of people or things snuggled together. *rare.* E20.
■ **snuggler** *noun* (*rare*) L19. **snuggly** *adjective* (*colloq.*) characterized by or inviting snuggling; snug: E20.

snum /snʌm/ *noun & verb intrans.* (*1 sing. pres. indic.*). *US dial.* E19.
[App. fanciful alt. of SWEAR *verb*. Cf. VUM.]
I snum, †***by snum***, I declare!: expr. surprise, asseveration, etc.

snurge /snəːdʒ/ *noun. slang.* M20.
[Origin unkn.]
A toady; a tell-tale; an obnoxious person.

snurt /snəːt/ *verb intrans. obsolete* exc. *dial.* LME.
[Prob. imit.: cf. SNIRT, SNORT *verb*[2].]
Snort; snore.

†**snush** *noun.* L17–E19.
[Origin uncertain: cf. Danish, Swedish *snus*.]
Snuff.

snuzzle /ˈsnʌz(ə)l/ *verb intrans. obsolete* exc. *dial.* M18.
[Var. of NUZZLE *verb*[1].]
Root or sniff about with the nose; nuzzle; snuggle.

sny /snʌɪ/ *noun & verb.* E18.
[Origin unkn.]
SHIPBUILDING. ▶**A** *noun.* An upward curve of the lines of a ship from amidships to the bow or stern. E18.
▶ **B** *verb intrans.* Have an upward curve. Chiefly as ***snying*** *verbal noun & ppl adjective.* E18.

snye /snʌɪ/ *noun. Canad. & US (local).* E19.
[Canad. French *chenail*, French *chenal* channel.]
A side-channel, esp. one creating an island.

so *noun* see SOL *noun*[1].

so /səʊ/ *adverb, conjunction, & adjective.* Also (*colloq.*) **s'** /s/.
[Old English *swa*, *swā*, *swǣ*, *swē*, *se*, corresp. to Old Frisian *sa*, *so*, Old Saxon *sō*, Old High German *sō* (Dutch *zo*, German *so*), Old Norse *svá*, Gothic *swa*, *swe*, from Germanic. Cf. SOH *interjection*.]

▶ **A** *adverb.* (Not always distinguishable from the conjunction.)
1 In the way or manner described, indicated, or implied contextually; in that style or fashion; in the same way, by that means; in this way, thus, as follows. OE.
2 a Acting as predicate with *be*, *become*, etc., or as object with *do*, *say*, *think*, *imagine*, etc.: what has been or is to be mentioned; of that nature, in that condition; that, thus, such. OE. ▸**b** With verbal ellipsis: as or what has been mentioned, described, or indicated (freq. used in questioning, commenting on, or expressing approval or confirmation of something); *spec.* (*a*) so says or writes —; †(*b*) let it be so. ME. ▸**c** Adding emphasis to a statement contradicting another's negative assertion. *colloq.* E20.
3 To the extent or degree stated or implied; to that extent (with adjective & noun now usu. with indef. article). Passing into intensive: to a large extent, very, much, quite, such; *colloq.* absolutely (right etc.). OE. ▸**b** Followed by *as*: to the same extent *as*, in the same degree *as*. Now usu. with neg.; in affirmative now *arch. & dial.* (**as . . as** being usual). ME.
4 With consequence expressed by clause or by *as* + inf.: in such a manner (*that*), to such an extent (*that*). OE.
5 With correspondence, similarity, or analogy of fact, condition, or action. OE. ▸†**b** Equally. ME–L17.
6 For that reason, on that account, accordingly, consequently, therefore. Passing into: as the next step, then, thereafter, subsequently. ME. ▸**b** As an introductory particle or *interjection* expr. surprise, incredulity, scorn, etc., or simply used in resuming: well then, at any rate. Also *ellipt.* = ***so what?*** below. L16.
†**7** After rel. pronoun: soever. ME–L16.

> 📖 **1** T. HARDY 'You don't hold the shears right, miss . . Incline the edge so,' he said. M. DRABBLE He had not sat so, in a cinema, for . . years. A. H. SOMMERSTEIN So to express it, however, would result in great inelegance of presentation. **2a** STEELE Yet so it is, that People can bear any Quality . . better than Beauty. J. RUSKIN England may, if it so chooses, become one manufacturing town. L. P. HARTLEY Persons using the bridge do so at their own risk. S. BEDFORD Putnitz testified that this was not so. D. M. DAVIN He was at all times excitable, and alcohol made him more so. J. SIMMS He never said so, but I could tell he thought I was pretty. **b** SHAKES. *Two Gent.* If it please you, so; if not, why, so. SIR W. SCOTT He will not die unless we abandon him; and if so, we are indeed answerable for his blood. G. BOOTHBY 'I know China as well as any living Englishman.' 'Quite so.' W. T. WATTS-DUNTON My father's birthday? Why, so it is! G. GREENE So Henry James in the preface to his first novel. **c** K. TENNANT 'How old are you?' 'Eighteen.' 'Eighteen, my fat aunt.' . . 'I am so eighteen.' **3** SHAKES. *Jul. Caes.* Who so firm that cannot be seduc'd? WORDSWORTH A voice so thrilling ne'er was heard. SIR W. SCOTT So short time have I been absent. R. H. BARHAM So barefaced a blunder. C. GIBBON I held back because I loved you so. W. S. MAUGHAM Why did he not ask what she was so willing to grant? D. EDEN Why are you so sure Nurse Ellen won't come back? O. NORTON 'It'll only make trouble. You'll see.' She was so right. H. SECOMBE It won't look so attractive in a truss. **b** J. IMISON This planet being but a fifth part so big as the earth. TENNYSON I never saw . . So great a miracle as yonder hilt. M. PATTISON So distant a quarter as Moravia. J. DAWSON Mother . . was not so young as she used to be. **4** M. EDGEWORTH So ill that she could hardly speak. R. DUPPA So broken into small fragments as to be useless. J. STEINBECK His suit was . . so new that there were creases in the trousers. I. MURDOCH She cannot be so naive as not to have some . . appreciation of what is going on. K. AMIS You're so ignorant it isn't true. **5** BROWNING The Mayor looked blue; So did the Corporation too. M. DICKENS Mr. Askey can go to hell, and so can you. J. FOWLES She liked it and so me for buying it. **6** SIR W. SCOTT Thence by a whaling vessel to Lerwick, and so to Jarlshof. A. J. BUTLER We marched out . . to the drum, and so to bed. G. BOOTHBY We leave at daybreak . . , so I will wish you good-bye now. F. BRANSTON 'Impossible to do more than make a wild guess.' 'So make a wild guess.' **b** BYRON So Lord G* is married to a rustic! B. MALAMUD 'So where did you go?' Feld asked. A. MORICE 'He's an estate agent.' . . 'So?' O. MANNING So here he was, obliged to attend an office at fixed hours. TIRESIAS I suddenly realised one day that DORMAR is RAMROD backwards. So?

▶ **B** *conjunction.* **1** With the result that, in such a way that, to such an extent that; in order that. Usu. with *that*. OE.
2 On condition that, provided that; so long as, if only. Usu. with *that*. *arch.* OE. ▸**b** In the event *that*, in case. *rare.* OE.
†**3** In the way that; as much as; as. Also, as if. OE–L16.
4 Introducing an adjuration or asseveration: and in this matter, and to that extent. Chiefly in ***so help me (God)*** etc. OE.
5 Used to introduce a clause or phr. following *as*, indicating correspondence, similarity, or proportion: and in the same way, and correspondingly. ME.

> 📖 **1** A. THWAITE I shall make it simple so you understand. R. MACAULAY I wish every one would shut up, so that we could hear ourselves think. R. D. EDWARDS Sir Nicholas fixed it so Nixon had to turn up. **2** STEELE It is no Matter how dirty a Bag it is conveyed to him in, . . so the Money is good. M. EDGEWORTH It was . . indifferent who was found guilty, so that he could recover his money. **b** TENNYSON But, So thou dread to swear, Pass not beneath this gateway. **4** SIR W. SCOTT This seat . . I claim as my right so prosper me God. R. KIPLING Slane . . murmured: 'S'elp me, I believe 'e's dead.' **5** AV *Prov.* 23 For as he thinketh in his heart, so is he. ADDISON In proportion as there are more Follies discovered, so there is more Laughter raised. B. JOWETT As in the arts, so also in politics, the new must . . prevail. A. T. ELLIS As their sorrow increased so they grew bolder.

▶ **C** *adjective.* **1** *attrib.* The specified or implied —; this, that. *dial.* M19.
2 Homosexual. *arch. slang.* M20.

> 📖 **1** R. FROST I'll knock so-fashion . . When I come back. **2** J. R. ACKERLEY A young 'so' man, picked up . . in a . . urinal.

Phrases: **and so on, and so forth** and in other similar ways, and others of the same kind, et cetera. *EVER* ***so***. ***how so?***: see HOW *adverb*. ***if so be (that)***: see IF *conjunction*. ***in so far as***: see IN *adverb*. ***I suppose so***: see SUPPOSE *verb* 11a. ***I told you so***: see TELL *verb*. ***just so***: see JUST *adverb*. †**neither so nor so** neither one thing nor the other. ***never so***: see NEVER 2. ***not so as you'd notice***: see NOTICE *verb*. ***not so bad***: see BAD *adjective*. **or so** or something of that kind; or the like; or about that amount or number; or thereabout. **so as** (*a*) (*obsolete exc. dial.*) so that; (*b*) *arch.* in the manner that, in such a way that; (*c*) (now *colloq.*) provided that; (see also senses A.3b, 4 above). **so being** (chiefly *Scot.*) (*a*) provided that; (*b*) seeing that, since. ***so far (as)***: see FAR *adverb*. ***so far so good***: see FAR *adverb*. ***so help me (God)***: see HELP *verb* 1. ***so long (as)***: see LONG *adverb*. **so many** such a (large) number (of); as many; an equal number (of); a large or unspecified number (of), many, several. **so much** *adjectival, noun, & adverbial phr.* (*a*) *adjectival & noun phr.* so large a quantity or amount (of); a large or unspecified quantity or amount (of); an equal quantity or amount (of); (*b*) *adverbial phr.* to such an extent, in such a degree; (followed by *the* + compar.) to that extent, in that degree; (with neg.) less than, to a lesser extent; not even. **so much for** that is all that need be said or done about; (freq. *iron.*) **so muckle** *Scot.* so much. **so or so** *arch.* after this or that manner; this or that. ***so PLEASE you***. ***so there!***: see THERE. ***so to say***: see SAY *verb*[1]. ***so to speak***: see SPEAK *verb*. **so what?** *colloq.* why should that be considered significant? †**than so** than that. ***why so***: see WHY *interjection*.

Comb.: **so-called** *adjective* commonly called or designated by the name or term specified, often incorrectly; **so so** *adverbial & adjectival phr.* (*a*) *adverbial phr.* indifferently; only moderately; (*b*) *adjectival phr.* (usu. *pred.*) indifferent, mediocre; not very good; **so-soish** *adjective* rather indifferent.

So. *abbreviation.*
South.

soak /səʊk/ *noun*[1]. LME.
[from the verb.]
1 The process of soaking or state of being soaked; an instance of this. Earliest in ***in soak***. LME. ▸**b** A liquid used for maceration; a steep. M19. ▸**c** A vat in which hides are macerated. L19. ▸**d** A heavy drenching rain. L19.
2 A percolation of water; water which has seeped through the ground etc. E18. ▸**b** A hollow where rainwater collects, a water-hole. *Austral. & NZ.* M19.
3 A heavy drinker; a drunkard. *colloq.* E19.
4 A drinking-bout. M19.

> 📖 **1** P. MONETTE Roger took a soak in the tub. **2b** DOUGLAS STUART A soak is dug for water a yard or so from the . . pool. **3** J. FENTON Old soaks from . . pubs And . . drinking clubs.

soak *noun*[2] var. of SOKE.

soak /səʊk/ *verb.* Pa. pple **-ed**, (now *rare*) **-en** /-ən/.
[Old English *socian* from weak grade of *sūcan* SUCK *verb* (cf. *soc* sucking at the breast).]
▶ **I** *verb intrans.* **1 a** Become saturated with a liquid by being immersed in it; become thoroughly wet or soft in this manner. OE. ▸**b** Of a metal ingot or ceramic object: become heated uniformly in a furnace or kiln. M19.
2 a Percolate; penetrate *into* by saturation, filter *through*, seep *out*, *up*, etc. LME. ▸**b** Of heat: penetrate *through* the mass of a metal ingot or ceramic object until it is at a uniform temperature. E20.
3 Drink heavily or to excess. Cf. earlier SOAKER 2. *colloq.* L17.

> 📖 **1a** M. WESLEY She ran a bath and . . soaked in the hot water. **2a** G. GREENE The rain . . soaked through the brown leaves in the square. M. DUFFY Sweat had soaked up into his clothes. **3** WILFRID GIBSON He liked his drink, but he had never cared For soaking by himself.

▶ **II** *verb trans.* **4** Saturate by immersion in a liquid; wet or permeate thoroughly; drench. ME. ▸**b** *fig.* Imbue thoroughly with a quality etc., make profoundly acquainted with a subject of study etc., (usu. in *pass.*); *refl.* immerse (oneself) in a subject of study etc. ME.
5 a Draw or suck *out*; cause to seep *out* by means of soaking. LME. ▸**b** Drain, exhaust. *obsolete exc. dial.* L16.
6 Allow (liquid) to sink in; absorb; *fig.* receive into the mind easily or copiously as by absorption. Usu. foll. by *up*. M16. ▸**b** Drink (liquor), esp. to excess. Also foll. by *up*. L17.
7 a Bake (bread etc.) thoroughly. L17. ▸**b** Maintain a (metal ingot or ceramic object) at a constant temperature for a period to ensure uniform heating. E20.
8 Make drunk; *refl.* drink heavily or to excess. *colloq.* M18.
9 Put (something) in pawn. *slang.* L19.
10 Punch, hit hard; punish; criticize harshly. *US slang.* L19.
11 Impose an extortionate charge or tax on; extort money from. *colloq.* L19.

> 📖 **4** L. CHAMBERLAIN Soak the herring in milk. WILBUR SMITH The dressing was soaked with fresh blood. **b** GEO. ELIOT We soak our children in habits of contempt. *Motorboats Monthly* Wells is soaked in tradition. **soaked to the skin** (of a person) drenched by rain, thoroughly wet. **6** E. DAVID There is a good deal of . . juice; for soaking it up one needs plenty of bread. E. PAWEL They had come to soak up sun rather than culture. **8** E. O'NEILL Like a rum-soaked trooper . . on a Saturday. **9** D. HAMMETT The banks were closed, so he soaked his watch. **10** H. L. WILSON If he gets fancy with you, soak him again. **soak it to** = *sock it to* s.v. SOCK *verb*[1]. **11** M. FRENCH She was angry, so she really soaked him. She asked for fifteen thousand.

Comb.: **soakaway** a pit into which waste water flows in order to drain slowly out into the surrounding soil; **soak-hole** (*a*) *Austral.* an enclosed place in a stream, used for washing sheep; (*b*) a hole into or from which water etc. soaks or drains away; **soak-the-rich** *adjective* designating a policy of progressive taxation; **soakway** = *soakaway* above.

soakage /ˈsəʊkɪdʒ/ *noun.* M18.
[from prec. + -AGE.]
1 a Liquid which has filtered or seeped out. M18. ▸**b** = SOAK *noun*[1] 2b. *Austral.* L19.
2 Liquid or moisture collected or absorbed. M19.
3 The process of percolating or soaking through something. M19.
4 The state or process of being soaked. M19.

soaken *verb pa. pple*: see SOAK *verb*.

soaker /ˈsəʊkə/ *noun.* L16.
[formed as prec. + -ER[1].]
†**1** A drainer, an exhauster. L16–M17.
2 A heavy drinker; a drunkard. *colloq.* L16.
3 a A person who soaks something. E17. ▸**b** A heavy drenching rain. L18. ▸**c** A soaking pit. E20.
4 A sheet of metal used in roofing to keep out rain. L19.

Phrases: **old soaker** *colloq.* (*a*) an old hand at something, an old stager; (*b*) a regular or heavy drinker.

soaking /ˈsəʊkɪŋ/ *verbal noun.* LME.
[from SOAK *verb* + -ING[1].]
The action of SOAK *verb*; an instance of this.
Comb.: **soaking pit** a furnace in which metal ingots are reheated to a uniform temperature required for rolling.

soaking /ˈsəʊkɪŋ/ *adjective & adverb.* LME.
[formed as prec. + -ING[2].]
▶ **A** *adjective.* **1** Taking in moisture, absorbent; *fig.* weakening, exhausting. *obsolete exc. dial.* LME.
2 †**a** Of a fire: slow. LME–E17. ▸**b** PRINTING. Of a pull on the bar of a press: long and slow, gradual. Now *rare* or *obsolete*. L17.
3 Percolating; sinking in; flowing slowly. L16.
4 Esp. of rain: drenching, wetting thoroughly. M17.
5 Saturated, drenched, very wet. M19.
▶ **B** *adverb.* ***soaking wet***, very wet. M19.
■ **soakingly** *adverb* †(*a*) slowly, gradually; (*b*) so as to saturate or drench: LME.

soam /səʊm/ *noun. Scot. & north.* LME.
[Prob. from Old French *some* pack-saddle, horse-load, but the difference in sense is unexplained.]
1 A rope or chain attaching a draught horse or other animal to a wagon, plough, etc. LME.
2 MINING. Either of a pair of cords used to pull a tub of coal. L18.

so-and-so /ˈsəʊənsəʊ/ *noun, adjective, & adverb.* Also **so and so.** L16.
[from SO *adverb* + AND *conjunction*[1] + SO *adverb*.]
▶ **A** *noun.* **1** A person or thing whose name does not need to be specified, or whose name one does not know or remember. L16.
2 *euphem.* A person or thing regarded with disfavour or criticism. L19.

> 📖 **1** E. TAYLOR His father had only vaguely spoken of . . 'having a chat with so-and-so some time.' **2** M. BINCHY He was a selfish . . ungrateful so and so.

▶ **B** *adjective.* **1** Paltry, worthless; indifferent; poor in health or circumstances. Now *dial.* M17.
2 *euphem.* Bloody, damned, etc. E20.

> 📖 **2** *Listener* Some [clients] are good, some are indifferent, some are a so-and-so nuisance.

▶ **C** *adverb.* Now *rare.*

1 To a certain (unspecified) number or degree; in a certain manner. **M17.**
2 Indifferently, moderately. **M19.**
3 *euphem.* Bloody, damnedly, etc. **M20.**

Soanean /ˈsəʊnɪən/ *adjective.* **M19.**
[from *Soane* (see below) + **-AN**.]
Of, pertaining to, or characteristic of the British architect Sir John Soane (1753–1837) or the buildings designed by him.
■ Also **Soaˈnesque**, **Soanic** *adjectives* (*rare*) **M20.**

soap /səʊp/ *noun*¹.
[Old English *sāpe* = Middle & mod. Low German *sēpe*, Middle Dutch *seepe* (Dutch *zeep*), Old High German *seif(f)a* (German *Seife*), from West Germanic, whence also Finnish *saip(p)io*, *saip(p)ua*, Lappish *saipo*, Latin *sapo(n-)*.]
1 A cleansing or emulsifying agent formed by reacting natural oils and fats with sodium hydroxide or any strong alkali, usu. with added colouring matter and perfume; a particular type of this. Also, a heavy metal salt of a fatty acid, producing an insoluble soap used in lubricating grease etc. Cf. **DETERGENT** *noun*. **OE.**
2 *slang.* **a** Flattery. **M19.** ▸**b** Money. Now *esp.*, that used in bribery. *US.* **M19.**
3 [So called because orig. sponsored in the US by soap manufacturers.] In full ***soap opera***. A television or radio serial dealing with sentimental and melodramatic domestic themes and usu. broadcast in many episodes; this type of serial considered as a genre. **M20.**

> 🕮 **1** GEO. ELIOT A great ceremony with soap and water, from which baby came out in new beauty. D. PROFUMO The water's so soft you can hardly wash the soap off your face. ***Castile soap***, ***lavender soap***, ***marine soap***, ***Naples soap***, ***toilet soap*** etc. ***invert soap***: see **INVERT** *noun & adjective*. ***metallic soap***: see **METALLIC** *adjective*. **3** *attrib.*: *Times* The dedication of soap viewers is astonishing.

Phrases: **no soap** *slang* (orig. & chiefly *US*) it's no good; I refuse, nothing doing. **not know from a bar of soap** *colloq.* (chiefly *Austral.*) not have the slightest acquaintance with. **soap of glass**, **glass-maker's soap** *arch.* manganese dioxide. ***wash a person's head without soap***, ***wash one's mouth out with soap***: see **WASH** *verb*.

Comb.: †**soap-ashes** wood ashes used in forming a lye in soap-making; **soapbark** the bark of certain trees containing saponin and used as a substitute for soap; ***soapbark tree***, a Chilean tree of the rose family, *Quillaja saponaria*, which has such bark; **soapberry** (*a*) the fruit of any of various trees of the genus *Sapindus* (family Sapindaceae), esp. *S. saponaria*, or of the leguminous tree *Acacia concinna*, used in certain countries as a substitute for soap; any of the trees bearing such a fruit; (*b*) *N. Amer.* the edible fruit of a buffalo berry, *Shepherdia canadensis*, which forms a soapy froth when crushed; the shrub bearing this fruit; **soap-boiler** (*a*) a person who boils (the ingredients of) soap, a soap manufacturer; (*b*) a pot used for boiling (the ingredients of) soap; **soap-bubble** an iridescent bubble composed of a thin film of soap and water; *fig.* a (usu. attractive) thing which does not last; **soap cerate** (now *rare*) MEDICINE a mixture containing soap, lead acetate, wax, and oil, applied externally to sprains, inflammations, etc.; **soapfish** any of numerous tropical marine fishes of the family Grammistidae, which produce large amounts of toxic mucus from the skin and have a soapy feel when handled; **soap flakes** soap in the form of thin flakes, used for washing clothes etc.; **soap-house** a place where soap is manufactured; **soap-lees** (*obsolete* exc. *Hist.*) spent soap-lye; **soap-lye** (now *rare*) a caustic alkaline lye obtained by running water over alternate layers of soda ash and quicklime, and used in soap-making; **soap-nut** = ***soapberry*** (a) above; ***soap opera***: see sense 3 above; **soap-operatic**, **soap-operatical** *adjectives* characteristic of a soap opera; **soap-plant** (*a*) a Californian plant of the lily family, *Chlorogalum pomeridianum*, used as a substitute for soap; (*b*) = ***soapberry*** (a) above; **soap powder** detergent in the form of a powder; **soap-rock**, **soapstone** (*a*) MINERALOGY steatite, massive talc; (*b*) GEOLOGY a soft metamorphic rock with a smooth greasy feel, composed of talc with micas etc., and readily sawn into slabs, carved, etc.; **soap-stock** a crude, partially saponified mixture of fatty acids formed as a by-product in the refining of natural fats; **soapsuds** froth or lather made from soap; *esp.* water in which clothes have been washed; **soap-suddy**, **soap-sudsy** *adjectives* (*rare*) of the nature of soapsuds; **soap-tree** any of various trees of which the roots, leaves, or fruits can be used as a substitute for soap; **soapweed** any of several yuccas or allied plants of the southern US with detergent properties, esp. *Yucca elata* and *Y. glauca*; **soap-work(s)** a soap factory; **soapwort** (*a*) any of various pink-flowered Eurasian plants constituting the genus *Saponaria*, of the pink family, with a juice which forms a lather with water; esp. *S. officinalis*, an old garden flower, (also called ***bouncing Bet***); (*b*) any plant of the Sapindaceae or soapberry family.
■ **soapie** *noun* (*colloq.*) a soap opera **M20.** **soapless** *adjective* (*a*) unwashed, dirty; (*b*) (of shampoo, detergent, etc.) not containing soap: **E19.** **soaplike** *adjective* resembling (that of) soap **M19.**

soap /səʊp/ *noun*². *slang.* **L20.**
[Contr. of *sodium Pentothal*, after prec.]
Thiopentone, or a mixture of this and an amphetamine, used as a truth drug.

soap /səʊp/ *verb trans.* **M16.**
[from **SOAP** *noun*¹.]
1 Rub, lather, or wash with soap; apply soap to. **M16.**
2 Flatter; compliment insincerely. Cf. ***soft-soap*** s.v. **SOFT** *adjective*. *arch. slang.* **M19.**

soapbox /ˈsəʊpbɒks/ *noun & verb.* **M17.**
[from **SOAP** *noun*¹ + **BOX** *noun*².]
▶ **A** *noun.* **1** A box or crate for holding soap. **M17.**
2 A crate or case used as a makeshift stand for a public speaker. **E20.**

> 🕮 **2** V. GORNICK She had stood on soapboxes . . pleading for economic and social justice.

Comb.: **soapbox cart** a child's cart made from a soapbox.
▶ **B** *verb intrans.* Speak from or as from a soapbox. Orig. *US.* **E20.**
■ **soapboxer** *noun* a person who speaks from a soapbox **E20.**

soaper /ˈsəʊpə/ *noun.* **ME.**
[from **SOAP** *noun*¹ + **-ER**¹.]
1 A soap manufacturer. Formerly also, a person selling soap. **ME.**
2 A soap opera. *N. Amer. colloq.* **M20.**
■ **soapery** *noun* a soap-works **L17.**

soapolallie /ˈsəʊpəlali/ *noun. N. Amer.* Also **soop-** /ˈsuːp-/. **L19.**
[from **SOAP** *noun*¹ + Chinook Jargon *olallie* berry.]
1 A thick drink made from crushed soapberries. **L19.**
2 More fully ***soapolallie bush***. The shrub which bears soapberries, *Shepherdia canadensis*. **M20.**

soapy /ˈsəʊpi/ *adjective.* **L16.**
[from **SOAP** *noun*¹ + **-Y**¹.]
1 Smeared or covered with soap; containing soap or lather. **L16.**
2 Resembling soap in texture, appearance, or taste; soaplike. **E18.**
3 Ingratiating, unctuous, flattering. **M19.**
4 a Of a style, manner, etc.: smooth, bland, sentimental. **L19.** ▸**b** Characteristic of a soap opera. *colloq.* **M20.**
■ **soapily** *adverb* in a soft or easy manner; smoothly: **M19.** **soapiness** *noun* the quality of being soapy **E18.**

soar /sɔː/ *noun.* **L16.**
[from the verb, perh. after Old & mod. French *essor*, from *essorer*: see next.]
1 The altitude attained in soaring; range of flight upwards. **L16.**
2 The action or an act of soaring or rising high. **E19.**

soar *adjective* var. of **SORE** *adjective*².

soar /sɔː/ *verb.* **LME.**
[Aphet. from Old & mod. French *essorer* fly up, soar, from Proto-Romance, formed as **EX-**¹ + Latin *aura* air in motion.]
▶ **I** *verb intrans.* **1 a** Of a bird etc.: fly upwards, ascend; maintain height without flapping the wings; fly at a great height. Also foll. by *up*. **LME.** ▸**b** Of a mountain, building, etc.: reach or rise up majestically to a great height; tower imposingly. Also foll. by *up*. **E19.** ▸**c** Of an aircraft: fly without engine-power; glide. **L19.**
2 *fig.* Rise to a higher level, better position, etc.; (of an amount, price, etc.) increase rapidly. **L16.**

> 🕮 **1a** J. FIELD I was idly watching some gulls as they soared high overhead. **b** J. BETJEMAN Where the tower of Tewkesbury soars to heaven. B. ENGLAND The flames soared up in a sudden gust of wind. **2** E. P. THOMPSON The exceptionally severe winter . . sent the price of provisions soaring. V. S. PRITCHETT The simple lady who . . wished to soar socially. ANNE STEVENSON Her moods seemed to soar and sink with alarming rapidity.

▶ **II** *verb trans.* **3** Exalt. *rare.* **L16.**
4 Perform or accomplish (a flight) by rising high. **M17.**
5 Reach (a height); fly up through (the air etc.). **M17.**
6 Cause to rise or soar. **M17.**
Comb.: **soaraway** *adjective* soaring, making rapid or impressive progress.
■ **soaraˈbility** *noun* (*rare*) the condition of being soarable **E20.** **soarable** *adjective* suitable for soaring flight **E20.** **soarer** *noun* a person who or thing which soars; *spec.* an aircraft designed for soaring, a glider: **M19.**

soarage *noun* var. of **SORAGE**.

soaring /ˈsɔːrɪŋ/ *verbal noun.* **LME.**
[from prec. + **-ING**¹.]
The action of **SOAR** *verb*; an instance of this.

soaring /ˈsɔːrɪŋ/ *ppl adjective.* **L16.**
[formed as prec. + **-ING**².]
1 That soars; *fig.* ambitious, aspiring. **L16.**
2 Tall and imposing, lofty, towering. **L16.**
■ **soaringly** *adverb* **E19.**

Soave /ˈswɑːveɪ/ *noun.* **M20.**
[A town in northern Italy.]
A dry white wine produced in the region around Soave; a drink of this.

soave /səʊˈɑːveɪ/ *adverb.* **M18.**
[Italian.]
MUSIC. A direction: gently, delicately, sweetly.
■ Also **soavemente** /səʊˌɑːvəˈmenteɪ/ *adverb* **M18.**

Soay /ˈsəʊeɪ/ *noun.* **E20.**
[An island in the St Kilda group, Scotland.]
In full ***Soay sheep***. (An animal of) a small brown short-tailed breed of sheep, formerly only found on Soay.

SOB *abbreviation. slang*, chiefly *N. Amer.*
Son of a bitch.

sob /sɒb/ *noun*¹. **LME.**
[from **SOB** *verb*¹.]
1 a An act of sobbing; an audible convulsive drawing and expelling of breath when weeping or from distress, pain or exertion, etc. **LME.** ▸**b** A sound resembling that of a sob. **M18.**
2 An act of a horse recovering its wind after exertion; an opportunity of doing this; *fig.* a rest, a respite. Chiefly in ***give a sob***. Long *rare* or *obsolete*. **L16.**

> 🕮 **1a** U. LE GUIN His companion was breathing in sobs, gulping for air as he struggled along. A. COHEN Her chest heaving with the deepest kind of wretched sobs. L. SPALDING Little Paul . . burst into wails and sobs. **b** D. H. LAWRENCE Love . . tries to put her ear to the painful sob of my blood.

Comb.: **sob sister** (*a*) a female journalist who writes sentimental reports or articles or who gives advice on readers' problems; (*b*) an actress who plays sentimental roles; **sob story** a story of misfortune etc., esp. as an explanation or excuse for something, designed to appeal to the emotions; **sob-stuff** *colloq.* sentimental speech or writing.

sob /sɒb/ *noun*². *slang.* **L20.**
[Prob. alt. of **SOV** *noun*¹.]
A pound.

sob /sɒb/ *verb*¹. Infl. **-bb-**. **ME.**
[Perh. of Low Dutch origin: cf. West Frisian *sobje*, Dutch dial. *sabben* suck.]
1 *verb intrans.* **a** Draw and expel breath audibly and convulsively when weeping or from distress, pain, exertion, etc.; weep in this way. **ME.** ▸**b** Make a sound or sounds resembling sobbing. **L17.**
2 *verb refl.* Bring (oneself) into a specified state by sobbing. **M17.**
3 *verb trans.* **a** Get rid of, expel, or send out, by sobbing. Foll. by *away*, *off*, *out*, etc. **E18.** ▸**b** Utter with sobs. Also foll. by *out*. **L18.**

> 🕮 **1a** G. GREENE She sobbed without tears, a dry, breathless sound. DAY LEWIS I began sobbing in hysterical despair. **b** R. BROOKE Hear the breeze Sobbing in the little trees. **2** A. CARTER His terrors were too great to be soothed . . and so he sobbed himself to sleep. **3a** D. F. GALOUYE He sat in the dirt . . uncontrollably sobbing off the effects of the attack. **b** D. H. LAWRENCE 'You're a lost girl,' sobbed Miss Pinnegar, on a final note of despair.

■ **sobber** *noun* **L19.** **sobbing** *verbal noun* the action of the verb; an instance of this: **ME.** **sobbingly** *adverb* in a sobbing manner, with sobs **M16.**

sob /sɒb/ *verb*² *trans.* Now *Scot.*, *dial.*, & *US.* Infl. **-bb-**. **E17.**
[Origin unkn.]
Soak, saturate. Chiefly as ***sobbed*** *ppl adjective.*
■ **sobby** *adjective* soaked, saturated with moisture **E17.**

soba /ˈsəʊbə/ *noun* (treated as *sing.* or *pl.*). **L19.**
[Japanese.]
Japanese noodles made from buckwheat flour.

sobeit /səʊˈbiːɪt/ *conjunction. arch.* Also **so be it**. **L16.**
[from **SO** *adverb* + **BE** + **IT** *pronoun*.]
Provided that.

> 🕮 LONGFELLOW His friend cared little whither he went, so be it he were not too much alone.

sober /ˈsəʊbə/ *adjective.* **ME.**
[Old & mod. French *sobre* from Latin *sobrius* opp. to *ebrius* (see **EBRIOUS**).]
▶ **I 1** Moderate, avoiding excess, esp. in eating and drinking; characterized by lack of indulgence. **ME.**
2 Abstaining from drinking alcohol; temperate, abstemious. **LME.**
3 Free from the influence of alcohol; not drunk. **LME.**

> 🕮 **3** A. ALVAREZ He felt perfectly sober, but technically he was far over the legal alcohol limit. **(as) sober as a judge** completely sober. ***stone-cold sober***: see **STONE** *adverb*.

▶ **II 4** Serious, solemn, staid; quiet or sedate in demeanour or bearing. **ME.** ▸**b** Of wind, rain, a river, etc.: quiet, gentle, not violent. Now *poet.* **LME.**
5 Characterized by a moderate disposition; calm, dispassionate, not readily excited. **M16.** ▸**b** Humble, unambitious. **M17.**
6 a Of colour, dress, etc.: subdued in tone; not bright or showy. **L16.** ▸**b** Unexciting, uneventful, dull. **M19.**
7 a Free from extravagance or excess. **E17.** ▸**b** Unexaggerated, sensible; not fanciful or imaginative. **E17.**
8 Guided by sound reason; sane, rational. Now only of the mind, speech, etc. *arch.* **M17.**

> 🕮 **4** J. C. OATES Even the boldest of the girls grew sober. **5** F. W. FARRAR Some of the most profound and sober intellects in Europe. M. KLINE A man of even temper, sober judgement, and serenity. **6a** SHAKES. *Rom. & Jul.* Come, civil night, Thou sober-suited matron, all in black. **7b** *Honey* The sober facts on a controversial issue.

▶ **III 9** Small, insignificant, slight; paltry, trifling, poor. Chiefly *Scot.* **LME.**
10 In poor health; not very well. *Scot.* **E19.**
Comb.: **sober-minded** *adjective*, **sober-sided** *adjectives* sedate, serious; **sobersides** a sedate serious person.
■ **soberly** *adverb* **ME.** **soberness** *noun* **ME.**

sober /ˈsəʊbə/ *verb.* LME.
[from the adjective.]
▶ **I** *verb trans.* **1** Reduce to a quiet or gentle condition; appease, pacify; moderate. Long *arch. rare.* LME.
2 a Make grave, serious, or thoughtful. Freq. as ***sobering*** *ppl adjective.* E18. ▸**b** Make less bright or conspicuous. M19.
3 Make (a drunk person) sober; free from intoxication. Now usu. foll. by *up.* E18.
4 Bring *down* to a sober condition. E19.

📖 **2** D. FRASER The sobering experiences of the Boer War. **4** G. GREENE Kay Francis . . does her best to sober down this sentimental version of Florence Nightingale's character.

▶ **II** *verb intrans.* **5** Become sober. Usu. foll. by *up.* E19.
6 Settle or quieten *down.* E19.

📖 **5** M. HOCKING I feel quite squiffy. I'd better sober up before I see Mummy.

■ **soberer** *noun* (*rare*) M19. **soberingly** *adverb* in a sobering manner E20. **soberize** *verb trans. & intrans.* make or become sober E18.

Soberano /səʊbəˈrɑːnəʊ/ *noun.* Pl. **-os.** M20.
[Spanish, lit. 'sovereign'.]
A type of Spanish brandy; a drink of this.

sobful /ˈsɒbfʊl, -f(ə)l/ *adjective. rare.* E20.
[from SOB *noun*[1] or *verb*[1]: see -FUL.]
Given to or provoking sobbing.

Sobieski /sɒˈbjɛski/ *noun. obsolete* exc. *Hist.* L18.
[John III *Sobieski* (1629–96), Polish king and warrior.]
ASTRONOMY. ***Scutum Sobieski***, ***Sobieski's shield***, the constellation Scutum.

sobole /ˈsɒbəʊl/ *noun.* Also (earlier) in Latin form as **-boles** /-bə(ʊ)liːz/, pl. same. E18.
[Latin *soboles, suboles*, from *sub* under + base of *alescere* grow up.]
BOTANY. A shoot, esp. from near the base of a plant; a creeping underground stem.
■ **sobo'liferous** *adjective* bearing (vigorous) basal shoots M18.

sobornost /soˈbornost/ *noun.* M20.
[Russian *sobornost'* conciliarism, catholicity.]
THEOLOGY. A unity of people in a loving fellowship in which each member retains freedom and integrity without excessive individualism.

Sobranye /səˈbrɑːnjeɪ/ *noun.* Also **-je.** L19.
[Bulgarian *săbrânie* assembly.]
The parliament or national assembly of Bulgaria.

sobriety /səˈbrʌɪ(ə)ti/ *noun.* LME.
[Old & mod. French *sobriété* or Latin *sobrietas*, from *sobrius* SOBER *adjective*: see -ITY.]
1 The quality of being sober or moderate; avoidance of excess; *spec.* moderation in drinking alcohol. LME.
2 Staidness, seriousness; soundness of judgement. M16.

sobriquet /ˈsəʊbrɪkeɪ/ *noun.* M17.
[French, orig. 'a tap under the chin'.]
An epithet, a nickname. Cf. SOUBRIQUET.

📖 D. ACHESON Gromyko's sobriquet 'Old Stone Face', belied a dry, sardonic humor.

soc *abbreviation. N. Amer. colloq.*
In an academic context: sociology.

soc *noun* see SOKE.

Soc. *abbreviation.*
1 Socialist.
2 Society.

soca /ˈsəʊkə/ *noun.* L20.
[from SO(UL *noun* + CA(LYPSO.]
A type of calypso music, originating in Trinidad, which incorporates etc. elements from other regional music types, as Afro-Caribbean soul and French Caribbean music.

socage /ˈsɒkɪdʒ/ *noun.* Also **soccage.** ME.
[Anglo-Norman, from *soc* var. of SOKE: see -AGE. Cf. Anglo-Latin *socagium.*]
Hist. **1** A feudal tenure of land involving payment of rent or other non-military services to a superior. Freq. in ***in free and common socage***. ME.
2 a An estate held in socage. *rare.* LME. ▸**b** A payment made by a person holding land in socage. *rare.* M19.
■ **socager** *noun* a person holding land in socage M17.

soccer /ˈsɒkə/ *noun.* L19.
[Aphet. from *Assoc.* (abbreviation of *Association*) + -ER[6].]
Football as played under Association rules; Association Football.
Comb.: ***soccer fan***, ***soccer field***, ***soccer hooligan***, ***soccer match***, etc.; **soccer mom** *US* a middle-class suburban housewife, typically having children who play soccer rather than a traditional American sport.
■ **soccerite** *noun* (now *rare*) a player of soccer M20.

sociability /səʊʃəˈbɪlɪti/ *noun.* L15.
[from next + -ITY.]
1 The quality of being sociable; friendly disposition or interaction. Also, an instance of this. L15.
2 ECOLOGY. The extent to which plants of a given species grow in close proximity. E20.

sociable /ˈsəʊʃəb(ə)l/ *adjective & noun.* M16.
[French, or Latin *sociabilis*, from *sociare* unite, ASSOCIATE *verb*, from *socius* companion, ally, fellow: see -ABLE.]
▶ **A** *adjective.* **1** Naturally inclined to be in company with others of the same species. M16. ▸**b** Of a bird: nesting in colonies. Cf. SOCIAL *adjective* 2b. E19.
2 Inclined to seek and enjoy the company of others; disposed to be friendly, affable, or conversational in company. (Foll. by †*to.*) L16.
3 Of or pertaining to companionship or friendliness with others; (of manner, behaviour, etc.) friendly, pleasant, companionable; (of a meeting etc.) marked by friendliness, not stiff or formal. L16.
4 MATH. Designating a cycle of three or more integers such that each is the sum of the factors of the previous one. Cf. PERFECT *adjective* 7. L20.

📖 **1** W. TEMPLE What it is that makes some Creatures sociable, and others live and range more alone. **2** N. LOWNDES He was such a sociable man . . made friends wherever he went. **3** W. COWPER Comfortably situated by a good fire, and just entering on a sociable conversation. J. BERNARD He . . shouted an invitation to alight and take a drop of something sociable.

Special collocations: †**sociable coach** = sense B.2a below. **sociable grosbeak** = *sociable weaver* below. **sociable plover** a lapwing, *Vanellus gregarius*, which has a black crown and white eyestripe, and nests colonially on the central Russian steppe. **sociable weaver** a sparrow-like weaver-bird, *Philetairus socius*, which breeds in large communal nests and is common in southern Africa.
▶ **B** *noun.* **1** †**a** A social being. Only in E17. ▸**b** A sociable person. *rare.* E20.
2 a An open four-wheeled carriage with facing side seats. Cf. ***sociable coach*** above. L18. ▸**b** An S-shaped couch for two people who sit partially facing each other. M19. ▸**c** A tricycle with two seats side by side. L19.
3 An informal evening party, a social. *US.* E19.
■ **sociableness** *noun* L16. **sociably** *adverb* L16.

social /ˈsəʊʃ(ə)l/ *adjective & noun.* LME.
[Old & mod. French, or Latin *socialis* allied, confederate, etc., from *socius*: see SOCIABLE, -AL[1].]
▶ **A** *adjective.* **1** Designating a war between traditional allies or confederates; *spec.* (**a**) ROMAN HISTORY the war of 90–89 BC between Rome and the Italian allies; (**b**) GREEK HISTORY the war of 357–355 BC between the Athenians and their confederates. LME.
2 a Living or disposed to live in companies or communities; desirous of the pleasant society or companionship of others. Formerly also, devoted to home life, domestic. LME. ▸**b** ZOOLOGY. Gregarious, colonial; breeding or nesting in colonies. Cf. SOCIABLE *adjective* 1b. L18. ▸**c** ENTOMOLOGY. Living together in more or less organized communities, freq. with specialized castes; belonging to such a community. M19. ▸**d** BOTANY. Of a plant: tending to grow in large numbers where it occurs, esp. so as to cover a large area. M19.
†**3** Associated, allied, combined. Only in 17.
4 a Marked or characterized by mutual friendliness or geniality; (of an activity, occasion, etc.) enjoyed, spent, etc., in company with others; consisting of people associated together for friendly interaction or companionship. M17. ▸**b** Inclined to friendly interaction or companionship; sociable. E18. ▸**c** Of or pertaining to (the activities of) fashionable or wealthy society (cf. SOCIETY 3b). L19.
5 a Of or pertaining to society or its organization as a natural or ordinary condition of human life. L17. ▸**b** *spec.* in SOCIAL SCIENCES. Of or pertaining to the mutual relationships of human beings or of classes of human beings; connected with the functions and structures necessary to membership of a group or society. M19.
6 Concerned with or interested in the constitution of society and the problems and issues presented by this. E19. ▸**b** Of an activity etc.: performed to benefit or improve the condition of society. M20.

📖 **2a** T. LILLEY Nathan was . . very much the social animal. He liked people, and he liked to be liked. **4a** LD MACAULAY The contest went on in . . every social circle. *Practical Wireless* You get . . sports, games, and a great social life. *Highland News* She had gone out for a social drink. P. DALLY Almost her only social activity at this time was to go with Arabel to see Boyd. **b** M. WESLEY John seems to know everybody, he's very social. **c** G. B. SHAW The King's displeasure is still a sentence of social death. **5a** *Times* The sense of social identity which comes from group membership. *Oxford Mail* It . . appeals to . . doctors, nurses, teachers, secretaries—it cuts right across the social spectrum. G. PHELPS As he matured Dickens's social criticism became more searching and profound. **b** *American Journal of Sociology* Past and present social methods of dealing with . . intemperance. J. A. C. BROWN The social function of industry is no less important than its technical efficiency. N. FREELING A . . piece of social legislation . . in line for repeal. **6** *Burlington Magazine* The books of . . Rabelais, with their rollicking social satire. J. CAMPLIN The social ideals of any society take . . time to catch up with . . economic realities. **b** *Spare Rib* Cuts in social spending continue.

Special collocations & comb.: **social action** action that takes place in a social context; action oriented to other members of a society. *social* ANTHROPOLOGY. **social benefit** (**a**) a benefit to society resulting from technological innovation etc.; (**b**) a benefit payable under a social security system. **social butterfly** a person who goes to many social entertainments; a socialite. **social casework**, **social caseworker** = *casework*, *caseworker* s.v. CASE *noun*[1]. **social causation** explanation of phenomena in terms of social causes. **social centre** a place, esp. a building, where people gather for communal activities, recreation, etc. **social change** change in the customs, institutions, or culture of a society. **social chapter** a social charter forming part of the Maastricht Treaty. **social character** the collective essential traits of a group of people, drawn from their common experience, feelings, etc. **social charter** a document dealing with social policy, esp. workers' rights and welfare; *spec.* that signed in December 1989 by eleven EU member states and later forming the basis of the social chapter of the Maastricht Treaty. **social climber** a person anxious to attain a higher social status. **social climbing** *noun & adjective* (**a**) *noun* the action or process of raising one's social status; (**b**) *adjective* (of a person) anxious to attain a higher social status. **social column** a column in a newspaper or magazine that reports the activities of fashionable, famous, and wealthy people. **social comment** something, as a picture, play, symbol, etc., which makes a point about human society and the distinctions within it; such things collectively. **social compact** = ***social contract*** below. **social conscience** a sense of responsibility for or preoccupation with the problems and injustices of society. **social contract** mutual agreement as the basis of human society. **social control** control of an individual or group by the wider society (as through laws, policing, etc.). **social cost** the cost to society in terms of effort, ill health, inconvenience, etc., as well as the cost to the individual, of some enterprise or innovation. **social credit** the economic theory that consumer purchasing power should be increased either by subsidizing producers so they can reduce prices, or by distributing the profits of industry to consumers; ***Social Credit League***, a New Zealand political party, or Canadian non-political organization, advocating social credit; ***Social Credit Party***, a Canadian political party advocating social credit. **social Darwinism** the application of aspects of Darwinian theory to the analysis of society. **social democracy** POLITICS (**a**) (the advocacy of) a socialist system achieved by democratic means; †(**b**) *gen.* socialism, Communism. **social democrat** POLITICS an advocate of social democracy; a member of a political party with socialistic views; *Hist.* a member of the Social Democratic Party. **social democratic** *adjective* of or pertaining to social democracy; ***Social Democratic Party*** (*Hist.*), a British political party founded in 1981 by a group of former Labour MPs (later merged with the Liberal Party to form the Social and Liberal Democrats, afterwards the Liberal Democrats). **social deprivation** deprivation of the ordinary material benefits of life in society. **social dialect** a dialect spoken by a particular social group. **social dialectology** the study of the dialects spoken by particular social groups. **social differentiation** the process whereby a group or community becomes separate or distinct. **social disease** (**a**) a social evil; (**b**) *N. Amer.* a venereal disease. **social distance** SOCIAL PSYCHOLOGY (**a**) the perceived or desired degree of remoteness between a member of one social group and the members of another, as evidenced in, for example, the relationships to which he or she might admit them; (**b**) the physical distance between individuals that they find acceptable in a given social context. **social document** a literary work embodying an authentic and informative description of the social conditions of its time. **social drinker** a person who drinks alcoholic liquor chiefly on social occasions. **social drinking** the drinking of alcoholic liquor as a feature or accompaniment of social occasions. **social dynamics** (the study of) the forces that results in social change. **social élite** an exclusive section of fashionable society. **social engineering** the application of sociological principles to specific social problems. **social ethic** a set of moral principles for the proper and efficient running of society. **social evening** an informal evening gathering or party, freq. with some form of entertainment; an evening on which this is held. **social evil** a thing which has a negative effect on the running or standard of society, as starvation, poverty, etc.; ***the social evil*** (*arch.*), prostitution. **social fact** something originating in the institutions or culture of a society which affects the behaviour or attitudes of an individual member of that society. **social fascist** in Communism, a member of any other left-wing party. **social fund** a social security fund from which loans or grants are made to people in need. **social geography** the study of people and their environment with particular emphasis on social factors. **social gospel** (**a**) CHRISTIAN THEOLOGY the Gospel interpreted as having a social application, formerly used esp. in the US to advocate social reform; (**b**) *gen.* a message of salvation for society. **social-historical** *adjective* of or pertaining to social history. **social history** (**a**) the history of society or of social behaviour; history with an emphasis on social structures; (**b**) the background and circumstances of a social worker's client. **social inquiry report** a report made by a probation officer or social worker on a person's character and circumstances, which may be required by a court before sentencing. **social insurance** a system of compulsory contribution to provide State assistance in sickness, unemployment, etc. **social ladder** = *social scale* below. **social market (economy)** an economic system based on a free market operated in conjunction with state provision for those unable to sell their labour, such as the elderly or unemployed. **social medicine** *collect.* those areas of medicine which aim to assist people with social or emotional problems, as psychology, psychiatry, etc. ***social mobility***: see MOBILITY *noun*[1] 3. **social morphology** (the study of) the various forms of social structure and the changes that take place in them or govern them. **social order** (**a**) orderliness within society; (**b**) SOCIOLOGY the way in which society is organized, the network of human relationships in society. **social ownership** a form of collective ownership in which organization and control are shared; *esp.* ownership and control of an industry, company, etc., by its workers or by the community at large. **social partner** POLITICS an individual or organization, such as an employer, trade union, or employee, participating in a cooperative relationship for the mutual benefit of all concerned. ***social position***: see POSITION *noun* 6b. **social process** the pattern of growth and change in a society over the years. **social psychiatry** the branch of psychiatry that deals with the social causes, social consequences, and social methods of treatment of mental illness. **social psychology** the branch of psychology that deals with social interactions, including their origins and effects on the individual. **social realism** the realistic depiction of social conditions or political views in art and literature. **social reality** a conception of what exists that is affected by the customs and beliefs of the social group holding the conception. **social register** (orig. *US*) a register or directory of those in the upper or wealthy classes. **social revolution** a revolution in the structure and nature of society, *esp.* one anticipated or advocated by socialists and communists. **social revolutionary** *adjective & noun* (a person) advocating or supporting social revolution, formerly esp. in the USSR. **social scale** the hierarchical structure of human society. **social science** the scientific study of the structure and functions of society and social relationships; any discipline, as politics, economics, etc., that attempts to study human society in a systematic way. **social scientist** an expert in or student of social science. **social secretary** a secretary whose role is to make arrangements for the social activities of a person or club etc. **social security** a system of State assistance for people on a low or non-existent income, as the unemployed, the aged, etc.; the money paid out under this system. **social service** (*a*) service to society or to one's fellows; philanthropic work, esp. on behalf of the poor or underprivileged; (*b*) a service provided esp. by the State for the benefit of the community, esp. education, health, and housing. (freq. in *pl.*). **social space** social distance. ***social status***: see STATUS 3. **social stratification** the division of society into strata based on social position or class. **social structure** the customs, relationships, and institutions of which a social system is composed. **social studies** *collect.* various aspects or branches of the study of human society. **social survey** a comprehensive survey of some aspect of the social life, history, problems, etc., of a particular locality. **social system** a set of interdependent relationships, customs, institutions, etc., which together form a functioning society. **social unit** an individual considered as a constituent of a society or group; a community or group considered as having a separate identity within a larger whole. **social wage** (*a*) the cost per person of the amenities provided within a society from public funds; (*b*) a social security payment. **social weaver** (*a*) either of two E. African sparrow-weavers of the genus *Pseudonigrita*, which breed in colonies of closely-packed domed nests; (*b*) = ***sociable weaver*** s.v. SOCIABLE *adjective*. **social whale** = ***pilot whale*** s.v. PILOT *noun*. **social work** work of benefit to those in need of help or welfare; *esp.* such work provided by trained personnel for those with family or social problems often arising from poverty, handicap, etc. **social worker** a person who undertakes social work, esp. on a professional basis.

▶ **B** *noun*. †**1** A companion, an associate. *rare*. E–M17.

2 A social gathering or party, *esp.* one organized by a club, association, etc. L19.

3 *ellipt.* = ***social security*** above. *colloq.* M20.

socialisation *noun* var. of SOCIALIZATION.

socialise *verb* var. of SOCIALIZE.

socialism /ˈsəʊʃəlɪz(ə)m/ *noun*. Also **S-**. E19.

[French *socialisme*, formed as SOCIAL: see -ISM.]

A political and economic theory or policy of social organization which advocates that the community as a whole should own and control the means of production, capital, land, property, etc. Also *spec.* in Marxist theory, a transitional social state between the overthrow of capitalism and the realization of Communism.

Christian Socialism: see CHRISTIAN *adjective*. ***National Socialism***: see NATIONAL *adjective*.

socialist /ˈsəʊʃəlɪst/ *noun & adjective*. Also **S-**. E19.

[from SOCIAL *adjective* + -IST. Cf. French *socialiste*.]

▶ **A** *noun*. An advocate of or believer in socialism; an adherent or supporter of socialism. Also, a member of a socialist political party. E19.

Christian Socialist: see CHRISTIAN *adjective*. ***National Socialist***: see NATIONAL *adjective*.

▶ **B** *attrib.* or as *adjective*. (Of a person, party, etc.) supporting, advocating, or practising socialism; (of an idea, theory, etc.) in accordance with socialism. M19.

📖 A. G. FRANK Food production in Asia, Africa, and Latin America (excluding . . socialist countries) has fallen. ***primitive socialist accumulation***: see PRIMITIVE *adjective*. **socialist realism** [translating Russian *sotsialisticheskiĭ realizm*] the official theory of art and literature of the former Soviet Communist Party, by which an artist's or writer's work should reflect and promote (the ideals of) socialist society. **socialist-realist** *noun & adjective* (*a*) *noun* an advocate of socialist realism; (*b*) *adjective* reflecting or promoting socialist realism.

■ **socia'listic** *adjective* (*a*) of, pertaining to, or characteristic of socialism; in accordance with socialism; (*b*) advocating or favouring socialism: M19. **socia'listically** *adverb* L19.

socialite /ˈsəʊʃəlʌɪt/ *noun*. *colloq.* E20.

[from SOCIAL + -ITE[1].]

A person prominent in fashionable society; a person fond of social activities and entertainments.

sociality /səʊʃɪˈalɪti/ *noun*. M17.

[Latin *socialitas*, from *socialis*: see SOCIAL, -ITY.]

1 The state or quality of being social; social interaction or companionship with one's fellows; the enjoyment of this. M17. ▸**b** A social act or entertainment. E19.

2 The action or fact of forming a society or associating together; the disposition, impulse, or tendency to do this. L18.

3 Companionship or fellowship *in* or *with* some thing or person. E19.

📖 **2** *New Scientist* Nearly all bees are solitary but in three groups there is a . . degree of sociality.

socialization /səʊʃəlʌɪˈzeɪʃ(ə)n/ *noun*. Also **-isation**. M19.

[from next + -ATION.]

The action or fact of socializing something or someone; *spec.* in SOCIOLOGY, the process of forming or adapting oneself to associations, *esp.* the process of acquiring the necessary values and behaviour modifications for the stability of the social group of which one is a member.

socialize /ˈsəʊʃəlʌɪz/ *verb*. Also **-ise**. E19.

[from SOCIAL + -IZE.]

1 *verb trans.* Make social; make fit to live in society; *spec.* in SOCIOLOGY, transmit to (an individual) the cultural values and behaviour standards of the social group of which he or she is a member. E19.

2 *verb trans.* Make socialistic; establish, organize, or run on a socialistic basis; *gen.* finance with public funds, bring under public control. M19.

3 *verb intrans.* Be sociable, participate in social activities. Freq. foll. by *with*. L19.

📖 **1** *Daily Telegraph* The father is prepared to take . . part in socialising a child. *Independent* Women are still socialised to defer to men. **2 socialized medicine** *US* (freq. *derog.*) a system of medical care that is financed and administered by the State. **3** G. SAYER He was willing to socialize with his pupils outside . . college.

■ **socializer** *noun* M20.

socially /ˈsəʊʃ(ə)li/ *adverb*. E16.

[from SOCIAL *adjective* + -LY[2].]

†**1** In company. *Scot. rare*. Only in E16.

†**2** As a member of a body or society. *rare*. Only in M17.

3 In a social manner; sociably. M18.

4 In respect of or with regard to society. L19.

📖 **3** R. G. CUMMING These remarkable birds . . live socially together under one common roof. **4** D. JENKINS Public schools and socially-privileged private schools. M. GIROUARD To marry someone who was not a lady was socially unthinkable. *City Limits* The socially conscious earnestness of much black American theatre.

socialness /ˈsəʊʃ(ə)lnɪs/ *noun*. E18.

[from SOCIAL *adjective* + -NESS.]

Social quality or character; social interaction, sociality.

†**sociate** *noun*. LME–L18.

[Aphet. from ASSOCIATE *noun*.]

An associate, a colleague; a companion, a comrade.

sociate /ˈsəʊʃɪət, -sɪət/ *adjective*. Long *arch. rare*. LME.

[Latin *sociatus* pa. pple of *sociare* unite, associate, from *socius* companion: see -ATE[2].]

Associated with a thing or person (foll. by *to*, *with*); joined or united *together*.

†**sociate** *verb*. L15.

[Latin *sociat-* pa. ppl stem of *sociare*: see prec., -ATE[3].]

1 *verb trans.* Associate, join, or unite together; form into an association. L15–M17.

2 *verb intrans.* Associate, mix, or keep company *with* others. M17–E18.

sociation /səʊʃɪˈeɪʃ(ə)n, səʊsɪ-/ *noun*. L17.

[Late Latin *sociatio(n-)*, formed as SOCIATE *adjective*, or directly from SOCIATE *verb* after ASSOCIATION: see -ATION.]

†**1** Association, conjunction, union. *rare*. L17–E18.

2 ECOLOGY. = SOCIETY 8. M20.

sociative /ˈsəʊʃɪətɪv/ *adjective*. L19.

[French *sociatif, -ive*, formed as SOCIATE *adjective*: see -IVE.]

GRAMMAR. Denoting or expressing association.

sociétaire /sɔsjetɛːr/ *noun*. Pl. pronounced same. L19.

[French, from *société* SOCIETY: see -ARY[1].]

An actor who is a full member of the Comédie Française, Paris, and so has a share in its management and profits.

societal /səˈsʌɪɪt(ə)l/ *adjective*. L19.

[from SOCIETY + -AL[1].]

Societary; social.

■ **societally** *adverb* M20.

societarian /səsʌɪˈtɛːrɪən/ *adjective & noun*. E19.

[from SOCIETY + -ARIAN, after *antiquarian*, *humanitarian*, etc.]

▶ **A** *adjective*. Societary; socialistic. E19.

▶ **B** *noun*. **1** A believer in or advocate of socialism; a socialist. M19.

2 A person who moves in or is a member of fashionable society. L19.

societary /səˈsʌɪɪt(ə)ri/ *adjective*. M19.

[from SOCIETY + -ARY[1].]

Of, pertaining to, or concerned with society or social conditions; social.

society /səˈsʌɪɪti/ *noun*. M16.

[French *société* from Latin *societas, -tat-*, from *socius*: see SOCIABLE, -ITY.]

▶ **I 1 a** Association with one's fellows, esp. in a friendly or intimate manner; companionship, the company of others. Also (*rare*), an instance of this. (Foll. by *between*, *with*.) M16. ▸**b** People with whom one has companionship or friendly association. *arch.* E17.

2 The system of customs and organization adopted by a body of (esp. human) individuals for harmonious and interactive coexistence or for mutual benefit, defence, etc. M16.

3 a The aggregate of people living together in a more or less ordered community. Also (with qualifying adjective), a part of this. M17. ▸**b** The aggregate of fashionable, wealthy, or otherwise prominent people regarded as forming a distinct class or body in a community. Also, a group of such people. E19.

📖 **1a** E. STILLINGFLEET An Island, where he may have no society with mankind. H. JAMES It was . . natural he should seek her society. JULIA HAMILTON The society of women and the young all morning has tired him. **b** C. READE They have plenty of society. **2** J. BULWER A due reverence . . towards Society wherein we live. **3a** J. C. RANSOM The failure of society and state to sympathize with the needs of the individual. J. AIKEN *Nobody* in polite society *ever* picked their nose. **the alternative society** (those people embracing) a way of life with values and habits which purport to be preferable to those of established society.

▶ **II** †**4** The fact or condition of taking part with others or another in some action; participation; partnership. M16–M18.

†**5** The fact or condition of being connected, related, or allied; relationship; alliance. M16–L18.

▶ **III 6 a** An association or body of people united by a common aim, interest, belief, profession, etc. M16. ▸**b** A group of people meeting together, esp. for discussion, conviviality, or worship. L17.

7 A body of people forming a community or living under the same government. L16. ▸**b** A company; a small party. Now *rare* or *obsolete*. L16. ▸**c** ZOOLOGY. A group of animals of the same species, esp. social insects, organized in a cooperative manner. E20.

8 ECOLOGY. A community of plants within a mature consociation characterized by a particular subdominant species. L19.

📖 **6a** DAY LEWIS Honorary membership of the Incorporated Society of Musicians. ***building society***, ***cooperative society***, etc. **Society of Friends** the Quakers (see QUAKER *noun* 2). ***society of Jesus***: see JESUIT *noun* 1. **b** ***choral society***, ***debating society***, etc. **7** R. G. COLLINGWOOD A society consists in the common way of life which its members practise. ***closed society***, ***open society***, ***plural society***, etc.

socii *noun pl.* see SOCIUS.

Socinian /səˈsɪnɪən/ *noun & adjective*. M17.

[mod. Latin *Socinianus*, from *Socinus* Latinized form of Italian surname *Soz(z)ini* (see below): see -IAN.]

▶ **A** *noun*. A member of a sect founded by Laelius and Faustus Socinus, two 16th-cent. Italian theologians who denied the divinity of Christ. M17.

▶ **B** *adjective*. Of or pertaining to the Socinians or their creed. M17.

■ **Socinianism** *noun* the doctrines or views of the Socinians M17. **Socinianize** *verb* (*a*) *verb intrans.* (*rare*) adopt or express Socinian views; (*b*) *verb trans.* imbue with Socinian doctrines: L17.

socio- /ˈsəʊsɪəʊ, ˈsəʊʃɪəʊ/ *combining form*.

[from Latin *socius* (see SOCIABLE) + -O-.]

Forming combs. in various relations and with various senses as 'of or pertaining to society or the composition, study, etc., of society', 'social(ly) and —'.

■ **socio'centric** *adjective* tending to focus one's interest on one's own community or group L19. **soci'ocracy** *noun* government by society as a whole M19. **socio-'cultural** *adjective* combining social and cultural factors E20. **socio-'culturally** *adverb* in a sociocultural manner M20. **socio-demo'graphic** *adjective* combining social and demographic features L20. **socio'drama** *noun* (PSYCHOLOGY) an improvised play acted by or for people in a socially tense situation in order to portray different perceptions and experiences of the same situation; a form of group psychotherapy based on role-play: M20. **sociodra'matic** *adjective* of or pertaining to sociodrama M20. **sociody'namic** *adjective* tending to produce change in a society or group M20. **socioeco'logical** *adjective* of or pertaining to socioecology M20. **socioe'cology** *noun* the branch of science that deals with the interactions among the members of a species, and between them and the environment L20. **sociogram** *noun* (SOCIOLOGY) a diagrammatic representation of the ratings for popularity, leadership, etc., that members of a small group give each other M20. **soci'ography** *noun* a (method of) sociological analysis that uses both quantitative and qualitative data L19. **socio-his'torical** *adjective* combining social and historical factors M20. **socio-'legal** *adjective* of or pertaining to the relationship between law and society; combining social and legal factors: L20. **sociolect** *noun* a variety of a language that is characteristic of the social background or status of its user L20. **socio'lectal** *adjective* of or pertaining to a sociolect L20. **socio-'medical** *adjective* of or pertaining to the relationship between medicine and society M20. **socio'nomic** *adjective* relating to the environmental conditions affecting the formation and development of social groups;

socionomic sex ratio, the ratio of females to males in relatively stable social groups: E20. **socio-poˈlitical** *adjective* combining social and political factors L19. **sociopsychoˈlogical** *adjective* combining social and psychological factors L19. **socio-reˈligious** *adjective* pertaining to or affected by the influence and effect of religion on society L19. **socio-ˈtechnical** *adjective* pertaining to the interaction between society or social factors and technology M20.

sociobiology /ˌsəʊsɪəʊbʌɪˈɒlədʒi, ˌsəʊʃɪəʊ-/ *noun*. M20.
[from SOCIO- + BIOLOGY.]
The branch of science that deals with the biological, esp. ecological and evolutionary, aspects of social behaviour.
■ **ˌsociobioˈlogical** *adjective* E20. **ˌsociobioˈlogically** *adverb* L20. **sociobiologist** *noun* L20.

socio-economic /ˌsəʊsɪəʊiːkəˈnɒmɪk, ˌsəʊʃɪəʊ-/ *adjective*. L19.
[from SOCIO- + ECONOMIC.]
Deriving from both social and economic factors; combining such factors to provide an indication of a person's or group's effective social situation.
■ **socio-economically** *adverb* M20.

sociolinguistic /ˌsəʊsɪəʊlɪŋˈɡwɪstɪk, ˌsəʊʃɪəʊ-/ *adjective*. M20.
[from SOCIO- + LINGUISTIC.]
Of or pertaining to sociolinguistics.
■ **sociolinguistically** *adverb* M20.

sociolinguistics /ˌsəʊsɪəʊlɪŋˈɡwɪstɪks, ˌsəʊʃɪəʊ-/ *noun*. M20.
[from SOCIO- + LINGUISTICS.]
The branch of linguistics that deals with language and linguistic structures in relation to social factors.
■ **socioˈlinguist** *noun* an expert in or student of sociolinguistics M20.

sociologese /ˌsəʊsɪɒləˈdʒiːz, ˌsəʊʃɪ-/ *noun*. *derog*. M20.
[from SOCIOLOGY + -ESE.]
Writing of a style supposedly typical of sociologists, *esp*. excessively complicated or jargonistic and abstruse writing.

sociologism /səʊsɪˈɒlədʒɪz(ə)m, səʊʃɪ-/ *noun*. M20.
[from next + -ISM.]
The tendency to ascribe a sociological basis to other disciplines.
■ **socioloˈgistic** *adjective* M20.

sociology /səʊsɪˈɒlədʒi, səʊʃɪ-/ *noun*. M19.
[French *sociologie*, formed as SOCIO-: see -LOGY.]
1 The branch of knowledge that deals with the development, structure, and collective behaviour and interaction of human society. M19. ▸**b** The application of sociological concepts and analysis to other disciplines or fields. E20.
2 With specifying word(s): the study of plant or animal communities. Cf. PHYTOSOCIOLOGY. M20.

📖 **1** L. F. WARD Man, whose associative habits form the . . subject of sociology. **b** *English World-Wide* The sociology of language . . uses linguistic information as a means of describing social phenomena. **2** N. POLUNIN Plant sociology, where considerations of life-forms may help in the description of the structure of the communities.

■ **socioˈlogic** *adjective* = SOCIOLOGICAL M19. **socioˈlogical** *adjective* of or pertaining to sociology; concerned or connected with the organization, functioning, or study of society: M19. **socioˈlogically** *adverb* L19. **sociologist** *noun* an expert in or student of sociology M19. **sociologize** *verb* (**a**) *verb intrans*. make a study of social questions; (**b**) *verb trans*. make sociological in character; study from a sociological standpoint: L19.

sociometry /səʊsɪˈɒmɪtri, səʊʃɪ-/ *noun*. E20.
[from SOCIO- + -METRY.]
SOCIOLOGY & PSYCHOLOGY. The branch of knowledge that deals with the structure of groups, esp. the relationships between the members of a group.
■ **socioˈmetric** *adjective* of or pertaining to sociometry M20. **socioˈmetrically** *adverb* M20. **sociometrist** *noun* an expert in or student of sociometry M20.

sociopath /ˈsəʊsɪə(ʊ)paθ, ˈsəʊʃɪə(ʊ)-/ *noun*. M20.
[from SOCIO-, after *psychopath*.]
PSYCHOLOGY. A person with a personality disorder manifesting itself in extreme anti-social attitudes and behaviour.
■ **socioˈpathic** *adjective* M20. **sociˈopathy** *noun* the disorder suffered by a sociopath M20.

socius /ˈsəʊʃɪəs/ *noun*. Pl. **-cii** /-sɪʌɪ/, **-ciuses**. E18.
[Latin.]
1 An associate, a colleague. E18.
2 SOCIOLOGY. An individual person, regarded as a unit of human society. L19.

sock /sɒk/ *noun*[1]. Pl. **socks**, (in sense 2 also *informal*) **sox**.
[Old English *socc* corresp. to Middle Low German, Middle Dutch *socke* (Dutch *zok*), Old High German *soc* (German *Socke*), Old Norse *sokkr*, from Germanic, from Latin *soccus* light low-heeled shoe or slipper from Greek *sukkhos*.]
1 A light shoe, a slipper, a pump. Now only *spec*. a light shoe worn by a comic actor on the ancient Greek and Roman stage; *transf.* (*arch*.) comic drama, comedy. OE.
2 A knitted covering for the foot, usually reaching to the ankle or calf of the leg. ME. ▸**b** A sock used as a receptacle for money; *transf.* a store of money. *colloq*. M20. ▸**c** The wool between the knee and foot of a sheep. *NZ*. M20.
3 A removable insole put into a shoe or boot for warmth etc. M19.
4 = ***wind-sock*** s.v. WIND *noun*[1]. M20.
Phrases: **in one's socks** without shoes (with ref. to a person's height). **knock the socks off** *informal* beat (a person) thoroughly, trounce. **old socks** *colloq*. (orig. *US*) a familiar form of address. **pull one's socks up** *colloq*. make an effort to improve. **put a sock in it** *colloq*. be quiet, desist from an annoying action. **sock and buskin** *arch*. the theatrical profession, comedy and tragedy, drama. **white sock** a white portion on a horse's fetlock joint.
■ **socked** *adjective* wearing socks L18. **sockette** /sɒˈkɛt/ *noun* a short sock M20. **sockless** *adjective* without socks, wearing no socks E17.

sock /sɒk/ *noun*[2]. Long *obsolete* exc. *dial*.
[Old English *sūcan* to suck (cf. Middle Dutch *soc, zok* suck, West Frisian *sok* the suck of water in the wake of a ship). Cf. SOCK-LAMB.]
†**1** Suck given to a child. OE–LME.
2 Moisture that collects in or percolates through soil. Also, the drainage of a dunghill, liquid manure. L18.

sock /sɒk/ *noun*[3]. *colloq*. L17.
[Origin uncertain: rel to SOCK *verb*[1].]
1 A forceful blow; *arch*. a beating. L17.
2 (Power to make) a strong impact; emphasis. *US*. M20.

📖 **1** J. DOS PASSOS One of the brakeman . . got such a sock in the jaw that he fell clear off the front porch. **2** T. K. WOLFE The old argument . . didn't have much sock to it any more.

Comb.: **sock chorus** JAZZ the last chorus of an arrangement; **sock cymbal** JAZZ = HIGH-HAT *noun* 2.
■ **sockeroo** /sɒkəˈruː/ *noun* (orig. *US*) a show, play, etc., with an overwhelming impact; a great success: M20.

sock /sɒk/ *noun*[4]. *School slang*. E19.
[Origin unkn.]
Food; *esp*. sweets, cakes.

sock /sɒk/ *noun*[5]. *rare*. M19.
[Perh. ellipt. for SOCK-LAMB.]
An indulged child; a pet.

sock /sɒk/ *verb*[1]. *colloq*. L17.
[Origin uncertain: rel. to SOCK *noun*[3].]
1 *verb trans*. Beat, strike, or hit forcefully. L17. ▸**b** Drive or thrust *in(to)* something. Chiefly *US*. M19. ▸**c** JAZZ. Perform (music) in a swinging manner. Freq. foll. by *out*. E20.
2 *verb intrans*. Strike out; pitch *into* a person. M19.

📖 **1** B. CHATWIN The porter had socked him on the jaw, and he now lay, face down on the paving. *Smash Hits* The tiff resulted in fisticuffs—Mimi socked Tom, Tom socked her back. *fig.*: *USA Today* College students . . may be socked with a new batch of exams. **sock it to** strike or attack (a person) forcefully; *fig*. make a powerful impression on (a person). **c** *New Yorker* From the top—'Watermelon Man'. Let's sock it out.

sock /sɒk/ *verb*[2] *trans*. L19.
[from SOCK *noun*[1].]
1 Provide with socks; put socks on the feet of (a person). L19.
2 Put (money) aside as savings. Usu. foll. by *away*. *colloq*. (orig. *US*). M20.
3 Of fog, cloud, etc.: close *in*, enshroud. *N. Amer*. M20.

📖 **2** R. DOLINER He's got to have money . . . How much you figure he socked away? **3** *High Times* Pilots . . are often completely socked in by fog and haze.

sockdolager /sɒkˈdɒlədʒə/ *noun*. *US slang*. Also **-loger**. M19.
[Prob. fanciful formation from SOCK *noun*[3].]
1 A forceful or decisive blow. M19.
2 An exceptional person or thing. M19.

socket /ˈsɒkɪt/ *noun & verb*. ME.
[Anglo-Norman *soket* (Anglo-Latin *sokettus* spearhead) dim. of Old & mod. French *soc* ploughshare, prob. of Celtic origin: see -ET[1].]
▸ **A** *noun*. †**1** The head of a lance or spear, resembling a ploughshare. ME–M16.
2 A hollow part or piece constructed to receive some part or thing fitting into it. LME.
3 *spec*. **a** The part of a candlestick or chandelier in which the candle is placed. LME. ▸**b** ANATOMY. A hollow or cavity in which a part (as a tooth, an eye, the end of a bone, etc.) is situated. E17. ▸**c** A device receiving the pins of an electric plug, a light-bulb, etc., for connection to an electrical circuit; *esp*. one for an electric plug that is fixed to a wall. L19. ▸**d** GOLF. The part of the head of an iron club into which the shaft is fitted; a shot made off this. L19.
2c ***jack-socket***: see JACK *noun*[1] 13.
Comb.: **socket outlet** a socket for an electric plug that is fixed to a wall and connected to an electricity supply; **socket set** a number of detachable sockets of different sizes for use with a socket wrench; **socket spanner**, **socket wrench**: having a (detachable) socket which fits over the nut; a box spanner.
▸ **B** *verb*. **1** *verb trans*. Place in or fit with a socket. M16.
2 *verb trans. & intrans*. GOLF. Hit (the ball or a shot) off the socket. E20.
■ **socketer** *noun* a golfer who sockets the ball E20. **socketless** *adjective* M19.

sockeye /ˈsɒkʌɪ/ *noun*. L19.
[Salish *sukai* lit. 'fish of fishes'.]
A salmon, *Oncorhynchus nerka*, of the N. American Pacific coast. Also ***sockeye salmon***.

socking /ˈsɒkɪŋ/ *adverb & adjective*. *slang*. L19.
[Perh. from SOCK *verb*[1] or euphem. alt. of FUCKING.]
▸ **A** *adverb*. Exceedingly, very. L19.

📖 D. FRANCIS A brooch I had . . with a socking big diamond in the middle.

▸ **B** *adjective*. Confounded, damned. M20.

sock-lamb /ˈsɒklam/ *noun*. M19.
[Perh. from SOCK *noun*[2] + LAMB *noun*.]
A hand-reared lamb; a pet lamb.

socko /ˈsɒkəʊ/ *interjection, adjective, & noun*. *slang*. E20.
[from SOCK *noun*[3] + -O.]
▸ **A** *interjection*. Repr. the sound of a violent blow. Orig. & chiefly *US*. E20.
▸ **B** *adjective*. Stunningly effective or successful. M20.
▸ **C** *noun*. Pl. **-os**. A success, a hit. Orig. & chiefly *US*. M20.

socle /ˈsəʊk(ə)l, ˈsɒk-/ *noun*. E18.
[French from Italian *zoccolo* wooden shoe, socle, repr. Latin *socculus* dim. of *soccus* SOCK *noun*[1]. Cf. ZOCLE.]
A low plinth serving as a pedestal for a statue, column, vase, etc.

socman *noun* var. of SOKEMAN.

Socotrine /səˈkəʊtrɪn/ *adjective*. Also **s-**. LME.
[from *Socotra*, an island in the Indian Ocean near the mouth of the Gulf of Aden + -INE[5].]
Found in, originating from, or associated with Socotra. Chiefly in ***Socotrine aloes***, bitter aloes from the aloe *Aloe perryi* found in Socotra.

Socratic /səˈkratɪk/ *adjective & noun*. E17.
[Latin *Socraticus* from Greek *Sōkratikos*, from *Sōkratēs* Socrates (see below): see -IC.]
▸ **A** *adjective*. Of, pertaining to, or characteristic of the Athenian philosopher Socrates (d. 399 BC) or his philosophy or methods. E17.
Socratic elenchus refutation by short questions eliciting from the proponent of a thesis its absurd or unacceptable implications. **Socratic irony** a pose of ignorance by which a skilful questioner exposes the emptiness of the answerer's claims to knowledge.
▸ **B** *noun*. A follower or adherent of Socrates. L17.
■ **Socraˈtean** *adjective* (*rare*) = SOCRATIC *adjective* M20. **Socratical** *adjective* = SOCRATIC *adjective* L16. **Socratically** *adverb* E17. **ˈSocratist** *noun* (*rare*) = SOCRATIC *noun* M16. **ˈSocratize** *verb intrans*. philosophize or live like Socrates M19.

Socred /ˈsəʊkrɛd/ *noun*. *Canad. & NZ*. M20.
[Contr. of ***social credit*** s.v. SOCIAL *adjective*.]
A supporter of (a party advocating) social credit.

sod /sɒd/ *noun*[1]. LME.
[Middle & mod. Low German or Middle Dutch *sode* (Dutch *zode*) = Old Frisian *sātha, sāda*, of unkn. origin.]
1 a A usu. square or oblong piece or slice of earth together with the grass growing on it; (a) turf. LME. ▸**b** *spec*. A piece of turf used for fuel; a peat. *Scot*. E19. ▸**c** A usu. square piece of clay. *dial*. M19.
2 In *pl*. Two pieces of turf, or a piece of cloth stuffed with straw, forming a rough kind of saddle. Freq. in ***a pair of sods***. Cf. SUNK *noun* 2. *Scot. & north*. Now *rare*. L16.
3 *The* ground on which one is standing. *dial*. L17.
4 The surface of the ground, esp. when covered with grass (chiefly *poet*.); *N. Amer*. grass-covered soil, the surface of a lawn. E18.
5 ***the sod***: a cock-fighting pit; *transf*. cock-fighting. Formerly also, horse-racing. *colloq*. (now chiefly *Hist*.). M18.
Phrases: **the old sod** one's native district or country; *spec*. Ireland. **under the sod** dead and buried.
Comb.: **sodbuster** *N. Amer. colloq*. a farmer or farmworker, who ploughs the land, esp. virgin grassland; **sod corn** *N. Amer.* (whiskey made from) maize planted in ploughed-up grassland; **sod house**: made of sods; **sod planting** the sowing of seed in unploughed ground, herbicides being used to kill or control any existing vegetation; also called ***zero tillage***; **sod webworm**, **sod-worm** *N. Amer*. the larva of any of several pyralid moths of the genus *Crambus*, which form silk tunnels at the base of grasses; **sod widow**: whose husband is dead and buried (cf. GRASS WIDOW).

sod /sɒd/ *noun*[2]. M16.
[from SOD *adjective*.]
†**1** Boiled meat. M16–E17.
2 A damper or type of unleavened cake, *esp*. one that has failed to rise. *Austral*. M19.

sod /sɒd/ *noun*[3]. *slang*. E19.
[Abbreviation of SODOMITE.]
1 An unpleasant or despicable person, esp. a man; a person of a specified kind. E19. ▸**b** A difficult, awkward, or annoying thing. M20.
2 A person who commits sodomy. M19.

📖 **1** D. Welch 'Lucky sod!' he muttered. 'You get everything you want.' D. Francis The sods had missed that, at least. J. Diski The poor sod sits around brewing beer . . to pass the time. **b** *Business* Profits . . were marginally down on 1988, after . . 'a sod of a year'.

Phrases & comb.: ***odds and sods***: see ODDS noun 2b. **Sod's law** = ***Murphy's law*** s.v. MURPHY noun[2] 3. **not give a sod** = ***not give a damn*** s.v. DAMN noun 2. **sod-all** *noun & adjective* (**a**) *noun* nothing; (**b**) *adjective* no, not any.

sod /sɒd/ *adjective.* Long *rare* or *obsolete.* ME.
[Obsolete pa. pple of SEETHE *verb.* Cf. SODDEN *adjective*[1].]
†**1** Boiled; cooked by boiling. ME–M17.
2 Sodden, soaked through. E17.

sod /sɒd/ *verb*[1] *trans.* Infl. **-dd-**. LME.
[from SOD *noun*[1].]
Cover, build up provide, or lay with sods or turfs; turf.

sod /sɒd/ *verb*[2] *intrans.* Long *obsolete* exc. *dial.* Infl. **-dd-**. M17.
[from SOD *adjective.*]
Become sodden or soaked through.

sod /sɒd/ *verb*[3]. *coarse slang.* Infl. **-dd-**. L19.
[from SOD *noun*[3].]
1 *verb trans.* Sodomize. *rare.* L19.
2 *verb trans.* Curse, damn; = BUGGER *verb* 2. E20.
3 *verb intrans.* Foll. by *off*: go away. Usu. in *imper.* M20.

📖 **2** Alan Bennett Oh, sod it, what have I sat on?

†**sod** *verb*[4] *pa. t. & pple*: see SEETHE *verb.*

soda /ˈsəʊdə/ *noun.* LME.
[medieval Latin, prob. from Persian *šūrac(h)* saltwort, salt-marsh, misread as *sūda.*]
1 Sodium carbonate, an alkaline substance orig. obtained from the ashes of certain salt-impregnated plants, and found dissolved or deposited in certain lakes, but now usu. manufactured from common salt, and used esp. in the manufacture of glass and soap. Also ***washing soda***. LME.
2 Sodium monoxide. Now *rare.* E19. ▸**b** In names of compounds, minerals, etc.: = SODIUM. *arch.* in CHEMISTRY. M19. ▸**c** More fully ***baking soda***. Sodium bicarbonate, used in cooking or taken for relief from indigestion. M19.
3 a In full ***soda water***. Water made effervescent orig. with sodium bicarbonate, now by impregnation with carbon dioxide under pressure, used alone or with spirits etc. as a drink. E19. ▸**b** A glass or drink of soda water; *gen.* (chiefly *US*) a sweet effervescent soft drink. M20.
4 [Perh. from Spanish *sota* jack (in cards).] In full ***soda card***. In faro, the exposed top card at the beginning of a deal. M19.
5 A simple task; an easy victim. *Austral. slang.* E20.
2 ***caustic soda***: see CAUSTIC *adjective.* **3a** attrib.: ***soda bottle***, ***soda-siphon***, ***soda tumbler***, etc. **4** ***from soda card to hock***, ***from soda to hock***: see HOCK *noun*[5].
Comb.: **soda-acid** *adjective* designating a fire extinguisher containing sulphuric acid and sodium bicarbonate (or carbonate), which combine just before use to provide the gas for expelling the water; **soda alum** a hydrated double sulphate of sodium and aluminium; **soda ash** sodium carbonate as commercially manufactured; **soda biscuit**, **soda bread**, **soda cake**: leavened with baking soda; ***soda card***: see sense 5 above; **soda cellulose** cellulose heavily impregnated with soda, produced by the action of caustic soda on wood pulp esp. in the manufacture of paper or rayon; **soda counter** (chiefly *US*) a counter or bar where soft drinks, ice-cream, etc., are sold; **soda cracker** *N. Amer.* a thin crisp biscuit made with baking soda; **soda fountain** (chiefly *US*) a device for supplying soda water or soft drinks; a counter, bar, shop, etc., featuring this; **soda glass** (**a**) glass containing a high proportion of soda; (**b**) = ***soda-lime glass*** below; **soda jerk**, **soda jerker** *colloq.* (chiefly *US*) a person who mixes and sells soft drinks etc. at a soda fountain; **soda lake** a natron lake; **soda lime** a mixture of sodium hydroxide and calcium hydroxide, used esp. to absorb carbon dioxide; **soda-lime feldspar** a feldspar rich in sodium and calcium; **soda-lime glass** the standard form of glass, manufactured mainly from silica, soda, and lime; **soda-mint (tablet)** an indigestion tablet made from sodium bicarbonate and spearmint; **soda nitre** MINERALOGY native sodium nitrate, a highly soluble trigonal mineral worked as a source of nitrate; also called ***Chile nitre***, ***Chile saltpetre***; **soda-pop** flavoured soda water; **soda process** a method of pulping wood by boiling it with caustic soda; **soda pulp** wood pulp made by the soda process; ***soda water***: see sense 3a above.

sodalite /ˈsəʊdəlʌɪt/ *noun.* E19.
[from SODA + -LITE.]
MINERALOGY. A transparent or translucent vitreous cubic silicate of aluminium and sodium containing sodium chloride, usually azure-blue, and occurring esp. in alkaline igneous rocks.

sodality /səʊˈdalɪti/ *noun.* E17.
[French *sodalité* or Latin *sodalitas*, from *sodalis* companion: see -ITY.]
1 Companionship, fellowship; a society, a confraternity, an association. E17.
2 *spec.* (ROMAN CATHOLIC CHURCH). A religious guild or brotherhood established for purposes of devotion, charitable works, etc.; a chapel set apart for or used by such a guild. E17.
■ ˈ**sodalist** *noun* a member of a Roman Catholic sodality L18.

sodamide /ˈsəʊdəmʌɪd/ *noun.* M19.
[from SOD(IUM + AMIDE.]
CHEMISTRY. Sodium amide, $NaNH_2$, a flammable powder formed by passing ammonia gas over hot sodium, and used chiefly in the manufacture of sodium cyanide.

sodar /ˈsəʊdɑː/ *noun.* M20.
[from SO(UND *noun*[2] + RA)DAR.]
METEOROLOGY. An instrument for investigating the state of the atmosphere, working on the principle of radar but using ultrasonic sound waves.

sodden /ˈsɒd(ə)n/ *adjective*[1] *& noun.* ME.
[Obsolete pa. pple of SEETHE *verb.* Cf. SOD *adjective.*]
▸ **A** *adjective.* **1** Boiled; cooked by boiling. Earlier in UNSODDEN 1. Long *obsolete* exc. *dial.* ME.
2 Dull, stupid, expressionless, esp. through drunkenness; pale and flaccid. L16.
3 Of food: heavy, doughy; spoiled through overboiling or poor baking. Now *rare.* L18.
4 Saturated with liquid; soaked through. E19.

📖 **1** *fig.*: Shakes. *Tr. & Cr.* My business seethes . . . Sodden business! There's a stew'd phrase indeed! **2** O. Manning He spoke dully, sodden with boredom. **4** *Field* The ground . . so sodden with wet that it was quite unfit to ride over. J. Buchan The soles of his boots, thin . . and now as sodden as a sponge.

▸ **B** *noun.* Boiled meat. Long *rare* or *obsolete.* LME.
■ **soddenly** *adverb* E20. **soddenness** /-n-n-/ *noun* L19.

sodden /ˈsɒd(ə)n/ *adjective*[2]. *rare.* M17.
[from SOD *noun*[1] + -EN[4].]
Built of sods or turfs.

sodden /ˈsɒd(ə)n/ *verb*[1] *trans. & intrans.* E19.
[from SODDEN *adjective*[1].]
Make or become sodden.

†**sodden** *verb*[2] *pa. pple*: see SEETHE *verb.*

†**sodder** *noun & verb* var. of SOLDER.

sodding /ˈsɒdɪŋ/ *noun.* L17.
[from SOD *verb*[1] + -ING[1].]
1 The action of SOD *verb*[1]. L17.
2 Sods or turfs as a material for forming or strengthening embankments etc. M19.

sodding /ˈsɒdɪŋ/ *adjective & adverb. coarse slang.* L19.
[from SOD *verb*[3] + -ING[2].]
Used as an intensive: confounded(ly), cursed(ly).

soddish /ˈsɒdɪʃ/ *adjective. colloq. rare.* M20.
[from SOD *noun*[3] + -ISH[1].]
Unpleasant, despicable.
■ **soddishness** *noun* M20.

soddite *noun* var. of SODDYITE.

soddy /ˈsɒdi/ *adjective & noun.* L15.
[from SOD *noun*[1] + -Y[1].]
▸ **A** *adjective.* Composed of turfs or sods; of the nature of a sod or turf. L15.
▸ **B** *noun. N. Amer.*
1 A sod house. L19.
2 An occupant of a sod house. M20.

soddyite /ˈsɒdɪʌɪt/ *noun.* Also **soddite** /ˈsɒdʌɪt/. E20.
[from Frederick *Soddy* (1877–1956), English chemist and physicist + -ITE[1].]
MINERALOGY. A hydrated uranyl silicate occurring as yellow orthorhombic crystals.

sodger *noun, verb* var. of SOLDIER *noun, verb.*

sodian /ˈsəʊdɪən/ *adjective.* M20.
[from SOD(IUM + -IAN.]
MINERALOGY. Having a constituent element partly replaced by sodium.

sodic /ˈsəʊdɪk/ *adjective.* M19.
[from SOD(IUM + -IC.]
1 CHEMISTRY. Of or containing sodium. Now *rare* or *obsolete.* M19.
2 GEOLOGY. Of a mineral, rock, or soil: containing a higher proportion of sodium than usual. Also, pertaining to or designating a metamorphic process in which such minerals are formed. E20.

sodide /ˈsəʊdʌɪd/ *noun.* L20.
[from SOD(IUM + -IDE.]
CHEMISTRY. An alkalide in which the anion is sodium.

sodipotassic /ˌsəʊdɪpəˈtasɪk/ *adjective.* Also **sodo-** /ˌsəʊdəʊ-/. E20.
[from SODI(C + POTASSIC.]
GEOLOGY. Containing both sodium and potassium in appreciable quantities.

sodium /ˈsəʊdɪəm/ *noun.* E19.
[from SODA + -IUM.]
A soft waxlike silvery-white highly reactive chemical element, atomic no. 11, which is a member of the alkali metal group present in seawater as common salt and in numerous minerals, and whose salts are essential to biological processes. (Symbol Na.)
Comb.: **sodium-amalgam** a compound of mercury and sodium; **sodium bicarbonate** a white soluble solid, $NaHCO_3$, used in effervescent drinks, antacids, soda-acid fire extinguishers, baking powder, etc.; baking soda, sodium hydrogen carbonate; **sodium carbonate** a white solid Na_2CO_3, with many commercial applications including the manufacture of soap and glass, and obtained esp. by the Solvay process; **sodium chloride** a colourless crystalline compound, NaCl, occurring naturally as halite and in sea water; common salt; **sodium-cooled** *adjective* that employs liquid sodium as a coolant; **sodium hydroxide** a deliquescent compound, NaOH, which is strongly alkaline and is used in many industrial processes, e.g. the manufacture of soap and paper; caustic soda; **sodium lamp** a gas discharge lamp using sodium vapour and producing intense yellow light, used esp. for street lighting; **sodium lighting** the lighting of streets etc. by means of sodium lamps; **sodium nitrate** a white solid, $NaNO_3$, used in the manufacture of fertilizers and explosives and as a food preservative; **sodium pump** PHYSIOLOGY a pump (PUMP *noun*[1] 1c) which operates on sodium ions; **sodium-vapour lamp** *N. Amer. & techn.* = ***sodium lamp*** above.

sodoku /ˈsɒdəkuː/ *noun.* E20.
[Japanese, from *so* rat + *doku* poison.]
MEDICINE. The spirillary form of rat-bite fever, caused by *Spirillum minus* and prevalent in eastern countries.

Sodom /ˈsɒdəm/ *noun.* L16.
[Latin or Greek *Sodoma* from Hebrew *sĕdōm* an ancient city beside the Dead Sea, destroyed along with Gomorrah because of the depravity of the inhabitants (*Genesis* 18–19).]
An extremely or notoriously depraved or corrupt place. Also ***Sodom and Gomorrah***.
apple of Sodom, ***Sodom apple***: see APPLE *noun.*

Sodomic /ˈsɒdəmɪk/ *adjective. rare.* ME.
[from *Sodom* (see prec.) + -IC.]
Of or pertaining to Sodom; sodomitical.

sodomise *verb* var. of SODOMIZE.

sodomist /ˈsɒdəmɪst/ *noun.* L19.
[from SODOMY + -IST.]
A sodomite.

sodomite /ˈsɒdəmʌɪt/ *noun.* ME.
[Old & mod. French from late Latin *Sodomita* from Greek *Sodomitēs*, from *Sodoma* Sodom: see -ITE[1].]
†**1** Sodomy. Only in ME.
2 A person who practises or commits sodomy. LME.
3 *Hist.* (**S-**.) A native or inhabitant of Sodom. LME.

sodomitical /sɒdəˈmɪtɪk(ə)l/ *adjective.* M16.
[Late Latin *Sodomiticus*, from Latin *Sodomita*: see prec., -AL[1].]
1 Of a person: practising or guilty of committing sodomy. M16. ▸†**b** (Of a boy or man) sodomized; (of a place, institution, etc.) corrupted or degraded by the practice of sodomy. M16–M17.
2 Of the nature of, characterized by, or involving sodomy. M16.
■ **sodomitic** *adjective* (*rare*) = SODOMITICAL M17. **sodomitically** *adverb* (long *rare*) E17.

Sodomitish /ˈsɒdəmʌɪtɪʃ/ *adjective. rare.* OE.
[Prob. from late Latin *Sodomita*: see SODOMITE, -ISH[1].]
Sodomitical; of Sodom.

sodomize /ˈsɒdəmʌɪz/ *verb trans.* Also **-ise**. M19.
[from SODOMY + -IZE.]
Practise or commit sodomy on or with (a person).

sodomy /ˈsɒdəmi/ *noun.* ME.
[medieval Latin *sodomia*, from ecclesiastical Latin *peccatum Sodomiticum* sin of Sodom: see SODOM, -Y[3].]
Any form of sexual intercourse with a person of the same or opposite sex, except copulation; *spec.* anal intercourse. Also, bestiality.

sodopotassic *adjective* var. of SODIPOTASSIC.

sody /ˈsəʊdi/ *noun. Scot. & US dial.* Also (*Scot.*) **sodie**. E19.
[Alt. of SODA.]
Soda water; sodium bicarbonate.

soe /səʊ/ *noun.* Long *obsolete* exc. *dial.* ME.
[formed as SAY *noun*[3].]
A large tub, *esp.* one carried by two persons using a pole.

soe'er *adverb* see SOEVER.

Soerensen *noun* var. of SÖRENSEN.

soetkoekie /sʊtˈkʊki/ *noun. S. Afr.* E20.
[Afrikaans, lit. 'little sweet cake', from Dutch *zoet* sweet + *koek* cake + *-ie* dim. suffix.]
A spiced biscuit.

soever /səʊˈɛvə/ *adverb. literary.* Also (*poet.*) **-e'er** /-ˈɛː/. ME.
[Orig. two words, from SO *adverb* + EVER.]
Of whatever kind; to whatever extent; at all. Used with generalizing or emphatic force after words or phrs. preceded by *what*, *which*, *whose*, etc.

📖 Shakes. *John* Whose tongue soe'er speaks false, Not truly speaks. J. H. Newman To all who are perplexed in any way soever.

sofa /ˈsəʊfə/ *noun.* E17.
[French, ult. from Arab. *suffa* long (stone) bench.]
1 Esp. in Arab countries, a raised part of a floor, covered with rich carpets and cushions, and used for sitting. E17.

2 A long upholstered seat with a back and one or two arms, on which an individual may recline or two or more people may sit. E18.

Comb.: **sofa bed**, **sofa-sleeper** a sofa that can be converted to serve as a bed.

■ **sofa'd** *adjective* (*a*) (now *rare* or *obsolete*) seated as on a sofa; (*b*) furnished with a sofa or sofas: L18.

Sofar /ˈsəʊfɑː/ *noun*. M20.

[Acronym, from *Sound fixing and ranging*.]

A system in which the sound waves from an underwater explosion are detected and located by three or more listening stations.

soffit /ˈsɒfɪt/ *noun*. E17.

[French *soffite* or Italian *soffitto*, -*itta*, ult. from Latin *suffixus*: see SUFFIX *noun*.]

The underside of any architectural structure, as an arch, balcony, cornice, vault, etc.; *spec.* (the undersurface of) a board nailed to the underside of rafters under overhanging eaves. Now also, the uppermost part of the inside of a drainpipe, sewer-pipe, etc.

†**so-forth** *noun*. *rare* (Shakes.). Only in E17.

[from *and so forth* s.v. SO *adverb* etc.]

Such and such a thing.

S. of S. *abbreviation*.

Song of Solomon (or Songs) (in the Bible).

soft /sɒft/ *noun*. ME.

[from the adjective.]

1 An agreeable, pleasant, or easy thing; comfort, ease. *rare*. ME.

2 A soft or yielding thing; the soft part *of* something; softness. ME. ▸**b** Paper money, banknotes. *slang*. E19. ▸**c** COMMERCE. In *pl.* Soft commodities (cf. *soft goods* (b) s.v. SOFT *adjective*). M20.

3 A weak foolish person; a soft-hearted person. Chiefly *dial.* M19.

> 🕮 **2** W. S. MAUGHAM Isabel . . gave the soft of my arm a vicious pinch. **c** *Times* Softs were quiet, except for coffee, which weakened.

soft /sɒft/ *adjective*.

[Old English *sōfte*, earlier *sēfte* = Old Frisian *sefte*, Old Saxon *sāfti*, Old High German *semfti* (German †*senft*, *sanft*), from West Germanic.]

▸ **I** Pleasant, agreeable.

1 a Producing agreeable or gently pleasant sensations; peaceful, calm. OE. ▸**b** Of a taste or smell: pleasant, not acidic or sharp. LME. ▸**c** Pleasing to the eye; not rugged or harsh; (of colour or light) subdued, not glaring; (of an outline etc.) blurred, not sharply defined. E18. ▸**d** (Of a photographic film or paper) producing a low contrast image; (of a lens) having low resolving power. Cf. SOFT-FOCUS. E20.

2 a Causing little or no discomfort or hardship; easily endured. ME. ▸**b** Involving little or no exertion or effort; easy, undemanding. Now *informal*. M17.

3 a Of a sound or voice: low, gentle, subdued; melodious. ME. ▸**b** PHONETICS. Of a consonant: sibilant, palatal; voiced, unaspirated. Cf. HARD *adjective* 17. M17.

4 a Of weather, a day, etc.: free from storms, mild, balmy. Cf. sense 18 below. ME. ▸**b** Of the sun, rain, wind, etc.: gentle, not strong or violent. LME. ▸**c** Of the sea etc.: smooth, calm not rough or turbulent. LME.

5 a Of progression or movement: leisurely, easy, slow. *arch.* ME. ▸**b** Having a smooth easy motion. Long *rare*. L15.

†**6** Of a fire: burning slowly or gently; moderate in heat or intensity. LME–M18.

7 Of a slope, ascent, etc.: gentle, gradual. M17.

> 🕮 **1a** BYRON Joy could he from Night's soft presence glean. **b** P. V. PRICE The Sauvignon Blanc grape is used to make . . soft, even sweet wines. **2b** J. G. FARRELL Their soft and luxurious upbringing had not fitted them for this harsh reality. *Tennis World* Playing a soft second serve. **3a** P. SCOTT The sound, so soft, . . just audible. R. RENDELL He heard her voice again and the tone seemed infinitely soft and yearning. **4a** H. JAMES The day was so soft that the . . party had . . adjourned to the open air. **b** TENNYSON The soft river-breeze . . fann'd the gardens.

▸ **II** Gentle, mild.

8 a Of a person, disposition, feeling, etc.: gentle, tender; inclined to be merciful, compassionate, or considerate; not harsh or severe. OE. ▸**b** Of words, language, etc.: ingratiating, bland; sentimental; soothing. ME. ▸**c** Of an action, manner, etc.: gentle, conciliatory. ME. ▸**d** POLITICS. Designating a comparatively moderate or centrist section of a political party. Esp. in ***soft left***, ***soft right***. Cf. HARD *adjective* 12d. L20.

9 Of an animal: docile; lacking in spirit. ME.

10 Of the hand etc.: touching lightly or gently. M17.

> 🕮 **8a** THACKERAY He . . was very soft and gentle with the children. J. STEINBECK His eyes were soft and warm on her. *Times* He goes soft when he ought to stand firm. C. SIMMONS People say he's soft on murderers. **c** *Daily Progress* He expects a softer policy toward Cuba when . . Kennedy becomes president.

▸ **III 11** Yielding readily to tender emotions; easily moved or affected. ME.

12 a Easily influenced or swayed; facile, compliant. ME. ▸**b** Effeminate, unmanly. L16. ▸**c** Refined, delicate. *rare*. E17.

13 a Having a delicate constitution; not strong or robust. LME. ▸**b** Of the pulse: beating weakly because of low blood-pressure. E18.

14 Foolish, feeble; lacking common-sense; halfwitted. *colloq.* E17. ▸**b** Stupefied with drink. Chiefly *dial.* M19.

> 🕮 **11** CARLYLE The soft young heart adopts orphans. **12a** LD MACAULAY His soft mind had . . taken an impress from the society which surrounded him. **c** SHAKES. *Haml.* An absolute gentleman . . of very soft society. **14** U. HOLDEN Too much water made you soft in the head.

▸ **IV 15** Yielding to pressure; lacking hardness or firmness; (of a substance, material, etc.) easily folded, cut, moulded, or compressed; (of cloth, hair, etc.) having a smooth surface or texture, pleasant to the touch, not rough or coarse. ME. ▸**b** Of a substance: readily magnetized by an external magnetic field but retaining no permanent magnetization in the absence of such a field. M19. ▸**c** Of glass: softening at a relatively low temperature when heated. E20. ▸**d** MILITARY. (Of a potential target) vulnerable to attack, unprotected; (of a missile base) vulnerable to a nuclear explosion. M20.

16 Of stone: relatively deficient in hardness; readily crumbled, broken, or cut. L16.

17 Of water: low in or free from calcium and magnesium salts, and therefore good for lathering. Cf. HARD *adjective* 16b. M18. ▸**b** Of a detergent: biodegradable. M20.

18 Of the weather, a day, etc.: rainy, wet; thawing. Cf. sense 4a above. Chiefly *Scot.* & *dial.* E19.

19 a Of money: in banknotes as opp. to coin. Cf. HARD *adjective* 9. Chiefly *US*. M19. ▸**b** Of money: given as a research grant by a charitable foundation; (*US*) given as a contribution to a political party rather than a particular candidate, thus avoiding various legal limitations. M19. ▸**c** COMMERCE. Of a market, commodity, currency, etc.: depressed, likely to fall in value. M20.

20 a ELECTRONICS. Of a thermionic valve or discharge tube: not containing a hard vacuum, either due to the introduction of an inert gas during manufacture to modify its performance, or as a result of a leak or of outgassing by component parts. L19. ▸**b** PHYSICS. Of radiation, esp. X-rays and gamma rays: of low penetrating power, of relatively long wavelength. Of subatomic particles: of relatively low energy. E20.

21 Of (a) fact, information, etc.: insubstantial, imprecise (cf. HARD *adjective* 8b, c.). Also, of a science or its method: not amenable to precise mathematical treatment or to experimental verification or refutation. E20.

22 Of a drug: having a mild effect; not likely to cause addiction. M20.

23 Of pornography: = ***soft-core*** below. L20.

> 🕮 **15** DRYDEN More sleek thy Skin . . And softer to the touch, than down of Swans. SHELLEY Soft mossy lawns . . extend their swells. J. STEINBECK She began to eat soft food that required little chewing. *Woman* Sofas . . covered in soft Italian leather. P. ACKROYD The ground was still soft after a recent rainstorm. **d** T. MANGOLD Satellites are . . vulnerable to attack; in the jargon, they're soft. N. GORDIMER If the government goes on . . killing in the townships, in time . . we'll have to turn to soft targets as well. **19** J. YEOWELL A head . . rudely carved in a soft stone. **b** *Times* The US market for imported luxury cars remains very soft.

Special collocations, comb., & phrases: **be soft on**, **go soft on** *colloq.* be or become infatuated with. **soft answer** a good-natured answer to abuse or an accusation. ***soft as a brush***: see BRUSH *noun*² 3. **softback** *noun* & *adjective* (*a*) *US* = PAPERBACK *noun*, *adjective*; (*b*) a soft-shell turtle. **softball** (*a*) a game resembling baseball but played on a smaller field with a larger softer ball that is pitched underarm; a ball used in this game; (*b*) a stage in the boiling of sugar at which a drop of the syrup will form a soft ball when dropped into cold water. **soft-board** a relatively soft kind of fibreboard. **soft-boiled** *adjective* (*a*) (of an egg) lightly boiled with the yolk semi-liquid; not hard-boiled; (*b*) (of a person) mild, easygoing; naive, impractical. **soft box** PHOTOGRAPHY a frame with a cloth covering used to diffuse the light from a flash or floodlight. **soft brome** any of several bromes (grasses) with soft heavy panicles, esp. *Bromus hordeaceus*. **soft cancer**: in which the affected tissue is soft and yielding. ***soft*** CHANCRE. ***soft clam***: see CLAM *noun*² 1(c). **soft coal** (*a*) coal that is easily cut; (*b*) inferior coal. **soft copy** a legible version of a piece of information not printed on a physical medium, esp. as stored or displayed on a computer. **soft coral** a coral of the order Alcyonacea, members of which form soft leathery or fleshy colonies with calcareous spicules embedded in the connecting tissue. **soft-core** *adjective* (of pornography) less explicit or obscene than hard-core pornography. **soft corn** (*a*) a variety of maize, *Zea mays* var. *amylacea*, whose seeds are rich in soft starch; (*b*) maize containing a high quantity of moisture, making it unlikely to keep well; (*c*) *fig.* plausible speech or language, flattery. **soft-cover** *noun* & *adjective* = PAPERBACK *noun*, *adjective*. **soft crab** a crab that has shed its shell and is waiting for the new one to harden. **soft drink** a non-alcoholic drink. **soft food** (*a*) (a) food of a semi-liquid consistency, esp. as prepared for babies and invalids; (*b*) partly digested food regurgitated by pigeons to feed their young. **soft-foot** *verb intrans.* (*N. Amer.*) go with quiet footsteps, tiptoe. **soft-footed** *adjective* having feet which tread softly. **soft fruit** small stoneless fruit, as strawberries, blackberries, etc. **soft furnishing(s)** furnishings such as curtains, rugs, etc., as opp. to furniture. **soft goods** (*a*) textiles; articles made from textiles; (*b*) COMMERCE relatively perishable consumer goods, as clothes, foods, and drugs. **soft-grass** either of two softly downy grasses of the genus *Holcus*, (*a*) (more fully ***meadow soft-grass***) Yorkshire fog, *H. lanatus*, and (*b*) (more fully ***creeping soft-grass***) *H. mollis*, a rhizomatous species of acid soils. **soft ground** ART (*a*) a covering of wax and tallow on an etching plate; (*b*) (in full ***soft ground etching***) a print-making process using plates covered with soft ground working by applying pressure through a sheet of paper or from found objects; a print produced in this way. ***soft*** GROWAN. **soft hail**: consisting of snow pellets. **soft-head** a stupid or foolish person. **soft-headed** *adjective* feeble-minded, foolish, stupid. **soft-headedness** feeble-mindedness. **soft hyphen** a hyphen introduced into a word, formula, etc., not otherwise hyphenated, for reasons of page or column layout or onscreen formatting, as at the end of a line of text. **soft in the head** foolish, halfwitted (cf. sense 14 above). **soft iron** iron that has a low carbon content and is easily magnetized and demagnetized, used to make the cores of solenoids, transformers, etc. **soft-land** *verb trans.* & *intrans.* (cause to) make a soft landing. **soft-lander** a craft or vehicle that can make or has made a soft landing. **soft landing** (*a*) a landing of a spacecraft etc. that is slow enough for no serious damage to be incurred; (*b*) *fig.* a change that is gentle or trouble-free; *spec.* (ECONOMICS) the slowing down of economic growth at an acceptable degree relative to inflation and unemployment. **soft line** a flexible or conciliatory policy. **soft-line** *adjective* (of a policy etc.) flexible, conciliatory. **soft loan** a loan, esp. to a developing country, made on terms very favourable to the borrower. **soft maple** any of several maples with less durable wood, *esp.* red maple, *Acer rubrum*, and silver maple, *A. saccharinum*; the timber of such a tree. **soft-nosed** *adjective* (of a bullet) expanding. ***soft option***: see OPTION *noun* 1. ***soft palate***: see PALATE *noun* 1. **soft paste** the mixture of clay, ground glass, fired at a moderate temperature, from which a type of porcelain is made. **soft pedal** a foot lever on a piano which softens the tone. **soft-pedal** *verb trans.* & *intrans.* (usu. with *on*) (*a*) play with the soft pedal down; (*b*) *fig.* reduce the force or effect of (something); refrain from emphasizing (something); be restrained (about). ***soft roe***: see ROE *noun*². **soft rot** (*a*) any of various bacterial or fungal diseases of vegetables, fruit, and herbaceous plants in which the tissue becomes soft and pulpy; (*b*) a fungal condition of timber which makes it soft and friable. **soft rush** a common rush, *Juncus effusus*, with a leafless flexible pith-filled stem. ***soft sawder***: see SAWDER *noun*. **soft sculpture**: using pliable materials, as cloth, foam rubber, etc. **soft sell** (an instance of) subtly persuasive rather than aggressive selling or advertising. **soft-sell** *verb trans.* sell (goods) by this method. **soft-shoe** *noun*, *adjective*, & *verb* (*a*) *noun* & *adjective* (designating or pertaining to) a kind of tap-dance performed in soft-soled shoes; (*b*) *verb intrans.* perform this dance, move in soft-soled shoes. **soft-shoulder** (chiefly *N. Amer.*) an unmetalled strip of land at the side of a road. **soft-skinned** *adjective* (*a*) having a soft skin; (*b*) MILITARY (of a vehicle) unprotected, unarmoured. **soft soap** (*a*) a semi-liquid soap made with potash; (*b*) *colloq.* persuasive flattery; blarney. **soft-soap** *verb trans.* *colloq.* flatter, persuade with flattery. **soft-soaper** a person who persuades by flattery. ***soft solder***: see SOLDER *noun* 1. **soft sore** a chancroid. **soft-spoken** *adjective* (of a person) speaking with a soft or gentle voice; (of words) spoken softly or affably; persuasive. **soft spot** a weak or vulnerable place; ***have a soft spot for***, have a tender regard for, be fond of. **soft sugar** granulated or powdered sugar. **soft tack** bread or other good food (opp. hard tack). **soft tick** a tick of the family Argasidae, lacking a dorsal shield. **soft tissue(s)** body tissue other than bone or cartilage. ***soft Tommy***: see TOMMY *noun*¹. **soft-top** a motor-vehicle roof that is made of soft material and can be folded back; a vehicle having such a roof. ***soft touch***: see TOUCH *noun*. **soft toy** a figure made of fabric stuffed with a soft filling. **soft wart** a small soft rounded growth on the skin, *esp.* a nodule typical of molluscum. **soft wheat** any of several varieties of wheat having a soft grain rich in starch. **soft wicket** a wicket with moist or sodden turf. **softwood** wood which is relatively soft or easily cut; *esp.* (*a*) the timber of coniferous trees; (*b*) sapwood; *ellipt.* a tree with such wood. **soft-wooded** *adjective* having relatively soft wood. ***the softer sex***, ***the soft sex***: see SEX *noun*.

■ **softish** *adjective* somewhat soft L16.

soft /sɒft/ *verb trans.* & *intrans.* Now *rare* or *obsolete*. ME.

[from the adjective.]

Make or become soft; soften.

soft /sɒft/ *adverb* & *interjection*. OE.

[from the adjective.]

▸ **A** *adverb*. Softly. OE.

> 🕮 W. COWPER Now murm'ring soft, now roaring. KEATS By the bed-side . . soft he set A table.

▸ **B** *interjection*. Used to urge silence or caution, or to discourage haste. *arch.* M16.

> 🕮 BYRON A rabble who know not — But soft, here they come!

softa /ˈsɒftə/ *noun*. E17.

[Turkish, from Persian *sūkta* burnt, parched, scorched.]

Hist. In Turkey, a Muslim student or practitioner of sacred law and theology.

soft centre /sɒf(t) ˈsɛntə/ *noun phr.* Also ***soft center**. M20.

[from SOFT *adjective* + CENTRE *noun*.]

1 a A soft filling inside a chocolate. M20. ▸**b** A chocolate with a soft filling. L20.

2 *fig.* A tender or compassionate heart, esp. when concealed; a vulnerable or weak core. M20.

■ **soft-centred** *adjective* (*a*) soft-hearted; (of a literary or artistic work) having a weak or sentimental core; (*b*) (of a chocolate) having a soft centre: M20. **soft-centredness** *noun* M20.

soften /ˈsɒf(ə)n/ *verb*. LME.
[from SOFT *adjective* + -EN⁵.]
▶ **I** *verb trans*. **1** Mitigate; make more bearable. Also foll. by *off*. LME.
2 a Make more impressionable or tender; affect emotionally. LME. ▸**b** Make weak or effeminate. L16. ▸**c** Make more gentle or refined. Also foll. by *into*. E18.
3 Mollify, appease; make less harsh or severe. LME.
4 a Make physically soft or softer; lessen the hardness of. LME. ▸**b** *spec*. Make (water) soft. L18.
5 Modify, tone down; make less pronounced or prominent. Also foll. by *down*, *into*, *to*, etc. L17.
6 Make (a sound) quieter or less harsh. M18.
7 MILITARY. Reduce the strength of (defences) by bombing or other preliminary attack; *fig*. undermine the resistance of (a person). Also foll. by *up*. *colloq*. M20.

📖 **1** S. LOVER The lapse of a few days had softened the bitter grief. **2a** J. B. MOZLEY Misfortune, adversity, soften the human heart. **3** LD MACAULAY That good prelate used all his influence to soften the gaolers. G. GREENE No charm softens the brutality of Mr Tod. **5** M. GIROUARD Rectangularity was softened by ornament. T. MORRISON She pulled a few strands over her ears . . to soften the look. **6** B. PYM A band was playing, its brassiness softened by distance. **7** M. M. R. KHAN The old fox was softening me up.

▶ **II** *verb intrans*. **8** Become more bearable, tender, or gentle; become less harsh or pronounced. Also foll. by *away*, *down*, *into*, *off*. E17. ▸**b** COMMERCE. Of a commodity, currency, etc.: lose firmness, fall in value. M20.
9 Become physically soft or softer; become less hard. E17.

📖 **8** E. WAUGH Seeing their discomfort, Mrs Ape softened and smiled. S. TROTT The day softening into dusk. J. M. COETZEE The lines of his face softened, his raving ended. **b** *Daily Telegraph* The whole personal computer market has softened since Christmas. *Times* The authorities appear to be willing to allow the pound to soften.

■ **softener** *noun* E17.

softening /ˈsɒf(ə)nɪŋ/ *verbal noun*. LME.
[from prec. + -ING¹.]
The action of SOFTEN *verb*; an instance of this. Also foll. by *up*.
softening of the brain degeneration of the brain tissue with loss of firmness; *colloq*. senile dementia, esp. with paralysis.

soft-focus /sɒf(t)ˈfəʊkəs/ *adjective & noun*. E20.
[from SOFT *adjective* + FOCUS *noun*.]
▶ **A** *adjective*. **1** PHOTOGRAPHY. Characterized by or producing a deliberate slight blurring or lack of definition in a photograph. E20.
2 *fig*. Deliberately diffuse, unclear, or imprecise. M20.
▶ **B** *noun*. A deliberate slight blurring or lack of definition in a photograph; *fig*. deliberate diffuseness or imprecision. M20.
■ **soft-focused** *adjective* L20.

soft-hearted /sɒftˈhɑːtɪd/ *adjective*. L16.
[from SOFT *adjective* + HEARTED.]
Tender, compassionate, easily moved.
■ **soft-heartedness** *noun* L16.

softie /ˈsɒfti/ *noun*. *colloq*. Also **softy**. M19.
[from SOFT *adjective* + -IE.]
A weak-minded, silly, or cowardly person; a very soft-hearted person.

📖 D. HALLIDAY He was an awful old softie inside. *Beano* Those softies playing soppy games.

softling /ˈsɒftlɪŋ/ *noun*. Now *rare*. M16.
[from SOFT *adjective* + -LING¹.]
1 An effeminate or cowardly person; a weakling. M16.
2 A small soft thing. E19.

softly /ˈsɒftli/ *adjective*. Now *dial*. & *US*. L16.
[from SOFT *adjective* + -LY¹.]
1 Of sound etc.: quiet, soft. L16.
†**2** Of pace: easy, slow, gentle. L16–M17.
†**3** Of manner, disposition, etc.: gentle, weak, simple. E17–M18.
4 Of a person: slow in action; lacking in energy. Also, simple, foolish. M17.

softly /ˈsɒftli/ *adverb & interjection*. ME.
[from SOFT *adjective* + -LY².]
▶ **A** *adverb*. **1** Gently, tenderly. ME.
2 With a soft or subdued voice or utterance; in a low or gentle tone. ME.
3 Quietly, noiselessly; lightly. Also, unobtrusively, stealthily. ME.
4 Slowly, with an easy pace or motion. LME.
5 Comfortably, luxuriously. LME.
6 Gradually; gently. LME.
7 In a subdued manner. E19.

📖 **1** M. CALLAGHAN He . . stroked her hair softly. **2** I. MURDOCH I spoke softly, but the words seemed like thunder. **3** J. BARTH I . . opened the door softly, and tiptoed inside. **softly softly (catchee monkey)** cautiously; discreetly and with cunning.

▶ **B** *interjection*. = SOFT *interjection*. *arch*. LME.

softness /ˈsɒf(t)nɪs/ *noun*. OE.
[from SOFT *adjective* + -NESS.]
The quality or state of being soft.
softness of the pulse a condition of low blood-pressure, so that the radial artery at the wrist feels soft and easily compressible.

softnomics /sɒf(t)ˈnɒmɪks/ *noun*. *colloq*. L20.
[from SOFT(WARE *noun* + ECO)NOMICS.]
ECONOMICS. The branch of knowledge that deals with the shift of the economic basis of developed countries from manufacturing industry to service industry, esp. information technology.

soft-shell /ˈsɒf(t)ʃɛl, sɒf(t)ˈʃɛl/ *adjective & noun*. E19.
[from SOFT *adjective* + SHELL *noun*.]
▶ **A** *adjective*. **1** Having a soft shell. E19.
2 POLITICS. Adopting or advocating a moderate course or policy. *US*. M19.
soft-shell clam a soft clam. **soft-shell crab** a soft crab. **soft-shell turtle** a turtle of the mainly freshwater family Trionychidae, having a leathery covering to the body.
▶ **B** *noun*. **1** POLITICS. A person with moderate views. *US*. E19.
2 A soft-shell crab or turtle. *US*. M19.
■ **soft-shelled** *adjective* having a soft shell E17.

software /ˈsɒf(t)wɛː; *in sense 1 also* sɒf(t)ˈwɛː/ *noun*. In sense 1 **soft-ware**. M19.
[from SOFT *adjective* + WARE *noun*².]
1 In *pl*. = ***soft goods*** s.v. SOFT *adjective*. M19.
2 COMPUTING. The programs and other operating information used by a computer (opp. ***hardware***); *esp*. the body of system programs specific to a particular computer. M20.

📖 **2** *Which Micro?* Extra memory means a greater range of software can be run.

Comb.: **software engineering** COMPUTING the professional development, production, and management of system software; **software house** a company that specializes in producing and testing software.

softy *noun* var. of SOFTIE.

sog /sɒɡ/ *noun*¹. *obsolete* exc. *dial*. M16.
[Rel. to SOG *verb*.]
A soft or marshy piece of ground; a swamp, a quagmire.

sog /sɒɡ/ *noun*². *dial*. & *US*. L18.
[Origin unkn.]
A drowsy or lethargic state; a sleep, a doze.

†**sog** *noun*³. Only in M19.
[Origin unkn.]
A large whale.

sog /sɒɡ/ *verb*. *obsolete* exc. *dial*. Infl. **-gg-**. LME.
[Perh. from Old Norse.]
1 *verb trans*. & *intrans*. Make or become soaked or saturated. LME.
2 *verb intrans*. Sink or soak *in*. M19.

soga /ˈsəʊɡə/ *noun*. *rare*. M19.
[Spanish, of unkn. origin.]
A rope, a halter.

SOGAT /ˈsəʊɡat/ *abbreviation*.
Hist. Society of Graphical and Allied Trades.

Sogdian /ˈsɒɡdɪən/ *noun & adjective*. M16.
[Latin *Sogdianus* from Greek *Sogdianos*, from Old Persian *Suguda*.]
Hist. ▶**A** *noun*. **1** A native of Sogdiana, an ancient Persian province centred on Samarkand (now in Uzbekistan). M16.
2 The Iranian language of Sogdiana. E20
▶ **B** *adjective*. Of or pertaining to Sogdiana. E18.

sogged /sɒɡd/ *adjective*. M19.
[from SOG *verb* + -ED¹.]
Soaked, saturated.

soggy /ˈsɒɡi/ *adjective*. Orig. *dial*. & *US*. E18.
[from SOG *noun*¹ + -Y¹.]
1 Of land: boggy, swampy, marshy. E18.
2 Saturated with wet, soaked, sodden; *spec*. (of bread, cake, etc.) overly heavy and moist. E19. ▸**b** Resulting from or caused by moistness or wetness. L19. ▸**c** Of weather etc.: moist, close, dank. L19.
3 *fig*. Dull, lifeless; lacking in firmness or vigour, feeble, sluggish. L19.

📖 **1** B. MASON The lawn was soggy in wet weather. **2b** *Harper's Magazine* Every footstep giving out a soggy wheeze from . . wet boots. **3** *Guardian* A Tory . . whose . . complaint about the wets is that they are too soggy to stand firm. *Literary Review* Books like this . . are soggy, formless soap operas.

■ **soggily** *adverb* M20. **sogginess** *noun* L19.

sogo shosha /səʊɡəʊ ˈʃəʊʃə/ *noun phr*. Pl. same, **-s**. M20.
[Japanese *sōgō shōsha*, from *sōgō* comprehensive + *shōsha*: see SHOSHA.]
A very large Japanese company that trades internationally in a wide range of goods and services.

soh *noun* see SOL *noun*¹.

soh /səʊ/ *interjection*. M18.
[Var. of SO *adverb*, or natural exclam.]
1 Expr. anger, scorn, reproof, surprise, etc. M18.
2 Calming a restive horse: quiet!, easy! M18.

SOHO /ˈsəʊhəʊ/ *abbreviation*. Also **SoHo**.
Small office, home office: denoting (a market for) computers and other information technology products used by home-based individuals and small companies.

Soho /ˈsəʊhəʊ/ *adjective*. L19.
[See below.]
1 Situated in, connected with, or characteristic of Soho, a district in the West End of London noted for its restaurants, nightclubs, striptease shows, pornography shops, etc. L19.
2 *Hist*. Designating a type of tapestry produced in England after 1685, usu. in Soho. M20.

📖 **1** *Times Lit. Suppl.* Harris . . wrote about sex in the . . style of the cheapest Soho trash.

soho /səʊˈhəʊ/ *interjection, noun, & verb*. Also **so-ho**, (as *interjection*) **so ho**. ME.
[Anglo-Norman, prob. natural exclam. Cf. SA-HA, SEE-HO.]
▶ **A** *interjection*. **1** Orig., directing the attention of dogs or other hunters to a hare which has been discovered or started, or encouraging them in the chase. Later *gen*., attracting attention, announcing a discovery, etc. ME.
2 = SOH *interjection*. E19.
▶ **B** *noun*. A cry of 'soho'. L16.
▶ **C** *verb*. **1** *verb intrans*. Cry 'soho!' L16.
2 *verb trans*. Announce the discovery or starting of (a hare) with this cry. M19.

soi-disant /swadizɑ̃/ *adjective*. M18.
[French, from *soi* oneself + *disant* pres. pple of *dire* say.]
1 Of a person: self-styled, would-be. M18.
2 Of a thing: so-called, pretended. M19.

soigné /swaɲe, ˈswɑːnjeɪ/ *adjective*. Fem. **-ée**. E19.
[French, pa. ppl adjective of *soigner* care for, from *soin* care.]
Meticulously dressed, prepared, or arranged; well-groomed.

soigneur /swaɲœːr/ *noun*. Pl. pronounced same. L20.
[French, from *soigner* (see prec.) + *-eur* -OR.]
In cycling, a person who gives training, massage, and other assistance to a team.

soil /sɔɪl/ *noun*¹. Also (earlier) †**soyle**. LME.
[Anglo-Norman = land, perh. repr. Latin *solium* seat, by assoc. with *solum* ground.]
1 The face or surface of the earth; the ground, esp. considered as the source of vegetation or with ref. to its composition, quality, etc. LME.
†**2** A piece or stretch of ground; a site. LME–L18.
3 A land, a country, a region; *spec*. (*a*) one's native land; †(*b*) one's domicile. Now also, national territory. LME.
4 The material comprising the thin top layer of much of the earth's land surface, composed of fragmented rock particles with humus, water, and air; *esp*. such material as will support the growth of plants, as contrasted with subsoil. Also, a particular kind of this. LME. ▸**b** Fragmentary or unconsolidated material occurring naturally at or near the surface of the earth, or of another planet or moon. Also, a particular kind of this. Cf. REGOLITH. M20.

📖 **1** E. LANGLEY The marble head . . lying deep in the soil. P. S. BUCK The . . beans lifted their . . heads from the soil. *fig*.: R. DAVIES Boredom is rich soil for . . rancour. **2** T. WRIGHT If I could purchase a soil anywhere nigh . . to build the house. **3** MILTON Is this . . the Soil . . That we must change for Heav'n? C. THIRLWALL Outcasts whom the . . Athenians had . . deprived of their native soils. JULIA HAMILTON The Germans had to be removed from foreign soil. **4** J. GRIGSON Run them under the cold tap and scrub away any soil with a small . . brush. *Practical Gardening* Easy-to-use . . even in heavy clay soils.

Phrases: **child of the soil** (*a*) a native of a place or country; (*b*) a person closely connected with or engaged in agriculture. ***free soil***: see FREE *adjective*. **lord of the soil** the owner of an estate or domain. ***mineral soil***: see MINERAL *adjective*. ***organic soil***: see ORGANIC *adjective*. ***racy of the soil***: see RACY *adjective*¹ 1b. **son of the soil** = *child of the soil* above.

Comb.: **soil air**: present in the soil; **soil amendment** a substance added to the soil to improve its properties, esp. physical ones; the use of such substances; **soil association** a group of soils that are related geographically or topographically, or esp. derived from a common parent material; **soil auger**: for boring into or taking samples of soil; **soil bank** *US* land taken out of use for agricultural production; **soil catena** = ***soil association*** above; **soil cement** material composed of soil or a soil substitute strengthened and stabilized by the admixture of cement (freq. *attrib*. with hyphen); **soil class** a group of soils similar to one another, esp. in texture; **soil climate** the prevailing physical conditions in the soil, esp. as they affect soil organisms and plant life; **soil colloid** a substance present in the soil as a colloid; **soil conditioner** a substance added to the soil to improve its physical characteristics; **soil conservation** protection of soil against erosion, loss of fertility, and damage; **soil-creep** the slow creeping movement of surface soil down a slope; **soil deficiency**: of some substance necessary in the soil for the proper growth of plants; **soil exhaustion** the loss of fertility from the soil; **soil extract** a mixture of dissolved substances extracted from a soil; **soil group** a group of types of soil; *spec.* in SOIL SCIENCE (also ***great soil group***), each of the small number of groups into which soils are divided on the basis of their profiles and the climate in which they form; **soil mantle** the soil as a covering of the underlying rock; **soil map**: showing the distribution of various kinds of soil in a region; **soil mark** ARCHAEOLOGY a trace of a buried feature indicated by differences in the colour or texture of the soil, usu. on ploughed land; **soil mechanics** ENGINEERING the science that deals with the mechanical properties and behaviour of soil; **soil phase** any of a number of soils that belong to the same soil series but differ in some feature such as stoniness, slope, etc.; **soil polygon** = POLYGON 2b; **soil profile** = PROFILE *noun* 8a; **soil resistivity** the electrical resistivity of the soil (usu. *attrib.*); **soil sample**: of soil taken for scientific investigation; **soil sampler** a device for taking soil samples; **soil science** = PEDOLOGY; **soil scientist** = PEDOLOGIST; ***soil separate***: see SEPARATE *noun* 4; ***soil series***: see SERIES *noun* 17; **soil sickness** a condition of soil in which it has become unable to support the healthy growth of a crop; **soil solution** the water present around and between soil particles as a dilute solution of mineral salts; **soil stabilization** the treatment of soil to increase its resistance to movement, esp. under load, and erosion; **soil stripe** PHYSICAL GEOGRAPHY each of the low ridges of stony soil which occur in periglacial environments and form parallel evenly spaced lines; **soil survey** a systematic examination and mapping of the different kinds of soil present in a region or on a site; **soil type** a particular kind of soil; *spec.* in SOIL SCIENCE, a subdivision of a soil series made according to the texture of the surface horizon; **soil wash** the erosion of soil by groundwater; **soil water** the water present in soil.

■ **soilless** /-l-l-/ *adjective* (*a*) devoid of soil; (*b*) hydroponic: E19.

soil /sɔɪl/ *noun*[2]. LME.

[Old & mod. French *souille* muddy place (mod. dial. *souil* pond, ordure), from *souiller*: see SOIL *verb*[1].]

†**1** A miry or muddy place used by a wild boar for wallowing in. LME–E17.

2 HUNTING. A pool or stretch of water used as a refuge by a hunted animal, esp. a deer. Freq. in ***take soil***, reach such a refuge. LME.

3 Staining, soiling; a stain, a discolouring mark. E16. ▸**b** Dirt or discolouring matter on cloth. M20.

4 *fig.* Moral stain or blemish. L16.

5 a Dirty or refuse matter; sewage; *spec.* liquid matter likely to contain excrement (cf. WASTE *noun* 11). E17. ▸**b** Excrement, night-soil; animal dung used as compost; manure. E17.

> 📖 **3** JANE TAYLOR This dress is less liable to take a soil. **4** R. KANE Let no soil of sin . . sully the . . innocence of your soul.

Comb.: **soil pipe** a sewage or waste-water pipe; *spec.* a drainage pipe carrying away human excrement from a water-closet; **soil release** *noun & adjectival phr.* (a substance) causing the loosening of dirt from cloth during washing; **soil stack** a downpipe which takes all the waste water from the upstairs plumbing system of a building.

†**soil** *noun*[3]. *rare* (Shakes.). Only in L16.

[from SOIL *verb*[2].]

The solution, the answer.

soil /sɔɪl/ *noun*[4]. Now *local*. E17.

[Rel. to SOIL *verb*[4].]

†**1** The feeding of horses on cut green fodder as a laxative. Only in E17.

2 Freshly cut grass or other green fodder. M19.

soil /sɔɪl/ *verb*[1]. Also †**soyle**. ME.

[Old French *soill(i)er*, *suill(i)er* (mod. *souiller*) from Proto-Romance verb based on Latin *suculus*, *-ula* dim. of *sus* pig: see SOW *noun*[1].]

1 *verb trans.* Defile or pollute with sin, corrupt. ME.

2 *verb trans.* Make dirty, esp. on the surface; smear or stain with dirt; tarnish. Now also *spec.*, (esp. of a child or patient) make dirty by (usu. involuntary) defecation. ME. ▸**b** *fig.* Sully; bring disgrace or discredit on (a person or thing). L16.

3 *verb intrans.* Become dirty or stained, tarnish. Now also *spec.*, (esp. of a child or patient) make oneself, bedclothes, etc., dirty by defecation. ME.

4 a *verb intrans.* & †*refl.* Of a wild boar or deer: roll or wallow in mud or water. Cf. SOIL *noun*[2] 1. Long *rare* or *obsolete*. LME. ▸**b** *verb intrans.* Of a hunted deer: take to water or marshy ground. Cf. SOIL *noun*[2] 2. LME.

> 📖 **1** H. E. MANNING The lusts of the flesh soiled his spiritual being. **2** H. JOLLY A child . . may soil his pants by accident. *fig.*: O. MANNING Money . . soiled any relationship it touched. **b** CARLYLE Black falsehood has . . soiled her name. **3** *New Society* When she started school she still wet and soiled by day and night. A. LURIE The sack suit . . soiled easily.

■ **soiling** *ppl adjective* that stains or soils; polluting, defiling: E19.

†**soil** *verb*[2] *trans.* ME.

[Old French *soil-* pres. stem of *soudre*, *soldre* from Latin *solvere* release, loosen. Cf. ASSOIL.]

1 Absolve (a person) from sin; (foll. by *of*) release from a duty, an obligation, etc. ME–M16.

2 Resolve or explain (a doubt, problem, etc.); refute (an argument or objection). LME–E17.

†**soil** *verb*[3] *trans.* L16–L17.

[from SOIL *noun*[2].]

Cover or treat (land) with manure.

■ †**soiling** *noun* (*a*) the action of the verb; (*b*) manure, animal droppings: E17–L18.

soil /sɔɪl/ *verb*[4] *trans.* Now *rare*. E17.

[Perh. from SOIL *noun*[2].]

Feed (horses, cattle, etc.) on freshly cut green fodder, orig. for laxative purposes.

soil /sɔɪl/ *verb*[5] *trans.* L18.

[from SOIL *noun*[1].]

Cover with soil, earth *up*.

soilage /ˈsɔɪlɪdʒ/ *noun*. L16.

[from SOIL *noun*[2] or *verb*[1] + -AGE.]

†**1** Rubbish, dirt, filth; manure. L16–M18.

2 The process of becoming or condition of being soiled. *US. rare*. E20.

soiled /sɔɪld/ *adjective*[1]. ME.

[from SOIL *verb*[1] + -ED[1].]

Defiled; stained, dirtied.

soiled dove *N. Amer. & Austral. slang* a prostitute.

soiled /sɔɪld/ *adjective*[2]. M17.

[from SOIL *noun*[1] + -ED[2].]

Having a specified kind of soil.

soilure /ˈsɔɪljʊə/ *noun*. Now *arch.* or *literary*. ME.

[Old French *soilleure* (mod. *souillure*), from *soillier*: see SOIL *verb*[1], -URE.]

1 Soiling, staining, (*lit. & fig.*). ME.

2 A stain, a blot, a blemish, (*lit. & fig.*). E19.

soily /ˈsɔɪli/ *adjective*[1]. LME.

[from SOIL *noun*[2] or *verb*[1] + -Y[1].]

Soiled, dirty; impure.

soily /ˈsɔɪli/ *adjective*[2]. M18.

[from SOIL *noun*[1] + -Y[1].]

Pertaining to or of the nature of soil.

soirée /ˈswɑːreɪ, *foreign* sware (*pl. same*)/ *noun*. See also SWARRY. L18.

[French, from *soir* evening.]

An evening party, gathering, or social meeting, esp. in a private house.

soirée dansante /sware dɑ̃sɑ̃ːt/ *noun phr.* Pl. **-s -s** (pronounced same). M19.

[French, formed as prec. + *dansante* fem. of pres. pple of *danser* dance.]

An evening party with dancing.

soit /swa/ *interjection*. L19.

[French, 3rd person sing. pres. subjunct. of *être* be.]

So be it.

soixante-neuf /swasɑ̃t nœf/ *noun*. L19.

[French = sixty-nine, after the position of the couple involved.]

Sexual activity between two people involving mutual oral stimulation of the genitals; a position enabling this. Cf. ***sixty-nine*** s.v. SIXTY.

sojourn /ˈsɒdʒ(ə)n, -dʒəːn, ˈsʌd-/ *noun*. ME.

[Anglo-Norman *su(r)jurn* or Old French *sojor(n)* (mod. *séjour*), from Old French *sojourner*: see next.]

1 A temporary stay at a place. ME. ▸†**b** A delay; a digression. ME–E16.

2 A place of temporary stay. ME.

> 📖 **1** C. THIRLWALL Here . . he made a sojourn of sixty days.

sojourn /ˈsɒdʒ(ə)n, -dʒəːn, ˈsʌd-/ *verb*. ME.

[Old French *so(r)journer* (mod. *séjourner*), ult. from Latin *sub-* SUB- + late Latin *diurnum* day. Cf. JOURNAL *noun & adjective*.]

1 *verb intrans.* Stay temporarily; reside for a time. ME.

†**2** *verb intrans.* Tarry, delay. LME–L16.

†**3** *verb trans.* Lodge (a person); rest or quarter (horses). LME–L17.

■ **sojourner** *noun* (*a*) a visitor, a guest; a lodger; †(*b*) *spec.* a boarder living in a house, school, or college to receive instruction: LME. **sojourning** *noun* (*a*) the action or fact of making a sojourn; (*b*) the time or period of a sojourn: ME. **sojournment** *noun* the action of sojourning; a temporary stay: L17.

Soka Gakkai /səʊkə ˈɡakʌɪ/ *noun phr.* Also **Sōka gakkai**. M20.

[Japanese, from *sō* create + *ka* value + *gakkai* (learned) society.]

A lay religious group founded in Japan in 1930 and based on the teachings of a Buddhist order named after the religious teacher Nichiren (1222–82).

sokaiya /ˈsəʊkʌɪjə/ *noun*. Pl. same. L20.

[Japanese, from *sōkai* general meeting + *-ya* dealer.]

A holder of shares in a company who tries to extort money from it by threatening to cause trouble for executives at a general meeting of the shareholders.

soke /səʊk/ *noun*. Also **soak**, (esp., & the usual form, in sense 1) **soc**. LOE.

[Back-form. from SOKEN. Repr. earliest in Anglo-Latin *soca*.]

Hist. **1** A right of local jurisdiction. Chiefly in ***sac and soc*** s.v. SAC *noun*[1]. LOE.

2 A district under a particular jurisdiction; a minor administrative district. LOE.

3 An exclusive right of a mill to grind corn used in the local soke. E17.

sokeman /ˈsəʊkmən/ *noun*. Also **socman**. Pl. **-men**. ME.

[Anglo-Norman, or from Anglo-Latin *sokemannus*, *socamannus*, formed as prec. + MAN *noun*.]

Hist. A tenant holding land in socage.

■ **sokemanry** *noun* (*a*) a tenancy of a sokeman; (*b*) sokemen collectively: E17.

soken /ˈsəʊk(ə)n/ *noun*. See also SUCKEN.

[Old English *sōcn* = Old Norse *sókn*, Gothic *sōkns* search, inquiry, from Germanic.]

†**1** An attack, an assault. *rare*. Only in OE.

†**2** (Habitual) resort to or visiting of a place. OE–LME. ▸**b** *spec.* Resort of local tenants etc. to a particular mill to have their corn ground; the right of the mill to such custom. Cf. SOKE 3. LME–L16.

†**3** = SOKE 1. OE–ME.

4 *Hist.* = SOKE 2. OE.

Sokol /ˈsɒkɒl/ *noun*. E20.

[Czech, lit. 'falcon' (after the emblem of the society).]

A Slav gymnastic society aiming to promote a communal spirit and physical fitness, originating in Prague in 1862. Also, (a member of) a club in this society.

sol /sɒl, səʊl/ *noun*[1]. Also (later) **so**, **soh** /səʊ/. ME.

[Latin *sol(ve)*: see UT.]

MUSIC. The fifth note of a scale in a movable-doh system; the note German in the fixed-doh system.

sol /sɒl/ *noun*[2]. LME.

[Latin = sun.]

1 (**S-**.) Without article: the sun personified. LME.

2 †**a** ALCHEMY. The metal gold. LME–M18. ▸**b** HERALDRY. The tincture or in the fanciful blazon of arms of sovereign houses. Long *obsolete* exc. *Hist.* E17.

3 ASTRONOMY. A solar day on the planet Mars (24 hours 39 minutes). L20.

sol /sɒl/ *noun*[3]. *obsolete* exc. *Hist.* L16.

[Obsolete French (now *sou*) from Latin *solidus*: see SOU.]

A former coin and monetary unit in France and some other countries, notionally equivalent to a twentieth of a livre but varying in actual value.

sol /sɒl/ *noun*[4]. Pl. **soles** /ˈsɒlɛs/. L19.

[Spanish = sun, formed as SOL *noun*[2].]

Orig., a Spanish-American gold or silver coin. Later, a Peruvian bronze coin and monetary unit, replaced as the basic monetary unit by the inti. Now (also ***new sol***), a monetary unit (worth one million intis) which replaced the inti in 1991.

sol /sɒl/ *noun*[5]. L19.

[Abbreviation of SOLUTION. Cf. earlier HYDROSOL.]

PHYSICAL CHEMISTRY. A liquid colloidal solution or dispersion of a solid. Cf. GEL *noun*.

-sol /sɒl/ *suffix*.

[from Latin *solum* floor, ground, soil.]

SOIL SCIENCE. Forming the names of different kinds and states of soil, as ***latosol***, ***lithosol***, ***planosol***, etc.

sola /ˈsəʊlə/ *noun*[1] & *adjective*[1]. Also **solah**, **shola** /ˈʃəʊlə/, (as adjective) **solar**. M19.

[Bengali *solā*, Urdu *śolā*.]

▶ **A** *noun*. Either of two tall leguminous swamp plants, *Aeschynomene aspera* and *A. indica*, of tropical Asia; the lightweight pith of such a shrub, used to make sun-helmets etc. M19.

▶ **B** *attrib.* or as *adjective*. Made of the pith of a sola. M19.

sola *noun*[2] *pl.* see SOLUM.

sola /ˈsəʊlə/ *adverb & adjective*[2]. M18.

[Latin, fem. of *solus* SOLUS, or Italian, fem. of *solo* SOLO *adjective*.]

1 *adverb & pred. adjective.* Of a woman: solitary; alone. M18.

2 *adjective*. COMMERCE. Of a bill of exchange: single (as opp. to one of a set). M18.

†**sola** *interjection*. *rare* (Shakes.). Only in L16.

[Perh. blend of SOHO *interjection* and HOLLA *interjection*.]

Calling for or trying to attract attention.

solace /ˈsɒləs/ *noun*. ME.

[Old French *solas*, *-atz* (mod. dial. *soulas*) from Latin *solatium*, from *solari* relieve, console.]

1 (A thing that gives) comfort or consolation in sorrow, distress, disappointment, or tedium. ME.

†**2** (A thing that gives) pleasure or enjoyment; entertainment, recreation. ME–M17.

3 PRINTING. A penalty imposed by a chapel for a breach of its rules. Now *rare* or *obsolete*. L17.

📖 1 R. K. NARAYAN I saw Rosie suffer and my only solace was that I suffered with her. M. COREN He sought solace in the company of friends.

■ **solaceful** *adjective* (*rare*) full of solace E17. **solacement** *noun* (now *rare*) solace, consolation E18.

solace /ˈsɒləs/ *verb*. ME.
[Old French *solacier* (mod. dial. *soulasser*), formed as prec.]
1 *verb trans. & refl.* Give solace to (a person), console. Formerly also, entertain, amuse. ME.
†**2** *verb intrans.* Take solace, find recreation, enjoy oneself. ME–E18.
3 *verb trans.* Make (a place) cheerful or pleasant; alleviate, assuage, soothe, (distress etc.). Chiefly *poet.* M17.
4 *verb trans.* PRINTING. Punish for non-payment of a solace. Now *rare* or *obsolete*. L17.

📖 1 J. WILSON Such dreams are given . . To solace them that mourn. 3 J. HERVEY Birds . . who . . solace the groves with your artless song. SHELLEY Solacing our despondency with tears.

■ **solacer** *noun* E17. **solacing** *ppl adjective* conveying solace, consoling E18.

Solacet /ˈsɒləsɛt/ *noun*. Also **s-**. M20.
[from SOL(UBLE *adjective* + ACET(ATE.]
Any of a range of azo dyes which contain sulphate ester groups and were formerly much used for direct dyeing of man-made fibres.
¶ Proprietary name in the US.

solah *noun & adjective* var. of SOLA *noun*¹ & *adjective*¹.

solan /ˈsəʊlən/ *noun*. Also **S-**, †**soland**. LME.
[Prob. from Old Norse *súla* gannet + *and-*, nom. *ǫnd* duck.]
More fully ***solan goose***. The northern gannet, *Sula bassana*.

solanaceous /sɒləˈneɪʃəs/ *adjective*. E19.
[from mod. Latin *Solanaceae* (see below), from Latin SOLANUM: see -ACEOUS.]
BOTANY. Of or pertaining to the Solanaceae or nightshade family, which includes potatoes, nightshades, tobacco, sweet and chilli peppers, and tomatoes.

†**soland** *noun* var. of SOLAN.

solander /səˈlandə/ *noun*. L18.
[D. C. *Solander* (1736–82), Swedish botanist.]
A box made in the form of a book, for holding botanical specimens, maps, etc. Also ***solander box***, ***solander case***.

solandra /səˈlandrə/ *noun*. M19.
[mod. Latin (see below), from D. C. *Solander*: see prec.]
Any of various tropical American climbing shrubs constituting the genus *Solandra*, of the nightshade family, with very long trumpet-shaped flowers; *esp.* the chalice vine, *S. maxima*.

solanine /ˈsɒləniːn/ *noun*. Also **-in** /-ɪn/. M19.
[French, formed as SOLANUM + -INE⁵.]
CHEMISTRY. A poisonous steroid glycoside of the saponin group present in many solanaceous plants.
■ **solanidine** /səˈlanɪdiːn/ *noun* a steroid alkaloid which is the aglycone of solanine M19.

solano /soˈlano/ *noun*. L18.
[Spanish from Latin *solanus* from *sol* sun.]
In Spain: a hot south-easterly wind.

solanum /səˈleɪnəm/ *noun*. L16.
[Latin.]
Any plant of the genus *Solanum* (family Solanaceae), marked by rotate corollas and protruding anthers often united in a cone; a preparation of such a plant used for medicinal purposes. Now freq., a plant of this genus grown for its flowers or ornamental fruits.

solar *noun*¹ see SOLLAR.

solar /ˈsəʊlə/ *adjective*¹ & *noun*². LME.
[Latin *solaris*, from *sol* sun: see -AR¹.]
► **A** *adjective*. **1** Of or pertaining to the sun; proceeding or emanating from the sun. LME. ▸**b** (Of time etc.) determined by the course of the sun; fixed by observation of the sun; indicating time in relation to the sun. L16. ▸**c** Utilizing the sun as a source of radiant light or heat. Now *esp.* of or pertaining to the generation of power or energy more or less directly from the sun's radiation. M18.
2 a ASTROLOGY. Influenced by or dependent on the sun, esp. as opp. to the moon. E17. ▸**b** Sacred to the sun; connected or associated with sun-worship; representing or symbolizing the sun; MYTHOLOGY descended from the sun. L18.
3 Like that of the sun; comparable to the sun. M18.
4 [So called because the class includes *š*, the initial letter of Arab. *šams* sun.] Of an Arabic consonant: before which the *l* of the article is assimilated. Opp. LUNAR *adjective* 3. L18.
Special collocations & comb.: ***solar apex***: see APEX *noun*¹ 4. **solar battery** a solar cell or (more usu.) a device consisting of several solar cells. **solar cell** a photovoltaic device which converts solar radiation into electrical energy. **solar constant** the mean rate per unit area at which energy is received at the earth from the sun, equal to 1388 watts per square metre. **solar day** the interval between successive meridional transits of the sun at a place, a day reckoned from noon to noon. ***solar eclipse***: see ECLIPSE *noun* 1. **solar energy**: derived more or less directly from the sun's radiation. ***solar flare***: see FLARE *noun*¹ 1c. **solar furnace**: in which high temperatures are achieved by focusing sunlight using a system of reflectors. **solar-heated** *adjective* heated by means of the sun's rays; equipped with a solar heating system. **solar heating** heating by means of the sun's rays, esp. when utilized for water or space heating. **solar hour** one twenty-fourth of a solar day. **solar lamp** (*a*) an argon lamp; (*b*) a grade of electric lamp. **solar mass** ASTRONOMY the mass of the sun (= 1.989×10^{30} kg) used as a unit of mass. **solar month** one twelfth of a solar year; the time taken by the sun to pass through a sign of the zodiac. **solar myth**: ascribing the course or attributes of the sun to some god or hero. **solar neutrino unit** a unit used in expressing the detected flux of neutrinos from the sun, equal to 10^{-36} neutrino captures per target atom per second; abbreviation ***SNU***. **solar panel** a panel designed to absorb the sun's rays for the purpose of generating electricity (using solar cells) or heating. **solar plexus** ANATOMY a complex of radiating nerves situated behind the stomach; *loosely* the region of the chest in front of this, *esp.* as regarded as vulnerable to a blow. **solar pond**, **solar pool** a pool of very salty water in which convection is inhibited, allowing considerable heating of the bottom water by solar radiation. **solar power**: derived more or less directly from solar radiation. **solar-powered** *adjective* using power derived directly from the sun's rays. ***solar prominence***: see PROMINENCE 4. ***solar regular***: see REGULAR *noun* 4. **solar salt** salt obtained by allowing seawater to evaporate in sunlight. **solar still**: in which solar radiation is employed to evaporate salty or impure water and produce fresh water. **solar system** the sun together with all the planets and other bodies connected with it. **solar time**: determined with reference to the position of the sun (***apparent solar time***: see APPARENT *adjective* 4; ***mean solar time***: see MEAN *adjective*²). **solar wind** the stream of ions and electrons which constantly emanates from the sun and which permeates the solar system. ***solar year***: see YEAR *noun*¹ 1.
► **B** *noun*. **1** A solar lamp. M19.
2 Solar energy, esp. as used for domestic or industrial purposes. L20.
■ **solarism** *noun* the belief that (most or all) myths can be explained as solar myths L19. **solarist** *noun* an adherent of solarism L19.

solar *adjective*² var. of SOLA *adjective*¹.

solaria *noun pl.* see SOLARIUM.

solarimeter /səʊləˈrɪmɪtə/ *noun*. E20.
[from SOLAR *adjective*¹ + -IMETER.]
An instrument for measuring the total intensity of (solar) radiation incident on a surface.

solarisation *noun*, **solarise** *verb* vars. of SOLARIZATION, SOLARIZE.

solarium /səˈlɛːrɪəm/ *noun*. Pl. **-ia** /-ɪə/, **-iums**. M19.
[Latin, from *sol* sun: see -ARIUM.]
1 A sundial. Now *rare* or *obsolete*. M19.
2 a A room, balcony, etc., built (esp. with large areas of glass) to provide exposure to the rays of the sun; a sun lounge or parlour. L19. ▸**b** A room equipped with sun-lamps for giving an artificial suntan; an establishment providing sun-lamps. M20.

solarization /səʊlərʌɪˈzeɪʃ(ə)n/ *noun*. Also **-isation**. M19.
[from next + -ATION.]
► **I 1** PHOTOGRAPHY. Reversal or other change in the relative darkness of an image due to overexposure; the progressive reduction in the developable density of an emulsion following initial exposure beyond a certain light intensity. Also, the Sabatier effect (cf. PSEUDOSOLARIZATION). M19.
2 BOTANY. The inhibition of photosynthesis as a result of prolonged exposure to high light intensities. E20.
3 The alteration of the opacity of glass as a result of prolonged exposure to light. E20.
► **II** *gen.* **4** (Change produced by) excessive or prolonged exposure to sunlight or other bright light. L19.

solarize /ˈsəʊlərʌɪz/ *verb*. Also **-ise**. M19.
[from SOLAR *adjective*¹ + -IZE.]
1 *verb trans.* Affect, modify, or injure by (excessive or prolonged) exposure to sunlight or other bright light; affect by or cause to undergo solarization. M19.
2 *verb intrans.* Undergo or be affected by solarization. M19.

†**solary** *adjective*. L16–E18.
[medieval Latin *solarius*, from Latin *sol* sun: see -ARY².]
Of or pertaining to the sun; solar.

Solas /ˈsəʊləs/ *noun*. Also **SOLAS**. M20.
[Acronym, from *Safety of Life at Sea*.]
Used *attrib.* to designate (the provisions of) a series of international conventions governing maritime safety.

solaster /səˈlastə/ *noun*. M19.
[mod. Latin (see below), from Latin *sol* sun + *aster* star (from Greek *astēr*).]
A starfish of the genus *Solaster*, typically having more than five arms; a sunstar.

solate /səˈleɪt/ *verb trans. & intrans.* E20.
[from SOL *noun*⁵ + -ATE³.]
PHYSICAL CHEMISTRY. Convert or be converted from a gel into a sol.

solatia *noun pl.* of SOLATIUM.

†**solation** *noun*¹. *rare*. LME–M18.
[Old French *solacion*, *-tion*, ult. from Latin *solari* console: see -ATION.]
Rejoicing, joy; (a) consolation.

solation /səˈleɪʃ(ə)n/ *noun*². E20.
[from SOL *noun*⁵ + -ATION.]
PHYSICAL CHEMISTRY. The change of a gel into a sol.

solatium /səˈleɪʃɪəm/ *noun*. Pl. **-ia** /-ɪə/. E19.
[Latin: see SOLACE *noun*.]
A sum of money or other compensation given to a person to make up for loss, inconvenience, injured feelings, etc.; *spec.* in LAW, such an amount awarded to a litigant over and above the actual loss.

sold /səʊld/ *noun*. ME.
[Old French *sou(l)de* from Latin SOLIDUS.]
†**1** Pay, esp. of soldiers; wages, salary. ME–M17.
2 A sum or quantity, orig. of money etc. *Scot.* E16.

sold *verb pa. t. & pple* of SELL *verb*.

soldado /sɒlˈdɑːdəʊ/ *noun*. Now *rare* or *obsolete*. Pl. **-o(e)s**. L16.
[Spanish, Portuguese = Italian *soldato*, from *soldo* military pay, SOLD *noun*: see -ADO.]
A soldier.

soldan /ˈsɒldən/ *noun*. Now *arch.* or *Hist.* Also **S-**. ME.
[Old French *soudan*, *soldan* (medieval Latin *soldanus*), ult. from Arab. *sulṭān* SULTAN.]
= SULTAN *noun* 1; *spec.* (*Hist.*) the Sultan of Egypt.

soldanella /sɒldəˈnɛlə/ *noun*. In sense 1 also Anglicized as †**soldanel**. M16.
[mod. Latin (see below), from Italian, of unkn. origin.]
†**1** The sea bindweed, *Calystegia soldanella*. M16–L18.
2 Any of several small alpine plants constituting the genus *Soldanella*, of the primrose family, with bell-shaped lilac flowers. E17.

soldatesque /sɒldəˈtɛsk/ *noun & adjective*. *rare*. M17.
[French from Italian *soldatesco*, from *soldato*: see SOLDADO, -ESQUE.]
► †**A** *noun*. The military. Only in M17.
► **B** *adjective*. Of or pertaining to a soldier or soldiers; soldierly. M19.

solder /ˈsəʊldə, ˈsɒldə/ *noun & verb*. Also †**sodder**. ME.
[Old & mod. French *soudure*, from *souder*, †*solder* from Latin *solidare* fasten together, from *solidus* SOLID *adjective*. Cf. SAWDER.]
► **A** *noun*. **1** A fusible metallic alloy used for uniting less fusible metal surfaces or parts. ME.
2 *fig.* Something which unites things; *esp.* a unifying quality or principle. L16.
1 hard solder: fusible at a relatively high temperature and typically containing brass and silver. ***silver solder***: see SILVER *noun & adjective*. **soft solder** (*a*) solder fusible at a relatively low temperature, typically containing lead and tin; (*b*) *fig.* (*arch.*) flattery (cf. SAWDER *noun*). ***spelter solder***: see SPELTER 2.
► **B** *verb*. **I** *verb trans.* **1** Unite, fasten, or repair by means of metallic solder. Foll. by *to*, *on*, *together*, etc. LME.
†**2** MEDICINE. Cause (a wound) to close up and become whole; reunite (tissues or bones). L15–L18.
3 *transf. & fig.* Unite firmly or closely, join, cause to adhere. Also, restore to a sound condition, patch *up* again. M16.

📖 3 CARLYLE The sad Varennes business has been soldered up. E. MUIR Walking by / With frozen fingers soldered to her basket.

► **II** *verb intrans.* **4** Adhere, unite, grow together. Chiefly *fig.* L15.
■ **soldera'bility** *noun* the property of being solderable M20. **solderable** *adjective* able to be joined by means of solder M20. **solderer** *noun* a person who works with solder M16. **soldering** *noun* (*a*) the action of the verb; (***soldering iron***, a tool for applying molten solder); (*b*) solder: LME. **solderless** *adjective* made without solder; not requiring solder: E20.

soldi *noun* pl. of SOLDO.

soldier /ˈsəʊldʒə/ *noun*. Also (*dial.*) **sodger** /ˈsɒdʒə/. ME.
[Old French *soud(i)er*, *so(l)dier* (medieval Latin *sol(i)darius*), from *sou(l)de* SOLD *noun*: see -IER.]
► **I 1** A person who serves or has served in an army; *esp.* (more fully ***common soldier***) a member of the ordinary rank and file, a private, a non-commissioned officer. ME. ▸**b** A person of military skill and experience. E17. ▸**c** A small model of a soldier, esp. as a child's toy; = ***toy soldier*** (a) s.v. TOY *noun*. L19.
2 *fig.* A person who fights for a cause (usu. specified or understood contextually). ME.
3 a A worthless seaman; a loafer, a shirker. *Nautical slang* (orig. and chiefly *US*). M19. ▸**b** A member of the Salvation Army. L19. ▸**c** A rank-and-file member of the Mafia. M20.

📖 2 SHAKES. *Per.* Be A soldier to thy purpose. J. W. WARTER No mean soldier of the Church Militant.

► **II 4** ***water soldier***, †***freshwater soldier***, an aquatic plant, *Stratiotes aloides*, of the frogbit family, with white flowers and rosettes of sword-shaped spiny serrate leaves. L16.

5 a More fully ***soldier-crab***. A hermit crab. **M17.** ▸**b** Any of various fishes likened to soldiers, esp. because of red colouring; *esp.* (in full ***soldier-fish***) = **SQUIRREL** *noun* 3. **E18.** ▸**c** More fully ***soldier ant***, ***soldier termite***. A wingless ant or termite with a large head and jaws, specialized for fighting in defence of its colony. **L18.** ▸**d** A red spider, beetle, or similar animal; *spec.* (in full ***soldier beetle***) any of various reddish carnivorous beetles of the family Cantharidae. **M19.**

6 a A red smoked herring. *arch. slang.* **E19.** ▸**b** A strip or finger of bread or toast. *colloq.* **M20.**

7 *BUILDING* etc. Each of an orderly series of upright bricks, timbers, etc., suggestive of a line of soldiers on parade. **E20.**

🕮 **6b** P. SCOTT He cut his buttered bread into soldiers.

Phrases: **blow that for a game of soldiers** & vars., *colloq.* in *imper.*, expr. impatience or exasperation with, or rejection of, a situation, course of action, etc. ***common soldier***: see sense 1 above. **dead soldier** *N. Amer. slang* an empty bottle. ***foot-soldier***: see **FOOT** *noun*. ***freshwater soldier***: see sense 4 above. **old soldier** *fig.* a person who is or pretends to be practised or experienced in something (***come the old soldier over***: see **COME** *verb*). ***private soldier***: see **PRIVATE** *adjective*. ***regular soldier***: see **REGULAR** *adjective*. **soldier of Christ** an active or proselytizing Christian. ***soldier of fortune***: see **FORTUNE** *noun*. ***tin soldier***: see **TIN** *noun & adjective*. ***toy soldier***: see sense 1c above. ***Unknown Soldier***: see **UNKNOWN** *adjective*. ***water soldier***: see sense 4 above.

Comb.: ***soldier ant***: see sense 5c above; **soldier arch** *BUILDING* a flat or gently curved arch made from upright bricks; ***soldier beetle***: see sense 5d above; **soldier bird** *Austral.* = ***noisy miner*** s.v. **NOISY** 1; **soldier-bug** a predacious N. American pentatomid bug of the genus *Podisus*, *esp.* the yellowish-brown *P. maculiventris*; **soldier course** *BUILDING* a course of bricks set on end with their narrower long face exposed; ***soldier-crab***: see sense 5a above; ***soldier-fish***: see sense 5b above; **soldier-fly** (orig. *US*) any of various often brightly coloured dipteran flies constituting the family Stratiomyidae; **soldier orchid**, **soldier orchis** = ***military orchid*** s.v. **MILITARY** *adjective*; **soldier palmer** a kind of artificial fly used in angling; ***soldier-termite***: see sense 5c above; **soldier's farewell** *slang* an abusive farewell (cf. ***SAILOR'S farewell***); **soldier's heart** *MEDICINE* a psychosomatic syndrome characterized by throbbing in the chest, shortness of breath, fatigue, etc; **soldier's wind** *Nautical slang* a wind which serves either way.

▪ **soldieress** *noun* (*rare*) a female soldier **E17.** **soldierhood** *noun* the essential qualities of a soldier; the condition of being a soldier: **M19.** **soldierize** *verb* (*rare*) (*a*) *verb intrans.* & †*trans.* (with *it*) = **SOLDIER** *verb* 1; (*b*) *verb trans.* make into a soldier: **L16.** **soldierlike** *adjective & adverb* soldierly **M16.** **soldiership** *noun* the state or condition of being a soldier; the qualities of a soldier; military experience or skill: **M16.**

soldier /ˈsəʊldʒə/ *verb*. Also (*dial.*) **sodger** /ˈsɒdʒə/. **E17.**
[from the noun.]

1 *verb intrans.* & †*trans.* (with *it*). Act or serve as a soldier. Freq. as ***soldiering*** *verbal noun*. **E17.**

2 *verb intrans.* Feign illness, malinger; merely pretend to work, shirk. *slang.* **E19.**

3 *verb intrans.* Foll. by *on*: persevere, carry on doggedly. **M20.**

🕮 **1** SIR W. SCOTT This comes o' letting ye gang a-sodgering for a day. T. PARKER I enjoy soldiering enormously. **2** F. G. SLAUGHTER Has my staff taken advantage of my absence to soldier on the job? **3** P. LIVELY You pick yourself up and soldier on.

soldierly /ˈsəʊldʒəli/ *adjective*. **L16.**
[from **SOLDIER** *noun* + **-LY**¹.]

1 Appropriate to or befitting a soldier or soldiers. **L16.**

2 Having the qualities of a soldier. **E17.**

🕮 **1** R. L. STEVENSON A . . Pennsylvania Dutchman, with a soldierly smartness in his manner. A. BURGESS Sergeants, whose sole soldierly quality had been a capacity for . . liquor.

▪ **soldierliness** *noun* **L19.**

soldierly /ˈsəʊldʒəli/ *adverb*. **L16.**
[from **SOLDIER** *noun* + **-LY**².]
In the manner of a soldier, as befits a soldier.

soldiery /ˈsəʊldʒ(ə)ri/ *noun*. **L16.**
[from **SOLDIER** *noun* + **-Y**³. Cf. **-ERY**.]

1 Soldiers collectively; the military; a military class or body. **L16.**

2 The business of soldiers; military training or knowledge. **L16.**

🕮 **1** SIR W. SCOTT These mercenaries were . . a fierce . . soldiery. R. PILCHER It's . . a problem to know what to do with randy soldiery. **2** I. MURDOCH Whenever . . talking soldiery you seem to . . become utterly stupid.

soldo /ˈsɒldəʊ, *foreign* ˈsoldo/ *noun*. Pl. **-di** /-di/. **L16.**
[Italian from Latin **SOLIDUS**.]
Orig. (now *Hist.*), a former Italian coin and monetary unit worth the twentieth part of a lira. Now also, (in Italy) a very small sum of money (cf. **SOU**).

sole /səʊl/ *noun*¹. *obsolete* exc. *dial.*
[Old English *sāl* = Old Saxon *sēl* (Low German *seil*), Middle Dutch *seel* (Dutch *zeel*), Old High German *seil* (German *Seil*), Old Norse *seil*, etc.]
A rope or cord, now *spec.* one for tethering cattle. Also, a wooden collar used to fasten a cow etc. in the stall.

sole /səʊl/ *noun*². **ME.**
[Old French from Latin *solea* sandal, sill, from *solum* bottom, pavement, sole; prob. already in Old English, corresp. to Old Saxon, Old High German *sola* (Dutch *zool*, German *Sohle*). Cf. **SOLE** *noun*³.]

1 The undersurface of a foot; that part of the foot which normally rests or is placed on the ground. Also ***sole of the foot***, ***sole of his or her foot***, etc. **ME.** ▸**b** *FARRIERY.* The concave horny underside of a horse's hoof. **E17.**

2 The part of a boot, shoe, sock, etc., corresponding to the sole of the foot; that part of a boot, shoe, sock, etc., on which the wearer treads, freq. exclusive of the heel; a piece of leather etc. from which this is made. Also, a shaped piece of material worn in the bottom of a boot, shoe, etc. **LME.**

3 †**a** The foundation or site of a building etc. *rare.* **LME–M17.** ▸**b** The sill of a window; a threshold. Now *Scot.* & *dial.* **LME.** ▸**c** The bottom, floor, or hearth of an oven or furnace. **E17.** ▸**d** *NAUTICAL.* The floor of a ship's cabin. **M19.** ▸**e** A flat tile used as a support for a drainpipe etc. **M19.**

4 The rim of a wheel. Now only, the inner circle of a water-wheel. **LME.**

5 The lower part, bottom, or undersurface of an implement or other object, e.g. of a plane stock, plough, rudder, golf club head, etc. **E17.**

6 a *MINING.* The bottom or floor of a vein, working, etc. **M17.** ▸**b** The undersurface of the ground, the subsoil. Also, a (good etc.) surface or bottom in a field etc. *obsolete* exc. *dial.* **L17.** ▸**c** The bottom or lowest part *of* a valley etc. **L19.** ▸**d** *GEOLOGY.* The underside or lowest plane or layer in a stratum, glacier, etc. **L19.**

🕮 **1** B. TAYLOR Our shoes are . . danced out . . . We've but naked soles to run with. J. AGEE He felt the ground against the bare soles of his feet. **2** A. CARTER He moved as softly as if . . his shoes had soles of velvet. ***crêpe sole***, ***clump-sole***, ***half-sole***, ***lug sole***, ***platform sole***, etc. **5** C. FORD On . . convex surfaces a plane with a flat sole . . is best. **6c** R. F. BURTON His men . . fled along the sole of the Wady. **d** A. HOLMES Along the sole of a . . thrust severe crushing . . of the rocks is to be expected.

Comb.: **solebar** a longitudinal member forming part of the underframe of a railway carriage etc.; **sole-leather**: of a thick or strong kind suitable for the soles of boots, shoes, etc.; **sole-plate** (*a*) the bedplate of an engine; (*b*) the metal plate forming the base of an electric iron; **sole-tree** (*a*) a beam, plank, or piece of timber forming a support, base, or foundation to something; (*b*) *spec.* in *MINING*, a wooden beam forming part of a stowce or windlass.

▪ **soleless** /-l-l-/ *adjective* having no sole, without soles **L18.**

sole /səʊl/ *noun*³. Pl. same. **ME.**
[Old & mod. French from Provençal *sola* from Proto-Romance from Latin *solea*: see prec.]
Any of various mainly tongue-shaped flatfishes; *esp.* a member of the family Soleidae; spec. *Solea solea* (more fully ***common sole***, ***European sole***), a highly valued food fish of Mediterranean and NE Atlantic waters. Also, the flesh of any of these fishes as food.
Dover sole, ***lemon sole***, ***thickback sole***, etc.

sole /səʊl/ *adjective & adverb*. **LME.**
[Old French *soule* (mod. *seule*) from Latin *sola* fem. of *solus*.]

▸ **A** *adjective.* **1** Esp. of a woman: single, unmarried. Formerly also, celibate. *arch.* & *LAW.* **LME.**

2 Usu. (now only) of a person: unaccompanied by another or others; alone; solitary. *arch.* **LME.** ▸**b** Of a place: lonely, secluded. *rare.* **L16.**

3 Being or consisting of one person only. Now only (*LAW*) in ***corporation sole*** s.v. **CORPORATION** 2. **LME.**

4 *attrib.* One and only, single; only. Also, singular, unique, unrivalled. **LME.**

5 Pertaining to, possessed or exercised by, or vested in one person or body to the exclusion of all others; exclusive. **M16.**

6 Uniform, unvaried. *rare.* **M19.**

🕮 **2** POPE Sole should he sit, with scarce a God to friend. **4** H. JAMES The theatre is my sole vice. C. HARE We are the sole witnesses. G. GREENE You . . have come . . with the sole purpose of making trouble. G. VIDAL You deny that the . . Lord is the sole creator of all things? **5** T. REID A theory of which he claims the sole invention. J. RUSKIN Judges . . exercising sole authority in courts. *Guardian* BR agreed to take sole charge of a rail link scheme after private-sector partners pulled out.

▸ **B** *adverb.* †**1** = **SOLELY** *adverb* 1. **LME–L17.**

2 = **SOLELY** *adverb* 2. *non-standard.* **M16.**

sole /səʊl/ *verb trans.* **L16.**
[from **SOLE** *noun*².]

1 Provide (esp. a boot, shoe, etc.) with a sole; renew the sole of. **L16.**

2 Form the base or bottom of. *rare.* **M17.**

▪ **soled** *ppl adjective* having a sole or soles (of a specified kind) **L15.** **soler** *noun* a person who soles footwear **L19.** **soling** *noun* (*a*) the action of putting a (new) sole on a boot, shoe, etc.; (*b*) a foundation laid down in constructing a road over boggy or marshy ground: **LME.**

solea /ˈsəʊlɪə/ *noun*. **M19.**
[Byzantine Greek from Proto-Romance.]
ARCHITECTURE. A raised part of the floor in front of a door, chapel, etc., esp. in an Orthodox church.

solecism /ˈsɒlɪsɪz(ə)m/ *noun*. **M16.**
[French *solécisme* or Latin *soloecismus* from Greek *soloikismos*, from *soloikos* speaking incorrectly, said by ancient writers to refer to the corrupted Attic dialect spoken by Athenian colonists at Soloi in Cilicia: see **-ISM**.]

1 A violation of rules or conventions; a mistake, a blunder; an incongruity, an inconsistency; *esp.* (*a*) a mistake of grammar or idiom, a blunder in speaking or writing; (*b*) a breach of good manners, a piece of incorrect behaviour. **M16.**

2 Violation of rules or conventions, error; *esp.* incorrect or ungrammatical speech or writing. **L16.**

🕮 **1** SIR W. SCOTT The slightest solecism in politeness . . was agony. A. PRYCE-JONES To carve a ham in any house but one's own was an appalling solecism. P. LIVELY To encourage freedom of expression he preferred not to jump on every solecism. **2** DRYDEN A wary man . . in grammar, very nice as to solecism.

▪ **solecist** *noun* (*rare*) a person who uses solecisms **E18.** **soleˈcistic** *adjective* of the nature of or involving solecism **E19.** **soleˈcistical** *adjective* (now *rare* or *obsolete*) solecistic **M17.** **soleˈcistically** *adverb* (*rare*) in the manner of a solecism, with solecisms **E18.** **solecize** *verb intrans.* (now *rare* or *obsolete*) make use of or commit solecisms **E17.**

Soledon /ˈsɒlɪd(ə)n/ *noun*. **E20.**
[from **SOL**(**UBLE** + *Caledon* proprietary name (formed as **CALEDONIAN**).]
(Proprietary name for) any of a range of water-soluble vat dyes derived mainly from anthraquinones.

solely /ˈsəʊlli/ *adverb*. **LME.**
[from **SOLE** *adjective* + **-LY**².]

1 As a single person or thing; without any other as an associate, partner, etc.; alone. **LME.**

2 Only, merely, exclusively. Also (contextually), entirely, altogether. **LME.**

🕮 **1** B. LOPEZ We are not solely responsible for every extinction. **2** M. LAVIN He valued the country solely for . . protection . . from people. A. TYLER They used to exist solely on baked potatoes.

solemn /ˈsɒləm/ *adjective*. **ME.**
[Old French *solem(p)ne* from Latin *sol(l)emnis*, *-ennis*, *-empnis* celebrated ceremonially and at a fixed date, festive, customary, from *sollus* whole, entire: the terminal element is unexplained.]

1 Associated or connected with religious rites or observances; performed with due ceremony and reverence; having a religious character; sacred. **ME.**

2 Of a day or season: marked by the celebration of special observances or rites, esp. of a religious character; distinguished by or set apart for special ceremonies. Now *rare* or *obsolete.* **ME.**

†**3 a** Grand, imposing; sumptuous. **ME–L16.** ▸**b** Famous, renowned. **LME–L16.**

4 Of a vow, oath, document, etc.: of a formal and serious or significant character. **LME.**

5 Performed with or accompanied by due ceremony or dignity; of a ceremonious or dignified character. Formerly also, of great importance. **LME.** ▸†**b** Formal; regular; uniform. **M17–E18.**

6 Of a sober, grave, or earnest character; slow and deliberate in movement or action; serious or cheerless in manner or appearance. **LME.**

7 a Mysteriously impressive, awe-inspiring. **LME.** ▸†**b** Gloomy, dark, sombre. Only in **E17.**

🕮 **1** MILTON His holy Rites, and solemn Feasts profan'd. ***solemn mass***: see **MASS** *noun*¹. **2** J. FRITH The Jews . . were commanded to keep the seventh day solemn. **3a** G. PUTTENHAM The players garments were made more rich and costly and solemne. **4** ALBAN BUTLER The Oblates make no solemn vows, only a promise of obedience. *Which?* Saray gave a solemn undertaking to mend their ways. ***Solemn League and Covenant***: see **COVENANT** *noun* 6. **5** EVELYN Being the King's birth day, there was a solemne ball at Court. **6** J. BROWN Our parochial Music . . is solemn and devout. A. BROOKNER He had an owlish and solemn air. *Harpers & Queen* A little girl with wide, solemn eyes. **7a** J. CONRAD The solemn hush of the deep Golfo Placido.

▪ **solemness** *noun* **M16.** **solemnly** *adverb* **ME.**

solemncholy /ˈsɒləmk(ə)li/ *adjective*. *joc. rare.* **L18.**
[from prec. after *melancholy*.]
Excessively solemn or serious.

solemnify /səˈlɛmnɪfʌɪ/ *verb trans.* **LME.**
[formed as prec. + **-I-** + **-FY**.]
Solemnize (a marriage); make solemn.

solemniously /səˈləmnɪəsli/ *adverb*. *rare.* **L16.**
[formed as prec. + **-IOUS** + **-LY**².]
Solemnly.

solemnisation *noun* var. of **SOLEMNIZATION**.

solemnise *verb & noun* var. of **SOLEMNIZE**.

solemnity /səˈlɛmnɪti/ *noun*. **ME**.
[Old French *solem(p)nité* (mod. *solennité*) from Latin *sollem(p)nitas*: see **SOLEMN**, **-ITY**.]
1 Observance of ceremony or due formality, esp. during religious rites or on other important occasions. Freq. in †***in solemnity***, ***with solemnity***. **ME**.
2 A ceremonial occasion; an observance or rite of special importance; a festival, a celebration. **ME**. ▸†**b** A ceremonial procession. **M17–M18**.
3 †**a** Proper performance; due process. Only in **LME**. ▸**b** *LAW*. Necessary formality; a formal procedure such as is necessary to validate an act or document. **L16**.
4 The state or character of being solemn or serious; impressiveness; gravity. Also, a solemn utterance or statement; a solemn feeling. **E18**.

> 🕮 **2** J. BROWN *Hymns* . . Sung by their Composers at their festal Solemnities. **3b** K. E. DIGBY No solemnity short of a deed is regarded by our law as sufficient. A. MACLEAN The almost complete silence . . didn't stem entirely from the solemnity of the occasion. **4** *Scientific American* The U.S. Government has acknowledged the solemnity of the AIDS crisis. R. FRAME A solemnity had taken over and the gaiety was a thing of the past.

solemnization /sɒləmnʌɪˈzeɪʃ(ə)n/ *noun*. Also **-isation**. **LME**.
[Old French *solem(p)nisation*, *-ization* or medieval Latin *solempnizatio(n-)*: see next, **-ION**.]
The action of solemnizing or celebrating something in a ceremonial or formal manner; *spec.* the celebration of a marriage, the due performance *of* a marriage ceremony.

solemnize /ˈsɒləmnʌɪz/ *verb & noun*. Also **-ise**. **LME**.
[Old French *solem(p)niser* from medieval Latin *solem(p)nizare*, from Latin *solem(p)nis*: see **SOLEMN**, **-IZE**.]
▸ **A** *verb*. **1** *verb trans*. Dignify or honour by a ceremony or ceremonies; celebrate or commemorate (an occasion etc.) by special observances or with special formality. **LME**.
2 *verb trans*. Celebrate (a marriage) with proper ceremonies and in due form; duly perform the ceremony of (marriage). **LME**. ▸**b** *verb intrans*. Marry. *rare*. **M18**.
3 *verb trans*. Hold or observe with a degree of ceremony or formality. Formerly also, proclaim formally. **LME**.
†**4** *verb trans*. Celebrate with praise or commendation; glorify. **LME–L17**.
5 *verb trans*. Make solemn; render serious or grave. **E18**.
6 *verb intrans*. Speak or meditate solemnly. *rare*. **M19**.

> 🕮 **1** C. THIRLWALL The king solemnized his triumph with great magnificence. **2** D. MADDEN The priest who had solemnized the marriage now said the prayers. **3** G. ALLEN Dinner solemnised, we withdrew to . . the balcony. **5** J. BUCHAN Half the audience in tears and the rest too solemnised to shout.

▸†**B** *noun*. Solemnization; solemn rite. *rare* (Spenser). Only in **L16**.
▪ **solemnizer** *noun* (*rare*) **L16**.

solemnsides /ˈsɒləmsʌɪdz/ *adjective & noun*. **E20**.
[from **SOLEMN** + *-sides*, after *sobersides*.]
▸ **A** *adjective*. Excessively solemn or serious. **E20**.
▸ **B** *noun*. An excessively solemn or serious person. **M20**.

solen /ˈsəʊlən/ *noun*. **M17**.
[Latin from Greek *sōlēn* channel, pipe, syringe, shellfish.]
1 *ZOOLOGY*. Any of several common razor-shells, esp. *Ensis ensis* and the pod razor *E. siliqua*. Now chiefly as mod. Latin genus name. **M17**.
2 *MEDICINE*. = **CRADLE** *noun* 8. Now *rare*. **L17**.

soleness /ˈsəʊlnɪs/ *noun*. Now *rare*. **LME**.
[from **SOLE** *adjective* + **-NESS**.]
†**1** Solitude; solitariness. **LME–E17**.
2 The state or condition of being sole, alone, or apart. **L16**.

solenette /səʊlˈnɛt, sɒləˈnɛt/ *noun*. **M19**.
[Irreg. from **SOLE** *noun*[3] + *-n-* + **-ETTE**.]
A small sole, *Buglossidium luteum*, found in offshore waters of the NE Atlantic.

Solenhofen /ˈsəʊl(ə)nhəʊf(ə)n/ *noun*. **M19**.
[*Solnhofen*, a village in Bavaria, Germany.]
GEOLOGY. **1** ***Solenhofen slate***, ***Solenhofen stone***, a thinly stratified lithographic limestone. **M19**.
2 ***Solenhofen bed***, any of the Upper Jurassic deposits at Solnhofen that yield Solenhofen stone, noted as the chief source of *Archaeopteryx* fossils. **M19**.

solenium /sə(ʊ)ˈliːnɪəm/ *noun*. Pl. **-nia** /-nɪə/. **E20**.
[mod. Latin from Greek *sōlēnion* dim. of *sōlēn*: see **SOLEN**.]
ZOOLOGY. Any of various endoderm-lined canals which are diverticula from the coelenteron of a colonial coelenterate.

soleno- /səˈliːnəʊ/ *combining form* of Greek *sōlēn*: see **SOLEN**, **-O-**.
▪ **solenocyte** *noun* (*ZOOLOGY*) any of the cells with single flagellae found in the nephridia of some polychaetes **E20**. **solenoglyph** *noun* (*ZOOLOGY*) any of various venomous snakes which have folding fangs with a longitudinal canal to inject the venom **E20**. **solenoˈglyphous** *adjective* of or pertaining to a solenoglyph **M20**.

solenodon /səˈlɛnədən, səˈliːn-/ *noun*. Also earlier **-dont** /-dɒnt/. **M19**.
[mod. Latin *Solenodon* (see below), from prec. + **-ODON**.]
ZOOLOGY. Either of two endangered nocturnal mammals (insectivores) of the genus *Solenodon*, which resemble very large shrews with elongated snouts and are confined to the Caribbean islands of Cuba and Hispaniola.

solenoid /ˈsɒlənɔɪd, ˈsəʊl-/ *noun*. **E19**.
[French *solénoïde*, from Greek *sōlēn* (see **SOLEN**) + **-OID**.]
1 *ELECTRICITY*. A cylindrical coil of wire which sets up a magnetic field when an electric current is passed through it; *esp.* such a coil surrounding a moving iron core and used to operate an electrical switch or relay. **E19**.
2 *MEDICINE*. A cage for enclosing a patient during treatment. Now *rare* or *obsolete*. **E20**.
1 attrib.: ***solenoid brake***, ***solenoid lock***, etc.
▪ **soleˈnoidal** *adjective* of or pertaining to a solenoid; of the nature, or having the properties, of a solenoid; *spec.* (of a vector field) having no divergence anywhere and hence expressible as the curl of another vector field: **L19**.

solera /səˈlɛːrə, *foreign* soˈlera/ *noun*. **M19**.
[Spanish, lit. 'crossbeam, stone base' from *suelo* ground, floor, dregs from Latin **SOLUM**.]
1 A blend of sherry or Malaga wine produced by the Spanish solera system (see sense 3 below). Also ***solera wine***. **M19**.
2 A wine-cask, usu. with a capacity of four hogsheads; a set of such casks arranged in tiers so as to produce wine by the solera system. **M19**.
3 ***solera system***, a method of producing wine, esp. sherry and Madeira, whereby small amounts of younger wines stored in an upper tier of casks are systematically blended with the more mature wine in the casks below. **M20**.

soles *noun* pl. of **SOL** *noun*[4].

soleus /sə(ʊ)ˈliːəs, ˈsəʊlɪəs/ *noun*. **L17**.
[mod. Latin from Latin *solea* **SOLE** *noun*[2].]
ANATOMY. A muscle of the calf of the leg, situated under the gastrocnemius.

†**solf** *verb*. **ME**.
[from (the same root as) **SOL-FA**. Cf. **SOWFF**.]
1 *verb intrans*. = **SOL-FA** *verb* 2. **ME–L16**.
2 *verb trans*. = **SOL-FA** *verb* 1. **LME–L16**.

sol-fa /ˈsɒlfɑː/ *verb & noun*. **E16**.
[from the syllables *sol* **SOL** *noun*[1] and *fa* **FAH**: see **UT**. Cf. earlier **SOLF** *verb*.]
MUSIC. ▸**A** *verb*. **1** *verb trans*. Sing (a tune etc.) to the sol-fa syllables. **E16**.
2 *verb intrans*. Sing using the sol-fa syllables. **L16**.
▸ **B** *noun*. The set of syllables 'doh (or ut), ray, mi, fah, sol, lah, te (or si)', sung to the respective notes of the major scale; the system of notating music for singers using these syllables; solmization; a musical scale or exercise thus sung. **M16**.
tonic sol-fa: see **TONIC** *adjective* 4.

solfatara /sɒlfəˈtɑːrə/ *noun*. Also earlier **-terra** /-ˈtɛrə/. **L18**.
[A sulphurous volcano near Naples, from Italian *solfo* sulphur.]
GEOLOGY. A fumarole which emits sulphurous gases, encrusting the edge with sulphur etc. Cf. **SOUFRIÈRE**.
▪ **solfataric** *adjective* of or pertaining to solfataras; designating (the stage of) volcanic activity in which sulphurous gases are emitted from vents: **L19**.

solfège /sɒlfɛʒ/ *noun*. Pl. pronounced same. **E20**.
[French.]
MUSIC. = **SOLFEGGIO**. Also (*gen.*), rudimentary musical instruction, esp. using textless exercises for the voice.

solfeggio /sɒlˈfɛdʒɪəʊ/ *noun*. Pl. **-ggi** /-dʒi/, **-ggios**. **L18**.
[Italian, from *sol-fa* **SOL-FA**.]
MUSIC. An exercise for the voice (formerly also for a musical instrument), using the sol-fa syllables. Also, solmization.

solferino /sɒlfəˈriːnəʊ/ *noun & adjective*. **M19**.
[A town in Italy, site of a battle (1859) shortly before the dye was discovered.]
▸ **A** *noun*. A bright crimson aniline dye, rosaniline; the colour of this dye. **M19**.
▸ **B** *attrib*. or as *adjective*. Coloured with or like solferino. **L19**.

soli *noun* pl. of **SOLO** *noun*[1].

solicit /səˈlɪsɪt/ *verb & noun*. **LME**.
[Old & mod. French *solliciter* from Latin *sollicitare* stir, agitate, (in medieval Latin) look after, from *sollicitus* agitated, from *sollus* whole, entire + *citus* pa. pple of *ciere* (see **CITE**) set in motion.]
▸ **A** *verb*. **I** *verb trans*. †**1** Disturb, disquiet; make anxious, fill with concern. **LME–L18**.
2 Entreat, petition, urge, (a person); ask earnestly or persistently *for*, *that*, *to do*. **LME**.
3 †**a** Manage, pursue, attend to, (business etc.). **LME–L18**. ▸**b** Conduct (a lawsuit etc.) as a solicitor; transact or negotiate in the capacity of a solicitor. Now *rare* or *obsolete*. **E17**.
†**4** Urge or plead (one's case etc.); press (a matter). **M16–M18**.
5 Incite or persuade (a person) to commit an illegal or insubordinate act. Freq. foll. by *to*, *to do*. **M16**.
6 **a** Entice or lead (a person) on by a specious representation or argument. **L16**. ▸**b** Try to win the affection or gain the favour of (a woman), esp. with sexual intent. **L16**. ▸**c** Attempt to force one's unwelcome sexual attentions on. *rare*. **M17**. ▸**d** Accost (a person) and offer oneself or another as a prostitute. **E18**.
7 Seek assiduously to obtain (business, a favour, etc.); ask earnestly or persistently for, request, invite. **L16**.
8 Of a thing: call or ask for, demand, (action, attention, etc.). **L16**.
9 **a** Of a thing: affect by some form of physical influence or attraction. Now *rare*. **E17**. ▸**b** Of a thing: tempt, allure; attract by enticement etc. **M17**.
†**10** Endeavour to ease (a weapon etc.) gently from a wound. *poet*. **L17–L18**.
11 *MEDICINE*. Seek to induce or bring on, esp. by gentle means. Now *rare* or *obsolete*. **M18**.

> 🕮 **2** W. ROBERTSON Henry had been soliciting the pope . . in order to obtain a divorce. LD MACAULAY He had been solicited to accept indulgences. **3a** STEELE I am going . . to solicit some matters relating to our commission. **5** E. CHRISTIAN Higgins was indicted . . for having . . solicited a servant to steal. **6a** SHAKES. *1 Hen. VI* Solicit Henry with her wondrous praise. **d** M. SPARK He had served a sentence for soliciting. **7** L. NAMIER He sent out another circular soliciting . . the support of his own friends. **8** JAS. MILL The formation of a new government solicited his attention. **9b** MILTON That Fruit, which with desire . . Solicited her longing eye.

▸ **II** *verb intrans*. **12** Make request or petition; ask earnestly or persistently, beg. Freq. foll. by *for*, *to do*. **E16**.
13 Act or practise as a solicitor. Long *rare* or *obsolete*. **L16**.
†**14** Petition *against* or intercede *for* a person or thing. **E17–M18**.
▸†**B** *noun*. An entreaty, a solicitation. *rare*. **E–M17**.
▪ **solicitee** *noun* (*rare*) a person who is solicited **L19**.

solicitancy /səˈlɪsɪt(ə)nsi/ *noun*. *rare*. **M17**.
[from prec. + **-ANCY**.]
Soliciting.

solicitant /səˈlɪsɪt(ə)nt/ *noun & adjective*. **E19**.
[from **SOLICIT** + **-ANT**[1].]
▸ **A** *noun*. A person who solicits or requests something earnestly. **E19**.
▸ **B** *adjective*. That solicits or requests something earnestly; making petition or request. **L19**.

solicitation /səlɪsɪˈteɪʃ(ə)n/ *noun*. **L15**.
[French *sollicitation* from Latin *sollicitatio(n-)*: see **SOLICIT**, **-ATION**.]
†**1** Management, transaction, or pursuit of business, legal affairs, etc. **L15–E18**.
2 The action of soliciting or seeking to obtain something; entreaty, petition; an instance of this. **E16**. ▸**b** The action of soliciting a person with sexual intent or as a prostitute. **E17**.
3 The exertion or operation of a physically attracting influence or force; an instance of this. **E17**.
4 The action of some attractive, enticing, or alluring influence; an instance of this. **L17**.
†**5** Anxiety; solicitude. **L17–E18**.

> 🕮 **2** M. HOLROYD He bowed to their solicitations to become president of societies. **b** T. OTWAY She cannot be free from the insolent Sollicitations of such Fellows. **3** *North American Review* The solicitations of Jupiter's attractive force . . on a swiftly rushing body. **4** T. BROWN The duty that is exercised in resisting the solicitations of evils.

†**soliciter** *noun*. **LME**.
[from **SOLICIT** *verb* + **-ER**[1].]
1 A person who transacts or manages affairs on behalf of another; *spec.* = **SOLICITOR** 2. **LME–M17**.
2 A person who takes charge *of* or part *in* an affair or activity. **E16–M17**.
3 = **SOLICITOR** 3. **E16–M17**.

solicitor /səˈlɪsɪtə/ *noun*. **LME**.
[Old & mod. French *solliciteur*, from *solliciter*: see **SOLICIT**, **-OR**. Cf. late Latin *sollicitator*.]
†**1** A person who or thing which urges, prompts, or incites someone or something. **LME–E18**.
†**2** A person who conducts, negotiates, or transacts matters on behalf of another or others; a representative, an agent, a deputy; *spec.* an official representing a sovereign's interests. **LME–M18**.
3 A person who or (long *rare*) thing which entreats, requests, or petitions; a person who begs favours; a petitioner, an intercessor. **LME**.
4 A legal practitioner properly qualified to deal with conveyancing, draw up wills etc., advise clients and instruct barristers, and represent clients in the lower courts; *Hist.* a legal practitioner practising in a court of equity. Also (*US*), the chief law officer of a city etc. **M16**.
†**5** A tempter; a source of temptation, an enticement. **L16–M17**.

6 A person who solicits business orders, advertising, etc.; a canvasser. *US*. **L19**.

📖 **2** T. FULLER The Presbyterian party . . applied . . by their secret solicitors to James King of Scotland. **3** S. SMILES A mere crowd of servile solicitors for place. **4 Official Solicitor** (*a*) *Hist*. an officer of the Court of Chancery; (*b*) an officer of the Supreme Court who acts as next friend or guardian *ad litem* for those under a disability with no one else to act for them, or who intervenes to protect the interest of children. **Solicitor-General** (*a*) the Crown law officer (in England ranking next to the Attorney-General, in Scotland to the Lord Advocate), who acts for the State or Crown in cases affecting the public interest and who is usually a member of the House of Commons; (*b*) *US* a law officer whose main function is to assist an Attorney-General.

■ **solici'torial** *adjective* of or pertaining to a solicitor, esp. a legal practitioner **M20**. **solicitorship** *noun* the official post, duty, or calling of a solicitor **L16**.

solicitous /səˈlɪsɪtəs/ *adjective*. **M16**.
[from Latin *sollicitus*: see SOLICIT, -OUS.]
1 Characterized by or showing anxiety, care, or concern. **M16**.
2 Troubled, anxious, or deeply concerned on some specified account. Usu. foll. by *about, for, of* or with subord. clause. **L16**.
†**3** Apprehensive, uneasy, disturbed. **E17–M18**.
4 Particularly careful or attentive; taking the utmost care. **E17**.
5 Anxious, eager, or desirous *to do* something. Formerly also foll. by *in*. **E17**.

📖 **1** *Washington Post* The service has been both quick and solicitous. **2** J. GALSWORTHY They were solicitous of each other's welfare. **3** MILTON There without sign of boast, or sign of joy, Sollicitous and blank he thus began. **4** L. GRANT-ADAMSON She recommended whisky and a warm bed. Maddening how solicitous women were. **5** JAS. MILL Whose alliance Hyder was solicitous to gain.

■ **solicitously** *adverb* **E17**. **solicitousness** *noun* **M17**.

solicitress /səˈlɪsɪtrɪs/ *noun*. Now *rare*. **M17**.
[from SOLICITOR + -ESS¹.]
1 A woman who solicits or petitions for something. **M17**.
†**2** = SOLICITRIX 1. Only in **M17**.

solicitrix /səˈlɪsɪtrɪks/ *noun*. Long *rare*. **E17**.
[mod. Latin, formed as prec. + -TRIX.]
1 A female prostitute; a woman who entices a person with sexual intent. **E17**.
2 = SOLICITRESS 1. **M17**.

solicitude /səˈlɪsɪtjuːd/ *noun*. **LME**.
[Old & mod. French *sollicitude* from Latin *sollicitudo*, formed as SOLICITOUS: see -TUDE.]
1 The state of being solicitous; anxiety; care, concern; solicitous behaviour. **LME**.
2 Anxious or particular care or attention. Formerly also, diligence, industry. Foll. by †*of, about, for, to do*. **LME**.
3 In *pl*. Cares, troubles, anxieties. **L15**.

📖 **1** J. LONDON Now, out of sisterly solicitude, she grew anxious. **2** L. NKOSI Such solicitude for the comforts of a black man is . . unheard of. **3** GEO. ELIOT The solicitudes of feminine fashion appear an occupation for Bedlam.

solicitudinous /səlɪsɪˈtjuːdɪnəs/ *adjective*. *rare*. **L17**.
[from Latin *sollicitudin-, -tudo* SOLICITUDE + -OUS.]
†**1** Filled with anxiety, care, or concern. *rare*. **L17**.
2 Characterized by solicitude or anxiety. **E19**.

solid /ˈsɒlɪd/ *noun*. **LME**.
[After French *solide*, Latin *solidum* use as noun of neut. of *solidus* SOLID *adjective*.]
1 GEOMETRY. A closed surface in three-dimensional space; the volume bounded by such a surface. **LME**.
2 A solid substance or body. **L17**. ▸†**b** PHYSIOLOGY. In *pl*. A solid constituent of the body. **E18–E19**. ▸**c** BUILDING. An unbroken mass of masonry etc. (as that between windows or doors) as distinct from a void or gap; a pier of a bridge. **M18**. ▸**d** PRINTING. A printed area with total ink coverage. Freq. in *pl*. **L19**.
3 a In *pl*. Solid or substantial food, esp. as opp. to *liquids*. **L18**. ▸**b** In *pl*. Self-coloured textiles or garments. *US*. **L19**.
4 A solid rubber tyre. **E20**.

📖 **1** *Platonic solid*: see PLATONIC *adjective* 1. **2 the solid** the unbroken mass or the main part or body of something. **3a** *Mother & Baby* Make the transition from milk to solids . . the most natural thing.

Comb.: **solids-not-fat** in dairy farming, (the proportion of) the components of milk other than water and lipids; **solids pump** a machine for forcing fragmentary solid material, or liquid containing it, through a pipe or chamber against the force of gravity.

solid /ˈsɒlɪd/ *adjective & adverb*. **LME**.
[Old & mod. French *solide* or Latin *solidus* rel. to *salvus* safe, *sollus* whole, entire.]
▶ **A** *adjective*. **I 1** Free from empty spaces or cavities; having the interior completely filled in or up; not hollow. **LME**. ▸**b** PRINTING. (Of printed matter) having no extra spacing between the lines of type; (of a word comprised of two or more elements) printed or written as a single unit rather than with a hyphen or as separate words; (of a printed area) having total ink coverage. **E19**. ▸**c** Of a wall etc.: having no opening or window; unbroken, blank. **M19**. ▸**d** Of a tyre: without a central air space. **L19**.
2 MATH. **a** Of a body or figure: having three dimensions. **LME**. ▸†**b** Of number or measure: = CUBIC *adjective* 1. **LME–E18**. ▸**c** Of, pertaining to, or designating a geometrical solid or solids. **L16**.
3 a Of a material substance: of a dense or massive consistency; firmly coherent; hard and compact. **M16**. ▸**b** Solidified; frozen. **L17**. ▸**c** Of cloud etc.: having the appearance of an unbroken mass; dense, thick, compact. **E19**. ▸**d** ASTRONAUTICS. Using solid fuel. **M20**.
4 Of a state, a condition, etc.: characterized by solidity or compactness. **L16**.
5 Of rain etc.: steady, drenching; continuous. Also, (of a day) characterized by rain of a steady nature. **E17**.
6 Having the property of occupying a certain amount of space. Now *rare*. **L17**.

📖 **1** P. BARRY Mr Fawcett introduced the . . improvement of casting the guns solid and boring them. **3a** A. RADCLIFFE Steps cut in the solid rock.

▶ **II 7** Of a strong, firm, or substantial nature or quality; not slight or flimsy; of strong construction or material; (of food) substantial or fortifying, not liquid. **L16**. ▸**b** BRIDGE. Of a suit: of sufficient strength to be relied on to win every trick in the suit. **E20**.
8 a Combined; consolidated; united. *rare*. **E17**. ▸**b** Unanimous, undivided; united in approval or opposition; (foll. by *for*) united in favour of. Orig. *US*. **M19**. ▸**c** Of a person: steady and dependable as to politics, voting habits, etc.; regular in attendance. Orig. *US*. **L19**. ▸**d** Intimately or closely allied, on friendly terms, *with* another. Orig. *US*. **L19**.
9 Of time, a day, etc.: whole, entire; uninterrupted, continuous. Formerly also (*rare*), consecutive. **M17**.
10 a Entirely of the same substance or material; of the specified material (as gold, silver, etc., or a legitimate alloy) and nothing else. **E18**. ▸**b** Of colour: of a uniform tone or shade throughout; self. **L19**. ▸**c** Of liquor: neat, undiluted. *US*. **L19**.
11 Of a person, a person's constitution, etc.: strong, healthy, sturdy. **M18**.

📖 **7** S. ROSENBERG Built of such solid masonry that it had survived the Moscow fire. *fig*.: J. JORTIN Faith is gone, having no solid support. **8b** *Times* The strike remained solid until November . . when some union members . . returned to work. **9** D. HALLIDAY Someone . . started jogging me up and down . . for ten solid minutes.

▶ **III 12 a** Sound in scholarship; of sober judgement in matters of learning or speculation. **E17**. ▸**b** Fully possessed of the mental faculties; of sound mind, sane. *Scot*. **E17**. ▸**c** Sober-minded; steadily impressive or reliable in performance, actions, etc.; sensible but not brilliant; sedate, staid. **M17**. ▸**d** Financially sound; possessing capital, property, or means. Orig. *US*. **L18**.
13 (Of a quality) well founded or established, of real value or importance; (of learning or knowledge) thorough, substantial. **E17**.
14 Of an argument, discourse, etc.: having a sound or substantial foundation; based on sound principles or indisputable facts. **E17**.
15 Marked by or involving serious study or intention; not frivolous or merely amusing. **M17**.
16 Of judgement etc.: of a sober, sound, or practical character. **M17**.
17 Esp. among the Society of Friends: marked or characterized by a high degree of religious fervour or seriousness. **M18**.
18 With intensive force: thorough, downright, vigorous. Freq. with *good* or *right*. *colloq*. **M19**.
19 Severe, difficult; unfair. *Austral. & NZ colloq*. **E20**.
20 Excellent, first-rate; (of a player) having a good rapport with the band when improvising. *Jazz slang*. **M20**.

📖 **12a** LEIGH HUNT He has . . become a solid student in Butler. **c** *Cornish Guardian* This position was achieved by a solid performance by club members. *Observer* The solid citizens . . have futures as pillars of the great and the good. **13** E. A. FREEMAN He undoubtedly owed William a debt of solid gratitude. **14** *on solid ground*: see GROUND *noun*. **15** W. A. BUTLER Romances debauch the taste for solid reading. **18** R. L. STEVENSON Swear your innocency with a good solid oath.

▶ **B** *adverb*. **1** Solidly, firmly, completely; certainly, surely. Now chiefly *dial. & US colloq*. **M17**.
2 Esp. of voting or political support: in a body, as a whole; unanimously. Freq. in ***go solid*** (foll. by *for* or *against* a person or thing). **L19**.
3 Of time: consecutively, without a break. **M20**.

📖 **1** *American Speech* 'Are you taking Amelia to the Charcoal Dance?' 'I solid am.' **3** L. DEIGHTON He'll be out for eight hours solid. **be booked solid** (of a theatre, cinema, etc.) be fully booked for a (specified) continuous period of time.

Special collocations & comb.: **solid angle** MATH. a vertex of a three-dimensional body; a measure of this as a proportion of a sphere centred on it (see STERADIAN). **solid-bodied** *adjective* = ***solid-body*** below. **solid body** a solid-body guitar. **solid-body** *adjective* designating an electric guitar without a soundbox, the strings being mounted on a solid shaped block forming the guitar body. **solid circuit** ELECTRONICS (now *rare*) = ***integrated circuit*** s.v. INTEGRATED 1b. **solid colour** *noun & adjective* (of) uniform colour covering the whole of an object. **solid diffusion** GEOLOGY migration of atoms within the crystal lattice of a mineral or rock, esp. as a possible mechanism of metasomatism. **solid-drawn** *adjective* (of a tube etc.) pressed or drawn out from a solid bar of metal. **solid fuel** fuel that is solid; *spec*. (*a*) coal, coke, etc., used for domestic heating; (*b*) rocket propellant in which the fuel and oxidizer are combined to form a plastic solid. **solid-fuel**, **solid-fuelled** *adjectives* that uses solid fuel. **solid geology** the geological structure of a region, excluding superficial deposits of clay, sand, gravel, etc. **solid geometry**: in three dimensions. **solid-hoofed**, **-hooved** *adjective* having the hoof whole or undivided; solidungulate. **solid injection** in diesel engines, the use of a pump to spray fuel into the cylinder at high pressure, without the use of compressed air. ***solid newel***: see NEWEL 1. ***solid sender***: see SENDER 3. **solid solution** a solid phase consisting of two or more substances uniformly mixed, esp. with atoms of the minor constituent(s) within the crystal lattice of the major constituent. **solid South** (chiefly *Hist*.) the politically united Southern States of America, esp. as giving unanimous electoral support to the Democratic party. **solid state** the state of matter which retains its boundaries without support. **solid-state** *adjective* (*a*) PHYSICS concerned with the structure and properties of solids, esp. with their explanation in terms of atomic and nuclear physics; (*b*) ELECTRONICS (employing devices) utilizing the electronic properties of solids (as in transistors and other semiconductors, in contrast to the use of thermionic valves). **solid stowing** MINING the process of filling abandoned workings with solid spoil etc., esp. to prevent subsidence. **solid system** ELECTRICAL ENGINEERING a system of cable-laying in which insulated cables are laid in a trough which is then filled with bitumen.

■ **solidly** *adverb* **E17** **solidness** *noun* **E17**

solidago /sɒlɪˈdeɪɡəʊ/ *noun*. Pl. **-os**. **L18**.
[medieval Latin, alt. of late Latin *consolida* CONSOUND.]
= ***goldenrod*** s.v. GOLDEN *adjective*. Now chiefly as mod. Latin genus name.

solidaire /sɒlɪˈdɛː/ *adjective*. **M19**.
[French.]
= SOLIDARY 2.

†**solidare** *noun*. *rare* (Shakes.). Only in **E17**.
[Irreg. from Latin SOLIDUS.]
= SOLIDUS 1.

solidarism /ˈsɒlɪd(ə)rɪz(ə)m/ *noun*. *rare*. **E20**.
[from SOLIDAR(ITY + -ISM.]
A theory of social organization based on solidarity of interests.

solidarist /ˈsɒlɪd(ə)rɪst/ *noun & adjective*. **L19**.
[formed as prec. + -IST.]
▶ **A** *noun*. A believer in or advocate of solidarism. **L19**.
▶ **B** *attrib*. or as *adjective*. Of or pertaining to solidarism or solidarists. **M20**.
■ **solida'ristic** *adjective* **M20**.

solidarity /sɒlɪˈdarɪti/ *noun*. **M19**.
[French *solidarité*, from *solidaire* SOLIDARY *adjective*.]
1 Unity or accordance of feeling, action, etc., esp. among individuals with common interest, sympathies, or aspirations, as the members of a trade union, social class, etc.; mutual support or cohesiveness within a group. Freq. foll. by *among* or *of* (a group), *between* or *with* (others). **M19**. ▸**b** [translating Polish *Solidarność*.] In Poland, an organization of independent trade unions, founded in September 1980. **L20**.
2 Complete or exact coincidence *of* (or *between*) interests. **L19**.
3 LAW. A form of obligation involving joint and several responsibilities or rights. Cf. SOLIDITY 6. **L19**.

solidary /ˈsɒlɪd(ə)ri/ *adjective*. **E19**.
[French *solidaire*, from *solide* SOLID *adjective*: see -ARY¹.]
1 LAW. Of an obligation: joint and several. **E19**.
2 Characterized by or having solidarity or coincidence of interests. **M19**.

solidate /ˈsɒlɪdeɪt/ *noun*. **E17**.
[medieval Latin *solidata (terrae)* a shilling's worth (of land), from Latin SOLIDUS *noun*: see -ATE¹.]
Hist. A piece of land worth a solidus or shilling a year.

solidate /ˈsɒlɪdeɪt/ *verb trans*. Now *rare*. **M17**.
[Latin *solidat-* pa. ppl stem of *solidare* make solid, from *solidus* SOLID *adjective*: see -ATE³.]
1 Make solid or firm; consolidate. **M17**.
†**2** = CONSOLIDATE 1b. **M–L17**.

solidi *noun* pl. of SOLIDUS *noun*.

solidification /səˌlɪdɪfɪˈkeɪʃ(ə)n/ *noun*. **E19**.
[from next + -ATION, or from French *solidification*.]
1 The action or process of solidifying or becoming solid. **E19**.
2 Consolidation, concentration. **L19**.

solidify /sə'lɪdɪfʌɪ/ *verb.* L18.
[French *solidifier*, from *solide* SOLID *adjective*: see -FY.]
1 *verb trans.* Make solid; convert into a solid body; make firm, hard, or compact. L18. ▸**b** Concentrate, consolidate. L19.
2 *verb intrans.* Become solid; change or pass from a liquid or gaseous to a solid state. M19.
■ **solidi'fiable** *adjective* M19. **solidifier** *noun* M19.

solidism /'sɒlɪdɪz(ə)m/ *noun.* M19.
[from SOLID *noun* + -ISM.]
MEDICAL HISTORY. The doctrine or theory which attributed diseases to a disordered state of the body solids. Cf. HUMORISM.
■ **solidist** *noun* M19.

solidity /sə'lɪdɪti/ *noun.* LME.
[Latin *soliditas*, from *solidus* SOLID *adjective*: see -ITY.]
1 The quality or condition of being materially solid; compactness, density, or firmness of texture or structure; substantiality or strength of construction. LME.
2 The quality of being solid or substantial in character; soundness or reliability of learning, judgement, argument, etc.; financial soundness. M16.
3 a GEOMETRY. The volume occupied by a solid body. Now *rare* or *obsolete*. L16. ▸**b** Relative density or mass. Now *rare* or *obsolete*. L17. ▸**c** ENGINEERING. The ratio of the area of the blades of a propeller (counting one side only) to the area of the circle they turn in. E20.
4 A solid thing or body. E17.
5 a The property of occupying a certain amount of space. L17. ▸**b** PSYCHOLOGY. The three-dimensional nature of an object, esp. as perceived optically. M19.
6 LAW. = SOLIDARITY 3. *rare*. E18.

🕮 **1** L. RITCHIE The château . . strikes the spectator by its solidity and magnificence. S. LOVER When they came to take the hay-stack to pieces, the solidity of its centre rather astonished them. **2** E. B. PUSEY Objecting to the decree with much solidity and clearness. J. R. SEELEY Human relations gained a solidity . . which they had never before seemed to have.

solidungulate /sɒlɪ'dʌŋgjʊlət/ *noun & adjective.* M19.
[from Latin *solidus* SOLID *adjective* + *ungulatus* UNGULATE. Cf. SOLIPED.]
ZOOLOGY. ▸**A** *noun.* Any of a group of ungulates which have single undivided hoofs, comprising members of the horse family. M19.
▸**B** *adjective.* Of, pertaining to, or designating the solidungulates. M19.
■ **solidungular** *adjective* (*rare*) = SOLIDUNGULATE *adjective* E19. **solidungulous** *adjective* (**a**) = SOLIDUNGULATE *adjective*; (**b**) designating a solid-hoofed variety of a normally cloven-hoofed ungulate: M17.

solidus /'sɒlɪdəs/ *noun.* Pl. **-di** /-dʌɪ/. ME.
[Latin *solidus* SOLID *adjective* used as noun. In branch I from Latin *solidus (nummus)* a gold coin: cf. SOU.]
▸**I 1** *Hist.* A gold coin of the later Roman Empire, originally worth about 25 denarii. Formerly also, in medieval England, a shilling. ME.
2 An oblique stroke formerly written to separate shillings from pence, and now used in writing fractions, to separate figures and letters, or to denote alternatives or ratios. Cf. VIRGULE 1. L19.
▸**II 3** A line or surface in a binary or ternary phase diagram respectively, or a temperature (corresponding to a point on the line or surface), below which a mixture is entirely solid and above which it consists of solid and liquid in equilibrium. E20.
3 attrib.: ***solidus curve***, ***solidus temperature***, etc.

solifidian /sɒulɪ'fɪdɪən/ *noun & adjective.* L16.
[mod. Latin *solifidius*, from Latin *soli-* combining form of *solus* sole, alone + *fides* faith: see -IAN.]
CHRISTIAN THEOLOGY. ▸**A** *noun.* A person who holds that faith alone, without works, is sufficient for justification. L16.
▸**B** *adjective.* Of, pertaining to, or accepting the doctrine of justification by faith alone. E17.
■ **solifidianism** *noun* the doctrine of justification by faith alone E19.

soliflual /sə'lɪfl(j)ʊəl/ *noun & adjective.* M20.
[from SOLIFLU(CTION + -AL[1].]
PHYSICAL GEOGRAPHY. ▸**A** *noun.* Material that has moved by solifluction. *rare*. M20.
▸**B** *adjective.* Pertaining to or produced by solifluction, solifluctional. M20.

solifluction /sɒlɪ'flʌkʃ(ə)n/ *noun.* Also **-fluxion**. E20.
[from Latin *solum* ground, earth + -I- + *fluct-* pa. ppl stem of *fluere* flow: see -ION.]
PHYSICAL GEOGRAPHY. The gradual movement of waterlogged soil etc. down a slope, esp. where the subsoil is frozen and acts as a barrier to the percolation of water. Cf. SLUDGING 3.
■ **solifluctional** *adjective* pertaining to or produced by solifluction E20. **solifluctеd** *adjective* that has moved by solifluction M20.

soliform /'sɒulɪfɔːm/ *adjective.* L17.
[from Latin *sol* or SOL *noun*[2] + -I- + -FORM.]
Resembling the sun, sunlike.

solifuge /'sɒlɪfjuːdʒ/ *noun.* M17.
[Latin *solifuga* (also as mod. Latin genus name), var. of *sol(i)puga*: cf. SOLPUGA.]
†**1** = SOLPUGA 1. Only in M17.
2 ZOOLOGY. = next. E20.

solifugid /sɒlɪ'fjuːdʒɪd/ *noun.* M20.
[from prec. + -ID[3].]
ZOOLOGY. Any of various fast-moving desert arachnids of the order Solifugae (or Solpugida), which have massive paired chelicerae. Also called ***solpugid***, ***camel-spider***, ***sun-spider***, ***wind-scorpion***.

soligenous /sɒ'lɪdʒɪnəs/ *adjective.* M20.
[Latin *solum* ground + -I- + -GENOUS.]
ECOLOGY. Of a bog, peat, etc.: dependent on groundwater for its formation. Cf. OMBROGENOUS, TOPOGENOUS.

Solignum /sə'lɪgnəm/ *noun.* Also **s-**. E20.
[from unkn. 1st elem. + Latin *lignum* wood.]
(Proprietary name for) a preparation for preserving timber.

soliloquacity /səlɪlə'kwasɪti/ *noun.* L19.
[Blend of SOLILOQUY and LOQUACITY.]
Soliloquizing at great length.

soliloquia *noun* pl. of SOLILOQUIUM.

soliloquise *verb* var. of SOLILOQUIZE.

soliloquium /sɒlɪ'ləʊkwɪəm/ *noun.* Long *rare*. Pl. ***-quia*** /-kwɪə/. E17.
[Late Latin: see SOLILOQUY.]
A soliloquy, *esp.* a written one.

soliloquize /sə'lɪləkwʌɪz/ *verb.* Also **-ise**. M18.
[from next: see -IZE.]
1 *verb intrans.* Engage in soliloquy; talk to oneself. M18.
2 *verb trans.* Utter in soliloquy. E19.

🕮 **2** E. BOWEN 'Who's in here, I wonder?' she soliloquized.

■ **soliloquist** *noun* a person who soliloquizes, a writer of soliloquies E19. **soliloquizer** *noun* E19.

soliloquy /sə'lɪləkwi/ *noun.* ME.
[Late Latin *soliloquium*, from Latin *soli-*, *solus* sole, alone + *loqui* speak: see -Y[4].]
1 (A literary representation or imitation of) an instance of talking to oneself or regardless of any audience; *spec.* a part of a play involving this. ME.
2 The action of soliloquizing; monologue. M17.

🕮 **1** M. PRIOR The . . poem is a soliloquy: Solomon . . speaks. **2** W. F. BUCKLEY He did . . his thinking by soliloquy, preferably in the presence of one other person.

¶ Rare before E19.

soli-lunar /səʊlɪ'luːnə/ *adjective.* L17.
[Latin *soli-*, *sol* sun + LUNAR.]
Of or pertaining to both sun and moon. Cf. SOLUNAR.

solion /'sɒlɪən/ *noun.* M20.
[from SOL(UTION + ION.]
ELECTRONICS (now *Hist.*). An electrochemical device consisting of two or more electrodes sealed in an electrolyte in which a reversible electrochemical reaction is monitored, used in amplifiers, integrators, and pressure transducers.

soliped /'sɒlɪpɛd/ *noun & adjective.* Now *rare*. Also **-pede** /-piːd/. M17.
[mod. Latin *soliped-*, *-pes* from Latin *solidipes*, from *solidus* SOLID *adjective* + *-ped-*, *pes* foot.]
= SOLIDUNGULATE.

solipsism /'sɒlɪpsɪz(ə)m/ *noun.* L19.
[from Latin *solus* sole, alone + *ipse* self: see -ISM.]
In philosophy, the view or theory that only the self really exists or can be known. Now also, isolation, self-centredness, selfishness.
■ **solip'sismal** *adjective* (*rare*) L19.

solipsist /'sɒlɪpsɪst/ *noun & adjective.* L19.
[formed as prec.: see -IST.]
▸**A** *noun.* An adherent of solipsism; a person characterized by solipsism. L19.

🕮 A. CROSS He was a solitary solipsist: he thought he was the only person . . who mattered.

▸**B** *adjective.* Favouring or characterized by solipsism. E20.
■ **solip'sistic** *adjective* = SOLIPSIST *adjective* L19. **solip'sistically** *adverb* L19.

solipugid *noun* var. of SOLPUGID.

solitaire /'sɒlɪtɛː, sɒlɪ'tɛː/ *noun.* E18.
[Old & mod. French, from Latin *solitarius*: see SOLITARY *adjective*.]
1 A person who lives in seclusion or solitude; a recluse. E18.
2 (A ring with) a diamond or other gem set by itself. E18.
3 A game for one player; *spec.* (**a**) (chiefly *N. Amer.*) = PATIENCE *noun* 4; (**b**) a board game in which marbles or pegs have to be successively captured as in draughts until only one is left. M18.
4 *Hist.* A man's loose necktie of black silk or broad ribbon, worn in the 18th cent. M18.
5 ORNITHOLOGY. **a** Either of two large flightless birds related to the dodo and formerly found in the Mascarene Islands, *Pezophaps solitaria* (in full ***Rodriguez solitaire***) and *Ornithaptera solitaria* (more fully ***Réunion solitaire***), exterminated in the 18th and 17th cents. respectively. L18. ▸**b** Any of various mainly tropical New World thrushes of the genera *Myadestes* and *Entomodestes*, some of which are noted for their beautiful songs. M19.

solitary /'sɒlɪt(ə)ri/ *adjective & noun.* ME.
[Latin *solitarius* from *solus* sole, alone: see -ARY[1].]
▸**A** *adjective.* **1** Of a person or animal: unaccompanied; deprived of or avoiding the society of others; keeping apart or aloof; living alone. ME. ▸**b** Sole, single; unsupported, unparalleled. M17.
2 Of a place: remote, unfrequented, secluded, lonely. ME.
3 Of an action, state, etc.: characterized by the absence of all companionship or society. LME.
4 ZOOLOGY. (Of a bird etc.) that lives alone or in pairs only; (of an insect) not cooperating to form social colonies. M18.
5 BOTANY. Of a flower or other part of a plant: borne singly. L18.

🕮 **1** A. N. WILSON He had felt alienated, cut off, solitary. I. MURDOCH Gildas was said to be a solitary man, but he depended . . upon his few close friends. **b** S. JOHNSON The result, not of solitary conjecture but of . . experience. E. BLAIR Not one solitary cottage had survived. **2** GOLDSMITH They keep chiefly in the most solitary and inaccessible places.

Special collocations: **solitary confinement** isolation of a prisoner in a separate cell etc., esp. as a punishment. **solitary dodo** = SOLITAIRE 5a. **solitary sandpiper** an American sandpiper, *Tringa solitaria*, which breeds in Canada. **solitary thrush** the blue rock thrush, *Monticola solitarius*, occurring in southern Europe and throughout much of Asia. **solitary vireo** a vireo, *Vireo solitarius*, found in various forms in North and Central America. **solitary wave** a travelling non-dissipative wave which is neither preceded nor followed by another such disturbance.
▸**B** *noun.* **1** A person who retires into or lives in solitude for religious reasons; a hermit, an anchorite. Now also, any person who avoids or is deprived of the society of others. LME.
2 *ellipt.* Solitary confinement. *colloq.* M19.

🕮 **1** E. A. FREEMAN Wythmann . . , after a pilgrimage to Jerusalem, died a solitary. I. MURDOCH Tallis is . . better off on his own . . . He's a natural solitary. **2** D. CAUTE I was kept in solitary . . not allowed to communicate with any other prisoner.

■ **solitarily** *adverb* LME. **solitariness** *noun* LME.

soliton /'sɒlɪtɒn/ *noun.* M20.
[from SOLIT(ARY *noun* + -ON.]
PHYSICS. A solitary wave; a quantum or quasiparticle propagated in the manner of a solitary wave.

solitude /'sɒlɪtjuːd/ *noun.* ME.
[Old & mod. French, or Latin *solitudo*, *solitudin-*, from *solus* sole, alone: see -TUDE.]
1 The state of being or living alone, solitariness. Later also, absence of life or disturbance. ME.
2 A lonely, unfrequented, or uninhabited place. LME.
3 A complete absence or lack. *rare*. E17.

🕮 **1** SIR W. SCOTT The solitude of the early morning. H. JAMES The agreeable sense of solitude, of having the house to herself. J. BARNES They were alone on the mountain and found their solitude exalting. **3** BACON Princes find a solitude, in regard of able men.

■ **ˌsolitudi'narian** *noun* a person who seeks solitude, a recluse L17. **soli'tudinous** *adjective* characterized by solitude E19.

solity /'səʊlɪti/ *noun.* *rare*. L19.
[Latin *solitas*, from *solus* sole, alone: see -ITY.]
Soleness.

solivagant /sə'lɪvəg(ə)nt/ *noun & adjective.* Now *literary*. E17.
[from Latin *solivagus*, from *solus* sole, alone + *vagari* wander: see -ANT[1].]
▸**A** *noun.* A person who wanders about alone. E17.
▸**B** *adjective.* (Characterized by) wandering about alone. M17.

sollar /'sɒlə/ *noun & verb.* In sense A.1 also **solar**. ME.
[Anglo-Norman *soler* or Old French *solier*, from Latin *solarium* sundial, gallery, terrace, from *sol* sun.]
▸**A** *noun.* **1** An upper room, a garret; *spec.* (**a**) a loft open to the sun; (**b**) a loft in the steeple or belfry of a church. Now *arch. & dial.* exc. *Hist.* ME.
2 MINING. A raised floor or platform in a mine, *esp.* one supporting a ladder. *dial.* L18.
▸**B** *verb trans.* Provide with a sollar or flooring. Long *rare* or *obsolete*. M16.

solleret /'sɒlərɛt/ *noun.* E19.
[Old French *sol(l)eret* dim. of *sol(l)er* (mod. *soulier* shoe), from medieval Latin *subtelaris* (sc. *calceus* shoe), from late Latin *subtel* arch of the sole: see -ET[1].]

Hist. A shoe made of steel plates or scales, forming part of a knight's armour in the 14th and 15th cents.

†sollevation *noun.* E17–M18.
[Italian *sollevazione*, from *sollevare* from Latin *sublevare* raise, formed as SUB- + *levare* lift.]
An insurrection.

sollicker /ˈsɒlɪkə/ *noun. Austral. slang.* L19.
[Origin unkn.]
Something very big of its kind.

†sol-lunar *adjective* var. of SOLUNAR.

solmization /sɒlmɪˈzeɪʃ(ə)n/ *noun.* Also **-isation.** M18.
[French *solmisation*, from *solmiser* solmizate, from *sol* SOL *noun*[1] + *mi* MI *noun*: see -IZE, -ATION.]
MUSIC. The action or practice of sol-faing, the notation of music for singers using these syllables.
■ **ˈsolmizate** *verb trans. & intrans.* express by or employ solmization, sol-fa L19.

solo /ˈsəʊləʊ/ *noun*[1], *adverb, adjective, & verb.* L17.
[Italian, from Latin *solus* sole, alone.]
▶ **A** *noun.* Pl. **solos**, (in sense 1 also) **soli** /ˈsəʊli/.
1 *MUSIC.* A vocal or instrumental piece or passage (to be) performed by one person with or without accompaniment. L17. ▸**b** Performance by one singer or player. L18.
2 A dance by one person. L18.
3 *CARDS.* Any of various games, esp. solo whist, in which each player plays independently rather than in partnership. Also, a bid by a player to take a certain number of tricks, esp. five out of the thirteen in solo whist, or to play solely with the hand dealt him or her. E19.
4 A solo flight. E20.
5 A bicycle or motorcycle designed for one rider. E20.

> 🕮 **1** *Jazz Journal International* Contributing to an outstanding trombone section, and taking some solos. *transf.*: F. F. MOORE There came . . a loud peal of laughter—not a solo, but a duet.

▶ **B** *adverb & adjective.* **1** *adverb & pred. adjective.* Alone; without a companion or partner, unaccompanied. E18.
2 *attrib. adjective.* **a** Orig., (of a vehicle) accommodating or seating one person. Now also *gen.*, designed or intended for one person. L18. ▸**b** Acting or performing alone or unassisted; *spec.* (*MUSIC*) playing or taking the solo part. M19. ▸**c** Made, carried out, or performed alone or unassisted. E20.

> 🕮 **1** *Times* Lindbergh took 33 hr. 30 min . . . to fly solo . . from New York to Paris. G. LEES He . . plays the tune, twice, solo. **2a** *Motor Cycle News* A . . Russian solo motor cycle . . the two-stroke Moskva. *Games Machine: Lone Wolf* became the world's biggest selling solo games book. **b** A. MACRAE It can't be easy to be a solo parent. **c** *Glasgow Herald* The longest solo flight . . achieved by an airman.

Special collocations & comb.: **solo stop** an organ-stop of special quality or position for the performance of solos; **solo whist** *CARDS* a form of whist in which each of the four players may bid independently to win or lose a certain number out of the thirteen possible tricks.
▶ **C** *verb.* **I** *verb trans.* **1** Perform (a piece of music) as a solo. *rare.* M19.
2 Climb (a mountain etc.) without a partner. M20.
▶ **II** *verb intrans.* **3** Perform a solo; *spec.* make one's first solo flight. L19.

> 🕮 **3** *New Yorker* I love flying and . . can hardly wait to solo. *Rhythm* The . . group would be keeping one rhythm while one person would . . solo over it.

Solo /ˈsəʊləʊ/ *noun*[2]. M20.
[A river in Java.]
Used *attrib.* with ref. to a fossil hominid known from skull fragments found near Ngandong in Java in 1931–3, now considered to be either a late form of *Homo erectus* or an early form of archaic *H. sapiens*.

Solochrome /ˈsəʊləkrəʊm/ *noun.* E20.
[Invented word, from unkn. 1st elem. + Greek *khrōma* colour.]
(Proprietary name for) a range of synthetic mordant dyes used chiefly in colour tests for various metals, esp. aluminium.
attrib.: ***Solochrome cyanin***, ***Solochrome red***, ***Solochrome violet***.

solod /ˈsɒlɒt/ *noun.* Also **soloth** /ˈsɒləθ/. Pl. **solodi** /ˈsɒlədi/, **soloti** /ˈsɒləti/, **solods** /ˈsɒləts/. E20.
[Russian *solod'* from *sol'* salt.]
SOIL SCIENCE. A type of soil derived from a solonetz by leaching of saline or alkaline constituents, having a pale leached subsurface horizon and occurring in arid regions.
■ **solodic** /səˈlɒdɪk/ *adjective* being, resembling, or characteristic of a solod M20. **solodiˈzation**, **solot-** *noun* the formation of a solod by the leaching of salts from a solonetz M20. **solodize**, **solot-** *verb intrans.* change into a solod M20. **solodized**, **solot-** *ppl adjective* altered by solodization E20.

soloist /ˈsəʊləʊɪst/ *noun.* M19.
[from SOLO *noun*[1] + -IST.]
A performer of a solo, esp. in music.
■ **soloˈistic** *adjective* of, pertaining to, or of the nature of a soloist or solo part M20.

Solomon /ˈsɒləmən/ *noun.* Orig. **†Sal-.** M16.
[A king of Israel *c* 970–930 BC, famed for his wisdom and justice.]
A profoundly wise person, a sage. Also (*iron.*), a would-be clever person, a know-all.
Comb.: **Solomon's seal** [perh. with ref. to the plant's reputed ability to heal wounds] (*a*) a woodland plant, *Polygonatum multiflorum*, of the lily family, which bears drooping tubular white flowers in the axils of broad sessile leaves; (with specifying word) any of several other plants of this genus; (*b*) ***false Solomon's seal***, any smilacina with similar leaves but flowers in terminal clusters.

Solomon-gundy /ˌsɒləmənˈɡʌndɪ/ *noun.* M18.
[Alt.]
= SALMAGUNDI.

Solomonic /sɒləˈmɒnɪk/ *adjective.* Orig. **†-ick.** E18.
[formed as SOLOMON + -IC.]
1 Ascribed or pertaining to or originating with King Solomon. E18.
2 Characteristic of Solomon; profoundly wise. M19.
■ Also **Solomonian** /sɒləˈməʊnɪən/ *adjective* M19.

Solomon Islander /ˈsɒləmən ˈʌɪləndə/ *noun phr.* M19.
[from *Solomon Islands* (see below) + -ER[1].]
A native or inhabitant of the Solomon Islands in the SW Pacific.

Solon /ˈsəʊlɒn/ *noun.* Also ***s-.** E17.
[An early Athenian legislator and sage.]
A sage, a wise statesman. Also (*US*), a legislator, *esp.* a congressman.

solonchak /ˈsɒləntʃak/ *noun.* E20.
[Russian = salt-marsh, salt lake, from *sol'* salt.]
SOIL SCIENCE. A type of salty alkaline soil that has little or no structure, is typically pale in colour, and occurs in poorly drained arid regions.

solonetz /ˈsɒlənɛts/ *noun.* E20.
[Russian *solonets* salt-marsh, salt lake, from *sol'* salt.]
SOIL SCIENCE. A type of alkaline soil that is rich in carbonates, consists typically of a hard dark columnar subsoil overlain by a thin friable surface layer, and occurs in better-drained areas than solonchaks.
■ **soloˈnetzic** *adjective* being, resembling, or characteristic of a solonetz M20.

Solonian /səˈləʊnɪən/ *adjective.* M19.
[formed as SOLON + -IAN.]
Of, pertaining to, or connected with Solon.
■ Also **Solonic** *adjective* L18.

solonization /ˌsɒlənʌɪˈzeɪʃ(ə)n/ *noun.* Also **-isation.** M20.
[from SOLON(ETZ + -IZATION.]
SOIL SCIENCE. The formation of a solonetzic soil by the leaching of salts from a solonchak.
■ **ˈsolonized** *adjective* altered by this process M20.

soloth *noun* var. of SOLOD.

soloti *noun pl.* see SOLOD.

solpuga /sɒlˈpjuːɡə/ *noun.* Also **S-.** Pl. **-gae** /-ɡiː/. E17.
[Latin *sol(i)puga*, *solifuga*. Cf. SOLIFUGE.]
†1 A venomous ant or spider. E17–E18.
2 *ZOOLOGY.* A solifugid. Now chiefly as mod. Latin genus name. E19.

solpugid /sɒlˈpjuːdʒɪd/ *noun.* Also **soli-** /sɒlɪ-/. M19.
[mod. Latin *Solpugidae* family name or *Solpugida* former order name, from *Solpuga* genus name: see prec., -ID[3].]
ZOOLOGY. = SOLIFUGID.

solstice /ˈsɒlstɪs/ *noun.* ME.
[Old & mod. French from Latin *solstitium*, from *sol* sun + *stit-* pa. ppl stem of *sistere* stand still.]
1 Either of the two occasions in the year when the sun reaches its highest or lowest point in the sky at noon, and is directly overhead at noon along one or other of the tropics, the day then being of maximum or minimum length according to hemisphere. ME. ▸**b** A solstitial point. Now *rare.* E17. ▸**c** (The heat of) the summer solstice. Now *rare.* M17.
2 *fig.* A turning-point, a crisis; a stopping-point, a limit. E17.

> 🕮 **1 summer solstice** the solstice occurring in midsummer at the time of the longest day (about 21 June in the northern hemisphere, 22 December in the southern); *ASTRONOMY* the solstice occurring in June. **winter solstice** the solstice occurring in midwinter at the time of the shortest day (about 22 December in the northern hemisphere, 21 June in the southern); *ASTRONOMY* the solstice occurring in December. **2** DONNE A Christian hath no solstice . . where he may . . go no further.

solstitia *noun pl.* see SOLSTITIUM.

solstitial /sɒlˈstɪʃ(ə)l/ *adjective & noun.* Also **-icial.** LME.
[Old & mod. French *solsticial*, †*-tial*, or Latin *solstitialis*, from *solstitium*: see prec., -AL[1].]
▶ **A** *adjective.* **1** Of or pertaining to (the time of) a solstice or the solstices. LME.
2 Of heat, sunlight, etc.: characteristic of the summer solstice. M17.
3 a Of a plant: coming up at the summer solstice; growing or fading rapidly. M17. ▸**b** Of insects etc.: appearing about the time of the summer solstice. E19.
4 Pertaining to or used for the observation of the solstices. M19.
1 solstitial point *ASTRONOMY & ASTROLOGY* either of the two points on the ecliptic midway between the two equinoxes, which the sun reaches at the solstice. **4** ***solstitial armilla***: see ARMILLA 1.
▶**†B** *noun.* = SOLSTICE 1. *rare.* LME–E17.
■ **solstitially** *adverb* (*rare*) towards the solstices M17.

solstitium /sɒlˈstɪʃ(ɪ)əm/ *noun.* Now *rare* or *obsolete.* Pl. **-tia** /-ʃ(ɪ)ə/, **-iums.** E16.
[Latin: see SOLSTICE.]
= SOLSTICE 1.

solubility /sɒljʊˈbɪlɪti/ *noun.* M17.
[from SOLUBLE *adjective* + -ITY: see -ILITY.]
The quality or property of being soluble; the degree to which a substance is soluble in a solvent.
Comb.: **solubility curve** *CHEMISTRY* a curve showing how the solubility of a substance varies with temperature; **solubility product** *CHEMISTRY* the product of the concentrations (strictly, the activities) of each of the component ions present in a saturated solution of a sparingly soluble salt.

solubilize /ˈsɒljʊbɪlʌɪz/ *verb trans.* Also **-ise.** E20.
[from SOLUBIL(ITY + -IZE, after *stability*, *stabilize*. Cf. earlier INSOLUBILIZE.]
Increase the solubility of; convert into a soluble form.
■ **solubiˈlizable** *adjective* able to be solubilized L20. **ˌsolubiliˈzation** *noun* M20. **solubilizer** *noun* a solubilizing agent M20.

soluble /ˈsɒljʊb(ə)l/ *adjective & noun.* LME.
[Old & mod. French from late Latin *solubilis*, from Latin *solvere* SOLVE: see -UBLE.]
▶ **A** *adjective.* **1** *MEDICINE.* **a** Of the bowels etc.: free from constipation. Now *rare* or *obsolete.* LME. ▸**†b** Laxative. E16–E18.
2 Able or intended to be dissolved, esp. in water. Formerly also, able to be melted. LME.
3 Able to be untied or loosed. *rare.* E17.
4 Able to be solved or explained. E18. ▸**b** *MATH.* = SOLVABLE 2b. E20.
5 Able to be resolved, reducible. E19.

> 🕮 **2** E. AMBLER I gave her some soluble aspirin and left. **soluble blue** any of various water-soluble dyes that are di- and trisulphonic acid derivatives of aniline blue, now used chiefly in papers and inks. **soluble RNA** = ***transfer RNA*** s.v. TRANSFER *noun.* **5** O. W. HOLMES Love is sparingly soluble in the words of men.

▶ **B** *noun.* A soluble constituent, esp. of a foodstuff. M20.

solum /ˈsəʊləm/ *noun.* Pl. (in sense 2) **sola** /ˈsəʊlə/, **solums.** M18.
[Latin.]
1 Soil, ground. Chiefly *SCOTS LAW.* M18.
2 *SOIL SCIENCE.* The upper part of a soil profile, in which the soil-forming processes predominantly occur; *spec.* the A and B horizons. E20.

solunar /sɒˈluːnə/ *adjective.* Also **†sol-lunar.** L18.
[from SOL *noun*[2] + LUNAR *adjective*.]
Due to or pertaining to the combined influence, esp. the conjunction, of the sun and moon. Cf. SOLI-LUNAR.

solus /ˈsəʊləs/ *adverb & adjective.* L16.
[Latin: cf. SOLA *adverb & adjective*[2].]
1 *adverb & pred. adjective.* Of a male (occas. a female) person: alone, by oneself. Freq. as a stage direction. L16.
2 *adjective.* **a** Of an advertisement: standing alone on a page etc.; dealing with one item only. Also, pertaining to such an advertisement. M20. ▸**b** *COMMERCE.* Of a petrol station etc.: selling the products of one company only. Also, of or pertaining to such an arrangement. M20.

solute /ˈsɒljuːt, sɒˈljuːt/ *noun.* E17.
[from (the same root as) next.]
†1 A sum to be received in payment. Only in E17.
2 The minor component in a solution, which is dissolved in the solvent. L19.

solute /sɒˈljuːt/ *adjective.* LME.
[Latin *solutus* pa. pple of *solvere* SOLVE.]
†1 Of loose open texture or composition. LME–M17.
†2 Of discourse: free, loose, discursive. Only in 17.
3 *BOTANY.* Not adhering; separate. *rare.* M18.
4 Dissolved. Now *rare.* L19.

solution /səˈluːʃ(ə)n/ *noun, adjective, & verb.* LME.
[Old & mod. French from Latin *solutio(n-)*, from *solut-* pa. ppl stem of *solvere* SOLVE: see -ION.]
▶ **A** *noun.* **I** Bringing to an end.
1 The action or an act of solving a problem, difficulty, etc.; a means or method of doing this; the condition of being solved. Also, an explanation, an answer, a decision; *spec.* in *MATH.*, the value of an unknown or variable that satisfies an equation or set of equations. LME.
†2 The action of paying a bill or amount. Also, a payment. L15–E18.
†3 The action of releasing a person or thing; deliverance, release. E16–M17.
4 The action or an instance of bringing something to an end. M17.

> 1 A. De Morgan The solution of complicated questions. Saki The problem which . . hard thinking . . had brought no nearer to solution. J. Thurber My solutions to marital problems may seem a little untidy. J. Barnes He shrugged as if the dilemma were insoluble, then found a solution.

▸ **II** The action of dissolving something; the state of being dissolved.

5 The action of dissolving or uniformly dispersing a solid, liquid, or gas in a liquid, or a solid in a solid; the fact of becoming dissolved. LME.

6 A homogeneous liquid, semi-liquid, or solid mixture produced by this process. Also, a liquid colloidal dispersion. L16. ▸**b** = ***rubber solution*** s.v. RUBBER *noun*[1]. L19.

7 A dissolved state or condition. Freq. in ***in solution***. E19.

Phrases & comb.: ***conjugate solution***: see CONJUGATE *adjective*. ***final solution***: see FINAL *adjective*. ***Lugol's solution***. ***Ringer solution***, ***Ringer's solution***: see RINGER *noun*[3]. ***saline solution***: see SALINE *adjective* 4. ***solid solution***: see SOLID *adjective & adverb*. **solution heat treatment** METALLURGY = ***solution treatment*** below. ***solution of continuity***: see CONTINUITY 1. **solution set** MATH. the set of all the solutions of an equation or condition. **solution-treat** *verb trans.* (METALLURGY) subject (an alloy) to solution treatment. **solution treatment** METALLURGY a process in which an alloy is made susceptible to age-hardening by heating it to make a hardening constituent enter into solid solution, followed by quenching.

▸ **B** *attrib.* or as *adjective*. PHYSICAL GEOGRAPHY. Designating features and phenomena resulting from the solvent action of water, esp. in karst environments. L19.

▸ **C** *verb trans.* Treat with or secure by a solution. *rare*. L19.

■ **solutional** *adjective* pertaining to a solution; *spec.* in PHYSICAL GEOGRAPHY, pertaining to solution phenomena: E20. **solutionist** *noun* a person who solves problems or puzzles; *spec.* an expert solver of crossword puzzles: L19. **solutionized** *ppl adjective* (METALLURGY) that has been subjected to solution treatment L20. **solutionizing** *verbal noun* the process of forming a solution; *spec.* in METALLURGY = ***solution treatment*** above: M20.

†solutive *adjective & noun*. LME.
[medieval Latin *solutivus*, from Latin *solutio* SOLUTION: see -IVE.]
▸ **A** *adjective*. Laxative, relaxing. LME–M18.
▸ **B** *noun*. **1** A laxative. Only in 17.
2 = SOLVENT *noun* 1. Only in E18.

solutizer /'sɒljʊtʌɪzə/ *noun*. Also **-iser**. M20.
[from Latin *solut-* pa. ppl stem of *solvere* SOLVE + -IZE + -ER[1].]
= SOLUBILIZER.

Solutrean /sə'luːtrɪən/ *adjective & noun*. Also **-trian**. L19.
[French *solutréen*, from *Solutré* (see below).]
ARCHAEOLOGY. ▸**A** *adjective*. Designating or pertaining to a type of flint implement found in a cave at Solutré in eastern France, or the period or culture in which such implements were produced, between the Aurignacian and the Magdalenian. L19.
▸ **B** *noun*. (A person of) the Solutrean period or culture. M20.

solvability /sɒlvə'bɪlɪti/ *noun*. E18.
[from next: see -ITY.]
1 Solvency. E18.
2 The degree to which a problem etc. is solvable; solubility. M19.

solvable /'sɒlvəb(ə)l/ *adjective*. M17.
[from SOLVE + -ABLE, in sense 1 after French.]
†**1** Able to pay one's debts etc.; solvent. M17–L18.
2 Of a problem etc.: able to be solved. L17. ▸**b** MATH. Of a group: that may be regarded as the last of a finite series of groups of which the first is trivial, each being a normal subgroup of the next and each of the quotients being abelian. L19.

solvate /'sɒlveɪt/ *noun*. E20.
[Irreg. from SOLVE + -ATE[2].]
CHEMISTRY. A more or less loosely bonded complex formed between a solvent and a solute or colloidal dispersion.

solvate /sɒl'veɪt/ *verb trans*. E20.
[from SOLVE + -ATE[3].]
CHEMISTRY. Form a solvate with (a solute). Chiefly as ***solvated*** *ppl adjective*.
■ **solvation** *noun* the process or state of being solvated E20.

Solvay /'sɒlveɪ/ *noun*. L19.
[Ernest *Solvay* (1838–1922), Belgian chemist.]
CHEMISTRY. Used *attrib.* with ref. to a process for manufacturing sodium carbonate, in which carbon dioxide is passed through ammonia-saturated brine and the resulting bicarbonate is heated.

solve /sɒlv/ *verb trans*. LME.
[Latin *solvere* unfasten, free, pay.]
†**1** Loosen; break. Only in LME.
2 Dissolve; melt. LME.
†**3** Unbind, untie. LME–M17.
4 Find an answer to or a means of removing or dealing with (a problem, difficulty, etc.); explain, clear up, resolve; *spec.* (MATH.) find the solution to (an equation etc.). M16. ▸†**b** Save (appearances). E17–M18.
5 Pay or discharge (money, a debt, etc.). M16.
6 Put an end to (conflict etc.). Now *rare*. M17.

> 4 H. P. Gurney Anyone who can solve a spherical triangle will have no difficulty. *Scientific American* Nilsson solved the paradox with . . a spectrophotometer. P. D. James Problems could be solved, evils overcome.

■ †**solvend** *noun* a substance to be dissolved M18–M19. **solver** *noun* a person who solves a problem, difficulty, etc. E18.

solvency /'sɒlv(ə)nsi/ *noun*. E18.
[from next + -ENCY.]
The state of being financially solvent.

solvent /'sɒlv(ə)nt/ *adjective & noun*. M17.
[Latin *solvent-* pres. ppl stem of *solvere*: see SOLVE, -ENT.]
▸ **A** *adjective*. **1** Able to pay one's debts or meet one's liabilities; financially sound. M17.
2 Capable of dissolving something; causing solution. L17.

> 1 A. C. Amor Hunt had pawned everything . . in a desperate attempt to remain solvent.

▸ **B** *noun*. **1** A substance having the power of dissolving other substances; *esp.* any of various volatile organic liquids used commercially in paints, glues, etc. Also, the major component in a solution, in which the solute is dissolved. L17.
2 An explanation, a solution. M19.

Comb.: **solvent abuse** a form of drug abuse in which volatile organic solvents are inhaled; **solvent extract** *verb & noun* (**a**) *verb trans.* purify by means of solvent extraction; (**b**) *noun* a fraction extracted from a mixture by this process; a spell of solvent extraction; **solvent extraction** the partial removal of a substance from a solution or mixture by utilizing its greater solubility in another liquid, sometimes via a permeable membrane.
¶ Earlier in INSOLVENT.
■ **solventless** *adjective* without a chemical solvent M20.

solvi *noun* pl. of SOLVUS.

solvolysis /sɒl'vɒlɪsɪs/ *noun*. Pl. **-lyses** /-lɪsiːz/. E20.
[formed as SOLVENT *noun* + -O- + -LYSIS.]
CHEMISTRY. The decomposition or dissociation of a solute brought about by the action of the solvent.
■ **'solvolyse** *verb* (**a**) *verb trans.* bring about the solvolysis of (a solute); (**b**) *verb intrans.* undergo solvolysis: E20. **solvo'lytic** *adjective* pertaining to or of the nature of solvolysis E20. **solvo'lytically** *adverb* L20.

solvus /'sɒlvəs/ *noun*. Pl. **solvi** /'sɒlvi/. M20.
[mod. Latin from Latin *solvere* dissolve, after LIQUIDUS, SOLIDUS.]
A line or surface in a phase diagram delimiting the region of stability of a solid solution.

solyanka /sə'ljankə/ *noun*. M20.
[Russian.]
A soup made of vegetables and meat or fish.

sol y sombra /sol i 'sombra/ *noun*. M20.
[Spanish, lit. 'sun and shade'.]
A drink of brandy mixed with anisette or gin.

som /səʊm/ *noun*. Pl. same. L20.
[Kirghiz, = crude iron casting, rouble.]
The basic monetary unit of Kyrgyzstan, equal to 100 tiyin.

Som. *abbreviation*.
Somerset.

soma /'səʊmə/ *noun*[1]. Orig. †**som**. L18.
[Sanskrit. Cf. HOM.]
1 More fully ***soma plant***. A plant of uncertain identity, probably an ephedra, whose juice was used in India etc. to prepare an intoxicating drink. L18.
2 The drink itself, used in Vedic ritual. L18.
3 [After a drug in Aldous Huxley's novel *Brave New World* (1932).] A narcotic drug which produces euphoria and hallucination, distributed by the State in order to promote social harmony. M20.

soma /'səʊmə/ *noun*[2]. L19.
[Greek *sōma* body.]
1 The body of an organism as distinct from the reproductive cells. L19.
2 ANATOMY. The compact portion of a nerve cell, excluding the axon and dendrites. M20.
3 The body in contrast to the mind or the soul. Opp. ***psyche***. M20.

somaesthetic /səʊmiːs'θɛtɪk/ *adjective*. Also ***-mes-**. L19.
[formed as prec. + Greek *aisthētikos* perceptive, AESTHETIC.]
PHYSIOLOGY. Of, pertaining to, or designating a sensation (as of pressure, pain, or warmth) which can occur anywhere in the body, in contrast to one localized at a sense organ (as sight, balance, or taste).
■ **somaesthesis** /-'θiːsɪs/ *noun* the perception of somaesthetic sensations E20.

somal /'səʊm(ə)l/ *adjective*. E20.
[formed as prec. + -AL[1].]
1 Of or pertaining to the body. E20.
2 ANATOMY. Of or pertaining to the soma of a nerve cell. M20.

Somali /sə'mɑːli/ *noun & adjective*. E19.
[African name.]
▸ **A** *noun*. Pl. same, **-s**.
1 A member of a chiefly Muslim Hamitic people living in the Horn of Africa, esp. in the Republic of Somalia. E19.
2 The Cushitic language of this people. M19.
▸ **B** *attrib.* or as *adjective*. Of or pertaining to the Somali or their language; of or pertaining to Somalia. M19.
■ **Somalian** *adjective* = SOMALI *adjective* M20.

Soman /'səʊmən/ *noun*. M20.
[German, of unkn. origin.]
An organophosphorus nerve gas, $(C_6H_{13}O)(CH_3)FPO$.

Somasco /sə'maskəʊ/ *noun*. Pl. **-chi** /-ki/. Orig. (after French) †**Somasque**. L17.
[Italian, from *Somasca* a town in N. Italy.]
Hist. A member of a charitable religious order founded at Somasca by Gerolamo Emiliani about 1530. Usu. in *pl.*
■ Also **Somaschan** *noun* L19.

somasteroid /sə'mastərɔɪd/ *adjective & noun*. M20.
[from mod. Latin *Somasteroidea* (see below), from Greek *sōma* body + mod. Latin *Asteroidea* (see ASTEROID *noun* 2): see -OID.]
ZOOLOGY. ▸**A** *adjective*. Of or pertaining to the subclass or class Somasteroidea of star-shaped echinoderms, mainly comprising extinct forms having broad petal-like arms. M20.
▸ **B** *noun*. A somasteroid echinoderm. M20.

somat- *combining form* see SOMATO-.

somatic /sə'matɪk/ *adjective*. L18.
[Greek *sōmatikos*, from *sōmat-*, *sōma* body: see -IC.]
Of, pertaining to, or affecting the body, esp. as distinct from the mind; bodily, corporeal, physical; *spec.* pertaining to the soma.
somatic cell any of the cells of an organism other than a germ cell.
■ **somatically** *adverb* M19.

somatisation *noun* var. of SOMATIZATION.

somatism /'səʊmətɪz(ə)m/ *noun*. *rare*. E18.
[from Greek *sōmat-*, *sōma* body + -ISM.]
Materialism.
■ **somatist** *noun & adjective* L17.

somatization /ˌsəʊmətʌɪ'zeɪʃ(ə)n/ *noun*. Also **-isation**. E20.
[formed as prec. + -IZATION.]
The occurrence of bodily symptoms in consequence of or as an expression of emotional or mental disorder.
■ **somatize** *verb trans.* express (a mental state) in the form of bodily symptoms (chiefly as ***somatizing*** *verbal noun & ppl adjective*) M20.

somato- /'səʊmətəʊ/ *combining form* of Greek *sōmat-*, *sōma* body: see -O-. Before a vowel **somat-**.
■ **soma'talgia** *noun* (*rare*) bodily pain or suffering E17. **somatocoel** *noun* (ZOOLOGY) either of a pair of cavities in an echinoderm embryo that develop into the main body cavity of the adult M20. **somatogamy** /səʊmə'tɒgəmi/ *noun* (BOTANY) = PSEUDOGAMY M20. **somato'genic** *adjective* (BIOLOGY) originating in the somatic cells L19. **somatomedin** /-'miːdɪn/ *noun* [-*med*- from INTERMEDIARY] PHYSIOLOGY a peptide hormone which acts as an intermediate in the stimulation of growth by growth hormone L20. **somatoplasm** *noun* (BIOLOGY) somatic cytoplasm, somatic cells collectively L19. **somatopleure** *noun* [Greek *pleura* side] EMBRYOLOGY a layer of tissue in a vertebrate embryo comprising the ectoderm and the outer layer of mesoderm, and giving rise to the amnion, chorion, and part of the body wall (opp. ***splanchnopleure***) L19. **somato'pleuric** *adjective* (EMBRYOLOGY) of or pertaining to the somatopleure L19. **somato'psychic** *adjective* (PSYCHOLOGY) †(**a**) of or pertaining to awareness of one's own body; (**b**) arising from or pertaining to the effects of bodily illness on the mind: E20. **somato'sensory** *adjective* (PHYSIOLOGY) = SOMAESTHETIC M20. **somatostatin** /-'statɪn/ *noun* [-STAT] PHYSIOLOGY a peptide hormone secreted in the pancreas and pituitary which inhibits gastric secretion and somatotropin release L20. **somato'tonic** *adjective & noun* (**a**) *adjective* designating or characteristic of an extroverted and aggressive personality type, thought to be associated esp. with a mesomorphic physique; (**b**) *noun* a person having this type of personality: M20. **somato'topic**, **somato'topical** *adjectives* (PHYSIOLOGY) characterized by, pertaining to, or designating a relationship between the locations of neurones in the central nervous system and in the tissues they serve M20. **somato'topically** *adverb* in a manner which preserves a somatotopic relationship M20. **somatotrophic** /-'trəʊfɪk, -'trɒfɪk/ *adjective* (PHYSIOLOGY) pertaining to or having the property of stimulating body growth M20. **somatotrophin** /-'trəʊfɪn/ *noun* (PHYSIOLOGY) a hormone secreted by the anterior pituitary which promotes the release of somatomedins; growth hormone; (***bovine somatotrophin***: see BOVINE *adjective* 1): M20. **somatotropic** /-'trəʊpɪk, -'trɒpɪk/ *adjective* (PHYSIOLOGY) = SOMATOTROPHIC M20. **somatotropin** /-'trəʊpɪn/ *noun* (PHYSIOLOGY) = SOMATOTROPHIN M20. **somatotype** *noun & verb* (**a**) *noun* a person's physique, esp. as it relates to personality, often expressed numerically in terms of a ratio of three extreme types (endomorph, mesomorph, and ectomorph); (**b**) *verb trans.* assign to a somatotype: M20.

somatology /səʊmə'tɒlədʒi/ *noun*. M17.
[from prec. + -LOGY.]
The branch of science that deals with (esp. human) bodies; *spec.* the branch of anthropology that deals with

the human body, physical anthropology. Also (*rare*), a treatise on bodies.

■ **somato'logical** *adjective* E19. **somato'logically** *adverb* L19. **somatologist** *noun* L19.

sombre /'sɒmbə/ *adjective, noun, & verb.* Also *-**ber**. M18.
[Old & mod. French use as adjective of Old French noun (= Catalan, Spanish, Portuguese *sombra* shade), ult. from Latin *sub* SUB- + *umbra* shade, shadow.]

▸ **A** *adjective.* **1** Characterized by the presence of gloom or shadow; depressingly dark. M18.
2 Gloomy in spirit or mood; oppressively solemn or sober, grave; dismal, foreboding. M18.
3 (Of colouring) dark, dull; of a dark or dull shade. E19.

📖 **1** M. F. MAURY The sombre skies and changeable weather of our latitudes. QUILLER-COUCH For many miles nothing but sombre moors . . stretching away. **2** M. SINCLAIR Looking at the graves . . with a sombre . . interest. L. STRACHEY Victoria . . succeeded in instilling . . cheerfulness into her uncle's sombre court. *Observer* We stand on the threshold of a sombre decade. **3** J. WILKES The olive-tree . . is a sombre brown.

▸ **B** *noun.* Sombre character; sombreness. *rare.* L18.
▸ **C** *verb trans. & intrans.* Make or become sombre. *literary.* L18.

📖 J. G. WHITTIER This lake . . Walled round with sombering pines.

■ **sombrely** *adverb* M19. **sombreness** *noun* M19. **sombrous** *adjective* (now *rare*) = SOMBRE *adjective* E18.

sombrero /sɒm'brɛːrəʊ/ *noun.* Pl. **-os**. L16.
[Spanish, from *sombra* shade.]
†**1** An oriental umbrella or parasol. L16–E18.
2 A broad-brimmed hat of felt or other soft material, of a type common in Mexico and the south-western US. L18.
2 *TEN-gallon sombrero.*
■ **sombreroed** *adjective* wearing a sombrero L19.

some /sʌm, *unstressed* s(ə)m/ *pronoun, adjective* (in mod. usage also classed as a *determiner*), *& adverb.*
[Old English *sum* = Old Frisian, Old Saxon, Old High German *sum*, Old Norse *sumr*, Gothic *sums*, from Germanic from Indo-European, from base also repr. by Greek *hamōs* somehow, *hamothen* from some place, Sanskrit *sama* any, every.]

▸ **A** *pronoun.* **1** Treated as *sing.* ▸†**a** One or other of a number of people or things; someone, somebody, one. Also foll. by *of.* OE–M19. ▸**b** A certain indeterminate part of something; a portion. Also foll. by *of.* OE.
2 Treated as *pl.* An indefinite or unspecified (but not large) number of people or things; certain people or things not named or enumerated. Also foll. by *of.* OE.

📖 **1a** J. H. NEWMAN We shall have you a papist some of these fine days. **b** E. J. HOWARD Give me some. You'll be drunk if you drink all that. E. BAKER Becoming familiar with some of his work. **2** T. HARDY Some believe in it; some don't. SCOTT FITZGERALD They were . . in uniform, some sober, some . . drunk. R. P. JHABVALA If it rained . . heavily, some of the older houses would collapse. C. P. SNOW He was . . less of a fool than some.

▸ **B** *adjective.* **I** With sing. nouns.
1 A certain, a particular. Now only with *certain* or *one.* OE.
2 One or other; an undetermined or unspecified. Freq. with the indefiniteness emphasized by *or other* (cf. OTHER *pronoun & noun* 5a). OE.
†**3** With generalizing force: = sense 6 below. OE–M17.
4 A certain amount, part, degree, or extent of; at least a small amount of, no little amount of, a considerable. OE. ▸**b** Quite a; a remarkable. *colloq.* Freq. *iron.* E19. ▸**c** *pred.* Of some account, deserving of consideration. *US.* M19.
5 With a singular quantity or amount: = sense 8 below. L16.

📖 **1** J. RUSKIN She should . . follow at least some one path of scientific attainment. **2** SHELLEY His Grace . . expects to enter . . Jerusalem some Palm Sunday in triumph. C. P. SNOW I achieved some sort of calm. SCOTT FITZGERALD He was the head of some combine. W. GOLDING I was . . quoting from some play or other. A. S. BYATT Outside, for some reason, Oxford bells were pealing. **3** COVERDALE *Ecclus* 20:5 Some man kepeth sylence, and is founde wyse. **4** SHAKES. *Haml.* Rest here in our court Some little time. STEELE He . . calls for some Posset-drink. G. MILLERSON The camera has to be positioned some way from the subject. I. MURDOCH He was prepared to put up some money. J. SIMMS You have known for some time that we are here. **b** A. PRICE 'David has us to console him.' . . 'Some consolation!' murmured Frances. A. TYLER Watch . . . This man here is some operator. **c** M. TWAIN Smarty! You think you're *some*, now, don't you. **5** THOMAS HUGHES Distant some mile or so from the school.

▸ **II** With pl. nouns.
6 Certain (taken individually). OE.
7 An unspecified number of; a few (at least). OE.
8 (With following numeral adjective) that is an approximate amount; passing into adverb use: about, nearly, approximately. Formerly also, with numerals denoting the time of day. OE.

📖 **6** GOLDSMITH There is Seneca, and Bolingbroke, and some others. JOHN PHILLIPS Oligoclase occurs in some granites. R. MACNEIL Some boys . . wore . . buckled overshoes. **7** J. MARQUAND There were some men . . half-way down the steps. W. SANSOM A small . . church some kilometres away. A. N. WILSON In this way, for some years, Giles's life had passed. **8** G. GREENE I found myself in a . . cave some eight feet high. M. SCHAPIRO In Arles, Vincent painted some forty-six portraits.

▸ **C** *adverb.* (See also sense B.8 above.)
1 A certain amount; a little; slightly; somewhat. Now *colloq. & dial.* exc. in ***some more***. ME.
2 Very much, very well, a lot. Chiefly in ***go some*** below. *colloq.* (orig. *US*). M19.

📖 **1** W. FAULKNER We got to eat and then sleep some. T. HEGGEN When he left . . , Roberts felt some better. I. MURDOCH Let's meet tomorrow and discuss it some more. R. MACDONALD 'Has Luster been talking?' 'Some. But not enough.' M. MACHLIN He's going to be some pissed off when he finds out.

Phrases: ***all and some***: see ALL *pronoun* 4. **and then some** *slang* and (plenty) more in addition. **get some** *US slang* have sexual intercourse, find a sexual partner. **go some** (*colloq.*, orig. *US*) go well or fast, do well, work hard. ***other some***: see OTHER *adjective.* †**some and some** a few at a time, gradually. ***some FEW***. ***some hope!***, ***some hopes!***: see HOPE *noun*[1]. ***to some tune***: see TUNE *noun.*

-some /s(ə)m/ *suffix*[1].
[Old English *-sum* = Old Frisian *-sum* rel. to Old Saxon, Old High German *-sam* (German *-sam*, Dutch *-zaam*), Old Norse *-samr* (Swedish *-sam*, Danish *-som*), Gothic *-sams*.]
Forming adjectives from nouns, adjectives, and verbs, with the senses (***a***) characterized by being, as ***fulsome***, ***lithesome***, ***wholesome***; (***b***) adapted to, productive of, as ***cuddlesome***, ***fearsome***, ***handsome***; (***c***) apt to, as ***cumbersome***, ***tiresome***.

-some /*in sense* 1 s(ə)m, *in sense* 2 sʌm/ *suffix*[2].
[Old English *sum* SOME *pronoun*, used after numerals in genit. pl. In sense 2 from SOME *adjective*.]
1 Forming nouns from numerals, with the sense 'a group of (so many)', as ***foursome***, ***twosome***, etc.
2 Affixed to numerals with the sense 'about, approximately, or so' (cf. SOME *adjective* 8). *US.*

📖 **2** G. KEILLOR Lake Wobegon babies are born in a hospital thirty-some miles away.

-some /səʊm/ *suffix*[3].
[Greek *sōma* body.]
Used in *BIOLOGY* to form nouns denoting a small body, esp. an intracellular particle, as ***chromosome***, ***ribosome***, etc. Freq. *spec.* repr. ***chromosome***, as ***disome***, ***monosome***.

somebody /'sʌmbədi/ *pronoun & noun.* Orig. two words. ME.
[from SOME *adjective* + BODY *noun.*]
1 An unknown, indeterminate, or unnamed person; someone, some person. ME.
2 A person of note or importance. M16.
3 A person whose name is intentionally suppressed. E17.

📖 **1** BROWNING Take the pipe out of his mouth, somebody. J. AGATE Invited by two somebodies I don't know to attend a welcome lunch. E. J. HOWARD It is much more exhausting seducing somebody one has known for a long time. **somebody else** some other person, someone else; *spec.* a rival for a person's affections. **2** P. MARSHALL A year of college and she thought she was somebody.

someday /'sʌmdeɪ/ *adverb.* Orig. two words. OE.
[from SOME *adjective* + DAY *noun.*]
At some future time.
¶ Not recorded as one word before L19.

somedeal /'sʌmdiːl/ *noun & adverb.* Now *arch. & dial.* Orig. two words. OE.
[from SOME *adjective* + DEAL *noun*[1].]
▸ **A** *noun.* Some part or portion *of*; some, somewhat. OE.
▸ **B** *adverb.* To some extent; somewhat; partly. OE.

somegate /'sʌmgeɪt/ *adverb. Scot. & north.* Also as two words. E19.
[from SOME *adjective* + GATE *noun*[2].]
1 In some place, somewhere. E19.
2 In some way, somehow. E19.

somehow /'sʌmhaʊ/ *adverb.* M17.
[from SOME *adjective* + HOW *adverb.*]
In some unspecified or unknown way; one way or another; no matter how; for some reason or other.

📖 H. JAMES Somehow or other one can always arrange one's life. V. WOOLF She must escape somehow. G. VIDAL It seemed, somehow, grossly unfair.

someone /'sʌmwʌn/ *pronoun & noun.* Orig. two words. ME.
[from SOME *adjective* + ONE *noun & pronoun.*]
Some unspecified or unnamed person; = SOMEBODY.
¶ Not recorded as one word before M19.

someplace /'sʌmpleɪs/ *adverb & pronoun. dial. & N. Amer.* Orig. two words. L19.
[from SOME *adjective* + PLACE *noun*[1].]
Somewhere; (at, in, to, etc.) a particular or unspecified place.

somersault /'sʌməsɒlt, -sɔːlt/ *noun & verb.* Also **summer-**. M16.
[Old French *sombresau(l)t* alt. of *sobresault* (mod. *soubresaut*) from Provençal, from *sobre* above (from Latin *supra*) + *saut* leap (from Latin *saltus*). Cf. next.]
▸ **A** *noun.* An acrobatic leap or spring in which a person turns head over heels in the air or on the ground and alights on the feet. Also (*transf. & fig.*), an acrobatic roll or turn; a complete overturn or upset; a reversal of opinion, policy, etc. M16.

📖 J. G. WHITTIER Dr Lord . . professedly in favor of emancipation, but who afterwards turned a moral somersault. *Strength & Health* He . . did a very nice back somersault. J. CAREW A famous acrobat . . who could do eighty somersaults. R. ALTER Pnin, through a somersault of etymology, connects squirrel fur with Cinderella's slippers.

▸ **B** *verb intrans.* Perform a somersault or somersaults; turn over and over acrobatically. M19.

📖 A. DILLARD The wing went down and we went somersaulting over it. *fig.*: *Business* The . . dream of cheap . . air travel somersaulted into a series of financial crashes.

■ **somersaulter** *noun* M19.

somerset /'sʌməsɛt/ *noun & verb.* Now *dial. & colloq.* L16.
[Alt. of prec.]
▸ **A** *noun.* = SOMERSAULT *noun.* L16.
▸ **B** *verb.* Infl. **-tt-**.
1 *verb trans.* †**a** With *it.* Perform a somersault. Only in L16. ▸**b** Cause to turn a somersault. *rare.* E19.
2 *verb intrans.* = SOMERSAULT *verb.* M19.

Somervillian /sʌmə'vɪlɪən/ *adjective & noun.* L19.
[from *Somerville* College, from Mary *Somerville* (1780–1872), Scot. scientist: see -IAN.]
▸ **A** *adjective.* Of or pertaining to Somerville College, Oxford (founded as a women's college in 1879), or its members. L19.
▸ **B** *noun.* A member of Somerville College. L19.

somesthetic *adjective* see SOMAESTHETIC.

something /'sʌmθɪŋ/ *pronoun, noun, adverb, & verb.* OE.
[from SOME *adjective* + THING *noun*[1].]
▸ **A** *pronoun & noun.* Orig. two words.
1 Some unspecified or unknown thing (material or immaterial). Freq. used as a substitute for a forgotten, unknown, or immaterial name, description, etc. OE.
2 A certain part, amount, or share *of* some thing, quality, etc.; *esp.* a small amount, a slight trace. ME.
3 a A thing, fact, person, etc., of some value, consideration, or regard. L16. ▸**b** The holder of an unspecified position *in* some field of business. M19.

📖 **1** G. BORROW I passed by a place called Llan something. H. JAMES There's something the matter with you. E. WAUGH There was something . . voluptuous in the beauty of Malfrey. D. EDEN Do something, Fergus. Why doesn't somebody do something? M. HUNTER That something in . . us which creates the need for fairy stories. P. D. JAMES I cook a little something . . in the evenings. S. ROSENBERG I dropped in to see if I could buy something for tea. **2** SIR W. SCOTT Something of the tone . . and feeling of a gentleman. G. GREENE You see something of each other then? S. CONN Neither Freak nor fossil but something Of each. **3a** M. EDGEWORTH If he could even recover five guineas . . , it would be something. *New Yorker* The quality of the tennis . . has been something to behold. F. WELDON I am good at it. I'm really something. **b** W. E. GOSSE My uncles . . earned a comfortable living . . as 'something in the City.'

Phrases & comb.: **have got something**, **have something** have a valuable or noteworthy idea or attribute. **have something going** have a romantic or sexual relationship (*with*). ***make something of***: see MAKE *verb.* **or something** or some unspecified alternative or possibility. ***quite something***: see QUITE *adverb.* **something else** (*a*) a different thing; (*b*) *colloq.* an exceptional or extraordinary person, event, etc. ***something like***: see LIKE *adjective* etc. **something of** to a certain extent or degree a (person or thing of the kind specified); see also sense 2 above. **something of the kind**, **something of the sort** something similar to that previously indicated or specified; (expr. agreement) to some extent, in some ways. **something or other** = sense 1 above. **twenty-something**, **thirty-something**, etc. *colloq.* an undetermined age between twenty and thirty, thirty and forty, etc.

▸ **B** *adverb.* In some degree; to some extent; somewhat; rather, a little. *arch.* exc. in constructions in which the word can be understood as a noun or pronoun. ME.

📖 SHAKES. *Wint. T.* Please you come something nearer. G. MEREDITH The *dulness* is something frightful. DICKENS 'O!' said I, something snappishly. R. L. STEVENSON This song . . is something less than just. DOUGLAS CLARK It does sting something chronic.

▸ **C** *verb trans. euphem.* Confound, damn. Usu. in *pass.* M19.

📖 H. KINGSLEY He said that he would be somethinged if he gave way.

■ **somethingness** *noun* the fact or state of being something; real or material existence: L17.

sometime /ˈsʌmtʌɪm/ *adverb & adjective.* ME.
[from SOME *adjective* + TIME *noun.*]
▶ **A** *adverb.* Formerly also as two words.
1 At one time (or another); sometimes, now and then, occasionally. Now *rare.* ME.
2 †**a** At a certain time, on a particular occasion, once. ME–M17. ▸**b** At one time, formerly. Now only with omission of relative and verb (passing into adjectival use: cf. sense B.1 below). ME.
3 At some future time; on a future occasion. LME.
4 At some indefinite or unspecified time; at some time or other. L16.

> **1** SHAKES. *3 Hen. VI* Sometime the flood prevails, and then the wind. S. GREENLEE Rhoda would fuss sometime about her no-good man. **2b** EVELYN A . . gentleman, with whom my son was sometime bred in Arundel House. **3** G. BERKELEY You may sometime or other come to Bath. B. PYM I might ask her in to coffee sometime. **4** R. LEHMANN Rollo would think about ringing up, sometime to-morrow maybe. R. COBB It was sometime in the spring of 1950.

▶ **B** *adjective.* **1** Former. L15.
2 Future. *rare.* M17.
3 Transient, occasional. M20.

> **1** J. I. M. STEWART There she was, my sometime wife. **2** A. SEWARD The sometime resurrection of the body. **3** G. GERSHWIN A woman is a sometime thing.

■ **sometimey** *adjective* (*US slang*) variable, unstable M20.

sometimes /ˈsʌmtʌɪmz/ *adverb & adjective.* LME.
[from SOME *adjective* + TIME *noun* + -S[3], later identified with -S[1].]
▶ **A** *adverb.* **1** On some occasions; at times; now and then, occasionally. Cf. SOMETIME *adverb* 1. LME.
†**2** Once; formerly; = SOMETIME *adverb* 2. L15–E18.

> **1** R. W. CHURCH Shrewd and sometimes cynical epigrams. M. SINCLAIR They quarrelled sometimes but they didn't hate each other. J. BUCHAN Sometimes I wanted to cry and sometimes I wanted to swear. O. MANNING Sometimes . . Hugh would persuade her to go down to the harbour.

▶ **B** *adjective.* †**1** = SOMETIME *adjective* 1. L16–L18.
2 = SOMETIME *adjective* 3. M20.

†**somever** *adverb.* ME–E17.
[from Scandinavian *sum, som* rel. adverb + EVER.]
= SOEVER.

someway /ˈsʌmweɪ/ *adverb.* Now chiefly *dial.* & *US colloq.* Also **-ways** /-weɪz/. Formerly also as two words. LME.
[from SOME *adjective* + WAY *noun.*]
In some way or manner; by some means; somehow.

somewhat /ˈsʌmwɒt/ *pronoun, noun, & adverb.* ME.
[from SOME *adjective* + WHAT *pronoun.*]
▶ **A** *pronoun & noun.* **1** = SOMETHING *pronoun & noun* 1, 2. *arch.* ME.
†**2** = SOMETHING *pronoun & noun* 3a. LME–M19.
▶ **B** *adverb.* To some (slight or small) extent; slightly, a little; rather. ME.

> W. WHEWELL I . . acknowledge myself somewhat an idle correspondent. DAY LEWIS We were . . somewhat isolated . . , a Protestant enclave in a Catholic community. R. JAFFE The shock had sobered her somewhat. A. J. AYER The house . . was severely functional, somewhat in the Bauhaus style. **more than somewhat** *colloq.* very, extremely, very much. **somewhat as** in much the same way as, to some extent as.

■ †**somewhatly** *adverb* (*rare*) LME–E18.

somewhen /ˈsʌmwɛn/ *adverb. colloq. & dial.* OE.
[from SOME *adjective* + WHEN *adverb.*]
At some (indefinite or unknown) time; sometime or other. Freq. coupled with *somewhere* or *somehow.*
¶ Not recorded between LME and M19.

somewhence /ˈsʌmwɛns/ *adverb. rare.* M16.
[from SOME *adjective* + WHENCE *adverb.*]
From some unspecified place; from somewhere or other.

somewhere /ˈsʌmwɛː/ *adverb, pronoun, & noun.* ME.
[from SOME *adjective* + WHERE *adverb.*]
▶ **A** *adverb.* **1** In, at, or to some unspecified, indeterminate, or unknown place. ME. ▸**b** In some part or passage of a book etc.; in some work or other. LME. ▸**c** At or in an indefinite place in a quantitative scale, esp. of time; at or for some time *about* or *in* a certain period, date, etc. M19.
†**2** In some places; here and there. *rare.* M16–E17.

> **1** GEO. ELIOT Arthur must be somewhere in the back rooms. J. STEINBECK Somewhere he had a . . hoard of money. S. BEDFORD He inherited some land in Bavaria or somewhere. O. MANNING When this is over, let's go away somewhere. J. KOSINSKI He had seen this man before somewhere. **b** G. VIDAL Somewhere Thomas Hardy had written . . on this theme. **c** R. FRY The picture . . could . . be got for somewhere between 3 and 4 thousand pounds. S. O'FAOLÁIN Macroom Castle was built somewhere in the sixteenth century.

▶ **B** *pronoun & noun.* Some unspecified or indefinite place. M17.

> S. BECKETT He looked for somewhere to sit down. W. FAULKNER A hound with a strain of mastiff from somewhere.

Phrases: **get somewhere** *colloq.* achieve success. **go somewhere**: see GO *verb.* **somewhere about** approximately. **somewhere along the line**: see LINE *noun*[2]. **somewhere else** (in) some other place, elsewhere. **somewhere in** at a place within (a specified area, esp. a theatre of war) which cannot be more precisely identified for reasons of security or censorship.

■ **somewheres** *adverb* (*dial.*) somewhere M19.

somewhile /ˈsʌmwʌɪl/ *adverb.* Now *rare.* Also (now *dial.*) **-whiles** /-z/. ME.
[from SOME *adjective* + WHILE *noun.*]
†**1** At or in some former time; formerly. ME–L19.
†**2** Once; at one time. ME–M17.
3 At some unspecified time; at one time or other; at times, sometimes. ME.
4 For some time. M19.

somewhither /ˈsʌmwɪðə/ *adverb. arch.* LME.
[from SOME *adjective* + WHITHER *adverb.*]
In some direction; to some unspecified place.

somewhy /ˈsʌmwʌɪ/ *adverb. rare.* M19.
[from SOME *adjective* + WHY *adverb.*]
For some reason or reasons.

somewise /ˈsʌmwʌɪz/ *adverb & noun. arch.* LME.
[from SOME *adjective* + -WISE.]
▶ **A** *adverb.* In some way or manner, to some extent, somehow. LME.
▶ **B** *noun.* ***in somewise***, somehow. M19.

somite /ˈsəʊmʌɪt/ *noun.* M19.
[from Greek *sōma* body + -ITE[1].]
ZOOLOGY. A body segment of a metameric organism; = METAMERE.
■ **somitic** /səˈmɪtɪk/ *adjective* L19.

somma /ˈsɒmə/ *noun & adjective.* E20.
[Italian (*Monte*) *Somma*, Vesuvius.]
PHYSICAL GEOGRAPHY. ▶**A** *noun.* A remnant of an older volcanic crater which partly or wholly encircles a younger cone; the rim of a caldera. E20.
▶ **B** *adjective.* Of or pertaining to a somma. E20.

sommelier /ˈsɒm(ə)ljeɪ, səˈmɛljeɪ; *foreign* sɔməlje (*pl. same*)/ *noun.* E19.
[French.]
A wine waiter.

sommer /ˈsɒmə/ *adverb. S. Afr. colloq.* M19.
[Afrikaans *somaar, sommer.*]
Just, for no specific reason, without further ado.

sommité /sɔmite/ *noun.* Pl. pronounced same. M19.
[French = summit, top, tip.]
A person of great eminence or influence.

somn- /sɒmn/ *combining form* of Latin *somnus* sleep, forming words with a second elem. based on Latin *ambulare* to walk.

■ **somˈnambulance** *noun* sleepwalking, somnambulism L19. **somˈnambulant** *adjective & noun* (*a*) *adjective* walking in sleep, somnambulic; (*b*) *noun* a somnambulist: M19. **somˈnambulantly** *adverb* in a somnambulant manner E20. **somˈnambular** *adjective* of or pertaining to sleepwalking M19. **somˈnambulate** *verb* (*a*) *verb intrans.* walk during sleep; (*b*) *verb trans.* walk along (a place) while asleep: M19. **somnambuˈlation** *noun* [mod. Latin *somnambulatio(n-)*] sleepwalking L18. **somˈnambule** *noun* [French] a somnambulist M19. **somˈnambulic** *adjective* of the nature of or pertaining to somnambulism; walking during sleep: M19. **somˈnambulism** *noun* [French *somnambulisme*] (*a*) the fact or habit of walking about etc. while asleep; sleepwalking; (*b*) a condition of the brain inducing this; (*c*) a hypnotic state in which the subject is alert but has no subsequent recollection: L18. **somˈnambulist** *noun* a person who walks etc. while asleep L18. **somnambuˈlistic** *adjective* somnambulic M19. **somnambuˈlistically** *adverb* in a somnambulistic manner M19.

somnial /ˈsɒmnɪəl/ *adjective. rare.* L17.
[Obsolete French; or late Latin *somnialis*, from Latin *somnium* dream: see -AL[1].]
Of or relating to dreams.

somniculous /sɒmˈnɪkjʊləs/ *adjective. rare.* M17.
[from Latin *somniculosus*, from *somnium* dream: see -ULOUS.]
Drowsy, sleepy. Also, inducing sleep.

somniferous /sɒmˈnɪf(ə)rəs/ *adjective.* E17.
[Latin *somnifer*, from *somnium* dream: see -FEROUS.]
1 Inducing sleep; soporific. E17.
2 Somnolent, sleepy. *rare.* L18.
■ **somniferously** *adverb* M19.

somnific /sɒmˈnɪfɪk/ *adjective.* Now *rare.* E18.
[Latin *somnificus*, from *somnus* sleep: see -I-, -FIC.]
Causing sleep; somniferous.

somniloquism /sɒmˈnɪləkwɪz(ə)m/ *noun. rare.* E19.
[from Latin *somnus* sleep + -I- + LOQU(ACIOUS + -ISM.]
The action or habit of talking while asleep.
■ **somniloquent** *adjective* talking in sleep E19. **somniloquist** *noun* a person who talks while asleep M19.

somnolence /ˈsɒmnələns/ *noun.* LME.
[Old French *sompnolence* (mod. *somn-*) or late Latin *somnolentia* (medieval Latin *somp-*) from Latin *somnolentus*: see next, -ENCE.]
Inclination to sleep; sleepiness, drowsiness.
■ Also **somnolency** *noun* E17.

somnolent /ˈsɒmnələnt/ *adjective.* LME.
[Old French *sompnolent* (mod. *somn-*) or Latin *somnolentus* (medieval Latin *somp-*) from *somnus* sleep: see -ENT.]
1 Tending to cause sleepiness or drowsiness; inclining to sleep. LME. ▸**b** Marked by sleepiness or slowness. E19.
2 Of a person etc.: inclined to sleep; heavy with sleep; drowsy; *spec.* in MEDICINE, unnaturally drowsy; in a state between sleeping and waking. M16.

> **1b** M. ROBERTS That peaceful, somnolent, after-lunch time. **2** R. P. WARREN Twitching like . . a somnolent beast that may wake to leap.

■ **somnolently** *adverb* E17.

somnolescent /sɒmnəˈlɛs(ə)nt/ *adjective.* M19.
[from prec.: see -ESCENT.]
Drowsy, sleepy; inert.

> H. BELLOC I was dozing . . in somnolescent bliss.

■ **somnolescence** *noun* sleepiness, drowsiness M19.

Somocista /sɒmə(ʊ)ˈsiːstə, -ˈsɪstə/ *noun & adjective.* Also **Somocist** /sɒˈməʊsɪst/. L20.
[Spanish, from Anastasio *Somoza* Portocarrero (1896–1956) and his sons Luis and Anastasio Somoza Debayle (see below) + *-ista* -IST.]
▶ **A** *noun.* A follower of the Somozas, who between them held the presidency of Nicaragua almost continuously from 1937 to 1979; a member or supporter of the family's regime. Cf. SANDINISTA. L20.
▶ **B** *adjective.* Of or belonging to the Somozas or their followers. L20.

Somogyi unit /səˈməʊgi/ *noun.* M20.
[Michael *Somogyi* (1883–1971), Hungarian-born US biochemist.]
BIOCHEMISTRY. A unit used to express the effectiveness of an enzyme solution at catalysing the hydrolysis of starch.

son /sʌn/ *noun*[1].
[Old English *sunu* = Old Frisian, Old Saxon, Old High German *sunu* (Dutch *zoon*, German *Sohn*), Old Norse *sunr, sonr*, Gothic *sunus*, from Germanic, rel. to Greek *huios*.]
1 a A male human being in relation to either or both of his parents. Also, a male offspring of an animal. OE. ▸**b** A son-in-law. Long *rare.* M16.
2 CHRISTIAN CHURCH. (Usu. **S-**.) Jesus Christ; the Second Person of the Trinity. OE.
3 a A person who is regarded as, or takes the place of, a son. OE. ▸**b** Used as a term of affectionate or familiar address to a man or boy by an older person or (also ***my son***) by a person in a superior, esp. ecclesiastical, relation. OE.
4 a A male descendant; a male member *of* a family, race, etc. OE. ▸**b** A member, follower, or founder of a religious body or order. LME.
5 A person who is characterized by or regarded as inheriting a certain quality, trait, occupation, etc.; a person who is associated with a particular attribute or is the product of a certain place. L16.
6 COMPUTING. An updated file, usu. on a removable magnetic medium, which has been created from a corresponding father (see FATHER *noun* 7). M20.

> **1a** *Times* D. Illingworth and Son, Leeds, mungo manufacturers. G. F. NEWMAN The maintenance of his ex-wife and her mongol son. M. ESSLIN Samuel Beckett was . . the son of a quantity surveyor. **3b** SIR W. SCOTT 'Prove thy strength, my son . . ' said the preacher. K. WATERHOUSE Come in, son, sit yourself down. L. GRIFFITHS Wisdom, shrewdness . . nothing goes further than this, my old son. **4a** SHAKES. *Much Ado* Adam's sons are my brethren. **b** *Friend* A loyal son of the Roman Church. **5** POPE All the sons of warlike Greece. J. ADAMS A staunch, zealous son of liberty.

Phrases & comb.: ***favourite son***: see FAVOURITE *adjective.* ***God the Father, God the Son, and God the Holy Spirit, God the Father, God the Son, and God the Holy Ghost***: see GOD *noun.* **horny-handed son of toil**, **son of toil** (now often *iron.*) a manual labourer. ***native son***: see NATIVE *adjective.* ***prodigal son***: see PRODIGAL *adjective.* **son and heir** a usu. eldest son who stands to succeed to an inheritance. **son-before-the-father** (now *dial.*) any of several plants with flowers appearing before the leaves, e.g. coltsfoot, *Tussilago farfara*. **son-in-law**, pl. **sons-in-law**, (*a*) the husband of one's daughter; †(*b*) a stepson. **son of** — a formula for the title of a sequel to a book or film; *joc.* a programme, product, institution, etc., that is a derivative *of* its predecessor. **son of a bitch**, **sonofabitch** *slang* (*a*) a despicable or hateful man; (*b*) used as a general term of contempt or abuse. ***son of a gun***: see GUN *noun.* **Son of God** (*a*) Jesus Christ; (*b*) a divine being; an angel; (*c*) (**s-**) a person spiritually attached to God. **Son of Heaven** [translating Chinese *tiānzǐ*] *Hist.* the Emperor of China. **son of man** (*a*) a member of the human race; a mortal; (*b*) *spec.* (*Son of Man*) Jesus Christ. ***son of the house***: see HOUSE *noun*[1]. ***son of the manse***: see MANSE 2. ***son of the soil***: see SOIL *noun*[1]. ***son of toil***: see ***horny-handed son of toil*** above.

son /səʊn/ *noun*[2]. M20.
[Spanish = sound.]
A slow Cuban dance and song in 2/4 time.
son Afro-Cubano /-kuːˈbɑːnəʊ/ a form of the son influenced by Afro-American dances.

so-na /ˈsəʊna/ *noun.* **E20.**
[Chinese *suǒnà*.]
MUSIC. A Chinese wind instrument with a reed mouthpiece.

Sonagraph *noun* see SONOGRAPH.

sonance /ˈsəʊnəns/ *noun.* **L16.**
[from Latin *sonare* to sound + -ANCE.]
Sound; the quality of sounding.
■ **sonancy** *noun* (*rare*) the quality of being sonant **L19.**

sonant /ˈsəʊnənt/ *adjective & noun.* **M19.**
[Latin *sonant-* pres. ppl stem of *sonare* to sound: see -ANT[1].]
PHONETICS. ▶**A** *adjective.* **1** Uttered with vocal sound, voiced. **M19.**
2 Syllabic; forming or capable of forming a syllable. **L19.**
▶**B** *noun.* **1** A voiced sound or letter. **M19.**
2 A syllabic sound; *esp.* a syllabic consonant. **L19.**
3 A consonant that can be either syllabic or non-syllabic; a continuant or nasal, as /l, m, n, ŋ, r/. **M20.**
■ **soˈnantal** *adjective* (*a*) syllabic; (*b*) *rare* that is or contains a sonant: **L19.**

sonar /ˈsəʊnɑː/ *noun.* **M20.**
[Acronym, from sound *navigation* (and) *ranging*, after *radar*.]
1 A system for detecting the presence of objects under water and determining their position and motion by emitting sound pulses and detecting or measuring their return after being reflected; a similar method of (freq. ultrasonic) echolocation used in air or water by bats, whales, etc.; in MEDICINE, a system for examining a foetus etc. inside the body, using reflected ultrasound. Cf. ASDIC. **M20.**
2 (An) apparatus or an installation used for any of these systems. **M20.**

sonata /səˈnɑːtə/ *noun.* **L17.**
[Italian, fem. pa. pple of *sonare* to sound.]
A musical composition for one or two instruments (one usu. being the piano), usu. in several movements with one (esp. the first) or more in sonata form (see below).
Comb.: **sonata form** the musical form of a sonata; *spec.* a type of composition in three main sections (exposition, development, and recapitulation) in which the thematic material is explored, being characteristic of the first movement in a sonata, symphony, concerto, etc.

sonata da camera /soˌnaːta da ˈkamera/ *noun phr.* Pl. ***sonate da camera*** /soˌnaːte/. **E19.**
[Italian, lit. 'chamber sonata'.]
A musical composition for one or more solo instruments and continuo, popular in the 17th and 18th cents., usu. consisting of a suite of dance movements.

sonata da chiesa /soˌnaːta da kiˈeːza/ *noun phr.* Pl. ***sonate da chiesa*** /soˌnaːte/. **E19.**
[Italian, lit. 'church sonata'.]
A musical composition for one or more solo instruments and continuo, popular in the 17th and 18th cents., usu. consisting of four alternately slow and fast movements.

sonate da camera, ***sonate da chiesa*** *noun phrs.* pls. of SONATA DA CAMERA, SONATA DA CHIESA.

sonatina /sɒnəˈtiːnə/ *noun.* **M18.**
[Italian, dim. of SONATA.]
A short or simple sonata.

sondage /sɒnˈdɑːʒ/ *noun.* Pl. **-dages** /-ˈdɑːʒɪz, -ˈdɑːʒ/. **M20.**
[French = sounding, borehole.]
ARCHAEOLOGY. A trench dug to investigate the stratigraphy of a site.

sonde /sɒnd/ *noun.* **E20.**
[French = sounding-line, sounding.]
1 A radiosonde or similar device that is sent aloft to transmit or record information on conditions in the atmosphere. Orig. only in comb. with specifying word, as ***ballon-sonde*** etc. **E20.**
2 An instrument probe for transmitting information about its surroundings underground or under water. **M20.**

sonder /ˈzɒndə/ *adjective & noun. US.* **E20.**
[Abbreviation of German *Sonderklasse* special class.]
▶**A** *adjective.* Of, pertaining to, or designating a class of small racing yachts. **E20.**
▶**B** *noun.* A yacht of this class. **E20.**

Sonderbund /ˈzɒndəbʊnt/ *noun.* **M19.**
[German = special league, separate association.]
Hist. A league formed by the Roman Catholic cantons of Switzerland in 1843 and defeated in a civil war in 1847.

Sonderkommando /ˈzɔndərkɔˌmando/ *noun.* Pl. **-os** /-oz/. **M20.**
[German = special detachment.]
Hist. In Nazi Germany, a detachment of prisoners in a concentration camp responsible for the disposal of the dead; a member of such a detachment.

sone /səʊn/ *noun.* **E17.**
[Latin *sonus* sound.]
†**1** Sound. Only in **E17.**
2 A unit of subjective loudness such that the number of sones is proportional to the loudness of a sound, a tone of frequency 1000 Hz and 40 dB above the listener's audibility threshold producing a loudness of one sone. **M20.**

sonerila /sɒnəˈriːlə/ *noun.* **M19.**
[mod. Latin (see below), from Javanese *sonerila*.]
Any of various tropical Asian plants constituting the genus *Sonerila* (family Melastomataceae), with scorpioid racemes of showy, chiefly purple, trimerous flowers; esp. *S. margaritacea*, grown for its variegated leaves.

Soneryl /ˈsɒnərɪl/ *noun.* **E20.**
[Invented word.]
PHARMACOLOGY. (Proprietary name for) the drug butobarbitone.

son et lumière /sɒn eɪ ˈluːmjɛː, *foreign* sɔ̃ e lymjɛːr/ *noun phr.* Pl. **son et lumières** /ˈluːmjɛːz, *foreign* lymjɛːr/. **M20.**
[French, lit. 'sound and light'.]
1 An entertainment using recorded sound and lighting effects, usu. presented at night at a historic building or other site to give a dramatic narrative of its history. **M20.**
2 *fig.* Writing or behaviour resembling a son et lumière presentation, esp. in its dramatic qualities. **M20.**

song /sɒŋ/ *noun*[1].
[Old English *sang* (*song*) = Old Frisian *sang* (*song*), Old Saxon *sang* (Dutch *zang*), Old High German *sanc* (German *Sang*), Old Norse *songr*, Gothic *saggws*, from Germanic base also of SING *verb*[1].]
1 An act or the art of singing; vocal music; that which is sung. Also (*occas.*), poetry. **OE.**
2 a A metrical composition or other set of words adapted for singing or intended to be sung. Also, a poem, *esp.* a short poem in rhymed stanzas. **OE.** ▸**b** *transf.* A sound as of singing. **E19.** ▸**c** MUSIC. A musical setting or composition adapted for singing or suggestive of a song. **L19.**
3 The musical call or sound made by certain birds, insects, etc., usu. uttered repeatedly in order to establish territory, attract a mate, etc. **OE.**
4 *transf. & fig.* **a** A subject, a theme, a sentiment. **OE.** ▸**b** A trifling sum, amount, or value; a thing of little worth or importance. Also ***an old song***. Freq. in ***for a song***, ***for an old song***, very cheaply, for little or nothing. **E17.** ▸**c** More fully ***song and dance***. A fuss, an outcry, a commotion. *colloq.* **M18.**

> 🕮 **1** MILTON This Subject for Heroic Song Pleas'd me. **2a** E. J. TRELAWNY Inspiring it towards songs and other poetry. DAY LEWIS A . . book of Irish patriotic songs. **4a** EDWARD WARD The same old Song of . . Love . . which they have pip'd to each other these many Years. **c** N. MARSH This is all nonsense. You're making a song about nothing. J. WILCOX She gave me a big song and dance about the article.

Phrases: ***an old song***: see sense 4b above. **a song in one's heart** a feeling of joy or pleasure. ***birdsong***: see BIRD *noun*. ***for a song***, ***for an old song***: see sense 4b above. **on song**, **on full song** *colloq.* in good form, performing well. ***sing another song***, ***sing the same song***: see SING *verb*[1]. **song and dance** (*a*) an entertainment consisting of singing and dancing; (*b*) see sense 4c above. **Song of Ascents**, **Song of Degrees** each of the gradual psalms (see GRADUAL *adjective*). **Song of Solomon**, **Song of Songs** (the name of) a poetic book of the Old Testament and Hebrew Scriptures traditionally attributed to Solomon.
Comb.: **song-ballet** (*a*) *US dial.* a ballad; (*b*) a theatrical work combining songs and ballet; **songbook** (*a*) *Hist.* a service-book of the Anglo-Saxon church; (*b*) a book of songs; **song cycle** a series of related songs, often on a romantic theme, intended to form one musical entity; **songfest** (chiefly *N. Amer.*) an informal session of group-singing; a festive singsong; **song-flight** (a) characteristic flight made by a singing bird in a territorial display; **song-form** MUSIC a form used in the composition of a song; *spec.* a simple melody and accompaniment or a three-part work in which the third part is a repetition of the first; **song-grosbeak** any of several American grosbeaks of the genus *Pheucticus*, which are known for their melodious songs; **song-hit** *colloq.* (now *rare*) a song which is a popular success; **songman** a man accustomed to sing songs, *spec.* one who sings in a church choir; **song-motet** a simple type of motet; **song-perch** a place where a bird regularly perches to sing; **song period** the part of the year during which the birds of a species sing; **song-plug** *verb trans. & intrans.* popularize (a song), esp. by repeated performances; **song-plugger** (orig. *US*) a person employed to popularize songs, esp. by performing them repeatedly; **song-post** = ***song-perch*** above; **song-school** (orig. chiefly *Scot.*) a school for the teaching of (ecclesiastical or secular) singing and music; **songsmith** a writer of songs; **song sparrow** any of three common N. American sparrow-like birds of the genus *Melospiza* (family Emberizidae); esp. *M. melodia*, which occurs in numerous colour varieties; **song stylist** a singer admired for his or her style; ***song thrush***: see THRUSH *noun*[1] 1.
■ **songlet** *noun* a little song **M19.** **songlike** *adjective* resembling (that of) a song **M19.**

Song /sʊŋ/ *noun*[2] *& adjective.* Also **Sung**. **L17.**
[Chinese *sòng*.]
(Designating or pertaining to) a dynasty ruling in China from the 10th to the 13th cent.

songbird /ˈsɒŋbəːd/ *noun.* **L18.**
[from SONG *noun*[1] + BIRD *noun*.]
1 Any bird having a musical song; a singing bird; *spec.* in ORNITHOLOGY, any passerine bird of the suborder Oscines; (in Europe) a perching bird. **L18.**
2 *transf.* A superb (female) singer. **L19.**

songful /ˈsɒŋfʊl, -f(ə)l/ *adjective.* **LME.**
[formed as prec. + -FUL.]
Having much song; musical, melodious.
■ **songfully** *adverb* **L19.** **songfulness** *noun* **M19.**

Songhai /sɒŋˈgʌɪ/ *noun & adjective.* Also **Songhay**, †**Sungai**. **M18.**
[Songhai.]
▶**A** *noun.* Pl. same, **-s**. A member of a people of W. Africa living mainly in Niger and Mali; the language of this people. **M18.**
▶**B** *attrib.* or as *adjective*. Of or pertaining to the Songhai or their language. **M19.**

Songish /sɒŋˈgiːʃ/ *noun & adjective.* Also **Songhies** & other vars. **M19.**
[Songish.]
▶**A** *noun.* Pl. same, **-es**. A member of N. American Indian people of Vancouver Island, British Columbia; the language of this people, a dialect of Salish. **M19.**
▶**B** *attrib.* or as *adjective*. Of or pertaining to the Songish or their language. **M19.**

songket /ˈsɒŋkɛt/ *adjective.* **L19.**
[Malay.]
Of fabric: decorated with short interwoven gold or silver threads.

songkok /ˈsɒŋkɒk/ *noun.* **L19.**
[Malay.]
A kind of skullcap worn by Malay men.

songless /ˈsɒŋlɪs/ *adjective.* **L18.**
[from SONG *noun*[1] + -LESS.]
1 Devoid of song; not singing. **L18.**
2 ORNITHOLOGY. Lacking a musical song. Now *rare*. **E19.**
■ **songlessly** *adverb* **M19.** **songlessness** *noun* **E20.**

songster /ˈsɒŋstə/ *noun.*
[Old English *sangestre*: see SONG *noun*[1], -STER.]
1 A person who sings, a singer, *esp.* a versatile and skilful one. **OE.**
2 A poet; a writer of songs or verse. **L16.**
3 A songbird. **E18.**

> 🕮 **1** P. OLIVER The . . traditions of the blues singers, the songsters . . and guitarists.

songstress /ˈsɒŋstrɪs/ *noun.* **E18.**
[Cf. prec.: see -ESS[1].]
A female songster.

sonhood /ˈsʌnhʊd/ *noun.* **LME.**
[from SON *noun*[1] + -HOOD.]
The condition or relation of being a son.

sonic /ˈsɒnɪk/ *adjective.* **E20.**
[from Latin *sonus* sound + -IC.]
1 Employing or operated by sound waves; *esp.* designating devices and techniques which make use of the reflected echo of a sound pulse. **E20.**
2 Of or pertaining to sound or sound waves, esp. within the audible range. **M20.**
2 sonic bang = ***sonic boom*** below. **sonic barrier** = ***sound barrier*** s.v. SOUND *noun*[2]. **sonic boom** a sudden loud bang heard when the shock wave from an aircraft etc. travelling faster than sound reaches the ears. **sonic mine**: detonated by the sound of a passing ship etc. **sonic speed**, **sonic velocity** the speed at which sound waves travel in a particular medium, esp. air.
■ **sonically** *adverb* **M20.**

sonicate /ˈsɒnɪkeɪt/ *noun & verb.* **M20.**
[from prec. + -ATE[2], after *filtrate*, *precipitate*.]
▶**A** *noun.* A (biological) sample which has been subjected to ultrasonic vibration so as to fragment the macromolecules and membranes in it. **M20.**
▶**B** *verb trans.* Subject to such treatment. **M20.**
■ **soniˈcation** *noun* treatment with ultrasonic vibration **M20.** **sonicator** *noun* an apparatus for performing sonication **M20.**

sonics /ˈsɒnɪks/ *noun pl.* **M20.**
[from SONIC: see -ICS.]
Sonic techniques and equipment generally or collectively.

soniferous /sə(ʊ)ˈnɪf(ə)rəs/ *adjective. rare.* **E18.**
[from Latin *soni-*, *sonus* sound + -FEROUS.]
Sound-bearing; conveying or producing sound.

Sonifier /ˈsɒnɪfʌɪə/ *noun.* **M20.**
[formed as SONIC + -FY + -ER[1].]
(Proprietary name for) a make of sonicator.

Soninke /səˈniːŋkeɪ/ *noun & adjective.* **L19.**
[Soninke.]
▶**A** *noun.* Pl. same, **-s**. A member of a W. African people living in Mali and Senegal; the Mande language or dialects of this people. **L19.**
▶**B** *attrib.* or as *adjective*. Of or pertaining to the Soninke or their language. **L19.**

sonless /ˈsʌnlɪs/ *adjective.* LME.
[from SON *noun*¹ + -LESS.]
Having no son; without a son or sons.

sonlike /ˈsʌnlʌɪk/ *adjective.* L16.
[from SON *noun*¹ + -LIKE.]
Resembling that of a son; filial.

sonly /ˈsʌnli/ *adjective. rare.* LME.
[from SON *noun*¹ + -LY¹.]
Sonlike, filial.

Sonne /ˈsɒnə/ *noun.* E20.
[Carl Olaf *Sonne* (1882–1948), Danish bacteriologist.]
BACTERIOLOGY. Used **attrib.** and formerly in **possess.** with ref. to the Gram-negative bacterium *Shigella sonnei* and the mild form of dysentery which it causes.

sonnet /ˈsɒnɪt/ *noun & verb.* M16.
[French, or its source Italian *sonetto* dim. of *suono* sound.]
▶ **A** *noun.* A poem of fourteen decasyllabic lines, using any of various formal rhyme schemes and usu. having a single theme. More widely (now *rare*), a short poem or piece of esp. lyrical and amatory verse. M16.
Comb.: **sonnet-sequence** a set of sonnets with a common theme or subject.
▶ **B** *verb.* **1** *verb intrans.* Compose sonnets. L16.
2 *verb trans.* Address sonnets to; celebrate in a sonnet or sonnets. L16.
■ **sonnetize** *verb intrans. & trans.* = SONNET *verb* L18. **sonnetry** *noun* sonnet-making L16.

sonneteer /sɒnɪˈtɪə/ *noun & verb.* M17.
[Italian *sonnettiere* (from *sonetto*) or from SONNET *noun* + -EER.]
▶ **A** *noun.* A writer of sonnets; *derog.* a minor or indifferent poet. M17.
▶ **B** *verb trans. & intrans.* = SONNET *verb.* E19.

sonny /ˈsʌni/ *noun. colloq.* M19.
[from SON *noun*¹ + -Y⁶.]
A familiar form of address to a boy or man who is one's junior. Also, a small boy.
Comb.: **sonny boy** [title of a song] a boy; (a form of address to) a man or boy who is one's junior; **Sonny Jim** a familiar form of address to a man or (usu.) a boy who is one's junior.

sono- /ˈsəʊnəʊ/ *combining form* of Latin *sonus* sound: see -O-. Before a vowel also **son-**.
■ **sonobuoy** *noun* a buoy equipped to detect underwater sounds and transmit them automatically by radio M20. **sonoˈchemical** *adjective* of or pertaining to sonochemistry M20. **sonoˈchemistry** *noun* (the branch of science that deals with) the chemical action of sound waves M20. **sonogram** *noun* (*a*) a graphical representation produced by a sonograph of the distribution of sound energy at different frequencies, esp. as a function of time; (*b*) MEDICINE the visual image produced by reflected sound waves in a diagnostic ultrasound examination: M20. **sonolumiˈnescence** *noun* (CHEMISTRY) luminescence excited in a substance by the passage of sound waves through it M20. **sonolumiˈnescent** *adjective* of or pertaining to sonoluminescence L20. **soˈnometer** *noun* (*a*) an instrument for determining the frequency of a musical note, *esp.* one consisting of a resonance box supporting a string over a movable fret; (*b*) = AUDIOMETER; (*c*) a telephone attached to an apparatus for testing metals by means of an induction coil: E19. **sonoˈrescence** *noun* (now *rare*) the conversion of intermittent radiations into sound L19.

sonograph /ˈsəʊnəgrɑːf/ *noun.* In sense 1 also (proprietary name in the US) **Sona-**. M20.
[from prec. + -GRAPH.]
1 An instrument which analyses sound into its component frequencies and produces a graphical record of the results. M20.
2 An image of a tract of seabed obtained by means of side-scan sonar. L20.

sonolysis /sə(ʊ)ˈnɒləsɪs/ *noun.* M20.
[from SONO- + -LYSIS.]
CHEMISTRY. The chemical breakdown of a liquid or solution by ultrasound as a result of the high temperatures generated within the cavitation bubbles formed.
■ **sonoˈlytic** *adjective* M20. **sonoˈlytically** *adverb* M20. **ˈsonolyse** *verb trans.* subject to sonolysis M20.

Sonoran /səˈnɔːrən/ *adjective.* L19.
[from *Sonora* a State in NW Mexico + -AN.]
1 Of or pertaining to a biogeographical region including desert areas of the south-western US and central Mexico. L19.
2 Of, pertaining to, or characteristic of a grouping of related Indian languages spoken in southern Arizona and northern Mexico. L19.

sonorant /ˈsɒn(ə)r(ə)nt, səˈnɔːr(ə)nt/ *noun.* M20.
[from SONOR(OUS + -ANT¹.]
PHONETICS. A resonant; a sound produced with the vocal cord so positioned that spontaneous voicing is possible; a vowel, a glide, or a liquid or nasal consonant.

sonority /səˈnɒrɪti/ *noun.* E17.
[French *sonorité* or late Latin *sonoritas*, from *sonorus*: see next, -ITY.]
The quality of being sonorous; an instance of this.

📖 V. BROME A biblical sonority in the language. *Gramophone* It is no masterpiece though there are some rich sonorities.

sonorous /ˈsɒn(ə)rəs, səˈnɔːrəs/ *adjective.* E17.
[Latin *sonorus*, from *sonor*, *sonor-* sound: see -OUS.]
1 a Of a thing: emitting or capable of emitting an esp. deep or ringing sound. E17. ▸**b** Of a place etc.: resounding, roaring, noisy. E18.
2 Of a sound: loud, deep, resonant. M17.
3 Of language, diction, etc.: having a full, rich sound; imposing, grand; harmonious. L17.
4 PHYSICS. Of or pertaining to sound. Now *rare.* M19.

📖 **1a** C. ENGEL Instruments consisting of a series of pieces of sonorous wood. **2** B. CHATWIN A funeral march composed of the two sonorous chords he had learned. **3** H. WOUK Announcers . . tended to use sonorous doom-filled voices.

■ **sonoˈrosity** *noun* (*rare*) L18. **sonorously** *adverb* M17. **sonorousness** *noun* L17.

sons bouchés /sɔ̃ buʃe/ *noun pl.* E20.
[French, lit. 'blocked sounds'.]
In horn-playing, notes stopped by the insertion of the hand into the bell of the instrument; a direction indicating this.

sonse /sɒns/ *noun. Scot. & Anglo-Irish.* ME.
[Irish, Gaelic *sonas* good fortune, from *sona* fortunate, happy.]
Abundance, plentifulness, plenty; prosperity.

sonship /ˈsʌnʃɪp/ *noun.* L16.
[from SON *noun*¹ + -SHIP.]
The position, state, or relation of a son; sonhood.

sonsy /ˈsɒnsi/ *adjective.* Chiefly *Scot., Anglo-Irish, & north.* M16.
[from SONSE + -Y¹.]
1 Bringing luck or good fortune; lucky, fortunate. M16.
2 Having an agreeably healthy or attractive appearance; plump, buxom, comely. M16.
3 Of an animal: tractable, manageable. L18.

📖 **2** *Daily Telegraph* The delicious Miss Scales, as sonsy and cuddlesome as ever.

sontag /ˈsɒntag, *foreign* ˈzɔntak/ *noun.* M19.
[Henriette *Sontag* (1806–54), German singer.]
A type of knitted or crocheted jacket or cape, with long ends which cross in front and tie behind, worn by women in the second half of the 19th cent.

†sontie, sonty *nouns* vars. of SANTY.

sooey /ˈsuːi/ *interjection. US dial.* L19.
[Origin uncertain: perh. alt. of SOW *noun*¹. Cf. SHOO.]
Calling or driving pigs.

soogan *noun* see SUGGAN.

soogee /ˈsuːdʒiː/ *verb & noun. Nautical slang.* E20.
[from next.]
▶ **A** *verb trans.* Pa. t. & pple **-geed**. Clean (wood and paintwork) with soogee-moogee. E20.
▶ **B** *noun.* = next. M20.

soogee-moogee /ˈsuːdʒɪmuːdʒiː/ *noun. Nautical slang.* L19.
[Origin unkn.]
A mixture containing caustic soda used to clean paintwork and woodwork on a ship or boat. Also, a cleaning operation in which soogee-moogee is used.

soojee /ˈsuːdʒiː/ *noun.* Also **-ji**. L18.
[Hindi *sūjī*.]
A flour obtained by grinding Indian wheat; fine semolina; a nutritious food prepared from this.

sook /sʊk/ *noun*¹. *colloq.* Now chiefly *Scot., Austral., & NZ.* Also (earlier) **souk**. M19.
[Dial. var. of SUCK *noun.*]
A stupid or timid person; a coward; a softie.
■ **sookey, sooky** *adjective* cowardly, soft, stupid M20.

sook /suːk/ *noun*² *& interjection. Scot. & US dial.* Also **suke**. M19.
[Prob. from SUCK *verb.*]
▶ **A** *noun.* (A familiar name for) a cow. M19.
▶ **B** *interjection.* Calling or driving cattle. Freq. in ***sook cow***. M19.
■ Also **sookie, sukey** *noun & interjection* M19.

sook /suːk/ *noun*³. *US.* M20.
[Origin unkn.]
A mature female of the blue crab, *Callinectes sapidus*.

sool /suːl/ *verb.* Chiefly *Austral. & NZ.* L19.
[Var. of SOWL *verb.*]
1 *verb trans. & intrans.* Of a dog: attack, worry. Freq. as *imper.* L19.
2 *verb trans.* Urge, goad. Also foll. by *after, on.* L19.
■ **sooler** *noun* an inciter; an agitator: E20.

soon /suːn/ *adjective.* ME.
[Attrib. use of the adverb.]
Taking place, coming about, happening, etc., soon or quickly; early, speedy.

soon /suːn/ *adverb.*
[Old English *sōna* = Old Frisian *sōn*, Old Saxon *sāno*, *sān(a*, Old High German *sān*, from West Germanic, perh. rel. to Gothic *suns* immediately.]
1 Within a short time, before long, quickly. Formerly also, without delay, straightaway, immediately. OE.
2 a Early; before the time specified or referred to is much advanced. ME. ▸**b** At an early stage, date, period, etc. E17.
3 In compar.: more quickly, readily, or easily (*than*); earlier (*than*); preferably, rather. ME.
4 In superl.: most quickly, readily, etc. Now freq., as soon as possible. ME.

📖 **1** F. SWINNERTON One day soon she would refurnish the entire flat. I. MURDOCH I must go back soon, perhaps tomorrow. **2a** E. PEACOCK It was not a moment too soon. H. HORNSBY I'll come back soon in the morning. **3** W. S. MAUGHAM I'd much sooner call you Edward. H. JAMES He hasn't broached the question sooner because their return was uncertain. G. VIDAL She had come away from Rome sooner than planned. **4** C. SIMMONS Get a wire off to Tony soonest.

Phrases: **as soon (as)** (*a*) as quickly (as), as early (as); (*b*) as readily (as); (*c*) (now *rare*) with as much reason or likelihood (as). **as soon as** at the very time or moment when; see also *soon as* below. **at soonest, at the soonest** at the earliest. ***least said, soonest mended***. **no sooner** not earlier. **no sooner . . but, no sooner . . than** = *as soon as* above. **soon after** (*a*) shortly after, before long; (*b*) not long after, within a short time from. **soon afterwards** = *soon after* above. **soon as** (*poet.* or *colloq.*) = *as soon as* above. **sooner or later** at some time or other, eventually. **soon or late** = *sooner or later* above. ***soon or syne***: see SYNE *adverb* 2. **so soon** so quickly, so early. **so soon as** = *as soon as* above. **the sooner** the more quickly, the earlier.
■ **soonish** *adverb* L19. **soonly** *adverb* (now *rare*) soon, quickly, speedily L15. **soonness** /-n-n-/ *noun* (now *rare*) M17.

sooner /ˈsuːnə/ *noun*¹. *US slang.* L19.
[from prec. + -ER¹.]
A person who acts prematurely; *spec.* (*Hist.*) a person trying to settle Government territory in the western US (esp. in Oklahoma) before the appointed time. Also (**S-**), an Oklahoman.

sooner /ˈsuːnə/ *noun*². *slang* (chiefly *Austral.*). L19.
[Perh. formed as prec.]
An idler, a shirker; *contempt.* an ineffectual or obstructive person, object, etc.

soop /suːp/ *verb trans. Scot. & north.* L15.
[Old Norse *sópa* rel. to Old English *swāpan*: see SWEEP *verb.*]
1 Sweep (a house etc.). L15.
2 CURLING. Assist the progress of (a curling-stone) by sweeping the ice in front of it. Also foll. by *up.* E19.

soopolallie *noun* var. of SOAPOLALLIE.

soor /ˈsuːə/ *noun*¹. *Indian subcontinent.* M19.
[Hindi *sūar*, *sūr* from Sanskrit *sūkara* pig.]
A term of abuse for a person: pig, swine.

soor /sʊə/ *noun*². Now *rare* or *obsolete.* L19.
[Origin unkn.]
MEDICINE. = THRUSH *noun*² 1.

sooranjee /sʊəˈrandʒiː/ *noun.* Also **-ngie**. M19.
[Sanskrit *surañgī*.]
The root of a tropical Asian shrub, *Morinda citrifolia*, of the madder family; the dye morindin obtained from this.

soorma *noun* var. of SURMA.

soosy /ˈsuːsi, ˈsʊsi/ *noun.* Now *rare* or *obsolete.* Also (earlier) **†sooseys**. E17.
[Portuguese *soajes* from Persian & Urdu *sūsī*.]
A striped Indian fabric of silk and cotton.

soot /sʊt/ *noun & verb.*
[Old English *sōt* = Middle Low German *sōt* (German dial. *Sott*), Middle Dutch *soet*, (also mod. dial.) *zoet*, Old Norse *sót*, from Germanic from Indo-European base also of SIT *verb.*]
▶ **A** *noun.* A black carbonaceous substance rising as fine particles in the smoke from the combustion of coal, wood, oil, etc., and deposited on the sides of a chimney etc.; a deposit or particular kind of soot; the colour of soot. OE.

📖 R. WEST The winter countryside . . the soot-black coppices. U. BENTLEY Buildings . . charred with two hundred years of industrial soot.

▶ **B** *verb trans.* **1** Cover or darken (as) with soot; deposit soot on. E17.
2 Sprinkle or manure with soot. E18.
3 Foll. by *up*: fill or choke with a sooty deposit. E20.

sooterkin /ˈsuːtəkɪn/ *noun.* Now *rare.* M16.
[Sense 1 app. from early Dutch or Flemish *soet* sweet (see -KIN); sense 2 perh. from prec.]
†1 Sweetheart, mistress. Only in M16.
2 A kind of afterbirth formerly attributed to Dutch women. *obsolete* exc. *Hist.* E17. ▸**b** An imperfect or supplementary literary composition. M17. ▸**c** A Dutch person. Also, a blackened or black person. Now *rare* or *obsolete.* L17.

sooth /suːθ/ *adjective, noun, & adverb. arch.*
[Old English *sōþ* = Old Saxon *sōð*, Old Norse *sannr*, *saðr*, from Germanic from Indo-European. Cf. Sanskrit *satya*. See also next.]
▶ **A** *adjective.* **†1** Veritable, real, genuine. OE–ME.
2 Of a statement etc.: true, not false or fictitious. OE.
3 Of a person etc.: telling or speaking the truth, truthful. ME.

4 Soothing, soft; smooth. *poet.* **E19.**
▶**B** *noun.* **1** (The) truth, the facts; fact, verity. **OE.**
2 A true thing or saying; a truth. Long *obsolete* exc. *Scot.* **ME.**
†**3** Flattery, blandishments; a smooth or plausible word or speech. **L16–E17.**

📖 **1** W. HAIG How far my accuser is from the sooth in charging me with this imputation. TENNYSON Was there sooth in Arthur's prophecy? **by my sooth**, **by my good sooth**, **by your sooth**, **by your good sooth** my word!, my goodness! **in sooth**, **in good sooth**, **in very sooth** in truth, truly, really.

▶**C** *adverb.* Truly, truthfully, in truth. **OE.**
¶ Rare or obsolete (exc. in **by my sooth**, **by your sooth**, etc.) by **M17**; revived **E19.**

soothe /suːð/ *verb & noun.*
[Old English (*ġe*)*sōþian*, from *sōþ* **SOOTH** *adjective.*]
▶**A** *verb trans.* Also †**sooth.**
†**1** Prove or show (a fact etc.) to be true, verify. **OE–L16.**
†**2** Declare or maintain (a statement) to be true; put forward (a lie or untruth) as being true; uphold as the truth. **M16–E18.**
†**3** Support or encourage (a person) *in* an activity, assertion, etc. Also foll. by *up.* **M16–E18.**
†**4** Flatter or humour (a person). Also foll. by *up.* **L16–E19.**
†**5** Smooth or gloss over (an offence etc.). Also foll. by *up.* **L16–M17.**
6 Bring or restore (a person, feelings, etc.) to a peaceful or tranquil condition; calm, pacify, comfort; appease, placate. **L17.** ▶**b** Say in a soothing manner. **M20.**
7 Reduce the force or intensity of (an emotion, pain, etc.); soften, allay, assuage. **E18.** ▶**b** Drive *away* or dispel by soothing. **M18.**

📖 **6** L. STEFFENS He is satisfying the people, soothing their ruffled pride. G. STEIN The little girl . . cried, and . . Lena had to soothe her. M. WARNER It seems to soothe her to think of him in heaven. **b** *Punch* 'The neighbours need know nothing . . ,' soothed Dr Snodgrass. **7** L. STEPHEN Coffee . . seems to have soothed his headaches. J. SUTHERLAND Humphry soothed his grief by composing an inscription for RR's gravestone. *absol.*: A. B. GARROD The decoction . . is employed as an external application to allay pain and soothe.

▶**B** *noun.* A soothing feeling or effect. *rare.* **M20.**
■ **soothing** *noun* the action of the verb; an instance of this: **LME.** **soothing** *adjective* †(*a*) flattering; specious, plausible; (*b*) serving or intended to soothe, calm, or comfort a person or thing; *soothing syrup*, a medicinal preparation supposed to calm fretful children; *fig.* flattery; empty reassurance; merely palliative remedies: **L16.** **soothingly** *adverb* **E17.** **soothingness** *noun* (*rare*) **E19.**

soother /ˈsuːðə/ *noun.* **M16.**
[from **SOOTHE** *verb* + **-ER**[1].]
†**1** A flatterer. **M16–M17.**
2 A person who or thing which soothes, calms, or comforts someone or something; a soothing influence; now *spec.* a baby's dummy. **L18.**

soother /ˈsuːðə/ *verb trans. Scot., Anglo-Irish, dial., & US.* **M19.**
[formed as prec. + **-ER**[5].]
Cajole, flatter; soothe, calm. Freq. as ***soothering*** *ppl adjective.*

soothfast /ˈsuːθfɑːst/ *adjective & adverb. arch.*
[Old English *sōþfæst*: see **SOOTH** *noun*, **FAST** *adjective.*]
▶**A** *adjective.* **1** Of a person: speaking or adhering to the truth, truthful; faithful, loyal. **OE.**
2 In accordance or conformity with the truth, true. **OE.** ▶†**b** Reliable, certain, sure. **LME–L16.**
†**3** Correctly so called, genuine, real. **ME–L15.**
▶**B** *adverb.* Soothfastly. **ME.**
¶ Obsolete exc. **SCOTS LAW** by **E17**; revived **E19.**
■ **soothfastly** *adverb* **OE.** **soothfastness** *noun* **OE.**

soothful /ˈsuːθfʊl, -f(ə)l/ *adjective. arch.* **ME.**
[from **SOOTH** *adjective* + **-FUL.**]
True, truthful.
¶ Obsolete by **L16**; revived **E19.**
■ †**soothfully** *adverb*: only in **ME.**

†**soothly** *adjective. rare.* **OE–L18.**
[formed as prec. + **-LY**[1].]
Truthful; true, real.

soothly /ˈsuːθli/ *adverb. arch.* **OE.**
[formed as prec. + **-LY**[2].]
Truly, verily; assuredly, certainly, really; indeed.
¶ Rare or obsolete by **18**; revived in **E19.**

soothsay /ˈsuːθseɪ/ *noun & verb.* **M16.**
[Back-form. from **SOOTHSAYER** or **SOOTHSAYING.**]
▶**A** *noun.* †**1** A true or wise saying; a proverb. Only in **M16.**
2 A prediction, a prophecy; an omen, a portent. **L16.** ▶**b** (Good) omen; soothsaying, prophesying. *rare.* **L16.**
▶**B** *verb intrans. & trans.* (with *it*) (*inf. & pres.*). Make predictions, foretell future events; predict, prophesy. **L16.**

soothsayer /ˈsuːθseɪə/ *noun.* **ME.**
[from **SOOTH** *noun, adjective* + **SAYER** *noun*[1].]
†**1** A speaker of the truth, a truthful person. **ME–M17.**
2 A person claiming to be able to foretell future events; a prophet, a seer, a diviner. **LME.**
3 A praying mantis. **M19.**

📖 **2** P. LOMAS A soothsayer revealed . . that they would never defeat the Trojans without . . Philoctetes.

■ **soothsayeress** *noun* (*rare*) a female soothsayer **M17.**

soothsaying /ˈsuːθseɪɪŋ/ *noun & adjective.* **LME.**
[formed as prec. + **SAYING.**]
▶**A** *noun.* †**1** The action or practice of telling the truth. Only in **LME.**
2 The action or practice of foretelling future events; an instance of this; (a) prediction, (a) prophecy, (a) divination. **LME.**
▶**B** *adjective.* Acting as a soothsayer, foretelling the future, prophesying. Now *rare.* **M16.**

sootless /ˈsʊtlɪs/ *adjective.* **L19.**
[from **SOOT** *noun* + **-LESS.**]
Free from soot.

sooty /ˈsʊti/ *adjective & noun.* **ME.**
[formed as prec. + **-Y**[1].]
▶**A** *adjective.* **1** Covered or smeared with soot, full of soot; consisting, characteristic, or of the nature of soot. **ME.**
2 Resembling soot in colour; dusky, blackish, brownish black. **L16.**

📖 **1** P. DALLY The air was raw and sooty. **2** A. HALL A grey face and sooty bags under his eyes.

Special collocations: **sooty albatross** either of two albatrosses of the genus *Phoebetria*, which have mainly dark grey plumage and breed on islands in the southern oceans. **sooty blotch** a disease of apples, pears, and citrus fruit, caused by the fungus *Gloeodes pomigena*, which gives rise to darkish blotches on the skin of the fruit. **sooty mangabey** a white mangabey, *Cercocebus torquatus*, of a race which has dusky grey fur. **sooty mould** a black velvety deposit on leaves, fruit, etc., formed by the mycelium of any of various fungi of the family Capnoidaceae; any of such fungi. **sooty shearwater** a southern shearwater, *Puffinus griseus*, which has mainly dark grey plumage and breeds from New Zealand to Chile and the Falklands. **sooty tern** a large oceanic tern, *Sterna fuscata*, which is blackish above and white below, and breeds throughout the tropical oceans.

▶**B** *noun.* A black person. *slang* (*derog.* & considered *racially offensive*). **M19.**
■ **sootily** *adverb* **L19.** **sootiness** *noun* **E17.**

SOP *abbreviation. US.*
Standard operating procedure.

sop /sɒp/ *noun*[1].
[Late Old English *sopp* corresp. to Middle Low German *soppe*, Old High German *sopfa* bread and milk, Old Norse *soppa*, prob. from weak grade of base of Old English *sūpan* **SUP** *verb*[1].]
1 A piece of bread etc. dipped or steeped in water, wine, gravy, etc. **LOE.** ▶**b** A dish composed of steeped bread. **M19.**
2 *transf. & fig.* †**a** A thing of small value. **LME–E16.** ▶**b** A person or thing soaked in a liquid or (formerly) imbued with a quality etc. **L15.** ▶**c** A dull or foolish person; a milksop. *colloq.* **E17.**
3 A thing given or done to appease or pacify a person; a meaningless concession; a bribe. **M17.**
4 An accumulation of liquid; a soaked state or condition; a thorough wetting or soaking. **E18.**

📖 **3** *Times* This lavish expenditure . . is intended as a sop to the disaffected. J. COLVILLE The necessity of throwing occasional sops to public opinion.

Comb.: **sops-in-wine** *arch.* (*a*) the clove pink, *Dianthus carophyllus*, esp. a variety with red-striped petals; (*b*) a crimson-flushed variety of apple.

sop /sɒp/ *noun*[2]. Now *north.* **LME.**
[Perh. from Old Norse *soppr* ball.]
†**1** A compact body or group, esp. of troops. **LME–E16.**
2 †**a** A cloud *of* mist or smoke. Only in **E16.** ▶**b** A small cloud. **E19.**
3 a A tuft, a clump, esp. of wet green grass among hay. **M17.** ▶**b** A lump or mass of blacklead in the ground. **L18.**

sop /sɒp/ *verb.* Infl. **-pp-.**
[Old English *soppian*, from **SOP** *noun*[1].]
1 *verb trans.* **a** Dip, soak, or steep (bread etc.) in liquid. **OE.** ▶**b** Drench with moisture, soak; *fig.* intoxicate. **L17.** ▶**c** Soak *up*, absorb. **L19.**
2 *verb intrans.* **a** Be or become soaking wet. See also **SOPPING** *ppl adjective.* **M19.** ▶**b** Of moisture: soak *in* or *through.* **M19.**

📖 **1a** M. MITCHELL Scarlett sopped the wheat cake in the gravy. **c** *fig.*: B. CHATWIN He travelled all over the subcontinent, sopping up impressions.

sopaipilla /sopaiˈpiʎa, səʊpʌɪˈpiːljə/ *noun.* Pl. **-as** /-əs, -əz/. **M20.**
[Amer. Spanish, dim. of Spanish *sopaipa* a kind of sweet fritter.]
Esp. in New Mexico, a deep-fried usu. square pastry eaten with honey or sugar or as a bread.

sope /səʊp/ *noun. obsolete* exc. *north.*
[Old English *sopa* (from weak grade of *sūpan* **SUP** *verb*[1]) = Old Norse (Icelandic) *sopi*, Middle Low German *sope*, Middle Dutch *sope*, *soop* (Dutch *zoop*).]
A small amount of liquid, esp. drink; a sup, a draught.

soph /sɒf/ *noun. colloq.* **M17.**
[Abbreviation.]
1 = **SOPHISTER** 2a. Now *Hist.* **M17.**
2 = **SOPHOMORE.** Chiefly *US.* **L18.**

Sophia /ˈsɒfɪə/ *noun.* **M17.**
[Latin from Greek, from *sophos* wise.]
Wisdom, knowledge (freq. personified).
■ **Sophian** *adjective* **E20.**

sophianic /səʊfɪˈanɪk/ *adjective.* **M20.**
[from prec. after *Messianic*: see **-IC.**]
THEOLOGY. Of or pertaining to wisdom.

sophic /ˈsɒfɪk/ *adjective.* **E18.**
[Greek *sophikos*, from *sophia* wisdom: see **-IC.**]
†**1** Obtained by some secret process. Only in **E18.**
2 Full of or conveying wisdom, learned. **L18.**
3 Pertaining to knowledge or speculation. **L19.**
■ **sophical** *adjective* sophic **E17.** **sophically** *adverb* **L19.**

†**sophimore** *noun* var. of **SOPHOMORE.**

sophiology /sɒfɪˈɒlədʒi/ *noun.* **L19.**
[Greek *sophia*: see prec., **-OLOGY.**]
1 The science of educational activities. *rare.* **L19.**
2 **THEOLOGY.** The doctrine of the Divine Wisdom, as serving to explain the relations between God and the world. **M20.**
■ **sophioˈlogical** *adjective* **M20.** **sophiologist** *noun* **M20.**

sophism /ˈsɒfɪz(ə)m/ *noun.* Also †**sophom**, †**sophum.** **LME.**
[Old French *sophime* (mod. *sophisme*) from Latin from Greek *sophisma* clever device, trick, argument, from *sophizesthai* devise, become wise, from *sophos* wise, clever: see **-ISM.**]
1 A plausible but fallacious argument, *esp.* one intended to deceive or to display ingenuity in reasoning. **LME.**
2 Specious or oversubtle reasoning, sophistry, casuistry. **M18.**

sophist /ˈsɒfɪst/ *noun.* **LME.**
[Latin *sophista*, *-tes* from Greek *sophistēs*, from *sophizesthai*: see prec., **-IST.**]
In ancient Greece, a scholar, a teacher; *spec.* a paid teacher of philosophy and rhetoric, *esp.* one associated with specious reasoning and moral scepticism; *gen.* (now *rare*) a wise or learned person. Now, a person using clever but fallacious arguments; a specious reasoner, a casuist.

sophister /ˈsɒfɪstə/ *noun.* **LME.**
[Old French *sophistre*, formed as prec.: see **-ER**[2].]
1 A person reasoning with specious arguments. Formerly also, a sophist of ancient Greece. **LME.**
2 a A student in his second or third year at Cambridge or (*occas.*) Oxford University. Now *Hist.* **L16.** ▶**b** A similar (male or female) student at Harvard or Dartmouth University. *US.* **M17.** ▶**c** A student in his or her third or fourth year at Trinity College, Dublin. **M19.**

sophistic /səˈfɪstɪk/ *adjective & noun.* **L15.**
[Old & mod. French *sophistique* or Latin *sophisticus*, from *sophista*: see **SOPHIST**, **-IC.**]
▶**A** *adjective.* **1** Of or pertaining to sophistry or sophists; of the nature of sophistry, specious, oversubtle. **L15.** ▶**b** Pertaining to or characteristic of sophists of ancient Greece. **M19.**
2 Of a person: given to or using sophistry or specious reasoning. **M16.**

📖 **1** *Music & Letters* Criticism . . that used to appear . . oversophisticated, even sophistic.

▶**B** *noun.* **1** *sing.* & in *pl.* Sophistic argument or speculation, esp. as a subject of instruction. **L15.**
2 Sophistry, deceptiveness. **M19.**

sophistical /səˈfɪstɪk(ə)l/ *adjective.* **LME.**
[formed as prec.: see **-ICAL.**]
1 = **SOPHISTIC** *adjective.* **LME.**
†**2** Used for the purpose of adulteration or deception. **M16–L17.**
■ †**sophisticalness** *noun* **M17–E18.** **sophistically** *adverb* **LME.**

sophisticate /səˈfɪstɪkət/ *noun.* Orig. *US.* **E20.**
[Back-form. from the verb.]
A sophisticated person, a person with sophisticated tastes.

📖 F. ASTAIRE It was not exactly a fashionable . . event but still drew the important mob of Broadway sophisticates. CLIVE JAMES Naïveté leads him closer to the truth than many sophisticates have been able to go.

sophisticate /səˈfɪstɪkət/ *adjective.* **LME.**
[medieval Latin *sophisticatus* pa. pple of *sophisticare*: see next, **-ATE**[2].]
†**1** = **SOPHISTICATED** 1. **LME–L17.**
†**2** = **SOPHISTICATED** 3. **M16–L17.**
3 = **SOPHISTICATED** 2. **L16.**

sophisticate /səˈfɪstɪkeɪt/ *verb.* **LME.**
[medieval Latin *sophisticat-* pa. ppl stem of *sophisticare* tamper with, adulterate, quibble, from Latin *sophisticus*: see **SOPHISTIC**, **-ATE**[3].]

1 *verb trans.* Mix with a foreign or inferior substance, make impure; adulterate (wine etc.). Now *rare*. LME.
2 a *verb trans.* Corrupt, spoil; mislead, overcomplicate, or distort (a person, argument, the mind, etc.) by sophistry. L16. ▸**b** *verb intrans.* Use sophistry. M17.
3 *verb trans.* Falsify (a text etc.) by misrepresentation, interpolation, alteration, etc.; alter deceptively, tamper with. L16.
4 *verb trans.* **a** Make artificial, deprive of natural simplicity or innocence; convert *into* something artificial. E17. ▸**b** Make cultured, worldly, or experienced; refine; make (a technique, theory, piece of equipment, etc.) highly developed and complex. M20.

> 📖 **4a** L. CARR They spoke out their thoughts with a rude freedom which . . proved that they had not been sophisticated into prigs. **b** M. STEWART Three years of . . Nicholas . . would sophisticate a Vestal Virgin.

sophisticated /sə'fɪstɪkeɪtɪd/ *adjective.* E17.
[from prec. + -ED^1.]
1 Mixed with a foreign substance, adulterated, impure. E17.
2 Altered from or deprived of natural simplicity or innocence; (of a text) altered in the course of being copied or printed. E17.
3 Falsified to a greater or lesser extent; not plain, honest, or straightforward. L17. ▸**b** Of a book: having the content, binding, etc., altered so as to deceive. M19.
4 a Experienced, worldly, cultured; discriminating in taste or judgement, subtle; showing awareness of the complexities of a subject etc. Also, associated with or appealing to sophisticated people or tastes. L19. ▸**b** Of a technique, theory, piece of equipment, etc.: involving advanced or refined methods or concepts, highly developed and complex. M20.

> 📖 **4a** D. MACDONALD The kind of sophisticated audience . . that can appreciate and discriminate on its own. *Rolling Stone* A sophisticated cabaret artist whose vocal mimicry and jazz-man scat account for . . his onstage success. R. JAFFE A camel's hair coat . . understated, sophisticated. **b** *New Left Review* The more sophisticated elaboration of post-Keynesian evolutionary theory. *Keyboard Player* Sophisticated edit facilities allow complicated musical forms to be created. *New Yorker* A technologically sophisticated cartoon with . . simpering old Disney values.

■ **sophisticatedly** *adverb* M20.

sophistication /səfɪstɪ'keɪʃ(ə)n/ *noun.* LME.
[Old French, or medieval Latin *sophisticatio(n-)*, formed as SOPHISTICATE *verb*: see -ATION.]
1 The use of sophistry, the process or an act of reasoning with specious arguments or of misleading with these; a sophism, a specious argument. LME.
2 a Adulteration of or *of* a commodity etc.; something adulterated. Also, a substance used in adulteration. LME. ▸**b** Deceptive alteration or corruption *of* something, conversion into a less genuine form; *spec.* the alteration of a text in the course of copying or printing. M16.
3 a The quality or fact of being sophisticated, worldly, or experienced; subtlety, discrimination, refinement; awareness of the complexities of a subject. M19. ▸**b** The property or condition of being highly developed and complex, technical refinement; an instance of this, a technically advanced characteristic. M20.

> 📖 **3a** *Guardian* Off camera Garbo . . would display a . . naiveté very different from the sophistication of the rôles she played. I. COLEGATE Catherine . . felt conscious of her . . lack of sophistication. **b** *Listener* The Trombay establishment is the last word in nuclear sophistication. *Early Music* Instamatics . . with built-in light meter and other sophistications.

sophisticator /sə'fɪstɪkeɪtə/ *noun.* E17.
[from SOPHISTICATE *verb* + -OR.]
A person who sophisticates or adulterates something.

†**sophistress** *noun.* M17–E18.
[from SOPHIST or SOPHISTER: see -ESS^1.]
A female sophist.

sophistry /'sɒfɪstri/ *noun.* ME.
[Old French *sophistrie* (mod. *-erie*) or medieval Latin *sophistria*, formed as SOPHIST: see -RY.]
1 Specious or oversubtle reasoning, the use of intentionally deceptive arguments; casuistry; the use or practice of specious reasoning as an art or dialectic exercise. ME. ▸**b** An instance of this, a sophism. L17.
†**2** Cunning, trickery, craft. LME–M17.
3 The type of learning characteristic of the ancient sophists; the profession of a sophist. M19.

Sophoclean /sɒfə'kliːən/ *adjective.* M17.
[from Latin *Sophocleus* from Greek *Sophokleios*, from *Sophoklēs*, *-klees* (see below): see -EAN.]
Of, pertaining to, or characteristic of the Athenian tragic poet Sophocles (496–406 BC), or his works, style, etc.

†**sophom** *noun* var. of SOPHISM.

sophomore /'sɒfəmɔː/ *noun.* Now chiefly *N. Amer.* Also †**sophimore**. M17.
[from *sophum*, *sophom* obsolete vars. of SOPHISM + -ER^1.]
Orig. (now *rare*), a second-year student at Cambridge University. Now usu., such a student at an American university, college, or high school.

> 📖 *attrib.*: *New Yorker* Stedman entered Yale . . but was invited to leave at the end of his sophomore year.

sophomoric /sɒfə'mɒrɪk/ *adjective.* Chiefly *N. Amer.* E19.
[from prec. + -IC.]
Of, befitting, or characteristic of a sophomore; pretentious; immature, juvenile; crude, superficial.

> 📖 *National Observer (US)* The sophomoric skepticism of the man who has read one book . . only.

■ **sophomorical** *adjective* = SOPHOMORIC M19. **sophomorically** *adverb* L19.

sophora /sə'fɔːrə/ *noun.* M18.
[mod. Latin (see below), from Arab. *ṣufayrāʼ*.]
Any of numerous leguminous trees and shrubs constituting the genus *Sophora*, characterized by pinnate leaves and racemose or paniculate flowers, and including a number grown for ornament, esp. the pagoda-tree, *S. japonica*, and the kowhai, *S. tetraptera*.

sophrosyne /sə(ʊ)'frɒzɪni/ *noun.* L19.
[Greek *sōphrosunē*, from *sōphrōn* of sound mind, prudent.]
Soundness of mind; moderation, prudence, self-control.

†**sophum** *noun* var. of SOPHISM.

Sophy /'səʊfi/ *noun.* E16.
[Arab. *Ṣafī-al-Dīn* pure of religion, epithet given to the ancestor of the dynasty of Persia *c* 1500–1736. Cf. SAFAVID.]
Hist. **1** (A former title of) the supreme ruler of Persia, the Shah. Also ***Grand Sophy***. E16.
2 *gen.* A Persian monarch or king. E17.

sopie /'suːpi/ *noun.* Chiefly *S. Afr.* L17.
[Afrikaans, from Dutch *zoopje* dim. of *zope* SOPE.]
A drink of spirits, a dram, a tot.

sopite /sə(ʊ)'pʌɪt/ *verb trans.* Now *rare*. Pa. pple **-ed**, (*rare*) **-ite**. LME.
[Latin *sopit-* pa. ppl stem of *sopire* deprive of sense or consciousness, formed as next.]
1 Put an end to, settle, (a dispute etc.). Also, pass over, suppress, (something discreditable). LME.
2 Put or lull to sleep; make drowsy, dull, or inactive. M16.

sopor /'səʊpə/ *noun.* M16.
[Latin, rel. to *somnus* sleep.]
1 An abnormally deep sleep; a coma, a stupor. M16.
†**2** A state of mental or moral lethargy or deadness. M–L17.

soporiferous /sɒpə'rɪf(ə)rəs/ *adjective.* Now *rare*. L16.
[from Latin *soporifer* (formed as prec.) + -OUS: see -FEROUS.]
†**1** Of a disease etc.: characterized by abnormal or excessive sleep. L16–L17.
2 = SOPORIFIC *adjective* 1. E17.
3 = SOPORIFIC *adjective* 3. *rare*. E17.
■ **soporiferously** *adverb* M19. **soporiferousness** *noun* L16.

soporific /sɒpə'rɪfɪk/ *adjective & noun.* M17.
[formed as SOPOR + -FIC.]
▸**A** *adjective.* **1** Inducing or tending to produce sleep; *transf.* very tedious or boring. M17.
2 Of the nature of, characterized by, or resembling sleep or sleepiness. M18.
3 Of a person: drowsy, sleepy, somnolent. M19.

> 📖 **1** J. MCCARTHY Those who tried to listen found the soporific influence irresistible. O. SACKS Gentle . . motion is normally soothing and soporific.

▸**B** *noun.* **1** A drug, influence, etc., which induces sleep. E18.
2 A sleepy or somnolent person. *rare*. E19.

> 📖 **1** R. CHURCH Intellectuals using crime-stories as bedtime soporifics.

■ **soporifical** *adjective* = SOPORIFIC *adjective* E19. **soporifically** *adverb* E19.

soporose /'sɒpərəʊs/ *adjective.* Now *rare*. E18.
[from SOPOR + -OSE^1.]
MEDICINE. Of diseases etc.: characterized by abnormally deep sleep or stupor; comatose.
■ Also **soporous** /-rəs/ *adjective* (*rare*) L17.

sopper /'sɒpə/ *noun. rare.* LME.
[from SOP *verb* + -ER^1.]
A person who sops something.

sopping /'sɒpɪŋ/ *noun.* M16.
[from SOP *verb* + -ING^1.]
The action of SOP *verb*; a thorough soaking or wetting.

sopping /'sɒpɪŋ/ *ppl adjective & adverb.* M19.
[formed as prec. + -ING^2.]
▸**A** *adjective.* Soaked with water or moisture, drenched, sodden. M19.
▸**B** *adverb.* ***sopping wet***, very wet, sodden. L19.

soppy /'sɒpi/ *adjective.* E17.
[from SOP *noun*^{1}, *verb* + -Y^1.]
†**1** Full of or containing sops. Only in E17.
2 Soaked with water or moisture, saturated with rain; drenched, sodden. E19.
3 Of the season or weather: very wet or rainy. L19.
4 Mawkishly sentimental. Also, foolishly affectionate; feeble, silly, inane, esp. in a self-indulgent way. *colloq.* E20.

> 📖 **4** A. DRAPER I felt 10 feet tall and there was a soppy grin on my face. *Beano* The softies are playing . . soppy games! I. MURDOCH In England a drawing of a cat will always sell if it is soppy enough. **be soppy on** be infatuated with.

■ **soppily** *adverb* L20. **soppiness** *noun* L19.

sopra bianco /sopra 'bjanko/ *noun phr.* M19.
[Ellipt.]
= BIANCO SOPRA BIANCO.

soprani *noun pl.* see SOPRANO.

sopranino /sɒprə'niːnəʊ/ *noun & adjective.* Pl. **-os**. E20.
[Italian, dim. of next.]
(Designating) an instrument (usu. wind) of higher pitch than a soprano instrument.

soprano /sə'prɑːnəʊ/ *noun & adjective.* M18.
[Italian, from *sopra* above from Latin *supra*.]
▸**A** *noun.* Pl. **-nos**, **-ni** /-ni/.
1 The highest singing voice; the quality or range of this voice. M18. ▸**b** A part for or sung by such a voice. E19.
2 A female or boy singer having such a voice; a person singing a soprano part. M18. ▸**b** (The player of) an instrument of a high pitch, *spec.* of the highest pitch in a family. L19.
▸**B** *attrib.* or as *adjective.* Of, pertaining to, or designating the highest singing voice or instrumental pitch. M18.
soprano clef an obsolete clef placing middle C on the lowest line of the staff.
■ **sopranist** *noun* a soprano singer M19.

sora /'sɔːrə/ *noun.* E18.
[Perh. from an Amer. Indian lang.]
A common New World crake, *Porzana carolina*, which frequents marshy ground. Also ***sora crake***, ***sora rail***.

Sorabian /sə'reɪbɪən/ *adjective & noun.* Now *rare* or *obsolete*. L18.
[from medieval Latin *Sorabi*: see -IAN. Cf. SORB *noun*^{2} & *adjective*.]
= SORB *noun*^{2} & *adjective*.

sorage /'sɔːrɪdʒ/ *noun.* Now *rare*. Also **soarage**. LME.
[Old French (mod. *saurage*), formed as SORE *adjective*^{2}: see -AGE.]
FALCONRY. The first year of a hawk's life; a hawk in its first year. Cf. SORE *noun*^{2}, *adjective*^{2}.

soral /'sɔːr(ə)l/ *adjective.* L19.
[from SORUS + -AL^1.]
BOTANY. Of or pertaining to the sori of ferns.

soralium /sə'reɪlɪəm/ *noun.* Pl. **-ia** /-ɪə/. E20.
[mod. Latin, formed as prec. + -IUM.]
BOTANY. A swollen area of a lichen thallus in which soredia occur.

†**sorance** *noun.* E16–M18.
[from SORE *adjective*^{1} + -ANCE, prob. after GRIEVANCE.]
A sore, or a disease producing a sore, in an animal, esp. a horse.

sorb /sɔːb/ *noun*^{1}. E16.
[French *sorbe* or Latin *sorbum*, from SORBUS.]
1 The fruit of the service tree, *Sorbus domestica*. E16.
2 The service tree, *Sorbus domestica*. Also (*rare*), the wild service, *S. torminalis*; the mountain ash, *S. aucuparia*. M16.

Sorb /sɔːb/ *noun*^{2} & *adjective.* M19.
[German *Sorbe* var. of *Serbe* formed as SERB.]
▸**A** *noun.* **1** A member of a Slavonic people inhabiting the area of Lusatia in eastern Germany. Also called ***Wend***. M19.
2 = SORBIAN *noun* 2. M19.
▸**B** *adjective.* = SORBIAN *adjective*. E20.

sorb /sɔːb/ *verb.* E20.
[Back-form. from SORPTION, after *absorb*, *absorption*.]
PHYSICAL CHEMISTRY. **1** *verb trans. & intrans.* Take up (a substance) by sorption. E20.
2 *verb intrans.* Be taken up by sorption. L20.
■ **sorbate** *noun*^{1} a substance that is sorbed E20.

sorb-apple /'sɔːbap(ə)l/ *noun.* M16.
[German *Sorbapfel*, older Low German, Flemish *sorbappel*: see SORB *noun*^{1}.]
(The fruit of) the service tree, *Sorbus domestica*.

sorbefacient /sɔːbɪ'feɪʃ(ə)nt/ *adjective & noun.* M19.
[from Latin *sorbere* absorb + -FACIENT.]
Chiefly *MEDICINE.* ▸**A** *adjective.* Causing or promoting absorption. M19.
▸**B** *noun.* A sorbefacient drug or substance. M19.

sorbent /'sɔːb(ə)nt/ *adjective & noun.* E20.
[from SORB *verb*, after *absorbent*.]
PHYSICAL CHEMISTRY. ▸**A** *adjective.* Having the property of collecting molecules of a substance by sorption. E20.
▸**B** *noun.* A sorbent substance. E20.

sorbet /ˈsɔːbeɪ, -bɪt/ *noun*. **L16.**
[French, from Italian *sorbetto* formed as SHERBET.]
Orig., an Eastern sherbet. Now usu., a water-ice.

sorbetière /sɔːˈbɛtɪɛː, *foreign* sɔrbətjɛːr/ *noun*. **M20.**
[French, formed as prec.]
A domestic ice-cream-making machine, in which the mixture is stirred as it is being frozen.

Sorbian /ˈsɔːbɪən/ *noun & adjective*. **M19.**
[from SORB *noun*² & *adjective* + -IAN.]
▶ **A** *noun*. **1** A Sorb. **M19.**
2 The W. Slavonic language of the Sorbs. Also called ***Wendish***. **L19.**
▶ **B** *adjective*. Of or pertaining to the Sorbs or their language. **L19.**

sorbic /ˈsɔːbɪk/ *adjective*. **E19.**
[formed as SORB *noun*¹ + -IC.]
CHEMISTRY. ***sorbic acid***, a weak carboxylic acid originally obtained from the berries of mountain ash, *Sorbus aucuparia*, and used as a fungicide, food preservative, and in synthetic coatings etc.; 2,4-hexadienoic acid, $CH_3CH{=}CH{\cdot}CH{=}CHCOOH$.
■ **sorbate** *noun*² a salt or ester of sorbic acid **E19.**

sorbile /ˈsɔːbɪl/ *adjective*. Now *rare*. **LME.**
[Latin *sorbilis*, from *sorbere* drink: see -ILE.]
That may be drunk or sipped; liquid, semi-liquid.

Sorbish /ˈsɔːbɪʃ/ *noun & adjective*. **L19.**
[from SORB *noun*² after German *Sorbisch*, *Serbisch*.]
(Of) the language of the Sorbs, Sorbian.

sorbitan /ˈsɔːbɪtan/ *noun*. **M20.**
[from SORBIT(OL + AN(HYDRIDE.]
CHEMISTRY. Any of several cyclic ethers which are monoanhydrides of sorbitol; *spec*. the 1,4-anhydride, $C_6H_8O(OH)_4$, the fatty-acid esters of which are used as emulsifiers and surfactants.

sorbite /ˈsɔːbʌɪt/ *noun*. **L19.**
[Henry Clifton *Sorby* (1826–1908), English geologist + -ITE¹.]
METALLURGY. **1** A nitride and carbide of titanium found as red microscopic crystals in pig-iron. Now *rare* or *obsolete*. **L19.**
2 A constituent of steel or cast iron consisting of microscopic granules of cementite in a ferrite matrix, produced esp. when hardened steel is tempered above about 450°C. **E20.**
■ **sor'bitic** *adjective* (of cast iron or steel) that contains sorbite, or that has the microstructure of sorbite **E20.** **sorbiti'zation** *noun* the process of sorbitizing steel **M20.** **sorbitize** *verb trans*. convert (steel) into a form containing sorbite (chiefly as ***sorbitized*** *ppl adjective*, ***sorbitizing*** *verbal noun*) **E20.**

sorbitol /ˈsɔːbɪtɒl/ *noun*. **L19.**
[from SORB *noun*¹ + -ITOL.]
CHEMISTRY. A crystalline sweet-tasting hexahydric alcohol, $C_6H_8(OH)_6$, found in various fruits and berries, which has many uses in industry and as a food additive.

Sorbo /ˈsɔːbəʊ/ *noun*. **E20.**
[App. from ABSORB + -O-.]
(Proprietary name for) a type of sponge rubber. Also ***Sorbo rubber***.

Sorbonist /ˈsɔːb(ə)nɪst/ *noun*. **M16.**
[mod. Latin *Sorbonista* or French *Sorboniste*, from *Sorbonne* (see below): see -IST.]
A doctor, graduate, or student at the Sorbonne, orig. a theological college and now part of Paris University.

sorbose /ˈsɔːbəʊz, -s/ *noun*. **L19.**
[from SORB *noun*¹ + -OSE².]
CHEMISTRY. A ketohexose sugar, obtained esp. from mountain ash berries as a bacterial fermentation product of sorbitol, and used in the manufacture of ascorbic acid etc.

sorbus /ˈsɔːbəs/ *noun*. **L16.**
[mod. Latin *Sorbus* (see below) from Latin *sorbus* service tree: cf. SORB *noun*¹.]
Orig. = SORB *noun*¹ 1. Later, any of various north-temperate trees and shrubs constituting the genus *Sorbus*, of the rose family, which includes the service tree, the whitebeam, and the mountain ash.

sorcerer /ˈsɔːs(ə)rə/ *noun*. **LME.**
[from Old & mod. French *sorcier* ult. from Latin *sort-* *sors* lot: see -ER².]
A person claiming magic powers, a practitioner of sorcery; a wizard, a magician.
sorcerer's apprentice [translating French *l'apprenti sorcier*, a symphonic poem by Paul Dukas (1897) after *der Zauberlehrling*, a ballad by Goethe (1797)] a person instigating but being unable to control a process etc.

sorceress /ˈsɔːs(ə)rɪs/ *noun*. **LME.**
[Anglo-Norman *sorceresse* fem. of Old & mod. French *sorcier*: see prec., -ESS¹.]
A female sorcerer, a witch.

sorcerize /sɔːsərʌɪz/ *verb trans*. *rare*. Also **-ise**. **M19.**
[from SORCERER + -IZE.]
Transform by sorcery.

sorcerous /ˈsɔːs(ə)rəs/ *adjective*. **M16.**
[formed as prec. + -OUS.]
Of the nature of or connected with sorcery; dealing in or practising sorcery.

sorcery /ˈsɔːs(ə)ri/ *noun*. **ME.**
[Old French *sorcerie*, formed as SORCERER: see -ERY.]
The art or practice of magic or enchantment, esp. to cause harm; witchcraft; a form or instance of this (usu. in *pl*.).

> 🕮 E. SANDYS They labour . . by . . magic, sorcery and witchcraft, to consume, kill, and destroy. *fig*.: OUIDA Personal beauty is a rare sorcery.

sord /sɔːd/ *verb & noun*. Long *arch*. **LME.**
[Old French *so(u)rdre* from Latin *surgere* rise.]
▶†**A** *verb intrans*. Rise or soar *up* in flight. Only in **LME.**
▶ **B** *noun*. A flight or flock *of* mallards. *rare*. **LME.**

sordes /ˈsɔːdiːz/ *noun pl*. (treated as *sing*. or *pl*.). Now *rare*. **LME.**
[Latin (pl., rare in sing.), dirt, filth, rel. to *sordere* be dirty or foul.]
1 Dirty deposits, purulent discharges, etc., collecting on or in the bodies of people or animals; gut contents. **LME.** ▸**b** MEDICINE. Whitish deposits containing bacteria etc. on the teeth or gums; crusted sores formed about the lips etc. in severe fevers. **M18.**
2 Dirt, filth, refuse; domestic or industrial waste. **M17.**

sordid /ˈsɔːdɪd/ *adjective*. **LME.**
[French *sordide* or Latin *sordidus*, from *sordere* be dirty or foul: see -ID¹.]
▶ **I 1** MEDICINE. (Of discharges etc.) purulent, foul; (of an ulcer, wound, etc.) discharging matter of this kind. Now *rare* or *obsolete*. **LME.**
2 Of a place, condition, appearance, etc.: dirty, foul, filthy; mean and squalid. **E17.**
3 †**a** Of a person etc.: dirty in habits or appearance. **E17–E18.** ▸**b** ZOOLOGY. In the names of fishes etc.: of a dirty colour. Now *rare*. **E19.**

> 🕮 **2** *Harpers & Queen* The couture world was very sordid backstage . . the cabinets were filthy. **3 sordid dragonet** the dull brown female of the dragonet, *Callionymus lyra*, formerly regarded as a different species to the brightly coloured male.

▶ **II** †**4** Of or befitting a low status; humble, menial. **L16–M18.**
5 Esp. of a situation: degraded, base, distasteful; sleazy, gross. Also, characterized by or proceeding from ignoble motives; *spec*. self-interested, mercenary. **E17.** ▸**b** Lacking in refinement; coarse, rough. **M17.**

> 🕮 **5** R. ALI They . . sacrificed their own political principles . . for the sake of sheer opportunism and sordid careerism. C. MCWILLIAMS The . . sordid aftermath, involving jury-fixing, bribery, and murder.

■ **sor'didity** *noun* sordidness **L16.** **sordidly** *adverb* **M17.** **sordidness** *noun* the state or quality of being sordid; dirtiness, squalor; baseness, meanness: **M17.**

sordino /ˈsɔːdɪnəʊ/ *noun*. Pl. **-ini** /-iːni/. Also **-ine** /-iːn/. **L16.**
[Italian, from *sordo*, from Latin *surdus* deaf, mute.]
A mute for a wind or bowed instrument; a damper for a piano.
CON SORDINO.

sordor /ˈsɔːdə/ *noun*. **E19.**
[from SORDID after *squalor*, *squalid*.]
Physical or moral sordidness.

sordun /sɔˈduːn/ *noun*. Also **-une**. **L19.**
[German.]
An early form of bassoon, having a cylindrical bore with double reeds.

sore /sɔː/ *noun*¹.
[Old English *sār* = Old Frisian, Old Saxon, Old High German *sēr* (Dutch *zeer*, German †*Sehr*), Old Norse *sár*, Gothic *sair*, from Germanic.]
†**1** Physical pain or suffering. **OE–L16.**
†**2** (A) sickness, (a) disease. **OE–M17.**
3 A bodily injury; a wound. *obsolete* exc. *dial*. **OE.**
4 A raw or tender place on the body, now *esp*. one caused by pressure or friction. **OE.**
†**5** Mental pain or suffering; sorrow, anxiety; grievous state, misery. **OE–L16.**
6 *fig*. A source of distress or annoyance. **LME.**
4 pressure sore, ***running sore***, ***soft sore***, etc.

†**sore** *noun*². **LME.**
[from SORE *adjective*².]
1 A buck in its fourth year. **LME–M19.**
2 FALCONRY. A hawk with immature plumage. Only in 17.

sore /sɔː/ *adjective*¹.
[Old English *sār* = Old Saxon, Old High German *sēr* (Dutch *zeer*, German *sehr*), Old Norse *sárr*, from Germanic word repr. also in Finnish *sairas* sick, ill.]
▶ **I 1** Of a sickness, wound, blow, etc.: causing physical pain; severe in this respect. *arch*. **OE.**
2 Causing, characterized by, or expressive of mental pain; sorrowful; bitter. *arch*. **OE.** ▸**b** Sorry, pitiful, contemptible. Long *dial*. **LME.**
3 Involving great hardship, exertion, or difficulty. Long *obsolete* exc. *Scot*. **OE.**
4 Of a trouble, affliction, etc.: difficult to endure, grievous; (as an intensive) very great, serious. Chiefly *arch*. **ME.**
5 (Of a feeling) intense, strong, violent; (of weather) severe, stormy. Now *arch*. & *Scot*. **LME.**
6 Of a person (formerly also of language, a command, etc.): stern, hard, harsh. Now *dial*. **E16.**

> 🕮 **4** J. JOHNSTON We haven't cut the cake yet. It's been a sore temptation though.

▶ **II 7** Of a part of the body: painful, aching; raw, tender, inflamed. **OE.**
8 Of a person: suffering pain. **ME.**
9 Now esp. of the conscience, heart, etc.: afflicted with sorrow or grief; distressed. *arch*. **ME.**
10 Irritated; angry; resentful. Now *colloq*. (chiefly *N. Amer*.). **L17.**

> 🕮 **7** F. MARRYAT My shoulder is quite sore with the rope. A. SILLITOE His eyes were sore from little sleep. A. N. WILSON She . . sobbed till her throat was sore. **8** E. BLAIR Curling up . . she sank into gorgeous oblivion! She awoke stiff and sore. **10** J. VAN DRUTEN I'm a little sore at her for letting me down. S. BELLOW I'm still sore because he cheated on me. *Superbike* I'm not being a sore loser.

Phrases: **done up like a sore finger**, **done up like a sore toe** *Austral*. & *NZ colloq*. overdressed. ***like a bear with a sore head***: see BEAR *noun*¹. ***sight for sore eyes***: see SIGHT *noun*. **stand out like a sore thumb**, **stick out like a sore thumb** *colloq*. be very conspicuous.
Special collocations: **sore point** a subject causing distress or annoyance. **sore throat** an inflammation of the mucous membrane lining the back of the mouth, or of the tonsils.

sore /sɔː/ *adjective*². *obsolete* exc. *Hist*. Also †**soar**. **ME.**
[Anglo-Norman, Old French *sor* (mod. *saur*): see SORREL *adjective*.]
†**1** Of a horse: sorrel. **ME–L17.**
2 FALCONRY. Designating a hawk (untrained) that has not moulted and still has its red plumage. **LME.**

sore /sɔː/ *verb trans*. **LME.**
[from SORE *adjective*¹.]
1 Make sore; pain. *arch*. **LME.**
2 Foll. by *up*: annoy. *US colloq*. *rare*. **E20.**

sore /sɔː/ *adverb*. Now *arch*. & *dial*.
[Old English *sāre* = Old Frisian *sēre*, Old Saxon, Old High German *sēro* (Dutch *zeer*, German *sehr* greatly, very).]
1 = SORELY. **OE.**
2 With great effort or exertion; with force or vigour. **ME.**

soredium /sɔˈriːdɪəm/ *noun*. Pl. **-ia** /-ɪə/. **E19.**
[mod. Latin, from Greek *sōros* heap.]
BOTANY. In lichens, any of a number of minute granules (each consisting of a group of algal cells surrounded by hyphae) which appear as powdery dust on the upper surface of the thallus and are dispersed by the wind, giving rise to new plants. Usu. in *pl*.
■ **soredial** *adjective* of the nature of or pertaining to a soredium **L19.** **sorediate** *adjective* bearing soredia **M19.** **sore'diferous** *adjective* = SOREDIATE **E19.** **soredioid** *adjective* having the appearance or character of a soredium or soredia **M19.**

sorehead /ˈsɔːhɛd/ *noun & adjective*. *N. Amer. colloq*. **M19.**
[from SORE *adjective*¹ + HEAD *noun*.]
▶ **A** *noun*. An irritable or disgruntled person. **M19.**
▶ **B** *adjective*. Irritable; disgruntled. **M19.**
■ **soreheaded** *adjective* = SOREHEAD *adjective* **M19.** **soreheadedly** *adverb* **L19.** **soreheadedness** *noun* **M19.**

sorel *adjective & noun* see SORREL *adjective & noun*².

Sorelian /sɔˈrɛlɪən, -ˈriːlɪən/ *adjective*. **E20.**
[from *Sorel* (see below) + -IAN.]
Of, pertaining to, or characteristic of Georges Sorel (1847–1922), French political philosopher, or his views on the regeneration of society through proletarian or syndicalist violence.

sorely /ˈsɔːli/ *adverb*. **OE.**
[from SORE *adjective*¹ + -LY².]
1 So as to cause, or in a manner expressive of, physical or mental pain. *obsolete* exc. as passing into sense 2. **OE.**
2 Severely, grievously; greatly; extremely. **ME.**

> 🕮 **2** R. ANGELL The Dodgers, sorely afflicted with injuries, floundered along . . eight games back. M. FORSTER What Wilsen began to long for and what was sorely lacking: variety.

soreness /ˈsɔːnɪs/ *noun*. **OE.**
[from SORE *adjective*¹ + -NESS.]
The condition of being sore; (physical or mental) pain; (*colloq*., chiefly *N. Amer*.) irritability.

Sörensen /ˈsɔːr(ə)ns(ə)n/ *noun*. Also **Soer-**, **Sor-** /sɒr-/. **E20.**
[Søren Peer Lauritz *Sørensen* (1868–1939), Danish biochemist.]
CHEMISTRY. Used *attrib*. and in *possess*. to designate a titration method for the estimation of amino acids, consisting in treating the sample with formaldehyde and then titrating the resulting carboxylic acid groups against a base.

sorgho *noun* var. of SORGO.

sorghum /ˈsɔːɡəm/ *noun.* L16.
[mod. Latin (see below) from Italian *sorgo*, perh. from Proto-Romance var. of medieval Latin *sur(i)cum* (sc. *gramen*) Syrian (grass).]
1 A cereal grass, *Sorghum bicolor*, similar to maize and extensively grown in Africa, southern India, and elsewhere (different strains being known as ***durra***, ***Guinea corn***, ***Indian millet***, ***Kaffir corn***, ***milo***, etc.). Also, any variety of this or other species of the genus *Sorghum*. L16. ▸**b** More fully ***sweet sorghum***. A variety of this grass, *Sorghum bicolor* var. *saccharatum*, with a sweet juicy pith, grown as fodder or for syrup manufacture. M19.
2 A kind of molasses made from the juice of sweet sorghum. *US.* L19.

sorgo /ˈsɔːɡəʊ/ *noun.* Also **sorgho**. M18.
[French *sorgho*, Italian *sorgo*: see prec.]
Sorghum; *esp.* sweet sorghum.

sori *noun* pl. of SORUS.

soricine /ˈsɒrɪsʌɪn/ *adjective.* L18.
[Latin *soricinus*, from *sorex* rel. to Greek *urax* a shrew; in sense 2 from mod. Latin *Soricinae* (see below): see -INE[1].]
1 Resembling a shrew. L18.
2 *ZOOLOGY.* Of, pertaining to, or designating shrews, esp. those of the subfamily Soricinae. L20.

sorites /səˈrʌɪtiːz/ *noun.* M16.
[Latin from Greek *sōreitēs*, from *sōros* heap.]
1 *LOGIC.* A series of propositions in which the predicate of each is the subject of the next; an instance of this. M16.
2 *transf.* A series or succession *of* things. Now *rare.* M17.
3 A form of sophism leading by gradual steps from truth to absurdity and based on the absence of precise, esp. numerical, limits to terms such as 'heap'. *rare.* L18.
■ **soritic** /-ˈrɪtɪk/ *adjective* M17. **soritical** /-ˈrɪtɪk(ə)l/ *adjective* L17.

sorn /sɔːn/ *verb. Scot.* E16.
[from SORREN.]
1 *verb intrans.* Take up free lodging or maintenance by use of force or threats (*Hist.*); sponge *on.* E16.
2 *verb trans. Hist.* Exact free lodging and maintenance from by use of force or threats. M16.
■ **sorner** *noun* LME.

soroban /ˈsoroban/ *noun.* L19.
[Japanese, from Chinese *suànpan* SUAN-PAN.]
A kind of abacus used in Japan.

Soroptimist /səˈrɒptɪmɪst/ *adjective & noun.* E20.
[from Latin *soror* sister + OPTIMIST.]
▸**A** *adjective.* Designating a branch of an international service club for professional women and businesswomen, founded in California in 1921. E20.
▸**B** *noun.* A member of a Soroptimist club. E20.

sororal /səˈrɔːr(ə)l/ *adjective.* M17.
[from Latin *soror* sister + -AL[1].]
†**1** Of a relative: by one's sister. *rare.* Only in M17.
2 Sisterly. M19.
2 sororal polygyny (*ANTHROPOLOGY*) polygamous marriage to two (or more) sisters.

sororate /sɒˈrɔːrət/ *noun.* E20.
[from Latin *soror* sister + -ATE[1], after LEVIRATE.]
ANTHROPOLOGY. In some kinship systems, a custom whereby, on the death of his wife, a man is expected to marry her (unmarried) sister.

sororial /səˈrɔːrɪəl/ *adjective.* E19.
[from Latin *sororius* sisterly, formed as prec.: see -AL[1].]
= SORORAL 2.

sororicide /səˈrɒrɪsʌɪd/ *noun.* M17.
[from Latin *soror* sister + -CIDE.]
1 A person who kills his or her sister. M17.
2 The action of killing one's sister. E18.
■ **sororiˈcidal** *adjective* L19.

sororise *verb* var. of SORORIZE.

sorority /səˈrɒrɪti/ *noun.* M16.
[medieval Latin *sororitas*, or from Latin *soror* sister + -ITY, after FRATERNITY.]
1 A group of women united for a common (esp. religious) purpose. Now *rare.* M16.
2 A female students' society at a college or university. *N. Amer.* E20.

sororize /səˈrɒrʌɪz/ *verb intrans. rare.* Also **-ise**. L19.
[from Latin *soror* sister + -IZE, after FRATERNIZE.]
Associate *with* as a sister or sisters; form a sisterly friendship.

sorosilicate /sɒrəʊˈsɪlɪkeɪt/ *noun.* M20.
[from Greek *sōros* heap + SILICATE.]
MINERALOGY. Any of a group of silicates characterized by isolated pairs of SiO_4 tetrahedra that share an oxygen atom at a common apex.

sorosis /səˈrəʊsɪs/ *noun.* Pl. **-roses** /-ˈrəʊsiːz/. M19.
[mod. Latin, from Greek *sōros* heap.]
1 *BOTANY.* A multiple fruit, e.g. a pineapple or a mulberry, derived from the ovaries of several flowers. M19.
2 A women's society or club. *US.* M19.

sorption /ˈsɔːpʃ(ə)n/ *noun.* E20.
[Extracted from *absorption* + *adsorption*.]
PHYSICAL CHEMISTRY. The combined or undifferentiated action of absorption and adsorption.
■ **sorptive** *adjective* of, pertaining to, or exhibiting sorption E20.

sorrel /ˈsɒr(ə)l/ *noun*[1]. LME.
[Old French *sorele*, *surele* (mod. dial. *surelle*), from *sur* from Germanic base of SOUR *adjective*: see -EL[2].]
1 Any of several plants with acid leaves, allied to the docks; spec. *Rumex acetosa*, a plant of meadows with hastate leaves sometimes used in salads etc. Also, the leaves of this plant. LME.
2 Chiefly with specifying word: any of several plants of other genera and families resembling sorrel, esp. in their acidity; *W. Indies* (in full ***French sorrel***, ***Jamaica sorrel***, ***red sorrel***) a hibiscus, *Hibiscus sabdariffa*, whose leaves are used in salads and whose red fleshy calyx is used to make cooling drinks, jam, etc. E16.
Phrases & comb.: **French sorrel** (*a*) a small sorrel of central and southern Europe, *Rumex scutatus*, sometimes cultivated as a salad plant; (*b*) see sense 2 above. ***Jamaica sorrel***: see sense 2 above. **mountain sorrel** a plant of damp rocky places on mountains, *Oxyria digyna*, of the dock family, with rosettes of kidney-shaped leaves. ***red sorrel***: see sense 2 above. **salt of sorrel** potassium hydrogen oxalate. **sheep sorrel**, **sheep's sorrel** a small reddish European sorrel, *Rumex acetosella*, of heaths and acid sandy soils. **sorrel tree** a N. American tree of the heath family, *Oxydendrum arboreum*, with sour-tasting leaves. ***wood sorrel***: see WOOD *noun*[1] & *adjective*[1].

sorrel /ˈsɒr(ə)l/ *adjective & noun*[2]. Also (now only and the usual form in sense B.2) **sorel**. ME.
[Old French *sorel*, from *sor* yellowish from Frankish adjective meaning 'dry': see -EL[2].]
▸**A** *adjective.* Of a light chestnut colour; reddish-brown. ME.
sorrel-top *US colloq.* a red-haired person.
▸**B** *noun.* **1** A sorrel horse. ME.
2 (**sorel**.) A male fallow deer in its third year. L15.
3 A sorrel or light reddish-brown colour. M16.

sorren /ˈsɒrən/ *noun.* ME.
[Irish †*sorthan* free quarters, living at free expense. Cf. SORN *verb*.]
IRISH & SCOTTISH HISTORY. A service formerly required of vassals in Ireland and Scotland, consisting in providing free lodging or maintenance for a feudal superior or his men; money etc. given in lieu of this.

sorrow /ˈsɒrəʊ/ *noun.*
[Old English *sorh*, *sorg* = Old Saxon *sorga* (Dutch *zorg*), Old High German *sor(a)ga* (German *Sorge*), Old Norse *sorg*, Gothic *saurga*, from Germanic.]
1 Mental distress caused by bereavement, suffering, disappointment, etc.; grief, deep sadness. OE. ▸**b** Used in imprecatory phrs. expr. impatience, anger, regret, etc., or with emphatic or negative force. Cf. DEVIL *noun* 1. Now *arch.*, *Scot.*, & *dial.* OE. ▸**c** As a term of abuse: an unpleasant or mischievous person; a devil, a rascal. Chiefly *Scot.* & *north.* LME.
2 An instance or cause of grief or sadness. OE.
3 The outward expression of grief; lamentation, mourning; *sing.* & in *pl.* (*poet.*), tears. ME.
4 Physical pain or suffering. *obsolete* exc. *dial.* ME. ▸†**b** Harm, damage. ME–L16.

> 1 D. LEAVITT She felt no pleasure, only sorrow that her anger had . . won her nothing. *Japan Journal* Their deep-felt sorrow on the anniversaries of the deaths of their loved ones. **b** TENNYSON Sorrow seize me if ever that light be my leading star! L. A. G. STRONG Dusk was coming on . . and sorrow a curlew had we shot. **2** N. HERMAN Accustomed to the blows of fate, he bore his sorrows stoically. **3** POPE Down his white beard a stream of sorrow flows.

Comb.: **sorrow song** a lament; *spec.* a song expressing the sorrows of the American black people.
■ **sorrowless** *adjective* OE. **sorrowy** *adjective* (*rare*) sorrowful LME.

sorrow /ˈsɒrəʊ/ *verb.*
[Old English *sorgian*: cf. Old Saxon *sorgon*, Old High German *sorgēn* (Dutch *zorgen*, German *sorgen*), Old Norse *syrgja*, Gothic *saurgan*, from Germanic.]
1 *verb intrans.* Feel sorrow or sadness; grieve. Also, mourn. (Foll. by *at*, *for*, *over*.) OE.
2 *verb trans.* Feel sorrow on account of; lament, regret. Also foll. by subord. clause OE.
3 *verb trans.* Bring grief or pain to; make sorrowful. ME.

> 1 LYTTON They who have sorrowed may . . be reluctant to sadden . . those to whom sorrow is yet unknown. D. M. THOMAS The Council Officer had been shot dead . . . I sorrowed for his wife and children. **2** E. LANGLEY I remembered the dead and sorrowed that they should not see this day.

■ **sorrower** *noun* E18. **sorrowing** *verbal noun* the action of the verb; an instance of this: OE. **sorrowingly** *adverb* (*rare*) in a sorrowing manner LME.

sorrowful /ˈsɒrə(ʊ)fʊl, -f(ə)l/ *adjective & adverb.* OE.
[from SORROW *noun* + -FUL.]
▸**A** *adjective.* **1** Feeling sorrow; unhappy, sad. OE.
2 Characterized by or causing sorrow; distressing, lamentable. OE.
3 Expressing sorrow. ME.

> 1 *ellipt.*: H. F. TOZER [Death] coming with a friendly aspect to relieve the sorrowful. **2** SHELLEY Sounds and odours, sorrowful Because they once were sweet. **3** SIR W. SCOTT Her lovely brow, though sorrowful, bore . . a cast of reviving hope.

▸**B** *adverb.* Sorrowfully. *rare.* ME.
■ **sorrowfully** *adverb* ME. **sorrowfulness** *noun* ME.

sorry /ˈsɒri/ *noun*[1]. *dial.* L18.
[Alt. of SIRRAH *noun*[1].]
A familiar form of address to a man or boy.

> D. H. LAWRENCE 'Shall ter finish, Sorry?' cried Barker, his fellow butty.

sorry /ˈsɒri/ *adjective & noun*[2].
[Old English *sārig* = Old Saxon, Old High German *sērag* (German dial. *serich*), from West Germanic, from Germanic base of SORE *noun*[1]: see -Y[1]. The change and shortening of the vowel have given the word an apparent connection with unrelated SORROW *noun*.]
▸**A** *adjective.* **1** *pred.* Pained, distressed, sad. Now *esp.* regretful, penitent. (Foll. by †*at*, *for*, *that*, *to do*, *to be*.) OE. ▸**b** *pred.* Feeling pity or sympathy *for.* LME. ▸**c** *ellipt.* = ***I am sorry*** below. *colloq.* E20.
†**2** Expressing distress or sorrow; sorrowful. OE–M16.
3 Orig., causing distress or sorrow. Now, wretched, mean; pitiful, poor; deplorable. ME.

> 1 P. NORMAN She often smacked him, but was sorry soon afterwards. A. THWAITE Gosse was extremely vexed and sorry about his mistake. P. D. JAMES I'm sorry she's dead. A. C. AMOR Nobody was particularly sorry to see him go. **b** R. C. HUTCHINSON She did things for invalids, but she wouldn't let us be sorry for them. I. WALLACE Here he was . . suffocated with nausea . . and sorry for himself. **c** A. LURIE Dr. Einsam held open the door . . . 'Sorry to keep you waiting.' **3** *Blackwood's Magazine* A sorry sight . . with our dirty torn uniforms and unshaven chins. JANET MORGAN Frederick's business affairs had fallen into a sorry state. *Banker* The document . . reveals a sorry set of nine-month figures.

Phrases etc.: **I am sorry** (*a*) expr. apology or regret; (*b*) *interrog.* (*colloq.*) (as a request for a question etc. to be repeated) what did you say?
▸**B** *noun.* An utterance of 'sorry' in apology etc. *rare.* M19.

> N. HINTON Look—I don't want to hear no sorries about nuffin'.

Comb.: **sorry-go-round** *rare* [after *merry-go-round*] a depressing cycle of events.
■ **sorrily** *adverb* ME. **sorriness** *noun* (*a*) (now *rare*) the state of being sorry; †(*b*) an instance of this: OE. **sorryish** *adjective* somewhat sorry L18.

†**sort** *noun*[1]. ME.
[Old & mod. French, or Latin *sort-*, *sors*: see next.]
1 Destiny, fate; (with *possess.*) the destiny of a particular person. ME–L16.
2 = LOT *noun* 1, 2, 2b. LME–E17.

sort /sɔːt/ *noun*[2]. LME.
[Old & mod. French *sorte* = Italian *sorta* from Proto-Romance alt. of Latin *sort-*, *sors* wooden voting tablet, lot, share, condition, rank (Anglo-Latin *sorta* sort, kind).]
▸**I 1** Pl **-s**, (before *of*, now *rare* exc. in ***these sort of***, ***those sort of***) same. A class of or *of* people or things determined on the basis of common attributes; a kind, a type, (of). LME.
2 Character, disposition; rank. Formerly also *spec.*, high rank. LME.
3 a *The* people of a specified character, type, or rank collectively. M16. ▸**b** A person of a specified character. *colloq.* M19. ▸**c** A girl, a woman. *slang* (chiefly *Austral.*). M20.
4 *PRINTING.* A letter etc. from a font of type. Usu. in *pl.* M17.

> 1 D. L. SAYERS I thought those sort of people knew every boat . . by sight. E. F. BENSON I should condemn myself for doing that sort of thing. J. MARQUAND Major Best was the sort to die by violence. R. N. CURREY This is a damned inhuman sort of war. R. FRAME She hadn't any qualifications of the secretarial sort. D. LEAVITT Upheavals of various sorts had ravaged their faces. *Bird Watching* More than 100 different sorts of . . call by birds have . . been identified. **2** SHAKES. *Mids. N. D.* None of noble sort Would so offend a virgin. SHELLEY They are too mad for people of my sort. **3a** GOLDSMITH The better sort here pretend to the utmost compassion for animals. **b** T. PARKS She seems a sociable sort.

▸**II 5** A group or company of people or animals. Now only (*arch.*) foll. by *of.* LME. ▸†**b** A collection or set *of* things. M16–E17.
6 A (great, good, etc.) number of people or things; a large number or quantity, a multitude. Formerly also foll. by *of.* Now *Scot.* & *dial.* L15.

†**7** A part *of* a thing or group. **M16–M17.**

📖 **5** Sir W. Scott Here are a sort of knaves breaking peace within burgh.

▶ **III 8** A manner, a method, a way. *arch.* exc. in phrs. below. **M16.**

▶ **IV** *COMPUTING.* [from **SORT** *verb*.]

9 The action of arranging items of data in a prescribed sequence. **M20.**

Phrases: **after a sort** after a fashion, in some way or other. ***all-sorts***: see **ALL** *adjective* 2. **a sort of** a type resembling or roughly equivalent to the person or thing specified. **in a sort** *arch.* in some (esp. unsatisfactory) manner. **in a sort of way** imperfectly; not properly. **in some sort** to a certain extent. †**in sort** in a body or company. ***NOTHING of the sort.*** **of a sort** (*a*) (now *dial.*) of the same kind; (*b*) *colloq.* = **of sorts** (b) below. **of sorts** (*a*) (now *rare*) of different or various kinds; (*b*) *colloq.* of an inferior or unusual kind, not fully deserving the name. **out of sorts** (*a*) slightly unwell; (*b*) in low spirits; irritable, peevish. ***SOMETHING of the sort.*** **sort of** *colloq.* to some extent, somewhat; in some way, somehow. ***these sort of***: see **THESE** *demonstr. adjective* 1. ***those sort of***: see **THOSE** *demonstr. adjective* 2.

Comb.: **sort key** *COMPUTING* a characteristic feature of items of data according to which the data may be arranged; **sort program** *COMPUTING* a program written to perform a sort; **sort routine** *COMPUTING* a routine written to perform a sort.

sort /sɔːt/ *verb.* **LME.**

[Old French *sortir* or Latin *sortiri* divide or obtain by lot, from *sort-*, *sors*: see prec. Later from the noun or aphet. from **ASSORT**.]

▶ **I** †**1** *verb trans.* Allot, assign. Usu. foll. by *to*, *for*. **LME–L16.** ▸**b** Dispose, ordain. *rare.* Only in **L16.**

†**2** *verb intrans.* Of an event etc.: come about; turn out well, badly, etc. Also foll. by *out*. **L15–M17.**

†**3** *verb trans. & intrans.* (with *to*). Arrive at or result in (an effect, end, etc.). **M16–M17.**

†**4** *verb intrans.* Foll. by *to*: end in a specified result; turn out according to one's wish, desire, etc. **M16–M17.** ▸**b** Fall *to* a person as a right or duty. Only in **17.**

5 *verb trans.* Correspond to; befit, suit. Now *rare* or *obsolete.* **L16.**

▶ **II 6** *verb trans.* Arrange systematically or according to type, class, etc.; separate and put into different sorts. **LME.**

7 *verb trans.* Place in a class or sort. Usu. foll. by *together, with*. *arch.* **L15.**

8 *verb trans.* Foll. by *out*: ▸**a** Separate into sorts; remove (certain sorts) *from* others. **M16.** ▸**b** Choose or select by separating into sorts. Now *rare* or *obsolete.* **M16.** ▸**c** Arrange according to sort. **E18.**

9 a *verb trans.* Adapt, fit, make conformable. Foll. by *to*, *with*. Now *rare* or *obsolete.* **M16.** ▸**b** *verb intrans.* Be suitable; accord or be in harmony (foll. by *with*, †*to*, †*together*); *Scot.* come to an agreement. *arch.* **L16.**

†**10** *verb trans.* Choose, select, esp. as fitting or suitable. **L16–M17.**

11 *verb trans.* Provide or supply (a person or thing) *with*; *spec.* give (an animal) food and shelter. Long *obsolete* exc. *Scot.* **L16.**

12 *verb intrans. & refl.* Associate or consort with another or others. Usu. foll. by *with*. Now *dial.* **L16.**

13 *verb trans.* Arrange or put in order; put to rights. Also foll. by *up*. *Scot. & north.* **E19.**

14 *verb trans.* **a** Resolve (a problem or difficulty); solve the problems of (a person); deal with. Usu. foll. by *out*. **E19.** ▸**b** Reprimand (a person); put right or deal with by means of force, violence, etc. Usu. foll. by *out*. *colloq.* **M20.**

📖 **6** E. Bowen Helping her sort the apples and range them in . . rows. G. Gorer They had been sorted into six groups (dependent on sex and marital status). *Stamps* Postal Corps personnel sorting mail. **7** W. Burkitt It had been sufficient disparagement to our . . Saviour to have been sorted with the best of men. **8a** J. N. Lockyer Not yet . . time to sort out the real from the apparent nebulae. R. Lardner From the pile he sorted out three letters. ***sort out the men from the boys***: see **MAN** *noun.* **c** M. Cox He spent hours sorting out his books. **9b** H. Allen A nostalgic aspect which sorted well with his own mood within. **14a** B. Bainbridge He could just lie there for several days . . trying to sort himself out. P. Fitzgerald Sorting out administrative and technical problems since five in the morning. R. Rendell Time had sorted things out for us. *Rally Sport* Mud . . clogging the radiator . . causing the engine to overheat, but this was sorted at Harrogate. **b** M. Gee I'll send the police round to sort you out.

Comb.: **sort-out** an act of sorting out or ordering something; *colloq.* a fight, a dispute.

■ **sortable** *adjective* (*a*) (*obsolete* exc. *dial.*) suitable, appropriate; accordant; (*b*) able to be sorted or arranged: **L16.** †**sortance** *noun* (*rare*, Shakes.) agreement, correspondence: only in **L16.** **sorter** *noun* a person who or machine which sorts, arranges, or classifies things **M16.** **sorting** *verbal noun* the action of the verb; an instance of this: **LME.** †**sortment** *noun* (*a*) the action of sorting or arranging things; (*b*) a collection of assorted things, an assortment: **L16–M18.**

sortal /ˈsɔːt(ə)l/ *adjective & noun.* **L17.**

[from **SORT** *noun*² + **-AL**¹.]

PHILOSOPHY. ▶**A** *adjective.* Designating a generic term classifying a thing as being of a particular kind. **L17.**

▶ **B** *noun.* A sortal term. **L20.**

sortation /sɔːˈteɪʃ(ə)n/ *noun.* **M19.**

[from **SORT** *verb* + **-ATION**.]

Now chiefly *COMPUTING.* The action or process of arranging or sorting something.

sorted /ˈsɔːtɪd/ *adjective.* **M16.**

[from **SORT** *verb* + **-ED**¹.]

1 Chosen, selected. Now *rare.* **M16.**

2 Put in order or categories according to kind, size, etc.; arranged, classified. **L17.**

3 Of a state of affairs, etc.: fixed, settled, secure; arranged, prepared, dealt with. Also as *interjection*, expr. agreement, satisfaction, or readiness to act. *slang.* **M20.** ▸**b** Supplied with or under the influence of illegal drugs. *slang.* **L20.** ▸**c** Of a person: confident, organized, and emotionally well balanced; streetwise, cool. *slang.* **L20.**

📖 **2** *Wastes Management* The primary role of the . . hook loader is to take sorted waste . . from the recycling station to the landfill sites. **sorted circle**, **sorted polygon** (*PHYSICAL GEOGRAPHY*): formed on patterned ground by stones distributed in such a way as to suggest their having been sorted according to size. **3** D. McLean Who's in control here? . . Come on, let's get this sorted! R. T. Davies On the house! Sorted! **b** J. Cocker Sorted for E's and wizz. **c** M. Burgess When you're in the state I was in, even someone like Gemma looks sorted.

sortes /ˈsɔːtiːz, ˈsɔːteɪz/ *noun pl.*, also treated as *sing.* **L16.**

[Latin, pl. of *sors* lot, chance.]

Divination, or the seeking of guidance, by chance selection of a passage in Virgil (in full ***sortes Virgilianae*** /ˌvəːdʒɪlɪˈɑːniː/), Homer (in full ***sortes Homericae*** /həʊˈmɛrɪkiː/), or the Bible (in full ***sortes Biblicae*** /ˈbɪblɪkiː/).

sortie /ˈsɔːtiː/ *noun & verb.* **L17.**

[French, fem. pa. pple of *sortir* go out.]

▶ **A** *noun.* †**1** A half-concealed decorative knot etc. on a garment. Only in **L17.**

2 A dash or sally, *esp.* one made by troops from a besieged garrison; the body of troops making such a sally. Also *transf.*, an outing, an excursion. **L18.**

3 An outlet of a river. **E19.**

4 An operational flight by a single military aircraft. **E20.** ▸**b** *PHOTOGRAPHY.* A series of aerial photographs taken during one flight. **M20.**

📖 **2** A. Brookner Every sortie he proposed—to the theatre, the cinema—she declined.

▶ **B** *verb intrans.* Pres. pple & verbal noun **-ieing**. Make a sortie; sally. **L19.**

sortie de bal /sɔrti də bal/ *noun phr.* Pl. ***sorties de bal*** (pronounced same). **M19.**

[French, lit. 'departure from (the) ball'.]

Hist. A woman's hooded evening cloak with a quilted lining.

sortilege /ˈsɔːtɪlɪdʒ/ *noun.* **LME.**

[Old & mod. French *sortilège* from medieval Latin *sortilegium* sorcery, divination, from Latin *sortilegus* sorcerer, diviner, from Latin *sors*, *sort-* (**SORT** *noun*²) + *legere* choose; in sense 2 directly from Latin *sortilegus*.]

1 The action or an act of divining or deciding something by casting lots. Also, sorcery, magic. **LME.**

2 A person who practises sortilege. *rare.* **L15.**

■ **sortileger** *noun* (now *rare*) a person who practises sortilege **LME.** **sortiˈlegious** *adjective* (now *rare*) of, pertaining to, or of the nature of sortilege **E17.** **sortilegy** *noun* [medieval Latin *sortilegium*] = **SORTILEGE** 1 **LME.**

sortition /sɔːˈtɪʃ(ə)n/ *noun.* **L16.**

[Latin *sortitio(n-)*, from *sortit-* pa. ppl stem of *sortiri*: see **SORT** *verb*, **-ION**.]

The action or an act of selecting or determining something by the casting or drawing of lots.

sorus /ˈsɔːrəs/ *noun.* Pl. **sori** /ˈsɔːrʌɪ/. **M19.**

[mod. Latin from Greek *sōros* heap.]

BOTANY. **1** Any of the clusters of sporangia on the underside of the frond of a fern. **M19.**

2 Any of the groups of antheridia or oogonia in certain algae; any of the groups of fruiting bodies in rust fungi. **M19.**

sorva /ˈsɔːvə/ *noun.* **E20.**

[Portuguese *sôrva* (the fruit), ult. from Latin *sorbum* service berry: see **SORB** *noun*¹.]

The edible fruit of the Amazonian tree *Couma utilis*. Also, the tree itself; the sap of this, used as a substitute for chicle.

SOS /ɛsəʊˈɛs/ *noun & verb.* **E20.**

[The letters *s*, *o*, and *s*, chosen as being easily transmitted and recognized in Morse code; by folk etym. an abbreviation of *save our souls*.]

▶ **A** *noun.* **1** An international radio code-signal of extreme distress, used esp. by ships at sea. **E20.**

2 *transf.* An urgent appeal for help. Also, a broadcast message intended to contact an otherwise untraceable person in an emergency. **E20.**

Comb.: **SOS redouble** *BRIDGE*: made to indicate weakness rather than strength.

▶ **B** *verb intrans.* Pa. t. & pple **-ed**, **-'d**.

1 Send an SOS. **E20.**

2 *BRIDGE.* Make an SOS redouble. **M20.**

sosatie /sɔˈsɑːti, sə-/ *noun.* *S. Afr.* **M19.**

[Afrikaans, ult. from Malay *sesate*. Cf. **SATAY**.]

(A dish of) marinaded spiced meat grilled on a skewer.

soshi /ˈsəʊʃi/ *noun.* Pl. same. **L19.**

[Japanese *sōshi* lit. 'strong man'.]

A mercenary political agitator.

soss /sɒs/ *noun*¹. Long *obsolete* exc. *Scot. & dial.* **LME.**

[Perh. imit. of the sound of lapping. Cf. **SOZZLE** *noun*.]

1 A sloppy mess of food (orig. for dogs); any sloppy mess or mixture. **LME.**

2 A slattern. **E17.**

soss /sɒs/ *noun*². Chiefly *dial.* **L17.**

[Imit.]

1 A sound made by the impact of a body on water; a splash. **L17.**

2 A muffled sound (as) made by the impact of a heavy soft body; a thud; a heavy fall. Chiefly in ***with a soss***. **E18.**

soss /sɒs/ *verb*¹. Long *obsolete* exc. *Scot. & north.* **M16.**

[from **SOSS** *noun*¹. Cf. **SOZZLE** *verb*.]

1 *verb trans.* Make dirty; make a mess of. **M16.**

2 *verb intrans.* Splash in mud or dirt. Also, make a mess. **L16.**

3 *verb trans.* Lap (*up*). **L16.**

soss /sɒs/ *verb*² *intrans.* Now *Scot. & dial.* **E18.**

[Cf. **SOSS** *noun*².]

†**1** Move gently; lounge. *rare.* Only in **E18.**

2 Fall with a thud; sit *down* heavily. **L18.**

soss /sɒs/ *adverb.* Now *dial.* **M18.**

[Cf. **SOSS** *noun*², *verb*².]

With a heavy fall or dull thud.

sostenuto /sɒstəˈnuːtəʊ/ *adverb, adjective, & noun.* **E18.**

[Italian, pa. pple of *sostenere* sustain.]

MUSIC. ▶**A** *adverb & adjective.* A direction: in a sustained or prolonged manner. **E18.**

▶ **B** *noun.* Pl. **-os**. A passage (to be) played in a sustained or prolonged manner. Also, a sustained sound or note. **M18.**

sot /sɒt/ *noun & adjective.*

[Late Old English *sott* from medieval Latin *sottus*, of unkn. origin. Reinforced from Old & mod. French *sot*.]

▶ **A** *noun.* **1** A foolish or stupid person; a dolt. Long *rare* exc. *dial.* **LOE.**

2 A habitual drunkard. **L16.**

Comb.: **sot-weed** (*obsolete* exc. *Hist.*) tobacco.

▶†**B** *adjective.* Foolish, stupid. **LOE–M17.**

sot /sɒt/ *verb.* Infl. **-tt-**. **ME.**

[from the noun, or aphet. from **ASSOT**.]

1 †**a** *verb intrans.* Be or become foolish. Only in **ME.** ▸**b** *verb trans.* Make foolish; stupefy, besot. Long *rare.* **ME.**

2 *verb intrans.* Act like a sot; drink to excess. **M17.**

3 *verb trans.* Foll. by *away*: waste (money or time) in drinking to excess. Now *rare.* **M18.**

Sotadean /səʊtəˈdiːən/ *adjective.* **L18.**

[from Latin *Sotadeus*, from *Sotades*: see next, **-EAN**.]

PROSODY. = **SOTADIC** *adjective* 3.

Sotadic /səʊˈtadɪk/ *adjective & noun.* **M17.**

[Latin *Sotadicus*, from *Sotades* from Greek *Sōtadēs*: see below, **-IC**.]

▶ **A** *noun.* **1** A satire in the style of Sotades, a Greek poet (3rd cent. BC) noted for his licentious and scurrilous writings. **M17.**

2 *PROSODY.* A catalectic tetrameter composed of major ionics. **M19.**

▶ **B** *adjective.* **1** Licentious; scurrilous. *rare.* **E18.**

2 Palindromic. *rare.* **E19.**

3 *PROSODY.* Designating verse comprised of catalectic tetrameters composed of major ionics. **M19.**

sotalol /ˈsəʊtəlɒl/ *noun.* **M20.**

[Origin unkn.: see **-OL**.]

PHARMACOLOGY. A sulphonamide used as a beta-adrenergic blocking agent in the treatment of cardiac arrhythmias.

†**sotana** *noun.* **E17–L19.**

[Spanish.]

A gown, a cassock.

sotch /səʊtʃ/ *noun.* Pl. **-s**, **-es** /-ɪz/. **E20.**

[French dial.; ult. origin unkn.]

PHYSICAL GEOGRAPHY. A sink-hole, esp. one in the Causses region of France.

soteriology /sə(ʊ)ˌtɪərɪˈɒlədʒi/ *noun.* **M19.**

[from Greek *sōtēria* salvation + **-OLOGY**.]

THEOLOGY. The doctrine of salvation.

■ **soterioˈlogical** *adjective* **L19.**

Sothiac /ˈsəʊθɪak/ *adjective.* **M19.**

[French *sothiaque*, formed as next + *-aque* **-AC**.]

= **SOTHIC**.

■ Also **Soˈthiacal** *adjective* (*rare*) **L18.**

Sothic /ˈsəʊθɪk, ˈsɒθ-/ *adjective.* E19.
[from Greek *Sōthis*, an Egyptian name for Sirius, the dog-star: see -IC.]
1 *Sothic cycle*, *Sothic period*, a period of 1460 full years, containing 1461 of the ancient Egyptian ordinary years of 365 days. E19.
2 *Sothic year*, a year of 365¼ days, fixed according to the heliacal rising of the dog-star. E19.

Sotho /ˈsuːtuː/ *noun & adjective.* In sense A.1 sing. also **Mosotho** /mʊˈsuːtuː/. E20.
[Bantu.]
► **A** *noun.* Pl. BASOTHO *noun*, **Sotho(s)**.
1 A member of a Bantu-speaking people chiefly inhabiting Lesotho, Botswana, and Transvaal. E20.
2 The language of this people, Sesotho. E20.
► **B** *attrib.* or as *adjective.* Of or pertaining to the Basotho or their language. E20.

sotie /ˈsɔːtiː/ *noun.* LME.
[Old French *sot(t)ie* (mod. *sotie*), from *sot*: see SOT *noun & adjective.*]
†**1** Foolishness, folly. LME–L15.
2 *Hist.* A type of satirical farce, popular in France in the 15th and 16th cents. E19.

Soto /ˈsəʊtəʊ/ *noun.* M19.
[Japanese *Sōtō*, from Chinese *Ts'ao Tung* (see below).]
One of the three branches of Zen Buddhism (the others being Obaku and Rinzai) founded in the 9th cent. in the Ts'ao and Tung monasteries in China, and transmitted to Japan in 1227 by Dōgen (1200–53).

sotol /ˈsəʊtəʊl/ *noun.* L19.
[Amer. Spanish from Nahuatl *tzotolli*.]
Any of several desert plants of the genus *Dasylirion*, of the agave family, native to south-western N. America, with linear spiny-edged leaves and small white flowers. Also, the fibre from the leaves of this plant; an alcoholic drink made from its sap.

sotter /ˈsɒtə/ *verb intrans. Scot. & north.* L18.
[Origin unkn.: cf. German dial. *sottern*.]
1 Boil slowly or with a sputtering sound. L18.
2 Bubble. M19.

†**sottery** *noun.* L16–M18.
[French (now dial.) *sotterie*, from *sot*: see SOT *noun & adjective*, -ERY.]
An instance of foolishness or folly.

sottise /sɔtiːz/ *noun.* Pl. pronounced same. L17.
[French, from *sot*: see SOT *noun & adjective*, -ISE[1].]
A foolish remark or action.

sottish /ˈsɒtɪʃ/ *adjective.* M16.
[from SOT *noun & adjective* + -ISH[1].]
1 Foolish, stupid. Long *rare* or *obsolete.* M16.
2 Given to or characterized or affected by excessive or habitual drinking. M17.
■ **sottishly** *adverb* M16. **sottishness** *noun* L16.

sottisier /sɔtizje/ *noun.* Pl. pronounced same. E20.
[French, formed as SOTTISE: see -IER.]
A collection or (esp.) a written list of *sottises*.

sottoportico /sotoˈpɔrtiko, sɒtəʊˈpɔːtɪkəʊ/ *noun.* Pl. ***-chi*** /-ki/, ***-cos***. Also ***-tego*** /-tego, -teɪgəʊ/, pl. ***-ghi*** /-gi/, ***-gos***. E20.
[Italian, from *sotto* under + PORTICO.]
ARCHITECTURE. The passage formed by a portico.

sotto voce /sotto ˈvotʃe, sɒtəʊ ˈvəʊtʃi/ *adverbial & adjectival phr.* M18.
[Italian *sotto* under + *voce* voice.]
► **A** *adverb.* In an undertone or aside. M18.

> A. MILLER I heard Churchill growl *sotto voce* but audibly enough.

► **B** *adjective.* Uttered in an undertone; *transf.* muted, understated. E19.

> *Classical Music* The irritation of having an audience . . coughing during *sotto voce* passages.

sou /suː/ *noun.* L15.
[French, sing. form deduced from *sous*, †*soux* pl. of Old French *sout* from Latin *solidus* (sc. *nummus* coin) use as noun of *solidus* SOLID *adjective*: see SOLIDUS. Cf. SOL *noun*[3], SOUSE *noun*[4].]
Hist. A French coin, at one time a twentieth of a livre, later a five-centime piece. Cf. SOLDO.
not a sou *colloq.* no money at all.

souari *noun* var. of SAOUARI.

soubah *noun* var. of SUBAH.

Soubise /subiz/ *noun.* Pl. pronounced same. L18.
[Charles de Rohan *Soubise* (1715–87), French general and courtier.]
†**1** A kind of cravat. Only in L18.
2 A white onion sauce. Also ***Soubise sauce***. E19.

soubresaut /subrəso/ *noun.* Pl. pronounced same. M19.
[French: see SOMERSAULT.]
1 A jumping motion seen in some liquids when boiling. Now *rare* or *obsolete.* M19.
2 BALLET. A straight-legged jump from both feet with the toes pointed and feet together, one behind the other. E20.

soubrette /suːˈbrɛt/ *noun.* M18.
[French, from mod. Provençal *soubreto* fem. of *soubret* coy, from *soubra* (Provençal *sobrar*) from Latin *superare* be above.]
1 A maidservant or lady's maid as a character in a play or opera, *esp.* one of a pert or coquettish character; an actress or singer playing the role of a pert or coquettish female in any light entertainment. M18.
2 A lady's maid; a maidservant. E19.
■ **soubrettish** *adjective* of the nature of a soubrette L19.

soubriquet /ˈsuːbrɪkeɪ/ *noun.* E19.
[French, older var. of *sobriquet*.]
= SOBRIQUET.

soucar /ˈsaʊkɑː/ *noun.* L18.
[Urdu *sāhūkār*.]
In the Indian subcontinent, a banker, broker, or moneylender.

souchong /ˈsuːʃɒŋ/ *noun.* M18.
[Chinese (Cantonese) *siú chúng* small sort.]
A fine black variety of China tea.

soucouyant /suːkuːˈjɒ̃/ *noun. W. Indies.* Also **soucriant** /suːkriːˈjɒ̃/ & other vars. M20.
[W. Indian creole, prob. rel. to Fulfulde *sukunyadyo* sorcerer, witch.]
In eastern Caribbean folklore, a malignant witch believed to shed her skin by night and suck the blood of her victims.

souffle /ˈsuːf(ə)l/ *noun.* L19.
[French = breath, from *souffler*: see next.]
MEDICINE. A low murmuring or breathing sound, audible in a stethoscope, caused chiefly by the flow of blood.

soufflé /ˈsuːfleɪ, *foreign* sufle (*pl. same*)/ *noun & adjective.* E19.
[French, pa. pple of *souffler* from Latin *sufflare*, from *sub* under + *flare* blow.]
► **A** *noun.* A light spongy dish made by mixing egg-yolks and other ingredients with stiffly beaten egg-whites, usu. baked in an oven until puffy. E19.
OMELETTE ***soufflé***.
► **B** *adjective.* Of ceramic ware: having liquid colour applied by means of blowing. L19.

souffrante /sufrɑ̃ːt/ *adjective.* E19.
[French, fem. sing. pres. ppl adjective of *souffrir* suffer.]
Of a woman: delicate; prone to illness, anxiety, or depression.

souffre-douleur /sufrədulœːr/ *noun.* Pl. pronounced same. M19.
[French, lit. 'suffer sorrow'.]
A person who is in a subservient position and must listen to or share another's troubles; *spec.* a woman who acts as a paid companion to an older woman.

soufrière /suːfrɪˈɛː/ *noun.* M19.
[French, from *soufre* SULPHUR *noun* + *-ière* -IER.]
= SOLFATARA.

sough /saʊ, sʌf/ *noun*[1]. See also SWOOF *noun.* ME.
[Ult. formed as SOUGH *verb*[1].]
1 A usu. gentle rushing or murmuring sound as of wind, water, etc. ME. ▸**b** A hypocritical or overly pious manner of speaking, esp. in preaching or praying. *Scot.* E18.
2 A deep sigh or breath. LME.
3 A rumour; a report. E18.
Phrases: **keep a calm sough**, **keep a quiet sough** *Scot.* keep quiet, say little or nothing.
¶ From 16 chiefly *Scot. & north.*, but revived in literary use in 19.
■ **soughfully** *adverb* (*rare*) with a murmuring sound L19. **soughless** *adjective* (*rare*) silent, noiseless M19.

sough /sʌf/ *noun*[2]. See also SHEUGH. ME.
[Origin unkn. Cf. SOW *noun*[2].]
1 A boggy or swampy place; a small pool. ME.
2 A gutter for draining off water; a drain, a sewer, a trench. LME.
3 An underground drain to carry off the water in a mine; an adit of a mine. E17.

sough /saʊ, sʌf/ *verb*[1]. See also SWOOF *verb.*
[Old English *swōgan* = Old Saxon *swōgan* resound, rel. to Old English *swēgan* sound, Gothic *ga-, uf)swōgjan, swōgatjan, swēgnjan* sigh.]
1 a *verb intrans.* Make a rushing, rustling, or murmuring sound, as of the wind in trees etc. OE. ▸**b** *verb trans.* Utter in this manner. E19.
2 *verb intrans.* **a** Draw breath heavily or noisily; sigh deeply. ME. ▸**b** Foll. by *away*: breathe one's last; die. E19.
3 *verb trans.* **a** Hum (a tune). E18. ▸**b** Utter, preach, or pray in a hypocritical manner. E19.

> **1a** W. GOLDING The jets soughing down every minute to London airport. C. MUNGOSHI The sound of . . leaves calmly soughing in the slight wind.

sough /sʌf/ *verb*[2]. L17.
[from SOUGH *noun*[2].]
1 *verb trans.* **a** Face or build up (a ditch) with stone etc. L17. ▸**b** Make drains in (land); drain by constructing proper channels. L18.
2 *verb intrans.* Reach or get into a sough. *rare.* L19.

sought /sɔːt/ *ppl adjective.* ME.
[pa. pple of SEEK *verb.*]
That is or has been searched for, desired, etc.
Comb.: **sought-after**, **sought-for** *adjectives* much desired, coveted.

sought *verb pa. t. & pple of* SEEK *verb.*

souk /suːk/ *noun*[1]. Also **suk**, **sukh**, **suq**. E19.
[Arab. *sūk* market, prob. through French *souk*.]
An Arab market or market-place, a bazaar.

souk *noun*[2] see SOOK *noun*[1].

soukous /ˈsuːkuːs/ *noun.* L20.
[Congolese alt. of French *secouer* to shake.]
A style of African popular music characterized by syncopated rhythms and intricate contrasting guitar melodies, originating in the Democratic Republic of Congo (Zaire).

soul /səʊl/ *noun.*
[Old English *sāwol*, *sāw(e)l* = Gothic *saiwala* corresp. to Old Frisian *sēle*, Old Saxon *sēola* (Dutch *ziel*), Old High German *sē(u)la* (German *Seele*) from Germanic, corresp. formally to Greek *aiolos* quick-moving, easily moved.]
► **I** †**1** The principle of life in humans or animals; animate existence. OE–L17.
2 The principle of thought and action in a person, regarded as an entity distinct from the body; a person's spiritual as opp. to corporeal nature. Also (*rare*), an analogous principle in animals. OE.
3 a The spiritual part of a human being considered in its moral aspect or in relation to God and his precepts, *spec.* regarded as immortal and as being capable of redemption or damnation in a future state. OE. ▸**b** The disembodied spirit of a dead person, regarded as invested with some degree of personality and form. OE.
4 a The seat of the emotions or sentiments; the emotional part of human nature. OE. ▸**b** Intellectual or spiritual power; high development of the mental faculties. Also, deep feeling, sensitivity, esp. as an aesthetic quality; zest, spirit. E17.
5 PHILOSOPHY. The vital, sensitive, or rational principle in plants, animals, or human beings. *arch.* ME.
6 a A person, an individual. Usu. in *pl.* or in neg. contexts. ME. ▸**b** *Hist.* In tsarist Russia, a serf. E19.
7 a A person regarded with familiarity, affection, pity, etc. Freq. with defining adjective. E16. ▸**b** A person regarded as the personification *of* a certain quality; a person regarded as embodying certain moral, spiritual, or intellectual qualities. E17. ▸**c** A person regarded as the inspirer or leader *of* some activity, cause, etc.; the chief agent, the prime mover, the animating spirit. M17.
8 a The essential or animating element or quality *of* something. L16. ▸**b** An element or trace *of* something. *rare.* L16.
9 a The emotional or spiritual quality of black American life and culture, manifested esp. in music. M20. ▸**b** *ellipt.* = ***soul music*** below. M20.

> **2** P. KAVANAGH Weary in body and mind, but in soul perhaps as fresh as rain-green grass. R. A. KNOX Soul and body can exist without one another. **3a** A. C. BENSON He [Newman] had little of the priestly hunger to save souls. *New Age Journal* Spiritual pessimism is the ultimate statement of fear, because our very soul is in danger. **b** R. MACAULAY Prayed that all the souls in those cemeteries might rest in peace. **4a** D. H. LAWRENCE One doesn't really want them, in one's soul—only superficially. **b** S. RICHARDSON I never saw so much soul in a lady's eyes, as in hers. *City Limits* One wishes for . . more of the soul shown in 'Raging Bull'. **6a** DYLAN THOMAS Less than five hundred souls inhabit the three . . streets. R. DAHL A countryside of green fields . . with not a soul in sight. **7a** SHAKES. *Mids. N. D.* My love, my life, my soul, fair Helena! L. EGAN Poor soul, this awful cancer. She . . died inside of three months. **b** R. LEHMANN He's the soul of courtesy but he can be . . difficult. *Which?* Thanks . . to the 24,269 stalwart souls. **c** LD MACAULAY He was the . . soul of the European coalition. **9a** *Sound Choice* The guy's got soul . . wrenches sounds out of his guitar that'll . . have your dog convulsing. **b** *Thames Valley Now* Loud . . music from soul to blues to house. *attrib.*: A. ALI A fanatical collector of soul records.

► **II** *techn.* **10** The lungs of a goose, forming a spongy lining to the ribcage esp. when cooked. Now *dial.* L15.
†**11** The bore of a cannon. L16–M17.
12 The sound-post of a violin. M19.
Phrases: ***All Souls' Day***: see ALL *adjective* 2. ***bless my soul***: see BLESS *verb*[1]. **call one's soul one's own** be free from interference with one's privacy or independence (usu. in neg. contexts). ***dark night of the soul***: see DARK *adjective*. ***flow of soul***: see FLOW *noun*[1]. **for the soul of me** even if my soul depended on it (I could not etc.). ***God bless my soul***: see BLESS *verb*[1]. **have a soul above** *arch.* be superior to or have higher aspirations than. **have no soul** be lacking in sensitivity, spirit, or appreciation for something.

heart and soul: see HEART *noun*. ***holy souls***: see HOLY *adjective*. ***keep body and soul together***: see BODY *noun*. ***Lord bless my soul***: see BLESS *verb*¹. ***make one's soul***: see MAKE *verb*. ***sell one's soul to the Devil***: see SELL *verb*. **soul and body lashing** NAUTICAL rope yarn tied round open parts of oilskin clothing to keep out water and wind. **soul and conscience** SCOTS LAW the formula by which medical testimony in writing is authenticated. ***the iron entered into his soul***: see IRON *noun*. **the soul of discretion**, **the soul of honour**, etc., a person of extreme discretion, honour, etc. **the soul of the world** *arch.* [after Latin *anima mundi*, Greek *psukh tou kosmou*] the animating principle of the world, according to early philosophers. **The Souls** a late 19th-cent. aristocratic circle with predominantly cultural and intellectual interests. ***twin soul***: see TWIN *adjective & noun*. **upon my soul!** *arch.*: expr. of asseveration. **with all one's soul** deeply, sincerely.

Comb.: **soul bell** = ***passing-bell*** s.v. PASSING *noun*; **soul-body** SPIRITUALISM a spiritual body; **soul brother** (*a*) a spiritual brother; (*b*) (orig. *US Black slang*) a fellow black man; **soul-cake** (now *Hist.* or *dial.*) a specially prepared cake or bun distributed esp. to parties of children in various northern or north-midland counties of England on All Souls' Day; **soul-candle** [translating Yiddish *neshome licht* 'soul light'] JUDAISM a candle lit on the eve of the anniversary of a parent's death, and also on the eve of Yom Kippur; **soul-case** *slang* (*obsolete* exc. *US & Austral.*) the body; now esp. in ***work the soul-case off***, ***worry the soul-case off***, ***work the soul-case out of***, ***worry the soul-case out of***, put under severe stress; **soul-catcher** among various N. American Indian peoples, a hollowed bone tube used by a medicine man to contain the soul of a sick person; **Soul City** the Harlem area of New York City; **soul-destroying** (of an activity etc.) deadeningly monotonous; **soul-doctor** *slang* (*a*) (now *rare*) a clergyman; (*b*) a psychiatrist; †**soul-driver** (*a*) a clergyman; (*b*) *US* a person trading the services of convicts, indentured servants, or slaves; **soul food** (*a*) *fig.* spiritual nourishment; (*b*) (orig. *US Black slang*) food traditionally eaten by American black people, *spec.* foodstuffs originating in the States of the southern US; **soul-force** = SATYAGRAHA; **soul-friend** a confessor; a person giving spiritual guidance; **soul-house** a model or representation of a house placed by the ancient Egyptians in a tomb to receive the soul of a dead person; **soul kiss** = ***deep kiss*** s.v. DEEP *adjective*; **soul-mass** (now *Hist.* or *dial.*) (*a*) (orig. *Scot. & north.*) a mass for the soul of a dead person; (*b*) ***Soul-mass Day***, All Souls' Day; **soul mate** a person ideally suited to another; **soul music**: popularized by black American singers and musicians and incorporating elements of rhythm and blues and gospel music; **soul-scot** *Hist.* a due paid on behalf of a deceased person to the church of the parish to which he or she belonged; a mortuary; **soul-search** *verb & noun* [back-form.] (*a*) *verb intrans.* engage in examination of one's thoughts or conscience, reflect deeply (chiefly as ***soul-searching*** *verbal noun*); (*b*) *noun* an act of soul-searching; **soul-searching** *adjective* that examines a person's thoughts and emotions deeply; penetrating the conscience; **soul-searchingly** *adverb* in a soul-searching manner; **soul-shot** *Hist.* = ***soul-scot*** above; **soul-sick** *adjective* (*a*) suffering from spiritual unease or distress; dejected, depressed; (*b*) characterized by dejection of spirit; **soul-sickening** *adjective* extremely depressing; **soul-sickness** spiritual distress; depression; **soul sister** (orig. *US Black slang*) a fellow black woman; **soul stuff**, **soul-substance** a hypothetical immaterial substance believed in some cultures to form the spirit of each person (also occas. of animals and objects) and to be independent of the physical body, continuing to exist after death.

■ **soulhood**, **soulship** *nouns* the condition or state of being a soul; soulful quality: L19. **soul-like** *adjective & adverb* (*a*) *adjective* resembling (that of) a soul; (*b*) in a manner suggestive of a soul: M17. **soulster** *noun* (*colloq.*) a singer of soul music L20. **souly** *adjective* †(*a*) of or pertaining to the soul; (*b*) *rare* = SOULFUL *adjective* 1: LME.

soul /səʊl/ *verb*. LME.
[from the noun.]
1 *verb trans.* †**a** Endow with a soul. *rare*. LME–M17. ▸**b** Inspire, animate. *rare*. L19.
2 *verb intrans.* Go about asking for donations of food etc., traditionally on the eve of All Souls' Day. Chiefly in ***go souling***, ***go a-souling***. Now *Hist.* or *dial.* L18.
3 *verb intrans.* Capture or catch souls. *rare*. E19.
■ **souler** *noun* (*dial.*) a person who goes souling E19.

soulagement /sulaʒmɑ̃/ *noun*. L18.
[French.]
Solace, relief.

souled /səʊld/ *ppl adjective*. LME.
[from SOUL *noun* + -ED².]
†**1** Conferred on the soul. Only in LME.
2 Having a soul, esp. one of a specified kind. LME.
2 high-souled, ***large-souled***, ***mean-souled***, etc.

†**soulein** *adjective, noun, & adverb* see SULLEN *adjective, noun, & adverb*.

soulful /ˈsəʊlfʊl, -f(ə)l/ *noun & adjective*. M17.
[from SOUL *noun* + -FUL.]
▸**A** *noun*. As much as a soul will contain. *rare*. M17.
▸**B** *adjective*. **1** Full of soul or feeling; of a highly emotional, spiritual, or aesthetic nature; expressing or evoking deep feeling. Also, affectedly or unduly emotional. M19.
2 Expressive of black American feeling; characteristic of soul music. M20.

📖 **1** JUNE ROSE A mysterious young woman with soulful blue eyes. A. N. WILSON The soulful poet who loved to be alone and to confront the mystery of things.

■ **soulfully** *adverb* L19. **soulfulness** *noun* L19.

soulical /ˈsəʊlɪk(ə)l/ *adjective*. *rare*. M19.
[Irreg. from SOUL *noun* + -ICAL.]
= SOULISH *adjective* 1.

soulie /ˈsəʊli/ *noun*. *slang*. L20.
[from SOUL *noun* + -IE.]
A fan of soul music.

Souliote *noun & adjective* var. of SULIOTE.

soulish /ˈsəʊlɪʃ/ *adjective*. M16.
[formed as next + -ISH¹.]
1 Of or pertaining to the soul. M16.
2 Of the nature of the soul; soul-like. *rare*. L16.

soulless /ˈsəʊllɪs/ *adjective*. LME.
[from SOUL *noun* + -LESS.]
1 Having no soul; from whom or which the soul has departed. LME.
2 Of a person: lacking spirit, courage, sensitivity, or other elevated qualities. L16.
3 Of a thing, quality, etc.: lacking animation, ardour, or zest; dull, uninteresting. M17. ▸**b** *spec.* Of writing, art, etc.: devoid of inspiration or feeling. M19.

📖 **3** E. FEINSTEIN The soulless search for amusement of those who have no work to do. **b** G. DALY The soulless state of contemporary architecture.

■ **soullessly** *adverb* L19. **soullessness** *noun* L19.

soum /suːm/ *noun & verb*. *Scot.* Now chiefly *Hist.* As noun also **sum**. E16.
[Scot. var. of SUM *noun*.]
▸**A** *noun*. The amount of pasturage which will support one cow or a proportional number of sheep or other stock; the number of livestock that can be maintained on this amount of pasturage. E16.
▸**B** *verb trans.* Estimate the amount of (pasturage) in terms of the number of livestock the land can support. L17.

Soumak /ˈsuːmak/ *noun & adjective*. E20.
[Origin uncertain: perh. alt. of *Shemakha* (see below).]
(Designating or pertaining to) a rug or carpet made in the neighbourhood of Shemakha in Azerbaijan, distinguished by a flat, napless surface and loose threads at the back. Also called ***Kashmir***.

sou markee /suː mɑːˈkiː/ *noun*. M17.
[French *sou marqué* lit. 'marked sou'.]
A small 18th-cent. French coin issued for the colonies and circulating esp. in the W. Indies and N. America (*Hist.*); *gen.* something of little value.

sound /saʊnd/ *noun*¹.
[Old English *sund* = Old Norse *sund* swimming, strait (Norwegian *sund* swimming, swimming bladder, strait, ferry, Swedish, Danish *sund* strait), from Germanic base also of SWIM *verb*.]
†**1** The action or power of swimming. OE–LME.
2 The swim-bladder of certain fishes, esp. cod. Now chiefly *dial.* ME.
3 A narrow channel or stretch of water, esp. one between the mainland and an island, or connecting two large bodies of water; a strait. Also, a sea inlet. ME.

sound /saʊnd/ *noun*². ME.
[Anglo-Norman *sun*, *soun*, Old & mod. French *son* from Latin *sonus*. The intrusive *d* appears in 15.]
1 The sensation produced in the ear or other organ of hearing by the vibration of the surrounding air or other medium; that which is or may be heard; the phenomenon of vibration by which this is produced. Also, pressure waves outside the range of audible frequencies, as infrasound, ultrasound. ME. ▸†**b** Music, melody. ME–M16. ▸**c** The music, speech, etc., accompanying a film, television programme, or other visual presentation. E20. ▸**d** PHYSICS. Any of various kinds of wave motion predicted or observed to occur in superfluid helium and propagated in a way analogous to ordinary sound. M20.
2 a A particular cause of auditory effect; the sensation resulting from this. Also, a similar phenomenon that is beyond the range of hearing. ME. ▸**b** The distance or range over which the sound of something is heard. Chiefly in ***within the sound of***, ***in the sound of***. Now *rare*. E17.
3 a The auditory effect produced by the operation of the human voice; speech, utterance; any of a series of articulate utterances. LME. ▸**b** Rich, euphonious, or harmonious auditory effect produced by certain articulations. L16. ▸**c** Mere audible effect of words, without significance or real importance. E17. ▸†**d** Meaning, sense, significance. M17–E18. ▸**e** The mental impression produced by a statement, report, etc. Freq. in ***like the sound of***. M19.
4 Knowledge, gossip, news (*of* a person or thing); a rumour, a report. *obsolete* exc. *Scot. & dial.* LME.
5 a CINEMATOGRAPHY & BROADCASTING. The department in charge of recording sound; (equipment used by) an engineer in this department. M20. ▸**b** (Broadcasting by) radio as distinct from television. Freq. *attrib.* M20.
6 a A tune, a record; in *pl.*, popular music. *slang* (orig. *US*). M20. ▸**b** A specified characteristic style of (usu. popular) music. M20.

📖 **1** M. TIPPETT My sharpest sense is that of sound. **c** A. LEE A big television with . . the sound off. **d** ***zero sound***, ***second sound***, ***third sound***, etc. **2a** M. MITCHELL The sounds of hooves, the jingling of harness chains. D. EDEN She . . awoke suddenly to the sound of Uncle . . shouting. C. HARKNESS No sound except for the chirping of birds. I. MURDOCH Camilla's . . shoes with medium-high heels made a sharp clacking sound. **3a** B. BRYSON In a relatively short period the long vowel sounds of English . . changed their values. **c** SHAKES. *Macb.* A tale Told by an idiot, full of sound and fury, Signifying nothing. **6b** *Sunday Express* That great musical sound of the Beatles which . . shook the world.

Phrases: **first sound** ordinary sound as distinct from other waves in superfluid helium. **sound and light** designating a *son et lumière* production or show. ***WIRED for sound***.

Attrib. & comb.: In the sense 'pertaining to the transmission, broadcasting, or reproduction of sound', as ***sound boom***, ***sound engineer***, ***sound studio***, ***sound system***, ***sound recording***, etc. Special combs., as **sound archive** a library in which sound recordings are preserved; **sound barrier** the increased drag, reduced controllability, etc., which occurs when an aircraft approaches the speed of sound, formerly regarded as an obstacle to supersonic flight; ***break the sound barrier***, travel faster than, or accelerate past, the speed of sound; **sound bite** (orig. *US*) a short extract from a recorded interview, speech, etc., chosen for its succinctness or appropriateness and edited into a news broadcast; **sound-boarding** CARPENTRY short boards placed between floor joists to hold pugging for sound insulation; **sound-bow** the thickest part of a bell, against which the hammer strikes; **soundbox** MUSIC (*a*) the hollow part of a stringed instrument which increases its resonation; (*b*) in a gramophone, the box which carries the reproducing or recording stylus; **sound camera** CINEMATOGRAPHY: that records sound as well as optical images on the film; **sound card** COMPUTING a printed circuit board which can be slotted into a computer to allow the use of audio components for multimedia applications; **sound cell** a crystal microphone in which sound acts directly on the crystal, without the use of a diaphragm; **sound channel** OCEANOGRAPHY a layer of water in which sound is propagated over long distances with minimum energy loss, usu. because of refraction back into this layer by temperature or pressure gradients; **sound check** a test of sound equipment before a musical performance or recording to ensure that the sound level is correct; **sound-conditioned** *adjective* insulated against sound; having improved acoustic qualities; **sound conditioner** a device designed to mask or block out undesirable sounds by generating white noise or some other continuous, unobtrusive sound; **sound conditioning** insulation against sound; **sound effect** (*a*) a sound typical of an event or evocative of an atmosphere, produced artificially in a play, film, etc. (usu. in *pl.*); (*b*) the effect produced by the sound of a word; **sound-film** CINEMATOGRAPHY a cinematic film with accompanying recorded sound; **sound gate** CINEMATOGRAPHY the part of a sound head where the sound-track is scanned as the film passes through it; **sound generator** an electronic device that generates sound, *spec.* a chip for doing this in a computer, musical keyboard, etc.; **sound head** CINEMATOGRAPHY the part of a film projector that produces an electrical signal from the soundtrack; **sound-hole** (*a*) MUSIC an opening in the belly of most stringed instruments; (*b*) ARCHITECTURE an opening in a belfry filled with tracery but not glazed, found esp. in Norfolk, Somerset, and Gloucestershire; **sound-insulated** *adjective* = ***sound-conditioned*** above; **sound insulation** = ***sound-conditioning*** above; **sound-law** PHILOLOGY [translating German *Lautgesetz*] a rule stating the regular occurrence of a phonetic change in the history of a language or language family; **sound meter** an instrument for measuring the intensity of sound; **sound mixer** a mixer for combining sound signals (see MIXER *noun* 4a); **sound moderator** a silencer on a firearm; **sound-on-film** CINEMATOGRAPHY the incorporation of a soundtrack with a film; **sound picture** = ***sound-film*** above; **sound-post** MUSIC a small peg of wood fixed as a support beneath the bridge of a violin or similar stringed instrument, connecting the belly and the back; **sound pressure** the difference between the instantaneous pressure at a point in the presence of a sound wave and the static pressure of the medium; **sound print** = SONOGRAM; **soundproof** *adjective & verb* (*a*) *adjective* impervious to sound, preventing noise from being heard; (*b*) *verb trans.* make soundproof (chiefly as ***soundproofed*** *ppl adjective*); **sound-ranger** MILITARY a person trained in sound-ranging; **sound-ranging** MILITARY calculation of the source of a sound based on the time lapse between the reception of the sound at different positions; **soundscape** (*a*) a musical composition consisting of a texture of sounds; (*b*) the sounds which form an auditory environment; **Soundscriber** (US proprietary name for) a machine for the recording and subsequent reproduction of speech; ***sound shift***: see SHIFT *noun* 11C; **sound spectrogram** = SONOGRAM; **sound spectrograph** = SONOGRAPH 1; **sound stage**: having acoustic properties suitable for the recording of sound (*spec.* one used for filming); **sound stripe** CINEMATOGRAPHY a narrow band of magnetic material on the edge of a film, which contains the soundtrack; **sound-substitution** LINGUISTICS the replacement of one sound by another; **sound-symbolic** *adjective* (LINGUISTICS) pertaining to or manifesting sound-symbolism; **sound-symbolism** LINGUISTICS the (partial) natural representation of the sense of a word by its sound; **sound synthesis** the generation of sound by electronic means, as in a computer, synthesizer, etc.; **sound system** = HI-FI *noun*; **soundtrack** *noun & verb* (*a*) *noun* the sound element of a film or video, recorded optically or magnetically; such a recording made available separately; any constituent single track in a multi-track recording; (*b*) *verb trans.* provide with a soundtrack, serve as a soundtrack for; **sound truck** (*a*) *N. Amer.* a van equipped with a loudspeaker; (*b*) CINEMATOGRAPHY a mobile sound recording unit; **sound wave** a longitudinal pressure wave in an elastic medium, *esp.* one that propagates audible sound.

■ **soundful** *adjective* (*rare*) full of sound **E17.**

sound /saʊnd/ *noun*³. **LME.**
[Var. of **SWOON** *noun*, with parasitic *d*.]
1 A swoon, a fainting fit; faintness. Esp. in ***fall in a sound***. Now *Scot. & dial.* **LME.**
2 A deep sleep. *dial. rare.* **M19.**

sound /saʊnd/ *noun*⁴. **L16.**
[Partly from **SOUND** *verb*², partly from French *sonde* in same sense.]
1 An act of sounding with a lead; *fig.* the power of sounding or investigating. Long *rare.* **L16.** ▸†**b** A sounding-line, a sounding-lead. *rare.* **L16–E17.**
†**2** A hole, an excavation. Only in **E17.**
3 *MEDICINE.* A long rodlike instrument for probing body cavities or dilating strictures. **L18.**

sound /saʊnd/ *adjective.* **ME.**
[Repr. Old English *gesund* = Old Saxon *gisund* (Dutch *gezond*), Old High German *gisunt* (German *gesund*), from West Germanic.]
▶ **I 1 a** Of a person, animal, etc.: free from disease or injury; physically healthy, strong, well. Also foll. by *in*, *of* (the limbs, mind, etc.). **ME.** ▸**b** Of a person's health, appetite, etc.: good, not impaired. **L16.**
2 a Of a part of the body: not affected by disease, decay, or injury. Formerly also (freq. of a wound or illness), healed, cured. **ME.** ▸**b** Of the mind, heart, etc.: strong (in intellectual or moral qualities), steadfast. **M16.**
3 a Of a thing: free from any decay or defect; undamaged, unbroken; in good condition. **ME.** ▸**b** Of air, alcohol, or food: unspoiled; wholesome, good. **LME.** ▸**c** Financially secure. Also *spec.* (of currency): having a fixed or stable value, esp. based on gold. Freq. in ***sound money***. **E17.**
†**4** Safe, secure; protected, free from danger. **ME–M16.**
5 a Of land: dry, not boggy or marshy. Now *dial.* **ME.** ▸**b** Of a thing or substance: solid, dense, compact. **LME.**
6 a Of sleep: deep; unbroken, undisturbed. **M16.** ▸**b** Of a sleeper: tending to sleep deeply and unbrokenly. **L19.**
7 a Of a solid, substantial, or thorough nature. **M16.** ▸**b** Of a blow, beating, etc.: severe, hard. **E17.**

> 🕮 **1a** V. WOOLF Men in the prime of life, sound of wind and limb. C. P. SNOW Doctors . . overhauled him and found him pretty sound. ***sound as a bell***, ***sound as a nut***, ***sound as a pippin***, ***sound as a roach***, etc. **2a** J. HERRIOT My teeth were perfectly sound. *Carriage Driving* Any animal with only three sound legs would be unbalanced. **b** B. BAINBRIDGE A man of sound mind, capable of exercising his judgement. **3a** E. HUXLEY The property's . . sound enough to be repaired. **c** J. CHEEVER She . . read somewhere that diamonds were a sound investment. **7a** M. KEANE Happiness was restored to me, sounder, more assured than it had been. *Modern Maturity* Older Americans who . . have . . acquired sound educations.

▶ **II 8 a** Of advice, judgement, a course of action, etc.: in full accordance with fact or reason, based on well-grounded principles; sensible, judicious; valid, correct. **LME.** ▸**b** Theologically correct; orthodox. **L16.** ▸†**c** Of a text: accurate. **L16–E18.**
9 Of a person: holding approved, solid, or well-founded opinions, esp. with regard to religious belief; orthodox. Also foll. by *on* (something). **E16.**
10 a Of a person, disposition, principle, etc.: morally good, honourable; honest, sincere; trusty, loyal. **L16.** ▸**b** Esp. of the public: dependable, loyal; trustworthy in terms of national character. **M19.**
11 Of a person: of sober or solid judgement; well grounded in principles or knowledge; experienced, reliable. **E17.**

> 🕮 **8a** *Times*: Sound advice would . . be . . moderation in all things. G. E. HUTCHINSON The adjective planktic would be etymologically sounder than planktonic. R. FRAME A man of rational and sound reasoning. **10a** W. COWPER The requisites that form a friend, A real and a sound one. **11** W. GERHARDIE She was still a sound business woman.

■ **soundly** *adverb* **LME.** **soundness** *noun* **LME.**

sound /saʊnd/ *verb*¹. **ME.**
[Anglo-Norman *suner*, Old French *soner* (mod. *sonner*) from Latin *sonare*, from *sonus*: see **SOUND** *noun*².]
▶ **I** *verb intrans.* **1** Of a thing: make or emit a sound; resound (*to*, *with* something); be filled with sound. **ME.** ▸**b** *spec.* Of a trumpet or other instrument: give a call or summons *to* arms, battle, etc; make a signal. **ME.**
2 †**a** Utter vocal sounds; speak, cry, sing. **ME–L16.** ▸**b** Of a person: make a sound or signal by blowing or playing an instrument. **ME.**
†**3** Have a suggestion of, a tendency towards, or a connection with a specified thing. Foll. by *against*, *in(to)*, *to*, etc. **ME–M17.**
4 Strike the ears, be heard as a particular type of sound; be emitted or mentioned. Freq. foll. by adjective compl., adverb. **LME.**
5 Convey a certain impression by sound; seem to the ear to be. Foll. by noun or adjective compl., inf., adverb (now chiefly *well*, *ill*, or indefinite in *how*). **LME.**

> 🕮 **1** T. HARDY A bell began clanging, and he listened till a hundred . . strokes had sounded. A. E. HOUSMAN The street sounds to the soldiers' tread. A. SCHLEE A gun sounded from the bank. **4** G. GREENE The feminine question sounded oddly in Miss Warren's . . masculine voice. J. STEINBECK The music . . sounded in his head with a steely tone. G. VIDAL Footsteps sounded . . loud on the pavement. **5** P. CAMPBELL She sounded . . a little guarded on the telephone. M. GEE He had his own plane, which sounded fun. M. SEYMOUR Life at Brede sounds to have come . . out of a novel.

▶ **II** *verb trans.* **6 a** Utter, state; pronounce, esp. loudly or deliberately; repeat. Also foll. by *forth*, *out*. **ME.** ▸**b** Reproduce or express in words. Long *rare*. **LME.**
7 Cause (an instrument etc.) to make a sound; blow, strike (an instrument etc.); play (a note or notes). **LME.**
8 Declare, announce, proclaim; celebrate. **LME.**
†**9** Of words: signify, mean; imply. **LME–L17.**
10 a Give a signal or order for (something) by the sound of a trumpet or other instrument; *fig.* give intimation of. **M16.** ▸**b** Blow (a blast). *poet.* **E19.**
11 Taunt. Cf. ***sound on*** below. *US slang. rare.* **M20.**

> 🕮 **6a** J. K. JEROME But I thought . . you did not sound the 'e' at the end of h-a-v-e. **7** G. GREENE The driver . . sounded his horn. M. LEITCH An ice-cream van sounded its chimes. *fig.*: *Observer* Reluctance to sound the trumpet for his own measures. **8** LD MACAULAY The Tories still continued . . to sound the praise of a national militia. **10a** G. GREENE The sirens were sounding the All Clear. P. DALLY He sounded a warning in August.

With adverbs & prepositions in specialized senses, & phrases: ***sound a note of caution***, ***sound a note of warning***: see **NOTE** *noun*². **sound in damages**, **sound in tort**, **sound in contract**, etc. *LAW* be concerned only with damages; give rise to a claim for damages. **sound off** (*a*) *US MILITARY* (of a band) strike up, start playing; (*b*) *colloq.* (orig. *US*) speak loudly, express one's opinions forcefully; complain; brag. **sound on** *Black slang* taunt, criticize.

sound /saʊnd/ *verb*². **LME.**
[Old & mod. French *sonder*, corresp. to Spanish, Portuguese *sondar* use the sounding-lead from Proto-Romance, from Latin *sub* **SUB-** + *unda* wave.]
†**1** *verb intrans.* Sink in, penetrate. Only in **LME.**
2 *verb trans. & intrans.* Use a line and lead or (now usu.) an echo-sounder to test the depth or quality of the bottom of (the sea, a river, etc.); measure or examine (water). **LME.**
3 *fig.* **a** *verb trans.* Measure or test as by sounding. **L16.** ▸**b** *verb intrans.* Make an inquiry or investigation. **L18.**
4 *verb trans.* **a** Inquire (esp. cautiously or indirectly) into the opinions or feelings of (a person); examine or question in an indirect manner. Also foll. by *out*. **L16.** ▸**b** Investigate, attempt to find out (a matter, a person's views, etc.), esp. by cautious or indirect questioning. Also foll. by *out*. **L16.**
†**5** *verb trans.* Understand; fathom. **L16–M17.**
6 *verb trans. MEDICINE.* Orig., probe (a wound etc.). Now, examine (a body cavity, esp. the bladder) using a sound (**SOUND** *noun*⁴ 3). **L16.**
7 *verb intrans.* **a** Of a sounding-lead: go down; touch bottom. **E17.** ▸**b** Of a whale: go deep under water; dive. **M19.**

> 🕮 **2** T. MO Let us go to the bow and see the linesman sounding. **3a** G. GREENE There was a depth of bitterness . . in Mrs Baines you couldn't sound. **4a** J. CARY His real purpose was to sound the . . governor about the political situation. P. GROSSKURTH To sound him out on Melanie's suggestion. **b** N. SYMINGTON He spoke to Brücke . . to sound out whether there was any likelihood of promotion.

sound /saʊnd/ *verb*³ *intrans.* Now only *Scot. & dial.* **LME.**
[Var. of **SWOON** *verb*. Cf. **SOUND** *noun*³.]
Swoon, faint.

sound /saʊnd/ *adverb.* **ME.**
[from the adjective.]
1 Without harm or injury; safely, securely. Long *rare* or *obsolete*. **ME.**
2 In a sound manner; heartily, soundly; thoroughly. Now only in phrs. (see below) or comb., as ***sound-judging***, ***sound-thinking***. **LME.**
2 sleep sound sleep deeply and unbrokenly; be in a deep sleep. **sound asleep** sleeping deeply, fast asleep.

sound-alike /ˈsaʊndəlʌɪk/ *noun & adjective.* **L20.**
[from **SOUND** *verb*¹ + **ALIKE** *adjective*.]
▶ **A** *noun.* A person or thing closely resembling another in sound or name. **L20.**
▶ **B** *adjective.* Closely similar in sound or name. **L20.**

> 🕮 *Independent on Sunday* The *Minder* soundalike theme song which suggests they are actively seeking the comparison.

soundboard /ˈsaʊn(d)bɔːd/ *noun.* **E16.**
[from **SOUND** *noun*² + **BOARD** *noun*.]
1 *MUSIC.* A thin board of wood placed in a musical (esp. keyboard) instrument in such a position as to increase its sound. **E16.** ▸**b** A shallow grooved box having the same function in an organ. **E17.**
2 A sounding-board placed over or behind a pulpit etc. **M18.**

sounder /ˈsaʊndə/ *noun*¹. **LME.**
[Old French *sundre*, (also mod. dial.) *sonre*, from Germanic.]
1 A herd of wild swine. **LME.**
2 A boar in its first or second year. **E19.**

sounder /ˈsaʊndə/ *noun*². **LME.**
[from **SOUND** *verb*¹ + **-ER**¹.]
1 A person who makes or utters a sound or sounds; a person who plays a musical instrument. *arch.* **LME.**
2 A telegraphic device which enables communications to be received audibly; a telegraphist who operates such a device. **M19.**
3 A device or instrument which gives an audible signal or alarm; a signal so given. **L19.**

sounder /ˈsaʊndə/ *noun*³. **L16.**
[from **SOUND** *verb*² + **-ER**¹.]
1 a A person who sounds the depth of water etc. **L16.** ▸**b** A person who sounds the opinions or feelings of others. *rare.* **L16.**
2 A device or instrument for sounding the sea. **E19.**

Soundex /ˈsaʊndɛks/ *adjective & noun.* **M20.**
[from **SOUND** *noun*² + *-ex* (arbitrary ending).]
(Designating) a phonetic coding system intended to suppress spelling variations, used esp. to encode surnames for the linkage of medical records; (designating) material encoded using this code.
Comb.: **Soundex-code** *verb trans.* encode (a name or other data) using the Soundex code.

sounding /ˈsaʊndɪŋ/ *noun*¹. **ME.**
[from **SOUND** *verb*² + **-ING**¹.]
1 a The action or process of sounding the depth of water; an instance of this. **ME.** ▸**b** The determination of a physical property at a depth in the sea or at a height in the atmosphere; an instance of this. **L19.** ▸**c** *ARCHAEOLOGY.* A trial excavation of limited scale made on a site to gain preliminary information. **M20.**
2 a In *pl.* & †*sing.* A position at sea where it is possible to reach the bottom with an ordinary deep-sea lead; a depth of water able to be sounded. Freq. in ***in soundings***, ***off soundings***. **L15.** ▸**b** In *pl.* Depths of water, esp. of the sea along a coast or in a harbour, ascertained by sounding; entries in a logbook etc. giving details of these. **L16.**
3 Investigation, inquiry. Also ***sounding out***. **M16.**
4 *MEDICINE.* The action of examining with a sound (**SOUND** *noun*⁴ 3) or probe. **L16.**
Phrases: ***strike soundings***: see **STRIKE** *verb*. **take soundings** try to find out how matters stand, esp. cautiously or indirectly.
Comb.: **sounding balloon**: used to obtain information about the upper atmosphere; **sounding-lead** the lead or plummet attached to a sounding-line; **sounding-line** a line used in sounding the depth of water; **sounding rocket**: designed to carry scientific instruments into the upper atmosphere in order to make measurements during its flight; **sounding-rod**: used in finding the depth of water in a ship's hold.

sounding /ˈsaʊndɪŋ/ *noun*². **LME.**
[from **SOUND** *verb*¹ + **-ING**¹.]
1 The fact of emitting or capacity to emit a sound or sounds; the sound produced by something, esp. a bell or trumpet. **LME.**
2 a Vocal utterance or pronunciation; the resonant or sonorous quality of the voice. Long *rare*. **LME.** ▸**b** The exchange of ritual insults among black Americans, playing the dozens (see **DOZEN** *noun* 1d). **M20.**
3 An act of causing a trumpet, bell, etc., to sound; the blowing *of* a bugle or trumpet, esp. as a signal. **E16.**
4 *MEDICINE.* The action or an act of examining the chest, abdomen, etc., by percussion or auscultation. **L19.**
Comb.: **sounding-board** (*a*) a board or screen placed over or behind a pulpit etc. to reflect the speaker's voice towards the audience or congregation; (*b*) *MUSIC* = **SOUNDBOARD** *noun* 1; (*c*) a means of making opinions etc. more widely known; (*d*) a person or group used as a trial audience.

sounding /ˈsaʊndɪŋ/ *noun*³. Long *rare* or *obsolete*. **LME.**
[from **SOUND** *verb*³ + **-ING**¹.]
1 Swooning, fainting. **LME.**
2 A swoon; a fainting-fit. **L16.**
1 *sounding fit* etc.

sounding /ˈsaʊndɪŋ/ *adjective.* **ME.**
[from **SOUND** *verb*¹ + **-ING**².]
1 Having or emitting a sound or sounds; resonant, sonorous; reverberant. Freq. with qualifying adjective, as ***clear sounding***, ***deep sounding***, ***loud sounding***, etc. **ME.**
2 a Of language, a name, etc.: having a full, rich, or imposing sound; pompous, bombastic. **L17.** ▸**b** Of a person: loudly demonstrative. *rare.* **E19.**
1 sounding sand = ***singing sand*** s.v. **SINGING** *ppl adjective*.
■ **soundingly** *adverb* so as to emit or produce a (loud) sound; sonorously, imposingly: **L17.** **soundingness** *noun* (*rare*) the quality or character of being sonorous **E18.**

soundless /ˈsaʊndlɪs/ *adjective*¹. **L16.**
[from **SOUND** *verb*² + **-LESS**.]
That cannot be sounded; unfathomable (*lit.* & *fig.*).

soundless /ˈsaʊndlɪs/ *adjective*[2]. E17.
[from SOUND *noun*[2] + -LESS.]
1 Having or making no sound; quiet, silent. E17.
2 In which no sound is heard; still. E19.
■ **soundlessly** *adverb* M19. **soundlessness** *noun* M19.

soup /suːp/ *noun*. ME.
[Old & mod. French *soupe* sop, broth poured on slices of bread, from late Latin *suppa*, from verb meaning 'soak', ult. from Germanic. Cf. SOP *noun*[1], SUP *verb*[1].]
1 A usu. savoury liquid food made by boiling meat, fish, or vegetables, etc., with seasoning in stock or water, and freq. served as a first course; a dish or variety of this. ME. ▸**b** BIOLOGY. A solution rich in organic compounds which made up the primitive oceans of earth and was the environment in which cellular life originated. Also ***primordial soup***. M20.
2 a LAW. *sing.* & (occas.) in *pl.* Dock briefs. *slang*. M19. ▸**b** Fog; thick cloud. Cf. PEA-SOUP 2. *colloq.* E20. ▸**c** Nitroglycerine or gelignite, esp. as used for safe-breaking. *US slang*. E20. ▸**d** The chemical mixture used to develop photographic film. *slang*. E20. ▸**e** SURFING. Foam produced by a broken wave. M20.

📖 **1** *Vogue* For a more elegant soup, the chopped herb can be mixed with the sour cream. ***chicken soup***, ***onion soup***, ***tomato soup***, etc. **2b** J. GORES Ballard watched the taillights recede into the soup.

Comb. & phrases: **from soup to nuts** *N. Amer. colloq.* from beginning to end; completely; **in the soup** *colloq.* in difficulties, in trouble; **soup and fish** *colloq.* men's evening dress, a dinner suit; **soup-bone** a bone used to make stock for soup; **soup bunch** *US dial.* a bundle of vegetables sold for making soup; **soupfin (shark)** any of several slender grey sharks having a large dorsal fin, of the genus *Galeorhinus*; esp. *G. zyopterus*, found off the Pacific coast of N. America and once hunted for its liver and fins; **soup-kitchen** a place dispensing free soup etc. to the poor or unemployed; **soup line** *US* a queue for food at a soup-kitchen; **soup maigre** [French *soupe maigre*] thin (esp. vegetable or fish) soup; **soup man** *slang* a safe-breaker using nitroglycerine etc.; **soup-plate** a deep wide-rimmed plate in which soup is served; **soup-spoon** a large round-bowled spoon for drinking soup; **soup-stock**: used as a base for making soup; **soup-strainer** *colloq.* a long moustache; **soup-ticket**: entitling a person to receive soup from a soup-kitchen.

soup /suːp/ *verb trans.* M19.
[from the noun.]
1 Provide with soup. *rare*. M19.
2 Place in trouble or difficulties. Usu. in *pass. colloq.* L19.
3 Foll. by *up*: modify (an engine, vehicle, etc.) so as to increase its power and efficiency; *transf.* revise (writing, music, etc.) so as to increase its power or impact; enhance (an existing product etc.). Freq. as ***souped-up*** *ppl adjective. colloq.* M20.

📖 **2** *Daily Telegraph* If he accepted a junior Ministry he would be 'souped'. **3** T. KENEALLY Two Terrots which had been souped up with English Blackburne engines. *Verbatim* This edition . . baited with a 31-page preface by Shaw and a souped-up title.

soupçon /ˈsuːpsɒn, *foreign* supsɔ̃/ *noun*. M18.
[French from Old French *sous(s)peçon*, from medieval Latin *suspectio(n-)*: see SUSPICION *noun*.]
A suspicion, a suggestion; a very small quantity, a trace.

📖 *Time* Life was filled with laughter . . a soupçon of scandal and . . money. *Country Living* Season with salt and pepper, and add a soupçon of garlic.

soupe /sup/ *noun*. Pl. pronounced same. M18.
[French: see SOUP *noun*.]
Soup, esp. in French cooking. Chiefly in phrs., as ***soupe à l'oignon*** /alɔɲɔ̃/, onion soup.

souper /supe/ *noun*[1]. Pl. pronounced same. L18.
[French.]
Esp. in France: an evening meal, supper.

souper /ˈsuːpə/ *noun*[2]. Now chiefly *Hist.* M19.
[from SOUP *noun* or *verb* + -ER[1].]
1 In Ireland, a member of the Protestant clergy seeking to make converts by dispensing free soup etc. M19.
2 A convert to Protestantism by the receipt of free soup etc. L19.

souper *noun*[3] see SUPER *noun*[1].

soupirant /supirɑ̃/ *noun*. Pl. pronounced same. M19.
[French, pres. pple of *soupirer* sigh.]
A male admirer, a suitor.

souple /supl/ *noun*. L19.
[French.]
More fully ***souple silk***. A fabric made of partially degummed silk.

soupy /ˈsuːpi/ *noun*. *US Military slang*. L19.
[from SOUP *noun* + -Y[6].]
(A summons to) a meal.

soupy /ˈsuːpi/ *adjective*. M19.
[from SOUP *noun* + -Y[1].]
1 Of, pertaining to, or resembling soup, esp. in consistency; *colloq.* (of weather) foggy. M19.
2 Sentimental; mawkish. *colloq.* M20.

📖 **1** H. MANTEL A soupy lemon-brown dust haze hung over Ghazzah Street. **2** E. JONG A sleazy rendition of 'Stardust'—all tinny strings and soupy nasal horns.

■ **soupily** *adverb* L20. **soupiness** *noun* M20.

sour /saʊə/ *adjective, noun, & adverb*.
[Old English *sūr* = Old Saxon, Old High German *sūr* (Dutch *zuur*, German *sauer*), Old Norse *súrr*, from Germanic.]
▶ **A** *adjective*. **I 1** Having a tart or acid taste, as of unripe fruit, lemon, vinegar, etc. Opp. ***sweet***. OE. ▸**b** Of a tree: producing tart or acid fruit. OE.
2 a Of food (esp. milk or bread): acidic as a result of fermentation; bad, fermented. ME. ▸**b** Of a smell, breath, etc.: bad, rancid. ME.
3 a (Of wood, hay, etc.) green; (of pasture) harsh to the taste, rank. Now *dial.* L15. ▸**b** Of soil, land, etc.: cold and wet; deficient in lime. M16.
4 Of petroleum, natural gas, etc.: containing a relatively high proportion of sulphur. Opp. SWEET *adjective* 3b. E20.

📖 **1** E. HYAMS No matter how sour and sharp the apples. **2a** S. CLOETE He ate . . maas, the sour thickened milk of the indigenous people. **b** M. GORDON The smell of his sickness . . a sour male smell.

▶ **II** *fig.* **5** Distasteful, disagreeable; unpleasant. ME. ▸**b** Of weather etc.: cold and wet; inclement. L16. ▸**c** Of music: out of tune. M20.
6 Of a person, a person's disposition, etc.: harsh; sullen, morose; discontented, embittered. ME.
7 Of a comment, facial expression, etc.: indicating or expressing discontent; peevish, cross. LME.
8 Of an animal: heavy, gross. Chiefly *dial.* E17.

📖 **5** *Videographic* The . . Center is located in an especially sour part of town. **6** V. ALCOCK In one of those sour, angry moods when you hug your misery to yourself. **7** L. M. MONTGOMERY Would you want to . . wear a sour look all your life? *Times* He described the preface as scurrilous, sour and vindictive.

Phrases: **go sour**, **turn sour** (of food) become sour, go bad; *fig.* become corrupt. **go sour on**, **turn sour on** turn out badly for; turn against.
Special collocations: **sourball** *US* = **sourpuss** below. **sour beef** *US* = SAUERBRATEN. **sour bread** †(*a*) leavened bread; (*b*) *US* sourdough bread. **sour cherry** an acid type of cherry used in cooking, the fruit of *Prunus cerasus*; the small bushy tree which bears this fruit. **sour cream** cream intentionally fermented by the addition of bacteria. **sour crop** VETERINARY MEDICINE (*a*) candidiasis of poultry, producing a crop filled with foul-smelling liquid and often thickened and ulcerated; (*b*) impacted crop. **sour crout** (now *rare* or *obsolete*) = SAUERKRAUT. **sour dock** (now *dial.*) sorrel, *Rumex acetosa*. **sour gourd** (the fruit of) the baobab, *Adansonia digitata*, or the related Australian tree *A. gregorii*. ***sour grapes***: see GRAPE *noun* 2. **sour grass** (*a*) a coarse W. Indian grass, *Paspalum conjugatum*; (*b*) *S. Afr.* the coarse grass of poor nutritional value characteristic of sour veld; (*c*) any of several sour-tasting plants, esp. sorrel, *Rumex acetosa*, and various oxalises. **sour gum** *US* = ***black gum*** s.v. BLACK *adjective*. **sour-mash** *US* (whiskey etc. made from) a mash for brewing or distilling which is acidifed to promote fermentation. **sour orange** (the fruit of) the Seville orange, *Citrus aurantium*. **sour plum** (the fruit of) the emu-apple, *Owenia acidula*. **sourpuss** *colloq.* a peevish or sour-tempered person; a grumbler, a killjoy. **sour-sweet** *adjective* & *noun* (a thing which is) sweet with an admixture or aftertaste of sourness. **sour veld** *S. Afr.* veld of sour grass, edible for only a few months of the year. **sourwood** the sorrel tree, *Oxydendrum arboreum*.
▶ **B** *noun*. **1** That which is sour (*lit.* & *fig.*); a sour thing, experience, etc. OE.
2 An acid solution used in bleaching, tanning, etc. M18.
3 An alcoholic drink, esp. of a specified kind, mixed with lemon-juice or lime-juice. *N. Amer.* M19.

📖 **1** SHAKES. *Lucr.* The sweets we wish for turn to loathed sours. **3** T. PYNCHON Metzger came up with an enormous Thermos of tequila sours.

▶ **C** *adverb*. †**1** Bitterly, dearly; severely. Only in ME.
2 In a sour manner; crossly, unfavourably. Chiefly in ***look sour on***. Now *rare*. E16.
■ **sourish** *adjective* LME. **sourly** *adverb* LME. **sourness** *noun* OE.

sour /saʊə/ *verb*. ME.
[from the adjective.]
1 *verb intrans.* **a** Become sour; acquire a sour or acid taste; *fig.* become unpleasant or disagreeable. ME. ▸**b** Develop a sour temper or disposition; assume a sour expression; become embittered. M18.
2 *verb trans.* Make sour; cause to turn acid, spoil in this way; *fig.* cause to become unpleasant or disagreeable. ME. ▸**b** Of leaven: cause fermentation in (dough etc.). ME. ▸**c** Apply diluted acid to (cloth etc.) in bleaching. M18.
3 *verb trans.* Cause to be sour in disposition; embitter. L16.

📖 **1a** H. E. BATES A bowl of milk was souring in the sun. *New Yorker* When Dick left the Air Force the marriage soured. **b** A. PRICE The Brigadier's expression soured, as though the thought . . was distasteful to him. A. S. BYATT His mother soured rapidly and ungracefully, and spent much of her time complaining. **2** S. BRETT One of his little tantrums . . It . . soured the atmosphere. *Rugby World & Post* The incident sparked off a general punch-up and soured the rest of the match. **3** B. VINE She . . had been permanently soured by her disillusionment.

Phrases: **sour on** *colloq.* (chiefly *US*) take a dislike or distaste to. **soured on** *N. Amer. & Austral. colloq.* embittered with.
■ **souring** *noun* (*a*) the action of the verb; (*b*) (now chiefly *dial.*) a substance which causes sourness or fermentation; (*c*) *dial.* a sour variety of apple, a crab-apple: LME.

source /sɔːs/ *noun & verb*. ME.
[Old French *sours, sors* masc., and *source* (also mod.), *sourse* fem., use as noun of pa. pple of *sourdre* rise, spring, from Latin *surgere* SURGE *verb*.]
▶ **A** *noun*. **1** = SOUSE *noun*[2] 1. Long *obsolete* exc. *Hist.* ME.
†**2** FALCONRY. The upward flight of a hawk etc. LME–E17.
3 The fountain-head of a river or stream; the place from which a flow of water begins. LME. ▸**b** A spring, a fountain. L15.
4 A person who or thing which is the chief or prime cause *of* a specified condition, quality, emotion, etc.; a place where such a condition etc. originates. LME. ▸**b** *spec.* The genealogical origin *of* a person or family. M17. ▸**c** A document, person, etc., supplying esp. original information or evidence in support of some fact or event; a spokesperson, *esp.* one who gives unattributable statements to the media. L18.
5 a The derivation of a material thing; a place or thing from which something material is obtained or originates; the originating cause of a physical agency; a body which emits radiation, energy, etc. E19. ▸**b** PHYSICS. A place where, or process by which, energy or some specific component enters a system; a point or centre from which a fluid or current flows. Opp. SINK *noun* 7. M19. ▸**c** ELECTRONICS. (The material forming) the part of a field-effect transistor which acts as an emitter of charge-carriers. Opp. DRAIN *noun* 1c. M20.

📖 **3** JULIA HAMILTON An expedition searching for the source of the river Niger. *fig.*: J. AIKEN Being given permission to cry ad lib had the effect of drying up the source. **b** TENNYSON Like torrents from a mountain source. **4** E. ROOSEVELT Religion was an anchor and a source of strength and guidance. T. CAPOTE The source of her misery . . was . . in her spine. **c** *Times Educ. Suppl.* Pupils should be able to . . read with a large degree of independence using . . reference sources. *Guardian* According to . . diplomatic sources, . . they may issue a joint statement calling for a peace conference. **5a** P. L. FERMOR Transylvania was the oldest source of gold in the classical world. *Which?* Toothpaste is only one source of fluoride. *Scientific American* The major commercial application for his superbulbs was as a source of heat rather than of light.

Phrases: **at source** at the point, place, etc., of origin.
Comb.: **sourcebook** a collection of documentary sources for the study of a subject; **source code** COMPUTING (a program, procedure, etc., written in) a source language; **source-criticism** THEOLOGY analysis and study of the sources used by biblical authors; **source language** (*a*) a language from which a translation is made; (*b*) COMPUTING a language in which a program or procedure is written; **source program** COMPUTING a program written in a language other than machine code, usu. a high-level language; **source rock** GEOLOGY (*a*) a rock formation from which later sediments are derived, or in which a particular mineral originates; (*b*) sediment in which hydrocarbons originate and with sufficient organic content to generate petroleum.
▶ **B** *verb*. †**1** *verb intrans.* Of a bird of prey: fly upwards. *rare*. Only in E16.
†**2** *verb intrans.* Arise *from* something. L16–M17.
3 *verb trans.* **a** In *pass.* Have as a source, originate in or from, (foll. by *in*); be cited as a source of evidence etc. M20. ▸**b** Of a manufacturer: obtain (components etc.) *in* or *from* a specified place. Usu. in *pass.* L20.

📖 **3** *Times Lit. Suppl.* A scientific paper . . by the Chicago psychoanalyst . . which is sourced in my notes. *Achievement* The . . error is sourced either in the design team or in the construction management team. **b** *Grocer* A range of savoury peanut snacks sourced from Belgium.

■ **sourceless** *adjective* M19.

sourdine /sʊəˈdiːn/ *noun & adjective*. E17.
[French, from *sourd* deaf, dull.]
▶ **A** *noun*. MUSIC.
1 = SORDUN. E17.
2 A mute; a damper. L18.
▶ **B** *adjective*. Muffled, subdued. *rare*. L19.

sourdough /ˈsaʊədəʊ/ *noun*. LME.
[from SOUR *adjective* + DOUGH *noun*.]
1 a Leaven. Long *obsolete* exc. *dial.* LME. ▸**b** Fermenting dough, esp. that left over from a previous baking, used as leaven; bread made from this (also ***sourdough bread***). *N. Amer.* M19.
2 An experienced prospector in Alaska, the Yukon, etc. (in allusion to the use of sourdough to raise bread baked during the winter). *N. Amer.* L19.

sourock /ˈsʊərək/ *noun*. *Scot.* LME.
[from SOUR *adjective*: cf. Middle Dutch *zuric*, Middle Low German *sureke*.]
1 Sorrel, *Rumex acetosa*. Also, sheep's sorrel, *R. acetosella*. LME.
2 *fig.* A sour-tempered person. E18.

soursop /ˈsaʊəsɒp/ *noun*. Also (in sense 2) **soursob** /-sɒb/, **-sobs** /-sɒbz/. M17.
[from SOUR *adjective* + SOP *noun*[1].]
1 The large spiny slightly acid fruit of a W. Indian tree, *Annona muricata* (family Annonaceae); the tree bearing this fruit. M17.
2 The Bermuda buttercup, *Oxalis pes-caprae*. *Austral.* L19.

sous- /su, suz/ *prefix*. ME.
[Old & mod. French *sous*, from Latin *subtus* under.]
Used in words adopted from French with the sense 'under', 'sub-', as ***sous-chef***, ***sous-lieutenant***, etc.

sousaphone /ˈsuːzəfəʊn/ *noun*. E20.
[from John Philip *Sousa* (1854–1932), US bandmaster and composer, after *saxophone* etc.]
A large brass bass wind instrument encircling the player's body.
■ **souˈsaphonist** /suːˈzaf(ə)nɪst/ *noun* a performer on the sousaphone M20.

souse /saʊs/ *noun*[1]. LME.
[Old French *sous*, *souz*, from Old Saxon *sultia*, Old High German *sulza* (German *Sülze*) brine, from Germanic, from base also of SALT *noun*. In branch II directly from SOUSE *verb*[1].]
► **I 1** Pickled meat, esp. pig's feet and ears. Now *dial.*, *US*, & *W. Indies*. LME. ▸**b** An ear. Now *dial.* M17.
2 A liquid, esp. one with salt, used in pickling. E16.
► **II 3** The action or an act of sousing or soaking something; *dial.* a wash. M18.
4 A heavy drinking-bout. Also, a drunkard. *colloq.* (chiefly *US*). E20.

souse /saʊs/ *noun*[2]. LME.
[Anglo-Norman, app. alt. of SOURCE *noun*.]
1 ARCHITECTURE. A corbel, a bracket. Long *obsolete* exc. *Hist.* LME.
†**2** FALCONRY. **a** = SOURCE *noun* 2. Only in ***at souse***, ***at the souse***. L15–L17. ▸**b** = QUARRY *noun*[1] 4. L16–M17.

souse /saʊs/ *noun*[3]. Now *Scot.* & *dial.* L15.
[Prob. imit.]
A heavy blow or fall; a thump.

†**souse** *noun*[4]. E16–E19.
[Old French *sous* (pl.): see SOU.]
= SOU.

souse /saʊs/ *verb*[1]. LME.
[from SOUSE *noun*[1].]
► **I** *verb trans.* **1** Preserve (food) in pickle, esp. vinegar. LME. ▸**b** *transf.* Steep (food) *in* liquid; marinate. M17.
2 Plunge or immerse in water etc.; soak. Freq. foll. by *in*. L15.
3 Drench with water, rain, etc. Formerly also *fig.*, impose on, swindle. M16. ▸**b** *fig.* Make thoroughly drunk. Chiefly as ***soused*** *ppl adjective*. Now *slang*. E17.
4 Splash, dab, (water etc.). *rare*. M19.

> 📖 **1** B. FUSSELL The head was also a valued part of soused pig. **2** H. ALLEN Pounded their linen garments . . and soused them in the fountain till they were spotless. **3** J. K. JEROME He has just soused a dog, and now he's busy watering a signpost. **b** L. ARMSTRONG I could see that mother was getting soused.

► **II** *verb intrans.* **5 a** Soak; be drenched; plunge into or immerse oneself in water etc. LME. ▸**b** Wash thoroughly. *dial.* L19. ▸**c** Become thoroughly drunk. *slang*. E20.
†**6** Of water, rain, etc.: flow or fall copiously. L16–M17.
■ **sousing** *ppl adjective* (*a*) *rare* (of ears) suitable for sousing, unusually large; (*b*) that souses; drenching, soaking; (*c*) (now *dial.*) strong, vigorous: M16.

souse /saʊs/ *verb*[2]. Now *Scot.* & *dial.* E16.
[from SOUSE *noun*[3].]
1 *verb trans.* Strike forcefully or heavily; knock *down* with a heavy blow. E16.
†**2** *verb intrans.* Deliver heavy blows. *rare* (Spenser). Only in L16.
3 *verb intrans.* Fall heavily. L16.

souse /saʊs/ *verb*[3]. *arch.* L16.
[from SOUSE *noun*[2].]
1 *verb intrans.* Esp. of a bird of prey: swoop down. Freq. foll. by *on*, *upon*, etc. L16.
2 *verb trans.* Swoop or pounce on (a quarry). L16.

souse /saʊs/ *adverb*[1]. Now *arch.* & *dial.* L17.
[from SOUSE *noun*[3] or *verb*[2].]
Suddenly; with a swift course; headlong. Also, forcefully; heavily.

souse /saʊs/ *adverb*[2]. E18.
[from SOUSE *noun*[1] or *verb*[1].]
With a sudden or deep plunge into water etc.

sous-entendu /suzɑ̃tɑ̃dy/ *noun*. Pl. pronounced same. M19.
[French.]
Something implied or understood but not expressed.

souslik /ˈsuːslɪk/ *noun*. Also **sus-** /ˈsʌs-/. L18.
[French from Russian *suslik*.]
Any of several European, Asian, and Arctic ground squirrels of the genus *Spermophilus*. Also called ***zizel***.

sous vide /su vid, suː ˈviːd/ *adjectival & adverbial phr.* L20.
[French, from *sous* under + *vide* vacuum.]
Of food: (prepared) by partial cooking followed by vacuum-sealing and chilling.

soutache /suːˈtaʃ/ *noun*. M19.
[French from Hungarian *sujtás*.]
More fully ***soutache braid***. A narrow flat ornamental braid used for decorative trimming. Also called ***Russia braid***.

soutane /suːˈtɑːn/ *noun*. M19.
[French from Italian *sottana*, from *sotto* from Latin *subtus* under.]
ROMAN CATHOLIC CHURCH. A cassock, *esp.* a cassock with scarf and cincture worn by a priest.

souteneur /sutənœːr/ *noun*. Pl. pronounced same. E20.
[French = protector, from *soutenir* sustain + *-eur* -OR.]
A pimp.

soutenu /sutəny/ *adjective & noun*. M20.
[French, pa. pple of *soutenir* sustain.]
BALLET. ▸**A** *adjective*. Of a movement: sustained, performed slowly. M20.
► **B** *noun*. Pl. pronounced same. A sustained or slow movement; *esp.* a complete turn on point or half point. M20.

souter /ˈsuːtə/ *noun*. Now *Scot.* & *north.*
[Old English *sūtere* corresp. to Old High German *sūtāri*, Old Norse *sútari*, from Latin *sutor*, from *suere* sew, stitch: see -ER[1].]
A shoemaker, a cobbler. Formerly also (*derog.*), a stupid or uneducated person.

souterrain /ˈsuːtəreɪn/ *noun*. M18.
[French, from *sous* under + *terre* earth, after Latin *subterraneus*.]
Chiefly ARCHAEOLOGY. An underground chamber or passage.

south /saʊθ/ *adverb, adjective, noun, & verb*.
[Old English *sūþ* = Old Frisian *suth*, Old Saxon *sūþ* (Low German *sud*), Old High German *sunt*, *sund-*, Old Norse *suðr*.]
► **A** *adverb*. **1** In the direction of the part of the horizon on the right-hand side of a person facing east; towards the point or pole on the earth's surface where it is cut by the earth's axis of rotation and where the heavens appear to turn clockwise about a point directly overhead; towards the magnetic pole near this point. OE. ▸**b** Foll. by *of*: further in this direction than. E18.
2 From the south; southerly. *rare*. E17.

> 📖 **1** SHAKES. *Rich. III* His regiment lies half a mile at least south from the mighty power of the King. G. JONES The upturned keel of mountains running south from Finnmark. L. DEIGHTON We'll go south until we find the end of the rafted ice. *American Speech* As one moves north or south through Indiana there are changes in dialect. **b** P. MAILLOUX A tiny . . village located . . south of Prague.

► **B** *adjective*. Compar. †**souther**, superl. †**southest**.
1 (Also **S-**.) Designating (a person or the people of) the southern part of a country, region, city, etc. OE.
2 Situated in or lying towards the south or southern part of something; on the southerly side. OE. ▸**b** Facing south. E16.
3 Of or pertaining to the south; (of a wind) coming from the south. OE.

> 📖 **1** ***South America***, ***South Atlantic***, ***South Kensington***, ***South Korea***, ***South London***, ***South Pacific***, etc. ***South American***, ***South Korean***, etc. **2** *Farmer's Magazine* Elgin . . situated on the south bank of the Lossie. C. E. PASCOE Within a few steps of Hanover Square, in a south direction. **b** A. J. WILSON Carnations . . blooming in the south window. **3** N. DOUGLAS Nepenthe was famous . . for its south wind.

► **C** *noun*. In senses 1, 2, 3 usu. with *the*.
1 (The direction of) the part of the horizon on the right-hand side of a person facing east; *spec.* the cardinal point opposite to the north point. ME.
2 (Freq. **S-**.) The southern part of the world relative to another part, or of a (specified) country, region, town, etc.; *spec.* (*a*) the southern part of England, regarded as extending south from the Wash; (*b*) England regarded as the southern part of Britain; (*c*) the Republic of Ireland; (*d*) the southern countries of Europe; (*e*) the southern US States, bounded on the north by Maryland, the Ohio River, and Missouri; *Hist.* the States upholding slavery; (*f*) the underdeveloped or non-industrialized nations of the world. Also (*transf.*), the inhabitants of such a part of the world, such a region, country, etc. ME.
3 A south wind, *esp.* one that brings warm weather. Also, a southerly gale in the W. Indies (usu. in *pl.*). ME.
4 (**S-**.) In bridge, (formerly) whist, or other four-handed partnership game, the player occupying the position so designated, who sits opposite 'North'. In mah-jong, = ***south wind*** (b) below. E20.

> 📖 **1** J. THOMSON The winds at eve . . Blow, hollow-blustering from the south. SHELLEY The rainbow hung over the city . . from north to south. **2** I. MURDOCH Soho in summer was his South of France. *Country Life* The traditional white-columned porticos of the South. *Journal of Refugee Studies* The South has suffered disasters almost beyond comprehension.

► **D** *verb intrans.* **1** Of a celestial object etc.: cross or approach the meridian of a place. *rare*. M17.
2 Move southward; (of a wind) shift or veer southward. *rare*. E18.

Special collocations, comb., & phrases: ***Deep South***: see DEEP *adjective*. ***down south***: see DOWN *adverb* & *adjective*. ***Empire State of the South***: see EMPIRE. **go south** *colloq.* (chiefly *US*) deteriorate, fail; fall in value. ***Old South***: see OLD *adjective*. ***solid South***: see SOLID *adjective*. **southabout** *adverb* (NAUTICAL) by a southerly route; southwards. **South African** *noun* & *adjective* (*a*) *noun* a native or inhabitant of South Africa, a country occupying the southernmost part of the African continent; (*b*) *adjective* of or pertaining to South Africa or its inhabitants; ***South African Dutch***, = AFRIKAANS. **South Africanism** (*a*) South African character or quality; (*b*) a South African characteristic, idiom, etc. **South American** *noun* & *adjective* (*a*) *noun* a native or inhabitant of South America, the southern half of the American land-mass; (*b*) *adjective* of or pertaining to South America or its inhabitants. **south and north** = ***north and south*** (a) s.v. NORTH. **South Bank** (the area adjacent to) the southern bank of the River Thames; now *esp.* the cultural complex located between Westminster and Blackfriars bridges in London. **southbound** *adjective* & *noun* (*a*) *adjective* travelling or heading southwards; (*b*) *noun* (chiefly *N. Amer.*) a southbound train. **south-by-east**, **south-by-west** *noun* & *adverb* (in the direction of) those compass points 11¼ degrees or one point east, west, of the south point. **south country** the southern part of a country; *spec.* (*a*) England south of the Wash; (*b*) Scotland south of the Forth. **South Devon** (an animal of) a large breed of cattle with a light red or fawn coat. ***South Downs***: see DOWN *noun*[1] 2. **South Islander** a native or inhabitant of the South Island of New Zealand. **southland** (now chiefly *poet.*) the southern part of a country, region, etc., or of the world; in *pl.*, lands lying in the south. **southlander** a southerner. **southpaw** *noun* & *verb* (*colloq.*) (*a*) *noun* the left hand; a left-handed person, esp. a baseball pitcher or a boxer; (*b*) *verb trans.* (*US*) pitch with the left hand. ***south pole***: see POLE *noun*[1]. **South Sea(s)** the seas of the southern hemisphere; *esp.* the southern Pacific Ocean. **South Sea bubble**, **South Sea scheme** *Hist.* a stockjobbing scheme for trading in the southern hemisphere to repay the British National Debt, which started and collapsed in 1720. **South sea rose** *W. Indies* the oleander, *Nerium oleander*. ***South Sea scheme***: see ***South Sea bubble*** above. **south-side** the side situated in or lying towards the south. **south-south-east**, **south-south-west** (in the direction) midway between south and south-east, south-west. **South Spainer** *Hist.* (a sailor on) a ship trading with Spain. **South Suffolk** (an animal of) a breed of sheep developed in New Zealand by crossing Suffolk and Southdown sheep. ***south transept***. **south wind** (*a*) (usu. with cap. initials) one of the four players in mah-jong, the player who takes the next four tiles after East Wind and preceding West Wind at the outset of the game; (*b*) each of four tiles so designated, which with east, west, and north winds make up the suit of winds in mah-jong; (see also sense B.3 above). **to the south (of)** in a southerly direction (from).
■ **southmost** *adjective* (now *rare*) southernmost OE. **southness** *noun* (*rare*) M19.

southard *adverb, noun, & adjective* see SOUTHWARD.

Southcottian /saʊθˈkɒtɪən/ *noun & adjective*. M19.
[from *Southcott* (see below) + -IAN.]
► **A** *noun*. An adherent or follower of the teaching of Joanna Southcott (1750–1814), who claimed to be the woman spoken of in *Revelation* 12. M19.
► **B** *adjective*. Of or pertaining to (the claims of) Joanna Southcott or her followers. M19.

Southdown /ˈsaʊθdaʊn/ *noun*. L18.
[from the *South Downs*: see DOWN *noun*[1] 2.]
(An animal of) a breed of sheep with short fine wool originally reared on the South Downs.

south-east /saʊθˈiːst/ *adverb, noun, & adjective*. OE.
[from SOUTH + EAST.]
► **A** *adverb*. In the direction midway between south and east. Foll. by *of*: further in this direction than. OE.

> 📖 DEFOE We . . stood off to sea, steering still south-east. *Geographical Journal* 50 kilometres south-east of Bamako.

► **B** *noun*. **1** (The direction of) the point of the horizon midway between south and east; the compass point corresponding to this. Also (freq. **South-East**), *the* south-eastern part of a country, region, etc., *spec.* the area of England regarded as consisting of the London area, Berkshire, Hampshire, Surrey, Sussex, and Kent. ME.
2 A south-east wind. LME.

> 📖 **1** T. KENEALLY Far out to the south-east. *Daily Telegraph* The promotional campaign, which will be launched in London and the south-east this month.

► **C** *adjective*. Of or pertaining to the south-east; (esp. of a wind) coming from the south-east; situated in, directed towards, or facing the south-east. LME.

> 📖 JOHN PHILLIPS Other ramifications run both on the south-east and north-west sides of Snowdonia. H. TREVELYAN The Deputy Minister in charge of South-east Asian affairs spoke to me.

■ **south-easter** *noun* a south-east wind L18. **south-easterly** *adjective & adverb* (*a*) *adjective* situated towards or facing the south-east; directed towards the south-east; (esp. of a wind) coming (nearly) from the south-east; (*b*) *adverb* in a south-easterly position or direction; towards the south-east: E18.

south-eastern /saʊθ'iːst(ə)n/ *adjective.* L16.
[from SOUTH + EASTERN.]
1 Situated in or directed towards the south-east; of, pertaining to, or characteristic of the south-east. L16.
2 Esp. of a wind: coming from the south-east. M19.
■ **south-easterner** *noun* a native or inhabitant of the south-eastern part of a country M20. **south-easternmost** *adjective* situated furthest to the south-east M19.

south-eastward /saʊθ'iːstwəd/ *adverb, noun, & adjective.* E16.
[from SOUTH-EAST + -WARD.]
▶ **A** *adverb.* Towards the south-east (*of*); in a south-easterly direction. E16.
▶ **B** *noun.* The direction or area lying to the south-east or south-east *of* a place etc. M16.
▶ **C** *adjective.* Situated or directed towards the south-east; moving or facing towards the south-east. M18.
■ **south-eastwardly** *adjective & adverb* (*a*) *adjective* moving, lying, or facing towards the south-east; (of a wind) blowing (nearly) from the south-east; (*b*) *adverb* in or from a north-easterly direction: L18. **south-eastwards** *adverb* = SOUTH-EASTWARD *adverb* L19.

southen /'ʃəʊð(ə)n/ *adjective. Scot. arch.* OE.
[from SOUTH + -EN[4].]
Orig., (of the wind) south, southerly. Later, southern.

souther /'saʊθə/ *noun.* M19.
[from SOUTH + -ER[1].]
A (strong) southerly wind.

†**souther** *adjective* compar. of SOUTH *adjective.*

souther /'sʌðə/ *verb intrans.* Chiefly *poet. rare.* E17.
[from SOUTH + -ER[5].]
= SOUTH *verb* 2.

southerly /'sʌðəli/ *adjective, adverb, & noun.* M16.
[from †*souther* compar. of SOUTH *adjective* + -LY[2], -LY[1]; partly from SOUTH after *easterly*.]
▶ **A** *adjective.* **1** Situated towards or facing the south; directed towards the south. M16.
2 Esp. of a wind: coming (nearly) from the south. E17.

> 📖 **1** *Flintshire Leader* The . . Chester southerly bypass will be opened . . on December 22nd. *West Briton* Surrounded by farmland. Extensive southerly rural views.

▶ **B** *adverb.* **1** In a southward position or direction. L16.
2 Esp. of a wind: (nearly) from the south. M17.
▶ **C** *noun.* A southerly wind. Freq. in *pl.* Chiefly *Austral. & NZ.* L19.
■ **southerliness** *noun* (*rare*) E18.

southermost /'sʌðəməʊst/ *adjective.* Now *rare.* M16.
[from †*souther* compar. of SOUTH *adjective* + -MOST.]
= SOUTHERNMOST.

southern /'sʌð(ə)n/ *adjective, noun, & verb.*
[Old English *superne* = Old Frisian *sūthern*, Old Saxon *sūprōni*, Old High German *sundrōni*, Old Norse *suðrœnn*, from Germanic base of SOUTH. See also SOUTHRON.]
▶ **A** *adjective.* **1** (Freq. **S-**.) Living in or originating from the south. OE. ▸**b** *spec.* Living in or originating from (any of) the States in the south of the US. L18.
2 Of a wind: blowing from the south. OE.
3 Situated in the south; directed, facing, or lying towards the south; having a position relatively south. OE.
4 (Freq. **S-**.) Of, pertaining to, or characteristic of the south or its inhabitants; *spec.* of or pertaining to (any of) the States in the south of the US. E19.

> 📖 **1** W. W. SKEAT The southern forms in the poem being due to a southern scribe. R. MACNEIL A Southern belle transplanted to colder climes. **3** R. WEST A nice room with a southern exposure. **4** *Farmer's Magazine* The great demand for the southern markets in the Autumn. W. A. PERCY The old Southern way of life . . existed no more.

Special collocations & comb.: ***Southern Alps***: see ALP *noun*[1] 2. **Southern Baptist** (*a*) ***Southern Baptist Convention***, a body of Baptist churches in the US, established in 1845; (*b*) a member of any of these churches. **southern beech** = NOTHOFAGUS. **Southern Comfort** (proprietary name for) a whiskey-based alcoholic drink. **Southern Cone** the S. American countries of Uruguay, Paraguay, and Chile. ***Southern Cross***: see CROSS *noun* 13. ***Southern Crown***: see CROWN *noun* 8. **Southern Fish** *the* constellation Piscis Austrinus. **southern-fried** *adjective* (orig. & chiefly *US*) (esp. of chicken) coated in batter and deep-fried. **southern hake** a tomcod, *Urophycis floridana*. ***Southern hemisphere***: see HEMISPHERE 1b. **southern hornworm** = TOBACCO ***hornworm***. **Southern Irish** *noun pl. & adjective* (the people) of the south of Ireland or of the Republic of Ireland. **southern lights** the Aurora Australis. **Southern Ocean** the southernmost parts of the Atlantic, Indian, and Pacific Oceans, surrounding Antarctica; also called ***Antarctic Ocean***. ***Southern Paiute***: see PAIUTE *noun* 1. ***southern* REEDBUCK**. **Southern States** the States in the south of the US; *Hist.* the States upholding slavery. **Southern Triangle** *the* constellation Triangulum Australe. **southernwood** (*a*) an aromatic shrubby plant of southern Europe, *Artemisia abrotanum*, of the composite family, formerly much cultivated for medicinal purposes; (*b*) (with specifying word) any of various other plants of this genus.
▶ **B** *noun.* **1** *pl. & collect. sing.* Southern people; southern men. Now *arch. rare.* LME.
2 A native or inhabitant of the south; a southerner. E18.
3 The dialect of English spoken in the southern States. *US.* M20.

> 📖 **1** SIR W. SCOTT A sturdy Scotsman, with . . prejudices against the southern, and the spawn of the southern. **2** HARTLEY COLERIDGE The Southerns . . have a strange idea of the lakes. **3** *New Yorker* Her South Delaware friends . . *were* talking Southern.

▶ **C** *verb intrans.* Of a wind: shift or veer southward. *rare.* L19.
■ **southerner** *noun* a native or inhabitant of the south, esp. of southern England; (freq. **S-**) a person belonging to the States in the south of the US: M19. **southernism** *noun* (*a*) southern character or quality; (*b*) a southern characteristic, idiom, etc.: M19. **southernize** *verb trans.* make southern in character, quality, form, etc. M19. **southernly** *adjective & †adverb* = SOUTHERLY *adjective, adverb* L16. **southernmost** *adjective* situated furthest to the south, most southerly E18. **southernness** /-n-n-/ *noun* L19.

Southern blot /sʌð(ə)n 'blɒt/ *noun phr.* L20.
[Edwin M. *Southern* (b. 1938), Brit. biochemist.]
BIOCHEMISTRY. A procedure for identifying specific sequences of DNA, in which fragments separated on a gel are transferred directly to a second medium on which assay by hybridization etc. may be carried out. Also called ***Southern hybridization***.

†**southest** *adjective* superl. of SOUTH *adjective.*

Southeyan /'sʌðɪən/ *adjective.* E19.
[from *Southey* (see below) + -AN.]
Of, pertaining to, or characteristic of the work of the English writer Robert Southey (1774–1843).

southing /'saʊθɪŋ/ *noun.* M17.
[from SOUTH + -ING[1].]
1 Chiefly *NAUTICAL.* (A measurement of) progress or deviation made towards the south. Freq. in ***make (so much) southing***. M17.
2 *ASTRONOMY.* The transit of a celestial body across the meridian, due south of the observer. M17.
3 *CARTOGRAPHY.* Distance southward from a point of origin; a figure representing this. Also in *ASTRONOMY*, angular distance south of the celestial equator. M18.

Southron /'sʌðr(ə)n/ *adjective & noun.* Orig. & chiefly *Scot. & north.* LME.
[Var. of SOUTHERN *adjective.*]
▶ **A** *adjective.* **1** Of, pertaining to, or characteristic of England or the English; situated or living in England. *arch.* LME.
2 *gen.* Southern. E19.
▶ **B** *noun.* **1** An Englishman or Englishwoman; *the* English collectively. *arch.* LME. ▸†**b** The English as opp. to Scots language. Only in 16.
2 *gen.* A southerner. M19.

south-southerly /saʊθ'sʌðəli/ *noun. N. Amer.* E19.
[Imit. of the bird's call.]
The long-tailed duck, *Clangula hyemalis*.

Southumbrian /saʊ'θʌmbrɪən/ *noun & adjective.* E19.
[from SOUTH + *Humber* a river in NE England (repr. Old English *Sūp(an)hymbre*) + -AN, -IAN, after *Northumbrian*.]
Hist. ▶**A** *noun.* A native or inhabitant of the northern part of the early English kingdom of Mercia. E19.
▶ **B** *adjective.* Of or pertaining to northern Mercia. L19.

southward /'saʊθwəd, *NAUTICAL* 'sʌðəd/ *adverb, noun, & adjective.* Also (*NAUTICAL & colloq.*) **southard** /'sʌðəd/. OE.
[from SOUTH + -WARD.]
▶ **A** *adverb.* Towards the south (*of*); in a southerly direction. OE.

> 📖 TENNYSON Southward they set their faces. R. BADEN-POWELL Half a mile southward of the town lies a bush-covered rising ground.

▶ **B** *noun.* The direction or area lying to the south or south *of* a place etc. ME.

> 📖 R. ADAMS He . . was gone to the southward.

▶ **C** *adjective.* Situated or directed towards the south; moving or facing towards the south. LME.

> 📖 L. MACNEICE The Southward trains are puffing.

■ **southwardly** *adverb & adjective* (*a*) *adverb* in or from a southerly direction; (*b*) *adjective* moving, lying, or facing towards the south; (of a wind) blowing (nearly) towards the south: L16. **southwards** *adverb* & (now *rare*) *noun* = SOUTHWARD *adverb, noun* OE.

south-west /saʊθ'wɛst/ *adverb, noun, & adjective.* OE.
[from SOUTH + WEST *adverb.*]
▶ **A** *adverb.* In the direction midway between south and west. Foll. by *of*: further in this direction than. OE.

> 📖 W. MORRIS The rook still flies South-west before the wind. *Navy News* The . . trawler Aran Lass, 25 miles south west of the Isle of Man.

▶ **B** *noun.* **1** (The direction of) the point of the horizon midway between south and west; the compass point corresponding to this. Also, (freq. **South-West**) the south-western part of a country, region, etc.; *spec.* (*a*) *N. Amer.* the south-western States of the US; (*b*) Namibia (formerly South West Africa); (*c*) the part of England regarded as consisting of Cornwall, Devon, Dorset, Somerset, and Wiltshire. OE.
2 A south-west wind. LME.

> 📖 **1** C. KINGSLEY The vast forest which ringed London round from north-east to south-west. *Observer* The University College of the South-west is the youngest of our University institutions. **2** SHAKES. *Temp.* A south-west blow on ye.

▶ **C** *adjective.* Of or pertaining to the south-west; (esp. of a wind) coming from the south-west; situated in, directed towards, or facing the south-west. LME.

> 📖 M. LINSKILL The south-west wind blew revivingly. *Here's Health* Malvern lies at the foot of a range of hills in south-west Worcestershire.

■ **south-wester** *noun* (*a*) a south-west wind; (*b*) = SOU'WESTER; (*c*) a white inhabitant of Namibia (formerly South West Africa): M19. **south-westerly** *adjective & adverb* (*a*) *adjective* situated towards or facing the south-west; directed towards the south-west; (esp. of a wind) coming (nearly) from the south-west; (*b*) *adverb* in a south-westerly position or direction, towards the south-west: E18.

south-western /saʊθ'wɛst(ə)n/ *adjective.* OE.
[from SOUTH + WESTERN *adjective.*]
1 Esp. of a wind: coming from the south-west. OE.
2 Situated in or directed towards the south-west; of, pertaining to, or characteristic of the south-west. E19.
■ **south-westerner** *noun* a native or inhabitant of the south-western part of a country L19. **south-westernmost** *adverb* situated furthest to the south-west M19.

south-westward /saʊθ'wɛstwəd/ *adverb, noun, & adjective.* M16.
[from SOUTH-WEST + -WARD.]
▶ **A** *adverb.* Towards the south-west (*of*); in a south-westerly direction. M16.
▶ **B** *noun.* The direction or area lying to the south-west or south-west *of* a place etc. L18.
▶ **C** *adjective.* Situated, directed, or moving towards the south-west. L18.
■ **south-westwardly** *adjective & adverb* (*a*) *adjective* moving, lying, or facing towards the south-west; (of a wind) blowing (nearly) from the south-west; (*b*) *adverb* in or from a south-westerly direction: L18. **south-westwards** *adverb* = SOUTH-WESTWARD *adverb* M18.

souvenir /suːvə'nɪə/ *noun & verb.* L18.
[French, use as noun of verb = remember from Latin *subvenire* come into the mind, formed as SUB- + *venire* come.]
▶ **A** *noun.* **1** A remembrance, a memory. Now *rare.* L18.
2 A token of remembrance; *esp.* an article given or purchased as a reminder *of* a particular person, place, or event; a keepsake. L18. ▸**b** *spec.* A usu. illustrated publication designed to be purchased as a gift. E19. ▸**c** In the war of 1914–18, a bullet, a shell. *Military slang.* E20.

> 📖 **2** N. ALGREN Paused in front of the curio shop to admire the little fringed souvenirs.

▶ **B** *verb trans.* **1** Provide with or constitute a souvenir of. *rare.* E20.
2 Take as a souvenir; (esp. *MILITARY*) pilfer, steal. *slang.* E20.

souvlaki /suː'vlɑːki/ *noun.* Pl. **-kia** /-kɪə/. M20.
[mod. Greek *soublaki* from *soubla* skewer.]
A Greek dish of small pieces of meat grilled on a skewer.

sou'wester /saʊ'wɛstə/ *noun.* M19.
[Reduced form of SOUTH-WESTER.]
1 A south-west wind, a south-wester. M19.
2 A (usu. oilskin) waterproof hat with a broad rim covering the back of the neck, worn esp. at sea. Also ***sou'wester hat***. M19.

sov /sɒv/ *noun*[1]. *colloq.* E19.
[Abbreviation. Cf. SOB *noun*[2].]
= SOVEREIGN *noun*; *spec.* (*Hist.*) a British gold coin of the nominal value of one pound.

Sov /sɒv/ *noun*[2]. *colloq.* M20.
[Abbreviation.]
= SOVIET *noun* 2. Usu. in *pl.*

sov. *abbreviation.*
Sovereign.

†**sovenance** *noun.* LME–E17.
[Old French *sovenance*, (also mod.) *souvenance*, from *so(u)venir*: see SOUVENIR *noun*, -ANCE.]
Remembrance; memory.

sovereign /'sɒvrɪn/ *noun & adjective.* ME.
[Old French *so(u)verain, -ein* (mod. *souverain*) from Proto-Romance: cf. Latin *super* above. Forms in *-gn* (after *reign*) appear in Late Middle English (cf. FOREIGN). Cf. SUZERAIN, SOVRAN.]

▸ **A** *noun.* **1** A person who has supremacy or authority over another or others; a superior; a governor, a master; *spec.* God. **ME.** ▸**b** A person who or thing which surpasses others of the same kind. Now *rare.* **E16.**

2 The recognized supreme ruler of a people or country under monarchical government; a monarch. **ME.**

†**3 a** A mayor or provost of a town, later esp. in Ireland. **ME–E19.** ▸**b** The superior of a monastery, convent, etc. **LME–M16.**

4 *Hist.* **a** A gold coin minted in England from the time of Henry VII to Charles I, originally of the value of 22*s.* 6*d.* but later worth only 10*s.* or 11*s.* **E16.** ▸**b** A British gold coin of the nominal value of one pound. **E19.**

> **1** SHAKES. *Tam. Shr.* Thy husband is thy lord, . . thy sovereign. **2** L. STRACHEY Since Charles the Second . . sovereigns of England had . . always been unfashionable. **4b** *Times* They fined . . Keith Ford 100 sovereigns for negligence.

Phrases: ***constitutional sovereign***: see CONSTITUTIONAL *adjective* 4. ***Royal Sovereign***: see ROYAL *adjective*.

▸ **B** *adjective.* †**1** Of a person: surpassing others, excelling in some respect. **ME–L17.**

2 Of a thing, quality, power, etc.: supreme; paramount; principal, greatest. **ME.** ▸**b** Of contempt: unmitigated. **M18.**

3 a Of a person: having superior or supreme rank or power; *spec.* holding the position of a ruler or monarch, royal. Freq. in ***sovereign lady***, ***sovereign lord***. **ME.** ▸**b** Of a State, community, etc.: possessing sovereign power. **L16.** ▸**c** COMMERCE. Designating or pertaining to a commercial loan made to a sovereign State. **L20.**

4 Of a remedy etc.: excellent, extremely effective. **LME.**

5 Pertaining to or characteristic of supremacy or superiority. **L16.**

> **2** L. STRACHEY This principality . . enjoyed independence and sovereign rights. *Chess* Karpov dominated a powerful event . . turning in a sovereign performance. **the sovereign good** the greatest good, esp. for a State, its people, etc. **3a** A. N. WILSON Perhaps at all public schools . . the housemasters were sovereign. ***sovereign pontiff***: see PONTIFF 3. **b** *New York Times* The first duty of a sovereign nation is to control its borders. **4** BARONESS ORCZY The smell of burnt paper was a sovereign remedy against giddiness. A. BURGESS Mineral oil was a sovereign preservative of metals.

■ **sovereignship** *noun* (*rare*) (*a*) (with possess. adjective, as ***his sovereignship*** etc.) a title of respect given to a sovereign; (*b*) sovereignty: **M17.**

†**sovereignity** *noun.* **M16–L18.**
[from SOVEREIGN *adjective* + -ITY.]
= SOVEREIGNTY.

sovereignly /ˈsɒvrɪnli/ *adjective. rare.* **L19.**
[from SOVEREIGN *noun* + -LY¹.]
Befitting a sovereign.

sovereignly /ˈsɒvrɪnli/ *adverb.* **ME.**
[from SOVEREIGN *adjective* + -LY².]
1 To a supreme degree; in a pre-eminent manner. **ME.**
2 With supremacy or supreme power; royally; as a sovereign. **LME.**

sovereignty /ˈsɒvrɪnti/ *noun.* **LME.**
[Old French *so(u)vereineté* (mod. *souveraineté*), formed as SOVEREIGN: see -TY¹.]
1 Supremacy in respect of excellence or efficacy; pre-eminence. **LME.**
2 Supremacy in respect of power or rank; supreme authority. **LME.**
3 The position, rank, or power of a supreme ruler or monarch; royal dominion. **LME.** ▸**b** *transf.* The supreme controlling power in a community not under monarchical government; absolute and independent authority of a State, community, etc. **E17.**
4 A territory under the rule of a sovereign or existing as an independent State. **E18.**

> **2** M. L. KING God relinquished a measure of his own sovereignty. **3b** *New York Times* The United States cannot . . disregard . . the sovereignty of South Africa's neighbors.

Soviet /ˈsəʊvɪət, ˈsɒv-/ *noun & adjective.* Also **s-**. **E20.**
[Russian *sovet* council.]
▸ **A** *noun.* **1 a** *Hist.* Any of a number of elected local, district, or national councils in the former USSR with legislative and executive functions; any of various revolutionary councils of workers, peasants, etc., set up in Russia etc. before 1917. **E20.** ▸**b** In other countries: a similar council organized on socialist principles. **E20.**
2 A citizen of the former USSR. Usu. in *pl.* **E20.**
1a ***Supreme Soviet***: see SUPREME *adjective* 2.
▸ **B** *adjective.* Belonging or pertaining to the former USSR; *gen.* pertaining to or having a system of government based on Soviets. **E20.**
the Soviet Zone: see ZONE *noun* 6d.
■ **Soviˈetic** *adjective* (now *rare*) of or pertaining to the (Russian) Soviet system **E20.** **Sovietism** *noun* the (Russian) Soviet system **E20.** **Sovietist** *noun* (*rare*) an adherent of the Soviet system **E20.** **Sovietophile** *adjective & noun* (a person who is) friendly to the USSR or fond of Soviet things **M20.** **Sovietoˈphobia** *noun* dread or dislike of the USSR **M20.** **Sovietophobe** *adjective & noun* (a person who is) affected with Sovietophobia **L20.**

Sovietize /ˈsəʊvɪətʌɪz, ˈsɒv-/ *verb trans.* Also **-ise**. **E20.**
[from prec. + -IZE.]
Convert to a Soviet system of government; *Hist.* subject to the influence or control of the USSR.
■ **Sovietiˈzation** *noun* **E20.** **Sovietizer** *noun* **M20.**

Sovietology /səʊvɪəˈtɒlədʒi, sɒv-/ *noun.* **M20.**
[formed as prec. + -OLOGY.]
The study and analysis of affairs and events in the former USSR.
■ **Sovietoˈlogical** *adjective* **M20.** **Sovietoˈlogically** *adverb* **M20.** **Sovietologist** *noun* **M20.**

sovkhoz /ˈsɒvkɒz, sʌvˈkɔːz/ *noun.* Pl. same, **-es** /-ɪz/, **-y** /-i/. **E20.**
[Russian, from *sov(etskoe khoz(yaĭstvo* Soviet farm.]
A State-owned farm in countries of the former USSR.

sovnarkhoz /ˈsɒvnəkɒz, sʌvnɑːˈkɔːz/ *noun.* Pl. same, **-es**, **-y** /-i/. **M20.**
[Russian, from *sov(et nar(odnogo khoz(yaĭstva* council of national economy.]
Hist. Any of a number of regional councils for the local regulation of the economy in the USSR.

Sovnarkom /ˈsɒvnɑːkɒm/ *noun.* **M20.**
[Russian, from *sov(et nar(odnykh kom(issarov* council of people's commissars.]
Hist. The highest executive and administrative organ of government of the USSR (renamed the Council of Ministers in 1946). Also, a council having analogous functions in any of the republics of the USSR.

sovran /ˈsɒvrən/ *noun & adjective.* Chiefly *poet.* **M17.**
[Alt. of SOVEREIGN after Italian *sovrano*.]
= SOVEREIGN.
■ **sovranly** *adverb* = SOVEREIGNLY *adverb* **M19.** **sovranty** *noun* = SOVEREIGNTY **M17.**

sow /saʊ/ *noun*¹.
[Old English *sugu* = Old Saxon *suga*, Middle Low German, Middle Dutch *soge* (Dutch *zeug*) rel. to Old English *sū*, Old High German *sū* (German *Sau*), Old Norse *sýr* (accus. *sú*); from Indo-European base, repr. also by Latin *sus* (*suis*) pig, Greek *hus*.]
▸ **I 1** A female pig, *esp.* an adult or full-grown female one, *spec.* a domestic one after farrowing. **OE.** ▸**b** The (full-grown) female of certain other animals, esp. the bear, badger, guinea-pig, and hedgehog. **L17.**
2 A movable structure with a strong roof, spec. (*a*) *Hist.* a protective structure used in siege warfare forces; (*b*) a protective structure for miners working underground. **ME.**
3 = ***sowbug*** below. Now *rare.* **L15.**
4 As a term of abuse: a contemptible person, *esp.* a fat, clumsy, or slovenly woman. **E16.**
▸ **II 5** A large bar or mass of metal (orig. lead, now usu. iron), esp. from a smelting-furnace. Cf. PIG *noun*¹ 6. **LME.** ▸**b** Any of the larger channels in a smelting-furnace, serving as a feeder to the smaller channels. Cf. PIG *noun*¹ 6b. **M19.**
6 A large oblong-shaped rick or stack, esp. of hay. *Scot. & north.* **M17.**
Phrases: **as drunk as David's sow** (now *arch. & dial.*) extremely drunk. **get the right sow by the ear**, **get the wrong sow by the ear** get hold of the right (or wrong) person or thing; take a correct (or incorrect) view. ***grease the fat sow***: see GREASE *verb* 3. **have the right sow by the ear**, **have the wrong sow by the ear** have hold of the right (or wrong) person or thing; have a correct (or incorrect) view. **my sow's pigged** *Hist.* a former card-game.
Comb.: **sow-back** (chiefly *Scot.*) (*a*) a woman's cap or head-dress with a ridge or fold running from front to back; (*b*) GEOLOGY a long low hill or ridge resembling the back of a sow, usu. of glacial origin; **sow-backed** *adjective* (*a*) having a back like that of a sow; (*b*) ridged like a sow's back; **sowbane** orig., any of several goosefoots (genus *Chenopodium*); now *spec.* maple-leaved goosefoot, *C. hybridum*; **sow-belly** *US slang* (salted) side of pork; **sowbread** *arch.* a cyclamen of southern Europe, *Cyclamen hederifolium*, whose roots are reputedly eaten by wild boars in Sicily; **sowbug** a woodlouse, *esp.* one of the genus *Oniscus*; **sow-drunk** *adjective* (now *arch. & dial.*) extremely drunk; **sow-gelder** a person whose business it is to geld or spay sows; **sow-louse** (now *rare*) = ***sowbug*** above; **sow-metal** cast iron in sows or large ingots as obtained from a smelting-furnace; **sow-pig** a young female pig, *esp.* one which has been spayed; a sow; **sow's-baby** *slang* (*a*) a (young) pig; (*b*) sixpence; **sowthistle** [perh. alt. of THOWTHISTLE] (*a*) any of various composite plants constituting the genus *Sonchus*, having yellow flower-heads, sharply-toothed leaves, and milky juice; esp. either of the common weeds *S. oleraceus* and *S. asper* (also called ***milk-thistle***); (*b*) (with specifying word) any of various plants of several genera allied to *Sonchus*; ***blue sowthistle***, a lilac-flowered Caucasian plant, *Cicerbita macrophylla*, grown in gardens and increasingly naturalized.

sow /saʊ/ *noun*². *obsolete* exc. *dial.* **ME.**
[Perh. identical with Flemish dial. *zou* drain; app. distinct from SOUGH *noun*².]
A drain; a channel of water.

sow /saʊ/ *noun*³. *obsolete* exc. *dial.* **LME.**
[Origin unkn.]
A blow, a stroke.

sow /saʊ/ *noun*⁴. *Scot. rare.* **L17.**
[Origin unkn.]
1 A bride's outfit of clothes; a trousseau. **L17.**
2 A burial garment; a shroud. **M18.**

sow /səʊ/ *verb*¹. Pa. t. **sowed** /səʊd/; pa. pple **sowed**, **sown** /səʊn/.
[Old English *sāwan* corresp. to Old Saxon *sāian*, Old High German *sāwen*, *sājen*, *sā(h)en* (Dutch *zaaien*, German *säen*), Old Norse *sá*, Gothic *saian*, from Germanic, from Indo-European base repr. also by Latin *serere* (pa. t. *sevi*): cf. SEED *noun*, SEMEN.]
1 *verb intrans. & trans.* Scatter, sprinkle, or deposit (seed) on or in the ground so that it may grow; plant (a crop) in this way. **OE.** ▸**b** *verb trans.* MILITARY. Lay or plant (an explosive mine); *spec.* drop (mines etc.) esp. by aircraft into the sea. **M20.**
2 *verb trans.* **a** Scatter seed on (land etc.) in order that it may grow; supply with seed. (Foll. by *to*, *with*.) **OE.** ▸**b** Of seed: be sufficient for (a certain area). **LME.**
3 *verb trans.* Disseminate, spread, propagate; initiate, introduce, arouse. **OE.**
4 *verb trans.* Cover or strew (a place etc.) *with* something, esp. thickly; sprinkle, dot. Chiefly as ***sown ppl adjective***. **OE.**
†**5** Beget (a child). *rare.* Only in **ME.**

> **1** L. M. MONTGOMERY Thomas . . was sowing his late turnip seed. *transf.*: C. SINGER A fragment of spleen of a mouse . . sown in a drop of blood serum. **2a** *Morning Star* About 75,000 acres sown to grain. **3** *Time* The range of cuts under discussion grows larger by the week, sowing panic in executive suites. **4** *Scientific American* Sowing areas of the ocean floor with acoustic beacons.

Phrases: SOW GAPE-SEED. **sow the seed of**, **sow the seeds of** first give rise to; implant (an idea etc.).
■ **sowable** *adjective* able to be sowed; fit for sowing: **E18.** **sower** *noun* (*a*) a person who sows (seed etc.); (*b*) a person who spreads or propagates something, esp. discord, sedition, etc.; (*c*) a machine or apparatus for sowing seed: **LOE.**

sow /səʊ/ *verb*². Long *obsolete* exc. *Scot. & north.* **LME.**
[Origin unkn.]
1 *verb trans.* Affect (a person) with pain; hurt, grieve. Usu. with *sore*. **LME.**
2 *verb intrans.* Thrill or tingle with pain or exertion; ache, throb. **LME.**

sowans *noun pl.* var. of SOWENS.

sowar /səʊˈwɑː/ *noun.* **E19.**
[Persian & Urdu *suwār*, *sawār* horseman.]
Chiefly *Hist.* In the Indian subcontinent: a non-European cavalryman, trooper, or mounted orderly.

sowarry /səʊˈwɑːri/ *noun.* **L18.**
[Persian & Urdu *suwārī*, *sawārī* formed as prec.]
Chiefly *Hist.* In the Indian subcontinent: a body of mounted attendants of a State official or other person of high rank, esp. as forming a cavalcade.

sowel /ˈsaʊəl/ *noun.* Now *dial.*
[Old English *sāgol* = Middle High German (now Swiss German) *seigel* rung of a ladder.]
†**1** A stout stick or staff; a pole, a cudgel, etc. **OE–ME.**
2 A stake sharpened at one end, used orig. esp. in the construction of a hedge or fence, later esp. to fasten up hurdles. **OE.**

sowens /ˈsəʊənz, ˈsuːənz/ *noun pl.* (treated as *sing.* or *pl.*). *Scot. & Anglo-Irish.* Also **-ans**. **L16.**
[App. from Gaelic *súghan*, *súbhan* (Irish *subh'án*, *súghán*) the liquid used in preparing sowens, from *súgh*, *súbh* sap.]
A kind of porridge made from oat husks and fine meal steeped in water and allowed to ferment slightly.

Sowetan /səˈwɛt(ə)n, -ˈweɪt(ə)n/ *noun & adjective.* **L20.**
[from *Soweto* acronym, from South Western Townships (see below): see -AN.]
▸ **A** *noun.* A native or inhabitant of Soweto, a group of black African townships outside Johannesburg, South Africa. **L20.**
▸ **B** *adjective.* Of or pertaining to Soweto or its inhabitants; native to or residing in Soweto. **L20.**

sowff /saʊf/ *verb trans. Scot.* **E18.**
[Alt. of SOLF. Cf. SOWTH.]
Sing, hum, or whistle (a tune) softly.

sowing /ˈsəʊɪŋ/ *noun & adjective.* **ME.**
[from SOW *verb*¹ + -ING¹.]
▸ **A** *noun.* **1** The action of SOW *verb*¹; an instance of this. **ME.**
2 That which is sown; the quantity of seed sown at one time. **M18.**
▸ **B** *attrib.* or as *adjective.* Of seed, an implement, etc.: suitable or used for sowing. **E17.**

sowl /saʊl/ *noun.* Now *dial.*
[Old English *sufel*, *sufol* = Middle Dutch *sufel*, *zuvel* (Dutch *zuivel*), Middle Low German *suvel*, Old High German *sufil*, Old Norse *sufl* (Norwegian *suvl*, *sovl*, *sul*, etc., Swedish *sofvel*, Danish *sul*), of unkn. origin.]
Any food eaten with bread, as meat, cheese, etc.; seasoned food added to liquid; soup, broth.

sowl /saʊl/ *verb trans.* Now *dial.* See also SOOL. **E17.**
[Origin unkn.]
1 Pull roughly by the ear or ears; *esp.* (of a dog) seize (a pig) by the ears. **E17.**
2 Pull or lug (the ears). **M17.**
†**3** = SOOL. *Austral.* Only in **M19.**

sowlth /saʊlt/ *noun.* E19.
[Irish *samhailt* likeness, apparition.]
A formless luminous spectre.
¶ Chiefly in the writings of W. B. Yeats.

sown /səʊn/ *noun.* Chiefly *literary.* M19.
[from pa. pple of SOW *verb*[1].]
The cultivated land or grassland as opp. to the desert.

sown *verb pa. pple* of SOW *verb*[1].

sowp /saʊp/ *noun. Scot. & north.* E16.
[Old Norse *saup* (cf. Norwegian *saup* whey, buttermilk, Icelandic *saup* soup), rel. to *súpa* sup, sip.]
A sup, a sip; a drink.

sowp /saʊp/ *verb trans. obsolete* exc. *dial.* E16.
[App. rel. to the noun.]
Soak, saturate.

sowth /saʊθ/ *verb trans. Scot.* Also **south**. L18.
[Alt. of SOWFF.]
= SOWFF.

sox *noun pl.* see SOCK *noun*[1].

Soxhlet /ˈsɒkslət/ *noun.* L19.
[Franz *Soxhlet* (1848–1926), Belgian chemist.]
CHEMISTRY. Used ***attrib.*** to designate an apparatus and method for the continuous solvent extraction of a solid.

soy /sɔɪ/ *noun.* L17.
[(Prob. through Dutch) from Japanese var. of *shōyu* from Chinese *jiàngyóu* (Wade–Giles *chiang-yu*), from *jiàng* bean paste + *yóu* oil. Cf. next, SHOYU.]
1 More fully ***soy sauce***. A sauce made from fermented soya beans. Also called ***shoyu***. L17.
2 More fully (earlier, now chiefly *N. Amer.*) ***soybean***. = *SOYA* ***bean***. L18.
Comb.: ***soybean*** see sense 2 above; **soy frame** an ornamental stand with a ring frame used for holding a bottle of soya sauce; ***soy sauce***: see sense 1 above.

soya /ˈsɔɪə/ *noun.* L17.
[Dutch *soja* from Japanese *shōyu*: see prec. Cf. SHOYU.]
1 More fully ***soya sauce***. Soy sauce. L17.
2 More fully ***soya bean***. (The fruit of) a leguminous plant, *Glycine max*, grown as a vegetable or for its protein-rich seeds which yield an edible oil, a flour, etc. M19.
Comb.: ***soya bean***: see sense 2 above; **soya meal** the residue of soya bean seeds after the extraction of the oil, used as animal feed; **soya milk** the liquid obtained by suspending soya bean flour in water, used as a fat-free substitute for milk; ***soya sauce***: see sense 1 above.

Soyer stove /ˈsɔɪə stəʊv/ *noun phr.* Also **Soyer's stove** /ˈsɔɪəz/. M19.
[Alexis Benoît *Soyer* (1809–58), French-born cook to fashionable society in England, subsequently working for Irish famine-relief and with the British army in the Crimea.]
A tabletop cooking-range or field stove of types developed by Alexis Soyer.

†soyle *noun, verb*: see SOIL *noun*[1], *verb*[1].

sozzle /ˈsɒz(ə)l/ *noun & verb.* E19.
[Perh. imit.: cf. SOSS *noun*[1], *verb*[1].]
▶ **A** *noun.* **1** A sloppy spoon-meat or medicine. *dial.* E19.
2 A slattern; a state of sluttish confusion or disorder. *US.* M19.
▶ **B** *verb.* **1** *verb trans.* Mix in a sloppy manner. *dial.* M19.
2 *verb trans.* Wash by splashing; douse. *US.* M19.
3 *verb intrans.* Lounge, loll. *US.* M19.
4 *verb intrans.* [Back-form. from SOZZLED.] Imbibe intoxicating drink. *slang.* M20.
■ **sozzled** *adjective* (*slang*) intoxicated, drunk; drunken: L19.

SP *abbreviation.*
Starting price.

sp. *abbreviation.*
BIOLOGY. Species (*sing.*).

spa /spɑː/ *noun & verb.* E17.
[A watering-place in the province of Liège, Belgium, celebrated for the curative properties of its mineral springs.]
▶ **A** *noun.* **1** A medicinal or mineral spring; a place or resort with such a spring. E17.
2 A commercial establishment offering health and beauty treatment through steam baths, exercise equipment, massage, etc. *N. Amer.* M20.
3 A bath containing hot aerated water. Also ***spa bath***, ***spa pool***. *US.* L20.
1 ***spa town***, ***spa water***, etc.
▶ **B** *verb. rare.*
1 *verb trans.* Subject to treatment at a spa. M19.
2 *verb intrans.* Visit a spa or spas. M19.

†spaad *noun.* L16–M18.
[German †*Spad*, †*Spade* vars. of *Spat*: see SPATH. Cf. FELDSPAR.]
MINERALOGY. (A powder prepared from) talc, gypsum, or spar, formerly used to form moulds for casting metal objects.

space /speɪs/ *noun.* ME.
[Aphet. from Old & mod. French *espace* from Latin *spatium*.]
▶ **I** With ref. to time.
1 a Lapse or extent of time between two points, events, etc. Usu. with qualifying adjective, as *long, short, small*, etc. ME. ▸**†b** Delay, deferment. *rare.* LME–M16.
2 Time that is not committed or limited, the opportunity to do something. Chiefly in ***have space to***. Now *rare.* ME.
3 The amount of time contained in a specified period. ME.
4 A (short) period of time. ME.

📖 **1** DRYDEN To her Father's Court in little space Restor'd anew. W. COWPER The turnpike gates again Flew open in short space. **2** JONSON Give unto the flying hart Space to breathe. **3** C. PRIEST These misfortunes . . came together in the space of a few weeks. **4** A. H. SAYCE The number of . . vibrations in any given space of time. P. G. WODEHOUSE Even Comrade Butt cast off his gloom for a space.

▶ **II** With ref. to area.
5 a Extent, area; *spec.* area sufficient for some purpose; capacity to accommodate a person or thing or allow a particular action (foll. by *for, to do*). ME. ▸**b** That part of the page area of a letter, periodical, book, etc., available for or occupied by written or printed matter. M16.
6 An interval between two or more points; a length of way; a distance. ME. ▸**b** *spec.* A short distance. E19.
7 A certain stretch, extent, or area of ground, sea, sky, etc.; an expanse. ME. ▸**b** The place where one takes up a position, residence, etc. LME. ▸**c** = ***living space*** (a) s.v. LIVING *noun*[1]. *slang* (chiefly *N. Amer.*). L20.
8 a A limited area or extent; a portion of room or space; a gap, an empty place. LME. ▸**b** A portion or gap marked off in some way; a division, a section. Later also (*spec.*), a (vacant) place among a number of other places in which a person, car, etc., is or may be accommodated. LME.
9 *MUSIC.* Any of the degrees between the lines of a stave. L15.
10 The dimensional extent occupied by a body or enclosed within specified limits. M16.
11 *METAPHYSICS.* Continuous, unbounded, or unlimited extension in every direction, regarded as void of, or without reference to, matter. M17.
12 a The immense expanse of the universe beyond the earth's atmosphere; the near vacuum occupying the regions between stars, planets, etc. M17. ▸**b** Extension in all directions, esp. from a given point. E19.
13 a An interval or blank between printed or written words or lines. L17. ▸**b** *TYPOGRAPHY.* Any of certain small pieces of cast metal shorter than a type, used to separate words (or letters in a word) and to justify the line. L17. ▸**c** *TELECOMMUNICATIONS.* An interval between consecutive marks in a mark-space signalling system such as telegraphy. Opp. ***mark***. M19.
14 A portion of a newspaper etc. available for a specific purpose, esp. for advertising; room which may be acquired for this. Also, a period or interval of broadcasting time available to or occupied by a particular programme or advertising slot. Esp. in ***watch this space!*** E20.
15 *MATH.* An instance of any of various mathematical concepts, usu. regarded as a set of points having some specified structure. E20.

📖 **5a** M. MEYER A tiny room with space for only two beds. N. LOWNDES These . . hunting dogs, they need space, . . they want the wild moor to roam. **b** H. JAMES I shall not take up space with attempting to explain. **6** SIR W. SCOTT It corresponds . . with the proper and usual space between comma and comma. **7** E. F. BENSON Beyond lay the dark grey spaces of the downs. *fig.*: SHAKES. *Jul. Caes.* The mighty space of our large honours. **b** E. JONG Living apart . . maintaining separate spaces. **c** *Mother & Baby* The last child . . has to find their own space in the family. **8a** J. IRVING A . . thick hedgerow, but . . I can find spaces to look through. J. HERBERT Ash had no trouble in finding space at the bar. *fig.*: R. LINDNER The space in his life left by her death. **b** D. JOHNSON There were no spaces on the flights. W. MCILVANNEY She treated his questions like spaces in an official form. P. D. JAMES Cars cruised . . past, the drivers peering for a parking space. **11** P. DAVIES Space and time will go on distorting indefinitely. **14** H. EVANS One salesman would sell space for both papers. **15** ***metric space***, ***null space***, ***projective space***, ***topological space***, ***vector space***.

Phrases: ***Crookes dark space***, ***Crookes space***: see CROOKES. ***dark space***: see DARK *adjective.* ***deep space***: see DEEP *adjective.* ***EUCLIDEAN space***. **from space to space** at (regular) intervals. ***inner space***: see INNER *adjective.* **†in the mean space** meanwhile. **look into space**, **stare into space**, etc., look, stare, etc., straight ahead, usu. while daydreaming. **on space** (orig. *US*) paid according to the extent occupied by accepted contributions. ***open space***: see OPEN *adjective.* ***outer space***: see OUTER *adjective.* ***PERMEABILITY of free space***. ***PERMITTIVITY of free space***. ***personal space***: see PERSONAL *adjective.* ***plenum space***: see PLENUM *adjective.* ***rid space***: see RID *verb*[1]. ***social space***: see SOCIAL *adjective.* ***stare into space***: see ***look into space*** above. ***Tenon's space***: see TENON *noun*[2]. ***thick space***: see THICK *adjective.* ***thin space***: see THIN *adjective* etc. ***wide open spaces***: see WIDE *adjective.*

Comb.: **space age** the present period when human exploration of space has become possible; **space-age** *adjective* characteristic of the space age; extremely modern; **space-ager** a person living in the space age; **space astronomy**: that is based on data obtained in space, not from earth; **space-averaged** *adjective* (*PHYSICS*) averaged over a region of space; **space-bar** a long horizontal key on a typewriter or computer keyboard for making a space between letters; **space blanket** a light metal-coated plastic sheet designed to retain heat; **space-borne** *adjective* carried through space; carried out in space or by means of instruments in space; **spacebound** *adjective* (***a***) (of an activity or procedure) bound or limited by the properties of space; (***b***) (of a person or spacecraft) bound for space; **space cabin** a chamber designed to support human life in space; **space cadet** (***a***) a trainee astronaut; a (young) enthusiast for space travel; (***b***) a drug addict; *transf.* an eccentric person; **space capsule** a small spacecraft containing the instruments or crew; **space chamber**: in which conditions in space or in a spacecraft can be simulated; **space charge** *ELECTRONICS* a collection of particles with a net electric charge occupying a region, either in free space or in a device; **space-charge** *adjective* (*ELECTRONICS*) of or pertaining to space charge; **space club** (***a***) those nations that have successfully launched a rocket into space; (***b***) a consortium of nations formed to cooperate in space research and development; **spacecraft** any vehicle designed to travel in space; **space curve** *GEOMETRY* a curve that is not confined to any one plane; **space density** *ASTRONOMY* frequency of occurrence of stars, particles, etc., per specified volume of space; **spacefaring** *noun & adjective* (engaging in) space travel; **spacefarer** a person who travels in space; **space fiction** science fiction set in space or on other worlds, or involving space travel; **space flight** a journey into or through space, travel through outer space; **space flyer** (***a***) (now *rare*) a spacecraft; (***b***) an astronaut; **space frame** *ENGINEERING* a three-dimensional structural framework which is designed to behave as an integral unit and to withstand loads applied at any point; **space group** *CRYSTALLOGRAPHY* any of the 230 sets of symmetry operations, derived from the point groups by the inclusion of translations, glide planes, and screw axes, which are used to classify crystal structures; **space gun** (***a***) a hypothetical large gun for the propulsion of a spacecraft into space; (***b***) a hand-held gun whose recoil is used to propel an astronaut; **space heater** any self-contained appliance for heating an enclosed space within a building; **space helmet** a pressurized helmet worn in space to protect the head and provide air, communications, etc. to the wearer; **space industry** the sector of industry which manufactures goods and materials in connection with space travel; **Space Invaders** (proprietary name for) a computer game in which a player attempts to defend against a fleet of enemy spaceships; **space lab**, **space laboratory** a laboratory in space, *esp.* a spacecraft equipped as a laboratory; **space lattice** *CRYSTALLOGRAPHY* a regular, indefinitely repeated array of points in three dimensions in which the points lie at the intersections of three sets of parallel equidistant planes; a three-dimensional Bravais lattice; **space launcher** a rocket used to lift spacecraft into space; **space lift** an act of transporting goods or personnel in space; **space-line** *TYPOGRAPHY* = LEAD *noun*[1] 7; **spaceman** (***a***) a journalist paid according to the extent of space occupied by his or her writing; (***b***) a person who travels in space or comes from another planet; **spacemanship** the activity or skill of travelling in space; **space medicine** the branch of medicine that deals with the effects of being in space; **space mine** an artificial satellite containing an explosive charge capable of damaging or destroying another satellite, space station, etc.; **space myopia** the tendency of the eye to focus at a close distance when looking into featureless space; **space needle** any of a large number of metallic rods placed in orbit and intended to act as radio reflectors or dipoles; **space observatory** an astronomical observatory in space; **space-occupying lesion** *MEDICINE* a mass, freq. a tumour, which has displaced brain tissue; **space opera** (chiefly *US*) space fiction, esp. of a primitive and extravagant kind; **space-order** an ordering of points or events in space; **space physics** the branch of physics that deals with extraterrestrial phenomena and bodies, esp. within the solar system; **spaceplane** (***a***) an aircraft that takes off and lands conventionally but is capable of entry into orbit or travel through space; (***b***) = SHUTTLE *noun*[1] 5b; **space platform** = ***space station*** below; **spaceport** a base from which spacecraft are launched; **space probe** = PROBE *noun* 4; **space programme**: of exploration of space and development of space technology; **space race** competition between nations in developments and achievements in space exploration; **space-reddening** *ASTRONOMY* the reddening of starlight due to wavelength-dependent absorption and scattering by interstellar dust; **space-reddened** *adjective* that has been subjected to space-reddening; **space rocket**: designed to travel in space or to launch a spacecraft; **space satellite** = SATELLITE *noun* 2c; **space-saving** *adjective* that uses space economically, occupying little space; **spacescape** a view, picture, or expanse of scenery in outer space; **space shot** the launch of a spacecraft and its subsequent progress in space; ***space shuttle***: see SHUTTLE *noun*[1] 5b; **space-sick** *adjective* affected with space-sickness; **space-sickness** sickness from the effects of space flight; **space simulator** a device which simulates the conditions of space, or of the interior of a spacecraft; **space stage** *THEATRE & TELEVISION* a large open stage on which the significant action alone is lighted, the rest remaining in darkness; **space station** a large artificial satellite used as a long-term base for manned operations in space; **spacesuit** a garment designed to protect an astronaut in space; **space telescope** an astronomical telescope that operates in space by remote control, to avoid interference by the earth's atmosphere; **space travel** travel through outer space; **space traveller** a person who undertakes space travel; **space vehicle** a spacecraft, *esp.* one travelling in interplanetary space or beyond; **space velocity** *ASTRONOMY* the velocity in space of a star relative to the sun, equal to the vector sum of its proper motion and its radial velocity; **space walk** *noun & verb* (***a***) *noun* any physical activity undertaken by an astronaut in space outside a spacecraft; (***b***) *verb intrans.* undertake a space walk; **space warp** an imaginary or hypothetical distortion of space–time that enables space travellers to travel faster than light or otherwise make journeys contrary to the known laws of nature; **space wave** (RADIO etc.) a ground wave that passes from a transmitter to a receiver directly in line-of-sight or with a single reflection from the ground; **spaceway** in science fiction, an established route for space travellers (usu. in *pl.*); **spacewoman** a female traveller in space, a female astronaut; a woman who comes from another planet.

■ **spaceful** *adjective* (*rare*) spacious, roomy; wide, extensive: **E17**. **spacelike** *adjective* (PHYSICS) resembling or having the properties of space; *spec.* being or related to an interval between two points in space–time that lie outside one another's light cones (so that no signal or observer can pass from one to the other): **E20**.

space /speɪs/ *verb.* **LME**.
[Aphet. from Old & mod. French *espacer*, from *espace* (see prec.), or directly from the noun.]
†**1** *verb intrans.* Walk, pace; ramble, roam. **LME–L16**.
2 *verb trans.* Measure (an area) by pacing; pace *out*. *Scot. & dial.* **LME**.
3 *verb trans.* Limit or bound in respect of space; make of a certain extent. Now *rare*. **M16**.
†**4** *verb trans.* Divide into spaces or sections. *rare*. Only in **L16**.
5 *verb trans.* TYPOGRAPHY. ▸**a** Foll. by *out*: extend to a required length by inserting additional space between the words or lines. **L17**. ▸**b** Separate (words, letters, or lines) by means of a space or spaces. **L18**.
6 *verb trans.* Set, arrange, or place at determinate intervals in space or time; make more or wider spaces between. Also foll. by *out*. **E18**.
7 *verb intrans.* Foll. by *out*: experience a drug-induced state of euphoria; hallucinate. *slang* (orig. *US*). **M20**.

> **6** *Which?* If you can't water your vegetables regularly, it's best to space them further apart.

spacearium /speɪˈsɛːrɪəm/ *noun.* Pl. **-iums**, **-ia** /-ɪə/. **M20**.
[from SPACE *noun* + -ARIUM.]
A large room arranged so that space scenes may be projected on to its interior. Cf. PLANETARIUM.

spaced /speɪst/ *adjective.* **E19**.
[from SPACE *verb* + -ED[1].]
1 Of printed or typed matter: having the words or lines separated by (a specified mode of) spacing. **E19**.
2 Set or occurring at intervals in space or time; *fig.* measured, regulated. Also with *out*. **L19**. ▸**b** *spec.* Of children: born at certain intervals. **M20**.
3 In a state of drug-induced euphoria, out of touch with reality, disoriented. Freq. foll. by *out*. *slang* (orig. *US*). **M20**.

> **1** ***double-spaced***, ***single-spaced***, etc. **2** W. S. BURROUGHS Two pairs of sandals . . were spaced eighteen inches apart. G. CLARE Migraine attacks were . . intermittent and spaced out over . . long periods. **b** *Times* A smaller or adequately spaced family. **3** J. O'FAOLAIN Jame's mind moved as though he were spaced out: slowly, repetitively. M. PIERCY You're spaced. Do you take downers?

spaceless /ˈspeɪslɪs/ *adjective.* **E17**.
[from SPACE *noun* + -LESS.]
1 That is not subject to or limited by space; infinite, boundless. **E17**.
2 Occupying no space. **E19**.
■ **spacelessly** *adverb* **L19**. **spacelessness** *noun* **E20**.

spacer /ˈspeɪsə/ *noun*[1]. **M19**.
[from SPACE *verb* + -ER[1].]
1 a A device used for making a space, interval, or division; *spec.* a mechanism for spacing words. **M19**. ▸**b** ARCHAEOLOGY. More fully ***spacer-plate***. A flat bead perforated with several holes in the same plane, by which the threads of a necklace with several strands are held apart. **E20**.
2 A person who or thing which spaces things in a particular manner. *rare*. **L19**.
3 BIOLOGY. A section of DNA which is not represented in the final RNA transcript, separating two sections which are. **L20**.
Comb.: **spacer gel** a part of the gel used in electrophoresis, which functions to concentrate the sample prior to separation; ***spacer-plate***: see sense 1b above.

spacer /ˈspeɪsə/ *noun*[2]. **M20**.
[from SPACE *noun* + -ER[1].]
1 = ***spaceman*** (b) s.v. SPACE *noun*. **M20**.
2 A spaceship, a spacecraft. **M20**.

spaceship /ˈspeɪsʃɪp/ *noun.* **L19**.
[formed as prec. + SHIP *noun*.]
A spacecraft, *esp.* a manned one controlled by its crew.
Comb.: ***spaceship earth***: see EARTH *noun*[1].

space–time /speɪsˈtʌɪm/ *noun & adjective.* **E20**.
[from SPACE *noun* + TIME *noun*.]
▸ **A** *noun.* PHYSICS. Time and three-dimensional space regarded as fused in a four-dimensional continuum containing all events. **E20**.
▸ **B** *attrib.* or as *adjective.* Pertaining to or situated in both space and time; *spec.* in PHYSICS, pertaining to or designating the space–time continuum. **E20**.

spaceworthy /ˈspeɪswəːði/ *adjective.* **M20**.
[from SPACE *noun* + -WORTHY.]
In a fit condition for space travel.
■ **spaceworthiness** *noun* **M20**.

spacey *adjective* var. of SPACY.

spacial *adjective* var. of SPATIAL.

spacing /ˈspeɪsɪŋ/ *noun.* **L17**.
[from SPACE *verb* + -ING[1].]
The action of SPACE *verb*; an instance or the result of this. Also foll. by *out*.
spacing machine, ***spacing washer***, etc. ***double spacing***: see DOUBLE *adjective & adverb*. ***single spacing***: see SINGLE *adjective & adverb*. ***triple spacing***: see TRIPLE *adjective & adverb*.

spacious /ˈspeɪʃəs/ *adjective & adverb.* **LME**.
[Old French *spacios* (mod. *spacieux*) or Latin *spatiosus*, from *spatium*: see SPACE *noun*, -IOUS.]
▸ **A** *adjective.* **1** Of land etc.: of vast or indefinite extent or area; covering a wide area, extensive. **LME**. ▸**b** Covering a considerable distance. Long *rare* or *obsolete*. **E17**.
2 Of a house, room, street, etc.: having ample space or room; large, roomy. **LME**.
3 *gen.* Great, extensive, ample; large, expansive. **L16**. ▸**b** Large in size; bulky. **M17**.
4 Characterized by breadth or comprehensiveness of views or sympathies. **L16**.
5 Prolonged; occupying a considerable time. **M17**.

> **2** *She* Bright and spacious stores. **4** J. R. LOWELL This eclogue . . hints of that spacious style. **5** R. K. NARAYAN A slow, spacious way of handling a story.

▸†**B** *adverb.* In a spacious manner, spaciously. *rare* (Milton). Only in **M17**.
■ **spaciousness** *noun* **E17**.

spaciously /ˈspeɪʃəsli/ *adverb.* **LME**.
[from prec. + -LY[2].]
1 In a spacious house or place. **LME**.
2 Amply; largely. **E17**.
3 At great length; fully. **E17**.
4 So as to cover much space; extensively. **E17**.
5 With largeness of manner. **M19**.

spacistor /speɪˈsɪstə/ *noun.* **M20**.
[from SPACE *noun* + TRANS)ISTOR.]
ELECTRONICS. A kind of semiconductor in which electrons are injected directly into the space-charge region of a reverse-biased junction.

spack /spak/ *adjective.* *obsolete* exc. *dial.* **ME**.
[Old Norse *spakr* (Middle Swedish *spaker*, Norwegian, Swedish *spak*, Danish *spag*) quiet, gentle, wise, clever.]
1 Of a person: quick, prompt, ready; intelligent, clever. **ME**.
†**2** Gentle, quiet, tame. *rare*. Only in **ME**.

Spackle /ˈspak(ə)l/ *noun & verb.* *N. Amer.* **E20**.
[Origin uncertain: perh. blend of SPARKLE *verb*[2] and German *Spachtel* putty-knife, mastic, filler.]
▸ **A** *noun.* (Proprietary name for) a compound used to fill cracks in plaster and produce a smooth surface before decoration. **E20**.
▸ **B** *verb trans. & intrans.* Repair (a wall) or fill (a crack) with Spackle. **E20**.

spacy /ˈspeɪsi/ *adjective.* Also **spacey**. **L19**.
[from SPACE *noun* + -Y[1].]
1 Large, roomy; spacious. **L19**.
2 Out of touch with reality, disoriented; spaced out. *slang* (chiefly *N. Amer.*). **M20**.
3 Freq. with ref. to electronic music: pertaining to or characteristic of (conditions in) outer space. **L20**.

> **1** S. BELLOW The U.S. Heartland (the spacy continent between Pennsylvania and the Pacific). **2** R. SILVERBERG Vivid visionary dreams, very spacy stuff. *Parenting* I was . . tired and spacy. **3** *New York Times* Neon tubes and spacy saucer-shaped lights. *Los Angeles Times* A musical legacy of spacey but melodic rock.

■ **spaciness** *noun* (*rare*) **L19**.

SPAD /spad/ *abbreviation.*
RAILWAYS. Signal passed at danger.

spad /spad/ *noun*[1]. **E20**.
[Var. of SPUD *noun*.]
A spike with a perforated end to carry a plumb-line, used as a marker in mining etc.

Spad /spad/ *noun*[2]. **E20**.
[Acronym from *Société pour Aviation et ses Dérivés*, the designers.]
Any of several types of French aircraft; *spec.* (*Hist.*) a biplane fighter used in the war of 1914–18.

spaddle /ˈspad(ə)l/ *noun.* *rare*. **M17**.
[Alt. of PADDLE *noun*[1] after *spade*.]
†**1** A small spade. **M17–M19**.
2 A spatula. **M19**.

spade /speɪd/ *noun*[1] & *verb*[1].
[Old English *spadu*, *spada*, *spade* = Old Frisian *spada*, Old Saxon *spado* (Dutch *spade*, *spa*); rel. to Greek *spathē* blade, paddle, shoulder-blade, broadsword (cf. next).]
▸ **A** *noun.* **1** A tool for digging or cutting the ground, now usu. consisting of a sharp-edged rectangular metal blade fitted on a long handle with a grip or crossbar at the upper end. **OE**. ▸**b** = SPIT *noun*[3] 1. **L17**. ▸**c** The length of a spade with the handle as a measure. **E19**.
2 An implement resembling a spade in shape or function; *esp.* a knife with an oblong blade for removing whale blubber. **E19**.
Phrases: **call a spade a bloody shovel**, **call a spade a shovel** *colloq.* speak with exaggerated or unnecessary bluntness. **call a spade a spade** speak plainly or bluntly; not use euphemisms.
Comb.: **spade-beard** an oblong-shaped beard; **spade-bone** (chiefly *dial.*) the shoulder-blade; **spade-farm**: cultivated by manual labour; **spadefish** a fish having a spadelike body or organ; *spec.* any of various very deep-bodied fishes of warm seas, of the small family Ephippidae, esp. the large grey or black *Chaetodipterus faber* of the W. Atlantic; **spade-foot** (*a*) the foot used to press a spade into the ground; (*b*) a square spade-shaped enlargement at the end of a chair-leg; (*c*) (in full ***spade-foot toad***) any of several toads of the genera *Pelobates* and *Scaphiopus* having hind feet adapted for burrowing; **spade-graft** = SPIT *noun*[3] 1; **spade-guinea** *Hist.*: coined from 1787 to 1799, bearing a spade-shaped shield on the reverse; **spade lug** any of several metal lugs bolted to the rim of a tractor wheel to improve grip; **spademan** a spadesman; **spade-money** *Hist.* early Chinese money consisting of spade-shaped pieces of bronze; **spade-press** *Austral.* a wool-press using a spade to compress fleeces; **spade-shaped** *adjective* shaped like (the blade of) a spade, rectangular; **spadesman** a person who uses or works with a spade; **spade terminal**, **spade tip** ELECTRICITY a small flat broad piece of metal with a slot or hole in it for fixing under a nut or bolt to make an electrical connection; **spade-tree** (now chiefly *dial.*) the shaft of a spade; **spade-wheel**: to which the blades are attached in a spader; **spadewise** *adverb* (*literary*) in the shape of a spade; **spadework** (*a*) digging etc. done with a spade; (*b*) *fig.* hard or routine preliminary work.
▸ **B** *verb.* †**1** *verb trans.* Shape like a spade. *rare*. Only in **L16**.
2 *verb trans.* Dig up or remove with a spade; dig over (ground) with a spade. Also foll. by *out*, *up*. **M17**.
3 *verb intrans.* Work or dig with a spade. **M19**.

> **2** W. H. AUDEN In Spring we shall spade the soil on the border. R. BRADBURY At the graveyard . . two men were . . spading out the earth. **3** *New Yorker* Her husband forked and spaded.

■ **spadeful** *noun* as much as a spade can hold or lift at one time **M17**. **spadelike** *adjective* resembling a spade in shape or function **E17**. **spader** *noun* (*a*) a person who uses or works with a spade; (*b*) a rotary digging implement with several spadelike blades: **M17**. **spading** *noun* (*a*) the action of the verb; (*b*) the depth of a spade; a spadeful, a spit: **M17**.

spade /speɪd/ *noun*[2]. Now *dial.* **OE**.
[Origin unkn.]
Gum secreted at the corner of the eye.

spade /speɪd/ *noun*[3] & *adjective.* **L16**.
[Italian, pl. of *spada* from Latin *spatha* from Greek *spathē*: see SPADE *noun*[1].]
▸ **A** *noun.* **1** CARDS. A black inverted heart-shape with short stalk on the face of a playing-card; in *pl.* (occas. treated as *sing.*), one of the four suits into which a pack of playing-cards is divided, distinguished by such markings; *sing.* a card of this suit. **L16**.
2 A black person (esp. a man). *slang* (*derog.* & considered *racially offensive*). **E20**.
1 in spades *colloq.* (chiefly *N. Amer.*) to a considerable degree, extremely.
▸ **B** *attrib.* or as *adjective.* That is a spade, that consists of spades (CARDS). Also (*slang*, *derog.* & considered *racially offensive*), black; of or pertaining to black people. **E20**.

spade /speɪd/ *verb*[2] *trans.* Now *rare* or *obsolete*. **E17**.
[from alt. of pa. pple of SPAY *verb*.]
= SPAY *verb* 2.

spadger /ˈspadʒə/ *noun & verb.* *dial.* & *slang*. **M19**.
[Fanciful alt. of SPARROW.]
▸ **A** *noun.* A sparrow; *transf.* a young boy. **M19**.

> D. HEWETT Head cocked sideways like a cheeky spadger.

▸ **B** *verb intrans.* Catch sparrows etc. in a net; *fig.* play or frolic *about*. *rare*. **M20**.

spadiceous /speɪˈdɪʃəs/ *adjective.* **M17**.
[from Latin *spadic-*, SPADIX + -EOUS.]
Now BOTANY. **1** Having the colour of dates; deep reddish-brown. **M17**.
2 Having the nature or form of a spadix. **M18**.

spadices *noun pl.* see SPADIX.

spadille /spəˈdɪl/ *noun.* Also (earlier) †**spadillo**. **L17**.
[(French from) Spanish *espadilla* dim. of *espada* sword from Latin *spatha* from Greek *spathē*: see SPADE *noun*[1].]
The ace of spades, esp. in ombre and quadrille. Also, the highest trump.

spadix /ˈspeɪdɪks/ *noun.* Pl. **-dices** /-dɪsiːz/, **-dixes**. **M18**.
[Latin, lit. 'palm branch with its fruit', from Greek.]
1 BOTANY. A form of spike which has the flowers arranged on a thick fleshy axis and is usu. enclosed in a spathe, characteristic esp. of the arums. **M18**.
2 ZOOLOGY. In various invertebrates, an organ or part of more or less conical shape. **L19**.

spadona /spəˈdəʊnə/ *noun. S. Afr.* L19.
[Italian *spadone* large sword, from *spada*: see SPADE *noun*[3].]
An imperfectly developed feather from a young ostrich.

spadroon /spəˈdruːn/ *noun.* L18.
[Swiss French *espadron* = French ESPADON.]
Hist. A light cut-and-thrust sword with a flat pointed blade, originating in Germany in the 18th cent.

spae /speɪ/ *verb & noun.* Chiefly *Scot.* ME.
[Old Norse *spá*, of unkn. origin.]
▶ **A** *verb trans. & intrans.* Pres. pple & verbal noun **spaeing**. Prophesy, predict. ME.
▶ **B** *noun.* Orig., a prophecy, an omen. Now, an enchantment, a spell. ME.
Comb.: **spae-craft** prophecy, fortune-telling; **spaeman** a soothsayer; a fortune-teller; a wizard; **spaewife** a female fortune-teller; a witch.

spag /spag/ *noun. colloq.* M20.
[Abbreviation.]
= SPAGHETTI 1.
spag bol /bɒl/ = *SPAGHETTI Bolognese.*

spaggers /ˈspagəz/ *noun. slang.* M20.
[from next: see -ER[6].]
= SPAGHETTI 1.

spaghetti /spəˈgɛti/ *noun.* M19.
[Italian, pl. of dim. of *spago* string.]
1 Pasta in the form of long solid threads, between macaroni and vermicelli in thickness; an Italian dish consisting largely of this and usu. a sauce. M19.
2 Complex roadways forming a multi-level junction, esp. on a roadway. *colloq.* M20.
3 An Italian. *slang. derog.* M20.

📖 **1** *transf.*: *Times* The complicated spaghetti of wires inside a telephone cable. ***vegetable spaghetti***: see VEGETABLE *adjective*. **2** *Canal & Riverboat* Under the motorway spaghetti is a canal crossroads.

Comb. & phrases: **spaghetti Bolognese** spaghetti served with a sauce of minced beef, tomato, onion, etc.; **spaghetti bowl** a network of pipelines constructed to carry materials between petrochemical companies on the Gulf Coast of the US; **spaghetti house**, (*US*) **spaghetti joint** *colloq.* a restaurant serving varieties of pasta, esp. spaghetti; **spaghetti junction** *colloq.* a complex multi-level road junction, esp. on a motorway; **spaghetti shoulder-strap** a thin shoulder-strap on a dress etc.; **spaghetti squash** = ***vegetable spaghetti*** s.v. VEGETABLE *adjective*; **spaghetti strap** = ***spaghetti shoulder-strap*** above; **spaghetti tongs**: having small teeth on the end to lift and separate strands of cooked spaghetti; **spaghetti tubing** *colloq.* tubular insulation for electrical wire; **spaghetti western** a western film made cheaply in Europe by an Italian director.

spaghettification /spəˌgɛtifɪˈkeɪʃ(ə)n/ *noun.* L20.
[from prec. + -FICATION.]
PHYSICS. The process by which (in some theories) an object would be stretched and ripped apart by gravitational forces on falling into a black hole.

spaghettini /spagɛˈtiːni/ *noun.* M20.
[Italian, dim. of SPAGHETTI.]
Pasta in the form of strings of thin spaghetti; an Italian dish consisting largely of this and usu. a sauce.

spagyric /spəˈdʒɪrɪk/ *noun & adjective. obsolete* exc. *Hist.* L16.
[mod. Latin *spagiricus*, used and prob. invented by Paracelsus.]
▶ **A** *noun.* †**1** The science of alchemy. L16–E17.
2 An alchemist. L16.
▶ **B** *adjective.* Alchemical. L16.
■ **spagyrical** *adjective* alchemical; (of a person) practising or believing in alchemy: L16.

spagyrist /ˈspadʒərɪst/ *noun. obsolete* exc. *Hist.* M17.
[mod. Latin *spagirista*, formed as prec.: see -IST.]
An alchemist.

spahi /ˈspɑːhiː/ *noun.* M16.
[(French from) Turkish *sipahi* from Persian *sipāhī*: see SEPOY.]
Hist. **1** A member of a cavalry corps within the Ottoman Turkish army. M16.
2 A member of a corps of Algerian cavalry serving under the French government from 1834 to 1962. M19.

spake /speɪk/ *noun.* M20.
[Origin unkn.]
An underground train for transporting men in a coalmine, esp. in S. Wales.

spake *verb pa. t.*: see SPEAK *verb*.

spald /spɔːld/ *verb trans. & intrans. Scot. & north.* LME.
[Middle Low German *spalden* = Old High German *spaltan* (Middle High German & German *spalten*). Cf. SPALT *verb*, SPELD *verb*, SPELT *verb*[1].]
Splinter, split; break up or open.
Comb.: **spalding-knife** a knife for splitting dried fish.
■ **spalding** *noun* a split dried fish (esp. whiting) L18.

spale /speɪl/ *noun. Scot. & north.* LME.
[Origin unkn.]
1 A splinter, a chip; a thin strip of wood, *esp.* one used in basket-making. LME.
2 *transf.* A curl of wax on a burning candle. L18.

spall /spɔːl/ *noun*[1]. LME.
[Origin unkn.]
A splinter or chip, esp. of wood, stone, etc.

spall /spɔːl/ *noun*[2]. *Scot. & poet. rare.* L16.
[Italian *spalla* from medieval & mod. Latin *spatula* (see SPAULD) or var. of SPAULD.]
The shoulder; the shoulder-bone.

spall /spɔːl/ *verb.* M18.
[Rel. to SPALL *noun*[1].]
1 *verb trans.* **a** *MINING.* Break (ore) into smaller pieces. M18. ▸**b** Dress (stone) roughly. L18.
2 *verb trans. & intrans.* Break off or *off* in fragments; splinter, chip. M19.
3 *verb trans. NUCLEAR PHYSICS.* Cause spallation of (a nucleus). L20.
■ **spaller** *noun* (*MINING*) a person who or machine which spalls ore M19.

spallation /spəˈleɪʃ(ə)n/ *noun.* M20.
[from prec. + -ATION.]
1 *NUCLEAR PHYSICS.* The detachment of a number of nucleons, esp. neutrons, from a larger nucleus, esp. as a result of the impact of an energetic particle. M20.
2 *GEOLOGY.* Separation of fragments from the surface of a rock by interaction with a compression wave (esp. by micrometeoritic impact). L20.

spalpeen /spalˈpiːn/ *noun. Anglo-Irish.* L18.
[from Irish *spailpín*, ult. origin unkn.: see -EEN[2].]
1 A migratory agricultural labourer; a harvester, a reaper. L18.
2 A worthless or disagreeable person. E19.
3 A young boy. L19.

spalt /spɔːlt/ *adjective.* Now *dial.* M16.
[Origin uncertain: perh. rel. to next.]
Of wood: brittle, breaking easily through dryness or decay. Also = SPALTED.

spalt /spɔːlt/ *verb intrans. & trans. dial.* M18.
[App. var. of SPALD. Cf. prec., SPELT *verb*[1].]
Split, tear, splinter.

spalted /ˈspɔːltəd/ *adjective.* L20.
[from SPALT *verb* + -ED[1]. Cf. SPALT *adjective*.]
Of wood: having a distinctive lined grain caused by bacterial decay, esp. as producing a decorative surface when finely sanded.

Spam /spam/ *noun*[1]. Also **s-**. M20.
[App. from SP(ICED + H)AM *noun*[1].]
(Proprietary name for) a tinned meat product consisting chiefly of ham. Also *loosely*, any tinned luncheon meat.
Comb.: **Spam can** *slang* a kind of streamlined steam locomotive formerly used on British Rail; **Spam medal** *Military slang* a medal awarded to all the members of a force.
■ **spammy** *adjective* consisting chiefly of or resembling spam; *fig.* bland, mediocre: M20.

spam /spam/ *verb & noun*[2]. *slang.* L20.
[from SPAM *noun*[1], app. with ref. to a sketch in the TV comedy series *Monty Python's Flying Circus*, set in a café where Spam was the main ingredient of every dish and featuring a song containing the word 'Spam' repeated many times.]
COMPUTING. ▸**A** *verb trans.* Infl. **-mm-**. Send the same message indiscriminately to (a large number of newsgroups or users) on the Internet. L20.
▶ **B** *noun.* Irrelevant or inappropriate messages sent on the Internet to a large number of newsgroups or users. L20.
■ **spammer** *noun* L20.

span /span/ *noun*[1].
[Old English *span(n* = Middle Low German *spen(ne*, Middle & mod. Dutch *spanne*, Old High German *spanna* (German *Spanne*), Old Norse *spǫnn*, *spann-*, reinforced in Middle English by Old French *espan(n)e*, *espan* (mod. *empan*), of Germanic origin.]
1 The distance between the tips of the thumb and little finger or (occas.) forefinger, when the hand is fully extended; this as a measure of length, regarded as averaging nine inches. OE.
2 (A thing encompassing) a short distance, space, or time. *arch.* ME.
3 The full extent of a thing from end to end in space or time; *spec.* (***a***) (a measure of) the distance between the piers of a bridge; (***b***) the duration of life of a person or thing. E17. ▸**b** *PSYCHOLOGY.* Mental extent; the amount of information of which the mind can be conscious at a given moment, or can recall after one presentation. Also, the length of time for which attention, concentration, etc. can be maintained. L19. ▸**c** The maximum lateral extent of an aircraft or its wing(s), a bird's wing(s), etc., from tip to tip. More fully ***wingspan***. E20. ▸**d** A range of numerical values; the difference between the highest and lowest values in a range. M20.
4 Any of the arches or sections of a bridge between piers. E19.
5 *MATH.* A region or subspace generated or encompassed by the elements of some set. Cf. SPAN *verb*[1] 5. M20.

📖 **1** I. WATSON The top stone platform . . was . . about seventy spans across. J. C. OATES Fairchild's finger span is such that . . he can grip a basketball in his . . hand. **2** SHAKES. *Hen. VIII* Scarce time To steal from spiritual leisure a brief span. TENNYSON Every grain of sand that runs, And every span of shade that steals. **3** J. T. MICKLETHWAITE York Minster, with its choir of fifty feet span. J. HELLER He was working hard at increasing his life span. L. VAN DER POST The span of years between us. **b** ***attention span***, ***span of attention***, etc. **4** P. L. FERMOR We . . sailed under . . the spans of the first bridge.

Phrases: **span of control** the area of activity, number of functions, people, etc., for which an individual or organization is responsible. ***MEMORY span***.
Comb.: **span-counter** a game with the object of throwing a coin etc. within a span's distance of that of one's opponent; **span-farthing** *Hist.* a game similar to span-counter, played with farthings; **span loading** *AERODYNAMICS* the gross weight of an aircraft, bird, etc., divided by its wingspan or, more usu., by the square of the wingspan; **span-long** *adjective* (*poet.*) brief, short; **span wire** any of a series of overhead wires crossing a tram route to carry the electric cable; **span-worm** *US* = LOOPER *noun*[1] 1.

span /span/ *noun*[2]. M18.
[Low German & Dutch, from *spannen* SPAN *verb*[2].]
1 *NAUTICAL.* A rope or chain with both ends fastened to take a purchase where no other convenient point is available. M18.
2 A pair of harnessed horses, *esp.* one matched in colour and size. Chiefly *N. Amer.* M18.
3 *S. Afr.* **a** A team of two or more pairs of oxen etc. E19. ▸**b** A team or gang of workers. E20.
Comb.: **span-roof**: consisting of two inclined sides.

span /span/ *verb*[1] *trans.* Infl. **-nn-**. OE.
[Partly formed as next, partly from SPAN *noun*[1].]
▶ **I** *verb trans.* **1** Orig., join, fasten, clasp. Later, grasp, seize. Long *obsolete* exc. *Scot.* OE.
2 Measure or cover (as) with the span of the hand; encircle (as) with the hand or hands. Formerly also, take measure of or encompass with the mind. OE.
3 Reach or extend over (a distance, period of time, etc.); arch across from side to side; encompass or range over in subject etc. E17.
4 Construct a bridge across. M19.
5 *MATH.* Generate. Cf. SPAN *noun*[1] 5. M20.

📖 **2** KEATS She spann'd The quick invisible strings [of the lute]. BROWNING How your plump arms . . have dropped away! Why, I can span them! **3** M. MEYER His . . career . . spanned fifty years. G. SWIFT The footbridge . . spanned . . the river. *Antique Collector* The exhibits span the Zapotec to the Aztec cultures. **4** S. SMILES Telford spanned . . these straits with suspension road bridges. *transf.*: B. JOWETT He is the mediator who spans the chasm which divides them.

▶ **II** *verb intrans.* **6** Extend or reach *over* a distance, period of time, etc.; stretch or range *from* one place or thing *to* another. M16.
■ **spanning** *ppl adjective* (***a***) that spans or extends across something; (***b***) *MATH.* (of a subgraph, esp. one that is a tree) that includes and connects every vertex of a graph: E19.

span /span/ *verb*[2]. Infl. **-nn-**. E16.
[Middle & mod. Dutch, Middle & mod. Low German *spannen*, from Germanic. Cf. prec.]
1 *verb trans.* **a** Stretch, extend; make taut, tighten. *arch.* E16. ▸**b** *NAUTICAL.* Fix, fasten; draw tight. Also foll. by *in*. L18.
2 *verb trans. & intrans.* Harness or yoke (oxen, horses, etc.) to a vehicle. Also foll. by *in*. Cf. INSPAN, OUTSPAN *verb*[1]. Now chiefly *S. Afr.* M16. ▸**b** *verb trans.* Fetter or hobble (a horse). *dial.* M19.
3 *verb intrans.* Of horses: match in colour and size. Cf. SPAN *noun*[2] 2. *US.* E19.

span *verb*[3] *pa. t.*: see SPIN *verb*.

spanaemia /spaˈniːmɪə/ *noun.* Now *rare* or *obsolete*. M19.
[mod. Latin from Greek *spanos*, *spanios* scarce, scanty + *haima* blood + -IA[1].]
MEDICINE. = ANAEMIA.

spanakopita /spanəˈkɒpɪtə/ *noun.* M20.
[mod. Greek, from *spanaki* spinach + *pita* pie.]
In Greek cookery: a filo pastry stuffed with spinach and feta cheese.

spanandry /ˈspanandri/ *noun.* E20.
[French *spanandrie* from patristic Greek *spanandria* scarcity of population, from Greek *spanis* scarcity + *andr-*, *anēr* man: see -Y[3].]
ZOOLOGY. Lack or extreme scarcity of males in a population.
■ **spaˈnandric** *adjective* of, pertaining to, or characterized by spanandry L20.

spancel /ˈspansɪl/ *noun & verb.* Now *dial.* E17.
[Flemish, Dutch, or Low German *spansel*, from *spannen*: see SPAN *verb*[2].]
▶ **A** *noun.* An animal fetter, *esp.* one used to hobble a cow during milking. E17.
▶ **B** *verb trans.* Infl. **-ll-**. Fetter or hobble with a spancel or spancels. E17.

Spandau /ˈspandaʊ/ *noun*. **E20**.
[A district in West Berlin, Germany.]
A German machine-gun used during the war of 1914–18; *transf.* any of various types of German machine-gun used in the war of 1939–45. Also more fully ***Spandau gun***.

spander-new /spandəˈnjuː/ *adjective*. Now *dial.* **E18**.
[Alt. Cf. SPANDY.]
= SPAN-NEW.

Spandex /ˈspandɛks/ *noun*. **M20**.
[Arbitrary formation from EXPAND.]
(Proprietary name for) a man-made elastomeric fibre composed largely of polyurethane; a fabric made from this fibre.

spandrel /ˈspandrɪl/ *noun*. **LME**.
[Origin uncertain: perh. from Anglo-Norman *spaund(e)re*, or from *espaundre* expand.]
ARCHITECTURE. **1** Orig., a space between timbers supporting a building. Later, the almost triangular space between one side of the outer curve of an arch and the rectangle formed by the mouldings enclosing it (esp. a wall and ceiling), freq. filled in with ornamental work. Also, the space between the shoulders of adjoining arches and the ceiling or moulding above. **LME**.
2 *transf.* **a** The area of support between a set of steps and the ground. **M19**. ▸**b** Any of the spaces between the central field and border on an oriental rug. **E20**.
■ **spandrelled** *adjective* having a spandrel or spandrels **E19**.

spandy /ˈspandi/ *adjective & adverb*. *US colloq.* **M19**.
[Perh. var. of 1st elem. of SPANDER-NEW.]
▶ **A** *adjective*. Very good or fine; smart. **M19**.
▶ **B** *adverb*. Quite, entirely. Esp. in ***spandy new***. **M19**.

spane /speɪn/ *verb*. **ME**.
[Middle Low German, Middle Dutch *spanen*, corresp. to Old High German *spanan* entice, ult. from Germanic base also of Middle Dutch, Middle Low German *spenen*: see SPEAN *verb*.]
1 *verb trans.* Wean; *fig.* separate or draw away from something. *Scot. & north.* **ME**.
2 *verb intrans.* Of corn: germinate, take root. *north.* **M19**.

spang /spaŋ/ *noun*¹ & *verb*¹. Now *arch. & Scot.* **LME**.
[Middle Dutch *spange* (Dutch *spang*) = Old High German *spanga* (German *Spange*), Old Norse *spang-*, *spǫng* clasp, brooch, from Germanic.]
▶ **A** *noun*. †**1** A glittering ornament; a spangle. **LME–E17**.
2 A clasp, a buckle. **L19**.
▶† **B** *verb trans.* = SPANGLE *verb* 1. **L16–E17**.

spang /spaŋ/ *noun*² & *verb*². Chiefly *Scot. & north.* **E16**.
[Origin unkn. Cf. SPANG *adverb*.]
▶ **A** *noun*. **1** A jerk; a sudden violent movement. **E16**.
2 A smart rap or blow. **L16**.
3 A spring, a bound; a vigorous stride. **E18**.
▶ **B** *verb*. **1** *verb intrans.* Stride briskly; spring, bound; ricochet *off* a surface etc. **E16**.
2 *verb trans.* Throw with a jerk; pitch, fling. Also, eat *up* (food) rapidly. **E16**.

†**spang** *noun*³. *rare*. See also SPONG. **E17–M18**.
[Origin uncertain: perh. rel. to SPANG *noun*¹.]
A long narrow strip (*of* land).

spang /spaŋ/ *adverb*. *colloq.* (chiefly *US*). **M19**.
[Origin uncertain: prob. rel. to SPANG *noun*² & *verb*² or alt. of SPAN(-NEW.]
Directly; entirely, quite.

> M. MITCHELL You needs a spang new pretty dress.

spangle /ˈspaŋɡ(ə)l/ *noun & verb*. **LME**.
[from SPANG *noun*¹ + -LE¹. Cf. SPANKLED.]
▶ **A** *noun*. **1** A small thin piece of glittering metal, usu. round and pierced in the centre, for sewing as ornamentation on to fabric, a dress, etc.; a sequin. **LME**.
2 *transf.* Any small sparkling object or particle; a glittering point of light; *spec.* (**a**) *poet.* a star; (**b**) LACE-MAKING any of the beads attached to the end of a bobbin. **L16**. ▸**b** Glitter, sparkle; an instance of this. **M19**.
3 A mark, speckle, gall, etc., on an animal or plant; *spec.* (also ***spangle gall***) = OAK-*spangle*. **L18**. ▸**b** A bird (esp. a pigeon) with speckled plumage. **M19**.

> **1** M. ATWOOD She wears . . a scarf with spangles on it. **2** R. BOYLE We took notice of the icy spangles in the air, flying about like atoms in the sun's beams. W. BOYD Spangles of light exploding off . . the parked cars. **b** H. WILLIAMSON The walls were red . . with a spangle of tiny gold stars.

▶ **B** *verb*. **1** *verb trans.* Cover or decorate (as) with spangles; cause to glitter (as) with spangles. Also foll. by *with*. Freq. as ***spangled*** *ppl adjective*. **LME**.
2 *verb intrans.* Glitter or sparkle (as) with spangles. Freq. as ***spangling*** *ppl adjective*. **E17**.

> **1** D. SHIELDS Instead of spilling the coins slowly, I . . spun around . . and spangled the floor with silver. J. C. OATES Smoky spangled stockings and three-inch heels. **2** SHELLEY Upon whose floor the spangling sands were thrown. R. ADAMS Fast-flowing and smooth, spangling and dazzling in the . . sun.

■ **spangler** *noun* **M17**. **spanglet** *noun* a little spangle **E17**. **spangly** *adjective* (as if) covered with spangles; sparkling, glittery: **E19**.

Spanglish /ˈspaŋɡlɪʃ/ *noun*. **M20**.
[Blend of SPANISH *noun* + ENGLISH *noun*.]
A corrupt version of Latin American Spanish marked by the use of words and phrases of English or American origin.

Spaniard /ˈspanjəd/ *noun & adjective*. **ME**.
[Aphet. from Old French *Espaignart*, *-niard*, from *Espaigne* (mod. *Espagne*) Spain: see -ARD.]
▶ **A** *noun*. **1** A person of Spanish birth, nationality, or descent. Also (*arch.*) *the* Spanish people, forces, etc., collectively. **ME**.
2 A Spanish ship or vessel. **M16**.
3 An umbelliferous New Zealand plant, *Aciphylla colensoi*, characterized by long spine-tipped leaflets. Also called ***bayonet-grass***, ***spear-grass***. **M19**.
▶ **B** *adjective*. Spanish. Now *rare* or *obsolete*. **ME**.
■ **Spaniardize** *verb trans.* (*rare*) make Spanish, hispanize **L19**.

spaniel /ˈspanj(ə)l/ *noun, verb, & adjective*. **ME**.
[Old French *espaigneul* (mod. *épagneul*) from Proto-Romance, from Latin *Hispaniolus* Spanish, from *Hispania* Spain.]
▶ **A** *noun*. **1** (An animal of) any of various breeds of small or medium-sized dog characterized by a long silky coat and drooping ears, and originally bred mainly as gun dogs. **ME**.
2 *fig.* A person who investigates a matter on another's behalf; a loyal follower or servant; now *esp.* an obsequious or fawning person. **M16**.
1 ***Blenheim spaniel***, ***cocker spaniel***, ***Japanese spaniel***, ***King Charles's spaniel***, ***Norfolk spaniel***, ***springer spaniel***, etc.
▶ **B** *verb*. Infl. **-l(l)-**.
1 *verb intrans. & trans.* (with *it*). Act like a spaniel; be obsequious, fawn. **L16**.
†**2** *verb trans.* Follow like a spaniel; fawn on. *rare* (Shakes.). Only in **E17**.

> **1** J. GALSWORTHY Fawningly spaniel'd to bestow her hand.

▶ **C** *adjective*. Of, pertaining to, or characteristic of a spaniel or spaniels; *fig.* obsequious, fawning. **E17**.

> SHAKES. *Jul. Caes.* Low-crooked curtsies, and base spaniel fawning.

spaniolize /ˈspanɪəlʌɪz/ *verb trans.* Now *rare*. Also **-ise**. **L16**.
[Aphet. from HISPANIOLIZE, perh. after French †*espagnoliser*.]
= HISPANIZE. Chiefly as ***spaniolized*** *ppl adjective*.
■ Also **spaniolate** *verb trans.* (*rare*) **L16**.

Spanish /ˈspanɪʃ/ *adjective, noun, & adverb*. **ME**.
[from *Spain* (see below) + -ISH¹, with later shortening of 1st elem.]
▶ **A** *adjective*. **1** Of or pertaining to Spain, a country in SW Europe occupying the greater part of the Iberian peninsula, or its inhabitants; native to or originating in Spain; associated with or characteristic of Spain or Spaniards. Also, of, pertaining to, or characteristic of Spanish America or its inhabitants. **ME**.
2 Of or pertaining to Spanish. **LME**.
1 **old Spanish custom**, **old Spanish practice** *joc.* a long-standing though unauthorized or irregular practice.
Special collocations: **Spanish America** those parts of Central and S. America, the W. Indies, and sometimes more widely the south-western US, which were colonized by Spain. **Spanish American** a native or inhabitant of Spanish America; a Spanish-American person. **Spanish-American** *adjective* of or pertaining to Spanish America; of or belonging to both Spain and America. **Spanish Armada** *Hist.* the Spanish war fleet sent against England in 1588. **Spanish bayonet** any of several yuccas, so called from the sharp rigid leaves; esp. *Yucca aloifolia*, of south-western N. America. **Spanish beard** *US* = *Spanish moss* below. **Spanish bluebell** a freq. cultivated bluebell of the Iberian peninsula, *Hyacinthoides hispanica*, with broader leaves than the English bluebell and upright flowers. **Spanish bowline** a double loop knot used esp. to hoist or lower a person. **Spanish broom** a leguminous shrub, *Spartium junceum*, of the Mediterranean region, with fragrant yellow flowers and green rushlike almost leafless branches which are used in basket-work. **Spanish brown** a reddish-brown earth containing iron oxides, used as a pigment; the colour of this. **Spanish burton** NAUTICAL a tackle with two single blocks. **Spanish cedar** the wood of a tropical American tree, *Cedrela odorata*, which is soft, light, and fragrant like that of the cedar; the tree yielding this wood. ***Spanish chestnut***: see CHESTNUT *noun* 1a. **Spanish-Colonial** *adjective & noun* (designating) a style of architecture characteristic of Spanish America. **Spanish comb** a decorative comb with a deep top, worn in the hair. **Spanish dagger** any of several yuccas (cf. *Spanish bayonet* above); esp. *Yucca gloriosa*, of the south-eastern US. **Spanish dance** a flamenco dance, flamenco dancing. **Spanish dancing** flamenco dancing. **Spanish elm** = ***prince-wood*** s.v. PRINCE *noun*. **Spanish flu** *colloq.* = *Spanish influenza* below. **Spanish fly** a bright green blister-beetle, *Lyssa vesicatoria*; a dried preparation of these beetles (see CANTHARIS). **Spanish foot** a foot on a chair etc. in the form of a scroll with vertical ribs. **Spanish garlic** the sand leek or rocambole, *Allium scorodoprasum*. **Spanish guitar** the standard six-stringed acoustic guitar, used for both folk and classical music. **Spanish influenza** influenza caused by an influenza virus of type A, *esp.* that of the pandemic which began in 1918. ***Spanish Inquisition***: see INQUISITION *noun* 3. **Spanish iris** any garden iris belonging to a group having bulbs without storage roots, hybrids of *Iris xiphium* and its close allies. **Spanish lime** = GUINEP. **Spanish mackerel** any of several large Atlantic game-fishes mainly of the genus *Scomberomorus*, esp. *Scomberomorus maculatus*; (***Monterey Spanish mackerel***: see MONTEREY 3). **Spanish Main** *Hist.* the northern coast of S. America adjacent to the Caribbean Sea esp. between Panama and the Orinoco river. **Spanish Mission** *adjective & noun* (designating) a style of architecture characteristic of the Catholic missions in Spanish America. **Spanish moss** an epiphytic bromeliad of tropical America, *Tillandsia usneoides*, forming silvery festoons on trees. **Spanish needles** (the prickly fruits of) an American bur-marigold, *Bidens bipinnata*. **Spanish nut** a Mediterranean plant of the iris family, *Gynandriris sisyrinchium*, with an edible corm. **Spanish omelette**: containing various chopped vegetables and freq. served unfolded. **Spanish onion** a large mild-flavoured variety of onion. **Spanish opening** CHESS = RUY LOPEZ. **Spanish plum** *W. Indies* a kind of hog plum, *Spondias purpurea*. **Spanish rice** a dish of rice with onions, peppers, tomatoes, and other vegetables, typically coloured and flavoured with saffron. **Spanish sheep** (**a**) a merino sheep; (**b**) = JACOB 4. **Spanish squill** = *Spanish bluebell* above. **Spanish stitch** an embroidery stitch worked as two adjacent rows of straight stitches slanting in opposite directions. **Spanish tile** (**a**) a curved roof tile, laid alternately convex and concave so as to overlap at both sides; (**b**) *US* a curved roof tile with an overlapping straight projection at one side. ***Spanish toothpick***: see TOOTHPICK *noun* 2. **Spanish topaz** a reddish- or brownish-orange form of quartz, resembling topaz; *esp.* a variety of citrine occurring naturally in Spain. **Spanish tummy** *colloq.* diarrhoea suffered by visitors to Spain. **Spanish white** finely powdered chalk used as a pigment or for its cleansing properties; pigment made from this. **Spanish windlass** NAUTICAL a device for tightening a rope etc. using a stick as a lever. **Spanish wood** Spanish mahogany.
▶ **B** *noun*. **1** Orig., a Spaniard. Later only, *the* Spanish people collectively. **LME**.
2 The principal language of Spain and of most of Central and S. America, a Romance language with many Arabic words; a particular variety of this. **L15**.
3 †**a** More fully ***plain Spanish***. Spanish snuff. **L17–M18**. ▸**b** *The* cash, *the* money. *slang*. **M18**. ▸**c** (A variety of) Spanish wine. **L20**.

> **1** C. PHILLIPS The Spanish press home a full claim to sovereignty. **2** C. PHILLIPS The British make no effort to acquire any Spanish. *Word* These usages are not . . similar to coastal Peruvian Spanish. ***Mexican Spanish***: see MEXICAN.

▶ **C** *adverb*. ***walk Spanish***, (cause to) walk under compulsion, esp. with a person holding the collar and the seat of the trousers of the person made to walk. *US slang*. **M19**.
■ **Spanishly** *adverb* (**a**) *rare* towards Spain or the Spanish; (**b**) resembling (the) Spanish; in a characteristically Spanish manner: **M17**. **Spanishness**, **Spanishry** *nouns* the quality of being Spanish or having Spanish characteristics **M20**. **Spanishy** *adjective* of a Spanish type or character **E20**.

spank /spaŋk/ *verb*¹ & *noun*¹. **E18**.
[Prob. imit.]
▶ **A** *verb*. **1** *verb trans.* Slap or smack, esp. (repeatedly) on the buttocks with the open hand, a slipper, etc., administer a spanking to; *fig.* criticize or defeat heavily, trounce. **E18**. ▸**b** Milk (a cow). *NZ colloq.* **L19**.
2 *verb intrans.* Beat on or against a surface with a slapping sound. *rare*. **E19**.

> **1** E. WALLACE She . . left him feeling like a spanked child. *Chicago Tribune* Payton scored . . to spank the Mustang's 35–7.

▶ **B** *noun*. (The sound of) a slap or smack, esp. on the buttocks with the open hand etc. **L18**.

spank /spaŋk/ *verb*² & *noun*². **E19**.
[Prob. back-form. from SPANKING *adjective*.]
▶ **A** *verb*. **1** *verb intrans. & trans.* (with *it*). Move or travel quickly or briskly; *esp.* (of a horse) move at a brisk trot. Freq. foll. by *along*. **E19**.
2 *verb trans.* Drive (a horse) at a brisk pace. *rare*. **E19**.

> **1** L. G. GIBBON A gig came spanking along from the station.

▶ **B** *noun*. **1** The action or an act of spanking or moving along briskly. *rare*. **E19**.
2 A light jump; a bound, a spring. Chiefly *Scot.* **L19**.

spanker /ˈspaŋkə/ *noun*¹. **M17**.
[Rel. to SPANKING *adjective*, later also from SPANK *verb*²: see -ER¹. Cf. SPINNAKER.]
1 A coin, *esp.* a gold one; in *pl.*, money. *slang*. Long *rare* or *obsolete*. **M17**.
2 A person or thing of exceptional size or quality. *dial. & colloq.* **M18**. ▸**b** A heavy blow or smack. **L18**.
3 NAUTICAL. **a** A fore-and-aft sail set on the after side of the mizzen-mast. **L18**. ▸**b** In full ***spanker mast***. The fourth (or fifth) mast of a ship with four or more masts. **M19**.
4 **a** A person who walks briskly. *Scot. & dial.* **E19**. ▸**b** A fast horse. *Scot., dial., & colloq.* **E19**.
Comb.: **spanker-boom** NAUTICAL: on which the spanker is set.

spanker /ˈspaŋkə/ *noun*². **L19**.
[from SPANK *verb*¹ + -ER¹.]
A person who or thing which spanks or slaps someone or something.

spanking /ˈspaŋkɪŋ/ *verbal noun*. **M19**.
[from SPANK *verb*¹ + -ING¹.]
The action of SPANK *verb*¹; an instance of this, esp. as a punishment for children.

spanking /ˈspaŋkɪŋ/ *adjective & adverb.* Chiefly *dial. & colloq.* **M17.**
[Perh. of symbolic origin: cf. *thumping, whacking*, etc.]
▶ **A** *adjective.* **1** Exceptionally large or fine; excellent; showy, striking. **M17.**
2 (Esp. of a horse) moving at a brisk pace; smart; lively; (of a person) dashing. **M18.** ▸**b** Of pace etc.: brisk, vigorous. **M19.**

> **1** *Times* Sir Leslie expects BOC to show a spanking profits performance. **2** *Prima* A story told at a spanking pace. A. UTTLEY The horse was a spanking beast, a high stepper.

▶ **B** *adverb.* Very, exceedingly. Chiefly in ***spanking new***, brand-new. *colloq.* **L19.**
■ **spankingly** *adverb* **E19.**

†**spankled** *adjective.* **E18–M19.**
[Alt. of pa. pple of SPANGLE *verb*.]
Spangled.

spanned /spand/ *adjective.* **M20.**
[from SPAN *verb*[1] + -ED[1].]
BIOLOGY. Of a culture of cells or micro-organisms: having a restricted lifespan; unable to propagate asexually without limit.

spanner /ˈspanə/ *noun*[1]. **M17.**
[German, from *spannen*: see SPAN *verb*[2].]
1 A device for winding the spring of a wheel-lock gun. Long *rare* or *obsolete*. **M17.**
2 A hand-held tool with a fixed or adjustable opening or jaw at one end which fits over or around a nut, bolt, etc. **L18.**
3 *MECHANICS.* A lever in a steam engine, esp. one which opens a valve. **L18.**
2 *shifting spanner*: see SHIFTING *adjective* 1. **spanner in the works** *colloq.* a disruption or impediment (freq. in ***throw a spanner in the works***).
Comb.: **spanner tight** *adjective* (of a nut) secured as tight as is possible with a spanner; **spanner wrench** *US* a non-adjustable spanner.

spanner /ˈspanə/ *noun*[2]. *rare.* **M19.**
[from SPAN *verb*[1] + -ER[1].]
A supportive rib or brace spanning a roof, bridge, etc.

span-new /ˈspannjuː/ *adjective.* Now *Scot. & dial.* **ME.**
[Old Norse *spán-nýr*, from *spánn* chip + *nýr* new. Cf. SPANDER-NEW, SPANG *adverb*, SPICK AND SPAN.]
Completely new.

spanspek /ˈspanspɛk/ *noun. S. Afr.* **L19.**
[Afrikaans.]
= CANTALOUP.

Spansule /ˈspansjuːl/ *noun.* **M20.**
[from SPAN *noun*[1] + CAP)SULE *noun*.]
PHARMACOLOGY. (Proprietary name for) a capsule that when swallowed releases a drug steadily for several hours, or releases several drugs sequentially.

spanwise /ˈspanwʌɪz/ *adjective.* **M20.**
[from SPAN *noun*[1] + -WISE.]
AERODYNAMICS. Following the direction of the span of a wing or other aerofoil.

spar /spɑː/ *noun*[1]. **ME.**
[Old Norse *sperra*, or aphet. from Old French *esparre* (mod. *épar(e)*) or its Germanic source (of unkn. origin), repr. by Middle Low German, Middle Dutch *sparre* (Dutch *spar*), Old High German *sparro* (German *Sparren*), Old Norse *sparri*.]
1 A stout pole or piece of timber, esp. (*NAUTICAL*) a pole (now of any material) used as a mast, yard, boom, etc. **ME.**
2 A rafter or beam in a roof. Now *dial.* **ME.**
3 A wooden bar for fastening a door etc.; a crossbar or rail of a gate; a rung. Now *Scot.* **L16.**
4 The main longitudinal beam of an aeroplane wing. **M19.**
Comb.: **spar-buoy**: made of a spar with one end moored so that the other stands up; **spar-deck** the light upper deck of a vessel; **spar tree** *FORESTRY* a tree or other tall structure to which cables are attached for hauling logs.

spar /spɑː/ *noun*[2]. **LME.**
[from SPAR *verb*[1].]
†**1** A thrust. Only in **LME.**
2 A boxing-match, *esp.* a non-aggressive one for practice or exhibition; a sparring movement. **E19.**
3 A cock-fight. **M19.**
4 *transf.* An argument, a dispute. **M19.**
Comb.: **sparmate** *US* a sparring partner.

spar /spɑː/ *noun*[3]. **L16.**
[Middle Low German, rel. to base of SPAR-STONE. Cf. SPAT *noun*[3], SPATH.]
MINERALOGY. **1** Any of various crystalline transparent or translucent minerals, usu. more or less lustrous and readily cleavable. **L16.**
2 A fragment or particle of spar; *rare* an ornament made of spar. **M19.**
1 ***Derbyshire spar, feldspar, fluorspar, iceland spar, pearl spar, tabular spar***, etc.

spar /spɑː/ *noun*[4]. *dial.* Also **spear**. **M18.**
[Origin unkn.]
A pointed and doubled rod for securing thatch.

spar /spɑː/ *verb*[1]. Infl. **-rr-**.
[Old English *sperran, spyrran*, corresp. to Old Norse *sperrask* kick out, of unkn. origin.]
†**1** *verb intrans.* Dart, spring; strike or thrust rapidly. **OE–LME.**
2 *verb intrans.* Of a cock: fight with the feet or spurs. **L16.** ▸**b** *verb trans.* Make (a cock) fight in this way. **L17.**
3 *verb intrans.* Engage in argument, dispute. **L17.**
4 *verb intrans.* Make the movements of boxing without landing heavy blows; box in this way as practice or training. **M18.**
4 **sparring partner** (*a*) a boxer employed to spar with another as training; (*b*) a person with whom one enjoys arguing.

spar /spɑː/ *verb*[2] *trans. arch.* Infl. **-rr-**. **ME.**
[Middle Dutch, Old High German *sperren*, ult. from Germanic base of SPAR *noun*[1]. Cf. SPEAR *verb*[1].]
1 Fasten (a door or gate) with a bar or bolt. **ME.**
†**2** Close; fasten; secure. **ME–E18.**
†**3** Confine or imprison *in* a place. **ME–L16.**
†**4** Shut *out* or *in*. **LME–M16.**

spar /spɑː/ *verb*[3] *trans.* Infl. **-rr-**. **M17.**
[from SPAR *noun*[1].]
1 Provide, make, or close *in* (a gate, roof, etc.) with a spar or spars. **M17.**
2 *NAUTICAL.* Provide or fit (a vessel) with spars. **M19.** ▸**b** Guide (a vessel) over a shallow bar by using spars. *US.* **M19.**

sparable /ˈsparəb(ə)l/ *noun.* **E17.**
[Contr. of SPARROW-BILL.]
A small headless wedge-shaped nail, used for the soles and heels of shoes.

†**sparadrap** *noun.* **M16–E18.**
[Old & mod. French from Italian *sparadrappo*, of unkn. origin.]
MEDICINE. A piece of linen etc. dipped in, or spread with, an ointment or medicament for use as a bandage or plaster.

†**sparage** *noun* var. of SPERAGE.

sparagmite /ˈsparəgmʌɪt/ *noun.* **L19.**
[Greek *sparagma* fragment, piece torn off: see -ITE[1].]
GEOLOGY. Any of the feldspathic sandstones, conglomerates, and other fragmental rocks which occur in late Precambrian formations in Scandinavia; such rocks collectively.

sparagmos /spəˈragmɒs/ *noun.* **M20.**
[Greek = tearing, rending.]
The ritual tearing to pieces of a victim, as represented in some Greek tragedies.

†**sparagus** *noun* see ASPARAGUS.

sparaxis /spəˈraksɪs/ *noun.* **E19.**
[mod. Latin (see below), from Greek = tearing, laceration.]
Any of several ornamental southern African plants constituting the genus *Sparaxis*, of the iris family, which are allied to the genus *Ixia* but have a lacerate spathe.

spare /spɛː/ *noun*[1]. **ME.**
[from SPARE *verb, adjective.*]
†**1** The fact of leaving unharmed; leniency, mercy. **ME–M17.**
2 (The exercise of) economy or frugality. *arch.* **LME.**
3 *ellipt.* A reserve sum of money (*rare*); a spare room; *esp.* a spare part, a spare tyre. **M17.**
4 In ten-pin bowling etc., the knocking down of all the pins with the first two bowls (leaving one 'to spare'); the score for doing this. **M19.**

> **3** *Which?* Poor or tardy supply of spares from the makers. *Rally Car* A car may carry only 2 spares. **bit of spare** *slang* (*derog.*) an unattached woman, *esp.* one regarded as available for casual sex.

spare /spɛː/ *noun*[2]. Long *obsolete* exc. *Scot.* **ME.**
[Perh. rel. to Old Norse *spjǫrr* rag, tatter, Norwegian *spjær* rent, tear.]
A slit or opening in a garment.

spare /spɛː/ *adjective & adverb.*
[Old English *spær* sparing, frugal = Old High German *spar*, Old Norse *sparr*, rel. to next.]
▶ **A** *adjective.* **I 1** Characterized by meanness or frugality; (of diet etc.) meagre and plain; scanty; not abundant or plentiful. **OE.** ▸†**b** Of a person: not lavish in expenditure or living; frugal; moderate, esp. in eating habits or speech; sparing. **M16–L17.**
2 Having little fat; lean, thin. **M16.** ▸**b** Of style: unadorned, restrained, simple. **M20.**

> **1** W. COWPER Patriots . . Enjoy'd—spare feast!—a radish and an egg! GEO. ELIOT To order the whole establishment on the sparest footing possible. **2** P. KAVANAGH He was spare of flesh and slight of build. B. W. ALDISS His tall, spare figure. **b** *Times* A frighteningly spare performance in One Day in the Life of Ivan Denisovich. *New Yorker* The watercolours themselves . . are utterly spare, . . sometimes sparse.

▶ **II 3 a** Not presently in use; reserved for future or emergency use; additional, extra. **LME.** ▸**b** Of land, etc.: uncultivated; vacant. *obsolete* exc. as in senses 3, 4. **LME.**
4 In excess of present requirements; superfluous. **M16.** ▸**b** *spec.* Of time: not taken up by one's usual work or duties; free. **L16.**

> **3a** R. G. CUMMING A horseman . . accompanied by an after-rider leading a spare horse. E. SIMON The spare room . . was frequently inhabited by . . distinguished visitors. DOUGLAS CLARK Doris will stay . . The spare bed is made up. **b** *Lancashire Life* Anti-apartheid marchers heading for their meeting place on spare ground. **4** J. WAIN There wasn't the spare cash for him to go on being a non-earner. *Times* With unemployment of over 600,000 there is excessive spare capacity in industry. F. WELDON Irma . . asked her to dinner, to sit opposite a spare man. **b** D. LODGE I teach English literature . . and write novels in my spare time. D. CECIL Whenever he had a spare moment he turned to scribble a letter.

Phrases: **go spare** *colloq.* (*a*) become infuriated or distraught; (*b*) not be required or wanted by others.
Special collocations: **spare part** (*a*) a duplicate part to replace a lost or damaged part of a machine (freq. in *pl.*); (*b*) *colloq.* (*SURGERY*) a visceral organ or other bodily part from a donor, or a prosthetic device, which is to be used to replace a defective organ etc. **spare tyre** (*a*) an extra tyre carried in a motor vehicle for emergencies; (*b*) *colloq.* a roll of fat round the waist.
▶ **B** *adverb.* Sparely. *Scot.* **E19.**
■ **sparely** *adverb* in a sparing manner; frugally; simply; sparsely: **OE. spareness** *noun* **M17.**

spare /spɛː/ *verb.*
[Old English *sparian* = Old Frisian *sparia*, Old Saxon, Old High German *sparōn* (Dutch, German *sparen*), Old Norse *spara*, from Germanic.]
▶ **I 1** *verb trans.* Refrain from killing, injuring or punishing (a person); refrain from destroying or damaging (a thing). **OE.** ▸**b** Forgive or pardon (a sin, etc.). Now *rare.* **LME.** ▸**c** Refrain from ending (a person's life). **L16.**
2 *verb intrans.* Exercise or show mercy or leniency. *arch.* **ME.**
3 *verb trans.* **a** Allow to be free or exempt *from* a task etc.; save or relieve from. **LME.** ▸**b** Refrain from denouncing; deal leniently with. **M16.**

> **1** SHAKES. *Lear* Spare my grey beard, you wagtail? J. M. COETZEE He and Friday, none but they having been spared when their ship went down. B. W. ALDISS Successive owners had spared the . . Victorian fireplace. **2** AV *Prov.* 6:34 He will not spare in the day of vengeance. **3a** J. C. POWYS Johnny was spared the embarrassment of explaining . . by the entrance of the Marquis. S. BELLOW I wanted to be . . spared from knowing what . . my generation is undergoing. R. GORDON To spare my feelings I was allowed to slip away. J. WAIN Now was my chance to spare him . . further anxiety. A. DILLARD He spares his readers a report of his experience. **b** H. WILSON The Prime Minister spared no one, . . and reserved his most cutting quips for his most powerful colleagues.

▶ **II 4** *verb trans.* Refrain from using or (now *rare*) consuming; use with moderation or restraint; (now *rare*) forbear *to do*. Formerly also, save, hoard. **OE.** ▸**b** *verb intrans.* Refrain from doing something; *spec.* use or practise economy, be frugal. *arch.* **ME.** ▸**c** *verb trans.* In *pass.*: be left over or unused. Now *dial.* **L16.**
5 a *verb trans.* Avoid incurring or be grudging of (expense etc.). **ME.** ▸**b** *verb trans.* Avoid, shun. Now *rare.* **LME.**
6 *verb trans.* Afford to give or do without; part or dispense with. **ME.** ▸**b** Reserve or retain *for* a particular use. Now *rare.* **ME.** ▸**c** Give, grant; supply (a person) with something. **L16.** ▸**d** Save or relieve (a person, a person's feelings, etc.) from something. **L17.**

> **4** SWIFT Resolved to spare my provisions as much as I could. R. L. STEVENSON Of my nightmare wanderings . . I spare to tell. P. G. WODEHOUSE Home, James, and don't spare the horses. *Proverb*: Spare the rod and spoil the child. **5a** B. MONTGOMERY No effort was spared in standardising the experimental conditions. M. FORSTER A good party, no expense spared. **6** D. CUSACK Could you spare a moment? I am so sorry to disturb you. G. GREENE They could spare Joseph easily because of his damaged hip. G. BATTISCOMBE Where money for necessities was short, little . . could be spared for amusement. **c** J. CONRAD No one spared him a glance. **d** A. RADCLIFFE Spare me the necessity of mentioning those circumstances.

Phrases: **not spare oneself** exert one's utmost efforts. ***spare a person's blushes***: see BLUSH *noun* 2. **spare for** *arch.* refrain from doing; be economical (usu. in neg. contexts). **to spare** left over; free; additional.
■ **spareable** *adjective* (earlier in UNSPAREABLE) **L17. sparer** *noun* **LME.**

spareless /ˈspɛːlɪs/ *adjective.* **LME.**
[from SPARE *noun*[1] or *verb*: see -LESS.]
†**1** Unlimited. Only in **LME.**
2 Merciless. *arch.* **L16.**

spare-rib /spɛːˈrɪb/ *noun.* **L16.**
[Prob. from Middle Low German *ribbesper*, with transposition of the two elems. and assoc. with SPARE *adjective*.]
A cut of meat, esp. pork, consisting of closely-trimmed ribs. Usu. in *pl.*

spargana *noun* pl. of SPARGANUM.

sparganosis /spɑːgəˈnəʊsɪs/ *noun*. Pl. **-noses** /-ˈnəʊsiːz/ L17.
[Greek *sparganōsis* swathing, used for *spargēsis* swelling, distension, from *spargan* be full to bursting, swell: see -OSIS. In sense 3 from SPARGANUM.]
MEDICINE. †**1** Distension of the breasts with milk. Only in L17.
†**2** Puerperal swelling of the legs. Only in E19.
3 Infection with spargana. E20.

sparganum /ˈspɑːgənəm/ *noun*. Pl. **-na** /-nə/. E20.
[Use as mod. Latin genus name of medieval Latin = swaddling-band from Greek *sparganōsis*: see prec.]
ZOOLOGY & MEDICINE. A migrating plerocercoid larva of tapeworms of the genera *Spirometra* and *Diphyllobothrium*, which are parasites of various vertebrates.

sparge /spɑːdʒ/ *noun*. E19.
[from the verb.]
1 The action of sprinkling or splashing; a splash or dash. E19.
2 BREWING. A spray of hot water sprinkled over the malt. E19.
Comb.: **sparge arm** BREWING a (usu. rotating) sparge pipe used to sprinkle hot water over the malt; **sparge pipe** a horizontal perforated pipe used to sprinkle or spray water etc.; *esp.* one used to flush a urinal.

sparge /spɑːdʒ/ *verb trans.* Also (earlier) †**sparget**. LME.
[In sense 1 from PARGET, prob. infl. by Old French *espargier* sprinkle; in senses 2, 3 prob. from Latin *spargere* sprinkle.]
1 Plaster; roughcast. LME.
2 Splash or sprinkle (water etc.) about. L16.
3 Bespatter, besprinkle. L18.
4 BREWING. Sprinkle (malt) with hot water. E19. ▸**b** Aerate (a liquid) with air. L20.
■ **sparger** *noun* an appliance for sprinkling water etc. (esp. in brewing) or for aerating a liquid with air M19.

spargefication /ˌspɑːdʒɪfɪˈkeɪʃ(ə)n/ *noun*. *rare*. M19.
[from Latin *spargere* sprinkle + -I- + -FICATION.]
The action of sprinkling something.

†**sparget** *verb* var. of SPARGE *verb*.

spargosis /spɑːˈgəʊsɪs/ *noun*. Now *rare*. Pl. **-goses** /-ˈgəʊsiːz/. M19.
[Greek *spargōsis*, var. of *spargēsis*: see SPARGANOSIS.]
MEDICINE. Swelling or distension, *spec.* of the breasts (with milk), or of the skin.

sparhawk /ˈspɑːhɔːk/ *noun*. Now *arch.* & *dial.*
[Old English *spearhafoc* (= Old Norse *sparrhaukr*), from stem of *spearwa* SPARROW + HAWK *noun*[1].]
A sparrowhawk.

spari *noun* pl. of SPARUS.

sparid /ˈsparɪd/ *adjective* & *noun*. L20.
[mod. Latin *Sparidae* (see below), from Latin SPARUS: see -ID[3].]
ZOOLOGY. ▶**A** *adjective*. Of, pertaining to, or designating the percoid family Sparidae of mainly tropical and subtropical deep-bodied marine fishes with long spiny dorsal fins, which includes several species caught for food. L20.
▶**B** *noun*. A fish of the family Sparidae; a sea bream, a porgy. L20.

Sparine /ˈspɛːriːn/ *noun*. M20.
[Origin unkn.: see -INE[5].]
PHARMACOLOGY. (Proprietary name for) promazine hydrochloride.

sparing /ˈspɛːrɪŋ/ *noun*. LME.
[from SPARE *verb* + -ING[1].]
1 The action of SPARE *verb*. LME.
2 In *pl.* & (*rare*) *sing.* That which is saved by economy; savings. LME.

sparing /ˈspɛːrɪŋ/ *adjective* & *adverb*. LME.
[from SPARE *verb* + -ING[2].]
▶**A** *adjective*. **1** Merciful, forbearing. *arch.* LME.
2 Inclined to save; economical. LME. ▸**b** Moderate or avoiding excess in a specified respect. Foll. by *in*, *of*. E17.
3 Reticent, restrained. M16.
4 Small in amount or extent; scanty, limited; slight. E17.
▶†**B** *adverb*. Sparingly. E17–M18.
■ **sparingly** *adverb* LME. **sparingness** *noun* L16.

spark /spɑːk/ *noun*[1].
[Old English *spærca*, *spearca* = Middle & mod. Low German, Middle Dutch *sparke*, of unkn. origin.]
1 A small fiery particle or a tiny burning fragment, thrown off from a burning object, alight in ashes, or produced by friction between two hard objects. Also ***spark of fire***. OE. ▸**b** *fig.* Anything acting as an incitement or inspiration to action, or which excites emotion; a catalyst. ME.
2 A tiny indication or trace *of* a (latent) quality, feeling, etc.; a tiny piece or amount *of* a thing. Freq. in neg. contexts. OE. ▸**b** *spec.* The life-giving principle in humankind or a living creature; a trace or small sign *of* life. LME. ▸**c** A speck or spot of contrasting colour. *rare*. L17. ▸**d** A trace or flash of spirit, courage, wit, etc. M20.
3 A small diamond or (formerly) other precious stone. Orig with specifying word. E16. ▸**b** A glittering fragment *of* a metal, ore, or mineral. *arch.* M16.
4 A bright flash of light; a gleam. M16.
5 ELECTRICITY. A brilliant streak or flash of light accompanied by a crackling sound, produced by an abrupt discharge of electricity between two conductors a short distance apart. Also, the discharge itself, *esp.* that which ignites the mixture in an internal-combustion engine. M18. ▸**b** *ellipt.* = ***spark telegraphy*** below. E20.
6 (A nickname for) a radio operator or an electrician. Usu. in *pl.* (treated as *sing.*). *slang*. E20.

> 🕮 **1** SWIFT The smallest spark of fire . . would kindle the whole. A. BRINK I added more logs . . sending up a spray of red sparks. G. MCCAUGHREAN The two ships grazed together with a flurry of sparks from the iron bolts clashing. **b** S. BOOTH One of their people had been kicked, and that was the spark. *Dateline Magazine* We obviously felt the same for each other—the spark was there . . and we confessed our feelings. **2** R. GODDEN 'Shaken into life'; that is what dancing does to all . . who have any spark of gaiety. A. BRINK I . . introduced them . . . There was an immediate spark of recognition between them. **b** A. PATON There is a spark of life in the eyes, of some hope.

Phrases: **a spark in one's throat** *arch. slang* a raging thirst. **divine spark** a trace of the divine nature in a human being. **get a spark up** *NZ colloq.* fortify one's spirits with alcohol. **sparks will fly** *colloq.* there will be heated words or friction. ***vital spark***: see VITAL *adjective*.
Comb.: **spark-arrester** a device resembling a wire or perforated metal cage used to prevent the escape of sparks from a locomotive funnel or a chimney; **spark ball** ELECTRICITY a sphere forming one side of a spark gap; **spark chamber** PHYSICS a form of spark counter in which many closely spaced electrodes are used to enable the path of an ionizing particle to be determined; **spark coil** ELECTRICITY an induction coil that generates high-voltage pulses from an interrupted low-voltage source, used esp. to energize the sparking plugs in an internal-combustion engine; **spark counter** PHYSICS a detector for charged particles consisting of two charged electrodes separated by a gas that is ionized by the passage of the particle; **spark-erode** *verb trans.* (ENGINEERING) machine (a piece) by spark erosion; **spark erosion (machining)** ENGINEERING a method of machining metal in which a series of electric sparks is used to remove droplets from the piece; **spark gap** ELECTRICITY the space between two conductors across which a transient discharge passes; **spark-gap** *adjective* (ELECTRICITY) of or pertaining to a spark gap; **spark guard** = ***spark-arrester*** above; **spark line** PHYSICS a spectral line corresponding to an atom in a given state of ionization; **spark machining** ENGINEERING = ***spark erosion*** above; **spark-plug** a device fitted to the cylinder head of an internal-combustion engine, used to ignite the explosive mixture by the discharge of a spark between two electrodes at its end; *colloq.* (chiefly *N. Amer.*) a person who or thing which initiates, inspires, or encourages an activity or undertaking; **sparkplug** *verb trans.* (*colloq.*, chiefly *N. Amer.*) initiate, inspire, encourage; **spark spectrum** PHYSICS a spectrum produced by an atom in a given state of ionization, usu. induced under laboratory conditions by an electric spark; **spark telegraphy** an early method of radio-telegraphy in which high-frequency oscillations are set up by the discharge of a capacitor through a spark gap in series with an inductor; **spark transmitter**: that is used for spark telegraphy.
■ **sparklike** *adjective* resembling (that of) a spark E19.

spark /spɑːk/ *noun*[2]. E16.
[Prob. a fig. use of prec.]
1 An elegant, fashionable, or lively young woman or (usu.) man; a gallant, a fop. Now chiefly (freq. *iron.*), a clever or witty person (esp. in ***bright spark***). E16.
2 A lover; a suitor. *arch.* E18.

> 🕮 **1** *Toronto Star* Who was the bright spark who convinced Wilson he should tax one portion of the . . industry?

spark /spɑːk/ *verb*[1]. ME.
[from SPARK *noun*[1].]
▶**I 1** *verb intrans.* Emit a spark or sparks; *spec.* in ELECTRICITY, produce or emit an electric spark or sparks by ionization of the medium separating two conductors at different potentials. ME. ▸**b** ELECTRICITY. Foll. by *over*: be crossed or connected by a spark as a result of a breakdown in insulation. E20.
2 *verb intrans.* Issue or flash like a spark or sparks. Also foll. by *off*, *out*. E16. ▸**b** Foll. by *out*: be extinguished like a spark. Cf. SPARK OUT. *rare*. M19.
3 *verb trans.* **a** Emit or send *out* as sparks. L16. ▸**b** ELECTRICITY. Affect, act, or operate on, by the emission or transmission of electrical sparks. L19.
4 *verb trans. fig.* Stir into activity, stimulate, inspire; provide the immediate instigation for (a process etc.). Freq. foll. by *off*. E20.

> 🕮 **2** S. R. CROCKETT The anger fair sparked . . from her dark, indignant eyes. A. TAYLOR A love of sorts . . sparked between them. **4** JULIETTE HUXLEY A word could spark off a brilliant discussion. H. S. STREAN My academic success sparked envy.

▶**II 5** *verb trans.* Spatter (dirt etc.); spatter with dirt etc. *Scot.* & *north.* M17.

Comb.: **sparking coil** = ***spark coil*** s.v. SPARK *noun*[1]; **sparking plug** = ***spark-plug*** s.v. SPARK *noun*[1]; **sparkover** = ***flash-over*** s.v. FLASH *verb*.

spark /spɑːk/ *verb*[2]. Now *US*. L17.
[from SPARK *noun*[2].]
†**1** *verb trans.* with *it*. Make a display, show off. L17–E18.
2 *verb intrans.* & *trans.* (with *it*). ▸**a** Engage in courtship. L18. ▸**b** *verb trans.* Court. L19.

> 🕮 **2b** B. GRAEME Erskine had been sparking Olive for well over a year.

sparker /ˈspɑːkə/ *noun*. LME.
[from SPARK *noun*[1] or *verb*[1] + -ER[1].]
†**1** A spark. Only in LME.
2 A spark-arrester. *rare*. M19.
3 A miniature firework. *rare*. E20.
4 A powerful form of sonar apparatus used to investigate solid structures underlying sediment on the seabed. M20.

sparkish /ˈspɑːkɪʃ/ *adjective*. M17.
[from SPARK *noun*[2] + -ISH[1].]
1 Having the character or manners of a spark or gallant; lively; witty. M17.
2 Characteristic of or appropriate to a spark; smart, elegant. M17.
■ **sparkishly** *adverb* L17. **sparkishness** *noun* L17.

sparkle /ˈspɑːk(ə)l/ *noun*. ME.
[from SPARK *noun*[1] + -LE[1].]
1 A small spark or burning fragment. ME. ▸**b** *fig.* = SPARK *noun*[1] 1b. *arch.* LME.
2 = SPARK *noun*[1] 2. *arch.* ME.
†**3** A small ruby or diamond. *rare*. L15–E18.
4 A glittering or flashing point of light. L15. ▸**b** *fig.* A flashing glance. L16.
5 A tiny piece or spot *of* something. Now chiefly, a glittering particle. M16.
6 Glittering or flashing appearance or quality. L16. ▸**b** *fig.* Vivacity, liveliness of spirit. E17.
7 Effervescence. M19.

> 🕮 **1** SIR W. SCOTT The sparkles which flew from the horses' hoofs. **4** J. RUSKIN The sparkles streaming from their . . wings like the glitter of many suns. W. LEWIS The excellent cognac . . put a . . sparkle in her eye. **6** I. MURDOCH The fountain . . whose sparkle they had seen from across the lake. **b** L. BLUE The conversation lacked sparkle.

Comb.: **sparkleberry** the farkleberry, *Vaccinium arboreum*, a large shrub of the southern US.

sparkle /ˈspɑːk(ə)l/ *verb*[1]. ME.
[from SPARK *noun*[1] or *verb*[1] + -LE[3].]
1 *verb intrans.* Issue or fly *out* in or as sparks of fire; emit or send out sparks of fire. *arch.* ME. ▸**b** *verb trans.* Emit (fire etc.) as sparks. Now *rare* or *obsolete*. L16.
2 *verb intrans.* Reflect or emit sparkles or numerous separate points of light; glitter, glisten. ME. ▸**b** *verb trans.* Cause to glitter or glisten. (Not always clearly distinguishable from SPARKLE *verb*[2] 2.) *arch.* M16. ▸**c** *verb intrans.* Move in a glittering manner. E19.
3 *verb intrans.* Of wine etc.: effervesce. Chiefly as SPARKLING *adjective*. LME.
4 *verb intrans.* (Of the eyes) flash or shine with a (specified) feeling or quality; (of a feeling or quality) be indicated by a shine or brightness *in* the eyes. L16. ▸**b** *verb trans.* Of the eyes: indicate (a feeling) by shine or brightness. E17.
5 Be vivacious, lively or witty; scintillate. L17.

> 🕮 **1** TENNYSON When some heat of difference sparkled out. **2** J. OXENHAM They saw Guernsey . . sparkling in the sun. E. MITTELHOLZER On her bosom sparkled a necklace of fake emeralds. **c** C. LAMB To trace your . . waters sparkling through . . Hertfordshire. **4** DICKENS Intense abhorrence sparkling in her eyes. J. CONRAD Her little black eyes sparkled venomously. G. GREENE The young man's . . eyes sparkled with his interest. **b** C. IRVINE Our eyes sparkled gladness. **5** F. KAPLAN At parties he sparkled with all the wit . . he could muster.

■ **sparkling** *noun* (*a*) the action of the verb; an instance of this; (*b*) a spark: LME. **sparkling** *adjective* (*a*) that sparkles; bright, glittering; scintillating; vivacious; (*b*) (of wine) effervescent (opp. ***still***); (*c*) *transf.* very clean, spotless: ME. **sparklingly** *adverb* M17.

sparkle /ˈspɑːk(ə)l/ *verb*[2]. *obsolete* exc. *dial.* LME.
[Alt. of SPARPLE.]
1 *verb trans.* & *intrans.* (Cause to) scatter or disperse. LME.
2 *verb trans.* Sprinkle, spatter, or daub *with* something; spatter (liquid etc.) *over*. LME.

sparkled /ˈspɑːk(ə)ld/ *ppl adjective*. L15.
[from SPARKLE *noun* or *verb*[1]: see -ED[2], -ED[1].]
1 Speckled, spotted. Now *dial.* L15.
2 Sparkling, shining. *rare*. M16.

sparkler /ˈspɑːklə/ *noun*. E18.
[from SPARKLE *verb*[1] + -ER[1].]
1 A person (esp. a young woman) who sparkles or is vivacious or witty. E18.
2 A bright or sparkling eye. Usu. in *pl.* *arch. slang*. M18.
3 A sparkling jewel, *esp.* a diamond. *colloq.* E19.

4 A sparkling wine. *colloq.* **M19.**
5 A sparkling firework designed to be hand-held. **L19.**

sparkless /ˈspɑːklɪs/ *adjective.* **E19.**
[from SPARK *noun*[1] + -LESS.]
Without a spark or sparks; emitting no sparks; (of an electrical connection) that is made, broken, or changed without sparking.
■ **sparklessly** *adverb* **L19.**

sparklet /ˈspɑːklɪt/ *noun.* **L17.**
[from SPARK *noun*[1] + -LET.]
1 A small spark or sparkle. **L17.**
2 (Also **S-**.) A device used to carbonate the water in a siphon (freq. *attrib.*); the carbonated water so produced. **L19.**
¶ Sparklets is a proprietary name.

sparkly /ˈspɑːkli/ *adjective.* **L15.**
[from SPARKLE *noun* or *verb*[1] + -Y[1].]
Sparkling; that sparkles.
¶ Rare before 20.

spark out /spɑːk ˈaʊt/ *pred. adjectival phr.* **L19.**
[Perh. from SPARK *noun*[1] + OUT *adverb*.]
1 Completely extinguished or eliminated. Cf. SPARK *verb*[1] 2b. *dial.* **L19.**
2 Completely unconscious. *slang.* **M20.**

sparky /ˈspɑːki/ *adjective.* **E17.**
[from SPARK *noun*[1] or *verb*[1] + -Y[1].]
1 †**a** Of a fabric: spotted with gold. Only in **E17.** ▸**b** Of a cow: mottled. *dial.* **L18.**
2 Emitting sparks (*lit.* & *fig.*); now *esp.* vivacious, spirited, lively. *colloq.* **E19.**

> 📖 **2** H. JACOBSON She had recovered from . . despondency and was looking sparky. *Listener* Reassuring in intent, but sparky in style.

■ **sparkiness** *noun* (*rare*) †(*a*) effervescence; (*b*) the quality of being sparky: **M17.**

sparling /ˈspɑːlɪŋ/ *noun.* Now chiefly *Scot.* & *north.* **ME.**
[Aphet. from Old French *esperlinge* (mod. *éperlan*), of Germanic origin (cf. Middle Low German, Middle Dutch *spirlinc*, German *Spierling*). Cf. SPIRLING.]
The smelt, *Osmerus eperlanus*. Formerly also, any of various other fishes resembling small herring.

sparmannia /spɑːˈmanɪə/ *noun.* **E19.**
[mod. Latin (see below), from Andres *Sparmann* (1748–1820), Swedish traveller + -IA[1].]
Any of several southern African shrubs constituting the genus *Sparmannia*, of the linden family, with hairy heart-shaped leaves and clusters of white flowers; *esp.* African hemp, *S. africana*, grown as a house-plant.

sparoid /ˈsparɔɪd, ˈspeɪrɔɪd/ *adjective* & *noun.* **M19.**
[from mod. Latin *Sparoides* former taxonomic name, from SPARUS: see -OID.]
▶ **A** *adjective.* **1** = SPARID *adjective.* **M19.**
2 Of a fish-scale: thin and broad, with a spiny surface. **M19.**
▶ **B** *noun.* = SPARID *noun.* **M19.**

†**sparple** *verb trans.* & *intrans.* **ME–M19.**
[Old French *esparpeillier* (mod. *éparpiller*).]
= SPARKLE *verb*[2] 1.

sparred /spɑːd/ *adjective.* **E19.**
[from SPAR *noun*[1] or *verb*[3]: see -ED[2], -ED[1].]
Having a spar or spars; made or fitted with spars.

sparrer /ˈspɑːrə/ *noun*[1]. *colloq.* **E19.**
[from SPAR *verb*[1] + -ER[1].]
A person who spars or boxes.

sparrer /ˈsparə/ *noun*[2]. *dial.* **L19.**
[Repr. a pronunc.]
A sparrow.

sparrow /ˈsparəʊ/ *noun.*
[Old English *spearwa* = Old High German *sparo*, Old Norse *spǫrr*, Gothic *sparwa*, from Germanic.]
1 a Any of various small Old World finchlike birds of the genus *Passer* and related genera (family Ploceidae); *esp.* the house sparrow. **OE.** ▸**b** With specifying word: any of several other small sparrow-like birds of the Old World which are unrelated to the true sparrows. **M17.** ▸**c** Any of various small New World birds of the family Emberizidae, resembling sparrows or buntings. **L18.**
2 A chirpy quick-witted person. Freq. in ***cockney sparrow***. **M19.**
1a *rock sparrow*, *tree sparrow*, etc. **b** *hedge sparrow*, *java sparrow*, *reed-sparrow*, etc. **c** *fox sparrow*, *savannah sparrow*, *song sparrow*, etc.
Comb.: **sparrow-brain** *colloq.* (a person of) limited intelligence or perception; **sparrow-fart**, **sparrow's-fart** *dial.* & *slang* daybreak, very early morning; **sparrow owl** = PYGMY *owl*; ***sparrow's-fart***: see *sparrow-fart* above; **sparrow-tail** a long narrow coat-tail.
■ **sparrow-like** *adjective* resembling (that of) a sparrow **E17.** **sparrowy** *adjective* (*a*) characteristic of or resembling a sparrow; (*b*) having many sparrows: **L19.**

sparrow-bill /ˈsparəʊbɪl/ *noun.* **E17.**
[from prec. + BILL *noun*[2].]
= SPARABLE.

sparrow-grass /ˈsparəʊɡrɑːs/ *noun.* Now *dial.* & *colloq.* Also **sparrowgrass.** **M17.**
[Alt. of SPARAGUS by assim. to *sparrow* and *grass*.]
Asparagus.

sparrowhawk /ˈsparəʊhɔːk/ *noun.* Also **sparrow hawk**, **sparrow-hawk.** **LME.**
[from SPARROW + HAWK *noun*[1], repl. SPARHAWK.]
1 Any of various small Old World hawks of the genus *Accipiter* which prey on small birds etc.; *esp.* (more fully ***northern sparrowhawk***, ***European sparrowhawk***) *A. nisus*, which occurs throughout much of Eurasia. **LME.** ▸**b** Any of several other small birds of prey; *esp.* (more fully ***American sparrowhawk***) *Falco sparverius*, also called ***American kestrel***. **L18.**
2 A small anvil used in silversmithing. **M19.**

sparry /ˈspɑːri/ *adjective.* **L17.**
[from SPAR *noun*[3] + -Y[1].]
1 Consisting of, rich in, or containing spar; of the nature of spar. **L17.**
2 Of lustre etc.: resembling that of spar. **L18.**
1 sparry iron (ore) = SIDERITE 3(a).

sparse /spɑːs/ *adjective* & *adverb.* **E18.**
[Latin *sparsus* pa. pple of *spargere* scatter.]
▶ **A** *adjective.* †**1** Of writing: widely spaced or spread out. *Scot.* **E18–E19.**
2 Separated or characterized by wide intervals or spaces; thinly dispersed, distributed, or scattered; not dense. Also, scanty, meagre. **M18.**

> 📖 **2** M. HOWITT Nearly the whole of our way led through sparse olive-woods. A. CARTER A sparse breakfast had been set out . . just a packet of cornflakes, a can of dried milk. K. ISHIGURO At other times of the day the clientele became sparse. N. LOWNDES His pink scalp glistening amidst the sparse hair.

▶ **B** *adverb.* Sparsely. Chiefly in comb. *poet.* **E18.**
■ **sparsely** *adverb* **L18.** **sparseness** *noun* **M19.** **sparsity** *noun* the state or condition of being sparse **M19.**

†**sparse** *verb.* See also SPARSED. **M16–E17.**
[Latin *spars-* pa. ppl stem of *spargere* scatter.]
1 *verb trans.* Disperse, scatter; distribute at wide intervals; spread or disseminate (a rumour etc.). **M16–M17.**
2 *verb intrans.* Foll. by *abroad*: distribute gifts etc. widely. **M16–E17.**

sparsed /spɑːst/ *ppl adjective.* Now *rare* or *obsolete.* **L16.**
[from prec. + -ED[1].]
Dispersed, scattered, or spread about, esp. thinly.
■ **sparsedly** *adverb* **L16.**

sparsim /ˈspɑːsɪm/ *adverb.* Chiefly *literary.* **L16.**
[Latin, formed as SPARSE *verb*.]
Here and there; sparsely.

spar-stone /ˈspɑːstəʊn/ *noun.* Long *obsolete* exc. *dial.*
[Old English *spærstān*, from base recorded also in Old English *spæren* of plaster or gypsum: see STONE *noun* & cf. SPAR *noun*[3]. In sense 2 directly from SPAR *noun*[3].]
†**1** Gypsum; plaster. **OE–L15.**
2 MINERALOGY. = SPAR *noun*[3] 1. **L17.**

spart /spɑːt/ *noun.* Also (*rare*) in Latin form **spartum** /ˈspɑːtəm/. **E17.**
[Latin *spartum* or Spanish ESPARTO.]
1 Esparto grass, *Stipa tenacissma*. **E17.**
†**2** Spanish broom, *Spartium junceum*. **E17–E18.**

Spartacist /ˈspɑːtəsɪst, -kɪst/ *noun* & *adjective.* **E20.**
[German *Spartakist*, from *Spartacus* pen-name of one of the founders of the party (see below), after the leader of the slave revolt against Rome 73–71 BC.]
Hist. (Designating) a member of a German radical socialist party formed in 1916 and dedicated to ending the war of 1914–18 through revolution.
■ **Spartacism** *noun* the policy and principles of the Spartacists **E20.**

spartakiad /spɑːˈtakɪad/ *noun.* **E20.**
[Russian *spartakiada*, from *Spartacus*: see prec. Cf. OLYMPIAD.]
A sporting competition involving a large number of participants and a wide range of events.

Spartan /ˈspɑːt(ə)n/ *noun* & *adjective.* **LME.**
[Latin *Spartanus*, from *Sparta* (Greek *Sparta*, *-tē*), capital of the ancient Doric State of Laconia: see -AN.]
▶ **A** *noun.* **1** A native or inhabitant of Sparta. **LME.**
2 A crisp red-skinned eating apple of a variety originally bred in Canada to withstand cold winters. **M20.**
▶ **B** *adjective.* **1** Of or pertaining to Sparta or its inhabitants. **L16.**
2 (Also **s-**.) Characteristic of a Spartan; possessing the qualities of courage, endurance, frugality, etc., associated with the inhabitants of Sparta; *esp.* austere, strictly disciplined. **M17.**

> 📖 **2** G. MARKSTEIN Ulbricht . . prided himself on his Spartan fitness. I. D. YALOM Saul's bedroom was Spartan—bare stucco walls and wooden floors. HELEN FIELDING Tomorrow new Spartan health and beauty regime will begin.

■ **Spartanism** *noun* discipline, principles, or methods resembling those of Sparta **L19.** **Spartanize** *verb trans.* (*rare*) make Spartan in character **M19.** **Spartanly** *adverb* **L19.**

sparteine /ˈspɑːtɪʌɪn/ *noun.* Also †**-ein.** **M19.**
[Irreg. from mod. Latin *Spartium* genus name from Latin *spartum* broom from Greek *sparton* esparto, perh. after *coneine* CONIINE: see -INE[5].]
An oily alkaloid obtained from common broom and lupin seeds, formerly used to treat heart conditions.

sparth /spɑːθ/ *noun.* *obsolete* exc. *Hist.* **ME.**
[Old Norse *sparða*.]
1 A long-handled battleaxe, used esp. by the Irish until the 16th cent. **ME.**
2 A soldier armed with such an axe. **E16.**

Spartiate /ˈspɑːʃɪət/ *noun.* *rare.* **LME.**
[Latin *Spartiates* from Greek *Spartiatēs*, from *Spartē* Sparta.]
A Spartan.

spartina /spɑːˈtʌɪnə, -ˈtiːnə/ *noun.* **M19.**
[mod. Latin (see below), from Greek *spartinē* rope.]
Any of several grasses of coastal mud-flats constituting the genus *Spartina*; also called ***cord-grass***.

spartle *verb* see SPROTTLE.

sparus /ˈspɛːrəs/ *noun.* Pl. **spari** /ˈspɛːrʌɪ/. **M17.**
[Latin from Greek *sparos* a sea bream.]
A sea bream, *esp.* the gilt-head, *Sparus aurata*. Now only as mod. Latin genus name.

spasm /ˈspaz(ə)m/ *noun.* **LME.**
[Old & mod. French *spasme* or Latin *spasmus*, *spasma* from Greek *spasmos*, *spasma*, from *span* draw, pull.]
1 Sudden and violent involuntary muscular contraction, esp. of a convulsive or painful nature. **LME.**
2 An instance of this; a convulsive twitch. **L15.**
3 *fig.* Any sudden violent or convulsive movement; a sudden brief burst of activity or emotion; a convulsion. **E19.**

> 📖 **2** I. ASIMOV Her hands became fists . . held . . in a tight spasm. **3** J. GALSWORTHY Moved by an uncontrollable spasm of curiosity. *Globe & Mail (Toronto)* The latest spasm of violence in the Soviet Caucasus.

Comb.: **spasm band** *US* (now *Hist.*): playing jazz on home-made musical instruments; **spasm music** *US* (now *Hist.*): played by spasm bands; **spasm war**: in which the combatants would use their complete thermonuclear capabilities.
■ **spasmed** *adjective* affected with or accompanied by spasms **L18.** **spasmic** *adjective* spasmodic; convulsive: **E18.** **spasmous** *adjective* (*rare*) characterized by spasms **M16.** **spasmy** *adjective* (*rare*) affected by spasms **M19.**

spasm /ˈspaz(ə)m/ *verb.* **E20.**
[from the noun.]
1 *verb intrans.* Twitch convulsively; suffer a spasm. **E20.**
2 *verb trans.* Cause to move convulsively. *rare.* **M20.**

†**spasma** *noun.* **M16–E18.**
[Latin, Greek: see SPASM *noun*.]
= SPASM *noun* 1, 2.

spasmatic /spazˈmatɪk/ *adjective.* Now *rare* or *obsolete.* **E17.**
[French †*spasmatique* or Greek *spasmat-* stem of *spasma* SPASM *noun*: see -ATIC.]
1 Spasmodic. **E17.**
2 Suffering from spasms. **E17.**
■ Also **spasmatical** *adjective* **M17.**

spasmi *noun* pl. of SPASMUS.

spasmodic /spazˈmɒdɪk/ *adjective* & *noun.* **L17.**
[mod. Latin *spasmodicus*, from Greek *spasmōdēs*, from *spasma* SPASM *noun*: see -ODE[1], -IC.]
▶ **A** *adjective.* **1** Of the nature of a spasm; characterized by spasms or convulsive twitches; marked by jerkiness or suddenness of muscular movement. **L17.**
2 Employed against spasms; antispasmodic. *rare.* **E18.**
3 Occurring or proceeding in brief, irregular bursts; intermittent; unsustained. **M19.**
4 Agitated, given to outbursts of excitement; highly strung; characterized by a disjointed style of expression. **M19.**

> 📖 **1** S. CISNEROS The dog was eating something, jaws working in spasmodic gulps. **3** S. NAIPAUL The news . . filtered through in a spasmodic fashion. P. ANGADI Mim's acting career was only spasmodic.

▶ **B** *noun.* *rare.*
†**1** An antispasmodic medicine. Only in **E18.**
2 In *pl.* Spasmodic utterances. **M19.**
■ **spasmodical** *adjective* = SPASMODIC *adjective* **M18.** **spasmodically** *adverb* (*a*) MEDICINE by or with a spasm or spasms; (*b*) in a jerky, convulsive, or sudden violent manner; (*c*) irregularly, intermittently: **E18.** **spasmodicalness** *noun* (*rare*) the quality or state of being spasmodic **L19.** ˈ**spasmodism** *noun* (*rare*) spasmodic feeling or emotion **L19.** ˈ**spasmodist** *noun* a person whose work is of a spasmodic character or who affects a disjointed style **M19.**

spasmogenic /spazmə(ʊ)ˈdʒɛnɪk/ *adjective.* **L19.**
[from SPASM *noun* + -O- + -GENIC.]
†**1** MEDICINE. Having the potential to cause a hysterical fit. *rare.* Only in **L19.**
2 PHARMACOLOGY. Of a drug or other substance: promoting the contraction of smooth muscle. **E20.**
■ ˈ**spasmogen** *noun* (PHARMACOLOGY) a spasmogenic drug **M20.**

spasmolytic /spazmə'lɪtɪk/ *adjective & noun.* M20.
[from SPASM *noun* + -O- + -LYTIC.]
PHARMACOLOGY. ▶**A** *adjective.* That relieves spasm of smooth muscle. M20.
▶**B** *noun.* A spasmolytic drug. M20.
■ **spas'molysis** *noun* the action of a spasmolytic drug M20.

spasmoneme /'spazmə(ʊ)niːm/ *noun.* E20.
[from SPASM *noun* + -O- + Greek *nema* thread.]
ZOOLOGY. Each of the three strands (myonemes) in the stalk of a vorticellid protozoan whose sudden contraction causes the stalk to coil tightly, withdrawing the animal from danger.

spasmophilia /spazmə(ʊ)'fɪlɪə/ *noun.* M19.
[from SPASM *noun* + -O- + -PHILIA.]
MEDICINE. Undue tendency of the muscles to contract, *esp.* as caused by a deficiency of ionic calcium in the blood of patients with tetany.
■ **'spasmophile** *noun* (*rare*) a person affected with spasmophilia M20. **spasmophilic** *adjective* of, pertaining to, or affected with spasmophilia E20.

†**spasmus** *noun.* Pl. **spasmi.** LME–E18.
[Latin from Greek *spasmos* SPASM *noun.*]
= SPASM *noun* 1, 2.

spastic /'spastɪk/ *adjective & noun.* M18.
[Latin *spasticus* from Greek *spastikos*, from *span* draw, pull: see -IC.]
▶**A** *adjective.* **1** MEDICINE. Of the nature of a spasm or sudden involuntary contraction; characterized or affected by such symptoms or movements. M18.
2 Affected with spastic paralysis. Now considered *offensive.* E20.
3 Uncoordinated, incompetent; weak, feeble; stupid. *slang. offensive.* L20.
Special collocations: **spastic paralysis** a condition in which some muscles undergo tonic spasm and resist passive displacement, esp. due to a disorder of the motor neurones, so that voluntary movement of the part affected is difficult and poorly coordinated.
▶**B** *noun.* **1** A person with spastic paralysis, esp. associated with cerebral palsy. Now considered *offensive.* L19.
2 A person who is uncoordinated, incompetent, or stupid; a fool. *slang. offensive.* L20.
■ **spastically** *adverb* M19. **spas'ticity** *noun* the condition or quality of being spastic E19.

spat /spat/ *noun*¹. M17.
[Anglo-Norman, of unkn. origin.]
1 *sing.* & in *pl.* The spawn of an oyster or other shellfish. M17.
†**2** The eggs of bees. Only in M17.
Comb.: **spatfall** the settling of the planktonic larvae of bivalves at the sites where they will develop as adults; the extent of such settling.

spat /spat/ *noun*². *rare.* M17.
[App. abbreviation of SPATULA.]
†**1** A spatula for spreading ointment. Only in M17.
2 A flat implement used in ball-games. M19.

†**spat** *noun*³. *rare.* E–M18.
[German *Spat* SPATH *noun.*]
MINERALOGY. = SPAR *noun*³.

spat /spat/ *noun*⁴. Chiefly *dial.* & *colloq.* E19.
[Prob. imit.: cf. SPAT *verb*².]
1 A dispute; a petty quarrel, a tiff. Orig. *US.* E19.
2 A smart blow, a smack, a slap. E19.
3 A sharp, smacking sound. L19.
📖 **1** *Times* He was mobilizing support for Israel in its latest spat with the U.S. *Arizona Daily Star* We spotted Tony and his wife embroiled in a bitter spat.

spat /spat/ *noun*⁵. E19.
[Abbreviation of SPATTERDASH.]
1 A short gaiter worn over the instep and reaching only a little way above the ankle. Usu. in *pl.* E19.
2 AERONAUTICS. A streamlined covering for the upper part of the wheel of an aircraft, usu. of one with fixed landing gear. M20.
■ **spatted** *adjective* (**a**) possessing or wearing spats or short gaiters; (**b**) (of an aircraft or its undercarriage) equipped with spats: L19. **spa'ttee** *noun* (*Hist.*) an outer stocking or legging worn by women for protection against wet and cold E20.

spat /spat/ *noun*⁶. L19.
[App. from Dutch *spat* in same sense.]
A small splash *of* something.

spat /spat/ *verb*¹. Infl. **-tt-**. M17.
[from SPAT *noun*¹.]
1 *verb intrans. & trans.* Of an oyster: spawn. M17.
†**2** *verb intrans.* Of bees: produce young. Only in M17.

spat /spat/ *verb*² & *adverb.* E19.
[Prob. imit.: cf. SPAT *noun*⁴.]
▶**A** *verb.* Infl. **-tt-**.
1 *verb intrans.* Speak *up* angrily; engage in a dispute; quarrel pettily (*with*). *US colloq.* E19.
2 *verb trans.* Clap (one's hands), stamp (one's feet); slap, smack. *colloq.* M19. ▶**b** Beat *down* with a spade etc. *colloq.* M19.
3 *verb intrans.* Make a slapping or smacking sound or action; spatter. M19.
📖 **3** C. THUBRON Frogs . . plopped and spatted among reed-filled pools.
▶**B** *adverb.* With a slapping or smacking sound or action. L19.

spat *verb*³ *pa. t. & pple*: see SPIT *verb*¹.

spatangoid /spa'taŋgɔɪd/ *noun & adjective.* M19.
[from mod. Latin *Spatangoides* (now *Spatangoida*: see below), from *Spatangus* genus name, from late Latin *spatangius*, Greek *spataggēs* a kind of sea urchin: see -OID.]
ZOOLOGY. ▶**A** *noun.* An irregular heart-shaped sea urchin of the order Spatangoida; a heart-urchin. M19.
▶**B** *adjective.* Of, pertaining to, or characteristic of the heart-urchins or a heart-urchin. M19.

spatchcock /'spatʃkɒk/ *noun & verb.* Orig. *Anglo-Irish.* L18.
[Perh. rel. to DISPATCH *noun* + COCK *noun*¹, but cf. SPITCHCOCK.]
▶**A** *noun.* A chicken or esp. a game-bird split open and grilled after a simple and speedy method of preparation. L18.
▶**B** *verb trans.* **1** Cook as or in the manner of a spatchcock. Chiefly as ***spatchcocked*** *ppl adjective.* M19.
2 Insert, interpolate, or sandwich (an extra piece of writing etc.) *in* or *into.* E20. ▶**b** Add to or modify by interpolation. E20.
📖 **1** J. MAY Turning a long spit crowded with spatchcocked birds. **2** *London Review of Books* Foulkes . . was able to spatchcock into the debate some . . sentences of disquiet. **b** *Listener* It read like a hurried and spatchcocked solution.

spate /speɪt/ *noun & verb.* Orig. *Scot. & north.* LME.
[Origin unkn.]
▶**A** *noun.* **1** A flood, an inundation; *esp.* a sudden flood in a river or stream caused by heavy rains or melting snow. LME. ▶**b** A sudden heavy downpour or storm *of* rain. Chiefly *Scot.* E18.
2 Flooding, inundation of water; copious rain. E16. ▶**b** Turbulent water characteristic of a river in flood. *rare.* L19.
3 A sudden or violent outburst *of* some quality, feeling, etc.; a large series or sudden excessive amount *of* words, events, etc. E17.
📖 **1** H. BELLOC A . . spate roaring a furlong broad after the rains. **3** *Japan Times* The original plan had drawn a spate of criticism. *Daily Telegraph* After a spate of development in the 1980s, the county council wants to restrict it.
Phrases: **in spate** (of a river) in flood.
▶**B** *verb. Scot.*
1 *verb trans.* Flood, swell. E19.
2 *verb intrans.* Rain heavily. M19.

spath /spaθ/ *noun.* Now *rare.* M18.
[German *Spat(h).*]
= SPAR *noun*³.

spatha /'speɪθə/ *noun.* Pl. **-thae** /-θiː/. M18.
[Latin: see SPATHE.]
1 BOTANY. A spathe. Now *rare.* M18.
2 A flat blade-shaped instrument; *esp.* (*Hist.*) a broadsword with a blunt point. L19.

spathaceous /spə'θeɪʃəs/ *adjective.* M18.
[mod. Latin *spathaceus*, from SPATHA: see -ACEOUS.]
BOTANY. Provided with or enclosed by a spathe; of the nature of or resembling a spathe.

spathae *noun* pl. of SPATHA.

spathe /speɪð/ *noun.* L18.
[Latin *spatha* from Greek *spathē*: see SPADE *noun*¹.]
BOTANY. A large sheathing bract enclosing the inflorescence of certain plants, esp. the spadix of arums and palms.

spathic /'spaθɪk/ *adjective.* L18.
[from SPATH *noun* + -IC.]
MINERALOGY. Of the nature of or resembling spath or spar; consisting of or containing much spar; foliated or lamellar in structure or texture; spathose, sparry.

spathodea /speɪ'θəʊdɪə, spə-/ *noun.* L19.
[mod. Latin *Spathodea* (see below), from (the same root as) Latin SPATHA + Greek *-ōdēs* (cf. -ODE¹), with ref. to the shape of the calyx.]
An African tree, *Spathodea campanulata* (family Bignoniaceae), with large orange-red or scarlet cup-shaped flowers, widely planted for ornament in the tropics. Also called ***African tulip tree***.

spathose /spa'θəʊs/ *adjective.* L18.
[from SPATH *noun* + -OSE¹.]
= SPATHIC.
spathose iron (ore) siderite (ferrous carbonate).

spathula /'spaθjʊlə/ *noun. rare.* E18.
[Latin, var. of SPATULA.]
A spatula.

spathulate /'spaθjʊlət/ *adjective.* E19.
[from prec. + -ATE².]
BOTANY & ZOOLOGY. Broad at the apex and tapered to the base; spatulate.
■ Also **spathulated** *adjective* (*rare*) E19.

spatial /'speɪʃ(ə)l/ *adjective.* Also **spacial.** M19.
[from Latin *spatium* SPACE *noun* + -AL¹.]
1 Having extension in space; occupying space; consisting of or characterized by space. M19.
2 Of or relating to space; subject to or governed by the conditions of space, freq. as opp. to those of time. M19.
3 Happening in or caused by space. M19.
4 Of a faculty or sense: apprehending or perceiving space or extension. L19.
📖 **2** H. MOORE They do not . . comprehend form in its full spatial existence. **2** N. S. MOMADAY This valley alone could reflect the great spatial majesty of the sky. A. LIVINGSTONE She saw her life as spatial, not temporal.
Special collocations & comb.: **spatial ability** PSYCHOLOGY the (measured) aptitude for perceiving and comprehending relations involving space or extension. **spatial-temporal** *adjective* = SPATIO-TEMPORAL.
■ **spati'ality** *noun* spatial character, quality, or property L19. **spatially** *adverb* with reference to space; by means of space: M19.

spatialise *verb* var. of SPATIALIZE.

spatialism /'speɪʃ(ə)lɪz(ə)m/ *noun.* M20.
[In sense 1 from prec. + -ISM; in sense 2 from French *spatialisme.*]
1 PHILOSOPHY. The theory that matter has only spatial, temporal, and causal properties. *rare.* M20.
2 A mid-20th-cent. movement in experimental French poetry. M20.
■ **spatialist** *noun & adjective* (**a**) *noun* an adherent or practitioner of spatialism; (**b**) *adjective* of or pertaining to spatialism or spatialists: M20.

spatialize /'speɪʃ(ə)lʌɪz/ *verb trans.* Also **-ise.** E20.
[from SPATIAL + -IZE.]
Make spatial; consider as spatial; apply spatial qualities or relations to.
■ **spatiali'zation** *noun* L19.

spatiate /'speɪʃɪeɪt/ *verb intrans.* Now *rare.* E17.
[Latin *spatiat-* pa. ppl stem of *spatiari*, from *spatium* SPACE *noun*: see -ATE³.]
Walk about; stroll, wander, roam.

spatiography /speɪʃɪ'ɒgrəfi/ *noun. rare.* M20.
[from *spatio-* (after *spatio-temporal*) + -OGRAPHY.]
The scientific description of the features of (outer) space; the topography of space.

spatio-temporal /ˌspeɪʃɪəʊ'temp(ə)r(ə)l/ *adjective.* E20.
[from *spatio-* combining form of Latin *spatium* SPACE *noun* + TEMPORAL *adjective*¹.]
Belonging to both space and time or to space–time.
■ **spatio-tempo'rality** *noun* E20. **spatio-temporali'zation** *noun* the fact of making or applying spatio-temporal qualities or relations M20. **spatio-temporalize** *verb trans.* apply spatio-temporal qualities or relations to M20. **spatio-temporally** *adverb* in space and time, with reference to both space and time E20.

Spätlese /'ʃpɛtleːzə/ *noun.* Pl. ***-sen*** /-zən/, ***-ses.*** M20.
[German, from *spät* late + *Lese* picking, vintage.]
A white wine made (esp. in Germany) from grapes picked later than the general harvest.

spatter /'spatə/ *noun.* L18.
[from the verb.]
1 A slight splash, a sprinkle. Also, a pattering sound. L18.
2 GEOLOGY. Magmatic material emitted as small fluid fragments by a volcanic vent or fissure; a fragment of this. M20.
📖 **1** F. POHL The screen lit up . . with a sprinkling of black dots, like ink spatters on a blotter. N. LOWNDES A spatter of rain dashed at the window.
Comb.: **spatterdock** *N. Amer.* any of several yellow water lilies, esp. *Nuphar advena*; **spatter rampart** GEOLOGY a wall or ridge formed of spatter along the edge of a volcanic fissure.

spatter /'spatə/ *verb.* M16.
[Frequentative of imit. base repr. also by Low German, Dutch *spatten* burst, spout, Western Flemish *spatteren*, West Frisian *spatterje*: see -ER⁵.]
▶**I** *verb intrans.* **1** Spit drops of saliva or particles of food etc. from the mouth; splutter while speaking. Now *rare.* M16.
2 a Fly or spurt in drops or particles; throw off or scatter drops or small fragments. E17. ▶**b** Fall or strike in heavy drops or with a sound suggestive of these. Usu. foll. by preposition. L17.
3 Walk through or tread in a splashy substance. E19.
📖 **2a** W. BOYD He . . drove off with gravel spattering from his rear wheels. J. WILCOX Margarine spattered out of the frying pan. **b** P. BARKER The rain spattered against the glass.
▶**II** *verb trans.* **4** Scatter or send flying in drops or small fragments; sprinkle (drops, small fragments, etc.). (Foll. by *on*, *out*, etc.) L16.
5 Splash or stain with spots of liquid etc.; *fig.* assail with abuse or detraction, vilify, defame. Freq. foll. by *with.* M17.
6 Cover (a surface) with a sprinkling of something; fall on or strike (something) in scattered drops. M17.

📖 **4** M. FRAYN Cleaning his teeth and spattering specks of toothpaste over . . walls and carpet. **5** J. A. FROUDE Praise the man whom . . he had spattered with ignominy. P. ACKROYD The cabs . . pass by and spatter him with mud. R. BANKS A furious small man spattering us with his words. **6** E. FIGES Drops of rain will spatter the pane. V. GLENDINNING Her manuscript is spattered with . . notes to herself.

Comb.: **spatterware** earthenware decorated with colours applied with a sponge to give a blotchy effect.

■ **spatteˈration** *noun* (*rare, US*) spattering M19. **spattered** *ppl adjective* (*a*) dispersed or scattered in drops or small particles; (*b*) sprinkled, splashed, or covered with spots of liquid etc.: M17.

spatterdash /ˈspatədaʃ/ *noun.* L17.
[from prec. + DASH *verb*[1].]
Hist. A long gaiter or legging of leather, cloth, etc., worn to keep trousers or stockings clean, esp. when riding. Usu. in *pl.*
■ **spatterdashed** *adjective* wearing spatterdashes M19.

spattering /ˈspat(ə)rɪŋ/ *noun.* M16.
[from SPATTER *verb* + -ING[1].]
1 The action of SPATTER *verb*; an instance of this. M16.
2 A smattering. *rare.* M17.
3 A noise suggestive of the fall or impact of heavy drops; a pattering sound. M19.

spattle /ˈspat(ə)l/ *noun*[1]. *obsolete exc. dial.*
[Old English *spātl*, from *spāt-* stem of *spǣtan* to spit. Cf. SPITTLE *noun*[3].]
Spittle.

spattle /ˈspat(ə)l/ *noun*[2]. *obsolete* exc. *dial.* LME.
[Contr. of SPATULE.]
A spatula.

spattle /ˈspat(ə)l/ *verb*[1] *intrans. & trans.* Now *arch. & dial.* OE.
[from SPATTLE *noun*[1]. Cf. SPITTLE *verb*[1].]
Spit. Now only in ***spattling poppy***, the bladder campion, *Silene vulgaris* (said to be freq. covered with cuckoo-spit).

spattle /ˈspat(ə)l/ *verb*[2] *trans.* Now *dial. & techn.* E17.
[Rel. to SPATTER *verb*.]
Spatter, sprinkle; mottle.

spatula /ˈspatjʊlə/ *noun.* E16.
[Latin, var. of *spathula* dim. of SPATHA: see -ULE.]
A blunt knifelike implement with a broad flat blade used for stirring, spreading, or spooning powdered or pasty substances, or for various technical (esp. medical) operations, as holding down the tongue to examine the throat.
■ **spatular** *adjective* having the form of a spatula L19.

spatulamancy /ˈspatjʊləmansi/ *noun. rare.* E18.
[medieval or mod. Latin *spatulamancia*, from *spatula* shoulder-blade: see -MANCY.]
Divination by means of the shoulder-blade of an animal.

spatulate /ˈspatjʊlət/ *adjective.* M18.
[from SPATUL(A + -ATE[2].]
Spatula-shaped; having a broad rounded end; *BOTANY & ZOOLOGY* = SPATHULATE.
■ Also **spatulated** *adjective* L18.

spatulate /ˈspatjʊleɪt/ *verb trans.* E20.
[formed as prec. + -ATE[3].]
1 Chiefly *DENTISTRY.* Stir or mix with a spatula. E20.
2 *SURGERY.* Give a spatulate form to (a tubular vessel). M20.

spatulation /spatjʊˈleɪʃ(ə)n/ *noun.* L19.
[In sense 1 from SPATULATE *adjective*; in other senses from prec.: see -ION.]
1 *ZOOLOGY* etc. The condition of being spatulate; a spatulate formation. *rare.* L19.
2 Chiefly *DENTISTRY.* The process of stirring or mixing with a spatula. M20.
3 *SURGERY.* The procedure of spatulating a tubular vessel; a spatulated portion. L20.

spatule /ˈspatjuːl/ *noun.* LME.
[Old & mod. French from Latin SPATULA.]
1 = SPATULA *noun.* LME.
†**2** The shoulder-bone of an animal. Only in LME.
3 *ZOOLOGY* etc. A spatulate formation or part; *esp.* a broad flat portion at the end of a bird's tail feather. L19.
■ **spatuliform** *adjective* (*rare*) spatula-shaped E19.

spatulous /ˈspatjʊləs/ *adjective.* E19.
[from SPATUL(A + -OUS.]
Spatula-shaped; spatulate.
■ Also **spatulose** *adjective* M19.

Spätzle /ˈʃpɛtslə, ˈʃpɛts(ə)l/ *noun pl.* L19.
[German dial., lit. 'little sparrows'.]
Noodles of a type made in southern Germany.

spaug /spɔːg/ *noun. Anglo-Irish.* E20.
[Irish *spág*.]
A clumsy, awkward foot.

spauld /spɔːld/ *noun.* Now *Scot. & north.* ME.
[Old French *espalde* etc. (mod. *épaule*) from medieval or mod. Latin *spatula* shoulder-blade. Cf. SPALL *noun*[2], SPULE.]
1 The shoulder; a shoulder of an animal used as food. ME.
2 A limb; any joint of the carcass of an animal or bird. E16.
Phrases: **black spauld** *Scot.* a bacterial disease of cattle; black-leg.

spaulty /ˈspɔːlti/ *adjective. dial.* L19.
[from SPALT *adjective* + -Y[1].]
Dry and brittle.

spave /speɪv/ *verb trans. Scot. & north.* L17.
[Alt. of SPAY.]
Spay (a female animal).
■ **spaver** *noun* a spayer E19.

spavie /ˈspeɪvi/ *adjective & noun. Scot.* L17.
[Alt. of next.]
▶ **A** *adjective.* Spavined. *rare.* L17.
▶ **B** *noun.* Spavin. E18.
■ **spavied** *adjective* spavined L18.

spavin /ˈspavɪn/ *noun*[1] *& verb.* LME.
[Aphet. from Old French *espavin* var. of *esparvain* (mod. *éparvin*) from Germanic, from base repr. by East Frisian *spadde, sparre*.]
▶ **A** *noun. VETERINARY MEDICINE.* (A) swelling or inflammation of the carpal or tarsal (hock) joint in a horse's leg; *esp.* (in full ***bone spavin***) (a swelling due to) osteoarthritis or osteitis of the hock. LME.
blood spavin (a) soft swelling of the hock due to distension of the main vein. **bog-spavin** (a) swelling of the capsule of the hock joint. **occult spavin**: without visible swelling.
▶ **B** *verb trans.* Affect with the spavin. *rare.* M19.
■ **spavined** *adjective* (of a horse etc.) affected with spavin, having a spavin; *fig.* lame, maimed: LME.

spavin /ˈspavɪn/ *noun*[2]. *rare.* L19.
[Origin unkn.]
MINING. Underclay.

spawl /spɔːl/ *verb. arch.* L16.
[Origin unkn.]
1 *verb intrans.* Spit copiously or coarsely; expectorate. Freq. in ***spit and spawl***. L16.
2 *verb trans.* Utter in a coarse manner. E17.
■ **spawling** *noun* (*a*) the action of the verb; (*b*) (in *pl.*) spittle, saliva: E17.

spawn /spɔːn/ *noun.* Pl. same, †-S. LME.
[from the verb.]
†**1** The milt of a fish. Only in LME.
2 *collect.* & †in *pl.* The minute eggs of fishes and various other oviparous animals (chiefly aquatic or amphibian), usually extruded in large numbers and forming a more or less coherent or gelatinous mass; the very young brood hatched from such eggs. L15. ▸†**b** A fish-egg; an undeveloped fish. M16–E17.
3 A brood, many offspring; *transf.* a large quantity. Now *rare.* L16.
4 The offspring of a specified parent or stock; a person or group regarded as such, or as imbued with some quality or principle. Chiefly *derog.* L16.
5 The source or origin of something. Now *rare.* L16.
6 A product, result, or effect of something. M17.
7 The mycelium of mushrooms or other fungi. M18.

📖 **2** J. DUNCUMB The spawn . . are in some parts termed salmon-fry. *Guardian* Herring spawn is relatively vulnerable and . . few survive. ***frog-spawn***: see FROG *noun*[1]. **4** R. S. HAWKER Wretched Heretics, the spawn of that miscreant John Wesley. **6** J. RUSKIN Misbegotten fantasies which are the spawn of modern licence. **7** J. C. LOUDON Spawn is a white fibrous substance, . . like broken threads. ***mushroom spawn***: see MUSHROOM *noun & adjective.*

■ **spawny** *adjective* resembling spawn; spawning: M17.

spawn /spɔːn/ *verb.* LME.
[Aphet. from Anglo-Norman *espaundre* shed roe, var. of Old French *espandre* (mod. *épandre*) shed, spill, pour out from Latin *expandere* EXPAND.]
▶ **I** *verb intrans.* **1** Of fish etc.: cast spawn. LME.
2 Increase, develop, grow; become reproductive. Also foll. by *into*. E17.
3 Appear, arise, result; come *out* in large numbers. M17.
4 Swarm or teem *with* something. *rare.* E19.

📖 **1** *New Scientist*: *Acanthaster*, like other starfish, spawns directly into the water. *transf.*: G. GREENE A wretched father, whose wife spawns by calendar every fall. **3** H. E. BATES Continually new roofs spawned along clay hill-sides, encrusting new land.

▶ **II** *verb trans.* **5** Produce, generate; result in, give rise to. Freq. *derog.* L16. ▸**b** *spec.* Produce or generate as spawn; *derog.* give birth to (a person). E17.
6 Supply with mushroom spawn. L18.
7 Extract spawn from (a fish). L19.

📖 **5** *Scientific American* Novel consumer products that are spawned by developments in microelectronics. *Arizona Daily Star* The hot air spawned thunderstorms that rained golfball-size hail. *Country Walking* Walking . . has spawned a whole new range of literature. **b** W. COWPER A race obscene, Spawn'd in the muddy beds of Nile, came forth, Polluting Egypt.

■ **spawned** *ppl adjective* (*a*) cast or deposited as spawn; (*b*) that has emitted spawn, spent (freq. foll. by *out*): M19. **spawning** *ppl adjective* (*a*) (of fish etc.) engaged in casting spawn; (*b*) fertile; teeming; prolific: L16.

spawner /ˈspɔːnə/ *noun.* E17.
[from SPAWN *noun* or *verb* + -ER[1].]
1 A female fish, esp. at spawning time. E17. ▸†**b** A woman, *esp.* one considered with respect to child-bearing. Chiefly *derog.* Only in 17.
2 A person who or thing which spawns a thing or things. Chiefly *derog.* E17.

spay /speɪ/ *verb trans.* Also (*rare*) **spey**. LME.
[Aphet. from Anglo-Norman *espeier*, Old French *espeer*, from *espee* (mod. *épée*) sword from Latin *spatha*: see SPATHE. Cf. SPLAY *verb*[2].]
†**1** Stab or cut (a deer). Only in LME.
2 Sterilize (a female animal) by removing the ovaries. LME.

spayad /ˈspeɪəd/ *noun. arch.* Also **spayard** /ˈspeɪɑːd/, **spayd** /speɪd/. LME.
[Origin unkn.]
A male deer in its third year.

spaz /spaz/ *noun. slang. offensive.* Pl. **spaz(z)es**. M20.
[Abbreviation of SPASTIC.]
= SPASTIC *noun* 2.

spazz /spaz/ *verb intrans. US slang.* L20.
[formed as prec.]
Foll. by *out*: lose physical or emotional control; be overcome, esp. as the result of an intense emotional experience; display the symptoms of this.

SPCK *abbreviation.*
Society for Promoting Christian Knowledge.

speak /spiːk/ *noun.* Chiefly *Scot. & north.* ME.
[Partly from north. repr. Old English *spǣc*, *sprǣc* SPEECH *noun*; later partly from next.]
1 †**a** The action of speaking; a manner of speaking. Only in ME. ▸†**b** The power or faculty of speech. Only in LME. ▸**c** (A) language. Long only with specifying word (see also -SPEAK). LME.
2 Talk, conversation; a chat. ME.
3 A formal discourse; a speech, a statement. M16.
4 A speakeasy. *US slang.* M20.

📖 **2** L. G. GIBBON It was fair the speak of the place that happening early in April.

speak /spiːk/ *verb.* Pa. t. **spoke** /spəʊk/, (*arch. & poet.*) **spake** /speɪk/. Pa. pple **spoken** /ˈspəʊk(ə)n/, (*arch.*) **spoke**.
[Late Old English *specan*, superseding parallel Old English *sprecan* which did not survive beyond early Middle English, = Old Frisian *spreka*, Old Saxon *sprekan*, Old High German *sprehhan* (Dutch *spreken*, German *sprechen*), from West Germanic strong verb with which cf. Old Norse *spraki* rumour, *forsprakki* spokesman.]
▶ **I** *verb intrans.* **1 a** Pronounce words, make articulate verbal utterances with the voice; express one's thoughts by words. (Foll. by *about*, *on* a subject, *to* a person, etc.) LOE. ▸**b** Converse; talk *with* others, *with* each other, etc. Later also, be on speaking terms. LOE. ▸**c** Deliver a speech or formal address; express one's views in an assembly or to an audience. L16. ▸**d** Propose marriage. *arch.* E17.
2 Of a writer, literary composition, etc.: make a statement or declaration in words. ME.
3 a Of thunder etc.: make a noise; resound, reverberate. LME. ▸**b** Of a musical instrument etc.: make a sound; *spec.* emit a full and proper note. E17. ▸**c** Of a firearm: emit a report on being fired. E18. ▸**d** Of a hound: bay or bark; give tongue on finding a scent. E19.
4 a Of a thing: be expressive or significant; make some revelation or disclosure. (Foll. by *to*.) M16. ▸**b** Take effect legally; be valid. M19.

📖 **1a** J. WAIN The one who spoke had a broad Lancashire accent. G. BATTISCOMBE William found her very weak and unable to speak distinctly. *Encounter* No one spoke except about the weather. P. FITZGERALD He must speak to this woman. **b** *People* We didn't speak for two years. **c** C. V. WEDGWOOD The King, . . allowed to speak before an audience of his people, uttered a . . solemn farewell. E. SEGAL The defence had to speak first and allow the prosecution the last word. **4a** I. MURDOCH There was something . . oriental in their mood, something which spoke . . in the subtly curving mouth.

▶ **II** *verb trans.* **5 a** Articulate, utter (a word, remark, sentence, etc.); make, recite, deliver (a speech or statement); direct or address (words) *against*, *to*, etc. LOE. ▸†**b** Use (one's voice) to make an utterance. LME–L16.
6 Utter or express (truth, falsehood, etc.) in words or speech. LOE.
7 a Declare or tell of in words; make known by speech or writing; state *that*. LOE. ▸**b** Of a musical instrument: announce or proclaim by sound. Chiefly *literary.* E18.
8 a Talk or converse with; address (a person). *arch.* LOE. ▸**b** Communicate with (a passing vessel) at sea by signal etc. L18.
9 Use or be able to use as a language; talk (a particular language). ME.

10 †**a** Mention (a person); speak of in a certain way; commend (a person) *to* another. ME–M17. ▸**b** Bespeak, order. *rare.* E16.

11 Of a thing: be a sign of, indicate, express; reveal, make known. L16. ▸**b** *spec.* Of the face, eyes, etc.: indicate or manifest by expression. E17.

12 a Show (a person or thing) to be or do a certain thing or to possess a certain quality. *arch.* E17. ▸**b** Term, call; describe (as). *arch.* E17.

13 a Create by speaking. Also foll. by *out*. *rare.* M17. ▸**b** Cause to change or enter into another state, condition, or position by speaking. Foll. by *into*, *to*, or adjective compl. L17.

> 📖 **5a** SHAKES. *Meas. for M.* Certain words he spoke against your Grace. P. MORTIMER 'You're tired,' he said, the first words he had spoken directly to me for . . weeks. **6** G. GREENE How can I tell that you are speaking the truth? **7a** H. BROOKE You have, in a few words, spoke the whole of the matter. **b** N. ROWE These Trumpets speak his Presence. **9** R. MACAULAY She . . could speak enough Turkish to get about. D. M. THOMAS Anna could speak three languages besides her native Ukrainian. **10a** SHAKES. *Hen. VIII* Griffith, give me leave to speak him, And yet with charity. **11** GOLDSMITH The loud laugh that spoke the vacant mind. **b** DRYDEN His face spake hope, while deep his sorrows flow. **12a** SIR W. SCOTT His acquaintance with the English language . . plainly spoke him to be an Englishman. **b** TENNYSON To speak him true, . . No keener hunter after glory breathes. **13b** *refl.*: *New Monthly Magazine* He spoke himself into the Common Council.

Phrases: **as they speak** *arch.* as the phrase is. **know to speak to** have a slight acquaintance with (a person). ***know whereof one speaks***: see WHEREOF 3. †**not to be spoken of** (be) beyond all description. **so to speak** as it were, to a certain extent, in some sense. ***speak (a person) fair***: see FAIR *adverb* 2. ***speak daggers***: see DAGGER *noun*[1]. **speak evil of**, **speak ill of** mention unfavourably, criticize. ***speak extempore***: see EXTEMPORE *adverb* 1. **speak for itself** be significant or self-evident. **speak for oneself** give one's own opinions; ***speak for yourself***, do not presume to speak for others. ***speak ill of***: see ***speak evil of*** above. **speak in a person's ear** whisper, speak privately. — **speaking** used by a speaker on the telephone to announce his or her identity. ***speak in tongues***: see TONGUE *noun*. ***speak like a book***: see BOOK *noun*. ***speak one's mind***: see MIND *noun*[1]. ***speak out of turn***: see TURN *noun*. ***speak the truth***: see TRUTH *noun*. ***speak volumes***: see VOLUME *noun*. **speak well of** mention favourably, praise. ***speak with tongues***: see TONGUE *noun*. **speak-your-weight machine** a weighing machine which announces one's weight in spoken words. **to speak of** worth mentioning (usu. in neg. contexts).

With adverbs & prepositions in specialized senses: (See also Phrases above.) **speak for** (*a*) make a speech or plea in place of or on behalf of (a person); plead for or concerning; (*b*) (now *rare*) beg, request; (*c*) (now usu. in *pass.*) order; bespeak; engage; (*d*) indicate, betoken. †**speak forth** utter, declare, proclaim. **speak of** (*a*) mention or discuss in speech or writing; †(*b*) *rare* (Shakes.) bespeak, order; (*c*) suggest, propose, hint at (doing something). **speak out** (*a*) utter; make known in words; declare openly or clearly, manifest; (*b*) talk distinctly or in a loud voice; (*c*) talk freely or unreservedly; see also sense 13a above. **speak past** talk at cross purposes with; speak incomprehensibly to. **speak to** (*a*) approach (a person) for help, service, etc.; bribe; *spec.* propose marriage to; (*b*) influence, affect, touch; (*c*) deal with, discuss, or comment on (a subject) in speech or writing; (*d*) give evidence regarding (a thing), attest; (*e*) address with censure or reproof, admonish; (*f*) (of a hound) give indications of (a fox, scent, etc.) by baying or barking. **speak together** hold consultation; confer. **speak up** (*a*) raise one's voice; (begin to) talk boldly or unreservedly; (*b*) ***speak up for***, speak firmly on behalf of or in defence of. **speak with** NAUTICAL communicate with (another vessel); see also sense 1b above.

Comb.: **speak-back** = ***talkback*** s.v. TALK *verb*; **speak-box** an intercom device which allows a caller to speak to someone elsewhere in a building; **speakeasy** *slang* (chiefly *US*, now *Hist.*) a shop or drinking club selling alcoholic liquor illegally during Prohibition; **speak-house** (*a*) *Hist.* a room in a convent or monastery where conversation was permitted or visitors received; (*b*) in the S. Pacific islands, a large hut used as a place of council.

-speak /spiːk/ *suffix.* M20.
[from prec. after NEWSPEAK, OLDSPEAK.]
Forming nouns denoting a particular variety of language or characteristic mode of speaking, as ***computerspeak***, ***marketing-speak***, ***military-speak***, ***union-speak***, etc.

speakable /ˈspiːkəb(ə)l/ *adjective.* L15.
[from SPEAK *verb* + -ABLE.]
1 That can be spoken; fit or possible to be expressed in words. Earlier in UNSPEAKABLE 1. L15.
†**2** Capable of speech; having the faculty of speech. *rare.* M–L17.
3 Able or fit to be spoken *to*. *colloq.* M20.
■ **speakably** *adverb* (*rare*) (earlier in UNSPEAKABLY) M19.

speaker /ˈspiːkə/ *noun.* ME.
[from SPEAK *verb* + -ER[1].]
1 A person who speaks or talks; *spec.* a person who speaks formally in public, an orator; a person who speaks on behalf of another or others. Freq. with qualifying adjective. ME.
2 (**S-**.) ▸**a** The member of the British House of Commons who is chosen by the House itself to act as its representative and to preside over its debates. Also ***Madam Speaker***, ***Mr Speaker***, †***Speaker of Parliament***, †***Speaker of the Parliament***. LME. ▸**b** The presiding officer or chairman of the British House of Lords (now the Lord Chancellor). M17. ▸**c** *gen.* The president in any legislative assembly. M17.
†**3** A person who proclaims or celebrates something. *rare* (Shakes.). Only in E17.
4 A book containing texts adapted for reading aloud. Now *rare.* L18.
5 A person who speaks a specified language. L19.
6 = ***loudspeaker*** s.v. LOUD *adjective.* E20.

> 📖 **1** P. FUSSELL Amis's poem, what class is the speaker in it? S. ROSENBERG A splendid speaker, with a strong, well-modulated voice. A. S. BYATT She was a fervent speaker for the Emancipation of Women. **5** *Guardian* The rights of the Welsh speaker. ***native speaker***: see NATIVE *adjective*. **6** S. NAIPAUL The heavy pound of rhythm and blues from scattered speakers.

Comb.: **speaker-hearer** a person regarded as a user of language; **speaker-key**: fitted to a wind instrument to enable the playing of notes an octave or a twelfth higher; **speaker-listener** = ***speaker-hearer*** above; **speakerphone** *N. Amer.* a telephone receiver which does not need to be held in the hand; **Speaker's Conference**: first convened in 1916, with the purpose of examining electoral law and reform under the chairmanship of the Speaker of the British House of Commons.

■ **speakeress** *noun* a female speaker; (**S-**) a woman acting as a president or Speaker: L18. **Speakership** *noun* (*a*) the office of Speaker in a legislative assembly; (*b*) (**s-**) oratory: M17.

speakerine /spiːkəˈriːn/ *noun.* M20.
[French, from *speaker* announcer + *-ine* fem. suffix.]
A female announcer on radio or television; a television hostess.

speakie /ˈspiːki/ *noun.* Now *rare.* E20.
[from SPEAK *verb* + -IE. Cf. MOVIE.]
A stage play in contrast to a (silent) film. Also = TALKIE. Usu. in *pl.*

speaking /ˈspiːkɪŋ/ *verbal noun.* ME.
[from SPEAK *verb* + -ING[1].]
1 a The action of SPEAK *verb*; speech, talk; conversation, discourse. ME. ▸**b** The delivery of speeches; speech-making. M18.
2 a An instance or occasion of speech or talk; a discourse, a discussion. Now chiefly *US.* ME. ▸†**b** In *pl.* Things spoken; sayings, statements, words. ME–M17.
†**3** The faculty or power of speech. LME–E16.

Phrases: **at that present speaking** *US* at that moment. **at the present speaking**, **at this present speaking** *US* at this moment. ***in a manner of speaking***: see MANNER *noun*[1]. **on speaking terms** (*a*) slightly acquainted; (*b*) on friendly terms.

Attrib. & comb.: In the sense 'used for producing or conveying articulate sounds', as ***speaking-machine***, ***speaking-pipe***, etc.; in the sense 'pertaining to speech', as ***speaking skills***, ***speaking voice***, etc. Special combs., as **speaking acquaintance** (*a*) a person one knows slightly; (*b*) this degree of familiarity; **speaking front** MUSIC an organ-front composed of pipes which actually sound, as opp. to dummy pipes; **speaking-trumpet** *Hist.* an instrument used (formerly esp. at sea) to make the voice carry; **speaking-tube** a tube or pipe for communicating by voice from one room, building, etc., to another.

speaking /ˈspiːkɪŋ/ *ppl adjective.* ME.
[formed as prec. + -ING[2].]
▸ **I 1 a** That speaks; capable of articulate speech. Also as 2nd elem. of comb. ME. ▸**b** (Capable of) speaking a specified language. M19.
2 Significant; eloquent; (esp. of the eyes or face) highly expressive. L16.
3 (Of a likeness) striking, true; (of a portrait) lifelike. L16.

> 📖 **1a** ***evil-speaking***, ***public-speaking***, ***true-speaking***, etc. **b** *Guardian* The Urdu-speaking immigrants. **2** E. BOWEN Speaking looks were cast by the . . children at the place where Hermione did not sit.

▸ **II 4** With regard to a limitation or sense specified; from a particular point of view. L17.
4 *broadly speaking*, ***generally speaking***, ***professionally speaking***, ***strictly speaking***, etc.

Special collocations: **speaking clock** a telephone service giving the correct time in words. **speaking stop** an organ-stop key which controls the sounding of a rank of pipes.

■ **speakingly** *adverb* in an eloquent or expressive manner; strikingly: LME. **speakingness** *noun* (*rare*) the quality of being eloquent or expressive M19.

spean /spiːn/ *noun*[1]. Now *dial.* E16.
[Middle Dutch or Middle Low German *spene* (Dutch, Flemish *speen*, West Frisian *spien*, Low German *spene*, *späne*) = Old Norse *speni* (Middle Swedish *spene*, *späne*, etc. Norwegian, Swedish *spene*, Danish †*spene*), ult. from Germanic base also of SPANE.]
†**1** Swelling of the uvula. Only in E16.
2 A teat, a nipple, *esp.* that of a cow. L16.

spean /spiːn/ *noun*[2]. *dial.* L18.
[Origin unkn.]
A prong of a fork.

spean /spiːn/ *verb trans.* *Scot. & north.* L16.
[Partly var. of SPANE, partly from Middle Dutch or Middle Low German *spenen* (Dutch, Flemish *spenen*, Low German *spenen*, *spänen*) = Middle High German *spenen* (German dial. *spänen*), from *spene* SPEAN *noun*[1].]
Wean (an infant, lamb, etc.).

spear /spɪə/ *noun*[1].
[Old English *spere* = Old Frisian *spiri*, *spere*, Old Saxon, Old High German *sper* (Dutch, German *Speer*), Old Norse (pl.) *spjǫr*, doubtfully rel. to Latin *sparus* hunting-spear.]
1 a A thrusting or throwing weapon with a long shaft and a sharp-pointed usu. steel tip; a lance. OE. ▸**b** MILITARY. Any of the transverse spikes in *chevaux de frise*. E19.
2 *fig.* **a** A quality, condition, etc., regarded as being sharp or severe. OE. ▸**b** Dismissal from employment. *Austral. slang.* L19.
3 a A soldier armed with a spear; a spearman. *arch.* ME. ▸**b** A hunter who uses a spear; *spec.* a pigsticker. M19.
4 a A sharp-pointed or barbed instrument used for catching fish etc.; a leister; *gen.* any instrument with a sharp end. LME. ▸**b** A prong *of* a fork. *rare.* M18.
5 a The sting of a reptile or insect, esp. of a bee. Now *dial.* LME. ▸**b** In *pl.* The thorns or prickles of a plant; the spines of a hedgehog; the sharp fins of a fish. Chiefly *poet.* E17.
6 A beam or ray *of* light. *literary.* M19.

> 📖 **1a** F. HOYLE Chipped pieces of stone could . . be attached to sticks to form spears. **2a** M. ARNOLD The spear of Butler's reasoning. R. CAMPBELL A thrilling spear of pain. **3a** T. H. WHITE He sent only a small troop of forty spears to start the work. **4a** ***eel-spear***, ***fish-spear***, ***salmon-spear***, etc.

Phrases: †**put under the spear**, †**sell at the spear**, etc., sell by auction.

Comb.: **spear-carrier** (*a*) a carrier of a spear, a spearman; (*b*) an actor with a walk-on part; *gen.* any unimportant participant; (*c*) *US colloq.* a proponent of something, a standard-bearer; **spearfish** *noun & verb* (*a*) *noun* any of several N. American fishes with a spine on the jaw or fin, esp. a marlin or a quillback; (*b*) *verb intrans.* fish using a spear under water (chiefly as ***spearfishing*** *verbal noun*); **spear gun** a weapon used in spearfishing which operates by firing a detachable harpoon; **spear-play** exercise or fighting with spears; **spear-running** *arch.* jousting with spears; **spear-shaft** the long shaft or handle to which a spearhead is fixed; **spear side** the male line of descent, the male side of a family; **spearsman** = SPEARMAN *noun*[1]; **spear tackle** *Austral.* an illegal tackle in rugby football in which a player is lifted and thrown to the ground head first; **spear thistle** the thistle *Cirsium vulgare*, a common weed of pastures, with large ovoid heads and deeply lobed spiny leaves; **spearwood** any of various Australian trees and shrubs used to make Aboriginal spears, esp. the yarran, *Acacia homalophylla*.

■ **speared** *adjective* armed with a spear or spears E19. **spearlike** *adjective* resembling or shaped like a spear M16. **speary** *adjective* †(*a*) (of grass) hard and stiff; (*b*) resembling a spear or spears; slender and sharp-pointed; (*c*) *rare* consisting of or involving spears: L16.

spear /spɪə/ *noun*[2]. L15.
[Irreg. var. of SPIRE *noun*[1], perh. infl. by prec.]
†**1** A spire of a church or other building; a pyramid. Cf. SPIRE *noun*[1] 5. L15–M18.
2 a The plumule of an embryo plant; *spec.* the acrospire of grain. Cf. SPIRE *noun*[1] 3. M17. ▸**b** A blade of grass; a plant shoot. M19.
3 A stem of a reed, osier, etc.; *collect.* reeds, esp. as a thatching material. Cf. SPIRE *noun*[1] 2. *dial.* L18.
4 The edible shoot, including stem and tip or head, of asparagus or of sprouting broccoli. M19.

spear /spɪə/ *noun*[3]. E16.
[Var. of SPIRE *noun*[2].]
1 †**a** A stripling, a youth. Only in E16. ▸**b** A young tree, *esp.* a young oak; a sapling. M16.
2 A pump-rod. Now *rare.* E18.
1b *spear oak*, ***spear tree***.

spear /spɪə/ *noun*[4]. *rare.* E20.
[from SPEAR *verb*[2].]
An act of piercing or striking someone or something with a spear, *spec.* in pigsticking.

spear *noun*[5] var. of SPAR *noun*[4].

spear /spɪə/ *verb*[1]. *obsolete* exc. *dial.* ME.
[Middle Low German *speren* (Low German *speren*, *speeren*, *speiren*) rel. to Middle Dutch *sperren*, Old High German *sperran*: see SPAR *verb*[2].]
1 *verb trans. & intrans.* Shut, close, esp. firmly or securely. (Foll. by *out*, *up*.) ME.
2 *verb trans.* Shut up, confine (a person); put away, enclose (a thing). Long *rare* or *obsolete.* ME.

spear /spɪə/ *verb*[2]. LME.
[from SPEAR *noun*[1].]
▸ **I** *verb trans.* **1** Pierce or strike with a spear or other pointed object. LME.
2 Cause to move like a spear; spearhead (an attack etc.). E20.
3 Dismiss from employment. Cf. SPEAR *noun*[1] 2b. *Austral. slang.* E20.
4 Beg; obtain by begging. *US slang.* E20.

> 📖 **1** E. BOWEN She took her fork up, speared the eclair, and watched the cream ooze forth. G. SWIFT My ancestors were water people. They speared fish and netted ducks. *fig.*: S. KEYES A stormy day, a granite peak Spearing the sky.

▸ **II** *verb intrans. rare.*
5 Rise *up* like a spear. E19.

6 Move like a spear. M20.

> 📖 **5** CLIVE JAMES The plane went spearing up through the heat-wobble.

spear /spɪə/ *verb*[3] *intrans.* L16.
[Irreg. var. of SPIRE *verb*[1].]
Of corn, a shoot, etc.: sprout, germinate.

spearer /ˈspɪərə/ *noun.* L16.
[from SPEAR *noun*[1] or *verb*[2] + -ER[1].]
A person who is armed with or strikes someone or something with a spear. Chiefly as 2nd elem. of comb., as ***eel-spearer*** etc.

spear-grass /ˈspɪəgrɑːs/ *noun.* M16.
[from SPEAR *noun*[1] + GRASS *noun.*]
†**1** = SPEARWORT 2. M–L16.
2 Any of several kinds of meadow-grass, esp. *Poa pratensis. US.* M18.
3 Any of several British grasses occurring as weeds, *esp.* couch grass, *Elytrigia repens.* L18.
4 Any of various grasses of the genera *Stipa, Heteropogon*, and *Aristida*, with pointed seeds and twisted awns. Chiefly *Austral.* M19.
5 = SPANIARD *noun* 3. M19.
6 Any of several sharp-pointed Asiatic grasses or plants. M19.

spearhead /ˈspɪəhɛd/ *noun & verb.* LME.
[from SPEAR *noun*[1] + HEAD *noun.*]
► **A** *noun.* **1** The sharp-pointed head or blade on the end of a spear; *transf.* anything with a pointed end characteristic of the head of a spear. LME.
2 The leading element of a thrust, movement, etc.; a person or group leading an attack. L19.

> 📖 **2** C. R. ATTLEE The spearheads of the Panzer Divisions penetrated further . . toward the Channel Ports.

► **B** *verb trans.* Act as the spearhead of; lead (a movement, attack, etc.). M20.

> 📖 *Japan Times* The man spearheading many of the reforms.

spearing /ˈspɪərɪŋ/ *noun.* Chiefly *US.* M19.
[App. from Dutch, German *Spiering* smelt.]
Any of several small fishes, as a silverside or an anchovy.
ground spearing a small lizardfish, *Trachinocephalus myops*.

spearman /ˈspɪəmən/ *noun*[1]. Pl. **-men**. ME.
[from SPEAR *noun*[1] + MAN *noun.*]
1 A soldier or warrior armed with a spear; a person who carries or uses a spear. *arch.* ME.
2 A royal or civic officer bearing a spear. Long *rare.* M17.

Spearman /ˈspɪəmən/ *noun*[2]. E20.
[Charles Edward *Spearman* (1863–1945), English psychologist.]
STATISTICS. Used *attrib.* and in *possess.* to designate a product-moment correlation coefficient devised by Spearman as a measure of the degree of agreement between two rankings (symbol ρ or *R*).

spearmen *noun* pl. of SPEARMAN *noun*[1].

spearmint /ˈspɪəmɪnt/ *noun.* M16.
[from SPEAR *noun*[1] + MINT *noun*[2].]
1 A garden mint, a glabrous form of *Mentha spicata*, commonly grown as a flavouring, esp. for use in mint sauce. M16.
2 In full ***spearmint oil***. An aromatic oil extracted from the spearmint. M19.
3 A sweet or piece of chewing-gum flavoured with spearmint oil. E20.
■ **spearminty** *adjective* of, pertaining to, or resembling spearmint; that tastes or smells of spearmint: M20.

spearwort /ˈspɪəwəːt/ *noun.* OE.
[from SPEAR *noun*[1] + WORT *noun*[1].]
†**1** The plant elecampane, *Inula helenium.* OE–ME.
2 Either of two yellow-flowered marsh plants (allied to the buttercups) with spear-shaped leaves, *Ranunculus flammula* (more fully ***lesser spearwort***) and *R. lingua* (more fully ***great spearwort***). LME.

spec /spɛk/ *noun*[1]. *colloq.* L18.
[Abbreviation of SPECULATION.]
A commercial speculation or venture.

> 📖 J. FOWLES I was rich, a good spec as a husband. **on spec** in the hope of gaining some advantage or profit etc.; as a gamble, on the off chance.

spec /spɛk/ *noun*[2]. *US slang.* E20.
[Abbreviation of SPECTACLE *noun*[1].]
An elaborate or expensive show; a spectacle.

spec /spɛk/ *noun*[3]. *colloq.* M20.
[Abbreviation of SPECIFICATION.]
A detailed working description; a specification.

spec /spɛk/ *noun*[4]. *US colloq.* M20.
[Abbreviation.]
= SPECIALIST 2b.

spec /spɛk/ *adjective. colloq.* M20.
[Abbreviation of SPECULATIVE.]
Designating or pertaining to the building of houses without prior guarantee of sale.

speccy *adjective* var. of SPECKY *adjective*[2].

special /ˈspɛʃ(ə)l/ *adjective, adverb, noun, & verb.* ME.
[Aphet. from Old French *especial* (mod. *spécial*) ESPECIAL, or from Latin *specialis*, formed as SPECIES: see -AL[1].]
► **A** *adjective.* **1** Exceptional in quality or degree; unusual; out of the ordinary; *esp.* excelling in some (positive) quality; exceptionally good, talented, etc. ME. ▸†**b** Of a person: important, distinguished. L16–M17.
2 Orig. *spec.* of a friend: held in particular esteem or affection; of particular value or importance *to*. ME.
3 Distinguished from others of the kind by a particular quality or feature; distinctive in some way; *spec.* pertaining to or designating education for children with particular needs (as the mentally handicapped etc.). ME. ▸**b** Additional to the usual, extra. M19.
4 Appointed or employed for a particular purpose or occasion. ME.
5 Having an individual or limited application or purpose; affecting or concerning a single person, thing, or set. Also, designating or pertaining to something in which a person specializes. LME. ▸**b** Containing details; precise, specific. L17.
6 Having a close or exclusive connection with a single person, thing, or set; peculiar. LME.
7 *MATH.* Of a group: that can be represented by matrices of unit determinant. E20.

> 📖 **1** J. SIMMS We deliberated over a rather special bottle of wine. *Punch* The special excellence of this novel lies in its . . subtle depiction. A. HOLLINGHURST I used to take photographs . . but they're nothing special. J. HALPERIN Hardy paid special attention to passages of . . description. **2** J. B. HILTON He was somehow special to me . . . I would put my head against his tweedy chest. **3** E. M. FORSTER The doctor has ordered her special digestive bread. *Which?* Some special wood paints . . allow water vapour . . to escape. A. N. WILSON He opted to be taught medieval Welsh as a special subject. **b** J. JOHNSTON Two special trains have to be put on . . to bring them back. **5** M. MARRIN A special language, to prevent you from thinking that just anyone can look at pictures. F. TOMLIN He would not have approved of being singled out for special treatment. *Model Engineer* A range of bargain lines on special offer. **6** J. MCCOSH Every intuitive principle . . has its special truth to reveal. J. YEATS Each region has its special treasures.

Phrases: ***SATURDAY NIGHT special. Site of Special Scientific Interest***: see SITE *noun*.
Special collocations: **special area**, **special development area** in the UK, a district for which special economic provision is made in legislation. **Special Branch** a police department in Britain and S. Africa dealing with political security. **special buyer** the bill-broker of the Bank of England in the discount market. **special case** (*a*) *LAW* a written statement of fact presented by litigants to a court, raising a matter to be tried separately from the main action; (*b*) an exceptional or unusual case. ***special constable***: see CONSTABLE 4. **special correspondent** a journalist writing for a newspaper on special events or a special area of interest. **special delivery** a delivery of mail in advance of the regular delivery. ***special development area***: see ***special area*** above. **special drawing rights** the right to purchase extra foreign currency from the International Monetary Fund. **special edition** an extra edition of a newspaper including later news than the ordinary edition. **special effects** in film and television, scenic or other illusions created by props, camera work, computer graphics, etc. **Special Forces** an elite body within the US Army specializing in guerrilla warfare and counter-insurgency. ***special INTENTION***. **special interest** *N. Amer.* a group of people or a corporation seeking or receiving special advantages, esp. by political means. **special jury** *Hist.*: consisting of people of a particular social standing. **special licence** a marriage licence allowing immediate marriage without banns, or at an unusual time or place. **special needs** (in the context of children at school) particular educational requirements resulting from learning difficulties, physical disability, or emotional and behavioural difficulties. **special partner** *US* = ***limited partner*** s.v. LIMITED *adjective*. **special pleader** *LAW* (now *Hist.*) a member of an Inn of Court whose business was to draw the written proceedings of a lawsuit. ***special plea(-in-bar)***: see PLEA *noun*. **special pleading** (*a*) *LAW* the art of drawing pleadings; pleading with reference to a particular case or to new facts in a case; (now *rare* or *obsolete*) an instance of this; (*b*) *fig.* specious or unfair argument favouring the speaker's point of view. ***special providence***: see PROVIDENCE 4. ***special relativity***: see RELATIVITY 2. **special school**: catering for children with special needs. ***special service***: see SERVICE *noun*[1]. ***special sessions***: see SESSION *noun*. **special sort** *PRINTING* a character that is not normally included in a font, such as an accented letter or a symbol. **special team** *AMER. FOOTBALL* a squad that is used for kick-offs, punts, and other special plays. ***special theory of relativity***: see RELATIVITY 2. **special verdict** *LAW* (*a*) a verdict stating the facts as proved but leaving the court to draw conclusions from them; (*b*) a verdict that an accused is not guilty by reason of insanity. ***special vert***: see VERT *noun*[1] *& adjective*.
► **B** *adverb.* In a special manner; especially, particularly. Now *colloq. & dial.* ME.
► **C** *noun.* †**1** A particularly close friend or follower. ME–M17. ▸**b** A sweetheart, a lover. LME–M16.
†**2** A particular point, part, object, etc. LME–E17.
†**3** A species, a kind. M16–M17.
4 *ellipt.* A special person or thing; a special constable, correspondent, train, examination, dish on a menu, offer, programme, etc. M19.

> 📖 **4** E. WAUGH All the papers are sending specials. *Rail Enthusiast* Chartered specials were run, as well as . . service trains. *Truck & Driver* Shepherd's pie was the special of the day.

► **D** *verb.* Infl. **-l(l)-**.
1 *verb intrans.* Work as a special correspondent for a newspaper. *slang. rare.* E20.
2 *verb trans.* Of a nurse etc. in a hospital: attend continuously to (a single patient). *slang.* M20.
■ **specialness** *noun* M16.

specialise *verb* var. of SPECIALIZE.

specialist /ˈspɛʃ(ə)lɪst/ *noun & adjective.* M19.
[from SPECIAL *adjective* + -IST.]
► **A** *noun.* **1** A medical practitioner having advanced training in and dealing exclusively with the study or treatment of a particular disease or a class of diseases affecting a particular part or system of the body or a particular group of people. M19.
2 A person who specially or exclusively studies a subject or a particular branch of a subject. Opp. GENERALIST. M19. ▸**b** An enlisted person in the US army employed on technical or administrative duties but not having command responsibilities. Cf. SPEC *noun*[4]. M20.
3 *ECOLOGY.* A species which is closely adapted, and largely restricted, to a particular mode of life. M20.

> 📖 **1** *Lancet* This is . . because of the range of specialists involved, including . . interventional radiologists. *Reader's Digest* Dr Howard Flaks, a bariatric (obesity) specialist. **2** D. HALBERSTAM Reporters who were often highly trained specialists . . wrote of national implications. *Which Micro?* A . . computer of limited usefulness to anyone other than a specialist. *Boston* Specialists in international financial services.

► **B** *attrib.* or as *adjective.* Of, pertaining to, or suitable for a specialist or specialists. L19.

> 📖 *Punch* Dick . . runs the London specialist bookshop Forbidden Planet. G. BODDY Despite specialist opinion that such treatment was her only chance.

■ **specialism** *noun* (*a*) restriction or devotion to one aspect of a subject or area of study; (*b*) a specialized area of study or work: M19. **speciaˈlistic** *adjective* L19.

speciality /spɛʃɪˈalɪti/ *noun & adjective.* Also in French form ***spécialité*** /spesjalite (*pl. same*)/. LME.
[Old French *especialté* (mod. *spécialité*) or late Latin *specialitas*, from Latin *specialis*: see SPECIAL, -ITY. Cf. SPECIALTY.]
► **A** *noun.* **1** The quality of being special, distinctive, or limited in some respect. LME.
2 A special or particular point or matter; in *pl.*, particulars, details. *arch.* LME.
3 A special or distinctive feature or characteristic. E17.
4 *LAW.* = SPECIALTY *noun* 5. Now *rare.* L17.
5 A special or particular branch of a subject, profession, etc., which one studies or in which one works; a particular activity or interest to which one devotes oneself; = SPECIALTY *noun* 6. M19. ▸**b** An article or service specially characteristic of, dealt in, or produced by, a particular place, firm, etc; = SPECIALTY *noun* 6b. M19.
6 An unusual or distinctive thing. M19.

> 📖 **1** J. G. MURPHY In the general ordinances . . it would have been out of place because of its speciality. **5** L. WOOLF Jean Thomas . . made a speciality of taking nerve or mental patients. *Vanity Fair* An elite corps of marksmen . . whose speciality is apprehending barricaded suspects. **b** DICKENS Romantic drama . . is the speciality of your theatre. L. CHAMBERLAIN Smoked sprats, a speciality of the Baltic states.

► **B** *attrib.* or as *adjective.* Of or pertaining to a speciality or specialities; of the nature of a speciality, *esp.* unusual, distinctive. E20.

> 📖 *Times Review of Industry* Three different markets—household and pharmaceutical products and speciality foods. *Bon Appetit* The cookies . . are available in speciality food stores. *New Scientist* A substance derived from oranges, now used for speciality beers in Belgium.

specialize /ˈspɛʃ(ə)lʌɪz/ *verb.* Also **-ise**. E17.
[French *spécialiser*, from *spécial*: see SPECIAL, -IZE.]
1 *verb trans.* Mention specially; particularize, specify. Chiefly *arch.* E17.
2 *verb trans.* Make special or distinctive; invest with a special function or character; modify or limit (an idea, statement, etc.). E17.
3 *verb trans.* (usu. in *pass.*) *& intrans.* *BIOLOGY.* Adapt or be adapted to a special function or environment; modify or be modified by development tending towards this end. M19.
4 *verb intrans.* Be or become a specialist; deal in or have a speciality. Freq. foll. by *in*. L19.

📖 **1** J. S. BLACKIE I will . . specialize a few of those virtues. **2** J. P. MAHAFFY Specialising its courts . . provided for a prompt . . treatment of disputes. W. T. MILLS Work which . . has been specialized into not fewer than sixty trades. **4** G. GREENE An auction-room which specialised in books. E. BOWEN He specialized in iniquity: off his subject, he objected to being . . a confidant. A. PHILLIPS He was a qualified doctor specializing in . . children's medicine.

■ **speciali'zation** *noun* (*a*) the action of the verb; an instance of this; (*b*) BIOLOGY a specialized character or adaptive feature in an organism: M19.

specially /'spɛʃ(ə)li/ *adverb*. ME.
[from SPECIAL *adjective* + -LY².]
1 In a special manner; in a degree or to an extent beyond what is usual or customary; particularly; pre-eminently. ME.
2 For a special purpose; expressly. ME.
†**3** In detail; specifically, not generally or vaguely. ME–E17.

📖 **1** R. LEHMANN Give everybody my love—specially your mother. N. FARAH Is there anything you specially want me to get? J. C. OATES Your daddy had a specially worrisome week last week. **2** J. B. PRIESTLEY He did not come down specially. P. G. WODEHOUSE Came here specially to see him. M. WESLEY Joyce had scent specially made for her in Paris.

specialogue /'spɛʃəlɒg/ *noun*. Orig. *N. Amer.* L20.
[from SPECIAL *adjective* + CAT)ALOGUE *noun*.]
(Proprietary name for) a specialized catalogue, intended to promote a specific brand or type of product and aimed at a particular market segment.

specialty /'spɛʃ(ə)lti/ *noun & adjective*. ME.
[Old French (*e*)*specialté*, from (*e*)*special* SPECIAL: see -TY¹. Cf. SPECIALITY.]
▶ **A** *noun*. †**1** Special affection or favour. Only in ME.
†**2** Detail in description or discussion. LME–L16.
3 Special or distinctive character or quality; a special feature or characteristic. LME. ▸**b** The quality of being special or limited in some respect. E17.
4 A special or particular point or matter. LME. ▸†**b** A thing specially belonging to or conferred on a person. LME–E17.
5 LAW. A special contract, obligation, or bond, expressed in an instrument under seal. LME.
6 = SPECIALITY *noun* 5. M19. ▸**b** = SPECIALITY *noun* 5b. M19.
7 = SPECIALITY *noun* 6. Usu. *attrib.* (see B. below). Chiefly *N. Amer.* L19.

📖 **3** DICKENS The specialty of the occasion caused our talk to be less dry. **4** CARLYLE Amid these specialties, let us not forget the great generality. **6** M. GORDON An . . art historian . . whose specialty was nineteenth century French painting. G. LEES His specialty had been shoplifting. **b** D. DELILLO A restaurant . . stuffed pigeon was the specialty.

▶ **B** *attrib.* or as *adjective*. = SPECIALITY *adjective*. Chiefly *N. Amer.* L19.

📖 J. STEINBECK Department stores and specialty shops. *British Medical Journal* Plans to include . . American and British specialty journals.

speciation /spiːʃɪ'eɪʃ(ə)n, spiːs-/ *noun*. E20.
[from SPECIES + -ATION.]
BIOLOGY. The formation of new and distinct species in the course of evolution.
■ **'speciate** *verb intrans.* [back-form.] (of a population of plants and animals) exhibit evolutionary development leading to the formation of a new species M20.

specie /'spiːʃiː, 'spiːʃi/ *noun*. M16.
[Latin, abl. sing. of SPECIES. Orig. in phr. *in specie*.]
1 Form. Long only in ***in specie*** (*Law*), in the real, precise, or actual form. M16.
2 Kind. Only in ***in specie***. Now *rare* or *obsolete*. M16.
3 Coin money as opp. to paper money. Freq. *attrib.* E17.
4 †**a** A subordinate division. *rare*. L17–M18. ▸**b** = SPECIES 3, 3b. Long *non-standard*. M18.
Comb.: **specie jar** a large glass or china jar formerly used for storage (now for display) in chemists' shops; **specie-room** *Hist.* a strongroom on a ship in which gold coin was deposited.

species /'spiːʃiːz, -ɪz, 'spiːs-/ *noun*. Pl. same. LME.
[Latin (sing. & pl.) = appearance, form, kind, etc., from *spec-* base of *specere* look, behold. Cf. prec., SPICE *noun*.]
▶ **I 1 a** A class of things having some common qualities or characteristics. LME. ▸**b** A kind, a sort, (*of*). L16. ▸†**c** *pl.* (NAUTICAL). Sorts of provisions. E18–E19.
2 LOGIC. A class of things subordinate to a genus and containing individuals sharing an attribute or attributes absent from other members of the genus and called by a common name; the second of the five predicables. M16. ▸†**b** The essential quality or specific properties *of* a thing. L16–M17.
3 a BIOLOGY. A taxonomic grouping ranking next below genus and subgenus, which contains organisms that are uniquely distinguished from others by certain shared characteristics and usu. by an inability to interbreed with members of other such groupings; such a grouping as denoted by a Latin binomial, and freq. subdivided into subspecies, races, varieties, etc.; the organisms of such a grouping. E17. ▸**b** MINERALOGY. A distinct kind of mineral with a unique set of physical and chemical properties. M17. ▸**c** CHEMISTRY & PHYSICS. A particular kind of molecule, ion, free radical, etc.; a distinct kind of atom (esp. a radioactive one) or subatomic particle. L19. ▸**d** HORTICULTURE. A garden flower, shrub, etc., that represents the plant in its pure or natural state and is not a cultivar or garden hybrid. Cf. ***species rose*** below. L20.
†**4 a** A particular kind of coin or money. E17–M18. ▸**b** Coin, coin money. (Not always clearly distinguishable from SPECIE 3.) E17–E19.
†**5 a** *pl.* The separate ingredients used in compounding a perfume, drug, etc. Only in 17. ▸†**b** A mixture used in embalming. Only in M18.

📖 **1a** *Independent* The 'new man', . . who is happy to . . look after the children, is still a rare species. **b** LD MACAULAY No species of fiction is so delightful . . as . . old English drama. J. G. FARRELL He saw them as a species of game that one could shoot. **3a** J. HERSEY I wondered what vile excuse for the species *Homo sapiens* could have done such a thing? *Choice* Most of the species that were declining are now holding their own in our conservation areas.

▶ **II 6** Appearance; outward form. Now only (LAW), a form or shape into which materials are converted (cf. SPECIFICATION 2b). LME. ▸**b** GEOMETRY. Form, irrespective of size. M19.
†**7** The visible form or image *of* a thing. L16–L17. ▸**b** The reflected image of a thing, a reflection. M17–L18.
8 ECCLESIASTICAL. The visible form of each of the elements of consecrated bread and wine used in the Eucharist; either of these elements. L16.
†**9** METAPHYSICS. A supposed emanation from a thing, forming the direct object of cognition for the senses. L16–M18. ▸**b** A mental impression. M17–E18.
†**10** A thing seen; *esp.* an unreal vision, an illusion. M–L17.
†**11** PHILOSOPHY. = IDEA *noun* 1. L17–L18.
Phrases: ***endangered species***: see ENDANGER 2. ***pioneer species***: see PIONEER *noun* 3b. ***protected species***: see PROTECT 1c. **the species** the human race. ***twin species***: see TWIN *adjective & noun*.
Comb.: **species pair** BIOLOGY a pair of species which are similar, sympatric, and closely related, but distinct; **species-poor** *adjective* (of a habitat or site) containing only a small range of species; **species-rich** *adjective* (of a habitat or site) containing a great diversity of species; **species richness** species-rich quality; **species rose**: belonging to a distinct species and not to one of the many varieties produced by hybridization; **species sanitation** MEDICINE measures taken against a particular species of insect vector in order to reduce the incidence of disease; **species-specific** *adjective* confined to, or characteristic of, the members of one species only.
■ **specieshood** *noun* (chiefly PSYCHOLOGY & SOCIOLOGY) the condition of being (a member of) a species, esp. of being or perceiving oneself as a member of the human species M20.

speciesism /'spiːʃiːzɪz(ə)m, 'spiːs-/ *noun*. L20.
[from prec. + -ISM.]
Discrimination against or exploitation of certain animal species by humans, based on an assumption of human superiority.
■ **speciesist** *adjective & noun* (*a*) *adjective* of, pertaining to, or characterized by speciesism; (*b*) *noun* an advocate of speciesism: L20.

specific /spə'sɪfɪk/ *adjective & noun*. M17.
[Late Latin *specificus*, from Latin SPECIES: see -FIC.]
▶ **A** *adjective*. **1** Having a special determining quality. Now *rare* or *obsolete*. M17.
2 Specially or peculiarly pertaining to a particular thing or person, or a class of these; peculiar (*to*). Also as 2nd elem. of comb. M17. ▸**b** PHYSICS. Of or designating a number equal to the ratio of the value of some property of a given substance to the value of the same property of some reference substance (as water), or of a vacuum, under equivalent conditions. Also, of or designating a physical quantity expressed in terms of a unit mass, volume, etc., in order to give a value independent of the properties or scale of the particular system studied. M19.
3 MEDICINE. **a** Of a remedy or medicine: specially or exclusively efficacious for, or acting on, a particular disease or part of the body. L17. ▸**b** Of a disease, condition, etc.: of a distinct or characteristic kind; caused by one identifiable agent. E19.
4 Of, pertaining to, or connected with, a particular species of organism. M18.
5 a Clearly or explicitly defined; precise, exact; definite. M18. ▸**b** Of a duty or tax: assessed according to the quantity or amount of goods, not the value. L18.

📖 **2** J. ABERNETHY The specific operation of mercury on the constitution. *Times Educ. Suppl.* The training is not necessarily job-specific. G. K. WOLFE A number of narrative formulas specific to both fantasy and science fiction. **5a** J. WAIN A fairly big sum of money . . to put to a specific use. R. D. LAING He is taught to move in specific ways. D. JACOBSON The message . . was specific and unambiguous.

Special collocations: ***specific acoustic*** IMPEDANCE. **specific activity** PHYSICS the activity of a given radioisotope per unit mass. **specific character** BIOLOGY any of various characters that distinguish a species from related forms. **specific charge** PHYSICS the ratio of the charge of an ion or subatomic particle to its mass. **specific conductance**, **specific conductivity** (now *rare*) = ELECTRICAL *conductivity*. **specific consumption** = *specific fuel consumption* below. **specific difference** a factor that differentiates a species. **specific epithet** (chiefly BOTANY & MICROBIOLOGY) the second (adjectival) element in the binomial Latin name of a species, which follows the generic name and distinguishes the species from others in the same genus (cf. ***specific name*** below). **specific fuel consumption** the weight of fuel consumed by an engine per unit time per unit of power or thrust developed; the reciprocal of specific impulse. **specific gravity** = RELATIVE *density*. **specific heat** (now *rare*) = ***specific heat capacity*** below. **specific heat capacity** PHYSICS the heat required to raise the temperature of the unit mass of a given substance by a given amount (usu. one degree Celsius), under specified conditions. ***specific impulse***: see IMPULSE *noun* 3b. **specific inductive capacity** = ***dielectric constant*** s.v. DIELECTRIC *adjective* 1. **specific ionization** PHYSICS the number of ion pairs produced by an ionizing particle per unit path length. **specific name** (*a*) (now chiefly ZOOLOGY) = ***specific epithet*** above; (*b*) (now chiefly BOTANY & MICROBIOLOGY) the binomial Latin name of a species, which comprises a generic name and a specific epithet. **specific performance** LAW the judicially compelled performance of a contractual duty, in a case where damages would not be adequate remedy. **specific refraction**, **specific refractive constant** PHYSICS a constant relating the refractive index (n) of a material to its density (ρ), given by $(n^2 - 1)/\rho(n^2 + 2)$. ***specific*** RESISTANCE. ***specific*** RESISTIVITY. **specific rotation**, **specific rotary power** PHYSICS the angle through which the plane of polarization of light of a specified wavelength is rotated by passage through a column of an optically active substance of given length (usu. 10 cm, approx. 3.9 inches) and at unit concentration. **specific surface** PHYSICS the surface area per unit volume of a finely-divided substance. **specific thrust** = ***specific impulse*** above. **specific viscosity** PHYSICS the difference between the viscosity of a solution of a given concentration and that of the pure solvent, divided by the viscosity of the pure solvent. **specific volume** PHYSICS the volume of a substance per unit mass; the reciprocal of density.
▶ **B** *noun*. **1** A specific medicine or remedy. Now chiefly *fig. arch.* M17.
2 *ellipt.* A specific difference or quality; *esp.* a specific aspect or factor, a detail. Usu. in *pl.* L17.
3 A specific word or name, esp. in taxonomy and toponymy. M20.

📖 **1** P. D. JAMES A cup of tea, the British specific against disaster. R. ELLMANN He adopted mercury . . as the specific for his dreadful disease. **2** F. BRANSTON He had been investing in property . . but he was . . vague about the specifics. M. DORRIS Experiences . . which he would . . recollect in essence rather than in specifics.

■ **specifical** *adjective & noun* (now *rare*) (*a*) *adjective* = SPECIFIC *adjective*; (*b*) *noun* = SPECIFIC *noun* 1: LME. **specifi'cality** *noun* (*rare*) the quality of being specific M17. **specifically** *adverb* (*a*) in respect of specific or distinctive qualities; (*b*) peculiarly; (*c*) in a clearly defined manner, definitely, precisely: E17. **speci'ficity** *noun* (*a*) the quality or fact of being specific; (*b*) (MEDICINE & BIOLOGY etc.) the narrowness of the range of substances with which an antibody, enzyme, or other agent acts or is effective; (*c*) BIOLOGY the degree to which a parasite or symbiote is restricted in its range of hosts: L19. **specificness** *noun* the quality of being specific L17.

specificate /spə'sɪfɪkeɪt/ *verb trans*. Now *rare* or *obsolete*. E17.
[Late Latin *specificat-* pa. ppl stem of *specificare* SPECIFY: see -ATE³. Cf. SPECIFY.]
†**1** Distinguish as belonging to a particular variety, kind, etc. Only in 17.
†**2** Apply specifically *to*; limit *to*. M–L17.
3 = SPECIFY 2. M17.
4 Make specific in character or qualities. M17.
■ †**specificative** *adjective* serving to specify; specific: L16–E18. †**specificatively** *adverb* specifically L16–E18.

specification /ˌspɛsɪfɪ'keɪʃ(ə)n/ *noun*. L16.
[medieval Latin *specificatio(n-)*, formed as prec.: see -ATION.]
1 An explicit or detailed enumeration or statement (*of*). L16. ▸**b** A document drawn up by the applicant for a patent, describing the construction and use of his or her invention. L18. ▸**c** A specified item, detail, etc. E19. ▸**d** *sing.* & in *pl.* A detailed description of the dimensions, construction, workmanship, materials, etc., of work done or to be done, prepared by an architect, engineer, etc. M19.
2 †**a** The action of investing something with a specific or distinguishing quality; conversion to something specific. E17–E18. ▸**b** LAW. The conversion of materials into a new product not held to be the property of the owner of the materials. Cf. SPECIES 6. M17.
†**3** A specific character or nature. E17–E18.
4 The action or an act of defining or describing a thing by reference to its specific or peculiar characteristics. M17.

📖 **1** J. SUTHERLAND His distilled advice . . was . . 'Work!', without any specification as to what the work should be. **d** M. MUGGERIDGE A new house . . built in accordance with my father's specifications. A. S. BYATT His slippers . . made in London, to his specification.

specify /'spɛsɪfʌɪ/ *verb*. ME.
[Old & mod. French *spécifier* or late Latin *specificare*: see -FY. Cf. prec., SPECIFICATE.]
1 *verb intrans.* Speak or treat of a matter etc. in detail; give details or particulars. Formerly foll. by *of*. ME.

2 *verb trans.* Mention or name (a thing, *that*) explicitly; state categorically or particularly. Also, include in an architect's, engineer's, etc. specification. **ME.**
3 *verb trans.* Chiefly *LOGIC.* Invest with a specific character. **M17.**

> 🕮 **1** N. FARAH 'Did Father say where I would go?' 'No. He wouldn't specify'. **2** *Nursing Times* General administrative duties . . as specified by the Whitley Council. E. SEGAL They failed to specify that taking Saranac . . during pregnancy could cause birth defects. D. JUDD Robert requests . . that I read him a story. He specifies *Snow White*.

■ **speci'fiable** *adjective* **M17.** **specifier** *noun* **M18.**

specimen /ˈspɛsɪmɪn/ *noun & adjective.* **E17.**
[Latin, from *specere* look (at).]
▸**A** *noun.* †**1** A pattern, a model. Only in 17.
2 A single thing or part taken as an example of a class or as representative of the whole. **M17.**
3 *spec.* An individual animal or plant, a piece of a mineral, etc., taken for scientific study or display; *MEDICINE* a small quantity of blood, urine, tissue, etc., taken for scientific analysis; *ellipt.* (*MEDICINE*) a specimen of urine. **L17.**
4 A person as an example of or *of* a certain quality or of the human race; (*colloq.*, freq. *derog.*) a person of a specified sort. **E19.**

> 🕮 **2** O. HENRY His wardrobe represented the . . specimens of half a dozen fashions. *Raritan* I take this . . piece of irony as a specimen of religious awe. **3** H. JAMES Glass cases containing specimens of butterflies. B. BAINBRIDGE Going into a . . cubicle to provide a cloudy specimen. P. CAREY He was a naturalist . . and . . would collect specimens. **4** P. H. GIBBS Seeing some remarkable . . specimen of mankind. I. WATSON The two men . . were less savoury specimens.

▸**B** *attrib.* or as *adjective.* Serving as or intended for a specimen. **M19.**
Comb. & special collocations: **specimen-book** a book of specimens or samples; **specimen-box** a portable box for carrying botanical etc. specimens; **specimen page**: submitted by a printer as a sample setting for a book etc.; **specimen shrub**, **specimen tree**, etc.: planted on its own, away from other plants of a similar size.

speciose /ˈspiːsɪəʊs, ˈspiːʃɪ-/ *adjective.* **L20.**
[from SPECIES + -OSE[1].]
BIOLOGY. Of a taxon or other group of organisms: comprising many species, species-rich.

speciosity /spiːʃɪˈɒsɪti/ *noun*[1]. Now *rare.* **LME.**
[Late Latin *speciositas* beauty etc., formed as next; in sense 2 directly from next: see -ITY.]
†**1** Beauty. Also, a beautiful thing. **LME–M17.**
2 The quality of being specious; speciousness. **E17.**

speciosity /spiːsɪˈɒsɪti, spiːʃɪ-/ *noun*[2]. **L20.**
[from SPECIOSE + -ITY.]
BIOLOGY. Abundance of species, esp. in a taxonomic grouping.

specious /ˈspiːʃəs/ *adjective.* **LME.**
[from Latin *speciosus* fair, fair-seeming, etc., formed as SPECIES + -OUS.]
†**1** Pleasing to the eye; beautiful, handsome. Later also, (of a flower or bird) having brilliant colouring. **LME–M19.**
2 Deceptively attractive in appearance or character; merely apparent. **E17.**
3 Superficially genuine or correct but in reality wrong or false; (of an argument, reasoning, etc.) misleadingly sound or convincing. **M17.** ▸**b** Of a person: characterized by speciousness in behaviour, reasoning, etc. **M18.**
†**4** Of algebra: performed by means of, or expressed in, letters. **L17–E18.**

> 🕮 **2** G. CRABBE What are these specious gifts, these paltry gains? LD MACAULAY A policy which had a specious show of liberality. R. C. HUTCHINSON The specious self-assurance of those . . conscious of inferior birth. **3** J. LE CARRÉ For reasons which I regarded . . as specious and insulting, the Americans objected to your husband. G. STEINER Specious pretensions to technicality which make the bulk of . . deconstructive theory . . unreadable.

■ **speciousness** *noun* **M17.**

speciously /ˈspiːʃəsli/ *adverb*[1]. **M17.**
[from prec. + -LY[2].]
In a specious manner.

speciously /ˈspiːʃəsli/ *adverb*[2]. Long *obsolete* exc. *dial.* **L16.**
[Alt.]
Specially.

speck /spɛk/ *noun*[1].
[Old English *specca*: no cognates but cf. SPECKLE *noun.*]
1 A small spot or mark of a different colour or shade; a minute discoloration or stain. (Foll. by *of.*) **OE.** ▸**b** A very small or distant cloud. Chiefly *fig.* **M18.**
2 A minute particle (*of*); *spec.* (**a**) *Austral.* a small fragment of gold; (**b**) a small piece of land. **LME.**
3 A small spot or lesion indicative of a defect or disease. Now chiefly *spec.*, a rotten or bruised spot in fruit; in *pl.*, (*slang*) rotten or bruised fruit. **LME.**

> 🕮 **1** J. STEINBECK Specks of green and red light swarmed on his vision. P. L. FERMOR His flock was a blur of white specks and faraway tinklings. **2** H. CARPENTER He could not bear even a speck of dirt on his clothes. **not a speck** *US* not at all. **b the Speck** *Austral. colloq.* Tasmania. **3** J. AUSTEN Lizzy was going to be very ill one day; she had specks & a great deal of fever.

■ **speckless** *adjective* having no speck or specks; *esp.* spotlessly clean: **L18.** **specklessly** *adverb* **M19.** **specklessness** *noun* **L19.**

speck /spɛk/ *noun*[2]. Now *US & S. Afr.*
[Old English *spec* (once) var. of SPICK *noun*[1]. Reintroduced in 17 from Dutch *spek* (from Middle Dutch *spec*) or German *Speck* (Old High German *spec*). Cf. SPETCH.]
1 Fat meat, *esp.* strips of bacon for larding meat etc. **OE.**
2 The fat or blubber of a whale. **M18.**

speck /spɛk/ *verb.* **L16.**
[from SPECK *noun*[1] or back-form. from SPECKED.]
1 *verb trans.* Mark with a speck or specks; in *pass.*, be covered or marked *with* specks (cf. SPECKED). **L16.**
2 *Austral.* **a** *verb intrans.* Search for small particles of gold or opal on the surface of alluvial deposits. **L19.** ▸**b** *verb trans.* Search the surface of (the ground) for particles of gold or opal; find (particles of gold or opal) in this way. **L19.**

> 🕮 **1** S. WYNTER Above the church a vulture specked the blue sky. **2a** E. WALLER Tourists specking for bits of potch and opal.

speck and span *adjectival phr.* see SPICK AND SPAN.

specked /spɛkt/ *adjective.* **LME.**
[from SPECK *noun*[1]. Cf. prec.]
Covered or marked with specks or spots; speckled; dappled; variegated.

> 🕮 J. CLARE The spekt throstle never wakes his song.

speckle /ˈspɛk(ə)l/ *noun.* **LME.**
[Middle Dutch *spekkel* (Dutch *spikkel*). Cf. SPECKLED.]
1 A speck, a small mark or patch of colour, *esp.* one occurring naturally and in quantity on the skin, a bird's egg, etc. **LME.**
2 a Speckled marking, speckling. *rare.* **M19.** ▸**b** *OPTICS* etc. A granular appearance seen in images formed by originally coherent light as a result of the interference of waves that have been reflected at a rough surface or have passed through an inhomogeneous medium; each of the light or dark areas giving rise to this appearance. **M20.**

> 🕮 **1** J. C. MORTON Seeds of a grayish colour, with purple speckles.

Comb.: **speckle interferometry** the analysis of speckle in two or more images, differing only in the instant of exposure, as a means of obtaining information about the source of light or the agent that caused the speckle.
■ **speckly** *adjective* covered or marked with speckles, speckled **LME.**

speckle /ˈspɛk(ə)l/ *verb.* **L16.**
[from the noun or back-form. from next.]
1 *verb trans.* Mark or cover (as) with speckles. **L16.**
2 *verb intrans.* Form speckles; become speckled. *rare.* **E18.**

> 🕮 **1** R. ADAMS A green, faint light . . shone down from the under-sides of the leaves, speckling the bare ground. A. TYLER Flakes of lint speckled the rug. **2** R. ADAMS The sunlight dappled and speckled . . over the brown soil.

■ **speckling** *noun* (**a**) the action of the verb; (**b**) speckled marking or marks, an instance of this: **E17.**

speckled /ˈspɛk(ə)ld/ *adjective.* **LME.**
[from SPECKLE *noun* + -ED[2] (cf. Middle Dutch *spekelde*, *gespekeld* (Dutch *gespikkeld*)). Cf. prec.]
Covered or marked with (numerous) speckles; variegated or flecked with spots of a contrasting colour.

> 🕮 D. MADDEN The smooth, speckled sea shell. K. MANSFIELD His black hair was speckled all over with silver. **speckled belly** *N. Amer.* the white-fronted goose, *Anser albifrons*. **speckled diver** the red-throated diver, *Gavia stellata*. **speckled trout** *N. Amer.* the brook trout, *Salvelinus fontinalis*. **speckled wood** (**a**) any of several timbers having speckled markings, *esp.* that of the S. American letter-wood, *Brosimum aubletii*; any of the trees yielding such wood; (**b**) a brown satyrid butterfly with yellowish spots, *Pararge aegeria*, found in lightly shaded places in much of Europe. **speckled yellows** a disease of sugar beet characterized by distorted and discoloured leaves, caused by a deficiency of manganese.

specksioneer /spɛkʃəˈnɪə/ *noun.* **E19.**
[Dutch *speksnijer* colloq. var. of *speknijder*, from *spek* SPECK *noun*[2] + *snijden* to cut.]
WHALING. The chief harpooner on a whaler, who directs the flensing of the whale.

specky /ˈspɛki/ *adjective*[1]. **LME.**
[from SPECK *noun*[1] + -Y[1].]
Covered or marked with specks.

specky /ˈspɛki/ *adjective*[2]. *colloq.* Also **speccy**. **M20.**
[from SPEC(S + -Y[1].]
Spectacled, wearing spectacles.

specs /spɛks/ *noun pl. colloq.* **E19.**
[Abbreviation.]
(A pair of) spectacles.

spect /spɛkt/ *verb intrans. & trans.* (*1 sing. pres.*). *non-standard.* **M19.**
[Repr. a pronunc.]
I expect.

spectacle /ˈspɛktək(ə)l/ *noun*[1] *& verb.* **ME.**
[Old & mod. French from Latin *spectaculum* public show, from *spectare*: see SPECTATE *verb*. Cf. next.]
▸**A** *noun.* **I 1** An organized (usu. public) display or entertainment, *esp.* one on a large or splendid scale; splendid display or ceremony. **ME.**
2 A person or thing as an object of public curiosity, contempt, or admiration. Now chiefly in ***make a spectacle of oneself*** below. **LME.**
3 A thing seen or able to be seen, a sight, esp. of a striking or unusual character; a manifestation *of* a quality or condition. **LME.**

> 🕮 **1** J. W. KRUTCH The million-dollar TV spectacle, with . . highly paid comedians and singers. *San Antonio Express* A taco-eating, tortilla-tossing and chile-cooking spectacle. A. BROOKNER He wanted noise, spectacle. **2** AV *1 Cor.* 4:9 For wee are made a spectacle vnto the world, and to Angels, and to men. **3** J. AGATE The horrid spectacle of intellectuals consuming cocoa. D. LEAVITT He was unmoved by the spectacle of the Grand Canyon. H. CARPENTER Their attention diverted by a curious spectacle.

▸**II** †**4** A means of seeing; something made of glass; a window; a mirror; *fig.* a model, a standard, an example. **LME–M17.**
5 In *pl.* & (now only attrib. & in comb.) *sing.* A pair of glass (now also plastic) lenses set in a metal, plastic, etc., frame resting on the nose and usu. on the ears, used to correct or assist defective eyesight. Also ***pair of spectacles***. **LME.** ▸**b** *fig.* A medium through which something is regarded; a point of view. **LME.** ▸**c** *CRICKET.* In *pl.* A batsman's score of zero in each innings of a match. Chiefly & now only ***pair of spectacles***. **M19.** ▸**d** *ZOOLOGY.* A marking resembling a pair of spectacles, round the eyes or elsewhere. **L19.** ▸**e** A frame containing a red and a green light in a railway signal. **L19.**
6 Either of two brownish noctuid moths of the genus *Abrostola*, which have two round pale dark-edged marks on the front of the thorax. **E19.**
7 *ZOOLOGY.* A fixed transparent eyelid covering the eye of snakes and some lizards. **M20.**

> 🕮 **5** D. PROFUMO Looking at him . . through round, wire-rimmed spectacles. **b** A. COOKE The British monarchy, which now—through American spectacles—seemed impressive but quaint.

Phrases: **make a spectacle of oneself** make oneself an object of ridicule. ***pair of spectacles***: see senses 5, 5c above. ***see through rose-coloured spectacles***: see ROSE-COLOURED 2.
Comb.: **spectacle-case**: for keeping spectacles when not in use; **spectacle clew** a form of double clew for a sail; **spectacle-glass** a lens of a pair of spectacles.
▸**B** *verb trans.* Scrutinize through spectacles. *rare.* **M18.**

spectacle /spɛktakl/ *noun*[2]. Now *rare.* Pl. pronounced same. **M18.**
[French: see prec.]
= SPECTACLE *noun*[1] 1; *spec.* a theatrical display or pageant.

spectacled /ˈspɛktək(ə)ld/ *adjective.* **E17.**
[from SPECTACLE *noun*[1] + -ED[2].]
1 Provided with or wearing spectacles. **E17.**
2 In names of animals: having markings shaped like spectacles, esp. as pale or dark rings or patches around the eyes. **M19.**
2 spectacled bear a small S. American bear, *Tremarctos ornatus*, which has white markings around the eyes and occurs in the tropical forests of the Andes. **spectacled cayman** a small S. American alligator, *Caiman sclerops*, which is freq. kept as a pet. **spectacled cobra** the Asian cobra, *Naja naja*, which often has a double loop-shaped marking on the expanded hood. **spectacled owl** a Central and S. American owl, *Pulsatrix perspicillata*, which has dark plumage with creamy white underparts and a striking white facial pattern. **spectacled salamander** a small slender Italian salamander, *Salamandrina terdigitata*, which is blackish above and bright red under the legs and tail. **spectacled serpent**, **spectacled snake** = ***spectacled cobra*** above. **spectacled warbler** a Mediterranean and N. African warbler, *Sylvia conspicillata*, which resembles a small whitethroat and occurs in scrub in arid areas.

spectacular /spɛkˈtakjʊlə/ *adjective & noun.* **L17.**
[from SPECTACLE *noun*[1] after pairs like *oracle*, *oracular*: see -ULAR.]
▸**A** *adjective.* Of the nature of a spectacle, resembling that of a spectacle; striking, amazing, lavish; *fig.* strikingly large or obvious. **L17.**

> 🕮 **1** E. MELLOR It is easy . . to surround any ceremony . . with a spectacular splendour which captivates the imagination. A. BROOKNER She could have made a spectacular entrance and stunned everyone. D. M. THOMAS With spectacular meanness, I kept the College Library copy of Klaeber's *Beowulf* for two years. Q. HOGG The view was spectacular, especially in the evening as the lights came out across the valley.

▸**B** *noun.* A spectacular display; *esp.* a theatrical show, television programme, etc., produced on a lavish scale. **L19.**

📖 *Daily Star* Their live music show is an action-packed spectacular.

■ **spectacularism** *noun* (*rare*) spectacular character or quality L19. **spectacu'larity** *noun* spectacular character or quality L19. **spectacularly** *adverb* M19.

spectate /spɛk'teɪt/ *verb*. E18.
[In sense 1 from Latin *spectat-* pa. ppl stem of *spectare* to look, frequentative of *specere* look at, in sense 2 back-form. from SPECTATOR: see -ATE³.]
1 *verb intrans. & trans.* Look or gaze (at). *rare*. E18.
2 *verb intrans.* Be a spectator, esp. at a sporting event. E20.

📖 **2** R. FRAME Fairs were held on Pack Street: later I went to spectate at some. C. HARMAN A . . preference for spectating rather than partaking in sports.

■ **spectation** *noun* (*rare*) [Latin *spectatio(n-)*, from *spectat-*] the action of looking or gazing at something M17.

spectator /spɛk'teɪtə/ *noun*. L16.
[French *spectateur* or Latin *spectator*, from *spectat-*: see prec., -OR.]
1 A person who looks on at a scene or incident, esp. a show or sporting event. Also in the titles of periodicals. L16.
†**2** *spec.* A scientific observer. *rare*. M17–L18.
Comb.: **spectator sport** (a) sport affording good entertainment for spectators as well as for participants (cf. PARTICIPATION *sport*).
■ **spectatordom** *noun* (*rare*) spectators collectively M19. **specta'torial** *adjective* of, pertaining to, or characteristic of, a spectator E18. **specta'torially** *adverb* M20. **spectatorism** *noun* (*rare*) the practice of being a spectator L19. **spectatorship** *noun* †(*a*) *rare* presentation to view; (*b*) the state or fact of being a spectator: E17. **spectatory** *noun* (*arch.*) the part of a building set aside for spectators E19. **spectatress** *noun* (now *rare*) a female spectator M17. **spectatrix** *noun* (now *rare*) = SPECTATRESS E17.

specter *noun* see SPECTRE.

spectinomycin /ˌspɛktɪnə'mʌɪsɪn/ *noun*. M20.
[from mod. Latin use as specific epithet (see below) of Latin *spectabilis* visible, remarkable, from *spectare* (see SPECTATE): see -O-, -MYCIN.]
PHARMACOLOGY. An antibiotic obtained from the bacterium *Streptomyces spectabilis* and used esp. to treat gonorrhoea that is resistant to penicillin.

spectra *noun* pl. of SPECTRUM.

spectral /'spɛktr(ə)l/ *adjective*. E18.
[from next or directly from SPECTRUM + -AL¹.]
†**1** Capable of seeing spectres. *rare*. Only in E18.
2 Of the nature of a spectre; resembling (that of) a spectre; ghostly. E19.
3 Of or pertaining to the spectrum, appearing or observed in the spectrum. Also, designating a property or parameter which is being considered as a function of frequency or wavelength, or which pertains to a given frequency range or value within the spectrum. Cf. SPECTRUM 3a, b. M19.

📖 **2** W. BLACK A pair of spectral horses apparently in mid-air. O. MANNING The promenade was a spectral grey in the moon glimmer. R. FRAME Houses . . becoming paler and more spectral as the moon sailed clear.

Special collocations: **spectral analysis** (*a*) *CHEMISTRY* the chemical analysis of substances by means of their spectra; (*b*) *PHYSICS* the analysis of light or another oscillating system into a spectrum. **spectral class** *ASTRONOMY* = *spectral type* below. **spectral index** *ASTRONOMY* an exponential factor relating the flux density of a radio source to the frequency. **spectral-luminosity class** *ASTRONOMY* the group in which a star is classified, relating its spectral characteristics to its luminosity. **spectral luminous efficiency** a measure of the ability of the eye to judge the power of monochromatic light of a given wavelength. ***spectral series***: see SERIES *noun* 16. **spectral tarsier** a tarsier, *Tarsius spectrum*, which is distinguished by a scaly tail with a long bushy tuft, and occurs in forests in Sulawesi. ***spectral term***: see TERM *noun* 13c. **spectral type** *ASTRONOMY* the group in which a star is classified according to its spectrum, esp. using the Harvard classification in which letters are used to represent particular surface temperatures.
■ **spec'trality** *noun* (*a*) a ghost; (*b*) ghostliness; (*c*) *MATH.* the state of being expressible as a spectral function: M19. **spectrally** *adverb* M19.

spectre /'spɛktə/ *noun*. Also *-ter. E17.
[French, or Latin *spectrum*, from *specere* look, see. Cf. SPECTRUM.]
1 An apparition, a ghost, *esp.* one of a terrifying nature or aspect. E17. ▸**b** In Epicurean philosophy, an image supposed to emanate from a corporeal thing. *arch.* L18.
2 *fig.* A haunting or terrifying presentiment. Freq. foll. by *of*. L18. ▸**b** A person resembling a ghost in appearance. E19.
3 *ENTOMOLOGY*. A stick insect. Also ***spectre-insect***. L18.
4 An image produced by reflection or other natural cause. E19.

📖 **2** E. YOUNG-BRUEHL The . . frightening specter of a mortal illness. E. S. PERSON The spectre overshadowing love is the fear that it will end. **4** ***BROCKEN spectre***, ***spectre of the BROCKEN***.

Comb.: ***spectre-insect***: see sense 3 above; **spectre-lemur**, **spectre tarsier** = *SPECTRAL* ***tarsier***.
■ **spectred** *adjective* (now *rare*) (*a*) filled with spectres; (*b*) resembling a spectre: L18. **spectredom** *noun* the realm of spectres L19. **spectrous** *adjective* (now *rare*) spectral M17.

spectrin /'spɛktrɪn/ *noun*. M20.
[from SPECTRE + -IN¹, so called because it was isolated from red blood cell ghosts (see GHOST *noun* 11).]
BIOCHEMISTRY. A fibrous protein constituent of the membranes of red blood cells, forming a network on the inside of the plasma membrane.

spectro- /'spɛktrəʊ/ *combining form* (on Greek analogies) of SPECTRUM: see -O-.
■ **spectrobo'lometer** *noun* a combination of a spectroscope and a bolometer, designed to determine the wavelength distribution of radiant energy emitted by a source E20. **spectro'heliogram** *noun* a photograph obtained with a spectroheliograph E20. **spectro'heliograph** *noun* (*a*) an instrument which photographs the sun using light of a particular wavelength, esp. that of the Balmer α emission line of hydrogen; (*b*) *rare* a spectroheliogram: L19. **spectrohelio'graphic** *adjective* of, pertaining to, or employing a spectroheliograph E20. **spectroheli'ometer** *noun* a spectrophotometer for use in observing the sun L20. **spectro'helioscope** *noun* an instrument which provides a directly observable monochromatic image of the sun by means of a rapidly scanning device which transmits light of only one wavelength E20. **spectrophone** *noun* a device in which a body of gas may be caused to emit sound waves when illuminated by a periodically interrupted beam of electromagnetic radiation (usu. visible or infrared) L19. **spectro'phonic** *adjective* of, pertaining to, or employing a spectrophone L19. **spectrophospho'rimeter** *noun* a spectrometer designed for the observation of phosphorescence M20. **spectrophosphori'metric** *adjective* of, pertaining to, or employing spectrophosphorimetry M20. **spectrophospho'rimetry** *noun* spectrometry as applied to the observation of phosphorescence M20. **spectrophotofluo'rometer** *noun* a spectrophotometer designed for the observation of fluorescence M20. **spectrophotofluoro'metric** *adjective* of, pertaining to, or employing a spectrophotofluorometer M20. **spectropola'rimeter** *noun* an instrument designed to measure rotation of the plane of polarized light as a function of wavelength E20. **spectropolari'metric** *adjective* of, pertaining to, or employing spectropolarimetry M20. **spectropola'rimetry** *noun* the use of a spectropolarimeter M20. **spectroradi'ometer** *noun* a combination of a spectroscope and a radiometer, designed to measure the intensity of electromagnetic radiation over a range of wavelengths E20. **spectroradio'metric** *adjective* of, pertaining to, or employing spectroradiometry E20. **spectroradi'ometry** *noun* the scientific investigation of electromagnetic radiation at different wavelengths E20. **spectrotype** *noun* (*IMMUNOLOGY*) the range of antigens to which a given antibody is reactive L20.

spectrochemistry /spɛktrə(ʊ)'kɛmɪstri/ *noun*. L19.
[from SPECTRO- + CHEMISTRY.]
The branch of chemistry that deals with the chemical application of spectroscopy, esp. in analysis, and with the interpretation of spectra in chemical terms.
■ **spectrochemical** *adjective* of or pertaining to spectrochemistry; ***spectrochemical series***, a series of ligands arranged in order of magnitude of the ligand field splitting that they cause in the electronic orbitals of a central atom: L19. **spectrochemically** *adverb* as regards spectrochemistry; by spectrochemical methods: E20.

spectrofluorimetry /ˌspɛktrə(ʊ)flʊə'rɪmɪtri/ *noun*. Also **-rometry** /-'rɒmɪtri/. M20.
[from SPECTRO- + FLUORIMETRY.]
The spectrometric observation of fluorescence.
■ **spectrofluorimeter** *noun* a spectrometer designed for this M20. **spectrofluori'metric** *adjective* of, pertaining to, or employing spectrofluorimetry M20. **spectrofluori'metrically** *adverb* by means of spectrofluorimetry M20.

spectrograph /'spɛktrəgrɑːf/ *noun*. L19.
[from SPECTRO- + -GRAPH.]
1 An instrument for photographing a spectrum; any apparatus for producing a visual record of a spectrum (optical or otherwise). L19.
2 = SPECTROGRAM. Now *rare* or *obsolete*. L19.
1 ***mass spectrograph***, ***sound spectrograph***, etc.
■ **spectrogram** *noun* a photograph of a spectrum; any visual representation of a spectrum: L19. **spec'trographer** *noun* a person who uses a spectrograph M20. **spectro'graphic** *adjective* of, pertaining to, or employing spectrography L19. **spectro'graphically** *adverb* by means of a spectrograph E20. **spec'trography** *noun* the technique of using a spectrograph E20.

spectrology /spɛk'trɒlədʒi/ *noun*. *rare*. E19.
[from (the same root as) SPECTRO- + -OLOGY.]
1 The branch of knowledge that deals with spectres. E19.
2 The branch of science that deals with spectra. M19.
■ **spectro'logical** *adjective* E19.

spectrometer /spɛk'trɒmɪtə/ *noun*. L19.
[from SPECTRO- + -METER.]
Orig., an instrument for measuring a refractive index. Now, any of a wide range of instruments for producing spectra and measuring the positions etc. of spectral features.
mass spectrometer: see MASS *noun*² & *adjective*.
■ **spectro'metric** *adjective* of, pertaining to, or employing spectrometry L19. **spectro'metrically** *adverb* by means of spectrometry M20. **spectrometrist** *noun* an expert in spectrometry; a person employed to operate a spectrometer: M20. **spectrometry** *noun* the branch of science that deals with spectra E20.

spectrophotometer /ˌspɛktrə(ʊ)fəʊ'tɒmɪtə/ *noun*. L19.
[from SPECTRO- + PHOTOMETER.]
An instrument incorporating a photometer and designed to measure the relative intensity of light (usu. transmitted or emitted by a substance under study) at different wavelengths in a particular region of the spectrum.
■ **spectrophoto'metric** *adjective* of, pertaining to, or employing spectrophotometry L19. **spectrophoto'metrically** *adverb* by means of spectrophotometry L19. **spectrophotometry** *noun* the technique of using a spectrophotometer L19.

spectroscope /'spɛktrəskəʊp/ *noun & verb*. M19.
[from SPECTRO- + -SCOPE.]
▸ **A** *noun*. An instrument for the production and examination of spectra. M19.
mass spectroscope: see MASS *noun*² & *adjective*.
▸ **B** *verb trans.* Examine by means of a spectroscope. Now *rare*. L19.
■ **spectro'scopic** *adjective* of, pertaining to, or employing the spectroscope; ***spectroscopic binary*** (*ASTRONOMY*), a star whose binary nature is revealed only by a study of its spectrum: M19. **spectro'scopical** *adjective* = SPECTROSCOPIC L19. **spectro'scopically** *adverb* by means of the spectroscope; in respect of spectroscopic qualities etc.: L19.

spectroscopy /spɛk'trɒskəpi/ *noun*. L19.
[formed as prec.: see -SCOPY.]
The technique of using the spectroscope; the branch of science which involves the use of the spectroscope; the investigation of spectra by any of various instruments.
■ **spectroscopist** *noun* an expert in spectroscopy; a person employed to operate a spectroscope: M19.

spectrum /'spɛktrəm/ *noun*. Pl. **-tra** /-trə/, **-trums**. E17.
[Latin = image of a thing, apparition: see SPECTRE.]
1 An apparition, a spectre. *arch.* E17.
2 An image. *rare*. L17.
3 a The coloured band into which a beam of light is split by means of a prism or diffraction grating. Also, such a band containing bright or dark lines corresponding to the frequencies emitted or absorbed, and characteristic of the light source; the pattern of absorption or emission of any electromagnetic radiation over a range of wavelengths characteristic of a body or substance. L17. ▸**b** (Any part of) the entire range of wavelengths of electromagnetic radiation, from the longest radio waves to the shortest gamma rays. L19. ▸**c** An actual or notional arrangement of the component parts of any phenomenon according to frequency, energy, mass, etc. L19. ▸**d** *fig.* The entire or a wide range of something arranged by degree, quality, etc. M20.
4 A visual after-image. Now *rare* or *obsolete*. L18.

📖 **3a** *RAMAN* ***spectrum***. ***visible spectrum***: see VISIBLE *adjective*. **b** *ELECTROMAGNETIC* ***spectrum***. **c** ***mass spectrum***: see MASS *noun*² & *adjective*. ***power spectrum***: see POWER *noun*. **d** A. C. CLARKE A whole spectrum of shifting overtones covering the range of hearing. *Business Tokyo* Tastings . . covering almost the entire spectrum of quality wines.

Comb.: **spectrum analyser** an instrument which analyses a system of oscillations into its spectral components; **spectrum analysis** the determination of the spectral components of a system of oscillations.

specula *noun pl.* see SPECULUM.

specular /'spɛkjʊlə/ *adjective*. L16.
[Latin *specularis*, from SPECULUM. In branch II from Latin *speculari* spy, observe, *specula* watch-tower.]
▸ **I 1** ***specular stone*** [after Latin *specularis lapis*], a transparent or semi-transparent substance formerly used as glass or for ornamental purposes; (a piece or flake) of mica, selenite, or talc. *arch.* L16.
†**2** Of (spiritual) vision: indirect, unclear, not immediate (with allus. to 1 *Corinthians* 13:12 (Vulgate) *per speculum in aenigmate*, (AV) 'through a glasse, darkely'). E17–E18.
3 a Now chiefly *MINERALOGY*. Having the reflecting property of a mirror; presenting a smooth, polished, reflective surface; of a brilliant glassy or metallic lustre. M17. ▸**b** Designating or pertaining to reflection by a surface in which incident light is reflected as in a mirror. M19.
▸ **II 4** Of or pertaining to sight or vision. Now *rare* or *obsolete*. M17.
5 Of a hill, a tower, etc.: giving a wide or extensive view. *literary*. L17.
Special collocations: **specular iron (ore)** a grey or black variety of haematite with a bright metallic lustre. **specular orb** *poet.* the eye. ***specular stone***: see sense 1 above.
■ **specularly** *adverb* E18.

specularite /'spɛkjʊlərʌɪt/ *noun*. L19.
[from prec. + -ITE¹.]
MINERALOGY. = *SPECULAR* ***iron (ore)***.

speculate /'spɛkjʊleɪt/ *verb*. L16.
[Latin *speculat-* pa. ppl stem of *speculari* spy out, watch, from *specula* lookout, watch-tower, from *specere* see, look: see -ATE³.]
1 *verb trans.* Orig., reflect or theorize on, contemplate, (a theory, subject, etc.). Now usu., consider, conjecture, wonder, (*that*, *how*, *what*, etc.). L16.

2 *verb trans.* Look or gaze at (a thing); examine or inspect closely; *spec.* observe (the stars, heaven, etc.), esp. for the purpose of study. Now *rare* or *obsolete.* **E17.**

3 *verb intrans.* Engage in reflection or conjecture, form a theory, meditate, esp. without a firm factual basis. (Foll. by *on, upon, about,* etc.) **L17.**

4 a *verb intrans.* Invest in stocks, property, etc., in the hope of profit from a rise or fall in market value but with the possibility of a loss; enter into a risky enterprise in the hope of considerable gain; gamble. (Foll. by *on, in.*) **L18.** ▸**b** *verb trans.* Invest (funds) in a risky enterprise, gamble (money). **E20.**

> **1** *Scientific American* Some physicists have speculated that in nature all particles may be colorless. **3** R. LINDNER I speculated on what could be wrong with my patient. M. MOORCOCK Nobody was able to speculate . . as to the identity of the antagonists. **4a** R. MACAULAY Their brother . . made a fortune by speculating in . . gold mine shares. P. G. WODEHOUSE If you don't speculate . . you can't accumulate. **b** P. KAVANAGH A roulette-table on which I speculated three pennies without any return.

speculation /spɛkjʊˈleɪʃ(ə)n/ *noun.* **LME.**
[Old & mod. French *spéculation* or late Latin *speculatio(n-)*, formed as prec.: see **-ATION.**]
▸ **I 1** A spectacle, a sight; a spectacular entertainment or show. *rare. obsolete* exc. *Scot.* **LME.**

2 The faculty or power of seeing, esp. with comprehension; sight, vision. *arch.* **L15.**

†**3** The action or an act of seeing or looking at something, *spec.* the stars; examination, observation. **E16–L18.**

▸ **II 4** Contemplation, consideration, or study of a subject etc. (Foll. by *of, in, into, concerning.*) Now *rare* or *obsolete.* **LME.**

5 The action of speculating or theorizing; abstract or hypothetical reflection or meditation; conjecture, surmise; an instance of this. Also, a theory, work, etc., reached by speculating. **LME.**

6 The action or practice of investing in stocks, property, etc., in the hope of profit from a rise or fall in market value but with the possibility of a loss; engagement in a venture offering the chance of considerable gain but the possibility of loss; an instance of this. Also, an investment or enterprise of this kind. **L18.**

7 *CARDS* (now *Hist.*). A round game in which trump cards are bought and sold. **E19.**

> **5** H. P. BROUGHAM Mere romantic speculation of political dreamers. LYNDON B. JOHNSON Speculation increased that we might . . devalue the dollar. I. A. RICHARDS Speculations as to what went on in the artist's mind are unverifiable. **6** E. F. BENSON Mad speculation had lost him . . his . . fortune. L. STRACHEY A joint-stock company . . built, as a private speculation, the Albert Hall. F. ZWEIG Public concern . . over land and property speculation.

speculatist /ˈspɛkjʊlətɪst/ *noun.* **E17.**
[from **SPECULATE** + **-IST.**]

1 A person engaging in abstract or hypothetical reasoning or speculation, a theorist. **E17.**

2 A person speculating in stocks, property, etc., a speculative investor. **E19.**

speculative /ˈspɛkjʊlətɪv/ *adjective & noun.* **LME.**
[Old & mod. French *spéculatif, -ive* or late Latin *speculativus*, formed as **SPECULATE**: see **-ATIVE.**]
▸ **A** *adjective.* **1** Of the nature of, based on, or characterized by speculation or theory rather than practical or positive knowledge; conjectural. **LME.**

2 Of a person etc.: given to abstract speculation, inclined to theorize or engage in conjecture, meditative. Of time, a faculty, etc.: spent in, used for, or devoted to such speculation. **M16.**

3 Suitable for observation, providing a vantage-point. Chiefly *poet.* **E18.**

4 Of a person: given to or engaging in speculation in stocks, property, etc. Also, of the nature of or based on such speculation, involving the risk of loss; *gen.* performed more in the hope than the anticipation of success. **M18.**

> **1** COLERIDGE Philosophy must have a practical . . as well as a theoretical or speculative side. C. P. SNOW All this is speculative, . . a dubious guess. N. SHERRY His . . speculative eyes, the eyebrows raised in a perpetual questioning. **speculative fiction** literature, as science fiction or fantasy writing, dealing with imaginary or hypothetical worlds or environments. **speculative grammar** *Hist.* a late medieval scholastic grammar system interpreting the structure of language as mirroring reality; a grammatical theory arising from this. **2** A. S. BYATT A fellow-scholar, erudite and speculative. **4** *Hull Advertiser* The price of corn which speculative men were trying to advance. **speculative builder** a person who has houses erected without securing buyers in advance.

▸ **B** *noun.* †**1 a** Speculation; hypothetical reasoning; theory. **LME–E16.** ▸**b** In *pl.* Speculative matters; the speculative sciences. **M–L17.**

2 A speculator, a speculatist. *rare.* **M17.**

■ **speculatively** *adverb* **L16.** **speculativeness** *noun* **E18.** **speculativism** *noun* (excessive) practice of or tendency towards speculation **M19.**

speculator /ˈspɛkjʊleɪtə/ *noun.* **M16.**
[Latin, formed as **SPECULATE**: see **-OR.**]

1 A person engaged in abstract speculation or in conjecture; a theorist. **M16.**

2 A sentry, a lookout. Now *rare.* **E17.**

†**3** A person engaged in occult observations or studies. **M–L17.**

4 A person speculating in stocks, property, etc. **L18.**

> **4** LYNDON B. JOHNSON Speculators willing to gamble that . . we would . . raise the official price of gold.

■ **speculatrix** *noun* (*rare*) a female speculator **E17.**

speculatory /ˈspɛkjʊlət(ə)ri/ *noun & adjective.* Now *rare.* **M16.**
[Latin *speculatorius* pertaining to spies or scouts, formed as **SPECULATE**: see **-ORY**[1], **-ORY**[2].]
▸†**A** *noun.* **1** The observation or study of occult phenomena. **M16–L17.**

2 A place of observation. Only in **E17.**

3 A sentry, a lookout. Only in **L18.**

▸ **B** *adjective.* †**1** Of the nature of or pertaining to observation or study of the occult. **L16–L17.**

2 Serving as a vantage-point, providing an outlook or view. **L18.**

speculist /ˈspɛkjʊlɪst/ *noun.* **E18.**
[from **SPECULATE** + **-IST.**]
= **SPECULATIST.**

speculum /ˈspɛkjʊləm/ *noun.* Pl. **-la** /-lə/, **-lums.** **LME.**
[Latin, from base of *specere* look, see: see **-ULE.**]

1 *MEDICINE.* An instrument, usu. of metal, used to dilate an orifice or canal in the body to allow inspection. **LME.**

2 Chiefly *SCIENCE.* A mirror or reflector of glass or metal; *spec.* a metallic mirror forming part of a reflecting telescope. **M17.**

3 *ORNITHOLOGY.* A bright patch of plumage on the wings of certain birds, esp. the strip of metallic sheen on the secondary flight-feathers of many ducks. **E19.**

4 An alloy of copper and tin in a ratio of around 2:1, formerly used to make mirrors for scientific instruments. Also more fully ***speculum metal.*** **E20.**

sped *verb pa. t. & pple*: see **SPEED** *verb.*

speech /spiːtʃ/ *noun.*
[Old English *spǣc*, (West Saxon) *spǣc* rel. to *specan* speak repl. earlier *sprǣc* = Old Frisian *sprēke, sprētze*, Old Saxon *sprāka* (Dutch *spraak*), Old High German *sprāhha* (German *Sprache*), from West Germanic base also of **SPEAK** *verb.*]
▸ **I 1** The action or faculty of speaking; the ability to express thoughts or feelings by articulate sounds, the utterance of words or sentences. **OE.** ▸**b** *transf.* The sounding of a musical instrument, esp. an organ. **M19.** ▸**c** *spec.* in *LINGUISTICS.* = **PAROLE** *noun* 4. **M20.**

2 The language or dialect of a nation, people, group, etc. **OE.**

3 Manner of speaking, *esp.* that habitual to or characteristic of a particular person, group, etc. Usu. with *possess.* **OE.**

4 Talk, conversation, discourse. (Foll. by *with,* (*arch.*) *of* a person.) **OE.** ▸**b** With *possess.* & *the.* The opportunity of speaking to, an audience or interview with. Now *rare* or *obsolete.* **OE.** ▸**c** Mention *of* a thing. Now *rare.* **ME.**

> **1** H. REED Speech, even more than reason, distinguishes man from the brute. J. MARQUAND I wanted to shout . . but I seemed incapable of speech. G. DALY A swelling in his throat . . had begun to affect his power of speech. **2** R. G. COLLINGWOOD The common speech of European civilisation. **3** *American Speech* Bermudians . . taking pride in their speech. M. SCHORER The prevalence of American slang in British speech. M. EDELMAN The conventional speech of the working class. B. TRAPIDO Jonathan enacted the episode . . catching his grandmother's speech and gesture.

▸ **II 5 a** That which is spoken or uttered; the talk or words *of* a person; an utterance, a statement, a remark. Also, a group of lines spoken by a character in a play etc. **OE.** ▸**b** A more or less formal address or discourse delivered to an audience or assembly, an oration; a written or printed copy or report of this; *LAW* a judgement given by a Law Lord. **L16.**

6 General talk or discussion, rumour. Formerly also, a report, a rumour. Now *rare* or *obsolete.* **OE.**

†**7** A legal claim, cause, or suit; a plea. **OE–LME.**

> **5a** MILTON They who to States . . direct their Speech. A. RADCLIFFE His quivering lip . . made her . . repent the boldness of her speech. **b** H. KELLER Burke's masterly speech rolled on in . . surges of eloquence. J. HALPERIN Making a socialist speech in Trafalgar Square.

Phrases: ***direct speech***: see **DIRECT** *adjective.* ***free speech***: see **FREE** *adjective.* ***inner speech***: see **INNER** *adjective.* ***in STRICTNESS of speech.*** ***maiden speech***: see **MAIDEN** *adjective.* ***oblique speech***: see **OBLIQUE** *adjective.* ***part of speech***: see **PART** *noun.* ***reported speech***: see **REPORT** *verb* 3. **the King's speech, the Queen's speech** a statement including details of the Government's proposed measures, read by the sovereign at the opening of Parliament. ***visible speech***: see **VISIBLE** *adjective.*

Comb.: **speech act** an utterance regarded as an act performed with a particular purpose and effect; **speech area** (*a*) a region of the brain involved in the comprehension or production of speech; (*b*) a geographical area with a distinct speech type; **speech-centre** = ***speech area*** (a) above; **speech chain** the sequence of sounds forming an utterance; **speech coil** a coil that drives the cone of a loudspeaker according to the signal current flowing in it; **speech community** a group of people sharing a language or variety of a language; **speech day** an annual prize-giving day at the end of the year in many (esp. public) schools, traditionally marked by the making of speeches; **speech-house** *Hist.* a hall, room, or building set apart for discussion, conference, etc.; a court-house; ***speech island***: see **ISLAND** *noun*[1] 2e; **speech pathologist** a practitioner of speech pathology; **speech pathology** the branch of medicine that deals with defective speech; **speech physiology** the branch of physiology that deals with the physical production of speech sounds; **speech-reading** lip-reading; **speech recognition** the process of identifying and interpreting or responding to the sounds produced in human speech; **speech recognizer** a machine capable of responding to the content of speech; **speech-song** = **SPRECHGESANG**; **speech sound** a phonetically distinct unit of speech; **speech stretcher** a device to slow down recorded speech without altering its pitch; **speech synthesis** the process of generating spoken language by machine on the basis of written input; **speech synthesizer** a machine designed to generate sounds imitative of the human voice and recognizable as meaningful speech; **speech therapist** a practitioner of speech therapy; **speech therapy**: designed to improve defective speech; **speech-writer** a person employed to write speeches for a politician etc. to deliver.

■ **speeched** *adjective* having or using speech of a specified kind **L15.** **speechful** *adjective* possessing the power of speech; talkative; (of the eyes etc.) expressive: **E19.** **speechfulness** *noun* **L19.** **speechlet, speechling** *nouns* a short speech **L19.**

speech /spiːtʃ/ *verb.* Now *rare.* **M17.**
[from the noun.]
†**1** *verb trans.* Drive *out* by means of speech. Only in **M17.**

2 *verb trans.* Say or state in a speech or speeches. **L17.**

3 *verb intrans. & trans.* (with *it*). Make or deliver a speech or speeches; *dial.* speak (*with*). **L17.**

4 *verb trans.* Make a speech to, address in a speech; *dial.* speak or talk to. **E19.**

■ **speeching** *noun* the action or practice of making speeches; an instance of this, a speech: **M17.**

speecher /ˈspiːtʃə/ *noun.* **M18.**
[from **SPEECH** *noun* or *verb* + **-ER**[1].]
A person who makes a speech or speeches, a speaker.

speechify /ˈspiːtʃɪfʌɪ/ *verb.* Now chiefly *joc.* or *derog.* **E18.**
[from **SPEECH** *noun* + **-I-** + **-FY.**]

1 *verb intrans.* Make or deliver a speech or speeches, esp. tediously, pompously, or at length. **E18.**

2 *verb trans.* Address in a speech or speeches. *rare.* **M19.**

> **1** H. JAMES She speechified as a bird sings. R. F. HOBSON I could spell all this out . . but I do not want to speechify.

■ **speechifiˈcation** *noun* = **SPEECHIFYING** **E19.** **speechifier** *noun* **L18.** **speechifying** *noun* the action of speechifying; an instance of this, a (lengthy or tedious) speech: **E18.**

speechless /ˈspiːtʃlɪs/ *adjective.* **OE.**
[from **SPEECH** *noun* + **-LESS.**]

1 Lacking the faculty of speech; naturally or permanently mute or dumb. **OE.**

2 a Unable to speak on account of illness, injury, or exhaustion. **ME.** ▸**b** Temporarily deprived of the power of speech through strong emotion etc. (freq. foll. by *with*); amazed, astonished; very angry, outraged. **LME.** ▸**c** Deprived of speech through excessive drinking; *colloq.* dead drunk. **L19.**

3 Refraining from speech, keeping silence. Also, reticent, taciturn. **LME.**

4 †**a** Not uttered or expressed in speech. **L16–E17.** ▸**b** Incapable of expression in or by speech. *poet.* **E19.**

5 (Of a state or condition) characterized by loss or absence of speech; unaccompanied or undisturbed by speech; (of an emotion etc.) tending to deprive one temporarily of speech. **L16.**

> **1** LONGFELLOW Like a ghost that is speechless. **2b** *Observer* This proposal leaves me speechless. E. SEGAL I'm absolutely speechless You mean that creep is gonna get away scot-free? W. HORWOOD Spindle seemed struck speechless with fright. **3** L. GORDON They could sit speechless, well knowing that it was . . drizzling and their guests . . bored. **5** SHELLEY She is as pure as speechless infancy! E. LYALL A stony speechless sorrow.

■ **speechlessly** *adverb* **M19.** **speechlessness** *noun* **L16.**

speed /spiːd/ *noun.*
[Old English *spēd*, earlier *spœ̄d* = Old Saxon *spōd*, Old High German *spuot*, from Germanic base of **SPEED** *verb.*]
▸ **I** †**1** Abundance. **OE–ME.**

†**2** Power, might. **OE–LME.**

3 Success, prosperity, profit; fortune, lot. *arch.* exc. *Scot.* **OE.**

†**4 a** Assistance, aid, help. **ME–L15.** ▸**b** A person or thing promoting success or prosperity. **LME–L17.**

> **3** DEFOE The king wished us good speed.

▸ **II 5** The action, quality, or capability of moving quickly; rapidity of travel or movement, swiftness. Also, rate of progress or motion. Freq. as 2nd elem. of comb. **OE.** ▸**b** Each of the possible gear ratios of a bicycle, (now chiefly *US*) motor vehicle, etc.; the equipment associated

with this; *ellipt.* a bicycle etc. having a specified number of gears. Also, each of the various possible rates of operation of a machine, appliance, etc.; a particular setting of a machine etc. Freq. as 2nd elem. of comb. **M19.**
6 Quickness or promptness in the performance of an action, operation, etc. **OE.** ▸**b** *PHOTOGRAPHY.* The degree of sensitivity to light or a developer of a film, plate, etc. Also = *SHUTTER* ***speed***. **L19.** ▸**c** The rate in words per minute at which a person can write shorthand or can type. **L19.**
7 An inflammatory disease of cattle. **E18.**
8 An amphetamine drug, *esp.* methamphetamine. *slang.* **M20.**

📖 **5** R. L. STEVENSON It was vain . . to contend in speed with such an adversary. ALAN ROSS We covered the . . miles at an average speed of 91 . . miles an hour. C. EASTON The Jaguar automobile she drove at terrifying speed. *Which?* Jigsaws . . operate at maximum speeds of . . 3,500 strokes per minute. **b** P. LIVELY A shiny new bike with three speeds. **6** F. W. FARRAR The execution . . was . . hurried on with all speed. *Vogue* The indecent speed of the guided tour . . detracted . . from the impact of the site. **8** *Twenty Twenty* A weirdo wired up on speed and brandy.

Phrases: **at full speed** as quickly as possible. **at speed** at a rapid rate of movement. **be one's speed** *colloq.* (chiefly *N. Amer.*) suit one's tastes, interests, or abilities. **full speed** = *at full speed* above (*full speed ahead*: see **FULL** *adjective*). *high speed*: see **HIGH** *adjective*. *idling speed*: see **IDLE** *verb* 5. **make good speed** make good progress, travel quickly. **make speed** hurry, make haste. *more haste, less speed*: see **HASTE** *noun*. *second speed*: see **SECOND** *adjective*. *sonic speed*: see **SONIC** 2. *thermal speed*: see **THERMAL** *adjective*. *turn of speed*: see **TURN** *noun*. **up to speed** (*a*) operating at full or working speed; (*b*) (of a person or company) performing at an anticipated rate or level; (*c*) *colloq.* (of a person) fully informed or up to date.
Attrib. & comb.: Designating a device or apparatus for regulating or indicating speed, as *speed clock*, *speed cone*, *speed gauge*, etc.; in the sense 'pertaining to the achievement of or capacity for high speed', as *speed-bowler*, *speed-skating*, etc. Special combs., as **speed bag** *N. Amer.* a small punchbag used by boxers for practising quick punches; **speedball** (*a*) *slang* a mixture of cocaine with morphine or heroin; (*b*) *US slang* a glass of wine, *spec.* one strengthened by additional alcohol or spirits; (*c*) *US* a ball game which resembles soccer but in which the ball may be handled; (*d*) *BOXING* a type of small fast punchball; **speedboat** a high-speed motor boat; **speed bug** *slang* a person who enjoys travelling at high speed, an enthusiast for speed sports; **speed bump** *colloq.* = *speed hump* below; **speed camera** a roadside camera triggered by speeding vehicles, taking either video footage or a photograph of the vehicle with a record of its speed; **speed cop** *slang* a police officer detailed to enforce speed limits, *esp.* one riding a motorcycle; **speed demon** *slang* = *speed bug* above; **speed dial** a function on some telephones which allows frequently called telephone numbers to be entered into a memory and dialled with the push of a single button; **speed freak** *slang* a habitual user of an amphetamine drug; **speed hog** *slang* a person who causes annoyance by driving excessively fast; **speed hump** a ramp or ridge in a road surface designed to slow down vehicles; also called *sleeping policeman*; **speed king** *slang* (*a*) a motor-racing champion; (*b*) = *speed bug* above; **speed limit** (*a*) the maximum speed attainable by a particular vehicle; (*b*) the maximum speed permitted by law on a particular type of road or to a specified class of vehicle; **speed limiter** a device which prevents a vehicle from being driven above a specified speed; **speed merchant** *colloq.* a person concerned with the use of speed; *spec.* (*a*) *CRICKET* a fast bowler; (*b*) a person who enjoys driving etc. at high speed; **speed-read** *verb trans. & intrans.* read rapidly by assimilating several phrases or sentences at once; **speed-reader** a person who speed-reads; *speed trap*: see **TRAP** *noun*[1] 1e; **Speed-walk** *US* (proprietary name for) a moving walkway for conveying passengers; **speedway** (*a*) *N. Amer.* a road or track used for fast motor or (*Hist.*) horse traffic; *gen.* a motorway, a raceway; (*b*) a sport in which motorcyclists race several laps around a short oval dirt track; a stadium or track used for this; **speedwriter** a practitioner of Speedwriting; **Speedwriting** (proprietary name for) a form of shorthand using the letters of the alphabet.
■ **speedless** *adjective* **LME.**

speed /spiːd/ *verb*. Pa. t. & pple **sped** /spɛd/, (esp. senses 8c, 8d, 9) **speeded**.
[Old English (*ge*)*spēdan* = Old Saxon *spōdian* (Dutch *spoeden*), Old High German *spuoten* (German *spuden*, *sputen* from Low German), from Germanic base also of Old English *spōwan*, Old High German *spuo(e)n* prosper, succeed.]
▸**I 1** *verb intrans.* Succeed, prosper, meet with good fortune. (Foll. by †*of* an aim, object, etc.) *arch.* **OE.**
2 *verb intrans.* Meet with fortune of a specified kind; progress or fare *well*, *ill*, etc. Also *impers.* (foll. by *with*, †*to*). *arch.* **OE.**
3 *verb trans.* Esp. of God: help, assist, cause to succeed or prosper. *arch.* **ME.**
4 *verb trans.* Bring (a person etc.) to a condition or situation, *spec.* (*a*) a desired one, (*b*) a hazardous or unpleasant one. Only as ***sped*** *ppl adjective*. *arch.* **ME.** ▸**b** Appoint or elect (a person) *to* or *as* something. Only as ***sped*** *ppl adjective*. Now *rare* or *obsolete*. **LME.**
5 *verb trans.* Promote, further, or assist in (a matter); accomplish, carry out, commit; *spec.* expedite or prosecute (a bill, plea, etc.) as a matter of official or legal business. *arch.* **ME.**
6 *verb trans.* **a** Bring to an end, finish. *arch.* **ME.** ▸**b** Kill, dispatch (a person etc.). *arch.* **L16.**

📖 **2** W. COWPER For boldest men Speed ever best. **3** T. BIRCH God speed him and send him a better voyage.

▸**II 7** *verb trans.* Send or convey with speed; hurry (a person etc.) *out* or *away*; send out, discharge, or direct with speed and (freq.) force. **ME.** ▸**b** *refl.* Go, move, or act with speed. *arch.* **ME.** ▸**c** Enable (a person) to depart or travel speedily, assist in travel or departure; *gen.* say goodbye to. **E18.**
8 *verb trans.* **a** Give speed to (a course etc.); cause to be rapid in movement. Formerly also, make haste *to do* something. **ME.** ▸**b** Press or urge on, esp. to completion etc.; expedite. **LME.** ▸**c** Increase the speed or working rate of. Usu. foll. by *up*. **M19.** ▸**d** Cause (a machine) to go at a specified speed. **L19.**
9 *verb intrans.* Go or move with speed; (foll. by *up*) move or work with greater speed; (of time) advance or pass quickly (freq. foll. by *by*). **ME.** ▸**b** Drive a motor vehicle at an illegal or dangerous speed, break the speed limit in a motor vehicle. Freq. as ***speeding*** *verbal noun*. **M20.** ▸**c** (Seem to) be under the influence of an amphetamine drug. Usu. in the progressive, ***be speeding***. *slang.* **L20.**

📖 **7** TENNYSON His last arrow is sped. H. HERMAN The glance he sped towards his betrothed. N. HERMAN G would spend her holidays speeding Cynthia back to health. A. BROOKNER They struggle into a taxi and are speeded towards the Hôtel. **c** A. THIRKELL To help with coats and speed the parting guests. **8a** F. CHAMIER Traveller after traveller . . speeding his way to the hotel. **b** W. C. BRYANT Command thy maids to speed the work. **c** A. BRIGGS Reformers . . wished to speed up the processes of change. *Listener* A speeded-up film of a flower opening. **9** KEATS I sped to meet them. SCOTT FITZGERALD We sped along . . at fifty miles an hour. R. S. THOMAS His shadow lengthened, and the years speed by. V. GLENDINNING Everything had speeded up. Before Charlotte knew it spring had come. **b** *Harper's Magazine* I was speeding on the road to Norfolk, doing seventy. **c** *Melody Maker* I can't go on stage speeding out of my head and still cut it.

Comb.: **speed-up** an increase in speed or rate of working; (chiefly *US*) the increasing of industrial productivity, esp. without raising rates of pay.

speeder /ˈspiːdə/ *noun*. **ME.**
[from prec. + -ER[1].]
1 A person who aids or assists, a helper. *arch.* **ME.**
†**2** A person who prospers or is successful. **L16–L17.**
3 A device or contrivance for quickening or regulating the speed of machinery. Also, a kind of machine for roving cotton. **M19.**
4 A person who drives etc. at high speed; *spec.* a person who exceeds the speed limit in a vehicle; a fast car, horse, etc. **L19.**
5 A small vehicle running on railway tracks used for line maintenance etc., orig. manually propelled. *N. Amer.* **E20.**

speedful /ˈspiːdfʊl, -f(ə)l/ *adjective*. Now *rare*. **ME.**
[from SPEED *noun* + -FUL.]
1 Advantageous, helpful, efficacious. Long *obsolete* exc. *Scot.* **ME.**
2 Quick, swift, rapid. **LME.**

speedo /ˈspiːdəʊ/ *noun*. *colloq.* Pl. **-os**. **M20.**
[Abbreviation.]
= next.

speedometer /spiːˈdɒmɪtə/ *noun*. **E20.**
[from SPEED *noun* + -OMETER.]
1 An instrument, usu. in the form of a dial, on a motor vehicle etc. indicating the speed to the driver. **E20.**
2 A milometer, an odometer, (freq. incorporated in the speedometer of a motor vehicle). *US.* **E20.**

speedster /ˈspiːdstə/ *noun*. **E20.**
[formed as prec. + -STER, after *roadster*.]
1 A fast motor vehicle; a speedboat. **E20.**
2 A person who drives etc. fast; a person etc. who moves or acts very quickly, a fast runner, bowler, etc. **E20.**

speedwell /ˈspiːdwɛl/ *noun*. **L16.**
[App. from SPEED *verb* + WELL *adverb*.]
Any of numerous small herbaceous plants constituting the genus *Veronica*, of the figwort family, which have small usu. blue flowers, often in axillary or terminal racemes.
germander speedwell, ***heath speedwell***, ***ivy-leaved speedwell***, etc.

speedy /ˈspiːdi/ *adjective*. **LME.**
[from SPEED *noun* + -Y[1].]
†**1** Advantageous, expedient, helpful. Only in **LME.**
2 Moving or able to move with speed, swift, acting or operating quickly. **LME.**
3 Characterized by or facilitating speed of operation or motion. **LME.**
4 Performed or taking place rapidly; done without delay, prompt. **E16.**

📖 **2** A. FLEMING Foure swifte and speedie legions. **3** H. MAUNDRELL The nearest and speediest way. **4** C. S. FORESTER They will die unless they receive speedy aid. V. GLENDINNING Sent her best wishes for a speedy recovery.

Phrases: **speedy cut** an injury on the inner side of a horse's foreleg or hind leg just below the knee or hock joint, caused by the foot of the opposite leg when in motion. **speedy trial** *LAW* a criminal trial held after minimal delay, esp. (in N. America) as considered to be a citizen's right.
■ **speedily** *adverb* **LME.** **speediness** *noun* **LME.**

speel /spiːl/ *noun*[1]. Now *dial.* **LME.**
[Of Scandinavian origin: cf. Norwegian *spela*, *spila*, Swedish *spjela*, *spjele*.]
A splinter or strip of wood, iron, etc.

speel /spiːl/ *noun*[2]. *Scot.* **E19.**
[from next.]
The action or an act of clambering or climbing.

speel /spiːl/ *verb*[1]. *Scot. & north.* **E16.**
[Origin uncertain: perh. back-form. from SPEELER *noun*[1]. Cf. next.]
1 *verb intrans.* Mount or ascend to a height by climbing; climb *up* or *down*. **E16.**
2 *verb trans.* Climb or clamber up (a hill, tree, etc.). **L16.**

speel /spiːl/ *verb*[2]. Now *dial. & colloq.* Also **spiel**. **E19.**
[Origin uncertain: perh. the same word as prec.]
1 *verb intrans.* Go fast, gallop quickly; run *away*, make off. Now chiefly *Austral.* **E19.**
†**2** *verb trans.* ***speel the drum***, make off with stolen property. Only in **M19.**

speeler /ˈspiːlə/ *noun*[1]. *Scot.* Also **spieler**. **L15.**
[Partly from Middle Dutch, Low German *speler* (German *Spieler*) actor, player, from Middle Dutch *spelen* play, perform tricks, partly from SPEEL *verb*[1]: see -ER[1].]
1 Orig., an acrobat, a performer. Now, a climber. **L15.**
2 Either of a pair of spiked irons used in climbing poles or trees. **M18.**

speeler /ˈspiːlə/ *noun*[2]. *Austral. slang.* **L19.**
[Prob. from SPEEL *verb*[2]: see -ER[1].]
A swift horse.

Speenhamland /ˈspiːnəmland/ *noun*. **M19.**
[See below.]
Hist. Used **attrib.** to designate a system of poor relief first adopted in Speenhamland, an English village near Newbury in the county of Berkshire, and subsequently established throughout most of rural England.

speer /spɪə/ *noun*[1]. Now *dial.* **ME.**
[Origin uncertain: perh. from Middle Low German *speer*, *sper* sparwork.]
A screen or partition for warding off a draught, shielding a fire, etc. Also, a post on either side of a fireplace.

†**speer** *noun*[2]. **E17–L18.**
[Var. of SPIRE *noun*[1].]
A branch or prong of a deer's horn.

speer /ˈspɪə/ *noun*[3]. *Scot. rare.* **L18.**
[from SPEER *verb*[1].]
An inquiry, a questioning.

speer /ˈspɪə/ *noun*[4]. *rare.* **E19.**
[Origin unkn.]
Spray.

speer /spɪə/ *verb*[1]. Chiefly *Scot. & north.* Also **speir**.
[Old English *spyrian* = Old Frisian *spera*, Old High German *spur(r)en* (German *spüren*), Old Norse *spyrja*, from Germanic base also of SPOOR.]
1 *verb intrans.* Ask a question or questions, make inquiries. (Foll. by *about*, *for*, *of* a thing, *at* a person.) **OE.** ▸†**b** Inquire one's way; proceed or go *to* a place etc. **LME–E17.**
2 *verb trans.* Inquire or ask *how*, *what*, *who*, etc.; make inquiries concerning, ask questions regarding, (a thing or fact); ask (a question or questions). (Foll. by *at* or *of* a person.) **OE.**
3 *verb trans.* Question or interrogate (a person); ask (a person) a question. **ME.**
4 *verb trans.* Find out by inquiry. Usu. foll. by *out*. **LME.**
■ **speering** *noun* the action of questioning or inquiring, inquiry; *sing.* & in *pl.* information: **LOE.**

speer /spɪə/ *verb*[2] *intrans. dial. & US.* **M19.**
[Perh. from prec., infl. by PEER *verb*[2].]
Peer. Foll. by *at*, *into*, *out*.

†**speight** *noun*. Also **spight**. **LME–M17.**
[Middle Low German, Middle & mod. Dutch *specht*, Old High German *speht* (German *Specht*), perh. from an unrecorded Old English form. Cf. WOODSPITE.]
A woodpecker, *esp.* the green woodpecker, *Picus viridis*.

speir *verb* var. of SPEER *verb*[1].

speisesaal /ˈʃpʌɪzəzaːl/ *noun*. **L19.**
[German, from *Speise* food + *Saal* hall.]
In Germany and German-speaking countries, a dining-room or hall.

speiss /spʌɪs/ *noun.* L18.
[German *Speise* in same sense, spec. use of *Speise* food.]
METALLURGY. **1** A mixture of impure arsenides and antimonides of nickel, cobalt, iron, etc., produced in the smelting of esp. cobalt ores. L18.
2 *speiss-cobalt*, = SMALTITE. L19.

spekboom /ˈspɛkbʊəm/ *noun. S. Afr.* M19.
[Afrikaans, from *spek* SPECK *noun*² + *boom* tree.]
A shrub with succulent leaves, *Portulacaria afra*, of the purslane family, used for fodder in dry areas.

spelaean /spɪˈliːən/ *adjective.* M19.
[from Latin *spelaeum* (from Greek *spēlaion* cave) + -AN.]
1 Inhabiting a cave or caves, cave-dwelling. M19.
2 Of the nature of a cave. L19.

spelaeology *noun* var. of SPELEOLOGY.

†speld *noun.* OE–LME.
[Old English *speld* = Old Norse *speld*, *spjald* (Norwegian *spjeld*, Swedish *spjell*) rel. to Gothic *spilda*, Middle High German & German dial. *spelte* tablet, splinter, chip, from Germanic.]
A glimmer of fire, a spark; a chip, a splinter.
¶ Perh. earlier form of SPELL *noun*².

speld /spɛld/ *verb trans. Scot.* L15.
[Rel. to SPALD. Cf. SPELT *verb*¹.]
Lay flat or extended; spread out; split open.

spelder /ˈspɛldə/ *verb. Scot.* E18.
[from SPELD *verb* + -ER⁵.]
1 *verb intrans.* Spread or stretch oneself out. E18.
2 *verb trans.* Spread or stretch out; split and spread open (a fish etc.). E18.

spelding /ˈspɛldɪŋ/ *noun. Scot.* E16.
[from SPELD *verb* + -ING¹.]
A small split fish preserved by being dried in the sun.
■ Also **speldring** *noun* E19.

spele /spiːl/ *verb trans.* Now *dial. rare.* See also SPELL *verb*³. OE.
[Origin unkn.]
1 Take the place of or represent (a person). OE.
2 a Spare or save (a thing); leave over; use sparingly or frugally. ME. ▸**†b** Spare (a person) from punishment or harm. Only in ME.

speleology /spiːlɪˈɒlədʒi, spɛl-/ *noun.* Also **spelae-**. L19.
[French *spéléologie*, formed as SPELAEAN + -OLOGY.]
The branch of knowledge that deals with caves; the sport or pastime of exploring caves.
■ **speleoˈlogical** *adjective* of or pertaining to speleology L19. **speleologist** *noun* a student of or authority on speleology; an explorer of caves: L19.

speleothem /ˈspiːlɪə(ʊ)θɛm/ *noun.* M20.
[from Greek *spēlaion* cave (after prec.) + *thema* that which is laid down, deposit.]
GEOLOGY. A structure formed in a cave by the deposition of minerals from water, as a stalactite, a stalagmite, etc.

spelk /spɛlk/ *noun & verb.* Chiefly *Scot. & north.* OE.
[Corresp. to Low German *spalke*, Old Norse *spelkur* (pl.).]
▶ **A** *noun.* **1** A surgical splint. OE.
2 A splinter, a chip; a small strip of wood. LME.
3 A rod, esp. as used in thatching. M16.
▶ **B** *verb trans.* Fasten with a spelk; *esp.* bind or join (a broken limb or bone) with splints. OE.

spell /spɛl/ *noun*¹.
[Old English *spel(l)* = Old Saxon, Old High German *spel*, Old Norse *spjall*, Gothic *spill* recital, tale, from Germanic base also of SPELL *verb*¹, *verb*². Cf. GOSPEL *noun*.]
1 Talk, narration, speech; a story, a narrative, a tale. Long *obsolete* exc. *Scot. & dial.* OE.
2 A verse or form of words, sometimes accompanied by actions, sometimes supposedly possessing magical powers and able to bring about a desired end; a charm, an incantation. Earliest in ***night-spell*** s.v. NIGHT *noun.* LME. ▸**b** An attraction or fascination exercised by a person, activity, quality, etc.; a mysterious power or influence. Also, a state of enchantment or trance (as) produced by a magic spell. L16.

> 📖 **2** R. FINLAYSON She was sure someone had put a makutu spell on her and the evil spirit was eating her life away. **b** *Times* Music casts a spell of enchantment. B. TRAPIDO I was so under his spell I believed him. B. BETTELHEIM As soon as the lights are turned on, the spell is . . broken.

■ **spellful** *adjective* full of spells or magical power, bewitching L18.

spell /spɛl/ *noun*². Now *dial.* LME.
[Perh. var. of SPELD *noun*.]
1 A splinter, chip, or fragment of wood etc. LME.
2 A bar, a rail, a rung. M16.
3 The trap used in the game of knur and spell. L18.

spell /spɛl/ *noun*³. L16.
[from SPELL *verb*³.]
1 A set of workers taking a turn of work to relieve others; a relay, a shift. Now *rare.* L16.
2 A turn of work taken by one person or group to relieve another. E17.
3 A continuous period, bout, or turn of an occupation or activity. (Foll. by *of*, *at*.) E18. ▸**b** An interval or period of repose or relaxation, a rest from work etc. Now *dial. & Austral.* L18.
4 A period or space of time, esp. of a short or fairly short duration; (with specifying word) a period having a certain character or spent in a particular way; *spec.* a continuous period or stretch of a specified kind of weather. E18. ▸**b** Each of the periods into which a game of rugby is divided. *NZ.* E20. ▸**c** CRICKET. A series of overs during a session of play in which a particular bowler bowls. L20.
5 A period of being unwell or out of sorts, an attack or fit of illness or nervous excitement. *US.* M19.

> 📖 **3** D. LESSING Had recently done spells of hard labour for simply being in possession of seditious literature. G. SAYER His first spell of duty began at half past one. **4** E. WAUGH He looked forward to a spell of solitude. E. O'BRIEN Spells of calmness and then an outburst. A. HIGGINS The hot days of the long dry spell. B. TRAPIDO Required . . to spend occasional week-long spells in hospital. P. DALLY A high state of tension . . with headaches and dizzy spells. **for a spell** for a while. **5** E. K. KANE An attack of partial epilepsy; one of those strange indescribable spells, fits, seizures.

spell /spɛl/ *noun*⁴. *colloq.* E18.
[from SPELL *verb*².]
A way of spelling a word.

spell /spɛl/ *noun*⁵. *slang.* Now *rare* or *obsolete.* E19.
[from Dutch or Flemish *spel* (German *Spiel*), or abbreviation of SPELLKEN.]
A playhouse, a theatre.

spell /spɛl/ *verb*¹. Long *obsolete* exc. *dial.*
[Old English *spellian* = Middle Low German, Middle Dutch *spellen*, Old High German *-spellōn*, Old Norse *spjalla*, Gothic *spillōn*, from Germanic base also of SPELL *noun*¹, *verb*².]
1 *verb intrans.* Talk, converse, speak; preach. OE.
2 *verb trans.* Utter, relate, tell. OE.

spell /spɛl/ *verb*². Pa. t. & pple **spelled**; **spelt** /spɛlt/. ME.
[Aphet. from Old French *espel(l)er* (mod. *épeler*) repr. *espeaudre* from Frankish, from Germanic base also of SPELL *verb*¹.]
▶ **I** *verb trans.* **1** Read (words, writing, a book, etc.) letter by letter; peruse or make out slowly or with difficulty. *arch.* ME. ▸**b** Consider, contemplate, scan intently. *arch.* M17.
2 Interpret, understand; comprehend or discern by close study or observation. *arch.* ME.
3 †a Mean, signify. Only in ME. ▸**b** Amount to, lead inevitably to, imply, indicate, give warning of; result in. M17.
4 Write or name in sequence the constituent letters of (a word, syllable, etc.), esp. correctly. LME. ▸**b** Of letters: form (a word) when placed in a particular order. M19.

> 📖 **1** THACKERAY He was spelling the paper, with the help of his lips. **2** MILTON By what the Stars . . in thir conjunction met, give me to spell. **3b** E. F. BENSON Responsibilities really spelled opportunities. *Today* A wife's self-neglect . . spells DANGER. K. GIBBONS She will not let more than three of us go . . because that spells trouble. **4** J. BARTH Todd . . is my name. You can spell it with one or two *d*'s. L. HELLMAN She . . could spell very few words. J. HARVEY Workshops . . with the firm's name spelt across them. **b** F. MARRYAT What doth *c-a-t* spell then?

▶ **II** *verb intrans.* **5** Write or name in sequence, esp. correctly, the constituent letters of a word, syllable, etc. LME.
6 Engage in study or contemplation *of*. *poet. rare.* M17.
7 Indicate a wish for, ask, hint. (Foll. by *for*, *at*.) Now *arch. & dial.* L18.

> 📖 **5** M. TWAIN Foreigners always spell better than they pronounce. H. W. FOWLER The uneasy half-literates who like to prove that they can spell. **6** T. GRAY Then let me rightly spell of nature's ways. **7** J. H. NEWMAN Before I had given him anything, he had begun to spell for something.

With adverbs in specialized senses: **spell down** *US* defeat or test (a person) in a spelling contest. **spell out** (*a*) read (words etc.), esp. slowly and with difficulty, give the constituent letters of (a word etc.) in sequence, esp. correctly; (*b*) *fig.* explain or state (a thing) explicitly or in detail.
Comb.: **spell-check** *verb trans.* (*colloq.*) correct (text) using a spelling checker; **spell-checker** = *SPELLING checker*; **spelldown** *US* an eliminating contest in spelling.
■ **spellable** *adjective* able to be (easily) spelt M19. **spellingly** *adverb* (now *rare*) by means of spelling, letter by letter M17.

spell /spɛl/ *verb*³. L16.
[Var. of SPELE.]
1 *verb trans.* Take the place of or relieve (a person) in a task or undertaking, alternate with in an activity. Now chiefly *N. Amer.* L16. ▸**b** Allow (esp. a horse) to rest briefly. Chiefly *Austral.* M19.
2 *verb trans.* NAUTICAL. Take a turn or turns of work at (esp. a pump). M18.
3 *verb intrans.* **a** Of sets of workers: replace one another at set intervals; take turns. *rare.* M19. ▸**b** Take a brief rest. Chiefly *Austral.* M19.

> 📖 **1** W. STEGNER 'Here,' Oliver said, reaching. 'Let me spell you.'

spell /spɛl/ *verb*⁴ *trans.* E17.
[from SPELL *noun*¹.]
Charm, bewitch, or bind (as) with a spell; drive *away* with a spell; invest with magical properties.

spellbind /ˈspɛlbʌɪnd/ *verb trans.* Infl. as BIND *verb*; pa. t. & pple usu. **-bound** /-baʊnd/. E19.
[from SPELL *noun*¹ + BIND *verb*, after *spellbound*.]
Bind (as) with a spell; fascinate, enchant, bewitch.
■ **spellbinding** *adjective* fascinating, enchanting, bewitching M20. **spellbindingly** *adverb* in a spellbinding manner L20.

spellbinder /ˈspɛlbʌɪndə/ *noun.* Orig. *US.* L19.
[from prec. + -ER¹.]
A person, orig. *spec.* a political speaker, capable of holding an audience etc. spellbound.

spellbound /ˈspɛlbaʊnd/ *adjective.* L18.
[from SPELL *noun*¹ + *bound* pa. pple of BIND *verb*.]
Bound (as) with a spell; fascinated, enchanted, entranced, esp. as by a speaker, activity, quality, etc.

> 📖 W. C. WILLIAMS A great silence followed as the crowd stood spellbound. S. RUSHDIE She appeared to be spellbound by the sorceries of the drug.

spellbound *verb pa. t. & pple*: see SPELLBIND.

speller /ˈspɛlə/ *noun*¹. LME.
[from SPELL *verb*² + -ER¹.]
1 A person who spells words etc., esp. correctly; an authority on spelling. LME.
2 A spelling-book. *N. Amer.* M19.

speller /ˈspɛlə/ *noun*². Long *arch.* L16.
[Aphet. from ESPELER. Cf. SPILLER *noun*².]
= SPILLER *noun*².

spellican *noun* var. of SPILLIKIN.

spelling /ˈspɛlɪŋ/ *noun.* LME.
[from SPELL *verb*² + -ING¹.]
1 The action of SPELL *verb*², *esp.* the process or activity of (correctly) naming or writing the letters of a word etc.; a person's ability to spell. LME. ▸**b** A spelling-bee, a spelling-test. *US. rare.* M19.
2 The manner of expressing or writing words with letters; a particular way of spelling a word. M17.

> 📖 **1** M. LANE Spelling remained a weak point all his life. **2** W. M. LINDSAY However natural it may appear for the Romans to have adopted Greek spelling. *American Speech* By 1890 the name had become Apalousey, but today's accepted spelling is Appaloosa. *Times Educ. Suppl.* Many words have alternative spellings. ***inverse spelling***: see INVERSE *adjective & noun.* INVERTED ***spelling***.

Comb.: **spelling-bee** a contest in spelling; **spelling-book** a book designed to teach spelling; **spelling checker** a computer program for checking the spelling of entered text against a wordlist in the memory; **spelling pronunciation** the pronunciation of a word according to its written form; an instance of this; **spelling school** *US* a contest in spelling.

†spellken *noun. slang.* L18–E19.
[Origin uncertain: perh. formed as SPELL *noun*⁵ + KEN *noun*².]
A theatre, a playhouse.

spelt /spɛlt/ *noun*¹. LOE.
[Old Saxon *spelta*, Middle Low German, Middle Dutch *spelte*, Dutch *spelt* = Old High German *spelza*, *spelta* (German *Spelz*). Readopted at different times from Middle Dutch and Dutch.]
A primitive form of wheat, *Triticum spelta*, now rarely grown, in which the rhachis of the spike disarticulates at maturity.
¶ Rare before 16.

spelt /spɛlt/ *noun*². Now *dial. rare.*
[Rel. to SPELT *verb*¹. Cf. SPELD *noun*, German *Spelze* husk.]
A thin piece of wood or metal, *spec.* as a plate on the toe or heel of a boot or shoe.

spelt /spɛlt/ *verb*¹ *trans.* Now *dial.* L16.
[Rel. to SPELD *verb.* Cf. SPALT *verb*.]
Husk, pound (grain); bruise, split (esp. beans).

spelt *verb*² *pa. t. & pple*: see SPELL *verb*².

spelter /ˈspɛltə/ *noun.* M17.
[Corresp. to Old French *espeautre*, Middle Dutch *speauter* (Dutch, German *Spiauter*), German *Spialter*, ult. rel. to PEWTER.]
1 Zinc; now *esp.* commercial crude smelted zinc. Also (now *rare*), any of various ores of tin, zinc, or (by confusion) bismuth. M17.
2 In full ***spelter solder***. An alloy or solder of which zinc is the main constituent, and copper usu. the second. L17.

speltoid /ˈspɛltɔɪd/ *adjective & noun.* E20.
[from SPELT *noun*¹ + -OID.]
BOTANY. (A wheat) resembling or having certain characteristics of spelt.

speluncar /spɛˈlʌŋkɑː/ *adjective.* M19.
[from Latin *spelunca* cave + -AR¹. Cf. next.]
Of, pertaining to, or resembling a cave; of the nature of a cave.

spelunker /spɛˈlʌŋkə/ *noun. N. Amer. slang.* M20.
[Joc. formation, from (the same root as) prec. + -ER[1].]
A person who explores caves, esp. as a sport or pastime; a caver, a speleologist.
■ **spelunk** *verb intrans.* explore caves as a sport or pastime (chiefly as *spelunking verbal noun*) M20.

spence /spɛns/ *noun.* LME.
[Aphet. from Old French *despense* (mod. *dépense*) use as noun of fem. pa. pple of Latin *dispendere* DISPENSE *verb*.]
1 A room or cupboard in which food and drink are kept; a buttery, a pantry; a larder. Now *arch. & dial.* LME.
2 An inner room; a parlour. *Scot.* E18.

Spencean /spɛnˈsiːən/ *adjective & noun.* E19.
[Thomas *Spence* (1750–1814), political theorist.]
▶ **A** *adjective.* Of or pertaining to Thomas Spence or his views. E19.
▶ **B** *noun.* A follower or adherent of Thomas Spence. E19.

spencer /ˈspɛnsə/ *noun*[1]. E18.
[Family name: sense 1 prob. from Charles (1674–1722), third Earl of Sunderland; sense 2 from George John (1758–1834), second Earl Spencer; sense 3 from Mr Knight (early 19th cent.); sense 4 from Christopher Miner (1833–1922), US inventor and manufacturer.]
1 More fully ***spencer wig***. A man's wig. *obsolete* exc. *Hist.* E18.
2 A short double-breasted overcoat without tails worn by men during the late 18th and early 19th cents. L18. ▸**b** A close-fitting jacket or bodice, esp. as worn by women and children in the early 19th cent. L18. ▸**c** A woman's usu. woollen underbodice worn for extra warmth in winter. L19.
3 A form of lifebelt. E19.
4 (**S-**.) A type of rimfire repeating rifle or carbine used esp. during the US Civil War. Also ***Spencer carbine***, ***Spencer rifle***. M19.

spencer /ˈspɛnsə/ *noun*[2]. M19.
[Perh. formed as sense 3 of prec.]
NAUTICAL. A fore-and-aft sail, set with a gaff, serving as a trysail to the foremast or mainmast of a vessel.

Spencerian /spɛnˈsɪərɪən/ *adjective & noun.* M19.
[In sense 1 from Herbert *Spencer* (1820–1903), English philosopher; in sense 2 from Platt Rogers *Spencer* (1800–64), US calligrapher: see -IAN.]
▶ **A** *adjective.* **1** Of or pertaining to Herbert Spencer or his philosophical views, esp. as relating to the unification of physical and social science through a concept of evolution. M19.
2 a Designating a system of handwriting developed by P. R. Spencer. M19. ▸**b** Of, pertaining to, or characteristic of the cursive script developed by Spencer and used in the system developed by him. L19.
▶ **B** *noun.* A follower or adherent of Herbert Spencer or his philosophical views. L19.
■ **Spencerianism** *noun* = SPENCERISM L19.

Spencerism /ˈspɛnsərɪz(ə)m/ *noun.* L19.
[from Herbert *Spencer* (see prec.) + -ISM.]
The philosophy or beliefs of Herbert Spencer.
■ **Spencerite** *noun* a Spencerian L19.

spend /spɛnd/ *noun.* L17.
[from the verb.]
1 a The action or an act of spending money; an amount spent; expenditure. L17. ▸**b** A sum of money given for spending, esp. pocket money. Usu. in *pl. colloq. & dial.* M20.
†**2** Semen; vaginal secretion; ejaculation. *slang.* Only in L19.

spend /spɛnd/ *verb.* Pa. t. & pple **spent** /spɛnt/.
[Old English *spendan* corresp. to Middle Low German, Middle Dutch *spenden*, Old High German *spentōn* (German *spenden*), Old Norse *spenna*, from Latin *expendere* EXPEND. Partly also aphet. from DISPEND.]
▶ **I** *verb trans.* **1** Of a person: pay out (money), disburse, expend; dispose of (wealth, property, etc.) by paying out money. Also foll. by *for, on, upon* (a thing bought), *on* (a person for whom a thing is bought). OE.
2 a Expend or use (effort, material, thought, etc.) in a specified way; *spec.* use (speech), utter (a word, sound, etc.). (Foll. by *in, on,* or *upon* a subject, activity, etc.) OE. ▸**b** Express (an opinion). Now *dial. rare.* E17.
3 a Occupy, use, or pass (time, one's life, etc.) in some activity, occupation, place, or state. (Foll. by *in, on,* †*out*.) OE. ▸**b** Stay for (a period of time) as a guest. L17.
4 a Use up; exhaust by use; wear out. Also *refl.*, become used up or incapable of further activity. OE. ▸**b** Bring to a violent end; destroy. *arch.* LME.
5 a Use for food or drink; consume; eat, drink. Now *dial.* OE. ▸**b** AGRICULTURE. Use (a crop etc.) as fodder for cattle; eat off. M18.
6 Make use of (goods, possessions, etc.); utilize, employ. Now *rare.* OE.
7 Use wastefully, squander; throw away. OE.
8 a Suffer the loss of (blood, life, etc.); allow or cause to flow or be shed. LME. ▸†**b** NAUTICAL. Lose (a mast, sail, etc.) through bad weather or by some accident. L16–L17.
†**9** Require or involve expenditure or use of (money, material, time, etc.). E17–E18.

📖 **1** L. STEFFENS Magee spent his wealth for more power. S. DELANEY He spends his money like water. M. AMIS I spent . . half my wages on nude magazines. **2a** H. L. MENCKEN He spends immense energy on work that cannot . . get him any reward. **3a** W. CATHER Father . . spent all his time at his office. S. RAVEN I shall spend the summers in England. LD BRAIN Flaubert would spend a day on a line. *Punch* I've spent much of my life working with photographers. **4a** T. HARDY Her grief had . . spent itself. K. AMIS The deflationary aspect of the episode had . . spent its force. W. CATHER The storm had spent itself . . . The downpour had died into . . soft, dripping rain. **7** SIR W. SCOTT I am a fool . . to spend my words upon an idle . . boy. MRS ALEXANDER The horror . . of the creature on whom you spent your life!

▶ **II** *verb intrans.* **10** Pay out money for goods etc.; incur expenditure. OE.
†**11** Of a hunting dog: give tongue on finding a scent or seeing game. E17–M18.
12 Of time, a season, etc.: pass, elapse. Long *obsolete* exc. *Scot.* E17.
13 †**a** Be consumed or used up; disperse, pass off. E17–E18. ▸**b** Ejaculate; have an orgasm. *slang.* E17.
14 Esp. of a crop, foodstuff, etc.: prove in use to be of a certain quality; last or hold out *well* etc. Now *dial.* E17.
15 Of a liquid: flow, run. Now *rare* or *obsolete.* M18.
Phrases: ***spend a penny***: see PENNY *noun*. ***spend money like water***: see WATER *noun*. †**spend the mouth** = sense 11 above. ***spend the night***: see NIGHT *noun*. †**spend the tongue** = sense 11 above.
Comb.: **spend-all** (now *rare*) a spendthrift; **spendthrift** *noun & adjective* (*a*) *noun* a person who spends money profusely or wastefully; an extravagant or wasteful person; (*b*) *adjective* extravagant, wasteful; **spendthriftiness** *rare* the quality of being spendthrift.
■ **spendable** *adjective* †(*a*) that may be consumed or used for ordinary purposes; *spec.* (of paper) used for wrapping etc. as opp. to writing on; (*b*) (of income etc.) that may be spent: LME. **spender** *noun* (*a*) a person who spends money etc.; *spec.* a spendthrift; (*b*) a person who or thing which consumes or uses up something; (*c*) TANNING a pit in which the bark is leached (also ***spender pit***): LME.

spending /ˈspɛndɪŋ/ *noun.* OE.
[from prec. + -ING[1].]
1 The paying out of money etc.; expenditure. OE. ▸**b** An instance of this; an amount spent. E17.
†**2** That which may be spent; means of support; goods, money. ME–M17.
3 The action of using or consuming something; in later use esp. as food. LME.
4 The action or fact of losing, destroying, or exhausting something. LME.
†**5** An orgasm; an ejaculation. *slang.* M–L19.

📖 **1** *Japan Times* The added military spending went toward putting down the . . uprising. *attrib.*: *Wine Spectator* The company was on a spending spree, buying vineyards, wineries and companies.

Comb.: **spending money**. †**spending silver** money available or provided for spending; pocket money.

Spenglerian /ʃpɛŋˈɡlɪərɪən/ *adjective.* E20.
[from *Spengler* (see below) + -IAN.]
Of, pertaining to, or characteristic of the philosophy of the German philosopher Oswald Spengler (1880–1936), esp. as expressed in his work *Der Untergang des Abendlandes* ('The Decline of the West').
■ ˈ**Spenglerism** *noun* (*rare*) the philosophy of Spengler E20.

spense /spɛns/ *noun.* Now *dial.* ME.
[Aphet. from Old French *espense* = Anglo-Norman *expense* EXPENSE.]
1 †**a** Expense; expenditure *of* goods, income, etc.; cost. Later also, the consuming or using up *of* something. ME–L16. ▸**b** In *pl.* Charges, costs, items of expense or expenditure; expenses. LME.
2 That which may be spent; money, supplies; pocket money. ME.

Spenserian /spɛnˈsɪərɪən/ *adjective & noun.* E19.
[from *Spenser* (see below) + -IAN.]
▶ **A** *adjective.* Of, pertaining to, or characteristic of the English poet Edmund Spenser (d. 1599) or his work. E19.
Spenserian stanza the form of stanza used by Spenser in the *Faerie Queene*, consisting of eight iambic pentameters and a final alexandrine, with the rhyming scheme *ababbcbcc*.
▶ **B** *noun.* **1** A Spenserian stanza; a poem in this metre. E19.
2 A follower or imitator of Spenser; a poet of Spenser's school. *rare.* L19.

spent /spɛnt/ *adjective & noun.* LME.
[pa. pple of SPEND *verb*.]
▶ **A** *adjective.* **1 a** Of a thing: consumed, exhausted, used up completely; no longer active, effective, or serviceable. LME. ▸†**b** Wrecked; drowned. *rare.* L15–E17.
2 Past, gone; at an end, over. E16.
3 Of a person or animal: deprived of strength, worn out by exertion, hardship, etc.; *spec.* (of a fish) exhausted by spawning. Also foll. by *with* effort, fatigue, etc. M16.

📖 **1a** K. WATERHOUSE He was slowing down, like a spent volcano. *Time* Facilities for separating plutonium from spent reactor fuel. *Guns & Weapons* His gun was uncocked, with a spent cartridge in the chamber. ***spent tan***: see TAN *noun*[1] 1b. **2** B. MAGEE The Romantic Movement in Literature was already spent. **3** B. BAINBRIDGE Utterly spent, he dribbled to a standstill. **spent gnat** ANGLING (an artificial trout fly imitating) a floating mayfly exhausted after mating.

▶ **B** *noun.* A fish (esp. a herring) that has just spawned. M19.

spent *verb pa. t. & pple* of SPEND *verb*.

speos /ˈspiːɒs/ *noun.* M19.
[Greek = cave, grotto.]
EGYPTOLOGY. A cave temple or tomb, *esp.* one of some architectural importance.

sperage /ˈspəːrɪdʒ/ *noun. obsolete* exc. *dial.* Also †**sparage**. LME.
[Old French *sperage*, *sparage* from Latin ASPARAGUS.]
Asparagus.

sperate /ˈspɛrət/ *adjective.* Long *rare* or *obsolete.* LME.
[Latin *speratus* pa. pple of *sperare* hope: see -ATE[2].]
1 Orig. (of a debtor), able to repay a debt. Later (of a debt), having some likelihood of being repaid. LME.
2 *gen.* Of a promising nature; hopeful. E19.

spergula /ˈspəːɡjʊlə/ *noun.* LME.
[medieval Latin, of unkn. origin.]
Corn spurrey, *Spergula arvensis*.

sperm /spəːm/ *noun.* Pl. same, **-s**. LME.
[Late Latin *sperma* from Greek = sperm, seed, from base of *speirein* to sow. Cf. next.]
1 (The fluid which includes) the male reproductive cells or gametes of humans and animals; semen. LME. ▸**b** A spermatozoon. Also ***sperm cell***. E20.
†**2** *collect.* The eggs of an insect. E17–M18.
3 The generative matter or source from which any plant, material thing, quality, etc., is formed or takes its origin. *literary.* E17.
4 A sperm whale. M19.
5 Spermaceti. M19.
Comb.: **sperm-aster** BIOLOGY a star-shaped configuration which in some species forms ahead of the sperm nucleus as it enters the egg in fertilization; **sperm bank** a supply of semen stored for use in artificial insemination; **sperm candle** a spermaceti candle; ***sperm cell***: see sense 1b above; **sperm count** the approximate number of spermatozoa in one ejaculation or in a measured amount of semen; **sperm morula** a ball of spermatozoa; **sperm oil** an oil found with spermaceti in the heads of various whales, and used as a lubricant. See also SPERM WHALE.
■ **spermic** *adjective* (*rare*) of or pertaining to sperm or seed M19. **spermous** *adjective* (*rare*) = SPERMY E19. **spermy** *adjective* (*rare*) resembling or of the nature of sperm; spermatic; full of sperm: LME.

sperma /ˈspəːmə/ *noun. obsolete* exc. *Hist.* Pl. **spermata** /spəːˈmɑːtə/. LME.
[Late Latin or Greek: see prec.]
Sperm; seed.

sperma- /ˈspəːmə/ *combining form.*
[from (the same root as) SPERM with connective *-a-*. Cf. SPERMATO-, SPERMO-.]
Forming words with the sense 'of or pertaining to sperm, seed, or reproductive processes', as ***spermaduct***, ***spermalege***, etc.

spermaceti /spəːməˈsiːti, -ˈsɛti/ *noun.* L15.
[medieval Latin, formed as SPERM + *ceti* genit. of *cetus*, Greek *kētos* whale (from its appearance or the belief that it represents whale-spawn).]
A soft white waxy substance used in the manufacture of candles, ointments, etc., found in the sperm whale and some other cetaceans, chiefly in a rounded organ in the head which focuses acoustic signals and aids control of buoyancy.
Attrib. & comb.: In the sense 'made or consisting of spermaceti', as ***spermaceti candle***, ***spermaceti oil***, etc.; **spermaceti whale** (now *rare*) = SPERM WHALE.
■ **spermacetic** *adjective* (*rare*) E20.

spermaduct /ˈspəːmədʌkt/ *noun.* L19.
[from SPERMA- + DUCT *noun*.]
ZOOLOGY. A duct for the passage of sperm.

spermagone, **spermagonium** *nouns* vars. of SPERMOGONE etc.

spermal /ˈspəːm(ə)l/ *adjective. rare.* M17.
[from SPERM + -AL[1], or medieval Latin *spermalis*.]
Spermatic.

spermalege /ˈspəːməlɪdʒ/ *noun.* M20.
[from SPERMA- + Latin *legere* gather, collect.]
ENTOMOLOGY. In female bedbugs, a cuticular structure in which sperm is received and stored.

spermarium /spəːˈmɛːrɪəm/ *noun. rare.* Pl. **-ria** /-rɪə/. M19.
[mod. Latin, formed as SPERM + -ARIUM.]
= next.

spermary /ˈspəːməri/ *noun. rare.* M19.
[Anglicized from prec.: see -ARY[1].]
An organ in which sperms are generated, esp. in certain invertebrates.

spermata *noun* pl. of SPERMA.

spermatheca /spəːməˈθiːkə/ *noun.* Pl. **-cae** /-kiː/. E19.
[from SPERMA- + THECA.]
ZOOLOGY. A receptacle in a female or hermaphrodite animal in which sperm is stored.
■ **spermathecal** *adjective* of or pertaining to a spermatheca L19.

spermatia *noun* pl. of SPERMATIUM.

spermatic /spəːˈmatɪk/ *adjective & noun.* LME.
[Late Latin *spermaticus* from Greek *spermatikos*, from *sperma* SPERM: see -ATIC.]
▶ **A** *adjective.* **1 a** *ANATOMY.* Containing or conveying sperm; bearing or producing semen. LME. ▸**b** Full of or rich in sperm; generative, productive. *arch.* E17.
2 a *PHYSIOLOGY.* Of the nature of sperm; occurring in sperm. LME. ▸**b** *fig.* Resembling sperm, esp. in generative or reproductive power. *arch.* M17.
†**3** Directly derived from the united semen of male and female (according to former physiological theory). LME–E18.
4 Of a quality: characteristic of or derived from sperm, generative. M17.
Special collocations: **spermatic cord** *ANATOMY* a bundle of nerves, ducts, and blood-vessels running to and from each testis within the scrotum.
▶ **B** *noun.* In *pl.* The blood-vessels supplying the gonads. Also, the ducts which convey sperm. LME.
■ **spermatically** *adverb* in a way or form characteristic of a sperm or seed; seminally: M17.

spermaticide /spəːˈmatɪsʌɪd/ *noun.* Now *rare.* E20.
[from SPERMATO-: see -CIDE.]
= SPERMICIDE.
■ **spermatiˈcidal** *adjective* = SPERMICIDAL M20.

spermatid /ˈspəːmətɪd/ *noun.* L19.
[from SPERMAT(O- + -ID[2].]
BIOLOGY. An immature male sex cell formed from a spermatocyte, which may develop into a spermatozoon without further division.
■ **spermatidal** /-ˈmat-/ *adjective* L20.

spermatiferous /spəːməˈtɪf(ə)rəs/ *adjective.* M19.
[from SPERMAT(O-: see -FEROUS.]
MYCOLOGY. Bearing spermatia.

spermatise *verb* var. of SPERMATIZE.

spermatist /ˈspəːmətɪst/ *noun.* M19.
[from SPERMAT(O- + -IST.]
BIOLOGY (now *Hist.*). An advocate of the theory that the sperm alone is the essential source of animal life. Cf. OVIST.
■ **spermatism** *noun* (*rare*) the theory of the spermatists M19.

spermatium /spəːˈmeɪʃɪəm/ *noun.* Pl. **-tia** /-ʃɪə/. M19.
[mod. Latin from Greek *spermation* dim. of *sperma* SPERM: see -IUM.]
BOTANY. A non-motile cell acting as a male gamete in fungi lacking antheridia, esp. rust fungi and certain ascomycetes. In red algae, a non-flagellated male gamete.
■ **spermatiophore** *noun* (*MYCOLOGY*) a special hypha bearing spermatia L19.

spermatize /ˈspəːmətʌɪz/ *verb.* Also **-ise.** E17.
[French *spermatiser* or medieval Latin *spermatizare*, from Greek *spermatizein* to sow, from *spermat-*, *sperma* SPERM.]
†**1** *verb intrans.* Emit or produce sperm. E17–L18.
2 *verb trans. MYCOLOGY.* Fertilize by means of spermatia. *rare.* M20.
■ **spermatiˈzation** *noun* (*MYCOLOGY*). M20.

spermato- /ˈspəːmətəʊ, spəˈmatəʊ/ *combining form.*
[Greek, from *spermat-*, *sperma* SPERM: see -O-.]
BIOLOGY. Relating to the reproductive organs or processes of animals or plants, esp. to sperm or seeds.
■ **spermatoˈcidal** *adjective* = SPERMICIDAL *adjective* E20. **sperˈmatocide** = SPERMICIDE M20. **spermatocyte** *noun* a cell produced from a spermatogonium which may give rise to spermatids by meiosis L19. **spermatoˈgenesis** *noun* the production or development of spermatozoa L19. **spermatogeˈnetic**, **spermatoˈgenic** *adjectives* of or relating to spermatogenesis L19. **spermatoˈgonium** *noun*, pl. **-nia**, (*ANATOMY*) a cell in the wall of a seminiferous tubule which gives rise by mitosis to spermatocytes L19. **spermaˈtology** *noun* = SPERMOLOGY E20. **spermatoˈrrhoea** *noun* (*MEDICINE*) involuntary ejection of semen without orgasm M19. **spermatozoid** /-ˈzəʊɪd/ *noun* (*BOTANY*) an antherozoid M19.

spermatophore /ˈspəːmətə(ʊ)fɔː, spəˈmat-/ *noun.* M19.
[from SPERMATO- + -PHORE.]
ZOOLOGY. A protein capsule containing a mass of spermatozoa, transferred during mating in various insects and other invertebrates.
■ **spermatoˈphoric** *adjective* M20.

spermatophyte /ˈspəːmətə(ʊ)fʌɪt, spəˈmat-/ *noun.* L19.
[from SPERMATO- + -PHYTE.]
BOTANY. Any vascular plant of the division Spermatophyta, which comprises the seed-bearing plants and is divisible into angiosperms and gymnosperms. Cf. *pteridophyte*.

spermatozoon /spəːmətə(ʊ)ˈzəʊɒn, spəˌmat-/ *noun.* Pl. **-zoa** /-ˈzəʊə/. M19.
[from SPERMATO- + Greek *zōion* animal.]
The mature motile male sex cell of an animal by which the ovum is fertilized, usu. having a compact head and one or more flagella.
■ **spermatozoal** *adjective* of or pertaining to spermatozoa; of the nature of a spermatozoon: M19. **spermatozoan** *adjective* = SPERMATOZOAL M20.

spermicide /ˈspəːmɪsʌɪd/ *noun.* E20.
[from SPERM + -I- + -CIDE.]
A substance which kills spermatozoa, *esp.* one used as a contraceptive.
■ **spermiˈcidal** *adjective* E20.

spermidine /ˈspəːmɪdiːn/ *noun.* E20.
[from SPERM + -IDINE.]
BIOCHEMISTRY. A colourless amine, $H_2N(CH_2)_3NH(CH_2)_4NH_2$, having a similar distribution and function to spermine.

spermine /ˈspəːmiːn/ *noun.* L19.
[from SPERM + -INE[5].]
BIOCHEMISTRY. A deliquescent polyamine, $[H_2N{\cdot}(CH_2)_3{\cdot}NH{\cdot}(CH_2)_2{\cdot}]_2$, which acts to stabilize various components of living cells and is widely distributed in living and decaying tissues.

spermiogenesis /ˌspəːmɪə(ʊ)ˈdʒɛnɪsɪs/ *noun.* E20.
[from SPERM + *-i-* + -O- + -GENESIS.]
BIOLOGY. The development of spermatozoa; *spec.* the last phase of spermatogenesis, in which spermatids become mature spermatozoa.

spermo- /ˈspəːməʊ/ *combining form.*
[from SPERM + -O-. Cf. SPERMATO-.]
Of or pertaining to sperm or (esp.) seeds.
■ **spermoderm** *noun* (*BOTANY*) the testa or outer coat of a seed M19.

spermogone /ˈspəːməgəʊn/ *noun.* Also **sperma-.** M19.
[Anglicized from next.]
= next.

spermogonium /spəːməˈgəʊnɪəm/ *noun.* Also **sperma-.** Pl. **-nia** /-nɪə/. M19.
[from SPERMO- + Greek *gon-* stem of *gonē*, *gonos* offspring + -IUM.]
MYCOLOGY. A hollow hyphal structure in which spermatia are produced.

spermology /spəːˈmɒlədʒi/ *noun. rare.* L19.
[In sense 1 from SPERMO- + -LOGY; in sense 2 from Greek *spermologia*.]
1 The branch of science that deals with the investigation of sperm. L19.
2 An instance of babbling or trifling talk. L19.
■ **spermologist** *noun* E18.

spermophile /ˈspəːməfɪl, -fʌɪl/ *noun.* E19.
[mod. Latin *Spermophilus* (see below), lit. 'seed-lover': see SPERMO-, -PHILE.]
Any of various (mainly N. American) ground squirrels of the genus *Spermophilus* or related genera.

sperm whale /ˈspəːm weɪl/ *noun phr.* M19.
[Abbreviation from *SPERMACETI whale*.]
1 A large toothed whale, *Physeter macrocephalus*, found in warm oceans worldwide, feeding on squid and having a massive oblong head containing a spermaceti-organ. Also called *cachalot*. M19.
2 Either of two smaller related whales of the genus *Kogia*. L19.

speromagnetic /spɪərəmagˈnɛtɪk/ *adjective.* L20.
[from Greek *dia*)*speirein* scatter + -O- + MAGNETIC *adjective* (after *antiferromagnetic* etc.).]
PHYSICS. Designating an amorphous magnetic material in which the individual electron spins are aligned more or less antiparallel to their closest neighbours but with an overall statistical distribution of orientations with no preferred direction.
■ **speroˈmagnetism** *noun* the property characterizing a speromagnetic material L20.

speronara /spɛrəˈnɑːrə/ *noun.* L18.
[Italian.]
A large rowing and sailing boat used in southern Italy and Malta.

sperse /spəːs/ *verb.* Now *rare.* L16.
[Aphet. from DISPERSE *verb*, prob. partly after Italian *sperso* pa. pple of *spergere* scatter.]
1 *verb trans.* Cause to scatter or disperse; drive in different directions. L16.
2 *verb intrans.* Take different directions. E19.

spes /speɪz/ *noun.* E19.
[Latin.]
LAW. A hope, an expectation, esp. of some future benefit.
spes recuperandi /rɪˌkuːpəˈrandiː, -dʌɪ/ hope of recovery. ***spes successionis*** /sʌkˌsɛsɪˈəʊnɪs/ an expectation (as opp. to a right) of succession.

spessartine /ˈspɛsətiːn/ *noun.* M19.
[French, from *Spessart* a district in NW Bavaria: see -INE[5].]
MINERALOGY. Garnet in which the chief cations are manganese and aluminium, occurring as orange-red to dark brown crystals; manganese-aluminium garnet.

spessartite /ˈspɛsətʌɪt/ *noun.* M19.
[formed as prec. + -ITE[1].]
1 *MINERALOGY.* = SPESSARTINE. Chiefly *N. Amer.* M19.
2 *GEOLOGY.* A porphyritic rock consisting of phenocrysts of an amphibole or pyroxene, usu. green hornblende, in a groundmass of sodic plagioclase. E20.

spet /spɛt/ *noun.* Long *obsolete* exc. *dial.* LME.
[from SPET *verb*.]
An act of spitting; spit, spittle.

spet /spɛt/ *verb intrans. & trans.* Long *obsolete* exc. *dial.* Infl. **-tt-.** Also †**spete.**
[Old English *spǣtan* from base also of SPIT *verb*[1].]
Spit; expectorate.

spetch /spɛtʃ/ *verb & noun.* L16.
[Rel. to SPECK *noun*[2].]
▶ **A** *verb trans.* Patch or mend (shoes etc.) with leather; patch (a garment) with cloth. *north.* L16.
▶ **B** *noun.* A strip or patch of leather used in making glue or size, later also (*north.*) for making or mending boots or shoes. E17.

†**spete** *verb* var. of SPET *verb.*

Spetsnaz /ˈspɛtsnaz/ *noun.* L20.
[Russian, from *voĭska spetsial'nogo naznacheniya* = special purpose force.]
In the former Soviet Union, an elite highly-trained armed force freq. involved in international security operations.

spew /spjuː/ *noun.* Also (*arch.*) **spue.** L15.
[from the verb.]
1 a Orig., the action of vomiting. Later, contents of the stomach brought up through the mouth; vomit. L15. ▸**b** Excess material forced out between the halves of a mould as they close during the manufacture of plastic objects. M20.
2 *dial.* **a** The fourth swarm of bees in a season. M18. ▸**b** A wet, marshy piece of ground; a place in a field etc. where water oozes up. L18.
Comb.: **spew frost** = *needle ice* s.v. NEEDLE *noun*.

spew /spjuː/ *verb.* Also (*arch.*) **spue.**
[Old English *spīwan* (strong) = Old Frisian *spīa*, Old Saxon, Old High German *spīwan* (German *speien*), Old Norse *spýja*, Gothic *speiwan*; partly Old English *spēowan*, *spīowan* (weak) corresp. to Latin *spuere*, Greek *ptuein*, and Balto-Slavonic formations on an Indo-European base of imit. origin.]
1 *verb intrans.* Bring up the contents of the stomach through the mouth; vomit. OE.
2 *verb trans.* **a** Bring up (food or drink) from the stomach and eject through the mouth; vomit; eject or emit (blood, poison, etc.) from the mouth. Also foll. by *forth*, *out*, *up*. OE. ▸**b** Utter (abusive or objectionable language). Usu. foll. by *forth*, *out*, etc. ME. ▸**c** *fig.* Cast out, reject; drive *out* with abhorrence or contempt. *arch.* ME.
3 *verb trans.* Eject as if by vomiting; *spec.* (*NAUTICAL*) force (oakum) out of the seams of a vessel by pressure. Also foll. by *forth*, *out*, *over*, *up*. L16.
4 *verb intrans.* **a** Of liquid etc.: flow or issue in a stream; ooze *out*, pour *over*, be forced *up*. E17. ▸**b** Of ground: swell through excess of moisture; slip when left unsupported. E17.
5 *verb intrans.* Of people, animals, etc.: swarm; spill *out* in large numbers. M18.

> 📖 **2a** O. MANNING Hadjimoscos . . had spewed out his false teeth. ***spew one's ring***: see RING *noun*[1]. **b** J. WAINWRIGHT Where was the object of spewing out untruths. **c** BACON He was thus justly spewed out of the realm. **3** D. ATTENBOROUGH Volcanoes . . spewing ash and lava. **5a** *New Scientist* Poisonous fumes . . spewed over parts of Cambridgeshire. J. HERBERT Film was spewing from the camera's mouth. **6** D. ADAMS Noisy revellers spewed out onto the platform.

■ **spewer** *noun* OE.

spewy /ˈspjuːɪ/ *adjective.* M17.
[from prec. + -Y[1].]
Of ground: excessively moist, boggy; from which water oozes out.
■ **spewiness** *noun* M17.

spey *verb* see SPAY.

SPF *abbreviation.*
Sun protection factor (with ref. to the effectiveness of suntan oils etc.).

SPG *abbreviation.*
Hist. Special Patrol Group (a division of the Police Force).

sp. gr. *abbreviation.*
Specific gravity.

sphacelia /sfəˈsiːlɪə/ *noun*. L19.
[mod. Latin, from SPHACELUS, with ref. to its effects when eaten: see -IA[1].]
BOTANY. The whitish hymenium or conidial stage of an ergot fungus.
■ **sphacelial** *adjective* E20

sphacelus /ˈsfasɪləs/ *noun*. Now *rare* or *obsolete*. L16.
[mod. Latin from Greek *sphakelos* gangrene.]
MEDICINE. Necrosis, the terminal stage of gangrene; an instance of this; a mass of necrotic tissue.
■ **sphacelate** *adjective & verb* (*a*) *adjective* = SPHACELATED; (*b*) *verb intrans. & trans.* make or become gangrenous or necrotic: E17. **sphacelated** *adjective* affected with sphacelus, gangrenous, necrosed; BOTANY dark and withered: E17. **sphaceˈlation** *noun* necrosis M17. **sphacelous** *adjective* gangrenous, necrotic L17.

sphaeridium /sfɪəˈrɪdɪəm/ *noun*. Pl. **-dia** /-dɪə/. L19.
[mod. Latin, from *sphaera* SPHERE *noun*: see -IDIUM.]
ZOOLOGY. In sea urchins, each of numerous minute rounded modified spines thought to be organs of orientation.

sphaero- /ˈsfɪərəʊ/ *combining form*.
[mod. Latin from Greek *sphairo-* combining form of *sphaira* SPHERE *noun*: see -O-. Cf. SPHERO-.]
= SPHERO-.
¶ Now mainly superseded by forms in *sphero-* exc. in some TAXONOMY, PALAEONTOLOGY, & MINERALOGY contexts.
■ **sphaerocone** *noun* (PALAEONTOLOGY) an ammonoid with a very involute shell in which the outer whorl conceals the inner one, the whole having a globular form E20. **sphaeroˈcobaltite** *noun* (MINERALOGY) a rare trigonal cobalt carbonate mineral occurring as spherical masses of rose-red crystals L19. **sphaeroˈsiderite** *noun* (MINERALOGY) siderite occurring as knoblike masses of radial crystals M19.

sphagna *noun pl.* see SPHAGNUM.

sphagnous /ˈsfagnəs/ *adjective*. E19.
[from next + -OUS.]
Of the nature of, consisting in, or full of, sphagnum.
■ Also **sphagnose** *adjective* (*rare*) E18.

sphagnum /ˈsfagnəm/ *noun*. Pl. **-na** /-nə/, **-nums**. M18.
[mod. Latin (see below), from Greek *sphagnos* a kind of moss.]
Any of various mosses constituting the genus *Sphagnum*, which freq. dominate acid bogs and are spongy and absorbent from the presence of numerous hollow porous cells in the leaves and stem cortex; plants of this kind massed together, freq. used as a medium for growing orchids etc. Also ***sphagnum moss***.
Comb.: **sphagnum bog**, **sphagnum swamp**: in which the plant life consists chiefly of mosses of the genus *Sphagnum*.

sphairistic /sfɛːˈrɪstɪk/ *adjective*. *rare*. L19.
[Greek *sphairistikos* playing at ball: see -IC. Cf. next.]
Tennis-playing.

sphairistike /sfɛːˈrɪstɪki/ *noun*. L19.
[Greek *sphairistikē* (*tekhnē*) skill in playing at ball, formed as prec. Cf. STICKÉ.]
Hist. An early form of lawn tennis.

sphalerite /ˈsfaləraɪt/ *noun*. M19.
[from Greek *sphaleros* deceptive + -ITE[1].]
MINERALOGY. Native zinc sulphide, crystallizing in the cubic system and occurring as yellow, brown, or black prisms often also containing iron; zinc blende.

sphecid /ˈsfiːsɪd, ˈsfɛ-, -kɪd/ *noun & adjective*. L19.
[mod. Latin *Sphecidae* (see below), from Greek *sphek-*, *sphex* wasp: see SPHEX, -ID[3].]
ENTOMOLOGY. ▶**A** *noun*. Any hymenopteran insect of the family Sphecidae of solitary, mainly fossorial wasps. L19.
▶ **B** *adjective*. Of, pertaining to, or designating this family. L19.

sphecoid /ˈsfiːkɔɪd/ *adjective*. E19.
[from Greek *sphek-*, *sphex* wasp, SPHEX + -OID.]
ENTOMOLOGY. Resembling a sphex; *spec.* belonging to or characteristic of the superfamily Sphecoidea, including sphecids.

spheges *noun pl.* see SPHEX.

sphen- *combining form* see SPHENO-.

sphendone /ˈsfɛndəni/ *noun*. M19.
[Greek *sphendonē*.]
ARCHAEOLOGY. **1** A headband or fillet shaped like a form of sling, worn by women in ancient Greece. M19.
2 An area composed of elongated sloping sides with a rounded end. M19.

sphene /sfiːn/ *noun*. E19.
[French *sphène* from Greek *sphēn* wedge.]
MINERALOGY. Calcium titanium silicate, occurring as wedge-shaped monoclinic crystals, usu. greenish-yellow or brown, as an accessory mineral in granitic and metamorphic rocks. Also called ***titanite***.

spheno- /ˈsfiːnəʊ/ *combining form*. Before a vowel also **sphen-**.
[from Greek *sphēn* wedge: see -O-.]
1 Wedge-shaped; having or pertaining to wedge-shaped parts or things.
2 ANATOMY & ZOOLOGY. Of, pertaining to, or homologous with the sphenoid bone together with another part, as *sphenethmoid*, *sphenomandibular*, *sphenopalatine*, etc.
■ **sphenochasm** *noun* (GEOLOGY) a triangular region of oceanic crust separating two cratons M20.

sphenoid /ˈsfiːnɔɪd/ *adjective & noun*. M18.
[mod. Latin *spheno(e)ides* from Greek *sphēnoeidēs*, from *sphēn* wedge: see -OID.]
▶ **A** *adjective*. Designating, of, or pertaining to a bone of irregular shape situated at the base of the skull, in front of the temporal and occipital bones. M18.
▶ **B** *noun*. **1** ANATOMY & ZOOLOGY. The sphenoid bone; each of the separate parts of this. E19.
2 CRYSTALLOGRAPHY. A long wedge-shaped prismatic crystal form of the sphenoidal class. Also = DISPHENOID. M19.

sphenoidal /sfɪˈnɔɪd(ə)l/ *adjective*. E18.
[from (the same root as) prec. + -AL[1].]
1 ANATOMY. Of or pertaining to the sphenoid bone. E18.
2 CRYSTALLOGRAPHY. Of or designating an open crystal form with two non-parallel faces and an axis of two-fold symmetry. M20.

sphenotic /sfɪˈnɒtɪk/ *adjective & noun*. L19.
[from SPHEN(O- + OTIC *adjective*.]
ZOOLOGY. ▶**A** *adjective*. Of, pertaining to, or formed by the sphenoid bone and otic structures. L19.
▶ **B** *noun*. A sphenotic bone, found in birds and certain fishes. L19.

spheral /ˈsfɪər(ə)l/ *adjective*. M16.
[Late Latin *spheralis*, *sphaeralis*, from *sphaera* SPHERE *noun*: see -AL[1].]
1 Of or pertaining to a sphere or round body; having the rounded form of a sphere; spherical. M16.
2 Of or pertaining to the cosmic spheres or celestial objects. E19.

sphere /sfɪə/ *noun*. ME.
[Old French *espere*, later (with assim. to Greek or Latin) *sphère* from late Latin *sphera*, earlier *sphaera*, from Greek *sphaira* ball, globe.]
▶ **I 1** The apparent outward limit of space, conceived as a hollow globe enclosing the earth; the sky perceived as a vault on or in which celestial objects are represented as lying; *poet.* the heavens, the sky. ME. ▸**b** A material representation of the apparent form of the heavens; a globe or other construction illustrating the place and motions of celestial objects. LME.
2 *Hist.* Each of a series of concentric transparent hollow globes envisaged by medieval astronomers as revolving round the earth and respectively carrying with them the moon, sun, planets, and fixed stars. Freq. in ***harmony of the spheres***, ***music of the spheres*** below. Also ***celestial sphere***. Cf. ORB *noun*[1] 5. ME. ▸**b** *Hist.* Any of the concentric globes formerly supposed to be formed around the world by the four elements, earth, water, air, and fire. LME.
3 With possess.: a particular sphere (sense 2) appropriate to or occupied by each of the planets or the fixed stars; *fig.* a sphere occupied or imagined as occupied by a deity, person, or thing. LME.
4 A place of abode different from the present earth or world; a heaven. L16.
5 a A place, position, or station in society; a body of people of a certain (orig. only high) rank or standing. E17. ▸**b** A measure of comparison used to denote a great difference in rank, intelligence, etc. M17. ▸**c** With possess.: the group of people with whom one is directly in contact in society. M19.
6 A province or domain in which one's activities or faculties find scope, or within which they are naturally confined; the whole field or range of some quality, thing, activity, operation, etc. E17.

🕮 **3** SHAKES. *Haml.* Thy . . eyes, like stars, start from their spheres. **4** W. E. H. LECKY A future sphere, where . . injustices . . shall be rectified. **5a** J. RUSKIN The change . . was into a higher sphere of society. **b** S. MARMION A civil gentleman, ten spheres below a fool. **c** P. G. WODEHOUSE The only person in his immediate sphere over whom he had no . . hold. **6** W. S. CHURCHILL The need for . . reforms in the sphere of government. B. MONTGOMERY Each was an expert in his own particular sphere. M. ESSLIN In the social and political sphere, Adamov finds the solution in Communism.

▶ **II 7 a** GEOMETRY. A body the surface of which is at all points equidistant from the centre; a figure formed by the revolution of a circle about its diameter. LME. ▸**b** MATH. The set of all points at (or within) a specified distance from a specified point. Also (with preceding numeral or symbol), a figure analogous to a sphere in a higher dimension. M20.
8 A globe, a ball; the rounded mass *of* such a body. LME.
9 A planet, a star; *spec.* the earth. L16.

🕮 **8** A. HARDY Plaice lay floating eggs: little spheres of glass-like transparency.

Phrases: ***armil sphere***: see ARMIL 3a. ***armillary sphere***: see ARMILLARY *adjective*. ***celestial sphere***: see sense 2 above. CO-PROSPERITY ***sphere***. ***crystalline sphere(s)***: see CRYSTALLINE *adjective* 1. **harmony of the spheres** *Hist.* = ***music of the spheres*** below. **in one's sphere** at home in one's surroundings or environment. **music of the spheres** *Hist.* the natural harmonic tones supposedly produced by the movement of the series of concentric transparent hollow globes envisaged by medieval astronomers as revolving round the earth. ***oblique sphere***: see OBLIQUE *adjective*. **out of one's sphere** not at home in one's surroundings or environment. ***right sphere***: see RIGHT *adjective*. ***Schwarzschild sphere***: see SCHWARZSCHILD 2. ***sector of a sphere***: see SECTOR *noun*. ***segment of a sphere***: see SEGMENT *noun* 1a. **sphere of action**, **sphere of influence**, **sphere of interest** (*a*) a region or territory within which a particular nation claims or is recognized to have a special interest for political or economic purposes; (*b*) the area of an individual's control, interest, etc.
Comb.: **sphere gap** ELECTRICITY a form of spark gap with two spherical electrodes, used esp. in devices for measuring high voltages.
■ **sphereless** *adjective* (*rare*) E19. **spheriform** *adjective* = SPHERICAL *adjective* 1 L17. **spherify** *verb trans.* (*rare*) give a spherical form to M19. **sphery** *adjective* (*a*) pertaining to or connected with the spheres or celestial objects; (*b*) *rare* having the form of a sphere: L16.

sphere /sfɪə/ *verb*. Chiefly *poet.* E17.
[from the noun.]
1 *verb trans.* Enclose in or as in a sphere; encircle, surround. E17.
2 *verb trans.* Make into a sphere; *fig.* form into a rounded or perfect whole. E17.
3 *verb trans.* Place among the planets, set in the sky; *fig.* place high or aloof above the common reach. E17.
4 *verb trans. & intrans.* Turn *about* or *round* in a circle. M17.
5 *verb intrans.* Centre *in* something. M19.

-sphere /sfɪə/ *suffix*.
[from SPHERE *noun*, after *atmosphere*.]
Forming names of more or less spherical structures or regions, esp. forming part of or associated with the earth (or any celestial object), as ***biosphere***, ***chromosphere***, ***ionosphere***, ***lithosphere***, ***magnetosphere***, etc.

spheric /ˈsfɛrɪk/ *adjective & noun*. LME.
[Late Latin *sphericus*, *sphae-* from Greek *sphairikos*, from *sphaira* SPHERE *noun*: see -IC. In sense A.II var. of SFERIC.]
▶ **A** *adjective*. **I 1** = SPHERICAL *adjective* 1. LME.
2 Of or relating to the sphere as a geometrical figure. M16.
3 Of or pertaining to the celestial spheres. *poet.* M17.
▶ **II** See SFERIC.
▶† **B** *noun*. = SPHERICS 1. *rare*. Only in 17.

spherical /ˈsfɛrɪk(ə)l/ *adjective*. L15.
[formed as prec.: see -ICAL.]
1 (Of a body) having the form of a sphere; (of shape or form) characteristic of a sphere; globular. L15. ▸†**b** Circular. *rare*. E17–M18.
2 MATH. **a** Of a line, figure, etc.: drawn in or on, or forming part of, the surface of a sphere. L16. ▸**b** Dealing with the properties of the sphere or spherical figures. E18. ▸**c** Pertaining to or arising from the sphere or its properties. M19.
3 Of or pertaining to the celestial spheres. E17.
Special collocations: ***spherical aberration***: see ABERRATION 2. **spherical angle**: between arcs of great circles on a sphere. **spherical coordinates** = ***spherical polar coordinates*** below. †**spherical number** each of the numbers (5, 6, and 10) whose powers always terminate in the same digit as the number itself. ***spherical pendulum***: see PENDULUM *noun*. **spherical polar coordinates** GEOMETRY three coordinates describing the position of a point in space, one indicating the radial distance of the point from the origin or pole and the others indicating its latitude and longitude relative to a fixed reference axis. **spherical projection**: of points on a surface (esp. points at the centre of each face of a crystal) on to an imaginary enclosing sphere. **spherical triangle**: formed by three arcs of great circles on a sphere. ***spherical* TRIGONOMETRY**. **spherical wave**: in which the wave fronts are concentric spheres. ***spherical wedge***: see WEDGE *noun* 6.
■ **spheriˈcality** *noun* M17. **spherically** *adverb* L16. **sphericalness** *noun* (*rare*) M17.

sphericity /sfɛˈrɪsɪti/ *noun*. E17.
[from SPHERIC + -ITY.]
†**1** A spherical body or figure. Only in E17.
2 The quality or degree of being spherical or having the (exact) form of a sphere. E17.

spherics /ˈsfɛrɪks/ *noun pl.* M18.
[In sense 1 from SPHERIC *noun*; in sense 2 var. of SFERICS.]
1 The branch of mathematics that deals with the properties of spheres. M18.
2 See SFERICS.

sphero- /ˈsfɪərəʊ/ *combining form*.
[Var. of SPHAERO-, alt. after SPHERE *noun*, or directly from SPHERE *noun* + -O-.]
Spherical or partly spherical in form; having or consisting of spherical parts; pertaining to spheres.
■ **sphero-cyˈlindrical** *adjective* (of a lens) having a spherical and a cylindrical surface L19. **spherograph** *noun* (NAUTICAL) a device designed to facilitate the calculation of spherical problems M19. **spheˈrometer** *noun* an instrument for measuring the sphericity or curvature of bodies or surfaces E19. **spheroplast** *noun* (BIOLOGY) a bacterium or plant cell bound by its plasma membrane, the

cell wall being deficient or lacking and the whole having a spherical form M20. **spheroplasting** *verbal noun* treatment (as with an enzyme) that converts cells to spheroplasts M20.

spherocyte /ˈsfɛrəsʌɪt, ˈsfɪərə-/ *noun.* E20.
[from SPHERO- + -CYTE.]
MEDICINE. A spherical cell; *esp.* a red blood cell which is biconvex instead of biconcave.
■ **spherocytic** /-ˈsɪtɪk/ *adjective* of, pertaining to, or characterized by the presence of spherocytes M20. **spherocyˈtosis** *noun*, pl. **-toses** /-ˈtəʊsiːz/, a spherocytic condition M20.

spheroid /ˈsfɪərɔɪd/ *noun & adjective.* L16.
[Latin *sphaeroides* from Greek *sphairoeidēs*, from *sphaira*: see SPHERE *noun*, -OID.]
▶ **A** *noun.* A body resembling or approximating to a sphere in shape; *esp.* one formed by the revolution of an ellipse about one of its axes. L16.
> D. BREWSTER The earth is an oblate spheroid.

▶ **B** *adjective.* = SPHEROIDAL *adjective* 1. M18.
■ **spheˈroidical** *adjective* (now *rare*) = SPHEROIDAL *adjective* 1 L17. **spheroiˈdicity** *noun* (*rare*) the state or character of being spheroidal M19. **spheroidism** *noun* (*rare*) the fact of being a spheroid E18.

spheroidal /sfɪəˈrɔɪd(ə)l, sfɛ-/ *adjective.* L18.
[from prec. + -AL¹.]
1 Resembling or approximating to a sphere in shape. L18.
2 Composed of or involving roughly spherical structures; spherulitic; *METALLURGY* = NODULAR *adjective* 3. E19.
3 Concerning the properties of spheroids. *rare.* L19.
2 spheroidal condition, **spheroidal state** a state in which a liquid on a hot surface forms small globules insulated by the Leidenfrost phenomenon.
■ **spheroidally** *adverb* L19.

spheroidize /ˈsfɪərɔɪdʌɪz/ *verb.* Also **-ise**. E20.
[from SPHEROID *noun* + -IZE.]
METALLURGY. **1** *verb intrans.* Of grains, esp. of graphite in cast iron or steel: undergo conversion into spheroids. E20.
2 *verb trans.* Convert into spheroids or to a spheroidal form. E20.
■ **spheroidiˈzation** *noun* the process of converting to spheroidal or nodular form E20.

spherosome /ˈsfɪərəsəʊm/ *noun.* M20.
[from SPHERO- + -SOME³.]
BIOLOGY. A cytoplasmic liquid droplet or cell organelle found in plant tissues, often associated with hydrolytic enzymic activity and corresponding to the lysosome in animal tissues.
■ **spherosomal** *adjective* M20.

spherule /ˈsfɛruːl/ *noun.* M17.
[Late Latin *spherula*, *sphaerula* dim. of Latin *sphaera* SPHERE *noun.*]
A little sphere; a small spherical or globular body.
■ **spherular** *adjective* having the form of a spherule E19.

spherulite /ˈsfɛrjʊlʌɪt/ *noun.* E19.
[from SPHERULE *noun* + -ITE¹.]
†**1** *MINERALOGY.* A concretionary substance occurring in small spherular masses in certain rocks. Only in 19.
2 *GEOLOGY.* A small spheroidal mass found in rock; *spec.* one consisting of many crystals grouped radially around a point. E19.
3 A small spheroidal mass of crystals or fibrils of any substance, esp. a polymer. L19.

spherulitic /sfɛrjʊˈlɪtɪk/ *adjective.* E19.
[formed as prec.: see -IC.]
GEOLOGY & MINERALOGY. **1** Pertaining to or characterized by spherulites. E19.
2 Of rocks and other substances: containing or composed of spherulites. Also (*METALLURGY*), = NODULAR *adjective* 3. M19.
3 Having the form of a spherulite. M19.
■ **spherulitically** *adverb* L20. **ˈspherulitize** *verb trans.* (*GEOLOGY*) make spherulitic (in texture) L19.

spheterize /ˈsfɛt(ə)rʌɪz/ *verb trans. rare.* Also **-ise**. L18.
[Greek *spheterizein*, from *spheteros* one's own: see -IZE.]
Make one's own; appropriate.

sphex /sfɛks/ *noun.* Pl. **spheges** /ˈsfiːdʒiːz/, **sphexes**. L18.
[mod. Latin from Greek *sphēx* (pl. *sphēkes*) wasp.]
ENTOMOLOGY. A fossorial solitary wasp of the genus *Sphex* (family Sphecidae). Now *rare* or *obsolete* exc. as mod. Latin genus name.

sphincter /ˈsfɪŋktə/ *noun.* L16.
[Latin from Greek *sphigktēr* band, contractile muscle, from *sphiggein* bind tight.]
1 *ANATOMY.* A contractile muscular ring by which an orifice of the body is normally kept closed. Also with mod. Latin specifying word, as ***sphincter ani***, ***sphincter vaginae***, etc. L16.
2 A narrow esp. contractile circular opening. M18.
1 *sphincter of* ODDI.
Comb.: **sphincter control** voluntary control of the sphincter of the anus and hence of defecation; **sphincter muscle** = sense 1 above.
■ **sphinctered** *adjective* possessing a sphincter (of a specified kind) M20. **sphincterial** /-ˈtɪərɪəl/, **sphincteric** /-ˈtɛrɪk/ *adjectives* of, pertaining to, or of the nature of, a sphincter L19. **sphincterotomy** /-ˈrɒtəmi/ *noun* (an instance of) surgical cutting of or into a sphincter L19.

sphinges *noun pl.* see SPHINX.

sphingid /ˈsfɪndʒɪd, ˈsfɪŋgɪd/ *noun & adjective.* E20.
[mod. Latin *Sphingidae* (see below), from SPHINX: see -ID³.]
ENTOMOLOGY. (Of, pertaining to, or designating) a moth of the family Sphingidae (the hawkmoths).

sphingo- /ˈsfɪŋgəʊ/ *combining form.*
[from Greek *Sphigg-*, *Sphigx* SPHINX, orig. in *sphingosine*, with ref. to the enigmatic nature of the compound: see -O-.]
BIOCHEMISTRY. Used in the names of a number of related compounds isolated from the brain and nervous tissue.
■ **sphingolipid** *noun* any naturally occurring fatty acid derivative of a sphingosine M20. **sphingolipiˈdosis** *noun*, pl. **-doses** /-ˈdəʊsiːz/, a hereditary disorder involving accumulation of sphingolipids in the tissues M20. **sphingoˈmyelin** *noun* any of a number of complex phospholipids which are phosphoryl choline derivatives of *N*-acyl sphingosines L19. **sphingosine** *noun* a colourless crystalline base, $C_{18}H_{37}NO_2$, or any of various homologues and derivatives of this, which combined as sphingolipids occur in the cell membranes of the brain and nervous tissue L19.

sphinx /sfɪŋks/ *noun.* Pl. **sphinxes**, **sphinges** /ˈsfɪndʒiːz/. LME.
[Latin from Greek *Sphigx*, *Sphigg-*, app. from *sphiggein* draw tight.]
1 *GREEK MYTHOLOGY.* (**S-**.) A hybrid monster, usu. described as having a woman's head and a (winged) lion's body, which plagued Thebes until Oedipus solved its riddle. Also, any monster resembling this. LME. ▸**b** *fig.* An inscrutable or enigmatic person or thing; a mystery. E17.
2 Any of several ancient Greek or (esp.) Egyptian stone figures of a creature with a human or animal head and (occas.) breast and a lion's body; *spec.* (**S-**) *the* colossal figure of this kind near the pyramids at Giza in Egypt. L16.
3 A baboon, *esp.* a mandrill. Also ***sphinx-baboon***. Now *rare.* E17.
4 A moth of the genus *Sphinx*, or of the family Sphingidae, so called from the typical attitude of the caterpillar; a hawkmoth. Also ***sphinx-moth***. Chiefly *US.* M18.
> **1b** R. A. VAUGHAN History fairly questioned is no Sphinx. *Bath Herald* Mr Dodson has . . been a political sphinx.

■ **sphinxian** *adjective* of or pertaining to the Sphinx; sphinxlike: L16. **sphinxlike** *adjective* resembling the Sphinx; enigmatic, mysterious, inscrutable: M19.

†**sphondyl(e)** *nouns* vars. of SPONDYLE.

sphragistes /sfrəˈdʒɪstiːz/ *noun.* M19.
[Greek *sphragistēs*, from *sphragis* a seal.]
In Ancient Egypt, a priest in charge of the official seal of a temple.

sphygmo- /ˈsfɪgməʊ/ *combining form.*
[from Greek *sphugmo-* combining form of *sphugmos* pulse: see -O-.]
MEDICINE & PHYSIOLOGY. Of or pertaining to the pulse.
■ **sphygmogram** *noun* a record made by a sphygmograph L19. **sphygmograph** *noun* an instrument which continuously records the force and rate of the pulse in a blood-vessel M19. **sphygmoˈgraphic** *adjective* of, pertaining to, or produced by a sphygmograph M19. **sphygmoˈgraphically** *adverb* with regard to a sphygmographic trace M19. **sphygˈmography** *noun* the scientific measurement and description of the pulse M19. **sphygmomaˈnometer** *noun* an instrument for measuring arterial blood-pressure by means of a manometer and an inflatable cuff L19. **sphygmomaˈnometry** *noun* the use of a sphygmomanometer E20. **sphygˈmometer** *noun* an instrument for measuring the force or rate of the pulse M19. **sphygmoˈmetric** *adjective* of or pertaining to (the use of) a sphygmometer L19. **sphygˈmometry** *noun* measurement of the pulse or of blood-pressure M19. **sphygmophone** *noun* an instrument by which pulsations are rendered audible L19. **sphygmoscope** *noun* a device for displaying the pulse or heartbeat visibly, now esp. on a cathode-ray screen M19.

sphygmology /sfɪgˈmɒlədʒi/ *noun.* L19.
[from prec. + -LOGY.]
MEDICINE. The branch of (esp. diagnostic) medicine concerned with the pulse.
■ **sphygmoˈlogical** *adjective* M20.

Sphynx /sfɪŋks/ *noun.* L20.
[Origin uncertain: presumably a var. of SPHINX.]
A cat of a hairless breed, orig. from N. America.

sphyrelaton /sfʌɪˈriːlət(ə)n/ *noun.* M19.
[Greek *sphurēlaton*, from *sphura* hammer + *elatos*, from *elaunein* beat out.]
Repoussé work, esp. in Minoan or Etruscan art.

spial /ˈspʌɪəl/ *noun.* LME.
[Aphet. from ESPIAL.]
†**1** Espial; observation, watch. LME–E17.
2 A spy; a scout. *arch.* M16.

spianato /spɪəˈnɑːtəʊ/ *adjective & adverb.* L19.
[Italian.]
MUSIC. (Played) in a smooth, even, level-toned style.

spic /spɪk/ *noun & adjective. US slang* (*derog.* & considered *racially offensive*). E20.
[Abbreviation of SPIGGOTY.]
1 (Of, pertaining to, or designating) a Spanish-speaking person from Central or S. America or the Caribbean; *esp.* (a) Mexican. E20.
2 (Of or pertaining to) the Spanish language, esp. as spoken in Central or S. America or the Caribbean. M20.

spica /ˈspʌɪkə/ *noun.* LME.
[Latin = ear of grain. In sense 3 after Greek *stakhus*.]
†**1** ***oil of spica***, = ***oil of spike*** s.v. SPIKE *noun*². Only in LME.
2 *BOTANY.* A flower-spike. Now *rare* or *obsolete.* L17.
3 *MEDICINE.* A bandage folded into a spiral arrangement resembling an ear of wheat or barley. M18.

spic and span *adjectival, noun, & adverbial phr.* var. of SPICK AND SPAN.

spicate /ˈspʌɪkeɪt, -kət/ *adjective.* M17.
[Latin *spicatus* pa. pple of *spicare* furnish with spikes, from *spica* SPIKE *noun*²: see -ATE². In sense 2 infl. by SPIKE *noun*¹.]
1 *BOTANY.* (Of flowers) arranged in a spike; (of a plant) having its flowers so arranged. M17.
2 *ZOOLOGY.* Having the form of a spike; pointed. M19.

spicated /spɪˈkeɪtɪd, spʌɪ-/ *adjective.* Now *rare.* M17.
[formed as prec. + -ED². In sense 2 infl. by SPIKE *noun*¹.]
1 *BOTANY.* = SPICATE 1. M17.
2 Chiefly *BOTANY.* Spiky, bristly. E18.

spiccato /spɪˈkɑːtəʊ/ *adjective, adverb, & noun.* E18.
[Italian, = detailed, distinct.]
MUSIC. ▶**A** *adjective & adverb.* (Played) in a staccato style performed by bouncing the bow on the strings of a violin etc. E18.
▶ **B** *noun.* Spiccato playing; a passage played in this style. L19.

spice /spʌɪs/ *noun.* ME.
[Aphet. from Old French *espice* (mod. *épice*), from Latin *species* appearance, kind, SPECIES, (late) pl. wares, merchandise (after late Greek use of pl. of *eidos* form, in senses 'goods', 'groceries', 'spices').]
▶**I** †**1** A sort, a kind; a species. Also foll. by *of*. ME–E17.
†**2** Appearance, semblance. *rare.* LME–M16.
▶**II 3** Any of various strongly flavoured or aromatic vegetable substances, used esp. to flavour or scent food, or as medicines etc.; such substances collectively; *spec.* (*Scot.*) pepper. ME. ▸**b** Dried fruit. *dial.* L17. ▸**c** A medication formerly added to animal feed. *obsolete* exc. *Hist.* E18.
4 *fig.* **a** A person who or thing which adds interest or piquancy to something. ME. ▸**b** A slight flavour or suggestion *of* something; a trace; a touch *of* a particular illness (now *dial.*). L15.
5 An odour (as) of spice; spicy fragrance. *rare. poet.* M16.
> **3** B. FUSSELL Beef marinated in wine, vinegar, and spices. **4a** *Dogworld* If you . . enjoy the added spice of a little danger, this can be an exciting career. **b** W. IRVING The horse . . had a considerable spice of devil in his composition.
> **5** TENNYSON A summer fann'd with spice.

Comb.: **spice bag** a bundle of spices tied in muslin etc. to flavour food during cooking; **spice-berry** *N. Amer.* the checkerberry or wintergreen, *Gaultheria procumbens*; **spice-box** a lidded box for keeping spices, usu. divided into compartments; **spicebush** a pungently aromatic N. American shrub, *Lindera benzoin*, of the laurel family; **spice-cake** (*a*) a cake flavoured with sweet spices; (*b*) *dial.* a rich fruit cake; **spice-islands** *Hist.* the Moluccas; **spice mill** a small device for grinding spices by hand; **spice-plate** *Hist.* a small dish on which spices were formerly served separately at table; **spice rack** a freq. wooden rack with holes or shelves for holding separate jars of spices; **spicewood** *US* = ***spicebush*** above.

spice /spʌɪs/ *verb trans.* LME.
[Aphet. from Old French *espicer* (mod. *epicer*), formed as prec.]
1 Add a spice or spices to; flavour *with* spice. Formerly also *spec.*, embalm (a body) with spices. LME.
2 *fig.* Add interest or piquancy to; enliven; make more sensational. Freq. foll. by *up*. E16.
> **1** T. H. WHITE The . . saffron, aniseed, and tarragon . . were used to spice the savouries. BEVERLEY CLEARY A . . juicy hamburger spiced with relish. **2** *People* Johnson spices his text with lively . . photographs. *Los Angeles Times* An infectious musical stew that spices up familiar Western pop.

■ **spiced** *ppl adjective* (*a*) (as if) flavoured with spices; pungent, aromatic; †(*b*) delicate, tender; excessively particular or scrupulous: ME.

spicer /ˈspʌɪsə/ *noun. obsolete* exc. *Hist.* ME.
[Aphet. from Old French *espicier* (mod. *épicier* grocer), formed as SPICE *noun*: see -ER².]
A dealer in spices; an apothecary.

spicery /ˈspʌɪsəri/ *noun.* ME.
[Aphet. from Old French *espicerie* (mod. *épicerie*), formed as SPICE *noun*: see -ERY.]
1 *sing.* & in *pl.* Spices collectively. *arch.* ME.
2 †**a** A shop selling spices. ME–E16. ▸**b** A place for storing spices; *spec.* a department responsible for this in the royal household. *obsolete* exc. *Hist.* LME.

spicey *adjective* var. of SPICY.

spick /spɪk/ *noun*¹. Long *obsolete* exc. *Scot.*
[Old English *spic* (= Old Norse, Middle Swedish *spik*) var. of *spec*: see SPECK *noun*².]
= SPECK *noun*².

spick /spɪk/ *noun*². Now *dial.* M16.
[Old French *spic*, *espic*, formed as SPIKE *noun*². Cf. ASPIC *noun*².]
(Spike) lavender. Cf. SPIKE *noun*² 4.

spick /spɪk/ *noun*³. Long *obsolete* exc. *Scot.* E17.
[Var. of SPIKE *noun*¹.]
A large nail, a spike-nail.

spick /spɪk/ *adjective*. L19.
[Abbreviation.]
= SPICK AND SPAN *adjective*.

📖 *Listener* An allegedly sleazy joint, though it looked spick enough to me.

spick and span /spɪk (ə)nd ˈspan/ *adjectival, noun, & adverbial phr.* Also **spic and span**, (as *adjectival phr.*) **speck and span** /spɛk/. L16.
[(Shortened from) emphatic extension of SPAN-NEW; 1st elem. is prob. due to synon. Dutch *spikspelldernieuw*, *-splinternieuw* lit. 'spike-, splinter-new' (cf. German *nagelneu* lit. 'nail-new').]
▶ **A** *adjective*. (Freq. with hyphens, esp. when *attrib.*)
1 Absolutely new or fresh; brand-new; unused. Also more fully ***spick and span new***. L16.
2 Particularly neat and clean; trim, smart. M19.

📖 **1** M. HOLROYD A brand new spick-and-span school which had recently opened. **2** G. PALEY In a white shirt and blue-striped tie, spick-and-span, a Sunday-school man. O. A. BURNS It had never been a spic-and-span house. Granny wasn't much for cleaning.

▶ **B** *noun*. That which is spick and span. *rare*. M18.
▶ **C** *adverb*. In a spick and span manner; smartly, neatly. *rare*. E19.
■ **spick-and-spanness** /-n-n-/ *noun* E20.

spicket /ˈspɪkɪt/ *noun*. Now *Scot.*, *US*, & *dial.* LME.
[Alt. of SPIGOT.]
A spigot; a water-tap.

spick-span /ˈspɪkspan/ *adjective*. E19.
[Abbreviation.]
= SPICK AND SPAN *adjective*.

spicula /ˈspɪkjʊlə/ *noun*¹. Pl. **-lae** /-liː/. M18.
[mod. Latin, dim. of Latin *spica* SPIKE *noun*¹: see -CULE.]
1 A sharp-pointed or needle-like crystal etc.; *esp.* a minute ice-crystal. M18.
2 A small spine on part of a plant or animal; a prickle, a spicule. M18.
†**3** BOTANY. A spikelet of a grass or sedge. M18–M19.
4 = SPICULE 5. M19.

spicula *noun*² pl. of SPICULUM.

spicular /ˈspɪkjʊlə/ *adjective*. L18.
[from prec. + -AR¹.]
Of the nature of a spicule or spicula; slender and sharp-pointed. Also, characterized by the presence of spicules.

spiculate /ˈspɪkjʊlət/ *adjective*. M19.
[from SPICULE or SPICULA *noun*¹ + -ATE².]
BOTANY. Covered with spicules or small pointed processes. Also, divided into spikelets; having spikelets of a specified kind.

spiculated /ˈspɪkjʊleɪtɪd/ *adjective*. M18.
[from SPICULA *noun*¹ + -ATE² + -ED¹.]
1 Containing or involving spiculae. M18.
2 Having the form of a spicula; slender and sharp-pointed. M18.
3 Bearing many sharp points or spines. M18.
■ **spicuˈlation** *noun* formation of or into a spicule or spicules M19.

spicule /ˈspɪkjuːl/ *noun*. L18.
[Anglicized from SPICULA *noun*¹, SPICULUM.]
1 BOTANY. = SPICULA *noun*¹ 3. Now *rare* or *obsolete*. L18.
†**2** MYCOLOGY. A sterigma of a basidium. M19–L19.
3 ZOOLOGY. A needle-like or sharp-pointed process or part; *esp.* each of the small pointed structures of calcite or silica which make up the skeleton of a sponge. M19.
4 A fine-pointed piece, splinter, or fragment of some hard substance; *esp.* in MEDICINE, a splinter of bone. M19.
5 ASTRONOMY. Any of numerous short-lived, relatively small radial jets of gas observed in the chromosphere and lower corona of the sun. M20.

spiculum /ˈspɪkjʊləm/ *noun*. Pl. **-la** /-lə/. M18.
[mod. Latin, irreg. dim. of Latin *spica* SPIKE *noun*¹: see -ULE.]
1 = SPICULA *noun*¹ 1. M18.
2 = SPICULE 3. M18.
3 = SPICULE 5. L19.

spicy /ˈspʌɪsi/ *adjective*. Also **spicey**. M16.
[from SPICE *noun* + -Y¹.]
1 Of, pertaining to, or characteristic of spice; of the nature of spice. M16. ▸**b** Producing or carrying spices, esp. for trade. Chiefly *poet.* M17.
2 (As if) flavoured or fragranced with spice; pungent, aromatic; piquant. M17.
3 *fig.* **a** Proud, conceited. *Scot.* M18. ▸**b** Spirited; smart, neat. *colloq.* Now *rare*. E19. ▸**c** Of writing, humour, etc.: pointed, sharp; sensational, improper. M19.

📖 **1** DEFOE The herbs were of a spicy kind. **2** J. FRAME Mattina breathed the sweet, spicy fragrance. *Holiday Which?* Rice . . dishes and little spicy kebabs. **3c** W. S. MAUGHAM The dry and spicy humour of his yokels. J. HELLER I want something racier . . on that subject, spicier.

■ **spicily** *adverb* M19. **spiciness** *noun* M17.

spider /ˈspʌɪdə/ *noun & verb*.
[Late Old English *spīpra*, from *spinnan* SPIN *verb*. Cf. Old High German *spinna*, German *Spinne* (lit. 'female spinner'), SPINNER 1.]
▶ **A** *noun*. **I 1** An arachnid of the order Araneida, having a narrow-waisted body and eight jointed legs, and typically feeding on the fluids of insect prey caught by hunting or in webs and immobilized with poison. LOE. ▸**b** *fig.* A person who or thing which entraps or ensnares others. M16.
2 a Any of various arachnids resembling spiders, as harvestmen, sun-spiders, etc. Usu. with specifying word. M17. ▸**b** A spider-like animal, as a long-legged crab. *colloq.* M19. ▸**c** ANGLING. A hackle fly. M19.

📖 **1** V. GLENDINNING Spiders waited for her on the bottom of the bath. ***crab-spider***, ***diadem spider***, ***funnel-web spider***, ***jumping spider***, ***money spider***, ***trapdoor spider***, etc. **b** V. NABOKOV A palace intrigue is a spectral spider that entangles you. **2** ***HARVEST-spider***. ***SEA-spider***.

▶ **II** *transf.* **3** An iron frying-pan, *esp.* and orig. one with long legs and handle. Chiefly *US*. L18.
4 A mixed alcoholic drink usu. of lemonade and brandy. Also = FLOAT *noun* 9. *Austral. slang*. M19.
5 Any of various mechanical devices with radiating arms or spokes. M19. ▸**b** NAUTICAL. = ***spider-hoop*** below. M19. ▸**c** BILLIARDS & SNOOKER. A long-legged rest that can be placed over a ball without touching it. Also more fully ***spider-rest***. L19. ▸**d** A spiked candle-holder used esp. in opal-mining. *Austral.* E20. ▸**e** ENGINEERING. A metal sleeve, orig. at the end of a hanging cable, within which an object may be gripped by screws or wedges. E20. ▸**f** ELECTRONICS. A flexible linkage formerly placed between the moving cone and the fixed magnet assembly of a loudspeaker. E20.
6 CARDS. A form of patience using two packs. L19.
7 a A light cart or carriage with high body and very large narrow wheels. Also (*Austral.*), a trotting gig. L19. ▸**b** *Hist.* An early bicycle with steel as opp. to wooden wheels. Also (*Scot.*), a pennyfarthing bicycle. L19.
8 = ***spider-naevus*** below. M20.
9 COMPUTING. = CRAWLER 8. L20.
Comb.: **spider angioma** MEDICINE = ***spider-naevus*** below; **spider-band** NAUTICAL = ***spider-hoop*** below; **spider beetle** a long-legged beetle of the family Ptinidae, many of which are pests of stored products; **spider-catcher** †(*a*) a person who catches spiders (freq. as a general term of abuse); (*b*) any of various birds which catch or eat spiders, as a spider-hunter; **spider-cell** BIOLOGY a cell having numerous delicate processes resembling the legs of a spider, esp. as found characteristically in glia; **spider crab** any of various crabs of the family Majidae, having long slender legs; **spider flower** a cleome, *Cleome hassleriana*, with white or pink flowers, grown for ornament; **spider hole** MILITARY a small foxhole; **spider-hoop** NAUTICAL a small metal band put around a mast, to which the gooseneck of the main boom is attached, used to hold belaying pins; **spider-hunter** any of several sunbirds of the genus *Arachnothera*, native to parts of the Indian subcontinent and SE Asia; **spider-hunting wasp** = ***spider-wasp*** below; **spider-leg** (*a*) any of the legs of a spider; *transf.* a long thin leg or other object resembling this; (*b*) *Scot.* (in *pl.*) a crane-fly; **spider lily** any of various bulbous plants having lily-like flowers with long narrow perianth segments, esp. plants of the genera *Hymenocallis* and *Crinum*, both of the amaryllis family; **spider-line** a slender thread or wire used to form a cross-wire in an optical instrument, esp. a micrometer; **spiderman** *colloq.* a construction worker etc. employed on a high building; a steeple-jack; **spider monkey** any of several monkeys of Central and S. America, esp. of the genera *Ateles* and *Brachyteles*, having long slender limbs and a prehensile tail; **spider-naevus** MEDICINE a cluster of minute red blood-vessels visible under the skin, occurring esp. during pregnancy or as a symptom of cirrhosis, acne rosacea, etc.; **spider orchid** any of several orchids with flowers thought to resemble a spider; *esp.* (*a*) (in full ***early spider orchid***) a rare British orchid, *Ophrys sphegodes*, of chalk grassland, with a velvety labellum; (*b*) *Austral.* any of several orchids of the genus *Caladenia*, with very long filiform petals and sepals; **spider plant** a southern African plant *Chlorophytum comosum*, of the lily family, with long narrow leaves, which spreads by producing plantlets and in its variegated form is a popular house-plant; ***spider-rest***: see sense 5c above; **spider-stitch** EMBROIDERY a stitch producing a weblike motif, worked by darning in a spiral on a base of crossed straight stitches; ***spider's web***: see SPIDERWEB; **spider-table** a light table with thin elongated legs; **spider-wasp** = POMPILID *noun*; **spider-wheel** (*a*) a type of water-wheel; (*b*) EMBROIDERY = ***spider-stitch*** above; (*c*) a spoked metal wheel, *esp.* a bicycle-wheel; **spider-work** EMBROIDERY = OPUS ARANEUM; **spiderwort** (*a*) (in full ***mountain spiderwort***) the Snowdon lily, *Lloydia serotina*; (*b*) a tradescantia, *esp.* a cultivated form or hybrid of *Tradescantia virginiana*.
▶ **B** *verb*. **1** *verb trans.* Entrap, ensnare. *rare*. L19.
2 *verb intrans.* & *trans.* Move or spread (along) in a manner suggestive of a spider. M20.

📖 **2** T. PYNCHON A glimmering map, . . written names and spidering streets. *Wilderness Odyssey* We scuttled up a . . ramp and spidered some cracks to a clutter of big ledges.

■ **spidered** *adjective* (*rare*) (*a*) resembling a spider or spiderweb; (*b*) = SPIDERY 3: M17. **spiderish** *adjective* spider-like, spidery M20. **spider-like** *adverb & adjective* (*a*) *adverb* in the manner of a spider; (*b*) *adjective* resembling a spider, spidery: E17. **spiderling** *noun* a young or small spider L19. **spiderly** *adjective* (*rare*) like a spider L19.

spiderweb /ˈspʌɪdəwɛb/ *noun & verb*. Also **spider-web**, (as noun) **spider's web** /ˈspʌɪdəz wɛb/. M16.
[from SPIDER *noun* + WEB *noun*.]
▶ **A** *noun*. **1** The web of a spider; a cobweb. M16.
2 *fig.* A thing resembling a cobweb in form or function; a network, a mesh; a snare. L17. ▸**b** In full ***spiderweb turquoise***. A variety of turquoise run through with fine dark lines. M20.

📖 **2** P. CAREY Below him . . the yellow spiderweb of lighted streets.

▶ **B** *verb*. Infl. **-bb-**.
1 *verb intrans.* Move in, or present, a pattern resembling a spiderweb. E19.
2 *verb trans.* Cover with a pattern resembling a spiderweb; enmesh. L19.

📖 **1** I. L. IDRIESS Others have spider-webbed from the . . coasts far . . inland. **2** B. BOVA That handsome face was sagging now; gravity was pulling at it, spiderwebbing it with wrinkles.

■ **spiderwebby** *adjective* resembling a spiderweb; having many spiderwebs: M19.

spidery /ˈspʌɪd(ə)ri/ *adjective*. E19.
[from SPIDER *noun* + -Y¹.]
1 Of, pertaining to, or characteristic of a spider or spiders; of the nature of spiders; *fig.* entangling, ensnaring. E19.
2 Resembling (that of) a spider in appearance or form; elongated and thin. Also, resembling a spiderweb in form. M19.
3 Full of cobwebs; infested with spiders. L19.

📖 **1** COLERIDGE The World, that spidery Witch, spins it's threads narrower . . , still closing in on us. A. LEE The spidery gait of little girls who are rapidly growing taller. **2** A. TYLER His spidery hands twisted in front of him. N. ANNAN His . . handwriting grew spidery and difficult to read.

spied *verb pa. t. & pple* of SPY *verb*.

spiegel /ˈspiːg(ə)l/ *noun*. L19.
[German = mirror.]
A white alloy of iron with carbon and manganese used in the Bessemer process for the manufacture of steel. Also ***spiegel-iron***.
■ Also **spiegeleisen** /ˈspiːg(ə)lʌɪz(ə)n/ *noun* [German *Eisen* iron] M19.

spiel /spiːl/ *noun*¹. *Scot.* L18.
[Middle Dutch, Middle Low German *spel*, from *spelen* to play. Cf. next.]
A play, a game; *esp.* a curling-match.

spiel /ʃpiːl, spiːl/ *noun*². *slang* (orig. *US*). L19.
[German = play, game.]
1 Talk, a story; a glib speech, *esp.* one intended to persuade or impress; a salesperson's patter. L19.
2 A swindle, a dishonest enterprise. E20.

📖 **1** S. BELLOW His spiel took in Freud, Heine, Wagner, Goethe in Italy. **2** T. A. G. HUNGERFORD This isn't a spiel, Colonel . . . I know this bloke, and he's on the level.

spiel /ʃpiːl, spiːl/ *verb*¹. *slang* (orig. *US*). M19.
[German *spielen* play, gamble.]
1 *verb intrans.* **a** Gamble. M19. ▸**b** Play music. L19.
2 *verb intrans.* Talk, esp. volubly or glibly; patter. Also foll. by *away*. L19.
3 *verb trans.* Recite or announce glibly; reel *off*. E20.

📖 **2** *Independent* The guides . . spieling away about history. **3** A. TOFFLER Each participant spieled off his reason for attending.

spiel *verb*² var. of SPEEL *verb*².

spieler /ˈʃpiːlə, ˈspiːlə/ *noun*¹. *slang* (orig. *US*). M19.
[German = player, gambler.]
1 A gambler; a card-sharp; a swindler. Now chiefly *Austral.* & *NZ*. M19.
2 A voluble or glib speaker. L19.
3 A gambling club. M20.

spieler *noun*² var. of SPEELER *noun*¹.

Spielraum /ˈʃpiːlraʊm/ *noun*. Pl. **-räume** /-rɔymə/. E20.
[German, formed as SPIEL *noun*² + *Raum* room.]
PHILOSOPHY. The range of possibilities within which the probability of an outcome or likelihood of a hypothesis is to be assessed.

spier /ˈspʌɪə/ *noun*. ME.
[from SPY *verb* + -ER^{1}, or from Old French *espierre*, *espieur* (mod. *épieur*).]
A watcher, an observer; a spy.

spiff /spɪf/ *noun*. *slang*. M19.
[Origin unkn.]
A money bonus given to an employee for selling old or unwanted stock. Usu. in *pl*.

spiff /spɪf/ *verb trans*. *slang*. L19.
[Origin unkn. Cf. next.]
Smarten in appearance; make neat or spruce. Now only foll. by *up*. Freq. as ***spiffed (up)*** *ppl adjective*.

> A. LURIE I . . got all spiffed up . . to look like I was related to a lord. *Sunday Mail (Brisbane)* About 300 cars were spiffed up for the occasion.

spiffing /ˈspɪfɪŋ/ *adjective*. *slang* (now *joc*.) & *dial*. L19.
[Origin unkn.: of pres. ppl form, as *ripping*, *topping*, etc., and rel. to SPIFFY.]
Excellent, splendid, very good (also as ***interjection***); smart in appearance, spruce.

> R. BARNARD 'We could have a . . chat, Aunt Kate' . . 'Oh, spiffing!' *Weekly News (Cambridge)* A spiffing idea . . to involve the audience more with the programme.

spifflicate *verb* var. of SPIFLICATE.

spiffy /ˈspɪfi/ *adjective*. *slang* (chiefly *N. Amer*.) & *dial*. M19.
[Origin unkn. Cf. SPIFFING.]
Smart, spruce.

> *Weekly World News (US)* Nattily dressed in a spiffy three-piece suit.

spiflicate /ˈspɪflɪkeɪt/ *verb trans*. *joc*. & *colloq*. Also **-ff-**. M18.
[Fanciful.]
Treat roughly or severely, *esp*. beat heavily in a fight; crush, destroy.

> *Listener* The mosquito . . spiflicated by whatever means science now kills them.

■ **spiflicated** *ppl adjective* (chiefly *US*) intoxicated, drunk E20. **spifli'cation** *noun* M19.

spigelia /spʌɪˈdʒiːlɪə/ *noun*. E19.
[mod. Latin (see below), from Adrian *Spigelius* (1578–1625), Flemish anatomist and botanist: see -IA^{1}.]
Any plant of the genus *Spigelia* (family Loganiaceae); a pinkroot, esp. *S. marilandica* or *S. anthelmia*.

spigelian /spʌɪˈdʒiːlɪən/ *adjective*. Now *rare*. E19.
[from *Spigelius* (see prec.) + -IAN.]
ANATOMY. ***spigelian lobe***, part of the right lateral lobe of the liver in mammals.

spiggoty /ˈspɪɡəti/ *noun* & *adjective*. *US slang* (*derog*. & considered *racially offensive*). E20.
[Origin uncertain: perh. alt. of *speak the* in 'no speak the English'.]
= SPIC.

†**spight** *noun*^{1} & *verb* var. of SPITE *noun*, *verb*.

†**spight** *noun*^{2} var. of SPEIGHT.

spignel /ˈspɪɡn(ə)l/ *noun*. E16.
[Origin uncertain: perh. from Anglo-Norman *spigurnelle* an unidentified plant.]
A fine-leaved aromatic umbelliferous plant of mountain pastures, *Meum athamanticum*, the root of which was chewed in the Highlands as a carminative; also called ***baldmoney***, ***meu***. Formerly, the root of this plant.

spigot /ˈspɪɡət/ *noun* & *verb*. ME.
[Perh. with change of suffix from Provençal *espigou(n)* = Spanish *espigón*, Italian *spigone* ladder rung, bar of a chair, bung: cf. Portuguese *espicho* spigot from Latin *spiculum* dim. of *spicum* var. of *spica* SPIKE *noun*^{2}.]
▶ **A** *noun*. **1** A small peg or plug inserted into the vent-hole of a barrel or cask; a small tap or outlet controlling the flow of liquid from a container. Also (*US*), a tap. ME.
2 The plain end of a pipe-section fitting into the socket of another to form a joint. L18.

> **1** M. BRADBURY There were spigots for iced tea. *fig*.: *Time* Government agencies did not open the funding spigot.
> **knight of the spigot**, **man of the spigot**, etc., *arch*. a seller of alcohol, an alehouse-keeper.

▶ **B** *verb trans*. Stop (as) with a spigot; insert in the manner of a spigot. E19.

spike /spʌɪk/ *noun*^{1}. ME.
[Origin uncertain: perh. shortened from Middle & mod. Low German, Middle Dutch *spiker* (Dutch *spijker*), or Middle Dutch *spiking*; rel. to SPOKE *noun*. Cf. Old Swedish *spīk*, *spijk* (Swedish, Norwegian *spik* nail).]
1 A sharp-pointed piece of metal or wood used as a strong fastener or nail, now *esp*. one used to secure a rail on a railway. ME. ▶**b** A pointed steel plug driven into the touch-hole to disable a cannon. *obsolete* exc. *Hist*. E17.
2 A pointed piece of metal etc. projecting from a surface or fixed in the ground; *esp*. the top of an iron railing. LME. ▶**b** Any stiff point or pointed object; *transf*. a sharp increase (as) represented by a rise on a graph. E18.
3 *spec*. **a** Any of several pointed metal studs set into the sole of a sports shoe to prevent slipping; *transf*. (in *pl*.) a pair of sports shoes with spikes. M19. ▶**b** A young mackerel. *US*. L19. ▶**c** A pointed metal rod fixed on a base on which loose pieces of paper are filed, esp. newspaper stories rejected for publication. M20. ▶**d** A hypodermic needle or syringe; *transf*. a drug injected with this. *slang*. M20. ▶**e** A pulse of very short duration in which a rapid increase in voltage, intensity of radiation, etc., is followed immediately by a rapid decrease; a graphic representation of this. M20.
4 The casual ward of a hostel or (formerly) workhouse offering temporary accommodation for the homeless. *slang*. M19.
5 A quantity of alcohol (esp. spirits) added to a drink. *US slang*. E20. ▶**b** A small quantity *of* a radioisotope or other substance added to a material as a tracer, a reference, etc. E20.

> **1** K. VONNEGUT I . . nailed the doors . . with six-inch spikes. **2** *Hi-Fi News* The baseplate . . incorporates 6mm spikes. **b** *Hairdo Ideas* Hair is cut into spikes that take off with the addition of gel. *Times* Supply problems . . could even bring a . . crisis and a new price spike. **3a** *Running* She has . . never worn a pair of spikes. W. MCILVANNEY Hardened dirt from the spikes of his golf-shoes. **4** *Sunday Correspondent* The Spike in Peckham which slept 1,000 men in . . bunk beds.

Phrases: **get the spike**, **have the spike** become or be angry or offended.
Comb.: **spike-buck** *N. Amer*. a young male deer with unbranched antlers; **spike-fiddle** a bowed stringed instrument with a neck that passes through the body and projects as a spike at the base; **spike-fish** *US* (**a**) the sailfish *Istiophorus platypterus*; (**b**) a spiny fish of the family Acanthodidae; **spike heel** (a shoe with) a stiletto heel; †**spike-hole** a small opening in a wall, esp. for shooting from; **spike-horn** *N. Amer*. (**a**) a deer's unbranched antler; (**b**) = ***spike-buck*** above; **spike microphone**, (*colloq*.) **spike mike** a small microphone that can be driven through a wall etc. as a bug; **spike-nail** a large strong nail, *esp*. one over three inches long with a small head; **spike-team** *US* a team of three draught animals, two abreast and one leading.
■ **spikelike** *adjective*^{1} resembling (that of) a spike, spiky M19.

spike /spʌɪk/ *noun*^{2}. LME.
[Latin *spica* (*spicus*, *spicum*) rel. to *spina* SPINE.]
▶ **I 1** An ear of corn. Chiefly *poet*. LME.
2 BOTANY. A flower-cluster or form of inflorescence consisting of sessile flowers borne on an elongated simple axis. Cf. RACEME. L16.
▶ **II** †**3** Any of several kinds of valerian, *esp*. Celtic nard, *Valeriana celtica* (more fully ***spike Celtic***), and common valerian, *V. officinalis*, used medicinally. LME–L16.
4 Lavender; *spec*. spike lavender. Now *dial*. exc. in ***oil of spike*** below. M16.
Phrases & comb.: **oil of spike** an essential oil distilled from spike lavender, used in paints and in veterinary medicine. ***spike Celtic***: see sense 3 above. **spike lavender** a garden or cultivated lavender. **spikemoss** a chiefly tropical creeping clubmoss of the genus *Selaginella*, which has branching stems with hair-like spines on the leaf margins and small spore-bearing cones. **spike-rush** any of various small marsh plants constituting the genus *Eleocharis*, of the sedge family, having flowers in dense solitary terminal spikelets on leafless stems. ***Virgin's spike***: see VIRGIN *noun*.
■ **spikelike** *adjective*^{2} (BOTANY) (of an inflorescence) resembling a spike M19.

spike /spʌɪk/ *noun*^{3}. *slang*. E20.
[Back-form. from SPIKY *adjective*^{2}.]
noun. A High Church Anglican; an Anglo-Catholic.
■ **spikery** *noun* High Church character or behaviour E20.

spike /spʌɪk/ *verb*^{1}. E17.
[from SPIKE *noun*^{1}.]
1 *verb trans*. Fasten or nail securely with a spike or spikes. Usu. foll. by *on*, *to*, *up*, etc. E17. ▶**b** Disable (a cannon etc.) by plugging the touch-hole with a spike (*obsolete* exc. *Hist*.); *fig*. make useless or ineffective, thwart. L17.
2 *verb trans*. **a** Form into a spike or spikes. L17. ▶**b** Provide or cover with a spike or spikes. E18.
3 *verb trans*. Pierce (as) with a spike or spikes; fix on to a spike; *spec*. (**a**) injure (a competitor) with the spikes of a sports shoe; (**b**) reject (a newspaper story etc.) for publication (as) by filing on a spike. L17.
4 *verb trans*. Lace (a drink) with alcohol, a drug, etc.; contaminate with an added substance; *transf*. sharpen or enliven the taste of (food etc.) with an added ingredient. Freq. foll. by *with*. *colloq*. L19. ▶**b** Enrich (a nuclear reactor or its fuel) *with* a particular isotope; add a small proportion of some distinctive material to. M20.
5 *verb intrans*. & *trans*. Inject (oneself or another) with a narcotic drug. *slang*. M20.
6 *verb intrans*. Form or rise in a spike; protrude angularly. M20. ▶**b** Of a temperature, price, etc.: rise or fall sharply. Freq. foll. by *up*, *down*. L20.

> **1b** J. G. FARRELL: 'Spike the twelve-pounder!' shouted Harry. *Video for You* Her brother . . is intent on spiking his chances in the big race. **2a** *Amateur Photographer* I got Kit to spike Beverley's hair with gel. **b** W. H. CANAWAY The cypresses spiking the lower slopes. **3** *New York Times* One runner was knocked down and another was spiked. D. CAUTE That was the story your boss . . spiked? G. GREENE To cook sausages . . you had to spike them before putting them in the pan. **4** D. BOLGER Mary . . bought me an orange juice and then spiked it with vodka when my back was turned. **6** C. HOLME Long 's's' spiking up and down the page. **b** *Times* I could envisage interest rates spiking down even further.

Comb.: **spiking curb** MINING a ring of wood to which planks of wood are spiked before sinking.

spike /spʌɪk/ *verb*^{2} *intrans*. E18.
[from SPIKE *noun*^{2}.]
Of a plant: form a spike of flowers. Also foll. by *up*.

spike /spʌɪk/ *verb*^{3} *trans*. *slang*. E20.
[from SPIKE *noun*^{3}.]
Foll. by *up*: make more High Church in character.

spike-bozzle /spʌɪkˈbɒz(ə)l/ *verb trans*. *slang* (orig. MILITARY). Now *rare*. E20.
[from SPIKE *verb*^{1}; 2nd elem. obscure.]
Render ineffective; sabotage, destroy.

spiked /spʌɪkt/ *adjective*^{1}. L16.
[from SPIKE *noun*^{2} + -ED^{2}.]
(Of a plant) having an inflorescence in the form of a spike; (of a cereal grass) bearing ears.
spiked loosestrife, ***spiked rampion***, ***spiked speedwell***, etc.

spiked /spʌɪkt/ *adjective*^{2}. L17.
[from SPIKE *noun*^{1}, *verb*^{1}: see -ED^{2}, -ED^{1}.]
1 Having a spike or spikes; sharp-pointed, spiky. L17.
2 Laced with alcohol etc.; contaminated or enlivened with an added substance. E20. ▶**b** Containing a small addition of a radioactive or otherwise distinctive material. M20.

> **1** P. D. JAMES Bright-eyed beneath the spiked . . lashes. **spiked buck** *US* = ***spike-buck*** s.v. SPIKE *noun*^{1}. **2** B. FUSSELL Serve with a mayonnaise spiked with lime juice. N. HINTON Tea . . they reckoned . . was spiked with tranquillisers.

spikelet /ˈspʌɪklɪt/ *noun*^{1}. L18.
[from SPIKE *noun*^{2} + -LET.]
BOTANY. A diminutive or secondary spike; *esp*. the basic unit of a grass inflorescence, consisting of two glumes or outer bracts at the base and one or more florets above.

spikelet /ˈspʌɪklɪt/ *noun*^{2}. M19.
[from SPIKE *noun*^{1} + -LET.]
A small spike; a prickle, a thorn.

spikenard /ˈspʌɪknɑːd/ *noun*. ME.
[medieval Latin *spica nardi* (see SPIKE *noun*^{2}, NARD), translating Greek *nardou stakhus*, *nardostakhus*; or more directly from Old French *spicanard(e* or Middle Low German *spīkenard*, Middle Dutch *spīkenaerde* (Dutch *spijknardus*).]
1 A costly perfumed ointment much valued in ancient times; the plant from whose fragrant rhizome this was prepared, prob. *Nardostachys grandiflora*, a Himalayan plant of the valerian family. ME.
2 Any of various plants resembling spikenard in fragrance; *esp*. (**a**) any of several kinds of valerian, *esp*. (more fully ***Celtic spikenard***) Celtic nard, *Valeriana celtica*; (**b**) (now *dial*.) lavender (cf. SPIKE *noun*^{2} 4); (**c**) *US* (more fully ***American spikenard***) a plant of the ginseng family with an aromatic root, *Aralia racemosa*. LME.
2 PLOUGHMAN'S ***spikenard***.

spiker /ˈspʌɪkə/ *noun*^{1}. *obsolete* exc. *Scot*. L16.
[Middle Dutch or Middle Low German *spīker* SPIKE *noun*^{1}.]
= SPICK *noun*^{3}.

spiker /ˈspʌɪkə/ *noun*^{2}. M19.
[from SPIKE *verb*^{1} + -ER^{1}.]
1 A device for spiking a cannon. M19.
2 A person charged with spiking a cannon. L19.

spikey *adjective* var. of SPIKY *adjective*^{2}.

spiking /ˈspʌɪkɪŋ/ *noun*. Long *obsolete* exc. *dial*. ME.
[Prob. from Middle Dutch: see SPIKE *noun*^{1}.]
A spike-nail.

spiky /ˈspʌɪki/ *adjective*^{1}. L16.
[from SPIKE *noun*^{2} + -Y^{1}.]
Having the form of a flower-spike; characterized by the production of spikes or ears.

spiky /ˈspʌɪki/ *adjective*^{2}. Also **spikey**. E18.
[from SPIKE *noun*^{1} + -Y^{1}.]
1 Having (the form of) a spike or spikes; sharp-pointed; prickly. E18. ▶**b** *fig*. Having a sharp nature or disposition; prickly; acerbic. L19.
2 High Church in character; ritualistic. *slang*. L19.

> **1** J. WINTERSON He . . rubbed his spiky chin against my face. J. C. OATES Spiky weeds the color of grit. **b** *New Yorker* We find ourselves becoming spiky and bloody-minded.

■ **spikily** *adverb* L19. **spikiness** *noun* E18.

spile /spʌɪl/ *noun*[1] & *verb*[1]. **E16.**
[Middle Low German, Middle Dutch (Northern Frisian *spīl*, German dial. *Speil*) = splinter, wooden peg or pin, skewer, etc.; rel. to **SPILL** *noun*[1].]
▶ **A** *noun.* **1** A splinter or chip of wood; a spill. *Scot. & north.* **E16.**
2 a A small wooden peg or plug; a spigot. Chiefly *Scot. & dial.* **E18.** ▸**b** A small spout for tapping the sap from a sugar maple etc. *N. Amer.* **L18.**
▶ **B** *verb trans.* **1** Stop up (a hole) with a spile. Also foll. by *up*. **L17.**
2 Broach (a cask, liquid, etc.) with a spile. Now *dial. & US.* **L18.**

spile /spʌɪl/ *noun*[2] & *verb*[2]. **E16.**
[App. alt. of **PILE** *noun*[1] after prec., or by wrong analysis of combination.]
▶ **A** *noun.* **1** = **PILE** *noun*[1] 3. **E16.**
2 *MINING.* A sharp-pointed post used in sinking with cribs. **M19.**
▶ **B** *verb trans.* = **PILE** *verb*[1] 1. Now *dial.* **E19.**

spiling /ˈspʌɪlɪŋ/ *noun*[1]. Now chiefly *Scot.* **M19.**
[from **SPILE** *verb*[2] + **-ING**[1].]
The action of **SPILE** *verb*[2]. Also, spiles collectively.

spiling /ˈspʌɪlɪŋ/ *noun*[2]. **M19.**
[Origin unkn.]
NAUTICAL. The measure of the curve of a plank's edge.

spilite /ˈspʌɪlʌɪt, ˈspɪlʌɪt/ *noun.* **M19.**
[French *spillite*, from Greek *spilos* spot, stain: see **-ITE**[1].]
GEOLOGY. An altered basalt, rich in albite and commonly amygdaloidal in structure, typically produced by the reaction of molten basaltic lavas with seawater.
■ **spilitic** /-ˈlɪtɪk/ *adjective* of, pertaining to, of the nature of, or containing spilite **E20.** **spiliti'zation** *noun* conversion into spilite **M20.** **spilitized** *adjective* converted into spillite **M20.**

spill /spɪl/ *noun*[1]. **ME.**
[Obscurely rel. to **SPILE** *noun*[1].]
1 A sharp-pointed fragment of wood, bone, etc.; a splinter, a sliver. **ME.**
2 A thin strip of wood or a folded or twisted piece of paper used for lighting a fire, candle, pipe, etc. **E19.** ▸**b** *ellipt.* A cylindrical jar, vase, etc., (as) used for holding spills. **L19.**
3 *METALLURGY.* A cavity at the surface of an ingot, which forms a surface oxide lamination. **M19.**
4 A small peg used to plug a hole. **L19.**

> 🕮 **2** P. L. FERMOR A . . maid with a spill was lighting lamps.

■ **spilly** *adjective* (*METALLURGY*) (of iron) exhibiting spills (surface cavities) **M19.**

spill /spɪl/ *noun*[2]. **L16.**
[Prob. from Middle & mod. Low German, Middle & mod. Dutch *spil(l)e* = Old High German *spilla* (German *Spille* spindle, axis, stalk), from West Germanic word rel. to base of **SPIN** *verb*.]
1 A spool or small cylinder on which yarn is wound. Long *obsolete* exc. *N. Amer. dial.* **L16.**
2 A rod or stalk of wood, metal, etc. **L16.**
3 A pin or slender rod on which something turns. **M18.**

†**spill** *noun*[3]. *slang.* **L17–E19.**
[Origin uncertain: perh. from the verb.]
A small gift of money, a tip.

spill /spɪl/ *noun*[4]. **M19.**
[from the verb.]
1 The action or an instance of spilling or being spilled; a fall or tumble from a horse, vehicle, etc. Freq. in ***thrills and spills***. **M19.**
2 A quantity of liquid etc. spilled; *spec.* (*a*) = ***oil spill*** s.v. **OIL** *noun*; (*b*) a diffusion of light, esp. beyond the area intended to be illuminated. **M19.** ▸**b** = ***spillway*** below. **E20.**
3 *NAUTICAL.* A slight breeze. **L19.**
4 A vacating of all or several posts of a parliamentary party to allow reorganization after an important change of office. *Austral.* **M20.**

> 🕮 **1** *Sun (Baltimore)* Virginia . . takes a spill in the snow during a practice run. **2** *Which?* Wipe up spills to stop children . . slipping.

Comb.: **spill burner** a burner used in some gas turbines which allows excess fuel to be recirculated; **spill valve** a valve which serves to allow the escape of surplus fluid; **spillway** (*a*) a channel or slope built to carry away surplus water from a reservoir; (*b*) *PHYSICAL GEOGRAPHY* a natural drainage channel cut by water during glaciation.

spill /spɪl/ *verb.* Pa. t. & pple **spilled**, **spilt** /spɪlt/.
[Old English *spillan* = Middle & mod. Low German, Middle & mod. Dutch *spillen* rel. to Old English *spildan* destroy = Old Saxon *spildian*, Old High German *spilden*, Old Norse *spilla*, of unkn. origin.]
▶ **I 1 a** *verb trans.* Put to death, kill; put an end to (life). Long *arch.* **OE.** ▸†**b** *verb intrans.* Cause death or slaughter. **ME–E17.**
†**2** *verb trans.* Bring (a person) to ruin or misery; wreck, destroy, devastate, (a thing). **OE–M17.**
†**3** *verb trans.* Waste, squander; use wastefully; spend (time, effort, etc.) fruitlessly or unprofitably. **OE–L18.**
4 *verb trans.* Spoil, damage, make imperfect or useless, destroy the goodness or value of. Long *Scot. & dial.* **ME.**
5 *verb intrans.* †**a** Die; be destroyed, go to ruin. **ME–L16.** ▸**b** Decline in quality, degenerate, deteriorate. *obsolete* exc. *Scot. & dial.* **ME.**
▶ **II 6** *verb trans.* Shed (blood), esp. in killing or wounding a person or persons. **OE.**
7 *verb trans.* Allow or cause (a liquid, powder, etc.) to flow or run out over the edge of a container or vessel, esp. accidentally or wastefully; lose or waste in this way. **ME.** ▸**b** Scatter, esp. by emptying from a receptacle etc.; disperse. **ME.** ▸**c** *SPORT.* Drop (the ball); *esp.* in *CRICKET*, put down (a catch). *colloq.* **L20.**
8 *verb intrans.* Of a liquid, powder, etc.: flow, spread, or run over the edge of a container or vessel; be wasted in this way; *fig.* (of a crowd etc.) tumble out quickly from a place. **ME.**
9 *verb trans.* Cover or overlay *with* something (as) by spilling. *rare.* **L16.**
10 *NAUTICAL.* **a** *verb trans.* Empty (a sail) of wind. **E17.** ▸**b** *verb intrans.* Of a sail: become empty of wind. **M18.** ▸**c** *verb trans.* Discharge (wind) from a sail etc. **L19.**
11 *verb trans.* Throw or cause to fall from a horse, vehicle, etc. *colloq.* **M19.**
12 *verb trans.* Confess, divulge, (information etc.). *slang.* **E20.**

> 🕮 **6** A. BURGESS The blood of our sons . . must not be spilt to no end. **7** J. GARDNER In his clumsy excitement he bumped Willard's coffee and spilled it. P. MARSHALL Holding the glass . . as if fearful of spilling a drop. P. CHAPLIN 'Has someone spilled perfume in here?' she asked . . . almost stifled. U. HOLDEN I had spilled ink on my . . sleeve. ***cry over spilt milk***: see **MILK** *noun*. **b** G. NAYLOR The box spilled out piles of photographs. **8** A. WILSON Swilling her whisky . . , letting it slop to the brim but never spill. G. LORD Cops spilled from the squad car. C. PRIEST Her . . bag . . , its contents spilling out over the worn linoleum. *Company* A crowded cafe with tables spilling onto the street. **spill over** overflow; *spec.* (of a surplus population) move from an overcrowded area, esp. a city. **12 spill one's guts (out)** *slang* divulge as much as one can, confess completely. **spill the beans** *colloq.* reveal a secret, divulge information, esp. unintentionally or indiscreetly.

■ **spilling** *noun* the action of the verb; an instance of this; (*sing.* & in *pl.*) something spilled: **OE.**

spillage /ˈspɪlɪdʒ/ *noun.* **M20.**
[from prec. + **-AGE**.]
The action or fact of spilling; something which spills, a quantity of liquid etc. spilled.

spiller /ˈspɪlə/ *noun*[1]. **LME.**
[formed as prec. + **-ER**[1].]
A person etc. who spills something; *esp.* a shedder of blood.

spiller /ˈspɪlə/ *noun*[2]. *arch.* **L16.**
[Alt. of **SPELLER** *noun*[2].]
A branchlet on a deer's horn.

spiller /ˈspɪlə/ *noun*[3]. Chiefly *dial., Anglo-Irish, & N. Amer.* **E17.**
[Origin unkn.]
1 A long fishing-line with a number of hooks. Cf. **SPILLET. E17.**
2 A net inserted into a larger net to take out caught fish. **L19.**

spiller /ˈspɪlə/ *noun*[4]. *rare.* **M20.**
[from **SPILL** *noun*[1] + **-ER**[1].]
= **SPILL** *noun*[1] 2.

spillet /ˈspɪlɪt/ *noun. Scot. & Anglo-Irish.* **M19.**
[Alt.]
= **SPILLER** *noun*[3] 1.

spillikin /ˈspɪlɪkɪn/ *noun.* Also **spellican** /ˈspɛlɪk(ə)n/. **M18.**
[from **SPILL** *noun*[1] + **-KIN**.]
1 a In *pl.* (treated as *sing.*). A game played with a heap of slips or small rods of wood, bone, etc., the object being to remove each one without disturbing the rest; jackstraws. **M18.** ▸**b** A rod or slip used in this game. **L19.**
2 *fig.* A splinter, a fragment. Usu. in *pl.* **M19.**

spillover /ˈspɪləʊvə/ *noun & adjective.* **M20.**
[from **SPILL** *verb* + **OVER** *adverb*.]
▶ **A** *noun.* That which spills over; the process of spilling over; an instance of this; (an) incidental development; a consequence, a repercussion, a by-product. **M20.**

> 🕮 *Forbes* No spillover of technology from the military to the civilian sector.

▶ **B** *attrib.* or as *adjective.* Resulting from spilling over; arising or developed incidentally. **M20.**

spilt *verb pa. t. & pple*: see **SPILL** *verb*.

spilth /spɪlθ/ *noun. arch.* **E17.**
[from **SPILL** *verb* + **-TH**[1].]
Material, liquid, etc., which is spilled; the action or an instance of spilling; an excess, a surplus.

spin /spɪn/ *noun*[1]. **M19.**
[from the verb.]
1 An act or spell of spinning or drawing out thread from wool etc.; ability to be twisted or spun; the product resulting from spinning, thread, yarn. **M19.**
2 Spinning motion, rapid rotation; an instance or spell of this, a whirl; *spec.* a spell of spin-drying. **M19.** ▸**b** A revolving motion through the air given to a rifle bullet etc.; a quality imparted in bowling or striking a ball in cricket etc., causing it to change direction or speed on contact with the ground, a surface, etc. Also, the ability to impart such a motion to the ball; spin-bowling. **M19.** ▸**c** A steep descent in which an aircraft describes a helix at an angle of attack greater than the stalling angle. **E20.** ▸**d** = ***wheel-spin*** s.v. **WHEEL** *noun*. Also, the continued revolving of the clutch of a motor after being disengaged. **E20.** ▸**e** The action or an act of playing a gramophone record or piece of recorded music, esp. for public entertainment; a session of playing records. *colloq.* **L20.**
3 The action or an act of causing something to spin. **M19.**
4 A fairly rapid ride or run; a brief drive in a motor vehicle, aircraft, etc., now esp. for pleasure. **M19.**
5 *MATH.* The local rotation of a continuous medium, as expressed by the curl of the local velocity; vorticity. **L19.**
6 *PHYSICS.* An intrinsic property of certain elementary particles which is a form of angular momentum, usu. pictured as a rotation; a vector representing this in the case of a particular particle. **E20.**
7 A (good, bad, etc.) experience or piece of luck. *Austral. & NZ slang.* **E20.**
8 Five pounds, a five-pound note. *Austral. slang* (now *Hist.*). **M20.**
9 A bias or slant on information, intended to create a favourable impression when it is presented to the public; an interpretation, a viewpoint. Freq. in ***put a spin on***. *colloq.* (orig. *US POLITICS*). **L20.**

> 🕮 **2b** P. NORMAN There was always a good spin on his ball. *Times* Short of spin . . our pace attack will be as formidable as . . four years ago. ***back-spin***, ***off spin***, ***topspin***, etc. **c** W. GREATOREX A stall that would have turned into a spin . . with a less-experienced pilot. ***flat spin***: see **FLAT** *adjective*. **in a spin** *colloq.* in a state of nervous excitement or confusion. **4** A. CHRISTIE He took his car and went for a spin down to the front. **6** ***isobaric spin***: see **ISOBARIC** *adjective* 2. ***isotopic spin***: see **ISOTOPIC** 2. **7** ***rough spin***: see **ROUGH** *adjective*. **9** *Washington Post* American spokesman Jody Powell . . put a negative spin on the talks. C. BROOKMYRE It doesn't matter what the evidence says, . . it's how you present it, and how your opponent responds. It's spin.

Comb.: **spin-allowed** *adjective* (*PHYSICS*) consistent with the selection rules describing changes in spin quantum number; **spin bowler** *CRICKET* a slow bowler who imparts spin to the ball on delivery; **spin-bowling** *CRICKET* the action or technique of bowling with spin; spin bowlers collectively; **spin control** *N. Amer. colloq.* the attempt to give a particular slant or bias to (esp. political) news coverage; **spin doctor** *colloq.* (orig. *US*) a political spokesperson employed to promote a favourable interpretation of events to journalists; **spin-down** *adjective* (*PHYSICS*) being or pertaining to a particle whose spin points downwards; **spin-dye** *verb trans.* (*TEXTILES*) dye (textiles) by a process incorporating the colouring matter before the filament is formed; **spin echo** *PHYSICS* a radio-frequency signal induced in a (nuclear magnetic resonance) coil following the application of two radio-frequency pulses; **spin flip** *PHYSICS* the quantum jump of a particle from one spin state to another; **spin glass** a dilute solid solution of a magnetic substance in a non-magnetic host; **spin label** *CHEMISTRY* a radical or compound used in spin-labelling; **spin-label** *verb trans.* (*CHEMISTRY*) label (**LABEL** *verb* 2) with stable paramagnetic radicals which can be studied using electron spin resonance techniques (freq. as ***spin-labelled*** *ppl adjective*, ***spin-labelling*** *verbal noun*); **spin-lattice** *adjective* (*PHYSICS*) of or pertaining to the interaction between a crystal lattice and a particle possessing spin; **spin-orbit** *adjective* (*PHYSICS*) of or pertaining to the interaction between spin and orbital motion, esp. of an electron in an atom; **spin polarization** *PHYSICS* = **POLARIZATION** 3; **spin-polarized** *adjective* (*PHYSICS*) subjected to or displaying spin-polarization; **spin-spin** *adjective* (*PHYSICS*) of or pertaining to the interaction between two or more particles possessing spin; **spin-stabilization** *ASTRONAUTICS* the production or maintenance of a spin-stabilized state; **spin-stabilized** *adjective* (*ASTRONAUTICS*) (of a satellite, spacecraft, etc.) stabilized in a desired orientation by being made to rotate about an axis; **spin tunnel** *AERONAUTICS* = ***spinning tunnel*** s.v. **SPINNING** *noun*; **spin-up** *adjective* (*PHYSICS*) being or pertaining to a particle whose spin points upwards; **spin vector** *MATH.* & *PHYSICS* a vector representing rotation; *spec.* one which by its magnitude and direction represents the intrinsic angular momentum of a particle; **spin wave** *PHYSICS* a cooperative oscillation in the alignment of electron spins, propagated through a magnetic material in the form of a wave.
■ **spinless** *adjective* having no (tendency to) spin **M20.**

spin /spɪn/ *noun*[2]. *Anglo-Indian.* **M19.**
[Abbreviation.]
= **SPINSTER** 3.

spin /spɪn/ *verb.* Infl. **-nn-**. Pa. t. **spun**, /spʌn/, **span** /span/; pa. pple **spun**.
[Old English *spinnan* = Middle & mod. Dutch *spinnen*, Old High German, Gothic *spinnan* (German *spinnen*), Old Norse *spinna*, from Germanic.]
▶ **I 1 a** *verb trans. & intrans.* Draw out and twist (wool, cotton, flax, etc.) by hand or with machinery so as to

form thread; make a similar type of thread from (a synthetic substance, glass, etc.). Also foll. by *into*. **OE.** ▸**b** *verb trans.* Form (thread etc.) by drawing out and twisting wool etc.; prepare the material for (a fabric or garment) by this process. **ME.** ▸**c** *verb trans. & intrans.* Of an insect, spider, etc.: produce (glutinous silken threads) from the body by means of special organs; construct (a web, cocoon, etc.) using silken threads. **E16.** ▸**d** *verb intrans.* Admit of being converted into thread etc. by spinning. Also foll. by *into*. **L18.**

2 *verb trans. fig.* ▸**a** Of the Fates etc.: determine or appoint (a person's destiny or fortune) by spinning. **LME.** ▸**b** Tell, write, devise, (a story, plan, etc.), esp. fancifully or lengthily. **M16.** ▸**c** = ***spin out*** (a), (b), (d) below. **E17.**

> 🕮 **1a** G. R. PORTER Glass may be spun into very long and minute threads. L. D. B. GORDON Factories in which raw silk is spun into silk-thread for weaving. J. R. GREEN To spin their wool from their own sheeps' backs. OUIDA She sat at home and span. **b** P. S. BUCK Thread that she herself spun on a bamboo spindle from a wad of cotton. **d** R. OASTLER It will not spin into good yarn. **2a** M. ARNOLD That doom, which long ago The Nornies, when his mother bare him, spun. **b** J. HALPERIN Spinning fantastic yarns whose action . . took place at sea.

▶ **II 3** *verb intrans.* Of blood etc.: issue in a rapid stream; gush, spurt. Freq. foll. by *out*. **LME.**

4 a *verb intrans.* Move or travel quickly. Now *esp.*, drive or ride at a rapid and even rate. **LME.** ▸**b** *verb trans.* Cause (time) to pass; convey rapidly, carry *away*. **L17.** ▸**c** *verb intrans.* Pass or be spent quickly. **M19.**

5 *verb trans.* Cause to turn or revolve rapidly, as on an axis. **E17.** ▸**b** Shape (metal) by pressure applied during rotation on a lathe. **M19.** ▸**c** Impart spin to (a ball) in cricket etc., cause (a ball) to change direction or speed on striking the ground etc. **E20.** ▸**d** Make (an aircraft, car, etc.) perform a spin. **E20.** ▸**e** = ***spin-dry*** (a) below. **M20.** ▸**f** Play (a gramophone record), esp. for public entertainment. **M20.**

6 *verb intrans.* Turn or revolve rapidly, as on an axis; whirl *round*. **M17.** ▸**b** Of the brain or head: be dizzy, dazed, or confused through excitement, astonishment, etc. **E19.** ▸**c** CRICKET etc. Of a ball: travel through the air etc. with spin. **M19.** ▸**d** Of an aircraft, car, pilot, etc.: perform or undergo a spin. **E20.** ▸**e** (Of a wheel etc.) revolve without providing traction; (of a motor clutch) continue to revolve after being disengaged. **E20.**

7 ANGLING. **a** *verb trans.* Cause (a spinner or bait) to revolve when drawn through the water by fastening to a hook in a particular manner. **E19.** ▸**b** *verb intrans.* Fish with a spinning bait. **M19.** ▸**c** *verb trans.* Fish (a pool, stream, etc.) with a spinning bait. **L19.**

8 a *verb trans.* Reject (a candidate) as not reaching the pass standard in an examination. Usu. in *pass*. *slang*. **M19.** ▸**b** *verb intrans.* Fail an examination. *slang*. **M19.**

> 🕮 **4a** F. M. CRAWFORD A cab at the door, . . and in a minute . . he was spinning along Fifth Avenue. **5** R. HODGSON When stately ships are twirled and spun Like whipping tops. R. RAYNER He fiddled with the radio, spinning the dial. L. KENNEDY Billy and I . . spun a coin as to who would go first. **f** *New Yorker* Nancy . . , who spins the platters . . , organised the event. **6** E. J. HOWARD They nailed the catherine wheels . . so that they could spin freely. C. SAGAN Our tiny planet, spinning in an almost circular orbit. P. FARMER When the sneeze came from behind me I spun round. **b** K. A. PORTER Little Sophie's head would spin . . trying to follow her brilliant schoolmate's mind. **d** H. MANTEL She sees the vehicle spin out of control. **e** A. LURIE The rear wheels spun violently.

With adverbs in specialized senses: **spin down** (*a*) *verb phr. trans.* (BIOLOGY) centrifuge so as to cause the separation of components; (*b*) *verb phr. intrans. & trans.* (ASTRONOMY) (of a celestial object, esp. a star) rotate more slowly, usu. because of decreasing angular momentum. **spin off** (*a*) *verb phr. trans.* finish or clear off (a distaff etc.) by spinning; (*b*) *verb phr. trans.* throw off (as) by centrifugal force in spinning; (*c*) *verb phr. trans.* distribute (stock of a new company) to shareholders of a parent company, create (a company) in this way (*US*); produce as a spin-off or indirect benefit from a large project etc.; (*d*) *verb phr. intrans.* be thrown or move off (as) by centrifugal force in spinning. **spin out** (*a*) *verb phr. trans.* make (a story, discussion, period, etc.) lengthy or protracted; prolong, draw out, extend; (*b*) *verb phr. trans.* spend or occupy (time) fruitlessly or in a specified way; (*c*) *verb phr. trans.* evolve or devise by mental effort, express at length; (*d*) *verb phr. trans.* bring to an end, consume, exhaust, (usu. in *pass.*); (*e*) *verb phr. trans.* use (money, a resource, etc.) sparingly, eke out; (*f*) *verb phr. intrans.* run out; extend; last out; (*g*) *verb phr. trans.* (CRICKET) dismiss (a batsman or side) by spin-bowling; (*h*) *verb phr. intrans.* (*N. Amer. slang*) (of a vehicle) skid out of control. **spin up** *verb phr. intrans. & trans.* (ASTRONOMY) (of a celestial object, esp. a star) rotate more quickly because of a gain in angular momentum or a redistribution of matter.

Comb.: **spin-down** (chiefly ASTRONOMY) a decrease in the speed of rotation of something; **spin-drier** a machine for drying washing by spinning it rapidly in a rotating perforated drum; **spin-dry** *verb & noun* (*a*) *verb trans.* dry (washing) by spinning it rapidly in a (washing machine with a) spin-drier; (*b*) *noun* an instance or spell of spin-drying washing; **spin-out** *N. Amer. slang* a skidding spin by a vehicle out of control; **spin-rinse** a rinsing of washing in a rotating perforated drum which draws off water; a combined rinse and partial spin-dry; **spin-scan** *adjective & noun* (*a*) *adjective* designating a device having a scanning motion provided by the rotation of the craft carrying it; (*b*) *noun* a scan performed or produced by such a device; **spintext** *arch.* a clergyman, a parson, *esp.* one who preaches long or weak sermons; **spin-up** an increase in the speed of rotation of something.

■ **spinna'bility** *noun* ability to be spun or drawn into a fibre **M20.** **spinnable** *adjective* able to be spun **L19.**

spina /ˈspʌɪnə/ *noun*. Pl. **-nae** /-niː/. **LME.**
[Latin = spine.]

1 The backbone. Now only MEDICINE in mod. Latin phrs. **LME.**

2 ROMAN ANTIQUITIES. The barrier running up the middle of a Roman circus. **M18.**

1 spina bifida /ˈbɪfɪdə/ [fem. of *bifidus*: see BIFID] a congenital malformation in which one or more vertebrae fail to close fully over the meninges of the spinal cord, freq. causing lower limb paralysis and hydrocephalus. **spina ventosa** /vɛnˈtəʊzə/ [= windy] a condition caused by tuberculosis or cancer in which bone is eroded and sinuses are formed, causing enlargement of the fingers or toes.

spinach /ˈspɪnɪdʒ, -ɪtʃ/ *noun*. **ME.**
[Prob. from Old French *espinache*, *-age* (mod. *épinard*) from Spanish *espinaca* from Hispano-Arab. *isbinākh*, Arab. *isbānākh* from Persian *aspānākh*, *aspanākh*.]

1 A plant of the goosefoot family, *Spinacia oleracea*, cultivated for its edible dark green succulent leaves; the leaves of this plant used as a vegetable. **ME.** ▸**b** With specifying word: any of various plants of other genera and families resembling spinach or used in a similar way. **E18.**

2 Any of three geometrid moths of the genera *Eulithis* and *Pelurga*, which have brown and yellow patterned forewings; esp. *E. mellinata*, the larvae of which feed on the leaves of currants. **M19.**

3 Nonsense, rubbish. *US colloq.* (now *rare*). **E20.**

b *Malabar spinach*, *New Zealand spinach*, etc. **3 *gammon and spinach***: see GAMMON *noun*[3] 3.

Comb.: **spinach beet** a form of beet, *Beta vulgaris* subsp. *cicla*, eaten as a green vegetable; **spinach-green** *noun & adjective* (of) a dark green colour; **spinach jade** a dark green nephrite; **spinach moth** = sense 2 above.

■ **spinachy** *adjective* characteristic or suggestive of spinach **M20.**

spinae *noun* pl. of SPINA.

spinal /ˈspɪn(ə)l/ *noun*[1]. **LME.**
[Origin uncertain: sense 2 app. from German *Spinal* (Dutch *spinaal*) thread, yarn.]

Hist. †**1** A textile fabric. Only in **LME.**

2 A kind of bleached linen yarn. **L17.**

spinal /ˈspʌɪn(ə)l/ *adjective & noun*[2]. **L16.**
[Late Latin *spinalis* from Latin *spina* SPINE: see -AL[1].]

▶ **A** *adjective*. **1** Of, pertaining to, forming part of, or located in, the vertebral column or spinal cord or both. **L16.**

2 Of a disease etc.: affecting the spine. **M19.**

3 Resembling a spine or backbone in form or function. **M19.**

4 Of a quality: arising from, or seated in, the spine. **M19.**

5 Of an appliance: adapted to, or intended for, application to the spine. Formerly also (of a seat or carriage), designed to support the spine. **M19.**

6 PHYSIOLOGY. Involving the spinal cord as part of the central nervous system. **L19.** ▸**b** Of an animal: whose spine has been severed from its brain. **E20.**

Special collocations: **spinal anaesthesia**, **spinal analgesia** anaesthesia or analgesia induced by an injection into the spine. **spinal block** (*a*) an obstruction to the flow of the cerebrospinal fluid; (*b*) spinal anaesthesia or analgesia. **spinal canal** the channel containing the spinal cord that runs down the centre of the spinal column. **spinal column** the series of connecting vertebrae that support and protect the spinal cord; the spine or backbone. **spinal cord** the part of the central nervous system which is posterior to the brain, extending down the spinal canal and giving rise to the spinal nerves. ***spinal marrow***: see MARROW *noun*[1] 3. **spinal nerve** any of several paired nerves that arise from the spinal cord and innervate the trunk or limbs. **spinal puncture** = ***spinal tap*** below. **spinal reflex** a reflex involving the spinal cord but not the brain. **spinal shock** a temporary flaccid paralysis and loss of reflexes in some muscles that may follow an injury to the spine above the part controlling the affected area. **spinal tap** the insertion of a needle into the subarachnoid space of the spine, usu. in the lumbar region, so that cerebrospinal fluid may be withdrawn or something introduced.

▶ **B** *noun*. MEDICINE. = EPIDURAL *noun*. *US colloq.* **M20.**

spinar /ˈspɪnɑː/ *noun*. **L20.**
[from *spin(ning st)ar*, after *quasar*, *pulsar*.]

ASTRONOMY. A hypothetical, supermassive, rapidly rotating celestial object which may be located in the nuclei of some active galaxies and quasars, and which could help to account for the huge energy output of quasars.

spination /spɪˈneɪʃ(ə)n, spʌɪ-/ *noun*. **M19.**
[from Latin *spina* SPINE: see -ATION.]

ZOOLOGY. The condition of having spines; the manner of formation or arrangement of spines.

spindlage *noun* var. of SPINDLEAGE.

spindle /ˈspɪnd(ə)l/ *noun & adjective*.
[Old English *spinel* corresp. to Old Frisian *spindel*, Old Saxon *spinnila*, Middle & mod. Dutch *spindel*, Old High German *spin(n)ila* (German *Spindel*), from base of SPIN *verb*: see -LE[1].]

▶ **A** *noun*. **I 1 a** A slender rounded rod, usu. tapering at each end, used in hand-spinning to twist and wind thread from a mass of wool, flax, etc., held on a distaff etc. **OE.** ▸**b** A pin or rod used on a spinning-wheel to twist and wind the thread; a pin bearing the bobbin of a spinning-machine. **L18.** ▸**c** A spool or bobbin for thread etc. **M19.**

2 As much thread or yarn as can be wound on to a spindle; a varying measure of length for yarn. **LME.**

3 a A figure, esp. a heraldic bearing, in the form of an elongated lozenge; a fusil. **L15.** ▸**b** CYTOLOGY. A bipolar configuration of fibres to which the chromosomes become attached by their centromeres at the metaphase of mitosis, before being pulled towards its poles. **L19.** ▸**c** ANATOMY. Any of numerous small sensory organs within muscles, tendons, etc., which consist of a spindle-shaped body containing nerve endings and enclosed in a capsule. Also ***neuromuscular spindle***, ***neurotendinous spindle***. **L19.** ▸**d** MEDICINE. A configuration of waves seen in an electroencephalogram. **M20.**

4 *ellipt.* **a** = ***spindle tree*** below. **E18.** ▸**b** = ***spindle-shell*** below. **M19.**

▶ **II 5** A rod or pin serving as an axis which revolves or on which something revolves or is turned. **ME.** ▸**b** *spec.* The vertical rod at the centre of a record turntable which keeps the record in place during play. **M20.**

6 a A grooved cylindrical rod or bar acting as a screw, *spec.* to lower and raise the platen of a hand printing-press. **LME.** ▸**b** In full ***spindle machine***, ***spindle moulder***. A machine consisting of one or more cutters on a spindle, used to shape wooden mouldings. **E20.**

7 The stalk or young shoot of a plant, esp. a cereal grass (now *dial.*). Also (*US*), the tassel of maize. **L16.**

8 A fixed rod or bar, *esp.* one of cylindrical section; *spec.* (*a*) NAUTICAL the upper part or section of a wooden mast; (*b*) (long *dial.*) a rod or bar forming part of a plough or harrow; (*c*) a turned piece of wood used as a banister, chair leg, etc.; (*d*) *US* a stout metal rod or pole fixed on a rock as a guide to shipping. **L16.**

9 The third swarm of bees from a hive in one year. *dial.* **E19.**

▶ **B** *attrib.* or as *adjective*. **1** Long or tall and slender, thin and lacking robustness, spindly. **L16.**

2 Shaped like a spindle, cylindrical with tapered ends. **M17.**

Comb. & special collocations: **spindle-back** *adjective* designating a chair with a back consisting of framed cylindrical bars; **spindle berry** the fruit of the spindle tree; **spindle cell** a narrow, elongated cell; *spec.* (*a*) BIOLOGY such a cell in the blood of some lower vertebrates analogous to the thrombocyte; (*b*) MEDICINE such a cell characteristic of a type of sarcoma; **spindle cross** HERALDRY a cross having limbs shaped somewhat like a spindle; **spindle fibre** CYTOLOGY any of the microtubular strands which form the visible structure of a spindle (sense 3b above); **spindle-legged** *adjective* (chiefly *derog.*) (of a person etc.) having long thin legs; ***spindle machine***, ***spindle moulder***: see sense 6b above; **spindle-shank** (chiefly *derog.*) (*a*) a long thin leg (usu. in *pl.*); (*b*) *sing.* & (usu.) in *pl.* a spindle-legged person; **spindle-shanked** *adjective* = ***spindle-legged*** above; **spindle-shaped** *adjective* cylindrical with tapered ends, fusiform; **spindle-shell** (*a*) (the shell of) any of various gastropod molluscs having shells with long slender spires and siphonal canals, esp. the rare Indo-Pacific *Tibia fusus* and members of the family Fusinidae; (*b*) (the rounded tapering shell of) a large gastropod mollusc related to whelks, *Neptunea antiqua*, of northern seas; **spindle side** the female line of descent (cf. DISTAFF *noun* 2); **spindle tree** any of various shrubs and small trees of the genus *Euonymus* (family Celastraceae), with small tetramerous flowers and fruits which open to disclose orange arils *esp.* the Eurasian shrub *E. europaeus*; **spindle-whorl** (chiefly ARCHAEOLOGY) a whorl or small pulley used to weight a spindle; **spindle-wood** the wood of the spindle tree, formerly used for making spindles.

■ **spindleful** *noun* as much yarn or thread as will fill a spindle **E17.** **spindleless** /-l-l-/ *adjective* **M20.**

spindle /ˈspɪnd(ə)l/ *verb*. **L16.**
[from the noun.]

1 *verb intrans.* Of a cereal grass or flowering plant: develop its stem or stalk, shoot up; *esp.* grow excessively long and slender. Freq. foll. by *up*. **L16.**

2 *verb intrans.* Grow into or have a long and slender form, be or become thin and unsubstantial. (Foll. by *into*.) **L18.**

3 *verb trans.* Fit with or fix on a spindle or axis. **M19.**

4 *verb trans.* Spin (a garment). *rare*. **L19.**

5 *verb trans.* Recess and taper (a spar) for an aeroplane's wing; cut *out* (a recess) in a spar. **E20.**

spindleage /ˈspɪnd(ə)lɪdʒ/ *noun*. Also **spindlage**. **E20.**
[formed as prec. + -AGE.]

The total number of spindles in use at a given time in a particular mill, district, etc.

spindled /ˈspɪnd(ə)ld/ *ppl adjective*. **L16.**
[from SPINDLE *noun*, *verb*: see -ED[2], -ED[1].]

1 Long and slender, esp. in the stalk; thin and insubstantial. Also ***spindled up***. **L16.**

2 Of a cereal grass etc.: that has developed its stem. E17.
3 Spindle-shaped, cylindrical with tapered ends. E18. ▸**b** Of a spar or strut for an aeroplane wing: recessed and tapered. Also foll. by *out*. E20.
4 Twisted or wound on a spindle. M19.

spindling /ˈspɪndlɪŋ/ *noun*. LME.
[formed as prec. + -ING¹.]
1 The action or process of SPINDLE *verb*. LME.
2 A thin or spindly plant, animal, etc. M19.
3 MEDICINE. The occurrence of fairly regular alternating increases and decreases of amplitude in an electroencephalogram. M20.

spindling /ˈspɪndlɪŋ/ *adjective*. M18.
[from SPINDLE *verb* + -ING².]
1 Of a plant: growing or shooting out into a (long) stalk, esp. of a slender or weakly kind. M18.
2 Of a thing: long and slender, spindly. E19.

spindly /ˈspɪndli/ *adjective*. M17.
[from SPINDLE *noun* + -Y¹.]
1 a Of a plant: of a slender and weakly growth. M17. ▸**b** Of growth: characterized by slimness and weakness. M19.
2 Long or tall and slender, thin and weak or insubstantial. E19.

> **1a** E. O'BRIEN The pines were young and spindly. **2** B. PYM His . . spindly jean-clad legs.

spindrift /ˈspɪndrɪft/ *noun*. Orig. *Scot*. E17.
[Alt. of SPOONDRIFT.]
1 Spray swept from waves by a strong wind and driven along the surface of the sea. E17.
2 *transf.* Driving snow, sand, etc. M20.

spine /spʌɪn/ *noun*. LME.
[Aphet. from Old French *espine* (mod. *épine*), or from its source Latin *spina* thorn, prickle, backbone, rel. to *spica* SPIKE *noun*².]
▸**I 1** BOTANY. A stiff sharp-pointed outgrowth arising esp. from the wood of a plant; *spec.* one that represents a modified leaf, part of a leaf, or stipule. Cf. PRICKLE *noun*¹ 3, THORN *noun* 1. LME. ▸**b** = NEEDLE *noun* 10. M19.
2 ANATOMY. Any of several sharp-pointed slender processes of certain bones. E18.
3 ZOOLOGY. A stiff, pointed, thornlike process or appendage developed on the integument or shell of certain insects and other invertebrates. E18. ▸**b** Any of the prickles of a hedgehog, the quills of a porcupine, or similar growth on other mammals. M18. ▸**c** Any of the rigid, often sharp-pointed rays or spines in the fins of a fish. L18.
4 a Any natural formation having a slender sharp-pointed form. M18. ▸**b** A tall mass of lava projecting upwards from the mouth of a volcano. E20.
▸**II 5** The spinal column or backbone, freq. also including the spinal cord. LME.
6 *transf.* & *fig.* A part or formation having the function of a spine in a structure, object, etc.; a central feature, a main support; a source of strength. Also, strength of character, firmness. M17. ▸**b** In full ***pay spine***. A linear pay scale operated in some large bodies such as the civil service and allowing flexibility for local and specific conditions. L20.
7 The heartwood of a tree. M17.
8 A sharp ridge or projection of ground, rock, etc., esp. of a mountain range or hill. L18.
9 The part of a book's jacket or cover that encloses the back, usu. facing outwards on a shelf and bearing the title, author's name, etc. Also, the inner back of a book, the seam edge or glued edge of a book. E20.

> **5** WILBUR SMITH Sean felt a cold wind blow down his spine. **6** TENNYSON The shock Of cataract seas that snap The three decker's oaken spine. *Tucson Magazine* No one cares or has the spine to sound off. *Construction News* Constructing a main spine with four spur blocks radiating east and west. **8** N. WEST He . . climbed across the spine of the hill to look down on the other side. **9** R. FRAME The gilt letters on the red spine of one of the . . books. *transf.*: T. C. BOYLE He . . crossed the room to the stereo, ran a . . finger along the spines of the albums.

Phrases: ***neural spine***: see NEURAL *adjective* 1. ***radiole spine***. ***railway spine***: see RAILWAY *noun*.
Comb.: **spine-basher** *Austral. slang* a loafer, an idler; **spine-bashing** *Austral. slang* idling, loafing; **spinebill** either of two small Australian honey-eaters of the genus *Acanthorhynchus*, which have long narrow down-curved bills; **spine-chiller** a thing or (occas.) person inspiring excitement and terror; *esp.* a horror or suspense story, film, etc.; **spine-chilling** *adjective* (of a story, film, etc.), inspiring excitement and terror, frightening; **spinefoot** any of several tropical marine fishes of the genus *Siganus* (family Siganidae), which bear several sharp venomous spines on the fins and occur in inshore waters of the Indo-Pacific; **spine-freezer** = *spine-chiller* above; **spine-freezing** *adjective* = *spine-chilling* above; **spine-oak** the heartwood of an oak; **spine point** each of the pay levels on a pay spine (see sense 6b above); **spine road** a major road linking other important routes or points; **spinetail** any of various birds that have stiff, pointed tail feathers; *esp.* (*a*) any Central or S. American ovenbird of the subfamily Synallaxinae (family Furnariidae), inhabiting marshy areas and building complex covered nests; (*b*) = ***spine-tailed swift*** below; (*c*) *Austral.* a spine-tailed logrunner, *Orthonyx temminckii*; (*d*) *N. Amer.* = RUDDY ***duck***; **spine-tailed** *adjective* having spinelike tail feathers; ***spine-tailed swift***, any of various swifts of the tribe Chaeturini, which have the shafts of the tail feathers projecting beyond the tail; **spine-tingler** something thrilling or pleasurably frightening; *esp.* an exciting story etc.; a spine-chiller; **spine-tingling** *adjective* thrilling or pleasurably frightening, spine-chilling.
■ **spined** *adjective* (*a*) covered with spines, having spines of a specified kind or number; spinous, spiny; ***spined loach***, a common Eurasian loach, *Cobitis taenia*, which bears a backward-pointing spine below each eye; (*b*) having a spinal column: L18. **spinelike** *adjective* resembling a spine M19.

spinel /ˈspɪn(ə)l/ *noun*. Also †**-ell(e)**. E16.
[French *spinelle* from Italian *spinella* dim. of Latin *spina* SPINE: see -EL².]
MINERALOGY. **1** A hard glassy cubic mineral, $MgAl_2O_4$, occurring usu. as octahedral crystals of variable colour; *esp.* (more fully ***spinel ruby***, ***ruby spinel***) a gemstone of a red or scarlet colour, resembling the true ruby. E16.
2 Any of a group or series of minerals related to typical spinel which are oxides of magnesium, iron, zinc, or manganese, with aluminium. Also, any of various artificial minerals having similar structures. E19.

spineless /ˈspʌɪnlɪs/ *adjective*. E19.
[from SPINE + -LESS.]
1 Of an animal, plant, etc.: having no spines, not spinous. E19.
2 Having no spine, invertebrate; having a weak or diseased spine. Now chiefly *fig.*, (of a person etc.) lacking resolution, energy, or strength of character; feeble, weak, irresolute. L19.

> **2** P. G. WODEHOUSE A . . poor, spineless sheep who can't say boo to a goose. *Sunday Telegraph* A spineless exhibition by the early Yorkshire batting.

■ **spinelessly** *adverb* L20. **spinelessness** *noun* E20.

†**spinell(e)** *noun* var. of SPINEL.

spinescent /spʌɪˈnɛs(ə)nt/ *adjective*. L18.
[Late Latin *spinescent-* pres. ppl stem of *spinescere* grow thorny, from Latin *spina* thorn: see -ESCENT.]
1 BOTANY. Terminating in a spine; more or less spiny. L18.
2 ZOOLOGY. Tending to become a spine or spinous process; spinous, spinulose. M19.
■ **spinescence** *noun* M19.

spinet /spɪˈnɛt, ˈspɪnɪt/ *noun*¹. Also **-ette**. M17.
[Aphet. from French †*espinette* (now *épinette*) from Italian *spinetta* virginal, spinet, dim. of *spina* SPINE (the strings of both instruments being plucked by quills): see -ET¹.]
1 A kind of small harpsichord with the strings set obliquely to the keyboard, popular esp. in the 18th cent. M17.
2 In full ***spinet piano***. A type of small piano. *US*. M20.

spinet /ˈspɪnɪt/ *noun*². *arch.* E17.
[Latin *spinetum* from *spina* SPINE: see -ET¹. Cf. SPINNEY.]
A thicket, a spinney.

spinette *noun* var. of SPINET *noun*¹.

spin-house /ˈspɪnhaʊs/ *noun*. L17.
[Dutch *spinhuis* spinning-house.]
Hist. Esp. in Continental Europe: a women's prison or reformatory; a workhouse. Cf. ***spinning-house*** s.v. SPINNING *noun*.

spini- /ˈspʌɪni/ *combining form*.
[from Latin *spina* SPINE: see -I-.]
Forming adjectives with ref. to (*a*) in BOTANY & ZOOLOGY, a spine or spines, as ***spinidentate***, ***spinituberculate***; (*b*) in ANATOMY, the spinal column, or the spine of a bone, as ***spinirector***, ***spinideltoid***. Cf. SPINO-.
■ **spiˈniferous** *adjective* (chiefly BOTANY) bearing spines; spinose: M17. **spiniform** *adjective* (BOTANY & ZOOLOGY) having the form of a spine M19. **spiˈnigerous** *adjective* spiniferous; *spec.* in ENTOMOLOGY, (of a beetle etc.) bearing a dorsal spine common to both elytra: E19.

spinifex /ˈspɪnɪfɛks/ *noun*. E19.
[mod. Latin (see below), from Latin *spina* SPINE + *-fex* maker, from *facere* to make.]
1 Any of various tussock-forming spiny-leaved grasses, chiefly of the genera *Triodia* and *Plectrachne*, abundant in the deserts of the Australian interior; *esp.* the porcupine grass, *Triodia irritans*. Also, the mass formed by such a grass. E19.
2 Any of several grasses constituting the genus *Spinifex*, esp. *S. hirsutus*, which are common on Australasian seashores and characterized by the elastic spines of the seeds. L19.
Comb.: **spinifex texture** PETROGRAPHY a texture of criss-crossing olivine crystals characteristic of komatiites.

spiniken /ˈspɪnɪkɪn/ *noun*. *slang* (now *Hist.*). Also **-nn-**. M19.
[from SPIN *verb* + KEN *noun*². Cf. SPIN-HOUSE.]
A workhouse.

spink /spɪŋk/ *noun*¹. Now *dial.* LME.
[Prob. imit. of the chaffinch's call.]
1 The chaffinch. Formerly also (with specifying word), any of several other finches etc. LME.
2 Used to imitate or represent the call of certain birds. L19.

spink /spɪŋk/ *noun*². *Scot.* & *north*. L18.
[Origin unkn.]
The cuckoo-flower, *Cardamine pratensis*.

spinks /spɪŋks/ *noun*. *Austral.* M20.
[from SPINK *noun*¹ + -S⁴.]
= JACKY ***Winter***.

spinmeister /ˈspɪnmʌɪstə/ *noun*. *colloq.* L20.
[from SPIN *noun*¹ + -MEISTER.]
POLITICS. An accomplished or politically powerful spin doctor; an expert at presenting information or events to the media in a favourable light.

spinnaker /ˈspɪnəkə/ *noun*. M19.
[App. fanciful formation from *spinx* mispronunc. of *Sphinx* name of the first yacht to use the sail, perh. infl. by SPANKER *noun*¹.]
A large triangular sail carried forward of or opposite the mainsail of a racing yacht etc. running before the wind.

spinnbar /ˈʃpɪnbɑː/ *adjective*. M20.
[German.]
Of a viscous liquid: able to be drawn into strands; spinnable.
■ **spinnbarkeit** *noun* the capacity of a viscous liquid, esp. (in PHYSIOLOGY) the cervical mucus, for being drawn into strands; spinnability: M20.

spinner /ˈspɪnə/ *noun*. ME.
[from SPIN *verb* + -ER¹.]
▸**I 1** A spider, *esp.* one which spins a web. Now *arch.* & *dial.* ME. ▸**b** A caterpillar which spins a cocoon; a silkworm. *rare*. L16.
2 A person engaged or occupied in spinning cotton, wool, etc. ME. ▸**b** A manufacturer or merchant engaged in spinning, esp. cotton-spinning. M19.
3 A person spinning or telling a story etc. L18.
4 a ZOOLOGY. = SPINNERET 1. Now *rare*. E19. ▸**b** A spinning-machine. L19.
5 Each of the principal supporting threads of a spider's web. M19.

> **2** ADAM SMITH The spinner is . . a distinct person from the weaver. ***cotton-spinner***: see COTTON *noun*¹. **3** L. STEPHEN An accomplished spinner of boyish stories.

▸**II 6** An adult mayfly, *esp.* a male one; *dial.* a crane-fly (also ***spinner-fly***). In ANGLING also, any of various artificial flies used esp. in trout-fishing. L18. ▸**b** ANGLING. A real or artificial bait or lure fixed so as to revolve when pulled through the water. Also, an angler using such a bait or lure. M19.
7 a A thing which spins round or revolves; *spec.* (*a*) a top; (*b*) CRICKET a ball bowled with spin; (*c*) AGRICULTURE a rotating device for lifting potatoes out of the ground; (*d*) a spin-drier. L18. ▸**b** A person who spins something round; *spec.* (*a*) (chiefly *Austral.*) the person who tosses the coins in the game of two-up; (*b*) CRICKET a spin bowler. E20.
8 A thing which moves rapidly. L19.
9 A metal fairing that is attached to and revolves with the propeller boss of an aircraft in order to streamline it. E20.

> **6** JENNY ***spinner***. ***red spinner***: see RED *adjective*. **b** F. FRANCIS The very best spinners for large trout . . are Thames fishermen.

Comb.: **spinner dolphin** a dolphin of warm seas, *Stenella longirostris*, noted for rotating several times while leaping out of the water; **spinner magnetometer** GEOLOGY & ARCHAEOLOGY a magnetometer used to measure the remanent magnetism of rocks, baked clay, etc., in which the sample is spun between coils and induces in them a current dependent on the strength and direction of the magnetic field.

spinneret /ˈspɪnərɛt/ *noun*. E19.
[Dim. of prec.: see -ET¹.]
1 ZOOLOGY. Any of various organs through which the silk, gossamer, or thread of spiders, silkworms, and certain other insects is produced. E19.
2 A cap or plate having a number of small holes through which a spinnable solution is forced in the production of man-made fibres; an individual hole or channel in such a plate. L19.

spinnery /ˈspɪnəri/ *noun*. M19.
[from SPIN *verb* + -ERY.]
A spinning factory or establishment.

spinney /ˈspɪni/ *noun*. Also **spinny**. LME.
[Aphet. from Old French *espinei* (mod. *épinaie*) from Proto-Romance alt. of Latin *spinetum* SPINET *noun*²: see -Y⁶.]
†**1** A thorn hedge. *rare*. Only in LME.
2 A small wood or copse, *esp.* one planted or preserved for sheltering game-birds; a small clump or plantation of trees. L16.

spinniken *noun* var. of SPINIKEN.

spinning /ˈspɪnɪŋ/ *noun.* ME.
[from SPIN *verb* + -ING[1].]
1 The action or process of SPIN *verb*; an instance of this. ME.
2 The product of the operation of spinning; thread or yarn spun. E16.
Attrib. & comb.: In the sense 'of or pertaining to spinning thread', as ***spinning process***, ***spinning room***, etc. Special combs., as **spinning-frame** a kind of spinning-machine; **spinning-house** (*a*) a room or building set apart or used for spinning; (*b*) *Hist.* a women's prison or reformatory (cf. SPIN-HOUSE); **spinning-jenny** *Hist.* an early form of spinning-machine in which several spindles were set in motion by a band from one wheel; **spinning-machine** a machine for spinning fibres continuously; **spinning magnetometer** = ***SPINNER magnetometer***; **spinning-top** = TOP *noun*[2] 1; **spinning tunnel** AERONAUTICS a wind tunnel with a vertical airflow for testing the behaviour of models of aircraft in simulated spins; **spinning-wheel** a simple household apparatus for spinning thread or yarn with a spindle driven by a wheel attached to a crank or treadle.

spinning /ˈspɪnɪŋ/ *adjective.* L16.
[formed as prec. + -ING[2].]
That spins, revolves, or produces thread; *colloq.* rapid, fast.
spinning reserve ELECTRICAL ENGINEERING reserve power-generating capacity which is available to meet sudden increases in load.
■ **spinningly** *adverb* E20.

spinny *noun* var. of SPINNEY.

spino- /ˈspʌɪnəʊ/ *combining form.*
[from Latin *spina*: see -O-.]
Forming adjectives with ref. to (*a*) BOTANY & ZOOLOGY a spine or spines, as ***spinocarpous***, ***spinotuberculous***; (*b*) ANATOMY the spinal column, or the spine of a bone, as ***spinocerebellar***, ***spinothalamic***. Cf. SPINI-.

spinode /ˈspʌɪnəʊd/ *noun.* M19.
[Irreg. from Latin *spina* SPINE + NODE.]
GEOMETRY. A stationary point on a curve; a cusp.
■ **spiˈnodal** *noun & adjective* (PHYSICAL CHEMISTRY) (*a*) *noun* a curve which is the locus of stationary points in a system of curves; *spec.* such a curve in a pressure-volume diagram etc. which delimits a region of thermodynamic metastability from one of instability; (*b*) *adjective* pertaining to or of the nature of a spinodal; involving a metastable condition described by such a curve: M20.

spin-off /ˈspɪnɒf/ *noun & adjective.* Also **spinoff**. M20.
[from ***spin off*** s.v. SPIN *verb*.]
▶ **A** *noun.* **1** COMMERCE. A distribution of stock of a new company to shareholders of a parent company; a company so created. M20.
2 A by-product or an incidental development from a larger project; the production or accrual of by-products; *spec.* (*a*) an incidental benefit arising from industrial or military technology; (*b*) a business, organization, etc., developed out of or by (former) members of another; (*c*) a television programme etc. derived from another or from a film etc.; (*d*) a product or range of goods marketed by association with a popular personality, show, etc. M20.

> 📖 **2** *Graphics World* ADC . . working on a range of spin-offs including a record . . and a . . film. *Nature* All governments worry about the civil spin-off from defence research.

▶ **B** *attrib.* or as *adjective.* Developing or created as a spin-off. M20.

> 📖 *Boston Globe* Shares of the spin-off company will be distributed tax free.

spinone /spɪˈnəʊni/ *noun.* M20.
[Italian.]
(An animal of) a wire-haired Italian breed of gun dog, usu. white with tan or brown markings, drooping ears, and a docked tail.

spinor /ˈspɪnə/ *noun.* M20.
[from SPIN *verb* + -OR, after *tensor*, *vector*.]
PHYSICS. Any quantity existing in a space and having the property that rotation through 360° reverses its sign and leaves it otherwise unchanged; also, quantities constructed from two or more of these in the way that tensors may be constructed from vectors.
■ **spiˈnorial** *adjective* involving spinors, described by means of spinors M20.

spinose /spʌɪˈnəʊs/ *adjective.* M17.
[Latin *spinosus*, from *spina* SPINE: see -OSE[1].]
Chiefly BOTANY & ZOOLOGY. = SPINOUS.
■ **spinosely** *adverb* M19.

spinosity /spʌɪˈnɒsɪti/ *noun.* E17.
[Late Latin *spinositas*, formed as prec.: see -ITY.]
Chiefly *fig.* †**1** The quality of being spinous or thorny. E–M17.
2 A rude or disagreeable remark; an argument or theory of a difficult and unprofitable character. Now *rare* or *obsolete.* M17.

spinous /ˈspʌɪnəs/ *adjective.* LME.
[Latin *spinosus*, from *spina* SPINE: see -OUS.]
1 BOTANY. Having spines or thorns; spiny. Also, of the nature of a spine. LME.
2 *fig.* Resembling or suggestive of a thorn or thorns in respect of sharpness and aridity; unpleasant and difficult or unprofitable to handle or deal with. M17.
3 Chiefly ZOOLOGY. Armed or covered with spines; spinigerous. M18.
4 Having the form of a spine or thorn; slender and sharp-pointed. M18.
4 spinous process a process or apophysis in the form of a spine, esp. on a vertebra.
■ **spinousness** *noun* M19.

Spinozan /spɪˈnəʊz(ə)n/ *adjective.* L19.
[from *Spinoza* (see next) + -AN.]
PHILOSOPHY. Of, pertaining to, or originating with Spinoza.

Spinozism /spɪˈnəʊzɪz(ə)m/ *noun.* E18.
[from *Spinoza* (see below) + -ISM.]
The doctrines and principles of the Dutch philosopher of Jewish descent, Baruch (Benedict) de Spinoza (1632–77), esp. that there is one infinite substance of which extension and thought are attributes and human beings are changing forms; pantheism as represented by Spinoza.

Spinozist /spɪˈnəʊzɪst/ *noun.* E18.
[formed as prec. + -IST.]
PHILOSOPHY. An expert in or student of the doctrines of Spinoza, an advocate of Spinozism.
■ **Spinoˈzistic** *adjective* of, pertaining to, or characteristic of Spinoza or his views E19. **Spinozite** *noun* = SPINOZIST L17.

spinster /ˈspɪnstə/ *noun.* LME.
[from SPIN *verb* + -STER, perh. after Middle & mod. Dutch *spinster* (cf. Middle Low German *spinsterinne*).]
1 A person, usu. a woman, who spins cotton, wool, etc., esp. as an occupation. LME. ▸**b** A spider; an insect that spins. *rare.* M17.
2 Used as a title following the name of a woman, orig. to denote occupation but later as the legal designation of an unmarried woman. LME.
3 An unmarried woman, esp. an older woman thought unlikely to marry. E18.

> 📖 **3** G. DALY While she liked Mr Woolner . . , she would be perfectly happy to live . . as a spinster. *attrib.*: J. R. ACKERLEY My father entirely supported his three spinster sisters.

■ **spinsterdom** *noun* = SPINSTERHOOD L19. **spinsterhood** *noun* the condition of being an unmarried woman; spinsters collectively: E19. **spinˈsterial** *adjective* = SPINSTERISH M19. **spinˈsterian** *adjective* = SPINSTERISH E19. **spinsterish** *adjective* of, pertaining to, or characteristic of a spinster; old-maidish: L19. **spinsterishness** *noun* E20. **spinsterism**, **spinstership** *nouns* = SPINSTERHOOD E19. **spinsterly** *adjective* = SPINSTERISH E19.

spinstress /ˈspɪnstrɪs/ *noun.* M17.
[from prec. + -ESS[1].]
1 A female spinner. M17.
2 = SPINSTER 3. E18.

spinstry /ˈspɪnstri/ *noun.* Now *rare.* E17.
[formed as prec. + -Y[3].]
1 The art or occupation of spinning; the product of spinning. E17.
2 Spinsterhood. *rare.* L18.

spinthariscope /spɪnˈθarɪskəʊp/ *noun. obsolete* exc. *Hist.* E20.
[Irreg. from Greek *spintharis* spark: see -SCOPE.]
An instrument in which ionizing radiation is observable as light pulses on a phosphorescent screen.

spinto /ˈspɪntəʊ/ *noun & adjective.* Pl. of noun **-os**. M20.
[Italian, pa. pple of *spingere* push.]
MUSIC. (Designating) a lyric soprano or tenor voice of powerful dramatic quality; (designating) a singer with such a voice.

spintrian /ˈspɪntrɪən/ *adjective. rare.* M17.
[from Latin *spintria* male prostitute + -AN.]
Pertaining to or of the nature of (esp. homosexual) sexual activity involving three or more people.

spinule /ˈspɪnjuːl/ *noun.* M18.
[Latin *spinula* dim. of *spina* SPINE: see -ULE.]
ZOOLOGY & BOTANY. A small or minute spine or spinelike process, esp. in invertebrates.
■ **spinulate** *adjective* bearing spinules or small spines M19. **spinuˈlation** *noun* the form or arrangement of spinules L19. **spinuˈlescent** *adjective* tending to produce small spines E19. **spinuˈliferous** *adjective* = SPINULATE M19. **spinulose** *adjective* (*a*) = SPINULATE; (*b*) BOTANY (of the tooth of a fern pinnule etc.) prolonged into a hairlike point: E19. **spinulous** *adjective* = SPINULATE M19.

spiny /ˈspʌɪni/ *adjective.* L16.
[from SPINE + -Y[1].]
1 Having the characteristics of a thorn or thorns; resembling a thorn in form or qualities. L16. ▸†**b** Thin and hard or dry; spare, lean. L16–E18.
2 Chiefly BOTANY. Covered with thorns or spines; thorny. E17.
3 ZOOLOGY. Bearing or set with spines; covered with slender sharp-pointed processes. E17.
4 Having the form of a spine; stiff and sharp-pointed. E19.
Special collocations: **spiny anteater** = ECHIDNA. **spiny cocklebur** a S. American cocklebur, *Xanthium spinosum*, which is widely naturalized. **spiny dogfish** = ***spur-dog*** s.v. SPUR *noun*[1]. **spiny eel** any of various eel-like fishes with dorsal and ventral spines; *esp.* (*a*) a deep-water marine fish of the family Notacanthidae; (*b*) an Old World freshwater fish of the family Mastacambelidae. **spiny lizard** *Austral.* = MOLOCH 2. **spiny lobster** any of various large marine lobsters of the family Palinuridae, which lack large pincers; *esp.* the European species *Palinurus elephas*; also called ***crawfish***, ***rock lobster***. **spiny mouse** any of several African and SW Asian mice of the genus *Acomys*, which have bristly fur. **spiny pocket-mouse** any of several pocket-mice of the genera *Liomys* and *Heteromys*, which have bristly fur and occur from Mexico to Ecuador. **spiny rat** any of various ratlike rodents with bristly fur, esp. Central and S. American rodents of the family Echimyidae or SE Asian rats of the genus *Maxomys*. **spiny shark** any of various small sharks of the superfamily Squaloidea, most of which have spines in front of the dorsal fins.
■ **spininess** *noun* E17.

spir-, **spira-** *combining forms* see SPIRO-.

†**spirable** *adjective.* M16.
[Latin *spirabilis*, from *spirare* breathe: see -ABLE.]
1 Pertaining to breathing; respiratory. M16–L17.
2 Able to be breathed; respirable. L16–E18.

spiracle /ˈspʌɪrək(ə)l/ *noun.* Also (in senses 2, 3) in Latin form **spiraculum** /spʌɪˈrakjʊləm/, pl. **-la** /-lə/. LME.
[Latin *spiraculum*, from *spirare* breathe.]
†**1** Breath, spirit. LME–M17.
2 A small opening allowing air, light, etc., into or smoke, volcanic matter, etc., out of a confined space; a vent-hole. Now *rare.* LME.
3 a A pore of the skin. *rare.* M17. ▸**b** A stoma in the epidermis of a plant. *rare.* L18. ▸**c** ZOOLOGY. An aperture, orifice, or pore in an animal by which air or water can circulate for respiration; *esp.*: (*a*) a pore leading into the tracheae of an insect; (*b*) a rounded opening in front of the gills in various (esp. cartilaginous) fishes; (*c*) the blow-hole of a whale, dolphin, etc. L18.
■ **spiracular** /spʌɪˈrakjʊlə/ *adjective* (ZOOLOGY) of, pertaining to, or serving as a spiracle or spiracles M19. **spiraculate** /spʌɪˈrakjʊleɪt/ *adjective* (ZOOLOGY) possessing a spiracle or spiracles E20.

spiraea /spʌɪˈriːə/ *noun.* Also ***-rea**. M17.
[mod. Latin *Spiraea* (see below) from Latin *spiraea* privet from Greek *speiraia*, app. from *speira* SPIRE *noun*[3].]
Any plant of the genus *Spiraea*, of the rose family, which contains many ornamental shrubs with corymbs or panicles of small white, pink, or crimson flowers, and formerly included also meadowsweet and dropwort (now genus *Filipendula*).
Phrases: †**oil of spiraea** salicylic acid.

spiral /ˈspʌɪr(ə)l/ *noun.* M17.
[from SPIRAL *adjective*[1].]
1 A continuous flat curve traced by a point moving round a fixed point in the same plane at a steadily increasing or diminishing distance. M17.
2 A three-dimensional curve traced by a point moving round and simultaneously advancing along a cylinder or cone; a helix. L17. ▸**b** The pitch of such a curve, esp. in the rifling of a gun barrel. M19. ▸**c** AMER. FOOTBALL. A kick or pass in which the ball in flight spins round its long axis. L19. ▸**d** AERONAUTICS. A continuous banking turn accompanying a descent or (rarely) ascent. E20.
3 Each of the separate turns or coils of a spiral object. Cf. SPIRE *noun*[3] 1. E18.
4 A thing having a spiral form; *spec.* (*a*) a spiral spring; (*b*) ASTRONOMY a spiral galaxy. E19.
5 A progressive increase or decrease, *esp.* one in which two factors each respond to the stimulus provided by the other. L19.

> 📖 **1** ***equiangular spiral***, ***loxodromic spiral***, ***parabolic spiral***, etc. **4** M. ATWOOD The peel falls from her . . hands in a long pale spiral. N. SHERRY They climbed in long spirals, up into the mountains. **5** B. BAINBRIDGE The downward spiral in prices. *Community Librarian* The . . spiral of low use, opening hours reduction, further decreasing use. ***vicious spiral***: see VICIOUS *adjective*.

spiral /ˈspʌɪr(ə)l/ *adjective*[1] & *adverb.* M16.
[French, or medieval Latin *spiralis*, from Latin *spira* SPIRE *noun*[3]: see -AL[1].]
▶ **A** *adjective.* **1** Winding continuously round a fixed point at a steadily increasing or decreasing distance in the same plane. M16.
2 Forming a continuous curve which winds like the thread of a screw in a cylindrical or conical manner; helical. M16. ▸**b** MEDICINE. Of a fracture: curving round a long bone lengthwise. L19.
3 = ***spiral-bound*** below. L20.

> 📖 **2** A. BURGESS Spiral stone steps worn by a century . . of monkish feet.

Special collocations: **spiral arm** an arm of a spiral galaxy. **spiral balance** a device for measuring weight by the torsion of a spiral spring. **spiral bevel gear** a bevel gear that is also a spiral gear. **spiral binding**: in which a helical wire passes through a closely spaced row of holes near the inside edge of each leaf. **spiral-bound** *adjective* (of a notebook etc.) having spiral binding. **spiral cleavage** ZOOLOGY a pattern of embryogenesis characteristic of certain phyla of protostomes, in which the third cell division is asymmetrical and destroys all but four-fold rotational symmetry. **spiral divergence** AERONAUTICS = *spiral instability* below. **spiral galaxy** a galaxy in which stars and gas clouds are concentrated along arcs or arms that appear to spiral from a central nucleus. **spiral gear** a gear wheel with teeth cut obliquely to the axis and curved to form part of a spiral; *esp.* a skew gear of this kind. **spiral instability** AERONAUTICS: in which an aeroplane undergoing a banked turn tends to enter a descending spiral as a result of side-slipping and reduction of the radius of turn. **spiral nebula** (now chiefly *Hist.*) a spiral galaxy. **spiral stability** AERONAUTICS the capacity of an aeroplane not to enter a spiral while executing a banked turn, or to recover from a steeply-banked spiral path. **spiral staircase** a staircase rising in a spiral round a central axis. **spiral thickening** BOTANY (in the tracheary elements of the xylem, esp. the protoxylem) a thickening of the cell wall in which the secondary wall is laid down in the form of a continuous helix.

▶ **B** *adverb.* Spirally. *rare.* E18.

▪ **spi'rality** *noun* spiral character; the degree of a spiral curve: M19. **spirally** *adverb* so as to form a spiral; in a spiral course: E17.

spiral /'spʌɪr(ə)l/ *adjective*². Now *rare.* M17.
[from SPIRE *noun*¹ + -AL¹.]
Shaped like a spire; tall and tapering or pointed.

spiral /'spʌɪr(ə)l/ *verb.* Infl. **-ll-**, ***-l-**. M19.
[from the noun.]
1 *verb intrans.* Wind in a spiral manner; move, esp. ascend or descend, in a spiral course; form a spiral shape. M19. ▸**b** Increase or decrease, esp. in response to the same movement in another factor. E20.
2 *verb trans.* Twist so as to form a spiral; coil. L19.

> 🕮 **1** R. MACAULAY A narrow stairway spiralled up to the tower. *Times* All . . on board a . . Boeing 737 died when it spiralled into the sea. *New Quarterly (Canada)* That shadow falling, like a leaf spiralling down. *fig.*: O. MANNING Hope spiralled up from the pit of her stomach. **b** *What Mortgage* You could be in for a shock if interest rates spiral.

spiraliform /spʌɪ'ralɪfɔːm/ *adjective. rare.* L19.
[from SPIRAL *noun* + -I- + -FORM.]
Having or taking the form of spiral lines.

spiralize /'spʌɪrəlʌɪz/ *verb intrans & trans.* Also **-ise**. M19.
[from SPIRAL *noun or adjective*¹ + -IZE.]
Move in a spiral course; form into a spiral shape.
▪ **spirali'zation** *noun* (*a*) *rare* a spiral coil; (*b*) the acquisition of spiral form: M19.

spiralled /'spʌɪr(ə)ld/ *adjective.* Also ***-aled**. M17.
[from SPIRAL *noun* + -ED².]
Shaped like a spiral.

spiraloid /'spʌɪrəlɔɪd/ *adjective.* M19.
[from SPIRAL *noun* + -OID.]
Resembling the form of a spiral.

spiramycin /spʌɪrə'mʌɪsɪn/ *noun.* M20.
[Prob. from mod. Latin *spira* a morphological type of bacterial spore chain + -MYCIN.]
PHARMACOLOGY. (Each of the three components of) a mixture of related macrolide antibiotics obtained from *Streptomyces ambofaciens*.

spirane /'spʌɪreɪn/ *noun.* E20.
[German *Spiran*: see SPIRO-, -ANE.]
CHEMISTRY. Any organic compound having two rings in its molecule with a single atom (usu. of carbon or nitrogen) common to both; a spiro-compound.

spirant /'spʌɪr(ə)nt/ *noun & adjective.* M19.
[Latin *spirant-* pres. ppl stem of *spirare* breathe: see -ANT¹.]
PHONETICS. ▶**A** *noun.* = FRICATIVE *noun.* M19.
▶ **B** *adjective.* = FRICATIVE *adjective.* L19.
▪ **spi'rantal** *adjective* = SPIRANT *adjective* L19.

spirantize /'spʌɪr(ə)ntʌɪz/ *verb trans.* Also **-ise**. L19.
[from prec. + -IZE.]
Pronounce as a spirant; make into a spirant.
▪ **spiranti'zation** *noun* E20.

spirated /'spʌɪrətɪd/ *adjective. rare.* L19.
[from SPIRE *noun*³ + -ATE² + -ED¹.]
Spirally twisted.

spiration /spʌɪ'reɪʃ(ə)n/ *noun.* LME.
[Latin *spiratio(n-)*, from *spirat-* pa. ppl stem of *spirare* breathe: see -ATION.]
1 THEOLOGY. **a** The procession of the Holy Spirit. LME. ▸†**b** The action of breathing regarded as the creative means of God. M16–M18.
†**2** The action of breathing in humans and animals. M16–L17.
†**3** A spiritual influence. Only in 17.

spire /spʌɪə/ *noun*¹.
[Old English *spīr* = Middle Low German, Middle Dutch *spier*, *spīr*, Middle High German *spir* (German *Spier* tip of blade of grass). Cf. SPEAR *noun*², SPEER *noun*².]
1 a A stalk or stem of a plant, *esp.* a tall and slender one. Now *rare.* OE. ▸**b** The tapering top of a tree; the continuation of a tree-trunk above the point where branching begins. M17. ▸**c** A long flower-spike. M19.
2 A reed or reedlike plant; *collect.* reeds. Cf. SPEAR *noun*² 3. Now *dial.* ME.
3 A young or tender shoot or sprout; *spec.* = SPEAR *noun*² 2a. ME. ▸**b** A blade *of* grass. Now *rare.* M17.
4 A conical, tapering, or pointed object. Now chiefly *fig.* of sense 5 below. LME.
5 A tall conical or pyramid-shaped structure built on the roof or tower of a building, esp. a church. Cf. SPEAR *noun*² 1. M16. ▸**b** *fig.* The highest point *of* something. E17.

> 🕮 **4** SHELLEY Icicles . . their white and glittering spires. TENNYSON Crags that wall the dell With spires of silver shine. **5** A. BURGESS You could just see the church spire . . on the . . horizon.

Comb.: **spire-grass** (now *dial.*) any of various reeds or sedges; **spire-shell** any of various marine or freshwater snails of the superfamily Rissoacea, which have long conical spiral shells; †**spire-steeple**: surmounted by a spire.
▪ **spireless** *adjective* (of a building etc.) having no spire M19. **spirelet** *noun* a small spire, *esp.* one on a tower M19.

spire /spʌɪə/ *noun*². Chiefly *Scot. & north.* ME.
[Origin uncertain: corresp. in sense 1 to Old Norse *spíra*, Low German *spier(e)*. Cf. SPEAR *noun*³.]
†**1** A wooden beam, pole, or plank; a spar. ME–E17.
2 A young tree suitable for making into a spar; a sapling. LME.

spire /spʌɪə/ *noun*³. M16.
[French, or Latin *spira* from Greek *speira* coil, winding.]
1 A spiral. M16.
2 Each of the complete turns forming a coil or spiral. Usu. in *pl.* L16.
3 A curl or wreath of smoke etc. L17.
4 CONCHOLOGY. The upper convoluted portion of a spiral shell, consisting of all the whorls except the body-whorl. E19.

spire /spʌɪə/ *verb*¹. ME.
[from SPIRE *noun*¹. Cf. SPEAR *verb*³.]
1 *verb intrans.* Of a seed etc.: germinate, sprout. Now *rare* or *obsolete.* ME. ▸†**b** *verb trans.* Produce; put *forth. rare* (Spenser). Only in L16.
2 *verb intrans.* Of a plant: shoot up into a tall stem or spike. Now *dial.* LME.
3 *verb intrans.* Rise or shoot up into a spire-shaped form or to a great height. Also foll. by *up.* LME.
4 *verb trans.* Cause to rise up in a spire-shaped form. *rare.* M18.

spire /spʌɪə/ *verb*² *intrans.* E17.
[from SPIRE *noun*³.]
Twist or wind in a spiral; *esp.* ascend in a spiral.
¶ Not always distinguishable from SPIRE *verb*¹.

spirea *noun* see SPIRAEA.

spired /'spʌɪəd/ *adjective.* L16.
[from SPIRE *noun*¹ + -ED².]
1 Of a steeple, tower, etc.: having a spire, esp. of a specified kind. L16. ▸**b** Having a tapering or pointed top. L16.
2 Of a plant: having a stem of a specified kind. *rare.* L18.

†**spireme** *noun.* L19–M20.
[German *Spirem* from Greek (Ionic) *speirēma* a coil, convolution.]
CYTOLOGY. The tangled strands of chromosomal material seen in the early stages of cell division, formerly believed to be a single strand.

spirifer /'spʌɪrɪfə/ *noun.* M19.
[mod. Latin (see below), from Latin *spira* SPIRE *noun*³: see -FER.]
PALAEONTOLOGY. A fossil brachiopod of the genus *Spirifer* or the family Spiriferidae, found in Silurian, Devonian, and Carboniferous formations and having long spiral appendages. Now chiefly as mod. Latin genus name.

spiriform /'spʌɪrɪfɔːm/ *adjective.* M19.
[mod. Latin *spiriformis*, from Latin *spira* SPIRE *noun*³: see -FORM.]
Having the form of a spiral.

spirillum /spʌɪ'rɪləm/ *noun.* Pl. **-lla** /-'lə/. L19.
[mod. Latin genus name (see below), irreg. dim. of Latin *spira* SPIRE *noun*³.]
BACTERIOLOGY & MEDICINE. A bacterium having a spiral structure; *spec.* any of the genus *Spirillum* of rigid helical motile mainly saprophytic bacteria, including *S. minus*, a cause of rat-bite fever.
▪ **spirillar** *adjective* of or belonging to the genus *Spirillum*; resembling a spirillum; characterized by the presence of spirilla: L19. **spiri'llosis** *noun*, pl. **-lloses** /-'ləʊsiːz/, MEDICINE infection with spirilla E20.

spirit /'spɪrɪt/ *noun.* ME.
[Anglo-Norman, aphet. from *espirit*, Old French *esperit*, (also mod.) *esprit* from Latin *spiritus* breathing etc. (in Christian use, incorporeal being), from *spirare* breathe. Cf. SPRITE.]
▶ **I 1** The animating or life-giving principle in humans and animals. ME.
2 The immaterial part of a corporeal being, esp. considered as a moral agent; the soul. ME. ▸**b** This as a disembodied and separate entity esp. regarded as surviving after death; a soul. LME. ▸**c** Immaterial substance, as opp. to body or matter. LME.
3 A supernatural, immaterial, rational or intelligent being, usu. regarded as imperceptible to humans but capable of becoming visible at will, as an angel, demon, fairy, etc. Usu. with specifying word. ME.
4 THEOLOGY. (Usu. **S-**.) The divine nature or essential power *of* God, regarded as a creative, animating, or inspiring influence; *spec.* = **Holy Spirit** s.v. HOLY *adjective.* LME.
5 The active power *of* an emotion, attitude, etc., as operating on or in a person; an inclination or impulse *of* a specified kind. LME.
6 a A particular (specified) character or attitude existing in or animating a person or set of people; a person with a specified kind of character or attitude. M16. ▸**b** The attitude or feeling with which something is done or viewed. E17.
7 a The essential character *of* a thing, esp. a place, regarded as exerting an influence. L17. ▸**b** The prevailing tendency or mood *of* a particular period of time. E19. ▸**c** The general intent or true meaning *of* a statement etc. as opp. to its strict verbal interpretation. Cf. LETTER *noun*¹ 5. E19.

> 🕮 **1** SHAKES. *Ant. & Cl.* My spirit is going; I can no more. **2** AV *Luke* 23:46 Into thy hands I commend my spirit. **b** S. LEACOCK Devices by which the spirits now enter into communication with us. R. J. CONLEY He must be apologising to the spirit of the dead animal. **3** T. KENEALLY Jimmie seemed taken over by a bad spirit. H. NORMAN Hermits, ranging from benevolent spirits to . . horrific cannibal giants. A. STEVENS Emilie sat behind him to ward off evil spirits. **4** D. MADDEN God's spirit would descend upon her. *Methodist Recorder* They will have their sins forgiven and receive the Spirit. **5** W. S. CHURCHILL He had built up a spirit of resistance among the townsfolk. C. HILL Charles I had been executed in no spirit of republican doctrinairism. *New Yorker* The spirit of adventure seems to have disappeared . . from modern life. **6a** J. A. FROUDE The money-making spirit was . . driven back. CLIVE JAMES Some of the more adventurous spirits even dared to immerse themselves in the sea. **b** J. G. FARRELL There was an excellent spirit at these games: an air of gaiety. G. F. NEWMAN '. . I'll be completely vindicated.' 'That's the spirit'. P. FITZGERALD She wasn't saying this . . bitterly, and she wanted him to take it in the same spirit. **7a** J. RUSKIN The spirit of the hills is action. G. PRIESTLAND One can't . . maintain that episcopacy is alien to the spirit of Wesley. **b** J. CARTWRIGHT A . . mission to keep alive . . the spirit of the old days. *Art* The 'spirit of the age' is best revealed by its young progressive artists. **c** *Scotsman* It could be . . violated in the spirit even if . . kept in the letter.

▶ **II 8** The immaterial intelligent or sentient part of a person as the seat of action and feeling. Formerly also (usu. in *pl.*), the mind, mental faculties; something in the mind, a thought. ME. ▸**b** In *pl.* The emotional faculties, esp. as liable to be exalted or depressed. LME.
9 a Orig., anger, hostility; lack of humility, undue zeal. Later, courage; assertiveness. ME. ▸**b** *sing.* & in *pl.* Liveliness, vivacity, dash. L17.

> 🕮 **8** W. COWPER The cordial thought her spirit cheer'd. LD MACAULAY The slaughter . . had broken the spirit of the army. ALDOUS HUXLEY The spirit is willing, but the flesh is weak. **b** D. EDEN Her spirits would . . sink lower and lower. S. RUSHDIE Whistling . . showed that he was keeping his spirits up. P. DALLY Opium was essential to Elizabeth's tranquillity and evenness of spirits. **9a** G. STEIN He is just the way . . his mother wants him, . . got no spirit in him. **b** J. RUSKIN She danced . . with . . spirit, sweetness, and self-forgetfulness. R. W. EMERSON The cramping influence of a hard formalist on a young child in repressing his spirits and courage.

▶ **III 10** A wind; a breath of wind or air. Later *poet.* & passing into other senses. ME. ▸†**b** The action of breathing; a breath. LME–L17. ▸**c** GRAMMAR. An aspirate, a breathing; a conventional mark indicating this. M16.
11 a In *pl.* & †*sing.* A subtle highly refined substance or fluid formerly supposed to permeate and animate the blood and chief organs of the body. Freq. with specifying word, as ***animal spirit(s)***, ***natural spirit(s)***, ***vital spirit(s)***. *arch.* LME. ▸**b** *fig.* In *pl.* Vital power or energy. *arch.* LME. ▸†**c** An intangible element in a material thing. E17–E18.
▶ **IV** †**12** ALCHEMY. Each of four substances: sulphur, orpiment, sal ammoniac, and (esp.) mercury. Also, any volatile substance or vapour. LME–E18.
13 In *pl.* & *sing.* ▸**a** A liquid essence extracted from some substance, esp. by distillation; a solution in alcohol *of* a specified substance. E17. ▸**b** Without article: liquid such as is obtained by distillation, esp. of an alcoholic nature. E17. ▸**c** Strong distilled alcoholic liquor for drinking. L17. ▸**d** DYEING. A mordant, *esp.* one containing tin. Now *rare* or *obsolete.* L19.

> 🕮 **13a** ***spirit of hartshorn***, ***spirit of Mindererus***, ***spirit of turpentine***, etc. ***spirits of hartshorn***, ***spirits of Mindererus***, ***spirits of turpentine***, etc. **c** P. V. PRICE Old . . casks . . in which the spirit was matured. *New Statesman* Wine and spirit drinking is rising.

Phrases: ***animal spirits***: see ANIMAL *adjective.* ***astral spirits***: see ASTRAL *adjective* 1. **baptism in the Spirit**, **baptism of the Spirit** a religious experience subsequent to conversion to Christianity, freq. evidenced by speaking in tongues. **enter into the spirit (of)** act in accordance with the prevailing (cheerful) mood (of an event etc.); participate enthusiastically (in). ***familiar spirit***: see FAMILIAR *adjective* 1. ***flow of spirits***: see FLOW *noun*¹. ***Great Spirit***: see GREAT *adjective.* ***high spirits***: see HIGH *adjective, adverb, & noun.* ***Holy Spirit***: see HOLY *adjective.* ***in letter and in spirit***: see LETTER *noun*¹. **in spirit** (*a*) inwardly, as a presence felt but not seen; (*b*) *arch.* in one's mind or imagination. **in spirits** in a cheerful mood; happy. ***kindred spirit***: see KINDRED *adjective* 1. ***low spirits***: see LOW *adjective*. ***methylated spirit***: see METHYLATE *verb*. ***natural spirit(s)***: see NATURAL *adjective*. **out of spirits** low-spirited. *PUBLIC spirit*. *PYROXYLIC spirit*. ***raise a person's spirits***: see RAISE *verb*. **receive the Spirit** experience religious conversion, esp. as evidenced by speaking in tongues. ***spirit of the staircase***: see STAIRCASE *noun* 1. **spirit of salt, spirits of salt** *arch.* hydrochloric acid. **spirit of wine, spirits of wine** *arch.* purified alcohol. ***surgical spirit***: see SURGICAL *adjective* 1a. **the spirit moves one** one feels inclined (to do something); orig. in Quaker use. *UNCLEAN spirit*. ***vital spirit(s)***: see sense 11a above. ***white spirit***: see WHITE *adjective*.

Comb.: **spirit duplicator**: using an alcoholic solution to reproduce copies from a master sheet; **spirit fresco** a method of fresco-painting in which the colours are ground in a medium containing oil of spike or spirits of turpentine; **spirit gum** a quick-drying solution of gum used esp. for attaching false hair; **spirit-lamp**: burning methylated or other volatile spirits instead of oil; **spirit-level** a slightly bent hermetically-sealed glass tube filled with spirit or other liquid and containing an air-bubble whose position is used to determine horizontality; **spirit-rapper** *colloq.* a person who claims to be able to receive communications from spirits in the form of raps; **spirit-rapping** *colloq.* (a) professed communication from or with spirits in the form of raps; **spirit varnish**: prepared by dissolving a resin in spirit; **spirit-weed** *W. Indies* an eryngo, *Eryngium foetidum*, with a pungent smell, used to revive people having fits; **spirit world** the world of disembodied spirits.

■ **spiritful** *adjective* (*obsolete* exc. *dial.*) (*a*) spirited, lively; †(*b*) having a spiritual character; †(*c*) (of liquor) spirituous: M16. **spiritism** *noun* = SPIRITUALISM 2 M19. **spiritist** *noun & adjective* (*a*) *noun* a spiritualist; (*b*) *adjective* spiritualistic: M19. **spiri'tistic** *adjective* spiritualistic M19. **spiritize** *verb trans.* (*rare*) invest with spirit or spiritual power M17. **spirit-like** *adjective* resembling (that of) a spirit M17.

spirit /ˈspɪrɪt/ *verb trans.* L16.
[from the noun.]
▶ **I 1** Make (the blood, a liquor) more active. *arch.* L16.
2 Invest with spirit, life, vigour, or energy; invest with a particular spirit; animate, encourage, (also foll. by *up*). *arch.* E17. ▸**b** Urge *on* by encouragement. L17. ▸**c** Excite; stir *up*. L17.

> 📖 **2** PATRICK WALKER They were . . fitted and spirited for Trials. H. ROGERS He was further spirited to it by an anonymous letter. R. L. STEVENSON One . . boy . . had to spirit himself up, whenever he came to play. **c** P. EGAN Why . . meet?—to spirit up others to a breach of the peace.

▶ **II †3** Kidnap for transportation to a plantation in the W. Indies or America. M–L17.
4 Convey rapidly and mysteriously or secretly (as) by a spirit or supernatural being. Foll. by *away*, *off*, *out of*, etc. L17.

> 📖 **4** *Times* Fusilier Moody had . . been spirited out of the country. M. FORSTER Browning . . married and secretly spirited her away to Italy.

▶ **III †5** Extract spirit from; distil. *rare*. Only in L17.
6 Treat with a solution of spirits. L19.

†spirital *adjective*. LME.
[Aphet. from Old French *esperital*, *espirital*, or from Late Latin *spiritalis*, from Latin *spiritus*: see SPIRIT *noun*, -AL¹.]
1 = SPIRITUAL *adjective* 2. Only in LME.
2 Of the nature of spirit; of or pertaining to the spirit in contrast to the body or matter. L16–E18.

spirited /ˈspɪrɪtɪd/ *adjective*. L16.
[from SPIRIT *noun* + -ED².]
†1 Impregnated with spirit or active properties. L16–L17.
2 Full of spirit or animation; lively, animated; vigorous, energetic. L16.
3 Having a spirit or spirits of a specified kind. L16.
4 Occupied or possessed by a (good or evil) spirit. *rare*. M17.

> 📖 **2** H. F. TOZER A man . . seated on a spirited charger. P. PEARCE The geese had goslings . . and . . fought a spirited rearguard action in their defence. M. MEYER A spirited production . . of Büchner's *Danton's Death*. **3 *high-spirited, low-spirited, mean-spirited, poor-spirited, public-spirited***, etc.

■ **spiritedly** *adverb* L18. **spiritedness** *noun* †(*a*) *rare* a spiritual state or condition; (*b*) the quality of being spirited, liveliness: L17.

spiriting /ˈspɪrɪtɪŋ/ *noun*. M18.
[from SPIRIT *noun*, *verb*: see -ING¹.]
1 The activity or work of a spirit. M18.
2 a A solution of spirits used in the manufacture of carpets etc. L19. ▸**b** The application of a spirit as a finishing process in French polishing. M20.

spiritless /ˈspɪrɪtlɪs/ *adjective*. L16.
[from SPIRIT *noun* + -LESS.]
1 Deprived of the spirit or life-giving principle; lifeless. L16.
2 Lacking courage, vigour, or animation; characterized by lack of animation or energy. Also, low-spirited, depressed, dejected. L16.

> 📖 **2** GIBBON The infantry was a half-armed spiritless crowd of peasants. F. BURNEY The evening was passed in spiritless conversation.

■ **spiritlessly** *adverb* M17. **spiritlessness** *noun* M17.

spiritous /ˈspɪrɪtəs/ *adjective*. E17.
[from SPIRIT *noun* + -OUS.]
1 Of the nature of a spirit or distilled product; highly refined. E17. ▸**b** Of liquor: alcoholic, *spec.* distilled. L18.
†2 Lively, animated, high-spirited. E17–M18.

spiritual /ˈspɪrɪtʃʊəl, -tjʊəl-/ *adjective & noun*. ME.
[Old & mod. French *spirituel* from Latin *spiritualis*, from *spiritus*: see SPIRIT *noun*, -AL¹.]
▶ **A** *adjective*. **I 1** Of, pertaining to, or affecting the spirit or soul, esp. from a religious aspect. ME. ▸**b** Standing in a relationship to another based on matters of the soul. LME. ▸**c** Of a person: devout, pious; morally good. LME. ▸**d** Of a song, music, etc.: devotional; *spec.* designating or in the style of a Negro spiritual (see NEGRO). LME.
2 Of, pertaining to, or concerned with sacred or religious things, holy, divine, prayerful; of or pertaining to the church or the clergy; ecclesiastical. ME. ▸**†b** Of law: canonical. L15–M17.
3 Pertaining to or consisting of spirit, immaterial. ME. ▸**†b** Of or appropriate to a spirit or immaterial being. *rare* (Milton). Only in M17.
4 Of or pertaining to the intellect; intellectual. M17. ▸**b** Of the mind etc.: highly refined; sensitive; not concerned with material things. Cf. SPIRITUEL. L18. ▸**c** Clever, witty. Cf. SPIRITUEL. E19.
5 Concerned with spirits or supernatural beings. M19.

> 📖 **1** G. SANTAYANA He has no soul, because he feels no need of spiritual things. V. A. DEMANT The field in which spiritual direction is best known . . is . . prayer. *Woman* The spiritual rewards made up for the lack of material rewards. **spiritual healing** faith-healing. ***spiritual home***: see HOME *noun* 4. **b** *Tablet* A letter I wrote . . to my spiritual children. **2 spiritual court** an ecclesiastical court. ***the Lords spiritual***: see LORD *noun*. **3** MILTON Spiritual Creatures walk the Earth Unseen. **4** HENRY FIELDING Platonic affection which is . . purely spiritual.

▶**†II 6** Of or pertaining to breathing; respiratory. LME–L16.
▶ **III 7** Consisting of a spirit or essence; volatile; alcoholic. Now *rare* or *obsolete*. L15.
▶ **B** *noun*. **I †1** (A member of) the clergy. *rare*. LME–L17.
2 †a A spiritual or devout person. Only in M16. ▸**b** ECCLESIASTICAL HISTORY. (**S-**.) A member of a branch of Franciscans which advocated simple attire and strict observance of the rule of poverty. L18.
3 In *pl.* ▸**a** Matters concerning the spirit or soul. L16. ▸**b** Matters concerning religion or the church. Also, ecclesiastical possessions. M17.
4 A spiritual or immaterial thing; spiritual quality; that which is spiritual. M17.
5 = *NEGRO* ***spiritual***. M19.
▶**†II 6** In *pl.* The respiratory organs. LME–E17.
■ **spiritually** *adverb* (*a*) in respect of spiritual things; †(*b*) in a spiritual as opp. to a literal sense; (*c*) *poet.* like a spiritual being: ME. **spiritualness** *noun* the fact, quality, or state of being spiritual, spirituality M16.

spiritualise *verb* var. of SPIRITUALIZE.

spiritualism /ˈspɪrɪtʃʊəlɪz(ə)m, -tjʊəl-/ *noun*. L18.
[from SPIRITUAL *adjective* + -ISM.]
1 PHILOSOPHY. The doctrine that the spirit exists as distinct from matter, or that spirit is the only reality; any philosophical or religious doctrine stressing the importance of spiritual as opp. to material things. L18. ▸**b** Spiritual nature or quality. M19.
2 The belief that the spirits of the dead can communicate with the living, esp. through a medium; the practice of this belief. Cf. SPIRITISM. M19.
3 Belief in the existence and influence of supernatural beings. M19.

spiritualist /ˈspɪrɪtʃʊəlɪst, -tjʊəl-/ *noun & adjective*. M17.
[formed as prec. + -IST.]
▶ **A** *noun*. **1** A person who regards or interprets things from a spiritual point of view; PHILOSOPHY an adherent of spiritualism. M17. ▸**b** ECCLESIASTICAL HISTORY. (**S-**.) = SPIRITUAL *noun* 2b. E18.
2 A believer in or practitioner of spiritualism. M19.
▶ **B** *adjective*. Spiritualistic. M19.
■ **spiritua'listic** *adjective* of or pertaining to spiritualism M19. **spiritua'listically** *adverb* L19.

spirituality /ˌspɪrɪtʃʊˈalɪti, -tjʊ-/ *noun*. LME.
[Old & mod. French *spiritualité* or late Latin *spiritualitas*, from *spiritualis*: see SPIRITUAL, -ITY.]
1 The clergy. Now *arch.* or *Hist.* LME.
2 Ecclesiastical property or revenue held or received in return for spiritual services. *arch.* LME. ▸**b** In *pl.* Ecclesiastical possessions, rights, etc., of a purely spiritual character. Now *Hist.* LME.
3 The quality or condition of being spiritual; regard for spiritual as opp. to material things; *spec.* the study and practice of prayer, esp. as leading to union with God. LME. ▸**b** A spiritual as opp. to a material thing or quality. Formerly *spec.*, a pious remark. L17.
4 The fact or condition of being immaterial. Formerly also, an immaterial being or substance. E17.
†5 The fact of being or containing pure spirit or essence; a volatile state or quality. M–L17.

spiritualize /ˈspɪrɪtʃʊəlʌɪz, -tjʊəl-/ *verb trans.* Also **-ise**. M17.
[from SPIRITUAL *adjective* + -IZE.]
1 Make spiritual; give a spiritual character to; elevate. M17. ▸**b** Attach a spiritual as opp. to a literal meaning to. M17. ▸**c** Give an immaterial appearance to; refine. M19.
2 Invest with the immaterial qualities of a spirit. *rare*. M17.
†3 Change into or reduce to spirit; make volatile or alcoholic. M17–L18.
■ **spirituali'zation** *noun* M17. **spiritualized** *adjective* †(*a*) *rare* containing an infusion of spirits; (*b*) that has been spiritualized: L16. **spiritualizer** *noun* L17.

spiritualty /ˈspɪrɪtʃʊəlti, -tjʊəl-/ *noun*. LME.
[Old French *spiritualté* from late Latin *spiritualitas*: see SPIRITUALITY, -TY¹.]
†1 = SPIRITUALITY 3. LME–L15.
2 †a = SPIRITUALITY 2. LME–E18. ▸**b** In *pl.* = SPIRITUALITY 2b. Now *Hist.* LME.
3 The clergy. Formerly also, a body of clergy. LME.

spirituel /spirityɛl, ˌspɪrɪtjʊˈɛl/ *adjective*. Also **-elle**. L17.
[French: see SPIRITUAL.]
Highly refined and lively; witty.

spirituous /ˈspɪrɪtjʊəs/ *adjective*. L16.
[from Latin *spiritus* SPIRIT *noun* or from French *spiritueux*: see -OUS.]
1 Spirited, lively. Now *rare*. L16.
2 Of the nature of spirit; volatile. Now *rare*. E17.
3 Of or pertaining to spirit or alcohol; containing (much) spirit or alcohol; alcoholic; *spec.* distilled. M17.
†4 = SPIRITUAL *adjective* 3. M17–M18.
3 *spirituous liquor*.
■ **spiritu'osity** *noun* the state or quality of containing spirit, esp. through distillation M17. **spirituousness** *noun* (now *rare*) M17.

spiritus /ˈspɪrɪtʊs/ *noun*. M19.
[Latin = breath, aspiration, spirit.]
1 GREEK GRAMMAR. **a *spiritus lenis***, smooth breathing (see BREATHING 5). M19. ▸**b *spiritus asper***, rough breathing (see BREATHING 5). L19.
2 *spiritus rector* /ˈrɛktɔː/, a ruling or directing spirit. E20.

spirity /ˈspɪrɪti/ *adjective*. Chiefly *dial.* & *colloq.* M17.
[from SPIRIT *noun* + -Y¹.]
1 Full of spirit or animation; spirited. M17.
2 Of the nature of spirit; spirituous. *rare*. E18.

spirketting /ˈspəːkɪtɪŋ/ *noun*. Also ***-eting**. M18.
[Perh. from SPURKET + -ING¹.]
NAUTICAL. The extra thick line of planking fitted inside between the waterways and the ports of a wooden ship for additional strength.

spirling /ˈspəːlɪŋ/ *noun*. Now only *Scot.* LME.
[Middle Low German *spirling*, Middle Dutch *spierling* (Anglo-Latin *sper*, *lingus*, *spir-*). Cf. SPARLING.]
The smelt, *Osmerus eperlanus*.

spiro- /ˈspʌɪrəʊ/ *combining form*. Before a vowel also **spir-**. In sense 2 also **spira-** /ˈspʌɪrə/ and as attrib. adjective **spiro**. L19.
[from Latin *spira*, Greek *speira* SPIRE *noun*³: see -O-.]
1 Having or pertaining to a spiral shape.
2 CHEMISTRY. Forming names of organic compounds whose molecular structure includes two rings having a single atom (usu. of carbon or nitrogen) in common. Cf. SPIRANE.
■ **spiro'lactone** *noun* (CHEMISTRY & PHARMACOLOGY) a spirane in which one of the rings is a lactone; *spec.* any of the series of steroid derivatives to which spironolactone belongs: M20. **spiroplasma** *noun* (BIOLOGY) any of a group of pathogenic prokaryotes lacking a cell wall and related to the mycoplasmas, distinguished by helical structure and rotatory movement L20.

spirochaete /ˈspʌɪrə(ʊ)kiːt/ *noun*. Also **-chete**. L19.
[from SPIRO- + mod. Latin CHAETA.]
A bacterium of a type having a highly twisted spiral form; *spec.* any of the order Spirochaetales, comprising motile non-spore-forming flexible micro-organisms including the pathogens of syphilis and other diseases.
■ **spiro'chaetal** *adjective* that is a spirochaete; caused by spirochaetes: E20. **spirochaeti'cidal** *adjective* lethal to spirochaetes E20. **spiro'chaeticide** *noun* a spirochaeticidal substance E20. **spirochae'tosis** *noun*, pl. **-toses** /-ˈtəʊsiːz/, infection with, or a disease caused by, spirochaetes E20.

spirograph /ˈspʌɪrəɡrɑːf/ *noun*. L19.
[formed as SPIROMETER: see -GRAPH.]
MEDICINE. An instrument which provides a continuous tracing of the movements of the lungs during respiration.
■ **spirogram** *noun* the tracing produced by a spirograph M20. **spiro'graphic** *adjective* pertaining to or observed by means of a spirograph M20. **spiro'graphically** *adverb* M20. **spi'rography** *noun* the use of a spirograph M20.

spirogyra /spʌɪrəˈdʒʌɪrə/ *noun.* L19.
[mod. Latin (see below), formed as SPIRO- + Greek *gura*, *guros* round.]
Any of various minute green filamentous freshwater algae constituting the genus *Spirogyra*.

spiroid /ˈspʌɪrɔɪd/ *adjective.* M19.
[from SPIRAL *adjective*¹ + -OID.]
More or less spiral in form.
■ Also **spiroidal** /spʌɪˈrɔɪd(ə)l/ *adjective* E20.

spirometer /spʌɪˈrɒmɪtə/ *noun.* M19.
[from Latin *spirare* breathe + -OMETER.]
MEDICINE. An instrument for measuring the volume of inhaled or exhaled air. Also called ***pulmometer***.
■ **spiroˈmetric**, **spiroˈmetrical** *adjectives* pertaining to (the use of) a spirometer L19. **spiˈrometry** *noun* measurement of lung-capacity with a spirometer M19.

spironolactone /spʌɪrənəˈlaktəʊn/ *noun.* M20.
[from *spirolactone* (see SPIRO-) with inserted -ON(E).]
PHARMACOLOGY. A steroid spirolactone derivative, $C_{24}H_{32}O_4S$, which is an aldosterone antagonist promoting sodium excretion, used esp. to treat certain types of oedema and hypertension.

†**spirt** *noun*¹. LME–L18.
[Reduced form of SPIRIT *noun*.]
The spirit of a person or thing; a supernatural spirit.

spirt /spəːt/ *noun*². Now *dial.* M17.
[Metathetic var.]
= SPRIT *noun*².

spirt *noun*³ see SPURT *noun*.

spirt /spəːt/ *verb*¹ *intrans.* Now *dial.* L16.
[Metathetic alt.]
= SPRIT *verb*¹.

spirt *verb*² see SPURT *verb*.

spirtle *noun*¹ var. of SPURTLE *noun*¹.

spirtle *verb & noun*² see SPURTLE *verb & noun*².

spirula /ˈspʌɪrjʊlə/ *noun.* *rare* exc. as mod. Latin genus name. M19.
[mod. Latin (see below), dim. of Latin *spira* SPIRE *noun*³.]
ZOOLOGY. (The shell of) a cephalopod of the genus *Spirula* having a white flat open spiral shell embedded in the body.

spirulina /spɪrʊˈlʌɪnə, spʌɪr-/ *noun.* L20.
[mod. Latin genus name (see below), formed as prec. + *-ina* -INA².]
An alga of the genus *Spirulina*, which forms tangled masses in warm alkaline lakes in Africa and Central and South America. Also, the substance of these growths, which when dried is prepared as a food or food additive.

spiry /ˈspʌɪri/ *adjective*¹. E17.
[from SPIRE *noun*¹ + -Y¹.]
1 Esp. of a plant: having the form of a spire; tapering to a point. Also *loosely*, slender, tall. E17. ▸**b** *fig.* Highly distinguished. *slang. rare.* E19.
2 Of a place: having many buildings with spires. M18.

spiry /ˈspʌɪri/ *adjective*². *poet.* L17.
[from SPIRE *noun*³ + -Y¹.]
Spiralling, coiling.

spiss /spɪs/ *adjective. arch.* LME.
[Latin *spissus*.]
Thick, dense, compact.

spissated /spɪˈseɪtɪd/ *adjective. rare.* E18.
[from Latin *spissatus* pa. pple of *spissare* thicken, formed as prec.: see -ED¹.]
Thickened.

spissitude /ˈspɪsɪtjuːd/ *noun.* LME.
[Latin *spissitudo*, formed as SPISS: see -TUDE.]
Density, thickness, compactness.

spit /spɪt/ *noun*¹.
[Old English *spitu* = Middle Low German, Middle Dutch *spit*, *spet* (Dutch *spit*), Old High German *spiz* (German *Spiess*), from West Germanic.]
1 A slender pointed rod on which meat is skewered and set over a fire or next to a grill etc. for roasting. Also ***roasting-spit***. OE.
2 *gen.* Any pointed rod or stick; a skewer, a broach; *spec.* (*a*) *joc. arch. derog.* a sword; (*b*) PRINTING the axle of the carriage wheels of a hand-press; (*c*) (now *Scot. & dial.*) a stick for hanging up fish to dry. ME.
3 *transf.* †**a** = OBELUS. LME–E17. ▸**b** A small projecting point of land; a narrow reef or sandbank extending from the shore. L15.

📖 **1** V. S. REID Wild hogs turn on spits all day. *Which?* Five of the cookers had roasting spits. **beat with the spit** (now *dial.*) treat harshly, esp. without cause. **3b** *US Air* Along its grassy spit, you're . . likely to find artists at work on their seascapes.

Comb.: **spit dog** a firedog with a hook on its upright for supporting a spit; **spit-jack** a mechanical device for rotating a spit; **spit-roast** *verb trans.* cook on a spit.

spit /spɪt/ *noun*². ME.
[from SPIT *verb*¹.]
1 Saliva; *esp.* saliva, or a mixture of saliva and other matter, when ejected from the mouth; a clot of this. ME.
2 The action or an act of spitting. M17.
3 The exact likeness or counterpart *of* a person or thing. Freq. in ***the dead spit of***, ***the very spit of***. *colloq.* E19.
4 A light drop or shower of rain or snow. M19.

📖 **1** R. DAHL It's your spit that makes a Gobstopper change colour. **2** C. JOHNSTON To hope that I should come off with a spit in the face . . at worst. **3** J. R. ACKERLEY He's the spit of what Johnny was as a baby. **4** W. HORWOOD Wharfe felt the first spits of rain.

Phrases etc.: **a spit and a stride** a very short distance. ***cuckoo-spit***: see CUCKOO *noun*. ***frog-spit***: see FROG *noun*¹. **go for the big spit** *Austral. slang* vomit. **spit and image** = sense 3 above; cf. ***spit image*** below, ***spitting image*** s.v. SPIT *verb*¹. **spit and polish** the cleaning and polishing duties of a soldier etc.; *transf.* exaggerated neatness or smartness. **spit and sawdust** *noun & adjective* (*arch.*) (*a*) *noun* (the floor covering of) the general bar of a public house; (*b*) *adjective* (of a public house etc.) having such a covering.
Comb.: **spit-box** *colloq.* a spittoon; **spit-curl** a curl of hair stuck on to the forehead, cheek, etc., with saliva; **spit image** = sense 3 above; cf. ***spit and image*** above, ***spitting image*** s.v. SPIT *verb*¹; **spit-insect** a frog-hopper, a spittle-bug.
■ **spitty** *adjective* (*a*) resembling spit; (*b*) spitting, inclined to spit: M18.

spit /spɪt/ *noun*³. Pl. **-s**, (sense 1 also) same. E16.
[Middle & mod. Low German & Middle & mod. Dutch, rel. to SPIT *verb*².]
1 A depth of earth etc. equal to the length of the blade of a spade. E16. ▸**b** A layer of earth etc. of this depth. M17.
2 The amount a spade can hold, a spadeful. L17. ▸**b** A row dug in spadefuls. E18.
3 A kind of spade with a concave blade used for draining. *dial.* E19.
■ **spitful** *noun* a spadeful M19.

Spit /spɪt/ *noun*⁴. *colloq.* M20.
[Abbreviation.]
= SPITFIRE *noun* 1b.

spit /spɪt/ *verb*¹. Infl. **-tt-**. Pa. t. & pple **spat** /spat/, **spit**.
[Old English (late Northumbrian) (*ge*)*spittan* = German dial. *spützen*, from imit. base. Cf. SPET *verb*.]
▶ **I** *verb intrans.* **1** Eject saliva forcefully from the mouth; do this as an expression of hatred or contempt; *fig.* scorn, despise. Usu. foll. by *at*, *in*, *on*, etc. OE. ▸**b** Of an animal, esp. a cat: hiss or eject saliva when angry. Also foll. by *at*. M17.
2 *transf.* **a** Of rain etc.: fall lightly. M16. ▸**b** Emit sparks or light quick bursts of fire, hot fat, etc.; sputter. E17. ▸**c** Foll. by *out*. Of a ceramic glaze: blister during firing. E20.

📖 **2** E. WAUGH He . . spat at Miles' friend. *Independent* You can get a fine for smoking or spitting in the wrong places. **b** M. HOCKING The cat spat at her. **2a** S. O'FAOLÁIN I looked at the rain spitting on the dark window. **b** J. G. FARRELL The candle coughed, spat, and went out. *Hot Car* The car spat and coughed badly.

▶ **II** *verb trans.* †**3** Spit at (a person) as a sign of contempt. OE–ME.
4 Eject (saliva, blood, food, etc.) from the mouth with force. Freq. foll. by *out*, *up*. ME. ▸**b** *fig.* Utter or express with vehement anger, malice, etc. Freq. foll. by *out*. LME.
5 *transf.* Emit or throw forcefully in a manner resembling spitting. Freq. foll. by *out*. ME. ▸**b** Lay (eggs or spawn). M19.

📖 **4** B. BAINBRIDGE He . . spat a gob of saliva at the photograph. **b** A. COHEN I . . spat out curses I had forgotten I knew. E. SEGAL She looked fiercely at Rhodes and spat out, 'You are one slimy bastard.' **5** *Time* The computer . . spit out the names of ten people. B. VINE It was a grey day, the low clouds sometimes spitting rain.

Phrases & comb.: **spit blood** (*a*) *colloq.* express vehement anger; rage; (*b*) *slang* (of a spy etc.) fear exposure. **spit chips** *Austral. slang* (*a*) feel acute thirst; (*b*) feel or express extreme anger or vexation. **spit in the eye of**, **spit in the face of** show contempt or scorn for. **spit-out** accidental blistering of a ceramic glaze during firing caused by air bubbles (cf. sense 2c above). **spit-shine** *verb trans.* polish after spitting on. **spit something out** *colloq.* confess or disclose something; say what is on one's mind. **spitting cobra** any of various cobras which can spray venom several feet when threatened; *esp.* (*a*) the black-necked cobra, *Naja nigricollis*, of southern Africa; (*b*) = RINKHALS. **spitting image** *colloq.* the exact likeness or double of another person or thing; cf. ***spit and image***, ***spit image*** s.v. SPIT *noun*². **spitting snake** = ***spitting cobra*** above.
■ **spitting** *noun*¹ (*a*) the action of the verb; ***spitting distance***, a very short distance; (*b*) ejected saliva, spittle; (*c*) (now *dial.*) a light shower of rain: ME.

spit /spɪt/ *verb*². Now *dial.* Infl. **-tt-**. OE.
[Prob. ult. rel. to SPIT *noun*¹. Cf. SPIT *noun*³.]
1 *verb intrans. & trans.* Dig (*up*) with a spade. OE.
2 *verb trans.* Plant with a spade. E17.
■ **spitting** *noun*² (*a*) the action of the verb; (*b*) a small trench dug with a spade: L16.

spit /spɪt/ *verb*³ *trans.* Infl. **-tt-**. ME.
[from SPIT *noun*¹.]
1 Put on a spit; thrust through with a spit; skewer. ME.
2 *transf.* Pierce or transfix with a sharp weapon, esp. a sword; impale *on* or *upon* something sharp. LME.

📖 **2** I. WATSON A bundle of rags was spitted on a nail.

spital /ˈspɪt(ə)l/ *noun.* Also **spittal**. ME.
[Partly respelling of SPITTLE *noun*², partly aphet. from HOSPITAL *noun*.]
1 = HOSPITAL *noun* 2. Now *arch. & poet.* ME.
2 A shelter for travellers. Chiefly *Scot.* E18.

Spitalfields /ˈspɪt(ə)lfiːldz/ *adjective & noun.* E19.
[See below.]
(Designating or made of) woven fabric (esp. silk or velvet) formerly produced in Spitalfields, a district of east London.

spitball /ˈspɪtbɔːl/ *noun & verb.* *N. Amer. colloq.* M19.
[from SPIT *noun*³ + BALL *noun*¹.]
▶ **A** *noun.* **1** = ***spittle-ball*** s.v. SPITTLE *noun*³. M19.
2 BASEBALL. A swerving pitch made with a ball moistened with saliva or sweat. E20.
▶ **B** *verb intrans.* Throw out suggestions for discussion. M19.
■ **spitballer** *noun* a person who throws or pitches spitballs E20.

spitchcock /ˈspɪtʃkɒk/ *noun & verb.* L15.
[Origin unkn. Cf. SPATCHCOCK.]
▶ **A** *noun.* (A dish of) an eel grilled or fried, cut into sections, and dressed with breadcrumbs and herbs. L15.
▶ **B** *verb trans.* Cut into pieces (as if) to make a spitchcock; *fig.* treat harshly or severely. M17.

spitchered /ˈspɪtʃəd/ *adjective. slang* (orig. NAUTICAL). E20.
[from Maltese *spicca* finished, perh. ult. from Italian *spezzare* fragment; assim. to English ppl adjectives in *-ered*: see -ED¹.]
Made inoperative, ruined.

spite /spʌɪt/ *noun.* Also †**spight**. ME.
[Aphet. from (the same root as) DESPITE *noun*.]
†**1** (A) hostile or malevolent action; (a) deliberate injury or insult. ME–M17.
2 Malice, ill will, *esp.* such as arises from offended pride, jealousy, or a desire for revenge. Formerly also, contempt for a person. ME. ▸**b** An instance of this; a grudge. LME.
3 †**a** Matter for regret. *rare.* Only in LME. ▸**b** An annoying or regrettable thing, a disappointment. Long *obsolete* exc. *Scot.* L16. ▸†**c** A feeling of annoyance. L16–L17.

📖 **2** J. GALSWORTHY He . . added, with an uncontrollable burst of spite: 'June's got a temper of her own.' I. MURDOCH Why should he be so troubled by a girl's spite?

Phrases & comb.: **in spite of** in defiance of; notwithstanding. **in spite of oneself** though one would rather have done otherwise. ***in spite of one's teeth***: see TOOTH *noun*. **spite and malice** a form of the card-game Russian Bank. **spite fence** (chiefly *US*) a wall, fence, etc., erected to cause annoyance. **spite of** = ***in spite of*** above. **spitework** *US* = sense 2 above.
■ **spiteless** *adjective* (*rare*) L19. **spitish** *adjective* spiteful, snappish E17.

spite /spʌɪt/ *verb.* Also †**spight**. LME.
[Aphet. from (the same root as) DESPITE *verb*.]
1 *verb trans.* Despise. Long *obsolete* exc. *Scot.* LME.
2 *verb trans.* Treat spitefully or maliciously; annoy or thwart out of spite. M16.
3 *verb trans.* Fill with spite or malice; annoy, offend. Freq. in *pass.* M16.
†**4** *verb intrans.* Be angry or annoyed. Usu. foll. by *at*. M16–M17.

📖 **2** C. STEAD I hung on to spite him. I didn't want him. ***cut off one's nose to spite one's face***: see NOSE *noun*. **3** SIR W. SCOTT One so spited against humanity.

spiteful /ˈspʌɪtfʊl, -f(ə)l/ *adjective & adverb.* LME.
[from SPITE *noun* + -FUL.]
▶ **A** *adjective.* †**1** Expressing contempt or disdain; opprobrious. LME–L17. ▸**b** Worthy of contempt, shameful. LME–L16.
2 Motivated by or expressing spite; malicious, malevolent. LME.
†**3** Distressing; vexing. M16–M17.

📖 **2** M. HOCKING She saw nothing spiteful in his face, . . no real viciousness. A. CRAIG Teachers made spiteful little jokes about me.

▶†**B** *adverb.* Excessively, extremely. LME–M16.
■ **spitefully** *adverb* LME. **spitefulness** *noun* M16.

spitfire /ˈspɪtfʌɪə/ *adjective & noun.* E17.
[from SPIT *verb*¹ + FIRE *noun*.]
▶ **A** *adjective.* That spits fire or sparks; *fig.* fiery-tempered. E17.
▶ **B** *noun.* **1** A thing which emits fire or sparks; *esp.* a cannon. E17. ▸**b** (**S-**.) A British single-engine fighter plane used in the war of 1939–45. M20.
2 A fiery-tempered person or animal. L17.

2 R. RENDELL I love her, temperamental little spitfire that she is.

Comb.: **spitfire-jib** NAUTICAL = ***storm-jib*** s.v. STORM *noun*.

Spithead pheasant /ˈspɪthɛd ˈfɛz(ə)nt/ *noun phr. Nautical slang*. M20.
[from *Spithead*, a strait lying off Portsmouth + PHEASANT.]
A bloater; a kipper.

spitlock /ˈspɪtlɒk/ *verb trans.* M19.
[Prob. from SPIT *noun*³ + LOCK *verb*¹.]
MILITARY. Trace (a line) on the ground with the point of a pickaxe.

spitskop /ˈspɪtskɒp/ *noun. S. Afr.* L19.
[Afrikaans, from Dutch *spits* pointed + KOP.]
A sharp-pointed hill.

spitsticker /ˈspɪtstɪkə/ *noun.* M19.
[Flemish *spitsteker* = German *Spitzstichel*.]
An engraving tool with a rounded convex blade.
■ Also **spitstick** *noun* E20.

spittal *noun* var. of SPITAL.

spitter /ˈspɪtə/ *noun*¹. LME.
[from SPIT *verb*¹ + -ER¹.]
1 A person who spits. LME.
2 = SPITBALL *noun* 2. *US*. E20.

spitter /ˈspɪtə/ *noun*². Now *dial.* E17.
[from SPIT *verb*² + -ER¹.]
1 A spade. E17.
2 A person who uses a spade. M17.

spittle /ˈspɪt(ə)l/ *noun*¹. Now *dial.* LOE.
[Rel. to SPIT *noun*³, *verb*².]
1 A spade, *esp.* a small one. LOE.
2 A hoe; a scraper. M19.
3 A baker's shovel; a peel. M19.
Comb.: **spittle-staff** a long-handled spade or hoe.

†**spittle** *noun*². ME–M19.
[Aphet. from HOSPITAL *noun*, after words in *-el*, *-le*.]
= SPITAL 1; an almshouse. Also ***spittle house***.
rob the spittle profit in a particularly mean manner.

spittle /ˈspɪt(ə)l/ *noun*³. L15.
[Alt. of SPATTLE *noun*¹, by assoc. with SPIT *noun*².]
1 Saliva. L15. ▸**b** A quantity of saliva spat out at one time; *fig.* a worthless thing. *Scot.* E18.
2 A frothy secretion produced by an insect; *esp.* = ***cuckoo-spit***. E19.

1 P. BAILEY They backed away .. to avoid the spittle that cascaded from him whenever he spoke.

Comb.: **spittle-ball** a ball of chewed paper moistened with saliva for use as a missile; **spittle-bug** = *froghopper* s.v. FROG *noun*¹; *esp.* a larva of such an insect.
■ **spittled** *adjective* covered with spittle E20. **spittly** *adjective* containing or covered with spittle E17.

spittle /ˈspɪt(ə)l/ *verb*¹ *intrans. rare.* ME.
[Alt. of SPATTLE *verb*¹, by assoc. with SPIT *verb*¹; later from SPITTLE *noun*³.]
Eject spittle; spit.

spittle /spɪt(ə)l/ *verb*² *trans.* Now *dial.* E18.
[from SPITTLE *noun*¹.]
Dig or pare (ground) with a small spade. Also foll. by *in*.

spittoon /spɪˈtuːn/ *noun.* E19.
[from SPIT *verb*¹ + -OON.]
A vessel for spitting into, usu. round and shallow and sometimes with a funnel-shaped cover.

Spitz /spɪts/ *noun.* M19.
[German (also *Spitzhund*), special use of *spitz* pointed, peaked.]
(A dog of) a thick-coated breed with pointed muzzle, pricked ears, and a tail curling over the back; *esp.* a Pomeranian. Also ***Spitz dog***.
■ **spitzy** *adjective* characteristic of or resembling (that of) a Spitz; pointed: M20.

Spitzenberg /ˈspɪts(ə)nbəːg/ *noun.* Also **-burg**. L18.
[Origin unkn.]
Any of several N. American varieties of apple with red and yellow skins.

Spitzflöte /ˈspɪtsflɔːtə/ *noun.* M19.
[German, from *spitz* pointed + *flöte* flute.]
MUSIC. An organ-stop of the gemshorn type, with a tone resembling a flute's.

spiv /spɪv/ *noun & verb. colloq.* M20.
[Origin uncertain: perh. from SPIFF *verb*, SPIFFY *adjective*.]
▶ **A** *noun.* A man who makes a living by dishonest or unscrupulous dealings, *esp.* one who dresses in a flashy manner. M20.
▶ **B** *verb.* Infl. **-vv-**.
1 *verb intrans.* Make one's living as such a person. M20.
2 *verb trans.* Spruce (oneself) *up*. M20.

1 *Times* A land fit for bookies to spiv in. **2** B. W. ALDISS We spivved ourselves up, put on clean shirts.

■ **spivvery** *noun* behaviour characteristic of a spiv; the state of being a spiv: M20. **spivvish**, **spivvy** *adjectives* resembling or characteristic of a spiv M20.

splacknuck /ˈsplaknʌk/ *noun.* E18.
[Invented name.]
An imaginary animal of Brobdingnag in Swift's *Gulliver's Travels*; *transf.* a strange animal or person.

splake /spleɪk/ *noun. N. Amer.* M20.
[Blend of SPECKLED and LAKE *noun*².]
A hybrid trout produced by crossing the N. American lake trout, *Salvelinus namaycush*, and the speckled trout, *Salvelinus fontinalis*.

splanchnic /ˈsplaŋknɪk/ *adjective & noun.* L17.
[mod. Latin *splanchnicus* from Greek *splagkhnikos*, from *splagkhna* entrails: see -IC.]
ANATOMY. ▶ **A** *adjective.* Pertaining to or affecting the viscera, esp. the intestines and their associated blood-vessels; occupied by the viscera; *spec.* designating nerves of the sympathetic system which serve the viscera and major blood-vessels. L17.
▶ **B** *noun.* A splanchnic nerve. Usu. in *pl.* M19.

splanchno- /ˈsplaŋknəʊ/ *combining form.*
[from Greek *splagkhna* (see prec.) + -O-.]
ANATOMY & MEDICINE. Pertaining to the viscera and —.
■ **splanchnoˈcranial** *adjective* of or pertaining to the splanchnocranium L20. **splanchnoˈcranium** *noun* the part of the head, notably the lower jaw, derived from visceral arch elements E20. **splanchnoˈmegaly** *noun* (MEDICINE) an enlarged condition of the abdominal organs E20. **splanchnopleure** *noun* [Greek *pleura* side] EMBRYOLOGY a layer of tissue in a vertebrate embryo comprising the endoderm and the inner layer of mesoderm, and giving rise to the gut and lungs and the yolk sac (opp. SOMATOPLEURE) L19. **splanchnoˈpleuric** *adjective* (EMBRYOLOGY) of or pertaining to the splanchnopleure E20.

splanchnology /splaŋkˈnɒlədʒi/ *noun.* E18.
[from prec. + -LOGY.]
1 The branch of anatomy that deals with the viscera. E18.
2 (The structure and arrangement of) the viscera. M19.
■ **splanchnoˈlogical** *adjective* L19. **splanchnologist** *noun* E18.

splash /splaʃ/ *noun*¹ & *adverb.* M18.
[from SPLASH *verb*¹.]
▶ **A** *noun.* **1** A quantity of liquid dashed against or dropped on a surface. M18. ▸**b** An irregular area of shattered fragments; *spec.* (*sing.* & in *pl.*) fragments from exploded bullets. M19. ▸**c** A body of water suddenly released to carry down logs. *N. Amer.* L19. ▸**d** A small quantity of liquid as a drink; *esp.* a small amount of soda water etc. added to spirits. E20.
2 The action or an act of forcefully striking the surface of a liquid, esp. water; the noisy impact of a liquid against a surface; the sound produced by this. E19. ▸**b** MEDICINE. A sound produced by a mixture of air and liquid in the stomach or other body cavity when it is sharply displaced. Also ***splash sound***. L19.
3 A striking or ostentatious display or effect; an extravagant event etc. to attract publicity. E19. ▸**b** A prominent newspaper headline or feature; a dramatic or sensational news story. *colloq.* E20.
4 A daub or patch of colour or light; *esp.* a patch on an animal's coat. M19.
5 Amphetamine tablets. *US slang.* M20.

1 *Which?* Oven linings which vaporise splashes .. keep the oven clean. **b** K. KESEY The .. splash of broken glass all over her desk. **d** *Rolling Stone* A double vodka with a splash of tonic. **2** TENNYSON The splash and stir of fountains. C. MUNGOSHI The splash of a kingfisher as it flew away, fish in beak. **3** *Nature* The newly formed .. Association started .. with a suitably large splash. **cut a splash**, **make a splash** make a strong impression, attract much attention, esp. by extravagance. **b** *Observer* The .. attack on Mr Scargill was published as a front-page 'splash'. *attrib.*: *Independent* The first issue .. had a splash story on the .. bid. **4** M. DAS The sun had set .. with an unusually large splash of vermilion.

▶ **B** *adverb.* With or as with a splash. L18.

splash /splaʃ/ *noun*². M18.
[Alt., prob. by assoc. with prec. and next.]
= PLASH *noun*¹.

splash /splaʃ/ *verb*¹. E18.
[Expressive alt. of PLASH *verb*².]
1 *verb trans.* Dash liquid against (deliberately or inadvertently) in an irregular or spasmodic way; make wet or dirty by this action. E18. ▸**b** *transf.* Mark with irregular patches of colour or light. Chiefly as ***splashed*** *ppl adjective*. M19.
2 *verb trans.* & *intrans.* Cause (liquid) to spill, scatter, or fly about, esp. by sudden movement or agitation. Also, make (one's way) with this effect. E18. ▸**b** *verb intrans.* Foll. by *down*. Of a spacecraft: alight on the sea after flight. M20.
3 *verb intrans.* Of a liquid: scatter or fly about in some quantity, esp. because of sudden movement or agitation. M18.
4 *verb trans.* Throw into or move forcefully in liquid, so as to cause splashing. L19.
5 *fig.* **a** *verb trans.* Display (a newspaper story etc.) prominently or sensationally. *colloq.* M20. ▸**b** *verb trans.* & *intrans.* Spend (money) extravagantly or ostentatiously. Freq. foll. by *out*. *colloq.* M20.

1 E. FIGES She poured water into the bowl and began to splash her face. M. FORSTER Wilson was splashed by a .. cab going through a puddle. **2** S. RADLEY He .. splashed some water on his double whisky. R. K. NARAYAN We splashed about in the water. R. OWEN I was splashing through vast puddles of muddy water. **3** B. W. ALDISS Water gushes forth, splashing everywhere. **4** J. A. FROUDE Splashing their oars, and making as much noise as possible. **5** G. ADAIR The Langlois affair .. had been splashed over the front page. **b** M. AMIS You have to splash out big for everything over here. *Soccer Special* Venables has .. splashed out .. £6 million on new players.

Comb.: **splashback** a panel behind a sink, cooker, etc., to protect the wall from splashes; **splashboard** (*a*) a screen protecting the driver of a horse-drawn vehicle from splashes; (*b*) = ***splashback*** above; (*c*) NAUTICAL a screen above the deck-line of a vessel; **splash cymbal** a small light cymbal; **splash-dash** *adverb* headlong; **splashdown** the alighting of a spacecraft on the sea; **splashguard** a protective guard against splashes, a mudguard; **splash lubrication**: in which oil is distributed throughout an engine in the form of drops initially splashed from a reservoir by the working of certain moving parts; **splash-net** *noun & verb intrans.* (use) a small fishing net; **splash party** *US*: at which guests engage in swimming or water sports; **splashplate** = ***splashback*** above; **splash pool** a shallow paddling pool for children; **splash-proof** *adjective* impervious to splashes; **splash-work** spatter-work; **splash zone** an area adjoining the sea etc. that is continually splashed by water.
■ **splasher** *noun* a splashguard, a splashboard; *US* a protective piece of cloth etc. formerly hung behind a washstand: M19.

splash /splaʃ/ *verb*² *trans.* Chiefly *dial.* E19.
[Alt. of PLASH *verb*¹.]
Pleach (a hedge). Freq. as ***splashed*** *ppl adjective*.

splashy /ˈsplaʃi/ *adjective*¹. E18.
[Alt.]
= PLASHY *adjective*¹.

splashy /ˈsplaʃi/ *adjective*². M19.
[from SPLASH *noun*¹, *verb*¹ + -Y¹.]
1 That splashes; *esp.* (of rain) falling in splashes. M19.
2 Of a sound: resembling a splash. M19.
3 Attracting attention; ostentatious; sensational. M19.
4 Irregular, spasmodic. L19.
■ **splashily** *adverb* L19. **splashiness** *noun* (*rare*) E18.

splat /splat/ *noun*¹. M19.
[from SPLAT *verb*¹.]
A flat piece of wood forming the centre of a chair-back.

splat /splat/ *noun*². M20.
[from SPLAT *verb*².]
1 A sharp slapping or splashing sound. *colloq.* M20.
2 METALLURGY. A thin localized film of metal produced in splat-cooling. M20.

1 *Times* There was .. a loud splat, and a tomato was all over .. his suit.

Comb.: **splat-cool** *verb trans.* (METALLURGY) rapidly cool molten metal by propelling droplets of it in a shock wave against a (usu. rotating) metal surface; **splat-quench** *verb trans.* = ***splat-cool***.

splat /splat/ *verb*¹. Infl. **-tt-**. LME.
[Rel. to SPLET *verb*, SPLIT *verb*.]
1 *verb trans.* Cut up, split open. Later only *spec.*, split open (a pike) before cooking. Long *rare* or *obsolete*. LME.
†**2** *verb intrans.* Spread out, extend. *rare*. LME–E17.

splat /splat/ *adverb & verb*². *colloq.* L19.
[Shortening of SPLATTER *verb*.]
▶ **A** *adverb.* With a splat. Also as *interjection*. L19.

A. S. BYATT Simon .. dropped .. ice-cubes splat into his drink. J. O'FAOLAIN Suppose he were to push me now? Over that bannister? Splat!

▶ **B** *verb.* Infl. **-tt-**.
1 *verb intrans.* Hit a surface with a splat. E20.
2 *verb trans.* METALLURGY. Subject to splat-cooling. M20.

1 S. BELLOW Snowballs .. splatted on the black trunks.

splatch /splatʃ/ *noun & verb.* Now *Scot.* & *US*. M17.
[App. imit. Cf. SPLOTCH.]
▶ **A** *noun.* A large splash or spatter; a blot, a patch. M17.
▶ **B** *verb trans.* Splash, spatter. E19.
■ **splatchy** *adjective* spattered; patchy, blotched: E18.

splatter /ˈsplatə/ *verb & noun.* Chiefly *Scot.*, *dial.*, & *N. Amer.* L18.
[Imit.]
▶ **A** *verb.* **1** *verb intrans.* Splash noisily. L18.
2 *verb trans.* Cause to splatter; blurt *out*. L18.
3 *verb trans.* Make wet or dirty by splashing. (Foll. by *with*.) E19.
4 *verb trans.* Beat, batter. L19.
▶ **B** *noun.* **1** A heavy or loud splash. Also, a rattling noise, a clatter. E19.
2 A scattered arrangement; a sprinkling. L19.
3 A genre of films featuring the graphic depiction of gory violence and gruesome death; sensationalized violence depicted in such films. Cf. ***splatterpunk*** below. Freq. *attrib. colloq.* L20.
Comb.: **splatterdash** (*a*) *rare* = SPATTERDASH; (*b*) *Scot.* & *dial.* (an) uproar, (a) commotion; **splatterdock** *US* = ***spatterdock*** s.v.

SPATTER *noun*; **splatterpunk** a genre of fiction, cinema, etc., characterized by the explicit description of horrific, violent, or pornographic scenes.

splatter-faced /ˈsplatəfeɪst/ *adjective*. Now *dial.* E18.
[Alt.]
= *platter-faced* s.v. PLATTER *noun*.

splay /spleɪ/ *noun*. E16.
[from SPLAY *verb*¹.]
1 ARCHITECTURE. A surface set at an oblique angle to another; *esp.* a splayed or bevelled window, doorway, etc. Also, the degree of bevel or slant of a surface. E16.
2 A tapered widening of a road at an intersection to increase visibility. M20.

splay /spleɪ/ *verb*¹. ME.
[Aphet. from DISPLAY *verb*.]
†**1 a** *verb trans.* Unfurl, unfold to view. ME–L16. ▸**b** *verb intrans.* Appear; show oneself. LME–E16.
2 a *verb trans.* Spread *out*, esp. widely or awkwardly; expand, extend. Formerly also, expose to view, display. Freq. as ***splayed*** *ppl adjective*. LME. ▸†**b** *verb trans.* = DISPLAY *verb* 2. Chiefly as ***splayed*** *ppl adjective*. LME–M17. ▸**c** *verb intrans.* Spread out widely or awkwardly. M19.
3 a *verb trans.* Bevel, slant; *spec.* construct (a window, doorway, etc.) so as to be wider on one side of the wall than the other. L16. ▸**b** *verb intrans.* Move or lie at an oblique angle; slant. E18.

> **2a** E. BOWEN He splayed his hands out on the . . chair-arms. B. BAINBRIDGE Her hands over her mouth . . laughter spilled from her splayed fingers. **c** W. GOLDING Stems that splayed out in branches to support the roof.

Comb.: **splay-legged** *adjective* having legs wide apart; **splay-mouthed** *adjective* (now *rare* or *obsolete*) having a wide or wry mouth.

splay /spleɪ/ *verb*² *trans*. Now *dial.* E17.
[Alt.]
= SPAY.

splay /spleɪ/ *adverb & adjective*. M18.
[Back-form. from SPLAY-FOOTED.]
▸**A** *adverb*. *rare*.
1 = SPLAY-FOOT *adverb*. M18.
2 At an oblique angle; at a slant. E19.
▸**B** *adjective*. Oblique, slanted; awry. L19.
splay fault GEOLOGY a subsidiary fault diverging at an acute angle from a larger dislocation.

splay-foot /spleɪˈfʊt/ *noun & adverb*. Pl. **-feet** /-ˈfiːt/. M16.
[from SPLAY *verb*¹ + FOOT *noun*.]
▸**A** *noun*. A broad flat foot, *esp.* one turned outwards. M16.
▸**B** *adverb*. In a splay-footed manner. E17.
■ **splay-footed** *adjective* (*a*) having splay-feet; (*b*) *fig.* clumsy, awkward, sprawling: M16.

spleen /spliːn/ *noun & verb*. ME.
[Aphet. from Old French *esplen* from Latin *splen* from Greek *splēn*, prob. rel. to *splagkhnon* (see SPLANCHNIC), Latin *lien*, Sanskrit *plīhán*.]
▸**A** *noun*. **1** ANATOMY. An abdominal organ found in most vertebrates which serves as a reservoir for blood, and in humans is an ovoid structure situated on the left side below the stomach and forming part of the immune system. Also called ***lien***, ***milt***. ME. ▸†**b** *spec.* This organ regarded as (*a*) the seat of melancholy or moroseness (cf. sense 6 below); (*b*) the seat of passionate laughter or mirth. LME–M17.
†**2** Merriment, mirth; delight. *rare* (Shakes.). Only in L16.
†**3** (A) sudden impulse; (a) caprice. L16–E17.
†**4 a** Proud temper, passion; spirit, courage. L16–E17. ▸**b** Impetuosity, eagerness. *rare* (Shakes.). Only in L16.
5 a A fit of temper; a passion. *arch.* L16. ▸**b** Violent ill temper, spite; irritability, peevishness. Now chiefly in ***a fit of spleen***, ***vent one's spleen***. L16. ▸†**c** An instance of this; a grudge, a spite. E17–E18.
6 Extreme lowness or depression of spirits; moroseness, melancholy (cf. sense 1b above). *arch.* M17.

> **5b** D. HOGAN Mouthing spleen about the . . working-class cause. **6** C. CONNOLLY To read aloud . . Paradise Lost is the surest panacea for the spleen.

▸**B** *verb*. †**1** *verb trans*. **a** Regard with ill humour; bear a grudge towards. Only in 17. ▸**b** Make angry or ill-tempered. L17–E19.
2 *verb intrans*. Become angry or ill-tempered. *US*. L19.

> **2** H. L. WILSON I spleened against some of his ways.

Comb.: **spleen index**, **spleen rate** MEDICINE the proportion of the population having enlarged spleens (as determined by palpation), esp. as an indicator of the incidence of malaria; †**spleen-stone** a green stone formerly supposed to cure disorders of the spleen; **spleenwort** any of various small ferns of the genus *Asplenium* or the family Aspleniaceae; orig. *spec.* the rustyback fern, *Ceterach officinarum*.
■ **spleenful** *adjective* passionate; irritable, peevish: L16. **spleenish** *adjective* †(*a*) apt to disorder the spleen; (*b*) (now *rare*) somewhat splenetic: L16. **spleenless** *adjective* (*rare*) LME. **spleeny** *adjective* (now chiefly *Scot. & dial.*) spleenful, splenetic E17.

spleet /spliːt/ *verb & noun*. Now *Scot.* E17.
[Middle Dutch *spleet*, *splete* (Dutch *spleet*), or Middle & mod. Low German *splete*, Northern Frisian *splēt*; rel. to SPLIT *verb*.]
▸**A** *verb trans. & intrans.* Split. E17.
▸**B** *noun*. A small strip of split wood; a splinter, a chip. E17.

splen- *combining form* see SPLENO-.

†**splenatic** *adjective*. E17.
[medieval Latin *splenaticus* var. of late Latin *spleneticus* SPLENETIC: see -IC.]
1 Seated in the spleen. Only in E17.
2 Irritable, ill-tempered; caused by irritation or ill humour. M17–E18.

†**splenative** *adjective*. L16–M17.
[Irreg. formed as prec.: see -IVE. Cf. SPLENETIVE.]
Irritable; ill-tempered.

> SHAKES. *Haml.* I am not splenative and rash.

splendacious /splɛnˈdeɪʃəs/ *adjective*. M19.
[Fanciful from SPLEND(ID + -ACIOUS.]
Extremely splendid; magnificent.

splendent /ˈsplɛnd(ə)nt/ *adjective*. Now *formal*. L15.
[Latin *splendent-*, *-dens* pres. pple of *splendere* be bright, shine: see -ENT.]
1 Shining brightly or brilliantly. L15. ▸**b** Gleaming, lustrous; *fig.* magnificent, splendid. M16.
2 Pre-eminently beautiful or grand. E16.

splendid /ˈsplɛndɪd/ *adjective*. E17.
[French *splendide* or Latin *splendidus*, from *splendere*: see prec., -ID¹.]
1 Sumptuous, magnificent, grand, gorgeous; (of a person) living in a grand style. E17.
2 Of light or colour: brilliant, extremely bright. *rare*. M17.
3 Of a person: illustrious, distinguished. Long *rare* or *obsolete*. M17.
4 Imposing, impressive; dignified. M17.
5 Excellent; very good or fine. M17.

> **1** O. SITWELL The view is splendid . . across the . . Hudson to wooded heights. J. RATHBONE They looked splendid and the sun flashed on their . . accoutrements. G. VIDAL We were assigned splendid apartments in the new palace. A. THWAITE A splendid Victorian pile . . with vast conservatories. **4 splendid isolation** *spec.* (*Hist.*) the period 1890 to 1907 when Britain pursued a policy of diplomatic and commercial non-involvement. **5** T. HARDY I've a splendid fellow to superintend my business. E. M. FORSTER I'm thoroughly happy, and having a splendid time.

■ **splendidly** *adverb* M17. **splendidness** *noun* M17.

splendiferous /splɛnˈdɪf(ə)rəs/ *adjective*. Now *joc. & colloq.* L15.
[In sense 1 from medieval Latin *splendifer* alt. of late Latin *splendorifer*; in sense 2 fanciful formation from SPLENDOUR: see -FEROUS.]
†**1** Full of splendour. L15–M16.
2 Remarkably fine; magnificent. M19.
■ **splendiferously** *adverb* magnificently E20. **splendiferousness** *noun* magnificence M20.

splendour /ˈsplɛndə/ *noun & verb*. Also ***-or**. LME.
[Old & mod. French *splendeur*, *-or* or Latin *splendor*, from *splendere* be bright, shine: see -OUR.]
▸**A** *noun*. **1** Great or dazzling brightness, brilliance. LME.
2 Magnificence; sumptuous or ornate display; impressive or imposing character; a magnificent feature, object, etc. E17.
3 Distinction, eminence, glory. E17.

> **1** SIR W. SCOTT His bright blue eye . . shone with uncommon keenness and splendour. R. L. STEVENSON The sun rises with a different splendour in America. **2** N. HAWTHORNE Gold-laced cocked hats and other splendors. P. CAMPBELL The curtain material was almost royal in its splendour. M. MARRIN The château had been built in . . imitation of Versailles, but all its splendour had long since been lost.

Phrases: ***sun in his splendour***, ***sun in splendour***: see SUN *noun*¹ 7.
▸**B** *verb*. *rare*.
1 *verb intrans.* Move with splendour. M19.
2 *verb trans.* Make splendid. M19.
■ **splendorous** *adjective* full of splendour L16.

splenectomy /splɪˈnɛktəmi/ *noun*. M19.
[from SPLENO- + -ECTOMY.]
Surgical removal of the spleen; an instance of this.
■ **splenectomize** *verb trans.* perform splenectomy on L19.

splenetic /splɪˈnɛtɪk/ *noun & adjective*. LME.
[Late Latin *spleneticus*, from *splen*: see SPLEEN, -ETIC. Cf. SPLENATIC.]
▸**A** *noun*. **1** †**a** A person with a disease of the spleen. LME–E18. ▸**b** A peevish or ill-humoured person. E18.
†**2** A medicine for diseases of the spleen. M17–E18.
▸**B** *adjective*. **1** Of or pertaining to the spleen. M16. ▸†**b** Of a medicine: acting on the spleen. M17–E18.
†**2** Orig., affected with a disease of the spleen. Later, affected with melancholia or hypochondria. M16–M18. ▸**b** Characterized by or tending to cause melancholia. L17–L18.
3 Irritable, peevish, ill-tempered, testy; characterized by or exhibiting ill temper. L16.

> **3** GEO. ELIOT Her hostess who, though not a splenetic or vindictive woman, had her susceptibilities. W. E. GOSSE The poem closes with an outburst of splenetic raillery.

■ †**splenetical** *adjective* = SPLENETIC *adjective* 1 L16–E18. **splenetically** *adverb* L18.

splenetive /ˈsplɛnətɪv/ *adjective*. *rare*. L17.
[Irreg. formed as prec.: see -IVE. Cf. SPLENATIVE.]
= SPLENETIC *adjective* 3.

splenial /ˈspliːnɪəl/ *adjective & noun*. M19.
[from Latin *splenium*, Greek *splēnion* bandage, compress: see -AL¹.]
ANATOMY & ZOOLOGY. ▸**A** *noun*. A splenial bone or process. M19.
▸**B** *adjective*. **1** Resembling a splint; *esp.* designating or pertaining to a bone or bony process extending along the inside of the lower jaw in some lower vertebrates. M19.
2 Of or pertaining to the splenium. L19.

splenic /ˈsplɛnɪk/ *adjective*. E17.
[French *splénique* or Latin *splenicus* from Greek *splēnikos*, from *splēn*: see SPLEEN, -IC.]
1 ANATOMY. Of, pertaining to, or situated in the spleen. E17.
2 MEDICINE. Of a disease: affecting the spleen. M19.
1 splenic flexure the bend of the colon near the spleen. **2 splenic fever** (now *rare*) anthrax.
■ Also †**splenical** *adjective* L17–E19.

spleniculus /splɪˈnɪkjʊləs/ *noun*. Pl. **-li** /-lʌɪ, -liː/. L19.
[mod. Latin, from Latin *splen* spleen: see -I-, -CULE.]
MEDICINE. A detached portion of the spleen, a small accessory spleen.

splenii *noun* pl. of SPLENIUS.

splenisation *noun* var. of SPLENIZATION.

splenitis /splɪˈnʌɪtɪs/ *noun*. M18.
[from SPLEN(O- + -ITIS.]
MEDICINE. Inflammation of the spleen.

splenium /ˈspliːnɪəm/ *noun*. M19.
[Latin: see SPLENIAL.]
ANATOMY. The thick posterior part of the corpus callosum of the brain.

splenius /ˈspliːnɪəs/ *noun*. Pl. **-nii** /-nɪʌɪ/. M18.
[mod. Latin from Greek *splēnion*: see SPLENIAL.]
ANATOMY. A broad muscle in the upper part of the back of the neck, attached to the occipital bone and serving to draw back the head; either of the two portions of this.

splenization /splɛnʌɪˈzeɪʃ(ə)n/ *noun*. Also **-isation**. M19.
[from SPLEN(O- + -IZATION.]
MEDICINE. Conversion into blood-filled tissue resembling that of the spleen; *esp.* the diseased condition of the lungs when this has taken place.

spleno- /ˈspliːnəʊ/ *combining form*. Before a vowel also **splen-**.
[Greek *splēno-*, from *splēn* SPLEEN: see -O-.]
ANATOMY & MEDICINE. Of, pertaining to, or involving the spleen.
■ **splenocyte** *noun* a mononuclear leucocyte of a type formerly thought characteristic of the spleen E20. **splenoˈmegaly** *noun* abnormal enlargement of the spleen E20. **splenoˈportogram** *noun* a radiograph obtained by splenoportography M20. **splenoporˈtography** *noun* radiography of the hepatic portal system following the introduction of a contrast medium into the spleen M20. **splenoˈrenal** *adjective* (of an anastomosis or shunt) connecting the splenic and left renal veins M20.

splenosis /splɪˈnəʊsɪs/ *noun*. M20.
[from SPLEN(O- + -OSIS.]
MEDICINE. The presence in the body of isolated pieces of living splenic tissue, esp. after rupture or removal of the spleen.

splenunculus /splɪˈnʌŋkjʊləs/ *noun*. Pl. **-li** /-lʌɪ, -liː/. L19.
[mod. Latin, from Latin *splen* spleen + *-unculus* -UNCLE.]
MEDICINE. = SPLENICULUS.

splet /splɛt/ *verb trans*. Now *dial.* Infl. **-tt-**. M16.
[Flemish or Low German *spletten* rel. to SPLAT *verb*¹, SPLIT *verb*.]
Split.

spleuchan /ˈspluːx(ə)n/ *noun*. *Scot. & Anglo-Irish*. L18.
[Gaelic *spliùchan*, Irish *spliúchán*.]
A tobacco pouch; a pouch used as a purse.

splib /splɪb/ *noun*. *US Black slang*. M20.
[Origin unkn.]
A black person.

splice /splʌɪs/ *verb & noun*. E16.
[Prob. from Middle Dutch *splissen*, whence also Dutch dial., German *splissen*, *spleissen* but agreeing in vowel sound with German *spleissen*.]
▸**A** *verb*. **1** *verb trans. & intrans.* Chiefly NAUTICAL. Join (ropes etc.) by untwisting and interweaving the strands of the ends so as to form one continuous length; form an eye or loop in (a rope) by interweaving the strands of one end

into an adjacent part; repair (rigging) in this way. Also foll. by adverb or preposition. E16. ▸**b** Form (an eye or knot) in a rope by splicing it. L18.

2 *verb trans.* Join (timbers) with a scarf joint; join (girders, beams, etc.) by partly overlapping the ends and fastening them together; join (pieces of film, tape, etc.) by sticking together the ends. Also foll. by *together*. E17. ▸**b** *gen.* Unite, join. Also *spec.* (BIOLOGY), join or insert (a gene or gene fragment). E19.

3 *slang.* **a** *verb trans.* Join in marriage. Usu. in *pass.* M18. ▸**b** *verb intrans.* Get married. (Foll. by *with*.) L19.

🕮 **1** T. HEGGEN He found Dowdy in the boatswain's locker, splicing a section of wire cable. ***splice the main-brace***: see ***main brace*** noun[1] s.v. MAIN *adjective*. **2b** R. FRAME She supplied—spliced into the narrative—some . . thoughts on character. A. MOOREHEAD Howitt shot . . wild pigeons and . . spliced their tail feathers on to his own birds. **3a** C. BROOKE-ROSE I worked in an office before I got spliced.

▸ **B** *noun.* **1** An act of splicing; a strong joint made by splicing. E17. ▸**b** *spec.* CRICKET. The wedge-shaped tang of a bat-handle, forming a joint with the blade; this joint. E20.

2 Union by marriage; a wedding. *slang.* M19.

🕮 **1** K. VONNEGUT The clumsy splice in the broken shoelaces. **b** *Daily Telegraph* Pringle and Burns were dismissed . . giving catches off the splice. **sit on the splice** *slang* play a cautious defensive game.

Comb.: **splice-bar**: for joining the ends of rails on a railway; **splice-grafting**: in which the scion and stock are cut obliquely and bound firmly together; **splice-piece** = ***splice-bar*** above.

■ **splicer** *noun* a person who or thing which splices; *spec.* a mechanical device used to splice film or tape: M19. **splicing** *noun* (*a*) the action of the verb; (*b*) the spliced part of a rope etc.; a splice: E16.

spliff /splɪf/ *noun. slang.* Also **splif**. M20.
[Origin unkn.]
A cannabis cigarette.

splinder *noun, verb* see SPLINTER *noun, verb*.

spline /splʌɪn/ *noun & verb.* M18.
[Orig. East Anglian dial.: perh. rel. to SPLINTER *noun*.]
▸ **A** *noun.* **1** A long thin narrow piece of wood, metal, etc.; a slat. M18. ▸**b** *spec.* A flexible strip of wood, rubber, etc., used in drawing curves. L19.

2 A rectangular key fitting into grooves in the hub and shaft of a wheel etc. so as to allow movement of the wheel on the shaft; *esp.* one formed integrally with the shaft. Also, a corresponding groove in a hub along which the key may slide. M19.

3 MATH. A continuous curve constructed so as to pass through a given set of points and have continuous first and second derivatives. Also ***spline curve***. M20.

▸ **B** *verb trans.* Fit or provide with a spline. L19.

splint /splɪnt/ *noun & adjective.* ME.
[Middle Low German *splente*, *splinte*, Middle Dutch *splinte* (Dutch *splint*): rel. to SPLINTER *noun*, but no cognates are recorded.]
▸ **A** *noun.* **1** *Hist.* Any of the plates or strips of overlapping metal making up a section of medieval armour; *spec.* either of a pair of armour plates for protecting the elbows. ME.

2 A long thin (rigid or flexible) strip of wood used in basketwork etc.; a lath; *spec.* a thin piece of wood or other material used to light a fire, pipe, etc. ME.

3 A fragment, a chip, a splinter. Now chiefly *north.* LME. ▸**b** *spec.* A fragment of diamond. *S. Afr.* L19.

4 SURGERY. A strip of rigid material used to support and immobilize an injury, esp. a broken limb etc. when set. LME.

5 VETERINARY MEDICINE. Growth or hardening due to damage of the ligaments attached to the splint-bones of a horse's leg, usu. on the inside of the leg along the line of union of the splint-bones with the cannon-bone; an instance of this. E16.

6 In full ***splint-coal***. A hard bituminous laminated coal which burns with great heat. L18.

Comb.: **splint-bone** †(*a*) = sense 5 above; (*b*) either of the two small metacarpal or metatarsal bones of the leg of a horse, lying behind and close to the cannon-bone or shank.

▸ **B** *attrib.* or as *adjective.* Of or made from splints. M19.

■ **splinty** *adjective* (now *rare*) of a splintery texture; of the nature of splint or splint coal: E17.

splint /splɪnt/ *verb.* LME.
[from the noun.]
1 *verb trans.* Fit a surgical splint to (a broken limb etc.); immobilize by means of a splint or splints. LME. ▸**b** *fig.* Strengthen or support as with a splint or splints. M17.

†**2** *verb trans.* Cover, provide, or make with splints or thin strips of wood etc. E16–M17.

†**3** *verb trans.* Cut (wood etc.) into splints; split apart or *in two*. L16–E17.

🕮 **1** *Daily Telegraph* She . . splinted the man's badly fractured legs with pieces of metal.

■ **splintage** *noun* the application or use of surgical splints L19. **splinting** *noun* (*a*) the action of the verb; (*b*) material for a splint or splints: LME.

splinter /ˈsplɪntə/ *noun & adjective.* ME.
[Middle & mod. Dutch (earlier also *splenter*), Low German *splinter*, *splenter* rel. to SPLINT *noun*.]
▸ **A** *noun.* Also (chiefly *Scot.*) **splinder** /ˈsplɪndə/.

1 A small thin sharp-edged piece of wood, glass, bone, etc., broken off from a whole, esp. as the result of impact; a tiny needle-like sliver of wood; a chip, a fragment, *esp.* one from a bursting shell or bomb. ME. ▸**b** *fig.* A very small piece or amount (*of* something). Usu. in neg. contexts. E17. ▸**c** A splinter group (see sense B. below). Chiefly *US*. M20.

2 = SPLINT *noun* 4. *obsolete* exc. *dial.* L16.

3 = SPLINT *noun* 2. Now *rare*. M17.

🕮 **1** J. HERSEY His desk was in splinters all over the room. A. CARTER A jagged splinter of glass. J. KOSINSKI A sharp splinter of broken bone protruded. H. NORMAN She ran her hand over the . . table, then acted as if she had picked up a splinter. **b** SHAKES. *Tr. & Cr.* Grecian dames are . . not worth The splinter of a lance. Z. N. HURSTON There was a splinter of regret in his voice.

Comb.: **splinter-bar** (*a*) a crossbar in a carriage etc. fixed across the head of the shafts and to which the traces are attached; (*b*) a swingletree; **splinter bid** BRIDGE an unusual jump bid showing a singleton or void in the suit bid; **splinter-deck** an armour-plated deck on a ship; **splinter haemorrhage** a narrow elongated bleeding cut, resembling one produced by a splinter; **splinter-netting** NAUTICAL HISTORY: of small rope spread on board a warship to give protection from falling splinters;

▸ **B** *adjective.* Designating or pertaining to a group, party, etc., which splits off from a larger political etc. group to form an independent entity. M20.

🕮 *Times* The Cabinet is made up of an uneasy coalition of splinter parties. *Cincinnati Enquirer* A terrorist splinter group of Palestinians.

splinter /ˈsplɪntə/ *verb.* Also (earlier, long *rare*) **splinder** /ˈsplɪndə/. LME.
[from the noun.]
1 *verb trans. & intrans.* Break into splinters or so as to leave a rough jagged edge. LME. ▸**b** *verb intrans.* Break away to form a splinter group. M20.

†**2** *verb trans.* = SPLINT *verb* 1. Also foll. by *up*. Long *obsolete* exc. *Canad. dial.* L16.

🕮 **1** G. R. SIMS The rotten woodwork splintered away from the bolt. R. HUGHES The furniture was splintered into matchwood. K. WATERHOUSE The chocolate covering splintered like an eggshell. *fig.*: P. L. FERMOR The sun splintered down through a colander of leaves.

splinter-proof /ˈsplɪntəpruːf/ *noun & adjective.* E19.
[from SPLINTER *noun*, *verb* + PROOF *adjective*.]
▸ **A** *noun.* MILITARY. A structure giving protection from the splinters of bursting shells. E19.

▸ **B** *adjective.* **1** MILITARY. Capable of withstanding the splinters of bursting shells. M19.

2 Of glass: that does not produce splinters when broken. M20.

splintery /ˈsplɪnt(ə)ri/ *adjective.* L18.
[from SPLINTER *noun*, *verb* + -Y[1].]
1 Of a mineral's fracture: characterized by the production of small splinters. L18.

2 Of stone, a mineral, etc.: breaking or separating easily into splinters; *spec.* having a splintery fracture. E19. ▸**b** Of a rock: rough, jagged. E19.

3 Resembling a splinter in shape or form. M19.

4 Full of splinters. M19.

splirt *verb* see SPLURT.

splish-splash /ˈsplɪʃsplaʃ/ *verb & noun. colloq.* E18.
[Redupl. of SPLASH *verb*[1] with vowel variation.]
▸ **A** *verb intrans.* Splash repeatedly. E18.

▸ **B** *noun.* A thing that makes a splashing noise; a large or noisy splash. E19.

■ **splishy-splashy** *adjective* sloppy, slushy M19.

split /splɪt/ *noun.* L16.
[from SPLIT *verb* or *adjective*.]
1 A narrow break or opening made by splitting; a cleft, a crack, a rent. L16. ▸**b** *techn.* An angular groove cut on a glass vessel. M19.

2 a A piece of wood separated or formed by splitting (now *US*); *spec.* (*a*) a split osier etc. used for parts of basketwork; (*b*) *Canad. dial.* a piece of kindling (usu. in *pl.*). E17. ▸**b** WEAVING. Each strip of steel, cane, etc., in the reed of a loom. Orig. *Scot.* M18. ▸**c** A single thickness of split hide. M19.

3 The action or process of splitting; an instance of this; the state of being split; *spec.* (*a*) a rupture or division in a party, sect, etc.; a party etc. formed by this; (*b*) BOTANY (*colloq.*) = SEGREGATE *noun* 1. E18. ▸**b** = ***split-up*** s.v. SPLIT *verb*. *US*. L20.

4 An informer; a police officer. *slang.* E19.

5 a In *pl.* & (*rare*) *sing.* A feat in which the legs are extended in opposite directions (to front and back, or to each side) and the body lowered to the floor. M19. ▸**b** WEIGHTLIFTING. The action or technique of thrusting forward with one foot and backward with the other during a lift; an exercise or lift during which this is done. M20.

6 A share of the proceeds from a legal or esp. illegal undertaking. *slang.* L19.

7 a A half-bottle of mineral water or other (fizzy) drink; a half-bottle *of* champagne; a half-glass of liquor. L19. ▸**b** A dessert consisting of sliced fruit (esp. banana, split open lengthways), ice-cream, syrup, etc. Usu. with specifying word. E20. ▸**c** A split roll or bun. E20. ▸**d** A split-level house. *N. Amer.* L20.

8 CROQUET. = ***split shot*** s.v. SPLIT *adjective*. L19.

9 SPORT. A draw. *US*. M20.

10 SPORT. The time taken to complete a recognized part of a race. M20.

🕮 **1** B. HINES Billy linked his fingers, placed his thumbs together and blew into the split between. **2a** *New Yorker* I lay a split of birch on the coals. **3** *Times* A dispute . . reflecting a deep split within the . . administration. **5** *Daily Telegraph* Backstage . . where dancers sit reading a novel while doing the splits.

split /splɪt/ *adjective.* M17.
[from SPLIT *verb*.]
1 That has split or been split; (of a surface) exposed by splitting. M17.

2 Deeply divided by a long narrow cleft; made or formed in two or more narrowly separated parts. M19.

🕮 **1** U. HOLDEN Their cases were cardboard, split and broken.

Special collocations & comb.: **split-arse** *adjective* (*Military slang*, *arch.*) (of an airman) reckless. **split beam** a beam of radiation etc. that has been split into two or more components, esp. as used in a radar technique in which a single aerial transmits alternately two beams slightly displaced from each other in order. **split bearing** MECHANICS: made in halves for ease of assembly. **split beaver** *slang* a picture or pose in which a woman's genitals are fully displayed. **split-brain** *adjective* (of a person or animal) having the corpus callosum severed or absent, so as to eliminate the main connection between the two hemispheres of the brain. **split decision** BOXING: made on points in which the judges and referee are not unanimous in their choice of a winner. **split-dose** *adjective* (MEDICINE) designating a technique of administering ionizing radiation in several exposures to reduce the harmful effects of a single large dose. **split end** (*a*) a hair which has split at the end through dryness etc. (usu. in *pl.*); (*b*) AMER. FOOTBALL an end positioned at some distance from the rest of the formation. **split-field** = ***split-image*** below. **split flap** AERONAUTICS: occupying only the lower part of the wing thickness. **split gear**, **split pulley**, **split wheel**: made in halves for removal from a shaft. **split graft** = ***split-skin graft*** below. **split-half** (STATISTICS) a technique of splitting a body of supposedly homogeneous data into two halves and calculating the results separately for each to assess their reliability. **split-image** an image in a rangefinder, camera focusing system, etc., that has been bisected by optical means, the halves being aligned only when the system is in focus. **split infinitive** a phrase consisting of an infinitive with an adverb etc. inserted between *to* and the verb (e.g. *to boldly go*). ***split jeté***. **split jump** a jump in skating during which the legs are momentarily kicked out into the splits position. **split-level** *adjective* (*a*) (of a building) having a room or rooms a fraction of a storey higher than other parts; (of a room) having a floor on two levels; (*b*) (of a cooker) having the oven and hob in separately installed units. **split mind** a mind holding contradictory or conflicting attitudes or desires. **split-minded** *adjective* having a split mind. **split page** *US* the front page of the second section of a newspaper. **split pea**: dried and split in half for cooking. **split personality** the alteration or dissociation of personality occurring in some mental illnesses, esp. schizophrenia and hysteria. **split-phase** *adjective* (ELECTRICITY) designating a device, esp. an induction motor, that utilizes two or more voltages at different phases produced from a single-phase supply. **split pin** a metal pin with two arms passed through a hole and held in place by the springing apart of the arms. ***split pulley***: see ***split gear*** above. **split rail** a fence rail split from a log (freq. in ***split-rail fence***). **split ring** a small steel ring with two spiral turns, such as a key-ring. **split run** a press run of a newspaper in which some issues contain copy, advertisements, etc., not carried by other parts. **split-screen**: on which two or more images are displayed simultaneously in different parts. **split shift**: comprising two or more periods of duty separated by an interval or intervals of several hours. **split shot**, **split stroke** CROQUET a stroke driving two touching balls in different directions. **split-skin graft** MEDICINE a skin graft which involves only the superficial portion of the thickness of the skin. **split stitch** an embroidery stitch in which the needle is passed through the thread. ***split stroke***: see ***split shot*** above. **split stuff** *Austral.* timber sawn into lengths and then split. **split ticket** *US*: on which the voter has voted for candidates of more than one party. **split time** SPORT = SPLIT *noun* 10. **split tin (loaf)** a long loaf of bread split lengthways on top. ***split wheel***: see ***split gear*** above.

split /splɪt/ *verb.* Orig. NAUTICAL. Infl. **-tt-**. Pa. t. & pple **split**, †**splitted**. L16.
[Middle & mod. Dutch *splitten* rel. to *spletten* (cf. SPLET), Old Frisian *splita*, Middle Low German, Middle Dutch *splīten*, Middle High German *splīzen* (German *spleissen* split, cleave): ult. origin unkn. Cf. SPLAT *verb*[1], SPLET *verb*.]
1 a *verb trans.* Of a storm, rock, etc.: break up (a ship). Usu. in *pass.* Now passing into sense 3. L16. ▸**b** *verb intrans.* Of a ship: break up or be wrecked on a rock or by the violence of a storm. Now passing into sense 3. L16. ▸**c** *verb intrans. & trans.* (in *pass.*). Suffer shipwreck. Now *rare* or *obsolete*. E17.

†**2** *verb intrans.* Go to pieces. L16–E17.

3 *verb intrans. & trans.* (Cause to) break into two parts, esp. lengthwise, as a result of or by means of force; (cause to) burst asunder. L16. **▸b** *verb trans.* NAUTICAL. (Of the wind) tear (a sail); (of a vessel or its occupants) have (a sail) torn by the wind. E17. **▸c** *verb trans.* AGRICULTURE. Plough (a ridge) so as to throw the furrow-slice outward. E19. **▸d** *verb intrans. fig.* Of the head: suffer great pain from a headache, noise, etc. M19.

4 a *verb trans.* Divide or share between two or more people etc. L17. **▸b** *verb trans. & intrans.* Divide or separate into parts. E18. **▸c** *verb trans. & intrans.* CARDS. Divide (a dealt pair) to start two new hands. M19. **▸d** *verb intrans. & trans.* SPORT. Draw, tie. *US.* L20.

5 *verb trans. & intrans.* Divide or separate into parties, factions, etc., esp. through discord or disagreement. E18. **▸b** *verb intrans.* Quarrel or cease association *with* a person. *slang.* M19. **▸c** *verb intrans.* Of a couple: separate, part. Freq. foll. by *up*. *colloq.* M20.

6 *slang.* **a** *verb intrans.* Betray secrets; inform (*on*). L18. **▸b** *verb trans.* Disclose, reveal. *rare.* M19.

7 *verb intrans.* Run, walk, etc., at great speed. *arch. colloq.* L18.

8 *verb intrans. & trans.* Leave, depart (from), esp. suddenly. *slang.* E20.

9 *verb trans.* Dilute (whisky etc.) with water. *US colloq.* M20.

> 📖 **3** S. P. WOODWARD The Stone that is Slaty . . will split only lengthways or horizontally. E. FERBER He reached for a hot biscuit and split it and placed . . butter in the centre. A. TYLER Two men were splitting logs. P. ABRAHAMS One . . knocked her down, splitting her lip. **4a** G. PALEY I'm taking a cab, said Livid. I'll split it with you, said Pallid. *New Yorker* We would . . split a litre of Chianti. **b** W. PALEY To facilitate the maintenance of families by . . splitting farms. F. O'CONNOR Mrs Watts's mouth split in a wide . . grin. I. MURDOCH The firm had split into two parts. J. RABAN The roomful of people split down the middle. B. MOORE The others split off and turned Proclamation Avenue. **5** D. FRASER Local insurgents were split into Communist and anti-Communist groups. P. CAREY The very basis of . . society . . cracked and split apart. **c** *Venue* His parents split up a year ago. **6** L. CODY If . . you ever split on me, I'll make you very sorry. **8** J. UPDIKE Mom, I got to split Where's your car keys?

Phrases: ***split hairs***: see HAIR *noun*. ***split one's sides***: see SIDE *noun*. **split one's vote** *US* = ***split the ticket*** below. ***split the atom***: see ATOM *noun* 6. ***split the difference***: see DIFFERENCE *noun*. **split the ticket** *US* vote for candidates of more than one party. **split the vote** (of a candidate or minority party) attract votes from another so that both are defeated by a third.

Comb.: **split-down** US STOCK EXCHANGE the combination of two or more stocks into one stock of the same total value (cf. ***split-up*** below); **split-up** an act of splitting up; *spec.* (US STOCK EXCHANGE) the division of a stock into two or more stocks of the same total value (cf. ***split-down*** above).

split-new /ˈsplɪtnjuː/ *adjective.* L17.
[App. from SPLIT *noun* or *verb*.]
Brand-new.

split-second /splɪtˈsɛk(ə)nd/ *adjective & noun.* As noun also **split second**. L19.
[Abbreviation of *split seconds hands*.]
▸ A *adjective.* **1** Designating a stopwatch with two second hands, each of which may be stopped independently of the other. L19.
2 Occurring, done in, or lasting a fraction of a second; extremely brief or short-lived. M20.

> 📖 **2** *City Limits* The split-second choice of saving her jazz collection or her photographs from the Blitz.

▸ B *noun.* A fraction of a second; a very brief moment of time. E20.

> 📖 M. DICKENS In a split second she saw it coming.

†splitted *verb pa. t. & pple*: see SPLIT *verb*.

splitter /ˈsplɪtə/ *noun.* E17.
[from SPLIT *verb* + -ER[1].]
1 A person who splits; *spec.* (*a*) a person employed in splitting fish; (*b*) *Austral.* a person whose occupation is cutting timber to make posts, rails, etc. E17. **▸b** A person (esp. a taxonomist) who attaches importance to differences rather than similarities in classification or analysis and so favours subdivision. Cf. LUMPER *noun* 3. L19.
2 A machine, instrument, etc., which splits something; *spec.* (*a*) an auxiliary set of gears that provides a set of ratios between those of the main gearbox; (*b*) a device for sending a received electric current or signal along two or more routes. M19.
3 A splitting headache. *colloq.* M19.
4 A first-rate hunt. *Hunting slang.* Now *rare.* M19.

splitter /ˈsplɪtə/ *verb intrans. rare.* M19.
[from SPLIT *verb* + -ER[5], or German *splittern*.]
Break into fragments.

splitting /ˈsplɪtɪŋ/ *noun.* L16.
[from SPLIT *verb* + -ING[1].]
1 The action of SPLIT *verb*. L16.
2 In *pl.* Pieces produced by splitting. M19.
Comb.: **splitting field** MATH. the least field which includes all roots of a specified polynomial.

splitting /ˈsplɪtɪŋ/ *ppl adjective.* L16.
[from SPLIT *verb* + -ING[2].]
1 Causing or undergoing splitting. L16.
2 Of a noise: very loud or piercing; ear-splitting. E19.
3 Of a headache: very painful, severe. E19.
4 Very fast. E19.

splittism /ˈsplɪtɪz(ə)m/ *noun.* M20.
[from SPLIT *noun* + -ISM, translating Chinese *fēnliè zhǔyì*.]
The pursuance of factional interests in opposition to official Communist Party policy.
■ **splittist** *noun & adjective* (*a*) *noun* a person who practises splittism; (*b*) *adjective* of or pertaining to splittists or splittism: M20.

splodge /splɒdʒ/ *noun.* M19.
[Imit., or alt. of SPLOTCH *noun*.]
A large irregular spot or patch of colour etc.; a blot, a smear, a stain.

> 📖 B. BAINBRIDGE There was a grey splodge on . . his hat where a pigeon had done its business.

splodge /splɒdʒ/ *verb.* M19.
[In sense 1 imit.; in sense 2 from the noun.]
1 *verb intrans.* Trudge or plod splashily through mud or water. Now *dial.* M19.
2 *verb trans. & intrans.* Make a splodge or splodges (on); cover with splodges. Cf. earlier SPLOTCH *verb*. M20.

> 📖 **2** *Daily Telegraph* It doesn't splodge or spill. P. D. JAMES Tears had started to flow . . splodging the packets of cereal.

splodgy /ˈsplɒdʒi/ *adjective.* M19.
[from SPLODGE *noun* + -Y[1].]
Covered with splodges.
■ **splodgily** *adverb* M20.

splore /splɔː/ *noun & verb. Scot.* L18.
[Origin unkn.]
▸ A *noun.* **1** A frolic, a revel. L18.
2 A commotion, a disturbance; a scrape, an escapade. L18.
▸ B *verb intrans.* Revel; riot; make a commotion. L18.

splosh /splɒʃ/ *noun, adverb, & verb.* M19.
[Imit.]
▸ A *noun.* **1** A dull splashing sound (as) of an object striking something wet and soft; an impact of this kind. Also, a splodge. *colloq.* M19.
2 Money. *slang.* L19.
3 Tea (the drink). *slang.* M20.

> 📖 **1** J. BARNES A discreet splosh as the eel-fishermen cast off. D. HOGAN Sploshes of freckles on her face.

▸ B *adverb.* With a dull splashing sound. *colloq.* L19.
▸ C *verb intrans. & trans.* Splash; move with a dull splashing sound. *colloq.* E20.

> 📖 W. FAULKNER The coffee sploshed out on to her hands. C. BUCHANAN Biscuit sploshed her glass down on the table.

■ **sploshy** *adjective* sloppy; splashy: M19.

splotch /splɒtʃ/ *noun & verb.* E17.
[Perh. blend of SPOT *noun* and PLOTCH *noun*. Cf. SPLATCH.]
▸ A *noun.* = SPLODGE *noun.* E17.

> 📖 B. BOVA Splotches of angry red appeared on his pallid cheeks. A. LURIE Pale-green splotches of paint . . could be meant for grass.

▸ B *verb trans.* Make a splotch or splotches on, cover with splotches. M17.

> 📖 J. DIDION His face and . . shirt were splotched with dust.

■ **splotchy** *adjective* covered with splotches; resembling a splotch: M19.

splunge /splʌn(d)ʒ/ *verb intrans. dial. & US.* M19.
[Imit.]
Plunge.

splurge /spləːdʒ/ *noun & verb.* Orig. *US.* E19.
[Symbolic.]
▸ A *noun.* **1** An ostentatious display or effort; *spec.* (JOURNALISM) a large or showy advertisement, feature, etc. E19.
2 A sudden extravagant indulgence, esp. in spending. E20.

> 📖 **1** E. POUND Chin Tsong lived soberly With no splurge of table or costumes. **2** N. MAILER Nicole went on a splurge and bought coloring books and crayons.

▸ B *verb.* **1 a** *verb intrans.* Make an ostentatious display. M19. **▸b** *verb intrans. & trans.* Spend (money) extravagantly (*on*). M20.
2 *verb intrans. & trans.* Splash heavily or clumsily. L19.

> 📖 **1b** D. ALDIS Mary had splurged on washable wall-papers. *Which?* If Christmas money isn't splurged . . on the latest craze. **2** JO GRIMOND Sunsets splurge across the sky colours . . no painter would dare to use.

■ **splurgy** *adjective* showy, ostentatious M19.

splurt /spləːt/ *verb intrans.* Chiefly *dial.* Also (earlier) **splirt**. L18.
[Imit.]
Spurt (*out*); spit *out* something.

> 📖 *fig.*: *Drive* Commentators splurting out . . accounts of football matches.

splutter /ˈsplʌtə/ *noun & verb.* L17.
[Imit. Cf. SPUTTER *noun, verb*.]
▸ A *noun.* **1** A commotion, a fuss. Now *dial.* L17.
2 Vehement and confused speech; an instance of this. L17.
3 A loud spitting or choking noise. E19.

> 📖 **2** T. H. HUXLEY Dinner . . with a confused splutter of German to . . my right. **3** R. FRAME 'She's barmy,' Margot said, . . stifling her splutters of laughter.

▸ B *verb.* **1** *verb trans. & intrans.* Utter or talk hastily and indistinctly with spitting or choking sounds. Also foll. by *out*. E18.
2 *verb intrans.* Make a loud spitting or choking noise. E19.
3 a *verb trans.* Scatter in small splashes; eject with a splutter. M19. **▸b** *verb trans.* Bespatter (a person). M19. **▸c** *verb intrans.* Of a pen: scatter ink when used. M19.

> 📖 **1** G. W. THORNBURY King James spluttered out his alarm at Jesuit plots. E. AMBLER I began to laugh . . 'My dear good Zaleshoff,' I spluttered. **2** F. KING She began to shake and splutter with laughter. G. GREENE The kettle was beginning to splutter. *Classic Racer* His engine splutters, then cuts dead. **3a** R. S. SURTEES Twirling the pen . . and spluttering the ink over the paper. L. GRANT-ADAMSON If Joseph had not swallowed quickly he might have spluttered his wine.

■ **splutterer** *noun* M19. **splutteringly** *adverb* in a spluttering manner M20. **spluttery** *adjective* suggestive of spluttering M19.

spod /spɒd/ *noun. slang. derog.* L20.
[Origin unkn.]
A dull or socially inept person, esp. someone who is excessively studious; a nerd.
■ **spoddy** *adjective* L20.

Spode /spəʊd/ *noun.* M19.
[Josiah *Spode* (1754–1827), English maker of china.]
(Proprietary name for) a make of fine pottery or porcelain.

spodic /ˈspɒdɪk/ *adjective.* M20.
[from Greek *spodos* ashes, embers + -IC.]
SOIL SCIENCE. Designating an illuviated soil horizon that is rich in aluminium oxide and organic matter and usu. also contains iron oxide.

spodium /ˈspəʊdɪəm/ *noun.* Now *rare* or *obsolete.* LME.
[Latin from Greek *spodion* = *spodos* ashes, embers.]
A fine powdery ash obtained from various substances by calcination.

spodomancy /ˈspɒdəmansi/ *noun. rare.* M19.
[formed as SPODIC + -O- + -MANCY.]
Divination by ashes.

Spodosol /ˈspɒdəʊsɒl/ *noun.* M20.
[formed as SPODIC + -SOL.]
SOIL SCIENCE. A soil of an order characterized by a spodic horizon and including most podzols and podzolic soils.

spodumene /ˈspɒdjʊmiːn/ *noun.* E19.
[French *spodumène*, German *Spodumen*, from Greek *spodoumenos* pres. pple of *spodousthai* be burnt to ashes, from *spodos* ashes, embers.]
MINERALOGY. A monoclinic lithium aluminosilicate occurring as translucent, usu. greyish-white, crystals and important as a source of lithium.

spoffish /ˈspɒfɪʃ/ *adjective. arch. slang.* M19.
[Origin unkn.: see -ISH[1].]
Fussy, officious.

spoil /spɔɪl/ *noun.* ME.
[Aphet. from Old French *espoille*, from *espoiller*: see next.]
1 *sing.* & (now usu.) in *pl.* Goods, valuables, territory, etc., taken forcibly from an enemy or place, as in war; property etc. seized by force or acquired by confiscation; booty, loot, plunder; *spec.* weapons and armour stripped from a dead or defeated enemy. Freq. in ***the spoils of war***. ME. **▸b** *transf. sing.* & (now usu.) in *pl.* That which has been acquired or collected by special effort or endeavour. M18. **▸c** *sing.* & (usu.) in *pl.* Profit, advantage, advancement, etc., gained by succession to or connection with public office or high position. Chiefly *US.* L18.
2 a The action or practice of pillaging; rapine, spoliation. *arch.* ME. **▸†b** An act or occasion of pillaging; a raid or incursion for the sake of booty. M16–M17.
3 †a An act or instance of spoiling or damaging something; an injury. (Foll. by *of*.) M16–E18. **▸b** The action or fact of spoiling or damaging something; damage, destruction. (Foll. by *of*.) Now *rare.* L16. **▸c** A thing that is spoiled, damaged, or imperfectly made. L19.
4 An object of pillage; a plundered article. *arch.* L16.
5 a *sing.* & in *pl.* The cast or stripped-off skin of an animal, esp. a snake; a pelt; a slough. *arch.* E17. **▸b** In *pl.* The remains of an animal body; the parts left intact or uneaten. *arch.* L17.
6 Waste material thrown or brought up in excavating, mining, dredging, etc. M19.

📖 **1** DRYDEN Mighty Caesar . . Seeks . . the Spoils of War. W. H. PRESCOTT Their galleys . . freighted with the spoils of the infidel. A. DUGGAN The spoil comes to very little when . . divided among a whole army. **b** *Liverpool Daily Post* Grasping . . the weedy spoils of the hedgerow. **5a** *Saturday Review* Enclad in the spoils of wolf and . . wild cat. **6** *attrib.*: *Times* Abandoned slurry ponds and spoil tips.

Comb.: **spoilsman** *US* (esp. POLITICS) (*a*) an advocate or supporter of the spoils system; (*b*) a person who obtains or seeks to obtain a share of political spoils; **spoils system** (chiefly *US*) the system or practice of a successful political party giving government or public positions to its supporters.

■ **spoilless** /-l-l-/ *adjective* (*rare*) unaccompanied by spoil or plunder E19.

spoil /spɔɪl/ *verb*. Pa. t. & pple **spoiled**, **spoilt** /spɔɪlt/. ME.
[Aphet. from Old French *espoillier* from Latin *spoliare*, from *spolium* skin stripped from an animal, booty, or aphet. from DESPOIL *verb*.]
1 *verb trans.* Rob or plunder (a person or place) forcibly of goods or valuables, as in war; pillage, ransack; *spec.* strip (a dead or defeated enemy) of weapons and armour; *gen.* deprive or strip of possessions, clothes, etc., esp. illicitly or stealthily. (Foll. by *of*.) *arch.* or *literary*. ME.
2 *verb trans.* Seize (goods) by force or violence, carry off as booty; steal. *arch.* LME.
3 *verb intrans.* Engage in pillage. *arch.* LME.
†**4** *verb refl.* Divest or rid oneself *of* sins etc. LME–L16.
†**5** *verb trans.* Carve, cut up, (a hen). LME–M18.
6 *verb trans.* Damage, esp. so as to make unfit or useless; diminish or destroy the value or quality of; prevent full enjoyment or development of; mar, ruin. M16. ▸**b** Make (a ballot paper) invalid, by improper marking, defacing, etc. L19.
7 *verb trans.* †**a** Destroy, bring to an end, kill. L16–E18. ▸**b** Inflict serious bodily injury on. Now *slang*. L16.
8 a *verb trans.* Injure the character of (esp. a child) by overindulgence or undue lenience (freq. as ***spoiled*** *ppl adjective*); *gen.* treat with great or excessive consideration or kindness. L17. ▸**b** *verb trans.* & *intrans.* Prevent or obstruct the success of (a person, undertaking, etc.) in sport etc. Freq. in ***spoiling tactics***. E19.
9 *verb intrans.* Esp. of food: become unfit for use; deteriorate, go bad, decay. L17. ▸**b** Be very eager *for* a fight etc., desire greatly *to do* something. M19.

📖 **1** G. MACDONALD They proceeded, by spoiling the country houses . . , to make a quite luxurious provision. W. C. BRYANT So did . . Ajax spoil the corpse of Simoïsus. **3** SIR W. SCOTT A soldier! then you have . . sacked and spoiled? **6** G. GREENE He would get wet . . and spoil his only suit. P. PEARCE He resolved not to let . . disappointment spoil his enjoyment. L. HELLMAN A handsome old house . . , the windows spoiled with ugly draperies. E. NORTH Whitby was spoiled, . . full of amusement arcades. *Proverb*: Too many cooks spoil the broth. **8a** J. GALSWORTHY Fleur does what she likes. You've always spoiled her. **9** M. GARDINER She had made the supper and refused to let it spoil. **b** E. M. FORSTER Durham . . would be found . . in his room and spoiling to argue. R. FRAME I was spoiling for a fight.

Phrases: ***make a spoon or spoil a horn***: see SPOON *noun*. **spoil a person for** impair a person's appreciation of by making accustomed to something better. ***spoil a person rotten***: see ROTTEN *adverb*. **spoilt for choice** having so many choices as to make it difficult to choose.

Comb.: **spoil-five** CARDS = ***twenty-five*** (b) s.v. TWENTY.

■ **spoilable** *adjective* able to be spoiled, capable of spoiling M17. **spoiled** *ppl adjective* that has been spoiled, damaged, or (*arch.*) plundered; ***spoiled nun***, ***spoiled priest***: that has repudiated her or his vocation: LME. **spoilt** *ppl adjective* = SPOILED E19.

spoilage /ˈspɔɪlɪdʒ/ *noun*. L16.
[from prec. + -AGE.]
†**1** The action or fact of plundering or robbing. L16–E17.
2 The action of spoiling, the fact of being spoiled or ruined; *esp.* the deterioration or decay of foodstuffs and perishable goods. E19.
3 Paper spoiled in printing. L19.

spoiler /ˈspɔɪlə/ *noun*. LME.
[formed as prec. + -ER¹.]
1 A person who or thing which pillages or robs. LME.
2 A person who or thing which spoils or damages something. M16. ▸**b** A person who obstructs or prevents an opponent's success while not being a potential winner. M20.
3 a A flap able to be projected from the upper surface of an aircraft wing to break up a smooth airflow and so reduce speed. E20. ▸**b** A similar (usu. fixed) structure on a motor vehicle intended to reduce lift and so improve road-holding at high speed. M20.

†**spoilful** *adjective*. L16–L17.
[from SPOIL *noun* + -FUL.]
Causing or characterized by destruction or pillage; plundering.

spoilsport /ˈspɔɪlspɔːt/ *noun*. E19.
[from SPOIL *verb* + SPORT *noun*.]
A person who spoils the enjoyment or plans of others by his or her actions or attitudes.

📖 P. H. GIBBS Patricia did not want to be a spoilsport and laughed . . at these antics.

spoilt *verb pa. t. & pple*: see SPOIL *verb*.

Spokane /spəʊˈkan/ *noun & adjective*. Also **-an**. M19.
[Spokane.]
▶ **A** *noun*. Pl. **-s**, same. A member of a Salish people of eastern Washington State; the language of this people. M19.
▶ **B** *attrib.* or as *adjective*. Of or pertaining to the Spokanes or their language. M19.

spoke /spəʊk/ *noun & verb*¹.
[Old English *spāca* = Old Frisian *spēke*, *spāke*, Old Saxon *spēca*, Old High German *speihha* (Dutch *speek*, German *Speiche*), from West Germanic, from Germanic base of SPIKE *noun*¹.]
▶ **A** *noun*. **1** Each of the bars or rods radiating from the hub of a wheel to support the rim. OE. ▸**b** Each of a set of radial handles projecting from a wheel or cylinder, esp. a ship's wheel. M17. ▸**c** BASKET-MAKING. = STAKE *noun*¹ 4c. L19.
2 A bar or rod of wood etc., esp. as used for a particular purpose; a stake, a pole; *spec.* (*a*) a rung of a ladder; (*b*) SCOTTISH HISTORY each of the poles used for carrying a coffin to the graveside. LME.
†**3** BOTANY. A pedicel of an umbel; a ray. *rare*. L16–L18.
Phrases: **a spoke in a person's wheel** a thing that thwarts or hinders a person, an impediment, an obstacle, (now chiefly in ***put a spoke in a person's wheel***, thwart or hinder a person). **put one's spoke in** = ***put one's oar in*** s.v. OAR *noun*.
Comb.: **spokeshave** a kind of draw-knife consisting of a blade set between two handles placed lengthwise, used for planing spokes and other work unsuitable for an ordinary plane.
▶ **B** *verb trans.* **1** Provide or construct with spokes; *fig.* mark *with* radial lines like spokes. E18.
2 Thrust a spoke into (a wheel etc.) to check movement; *fig.* block, impede, obstruct. M19.
3 Drive or force (a wheel or vehicle) *forward* by pushing the spokes. M19.
■ **spokeless** *adjective* LME. **spokewise** *adverb* in the manner of the spokes of a wheel M19.

spoke *verb*² *pa. t. & pple*: see SPEAK *verb*.

spoked /spəʊkt/ *adjective*. L16.
[from SPOKE *noun*, *verb*¹: see -ED², -ED¹.]
†**1** Arranged radially, radiating from a centre. L16–M17.
2 Made or provided with spokes. L19.

spoken /ˈspəʊk(ə)n/ *ppl adjective*. LME.
[pa. pple of SPEAK *verb*: see -EN⁶.]
1 Of a person etc.: speaking in a specified way, having a particular way of speaking. LME.
2 That is or has been spoken *about*, *of*, *to*, etc. L16.
3 a Of language, words, etc.: uttered in speech; oral. Also, colloquial as opp. to literary. M19. ▸**b** Expressed, declared, or made known by speech or utterance. M19.

📖 **1** ***fair-spoken***, ***plain-spoken***, ***soft-spoken***, ***well-spoken***, etc. **3a** *Multilingua*: *Ehrlich*, a lexeme which is infrequently used in written German but . . frequently occurs in the spoken language. JULIA HAMILTON Words on a page would . . make the impact that spoken protestations . . failed to do. **b** B. TAYLOR A vast difference between the silent and the spoken protest.

Phrases: **the spoken word** speech as opp. to music, written language, etc., esp. in the context of radio broadcasting. **spoken for** *colloq.* claimed, reserved, engaged; *spec.* (of a person) already involved in a romantic relationship.
■ **spokenness** /-n-n-/ *noun* the fact or quality of having been spoken or uttered E19.

spoken *verb* pa. pple: see SPEAK *verb*.

spokeslady /ˈspəʊksleɪdi/ *noun*. M20.
[formed as SPOKESWOMAN + LADY *noun*.]
A spokeswoman.

spokesman /ˈspəʊksmən/ *noun*. Pl. **-men**. E16.
[from *spoke* pa. pple of SPEAK *verb* + MAN *noun*, after *craftsman* etc.]
†**1** An interpreter. *rare*. E–M16.
2 A person who speaks on behalf of another or others, *esp.* one chosen or deputed to represent the views of an organization, group, etc. M16. ▸**b** *transf.* The chief representative or exponent *of* a movement, period, etc. E19.
3 A public speaker, *esp.* one formally addressing a deliberative or legislative assembly. M17.

📖 **2** *Times* A Post Office spokesman said . . the mailvan had previously collected three bags from . . Bell Street. L. GORDON The role of God's spokesman was . . daunting. J. BARNES If I'm the passengers' spokesman, how do I . . pass on the passengers' demands? **b** CARLYLE Dante is the spokesman of the Middle Ages.

■ **spokesmanship** *noun* (*a*) the position or office of spokesman; (*b*) skilful use of the position of spokesman: L19.

spokesmodel /ˈspəʊksmɒd(ə)l/ *noun*. *colloq.* (chiefly *N. Amer.*). L20.
[formed as prec. + MODEL *noun*.]
An attractive, elegant, and stylishly dressed person appearing in advertising for a particular product or service.

spokespeople /ˈspəʊkspiːp(ə)l/ *noun pl.* L20.
[formed as prec. + PEOPLE *noun*.]
Two or more spokespersons.

spokesperson /ˈspəʊkspəːs(ə)n/ *noun*. Pl. **-persons**. L20.
[formed as prec. + PERSON *noun*.]
A spokesman. (Used to avoid sexual distinction.)

spokeswoman /ˈspəʊkswʊmən/ *noun*. Pl. **-women** /-wɪmɪn/. M17.
[formed as prec. + WOMAN *noun*.]
A female spokesman.
■ **spokeswomanship** *noun* L19.

spoky /ˈspəʊki/ *adjective*. M16.
[from SPOKE *noun* + -Y¹.]
†**1** BOTANY. Having or consisting of parts arranged radially like the spokes of a wheel; radiate. M16–E18.
2 Of a wheel: having spokes. *rare*. M19.

spoliate /ˈspəʊlɪeɪt/ *verb trans.* E18.
[Latin *spoliat-* pa. ppl stem of *spoliare* SPOIL *verb*: see -ATE³.]
Spoil; pillage; rob or deprive *of* something.
■ **spoliative** *adjective* (MEDICINE) having the effect of seriously diminishing the blood volume L19. **spoliator** *noun* M19. **spoliatory** *adjective* of the nature of or characterized by spoliation or robbery; pillaging, plundering: L18.

spoliation /spəʊlɪˈeɪʃ(ə)n/ *noun*. LME.
[Latin *spoliatio(n-)*, formed as prec.: see -ATION.]
1 The action or an act of pillaging; (a) seizure of goods or property by violent means. Also, the condition of being pillaged. LME.
2 ECCLESIASTICAL. The taking of the fruits of a benefice properly belonging to another; a writ or suit brought by one incumbent against another holding the same benefice in such a situation. LME.
3 LAW. The action of destroying, mutilating, or altering a document so as to prevent its being used as evidence. M18.

spondaic /spɒnˈdeɪk/ *adjective & noun*. L16.
[French *spondaïque* or late Latin *spondaicus* alt. of *spondiacus* from Greek *spondeiakos*, from *spondeios* SPONDEE: see -IC.]
▶ **A** *adjective*. **1** Of or pertaining to spondees; composed of or characterized by a spondee or spondees. Also, having a spondee in positions where a different foot is normal; *esp.* (of a hexameter) having a spondee in the fifth foot. L16.
2 Of a word: consisting of two long syllables. M19.
▶ **B** *noun*. A spondaic foot or line. M19.

spondean /spɒnˈdiːən/ *adjective*. *rare*. L18.
[from Latin *spondeus* (see next) + -AN.]
= SPONDAIC *adjective* 1.

spondee /ˈspɒndiː/ *noun*. LME.
[Old & mod. French *spondée* or Latin *spondeus* from Greek *spondeios* (sc. *pous* foot) use as noun of adjective from *spondē* libation, the spondee being characteristic of melodies accompanying libations.]
PROSODY. A metrical foot consisting of two long or (in English etc.) two stressed syllables; a verse composed of or containing such feet.

spondulick /spɒnˈdjuːlɪk/ *noun*. *slang*. Also **-ik**. Pl. **-i(c)ks**, **-ix**. M19.
[Origin unkn.]
In *pl.*, money, cash. Also occas. *sing.*, a piece of money, a coin.

spondyle /ˈspɒndɪl/ *noun*. Now *rare*. Also †**sphon-**, †**-yl**. LME.
[Old & mod. French *spondyle* or Latin *spondylus* from Greek *spondulos*, *sph-*.]
†**1** A vertebra. LME–M17.
2 ZOOLOGY. = SPONDYLUS. M17.

spondylitis /spɒndɪˈlʌɪtɪs/ *noun*. M19.
[from Latin *spondylus* vertebra + -ITIS.]
MEDICINE. Inflammation of the synovial joints of the vertebral column.
ankylosing spondylitis: see ANKYLOSE.
■ **spondylitic** /-ˈlɪt-/ *noun & adjective* (*a*) *noun* a person affected with spondylitis; (*b*) *adjective* of, caused by, or associated with, spondylitis: L19.

spondylo- /ˈspɒndɪləʊ/ *combining form*.
[from Greek *spondulos* or Latin *spondylus* vertebra: see -O-.]
MEDICINE. Forming nouns and adjectives with the sense 'of or pertaining to the spinal column or vertebrae'.
■ **spondylolisˈthesis** *noun*, pl. **-theses** /-ˈθiːsiːz/, [Greek *olisthēsis* slipping] the forward displacement of a vertebra relative to the one below it, or of the lowest lumbar vertebra relative to the pelvis M19. **spondylolisˈthetic** *adjective* of, pertaining to, or affected by spondylolisthesis L19. **spondylolysis** /-ˈlɒl/ *noun* the splitting or partial disintegration of a vertebra L19. **spondyloˈlytic** *adjective* of, pertaining to, or affected by spondylolysis M20. **spondyˈlosis** *noun* ankylosis or degenerative change in the spine or a vertebral joint E20. **spondyˈlotic** *adjective* of, pertaining to, or affected by spondylosis M20.

spondylus /ˈspɒndɪləs/ *noun*. Pl. **-li** /-lʌɪ, -liː/ E17.
[mod. Latin (see below) from Latin: see SPONDYLE.]
ZOOLOGY. Any of several bivalve molluscs of the genus *Spondylus* (family Spondylidae), which bear long spatulate or pointed spines. Also called ***thorny oyster***.

spong /spɒŋ/ *noun*. Now *dial.* M17.
[Alt. of SPANG *noun*³.]
A long narrow strip (*of* land).

sponge /spʌn(d)ʒ/ *noun*¹. Also †**spunge**.
[Old English *sponge* corresp. to Old Saxon *spunsia* (Dutch *spons*) from Latin *spongia* from Greek *spoggia* from *spoggos*, *sphoggos*, reinforced in Middle English by Old French *esponge* (see next). Senses 7 & 8 from the verb.]

1 A soft light porous absorbent substance or object used in bathing, cleaning surfaces, etc., orig. consisting of the dried skeleton of a marine sponge (sense 3) but now freq. of synthetic material. OE.

2 †**a** The matted tuft formed by asparagus roots. LME–L16. ▸**b** = BEDEGUAR. E17.

3 *ZOOLOGY*. Any of various primitive sessile aquatic (chiefly marine) animals of the phylum Porifera, which have porous baglike bodies with a skeleton of hard spicules or elastic fibres. M16.

4 A moistened piece of sponge as used for wiping a surface to obliterate writing etc. Freq. *fig.*, a thing that effaces a memory, wipes out a debt, etc. M16. ▸**b** *Hist.* A kind of mop or swab for cleaning a cannon bore. E17.

5 A person or thing likened to a sponge in absorbency etc.; *spec.* (*a*) *colloq.* a heavy drinker; (*b*) a person etc. soaking up or acting as a source of wealth, knowledge, etc.; (*c*) a parasite, a sponger. L16.

6 A thing or substance having the appearance or consistency of a sponge; *spec.* (*a*) soft fermenting bread dough (freq. in ***set the sponge***, ***lay the sponge***); (*b*) a stretch of swampy ground (also ***sponge swamp***); (*c*) *METALLURGY* metal in a porous form, usu. obtained by reduction without fusion, or in a loose form, produced by electrolysis; (*d*) a type of thick jelly (of a specified kind) eaten as a dessert. L17. ▸**b** In full ***sponge cake***. A very light sweet cake of spongelike consistency, esp. as made with little or no fat. Also, the mixture from which such a cake is made. L19.

7 The action of sponging or living parasitically on others. Freq. in ***on the sponge***. *colloq.* L17.

8 An act of wetting, wiping, or removing something (as) with a sponge. E18.

> **1** RIDER HAGGARD He mopped up the . . blood with a sponge. E. SEGAL Nurses . . bathed him with alcohol-soaked sponges. ***glass sponge***, ***Turkey sponge***, ***vegetable sponge***, ***velvet sponge***, etc. **throw in the sponge** *colloq.* abandon a contest or struggle, submit, give in. **4** *Times* I advocate 'drawing the sponge across the crimes . . of the past.' **6b** *attrib.*: *Times* The mixture can be baked . . as a sponge flan. ***GENOESE sponge***. ***Victoria sponge***: see VICTORIA *noun* 6. **8** M. STEWART I took a quick cool sponge down.

Comb.: **sponge bag** a small waterproof bag for toilet articles; ***sponge-bag trousers***, checked trousers patterned in a style formerly associated with sponge bags; **sponge biscuit** a biscuit of a similar composition to sponge cake; ***sponge cake***: see sense 6b above; **sponge-cakey** *adjective* resembling a sponge cake; **sponge cloth** (*a*) a type of soft lightly woven cloth with a slightly wrinkled surface; (*b*) a thin spongy material used for cleaning; **sponge crab** (*a*) any of several crabs of the genus *Dromius* and related genera, which decorate the carapace with a living sponge; (*b*) *US* a spawning female crab, which bears a large spongelike mass of eggs on the underside; **sponge-finger** an elongated sponge biscuit; **sponge gourd** = ***dishcloth gourd*** s.v. DISH *noun*; **sponge mixture** (*a*) a packet of prepared dry ingredients for making a sponge cake; (*b*) the ingredients of a sponge cake mixed together ready for baking; **sponge pudding** a steamed or baked pudding of flour, eggs, and fat; **sponge rubber** *noun & adjective* (of) liquid rubber latex processed into a spongelike substance; **sponge sandwich** a sponge cake consisting of two halves sandwiched together with a filling of jam, cream, etc.; ***sponge-swamp***: see sense 6 above; **sponge tree** the opopanax tree, *Acacia farnesiana*.

■ **spongeful** *noun* as much as will fill a sponge M19. **spongeless** *adjective* M19. **spongelike** *adjective* resembling a sponge, spongy L16.

†**sponge** *noun*². L16–E18.
[Old French *esponge* (mod. *éponge*) alt. of *esponde* from Latin *sponda* frame of a bed etc.]
A heel of a horseshoe.

sponge /spʌn(d)ʒ/ *verb*. Also †**spunge** LME.
[from SPONGE *noun*¹, perh. partly after Old French *esponger* (mod. *éponger*).]

1 *verb trans.* Wipe, rub, or dab with a wet sponge or cloth so as to clean etc. (freq. foll. by *down*, *over*, *up*); wipe or moisten *with* liquid applied by means of a sponge. LME. ▸**b** *Hist.* Swab the bore of (a cannon), esp. after a discharge. E17. ▸**c** Apply paint with a sponge to (walls, furniture, pottery, etc.); apply (paint) in this way to achieve a mottled effect. E20.

2 *verb trans.* Remove, wipe away, or absorb (as) with a sponge; efface, obliterate, (writing, a memory, etc.); wipe out (a debt etc.). (Foll. by *away*, *off*, *out*, *up*.) M16.

†**3** *verb trans.* Foll. by *up*: make spruce, smart, or trim. M16–E17.

4 *verb trans.* **a** Drain, empty, clear; divest *of* money, goods, etc. *rare.* L16. ▸**b** Press (a person) *for* money etc.; deprive (a person) *of* something in this way. Now *rare.* M17.

5 *verb trans.* Obtain (money, drink, etc.) from another parasitically or by scrounging. L17.

6 *verb intrans.* Act in a parasitic manner, live off another (foll. by *on* or *off* a person); (foll. by *for*) seek to obtain by cadging. L17.

7 **a** *verb trans.* Convert (flour or dough) into sponge in bread-making. L18. ▸**b** *verb intrans.* Esp. of dough: take on spongy form, rise. L18.

8 *verb intrans.* Gather sponges from the sea. L19.

> **1** V. WOOLF She . . began sponging her cheeks with . . water. DODIE SMITH We sponged and pressed our winter coats. **2** F. S. OLIVER The old accounts were sponged off the slate. R. MACAULAY I was lying . . with someone sponging blood from my face. P. D. JAMES He had made an attempt to sponge off the stain. **6** R. L. STEVENSON I'm to be a poor, crawling beggar, sponging for rum! S. LEACOCK A sort of ne'er-do-well, always . . sponging on other people, and never working.

■ **spongeable** *adjective* able to be wiped (clean) with a sponge L20. **sponging** *verbal noun* the action of the verb; an act or instance of this; ***sponging house*** (*Hist.*), a preliminary detention centre for debtors: L16.

spongelet /ˈspʌn(d)ʒlɪt/ *noun*. Now *rare* or *obsolete*. M19.
[from SPONGE *noun*¹ + -LET.]
BOTANY. = SPONGIOLE.

spongeous /ˈspʌn(d)ʒəs/ *adjective*. LME.
[from Latin *spongeosus*, from *spongea* SPONGE *noun*¹: see -EOUS. Cf. SPONGIOUS.]
Of the nature or character of a sponge; spongy.

sponger /ˈspʌn(d)ʒə/ *noun*. Also †**spunger**. L17.
[from SPONGE *verb* or *noun*¹ + -ER¹.]

1 A person who contrives to live at another's expense; a parasite, a scrounger. (Foll. by *on*.) L17.

2 A person who uses a sponge, *spec.* (*a*) *Hist.* to clean the bore of a cannon, (*b*) to apply paint to pottery. E19.

3 A person or vessel engaged in fishing for or gathering sponges. L19.

> **1** M. SEYMOUR Spongers who looked on his new home as a free hotel.

spongey *adjective* var. of SPONGY.

spongi- /ˈspʌn(d)ʒi/ *combining form* of SPONGE *noun*¹, after Latin types: see -I-.

■ **spongiculture** *noun* the commercial culture of sponges E20. **spon'giferous** *adjective* (of a rock or stratum) yielding or bearing fossil sponges M19.

spongiform /ˈspʌn(d)ʒɪfɔːm/ *adjective*. E19.
[from prec. + -FORM.]

1 Spongelike, spongy; light and porous. E19.

2 *ZOOLOGY*. Of or resembling the poriferan sponges. M19.

1 spongiform encephalopathy any of several slow viral encephalopathies in which the brain tissue becomes spongy (***bovine spongiform encephalopathy***: see BOVINE *adjective* 1).

spongin /ˈspʌn(d)ʒɪn/ *noun*. M19.
[from SPONGE *noun*¹ + -IN¹.]
The horny or fibrous substance found in the skeleton of many sponges.

spongio- /ˈspɒn(d)ʒɪəʊ/ *combining form* of Latin *spongia* or SPONGE *noun*¹: see -O-.

■ **spongioblast** *noun* (*BIOLOGY*) one of the embryonic cells of the brain and spinal cord from which the glia is formed E20. **spongioblas'toma** *noun*, pl. **-mas**, **-mata** /-mətə/, *MEDICINE* a kind of malignant tumour, usu. of the brain or optic nerve E20. **spongi'ologist** *noun* an expert in or student of spongiology L19. **spongi'ology** *noun* the branch of zoology that deals with sponges L19. **spongiopiline** /-ˈpʌɪlʌɪn/ *noun* (now *rare* or *obsolete*) a material made from sponge and wool or cloth felted together, formerly used for poultices etc. M19. †**spongioplasm** *noun* (*BIOLOGY*) a fibrillar or protoplasmic network within the cell, forming the reticulum L19–M20. **spongi'osis** *noun*, pl. **-oses** /-ˈəʊsiːz/, *MEDICINE* accumulation of fluid between (formerly, within) epidermal cells E20.

spongiole /ˈspʌn(d)ʒɪəʊl/ *noun*. Now *rare* or *obsolete*. M19.
[French from Latin *spongiola* matted tuft of asparagus roots, dim. of *spongia* SPONGE *noun*¹.]
BOTANY. The tender extremity of a young root (formerly regarded as a distinct organ), which is characterized by loose spongelike cellular tissue.

spongiosa /spʌn(d)ʒɪˈəʊzə/ *noun*. M20.
[Latin, fem. of *spongiosus* (sc. *substantia* substance): see next.]
ANATOMY. **1** The tissue constituting the bulk of the posterior grey column of the spinal cord. Now *rare*. M20.

2 Cancellous or spongy bone tissue, such as that within the ends of long bones. M20.

spongiose /ˈspʌn(d)ʒɪəʊs/ *adjective*. M18.
[from Latin *spongiosus*, from *spongia* SPONGE *noun*¹: see -OSE¹.]
Of a spongy texture; porous.

spongious /ˈspʌn(d)ʒəs/ *adjective*. Now *rare*. LME.
[formed as prec.: see -OUS. Cf. SPONGEOUS.]
Of, pertaining to, or of the nature of a sponge; spongy.

spongo- /ˈspɒŋgəʊ/ *combining form* of Greek *spoggos* SPONGE *noun*¹: see -O-.

■ **spongolite** *noun* (*GEOLOGY*) a rock formed almost entirely of siliceous sponge spicules M20. **spon'gologist** *noun* = SPONGIOLOGIST L19. **spon'gology** *noun* = SPONGIOLOGY L19.

spongoid /ˈspɒŋgɔɪd/ *adjective*. Now *rare* or *obsolete*. E19.
[from Greek *spoggos* SPONGE *noun*¹ + -OID.]

1 = SPONGIFORM 1. E19.

2 *ZOOLOGY*. = SPONGIFORM 2. M19.

spongy /ˈspʌn(d)ʒi/ *adjective*. Also **spongey**, †**spungy**. LME.
[from SPONGE *noun*¹ + -Y¹.]

1 Resembling a sponge in being soft and porous, compressible, or elastic. LME. ▸**b** Of a motor vehicle's suspension or braking system: lacking firmness. M20.

2 Of a hard substance: having an open porous structure like that of a sponge. L16.

3 Sodden with or yielding up moisture; absorbent like a sponge. L16. ▸**b** Of moisture: resembling that pressed from a sponge. E17.

4 *fig.* Lacking definition or substance; vague, inexact. E17.

> **1** H. STEPHENS Flour that rises . . with yeast into a spongy dough. I. COLEGATE Her wrinkled spongy face fell into an expression of brooding discontent.

■ **spongily** *adverb* L19. **sponginess** *noun* E17.

sponsal /ˈspɒns(ə)l/ *adjective*. *literary*. M17.
[Latin *sponsalis*, from *sponsus*, *-a* spouse: see -AL¹.]
Of or pertaining to marriage or a wedding, nuptial.

sponsalia /spɒnˈseɪlɪə/ *noun pl.* *literary*. *rare*. M16.
[Latin, use as noun of neut. pl. of *sponsalis*: see prec.]
Nuptials, marriage.

sponsible /ˈspɒnsɪb(ə)l/ *adjective*. Now *dial.* E16.
[Aphet. from RESPONSIBLE.]
Responsible, reliable, respectable.

sponsion /ˈspɒnʃ(ə)n/ *noun*. M17.
[Latin *sponsio(n-)* from *spons-*: see SPONSOR *noun*, -ION.]

1 *ROMAN LAW*. A pledge to pay a certain sum to the other party in a suit in the event of not proving one's case. M17.

2 A solemn or formal promise, *esp.* one made on behalf of another; the action or an act of standing surety for another. L17. ▸**b** A promise made on behalf of the State by an agent not authorized to do so. L18.

sponson /ˈspɒns(ə)n/ *noun & verb*. M19.
[Origin unkn.]

▶ **A** *noun*. **1** Each of the triangular platforms fitted as supports fore and aft of the paddle-boxes of a paddle-steamer. M19.

2 A platform projecting from the side of a warship or tank to enable a gun to be trained forward and aft. M19.

3 **a** An air-filled buoyancy chamber in a canoe, intended to reduce the risk of sinking. Freq. in ***sponson canoe***. *Canad.* E20. ▸**b** A projection from the hull or body of a seaplane, intended to increase lateral stability in the water. Also, a stabilizer in the form of a float at the end of a wing. E20.

▶ **B** *verb trans.* Support or set out on a sponson. L19.

sponsor /ˈspɒnsə/ *noun*. M17.
[Latin, from *spons-* pa. ppl stem of *spondere* promise solemnly: see -OR.]

1 *CHRISTIAN CHURCH*. A godparent at a person's baptism; (esp. *ROMAN CATHOLIC CHURCH*) a person presenting a candidate for confirmation. M17.

2 A person taking responsibility or standing surety for another. Also, a person etc. putting a person or thing forward; *spec.* (*a*) a person introducing a proposal for legislation; (*b*) an organization supporting a candidate in an election. L17.

3 An organization or person supporting or promoting a sporting, artistic, etc., activity or performer, esp. in return for advertising; *spec.* (esp. *US*) a business etc. paying or contributing to the costs of a radio or television programme in return for air-time. M20.

4 A person etc. supporting a fund-raising (esp. charitable) activity by pledging money in advance, freq. as a certain amount for each unit completed. M20.

> **1** L. STRACHEY He stood as sponsor her son Arthur. **2** D. G. MITCHELL I found it requisite . . to become sponsor for his good conduct. **3** *Punch* National Broadcasting Company found a sponsor willing to put the . . Election up on prime time. **4** *Tuscaloosa News* A month-long read-a-thon . . in which each child obtained sponsors and pledges for each book . . read.

■ **sponsoress** *noun* (*rare*) a female sponsor L19. **spon'sorial** *adjective & noun* (*a*) *adjective* of or pertaining to a sponsor; (*b*) *noun* (*rare*) a godparent: L18. **sponsorship** *noun* (*a*) the state of being a sponsor; (*b*) money received from a sponsor: E19.

sponsor /ˈspɒnsə/ *verb trans.* L19.
[from the noun.]

1 Be surety for; favour or support strongly; *spec.* promote and support (a proposal) in a legislative assembly etc. M20.

2 Contribute to or bear the expenses of (an event or performer), esp. in return for advertising. M20.

3 Support (a person) in a fund-raising activity by pledging money in advance. **M20.**

> 📖 **1** *Planet* Early day motions sponsored by the Liberal Democrats . . have been signed by . . thirty MPs. **2** F. A. ARNOLD The travelogue . . program, sponsored by a tourist agency. **3** *Oxfam News* £35,000 was raised by young people . . sponsored by friends at a penny a mile. *Oxford Times* School's sponsored swim raises £920.

spontaneity /spɒntəˈniːɪti, -ˈneɪɪti/ *noun*. **M17.**
[from next + -ITY.]
The fact or quality of being spontaneous; spontaneous action or movement.

> 📖 *Times* The . . grainy photograph which . . was a sign of spontaneity and originality. J. CARTWRIGHT She possessed a spontaneity . . rare in our self-conscious times.

spontaneous /spɒnˈteɪnɪəs/ *adjective & adverb*. **M17.**
[from late Latin *spontaneus*, from Latin (*sua*) *sponte* of (one's) own accord: see -OUS.]
▸ **A** *adjective*. **1** Performed or occurring without external cause or stimulus; coming naturally or freely, unpremeditated; voluntary, done of one's own accord; (of literary style etc.) gracefully natural and unconstrained. **M17.** ▸**b** Of a person: acting voluntarily or without premeditation; tending to act in this way; unconstrained, uninhibited, natural. **M18.**
2 (Of movement or activity in an organism) instinctive, prompted by no motive; (of sudden movement etc.) involuntary, not due to conscious volition. **M17.**
3 Of a natural process: occurring without apparent external cause; having a self-contained cause or origin. **M17.**
4 Growing or produced naturally without cultivation or labour. **M17.** ▸**b** Produced, developed, or coming into existence by natural processes or changes. **M18.**

> 📖 **1** J. LONDON Stories and poems were springing into spontaneous creation in his brain. G. GORDON Edward clapped his hands briskly, . . a spontaneous gesture. W. F. BUCKLEY The applause was spontaneous, even heartfelt. D. MADDEN When they met for the first time it was with spontaneous and mutual antipathy. **b** W. CATHER She was not as spontaneous and frank as she used to be. M. SPUFFORD You are . . less spontaneous with your children if . . observed. **3 spontaneous combustion** the ignition or burning away of a substance or body as a result of heat engendered within itself, usu. by rapid oxidation. **4 spontaneous generation** HISTORY OF SCIENCE the supposed development of living organisms without the agency of pre-existing living matter, as of micro-organisms in water.

▸ **B** *adverb*. Spontaneously. *poet.* **M17.**
■ **spontaneously** *adverb* **M17.** **spontaneousness** *noun* **M17.**

spontoon /spɒnˈtuːn/ *noun*. **M18.**
[French †*sponton* (now *esponton*) from Italian *spuntone*, from *spuntare* to blunt, from *s-* ES- + *punto* POINT *noun*[1].]
Hist. A kind of half-pike or halberd used by infantry officers in the 18th cent.

spoof /spuːf/ *noun & adjective*. *colloq.* **L19.**
[Invented by Arthur Roberts (1852–1933), English comedian.]
▸ **A** *noun*. **1** A game involving bluff; a card-game in which certain cards when occurring together are denominated 'spoof'. **L19.**
2 a A hoax, a swindle; *rare* trickery, deception. **L19.** ▸**b** A parody; *spec.* a film, play, etc., that satirizes a particular genre. **M20.**

> 📖 **2b** *Daily News (New York)* A spoken spoof on Agatha Christie's style of mystery writing.

▸ **B** *adjective*. Bluffing, hoaxing; serving as a parody. **L19.**

> 📖 G. B. SHAW How am I to know how to take it? Is it serious, or is it spoof?

spoof /spuːf/ *verb*. *colloq.* **L19.**
[from the noun.]
1 *verb trans. & intrans.* Hoax, swindle. **L19.**
2 *verb trans.* Mock or satirize by parody. **E20.**
3 *verb trans.* Interfere with (radio or radar signals) so as to make them useless; jam deliberately. **L20.**
■ **spoofer** *noun* **E20.** **spoofery** *noun* †(*a*) in *pl.* (treated as *sing.*), a low sporting club; (*b*) trickery, hoaxing: **L19.**

spook /spuːk/ *noun*. Orig. *US.* **E19.**
[Dutch = Middle & mod. Low German *spōk* (whence German *Spuk*), of unkn. origin.]
1 An apparition, a ghost. *colloq.* Freq. *joc.* **E19.**
2 An undercover agent; a spy. *slang* (chiefly *US*). **M20.**
3 A black person. *slang* (chiefly *US*). *derog.* & considered *racially offensive*. **M20.**
■ **spookery** *noun* (*colloq.*) spookiness, eeriness; a spooky thing: **L19.** **spookish** *adjective* (*rare*) spooky **L19.** **spookist** *noun* a spiritualist, a medium **E20.**

spook /spuːk/ *verb*. **M19.**
[from the noun.]
1 a *verb intrans. & trans.* (with *it*). Act like a spook; walk *about* or *around* as a ghost. **M19.** ▸**b** *verb trans.* Haunt (a person or place). **L19.**
2 *slang* (chiefly *N. Amer.*). ▸**a** *verb intrans.* Take fright; become alarmed. **E20.** ▸**b** *verb trans.* Frighten, unnerve; *spec.* (of a hunter etc.) alarm (a wild animal). **M20.**

> 📖 **1b** *Publishers Weekly* The ghost of the highwayman . . spooks Flora with regular visitations. **2b** R. PILCHER He hated the horses and constantly spooked them into a frenzy.

■ **spooked** *ppl adjective* (*N. Amer. slang*) frightened, nervy; **spooked up**, excited: **M20.** **spooking** *verbal noun* (*a*) the action of calling spirits, as at a seance; (*b*) the action of haunting, frightening, or spying: **E20.**

spooky /ˈspuːki/ *adjective*. **M19.**
[from SPOOK *noun* + -Y[1].]
1 a Pertaining to or characteristic of ghosts or the supernatural; frightening, eerie. *colloq.* **M19.** ▸**b** SURFING. Of a wave: dangerous, frightening. **M20.**
2 Of a person or animal: nervous; easily frightened. *colloq.* (chiefly *N. Amer.*). **E20.**
3 Of or pertaining to spies or espionage. *US slang.* **L20.**

> 📖 **1a** A. TYLER She was thought to be unfriendly, even spooky—the witch of Calvert Street. J. BARNES Coincidences. There's something spooky about them. **2** M. MAHY I'm the one who feels spooky about Kate going out.

■ **spookily** *adverb* **M20.** **spookiness** *noun* **L19.**

spool /spuːl/ *noun & verb*. **ME.**
[Aphet. from Old French *espole* or its source Middle Low German *spōle* = Middle Dutch *spoele* (Dutch *spoel*), Old High German *spuolo*, *-a* (German *Spule*), from West Germanic, of unkn. origin.]
▸ **A** *noun*. **1** A small cylinder for winding thread on as it is spun, esp. for use in weaving. **ME.** ▸**b** Any cylinder on which thread, tape, wire, etc., is wound; *spec.* = REEL *noun* 2. **M19.**
2 A pin used in net-making. **M19.**
3 The sliding part of a spool valve. **M20.**
4 COMPUTING. [from sense B.3 below.] A file in which data is stored temporarily in readiness for printing. **L20.**

> 📖 **1b** J. HERBERT The spools of the . . tape recorder slowly revolved. *fig.*: M. TWAIN Reeling off his tranquil spool of lies.

Comb.: **spool valve**: in which a shaft with channels in its surface slides inside a sleeve with ports in it, the flow through the valve depending on the position of the shaft in the sleeve.
▸ **B** *verb*. **I 1** *verb intrans.* Wind a spool or spools. **E17.**
2 *verb trans.* Wind on to a spool. **E17.**
▸ **II 3** *verb trans.* COMPUTING. [Acronym, from simultaneous peripheral operation online.] Process, esp. print, on a peripheral device while the system that sent the data there carries out other processes. **M20.**
■ **spooler** *noun* (*a*) a person who winds thread on spools; (*b*) COMPUTING = **print spooler** s.v. PRINT *noun*: **M16.**

spoom /spuːm/ *verb intrans. & (rare) trans.* **E17.**
[Expressive alt. of SPOON *verb*[1].]
NAUTICAL. Run (a ship) *before* the wind or sea; scud.
■ **spooming** *ppl adjective* (*a*) running before the wind; (*b*) [by assoc. with *spume*] foaming: **M18.**

spoon /spuːn/ *noun*.
[Old English *spōn* = Middle Low German *spān*, Middle Dutch *spaen*, Old High German *spān* (German *Span* shaving), Old Norse *spónn*, *spánn*. Sense 2 is specifically Scandinavian (Norwegian and Icelandic).]
†**1 a** A thin piece of wood; a chip, a splinter. **OE–E16.** ▸**b** A roofing shingle. **ME–L15.**
2 An implement consisting of an oval or round bowl with a long straightish handle, used for conveying food (esp. liquid) to the mouth or plate, and for stirring, mixing, etc. (Freq. with specifying word.) **ME.** ▸†**b** A gift (in allus. to the traditional gift of a spoon to a child at his or her baptism). *rare* (Shakes.). Only in **E17.** ▸**c** The contents of a spoon, a spoonful; *spec.* a teaspoonful of sugar. **E20.** ▸**d** A dose or measure of an intoxicating drug; *spec.* two grams of heroin. *US.* **M20.** ▸**e** In *pl.* A pair of spoons held in the hand and beaten together rhythmically as a percussion instrument. **L20.**
3 a A spoon-shaped instrument used in surgery for scraping, or in heating or testing substances. **LME.** ▸**b** A golf club with a slightly concave wooden head (*Hist.*); a lofted stroke played with such a club. **L18.** ▸**c** ANGLING. An artificial bait in the shape of the bowl of a spoon, used in spinning or trolling. Also ***spoon-bait***. **M19.** ▸**d** CRICKET. A ball lofted by a soft or weak shot; a weak stroke which lifts the ball in the air. **L19.** ▸**e** SURFING. The slight upward slope of a surfboard. **M20.**
4 ZOOLOGY. A spoon-shaped part or process. *rare.* **E18.**
5 A shallow or foolish person; a simpleton. *colloq.* **L18.**
6 The student lowest in each class in the list of mathematical honours at Cambridge (the recipient of a wooden spoon). **E19.**
7 In *pl.*, sentimental or silly fondness; *sing.*, an instance of sentimental love-play; a fond lover. **M19.**

> 📖 **2** *Proverb*: Who sups with the devil will need a long spoon. ***dessertspoon***, ***soup spoon***, ***teaspoon***, etc. ***slotted spoon*** etc.

Phrases: **be spoons about**, **be spoons on**, **be spoons with** *slang* be in love with. **born with a silver spoon in one's mouth** born in affluence or under lucky auspices. ***deflagrating spoon***: see DEFLAGRATE. GREASY ***spoon (restaurant)***. **make a spoon or spoil a horn** (orig. *Scot.*) make a determined effort to achieve something. ***silver spoon***: see SILVER *noun & adjective*. †**spoon of the brisket** the hollow at the lower end of the breastbone of an animal. **wooden spoon**: see WOODEN *adjective*.
Comb.: **spoon-back** *noun & adjective* (*a*) *noun* (the back of) a chair curved concavely to fit a person's shape (popular in the late 18th and 19th centuries); (*b*) *adjective* designating a chair of this type; **spoon-backed** *adjective* (of a chair) having a spoon-back; ***spoon-bait***: see sense 3c above; **spoon-bender** a person who practises spoon-bending; **spoon-bending** the distortion of a spoon-handle or similar object by apparently psychokinetic means; **spoon-billed** *adjective* (ORNITHOLOGY) having a spatulate or spoon-shaped bill; ***spoon-billed sandpiper*** = ***spoonbill sandpiper***; **spoon bow** a boat's bow with full round sections resembling the bowl of a spoon; **spoon-bread** *US* soft maize bread; **spoon canoe** *Canad.*: having a spoon bow; **spoon drain** *Austral.* a shallow drain running across a street; **spoon-fashion** *adverb* fitting into each other after the manner of spoons; **spoonfeed** *verb trans.* (*a*) feed (a baby etc.) with a spoon; (*b*) provide (a person) with help, information, etc., so that no thought or effort is required by the recipient; (*c*) artificially encourage (an industry) by subsidies or import duties; **spoon-hook** ANGLING a spoon-bait; **spoon-meat** soft or liquid food for eating with a spoon, esp. by infants or invalids; **spoonwood** the mountain laurel, *Kalmia latifolia*; **spoonworm** = ECHIUROID *noun*.
■ **spooner** *noun*[1] (*rare*) †(*a*) a person who makes spoons; (*b*) a spoon-holder: **ME.** **spoonful** *noun* as much as a spoon will hold, as much as may be lifted in a spoon; *transf.* a very small quantity: **ME.** **spoonish** *adjective* (*rare*) foolish **M19.** **spoonist** *noun* the recipient of a spoon (only with specifying word); ***wooden spoonist***: see WOODEN *adjective*: **L20.** **spoonless** *adjective* (*rare*) **M19.**

spoon /spuːn/ *verb*[1] *intrans. arch.* **L16.**
[Origin unkn. Cf. SPOOM.]
NAUTICAL. Run *before* the wind or sea; scud.

spoon /spuːn/ *verb*[2]. **E18.**
[from the noun.]
▸ **I 1** *verb trans.* Lift or transfer by means of a spoon. Chiefly with prepositions or adverbs, as *into*, *off*, *out*, *up*. **E18.**
2 *verb trans.* **a** CROQUET. Push (a ball) without an audible knock. **M19.** ▸**b** CRICKET. Lift (the ball) up in the air with a soft or weak stroke; hit (an easy catch). **M19.**
3 a *verb intrans.* Lie close together or fit into each other in the manner of spoons. **M19.** ▸**b** *verb trans.* Lie with (a person) spoon-fashion. **L19.**
4 *verb trans.* Catch (fish) by means of a spoon-bait. **L19.**
5 *verb trans.* Hollow out, make concave like a spoon. **L19.**

> 📖 **1** J. C. OATES St. Dennis is spooning out mushrooms onto a platter. G. TINDALL An uncle . . let me spoon the cream from the top of his hot chocolate.

▸ **II 6** *verb intrans.* Cuddle, fondle, or talk amorously, esp. in a sentimental or silly fashion. *colloq.* **M19.**
7 *verb trans.* Try to win the affection of, court, esp. in a sentimental fashion. **L19.**

> 📖 **6** H. WILLIAMSON The Mecca coffee rooms . . where men go to spoon with the waitresses!

■ **spooned** *ppl adjective* shaped or hollowed out like a spoon **M19.** **spooner** *noun*[2] a person who spoons with another, a sentimental lover **L19.**

spoonbill /ˈspuːnbɪl/ *noun*. **L17.**
[from SPOON *noun* + BILL *noun*[2], after Dutch *lepelaar* (from *lepel* spoon).]
1 Any of various wading birds which with ibises constitute the family Threskiornithidae, and have a long spatulate or spoon-shaped bill specialized for feeding in water; *esp.* the Old World species *Platalea leucorodia*. **L17.**
2 A spatulate or spoon-shaped bill. **E19.**
3 = ***spoonbill duck*** below. *rare.* **L19.**
1 *roseate spoonbill*: see ROSEATE *adjective* 1.
Comb.: **spoonbill duck** a shoveller duck; **spoonbill sandpiper** a sandpiper, *Eurynorhynchus pygmeus*, of eastern Asia having a broad flat end to its bill.

spoondrift /ˈspuːndrɪft/ *noun*. **M18.**
[from SPOON *verb*[1] + DRIFT *noun*.]
= SPINDRIFT.

spoonerism /ˈspuːnərɪz(ə)m/ *noun*. **M19.**
[from *Spooner* (see below) + -ISM.]
†**1** The theory or opinions of the Revd W. A. Spooner (1844–1930), English educationist. Only in **M19.**
2 [from Spooner's tendency to make such transpositions.] A (usu. accidental) transposition of the initial sounds, or other parts, of two or more spoken words, as *fighting liars* from *lighting fires*. **E20.**
■ **spoonerize** *verb trans.* alter (a word or phrase) by a spoonerism **E20.**

spoony /ˈspuːni/ *noun & adjective*. Also **-ney**. **L18.**
[from SPOON *noun* + -Y[1].]
▸ **A** *noun*. **1** A silly or foolish person; a simpleton. **L18.**
2 A person who behaves in a sentimentally or foolishly amorous manner. **M19.**
▸ **B** *adjective*. **1** Foolish, silly, soft. **E19.**
2 Sentimentally or foolishly amorous; expressive of sentimental fondness; sweet *on* a person. **E19.**
■ **spoonily** *adverb* (*rare*) **M19.** **spooniness** *noun* (*a*) foolishness, silliness; (*b*) the condition of being sentimentally in love: **E19.** **spoonyism** *noun* the state or quality of being spoony **M19.**

spoor /spʊə, spɔː/ *noun & verb.* E19.
[Afrikaans, repr. Middle Dutch *spo(o)r* = Old English, Old High German, Old Norse *spor* (German *Spur*); rel. to SPEER *verb*[1].]
▶ **A** *noun.* The track, trail, or scent of a person or animal; *esp.* (*collect.*) the footprints of a wild animal hunted as game. E19.

📖 C. FULLER His party set out . . to follow exactly along Van Rensburg's spoor. W. HORWOOD Both vole and weazel had left spoor at the entrance.

▶ **B** *verb.* **1** *verb trans.* Trace (an animal) by spoor. M19.
2 *verb intrans.* Follow a spoor or trail. M19.
■ **spoorer** *noun* a person who follows an animal etc. by its spoor; a tracker: M19.

sporadic /spəˈradɪk/ *adjective & noun.* L17.
[medieval Latin *sporadicus* from Greek *sporadikos*, from *sporas, sporad-* scattered, dispersed, from base of *spora* sowing, seed.]
▶ **A** *adjective.* **1** MEDICINE. Of a disease: occurring in isolated instances, or in a few cases only; not epidemic. L17.
2 a Scattered or dispersed, occurring singly or in very small numbers. E19. ▸**b** Of a single person or thing: separate, isolated. E19. ▸**c** Appearing or happening only now and again or at intervals; occasional. M19. ▸**d** ASTRONOMY. Of a meteor: isolated, that does not appear to belong to a shower. E20.
3 MATH. Of a finite simple group: that does not fall into any of the infinite classes into which most such groups fall. M20.

📖 **2b** H. JAMES Think of the Baden episode as a mere sporadic piece of disorder. **c** O. SACKS Grimacing, which had been sporadic previously, had become frequent. INA TAYLOR Hunger brought unrest and . . there were sporadic outbreaks of violence.

Special collocations: **sporadic E-layer**, **sporadic E-region** a discontinuous region of ionization that occurs from time to time in the E-layer of the ionosphere and results in the anomalous reflection back to earth of VHF radio waves.
▶ **B** *noun.* **1** ASTRONOMY. A sporadic meteor. M20.
2 MATH. A sporadic group. L20.
■ **sporadical** *adjective* (now *rare* or *obsolete*) = SPORADIC *adjective* M17. **sporadically** *adverb* (*a*) in isolated cases; (*b*) in a scattered or dispersed manner; at intervals, occasionally; here and there: M18.

sporal /ˈspɔːr(ə)l/ *adjective.* L19.
[from SPORE + -AL[1].]
BOTANY. Consisting of or pertaining to spores.

sporangium /spəˈran(d)ʒɪəm/ *noun.* Pl. **-ia** /-ɪə/. Also Anglicized as **sporange** /spəˈran(d)ʒ/. E19.
[mod. Latin, from Greek *spora* (see SPORE) + *aggeion* vessel: see -IUM.]
BOTANY. A receptacle in which spores are formed; *esp.* an organ in various fungi producing endogenous asexual spores.
■ **sporangial** *adjective* of or pertaining to a sporangium M19. **sporanˈgiferous** *adjective* bearing sporangia M19. **sporangiolum** *noun*, pl. **-la**, a small sporangium usu. containing only a few spores E19. **sporangiophore** *noun* a structure or (MYCOLOGY) a specialized hypha bearing sporangia L19. **sporangiospore** *noun* a spore produced in a sporangium L19.

spore /spɔː/ *noun.* M19.
[mod. Latin *spora* from Greek *spora* sowing, seed: see SPORADIC.]
1 BIOLOGY. A small, usu. one-celled, reproductive unit capable of giving rise to a new individual without sexual fusion (cf. GAMETE), characteristic of cryptogamic plants, fungi, and protozoans; *spec.* (*a*) in a plant exhibiting alternation of generations, a haploid reproductive cell which gives rise to a gametophyte; (*b*) in bacteria, a rounded resistant form adopted by a bacterial cell in adverse conditions. Also, these collectively. M19.
2 *gen.* A germ, a seed. L19.
Comb.: **spore-case** BOTANY a structure containing spores, a sporangium; **spore print** BOTANY an image of the spore-producing structures of a fungal fruiting body, made by allowing spores to fall on to a plain surface.

sporeling /ˈspɔːlɪŋ/ *noun.* E20.
[from SPORE + -LING[1], after *seedling*.]
BOTANY. A young plant (e.g. a fern) developed from a spore.

Spörer /ˈʃpəːrə/ *noun.* E20.
[Gustav-Friedrich Wilhelm *Spörer* (1822–96), German astronomer.]
ASTRONOMY. Used *attrib.* and in *possess.* with ref. to phenomena investigated by Spörer.
Spörer minimum the interval between about 1400 and 1510 during which little activity is thought to have taken place on the sun. **Spörer's law** an empirical relationship according to which the mean latitude of sunspots tends to decrease as a sunspot cycle progresses.

sporidesmin /spɔːrɪˈdɛzmɪn/ *noun.* M20.
[from mod. Latin *Sporidesmium* genus name of the fungus from which first isolated (from SPORE + -i- + Greek *desmos* band, bundle): see -IN[1].]
BIOCHEMISTRY. Any of a class of toxins produced by some fungi which cause various diseases of animals, esp. sheep, when ingested.

sporidium /spəˈrɪdɪəm/ *noun.* Pl. **-dia** /-dɪə/. E19.
[mod. Latin, dim. of Latin *spora* SPORE: see -IDIUM.]
BOTANY. A small spore, esp. a basidiospore in a rust or smut fungus. Formerly also, a case or capsule containing such spores.
■ **sporiˈdiferous** *adjective* bearing sporidia M19. **sporidiole** *noun* = SPORIDIOLUM M19. **sporidiolum** *noun*, pl. **-la**, a small sporidium M19.

sporiferous /spɔːˈrɪf(ə)rəs/ *adjective.* M19.
[from mod. Latin *spora* SPORE + -I- + -FEROUS.]
BOTANY. Bearing spores.

Spork /spɔːk/ *noun.* E20.
[Blend of SPOON *noun* and FORK *noun*.]
(Proprietary name for) a piece of cutlery combining the features of a spoon, fork, and sometimes knife.

sporo- /ˈspɒrəʊ, ˈspɔːrəʊ/ *combining form.*
[from SPORE or directly from Latin, Greek *spora*: see -O-.]
BIOLOGY. Of or relating to the spores of plants or microorganisms or to elementary forms of animal life.
■ **sporoblast** *noun* a cell which gives rise to spores or similar structures, or sporozoites L19. **sporocarp** *noun* (BOTANY) an organ which bears spores; *esp.* (*a*) a fruiting body of a fungus; (*b*) a hard rounded body at the base of an aquatic pteridophyte, containing the sporangia: M19. **sporocyst** *noun* (ZOOLOGY) (*a*) a parasitic trematode in the initial stage of infection in a mollusc host, developed from a miracidium and in turn forming a redia; (*b*) in sporozoans etc., an encysted zygote in an invertebrate host: M19. **sporocyte** *noun* = SPOROBLAST L19. **sporoˈdochium** *noun*, pl. **-ia**, [Greek *dokhē* receptacle], MYCOLOGY a fruiting body composed of an exposed mass of conidia on a cushion-like layer of short conidiophores E20. **sporoˈgenesis** *noun* the formation of spores L19. **spoˈrogenous** *adjective* (of an organism, a tissue) producing spores L19. **sporoˈgonium** *noun*, pl. **-ia**, BOTANY the sporophyte of a bryophyte, represented by the capsule and its seta L19. **spoˈrogony** *noun* (ZOOLOGY) the asexual fission of a sporont to produce spores L19. **sporophore** *noun* (BOTANY) a spore-bearing process or structure, esp. a conidiophore M19. **sporophyll** *noun* (BOTANY) a modified leaf bearing sporangia; *esp.* any of the scalelike leaves in the terminal spike of a clubmoss: L19. **sporosac** *noun* (ZOOLOGY) in some hydrozoans, a stalked organ in which gametes develop M19.

sporonin /ˈspɒrənɪn/ *noun.* Now chiefly *Hist.* E20.
[from SPORO- + *-n-* + -IN[1].]
BIOCHEMISTRY. = SPOROPOLLENIN.

sporont /ˈspɒrɒnt, ˈspɔː-/ *noun.* L19.
[from SPORO- + -ONT.]
ZOOLOGY. A protozoan cell at a stage of the life cycle following syngenesis and preceding the formation of spores.
■ **sporontiˈcidal** *adjective* lethal to sporonts, esp. those of malaria parasites L20.

sporophyte /ˈspɒrəfʌɪt, ˈspɔː-/ *noun.* L19.
[from SPORO- + -PHYTE.]
BOTANY. In the alternation of generations: the asexual, usu. diploid phase in the life cycle of a plant (the dominant form in vascular plants but in bryophytes dependent on the gametophyte) which produces the spores from which the gametophyte arises. Cf. GAMETOPHYTE.
■ **sporophytic** /-ˈfɪtɪk/ *adjective* pertaining to or of the nature of a sporophyte L19. **sporoˈphytically** *adverb* L20.

sporopollenin /spɔːrə(ʊ)ˈpɒlənɪn/ *noun.* M20.
[from SPORO(NIN + POLLENIN.]
BIOCHEMISTRY. An inert substance, consisting largely of polysaccharides, that forms the resistant outer coating of spores and pollen grains.

sporotrichosis /ˌspɔːrə(ʊ)trɪˈkəʊsɪs, ˌspɒ-/ *noun.* E20.
[from mod. Latin *Sporotrichum* (orig. *Sporothricum*) former genus name of *Sporothrix* (see below), formed as SPORO- + -TRICH: see -OSIS.]
MEDICINE. A chronic disease caused by the fungus *Sporothrix schenckii*, common in soil and wood and freq. introduced by a superficial scratch, typically producing nodules and ulcers in the lymph nodes and skin.

sporozoan /spɔːrəˈzəʊən, spɒ-/ *noun & adjective.* L19.
[from mod. Latin *Sporozoa* (see below), formed as SPORO- + Greek *zōia* pl. of *zōion* animal: see -AN.]
BIOLOGY & MEDICINE. ▶**A** *noun.* A protozoan of the mainly parasitic phyla Apicomplexa (which includes class Sporozoa) and Microspora, having a complex life cycle with sexual and asexual generations and including the malaria parasites (genus *Plasmodium*). L19.
▶ **B** *adjective.* Of or pertaining to such protozoans. L19.
■ **sporozoon** *noun*, pl. **-zoa**, = SPOROZOAN *noun* (usu. in *pl.*) L19.

sporozoite /spɔːrəˈzəʊʌɪt, spɒ-/ *noun.* L19.
[from SPORO- + -ZOITE.]
BIOLOGY & MEDICINE. In certain protozoans, esp. sporozoans, a small motile individual produced by asexual fission of a sporont, usu. within a host.

sporran /ˈspɒr(ə)n/ *noun.* M18.
[Gaelic *sporan* = Irish *sparán* purse, Middle Irish *sboran* from Latin *bursa* PURSE *noun*.]
A pouch or large purse usu. made of leather or sealskin covered with fur and with ornamental tassels etc., worn by a Scottish Highlander in front of the kilt.

sport /spɔːt/ *noun.* LME.
[Aphet. from DISPORT *noun*.]
1 a Diversion, entertainment, fun; an activity providing this, a pastime. LME. ▸†**b** Lovemaking, esp. sexual intercourse, viewed as a game. M16–L18. ▸†**c** A theatrical performance; a show, a play. Only in L16.
2 a A matter providing amusement or entertainment; a joke. *arch.* LME. ▸**b** Jesting, joking; merriment. *arch.* L16.
3 a An activity involving physical exertion and skill, *esp.* one in which an individual competes against another or others to achieve the best performance. Later also, participation in such activities; such activities collectively. E16. ▸**b** In *pl.* A meeting consisting of various athletic and occas. other sporting contests. See also ***sports day*** below. L16. ▸**c** The recreation of hunting, shooting, or fishing. M17.
4 a A thing tossed about by natural forces as if a plaything. M17. ▸**b** An object of amusement, diversion, jesting, etc.; a laughing-stock, a plaything. L17.
5 BIOLOGY. A plant (or part of a plant), animal, etc., which exhibits some abnormal or striking variation from the parent stock or type, esp. in form or colour; a spontaneous mutation; a new variety produced in this way. (Earliest in ***sport of nature*** below.) Cf. SPORT *verb* 7b. M17.
6 a A gambler, a gamester. *US.* M19. ▸**b** A person who follows or participates in (a) sport; a sportsman or sportswoman. L19. ▸**c** A young man; a fellow. *US.* L19. ▸**d** A fair-minded, generous person; a lively, sociable person. See also ***good sport*** below. *colloq.* L19. ▸**e** Used as a familiar form of address, esp. between males. Chiefly *Austral. & NZ.* E20.
7 The sports section of a newspaper. Freq. in *pl.* (treated as *sing.*). *colloq.* E20.
8 In *pl.* (treated as *sing.*). A sports car; a sports model of a car. *colloq.* M20.

📖 **1a** S. PATRICK You can rest from your labours, and yet not spend your whole time in sport and play. D. C. PEATTIE The sport in taking life is a satisfaction I can't feel. G. DALY He tended to know . . almost everything, and it was . . great sport to catch him out. **c** SHAKES. *Rich. II* Mark . . the moral of this sport. **2b** F. BURNEY Dr. Johnson . . was . . lively and full of wit and sport. **3a** *Modern Painters* Establishments specifically devoted to indoctrination . . through activities such as sport and the arts. *Reader's Digest* Hang-gliding is a dangerous sport. ***racket sport***, ***water sport***, ***winter sport***, etc. **c** J. FOWLES Though he conceded enough to sport to shoot partridge . . , Charles . . refused to hunt the fox. **4a** CARLYLE Blown, like a . . rag, the sport of winds. **b** T. SOUTHERNE Am I then the sport, The Game of Fortune, and her laughing Fools? **5** *Australian House & Garden* A smaller flowered . . species, *Clematis montana*, and its pink sport *Clematis montana rubens*. **6d** P. MCGINLEY Will you come out this evening? . . Come on, be a sport.

Phrases: **a bad sport** a person who behaves unfairly, esp. regarding games, rules, etc.; a person unable to take a joke; a poor loser. **a good sport** a person who behaves fairly, esp. regarding games, rules, etc.; a person who takes a joke in good part or who reacts positively to a challenge or adversity. **a sport of terms**, **a sport of wit**, **a sport of words** (now *rare* or *obsolete*) a play on words; a piece of writing characterized by this. **have good sport** be successful in hunting, fishing, etc. **in sport** jestingly; for fun. **make a person sport** provide entertainment or diversion for a person. †**make a sport of** (*rare*, Shakes.) make a joke of. **make sport** find diversion, be amused *at* or *with*; make fun *of*. PARTICIPATION ***sport***. **show sport** (*a*) (of prey etc.) provide diversion by demonstrating spirit and courage; (*b*) (of a master of foxhounds) provide good hunting. **sport of nature** = LUSUS *naturae* (cf. sense 5 above). **the sport of kings** orig., warfare; now usu., horse-racing, hunting, or surfing. ***tinhorn sport***: see TINHORN *adjective*.
Attrib. & comb.: (usu. in *pl.*) in the sense 'designating clothing suitable for sport, physical activities, or informal wear', as ***sports shirt***, ***sports shoe***, etc.; (in *pl.*) in the sense 'used for, dealing with, or involving sport', as ***sports centre***, ***sports equipment***, ***sports ground***, ***sports reporter***, ***sports shop***, etc. Special combs., as **sportfish** a fish caught for sport rather than for food; **sportfisherman** a seagoing boat equipped for sportfishing; **sportfishing** fishing with a rod and line for sport or recreation; **sports bar** a bar where televised sport is shown continuously; **sports car** a low-built usu. open car designed for superior acceleration and performance at high speed; **sportscast** *N. Amer.* a broadcast of a sports event or information about sport; **sportscaster** (chiefly *N. Amer.*) a presenter of sports broadcasts on radio or television; a sports commentator; **sports coat**, **sports jacket** a man's jacket for informal wear; **sports day** a meeting at a school or college for competing in various sports, esp. athletics; **sports finder** PHOTOGRAPHY a direct-vision viewfinder usu. consisting of a simple frame which allows action outside the field of view of the camera to be seen, fitted esp. to twin-lens reflex cameras; ***sports jacket***: see ***sports coat*** above; **sports medicine** the branch of medicine that deals with injuries etc. resulting from activity in sports; **sports page**, **sports section** a page or section of a newspaper devoted to coverage of sports and games; **sportsperson** a sportsman or sportswoman; ***sports section***: see ***sports page*** above; **sports team** a team of players, freq. one belonging to a particular country or institution, competing in a particular sport or sporting event; **sportswear** clothes worn for sport or for casual use; **sportswoman** (*a*) a woman who takes part in sport; (*b*) a woman who behaves fairly and generously; **sports writer** a person, esp. a journalist, who writes on sports and games; **sport utility (vehicle)** a high-performance four-wheel-drive vehicle.

■ **sportless** *adjective* (*rare*) E17. **sportly** *adjective* (*rare*) connected with sport; sporting, sportsmanlike: L17.

sport /spɔːt/ *verb*. LME.
[Aphet. from DISPORT *verb*.]
▶ **I** With ref. to recreation or amusement.
†**1** *verb refl.* Amuse oneself; have a pleasant time. (Foll. by *with* a person, an activity, etc.) LME–L18.
2 a *verb intrans.* & (*rare*) *trans.* (with *it*). Amuse or entertain oneself, esp. by outdoor exercise or activity; play a game; frolic, gambol. L15. ▸**b** *verb intrans.* Take part in sport, esp. field sports; hunt or shoot for recreation. L18.
3 a *verb intrans.* & *trans.* (with *it*). Make fun of a person or thing; show ridicule. Foll. by *at*, *over*, *upon* (the person or thing). Now *rare*. M16. ▸**b** *verb intrans.* Deal *with* in a light or playful way; trifle or dally *with*. M17.
†**4** *verb trans.* Provide (a person) with sport or amusement; cheer, enliven. L16–M18.
5 *verb trans.* **a** Pass (time) with fun or amusement. Also foll. by *away*. *arch.* L16. ▸†**b** Play or toy with (something). *rare*. E18–E19.
6 *verb trans.* Foll. by *away*: remove or waste wantonly or recklessly; squander. Now *rare*. E18.
7 *verb intrans.* & (*rare*) †*refl.* †**a** Of nature: produce abnormal forms as if in sport. Cf. SPORTING *noun* 2. Only in M18. ▸**b** BIOLOGY. Of a plant, animal, etc.: deviate or vary abnormally from the parent stock or specific type; exhibit spontaneous mutation. Cf. SPORT *noun* 5. M18.

> 📖 **2a** E. WAUGH Clear air where doves sported with the butterflies. *fig.*: POPE When Sense subsides, and Fancy sports in sleep. **3b** C. READE My misery is too great to be sported with. **7a** E. BANCROFT The surrounding forests, where Nature sports in primaeval rudeness. **b** G. GORER A tree . . will grow misshapen or sport back to its wild origins if not timely treated.

▶ **II 8** †**a** *verb trans.* Stake (money) on the outcome of a race, game, etc.; bet, wager. E18–M19. ▸†**b** *verb intrans.* Engage in betting; speculate. M18–E19. ▸**c** *verb trans.* Spend (money) freely, extravagantly, or ostentatiously. *rare*. M19.
9 *verb trans.* **a** Display, exhibit, esp. ostentatiously; display on one's person, wear. E18. ▸**b** Set up, keep, maintain, use (a house etc.). Now *rare*. E19.
10 *verb trans.* Shut (a door), esp. from the inside and as a sign that one is busy; shut (a person) *in* by closing the door. Chiefly *Univ. slang*. E19.
11 *verb trans.* Entertain (a person) with food or drink; treat (a person) to (a drink etc.). *rare*. E19.

> 📖 **9a** *Argosy* A handsome . . youth who sported a fine moustache. S. WYNTER The fireflies hummed and . . sported their wings. G. KEILLOR My dad's car sported a compass on the dashboard. R. ELLMANN Wilde sported a new brownish-yellow coat. **10** ***sport one's oak***: see OAK *noun* 2b.

■ **sportaˈbility** *noun* (*rare*) ability to be sportive or playful M18. †**sportable** *adjective* able to be sportive: only in M18. **sportance** *noun* (*rare*) playful, sportive, or frolicsome activity LME.

sporter /ˈspɔːtə/ *noun*. M16.
[from prec. + -ER¹.]
†**1** A person who amuses or entertains others; a buffoon, a jester. *Scot.* M–L16.
2 A participant in sport of any kind; a sportsman or sportswoman. Also (*rare*), a gambler. E17. ▸**b** A sporting dog. E19. ▸**c** Any firearm designed for use in field sports. L20.
†**3** = SPORT *noun* 5. *rare*. Only in E18.
4 A person who trifles *with* something serious. *rare*. M19.
5 A person who sports a garment; a wearer *of* something. L19.

sportful /ˈspɔːtfʊl, -f(ə)l/ *adjective*. Now *rare*. LME.
[from SPORT *noun* + -FUL.]
1 Providing amusement or entertainment; enjoyable as a diversion or recreation. LME. ▸**b** Devised for fun, carried out in jest; not serious. E17. ▸**c** Of a movement: lively, frolicsome. L17.
2 Having an inclination to take part in sport, jest, or play; sportive, playful. L16.
■ **sportfully** *adverb* M16. **sportfulness** *noun* L16.

sportif /spɔrtif/ *adjective*. M20.
[French.]
Sportive; active or interested in athletic sports; (of a garment) suitable for sport or informal wear.

sporting /ˈspɔːtɪŋ/ *noun*. LME.
[from SPORT *verb* + -ING¹.]
1 The action of SPORT *verb*, participation in sport; amusement; recreation; (now *rare* or *obsolete*) an instance of this. LME.
2 The spontaneous producing by a plant (or formerly, by an animal, or by nature) of an abnormal form or variety; an instance of this, = SPORT *noun* 5. (Earliest in ***sporting of nature*** below.) L17.
2 †**sporting of nature** = LUSUS *naturae* (cf. ***sport of nature*** s.v. SPORT *noun*).
Attrib. & comb.: In the sense 'concerned with or suitable for sport', as ***sporting association***, ***sporting dog***, ***sporting equipment***, ***sporting event***, etc. Special combs., as **sporting editor** *US* a sports editor; **sporting house** †(*a*) a house or inn frequented by sportsmen; (*b*) *US* a brothel; **sporting picture**, **sporting print**: depicting a scene from a hunt or other field sport.

sporting /ˈspɔːtɪŋ/ *adjective*. E17.
[formed as prec. + -ING².]
1 †**a** Sportive; playful. *rare*. E17–E18. ▸**b** Engaged in sport or play. M17. ▸**c** Of a plant etc.: tending to produce abnormal varieties or sports. M19.
2 a Interested in or concerned in sport. M18. ▸**b** Designating an inferior sportsman or a person interested in sport from purely mercenary motives. Now *esp.* pertaining to or interested in betting or gambling. Chiefly in ***sporting man***. E19.
3 Orig., providing good sport or entertainment. Later, characterized by sportsmanlike conduct; fair-minded, generous. L18.

> 📖 **3** *New York Review of Books* It is not very sporting of her to hide behind them.

Special collocations: **sporting chance** a fair possibility of success. **sporting girl**, **sporting woman** *N. Amer.* a prostitute or promiscuous woman.
■ **sportingly** *adverb* L16.

sportive /ˈspɔːtɪv/ *adjective*. L16.
[from SPORT *noun* or *verb* + -IVE.]
1 Inclined to jesting or levity; playful, frolicsome; light, not serious. L16.
2 Lustful, amorous, sexually aroused or active. *arch.* L16.
3 Pertaining to, of the nature of, or providing, sport or amusement. E18.
4 a Produced (as) in sport or play; *spec.* of the nature of a sport or abnormal variation; anomalous. Now *rare* or *obsolete*. L18. ▸**b** BIOLOGY. Of a plant etc.: liable to sport or vary from the type. M19.
5 a Taking part in or interested in (athletic) sport or sports. L19. ▸**b** Of clothing: suitable for sporting or informal wear. M20.
■ **sportively** *adverb* playfully; with levity; in sport or jest: L16. **sportiveness** *noun* E17.

sportling /ˈspɔːtlɪŋ/ *noun*. Long *rare* or *obsolete*. E18.
[formed as prec. + -LING¹.]
1 A small playful animal or bird. E18.
†**2** = SPORT *noun* 5. Only in E18.

sportsman /ˈspɔːtsmən/ *noun*. Pl. **-men**. L17.
[from SPORT *noun* + -'S¹ + MAN *noun*.]
1 A person who takes part in sport; orig. *esp.* a person who hunts or shoots for pleasure. L17.
2 A better, a gambler. *US*. M18.
3 A person who behaves fairly and generously; a good sport. L19.
■ **sportsmanlike** *adjective* resembling (that of) a sportsman; *esp.* fair, honourable: M18. **sportsmanly** *adjective* worthy of or befitting a sportsman; sportsmanlike: L18. **sportsmanship** *noun* the performance or practice of a sportsman; skill in or knowledge of sport; sportsmanlike conduct: M18.

sportster /ˈspɔːtstə/ *noun*. M20.
[formed as prec. + -STER.]
1 A sports coat. *rare*. M20.
2 A sports car. L20.

sporty /ˈspɔːti/ *adjective*. *colloq.* L19.
[formed as prec. + -Y¹.]
1 Sportsmanlike; sporting; keen on sport. L19.
2 Of a motor car: resembling a sports car in appearance or performance. Also *gen.*, racy, showy. M20.

> 📖 **1** M. FORSTER He disapproves of smoking, being your sporty health-freak type.

■ **sportiness** *noun* L19.

sporulate /ˈspɒrjʊleɪt/ *verb*. L19.
[from SPORULE + -ATE³.]
1 *verb intrans.* Form spores or sporules. L19.
2 *verb trans.* Convert into spores. *rare*. L19.
■ **sporuˈlation** *noun* spore-formation L19.

sporule /ˈspɒrjuːl/ *noun*. E19.
[French, or mod. Latin *sporula*: see SPORE, -ULE.]
BIOLOGY. A (small) spore.
■ **sporular** *adjective* of, pertaining to, or of the nature of a sporule E19.

sposa /ˈspoːza/ *noun*. Pl. **-se** /-ze/. E17.
[Italian.]
A wife; a bride. Cf. SPOSO.
CARA SPOSA.

s'pose /spəʊz/ *verb intrans.* & *trans.* *colloq.* M19.
[Repr. a pronunc.]
= SUPPOSE *verb*.

sposh /spɒʃ/ *noun*. *US dial.* M19.
[Imit.]
Slush, mud.
■ **sposhy** *adjective* soft and watery M19.

sposo /ˈspoːzo/ *noun*. Now *rare*. Pl. **-si** /-zi/. L18.
[Italian.]
A husband. Cf. SPOSA.
CARO SPOSO.

spot /spɒt/ *noun*, *adjective*, & *adverb*. ME.
[Perh. from Middle Dutch *spotte*, Low German *spot*, corresp. to Old Norse *spotti* small piece, bit (Norwegian *spott* speck, spot, plot of land), obscurely rel. to Old English *splott* spot, plot of land.]
▶ **A** *noun*. **I 1** A small discoloration or disfiguring mark; a stain; a speck (*of*). ME.
2 *spec.* †**a** A mark on the eye symptomatic of a disease. ME–M17. ▸**b** A pimple. LME. ▸**c** Any of various plant diseases producing small round areas of discoloration on the leaves or fruit. Cf. ***leaf-spot*** s.v. LEAF *noun*¹. M19.
3 *fig.* A moral stain or blemish. ME.

> 📖 **1** SIR W. SCOTT Spots of dirt that we are about to wash from our hands. **2b** U. HOLDEN Ula had spots on her chin. **2c** ***coral spot***, ***dollar spot***, ***marsh spot***, etc. **3** SHELLEY Sublimely mild, a Spirit without spot.

▶ **II 4** A small mark on the surface of a thing visibly different in colour, texture, etc., and usually round or less elongated than a streak or stripe. ME. ▸†**b** A patch worn on the face; a beauty-spot. L16–M17. ▸**c** A pip on a playing-card, domino, or die. Now chiefly *US*. L16.
5 a A variety of the domestic pigeon with white plumage and a coloured mark above the beak. L17. ▸**b** A spotted fabric. L18. ▸**c** With specifying word: any of various moths having one or more prominent spots on the wings. M19. ▸**d** A dollar bill of a specified value; a playing-card with a specified number of pips. *N. Amer.* M19. ▸**e** Either of two marine food fishes of the family Sciaenidae, the red drum, *Sciaenops ocellatus* and esp. *Leiostomus xanthurus*. *US*. L19. ▸**f** More fully ***spot board***. A board for working plaster before application. E20.
6 a BILLIARDS & SNOOKER etc. Any of six positions on a table (orig. marked by a black patch) where a colour ball is to be placed at certain times. E19. ▸**b** BILLIARDS. In full ***spot-ball***. The white ball distinguished from the other by two black spots. M19.

> 📖 **4** H. JAMES The flush in Sarah's cheeks had . . settled to a small . . crimson spot. J. C. OATES Iris steps over the damp, shining spots in the linoleum. S. WYNTER A bald spot . . to the left of her widow's peak.

▶ **III 7** A small piece, amount, or quantity; *spec.* a small drink. Usu. foll. by *of*. Now *colloq.* LME. ▸†**b** A piece *of* work. L17–M19. ▸**c** A drop of or *of* rain. L19.
8 A particular place, esp. of limited extent. LME. ▸**b** A plot *of* land. Now passing into sense 7. LME. ▸**c** = SLOT *noun*² 4. E20. ▸**d** An awkward or difficult situation. Usu. with specifying word. *colloq.* E20. ▸**e** A place of entertainment; *spec.* = ***nightspot*** s.v. NIGHT *noun*. *colloq.* M20.
9 a A particular small area or definite point in a surface. E19. ▸**b** *transf.* A particular aspect of a person's character; a moment, feature, etc., of a specified kind. M19. ▸**c** CRICKET. The point at which a ball should pitch for optimum length and direction. M19. ▸**d** SOCCER. *The* place from which a penalty is taken. L20.
10 In *pl.* & (occas.) *sing.* Goods for immediate cash payment and delivery. L19.
11 = SPOTLIGHT *noun*. E20.

> 📖 **7** G. GREENE I asked you to come . . because there's a spot of trouble. S. J. PERELMAN How about a spot of whisky and soda? P. LIVELY There's a spot of dinner ready. *Sun* There was time for a spot of snooker. **c** B. PYM She had put on a raincoat, for a few spots were beginning to fall. **8** HUGH THOMAS Discussion as to the exact spot where the girls stopped. P. MARSHALL To stand in any one spot for too long. **b** T. CALLENDER He did own two spots o' land in St. George. **c** *Radio Times* Lynn . . of *Breakfast Time* will do a regular spot on pitfalls in the home. *Bowls International* To secure her semi-final spot with a 7–4 win. **d** E. BAKER Trying . . to determine just how serious a spot he was in. **9a** F. C. L. WRAXALL The Sea-snails have their gills at very different spots. **b** E. SEGAL The only . . bright spot for Barney had been Laura's weekly letters.

Phrases: BEAUTY ***spot***. ***blind spot***: see BLIND *adjective*. ***Great red spot***: see ***red spot*** s.v. RED *adjective*. ***have a soft spot for***: see SOFT *adjective*. ***high spot***: see HIGH *adjective*. **hit the spot** *colloq.* (chiefly *N. Amer.*) be exactly what is required. **in spots** *US* occasionally, at intervals. ***knock spots off***: see KNOCK *verb*. KOPLIK'S SPOT. ***Mongolian spot***: see MONGOLIAN *adjective*. **on-the-spot** *adjective* done, made, occurring, etc., on the spot or then and there. **on the spot** (*a*) at the scene of an action or event; (*b*) without delay or change of place, then and there; (*c*) competent, alert. **put on the spot** (*a*) *colloq.* put in a difficult or embarrassing position; (*b*) *US slang* arrange the murder of, kill. ***red spot***: see RED *adjective*. ***soft spot***: see SOFT *adjective*. **spot on** *adverbial & adjectival phr.* on target, precise(ly); absolutely correct(ly). ***sweet spot***: see SWEET *adjective & adverb*. ***tight spot***: see TIGHT *adjective* 7. ***touch the spot***: see TOUCH *verb*. ***weak spot***: see WEAK *adjective*. ***white spot***: see WHITE *adjective*. ***yellow spot***: see YELLOW *adjective*.
▶ **B** *adjective*. **1** (Of money) to be paid immediately after a sale; (of a price) involving immediate cash payment; (of a commodity) delivered immediately after a sale. L19.
2 Done, made, occurring, etc., on the spot or then and there. E20.

Comb. & special collocations: **spot advertisement**, **spot advertising**: occupying a short break during or between programmes; ***spot ball***: see sense 6b above; ***spot board***: see sense 5f above; **spot check** *noun & verb* (*a*) *noun* a check made on the spot or on a randomly selected sample; (*b*) *verb trans.* subject to a spot check; **spot commercial** = ***spot advertisement*** above; **spot effect** BROADCASTING a sound effect created in the studio; **spot height** the height of a point above mean sea level, esp. as marked on a map; **spot kick** SOCCER a penalty kick; **spot lamp** = SPOTLIGHT *noun*; **spot level** = ***spot height*** above; **spot-list** *verb trans.* place (a building) on a statutory preservation register; **spot map**: with spots indicating individual locations of a thing; **spot meter** a photometer that measures the intensity of light received within a cone of small angle, usu. 2° or less; **spot news** JOURNALISM news reported of events as they occur; **spot-nosed** *adjective* having a spot on the nose; ***spot-nosed monkey***, = HOCHEUR; **spot plate** CHEMISTRY a plate having several small depressions in which spot tests can be performed; **spot test** (*a*) a chemical test performed using a single drop of sample; (*b*) = ***spot check*** above; **spot weld**: made in spot welding; **spot-weld** *verb trans.* join by spot welding; **spot welder** a person or device that spot-welds something; **spot welding**: in which two surfaces are joined by a series of small discrete welds; **spot zoning** *US* the special rezoning of an area to meet a particular interest.

▶**C** *adverb.* For cash payment. L19.

spot /spɒt/ *verb.* Infl. **-tt-**. LME.

[from the noun.]

▶**I 1** *verb trans.* Mark with stains. LME.

2 *verb trans.* Stain or tarnish (a person's character etc.). LME. ▶**†b** Cast aspersions on. M16–E18.

3 *verb intrans.* Become marked with spots. M19.

4 *verb trans.* Remove small defects, marks, or stains from (a surface); remove (a mark or stain) from a surface. M19.

> 📖 **1** L. F. BAUM The tears will fall on your green silk gown, and spot it.

▶**II 5** *verb trans.* Cover or decorate with spots. LME. ▶**b** Mark (a tree) with a round blaze. *US.* M18. ▶**c** Moisten *with* a drop of liquid; place a drop of (liquid) *on* a surface etc. M20.

6 a *verb trans.* Appear as a spot on (a surface). E19. ▶**b** *verb intrans. impers.* in ***it spots***, ***it is spotting***, etc., it rains, it is raining, etc., slightly or in large scattered drops. Freq. in ***spot with rain***. M19.

7 *verb trans.* BILLIARDS & SNOOKER. Place (a ball) on a spot. M19.

8 *verb trans.* Place in a particular location; *esp.* position (a railway car) for loading or unloading. *N. Amer.* E20.

> 📖 **5** P. H. JOHNSON The ceiling was covered with a dark blue paper spotted with silver stars. **6b** M. DE LA ROCHE 'Is it raining?' asked Augusta. 'Just beginning to spot,' replied Mrs. Court. J. FOWLES It began to spot with rain.

▶**III 9** *verb trans.* Mark or note as a criminal or suspect. *slang.* E18.

10 *verb trans.* Guess or identify beforehand (the winner of a race etc.). *colloq.* M19.

11 *verb trans.* Catch sight of; notice; perceive. *colloq.* M19.

12 *verb trans. & intrans.* (also foll. by *for*). MILITARY. Locate and direct fire towards (an enemy position). E20.

13 *verb trans. & intrans.* Watch for and note types of or numbers on (trains, buses, etc.) as a hobby. E20.

> 📖 **11** BETTY SMITH Scouts . . watching . . games and spotting promising players. G. GREENE Someone spotted me and reported me. G. NAYLOR They finally spotted Parker . . in the dining room. F. SPALDING Spotting the comic in everyday exchange, overheard in the office or on the bus. **13** *Guardian* It is everyone's ambition to spot at Crewe.

spotless /ˈspɒtlɪs/ *adjective.* ME.

[from SPOT *noun* + -LESS.]

1 Free from stain (*lit.* & *fig.*); immaculate; absolutely clean or pure. ME.

2 In moth names: not bearing spots (in contrast to some related species). *rare.* E19.

> 📖 **1** C. MCCULLERS The kitchen was in a state of spotless order and cleanliness. E. SEGAL Your Honor, the defendant has a spotless record. B. CHATWIN All dressed up in spotless whites.

■ **spotlessly** *adverb* M19. **spotlessness** *noun* E17.

spotlight /ˈspɒtlʌɪt/ *noun & verb.* E20.

[from SPOT *noun* + LIGHT *noun.*]

▶**A** *noun.* **1** A narrow and intense beam of light directed on a small area, esp. on a particular part of a theatre stage or on the road in front of a vehicle; a lamp projecting this. E20.

2 *fig.* A close scrutiny; ***the spotlight***, public attention, the full glare of publicity. E20.

> 📖 **1** A. FRATER A spotlight flicked on and caught him, fair and square in mid-beam. N. SAHGAL Trees stepped into the spotlight and retreated into darkness as we passed. **2** *Oxford Star* They want to shift the spotlight to what they regard as the real problem. *Times Educ. Suppl.* He . . returned to the spotlight when he chaired an international symposium.

▶**B** *verb trans.* Pa. t. & pple **-lighted**, **-lit** /-lɪt/.

1 Illuminate with a spotlight; *fig.* subject to close scrutiny, bring to public attention. E20.

2 Hunt (game) by spotlight. Chiefly *US.* M20.

> 📖 **1** E. BOWEN A flower-bed . . spotlit by sunshine. *Omni* The AIDS epidemic has spotlighted discrimination against the disabled in the workplace.

■ **spotlighter** *noun* a person who hunts by spotlight M20.

spotted /ˈspɒtɪd/ *adjective.* ME.

[from SPOT *noun, verb*: see -ED², -ED¹.]

1 Marked or decorated with spots. ME. ▶**b** MINING. Having the ore irregularly distributed through the workings. L19.

2 Disfigured or stained with spots; *fig.* morally stained or tarnished. E16.

3 Of a disease etc.: characterized by the appearance of spots on the skin. Now chiefly in ***spotted fever*** below. M17.

> 📖 **1** W. WHITMAN Four light-green eggs spotted with brown. H. H. COLE A . . flower pattern on a spotted white ground.

Special collocations: ***spotted crake***: see CRAKE *noun*¹ 2. **spotted deer** = CHITAL. **Spotted Dick** a suet pudding made with currants or raisins. **spotted dog** (*a*) a white or light-coloured dog with black or dark spots, *esp.* a Dalmatian; (*b*) = ***Spotted Dick*** above. **spotted dogfish** = HUSS. **spotted fever** a fever characterized by the appearance of spots on the skin; now *spec.* (*a*) epidemic cerebrospinal meningitis; (*b*) typhus; (*c*) = ***ROCKY MOUNTAIN spotted fever***. **spotted flycatcher** a small Old World flycatcher, *Muscicapa striata*, with dull grey-brown plumage and a swerving flight. **spotted gum** any of various eucalypts, esp. *Eucalyptus maculata*, with spotted bark or leaves. ***spotted hyena***: see HYENA 1a. ***spotted LINSANG***. **spotted orchid**, **spotted orchis** either of two orchids with palmate tubers, spotted leaves, and lilac or mauve flowers, *Dactylorhiza fuchsii*, esp. of basic grassland, and *D. maculata*, esp. of acid soils. **spotted owl** a large, brown owl, *Strix occidentalis*, which inhabits forests from British Columbia to central Mexico and has white spots on the head, back, and underparts. ***spotted rat-fish***: see RAT *noun*¹. **spotted ray** = HOMELYN. ***spotted redshank***: see REDSHANK 1a. ***spotted SKAAPSTEKER***. **spotted wilt** a virus disease of herbaceous plants, esp. tomatoes, in which it causes curling and necrotic spotting of the leaves. ***spotted WINTERGREEN***. **spotted woodpecker** each of three woodpeckers of Eurasia and N. Africa with spotted plumage, of the genus *Dendrocopos* (or *Picoides*), *D. major*, *D. medius*, and *D. minor* (distinguished as ***greater spotted woodpecker***, ***middle spotted woodpecker***, ***lesser spotted woodpecker***).

■ **spottedness** *noun* E17.

spotter /ˈspɒtə/ *noun.* E17.

[from SPOT *verb, noun*: see -ER¹.]

1 A person who or thing which makes spots on something. E17.

2 A spy, a detective, *esp.* one employed by a company or business to keep watch on employees, customers, etc. *US.* L19.

3 A person who watches, looks out for, or identifies something; *spec.* (MILITARY) a person who or aircraft which locates enemy positions. E20.

4 A person who spots trains etc. Usu. as 2nd elem. of comb. M20.

4 ***bus-spotter***, ***plane-spotter***, ***train-spotter***, etc.

spotting /ˈspɒtɪŋ/ *noun.* LME.

[from SPOT *verb* + -ING¹.]

1 The action of SPOT *verb.* LME.

2 A set of spots; marking composed of spots. E17.

3 A slight discharge of blood via the vagina; light staining due to this. E20.

spotty /ˈspɒti/ *adjective & noun.* ME.

[from SPOT *noun* + -Y¹.]

▶**A** *adjective.* **1** Marked with spots; spotted; *esp.* pimply. ME.

2 Patchy; irregular; sporadic. Chiefly *N. Amer.* E19.

> 📖 **1** C. HARKNESS How they manage to be so conceited when they're all so spotty and uncouth. **2** M. HOWARD His attendance at school is spotty. *New Yorker* Ainge, who had not been hitting his . . shots consistently, continued his spotty shooting.

▶**B** *noun.* A small wrasse of New Zealand, *Labrichthys bothryocosmus*. L19.

■ **spottily** *adverb* L19. **spottiness** *noun* L16.

spoucher /ˈspaʊtʃə/ *noun.* Now *Scot. & Anglo-Irish.* ME.

[Old Northern French *espuchoir* (= Old French *espu(i)soir*), from *espu(i)chier* (= Old French *espuicier*, *-uis-*, mod. *épuiser*) drain, empty of water.]

A wooden vessel for baling out or conveying water.

spousage /ˈspaʊzɪdʒ/ *noun. arch.* ME.

[Aphet. from Anglo-Norman *esposage*, Old French *espousage*, from *espo(u)ser* SPOUSE *verb.*]

†1 = SPOUSAL *noun* 1. ME–M16.

2 = SPOUSAL *noun* 2. ME.

spousal /ˈspaʊz(ə)l/ *noun & adjective.* ME.

[Aphet. from Old French *espo(u)saille*: see ESPOUSAL.]

▶**A** *noun.* **†1** The state of being married; wedlock. ME–E17.

2 *sing.* & in *pl.* The action of marrying; an instance of this, a wedding. ME.

▶**B** *attrib.* or as *adjective.* **1** Of or pertaining to marriage. E16.

2 Of a hymn etc.: celebrating a marriage. L16.

■ **spousally** *adverb* (*rare*) (*a*) by marriage; (*b*) in the manner of a spouse: E16.

spouse /spaʊz, -s/ *noun.* ME.

[Old French *spus*, *spous* masc., *spuse*, *spouse* fem., aphet. vars. of *espous*, *espouse*, (mod. *époux*, *épouse*), from Latin *sponsus* bridegroom, *sponsa* bride, uses as nouns of masc. and fem. pa. pples of *spondere* betroth.]

1 A married person; a wife, a husband. Formerly also, a bride; a bridegroom. ME.

†2 A fiancé(e). ME–M16.

3 *fig.* God or Christ, or the Church or a woman who has taken religious vows, regarded as standing in a relationship of husband or wife respectively to each other. ME.

†4 Wedlock. Only in ME.

> 📖 **1** W. TREVOR With the help of her spouse . . cut into the wedding cake. C. HARKNESS Leave their respective spouses and be free to live with each other.

Comb.: **spouse-breach** (long *arch. rare*) adultery.

■ **spousehood** *noun* (*arch.*) marriage, wedlock ME. **spouseless** *adjective* LME. **spousy** *noun* (*arch. colloq.*) a spouse L18.

spouse /spaʊz/ *verb trans. arch.* ME.

[Aphet. from Old French *espo(u)ser*, *espus-*: see ESPOUSE *verb.*]

†1 Join in marriage (*to*). Usu. in *pass.* ME–M17.

†2 Give (esp. a woman) in marriage (*to*). ME–M16. ▶**b** Betroth. M–L16.

3 Take (esp. a woman) as a spouse; marry. ME. ▶**b** *fig.* Try (one's fortune). *Scot.* E19.

spout /spaʊt/ *noun.* LME.

[Corresp. to Flemish *spuyte*, Dutch *spuit*, but prob. immed. from the verb.]

▶**I 1** A pipe or trough for carrying off or discharging water; *spec.* (*a*) a downpipe; (*b*) a roof-gutter; (*c*) the part of a fountain, pump, etc., from which the water issues. LME. ▶**b** A syringe. Long *obsolete* exc. *Scot.* M16. ▶**c** More fully ***spout-hole***. The blow-hole of a whale etc. M17. ▶**d** MINING. A short passage connecting a ventilation shaft with a roadway in a pit. M19.

2 A projecting tube or lip on a vessel for facilitating the pouring of liquid. LME.

3 A sloping trough by which grain, coal, etc., is discharged from or conveyed to a receptacle; a chute. M16.

4 *Hist.* A lift in a pawnshop for taking pawned articles up for storage; *transf.* a pawnshop. E19.

5 A gun barrel. *slang.* M20.

▶**II 6** A shellfish which spouts or squirts out water, esp. a razor-fish (mollusc). Also ***spout-fish***. Chiefly *Scot.* E16.

7 A jet of water etc. discharged in quantity and with force. E16. ▶**b** A natural spring of water. L18.

8 a METEOROLOGY. A waterspout. Now chiefly *US.* M16. ▶**b** A heavy downpour (*of* rain). M17.

9 A cascade of falling water etc.; *esp.* a waterfall. L17.

10 A spurt; a rush; a sudden dart. *Scot.* L18.

Phrases: **put up the spout** *slang* pawn. **up the spout** *slang* (*a*) pawned; (*b*) useless, ruined, hopeless; (*c*) pregnant; (*d*) (of a bullet or cartridge) in the barrel and ready to be fired.

Comb.: **spout-bath** *NZ* a bath or pool producing massaging jets of water; **spout cup** (*a*) *Hist.* a cup with a spout; (*b*) the upper end of a downpipe; ***spout-fish***: see sense 6 above; ***spout-hole***: see sense 1c above.

¶ Earlier in place-names.

■ **spoutless** *adjective* L18.

spout /spaʊt/ *verb.* ME.

[Middle Dutch *spouten* (Dutch *spuiten*) from imit. Germanic base repr. also by Old Norse *spýta* to spit.]

1 *verb trans. & intrans.* Discharge (a liquid or other substance) in a copious jet or stream. ME. ▶**b** *verb trans.* Wet or drench by a stream of liquid. *rare.* L16. ▶**c** *verb trans. & intrans. spec.* Of a whale etc.: eject (water and air) through the blow-hole, blow. M17.

2 *verb intrans.* Of a liquid etc.: issue forcibly in a jet or stream. Also foll. by *out*, *up*. E16. ▶**b** Spring, bound. Now *dial.* M17.

3 *verb trans. & intrans.* Speak in a declamatory manner; utter (words) on a subject, esp. at great length or without much matter; recite (verses etc.) at length. M16.

4 *verb trans.* Pawn. *slang.* E19.

5 *verb trans.* Fit with a spout or spouts. M19.

> 📖 **1** POPE His arm falls spouting on the dust below. L. DURRELL A flame-swallower . . spouting a column of flame from his mouth. **2** RIDER HAGGARD A ribbon of white surf . . spouts up in pillars of foam. E. BOWEN A jet of white steam spouted across the kitchen. H. READ Ribbons of water, gushing and spouting in every direction. **3** N. ANNAN The gift of being able to spout thousands of lines of poetry by heart. C. LASSALLE Usually he spouted about death: the death of the family, the death of society.

■ **spouty** *adjective* given to spouting E18.

spouted /ˈspaʊtɪd/ *adjective.* E19.

[from SPOUT *noun, verb*: see -ED², -ED¹.]

1 Having or fitted with a spout or spouts. E19.

2 Discharged in a spout or stream. M19.

spouter /ˈspaʊtə/ *noun.* L15.
[from SPOUT *verb* + -ER[1].]
†**1** A person who spits. *rare.* Only in L15.
2 †**a** = SPOUT *noun* 1c. Only in E17. ▸**b** A spouting whale. M19. ▸**c** A whaling ship. M19.
3 †**a** An amateur actor. M18–E19. ▸**b** A person who spouts or speaks or recites at length. L18.
4 A spouting oil-well, a gusher. L19.

spouting /ˈspaʊtɪŋ/ *noun.* LME.
[from SPOUT *noun, verb*: see -ING[1].]
1 The action of SPOUT *verb*; an instance of this. LME.
2 Guttering on a roof; material for this. L19.

spp. *abbreviation.*
BIOLOGY. Species (*pl.*).

SPQR *abbreviation.*
1 *Hist.* Latin *Senatus Populusque Romanus* the Senate and People of Rome.
2 Small profits, quick returns. *colloq.*

Spr. *abbreviation.*
Sapper.

Sprachbund /ˈʃpraːxbʊnt/ *noun.* M20.
[German, from *Sprach* speech, language + *Bund* union.]
LINGUISTICS. A linguistic community containing members of different language families which have developed common characteristics through geographical proximity; the process of linguistic change producing this.

Sprachgefühl /ˈʃpraːxgəfyːl/ *noun.* E20.
[German, from *Sprache* speech + *Gefühl* feeling.]
Intuitive feeling for the essential character of a language, linguistic instinct; *gen.* the essential character of a language.

sprack /sprak/ *adjective.* Chiefly *dial.* ME.
[Origin uncertain: rel. to SPRAG *adjective.* Cf. SPRY *adjective.*]
In good health and spirits; brisk, lively, energetic.
■ Also **sprackish** *adjective* L19.

sprackle /ˈsprak(ə)l/ *verb intrans. Scot.* L18.
[Origin unkn.]
Clamber.

sprackly /ˈsprakli/ *adjective & adverb.* Long *dial. rare.* LME.
[from SPRACK + -LY[1], -LY[2].]
▸†**A** *adjective.* Lively, active. Only in LME.
▸**B** *adverb.* Actively, briskly, energetically. LME.

spraddle /ˈsprad(ə)l/ *verb.* Now chiefly *dial.* & *N. Amer.* M17.
[Perh. from *sprad* dial. pa. pple of SPREAD *verb*: see -LE[3].]
1 *verb intrans.* Sprawl. M17.
2 *verb trans.* Spread or stretch (one's legs etc.) wide apart. E20.
■ **spraddled** *ppl adjective.* E20.

sprag /sprag/ *noun*[1]. Now *dial.* L17.
[Origin unkn.]
A slip or cutting from a plant; a twig, a sprig.

sprag /sprag/ *noun*[2]. Chiefly *dial.* E18.
[Origin unkn.]
1 A lively young man. E18.
2 **a** A young salmon. L18. ▸**b** A young cod. L19.

sprag /sprag/ *noun*[3]. M19.
[Origin unkn.]
1 MINING. A prop used to support a roof or coal seam. M19.
2 A stout stick or bar inserted between the spokes of a wheel to check its motion; a similar device used as a simple brake on a vehicle. L19.

> 🕮 **2** *fig.*: R. DENTRY If you were in the President's shoes, how would you put a sprag in Ziauddin's wheel?

sprag /sprag/ *adjective. rare.* L16.
[App. repr. a mispronunc. of SPRACK. Cf. SPRY *adjective.*]
Smart, clever.

sprag /sprag/ *verb trans.* Infl. **-gg-**. M19.
[from SPRAG *noun*[3].]
1 MINING. Prop up (a roof or coal seam) with a sprag or sprags. M19.
2 Check or stop (a wheel or vehicle) by inserting a sprag. L19.
3 Accost aggressively, confront. *Austral. slang.* E20.
■ **spragger** *noun* L19.

sprain /spreɪn/ *verb*[1] & *noun.* E17.
[Origin unkn.]
▸**A** *verb intrans.* Wrench or twist the ligaments or muscles of (a wrist, ankle, etc.) violently so as to cause pain and swelling but not dislocation. E17.

> 🕮 J. B. PRIESTLEY Miss Callander . . fell and sprained her ankle. **sprain one's ankle** *euphem.* (*obsolete* exc. *Hist.*) (of a woman) be seduced (and become pregnant), lose one's virginity.

▸**B** *noun.* An instance or the condition of being sprained, a severe wrench or twist of a joint; the pain and swelling thus caused. E17.

sprain /spreɪn/ *verb*[2] *trans.* Now *rare* or *obsolete.* LME.
[App. back-form. from *spreynd(e)*, *spreynt(e)* pa. t. & pple of SPRENGE.]
Orig., sprinkle. Now only in AGRICULTURE, sow (seeds etc.) by hand.

spraing /spreɪŋ/ *noun & verb.* E16.
[App. of Scandinavian origin. Cf. early Icelandic & Norwegian *sprang* fringe, lace.]
▸**A** *noun.* **1** A glittering or brightly coloured stripe, streak, or ray. *Scot.* E16.
2 A disease of potatoes characterized by curved lines of discoloration inside the tuber. E20.
▸**B** *verb trans.* Variegate or decorate with coloured stripes or streaks. Chiefly as ***sprainged** ppl adjective. Scot.* M16.

spraint /spreɪnt/ *noun.* LME.
[Old French *espreintes* (mod. *épreintes*) use as noun of fem. pa. pple of *espraindre* squeeze out, ult. from Latin *exprimere* EXPRESS *verb*[1].]
In *pl.* & (now also) *sing.* The excrement of an otter.

sprang /spraŋ/ *noun. rare.* E16.
[Origin unkn. Cf. next.]
†**1** A rung of a ladder; a bar, a bolt. Only in 16.
2 A shoot, a branch. M19.

sprang *verb pa. t.* of SPRING *verb*[1].

sprangle /ˈspraŋg(ə)l/ *verb & noun.* Now *dial.* & *US.* LME.
[Origin unkn. Cf. prec.]
▸**A** *verb intrans.* **1** Spread out the limbs, sprawl; struggle. LME.
2 Straggle; spread out in branches or offshoots. L19.
▸**B** *noun.* A branch, a shoot; an offshoot; a sprawl. *US.* M19.
■ **sprangly** *adjective* (*US*) spreading, sprawling M19.

sprat /sprat/ *noun*[1] & *verb.* Earlier †**sprot**. Pl. **-s**, in sense 1 also same.
[Old English *sprot* = Middle Low German, Middle & mod. Dutch *sprot* (whence German *Sprotte*), of unkn. origin. Mod. form recorded from L16.]
▸**A** *noun.* **1** A small edible European marine fish, *Sprattus sprattus*, of the herring family; the flesh of this as food. Also, any of various other small fishes resembling a sprat. OE.
2 An insignificant or contemptible person. Also, a small (esp. lively) child. E17.
3 A sixpence. *slang.* (*obsolete* exc. *Hist.*) M19.
Phrases: **a sprat to catch a herring**, **a sprat to catch a mackerel**, **a sprat to catch a whale** a small expenditure made, or a small risk taken, in the hope of a large or significant gain.
▸**B** *verb intrans.* Infl. **-tt-**. Fish for sprats. Chiefly as ***spratting** verbal noun.* L19.

sprat /sprat/ *noun*[2]. *Scot.* & *north.* Also **sprot** /sprɒt/. L16.
[Cf. SPART *noun*, SPRET.]
A kind of coarse rush or rushlike grass.

sprat-barley /ˈspratbɑːli/ *noun.* E16.
[Origin of 1st elem. uncertain: perh. from SPRAT *noun*[2]. See BARLEY *noun.*]
An old variety of two-rowed barley, *Hordeum distichon*, with short broad ears and divaricate awns.

spratter /ˈspratə/ *noun.* M19.
[from SPRAT *verb* + -ER[1].]
1 A guillemot. *dial.* M19.
2 A person or a boat engaged in sprat-fishing. M19.

sprattle /ˈsprat(ə)l/ *verb*[1] & *noun. Scot. rare.* L18.
[Origin uncertain: cf. Swedish *sprattla* in same sense.]
▸**A** *verb intrans.* Scramble, struggle. L18.
▸**B** *noun.* A struggle, a scramble. E19.

sprattle *verb*[2] see SPROTTLE.

sprauncy /ˈsprɔːnsi/ *adjective. slang.* M20.
[Origin uncertain: perh. rel. to dial. *sprouncey* cheerful.]
Smart, showy, spruce.

> 🕮 OBSERVER The sprauncy part of the operation is the Premiere Dining Room on the second floor.

sprawl /sprɔːl/ *noun.* E18.
[from the verb.]
1 The action or an act of sprawling; an ungainly or awkward spreading out of the limbs. E18. ▸**b** A straggling array or display *of* something, an untidily spreading group or mass. E19. ▸**c** *spec.* The straggling expansion of an urban or industrial area into the adjoining countryside; the area of this advancement. M20.
2 A struggle. *rare.* M18.
3 Activity, energy, drive, initiative. *dial.* & *US.* M19.

> 🕮 **1** P. H. JOHNSON She . . fell into a sort of luxurious sprawl. **b** *Listener* The endless sprawl of . . lorries. **c** H. CARPENTER Birmingham . . had grown . . into one of the biggest industrial sprawls in the Midlands. ***urban sprawl***: see URBAN *adjective.*

sprawl /sprɔːl/ *verb.*
[Old English *spreawlian* rel. to Northern Frisian *spraweli*, Danish *sprelle*, *sprælle* kick or splash about, Swedish dial. *spral(l)a*, Norwegian dial. *sprala* struggle. Cf. SCRAWL *verb*[1].]
1 *verb intrans.* Orig., move the limbs in convulsive effort or struggle; toss about. Now, lie, sit, or fall with the limbs stretched out in an ungainly or awkward way; lounge, laze. Freq. as ***sprawled** ppl adjective.* OE. ▸**b** Of a thing: spread out or extend widely in a straggling way; be of untidily irregular form. Freq. as ***sprawling** ppl adjective.* L16.
2 *verb trans.* Spread out (a thing) widely or untidily, stretch out (the limbs) in an ungainly way. Usu. foll. by *out.* M16.

> 🕮 **1** R. GRAVES A child . . sprawling at ease On smooth turf. S. BRETT His foot caught in the grass, and he sprawled headlong. H. MANTEL Andrew had fallen asleep, sprawled on the sofa. **b** DISRAELI Travelling cases, directed in a boy's sprawling hand. *Daily Telegraph* An endless sprawling suburb without a centre. G. GREENE His short stories sprawl into the . . region of the novel. **2** SIR W. SCOTT Sprawling out his leg and bending his back.

■ **sprawler** *noun* (**a**) a person or thing which sprawls; (**b**) a noctuid moth of the genus *Brachionycha*, *esp.* the pale brown *B. sphinx*: M19. **sprawlingly** *adverb* in a sprawling manner E20.

sprawly /ˈsprɔːli/ *adjective.* L18.
[from prec. + -Y[1].]
Of a sprawling character, straggly, ungainly.

spray /spreɪ/ *noun*[1] & *verb*[1]. ME.
[Repr. late Old English *(e)sprei* in personal and place-names: ult. origin unkn.]
▸**A** *noun.* **1** *collect.* Small or fine twigs of trees or shrubs, either growing or as used for firewood etc. Freq. with *the.* ME.
2 A slender shoot or twig. Now *spec.* a branch or sprig of a flowering or attractively foliaged plant or tree used for decoration or ornament; an artificial imitation of this. ME. ▸**b** In *pl.* Hazel, birch, etc., twigs used in thatching. E16. ▸**c** A brooch or clip made in imitation of a bouquet of flowers or of a twig with fruit or foliage. Also ***spray brooch***. E19.
3 A metal casting resembling a set of twigs. M19.

> 🕮 **1** W. DE LA MARE Thrush and robin perched mute on spray. **2** E. BOWEN Three sprays of flowering cherry.

▸**B** *verb. rare.*
1 *verb trans.* Cover or provide with branches or twigs. L16.
2 *verb intrans.* Grow *out* into branches or twigs; ramify. L19.
■ **sprayey** *adjective*[1] having or resembling sprays or small twigs M19.

spray /spreɪ/ *noun*[2] & *verb*[2]. As noun also †**spry(e)**. E17.
[Immediate source unkn.: formally corresp. to Middle Dutch verb *spra(e)yen* = Middle High German *spræjen*, *spræwen*.]
▸**A** *noun.* **1** Water or other liquid blown or driven in the form of minute drops or fine mistlike particles from the force of wind, the dashing of waves, etc.; (a jet or cloud of) fine or liquid matter propelled through the air. E17.
2 A liquid preparation to be applied in the form of minute drops with an atomizer or aerosol, in medical treatment, cleaning, painting, etc.; (an instrument or apparatus for applying) a jet or cloud of such a preparation; the action or an act of spraying thus. L19.

> 🕮 **1** R. BUCHANAN The salt spray of the ocean was blown upon it. J. BARNES Another Renault flashed past and blinded the windscreen with spray. **2** *Amateur Gardening* Use insecticidal . . dusts instead of sprays. ***fly-spray***, ***hair-spray***, etc.

▸**B** *verb.* **1** *verb trans.* Propel, apply, or diffuse in the form of spray; scatter in minute drops. E19.
2 *verb trans.* Sprinkle or cover (as) with spray; wet with fine particles of water or other liquid, esp. by means of an atomizer or aerosol; *spec.* treat (a plant) thus with insecticide etc. M19. ▸**b** Shoot at or strike with a shower or rapid succession of bullets etc. E20.
3 *verb intrans.* Send out or diffuse spray. L19. ▸**b** *spec.* Of a male animal, esp. a cat: mark the environment with the smell of urine as an attractant to the female. M20.
4 *verb intrans.* Issue, rise, or fall as spray. L19.

> 🕮 **1** *Westminster Gazette* In the act of loud speaking, fine droplets of mucus are sprayed . . into the air. *Guardian* Mr Hardy sprayed on a sweet-smelling wave-setting lotion. **2** E. WAUGH 'We are being sprayed with liquid mustard-gas,' I said. M. ATWOOD Spraying ourselves from the cologne testers. **b** *Times* The CIA chief . . had his home . . sprayed with machine-gun fire. **3** M. SPARK She turned on the shower which creaked as it sprayed. **4** P. SCOTT Grass sprayed from the blades like a green fountain.

Comb.: **spray can** an aerosol can for applying paint, deodorant, etc., as a fine spray; **spraydeck** a flexible cover fitted to the opening in the top of a kayak to form a waterproof seal around the canoeist's body; **spray-dry** *verb trans.* dry (milk, ceramic material, etc.) by spraying as a fine powder into a current of hot air etc., the water in the particles being rapidly evaporated (freq. as ***spray-drying** verbal noun*); **sprayed-on** *adjective* (*colloq.*) (of clothing) very tight, esp. alluringly so; **spray gun** a device resembling a gun for applying a disinfectant, paint, etc., as spray; **sprayman** a person spraying crops with insecticide etc.; **spray-on** *adjective* (of a liquid) applied in the form of spray; **spray-paint** *verb & noun* (**a**) *verb trans.* paint (a surface) by means of a spray (freq. as ***spray-painting** verbal noun*); (**b**) *noun* paint applied thus; **spray refining** = ***spray steelmaking*** below; **spray region** the region at the top of the atmosphere where molecules are so far apart that their paths are determined by gravity and upward moving ones are likely to escape into space; **sprayskirt** = ***spraydeck*** above; **spray steelmaking** a method of making steel in which molten iron falling in a stream is atomized by jets of oxygen and flux that combine with impurities in the droplets; **spray tower** a hollow tower in which a liquid is made to fall as a spray, e.g. to cool it or to bring it into contact with a gas; **spray zone** the area near the sea or a waterfall frequently moistened by spray.

■ **sprayable** *adjective* M20. **sprayer** *noun* a person who or thing which sprays; *esp.* a machine, vehicle, or aircraft for diffusing insecticide etc. over plants and trees: L19. **sprayey** *adjective*² scattering or moistened with spray; of the nature of spray: M19. **spraying** *noun* the action or an act of diffusing as or sprinkling with spray; a liquid used as a spray: L19. **sprayless** *adjective* L19. **spraylike** *adjective* resembling water spray M19.

sprazer /ˈsprɑːzə/ *noun. slang* (*obsolete* exc. *Hist.*). M20.
[Shelta *sprazi*. Cf. SPROWSIE.]
Sixpence; a sixpenny piece.

spread /sprɛd/ *noun.* LME.
[from the verb.]
1 The action or an instance of spreading or extending in space; degree, or extent, or capability of spreading; *the* extent or expanse *of* something; breadth, width, compass. LME. ▸**b** In gem-cutting, the width of a stone considered in proportion to its depth. E19. ▸**c** The wing-span of a bird or aircraft. L19. ▸**d** (Degree of) divergence; *spec.* (***a***) ECONOMICS the difference between two rates or prices; (***b***) the degree or manner of variation of a quantity among the members of a population or sample; (***c***) *N. Amer.* SPORT the difference between the number of points, goals, etc. scored, *esp.* a winning margin; (***d***) = ***point spread*** s.v. POINT *noun*¹. E20. ▸**e** (An) increase in a person's girth, esp. at middle age; paunchiness. Usu. in ***middle-age spread*** s.v. MIDDLE AGE *adjective* 2. *colloq.* M20.
2 The fact of being spread abroad, diffused or made known; diffusion, dispersion; an instance of this. L17. ▸**b** BILLIARDS etc. A rebound of a cue-ball from the object ball at a considerable angle from its former course. *US.* M19.
3 An expanse, stretch, or display *of* something. E18. ▸**b** A large farm; a ranch, esp. for raising cattle. Chiefly *US.* E20. ▸**c** PHYSICAL GEOGRAPHY. A thin layer of alluvium. Also, an area of shallow water or marsh formed by the expansion of an obstructed stream. M20. ▸**d** CYTOLOGY. A microscopic preparation (as a smear, a squash) in which material is spread for observation rather than thin-sectioned, esp. so as to show chromosomes at metaphase. M20.
4 a Butter. *slang.* Now *rare.* E19. ▸**b** Any sweet or savoury paste, jam, etc., spread on bread; any oil- or fat-based substitute for butter, for spreading on bread. Orig. *US.* M19.
5 A large or elaborate meal or buffet, esp. as provided for a guest etc. *colloq.* E19.
6 a A bedspread, a coverlet. Orig. *US.* M19. ▸**b** A shawl. *slang.* Now *rare.* M19.
7 An article or advertisement displayed prominently in a newspaper or magazine, esp. on two facing pages. Cf. ***centre spread*** s.v. CENTRE *noun & adjective.* Orig. *US.* L19.
8 STOCK EXCHANGE. A contract combining the option of buying shares within a specified time at a specified price above that prevailing when the contract is signed, with the option of selling shares of the same stock within the same time at a specified price below that prevailing when the contract is signed. *US.* L19.
9 BRIDGE. (The revealing of) a hand able to win all the tricks of a round. E20.
10 a GEOLOGY. An array of seismometers used simultaneously to record disturbances resulting from a single shot in a geophysical survey. M20. ▸**b** OIL INDUSTRY. The total assemblage of men and equipment needed for a particular job, esp. laying a pipeline. L20.

> 🕮 **1** M. SPARK With a sardonic . . spread of his hands. *Accountant* To allow the spread of payment over eight years. D. ATTENBOROUGH A male may . . have arms with a spread of 2½ metres. **2** H. T. BUCKLE The influence of women and the spread of civilization have been nearly commensurate. *Scientific American* The mode of spread of histoplasmosis, a lung disease. J. UPDIKE The market for his . . portraits . . dried up with the spread, in the 1840s, of the daguerreotype. **3** B. VINE The green spread of the park lay bathed in soft sunshine. **b** *Daily Express* He is most content farming at his 300-acre spread. **4b** *Parents* Using a low fat spread on bread and toast would . . be sensible. **5** L. BLACK Kate goggled when she . . saw the food. 'What a spread!' she exclaimed.

Comb.: **spread bet**, **spread betting**: in which the bettor wins or loses money according to the margin by which the value of a score or other outcome varies from the spread of expected values quoted by the bookmaker.

spread /sprɛd/ *ppl adjective.* E16.
[pa. pple of prec.]
That has been spread; extended, expanded; displayed; diffused. In PHONETICS, pronounced with the lips drawn out rather than rounded, as for /iː/; unrounded.

> 🕮 MILTON A Bannerd Host Under spread Ensigns marching. R. ADAMS Four partridges . . sailed down, spread-winged, into the field. **spread-adder** *US* a hognose snake. **spread head** *US* a heading in printed matter intended to be particularly prominent.

spread /sprɛd/ *verb.* Pa. t. & pple **spread**, (*arch.* & *poet.*) **spreaded**. ME.
[from Old English *-sprǣdan* (in combs.), *sprǣdung* SPREADING *noun* = Old Saxon *tōspreidan*, Middle Low German, Middle Dutch *sprēden* (Dutch *spreiden*, *spreien*), Old High German *spreiten* (German *spreiten*), from West Germanic verb repr. by Old High German *sprītan* be extended. Earlier as SPREADING *noun.*]
▶ **I** *verb trans.* **1** Stretch or open out so as to extend the surface or width of; draw out to full extension, unfold; lay out or arrange so as to cover or occupy (more) space. Freq. foll. by *out.* ME. ▸**b** Display widely or fully to the eye or mind. E17. ▸**c** Flatten out, make flat. E18. ▸**d** *refl.* Exert oneself; make a display, show off. *US colloq.* M19. ▸**e** MUSIC. Play (notes, a chord) in arpeggio. L19.
2 Send out in various directions so as to extend over or cover a large or larger space. ME.
3 a Distribute or disperse (a material thing or things) over a certain area, scatter. ME. ▸**b** Apply (a substance) to a surface in a thin layer. M16. ▸**c** Place or distribute in a measured way *over* a certain space, time, etc. L16. ▸**d** Lay out (a meal) on a table etc. L18. ▸**e** Set down or enter *on* a documentary record. *US.* M19.
4 a In *pass.* Of people, animals, etc.: be scattered, dispersed, or distributed over or throughout some area. ME. ▸†**b** Cause to increase or multiply; beget. ME–E17.
5 Make (more) widely prevalent, known, felt, etc.; disseminate or diffuse. ME.
6 a Overlay, deck, or strew *with.* ME. ▸**b** Lay (a table) for a meal etc. LME. ▸**c** Cover *with* a thin layer of a soft substance, esp. butter. L16.
7 †**a** Overrun, overspread, (an area). LME–E18. ▸**b** Cover; extend over. *poet.* E18.

> 🕮 **1** C. MUNGOSHI You see rice spread out to dry. J. ROSSNER She . . spread out her pad, ballpoint pen, and a box of tissues. B. W. ALDISS He spread a tartan rug gently over her. R. RAYNER A cop got out of the car . . . 'OK . . . Spread those legs, lean over the hood.' ***spread one's wings***: see WING *noun.* **b** A. C. CLARKE Looking at the . . islands spread out below. **2** S. WYNTER A giant breadfruit tree spread out its broad leaves. **3a** W. S. BURROUGHS The atom bomb explodes over Hiroshima spreading radioactive particles. **b** B. MOORE The Abbot spread blackberry jam on his bread. ***spread it on thick***: see THICK *adverb.* **spread oneself too thin** dissipate one's time and energy through the diversity of one's activities. **c** *Times* This final stage of the repayment should be spread over the 12 months. **d** HOLME LEE Tea was spread on the round table. **4a** *Aquaculture* Rabbitfish are widely spread throughout the Indian and . . Pacific oceans. **5** LD MACAULAY His arrival spread dismay through the whole English population. H. S. STREAN This principal . . is also spreading malicious rumours about me. *Life* The five-year drought that spread famine from Ethiopia to Mali. **6a** W. H. PRESCOTT King Ferdinand's galleys were spread with rich carpets. **b** M. AYRTON A long table has been . . spread for the nine featured players. **c** A. ROUDYBUSH Spreading two slices of rye bread thickly with liverwurst.

▶ **II** *verb intrans.* **8** Become extended or expanded; cover or occupy a wide or wider space or area; stretch out widely or fully. Freq. foll. by *out.* ME. ▸**b** Become larger, increase in size. M17. ▸**c** Go apart, separate. M19. ▸**d** Make a display, show off. *US colloq.* M19.
9 Extend over a large or larger area by increase or separation, disperse, (freq. foll. by *out*). Now also (of butter etc.), admit of being spread. ME.
10 Of an immaterial thing: become diffused or disseminated, become more prevalent. ME.
11 Be displayed widely, extend. ME.
12 Extend by growth, grow outwards. ME.
13 BRIDGE. Reveal one's hand as a claim or concession of the remaining tricks. E20.

> 🕮 **8** DEFOE The water began to spread over the flat ground. *Manchester Examiner* A fire broke out and spread with great rapidity. C. MUNGOSHI Tendai had to get off the bed and spread out on the floor. INA TAYLOR Cancer had spread through the whole of Mrs Evans' body. **9** J. H. NEWMAN The Romans spread gradually from one central city. **10** V. WOOLF Somehow or other . . the fashion spread. S. WYNTER As his fame spread, disciples came to him. P. CAREY The word spread that the walls were finished. **11** P. LARKIN The lawn spreads dazzlingly wide.

Comb.: **spread-over** *noun & adjective* (in accordance with or designating) a system of distributing work or holidays over a period of time, *spec.* an arrangement allowing a fixed number of working hours to be performed at varying times within a given period.

■ **spreadaˈbility** *noun* ability to be (easily) spread M20. **spreadable** *adjective* (*esp.* of butter etc.) that can be (easily) spread M20.

spread-eagle /sprɛdˈiːɡ(ə)l/ *verb.* E19.
[formed as prec.]
1 *verb intrans.* SKATING. Perform a spread eagle. E19.
2 *verb trans.* Stretch out, hold, or secure in the position of a spread eagle, orig. esp. for punishment. Also, spread or splay apart, scatter; *esp.* (CRICKET) knock down (the wicket). Freq. as ***spread-eagled*** *ppl adjective.* E19.
3 *verb trans.* Defeat utterly, esp. in horse-racing. M19.
4 *verb intrans.* Speak or act in a grandiloquent or loudly patriotic way. Chiefly *US.* M19.

> 🕮 **2** E. WAUGH A dead child, like a broken doll, spread-eagled in the deserted roadway. *New Yorker* A detective . . spread-eagled Garreau against the wall.

spread eagle /sprɛd ˈiːɡ(ə)l/ *noun phr. & adjective.* Also **spread-eagle**. L16.
[from prec. + EAGLE *noun.*]
▶ **A** *noun phr.* **1** A representation of an eagle with legs and wings extended, esp. as an emblem or inn sign. L16. ▸**b** SKATING. A straight glide made with the feet turned outwards in one straight line. E19. ▸**c** A boastful or self-assertive person. L19.
2 A person held or secured with the arms and legs stretched out, orig. esp. to be flogged. L18.
3 A fowl flattened out for broiling. M19.
4 STOCK EXCHANGE. An operation by which a broker agrees to buy shares within a specified time at a specified price and sells the option of buying shares of the same stock within the same time at a higher price. Also = SPREAD *noun* 8. *US.* M19.
▶ **B** *attrib.* or as *adjective.* Usu. with hyphen.
1 High-sounding, grandiloquent. *rare.* M19.
2 Bombastic, extravagantly boastful; *esp.* loudly or aggressively patriotic. *US.* M19.
3 Having the position or appearance of a spread eagle. M19.

■ **spread-eagleism** *noun* (chiefly *US*) grandiloquence in speech, loud or aggressive patriotism M19. **spread-eagleist** *noun* (chiefly *US*) a person characterized by spread-eagleism L19.

spreader /ˈsprɛdə/ *noun.* L15.
[from SPREAD *verb* + -ER¹.]
1 A person who spreads, scatters, or disseminates something. Foll. by *of.* L15.
2 A thing spreading, growing, or branching outwards. M17.
3 A thing for spreading something; *spec.* (***a***) a bar for stretching out or keeping apart things or components (also ***spreader bar***); NAUTICAL a bar attached to the mast of a yacht in order to spread the angle of the upper shrouds; (***b***) an apparatus or device for spreading or scattering something, esp. manure on farmland or water issuing from a hose; (***c***) = ***lifting beam*** s.v. LIFTING *noun.* M19.
4 A surfactant. E20.

spreading /ˈsprɛdɪŋ/ *noun.*
[Old English *sprǣdung*: see SPREAD *verb*, -ING¹.]
The action of SPREAD *verb*; an instance of this.
Comb.: **spreading-board** (***a***) *rare* a board on which sheep are laid while being shorn; (***b***) a board to which insect specimens are fixed; **spreading factor** BIOLOGY = HYALURONIDASE.

spreading /ˈsprɛdɪŋ/ *adjective.* M16.
[from SPREAD *verb* + -ING².]
1 Extending or growing outwards; increasing in size or area. M16.
2 Tending to become (more) widely diffused or prevalent. M16.
1 spreading adder *US* a hognose snake.
■ **spreadingly** *adverb* (*rare*) E17. **spreadingness** *noun* (*rare*) L17.

spreadsheet /ˈsprɛdʃiːt/ *noun.* L20.
[from SPREAD *ppl adjective* + SHEET *noun*¹.]
COMPUTING. A program that allows any part of a table or rectangular array of positions or cells to be displayed on a screen, the contents of any cell being specifiable either independently or in terms of the contents of other cells.
■ **spreadsheeting** *verbal noun* the use of a spreadsheet L20.

spready /ˈsprɛdi/ *adjective. rare.* M16.
[from SPREAD *verb* + -Y¹.]
1 Tending to spread, expansive. M16.
2 Of a meal: substantial, lavish. M20.
3 Spreadable, easily spread. L20.

spreagh /sprɛk, -x/ *noun. Scot.* (now *arch.* or *Hist.*). E19.
[Alt. of SPREATH, prob. by assoc. with CREAGH.]
= SPREATH 2, 3.

spreaghery /ˈsprɛkəri, -x-/ *noun. Scot.* (now *arch.* or *Hist.*). Also **sprech-**. L18.
[from (the same root as) prec. + -ERY.]
Cattle-raiding; plunder, booty.

spreath /spriːθ/ *noun. Scot.* (now *arch.* or *Hist.*). LME.
[Gaelic *sprèidh* cattle from Old Irish *spréid* from Latin *praeda* booty.]
1 Booty, plunder, spoil. LME.
2 (A herd *of*) cattle carried or driven off in a raiding expedition. E16.
3 A cattle-raid. L18.

sprechery *noun* var. of SPREAGHERY.

Sprechgesang /ˈʃprɛçɡəzaŋ/ *noun.* E20.
[German, lit. 'speech song'.]
MUSIC. A style of dramatic vocalization intermediate between speech and song.

Sprechstimme /ˈʃprɛçʃtɪmə/ *noun.* E20.
[German, lit. 'speech voice'.]
MUSIC. = prec.

spreckle /ˈsprɛk(ə)l/ *noun. Scot. & north.* L15.
[Corresp. to Middle High German *spre(c)kel*, German dial. *Spreckel*, *Spräckel*, *Sprackel*, Swedish *spräckla*, Norwegian *sprekla*.]
A speck, a speckle.

spreckled /ˈsprɛk(ə)ld/ *adjective.* Now *dial.* LME.
[from (the same root as) prec.: see -ED². Cf. German dial. *gespreckelt*, Danish *spraglet*, Middle Swedish *spräklott*, Norwegian *spreklutt*, Icelandic *spreklóttur*.]
Speckled.

spree /spriː/ *noun & verb.* L18.
[Origin unkn.]
▶ **A** *noun.* **1** A period or occasion of extravagant or riotous indulgence; a bout of drinking or merrymaking, a revel, a binge. L18.
2 Riotous amusement or merrymaking, prolonged drinking. E19.
3 A spell or period of unrestrained activity of a specified kind. M19.

📖 **1** W. C. WILLIAMS They thought he would be on a spree and cause trouble. P. AUSTER He drank too much—stealing money . . to support his sprees. **on the spree** engaged in a spree, having a riotous time. **3** ***buying spree***, ***crime spree***, ***shopping spree***, ***spending spree***, etc.

Comb.: **spree killer** a person who murders several people in a sudden, apparently unpremeditated manner, often with no obvious motive. **spree killing** a murder carried out by a spree killer.
▶ **B** *verb.* Pa. t. & pple **spreed**.
1 *verb intrans. & trans.* (with *it*). Take part or indulge in a spree. M19.
2 *verb trans.* Spend (money etc.) recklessly, squander on a spree. L19.
■ **spreeish** *adjective* (*colloq.*) given to indulgence in sprees; slightly intoxicated: E19.

spreeu /ˈspriːuː/ *noun. S. Afr.* Also **sprew** /spruː/. L18.
[Dutch *spreeuw* (Afrikaans *spreeu*) starling.]
Any of various southern African starlings with variegated or iridescent plumage.

spreite /ˈʃprʌɪtə/ *noun.* Also **S-**. Pl. ***-ten*** /-tən/. M20.
[German = layer, lamina, esp. something extending between two supports.]
PALAEONTOLOGY. A banded pattern of uncertain origin found in the infill of the burrows of certain fossil invertebrates.

sprekelia /sprɛˈkiːlɪə/ *noun.* M19.
[mod. Latin (see below), from J. H. von *Spreckelsen* (d. 1764), German botanist + -IA¹.]
The Jacobean lily, ***Sprekelia formosissima***.

sprenge /sprɛn(d)ʒ/ *verb trans.* Long *arch. & poet.* Pa. t. & pple **sprent** /sprɛnt/.
[Old English *sprenġan* from base also of *springan* SPRING *verb*¹, corresp. to Old Frisian *sprendza*, Middle Low German, Old & mod. High German *sprengen*, Old Norse *sprengja*. Cf. SPRAIN *verb*², SPRINGE.]
1 Sprinkle (liquid etc.); scatter, disperse, distribute here and there. Chiefly as ***sprent ppl adjective***. OE.
2 Sprinkle with liquid etc., splatter, splash; mottle or fleck with colour etc. Freq. foll. by *with*. Chiefly as ***sprent ppl adjective***. OE.

Sprengel /ˈʃprɛŋ(ə)l, -ŋg(ə)l/ *noun.* M19.
[H. J. P. *Sprengel* (1834–1906), German-born English chemist.]
Used ***attrib.*** and in ***possess.*** to designate devices developed by Sprengel. Also *ellipt.*, a Sprengel pump.
Sprengel air pump, **Sprengel mercury pump**, **Sprengel pump**, **Sprengel's air pump**, **Sprengel's mercury pump**, **Sprengel's pump** = ***MERCURY vapour pump***. **Sprengel's tube**, **Sprengel tube** a glass U-tube that narrows to a capillary at each end, used to determine the specific gravity of a liquid by weighing the tube when filled with the liquid and then with water at the same temperature.

sprent /sprɛnt/ *noun. Scot. & north.* L15.
[from next. Cf. Old Norse *sprettr*, Icelandic *sprettur* short gallop, Norwegian *sprett* sprinkle, splash. Cf. SPRINT *noun*².]
1 †**a** A sprinkler for holy water. Only in L15. ▸**b** A sprinkle; a spot or stain caused by sprinkling. Chiefly *north.* M19.
2 a A spring of a lock etc. L15. ▸**b** A spring, a leap, a bound. E16.
3 The fastening or hasp of a chest, trunk, etc. E16.
4 A springe, a snare. E19.

sprent /sprɛnt/ *verb*¹. Now *Scot. & north.* ME.
[Of Scandinavian origin: cf. Old Norse *spretta* (Icelandic, Norwegian *spretta*, Swedish *spratta*, Danish *sprætte*) rel. to SPRINT *verb*. Cf. SPRUNT.]
1 *verb intrans.* Of a person, animal, etc.: spring, jump, leap; move quickly or with agility. ME.
2 *verb trans.* Sprinkle, spatter, splash. E17.

sprent *verb*² *pa. t. & pple* of SPRENGE.

spret /sprɛt/ *noun. Scot. & north.* LME.
[Obscurely rel. to SPRAT *noun*². Cf. SPRIT *noun*³.]
Any of various kinds of rush, esp. the jointed-leaved rush, *Juncus articulatus*; coarse rushlike grass; a stalk of such a plant.
■ **spretty** *adjective* of the nature of or full of spret E19.

sprew *noun* var. of SPREEU.

sprezzatura /sprettsaˈtuːra/ *noun.* M20.
[Italian.]
Ease of manner, studied carelessness, nonchalance, esp. in art or literature.

sprig /sprɪɡ/ *noun*¹ & *verb*¹. ME.
[Origin unkn.]
▶ **A** *noun.* **1** A small slender tapering nail or tack, usu. headless, esp. as used to hold glass in a window frame until the putty dries; a brad. ME.
2 A small projecting part or point; *spec.* (chiefly *NZ*) a stud or spike attached to the sole of a football boot, running shoe, etc. L17.
▶ **B** *verb trans.* Infl. **-gg-**. Fasten with sprigs or brads; *NZ* equip (a boot etc.) with sprigs. E18.
■ **sprigger** *noun*¹ L19.

sprig /sprɪɡ/ *noun*² & *verb*². ME.
[from or rel. to synon. Low German *sprick*: for the final *g* see SAG *verb*.]
▶ **A** *noun.* **1** A small branch, shoot, or spray of a plant, shrub, or tree; a spray *of* a particular plant etc. ME.
2 *fig.* **a** An offshoot or a minor development *of* something. L16. ▸**b** A scion or young representative *of* a class, institution, etc. Usu. *derog.* E17. ▸**c** A young lad, a youth. Usu. *derog.* M17.
3 a A brooch or piece of jewellery resembling a sprig or spray. L16. ▸**b** A representation of a sprig used in a design decorating fabric, ceramic ware, etc. L18. ▸**c** A small piece of lace made for use in composite work. M19.
4 †**a** A branch of a nerve, vein, etc. M17–M18. ▸**b** A piece of some substance or material resembling a sprig, spray, or twig of a plant. M17.

📖 **1** H. JAMES Gertrude . . plucked a small sprig from a lilac-bush. M. DRABBLE A sprig of parsley tucked jauntily behind one ear. **2b** J. KRANTZ These young sprigs of the old aristocracy had been reduced to working for their living.

Comb.: **sprigtail** (*a*) (now *rare*) a short pointed tail; (*b*) *US* the pintail duck; **sprig-tailed** *adjective* having a sharp-pointed tail.
▶ **B** *verb.* Infl. **-gg-**.
†**1 a** *verb intrans.* Form rootlets. Only in E17. ▸**b** *verb trans.* Divide into small branches. Only in M17.
2 *verb trans.* Ornament (fabric) with sprigs; decorate (ceramic ware) with sprigs or other designs in applied relief. M18.

📖 **2** A. SCHLEE Her frock, cotton, pink, sprigged with little brown flowers.

■ **sprigger** *noun*² L19. **spriglet** *noun* (*rare*) a little sprig L19.

spriggan /ˈsprɪɡ(ə)n/ *noun. dial.* M19.
[Prob. from Cornish.]
In Cornwall, a sprite, a goblin.

sprigged /sprɪɡd/ *adjective.* E17.
[from SPRIG *noun*², *verb*²: see -ED², -ED¹.]
1 Of fabric: decorated or patterned with sprigs. Of ceramic ware: ornamented with or forming sprigs or other designs in applied relief. E17.
2 Having the form of a sprig or sprigs; minutely branched. E18.

📖 **1** THACKERAY She insisted upon Rebecca accepting . . a sweet sprigged muslin.

sprigging /ˈsprɪɡɪŋ/ *noun.* L18.
[from SPRIG *verb*² + -ING¹.]
1 a The action or occupation of decorating fabric with sprigs. L18. ▸**b** The process of decorating ceramic ware with sprigs or other designs in applied relief. E20.
2 Decoration or needlework consisting of sprigs. L18.

spriggy /ˈsprɪɡi/ *adjective.* M16.
[from SPRIG *noun*² + -Y¹.]
Bearing or consisting of sprigs or small branches; suggestive of or decorated with a sprig or sprigs.

spright /sprʌɪt/ *noun & verb.* Now *rare.* M16.
[Var. of SPRITE after words in *-ight*.]
▶ **A** *noun.* †**1** Spirit, courage, cheer. In *pl.*, spirits. M16–E18.
2 A disembodied spirit, a ghost; a goblin, a fairy, an elf. M16.
▶†**B** *verb trans.* Haunt, bedevil. *rare* (Shakes.). Only in E17.
■ †**sprightless** *adjective* spiritless; lacking animation or vigour: L16–E18.

sprightful /ˈsprʌɪtfʊl, -f(ə)l/ *adjective.* Now *rare.* L16.
[from prec. + -FUL.]
Animated, lively, spirited; vigorous, sprightly.
■ **sprightfully** *adverb* L16. **sprightfulness** *noun* M17.

sprightly /ˈsprʌɪtli/ *adverb & adjective.* E16.
[formed as prec. + -LY¹, -LY².]
▶ **A** *adverb.* With vigour and animation, spiritedly, in a sprightly manner. Now *rare.* E16.
▶ **B** *adjective.* **1** Of a person (now esp. an older one) or thing: full of or characterized by animation or cheerful vitality; brisk, lively, vigorous; spirited, animated. L16.
†**2** Ghostly, spectral. *rare* (Shakes.). Only in E17.

📖 **1** J. G. FARRELL Old ladies who looked . . as sprightly and exuberant as young girls. E. SIMPSON His mood . . had been sprightly early in the evening. *Times* Smoked salmon salad . . nicely complemented by the sprightly Californian house wine.

■ **sprightlily** *adverb* (*rare*) L19. **sprightliness** *noun* E16.

spring /sprɪŋ/ *noun*¹.
[Old English *spring*, *spryng* from Germanic base of SPRING *verb*¹. In branch I cf. Middle & mod. Dutch, Middle & mod. Low German, Old High German *spring*.]
▶ **I 1** The source or head of a well, stream, or river. Freq. foll. by *of*. Now *rare.* OE.
2 A flow of water etc. rising or welling naturally from the earth; a similar flow of water, oil, etc., obtained by boring etc.; a place where such a flow rises. ME. ▸**b** Such a flow of water having special (esp. medicinal or curative) properties; in *pl.*, a town or locality having such springs, a spa, a watering-place. L18.
3 *fig.* A source or origin *of* something. ME.

📖 **2** H. BELLOC No good drinking water in that land, save . . at a rare spring. **b** E. BURRITT A mineral spring at which the visitors drink most voluminously. H. ALLEN Sitting in the hot springs at Royat with a half dozen other invalids. **3** T. C. WOLFE He had returned to the springs of innocence . . from whence he came. ***life-spring***: see LIFE *noun*.

▶ **II 4** The action or time of coming into being; the first sign *of* day etc., dawn; the beginning of a season. *obsolete* exc. *poet.* ME.
5 The first season of the year, between winter and summer, in which vegetation begins to appear: in the northern hemisphere freq. regarded as comprising March, April, and May or (ASTRONOMY) reckoned from the vernal equinox to the summer solstice; in the southern hemisphere corresponding in time to the northern autumn. LME. ▸**b** *fig.* The first or early stage or period *of* life etc. L16. ▸**c** *N. Amer.* In full ***spring salmon***. A Pacific salmon that returns to the river in spring, esp. the Chinook salmon. M19. ▸**d** *transf.* The initial stages of a period of political liberalization, esp. in a Communist state; the first steps in a programme of political and economic reform. Cf. ***PRAGUE Spring***. E20.

📖 **4** ***day-spring***: see DAY *noun*. **5** A. WILSON The promising early spring had turned to a wet summer. J. WRIGHT The Cyrenaicans lost heavily during tough fighting in the spring of 1914. *Daily Star* The . . 10-part series, is due to be screened next spring. **b** LYTTON Apæcides was in the spring of his years.

▶ **III** †**6** A young shoot of a tree, plant, etc.; a small branch, a twig. Also, a cutting, a slip. ME–M17. ▸**b** A young tree, a sapling. L15–M16.
7 A grove, wood, or plantation of young trees; a spinney (foll. by *of* wood etc.). Now *dial.* LME. ▸**b** Young growth or shoots, *esp.* the undergrowth of trees or shrubs. Now *dial.* L15.
8 A growth or crop of plants, vegetation, etc. Formerly also, a people, a race. Now *rare.* LME.
▶ **IV** †**9** Beginning, origin, birth, (*of* something). ME–L17.
10 †**a** The rising *of* the sea (to an exceptional height) at particular times. LME–L16. ▸**b** = ***spring tide*** (b) below. Usu. in *pl.* L16.
11 An act of springing; a bound, a jump, a leap. LME. ▸**b** A recoil or rebound of something bent or forced out of its normal position or form. L17. ▸**c** A distance able to be covered by a spring or leap. E19. ▸**d** An escape or rescue from prison. *slang.* E20.
12 A flock *of* teal. *arch.* LME.
13 A cut or joint of pork consisting of the belly or lower part of the forequarter. *obsolete* exc. *dial.* L16.
14 NAUTICAL. A crack or split in a mast, plank, spar, etc. E17.
15 The quality of springing; the ability of a thing to spring back strongly to its normal state or position on the removal of force or pressure; elasticity. M17. ▸**b** Liveliness in a person or *of* a person's mind, faculties, etc.; buoyancy and vigour in movement. Freq. in ***a spring in one's step***. L17.
16 a ARCHITECTURE. The point at which an arch rises from its abutment or impost; *rare* the rise of an arch, the ascent or slope of a bridge. E18. ▸**b** The upward curvature of a beam or plank from a horizontal line, esp. on a ship's deck. M19. ▸**c** The rise of the toe of a shoemaker's last above the ground-line. L19.

📖 **11** W. SCORESBY I made a spring towards a boat . . and caught hold of the gunwale. **b** E. K. KANE The spring of a well-drawn bow. **15** W. HOGARTH A small wire that has lost its spring.

▶ **V 17** A device, usu. of bent or coiled metal, having the ability to return to its normal shape on the removal of force or pressure and used esp. to drive clockwork or for cushioning in furniture or vehicles. LME. ▸**b** *fig.* The cause, motive, or agency *of* something; an impelling force. L15.

18 NAUTICAL. A rope put out from a vessel and made fast for anchorage or to aid movement or manoeuvring. Also ***spring line***. M18.

> 17 M. SHADBOLT The jangle of easing chair springs as his father stood up. *Woodworker* The invention of the coiled spring . . released a flood of small portable timepieces. **b** W. BAGEHOT The ordinary springs of progress . . begin their elastic action.

Attrib. & *comb.*: In the senses 'of, pertaining to, or characteristic of the season of spring', 'appearing or happening in spring', as ***spring fashion***, ***spring holiday***, ***spring lamb***, ***spring weather***, etc.; 'sown or suitable for sowing in spring', as ***spring barley***, ***spring corn***, etc.; 'fitted with, operated by, or acting like a spring', as ***spring bolt***, ***spring suspension***, ***spring trap***, etc. Special combs., as **spring balance**: that measures weight by the tension of a spring; **spring beauty** any of several succulent spring-flowering, chiefly N. American, pink- or white-flowered plants of the genera *Claytonia* and *Montia*, of the purslane family, esp. *C. virginica* and *C. perfoliata*; **spring bed** a bed with a spring mattress; **spring-beetle** = ***click-beetle*** s.v. CLICK *noun*[1]; **spring bows** = ***bow-compass*** s.v. BOW *noun*[1]; **spring cabbage** any variety of cabbage that matures in the spring; ***spring chicken***: see CHICKEN *noun*[1]; **spring-clean** *verb & noun* (*a*) *verb trans. & intrans.* perform thorough cleaning of (a house, room, etc.), esp. in spring (freq. as ***spring-cleaning*** *verbal noun*); (*b*) *noun* an act, spell, or instance of such cleaning; **spring collet** ENGINEERING a tapered collet that is slotted along much of its length, so that when moved in a similarly tapered seat the separate parts are pressed against the stock inside the collet; **spring equinox** = ***vernal equinox*** s.v. VERNAL *adjective* 1; **spring fever** a restless or lethargic feeling sometimes associated with spring; **spring garden** †(*a*) a public garden; (*b*) a garden containing many spring-flowering plants; **spring grass** sweet vernal grass, *Anthoxanthum odoratum*; **spring green** *noun & adjective* (of) a light green; **spring greens** the leaves of young non-hearting cabbage plants, used as a vegetable; also, a cabbage of a variety that matures in spring; **spring-gun** (*a*) a gun discharged by bodily contact or with a wire etc. attached to the trigger, formerly used as a trap for trespassers, poachers, etc.; (*b*) a toy gun in which the projectile is discharged by the release of a spring; **spring hare**, **springhare** [African SPRINGHAAS] a large nocturnal rodent, *Pedetes capensis* (family Pedetidae), resembling a miniature kangaroo, which is found on the grasslands of S. and E. Africa and is a pest of farmland; **springhead** = senses 2, 3 above; **spring herring** *N. Amer.* = ALEWIFE 2; **spring-house** *N. Amer.* an outhouse built over a spring or stream and used as a larder, dairy, etc.; **spring-jack** = ***click-beetle*** s.v. CLICK *noun*[1]; **spring line** (*a*) see sense 18 above; (*b*) a line where the water-table reaches the surface and along which springs are numerous; **spring-loaded** *adjective* containing a compressed or a stretched spring pressing one part against another; **spring lock** a self-locking form of lock featuring a spring-loaded bolt; **spring mattress** a mattress containing or consisting of springs; **spring onion** an onion taken from the ground before the bulb has formed, eaten in salads (esp. raw), in Chinese cookery, etc.; **spring peeper** a small brown tree frog, *Hyla crucifer*, that occurs throughout much of eastern N. America and has a high-pitched piping call; ***spring rate***: see RATE *noun*[1] 5c; **spring roll** a Chinese snack consisting of a pancake filled with vegetables (esp. bean sprouts), meat, etc., and fried; **spring salmon** *N. Amer.* = sense 5c above; ***spring snowflake***: see SNOWFLAKE 3; ***spring squill***: see SQUILL 1b; **springtide** (*a*) *arch. & poet.* the season of spring, springtime; (*b*) (usu. as two words) a tide occurring just after the new and full moon, in which there is the greatest difference between high and low water; **spring training** BASEBALL pre-season fitness and skills training taking place in spring; ***spring usher***: see USHER *noun* 4b; **spring water** water from a spring as opp. to that from rain or a river (freq. bottled and sold as being healthy); **spring-wood** (*a*) a copse of young trees; (*b*) = ***early wood*** s.v. EARLY *adjective*.

■ **springless** *adjective* L17. **springlet** *noun* †(*a*) a young sprout or shoot; (*b*) a small spring or fountain: M18. **springlike** *adverb & adjective* (*a*) *adverb* as in or in the manner of the season of spring; (*b*) *adjective* resembling (that of) spring, vernal: M16. **springling** *noun* (*rare*) (*a*) a youth; (*b*) a year-old salmon: M17.

spring /sprɪŋ/ *noun*[2]. Chiefly *Scot.* LME.

[Prob. rel. to Old French *espring(u)er*, *-ier* to dance: see SPRING *verb*[1].]

A tune, esp. a quick or lively one, played on the bagpipes etc.; a dance to such a tune.

spring /sprɪŋ/ *noun*[3]. *obsolete* exc. *dial.* E17.

[Alt.]

= SPRINGE *noun*.

spring /sprɪŋ/ *verb*[1]. Pa. t. **sprang** /spraŋ/, (now *arch. & non-standard* exc. *US*) **sprung** /sprʌŋ/; pa. pple **sprung**. See also SPRUNG *ppl adjective*[1], YSPRUNG.

[Old English *springan* = Old Frisian *springa*, Old Saxon, Old High German *springan* (Dutch, German *springen*), Old Norse *springa*, from Germanic.]

► **I 1 a** *verb intrans.* Come or rush out suddenly, issue, esp. in a jet or stream; (of water etc.) rise or flow in a stream, well up. Freq. foll. by *out*, *up*, *forth*. OE. ▸**b** *verb trans.* Sprinkle (a person or thing) *with* liquid etc. Cf. SPRENGE 2. *obsolete* exc. *dial.* ME. ▸†**c** *verb trans.* Sprinkle (a liquid etc.) in drops. Cf. SPRENGE 1. LME–L16. ▸†**d** *verb trans.* Cause to well up or flow out of the ground; cause to flow, pour. LME–M17.

2 *verb intrans.* Of vegetation etc.: begin to grow, sprout, develop by growth, esp. suddenly or quickly. Freq. foll. by *up*. OE. ▸**b** Of a horse or cow: swell *with* milk; give signs of foaling or calving. Now *dial.* E17.

3 *verb intrans.* Come into being, arise, appear, esp. suddenly; derive *from*. Freq. foll. by *up*. ME.

4 a *verb intrans.* Of dawn etc.: come above the horizon, begin to appear. *arch.* ME. ▸†**b** *verb trans.* Cause (the sun etc.) to appear or rise to view. LME–M17.

5 *verb intrans.* Originate through birth or descent, be descended. Usu. foll. by *from*, *of*, *out of*. ME. ▸**b** Come into being. Freq. in ***spring forth***, ***spring to life***. M17.

6 *verb trans.* Produce, bring forth, cause to grow. Long *obsolete* exc. *Scot.* ME.

7 *verb intrans.* Increase or extend in height or length; attain a certain height or point by growth; grow out *from*. LME. ▸**b** ARCHITECTURE. Of an arch etc.: rise in a curve *from* a point. M18.

8 *verb trans.* **a** ARCHITECTURE. Provide a foundation for or extend the curve of (an arch). E18. ▸**b** NAUTICAL. Move, haul, or swing (a vessel) by means of a spring or cable. M19. ▸**c** In shoemaking, raise (the toe or waist of a last) in relation to the line of the ground. E20.

> 1 P. HOLLAND Of one hill spring three great Rivers. SIR W. SCOTT The perspiration which sprung from his brow. **2** J. A. MICHENER Moisture in the ground, and from it sprang a million flowers. *Yankee* The alders had sprung up over the remains of two acres of pine. **3** S. HALE The wind soon sprung up. *Guardian* Englishy pubs . . have sprung up in New York. I. COLEGATE The friendship which had sprung up between them. M. ESSLIN The play springs from his darkest . . mood. **5** C. THIRLWALL A seer sprung from the gifted lineage of Iamus. J. BARZUN Distinguished men that have sprung . . from the Protestant clergy. *Listener* The Fabian Society sprang from an idealistic society . . called the Fellowship of the New Life. **b** *City Limits* The IBM machine . . suddenly sprang to noisy life. **8a** A. W. CLAPHAM The earlier stage consisted in springing a round arch across the nave between alternate bays.

► **II 9** *verb intrans.* Move with a sudden jerk or bound; move rapidly (as) from a constrained position or by the action of a spring. OE. ▸**b** Be resilient or elastic; shift or move on account of this. M17. ▸**c** Of emotion, expression, etc.: come suddenly *to* the eyes, face, etc. M19.

†**10** *verb intrans.* Of fame, rumour, etc.: spread, extend. OE–L16.

11 *verb intrans.* Jump, bound, leap; move rapidly or suddenly; rise quickly or with a bound from a sitting or lying position; *spec.* (of a game-bird, esp. a partridge) rise from cover. ME. ▸**b** Offer a higher price. *slang.* Now *rare* or *obsolete.* M19. ▸**c** Escape or be released from custody or imprisonment. *US slang.* E20. ▸**d** Pay for a treat. (Foll. by *for*.) *N. Amer. & Austral. slang.* E20.

12 a *verb intrans.* Break, crack, split; give way. ME. ▸**b** *verb trans.* NAUTICAL. Suffer the splitting or loss of (a mast etc.); have or make (a leak) open or start. L16. ▸**c** *verb trans.* Cause (a mine) to explode; sound (a rattle). M17. ▸**d** *verb intrans.* Of a mine: go off, explode. M17.

13 *verb trans.* Cause to move with a sudden springing or leaping motion; cause (a mechanism etc.) to operate suddenly, esp. by means of a spring; *spec.* (*a*) make (a horse, a coach team) gallop; (*b*) cause (a game-bird, esp. a partridge) to rise from cover. LME. ▸**b** MILITARY. Shift (a weapon etc.) smartly from one position to another. L18. ▸**c** Bend or deflect from a straight line. L19. ▸**d** Contrive the release or rescue of (a person) from custody or imprisonment. *slang.* E20.

14 *verb trans.* †**a** Start (a thing) going. L16–L18. ▸**b** Give out, pay, hand over, (money); buy (a thing). *colloq.* M19. ▸**c** Make known, reveal, or produce (news, an idea, etc.) suddenly or unexpectedly. Usu. foll. by *on* a person etc. L19.

15 *verb trans.* Leap over, clear with a spring. E19.

> 9 W. MORRIS He drew adown the wind-stirred bough . . then let it spring away. **c** S. KAUFFMANN Tears . . sprang into her eyes suddenly. **11** S. CRANE At the . . command the soldiers sprang forward. H. ROTH He sprang from the steps, three at a time. P. MORTIMER Holding the camera in both hands, he sprang athletically to his feet. *fig.*: A. WILSON The stockbroker's wife . . sprang to her husband's defence. **12b** ***spring a luff***, ***spring one's luff***: see LUFF *noun*[1]. **13** F. NORRIS Immediately after seven, this clock sprang its alarm with the abruptness of an explosion. H. KUSHNER When the maiden came . . he sprang the trap and caught her. **14c** L. P. HARTLEY Elspeth always springs a surprise or two. D. EDEN She's a bit upset. I did rather spring it on her. **15** J. H. PATTERSON If the lion could spring the twelve feet which separated me from the ground.

spring /sprɪŋ/ *verb*[2]. Pa. t. & pple **sprung** /sprʌŋ/, **springed**. See also SPRUNG *ppl adjective*[2]. L17.

[from SPRING *noun*[1].]

†**1** *verb trans.* Allow (ground) to send up shoots from the stumps of felled trees. Only in L17.

2 *verb trans.* Give spring or elasticity to. M19.

3 *verb trans.* Provide, fit, or cushion (furniture, a vehicle, etc.) with a spring or springs. Freq. as ***sprung*** *ppl adjective*. L19.

springal *noun*[1] var. of SPRINGALD *noun*[1].

springal *noun*[2] var. of SPRINGALD *noun*[2].

springald /ˈsprɪŋ(ə)ld/ *noun*[1]. *obsolete* exc. *Hist.* Also **springal** /-(ə)l/. ME.

[Old French *espringal(l)e* (cf. ESPRINGAL) or Anglo-Norman *springalde* (Anglo-Latin *springaldus*), from Old French *espringuer*, *-gier* from Frankish *springan* SPRING *verb*[1].]

A machine or engine used in medieval warfare for throwing heavy missiles; a missile thrown by such a machine.

springald /ˈsprɪŋ(ə)ld/ *noun*[2]. *arch.* Also **springal** /-(ə)l/. LME.

[App. from SPRING *verb*[1]: ending of unkn. origin.]

A young man, a youth, a stripling.

¶ Obsolete until revived in E19 by Sir Walter Scott.

springar /ˈsprɪŋə/ *noun*. M20.

[Norwegian.]

(A piece of music for) a Norwegian country dance in 3/4 time.

spring-back /ˈsprɪŋbak/ *noun*. L19.

[Sense 1 from SPRING *noun*[1] + BACK *noun*[1]; sense 2 from SPRING *verb*[1] + BACK *adverb*.]

1 A folder with a spring clip incorporated in the spine to hold the papers placed in it; the clip in such a folder. L19.

2 The capacity to spring flexibly back into position after subjection to pressure; the action or an act or springing back thus. M20.

springboard /ˈsprɪŋbɔːd/ *noun*. L18.

[from SPRING *noun*[1] or *verb*[1] + BOARD *noun*.]

1 A flexible board or plank projecting over water and used to gain impetus by a person jumping or diving; a similar board or platform used to give impetus in vaulting etc.; *fig.* a source of impetus or help in an activity. L18.

2 A platform fixed to the side of a tree and used by a lumberjack to stand on when working at some height from the ground. *N. Amer. & Austral.* L19.

> 1 *Glasgow Herald* New natural resources . . should be the springboard to economic expansion.

springbok /ˈsprɪŋbɒk/ *noun*. In sense 2 also **S-**. In sense 1 also Anglicized as **springbuck** /ˈsprɪŋbʌk/. L18.

[Afrikaans, from Dutch *springen* to spring + *bok* goat, antelope.]

1 A common and gregarious southern African gazelle, *Antidorcas marsupialis*, characterized by the habit of leaping (pronking) when excited or disturbed. L18.

2 A South African; *spec.* (*a*) a member of a South African national sporting (esp. rugby) team; (*b*) a South African soldier. Freq. in *pl.* E20.

> 2 *Country Life* The French . . lost both their matches against the Springboks.

springe /sprɪn(d)ʒ/ *noun & verb*. ME.

[Rel. to SPRENGE.]

► **A** *noun*. A snare or noose for catching small game, esp. birds. ME.

► **B** *verb*. Pres. pple **springeing**.

1 *verb trans.* Catch in a springe or snare. E17.

2 *verb intrans.* Set snares. L19.

springer /ˈsprɪŋə/ *noun*. ME.

[from SPRING *verb*[1] + -ER[1].]

1 A person who or thing which springs or leaps. ME. ▸**b** A physical-training instructor in the navy. *slang.* M20.

2 ARCHITECTURE. The part of an arch where the curve begins; the lowest stone of this; the bottom stone of the coping of a gable. E17.

3 †**a** A young sapling. *rare.* Only in E18. ▸**b** A tall variety of mushroom. *local.* M19.

4 a A fish which springs or leaps; now *spec.* a newly run salmon. E18. ▸**b** ZOOLOGY. The springbok. Also ***springer antelope***. Now *rare.* L18.

5 A snare, a springe. E19.

6 In full ***springer spaniel***. (An animal of) either of two breeds of sturdy spaniel (more fully ***English springer (spaniel)***, ***Welsh springer (spaniel)***) bred to spring game. E19.

7 A cow or heifer near to calving. M19.

8 A racehorse on which the betting odds suddenly shorten. *slang.* E20.

Springfield /ˈsprɪŋfiːld/ *noun*. E19.

[A town in Massachusetts, USA, site of a US government armoury.]

In full ***Springfield rifle***, ***Springfield gun***, etc. Any of various rifles formerly used by US troops.

springhaas /ˈsprɪŋhɑːs/ *noun*. *S. Afr.* L18.

[Afrikaans, from Dutch *spring* jump, leap + *haas* hare.]

= ***spring hare*** s.v. SPRING *noun*[1].

springhalt /ˈsprɪŋhɔːlt/ *noun*. E17.

[Unexplained alt. of STRINGHALT.]

= STRINGHALT.

springing /ˈsprɪŋɪŋ/ *noun*[1]. ME.

[from SPRING *verb*[1] + -ING[1].]

1 The action of SPRING *verb*[1]; an act or instance of this. ME.

2 †**a** The first appearance *of* the day, dawn. LME–E18. ▸**b** The beginning or early part of the year or a season. Long *dial.* E16.

3 a *ARCHITECTURE.* = SPRING *noun*[1] 16a. E18. ▸**b** The point of a branch's growth from the trunk. E19.

springing /ˈsprɪŋɪŋ/ *noun*[2]. L19.
[from SPRING *noun*[1] or *verb*[2] + -ING[1].]
The action or process of fitting a vehicle etc. with a spring or springs; the suspension of a vehicle etc., springs collectively.

Times The springing gives a comfortable ride for the passengers.

springing /ˈsprɪŋɪŋ/ *ppl adjective.* LME.
[from SPRING *verb*[1] + -ING[2].]
1 That springs; growing, rising, flowing; beginning to appear or come into being. LME.
2 Resilient, elastic, springy. M17.
3 *LAW* (now *Hist.*). = CONTINGENT *adjective* 7. M18.
4 Rising in or forming a curve. L18.
■ **springingly** *adverb* M19.

springle /ˈsprɪŋ(ə)l/ *noun*[1]. E17.
[Perh. from SPRING *noun*[3] + -LE[1].]
= SPRINGE *noun.*

springle /ˈsprɪŋ(ə)l/ *noun*[2]. Now *dial.* L17.
[Perh. from SPRING *noun*[1] + -LE[1].]
A thatching rod.

springle /ˈsprɪŋ(ə)l/ *verb trans.* Now *arch. rare.* E16.
[Var. of SPRINKLE *verb*. Cf. TINGLE *verb*, TINKLE *verb*.]
Sprinkle.

springtail /ˈsprɪŋteɪl/ *noun.* L18.
[from SPRING *noun*[1] or *verb*[1] + TAIL *noun*[1].]
Any of various small primitive wingless insects of the order Collembola, which leap by means of a forked posterior springing organ and are abundant in the soil.

springtime /ˈsprɪŋtʌɪm/ *noun.* L15.
[from SPRING *noun*[1] + TIME *noun*.]
1 The season of spring. L15.
2 The earlier part of life, youth; a time comparable to spring, the first stage or period *of* something. L16.

1 *attrib.*: L. M. BEEBE Wading pleasantly through springtime Arkansas meadows brave with daisies. **2** W. BLACK English girlhood in its sweetest springtime.

springy /ˈsprɪŋi/ *adjective.* L16.
[from SPRING *noun*[1], *verb*[1] + -Y[1].]
1 †**a** Growing in the season of spring. Only in L16. ▸**b** Characteristic of spring, springlike, vernal. M19.
2 Characterized by the presence of springs of water. M17.
3 Having or characterized by spring or elasticity, springing back on the removal of force or pressure; flexible, elastic, resilient; (of movement) buoyant and vigorous, bouncing. M17.

3 S. BELLOW The turf was springy, neither damp . . nor dry and hard. M. WESLEY Laura took off her hat and tossed back thick, springy hair. A. DAVIES She walked over to us with a long, springy stride.

■ **springily** *adverb* L19. **springiness** *noun* M17.

sprink /sprɪŋk/ *verb & noun. obsolete* exc. *dial.* LME.
[formed as SPRINKLE *verb*.]
▸ **A** *verb trans.* Sprinkle. LME.
▸†**B** *noun.* = SPRINKLE *noun* 1, 3. Only in M16.

sprinkle /ˈsprɪŋk(ə)l/ *noun.* LME.
[Rel. to SPRINKLE *verb*. Cf. Middle Low German, Middle Dutch *sprinkel*, Middle & mod. Dutch *sprenkel* speckle, spot, freckle.]
1 A sprinkler, *esp.* one for sprinkling holy water. Now only in ***holy-water sprinkle*** s.v. HOLY WATER. LME.
†**2** A spot, a speckle. *rare.* L15–L16.
3 The action or an act of sprinkling; a quantity sprinkled, a sprinkling, a small number or amount, (foll. by *of*); a light shower. L16. ▸**b** A colour effect produced by sprinkling; a mixture for producing this. M19.

3 C. MCCULLOUGH There had not been any rain . . , even a sprinkle to settle the dust. L. BLUE Dot with fat and a sprinkle of paprika.

sprinkle /ˈsprɪŋk(ə)l/ *verb.* LME.
[Perh. from Middle & mod. Dutch *sprenkelen* (cf. Middle Low German *sprinkelt* pa. pple 'spotted'): see -LE[3]. Cf. earlier STRINKLE.]
1 *verb trans.* Scatter or pour (liquid, powder, etc.) in small drops or particles, strew thinly or lightly; *fig.* disperse or distribute here and there. LME.
2 *verb trans.* Cover or spatter (a surface or object) *with* scattered drops or grains; powder or dust thinly or lightly; *fig.* dot or intersperse *with* (usu. in *pass.*). LME. ▸**b** Colour with small specks or spots. Freq. foll. by *with*. Usu. in *pass.* M18.
3 *verb intrans.* †**a** Spring or fly *up* in fine drops. *rare.* L16–E17. ▸**b** Rain or fall in fine or infrequent drops. Freq. *impers.* in ***it sprinkles***, ***it is sprinkling***, etc. L18.

1 H. SPENCER There are sprinkled throughout society men to whom active occupation is a need. P. CAREY Oscar was sprinkling sugar on his porridge. **2** P. H. JOHNSON The downs sprinkled with lights like a lawn with daisies. *National Observer (US)* Sprinkle the top with seasoning . . and sugar. ISAIAH BERLIN The French phrases with which this conversation is sprinkled. G. ADAIR He . . went into the bathroom to sprinkle his face with cold water. **b** C. G. W. LOCK Books may be sprinkled . . to resemble . . marble by using 2 or 3 different colours. **3b** *New Yorker* It began to sprinkle . . We began to hurry.

sprinkler /ˈsprɪŋklə/ *noun.* M16.
[from prec. + -ER[1].]
1 A thing that sprinkles something; *spec.* (***a***) a brush for sprinkling holy water; (***b***) a device or vehicle used for sprinkling water etc. on a lawn, road, etc., or to extinguish fires. M16.
2 A person who sprinkles something; *spec.* a person who favours baptism by sprinkling as opp. to immersion. E17.
Comb.: **sprinkler system** a system of sprinklers, *esp.* one in a building for extinguishing fires.
■ **sprinklered** *adjective* of or pertaining to a sprinkler system; *spec.* (chiefly *N. Amer.*), provided with or watered by a sprinkler system: M20.

sprinkling /ˈsprɪŋklɪŋ/ *noun.* LME.
[formed as prec. + -ING[1].]
1 The action of SPRINKLE *verb*; an act or instance of this. LME.
2 A quantity sprinkled; a small thinly distributed number or amount, a sprinkle. (Foll. by *of*.) L16.

2 E. GIBSON A sprinkling of gray hairs foretels the approaches of old age. E. DAVID A sprinkling of coarsely grated Gruyère.

sprinkling /ˈsprɪŋklɪŋ/ *ppl adjective.* M16.
[formed as prec. + -ING[2].]
1 That scatters small drops or particles. M16.
2 That falls in scattered drops. M17.
■ **sprinkingly** *adverb* (*rare*) E17.

sprint /sprɪnt/ *noun*[1]. L18.
[from the verb.]
1 A dart, a bound, a spring. *dial.* L18.
2 An instance of sprinting, a short burst or spell of running, driving, cycling, etc., at full speed; a short fast race; *transf.* a short spell of maximum speed or effort. M19.

2 E. MITTELHOLZER He covered the first hundred yards at a sprint. *attrib.*: *Times* The British sprint relay teams won their silver medals.

sprint /sprɪnt/ *noun*[2]. *dial.* L18.
[Var. of SPRENT *noun*.]
1 A snare, a springe. L18.
2 A spring of a lock etc. L19.

sprint /sprɪnt/ *verb.* M16.
[from Old Norse, ult. origin unkn. (cf. Swedish *spritta*, *sprätta*, Danish *sprætte*). Superseded SPRENT *verb*[1]. Cf. SPRUNT.]
†**1** *verb intrans.* Dart, bound, spring. Only in M16.
2 a *verb intrans.* Run on the spot. *dial.* M19. ▸**b** *verb intrans.* Run at full speed, esp. for a short distance; travel, drive, race, etc., in this manner. L19. ▸**c** *verb trans.* Traverse or cover (a certain distance or course) by sprinting. E20.
3 a *verb intrans.* Spurt out in small drops. *dial.* M19. ▸**b** *verb trans.* Sprinkle, spatter, (liquid etc.). *dial.* M19.
4 *verb intrans.* Sprout, grow. *Scot.* L19.

2b K. CROSSLEY-HOLLAND They sprinted over the grass as fast as their legs could carry them. E. SEGAL Too impatient to wait for the elevator, Barney sprinted up the stairs. *transf.*: *New Scientist* Thale cress . . sprints through its life cycle in five weeks. **c** *Time* When I trained, I wasn't used to sprinting the last two miles.

■ **sprinter** *noun* (***a***) a person who sprints, *spec.* a specialist at sprint racing; (***b***) a vehicle, esp. a type of passenger train, designed to travel at speed over short distances: L19.

sprit /sprɪt/ *noun*[1].
[Old English *sprēot* = Middle & mod. Low German, Middle & mod. Dutch *spr(i)et* (German *Spriet*), from Germanic base also of SPROUT *verb*[1].]
1 A pole, *esp.* one used for propelling a boat, a punting-pole. OE.
2 *NAUTICAL.* A small spar crossing diagonally from the mast to the upper rear or outer corner of a sail. Cf. BOWSPRIT. ME.

sprit /sprɪt/ *noun*[2]. Now *dial.* E17.
[from SPRIT *verb*[1].]
A young shoot of a plant or tree; a sprout from a seed or root.

sprit /sprɪt/ *noun*[3]. *Scot.* L18.
[Var. of SPRET.]
A rush, esp. the jointed rush, *Juncus articulatus*; such rushes collectively.

sprit /sprɪt/ *verb*[1] *intrans.* Now *dial.* Infl. **-tt-**. Pa. pple **sprit**, **spritted**.
[Old English *spryttan* from Germanic base also of SPROUT *verb*[1].]
Sprout, shoot, germinate.

sprit /sprɪt/ *verb*[2] *intrans.* Now *dial. rare.* Infl. **-tt-**. LME.
[Origin uncertain: perh. rel. to SPURT *verb*.]
Spring, dart.

sprite /sprʌɪt/ *noun & verb.* ME.
[Alt. with lengthened vowel of *sprit* contr. of SPIRIT *noun*. Cf. SPIRIT *noun*, SPRIGHT.]
▸ **A** *noun.* **1** Spirit, courage, cheer. *arch.* ME. ▸†**b** In *pl.* A person's spirits or emotional faculties. LME–L16.
2 A person's soul, a disembodied spirit, a ghost (*arch.*). Now usu., a goblin, a fairy, *esp.* a small freq. mischievous pixie or elf; *transf.* a small dainty person, esp. a child. ME.
3 *COMPUTING.* A graphical figure which may be moved onscreen and otherwise manipulated as a single entity. L20.

2 SHAKES. *Mids. N. D.* That shrewd and knavish sprite, called Robin Goodfellow.

▸†**B** *verb. rare.*
1 *verb trans.* Inspire (a person) *with* courage. Only in M16.
2 *verb intrans.* Act as a sprite or spirit. Chiefly as ***spriting*** *verbal noun.* M16–E17.
■ †**spriteful** *adjective* = SPRIGHTFUL E–M17. †**spritefully** *adverb* = SPRIGHTFULLY: only in E17. †**spritefulness** *noun* = SPRIGHTFULNESS: only in M17. **spritehood** *noun* (*rare*) the condition or state of being a sprite L19.

spritely /ˈsprʌɪtli/ *adjective & adverb.* L16.
[from prec. + -LY[2], -LY[1].]
▸ **A** *adjective.* = SPRIGHTLY *adjective* 1. L16.
▸ **B** *adverb.* = SPRIGHTLY *adverb.* E17.
■ **spriteliness** *noun* (now *rare*) = SPRIGHTLINESS M17.

spritsail /ˈsprɪts(ə)l, ˈsprɪtseɪl/ *noun.* LME.
[from SPRIT *noun*[1] + SAIL *noun*[1]. Cf. Dutch *sprietzeil*, West Frisian *-seil*.]
NAUTICAL. **1** A sail extended by a sprit; *Hist.* a sail attached to a yard slung under the bowsprit of a large vessel. LME.
2 *ellipt.* A ship or barge fitted with a spritsail. L19.
Comb.: **spritsail yard** a yard slung under the bowsprit to support a spritsail; **spritsail-yard** *verb trans.* (*slang*) disable (a shark, dogfish, etc.) by thrusting a spar or piece of wood through the snout or gills.

sprittle /ˈsprɪt(ə)l/ *verb trans.* Long *obsolete* exc. *dial.* L16.
[Origin unkn.]
Scrape *off* or dig *up* with a bladed instrument or tool.

spritty /ˈsprɪti/ *noun. colloq.* M20.
[from SPRIT(SAIL + -Y[6].]
A barge fitted with a spritsail.

spritty /ˈsprɪti/ *adjective. Scot.* L18.
[from SPRIT *noun*[3] + -Y[1].]
Full of sprits or rushes.

†**spritual** *adjective.* LME–L18.
[Contr.]
Spiritual.

sprity /ˈsprɪti/ *adjective.* Now *dial.* E16.
[from SPRITE + -Y[5].]
Spirited. Also, spirituous.

spritz /sprɪts/ *verb & noun. N. Amer.* E20.
[German *spritzen* to squirt, splash.]
▸ **A** *verb trans.* Sprinkle, squirt, spray. E20.
▸ **B** *noun.* The act or an instance of spritzing something; a squirt, a spray. M20.

spritzer /ˈsprɪtsə/ *noun.* M20.
[German = a splash, formed as prec.]
A mixture of (usu. white) wine and soda water; a drink or glass of this.

spritzig /ˈʃprɪtsɪç/ *adjective & noun.* M20.
[German, formed as SPRITZ.]
▸ **A** *adjective.* Of wine: sparkling. M20.
▸ **B** *noun.* Sparkle in wine. M20.

sprocket /ˈsprɒkɪt/ *noun.* M16.
[Origin unkn.]
1 A triangular piece of timber used in framing, esp. one fastened on the foot of a rafter in order to raise the level or change the slope of the eaves. M16.
2 a Any of several teeth projecting from the rim of a wheel and engaging with the links of a chain, a line of perforations in film or paper, tape, etc. M18. ▸**b** More fully ***sprocket-wheel***. A wheel bearing sprockets, esp. one that engages with a cycle chain, or that propels film through a projector or camera. M18.
3 *NAUTICAL.* Each of the teeth of a pawl-rim. Now *rare.* E20.
Comb.: **sprocket hole** each of a line of perforations in film, paper, tape, etc., with which sprockets can engage for propulsion or correct alignment; ***sprocket-wheel***: see sense 2b above.
■ **sprocketed** *adjective* possessing sprockets or sprocket holes L19. **sprocketless** *adjective* not having or requiring sprockets M20.

sprod /sprɒd/ *noun.* E17.
[Origin unkn.]
A salmon in its second year.

sprog /sprɒg/ *noun.* M20.
[Origin uncertain: perh. from SPRAG *noun*².]
1 A new recruit, a trainee, a novice; a person of inferior rank. Freq. *attrib.* Chiefly *Military slang.* M20.
2 A youngster; a child, a baby. *colloq.* (orig. *Nautical slang*). M20.

sprong /sprɒŋ/ *noun.* Now *Brit. & Canad. dial.* L15.
[Perh. var. of PRONG *noun.*]
(A prong of) a fork.

sprosser /ˈsprɒsə/ *noun.* L19.
[German.]
= ***thrush nightingale*** s.v. THRUSH *noun*¹.

sprot *noun*¹, *noun*² vars. of SPRAT *noun*¹, *noun*².

sprote /sprəʊt/ *noun.* Long *obsolete* exc. *dial.* Also **sprot** /sprɒt/.
[Old English *sprota* = Middle Dutch *sprote*, *sproot* (Dutch *sport*), Middle Low German *sprote*, *sprate*, Old High German *sprozzo* (Middle High German *sprosse*, German *Sprosse*), Old Norse *sproti*, from West Germanic, ult. rel. to SPROUT *verb*¹.]
†**1** A shoot, a sprout, a twig. OE–LME.
2 A chip, a splinter. LME.
3 In *pl.* Small sticks or twigs; bits of branches blown from trees. Also ***sprote-wood***. E19.

sprottle /ˈsprɒt(ə)l/ *verb intrans. dial.* Earlier (*Scot.*) **spartle** /ˈspɑːt(ə)l/, **sprattle** /ˈsprat(ə)l/. E18.
[Rel. to Middle & mod. Dutch, Middle & mod. Low German *spartelen*, Swedish *sprattla*.]
Sprawl, struggle helplessly, move the limbs in a struggling motion.

sprout /spraʊt/ *noun.* LME.
[from SPROUT *verb*¹, prob. after Middle Low German, Middle Dutch *sprūte*, Middle Dutch *spruyte* (Dutch *spruit*). Cf. SPROTE.]
1 A shoot from a plant, a bud; a new growth developing from a bud, seed, or other part of a plant. LME. ▸**b** A young tender shoot or side-growth of a plant, esp. a brassica, a bean, or (*N. Amer.*) alfalfa, eaten as a vegetable; *spec.* = ***Brussels sprout*** s.v. BRUSSELS 3. Usu. in *pl.* M17. ▸**c** A variety of potato. *US.* M19.
2 a MEDICINE. A small outgrowth. *rare.* L16. ▸†**b** A branch or mouth of a river; a creek; a section of a waterfall. *US.* L17–M19.
3 The action of sprouting or of putting forth new growths. *rare.* L16.
4 A scion, a descendant; *colloq.* a young person, a child. Now chiefly *Scot. & US.* E17.

🕮 **1b** ***bean sprouts***: see BEAN *noun.* **4** S. BELLOW He's not just a sprout any more, and we can't be watching him all his life.

Comb.: **sprout-land** *US* land covered with the sprouts of trees or shrubs.

sprout /spraʊt/ *verb*¹. ME.
[Corresp. to Old Saxon *sprūton*, Middle Low German *sprūten*, Middle & mod. Dutch *spruiten*, from West Germanic base repr. also by Old English *sprȳtan*, *spryttan*, Old High German *spriozan* (German *spriessen*). Prob. already in Old English. Cf. SPRIT *noun*¹, *verb*¹.]
1 *verb intrans.* Grow or emerge as a sprout or sprouts; shoot forth or spring up (as) by natural growth. (Foll. by *from*, *out of*, *forth*, *up*, etc.) ME.
2 *verb intrans.* Of a tree, a plant, a seed, etc.: put out a sprout or sprouts; develop new growths or shoots; bud. (Foll. by *out*, *up*, etc.) ME. ▸**b** *spec.* Of a seed, tuber, etc.: germinate or begin to grow shoots prematurely. L17.
3 *verb intrans.* Of earth, a surface, etc.: bear, bring forth, or produce sprouts or new growths. Freq. foll. by *with* (a growth). LME.
4 *verb trans.* Bear or develop (shoots, new growth, etc.); put *out* or produce as shoots or sprouts. L16.
5 *verb trans.* **a** Cause or induce (a plant, a seed, etc.) to develop sprouts or shoots, esp. before planting or sowing, or to eat. L18. ▸**b** Rub growing shoots off (a potato). *dial.* E19.

🕮 **1** J. BLUME Hotels and casinos are sprouting up all over the place. B. CHATWIN Burdocks were sprouting through cracks in the steps. E. SEGAL The fuzz he liked to call his 'beard' that sprouted on his face. **2** P. S. BUCK The wheat seed sprouted and pushed spears of delicate green above the . . earth. ***sprouting** BROCCOLI*. **b** K. VONNEGUT His potatoes would neither freeze nor sprout until he was ready to market them. **4** J. FANE The so-called Ruins . . just some unconnected flint walls sprouting weeds. **5a** *Health Now* The best beans to 'sprout' are the Mung beans.

▪ **sprouted** *ppl adjective* that has developed a sprout or sprouts; *spec.* (of corn) that has germinated prematurely: L15. **sprouter** *noun* (*a*) *rare* a person who or thing which causes plants etc. to sprout; (*b*) a container in which seeds (esp. of mung beans) are sprouted: L16. **sprouting** *noun* (*a*) the action of the verb; an instance of this; (*b*) a sprout, a shoot, a growth: M16.

sprout /sprəʊt/ *verb*² *trans. & intrans.* Long *obsolete* exc. *dial.* L16.
[Rel. to Norwegian *sprute*, Swedish *spruta*, Danish *sprude*, Low German *sprutten*, *sprütte*, Middle High German, German *sprützen*: perh. from stem of prec.]
(Cause to) run or pour out in a spout or gush, spurt.

sprowsie /ˈspraʊzi/ *noun. slang* (*obsolete* exc. *Hist.*). M20.
[Prob. var. of SPRAZER.]
= SPRAZER.

spruce /spruːs/ *noun & adjective*¹. LME.
[Alt. of early forms of *Prussia* (see PRUSSIAN) or from Old French *Prusse*, *Pruisse*. Cf. Anglo-Latin *Sprucia*.]
▸ **A** *noun.* †**1** (**S-**.) The country of Prussia. Also ***Spruce-land***. LME–M17.
2 *ellipt.* Something originating in or associated with Prussia, as leather, beer, a chest, etc. Now *rare* or *obsolete.* L15.
3 Any of various pyramidal evergreen coniferous trees constituting the genus *Picea*, of the pine family, with pendulous cones and with needles inserted in peglike projections; the wood of these trees. E17.
3 ***black spruce***, ***Norway spruce***, ***Sitka spruce***, etc.
▸ **B** *attrib.* or as *adjective.* **1** Prussian; of Baltic origin. *obsolete* exc. *Hist.* LME.
2 Of or pertaining to the spruce fir; made of the wood of the spruce fir. LME.
Comb. & special collocations: **spruce beer** †(*a*) beer from Prussia; (*b*) a fermented drink made with needles and twigs of spruce; **spruce budworm** the brown larva of a N. American tortricid moth, *Choristoneura fumiferana*, which is a serious pest of spruce and other conifers; **spruce fir** (now *rare*) = sense A.3 above; **spruce grouse** a grouse, *Dendragapus canadensis*, of N. American coniferous forests; **spruce hen** a female spruce grouse; †**spruce leather** a type of leather from Prussia, used esp. for jerkins; **spruce partridge** = ***spruce grouse*** above; **spruce pine** any of several N. American coniferous trees, now usu. the pines *Pinus glabra* and *P. virginiana*; **spruce tea** an infusion of tender spruce shoots.

spruce /spruːs/ *adjective*² *& adverb.* L16.
[Perh. from ***spruce leather*** s.v. SPRUCE *noun & adjective*¹.]
▸ **A** *adjective.* **1** Trim, neat, dapper; smart in appearance, dress, etc. L16.
†**2** Brisk, smart, lively. L16–M18.

🕮 **1** M. HOLROYD He appeared a very spruce . . figure, white-collared, clean-shaven. L. GRANT-ADAMSON The car . . was a . . family saloon, several years old, but spruce.

▸ **B** *adverb.* = SPRUCELY *adverb. arch.* E17.
▪ **sprucely** *adverb* in a spruce manner, smartly, trimly, neatly L16. **spruceness** *noun* E17.

spruce /spruːs/ *verb*¹. L16.
[from prec.]
1 *verb trans.* Make spruce, trim, or neat. Freq. foll. by *up*. L16.
2 *verb intrans.* Foll. by *up*, †*out*: make oneself spruce. E18.

🕮 **1** B. CHATWIN Photos show the building spruced up with a coat of whitewash. **2** F. FORSYTH He was still in a robe; there was little . . cause . . to rise early or spruce up.

Comb.: **spruce-up** *colloq.* (orig. *US*) the action of sprucing up; an instance of this, a tidying-up, a refurbishment.

spruce /spruːs/ *verb*². *slang* (orig. MILITARY). E20.
[Origin unkn.]
1 *verb intrans.* Lie, practise deception; evade a duty, malinger. E20.
2 *verb trans.* Deceive. E20.
▪ **sprucer** *noun* a person who tells tall stories, a trickster E20.

sprue /spruː/ *noun*¹. E19.
[Dutch *spruw*, perh. rel. to Flemish *spruwen* sprinkle.]
MEDICINE. **1** Thrush, candidiasis of the mouth. *rare* (only in Dicts.). E19.
2 More fully ***tropical sprue***. A condition caused by deficient absorption of food by a diseased small intestine, and characterized by ulceration of the mucous membrane of the mouth, anaemia, and diarrhoea, occurring esp. in visitors to tropical countries; psilosis. L19.
2 NON-TROPICAL ***sprue***.

sprue /spruː/ *noun*² *& verb.* E19.
[Origin unkn.]
▸ **A** *noun.* **1** A channel through which molten metal or plastic is poured into a mould cavity. E19.
2 A piece of metal or plastic attached to a casting, having solidified in the mould channel; *spec.* a stem joining a number of small items of moulded plastic. L19.
3 An object used to form a channel into a mould, e.g. by being withdrawn or by melting. L19.
▸ **B** *verb trans.* Chiefly DENTISTRY. Provide (a wax pattern) with a sprue or sprues. Freq. as ***sprued*** *ppl adjective*, ***sprueing*** *verbal noun*. M20.

sprue /spruː/ *noun*³. M19.
[Origin unkn.]
Long slender asparagus, often regarded as inferior in quality. Also ***sprue grass***.

spruik /spruːk/ *verb intrans. Austral. & NZ slang.* E20.
[Origin unkn.]
Esp. of a showman: hold forth, speak in public.
▪ **spruiker** *noun* a speaker employed to attract custom to a sideshow, a barker; a public speaker: E20.

spruit /spreɪt, *foreign* sprœyt/ *noun. S. Afr.* M19.
[Dutch = SPROUT *noun.*]
A small watercourse that is usually dry except in the rainy season.

sprung /sprʌŋ/ *ppl adjective*¹. L15.
[pa. pple of SPRING *verb*¹.]
1 That has been made to spring (out); *spec.* †(*a*) (of a horse) that has been made to gallop; (*b*) (of a game-bird) that has been made to rise from cover. L15.
2 Of a mast, a plank, a cricket bat, etc.: cracked, split. L16.
3 That has sprung up or arisen. Freq. as 2nd elem. in comb. Also foll. by *up*. L16.
4 Tipsy, drunk. *slang.* E19.
5 Of or in sprung rhythm (see below). L19.
6 Esp. of an alibi: produced unexpectedly in order to disconcert. M20.
3 ***first-sprung***, ***new-sprung***, etc. **5 sprung rhythm** a poetic metre used esp. by Gerard Manley Hopkins (1844–89), approximating to speech rhythm, in which each foot consists of one stressed syllable either alone or followed by a varying number of unstressed syllables; a similar rhythm in prose, speech, or music.

sprung /sprʌŋ/ *ppl adjective*². L19.
[Irreg. from SPRING *verb*², after prec.]
1 Provided with a spring or springs. L19.
2 Of a floor, esp. a timber dance-floor: suspended above a subfloor so as to be resilient. M20.

sprung *verb*¹ *pa. t. & pa. pple*: see SPRING *verb*¹.

sprung *verb*² *pa. t. & pa. pple*: see SPRING *verb*².

sprunt /sprʌnt/ *verb, adjective, & noun.* Now *rare* or *obsolete* exc. *dial.* E17.
[App. rel. to SPRENT *verb*¹ and SPRINT *verb.*]
▸ **A** *verb intrans.* Spring or start; move in a quick or convulsive manner; dart or run. E17.
▸ **B** *adjective.* Brisk, active; smart, spruce. M17.
▸ **C** *noun.* A convulsive movement; a spring or bound. L17.
▪ **spruntly** *adverb* E17.

†**spry** *noun* see SPRAY *noun*².

spry /sprʌɪ/ *adjective & adverb.* M18.
[Origin unkn.: cf. SPRACK, SPRAG *noun*², *adjective.*]
Active, nimble, smart, brisk; full of health and spirits. Also, alert, clever.
▪ **spryly** *adverb* E20. **spryness** *noun* M19.

†**sprye** *noun* see SPRAY *noun*².

spud /spʌd/ *noun.* See also SPAD *noun*¹. LME.
[Origin unkn.]
†**1** An inferior short knife or dagger. LME–E19.
†**2** An iron head or blade fixed to the foot of a staff. *rare.* Only in E17.
3 a A digging or weeding implement resembling a spade with a narrow chisel-shaped blade. M17. ▸**b** A digging fork with three broad prongs. E19. ▸**c** SURGERY. Any of various implements or instruments having a blunt chisel-shaped end; *esp.* (*a*) one used to remove the bark from timber; (*b*) one used in thatching; (*c*) a blunt needle used esp. to remove objects embedded in the cornea of the eye. M19 ▸**d** = ***spade lug*** s.v. SPADE *noun*¹. E20.
4 A short or stocky person or thing. *slang.* L17.
5 *colloq.* **a** = POTATO *noun* 1. M19. ▸**b** = POTATO *noun* 4a. M20.
6 Each of a number of poles that can be put out from a dredger and stuck into the bed or bank of a river to keep the vessel stationary. L19.
7 PLUMBING. A short length of pipe used to connect two components, or in the form of a projection from a fitting to which a pipe may be screwed. E20.
Comb. & phrases: **in the spud line** *slang* pregnant; **spud barber** *slang* a person who peels potatoes; **spud-bashing** *slang* (orig. MILITARY) the peeling of potatoes; **spud can** OIL INDUSTRY a structure that can be sunk into a soft sea bottom by temporary ballasting and used as the base of a platform extending above the water; **Spud Islander** *Canad. slang* a native or inhabitant of Prince Edward Island, which is noted for its potatoes; **spud wrench** a long bar with a socket on the end for tightening bolts.

spud /spʌd/ *verb.* Infl. **-dd-**. M17.
[from the noun.]
1 *verb trans.* Dig *up* or *out*, remove, by means of a spud. M17. ▸**b** *verb intrans.* Dig with a spud. E19.
2 *verb trans.* OIL INDUSTRY. Begin to drill (a hole for an oil well); make the initial drilling for (a well). (Foll. by *in*, occas. *out*.) L19.
3 *verb intrans.* Begin to drill an oil well. (Foll. by *in*.) E20.
▪ **spudder** *noun* a small drilling rig used for spudding in wells E20.

spuddle /ˈspʌd(ə)l/ *verb.* Now *dial.* E17.
[Alt. of PUDDLE *verb*; later partly from SPUD *noun.*]
1 *verb intrans.* = PUDDLE *verb* 1. E17.
2 *verb trans.* Dig up or work at lightly or superficially. E19.

spuddy /ˈspʌdi/ *adjective.* Now *rare.* E19.
[from SPUD *noun* + -Y¹. Cf. PUDDY *adjective.*]
Stumpy, thickset, pudgy.

spue *noun, verb* see SPEW *noun, verb.*

spule /spjuːl/ *noun. Scot. & north.* Also (earlier) **speal** /spiːl/. L18.
[App. var. of SPAULD *noun.*]
A shoulder-blade, esp. of an animal. Also more fully ***spule-bone***.

spulyie /ˈspuːl(j)i/ *noun & verb. Scot. arch.* Also **spulie**, **spuilzie**, **spulzie**. LME.
[Old French *espoillier* SPOIL *verb.*]
▶ **A** *noun.* **1** The action or an act of despoiling or plundering something; spoliation. LME. ▸**b** LAW. A taking away of another's movable goods without a legal warrant or the owner's consent; an action for the restitution of such goods. L17.
2 Spoil, booty, plunder. E16.
▶ **B** *verb.* **1** *verb trans.* Despoil, plunder; deprive *of* something. LME.
2 *verb trans.* Take as spoil or plunder; LAW take away without a legal warrant or the owner's consent. LME.
3 *verb intrans.* Commit spoliation. M19.

spumante /spuˈmanti/ *noun.* E20.
[Italian = sparkling.]
= ASTI ***spumante***.

spume /spjuːm/ *noun & verb.* LME.
[Old French (*e*)*spume* or Latin *spuma*.]
▶ **A** *noun.* **1** Foam, froth, frothy matter; *spec.* foam of the sea. LME.
†**2** Litharge *of* lead, silver. LME–M17.
▶ **B** *verb.* **1** *verb intrans.* Foam, froth. (Foll. by *out.*) LME.
2 *verb trans.* Send out like foam. (Foll. by *forth.*) M19.
■ **spuˈmescence** *noun* frothiness, foaminess L18.

spumoni /spuːˈməʊni/ *noun. N. Amer.* E20.
[Italian *spumone*, from *spuma* foam, SPUME *noun.*]
A rich dessert consisting of layered ice-cream with candied fruits, nuts, and sometimes brandy.

spumous /ˈspjuːməs/ *adjective.* LME.
[from Latin *spumosus*, from *spuma* SPUME *noun*: see -OUS.]
Of, pertaining to, producing, or resembling froth, foam, or spume; frothy, spumy, foaming.
■ Also **spuˈmose** *adjective* (*rare*) LME.

spumy /ˈspjuːmi/ *adjective.* L16.
[from SPUME *noun* + -Y¹.]
1 Of, covered with, or casting up sea-foam. L16.
2 Of a frothy nature or consistency; characterized by the presence of froth. E17.

spun /spʌn/ *noun. rare.* M19.
[from the adjective.]
Spun silk or yarn.

spun /spʌn/ *ppl adjective.* ME.
[pa. pple of SPIN *verb.*]
1 That has undergone the process of spinning; formed, fabricated, or prepared by spinning. ME.
2 *spec.* **a** Of sugar: boiled to a syrup and drawn out or worked up into a threadlike or fluffy form, esp. as a confection or decoration. M19. ▸**b** Of or designating vegetable protein, esp. soya, that has been spun into fibres to resemble meat. L20.
Phrases & comb.: ***fine-spun***: see FINE *adverb.* **spun gold** *noun & adjective* (*a*) *noun* = ***gold thread*** s.v. GOLD *adjective*; (*b*) *adjective* resembling gold thread. **spun-golden** *adjective* = ***spun gold*** (b) above. **spun out** unduly prolonged or protracted. **spunyarn** (*a*) yarn made by spinning; (*b*) *spec.* (NAUTICAL) (a) cord or line made of two or more rope-yarns not laid but simply twisted together.
¶ Earliest in comb. Not recorded in isolation until L15.

spun *verb pa. t. & pple*: see SPIN *verb.*

†**spunge** *noun, verb,* †**spunger** *noun,* etc. vars. of SPONGE *noun*¹ etc.

spunk /spʌŋk/ *noun.* M16.
[Perh. blend of SPARK *noun*¹ and FUNK *noun*¹, but cf. also Irish *sponc*, Gaelic *spong* tinder, ult. from Latin *spongia*, Greek *spoggia* SPONGE *noun*¹. Cf. PUNK *noun*² *& adjective.*]
1 A spark; *fig.* a glimmer, a vestige, (*of* some quality, light, etc.). Now chiefly *Scot. & dial.* M16. ▸**b** A small or feeble fire. Chiefly *Scot.* E19.
2 = TOUCHWOOD 1. Now *rare.* L16.
3 = TOUCHWOOD 2. Now *rare.* M17.
4 = MATCH *noun*² 4. Chiefly *Scot. & dial.* M18.
5 **a** Spirit, mettle; courage, pluck. *colloq.* L18. ▸**b** Seminal fluid. *coarse slang.* L19. ▸**c** A sexually attractive person. *Austral. slang.* L20.
■ **spunkless** *adjective* (*colloq.*) lacking courage or spirit L19.

spunk /spʌŋk/ *verb intrans.* E19.
[from the noun.]
1 Leak *out*, become known. *Scot.* E19.
2 **a** Stand *up* for oneself spiritedly or courageously. *US.* M19. ▸**b** Blaze *up* in anger or passion. *Scot.* L19.

spunkie /ˈspʌŋki/ *noun. Scot.* E18.
[from SPUNK *noun* + -IE.]
1 A will o' the wisp. E18.
2 Whisky, spirits. *rare.* L18.
3 A spirited or hot-tempered person. E19.

spunky /ˈspʌŋki/ *adjective.* L18.
[from SPUNK *noun* + -Y¹.]
1 Courageous, spirited. *colloq.* L18.
2 Irritable, irascible. *dial. & US.* E19.
■ **spunkily** *adverb* L19. **spunkiness** *noun* M20.

spur /spəː/ *noun*¹.
[Old English *spora, spura* = Old Saxon, Old High German *sporo* (Dutch *spoor*, German †*Sporen, Sporn*), Old Norse *spori*, from Germanic from Indo-European base also of SPURN *verb.* See also SPURN *noun*².]
▶ **I 1** A device for pricking the side of a horse in order to control it or urge it forward, consisting of a small (now usu. blunt) spike or spiked wheel on a U-shaped piece of metal which is attached by a strap to the counter of the rider's boot. OE. ▸**b** HERALDRY. A charge representing a spur. L17.
2 *fig.* A stimulus, an incentive, an incitement, a goad. (Foll. by *of* a particular influence etc., *to* a person, course of action, etc.) M16.

> 🕮 **1** SHAKES. *Wint. T.* You may ride's With one soft kiss a thousand furlongs ere With spur we heat an acre. J. DOS PASSOS General Miles . . dug in his spurs in an endeavor to control the horse. **2** A. BEVAN Fear of unemployment was the spur which compelled the worker to do his best. A. STORR A good deal of the world's great literature . . has been produced under the spur of economic necessity.

▶ **II 3** A short strut or stay set diagonally to support an upright timber; a piece of timber acting as a bracket; a sloping buttress. LME. ▸**b** A small support for ceramic ware during firing. M19.
4 a ZOOLOGY. A sharp hard claw present on the back of the foot or lower (usu. hind) leg of a bird or animal, esp. as a weapon in the male. LME. ▸**b** ANATOMY, MEDICINE, & ZOOLOGY. A short, somewhat pointed process or growth on a part of the body. L17.
5 †**a** FORTIFICATION. An angular projection from the face of a defensive wall. L16–E18. ▸**b** An artificial projection from a bridge or river-bank, serving to deflect the current. M18.
6 Each of the main roots of a tree. Cf. SPURN *noun*² 2. Long *obsolete* exc. *dial.* E17.
7 a *Hist.* A sharp-pointed projection from the prow of a warship. E17. ▸**b** A metal point fastened to the leg of a fighting cock. Now *rare.* L17. ▸**c** A climbing-iron. E19.
8 a A ridge, mountain, hill, range, or part of one, projecting for some distance from the main range or mass; an offshoot. M17. ▸**b** A short extension to the side; *spec.* a branch of a road, railway, etc. (cf. ***spur line***, ***spur road*** below). M19.
9 a A short lateral branch or side-shoot, *esp.* one bearing fruit. L17. ▸**b** BOTANY. A tubular projection from the base of a perianth-segment or corolla. M18. ▸**c** A disease of rye and other grasses, in which the blighted ear resembles a cock's spur; = ERGOT 1. M18.
10 *gen.* Any sharp or short projection or point resembling or suggestive of a spur. L19.

> 🕮 **4** A. NEWTON Snow-partridges are generally furnished with strong but blunt spurs. **b** F. SMYTH The laminal spurs on the thoracic vertebrae . . were very small. **8a** A. J. TOYNBEE The ruins of an Inca fortress on a spur of the eastern mountain-range. **b** *Environment Now* The proposal to drive an M4 spur road through the ancient Long Wood.

Phrases: ***gilded spurs***, ***gilt spurs***: see GILT *ppl adjective.* **on the spur** at full speed, in or with the utmost haste. **on the spur of the moment** without deliberation, on a sudden impulse, impromptu, instantly (cf. ***spur-of-the-moment*** below). **put spurs to**, **set spurs to** impel or urge on by spurring (*lit. & fig.*). **ride switch and spur**, **ride whip and spur** *arch.* ride at a furious pace. ***Scotch spur***: see SCOTCH *adjective.* ***set spurs to***: see ***put spurs to*** above. **win one's spurs** gain knighthood by an act of valour; *transf.* attain distinction, achieve one's first honours.
Comb.: **spur blight** a fungus disease of raspberries and loganberries causing discoloured patches on the stems, death of buds at the nodes, and weakening of the laterals; **spur-bow** (*Hist.*) = sense 7a above; **spur-dog** a grey and cream dogfish of the N. Atlantic and Mediterranean, *Squalus acanthias*, having a spine in front of the dorsal fin; also called ***spiny dogfish***; **spurfowl** any of a number of small Asian and African game birds, esp. of the genus *Galloperdix*, with spurs on the legs; **spur-gall** *verb trans.* (*arch.*) gall or injure (a horse) with the use of spurs in riding; *fig.* gall severely; **spur gear**, **spur gearing** MECHANICS: consisting of spur-wheels; **spur-leather** a leather strap for fastening a spur to a boot; ***under spur-leather*** (*arch.*), a subordinate, an attendant, a menial; **spur line** a short line branching off a railway line, *esp.* one making a connection to another line; **spur mark** a mark on the base of a glazed pot made by a spur or support during firing; **spur-of-the-moment** *adjective* impromptu, sudden, unpremeditated; **spur road** a side or minor road; *spec.* a connecting road branching off from a motorway or main highway; **spur-rowel** a rowel or spiked wheel forming part of a spur; **spur-royal** (*Hist.*) a gold coin worth fifteen shillings, chiefly struck in the reign of James I & VI and having on its reverse a sun with rays, resembling a spur-rowel; ***spur valerian***: see VALERIAN 1; **spur-wheel** a gear-wheel which has cogs or teeth arranged radially around its edge, a cog-wheel; **spur-wing** (*a*) ORNITHOLOGY a spur-winged bird; (*b*) ANGLING a mayfly of the genus *Centroptilum*; **spur-winged** *adjective* having one or more stiff claws or spurs projecting from the pinion-bone of the wing; ***spur-winged goose***, a black and white goose, *Plectropterus gambensis*, of sub-Saharan Africa; ***spur-winged plover***, a black and white plover, *Vanellus spinosus*, of N. Africa and the Middle East.
■ **spurless** *adjective* ME. **spurlike** *adjective* resembling (that of) a spur, esp. in shape L16.

spur /spəː/ *noun*². *rare.* L19.
[Origin unkn.]
A set of folded sheets of handmade paper, esp. as hung to dry.

spur /spəː/ *verb.* Infl. **-rr-**. ME.
[from SPUR *noun*¹.]
1 *verb trans.* Prick (a horse etc.) with a spur or spurs, in order to urge a faster pace; urge on by the use of spurs. Freq. foll. by *on.* ME.
2 *verb trans.* Drive on, hasten; incite, impel, stimulate; urge, prompt. Freq. foll. by *on, to, to do.* ME.
3 *verb trans.* Provide with a spur or spurs. ME.
4 a *verb intrans.* Hasten; proceed hurriedly. Long *obsolete* exc. *dial.* E16. ▸**b** *verb intrans. & trans.* (with *it*). Ride quickly by urging on one's horse with the use of spurs. L16.
5 a *verb intrans.* Strike out with the foot; kick. L16. ▸**b** *verb trans.* Esp. of a bird: strike or wound with a spur. M17. ▸**c** *verb intrans.* Fight (as) with spurs; strike *at.* E18.
6 *verb trans.* Support or prop up (a post etc.) by means of a strut or spur; strengthen with spurs. M18.
7 *verb trans.* Prune in (a side-shoot etc.) so as to form a spur close to the stem. Usu. foll. by *back, in.* M19.
■ **spurrer** *noun* (earlier in FORE-SPURRER) M17.

spurge /spəːdʒ/ *noun.* LME.
[Aphet. from Old French *espurge* (mod. *épurge*), from *espurgier* from Latin *expurgare* cleanse, EXPURGATE.]
Any of numerous plants constituting the genus *Euphorbia* (family Euphorbiaceae), which exude an acrid milky juice with purgative properties and have minute flowers grouped in a cup-shaped involucre.
caper spurge, ***petty spurge***, ***Portland spurge***, ***sun spurge***, etc.
Comb.: **spurge hawk**, **spurge hawkmoth** a grey-brown and pink hawkmoth, *Hyles euphorbiae*, whose caterpillars feed on spurges; **spurge laurel** a low early-flowering Eurasian shrub of the mezereon family, *Daphne laureola*, with glossy evergreen leaves and greenish flowers; **spurge nettle** a plant of the spurge family with stinging hairs, *Cnidoscolus stimulosus*, of the southern US; **spurge olive** the shrub mezereon, *Daphne mezereum*.

spurge /spəːdʒ/ *verb.* Long *obsolete* exc. *dial.* ME.
[Old French *espurgier*: see prec.]
†**1** *verb trans.* Cleanse or purify (a person, the body, etc.); free from or rid *of* impurity; *fig.* clear of guilt. ME–M16.
†**2** *verb trans.* Remove or clear *away* or *out* by cleansing or purifying. *rare.* LME–L15.
3 *verb intrans.* Of ale, wine, or other fermenting liquor: produce a deposit during fermentation; become clear; ferment. LME.
†**4** *verb intrans.* Empty the bowels. M16–M17.

spuria /ˈspjʊərɪə/ *noun pl.* E20.
[Latin, neut. pl. of *spurius* SPURIOUS. Cf. TRIVIA.]
1 Spurious works or words. E20.
2 ELECTRONICS. Spurious signals. L20.

spurii /ˈspjʊərɪiː/ *noun pl.* L20.
[Alt. of prec., after Latin pls. in *-ii*.]
ELECTRONICS. = SPURIA 2.

spurion /ˈspjʊərɪɒn/ *noun.* M20.
[from (the same root as) next + -ON.]
PHYSICS. A hypothetical subatomic particle introduced to facilitate mathematical calculations but having no physical reality.

spurious /ˈspjʊərɪəs/ *adjective.* L16.
[from Latin *spurius* illegitimate, false + -OUS.]
1 Of a person: conceived or born out of wedlock, illegitimate. Now *rare.* L16. ▸**b** Characterized by illegitimacy. Now *rare.* L18.
2 Having an unlawful or irregular origin; not properly qualified or constituted. Now *rare.* E17.
3 Superficially resembling or simulating something, but lacking its genuine character or qualities; not true or genuine; false, counterfeit; (of an electrical signal etc.) undesired, extraneous. E17.
4 Of a piece of writing, a word, etc.: not proceeding from the reputed origin, source, or author; not genuine or authentic. E17.
5 Of an imitation, counterfeit, etc.: characterized by spuriousness or falseness. M19.
■ **spuriˈosity** *noun* (*rare*) (*a*) the state or condition of being spurious; (*b*) a spurious thing or production: M19. **spuriously** *adverb* L17. **spuriousness** *noun* the state or quality of being spurious M17.

†**spurket** *noun.* E–M17.
[Origin unkn. Cf. SPIRKETTING.]
NAUTICAL. A space between a floor-timber and the side of a wooden ship. Usu. in *pl.*

spurling /ˈspəːlɪŋ/ *noun*. E19.
[Origin unkn.]
NAUTICAL. **1** ***spurling line***, a line running from a rudder to a wheel and operating a tell-tale indicating the position of the rudder. E19.
2 ***spurling gate***, ***spurling gate pipe***, ***spurling pipe***: a cast iron fitting in a deck through which the anchor chain passes. E20.

spurlos /ˈʃpuːrloːs/ *adjective*. E20.
[German = (sunk) without trace.]
In full ***spurlos versenkt*** /fɛrˈsɛŋkt/. Sunk without trace. Chiefly *fig.*, lost from sight, ruined.

spurn /spəːn/ *noun*¹. ME.
[from SPURN *verb*.]
†**1** A trip, a stumble. ME–M16.
2 A blow or thrust with the foot, a kick. ME. ▸**b** The action of kicking. M17.
3 The action of treating a person or thing with disdain or contemptuous rejection; an instance of this. E17.

spurn /spəːn/ *noun*². M16.
[Var. of SPUR *noun*¹, prob. after prec. or the verb.]
†**1 a** The beak of a war-galley. Only in M16. ▸**b** A sharp projection or edge on a horse-shoe. E18–M19.
2 An outward-growing root or rootlet; each of the main roots *of* a tree. Long *obsolete* exc. *dial.* E17.
3 A slanting prop or stay. E17.

spurn /spəːn/ *verb*.
[Old English *spurnan*, *spornan* corresp. to Old Saxon *spurnan*, Old High German *spornôn*, *spurnan*, from Germanic verb cogn. with Latin *spernere* scorn. Cf. SPUR *noun*¹.]
▶ **I** *verb intrans.* †**1** Strike against something with the foot; trip, stumble. OE–M18.
†**2** Strike or thrust with the foot; kick (*at*). LME–M18.
3 *fig.* Show opposition or antipathy towards something, esp. in a scornful or disdainful manner. (Foll. by *against*, *at*.) E16.
▶ **II** *verb trans.* **4** Reject with contempt or disdain; treat contemptuously; scorn, despise. OE.
†**5** Strike or tread on (something) with the foot; trample; kick. Now chiefly *literary* with implication of sense 4. ME.

> 🕮 **4** BARONESS ORCZY Her very limbs seemed to ache with longing for the love of a man who had spurned her. K. CROSSLEY-HOLLAND Iceland spurned kingship . . and was ruled . . by a union of chieftains. **5** LONGFELLOW With one touch of my . . feet, I spurn the solid Earth.

■ **spurner** *noun* M16.

spurred /spəːd/ *adjective*. LME.
[from SPUR *noun*¹, *verb*: see -ED², -ED¹.]
1 Wearing or provided with a spur or spurs. LME.
2 Having hard sharp spikes, claws, etc. E17.
3 Of rye etc.: affected with ergot or spur. M18.
4 BOTANY. Having a spur or projection of the flower. E19.

spurrey /ˈspʌri/ *noun*. Also **spurry**. L16.
[Dutch *spurrie*, †*sporie*, †*speurie*, prob. rel to medieval Latin *spergula*, whence German *Spergel*, *Spörgel*.]
1 More fully ***corn spurrey***. A cornfield weed, *Spergula arvensis*, of the pink family, with small white flowers and fleshy linear leaves. L16.
2 With specifying word: any of various similar plants of or formerly included in the genus *Spergula*. Now usu. *spec.*, any of several small pink-flowered plants constituting the genus *Spergularia*, esp. *S. rubra* (in full ***sand spurrey***), of sandy or gravelly ground, and *S. marina* (in full ***lesser sea spurrey***) and *S. media* (in full ***greater sea spurrey***), both of salt-marshes. L18.

spurrier /ˈspʌrɪə, ˈspəːr-/ *noun*. Now *rare*. ME.
[from SPUR *noun*¹ + -IER.]
A maker of spurs.

spurry *noun* var. of SPURREY.

spurry /ˈspəːri/ *adjective*. *rare*. E17.
[from SPUR *noun*¹ + -Y¹.]
†**1** Radiating like the points of a spur-rowel. Only in E17.
2 Of the nature of a spur or prop. M19.
3 Having spurlike projections. L19.

spurt /spəːt/ *noun*. Also (now chiefly in sense 4) **spirt**. M16.
[Origin unkn. Branches I and II may be separate developments. Cf. next.]
▶ **I 1 a** A short spell *of* something. Long only *spec.* (NAUTICAL), a short spell *of* wind. M16. ▸**b** A short space of time; a brief period. Freq. in ***for a spurt***. Now *dial.* or passing into sense 2. M16.
2 A brief and unsustained effort; a sudden spell of activity, exertion, or growth. L16. ▸**b** A marked or sudden increase of speed, esp. attained by special exertion. L18. ▸**c** *transf.* A marked increase or improvement, esp. in business; a sudden rise of prices etc. Also, the period during which this lasts. E19. ▸**d** A spell of gaiety; a frolic. *arch.* L19.
3 A small amount or quantity. *slang* or *dial.* M19.

> 🕮 **2** A. T. ELLIS He put on a spurt and he's nearly as tall as Henry. J. N. ISBISTER Freud continued to work in spurts upon the text. **b** B. VINE He couldn't put a spurt on . . because he had to keep in the slow lane to take the turn-off.

▶ **II 4** A stream or shower of water etc., ejected or thrown up with some force and suddenness; a jet of fire; a puff of smoke; *rare* the sound made by this. E18.
5 A sudden outbreak or outburst *of* feeling, action, etc. M19.

> 🕮 **4** P. THEROUX Great spurts of white steam from the hot springs. **5** TENNYSON A sudden spurt of woman's jealousy.

Phrases: **by spurts** in or with brief or spasmodic efforts, fitfully, spasmodically.

spurt /spəːt/ *verb*. Also (now chiefly in senses 1, 2) **spirt**. L16.
[Origin unkn. Branches I and II may be separate developments. Cf. prec.]
▶ **I 1** *verb intrans.* Of a liquid or a number of small objects: spring or burst out in a small quantity but with some force; issue in a jet. (Freq. foll. by *out*, *up*.) L16.
2 *verb trans.* Send out in a jet or rapid stream; squirt. (Foll. by *out*, *up*.) L16.

> 🕮 **1** E. BLYTON The jet of water spurted out at them. **2** S. BELLOW The buses were spurting the poisonous exhaust of cheap fuel.

▶ **II 3** *verb intrans.* Make a spurt; move rapidly or suddenly; put on speed or make greater exertion for a short time. L16.
4 *verb intrans.* Of a stock or share: rise suddenly in price or value. M20.

> 🕮 **4** *Time* Japanese imports spurted to 2.9 million sets.

■ **spurter** *noun* (*rare*) L19.

spurtle /ˈspəːt(ə)l/ *noun*¹. Chiefly *Scot.* & *north.* Also **spirtle**. E16.
[Origin unkn.]
1 †**a** A flat implement used for turning oatcakes etc. E16–L19. ▸**b** A wooden stick for stirring porridge etc. E16.
2 A sword. *joc.* Now *rare*. L17.

spurtle /ˈspəːt(ə)l/ *verb* & *noun*². Also (now *dial.*) **spirtle**. M17.
[from SPURT *verb* + -LE³.]
▶ **A** *verb*. **1** *verb trans.* Sprinkle, spurt, spatter. *rare*. M17.
2 *verb intrans.* **a** Burst or fly out in a small quantity or stream with some force; spurt. M17. ▸**b** Sputter. L17.
▶ **B** *noun*. **1** The action or an act of spurtling. *rare*. L19.
2 A small spurt or jet. *rare*. L19.

sputa *noun* pl. of SPUTUM.

sputcheon /ˈspʌtʃ(ə)n/ *noun*. *rare*. M19.
[Origin unkn.]
The metal lining of the mouth of a scabbard.

sputnik /ˈspʊtnɪk, ˈspʌt-/ *noun*. Also **S-**. M20.
[Russian, lit. 'travelling companion', from *s* with + *put'* way, journey + *-nik* -NIK.]
1 An unmanned artificial earth satellite, esp. a Russian one; *spec.* each of a series of such satellites launched by the Soviet Union between 1957 and 1961. M20.
2 BRIDGE. In full ***Sputnik double***. A take-out double of a suit overcall of one's partner's opening bid. M20.

sputter /ˈspʌtə/ *noun*. L17.
[from the verb.]
1 Noisy or confused speech; angry or excited argument or protest; (a) fuss, (a) clamour. L17.
2 Moisture or other matter expelled by sputtering. *rare*. M18.
3 The action or an act of sputtering or producing a slight explosive sound or series of sounds, esp. with the emission of small particles; such a sound or sounds. M19. ▸**b** A spattering, a sprinkling. L19.

> 🕮 **3** J. GALSWORTHY He heard the grinding sputter of a motor-cycle passing.

sputter /ˈspʌtə/ *verb*. L16.
[Dutch *sputteren*, of imit. origin. Cf. SPLUTTER.]
1 *verb trans.* Spit out in small particles or puffs with a slight explosive sound or a series of such sounds; scatter or spread in small drops or bits. L16.
2 *verb trans.* Utter hastily, with the emission of small drops of saliva, or in a confused, indistinct, or uncontrolled manner, esp. from anger or excitement; splutter. Also foll. by *out*. L17.
3 *verb intrans.* Spit out food or saliva in small particles with some force and in a noisy explosive manner. L17.
4 *verb intrans.* Speak agitatedly and disjointedly. L17.
5 *verb intrans.* Make or emit out a slight explosive sound or series of such sounds, esp. when hot or burning; move *away*, *off*, etc., with such a sound or sounds; *fig.* fizzle *out*. L17.
6 PHYSICS. **a** *verb intrans.* Remove atoms of (a metal) *from* a cathode by bombarding it with fast positive ions; deposit (metal removed in this way) *on* another surface. E20. ▸**b** *verb trans.* Cover (a surface) with metal by sputtering. E20.

> 🕮 **1** R. FRAME The car drove off, sputtering blue exhaust fumes behind it. **2** D. HALL I sputtered ponderous thanks. **4** M. MACHLIN A voice sputtered on the other end in apparent agitation. **5** K. DOUGLAS Occasionally a machine-gun would sputter for a few seconds. W. C. WILLIAMS Roasting hogs, sputtering, their drip sizzling in the fire. E. JONG It took another eight months . . for our marriage to sputter out completely.

Comb.: **sputter ion pump** PHYSICS a pump in which the gas is absorbed by a getter that is deposited by sputtering it from a cathode.
■ **sputterer** *noun* (*rare*) L17. **sputtering** *verbal noun* the action of the verb; an instance of this E18. **sputteringly** *adverb* in a sputtering manner; with a sputter or sputters: M19. **sputtery** *adjective* (*rare*) inclined to sputter M19.

sputum /ˈspjuːtəm/ *noun*. Pl. **-ta** /-tə/. L17.
[Latin, use as noun of neut. pa. pple of *spuere* spit.]
MEDICINE. Thick mucus coughed up from the respiratory tract esp. in certain diseases of the lungs, chest, or throat; a mass or quantity of this.

spuugslang /ˈspyːxslaŋ/ *noun*. *S. Afr.* L18.
[Afrikaans, lit. 'spit-snake'.]
= RINKHALS.

spy /spʌɪ/ *noun*. ME.
[Aphet. from Old French *espie* (mod. *espion*), from *espier*: see next. Cf. medieval Latin *spia*.]
1 A person who keeps watch on others secretly or stealthily. ME.
2 *spec.* A person employed by a State or organization to collect and report secret information on the esp. military activities of an enemy, hostile foreign State, etc., or on the activities of a rival organization. ME.
3 The action of spying; secret observation or watching; an instance or occasion of this. LME.
Phrases: **one's spies** *joc.* one's private or unofficial sources of information. **spy in the cab** *colloq.* = TACHOGRAPH. **spy in the sky** a satellite or aircraft used to gather intelligence (freq. *attrib.*, with hyphens).
Comb.: **spycatcher** an agent who seeks to detect and apprehend spies of another State or organization; **spymaster** the head of an organization of spies; **spy plane** an aircraft used to gather intelligence; **spy ring** an organization or network of people engaged in espionage; **spy satellite** a space satellite used to gather esp. military intelligence; **spy-ship** a vessel used for clandestine observation.
■ **spydom** *noun* the world of spies and espionage M19. **spyism** *noun* (*rare*) espionage M19. **spyship** *noun* the office or occupation of a spy L18.

spy /spʌɪ/ *verb*. Pa. t. & pple **spied** /spʌɪd/. ME.
[Aphet. from Old French *espier* ESPY *verb*, from Germanic base repr. also by Middle Low German *spêen*, Middle Dutch *spien* (Dutch *spieden*), Old High German *spehôn* (German *spähen*), Old Norse *speja*, *spæja*, from Indo-European base also of Latin *specere* look, behold.]
▶ **I** *verb trans.* **1 a** Watch in a secret or stealthy manner; keep under observation with hostile intent; act as a spy on (a person). Now *rare*. ME. ▸**b** Conduct secret or stealthy investigation or observation in (a country or place), esp. from hostile motives. Now chiefly in ***spy out the land***. ME. ▸**c** (Seek to) discover or ascertain by stealthy observation (something, *that*, *where*, etc.). Now *rare*. ME.
2 Seek an opportunity or look out for in a close or stealthy manner. Now *rare*. ME.
3 Look at, examine, or observe closely or carefully, esp. through a spy-glass or telescope. Now *rare*. ME.
4 Catch sight of; discern; discover. Cf. ESPY *verb* 1. ME.
5 Seek or find *out* by observation or scrutiny. LME.

> 🕮 **4** W. MARCH Miss Octavia, spying her through the blinds, came down . . to meet her.

▶ **II** *verb intrans.* **6** Make observations (esp. with a spy-glass); keep watch; be on the look out. Also foll. by *at*, *for* (a thing). ME.
7 Conduct secret or stealthy investigation or observation (*on*); act as a spy (*on*). Also, pry (*into*). LME.

> 🕮 **6** D. HART-DAVIS The stalkers . . stopped to spy for a stag they'd seen. **7** D. FRANCIS No one followed us . . or spied on us. A. COHEN Everyone spied, and reported to the police.

Phrases etc.: I-SPY. ***Northern Spy***: see NORTHERN *adjective*. **spying-glass** (now *rare* or *obsolete*) a spy-glass, an opera glass. ***spy strangers***: see STRANGER *noun*.
Comb.: **spyglass** a small telescope, a field-glass; **spyhole** a peep-hole.

SQ *abbreviation*.
Stereophonic-quadraphonic, a quadraphonic system of audio recording and reproduction (proprietary name in the US).

sq. *abbreviation*.
1 Latin *sequens*, *sequentes*, *-tia*, the following page(s) etc. (see ***ET sequens*** etc.).
2 Square.

SQL *abbreviation*.
COMPUTING. Structured Query Language, an international standard for database manipulation.

sqn *abbreviation.*
Squadron.

Sqn. Ldr. *abbreviation.*
Squadron Leader.

sqq. *abbreviation.*
Latin *sequentes*, *-tia*, the following pages etc. (see ET *sequentes* etc.).

squab /skwɒb/ *noun & adjective.* M17.
[Origin uncertain: cf. Swedish dial. *skvabb* loose flesh, *skvabba* fat woman, *skvabbig* flabby. Cf. QUAB *noun*², SQUAB *interjection*, SQUADDY *adjective*.]
▸ **A** *noun.* **1** †**a** A naive inexperienced person. Only in M17. ▸**b** A newly hatched or very young bird; *spec.* a young pigeon. L17.
2 a A settee, an ottoman, a couch. M17. ▸**b** A thick or soft cushion, *esp.* one on a chair or settee; a cushion forming part of the inside fittings of a carriage; the padded back or side of a car seat. L17.
3 A short fat person. L17.
▸ **B** *adjective.* **1** (Of a person) short and fat; having a thick clumsy form; squat. L17.
2 Young and undeveloped; *esp.* (of a young bird) not fully fledged, newly hatched. E18.
†**3** Abrupt, blunt, curt. Only in M18.
Special collocations & comb.: **squab chick** = sense 1b above. **squab cushion** = sense 2b above. **squab pie** (*a*) pigeon pie; (*b*) [perh. from a different word] a pie made of mutton, pork, apples, and onions, with a thick crust.
▪ **squabbish** *adjective* (*rare*) somewhat squab M17.

squab /skwɒb/ *verb.* Infl. **-bb-**. M17.
[Prob. rel. to prec.]
1 *verb trans.* Beat severely; squash, squeeze flat. Long *obsolete* exc. *dial.* M17.
2 *verb intrans.* Fall or hang in a full or heavy manner. M18.
3 *verb trans.* Stuff, stuff full. Now *rare.* E19.

squab /skwɒb/ *interjection & adverb.* E17.
[As interjection, perh. imit., but cf. SQUAB *noun*; as adverb, rel. to prec.]
▸ **A** *interjection.* Expr. the cry of a young bird. Long *rare* or *obsolete.* E17.
▸ **B** *adverb.* With a heavy fall. Long *obsolete* exc. *dial.* L17.

squabash /skwɒˈbaʃ/ *noun & verb. colloq.* Now *rare.* E19.
[Blend of SQUASH *noun*¹, *verb* and BASH *noun*, *verb*².]
▸ **A** *noun.* The action or an act of squashing or silencing someone. E19.
▸ **B** *verb trans.* Defeat, esp. in argument. E19.
▪ **squabasher** *noun* E19.

squabbed /skwɒbd/ *adjective.* L17.
[from SQUAB *noun*, *verb*: see -ED², -ED¹.]
Squat, dumpy.

squabble /ˈskwɒb(ə)l/ *noun & verb.* E17.
[Prob. imit.; cf. Swedish dial. *skvabbel*.]
▸ **A** *noun.* A petty or noisy quarrel; a wrangle, a dispute. E17.
▸ **B** *verb.* **1** *verb intrans.* Engage in a squabble (*with*); argue disagreeably or with heat (*over*, *about*, etc.) E17.
2 *verb trans.* PRINTING. Twist successive lines of (type) out of square so that the letters run into the wrong lines. L17.

> 1 B. PYM They had squabbled about who should get supper ready.

▪ **squabblement** *noun* squabbling, petty quarrelling M18. **squabbler** *noun* M17. **squabbling** *ppl adjective* (*a*) engaging in or given to squabbling; (*b*) of the nature of or characterized by squabbling: M17. **squabbly** *adjective* given to squabbling, of a squabbling character M19.

squabby /ˈskwɒbi/ *adjective.* M18.
[from SQUAB *noun & adjective* + -Y¹.]
= SQUAB *adjective* 1.

squacco /ˈskwakəʊ/ *noun.* Pl. **-os.** M18.
[Italian dial. *sguacco*.]
More fully ***squacco heron***. A small crested heron, *Ardeola ralloides*, of southern Europe and parts of Africa.

squad /skwɒd/ *noun*¹ *& verb.* M17.
[Aphet. (after *squadron*) from French *escouade*, †*esquade*, vars. of *escadre* from Spanish *escuadra*, Italian *squadra*, from Proto-Romance base also of SQUARE *noun*.]
▸ **A** *noun.* **1** MILITARY. A small number of soldiers assembled for drill or assigned to some special task. M17.
2 A small group of people with a common task, affiliation, etc.; a particular set or circle of people. L18.
3 SPORT. A group of players forming a team or from which a team is chosen. E20.
4 A specialized unit or division within a police force; *spec.* = ***flying squad*** s.v. FLYING *ppl adjective.* E20. ▸**b** = ***squad car*** below. *Police slang.* L20.

> **1 awkward squad**: composed of recruits and soldiers who need further training. **2** S. UNWIN The master . . gave him a squad of . . boys to help him. *Times* Apart from the attempts to kill . . Muhayshi in Tunisia, a . . hit squad sought him out in London. **4 bomb squad**, **drug squad**, **fraud squad**, etc.

Comb.: **squad car** a police car with a radio link to headquarters.
▸ **B** *verb trans.* Infl. **-dd-**. Divide into squads; draw up in a squad; assign to a squad. E19.

†**squad** *noun*². *rare.* L17–M19.
[Origin unkn.]
MINING. = SHOAD.

squad /skwɒd/ *noun*³. *dial.* M19.
[Origin unkn.]
Soft slimy mud.

squaddie /ˈskwɒdi/ *noun. Military slang.* Also **-ddy**. M20.
[from SQUAD *noun*¹ + -IE.]
A private soldier; a recruit.

squaddy /ˈskwɒdi/ *adjective.* Now *dial. & US.* L16.
[Perh. rel. to SQUAB *noun & adjective*.]
Of a person: short and thickset; squat.

squadra /ˈskwadra/ *noun.* Pl. ***-dre*** /-dre/. E20.
[Italian.]
Hist. In Italy: a paramilitary squad organized to support and promulgate Fascism; a Fascist cadre.
▪ ***squadrism***, ***squadrismo*** /skwaˈdrizmo/ *noun* the organization and activities of the *squadre* E20. ***squadrist*** *noun*, pl. ***squadrists***, ***squadristi*** /skwaˈdristi/, a member of a *squadra* M20.

†**squadrant** *noun & adjective.* L16.
[Italian *squadrante* pres. pple of *squadrare* to square.]
▸ **A** *noun.* A square piece of something. L16–E18.
▸ **B** *adjective.* Square. L16–M17.

†**squadrate** *adjective. rare.* M17–L18.
[Italian *squadrato* pa. pple of *squadrare* to square.]
Square; rectangular.

squadre *noun* pl. of SQUADRA.

squadrol /ˈskwɒdrəʊl/ *noun. US slang.* M20.
[from SQUAD *noun*¹ + PA)TROL *noun*.]
A small police van.

squadron /ˈskwɒdrən/ *noun.* M16.
[Italian *squadrone*, from *squadra* from Proto-Romance base also of SQUARE *noun*.]
1 MILITARY. †**a** A body of soldiers drawn up in square formation. M16–M17. ▸**b** A small body or detachment of soldiers. L16.
2 a A division of a fleet under the command of a flag-officer; a detachment of warships employed on a particular duty. L16. ▸**b** A principal division of an armoured or cavalry regiment, consisting of two troops. E18. ▸**c** A small operational unit in an air force, consisting of aircraft (10 to 18 in the Royal Air Force) and the personnel necessary to fly them. E20.
3 A large group or number of people or things; an organized body of people. E17.
†**4** A division or ward of a town, community, or district. *US.* M17–M18.
5 A body of cardinals not belonging to the main factions in a papal election. *rare.* L17.
Comb.: **squadron leader** the commander of a squadron of the Royal Air Force, a rank next below wing commander.
▪ **squadronal** *adjective* L19. **squadroned** *adjective* formed into squadrons; drawn up in a squadron: M17.

squail /skweɪl/ *noun.* M19.
[Origin uncertain: cf. next, KAYLES.]
1 In *pl.* Ninepins; skittles. *dial.* M19.
2 In *pl.*, a game in which counters placed at the edge of a table or board are struck with the open hand to send them near a central target; *sing.* a counter used in this game. M19.
Comb.: **squail-board**: used for playing squails.

squail /skweɪl/ *verb.* Chiefly *dial.* E17.
[Origin unkn. Cf. prec.]
1 *verb intrans.* Throw a (loaded) stick or similar missile (*at* something). E17.
2 *verb trans.* Strike or hit by throwing a stick. M19.
▪ **squailer** *noun* a loaded stick, used esp. for throwing at small game or apples M19.

squalamine /ˈskwɒləmiːn/ *noun.* L20.
[from mod. Latin *Squalus* (see below) + AMINE.]
BIOCHEMISTRY. A compound of the steroid type isolated from the dogfish *Squalus acanthias*, with antibiotic properties.

squalene /ˈskweɪliːn/ *noun.* E20.
[from SQUALUS + -ENE.]
CHEMISTRY. A triterpenoid hydrocarbon, $C_{30}H_{50}$, an oily liquid which occurs in shark liver oil and human sebum and is a precursor of sterols.

squali *noun* pl. of SQUALUS.

squalid /ˈskwɒlɪd/ *adjective.* L16.
[Latin *squalidus*, from *squalere* be dry, rough, or dirty: see -ID¹.]
▸ **I 1** Foul through neglect or lack of cleanliness; repulsively mean and filthy; characterized by filth, dirt, or squalor. L16.
2 Of land etc.: naturally foul and repulsive by the presence of slime, mud, etc., and the absence of cultivation. Now *rare.* L16.
3 Repulsive or loathsome to look at. E17.
4 *fig.* Wretched, miserable, morally repulsive or degraded. M17.

> 1 J. CONRAD A general air of squalid neglect pervaded the place. D. WELCH A narrow squalid street where people . . threw their filth into the gutters. **4** P. H. GIBBS She could never pardon Robin if he were . . having a squalid affair with Peggy.

▸ **II** †**5** Dry, parched; characterized by drought. E–M17.
†**6** Rough; shaggy; unkempt. E17–E18.
7 Having a pinched appearance; (of the complexion) having a dull unhealthy look. M17.
▪ **squaˈlidity** *noun* M17. **squalidly** *adverb* E18. **squalidness** *noun* E17.

squall /skwɔːl/ *noun*¹. L17.
[Perh. from next.]
1 Orig. NAUTICAL. A sudden short-lived strong wind, esp. with rain, sleet, or snow; a severe local storm. L17.
2 *fig.* A disturbance, a commotion; a quarrel. E19.
1 black squall: accompanied by dark clouds. **white squall**: unaccompanied by clouds.
Comb.: **squall line**: along which high winds and storms are occurring.

squall /skwɔːl/ *verb & noun*². M17.
[Prob. alt. of SQUEAL *verb* by assoc. with BAWL.]
▸ **A** *verb.* **1** *verb intrans.* Esp. of a child: scream loudly or discordantly. M17.
2 *verb trans.* Utter or sing in a loud discordant tone. E18.

> 1 S. MILLER Holding a squalling child huddled against his body.

▸ **B** *noun.* **1** A discordant scream; a loud harsh cry. E18.
2 The action or habit of squalling. M18.
▪ **squaller** *noun* a person, esp. a child, who squalls or is given to squalling L17.

squally /ˈskwɔːli/ *adjective*¹. L17.
[from SQUALL *noun*¹ + -Y¹.]
1 (Of the weather, a season, etc.) characterized by squalls; (of the wind) blowing in sudden strong gusts. L17.
2 *fig.* Threatening, stormy. E19.

squally /ˈskwɔːli/ *adjective*². M19.
[from SQUALL *verb & noun*² + -Y¹.]
Esp. of a child: that squalls; given to squalling, noisy.

squalmish /ˈskwɑːmɪʃ, ˈskwɔː-/ *adjective. US colloq.* M19.
[Alt. of QUALMISH, perh. infl. by SQUEAMISH.]
Nauseous, qualmish, queasy.

squaloid /ˈskweɪlɔɪd/ *adjective & noun.* M19.
[from SQUALUS + -OID.]
▸ **A** *adjective.* Of, pertaining to, or designating the family Squalidae (formerly Squaliformes) of mostly small sharks. M19.
▸ **B** *noun.* A shark of this family. M19.

squalor /ˈskwɒlə/ *noun.* E17.
[Latin, from *squalere*: see SQUALID, -OR.]
1 The state or condition of being physically squalid; a combination of misery and dirt. E17.
2 *fig.* The quality of being morally or mentally squalid. M19.

squalus /ˈskweɪləs/ *noun.* Pl. **-li** /-lʌɪ, -liː/. Now *rare.* M18.
[Latin = a marine fish of some kind.]
A shark.

squama /ˈskweɪmə/ *noun.* Pl. **-mae** /-miː/. E18.
[Latin = scale.]
1 ZOOLOGY. A scale as part of the integument of a fish, reptile, or insect. E18.
2 ANATOMY. A thin scaly portion of a bone, esp. the temporal bone; a platelike structure. E18.
3 BOTANY. Any of the scales of a catkin etc. M18.
4 MEDICINE. = SQUAME 3a. L19.

squamate /ˈskweɪmət/ *adjective.* E19.
[from prec., SQUAME + -ATE².]
ZOOLOGY & BOTANY. Covered with or having scales.
▪ **squaˈmation** *noun* the condition or character of being covered with scales; the mode or form of this: L19.

squame /ˈskweɪm/ *noun.* ME.
[Old French *esquame* or Latin SQUAMA.]
†**1** A scale of iron; a scale on the eye; a scab on the skin. ME–M17.
2 ZOOLOGY. = SQUAMA 1. L19.
3 a MEDICINE. A small flake of dead tissue shed from the surface of the skin in some disorders. E20. ▸**b** ANATOMY. A squamous cell. M20.

squameous /ˈskweɪmɪəs/ *adjective.* Now *rare* or *obsolete.* L17.
[from Latin *squamus*, formed as SQUAMA: see -EOUS.]
Covered with scales, scaly.

squamiform /ˈskweɪmɪfɔːm/ *adjective.* LME.
[medieval Latin *squamiformis*, formed as SQUAMA: see -FORM.]
ZOOLOGY & BOTANY. Having the shape of a scale or scales.
▪ **squaˈmiferous** *adjective* having scales M18. **squaˈmigerous** *adjective* = SQUAMIFEROUS M17.

Squamish /ˈskwɔːmɪʃ/ *noun & adjective.* **M19.**
[Alt. of Squamish name for themselves.]
▶ **A** *noun.* Pl. same. A member of a Salish people of SW British Columbia; the language of this people. **M19.**
▶ **B** *attrib.* or as *adjective.* Of or pertaining to the Squamish or their language. **E20.**

squamo- /ˈskweɪməʊ/ *combining form.*
[from SQUAMA, SQUAMOUS + -O-.]
ANATOMY & ZOOLOGY. Forming adjectives with the senses (*a*) pertaining to the squama of (the bone denoted by the 2nd elem.), as ***squamo-occipital***, ***squamo-temporal***; (*b*) squamous, as ***squamo-epithelial***. Cf. SQUAMOSO-.
■ **squamocoˈlumnar** *adjective* designating the junction between stratified squamous epithelium and columnar epithelium **M20.**

squamosal /skwəˈməʊs(ə)l/ *noun & adjective.* **M19.**
[from next + -AL¹.]
ANATOMY & ZOOLOGY. ▶**A** *noun.* The squamous portion of the temporal bone at the side of the skull, which in mammals articulates with the lower jaw. **M19.**
▶ **B** *adjective.* Designating, of, or pertaining to the squamosal. **M19.**

squamose /ˈskweɪməʊs, skwəˈməʊs/ *adjective.* **M17.**
[formed as SQUAMOUS.]
= SQUAMOUS 1, 2.
■ **squaˈmosity** *noun* (*rare*) the state or character of being covered with scales **L18.**

squamoso- /skwəˈməʊsəʊ/ *combining form.*
[from SQUAMOSE + -O-.]
= SQUAMO-.

squamous /ˈskweɪməs/ *adjective.* **LME.**
[Latin *squamosus*, formed as SQUAMA: see -OUS.]
1 Covered with or having scales, scaly; (of a substance) composed of scales; (of armour) laminated. **LME.** ▸**b** ANATOMY. Designating the thin scaly part of the temporal bone (the squamosal). **LME.**
2 ANATOMY. Of a suture: formed by thin overlapping parts resembling scales. **LME.**
3 (Of the skin) characterized by the development of scales; (of a disease) accompanied by skin of this kind. **LME.**
4 Containing scalelike particles. *rare.* **LME.**
5 ANATOMY & MEDICINE. Designating a layer of epithelium that contains or consists of very thin flattened cells; designating such a cell. **M19.**

> 🕮 **1** R. BROOKE There swimmeth One . . of fishy form and mind, Squamous, omnipotent and kind. **5** *Independent* Squamous cell carcinoma arises from the flat, squamous cells of the epidermis.

squamule /ˈskweɪmjuːl/ *noun.* Also (earlier) in Latin form **squamula** /ˈskweɪmjʊlə/, pl. **-lae** /-liː/. **M18.**
[Latin *squamula* dim. of *squama* scale: see -ULE.]
ZOOLOGY & BOTANY. A small scale.

squamulose /ˈskweɪmjʊləʊs/ *adjective.* **M19.**
[from prec. + -OSE¹.]
BOTANY. Covered with or having small scales.

squander /ˈskwɒndə/ *verb & noun.* **L16.**
[Origin unkn.]
▶ **A** *verb.* **1** *verb trans.* (usu. in *pass.*) & *intrans.* Scatter or disperse in various directions or over a wide area. **L16.** ▸†**b** *verb trans.* In *pass.* Brought to disintegration or dissolution. **E–M17.** ▸**c** *verb intrans.* Roam about, wander. **M17.**
2 *verb trans.* Spend recklessly or lavishly; use in a wasteful manner. Also foll. by *away.* **L16.**

> 🕮 **2** G. BORROW They considered the time occupied in learning as so much squandered away. H. JAMES He had squandered a substantial fortune. M. HOLROYD A thoughtless squandering of his natural gifts. M. LANE He squandered all the money . . on drink.

▶ **B** *noun.* (An instance of) reckless or lavish expenditure. **E18.**
Comb. (of verb & noun): **squander-bug** *colloq.* a symbol of reckless extravagance; a person who squanders money etc.; **squanderlust** *US slang* a strong desire to spend money or waste assets; squandermania; **squandermania** *colloq.* an obsession for squandering money etc.; wasteful use of assets.
■ **squanderer** *noun* **E17.** **squandering** *ppl adjective* (*a*) spending recklessly or lavishly; (*b*) (now *dial.*) straggling: **L16.**

square /skwɛː/ *noun.* Also †**squire**. **ME.**
[Aphet. from Old French *esquire*, *esquar(r)e* (mod. *équerre*) from Proto-Romance noun from verb whence also SQUARE *verb*.]
▶ **I 1** An L-shaped or T-shaped implement for measuring or setting out right angles. Freq. without article in ***by square*** below. **ME.**
†**2** Rectangular or square shape or form. Usu. without article in preposition phrs., as ***in square***, ***to square***. **LME–M17.**
†**3** A side of a rectilinear figure or a polygon; a face of a cube. **LME–M18.**
4 A plane figure with four right angles and four equal straight sides. Formerly also (usu. with specifying word, esp. *long* or *oblong*), a rectangle with unequal sides. **LME.**
5 a A square or four-sided space, *esp.* any of several marked out on paper, a board, etc., for playing a game or for purposes of measurement; a square or rectangular piece of ground; *Military slang* a parade ground. **LME.** ▸**b** An open, usu. four-sided, space enclosed by buildings in a town or city, *esp.* one containing a garden or laid out with trees; an open space resembling this, *esp.* one at the meeting of streets; the buildings surrounding an area of this kind. **L17.** ▸**c** A rectangular building or block of buildings; *US* a block of buildings bounded by streets. **L17.** ▸**d** A closer-cut area at the centre of a cricket ground, any strip of which may be prepared as a wicket. **L19.**
6 MATH. The product obtained by multiplying a number by itself; the second power *of* a quantity. **M16.**
7 *fig.* A canon, a criterion, a standard; a rule, a guiding principle; a pattern, an example. Now *rare* or *obsolete.* **M16.**
8 MILITARY. A body of troops drawn up in a square or rectangular formation. **L16.**
9 An object of a square or approximately square form; a square or rectangular piece, block, etc.; a square piece of material, *esp.* one used as a scarf or cravat, or (formerly) the breast of a dress; a rectangular pane of glass. **L16.** ▸†**b** A surveying instrument made in the form of a square. *rare.* **L16–E18.** ▸**c** A piece of wood or metal in the shape of a right-angled triangle used to transmit the motion of wires or rods through a right angle. **L17.** ▸**d** BOOKBINDING. In *pl.* The portion of the cover of a bound book which projects beyond the leaves. **L17.** ▸**e** US HISTORY. A square space in a newspaper column, considered as a unit of measurement for advertisements. **L17.** ▸**f** A square arrangement of letters, figures, etc. **M19.** ▸**g** (A group of bracts surrounding) the flower of a cotton plant. **L19.** ▸**h** = MORTARBOARD 1. **E20.**
10 An area of a hundred square feet as a unit of flooring, roofing, etc. **M17.**
11 ASTROLOGY. A quartile aspect. **M17.**
12 *ellipt.* A square meal (chiefly *N. Amer.*); a square piano; a square dance. **L19.**
13 A person considered to hold conventional or old-fashioned views or who is ignorant of or opposed to current trends. *slang.* **M20.**
14 A cigarette containing tobacco rather than marijuana. *US slang.* **L20.**

> 🕮 **5b** C. M. YONGE Sleeping every night in Bryanston Square. **6** A. KOESTLER The intensity of light diminishes with the square of distance. **7** R. WHITLOCK Let thy Actions be justified by the Square of Religion. **9** D. SIMPSON The square of carpet on the floor. T. TRYON He took out his pocket square and pressed his lips.

▶†**II 15** A quarrel, a dispute; discord, quarrelling. **M16–E17.**
Phrases: †**at square** in a state of disagreement, at variance. **back to square one** *colloq.* back to the starting-point, with no progress made. **by square** (*a*) using a square for measuring or setting out right angles; †(*b*) with extreme accuracy, precisely. ***hollow square***: see HOLLOW *adjective* & *adverb*. †**how squares go**, †**how the squares go** how matters are. ***inverse square***: see INVERSE *adjective*. ***Latin square***: see LATIN *adjective*. ***magic square***: see MAGIC *adjective*. ***mean square***: see MEAN *adjective*². **method of least squares**, **principle of least squares** the technique of estimating a quantity, fitting a graph to a set of experimental values, etc., so as to minimize the sum of the squares of the differences between the observed data and their estimated true values. **on the square** [from ellipt. use of SQUARE *adjective*] (*a*) (now *rare*) face to face; openly; (*b*) *colloq.* fair(ly), straightforward(ly), honest(ly); (*c*) at right angles; in a solid form; (*d*) having membership of the Freemasons. ***optical square***: see OPTICAL *adjective*. **out of square** out of the true or normal state; into irregularity or confusion. ***principle of least squares***: see ***method of least squares*** above. ***queening square***: see QUEEN *verb* 2a. ***set square***: see SET *adjective*. ***short square***: see SHORT *adjective*. ***T-square***: see T, T 2.
Comb.: **square-bashing** *Military slang* drill on a barrack-square; **square-free** *adjective* (MATH.) (of an integer) not divisible by a perfect square; **square-pushing** *arch. slang* the action or practice of going out with a woman; courting.

square /skwɛː/ *adjective & adverb.* **ME.**
[Old French *esquarré* pa. pple of *esquarrer* (mod. *équarrir*) from Proto-Romance, formed as EX-¹ + Latin *quadra* square.]
▶ **A** *adjective.* **I 1** Having a cross-section in the form of a square; approximately cubic in shape. **ME.**
2 Having the shape of a square; bounded by four equal straight sides at right angles to each other. **ME.** ▸**b** MATH. Of a quantity: equal to the product of a quantity multiplied by itself. Cf. ***square root*** below. **M16.** ▸**c** Designating an area equal to that of a square whose side is a specified unit of length. **E17.**
3 Of a square shape that is the specified length on each side. Usu. *postpositive.* **LME.**
4 Of the shoulders, body, etc.: approximating to a square outline, angular; stoutly and strongly built; solid, sturdy. **LME.**
5 Situated at right angles, perpendicular, (*to*). **L16.** ▸**b** SOCCER. Of a defence: positioned in a line at right angles to the direction of play (and so weak). **L20.**
6 a Even, straight, level. (Foll. by *with*.) **E19.** ▸**b** With all accounts settled, with no money owed; having equal scores in a game; (of scores) equal; GOLF having won the same number of holes as one's opponent. Also ***all square***. **M19.**
7 MUSIC. Of rhythm: simple, straightforward. **M20.**

> 🕮 **2** T. HARDY The . . house-door opened on the square yard or quadrangle. **c** ***square foot***, ***square inch***, ***square metre***, etc. **3** J. CLAVELL The room was forty paces square. **4** A. LURIE Today square shoulders and an athletic frame are in style. **5** C. FORD The lower and centre bouts . . are now . . filed perfectly square to the front surface.

▶ **II 8** †**a** Determined, obstinate; solid, steady, reliable. **L16–E18.** ▸**b** (Of a person) honest, straightforward, upright; (of an action) just, fair, honourable. (Earlier in SQUARELY 2.) **L16.** ▸**c** Out of touch with the ideas and conventions of a current trend; conventional, old-fashioned; conservative; unsophisticated. *slang.* **M20.**
9 a Precise, exact. **L16.** ▸†**b** Solidly or firmly constituted; free from flaw or defect. Only in **17.** ▸**c** Straight, direct, uncompromising. **E19.** ▸**d** On a proper footing, with things properly arranged. **E19.** ▸**e** Of a meal: full, solid, substantial, satisfying. **M19.**

> 🕮 **8c** J. LENNON They'd never seen us before, or heard—Vienna is a pretty square place.

Phrases: ***all square***: see sense 6b above. ***a square peg in a round hole***, ***a round peg in a square hole***: see PEG *noun*¹. ***fair and square***: see FAIR *adjective*. **get square with** pay or compound with (a creditor).
▶ **B** *adverb.* †**1** So as to be squared (by multiplication). Only in **M16.**
2 Steadily, copiously. Only in ***tipple square***, ***drink square***. *arch.* **L16.**
3 a Fairly, honestly; in a straightforward manner. Now *colloq.* **L16.** ▸**b** Completely, exactly, directly. Chiefly *N. Amer. colloq.* **M19.**
4 So as to be square; in a rectangular form or position; directly in line or in front. **M17.**
5 At right angles; CRICKET at right angles to the line of the delivery. (Foll. by *to*, *with*, etc.) **L17.**

> 🕮 **3a** O. HENRY Paisley . . told me I'd acted square and on the level with him. **b** *Daily Telegraph* Hubby gets his favourite sugared doughnut square in the kisser. **5** T. H. HUXLEY Shadows of objects are distorted when . . light does not fall square upon their surfaces.

Phrases: **square on** CRICKET (of a bowler) with the body square to the batsman; *fig.* directly, honestly.
Special collocations & comb.: **square bracket**: of the form [or]. **square-built** *adjective* of comparatively broad shape. **square cap** = MORTARBOARD 1. **square cut** CRICKET a cut hit square on the offside. **square-cut** *adjective* cut to or into a square form. **square-cut** *verb trans.* (CRICKET) hit (the ball) with a square cut. **square dance** (*a*) a dance in which four couples face inwards from four sides; (*b*) any country dance. **square deal** a fair bargain, fair treatment. ***square dinkum***: see DINKUM *adjective* & *adverb*. **square drive** CRICKET a drive hit square on the offside. **square-drive** *verb trans.* (CRICKET) hit (the ball) with a square drive. **square engine** an internal-combustion engine in which the length of the stroke is approximately equal to the bore of the cylinders. **square-eyed** *adjective* (*joc.*) affected by or given to excessive watching of television. **square eyes** *joc.* eyes supposedly affected by excessive watching of television. **square flipper** = BEARDED ***seal***. **squarehead** *slang* (*a*) an honest person; (*b*) *offensive* a foreigner of Germanic extraction, *esp.* a German or Scandinavian. **square-headed** *adjective* (*a*) having the head or top in a square or rectangular shape; (*b*) level-headed, sensible; (*c*) *slang* (*derog.*) of Germanic extraction. **square go** *Scot.* a brawl, a fight without weapons. **square Hebrew** the standard Hebrew script which displaced the Aramaic form towards the end of the biblical period, and has been adopted for use in printed texts. **square hit** CRICKET a hit at right angles to the wicket, esp. to square leg. **square John** *N. Amer. slang* an upright respectable person; *spec.* a person who is not a drug user. **square law** PHYSICS a law relating two variables one of which varies (directly or inversely) as the square of the other (***inverse square law***: see INVERSE *adjective*). ***square leg***: see LEG *noun*. ***square-lipped*** RHINOCEROS. **square measure** a unit of area consisting of a square of specified size; a system of measurement based on such units. **square piano**, **square pianoforte** an early type of piano of a rectangular form, superseded by the upright piano. **square pin** on an electrical plug, a pin with a rectangular rather than a circular cross-section. ***square pole***: see POLE *noun*¹ 2b. **square-rigged** *adjective* (of a vessel) having square sails placed at right angles to the length of the ship; opp. ***fore-and-aft rigged*** s.v. FORE AND AFT. **square-rigger** (a sailor on) a square-rigged vessel. **square root** a number which produces a specified quantity when multiplied by itself. **square-rooter** a device which produces the square root of an input variable. **square sail** a four-sided sail supported by a horizontal yard slung to a mast by the middle. **square serif** TYPOGRAPHY a style of type distinguished by serifs that are square-ended and generally as thick as the other parts of the letters. **square-shooter** *slang* (chiefly *US*) an honest dependable person. **square-shooting** *adjective* (*slang*, chiefly *US*) honest, respectable. **square-shouldered** *adjective* having broad shoulders that do not slope. **square-tail** (*a*) an oceanic fish, *Tetragonurus cuvieri*, of tropical and warm seas; (*b*) = **brook** TROUT. **square thread** MECHANICS a screw thread which in cross-section is castellated in form, with the width and height of the thread equal to the width of the valley between threads. **square-toed** *adjective* (*a*) (of shoes or boots) having square toes; (of a person)

wearing such shoes or boots; (*b*) old-fashioned, formal, prim. **square-toes** *arch.* an old-fashioned, formal, or prim person, or one who has strict ideas of conduct; chiefly as ***Old Square-toes***. **square wave** *ELECTRONICS* (a voltage represented by) a periodic wave that varies abruptly in amplitude between two fixed values, spending equal times at each.

■ **squareness** *noun* LME. **squarewise** *adverb* †(*a*) at right angles, rectangularly; (*b*) in the form of a square; squarely: M16. **squarish** *adjective* somewhat or approximately square M18. **squary** *adjective* square, squarish E17.

square /skwɛː/ *verb.* LME.
[Old French *esquarrer*: see SQUARE *adjective*.]
1 *verb trans.* **a** Make square, reduce to a square or rectangular form; shape by reduction to straight lines and right angles; give a square or rectangular cross-section to (timber). Also foll. by *out*, *up*. LME. ▸**b** Mark out as a square or in rectangular form; mark *off* or *out* in squares. LME. ▸**c** *verb trans.* Draw up (troops etc.) in a square. LME. ▸**d** Make by cutting (*out*) in square or rectangular form. L16.
†**2** *verb intrans.* Deviate, diverge, vary, (*from*). LME–E17.
†**3** *verb intrans.* Complain, grumble; fall out, disagree, quarrel; be at variance. LME–L18.
4 *verb trans.* **a** Multiply (a number) by itself once. M16. ▸**b** Reduce (measurements) to an equivalent square; calculate in square measure. M18.
5 *verb trans.* Regulate in accordance with a standard or principle. M16.
6 a *verb trans.* Adjust, adapt; cause to harmonize or be consistent *with*, reconcile; make appropriate or exact. L16. ▸**b** *verb intrans.* Correspond, harmonize, be consistent, (*with*). Formerly also foll. by *to*. L16.
7 *verb intrans.* & †*trans.* (with *it*). Strut, swagger. Long *obsolete* exc. *dial.* L16.
8 *verb trans.* **a** *NAUTICAL.* Set at right angles to or parallel with a part; *spec.* lay (the yards) at right angles to the line of the keel by trimming with the braces. E17. ▸**b** Adjust so as to set at right angles to something or to straighten. L17. ▸**c** *ASTROLOGY.* Stand in quartile aspect in relation to (another sign). L17. ▸**d** Set (a part of the body) squarely, *esp.* set (the shoulders) squarely facing forward; *refl.* put oneself into a posture of defence. E19. ▸**e** *FOOTBALL* etc. Pass (the ball) across the pitch, esp. towards the centre. L20.
9 *verb trans.* Of a tree: measure (a specified amount) on each of four sides forming a square; yield a square of (the dimensions specified). L18.
10 *verb trans.* Bring to an equality on both sides; balance (an account); (foll. by *up*) settle (a debt etc.) by means of payment. E19. ▸**b** *verb trans.* Put (a matter) straight; settle satisfactorily. *colloq.* M19. ▸**c** Satisfy or secure the acquiescence of (a person), esp. by bribery. *colloq.* M19. ▸**d** *verb trans.* & *intrans. SPORT.* Make the scores of (a match etc.) equal. E20.
11 *verb intrans.* Assume a defensive or aggressive posture. (Foll. by *at* or *up to* a person.) E19.
12 *verb intrans.* Become square in form. E20.

🕮 **5** HENRY FIELDING The bailiff had squared his conscience . . according to the law. **6a** J. ADAIR Attempting to square God's sovereignty with human freedom. **b** A. UPFIELD 'It doesn't square,' Alice . . admitted. I. COLEGATE None of these opinions seemed . . convincing, nor did they . . square with each other. **8d** *fig.*: J. I. M. STEWART I was squaring myself to the necessity of telling him. **10b** J. K. JEROME He squared the matter with . . a five-pound note. **c** E. BOWEN 'What's . . Willy going to think of us?' 'I'll square Willy.'

Phrases, & with adverbs in specialized senses: ***square accounts (with)***: see ACCOUNT *noun*. **square away** (*a*) *NAUTICAL* sail away with the yards squared; *fig.* (*US*) make ready, get moving; (*b*) *colloq.* (*US*) put in order, tidy up. **squared paper**: marked out in squares, esp. for plotting graphs. **square off** (*a*) assume an aggressive attitude; (*b*) *Austral. slang* placate, conciliate; apologize; (see also sense 1b above). **square the circle** construct a square equal in area to a given circle (a problem incapable of a purely geometrical solution); *fig.* do something impossible. **square up to** *fig.* face and tackle (a difficulty) resolutely.

■ **squarable** *adjective* able to be squared E18.

squarely /ˈskwɛːli/ *adverb.* M16.
[from SQUARE *adjective* + -LY².]
†**1** So as to be squared (by multiplication). M16–L17.
2 Honestly, fairly, in a straightforward manner. M16.
†**3** Precisely, exactly. Only in 17.
4 In a position directly square with or opposite to a line or object; in a straight or direct manner; at right angles to the length or height. E19. ▸**b** *fig.* Plainly, unequivocally, firmly. M19.
5 In a square form; so as to have a square shape. E19.

🕮 **2** ***fairly and squarely***: see FAIRLY *adverb*. **4** E. BAIRD A nice easy pace with the rider sitting squarely to the horse. **b** H. J. EYSENCK The blame for this . . must be squarely laid at the door of the analysts.

squareman /ˈskwɛːmən/ *noun. Scot.* Pl. **-men**. M17.
[from SQUARE *noun* + MAN *noun*.]
A carpenter, stone-cutter, or other worker who uses a square.

squarer /ˈskwɛːrə/ *noun.* LME.
[from SQUARE *verb* + -ER¹.]
1 a A person who reduces wood, stone, etc., to a square form. LME. ▸**b** A person who aims at squaring the circle. M19.
†**2** A contentious or quarrelsome person. *rare* (Shakes.). Only in L16.
3 *ELECTRONICS.* A device that converts a sinusoidal or other periodic wave into a square wave of the same period. M20.

Squaresville /ˈskwɛːzvɪl/ *noun & adjective.* Orig. *US.* M20.
[from SQUARE *noun*, *adjective* + -S¹ + -VILLE.]
▸ **A** *noun.* An imaginary town characterized by dullness and conventionality. M20.
▸ **B** *attrib.* or as *adjective*. = SQUARE *adjective* 8c. M20.

squark /skwɑːk, skwɔːk/ *noun*¹ & *verb.* M19.
[Imit. Cf. QUARK *verb*.]
▸ **A** *noun.* A harsh croak; a squawk. M19.
▸ **B** *verb.* **1** *verb intrans.* Of a bird: croak harshly; squawk. L19.
2 *verb trans.* Utter in croaks. L19.

squark /skwɑːk/ *noun*². L20.
[from S(UPER- + QUARK *noun*².]
PARTICLE PHYSICS. The supersymmetric counterpart of a quark, with spin 0 instead of ½.

squarrose /skwaˈrəʊs, skwɒ-/ *adjective.* M18.
[Latin *squarrosus* scurfy, scabby: see -OSE¹.]
BOTANY. Rough with spreading and divergent bracts, leaves, etc.; (of bracts, leaves, etc.) arranged so as to form a surface of this kind.

■ **squarrosely** *adverb* M19. **squarrulose** *adjective* minutely squarrose M19.

squarson /ˈskwɑːs(ə)n/ *noun.* Chiefly *joc.* L19.
[Blend of SQUIRE *noun*¹ + PARSON.]
Hist. An Anglican clergyman who also held the position of squire in his parish.

squash /skwɒʃ/ *noun*¹. L16.
[Rel. to or from SQUASH *verb*.]
1 The unripe pod of a pea; *derog.* a person likened to this. *arch.* L16.
2 a An act of squashing something; a thing which is squashed. E17. ▸**b** The impact of a soft heavy body falling on a surface; the sound produced by this, or by a soft substance being crushed. M17.
3 a A rugby scrum. M19. ▸**b** A social gathering, a party; an informal meeting. M19. ▸**c** A crowd, a large number. L19.
4 a A small soft rubber ball used in the game of squash. *arch.* L19. ▸**b** The game played with this ball, against the walls of a closed court. Also more fully ***squash rackets***. L19. ▸**c** = ***squash tennis*** below. *US.* L19.
5 Orig. = ***lemon squash*** s.v. LEMON *noun*¹. Now, a concentrated liquid made from crushed fruit, esp. oranges or lemons, to which water is added to make a drink; the diluted liquid as a drink. Freq. as 2nd elem. of comb. L19.
6 *BIOLOGY.* A preparation of softened tissue that has been made thin for microscopic examination by gently compressing or tapping. M20.

Comb.: **squash bite** an impression of the teeth made by biting the jaws together on a piece of plastic material. ***squash rackets***: see sense 4b above. **squash tennis** *US* a game similar to squash but played with a tennis ball.

squash /skwɒʃ/ *noun*². M17.
[Abbreviation of Narragansett *asquutasquash*, from *asq* raw, uncooked + *-ash* pl. suffix. Cf. QUASH *noun*, SUCCOTASH.]
The fruit of any of several kinds of gourd, cooked and eaten as a vegetable esp. in N. America; *esp.* that of *Cucurbita pepo* var. *melopepo*, eaten before the seeds and rinds have hardened (more fully ***summer squash***), and that of *C. maxima*, *C. moschata*, etc., stored and eaten when mature (more fully ***winter squash***). Also, any of the plants producing such a fruit.

Comb.: **squash-berry** the edible fruit of several N. American viburnums, *esp.* that of *Viburnum edule*, used to make jelly; **squash blossom** (*a*) the flower of the squash plant; (*b*) used *attrib.* to designate silver necklaces, earrings, etc., made by Navajos and characterized by designs resembling this flower; **squash-bug** *US* a N. American hemipteran insect, *Anasa tristis*, that is a pest of squashes, pumpkins, and melons.

†**squash** *noun*³. L17–E19.
[Aphet. from MUSQUASH.]
= MUSKRAT 1a.

squash /skwɒʃ/ *attrib. adjective.* M19.
[from the verb.]
Having the appearance of being squashed.

🕮 R. L. STEVENSON Admiring imbecility breathed from his squash nose and slobbering lips.

squash /skwɒʃ/ *verb & adverb.* M16.
[Expressive alt. of QUASH *verb*.]
▸ **A** *verb.* **I** Squeeze.
1 *verb trans.* Squeeze or crush into a pulp or flat mass; pack tight, crowd together. M16. ▸**b** *verb intrans.* Make one's way (*into*) by squeezing. M20.
2 *verb trans.* Suppress, stifle; dismiss (a proposal); quash (a rebellion); silence or discomfit (a person) with a crushing retort etc. M18.
3 *verb intrans.* Be pressed into a flat mass on impact; flatten *out* under pressure. M19.

🕮 **1** A. T. ELLIS He squashed all the rubbish into a . . box. W. TREVOR She squashed her cigarette butt on the ashtray. U. HOLDEN They liked being squashed together in bed. **squashed fly (biscuit)** *colloq.* a garibaldi biscuit. **b** P. G. WODEHOUSE The right of Countesses to squash into dinner ahead of the wives of Viscounts. **2** S. KNIGHT Word came that the project was to be squashed.

▸ **II** †**4** *verb trans.* Splash (water) *on* a person; wet by splashing. *rare.* E17–E19.
5 *verb intrans.* Make or move with a splashing sound. L17.
▸ **B** *adverb.* With or as with a squash. Freq. in ***go squash***. M18.

■ **squashaˈbility** *noun* ability to be squashed L19. **squashable** *adjective* E20.

squasher /ˈskwɒʃə/ *noun. US.* L20.
[from SQUASH *noun*¹ + -ER¹.]
A person who plays squash.

squashy /ˈskwɒʃi/ *adjective.* L17.
[from SQUASH *verb* or *noun*¹ + -Y¹.]
1 Having a soft or pulpy consistency; lacking firmness. L17.
2 Of ground etc.: soft with water; muddy; marshy. M18.
3 Of the nature of a squashing action. M19.

🕮 **1** A. LIVELY The low squashy seat seemed to suck me down.

■ **squashily** *adverb* E20. **squashiness** *noun* M19.

squat /skwɒt/ *noun*¹. LME.
[from SQUAT *verb*.]
1 a A heavy fall or bump; a violent jolt. Now *north.* LME. ▸**b** A bruise, a wound, *esp.* one caused by a fall; a dent. Long *obsolete* exc. *dial.* L16.
2 An act of squatting or crouching, esp. on the part of a hare. L16.
†**3** The place where an animal squats; *spec.* the form of a hare. L16–L17.
4 A squatting posture (*rare*); *WEIGHTLIFTING* an exercise or lift in which a person squats down and rises again while carrying a barbell behind the neck; *GYMNASTICS* an exercise involving a squatting movement or action. L19.
5 *NAUTICAL.* The increase in a vessel's draught arising from its motion through the water. E20.
6 An illegal occupation of otherwise unoccupied land or premises; a property occupied by squatters. M20.

Phrases: **at squat** (esp. of a hare) in a squatting posture.
Comb.: **squat board** a horizontal board fixed under the stern of a vessel to reduce squatting at high speed; **squat rack** *WEIGHTLIFTING* a pair of posts each with a support at the top for holding a barbell at a convenient height for a squat; **squat tag** *US* tag in which a player can gain temporary immunity by squatting on the ground; **squat thrust** an exercise in which the legs are thrust backwards to their full extent from a squatting position with the hands on the floor.

squat /skwɒt/ *noun*². *N. Amer. slang.* M20.
[Abbreviation of DOODLY-SQUAT.]
Nothing at all; (following a neg.) anything.

🕮 S. BELLOW You don't know squat about beautiful things.

squat *noun*³ var. of SQUATT.

squat /skwɒt/ *adjective.* LME.
[Obsolete pa. pple of SQUAT *verb*.]
▸ **I 1** *pred.* In a squatting posture. LME.
2 Hidden from sight; quiet, still. *dial.* M19.
▸ **II 3** Esp. of a person or building: short and thickset; disproportionately broad or wide; dumpy. M17. ▸**b** Characterized by squatness of form or structure. L18.

🕮 **3b** N. HAWTHORNE The roof . . gives a very squat aspect to the temple.

■ **squatly** *adverb* L19. **squatness** *noun* E19. **squattily** *adverb* somewhat squatly M19. **squattish** *adjective* E19. **squatty** *adjective* somewhat squat, squattish L19.

squat /skwɒt/ *verb.* Infl. **-tt-**. Pa. t. & pple **squatted**, †**squat**. ME.
[Old French *esquatir*, *-ter*, from *es-* EX-¹ + *quatir* press down, crouch, hide, from Proto-Romance verb from Latin *coactus* pa. pple of *cogere*: see COGENT. See also SWAT *verb*².]
▸ **I 1** *verb trans.* Dash down or thrust violently or with some force. Long *obsolete* exc. *dial.* ME.
2 *verb trans.* Crush, flatten, or beat out of shape; smash, squash; bruise severely. Now *dial.* LME.
†**3** *verb intrans.* Fall violently. LME–L16.
▸ **II 4** *verb intrans.* & *refl.* Of a person: sit with the hams resting on the backs of the heels, or with the knees drawn up and the heels close to or touching the hams; *esp.* sit on the ground in this way; *colloq.* sit (down). Also foll. by *down*. LME. ▸**b** *verb intrans.* Of an animal: crouch close to the ground, esp. to avoid observation or capture. LME. ▸**c** *verb trans.* Lower in the act of squatting. Also, (of

an animal) let (the tail) droop or fall. E18. ▸**d** *verb intrans. & trans.* WEIGHTLIFTING. Perform a squat while holding (a weight). M20.
5 *verb trans.* Cause to squat; put into a squatting posture. *rare.* E17.
6 *verb intrans.* **a** Sink in or down. Now *rare.* M17. ▸**b** (Of a vessel) settle lower in the water at the stern when at speed; (of a motor vehicle) undergo a lowering of the rear when travelling at speed. M20.
7 *verb intrans.* Settle on new, uncultivated, or unoccupied land without any legal title and without the payment of rent; live without legal right on land or in premises otherwise unoccupied; live as a squatter. E19. ▸**b** *verb intrans.* Take up government land for pasturage as a squatter. *Austral.* E19. ▸**c** *verb trans.* Install (a person) as a squatter; occupy as a squatter. L20.

📖 **7** S. TOWNSEND He was still squatting in the old tyre factory.

■ **squattage** *noun* (*a*) a property occupied by a squatter; (*b*) the occupation of property by squatting: M19. **squa'ttocracy** *noun* (AUSTRAL. HISTORY) the class of squatters as a body possessing social and political importance M19.

squatarole /ˈskwat(ə)rəʊl/ *noun. rare.* E19.
[mod. Latin *Squatarola* former genus name from Italian dial.]
The grey plover, *Pluvialis squatarola.*

squatt /skwɒt/ *noun.* Also **squat**. M20.
[Perh. from SQUAT *adjective.*]
ANGLING. The larva of the common house-fly, used as bait.

squatter /ˈskwɒtə/ *noun.* L18.
[from SQUAT *verb* + -ER¹.]
1 a US & AUSTRAL. HISTORY. A settler with no legal title to the land occupied, *esp.* one on land not yet allocated by a government. L18. ▸**b** A person occupying a tract of pastoral land as a tenant of the Crown (*Hist.*); a sheep-farmer or cattle-farmer, esp. on a large scale. *Austral. & NZ.* M19. ▸**c** An unauthorized or illegal occupant of otherwise unoccupied land or premises. M19.
2 A squatting or crouching person or animal. E19.
3 More fully ***squatter pigeon***. A bronzewing pigeon of the genus *Phaps*, esp *P. elegans* and *P. chalcoptera*. *Austral.* M19.
4 CRICKET. A ball which remains low on pitching; a shooter. M20.
Comb.: ***squatter pigeon***: see sense 3 above; **squatter sovereignty** US HISTORY the right claimed by settlers of newly formed territories to decide for themselves the question of slavery and other matters.
■ **squatterdom** *noun* (AUSTRAL. HISTORY) squatters collectively M19.

squatter /ˈskwɒtə/ *verb.* Now chiefly *Scot.* L16.
[Prob. imit. Cf. SWATTER *verb.*]
†**1** *verb intrans.* Be fussily busy. Only in L16.
†**2** *verb intrans.* = SQUITTER *verb* 2. L16–E17.
3 *verb trans. & intrans.* Scatter, disperse. Long *obsolete* exc. *Scot.* E17.
4 *verb intrans.* **a** Make one's way through water with much splashing or flapping. (Foll. by *away, out of, through*, etc.) L18. ▸**b** Flap or struggle in water or soft mud. E19.

squattle /ˈskwɒt(ə)l/ *verb. rare.* L18.
[from SQUAT *verb* + -LE³.]
1 *verb intrans.* Nestle. L18.
2 *verb trans.* Settle down squatly. L19.

squaw /skwɔː/ *noun.* M17.
[Narragansett *squaws*, Massachusetts Algonquian *squa* woman.]
1 A N. American Indian woman, esp. a married one; the wife of a N. American Indian. Cf. SANNUP. Now considered *offensive*. M17.
2 *transf.* An effeminate or weak man. E19.
Phrases: ***old squaw***: see OLD *adjective*. SUNCK ***squaw***.
Comb.: **squaw-berry** (the edible berry of) any of several shrubs, *esp.* bearberry, *Arctostaphylos uva-ursi*, and deerberry, *Vaccinium stamineum*; **squaw corn** soft corn, *Zea mays* var. *amylacea*, a staple crop of N. American Indians; **squaw duck** = ***old squaw*** s.v. OLD *adjective*; **squawfish** either of two large freshwater fish-eating cyprinid fishes, *Ptychocheilus oregonensis* and *P. lucius*, of the north-western US, formerly important food fishes for N. American Indians; **squaw-man** *derog.* a white or black man married to a N. American Indian woman; **squaw-root** a N. American plant of the broomrape family, *Conopholis americana*, parasitic on the roots of trees; **squaw-weed** any of several N. American ragworts, esp. *Senecio aureus*; **squaw winter** in Canada and the northern US, a short wintry spell before an Indian summer.

squawk /skwɔːk/ *verb & noun.* E19.
[Imit.]
▸ **A** *verb.* **1** *verb intrans.* Utter a loud harsh call or cry; give out a discordant high-pitched noise. E19. ▸**b** Turn informer. *US slang.* L19. ▸**c** Complain, protest. *N. Amer. slang.* L19.
2 *verb trans.* Utter with or as with a squawk. M19.
3 *verb trans.* Of an aircraft: transmit (a signal) as identification. *slang.* M20.

📖 **2** P. SCOBIE 'Exercise?' squawked Jackie. 'I can't move in this!'

▸ **B** *noun.* **1** A loud harsh call or cry, esp. of a bird; a discordant high-pitched noise. M19.
2 A complaint, a protest. Chiefly *N. Amer.* E20.
3 An identification signal transmitted by an aircraft. *slang.* L20.

📖 **2** P. KURTH Her plan provoked a loud squawk from . . other friends.

Comb.: **squawk box** *colloq.* a loudspeaker; an intercom.
■ **squawker** *noun* (*a*) a person who squawks; (*b*) a toy wind instrument for producing squawks; (*c*) a loudspeaker for reproducing sounds in the middle of the audible range: L19. **squawky** *adjective* (of a voice) loud and harsh; hoarsely squeaky: L19.

squdge /skwʌdʒ/ *verb trans. colloq.* L19.
[Perh. blend of SQUEEZE *verb* or SQUASH *verb* and PUDGE *noun*².]
Squash, squeeze; hug tightly.
■ **squdgy** *adjective* soft and moist or yielding, squashy L19.

squeak /skwiːk/ *noun.* E17.
[from the verb.]
1 The action of squeaking. Earliest in †***put to the squeak***, cause to squeak. E17.
2 a A short thin high-pitched cry made by a person or animal; a short squeal; *colloq.* (in neg. contexts) a single sound or communication. E18. ▸**b** A thin sharp high-pitched sound produced by a musical instrument, an unoiled hinge, etc. E19.
3 a A very slight chance *for* something. Now *rare.* E18. ▸**b** A narrow escape, a close shave; a success barely attained. Chiefly in ***narrow squeak*** s.v. NARROW *adjective.* E19.
4 *slang.* †**a** A criminal who informs on others. L18–L19. ▸**b** A piece of incriminating evidence offered to the police. Chiefly in ***put in the squeak***, turn informer. E20.

📖 **2a** A. WILSON Her little-girl's voice seemed higher than ever . . , almost a squeak. T. PARKS Graham phones regularly, while from Garry . . never a squeak. **b** I. MURDOCH He . . heard the squeak of the kitchen door. ***bubble and squeak***: see BUBBLE *noun* 4. **3b** H. L. WILSON A man who has had a narrow squeak from drowning.

squeak /skwiːk/ *verb.* LME.
[Imit.: cf. SQUEAL *verb*, SHRIEK *verb*, Swedish *skväka* croak.]
1 *verb intrans.* **a** Of a person or animal: emit a short thin high-pitched cry. LME. ▸**b** Of a thing: make a thin sharp high-pitched sound. M16.
2 *verb trans.* Utter, sing, or play in a squeaking manner or with a squeaky voice. Usu. *derog.* Freq. foll. by *out.* L16.
3 *verb intrans.* Confess; turn informer; give incriminating evidence. *slang.* L17.
4 *verb trans.* Cause (something) to squeak. E20.
5 *verb intrans.* Succeed with a narrow margin, barely manage. Foll. by *by, into, through*, etc. M20.

📖 **1b** W. MCILVANNEY The bed squeaked on its castors. **squeaking sand** sand that gives out a short high-pitched sound when disturbed. ***squeeze until the pips squeak***: see PIP *noun*² 2. **2** DICKENS Fiddles . . were squeaking out the tune. **3** E. AMADI Swear to secrecy. I have assured them that you will not squeak. **5** *Times* We are now holding just under 42 per cent . . . We are confident we will squeak home. *Boxing* McKinney just squeaked by . . by finishing more strongly.

■ **squeakery** *noun* squeaking character or quality E19.

squeaker /ˈskwiːkə/ *noun.* M17.
[from prec. + -ER¹.]
1 A person who makes or utters a squeaking sound. M17.
2 A bird or animal, esp. a young one, which squeaks; *spec.* (*a*) a young game-bird; (*b*) a swift; (*c*) any of various Australian birds having a squeaking call; (*d*) *colloq.* a (small) cicada. M17.
3 A device or toy which produces a squeaking sound. L18.
4 An informer. *slang.* E20.
5 A game won by a very narrow margin. *colloq.* (chiefly *N. Amer.*). M20.

squeaky /ˈskwiːki/ *adjective & adverb.* M19.
[from SQUEAK *noun* or *verb* + -Y¹.]
▸ **A** *adjective.* Characterized by a squeaking sound or sounds; tending to squeak. M19.

📖 J. WINTERSON His teeth stuck out, and his voice was squeaky. *Proverb*: The squeaky wheel gets the grease.

▸ **B** *adverb.* ***squeaky clean***: completely clean; *fig.* above criticism, beyond reproach. *colloq.* L20.
■ **squeakily** *adverb* L19. **squeakiness** *noun* E20.

squeal /skwiːl/ *noun.* M18.
[from the verb.]
1 A prolonged loud high-pitched sound; a shrill scream. M18.
2 *slang* (chiefly *US*). ▸**a** An act of informing against another. L19. ▸**b** A call for police assistance or investigation; a report of a case investigated by the police. M20.

📖 **1** A. LEE The bus slowed and halted, with a squeal of gears. F. KING He was joking with the two boys on duty, sending them into squeals of laughter.

squeal /skwiːl/ *verb.* ME.
[Imit. Cf. SQUALL *verb & noun*².]
1 *verb intrans.* Utter a prolonged loud high-pitched cry; scream shrilly; *fig.* complain, protest. ME.
2 *verb intrans.* Of a thing: emit or produce a prolonged loud high-pitched sound. L16.
3 *verb trans.* **a** Utter or produce a squeal. Also foll. by *out.* L17. ▸**b** Cause (esp. the tyres of a motor vehicle) to squeal. M20.
4 *verb intrans.* Turn informer; inform *on* a person. *slang.* M19.

📖 TOLKIEN He squealed, as if something had stabbed him. *Broadcast* Advertisers are squealing about the cost of commercial TV. **2** R. FRAME The groaning and screeching of traffic, . . brakes squealing, horns blaring. **4** T. TRYON The club required a sacred oath . . never to squeal on a fellow member.

■ **squealer** *noun* (*a*) a person who or thing which squeals; *spec.* any of several birds with a characteristic squealing cry, as the harlequin duck, the swift, the golden plover; (*b*) *slang* an informer: M19.

squeam /skwiːm/ *noun. rare.* L18.
[Back-form. from SQUEAMISH.]
A qualm, a scruple.

squeam /skwiːm/ *verb intrans. rare.* L16.
[formed as prec., or from SQUEAMOUS.]
Turn faint or squeamish.
■ **squeamer** *noun* L19.

squeamish /ˈskwiːmɪʃ/ *adjective.* LME.
[Alt. of next by substitution of -ISH¹ for -OUS.]
1 a (Of a person) easily turned sick or faint; (of the stomach) readily affected with nausea. LME. ▸**b** Slightly affected with nausea; queasy. M17.
†**2** Unwilling or backward *to do* something. M–L16.
3 Reserved, cold, coy; bashful, diffident. *obsolete* exc. *dial.* M16. ▸†**b** Averse to being free or generous with something. Foll. by *of.* M16–E17.
4 Easily shocked or offended by immodesty or indecency; prudish. Now *rare.* M16. ▸†**b** Sensitive; shrinking from contact with anything harsh or rough. Only in 18.
5 Excessively fastidious or scrupulous in questions of propriety, honesty, etc. L16. ▸**b** Fastidious or particular with respect to what one uses or comes in contact with. E17.

📖 **1a** R. RENDELL He was squeamish, he . . couldn't face the idea of seeing a dead body. **b** P. KAVANAGH The pigs were . . killed right beside our front door. Nobody felt sick or squeamish. **5** *absol.*: F. FORSYTH He had worked in Stalin's Public Prosecutor office, not a job for the squeamish.

■ **squeamishly** *adverb* L16. **squeamishness** *noun* L16. **squeamy** *adjective* (orig. & chiefly *US*) = SQUEAMISH M19.

squeamous /ˈskwiːməs/ *adjective. obsolete* exc. *north.* ME.
[Aphet. from Anglo-Norman *escoymos*, of unkn. origin.]
1 Distant, disdainful, fastidious. ME. ▸**b** Modest, shy. L15.
2 = SQUEAMISH *adjective* 1a. LME.
†**3** Feeling abhorrence or detestation *of* something. LME–E16.
†**4** = SQUEAMISH *adjective* 2. LME–M16.

squeege /skwiːdʒ/ *verb. arch. colloq.* Also **squeedge**. L18.
[Strengthened form of SQUEEZE *verb.*]
1 *verb intrans.* Press; make one's way by pressure or force. L18.
2 *verb trans.* Compress; squeeze. L18.

squeegee /ˈskwiːdʒiː/ *noun & verb.* M19.
[Arbitrary formation from prec.: see -EE².]
▸ **A** *noun.* **1** A scraping implement consisting of a rubber-edged blade attached to the end of a handle, used for removing water, mud, etc., now esp. in cleaning windows or windscreens. M19.
2 PHOTOGRAPHY. A rubber strip, pad, or roller used for squeezing or wiping moisture from a print, pressing a film closer to its mount, etc. L19.
Comb.: **squeegee band** *Nautical slang* an improvised musical band.
▸ **B** *verb.* Pa. t. & pple **-geed**.
1 *verb trans.* Press, squeeze, or scrape with or as with a squeegee. L19.
2 *verb intrans.* Use a squeegee. L20.

squeezable /ˈskwiːzəb(ə)l/ *adjective.* E19.
[from SQUEEZE *verb* + -ABLE.]
1 Able to be compressed or squeezed; extractable by pressure. E19.
2 Able to be constrained or coerced into yielding or granting something; *esp.* from which money may be exacted. M19.
■ **squeeza'bility** *noun* M19. **squeezableness** *noun* M19.

squeeze /skwiːz/ *noun.* E17.
[from the verb.]
1 The action or an act of squeezing; (an) application of strong pressure; the fact of being squeezed; pressure.

E17. ▸**b** Mental pressure, constraining influence, coercion. Chiefly in ***put the squeeze on***. *colloq.* E18. ▸**c** The pressure of a crowd of people; a crush. (Cf. sense 4 below.) E19. ▸**d** A strong financial demand or pressure, *esp.* a restriction on borrowing, investment, etc., in a financial crisis; *spec.* (STOCK EXCHANGE) pressure applied to a dealer who has sold short to settle at a loss. L19. ▸**e** BRIDGE. A tactic used to force an opponent to discard or unguard a potentially winning card; an end-play. E20.

2 a A strong or firm pressure of the hand as a sign of friendship or affection. M18. ▸**b** A close embrace; a hug. L18. ▸**c** A man's close female friend, *esp.* a girlfriend. *slang* (chiefly *US*). L20.

3 A (small) quantity squeezed out of something; a few drops pressed out by squeezing. M18. ▸**b** A sum of money extorted or exacted, *esp.* an illicit commission. M19.

4 A crowded assembly or social gathering. *colloq.* L18.

5 MINING. A gradual convergence of the floor and roof of a gallery or working; a place where this has occurred. L18.

6 *slang.* **a** The neck. E19. ▸**b** Silk; an article made of this, *esp.* a silk tie. E19. ▸**c** A plan; work. M19.

7 A moulding or cast of an object or an impression or copy of a design etc., obtained by pressing a pliable substance round or over it. M19. ▸**b** An impression of an object made for criminal purposes. *slang.* L19.

8 *colloq.* **a** An escape, a close shave. Chiefly in ***narrow squeeze***. M19. ▸**b** A difficult situation; a crisis, an emergency. E20.

9 BASEBALL. = ***squeeze play*** (a) below. E20.

> **1d** ***credit squeeze***: see CREDIT *noun*. **2c** ***main squeeze***: see MAIN *adjective*. **3** *Homes & Gardens* A good squeeze of lemon juice. **9b** ***at a squeeze*** at a pinch. ***a tight squeeze***: see TIGHT *adjective* 7.

Comb.: **squeeze bunt** BASEBALL the bunt made in a squeeze play; **squeeze-pidgin** *slang* a bribe; **squeeze play** (*a*) BASEBALL a tactic whereby the batter bunts so that a runner at third base can attempt to reach home safely and score; (*b*) BRIDGE the use of a squeeze; (*c*) *colloq.* (chiefly *N. Amer.*) an act of coercion or pressurizing.

squeeze /skwiːz/ *verb.* Also (earlier) †**squise**, †**squize**. M16.
[Intensive of QUEISE.]

1 *verb trans.* Exert pressure on from opposite or all sides, esp. so as to force together, extract moisture, or reduce in size; *spec.* compress with one's hand. M16. ▸**b** Bring into a specified condition or position by pressure. M17. ▸**c** Press (a person's hand) with one's own as a sign of sympathy or affection. L17.

2 *verb trans.* Press or force into a small or narrow space. Foll. by adverb or preposition. L16. ▸**b** *verb intrans. & trans.* Force (one's) way. Foll. by adverb or preposition. E18.

3 *verb trans.* Force out by pressure; extract (moisture); *transf. & fig.* extract with effort. Freq. foll. by *out*. L16.

4 *verb trans.* Extort, exact (money); obtain by force or pressure *from* or *out of* a person etc. E17.

5 *verb trans.* **a** Pressurize, constrain, esp. so as to exact or extort money. Also foll. by *of*. M17. ▸**b** Exert financial pressure on; impose financial hardship on; restrict (spending, borrowing, etc.); reduce the size of (profits); *spec.* (STOCK EXCHANGE) force (a dealer who has sold short) to settle at a loss. L19. ▸**c** BRIDGE. Force (an opponent) to discard a guarding or potentially winning card; subject to end-play. E20.

6 *verb intrans.* **a** Press hard; exert pressure, esp. with the hand. L17. ▸**b** Take a cast or facsimile impression. L19.

7 *verb intrans.* Yield to pressure; admit of being squeezed. L17.

8 *verb trans. colloq.* ▸**a** Fire *off* (a round, shot, etc.) from a gun. M20. ▸**b** Approach (a certain age). L20.

> **1** E. MITTELHOLZER Kattree's shoes squeezed her toes. Y. MENUHIN Klaxons . . with rubber bulbs which, when squeezed, emitted an almost animal sound. J. FULLER Cloths being dipped in the water and squeezed out. ***squeeze an orange***: see ORANGE *noun*. ***squeeze until the pips squeak***: see PIP *noun*² 2. **b** *fig.*: *City Limits* Multinational property developers squeeze the market dry. **2** L. ELLMANN She squeezes herself into her tightest pair of jeans. *fig.*: H. MOORE A two year examination course I squeezed into one. **b** C. PHILLIPS The sand . . had squeezed its way between shoe and sock. P. P. READ He squeezed through the crowd. **3** *Best Place* freshly squeezed orange juice and rind . . in a large saucepan. **5** *Sunday Mail (Brisbane)* She lent him money . . . Then. when he couldn't squeeze her for more he gave her the brush-off. **b** *Financial Weekly* Hard times for consumers, when spending is being squeezed.

Comb.: **squeeze bottle**: made of flexible plastic which is squeezed to extract the contents; **squeeze-box** *slang* †(*a*) NAUTICAL a ship's harmonium; (*b*) an accordion, a concertina; **squeeze cementing** OIL INDUSTRY the separation of permeable formations, sealing of casings, etc., by the forced introduction of cement slurry under pressure; **squeeze lens** CINEMATOGRAPHY an anamorphic lens attachment; **squeeze toy** a child's doll or similar toy which makes a sound when squeezed; **squeeze tube** a tube-shaped container which yields its contents when squeezed.

■ **squeezy** *adjective* (*a*) suggestive of or characterized by squeezing; compressed; (*b*) (esp. of a bottle) able to be squeezed: M18.

squeezer /ˈskwiːzə/ *noun.* E17.
[from prec. + -ER¹.]

1 A person who squeezes something. E17.

2 †**a** A crowded assembly. Only in M18. ▸**b** A squeezing pressure. E19. ▸**c** *The* hangman's rope; *the* noose. *slang.* E19.

3 An implement, mechanical device, etc., by which pressure can be applied; *spec.* an apparatus by which a ball of puddled iron is compacted. M19.

4 *Hist.* A playing-card with pips in the corner (as now usual), so that its value may be seen while the cards are held closely arranged. Usu. in *pl.* L19.

squegger /ˈskwɛgə/ *noun.* E20.
[Perh. alt. of *self-quench(ing* + -ER¹.]
ELECTRONICS. An oscillator whose oscillations build up to a certain amplitude and then temporarily cease; the production of such oscillations.

■ **squeg** *verb intrans.*, infl. **-gg-**, [back-form.] (of an electric circuit) undergo intermittent self-quenching oscillations M20.

squelch /skwɛltʃ/ *noun, verb, & adverb.* E17.
[Imit.: cf. QUELCH.]

▸ **A** *noun.* **1** Orig., a heavy crushing fall on to something soft or yielding. Later, the sound produced by this, *spec.* a sucking sound as made by falling or walking on wet muddy ground. E17. ▸**b** A disconcerting surprise. E19. ▸**c** A decisive argument; a crushing retort. *slang.* M20.

2 A thing or mass that has the appearance of having been crushed. M19.

3 The sound made by a liquid when subjected to sudden or intermittent pressure. L19.

4 ELECTRONICS. A circuit that suppresses all input signals except those of a particular kind; *spec.* in RADIO, a circuit that suppresses the noise output of a receiver when the signal strength falls below a predetermined level. Also ***squelch circuit***. M20.

▸ **B** *verb.* **1** *verb trans.* Fall or stamp on (something soft) so as to squash or crush flat. E17.

2 *verb intrans.* Make or emit a squelch or sucking sound. E18. ▸**b** Fall with a squelch. *obsolete* exc. *dial.* M18.

3 *verb intrans.* Walk or tread heavily in mud, on wet ground, or with water in the shoes, so as to make a sucking sound. M19.

4 *verb trans.* Squash or crush (a person, idea, etc.); put down, suppress completely; disconcert, silence. M19.

5 *verb trans.* ELECTRONICS. Subject to the action of a squelch. M20.

> **2** W. BOYD His feet squelched on the mud of his . . path. L. GRANT-ADAMSON The grass squelched beneath his feet. **3** BEVERLEY CLEARY She squelched off . . in her wet sneakers. L. ELLMANN I squelched through soggy grass. **4** P. ROTH Henry . . had to squelch all his doubts. D. LEAVITT Why . . do you always have to squelch me, to shut me up.

▸ **C** *adverb.* With a squelch. L18.

■ **squelcher** *noun* (*colloq.*) a person who or thing which squelches; a decisive or crushing blow, argument, etc.: M19. **squelchy** *adjective* (*a*) liable to squelch; emitting a squelching sound; (*b*) (of a sound) of the nature of a squelch: M19.

squench /skwɛn(t)ʃ/ *verb.* Now *dial.* LME.
[Intensive of QUENCH *verb*: cf. SQUEEZE *verb*.]

1 *verb trans.* Extinguish, put out (a fire etc.). LME.

2 *verb trans.* Suppress, put an end to; quell, stifle. L16.

3 *verb trans.* Satisfy (hunger, thirst, etc.). L16.

4 *verb intrans.* Of a fire: be extinguished. *rare.* M17.

■ **squencher** *noun* something which quenches thirst, a light, etc. L19.

squeteague /skwɛˈtiːg/ *noun. US.* E19.
[Southern New England Algonquian.]
= WEAKFISH.

squib /skwɪb/ *noun.* E16.
[Perh. imit. of a slight explosion.]

1 A small firework which burns with a hissing sound and usu. makes a final explosion. E16.

2 A sharp scornful or sarcastic remark; a short satirical composition; a lampoon. E16.

3 †**a** An explosive device used as a missile or means of attack. L16–L17. ▸**b** A gun. *slang. rare.* M19. ▸**c** MINING. A slow match; a safety fuse. L19.

4 A mean or insignificant person. Also, a short or thin person. *slang.* L16. ▸**b** A horse lacking courage or stamina; *transf.* a coward. *Austral. slang.* E20.

5 A syringe; a squirt. Now *dial.* L16.

6 A small measure or quantity (*of* strong drink). Now *dial.* M18.

7 AMER. FOOTBALL. A short kick on a kick-off. L20.

1 damp squib an unsuccessful attempt to impress; an anticlimax, a disappointment.

■ **squibbery** *noun* (*rare*) (*a*) satire in the form of squibs; (*b*) firework squibs collectively: E19. **squibbish** *adjective* of the nature of a squib L17.

squib /skwɪb/ *verb.* Infl. **-bb-**. L16.
[from the noun.]

▸ **I** *verb intrans.* **1** Use scornful, satirical, or sarcastic language; utter or write a squib or squibs. (Foll. by *against*, *at*, etc., a person.) L16.

2 a Let off a squib or squibs; make a report like that of a squib. *rare.* L17. ▸**b** Fire a gun etc.; shoot. M19.

3 a Dart *about* like a squib. M18. ▸**b** Behave in a cowardly manner; evade, wriggle *out of*; (foll. by *on*) betray, let down. *Austral. slang.* M20.

▸ **II** *verb trans.* **4** *arch.* **a** Utter (a remark, quip, etc.). Freq. foll. by *off*, *out*. L16. ▸**b** Lampoon, satirize. M17.

5 Let off (a squib); fire (a gun etc.). E17.

6 Avoid (a difficulty or responsibility); shirk through fear or cowardice. *Austral. slang.* E20.

7 AMER. FOOTBALL. Kick (the ball) a comparatively short distance on a kick-off; execute (a kick) in this way. *slang.* L20.

■ **squibber** *noun* (*arch.*) a person who writes or utters squibs E19.

squid /skwɪd/ *noun*¹ *& verb.* L16.
[Origin unkn.]

▸ **A** *noun.* Pl. same, **-s**.

1 Any of various fast-swimming marine cephalopods of the order Teuthoidea, having an elongated body with two stabilizing fins at the back, eight arms in a ring around two longer tentacles at the front, and a reduced internal horny shell (pen); *esp.* any of the common edible squid of the genera *Loligo* and *Illex*; *colloq.* a cuttlefish. L16.

2 An artificial bait for fish imitating a squid in form. L19.

3 A stable configuration of a parachute which is only partially extended. M20.

4 (Also **S-**.) A ship-mounted anti-submarine mortar with three barrels, developed in the war of 1939–45. M20.

5 A lead disc used as a puck in the game of octopush. M20.

Comb.: **squid fish** *arch.* = sense 1 above; **squid-hound** *N. Amer.* the striped bass; **squid jig**, **squid-jigger** a weight with hooks used in catching squid for bait; **squid-jigging** fishing for squid using a squid jig.

▸ **B** *verb intrans.* Infl. **-dd-**.

1 Fish using squid as bait. M19.

2 Of a parachute: achieve a stable configuration when only partially extended. M20.

SQUID /skwɪd/ *noun*². M20.
[Acronym, from *superconducting quantum interference device*.]
PHYSICS. A device, used esp. in sensitive magnetometers, consisting of a superconducting ring containing one or more Josephson junctions, a change in the magnetic flux linkage of the ring by one flux quantum producing a sharp change in the ring's impedance.

squidge /skwɪdʒ/ *noun*¹. L19.
[Imit.]
The sound made by soft mud yielding to sudden pressure.

squidge /skwɪdʒ/ *noun*². *US slang. rare.* E20.
[Origin unkn.]
A person given the worrying or troublesome duties of another.

squidge /skwɪdʒ/ *verb.* L19.
[Perh. imit.: for sense 1 cf. SQUIDGE *noun*¹.]

1 *verb trans. & intrans.* Squeeze; squelch, mix roughly; press together so as to make a sucking noise. *colloq.* L19.

2 *verb intrans.* In tiddlywinks, play (a wink) by snapping it with a larger counter. M20.

■ **squidger** *noun* in tiddlywinks, the larger wink used to flick a player's winks M20.

squidgy /ˈskwɪdʒi/ *adjective. colloq.* L19.
[Prob. from SQUIDGE *noun*¹ + -Y¹.]

1 Short and plump; podgy. L19.

2 Moist and pliant; squashy; soggy. L20.

> **2** *Under 5* Children love the . . squidgy feeling of modelling clay.

■ **squidgily** *adverb* M20.

squiffed /skwɪft/ *adjective. slang.* L19.
[Alt.]
= SQUIFFY *adjective* 1.

squiffer /ˈskwɪfə/ *noun. slang.* E20.
[Origin unkn.]
A concertina. Also, an organ-bellows, an organ.

squiffy /ˈskwɪfi/ *adjective. slang.* M19.
[Origin unkn.]

1 Intoxicated, drunk. M19.

2 Askew, skew-whiff. M20.

squiggle /ˈskwɪg(ə)l/ *noun*¹. *rare.* L19.
[Imit.]
A giggle, a snigger.

squiggle /ˈskwɪg(ə)l/ *verb & noun*². E19.
[Perh. blend of SQUIRM and WIGGLE or WRIGGLE *verb*, *noun*.]

▸ **A** *verb.* **1** *verb intrans.* Work wavy or intricate embroidery. *rare.* E19.

2 *verb intrans.* Writhe about; squirm, wriggle. Chiefly *dial.* & *US.* E19.
3 *verb trans.* Shake about (a liquid). *dial.* E19.
4 *verb trans.* Write or daub in waves or curves, scrawl. M20.

📖 2 R. SILVERBERG The car squiggled over the . . mud and slid to a stop. 4 *Observer* I watched a little girl squiggle . . red paint on a piece of white paper.

▶ **B** *noun.* A wriggly twist or curve; *esp.* a wavy line in handwriting or doodling. E20.

📖 P. LIVELY 'Best wishes from.' . . She cannot read the squiggle. M. FRAYN A squiggle of Worcester sauce across an open sandwich.

▪ **squiggly** *adjective* wavy, wriggly E20.

squilgee /ˈskwɪldʒiː/ *noun & verb.* M19.
[Alt. of SQUEEGEE.]
NAUTICAL. ▶**A** *noun.* An implement similar to a squeegee covered with leather and used to rub a ship's deck after washing. M19.
▶ **B** *verb intrans. & trans.* Pa. t. & pple **-geed**. Clean, swab, or rub with a squilgee. M19.

squill /skwɪl/ *noun.* LME.
[Latin *squilla* var. of SCILLA.]
1 a A Mediterranean plant of the lily family, *Drimia maritima*, with a long spike of white flowers and a large bulb. Also called ***sea onion***. LME. ▸**b** Any plant of the allied genus *Scilla*; *esp.* (*a*) (in full ***spring squill***) the spring-flowering *S. verna*; (*b*) (in full ***autumn squill***) the autumn flowering *S. autumnalis*. Also (more fully ***striped squill***), the related bulb plant *Puschkinia scilloides* (see PUSCHKINIA). L18.
2 a A bulb of the plant *Drimia maritima*, different varieties of which have respectively whitish or reddish-brown outer scales (distinguished as ***white squill*** and ***red squill***). Freq. in *pl.* LME. ▸**b** PHARMACOLOGY. An extract or preparation of (white) squill, used esp. in cough mixtures. Also, an extract of red squill, used as a rat poison. E18.
3 A mantis shrimp of the genus *Squilla*. E18.
Phrases: ***Spanish squill***: see SPANISH *adjective*.

squilla /ˈskwɪlə/ *noun.* Pl. **-llae** /-liː/. E16.
[Latin: see prec.]
†**1** (An extract of) squill, *Drimia maritima*. E16–E17.
2 = SQUILL 3. Now only as mod. Latin genus name. M17.

squillion /ˈskwɪljən/ *noun & adjective. colloq.* Pl. of noun same with specified number, **-s** when indefinite. M20.
[Arbitrary formation after *billion*, *trillion*: cf. ZILLION.]
A very large number of millions (of); an enormous number (of).

†**squillitic** *adjective.* LME–E18.
[medieval Latin *squilliticus* var. of Latin *scilliticus*, from *scilla* SQUILL: see -IC.]
MEDICINE. Of or containing squill.

squinacy /ˈskwɪnəsi/ *noun.* Long *dial.* ME.
[Var. of next.]
= QUINSY.

squinancy /ˈskwɪnənsi/ *noun.* Now *rare* or *obsolete* exc. in comb. below. ME.
[medieval Latin *squinantia*, app. formed by confusion of Greek *sunagkhē* and *kunagkhē* CYNANCHE, both denoting diseases of the throat. Cf. SQUINSY.]
= QUINSY.
Comb.: **squinancy-wort** a small trailing plant of chalk turf, *Asperula cynanchica*, of the madder family which has small pinkish-white flowers and is a reputed remedy for quinsy.
▪ Also †**squinance** *noun* LME–M18.

squinch /skwɪn(t)ʃ/ *noun*[1]. L15.
[Alt. of SCUNCH.]
ARCHITECTURE. †**1** A stone cut to serve as a scuncheon. L15.
2 A straight or arched support constructed across an interior angle of a square tower to carry a superstructure. M19.
3 A small structure, with two triangular faces, sloping back from an angle of a tower against the superimposed side of a spire. M19.

squinch /skwɪn(t)ʃ/ *noun*[2]. E17.
[Origin unkn.]
A narrow opening in a building; a slit, a crack.

squinch /skwɪn(t)ʃ/ *verb.* Chiefly *US.* E19.
[Perh. blend of SQUINT *verb* and PINCH *verb*.]
1 *verb trans.* Screw *up*, contort (one's face, features, etc.). E19.
2 *verb intrans.* Squeeze up so as to occupy less place; crouch. M19.
Comb.: **squinch-owl** *US local* a screech owl (of the genus *Otus*).

squinny /ˈskwɪni/ *adjective*[1]. M18.
[Origin unkn.]
Very thin; lean, meagre; narrow. Earliest in ***squinny-gut***.

squinny /ˈskwɪni/ *verb*[1], *adjective*[2], & *noun.* E17.
[Obscurely rel. to SQUINT *verb*.]
▶ **A** *verb.* **1** *verb intrans.* Squint, look askance; peer with partly closed eyes (*at*). E17.
2 *verb trans.* Direct (the eyes) obliquely; close (the eyes) *up* partly in a short-sighted manner. *rare.* E19.

📖 1 F. TUOHY Officials on the balcony . . began squinnying upwards into the sunlight.

▶ **B** *adjective.* Squinting; looking askance; peering. E19.
Comb.: **squinny-eyed** *adjective* = ***squint-eyed*** s.v. SQUINT *adjective*.
▶ **C** *noun.* A squint; a glance, esp. with partly closed eyes. L19.

squinny /ˈskwɪni/ *verb*[2] *intrans.* M19.
[Origin unkn.]
Weep, cry; fret.

squinsy /ˈskwɪnzi/ *noun.* Now *dial.* L15.
[Reduced form of SQUINACY.]
= QUINSY.

squint /skwɪnt/ *noun.* M17.
[from SQUINT *adjective*, *verb*.]
1 A permanent deviation in the direction of gaze of one eye; defective alignment of the eyes; strabismus. M17. ▸**b** RADAR. Lack of alignment between the axis of a transmitting aerial and the direction of maximum radiation, deliberately introduced in some systems. M20.
2 A sidelong look or glance; *colloq.* a hasty or casual look, a peep. L17.
3 An inclination or tendency towards something, a drift, a leaning; a covert aim. M18. ▸**b** An oblique or perverse bent or tendency. L18.
4 ARCHITECTURE. = HAGIOSCOPE. M19.

📖 1 W. H. AUDEN She'd a slight squint in her left eye. 2 E. NESBIT 'Let's have a squint,' and I looked but I couldn't see anything.

squint /skwɪnt/ *verb.* L16.
[from (the same root as) SQUINT *adverb & adjective*.]
1 *verb intrans.* Have a covert implication, bearing, or aim; refer or bear indirectly; incline, tend. Foll. by *at*, *towards*, etc. L16.
2 *verb intrans.* **a** Have the axes of the eyes not coincident, so that they look in different directions; be affected with strabismus. E17. ▸**b** Of the eyes: look in different directions; have a squint. M19.
3 *verb intrans.* **a** Look (*at*, *through*, etc.) with the eyes differently directed; look indirectly, with a sidelong glance, or with half-closed eyes; *colloq.* glance hastily or casually, peep *at*. E17. ▸**b** Look *at*, *on*, or *upon* with dislike or disapproval; look down on. M17. ▸**c** Have a private interest as a reason for doing something. Foll. by *at*, *upon*. M17.
4 *verb trans.* **a** Give a squint or cast to (the eyes); cause to look asquint or obliquely. E17. ▸**b** Cast (a glance etc.) in a sidelong manner. M17.
5 *verb intrans.* Move or branch off in an oblique direction. E18.

📖 1 *New York Evening Post* Paragraphs in the . . papers, squinting at the possibility of a scandal. 2a J. CONRAD He used to squint horribly. 3a E. BOWEN Veronica . . squinted down at the tip of her cigarette. S. KAUFFMANN The sun was behind him, so . . she had to squint up at him. M. KEANE As she prayed, Nicandra squinted through her fingers to watch. 4a J. HERBERT She squinted her eyes, peering intently.

▪ **squinter** *noun* M18. **squintingly** *adverb* in a squinting manner L16.

squint /skwɪnt/ *adverb & adjective.* LME.
[Aphet. from ASQUINT.]
▶ **A** *adverb.* With a squint, asquint, obliquely. *rare.* LME.
▶ **B** *adjective.* **1** Of eyes: squinting; affected with strabismus. Earliest & now chiefly in ***squint-eyed*** below. M16.
2 a Of a look: characterized by a squint. E17. ▸**b** *fig.* Of suspicion, the mind, etc.: oblique, perverse, aberrant. *poet.* M17.
†**3** Of a connection, attitude, etc.: indirect. Only in 17.
4 Off the straight; slanting, skew. Now chiefly *Scot.* E18.
Comb.: **squint-eye** a look, a glance; a point of view; **squint-eyed** *adjective* (*a*) (of a person) having squint eyes, affected with strabismus; (of a look) characterized by a squint; (*b*) *fig.* oblique, perverse; malignant, ill-willed; **squint-eyes** a person with squinting eyes.
▪ **squinty** *adjective* †(*a*) oblique; (*b*) squint-eyed, having a squint: L16.

squinted /ˈskwɪntɪd/ *adjective.* L16.
[from SQUINT *noun*, *verb*: see -ED[2], -ED[1].]
1 Affected with strabismus or a squint. L16.
2 RADAR. Of an aerial: having squint. M20.

squirarch *noun*, **squirarchy** *noun* vars. of SQUIREARCH, SQUIREARCHY *noun*[1].

squire /skwʌɪə/ *noun*[1]. ME.
[Aphet. from Old French *esquier* ESQUIRE *noun*.]
1 a *Hist.* A young nobleman who, in training for knighthood, acted as shield-bearer and attendant to a knight; a man ranking next below a knight under the feudal system of military service and tenure. ME. ▸†**b** A title placed after a man's surname as a designation of rank. LME–L16. ▸**c** A personal attendant or servant; a follower. LME.
2 A person in ancient history or mythology regarded as holding a position or rank similar to that of a medieval squire (sense 1a). Long *rare* or *obsolete*. LME.
3 A man who escorts a woman in public; a gallant, a lover. L16.
4 a A country gentleman, a landed proprietor, *esp.* the chief landowner in a village or district. Also (now chiefly *colloq.*) used as a title placed before the surname. E17. ▸**b** Used as a form of polite address to any gentleman not formally a squire. Now *esp.* (*colloq.*), a jocular form of address from one man to another. E19.
5 A magistrate; a lawyer, a judge; a local dignitary. Also used as a title placed before the surname. *US.* E19.
6 A young snapper fish. *Austral.* L19.

📖 **1c squire of the body** *Hist.* an officer who is personal attendant to a king, nobleman, or other high dignitary. 3 *Publishers Weekly* She has a date . . . Her squire is handsome Dave Townsend. **squire of dames** a man who devotes himself to the service of women or plays marked attentions to them. 4a GEO. ELIOT He had been mole-catching on Squire Cass's land. b M. DUFFY The duty sergeant picked among the contents . . . 'What's this lot then squire?'

▪ **squirage** *noun* (*rare*) the body of country squires; a book containing a list or account of these: M19. **squiral** *adjective* (*rare*) = SQUIRELY L18. **squiralty** *noun* (*rare*) the existence or class of squires; the position of a squire: M19. **squiredom** *noun* (*a*) the position or status of a squire; (*b*) squires collectively: M17. **squiˈreen** *noun* a petty squire; a small landowner, a country gentleman, esp. in Ireland: E19. **squirehood** *noun* = SQUIREDOM L17. **squireless** *adjective* E19. **squirelet** *noun* a petty squire, a small landowner; a squireling: E19. **squirelike** *adverb* & *adjective* (*a*) *adverb* (*rare*, Shakes.) in the manner of a squire or attendant; humbly, submissively; (*b*) *adjective* like (that of) a squire: E17 **squireling** *noun* (*a*) a petty squire, a squirelet; (*b*) a young squire: L17. **squirely** *adjective* belonging or relating to a squire or the squirearchy; befitting a squire: E17. **squireship** *noun* (*a*) the position or dignity of squire; squirehood; (*b*) (with possess. adjective, as ***his squireship*** etc.) a title of respect given to a squire: E17. **squiress** *noun* a female squire; the wife of a squire or country gentleman: E19. **squiret** *noun* (*rare*) = SQUIRELET M19. **squirish** *adjective* †(*a*) *slang* foolish; (*b*) characteristic of or befitting a squire; (*c*) having the appearance or character of a country squire: E18. **squirism** *noun* = SQUIREDOM E19. **squiˈrocracy** *noun* (*rare*) = SQUIREARCHY *noun*[1] M19.

†**squire** *noun*[2] var. of SQUARE *noun*.

squire /ˈskwʌɪə/ *verb.* LME.
[from SQUIRE *noun*[1].]
1 *verb trans.* Of a man: escort, accompany, conduct (a lady); go out with. LME.
2 *verb trans.* with *it*. Act as a squire; play the squire. L17.
3 *verb trans.* Entitle or address as 'Squire' or 'Esquire'. *rare.* M19.

📖 1 R. FRAME The girl he'd been squiring had abandoned him. G. DALY Millais squired his daughter to . . parties.

squirearch /ˈskwʌɪərɑːk/ *noun.* Also **-rarch.** M19.
[Back-form. from next, after *monarch* etc.]
A member of the squirearchy; a squire as a local magnate.
▪ **squiˈrearchal**, **squiˈrearchial**, **squiˈrearchical** *adjectives* belonging to or characteristic of the squirearchy or a squirearch M19.

squirearchy /ˈskwʌɪərɑːki/ *noun*[1]. Also **-rarchy.** L18.
[from SQUIRE *noun*[1] + -ARCHY, after *hierarchy*, *monarchy*, etc.]
1 a The collective body of squires, landed proprietors, or country gentry; the class to which squires belong, esp. with regard to its political or social influence. L18. ▸**b** A class or body of squires. M19.
2 The position or dignity of a squire. *rare.* M19.
3 Rule or government by a squire or squires. *rare.* M19.

Squirearchy /ˈskwʌɪərɑːki/ *noun*[2]. M20.
[Sir John Collings *Squire* (1884–1958), English poet and writer, punningly after prec.]
The influential literary circle of critics, poets, etc., which surrounded Squire, esp. during his editorship of the *London Mercury* (1919–34).

squirl /skwəːl/ *noun. colloq.* M19.
[Perh. blend of SQUIGGLE *noun*[2] and TWIRL *noun* or WHIRL *noun*.]
A flourish, a twirl, esp. in handwriting.

squirm /skwəːm/ *verb & noun.* L17.
[Of symbolic origin: prob. assoc. with *worm*.]
▶ **A** *verb.* **1** *verb intrans.* Wriggle, writhe. Also foll. by *along*, *out*, *round*, *up*, etc. L17.
2 *verb intrans.* Be painfully affected by a reproof, sarcasm, etc.; show or feel embarrassment or discomfiture. E19.
3 *verb trans.* Foll. by *out*: utter with a squirm. *rare.* L19.

📖 1 S. O'FAOLÁIN We fell upon . . the moss, squirming around like legless things. E. BIRNEY The roomful of . . sweating men . . squirmed on the benches. G. SWIFT He tries to squirm free but I catch him by the collar. 2 N. HORNBY I began to squirm when watching England games on TV.

▶**B** *noun.* **1** A squirming or writhing movement; a wriggle. **M19.**
2 *NAUTICAL.* A twist in a rope. **M19.**
3 A twisting or curving form of decoration characteristic of art nouveau; *colloq. the* style of such decoration. **E20.**
■ **squirmer** *noun* a person who squirms, esp. with embarrassment; an evasive person: **M20.** **squirmy** *adjective* (*a*) given to squirming or writhing, wriggly; (*b*) of the nature of a squirm: **M19.**

squirr /skwəː/ *verb trans.* Now *rare.* **E18.**
[Var. of **SKIRR** *verb.*]
Throw (*away*) with a rapid whirling or skimming motion.

squirrel /ˈskwɪr(ə)l/ *noun.* **ME.**
[Aphet. from Anglo-Norman *esquirel*, Old French *esquireul*, *escureul* (mod. *écureuil*) from Proto-Romance dim. of Latin *sciurus* from Greek *skiouros*, prob. from *skia* shade + *oura* tail.]
1 Any of various slender agile seed-eating arboreal rodents having a long bushy tail and furry coat, chiefly of the genus *Sciurus* and related genera, noted for hoarding nuts for food in winter. Also ***tree-squirrel***. **ME.** ▸**b** The skin or fur of the squirrel, esp. as dressed and used for clothing; a coat etc. made of this fur. **LME.** ▸**c** A person or animal regarded as displaying some characteristic of a squirrel. Usu. *contempt.* **M16.**
2 Any of various arboreal or ground-dwelling rodents, *esp.* one of the family Sciuridae. Usu. with specifying word. **L16.**
3 In full ***squirrel-fish***. A member of the family Holocentridae of mainly brightly coloured spiny nocturnal fishes of tropical reefs. **M18.**
†**4** The prairie dog. *US. rare.* Only in **E19.**

📖 **1** ***grey squirrel***: see **GREY** *adjective.* ***red squirrel***: see **RED** *adjective.* **c** *Today* He is a . . squirrel Even the ordered office . . bears signs of hoarding. **2** ***chipping squirrel***, ***flying squirrel***, ***ground squirrel***, ***palm squirrel***, ***Richardson's ground squirrel***, ***scaly-tailed squirrel***, etc.

Comb.: **squirrel cage** (*a*) a cage for a squirrel, *esp.* one containing a runged cylinder which revolves as the squirrel moves on it; (*b*) *ELECTRICITY* a small electric rotor or other device containing a series of bars, rods, etc., arranged parallel to the axis of a cylinder; **squirrel-corn** = ***turkey-corn*** s.v. **TURKEY** *noun*[2]; **squirrel-dog**: used for hunting squirrels; ***squirrel-fish***: see sense 3 above; ***squirrel hake***: see **HAKE** *noun*[1] 2a; **squirrel-headed** *adjective* shallow-brained; **squirrel monkey** any of several S. American monkeys of the genus *Saimiri*, esp. the common yellowish *Saimiri sciureus*.
■ **squirrelish** *adjective* resembling or of the nature of a squirrel **M19.** **squirrel-like** *adjective & adverb* (*a*) *adjective* resembling (that of) a squirrel; (*b*) *adverb* in the manner of a squirrel: **M19.** **squirrelly** *adjective* (*a*) resembling or characteristic of a squirrel; (*b*) inclined to bustle about; (of a person) unpredictable, crazy, nervy: **E20.**

squirrel /ˈskwɪr(ə)l/ *verb.* Infl. **-ll-**, *-**l**-. **L16.**
[from the noun.]
†**1 a** *verb intrans.* Hunt squirrels. Only in **L16.** ▸**b** *verb trans.* Hunt as one does a squirrel. **L16–M17.**
2 *verb intrans.* Go *round* in circles like a caged squirrel; run or scurry like a squirrel. **E20.**
3 *verb trans.* Store *away* in the manner of a squirrel; save, hoard. **M20.**

📖 **3** C. McCULLOUGH He had squirreled . . spare parts away, and painstakingly repaired the . . motor. J. SUTHERLAND Squirreling . . knowledge away for some future great work.

squirrel-tail /ˈskwɪr(ə)lteɪl/ *noun.* **LME.**
[from **SQUIRREL** *noun* + **TAIL** *noun*[1].]
1 The tail of a squirrel. **LME.**
†**2** A kind of lobworm. **M17–M19.**
3 In full ***squirrel-tail grass***. Any of several kinds of wild barley, *esp.* sea barley, *Hordeum marinum*. **L18.**
Comb.: ***squirrel-tail grass***: see sense 3 above; **squirrel-tail fescue** a European grass of dry places, *Vulpia bromoides*, resembling rat's-tail fescue but with a shorter panicle.

squirt /skwəːt/ *noun.* **LME.**
[from the verb.]
1 a (Usu. with *the.*) Diarrhoea; *sing.* & (*dial.*) in *pl.*, an attack of diarrhoea. **LME.** ▸†**b** Semi-liquid excrement. **L16–M19.**
2 a A small tubular instrument by which water etc. may be squirted; a syringe. **LME.** ▸**b** A larger instrument of the same type, used esp. as a fire extinguisher. **L16.**
3 a A small quantity of liquid squirted; a small jet or spray, a spatter; an act of squirting. **LME.** ▸**b** A burst of gunfire. *Air Force slang.* **M20.** ▸**c** A compressed radio signal transmitted at high speed. **M20.**
4 An insignificant but presumptuous or contemptible person; a fop. Also, a child, a young person. *colloq.* (orig. *US*). **M19.**
5 A display of rhetoric; a showy recitation. *US.* **M19.**

📖 **3a** M. ATWOOD A girl giving away free squirts of some . . new perfume.

squirt /skwəːt/ *verb.* **ME.**
[Imit.]
▶**I** *verb intrans.* **1 a** Eject water in a jetlike stream. **ME.** ▸**b** Have diarrhoea. **M16.**
2 Move swiftly or quickly; dart or frisk *about, up and down*, etc. **L16.**
3 Issue or be ejected in a jetlike stream; spurt. **M19.**

📖 **3** BEVERLEY CLEARY Toothpaste squirted all over the bathroom. D. ATTENBOROUGH Tread on one of these . . and a jet of water squirts up your leg.

▶**II** *verb trans.* **4** Inject (a liquid) esp. by means of a squirt or syringe. Usu. foll. by *in, into.* **M16.**
5 Cause (liquid) to issue in a jet from a squirt or syringe; eject or propel in a stream from a small opening. (Foll. by *in(to), on(to), out*, etc.) **L16.**
6 Wet (a surface) with liquid by means of spurting or squirting. **E17.**
7 Transmit (information) in highly compressed or speeded-up form. **L20.**

📖 **5** D. H. LAWRENCE She would have liked to squirt water down his . . neck. D. LEAVITT He . . squirted . . detergent onto a sponge. **7** C. McCARRY Radio equipment . . could squirt . . words from one continent to another via satellite.

Comb.: **squirt boat** a small, highly manoeuvrable kayak; **squirt can** a flexible oilcan that ejects oil when compressed; **squirt-gun** a toy syringe; a water-pistol.
■ **squirter** *noun* †(*a*) a person who shoots jerkily with the bow; (*b*) a person who squirts something; (*c*) a device for squirting water etc.; (*d*) *slang* a revolver: **M16.** **squirting** *adjective* (*a*) (esp. of a person) contemptible, insignificant; (*b*) that squirts something, *esp.* that ejects a jetlike stream of liquid (***squirting cucumber***: see **CUCUMBER** 3): **L16.**

†**squise** *verb* see **SQUEEZE** *verb.*

squish /skwɪʃ/ *verb & noun.* **M17.**
[Imit.]
▶**A** *verb.* **1** *verb trans.* Squeeze, squash. Now *dial.* & *colloq.* **M17.**
2 *verb intrans.* Make a gushing or splashing sound when walked in or on, yield easily to pressure thus when squeezed or squashed; gush up, squirt out. **L18.** ▸**b** *verb trans.* & *intrans.* Make (one's way) with a squishing sound. *colloq.* **M20.**

📖 **1** C. LASSALLE This elephant had trodden on its keeper's head. 'Squished . . like a tomato,' she explained. **2** G. BENFORD Melting snow . . squished under his boots.

▶**B** *noun.* **1** Marmalade. *arch. slang.* **L19.**
2 A squishing sound. **E20.**
3 *ENGINEERING.* In some internal-combustion engines, the forced radial flow of the fuel mixture into the combustion chamber as the piston approaches the cylinder head. Freq. *attrib.* **M20.**
4 *LINGUISTICS.* A continuum or linear progression held to exist between categories (esp. parts of speech) usu. considered discrete. **L20.**
¶ As noun recorded earlier in **SQUISH-SQUASH**.

squish-squash /ˈskwɪʃskwɒʃ/ *adverb, noun, & verb.* **L18.**
[Redupl. of **SQUISH**.]
▶**A** *adverb & noun.* (With) a squishing sound. **L18.**
▶**B** *verb intrans.* = **SQUISH** *verb* 2. **M19.**

squishy /ˈskwɪʃi/ *adjective.* **M19.**
[from **SQUISH** + **-Y**[1].]
Tending to squish; of a soft wet texture that yields easily to pressure.
■ **squishiness** *noun* **E20.**

squit /skwɪt/ *noun*[1]. *dial. & slang.* **E19.**
[Perh. rel. to **SQUIT** *verb*: cf. also **SKIT** *noun*[2], **SQUIRT** *noun* 5.]
1 A small or insignificant person. **E19.**
2 Silly talk; nonsense. **L19.**

squit /skwɪt/ *noun*[2]. *dial. & colloq.* **M19.**
[Prob. back-form. from **SQUITTER**.]
Diarrhoea. Now only in *pl.* (with *the*).

squit /skwɪt/ *noun*[3]. *US.* **L19.**
[App. reduced form of **SQUETEAGUE**.]
= **SQUETEAGUE**.

squit /skwɪt/ *verb trans. obsolete* exc. *dial.* Infl. **-tt-**. **L16.**
[Perh. imit.]
Squirt.

squitch /skwɪtʃ/ *noun.* See also **SCUTCH** *noun*[1]. **L18.**
[Alt. of **QUITCH**.]
Any of several rhizomatous grasses occurring as weeds, esp. couch grass, *Elytrigia repens*.

squitch /skwɪtʃ/ *verb.* Now *dial.* **L16.**
[Var. of **QUETCH**.]
†**1** *verb intrans.* Move suddenly and quickly; flinch, wince. Only in **L16.**
2 *verb trans.* Twitch or jerk (a thing *away*). **L17.**

squitter /ˈskwɪtə/ *verb & noun.* **L16.**
[Imit.]
▶**A** *verb.* **1** *verb trans. & intrans.* Squirt; spatter, splutter. Now *dial.* **L16.**
2 *verb intrans.* Have diarrhoea. Now *dial.* **E17.**
▶**B** *noun.* **1** Diarrhoea. Usu. in *pl.* (with *the*). Now *dial.* & *colloq.* **M17.**
2 *RADAR.* Random pulses produced by a transponder in the absence of interrogating signals. **M20.**

squiz /skwɪz/ *noun & verb. Austral. & NZ slang.* **E20.**
[Prob. from **QUIZ** *noun*[2] blended with **SQUINT** *noun.*]
▶**A** *noun.* Pl. **-zzes**. A look, a glance. **E20.**
▶**B** *verb trans. & intrans.* Infl. **-zz-**. Look or glance (at). **M20.**

†**squize** *verb* see **SQUEEZE** *verb.*

squizzed /skwɪzd/ *adjective. US slang. rare.* **M19.**
[Origin unkn.]
Drunk, tipsy.

squizzle /ˈskwɪz(ə)l/ *verb intrans. colloq. & dial.* Now *rare.* **M19.**
[Imit.]
Squirt *out*; squish.

squodgy /ˈskwɒdʒi/ *adjective. colloq.* **L20.**
[Imit.: cf. **SQUASHY**.]
Soft and soggy; squelchy.

squop /skwɒp/ *verb & noun.* **M20.**
[Origin unkn.]
▶**A** *verb trans. & intrans.* Infl. **-pp-**. In tiddlywinks, cover and immobilize (an opponent's wink) with one's own. **M20.**
▶**B** *noun.* The action of covering an opponent's wink with one's own; a wink covered in this way. **M20.**
■ **squopper** *noun* a player who squops **M20.**

squush /skwʌʃ/ *verb intrans. US colloq. & dial.* **L19.**
[Imit.: cf. **SQUASH** *verb*, **SQUDGE**, **SQUISH** *verb.*]
1 Collapse into a soft, pulpy mass. **L19.**
2 Squelch, squeeze messily. **E20.**

SR *abbreviation*[1].
Hist. Southern Railway.

sr *abbreviation*[2].
Steradian(s).

Sr *symbol.*
CHEMISTRY. Strontium.

Sr. *abbreviation.*
1 Senior.
2 Señor.
3 Signor.
4 *ECCLESIASTICAL.* Sister.

S-R *abbreviation.*
PSYCHOLOGY. Stimulus-response.

sraddha *noun* var. of **SHRADH**.

SRAM /ˈɛsram/ *abbreviation.*
COMPUTING. Static random access memory.

Sranan /ˈsrɑːnən/ *noun & adjective.* **M20.**
[Prob. from Taki-Taki, in full *Sranan Tongo* Suriname tongue.]
= **TAKI-TAKI**.

srang *noun* var. of **SANG** *noun*[3].

SRC *abbreviation.*
Science Research Council.

Sri *noun* var. of **SHRI**.

'sright /srʌɪt/ *interjection. colloq.* **M20.**
[Aphet.]
That's right!

Sri Lankan /ʃrɪ ˈlaŋk(ə)n, srɪ ˈlaŋk(ə)n/ *noun & adjectival phr.* **L20.**
[from *Sri Lanka* (see below) + **-AN**.]
▶**A** *noun phr.* A native or inhabitant of Sri Lanka, an island in the Indian Ocean formerly called Ceylon; a person of Sri Lankan descent. **L20.**
▶**B** *adjectival phr.* Of or pertaining to Sri Lanka or its people. **L20.**

SRMN *abbreviation.*
State Registered Mental Nurse.

SRN *abbreviation.*
State Registered Nurse.

sRNA *abbreviation.*
BIOCHEMISTRY. Soluble RNA.

SRO *abbreviation.*
1 Single-room occupancy. *US.*
2 *THEATRICAL.* Standing room only.

sruti /ˈʃrʊti/ *noun.* **L18.**
[Sanskrit *śruti* sound, microtone.]
MUSIC. A microtonal interval in Indian music.

SS *abbreviation.*
1 Saints.
2 *Hist.* German *Schutzstaffel*, the internal security force of Nazi Germany.
3 Steamship.

SSAFA *abbreviation.*
Soldiers', Sailors', and Airmen's Families Association.

SSB *abbreviation.*
RADIO. Single sideband (transmission).

SSC *abbreviation.*
(In Scotland) Solicitor to the Supreme Court.

SSE *abbreviation.*
South-south-east.

SSL *abbreviation.*
COMPUTING. Secure Sockets Layer, a computing protocol that ensures the security of data sent via the Internet by using encryption.

SSN *abbreviation.*
Severely subnormal.

SSP *abbreviation.*
Statutory sick pay.

SSR *abbreviation.*
1 Secondary surveillance radar.
2 *Hist.* Soviet Socialist Republic.

SSRC *abbreviation.*
Social Science Research Council.

SSSI *abbreviation.*
Site of Special Scientific Interest.

SST *abbreviation.*
Supersonic transport.

SSW *abbreviation.*
South-south-west.

ST *abbreviation*[1]. *colloq.*
Sanitary towel.

St *abbreviation*[2].
1 Saint.
2 PHYSICS. Stokes.

St *noun & adjective* see SAINT *noun & adjective.*

st /(ə)st/ *interjection.* M16.
[Repr. a checked sibilation. Cf. HIST, WHISHT *interjections.*]
Demanding silence or quiet: hush!, sh! Also, urging a dog etc.: get back! attack!

St. *abbreviation*[1].
Street.

st. *abbreviation*[2].
1 Stone(s) (in weight).
2 CRICKET. Stumped by.

-st *suffix* var. of -EST[2].

Sta. *abbreviation.*
Station.

Staatsoper /ˈʃtaːtsoːpər/ *noun.* E20.
[German, lit. 'State opera'.]
The principal opera-house in Vienna, partially subsidized by the Austrian government; the resident company of this opera-house.

stab /stab/ *noun*[1]. LME.
[from the verb.]
1 A wound produced by stabbing; *transf.* a pierced hole. LME.
2 An act or instance of stabbing; a thrust or blow with a pointed weapon or tool; *transf.* a vigorous thrust, a jabbing lunge or gesture; *fig.* a sharply painful (physical or mental) sensation, a sudden pang; a blow aimed at a person's feelings etc. M16. ▸**b** A flash *of* bright colour against dark surroundings. L19. ▸**c** A try, an attempt. Chiefly in ***make a stab at, have a stab at.*** *colloq.* L19.
3 BILLIARDS & SNOOKER etc. More fully ***stab stroke.*** A short stiff stroke causing the striker's ball to stop dead or travel slowly after striking the object ball. L19.
4 OIL INDUSTRY. The operation of guiding a length of pipe to connect with another. L20.

> **1** DICKENS You found me with this stab and an ugly bruise or two. **2** H. BROOKE Pulling out his butcher's knife from a sheath . . he . . made a stab at my heart. R. K. NARAYAN A momentary stab of suspicion that this man was at the back of it all. W. RAEPER He felt a violent stab of pain in . . his chest. **stab in the back** *colloq.* a treacherous attack, a betrayal. **c** J. COX One last stab at reconciliation.

Comb.: **stab-and-drag** *noun & adjective* (ARCHAEOLOGY) (designating) a technique of ceramic decoration in which the surface of a pot is pierced at intervals by a pointed instrument which is then partially withdrawn and drawn along the surface; **stab-culture** MICROBIOLOGY a culture which is inoculated by means of a needle thrust deeply into the medium; **stab-stitch** *noun & verb* (**a**) *noun* a stitch in which the needle is pushed through the fabric at right angles; (**b**) *verb trans. & intrans.* stitch in this way; ***stab stroke***: see sense 3 above.

stab /stab/ *noun*[2]. *Printers' slang* (now *rare*). M19.
[Abbreviation.]
= ESTABLISHMENT 2b.
Comb.: **stab-man** a printer on weekly wages rather than on piece-work.

stab /stab/ *noun*[3] *& adjective.* E20.
[German = rod (in *stabförmig* rod-shaped, *Stabkern* rod-nucleus): cf. STAFF *noun*[1].]
MEDICINE. (Designating) a type of white blood cell characterized by a nucleus in the form of a single bent or twisted rod.

stab /stab/ *verb.* Infl. **-bb-**. LME.
[Origin unkn.]
1 *verb intrans.* Wound or kill a person by a thrust with the point of a knife, dagger, etc.; pierce a surface with the point of a tool etc.; aim a stroke or blow (*at*) with such a weapon or tool; make a jabbing lunge or gesture. Also, cause a sharp physical or mental sensation, aim a blow *at* a person's reputation etc. LME. ▸**b** Make a hole *through*; cut *through* in the manner of a pointed weapon. L19.
2 *verb trans.* Thrust (a pointed weapon or tool) through or into; direct (the hand etc.) in a jabbing lunge or gesture. LME. ▸**b** Make (a hole) by stabbing. E20.
3 *verb trans.* Wound, pierce, or kill with a thrust of a pointed weapon; pierce with the point of a tool; make a jabbing lunge or gesture at. Also, cause sharp mental distress or pangs to (a person, feelings, conscience, etc.). M16.
4 *verb trans.* Prick. Now *dial.* L16.
5 *verb trans.* Roughen the surface of (a wall etc.) with a sharp tool etc. before applying plaster. M19.
6 *verb trans.* BOOKBINDING. Pierce (a set of sheets) to make a hole for a binding thread etc.; bind together the sheets (of a pamphlet etc.) with thread etc. inserted through pierced holes. M19.
7 *verb trans.* OIL INDUSTRY. Guide (a length of pipe) so as to make a connection with another. M20.

> **1** SHELLEY Let them ride among you there, Slash, and stab, and maim, and hew. C. WOOD He . . stabbed at the snow with his sticks. B. BOVA The news of Doris's death . . stabbed deep into his flesh. **2** M. RENAULT He yawned then, and died; but still I stabbed in the dagger. *transf.: Oxford Times* To stab home his 14th goal of the season. **3** J. R. LOWELL Her silence stabbed his conscience through and through. C. CHAPLIN She picks up the paper-knife . . and stabs the villain, who falls dead. M. SPARK Freddy's mother had been stabbed to death by an old servant. **stab in the back** attack treacherously or unfairly, betray.

■ **stabbed** *ppl adjective* (**a**) wounded by stabbing; perforated with punctured holes; (**b**) *rare* (of a wound or hole) made by stabbing: L16. **stabber** *noun* a person who or thing which stabs; a knife, a dagger, a harpoon: L16. **stabbing** *noun* the action of the verb; an act or instance of this, a wounding or killing with a knife or dagger: LME. **stabbing** *adjective* that stabs; (of pain) sharp and sudden, characterized by twinges comparable to the effect of a stab: L16. **stabbingly** *adverb* (*rare*) L17.

Stabat Mater /stɑːbat ˈmɑːtə, steɪbat ˈmeɪtə/ *noun phr.* M19.
[Latin, from the opening words *stabat mater dolorosa* stood the mother, full of grief.]
A Latin hymn on the sorrows of the Virgin Mary at the Crucifixion; a musical setting for this.

Stabex /ˈsteɪbɛks/ *noun.* Also **s-**. L20.
[Shortened from *stabilization of export prices.*]
COMMERCE. A scheme operated by the European Community guaranteeing developing countries in Africa, the Caribbean, and the Pacific a minimum price for staple commodities in the event of a shortfall in their export earnings.

stabilate /ˈsteɪbɪleɪt/ *noun & verb.* M20.
[from Latin *stabilis* STABLE *adjective* + -ATE[2].]
BIOLOGY. ▶**A** *noun.* A sample of a micro-organism from a homogeneous source which is preserved by freezing on a single occasion to serve as a standard. M20.
▶ **B** *verb trans.* Make into a stabilate. L20.

stabilator /ˈsteɪbɪleɪtə/ *noun.* M20.
[from STABIL(IZER + ELEV)ATOR.]
AERONAUTICS. An adjustable control surface at the tail of an aircraft combining the functions of an elevator and a horizontal tailplane.

stabile /ˈsteɪbʌɪl/ *noun.* M20.
[formed as next after MOBILE *noun*[3].]
A rigid free-standing (usu. abstract) sculpture or construction of wire, sheet metal, wood, etc.

stabile /ˈsteɪbɪl/ *adjective. rare.* L18.
[from Latin *stabilis* STABLE *adjective*: see -ILE.]
Firmly established, enduring, lasting.

stabilimentum /stəbɪlɪˈmɛntəm/ *noun.* Pl. **-ta** /-tə/. E20.
[Latin = a stay, a support, from *stabilire* make stable, from *stabilis* STABLE *adjective.*]
ZOOLOGY. A conspicuous broad band of silk running across the web of certain kinds of spider.

stabilimeter /stabɪˈlɪmɪtə/ *noun.* E20.
[from STABILITY + -METER.]
1 AERONAUTICS. A device for ascertaining the stability of a model aircraft. Now *rare.* E20.
2 BIOLOGY. A device attached to or forming an animal's cage, the movement of which is recorded as a measure of the animal's activity. M20.

stabilise *verb*, **stabiliser** *noun* vars. of STABILIZE, STABILIZER.

stabilism /ˈsteɪbɪlɪz(ə)m/ *noun.* L20.
[from Latin *stabilis* STABLE *adjective* + -ISM, after MOBILISM.]
GEOLOGY. (Belief in) the hypothesis that continents are not capable of lateral movement.

■ **stabilist** *noun & adjective* (**a**) *noun* a supporter of stabilism; (**b**) *adjective* of or pertaining to stabilism or stabilists: L20.

stabilitate /stəˈbɪlɪteɪt/ *verb trans. rare.* M17.
[medieval Latin *stabilitat-* pa. ppl stem of *stabilitare*, from Latin *stabilitas* STABILITY: see -ATE[3].]
Give stability to.

stability /stəˈbɪlɪti/ *noun.* ME.
[Old French *(e)stableté* from Latin *stabilitas*, formed as STABLE *adjective.*]
1 Firmness or steadiness of character, resolution, steadfastness. Now also, mental soundness. ME.
2 The quality of being firmly fixed or placed; (capacity for) resistance to displacement or overbalancing; maintenance of or ability to maintain equilibrium or an upright position. LME. ▸**b** Fixity of position, tendency to remain in place. M16. ▸**c** The capacity of a physical system, chemical compound, isotope, subatomic particle, etc., to resist disintegration, decomposition, or decay; an instance of this. M19.
3 Resistance of an immaterial thing to destruction or essential change, enduring quality; constancy in composition or nature; steadiness and continuity of a condition, institution, etc.; an instance of this. LME. ▸**b** A fixed or settled thing. M19.

> **1** *Review of English Studies* Men can create visions of . . ideal life, but lack . . stability to make such visions an enduring reality. **2** J. S. FOSTER The stability of the building involves the equilibrium of all the forces. *Which?* The stability affected by crosswinds and bumps in corners. **3** H. MACMILLAN An aggressive action by Nasser threatening the stability of the whole Middle East. *Dance* A production . . whose earnings will secure a measure of financial stability. ***spiral stability***: see SPIRAL *adjective*[1].

stabilize /ˈsteɪbɪlʌɪz/ *verb.* Also **-ise**. M19.
[from STABLE *adjective* infl. by the stem of STABILITY: see -IZE. Cf. French *stabiliser.*]
1 *verb trans.* Make (more) stable; give stability to (a ship, aircraft, etc.), fit stabilizers to; give a stable character or value to. M19.
2 *verb intrans.* Be stabilized; become stable. M20.

> **1** *Publishers Weekly* The government of France has succeeded in stabilizing the franc at 25.52 to the dollar. *Times* The rocket during the whole of its flight was stabilized, to prevent rotation. J. K. GALBRAITH Efforts . . to stabilize the economy. P. DALLY She soon began to eat more and stabilise her weight. **2** ANTHONY SMITH There are considerable brain-wave changes during childhood, but the patterns stabilize before adulthood is reached.

■ **stabiliˈzation** *noun* L19. **stabilized** *adjective* made stable; (of cloth) treated in order to prevent stretching or shrinking; (of a drug addict) able to live more or less normally on a repeated constant dose: L19.

stabilizer /ˈsteɪbɪlʌɪzə/ *noun.* Also **-iser**. E20.
[from prec. + -ER[1].]
1 A device or apparatus fitted to keep something stable; *spec.* (**a**) (chiefly *N. Amer.*) the horizontal tailplane of an aircraft; (**b**) a gyroscopic device to reduce the rolling of a ship in heavy seas; (**c**) (chiefly *N. Amer.*) a stabilizing device on a motor vehicle or tractor, *spec.* = ***sway-bar*** (b) s.v. SWAY *verb*; (**d**) (in *pl.*) two small supporting wheels fitted one at each side of the rear wheel of a child's bicycle. E20.
2 Orig., a substance added to an explosive to make it less liable to spontaneous decomposition. Now, an additive which inhibits chemical or physical change in a substance, *esp.* one used to prevent the breakdown of emulsions. E20.
3 ELECTRONICS. **a** A circuit or device for preventing unwanted feedback. E20. ▸**b** A circuit that holds the output voltage of a power supply at a constant level despite changes in supply voltage or load, by comparison with a fixed reference voltage. Also ***stabilizer circuit.*** E20.
4 Any of various financial mechanisms which resist variation in an economic system. M20.
5 MATH. A subgroup of a permutation group, being the group of elements that map some subset of the permuted elements on to itself. M20.

Stabit /ˈstabɪt/ *noun.* M20.
[Invented word, suggested by STABILITY.]
ENGINEERING. A large mass of concrete so shaped that when large numbers are placed together they tend to interlock and form a strong barrier that can act as a coastal breakwater.

stable /ˈsteɪb(ə)l/ *noun*[1]. ME.
[Aphet. from Old French *estable* stable, pigsty (mod. *étable* cowshed) from Latin *stabulum*, from Proto-Romance base also of Latin *stare* stand. Cf. next.]
1 A building set apart and adapted for the keeping of horses (and orig. other domestic animals), freq. divided into individual stalls and accommodating a number of horses. Freq. in *pl.* ME. ▸**b** A collection of horses belonging to one stable. L16.
2 a An establishment where racehorses are kept and trained. Also, the racehorses etc. of a particular stable;

the proprietors and staff of such an establishment. **E19.** ▸**b** *transf.* A group or collection of people, products, etc., having a common origin or affiliation; a person, establishment, or organization producing such types of people, products, etc. **L19.**

3 *MILITARY.* In *pl.* Duty or work in stables; the bugle-call for this duty. **L19.**

> **1** SHAKES. *Rich. II* I was a poor groom of thy stable. F. REYNOLDS Sending our horses to the stables, and seeing them well rubbed, and fed. **2a** *Times* Yorkshire stables did not enjoy a . . happy Ebor Handicap meeting. *transf.*: S. MOSS Returned to Europe at the head of a racing stable of mechanics. **b from the same stable** *colloq.* from the same source, of similar nature and origin.

Comb.: **stable block** a building housing stables; **stable-boy** a boy or man employed in a stable; **stable companion** = *stablemate* below; **stable door** the door of a stable (***shut the stable door when the horse has bolted***, take preventive measures too late); **stable-fly** a small biting fly, *Stomoxys calcitrans* (family Muscidae), the adults of which feed on the blood of domestic animals; **stable girl** a girl or woman employed in a stable; **stable-lad** a person employed in a stable; **stable-lass** = ***stable-girl*** above; **stableman** a person employed in a stable; **stablemate** (*a*) a horse from the same stable; (*b*) a person, product, etc., from the same source, a member of the same organization.

■ **stableful** *noun* as much or as many as will fill a stable **M19.**

stable /ˈsteɪb(ə)l/ *noun*^{2}. **E20.**
[Origin uncertain: perh. same word as prec.]
MINING. Also more fully ***stable hole***. An excavation in a face to accommodate a coal-cutting machine or loader working into it.

stable /ˈsteɪb(ə)l/ *adjective.* **ME.**
[Anglo-Norman *stable*, Old French *estable* (mod. *stable*) from Latin *stabilis*, from base of *stare* stand: see -BLE.]

1 Firmly fixed or placed, not easily displaced or overbalanced; maintaining or able to maintain equilibrium or an erect position; (of a support or foundation) not likely to give way or shift. **ME.** ▸**b** Firm in consistency, solid. Now *rare.* **M16.**

2 Keeping to one place, not shifting in position, stationary. **ME.**

3 Of a condition, institution, group, etc.: firmly established, not liable to destruction or essential change; fundamentally constant in composition or nature. Of a property, agency, etc.: continuing without essential or permanent change. **ME.** ▸†**b** Permanent, reliable, enduring; (of a law, promise, judgement, etc.) not to be repealed or retracted. **ME–M18.** ▸**c** Of a theory, conclusion, etc.: not likely to be disproved or found wanting. **L15.** ▸**d** Of a physical system, chemical compound, isotope, subatomic particle, etc.: not readily or spontaneously disintegrating, decomposing, or decaying. **M19.**

4 Of a person etc.: resolute, steadfast; of steady character, not fickle or wavering. Now also, mentally sound, well-adjusted, sane and sensible. **ME.** ▸†**b** Of a god: unchangeable. **LME–E18.**

†**5** Of a look or expression: steady, unabashed. **LME–M17.**

> **1** J. S. BLACKIE A stable physical platform to stand on. *Pilot* A very stable aircraft, laterally, directionally, and in pitch. ***stable** EQUILIBRIUM.* **3** J. A. FROUDE His kingdom demanded the security of a stable succession. S. UNWIN Absorption of small insolvent firms by financially stable publishers. *Nature* White sifaka and ringtailed lemur populations have remained stable since 1963. A. STORR A stable home in which continuing care is taken for granted. *Daily News (New York)* Awake and in stable condition after his bypass operation. **4** JO GRIMOND He was not stable; you could never be sure of his mood. C. EASTON A solid, stable young man—the sympathetic rock that Jackie needed.

■ **stableness** *noun* (now *rare*) stability **ME.**

stable /ˈsteɪb(ə)l/ *verb.* **ME.**
[from STABLE *noun*^{1}, or aphet. from Old French *establer*.]

1 *verb trans.* Put or keep (a horse) in a stable or shelter; *transf.* base or position (a train etc.) at a depot. **ME.** ▸**b** Of a building: provide stabling or shelter for. **E20.**

2 *verb intrans.* Of an animal etc.: live or shelter in a stable. **E16.**

Stableford /ˈsteɪb(ə)lfəd/ *adjective & noun.* Also **s-.** **M20.**
[Dr Frank B. *Stableford* (*c* 1870–1959), medical practitioner, who devised this method of scoring.]
GOLF. (Designating or pertaining to) a kind of stroke-play competition in which points are awarded according to the number of strokes taken to complete each hole.

stabler /ˈsteɪblə/ *noun.* Now *Scot.* **ME.**
[Old French *establier*, from *estable* STABLE *noun*^{1}: see -ER^2.]
A person owning or running a stable.

stabley *adjective* var. of STABLY *adjective.*

stabling /ˈsteɪblɪŋ/ *noun.* **LME.**
[from STABLE *noun*^{1} or *verb* + -ING^1.]
The action of putting or keeping horses etc. in a stable; accommodation for horses etc., stable-buildings collectively.

stablish /ˈstablɪʃ/ *verb trans. arch.* **ME.**
[Var. of ESTABLISH.]

1 Place (a thing) firmly in position, set up, establish, (a condition, institution, etc.); put (a person) in a place, office, or condition. **ME.**

2 Place beyond dispute; demonstrate, prove, ascertain. **ME.**

†**3** Ordain permanently (a law, rule, etc.). **LME–E17.**

†**4** Bring (a country etc.) into settled order. **LME–E17.**

5 Make secure, strengthen, reinforce; strengthen the faith etc. of. **LME.**

> **1** P. J. BAILEY Heaven's eternal base, Whereon God's throne is stablished.

■ **stablisher** *noun* (*rare*) **M16.**

stablishment /ˈstablɪʃm(ə)nt/ *noun. arch.* **LME.**
[Var. of ESTABLISHMENT.]

1 The action of establishing something; the condition of being established. **LME.**

2 Confirmed possession. *rare.* **E17.**

stably /ˈsteɪbli/ *adjective.* Also **-ley.** **M19.**
[from STABLE *noun*^{1} + -Y^1.]
Characteristic or reminiscent of a stable; pertaining to a stable or stables.

stably /ˈsteɪbli/ *adverb.* **ME.**
[from STABLE *adjective* + -LY^2.]
In a stable manner.

staboy /stəˈbɔɪ/ *interjection, noun, & verb. US.* Also **ste(e)boy** & other vars. **L18.**
[Perh. from ST + BOY *noun.*]
▸**A** *interjection.* Used in urging on hounds: go on! go forward! **L18.**
▸**B** *noun.* A cry of 'staboy'. *rare.* **M19.**
▸**C** *verb trans.* Urge on (hounds) with the cry 'staboy'. *rare.* **M19.**

stac *noun* see STACK *noun.*

†**staccado** *noun.* Pl. **-os.** **E17–L18.**
[Aphet. from Spanish *estacada* (whence French *estacade*) STOCKADE *noun*. Cf. STOCKADO *noun*.]
A stockade.

staccato /stəˈkɑːtəʊ/ *adjective, adverb, noun, & verb.* **E18.**
[Italian, pa. pple of *staccare* aphet. from *distaccare* DETACH.]
▸**A** *adjective & adverb.* With each note or sound sharply separated or detached from the next, with a clipped style. Opp. ***legato***. **E18.**

> J. AGATE One of those expensive mechanical dolls with a staccato utterance. M. HOCKING Half-finished sentences came staccato from her lips.

▸**B** *noun.* Pl. **-os.** A succession of disconnected notes or sounds; a staccato passage in music etc.; staccato delivery, playing, or speech. **L18.**

> P. BECKFORD The monotonous staccato of the guitar.

Comb.: **staccato mark** a dot or stroke above or below a note, indicating that it is to be played staccato.

▸**C** *verb trans.* Play or utter in a staccato manner. **E19.**

stachybotryotoxicosis /stakɪˌbɒtrɪə(ʊ)tɒksɪˈkəʊsɪs/ *noun.* Pl. **-coses** /-ˈkəʊsiːz/. **M20.**
[from mod. Latin *Stachybotrys* (see below) (from Greek *stakhus* ear of wheat + *botrus* cluster) + -O- + TOXICOSIS.]
VETERINARY MEDICINE. Toxicosis caused by toxins of the graminivorous fungus *Stachybotrys alternans*, affecting esp. horses and characterized by haemorrhage and necrosis.

stachyose /ˈstakɪəʊz, -s/ *noun.* **L19.**
[from STACHYS + -OSE^2.]
CHEMISTRY. A tetrasaccharide found in the roots of a number of plants of the genus *Stachys* and in the seeds of many legumes.

stachys /ˈsteɪkɪs/ *noun.* **M16.**
[Latin from Greek *stakhus* ear of wheat.]
Any of various labiate plants constituting the genus *Stachys*, with spiked whorls of often purple, reddish, or white flowers, including betony, *S. officinalis*, and hedge woundwort, *S. sylvatica*. Orig. *spec.*, marsh woundwort, *S. palustris*.

stack /stak/ *noun.* In sense 4 also **stac.** **ME.**
[Old Norse *stakkr* haystack from Germanic, prob. of Indo-European origin (cf. Russian *stog* haystack).]

1 A heap or pile of things, *esp.* one in an orderly arrangement. **ME.** ▸**b** *sing.* & in *pl.* A large quantity or amount, *spec.* of money. (Foll. by *of*.) *colloq.* **L19.** ▸**c** A tall set of shelving for books, esp. in a library; *sing.* & in *pl.*, a part of a library for the compact storage of books, *esp.* one to which public access is restricted. Also ***bookstack***. **L19.** ▸**d** A group or series of aircraft circling at different altitudes and awaiting landing instructions. **M20.** ▸**e** In a computer or calculator, a set of registers or storage locations which store data in such a way that the most recently stored item is the first to be retrieved; a list of items so stored, a push-down list. **M20.** ▸**f** A vertical arrangement of guitar amplification, public address, or hi-fi equipment. **L20.**

2 A circular or rectangular pile of grain in the sheaf or of hay, straw, etc., usu. with a sloping thatched top; a rick, a haystack. **ME.**

3 a A pile of sticks, firewood, etc.; *MILITARY* a pyramidal heap of rifles. **LME.** ▸**b** A measure of volume for wood and coal, usu. 108 cu. ft (approx. 3.06 cu. metres). **M17.**

4 [Cf. Faeroese *stakkur* high solitary rock in the sea.] A column of rock detached from the mainland by erosion and rising precipitously out of the sea, esp. off the coast of Scotland and the Orkneys. **L15.**

5 A number of chimneys or flues standing together; a tall chimney on a factory etc.; a chimney-stack; the chimney or funnel of a steam locomotive or ship, a smokestack. Now also (*slang*), a vertical overhead exhaust-pipe on a diesel-powered truck or similar vehicle. **M17.**

> **1** CECIL ROBERTS A large stack of unchopped firewood. D. PROFUMO She shuffled her postcards into a precise stack. **b** P. G. WODEHOUSE I'm a bit foggy as to what jute is, but . . Mr. Worple had made quite an indecently large stack out of it. C. MACINNES I've got stacks of foreign phone numbers in my diary. **c** *Cosmopolitan* 'Not on the open shelves.' . . Order it to be fetched . . from the stacks. **5** E. ROBINS The big yellow stack belched out clouds of smoke. ***blow one's stack***: see BLOW *verb*^{1}.

Comb.: **stack-garth** *north.* = ***stackyard*** below; **stack gas**: emitted by a chimney-stack; **stackyard** a rickyard.

■ **stackful** *noun* as much as a stack can contain **M19.** **stackless** *adjective* **L19.**

stack /stak/ *verb.* **ME.**
[from the noun.]

1 *verb trans.* Pile into a stack or stacks; make a stack or pile of. Also foll. by *up*. **ME.** ▸**b** Fill (a place etc.) *with* a stack or stacks of; fill generously. Also foll. by *up*. **M17.**

2 *verb intrans.* **a** Put corn or hay into stacks; make a stack or stacks. **E18.** ▸**b** Pile *up* one's chips at poker. Now chiefly *fig.*, present oneself, measure up; arise, build up. *colloq.* (chiefly *N. Amer.*). **L19.**

3 *verb trans.* **a** Shuffle or arrange (playing-cards) dishonestly to gain unfair advantage. Orig. *US.* **E19.** ▸**b** = PACK *verb*^{2} 4. **M20.**

4 a *verb trans.* Cause (aircraft) to fly around the same point at different levels while waiting to land; put (an aircraft) into a waiting stack. Freq. foll. by *up*. **M20.** ▸**b** *verb intrans.* Of (an) aircraft: fly in or enter a waiting stack. **M20.**

> **1** F. KING Stacking the chairs on top of each other in a corner. J. THURBER Everything . . was stacked on the counter in . . boxes. S. ELDRED-GRIGG The fruit was stacked up in big gleaming pyramids. **b** D. LODGE Morris helped her stack the dishwasher. C. PHILLIPS His new job stacking shelves at Vijay's Supermarket. **2b** *Sun (Baltimore)* My record stacks up favourably enough with that of any other pro. past or present.

Phrases: **stack arms** *Hist.* = ***pile arms*** s.v. PILE *verb*^{2}. **stack the cards, stack the deck**, etc., *fig.* manipulate circumstances to one's advantage. **stack the cards against**, **stack the odds against**, etc., *fig.* reduce or prejudice the chances of success of.

Comb.: **stacking fault** *CRYSTALLOGRAPHY* a break in the regular order of stacking of layers of atoms in a crystal; **stack-up** the arrangement of objects in a stack or pile; an instance of this; a build-up; *spec.* the stacking of aircraft waiting to land.

■ **stackaˈbility** *noun* ability to be stacked (easily) **M20.** **stackable** *adjective* (esp. of a chair etc.) able or designed to be stacked or piled up (easily) **M20.**

stacked /stakt/ *adjective.* **M19.**
[from prec. + -ED^1.]

1 That has been stacked, piled into a stack; piled with goods etc.; (of cards etc.) cheatingly set in a prearranged order; (of odds etc.) unfavourable. **M19.** ▸**b** *COMPUTING.* Of a task: placed in a queue for subsequent processing. Of (a stream of) data etc.: consisting of or stored in a stack. **M20.**

2 Of a woman or girl: having an attractively well-rounded figure; *esp.* having a prominent bosom. Also ***well-stacked***. *slang* (orig. *US*). **M20.**

> **1** P. O'DONNELL They worked alone . . and . . often went in against stacked odds. **stacked head** in a tape recorder, a head in which the gaps corresponding to the tracks in multi-channel recording are located one above another. **stacked heel** a heel (apparently) made from thin layers of wood etc. stacked together.

stacken-cloud /ˈstakənklaʊd/ *noun.* Now *rare* or *obsolete.* **E19.**
[App. arbitrarily from STACK *noun* + -EN^4.]
A cumulus cloud.

stacker /ˈstakə/ *noun.* **M18.**
[formed as prec. + -ER^1.]

1 A person building up a stack or pile. **M18.**

2 A machine for raising things and depositing them in a stack or pile; *spec.* a stacker crane. **L19.** ▸**b** A part of a data-processing machine in which punched cards are deposited in a stack after having passed through the machine. **M20.**

Comb.: **stacker crane** a hoist running on a fixed horizontal track for stacking and retrieving pallets etc.

stacker /ˈstakə/ *verb intrans. obsolete* exc. *dial.* ME.
[Old Norse *stakra* frequentative of *staka* push, stagger. Cf. STAGGER *verb*.]
1 Totter, reel in one's gait, stagger. ME.
†**2** Stammer, hesitate in speech. LME–M16.
†**3** *fig.* Be insecure or in danger; waver, hesitate. LME–M16.

stackfreed /ˈstakfriːd/ *noun*. E19.
[Origin uncertain: perh. from German or Dutch.]
Hist. A wheel or cam attached to the barrel of a watch to equalize the power of the mainspring.

stacte /ˈstaktiː/ *noun*. LME.
[Latin from Greek *staktē* fem. of *staktos* distilling in drops, from *stazein* to drip.]
Any of several fragrant spices referred to by ancient writers; *spec.* †(*a*) the oil exuded from the myrrh tree; (*b*) in biblical translations, one of the prescribed ingredients of incense, variously identified as opobalsamum, myrrh, storax, or tragacanth.

stactometer /stakˈtɒmɪtə/ *noun*. Now *rare*. Also **stakt-**. M19.
[from Greek *staktos*: see prec., -METER.]
= STALAGMOMETER.

stad /stat/ *noun*. *S. Afr.* Also **stadt**. L19.
[Dutch.]
A town, a village.

stadda /ˈstadə/ *noun*. Now *rare*. Also **-dow** /-dəʊ/. L17.
[Origin unkn.]
A double saw used in making combs.

staddle /ˈstad(ə)l/ *noun & verb*. Also **steddle**.
[Old English *staþol* base, support, tree-trunk, fixed position = Old Frisian *stathul*, Old Saxon *staþal* standing, Old High German *stadal* barn (German dial. *Stadel*), Old Norse *stǫðull* milking-place, from Germanic from base of STAND *verb*: see -LE[1].]
▶ **A** *noun*. †**1** A foundation. (*lit.* & *fig.*) OE–ME.
2 A platform or framework of timber, stone, etc., supporting a stack or rick; (in full ***staddle-stone***) each of the mushroom-shaped stones used to raise a stack, rick, granary, etc., from the ground, esp. to deter rodents; *gen.* a supporting framework. LME. ▸**b** The lower part of a stack of corn, hay, etc. Now *dial.* L15.
3 A young tree left standing when others are cut down; *dial.* the root or stump of a felled or coppiced tree. M16. ▸†**b** A tree-trunk, a staff. *rare* (Spenser). Only in L16.
4 A mark, an impression, *esp.* one left by a body lying on a surface; a scar. *dial.* L17.
▶ **B** *verb trans.* **1** Provide with staddles; cut (a wood) so as to leave some young trees standing. *dial.* L16.
2 Stain, mark, leave an impression on. *dial.* E19.
■ **staddling** *noun* (now *dial.*) (materials forming) the support or foundation of a stack, rick, etc. LME.

staddow *noun* var. of STADDA.

stade /steɪd/ *noun*. M16.
[Anglicized from STADIUM.]
1 = STADIUM 1. M16.
†**2** A stage in a journey or process. E17–E18.
3 GEOLOGY. A single period of colder climate or advancing ice, as a subdivision of a longer glacial period. M20.

stadholder *noun* var. of STADTHOLDER.

stadhouse *noun* var. of STADTHOUSE.

stadia /ˈsteɪdɪə/ *noun*[1] & *adjective*. M19.
[Prob. from (*stadia* pl. of) STADIUM.]
▶ **A** *noun*. An instrument or apparatus for measuring distance by observing the apparent height of or angle subtended by a distant rod or other object of known actual height through a graduated plate, a telescope with cross-hairs, etc. M19.
▶ **B** *adjective*. Of, pertaining to, or designating this method of measuring distance. M19.
■ **stadic** *adjective* (*rare*) = STADIA *adjective* E20.

stadia *noun*[2] *pl.* see STADIUM.

stadial /ˈsteɪdɪəl/ *adjective & noun*. LME.
[Latin *stadialis*, formed as STADIUM: see -AL[1].]
▶ **A** *adjective*. †**1** CLASSICAL ANTIQUITIES. Pertaining to a stadium in length. *rare*. Only in LME.
2 a GEOLOGY. Of or pertaining to a glacial stade. M20. ▸**b** ARCHAEOLOGY. Pertaining to or expressed in terms of a series of successive stages into which a culture or period can be divided. M20.
2a stadial moraine a recessional moraine.
▶ **B** *noun*. GEOLOGY. = STADE *noun* 3. M20.

stadiometer /steɪdɪˈɒmɪtə/ *noun*. M19.
[from Greek *stadion* STADIUM + -METER.]
1 Any of various instruments for measuring distance. Cf. STADIA *noun*[1]. Now *rare*. M19.
2 An apparatus for measuring a person's height. L20.

stadium /ˈsteɪdɪəm/ *noun*. Pl. **-iums**; **-ia** /-ɪə/. LME.
[Latin from Greek *stadion*. Cf. STADE *noun*.]
▶ **I 1** CLASSICAL ANTIQUITIES. A unit of length, usu. equal to 600 Greek or Roman feet, or one-eighth of a Roman mile (*c* 185 m.). LME.
2 CLASSICAL ANTIQUITIES. A course (orig. a stadium in length) for foot-racing or chariot-racing; a race on such a course. E17.
3 An athletic or sports ground or arena with tiered seats or terraces for spectators. M19.
3 football stadium, sports stadium, etc.
▶ **II 4** A stage of a process, disease, etc. M17. ▸**b** ZOOLOGY. An interval between moults in the growth of an insect, crustacean, etc. L19.
5 Any of various instruments for measuring distance; a levelling rod. Cf. STADIA *noun*[1]. M19.

stadt *noun* var. of STAD.

stadthaus /ˈʃtathaʊs, ˈstat-/ *noun*. Pl. ***-hauser*** /-hɔyzər/. M19.
[German, from *Stadt* town + *Haus* house.]
A town hall in a German-speaking country. Cf. STADTHOUSE.

stadtholder /ˈstathəʊldə/ *noun*. Also **stadholder** /ˈstadhəʊldə/. M16.
[Dutch *stadhouder* (= German *Statthalter*) translating LOCUM TENENS, from *stad* place + *houder* agent-noun from *houden* HOLD *verb*: see -ER[1].]
Hist. Orig., the viceroy or governor of a province or town in the Netherlands or (occas.) Germany or Scandinavia. Later also, the chief magistrate of the United Provinces of the Netherlands.
■ **stadtholderate** *noun* the office or position of a stadtholder; a State, province, etc. ruled by a stadtholder: L18. **stadtholderess** *noun* (*rare*) a female stadtholder; the wife of a stadtholder: M18. **stadtholdership** *noun* (*a*) the office or position of a stadtholder; †(*b*) *rare* a State, province, etc., ruled by a stadtholder: M17.

stadthouse /ˈstathaʊs/ *noun*. Also **stadhouse** /ˈstadhaʊs/. M17.
[Anglicized formed as STADTHAUS or Dutch *stadhuis*.]
A town hall in a German-speaking or (esp.) Dutch-speaking country.

staff /stɑːf/ *noun*[1]. Also **stave** /steɪv/ (now chiefly in sense 13, sense 5 (exc. *Scot.*), and in senses 11 and 12, where now the usual form). Pl. (in branch III the only form) **staffs**; (corresp. to the sing. form *stave*) **staves** /steɪvz/.
[Old English *stæf* = Old Frisian *stef*, Old Saxon *staf* (Dutch *staf*), Old High German *stap* (German *Stab*), Old Norse *stafr*, from Germanic. See also STAVE *noun*.]
▶ **I 1** A long stout stick or pole carried as an aid or support in walking or climbing; *fig.* a person or thing regarded or functioning as a main source of support. OE. ▸**b** A stick or rod of this kind employed in a particular occupation or for a particular purpose; *spec.* (*a*) a rod or sceptre of wood, ivory, etc., held as a mark of authority or office; (*b*) a bishop's crosier; (*c*) a shepherd's crook; (*d*) a rod or wand used in magic or divination. OE.
2 A long thick stick or pole used as a weapon and in self-defence. Cf. ***quarterstaff*** s.v. QUARTER *noun*. OE. ▸**b** The shaft of a spear, lance, or similar weapon. Formerly also, a weapon of this kind. *arch.* ME.
3 A strong rod or bar serving as a prop, support, or strut, esp. within a structure; *spec.* (*a*) (now *rare* or *obsolete*) a rung of a ladder; †(*b*) a bar or rail in a gate, grid, etc.; †(*c*) = ***bowstaff*** s.v. BOW *noun*[1]; (*d*) (HERALDRY, now *Hist.*) a spoke of a wheel; (*e*) an arbor or spindle in the mechanism of a watch. OE.
4 †**a** Orig., a measure of area, esp. for land; an enclosure or plot of pasturage. Later (long *obsolete* exc. *Hist.*), a measure of length, *esp.* one equal to 9 feet (approx. 2.743 m.) or half a perch (approx. 2.515 m.). ME. ▸**b** SURVEYING. A rod for measuring distances, heights, etc. M16.
5 Each of the thin narrow usu. curved pieces of wood which, when placed together side by side and hooped, form the side of a barrel, cask, pail, etc. LME.
6 A flagstaff, a flag-pole. E17.
7 The gnomon of a sundial. M17.
8 SURGERY. A grooved steel instrument used to guide a scalpel, esp. in lithotomy. L17.
9 ARCHITECTURE. A vertical beaded moulding or protective strip at the angle of two walls. L17.
10 A token, orig. a stick of wood, given to an engine-driver on a single-track railway as authority to proceed over a given section of line. L19.

> 🕮 **1** SIR W. SCOTT The blind fiddler struck the earth with his staff. J. TYNDALL I.. dug my staff deeply into the snow. *fig.*: W. IRVING They had one son, who had grown up to be the staff and pride of their age. **b** J. LANGHORNE They discovered .. the augural staff of Romulus. GEORGE IV You have sent me the Staff of a French Marshal, and I send you in return that of England. **2** W. COMBE But warrants, staves and mastiffs wait To guard the approaches to his gate. *New York Times* They brandished spears, staves and knobkerries. **5** W. SCORESBY Empty casks are .. taken to pieces, and the staves closely packed up.

▶ **II 11** A written character, a letter, *spec.* in a runic alphabet. Formerly also, a mark made (as) by writing. Freq. in *pl. arch.* OE.
12 †**a** A line of verse. L15–M16. ▸**b** A verse or stanza of a poem, song, etc. E16.
13 MUSIC. A set of (now usu. five) parallel horizontal lines, on any one or between any adjacent two of which a note is placed to indicate its pitch. M17.

> 🕮 **13** *Guitar Player* The next step is to relate the staff's notes to the fingerboard.

▶ **III 14** MILITARY. The body of officers assisting a commanding officer responsible for an army, regiment, fleet, air force, etc., or for special departmental duties. L18. ▸**b** *ellipt.* (Usu. **S-**.) A staff sergeant; a staff nurse. E20.
15 The body of people employed in a business, establishment, etc.; the employees of an organization etc. collectively; *spec.* (*a*) those responsible for advisory and ancillary services rather than directly concerned with production; those in authority within an organization, as teachers in a school; (*b*) salaried as opp. to wage-earning or freelance workers. M19. ▸**b** A member of staff, an employee. *rare*. M20.

> 🕮 **15** *Daily News* A large staff is necessary for the working of each 'general hospital'. J. AIKEN Our staff are highly efficient. M. HOCKING At our school there is an undeclared war between staff and pupils. N. SHERRY He needed experience .. to find a place on the staff of *The Times*. *Applied Linguistics* Ten staff were allocated to proctoring and moderation, leaving twenty available for actual testing.

Phrases: ***Chief of Staff***: see CHIEF *noun*. GENERAL ***staff***. ***go to sticks and staves***: see STICK *noun*[1]. ***have the better end of the staff***, ***have the worse end of the staff***: see END *noun*. ***levelling staff***: see LEVELLING *noun*. ***pastoral staff***: see PASTORAL *adjective*. ***ragged staff***: see RAGGED *adjective*. ***shamble-stave***: see SHAMBLE *noun*[1] 7. **staff of life** bread; a similar staple food of an area or people. ***tau-staff***: see TAU *noun*[1] 2. **tip a person a stave** *arch.* sing a song to a person. ***white staff***: see WHITE *adjective*.
Comb.: **staff and ticket (system)** (*obsolete* exc. *Hist.*) an elaboration of the staff system (below) allowing for the movement of several trains in one direction along a single line, whereby the last train carried the staff (sense 10 above) and the preceding trains carried tickets pertaining to this; **staff association** an association of employees which performs some of the functions of a trade union, such as representing its members in discussions with management; **staff college** MILITARY a college at which officers are trained for appointments to the staff; **staff corps** MILITARY a body of officers and ordinary soldiers etc. organized to assist the commanding officer and his or her staff in various special departments; **staff notation** MUSIC notation by means of a staff, esp. as distinct from tonic sol-fa; **staff nurse** a trained nurse in a hospital, ranking above a registered nurse and below a ward sister; **staff officer** MILITARY an officer serving on the general or departmental staff of an army etc.; **staff photographer** a photographer on the staff of a newspaper, magazine, etc.; **staff-room** a common-room for the use of the staff, esp. in a school; *transf.* the staff itself; **staff sergeant** (*a*) the senior sergeant of a non-infantry company; (*b*) *US* a non-commissioned officer ranking just above a sergeant; **staff-sling** (*obsolete* exc. *Hist.*) a sling with its cords or strings attached to the end of a staff to facilitate the hurling of large stones; **staff system** a block system on railways according to which a train driver may not proceed along a single line without carrying the staff giving authority to do so; **staff vine** the climbing bitter-sweet, *Celastrus scandens*; **staff writer** a writer employed on the staff of a newspaper, magazine, broadcasting organization, etc.; **stave-wood** any of several trees providing wood suitable for cask-staves, esp. (*W. Indies*) the paradise-tree, *Quassia simarouba*.
■ **staffless** *adjective* M17.

staff /stɑːf/ *noun*[2]. L19.
[Origin unkn.]
A mixture of plaster of Paris, cement, fibre, etc., used for temporary building work.

staff /stɑːf/ *verb trans.* M19.
[from STAFF *noun*[1].]
Provide (an institution, business, etc.) with staff, work as a member of staff in.

> 🕮 J. P. HENNESSY The Secretary's office was staffed by some fifty clerks. *Woman* Building new hospitals .. and staffing them with .. well-paid administrators.

staffage /stəˈfɑːʒ/ *noun*. L19.
[German, pseudo-French form. from *staffieren* fit out, decorate, perh. from Old French *estoffer*, from *estoffe* STUFF *noun*.]
Accessory items in a painting, esp. figures or animals in a landscape picture.

staffer /ˈstɑːfə/ *noun*. Orig. & chiefly *US*. M20.
[from STAFF *noun*[1] + -ER[1].]
A member of a staff; *spec.* (*a*) a staff writer on a newspaper, magazine, etc.; (*b*) a member of the US president's White House staff.

staffette /staˈfɛt/ *noun*. *obsolete* exc. *Hist.* M16.
[Italian *staffetta*: see ESTAFETTE.]
= ESTAFETTE.

†**staffier** *noun*. M16–M18.
[Italian *staffiero*, *-ere*, from *staffa*: see ESTAFETTE, -IER.]
An attendant, a footman.

†**staffish** *adjective*. E16–E19.
[from STAFF *noun*[1] + -ISH[1].]
Rigid, stiff, hard; *fig.* stubborn, unmanageable.

Stafford knot /ˈstafəd nɒt/ *noun phr.* L15.
[from family name of the Dukes of Buckingham in the 15th and 16th cents. + KNOT *noun*[1].]
Chiefly HERALDRY. A half-hitch or overhand knot used as a badge orig. by the Stafford family.

Staffordshire /ˈstafədʃə/ *noun.* M18.
[A county in the north midlands of England.]
▶ **I** **1** Used *attrib.* to designate things found in or associated with Staffordshire. M18.
Staffordshire bull-terrier (an animal of) a small stocky breed of terrier having a short broad head with dropped ears. **Staffordshire cone** a kind of pyrometric cone. **Staffordshire knot** = STAFFORD KNOT. **Staffordshire ware** earthenware and porcelain made in Staffordshire.
▶ **II** *ellipt.* **2** Staffordshire ware. M19.
3 A Staffordshire bull-terrier. E20.

Staffs. *abbreviation.*
Staffordshire.

stag /stag/ *noun, adjective*[1], *& adverb.* ME.
[Rel. to Old Norse *steggr, steggi* (Norwegian *stegg*) male bird, Icelandic *steggi* tom-cat, male bird, male fox (cf. STEG). Prob. already in Old English.]
▶ **A** *noun.* **1** The male of a deer, esp. of the red deer; *spec.* a male red deer after its fifth year. Also (now *rare*), any of various large deer of the genus *Cervus.* ME. ▸**b** The antler of a stag, esp. as a material for cutlery handles. L18.
2 A young, esp. unbroken, horse. *Scot. & north.* ME.
3 †**a** A young male swan. Only in M16. ▸**b** A cock; *spec.* one less than a year old used in cock-fighting. *dial.* M18. ▸**c** A turkey cock over one year old. E19. ▸**d** The wren. *dial.* E19.
4 A bull, ram, or pig castrated after reaching maturity. Freq. in ***bull-stag, ram-stag.*** L17.
5 A big romping girl or woman. *dial.* L17.
6 *slang.* An informer. L18. ▸**b** A spell of duty, esp. on watch. L19.
7 STOCK EXCHANGE. A person who applies for shares of a new issue with a view to selling at once for a profit. M19.
8 A man who attends a social gathering without a female partner. Chiefly *US.* E20. ▸**b** *ellipt.* = ***stag-night*** below. *N. Amer. colloq.* E20.
1 ***royal stag***: see ROYAL *adjective.*
▶ **B** *attrib.* or as *adjective.* **1** Of a horse: unbroken. E17.
2 Of an animal: male. E18.
3 Of, for, or composed of men only. *slang.* M19.

📖 **3** *Daily Telegraph* The spring lunch . . , which is declared to be '100 per cent stag'.

▶ **C** *adverb.* Without a female partner. Chiefly in ***go stag.*** E20.
Comb. & special collocations: **stag beetle** any of various large scarabaeoid beetles of the family Lucanidae, the males of which have enlarged toothed mandibles resembling the horns of a stag; esp. *Lucanus cervus*, of Europe, and *L. elaphus*, of N. America; **stag bush** a viburnum of the US, *Viburnum prunifolium*; **stag film** *slang* a pornographic film made for men; **stag head** = ***stag's head*** below; **staghound** a dog used for hunting deer; a deer-hound; **stag-hunt** a hunt for a stag with hounds; **stag-hunter** a person who takes part in a stag-hunt; **stag-hunting** the sport or action of hunting a stag with hounds; **stag movie** = ***stag film*** above; **stag night, stag party** an all-male celebration, *esp.* one held in honour of a man about to marry; **stag's head** the head and antlers of a stag; ***stag's head moss*** = ***stag-horn moss*** s.v. STAG-HORN 2b.
■ **staglike** *adjective* resembling (that of) a stag M19.

†**stag** *adjective*[2] var. of STAGE *adjective.*

stag /stag/ *verb*[1] *intrans.* Now *Scot. & dial.* Infl. **-gg-**. M16.
[Prob. rel. to STAGGER *verb.*]
†**1** Stagger, waver. Only in M16.
2 Walk with long strides. E19.

stag /stag/ *verb*[2]. Infl. **-gg-**. L18.
[from STAG *noun.*]
1 *slang.* **a** *verb trans.* Observe; watch; discover by observation. L18. ▸**b** *verb intrans.* Turn informer; inform *against.* M19.
2 *verb trans. & intrans.* STOCK EXCHANGE. Deal in (shares) as a stag. M19.
3 *verb intrans. & trans.* (with *it*). Attend a social gathering without a female partner. *US slang.* E20.
4 *verb trans.* Cut (a garment, esp. trousers) off short. Also foll. by *off. N. Amer. colloq.* E20.

stage /steɪdʒ/ *noun.* ME.
[Aphet. from Old French *estage* dwelling, stay, situation (mod. *étage* storey) from Proto-Romance, from Latin *stare* stand: see -AGE.]
▶ **I** A thing to stand on, & derived senses.
1 **a** A storey or floor of a building. Now *rare.* ME. ▸**b** A shelf in a cupboard etc. Now only *spec.*, a shelf or tier of shelves for plants in a greenhouse etc. LME. ▸**c** ARCHITECTURE. A transom dividing a window; a section of a window so divided. Also, the space between the set-offs of buttresses. LME. ▸**d** A level of water in a river or lake. *US.* E19. ▸**e** GEOLOGY. Orig., a level in the hierarchy of rock classification. Now, a division of a stratigraphic series, composed of a number of zones and corresponding to an age in time; the rocks deposited during any particular age. M19. ▸**f** GEOLOGY. A glacial or interglacial period. L19.
†**2** A (specified) position or step in a hierarchy. Long *rare.* ME.
3 A raised platform, now *esp.* one used as a landing place or for storing or drying food on; a scaffold, now *esp.* one used in building etc. ME. ▸**b** A raised plate or ledge on which an object is placed for inspection through a microscope etc. L18. ▸**c** *Hist.* A boxing ring. E19.
4 *spec.* The platform in a theatre on which plays etc. are performed; *fig.* the scene of action. M16. ▸**b** The acting or theatrical profession; the art of writing or presenting plays. Usu. with *the.* L16.

📖 **4** *Listener* From her first entry on stage . . she was radiant. P. FITZGERALD His life had to be acted out, as though on a stage. *Engineering* It was remarkable that the company was . . surviving on the world stage. **centre stage** = ***stage centre*** below. ***hold the stage***: see HOLD *verb.* ***on-stage***: see ON *preposition.* ***open stage***: see OPEN *adjective.* ***play off the stage***: see PLAY *verb.* ***revolving stage***: see REVOLVING. ***set the stage***: see SET *verb*[1]. **stage centre, stage left, stage right** (in) the centre or (on) the left side or (on) the right side of a stage, facing the audience. ***take the stage***: see TAKE *verb.* ***tread the stage***: see TREAD *verb.* **b** M. ALLINGHAM Someone bought a wreath. The Stage is very conventional. ***go on the stage***: see GO *verb.* ***lyric stage***: see LYRIC *adjective* 1.

▶† **II** **5** A period of time; an appointed date. ME–E16.
▶ **III** Division of a journey or process.
6 A stopping-place, esp. a regular one, on a journey *spec.* (*Hist.*) a regular stopping-place, esp. an inn, on a stagecoach route where horses were changed and travellers taken up and set down. ME. ▸**b** *fig.* A point in a journey through a subject, life, etc. E17.
7 The distance between two stopping-places on a journey. E17. ▸**b** Any of the sections into which a long-distance race is divided. M20.
8 *ellipt.* A stagecoach. L17.
9 A point or period in a process or in the development of a thing; *spec.* (**a**) MEDICINE a definite period in the development of a disease, marked by specific symptoms; (**b**) BIOLOGY each of the several periods in the development and growth of animals and plants; freq. with specifying word. M18.
10 *ellipt.* = ***fare-stage*** s.v. FARE *noun*[1]. E20.
11 **a** ELECTRONICS. A part of a circuit usu. comprising one transistor or valve, or two or more functioning as a single unit, and the associated resistors, capacitors, etc. E20. ▸**b** ASTRONAUTICS. Each of two or more sections of a rocket that have their own engines and propellant and are jettisoned when their propellant becomes exhausted. M20.

📖 **6** P. FRANCIS We . . must engage Th' unwilling Horse to pass his usual Stage. **7** A. J. CRONIN The final stage of his tedious journey. A. DUGGAN Daily we covered the usual legionary stage of twenty miles. **b** *Guardian* A mountain stage of the Tour de France. **8** Z. GREY A stage arrived twice a week . . and the driver . . had letters. E. JONG Thus . . I came to be riding in the London stage. **9** P. ACKROYD We can discuss . . editing and production at a later stage. D. MADDEN At this stage in her life Jane dressed badly. A. MACRAE It's just a stage she's going through. C. EASTON In its earliest stages multiple sclerosis is . . difficult to diagnose.

▶† **IV** **12** = STADIUM 1. *rare.* LME–M16.
Attrib. & comb.: Esp. in the senses 'of or pertaining to the theatrical stage', as ***stage design, stage lighting, stage version***, 'seen on the stage, represented in drama', as ***stage hero, stage heroine.*** Special combs., as **stage box**: over the proscenium of a theatre; **stagecoach** *Hist.* a large closed horse-drawn coach running regularly between two places with fixed stages along the route; **stagecoachman** *Hist.* the driver of a stagecoach; **stagecraft** skill or experience in writing or staging plays; **stage direction** (*a*) an instruction in the text of a play as to the movement, position, tone of delivery, etc., of an actor, or sound effects or lighting; (*b*) = ***stage-management*** below; **stage director** (*a*) a stage-manager; (*b*) = DIRECTOR 4; **stage-dive** *verb intrans.* perform an act of stage-diving; **stage-diver** a person who stage-dives; **stage-diving** the practice (esp. among audience members) of jumping from the stage at a rock concert or other event to be caught and carried aloft by the crowd below; **stage door** an entrance for use by actors, workmen, etc., giving access from the street to behind the stage of a theatre; ***stage-door Johnny*** (*slang*, chiefly *US*), a man who frequents stage doors seeking the company of actresses; **stage effect** (*a*) effect on the audience of what is shown on stage; (*b*) a spectacular effect produced on the stage; an artificial or theatrical effect produced in real life; **stage-entrance** = ***stage door*** above; **stage fright** nervousness on appearing before an audience, esp. for the first time; **stage hand** a person who moves scenery or props during the performance or production of a play etc.; **stage lighting** imitation lighting produced for the stage etc.; **stage-manage** *verb trans.* (*a*) be the stage-manager of; (*b*) arrange and control for effect; **stage-management** the job or craft of a stage-manager; **stage-manager** orig., the person responsible for the production and performance of a play, and the stage arrangements; now *spec.* the person responsible for lighting and other mechanical arrangements for a play etc.; **stage name**: assumed for professional purposes by a theatrical performer; **stage play** a play performed on stage, now esp. as opp. to being broadcast etc.; **stage-player** *arch.* an actor, a player; **stage-playing** *arch.* acting; **stage presence** the (forceful) impression made by a theatrical performer on an audience; **stage rights** exclusive rights to perform a particular play; **stage school** a drama school; **stage-set** = SET *noun*[1] 15; **stage-setting** the disposition of the actors and props on a stage; **stage-struck** *adjective* filled with a passionate desire to become an actor; **stage thunder** imitation thunder produced for the stage etc.; **stage whisper** (*a*) a loud whisper meant to be heard by others than the person addressed; (*b*) an aside; **stage-whisper** *verb trans.* say in a stage whisper.
■ **stageaˈbility** *noun* the ability of a play etc. to be presented on stage E20. **stageable** *adjective* (of a play etc.) able to be presented on stage E20. **stagelike** *adjective* resembling that produced on the stage M16. **stagery** *noun* (*rare*) exhibition on the stage M17. **stageworthy** *adjective* (of a play etc.) worthy of presentation on the stage E19.

†**stage** *adjective.* Also **stag**. LME–M19.
[Origin unkn.]
Of a fur or skin: raw, unseasoned.

stage /steɪdʒ/ *verb.* ME.
[from STAGE *noun.*]
†**1** *verb trans.* Erect, build. *rare.* Only in ME.
2 *verb trans.* Provide with a stage or staging. Foll. by *about.* Now *rare* or *obsolete.* E16.
3 *verb trans.* **a** Represent (a character or incident) on stage; put (a person) into a play. E17. ▸**b** Present (a play etc.) on stage. L19. ▸**c** *transf.* Arrange the occurrence of, esp. dramatically. E20.
†**4** *verb trans.* Bring (a person) to trial for an offence (esp. before the ecclesiastical courts). *Scot.* L17–E18.
5 *verb intrans.* **a** Travel by stages; *esp.* travel by stage or stagecoach. Now *rare.* L17. ▸**b** Of a pilot or aircraft: make a brief landing in the course of a long journey. L20.
6 *verb trans.* Put (plants) on a stage in a greenhouse etc.; exhibit (plants) at a show. M19.
7 *verb trans. & intrans.* ASTRONAUTICS. Separate (a section or stage) from the upper or remaining part of a rocket. M20.
8 *verb trans.* Cause to pass through stages; bring about in stages. M20.
9 *verb trans.* MEDICINE. Diagnose or classify as exhibiting a particular stage in the progression of a disease or condition, esp. cancer. M20.

📖 **3b** H. CARPENTER Columbia University's music department had agreed to stage the . . opera. P. DALLY He wrote five plays . . although only two were staged. **c** *Observer* The Stock Market staged a vigorous recovery. C. ACHEBE Protest marches were staged up and down the land.

staged /steɪdʒd/ *adjective.* M16.
[from STAGE *noun,verb*: see -ED[2], -ED[1].]
1 †**a** That acts (as) on a stage. M–L16. ▸**b** Of a play: that is staged. E20.
2 Of a building: having a series of floors or storeys. L19.
3 That is brought about in stages, that proceeds in stages. M20.

stager /ˈsteɪdʒə/ *noun.* L16.
[from STAGE *noun* + -ER[1]. Cf. Old French *estagier* (from *estage* STAGE *noun*) inhabitant, resident.]
1 A person with a specified amount of experience in a profession, life, etc. Orig. & chiefly in ***old stager***, a veteran, an old hand. L16.
2 An actor. *arch.* L16.
3 A stagecoach; a stagecoach driver or horse. Now *rare* or *obsolete.* M19.
4 A person who erects scaffolding in a shipyard. E20.

stagey *adjective* var. of STAGY.

stagflation /stagˈfleɪʃ(ə)n/ *noun.* M20.
[Blend of STAG(NATION and IN)FLATION.]
ECONOMICS. A state of economic depression in which stagnant demand is accompanied by severe inflation.
■ **stagflationary** *adjective* of, characterized by, or involving stagflation L20.

staggard /ˈstagəd/ *noun. arch.* ME.
[from STAG *noun* + -ARD.]
A stag in its fourth year.

staggeen /staˈgiːn/ *noun. Anglo-Irish.* E19.
[from STAG *noun* + -EEN[2].]
A colt.

stagger /ˈstagə/ *noun*[1]. L16.
[from STAGGER *verb.*]
1 An act of staggering; an unsteady tottering or reeling movement of the body as if about to fall. L16. ▸**b** *fig.* A wavering, a hesitation. E17.
2 In *pl.* (treated as *sing.*). ▸**a** VETERINARY MEDICINE. Any of various diseases or conditions affecting domestic animals, characterized by incoordination and a staggering gait. Freq. with specifying word. L16. ▸**b** *transf.* Inability to walk steadily. L16.
3 **a** An attempt, a try. *dial. & slang.* M19. ▸**b** A rough preliminary rehearsal or run-through of a play etc. Also ***stagger through.*** *slang.* M20.
4 A staggered or overlapping or alternating arrangement; *spec.* (AERONAUTICS) such an arrangement of the wings of a biplane, the extent of this. E20.
2a ***grass staggers***: see GRASS *noun.* ***PHALARIS staggers.***
Comb.: **stagger-bush** *US* a shrub of the heath family, *Lyonia mariana*, reputed to give sheep the staggers; **stagger-juice** *slang*

(chiefly *Austral.*) strong alcoholic drink; **stagger-tuned** *adjective* (ELECTRONICS) that has been subjected to stagger tuning; **stagger tuning** ELECTRONICS the tuning of different stages of an amplifier to slightly different frequencies so as to broaden the overall frequency response; **staggerwort** *dial.* the ragwort *Senecio jacobaea*.

stagger /ˈstagə/ *noun*². *rare*. M19.
[from STAG *noun* + -ER¹.]
A person who hunts stags.

stagger /ˈstagə/ *verb*. LME.
[Alt. of STACKER *verb*.]
▶ **I** *verb intrans*. **1** Sway or move unsteadily from side to side; walk with unsteady zigzagging steps; totter as a result of weakness, intoxication, the carrying of a heavy load, etc. LME. ▸**b** Of the senses: reel. *rare*. E19. ▸**c** Of a ship: move unsteadily and with difficulty. M19.
2 Begin to doubt or waver in an opinion, faith, or purpose; falter, hesitate *at*. Formerly also foll. by *that*. Now *rare*. E16.
3 Of an army, line of battle, etc.: waver, give way. M16.

🕮 **1** J. CONRAD A push made him stagger against the mizzen-mast. A. RANSOME Staggering along the pavement with baskets crammed to the brims. E. JOHNSON The drunken revellers staggering home at .. dawn. F. KING My father slowly rose, staggered a little, and then took a faltering step. *fig.*: J. BARNES Both .. recovered, and staggered on through the year.

▶ **II** *verb trans*. **4** Bewilder, confuse, nonplus; astonish, shock. Freq. in *pass*. M16. ▸**b** Cause to waver or falter. Formerly also, throw doubt upon. E17.
5 Cause to totter, esp. from a blow. L16. ▸**b** Shake the stability of (a country, government, etc.). E17.
6 Cause (a line or body of troops) to waver or give way. E18.
7 Arrange in a zigzag order or in positions which are not in line; *spec*. (**a**) arrange (a road junction) so that the side roads are not in line; (**b**) set (the spokes of a wheel) to incline alternately right and left from the hub. Freq. as ***staggered*** *ppl adjective*. M19.
8 Arrange (holidays, hours of work, etc.) so that the given times do not coincide exactly; arrange for the occurrence or implementation of (an event or action) to be spread over a period of time. Freq. as ***staggered*** *ppl adjective*. E20.

🕮 **4** M. SINCLAIR The naked impudence of it .. staggered him. *Broadcast* He was staggered at the quantity of programmes in which James .. had been involved. G. DALY The committee .. was staggered by the bill they ran up. L. KENNEDY I am staggered how easily it was all arranged. **b** R. L. STEVENSON Nothing can stagger a child's faith. **5** F. MARRYAT I received a blow on the head from behind, which staggered me. **7** J. B. BISHOP The lamps are staggered .. to illuminate both .. chambers. M. ANGELOU Forty people sat staggered in an auditorium which could hold seven hundred. **8** *Construction News* To keep down vibrations .. the charges were staggered to go off over six seconds.

■ **staggerer** *noun* (**a**) a person who staggers; (**b**) a thing that causes a person to stagger; *esp.* an astonishing or bewildering event etc.: M16. **staggerment** *noun* (*rare*) great astonishment M20.

staggering /ˈstag(ə)rɪŋ/ *adjective*. M16.
[from STAGGER *verb* + -ING².]
1 That staggers. M16.
2 Amazing, shocking, bewildering; enormous. M18.

🕮 **2** *Rail Enthusiast* The East Lancashire Railway .. has attracted a staggering 10,000 visitors. M. COREN Considering the .. alcohol consumed .. it is staggering he was hardly ever seen out of control.

Special collocations: **staggering bob** *dial.* & *Austral.* (veal from) a very young calf.
■ **staggeringly** *adverb* L16.

staggery /ˈstag(ə)ri/ *adjective*. *colloq*. L18.
[from STAGGER *noun*¹, *verb* + -Y¹.]
1 Of an animal: affected with staggers. L18.
2 Tending to stagger; unsteady. M19.

staggie /ˈstagi/ *noun*. *Scot*. L18.
[from STAG *noun* + -IE.]
A colt.

staggy /ˈstagi/ *adjective*. L19.
[from STAG *noun* + -Y¹.]
†**1** Of a vegetable: hard and woody. *rare*. Only in L19.
2 (Of an animal) having the characteristics or appearance of a mature male; (of meat) coming from such an animal. *N. Amer.* & *NZ*. M20.
3 Of a tree etc.: having bare branches. Cf. STAG-HEADED *adjective* 2. M20.

stag-headed /stagˈhɛdɪd/ *adjective*. L17.
[from STAG *noun* + HEADED.]
1 Of an animal: having a head shaped like that of a stag. L17.
2 Of a tree, esp. an oak: having the upper branches dead and leafless. M18.

stag-horn /ˈstaghɔːn/ *noun*. Also **staghorn**, **stag's horn**. E17.
[from STAG *noun* + HORN *noun*.]
1 The antlers of a stag (usu. in *pl.*); this as a material used to make knife-handles, snuffboxes, etc. E17.
2 a More fully ***stag-horn sumac***. A N. American sumac, *Rhus hirta*, with stout upright densely hairy branches forming a flat head, freq. grown for ornament. M18. ▸**b** More fully ***stag-horn moss***, ***stag's-horn moss***, ***stag's-horn clubmoss***. The clubmoss *Lycopodium clavatum*, so called from its paired terminal spikes, used in homoeopathic remedies. M18. ▸**c** More fully ***stag-horn fern***. Any of various tropical ferns constituting the genus *Platycerium*, having fertile fronds divided like a stag's antlers. L19.
3 NAUTICAL (**staghorn**). A bollard with two horizontal arms of the same strength as the upright. E20.

Comb.: **stag-horn calculus** MEDICINE a large stone in the kidney, having the branched form of the renal pelvis that it occupies; **stag-horn coral** a branching stony coral of the genus *Acropora*; ***stag-horn fern***: see sense 2c above; ***stag-horn moss***, ***stag's horn moss***, ***stag's horn clubmoss***: see sense 2b above; ***stag-horn sumac***: see sense 2a above.
■ **stag-horned** *adjective* that has parts which resemble the antlers of a stag; stag-headed: M19.

stagiary /ˈsteɪdʒɪəri/ *noun*. M19.
[medieval Latin *stagiarius*, from *stagium* term of residence of a canon from Old French *estage*: see STAGE *noun*, -ARY¹.]
ECCLESIASTICAL HISTORY. A canon residentiary.

staging /ˈsteɪdʒɪŋ/ *noun* & *adjective*. ME.
[from STAGE *noun*, *verb* + -ING¹.]
▶ **A** *noun*. **1 a** A platform or scaffold, *esp.* a temporary one; scaffolding. ME. ▸**b** Shelving for plants in a greenhouse. ME.
2 The action of travelling by stages or *spec.* by stagecoach. Chiefly ANGLO-INDIAN & US HISTORY. Now *rare*. E19.
3 The action or art of presenting a play etc. on stage. L19.
4 ASTRONAUTICS. The arrangement of stages in a rocket; the separation and jettisoning of a stage from the remainder of the rocket when its propellant is spent. M20.
5 MEDICINE. The determination of the particular stage which a progressive disease or condition has reached. M20.
▶ **B** *attrib*. or as *adjective*. Designating a stopping-place or assembly-point en route to a destination. M20.
staging post a regular stopping-place, now esp. on an air route.

stagione /staˈdʒoːne/ *noun*. Pl. **-ni** /-ni/. M20.
[Italian = season.]
An opera or ballet season, *esp.* an opera season in which one work is performed on several occasions in a limited period with no change of cast.

Stagirite /ˈstadʒɪrʌɪt, ˈstag-/ *noun*. *literary*. E17.
[Latin *Stagirites* from Greek *Stageiritēs*, from *Stageiros*: see -ITE¹.]
A native or inhabitant of Stagira, a city in ancient Macedonia; spec. *the* philosopher Aristotle.

stagnant /ˈstagnənt/ *adjective*. M17.
[Latin *stagnant-* pres. ppl stem of *stagnare*: see next, -ANT¹.]
†**1** Of a fluid: that is at rest in a vessel. M17–E18.
2 Of water, air, etc.: not flowing, having no current, motionless; stale or foul due to this. M17.
3 *fig*. Showing no activity, not developing; dull, sluggish. M18.

🕮 **2** T. HEGGEN The air was as .. stagnant as that of an attic .. on a summer day. P. LIVELY Mosquito larvae hatched in the stagnant pool. **3** C. MCCULLERS Business was stagnant There was not a single customer. J. K. GALBRAITH An advancing national community, not a stagnant or declining one.

■ **stagnance** *noun* (*rare*) = STAGNANCY (a) M19. **stagnancy** *noun* (**a**) the condition of being stagnant; (**b**) a stagnant thing: M17. **stagnantly** *adverb* M19.

stagnate /stagˈneɪt, ˈstagneɪt/ *verb*. Pa. pple & ppl adjective **-ated**, (now *rare*) **-ate** /-ət/. M17.
[Latin *stagnat-* pa. ppl stem of *stagnare*, from *stagnum* pool: see -ATE³.]
1 *verb intrans*. Be or become stagnant (*lit.* & *fig.*). M17.
2 *verb trans*. Cause to be or become stagnant (*lit.* & *fig.*). L17.
3 *verb trans*. Astonish, stagger. *dial.* & *US*. L18.

🕮 **1** J. RAY The Air .. stagnated in the Shaft. E. BANCROFT Water .. stagnates and corrupts during .. months in which the rains intermit. J. DAWSON I'm stagnating horribly away from .. things intellectual. J. TROLLOPE He let his shame stagnate into bitterness. **2** G. HUGHES We have neither bogs nor marshes to stagnate our waters. *Daily Chronicle* There is a tendency for age to stagnate a man's initiative.

stagnation /stagˈneɪʃ(ə)n/ *noun*. M17.
[from prec. + -ATION.]
The action of stagnating; an instance of this; *spec*. (**a**) MEDICINE a local retardation or cessation of blood flow etc.; (**b**) ECONOMICS (an) absence or low rate of growth.
Comb.: **stagnation point** AERONAUTICS a point on the leading edge of a moving aerofoil at which the air is at rest relative to the aerofoil.

■ **stagnationist** *adjective* & *noun* (chiefly ECONOMICS) (**a**) *adjective* characterized by or promoting stagnation; (**b**) *noun* a person who advocates or forecasts stagnation: M20.

stag's horn *noun* var. of STAG-HORN.

stagy /ˈsteɪdʒi/ *adjective*. Also **stagey**. E19.
[from STAGE *noun* + -Y¹.]
1 Of or pertaining to the stage; theatrical; dramatically artificial or exaggerated; affected. E19.
2 Of a seal or its skin: out of condition as a result of moulting. L19.

🕮 **1** N. BAWDEN His stagey behaviour, his need to turn every small .. event into drama. B. VINE He gave the address a stagey emphasis.

■ **stagily** *adverb* M19. **staginess** *noun* M19.

Stahlian /ˈstɑːlɪən/ *adjective* & *noun*. L18.
[from Georg Ernst *Stahl* (1660–1734), German chemist and physician + -IAN.]
▶ **A** *adjective*. Pertaining to Stahl or his doctrines, esp. his theory of vital action and of disease. L18.
▶ **B** *noun*. A follower of Stahl; an animist. L18.

staid /steɪd/ *adjective*. Also †**stayed**. M16.
[Obsolete pa. pple of STAY *verb*¹.]
1 Of a belief, institution, etc.: fixed, permanent; settled, unchanging. Formerly also, (of a person) settled in faith or purpose. Now *rare*. M16.
2 Settled in character and conduct; dignified and serious; sedate, sober, steady. M16.
3 Characterized by or indicating sedateness. M16.

🕮 **2** J. LONDON It was a staid, respectable magazine. L. KENNEDY Off duty, staid Scottish lawyers .. let their hair down. ANNE STEVENSON They were as close to bohemians as staid Northampton could produce. **3** LEIGH HUNT Prodigiously staid names are apt to .. disgust the possessor.

■ **staidly** *adverb* (*rare*) (**a**) fixedly; (**b**) sedately, soberly: L16. **staidness** *noun* M16.

†**staid** *verb pa. t.* & *pple*: see STAY *verb*¹.

stain /steɪn/ *noun*. M16.
[from the verb.]
†**1** The action of staining something; pollution, disgrace. M16–E17.
2 A discoloration produced by absorption of or contact with foreign matter; *esp.* one that is not easily removed. L16. ▸**b** A blemish or (now esp.) discoloration on the skin. L16. ▸†**c** A slight trace *of*. *rare* (Shakes.). Only in E17. ▸**d** Any patch of colour different from the ground. E18. ▸**e** HUNTING. = FOIL *noun*³ 1. Cf. STAIN *verb* 4c. *rare*. M19.
3 *fig*. A blemish on a person's character or reputation; a stigma. L16. ▸**b** A person or thing causing a disgrace. Now *rare* or *obsolete*. L16. ▸†**c** A person who casts another into the shade. L16–E17.
4 A dye or colouring matter used in staining. M18.

🕮 **2** JULIA HAMILTON The stain on the ceiling where a bath had overflowed upstairs. **3** G. B. SHAW She went to the stake without a stain on her character except the overweening presumption .. that led her thither. B. CHATWIN As if to wipe away the stain of having harboured the Laval administration. **4** *Woodworker* To get this effect only a very light antique pine stain is required. ***Golgi stain***, ***Leishman stain***, ***Leishman's stain***: see LEISHMAN 2. ***Nissl stain***, ***Nissl's stain***: see NISSL.

Comb.: **stain painting** a style of painting in which diluted acrylic paints are applied to unsized canvas; a painting in this style; **stain-resistant** *adjective* resistant to staining.
■ **stainy** *adjective* (*rare*) having or like a stain M19.

stain /steɪn/ *verb*. LME.
[Aphet. from DISTAIN.]
1 *verb trans*. Impart colour to (something in contact); alter the colour of. LME. ▸**b** *transf.* Of the blood: suffuse (the cheeks, neck, etc.) with colour. M16. ▸**c** *verb intrans*. Absorb colouring matter, take a stain. L19.
2 *verb trans*. Colour (now esp. wood or stone) by applying a penetrative dye or using a chemical reagent, rather than painting the surface; dye. LME. ▸**b** HISTOLOGY etc. Colour (tissue etc.) with a suitable dye so as to render the structure clearly visible. L19.
3 *verb trans*. Orig., ornament with coloured designs or patterns; depict in colour. Later, print colours on (wallpaper). LME.
4 *verb trans*. Discolour or damage the appearance of (a thing) with spots or streaks of foreign matter not easily removed. LME. ▸†**b** Spoil (a crop) with damp. L18–M19. ▸**c** HUNTING. Foil (ground, a track). L18.
5 *verb trans*. *fig*. Defile, taint, or sully (a reputation, character, etc.). LME. ▸†**b** Vilify, abuse. LME–L17. ▸†**c** Impair the beauty or excellence of. L16–M17.
†**6 a** *verb trans*. Deprive of colour or lustre; *fig*. make pale or dim by comparison, overshadow, eclipse. LME–M17. ▸**b** *verb intrans*. Lose colour or lustre. LME–E17.

🕮 **1** V. WOOLF His forefinger .. was stained with tobacco juice. A. C. CLARKE The great corpse staining the sea crimson. **b** H. SURREY Blood .. by shame .. staines again the chekes with flaming red. **2** I. MCEWAN We stained the wooden floor black. *fig.*: G. ORWELL Faces deeply stained by .. ferocious suns. **4** I. MURDOCH Green patches upon his .. trousers where .. grass had stained them.

■ **staina'bility** *noun* ability to be stained **L19**. **stainable** *adjective* able to be stained **L19**. **stainer** *noun* (*a*) a person employed in staining wood, paper, cloth, etc.; (*b*) a dye or colouring matter used in staining: **ME**. **staining** *noun* (*a*) the action of the verb; (*b*) the result of this, a stain: **LME**.

stained /steɪnd/ *ppl adjective*. **LME**.
[from STAIN *verb* + -ED^1.]

That has been stained; *spec.* that has been discoloured or damaged in appearance (freq. as 2nd elem. of comb.).
bloodstained, ***travel-stained***, ***wine-stained***, etc. **stained glass** dyed or coloured glass, esp. formed into decorative mosaics in a lead framework and used in windows (freq. *attrib.* in ***stained-glass window***).

stainless /ˈsteɪnlɪs/ *adjective & noun*. **L16**.
[from STAIN *noun* + -LESS.]

▶ **A** *adjective*. **1** Esp. *fig.*, of a reputation etc.: without stain or stains. **L16**.

2 Highly resistant to staining or corrosion. **L19**.
2 stainless steel a chromium-steel alloy, usu. containing about 14 per cent of chromium when used for cutlery etc., that does not rust or tarnish under oxidizing conditions.

▶ **B** *noun*. *ellipt.* Stainless steel; articles made of this. **L20**.

■ **stainlessly** *adverb* (chiefly *fig.*) **L19**. **stainlessness** *noun* (chiefly *fig.*) **M19**.

stair /stɛː/ *noun*.
[Old English *stǣger* = Middle & mod. Low German, Middle & mod. Dutch *steiger* scaffolding, quay, ult. from Germanic verbal base meaning 'climb'.]

1 In *pl.* (formerly also treated as *sing.*) & (earlier, now esp. *Scot.*) *sing.* A series of fixed steps leading from one level to another; *esp.* such a series leading from one floor to another inside a building. **OE**. ▸**b** Orig., a ladder. Later, anything resembling a stair in appearance or function. **LME**. ▸**c** *fig. sing.* & (now *rare* or *obsolete*) in *pl.* A means of ascending in rank, power, virtue, etc. **L16**.

2 †**a** A step in a scale of rank or dignity, a level, a degree. Also, a high rank or level. **ME–M17**. ▸**b** Each of a series of fixed steps leading from one level to another, esp. from one floor to another in a building. (In pl. not always distinguishable from sense 1 above.) **LME**.

3 In *pl.* & †*sing.* A landing-stage. **E16**.

> **1** DICKENS She . . climbed the winding stair. P. TURNBULL 27 Duntarvie Quad was a solid sandstone tenement . . . The stair was clean and smelled of disinfectant. *Which?* Risks . . caused by . . objects left on the stairs. **below stairs** the basement of a house, formerly esp. as the part occupied by servants. ***moving stair***: see MOVING *adjective*. ***pair of stairs***, ***two pair of stairs***, ***three pair of stairs***: see PAIR *noun*^{1}. **b** ***salmon stair***. **2b** *New Yorker* Climbing down and up a hundred stairs to go buy something. M. DIBDIN The stairs creaked . . as she started to climb them. M. HOCKING A flight of stairs receded into . . the private part of the house.

Comb.: **stairclimber** an exercise machine on which the user simulates the action of climbing a staircase; **stair-foot** the level space in front of the lowest step of a staircase; **stairhead** the level space at the top of a staircase; **stairlift** a lift in the form of a chair built into a domestic staircase for conveying disabled people up and down stairs; **stair-rod**: for securing a carpet in the angle between two steps; **stair-step** *noun, adjective, & verb* (*a*) *noun* each of the steps in a flight of stairs; (*b*) *adjective* resembling a stair-step; (*c*) *verb intrans.* resemble stair-steps; **stair-tower**: with a flight of stairs in it; **stairway** (*a*) a staircase; (*b*) PHYSICAL GEOGRAPHY a series of abrupt changes of level in the floor of a glaciated valley; **stairwell** the shaft containing a flight of stairs.

■ **staired** *adjective* (*rare*) (*a*) arranged like stairs; (*b*) supplied with stairs: **M17**. **stairless** *adjective* (*rare*) having no stairs **M19**. **stairy** *adjective* (long *obsolete* exc. *dial.*) ascending like a flight of stairs, steep **L16**.

staircase /ˈstɛːkeɪs/ *noun*. **E17**.
[from STAIR + CASE *noun*^{2}.]

1 A flight (or occas. a series of flights) of stairs and the supporting structure including the framework, balusters, etc.; the walls, doors, etc., enclosing this. Also, (esp. at Oxford and Cambridge Universities) a part of a building containing this and the rooms accessible from it; *transf.* the people living in those rooms. **E17**. ▸**b** In full ***staircase lock***. A series of closely adjacent canal locks; *spec.* one in which the top gate of one lock acts as the bottom gate of the next. **M20**.

2 More fully ***staircase shell***. Any of several marine gastropod molluscs having a shell likened to a spiral staircase, esp. of the families Epitoniidae (wentletraps) and Architectonicidae; the shell of such a mollusc. **E18**.

3 ELECTRONICS. A voltage that alters in equal steps to a maximum or minimum value. **M20**.

> **1** H. CARPENTER Auden got to know another occupant of his staircase in Meadow Building. M. GARDINER Her flat—three . . rooms up a steep and narrow staircase. ***spiral staircase***: see SPIRAL *adjective*^{1}. **spirit of the staircase** = ESPRIT ***de l'escalier***.

Comb.: **staircase generator** ELECTRONICS a signal generator whose output is a staircase (sense 3); ***staircase lock***: see sense 1b above; ***staircase shell***: see sense 2 above.

staircase /ˈstɛːkeɪs/ *verb*. **E18**.
[from the noun.]

1 *verb trans.* Provide or supply with a staircase or staircases. Chiefly as ***staircasing*** *verbal noun*. *rare*. **E18**.

2 *verb intrans.* Of a tenant: purchase a freehold incrementally through a shared ownership scheme. **L20**.

staithe /steɪð/ *noun & verb*. Now *local*.
[Old English *stæþ* = Old Saxon *staþ*, Old High German *stad*, Gothic *staþa*; in sense A.2 directly from cogn. Old Norse *stǫð*.]

▶ **A** *noun*. †**1** A bank, a shore. **OE–ME**.

2 A landing-stage, a wharf; *esp.* a waterside coal depot equipped for loading vessels. **ME**.

3 An embankment. **LME**.

▶ **B** *verb trans.* Embank. **M19**.

stake /steɪk/ *noun*^{1}.
[Old English *staca* corresp. to Old Frisian, Middle & mod. Low German, Middle Dutch *stake* (Dutch *staak*), from Germanic, from base of STICK *noun*^{1}. Cf. next.]

1 A stout stick or post, usu. of wood, sharpened at one end and driven into the ground as a support for a plant, boundary-marker, a part of the framework of a fence, etc. **OE**.

2 *Hist.* **a** A post to which a person was tied for execution, esp. by burning; *the* punishment of death by burning. **ME**. ▸**b** A post to which a bull or bear was fastened to be baited. **M16**.

3 Chiefly *Hist.* A post sharpened at both ends for use in military defensive work. **ME**.

4 *techn.* **a** A small anvil used in metalworking, *esp.* one with a tang for fitting into a socket on a bench. **M17**. ▸**b** Each of the posts fitted into sockets or staples on a wagon or boat to prevent a load from slipping off. *N. Amer. colloq.* **L19**. ▸**c** BASKET-MAKING. Any of the rods forming the upright supports of the sides of a basket. **E20**.

5 In the Mormon Church: a territorial division; the jurisdiction of a Mormon bishop. Also ***Stake of Zion***. **M19**.

Comb. & phrases: **pick up stakes**, **pull up stakes**, **pull stakes** *N. Amer.* depart; go to live elsewhere; ***PUNJI stake***; **stake and rice (fence)** *Scot.* & *north.*: a fence made of stakes and brushwood; **stake and rider (fence)** (chiefly *N. Amer.*) a fence made of stakes with a top bar; **stake-boat** a boat anchored to mark the start or course for racing boats; **stake-body** *US* a body for a truck or lorry, having a flat open platform with removable posts along the sides; **stake-driver** *US* the American bittern, *Botaurus lentiginosus*, which has a call resembling a mallet striking a stake; **stake-net** a fishing net hung on stakes; ***Stake of Zion***: see sense 5 above; **stake-truck**: with a stake-body.

stake /steɪk/ *noun*^{2}. **LME**.
[Perh. specialized use of prec., from placing an object as a wager on a post or stake.]

1 A thing, esp. a sum of money, wagered on the outcome of a game, race, or contest. **LME**. ▸**b** *fig.* An interest, a concern, *esp.* a financial one. **L18**.

2 **a** In *pl.* Money offered as a prize in a race esp. for horses or dogs. **L17**. ▸**b** *sing.* & (usu.) in *pl.* A race, esp. for horses or dogs, in which money is so offered. Freq. with specifying words. **M18**. ▸**c** *fig.* In *pl.* With specifying word: something involving competition in the activity or quality specified. *colloq.* **L19**.

3 A sum of money earned or saved; a store of provisions or money necessary to survive a certain period. *N. Amer. slang*. **M18**.

> **1** J. CHEEVER You can win . . a hundred dollars on a game, but the stakes are usually . . lower. **b** H. EVANS He . . bought a 40% stake in London Weekend Television. P. ROAZEN Freud had . . a . . professional stake in their marriage. **2b** P. LARKIN Faint afternoons Of Cups and Stakes and Handicaps. *Field* The Champion Stakes . . for . . all-aged greyhounds. **c** J. GALSWORTHY He was not going to enter for the slander stakes. *Spare Rib* Outdoing other girls in the beauty stakes.

Phrases: **at stake** (*a*) risked, to be won or lost; (*b*) at issue, in question. ***nursery stakes***: see NURSERY 7.

stake /steɪk/ *verb*^{1} *trans.* **ME**.
[from STAKE *noun*^{1}.]

1 Mark off (an area) with stakes (freq. foll. by *off*, *out*); *N. Amer.* & *Austral.* claim (land) by marking with stakes. **ME**. ▸**b** Protect or obstruct with stakes; keep *in* or *out*, shut *off* or *up*, with a barrier of stakes. **L15**.

2 Fasten or tie to a stake; support in this way. **ME**. ▸**b** Fasten (a thing) *down* or *on* with a stake or stakes. Formerly also *fig.*, fasten *down* securely as with a stake. **L16**.

3 Impale or transfix on a stake. **ME**.

4 In leather-making, stretch and smooth (a skin) against a blunt edge. **L17**.

5 Place under surveillance; in *pass.* set (a person) to maintain surveillance. Usu. foll. by *out*. *colloq.* **M20**.

> **1**: ***stake a claim***, ***stake out a claim***: see CLAIM *noun* 3. **2** N. GORDIMER A pet sheep staked to mow the grass within the radius of its rope. *Amateur Gardening* Stake tall plants on exposed plots.

Comb.: **stake-out** *colloq.* a period of surveillance.

■ **staker** *noun*^{1} (*a*) *rare* a person who uses a stake for some purpose; (*b*) *Canad.* a person who stakes a mining claim: **L15**.

stake /steɪk/ *verb*^{2}. **M16**.
[Prob. from STAKE *noun*^{2}.]

1 *verb trans.* & *intrans.* Wager (esp. a sum of money) on the outcome of a game, race, or contest. Also foll. by *down*. **M16**.

2 *verb trans.* *fig.* Risk the loss of. **L17**.

3 *verb trans.* Give financial or other support to. Also foll. by *to*, *with*. *colloq.* (chiefly *US*). **M19**.

> **1** P. KAVANAGH Bashford staked his . . estate and all his money on his . . horse. **2** P. LIVELY Learned blokes stake their . . reputation on this or that interpretation. **3** J. O'FAOLAIN Stay here and I'll stake you until you get another . . post. N. SHERRY Mexico was ahead, but it was not certain that a publisher would stake him for the trip.

■ **staker** *noun*^{2} a person who stakes money etc. **M17**.

stakeholder /ˈsteɪkhəʊldə(r)/ *noun*. **E18**.
[from STAKE *noun*^{2} + HOLDER *noun*^{1}.]

1 An independent party with whom each of those who make a wager deposits the money etc. wagered. **E18**.

2 A person who has an interest or concern in something, esp. a business. **M20**.

Comb.: **stakeholder economy** POLITICS an economy which provides all members of society with a stake in its success; **stakeholder pension** a pension plan, available to those who do not belong to a company pension scheme or who are self-employed, which invests the money a person saves and uses the fund on retirement to buy a pension from a pension provider.

stakey /ˈsteɪki/ *adjective*. *slang* (chiefly *Canad.*). **E20**.
[from STAKE *noun*^{2} + -Y^1.]

Well provided with money.

Stakhanovite /stəˈkɑːnəvʌɪt/ *noun & adjective*. **M20**.
[from Aleksei Grigor'evich *Stakhanov* (1906–1977), Russian coalminer whose exceptional output was publicized as part of a campaign in 1935: see -ITE^1.]

▶ **A** *noun*. A worker (esp. in the former USSR) whose productivity exceeds the norm and who thereby earns special rewards; *transf.* any exceptionally hard-working and productive person. **M20**.

▶ **B** *adjective*. Designating, pertaining to, or characteristic of a Stakhanovite. **M20**.

■ **Stakhanovism** *noun* (*Hist.*) a movement or programme to encourage hard work and maximize productivity **M20**. **Stakhanovist** *noun & adjective* = STAKHANOVITE *noun & adjective* **M20**.

staktometer *noun* var. of STACTOMETER.

stalactic /stəˈlaktɪk/ *adjective*. *rare*. **M18**.
[Greek *stalaktikos*, from *stalak-*: see STALACTITES, -IC.]

Deposited by dripping water; stalactitic.

■ Also **stalactical** *adjective* (now *rare* or *obsolete*) **E18**.

stalactitae *noun* pl. of STALACTITES.

stalactite /ˈstaləktʌɪt/ *noun*. **L17**.
[Anglicized from next.]

1 a A conical or tapering formation of dripstone that hangs from the roof of a cave, formed of calcite etc. deposited by water droplets that have percolated through the overlying limestone etc. **L17**. ▸**b** A similar formation of other material, as of volcanic lava. **E19**.

2 Calcite deposited on the roofs or walls of caves etc. **L18**.

3 ARCHITECTURE. Esp. in Islamic architecture, an ornamental downward projection from a roof or arch. **M19**.

■ **stalactiform** /stəˈlak-/ *adjective* having the form of a stalactite **M19**. **stalac'tital** *adjective* = STALACTITIC **L18**. **stalactited** *adjective* (now chiefly ARCHITECTURE) having stalactites **L19**. **stalactitic** /-ˈtɪtɪk/ *adjective* (*a*) having the form or structure of a stalactite, resembling or pertaining to stalactites; (*b*) covered with, containing, or consisting of stalactites: **L18**. **stalac'titical** *adjective* (now *rare*) = STALACTITIC **L18**.

stalactites /staləkˈtʌɪtiːz/ *noun*. Now *rare* or *obsolete*. Pl. **-titae** /-ˈtʌɪtiː/. **L17**.
[mod. Latin, from Greek *stalaktos* dropping, dripping, from *stalak-* base of *stalassein* drip, let drip: see -ITE^1.]

= STALACTITE.

Stalag /ˈstalag, ˈʃtalak/ *noun*. **M20**.
[German, contr. of *Stammlager* main camp. Cf. OFLAG.]

Hist. In Nazi Germany: a prisoner-of-war camp, esp. for non-commissioned officers and privates.

Comb.: **Stalag Luft** /lʊft/ [= air] a Stalag for Air Force personnel.

stalagma /stəˈlagmə/ *noun*. *rare*. **L17**.
[mod. Latin from Greek = drop, drip, from *stalak-*: see STALACTITES.]

1 A distilled liquor. **L17**.

2 = STALAGMITE 2. **E20**.

stalagmite /ˈstaləgmʌɪt/ *noun*. **L17**.
[mod. Latin *stalagmites*, from Greek *stalagma*: see prec., -ITE^1.]

1 A conical or columnar formation of dripstone that rises from the floor of a cave, formed of calcite etc. deposited by water droplets falling from the roof or from stalactites. **L17**.

2 Calcite deposited on the walls or floors of caves etc. **E19**.

■ **stalagmitic** /-ˈmɪtɪk/ *adjective* formed in the same way as a stalagmite; composed of stalagmites; having their form or character: **L18**. **stalag'mitical** *adjective* (*rare*) = STALAGMITIC **E19**.

stalagmometer /staləgˈmɒmɪtə/ *noun*. **M19**.
[from Greek *stalagmos* a dropping, from *stalak-*: see STALACTITES, -OMETER.]

An apparatus for measuring the size, number, etc., of drops of liquid.

■ **stalagmometric** /-ˈmɛtrɪk/ *adjective* of or pertaining to a stalagmometer **E20.**

stalch /staltʃ/ *noun. rare.* **M18.**
[Origin unkn.]
MINING. A mass of ore left uncut and worked around.

stalder /ˈstɔːldə/ *noun.* **E17.**
[App. from Old English *stal-* base of *stellan* to place.]
†**1** A woodpile. *rare.* Only in **E17.**
2 = **STILLAGE** *noun*[1]. *dial.* **M18.**

stale /steɪl/ *noun*[1]. Now *dial.*
[Old English *stalu* (corresp. to Flemish, Frisian *staal* handle), from Germanic base also of **STEAL** *noun*[1].]
1 Orig., either of the stiles of a ladder. Later, a rung of a ladder. **OE.**
2 The handle or shaft of a tool. Formerly also *spec.*, an arrow shaft. Cf. **STEAL** *noun*[1] 4. **ME.**
3 = **STEAL** *noun*[1] 1. **LME.**

stale /steɪl/ *noun*[2]. **LME.**
[Prob. from Anglo-Norman *estal(e)* applied to a pigeon used to lure a hawk into a net; of Germanic origin, prob. from base of Old English *steall* **STALL** *noun*[1], *stellan* to place. Cf. **STALL** *noun*[2].]
1 (A figure of) a bird used as a decoy; *fig.* a person or thing acting as a decoy or bait. *obsolete* exc. *dial.* **LME.** ▸**b** A prostitute, *esp.* one employed as a thieves' decoy. *obsolete* exc. *Hist.* **L16.**
†**2 a** A person or thing used as a cover or pretext for some action; a stalking-horse. **L16–L18.** ▸**b** A lover ridiculed to amuse a rival. **L16–M17.**

stale /steɪl/ *noun*[3]. **LME.**
[Perh. from **STALE** *verb*[2].]
Urine (now only of horses and cattle).

†**stale** *noun*[4]. **LME–M17.**
[Anglo-Norman *estale* position, from *estaler* be placed, from Germanic.]
= **STALEMATE** *noun.*

stale /steɪl/ *noun*[5]. *colloq.* **L19.**
[from next.]
A stale cake, loaf of bread, etc.

stale /steɪl/ *adjective & verb*[1]. **ME.**
[Prob. from Anglo-Norman & Old French adjective (mod. *étale* (of water) stationary), from *estaler* come to a stand. Cf. **STALL** *verb*[1].]
▶ **A** *adjective.* **1** Of alcoholic liquor: clear from long standing; aged, strong. *obsolete* exc. *dial.* **ME.**
2 Of food, drink, air, etc.: no longer new or fresh; musty, rancid. **LME.** ▸**b** Of ground: lying fallow after long use. Now *dial.* **E18.**
3 *fig.* Lacking novelty or interest; hackneyed, trite; out of date. **M16.** ▸**b** *LAW.* Of a claim or demand: having been dormant an unreasonable time. **M18.** ▸**c** *COMMERCE.* Of an account etc.: inactive for a considerable time; (of a cheque) out of date. **L19.**
4 †**a** Of a person: no longer youthful; middle-aged, ageing. **M16–M19.** ▸**b** Having ability or performance impaired through excessive exertion or practice; *spec.* (of an athlete, race-horse, etc.) out of condition through excessive training or competition. **M19.**

> 🕮 **2** J. Barnes The carafe of stale water that nobody had bothered to change. R. MacNeil A waft of stale body odour. **3** A. G. Gardiner His jokes may be old, but they are never stale. A. Taylor The church, for me, has become a repository of stale attitudes. **4b** M. Duffy You get stale teaching.

▶ **B** *verb.* **1** *verb trans.* Make stale. **ME.** ▸†**b** Lower (oneself, one's dignity) in estimation by excessive familiarity. **L16–M19.**
2 *verb intrans.* Grow or become stale. **M18.**

> 🕮 **1** *Daily Telegraph* Thirty years together have not staled the work of the Amadeus Quartet. R. F. Hobson Our experience, staled by custom.

■ **stalely** *adverb* **L16.** **staleness** *noun* **M16.** **staling** *ppl adjective* that makes stale; ***staling substance*** (*BOTANY*), a substance produced by a fungus which inhibits its growth: **E20.** **stalish** *adjective* somewhat stale **M18.**

stale /steɪl/ *verb*[2]. **LME.**
[Perh. from Old French *estaler* take up a position, in spec. sense: see **STALE** *noun*[4]. Cf. **STALE** *noun*[3].]
1 *verb intrans.* Esp. of a horse or cattle: urinate. **LME.**
†**2** *verb trans.* Pass (blood) in the urine. **M16–M17.**
■ **staling** *noun* (*a*) the action of the verb; (*b*) (now *rare* or *obsolete*) = **STALE** *noun*[3]: **LME.**

stale /steɪl/ *verb*[3]. *rare.* **LME.**
[Prob. from Anglo-Norman *estaler*: see **STALE** *noun*[4].]
CHESS. **1** *verb trans.* = **STALEMATE** *verb.* **LME.**
2 *verb intrans.* Be stalemated. **L19.**

stalemate /ˈsteɪlmeɪt/ *noun & verb.* **M18.**
[from **STALE** *noun*[4] + **MATE** *noun*[1].]
▶ **A** *noun.* **1** *CHESS.* A position, now counting as a draw, in which the player whose turn it is to move is not in check, but cannot move except into check. **M18.**
2 *fig.* A drawn contest; a deadlock, a standstill. **L19.**

> 🕮 **2** *Opera Now* I reached a stalemate with the New York City Opera.

▶ **B** *verb trans.* Subject or bring to a stalemate. **M18.**

> 🕮 *Scotsman* Negotiations . . have been stalemated for three weeks.

Stalinesque /stɑːlɪˈnɛsk/ *adjective.* **M20.**
[formed as **STALINISM** + **-ESQUE.**]
= **STALINIST** *adjective.*

Stalinise *verb* var. of **STALINIZE.**

Stalinism /ˈstɑːlɪnɪz(ə)m/ *noun.* **E20.**
[from *Stalin*, surname adopted by Joseph Vissarionovich Dzhugashvili (1879–1953), Soviet Communist Party leader and head of State + **-ISM.**]
The policies pursued by Stalin; the version of Marxism-Leninism based on these, associated esp. with centralization, totalitarianism, and objectivism.

Stalinist /ˈstɑːlɪnɪst/ *noun & adjective.* **E20.**
[formed as prec. + **-IST.**]
▶ **A** *noun.* A supporter or advocate of Stalin or Stalinism. **E20.**
▶ **B** *adjective.* Of, pertaining to, or characteristic of Stalin or Stalinism. **E20.**
*LENINIST–****Stalinist.***
■ Also **Stalinite** *noun & adjective* (*rare*) **E20.**

Stalinize /ˈstɑːlɪnʌɪz/ *verb trans.* Also **-ise.** **M20.**
[formed as **STALINISM** + **-IZE.**]
Make Stalinist in character; apply Stalinist policy or practice to.
■ **Staliniˈzation** *noun* **M20.**

Stalinoid /ˈstɑːlɪnɔɪd/ *adjective.* **M20.**
[formed as **STALINISM** + **-OID.**]
Resembling or characteristic of Stalinism.

Stalin organ /ˈstɑːlɪn ˈɔːg(ə)n/ *noun phr. Military slang.* **M20.**
[from *Stalin* (see **STALINISM**) + **ORGAN** *noun*[1].]
A type of multi-barrelled mobile rocket launcher of the former USSR.

stalk /stɔːk/ *noun*[1]. **ME.**
[Prob. dim. (with *k* suffix) of **STALE** *noun*[1].]
1 a The slender attachment or support of a leaf, flower, fruit, etc.; a petiole, pedicel, etc. **ME.** ▸**b** Chiefly *ZOOLOGY & MEDICINE.* A similar slender connecting part by which an animal, organ, or structure is attached or supported. **E19.**
2 The main stem of a herbaceous plant. **LME.** ▸**b** The woody core of hemp and flax. **L16.**
3 Any upright slender object; *spec.* (***a***) a tall chimney stack; (***b***) *coarse slang* a penis, *esp.* an erect one. **LME.**
4 The central or supporting shaft of something; a stem; *spec.* the stem of a wineglass. **LME.** ▸**b** A lever on the steering column of a motor vehicle controlling the indicators, lights, etc. (also ***stalk switch***). Also, a gear lever. *colloq.* **M20.** ▸**c** In a motor vehicle: a flexible arm holding the mounting by which a seat-belt latch is secured. **L20.**
2 eyes on stalks: see **EYE** *noun.*
Comb.: **stalk borer** *US* any of several moths which have larvae that bore into stems; *esp.* the noctuid *Papaipema nebris*, which is destructive to maize, vegetables, and flowers. **stalk-eyed** *adjective* (*ZOOLOGY*) having the eye at the end of a stalk, as in many crustaceans; ***stalk switch***: see sense 4b above.
■ **stalked** *adjective* (chiefly *BOTANY, ZOOLOGY, & MEDICINE*) having a stalk or stalks (opp. ***sessile***) **LME.** **stalkiness** *noun* the quality of being stalky **L20.** **stalkless** *adjective* **L17.** **stalklet** *noun* a small stalk **L18.** **stalklike** *adjective* resembling (that of) a stalk **M19.** **stalky** *adjective* (***a***) consisting of or having many stalks; (***b***) resembling (that of) a stalk, long and slender; (***c***) (of wine) retaining a tannic, unripe taste from excessive contact with the grape-stalks during production: **M16.**

stalk /stɔːk/ *verb*[1] *& noun*[2].
[Late Old English verb repr. in *bistealcian* and *stealcung* verbal noun, ult. from Germanic base also of **STEAL** *verb.*]
▶ **A** *verb.* †**1** *verb intrans.* Walk cautiously or stealthily. **LOE–L16.**
2 *verb intrans.* Pursue a quarry or game by stealthy approach, esp. under cover. **LME.**
3 *verb trans.* Pursue (game, an enemy, etc.) stealthily. Also, track *down* in this way. **LME.** ▸**b** Go through (an area) stalking or pursuing game. **M19.**
4 a *verb intrans.* Walk with long stiff strides, esp. in an imposing or haughty manner. **E16.** ▸**b** *verb trans.* Stride along or through in this way. **E17.**
5 *verb trans.* Harass or persecute (someone) with unwanted and obsessive attention. Cf. **STALKER** 4. **M20.**

> 🕮 **2** J. H. Patterson The roars . . ceased, and we knew . . [the lions] were stalking for their prey. **3** E. Welty Cat was stalking something at the . . edge of the ditch. R. Rendell That ever-present fear of an assassin stalking Sheila. **4a** E. Blishen In a rage, I . . stalked out. *Punch* Magazines . . told her to stalk around in shoulder-pads. **b** H. Ainsworth Like a hideous phantom stalking the streets. **5** Annie Wood If you keep popping up in the cafe she's gonna think you're stalking her.

▶ **B** *noun.* **1** The action or an act of stalking game. **LME.**
2 A stalking or striding gait. **L16.**
■ **stalkable** *adjective* **L19.** **stalking** *ppl adjective* (***a***) that stalks; (***b***) *fig.* pompous, grandiloquent: **LME.**

stalk /stɔːk/ *verb*[2]. *rare.* **M17.**
[from **STALK** *noun*[1].]
1 *verb intrans.* Of a plant: put out a stalk or stalks. **M17.**
2 *verb trans.* Remove the stalks from (fruit). **E20.**

stalker /ˈstɔːkə/ *noun.* **LME.**
[from **STALK** *verb*[1] + **-ER**[1].]
†**1** A kind of fishing net used by poachers. **LME–M17.**
2 Orig. (*Scot.*), a poacher. Later, a person who stalks game. **LME.**
3 A person who walks with a stalking gait. **L16.**
4 A person who pursues another, esp. as part of an investigation or with criminal intent; *spec.* a person who harasses or persecutes someone with unwanted and obsessive attention. **M20.**

stalking-horse /ˈstɔːkɪŋhɔːs/ *noun.* **E16.**
[from *stalking* verbal noun of **STALK** *verb*[1] + **HORSE** *noun.*]
1 A horse behind which or under whose coverings a fowler or stalker is concealed; a light portable screen, freq. in the shape of a horse, used similarly in stalking game. **E16.**
2 *fig.* A false expedient or pretext concealing a person's real intentions or actions; a participant in an action used to divert attention from the real object or design; a decoy, a spoiler. **L16.**

> 🕮 **2** G. B. Shaw The Gaelic movement has got a footing by using Nationalism as a stalking-horse. *attrib.*: *Independent* They would run a 'stalking-horse' candidate to test the level of party dissatisfaction with the Prime Minister's performance.

stall /stɔːl/ *noun*[1].
[Old English *steall* = Old Frisian, Middle & mod. Dutch, Old High German *stal* (German *Stall*), Old Norse *stallr* pedestal, stall for a horse, from Germanic, prob. from base also of **STAND** *verb*; in some senses also partly from Old French *estal* (mod. *étal*). In branch II from **STALL** *verb*[1].]
▶ **I** †**1** *gen.* Place, position. **OE–E17.**
2 A standing-place or shelter for domesticated animals, esp. horses or cattle (*sing.* & in *pl.*); a stable, a cowshed, etc.; any of the individual compartments into which this may be divided. Also, any of the partitioned compartments of a starting-gate on a racecourse (also ***starting stall***). **OE.** ▸**b** A marked-off parking space for a single motor vehicle, esp. under cover. *N. Amer.* **M20.** ▸**c** An individual cubicle in a shower-room, lavatory, etc. **M20.**
3 †**a** A chair of State or office; a throne. **ME–M17.** ▸**b** A fixed seat, wholly or partially enclosed at the back and sides; *esp.* such a seat, freq. canopied, in the choir or chancel of a church, reserved for (a specified member of) the clergy or the higher orders of knighthood; *transf.* the office or dignity associated with this, as a canonry etc. **LME.** ▸**c** A long bench or doorless pew in a church. **L16.** ▸**d** Any of the set of seats in front of the pit in a theatre or concert hall, or on the ground floor of a cinema etc. (usu. in *pl.*); *transf.* (in *pl.*) the people occupying this area. **E19.**
4 A bench or table in front of a shop etc. for displaying goods for sale (also ***stall-board***); a vendor's booth or stand in a market, street, etc. **ME.**
5 A sheath or receptacle for a single object; *spec.* (***a***) each of the fingers or thumb of a glove; (***b***) any of a line of loops on a garment for holding cartridges etc. **L15.**
†**6** = **STILLAGE** *noun*[1]. **M16–M17.**
7 Any of a line of bookcases set at right angles to the walls of a library. Long *obsolete* exc. *Hist.* **L16.**
8 A working in a coal seam. **M17.**

> 🕮 **2** B. Malamud Two teams of horses—leaving six horses in the stalls. *New Scientist* Concrete-floored sow stalls . . can make the animals cold and uncomfortable. **c** N. Mailer I went . . to the men's room, and in the stall, locked the door. B. T. Bradford He stepped into the shower stall. **3b** W. F. Buckley The monks, seated in the chair stalls beyond the rood screen . . responded in the Gregorian mode. *PREBENDAL* ***stall.*** **d** P. Scott In those days one dressed for stalls and dress circle. **4** L. Spalding Along the highway, fruit stalls would be deserted for the night. **set out one's stall** display or show off one's abilities, attributes, or experience in order to fulfil an objective. **5** ***finger-stall***: see **FINGER** *noun.* **8** ***pillar and stall***: see **PILLAR** *noun.*

▶ **II 9** A feeling of surfeit; satiety. *Scot.* **L18.**
10 a *AERONAUTICS.* The condition of an aircraft when there is a progressive breakdown of the airflow over the wings, usu. due to low air speed or high angle of attack; the sudden loss of lift and height resulting from this. **E20.** ▸**b** The sudden stopping or cutting out of an internal-combustion engine or vehicle, due to low revolutions, insufficient fuel, etc. **M20.**
Comb.: **stall-board** (***a***) see sense 4 above; (***b***) a partition between individual stalls in a stable etc.; †**stall boat** a kind of fishing boat anchored in a river mouth; **stall-fed** *adjective* (of an animal) kept and fed in a stall, esp. for fattening; **stall-feed** *verb trans.* feed (an animal) in a stall, esp. for fattening; **stall-holder** (***a***) the holder of an ecclesiastical stall; (***b***) a vendor with a stall at a market etc.; (***c***) a seat-holder in the stalls of a theatre etc.; **stall-keeper** †(***a***) a stable-owner; (***b***) = ***stall-holder*** (b) above; **stallout** *US* = sense 10a above; **stall plate** an engraved metal plate bearing the arms of a knight fixed in a church or chapel stall; **stall-reader** a person

who peruses the books on a bookstall; **stall seat**: in the stalls of a theatre etc.; **stall shower**: enclosed in a cubicle; **stall turn** AERONAUTICS a turn achieved by stalling one wing of an aircraft, causing increased drag on that wing and reduction of the radius of the turn; **stall-turn** *verb intrans.* (AERONAUTICS) achieve a turn in this manner.
■ **stallite** *noun* (*rare*) a ticket-holder for the stalls in a theatre etc. L19.

stall /stɔːl/ *noun*^{2}. L15.
[Anglo-Norman *estal* var. of *estale*: see STALE *noun*^{2}.]
†**1** A decoy-bird. L15–L16.
2 An accomplice used to create a diversion by a thief, esp. by a pickpocket. *slang*. L16.
3 An evasive trick or excuse; a pretence, a blind. Also more fully ***stall-off***. *colloq.* E19.
4 The action or an act of stalling for time; (a) prevarication. *colloq.* M20.

📖 **3** W. FAULKNER If it was a stall, dont common sense tell you I'd have invented a better one? **4** D. E. WESTLAKE This isn't a stall . . I do have the money.

stall /stɔːl/ *noun*^{3}. *Scot. & north.* E16.
[Prob. rel. to STADDLE *noun*.]
A hive or colony of bees; a beehive.

stall /stɔːl/ *verb*^{1}. ME.
[Partly from Old French *estaler* stop, sit in choir, from *estal* STALL *noun*^{1}; partly directly from STALL *noun*^{1}; partly aphet. from INSTALL. Cf. FORESTALL *verb*, ESTALL, STELL *verb*.]
▶ **I 1** *verb intrans.* Orig., reside, dwell. Now (*dial.*), put up *with*, tolerate a person. ME.
2 *verb trans.* Assign a particular place to. Long *obsolete* exc. *poet.* LME. ▸†**b** *verb trans.* Fix, appoint beforehand; *spec.* = ESTALL. LME–L19.
†**3** *verb trans.* Induct (a king, bishop, etc.) formally into a seat of rule or dignity; *spec.* install (a member of the clergy, knight, etc.) formally or ceremonially; enthrone. LME–M17.
4 *verb trans.* Keep or confine (an animal) in a stall, esp. for fattening. Also foll. by *up*. LME. ▸**b** Satiate (as) with overfeeding; surfeit. Now *Scot. & dial.* L16. ▸**c** Weary, fatigue. Usu. in *pass.* Chiefly *Scot. & north.* E19.
5 *verb trans.* Provide with a stall or stalls; divide into stalls. Chiefly as ***stalled*** *ppl adjective*. E16.
▶ **II 6** *verb trans. & intrans.* Bring or come to a standstill, esp. suddenly or unexpectedly; stick fast (as) in mud, snow, etc. Now chiefly *US*. LME. ▸**b** *verb trans.* Avert; frighten *off*. Now *rare* or *obsolete*. M17. ▸**c** *verb intrans.* Loiter; hang *around*. *US colloq.* E20.
7 a *verb intrans.* (Of an aircraft) enter a stall; (of an engine, vehicle, etc.) stop suddenly, cut out; (of a pilot or driver) cause this to happen. Also (*US*) foll. by *out*. E20. ▸**b** *verb trans.* Cause (an aircraft, vehicle, engine, etc.) to stall. E20.

📖 **6** J. CARROLL Curley . . stalled . . , not knowing where to go. P. MAILLOUX Emma was now unhappy . . , their relationship seemed stalled. **7a** A. DILLARD The plane looped the loop . . stalled, dropped, and spun. **b** L. GRANT-ADAMSON In her haste she stalled the engine.

Phrases: **stalled cairn** ARCHAEOLOGY a type of neolithic cairn found in the Orkneys, covering a burial-chamber and divided into cells by stone slabs projecting from the walls.
Comb.: **stall-in** *US* a form of protest using stationary vehicles to block a road.
¶ In sense 6 not always distinguishable from STALL *verb*^{2}.
■ **stalling** *noun* (*a*) the action of the verb; (*b*) (a place of) accommodation for an animal: LME.

stall /stɔːl/ *verb*^{2}. L16.
[from STALL *noun*^{2}.]
1 *verb trans. & intrans.* Act as an accomplice or decoy for (a pickpocket etc.). *slang*. L16.
2 *verb trans.* Foll. by *off*: evade or extricate from difficulty by artifice. *slang*. E19.
3 a *verb trans.* Put off; delay or postpone with an excuse etc. Also foll. by *off*. E19. ▸**b** *verb intrans.* Prevaricate; be evasive; temporize. E20.

📖 **3a** J. CROSBY Bargain some more. It's the only way left to stall him. **b** J. BLUME They were stalling, passing it back and forth. *Evening Press (Eire)* Do not let a friend stall on repaying a loan. **stall for time** = *play for time* s.v. PLAY *verb*.

¶ In sense 3 not always distinguishable from STALL *verb*^{1}.

stallage /ˈstɔːlɪdʒ/ *noun*. ME.
[Aphet. from Old French *estalage* (mod. *étalage*), from *estal*: see STALL *noun*^{1}, -AGE.]
1 (A tax or fee charged for) the right to erect and use a stall in a market etc. Also, space for such a stall or stalls. ME.
2 Orig. *gen.*, a stand, a stage. Now *spec.* (*dial.*) = STILLAGE *noun*^{1}. L15.

†**stallager** *noun* see STALLENGER.

stallar /ˈstɔːlə, ˈstal-/ *noun*. M16.
[medieval Latin *stallarius*, from *stallum*, *stalla* stall.]
SCOTTISH ECCLESIASTICAL HISTORY. A vicar serving in a cathedral as opp. to a parish.
■ **stallary** *noun* the office or position of stallar E17.

stallenger /ˈstɔːlɪndʒə, ˈstal-/ *noun*. *Scot. & north. obsolete* exc. *Hist.* Also (earlier) †**stallager**. ME.
[Aphet. from Old French *estalagier*, from *estalage* STALLAGE. For the intrusive *n* cf. *messenger*, *passenger*, etc.]
A stall-holder; *esp.* a small trader or craftsman paying a stallage fee, being neither a member of a merchant guild nor a freeman of a burgh.

staller /ˈstɔːlə/ *noun*^{1}.
[Late Old English *stallere*, *steallere*, from *steall* STALL *noun*^{1}, after medieval Latin *stabularius*.]
Hist. In the reign of Edward the Confessor, (the title of) a high-ranking officer in the service of the king; a constable.

staller /ˈstɔːlə/ *noun*^{2}. E19.
[from STALL *verb*^{2} + -ER^1.]
A person who stalls; a prevaricator.

stallion /ˈstaljən/ *noun*. ME.
[Anglo-Norman var. of Old French *estalon* (mod. *étalon*), from Proto-Romance deriv. of Germanic base also of STALL *noun*^{1}.]
1 A promiscuous person, esp. a man. ME.
2 An uncastrated adult male horse, *esp.* one kept for breeding. LME. ▸**b** More fully ***stallion hound***. A male dog kept for breeding. E19.

stalloy /stəˈlɔɪ/ *noun*. E20.
[App. arbitrarily from ST(EEL *noun*^{1} + ALLOY *noun*.]
METALLURGY. A high quality steel alloy containing silicon, used in electrical engineering for its high magnetic permeability.

†**stalment** *noun*. LME–E18.
[Anglo-Norman *estal(l)ement*, formed as ESTALL: see -MENT. Cf. ESTALMENT.]
(An) arrangement to pay by instalments; an instalment.

stalwart /ˈstɔːlwət, ˈstal-/ *adjective & noun*. LME.
[Scot. var. of next.]
▶ **A** *adjective*. **1** Strongly built; sturdy, robust. LME.
2 Resolute, determined; staunch, loyal. LME. ▸**b** Courageous in battle; valiant. Formerly also, (of a fight) strongly or bravely contested. *arch.* LME.
†**3** Of weather: violent, tempestuous. *literary. Scot.* E16–E19.

📖 **1** J. STEINBECK An old man . . riding on the stalwart shoulders of his nephew. **2** J. B. PRIESTLEY The most stalwart devotees of the . . old beer. F. SPALDING She respected the . . stalwart reliability of her neighbours.

▶ **B** *noun*. **1** A stalwart person; now *esp.*, a loyal uncompromising partisan, a staunch or doctrinaire supporter. LME.
2 (S-.) US HISTORY. A member of an extremist faction within the Republican Party. L19.
¶ Not recorded in 18; revived in E19 by Sir Walter Scott.
■ **stalwartism** *noun* (*rare*) (*a*) the principles of a stalwart or stalwarts; (*b*) the nature or character of a stalwart: L19. **stalwartly** *adverb* (now *rare*) LME. **stalwartness** *noun* (*rare*) M19.

stalworth /ˈstɔːlwəθ/ *adjective & noun*. *arch.*
[Old English *stælwierþe*, from *stæl* place + *weorþ*, *worþ* WORTH *adjective*.]
▶ **A** *adjective*. *arch.*
†**1** Of a thing: serviceable. Only in OE.
2 = STALWART *adjective* 1, 2. ME.
▶†**B** *noun*. A stalwart person. ME–L15.

Stambouline /stambuːˈliːn/ *adjective & noun*. E19.
[French or Italian, from *Stamboul* earlier form of *Istanbul* former capital of Turkey: see -INE^1.]
▶ **A** *adjective*. Of or pertaining to Istanbul. *arch.* E19.
▶ **B** *noun*. (Also s-.) A long usu. ornamental Turkish robe worn under a dolman. L19.

stamen /ˈsteɪmən/ *noun*. Pl. **-mens**, (now *rare*) **-mina** /-mɪnə/. M17.
[Latin = (thread of) warp, applied by Pliny to the stamens of a lily, corresp. to Greek *stēmōn* warp, *stēma* some part of a plant. Cf. STAMINA *noun*^{1}.]
†**1** The warp of a fabric. *rare*. M–L17.
2 BOTANY. The male reproductive organ of a flower, usu. consisting of an anther and a filament. M17.
†**3** In CLASSICAL MYTHOLOGY, the thread of a person's life, spun by the Fates at his or her birth; the measure of vitality supposedly allocated at birth, determining the length of a person's normal life. Also, the fundamental element or quintessence *of* a thing. Only in 18.

Stamford /ˈstamfəd/ *adjective*. M20.
[A town in Lincolnshire, England.]
ARCHAEOLOGY. Designating a kind of Saxo-Norman lead-glazed pottery made of estuarine clay from the area around Stamford.

†**stamin** *noun*. ME.
[Old French *estamine* (mod. *étamine*), from fem. of Latin *stamineus* 'consisting of threads', formed as STAMEN. Cf. TAMINE.]
1 (An undergarment made of) stammel. ME–L15.
2 = TAMMY *noun*^{1}. LME–L18.

stamina /ˈstamɪnə/ *noun*^{1}. L17.
[Latin, pl. of STAMEN. The senses arise partly from sense 'warp (of cloth)', partly from application of pl. to the threads spun by the Fates.]
†**1** *pl.* The original or essential elements or form of something, esp. an organism; rudiments. L17–E19.
†**2** *pl.* The innate strength or vitality of a person's constitution, formerly supposed to govern or affect length of life. E18–E19.
3 *sing.* & (orig.) †*pl.* The ability to endure esp. physical strain or fatigue; capacity for resistance or endurance; staying power, perseverance. E18.

📖 **3** S. J. PERELMAN Sightseeing at ninety-six degrees requires stamina. E. H. GOMBRICH He lacked the stamina for trying again and again.

stamina *noun*^{2} pl. of STAMEN.

staminal /ˈstamɪn(ə)l/ *adjective*. L18.
[from Latin *stamin-* stem of STAMEN + -AL^1.]
1 Of or pertaining to the stamina or natural constitution of a person or thing. L18.
2 BOTANY. Pertaining to or consisting of stamens. M19.

staminate /ˈstamɪnət/ *adjective*. M19.
[formed as prec. + -ATE^2.]
BOTANY. Of a flower: having stamens but no female organs. Opp. ***pistillate***.

stamineous /stəˈmɪnɪəs/ *adjective*. Now *rare* or *obsolete*. M17.
[formed as prec. + -EOUS.]
BOTANY. Consisting of or pertaining to a stamen or stamens.

staminiferous /stamɪˈnɪf(ə)rəs/ *adjective*. M18.
[formed as prec. + -FEROUS.]
BOTANY. Having or bearing stamens; *spec.* = STAMINATE.

staminode /ˈstamɪnəʊd/ *noun*. Also (earlier) in Latin form **staminodium** /-ˈnəʊdɪəm/, pl. **-dia** /-dɪə/. E19.
[from Latin *stamin-* stem of STAMEN + -ODE^1.]
BOTANY. A sterile or abortive stamen, (freq. resembling a stamen without its anther).

staminody /ˈstamɪnəʊdi/ *noun*. M19.
[formed as prec. + -Y^3 (cf. PETALODY).]
BOTANY. Abnormal metamorphosis of floral organs into stamens.

staminoid /ˈstamɪnɔɪd/ *adjective*. M19.
[from Latin *stamin-* stem of STAMEN + -OID.]
BOTANY. Of the nature of or resembling a stamen.

Stammbaum /ˈʃtambaʊm/ *noun*. Pl. **-bäume** /-bɔymə/. M20.
[German.]
LINGUISTICS. A family tree of languages.
Comb.: ***Stammbaumtheorie*** /-teoˌriː/ the linguistic theory likening relationships between languages to genetic relationships.

stammel /ˈstam(ə)l/ *noun*. *obsolete* exc. *Hist.* M16.
[Prob. alt. (with var. of suffix) of STAMIN.]
A coarse woollen cloth formerly used esp. for underwear. Also, the shade of red in which this cloth was usu. dyed.

stammer /ˈstamə/ *verb & noun*. Also (*dial.*) **staumer**.
[Late Old English *stamerian* = Old Saxon *stamaron*, Middle & mod. Low German, Middle & mod. Dutch *stameren*, from West Germanic base also of STUMBLE, repr. by Old English *stam(m*, Old High German *stamm*, Old Norse *stamr*, Gothic *stamms* stammering.]
▶ **A** *verb*. **1** *verb intrans.* Speak with halting articulation; *esp.* speak with repeated pauses or involuntary repetitions of the same consonant or vowel, freq. because of indecision, embarrassment, etc., or from a speech impairment. Cf. STUTTER *verb*. LOE.
2 *verb intrans.* Esp. of a horse: stagger or stumble in walking. Now *Scot. & dial.* LME.
3 *verb trans.* Say or express with stammering articulation. Also foll. by *forth*, *out*. L16.

📖 **1** P. LARKIN I . . stammered to the point of handing over little slips of paper. **3** H. JAMES He stammered out that it was for *her* he should like to buy something. D. ARKELL As she said . . 'A quoi bon?' she raised her head slightly on the stammered b-b-b.

▶ **B** *noun*. The action or an instance of stammering; a tendency to stammer in speech, a speech impairment. L18.

📖 M. MCCARTHY 'You never expected a *g*-grandson . . ,' pointed out Priss with her slight nervous stammer.

■ **stammerer** *noun* †(*a*) = STAMMER *noun*; (*b*) a person who stammers: LME.

Stammtisch /ˈʃtamtɪʃ/ *noun*. Pl. **-e** /-ə/. M20.
[German, from *Stamm* core, regular stock + *Tisch* table.]
In Germany, a table reserved for regular customers in a restaurant etc.

stamnos /ˈstamnɒs/ *noun*. Pl. **-noi** /-nɔɪ/. M19.
[Greek, from *(hi)stanai* cause to stand.]
GREEK ANTIQUITIES. A vessel resembling a hydria but with shorter neck.

stamp /stamp/ *noun*. LME.
[Partly from the verb, partly from Old & mod. French *estampe*, from *estamper*: see next.]
▶ **I 1** An instrument for stamping or impressing a pattern or lettering on a surface. LME. ▶†**b** A printing-press. M16–E17.
2 In *pl.* Legs. *slang*. M16.
3 Any of the blocks or pestles used to crush ore in a stamp-mill; in *pl.*, a stamp-mill. L17. ▶**b** Maize crushed or pounded with a pestle. More fully ***stamp mealies***. Cf. SAMP. *S. Afr.* E20.
1 ***rubber stamp***: see RUBBER *noun*[1] *& adjective*.
▶ **II** The result of stamping.
4 An impression made with an engraved block or die; *spec.* (*a*) an official mark validating a document or certifying the quality of goods etc.; (*b*) the impression unique to a particular issue of a coin; (*c*) a postmark. M16.
5 *fig.* **a** A characteristic mark or sign *of* some quality or influence. L16. ▶**b** Character; cast, type. L16. ▶**c** (A mark of) authoritative approval. E17.
†**6** A stamped coin or medal. L16–M17.
†**7** A printed picture; an engraving. E17–L18.
8 An embossed or impressed mark issued by a government office and placed on a deed, bill of exchange, etc., as evidence of payment of tax. L17. ▶**b** A small adhesive piece of paper indicating payment or credit of a specified amount; *spec.* (*a*) = POSTAGE ***stamp***; (*b*) = INSURANCE ***stamp***; (*c*) = TRADING ***stamp***. M19. ▶**c** In *pl.* Money, esp. paper money. *US slang*. M19.

> 🕮 **4** J. ARCHER You can see on the back of the canvas the stamp of the Berlin National Gallery. **5a** T. WILLIAMS I haven't noticed the stamp of genius . . on Stanley's forehead. A. STEVENS Freudian psychoanalysis . . bears the stamp of its creator's personality. **b** R. L. STEVENSON He is a hero of the old Greek stamp. **c** *Animal World* The only brand . . to get the WDCS's stamp of approval is Sainsbury's . . Skipjack Tuna. **8b** J. TROLLOPE 'Six first class stamps,' Janet . . said through the grille. FOOD ***stamp***.

▶ **III 9** A heavy downward blow with the foot; the sound produced by this. L16.

> 🕮 **9** *Sunday Express* The . . mechanic gave an impatient stamp of his foot.

Comb.: **Stamp Act** any of various Acts of Parliament regulating stamp-duty, esp. (*Hist.*) that imposing stamp-duty on the American colonies in 1765 and repealed in 1766; **stamp-album** a book for the preservation and display of a stamp collection; **stamp book** (*a*) = ***stamp-album*** above; (*b*) a book containing sheets of postage stamps for sale; **stamp booklet** a small folder containing postage stamps sold at a post office etc.; **stamp catalogue** a reference book for philatelists; **stamp-collecting** *noun & adjective* (practising) philately; **stamp collection** a philatelist's collection of postage stamps; **stamp-collector** (*a*) a collector of stamp-duty; (*b*) a philatelist; **stamp-duty** a duty imposed on certain kinds of legal document, collected by means of stamps; ***stamp-hinge***: see HINGE *noun* 1c; **stamp machine** a coin-operated machine for selling postage stamps; ***stamp mealies***: see sense 3b above; **stamp-mill** a mill for crushing ore etc. using a machine-operated pestle or pestles; **stamp office** an office issuing government stamps and receiving stamp-duty; **stamp paper** (*a*) paper with the government revenue stamp; (*b*) the gummed marginal paper of a sheet of postage stamps; **stamp war** competition amongst retailers supplying trading stamps to customers.

stamp /stamp/ *verb*. ME.
[Prob. from Old English unrecorded verb = Middle & mod. Low German, Middle & mod. Dutch *stampen*, Old High German *stampfōn* pound (German *stampfen* stamp with the foot, pound, crush), Old Norse *stappa*, from Germanic, prob. from nasalized var. of base of STEP *verb*; reinforced or infl. in sense by Old & mod. French *estamper* stamp, from Germanic. Cf. STOMP *verb*.]
▶ **I 1** *verb trans.* Beat to a pulp or powder; mash; now *spec.*, crush (ore) with a stamp. ME. ▶†**b** Crush or press to extract juice etc. LME–E17. ▶**c** Thresh. Long *obsolete* exc. *dial.* LME.
▶ **II 2** *verb intrans.* **a** Bring down one's foot heavily to crush something, esp. as an expression of anger; trample *on* or *upon*. Also *transf.* (now *US*), be very angry. LME. ▶**b** Walk with a heavy tread; pound, tramp. L15. ▶**c** Strike the ground heavily with one's foot making a noise, esp. as a signal or for emphasis etc. M16.
3 *verb trans.* **a** Bring into a specified state by stamping; trample *down*, shake *off*, etc., by this action. LME. ▶**b** Trample heavily on in order to crush. E17. ▶**c** Strike the ground noisily with (one's foot), esp. as an expression of annoyance, anger, etc. Also, stamp with (one's shoes etc.) to remove mud or snow. E19.

> 🕮 **2a** G. ORWELL Imagine a boot stamping on a human face. **b** E. WAUGH Everyone stamps up and down the bare boards to keep warm. **3a** G. GREENE He stamped the mud off his boots before entering the house. **b** Z. TOMIN Children spread and stamp the hay on the wagon. **c** S. SASSOON Disconsolate men who stamp their sodden boots. W. GOLDING She stamped her foot like a child.

▶ **III** *verb trans.* **4** Impress or print (a surface, esp. metal or paper) with or *with* a pattern or lettering by means of an embossed die or block; impress (a pattern, lettering, etc.) on a surface in this way. Also, mint (a coin etc.) by this process. LME. ▶†**b** Print (a book etc.). M16–E19. ▶**c** Make by cutting out with a die or mould. Also foll. by *out*. L18.
5 Impress with or *with* a mark as proof of genuineness, quality, or official inspection; impress (such a mark) on merchandise etc. M16.
6 *fig.* **a** Imprint *on* or fix *in* the mind or memory. M16. ▶**b** Declare or reveal to be, mark out *as*. L16. ▶**c** Assign (a specific character) to, impress (a characteristic) *on*, mark *with*; distinguish, characterize. M17. ▶**d** Give authoritative approval to. Now *rare*. L17.
7 Affix an adhesive stamp to as proof of payment of a tax etc.; now *esp.*, affix a postage stamp to. M18.

> 🕮 **4** I. MCEWAN A . . chest covered in brass with figures stamped upon it. **c** P. CAREY Lucy . . cut the scones into squares, although she knew Mrs Stratton liked them stamped out round. **5** P. L. FERMOR The yawning official stamped my passport. *Garbage* Merchandise stamped with Earth-friendly slogans. **6a** W. GOLDING What I saw . . will be stamped on my mind till my dying day. **b** N. PODHORETZ Criteria existed by which I and everyone I knew were stamped as inferior. **c** CARLYLE That frankness of speech which stamps the independent man. J. CONRAD His . . appearance was stamped with the mark of cold and hunger. *Time* The man in charge of foreign policy . . has stamped his distinctive style on it. **7** A. HOLLINGHURST Letters stamped for the post.

Phrases etc.: **stamp and go** *slang* (*a*) NAUTICAL (the performance of) an order to sailors to carry out certain duties; (*b*) in the W. Indies, a simple codfish fritter. **stamped addressed envelope** a self-addressed envelope with affixed stamp, enclosed with a letter for an expected reply. **stamped leather** leather covered with gold or silver leaf and embossed with an elaborate design, used esp. in wall-hangings in the 16th and 17th cents. **stamped mealies** *S. Afr.* = STAMP *noun* 3b. **stamp one's authority on** impose one's views, wishes, etc., on.
With adverbs & prepositions in specialized senses: **stamp on** (*a*) suppress, put an end to; (*b*) see senses 6a, b above. **stamp out** (*a*) see sense 4c above; (*b*) extinguish (a fire) by trampling on it; *transf.* put an end to, eradicate, suppress.
■ **stampable** *adjective* able to be stamped; liable to stamp-duty: E19. **stampage** *noun* (*a*) a stamped impression; (*b*) postage charged on a letter or parcel: L19.

stampede /stamˈpiːd/ *noun & verb*. E19.
[Mexican Spanish use of Spanish *estampida* crash, uproar, use as noun of fem. pa. pple of Proto-Romance verb, from Germanic base also of STAMP *verb*.]
▶ **A** *noun*. **1** A sudden rush or flight of panic-stricken animals, esp. cattle. E19.
2 *transf.* A sudden or impulsive rush, mass action or movement; *spec.* (*a*) *US* a sudden rush of support for a political candidate, esp. at a convention; (*b*) N. AMER. HISTORY a gold-rush. M19. ▶**b** An uproarious kind of dance. Chiefly *US*. M19.
3 A gathering or festival exhibiting cowboy skills; a rodeo. *N. Amer.* E20.

> 🕮 **1** P. L. FERMOR The pigs rushed out in a hysterical stampede. **2** B. POTTER There was suddenly a stampede of farmers into the . . refreshment room.

▶ **B** *verb*. **1** *verb intrans.* Move or rush in a stampede. E19.
2 *verb trans.* Cause a stampede amongst; cause to move or rush (as) in a stampede. M19.

> 🕮 **1** BEVERLEY CLEARY The whole class forgot the rules and went stampeding out the door.

■ **stampeder** *noun* (*N. Amer.*) a person who takes part in or causes a stampede M19.

stamper /ˈstampə/ *noun*. LME.
[from STAMP *verb* + -ER[1].]
1 A person who stamps with the feet. LME.
2 An instrument used for stamping; *esp.* any of the pestles in a stamp-mill (cf. STAMP *noun* 3). L15. ▶**b** An original recording of a gramophone record from which other copies are pressed. E20.
3 A person who uses a stamp or stamping machine; *spec.* a postal employee who stamps letters etc. M16.
4 In *pl.* Shoes; feet. *slang*. Now *rare* or *obsolete*. M16.

stamping /ˈstampɪŋ/ *noun*. LME.
[from STAMP *verb* + -ING[1].]
1 The action of STAMP *verb*. LME.
2 a In *pl.* Pounded or crushed matter. L16. ▶**b** A stamped object; stamped ornamentation. M19.
Comb. & phrases: ***blind stamping***: see BLIND *adjective*; **stamping-ground** a favourite place of resort, a haunt; **stamping tube** MUSIC a wooden (usu. bamboo) tube beaten rhythmically on the ground, played esp. in S. America and Pacific islands.

Stancarist /staŋˈkeːrɪst/ *noun*. *rare*. M17.
[from *Stancarus* Latinized form of the name of Francesco *Stancari* (see below) + -IST.]
Hist. A follower or adherent of Francesco Stancari (1501–74), Italian theologian, who taught that the atonement of Christ was attributable to his human nature as opp. to his divine origin.

stance /stɑːns, stans/ *noun*. ME.
[French, formed as STANZA. Cf. STANCHION.]
1 *gen.* A standing-place, a station, a position. Now *rare*. ME. ▶**b** The position of a player's feet when hitting a ball etc., esp. in playing a golf-stroke; *transf.* a standing attitude or position of the body. L18. ▶**c** A platform, a ledge; *spec.* (MOUNTAINEERING) a ledge or foothold on which a belay can be secured. E19. ▶**d** *fig.* A standpoint, an attitude of mind, esp. in relation to a specified object. M20.
2 *Scot.* **a** A site; *esp.* an area for building on. Also ***building-stance***. M17. ▶**b** A street-trader's pitch; a location for a fair or market. E19. ▶**c** A place where public vehicles wait for passengers; a bus-stop, a taxi-rank. E20.

> 🕮 **1** J. C. ATKINSON My lads . . shot fifteen of these depredators from one stance. **b** C. POTOK He walked . . almost in imitation of a boxer's ring stance. P. USTINOV The stance of his body is a . . mixture of affectation and arrogance. **c** *High Magazine* Sustained difficulties on ice with poor stances and bivouacs. **d** A. S. DALE Both men adopted the classic . . stance that they must be free to criticize.

stanch /stɑːn(t)ʃ, stɔːn(t)ʃ/ *noun*[1]. Also **staunch** /stɔːn(t)ʃ/. Long *obsolete* exc. *dial.* LME.
[from the verb.]
1 A substance that arrests bleeding, a styptic. LME.
†**2** *fig.* That which stops or allays something. LME–L18.
3 MINING. A form of after-damp. Also ***stanch-air***. L17.

stanch /stɑːn(t)ʃ, stɔːn(t)ʃ/ *noun*[2]. Also **staunch** /stɔːn(t)ʃ/. M18.
[Old French *estanche* rel. to *estanc* STANK *noun*.]
A lock or dam in a river.

stanch *adjective & adverb* var. of STAUNCH *adjective & adverb*.

stanch /stɑːn(t)ʃ, stɔːn(t)ʃ/ *verb*. Also **staunch** /stɔːn(t)ʃ/. ME.
[Old French *estanchier* (mod. *étancher*), from Proto-Romance word meaning 'dried up, weary' (whence also Old French *estanc*); ult. origin unkn. Cf. STANK *noun & verb*[1].]
1 †**a** *verb trans.* Restrict or exhaust one's supply of (wealth, strength, etc.). ME–M16. ▶†**b** *verb intrans.* Of water etc.: stop flowing. LME–L16. ▶**c** *verb trans.* Stop or restrict the flow of (water etc.). Now only *poet. rare*. L15.
2 *spec.* **a** *verb trans.* Stop or restrict the flow of (esp. blood) from a wound etc.; stop or restrict the flow of esp. blood from (a wound etc.). Formerly also, stop the bleeding of (a person). ME. ▶**b** *verb intrans.* (Of blood) stop flowing from a wound etc.; (of a wound etc.) stop bleeding. *arch.* L15.
3 *verb trans.* Quench or satisfy (thirst, desire, etc.). Formerly also, repress or extinguish (appetite, anger, etc.). *obsolete* exc. *Scot.* ME. ▶**b** Satisfy the appetite of. Formerly also, cure (a person) *of* a desire or passion. Long *obsolete* exc. *Scot.* ME.
4 †**a** *verb trans.* Put an end to (strife, enmity, etc.). ME–E19. ▶**b** *verb intrans.* (Of strife, enmity, etc.) come to an end, be allayed; (of a person) cease from violence. Long *obsolete* exc. *Scot.* LME. ▶†**c** *verb trans.* Restrain *from* violence; put down, suppress. *Scot.* Only in 16.
5 *verb trans.* Quench (a fire). *arch.* ME.
6 *verb trans.* Arrest the progress of (a disease). Also, relieve (pain). *arch.* LME.
7 *verb trans.* Stop up, make watertight or weatherproof. L16.

> 🕮 **1c** A. C. SWINBURNE A . . well of life nor stanched nor stained. **2a** P. V. WHITE The blood which had begun to run . . was . . stanched by the dry atmosphere. J. A. MICHENER His wound . . opened . . but Blue Leaf stanched the flow of blood with wet leaves. **b** F. W. ROBERTSON The heart will bleed, and stanch when it has bled enough.

■ **stanchless** *adjective* (chiefly *literary*) unable to be stanched E17.

stanchel /ˈstɑːnʃ(ə)l/ *noun*. Chiefly *Scot.* M16.
[Perh. from Old French *estanc(h)ele* dim. of *estance* (see STANCHION), recorded as name of an object used in a game.]
A stanchion.

stancher /ˈstɑːn(t)ʃə, ˈstɔːn-/ *noun*[1]. LME.
[from STANCH *verb* + -ER[1].]
A person who or thing which stanches something.

stancher /ˈstɑːnʃə/ *noun*[2]. Long only *Scot.* LME.
[Alt. of next.]
= STANCHION *noun* 1.

stanchion /ˈstɑːnʃ(ə)n/ *noun & verb*. ME.
[Anglo-Norman *stanchon* from Old French *estanchon*, *estanson*, from *estance* prop, support, from Proto-Romance base also of STANZA (cf. STANCE).]
▶ **A** *noun*. **1** An upright bar, prop, or support; a vertical strut; a post, a pillar; *spec.* (NAUTICAL) each of the upright supports along the sides of the upper deck of a ship which carry the guard-rail. ME.
2 An upright bar, pair of bars, or frame for restricting the movement of cattle, esp. by confinement in a stall. M19.
Comb.: **stanchion-gun** a gun mounted in a boat for wildfowl-shooting.
▶ **B** *verb trans.* **1** Provide with a stanchion or stanchions, strengthen or support thus. E16.

2 Fasten to a stanchion, restrict the movement of (cattle) by a stanchion or stanchions. L19.

stand /stand/ *noun*¹. OE.
[from the verb.]
▶ **I** †**1** A pause, a delay. *rare*. Only in OE.
2 a The action or an act of standing or stopping; a pause, a halt. Freq. in ***make a stand***. Now *rare* or *obsolete*. L16. ▶†**b** A stage in a statement or argument. Only in 17. ▶**c** THEATRICAL. Each halt made on a tour to give one or more performances; the place where such a halt is made; a performance given at such a halt (freq. in ***one-night stand*** s.v. ONE *adjective, noun, & pronoun*). L19. ▶**d** The mean sea level at a given epoch in the past. Also, the state of the tide when vertical movement has ceased at high or low water. M20.
†**3** An act of concealing oneself in ambush or in cover, an attack from concealment. L16–E17.
4 a An act of holding one's ground against an opponent or enemy; a halt made for the purpose of resistance. Freq. in ***make a stand***. L16. ▶**b** SPORT. A prolonged resistance; *spec.* (CRICKET) a prolonged stay at the wicket by two batsmen. E19.
5 A state of being unable to proceed in thought, speech, or action; a state of perplexity or bewilderment. Freq. in ***be at a stand***. *arch.* L16.
6 a A state of checked or arrested movement; *spec.* the rigid attitude assumed by a dog on finding game. Freq. in ***bring to a stand***, ***come to a stand***, ***put to a stand***. E17. ▶**b** (The performance of) a stallion or bull at stud. Also, a stud, a stud-farm. *US*. L18. ▶**c** An erection of the penis. *arch. slang*. M19. ▶**d** *Hist.* A hunter's opportunity to fire a number of shots into a herd *of* buffalo etc. Freq. in ***get a stand***. *US*. L19.
7 A state of arrested development or progress. Freq. in ***be at a stand***, ***come to a stand***. E17.
8 A manner of standing, esp. an upright as opp. to a crouching posture. *rare*. L17.

> 🕮 **2a** STEELE But by Heaven . . ! If you could—. Here he made a full Stand. WORDSWORTH He . . made a sudden stand. **c** D. BAKER He'd been making stands at . . picture houses all over the country. G. BORDMAN Haverly's . . Minstrels arrived for a week's stand. **3** SHAKES. *3 Hen. VI* Anon the deer will come And in this covert will we make our stand. **4a** SHAKES. *Coriol.* Neither foolish in our stands Nor cowardly in retire. R. SUTCLIFF We made our last stand . . and we were overwhelmed. **b** *Wisden Cricket Monthly* Dilley split the useful ninth-wicket stand of 54. **5** G. HERBERT The . . Parson . . is at a stand . . what behaviour to assume. **6a** CARLYLE For five-and-thirty minutes . . the Berline is at a dead stand. **7** E. LISLE My wheat, for want of rain, was at a stand in it's growth.

▶ **II 9** A place where a person or animal stands, a position, a station; *fig.* an attitude, a standpoint. Freq. in ***take a stand***, ***take one's stand***. ME. ▶**b** A station or position taken up for a particular purpose; *spec.* (*a*) the place where a hunter or sportsman waits for game; (*b*) (now *rare*) the post or station of a sentinel, watchman, etc.; (*c*) *Austral. & NZ* the area in a shearing shed where a sheep-shearer works. LME.
10 A stall, a booth. Also, a street-trader's habitual station or pitch. E16.
†**11** FALCONRY. A raised perch or roost used by a hawk. L16–L17.
12 a A raised structure for spectators, esp. at a racecourse or other sporting venue, or for a company of musicians or performers. E17. ▶**b** A raised platform for a speaker; a rostrum, a pulpit; *US* a witness-box (also ***witness-stand***). M19.
13 A place where public vehicles are authorized to wait for passengers; a row of such vehicles. L17.
14 a A position, site, or building for a business. *US*. L18. ▶**b** A (usu. urban) plot of land. *S. Afr.* L19.

> 🕮 **9** DRYDEN Watchful Herons leave their watry Stand. E. ROOSEVELT He was rarely inclined to take a stand, to say that this was right or wrong. **b** S. JOHNSON Thunders at the door . . brought the watchmen from their stands. I. COLEGATE Stands over which the birds . . fly high and fast. **10** A. TOFFLER A new small-circulation magazine on the stands. R. FRAME She bought postcards . . from a stand outside a bookshop. **12a** A. S. BYATT The stands that had lined the . . Coronation route. **b** HARPER LEE The witness made a hasty descent from the stand.

▶ **III 15 a** A set *of* objects of a specified kind. Chiefly *Scot.* LME. ▶**b** MILITARY. (Pl. after numeral often same.) In the British army: ***stand of arms***, a complete set of weapons for one person; ***stand of colours***, a regiment's colours. E18. ▶**c** A set of rolls and their auxiliary fittings for the shaping of metal in a rolling-mill. L19. ▶**d** OIL INDUSTRY. A number (usu. four or less) of lengths of drill pipe joined together. E20.
16 ***stand of pikes***, a compact group of pikemen. *obsolete* exc. *Hist.* L16.
17 A young tree left standing for timber. *obsolete* exc. *dial. rare*. L18.
18 An assemblage or group of birds, esp. game-birds of a specified kind. M19.
19 A group *of* growing plants of a specified crop, *spec.* one of trees. Orig. *US*. M19.

> 🕮 **19** *Farmers Weekly* Good stands of the crop are now evident. M. CHABON I stepped . . into a stand of oak.

▶ **IV 20** A base etc. on which a thing stands or by which a thing is supported; a rack, table, set of shelves, etc., on or in which things may be placed. Freq. with specifying word. M17.
20 ***hatstand***, ***music stand***, ***umbrella stand***, etc.
Comb.: **stand camera** a camera for use on a tripod as opp. to being hand-held.

stand /stand/ *noun*². *obsolete* exc. *dial.* ME.
[from or cogn. with Middle & mod. Low German, Flemish *stande* = Old High German *standa* (Middle High German *stande*, German dial. *Stande*), from base of next.]
1 An open tub; a barrel set on end. ME.
2 A unit of weight of pitch or coal. E18.

stand /stand/ *verb*. Pa. t. & pple **stood** /stʊd/.
[Old English *standan* = Old Frisian *standa*, *stonda*, Old Saxon *standan*, Old High German *stantan*, Old Norse *standa*, Gothic *standan*, from Germanic base also of STADDLE *noun & verb*, STOOL *noun*, STUD *noun*² *& adjective*, from Indo-European base also of STEAD *noun*, Latin *stare*, Greek *histanai*.]
▶ **I** *verb intrans.* **1** Of a person or animal: assume or maintain an erect attitude on the feet. OE. ▶**b** Be of a specified height. M19.
2 Remain motionless on the feet, esp. in a specified place, condition, etc.; cease to walk or move on. OE. ▶**b** In *imper.* Stop, halt. *arch.* E16. ▶**c** Of a game-dog: point, set. (Foll. by *on*.) E19.
3 Remain firm or steady in an upright position, support oneself erect on the feet. Usu. in neg. contexts. OE. ▶**b** *fig.* Maintain one's fixity of purpose, remain firm or unmoved. ME.
4 Take up an offensive or defensive position; present a firm front; hold one's ground; (of a body of troops) be drawn up in battle array. OE.
5 Be or remain in a specified condition, state, etc. OE. ▶**b** Act in a specified capacity. LME. ▶**c** CRICKET. Act as umpire. M19.
6 a Of a horse: be kept in a stable or stall. ME. ▶**b** Of a stallion: be available for breeding, esp. *at* a specified place. Orig. *US*. M18.
7 Move to and remain in a specified place or position. ME.
8 Of the penis: become or remain erect. E16.
9 Be or offer oneself as a candidate for or *for* an office, legislature, constituency, etc. Freq. in ***stand for parliament***. M16.
10 †**a** Stay, stop, or wait *to do*; insist on doing something. Usu. in neg. contexts. M16–M19. ▶†**b** Hesitate, refuse, or be slow *to do*. Usu. in neg. contexts. Chiefly *Scot.* M16–L18. ▶**c** Be in a position to win, gain, lose, etc., a specified object or amount, esp. as the result of betting or speculation. (Foll. by *to do*.) M19.
11 In poker etc.: be ready to play. Also, retain one's hand as dealt. E19.

> 🕮 **1** G. GREENE He . . stood . . , stiff and straight-backed. **b** J. WAIN He stood about six feet and had plenty of bulk. *Horse & Hound* Standing at 16.3 h.h., the gelding had . . ability. **2** G. CHAPMAN All but Nausicaa fled; but she fast stood. E. BLISHEN There, hands on his hips, stood the headmaster. **b** SIR W. SCOTT 'Bayard, stand!'—the steed obeyed. **3** H. PRIDEAUX He could scarce speake or stand. **b** *Times* They had stood true to the honour of Ireland. T. F. TOUT Eldon exhorted the king to stand firm. **4** CARLYLE The Felons . . stand on the offensive. **5** *Examiner* We stand . . alone in this expression of taste. E. A. FREEMAN Let the meeting stand adjourned. R. TINE A Royal wedding . . Captain Stanhope stood as best man. **b** GOLDSMITH To stand godfather to all the butler's children. **9** H. WILSON Ministers should stand and seek election. V. GLENDINNING He stood as the Liberal candidate for Scarborough. **10a** M. HALE I do not stand to justifie this Opinion. **c** E. WAUGH We stand to lose quite a lot.

▶ **II** *verb intrans.* **12 a** Of a thing: be in an upright position with the lower part resting on or fixed in the ground or some other support; be set or placed, rest, lie. Freq. foll. by prepositions. OE. ▶**b** (Of a plant) grow; (of a crop) be left uncut to ripen. Also, (of land) be covered thickly etc. with a crop. OE. ▶**c** Of the hair: grow stiff and erect like bristles. LME.
13 Of a building etc.: be situated or located in a specified position or aspect. OE. ▶†**b** Be fixed, set, or turned in a specified direction. L15–L17.
14 Be written, printed, or drawn; be set down in a specified context or form. Also *spec.*, (of a sum, price, or score) be registered *at* a specified figure. OE. ▶**b** Of an account: show a specified position of the parties with regard to debit and credit. Also, remain unpaid. E18.
15 (Of water etc.) have the surface at a specified level; (of mercury etc. in a thermometer, barometer, etc.) reach a certain height; (of a thermometer, barometer, etc.) give a specific reading. ME.

> 🕮 **12a** K. GRAHAME A garden-seat stood on one side of the door. H. ROTH In the . . room stood a . . glass-topped table. J. STEINBECK There, against the wall, stood four . . sacks of pink beans. **b** J. JACKSON The lands stand thick with corn. J. C. LOUDON If the tree is to stand four or more years. **13** R. MACAULAY The . . palace ruins standing among the little . . gardens. T. HARDY The Abbey . . stood in a lovely . . valley. **14** *Harper's Magazine* His name stood on the club list. *Oxford University Gazette* The balance at the Bank stands . . at £50. **b** OED The account stands greatly in my favour. **15** *National Review (US)* The thermometer now stood at 20 Fah.

▶ **III** *verb intrans.* **16 a** Be or remain in a specified condition, relation, situation, etc.; *spec.* (of a building etc.) remain erect and entire, resist destruction or decay. OE. ▶**b** Endure, last; continue unimpaired; flourish. OE. ▶**c** Be or remain valid or of force, hold good. OE. ▶†**d** Of the world: exist; last. ME–L16.
17 Of a condition, process, etc.: remain stationary or unchanged. Now *rare* or *obsolete*. LME.
18 Of a ceremony: be performed, take place. *Scot.* Now *rare* or *obsolete*. M17.
19 Of a pigment or dye: keep its colour; not blot or run. E19.

> 🕮 **16d** TINDALE *1 Cor.* 8:13 Whill the worlde stondeth.

▶ **IV** *verb intrans.* **20** Esp. of water: cease flowing; collect and remain motionless, be or become stagnant. OE. ▶**b** Foll. by *with*: (of land, a ditch, etc.) be full of stagnant water. E17.
21 (Of a liquid etc.) be held in a utensil without disturbance; (of tea) be left to infuse. OE.
22 †**a** Of a ship: ride at anchor. *rare*. Only in ME. ▶**b** (Of a machine etc.) remain still or motionless; not move or be operated; cease working; (of a clock, watch, etc.) cease to keep time, no longer be going. Now *rare*. LME. ▶**c** Of a vehicle: remain in a customary place waiting for passengers or the scheduled time of departure. M17. ▶**d** Of a mine, factory, etc.: stop working; be at a standstill. M18.
23 Of a star, planet, etc.: appear or be seen as motionless in the sky. ME.
24 Orig., (of blood or other fluid) collect and remain in a part of the body. Later, (of tears, sweat, etc.) collect and remain in drops in the eyes or on the skin. LME.

> 🕮 **20** T. S. ELIOT The pools that stand in drains. **b** T. HEARNE The Ditch about the Camp stands with water. **21** H. WOOLLEY Strain it [the Jelly], and so let it stand for your use. E. A. ROBERTSON Bring some fresh tea . . . This has been standing . . a long time. **22b** S. FOOTE The dog was mad, the parrot dead, and the clock stood. **23** TENNYSON Full-faced above the valley stood the moon. **24** LONGFELLOW A tear stood in his bright blue eye. *Strand Magazine* The sweat stood in beads on his forehead.

▶ **V** *verb intrans.* †**25** Esp. of light: issue in a beam or shaft. OE–LME.
†**26** Esp. of a weapon: be fixed *at* or *on* the place to which it penetrates in wounding; penetrate *through*, *to*. OE–LME.
27 Of the wind: blow from a specified quarter; blow favourably, continue to blow. Now *rare* or *obsolete*. ME.
28 a Of a person: go or proceed esp. in a specified direction. Long *rare* or *obsolete*. ME. ▶**b** NAUTICAL. Of a ship, crew, etc.: hold a specified course. E17.

> 🕮 **27** *London Gazette* Sail for the River, as soon as the Wind stands fair. **28a** J. SHIPP They bowed a hundred times . . ; then stood towards their village. **b** J. MASEFIELD The ship was standing north, the Horn was rounded. F. MOWAT In a few moments she was standing swiftly across the habour.

▶ **VI** *verb trans.* **29** Confront, face, oppose, encounter; resist, withstand, bear the brunt of. OE. ▶†**b** Be exposed to (harsh weather etc.). L16–E18.
30 †**a** Comply with or remain loyal to (an ordinance etc.). *rare*. LME–L16. ▶**b** Endure or undergo (a trial, test, etc.), esp. with a successful outcome; bear (a hardship etc.) without hurt or weakness. E17. ▶**c** Submit to or offer to comply with (a decision or vote); take part in (a contested election). L17.
31 Face, encounter (an issue, hazard, etc.) without flinching or retreating; be exposed or liable to (hazard, fortunes). L16.
†**32** Withstand or disobey (a command). *rare*. E17–E19.
33 a Put up with, tolerate; be willing to endure. E17. ▶**b** Reconcile oneself to, be favourably disposed to, feel a degree of liking for. Usu. in neg. contexts (chiefly in ***cannot stand***). *colloq.* L19.
34 Bear the expense of; pay for, esp. as a treat; contribute (a share of a larger amount). *colloq.* E19.
35 RACING etc. ▶**a** Bet or wager (a sum of money) *on* or *about* a specified result. Now *rare* or *obsolete*. E19. ▶**b** Bet on the success of, back, (a horse). L19.
36 Of a game-dog: point or set (game). M19.

29 SHAKES. *1 Hen. VI* Hundreds he sent to hell, and none durst stand him. CARLYLE Training . . thousands to stand fire and be soldiers. **30b** *New Monthly Magazine* He has stood the ordeal of a London audience. **33b** M. STEEN I can't stand him! He's the most ghastly clot! **34** *Daily Mirror* Are you going to stand me a drink?

▸ **VII** *verb trans.* **37** Cost, be of a specified expense to, (a person). *obsolete* exc. *Scot.* **LME.**

▸ **VIII** *verb trans.* **38** Cause to stand; place or leave standing; set (a thing) upright; place firmly or steadily in a specified position. Also foll. by *up*. **M19.**

Phrases: **as it stands** (*a*) (esp. of a house) in its present condition, unaltered, taken or considered as it is; (*b*) in the present circumstances. ***as much as the traffic will stand***: see TRAFFIC *noun*. ***it stands to reason***: see REASON *noun*¹. ***know where one stands (with someone)***: see KNOW *verb*. ***no leg to stand on***, ***not a leg to stand on***: see LEG *noun*. **stand a chance** have a prospect of success etc. **stand and deliver!** *Hist.* a highwayman's order to hand over valuables etc. ***stand a person in stead***, ***stand a person in good stead***: see STEAD *noun*. ***stand at bay***: see BAY *noun*¹ 2. ***stand at stud***: see STUD *noun*². ***stand buff***: see BUFF *noun*¹. **stand good** be and remain valid. ***stand guard***: see GUARD *noun*. ***stand in a person's light***: see LIGHT *noun*. ***stand in line***: see LINE *noun*². ***stand in stead***: see STEAD *noun*. ***stand in the breach***: see BREACH *noun* 8. ***stand mute (of malice)***: see MUTE *adjective* 2. ***stand neuter***: see NEUTER *adjective* 2. ***stand on ceremony***: see CEREMONY. **stand on end** (freq. *hyperbol.*) (of the hair) become erect through fright or astonishment. ***stand one's corner***: see CORNER *noun* 9. ***stand on one's points***, ***stand on points***: see POINT *noun*¹. **stand one's ground** maintain one's position, refuse to yield. **stand one's trial** be tried by a court for an offence. ***stand on one's dignity***: see DIGNITY 5. **stand on one's head** perform a gymnastic movement in which the body is supported vertically in an upside-down position by the head and hands. ***stand on one's own bottom***: see BOTTOM *noun*. ***stand on one's own feet***, ***stand on one's own two feet***: see FOOT *noun*. ***stand out like a sore thumb***: see SORE *adjective*¹. ***stand pad***: see PAD *noun*² 1a. ***stand Sam***: see SAM *noun*¹ 1. ***stand sentinel***: see SENTINEL *noun* 1. ***stand sentry***: see SENTRY *noun*¹ 2. **stand someone's friend** *arch.* act the part of a friend to another. ***stand surety***: see SURETY *noun*. **stand the market** *Scot. & north.* attend a market in order to sell goods or (*Hist.*) to hire oneself out. ***stand the pace***: see PACE *noun*¹. ***stand the racket***: see RACKET *noun*² 4. ***stand to one's tackle***: see TACKLE *noun*. ***stand treat***: see TREAT *noun*² 3b. ***stand upon one's points***, ***stand upon points***: see POINT *noun*¹. ***stand upon one's toes***: see TOE *noun*. ***stand up to the rack***: see RACK *noun*². **stand well** be on good terms (*with*), be in good repute. ***stand widdershins***: see WIDDERSHINS *adverb* 1. **will the real — please stand up?** *colloq.*: requesting that a specified person clarify his or her position or make himself or herself known (often rhetorical).

With adverbs in specialized senses: **stand about** remain standing in a place without a fixed position or definite object. **stand aloof** remain standing at, or withdraw to, some distance (*from*), keep away (*from*) (*lit. & fig.*). **stand apart** stand alone or at a distance (*from*) (*lit. & fig.*). **stand aside** draw back or retire and stand apart from the general company or from what is going on. **stand away** (*a*) withdraw to some distance; (*b*) NAUTICAL sail or steer away, esp. in a specified direction. **stand back** withdraw and take up a position further away from the front. **stand by** (*a*) stand nearby, be present, esp. without interfering or protesting; (*b*) = ***stand aside*** above; (*c*) be excluded (*from*); *spec.* withdraw from a jury, esp. on being challenged; (*d*) be laid aside; (*e*) NAUTICAL hold oneself in readiness, be prepared *for*, *to do* (freq. in *imper.*). **stand down** (*a*) leave the witness-box after giving evidence; (*b*) SPORT withdraw from a game, match, or race; give up one's place in a team; (*c*) NAUTICAL sail with the wind or tide; (*d*) MILITARY (cause to) come off duty; (cause to) relax after a state of alert. **stand forth** *arch.* (*a*) step forward; come resolutely to the front; (*b*) make a conspicuous appearance, be prominent. **stand in** †(*a*) go shares *with*, be a partner *with*; have a friendly or profitable understanding *with*; (*b*) NAUTICAL direct one's course towards the shore; (*c*) act in the place of another, deputize *for*; CINEMATOGRAPHY act as a substitute *for* a principal actor. **stand off** (*a*) remain at or retire to a distance; draw back, go farther away; †(*b*) remain apart, distinct, or separate *from* a thing; differ; (*c*) hold aloof, be unhelpful or unaccommodating; (*d*) project, protrude, jut out (*from* a surface etc.); appear as if in relief; *fig.* be conspicuous or prominent; (*e*) NAUTICAL direct one's course away from the shore; ***stand off and on***, direct one's course alternately away from and towards the shore; (*f*) *US colloq.* repel; put off, evade; keep off, keep at a distance; (*g*) lay off (an employee) temporarily. **stand on** NAUTICAL continue on the same course. **stand out** (*a*) move away and stand apart or in open view; (*b*) choose not to take part in an undertaking or joint venture; hold aloof; (*c*) persist in opposition or resistance, hold out; ***stand out for***, declare oneself for, persist in supporting; (*d*) haggle; make a determined demand *for* specified terms; (*e*) NAUTICAL direct one's course away from the shore (freq. in ***stand out to sea***); (*f*) jut out, project, protrude (*from*); be prominent or conspicuous; appear in contrast or relief (*against*); (*g*) endure to the end, hold out under or against (an ordeal, severe weather, etc.); (*h*) maintain or insist *that* (also ***stand it out that***). **stand over** (*a*) NAUTICAL direct one's course away from one shore and towards another; (*b*) be postponed, be left for later treatment, consideration, or settlement. ***stand pat***: see PAT *adverb*². **stand to** †(*a*) (*rare*, Shakes.) set to work, fall to; *esp.* begin eating; (*b*) MILITARY stand ready for an attack, esp. before dawn or after dark; come or remain on duty. **stand up** (*a*) assume an erect position; rise to one's feet; be set upright; be or become erect; (*b*) *arch.* take part in a dance; dance *with* a specified partner; (*c*) (*colloq. & dial.*) take shelter from the rain; (*d*) *colloq.* be dressed *in* (freq. in ***(only) the clothes one stands up in***); (*e*) (of an animal) hold out in a race or chase; (*f*) *poet.* (of flame, smoke, etc.) rise up, issue upwards; (*g*) remain bravely standing to confront an opponent; make a stand *against* (*lit. & fig.*); (*h*) ***stand up for***, defend, support, or take the part of (a person or cause); (*i*) ***stand up to***, meet, face, or withstand (an opponent) courageously; be resistant to the harmful effects of (wear, use, etc.); (*j*) *colloq.* fail to keep an appointment, esp. a romantic date, with (a person); (*k*) ***stand up and be counted*** (*colloq.*), make public one's (esp. political) conviction or sympathy; (*l*) (esp. of an argument) sustain close examination, be tenable or valid; (*m*) see sense 38 above.

With prepositions in specialized senses: **stand against** — (*a*) withstand, resist successfully, hold one's ground against; (*b*) oppose as an alternative candidate. **stand at** — *arch. colloq.* hesitate at; be deterred by. **stand before** — (*a*) come or be brought into the presence of; (*b*) confront, hold one's ground against (usu. in neg. contexts). **stand by** — (*a*) have or take up a position nearby, esp. while giving help, advice, or sympathy; *fig.* uphold the interests of, support, side with; (*b*) NAUTICAL be ready to take hold of or operate (an anchor etc.); (*c*) adhere to or abide by (a statement, agreement, etc.). **stand for** — (*a*) uphold or defend (a cause); support or take the part of (a person); (*b*) be counted or considered as; represent, signify, imply; (*c*) NAUTICAL sail or steer towards; (*d*) *colloq.* (orig. *US*) endure, put up with, tolerate (usu. in neg. contexts); (*e*) see sense 9 above. **stand in** — (*a*) (now *rare* or *obsolete*) be dressed in, be actually wearing; †(*b*) persevere or persist in; dwell on; (*c*) *arch.* rest or depend on as a basis for existence. **stand on** — (*a*) base one's argument on, take one's stand on; †(*b*) (of an argument) be grounded on; †(*c*) give oneself to or practise (action or behaviour of a specified kind); (*d*) be meticulously careful about, observe scrupulously; (*e*) assert, claim respect or credit for; †(*f*) (*rare*, Shakes.) value, set store by; (*g*) (now *rare* or *obsolete*) regard as essential or necessary, urge, press for, demand; †(*h*) *impers.* with *it*, behove, be incumbent on; (*i*) ***stand on me*** (*slang*), rely on me, believe me. **stand over** — stand close to (a person) to watch, control, threaten, etc. **stand to** — †(*a*) submit oneself to or abide by (a trial etc.); obey or be bound by (a decision, opinion, etc.); †(*b*) trust to, rely on; (*c*) ***stand to it*** (*arch.*), fight bravely; work hard without flagging; (*d*) (now *rare*) confront, present a bold front to (an enemy); (*e*) *arch.* endure the consequences of; †(*f*) make good or bear the expense of (damage or loss); be answerable for (expenses); accept liability for (a tribute or tax); (*g*) side with or support (a person); uphold (a cause); (*h*) adhere to or abide by (a promise, agreement, etc.); (*i*) persist in affirming or asserting (a statement); (*j*) be related to; (*k*) *Anglo-Irish* be to one's advantage, sustain. **stand under** — (*a*) be exposed or subject to; bear the burden of; (*b*) NAUTICAL make sail with (a specified display of canvas). **stand upon** — = ***stand on*** — above. **stand with** — †(*a*) withstand or dispute with; †(*b*) side with, make common cause with; (*c*) *arch.* be consistent or consonant with, agree or accord with.

Comb.: **stand-alone** *adjective* (COMPUTING) designating a part of a computer system (hardware or software) that can be used independently; **stand-down** MILITARY the action or state of standing down; the end of a spell of duty; **stand-easy** an assumption of the attitude directed by the command 'stand easy!' (see EASY *adverb* 3); *fig.* a period of relaxation; **stand-in** †(*a*) *US colloq.* a friendly or profitable understanding (*with* another), esp. for illicit purposes; (*b*) a deputy, a substitute (*for*); *spec.* (chiefly *N. Amer.*) a person substituting for a principal film actor while the cameras and lighting for a scene are set; **stand-over** *adjective* (*Austral. slang*) bullying, threatening; ***stand-over man***, a perpetrator of extortion by threat, a protection-racketeer; **stand-to** MILITARY the action or state of standing to; the beginning of a spell of duty; **stand-to-arms** MILITARY the action of standing to arms; the period during which a force etc. stands to arms.

standage /ˈstandɪdʒ/ *noun*. Orig. †**stannage**. **E17.**
[from prec. + -AGE.]

1 †**a** A place for standing, a stall. *rare*. Only in **E17.** ▸**b** Arrangements or accommodation for standing; a charge for this. **L18.**

2 A reservoir for water in a mine. **M19.**

standard /ˈstandəd/ *noun & adjective*. **ME.**
[Aphet. (in Anglo-Latin *standard(i)um*) from Anglo-Norman *estaundart*, Old French *estendart* (mod. *étendard*), from *estendre* extend: see -ARD. In branch III also infl. by STAND *verb*.]

▸ **A** *noun*. **I 1 a** A flag or figurehead attached to the upper part of a pole and raised to indicate a rallying-point; the distinctive ensign of a sovereign, commander, nation, etc.; *transf.* an army. **ME.** ▸**b** A distinctive military or naval flag; *spec.* the flag of a cavalry regiment as distinct from the colours of an infantry regiment. **LME.**

†**2** A body of troops; *spec.* a company of cavalry. **ME–L17.**

3 = ***standard-bearer*** below. **LME.**

4 BOTANY. The large freq. erect uppermost petal of a papilionaceous corolla (also called ***vexillum***). Also (in *pl.*), the inner petals of an iris flower, freq. erect (cf. FALL *noun*² 21). **L18.**

5 ORNITHOLOGY. Either of the two elongated wing-feathers characteristic of certain birds. Cf. STANDARDWING. **M19.**

1a T. ARNOLD Nations . . were ready to join his standard. E. B. PUSEY The black eagle is the standard of Prussia. **b** K. AMIS The regimental standard hung limply in the motionless air.

▸ **II 6 a** The authorized exemplar of a unit of measure or weight, as a measuring rod of unit length, a vessel of unit capacity, or a mass of metal of unit weight, providing permanent evidence of the legally prescribed magnitude of the unit. **ME.** ▸†**b** A uniform size or amount. *rare*. Only in **17.** ▸†**c** A unit of measurement. *rare*. **M17–M19.** ▸**d** BOWLS. A light reed or cane formerly used to measure the distance of a bowl from the jack. **L19.**

7 a Legal rate of intrinsic value of a currency, esp. as defined in terms of gold or silver or both. Also, the prescribed proportion of the weight of fine metal in gold or silver coins. **LME.** ▸**b** Orig. †***standard of commerce***. A commodity of officially invariable value, serving as a measure of value for all other commodities. Now *rare*. **L17.**

8 a A thing serving as a recognized example or principle to which others conform or should conform or by which the accuracy or quality of others is judged. **L15.** ▸**b** A rule, a means of judgement or estimation; a criterion. **M16.** ▸**c** A document embodying an official statement of a rule or rules; *spec.* (*a*) a book or document accepted by a Church as the authoritative statement of its creed (usu. in *pl.*); (*b*) a document specifying nationally or internationally agreed properties for manufactured goods, principles for procedure, etc. (esp. in ***British Standard*** s.v. BRITISH *adjective* 2). **M19.**

9 †**a** A fixed numerical quantity. *rare*. Only in **M16.** ▸**b** A measure of timber, *spec.* one equal to 165 cu. ft (approx. 4.67 cu. metres). **M19.**

10 a A required or specified level of excellence, attainment, wealth, etc. **E18.** ▸**b** *Hist.* A grade of classification in elementary schools. Also, the form or class for preparing pupils for a specified standard. **L19.**

11 The market price per ton of copper in the ore. **M19.**

12 a A standard book (sense B.5a below). **L19.** ▸**b** A standard form of a language (sense B.5c below). **E20.**

6a R. BURN The statute for ascertaining the measure of ale quarts . . according to the standard. C. DAVIES These standards were kept in the royal exchequer. **7a** EVELYN Finer than the standard, such as was old angel gold. JOSEPH HARRIS Trade requires . . an indelible standard of money. **b** J. R. MCCULLOCH Standards whereby to measure the relative value of different commodities. **8a** R. QUIRK In . . scrabble, it is usual . . to take the nearest available dictionary as the standard for admissible words. **b** J. BRYCE Applying . . English standards to the examination of the American system. J. RABAN By Gulf standards the weather was pleasantly cool. **10a** G. B. SHAW He guesses Broadbent's standard of comfort. **b** C. ACHEBE He had been my teacher in standard three.

▸ **III 13 a** An upright timber, bar, or rod; an upright support or pedestal. Later *spec.*, an upright water or gas pipe. **ME.** ▸**b** A tall candlestick; *spec.* a tall candlestick or candelabrum rising directly from the floor of a church. **LME.** ▸†**c** = SHEATH *noun*². **M17–E18.** ▸**d** NAUTICAL. An inverted knee-timber, having the vertical portion turned upwards. **M18.** ▸**e** = ***standard lamp*** below. **E20.**

14 a FORESTRY. A tree or shoot from a stump left standing when a coppice is cut down. **ME.** ▸**b** HORTICULTURE. A tree or shrub growing on an erect stem of full height and standing alone without support; now *esp.*, a shrub grafted on an upright stem and trained in tree form. **E17.**

†**15** A tall wooden or stone structure containing a vertical conduit pipe with spouts and taps, for the public supply of water. **LME–M19.**

16 A kind of collar of mail or plate armour. *obsolete* exc. *Hist.* **LME.**

†**17** A kind of service-book. **LME–E16.**

†**18** A large packing-case or chest. **LME–M17.**

19 A vessel, a utensil; *spec.* a large tub. Cf. STANDER 3. Long *obsolete* exc. *dial. rare*. **LME.**

†**20** A principal or main dish. **L15–E16.**

21 †**a** A permanent or long-lasting thing; in *pl.*, permanent or necessary furniture or equipment. **L15–M17.** ▸**b** More fully ***old standard***. A person who has been in a specified place or position for a long time; a long-standing resident, servant, etc. Cf. STANDER 2b. Long *obsolete* exc. *Scot. & dial.* **M17.** ▸**c** A (freq. jazz) tune or song of established popularity. **M20.**

13a W. J. M. RANKINE The . . table also carries the standard, F, which supports the main gearing. H. WYNDHAM At intervals . . rose the tall standards of the electric lights. **b** A. W. N. PUGIN This screen is surmounted by standards for wax tapers. **e** H. G. WELLS The light of the big electric standard in the corner. **14** T. HERBERT Towers . . terrassed near the top like the Standard in Cheap-side. **20a** JAS. ROBERTSON No standard should be left, except . . seedlings . . necessary to renew the stocks. **b** JOHN BAXTER The fig-tree may be grown either as a standard, espalier, or against a wall. *Amateur Gardening* Specimens such as standards must be kept frost free.

Phrases: ***British Standard***: see BRITISH *adjective* 2. ***double standard***: see DOUBLE *adjective & adverb*. **gold standard** a system by which the value of a currency is defined in terms of gold, for which the currency may be exchanged. **multiple standard** a standard value obtained by averaging the prices of a number of products. **raise a standard**, **raise the standard** take up arms (foll. by *of*), rally support for. ***royal standard***: see ROYAL *adjective*. **silver standard** a system by which the value of a currency is defined in terms of silver, for which the currency may be exchanged. ***single standard***: see SINGLE *adjective & adverb*. **standard of comfort**, **standard of living** the degree of material comfort available to a person, class, or community. ***the Received Standard***: see RECEIVE.

▸ **B** *attrib.* or as *adjective*. **I** †**1** Designating or pertaining to a type of mattress, prob. one on a fixed frame. *rare*. Only in **LME.**

2 Upright, set up on end or vertically. M16.
3 Of a tree or shrub: grown as a standard (sense A.20b above). L17.

> 🕮 **2** *Morning Star* The illumination is produced . . by standard gas-burners. **3** *Country Life* Standard hybrid tea roses budded on *rugosa* stems.

▶**II 4 a** Serving or used as a standard of measurement, weight, value, etc. E17. ▸**b** Of a prescribed or normal size, amount, quality, etc. Also, commonly used or encountered; (esp. of a practice) customary, usual; (of a maxim etc.) constantly repeated, standing, stock. E19.
5 a Of a book, author, etc.: ranking as an authority, having a recognized and long-lasting value. M17. ▸**b** (Capable of) serving as a standard of comparison or judgement. E18. ▸**c** Designating or pertaining to the form of a spoken or written language of a country or other linguistic area generally considered the most correct and acceptable. M19.
6 Of a precious metal, currency, etc.: conforming to the legal standard of fineness or intrinsic value. L17.
7 *MATH.* That does not involve infinitesimal quantities. M20.

> 🕮 **4a** W. S. JEVONS Gold is the standard money and the legal tender. **b** J. NICHOLSON The standard thickness of a brick wall is 1½ brick laid lengthwise. P. N. HASLUCK All . . parts . . made to some standard measurement. N. CHOMSKY They adopted the standard colonialist policy of using minorities or outsiders. **5a** *Saturday Review* A standard authority in every country where the English language runs. J. B. PRIESTLEY Purchases, mostly of standard poets. **b** C. BURNEY We may suppose this sound to be the standard pitch, and fundamental note of the . . lyre.

Special collocations & comb.: **standard administrative** *REGION*. **Standard American** *BRIDGE* the commonest system of bidding in the US. **standard assessment task** a standardized form of testing a pupil to assess his or her progress in a core subject of the national curriculum. **standard atmosphere** (*a*) a unit of atmospheric pressure, equal to 760 torr; (*b*) a hypothetical atmosphere with defined surface temperature and pressure and specified profile of temperature with altitude, used esp. in aviation and space research. **standard-bearer** (*a*) a soldier whose duty is to carry a standard, esp. in battle; *transf.* a person who carries a banner in a procession; (*b*) *fig.* a conspicuous advocate of a cause; a prominent teacher of a political or religious party. **standard book number** *Hist.* in the UK, an identification number allocated to each (edition or format of a) book published (replaced by the *international standard book number*). **standardbred** *adjective & noun* (*N. Amer.*) (*a*) *adjective* (of a horse) bred up to a specified standard of excellence prescribed by some authority, *esp.* bred to attain a specified speed; (*b*) *noun* a standard-bred horse, developed esp. for trotting as in harness-racing. **standard cable** a unit of attenuation formerly used in telephone engineering. **standard candle** a former unit of luminous intensity, defined as the intensity of the flame of a spermaceti candle of specified properties. **standard cell** any of several forms of voltaic cell designed to produce a constant and reproducible electromotive force as long as the current drawn is not too large. ***standard deviation***: see DEVIATION 3c. **standard cost** the estimated cost of a process, resource, or item used in a manufacturing enterprise, entered in an account and compared with the actual cost so that anomalies are readily detectable. **standard error** *STATISTICS* a measure of the statistical accuracy of an estimate, equal to the standard deviation of the theoretical distribution of a large population of such estimates. **standard gauge** a railway gauge of 4 ft 8½ inches (1.435 m), standard in Britain and many other parts of the world. **standard grade** a level of examination of the Scottish Certificate of Education, which is replacing the ordinary grade. **standard lamp** a lamp set on a tall upright with its base resting on the floor. **standard lens** *PHOTOGRAPHY* a lens with a focal length approximately equal to the diagonal of the negative (taken as 50 mm for a 35 mm camera), giving a field of view similar to that of the naked eye. **standard model** (*PHYSICS*) *the* currently accepted mathematical description of the elementary particles of matter and the electromagnetic, weak, and strong forces by which they interact. ***standard REGION***. **standard time** a uniform time for places in approximately the same longitude, established in a country or region by law or custom (***British Standard Time***: see BRITISH *adjective* 2, ***Eastern Standard Time***: see EASTERN *adjective* 1, ***Pacific Standard Time***: see PACIFIC *adjective*). **standard wire gauge** one of the series of standard thicknesses for wire and metal plates in the UK; any specific measure in this series; abbreviation *SWG*.
▪ **standardless** *adjective* having no standard or standards; unprincipled: E20. **standardness** *noun* (*rare*) L20.

standard /ˈstandəd/ *verb trans. rare.* L17.
[from prec.]
Assay (precious metal). Also, establish or deposit as a standard of measure or weight.

standardize /ˈstandədʌɪz/ *verb.* Also **-ise**. L19.
[formed as prec. + -IZE.]
1 *verb trans.* Cause to conform to a standard or uniform size, strength, form, etc., make standard. Freq. as ***standardized*** *ppl adjective.* L19. ▸**b** *verb intrans.* Conform to a standard or uniform size, strength, form, etc.; (foll. by *on*) take a specified example as one's model or standard. E20.
2 *verb trans.* Determine the properties of by comparison with a standard. L19.

> 🕮 **1** R. DAWKINS To standardize the price of petrol at some artificially high value. J. S. FOSTER This necessitates . . standardised designs. **b** *Daily Telegraph* Their airlines are trying to standardise on American-engined planes. **2** *Longman's Magazine* To standardise the poisonous principle contained in it.

▪ **standardizable** *adjective* able to be standardized E20. **standardiˈzation** *noun* the action or process of standardizing something L19. **standardizer** *noun* a person who or machine which standardizes something L19. **standardly** *adverb* in a standard manner; according to common practice; normally, generally: M20.

standardwing /ˈstandədwɪŋ/ *noun & adjective.* As adjective usu. **standard-wing**. M19.
[from STANDARD *noun* + WING *noun.*]
▶**A** *noun.* More fully ***Wallace's standardwing***. A bird of paradise, *Semioptera wallacei*, the male of which bears a long white pennant feather on each wing. M19.
▶**B** *attrib.* or as *adjective.* = STANDARD-WINGED. L19.
▪ **standard-winged** *adjective* having an elongated feather on each wing; ***standard-winged bird of paradise*** = STANDARDWING *noun*; ***standard-winged nightjar***, an African nightjar, *Macrodipteryx longipennis*, the male of which bears a long feather on each wing during the breeding season: L19.

stand-by /ˈstandbʌɪ/ *noun & adjective.* Also **standby**. L18.
[from *stand by* s.v. STAND *verb.*]
▶**A** *noun.* Pl. **stand-bys**.
1 a *NAUTICAL.* A ship etc. held in reserve or in a state of readiness. *rare.* L18. ▸**b** Orig. *NAUTICAL.* The state of being immediately available to come on duty if required; readiness for duty. Freq. in ***on stand-by*** below. M20.
2 A person ready to give assistance to another; a staunch adherent or partisan. E19.
3 A thing on which one can rely; a main support; a chief resource. M19.
4 *ellipt.* **a** A stand-by credit, loan, etc. (sense B.1d below). M20. ▸**b** A stand-by passenger; a stand-by fare or ticket (sense B.4 below). M20.
5 An operational mode of an electrical appliance in which the power is switched on but the appliance is not actually functioning; *spec.* a mode in which the appliance is capable of receiving and acting on a signal from another device (as a radio, telephone, remote control, etc.). Also, on a mobile phone: the amount of time available for use in this mode when the battery is fully charged. L20.
Phrases: **on stand-by** (*a*) immediately available or ready for duty; (*b*) (of an air traveller) in possession of a stand-by seat, waiting for a stand-by ticket.
▶**B** *attrib.* or as *adjective.* **1 a** *NAUTICAL.* Of a ship etc.: held in reserve, in a state of readiness. L19. ▸**b** Immediately available to come on duty if required; ready for duty. L19. ▸**c** Of machinery, equipment, etc.: for use in an emergency; held in reserve, *spec.* in the case of failure of a primary device or supply. E20. ▸**d** Designating or pertaining to an economic or financial measure prepared for implementation in specified circumstances. M20.
2 Of a charge for electricity: remaining constant, fixed; levied for the availability of an electrical supply in a given period, irrespective of the amount used. E20.
3 Designating or pertaining to a state, position, or condition of readiness. E20. ▸**b** Designating or relating to the operational mode of stand-by on an electrical appliance. M20.
4 Designating or pertaining to a system of air travel whereby seats are not booked in advance but allocated on the basis of earliest availability; (of a passenger) using or hoping to use this system; (of a fare, ticket, etc.) paid, bought, etc., under this system. M20.

standee /stanˈdiː/ *noun. colloq.* (orig. & chiefly *US*). M19.
[from STAND *verb* + -EE[1].]
A person who is forced to stand; *spec.* a standing passenger in a public vehicle.

standel /ˈstand(ə)l/ *noun.* M16.
[Perh. alt. of STADDLE, infl. by STAND *verb.*]
A young tree left standing for timber. Cf. STANDER 4, STANDARD *noun* 14a.

stander /ˈstandə/ *noun.* ME.
[from STAND *verb* + -ER[1].]
1 An upright support; a supporting pillar, stem, etc. Also, a candlestick. *obsolete* exc. *Scot.* (now *rare*). ME.
2 a A person who stands. LME. ▸**b** In full ***old stander***. A person of long standing in a profession, place, etc.; an old hand, an old resident. Cf. STANDARD *noun* 21b. Now *rare* or *obsolete.* L16.
3 A pan or barrel set on end; *dial.* = STANDARD *noun* 19. *rare.* LME.
†**4** A tree left standing for timber. Cf. STANDEL, STANDARD *noun* 14a. M16–E18.
Comb.: **stander-by** (now *rare*) a person who stands by, *esp.* a person who looks on and does not interfere or participate; a casual spectator, a bystander.

standing /ˈstandɪŋ/ *noun.* ME.
[from STAND *verb* + -ING[1].]
1 a The action of STAND *verb*; an instance of this; *spec.* †(*a*) the state of being without either forward or backward movement; the condition of being at a standstill; (*b*) an act of standing erect on one's feet; a period during which a standing position is maintained. ME. ▸**b** An erect position; the condition of not falling or being overthrown. Chiefly *fig.*, with possess. pronoun. Now *rare* or *obsolete.* E18.
†**2** Manner of standing; relative position; situation, site; posture, attitude; position. LME–E19.
3 a The place in or on which a person stands; a standing-place; standing room. Now *rare* or *obsolete.* LME. ▸†**b** A hunter's station or stand from which to shoot game. LME–E17. ▸**c** A shelter for cattle and horses; a stable, a stall; stable-accommodation for a horse or horses. Now *dial.* LME. ▸**d** *LAW.* A position from which a person has the right to prosecute a claim or seek legal redress; the right to do this; = LOCUS STANDI. Orig. *US.* L19.
4 A thing on which a person or thing is supported in a standing position; a stage; a base, a foundation. Long *rare* or *obsolete.* LME.
5 Orig., the occupying of a place for selling wares. Later, the place itself; a booth, a stall. Now *dial.* LME.
6 a Orig., an office or position of importance. Later, grade or rank in society, one's profession, etc.; reputation, status. LME. ▸**b** The relative position of a person or organization in a graduated table; a score indicating this. Usu. in *pl.* Chiefly *N. Amer.* L19.
†**7** A tree left standing after coppicing, a standard. Also, an upright pole. *rare.* L16–E19.
8 Length of service, experience, residence, etc.; position as determined by seniority in membership. L16.
9 †**a** Continuance in existence; duration. Only in 17. ▸**b** The state or fact of having existed for a specified period of time; degree of antiquity. Freq. in ***of old standing***, ***of ancient standing***. Cf. LONG STANDING. M17.

> 🕮 **1a** I. WALTON His former standing for a Proctors place, and being disappointed, must prove much displeasing. R. H. BARHAM He cursed him in sitting, in standing, in lying. *Edinburgh Review* The gentleman . . who could reel you off two hundred verses at a standing. **b** G. STANHOPE They . . not only recover their Standing, but even profit themselves of their Fall. **2** T. HERBERT Visible by reason of her high standing a good way distant. W. ELLIS The double Rows were apt to heat each other by their close standing. **3a** DRYDEN Your cavalcade the fair spectators view From their high standings. W. COWPER We have . . commodious standing here. **c** T. ELLWOOD Don't you forget to pay for your Horse's standing? **d** H. W. R. WADE Every citizen has standing to invite the court to prevent some abuse of power. **5** J. ENTICK The clothiers . . had their booths and standings within the churchyard. **6a** JOHN BROOKE He was . . concerned about his standing in European politics. J. P. STERN Those very few thinkers . . whose standing as modern masters is undoubted. **b** R. EARLE Class standing is affected in some measure by conduct. *Belfast Telegraph* He now leads the world drivers' championship standings with 13 points. **8** J. LAMONT They came in order to the king (from the youngest in standing to the eldest). STEELE I am a Practitioner in the Law of some standing. **9a** SHAKES. *Wint. T.* His folly . . pil'd upon his faith . . will continue The standing of his body. **b** JOSEPH STRUTT These privileges were of ancient standing. D. ATHILL I already had a lover of five years' standing.

Phrases: **be in good standing (with)** stand well (with), be in favour (with).
Comb.: **standing count**, **standing eight count** *BOXING* a count of eight taken by a boxer who has not been knocked down but who appears temporarily unfit to continue fighting; **standing-ground** ground on which a contest is or may be fought or a stand is or may be made; ground a person or thing may (safely) stand; **standing-place** (*a*) a place prepared or intended for a person or thing to stand in; a place to accommodate people standing; (*b*) a place where a person takes his or her stand; **standing point** = STANDPOINT; **standing room** space in which to stand; accommodation (esp. in a theatre etc.) for a person or persons in a standing position (freq. in ***standing room only***).

standing /ˈstandɪŋ/ *adjective.* ME.
[from STAND *verb* + -ING[2].]
▶**I 1 a** (Of a person, animal, etc.) that maintains an erect stationary position on the feet; (of a position) upright and on the feet. ME. ▸**b** Of an action: performed in a standing position. M17. ▸**c** *spec.* in *SPORT.* Of a race, jump, start, etc.: performed from rest or from a standing position, without a run-up or the use of starting blocks. L19.
2 Of an object: that stands up, upright, or on end; that is set in a vertical position. (Earliest in ***standing stone*** below.) ME. ▸**b** Of a bowl, cup, etc.: supported by a foot, base, or stem. *obsolete* exc. *Hist.* LME. ▸**c** Of a piece of furniture: that rests on its own base; not supported by another structure; free-standing. L15.
3 a Of growing corn etc.: that stands erect; unreaped, not felled; not blown or trampled down. LME. ▸**b** Of (part of) a building: that remains erect; not fallen or overthrown; not demolished or destroyed. L17.
4 *SHIPBUILDING.* Of a bevel or bevelling: forming an angle greater than a right angle; obtuse. M18.

1a AV *Lev.* 26:1 Ye shall make you no Idoles . . , neither reare you vp a standing image. J. MOORE All the audience . . remain in a standing posture till their sovereign sit down. **b** MILTON That Warr . . on firm ground A standing fight. **c** D. RUTHERFORD Making a standing start . . . The Norton Commando accelerates from 0 to 100 m.p.h. in 13 seconds. **2c** SWIFT A kind of wooden machine . . formed like a standing ladder. **3a** AV *Deut.* 23:25 Thou shalt not mooue a sickle vnto thy neighbours standing corne. T. HARDY Melbury had purchased some standing timber . . and . . the date had come for felling it. **b** M. AYRTON Three still standing temples, . . the most beautiful anywhere outside Greece.

▶ **II** †**5** Esp. of a limb: stiff, rigid. Also (*rare*), (of the eyes) projecting. **ME–M17.**
6 Of (a stretch of) water: still, not ebbing or flowing, stagnant. **LME.**
7 That remains in one spot; that is not moved or carried from place to place; stationary. *obsolete* exc. in ***standing camp*** below. **LME.** ▸**b** Of a forme of type: not yet distributed after use. **L16.**
8 Of a machine, device, etc.: at a standstill; not in operation, not working. **L16.**
9 a *NAUTICAL.* Of or pertaining to the part of a ship's rigging which is made fast and serves as a support; not to be hauled on; not running. **E17.** ▸**b** That is used in a fixed position; (of part of a mechanism etc. in which other parts move) that remains stationary. **M17.**

6 T. BEST Eels never breed in standing waters . . without springs. **8** DRYDEN Ixion . . leans attentive on his standing Wheel. **9b** D. BREWSTER Rotation should be effected round a standing axis by wheels and pinions.

▶ **III 10** Continuing without diminution or change; constant, permanent; (of a dye etc.) permanent, unfading. **LME.**
11 Esp. of terms of employment, a wage, a price, etc.: fixed, settled; not casual, fluctuating, or occasional. **L15.**
12 Habitually used; customary; stock. **L15.**
13 a Permanently and authoritatively instituted; established, organized, regular. **M16.** ▸**b** *spec.* Of a legislative, administrative, or similar body: permanently constituted. Esp. in ***standing committee*** below. **E17.** ▸**c** Of troops etc.: permanently maintained. Esp. in ***standing army*** below. **E17.** ▸**d** Of an official: holding permanent office. **M17.**
14 †**a** Of a building: permanent, not temporary. **E17–L18.** ▸**b** That continues in existence or operation; that continues to be something specified; that remains valid. **M17.**

10 ADDISON The Landlord . . worked up his complexion to a standing crimson by his zeal. **11** R. MONTAGU My standing allowance from Michaelmas last till Christmas. **12** T. TROLLOPE He was fain to plead the standing excuse of a bad headache. GLADSTONE The standing appellations of the army in the Iliad. **13a** BURKE This standing, unalterable, fundamental government would make . . that territory truly . . an whole. G. GROTE A standing caravan commerce with Phenicia. **b** J. BENTHAM Packing into a standing Board a set of dependent Commissioners. CARLYLE Five Judges; a standing Jury . . : they are subject to no Appeal. **c** EVELYN The King . . required the continuance of a standing force instead of a militia. P. RICHEY Germans . . maintained a standing patrol on their own side.

▶†**IV 15** *pred.* Consistent *with*. **L15–M16.**

Phrases: **all standing** (*a*) *NAUTICAL* without time to lower the sails; (*b*) taken by surprise. **leave standing** make far more rapid progress than.

Special collocations: **standing army** a permanently maintained army. **standing committee** a committee that is permanent during the existence of the appointing body. **standing crop** a growing crop, esp. of corn etc.; *spec.* in *ECOLOGY*, the total biomass of an ecosystem or any of its components at a given time. ***standing dish***: see DISH *noun* 3a. **standing iron** *Canad.* a metal spike on the collar of a sledge dog, to which a ribbon or similar decoration may be attached. **standing joke** something that is regarded as irremediably ridiculous. **standing martingale** a simple form of martingale consisting of a strap fastened at one end to the noseband of a horse and at the other end to the girth. ***standing order***: see ORDER *noun*. ***standing ovation***: see OVATION 3. **standing part** the end of a rope, sheet, etc., in a ship's rigging which is made fast as distinct from the end to be hauled upon. **standing pillar** (chiefly *Hist.*) the door post of a carriage. ***standing post***: see POST *noun*² 1. ***standing rigging***: see RIGGING *noun*² 2a. **standing ropes** the ropes composing the standing rigging. ***standing rule of court***: see RULE *noun*. **standing salt** *Hist.* a large, often ornate, saltcellar to be placed in the middle of a dining-table. **standing stone** a large block of stone set upright; *spec.* a menhir, a monolith. **standing wave** a wave in which the positions of maximum and minimum oscillation remain stationary.

standish /ˈstandɪʃ/ *noun*. Now chiefly *Hist.* **ME.**
[Origin uncertain: 1st elem. prob. from STAND *verb*.]
A stand containing ink, pens, and other writing materials; an inkstand; an inkpot.

stand-off /ˈstandɒf/ *adjective & noun*. Also **standoff**. **M19.**
[from ***stand off*** s.v. STAND *verb*.]
▶ **A** *adjective*. **1** That holds aloof; proud, disdainful; reserved. Now *rare*. **M19.**
2 *RUGBY FOOTBALL*. Designating or pertaining to (the position of) a half-back forming a link between the scrum-half and the three-quarters. **E20.**
3 Projecting or positioned a short distance away from a surface or another object; serving to hold something in such a position. **M20.**
4 *MILITARY*. Of a guided missile: designed to be launched against its target from an aircraft at long range. **M20.**
▶ **B** *noun*. Chiefly *N. Amer.*
1 Reluctance to associate with others; aloofness. Now *rare*. **M19.**
2 A draw, a tie, esp. in a sporting event. **M19.**
3 a A thing which counterbalances another. Chiefly *fig.* **L19.** ▸**b** A stalemate, a deadlock; an impasse. **M20.**
4 An extension of the time set for a creditor; a postponement of payment due. *slang*. Now *rare*. **L19.**
5 A rest; a temporary cessation from work. *rare*. **E20.**
6 *RUGBY FOOTBALL*. = ***stand-off half*** below. **E20.**
7 A thing serving to hold an object clear of a surface or another object. **M20.**

Phrases & comb.: *MEXICAN* ***stand-off***. **stand-off half** *RUGBY FOOTBALL* a half-back forming a link between the scrum-half and the three-quarters.
■ **standoffish** *adjective* holding aloof; proud, disdainful; reserved: **M19.** **standoffishly** *adverb* **M20.** **standoffishness** *noun* stand-off behaviour **L19.**

stand oil /ˈstand ɔɪl/ *noun phr.* **E20.**
[translating German *Standöl*.]
Linseed oil or another drying oil thickened by heating, used in paints, varnishes, and printing inks.

standout /ˈstandaʊt/ *noun & adjective*. Also **stand-out** and as two words. **L19.**
[from ***stand out*** s.v. STAND *verb*.]
▶ **A** *noun*. **1** A workers' strike. *rare*. **L19.**
2 A person who stands out from the crowd; an outstanding or conspicuous person or thing. *N. Amer. colloq.* **E20.**
▶ **B** *attrib.* or as *adjective*. That stands out from the crowd; outstanding, conspicuous. *N. Amer. colloq.* **M20.**

standpipe /ˈstan(d)pʌɪp/ *noun*. **M19.**
[from STAND *verb* + PIPE *noun*¹.]
1 A vertical pipe for the conveyance of water, gas, etc., to a higher level. **M19.**
2 *spec.* A vertical pipe extending from a water supply, *esp.* one connecting a temporary tap to the mains. **M19.**

2 *Times* Erecting standpipes in the streets . . so that no one shall be . . without water.

standpoint /ˈstan(d)pɔɪnt/ *noun*. **E19.**
[from STAND *verb* + POINT *noun*¹, after German *Standpunkt*.]
1 The position from which a person views an object, scene, etc.; a point of view. **E19.**
2 A mental point of view; a person's attitude in relation to an object of mental contemplation. **M19.**

1 J. N. LOCKYER We want to know the distance of this tower from our stand-point. **2** *New Scientist* To discuss infectivity mechanisms from the standpoint of viruses regarded as independent entities. R. SCRUTON The first-person standpoint can provide no knowledge of the nature of any mental process.

standstill /ˈstan(d)stɪl/ *noun & adjective*. **E18.**
[from STAND *verb* + STILL *adverb*.]
▶ **A** *noun*. **1** A state of cessation of movement; a halt, a stoppage. **E18.**
2 The state of being unable to proceed, esp. owing to exhaustion. **E19.**

1 *Daily Telegraph* The . . express train . . came to a standstill at the signals. *Scientific American* The times of moonrise and moonset, with planetary and solar standstills. *fig.*: A. KOESTLER He worked . . , but was brought to a standstill . . by lack of historical documentation. **2** *Sporting Magazine* Osbaldeston rode his horse to a stand-still. K. VONNEGUT A small band of Armenian civilians fought Turkish militiamen to a standstill.

▶ **B** *adjective*. **1** Characterized by the absence or restriction of movement. Also, that stands still; that is deficient in advancement or progress. **E19.**
2 *ECONOMICS*. (Of an agreement etc.) that seeks to maintain the present state of affairs, esp. by deferring the necessity to repay an international debt; (of a debt etc.) subject to such an agreement. **M20.**

1 J. REYNOLDS The cotillions, or stand still dances, were not then known. *Bookseller* Its publishing subsidiary . . had a virtually standstill year. **2** *Stage* Northern Arts . . may pay no more than standstill grants to . . clients.

stand-up /ˈstandʌp/ *noun & adjective*. Also **standup**. **L16.**
[from ***stand up*** s.v. STAND *verb*.]
▶ **A** *noun*. **1** †**a** In *pl.* Long boots. Cf. START-UP *noun* 1. Only in **L16.** ▸**b** A stand-up collar (sense B.1 below). **E20.**
2 A stand-up fight (sense B.2 below). **M19.**
3 A meal etc. which is taken standing; a cafeteria etc. providing refreshment to be taken standing. **L19.**
4 A failure to keep an engagement, esp. a date with a member of the opposite sex. *slang* (orig. *US*). **E20.**
5 A police indentification parade. *US slang*. **M20.**
▶ **B** *adjective*. **1** That stands erect; *esp.* (of a collar) upright, not folded over or turned down. **M18.**
2 *BOXING*. Of a fight: in which the combatants stand up fairly to one another without wrestling, flinching, or evasion; vigorous, thorough. **E19.**
3 Performed in a standing posture; (of a meal etc.) taken standing; (of a cafeteria etc.) providing refreshment to be taken standing. **M19.**
4 Of a comedian: performing by standing before an audience and telling a succession of jokes. **M20.**

staneraw /ˈsteɪnrɔː/ *noun*. *Scot.* **M18.**
[from Scot. var. of STONE *noun* + 2nd elem. derived from Old English *raġu* lichen.]
The lichen *Parmelia saxatilis*, formerly used for dyeing.

Stanford–Binet /stanfədˈbiːneɪ/ *noun*. **E20.**
[from *Stanford* University, California + Alfred *Binet* (1857–1911), French psychologist.]
PSYCHOLOGY. Used *attrib.* & *absol.* to designate a revision and extension of the Binet-Simon intelligence tests which established the concept of an intelligence quotient.

stang /staŋ/ *noun*¹. Long *obsolete* exc. *Scot.* & *dial.* **ME.**
[Old Norse *stǫng* (corresp. to Old English *steng* STING *noun*¹) = Old Saxon, Old High German *stanga* (Dutch *stang*, German *Stange*), from Germanic base also of STING *verb*. Cf. STANG *verb*¹.]
1 A pole, a stake, a wooden bar or beam. **ME.**
2 A measure of land; *spec.* (*a*) a rood; (*b*) in Wales, an acre. **ME.**
1 ride the stang *Hist.* be carried or paraded astride a pole as a punishment.

stang /staŋ/ *noun*². *obsolete* exc. *Scot.* & *north.* **ME.**
[from next.]
1 a A sting; *rare* the punctured wound caused by a sting. **ME.** ▸**b** A sharp pain like that of a sting. **E16.**
2 a A pipefish, *Syngnathus acus*. **E18.** ▸**b** The lesser weever, *Trachinus vipera*. Also ***stangfish***. **L19.**
3 The tongue of a jew's harp. **E19.**
4 An eel-spear. **M19.**

stang /staŋ/ *verb*¹. *obsolete* exc. *Scot.* & *dial.* **ME.**
[Old Norse *stanga* prick, goad, spear (fish), formed as STANG *noun*¹.]
1 *verb trans.* †**a** Pierce (a person) with a weapon. Only in **ME.** ▸**b** Spear (an eel), catch with an eel-spear. **M19.**
2 *verb trans.* & *intrans.* Sting (*lit.* & *fig.*). **ME.**
3 *verb intrans.* Shoot or throb with pain. **L18.**

stang /staŋ/ *verb*² *trans.* *obsolete* exc. *Scot. rare.* **L16.**
[from STANG *noun*¹.]
†**1** Fasten with a stang, bar. Only in **L16.**
2 Carry on a stang; *spec.* (*Hist.*) cause (a person) to ride the stang. **L17.**

stang *verb*³ *pa. t.*: see STING *verb*.

Stanhope /ˈstanəp, -həʊp/ *noun*¹. **E19.**
[Charles *Stanhope*, 3rd Earl Stanhope (1753–1816), English politician and scientist.]
Used *attrib.* to designate devices invented by Stanhope.
Stanhope lens a lens of small diameter with two convex faces of different radii, enclosed in a metal tube. **Stanhope press** an iron hand printing-press, exerting pressure by means of a screw to which a system of levers adds progressively increasing power.

stanhope /ˈstanəp, -həʊp/ *noun*². Also **S-**. **E19.**
[Fitzroy Henry Richard *Stanhope* (1787–1864), English clergyman.]
Chiefly *Hist.* A light open one-seated carriage with two (or later four) wheels, first made for Stanhope.
Comb.: **stanhope horse**: suitable for drawing a stanhope; **stanhope phaeton** a variety of the stanhope.

stanhopea /stanˈhəʊpɪə/ *noun*. **E19.**
[mod. Latin (see below), from Philip Henry *Stanhope* (1781–1855), 4th Earl Stanhope, President of the Medico-Botanical Society.]
Any of various epiphytic orchids constituting the genus *Stanhopea*, of tropical America, bearing large, often fragrant, flowers.

staniel /ˈstanj(ə)l/ *noun*. *obsolete* exc. *dial.* Also **stannel** /ˈstan(ə)l/.
[Old English *stān(e)ġella* lit. 'stone-yeller', from *stān* STONE *noun* + suffix rel. to *ġellan* YELL *verb*.]
The kestrel. Also as a term of contempt for a person, with allus. to the uselessness of the kestrel for falconry.

stanine /ˈstanʌɪn/ *noun*. **M20.**
[from STAN(DARD *noun* + NINE *noun*.]
PSYCHOLOGY. A nine-point scale on which test scores can be grouped in descending order of achievement, first developed by the US Air Force; a score on such a scale.

Stanislavsky /stanɪˈslavski/ *adjective*. **E20.**
[See below.]
THEATRICAL. Designating or pertaining to the style and technique of acting practised and taught by Konstantin Stanislavsky (1863–1938), Russian actor and director.
■ **Stanislavskian** *adjective* **M20.**

stanitza /staˈnɪtzə/ *noun*. **M17.**
[Russian *stanitsa* dim. of *stan* station, district.]
Chiefly *Hist.* A Cossack community or township.

stank /staŋk/ *noun & verb*[1]. ME.
[Old French *estanc* (mod. *étang*) from Proto-Romance, ult. from base of STANCH *verb*. Cf. STANCH *noun*[2].]
▶ **A** *noun*. **1** A pond, a pool. Also, a ditch or dyke with slowly moving water, a moat. Now *Scot. & dial.* ME.
2 A dam to hold back water, a weir, a floodgate. Now *dial. & techn.* E17.
Comb.: **stank-hen** *Scot. & dial.* the moorhen.
▶ **B** *verb trans.* Dam or strengthen the banks of (a stream); dam or hold back (water) (freq. foll. by *back*, *up*). Now *dial. & techn.* LME.

stank *verb*[2] *pa. t.*: see STINK *verb*.

Stanley /ˈstanli/ *noun*. M19.
[Edward Smith *Stanley* (1775–1851), 13th Earl of Derby, English zoologist.]
Used *attrib.* to designate certain African birds.
Stanley bustard a large black and brown bustard, *Neotis denhami*, found throughout Africa. **Stanley crane** a grey southern African crane, *Anthropoides paradisea*, which has a large head and long trailing secondary feathers; also (*S. Afr.*) called ***blue crane***.

stann- *combining form* see STANNO-.

†**stannage** *noun* see STANDAGE.

stannary /ˈstan(ə)ri/ *noun*. Also **S-**. LME.
[medieval Latin *stannaria* pl. from late Latin STANNUM: see -ARY[1].]
1 Any of a number of tin-mining districts in Cornwall and Devon, formerly having their own customs and privileges and regulating legal body (usu. in *pl.* with *the*). Also, a tin-mine. LME.
2 Tin; tinware; a locality in a market or fair for the sale of this. *obsolete* exc. *Hist.* M17.
Comb.: **stannary court** a legal body for the regulation of tin-miners in the stannaries.
■ **stannator** /staˈneɪtə/ *noun* (*obsolete* exc. *Hist.*) [medieval Latin *stannator*, *stagnator* irreg. from late Latin STANNUM] a member of the assembly or parliament established for the stannaries (cf. CONVOCATION 5) L17.

stannel *noun* var. of STANIEL.

stannic /ˈstanɪk/ *adjective*. L18.
[from STANNUM + -IC.]
CHEMISTRY. Of a compound: containing tin in the tetravalent state. Cf. STANNOUS.
■ **stannate** *noun* a salt or ester of stannic acid M19.

stanniferous /staˈnɪf(ə)rəs/ *adjective*. E19.
[from STANNUM + -I- + -FEROUS.]
Producing or containing tin.

stannite /ˈstanʌɪt/ *noun*. M19.
[from STANNUM + -ITE[1].]
1 CHEMISTRY. A salt of stannous acid. M19.
2 MINERALOGY. A steel-grey metallic tetragonal sulphide of tin, copper, and iron, which is an ore of tin. M19.

stanno- /stanəʊ/ *combining form*. Before a vowel also **stann-**.
[from STANNUM: see -O-.]
Forming nouns with the sense 'a compound that contains tin', as ***stannofluoride***, ***stannethyl***, etc.

stannotype /ˈstanəʊtʌɪp/ *noun*. L19.
[from STANNO- + -TYPE.]
A simplified form of the Woodbury process of photomechanical engraving, in which a mould obtained from a positive instead of a negative is coated with tinfoil.

stannous /ˈstanəs/ *adjective*. M19.
[from STANNUM + -OUS.]
CHEMISTRY. Of a compound: containing tin in the divalent state. Cf. STANNIC.

†**stannum** *noun*. *rare*. L18–E19.
[Late Latin, from classical Latin *stagnum* alloy of silver and lead, perh. of Celtic origin.]
CHEMISTRY. Tin.

stanol /ˈsteɪnɒl/ *noun*. M20.
[from ST(ER)OL with inserted *an* (see -ANE), orig. as element in chemical names of saturated derivatives of *cholesterol*, *ergosterol*, etc. Cf. STENOL.]
CHEMISTRY. A fully saturated sterol.

Stanton number /ˈstantən nʌmbə/ *noun phr.* M20.
[Sir Thomas Edward *Stanton* (1865–1931), English engineer.]
A dimensionless measure of heat transfer used in forced convection studies, equivalent to the ratio of the Nusselt number to the product of the Reynolds and Prandtl numbers.

stanza /ˈstanzə, *in sense 2 also* ˈstantsə/ *noun*. Pl. **-s**, (in sense 2 also) **stanze** /ˈstantsi/. L16.
[Italian = standing, stopping-place, room, strophe from Proto-Romance, from Latin *stant-* pres. ppl stem of *stare* STAND *verb*.]
1 A group of (usu. between four and twelve) lines of verse occurring as the basic metrical unit of a song or poem consisting of a series of such groups; a verse. Also, a group of four lines in some Greek and Latin metres. L16.
2 In Italy, an apartment, a chamber, a room; *spec.* a room in the Vatican (usu. in *pl.*). M17.
3 A half or other session of a game or sporting contest. M20.

> 📖 **1** TENNYSON She . . sang to me the whole Of those three stanzas. G. S. FRASER Chaucer . . is very fond of the seven-line stanza rhyming ababbcc. ***Spenserian stanza***: see SPENSERIAN *adjective*. **3** *Ice Hockey News Review* Tigers tried roughing it up in the second stanza.

Comb.: **stanza-form** the metrical form of a stanza; arrangement in stanzas.
■ **stanza'd, -zaed** *adjective* having stanzas of a specified kind or number M18.

stanzaic /stanˈzeɪɪk/ *adjective*. E19.
[from prec. + -IC.]
Of, designating, or pertaining to poetry composed in the form of stanzas.
■ **stanzaical** *adjective* (*rare*) = STANZAIC L19. **stanzaically** *adverb* E20.

stanze *noun pl.* see STANZA.

stap /stap/ *verb trans.* (*imper.*). *arch.* L17.
[Repr. an affected pronunc. of STOP *verb*, given to a character in Vanbrugh's play *The Relapse* (1696).]
Stop: only in interjections, esp. ***stap my vitals!***, ***stap me!***, expr. surprise, indignation, asseveration, etc.

stapedectomy /stapɪˈdɛktəmi/ *noun*. L19.
[from mod. Latin *staped-*, STAPES + -ECTOMY.]
MEDICINE. (An instance of) surgical excision of the stapes of the ear.

stapedes *noun pl.* see STAPES.

stapedial /stəˈpiːdɪəl/ *adjective*. L19.
[formed as next + -AL[1].]
ANATOMY. Of or pertaining to the stapes of the ear.

stapedius /stəˈpiːdɪəs/ *noun*. L18.
[mod. Latin use as noun (sc. *musculus*) of adjective, from *staped-*, STAPES.]
ANATOMY. The small muscle attached to the neck of the stapes of the ear. Also ***stapedius muscle***.

stapelia /stəˈpiːlɪə/ *noun*. L18.
[mod. Latin (see below), from Jan Bode van *Stapel* (d. 1636), Dutch botanist + -IA[1].]
Any of various succulent southern African plants constituting the genus *Stapelia* (family Asclepiadaceae), remarkable for the large size and fetid smell of the star-shaped flowers. Also called ***carrion-flower***, ***starfish-flower***.
■ **stapeliad** *noun* a plant belonging to any of a group of closely related genera including *Stapelia* and others formerly considered part of it M20.

stapes /ˈsteɪpiːz/ *noun*. Pl. same, **stapedes** /stəˈpiːdiːz/. M17.
[medieval Latin = stirrup (from its shape).]
ANATOMY & ZOOLOGY. The innermost of the three small bones which conduct sound through the mammalian ear, transmitting the vibrations of the incus to the inner ear. Also called ***stirrup***. Cf. INCUS, MALLEUS.

staph /staf/ *noun*. *colloq.* E20.
[Abbreviation.]
1 MEDICINE. = STAPHYLOCOCCUS. E20.
2 ENTOMOLOGY. = STAPHYLINID *noun*. M20.

> 📖 **1** *attrib.*: J. IRVING He . . went through . . a staph infection.

staphylinid /stafɪˈlɪnɪd, -ˈlʌɪn-/ *noun & adjective*. L19.
[mod. Latin *Staphylinidae* (see below), from *Staphylinus* genus name from Greek *staphulinos* some kind of insect, prob. from *staphulē* bunch of grapes: see -ID[3].]
ENTOMOLOGY. ▶ **A** *noun*. A beetle of the family Staphylinidae; a rove-beetle. L19.
▶ **B** *adjective*. Of, pertaining to, or designating this family. L19.

staphylococcus /ˌstafɪləˈkɒkəs/ *noun*. Pl. **-cocci** /-ˈkɒk(s)ʌɪ, -ˈkɒk(s)iː/. L19.
[mod. Latin (see below), from Greek *staphulē* bunch of grapes + *kokkos* berry.]
BACTERIOLOGY. A bacterium of the genus *Staphylococcus*, members of which typically occur in grapelike clusters and include many pathogenic bacteria which cause pus formation usu. in the skin and mucous membranes.
■ **staphylococcal**, **staphylococcic** /-ˈkɒk(s)ɪk/ *adjectives* of, pertaining to, or produced by a staphylococcus E20.

staphyloma /stafɪˈləʊmə/ *noun*. Pl. **-mas**, **-mata** /-mətə/. Also (earlier) Anglicized as †**staphylome**. L16.
[mod. Latin from Greek *staphulōma*, from *staphulē* bunch of grapes: see -OMA.]
MEDICINE. (A) hernial protrusion of the cornea or sclera of the eye, usu. as a result of inflammation.
■ **staphylomatous** *adjective* M18.

staphylorrhaphy /stafɪˈlɒrəfi/ *noun*. M19.
[from Greek *staphulē* bunch of grapes, swollen uvula + -O- + *rhaphē* sewing, suture.]
MEDICINE. (An instance of) surgical closure of a cleft palate.

staple /ˈsteɪp(ə)l/ *noun*[1].
[Old English *stapol* corresp. to Old Frisian *stapul*, *-el* rung, anvil, etc., Middle Low German, Middle & mod. Dutch *stapel* pillar, emporium, etc., Old High German *staffal* foundation, Old Norse *stọpull* pillar, steeple, from Germanic: see -LE[1].]
1 A post, a pillar, a column. Long *rare* or *obsolete*. OE.
2 A short metal rod or bar with pointed ends which has the form of a u-shape or of three sides of a rectangle and can be driven into wood etc. to act as a fastener, point of attachment, etc. OE. ▸†**b** A clasp or fastening for armour. LME–M16. ▸**c** A piece of thin wire bent into the form of three sides of a rectangle (to be) driven through papers etc. and clinched to bind them. L19.
3 MUSIC. A metal tube on to which the double reed of a wind instrument is tied. L19.
Comb.: **staple gun** a hand-held device for driving staples home.

staple /ˈsteɪp(ə)l/ *noun*[2]. ME.
[Old French *estaple* emporium, mart (mod. *étape* halting-place) from Middle & mod. Low German, Middle & mod. Dutch *stapel*: see prec.]
1 a *Hist.* A town or place, appointed by royal authority, in which a body of merchants had the exclusive right to purchase certain classes of goods destined for export. Also, the body of merchants so privileged. ME. ▸**b** A centre of trade (in a specified commodity); a commercial centre; the chief place of business in a region. *arch.* LME. ▸**c** An authorized trading establishment for merchants of a foreign country. *obsolete* exc. *Hist.* E17.
†**2** A depot or storehouse for provisions, war material, etc.; a stock of such material. E16–L17.
3 *ellipt.* A staple commodity; the principal or an important item of diet, production, trade, etc.; a major component or element; a raw material. E17.

> 📖 **1a** ***statute of the staple***: see STATUTE *noun* 3. ***statute staple***: see STATUTE *noun* 3. **b** *fig.*: LD MACAULAY Whitehall . . became the chief staple of news. **3** *Times* Maize (which was the staple of Rhodesia). E. WAUGH In the matter of drink, beer was the staple. P. ACKROYD The same scenes had been the staple of television for . . years. L. SPALDING Sugar replaced Hawaiian staples like taro and yams.

staple /ˈsteɪp(ə)l/ *noun*[3]. L15.
[Perh. from STAPLE *verb*[2].]
1 The fibre of wool, cotton, flax, etc., considered with regard to its length and fineness; a particular length and degree of fineness of a fibre. L15. ▸**b** A lock of sheep's wool. E19. ▸**c** Unmanufactured wool. L19.
2 The fibre of which a thread or a textile fabric is made; *gen.* a material, a fabric. L16.
3 The stratum of soil overlying rock or other strata; a particular depth or quality of this. E18.

> 📖 **1** *Art & Craft* Wool with a long staple . . is easiest to comb and spin. ***short staple***: see SHORT *adjective*. **2** *fig.*: C. MERIVALE The homely staple of his Latin style.

■ **stapled** *adjective* having a staple (of a certain kind) L16.

staple /ˈsteɪp(ə)l/ *adjective*. LME.
[Attrib. use of STAPLE *noun*[2].]
1 *Hist.* Of or pertaining to the staple; (of merchandise) that was the monopoly of the staple. LME.
2 (Of a commodity etc.) foremost among the products exported, manufactured, etc., by a country or place; that is a main component; (most) important, leading, principal; (of diet) usual, predominant (also *fig.*). E17. ▸†**b** Of a book, an author: standard. M17–M18.

> 📖 **2** LEIGH HUNT We confined ourselves to tea, because it is the staple drink. E. JONES Textile manufacture, the town's staple source of income. F. WELDON The staple food of the household was fish fingers . . and frozen peas. L. CHAMBERLAIN Cabbage, swede, . . and beetroot were the staple vegetables. JANET MORGAN The detective story . . formed part of the staple diet of the reading public.

staple /ˈsteɪp(ə)l/ *verb*[1] *trans.* ME.
[from STAPLE *noun*[1].]
†**1** As ***stapled*** *ppl adjective*: built with pillars. Only in ME.
2 Fasten (together) or secure (as) with a staple. LME.

> 📖 **2** J. GASKELL A clasp-knife . . went through Connor's boot and stapled his foot to the floor. P. B. YUILL The wad of stapled foolscap sheets. J. S. FOSTER The moisture barrier is provided by a building paper stapled to the sheathing.

staple /ˈsteɪp(ə)l/ *verb*[2] *trans. & intrans.* *obsolete* exc. *Hist.* L15.
[from STAPLE *noun*[2].]
Receive or deal with (goods) at a staple.

stapler /ˈsteɪplə/ *noun*[1]. LME.
[from STAPLE *noun*[2] + -ER[1].]
1 *Hist.* A merchant of the staple. Also ***merchant stapler***. LME.
2 A trader who buys wool from the grower to sell to the manufacturer. Also ***wool-stapler***. M16.

stapler /ˈsteɪplə/ *noun*[2]. M20.
[from STAPLE *verb*[1] + -ER[1].]
A device for fastening together papers etc. with a staple or staples.

star /stɑː/ *noun*¹ & *adjective*.

[Old English *steorra* = Old Frisian *stēra*, Old Saxon *sterro* (Dutch *ster*, *star*), Old High German *sterro*, from West Germanic *sterro*, with parallel forms in Old High German *sterno* (German *Stern*), Old Norse *stjarna*, Gothic *stairnō*, from Germanic, from Indo-European base repr. also by Latin *stella*, Greek *astēr*.]

▶ **A** *noun*. **I 1** Any of the many celestial objects appearing as luminous points in the night sky; *esp.* a fixed star (see FIXED) as opp. to a planet, comet, etc.; ASTRONOMY a large, coherent, roughly spherical gaseous body (such as the sun) which is luminous by virtue of internal nuclear reactions. OE. ▸**b** = LODESTAR 1. *poet.* L16.

2 Any celestial object; a planet, a world. Chiefly *poet.* ME.

3 A planet, constellation, etc., regarded as influencing or reflecting human affairs; (with possess. adjective) the planet or constellation which influences a person's fortunes, character, etc., through its position at the moment of his or her birth; a person's destiny, temperament, etc., viewed as determined in this way. Also, (in *pl.*) a horoscope or set of horoscopes published in a newspaper, magazine, etc. ME.

4 A small brightly burning piece of pyrotechnic material emitted by a firework, rocket, etc. M17.

5 *fig.* A famous or brilliant person or (less usu.) thing; a celebrity; *esp.* a famous actor or other entertainer; the principal or most prominent performer in a play, show, film, etc. E19.

1 W. COWPER Whence the stars; why some are fix'd, And planetary some. WORDSWORTH Thy soul was like a Star, and dwelt apart. TOLKIEN The innumerable stars, faint and far. P. DAVIES This galaxy contains about one hundred billion stars. **b** SHAKES. *Sonn.* Love . . is the star to every wand'ring bark. **2** DICKENS She wondered what star was destined for her habitation. **3** SHAKES. *Twel. N.* In my stars I am above thee. HOR. WALPOLE It costs, the stars know what! D. HEWETT Me stars said it was me lucky week. N. FREELING Superstitious. Went in for stars and horoscopes. D. NORDEN Telemann's star was in the ascendant. **5** G. B. SHAW You still want to be a circus star. *Nature* A galaxy of scientific stars, including 14 Nobel Prizewinners. R. JAFFE Emma . . was the star of her gymnastics class. T. BARR Only the audience can determine who is a star. J. COX Guess who's the star of all the plants on our property?

▶ **II 6** A starfish or similarly star-shaped echinoderm. Usu. with modifying word. Earliest as ***sea-star***. OE.

7 An image or figure of a star, conventionally represented by a number of rays diverging from a centre or by a geometrical figure with a number of radiating points; a printed mark of this form, an asterisk. ME. ▸**b** *spec.* An asterisk or other star-shaped mark indicating distinction, excellence, or (usu. by the number of such marks) rank in a grading system. M19. ▸**c** A (star-shaped) badge of rank or status. L19.

8 A white spot or patch on the forehead of a horse etc. LME.

9 A (natural or man-made) object or structure resembling a star; a star-shaped mark or blemish. M17. ▸**b** METALLURGY. A starlike crystalline pattern which appears on the surface of antimony during refining. M17. ▸**c** An ornament representing a star, worn as part of the insignia of an order, or as a military decoration; a military decoration with a medal of this kind. E18. ▸**d** ELECTRICAL ENGINEERING. A set of windings arranged in a star connection. Also called ***wye***. E20. ▸**e** PARTICLE PHYSICS. A photographic image consisting of a number of lines emanating from a central point, representing the paths of secondary particles produced by the impact of a primary. M20. ▸**f** In full ***star network***. A data or communication network in which all terminals are independently connected to one central unit. L20.

10 *ellipt.* A star prisoner (see below). *colloq.* M19.

7 T. PYNCHON Drew a great five-pointed star on the pavement. **b** E. M. FORSTER Giotto . . has painted two frescoes . . . That is why Baedeker gives the place a star. *Homes & Gardens* Two stars indicate . . 10 deg. F . . . and frozen food will last for up to four weeks. **c** C. J. TOLLEY I passed on . . with a second lieutenant's star in that regiment. **8** TENNYSON She Kiss'd the white star upon his noble front. **9** EVELYN A grove of tall elmes cutt into a starr, every ray being a walk. C. J. LEVER An ominous-looking star in the looking-glass bore witness to the bullet. **c** SWIFT The fools with stars and garters.

▶ **B** *attrib.* or as *adjective*. (Of a person) that is a star (sense A.5 above); outstanding, particularly brilliant; of, pertaining to, or characteristic of a star or stars. M19.

N. COWARD He must possess . . what is described in the theatre as 'star quality'. *Sport* Star players . . allowed to drift away from . . Swansea Town. J. GARDNER You're playing the star role. G. SWIFT Tom . . is a star pupil, who wins a scholarship.

Phrases: BINARY **star**. ***blazing star***: see BLAZING 1. ***double star***: see DOUBLE *adjective* & *adverb*. EVENING **star**. ***falling star***: see FALLING *ppl adjective*. ***film star***: see FILM *noun*. ***flare star***: see FLARE *noun*¹. ***hitch one's wagon to a star***: see HITCH *verb*. ***lone star***: see LONE *adjective* & *adverb*. MORNING STAR. MOVIE **star**. ***multiple star***: see MULTIPLE *adjective*. **my stars!** expr. astonishment. NEBULOUS **star**. NEUTRON **star**. ***new star***: see NEW *adjective*. ***North Star***: see NORTH. ***polar star***: see POLAR *adjective*. ***pop star***: see POP *adjective*. ***radio star***: see RADIO *noun*. ***red star***: see RED *adjective*. **see stars** *colloq.* see light before one's eyes as a result of a blow on the head. ***seven stars***: see SEVEN *adjective*. ***Silver Star (medal)***: see SILVER *noun* & *adjective*. **star of Bethlehem** any of various plants with starry, usu. greenish-white, flowers constituting the genus *Ornithogalum*, of the lily family, esp. *O. umbellatum*, a plant of southern Europe freq. grown for ornament; ***yellow star of Bethlehem***, a related, early flowering woodland plant, *Gagea lutea*, with yellow green-streaked flowers. **Star of David** a six-pointed figure consisting of two interlaced equilateral triangles, used as a Jewish and Israeli symbol. **Stars and Bars** *Hist.* the flag of the Confederate States of the US. **Stars and Stripes** the national flag of the US. **thank one's lucky stars**, **thank one's stars** give thanks to fortune, providence, etc.; count oneself fortunate. ***wandering star***: see WANDERING *ppl adjective*.

Comb.: **star-anise** a small Chinese evergreen tree, *Illicium verum* (family Illiciaceae), so called from the stellate arrangement of the carpels; the oil or spice obtained from the unripe fruit of this tree; **star-apple** *W. Indies* the fruit of a tropical evergreen tree, *Chrysophyllum cainito* (family Sapotaceae), which resembles a large purple apple and whose core forms a marked star shape in cross-section; the tree bearing this fruit (also ***star-apple tree***); **star atlas** a series of charts showing the positions of the stars etc. on the celestial sphere; **star-beam** *poet.* a ray of starlight; †**star-blasting** the pernicious influence of malign stars; **star-bright** *adjective* (*a*) *poet.* bright as a star; bright with stars; (*b*) (of wine, cider) perfectly clear and free from sediment; **starburst** (*a*) an explosion of a star or stars; an explosion producing an appearance of stars; ***starburst galaxy***, an infrared-emitting galaxy in which there is thought to be a very high rate of star formation; (*b*) a camera lens attachment which causes a bright light source to appear with starlike rays; the effect so produced; **star catalogue** a list of stars with their position, magnitude, etc.; **Star Chamber** [name of the apartment in the palace of Westminster in which the king's council sat] (*a*) *Hist.* (more fully ***Court of Star Chamber***) a court of civil and criminal jurisdiction in England, developed in the late 15th cent. from the judicial sittings of the King's Council and abolished in 1641, noted for its arbitrary and oppressive procedure; (*b*) an arbitrary or oppressive tribunal; **star chart**: showing the stars in a certain portion of the sky; **star cloud** a region where stars appear to be especially numerous and close together; **star connection** ELECTRICAL ENGINEERING an arrangement in a polyphase system in motors etc. by which one end of each phase winding is connected to a common point; **star coral** any of various stony corals of the genus *Orbicella* and related genera, in which the polyp body cavity is divided by radial septa; **star-crossed** *adjective* thwarted by a malign star, ill-fated; **star-cucumber** a N. American gourd, *Sicyos angulatus*; **star-cut** *adjective* (of a diamond) cut with star-facets; **star-delta** *adjective* (ELECTRICAL ENGINEERING) designating or pertaining to the use of star connection when an induction motor is started with a change to delta connection for continuous running; **star drag** ANGLING an adjustable tension device (with a star-shaped adjusting nut) in a reel; **star-facet** each of the eight small triangular facets which surround the table of a brilliant; **star-flower** any of various plants with starlike flowers, esp. a N. American chickweed wintergreen, *Trientalis borealis*; **star fruit** (*a*) a rare plant of ponds, *Damasonium alisma*, allied to the water plantain, with carpels spreading like a star; (*b*) the fruit of the carambola, *Averrhoa carambola*, which is star-shaped in cross-section; **star-grass** any of various grasslike plants with stellate flowers or stellate arrangement of leaves, *esp.* (*US*) *Hypoxis hirsuta* (family Amaryllidaceae) and the blazing star or colic-root, *Aletris farinosa*; (see also STAR *noun*²); **star-lighted** *adjective* starlit; **star-map**: showing the apparent positions of stars in a region of the sky; ***star network***: see sense A.9f above; **star-nosed mole** a mole, *Condylura cristata*, which is native to north-eastern N. America and has a number of fleshy projections around its mouth; also called ***radiated mole***; **star prisoner** *slang* in Britain, a convict serving a first prison sentence; **star-proof** *adjective* (*poet.*) impervious to starlight; **starquake** ASTRONOMY a sudden change of shape or structure undergone by a neutron star, pulsar, etc.; **star ruby**, **star sapphire** an opalescent ruby, sapphire, with a six-rayed asterism; **starscape** a view or prospect of a sky filled with stars; **star shell** a shell which on bursting releases a bright flare or flares to illuminate enemy positions at night; **star-shine** starlight; **starship** †(*a*) the southern constellation Argo; (*b*) SCIENCE FICTION a large manned spacecraft designed for interstellar travel; **star-shot** (*obsolete* exc. *dial.*) nostoc; **star sign** = ***sign of the*** ZODIAC; **star-spangled** *adjective* spangled with stars; ***Star-Spangled Banner*** (*a*) *rhet.* the national flag of the USA, the Stars and Stripes; (*b*) (the name of) the US national anthem; **star-stone** (*a*) a pentagonal segment of the stem of a fossil crinoid; (*b*) a precious stone which exhibits asterism; a star sapphire or star ruby; **star stream** ASTRONOMY a systematic drift of stars in the same general direction within the Galaxy; **starstruck** *adjective* greatly fascinated or impressed by stars and stardom; **star-studded** containing or covered with many stars; *esp.* featuring many famous performers; **star system** (*a*) the practice of promoting stars in leading roles in films etc.; (*b*) a large structured collection of stars, a galaxy; **star-thistle** any of several knapweeds with radiating spines on the involucral bracts, esp. *Centaurea calcitrapa* and (more fully ***yellow star-thistle***) St Barnaby's thistle, *C. solstitialis*; **star-tracker** an automatic navigational device for spacecraft etc. which maintains a fixed orientation relative to a given star; **star tulip** any of certain mariposa lilies with erect star-shaped flowers, e.g. *Calochortus nudus*; **star turn** the principal or most important item in an entertainment or performance; **star vehicle** a play or film designed especially to show off the talents of a particular star; **Star Wars** [title of a popular science-fiction film (1977)] aggression and defence in space; *colloq.* = ***Strategic Defense Initiative*** s.v. STRATEGIC *adjective*; **star-wheel** a gear-wheel with radial projections or teeth.

■ **stardom** *noun* the status of a celebrity or star; the world of stars: M19. **starful** *adjective* (*poet. rare*) full of stars E17. **starless** *adjective* having no visible star; destitute of stars or starlight: LME. **starlike** *adjective* & *adverb* (*a*) *adjective* like a star; shining like a star; shaped like a conventional star, stellate; (*b*) *adverb* (*poet.*) in the manner of a star: L16. **starward** *adverb* & *adjective* (moving or directed) towards the stars M19.

star /stɑː/ *noun*². Now chiefly *Scot.* ME.

[Old Norse *storr*.]

Any of various coarse seaside grasses and sedges, as *Ammophila arenaria* and *Carex arenaria*. Also ***star-grass***.

star /stɑː/ *verb*. Infl. **-rr-**. See also STARRED. L16.

[from STAR *noun*¹.]

▶ **I** *verb trans.* **1** Mark (as) with a star or stars; bespangle (as) with stars; adorn with or *with* an ornament like a star. L16. ▸**b** Distinguish by an affixed star or asterisk; single out for special notice or recommendation. E19.

2 Fix as a star in the heavens; transform into a star. *poet. rare.* E17.

3 Make a radiating crack or fracture in (glass, ice, etc.). L18.

4 †**a** With *it*: = sense 6 below. Only in 19. ▸**b** Advertise as a film etc. star; give a star part to; (of a film etc.) present in a leading role. L19.

1 E. YOUNG Like a sable curtain starr'd with gold. H. CORBY The pale wild roses star the banks. **b** G. B. SHAW Is the church a celebrated one? . . Baedeker stars it. HENRY MILLER The bad ones are starred in red ink. **3** B. GARFIELD The third bullet starred the windshield. **4b** G. GREENE It is an error . . to star this player above . . brilliant professionals. B. GUEST A play starring Katharine Hepburn.

▶ **II** *verb intrans.* †**5** Of a planet: be in the ascendant. Only in L16.

6 Appear as a star in a play, film, etc.; perform the leading part, feature as a leading performer. E19.

7 In pool and certain other games: buy (by placing a star against) an additional life or lives. M19.

8 Suffer a star-shaped crack or fracture. M19.

6 *Dumfries Courier* Carson starred on the right wing. **8** *Which?* Laminated glass . . merely 'stars' around the point of impact.

■ **starrer** *noun* (*a*) *rare* a person who marks something with stars; (*b*) *colloq.* a film etc. which provides a leading role for a (specified) star: L19.

starboard /ˈstɑːbɔːd, -bəd/ *noun*, *adjective*, *verb*, & *adverb*.

[Old English *stēorbord*, from *stēor* steering paddle, rudder, STEER *noun*² (as being the side from which Teutonic vessels were usu. steered) + *bord* BOARD *noun*.]

▶ **A** *noun*. The right-hand side of a ship, boat, or aircraft looking forward. Opp. ***port***, ***larboard***. OE.

▶ **B** *attrib.* or as *adjective*. Belonging to, situated on, or designating the right-hand side of a vessel or aircraft. L15.

bring the starboard tacks aboard, ***have the starboard tacks aboard***, ***on the starboard tack***: see TACK *noun*¹.

▶ **C** *verb trans.* Put or turn (the helm) to the starboard side of the vessel. L16.

▶ **D** *adverb*. To or on the starboard side. M17.

starbolins /ˈstɑːbəlmz/ *noun pl.* Also **-bowlines**. M18.

[Contr. from prec. + -LING¹ + -S¹. Cf. LARBOLINS.]

NAUTICAL. The crew members of the starboard watch.

starch /stɑːtʃ/ *noun* & *adjective*. LME.

[from the verb: cf. Middle Dutch *stercke*, Middle High German *sterke* (German *Stärke*), German *Stärkemehl*.]

▶ **A** *noun*. **1** A white tasteless odourless powder obtained esp. from potatoes or cereals and used (dissolved in water as a viscous solution) for stiffening fabric before ironing and for other purposes; a polysaccharide consisting of glucose residues which is the main constituent of this powder and occurs widely in plant tissues as a stored form of glucose; also, food containing much starch, as potatoes, rice, etc. LME.

2 *fig.* Stiffness, esp. of manner or conduct; formality, pomposity; strength, backbone, vigour. E18.

3 More fully ***starch-fish***. A jellyfish. *dial.* M19.

1 HARPER LEE She had put so much starch in my dress it came up like a tent. JONATHAN ROSS Bulky from a prison diet strong on starch. **2** J. HARVEY A slight starch of dignity stiffened in Bowditch's stoop. D. ANTHONY Professional pride had put some starch in her. **take the starch out of** remove the stiffness from, esp. by ridicule; deflate.

Comb.: **starch blocker** a dietary preparation that supposedly affects the metabolism of starch so that it does not contribute to a gain in weight; ***starch fish***: see sense A.3 above; ***starch*** HYACINTH; **starch-reduced** *adjective* (of food) processed so as to reduce the proportion of starch; **starch-water** a solution of starch and water.

▶ **B** *adjective*. Stiff and unbending in manner or bearing; formal, severe, prim. Cf. STARCHY 2. *arch.* E18.

■ **starchly** *adverb* (*arch.*) E18. **starchness** *noun* (*arch.*) L17.

starch /stɑːtʃ/ *verb trans.*

[Old English (only in *sterċedferhþ* fixed or resolute of mind) = Old Frisian *sterka*, *-ia*, Old Saxon *sterkian*, Old High German *sterken* (Dutch *sterken*, German *stärken*) strengthen, from West Germanic, from Germanic base of STARK *adjective*.]

1 Stiffen, make rigid; make formal, severe, or pompous. Long only as fig. use of sense 2. Also foll. by *up*. OE.

2 Stiffen (linen etc.) with starch. LME.

3 Fasten or stick with starch paste; apply starch paste to. Now *rare.* E17.

4 *BOXING.* Knock out, floor. *N. Amer. slang.* **L20.**

> 🕮 **1** SMOLLETT She starched up her behaviour with a double portion of reserve. **2** *absol.*: S. HOOD They . . learned to . . starch and iron.

■ **starched** *ppl adjective* stiffened with or as with starch; *fig.* stiff, formal, precise: **L16.** **starchedness** *noun* stiffness, formality, primness **L17.**

starcher /ˈstɑːtʃə/ *noun.* **E16.**
[from STARCH *noun, verb* + -ER[1].]
1 A person employed to starch laundry. **E16.**
2 A starched neckcloth. **E19.**
3 A machine for starching laundry. **L19.**

starchy /ˈstɑːtʃi/ *adjective.* **E19.**
[from STARCH *noun* + -Y[1].]
1 Of, pertaining to, or characteristic of starch; of the nature of starch, made of starch; *spec.* (of food) containing much starch. **E19.**
2 Stiffened with starch. Chiefly *fig.*, stiff in manner, bearing, or character; formal, precise, prim. **E19.**

> 🕮 **1** C. MCCULLOUGH Vast quantities of starchy food. **2** N. MAILER The paper was . . owned by the Church, so it tended to be a little starchy. T. MCGUANE Ray . . looked starchy in his . . working clothes.

■ **starchily** *adverb* **L19.** **starchiness** *noun* **M19.**

stardust /ˈstɑːdʌst/ *noun.* **M19.**
[from STAR *noun*[1] + DUST *noun.*]
1 Innumerable minute stars likened to shining or twinkling particles of dust. **M19.**
2 Cosmic dust. *rare.* **L19.**
3 *fig.* A shimmering, illusory, or insubstantial substance. Freq. in ***have stardust in one's eyes***, be dreamily romantic or mystical. **M20.**

stare /stɛː/ *noun*[1]. *arch. & dial.*
[Old English *stær* = Middle Low German *star(e)*, Old High German *star(a)* (German *Star*), Old Norse *stari*, from Germanic, cogn. with Latin *sturnus*. Cf. STARLING *noun*[1].]
A starling.

stare /stɛː/ *noun*[2]. **LME.**
[from the verb.]
†**1** Power of seeing. *rare.* Only in **LME.**
2 A condition of amazement, horror, admiration, etc., indicated by staring. Long *rare* or *obsolete.* **L15.**
3 An act of staring; a fixed gaze with the eyes wide open. **E18.**

> 🕮 **2** SHAKES. *Temp.* Why stand you In this strange stare? **3** I. COLEGATE He was greeted by stares which expressed . . unfriendliness.

stare /stɛː/ *verb.*
[Old English *starian* = Middle Low German *staren*, Old High German *starēn*, Old Norse *stara*, from Germanic base meaning 'be rigid'.]
1 *verb intrans.* Look fixedly with the eyes wide open, esp. as the result of curiosity, surprise, horror, bewilderment, admiration, etc.; open the eyes wide in astonishment etc.; (of the eyes) be wide open and fixed. Freq. foll. by *at.* **OE.** ▸**b** *fig.* Of a thing: be obtrusively conspicuous. Cf. STARING 3. **M19.**
†**2** *verb intrans.* Shine. Only in **ME.**
3 *verb intrans.* Of hair, an animal's coat, fibres, etc.: stand on end. **E16.**
4 *verb trans.* **a** Reduce to a specified condition by a prolonged stare. **L17.** ▸**b** Gaze fixedly at in a specified manner. Chiefly in ***stare in the face***, gaze fixedly at the face of; *fig.* (of a thing) be glaringly or apparently obvious to, be the evident or imminent fate of. **L17.** ▸**c** Convey (hostility, disapproval, etc.) with a stare. **M20.**

> 🕮 **1** J. WAIN They stared at him stonily. O. MANNING He stared down the length of the train. DAY LEWIS He stared aghast at the message. L. HELLMAN The man sitting . . staring out of the window. *fig.*: I. BANKS The . . window . . staring down-river like a huge handless clockface. **b** C. CLARKE Their subtleties of character stare out like the bones of a starved beast. **4a** R. ADAMS Sheldra . . stared him into silence. **stare down**, **stare out** stare at (a person) without being first to blink or lower one's gaze, usu. as an expression of resistance or hostility; outstare. **b** E. LAW Ruin and bankruptcy were staring him in the face. H. S. MERRIMAN They are staring me up and down like a wild animal. ALDOUS HUXLEY The fact had been staring everyone in the face. **c** M. DICKENS Mollie was shouting, . . her eyes staring hatred.

Comb.: **stare-cat** *slang* a person given to staring inquisitively.
■ **starer** *noun* (*a*) a person who stares; (*b*) in *pl.* (*colloq.*), eyeglasses with a long handle: **M17.**

stare decisis /ˌstɛːrɪ dɪˈsʌɪzɪs, ˌstɑːreɪ dɪˈsiːsɪs/ *noun phr.* **L18.**
[Latin = stand by things decided.]
LAW. The legal principle of determining points in litigation according to precedent.

starets /ˈstarjɛts/ *noun.* Also **-tz.** Pl. ***startsy***, ***-tzy***, /ˈstartsi/. **E20.**
[Russian = (venerable) old man, elder.]
In the Russian Orthodox Church, a spiritual leader or counsellor.

starey /ˈstɛːri/ *adjective.* Also **stary.** **L19.**
[from STARE *verb* + -Y[1].]
1 = STARING 4. **L19.**
2 Inclined to stare; giving the appearance of staring. **E20.**

starfish /ˈstɑːfɪʃ/ *noun.* Pl. **-es** /-ɪz/, (usu.) same. **M16.**
[from STAR *noun*[1] + FISH *noun*[1].]
Any echinoderm of the class Asteroidea, members of which have a flattened body normally with a number of lobes or arms (freq. five) radiating from a central disc. Also *loosely*, a brittle-star, a basket star. Cf. STAR *noun*[1] 6.
Comb.: **starfish flower** = STAPELIA; **starfish plant** any of several Brazilian bromeliads of the genus *Cryptanthus*, esp. *C. acaulis*, grown for their variegated leaves which spread like a star.

stargaze /ˈstɑːgeɪz/ *verb intrans.* **L16.**
[Back-form. from next.]
Gaze at or study the stars; gaze intently as if into space; daydream.
■ **stargazy** *adjective*: ***stargazy pie***, a kind of fish pie traditionally made in Cornwall, with the heads of the fish appearing through the crust **M19.**

stargazer /ˈstɑːgeɪzə/ *noun.* **M16.**
[from STAR *noun*[1] + GAZER.]
1 A person who gazes at the stars; *colloq.* an astrologer or astronomer. **M16.**
2 A fish of the family Uranoscopidae, members of which have small eyes set on the top of the head, electric organs, and a poisonous spine on the gill-covers; esp. *Uranoscopus scaber* of the Mediterranean and warmer coastal waters of the eastern Atlantic. Also (in full ***sand stargazer***), a fish of the related family Dactyloscopidae. **M17.**
3 A horse that holds its head well up when trotting. *slang.* **L18.**

staring /ˈstɛːrɪŋ/ *ppl adjective.* **LME.**
[from STARE *verb* + -ING[2].]
1 That stares, gazing fixedly with wide open eyes. Also, frantic, wild. **LME.**
†**2** Shining, bright. **LME–E16.**
3 Glaringly conspicuous; obtrusive. Formerly also, sensational, lurid. **E16.**
4 Of hair, feathers, etc.: upright, standing up, bristling. **M16.**

> 🕮 **1 staring mad** *colloq.* conspicuously deranged (see also STARK *adverb* 2). **3** GEO. ELIOT There are some staring yellow curtains. W. M. SPACKMAN What an utter staring lie.

■ **staringly** *adverb* **L16.**

Stark /stɑːk/ *noun.* **E20.**
[Johannes *Stark* (1874–1957), German physicist.]
PHYSICS. Used *attrib.* to designate or refer to an effect whereby spectrum lines are split into a number of components when the excited atoms giving rise to the spectrum are in an electric field.

stark /stɑːk/ *adjective & adverb.*
[Old English *stearc* = Old Frisian *stark*, Old Saxon, Old & mod. High German *stark*, Middle & mod. Dutch *sterk*, Old Norse *sterkr*, from Germanic base also of STORKEN.]
▸ **A** *adjective.* **1** Hard, unyielding. Later only of a person, character, etc.: obdurate, resolute, firm. Long *rare* or *obsolete.* **OE.**
2 Violent, harsh, severe. Now only (*a*) *arch.* fiercely opposed or ruthless *to* an enemy etc.; (*b*) *dial.* (of weather) inclement, rough. **OE.**
3 Strong, stout, powerful; robust; vigorous. Now *arch. & dial.* **ME.** ▸**b** Of liquor: strong, potent. *obsolete* exc. *Scot.* **M16.**
4 a Rigid, stiff; not supple or pliable, inflexible. Now *arch., poet., & dial.* **ME.** ▸**b** (Of landscape etc.) hard and rigid in appearance or outline, bare, barren, desolate; austere, plain, devoid of any elaboration or adornment; brutally simple, plainly evident. (Passing into sense 6.) **M19.**
5 Sheer, absolute, unqualified. Also, (of a person) arrant, unmitigated. **ME.**
6 *ellipt.* Stark naked. **M18.**

> 🕮 **2** TENNYSON He is . . stark as death To those that cross him. **4a** LONGFELLOW A frozen corpse . . all stiff and stark. R. W. EMERSON Stoic schemes are too stark and stiff. **b** H. MARTINEAU Snow . . tumbled . . among the stark, black rocks. F. HERBERT A single stark thought dominating his awareness. R. GITTINGS Poetry seemed to lose reality against the stark facts of life. O. MANNING The stark gloom of the passages. A. GRAY Her austere manner . . had made Lanark expect a stark room. **5** T. DE W. TALMAGE We make stark fools of ourselves. N. MONSARRAT Father Salvatore . . experienced his first moment of stark terror. B. BETTELHEIM A shallow optimism . . stood in stark contrast to his . . pessimistic view. **6** J. FOWLES In Soho, books of stark women.

▸ **B** *adverb.* **1** Starkly. Now *rare.* **ME.**
2 To the fullest extent or degree; absolutely, utterly, quite. Often (usu. with *staring* or *raving*) in expressions denoting conspicuous or complete madness, as ***stark raving mad***, ***stark staring bonkers***, etc. **ME.**

> 🕮 **2** EVELYN He was 86 years of age, stark blind. A. TYLER The car is setting stark still. **stark naked** *adjectival & noun phr.* (*a*) *adjectival phr.* absolutely unclothed; (*b*) *noun phr.* (*arch. slang*) undiluted liquor. **stark naught** *adjectival phr.* (*arch.*) utterly worthless, useless, bad.

■ **starken** *verb intrans. & trans.* (now *poet. & dial.*) become or make stark; stiffen, harden: **LME.** **starkly** *adverb* **LOE.** **starkness** *noun* **LME.**

stark /stɑːk/ *verb trans. & intrans.* *obsolete* exc. *dial.*
[Old English *stearcian*, formed as the adjective.]
Stiffen, harden, solidify. Formerly also, strengthen.

starkers /ˈstɑːkəz/ *adjective. slang.* **E20.**
[from STARK *adjective*: see -ER[6].]
Stark naked. Also (less commonly), stark raving mad.

starko /ˈstɑːkəʊ/ *adjective. slang.* **E20.**
[from STARK *adjective* + -O.]
Stark naked.

starlet /ˈstɑːlɪt/ *noun.* **M19.**
[from STAR *noun*[1] + -LET.]
1 A small star. Chiefly *poet.* **M19.**
2 A small short-armed starfish of the genus *Asterina.* **M19.**
3 A promising young performer in the world of entertainment or sport, *esp.* a young and glamorous actress. **E20.**

> 🕮 **1** *fig.*: J. S. BLACKIE Yellow starlet that peeps out from a grassy carpet in the spring. **3** M. KRAMER Good proportions are as self-evident in a wine as . . in a Hollywood starlet.

starlight /ˈstɑːlʌɪt/ *noun & adjective.* **ME.**
[from STAR *noun*[1] + LIGHT *noun.*]
▸ **A** *noun.* The light of the stars. Also (*rare*), the time when the stars begin to shine. **ME.**
Comb.: **starlight scope** *MILITARY* a gun sight or telescope incorporating an image intensifier for use when there is little light.
▸ **B** *attrib.* or as *adjective.* Starlit; of or like starlight. **L16.**

starling /ˈstɑːlɪŋ/ *noun*[1].
[Late Old English *stærlinc*, formed as STARE *noun*[1] + -LING[1].]
1 A common and gregarious short-tailed Eurasian passerine bird, *Sturnus vulgaris*, having glossy blackish-brown plumage speckled with white, chiefly inhabiting cultivated and built-up areas. Also, (freq. with specifying word), any bird of the family Sturnidae to which this bird belongs. **LOE.** ▸**b** A bird of the family Icteridae, *esp.* (in full ***red-winged starling***) the red-winged blackbird, *Agelaius phoeniceus*. *N. Amer.* Now *rare* or *obsolete.* **M18.**
2 (A bird of) a breed of pigeon with a white crescent on the upper breast. **M19.**
1 *rose-coloured starling*: see ROSE-COLOURED 1.

starling /ˈstɑːlɪŋ/ *noun*[2]. **L17.**
[Perh. alt. of STADDLING.]
An outwork of piles built around or upstream of the pier of a bridge, so as to provide protection against the current, floating objects, etc.

starlit /ˈstɑːlɪt/ *adjective.* **M19.**
[from STAR *noun*[1] + LIT *adjective.*]
Lit up or lighted by the stars; (of the sky, night) with stars visible.

starn /stɑːn/ *noun*[1]. Long *rare* exc. *dial.* Also †**stern.**
[Old English *stearn*. Cf. Old Frisian *stern* etc., tern.]
The black tern, *Chlidonias niger*, formerly common in East Anglia.

starn *noun*[2] var. of STERN *noun*[1].

starnie /ˈstɑːni/ *noun. Scot.* **L18.**
[from prec. + -IE.]
A little star.

starosta /ˈstarɒstə/ *noun.* Pl. **-sti** /-sti/. Orig. also Anglicized as †**starost(e)**, pl. **-s.** **L16.**
[Russian & Polish, lit. 'elder'.]
Hist. **1** In pre-revolutionary Russia, the head man of a village community. **L16.**
2 In the kingdom of Poland, a noble or an administrative and judicial officer holding a castle and domain bestowed by the Crown. **L17.**

starosty /ˈstarɒsti/ *noun.* **E18.**
[German *Starostei* or French *starostie*, from prec.]
Hist. In the kingdom of Poland, the domain of a starosta.

starover /starəˈvjɛr, -ˈvjɛː/ *noun.* Pl. **-y** /-i/, **-s.** **E19.**
[Russian.]
ECCLESIASTICAL HISTORY. = ***Old Believer*** s.v. OLD *adjective.*

starr /stɑː/ *noun.* **E17.**
[medieval Latin *starrum* from late Hebrew *šĕṭār* document.]
Hist. A Jewish deed or bond, *esp.* one of acquittance of debt.

starred /stɑːd/ *adjective.* **ME.**
[from STAR *noun*[1], *verb*: see -ED[2], -ED[1].]
1 Studded with stars, starry. **ME.**
2 Marked with one or more stars or asterisks; studded or adorned with starlike figures; distinguished as special by means of an asterisk etc.; decorated with the star of

an order. LME. ▸**b** Of glass etc.: cracked with a system of radiating cracks. M19.

3 With adverb or adjective in parasynthetic comb.: influenced in a specified way by the stars, having (specified) luck or fortune. E17.

4 Made into a star or constellation, elevated to the stars. *rare*. M17.

5 Chiefly BOTANY. Star-shaped; arranged in the form of a star; stellate. E18.

2 starred question: asked in the House of Lords to obtain a spoken answer, marked with an asterisk on the order paper (cf. UNSTARRED *question*). **3** *ill-starred*: see ILL *adjective & adverb*.

starry /ˈstɑːri/ *adjective*. LME.

[from STAR *noun*¹ + -Y¹.]

1 Of the sky, night, etc.: full of or lit up with stars. LME.

2 Of or relating to the stars; of the nature or consisting of stars. L16. ▸**b** Of, pertaining to, or characteristic of stars in entertainment etc. E20.

3 Shining like a star or stars, bright as a star. E17.

4 Shaped like a conventional star; arranged in the form of a star; stellate. E17.

5 Chiefly ZOOLOGY. Marked or studded with starlike forms. E17.

📖 **1** MILTON The Starrie Cope of Heav'n. **2** DISRAELI The bright moon with her starry court. **b** P. FIDDICK The story was romantic, the casting suitably starry. **3** A. CHRISTIE Gazing at him with wide, starry eyes. **4** J. TROLLOPE A riot of starry pale blue flowers. **5** I. MURDOCH White hawthorn starry with stamens.

Special collocations & comb.: **starry-eyed** *adjective* idealistic, romantic; euphoric; enthusiastic but impractical, naively optimistic, visionary. **starry ray** a ray of northern seas, *Raja radiata*, with numerous short prickles covering its back.

■ **starrily** *adverb* (*rare*) E19. **starriness** *noun* E18.

START /stɑːt/ *abbreviation*.

Strategic Arms Reduction Treaty (or Talks).

start /stɑːt/ *noun*¹.

[Old English *steort* = Old Frisian, Middle & mod. Low German *stert*, Middle Dutch *staert* (Dutch *staart*), Old & mod. High German *sterz*, Old Norse *stertr*, from Germanic.]

1 The tail (of an animal). Cf. REDSTART. Long *obsolete* exc. *dial.* in ***start naked***, stark naked. OE.

2 A handle. *obsolete* exc. *dial.* ME.

†**3** The footstalk of a fruit. LME–L17.

4 a The innermost segment of the bucket of a waterwheel. M16. ▸**b** The shaft or lever of a horse-mill. L18.

5 An outgrowth, a projection, a spike; *esp.* a point of a stag's horn. *obsolete* exc. *Canad.* L16.

start /stɑːt/ *noun*². ME.

[from the verb.]

1 A short space of time, a moment. Long *obsolete* exc. *Scot.* ME.

2 a Orig., a leap, a rush. Now, a sudden and transient movement; a sudden brief acceleration. ME. ▸**b** A sudden journey, *esp.* a decampment, a flight. *obsolete* exc. *Hist.* L16.

3 a A sudden involuntary bodily movement, esp. due to surprise, terror, grief, etc., or the recollection of something forgotten. ME. ▸**b** A sudden burst of energy or activity; an outburst of emotion, madness, etc.; a flight of humour. Also, a sudden broken utterance or sound. Now *rare* or *obsolete*. L16.

4 A beginning to move; a setting out on a journey, race, process, etc.; the beginning of a career, course of action, series of events, etc. M16. ▸**b** An act of setting something in motion; an impulse to movement; a signal for starting in a race etc. E17. ▸**c** An opportunity or assistance given for embarking on a career etc. Freq. in ***a start in life***. M19. ▸**d** The starting-point of a journey etc. L19. ▸**e** A race, a contest, a game. Chiefly *N. Amer.* M20.

5 An advantage or lead held over the other competitor(s) in a race, journey, or other competitive undertaking; *esp.* such an advantage given by agreement or obtained by effort at the beginning. Freq. with a specified time or distance. L16.

6 a A prison. *arch. slang*. M18. ▸**b** A surprising occurrence or incident. Freq. in ***queer start***, ***rum start***. *colloq.* M19.

📖 **3a** I. WALLACE With a start, Nat Abrahams became aware of Wanda's presence behind him. W. STYRON I fell asleep, only to wake with a start. **b** LEIGH HUNT A passionate start Of tears. **4** A. SILLITOE She was never happy about our life together, right from the start. K. M. E. MURRAY He disliked night travel and early starts. E. FEINSTEIN The children looked forward . . to the start of the summer holidays. T. PARKS He decides to make a start on the garden. **b** E. H. COLERIDGE Keble's sermon . . was the start . . of the Catholic revival. **c** P. G. WODEHOUSE Take him into your business and give him a fair start. **5** MRS ALEXANDER The hopelessness of the search in the face of nearly twenty-four hours' start. BARONESS ORCZY He has not landed yet . . we have an hour's start of him. **6b** R. LEHMANN You hear of some rum starts in Africa . . devilish queer things.

Comb.: **start button** a switch pressed in order to set a machine or process in action; **start-line** a starting-line; MILITARY a line from which infantry etc. advance.

Phrases: ***by fits and starts***: see FIT *noun*². ***by starts*** = ***by fits and starts*** s.v. FIT *noun*². ***cold start***: see COLD *adjective*. ***false start***: see FALSE *adjective*. **for a start** *colloq.* to begin with. ***from start to finish***: see FINISH *noun* 1. ***get off to a good start***, ***get off to a poor start***, etc.: see GET *verb*. **get the start of** gain an advantage over. **give a person a start** startle a person. ***in fits and starts***: see FIT *noun*². ***rum start***: see RUM *adjective*².

start /stɑːt/ *verb*.

[Old English unrecorded verb from Germanic base repr. also by Middle & mod. Low German *störten*, Middle & mod. Dutch *storten*, Old High German *sturzen* (German *stürzen*) overthrow, pour out, rush, fall headlong, gush out.]

▶ **I** *verb intrans.* †**1** Jump, caper; leap or spring *upon*, *into*. OE–M16.

2 a Move with a bound or sudden impulse from a position of rest; come suddenly *from* or *out of* a place of concealment; come suddenly or burst *into* an action etc. ME. ▸**b** Move suddenly to avoid a danger; flinch or recoil *from* something. (Foll. by *back*, *aside*, etc.) ME. ▸**c** Spring *on*, *upon*, or *to* one's feet. LME. ▸**d** Awake suddenly *from*, *out of*, (sleep, reverie, etc.); come *awake* with a start. LME.

3 Fly, flow, or be projected by a sudden impulse; issue suddenly and violently; (of tears) burst out suddenly. ME. ▸**b** Of the eyes: seem about to escape from their sockets. (Foll. by *from*, *out of*.) E16.

†**4** Go or come swiftly or hastily; rush, hasten; depart, pass away; escape. ME–M17.

5 Of a hunted animal: leave or be forced from its lair or resting-place. LME.

6 Undergo a sudden involuntary movement as a result of surprise, fright, sudden pain, etc.; (of a horse) swerve *aside* suddenly. E16.

7 Of a thing: break away from its place, be displaced by pressure or shrinkage, come loose. E16.

†**8** Turn away *from* (a leader, a party; a course, a purpose); withdraw *from* (a promise etc.); turn *aside*, *back*. M16–L18.

9 Begin to run etc. or otherwise set out in a race. M17.

10 Set out or begin a journey; begin to move, leave the point of departure; begin a career, course of action, process, etc.; (of a journey, process, etc.) begin, commence. L18. ▸**b** *spec.* Of an engine, vehicle, or other machine: begin to operate. E20.

📖 **2a** SIR W. SCOTT She had seen Meg . . start suddenly out of a thicket. BYRON At intervals, some bird . . Starts into voice. E. WELTY At the inevitable hour, Laurel started from her bed. **b** DRYDEN Nature her self start back when thou wert born. MRS H. WOOD There ensued a proposal to knight him. He started from it with aversion. **3** G. P. R. JAMES A . . cascade, starting from mass to mass of volcanic rock. *fig.*: G. GREENE Haggard's comment starts shockingly from the page. **b** C. MACKENZIE His eyes were starting out of his head. **4** SHAKES. *1 Hen. IV* You start away, And lend no ear unto my purposes. **6** JULIAN GLOAG The phone rang—Oliver started and dropped his pencil. R. FRAME She started at the question, she hadn't been expecting it. **7** J. SMEATON The mortar in the joints had started. J. S. DOBIE Greased my boots . . and found . . they are starting at the sole. **10** LD MACAULAY Near four hundred ships were ready to start. H. J. BYRON When I . . started in business I'd the finest stock in Lambeth. M. BARING He was starting for the Colonies to begin life afresh. J. BUCHAN The ladies started for home early. E. J. HOWARD He'd never told anyone about Violet and he wasn't starting now. S. BECKETT I lets him get . . ahead and then starts after him. **b** *Daily Telegraph* The engine would start . . without using the choke control.

▶ **II** *verb trans.* **11 a** Cause to move suddenly or flinch; startle. *obsolete* exc. *Scot.* LME. ▸**b** Awaken. M18.

12 Force (a hunted animal) to leave its lair or resting-place. LME.

13 Propound (a question, an objection); raise (a subject). M17.

14 Commence or initiate (an action, process, journey, etc.); begin, originate, establish; begin work on; give the signal for the start of (a race etc.). Also foll. by *doing*, *to do*. M17. ▸**b** Cause to begin or set out on a race, journey, etc.; cause to begin operating or working; enable (a person) to enter on some (specified) course of action; give a signal to (competitors) to set off in a race etc. E18. ▸**c** Enter (a horse etc.) for a race. L19. ▸**d** Conceive (a child). M20. ▸**e** Begin to suffer from or succumb to (an illness). M20.

15 Chiefly NAUTICAL. Discharge the contents of, empty, (a container); pour or empty out (liquid, powder, etc.) *from*, *into*. L17.

16 Cause to break away or come loose; displace by pressure or strain; (of a ship etc.) undergo the giving way of (a plank etc.). L17.

17 NAUTICAL. Chastise with a rope's end or other object. *obsolete* exc. *Hist.* E19.

📖 **13** F. W. ROBERTSON Many difficulties arose; such . . as the one here started. **14** R. TYRWHITT Nothing is easier than to start an art-club. ROBERT ANDERSON He starts to say something several times, then stops. TOLKIEN The falling of small stones that starts an avalanche. O. MANNING On the following Monday . . Nancy . . started work. G. SWIFT Harry started going off for months on end. **b** G. GREENE I started the car and drove home. *New Yorker* She played the piano, and started me in at four and a half. **d** E. BOWEN Irene had started Portia. **e** E. M. DELAFIELD I think Cecily's starting a cold. **15** J. BADCOCK Charcoal might be started . . from its charring place to close vessels. *fig.*: L. STEPHEN They start their cargo of classical lumber and fill the void with law. **16** F. MARRYAT She had started one of her planks, and filled. F. NORRIS He found his rubber coat . . and swung into it with a fierce movement . . that all but started the seams. **17** C. S. FORESTER A boatswain's mate . . was starting one of the hands with the . . clew-line.

Phrases, & with adverbs in specialized senses: **start a family** conceive (one's first child). ***start a hare***: see HARE *noun*¹. **start in** *colloq.* (orig. *US*) begin. **start in on**, **start on** *colloq.* attack; nag, bully. **start off** (*a*) *verb phr. trans.* begin, commence; initiate; (*b*) *verb phr. intrans.* begin to move, set off. ***start on***: see ***start in on*** above. **start out** (*a*) begin a journey; (*b*) *colloq.* proceed as intending *to do*; (*c*) project, become visible or conspicuous. **start over** *N. Amer. & Austral.* begin again, make a fresh start. **start school** attend school for the first time. **start something** *colloq.* cause trouble, agitation, activity, a craze, etc. ***start the ball rolling***: see BALL *noun*¹ 2. **start to school** *US* = ***start school*** above. **start up** (*a*) *verb phr. intrans.* rise suddenly, spring up, stir oneself; arise, occur; begin to operate, function, etc.; (*b*) *verb phr. trans.* cause to begin to operate, function, move, etc.; set going; establish, set up. ***start widdershins***: see WIDDERSHINS *adverb* 1. ***stop-and-start***: see STOP *verb*. **to start with** at the beginning, at first.

¶ The predominant sense is now that of beginning or initiating.

■ **starta'bility** *noun* the degree to which a fuel facilitates the starting of an engine; the degree to which an engine can be readily started: M20. **startingly** *adverb* †(*a*) impetuously, fitfully; (*b*) (now *rare*) with a start; by starts: LME.

starter /ˈstɑːtə/ *noun*. LME.

[from START *verb* + -ER¹.]

1 The person who starts or initiates something; an instigator. LME. ▸**b** A person or animal that starts game; *esp.* a dog trained for this purpose. E17.

†**2** A person who is liable to abandon or desert his or her position, purpose, cause, etc.; a fickle or inconstant person; a coward, a shirker. Freq. as ***no starter***, a resolute or reliable person. M16–M18.

3 a A person who gives the signal for the start of a race or other contest. E17. ▸**b** A person employed to give a signal for or control the starting of a lift, train, taxi, etc. Chiefly *US*. M19. ▸**c** A railway starting-signal. M20. ▸**d** BASEBALL. A player who plays at the beginning of a game; *spec.* the pitcher who starts the game. *N. Amer.* M20.

4 A person who or thing which makes a start, sets out, begins an undertaking etc.; (with qualifying adjective) a person or thing (esp. a motor vehicle or engine) viewed in terms of ability to start; *spec.* a person, animal, yacht, etc., that is to start or has started in a race; *fig.* a practicable idea, something worth considering (cf. NON-STARTER). E19.

5 An apparatus for starting a machine; *esp.* (*a*) an automatic device for starting the engine of a motor vehicle etc.; (*b*) an automatic switch forming part of the auxiliary circuit of a fluorescent lamp, the purpose of which is to heat the electrodes sufficiently to initiate a discharge. L19.

6 A thing with which to make a start; an initial contribution or action; *spec.* a dish eaten as the first course of a meal, before the main course (also in *pl.*). L19.

7 A culture used to initiate souring or fermentation in making butter, cheese, dough, etc. L19.

8 NAUTICAL (*Hist.*). A knotted rope's end etc. formerly used as an instrument of chastisement (cf. START *verb* 17). E20.

📖 **4** N. GOULD These [horses] comprised the six starters. *Country Life* I found the Lancia a good starter. K. M. E. MURRAY A project which . . seemed a very doubtful starter. **6** M. MEYER Everyone forewent starters and . . chose a main dish.

Phrases & comb.: **as a starter**, **for starters** *colloq.* to begin with, for a start. LIQUID ***starter***. NON-STARTER. ***no starter***: see sense 1 above. SELF-STARTER. **starter home** (a house or flat suitable to be) the first home bought by a young couple. **starter set** a small set (*spec.* of china) intended to be the basis of a larger collection. **under starter's orders** (of racehorses) in a position to start a race and awaiting the starting-signal; *fig.* (of a person) ready and eager to begin.

startful /ˈstɑːtfʊl, -f(ə)l/ *adjective*. Now *rare* or *obsolete*. L18.

[from START *noun*², *verb* + -FUL.]

1 Easily startled, timorous. L18.

2 Proceeding by starts, fitful. L18.

starting /ˈstɑːtɪŋ/ *verbal noun*. LME.

[from START *verb* + -ING¹.]

The action of START *verb*; an instance of this.

Comb.: ***starting-block***: see BLOCK *noun* 2e; **starting-gate** (*a*) a barrier used at the start of a race (esp. of horses) to ensure a simultaneous start for all competitors; (*b*) a point from which individual runs are timed in skiing etc.; **starting grid** = GRID *noun* 2c; **starting-handle** a handle used to start a machine; *spec.* a detachable crank for starting the engine of a motor vehicle; †**starting-hole** a hole in which a hunted animal takes refuge; a fugitive's hiding place; *fig.* a means of evasion, a loophole; **starting line** a real or imaginary line used to mark the place from which a race starts (freq. *fig.*); ***starting-off***, ***starting-up***, etc.; **starting pistol**: used to give the signal at the start of a race; **starting-place** the place occupied at starting by a competitor in a race; a starting-point; **starting-point**: from which a person or thing starts; a point of departure in a journey, narration, development, etc.; **starting post**: marking the place from which the competitors in a race should start; **starting price** (*a*) the price at which the bidding at an auction is started; (*b*) (esp. HORSE-RACING) the final odds on a horse etc. at the time of starting; **starting salary** the salary earned by an employee taking up a new post; **starting-signal** (*a*) a signal given to competitors to start a race etc.; (*b*) a railway signal controlling the starting of trains on a particular track; **starting stall** a compartment in which one horse may stand at the start of a race.

startle /ˈstɑːt(ə)l/ *verb & noun.*
[Old English *steartlian*, from base of START *verb*: see -LE[3].]
▶ **A** *verb.* †**1** *verb intrans.* Kick, struggle. Only in OE.
2 *verb intrans.* Rush, move swiftly; rush about, caper. *obsolete* exc. *dial.* ME.
3 *verb intrans.* Start, undergo a sudden involuntary movement caused by surprise, alarm, etc. (= START *verb* 6); feel sudden astonishment, take fright, be shocked (*at*). Also, awake with a start, move *up, back*, etc., suddenly in surprise or fright. Now *rare.* M16.
4 *verb trans.* Cause to start; give a shock or surprise to; frighten; surprise greatly; shock. L16.
†**5** *verb trans.* Cause to waver; shake (a person, belief, etc.). M17–L18.

📖 **3** SHAKES. *A.Y.L.* Patience herself would startle at this letter. COLERIDGE The river-swans have heard my tread, And startle from their reedy bed. **4** N. COWARD Your advanced views quite startle me. I. WALLACE The telephone . . rang out, startling him from his brooding. A. DILLARD The door used to blow open and startle me witless. *fig.*: L. BINYON Guns! . . They startle the still street. **5** H. MAUNDRELL It almost startles their Faith.

▶ **B** *noun.* **1** An experience of being startled; a start of surprise or alarm; something that startles. Now *rare.* E18.
2 A sudden rush *of* water. *rare.* E20.
■ **startled** *ppl adjective* that has been startled; (of an expression etc.) resulting from surprise: E17. **startlement** *noun* the state or condition of being startled, alarm; something causing this: E20. **startler** *noun* L17. **startling** *ppl adjective* that startles; now *esp.* very surprising, alarming: LME. **startlingly** *adverb* in a startling manner, to a startling extent, very surprisingly, alarmingly M19. **startlish** *adjective* (esp. of a horse) easily startled, apt to take fright M18. **startly** *adjective* = STARTLISH E18.

startsy *noun pl.* see STARETS.

start-up /ˈstɑːtʌp/ *noun & adjective.* Also **startup**. E16.
[from *start up* S.V. START *verb*.]
▶ **A** *noun.* **1** Orig., a kind of boot. Later, a kind of gaiter or legging. Usu. in *pl.* Cf. STAND-UP *noun* 1a. *obsolete* exc. *dial.* & *Hist.* E16.
2 An upstart; a parvenu. Long *obsolete* exc. *dial.* L16.
3 The action or an instance of starting up; *esp.* the starting up of a series of operations, a piece of machinery, a business, etc. Also, a business etc. that is starting up. M19.
▶ **B** *adjective.* †**1** Newly arisen; suddenly; upstart, parvenu. Freq. with adverbs. M16–E19.
2 That is starting up; of or pertaining to starting up. M20.

startzy *noun pl.* see STARETS.

starvation /stɑːˈveɪʃ(ə)n/ *noun & adjective.* L18.
[from next + -ATION.]
▶ **A** *noun.* The action of starving or depriving a person or animal of food; the condition of being starved or having too little food to sustain life or health; *transf.* deprivation or insufficient supply of some essential thing. L18.
night starvation: see NIGHT *noun*. ***starvation diet***, ***starvation point***, ***starvation rations***, etc.
Comb.: **starvation wage(s)**: below the level necessary for subsistence.
▶ **B** *pred. adjective.* Extremely cold, freezing. *dial.* & *colloq.* L19.

starve /stɑːv/ *verb.*
[Old English *steorfan* = Old Frisian *sterva*, Old Saxon *sterƀan* (Dutch *sterven*), Old High German *sterban* (German *sterben*), from Germanic, prob. ult. from base (= be rigid) of STARE *verb*.]
▶ **I** *verb intrans.* **1** Orig., die, esp. slowly from hunger, cold, grief, disease, etc. (foll. by *of, with*, or *for* (a cause of death), *for* (something lacking)). Now (*dial.*), be in danger of dying, suffer extremely, *from* cold. OE. ▸†**b** (Of a plant) wither; (of a thing) spoil, deteriorate. LME–E18.
2 Die or be in danger of dying from shortage of food, die of hunger (also ***starve to death***); suffer extreme malnourishment; *colloq.* be extremely hungry (usu. in the progressive, ***be starving***). LME.
3 Die of exposure to cold; suffer extreme cold, be freezing. Now only *north.* E17.

📖 **2** A. CHRISTIE 'Lunch,' cried Mrs. Allerton . . . 'I'm starving.' G. R. TURNER Two-thirds of the world starves. *fig.*: R. BROOKE As never fool for love, I starved for you. **3** S. E. FERRIER Pull down that window, . . for we are perfectly starving here.

▶ **II** *verb trans.* †**4** Cause to die, kill, destroy (foll. by *by, for, with*); cause to wither or perish. LME–E18.
5 Cause to die of hunger (also ***starve to death***); cause to suffer from lack of food; deprive of or keep insufficiently supplied with food; *colloq.* (in *pass.*) be very hungry. Also, force *into* (a course of action) or *out* by starvation. M16. ▸**b** Treat (a disease) by abstemious diet. E17.
6 *transf.* & *fig.* Withhold something necessary from; deprive *of* some essential commodity etc.; cause to wither or decay by such means; make suffer from mental or spiritual want. L16.
7 Cause to die of cold; benumb with cold; freq. in *pass.*, be very cold, freeze. *obsolete* exc. *dial.* L16.

📖 **4** SHAKES. *Two Gent.* The air hath starv'd the roses in her cheeks. **5** G. GREENE His parents had starved themselves that he might be a doctor. C. POTOK 'Are you hungry, Reuven?' . . 'I'm starved,' I said. B. BETTELHEIM Father Maximilian . . was . . starved to death. **starve the crows** *interjection* (*Austral. slang*): expr. surprise, impatience, etc. **6** M. HENRY The soul that is starved is . . certainly murdered. S. HOOD He was bored and starved of company. *Parents* I'm so starved of sleep that I get tense and angry.

■ **starved** *ppl adjective* (*a*) that is starving or has been starved; suffering from hunger or lack of food etc.; emaciated; deprived of necessary sustenance; (*b*) (now *dial.*) perished with cold; (*c*) HERALDRY (of a branch etc.) withered; (*d*) POTTERY (of a glaze) lacking the expected brilliance after firing: M16. **starvedly** *adverb* (*rare*) so as to starve, meagrely E17. **starver** *noun* (*a*) a person who or thing which starves; a person who causes or suffers starvation; (*b*) *Austral. slang* a saveloy: E18.

starveling /ˈstɑːvlɪŋ/ *noun & adjective.* M16.
[from prec. + -LING[1].]
▶ **A** *noun.* An undernourished or emaciated person or animal. Also, a meagre or flimsy specimen of something. M16.

📖 *Daily Telegraph* Well-nourished plants are less likely to become affected than starvelings.

▶ **B** *adjective.* **1** That lacks enough food; lean and weak for lack of nourishment, ill-fed, hungry. L16. ▸**b** *fig.* Poor in quality or quantity, lean, meagre, scanty. E17.
2 Poverty-stricken; characterized by or exhibiting poverty. M17.
3 Perishing with cold and exposure. *rare.* L17.

📖 **1** J. SCOTT The thin starveling look of a hungry repertory actress. **b** *Times Lit. Suppl.* These days of rather starveling novels. **2** M. ROBINSON Jane Austen's landscape teemed with starveling agricultural laborers.

starven /ˈstɑːv(ə)n/ *ppl adjective. obsolete* exc. *poet.* & *dial.* M16.
[Irreg. pa. pple of STARVE: see -EN[6].]
Starved.

starwort /ˈstɑːwəːt/ *noun.* LME.
[from STAR *noun*[1] + WORT *noun*[1].]
1 Any of various plants with starlike flowers or stellately arranged leaves; *esp.* (*a*) greater stitchwort, *Stellaria holostea*, with starry white flowers; (*b*) an aster, esp. (in full ***sea starwort***) the sea aster *Aster tripolium*; (*c*) (in full ***water starwort***) any of various small aquatic plants constituting the genus *Callitriche* (family Callitrichaceae), with star-shaped rosettes of leaves and inconspicuous flowers. LME.
2 A noctuid moth, *Cucullia asteris*, which lays its eggs on sea asters and related plants. E19.

stary *adjective* var. of STAREY.

stases *noun* pl. of STASIS.

stash /staʃ/ *noun*[1]. *colloq.* E20.
[from the verb.]
1 A thing or collection of things stashed away; a hoard, a cache. Also *spec.*, a cache or quantity of an esp. illegal drug; the drug itself. E20.
2 A hiding place, a hide-out; a dwelling, a pad. E20.

📖 **1** R. BANKS He had inadvertently come upon her secret stash of pornography.

stash /staʃ/ *noun*[2]. *N. Amer. colloq.* M20.
[Abbreviation.]
= MOUSTACHE 1.

stash /staʃ/ *verb trans. colloq.* L18.
[Origin unkn.]
1 Bring to an end, stop (a matter, a practice); quit (a place). L18.
2 Conceal, hide; put aside for safe keeping; stow, store, hoard. Freq. with *away.* L18.

📖 **2** *Judy For Girls* These old codgers always have money stashed away somewhere! P. CORNWELL My guess is he's stashing his wheels in some inconspicuous spot.

Stasi /ˈʃtɑːzi/ *noun.* M20.
[German acronym, from *Staatssicherheits(dienst)* 'State security (service)'.]
Hist. The internal security force of the German Democratic Republic, abolished in 1989.

stasigenesis /steɪsɪˈdʒɛnɪsɪs/ *noun.* M20.
[from STASIS + GENESIS: cf. ANAGENESIS, CLADOGENESIS.]
BIOLOGY. Lack of significant change over a long period of time during evolution.
■ **ˌstasigeˈnetic** *adjective* characterized by stasigenesis M20.

stasimon /ˈstasɪmɒn/ *noun.* Pl. **-ma** /-mə/, **-mons**. M19.
[Greek, use as noun (sc. *melos* song) of neut. of *stasimos* stationary, from *sta-* base of *histanai* STAND *verb*.]
In Greek drama, a song sung by the chorus after the parode.

stasiology /stasɪˈɒlədʒi/ *noun. rare.* M20.
[French *stasiologie*, from Greek STASIS: see -OLOGY.]
The branch of knowledge that deals with political parties.

stasipatric /stasɪˈpatrɪk/ *adjective.* M20.
[from Greek STASIS + *patra* fatherland (from *patēr* father) + -IC.]
BIOLOGY. Designating a form of speciation in which a number of new contiguous taxa arise within the geographical range of the parent species.
■ **stasipatrically** *adverb* L20.

stasis /ˈsteɪsɪs, ˈsta-/ *noun.* Pl. **stases** /ˈsteɪsiːz, ˈsta-/. M18.
[mod. Latin from Greek, lit. 'standing, stoppage; party, faction', from *sta-* base of *histanai* STAND *verb*.]
1 MEDICINE. A stagnation or stoppage of flow due usu. to obstruction, as of the blood or lymph, or of the intestinal contents. M18.
2 *gen.* Inactivity; stagnation; a state of equilibrium. E20.
3 PSYCHOANALYSIS. The presence of high energy or excitement in the libido caused esp. by repression and thought to produce neurosis. M20.
4 Party faction, civil strife. M20.

📖 **2** *Times Lit. Suppl.* We see him in the moment of stasis before action.

stat /stat/ *noun*[1]. *colloq.* M20.
[Abbreviation of PHOTOSTAT.]
A photocopy.

stat /stat/ *noun*[2]. *colloq.* Chiefly *N. Amer.* M20.
[Abbreviation.]
= STATISTIC *noun*, STATISTICS. Cf. STATS.

stat /stat/ *noun*[3]. *colloq.* L20.
[Abbreviation.]
= THERMOSTAT *noun*.

stat /stat/ *adverb.* L19.
[Abbreviation of Latin *statim*.]
PHARMACOLOGY. Esp. on a prescription: immediately.

stat- /stat/ *combining form.*
[from STATIC.]
ELECTRICITY. Used in names of the cgs electrostatic system of units, as ***statampere***, ***statcoulomb***, ***statfarad***, ***statgauss***, ***statohm***, ***statvolt***.

-stat /stat/ *suffix.*
[Partly the ending of HELIO)STAT, partly back-form. from -STATIC.]
Forming names of instruments, devices, and substances with the sense 'stationary, constant, level, straight'; *spec.* (*a*) holding at a constant value, as ***thermostat***, ***humidistat***; (*b*) inhibiting flow, as ***haemostat***; (*c*) inhibiting growth, as ***bacteriostat***.

statal /ˈsteɪt(ə)l/ *adjective.* M19.
[from STATE *noun* + -AL[1].]
1 Of or pertaining to a US or other federal State. *rare.* M19.
2 LINGUISTICS. Of a passive verbal form: expressing a state or condition rather than an action; not actional; stative. M20.

statant /ˈsteɪt(ə)nt/ *adjective.* L15.
[Irreg. from Latin *stat-* pa. ppl stem of *stare*: see STAND *verb*, -ANT[1].]
HERALDRY. Of an animal, esp. a lion: standing in profile with all four feet on the ground.

statary /ˈsteɪt(ə)ri/ *adjective.* L16.
[Latin *statarius*, from *stat-*: see prec., -ARY[1].]
†**1** Standing firm, established; fixed, stationary. L16–M17.
2 ENTOMOLOGY. Pertaining to or designating army ants during their non-nomadic phase, when they return to a fixed colony each day. M20.

state /steɪt/ *noun & adjective.* Also (esp. in senses A.25, 26, 28, B.1) **S-**. ME.
[Partly aphet. from ESTATE *noun*, partly directly from Latin *status* manner of standing, condition, from base of *stare* STAND *verb*.]
▶ **A** *noun.* **I** Condition, manner of existing.
1 a A combination of circumstances or attributes belonging for the time being to a person or thing; a particular way of existing, as defined by certain circumstances or attributes; a condition, esp. of mind or body or (now *rare*) of prosperity. ME. ▸**b** A dirty, disorderly, or untidy condition. Cf. sense 7b below. *colloq.* L19.
2 The mode of existence of a spiritual being; a particular mode or phase of (spiritual) existence. ME.
3 a Physical condition as regards internal constitution, molecular form or structure, etc. Also, any of several forms or conditions in which an object, animal, plant, etc., may exist; a phase or stage of existence. More widely, each of the possible modes of existence of a system; the condition of a device that determines what output it produces for a given input. ME. ▸**b** PHYSICS. A

condition of an atom or other quantized system described by a particular set of quantum numbers; *esp.* one characterized by the quantum numbers *n*, *L*, *S*, *J*, and *m*. Cf. LEVEL *noun* 4c. E20.

†4 Original, proper, or normal condition; a healthy or flourishing condition. Cf. ESTATE *noun* 2b. ME–M17.

†5 Existence. ME–E17.

†6 A person's proper form, shape, or nature. Also, stature, bodily form. *rare*. ME–E17.

7 a A mental or emotional condition, *esp.* one experienced by a person at a particular time. Formerly also, mental or emotional condition as evidenced in one's manner or conduct. LME. **▸b** An agitated, excited, or anxious condition of mind or feeling. Cf. sense 1b above. *colloq.* M19.

†8 *RHETORIC.* The point in question or under debate between contending parties, as it emerges from their pleadings; the issue, the main question. LME–L18.

9 The height or chief stage of a process; the peak; *spec.* in *MEDICINE*, the crisis of a disease. Cf. STATUS 1. Now *rare* or *obsolete*. LME.

10 *GRAMMAR.* Chiefly & now only in Semitic languages, a case, a syntactical role played by a noun, as the construct state (see CONSTRUCT *adjective*). E18.

11 *ENGRAVING.* An etched or engraved plate at a particular stage of its progress. L19.

12 *BIBLIOGRAPHY.* Any of various versions of a first edition of a book, distinguishable from one another by last minute pre-publication changes. M20.

> 📖 **1a** J. B. MORTON The state of discipline in the Army seems to be getting a bit lax. L. WOOLF I noted almost daily the state of her health. P. DALLY He could not . . tell Mary about the state of their finances. C. HARKNESS To be childless is not a happy state for any woman. **b** B. BAINBRIDGE Look at the state of you . . . Cobwebs in your hair. **2** F. WESTON A state of being that is quite inferior to the divine state. **7a** H. NICOLSON She was in quite a state of excitement at my arrival. E. CALDWELL Her confused and tormented state of mind.

▶ II Status; high rank; pomp.

13 a A person's condition or position in life; a person's status, profession, rank, etc. Now *rare*. ME. **▸b** *spec.* A person's status as married or single. Esp. in ***married state***. LME.

†14 A high rank or position; an office of power or importance. Also *gen.*, high rank, greatness, power. ME–M17.

15 Costly and imposing display; splendour, pomp, ceremony, magnificence. ME.

†16 A raised chair with a canopy etc.; a throne. LME–E18. **▸b** A canopy. E17–E19.

17 a Dignity of demeanour or presence; stateliness of bearing. Now *rare*. L16. **▸†b** Dignified observance of form or ceremony. Only in 17.

> 📖 **15** TENNYSON Ancient homes of lord and lady, Built for pleasure and for state.

▶ III A class, a rank; a person of rank.

†18 A class, rank, or body *of* people; a condition, a profession, an occupation; the members of a class or profession collectively. ME–E17.

†19 An order or class of people regarded as part of the body politic and as sharing in government; *spec.* an Estate of the Realm (see ESTATE *noun*). LME–E18.

20 In *pl.* An assembly of the governing classes of a country, as in the Netherlands until the 18th cent., France before the Revolution, Scotland before the Union, or the Holy Roman Empire. Now *Hist.* exc. as the legislative body in Jersey, Guernsey, and Alderney. Cf. ESTATE *noun* 6b, STATES GENERAL. LME.

†21 A person of standing or high rank; a dignitary; a noble, a prince. LME–M17.

†22 In *pl.* The dignitaries or authorities of a town or district. LME–E17.

†23 The governing body of a town, city, or realm. E16–M17.

> 📖 **20** H. P. BROUGHAM The French States at no time attained the regularity of the English Parliament.

▶ IV Commonwealth, polity; common weal.

†24 The condition of a country, the Church, etc., with regard to its welfare and polity; *esp.* a condition of prosperity or administrative order. ME–M17.

25 a *The* political organization or management which forms the supreme civil rule and government of a country or nation. Also, *the* supreme civil power of a country or nation. ME. **▸b** All that concerns the government or ruling power of a country; the sphere of supreme political administration. L16.

26 a A community of people occupying a defined area and organized under one government; a commonwealth, a nation. Also (*occas.*), the territory occupied by such a community. M16. **▸b** Any of a number of such communities which together make up a federal republic as the United States of America. M17.

†27 A particular form of polity or government. M16–E18.

28 In full ***State Department***. The federal department for US foreign affairs, presided over by the Secretary of State. *US*. L18.

> 📖 **25a** *Nineteenth Century* The railways . . in Prussia are now all in the hands of the State. M. TIPPETT The state may even suppress certain art as anti-social. **b** N. CARPENTER I speake . . of matters of state and policy. **26a** *Daily Telegraph* The lack of human rights in Communist states. A. BURGESS Weizmann was to become first President of the Jewish State of Israel in 1949. ***corporate State***, ***free State***, ***front-line States***, etc. **b** A. MACRAE Full Californian: born in the state whose culture dominates the Western world. ***Empire State***, ***Granite State***, ***Lone Star State***, ***Middle Atlantic States***, ***Northern States***, ***Pelican State***, ***Southern States***, etc.

▶ V Interest in property; possessions.

†29 Property, possessions; one's private means. ME–L19.

†30 *LAW.* Possession (of property). Chiefly *Scot.* LME–E19.

†31 *LAW.* The interest anyone has in land or other property; entitlement to property; = ESTATE *noun* 11. LME–M17.

▶ VI A statement.

32 a A statement, account, or description, esp. *of* a transaction, event, legal case, etc. Now *rare* or *obsolete*. E17. **▸†b** A detailed enumeration or report of particulars or items; *esp.* a statement of expenses. Cf. ***state an account*** s.v. STATE *verb*. L17–E19. **▸c** *MILITARY.* A report of the numbers of a corps, regiment, etc., in battle, with details of casualties. E19.

Phrases: **†bear great state**, **†bear state** hold (high) office; *fig.* (of a thing) be important or consequential. **Church and State** supreme civil and ecclesiastical organization and authority. ***civil state***: see CIVIL *adjective*. ***cloth of state***: see CLOTH *noun* 1. ***equation of state***: see EQUATION 3. ***head of State***: see ***of State*** below. **hold one's state** *arch.* appear in pomp and splendour. **in a fit state (to)**, **in a state (to)** fit, likely, ready, (to). **in state** with great pomp and ceremony; ***lie in state***, (of a dead body) be ceremoniously displayed before interment, cremation, etc. **keep one's state**, **keep state** (now *rare*) observe the pomp and ceremony befitting a high position; keep one's dignity. ***Minister of State***: see MINISTER *noun* 4a. ***mint state***: see MINT *noun*[1]. ***mystery of State***: see MYSTERY *noun*[1] 5c. ***Native State***: see NATIVE *adjective*. ***NEGRO State***. **of state** (*a*) for ceremonial use, for people of rank or wealth; (*b*) ***of State***, concerning politics or government (freq. in ***head of State***, ***officer of State***). OUT-OF-STATE. ***Papal States***: see PAPAL. ***princely States***: see PRINCELY *adjective* 1. ***PRISONER of State***. ***reason of State***: see REASON *noun*[1]. ***satellite State***: see SATELLITE *noun* 3a. ***Secretary of State***: see SECRETARY *noun* 3. ***ship of State***, ***ship of the State***: see SHIP *noun* 1b. ***Slave State***: see SLAVE *noun*[1] & *adjective*[1]. ***spheroidal state***: see SPHEROIDAL 2. **State Enrolled Nurse** a nurse on a State register with a qualification below that of a State Registered Nurse. ***state of affairs***: see ***state of things*** below. ***state of emergency***: see EMERGENCY *noun* 1d. ***state of grace***: see GRACE *noun*. **state of life** rank and occupation. ***state of nature***: see NATURE *noun*. ***state of play***: see ***state of things*** below. **state of the art** the current stage of development of a practical or technological subject. **state-of-the-art** *adjective* using the latest techniques or equipment. **State of the Union message** an annual address made by the US President to Congress, giving plans for legislation. **state of things**, **state of affairs**, **state of play** the way in which events or circumstances stand; the current situation. **†state of time(s)** a juncture or posture of affairs. **state of war** the situation when war has been declared or is in progress. **State Registered Nurse** a nurse on a State register and more highly qualified than a State Enrolled Nurse. ***stationary state***: see STATIONARY *adjective*. ***stroke of state***: see STROKE *noun*[1]. ***Sword of State***: see SWORD *noun*. **the state of the case** the facts and circumstances of a particular affair, question, etc. **the States** (*a*) the United States of America; (*b*) (*obsolete* exc. *Hist.*) the cities and territories in an Italian principality or republic. ***turn State's evidence***: see EVIDENCE *noun*. ***Volunteer State***: see VOLUNTEER *noun* & *adjective*.

Comb.: **state-cabin** = STATEROOM 1, 3a; **State capitalism** a socialist system whereby the State exerts exclusive control over production and the use of capital; **State-church** a church established by the State; **State Council** the highest administrative and executive body of the People's Republic of China; **statecraft** the art of conducting State affairs; statesmanship; ***State Department***: see sense 28 above; **State education**: funded and run by the State, and given in a State school; **state function** *PHYSICS* a quantity in thermodynamics, such as entropy or enthalpy, that has a unique value for each given state of a system; **State line** *US* the boundary line of a State; **state machine** *ELECTRONICS* a device which can be in any of a set number of stable conditions depending on its previous condition and on the present values of its inputs; **state-monger** (*contempt.*, now *rare*) a promoter of political constitutions; a pretender to political science; **State-paper** an official document on some matter concerning the government or the nation; **State pension**: paid by the State to a person of pensionable age; **State-prison** (*a*) a prison for political offenders; (*b*) *US & Austral.* a penal prison run by a State; ***State PRISONER***; **State rights** = ***States rights*** below; **State's attorney** *US* a lawyer representing a State in court; **State Scholarship**: awarded by the State for study at a university; **State school**: managed and funded by the public authorities; **state secret** a matter kept secret by the government; *joc.* an important secret; **states-monger** (*contempt.*, now *rare*) = ***state-monger*** above; **State socialism**: achieved by State ownership of public utilities and industry; **State socialist** *adjective* & *noun* (*a*) *adjective* of or pertaining to State socialism; (*b*) *noun* an advocate of State socialism; **States-righter**, **States'-righter** an advocate of States rights in the US or other federal governments; **States rights**, **States' rights** the rights and powers vested in the separate States under the federal constitution of the US and other federal governments; **State trial** a prosecution on behalf of the State; ***State trooper***: see TROOPER 3b; **State university** *US*: run by the public authorities of a State; **state vector** *PHYSICS* a vector in a space whose dimensions correspond to all the independent wave-functions of a system, the instantaneous value of the vector conveying all possible information about the state of the system at that instant; **State visit** a ceremonial visit to a foreign country by a head of State; **state-wide** *adjective* & *adverb* (*a*) *adjective* extending over or affecting a whole State; (*b*) *adverb* so as to extend over or affect a whole State.

▶ B *attrib.* or as *adjective*. **1** Of, belonging to, or concerned with the State or with civil government. More widely, relating to politics or the art of government. L15.

2 Belonging to, reserved for, or done on occasions of ceremony; involving or accompanied by ceremony. M16.

> 📖 **1** N. FARAH He has become state property. **2** *Independent* Chairs . . that used to grace the state drawing room at Chatsworth.

■ **statehood** *noun* the condition or status of a political State M19. **statelet** *noun* a small State M19.

state /steɪt/ *verb trans.* L16.

[from prec.]

1 Place, station. *rare*. L16.

†2 Give a certain rank or position to; in *pass.*, be ranked. L16–E18. **▸b** Assign a value to, have an opinion on. *rare* (Milton). Only in L17.

†3 Place in a specified condition; *esp.* settle in quietness or safety. E17–L18.

4 Place or install *in* a dignity, office, right, etc. Now *rare*. E17. **▸†b** Confer (a possession, right, etc.) *upon* or vest *in* a person etc. M–L17.

†5 Settle or regulate by authority. M17–E18.

6 Set out fully or in the correct form; express clearly and properly, esp. in speech or writing; *spec.* express in a manner or form allowing assessment of the content in terms of truth or validity. M17. **▸b** Specify (a number, price, etc.). L18. **▸c** *MUSIC.* Play (a theme etc.) so as to make it known to a listener. M20.

> 📖 **6** J. MARTINEAU A problem must be stated in order to be solved. L. STEFFENS The . . secretary stated authoritatively . . that the mayor would not sign that day. R. FRASER The parents were requested to state what diseases their children had had.

Phrases: **state a case** set out the facts of a matter or pleading for consideration by a court. **state an account**, **state accounts** *COMMERCE* set down formally the debits and credits arising in the course of business transactions on an account.

■ **statable** *adjective* able to be stated E19.

stated /ˈsteɪtɪd/ *adjective*. M17.

[from prec. + -ED[1]. In early use perh. rather from Latin *status* appointed, fixed, regular + -ED[1].]

1 Fixed, regular, established; settled by authority, agreement, custom, etc. M17. **▸b** Of a functionary or an employment: recognized, regular, official. M18.

2 a Of a law, penalty, etc.: formulated, explicitly set forth. L17. **▸b** Narrated, alleged as fact. L18.

> 📖 **1** J. WESLEY The Studious ought to have stated times for Exercise. *Harper's Magazine* One of their stated weekly meetings.

Special collocations: **stated account** *LAW* a statement of account that has been agreed to by the parties to a suit. **stated case** *LAW* an agreed summary of disputed points presented to a court or arbitrator in order to facilitate a speedy decision.

■ **statedly** *adverb* L17.

State-house /ˈsteɪthaʊs/ *noun*. In sense 4 **State house**. L16.

[from STATE *noun* + HOUSE *noun*[1].]

†1 A building used for State ceremonies. L16–E17.

†2 A town hall. E17–M18.

3 a A building used for government or administration. *N. Amer. obsolete* exc. *Hist.* M17. **▸b** A building in which the legislature of a State meets. *US*. L18.

4 A house owned and let by the Government. *NZ*. M20.

stateless /ˈsteɪtlɪs/ *adjective*. E17.

[from STATE *noun* + -LESS.]

1 Without a State or political community. Also, destitute of state or ceremonial dignity. E17.

2 Not belonging to any State; having no nationality. M20.

■ **statelessness** *noun* the condition of having no nationality M20.

stately /ˈsteɪtli/ *adjective* & *adverb*. LME.

[from STATE *noun* + -LY[1], -LY[2].]

▶ A *adjective*. **1** Of a person, a person's manner, appearance, etc., or (occas.) an animal: noble, majestic; imposingly dignified. LME.

2 Of a person, disposition, or action: dignified and remote, unapproachable, superior. Formerly also, haughty, domineering, arrogant. LME.

3 Of a thing, a ceremony, etc.: belonging to or befitting a person of high estate; magnificent, splendid. Also, (esp. of a structure) imposing or majestic in size and proportions. LME. **▸b** Of sound: impressive, majestic. M17.

†4 Powerful, effectual. LME–M17.

5 Of speech, writing, etc.: elevated in thought or expression, dignified, majestic. L16.

📖 **1** SHAKES. *Rich. II* The Duke . . With slow but stately pace kept on his course. J. LONDON A tall, blonde woman, slender, and stately. **3** P. HEYLIN A stately portico . . raised on Corinthian pillars. M. ELPHINSTONE Buried at Sahserám, where his stately mausoleum is still to be seen. W. W. FOWLER Meaningless as they were, the stately processions remained. R. FRAME A stately church, richly endowed in its past. **stately home** a large magnificent house, usu. set in considerable grounds and open to the public. **b** F. WYNDHAM Sybil had a low, musical voice and spoke in measured, stately tones. **5** WORDSWORTH Choice word and measured phrase, above the reach Of ordinary men; a stately speech.

▶ **B** *adverb.* In a stately manner. Now *rare.* LME.

■ **statelihood** *noun* stateliness M19. **statelily** *adverb* (now *rare*) in a stately manner E17. **stateliness** *noun* dignity, nobleness; loftiness: E16.

statement /ˈsteɪtm(ə)nt/ *noun.* L18.
[from STATE *verb* + -MENT.]
1 a The action or an act of stating, alleging, or enunciating something; the manner in which something is stated. L18. ▸**b** *MUSIC.* A presentation of a subject or theme in a composition. L19.
2 a A thing that is stated; an allegation, a declaration; *spec.* a verbal expression whose content is assessable in terms of truth or validity. L18. ▸**b** *COMPUTING.* An expression or command in a programming language that corresponds to one or more underlying machine instructions. M20.
3 a A formal written or oral account, setting down facts, an argument, a demand, etc.; *esp.* an account of events made to the police or in a court of law. L18. ▸**b** *COMMERCE.* More fully ***statement of account***. A document setting out the items of debit and credit between two parties. M19.
4 *COMMERCE.* A document setting down the amount to be paid to a tradesman etc. L19.

📖 **2a** *Daily Telegraph* The . . inaccurate statements made by various Labour politicians. *USA Today* We will strike again if that statement was not strong enough. **3a** J. COLVILLE The P.M. made a statement in the House. *Guardian* Yasser Arafat . . addressed a message disowning the PLO statement. J. WAINWRIGHT You . . telephoned the police, then made this statement to a Detective Sergeant. **b** *Which?* Banks will generally provide statements whenever you ask.

Phrases: ***bank statement***: see BANK *noun*[3]. ***make a statement*** *fig.* demonstrate one's attitude, point of view, etc., in a conspicuous way, esp. by dressing or behaving in a striking manner. *RECONCILIATION* ***statement***. ***statement of account***: see sense 3b above. **statement of affairs** a list of assets and liabilities not expressed as a formal balance sheet. **statement of claim** *ENGLISH LAW* a pleading served by the plaintiff in a High Court action containing the allegations made against the defendant and the relief sought by the plaintiff.

■ **stateˈmental** *adjective* M20. **statementing** *noun* (*a*) *US* the issuing of bank or other financial statements; (*b*) the formal stating of the special educational needs of a child or children: L20.

statement /ˈsteɪtm(ə)nt/ *verb trans.* L20.
[Back-form. from STATEMENTING.]
1 Make a statement of special educational needs. L20.
2 Set out as in a bank statement. *US. rare.* L20.

stater /ˈsteɪtə/ *noun*[1]. LME.
[Late Latin, from Greek *statēr*, from *sta-* base of *histanai* STAND *verb* in the sense 'weigh'.]
ANTIQUITIES. **1** An ancient weight equal to half an ounce. LME.
2 Any of various ancient coins, *esp.* a gold coin or daric of Persia, or a gold or silver coin of ancient Greece. LME.

stater /ˈsteɪtə/ *noun*[2]. E18.
[from STATE *verb* + -ER[1].]
A person who states something.

Stater /ˈsteɪtə/ *noun*[3]. E20.
[from STATE *noun* + -ER[1].]
IRISH HISTORY. A member of the Irish Free State army.

statera /stəˈtɪərə/ *noun. obsolete* exc. *Hist.* Pl. **-rae** /-riː/. M17.
[Latin, prob. from Greek *statēra* accus. of *statēr* STATER *noun*[1].]
A steelyard.

stateroom /ˈsteɪtruːm, -rʊm/ *noun.* M17.
[from STATE *noun* + ROOM *noun*[1].]
1 A captain's or superior officer's room on board ship. M17.
2 A state apartment or room for ceremonial occasions in a palace, hotel, etc. E18.
3 a A sleeping apartment on a passenger ship. L18. ▸**b** A private compartment in a train. *US.* M19.

States General /steɪts ˈdʒɛn(ə)r(ə)l/ *noun phr.* L16.
[Repr. French *états généraux*, Dutch *staten generaal*.]
Hist. A legislative assembly, esp. in the Netherlands from the 15th to 18th cents. or in France before the Revolution, representing the three estates, viz. the clergy, the nobility, and the common people. Cf. ESTATE *noun* 6b, STATE *noun* 20.

Stateside /ˈsteɪtsʌɪd/ *adjective & adverb. colloq.* (chiefly *US*). Also **s-**. M20.
[from STATE *noun* + -S[1] + SIDE *noun*.]
▶ **A** *adjective.* Of, in, or pertaining to the United States of America. M20.
▶ **B** *adverb.* Towards or in the continental United States of America. M20.

statesman /ˈsteɪtsmən/ *noun.* Pl. **-men**. L16.
[from STATE *noun* + -'S[1] + MAN *noun*.]
1 A person who takes an active and esp. skilful part in politics or affairs of State. Also, a distinguished and capable politician. L16.
2 A yeoman, a small landowner. *dial.* L18.

📖 **1** J. SINCLAIR The Count . . was not only an able speaker, but a real statesman. ***elder statesman***: see ELDER *adjective*.

■ **statesmanlike** *adjective* having the qualities characteristic of a statesman; befitting or worthy of a statesman (earlier in UNSTATESMANLIKE): E19. **statesmanly** *adjective* pertaining to, characteristic of, or befitting a statesman: M19. **statesmanship** *noun* the activity or skill of a statesman; skilful management of public affairs: M18.

statesperson /ˈsteɪtspəːs(ə)n/ *noun.* L20.
[from STATE *noun* + -'S[1] + PERSON *noun*.]
A statesman or a stateswoman.

stateswoman /ˈsteɪtswʊmən/ *noun.* Pl. **-women** /-wɪmɪn/. E17.
[from STATE *noun* + -'S[1] + WOMAN *noun*.]
A woman who takes part in politics or affairs of State; a woman with statesmanlike ability.

stathmokinesis /ˌstaθməʊkɪˈniːsɪs/ *noun.* M20.
[from Greek *stathmos* station, stage + *kinēsis* motion.]
BIOLOGY & MEDICINE. A type of cell division produced by substances such as colchicine, characterized by a halt or long delay at metaphase.
■ **stathmokinetic** *adjective* (of a drug) that produces stathmokinesis; also, designating the method of measuring rates of cell division by means of such a drug: L20.

static /ˈstatɪk/ *noun & adjective.* L16.
[As noun from mod. Latin *statica* from Greek *statikē* (sc. *tekhnē* art) science of weighing, use as noun of fem. of *statikos* adjective; as adjective from mod. Latin *staticus* from Greek *statikos* causing to stand, pertaining to weighing, from *histanai* cause to stand, weigh (see STAND *verb*).]
▶ **A** *noun.* **1** = STATICS. Now *rare.* L16.
2 a Electrical disturbances producing interference with the reception of telecommunications and broadcasts; atmospherics. E20. ▸**b** *fig.* Aggravation, interference, hassle; confusion, fuss, criticism. *slang* (orig. *US*). E20.
3 = ***static electricity*** below. E20.

📖 **2a** T. O'BRIEN A long-distance connection broken by static. **b** L. DEIGHTON Spare me the static.

▶ **B** *adjective.* †**1** = STATICAL 1. M17–M18.
†**2** Pertaining to the effect of weight or to the conditions of the equilibrium of weight; (of a power or principle) operative in the production of equilibrium. M17–L18.
3 a Of or relating to forces or systems in equilibrium or bodies at rest. M19. ▸**b** *ELECTRICITY.* = ELECTROSTATIC. M19. ▸**c** *ECONOMICS.* Of or pertaining to an economic system in a state of equilibrium. Cf. STATICS 2. L19.
4 Fixed, stable, stationary; not changing or moving. M19. ▸**b** *PHONETICS.* (Of a consonant) continuant; (of a tone) not changing pitch during utterance. M20. ▸**c** *COMPUTING.* Of a process, variable, etc.: not able to be changed during a set period, e.g. while a program is running. L20.
5 *MEDICINE & PHYSIOLOGY.* Physical or structural as opp. to functional or dynamic. Now *rare* or *obsolete.* M19.
6 a Of an electric transformer or generator: having all its parts stationary, non-rotary. E20. ▸**b** *COMPUTING.* Of a memory or store: orig., in which the data are held in fixed positions and any location can be accessed at any time; now usu., not needing to be periodically refreshed by an applied voltage. M20.

📖 **3a** *PITOT-static.* **4** P. BROOK Talent is not static, it ebbs and flows according to . . circumstances. K. CLARK A small static society that never looks outside or beyond. *Which?* Diesel prices . . remained more or less static.

Special collocations & comb.: **static characteristic (curve)** *ELECTRONICS* a graph showing the relationship between two parameters of a valve, transistor, etc., measured with all other parameters constant. **static cling** the adhering of a garment to the wearer's body or to another garment, caused by a build-up of static electricity. **static electricity** a stationary electric charge, usu. produced by friction, which causes sparks or crackling, or the attraction of dust, hair, etc. **static equilibrium** a state of balance between bodies at rest. **static friction** the friction which tends to prevent stationary surfaces from being set in motion. **static line**: connecting a parachute to an aircraft and causing the parachute to open automatically when the parachutist moves away from the aircraft. **static pressure** the pressure of a fluid on a body when the latter is at rest relative to it. **static test** a test of a device or object in a stationary position, or under conditions that are constant or change only gradually. **static-test** *verb trans.* perform a static test on (an object). **static thrust**: generated by a stationary aero-engine or rocket engine. **static tube** a pitot-static tube (see PITOT). **static water** unpressurized water available from an emergency source, esp. in the war of 1939–45.
■ **staticky** *adjective* (*US colloq.*) subject to or affected by static; resembling static: M20. **staticness** *noun* M20.

-static /ˈstatɪk/ *suffix.*
[from Greek *statikos* causing to stand, stopping: see prec.]
Forming adjectives and nouns with the senses (*a*) causing or pertaining to equilibrium, as ***hydrostatic***, ***isostatic***; (*b*) inhibiting flow, as ***haemostatic***; (*c*) inhibiting growth, as ***bacteriostatic***, ***fungistatic***.

statical /ˈstatɪk(ə)l/ *adjective.* L16.
[formed as prec.: see -ICAL.]
†**1** Of or pertaining to weighing. L16–L18.
2 Of or pertaining to statics. M17.
†**3** Of analysis etc.: gravimetrical. E18–E19.
4 a = STATIC *adjective* 3a. E19. ▸**b** *ELECTRICITY.* = ELECTROSTATIC. M19.
5 = STATIC *adjective* 4. M19.
6 *MATH.* Concerned with magnitude alone, without regard to direction. *rare.* M19.
7 *MEDICINE.* = STATIC *adjective* 5. Now *rare* or *obsolete.* L19.

statically /ˈstatɪk(ə)li/ *adverb.* M19.
[from STATIC or STATICAL: see -ICALLY.]
With reference to static conditions; by means of static electricity.

statice /ˈstatɪsi/ *noun.* M18.
[Latin from Greek *statikē* fem. of *statikos* causing to stand still (see STATIC *adjective*), in sense 'stopping the flow of blood'.]
Any plant of the former genus *Statice* (family Plumbaginaceae), which contained the sea-lavenders, genus *Limonium*, and formerly also thrift, *Armeria maritima*.

staticisor /ˈstatɪsʌɪzə/ *noun.* Now *rare.* M20.
[from STATIC + -ISE[1] + -OR.]
COMPUTING. A device which converts a succession of bits into an array of simultaneous states, thereby storing them.
■ **staticize** *verb trans.* store by means of a staticisor M20.

statics /ˈstatɪks/ *noun.* M17.
[from STATIC + -S[1]: see -ICS.]
1 Orig., the branch of science that deals with weight and its mechanical effects, and with the conditions of equilibrium resulting from the distribution of weight. Now, the branch of physical science that deals with the action of forces in producing equilibrium or relative rest (opp. ***dynamics*** or ***kinetics***). M17.
2 That part of any field of study (esp. economics) which considers the forces and conditions obtaining at a state of equilibrium or rest. Freq. in ***comparative statics***. M19.
1 graphical statics the investigation of statical problems by means of scale drawings.

statin /ˈstatɪn/ *noun.* L20.
[from *stat-* (as in -STAT) + -IN[1].]
1 *BIOCHEMISTRY.* A phosphoprotein which is present in the nuclei of non-replicating or senescent cells, but not in cells that are undergoing replication. L20.
2 *PHARMACOLOGY.* Any of a class of cyclic organic compounds that inhibit the synthesis of cholesterol in the bloodstream, and are used in the treatment of high blood cholesterol levels. L20.

station /ˈsteɪʃ(ə)n/ *noun.* ME.
[Old & mod. French from Latin *statio(n-)*, from *sta-* base of *stare* STAND *verb*: see -ION.]
▶ **I** Position, place.
1 A person's position in life as determined by outward circumstances or conditions; one's status; *spec.* a calling, an office, one's employment. Now *rare.* ME. ▸**b** Position in the social scale; *spec.* elevated position, high social rank. L17.
2 a A place etc. in which a thing stands or is appointed to stand. Now *rare.* LME. ▸**b** *fig.* A standing-place or position in a class, scale, ranking, etc.; a level. E17. ▸**c** *BOTANY & ZOOLOGY.* The environment to which an animal or a plant is adapted; a habitat. Now *rare* or *obsolete.* E18. ▸**d** Chiefly *BOTANY.* A particular site in which a species, esp. an interesting or uncommon one, is found. E19.
3 *NAUTICAL.* **a** More fully ***naval station***. Orig., a port, a harbour. Now, a place where naval ships are regularly stationed. LME. ▸**b** A place or region to which a government ship or fleet is assigned for duty. Also (*rare*), the period of this assignation. M17.
4 A place etc. where a person stands or is located, esp. habitually or for a purpose. M16. ▸**b** The locality to which an official is appointed to perform his or her duties. M17. ▸**c** The position in boat-racing (at one or other side of the river) occupied by a competing crew at starting. M19.
5 *SURVEYING.* Each of various selected points at which observations, measurements, etc., are taken. L16.
6 *MILITARY.* **a** A place where soldiers are garrisoned, a military post. E17. ▸**b** *Hist.* In India, a place where British officials, esp. the officers of a garrison, resided; the

inhabitants of such a place. M19. ▸**c** An airfield where personnel are employed or garrisoned. E20.

7 a A pioneer settlement. *US*. L17. ▸**b** A large sheep or cattle farm. *Austral. & NZ*. E19.

8 a A designated place or establishment set up with personnel and apparatus for a particular purpose, as industrial work, scientific research, etc. E19. ▸**b** A permanent establishment of missionaries in a country; a mission. M19. ▸**c** A police-station. L19. ▸**d** A subsidiary post office. *US*. L19. ▸**e** A broadcasting establishment; an organization transmitting radio or television signals. E20. ▸**f** A location in an automated system (e.g. for data processing or a manufacturing process) where a particular operation takes place. M20. ▸**g** The headquarters of an intelligence service. *colloq*. L20.

> 📖 **1** DICKENS It is their station to work. **b** L. WHISTLER Everything . . that a Victorian miss of her station could be expected to do. *Times* He gets ideas above his station. **2** SIR W. SCOTT Groups of alder-trees . . had maintained their stations in the . . valley. **3b** *Times* She was fit for service on the Australasian Station. **4** BROWNING Can there be a lovelier station than this spot where now we stand? C. S. FORESTER Hornblower was at his station at the starboard quarter-deck carronades. **6b** J. G. FARRELL Chapatis were appearing . . in stations all over northern India. **7b** *American Poetry Review* Grazing cattle on a station large as Cornwall. **8a** *Standard* Establish a wireless telegraph station at Barfleur. LYNDON B. JOHNSON We can build an Antarctica-type station on the moon. *Daily Telegraph* A pulse of ultrasound is sent . . to a receiving station on the opposite bank. **e** *Which?* Fine tuning control can make separating stations easier on the crowded short wave band. ***radio station***, ***television station***, etc.

▸**II** ECCLESIASTICAL. **9 a** *Hist*. Each of a number of holy places visited in fixed succession by pilgrims; *esp*. any of several Roman churches at which special services were held on prescribed days. Also, a visit to such a holy place. ME. ▸**b** A special service in a holy place; *esp*. (*Hist*.) one attended by the clergy of Rome at any of several churches in the city, each of which had its fixed day in the year for celebration. LME.

10 (Also **S-**.) More fully ***Station of the Cross***. Each of a series of usu. fourteen images or pictures representing successive incidents of Christ's passion, usu. located in a church and visited for devotions; each of these devotions. M16.

11 *Hist*. A bi-weekly fast observed on Wednesdays and Fridays. M17.

> 📖 **9b** W. REEVES A holy well where Roman Catholics of old held stations at midsummer. **10** M. B. SAUNDERS She would follow the Stations of the Cross . . and lean longer over her kneeler.

▸**III** Action or condition of standing.

12 ASTRONOMY & ASTROLOGY. = STATIONARY ***point***. LME.

13 The action or posture of standing on the feet; manner of standing. Now *rare*. E16.

14 The condition or fact of standing still; assumption of or continuance in a stationary condition. Also, a halt, a stand. Now *rare*. E17.

▸**IV** A stopping-place.

15 *Hist*. A stopping-place on a journey; a temporary resting-place when travelling. L16.

16 A regular public-transport stopping-place usu. with associated administrative buildings, esp. on a railway line (more fully ***railway station***), for taking up and setting down passengers or goods; *spec*. such a place at the beginning or end of a journey, a terminus. Also, the administrative buildings associated with such a place. L18.

> 📖 **16** P. THEROUX The station was small— . . just about room for all of us on the platform. B. VINE The Norwich express . . roared past and the whole station shook.

Phrases: **bus station**, **coach station** a centre, usu. in a town, where esp. long-distance buses and coaches depart and arrive. **go for one's stations**, **go for the stations** ECCLESIASTICAL perform successive prescribed acts of devotion at certain holy places, or at the Stations of the Cross. **keep one's station**, **keep station** keep one's place or proper position, esp. relative to another. **make one's stations**, **make the stations** ECCLESIASTICAL = ***go for one's stations*** above. ***naval station***: see sense 3a above. **on station** (esp. of a vessel) near or at a specific station or place of assignment. **perform one's stations**, **perform the stations** ECCLESIASTICAL = ***go for one's stations*** above. ***railway station***: see sense 16 above. ***Station of the Cross***: see sense 10 above. ***stock and station***: see STOCK *noun*[1]. **take station**, **take up station** take up one's proper or assigned position. TRIGONOMETRICAL ***station***.

Comb.: **station agent** (*a*) (chiefly *US*) a person in charge of a stagecoach or railway station; (*b*) a person working for an intelligence service; **station-bill** NAUTICAL a list showing the prescribed stations of a ship's crew for various drills or in an emergency; **station break** *N. Amer*. a break between items on a radio or television station, esp. for announcements or advertising; **station-day** ECCLESIASTICAL HISTORY (*a*) a day on which a station or special service occurred; (*b*) a day on which a bi-weekly fast occurred; **station-distance** SURVEYING the distance between stations; **station hand** *Austral. & NZ* a worker on a sheep or cattle station; **station head** the chief of an intelligence service headquarters; **station hospital**: attached to a military station; **station house** (*a*) (chiefly *US*) a police station; a lock-up adjoining a police station; (*b*) a railway station; *esp*. a small country station; (*c*) *Austral*. & *NZ* the house belonging to a sheep or cattle station; **station-keeping** NAUTICAL the maintenance of one's proper relative position in a moving body of ships etc.; **station-line** (*a*) DRAWING a vertical line representing the vertical plane between the point of station and the vanishing point; (*b*) SURVEYING a line between stations, from which distances, angles, etc., are measured; **stationman** (*a*) a platform attendant, porter, etc., on the railway or underground; (*b*) = ***station hand*** above; **stationmaster** the official in charge of a railway station; **stationmistress** a female stationmaster; **station-point** (*a*) DRAWING = ***point of station*** (c) s.v. POINT *noun*[1]; (*b*) SURVEYING a station; a point on a plan corresponding to a station; **station pointer** SURVEYING an instrument for positioning the observer relative to three objects of known position; *spec*. (NAUTICAL) a ship's navigational instrument for fixing one's position on a chart from the angle in the horizontal plane between two land- and sea-marks; **station pole**, **station rod** SURVEYING a sighting pole set up at a station, usu. graduated; **station-sergeant** the sergeant in charge of a police station; **station-sow** *verb trans*. (HORTICULTURE) plant (seeds) singly or in groups at set intervals along a row or drill; **station-staff** SURVEYING = ***station pole*** above; **station-wagon** †(*a*) *US* a horse-drawn covered carriage; a motor vehicle resembling this; (*b*) an estate car.

▪ **stational** *adjective* of or pertaining to a station or stations E17.

station /ˈsteɪʃ(ə)n/ *verb trans*. L16.
[from the noun or French *stationner*.]

1 Assign a post, position, or station to (a person, troops, ships, etc.); place, post. L16.

2 *refl*. Take up one's station, post oneself. L18.

> 📖 **1** J. REED Troops were stationed at all the doors. U. HOLDEN A regiment was stationed in our town. **2** A. F. LOEWENSTEIN He . . scuttled out, stationing himself outside the door.

stationary /ˈsteɪʃ(ə)n(ə)ri/ *adjective & noun*. LME.
[Latin *stationarius* (orig. 'belonging to a military station') from *statio(n-)*: see STATION *noun*, -ARY[1].]

▸**A** *adjective*. **1** Having a fixed station or place; not moving or movable; *spec*. (*a*) ASTRONOMY (of a planet) appearing motionless at its stationary point (see below); (*b*) (of a machine or machine-part) that remains in one spot when in operation; (*c*) (of a person etc.) residing or established in one place, settled; (*d*) (of an artificial satellite) geostationary. LME.

2 Of or belonging to a station or stations; *spec*. †(*a*) of or pertaining to a military post; (*b*) ECCLESIASTICAL of or relating to (a church holding) a special service in a holy place or (*Hist*.) a bi-weekly fast. L16.

3 *transf*. **a** Remaining unchanged in condition, quality, or quantity; neither advancing nor retreating. E17. ▸**b** MATH. That is not instantaneously changing; associated with a derivative whose value is zero. E20. ▸**c** STATISTICS. Designating a time-series with properties (such as mean, variance, etc.) that do not vary with time. M20.

> 📖 **1** *Daily News* A field hospital is a very different affair from a stationary base hospital. H. MANTEL Remain seated until the aircraft is stationary. **3a** B. F. WESTCOTT Man not as a stationary being but as advancing with a continuous growth.

Special collocations: **stationary air** air which remains in the lungs in ordinary respiration. **stationary bicycle**, **stationary bike** *N. Amer*. an exercise bike. **stationary disease**, **stationary fever** (now *rare* or *obsolete*) a disease which prevails in a district for a number of years and then dies out. **stationary motion** (PHYSICS, now *rare*) motion involving no net change in position over a period of time. **stationary point** ASTRONOMY & ASTROLOGY a point in the apparent orbit of a superior planet when it changes between direct and retrograde motion, appearing motionless. **stationary state** PHYSICS a steady state; *spec*. any of the stable orbits of the electrons in the Bohr model of the atom. **stationary wave** = ***standing wave*** s.v. STANDING *adjective*.

▸**B** *noun*. **I** †**1** An appraiser of books and other valuables. Cf. STATIONER 1. LME–L15.

2 *ellipt*. †**a** ECCLESIASTICAL. An indulgence for attending a station. *rare*. Only in M16. ▸†**b** A planet when stationary. *rare*. Only in E17. ▸**c** A member of a force of permanent or stationary troops. *obsolete* exc. ROMAN HISTORY, a member of a military constabulary. L17.

▸**II 3** = STATIONERY. Freq. *attrib*. Now considered *erron*. M17.

▪ **stationarily** *adverb* L18. **stationariness** *noun* E18. **statioˈnarity** *noun* (*a*) (PHYSICS, now *rare*) the condition of stationary motion; (*b*) the state of being stationary or unvarying; stationariness; constancy: E20.

stationer /ˈsteɪʃ(ə)nə/ *noun*. ME.
[medieval Latin *stationarius* tradesman having a regular station or shop (i.e. not itinerant), chiefly a bookseller: see prec., -ER[2].]

†**1** A bookseller. More widely, a person engaged in any aspect of the book trade. ME–L19.

2 A person who sells writing materials etc. M17.

Comb.: **Stationers' Hall** the hall of the Stationers' Company in London at which a book was formerly registered for purposes of copyright.

stationery /ˈsteɪʃ(ə)nəri/ *noun*. Also (*rare*) **-ary**. L17.
[from prec. + -Y[3].]

The articles sold by a stationer; writing materials etc. Also more fully ***stationery ware(s)***.
CONTINUOUS ***stationery***.

Comb.: **Stationery Office** an office in London through which Government offices are supplied with stationery, and which issues the reports etc. published by the Government.

stationnaire /steɪʃəˈnɛː/ *noun*. *obsolete* exc. *Hist*. L19.
[French.]

A naval guard-ship, stationed at a foreign port for the use of an ambassador.

statism /ˈsteɪtɪz(ə)m/ *noun*. E17.
[from STATE *noun* + -ISM.]

†**1** Subservience to political expediency in religious matters. *rare*. E–M17.

2 Government of a country by the State; *spec*. centralized State administration and control, etatism. L19.

> 📖 **2** *Daily Telegraph* Various forms of Marxist-inspired Statism are establishing themselves.

statist /ˈsteɪtɪst/ *noun & adjective*. L16.
[Italian *statista*, from *stato* state: see -IST.]

▸**A** *noun*. **1** A person skilled in State affairs; a person with political knowledge, power, or influence; a politician, a statesman. *arch*. L16.

2 A person who deals with statistics, a statistician. E19.

3 *Hist*. (**S-**.) A member of a conservative Belgian nationalist party which sought to maintain the provincial States' power in the late 18th cent. E20.

4 A supporter of statism. L20.

▸**B** *adjective*. Of, pertaining to, advocating, or based on statism. M20.

statistic /stəˈtɪstɪk/ *adjective & noun*. L18.
[German *statistisch* adjective, *Statistik* noun, whence also French *statistique* from mod. Latin *statisticus* after German *Statist* statist.]

▸**A** *adjective*. = STATISTICAL 2. L18.

▸**B** *noun*. **1 a** = STATISTICS 1. *rare*. L18. ▸**b** A quantitative fact or statement. L19. ▸**c** STATISTICS. Any of the numerical characteristics of a sample, as opp. to one of the population from which it is drawn. E20.

2 A statistician. E19.

> 📖 **1b** E. HYAMS Although the first dead was . . a tragedy, the ten thousandth was a statistic. *Daily Telegraph* A . . statistic shows that 54 per cent of . . women voted. **c** ***sufficient statistic***: see SUFFICIENT *adjective*.

statistical /stəˈtɪstɪk(ə)l/ *adjective*. E17.
[from prec. + -AL[1].]

†**1** Political. *rare*. Only in E17.

2 a Of or pertaining to statistics; consisting of or founded on collections of numerical facts. L18. ▸**b** Of a writer etc.: dealing with statistics. L18. ▸**c** Of a branch of science, or a physical process or condition: not absolutely precise but dependent on the probable outcome of a large number of small events, and so predictable. L19.

2a statistical significance = SIGNIFICANCE 3. **c statistical mechanics** the description of physical phenomena in terms of a statistical treatment of the behaviour of large numbers of atoms, molecules, etc., esp. as regards the distribution of energy among them.

▪ **statistically** *adverb* E19.

statistician /statɪˈstɪʃ(ə)n/ *noun*. E19.
[from STATISTIC + -IAN: see -ICIAN.]

A person who collects and tabulates statistics.

statisticize /stəˈtɪstɪsʌɪz/ *verb*. Also **-ise**. L19.
[from STATISTIC(S + -IZE.]

1 *verb trans*. Arrange in the form of statistics. L19.

2 *verb intrans*. Collect or use statistics. E20.

statistics /stəˈtɪstɪks/ *noun pl*. L18.
[from STATISTIC + -S[1]: see -ICS.]

1 Treated as *sing*. Orig., the area of political science dealing with the collection, classification, and discussion of esp. numerical facts relating to the condition of a State or community. Now, the field of study that involves the collection and analysis of numerical facts or data of any kind. L18.

2 Treated as *pl*. ▸**a** Numerical facts or data collected and analysed. M19. ▸**b** = ***vital statistics*** (b) s.v. VITAL *adjective*. *colloq*. M20.

3 PHYSICS. Treated as *pl*. The statistical description appropriate to the behaviour and properties of an ensemble of many atoms, molecules, etc., esp. as regards the distribution of energy among them. E20.

> 📖 **2a** S. LEACOCK He clamours for articles filled with statistics about illiteracy. ***vital statistics***: see VITAL *adjective*.

stative /ˈsteɪtɪv/ *adjective & noun*. M17.
[Latin *stativus*, from *stat-*: see STATUE, -IVE.]

▸**A** *adjective*. **1** Stationary, fixed. Now only ROMAN ANTIQUITIES in ***stative camp*** etc. M17.

2 GRAMMAR. Designating a verb or other part of speech which expresses a state or condition. L19.

▸**B** *noun*. GRAMMAR. A stative verb, adjective, etc. L19.

▪ **statively** *adverb* L20. **staˈtivity** *noun* stative quality L19.

stato- /ˈstatəʊ/ *combining form*.
[from Greek *statos* standing: see -O-.]

Chiefly BIOLOGY. Forming nouns and adjectives with the sense 'static, of or pertaining to statics'.

■ **stato-a'coustic** *adjective* (*ANATOMY*) pertaining to the senses or faculties of both balance and hearing; ***stato-acoustic nerve***, the vestibulocochlear nerve: M20. **statoblast** *noun* (*ZOOLOGY*) (*a*) a resistant reproductive body released by bryozoa; (*b*) = GEMMULE 2: M19. **statocone** *noun* = STATOCONIUM E20. **stato'conium** *noun*, pl. **-nia** (*a*) any of numerous granules in the statocyst of some invertebrates, similar to a statolith, but smaller; (*b*) = OTOLITH: M20. **statocyst** *noun* (*ZOOLOGY*) a small organ of balance and orientation consisting of a vesicle or cell containing statoliths E20. **statocyte** *noun* (*a*) *BOTANY* a plant cell containing starch statoliths, enabling geotropic response; (*b*) (now *rare*) *ZOOLOGY* = GEMMULE 2: E20. **stato'genesis** *noun* the (theoretical) origination of animal structures under static conditions L19. **statolith** *noun* (*a*) a calcareous particle in the statocysts of invertebrates, which stimulates sensory receptors in response to gravity, so enabling balance and orientation; (*b*) a starch-grain in the cell-sap of some plant cells (statocytes); (*c*) = OTOLITH: E20. **statoscope** *noun* (*AERONAUTICS*) a form of aneroid barometer adapted for recording small changes in altitude E20. **statospore** *noun* a resting cell, spore, or cyst produced by certain algae etc. L19.

statocracy /steɪˈtɒkrəsi/ *noun*. *rare*. M19.
[from STATE *noun*: see -CRACY.]
Government or rule by the State alone.

statolatry /steɪˈtɒlətri/ *noun*. *rare*. M19.
[from STATE *noun* + -OLATRY.]
Idolization of the State.

statolon /ˈstatəlɒn/ *noun*. M20.
[Prob. blend of -STAT and mod. Latin *st)olon(iferum* (see below), STOLONIFEROUS.]
BIOCHEMISTRY. A product obtained from the mould *Penicillium stoloniferum*, now known to contain a virus which is an antiviral agent, stimulating the release of interferon.

stator /ˈsteɪtə/ *noun*. L19.
[from STAT(IONARY + -OR, after *rotor*.]
1 *ELECTRICITY*. The stationary portion of an electric generator or motor, esp. of an induction motor. Now *rare*. L19.
2 Orig., any non-rotating part of a turbine. Now *spec.* a stator blade or a row of such blades. E20.
Comb.: **stator blade** a small stationary aerofoil fixed to the casing of an axial-flow turbine, rows of which are positioned between the rows of rotor blades.

stats /stats/ *noun*. *colloq.* M20.
[Abbreviation of STATISTICS.]
1 (**S-**.) (Without article.) A company department responsible for collecting or recording numerical facts or data. M20.
2 = STATISTICS 2a. M20.
3 = STATISTICS 1. L20.

statuarist /ˈstatjʊərɪst, -tʃʊə-/ *noun*. Now *rare*. L17.
[from next + -IST.]
= STATUARY *noun* 2.

statuary /ˈstatjʊəri, -tʃʊə-/ *noun* & *adjective*. M16.
[Use as noun of Latin *statuarius, -aria* (sc. *ars* art), from *statua*: see next, -ARY[1].]
▶ **A** *noun*. **1** The art of making statues, sculpture. M16.
2 A person who practises this art; a sculptor. M16.
3 Sculpture composed of statues, statues collectively. Formerly also (in *pl.*), works of sculpture. L17.

> 🕮 **2** D. PIPER Poets' busts . . could be bought from statuaries. **3** J. GALSWORTHY An elaborate group of statuary in Italian marble.

▶ **B** *adjective*. **1** Of or pertaining to the making of statues. E17.
2 Consisting of statues or a statue; sculptured. E17.
3 Of a material: suitable for statues or statuary work. E19.
3 statuary marble, **statuary vein** fine-grained white marble suitable for making statues.

statue /ˈstatjuː, -tʃuː/ *noun* & *verb*. ME.
[Old & mod. French, from Latin *statua*, from *stat-* pa. ppl stem of *stare* STAND *verb*.]
▶ **A** *noun*. **1** A representation of a living being, sculptured, moulded, or cast in marble, metal, plaster, etc.; *spec.* a usu. life-size or larger figure of a deity, mythical being, or eminent person. Also *transf.*, a type of silence, stillness, or emotional coldness. ME.
2 In *pl.* (treated as *sing.*). Any of various children's games which involve standing still in different postures. E20.

> 🕮 **1** G. SWIFT Statues, trapped in immovable poses. R. GODDEN The . . formal garden of . . paths, statues, small flower beds.

▶ **B** *verb trans.* Represent in a statue or in statuary; honour by erecting a statue of. Now only *joc.* E17.
■ **statued** *ppl adjective* (*a*) represented in a statue or in statuary; (*b*) furnished or ornamented with statues or statuary: M18. **statuefy** *verb trans.* (*rare*) turn into a statue; erect a statue to: M19. **statueless** *adjective* (*rare*) M19.

statuesque /statjʊˈɛsk, -tʃʊ-/ *adjective*. L18.
[from STATUE *noun* + -ESQUE, after *picturesque*.]
Having the qualities of a statue or of sculpture.
■ **statuesquely** *adverb* M19. **statuesqueness** *noun* M19.

statuette /statjʊˈɛt, -tʃʊ-/ *noun*. M19.
[French, dim. of STATUE: see -ETTE.]
A small statue; a statue less than life-size.

statuomania /statjʊəˈmeɪnɪə, -tʃʊə-/ *noun*. *rare*. *obsolete* exc. *Hist.* L19.
[from STATUE *noun* + -O- + -MANIA.]
A mania for the erection of statues.

stature /ˈstatʃə/ *noun*. ME.
[Old & mod. French from Latin *statura*, from *stat-* (see STATUE) + *-ura* -URE.]
1 The normal standing height of a human body, a tree, etc. ME.
†**2** Bodily form, build. LME–E17.
†**3** An effigy, a statue. LME–M17.
4 Degree or level of eminence, social standing, or advancement. M19.

> 🕮 **4** J. BARNES He wanted to give prose the strength and stature of poetry.

■ **statural** *adjective* (*rare*) M19.

stature /ˈstatʃə/ *verb trans. rare*. LME.
[from the noun.]
Give stature to. Chiefly as ***statured*** *ppl adjective*. ***middle-statured***, ***short-statured***, etc.

status /ˈsteɪtəs/ *noun*. Pl. **-uses**, (*rare*) same. L17.
[Latin, from *stat-*: see STATUE.]
1 *MEDICINE*. †**a** The crisis of a disease. *rare*. Only in L17.
▸**b** A state, a condition. Only with mod. Latin specifying word (see below). L19.
2 Chiefly *LAW*. A person's standing or position such as determines his or her legal rights or limitations, as citizen, alien, commoner, etc.; condition in respect of marriage or celibacy, minority or majority, etc. L18.
3 Position or standing in society; rank, profession; relative importance; *spec.* (a) superior social etc. position. Also ***social status***. E19.
4 Condition or position of a thing, esp. with regard to importance. M19.

> 🕮 **1b status asthmaticus** /asˈmatɪkəs/ a condition in which asthma attacks follow one another without pause. **status epilepticus** /ɛpɪˈlɛptɪkəs/ a condition in which epileptic fits follow one another without pause. **2** *American Sociological Review* People can spend more time in the statuses of child, parent, and spouse. *Japan Times* They remain . . without legal status. J. FANE Her marital status is uncertain—she refers to a late husband. **3** INA TAYLOR As merely the mother of the heir, Mrs. Newdigate had no real status. T. C. BOYLE My shoes . . no small attraction to . . status-hungry young women. **4** P. FUSSELL When an institution . . wants to elevate its status, it pretends to be a university.

Comb.: **status anxiety**: about one's social status, esp. the fear of losing it; **status bar** *COMPUTING* a horizontal bar, usu. at the bottom of the screen or window, showing information about a document being edited or a program running; **status group**, **status grouping** a group of people of similar social standing; **status-seeker** a person who is concerned with improving or demonstrating his or her social status; **status symbol** a possession or asset sought or acquired as a symbol of social prestige; **status system** a social system in which status derives from one's relative position or achievement in the system.
■ **statusful** *adjective* having or conferring (high) social status or distinction M20. **statusy** *adjective* (*colloq.*) possessing, indicating, or imparting a high status M20.

status quo /steɪtəs ˈkwəʊ/ *noun phr*. M19.
[Latin = the state in which.]
The existing state of affairs.
status quo ante [Latin = before] the state of affairs previously existing.

statutable /ˈstatjʊtəb(ə)l, -tʃʊ-/ *adjective*. M17.
[from STATUTE *noun* + -ABLE.]
1 Prescribed, authorized, or permitted by statute. M17.
2 Conformed to the requirements of a statute or statutes, esp. in quality, size, or amount. L17.
3 Of an offence: recognized by statute; legally punishable. L18.
■ **statutableness** *noun* (*rare*) L17. **statutably** *adverb* M17.

†**statutary** *adjective*. *rare*. M17–L18.
[from STATUTE *noun* + -ARY[1].]
= STATUTORY.

statute /ˈstatjuːt, -tʃuːt/ *noun* & *adjective*. ME.
[Old & mod. French *statut* from late Latin *statutum* decree, decision, law, use as noun of neut. pa. pple of Latin *statuere* set up, establish, decree, from STATUS.]
▶ **A** *noun*. Chiefly *LAW*.
▶ **I 1** A law or decree made by a monarch or legislative authority. *obsolete* exc. as below. ME. ▸**b** A divine law. LME.
▸**c** A law or rule of a guild, corporation, etc.; a by-law of a borough. LME.
2 A decree or enactment passed by a legislative body, and expressed in a formal document; an Act of Parliament; the document containing such an enactment. ME.
†**3** A statute merchant, a statute staple. Also ***statute of the staple***. LME–E18.
4 *Hist. sing.* & in *pl.* An annual fair or gathering held for the hiring of servants. Also ***statute fair***, ***statute hiring***. L16.

> 🕮 **1c** W. PALEY Statutes of some colleges forbid the speaking of any language but Latin. **2** J. DOWDEN Another Act was passed by Parliament strengthening the earlier statute.

▶ **II 5** [By confusion.] = STATUE *noun* 1. Now *rare*. LME.
Phrases: †**by statute**, †**by the statute** according to the measure, price, etc., appointed by statute; by fixed rule, strictly. ***statute of limitations***: see LIMITATION 6. ***statute of the staple***: see sense 3 above. **statutes at large** the statutes as originally enacted, regardless of later modifications.
Comb.: **statute-barred** *adjective* (of a case etc.) barred by the statute of limitations; **statute-book** (*a*) a book or books containing statutes; (*b*) the whole body of the statute law of a nation or State; ***statute fair***, ***statute hiring***: see sense 4 above; **statute labour** a specific amount of labour formerly required by statute to be performed on public roads by the inhabitants of a parish; **statute law** (*a*) a law contained in a statute; (*b*) more widely, the system of law and body of principles laid down in statutes, as distinguished from common law; **statute merchant** *Hist.* a bond acknowledged before the chief magistrate of a trading town, giving to an obligee power of seizure of the lands and property of an obligor until payment of an outstanding debt; ***statute mile***: see MILE 1; **statute-roll** the roll on which statutes are engrossed; a statute-book; **statute staple** *Hist.* a bond acknowledged before the mayor of the staple, conveying powers similar to those given by a statute merchant.
▶ **B** *attrib.* or as *adjective*. Chiefly *LAW*. Fixed or recognized by statute; statutory. Also, customary. L16.

†**statute** *verb trans*. Chiefly *Scot.* Pa. pple **-ute**, **-uted**. LME–L19.
[Latin *statut-* pa. ppl stem of *statuere*: see prec.]
Ordain, decree.

statutory /ˈstatjʊt(ə)ri, -tʃʊ-/ *adjective*. E18.
[from STATUTE *noun* + -ORY[2].]
†**1** Of a clause etc.: enacting. *Scot.* E–M18.
2 Pertaining to or consisting in statutes; enacted, appointed, or created by statute; required or permitted by statute. M18.
3 *transf.* Obligatory by custom; regular. Now *spec.* required for the sake of appearances; having only token significance. E19.

> 🕮 **2** B. CASTLE The constitutional position . . was . . that a Motion of this kind had no statutory force. **3** M. GEE The statutory Christmas phone call to his mother.

Special collocations: **statutory company** a company created by statute, as distinguished from a chartered company or a company incorporated by royal charter. **statutory declaration** *LAW* a prescribed declaration made under statutory authority before a justice of the peace, commissioner of oaths, or notary public which may in certain cases be substituted for a statement on oath. **statutory holiday** a public holiday established by statute. **statutory instrument** a common type of subordinate legislation. **statutory meeting** a general meeting of the members of a company, held in accordance with a statute; *spec.* the first such meeting. **statutory rape** *US* sexual intercourse with a person (esp. a girl) under the age of consent. **statutory tenant** a person who is legally entitled to remain in a property although his or her tenancy has expired.
■ **statutorily** *adverb* L19.

statuvolent /stəˈtjuːvəl(ə)nt, -ˈtʃuː-/ *adjective*. Now *rare* or *obsolete*. L19.
[from Latin *status* STATE *noun* + *volent-* pres. ppl stem of *velle* wish, will.]
Inducing or affected by statuvolism.

statuvolism /stəˈtjuːvəlɪz(ə)m, -ˈtʃuː-/ *noun*. L19.
[from prec. + -ISM.]
Self-hypnosis.

St Augustine grass /s(ə)nt ɔːˈɡʌstɪn ɡrɑːs/ *noun phr*. E20.
[*St Augustine*, a town in Florida, USA.]
A creeping grass, *Stenotaphrum secundatum*, of the southern US, used for lawns, as a sand-binder, etc.

staumer *verb* & *noun* see STAMMER.

staumrel /ˈstamr(ə)l/ *adjective* & *noun*. *Scot.* L18.
[from *staumer* var. of STAMMER *verb* + -EL[1].]
▶ **A** *adjective*. Stupid, halfwitted. L18.
▶ **B** *noun*. A stupid halfwitted person. E19.

staunch *noun*[1], *noun*[2] vars. of STANCH *noun*[1], *noun*[2].

staunch /stɔːn(t)ʃ, stɑːn(t)ʃ/ *adjective* & *adverb*. Also **stanch** /stɑːnʃ/. LME.
[Old French *estanche* fem. of *estanc* (mod. *étanche*) from Proto-Romance: see STANCH *verb*.]
▶ **A** *adjective*. **1** Impervious to water, not leaking; watertight. Also occas., airtight. LME.
2 Of strong or firm construction, in good or firm condition, substantial. LME.
3 Of a sporting dog: able to be relied on to find or follow the scent or to mark the game; dependable. L16.
4 (Of a person) standing firm and true to his or her principles or purpose, determined, trustworthy, loyal; (of a personal quality, action, etc.) showing determination or resolution, unwavering. E17.
†**5** Restrained in behaviour, guarded, reserved. Only in 17.

> 🕮 **1** G. SEMPLE Our Coffer-dam . . which we began to despair of ever getting . . stanch. **2** N. HAWTHORNE The wall of the tower is still stanch and strong. **4** P. L. FERMOR Later generations clung to their faith with staunch tenacity. J. TROLLOPE She was a staunch supporter of family life.

►†**B** *adverb.* Strictly, with reserve. *rare.* M–L17.
■ **staunchly** *adverb* E19. **staunchness** *noun* E17.

staunch *verb* var. of STANCH *verb.*

Staunton /ˈstɔːntən/ *noun.* L19.
[Howard *Staunton* (1810–74), English chess-player and writer.]
Used *attrib. & absol.* to designate chess-pieces of a design now accepted as standard.

stauro- /ˈstɔːrəʊ/ *combining form.* Before a vowel also **staur-**. E20.
[from Greek *stauros* cross: see -O-.]
Of or pertaining to a cross; cross-shaped.
■ **stauroscope** *noun* (CRYSTALLOGRAPHY) a type of polariscope used in determining crystal planes L19.

staurolite /ˈstɔːrəlʌɪt/ *noun.* L18.
[from STAURO- + -LITE.]
MINERALOGY. †**1** = HARMOTOME. L18–M19.
2 Aluminium iron silicate, crystallizing in the orthorhombic system as yellowish-brown to dark brown hexagonal prisms, frequently twinned in the shape of a cross, and found esp. in schists and gneisses. E19.
■ **stauroˈlitic** *adjective* of or containing staurolite L19.

staurotide /ˈstɔːrətʌɪd/ *noun.* E19.
[French, irreg. from Greek *staurōtos* cruciform (from *stauros* cross) + *-ide* (for -ITE[1]).]
MINERALOGY. = STAUROLITE 2.

stave /steɪv/ *noun.* ME.
[Back-form. from *staves* pl. of STAFF *noun*[1].]
►**I 1** See STAFF *noun*[1]. ME.
►**II 2** An alliterating letter in a line of Old English verse. Also ***head-stave***. L19.
►**III 3** [Cf. Norwegian *stav.*] A vertical wooden post forming part of the framework of a building, esp. a stave church (see below); a plank used in the walls of such a construction. E20.
Comb.: **stave church** [translating Norwegian *stavkirke*] a church of a type mainly built in Norway from the eleventh to the thirteenth century, the walls of which were constructed of upright planks or staves.

stave /steɪv/ *verb.* Pa. t. & pple **staved**, **stove** /stəʊv/, pa. pple also **stoven** /ˈstəʊv(ə)n/. M16.
[from prec.]
1 *verb trans.* Fit with a staff or handle. Long *rare* or *obsolete.* M16.
2 *verb trans.* Break up (a cask) into staves; break into (a cask) and let out the contents. L16. ►**b** Destroy (wine etc.) by breaking up the cask. E17.
3 *verb trans.* Break a hole in (a boat); break (a boat) *to pieces*; break (a hole) *in* a boat. Cf. STOVE *verb*[2]. E17. ►**b** *verb intrans.* Of a boat: break up; become holed. M18.
4 *verb trans.* Fit or provide (a cask, pail, etc.) with a staff or staves; renew the staves of. E17.
5 *verb trans.* Drive off or beat (as) with a staff or stave; beat off (orig. a dog in bear- or bull-baiting), keep or push back (a person or crowd). Usu. foll. by *off. arch.* exc. as passing into sense 6. E17.
6 *verb trans.* Foll. by *off*: ►†**a** Keep (a person) away or at a distance; repel. Only in M17. ►†**b** Prevent (a person) *from* doing something; divert (a person) *from* a practice or course of action. M–L17. ►**c** Put off as inopportune; treat (a person) with evasion. M17. ►**d** Ward off or avert (something undesirable or harmful); prevent the occurrence of; defer. M17.
7 *verb trans.* Crush inwards; force out of shape. Usu. foll. by *in.* E18.
8 *verb intrans. & trans.* Compress, thicken, or reshape (a metal bar or pipe), or form a metal joint, by hammering and usu. heating. Also foll. by *up.* L18. ►**b** *verb intrans.* Of metal: undergo staving in this way. Also foll. by *up.* E20.
9 *verb intrans.* Go with a rush or dash; advance or press onwards with vigour. Usu. foll. by adverb. *Scot., dial., & US.* E19.
10 *verb trans.* Sprain (esp. the thumb). *Scot.* E19.
11 *verb trans.* Drive or force with a heavy blow. *US.* M19.

📖 **3 stave in** crush by forcing inwards, make a hole in. **5** *fig.*: J. TRAPP God . . staves him [the devil] off, when he would worry his poor lambs. †**stave and tail** bring a bull- or bear-baiting to an end by beating back the baited animal and pulling back the dogs. **6b** HENRY MORE They may be . . staved off from committing Idolatry. **d** S. HASTINGS To stave off despair, Nancy threw herself into a febrile social life. P. QUILLIN There are . . life support systems that can stave off death almost indefinitely. **9** M. TWAIN Other pedestrians went staving by us with vigorous strides. **11** J. C. NEAL I'll stave my fist right through you.

staved /steɪvd/ *adjective.* ME.
[from STAVE *noun, verb*: see -ED[2], -ED[1].]
1 Fitted or provided with a stave or staves. ME.
2 Broken; crushed *in.* L17.

staver /ˈsteɪvə/ *noun*[1]. *dial.* & *US.* M19.
[from STAVE *verb* + -ER[1].]
An active energetic person; a person who is continually rushing about.

staver /ˈstavə/ *noun*[2]. Now *rare* or *obsolete.* L16.
[from the verb.]
In *pl.* (treated as *sing.*). In horses etc., the disease staggers.
Comb.: **staverwort** the ragwort *Senecio jacobaea*, which is toxic to livestock.

staver /ˈsteɪvə/ *verb intrans.* Chiefly *Scot.* LME.
[Perh. alt. of STAGGER *verb.*]
Stagger. Also, wander about aimlessly or in a restless manner.

staves *noun pl.* see STAFF *noun*[1].

stavesacre /ˈsteɪvzeɪkə/ *noun.* LME.
[Latin *staphisagria* from Greek *staphis agria* lit. 'wild raisin'.]
A kind of delphinium, *Delphinium staphisagria*, native to the Mediterranean region; the seeds of this plant, used as an insecticide and formerly as an emetic.

staving /ˈsteɪvɪŋ/ *noun.* LME.
[from STAVE *verb, noun* + -ING[1].]
1 The action of STAVE *verb.* Usu. foll. by *off, in.* LME.
2 Staves collectively; a casing of staves or planks. L15.

staving /ˈsteɪvɪŋ/ *adjective.* E17.
[Prob. from STAVE *verb* + -ING[2].]
†**1** Inclined to fight with staves. Only in E17.
2 Used with intensive force: very strong, excessive. *US colloq.* M19.

Stavka /ˈstafkə, ˈstɑːvkə/ *noun.* E20.
[Russian, from *stavit'* put, place.]
The general headquarters of the Russian army.

stay /steɪ/ *noun*[1].
[Late Old English *staeg* corresp. to Middle Low German *stach*, Dutch *stag* (whence German *Stag*), Old Norse *stag*, from Germanic verb meaning 'be firm' (see STEEL *noun*[1]).]
1 *NAUTICAL.* A large rope used to brace a mast, leading from the masthead to another mast or spar or down to another part of the ship. Also as 2nd elem. of combs., the first elem. denoting the mast to which the stay is attached. LOE.
2 A guy or rope supporting a flagstaff or other upright pole. M16.
3 A supporting wire or cable on an aircraft etc. L19.
1 ***forestay, jackstay, mainstay***, etc. **at a long stay** (of a cable) taut and leading to the anchor well away from the ship's bows, entering the water at an acute angle. **at a short stay** *NAUTICAL* (of a cable) taut and leading to the anchor at a steep angle. **be in stays** (of a ship) be head to the wind while tacking. ***martingale-stay***: see MARTINGALE *noun* 2. ***miss stays***: see MISS *verb*[1].
Comb.: **stay-wire** (*a*) a wire forming part of a stay for a telegraph pole; (*b*) a supporting wire on an aircraft.

stay /steɪ/ *noun*[2]. ME.
[Partly from Old French *estaye* (mod. *étai*), from *estayer* STAY *verb*[2]; partly from STAY *verb*[2].]
1 a A thing that supports, secures, or steadies something else; a prop, a buttress, a bracket. ME. ►**b** *fig.* A thing or a person that provides support; an object of reliance. L15. ►**c** Support. Formerly also, reliance. Now *rare.* E16.
2 Any of various types of support or member used for bracing; *spec.* †(*a*) the arm or back of a chair; †(*b*) a support for a climbing plant; †(*c*) either of the strings holding up the brim of a shovelhat; (*d*) a transverse piece in a link of a chain; (*e*) an iron rod or brace forming a connecting piece or providing support in various engineering applications. M16.
3 *Hist.* In *pl.* & (*rare*) *sing.* A corset made of two pieces laced together and stiffened by the insertion of strips of whalebone etc., worn to shape and support the figure. Also ***pair of stays***. E17.
†**4** A linen bag for applying a medicinal poultice. L17–E18.

📖 **1a** P. MATTHIESSEN They . . drive . . into a stall behind my tent, uprooting the tent stays. **b** *Expositor* The Temple was . . the centre and stay of Hebrew worship. **c** C. CARTWRIGHT The Popes not erring was but . . policy . . to give stay to the Laity. **3** DICKENS So upright . . she seemed to have put an additional bone in her stays.

Comb.: **stay-bar** (*a*) *ARCHITECTURE* a horizontal iron bar extending along the top of the mullions of a traceried window; (*b*) a bar for keeping a casement window open at a required angle; **stay-hook** a small hook on the front of a dress bodice to which a watch etc. may be attached; **stay-rod** a rod used as a support or a connecting brace in machinery etc.; **stay-stitch** *verb trans.* provide (a bias or curved seam) with a line of stitches to prevent the fabric of a garment from stretching whilst the garment is being made; **stay-stitching** a line of stitches placed along a bias or curved seam to prevent the fabric of a garment from stretching whilst the garment is being made.
■ **stayless** *adjective*[1] without stay or support, unsupported; *spec.* unsupported by stays, uncorseted: L16.

stay /steɪ/ *noun*[3]. E16.
[from STAY *verb*[1].]
1 A stationary condition; a state of neither advance nor retreat. Chiefly in ***at a stay, in a stay, at one stay, in one stay***. *arch.* E16. ►†**b** A permanent state or condition. Chiefly in ***in good stay, in quiet stay***, etc. M16–E17.
2 A cessation of progress or action; a stop, a pause. Also in ***make a stay, make stay***. E16. ►†**b** A cessation of hostility or dissension. Also, a means of reconciliation. *rare.* M–L16.
†**3 a** An appliance for preventing the blade of a plough from cutting too deep a furrow. Only in E16. ►**b** A cause of stoppage; an obstacle, a hindrance. Also (*rare*), a scruple, a hesitation. M16–M17.
4 The action of stopping someone or something or of bringing something to a temporary halt or pause; the fact of being brought to a temporary halt or delayed; an instance of this, a stoppage, a suspension of action. M16. ►**b** *LAW.* Suspension or postponement of a judicial proceeding, sentence, or judgement. M16.
†**5** Control; self-restraint. M16–E17.
†**6** Waiting, postponement. M16–E18.
7 The action or fact of staying, being present, or dwelling in one place; an instance of this, (the duration of) a period of temporary residence. M16. ►**b** A place of temporary or fixed residence. *arch.* M16. ►†**c** Continuance in a state, duration. L16–E18. ►**d** Staying power; power of endurance or resistance. L16.

📖 **1** J. A. FROUDE In this world of change the point of view . . never continues in one stay. **2** J. RUSKIN We can plunge . . without stay . . into the profundity of space. **3b** DRYDEN My Rage, like dam'd-up Streams swell'd by some stay. **4** J. SUTHERLAND A six-month stay during which Tom was to take no decision on his . . future. **b** F. SMYTH Stielow's defence attorneys managed to gain a stay of execution. **7** D. HAMMETT Mrs Jorgenson . . returned . . after a six-year stay in Europe. **d** C. H. SPURGEON Some men are always great at beginnings; but they have no stay in them.

Phrases: †**make stay of** (*a*) withhold for a time; postpone; (*b*) put a stop to (an action); arrest (a person); intercept. †**set in stay**, †**set at stay** reduce to order or quiet; settle. †**set stays** settle matters.
Comb.: **stay-law** *US* a legislative enactment establishing a general moratorium.
■ **stayless** *adjective*[2] (*a*) not to be stayed or stopped, evermoving, unceasing; (*b*) without stay or permanence, everchanging, unsettled: L16.

stay /steɪ/ *verb*[1]. Pa. t. & pple **stayed**, †**staid**. LME.
[Prob. from Anglo-Norman *estai-, estei-* pres. stem of Old French *ester* from Latin *stare* STAND *verb.* See also STAID *adjective.*]
►**I** *verb intrans.* **1 a** Cease going forward; come to a halt. *obsolete* exc. as in sense b below. LME. ►**b** Stop or pause so as *to do* something. L16.
2 a Linger where one is; delay, esp. as opp. to going on. Chiefly with neg. *arch.* L15. ►**b** Stand one's ground, stand firm. Long *rare.* L16.
3 †**a** Cease speaking, break off one's discourse; pause or hesitate before speaking. M16–L17. ►**b** Cease or desist from a specified activity. Usu. foll. by *from. arch.* L16. ►**c** In *imper.* Wait a moment; give me, us, etc., time to consider or decide. L16.
4 Of an action, activity, process, etc.: be arrested, stop or cease at a certain point, not progress. *arch.* M16.
5 Be present or dwell in a place for a (specified) period; reside *with* a person as a guest. M16. ►**b** Dwell or reside on a permanent or regular basis, live. *Scot., US, & S. Afr.* M18.
†**6** Remain inactive or quiet; wait, esp. without taking action or making progress; defer action *until.* M16–M18.
†**7** Be in doubt, raise difficulties (*at*); delay *in* (doing something); hesitate, scruple *to do.* M16–M17.
8 Continue to be in a place or in others' company; not depart; remain *and* do something. Also with adverbs. L16. ►**b** Wait long enough in order *to do* or *to* share a meal etc. L16.
9 Of a person or thing: continue to be in the same place or (a specified) condition; (foll. by *with*) remain in the mind or memory. L16. ►**b** Of food etc.: be retained by the stomach after swallowing. Also (*US colloq.*, foll. by *with*), give lasting satisfaction to hunger. M17.
†**10** Of a business or other matter: be deferred or postponed; be kept waiting. M17–E18.
11 a Show powers of endurance, esp. in a race or contest; hold out. M19. ►**b** Foll. by *with*: keep up with (a competitor in a race etc.); *fig.* concentrate on, apply oneself to, continue with. Orig. *US.* L19.
12 *POKER.* Raise one's ante sufficiently to remain in a round. M19.

📖 **1b** A. RADCLIFFE Emily scarcely stayed to thank him. **2a** AV *Josh.* 10:19 Stay ye not, *but* pursue after your enemies. **3b** SPENSER He hearkned, and did stay from further harmes. **c** SHAKES. *Com. Err.* Stay, stand apart, I know not which is which. **5** V. BRITTAIN I . . was . . going there for a week to stay with friends. **b** W. FAULKNER Mr Wimbush stays a solid eight miles from town. **6** BACON The Market; where . . if you can stay a little, the Price will fall. **8** E. J. HOWARD She had been fetching drinking water . . and she had stayed too long. J. F. HENDRY Although they had both been invited to Capri, Rilke had prevailed on her to stay behind. **b** D. EDEN They had decided to stay to lunch. **9** A. LEE The school grounds stayed green into November. D. LEAVITT Stay calm now. **11b** *Psychology Today* People need to stay with a healthy diet.

►**II** *verb trans.* **13** Stop, delay, prevent, (an action or process, something which is begun or intended); *spec.* in

LAW, postpone (a judgement etc.). **E16.** ▸**b** Arrest the course or growth of (something harmful or destructive, esp. a disease). *arch.* **M16.**

14 Detain, hold back; check the progress of, bring to a halt; keep in a fixed place or position. Also foll. by *from*. Now *literary*. **M16.** ▸†**b** *refl.* & in *pass.* Take up a settled residence, live *in* a place. **M–L16.** ▸**c** Imprison; hold in captivity. *poet. rare.* **L16.**

15 Prevent, hinder, or stop (a person or thing) *from* doing something; restrain, check, hold back. Freq. in ***stay one's hand***, ***stay a person's hand*** below. Now *arch.* or *literary*. **M16.** ▸†**b** Cause (a bell) to cease ringing. *rare.* **L16–M17.**

16 Leave off or discontinue (an activity etc.). Also, defer or withhold (one's good opinion or thanks). Now *rare* exc. *poet.* **M16.**

17 Appease or allay (disorder etc.). Formerly also, bring under control (rebellious elements). *arch. rare.* **M16.**

18 †**a** Cause to rest or remain *on* something; rest or fix (the eyes) *on* an object. **L16–L17.** ▸**b** Cause to remain motionless, keep immovable; fix. **E17.**

19 Remain for, remain and share in or assist at, (a meal, ceremony, etc.); remain throughout or during (a period of time). **L16.**

20 Wait for, await, (a person, his or her arrival, an event, etc.); wait on (a person's leisure). *arch.* **L16.** ▸†**b** Stay to make or offer. *rare* (Shakes.). Only in **L16.**

21 Assuage (hunger); satisfy (the stomach or appetite), esp. temporarily. **E17.**

22 Foll. by *out*: remain until the end of; remain and witness the end of. Also (*rare*), outstay. **M17.**

23 Show powers of endurance in (a race, contest, etc.); hold out for (a specified distance etc.). **M19.**

> 📖 **13** *Belfast Telegraph* Execution date was stayed by former . . Governor Calvin Rampton. **14** TENNYSON Thou shalt not wander . . I'll stay thee with . . kisses. **15** M. SINCLAIR No rain nor snow . . had stayed him in his . . visiting. **16** SHAKES. *Wint. T.* Stay your thanks a while, And pay them when you part. **18b** V. WOOLF 'Heavens, the front-door bell!' exclaimed Clarissa, staying her needle. **19** I. MURDOCH She'd come as far as letting me stay the night. **22** A. BELL It had been Sydney's intention . . to stay out his two years with Michael.

Phrases, & with adverbs & prepositions in specialized senses: **be here to stay**, **have come to stay** *colloq.* have become permanent or well established, have attained recognition or a secure position. ***stay a person's hand***: see ***stay one's hand*** below. ***stay a person's leisure***: see LEISURE *noun*. **stay for** (*a*) remain or wait in a place for; remain and share or join in (an activity, meal, etc.); await the arrival of; †(*b*) wait or linger for before doing or beginning to do something. **stay in** remain at home; remain in school after hours as a punishment. **staying power** endurance, stamina, esp. in a race or contest. **stay on** remain in a place or position. †**stay on** — (*a*) wait for; await the outcome of (an event etc.); be subject to (a person's will or pleasure); (*b*) dwell on (a subject); (of the eye) rest on, be arrested by, (something). **stay one's hand**, **stay a person's hand** (now *arch.* or *literary*) (cause to) refrain from activity or aggression. **stay over** (orig. *US*) stop overnight. **stay put** *colloq.* (orig. *US*) remain where or as placed; remain fixed or steady. ***stay shtoom***: see SHTOOM *adjective*. **stay the course**, **stay the distance** (*a*) hold out to the end of a race, boxing-match, etc.; (*b*) *fig.* pursue a course of action or endure a difficult situation to the end. **stay the night** lodge or remain with a person until the following day. ***stay the pace***: see PACE *noun*[1]. **stay up** not go to bed, esp. until late at night. **stay upon** — = ***stay on*** — above. ***stay upon a person's leisure***: see LEISURE *noun*.

Comb.: **stay-awake** *noun & adjective* (designating) a pill or other product designed to prevent or delay sleep; **stay-away** (*a*) a person who stays away, esp. from work, as a strike or protest action; (*b*) an act or instance of staying away, esp. from work as a protest action etc.; **stay-clean** *adjective* (of an oven) lined with a special material which greatly reduces the need for cleaning; **stay-down** *adjective* of, pertaining to, or designating a strike staged by miners remaining down a mine; **stay-in** *adjective & noun* (*a*) *adjective* of, pertaining to, or designating a strike in which the strikers remain in their place of work; (*b*) *noun* (a person who participates in) a strike of this kind; **stay-ship** *arch.* = REMORA 1; **stay-stomach** *arch.* a snack to assuage the appetite; **stay-up** *adjective & noun* (*a*) *adjective* of stockings: having elastic tops and thereby remaining in place without garters or suspenders; (*b*) *noun* a stocking which remains in place by this means (usu. in *pl.*).

stay /steɪ/ *verb*[2]. **LME.**

[Old French *estayer* (mod. *étayer*), from Germanic. Cf. STAY *noun*[1], *noun*[2].]

1 *verb trans.* Support, sustain, hold up. Foll. by *on*, †*unto*, (arch.) *up*. Now *rare* exc. as passing into sense 4. **LME.** ▸**b** *transf.* & *fig.* Give support or sustenance to (a person), comfort. *arch.* **E16.**

2 *verb trans. fig.* Cause to rest *on*, *upon*, or *in* (a firm support or basis), base *upon*, fix firmly *in*. *arch.* **M16.** ▸†**b** *refl.* Rely or build *upon*, take one's stand *upon*, rest or act *upon*. **M16–E18.**

†**3** *verb intrans.* Foll. by *on*, *upon*: ▸**a** Rely on, trust or have confidence in; look to for help or support. **M16–E18.** ▸**b** Lean on, support oneself by; (of a thing) be supported by. **L16–L17.**

4 *verb trans.* Support, strengthen, or secure with stays or braces. Also foll. by *up*. **M16.**

> 📖 **1** JOHN TAYLOR A Water-man . . hath his Soueraigne by the hand, to stay him in and out the Barge. **b** D. BRAY Some old dame, staying her with . . words of comfort. **2** TENNYSON A grief . . deep as life . . But stay'd in peace with God and man. **4** H. ALLEN Young ladies, dressed in . . prim costumes stayed with whalebone, sat bolt upright.

stay /steɪ/ *verb*[3]. **E17.**

[from STAY *noun*[1].]

NAUTICAL. **1** *verb trans.* Secure or steady (a mast etc.) by means of stays or ropes; incline (a mast) at a specified angle by means of stays. **E17.**

2 *verb trans.* Turn (a ship) to the windward in order to tack; put on the other tack. **E17.**

3 *verb intrans.* Of a ship: turn to the wind in order to tack. **E17.**

stay-at-home /ˈsteɪəthəʊm/ *adjective & noun*. **E19.**

[from STAY *verb*[1] + AT + HOME *noun*.]

▸ **A** *adjective*. Remaining habitually at home, not given to going out or travelling abroad; untravelled; *spec.* avoiding going abroad on military service. **E19.**

▸ **B** *noun*. **1** A stay-at-home person. **M19.**

2 An instance of staying at home; *spec.* a strike. **M20.**

Staybrite /ˈsteɪbrʌɪt/ *noun*. **E20.**

[from STAY *verb*[1] + respelling of BRIGHT *adjective*.]

(Proprietary name for) a type of stainless steel.

stayer /ˈsteɪə/ *noun*[1]. **L16.**

[from STAY *verb*[1] + -ER[1].]

1 A person who stays or remains, esp. in a specified location. **L16.** ▸**b** A person, animal, or thing having superior powers of endurance. **M19.**

2 A person who or thing which stops or restrains something. **L16.**

> 📖 **1** SWIFT The Stayer at home may be comforted by a Visit. **b** *Greyhound Star* We find . . 650 metres is . . the limit for our graded stayers.

stayer /ˈsteɪə/ *noun*[2]. Now *rare*. **L16.**

[from STAY *verb*[2] + -ER[1].]

A person who stays or supports something.

staylace /ˈsteɪleɪs/ *noun & verb*. Now chiefly *Hist.* **E18.**

[from STAY *noun*[2] + LACE *noun*.]

▸ **A** *noun*. A lace or cord used to fasten or tighten a pair of stays or a bodice. **E18.**

▸ **B** *verb trans.* Lace up (a garment etc.) with staylaces. **E19.**

Stayman /ˈsteɪmən/ *noun*. **M20.**

[Samuel M. *Stayman* (1909–93), an American authority on contract bridge.]

BRIDGE. Used *attrib.* & *absol.* to designate a convention used in contract bridge whereby the response to a one no-trump asking opener is an artificial bid of two clubs, inviting the no-trump bidder to show a four-card major.

stay-put /ˈsteɪpʊt/ *noun & adjective*. *colloq.* **M20.**

[from *stay put* s.v. STAY *verb*[1].]

▸ **A** *noun*. **1** An instance of remaining in one place or refraining from movement or travel. **M20.**

2 A person who refuses to move; a person who stands his or her ground, a person who stays at home. Chiefly *Austral.* **M20.**

▸ **B** *adjective*. Remaining where or as placed, remaining fixed; refusing to move, refraining from travel. **M20.**

■ **stay-putter** *noun* a person who refuses to move or who refrains from moving **E20.**

staysail /ˈsteɪseɪl, ˈsteɪs(ə)l/ *noun*. **M17.**

[from STAY *noun*[1] + SAIL *noun*[1].]

NAUTICAL. A triangular fore-and-aft sail extended on a stay.

stay-tape /ˈsteɪteɪp/ *noun*. Now *rare*. **L17.**

[from STAY *noun*[2] + TAPE *noun*.]

A lace or cord used by tailors etc. as a binding to a fabric.

St Bees Sandstone /s(ə)nt biːz ˈsandstəʊn/ *noun phr.* **M19.**

[from *St Bees* Head, a coastal headland in Cumbria, England.]

GEOLOGY. A pebbly red sandstone of the Lower Triassic, occurring in thick beds in NW England.

St Clements /s(ə)nt ˈklɛm(ə)nts/ *noun*. **L20.**

[The name of a London church, with ref. to the first line of the children's song *Oranges and lemons, say the bells of St Clements*.]

A non-alcoholic cocktail of orange juice mixed with lemonade or bitter lemon.

St Cloud /sɛ̃ kluː/ *adjective*. **E18.**

[See below.]

Designating porcelain or faience made in the late 17th and the 18th cents. at St Cloud on the western outskirts of Paris.

STD *abbreviation*.

1 Latin *Sanctae Theologiae Doctor* Doctor of Sacred Theology.

2 Sexually transmitted disease.

3 Subscriber trunk dialling.

stead /stɛd/ *noun*.

[Old English *stede* corresp. to Old Frisian *stede*, Old Saxon *stad*, *stedi* (Middle Low German *stad*, *stede* place, town), Middle Dutch *stad*, *stede*, Old High German *stat* (German *Statt* place, *Stätte* place, site, *Stadt* town), Old Norse *staðr*, Gothic *staþs* place, from Germanic from Indo-European base also of STAND *verb*.]

▸†**I** **1** Standing still, as opp. to movement; stoppage, delay. *rare.* **OE–LME.**

▸ **II** †**2** A particular part of the earth's surface, or of space generally, considered as defined by its situation; a particular locality or place. Freq. in ***in every stead*** below. **OE–L16.**

3 †**a** A definite spot on a surface, esp. on the surface of the body. **OE–L15.** ▸**b** A mark, an imprint of one object on another, an impression. Usu. in *pl.* *Scot.* **E16.**

4 **a** The place assigned to, belonging to, or normally occupied by a thing; appointed or natural place. Long *arch.* **OE.** ▸†**b** A space or place assigned to or occupied by a person; a seat. **OE–M18.** ▸†**c** The place where a body of soldiers is stationed, a military position. **ME–E17.**

†**5** An inhabited place; a city, a town, a village; *rare* a country, a land. **ME–L16.** ▸**b** ***the Steads*** [= Middle Low German *de Steden*], towns of the Hanseatic League. Also, the corporation of Hanse merchants in London. **E–M16.**

6 A landed property, an estate; a farm. Formerly also, a portion of an estate. Now chiefly *Scot.* & *dial.* **ME.**

7 A site, a foundation, *esp.* a site for a building; the land on which a building stands; an enclosure adjoining a building, a yard. (Cf. ***farmstead*** s.v. FARM *noun*, HOMESTEAD.) Now chiefly *Scot.* **ME.**

†**8** The framework of a bed, a bedstead. Now *rare*. **LME.**

> 📖 **2** SPENSER Great God it planted in that blessed sted. **4a** W. MORRIS The mast in its stead we 'stablished. **6** RIDER HAGGARD A Hottentot . . who lived on the stead.

▸ **III** †**9** An official position assigned to or held by a person. **OE–E17.**

†**10** **a** The seat or home of hope, passions, etc. Only in **ME.** ▸**b** A space of time. *rare* (Spenser). Only in **L16.**

†**11** A place or passage in the Bible or other writing. **ME–M16.**

12 The place or function of a person or thing as held by a substitute or a successor. Only in phrs. below. **ME.**

▸ **IV** **13** Advantage, avail, profit; service, support. Chiefly in ***do a person stead***, ***stand in stead*** below. *arch.* exc. *Scot.* **ME.**

> 📖 **13** MILTON Here thy sword can do thee little stead.

Phrases: **do a person stead** *arch.* be of advantage to a person. **fill the stead of** (now *rare*) serve as a substitute for. **in a person's stead** †(*a*) as a person's successor; †(*b*) as a person's deputy or representative; (*c*) as a substitute in the place occupied by a person; (*d*) instead of a person. **in a thing's stead** (*a*) as a substitute in the place occupied by a thing; (*b*) instead of a thing. ***in bad stead***: see ***in good stead*** below. †**in every stead** everywhere. †**in good stead**, †**in bad stead**, etc., *rare* in good, bad, etc., condition or circumstances (see also ***stand a person in good stead*** below). †**in the stead** instead of it, as a substitute. **in the stead of** (*a*) in succession to (a person who has died or has otherwise vacated an official position); †(*b*) in lieu of, instead of; (*c*) in exchange for; †(*d*) ***be in stead for*** (rare), make up for the lack of. †**serve a person in some stead**, †**serve a person in no stead** be of some, no, advantage or profit to a person. **serve the stead of** (now *rare*) = ***fill the stead of*** above. **stand a person in good stead**, **stand a person in stead** be advantageous, useful, or profitable to a person. †**stand in stead** be advantageous or profitable (also with indirect obj.). **stead of** (now *dial.* & *colloq.*) instead of. **supply the stead of** (now *rare*) = ***fill the stead of*** above.

stead /stɛd/ *verb*. Pa. t. & pple **stead**, **steaded**. **ME.**

[from prec.]

▸ **I** **1** *verb trans.* **a** Avail, profit, be of use to, (a person). Formerly also, help (a person) *to do* something. Usu. *impers.* *arch.* **ME.** ▸†**b** Suffice for, serve the needs of. *Scot.* **L15–M16.** ▸**c** Of a thing: be useful or advantageous to. *arch. rare.* **L16.** ▸**d** Of a person: succour, help, render service to. Now *rare.* **L16.** ▸†**e** Supply (a person) *with* something helpful. Also foll. by *of*. **L16–M17.**

†**2** *verb trans.* Serve (a person) *for*. *rare.* **M16–M17.**

> 📖 **1a** CARLYLE It steads not the doomed man that he have interviews with the King. **c** BROWNING The qualities required For such an office . . Would little stead me, otherwise employed. **d** G. GISSING Her power to stead him in his misery. **2** R. BROME You have . . a Brother May stead you for a . . Friend.

▸ **II** **3** *verb trans.* Establish, fix, place; in *pass.* be situated. *obsolete* exc. *Scot.* **ME.**

†**4** *verb trans.* In *pass.* **a** Be placed *in* a certain plight or condition, esp. a difficult one; be burdened *with* sickness or beset *with* enemies etc. **ME–M16.** ▸**b** With adverbs, esp. *hard*, *straitly*, *stiffly*, etc.: be hard put to it, be beset with difficulties or perils. **ME–E19.**

†**5** *verb intrans.* Stay, linger; stop, come to a stand; stand firm. **ME–E16.**

> 📖 **3** KEATS To honour thee . . To stead thee as a verse in English tongue. **4b** SIR W. SCOTT We are cruelly sted between God's laws and man's.

Phrases: †**stead up** (*rare*, Shakes.) fulfil in the place of another.

steadfast /ˈstɛdfɑːst, -fəst/ *adjective, adverb, & noun.* OE.
[from STEAD *noun* + FAST *adjective*.]
▶ **A** *adjective.* **1 a** Of a person, esp. a soldier in battle: standing firm, not giving ground. Now *rare* or *obsolete* exc. as passing into sense 2. OE. ▸**b** Of a thing: firmly or securely fixed, not to be moved or displaced. *obsolete* exc. *literary.* OE. ▸†**c** Solid; firm in substance. *rare.* L15–M16.
2 Of a person, a person's belief, loyalty, etc.: unshaken, constant, unwavering. ME. ▸†**b** Of God: unchanging. LME–E17. ▸†**c** Confirmed, incorrigible. *rare* (Milton). Only in M17.
3 Of a state of affairs, a law, an institution, etc.: firmly settled, established, unchangeable. ME.
4 Of sight, a person's gaze, etc.: fixed in intensity; steadily directed. ME.

> **1b** MILTON These Elements . . had from her Axle torn The stedfast Earth. **2** W. M. CLARKE He remained steadfast . . as an admirer of his brother's success. **3** E. R. CONDER The stedfast regularity of phenomena.

▶ **B** *adverb.* Steadfastly. *arch. rare.* ME.
▶†**C** *noun.* = PALMA CHRISTI. LME–M17.
■ **steadfastly** *adverb* ME. **steadfastness** *noun* OE.

Steadicam /ˈstɛdikam/ *noun.* L20.
[Alt. from STEADY *adjective* or *verb* + CAM(ERA.]
(Proprietary name for) a lightweight mounting for a film camera which keeps it steady for filming when hand-held or moving.

steading /ˈstɛdɪŋ/ *noun. Scot. & north.* L15.
[from STEAD *noun* + -ING[1].]
1 A farmhouse and outbuildings; the outbuildings in contrast to the farmhouse. L15.
2 A site for a building. L17.

steadite /ˈstɛdʌɪt/ *noun.* E20.
[from J. E. *Stead* (1851–1923), English metallurgist + -ITE[1].]
1 METALLURGY. A eutectic of austenite and iron phosphide (and sometimes cementite) occurring in phosphorus-rich irons and steels and containing dissolved phosphorus. E20.
2 MINERALOGY. A siliceous variety of apatite, usu. containing iron, occurring native and in basic slag as yellowish needles. E20.

steady /ˈstɛdi/ *noun.* L16.
[In sense 1 absol. use of STEADY *adjective*; in sense 2 from STEADY *verb*.]
1 A thing which steadies something; *spec.* a device for holding steady an object during a manufacturing process. L16.
2 a A thing which is steady; *spec.* (*Canad. dial.*), a part of a river which has little or no perceptible current. L18. ▸**b** A regular boyfriend or girlfriend. *colloq.* (orig. *US*). L19.

steady /ˈstɛdi/ *adjective, adverb, & interjection.* ME.
[from STEAD *noun* + -Y[1], after Middle Low German, Middle Dutch *stēdig, stādig* stable, constant.]
▶ **A** *adjective.* **1** Of a person, a person's actions, etc.: persistent or unwavering in resolution, loyalty, or in a course of action; constant in commitment *to* a cause etc. ME. ▸**b** Of a boyfriend or girlfriend, a relationship, or a job etc.: regular, settled, established. *colloq.* L19.
2 NAUTICAL. Of a ship: moving without deviation from its course; upright, esp. in a heavy sea. ME.
3 †**a** Fixed permanently, immovable; not liable to give way or become displaced. M16–L17. ▸**b** Of a state of affairs: stable; settled, established. Now *rare* exc. as passing into sense 1b. L16.
4 Regular in operation, frequency, or intensity; that is maintained at an even rate of action, output, etc.; uniform. M16. ▸**b** Of the wind: blowing equably in force and direction. E17. ▸**c** (Of the weather or temperature) settled in a particular pattern; (of climate) having little variation of temperature. Also, (of a barometer etc.) giving a constant reading. L17. ▸**d** CRICKET. Of a batsman or a batsman's play: consistent, safe, cautious. E19. ▸**e** COMMERCE. Of prices, the stock market, shares, etc.: free from sudden fluctuation. M19. ▸**f** PHYSICS. Of flow, motion, a state, etc.: in equilibrium, such that the effective condition at any point does not change over time. See also ***steady state*** below. L19.
5 Firmly fixed, standing, or supported; stable, securely balanced; not tottering, rocking, or shaking. L16. ▸†**b** Of a thing: securely or firmly held. L16–E18. ▸**c** Of a movement or action: free from tremulousness or faltering. L18.
6 Of a person: not easily perturbed or discomposed; balanced. Of the head: unaffected by giddiness. Of a person's gaze or the eye: not diverted from its object; unwavering. E17. ▸**b** Of a soldier, a soldier's actions, etc.: disciplined; not liable to panic or loss of self-control. L17. ▸**c** Of a hound: not easily diverted from the scent. Of a horse: not nervous, skittish, or excitable; proceeding at a moderate and even pace. M18.
7 Not given to frivolity; staid. M18.
8 Regular and self-restrained in habits; industrious and sober in conduct. M19.

> **1** SMOLLETT A trusty counsellor and steady friend. C. S. FORESTER In two years of steady application Hornblower had mastered Galician. **b** A. SILLITOE I wanted a steady job after leaving the army. **3a** P. SIDNEY Built upon the steddy Foundation of Law. **4** I. MURDOCH Traffic . . noise . . muted to a steady murmur. A. THWAITE The downpour venting to a steady drizzle. B. BETTELHEIM A gradual but steady decline of the Hapsburgs . . set in. **5** M. DE LA ROCHE His hand was steady enough until the glass was almost filled. **8** J. M. COETZEE Her father was not steady; there was a problem with drinking.

▶ **B** *adverb.* In a steady manner, steadily. E17.

> V. WOOLF The flame . . burns steady even in the wildest night.

▶ **C** *interjection.* Orig. NAUTICAL. Hold your course! Maintain your position! Keep calm! Take care! E17.

> G. GREENE 'Steady does it,' he said. He advanced the plank inch by inch.

Phrases: **go steady** *colloq.* (orig. *US*) keep regular company (*with* someone) as a boyfriend or girlfriend. **steady from hare** (of a foxhound) trained to disregard a hare. **steady on** take care! be more restrained *with* something. **steady the Buffs** (BUFF *noun*[2] 5) keep calm! be careful!
Comb.: **steady-going** *adjective* staid, sober; **steady pin**: used to secure the relative positions of two adjoining surfaces or prevent them from sliding on each other; **steady state** an unvarying condition, a state of equilibrium; **steady-state** *adjective* designating a cosmological theory or model which proposes that the universe is isotropic and essentially unchanging on a large scale, with matter continuously created to counteract expansion; **steady-stater** an advocate of a steady-state theory of the universe.
■ **steadily** *adverb* L15. **steadiness** *noun* M16. **steadyish** *adjective* M19.

steady /ˈstɛdi/ *verb.* M16.
[from STEADY *adjective*.]
1 a *verb trans.* Keep from rocking, shaking, or tottering. M16. ▸**b** *verb trans.* Support on the feet, keep upright or from falling. M19. ▸**c** *verb intrans.* Become steady; cease rocking, shaking, or tottering. M19.
2 *verb trans.* **a** Settle (one's mind); compose (one's thoughts etc.). M16. ▸**b** Bring (soldiers) to a steady and disciplined condition. E20. ▸**c** Make (a foxhound) steady *from hare* (see STEADY *adjective, adverb, & interjection*). E20.
3 *verb trans.* NAUTICAL. Keep (a ship) to a direct course; keep (a ship) upright, esp. in a heavy sea. E17.
4 *verb trans. & intrans.* (Cause to) go at a more regular or less impetuous pace; (cause to) adopt a more uniform or even rate of progress. E19.
5 *verb trans.* Keep (a person) from irregularity or frivolity of conduct; make more self-restrained or sober in habit. Also foll. by *down, up.* M19.
6 *verb intrans.* COMMERCE. Of prices, the stock market, shares, etc.: become more free from fluctuation. E20.

> **1a** J. C. OATES Persia takes a large . . swallow . . steadying the glass with both hands. **b** *refl.*: J. FRAME Mattina gripped the . . table as if to steady herself. **2a** J. AGATE Taking something to steady her nerves. **4** M. M. KAYE The wind . . now . . steadied and blew strongly. **5** A. MOOREHEAD His first wife appears to have been a steadying influence on him.

■ **steadier** *noun* a person who or thing which steadies something M19. **steadiment** *noun* (*rare*) a means of steadying something; the condition of being steadied: E19.

steak /steɪk/ *noun.* ME.
[Old Norse *steik* rel. to *steikja* roast on a spit, *stikna* be roasted.]
1 A thick slice of meat (esp. beef) cut for grilling, frying, etc., *esp.* a piece cut from the hindquarters of the animal; beef cut for stewing or braising. Freq. with specifying word indicating the part from which the meat is cut or the style of cooking. ME. ▸**b** A thick slice of fish, esp. cod, salmon, or halibut. L19.
2 *transf. & fig.* Something resembling a steak in shape or texture. E17.

> **1** *steak hammer*, *steak pie*, *steak restaurant*, etc. *braising steak*, *minute steak*, *pepper steak*, *porterhouse steak*, *rump steak*, *sirloin steak*, *stewing steak*, *Swiss steak*, *T-bone steak*, etc.

Comb. & phrases: **steak and kidney** a mixture of beefsteak and kidney used esp. as a pie or pudding filling; **steak au poivre** /əʊ ˈpwɑːvrə, *foreign* o pwavr/ [French] = ***pepper steak*** s.v. PEPPER *noun*; **steakburger** a beefburger made of minced steak; **steak Diane** /dʌɪˈan, *foreign* dian/ a dish consisting of thin slices of beefsteak fried with seasonings, esp. Worcestershire sauce; **steak-house** a restaurant specializing in serving beefsteak; **steak knife** (*a*) a butcher's knife; (*b*) a serrated table knife for eating steak; **steak tartare** a dish consisting of raw minced beefsteak mixed with raw egg, onion, and seasonings and shaped into small cakes or patties.

steak raid /ˈsteɪk reɪd/ *noun phr.* L18.
[Repr. Gaelic *staoig rathaid*, from *staoig* collop (from (the same root as) STEAK) + *rathaid* genit. of *rathad* road.]
SCOTTISH HISTORY. A portion of the cattle stolen in a foray which was paid by the robbers to the proprietor of the land through which the booty was driven.

steal /stiːl/ *noun*[1]. *obsolete* exc. *dial.*
[Old English *stela*, from Germanic base also of STALE *noun*[1].]
1 The stalk or stem of a plant, leaf, flower or fruit. Cf. STALE *noun*[1] 3. OE.
†**2** A supporting post or pillar. OE–M16.
†**3** Orig., each of the upright sides of a ladder. Later, a rung or step of a ladder. Cf. STALE *noun*[1] 1. ME–E17.
4 The handle of a tool or utensil (as a hammer, pot, spoon, etc.); *esp.* a long straight handle, as of a rake or broom. Formerly also, the shaft of an arrow or spear. Cf. STALE *noun*[1] 2. ME. ▸**b** The stem of a tobacco-pipe. L17.

steal /stiːl/ *noun*[2]. ME.
[from the verb.]
1 a The action or an act of stealing; a theft; a thing stolen, purloined, or plagiarized. Chiefly *US colloq.* ME. ▸**b** A piece of dishonesty or fraud on a large scale; a corrupt or fraudulent transaction in politics. *N. Amer.* L19. ▸**c** A bargain. *colloq.* M20.
2 a GOLF. A long putt unexpectedly holed. M19. ▸**b** BASEBALL. A stolen advance from one base to another. M19. ▸**c** BASKETBALL etc. An act of obtaining possession of the ball from an opponent. L20.

steal /stiːl/ *verb.* Pa. t. **stole** /stəʊl/; pa. pple **stolen** /ˈstəʊlən/, (now *dial. & non-standard*) **stole**. See also STOLE *ppl adjective*, STOLEN *ppl adjective*.
[Old English *stelan* = Old Frisian *stela*, Old Saxon, Old High German *stelan* (Dutch *stelen*, German *stehlen*), Old Norse *stela*, Gothic *stilan*, from Germanic base also of STALK *verb*[1] & *noun*[2].]
▶ **I** Take dishonestly or secretly.
1 *verb trans.* **a** Take away dishonestly or illegally (portable property, livestock, etc., belonging to another), esp. secretly and with no intention of returning it. (Foll. by *from* the owner or a place.) Also foll. by *away.* OE. ▸**b** Take or appropriate dishonestly (anything belonging to another, material or immaterial). Also foll. by *away.* ME. ▸**c** *spec.* Plagiarize; pass off (another's work or words) as one's own; appropriate improperly. M16.
2 *verb intrans.* **a** Commit or practise theft. OE. ▸**b** Commit or practise plagiarism. E18.
3 *verb trans.* **a** Take away by cunning or in secret; quietly or surreptitiously remove. Also foll. by *away.* OE. ▸**b** Take (young) from a mother animal. ME. ▸†**c** Capture (a fortress, a military position) by surprise. ME–E17. ▸**d** Carry off, abduct, or kidnap (a person) secretly. Now *rare.* LME.
4 *verb trans.* †**a** Conceal dishonestly (a fault etc.). Only in ME. ▸**b** Cause the loss of, take away, (something valued, as a person's life, happiness, etc.). LME. ▸**c** Take (a period of time) from its usual or proper employment to devote to some other purpose. E16. ▸**d** Gain possession of or entice away from another (a person's heart, affections, etc.). E16.
5 *verb trans.* Place, move, or convey (something) stealthily; smuggle *in*. Formerly *spec.* put *on* (one's clothes etc.) surreptitiously or unobtrusively. Now *rare.* ME. ▸**b** Of a hen: make (a nest) in a concealed place. Of a ewe: bear (a lamb) out of season. M18.
6 *verb trans.* Effect, gain, or accomplish clandestinely, artfully, or insidiously. LME. ▸**b** Obtain (a kiss etc.) without permission or by surprise. Formerly also, give (a kiss) unobtrusively *to* a person. LME. ▸**c** Direct (a look) unobtrusively, breathe (a sigh) furtively. L16. ▸**d** In various games, gain (an advantage, a run, possession of the ball, etc.) unexpectedly, by luck or by exploiting the distraction of the opponent; *esp.* in BASEBALL, run to (a base) while the pitcher is in the action of delivery. M19.
7 *verb trans.* NAUTICAL. Omit (a strake) where a vessel narrows at each end. *rare.* E18.

> **1a** A. DAVIS My purse had been stolen while I slept . . and I had no money. M. LANE Charles had been sent down from university for stealing books. **b** SIR W. SCOTT No man like you for stealing other men's inventions. L. P. HARTLEY An interloper who, like Jacob, had stolen the blessing from her. **2a** L. STEFFENS The politicians stole from the city treasury. **3a** AV *Matt.* 27:64 Lest his disciples come by night, & steale him away. **5** E. BOWEN He would . . steal an arm round her shoulders. **6c** B. VINE He . . found himself constantly stealing glances at her.

▶ **II** Go secretly or quietly.
†**8** *verb refl.* Move away or withdraw secretly or quietly. Also foll. by *away. rare.* ME–E18.
9 a *verb intrans.* Depart or withdraw secretly or surreptitiously; go or come secretly or stealthily; walk or creep softly to avoid observation. Foll. by adverb or preposition. ME. ▸**b** *verb intrans.* Come stealthily *on* or *upon* a person for the purpose of attack or injury. ME. ▸**c** *verb trans.* Make (one's way) stealthily or secretly. Now *rare.* LME. ▸**d** *verb intrans.* HUNTING. Foll. by *away*: (of a hunted animal) leave a lair unperceived and gain a start on pursuers. LME.
10 *verb intrans.* **a** Of a condition, as sleep, unconsciousness, daylight, etc.: come gradually or insidiously *over* or *on* (a person, a place, etc.). LME. ▸**b** Of time: pass *on* or *away* unobserved. L16. ▸†**c** Insinuate itself, gradually gain influence. Foll. by *into, on.* L16–E19. ▸**d** Move stealthily; glide gently and slowly. Foll. by adverb or preposition. E17. ▸**e** Of sound, fragrance, light, etc.: become gradually perceptible. Freq. foll. by *on, upon, over* (the senses).

M17. ▸†f Develop by insensible degrees *from*; pass or change insensibly *into* or *to* something else. M17–E19.

> 9a POPE Unlamented let me die, steal from the world. J. AGEE They stole barefoot on tiptoe from the room. J. MARSH The lovers steal away into the night. 10a C. BRONTË A kind of pleasant stupor was stealing over me. JANET MORGAN They did not notice that twilight was stealing over the terraces. d S. BARING-GOULD Shadows of the evening Steal across the sky. S. O'FAOLÁIN His hand stole to the revolver in his pocket.

Phrases: **beg, borrow, or steal**: see BEG *verb* 1. ***steal a march on***: see MARCH *noun*³. **†steal a marriage**, **†steal a match** get married secretly. **steal a person blind** *colloq.* rob or cheat a person totally or mercilessly. ***steal a person's thunder***: see THUNDER *noun*. **steal the picture**, **steal the scene**, **steal the show** in theatrical contexts, outshine the rest of the cast, esp. unexpectedly; *gen.* become or make oneself the centre of attention.

■ **stealable** *adjective* able to be stolen E19. **stealage** *noun* losses due to stealing M18. **stealer** *noun* (*a*) a thief (now only, of something specified); (*b*) *slang* a finger; (*c*) NAUTICAL a plate, plank, or strake joined at one end to two narrower ones near the end of a vessel: LME. **stealing** *ppl adjective* (*a*) that steals; (*b*) ***stealing step(s)*** (now *rare*), quiet and stealthy step(s); (*c*) ***stealing strake*** (NAUTICAL), = STEALER (c): L16. **stealingly** *adverb* stealthily, furtively, so as to elude observation ME.

stealth /ˈstɛlθ/ *noun & adjective*. ME.

[Prob. repr. an Old English word rel. to STEAL *verb*: see -TH¹.]

▸ **A** *noun*. †**1** The action or practice of stealing or taking something secretly and wrongfully; theft. Also, an instance of stealing; a theft. ME–L18. ▸**b** A stolen thing; plunder. Freq. in *pl.* LME–M17. ▸**c** Plagiarism M16–M17.

2 Furtive, covert, or underhand activity; secret or unobserved action; skill in such action. Formerly also, an instance of such action. ME.

3 The action of going furtively in or out of a place, or of stealing or gliding along unperceived; the ability so to move. L16.

4 *ellipt.* Stealth technology; a stealth bomber. L20.

> 2 LD MACAULAY Congregations which had hitherto met only by stealth and in darkness.

▸ **B** *attrib. adjective*. Designating, connected with, or designed in accordance with a branch of technology that deals with rendering aircraft difficult to detect by radar, or submarines by sonar. L20.

stealth aircraft, ***stealth bomber***, ***stealth technology***, etc.

¶ App. rare in 19th cent. exc. in phr. *by stealth*.

■ **stealthful** *adjective* (chiefly *poet.*) stealthy E17. **stealthfully** *adverb* E19.

stealthy /ˈstɛlθi/ *adjective*. E17.

[from prec. + -Y¹.]

1 Moving, acting, or taking place by stealth or secretly; proceeding by imperceptible degrees; furtive in movement or action. E17.

2 Designed to be difficult to detect by radar or sonar. L20.

> 1 G. ORWELL A stealthy step, lowering your foot as gently as a cat. A. MACLEAN No one had heard or seen the stealthy opening of the door.

■ **stealthily** *adverb* E19. **stealthiness** *noun* M19.

steam /stiːm/ *noun*.

[Old English *stēam* = West Frisian *steam*, Dutch *stoom*, of Germanic origin.]

1 A vapour or cloud of minute liquid droplets given out by a substance when heated or burned; an odorous hot vapour or gas. Formerly freq. in *pl.* Now *rare* exc. as passing into sense 3. OE.

†**2 a** A vapour or exhalation produced by the body or by a crowd of people, as hot breath or perspiration; the infectious effluvium of a disease. OE–M19. ▸**b** A noxious vapour generated in the digestive system, *esp.* that of alcoholic liquor as supposed to ascend to the brain. OE–E17.

3 a The vapour into which water is converted when heated, which in air forms a white cloud or mist of minute drops of liquid water; *spec.* in technical use, the invisible gaseous form of water, formed by boiling, from which this vapour condenses on cooling. Also *loosely*, the vapour arising from any liquid when heated. LME. ▸**b** Watery vapour condensed as drops on a surface, as a mirror, a window. E17.

4 A watery vapour rising from the earth or sea. E17.

†**5** CHEMISTRY. Matter in the gaseous state; an impalpable emanation. M17–E18.

6 The gas produced by boiling water as used to generate mechanical power by the force of its expansion in a confined space; (the application or use of) the mechanical power thus generated, esp. in railway engines. L17. ▸**b** *fig.* Energy, drive, stamina. E19. ▸**c** (Cheap wine laced with) methylated spirits as an intoxicant. *Austral. & NZ slang.* M20.

7 A journey by steamer. E19.

8 a In full ***steam-coal***. Coal suitable for heating water in steam boilers. L19. ▸**b** In full ***steam radio***. Sound radio, as considered outmoded by television; a radio receiver. *colloq.* M20.

9 A dish cooked by steaming. *colloq.* E20.

Phrases: **by steam** (travelling) by steamer. **dry steam** ENGINEERING steam containing no suspended droplets of water. **full steam** (the condition of a ship or machine) under full power or at top speed. ***full steam ahead***: see FULL *adjective*. **get up steam** (*a*) generate enough pressure to work a steam engine; (*b*) *fig.* accumulate energy or power before or in the early stages of some great effort or strenuous activity; become angry. **in steam** with the (steam) engine working or ready to start working. ***Joly's steam calorimeter***. **let off steam** relieve excess pressure in a steam engine through a valve; *fig.* relieve pent-up energy by vigorous activity, give vent to one's feelings, esp. harmlessly. **like steam** *Austral.* furiously. ***Norwegian steam***: see NORWEGIAN *adjective*. ***run out of steam***: see RUN *verb*. ***saturated steam***. **under one's own steam** unaided, without provision of assistance (esp. transport) by others. **under steam** (*a*) being worked by steam (opp. ***under sail***); (*b*) = ***in steam*** above. **wet steam** ENGINEERING steam containing suspended droplets of water.

Attrib. & comb.: In the senses 'powered or operated by steam', as ***steam carriage***, ***steam plough***, ***steam railway***, ***steam tractor***, ***steam winch***, etc., 'carrying or containing steam', as ***steam boiler***, ***steam cabinet***, ***steam chest***, ***steam pipe***, etc., 'by the action of steam', as ***steam-bent***, ***steam-drawn***, ***steam-powered***, etc. Special combs., as **steam age** *noun & adjective* (belonging to) the era when all trains were drawn by steam engines; **steam bath** (*a*) a room etc. filled with steam for bathing in, a sauna; (*b*) a metal box filled with steam for heating chemical reaction vessels; **steam beer** an effervescent beer brewed esp. in the western US (proprietary name in the US); **steam boiler** a vessel in which water is heated to generate steam, esp. for working a steam engine; ***steam*** CALLIOPE; **steam-car** a car, tram, etc., powered or drawn by steam; *US* a carriage used on a steam railway; ***steam-coal***: see sense 8a above; **steam cracking** the thermal cracking of petroleum using steam as an inert diluent which reduces polymerization and increases the yield of olefins; **steam-cure** *verb trans.* cure or stiffen a material by treatment with steam (chiefly as ***steam-cured*** *ppl adjective*, ***steam curing*** *verbal noun*); **steam-distil** *verb trans. & intrans.* perform steam distillation (on); **steam distillation** PHYSICAL CHEMISTRY distillation of a liquid in a current of steam, used esp. to purify liquids that are not very volatile and are immiscible with water; **steam engine** an engine in which the force of expansion or rapid condensation of steam is used to generate power for driving machinery etc.; *spec.* a locomotive engine propelled by steam; **steamfitter** a person employed to install the pipes of a steam-heating system; **steam fly** *colloq.* = ***German cockroach*** s.v. GERMAN *noun*¹ & *adjective*¹; **steam gauge** a pressure gauge attached to a steam boiler; **steam hammer** a forging-hammer powered by steam; **steam-heat** heat produced by steam, esp. by a central heating system which uses steam; **steam-heater**, **steam-heating**: using steam-heat; **steam-iron** an electric iron containing hot water emitted as steam from its flat surface to improve its ability to press clothes; **steam-jacket** a jacket or casing filled with steam in order to preserve the heat of a vessel around which it is placed; ***steam-launch***: see LAUNCH *noun*² 2; **steam line** a line in a phase diagram representing the conditions of temperature and pressure at which water and water vapour are in equilibrium in the absence of ice; ***steam navvy***: see NAVVY *noun* 2; **steam organ** = CALLIOPE; **steam-packet** a steamer on a regular run between two ports; **steam plough** a plough propelled by a steam engine; a ploughing engine; **steam point** (*a*) a temperature at which liquid water and water vapour are in equilibrium; *spec.* the boiling point of water under standard atmospheric pressure; (*b*) *N. Amer.* a metal pipe, driven into frozen earth, down which steam can be passed to thaw the ground for mining; **steam power** the force of steam applied to machinery etc.; ***steam radio***: see sense 8b above; **steam-raiser** a person employed to light the fires of steam engines; **steamship** a ship propelled by steam; **steam shovel** an excavator powered by steam; **steam table** (orig. *US*) in a cafeteria etc., a table with slots to hold food containers kept hot by steam circulating beneath them; **steam-tight** *adjective* [after *watertight*] impervious to steam; **steam train**: drawn or driven by a steam engine; **steam tug** a steamer for towing ships etc.; **steam turbine** a turbine in which a high-velocity jet of steam rotates a bladed disc or drum; **steam-vessel** (*a*) a vessel for holding steam, esp. one in which steam is condensed for working an engine; (*b*) a steamboat or steamship; †**steam-wheel** a rotary steam engine; **steam-whistle** a powerful whistle worked by a jet of steam (usually from a steam boiler) and used as a signal. See also STEAMBOAT, STEAMROLLER.

■ **steamless** *adjective* without steam; that has run out of steam or is not propelled by steam; (of a railway) not carrying steam engines: E20.

steam /stiːm/ *verb*.

[Old English *stēman*, *stȳman*, from Germanic base also of the noun.]

▸ **I** *verb intrans.* †**1** Emit a scent or odour; (of a scent) be emitted. (Foll. by *out*, *up*.) OE–M19.

†**2** Emit flame, glow. Only in LME.

3 Of vapour etc.: be emitted or rise up in the form of steam. L16.

4 Emit or give off steam or vapour. E17.

5 Of an engine or boiler: produce steam for mechanical purposes. M19.

6 Esp. of (passengers on) a ship or train: move or travel, orig. *spec.* by the agency of steam. Freq. with adverbs & prepositions. M19. ▸**b** Come, go, or move rapidly and directly. Freq. with adverbs & prepositions. *colloq.* M19. ▸**c** Foll. by *in*: start or join a fight. *slang.* M20.

7 Become covered, filled, or obscured by condensed vapour. Usu. foll. by *up*. L19.

8 Of a gang; pass rapidly through a public place, train, etc., robbing bystanders or passengers by force of numbers. Freq. as ***steaming*** *verbal noun*. *slang.* L20.

> 4 A. CARTER Their already wet clothes steamed in the heat. 6 M. MEYER His train steamed out of Uppsala. *Sea Breezes* We steamed slowly in a wide circle, sounding our siren. **steaming light** a white light carried on the masthead of a steamship under way at sea by night. b P. BARKER At that moment, steaming round the corner, came Mrs Bulmer. *fig.*: *Times* Shares in Woolworth Holdings continued to steam ahead.

▸ **II** *verb trans.* **9** Apply steam to, expose to the action of steam; treat with steam in order to soften, cook, heat, bend, etc. L15. ▸**b** Fill with a warm odour. *rare.* M19. ▸**c** Cover (a surface) or fill (a room) with droplets of condensed vapour. Usu. foll. by *up*. M19. ▸**d** Expose (gummed paper etc.) to steam in order to soften the gum; force (an envelope etc.) *open* or prise (a postage stamp, a label, etc.) *off* by this method. L19.

10 Exhale (steam or other vapour); emit, send out in the form of vapour. L16.

11 Convey on a steam-vessel. *colloq.* L19.

12 Foll. by *up*: rouse or excite (a person), esp. to anger; agitate, upset. Also (*rare*), stir up or rouse (ardour etc.). *colloq.* E20.

13 AGRICULTURE. Foll. by *up*: provide extra food to (farm animals) in preparation for reproduction. M20.

14 Subject to the activity of steaming (sense 8 above); make (one's way) by or while steaming. *slang.* L20.

> 9 *Toronto Star* Rutabaga disks can be steamed . . until tender. d M. BEERBOHM She might easily steam open the envelope and master its contents.

■ **steaming** *ppl adjective & adverb* (*a*) *adjective* that steams; *colloq.* blasted, damned; (*b*) *adverb* ***steaming hot***, so hot as to steam, very hot and humid: M16.

steamboat /ˈstiːmbəʊt/ *noun*. L18.

[from STEAM *noun* + BOAT *noun*.]

A boat propelled by steam; *esp.* a coasting or river steamer carrying passengers or goods. Also *fig.*, an energetically or stolidly persistent person or thing.

Comb.: **steamboat Gothic** *US* (designating) a mid-19th-cent. style of architecture with elaborate ornamentation imitating that of Mississippi steamboats. **steamboatman** *US* a person who works on a steamboat, esp. the owner or captain.

■ **steamboating** *verbal noun* (*a*) travelling by steamboat; the business of working a steamboat; †(*b*) *fig.* undue hurrying of work: E19.

steamed /stiːmd/ *adjective*. E19.

[from STEAM *verb* + -ED¹; in sense 3 partly from STEAM *noun* + -ED².]

1 That has been subjected to the process of steaming; *esp.* cooked by steaming. E19.

2 a Excited or roused, esp. to anger; agitated, upset. Freq. in ***steamed up***, ***all steamed up***. *colloq.* E20. ▸**b** Drunk, intoxicated. Usu. foll. by *up*. *slang.* E20.

3 ***steamed up***, (of a surface, a room, etc.) covered or filled with condensed vapour, misted over. Freq. *attrib.* with hyphen. L20.

steamer /ˈstiːmə/ *noun & verb*. E19.

[from STEAM *noun* or *verb* + -ER¹.]

▸ **A** *noun*. **1 a** An apparatus for steaming something; a vessel in which articles are subjected to the action of steam, as in washing, cookery, etc. E19. ▸**b** A device which generates steam. L19.

†**2** A tobacco-pipe. *slang*. Only in E19.

3 A dish of stewed kangaroo. *Austral. obsolete* exc. *Hist.* E19.

4 A vessel propelled by steam; a steamboat, a steamship. E19.

5 a Each of three sturdily built greyish ducks of the S. American genus *Tachyeres*, which churn the water with their wings when fleeing danger; *esp.* the flightless *T. brachypterus* of the Falkland Islands. Also ***steamer duck***. E19. ▸**b** The edible longneck clam *Mya arenaria*. Also ***steamer clam***. E20.

6 A person who steams; a person engaged in some process of steaming. M19. ▸**b** A member of a gang engaged in steaming (STEAM *verb* 8). *slang.* L20.

7 a A steam-propelled road-vehicle or traction-engine; a motor car driven by steam. *rare.* M19. ▸**b** (A train drawn by) a steam locomotive engine. M19.

8 a A fire engine with a pump worked by steam. *obsolete* exc. *Hist.* L19. ▸**b** A steam threshing-machine. Now *rare* or *obsolete*. L19.

9 [from rhyming slang *steam tug* for *mug*.] = MUG *noun*⁶. Also *spec.*, a male homosexual, *esp.* one who seeks passive partners. M20.

10 A wetsuit. *slang.* L20.

4 ***screw-steamer***: see SCREW *noun*¹ 8b.

Comb.: **steamer-chair** a deck-chair of a style used on the deck of a steamer; **steamer rug**, **steamer trunk**: designed or intended for use on board a steamer.

▸ **B** *verb intrans.* Travel by steamboat. Now *rare.* M19.

steamie /ˈstiːmi/ *noun*. *Scot.* Also **-my**. E20.

[from STEAM *noun* + -IE.]

A communal wash-house (now esp. as a place of gossiping).

steamroller /'sti:mrəʊlə/ *noun & verb*. M19.
[from STEAM *noun* + ROLLER *noun*¹.]
▶ **A** *noun*. **1** A heavy slow-moving vehicle (orig. & *spec*. a steam-powered one) with wide wheels or rollers, used for crushing road-metal and levelling roads. M19.
2 *fig*. A crushing or irresistible power or force. *colloq*. L19.
▶ **B** *verb*. **1** *verb trans*. Crush or level with a steamroller. E20.
2 *verb trans. fig*. ▸**a** Crush or break down (opposition etc.) as with a steamroller; ride roughshod over; overwhelm, squash. E20. ▸**b** Push (a measure or proposal) *through* (a legislative assembly, committee, etc.) by forcibly overriding opposition. M20. ▸**c** Force (a person) *into* a course of action, situation, etc. M20.
3 *verb intrans*. Proceed (esp. continue speaking) regardless of opposition or interruption. Freq. foll. by *in, on, through*. M20.
■ **steamroll** *verb trans*. = STEAMROLLER *verb* 1, 2 L19.

steamy *noun* var. of STEAMIE.

steamy /'sti:mi/ *adjective*. M16.
[from STEAM *noun* + -Y¹.]
1 Consisting of or emitting steam; resembling steam; full of steam; (of weather etc.) humid. M16.
2 (Apparently) covered with condensed vapour. M19.
3 Salacious, erotic, sexy, torrid. *colloq*. L20.
■ **steamily** *adverb* E20. **steaminess** *noun* M19.

stean /sti:n/ *noun*. Now *arch. & dial*. Also **steen**.
[Old English *stǣne* = Old High German *steinna* from Germanic base also of STONE *noun*.]
A jar or pitcher for liquids or bread, meat, fish, etc., usually of clay with two handles. Cf. STONE *noun* 9.

steapsin /sti:'apsɪn/ *noun*. L19.
[from Greek *stear* fat, after *pepsin*.]
BIOCHEMISTRY. An enzyme in the pancreatic juice which breaks down fats; pancreatic lipase.

stearic /'stɪərɪk, stɪ'arɪk/ *adjective*. M19.
[from Greek *stear* fat, tallow: see -IC.]
CHEMISTRY. Derived from or containing stearin.
stearic acid a colourless unsaturated fatty acid, $CH_3(CH_2)_{16}COOH$, which is solid at room temperature and is the commonest constituent acid of animal and vegetable fats.
■ **stearate** *noun* a salt or ester of stearic acid M19. **stearyl** *noun* the radical $CH_3(CH_2)_{16}CO\cdot$ M19.

stearin /'stɪərɪn/ *noun*. Also (esp. in sense 2) **-ine** /-i:n/. E19.
[formed as prec.: see -IN¹, -INE⁵.]
1 CHEMISTRY. Any of the glycerides formed by the combination of stearic acid and glycerine; *esp*. tristearin, the chief constituent of tallow or suet; a mixture of these. E19.
2 A commercial preparation of purified fatty acids, used for making candles and formerly also statuettes. M19.

steatisation *noun* var. of STEATIZATION.

steatite /'stɪətʌɪt/ *noun*. M18.
[Latin from Greek *steatitis*, *-itēs* (sc. *lithos* stone) stone resembling tallow, from *steat-*, *stear* tallow: see -ITE¹.]
MINERALOGY & GEOLOGY. A massive variety of talc, most commonly grey or greyish-green, with a soapy feel; a soft rock consisting largely of this; soapstone. Also ***steatite talc***. Also called ***soap-rock***, ***soapstone***.
■ **steatitic** /-'tɪtɪk/ *adjective* of, consisting of, containing, or resembling steatite L18.

steatization /stɪətʌɪ'zeɪʃ(ə)n/ *noun*. Also **-isation**. E20.
[from prec. + -IZATION.]
GEOLOGY. Conversion to or replacement by steatite, esp. by hydrothermal alteration of ultrabasic rocks.

steato- /'stɪətəʊ/ *combining form*.
[from Greek *steat-*, *stear* stiff fat, tallow, suet: see -O-.]
Chiefly MEDICINE. Of, pertaining to, or involving fatty matter or tissue.
■ **steatoma** /stɪə'təʊmə/ *noun*, pl. **-mas**, **-mata** /-mətə/, MEDICINE †(*a*) an encysted fatty tumour, a lipoma; (*b*) a tumour of a sebaceous gland, esp. a sebaceous cyst: L16. **steatorrhoea** /-'ri:ə/ *noun* MEDICINE (*a*) excretion of fat with the faeces; †(*b*) = SEBORRHOEA: M19. **steatosis** /stɪə'təʊsɪs/ *noun* (MEDICINE) fatty degeneration, esp. of the liver M19.

steatopygia /stɪətə(ʊ)'pɪdʒɪə/ *noun*. Also Anglicized as **steatopygy** /stɪə'tɒpɪdʒi/. E19.
[mod. Latin, formed as STEATO- + Greek *pugē* rump.]
Protuberance of the buttocks, due to accumulation of fat in and behind the hips and thighs, esp. as found (chiefly in women) among the Nama and Bushmen of southern Africa.
■ **steatopygial** *adjective* (*rare*) = STEATOPYGOUS L20. **steatopygic** *adjective* = STEATOPYGOUS E20. **steatopygous** /stɪə'tɒpɪgəs, stɪətə(ʊ)'pʌɪgəs/ *adjective* pertaining to or characterized by steatopygia L19.

steboy *interjection, noun, & verb* var. of STABOY.

stech /stɛk, -x/ *verb trans. & intrans. Scot. & north*. Also **stegh**. M18.
[Origin unkn.]
Fill (the stomach, oneself) to repletion; cram (food) into the stomach.

Stechkin /'stɛtʃkɪn/ *noun*. M20.
[I. Y. *Stechkin*, Soviet engineer.]
A 9 mm automatic or semi-automatic machine pistol of the former USSR.

steddle *noun & verb* var. of STADDLE.

Stedman /'stɛdmən/ *noun*. M18.
[Fabian *Stedman* (fl. 1670).]
CAMPANOLOGY. Used *absol*., *attrib*., and in *possess*. to designate a method of change-ringing devised by Stedman.
Stedman caters, ***Stedman cinques***, ***Stedman triples***.

steeboy *interjection, noun, & verb* var. of STABOY.

steed /sti:d/ *noun*.
[Old English *stēda*, from base also of STUD *noun*².]
†**1** A stud-horse, a stallion. Only in OE.
2 Orig. *spec*., a large powerful spirited horse used on state occasions, in war, or for jousting. Now *gen*. (chiefly *literary* or *joc*.), a horse, *esp*. one for riding. OE. ▸**b** *transf*. Any animal used for riding. LME. ▸**c** *joc*. A bicycle or other machine for riding. L19.
■ **steedless** *adjective* without a steed, horseless L18.

steek /sti:k/ *noun*. *Scot*. M18.
[North. form of STITCH *noun*¹.]
1 A stitch in needlework or knitting. M18.
2 A strenuous spell or turn of an occupation. L19.
Phrases: **every steek** every stitch of clothing etc. **keep steeks with** keep pace or time with.

steek /sti:k/ *verb*¹. *obsolete* exc. *Scot. & north*. ME.
[Prob. repr. unrecorded Old English form = Old Frisian *steka*, Old Saxon *stekan* (Low German, Dutch *steken*), Old High German *stehhan* (German *stechen*), from var. of Germanic base of STICK *verb*¹. Branch II perh. from sense of 'fix shut, fasten (a door)', or possibly a different word.]
▶ **I** Fix.
†**1** *verb trans*. Pierce, stab; transfix. ME–E17.
†**2** *verb intrans*. Be stuck *in* or *into* something. ME–M16.
▸**b** *fig*. Stick *in* one's mind, heart, etc. LME–L16.
†**3** *verb intrans*. Be hindered from proceeding. ME–E17.
4 *verb trans*. Fix (a thing) by thrusting a point into; fix on a point. Also *gen*., fasten in position. Long *rare* or *obsolete*. ME.
†**5** *verb intrans*. Foll. by *in, on, with*: remain fixed to, stick on or to something. Also, cling tenaciously *to*. LME–M16.
†**6** *verb intrans*. Demur, hesitate. L15–L16.
▶ **II** Shut.
7 *verb trans*. Shut up or *up*, enclose, imprison; shut out or *out*, exclude; lock *up* or close (a place) securely; shut or fasten (a door, window, etc.), stop *up* (a hole, passage, etc.). ME.
†**8** *verb intrans*. Close a place, lock a door. ME–E16.

steek /sti:k/ *verb*². *Scot. & north*. E16.
[Rel. to STEEK *noun*. Cf. STICK *verb*¹.]
1 *verb trans*. Stitch. E16.
2 *verb intrans*. Sew. M19.

steekgras /'stɪəkxras/ *noun*. *S. Afr*. M19.
[Afrikaans, from *steek* prick + *gras* grass.]
Any of several grasses, esp. of the genera *Aristida* and *Andropogon*, having spiky awns which can cut the skin or damage the fleeces of sheep.

steel /sti:l/ *noun*¹ *& adjective*.
[Old English *stēli*, *stǣli*, *style* = Old Saxon *stēhli*, from West Germanic adjective repr. by Middle Low German *stāl*, Middle Dutch *stael* (Dutch *staal*), Old High German *stahal* (German *Stahl*), prob. from Germanic base of STAY *noun*¹.]
▶ **A** *noun*. **1** Any of numerous artificially produced alloys of iron containing up to 3 per cent of other elements (including less than about 2.2 per cent carbon) and having great strength and malleability, much used for making tools, weapons, machinery, etc., and able to be tempered to many different degrees of hardness. OE. ▸**b** A particular variety of this. Freq. with defining word. E19. ▸**c** A cold shade of grey resembling the colour of steel. Also ***steel-grey***. L19.
2 Steel in the form of weapons, cutting tools, etc.; a weapon, a sword. Also, steel shot, steel shells. OE.
3 As a type of hardness, inflexibility, or strength, esp. in phrs. and combs. ME. ▸**b** Power of endurance or sustained effort. M19.
4 Steel as the material of defensive armour. Now *rare*. ME.
5 Any of various instruments made of steel, *esp*. (*a*) a piece of steel shaped for the purpose of striking fire with a flint; (*b*) a rod of steel, fluted or plain, fitted with a handle and used to sharpen knives; (*c*) (*obsolete* exc. *dial*.) a flat-iron; (*d*) *dial*. a needle, a knitting-needle. ME.
6 A piece of steel forming part of something. LME.
7 A strip of steel used to give stiffness or support, or to expand the skirt of a dress. E17.
8 Iron or steel as used medicinally, esp. in the form of iron chloride. Now *rare*. M17.
9 (An illustration printed from) an engraved steel plate. M19.
10 In *pl*. Shares in steel-manufacturing companies. E20.

> 📖 **1** A. H. COTTRELL About 80 per cent of steel in Britain is made by the open hearth process. **b** ***blister steel***, ***cast steel***, ***mild steel***, ***run steel***, ***stainless steel***, etc.; ***carbon steel***, ***chrome steel***, ***manganese steel***, etc.; ***maraging steel***, ***rimming steel***, ***structural steel***, etc. **2** BYRON Bury your steel in the bosoms of Gath. R. ALDINGTON The earth was rent and torn By bursting steel. **3** B. MONTGOMERY An army must be as hard as steel in battle.

Phrases: **cold steel** steel in the form of a weapon or weapons; swords, spears, etc., collectively. **draw one's steel**, **draw steel** draw one's sword or pistol. ***end of steel***: see END *noun* 7c. ***have nerves of steel***: see NERVE *noun*. †**salt of steel** a salt of iron, esp. iron chloride. **true as steel** thoroughly trustworthy, reliable.
Comb.: **steel band** (*a*) a band of musicians who play (chiefly calypso-style) music on steel drums; (*b*) *Austral*. a hard thin stratum of iron-bearing siliceous material lying above an opal deposit; **steel bandsman** a musician in a steel band; **steel-bender** a worker who bends steel rods or girders into shape for reinforced concrete; **steel-blue** *adjective & noun* (of) a dark bluish-grey colour; **steel-bow**, **steel-bowed** *adjectives* (*US*) (of spectacles) having steel frames; **Steel boy** *Hist*. a member of an Irish rebel society of the 1770s (cf. ***oak-boy*** s.v. OAK *adjective*); **steel-clad** *adjective* wearing steel armour; armour-plated; **steel driver** *US* a worker who makes holes for explosive charges, using a steel stake and a sledgehammer; **steel drum** a percussion instrument originating in the W. Indies, made out of an oil drum with one end beaten down and divided into grooved sections to give different notes; **steel drummer** a person who plays a steel drum; **steel engraving** the process of engraving on, or an impression taken from, a steel-coated copper plate; **steel-face** *verb trans*. cover (an engraved metal plate) with a film of steel to increase its durability (chiefly as ***steel-faced*** *ppl adjective*, ***steel-facing*** *verbal noun*); **steel fixer** a skilled steel worker in the construction industries; **steel frame** a framework, esp. of a building, made of steel; **steel-framed** *adjective* having a steel frame; **steel guitar** (*a*) ***Hawaiian guitar*** (*b*) = ***pedal steel (guitar)*** s.v. PEDAL *noun*¹; **steelhead** *N. Amer*. (*a*) the rainbow trout, *Salmo gairdneri* (also ***steelhead trout***); (*b*) the ruddy duck, *Oxyura jamaicensis*; **steelheader** *N. Amer*. a person who fishes for steelhead trout; **steel-iron** (*a*) native iron resembling steel; (*b*) iron suitable for converting into steel; **steel mill** †(*a*) a device for producing a stream of sparks from a revolving steel disc in contact with a flint, used for light in coalmines before the invention of the safety lamp; †(*b*) a small mill with steel parts for grinding corn; (*c*) a factory where steel is rolled into sheets; **steel pan** a steel drum; **steel pen** (*a*) a pen-nib made of steel, split at the tip; (*b*) *US colloq*. (*arch*.) a tail-coat; ***steel tape***: see TAPE *noun & verb*; **steel trap** a trap with jaws and spring of steel; **steel wool** fine strands of steel matted together, used as an abrasive, esp. for scouring; **steelwork** work in steel, that part of a building etc. that is made of steel; **steelworks** a place or building where steel is manufactured.
▶ **B** *attrib*. or as *adjective*. **1** Made or consisting of steel; containing steel; *fig*. resembling steel in strength or hardness. ME. ▸**b** Of the colour of steel. M19.
2 Of or pertaining to the manufacture of steel. E17.
2 *steel furnace*, ***steel plant***, ***steel town***, etc.

steel /sti:l/ *noun*². *slang*. E19.
[Abbreviation of BASTILLE *noun*, alt. after prec.]
Usu. ***the steel***. Prison.

steel /sti:l/ *verb trans*. ME.
[from STEEL *noun*¹.]
1 a Overlay, point, or edge with steel. Freq. in *pass*. Now chiefly *Hist*. ME. ▸†**b** Back (a mirror) with steel. E–M17. ▸**c** Cover (an engraved metal plate) with a film of protective iron by electrolysis. L19.
2 a *fig*. Make hard, unbending, or strong as steel, make determined or obdurate; nerve or strengthen (*to* do something, *for* something); fortify *against*. L16. ▸**b** Make like steel in appearance. *rare*. E19.
3 Iron (clothes). *dial*. M18.
4 Convert (iron) into steel. M19.
5 Sharpen (a knife) with a steel. L19.

> 📖 **2a** H. JAMES Olive had . . a sense of real heroism in steeling herself against uneasiness. E. WAUGH He was dangerously near to converting me to righteousness but . . I steeled my heart. *Scotsman* Citizens will probably steel themselves for a further levy.

steelbow /'sti:lbəʊ/ *noun*. *obsolete* exc. *Hist*. LME.
[from STEEL *noun*¹ (in fig. sense = rigidly fixed) + BOW *noun*².]
SCOTS LAW. A quantity of farm stock which a new tenant received from the landlord and was obliged to return undiminished at the end of the tenancy. Also, the kind of tenancy or contract under which such a condition was made. Freq. *attrib*., as ***steelbow goods***, ***steelbow lease***, ***steelbow tenant***, etc.

steeled /sti:ld/ *adjective*. OE.
[from STEEL *noun*¹, *verb*: see -ED², -ED¹.]
1 Made of steel; covered, edged, or tipped with steel. OE.
2 Armed or protected with steel. L16.
3 *transf*. Hardened like steel, insensible to impression, inflexible. L16.
4 Of wine etc.: containing an infusion of steel. M17.

steelify /ˈstiːlɪfʌɪ/ *verb trans.* M17.
[from STEEL *noun*[1]: see -FY.]
†**1** Add steel to, imbue with the properties of steel. Only in M17.
2 Convert (iron) into steel. Chiefly as ***steelified** ppl adjective*, ***steelifying** verbal noun & ppl adjective.* E19.
■ **steelifiˈcation** *noun (rare)* L19.

steeling /ˈstiːlɪŋ/ *noun.* L15.
[from STEEL *verb* + -ING[1].]
1 The action of STEEL *verb*; the process of strengthening, stiffening, or hardening with steel. L15.
2 Conversion into steel. M19.
3 A steel part of a machine. M19.

steely /ˈstiːli/ *adjective & adverb.* E16.
[from STEEL *noun*[1] + -Y[1].]
► **A** *adjective.* **1** Of a person: hard and cold as steel, unimpressionable, inflexible, obdurate. Also (in physical sense), strong as steel. E16.
†**2** Of a blow: given with a sword or spear. M16–M17.
3 Of, pertaining to, or made of steel; containing or consisting of steel. L16.
4 Resembling steel in appearance, colour, hardness, or some other quality. L16. ▸**b** *spec.* Of corn, esp. barley: very hard and brittle. L16.
► **B** *adverb.* In a steely manner, like steel, cold and hard. *rare.* E17.
■ **steeliness** *noun* L16.

steelyard /ˈstiːljɑːd/ *noun*[1]. L15.
[from STEEL *noun*[1] + YARD *noun*[1], mistranslating Middle High German *stālhof*, from *stāl* sample, pattern + *hof* courtyard.]
Hist. The place on the north bank of the River Thames above London Bridge where the Merchants of the Hanse had their establishment; *transf.* the merchants collectively. Also, a similar establishment in a provincial town; a tavern within the precincts of the London steelyard where Rhenish wine was sold.

steelyard /ˈstiːljɑːd/ *noun*[2]. M17.
[from STEEL *noun*[1] + YARD *noun*[2].]
sing. & in *pl.* A balance consisting of a lever with unequal arms which moves on a fulcrum, the article to be weighed being suspended from the shorter arm and a counterpoise slid along the longer arm until the lever balances, a graduated scale on this arm showing the weight. Also called ***Roman balance***.

steen *noun* var. of STEAN.

steen /stiːn/ *adjective. US slang.* Also **'steen**. L19.
[Aphet. from SIXTEEN. Cf. STEENTH.]
An indefinite (fairly) large number of; umpteen.

steen /stiːn/ *verb trans.* In sense 2 also **stein**.
[Old English *stǣnan* = Middle Low German *stēnen*, Old High German *gisteinen*, Gothic *stainjan*, from *stān* STONE *noun*.]
†**1** Stone (a person); put to death by stoning. OE–LME.
2 Line (a well etc.) with stone, brick, or other material. Freq. as ***steened** ppl adjective.* Also foll. by *up*. ME.

steenbok /ˈstiːnbɒk, ˈstɪən-/ *noun.* Pl. same. Also **-buck** /-bʌk/. L18.
[Dutch (orig. = wild goat), from *steen* STONE *noun* + *bok* BUCK *noun*[1]. Cf. STEINBOCK.]
A small red-brown antelope of eastern and southern Africa, *Raphicerus campestris*. Also called **steinbock**.

steenbras /ˈstiːnbras, ˈstɪən-/ *noun. S. Afr.* Also **-brass**. E17.
[Afrikaans, from Dutch *steen* STONE *noun* + *brasem* bream.]
Any of several South African marine fishes of the family Sparidae, *esp. Sparodon durbanensis*, an edible game-fish found in shallow waters.

steenbuck *noun* var. of STEENBOK.

steening /ˈstiːnɪŋ/ *noun.* M18.
[from STEEN *verb* + -ING[1].]
1 The action of STEEN *verb* 2; the lining of a well or other excavation. M18.
2 A paved ford across a river. *dial.* M19.

steenkirk /ˈstiːnkəːk/ *noun.* Also **steinkirk**. L17.
[French *(cravate à la) Steinkerke, Steinkerque*, from the victory of the French over the English at Steenkerke, Belgium, in 1692.]
Hist. A kind of neckcloth worn by both men and women around 1700, having long laced ends hanging down or twisted together and passed through a loop or ring.

steenth /stiːnθ/ *adjective. US slang.* Also **'steenth**. L19.
[Aphet. from SIXTEENTH.]
Orig., sixteenth. Now, latest in an indefinitely long series, umpteenth.

steentjie /ˈstiːnki, -tʃi, ˈstɪən-/ *noun. S. Afr.* L19.
[Afrikaans, dim. of Dutch *steen* STONE *noun*.]
Either of two small marine fishes of the family Sparidae, *Spondyliosoma emarginatum* and *Sarpa salpa*, used mainly as bait.

steep /stiːp/ *noun*[1]. LME.
[from STEEP *verb*[1].]
1 The action or process of steeping or soaking something; the state of being steeped. LME.
2 A vessel in which something is steeped. *rare.* Long *obsolete* exc. *Scot.* E17.
3 = RENNET *noun*[1] 2. L17.
4 The liquid in which a thing is soaked or macerated; *spec.* (AGRICULTURE) a bath in which seeds are washed. M18.
Comb.: **steep-grass** *Scot.* the plant butterwort, *Pinguicula vulgaris*, which acts like rennet.

steep /stiːp/ *adjective, adverb, & noun*[2].
[Old English *stēap* = Old Frisian *stāp*, from West Germanic word rel. to STEEPLE *noun*, STOOP *verb*[1].]
► **A** *adjective.* **1** Extending to a great height; elevated, lofty. Long *rare.* OE.
†**2** (Of the eyes) projecting, prominent, staring, glaring; (of a jewel, eyes, etc.) brilliant. OE–L16.
3 Sharply sloping; almost perpendicular, precipitous; having a high gradient or inclination. Now also, (of a rise or fall) rapid, sharp. ME. ▸†**b** Of water: having a headlong course, flowing precipitously. ME–M17.
4 *fig.* **a** Of an aim, undertaking, etc.: ambitious. *rare.* L16. ▸†**b** Reckless, precipitate, headlong. E–M17.
5 Excessive, unreasonable; (of a price, demand, etc.) exorbitant; (of a story etc.) exaggerated, incredible. *colloq.* M19.

> **3** A. MACLEAN The slope . . was . . very steep, perhaps one in four. B. ENGLAND The terrain grew steeper until, fifty feet below the crest, they were forced to crawl. **5** *Munsey's Magazine* Forty thousand marks . . is a pretty steep price even for a royal motor carriage. *Modern Painters* To lay the blame for the Fall of Man on the modernists seems a bit steep.

Comb.: **steep-down** *adjective* (long *obsolete* exc. *poet.*) sloping steeply downwards, precipitous; **steep-to** *adjective* (NAUTICAL) (of a shore etc.) descending almost perpendicularly into the water; **steep-up** *adjective* (long *obsolete* exc. *poet.*) sloping steeply upwards, precipitous.
Phrases: **method of steepest descent(s)** MATH. a method of finding a minimum of a function by repeatedly evaluating it at a point displaced from the previous point in the direction that locally involves the greatest drop in its value.
► **B** *adverb.* Steeply, *esp.* with a steep slope. Long *rare* or *obsolete* exc. in comb. LME.

> R. KIPLING Up rough banks . . down steep-cut dips.

► **C** *noun.* The slope of a mountain, hill, etc.; a steep slope or place; a precipice. M16.

> MILTON The steep Of echoing Hill. L. MORRIS Knowledge is a steep which few may climb.

■ **steepen** *verb intrans. & trans.* become or make steep or steeper M19. **steepish** *adjective* E19. **steeply** *adverb* L18. **steepness** *noun* (*a*) the quality or condition of being steep; (*b*) a steep part or slope of a hill etc.: LME.

steep /stiːp/ *verb*[1]. ME.
[Rel. to Swedish *stöpa*, Danish *støbe*, Norwegian *støypa* steep (seeds, barley for malting), from Germanic word rel. to base of STOUP. Perh. already in Old English.]
► **I** *verb trans.* **1** Soak, saturate, or bathe in or *in* water or other liquid; make thoroughly moist or wet (*with*). ME.
2 *transf. & fig.* **a** Make (a person) drunk or intoxicated; stupefy (the senses etc.) or deaden (sorrow etc.) *in* alcoholic liquor, sleep, etc. LME. ▸**b** Of mist, smoke, light, etc.: pervade, envelop. L16.
3 Foll. by *in*: involve (a person) deeply; imbue thoroughly with (a quality); make profoundly acquainted with (a subject). Usu. in *pass.* E17.

> **1** G. ROSE Distillers steep . . malt a fortnight before they . . use it. DICKENS I have steeped my eyes in cold water. P. MANN I took off my shirt, steeped it in . . water. **2a** SHAKES. *2 Hen. IV* O Sleep . . thou no more wilt . . steep my senses in forgetfulness. SIR W. SCOTT My memory fails . . (for I did steep it . . too deeply in the sack-butt). **b** SHELLEY Mist began to . . steep The orient sun in shadow. **3** W. IRVING The . . scholar, steeped to the lips in Greek. J. O. DYKES A language of devotion in which the minister does well to steep himself. E. JONES He had . . long been steeped in the German classics and frequently quotes them.

► **II** *verb intrans.* **4** Undergo the process of soaking. LME.
Comb.: **steep-water** = STEEP *noun*[1] 4.

steep /stiːp/ *verb*[2]. LME.
[from STEEP *adjective*.]
1 *verb intrans.* Slope steeply or precipitously. LME.
2 *verb trans.* Orig., place in a sloping position. Now only (*dial.*), tilt (a cask or barrel). E17.
3 *verb trans.* Make a slope on the top or side of a hedge or haystack. *dial.* M18.

steeper /ˈstiːpə/ *noun.* E17.
[from STEEP *verb*[1] + -ER[1].]
1 A person who steeps flax, wool, etc. E17.
2 A vessel used in steeping or infusing. M18.
3 A drenching rain. *dial.* L19.

steephead /ˈstiːphɛd/ *noun. US.* E20.
[from STEEP *adjective* + HEAD *noun*.]
PHYSICAL GEOGRAPHY. A nearly vertical slope, from the base of which springs emerge, at the head of a pocket valley.

steeping /ˈstiːpɪŋ/ *noun.* LME.
[from STEEP *verb*[1] + -ING[1].]
1 The action or process of STEEP *verb*[1]; an instance of this. LME.
2 A liquid in which grain etc. is steeped. L16.

steeple /ˈstiːp(ə)l/ *noun.*
[Old English *stēpel*, from Germanic word rel. to STEEP *adjective*.]
†**1** A tall tower; a building of great height in relation to its length and breadth. OE–M19.
2 A tower forming part of a church, temple, or other public building, and often housing bells; such a tower together with its spire or other superstructure. OE.
3 A spire on the top of the tower or roof of a church etc. L15. ▸**b** *transf.* Any of various usu. pointed structures above the roof of a building. E19. ▸**c** A steeple-shaped formation of the two hands, with the palms facing and the extended fingers meeting at the tips. M20.

> **2** L. STERNE The steeple, which has a spire to it, is placed in the middle of the church. **3** H. ADAMS Notice how the octagonal steeple is fitted on . . the square tower.

Comb.: **steeple-bush** the hardhack, *Spiraea tomentosa*; **steeple clock** (*a*) a clock fixed to the steeple of a church; (*b*) *US* an antique mantel or shelf clock with a case shaped like a steeple; **steeple-crowned** *adjective* (of a hat) having a tall pointed crown; **steeple cup** a large usu. silver goblet, fashionable in the early 17th cent., with an ornamental structure resembling a steeple on the top of its cover; **steeple-house** a building with a steeple, *esp.* (*derog.* in early Quaker use) a church; **steeplejack** a person who climbs steeples, tall chimneys, etc., to carry out repairs or maintenance.
■ **steeplewise** *adverb* (long *rare*) in the manner of a steeple; in a conical or pyramidal shape: M16.

steeple /ˈstiːp(ə)l/ *verb.* M17.
[from prec.]
1 *verb trans.* Place (a bell etc.) in a steeple. *rare.* M17.
2 *verb intrans.* Rise sharply like a steeple. Chiefly as ***steepling** ppl adjective.* L19.
3 *verb trans.* Place (the fingers or hands) together in the shape of a steeple. Cf. STEEPLE *noun* 3c. M20.

> **3** B. BOVA Steepling his fingers and resting his chin on their tips.

■ **steepler** *noun* (CRICKET) a ball hit high into the air, *esp.* one from which the batsman is caught out M20.

steeplechase /ˈstiːp(ə)ltʃeɪs/ *noun & verb.* L18.
[from STEEPLE *noun* + CHASE *noun*[1].]
► **A** *noun.* **1** A horse-race across country (orig. with a church steeple as the goal) or on a racecourse, with hedges, ditches, etc., to be jumped. L18. ▸**b** A board game in which the throwing of dice determines the progress of model horses over a representation of a steeplechase course. L19.
2 ATHLETICS. A race (across country or on the track) in which runners must clear hurdles, a water jump, etc. M19.
► **B** *verb intrans.* Ride or run in a steeplechase. E19.
■ **steeplechaser** *noun* a rider or runner in a steeplechase; *spec.* a horse trained for steeplechasing: M19.

steepled /ˈstiːp(ə)ld/ *adjective.* E17.
[from STEEPLE *noun, verb*: see -ED[2], -ED[1].]
1 Shaped like a steeple; (of hands etc.) placed together in a steeple. E17.
2 Of a building: having a steeple or steeples. E18.
3 Of a town etc.: having many steeples; conspicuous for its steeple or steeples. M19.

> **1** J. WAINWRIGHT Lyle rested the tips of his steepled fingers against his lips.

steepy /ˈstiːpi/ *adjective.* Long *arch.* M16.
[from STEEP *adjective* + -Y[1].]
Steep; full of steep places; (of movement) headlong, precipitous.

> *fig.*: SHAKES. *Sonn.* His youthful morn Hath travelled on to age's steepy night.

■ †**steepiness** *noun* E17–L18.

steer /stɪə/ *noun*[1].
[Old English *stēor* = Middle Low German *stēr*, Old High German *stior* (Dutch, German *Stier*), Old Norse *stjórr*, Gothic *stiur*, from Germanic.]
A young male ox, *esp.* one castrated and raised for beef; (chiefly *N. Amer. & Austral.*) any male ox raised for beef.

> *Farmers Weekly* Bulls will generally be heavier than steers.

Comb.: **steerhide** *N. Amer.* (leather made from) the hide of a steer.
■ †**steerish** *adjective* (*rare*) (*a*) having the qualities of a steer, brutish; (*b*) *dial.* (of an ox) young: LME–M19. **steerling** *noun* a young steer M17.

steer /stɪə/ *noun*[2]. *obsolete* exc. in comb.
[Old English *stēor* = Old Frisian *stiure*, Old Saxon *stior*, Middle Low German *stūre*, Middle Dutch *stūre*, *stiere* (Dutch *stuur*), Old Norse *stýri* rudder, stem, from Germanic: rel. to STEER *verb*[1].]
†**1** The action of directing or governing a thing or person; control, rule, government. Freq. in ***have the steer, take the steer***, assume control or command (*of* a country etc.). OE–L16.
†**2** A rudder, a helm, (*lit.* & *fig.*). ME–M17.
†**3** A plough-team. Only in E19.
Comb.: **steerman** (NAUTICAL, now *rare*) a steersman; **steer-oar**: used at the stern for steering a boat; †**steer-tree** (*a*) a tiller; (*b*) a plough-handle.

steer /stɪə/ *noun*³. *colloq.* (orig. *US*). L19.
[from STEER *verb*¹.]
A piece of advice or information; a tip, a lead; a direction.

Times The public must give a clear steer . . as to which route the [police] service should follow. **bum steer** *slang* (a piece of) false information or bad advice.

steer *noun*⁴ see STIR *noun*¹.

steer /stɪə/ *adjective*. Long *obsolete* exc. *Scot.* & *north.* ME.
[Prob. rel. to Old High German *stiuri*, *stūri* strong, proud, Middle Low German *stūr* stiff, stern. Perh. already in Old English: cf. STOUR *adjective* & *adverb*.]
Strong, stout.

steer /stɪə/ *verb*¹.
[Old English *stieran* = Old Frisian *stiūra*, Middle Low German *stūren*, Middle Dutch *stūren*, *stieren*, Old High German *stiuren* (German *steuern*), Old Norse *stýra*, Gothic *stiurjan*, from Germanic: rel. to STEER *noun*².]
1 a *verb trans.* & *intrans.* Guide (a vessel) by means of a rudder, helm, oar, etc. OE. ▸**b** *verb trans.* & *intrans.* Guide (a vessel) to a specified point or in a specified direction. LME. ▸**c** *verb intrans.* Of a ship: respond to the helm in a specified manner; be guided by the helm in a certain direction. E17.
2 a *verb trans.* Guide the course of, control the direction of, manoeuvre, (a person, animal, vehicle, etc.). OE. ▸**b** *verb intrans.* & *trans.* Direct (one's steps, journey, etc.); follow (a course, path, etc.); make (one's way). L15. ▸†**c** *verb trans.* Direct one's course towards (a place). *rare.* M17–L18.
†**3** *verb trans.* Check, restrain, control. OE–M17.
4 a *verb trans.* Guide (a person, action, etc.) by admonition, advice, or instruction. OE. ▸†**b** *verb trans.* Conduct (oneself or one's life). ME–L17. ▸**c** *verb intrans.* Regulate one's course of action (*by* guiding indications); find a safe course *between* two evils or extremes. M17.
5 *verb trans.* Govern, rule. Long *rare* or *obsolete.* OE. ▸†**b** Manage, administer (government); conduct (business, negotiations, etc.). OE–M17.

1a W. FALCONER Two skilful helmsmen on the poop to steer. R. MACNEIL The man who steers a nuclear-powered aircraft carrier. *fig.*: N. HERMAN That inner compass we require to steer our life. **b** C. THIRLWALL He set sail . . and steered direct for Athens. J. G. HOLLAND Jim steered his boat around a . . bend. **2a** G. C. DAVIES Steering a bicycle along rutty lanes. J. L. WATEN He . . tried to steer the . . mare away from the centre of the road. J. RABAN He steered her through the crowd. A. TAN Trying to steer the conversation away from . . the cookie woman down the street. **b** MILTON With expanded wings he stears his flight Aloft. WORDSWORTH She . . oft her steps had hither steered. A. H. CLOUGH Thou . . sunny river . . Through woodlands steering. J. N. ISBISTER I have attempted to steer a . . path between exposition and criticism in . . this book. **4a** *Fortune* Reaching children . . and steering them in a productive direction. **b** W. CAVE He . . gave them . . counsels for the steering themselves. **c** M. PRIOR Her Prudence did . . steer Between the Gay and the Severe. W. WOLLASTON Rational animals should use . . reason, and steer by it.

Phrases: **steer a middle course** adopt a moderate or mediating position or policy. **steer-by-wire** *adjective* & *noun* (designating) a semi-automatic and usu. computer-regulated system for controlling the engine, handling, suspension, and other functions of a motor vehicle. **steer clear of** avoid, shun, (chiefly *fig.*). **steering committee**, **steering group** (orig. *US*): set up to determine the priorities or order of business for another body or to manage the general course of an operation. **steer off** guide away *from* some opinion, subject, etc.
■ **steera'bility** *noun* the quality of being steerable E20. **steerable** *adjective* able to be steered or guided M19.

steer /stɪə/ *verb*² *trans. rare.* L19.
[from STEER *noun*¹.]
Make a steer of, castrate, (a calf).

steerage /ˈstɪərɪdʒ/ *noun.* LME.
[from STEER *verb*¹ + -AGE.]
1 The action, practice, or method of steering a boat, ship, etc. LME. ▸**b** The effect of the helm on a ship, steerability. M17.
2 Steering apparatus, esp. of a boat. LME.
3 The direction or government of affairs, the State, one's life, etc. L16. ▸**b** A course (esp. of conduct) held or steered. E17.
4 *NAUTICAL.* **a** The area in the rear of a ship immediately in front of the chief cabin (from which the ship was originally steered). Also, quarters assigned to midshipmen or passengers in this area. *obsolete* exc. *Hist.* E17. ▸**b** The part of a ship allotted to passengers travelling at the cheapest rate. *arch.* E19.

1 J. SMEATON The carriages . . [having] a draught-tree for steerage. *Quarterly Review* The problems of . . the steerage of such a body [*sc.* a balloon]. **3** SHAKES. *Rom. & Jul.* He that hath the steerage of my course Direct my sail! W. L. BOWLES Under the firm steerage of Walpole . . the vessel of state held its way.

Comb.: **steerage-way** *NAUTICAL* the amount of headway required for a vessel to be controlled by the helm.

steerer /ˈstɪərə/ *noun.* LME.
[from STEER *verb*¹ + -ER¹.]
1 *NAUTICAL.* A rudder. Long *obsolete* exc. *Scot.* LME.
2 A person who steers a boat; *spec.* a cox of a rowing boat. L16.
3 An intermediary who directs or entices a person to the premises of or a meeting with a swindler, racketeer, etc. *US slang.* L19.
4 A vessel or vehicle with regard to the mode or quality of its steering. L19.

steering /ˈstɪərɪŋ/ *noun.* ME.
[from STEER *verb*¹ + -ING¹.]
1 The action of STEER *verb*¹. ME. ▸**b** *METEOROLOGY.* The moving of pressure systems, precipitation belts, etc., by temperature gradients or winds. E20. ▸**c** *ELECTRONICS.* The switching of pulses from one part of a circuit to another. M20.
2 The apparatus for steering a vehicle etc. L19.
Comb.: **steering box** a housing attached to the body of a motor vehicle that encloses the end of the steering column and the gearing that transmits its motion; **steering-column** a shaft or column connecting the steering-wheel, handlebars, etc., of a vehicle to the rest of the steering gear; **steering compass**: by which a ship is steered; **steering lock** (*a*) see LOCK *noun*² 13; (*b*) a device for immobilizing the steering of a vehicle, esp. to prevent theft; **steering-oar**: for steering a boat; **steering post** the steering-column of an early motor vehicle; **steering sail** *NAUTICAL* a studding sail; **steering-wheel**: by which a vehicle etc. is steered.

steersman /ˈstɪəzmən/ *noun.* Pl. **-men**.
[Old English *stēoresman*, from *stēores* genit. of STEER *noun*² + MAN *noun*.]
1 A person who steers a boat or ship. OE.
2 *transf.* A person who drives or guides a machine. E19.

1 *fig.*: COLERIDGE The . . merit of Buonaparte has been that of a skilful steersman.

■ **steersmanship** *noun* E19. †**steersmate** *noun* (*rare*) = STEERSMAN 1 L16–L17. **steerswoman** *noun* (*rare*) a woman who steers a ship etc. E19.

steeve /stiːv/ *noun*¹. Also †**stive**. L18.
[from STEEVE *verb*¹.]
NAUTICAL. The (angle of) elevation of the bowsprit above the horizontal.

steeve /stiːv/ *noun*². Orig. *US.* M19.
[Perh. from STEEVE *verb*².]
NAUTICAL. A long derrick or spar, with a block at one end, used in stowing cargo.

steeve /stiːv/ *adjective* & *adverb. obsolete* exc. *Scot.* & *dial.* ME.
[Origin unkn.]
▶ **A** *adjective.* Firm, unyielding; strong. Formerly also, rigid, stiff. ME.
▶ **B** *adverb.* Firmly, unyieldingly. ME.
■ **steevely** *adverb* (*obsolete* exc. *Scot.*) = STEEVE *adverb* ME.

steeve /stiːv/ *verb*¹. M17.
[Origin unkn.]
NAUTICAL. **1** *verb intrans.* Of a bowsprit etc.: incline upwards at an angle. M17.
2 *verb trans.* Set (a bowsprit) at a certain upward inclination. L18.
■ **steeving** *noun* (*a*) the action of the verb; (*b*) = STEEVE *noun*¹: M17.

steeve /stiːv/ *verb*² *trans.* L15.
[Old & mod. Spanish *estibar* (Portuguese *estivar*, French *estiver*): see STEVEDORE. Cf. STIFF *adjective*, *noun*, & *adverb*, STIVE *verb*¹.]
Chiefly *NAUTICAL.* Compress and stow (wool, cotton or other cargo) in a ship's hold; stow with a steeve; pack tightly.

Stefan /ˈstɛfan/ *noun.* L19.
[Josef *Stefan* (1835–93), Austrian physicist.]
PHYSICS. ***Stefan constant***, ***Stefan's constant***, the Stefan–Boltzmann constant; ***Stefan law***, ***Stefan's law***, the Stefan–Boltzmann law.

Stefan–Boltzmann /stɛfanˈbəʊltsmən/ *noun.* L19.
[from prec. + BOLTZMANN.]
PHYSICS. Used *attrib.* with ref. to a law empirically formulated by Stefan and theoretically deduced (in the form correctly restricted to black bodies) by Boltzmann.
Stefan–Boltzmann constant the constant in the Stefan–Boltzmann law, equal to 5.67×10^{-8} J m^{-2} s^{-1} K^{-4}; **Stefan–Boltzmann law**: which states that the total radiation emitted by a black body is proportional to the fourth power of its absolute temperature.

steg /stɛg/ *noun. obsolete* exc. *dial.* L15.
[Old Norse *steggi*, *steggr* (masc.), male bird (Norwegian *stegg*), prob. rel. to STAG *noun*.]
A gander.

steganography /stɛgəˈnɒgrəfi/ *noun.* Now chiefly *Hist.* M16.
[mod. Latin *steganographia*, from Greek *steganos* covered: see -GRAPHY.]
The art of secret writing; cryptography. Also, cryptographic script, cipher.
■ **stegano'graphical** *adjective* pertaining to steganography M18.

stegh *verb* var. of STECH.

stego- /stɛgəʊ/ *combining form.*
[from Greek *steg-* base of *stegein* cover, *stegē* covering, *stegos* roof: see -O-.]
Roofed, ridged, covered. Chiefly in *ZOOLOGY* words derived via mod. Latin names.
■ **stegoce'phalian** *adjective* & *noun* (*a*) *adjective* of, pertaining to, or characteristic of (a member of) the order Stegocephalia; (*b*) *noun* a member of the former order Stegocephalia of fossil amphibians, characterized by having the skull protected by bony plates (now included mainly in Labyrinthodontia): L19. †**stegocephalous** *adjective* = STEGOCEPHALIAN *adjective* L19–E20.

stegomyia /stɛgə(ʊ)ˈmʌɪə/ *noun.* E20.
[mod. Latin (see below), formed as STEGO- + Greek *muia* fly.]
A mosquito of the genus *Stegomyia* (now usu. regarded as a subdivision of *Aedes*), which includes tropical and subtropical species that transmit yellow fever. Chiefly as mod. Latin genus (or subgenus) name.

stegosaurus /stɛgəˈsɔːrəs/ *noun.* Pl. **-ri** /-rʌɪ/, **-ruses**. L19.
[mod. Latin (see below), formed as STEGO-: see -SAUR.]
A large quadrupedal herbivorous ornithischian dinosaur of the Jurassic genus *Stegosaurus*, having a double line of bony plates along the back.
■ **'stegosaur** *noun* any stegosaurian reptile E20. **stegosaurian** *adjective* & *noun* (*a*) *adjective* of or pertaining to the Jurassic and Cretaceous order Stegosauria; (*b*) *noun* a stegosaurian reptile: E20. **stegosaurid** *adjective* & *noun* (*a*) *adjective* of or pertaining to the family Stegosauridae; (*b*) *noun* a stegosaurid reptile: L20.

stein /stʌɪn/ *noun.* M19.
[German = STONE *noun*.]
A (usu. earthenware) mug, esp. for beer. Also, the amount of beer a stein will hold, usu. about a pint.

steinbock /ˈstʌɪnbɒk/ *noun.* L17.
[German, from *Stein* STONE *noun* + *Bock* BUCK *noun*¹. Cf. STEENBOK.]
1 The ibex, *Capra ibex*, esp. as formerly occurring in western Europe. L17.
2 *S. Afr.* = STEENBOK. M19.

Steiner /ˈstʌɪnə, *foreign* ˈʃtaɪnər/ *noun*¹. M20.
[See below.]
MATH. Used *attrib.* and in *possess.* to designate various mathematical concepts suggested by the Swiss geometer Jakob Steiner (1796–1863), esp. with ref. to (*a*) the problem of finding the set of line segments of minimum total length needed to connect a given set of points in a metric space; (*b*) the Steiner system (see below).
Steiner system a generalization of the Steiner triple system to include other sizes of subset. **Steiner triple system**, **Steiner triplet** an arrangement of *n* elements in sets of three such that each pair occurs in only one set of three.

Steiner /ˈstʌɪnə, *foreign* ˈʃtaɪnər/ *noun*². M20.
[See below.]
Used *attrib.* to designate a school, educational system, etc., based on the anthroposophical ideas of the Austrian thinker Rudolf Steiner (1861–1925).

Steinert's disease /ˈstʌɪnəts dɪˌziːz, ˈʃtʌɪn-/ *noun phr.* M20.
[from H. G. W. *Steinert* (b. 1875), German physician.]
MEDICINE. = DYSTROPHIA ***myotonica***.

steinkirk *noun* var. of STEENKIRK.

Steinmann /ˈstʌɪnmən, ˈʃt-/ *noun.* E20.
[Fritz *Steinmann* (1872–1932), Swiss surgeon.]
MEDICINE. ***Steinmann pin***, ***Steinmann's pin***, †***Steinmann's nail***, a surgical pin that may be passed through one end of a major bone for traction or setting.

stela /ˈstiːlə/ *noun.* Pl. **-lae** /-liː/ L18.
[Latin, formed as STELE.]
ANTIQUITIES. An upright slab or pillar, usu. bearing a commemorative inscription or sculptured design and often serving as a gravestone.

stelae *noun*¹ pl. of STELA.

stelae *noun*² *pl.* see STELE.

stelar /ˈstiːlə/ *adjective.* E20.
[from STELE + -AR¹.]
BOTANY. Pertaining to the stele.

Stelazine /ˈstɛləziːn/ *noun.* M20.
[from *stel-* (of unkn. origin) + AZINE.]
PHARMACOLOGY. (Proprietary name for) trifluoperazine.

stele /stiːl, ˈstiːli/ *noun.* Pl. **-les**, (esp. in sense 1) **-lae** /-liː/. E19.
[Greek *stēlē* standing block. Cf. STELA.]
1 *ANTIQUITIES.* A stela. Also *loosely*, any prepared surface on the face of a building, rock, etc., bearing an inscription. E19.
2 *BOTANY.* The central core of the stem and root of a vascular plant, consisting of the vascular tissue (xylem and phloem) and associated ground tissue (pith, pericycle, etc.). Also called ***vascular cylinder***. L19.

stelk /stɛlk/ *noun. Anglo-Irish.* M19.
[Prob. from Irish *stailc* stubbornness, sulkiness, starch.]
A cooked vegetable dish made usu. with onions, mashed potatoes, and butter.

†stell *noun*[1]. M17–L19.
[Origin uncertain: perh. rel. to next.]
A stand for a barrel.

stell /stɛl/ *noun*[2]. *S. Afr.* E19.
[Dutch *stel*.]
A kind of trap for wild animals.

stell /stɛl/ *verb trans.*
[Old English *st(i)ellan*, *styllan* = Old Saxon *stellian*, Old & mod. High German *stellen*, ult. from Germanic base of STALL *noun*[1].]
†1 Set (an example); establish (a law). OE–ME.
2 Fix, post, place; *spec.* position (cannon). *Scot.* ME.
3 Portray, delineate. Long *arch.* L16.

stellacyanin /stɛləˈsʌɪənɪn/ *noun.* M20.
[*Estelle* Peisach, after *plastocyanin*.]
BIOCHEMISTRY. An intensely blue copper-containing protein found in the latex of the Japanese lacquer-tree, *Rhus vernicifera*.

Stella Maris /stɛlə ˈmarɪs/ *noun.* L19.
[Latin, lit. 'star of the sea', a title given to the Virgin Mary.]
A protectress, a guiding spirit.

stellar /ˈstɛlə/ *adjective.* M17.
[Late Latin *stellaris*, from Latin *stella* star: see -AR[1].]
1 Of or pertaining to the stars or a star; of the nature of a star; star-shaped, stellate. M17.
2 Having the quality of a star entertainer, performer, etc.; brilliant; outstanding. Orig. *N. Amer.* L19.

1 *Times* How pulsars fit into the picture of stellar evolution. **stellar wind** ASTRONOMY a continuous flow of charged particles from a star, analogous to the solar wind. **2** *American Notes & Queries* Hollywood . . has lured and made stellar personalities out of . . novelists. *Wall Street Journal* An established family man with a stellar reputation . . to attest to his success.

■ **stellardom** *noun* (orig. & chiefly *US*) stardom L19.

stellarator /ˈstɛləreɪtə/ *noun.* M20.
[from prec. with ref. to the fusion processes in stars + -ATOR after *generator* etc.]
PHYSICS. A toroidal apparatus for producing controlled fusion reactions in hot plasma, of a kind distinct in that all the controlling magnetic fields inside it are produced by external windings.

stellaria /stɛˈlɛːrɪə/ *noun.* L18.
[mod. Latin (see below), from Latin *stella* star.]
Any of various plants constituting the genus *Stellaria*, of the pink family, which are characterized by starry white flowers with bifid petals and include the greater stitchwort, *S. holostea*, and chickweed, *S. media*.

†stellary *adjective.* E17–L18.
[formed as STELLAR: see -ARY[2].]
ASTRONOMY. Stellar.

stellate /ˈstɛlət/ *adjective.* E16.
[Latin *stellatus*, from *stella* star: see -ATE[2].]
†1 Of the sky: studded with stars. *poet. rare.* Only in E16.
2 Star-shaped; arranged or grouped in the form of a star or stars; (chiefly SCIENCE) (having parts) radiating from a centre like the rays of a star. M17.

2 stellate ganglion ANATOMY the lowest of the three cervical ganglia of the sympathetic trunk, often incorporating the superior thoracic ganglion. **stellate hair** BOTANY a hair with radiating branches. **stellate reticulum** ANATOMY a layer of cells with long processes in the enamel organ of a developing tooth.

■ **stellately** *adverb* M19.

stellate /ˈstɛleɪt/ *verb trans.* M19.
[Latin *stellat-* pa. ppl stem of *stellare*, from *stella* star: see -ATE[3].]
GEOMETRY. Make stellate.

stellated /stɛˈleɪtɪd/ *adjective.* M17.
[from STELLATE *adjective* + -ED[1].]
1 a = STELLATE *adjective* 2. M17. **▸b** GEOMETRY. Of a polygon, polyhedron, or polytope: (able to be) generated from a convex polygon (polyhedron, etc.) by extending the edges (faces, etc.) until they meet at a new set of vertices. M19.
2 Studded with stars. M18.

stellation /stɛˈleɪʃ(ə)n/ *noun.* E17.
[Latin *stellare* diversify with stars, place among the stars, from *stella* star: see -ATION.]
†1 = SIDERATION 1. Only in E17.
†2 An act or instance of ornamentation with stars. Only in Dicts. M17–E18.
3 GEOMETRY. The generation of a stellated figure; an instance of this. M19.

stelled /stɛld/ *adjective.* Long *obsolete* exc. *poet.* E17.
[from Latin *stella* star + -ED[1].]
Stellar; starry, studded with stars.

Stellenbosch /ˈstɛlənbɒʃ/ *verb trans.* Orig. *Military slang.* Now chiefly *S. Afr.* E20.
[A town in Cape Province, South Africa.]
Transfer (a person, esp. a military officer) to a post of minimal responsibility as a response to incompetence or lack of success. Usu. in *pass.*

Steller /ˈstɛlə/ *noun.* E19.
[Georg Wilhelm *Steller* (1709–46), German naturalist and explorer.]
Used *attrib.* and in *possess.* to designate animals associated with Steller's explorations.

Steller jay = *Steller's jay* below. **Steller's duck**, **Steller's eider (duck)** a black and white duck with reddish underparts, *Polysticta stelleri*, found in Siberia, Alaska, and Canada. **Steller sea lion** = *Steller's sea lion* below. **Steller's jay** a blue jay with a dark crest, *Cyanocitta stelleri*, found in Central and western N. America. **Steller's sea cow** a large sirenian, *Hydrodamalis gigas*, found in the Bering Sea area until it was exterminated in the 18th cent. **Steller's sea lion** a large red-brown sea lion, *Eumetopias jubatus*, of the northern Pacific.

stellerid /ˈstɛlərɪd/ *noun.* Now *rare* or *obsolete.* M19.
[French *stelléride*, irreg. from Latin *stella* star: see -ID[3].]
ZOOLOGY. = STELLEROID.

stelleroid /ˈstɛlərɔɪd/ *noun.* E20.
[mod. Latin *Stelleroidea* (see below), from STELLERID: see -OID.]
ZOOLOGY. A star-shaped echinoderm, a starfish or a brittlestar (sometimes combined in a class Stelleroidea).

stelliferous /stɛˈlɪf(ə)rəs/ *adjective.* L16.
[Latin *stellifer*, from *stella* star: see -FEROUS.]
1 Esp. of the sky: bearing stars. Long *rare* or *obsolete.* L16.
2 BOTANY & ZOOLOGY. Having star-shaped markings. L16.

stelliform /ˈstɛlɪfɔːm/ *adjective.* L18.
[from Latin *stella* star + -I- + -FORM.]
Star-shaped; occurring in the form of star-shaped crystals.

stellify /ˈstɛlɪfʌɪ/ *verb trans.* Long *rare.* LME.
[Old French *stellifier* from medieval Latin *stellificare*, from Latin *stella* star: see -FY.]
1 Transform into a star or constellation; place among the stars. LME. **▸†b** *fig.* Extol. E16–E18.
†2 Set with stars or something compared to stars. LME–M17.

■ **stellifiˈcation** *noun* M17.

stelline /stɛˈliːni/ *noun pl.* Also **-ni.** M20.
[Italian, from *stellina* dim. of *stella* star.]
Small star-shaped pieces of pasta; an Italian dish consisting largely of this and usu. a sauce.

stelling /ˈstɛlɪŋ/ *noun.* M19.
[Dutch, from *stellen* to place.]
In Guyana and the Caribbean, a wooden pier or landing-stage.

stellini *noun pl.* var. of STELLINE.

stellion /ˈstɛlɪən/ *noun.* Also in Latin form **-io** /-ɪəʊ/, pl. **-os.** LME.
[Latin *stellio(n-)*, app. from *stella* star: see -ION.]
In early and heraldic use, a kind of lizard bearing starlike spots. In modern use, an agamid lizard of the former genus *Stellio*, esp. *Agama stellio* of NE Africa, SW Asia, and parts of Greece.

stellionate /ˈstɛlɪənət/ *noun.* E17.
[Latin *stellionatus*, from *stellio(n-)* fraudulent person: see prec., -ATE[1].]
LAW. Fraudulent sale of a thing, esp. property. Also (*Scot.*), any fraud not otherwise classified.

Stellite /ˈstɛlʌɪt/ *noun.* E20.
[App. from Latin *stella* star + -ITE[1].]
Any of various cobalt-based alloys, usu. containing chromium and small amounts of tungsten and molybdenum, used for their great hardness and their resistance to heat.
¶ Proprietary name in the US.

stellium /ˈstɛlɪəm/ *noun.* E19.
[mod. Latin, from Latin *stella* star.]
ASTROLOGY. = SATELLITIUM.

stellular /ˈstɛljʊlə/ *adjective.* L18.
[from late Latin *stellula* dim. of Latin *stella* star: see -ULAR.]
Shaped like a small star or small stars; set with small stars.

■ **stellularly** *adverb* L18.

Stellwag's sign /ˈstɛlvagz sʌɪn/ *noun phr.* L19.
[Carl *Stellwag* von Carion (1823–1904), Austrian ophthalmologist.]
MEDICINE. Orig., retraction of the upper eyelid indicating thyrotoxicosis. Now also, the diminished blinking that normally accompanies this.

STEM *abbreviation.*
Scanning transmission electron microscope (or microscopy).

stem /stɛm/ *noun*[1].
[Old English *stemn*, *stefn*: in branch I rel. to Germanic base repr. by Middle & mod. Low German, Middle & mod. Dutch, Old High German *stam* (German *Stamm*); in branch II corresp. to Old Frisian *stevene*, Low German, Dutch *steven*, Old Saxon *stamn*, Old Norse *stamn*, *stafn*.]
▶ I 1 The part of a plant axis which bears buds, flowers, and leaves and is usu. above ground (as opp. to the *root* or underground part of the axis); *spec.* the main part of this, the stalk, the trunk. OE.
2 a The stock or main line of descent of a family; an ethnic stock, a race; the descendants of a particular ancestor. Also, ancestry, pedigree. Now *arch.* or *literary.* M16. **▸†b** A branch of a family. L16–M17. **▸†c** The primal ancestor or founder of a family. *rare.* E17–L18.
3 a The stalk supporting a leaf, flower, or fruit; a pedicel, a petiole. L16. **▸b** ANATOMY. A stalk supporting or forming part of an organ or structure. M19.
4 LINGUISTICS. Orig., a word from which a derivative is formed. Now, the root or main part of an inflected word to which inflections are affixed; a part of a word that appears unchanged throughout the cases and derivatives of a noun, persons of a tense, etc. M17.
5 Any of various objects or parts resembling the stem of a flower or other plant, as (*a*) the vertical stroke of a letter or musical note; (*b*) the tube of a tobacco-pipe; (*c*) a slender part of a wineglass or other vessel between the body and the base; (*d*) the winding-shaft of a watch; (*e*) (more fully *drill stem*) a (freq. rotating) rod, cylinder, pipe, etc., to which a drill bit fits. L17.
6 a A main line of a railway as opp. to a branch line. M19. **▸b** A street, *esp.* (*a*) a main street; (*b*) one frequented by beggars and tramps. *US slang.* E20.
7 A pipe for smoking opium or crack. *US slang.* E20.

1 B. VINE Flowers were out, tall stems with pink bells hanging from them. **2a** AV *Isa.* 11:1 A rod out of the stemme of Iesse. CHARLES CHURCHILL Men who came From stems unknown. GLADSTONE This older race and the Hellenic tribes . . were derived from the Aryan stem. **3b** *brainstem*: see BRAIN *noun.* **5** *Silesian stem*: see SILESIAN *adjective.*

▶ II NAUTICAL. **†8** The timber at either extremity of a vessel, to which the ends of the side-planks were fastened. Also, either extremity of a vessel. OE–L15.
9 The main upright timber or piece of metal at the bow of a vessel, to which the ship's sides are joined at the fore end. Also *stem post.* M16.
10 The prow, bows, or whole forepart of a vessel. M16.

9 E. REED The stem of an iron ship . . is usually a prolongation of the keel.

Comb.: **stem analysis** FORESTRY (an) analysis of the past growth of a tree by studying cross-sections of the trunk taken at different heights; **stem borer** an insect larva that bores into plant stems; **stem cell** BIOLOGY (*a*) *rare* a cell in the stem of an organism; (*b*) a cell of a multicellular organism which is capable of giving rise to indefinitely more cells of the same type, and from which certain other kinds of cell arise by differentiation; **stem-composition** PHILOLOGY composition of word-stems (as opp. to syntactical combination of words); **stem-cup** a Chinese porcelain goblet of a type with a wide shallow bowl mounted on a short base, first made in the Ming dynasty; **stem family** SOCIOLOGY: in which property descends to a married son who remains within the household, other (esp. married) children achieving independence on receiving an inheritance; **stemflow** FORESTRY precipitation which reaches the ground after running down the branches and trunks of trees (cf. THROUGHFLOW); **stem-fly** = *gout-fly* s.v. GOUT *noun*[1]; **stem ginger** a superior grade of crystallized or preserved ginger; **stem-glass** (*a*) a tall narrow glass vase for display of a flower or flowers; (*b*) a drinking-glass mounted on a stem; **stem-line** (*a*) the upright line or edge of a stone in relation to which characters of an oghamic inscription are arranged; (*b*) (*stemline*) MEDICINE the group of cells having a chromosome number that is (one of) the most frequent in a mixed population, esp. of tumour cells; **stem mother** ENTOMOLOGY = FUNDATRIX 2; **stem piece** NAUTICAL a bracket-shaped piece, attached to the stem, supporting a bowsprit; *stem-post*: see sense 9 above; **stem root** a root that develops from the stem of a plant, esp. on a lily from just above the top of the bulb; **stem-rooting** *adjective* (of a lily etc.) producing roots from the stem; **stem rust** a disease of cereal and other grasses, caused by the fungus *Puccinia graminis*, which is marked by rows of black telia on the stems; also called *black rust*; **stem sawfly**: of the family Cephidae, whose larvae live in plant stems; **stem stitch** an embroidery stitch forming a continuous line by means of slightly oblique overlapping stitches, used esp. for flower-stems or outlines; **stem succulent** any succulent, e.g. a desert cactus, having a fleshy stem adapted to storing water and often with much reduced leaves; **stemware** stemmed glass drinking-vessels; **stem-winder** *US* (*a*) a watch wound by turning a head on the end of a stem rather than by a key; (*b*) *slang* a first-rate person or thing, *esp.* a rousing speaker or speech; **stem-winding** *adjective* (*US*, of a watch) that is a stem-winder.

■ **stemless** *adjective*[1] (of a plant etc.) having no stem L18. **stemlet** *noun* (BOTANY) a small stem M19. **stemmed** *adjective* having a stem or stems (of a specified kind) L16.

stem /stɛm/ *noun*[2]. Also (in sense 1) **†steven.**
[Old English *stemn*, *stefn* rel. to Old Norse *stef* fixed time, summons.]
1 A fixed (period of) time; a turn. Long *obsolete* exc. as in sense 2. OE.
2 MINING. A day's work, a shift. L18.

stem /stɛm/ *verb*[1] & *noun*[3]. ME.
[Old Norse *stemma* = Old & mod. High German *stemmen*, from Germanic.]
▶ A *verb.* Infl. **-mm-**.
▶ I *verb intrans.* **†1** Stop, delay. ME–L16.
2 SKIING. [German *stemmen*.] Move the tail of one ski or both skis outwards, usu. in order to turn or slow down. E20.
▶ II *verb trans.* **3** Stop, check, staunch, dam up, (*lit.* & *fig.*). ME. **▸b** MINING. Plug or tamp (a hole for blasting). L18.
4 Place or hold (a limb) firmly. E19.
▶ B *noun.* **1** Resistance, opposition; a check. *Scot.* ME.

2 A barrier erected in a stretch of water, esp. to trap fish. Orig. & chiefly *Scot.* E18.
3 SKIING. An act of stemming. E20.
Comb. (of verb & noun): **stem-Christiania** SKIING a turn made by stemming and lifting the lower ski parallel as the manoeuvre is completed; **stem-christie** *noun & verb intrans.* (SKIING) (perform) a stem-Christiania; **stem-turn** *noun & verb intrans.* (SKIING) (perform) an elementary turn made by stemming with one ski and then bringing the unweighted ski parallel.
■ **stemless** *adjective*[2] (of a flow) unable to be stemmed M19. **stemming** *noun* (*a*) the action of the verb; (*b*) MINING material used for tamping a hole: L18.

stem /stɛm/ *verb*[2]. Infl. **-mm-**. LME.
[from STEM *noun*[1].]
▶ **I** NAUTICAL. **1** **a** *verb intrans.* Head in a certain direction, keep a course. LME. ▸**b** *verb trans.* Make headway or hold one's own against, resist, (a tide, current, wind, etc.). L16. ▸**c** *verb trans.* Direct, maintain the direction of, (a vessel). L16.
†**2** *verb trans.* Dash against, ram, (a vessel). LME–L15.
3 *verb trans.* Provide (a ship) with a stem. *rare.* L16.
> **1a** MILTON They on the . . Flood . . Ply stemming nightly toward the Pole. **b** J. K. TUCKEY Though the current was running scarcely three miles an hour . . [the ship] . . barely stemmed it. *fig.*: SIR W. SCOTT Stemming the furious current of . . contending parties.

▶ **II** **4** *verb intrans.* Rise erect; grow (*up*). Now *rare.* L16.
†**5** *verb intrans.* Produce a stem. M17–L18.
6 *verb trans.* **a** Remove the fibrous stalks and midribs from (tobacco). E18. ▸**b** Remove the stalks from (currants, grapes, etc.). L19.
7 *verb intrans.* Beg on the street. Cf. STEM *noun*[1] 6b. *US slang.* E20.
8 *verb intrans.* Derive, originate, or spring *from*. Also, extend *back to* in origin. M20.
> **8** *Times Lit. Suppl.* Doubt and conflict . . stemming back to the ancient world. H. S. STREAN Desire for revenge stems from fury at being overcontrolled.

†**stem** *verb*[3] *trans. rare* (Spenser). Infl. **-mm-**. Only in L16.
[Perh. from Greek *stemma* garland.]
Encircle.

St Emilion /sãt eɪˈmiːljɔ̃/ *noun.* M19.
[A town in the department of Gironde in SW France.]
Any of various usu. red wines produced in the region of St Emilion.

stemma /ˈstɛmə/ *noun.* Pl. **stemmata** /ˈstɛmətə/. M17.
[Latin from Greek (= garland), from *stephein* to crown.]
1 **a** A recorded genealogy of a family, a family tree; a pedigree. M17. ▸**b** A diagram representing a reconstruction of the interrelationships between surviving witnesses in the (esp. manuscript) tradition of a text. Cf. STEMMATICS. M20.
2 ZOOLOGY. In arthropods, a simple eye, an ocellus. Now usu. *spec.*, a lateral eye in a holometabolous insect larva. E19.

stemmatic /stɛˈmatɪk/ *adjective.* M20.
[German *stemmatisch.* Cf. next.]
Of or pertaining to stemmatics or a textual stemma.

stemmatics /stɛˈmatɪks/ *noun.* M20.
[German *Stemmatik*, from Latin *stemma(t-)* STEMMA + -ICS. Cf. prec.]
The branch of scholarship that attempts to reconstruct the (esp. manuscript) tradition of texts on the basis of relationships between the variant readings of the surviving witnesses.
■ Also **stemmaˈtology** *noun* M20.

stemmer /ˈstɛmə/ *noun*[1]. M19.
[from STEM *noun*[1] + -ER[1].]
A shoot rising from the stock of a felled tree.

stemmer /ˈstɛmə/ *noun*[2]. L19.
[from STEM *verb*[2] + -ER[1].]
A person who stems tobacco.
■ **stemmery** *noun* a building where tobacco is stemmed M19.

stemmy /ˈstɛmi/ *adjective.* M16.
[from STEM *noun*[1] + -Y[1].]
1 Having long bare stems. M16.
2 Containing stems. M19.

stemple /ˈstɛmp(ə)l/ *noun.* M17.
[Perh. rel. to Middle High German *stempfel* (German *Stempel*).]
MINING. Any of several pieces of wood across a mine shaft serving as supports or steps.

stemson /ˈstɛms(ə)n/ *noun.* M18.
[from STEM *noun*[1] after KEELSON. Cf. STERNSON.]
NAUTICAL. An internal timber connecting the apron and keelson in a wooden vessel.

Sten /stɛn/ *noun.* M20.
[from R. V. Shepherd and H. J. Turpin, the designers, + Enfield a district of Greater London, after BREN.]
More fully ***Sten gun***. A type of light rapid-fire sub-machine-gun.
Comb.: **Stengunner** a person who operates a Sten gun.

stench /stɛn(t)ʃ/ *noun.*
[Old English *stenċ*, corresp. to Old Saxon, Old High German *stank* (Dutch *stank*, German (*Ge*)*stank*), from Germanic base also of STINK verb.]
†**1** An odour, a smell (pleasant or unpleasant). Only in OE.
2 A foul or disagreeable smell; a stink. OE. ▸**b** Evil-smelling quality. ME.
3 A thing that smells offensively. *rare.* L16.
> **2** H. GREEN A stench rose from the copper harsh enough to turn the proudest stomach. R. DAHL I smelled the sickly stench of chloroform and ether. **b** LD MACAULAY In the dungeon below all was darkness, stench, lamentation . . and death. **3** *Edinburgh Review* Brayton has long been a stench in the nostrils of all decent citizens.

Comb.: **stench-pipe** an extension of a soil pipe to a point above the roof of a house, to allow gases to escape; **stench trap** a trap in a sewer etc. to prevent the upward passage of gas.
■ **stenchful** *adjective* foul-smelling, stinking L16. **stenchy** *adjective* = STENCHFUL LME.

stench /stɛn(t)ʃ/ *verb.* Now *rare.*
[Old English (Northumbrian) *stenċan*, from Germanic base of prec.]
1 *verb intrans.* Have a disagreeable smell; stink. Chiefly as ***stenching*** *ppl adjective.* OE.
2 *verb trans.* Impart a stench to; make foul-smelling. L16.
> **2** E. FITZGERALD Dead sheep, stenching the air.

stencil /ˈstɛnsɪl, -s(ə)l/ *noun.* E18.
[App. from next.]
1 A thin sheet of metal, paper, etc., in which a pattern or lettering is cut, used to produce a corresponding pattern on the surface beneath by the application of ink, paint, etc. Also ***stencil plate***, ***stencil paper***, etc. E18.
2 The colouring matter used in stencilling (*rare*); CERAMICS a composition used in transfer-printing and enamelling, to protect from the oil the portions of the pattern that are to be left uncoloured. M19.
3 A pattern, lettering, etc., produced by stencilling. L19.

stencil /ˈstɛnsɪl, -s(ə)l/ *verb trans.* Infl. **-ll-**, ***-l-**. LME.
[In sense 1 from Old French *estanceler*, *estenceler* sparkle, cover with stars, from *estencele* (mod. *étincelle*) spark, from Proto-Romance alt. of Latin SCINTILLA. In sense 2 from the noun.]
†**1** Ornament with bright colours or pieces of precious metal. Only in LME.
2 **a** Produce (an inscription, design, etc.) by using a stencil; blot *out* by stencilling. M18. ▸**b** Mark or paint (a surface) with an inscription or design by means of a stencil. M19.
■ **stenciller** *noun* a person who stencils M19.

stend /stɛnd/ *noun & verb. Scot. & north.* LME.
[Origin unkn.]
▶ **A** *noun.* A leap, a bound; a long bouncy stride. LME.
▶ **B** *verb intrans.* Leap, bound, spring up. Of an animal: rear, be restive. M16.

Stender dish /ˈstɛndə dɪʃ, ˈʃtɛ-/ *noun phr.* E20.
[Wilhelm P. *Stender*, 19th-cent. German manufacturer.]
BIOLOGY & MEDICINE. A shallow glass dish.

Stendhalian /stɒnˈdɑːlɪən/ *adjective & noun.* E20.
[from *Stendhal* (see below) + -IAN.]
▶ **A** *adjective.* Of, pertaining to, or characteristic of the writings of the French novelist Stendhal (Henri Beyle) (1783–1842). E20.
▶ **B** *noun.* An admirer or student of Stendhal or his writing. E20.

stengah /ˈstɛŋə/ *noun.* Now *rare.* L19.
[Malay *sa-tengah* one half. Cf. STINGER *noun*[2].]
Among the British in Malaysia: a half measure of whisky with soda or water.

stenlock /ˈstɛnlɒk/ *noun. Scot. & Anglo-Irish.* L18.
[Origin unkn.]
The saithe or coalfish.

steno /ˈstɛnəʊ/ *noun. N. Amer. colloq.* Pl. **-os**. E20.
[Abbreviation.]
1 = STENOGRAPHER. Cf. STENOG. E20.
2 = STENOGRAPHY. M20.

steno- /ˈstɛnəʊ/ *combining form* of Greek *stenos* narrow: see -O-. Opp. EURY-.
■ **stenoˈbathic** *adjective* [Greek *bathos* depth] (of aquatic life) limited to a narrow range of depths E20. **stenoˈcardia** *noun* [Greek *kardia* heart] MEDICINE = ANGINA 2 L19. **stenocephalic** /-sɪˈfalɪk, -kɪ-/ *adjective* (of a skull) characterized by abnormal or excessive narrowness M19. **stenoˈcranial** *adjective* = STENOCEPHALIC E20. **stenoˈcrotaphy** *noun* [Greek *krotaphos* the temples] excessive narrowness of the temporal region of the skull L19. **stenohaline** /-ˈheɪlʌɪn, -ˈheɪliːn/ *adjective* [Greek *halinos* of salt] (of aquatic life) tolerating only a narrow range of salinity M20. **stenoˈhydric** *adjective* (BIOLOGY) tolerating only a narrow range of humidity M20. **stenoˈpaeic**, **-paic**, **-peic** *adjective* [Greek *opaios* perforated] (of spectacles, optical instruments, etc.) having a narrow slit or aperture; designating such a slit: M19. **steˈnophagous** *adjective* (ZOOLOGY) feeding on only a narrow range of items E20. **stenoˈpodium** *noun*, pl. **-ia**, ZOOLOGY a slender elongated limb of some crustaceans M20. **stenotherm**, **stenoˈthermal** *adjectives* (BIOLOGY) tolerating only a small range of temperature L19. **stenoˈthermic** *adjective* (BIOLOGY) = STENOTHERMAL E20. **stenotope** *noun* (ECOLOGY) a stenotopic organism L19. **stenoˈtopic** *adjective* (ECOLOGY) (of an organism) tolerant of only a restricted range of types of habitat or of ecological conditions M20.

stenog /stɛˈnɒg/ *noun. US colloq.* E20.
[Abbreviation.]
= STENOGRAPHER. Cf. STENO.

stenograph /ˈstɛnəgrɑːf/ *noun.* E19.
[from STENO- + -GRAPH.]
1 A shorthand report. *rare.* E19.
2 A shorthand typewriting machine. L19.

stenograph /ˈstɛnəgrɑːf/ *verb trans.* E19.
[Back-form. from next.]
Write in shorthand.

stenography /stɪˈnɒgrəfi/ *noun.* E17.
[from STENO- + -GRAPHY.]
The skill or occupation of writing in shorthand.
■ **stenographer** *noun* (now chiefly *N. Amer.*) a shorthand writer; a shorthand typist: L18. **stenoˈgraphic**, **stenoˈgraphical** *adjectives* of, pertaining to, or expressed in stenography L17. **stenoˈgraphically** *adverb* by means of shorthand M17. **stenographist** *noun* (*rare*) = STENOGRAPHER M19.

stenol /ˈstiːnɒl/ *noun.* M20.
[from ST(ER)OL with inserted *en* (see -ENE). Cf. STANOL.]
CHEMISTRY. Any sterol with one carbon–carbon double bond in its skeleton.

Stenonian /stɪˈnəʊnɪən/ *adjective.* Now *rare.* M18.
[mod. Latin (*ductus*) *Stenonianus*, from *Steno* (genit. *Stenonis*) Latinized form of STENSEN: see -IAN.]
ANATOMY. ***Stenonian duct***, Stensen's duct (the parotid duct).

Stenorette /stɛnəˈrɛt/ *noun.* M20.
[from STENO- + -r- + -ETTE.]
(Proprietary name for) a type of dictating machine.

stenosis /stɪˈnəʊsɪs/ *noun.* Pl. **-noses** /-ˈnəʊsiːz/. L19.
[mod. Latin from Greek *stenōsis* narrowing, from *stenoun* to narrow, from *stenos* narrow: see -OSIS.]
MEDICINE. The abnormal narrowing of a passage, duct or opening, esp. of an artery or a heart valve.
PYLORIC *stenosis*.
■ **stenosed** *adjective* affected with stenosis L19. **stenosing** *adjective* causing or characterized by stenosis E20. **stenotic** /-ˈnɒt-/ *adjective* pertaining to, characterized by, or resulting from stenosis L19.

stenotype /ˈstɛnə(ʊ)tʌɪp/ *noun.* L19.
[from STENO- + TYPE *noun.*]
1 A letter of the alphabet used as a shorthand character. L19.
2 = STENOTYPER. Also ***stenotype machine***. E20.

stenotypy /ˈstɛnə(ʊ)tʌɪpi/ *noun.* L19.
[from prec.: see -Y[3].]
1 A method of shorthand using letters of the alphabet, rather than symbols, to represent words or groups of words. L19.
2 The skill or occupation of using a stenotyper; phonetic shorthand typed on such a machine. L19.
■ **stenotyper** *noun* a typewriting machine producing phonetic shorthand L19. **stenotypic** *adjective* (*rare*) of, pertaining to, or printed by stenotypy L19. **stenotyping** *noun* the process of typing by stenotypy L19. **stenotypist** *noun* a person skilled in stenotypy L19.

Stensen /ˈstɛns(ə)n, ˈstiːn-/ *noun.* Also **-son**. M19.
[Niels *Stensen* or Steensen (1638–86), Danish anatomist, geologist, and cleric. Cf. STENONIAN.]
ANATOMY. Used in *possess.* to designate structures investigated by Stensen.
Stensen's canal either of two (sometimes four) canals through the bony palate, running from just behind the incisor teeth to each half of the nasal cavity. **Stensen's duct** the parotid duct. **Stensen's foramen**, pl. **-mina**, any of the orifices of Stensen's canals in the bony palate.

stent /stɛnt/ *noun*[1]. Chiefly *Scot. obsolete* exc. *Hist.* ME.
[Old French *estente* rel. to Anglo-Norman *extente* EXTENT noun.]
An assessment of property made for purposes of taxation; the amount or value assessed, a tax.
Comb.: **stentmaster** an official appointed to fix the amount of tax payable by the inhabitants of a town or parish; **stent-roll** an assessment roll.

stent /stɛnt/ *noun*[2]. L19.
[Charles Thomas *Stent* (1807–85), English dentist.]
MEDICINE. **1** A substance for taking dental impressions; an impression or cast of a part or body cavity made of this, used to maintain pressure so as to promote healing, esp. of a skin graft. Freq. *attrib.* and in *possess.* L19.
2 A tube implanted temporarily in a vessel or part. M20.

stent *noun*[3] see STINT *noun*[1].

stent /stɛnt/ *verb*[1] *trans. Scot.* Pa. pple **-ed**, same. LME.
[Perh. aphet. from EXTEND.]
1 Extend, stretch out or set (a tent, sail, net, etc.) in its proper position. LME.

†**2** Extend (a person) *on* an instrument of torture. LME–E18.
†**3** Keep in place, stiffen, (a garment etc.). L15–M16.
Comb.: **stent-net** a fishing net stretched on stakes across a river.

stent /stɛnt/ *verb*² *trans.* Chiefly *Scot. obsolete* exc. *Hist.* ME.
[from STENT *noun*¹.]
1 Assess (a person, a community, etc.) for purposes of taxation. ME.
†**2** Levy (a sum of money) as an assessment; determine the amount of (an assessment). M17–E18.

stent *verb*³ see STINT *verb*.

stenter /ˈstɛntə/ *noun & verb*. M16.
[from STENT *verb*¹ + -ER¹.]
► **A** *noun*. †**1** A person who sets up (a tent). *Scot.* Only in M16.
2 = TENTER *noun*¹ 1. Now also, a machine through which fabric is carried mechanically while under sideways tension. E18.
► **B** *verb trans.* Stretch (fabric) by means of a stenter. L19.

stenting /ˈstɛntɪŋ/ *noun*¹. *Scot.* L15.
[from STENT *verb*¹ + -ING¹.]
†**1** Material used to stiffen a garment. L15–L18.
2 The action of STENT *verb*¹. E16.

stenting *noun*² see next.

stenton /ˈstɛnt(ə)n/ *noun*. Also **stenting** /-tɪŋ/. E19.
[Origin unkn.]
MINING. A narrow passage connecting two main headings in a coalmine, used to provide ventilation etc.

stentor /ˈstɛntə/ *noun*¹. *Scot. obsolete* exc. *Hist.* L16.
[from STENT *verb*² + -OR.]
An assessor of taxes.

Stentor /ˈstɛntɔː/ *noun*². Also **s-**. E17.
[A Greek herald in the Trojan war famous for his powerful voice.]
1 A person with a powerful voice. E17.
2 A trumpet-shaped sedentary ciliate protozoan of the genus *Stentor*. M19.

stentorian /stɛnˈtɔːrɪən/ *adjective*. E17.
[from prec. + -IAN.]
1 Of the voice, uttered sounds, etc.: very loud and far-reaching. E17.
2 That utters stentorian sounds. E17.
■ **stentorial** *adjective* (*rare*) = STENTORIAN M18. **stentorianly** *adverb* L19.

stentorious /stɛnˈtɔːrɪəs/ *adjective*. E16.
[formed as prec. + -IOUS.]
= STENTORIAN.
■ **stentoriously** *adverb* L17.

stentorophonic /stɛnt(ə)rə(ʊ)ˈfɒnɪk/ *adjective*. L17.
[mod. Latin *Stentorophonicus* from Greek *Stentorophōnikos* having the voice of a Stentor, formed as prec. + *phōnē* voice.]
1 ***stentorophonic horn***, ***stentorophonic trumpet***, ***stentorophonic tube***, a speaking trumpet. Now *Hist.* L17.
2 Very loud, stentorian. Now *rare*. L17.

step /stɛp/ *noun*¹.
[Old English *stepe*, *stæpe*, from West Germanic, from base of STEP *verb*.]
► **I** Action of stepping.
1 A single movement made by raising the foot from the ground and bringing it down in a fresh position, esp. as one of a sequence of such acts forming the process of walking, running, etc. OE. ▸**b** Manner of stepping when walking etc. OE. ▸**c** The sound made by a foot in walking etc.; a footfall. E17. ▸**d** Any of the distinctive foot movements of a particular dance. Also, a person's manner of executing such movements. L17. ▸**e** MILITARY. Pace in marching. L18. ▸**f** Usu. in *pl.* Any of various children's games; *esp.* = ***grandmother's steps*** s.v. GRANDMOTHER *noun*. E20. ▸**g** In full ***step aerobics***. A type of aerobics that involves stepping up on to and down from a portable block. L20.
2 In *pl.* The course followed by a person in walking etc. OE.
3 The space traversed in an act of stepping; a pace. OE. ▸**b** *sing.* & in *pl.* A very short walking distance. Chiefly in neg. contexts. OE. ▸**c** ELECTRICAL ENGINEERING. The movement through a fixed linear or angular distance made by a stepping device in response to an applied voltage pulse (see STEPPING *ppl adjective*). M20.
4 A degree in an ascending scale; a grade in rank or promotion. Freq. in ***get one's step***, ***get the step*** below. OE. ▸**b** MUSIC. An interval equal to one degree (tone or semitone) of the scale. Freq. in ***by step***, by progression through such intervals. Cf. LEAP *noun*¹ 4. L19.
5 The mark made by the foot in stepping; a footprint. ME. ▸†**b** *fig.* A trace or mark left by a material or immaterial thing. LME–L16.
†**6** [translating Latin *vestigium*.] The sole of the foot. *rare.* LME–E17.
7 *fig.* An action, measure, or proceeding, esp. one of a series, which leads towards a result. Freq. in ***take a step***, ***take steps***. M16. ▸**b** A stage in a gradual (freq. learning) process. E19. ▸**c** ASTRONAUTICS. = STAGE *noun* 11b. M20.

> 📖 **1** A. SILLITOE She walked in short quick steps. *fig.*: M. HOCKING Life is an act of faith, each step a venture into uncharted territory. **b** H. JAMES She quickened her step and reached the portico. W. F. BUCKLEY His bearing was manly, . . his step firm. **c** A. RADCLIFFE The steps of travellers seldom broke upon the silence of these regions. **d** W. J. FITZPATRICK They never saw him dance, though his small feet seemed naturally formed for 'steps'. ***e goose-step***, ***quick step***, ***slow step***, etc. **2** T. HARDY Instead of coming further she . . retraced her steps. D. BARNES The doctor . . directed his steps back to the café. *fig.*: E. J. TRELAWNY Envy, malice and hatred bedogged his steps. **3** G. GISSING Miriam moved a few steps away and seated herself. *fig.*: C. HARMAN The European war came a step nearer. **b** C. EASTON The house was just steps away from Hampstead Village. **4** L. M. MONTGOMERY It'll be a step up for a Plummer if you marry a Mitchell. **7** T. S. ELIOT Our first step must be to question Mrs. Guzzard. B. MONTGOMERY Drastic steps would have to be taken if we were to organise any . . defence. N. HERMAN They had . . made a . . break from home through the acceptable step of marriage. **b** B. JOWETT The regularity with which the steps of the argument succeed one another.

► **II** A thing on which to place the foot in ascending or descending.
8 A flat-topped structure used, singly or as one of a series, for passing from one level to another; a stair. Also, in *pl.*, a flight of (esp. outdoor) stairs. OE. ▸**b** FORTIFICATION. = BANQUETTE 1. L17. ▸**c** A flat projecting foot-piece, fixed or movable, for entering or alighting from a vehicle etc.; a projecting bracket attached to a bicycle to rest the foot on when mounting. E19. ▸**d** A foothold cut in a slope of earth or ice. M19. ▸**e** In Eton Fives, the shallow step which divides the court into an inner and outer part. L19.
9 A rung of a ladder; each of the flat crosspieces of a stepladder. OE. ▸**b** In *pl.* A stepladder. Also ***pair of steps***, ***set of steps***. *colloq.* L17.

> 📖 **8** M. KEANE Stone steps . . plunged downwards to the basement.

► **III** Transferred uses of sense 8.
10 NAUTICAL. The block in which is fixed the heel of a mast or capstan. OE.
11 An offset part resembling a step in outline, singly or in a series, as in the bit of a key. L17. ▸**b** AERONAUTICS. An edge with the form of an inverted step built across the float or hull of a seaplane or flying boat, which facilitates its separation from the water. E20.
12 MINING. A fault or dislocation of strata. Chiefly *Scot.* L18.
13 MECHANICS. The lower bearing or block on which a pivot, shaft, etc., rotates. E19.
14 SCIENCE. An abrupt change in the value of a quantity, esp. voltage. M20.

Phrases: **a good step**, **a tidy step**, etc., *colloq.* a considerable walking distance. **break step** cease marching etc. in step. **change step** reverse the order in which the feet are put forward in marching etc. **follow a person's steps**, **follow in a person's steps** *fig.* follow a person's example. **get one's step**, **get the step** *arch.* (chiefly MILITARY) be promoted to the next highest grade. **go up the steps** *slang* be sent for trial at a higher court, esp. the Old Bailey. ***hop, step, and jump***: see HOP *noun*². **in step** (*a*) putting the right and left foot forward alternately at the same time as others in marching etc.; *fig.* conforming with others; (*b*) ELECTRICITY (of two or more alternating currents) having the same frequency and always in the same phase. **keep step** remain in step with others in a march etc. **make a step** *arch.* = ***take a step*** (a) below. **mind one's step** = ***watch one's step*** below. **out of step** not in step. ***pair of steps***: see PAIR *noun*¹. **step by step** (*a*) moving one foot forward after the other continuously; *fig.* by gradual and regular progress; (*b*) keeping pace with another; (see also ***step-by-step*** below). **take a step** (*a*) perform a single act of stepping; (*obsolete* exc. *Scot.*) take a short journey (*to* a place); (*b*) see sense 7 above. **walk in a person's steps** *arch.* = ***follow in a person's steps*** above. **watch one's step** *colloq.* be careful where one puts one's feet when walking or (*fig.*) how one conducts oneself.

Comb.: ***step aerobics***: see sense 1g above; **step-bearing** = sense 13 above; **step-by-step** *adjective* (*a*) that advances step by step; (of a mechanism) moving with pauses at regular intervals; *spec.* in TELEPHONY, designating switching gear which makes successive contacts by alternating vertical and horizontal (rotary) movements; (*b*) *fig.* that proceeds through or involves a series of distinct stages or operations; **step-cut** *noun & adjective* (*a*) *noun* a method of cutting gems in straight facets round the centre; (*b*) *adjective* (of a gem) cut in this way; **step-dance**: intended to display special steps by an individual performer; **step-dancer** a person who performs a step-dance; **step fault** GEOLOGY each of a series of closely spaced parallel faults with successive falls like steps; the compound fault comprising such a series; **step flaking** ARCHAEOLOGY secondary flaking of a flint tool which produces a strong, ridged cutting edge; **step function** MATH. & ELECTRONICS a function that increases or decreases abruptly from one constant value to another; **step-gable** = CORBIE-***gable***; **step-gabled** *adjective* (of a house) having step-gables; **step iron** an iron projection on a wall serving as a support for the foot when ascending; **stepladder** a ladder which has flat steps instead of rungs; **step motor** a stepping motor (see STEPPING *ppl adjective*); **step-pyramid** ARCHAEOLOGY: having its faces built to form a series of large steps; **step response** ELECTRONICS the output of a device in response to a step input (see sense 14 above); **step rocket** ASTRONAUTICS a rocket of two or more stages; **step saver (kitchen)** *US* a kitchen designed to reduce the necessity of walking between units etc.; **step-stool** a stool which can convert into a short stepladder; **stepway** a path up or down steps; **step wedge** PHOTOGRAPHY a series of contiguous, uniformly shaded rectangles, getting progressively darker from white (or light grey) at one end to black (or dark grey) at the other.
■ **steplike** *adjective* resembling a step or series of steps E19.

step /stɛp/ *noun*². L19.
[Abbreviation: cf. STEP-.]
A stepfather; a stepmother; a stepchild etc.

step /stɛp/ *verb*. Infl. **-pp-**.
[Old English *steppan*, *stæppan* = Old Frisian *stapa*, *steppa*, Middle & mod. Low German, Middle & mod. Dutch *steppen*, Old High German *stapfōn*, *stepfen* (German *stapfen*), from West Germanic strong verb. Cf. STAMP *verb*.]
► **I 1** *verb intrans.* Lift the foot and put it down again in a new position; *esp.* perform this action with either of the two feet alternately in walking. OE. ▸**b** *verb trans.* Execute (a step etc.) with the foot. OE. ▸**c** *verb intrans. & trans.* Go through the steps or special paces of (a dance). L17. ▸**d** *verb intrans.* Esp. of a horse: move at a fast pace. M19.
2 *verb intrans.* Go or proceed on foot. Now chiefly (esp. in polite formulas or directions), go a step or short distance for a particular purpose. OE. ▸†**b** *fig.* Advance, proceed (in an action, argument, etc.). L16–M17.
3 *verb intrans. & trans.* (with *it*). Depart, make off. *colloq.* LME.

> 📖 **1** J. BUCHAN A figure who might have stepped out of a Raeburn canvas. J. CAREW Alice was drunk and she stepped carefully along the passage. L. HELLMAN I . . caught him as he was stepping into a taxi. **c** G. GREENE Baron Samedi, a grotesque figure in a ballet, stepping it delicately in his top-hat. **2** WILKIE COLLINS Will you step this way, and see her at once? A. HOLLINGHURST Step across the street and look up at the floors above. **3** *Munsey's Magazine* Well, I must be stepping . . . It's getting late.

► **II 4** *verb trans.* Set (foot) in a given place as a result of taking a step. Now *US*. M16.
5 NAUTICAL & MECHANICS. **a** *verb trans.* Fix securely in a groove, on a support, etc.; *esp.* fit (a mast) in its step. E18. ▸**b** *verb intrans.* Be fixed securely in a groove, on a support, etc.; *esp.* (of a mast) be fitted in its step. L18.
6 *verb trans.* Measure (a distance) by counting the steps it takes to traverse it. Also foll. by *out*. M19.
7 *verb trans.* MECHANICS. Cut steps in (a key etc.). M19.
8 *verb intrans.* Of an electromechanical device: move a small fixed distance in response to an input pulse. M20.
9 *verb trans.* Cause to move or progress intermittently; cause to assume successively larger or smaller values. M20.

> 📖 **4** *Times* The hostage crisis . . prompted the US State Department to ban its nationals from stepping foot in Lebanon.

Phrases & comb.: **step-and-repeat** *adjective* (PHOTOGRAPHY) involving or pertaining to a procedure in which performance of an operation and progressive movement of something involved in it occur alternately. **step astray** move from the right path (*lit.* & *fig.*). ***step into the breach***: see BREACH *noun* 8. ***step into the shoes of***: see SHOE *noun*. ***step lively***: see LIVELY *adverb* 3. **step on it** *colloq.* (orig. *US*) = ***step on the gas*** s.v. GAS *noun*². ***step on the gas***: see GAS *noun*². ***step on the toes of***: see TOE *noun*. ***step out of line***: see LINE *noun*².
With adverbs in specialized senses: **step back** go one or more paces backwards without turning the body round; *fig.* withdraw from prominence. **step down** (*a*) *verb phr. intrans.* (*fig.*) retire from a senior office, esp. to make way for another; (*b*) *verb phr. trans.* reduce the voltage of (a current) by means of a transformer. **step forward** advance and present oneself for a task, office, etc. **step in** (*a*) enter a house etc. casually or for a short visit; (*b*) intervene in an affair, dispute, etc., esp. at a senior level. **step off** mark off (distances) by successive equal movements of a pair of dividers. **step out** (*a*) *verb phr. intrans.* leave a place, esp. a house, for a short time; (*b*) *verb phr. intrans.* lengthen the pace in marching; (begin to) walk with vigorous strides; (*c*) *verb phr. intrans.* appear in company or society; *spec.* (*N. Amer. dial.* & *colloq.*) go out with a lover, have a romantic relationship *with*; (*d*) *verb phr. trans.* = ***step off*** above; (see also sense 6 above). **step up** (*a*) *verb phr. intrans.* come forward for some purpose; leave one's place and come close to a person; (*b*) *verb phr. trans.* increase the voltage of (a current) by means of a transformer; *fig.* intensify, increase.
With prepositions in specialized senses: **step into** (*a*) succeed at short notice to (an estate, office, etc.); †(*b*) enter suddenly and incautiously into (a course of action etc.). **step over** walk across (an intervening space, cavity, or obstacle); *fig.* miss or neglect in passing; be promoted to a position above (another considered to have a prior claim).

step- /stɛp/ *combining form*.
[Old English *stēop-*, corresp. to Old Frisian *stiāp-*, Old Saxon *stiof-*, Middle & mod. Dutch *stief-*, Middle Low German *stēf-*, Old High German *stiof-* (German *stief-*), Old Norse *stjúp-* rel. to Old English *āstieped* bereaved, Old High German *stiufen* bereave.]
Forming words denoting a person in a familial relation but unrelated biologically, orig. through a marriage of or with a widower or widow with one or more children, later through any marriage or marital relationship between persons either or both of whom have a child or children by another partner.
■ **stepbairn** *noun* †(*a*) an orphan; (*b*) *Scot.* a stepchild: OE. **stepbrother** *noun* a son, by another marriage or relationship, of

one's step-parent LME. **stepchild** *noun* †(*a*) an orphan; (*b*) a stepson or stepdaughter: OE. **stepdame** *noun* (*arch.*) a stepmother (now chiefly *fig.*) LME. **stepdaughter** *noun* a daughter, by another marriage or relationship, of one's husband or wife or *loosely* the person with whom one lives as if married OE. **stepfamily** *noun* a family including a stepchild or stepchildren M20. **stepfather** *noun* the husband of one's mother by another marriage; *loosely* the man, not one's biological father, with whom one's mother lives as if married OE. **step-parent** *noun* a stepfather or stepmother L19. **stepsire** *noun* (*arch.*) a stepfather ME. **stepsister** *noun* a daughter, by another marriage or relationship, of one's step-parent L15. **stepson** *noun* a son, by another marriage or relationship, of one's husband or wife or *loosely* the person with whom one lives as if married OE.

step-down /ˈstɛpdaʊn/ *adjective & noun.* L19.
[from *step down* s.v. STEP *verb*.]
▶ **A** *adjective.* **1** Causing or pertaining to a reduction in voltage or some other quantity. L19.
2 From or in which one steps to a lower level. Chiefly *US.* M20.
▶ **B** *noun.* **1** A reduction, a decrease. E20.
2 The action of stepping down or withdrawing from a position. L20.

stephane /ˈstɛfani/ *noun.* M19.
[Greek *stephanē* var. of *stephanos* crown.]
CLASSICAL ANTIQUITIES. A kind of diadem or coronet, represented in statuary as worn by the goddess Hera and other deities and also worn by military commanders.

stephanion /stɪˈfeɪnɪən/ *noun.* Pl. **-phania** /-ˈfeɪnɪə/, **-phanions.** L19.
[mod. Latin from Greek, dim. of *stephanos* crown.]
ANATOMY. The point on the skull where the coronal suture crosses the temporal ridge.
■ **stephanic** /-ˈfan-/ *adjective* L19.

stephanite /ˈstɛf(ə)nʌɪt/ *noun.* M19.
[from Archduke *Stephan* (d. 1867), Austrian mining director + -ITE¹.]
MINERALOGY. An orthorhombic sulphide of silver and antimony that occurs as brittle black crystals and is an ore of silver.

stephanotis /stɛfəˈnəʊtɪs/ *noun.* M19.
[mod. Latin (see below), from Greek *stephanōtis* fem. adjective 'fit for a crown or wreath', from *stephanos* crown, wreath.]
1 Any of several tropical twining shrubs constituting the genus *Stephanotis* (family Asclepiadaceae), characterized by fragrant waxy white flowers; esp. *S. floribunda*, grown as a hothouse plant (also called ***Madagascar jasmine***). Also, the blossom of this shrub. M19.
2 A perfume prepared from the flowers of *Stephanotis floribunda.* L19.

step-in /ˈstɛpɪn/ *noun & adjective.* E20.
[from *step in* s.v. STEP *verb*.]
▶ **A** *noun.* A garment or shoe put on by stepping into it; *spec.* in *pl.*, loose drawers or (more recently) brief panties for women (chiefly *US*). E20.
▶ **B** *attrib.* or as *adjective.* Designating a garment or shoe of this type. E20.

stepless /ˈstɛplɪs/ *adjective.* E19.
[from STEP *noun*¹ + -LESS.]
1 Having no step or steps. E19.
2 Continuously variable; able to be given any value within a certain range. M20.
■ **steplessly** *adverb* M20.

stepmother /ˈstɛpmʌðə/ *noun.* OE.
[from STEP- + MOTHER *noun*¹.]
1 The wife of one's father by another marriage; *loosely* the woman, not one's biological mother, with whom one's father lives as if married. OE.
2 *fig.* A person resembling a stepmother, esp. in exercising the spite and meanness traditionally ascribed to stepmothers. LME.
■ **stepmotherly** *adjective* pertaining to or characteristic of a stepmother M19. **stepmotherliness** *noun* stepmotherly quality L19.

Stepney /ˈstɛpni/ *noun.* Also **s-**. E20.
[Said to be from *Stepney* Street, Llanelli, Wales, the place of manufacture.]
A spare wheel for a motor vehicle, consisting of a ready-inflated tyre on a spokeless metal rim, which could be clamped temporarily over a punctured wheel (now *Hist.*); *gen.* in Bangladesh, India, and Malta, any spare wheel. Also more fully ***Stepney wheel***.

step-on /ˈstɛpɒn/ *adjective. US.* M20.
[from STEP *verb* + ON *preposition*.]
Operated by pressure of the foot.

†**stepony** *noun.* M17–L18.
[Perh. from *Stepney*, a district of London.]
A kind of raisin-wine, made from raisins with lemon juice and sugar added.

step-out /ˈstɛpaʊt/ *noun.* M20.
[from *step out* s.v. STEP *verb*.]
OIL INDUSTRY. In full ***step-out well***. A well drilled beyond the established area of an oil or gas field to find out if it extends further.

steppage /ˈstɛpɪdʒ/ *noun.* L19.
[French, from *stepper* to step (racing term), from STEP *verb*: see -AGE.]
MEDICINE. A peculiar high-stepping gait characteristic of certain nervous diseases.

steppe /stɛp/ *noun.* L17.
[Russian *step'*.]
Any of the vast level grassy usu. treeless plains of SE Europe and Siberia. Also, any similar plain elsewhere.
Comb.: ***steppe lemming***: see LEMMING 1; **steppe polecat** a reddish-brown polecat, *Mustela eversmanni*, occurring on the steppes and semideserts of Russia and Mongolia.

stepped /stɛpt/ *adjective.* M19.
[from STEP *noun*¹, *verb*: see -ED², -ED¹.]
1 Having a step or steps; MECHANICS (esp. of the float or hull of a seaplane or hydroplane) formed like a step or series of steps. M19.
2 Carried out or occurring in stages or with pauses, rather than continuously. M20.
3 With *up*: raised by degrees to a higher level; increased, intensified. M20.
Phrases: †**far stepped** far advanced in an action, attainment, etc. **stepped in years**, **well stepped in years** (long *arch.*) very elderly.

stepper /ˈstɛpə/ *noun.* M19.
[from STEP *verb* + -ER¹.]
1 A person or animal that steps, esp. (with specifying adjective) that steps in a specified way; *spec.* (*a*) a horse with good etc. paces; (*b*) a dancer, *esp.* a step-dancer. M19.
†**2** The treadmill. *slang.* M–L19.
3 In full ***stepper motor***. A stepping motor. M20.
1 ***high-stepper***: see HIGH *adjective*.

stepping /ˈstɛpɪŋ/ *noun.* LME.
[from STEP *verb* + -ING¹.]
1 The action of STEP *verb*; an instance of this. LME. ▶†**b** In *pl.* Footsteps, footprints. L16–M17. ▶**c** The step-by-step movement of a stepping device (see STEPPING *ppl adjective*). M20.
2 †**a** In *pl.* Steps, stairs. Also, stone for making steps. Only in 17. ▶**b** NAUTICAL. A rabbet taken out of the deadwood, for the heels of the timbers to step on. E19.
Comb.: **stepping-off place** = ***jumping-off place*** s.v. JUMPING *verbal noun*; **stepping-stile**: formed by steps projecting from a wall; **stepping-stone** (*a*) a raised stone (usu. one of a series) placed in the bed of a stream, on muddy ground, etc., to facilitate crossing on foot; (*b*) *fig.* something used as a means of advancement in a career or of making progress towards some object.

stepping /ˈstɛpɪŋ/ *ppl adjective.* M20.
[from STEP *verb* + -ING².]
Of an electric motor or other electromechanical device: designed to make a rapid succession of small equal movements in response to a pulsed input.

step-up /ˈstɛpʌp/ *adjective & noun.* L19.
[from *step up* s.v. STEP *verb*.]
▶ **A** *adjective.* **1** Causing or pertaining to an increase in voltage. L19.
2 Of a room or building: containing a step to a higher level. M20.
▶ **B** *noun.* **1** An increase in rate or quantity; an intensification. E20.
2 A step taken on to a platform and back again, repeated as a fitness exercise. Usu. in *pl.* L20.

stepwise /ˈstɛpwʌɪz/ *adverb & adjective.* L19.
[from STEP *noun*¹ + -WISE.]
▶ **A** *adverb.* **1** Like or in a series of steps. L19.
2 In a series of distinct stages; not continuously. L20.
▶ **B** *adjective.* **1** MUSIC. Occurring or arranged regularly in steps (STEP *noun*¹ 4b); conjunct. E20.
2 = ***step by step*** s.v. STEP *noun*¹. M20.

-ster /stə/ *suffix.*
[Repr. Old English *-istræ*, *-istre*, *-estre*, corresp. to Middle Low German *-(e)ster*, Middle Dutch *-ster*, from Germanic.]
Forming nouns from nouns or adjectives (formerly also from verbs) denoting a person (orig. a woman) engaged in or associated with a particular activity, esp. as an occupation or profession (cf. -ER¹), as ***brewster***, ***maltster***, ***spinster***, ***tapster***, etc., or denoting a person associated with a particular quality, as ***oldster***, ***youngster***, etc.; occas. *derog.*, as in ***jokester***, ***rhymester***, ***trickster***, etc.

steradian /stəˈreɪdɪən/ *noun.* L19.
[from Greek *stereos* solid + RADIAN.]
GEOMETRY. The SI unit of solid angle, equal to the solid angle subtended at the centre of a sphere by an area on its surface equal to the square of the radius of the sphere. (Symbol sr.)

sterane /ˈstɪəreɪn, ˈstɛreɪn/ *noun.* M20.
[from STER(OID + -ANE.]
MINERALOGY & CHEMISTRY. Any of a class of saturated hydrocarbons with a steroid structure, which are found in crude oils and are derived from the sterols of ancient organisms.

sterco- /ˈstɔːkəʊ/ *combining form* of Latin *stercor-*, *stercus* dung. Before a vowel also **stercor-** /ˈstɔːkər/.
■ **stercoˈbilin** *noun* the colouring matter of faeces, a breakdown product of the bile pigment bilirubin L19. **stercolith** *noun* (MEDICINE) a faecal concretion E20. **stercoˈraceous** *adjective* (*a*) consisting of, containing, or pertaining to faeces; faecal; (*b*) ENTOMOLOGY (of an insect) living in or feeding on dung; coprophagous: M18. **stercoral** *adjective* = STERCORACEOUS (a) M18. **stercoˈrarious** *adjective* (now *rare*) = STERCORACEOUS M17. **stercorary** *adjective & noun* (*a*) *adjective* (now *rare*) = STERCORACEOUS; (*b*) *noun* (now *rare* or *obsolete*) a place where manure is stored, a dungheap: M17. **stercorate** *verb trans.* (now *rare* or *obsolete*) manure, cover (the ground etc.) with dung E17. **stercoˈration** *noun* (now *rare*) (*a*) the action or an act of manuring the ground etc. with dung; †(*b*) dung, manure: E17. **sterˈcorean**, **sterˈcoreous** *adjectives* (*rare*) = STERCORACEOUS (a) M17. **stercoˈricolous** *adjective* (*rare*) living in dung or excrement L19. **stercorous** *adjective* (*rare*) = STERCORACEOUS (a) M16.

Stercoranism /ˈstɔːk(ə)r(ə)nɪz(ə)m/ *noun.* E18.
[formed as next + -ISM.]
ECCLESIASTICAL HISTORY. The beliefs of the Stercoranists.

Stercoranist /ˈstɔːk(ə)r(ə)nɪst/ *noun.* L17.
[from medieval Latin *stercoranista* irreg. from Latin *stercor-*, *stercus* dung + -IST.]
ECCLESIASTICAL HISTORY. (A nickname for) a person who holds that the consecrated elements in the Eucharist undergo digestion in, and evacuation from, the body of the recipient.

stercorarian /stɔːkəˈrɛːrɪən/ *noun & adjective.* M17.
[from Latin *stercorarius* STERCORARY + -AN.]
▶†**A** *noun.* **1** A physician following obsolete methods of practice. *derog. rare.* Only in M17.
2 = STERCORANIST. *rare.* Only in E18.
▶ **B** *adjective.* BIOLOGY. Designating trypanosomes which occur in the digestive tract of the secondary host, and are transmitted in its faeces. Cf. SALIVARIAN. M20.

sterculia /stɔːˈkjuːlɪə/ *noun.* M19.
[mod. Latin (see below), from Latin *Sterculius* god of manuring, with ref. to the putrid smell of some species.]
Any of numerous tropical trees constituting the genus *Sterculia* (family Sterculiaceae), with panicles of apetalous flowers and freq. with palmate leaves.

stere /stɪə/ *noun.* L18.
[French *stère* from Greek *stereos* solid.]
A unit of volume equal to one cubic metre (approximately 35.3 cu. ft).

sterelminthous /stɛrɛlˈmɪnθəs/ *adjective.* Now *rare* or *obsolete.* M19.
[from mod. Latin *Sterelmintha* (see below), irreg. from Greek *stereos* solid + *helminth-*, *helmins* intestinal worm: see -OUS.]
ZOOLOGY. Of or pertaining to a former taxon Sterelmintha comprising parasitic flatworms lacking a body cavity.

stereo /ˈstɛrɪəʊ, ˈstɪərɪəʊ/ *noun*¹. Pl. **-os.** E19.
[Abbreviation.]
= STEREOTYPE *noun* (*lit.* & *fig.*).

stereo /ˈstɛrɪəʊ, ˈstɪərɪəʊ/ *noun*² & *adjective*¹. L19.
[Abbreviation.]
▶ **A** *noun.* Pl. **-os.** = STEREOSCOPE. L19.
▶ **B** *adjective.* = STEREOSCOPIC. L19.
Special collocations & comb.: **stereo card** a card on which are mounted a pair of stereoscopic photographs. **stereo pair** a pair of photographs showing the same scene from slightly different points of view, so that when viewed appropriately a single stereoscopic image is seen.

stereo /ˈstɛrɪəʊ, ˈstɪərɪəʊ/ *noun*³ & *adjective*². *colloq.* M20.
[Abbreviation.]
▶ **A** *noun.* Pl. **-os.**
1 = STEREOPHONY. M20.
2 A stereophonic record-player, tape recorder, etc. M20.
2 ***personal stereo***: see PERSONAL *adjective*.
▶ **B** *adjective.* = STEREOPHONIC. M20.

stereo- /ˈstɛrɪəʊ, ˈstɪərɪəʊ/ *combining form.*
[from Greek *stereos*: see -O-.]
Forming scientific and technical terms with the sense (*a*) 'solid, in three dimensions'; (*b*) 'of or pertaining to the stereoscope' (cf. STEREO *noun*²).
■ **stereo-aˈcuity** *noun* the sharpness of the eyes in discerning separation along the line of sight M20. **stereoblock** *noun* (CHEMISTRY) a segment of a polymer chain possessing stereoregularity; ***stereoblock polymer***, a polymer with chains that contain such segments: M20. **stereo-camera** *noun* (PHOTOGRAPHY) a camera for simultaneously taking two photographs of the same thing from adjacent viewpoints, so that they will form a stereoscopic pair M20. **stereoˈcilium** *noun*, pl. **-lia**, ANATOMY an immotile cell process of certain epithelial cells of the male reproductive tract and the labyrinth of the ear, resembling a cilium at low magnifications M20. **stereocomˈparator** *noun* an instrument enabling two photographs of the same region to be seen simultaneously, one by each eye, either to detect any change (chiefly ASTRONOMY) or to make measurements E20. **stereoconˈtrol** *noun* (CHEMISTRY) control of a chemical synthesis by the choice of reagents and reaction conditions so as to produce a product with a desired stereochemical conformation L20. **stereoconˈtrolled** *adjective* (CHEMISTRY) (of a synthesis) that has been subjected to stereocontrol M20. **stereodiagram** *noun* a

diagram showing the three-dimensional structure of something M20. **stereoelecˈtronic** *adjective* (CHEMISTRY) pertaining to the relative positions of the electron orbitals in reacting molecules M20. **stereofluoˈroscopy** *noun* (MEDICINE) stereoradiography in which the images are viewed on a fluorescent screen E20. **stereoˈfluoroscope** *noun* (MEDICINE) an instrument for producing stereofluoroscopic images M20. **stereofluoroˈscopic** *adjective* (MEDICINE) of or pertaining to stereofluoroscopy E20. **stereogˈnosis** *noun* [Greek *gnōsis* knowledge] the stereognostic sense or faculty E20. **stereogˈnostic** *adjective* pertaining to the mental perception of the forms of solid objects by touch L19. **stereoˈmicrograph** *noun* a micrograph that conveys a vivid impression of depth, such as one obtained with a scanning electron microscope M20. **stereoˈmicroscope** *noun* a binocular microscope that gives a relatively low power stereoscopic view of the subject M20. **stereoˈmonoscope** *noun* (*obsolete* exc. *Hist.*) an instrument with two lenses by which an image of an object is projected upon a screen so as to appear solid, as in a stereoscope M19. **stereomuˈtation** *noun* (CHEMISTRY) the conversion of a *cis-* to a *trans*-isomer or vice versa M20. **stereoˈphantascope** *noun* (*obsolete* exc. *Hist.*) a form of kinetoscope giving a stereoscopic effect L19. **stereophanˈtasmascope** *noun* (*obsolete* exc. *Hist.*) = STEREOPHANTASCOPE M19. **stereophoto** *noun & adjective* (*a*) *noun* a stereophotograph; (*b*) *adjective* stereophotographic: E20. **stereophotograˈmmetric** *adjective* of or pertaining to stereophotogrammetry M20. **stereophotoˈgrammetry** *noun* photogrammetry by means of stereophotography E20. **stereoˈphotograph** *noun* a stereoscopic photograph M19. **stereophotoˈgraphic** *adjective* pertaining to or involving the use of stereophotography E20. **stereophoˈtography** *noun* the making of stereoscopic photographs E20. **stereoˈplanigraph** *noun* (CARTOGRAPHY) a machine which plots a map of an area semi-automatically under the guidance of the operator as he or she views a stereoscopic pair of aerial photographs of it E20. **stereoplotter** *noun* an instrument for plotting maps of an area from stereoscopic aerial photographs that are projected on to the plotting table E20. **stereo-ˈplotting** *adjective* functioning as a stereoplotter E20. **stereoˈradiograph** *noun* (MEDICINE) a stereoscopic radiograph M20. **stereoradioˈgraphic** *adjective* (MEDICINE) of or pertaining to stereoradiography M20. **stereoradioˈgraphically** *adverb* (MEDICINE) by means of stereoradiography M20. **stereoradiˈography** *noun* (MEDICINE) the science or process of making stereoscopic radiographs M20. **Stereoscan** *noun* (proprietary name for) a scanning electron microscope; (**s-**) a picture obtained with a scanning electron microscope: M20. **stereoˈspondylous** *adjective* (ZOOLOGY) (of a vertebra) that has its parts fused into one piece; (of an animal) that has such vertebrae: E20. **stereoˈstatics** *noun* the statics of solid bodies M19. **stereoˈtactic** *adjective* †(*a*) *rare* (BIOLOGY) = THIGMOTACTIC; (*b*) BIOLOGY & MEDICINE = STEREOTAXIC: E20. **stereoˈtactically** *adverb* = STEREOTAXICALLY M20. **stereoˈtelescope** *noun* a binocular telescope with widely-spaced objectives E20. **stereˈotomy** *noun* the science or art of cutting, or making sections of, solids; the branch of geometry that deals with sections of solid figures; the art of cutting stone etc. into measured forms: E18. **stereotropic** /-ˈtrəʊpɪk, -ˈtrɒpɪk/ *adjective* (BIOLOGY) pertaining to stereotropism E20. **stereotropism** /-ˈtrəʊp-/ *noun* (BIOLOGY) the growth or movement of an organism in response to a contact stimulus E20. **stereoˈviewing** *verbal noun* stereoscopic viewing M20.

stereobate /ˈstɛrɪə(ʊ)beɪt/ *noun.* M19.
[French *stéréobate* from Latin *stereobata* from Greek *stereobatēs*, formed as STEREO- + *-batēs* base, from *bainein* to walk.]
ARCHITECTURE. A solid mass of masonry serving as a foundation for a wall or a row of columns. Cf. STYLOBATE.

stereochemistry /ˌstɛrɪə(ʊ)ˈkɛmɪstri, ˌstɪə-/ *noun.* L19.
[from STEREO- + CHEMISTRY.]
The branch of chemistry that deals with theoretical differences in the relative position in space of atoms in a molecule, in relation to differences in the optical and chemical properties of the substances. Also, the stereochemical properties *of* something; a stereochemical configuration or arrangement.
■ **stereochemical** *adjective* pertaining to stereochemistry L19. **stereochemically** *adverb* as regards the relative spatial positions of atoms L19. **stereochemist** *noun* an expert in or student of stereochemistry M20.

stereochrome /ˈstɛrɪə(ʊ)krəʊm, ˈstɪərɪə(ʊ)-/ *noun.* M19.
[German *Stereochrom*, formed as STEREO- + Greek *khrōma* colour.]
= next. Also, a picture produced by stereochromy.

stereochromy /ˈstɛrɪə(ʊ)krəʊmi, ˈstɪərɪə(ʊ)-/ *noun.* M19.
[German *Stereochromie*, formed as prec.: see -Y³.]
A process of fresco-painting in which water-glass is used either as a medium for the paint or as a final preservative coat against atmospheric influences.

stereogram /ˈstɛrɪə(ʊ)gram, ˈstɪərɪə(ʊ)-/ *noun*¹. M19.
[from STEREO- + -GRAM.]
1 A diagram giving a three-dimensional representation of a solid object or surface. M19.
2 = STEREOGRAPH *noun* 1. M19.

stereogram /ˈstɛrɪə(ʊ)gram, ˈstɪərɪə(ʊ)-/ *noun*². M20.
[from STEREO *adjective*² + RADIO)GRAM *noun*².]
A stereo radiogram; a combined radio and record-player with stereophonic sound reproduction.

stereograph /ˈstɛrɪə(ʊ)grɑːf, ˈstɪərɪə(ʊ)-/ *noun & verb.* M19.
[from STEREO- + -GRAPH.]
▶ **A** *noun.* **1** A picture (or pair of pictures) representing an object so that it appears solid; a stereoscopic photograph. M19.
2 An instrument for making projections or geometrical drawings of skulls or similar solid objects. L19.
▶ **B** *verb trans.* Take a stereograph or stereoscopic photograph of (something). M19.

stereographic /ˌstɛrɪə(ʊ)ˈgrafɪk, ˌstɪərɪə(ʊ)-/ *adjective.* E18.
[mod. Latin *stereographicus*: see STEREO-, -GRAPHIC.]
1 Delineating or representing a three-dimensional body on a two-dimensional surface. E18.
2 = STEREOSCOPIC. M19.
1 stereographic projection: in which the angular relationships of lines and planes of the object represented are drawn in terms of their relationship to the great circle formed by the intersection of the equatorial plane with the surface of an imaginary sphere containing the object.
■ **stereographical** *adjective* (now *rare*) = STEREOGRAPHIC L17. **stereographically** *adverb* L17. **stereˈography** *noun* the art of delineating or representing the forms of solid bodies on a two-dimensional surface E18.

stereoisomer /ˌstɛrɪəʊˈʌɪsəmə, ˌstɪərɪəʊ-/ *noun.* L19.
[from STEREO- + ISOMER.]
CHEMISTRY. Any of two or more compounds that exhibit stereoisomerism.
■ **stereoisoˈmeric** *adjective* (of two or more compounds, or of one compound in relation to another) exhibiting stereoisomerism L19. †**stereoisomeride** *noun* = STEREOISOMER L19–M20. **stereoiˈsomerism** *noun* isomerism in which the atomic sequence is the same but the spatial arrangement of the atoms in the molecule is different L19. **stereoiˌsomeriˈzation** *noun* the conversion of one stereoisomer into another M20. **stereoiˈsomerize** *verb* (*a*) *verb intrans.* undergo stereoisomerization; (*b*) *verb trans.* cause the stereoisomerization of (a compound): M20.

stereolithography /ˌstɛrɪəʊlɪˈθɒgrəfi, ˌstɪərɪəʊ-/ *noun.* L20.
[from STEREO- + LITHOGRAPHY.]
A technique or process for creating three-dimensional objects, in which a computer-controlled moving laser beam is used to build up the required structure layer by layer from a liquid polymer that hardens on exposure to light.
■ **stereolithoˈgraphic** *adjective* L20.

stereology /stɛrɪˈɒlədʒi, stɪərɪ-/ *noun.* M20.
[from STEREO- + -LOGY.]
The science of the reconstruction of three-dimensional structures from two-dimensional sections of them.
■ **stereoˈlogical** *adjective* M20. **stereoˈlogically** *adverb* L20. **stereologist** *noun* M20.

stereome /ˈstɛrɪəʊm, ˈstɪərɪ-/ *noun.* Also **-om** /-əm/. L19.
[Greek *stereōma* solid body or part, from *stereoun* make solid, strengthen, from *stereos* solid.]
1 BOTANY. The strengthening or supporting tissue (esp. sclerenchyma and collenchyma) in a fibrovascular bundle. Cf. MESTOME. L19.
2 ZOOLOGY. A component of the exoskeleton of an invertebrate. L19.

stereometer /stɛrɪˈɒmɪtə, stɪərɪ-/ *noun.* E19.
[from STEREO- + -METER.]
1 An instrument for measuring the specific gravity of porous bodies or powders. E19.
2 CARTOGRAPHY. Any of various instruments for measuring the parallax of a feature depicted in a stereoscopic pair of aerial photographs. E20.

stereometric /ˌstɛrɪə(ʊ)ˈmɛtrɪk, ˌstɪərɪə(ʊ)-/ *adjective.* M19.
[mod. Latin *stereometricus*, formed as next: see -METRIC.]
Pertaining to stereometry or solid geometry; relating to or existing in three dimensions of space.
■ **stereometrical** *adjective* (now *rare*) = STEREOMETRIC M17. **stereometrically** *adverb* E20.

stereometry /stɛrɪˈɒmətri, stɪərɪ-/ *noun.* Now *rare*. L16.
[mod. Latin *stereometria*, from Greek, formed as STEREO- + -METRY.]
The art or science of measuring solids; solid geometry; the practical application of this to the measurement of solid bodies.

stereophonic /ˌstɛrɪə(ʊ)ˈfɒnɪk, ˌstɪərɪə(ʊ)-/ *adjective.* E20.
[from STEREO- + PHONIC.]
Of sound recording and reproduction: employing two or more channels of transmission and reproduction so that the sound output seems to be spatially distributed and to come from more than one source. Opp. MONOPHONIC 3.
■ **stereophonically** *adverb* M20.

stereophonics /ˌstɛrɪə(ʊ)ˈfɒnɪks, ˌstɪərɪə(ʊ)-/ *noun pl.* (treated as *sing.* or *pl.*). M20.
[formed as prec.: see -ICS.]
Stereophonic techniques; stereophonic sound.

stereophony /stɛrɪˈɒf(ə)ni, stɪərɪ-/ *noun.* M20.
[formed as prec.: see -PHONY.]
Stereophonic reproduction; stereophonic sound.

stereopsis /stɛrɪˈɒpsɪs, stɪərɪ-/ *noun.* E20.
[formed as STEREO- + Greek *opsis* power of sight.]
The ability to perceive depth and relief by stereoscopic vision.
■ **stereoptic** *adjective* of or pertaining to stereopsis M20. **stereoptically** *adverb* with an appearance of depth; stereoscopically: L20.

stereopticon /stɛrɪˈɒptɪk(ə)n, stɪərɪ-/ *noun.* M19.
[formed as STEREO- + Greek *optikon*, neut. of *optikos* OPTIC *adjective*.]
A type of projector arranged to combine two images of the same object or scene on a screen, giving an effect of solidity as in a stereoscope, or to cause one image to dissolve gradually into another.

stereoregular /ˌstɛrɪəʊˈrɛgjʊlə, ˌstɪərɪəʊ-/ *adjective.* M20.
[from STEREO- + REGULAR.]
CHEMISTRY. Of a polymer: having each substituent atom or group on the main polymer chain oriented in the same manner with respect to the neighbouring atoms or groups. Of a reaction: giving rise to such a polymer.
■ **stereoreguˈlarity** *noun* the state of being stereoregular M20. **stereoregulate** *verb trans.* cause (a polymerization or its product) to be stereoregular M20. **stereoreguˈlation** *noun* the act or process of stereoregulating M20.

stereoscope /ˈstɛrɪə(ʊ)skəʊp, ˈstɪərɪə(ʊ)-/ *noun.* M19.
[from STEREO- + -SCOPE.]
An instrument for obtaining, from two pictures (usu. photographs) of an object taken from slightly different points of view, a single image giving the impression of solidity or relief.
lenticular stereoscope, *reflecting stereoscope*, *refracting stereoscope*.
■ **stereoˈscopic** *adjective* of, pertaining to, or adapted to the stereoscope; having an appearance of solidity or relief: M19. **stereoˈscopically** *adverb* in a stereoscopic manner; by means of the stereoscope; with an appearance of solidity: M19. **stereˈoscopy** *noun* the art or practice of using the stereoscope M19.

stereoselective /ˌstɛrɪəʊsɪˈlɛktɪv, ˌstɪərɪəʊ-/ *adjective.* M20.
[from STEREO- + SELECTIVE.]
CHEMISTRY. Of a reaction: producing a particular stereoisomeric form of the product preferentially, irrespective of the configuration of the reactant.
■ **stereoselection** *noun* = STEREOSELECTIVITY M20. **stereoselectively** *adverb* M20. **stereoselecˈtivity** *noun* the property or fact of being stereoselective M20.

stereospecific /ˌstɛrɪəʊspɪˈsɪfɪk, ˌstɪərɪəʊ-/ *adjective.* M20.
[from STEREO- + SPECIFIC *adjective*.]
CHEMISTRY. **1 a** Of a reaction: = STEREOSELECTIVE. Of a catalyst: causing a reaction to be (more) stereoselective. M20. ▸**b** Of a polymer, esp. rubber: = STEREOREGULAR. M20.
2 Of a reaction or process: yielding a product, or having a rate, that depends on the particular stereoisomeric form of the starting material. M20.
■ **stereospecifically** *adverb* M20. **stereospeciˈficity** *noun* the property or state of being stereospecific M20.

stereotaxis /ˌstɛrɪə(ʊ)ˈtaksɪs, ˌstɪərɪə(ʊ)-/ *noun.* L19.
[from STEREO- + -TAXIS.]
BIOLOGY & MEDICINE. †**1** = THIGMOTAXIS. *rare*. L19–E20.
2 Stereotaxic surgery. M20.
■ **stereotaxic** *adjective* involving or designed for the accurate three-dimensional positioning and movement of probes etc. inside the brain E20. **stereotaxically** *adverb* by means of a stereotaxic technique M20. **ˈstereotaxy** *noun* = STEREOTAXIS 2 M20.

stereotype /ˈstɛrɪə(ʊ)tʌɪp, ˈstɪərɪə(ʊ)-/ *noun & adjective.* L18.
[French *stéréotype* adjective, formed as STEREO- + TYPE *noun*.]
▶ **A** *noun.* **1** *Hist.* A method of replicating a relief printing surface (as a page of type or a wood-engraving) by taking a cast using a mould orig. of papier-mâché or plaster, later of rubber, plastic, etc. L18.
2 A stereotype plate. E19.
3 a A thing continued or constantly repeated without change, *esp.* a phrase, formula, etc.; stereotyped diction or usage. E19. ▸**b** A preconceived, standardized, and oversimplified impression of the characteristics which typify a person, situation, etc., often shared by all members of a society or certain social groups; an attitude based on such a preconception. Also, a person or thing appearing to conform closely to such a standardized impression. E20. ▸**c** ZOOLOGY. A stereotyped action or series of actions performed by an animal. M20.

> 🕮 **3b** *Motor Trend* The grasping corporate exec stereotype normally portrayed by the media. *Entertainment Weekly* This . . article . . perpetuates the stereotype of the mechanic as a macho Neanderthal.

▶ **B** *attrib.* or as *adjective*. **1** Of or pertaining to the method of printing in which a stereotype is made; *spec.* (of an edition) printed using stereotypes. E19.
2 Reproduced in an unchanging manner; fixed, stereotyped. Now *rare*. E19.

> 🕮 **2** CARLYLE He . . answers now always with a kind of stereotype formula.

stereotype /ˈstɛrɪə(ʊ)tʌɪp, ˈstɪərɪə(ʊ)-/ *verb trans.* E19.
[French *stéréotyper*, formed as prec.]
1 *Hist.* Produce a stereotype plate from (a page or forme of type); prepare (a manuscript etc.) for printing by means of stereotypes. E19.

2 Reproduce or perpetuate in an unchanging or standardized form; cause to conform to a fixed or preconceived type. Chiefly as STEREOTYPED *ppl adjective*. E19.

> **1** W. IRVING I have nearly stereotyped the third volume of my Miscellanies. **2** P. JENNINGS In the early days . . he had dictated individual replies, but gradually a stereotyped form had evolved. P. D. JAMES To resist the temptation to . . stereotype him as the handsome, experienced seducer of cheap fiction.

■ **stereotyped** *ppl adjective* (*a*) that has been stereotyped; (*b*) ZOOLOGY (of an animal's action or behaviour) repeated though serving no obvious purpose: E19. **stereotypedness** *noun* (*rare*) L20. **stereotyper** *noun* E19.

stereotypical /ˌstɛrɪəʊˈtɪpɪk(ə)l, ˌstɪərɪəʊ-/ *adjective*. M20.
[from STEREOTYPE *noun* + -ICAL.]
Of, pertaining to, or resembling a stereotype or preconceived, standardized impression or attitude; *spec.* in PSYCHOLOGY, designating behaviour which is repeated without variation irrespective of circumstances.
■ **stereotypic** *adjective* = STEREOTYPICAL E19. **stereotypically** *adverb* E19.

stereotypy /ˈstɛrɪə(ʊ)tʌɪpi, ˈstɪərɪə(ʊ)-/ *noun*. L19.
[French *stéréotypie*, from STEREOTYPE *adjective* + -Y³.]
1 The process of making stereotype plates; stereotyping. L19.
2 PSYCHOLOGY. Abnormal persistence of a fixed or stereotyped idea, mode of action, etc., esp. in cases of autism or catatonia. E20.
3 ZOOLOGY. The frequent repetition by an animal of an action that serves no obvious purpose. M20.
4 The state or quality of being characterized as conforming to a stereotype. M20.

steric /ˈstɛrɪk, ˈstɪərɪk/ *adjective*. L19.
[Irreg. from Greek *stereos* solid + -IC.]
CHEMISTRY. Of or pertaining to the three-dimensional arrangement of the atoms in a molecule. Cf. STEREOCHEMISTRY.
steric hindrance hindrance of a reaction due to the spatial arrangement of the atoms in the molecules of one of the reacting compounds.
■ **sterically** *adverb* E20.

stericks /ˈstɛrɪks/ *noun*. *colloq. rare*. M18.
[Aphet. from *hysterics* (see HYSTERIC *noun* 2).]
Hysterics; a hysterical fit.

sterigma /stəˈrɪɡmə/ *noun*. Pl. **-mata** /-mətə/. M19.
[mod. Latin from Greek *stērigma* a support, from *stērizein* to fix, support.]
MYCOLOGY. A projection from a cell bearing a spore; *esp.* such a projection (usu. one of four) from a basidium.
■ **sterigˈmatic** *adjective* L19.

sterilant /ˈstɛrɪl(ə)nt/ *noun*. M20.
[from STERIL(IZE + -ANT¹.]
1 An agent used to make something free of plant life or micro-organisms; a herbicide, a disinfectant. M20.
2 An agent used to render an organism incapable of producing offspring. M20.

sterile /ˈstɛrʌɪl/ *adjective*. LME.
[Old & mod. French *stérile* or Latin *sterilis* cogn. with Sanskrit *starī*, Greek *steira* barren cow, *steriphos* barren, Gothic *stairō* (fem.) barren.]
1 a Infertile; barren; incapable of producing offspring; incapable of producing fruit; (of a cell, seed, etc.) incapable of reproducing or germinating. LME. ▸†**b** Causing sterility. *rare* (Shakes.). Only in E17.
2 Of soil, a country, a period of time, etc.: unproductive of vegetation or crops; barren. L16.
3 Mentally or spiritually barren; lacking vitality or creativity. Also, unproductive of results; unfruitful. M17.
4 Esp. of a surgical instrument etc.: free from micro-organisms, aseptic. L19.
5 Screened or cleared by security forces; *spec.* (of a telephone line) not tapped. Orig. *US*. L20.

> **1a** S. RUSHDIE You will find no children on this rock, sterile, every manjack of us. **2** C. DARWIN An utterly sterile land possesses a grandeur which more vegetation might spoil. **3** A. E. STEVENSON Instead of fresh ideas . . , our approach to world affairs has remained sterile and timid. W. MCILVANNEY The imposition of sterile theory upon the most creatively fluid ball-game in the world. **4** *Which?* AIDS kits . . contain sterile syringes and dressings.

Comb.: **sterile-male** *attrib. adjective* (ZOOLOGY) designating the technique of controlling a natural population by releasing large numbers of sterile males into it, so that females that mate only with these do not reproduce.
■ **sterilely** *adverb* L19.

sterilisation *noun*, **sterilise** *verb* vars. of STERILIZATION, STERILIZE.

sterility /stəˈrɪlɪti/ *noun*. LME.
[Old & mod. French *stérilité* or Latin *sterilitas*, from *sterilis*: see STERILE, -ITY.]
The quality or condition of being sterile; barrenness; asepsis; unproductiveness; incapability of producing offspring or fruit.

> SHAKES. *Lear* Hear, Nature . . . Into her womb convey sterility. A. GEIKIE A tree . . to relieve the sterility of these lonely shores. *New Republic* Stoppard's plays have been marked by . . ultimate sterility.

sterilization /ˌstɛrɪlʌɪˈzeɪʃ(ə)n/ *noun*. Also **-isation**. L19.
[from next + -ATION.]
The action or process of sterilizing a person, animal, or thing; *spec.* in ECONOMICS, control of the economy by inhibiting the use of resources or holding down money supply.

> B. SPOCK When nappies are . . washed at home, there is no sterilization and some of the bacteria . . stay alive.

sterilize /ˈstɛrɪlʌɪz/ *verb trans*. Also **-ise**. L17.
[from STERILE + -IZE, or Old & mod. French *stériliser*.]
1 Make sterile; cause to be unfruitful or unproductive. L17.
2 Deprive of the ability to produce offspring. E19.
3 Make mentally or spiritually barren; render unproductive, unfruitful or useless; reduce the vitality or creativity of. L19.
4 Make aseptic; render free from living micro-organisms. L19.
5 ECONOMICS. Inhibit the use of (resources) in order to exercise control over the economy, *esp.* control the balance of payments by taking offsetting action to hold down (the money supply). M20.
6 Preserve (a piece of land) as green belt; discourage or prevent building or development on (a piece of land). M20.

> **1** ANTHONY HUXLEY May partly sterilize the sea, destroying its plankton, algae and fish. **2** R. CLAY I'm never going to have children. I'm thinking of getting myself sterilized. **3** F. HARRISON: M. Grévy being sterilised by office, . . power fell to M. Gambetta. **4** B. SPOCK Thoroughly sterilized in the process of being tinned, so it is free of germs.

■ **sterilizable** *adjective* E20. **sterilizer** *noun* a person who or thing which sterilizes something; *spec.* (*a*) a substance causing sterility in soil; (*b*) an apparatus for sterilizing surgical instruments etc. by destroying micro-organisms: M19.

sterks /ˈstəːks/ *noun*. *Austral. slang. rare*. Also **sturks**. M20.
[Perh. abbreviation of STERCORACEOUS.]
A fit of depression, irritation, or annoyance. Usu. in ***give a person the sterks***, irritate or annoy a person.

sterlet /ˈstəːlɪt/ *noun*. L16.
[Russian *sterlyad'*.]
A small and delicate sturgeon, *Acipenser ruthenus*, found widely in eastern Europe and western Asia.

sterling /ˈstəːlɪŋ/ *noun*¹ & *adjective*. ME.
[Prob. from unrecorded late Old English noun, from *steorra* STAR *noun*¹ + -LING¹ (because some early Norman pennies bore a small star). Recorded earlier in Old French *esterlin* and medieval Latin *sterlingus*, *librae sterlingorum*, *librae sterilensium* pounds of sterlings.]
▸ **A** *noun*. **1 a** An English penny of the Norman and subsequent dynasties; a silver coin of this value. Freq. in ***pound of sterlings***, orig. a pound weight of silver pennies, later the English pound (240 pence) as a money of account. Also in ***pound sterlings***, ***mark sterlings***, ***shilling of sterlings***, etc. Long *obsolete* exc. *Hist.* ME. ▸**b** A Scottish penny. *Scot.* LME.
†**2** A pennyweight; a unit of weight equal to 24 grains (1/20 troy ounce). L15–L18.
3 Money of the quality of a sterling or standard silver penny; genuine English money. Formerly also *gen.* (*poet.*), money. Long *obsolete* exc. *Hist.* M16.
4 a British money. Formerly contrasted with *currency*, local money used in British colonies. E17. ▸**b** *fig.* A British-born Australian. *Austral. arch.* E19.
†**5** Standard degree of fineness. L17–E18.
6 Sterling silver tableware. L20.

> **3** R. GREENE So hard to descrie the true sterling from the counterfeit coyne. **4a** B. CASTLE There had been no run on sterling, despite the expenditure implications of the Queen's Speech. *Which?* Take some sterling (say, £50), for emergencies.

Comb.: **sterling area** a group of countries (chiefly of the British Commonwealth) that from 1931 to 1972 pegged their exchange rates to sterling, or kept their reserves in sterling rather than gold or dollars; **sterling balances** deposits in sterling held by overseas creditors in British banks.
▸ **B** *adjective*. **1** Of or in British money. Usu. *postpostive*. LME. ▸**b** Of an Australian person: born in Britain. *Austral. arch.* E19.
2 a Of legal English money or coin (now *rare*). Formerly (*Scot.*), of legal Scots money. LME. ▸†**b** *fig.* That has course or currency. M16–L17.
3 Orig., (of silver) having the same degree of purity as the penny. Later, (of silver or other precious metal) of standard value or purity. Freq. *spec.* in ***sterling silver***, silver of 92 per cent purity. L15.
4 Of a person, a person's character, qualities, etc.: of solid worth; reliable; excellent, genuine. M17.

> **1** *Arizona Daily Star* Schrikker's charts show both the U.S. dollar and the pound sterling in important uptrends. ***pound sterling***: see POUND *noun*¹ 2. **2a** SIR W. SCOTT Three shillings of sterling money of this realm. **pass as sterling**, **pass for sterling** (chiefly *fig.*) be accepted as genuine; reach the required standard (as for legal currency. **b** SHAKES. *Rich. II* If my word be sterling yet in England, Let it command a mirror hither straight. **4** *Sport* George, a sterling full-back . . in his playing days. K. M. E. MURRAY Sterling qualities of generous good humour, diligence and accuracy.

■ **sterlingly** *adverb* L19. **sterlingness** *noun* E19.

Sterling /ˈstəːlɪŋ/ *noun*². M20.
[The *Sterling* Armament Company Limited of London.]
(Proprietary name for) a sub-machine-gun made by the Sterling Armament Company Limited.

stern /stəːn/ *noun*¹. Now only *Scot.* Also **starn** /stɑːn/. ME.
[Old Norse *stjarna* star: see STAR *noun*¹.]
A star; a thing resembling or representing a star.
■ **sterny** *adjective* starry L15.

stern /stəːn/ *noun*². ME.
[Prob. from Old Norse *stjórn* steering, from base of *stýra* STEER *verb*¹. The existence of Old Frisian *stiārne*, *stiōrne* stern, rudder, may indicate that there was a corresp. form in Old English.]
1 The rear part of a vessel (as distinguished from the bow and midships); *spec.* that part of the vessel built around the sternpost, from the counter up to the taffrail. Also, the rear part of an aircraft; the rear part of any object. ME.
†**2 a** The steering gear of a vessel, the rudder and helm together; the rudder only; *rare* the helm only. LME–L17. ▸**b** *fig.* [from ***ship of State*** s.v. SHIP *noun* 1b.] That which guides or controls affairs, actions, etc.; government, rule. LME–E18.
3 The tail of an animal, esp. of a hound. Formerly also, the fleshy part of a horse's tail; the tail feathers of a hawk. L16.
4 The buttocks of a person or animal (freq. *joc.*); the rear part of any creature. E17.

> **1** D. PROFUMO Gulls billowed and creaked around the stern of the . . vessel. **stern foremost** backwards, with the stern or rear first. **stern on** with the stern presented. ***by the stern***: see BY *preposition*. **2b** F. MORYSON To the hands of these 28 Familyes, the Stern of the Commonwealth was committed. †**sit at the stern** govern, control; occupy the seat of government. **4** A. MACRAE She marched out . . , her stern twitching like an indignant duck's.

Comb.: **stern-boat** (*a*) a boat carried at a ship's stern; (*b*) an attendant boat following astern; **sterndrive** NAUTICAL (chiefly *N. Amer.*) an inboard engine connected to an outboard drive unit at the rear of a powerboat; **stern-fast** a rope by which a vessel's stern is moored; **stern-gland** packing round a propeller-shaft where it passes through the hull; **stern-line** = ***stern-fast*** above; **sternman** †(*a*) a steersman, a pilot; (*b*) a man posted in the stern of a boat; **stern-piece** †(*a*) a gun mounted in a vessel's stern; (*b*) a flat piece of wood to which the side planks of a vessel are brought, so as to terminate the hull behind; **stern-port** a port or opening in the stern of a vessel for a gun, the loading of cargo, ventilation, etc.; **stern-rail** (*a*) an ornamental moulding on a vessel's stern; (*b*) a rail running around the deck at a vessel's stern; **stern speed** the speed of a vessel travelling stern foremost with engines reversed; **stern-trawler** a trawler whose nets are operated from the stern of the vessel; **stern tube** (*a*) the tube through which the propeller-shaft of a steamship is passed for connection to the propeller; (*b*) a tube fitted in the stern of a warship from which torpedoes are fired; **stern-walk** (now *Hist.*) a roofed platform, connecting with the main cabin and built around the stern of certain large ships, esp. warships, which allowed the captain to take exercise without coming on deck; **sternway** the movement of a vessel going stern foremost; motion backwards through the water, either by the use of engines running astern, or by laying a sail aback.
■ †**sternage** *noun* (*rare*, Shakes.) the sterns of a fleet collectively: only in L16.

†**stern** *noun*³ var. of STARN *noun*¹.

stern /stəːn/ *adjective* & *adverb*.
[Old English *styrne* from West Germanic, prob. from West Germanic base also of STARE *verb*.]
▸ **A** *adjective*. **1** Of a person: severe, inflexible; rigorous in punishment or enforcing discipline. Also foll. by *with*, *to*, *towards*. OE. ▸**b** Of a personal attribute, action, utterance, etc.: strict, grim, harsh. ME. ▸**c** Rigorous in adherence to morals or principles; uncompromising, austere. LME.
2 †**a** Of a blow, a weapon: inflicting severe pain or injury. OE–E19. ▸**b** Of grief or pain: oppressive, hard to bear. Now *arch. rare*. ME. ▸†**c** Of the weather: severe, causing hardship. LME–E17.
3 †**a** Resolute in battle, fiercely brave, bold. Only in ME. ▸**b** Of battle, a sporting contest, debate, etc.: stubbornly contested, fierce. ME.
†**4** Merciless, cruel. ME–E17.
5 †**a** Terrible or threatening in appearance. ME–L16. ▸**b** Expressing grave displeasure; severe, strict, austere, or gloomy in appearance or tone of voice. ME.
6 a Of a country, its landscape, etc.: desolate, austere, inhospitable; forbidding, gloomy. LME. ▸**b** Of a building: severe in style; gloomy or forbidding in appearance. E19.

7 Of circumstances and conditions: oppressive, compelling; hard, relentless, inexorable. **M19.**

> 📖 **1** J. A. MICHENER A stern judge who had sentenced numerous persons to death. **b** R. HARLING A stern reminder that my next day's stint was still to do. **3b** *Motor Trend* Stern opposition will come from BMW's . . handsome coupe. **5b** MILTON Gods and men Fear'd her stern frown. **6a** H. F. TOZER The wild stern regions of European Turkey. **7** LD MACAULAY The great enterprise to which a stern necessity afterwards drove him.

Phrases: **be made of sterner stuff** be more resolute; be less inclined to yield, esp. to self-indulgence, weakness, emotion, etc. ***the sterner sex***: see SEX *noun*.

▶ **B** *adverb.* Sternly, resolutely, severely, harshly. Chiefly *poet.* **ME.**

> 📖 MILTON He shook his Miter'd locks, and stern bespake.

■ **sternful** *adjective* (*arch.*) full of sternness, severe, bold **LME.** **sternly** *adverb* **OE.** **sternness** /-n-n-/ *noun* **LME.**

stern /stəːn/ *verb.* **ME.**
[from STERN *noun*².]
†**1** *verb trans. & intrans.* Steer; govern. **ME–M17.**
2 a *verb intrans.* Of a boat: go stern foremost. **M19.**
▸**b** *verb trans.* Propel (a boat) stern foremost. **L19.**
3 *verb trans.* Cut off the stern or tail of (a dog). **M19.**

stern- *combining form* see STERNO-.

sterna *noun pl.* see STERNUM.

sternad /ˈstəːnad/ *adverb.* Now *rare* or *obsolete.* **E19.**
[from STERNUM + -AD³.]
ANATOMY. Towards the sternum or the sternal aspect; anteriorly.

sternal /ˈstəːn(ə)l/ *adjective & noun.* **M18.**
[from STERNUM + -AL¹, after *dorsal*, *ventral*.]
ANATOMY & ZOOLOGY. ▶**A** *adjective.* **1** Of, pertaining to, or connected with the sternum. **M18.**
2 Situated on the same side as the sternum; anterior (in man), ventral (in other animals). Now *rare* or *obsolete.* **E19.**
3 Of or pertaining to a sternum or sternite in an arthropod. **M19.**
▶ **B** *noun.* A sternal bone. **E20.**

stern-board /ˈstəːnbɔːd/ *noun.* **E19.**
[from STERN *noun*² + BOARD *noun*.]
1 *NAUTICAL.* ***make a stern-board***, go backwards as the result of tacking; force a ship astern with the sails. **E19.**
2 A board forming the flat part of the stern of a small boat, punt, etc. **M19.**

stern-chase /ˈstəːntʃeɪs/ *noun.* **E17.**
[from STERN *noun*² + CHASE *noun*¹.]
NAUTICAL. **1** A chase in which the pursuing vessel follows directly in the wake of the vessel pursued. **E17.**
2 *Hist.* The chase-guns of a ship. **L17.**

stern-chaser /ˈstəːntʃeɪsə/ *noun.* **E19.**
[from STERN *noun*² + CHASER *noun*¹.]
NAUTICAL. **1** *Hist.* An aft-firing gun mounted in the stern of a ship. **E19.**
2 The last vessel in a race. *rare.* **L19.**

sternebra /ˈstəːnɪbrə/ *noun.* Pl. **-brae** /-briː/. **L19.**
[mod. Latin, from STERNUM + ending of VERTEBRA.]
Chiefly *ZOOLOGY.* Any of the segments of the sternum, which in mammals usu. fuse during development.

sterned /stəːnd/ *adjective.* **E17.**
[from STERN *noun*² + -ED².]
Having a stern; (as 2nd elem. of comb.) having a stern of a specified kind.
black-sterned, ***pink-sterned***, etc.

Stern Gang /ˈstəːn gaŋ/ *noun phr.* **M20.**
[from Avraham *Stern* (1907–42), its founder.]
An underground militant Zionist organization founded as an offshoot of Irgun in 1940 and suppressed after the creation of Israel in 1948.
■ **Sternist** *adjective & noun* (**a**) *adjective* of or pertaining to the Stern Gang, its supporters, or its aims; (**b**) *noun* a member of the Stern Gang; an adherent or supporter of the Stern Gang or its aims: **M20.**

sternite /ˈstəːnʌɪt/ *noun.* **M19.**
[from STERNUM + -ITE¹.]
ZOOLOGY. A sclerite of a sternum of an arthropod; a section of the ventral exoskeleton. Cf. PLEURITE, TERGITE.

sternmost /ˈstəːnməʊst/ *adjective.* **E17.**
[from STERN *noun*² + -MOST.]
1 Farthest in the rear, last in a line of ships. **E17.**
2 Nearest the stern. **M19.**

Sterno /ˈstəːnəʊ/ *noun. US.* **E20.**
[from *Sternau* & Co., New York, USA + -O.]
(Proprietary name for) flammable hydrocarbon jelly supplied in cans for use as fuel for cooking stoves etc.

sterno- /ˈstəːnəʊ/ *combining form* of Greek *sternon* breast or Latin STERNUM: see -O-. Before a vowel also **stern-**.
■ **sternalgia** /-ˈnaldʒə/ *noun* [Greek *algos* pain] *MEDICINE* pain in the region of the sternum; *spec.* angina pectoris: **E19.** **sternoclaˈvicular** *adjective* (*ANATOMY*) pertaining to or connecting the sternum and clavicle **M19.** **sternocleidoˈmastoid** *adjective* (*ANATOMY*) pertaining to or connecting the sternum, clavicle, and the mastoid process of the temporal bone; *esp.* designating either of two muscles of the neck which serve to turn and nod the head: **E19.** **sternoˈcostal** *adjective* [Latin *costa* rib] *ANATOMY* pertaining to or connecting the sternum and the ribs **L18.** **sternoˈhyoid** *adjective* (*ANATOMY*) pertaining to or connecting the sternum and the hyoid bone; *esp.* designating either of two muscles that depress the larynx: **L19.** **sternoˈmastoid** *adjective* (*ANATOMY*) pertaining to or connecting the sternum and the mastoid process of the temporal bone; *esp.* = STERNOCLEIDOMASTOID: **M19.** **sternomaˈxillary** *adjective* (*ZOOLOGY*) pertaining to or connecting the sternum and the mandible **L19.** **sternoperiˈcardial** *adjective* (*ANATOMY*) pertaining to or connecting the sternum and the pericardium **E20.** **sternoˈpleural** *adjective* (*ENTOMOLOGY*) of or pertaining to the sternopleuron **E20.** **sternoˈpleuron** *noun*, pl. **-ra** /-rə/, *ENTOMOLOGY* in flies etc., either of two thoracic sclerites to which the middle two legs are attached **L19.** **sternoˈthyroid** *adjective* (*ANATOMY*) pertaining to or connecting the sternum and the thyroid cartilage **M19.** **sternoˈvertebral** *adjective* pertaining to the sternum and the vertebrae **M19.**

sternpost /ˈstəːnpəʊst/ *noun.* Also **stern-post.** **L16.**
[from STERN *noun*² + POST *noun*¹.]
1 *NAUTICAL.* The aftermost vertical support of a vessel, joined to the keel and (in small vessels) usu. bearing the vessel's rudder. **L16.**
2 A structure in the hull of an aircraft or the float of a seaplane, analogous to the sternpost of a ship. **M20.**

sternsheet /ˈstəːnʃiːt/ *noun.* Also **stern-sheet.** **L15.**
[from STERN *noun*² + SHEET *noun*².]
NAUTICAL. **1** *sing.* & in *pl.* The stern section of an open boat; *spec.* that part between the stern and the after thwart. **L15.**
†**2** In *pl.* The ropes controlling the mizzen-sail. Only in **E17.**
3 In *pl.* The flooring planks in a boat's after section; the seats in this section. **M17.**

sternson /ˈstəːns(ə)n/ *noun.* **M19.**
[from STERN *noun*² after KEELSON. Cf. STEMSON.]
NAUTICAL. In a wooden vessel, a knee-shaped timber reinforcing the angle formed by the junction of the sternpost and the keelson.

sternum /ˈstəːnəm/ *noun.* Pl. **-na** /-nə/, **-nums.** **M17.**
[mod. Latin from Greek *sternon* chest, breast.]
ANATOMY & ZOOLOGY. **1** The breastbone; a long bone or cartilage, or series of bones, present in most vertebrates, extending along the midline of the front or ventral aspect of the thorax, usu. articulating with some of the ribs, and in most birds extended ventrally into a large keel. **M17.**
2 In arthropods, a sclerotized region forming the ventral part of each segment of the body. Cf. PLEURON, TERGUM. **M19.**

sternutation /stəːnjʊˈteɪʃ(ə)n/ *noun.* **LME.**
[Latin *sternutatio(n-)*, from *sternutare* frequentative of *sternuere* sneeze: see -ATION.]
1 The action of sneezing; a sneeze. Chiefly *MEDICINE* or *joc.* **LME.**
†**2** = STERNUTATORY *noun.* **M16–L17.**

sternutatory /stəːˈnjuːtət(ə)ri/ *adjective & noun.* **E17.**
[Late Latin *sternutatorius* adjective and medieval Latin *sternutatorium* sneezing powder, formed as prec.: see -ORY².]
▶ **A** *adjective.* **1** Causing or tending to cause sneezing. **E17.**
2 Of or pertaining to sneezing. Freq. *joc.* **M19.**
▶ **B** *noun.* An agent, esp. a drug, that causes sneezing. **M17.**
■ **sterˈnutative** *adjective & noun* (now *rare*) = STERNUTATORY **M17.** **ˈsternutator** *noun* an agent that causes sneezing; *esp.* a gas used in chemical warfare that causes irritation of the nose and eyes, pain in the chest, and nausea: **E20.** **ˈsternutory** *noun* (now *rare*) = STERNUTATORY *noun* **LME.**

sternward /ˈstəːnwəd/ *adjective & adverb.* **M19.**
[from STERN *noun*² + -WARD.]
Astern, (moving or directed) towards the stern.
■ **sternwards** *adverb* = STERNWARD *adverb* **L19.**

stern-wheel /ˈstəːnwiːl/ *noun & verb.* **E19.**
[from STERN *noun*² + WHEEL *noun*.]
▶ **A** *noun.* A paddle-wheel positioned at the stern of a small river or lake steamer. **E19.**

> 📖 *attrib.*: M. TWAIN You kick up the water like a stern-wheel boat.

▶ **B** *verb intrans.* Of a boat: move by the agency of a stern-wheel. **E19.**
■ **sternwheeler** *noun* a boat propelled by a stern-wheel **M19.**

steroid /ˈstɪərɔɪd, ˈstɛrɔɪd/ *noun.* **M20.**
[from STER(OL + -OID.]
BIOCHEMISTRY. Any of a large class of organic compounds characterized by a nucleus of three six-membered carbon rings and one five-membered carbon ring, the members of which include the sterols, most sex and adrenocortical hormones, bile acids, and many other compounds with important physiological effects. Freq. *attrib.*, as ***steroid chemistry***, ***steroid hormone***, ***steroid nucleus***.
ANABOLIC ***steroid***. *KETOGENIC* ***steroid***.
■ **steˈroidal** *adjective* of, pertaining to, or of the nature of a steroid **M20.** **steroidoˈgenesis** *noun* the biosynthesis of steroids **M20.** **steˌroidoˈgenic** *adjective* pertaining to or of the nature of steroidogenesis **M20.**

sterol /ˈstɪərɒl, ˈstɛrɒl/ *noun.* **E20.**
[The ending of CHOLESTEROL, ERGOSTEROL, etc., used as a separate word.]
BIOCHEMISTRY. Any of a class of solid, waxy, unsaturated steroid alcohols that occur naturally both free and in combination as esters or glycosides.

-sterol /stərɒl/ *suffix.*
[from CHOLE)STEROL.]
BIOCHEMISTRY. A formative element in the names of many sterols, as ***ergosterol***, ***phytosterol***.

-sterone /ˈstɪərəʊn, stərəʊn/ *suffix.*
[from STER(OL + KET)ONE.]
BIOCHEMISTRY. A formative element in the names of some steroids, as ***androsterone***, ***progesterone***.

sterro /ˈstɛrəʊ/ *adjective.* **M19.**
[Greek *sterros* stiff, hard.]
sterro alloy, ***sterro metal***, a high strength brass used for castings, containing a small amount of iron and manganese.

stertor /ˈstəːtɔː, ˈstəːtə/ *noun.* **E19.**
[mod. Latin (after *rigor* etc.), from Latin *stertere* to snore: see -OR.]
Chiefly *MEDICINE.* A heavy snoring sound, as that accompanying breathing in a deeply unconscious person.

stertorous /ˈstəːt(ə)rəs/ *adjective.* **E19.**
[from prec. + -OUS.]
Esp. of breathing: characterized by or of the nature of stertor; sounding like snoring; heavy.

> 📖 P. L. FERMOR A long stertorous note . . from the next bed woke me with a start.

■ **stertorously** *adverb* **M19.** **stertorousness** *noun* **M19.**

stet /stɛt/ *noun & verb.* **M18.**
[Latin, 3rd person sing. pres. subjunct. of *stare* = let it stand.]
▶ **A** *noun.* A direction in the margin of a proof-sheet etc. indicating that a correction or deletion should be ignored and that the original matter is to be retained. **M18.**
▶ **B** *verb trans.* Infl. **-tt-**. Cancel the correction or deletion of; write 'stet' against (an accidental deletion, miscorrection, etc.). **L19.**

stetho- /ˈstɛθəʊ/ *combining form.* Before a vowel also **steth-**.
[from Greek *stēthos* breast, chest: see -O-.]
MEDICINE. Of or pertaining to the chest.
■ **steˈthendoscope** *noun* (now *rare*) a fluoroscope for examining the chest **L19.** **stethogram** *noun* a stethographic tracing **L19.** **stethophone** *noun* a stethoscope, *esp.* one enabling several people to hear stethoscopic sounds simultaneously **M19.**

stethograph /ˈstɛθəgrɑːf/ *noun.* **L19.**
[from prec. + -GRAPH.]
MEDICINE. An instrument for recording the movements of the chest during breathing. Also called ***pneumograph***.
■ **stethographic** /-ˈgrafɪk/ *adjective* pertaining to or made by the stethograph **L19.** **stethography** /stɪˈθɒgrəfi/ *noun* the action or use of a stethograph **L19.**

stethometer /stɪˈθɒmɪtə/ *noun.* **M19.**
[from STETHO- + -METER.]
MEDICINE. An instrument for measuring the expansion of the chest in breathing.
■ **stethoˈmetric** *adjective* pertaining to or obtained by means of a stethometer **L19.** **stethometry** /stɪˈθɒmɪtri/ *noun* measurement by a stethometer; the use of a stethometer: **L19.**

stethoscope /ˈstɛθəskəʊp/ *noun & verb.* **E19.**
[from STETHO- + -SCOPE.]
▶ **A** *noun.* An instrument for examining the chest etc. by auscultation, conveying the sounds of the heart, lungs, etc. to the ear of the observer. **E19.**
▶ **B** *verb trans.* Apply a stethoscope to; examine with a stethoscope. Now *rare.* **M19.**
■ **stethoscoped** *adjective* equipped with a stethoscope **L20.** **stethoscopic** /-ˈskɒpɪk/ *adjective* pertaining to, of the nature of, observed or obtained by a stethoscope **E19.** **stethoˈscopical** *adjective* (now *rare*) = STETHOSCOPIC **M19.** **stethoˈscopically** *adverb* by means of the stethoscope **M19.** **steˈthoscopist** *noun* (now *rare*) a person who uses a stethoscope **E19.** **steˈthoscopy** *noun* examination of the chest or other part with a stethoscope; the use of a stethoscope: **M19.**

stet processus /stɛt prə(ʊ)ˈsɛsəs/ *noun phr.* **M19.**
[Latin = let process be stayed.]
LAW. An entry on the roll staying all further proceedings in an action by consent of the parties; an order granting a stay of this kind.

Stetson /ˈstɛts(ə)n/ *noun.* **L19.**
[John Batterson *Stetson* (1830–1906), Amer. hat manufacturer.]
(US proprietary name for) any of various hats made by the Stetson company; *spec.* a slouch hat with a broad brim and high crown associated with cowboys of the western US. Also ***Stetson hat***.
■ **Stetsoned** *adjective* wearing a Stetson **M20.**

Steuben /st(j)uːˈbɛn, ˈst(j)uːbən/ *noun & adjective*. **E20.**
[The *Steuben* Glass Works at Corning, New York, founded in 1903.]
(Designating) fine glassware made at the Steuben Glass Works, esp. the decorative engraved crystal produced there since 1933.

stevedore /ˈstiːvədɔː/ *noun & verb*. **L18.**
[Spanish *estibador* (Portuguese *estivador*), from Old & mod. Spanish *estibar* (Portuguese *estivar*, French *estiber*) stow a cargo from Latin *stipare* crowd or press together. Cf. STEEVE *verb*[2], STIVE *verb*[1].]
▶ **A** *noun*. A person employed in loading and unloading the cargoes of ships. **L18.**
▶ **B** *verb trans.* **1** Stow (cargo) in a ship's hold. **M19.**
2 Load or unload the cargo of (a ship). **L19.**
■ **stevedorage** *noun* (*rare*) (the charge made for) the loading and unloading of cargoes **M19.** **stevedoring** *noun* the action of the verb; the charge made for handling cargo: **L19.**

steven /ˈstɛv(ə)n/ *noun*[1]. *obsolete* exc. *dial.*
[Old English *stefn*, *stemn*, corresp. to Old Frisian *stifne*, *stemne*, Old Saxon *stemn(i)a*, *stemma*, Old High German *stimna*, *stimma* (German *Stimme*), Gothic *stibna*, from Germanic.]
1 The voice; now *esp.* a loud or strong voice. **OE.** ▶†**b** A cry, a petition, a prayer. **ME–L16.**
2 Outcry, tumult, din. Formerly also, sound, noise (of singing, music, etc.). **OE.**
📖 **1** G. E. MACKAY He . . lifted up his steven To keep the bulwarks of his faith secure. **2** JAS. HOGG All nature roar'd in one dire steven.

steven /ˈstɛv(ə)n/ *noun*[2]. *arch. slang*. **E19.**
[Origin unkn.]
Money.

†**steven** *noun*[3] see STEM *noun*[2].

steven /ˈstɛv(ə)n/ *verb*[1]. Long *obsolete* exc. *dial.*
[Old English *stefnan*, *stæfnan*, from *stefn* a time, turn, occasion, rel. to Old Norse *stefna* fix a time, summon.]
†**1** *verb intrans.* Alternate, take turns. Only in **OE.**
†**2** *verb trans.* Appoint, constitute. **OE–LME.**
†**3** *verb trans.* Specify, state, indicate. Only in **L15.**
4 *verb trans.* Order, ask for. *dial.* **L17.**

steven /ˈstɛv(ə)n/ *verb*[2]. Long *obsolete* exc. *dial.* **ME.**
[from STEVEN *noun*[1].]
1 *verb intrans.* Make an uproar, shout. **ME.**
2 *verb trans.* Deafen with noise. **M19.**

Stevengraph /ˈstiːv(ə)ngrɑːf/ *noun*. **L19.**
[from Thomas *Stevens* (1828–88), a ribbon weaver of Coventry + -GRAPH.]
(Proprietary name for) a type of coloured woven silk picture produced during the late 19th cent. by the firm founded by Stevens.

Stevensonian /stiːv(ə)nˈsəʊnɪən/ *adjective & noun*. **L19.**
[from *Stevenson* (see below) + -IAN.]
▶ **A** *adjective*. Of, pertaining to, or characteristic of the Scottish writer Robert Louis Stevenson (1850–94) or his writings. **L19.**
▶ **B** *noun*. An admirer or student of R. L. Stevenson or of his writings. **E20.**

Stevenson screen /ˈstiːv(ə)ns(ə)n skriːn/ *noun phr.* **L19.**
[Thomas *Stevenson* (1818–87), Scottish engineer and meteorologist.]
METEOROLOGY. A wooden box supported on a stand, usu. painted white, and made with doubly louvred sides and a double top with ventilation holes, so that thermometers etc. inside it effectively register the properties of the outside air.

stevioside /ˈstiːvɪəsʌɪd/ *noun*. **M20.**
[from mod. Latin *Stevia* (see below), from P. J. *Esteve* (d. 1566), Spanish botanist + -IA[1]: see -OSIDE.]
CHEMISTRY. A glycoside present in the leaves of the Paraguayan shrub *Stevia rebaudiana* (of the composite family), comparable in sweetness to saccharin.

stew /stjuː/ *noun*[1]. **ME.**
[Old French *estuve* (mod. *étuve*) rel. to *estuver*: see STEW *verb*. In branch II directly from the verb.]
▶ **I** †**1** A cauldron. **ME–E17.**
†**2 a** A heated room; a room with a fireplace. **LME–L16.** ▶**b** A hatter's drying room. *rare*. Only in **M19.**
3 A heated room used for hot steam baths: a hot bath. Now *arch.* or *Hist.* **LME.**
4 A brothel; a quarter or district occupied by brothels. Usu. in *pl.* Formerly also in *pl.* treated as *sing. arch.* **LME.** ▶†**b** *sing.* & in *pl.* A bawd; a prostitute. **M16–M17.**
📖 **3** A. HENRY Stews, . . or sweating-houses, are resorted to for cure of sickness. **4** J. HATTON He frequented the dens and fashionable stews of the metropolis.
▶ **II 5** A dish, usually consisting of meat or fish with various vegetables, cooked in a closed vessel by stewing. **M18.**
6 An agitated, anxious, or angry state. *colloq.* **E19.**
7 A state of being overheated or bathed in perspiration. *colloq.* **L19.**
📖 **5** *fig.*: R. SILVERBERG The cult was an international stew, a mix of Brazilian and Guinean stuff. ***Irish stew***: see IRISH *adjective*. **6** C. JACKSON Silly . . of her mother to get into such a stew about speaking to strangers.
Comb.: **stew-bum** *US slang* a tramp, *esp.* one who is habitually drunk; **stewpack** a selection of prepared vegetables packaged together and sold ready for use in a stew.

stew /stjuː/ *noun*[2]. **ME.**
[Old French *estui* place of confinement, fish-pond (mod. *étui* case, sheath), from *estoier* put into the sheath, shut up, conceal, reserve, from Proto-Romance, from Latin *studium* STUDY *noun*. Cf. ETUI, TWEEZE *noun*.]
1 A pond or tank in which edible fish are kept until needed for the table, (also ***stew-pond***). Formerly also (*rare*), a pond of any kind; a moat. **ME.**
2 An artificial oyster-bed. **E17.**
1 †**in stew** [Old French *en estui*] (of fish) kept in captivity until needed for the table.

stew /stuː, stjuː/ *noun*[3]. *N. Amer. colloq.* **L20.**
[Abbreviation.]
An air stewardess.

stew /stjuː/ *verb*. **LME.**
[Old French *estuver* (mod. *étuver*) from Proto-Romance, prob. ult. from EX-[1] + Greek *tuphos* smoke, steam, perh. also infl. by Germanic base of STOVE *noun & verb*[1]. Cf. STIVE *verb*[2].]
†**1** *verb trans.* Bathe (a person etc.) in a hot bath or a steam bath. **LME–M17.**
2 a *verb trans.* Cook (meat, fruit, etc.) slowly in simmering liquid in a closed vessel. Also, make (tea) strong or bitter due to prolonged brewing. **LME.** ▶**b** *verb intrans.* Of meat, fruit, etc.: undergo cooking by slow simmering in a closed vessel. Also, (of tea) become strong or bitter due to prolonged brewing. **L16.**
3 *transf.* **a** *verb trans.* Confine in an enclosed or poorly-ventilated space. Usu. foll. by *up*. *arch.* **L16.** ▶†**b** *verb trans.* Bathe in perspiration. Only in **17.** ▶**c** *verb trans. fig.* Soak, steep, imbue. Long *rare* or *obsolete*. **E17.** ▶**d** *verb intrans.* Stay excessively long in bed. Also, remain in a heated or stifling atmosphere. **L17.** ▶**e** *verb intrans.* Study hard. *colloq.* **M19.** ▶**f** *verb intrans.* Fret; be in an agitated, angry, or anxious state. Freq. foll. by *over*. **E20.**
📖 **2a** *Vogue* Soups . . made with a mixture of fresh and dried onions stewed in stock. **b** W. H. CANAWAY The tea stewed for fifteen minutes or so. **3a** J. SINCLAIR Cattle suffer much from being . . stewed close up in a low-roofed cow-house. **c** HAZLITT An opinion is vulgar that is stewed in the rank breath of the rabble. **d** P. H. NEWBY It was the height of summer, . . and in Port Said they'd be stewing. **f** *Tucson Magazine* City planners don't just sit around and stew over traffic congestion.
Phrases: **leave to stew**, **let stew** *fig.* keep in a state of uneasy anticipation or suspense. **leave to stew in one's own juice**, **let stew in one's own juice** *fig.* leave to suffer the likely consequences of one's own actions; leave to one's own devices.
■ **stewable** *adjective* **L19.** **stewy** *adjective* (*rare*) having a stewed or strong flavour; suggestive of being stewed: **L19.**

steward /ˈstjʊəd/ *noun & verb*. As noun also (*Scot. & north.*) **-art** /-ət/.
[Old English *stigweard*, *stīweard*, from *stig* (prob.) house, hall + *weard* WARD *noun*.]
▶ **A** *noun*. **1 a** An official appointed to control the domestic affairs of a household, esp. the supervision of servants and the regulation of household expenditure. *obsolete* exc. *Hist.* **OE.** ▶**b** Orig., an officer in a ship responsible for keeping the stores and arranging for the serving of meals. Now, a passengers' attendant on a ship. Freq. with specifying word. **LME.** ▶**c** An employee of a college or club responsible for the administration and supervision of catering arrangements. **E16.** ▶**d** At Oxford University, a member of a college elected to supervise the catering or to preside at table. **M18.** ▶**e** A person employed as a passengers' attendant on a train or aircraft. **E20.**
2 Orig., an officer of a royal household with similar functions to the steward of an ordinary household (see sense 1). Later, an (esp. hereditary) office in the household of an English medieval sovereign held only by a great noble of the realm. *obsolete* exc. *Hist.* **OE.**
3 *fig.* An administrator and dispenser of wealth, favours, etc.; *esp.* (after biblical use) a dispenser of wealth etc. regarded as the servant of God or of the people. **OE.**
4 a *Hist.* An officer in a guild, usually ranking next to the alderman and acting as his assistant. **OE.** ▶**b** In certain livery companies, each of two or more officers in charge of arrangements for the annual dinner. **E17.** ▶**c** (The title of) any of various officers of certain societies serving on an executive committee. **M19.**
†**5** A deputy-governor, a vice-gerent. **ME–M17.**
6 An overseer, a foreman; later *spec.*, a subordinate to the manager of a colliery, to whom the overmen and deputies report regarding the state of the mine. Also, a shop steward of a trade union. **ME.**
7 a A person employed to manage the affairs of an estate. Also, (the title of) the administrator, often with merely nominal duties, of certain estates of the Crown, as ***Steward of Blackburn Hundred***, ***Steward of the Chiltern Hundreds***, etc. **ME.** ▶**b** In Scotland: a magistrate formerly appointed by the sovereign to administer the crown lands forming a stewartry, a judicial office equivalent to that of a sheriff. *obsolete* exc. *Hist.* **LME.**
8 A corporation official, whose rank and duties vary widely in different municipalities. Freq. with specifying word. **LME.**
9 An official appointed to supervise the arrangements or maintain order at a race meeting, show, demonstration, etc. **E18.**
10 In the Methodist Church: a layman appointed to manage the financial affairs of a congregation or of a circuit. **M18.**
📖 **1b** ***cabin-steward***, ***chief steward***, ***deck-steward***, etc. **3** *Raritan* He saw himself as the steward of the whole nation.
Phrases: †**Great Steward of England** = ***Lord High Steward of England*** below. **high steward** (*a*) (in the universities of Oxford and Cambridge) a judicial officer, in whom is vested the jurisdiction belonging to the university in trials for treason or felony; (*b*) (in certain English cities) a municipal title of dignity, usually held by a nobleman or prince. **Lord High Steward of England** a high officer of State, appointed since the 15th cent. only on the occasion of a coronation, at which he presides, or formerly (prior to 1948), for the trial of a peer, at which he presided in the House of Lords. **Lord High Steward of Scotland** *Hist.* the principal officer of the Scottish sovereign in early times in charge of administering Crown revenues, supervising the royal household, and having the privilege of standing in the army in battle second only to the sovereign. **Lord Steward of the King's Household**, **Lord Steward of the Queen's Household** a peer in charge of the management of the sovereign's household and presiding at the Board of Green Cloth. **Steward of England** = ***Lord High Steward of England*** above. **Steward of Scotland** *Hist.* = ***Lord High Steward of Scotland*** above. **Steward of the King's Household** = ***Lord Steward of the King's Household*** above. **steward of the manor** *Hist.* a person who transacted the financial and legal business of a manor on behalf of the lord and whose chief functions were to hold the manor-court in the lord's absence, and to keep the court rolls. **Steward of the Queen's Household** = ***Lord Steward of the Queen's Household*** above. ***stipendiary steward***: see STIPENDIARY *adjective*.
Comb.: **steward boy** = *houseboy* s.v. HOUSE *noun*[1].
▶ **B** *verb*. **1** *verb trans.* Act as a steward of; manage, administer. **E17.**
2 *verb intrans.* Perform the duties of a steward. **L19.**
📖 **1** *Daily Telegraph* Many helpers are willing to steward the rooms. **2** *Times* Damage had been reduced . . [due] to better stewarding by the football clubs.
■ **stewardly** *adjective* (*a*) *rare* pertaining to or administered by a steward; of the nature of a stewardship; (*b*) *dial.* skilled in household management: **M17.**

stewardess /ˈstjuːədɪs, stjuːəˈdɛs/ *noun*. **M17.**
[from STEWARD *noun* + -ESS[1].]
A female steward, *esp.* a passengers' attendant on a ship, train, or aircraft.
📖 *Scots Magazine* The boat was crewed by the skipper . . and the stewardess. *fig.*: GLADSTONE Her [the Church's] high office as stewardess of divine truth.

stewardry *noun* var. of STEWARTRY.

stewardship /ˈstjuːədʃɪp/ *noun*. **LME.**
[from STEWARD *noun* + -SHIP.]
1 The position or office of steward. **LME.**
2 a Administration, supervision, or management (as) by a steward. **E16.** ▶**b** CHRISTIAN CHURCH. The responsible use of resources, esp. money, time, and talents, in the service of God; *spec.* the organized pledging of specific amounts of money etc. to be given regularly to the Church. **L19.**
📖 **1** *Manchester Examiner* Successor in the stewardship to the Marquis of Londonderry. **2a** M. ROBINSON The . . misery which has been the consequence of the stewardship of the governing classes. **b** *attrib.*: *Oxford Diocesan Magazine* Pastoral reorganisation and the stewardship movement foster a sense of responsibility in parishes.

stewart *noun* see STEWARD.

stewartry /ˈstjuːətri/ *noun*. Chiefly *Scot.* Also **-dry** /-dri/. **L15.**
[formed as prec. + -RY.]
1 Chiefly *Hist.* A former territorial division of Scotland (abolished in 1747) under the jurisdiction of a steward (STEWARD *noun* 7b). Now only in ***The Stewartry***, the Kirkcudbright district of Galloway. **L15.**
2 The office of steward in such an administrative division. *obsolete* exc. *Hist.* **L15.**

stewarty /ˈstjuːəti/ *noun*. *Scot. obsolete* exc. *Hist.* **E17.**
[from STEWARD *noun* + -Y[5].]
= STEWARTRY.

stewed /stjuːd/ *adjective*. **LME.**
[from STEW *verb* + -ED[1]; in sense 2 from STEW *noun*[1] + -ED[2].]
1 Of meat, fish, fruit, etc.: cooked by stewing in a closed vessel. Also, (of tea) strong or bitter due to prolonged brewing. **LME.**
2 Of or pertaining to a stew or brothel. Freq. *derog.* Long *rare*. **M16.**
3 Drunk. Freq. in ***stewed to the ears***, ***stewed to the eyebrows***, ***stewed to the gills***, etc. *colloq.* (orig. *US*). **M18.**

stewing /ˈstjuːɪŋ/ *verbal noun & adjective*[1]. LME.
[from STEW *verb* + -ING[1].]
▶ **A** *noun.* The action of STEW *verb*; *rare* an instance of this. LME.
▶ **B** *attrib.* or as *adjective.* Suitable for or used in stewing. E18.
stewing beef, stewing pan, stewing pear, stewing steak, etc.

stewing /ˈstjuːɪŋ/ *adjective*[2]. E18.
[from STEW *verb* + -ING[2].]
That stews; *colloq.* very hot, uncomfortably hot or stifling.

stewpan /ˈstjuːpan/ *noun.* M17.
[from STEW *noun*[1] or *verb* + PAN *noun*[1].]
A saucepan for stewing meat, fish, fruit, etc.
fig.: G. H. KINGSLEY That tideless stewpan of a harbour.

stewpot /ˈstjuːpɒt/ *noun.* M16.
[formed as prec. + POT *noun*[1].]
†**1** A dish of meat etc. cooked in a covered pot; a stew. M16–E17.
2 A covered pot for stewing meat etc. E17.

stey /steɪ/ *adjective. Scot.* LME.
[Origin uncertain: perh. rel. to Germanic base of STY *verb*[1].]
1 Of a mountain, cliff, etc.: almost perpendicular, difficult of ascent, steep. LME.
2 *transf.* Unbending, upright. Also, (of a person) reserved, haughty. *arch.* L16.

Steyr /ʃtʌɪə/ *noun & adjective.* E20.
[An industrial town in Upper Austria.]
(Designating) a kind of automatic pistol made in Steyr.

stg. *abbreviation.*
Sterling.

Sth. *abbreviation.*
South.

St Helenian /s(ə)nt hɛˈliːnɪən/ *noun & adjective.* M20.
[from *St Helena* (see below) + -IAN.]
▶ **A** *noun.* A native or inhabitant of St Helena, an island in the S. Atlantic (a British territory since 1834). M20.
▶ **B** *adjective.* Of or pertaining to St Helena. M20.

sthenic /ˈsθɛnɪk/ *adjective.* L18.
[from Greek *sthenos* strength, after ASTHENIC.]
MEDICINE. Orig. (now *rare* or *obsolete*), of a disease etc.: characterized by normal or excessive vital energy. Now, strong and active; having an athletic physique; PSYCHOLOGY having a strong and vigorous personality, with a tendency to aggressive behaviour. Cf. ASTHENIC.
■ **sthenia** *noun* (now *rare* or *obsolete*) a condition of normal or excessive strength and activity L18.

stiacciato /stjaˈtʃɑːtəʊ/ *noun.* Also **schia-** /skja-/. M19.
[Italian *schiacciato, stiacciato* pa. pple of *schiacciare, stiacciare* flatten.]
SCULPTURE. Very low relief. Also more fully ***stiacciato-relievo, relievo stiacciato***.

stib- *combining form* see STIBO-.

†**stibbler** *noun. Scot.* E18–E20.
[Origin unkn.]
A licensed probationer in the Presbyterian Church who has not yet received a call to a settled ministerial charge.

stibialism /ˈstɪbɪəlɪz(ə)m/ *noun. rare.* M19.
[from mod. Latin *stibialis* of antimony + -ISM.]
MEDICINE. Antimony poisoning.

†**stibiate** *adjective.* E17–M18.
[mod. Latin *stibiatus*, from Latin STIBIUM: see -ATE[2].]
PHARMACOLOGY. Impregnated or combined with antimony.
■ Also †**stibiated** *adjective*: only in M19.

stibic /ˈstɪbɪk/ *adjective. rare.* E17.
[from STIBIUM + -IC.]
= ANTIMONIAL *adjective.*

stibine /ˈstɪbiːn, -bʌɪn/ *noun.* M19.
[French, formed as STIBIUM + -INE[5].]
1 MINERALOGY. = STIBNITE. Now *rare* or *obsolete.* M19.
2 CHEMISTRY. Any of a group of antimony compounds including the hydride SbH_3 and its alkyl-substituted derivatives. M19.

stibio- *combining form* see STIBO-.

stibious /ˈstɪbɪəs/ *adjective. rare.* M19.
[from next + -OUS.]
= ANTIMONIAL *adjective.*

stibium /ˈstɪbɪəm/ *noun.* LME.
[Latin, from Greek *stibi, stimmi* from Egyptian *stm*.]
Black antimony or stibnite, esp. as calcined and powdered for use as a cosmetic for blackening the eyelids and eyebrows. Formerly also, the element antimony or any of its salts, esp. used as a poison or emetic.

stibnite /ˈstɪbnʌɪt/ *noun.* M19.
[from STIB(I)N(E) + -ITE[1].]
MINERALOGY. Native antimony trisulphide, the most common ore of the metal, occurring as lead-grey striated prismatic crystals of the orthorhombic system.

stibo- /ˈstɪbəʊ/ *combining form.* Also **stib-**, (esp. MINERALOGY) **stibio-** /ˈstɪbɪəʊ/.
[from STIBIUM + -O-.]
CHEMISTRY & MINERALOGY. Of or containing antimony.
■ **stiboˈcaptate** *noun* [*-capt-* from MERCAPTO-] PHARMACOLOGY a drug containing antimony and sulphur, used in the treatment of schistosomiasis M20. **stiboˈgluconate** *noun* (PHARMACOLOGY): ***sodium stibogluconate***, an antimony-containing drug used in the treatment of leishmaniasis M20. **stibophen** *noun* (PHARMACOLOGY) an antimony-containing catechol derivative used esp. in the treatment of schistosomiasis M20.

sticcado /stɪˈkɑːdəʊ/ *noun.* Pl. **-os.** L18.
[Perh. from Italian *steccato*.]
MUSIC. A kind of xylophone.

stich /stɪk/ *noun.* E18.
[Greek *stikhos* row, rank, line of verse.]
A measured or average portion or division of prose or verse writing; a line, a verse.
■ **stiˈchology** *noun* (*rare*) the science or theory of poetic metres M18.

stichic /ˈstɪkɪk/ *adjective.* M19.
[Greek *stikhikos*, formed as prec.: see -IC.]
1 Pertaining to or consisting of verses or lines. M19.
2 PROSODY. Consisting of successive lines of the same metrical form. L19.
■ Also **stichical** *adjective* L18.

stichidium /stɪˈkɪdɪəm/ *noun.* Pl. **-ia** /-ɪə/. M19.
[mod. Latin from Greek *stikhidion*, from *stikhos* row, rank.]
BOTANY. A branch of a thallus in certain red algae that resembles a pod and bears tetraspores.

stichoi *noun* pl. of STICHOS.

stichometry /stɪˈkɒmɪtri/ *noun.* M18.
[Late Greek *stikhometria* from Greek *stikhos* STICHOS: see -METRY.]
PALAEOGRAPHY. The measurement of a manuscript text by means of the number of stichoi or fixed or average lines into which it may be divided; a list or appendix stating this measurement. Also (*rare*), the composition of a prose text in lines of nearly equal length corresponding to divisions in the sense.
■ **stichoˈmetric** *adjective* stichometrical L19. **stichoˈmetrical** *adjective* of or pertaining to stichometry; characterized by measurement by stichoi or lines: M19. **stichoˈmetrically** *adverb* L19.

stichomythia /stɪkə(ʊ)ˈmɪθɪə/ *noun.* M19.
[mod. Latin from Greek *stikhomuthia*, from *stikhos* STICHOS + *muthos* speech, talk.]
Dialogue in alternate lines of verse, used in disputation in Greek drama, and characterized by antithesis and repetition. Also, a modern imitation of this.
■ **stichomythic** *adjective* M19.

stichos /ˈstɪkɒs/ *noun.* Pl. **-choi** /-kɔɪ/. M19.
[Greek *stikhos* STICH.]
1 A verse or versicle in the Greek Orthodox Church. M19.
2 PALAEOGRAPHY. A line of a stichometrically written text; a line of average length assumed in measuring the contents of a manuscript text. L19.

stick /stɪk/ *noun*[1].
[Old English *sticca* = Old Frisian *stekk*, Middle Dutch *stecke* (Dutch *stek* slip, cutting), Old High German *stecko* (German *Stecken* stick, staff), from West Germanic, synon. vars. of which are repr. by Old High German *stehho*, Old Norse *stika*, from Germanic, from base of STICK *verb*[1].]
▶ **I** A rod or staff of wood.
1 A short piece of wood, *esp.* (freq. with defining word) one cut and shaped for a special purpose; *spec.* such a piece used as †(*a*) a tally; (*b*) MINING an identity marker of a hewer. OE.
2 a A slender branch or twig of a tree or shrub esp. when cut or broken off. Now *rare.* OE. ▸**b** In *pl.* Pieces of cut or broken branches or pieces of cut and chopped wood used as fuel. ME. ▸**c** A slender bough or long rod used as a support for a plant. L16.
3 a A relatively long and slender piece of shaped or natural wood, cut or broken to a convenient length for handling; *spec.* a staff or club used as a weapon. ME. ▸**b** A walking-stick. E17. ▸**c** A rod or staff carried as a symbol of dignity or office, a baton; the bearer of such a rod. L17. ▸**d** A conductor's baton. M19.
4 A trunk or thick branch of a tree cut and trimmed for use as timber in building, fencing, etc.; a stave, a stake. LME.
5 *spec.* in GAMES. **a** A staff used to strike or propel the ball in various games, as hockey, polo, etc. L17. ▸**b** CRICKET. In *pl.* The stumps of a wicket, the wickets. M19. ▸**c** In *pl.* (Foul play committed by) raising the stick above the shoulder when swinging it back to strike the ball in hockey. L19. ▸**d** In *pl.* Goalposts. *slang.* Chiefly *Austral.* L19.
6 NAUTICAL. A mast, a portion of a mast. Also, a yard. L18.

2b A. MASON Although the fire was fading . . , no one moved to put any sticks on to it. **3a** CONAN DOYLE The turnip on a stick at which we used to throw at the fairs. DAY LEWIS He struck the ass . . with his stick. **b** P. MATTHIESSEN In this land without a tree, I regret . . the loss of my faithful stick.

▶ **II** A thing resembling, pertaining to, or used like a stick.
†**7** A spoon. OE–ME.
8 A piece of a substance (as cinnamon bark, liquorice, dynamite, sealing-wax, bread, etc.) rolled or formed into a long slender shape like that of a stick. L15. ▸**b** A cigarette, a cigar; *spec.* a marijuana cigarette. *slang.* E20. ▸**c** A ¼lb pack of butter or margarine. *US.* M20.
9 A candlestick. M16.
10 a A mallet with which a drum, dulcimer, or other musical instrument is struck; a drumstick. Also in *pl.* (*Nautical slang*), a drummer. M16. ▸**b** A violin bow. *rare.* L16.
11 a PRINTING. A composing-stick (see COMPOSE 4). L17. ▸**b** JOURNALISM. A measure (roughly two column-inches) of copy. L19.
12 A person, *esp.* (*a*) one who is dull, perverse, or anti-social (also ***old stick***); (*b*) a wooden actor; (*c*) *US slang* a shill. L17.
13 In *pl.* The thin struts of ivory, bone, etc., which support the folding material of a fan. E18.
14 The long slender stem of a culinary plant, as rhubarb, celery, etc., when trimmed and ready for use. M18.
15 A pistol. *slang.* L18.
16 Furniture, household goods. Usu. in *pl.* Also ***sticks of furniture***. *slang.* E19.
17 a Punishment, a beating, esp. with a stick (usu. ***the stick***). Also used with allus. to the traditional use of a stick to try and force a donkey to move, freq. opp. ***carrot***. M19. ▸**b** *fig.* Adverse criticism, censure, reproof. *colloq.* M20.
18 A jemmy, a crowbar. *Criminals' slang.* L19.
19 A joy-stick; a gear lever. E20.
20 A ski stick. M20.
21 MILITARY. **a** A number (usu. five or six) of bombs dropped in quick succession from an aircraft. M20. ▸**b** A group of parachutists jumping in quick succession. M20. ▸**c** A small group of soldiers assigned to a particular duty. M20.

8 THACKERAY She bought pink sticks of barley-sugar for the young ones. **10a** J. BLADES The tenor drum . . is played with soft sticks. **12** J. CARY James is such a stick He drives me mad with his fuss. A. WILSON She's not a bad old stick. **14** *Harpers & Queen* A French-bread sandwich . . with celery sticks. **16** M. ALLINGHAM The top floor 'asn't got a stick in it. **17a** M. GRAY He'll do what he is told now without the stick. **b** *Sunday Times* The candidate was getting unfair stick for having a foreign-sounding name. *Sunday Express* I took quite a bit of stick from my mates. **19** *Air International* The pilots are working hard with sticks and throttles to keep the aircraft in their . . positions. *Holiday Which?* Move the stick in your hands and the rudder under your feet smoothly.

Phrases: **a big stick to beat someone or something with, a stick to beat someone or something with** *fig.* something to hold over a person or thing; a threat; an advantage; an incentive (cf. sense 17a above). **beat all to sticks** overcome or surpass completely. ***better than a poke in the eye with a sharp stick***: see POKE *noun*[4] 1. ***big stick***: see BIG *adjective.* ***cut one's stick***: see CUT *verb.* ***dirty end of the stick***: see DIRTY *adjective.* **every stick** (*a*) every piece of furniture; (*b*) all the materials of a building. ***French stick***: see FRENCH *adjective.* **get hold of the wrong end of the stick, get the wrong end of the stick** get a story wrong, misunderstand, not know the facts; see also ***have the wrong end of the stick*** below. **go to sticks (and staves)** be ruined. **have the right end of the stick, get the right end of the stick** be at an advantage in a bargain or contest. **have the wrong end of the stick, get the wrong end of the stick** be at an advantage or disadvantage in a bargain or contest. ***hop the stick***: see HOP *verb*[1]. ***in a cleft stick***: see CLEFT *ppl adjective.* ***Land of Little Sticks, Land of the Little Sticks***: see LAND *noun*[1]. ***monkey on a stick***: see MONKEY *noun.* ***more than you can shake a stick at***: see SHAKE *verb.* ***old stick***: see sense 12 above. **over the sticks** in steeplechasing and hurdles. **play a good stick** (of a fiddler) play well or in a lively fashion; *gen.* play one's part well. ***pogo stick***: see POGO *noun* 1. ***pugil stick***: see PUGIL *noun*[2]. PUNJI **stick**. ***Silver Stick***: see SILVER *noun & adjective.* ***ski stick***: see SKI *noun & adjective.* ***sticks of furniture***: see sense 16 above. ***Thai stick***: see THAI *adjective.* **the sticks** a remote, thinly populated, rural area; the backwoods; a provincial or unsophisticated area. ***thick end of the stick***: see THICK *adjective.* **up stick(s)** *slang* (*a*) set up a boat's mast; (*b*) *fig.* prepare to move, pack up and go, remove oneself. **up the stick** *slang* pregnant. ***white stick***: see WHITE *adjective.* **with a stick in it** (of tea, coffee, etc.) with a dash of brandy in it.

Comb.: **stick-and-carrot** *adjective* characterized by both the threat of punishment and the offer of reward (cf. sense 17a above); **stick-back** *adjective* designating a kind of wooden chair having a back formed by upright rods or sticks; **stickball** *US* a game played with a stick and a ball; *spec.* (*a*) a kind of baseball; (*b*) a kind of lacrosse; **stick bean** a runner bean; **stick-bomb** *noun*[1] a bomb or grenade with a protruding rod or stick for firing or throwing; **stick chair** (*a*) a sedan chair; (*b*) a stick-back chair; **stick country** *Canad.* wooded countryside; **stick dance** any of various folk-dances in which the dancer holds a stick and (in some dances) beats it against the sticks of other dancers; **stick-fighter** a person who engages in stick-fighting; **stick-fighting** *W. Indies* a kind of martial art; **stick-figure** a matchstick figure, a figure drawn in thin simple lines; **stick fixed** *adjective* (AERONAUTICS) that occurs when the control column of an aircraft is held in one position; **stick force** AERONAUTICS the force or effort needed to move or hold steady the control column of an aircraft; **stick free** *adjective* (AERONAUTICS) that occurs when the control column of an aircraft is allowed to move freely, unguided by the pilot; **stick**

grenade, **stick hand-grenade** a grenade with a stick to hold it by; **stick-handle** *verb intrans.* (chiefly *N. Amer.*) control the puck in ice hockey with one's stick; **stick-handling** (chiefly *N. Amer.*) the control and handling of one's stick in ice hockey and other games; **stick insect** any of numerous long-legged and long-bodied, mainly tropical insects of the family Phasmatidae (order Phasmida), which resemble straws or twigs in shape and colour; ***stick-lac***: see LAC *noun*[1] 1; **stick-man** (*a*) *slang* a pickpocket's accomplice; (*b*) *US colloq.* a croupier; **stickseed** a plant of the genera *Hackelia* or *Lappula* (family Boraginaceae), bearing small barbed seeds; esp. *H. floribunda*, which resembles a forget-me-not; **stick-shaker** *colloq.* AERONAUTICS a device which causes the control column to vibrate when an aircraft is close to stalling; **stick shift** *N. Amer.* a gear lever; **stickwork** (*a*) in various ball games, the control of the stick; (*b*) something made from or by using sticks.

■ **stickful** *noun* (PRINTING) as much type as a composing-stick will hold L17.

stick /stɪk/ *noun*[2]. *obsolete* exc. *Hist.* LOE.

[Anglo-Latin *stica*, *sticha*, *sticka*, *estika*, perh. Latinized form of STICK *noun*[1].]

A measure of quantity in small eels (usu. twenty-five).

stick /stɪk/ *noun*[3]. M17.

[from STICK *verb*[1].]

1 A temporary stoppage, a hitch. *arch.* M17.

2 A thing which causes hindrance or delay, a difficulty, an obstacle. *arch.* M17.

3 The power of adhesion; adhesiveness. Also, something adhesive. M19.

4 CRICKET. A batsman who remains in batting for a long time. *rare.* M19.

5 STOCK EXCHANGE. A large quantity of unsold stock, *esp.* one which has to be taken up by underwriters after an unsuccessful share issue. L20.

Stick /ˈstɪk/ *noun*[4]. L20.

[Abbreviation.]

= STICKIE.

stick /stɪk/ *verb*[1]. Pa. t. & pple **stuck** /stʌk/, (now *Scot. & dial.*) **sticked**.

[Old English *stician* = Old High German *stehhan* prick, stab, with parallel forms in Middle & mod. Low German, Middle & mod. Dutch *stikken*, Old High German *sticchen*, *sticken* (German *sticken* embroider), from Germanic, from Indo-European base whence also Greek *stizein* prick, *stigma* STIGMA, Latin *instigare* spur on, INSTIGATE. Cf. STEEK *verb*[2].]

► **I** Pierce, thrust.

1 *verb trans.* Stab or pierce with a thrust of a spear, sword, knife, or other sharp instrument; kill (esp. a pig or other animal) by this means. OE. ▸**b** Of a horned animal: pierce or impale with the tusks or horns; gore. Now *Scot. & dial.* OE. ▸**c** Inoculate, inject with a hypodermic needle. *N. Amer. colloq.* M20.

2 *verb trans.* Make a thrust or stab with (a dagger, a spear, a pointed instrument) *in, into, through*. LME.

3 a *verb intrans.* Project, protrude. Now only foll. by *from, out of*. Cf. ***stick out*** below. L16. ▸**b** *verb trans.* Push forward, protrude, (one's head, hand, etc.) *in, into, out of*, etc. E17.

> 📖 **1** T. H. WHITE When the unicorn comes, we must all rush out and stick it. B. MALAMUD You clubbed the . . boy unconscious before you stuck him with your knife. **2** T. PARKS I can't force him to let them stick needles in him. **3b** P. P. READ He ran to the window . . and stuck his head out into the smutty air.

► **II** Remain fixed.

4 *verb intrans.* Of a pointed instrument: remain with its point embedded; be fixed by its pointed end. OE.

†**5** *verb intrans.* Of a thing: be fastened in position; be fixed (as) in a socket. OE–L17.

6 *verb intrans.* Chiefly of a person: stay or remain persistently in a place or situation. Now *colloq.* OE. ▸**b** *fig.* (Of a feeling, thought, fact, etc.) remain persistently in the mind; (of a habit etc.) be established. ME. ▸†**c** Dwell on a point in discourse. Foll. by *in, upon*. M16–M17. ▸**d** Decline to add to one's hand in pontoon. M20.

7 *verb intrans.* Be or become set fast or jammed because of some obstacle or obstruction; lose the power of motion or action by this means. OE. ▸**b** Of food etc.: lodge in the throat. M16.

8 a *verb intrans.* Of a thing: become or remain attached or fixed by adhesion; adhere, cling. (Foll. by *on, to*, etc.) Cf. ***stick together*** below. ME. ▸**b** *fig.* (Of an accusation etc.) be fastened on a person, be substantiated, be convincing; (of a legal or official ruling) be implemented or complied with. L17.

9 †**a** *verb intrans.* Of the mind: remain steadfastly or rest on a matter; adhere to an opinion etc. (Foll. by *in, upon*.) LME–L17. ▸**b** *verb trans.* Put up with, endure, tolerate. Also with *it*. *colloq.* L19.

10 *verb intrans.* Of a matter: be at a standstill, suffer delay or hindrance. (Foll. by *at, on*, etc.) M16. ▸**b** (Of a person or thing) remain in a static condition, be unable to progress; (of a commodity etc.) remain unsold. M17.

11 *verb intrans.* Hesitate, scruple, be reluctant *to do*. Only in neg. contexts. Now *rare*. M16.

12 *verb intrans.* Of a living creature: cling or hold tightly *to, on, upon*. L16.

13 *verb intrans.* Be unable to proceed through puzzlement, embarrassment, or lapse of concentration or memory; stop in a state of perplexity. L16.

> 📖 **6** T. HARDY I'll stick where I am, for here I am safe. **b** J. BUCHAN That hour in the African twilight . . stuck in my memory. **7** G. ANSON The ship stuck fast in the mud. W. MAXWELL The kitchen drawer . . has a tendency to stick. A. TYLER The pretzels were the varnished kind that stuck in his teeth. *fig.*: G. GREENE He tried to add 'father', but the word stuck on his tongue. **8a** E. DAVID Throw in the rice . . stirring so that it doesn't stick. **b** S. WOODS They couldn't make it stick . . No evidence. **9b** *Daily Telegraph* I resigned . . because I could stick the chief's bullying no longer. J. B. PRIESTLEY I took a job in the City . . and I only stuck it a week. **10b** W. BAGEHOT Most civilisations stuck where they first were. **12** TENNYSON On thy ribs the limpet sticks. **13** SIR W. SCOTT He was able to pronounce the words, 'Saunders Souplejaw'—and then stuck fast.

► **III** Fix, cause to adhere.

14 *verb trans.* Secure (a thing) in a specified place by thrusting in its pointed end. ME. ▸**b** Fix on a point or pointed thing. ME. ▸**c** Insert or thrust the end of (a thing) *in, into, through*, etc. M17.

15 *verb trans. gen.* Fasten in position; *loosely* place, set, put, (*down, on*, etc.), esp. quickly or haphazardly. ME. ▸**b** CARPENTRY. Work (moulding, a bead) with a moulding-plane. M18. ▸**c** Dispose of as unwanted. Usu. in imprecations or expressions of contempt. Freq. foll. by *in, up*. *colloq.* E20.

16 *verb trans.* Set (a surface) *with*; strew or cover all over *with*, esp. as an adornment. ME.

17 *verb trans.* Cause to adhere; fasten or attach (a thing) *on, to*, etc., a surface using adhesive, pins, etc. LME.

18 *verb trans.* **a** Cheat (a person) out of money or with inferior goods; encumber *with* something worthless. Also (in *pass.*), be saddled or encumbered *with*. Orig. *US*. L17. ▸**b** Land with an expense or loss; let in *for*. *slang*. L19.

19 *verb trans.* Break down in (a speech, song, etc.); be unable to proceed with or complete. *Scot.* E18.

20 *verb trans.* Bring to a standstill; make unable to progress. Chiefly as STUCK *adjective*. E19. ▸**b** Perplex, nonplus. Chiefly as STUCK *adjective*. L19.

> 📖 **14** T. HARDY Sticking his pitchfork into the ground . . , he came forward. **b** BURKE Their heads were stuck upon spears. **c** A. TROLLOPE Sitting, with a short, black pipe stuck into his mouth. H. DOOLITTLE They had stuck a great bundle of calla-lilies . . into a jam pot. **15** E. RAFFALD Stick curled parsley in it. H. JAMES A Greek bas-relief to stick over my chimney-piece. J. SUTHERLAND This . . courtyard where everyone sticks their garbage. **c** R. STOUT Take your name and stick it up your chimney and go to hell. *Daily Telegraph* They can stick their cottage. I shall not move into it. **16** DRYDEN Cloves enough to stick an Orange with. **17** D. LEAVITT The sea anemone was stuck to the rock. L. ELLMANN Materials . . stuck on to the canvas with glue. *fig.*: SHAKES. *All's Well* At first I stuck my choice upon her. **18a** R. JAFFE Getting stuck with all the short boys on blind dates. **b** *New Yorker* She stuck me for all of last month's rent.

Phrases, & with prepositions & adverbs in specialized senses: **as close as it can stick**, **as close as one can stick**, **as full as it can stick**, **as full as one can stick**, etc., as close, full, etc., as possible. **be stuck for** *colloq.* be at a loss how to obtain; be unable to think of. **be stuck on** *colloq.* be infatuated with. **get stuck in**, **get stuck into** (*a*) lay into, make a physical attack on; (*b*) make a serious start on, get down to in earnest. **make something stick** make something effective; clinch, substantiate. **stick around** *colloq.* linger, remain in the same place. **stick at** (*a*) scruple at; hesitate to accept or believe, be deterred by (usu. in neg. contexts): cf. sense 11 above; (*b*) be impeded or brought to a standstill by (a difficulty): cf. sense 10 above; (*c*) keep persistently at (an activity). **stick at it** *colloq.* persevere. ***stick at nothing***: see NOTHING. **stick by** (*a*) stay faithful to, stand by; †(*b*) remain in (a person's) memory, remain with; †(*c*) persist at, continue. **stick down** (*a*) = sense 17 above; †(*b*) fasten by the point; secure by driving the point of into the ground. **stick 'em up!**: ordering a person or persons to raise both hands to signify surrender; hands up! **stick in** (*a*) insert; *Scot.* plant (a tree); (*b*) remain obstinately in (an office, a community); refuse to budge. ***stick in one's craw***: see CRAW *noun*[1] 1. ***stick in one's gizzard***: see GIZZARD 2. ***stick in one's stomach***: see STOMACH *noun*. **stick in one's throat** (*a*) (of words) be unarticulable; (*b*) be against one's principles, be unacceptable. ***stick in the mire***: see MIRE *noun*[1]. **stick in the mud** remain content in a mean or abject condition. ***stick in the stomach***: see STOMACH *noun*. **stick it on** (*a*) make high charges; (*b*) tell an exaggerated story. ***stick it on (a person)***: see ***stick one on (a person)*** below. **stick it out** *colloq.* put up with or persevere with something to the end; see it through. †**stick off** show (something) to advantage. **stick one on (a person)**, **stick it on (a person)** *colloq.* hit (a person). **stick one's chin out** show firmness or fortitude. ***stick one's neck out***: see NECK *noun*[1]. ***stick one's nose into***: see NOSE *noun*. **stick out** (*a*) project, protrude; (*b*) *colloq.* be prominent or conspicuous; (*c*) *colloq.* resist, hold out; (*d*) *colloq.* maintain, assert (*that*); (*e*) **stick out for** (*colloq.*), persist in demanding. ***stick out a* MILE**. ***stick out like a sore thumb***: see SORE *adjective*. **stick pigs** engage in pig-sticking. **stick to** †(*a*) cling to for support; (*b*) remain faithful to, support; (*c*) adhere or hold to (an argument, opinion, etc.); refuse to renounce; (*d*) refuse to be enticed or turned from (a task etc.); (*e*) keep exclusively to (a subject, choice of item, etc.); (*f*) remain by or in (a place etc.); (*g*) keep close to, esp. in a race or pursuit; (*h*) keep possession of. **stick to a person's fingers** *colloq.* (of money) be embezzled by a person. **stick together** (*a*) (of things) adhere one to another, cling together; (*b*) (of people etc.) cling together; remain united or mutually loyal. **stick to it** persevere. ***stick to one's guns***: see GUN *noun*. ***stick to one's last***: see LAST *noun*[1] 3. ***stick to one's tackle***: see TACKLE *noun*. **stick up** (*a*) stand out from a surface; project; (*b*) **stick up for** (*colloq.*), defend the cause of, champion; (*c*) *colloq.* resist, withstand (foll. by *to*); (*d*) set up in position, set up (a stake etc.) on its own point, or (a head, body) by impalement; (*e*) affix or post (a notice, poster, etc.); (*f*) stop and rob by violence or threats, hold up; *Criminals' slang* (of the police) hold up (a suspect); (*g*) *Austral.* hinder from proceeding; puzzle, nonplus; †(*h*) CRICKET put a batsman on the defensive. **stick with** †(*a*) side or argue with persistently; †(*b*) be incredible or unacceptable to; (*c*) remain in touch with or faithful to.

Comb.: **stick-at-it** *colloq.* a plodding conscientious person; **stick-at-nothing** *adjective* who will stop at nothing in order to accomplish a purpose; **stick-bomb** *noun*[2] = ***sticky bomb*** s.v. STICKY *adjective*[2]; **stickfast flea** a small flea, *Echidnophaga gallinacea*, which embeds its mouthparts in the skin esp. of poultry; **stick-in-the-mud** *colloq.* an unprogressive or old-fashioned person; **stick-in-the-muddish** *adjective* (*colloq.*) dull, unadventurous, old-fashioned; **stick-jaw** *colloq.* toffee, a pudding, etc., which is difficult to chew; **stick-on** *adjective* that sticks on or can be stuck on; adhesive; **stick-out** *adjective & noun* (*a*) *adjective* that projects or stands out; *US slang* outstanding, excellent; (*b*) *noun* (*US slang*) an outstanding racehorse, sportsman or sportswoman; **stick-pin** (chiefly *N. Amer.*) any (ornamental) pin that is simply stuck in, freq. without a catch, as a tie-pin, lapel pin, etc.; **stick-slip** movement of one surface over another in a series of abrupt shifts against frictional forces; **sticktight** (*a*) *N. Amer.* (the seed of) any of several plants having fruits armed with hooked bristles, esp. beggar-ticks, *Bidens frondosa*; (*b*) ***sticktight flea***, = ***stickfast flea*** above; **stick-to-it-iveness** *colloq.* (orig. *US*) dogged perseverance; **stick-up** *adjective & noun* (*a*) *adjective* that sticks up; (*b*) *noun* something which sticks up; also (*colloq.*), an armed robbery; **stickwater** the liquid squeezed out when cooked fish are compressed during the manufacture of fishmeal and fish oil.

stick /stɪk/ *verb*[2]. L16.

[from STICK *noun*[1].]

1 *verb trans.* Lay sticks or stickers between (pieces of timber) when stacking. *rare.* L16.

2 *verb trans.* Support (a plant) with a stick. M17.

3 *verb intrans.* Gather sticks for firewood. Esp. in ***go sticking***. L19.

4 *verb trans.* Strike (a person) with a stick. M20.

stickability /stɪkəˈbɪlɪti/ *noun. colloq.* L19.

[from STICK *verb*[1] + -ABILITY.]

Capacity for endurance, persistence, perseverance, or staying power.

stickadove /ˈstɪkədʌv/ *noun*. Now *dial.* Also **stickadoor** /-dɔː/. L16.

[Ult. from medieval Latin *sticados*, *stechados*, etc., vars. of Latin *stoechados* genit. of STOECHAS.]

French lavender, *Lavandula stoechas*.

stickage /ˈstɪkɪdʒ/ *noun. rare.* M18.

[from STICK *verb*[1] + -AGE.]

Tendency to stick; adhesion, cohesion.

stické /ˈstɪki/ *noun*. E20.

[from SPHAIRI)STIKE.]

A game resembling a combination of lawn tennis and rackets, played indoors on a small wooden court.

sticker /ˈstɪkə/ *noun*[1]. LME.

[from STICK *noun*[1] or *verb*[2] + -ER[1].]

1 A person who gathers sticks for firewood. LME.

2 A thin strip of wood placed between stacked logs or pieces of timber to allow for ventilation. E20.

sticker /ˈstɪkə/ *noun*[2] & *verb*. L15.

[from STICK *verb*[1] + -ER[1].]

► **A** *noun*. **1** A person who sticks or stabs an animal or animals, *esp.* one who kills pigs by sticking. L15.

2 a A person who or thing which remains attached or constant; a determined, persistent person. (Foll. by *to*.) L17. ▸**b** A commodity which does not sell. *colloq.* E19. ▸**c** CRICKET. A batsman who scores slowly and is hard to get out. *colloq.* M19. ▸**d** A thorn, a bur. *US colloq.* L19.

3 A thing which brings a person to a nonplus; a poser. *colloq.* M19.

4 A weapon used for piercing or stabbing as opp. to cutting or slashing. Chiefly *colloq.* L19.

5 An adhesive label; a (usu. small but eye-catching) adhesive notice. L19.

> 📖 **5** L. DEIGHTON On the back window there was a sticker saying 'Nuclear Power—No Thanks.' J. TROLLOPE His . . car with its huge orange disabled stickers. **attrib.**: *Portfolio Magazine* Hard at work bill posting in a poster and sticker campaign.

Comb.: **sticker shock** *N. Amer. colloq.* dismay or anger experienced on discovering the high or increased price of a product; **sticker-up** *Austral.* (*a*) a method of cooking meat outdoors over a spit; (*b*) a bush-ranger.

► **B** *verb trans. & intrans.* Affix a sticker (to). L20.

Stickie /ˈstɪki/ *noun. Anglo-Irish slang.* Also **-y**. L20.

[from STICK *verb*[1]: see -IE, -Y[6].]

A member of the official IRA or Sinn Fein. Usu. in *pl.* Cf. STICK *noun*[4].

stickiness /ˈstɪkɪnɪs/ *noun*[1]. E18.

[from STICKY *adjective*[2] + -NESS.]

1 The quality of being sticky; adhesiveness, glutinousness. E18.

2 Hesitancy, stubbornness; awkwardness. M20.

stickiness /ˈstɪkɪnɪs/ *noun*[2]. E20.
[from STICKY *adjective*[1] + -NESS.]
Stiffness, woodenness, esp. of movement.

sticking /ˈstɪkɪŋ/ *noun*. LME.
[from STICK *verb*[1] + -ING[1].]
1 The action of STICK *verb*[1]; *spec.* (**a**) the action of piercing, stabbing, or thrusting with a weapon or pointed object; (**b**) the process or condition of adhering or clinging; (**c**) (a cause of) hesitation or delay (now *rare*). LME.
2 a *MINING*. = SELVAGE 4a. M17. **▸b** In *pl*. Inferior meat, *esp.* the portions damaged by a butcher's knife. M19.
Comb.: **sticking place** the place at which something stops, the limit; ***sticking-plaster***: see PLASTER *noun* 1; **sticking point** (**a**) = ***sticking place*** above; (**b**) a point over which there can be no yielding or compromise, an obstacle.

stickit /ˈstɪkɪt/ *adjective*. *Scot.* L18.
[Scot. form of *sticked* pa. pple of STICK *verb*[1].]
1 Of a task: imperfect, bungled, unfinished. L18.
2 Designating a trade or profession which a person has undertaken and then given up from lack of means or ability. E19.

stickle /ˈstɪk(ə)l/ *noun*[1]. *dial.* E17.
[from the adjective.]
A shallow fast-flowing place in a river; a rapid.

stickle /ˈstɪk(ə)l/ *noun*[2]. L17.
[from the verb.]
†**1** Persistent activity or endeavour *in* something. Only in L17.
†**2** Contention, strife. Only in L17.
3 An agitated state of mind; consternation, alarm, bewilderment. *dial.* M18.

stickle /ˈstɪk(ə)l/ *adjective*. Now *dial.*
[Old English *sticol* lofty, steep, difficult = Old Saxon *stecul*, Middle Low German *stekel*, Old High German *stechal*, from Germanic base of STICK *verb*[1].]
1 Of a hill or incline: steep. OE.
2 Of running water: rapid. L16.
3 Of the hair of an animal: rough, bristly. E17.

stickle /ˈstɪk(ə)l/ *verb*. M16.
[Alt. of STIGHTLE.]
†**1** *verb intrans.* Act as a referee or umpire; mediate, intervene. M16–L17.
†**2** *verb intrans.* Be active or energetic; strive hard *to do*; take an active part *in*. M16–M18. **▸b** Contend *against* or *that*. M17–E18.
†**3** *verb trans.* Calm (a dispute, disputants); stop, quell, (a strife or contest). L16–M17.
4 *verb intrans.* Make difficulties, raise objections (*about*); scruple, demur (*at*). E17.
5 *verb intrans.* **a** Strive or contend *for*. M17. **▸†b** Take the part of, stand up *for* (a person). Also with *up*. M17–M18.

> 🕮 **4** C. M. YONGE He did not stickle at Edward calling himself King of France and England. **5a** *Athenaeum* The plot . . will . . please those who stickle for happy endings.

stickleback /ˈstɪk(ə)lbak/ *noun*. LME.
[from Old English *sticel* sting, goad, thorn = Old High German *stihhil* goad, Old Norse *stikill* point of a horn, from Germanic base of STICK *noun*[1], *verb*[1] + BACK *noun*[1].]
Any member of the family Gasterosteidae of small bony fishes widespread in the northern hemisphere in both fresh and salt water, and characteristically having several spines along the back; *esp.* (more fully ***three-spined stickleback***) the common *Gasterosteus aculeatus*.

> 🕮 N. TINBERGEN A male stickleback in full spring colours (red underneath, greenish blue on the back). ***sea stickleback***: see SEA *noun*.

stickler /ˈstɪklə/ *noun*. M16.
[from STICKLE *verb* + -ER[1].]
1 A referee or umpire at a tournament or sporting match. Formerly also, a mediator *between* combatants or disputants. *obsolete* exc. *dial.* M16.
†**2** A person who takes an active or busy part (*in* a contest, affair, cause, etc.); an agent, an instigator. M16–E18. **▸†b** A meddler, a busybody. L16–L17.
†**3** A person who contends *against* or objects to another person, a cause, etc.; an opponent, an antagonist. E17–M19.
4 A person who contends for or advocates a cause, principle, party, etc.; a person who insists on or stands out for something. Usu. foll. by *for*. M17.
†**5** A supporter in a contest. L17–E19.

> 🕮 **4** B. T. BRADFORD She recalled that Francesca . . was a stickler about time. *TV Guide (Canada)* A brilliant . . actor who's such a stickler that nobody will hire him. P. DALLY A stickler for observing Christian practices and social conventions.

stickling /ˈstɪklɪŋ/ *noun*. Long *obsolete* exc. *dial.* LME.
[from base of STICKLEBACK + -ING[3]. Corresp. to Middle & mod. Dutch *stekeling*, Middle High German *stichelinc* (German *Stechling*, *Stichling*). Cf. STITLING.]
Any of various spiny fishes, now *spec.* a stickleback.

†**stick or snee** *verb & noun phr.* see SNICK OR SNEE.

stickum /ˈstɪkəm/ *noun*. *N. Amer. colloq.* E20.
[from STICK *verb*[1] + UM *pronoun*[1].]
A sticky or adhesive substance; gum, paste; pomade.

sticky /ˈstɪki/ *noun*[1]. *slang.* M19.
[from STICKY *adjective*[2].]
Something sticky; *spec.* (**a**) an adhesive material; (**b**) a sticky wicket.

Sticky *noun*[2] var. of STICKIE.

sticky /ˈstɪki/ *adjective*[1]. L16.
[from STICK *noun*[1] + -Y[1].]
Of a plant stem: like a stick; woody.

sticky /ˈstɪki/ *adjective*[2] & *verb*. M18.
[from STICK *verb*[1] + -Y[1].]
▸ A *adjective*. **1 a** Able to stick or adhere; adhesive; (of a substance) viscid, glutinous. M18. **▸b** *fig.* Sickly, mawkish, sentimental. M19. **▸c** Of a sound: resembling that made by movement of or in a viscid substance. L19.
2 Of ground: having a soft wet surface. L19.
3 a Of the weather: humid, muggy. L19. **▸b** Of a person, the skin, etc.: damp with sweat. M20.
4 *colloq.* **a** Of a person: awkward, uncooperative; strait-laced, particular, intransigent (*about* or *over*). L19. **▸b** Of a situation, issue, period of time, etc.: awkward, difficult, unpleasant. E20.
5 a *STOCK EXCHANGE.* Of stock, a share issue: not selling, selling badly. E20. **▸b** *ECONOMICS.* Of prices, interest rates, wages, etc.: slow to change or to react to change. M20.

> 🕮 **1a** B. CHATWIN The cook was . . a wizard at sticky cakes. *New Scientist* The sticky secretions of mucus that cause congestion. **3a** B. VINE It was warm and the still air had a sticky feel. **b** C. HARKNESS I felt nervous and awkward . . . My hands felt sticky, although I felt cold. **4b** *TV Times* It's a sticky subject, and Reeve stiffens perceptibly at the reference.

Special collocations & comb.: **sticky-back** *noun & adjective* (a small photograph or notice) having an adhesive back. **sticky bomb** an anti-tank grenade covered with adhesive to make it stick to its target. **sticky dog** *Cricket slang* a sticky wicket. **sticky end** (**a**) a violent or unpleasant ending or death; chiefly in ***come to a sticky end***; (**b**) *GENETICS* an end of a DNA double helix at which a few unpaired nucleotides of one strand extend beyond the other. **sticky-fingered** *adjective* apt to steal, light-fingered. **sticky-out** *adjective colloq.* protruding. **sticky tape** adhesive tape. **sticky wicket** *CRICKET* a wet and difficult surface to play on; *fig.* (*colloq.*) a difficult or awkward situation; chiefly in ***bat on a sticky wicket***, ***be on a sticky wicket***.
▸ B *verb trans.* Smear with something sticky. *colloq.* M19.
■ **stickily** *adverb* E20.

stickybeak /ˈstɪkɪbiːk/ *noun & verb*. *Austral. & NZ colloq.* E20.
[from STICKY *adjective*[2] + BEAK *noun*[1].]
▸ A *noun*. An inquisitive person; a nosy or interfering person. E20.
▸ B *verb intrans.* Pry, snoop. M20.

stiction /ˈstɪkʃ(ə)n/ *noun*. M20.
[Blend of STATIC *adjective* and FRICTION.]
= ***static friction*** s.v. STATIC *adjective*.

Stiegel /ˈstiːg(ə)l/ *noun*. E20.
[Henry William *Stiegel* (1729–85), German-born US manufacturer.]
Used *attrib.* to designate glassware made by Stiegel or resembling his work.

stieve *adjective & adverb* see STEEVE *adjective & adverb*.

stifado /stɪˈfɑːdəʊ/ *noun*. Pl. **-os**. M20.
[mod. Greek *stiphado* prob. from Italian STUFATO.]
A Greek dish of meat stewed with onions and sometimes tomatoes.

stife /stʌɪf/ *noun*. *dial.* M17.
[Origin unkn.]
Suffocating fumes or vapour.

stiff /stɪf/ *adjective, adverb, & noun*.
[Old English *stīf* corresp. to Middle Low German, Middle Dutch *stīf* (Dutch *stijf*), Old Norse *stífr*, from Germanic, from base of Latin *stipare* (cf. STEEVE *verb*[2], CONSTIPATE *verb*).]
▸ A *adjective*. **I 1** Rigid; not flexible or pliant. Also, taut, firm from tension. OE.
2 Of the body, a limb, a joint, etc.: lacking suppleness, hard or painful to bend, move, or turn. ME. **▸b** Rigid in death; dead. Now *slang*. ME. **▸c** Intoxicated, drunk. *US slang*. M18. **▸d** Of machinery etc.: working with much friction, apt to stick, hard to move. M19. **▸e** Penniless; unlucky; (of luck) hard, tough. *Austral. & NZ slang*. L19.
3 *fig.* **a** Inflexible of purpose, steadfast, resolute, firm; obstinate, stubborn. Now *rare*. ME. **▸b** (Of a battle, debate, etc.) stubbornly contested, hard; (of competition) keen, fierce. ME. **▸c** Esp. of a letter, note, etc.: severe, stern, angry. M19.
4 a Of a semi-liquid substance: thick, viscous; capable of retaining a definite shape. LME. **▸b** Of soil or ground: heavy, dense, hard to work. E16.
5 *NAUTICAL*. Of a ship: resistant to deflection from the vertical; stable, not crank. E17.
6 Formal, constrained; haughty; lacking spontaneity; lacking ease or grace, laboured; (of handwriting) not flowing. E17.
7 Foll. by *with*: closely packed or densely crowded with, abundantly provided with. *colloq.* L17.
8 (Of a price, rate, etc.) unyielding, firm, having an upward tendency; (of a commodity etc.) not falling in price. M19.
9 *MATH.* Of a differential equation: having a solution that shows completely different behaviour over widely different scales of time (or other independent variable). M20.

> 🕮 **1** B. BAINBRIDGE The starched napkin hung stiff as a board. S. ELDRED-GRIGG Her husband wore stiff collars. **2** K. A. PORTER Stiff from trying to sleep . . in their chairs. M. WESLEY 'I am stiff,' she said. 'Unused muscles ache.' **d** J. FRAME An old piano with stiff yellow keys. **e** *New Zealand Listener* Maybe they were a bit stiff to lose that. **3b** J. BUCHAN To withdraw through that area meant a stiff holding battle around Brest. E. PAWEL Despite stiff competition, the young peddler survived on his own. **c** W. S. MAUGHAM I wrote a pretty stiff letter to the librarian. **4a** H. GLASSE Work it up into a stiff paste. **6** SIR W. SCOTT The knight . . thanked him with the stiff condescension of the court. C. HARE 'If you wish it, my lady,' he said, with a stiff little continental bow. M. AYRTON They think me stiff because I cannot share their jokes. J. UPDIKE The . . rather stiff and sickly portrait of Mrs. Carl Meyer. **7** FLORA THOMPSON Their talk was stiff with simile. JAN MORRIS Oxford is stiff with law courts. *Campaign* An appalling chicken-and-vegetable concoction . . stiff with monosodium glutamate.

▸ II 10 Stout, stalwart, sturdy; strong, stoutly-built, massive; powerful. Long *obsolete* exc. *dial.* ME.
11 a Of a wind: severe, strong; *esp.* blowing steadily with moderate force. ME. **▸†b** Of news: grave. *rare* (Shakes.). Only in E17. **▸c** Of a drink, esp. of spirits: strong, potent. Also, of generous quantity. E19.
12 Of an ascent or descent: steep so as to be difficult; *gen.* requiring considerable effort, taxing, hard. LME.
13 Of a price, charge, demand, etc.: unusually high, severe, excessive. E19.

> 🕮 **11a** POPE When the stiffer gales Rise on the poop. D. MADDEN A stiff salt breeze blew her hair across her face. **c** J. WYNDHAM I was shaky . . and . . could have done with a stiff drink. J. HERBERT She poured herself a stiff measure of brandy. **12** M. A. STEIN Next day's climb proved a stiff one. D. ACHESON This was the stiffest fence on the course. N. SHERRY Once Greene was invited . . for a stiff medical examination he knew the B.A.T. wanted him. **13** J. WAIN Don't tell me he'll get away with anything short of a stiff sentence. *Listener* A mark-up on the product which is stiff even by brewers' standards.

Phrases, special collocations, & comb.: **bore stiff** *colloq.* bore (a person) to an extreme degree. **scare stiff** *colloq.* scare (a person) very much, terrify. **stiff-arm** *verb & noun* (chiefly *RUGBY & AMER. FOOTBALL*) (**a**) *verb trans.* tackle, fend off, or push with a rigid arm; (**b**) *noun* the action or an act of stiff-arming someone (usu. *attrib.*). **stiff-arsed** *adjective* (*coarse slang*) (**a**) supercilious, condescending; (**b**) formal. ***stiff as a poker***: see POKER *noun*[1] 1. **stiff-leaf** *noun & adjective* (*ARCHITECTURE*) (designating) foliage of conventional form with stiff leaf-stems, characteristic of Early English decoration. **stiff neck** a rheumatic condition in which the head cannot be turned without pain, often due to exposure to a draught; **stiff-neck** *colloq.* an obstinate, haughty, or self-righteous person. **stiff-necked** *adjective* having a stiff neck; *fig.* obstinate, stubborn, inflexible, haughty. **stiff one** *slang* (**a**) a corpse; (**b**) a racehorse certain not to win; (**c**) a forged note or cheque. **stiff-tail (duck)** any of a group of ducks typified by the ruddy duck, *Oxyura jamaicensis*, which often swim with the tail raised stiffly. **stiff upper lip** (**a**) calm fortitude or courage; †(**b**) obstinacy, hardness.
▸ B *adverb*. Stiffly, tightly, hard, severely. Now *poet. & non-standard*. ME.

> 🕮 KEATS Stiff-holden shields, far-piercing spears, keen blades.

▸ C *noun*. †**1** A stiffened article of women's clothing. *rare*. Only in L17.
2 a A corpse. *colloq.* L18. **▸b** A racehorse certain not to win; a hopeless competitor. *slang*. L19. **▸c** An unsuccessful venture, esp. in the entertainment business; a failure, a flop. *slang*. M20.
3 Paper; paper money; counterfeit money; a document, a certificate; a (forged) note or cheque; a clandestine letter. *slang*. E19.
4 A mean, disagreeable, or contemptible person (freq. in ***big stiff***); a drunkard; a tramp, a loafer; an itinerant worker, a labourer; a man, a fellow; in *FOOTBALL* etc., a member of the reserve team. *slang*. L19.
5 An erection of the penis. *coarse slang*. L20.

> 🕮 **2a** T. TRYON There's a stiff in that room . . a real live dead body. **4** J. DOS PASSOS Working stiffs ought to stick-together. P. G. WODEHOUSE This man was a . . good sort of old stiff. *Sun* Gunners sign Metchick for stiffs. S. BELLOW Some hand-hacked old kitchen stiff.

■ **stiffish** *adjective* somewhat stiff M18. **stiffly** *adverb* in a stiff manner, so as to be stiff: ME. **stiffness** *noun* (**a**) the state or quality of being stiff; (**b**) *MECHANICS* the force required to produce unit deflection or displacement of an object; the maximum deflection of a beam etc. divided by the length of the beam: LME. **stiffy** *noun* (*slang*) a stiff person or thing; *esp.* (**a**) a stupid or contemptible person; (**b**) a formal invitation card; (**c**) *coarse slang* an erection of the penis: M20.

stiff /stɪf/ *verb*. LME.
[from the adjective.]
†**1** *verb intrans.* Grow strong. Only in LME.
2 *verb trans.* Make stiff, stiffen. *obsolete* exc. *dial.* L15.
3 *verb trans.* Cheat; refuse to pay, *esp.* fail to tip (a waiter etc.). *slang* (chiefly *N. Amer.*). M20.
4 *verb trans.* Kill; murder. *slang*. L20.

stiffen /ˈstɪf(ə)n/ *verb*. L15.
[from STIFF *adjective* + -EN⁵.]
1 *verb trans.* Make (more) stiff or rigid; take away the flexibility, suppleness, or mobility of; make stiffer in consistency, thicken; strengthen; make more steadfast, resistant, or obstinate; increase the fighting value of (a force) by reinforcement esp. with seasoned troops. L15. ▸**b** NAUTICAL. Make (a ship) less liable to heel. E18. ▸**c** Make (more) formal or cold in manner; make (a composition etc.) pedantic or laboured. M18. ▸**d** Make (a price etc.) stiffer. L19.
2 *verb intrans.* Become (more) stiff or rigid; harden, solidify; become stronger. L17. ▸**b** Of a price, commodity, etc.: become stiffer (**STIFF** *adjective* 8). M19. ▸**c** Of wind etc.: increase in force. M19. ▸**d** Increase in difficulty or steepness. L19.

> **1** COLERIDGE His legs were stiffen'd with dismay. E. WILSON Filmy muslin . . stiffened with rice starch. *Illustrated London News* Units of the Afghan army have been stiffened by the addition of Soviet soldiers. P. BARKER Laughter bound them together and stiffened their courage. A. C. AMOR Humiliation merely served to stiffen his will to succeed **2** J. STEINBECK For a moment Crooks did not see him, but on raising his eyes he stiffened. J. MARSH Class attitudes stiffened during the century.

■ **stiffener** *noun* (*a*) a person who or thing which stiffens something; (*b*) *slang* a fortifying or reviving (alcoholic) drink: L17. **stiffening** *noun* (*a*) the action of the verb; an instance of this; (*b*) an object, substance, etc., that serves to stiffen something: E17.

stifle /ˈstʌɪf(ə)l/ *noun*¹. ME.
[Origin unkn.]
1 The joint at the junction of the hind leg and the body (between the femur and the tibia) in a horse or other quadruped, corresponding anatomically to the knee in humans. Also ***stifle-joint***. ME.
2 Dislocation of this joint. Also ***stifle-lameness***. L16.
Comb.: **stifle-bone** the bone in front of the stifle-joint, the patella; ***stifle-joint***: see sense 1 above.

stifle /ˈstʌɪf(ə)l/ *noun*². *rare*. LME.
[from STIFLE *verb*¹.]
1 Difficulty in breathing, asthma. Long *obsolete* exc. *Scot.* LME.
2 Fumes from a fire. *Scot.* L18.
3 The action of stifling; the condition of being stifled. E19.

stifle /ˈstʌɪf(ə)l/ *verb*¹. LME.
[Perh. from frequentative of Old French *estouffer* (mod. *étouffer*) from Proto-Romance: see -LE³.]
1 *verb trans.* **a** Cause to experience difficulty or constraint in breathing; produce a choking sensation in. LME. ▸†**b** Suffocate by immersion; drown. LME–E18. ▸**c** Kill or make unconscious by stopping respiration; smother, suffocate. Also (long *rare*), strangle, throttle. E16.
2 *verb trans.* Stop the passage of (the breath) or the use of (the voice); suppress or prevent the utterance of (a cry, a sob, laughter, etc.). L15. ▸†**b** Keep back (tears). L17–L18. ▸**c** Make (a sound) mute or inaudible. M19.
3 *verb trans. fig.* Suppress; constrain; keep (a feeling, mental faculty, etc.) from manifestation, expression, or activity; deprive (a movement, activity, etc.) of vitality, crush; keep from becoming known, withhold from circulation. L16. ▸**b** Put out, smother (a flame etc.). E18.
4 *verb intrans.* Be or become suffocated; die by stoppage of breath; feel in danger of suffocation, experience difficulty or constraint in breathing. L16.
†**5** *verb trans.* Impede the flow of (water); absorb (light). E17–L18.

> **1a** H. MARTINEAU He almost stifled her with caresses. W. GOLDING The air was stifling me and I longed for the open. **c** J. M. SYNGE To have you stifled on the gallows tree. C. HARMAN Her heroine . . had just stifled her husband with a bolster. **2** J. BUCHAN Stifling the voice of conscience. D. M. THOMAS One of her smiles turned into a yawn, which she stifled quickly. **c** R. KIPLING Fog . . stifled the roar of the traffic. **3** SIR W. SCOTT The rumour may stifle the truth. B. PYM Their creative powers stifled by poverty. S. RUSHDIE He knew how unprofessional his feelings were, but did nothing to stifle them. P. ROAZEN Stifled by small-town existence, she was entranced by . . the outside world. A. C. AMOR Maternal domination . . stifled his natural development. **4** C. BRONTË I was . . beginning to stifle with the fumes of conservatory flowers.

■ **stifled** *ppl adjective* (*a*) that has been stifled; (*b*) lacking fresh air, close, stuffy: M16. **stifler** *noun* M17. **stifling** *ppl adjective* suffocating, smothering, choking; *esp.* (of air, a room, etc.) in which breathing is difficult; oppressive, constraining: M16. **stiflingly** *adverb* so as to be stifling; oppressively: M19.

stifle /ˈstʌɪf(ə)l/ *verb*² *trans.* L16.
[from STIFLE *noun*¹.]
Affect (an animal) with dislocation of the stifle-joint. Usu. in *pass.*

Stift /ʃtɪft/ *noun*. *obsolete* exc. *Hist.* M17.
[German.]
The domain of a German prince-bishop. Also, a German religious house.

†**stight** *verb trans.* OE–LME.
[Old English *stihtan*, *stihtian* corresp. to Old Norse *stétta* support, help. Cf. next.]
Set in order, arrange, place.

†**stightle** *verb*. ME.
[Frequentative of prec.: see -LE³.]
1 *verb trans.* Arrange; make ready; control; direct; appoint; establish. Only in ME.
2 *verb intrans.* Bestir oneself; strive, fight. LME–L15.
¶ An earlier form of STICKLE *verb*.

stigma /ˈstɪgmə/ *noun*. Pl. **-mas**, **-mata** /-mətə, -ˈmɑːtə/. L16.
[Latin from Greek *stigma*, *-mat-*, from base of *stizein* to prick: see STICK *verb*¹.]
1 A mark made on the skin by pricking, cutting, or (esp.) branding, as a sign of disgrace or subjection. L16. ▸**b** In *pl.* Marks resembling the wounds on Jesus' crucified body, said to have appeared on the bodies of certain saints etc. M17.
2 a A mark or sign of disgrace or discredit, regarded as impressed on or carried by a person or thing. E17. ▸**b** A visible or apparent characteristic indicative of some (esp. undesirable or discreditable) quality, action, or circumstance (foll. by *of*); MEDICINE a visible sign *of* a disease or condition. M19.
3 MEDICINE. A mark or blemish on the skin indicating a disease or condition, *esp.* one which bleeds spontaneously. Now *rare* or *obsolete*. M17.
4 ZOOLOGY. **a** A small external opening or pore; *esp.* a spiracle. M18. ▸**b** A natural spot or mark; *esp.* a spot on the wing of a butterfly or other insect. E19.
5 BOTANY. That part of the pistil in flowering plants which receives the pollen in impregnation, very varied in shape, and situated either directly on the ovary (sessile) or at the summit (more rarely, the side) of the style. Also, an analogous structure in cryptogams. M18.

> **2a** J. HALPERIN Illegitimacy was an unambiguous stigma for the Victorians. **b** L. WOOLF He was indelibly marked with the hereditary stigmata of . . wealth and aristocracy. P. FUSSELL The upper class has its distinct stigmata. C. MCCULLOUGH Old and plain and marked forever with stigmata of years of toil.

■ **stigmal** *adjective* (chiefly ZOOLOGY) of, pertaining to, or of the nature of a stigma E20.

stigmaria /stɪgˈmɛːrɪə/ *noun*. Pl. **-riae** /-riː/. M19.
[mod. Latin (name of the form-genus to which such fossils are referred), formed as prec. with ref. to the scars (points of attachment of rootlets) covering the fossils.]
PALAEONTOLOGY. A fossilized root of a tree-fern esp. of the genus *Sigillaria*, found as a branching structure in coal. Freq. *attrib.*
■ **stigmarian** *adjective* of, pertaining to, of the nature of, or containing stigmariae M19.

stigmasterol /stɪgˈmastərɒl/ *noun*. E20.
[from mod. Latin PHYSO)STIGMA + STEROL.]
BIOCHEMISTRY. A phytosterol present in Calabar beans and soya beans.

stigmat *noun* var. of STIGMATE.

stigmata *noun pl.* see STIGMA.

stigmate /ˈstɪgmət/ *noun*. Long *rare*. Also **-at**. LME.
[Latin *stigmata* pl. of STIGMA.]
A mark, a wound; *esp.* (in *pl.*) = STIGMA 1b.

stigmatic /stɪgˈmatɪk/ *adjective & noun*. L16.
[from Latin *stigmat-*, STIGMA + -IC; in sense A.5 back-form. from ASTIGMATIC.]
▶**A** *adjective*. †**1** Marked with or having a deformity or blemish; deformed, ugly. L16–E19.
2 Constituting or conveying a stigma or sign of disgrace or discredit; ignominious; severely condemnatory. E17. ▸†**b** Carrying a stigma; branded; infamous. Only in E17.
3 ZOOLOGY & BOTANY. Of, pertaining to, or of the nature of a stigma; having a stigma or stigmata. E19.
4 Of, pertaining to, or accompanying stigmata like the wounds of Jesus. L19.
5 PHOTOGRAPHY. = ANASTIGMATIC. L19.
▶**B** *noun*. †**1** A person marked with a physical deformity or blemish. L16–M17.
†**2** A person marked with a stigma; a profligate, a villain. L16–M19.
3 ECCLESIASTICAL. A person (said to be) marked with stigmata like the wounds of Jesus, = STIGMATIST 2. L19.
4 PHOTOGRAPHY. An anastigmatic lens or lens-system. E20.
■ †**stigmatical** = STIGMATIC *adjective* L16–E18. **stigmatically** *adverb* (*rare*) in a stigmatic manner, by means of a stigma: E17.

stigmatiferous /stɪgməˈtɪf(ə)rəs/ *adjective*. M19.
[from Latin *stigmat-* STIGMA + -FEROUS.]
BOTANY. Bearing a stigma.

stigmatiform /stɪgˈmatɪfɔːm/ *adjective*. M19.
[from Latin *stigmat-* STIGMA + -I- + -FORM.]
BOTANY & ZOOLOGY. Having the form of a stigma.

stigmatise *verb* var. of STIGMATIZE.

stigmatist /ˈstɪgmətɪst/ *noun*. E17.
[formed as STIGMATIC + -IST.]
†**1** = STIGMATIC *noun* 2. *rare*. Only in E17.
2 ECCLESIASTICAL. A person (said to be) marked with stigmata like the wounds of Jesus, = STIGMATIC *noun* 3. L19.

stigmatize /ˈstɪgmətʌɪz/ *verb trans.* Also **-ise**. L16.
[French *stigmatiser* or medieval Latin *stigmatizare* from Greek *stigmatizein*, from *stigmat-* STIGMA: see -IZE.]
1 Mark with a brand. Also, tattoo. Now *rare*. L16. ▸**b** Mark, stain, blemish; MEDICINE mark with visible blemishes. Now *rare*. M17. ▸**c** Imprint as a brand (*lit.* & *fig.*). *rare*. M17. ▸**d** Mark with stigmata like the wounds of Jesus. M19.
2 Set a stigma on; give a reproachful name or description to; characterize *as* something (usu. discreditable or undesirable). E17.

> **2** V. WOOLF Ill-dressing, over-dressing she stigmatized . . with impatient movements of the hands. S. BECKETT He stigmatized every work as the end of them. K. VONNEGUT I cannot be stigmatized as an American fortune-hunter.

■ **stigmatiˈzation** *noun* the action or an instance of stigmatizing; the condition of being stigmatized: M19.

stigmatose /ˈstɪgmətəʊs/ *adjective*. M19.
[from Latin *stigmat-* STIGMA + -OSE¹.]
1 BOTANY. Of a style: bearing the stigma on a specified part, as along the side instead of (as usual) at the summit. M19.
2 MEDICINE. Covered or affected with stigmata. *rare*. L19.

stigmergy /ˈstɪgməːdʒi/ *noun*. M20.
[French *stigmergie*, from Greek *stigmos* pricking + *ergon* work: see -Y³.]
ENTOMOLOGY. The process by which the results of a worker insect's activity act as a stimulus to further activity.
■ **stigˈmergic** *adjective* L20.

Stijl /stʌɪl/ *noun & adjective*. M20.
[Ellipt.]
= DE STIJL.

stilb /stɪlb/ *noun*. M20.
[French, from Greek *stilbein* to glitter.]
PHYSICS. A unit of luminance equal to one candela per square centimetre.

stilbene /ˈstɪlbiːn/ *noun*. M19.
[from Greek *stilbein* to glitter + -ENE.]
CHEMISTRY. A synthetic crystalline bicyclic aromatic hydrocarbon used esp. in dye manufacture; *trans*-1,2-diphenylethene, $C_6H_5CH{=}CHC_6H_5$.

stilbestrol *noun* see STILBOESTROL.

stilbite /ˈstɪlbʌɪt/ *noun*. E19.
[from Greek *stilbein* to glitter + -ITE¹.]
MINERALOGY. A monoclinic hydrated silicate of aluminium, calcium and sodium that belongs to the zeolite group and usu. occurs as pearly white crystals in aggregates that resemble corn sheaves.

stilboestrol /stɪlˈbiːstrɒl/ *noun*. Also ***-bes-**. M20.
[from STILB(ENE + OESTR(US + -OL.]
PHARMACOLOGY. **1** Any synthetic stilbene derivative with oestrogenic properties. *rare*. M20.
2 *spec.* A powerful synthetic non-steroidal oestrogen, $HOC_6H_4{\cdot}C(C_2H_5){=}C(C_2H_5){\cdot}C_6H_4OH$, used in hormone therapy, as a postcoital contraceptive, and as a growth-promoting agent esp. in livestock. Also called ***diethylstilboestrol***. M20.

stil de grain /stil də grɛ̃/ *noun phr.* M18.
[French, app. from Dutch *schijtgroen*, from *schijt* excrement, SHIT *noun* + *groen* green.]
A yellow pigment formerly prepared from Persian berries (unripe fruit of *Rhamnus infectorius*).

stile /stʌɪl/ *noun*¹.
[Old English *stigel* corresp. to Old Saxon, Old High German *stigilla* (German dial. *Stiegel*), from Germanic base also of STY *verb*¹.]
An arrangement of steps, rungs, etc., made to allow people but not animals to pass over or through a fence or hedge. See also TURNSTILE.

> B. HINES A stile spanned the gap in the hedgerow.

stile /stʌɪl/ *noun*². L17.
[Prob. from Dutch *stijl* pillar, prop, doorpost.]
A vertical piece in the frame of a panelled door, wainscot, sash-window, or other similar wooden framework.

†**stile** *noun*³ & *verb* var. of STYLE.

stile antico /ˌstiːle anˈtiːko/ *noun phr.* M20.
[Italian = old style.]
MUSIC. The strict contrapuntal style of the sixteenth century, esp. as exemplified in the works of Palestrina.

stile concitato /ˌstiːle kontʃiˈtaːto/ *noun phr.* **E20.**
[Italian = excited style.]
MUSIC. A baroque style developed by Monteverdi, emphasizing dramatic expression and excitement.

stile rappresentativo /ˌstiːle ˌrapprezentaˈtiːvo/ *noun phr.* **L19.**
[Italian = representative style.]
MUSIC. The vocal style of recitative used by Italian musicians of the early seventeenth century.

stiletto /stɪˈlɛtəʊ/ *noun & verb.* **E17.**
[Italian, dim. of *stilo* dagger, ult. from Latin *stilus* STYLUS.]
▶ **A** *noun.* Pl. **-o(e)s.**
1 A short dagger with a thick blade. **E17.**
2 A small pointed instrument for making eyelet-holes. **E19.**
3 In full ***stiletto heel***. A very high tapering heel on a woman's shoe; a shoe with such a heel. **M20.**
▶ **B** *verb trans.* Stab or kill with a stiletto. *rare.* **E17.**

†**stilish** *adjective* see STYLISH.

still /stɪl/ *noun*¹. **ME.**
[from the adjective.]
1 A calm; a lull; a pause. Long *obsolete* exc. *Scot.* **ME.**
2 Stillness, quiet; deep silence, tranquillity. Formerly also, secrecy, stealth. Now *poet. & rhet.* **ME.**
3 A still pool. Long *obsolete* exc. *Canad. dial.* **L17.**
†**4** A stillborn child; a stillbirth. *slang.* **M–L19.**
5 An ordinary static photograph, as opp. to a motion picture; *spec.* a single shot from a film etc. for use in advertising etc. Freq. *attrib.* (often in *pl.*). **E20.**

📖 **2** E. TOPSELL In the still of the night, when every one . . were at rest. T. KENEALLY He was the only thing that broke up the still of the water. **5** C. WESTON The photo was a standard publicity still. B. GELDOF I . . filmed the Who and then took stills from a blow up. ***stills camera***, ***stills photography***, ***still picture***, etc.

still /stɪl/ *noun*². **M16.**
[from STILL *verb*².]
1 An apparatus for distilling (esp. spirituous liquor), consisting essentially of a vessel in which the substance to be distilled is heated, a condenser in which the vapour is liquefied, and a receiver in which the product is collected. **M16.**
2 A distillery. Formerly also, a still-room. **M16.**
3 A chamber or vessel for the industrial preparation of a gas or vapour by a chemical reaction. **M19.**
1 small-still (whisky) *Scot. & Anglo-Irish* whisky produced in a small still, supposedly of superior quality. ***patent still***, ***solar still***, etc.
Comb.: **still-head** the cap or upper compartment of a still; **still-house** a distillery; **still-room** (*a*) *Hist.* a room in a house in which a still was kept for the distillation of perfumes and cordials; (*b*) a room in which preserves, cakes, liqueurs, etc., are kept, and tea, coffee, etc., are prepared.

still /stɪl/ *adjective.*
[Old English *stille* = Old Frisian *stille*, Old Saxon, Old High German *stilli* (Dutch *stil*, German *still*), from West Germanic, from base meaning 'be fixed, stand'.]
1 Motionless; not or hardly moving, stationary. Usu. *pred.* **OE.** ▸**b** Of a drink: not sparkling or effervescing. **L18.**
2 Esp. of a person: silent, not speaking or making a noise. Now usu., habitually silent, taciturn. **OE.**
3 Of a voice, sound, utterance, or (formerly) of music, an instrument, etc.: subdued, soft, not loud. Now chiefly in ***still small voice*** (1 *Kings* 19:12). **OE.** ▸†**b** Secret; unobserved. **ME–L18.**
4 Free from commotion, disturbance, or activity; with little or no sound; tranquil, calm, peaceful, quiet; (of water) having an unruffled surface, without waves, ripples, or strong currents; (of the air) hardly moving, undisturbed by wind. **OE.** ▸†**b** Gentle in disposition; meek. **OE–LME.** ▸**c** Settled or unperturbed in mind. **ME.** ▸†**d** Uneventful, dull. Only in **18.**
†**5** Constant, continual; continued until now. **ME–E17.**
†**6** Born dead. Cf. STILLBIRTH, STILLBORN. *rare.* Only in **E17.**

📖 **1** SHELLEY Beneath the ray Of the still moon. H. CAINE The dance is over, but she can't keep her feet still. L. DURRELL In the corner . . so still that she was invisible at first sat a very old lady. **b** N. FREELING Old dears drinking . . still champagne. **2** SHAKES. *Com. Err.* Oh soft sir, hold you still. C. KINGSLEY A very still man . . as a mass-priest might be. **3** GIBBON The still voice of . . reason was seldom heard. L. DURRELL Perhaps at the bottom of the . . soul there is a still small voice forever whispering. **4** W. COWPER Stillest streams Oft water fairest meadows. E. WHARTON Those still November days. J. GARDNER For a long moment everything was still. A. N. WILSON The Brompton Road was completely deserted and still. *Proverb*: Still waters run deep. **c** G. MACDONALD My soul was not still enough for songs.

Special collocations, comb., & phrases: **keep a still tongue in one's head** be (habitually) silent or taciturn. **still-air** *adjective* (*a*) AERONAUTICS applicable or calculated for a state of no wind; (*b*) not employing forced draught. **still-fishing** *N. Amer.* fishing from one spot, esp. with a baited line. **still hunt** *US* a stealthy or concealed hunt for game, stalking; any stealthy or covert pursuit of something. **still-hunt** *verb trans. & intrans.* (*US*) hunt (for) stealthily or covertly; stalk. **still life**, pl. **still lifes**, [after Dutch *stilleven*] (a painting or drawing of) inanimate objects such as fruit, flowers, dead game, pots, etc.; the genre of painting such objects. **still-stand** a standstill; *spec.* (*a*) PHYSICAL GEOGRAPHY a condition or period in which there is a pause in a process such as crustal uplift, sea level change, or glacial advance or retreat; †(*b*) an armistice. **still water** (*a*) slack water; (*b*) (a piece of) water lacking turbulence or currents.
¶ Before **L16** only in *pred.* use.
■ **stillness** *noun* **OE.**

still /stɪl/ *verb*¹. Now *literary.*
[Old English *stillan* = Old Saxon (*gi*)*stillian* trans., *stillon* intrans., Old High German *stillen* trans., *stillēn* intrans., Old Norse *stilla*, from base of the adjective.]
1 *verb trans.* Make still or motionless; stop the motion or activity of; quiet, calm; subdue, allay; silence (a sound, (long *rare*) a person). Formerly also, soothe, lull, pacify. **OE.**
2 *verb intrans.* Become still or calm. **OE.**

📖 **1** A. E. STEVENSON We are . . grateful that the guns are stilled. S. WYNTER Hugh stole mangoes . . to still their hunger. E. WELTY The bartender stilled his cloth on the bar. G. SAYER He tried to still the incessant chatter. M. SPUFFORD Pain . . powerful enough to still me into immobility. **2** M. KEANE The air had stilled and frozen.

■ **stiller** *noun*¹ **E17.**

still /stɪl/ *verb*². **ME.**
[Aphet. from (the same root as) DISTIL.]
†**1** *verb intrans.* Trickle down or fall in minute drops. **ME–L17.**
†**2** *verb trans.* Exude, discharge, or let fall in minute drops. **LME–E18.**
3 *verb trans.* Subject to the process of distillation; extract or produce by distillation; distil. Now *rare.* **LME.**
■ **stiller** *noun*² a distiller **L16.** †**stillery** *noun* a still; a distillery: **L16–E19.**

still /stɪl/ *adverb.*
[Old English *stille*, Old Saxon, Old High German *stillo* (Dutch *stil*, German *still*), from West Germanic *stillō*, from base of the adjective.]
1 Without or almost without moving, motionlessly (*lit. & fig.*). **OE.**
†**2** Without noise or commotion; quietly, silently; softly. Also, secretly. **ME–E17.**
3 Continually, constantly; invariably; always. *arch.* **ME.**
4 Even now (or at a particular time) as formerly; at present, as yet; (now *rare*) in future as up to the present. **E16.** ▸†**b** Continuously in the same direction as before; further. **E17–M18.** ▸**c** In addition, after the apparent ending of a series. **L18.**
5 In a further degree; even (more), even (further); yet. Now chiefly with compar.; freq. *postpositive.* **L16.**
6 In spite of what has been stated or implied; even then, nevertheless, all the same. **L17.**

📖 **1** A. MOOREHEAD Time here had been standing still. I. MURDOCH I can't sit still these days, I'm too nervous. H. SECOMBE He groaned and lay still. J. TROLLOPE Human beings never stand still, . . nor do their relationships. **3** SIR W. SCOTT God rest the Baron . . he still was kind to me! **4** S. JOHNSON There still remain many words . . undefined. T. HARDY I wonder if she lives there still! J. STEINBECK His . . cap was so new that the visor was still stiff. E. JOHNSON At the age of thirty-one he still had no settled profession. **b** T. HERBERT Thence we sailed still South. **c** *Journal of Pediatrics* Full appreciation of the potential . . involved still another concept. **5** POPE Thus still his courage, with his toils encreas'd. V. WOOLF The Fabians were well worth hearing: still more worth seeing. P. FITZGERALD A follower of Tolstoy, still more so since Tolstoy died. R. MACNEIL Being lumped with *children* made me angrier still. **6** GOLDSMITH Though vanquished, he could argue still. D. H. LAWRENCE But still he took no notice. I. MURDOCH Otto might be a mess in every other way, but he was still a meticulous craftsman. C. FREMLIN Still, she might have told me.

Phrases: ***loud and still***: see LOUD *adverb.* **still and all**, **still and on** (*colloq. & dial.*) nevertheless, even so; after all. ***still less***: see LESS *adjective* etc.

stillage /ˈstɪlɪdʒ/ *noun*¹. **L16.**
[App. from Dutch *stellagie*, *stellaedsie* (now *stellage*) scaffold, stand, from *stellen* to place: see -AGE. Cf. STILLING, STILLION.]
A stand, orig. for casks; a pallet, frame, bench, etc., for keeping things off the floor while draining, drying, waiting to be packed, etc.; *collect.* storage structures of this kind.

stillage /ˈstɪlɪdʒ/ *noun*². Chiefly *US.* **M20.**
[from STILL *noun*² + -AGE.]
The residue remaining in a still after fermentation of grain, molasses, etc., and removal of the alcohol by distillation.

†**stillatitious** *adjective.* **M17.**
[from Latin *stillaticius*, from *stillat-*: see next, -ITIOUS¹.]
1 Falling in drops; issuing by drops. **M17–E19.**
2 Produced by distillation. **M17–E18.**

stillatory /ˈstɪlət(ə)ri/ *noun.* Now *rare* or *obsolete.* **LME.**
[medieval Latin *stillatorium*, from Latin *stillat-* pa. ppl stem of *stillare* drip, distil: see -ORY¹.]
1 A still. **LME.**
2 A still-room; a distillery. **E17.**

stillbirth /ˈstɪlbəːθ/ *noun.* **L18.**
[from STILL *adjective* + BIRTH *noun*¹.]
1 Birth of stillborn offspring; an instance of this. **L18.**
2 A stillborn child. **M20.**

stillborn /ˈstɪlbɔːn/ *adjective & noun.* **M16.**
[from STILL *adjective* + BORN *ppl adjective.*]
▶ **A** *adjective.* **1** Of a foetus: born lifeless, dead at birth or before the completion of delivery, *spec.* at a stage when normally viable. **M16.**
2 *fig.* Of an idea, plan, etc.: not able to succeed, abortive. **L16.**

📖 **2** SHAKES. *2 Hen. IV* Grant that our hopes (yet likely of fair birth) Should be stillborn. W. GREENER Numerous patents . . most of which have fallen stillborn.

▶ **B** *noun.* A stillborn foetus or (*fig.*) idea etc. **E20.**

stilleite /ˈstɪləʌɪt/ *noun.* **M20.**
[from Hans W. *Stille* (1876–1966), German geologist + -ITE¹.]
MINERALOGY. Native zinc selenide, usu. occurring as grey or black crystals of the cubic system.

stillicide /ˈstɪlɪsʌɪd/ *noun.* Now *rare.* **E17.**
[Anglicized from next.]
1 The falling of water etc. in drops; a succession of drops. **E17.**
2 LAW. = STILLICIDIUM 1. **M17.**

stillicidium /stɪlɪˈsɪdɪəm/ *noun.* Now *rare.* Pl. **-cidia** /-ˈsɪdɪə/. **E18.**
[Latin, from *stilla* drop + *cid-* weakened base of *cadere* to fall: see -IUM.]
1 LAW. (A right or duty relating to) the drainage of rainwater from the eaves of a building on to another's property. **E18.**
2 MEDICINE. Dropping or trickling of a discharge. **M18.**

stilling /ˈstɪlɪŋ/ *noun.* **E17.**
[Perh. from Dutch *stelling*, from *stellen* to place. Cf. STILLAGE *noun*¹, next.]
A stand for barrels.

stillion /ˈstɪljən/ *noun.* **E19.**
[Prob. var. of prec.]
1 A stand for barrels. **E19.**
2 A vessel in which yeast collects after fermentation of beer. **E19.**

Still's disease /ˈstɪlz dɪziːz/ *noun phr.* **E20.**
[Sir George *Still* (1868–1941), English physician.]
MEDICINE. A form of rheumatoid arthritis having its onset in childhood.

Stillson /ˈstɪls(ə)n/ *noun.* **E20.**
[Daniel C. *Stillson* (1830–99), US inventor.]
In full ***Stillson wrench***. A large adjustable wrench with jaws that tighten as pressure is increased.

stillwellite /ˈstɪlwɛlʌɪt/ *noun.* **M20.**
[from F. L. *Stillwell* (1888–1963), Australian geologist + -ITE¹.]
MINERALOGY. A trigonal borosilicate of calcium and lanthanide elements, usu. occurring as brown rhombohedral crystals.

stilly /ˈstɪli/ *adjective.* **ME.**
[from STILL *adjective* + -LY¹ or -Y¹.]
†**1** Secret. Only in **ME.**
2 Still, quiet. *poet.* **L18.**

stilly /ˈstɪli, -ll-/ *adverb. literary.* **OE.**
[from STILL *adjective* + -LY².]
In a still manner; silently, quietly; in a low voice.

stilpnomelane /stɪlpˈnɒmɪleɪn/ *noun.* **M19.**
[German *Stilpnomelan*, from Greek *stilpnos* glittering + *melan-*, *melas* black.]
MINERALOGY. A monoclinic or trigonal hydrated aluminosilicate of iron and potassium, usu. occurring as black or brown scales or as a velvety crust.

stilt /stɪlt/ *noun.* **ME.**
[Corresp. to Low German, Flemish *stilte*, from Germanic, and rel. to Swedish *stylta*, Norwegian, Danish *stylte* (from Germanic base of STOUT *adjective*), Middle Low German, Middle Dutch *stelte* (Dutch *stelt*), Old High German *stelza* (German *Stelze*).]
1 Each of the handles of a plough or other farm implement. Usu. in *pl. dial.* **ME.**
2 A crutch. *obsolete* exc. *dial.* **ME.**
3 Either of a pair of poles with supports for the feet, enabling a person to walk with the feet some distance above the ground. **LME.** ▸**b** *transf.* In *pl.* Long slender legs, esp. of a bird. **L16.**
4 a Any of a set of posts or piles on which a building is raised from the ground or above water-level. **E18.** ▸**b** POTTERY. A device for supporting and separating ceramic ware in a kiln, usu. consisting of three arms radiating from the centre with an upright point at each end. **E19.** ▸**c** ARCHITECTURE. A vertical masonry course from which an arch or vault springs at a height above the general level, or placed above or below a column to increase the height. **M19.**

5 Any of various wading birds of the genera *Himantopus* and *Cladorynchus*, having very long slender legs and slender sharp bills. Also more fully ***stilt-plover***. L18.

> 3 GEO. ELIOT Those mysterious giants were really men . . balancing themselves on stilts. *fig.*: H. CAINE Lifting himself into notoriety on the stilts of blasphemy. **on stilts** *fig.* bombastic(ally), stilted(ly). **4a** *Guardian* A Westbound motor road partly on stilts. P. MARSHALL Houses huddled on their stilts above the . . mud.

Comb.: **stilt bug** any insect of the heteropteran family Berytidae, whose members are characteristically long-legged and feed on plants; **stilt heel** (a shoe with) a high heel; **stilt-heeled** *adjective* (of a shoe) high-heeled; ***stilt-plover***: see sense 5 above; **stilt-root** an aerial root, arising from the trunk or lower branches of a tree, and acting to provide support; **stilt sandpiper** a long-legged N. American sandpiper, *Micropalama himantopus*.

▪ **stilty** *adjective* (*a*) resembling stilts; (of legs) long and stiff in action; (*b*) = STILTED 3. E19.

stilt /stɪlt/ *verb*. M17.
[from the noun.]
1 *verb trans.* Raise or build on stilts; elevate (*lit.* & *fig.*) as on stilts. M17. ▸**b** BOOKBINDING. Bind (a book) in projecting covers for the sake of uniformity with other volumes. E19. ▸**c** ARCHITECTURE. Raise (an arch, vault, etc.) above the ordinary level by a course of masonry. Cf. STILT *noun* 4c. M19.
2 *verb intrans.* Walk on or as if on stilts. L18.

> 1 TENNYSON That would stilt up York to twice himself. **2** P. QUENNELL Arches of an unfinished bridge, stilting across a wide . . river. W. MCILVANNEY She stilted awkwardly ahead of him.

▪ **stilter** *noun* a person who walks on stilts M19.

stilted /ˈstɪltɪd/ *adjective*. E17.
[from STILT *noun* or *verb*: see -ED², -ED¹.]
1 Having stilts or (orig., *rare*) crutches; built on stilts; raised artificially (as) on stilts; ARCHITECTURE (of an arch etc.) springing from stilts. E17.
2 Of a plough: having a specified number of handles (cf. STILT *noun* 1). *dial.* L18.
3 *fig.* Of language, style, etc.: artificially or affectedly lofty; stiff and unnatural; formal, pompous, bombastic. E19.

> 3 V. G. KIERNAN The irksomeness of artificially stilted manners. G. DALY Exchanging stilted sentences at long intervals.

▪ **stiltedly** *adverb* L19. **stiltedness** *noun* E19.

stiltified /ˈstɪltɪfʌɪd/ *adjective*. E19.
[formed as prec. + -FY + -ED¹.]
= STILTED 3.

Stilton /ˈstɪlt(ə)n/ *noun*. M18.
[A village in Huntingdonshire (now Cambridgeshire) where (at a coaching inn) the cheese was sold to travellers.]
In full ***Stilton cheese***. (Proprietary name for) a strong rich white cheese, often blue-veined, made in Leicestershire and neighbouring counties. Formerly also, a similar cheese made elsewhere.

stilyaga /stɪˈljaga/ *noun*. Pl. ***-gi*** /-gi/. M20.
[Russian colloq.]
Chiefly *Hist.* In the former Soviet Union, a young person dressing stylishly as an expression of rebellion, nonconformity, etc.

stim /stɪm/ *noun*. *slang*. L19.
[Abbreviation.]
A stimulating drink or drug.

stime *noun* var. of STYME.

Stimmung /ˈʃtɪmʊŋ/ *noun*. E20.
[German.]
Mood, spirit, atmosphere, feeling.

stimulable /ˈstɪmjʊləb(ə)l/ *adjective*. *rare*. E19.
[from STIMULATE *verb* + -ABLE.]
Able to be stimulated.
▪ **stimulaˈbility** *noun* E19.

stimulant /ˈstɪmjʊlənt/ *noun* & *adjective*. E18.
[Latin *stimulant-* pres. ppl stem of *stimulare*: see STIMULATE, -ANT¹.]
▸**A** *noun*. An agent that stimulates a person or thing; a stimulus. Now *esp.*, an alcoholic drink or drug that stimulates bodily or mental activity. E18.

> I. COMPTON-BURNETT Tea is a stimulant . . and helps one about one's business. D. ACHESON Public life is not only a powerful stimulant but a habit-forming one. ANTHONY HUXLEY Dryness at the roots . . is often a good stimulant to flower initiation.

▸**B** *adjective*. Having the property of stimulating, acting as a stimulus; *esp.* that stimulates bodily or mental activity. L18.
▪ **stimulancy** *noun* (now *rare*) stimulating quality L18.

stimulate /ˈstɪmjʊleɪt/ *verb*. M16.
[Latin *stimulat-* pa. ppl stem of *stimulare*, formed as STIMULUS: see -ATE³.]
†**1** *verb trans.* Sting, afflict. *rare*. Only in M16.
2 *verb trans.* Rouse to action or exertion as by pricking or goading; spur on; incite *to do* something; animate, excite, arouse; give more energy to (an activity, a process); BIOLOGY act as a stimulus to. E17.
3 *verb intrans.* Indulge in (alcoholic) stimulants. Chiefly *US colloq.* Now *rare*. E19.

> 2 C. J. LEVER You have stimulated my curiosity. GEO. ELIOT They . . stimulated their prisoners to beg. T. HARDY Our arrival stimulated them in the work of repair. B. SPOCK Filling of the stomach tends to stimulate the intestinal tract. D. ACHESON The President chose to raise prices as the principal method of stimulating . . agriculture. R. FRASER The home provided a wealth of material that would stimulate young minds. *absol.*: J. AUSTEN Where Miss Taylor failed to stimulate . . Harriet . . will do nothing.

▪ **stimulating** *ppl adjective* that stimulates someone or something; stimulant; *esp.* providing a stimulus to mental activity: M17. **stimulatingly** *adverb* in a stimulating manner, so as to stimulate E20.

stimulation /stɪmjʊˈleɪʃ(ə)n/ *noun*. E16.
[Latin *stimulatio(n-)*, formed as prec.: see -ATION.]
The action of stimulating someone or something, the effect of a stimulus; the condition of being stimulated; an instance of this.

stimulative /ˈstɪmjʊlətɪv/ *noun* & *adjective*. M18.
[from STIMULATE + -IVE.]
▸†**A** *noun*. A stimulus, an incentive. Also (*rare*), a stimulant. M18–E19.
▸**B** *adjective*. Stimulating. (Foll. by *of*, *to*.) L18.

stimulator /ˈstɪmjʊleɪtə/ *noun*. E17.
[Latin, formed as STIMULATE: see -OR.]
A person who or thing which stimulates someone or something; *spec.* an instrument for communicating a stimulus.

stimulatory /ˈstɪmjʊlət(ə)ri/ *adjective*. M18.
[from STIMULATE + -ORY².]
Stimulating.

stimulus /ˈstɪmjʊləs/ *noun*. Pl. **-li** /-lʌɪ, -liː/. L17.
[Latin = goad, spur, incentive, prob. from base also of *stilus* STYLUS.]
1 A thing that provokes, increases, or quickens bodily activity; *esp.* (BIOLOGY) a material agency that evokes a specific reaction in an organ or tissue. L17. ▸**b** *gen.* An agency or influence that rouses or spurs something or someone to action or quickens an activity or process; a spur, an incentive. (Foll. by *to* an action etc.) L18. ▸**c** Chiefly PSYCHOLOGY. Any change or event which excites a nerve impulse and gives rise to a physical reaction or response. L19.
2 The effect or property of producing such a reaction; stimulation; an instance of this. L17.
3 BOTANY & ZOOLOGY. A sting, a stinging hair. *rare* (only in Dicts. & Glossaries). M18.

> 1 W. S. HALL Forms of energy act as stimuli for . . cells. **b** G. BATTISCOMBE In bad need of mental stimulus. M. MEYER This reverse was the stimulus that provoked him to write his first play. *New York Review of Books* War . . was the stimulus to ambitious programmes of reform. **2** H. KELLER The child . . learns of himself, provided he is supplied with sufficient outward stimulus. W. S. CHURCHILL Under the stimulus of the enemy's fire . . our pace increased. H. CARPENTER Renowned . . for his . . stimulus to the young.

Comb.: **stimulus generalization** PSYCHOLOGY the phenomenon of a response elicited by one stimulus being also elicited by other stimuli associated with but not identical to the original.

stimy *noun* & *verb* var. of STYMIE.

sting /stɪŋ/ *noun*¹. *Scot.* & *north.*
[Old English *steng* corresp. to Old Norse *stǫng*: see STANG *noun*¹.]
1 A pole, a staff; the shaft of a pike or spear. OE.
2 A pointed instrument used in thatching. E19.

sting /stɪŋ/ *noun*². OE.
[from the verb.]
▸**I 1** An act or instance of stinging; (the pain of) a wound caused by this. OE.
2 A sharp-pointed organ in various insects and other animals (as bees, wasps, scorpions, etc.) capable of inflicting a painful or dangerous wound, esp. by injecting poison. Also (now *arch.* & *poet.*), the fang or the forked tongue of a poisonous snake. LME.
3 BOTANY. A stiff sharp-pointed tubular hair, which emits an irritating fluid when touched. Formerly also, a thorn. M16.
4 AERONAUTICS. A rodlike support used in wind-tunnel testing. M20.

> 1 SHAKES. *2 Hen. VI* Their softest touch as smart as lizards' stings. J. RUSKIN The pang of a nice deep wasp sting.

▸**II** *fig.* **5** (A thing causing) a sharp mental or emotional pain or wound; a goad, a stimulus. ME.
6 A wounding or painful quality or effect, capacity to hurt; pungency, sharpness, vigour. M19.
7 *Austral. slang.* **a** Strong drink. E20. ▸**b** A drug, *esp.* one illegally administered to a racehorse by injection. M20.
8 A carefully planned and swiftly executed theft; a swindle, a confidence trick. Also, a police undercover operation to trap a criminal. *slang* (orig. & chiefly *N. Amer.*). M20.

> 5 SHAKES. *All's Well* Ah, what sharp stings are in her mildest words! LD MACAULAY They felt the sting of hunger. **sting in the tail** an unexpected pain or difficulty at the end. **6** G. O. TREVELYAN This passage . . has been deprived of half its sting. J. BRAINE The smile . . took the sting from the reproof. **8** *Daily Telegraph* He was caught in a police 'sting' which videotaped him handing over $2,500. *attrib.*: R. BANKS LaCoy started dealing cocaine and got nabbed in a sting operation.

Comb.: **sting-fish** any of various fishes with poisonous spines, *esp.* the lesser weever, *Trachinus vipera*; **sting-tailed** *adjective* having a sting in the tail (*lit.* & *fig.*).

▪ **stinged** *adjective* having a sting (*lit.* & *fig.*) M16. **stingless** *adjective* M16. **stinglike** *adjective* resembling (that of) a sting L19.

sting /stɪŋ/ *verb*. Pa. t. **stung** /stʌŋ/, (now *dial.*) **stang** /staŋ/; pa. pple **stung**.
[Old English *stingan* = Old Norse *stinga*, from Germanic base also of Old Norse *stanga* pierce. Cf. STANG *noun*¹, *verb*¹.]
†**1** *verb trans.* Pierce with a sharp-pointed weapon or instrument. OE–L15.
2 a *verb trans.* & *intrans.* Of an animal: prick or wound with a (poisonous) sting. OE. ▸**b** *verb trans.* & *intrans.* Of a plant: cause by contact a smarting itching rash or inflammation in (the skin); affect the skin of (a person) in this way. M16. ▸**c** *verb refl.* Get stung by a plant. M17.
3 *transf.* & *fig.* **a** *verb trans.* Inflict a painful or fatal wound on (now *poet.*); cause or occasion irritation or a sudden sharp mental pain in (a person); provoke or goad *(in)to* anger, action, etc. LME. ▸**b** *verb trans.* & *intrans.* Affect (a person) with a tingling pain or smarting sensation. E17. ▸**c** *verb trans.* Swindle, cheat, overcharge; involve in financial loss. Freq. in *pass. slang.* E19.
4 *verb intrans.* Feel sharp pain or distress; smart; (of a wound or sore) throb with pain. M19.

> 2a A. S. NEILL Mary . . was stung by a wasp. T. HOOPER When the bee stings it injects a protein. **b** ***stinging nettle***: see NETTLE *noun* 1. **stinging tree** *Austral.* any of several trees and shrubs of the genus *Dendrocnide*, of the nettle family, having leaves etc. covered with virulent stinging hairs; esp. *D. excelsa*, a tall tree of tropical rainforest. **3a** LD MACAULAY The jurymen . . were stung by remorse. C. DAY Clarence kept taunting him and daring him until Frank was stung into doing it. *absol.*: G. DALY His recent rejection by Annie still stung. **b** C. STANFORD Stung by a spark of fire we start in agony. F. W. FARRAR He felt the . . lash . . come stinging round his body. **c** P. G. WODEHOUSE 'How much did you pay?' 'Three hundred dollars.' 'You were stung.' **4** P. CAREY His right ear was still . . stinging from the blow.

▪ **stingingly** *adverb* in a stinging manner M17.

stingaree /ˌstɪŋgəˈriː, ˈstɪŋgəriː/ *noun*. *US* & *Austral.* M19.
[Alt. of STINGRAY.]
A stingray, *esp.* the common Australian *Urolophus testaceus*.

stinge /ˈstɪn(d)ʒ/ *noun*. E20.
[Back-form. from STINGY *adjective*².]
A stingy person.

stinger /ˈstɪŋə/ *noun*¹. M16.
[from STING *verb* + -ER¹.]
1 A person who inflicts (mental) pain on another, *esp.* one whose behaviour or speech is provocative. Long *rare*. M16.
2 An animal or plant that stings. L16.
3 A thing that stings or smarts; *spec.* (*a*) a sharp blow; (*b*) a biting or pungent speech or piece of writing; (*c*) *US* an animal's stinging organ; (*d*) *Austral.* a period of exceptionally hot or cold weather. Now *colloq.* L16.
4 A long structure attached to the stern of a pipe-laying barge to support the pipe as it enters the water and prevent it from buckling. M20.
5 (**S-**.) MILITARY. A lightweight shoulder-launched heat-seeking anti-aircraft missile. L20.
6 (**S-**.) (US proprietary name for) a device consisting of a spiked metal ribbon that is placed across a road to stop vehicles by puncturing their tyres. L20.

stinger /ˈstɪŋə/ *noun*². E20.
[Alt.]
= STENGAH. Also, any of various other mixed drinks or cocktails.

stingle /ˈstɪŋg(ə)l/ *noun*. *rare*. Long *obsolete* exc. *dial.* LME.
[from STING *noun*² + -LE¹.]
= STING *noun*² 2.

stingo /ˈstɪŋgəʊ/ *noun*. *arch. slang*. Pl. **-os**. M17.
[from STING *verb* (with allus. to the sharp taste) + -O.]
1 Strong ale or beer. M17.
2 *fig.* Vigour, energy. L19.

stingray /ˈstɪŋreɪ/ *noun*. E17.
[from STING *noun*² + RAY *noun*².]
Any of various cartilaginous fishes of the families Dasyatidae and Urolophidae having a flattened, roughly diamond-shaped body and a tapering tail armed with a long poisonous serrated spine.

stingy /ˈstɪŋi/ *adjective*^{1}. E17.
[from STING *noun*^{2} or *verb* + -Y^{1}.]
1 Having a sting; stinging, virulent. Chiefly *fig.* Long *rare*. E17.
2 *spec.* Of weather etc.: sharp, biting, cold. *dial.* E19.

> **1** E. HICKERINGILL I know your meaning .. and your stingy .. Innuendo. OED Those are very stingy nettles. **2** S. RADLEY I was hoping for .. a warm-up .. it's stingy old weather out there.

stingy /ˈstɪn(d)ʒi/ *adjective*^{2}. M17.
[Perh. from dial. var. of STING *noun*^{2}: see -Y^{1}.]
1 Of a person, action, etc.: niggardly, parsimonious, mean. Also foll. by *of*. M17. ▸**b** Of food, a portion, supply, etc.: given sparingly or grudgingly; scanty, meagre. M19.
2 Bad-tempered, irritable, peevish. *dial.* L18.

> **1** J. A. SYMONDS He was never stingy of cash. *National Observer (US)* The .. Administration is stingy about the .. information it releases. B. BAINBRIDGE He was a penniless student forced by his stingy brother to seek employment. R. JAFFE His father had been very stingy with the divorce settlement.

■ **stingily** *adverb* L17. **stinginess** *noun* L17.

stink /stɪŋk/ *verb & noun*.
[Old English *stincan* = Middle & mod. Low German, Middle & mod. Dutch *stinken*, Old High German *stinkan* (German *stinken*), from West Germanic. Cf. STENCH *noun*.]
▸ **A** *verb*. Pa. t. **stank** /staŋk/, **stunk** /stʌŋk/; pa. pple **stunk**.
†**1** *verb intrans.* Emit or give off a smell. OE–ME.
2 *verb intrans.* **a** Emit a strong offensive smell; smell foully or disgustingly (*of*). OE. ▸**b** *fig.* Be offensive or abhorrent; have or appear to have plenty (esp. an offensive amount or degree) of something, esp. money (foll. by *of, with*). Now also, be or seem scandalous, despicable, inept or completely incompetent. Now *colloq.* ME.
3 *verb trans.* **a** Cause to stink. ME. ▸**b** *spec.* Cause (a place) to stink. Foll. by *up, out*. *colloq.* M20.
4 *verb trans.* Fill (an animal's earth) with suffocating fumes. Also, drive (an animal or person) *out* of a place by an offensive smell. L18.

> **2a** M. M. KAYE The oil lamp .. stank abominably. P. BAILEY My father compained that his suit stank of mothballs. **b** I. BROWN He stinks of money. J. T. FARRELL I watched you guys go through signal practice. You stunk! *Creative Review* This advert .. stinks, but apparently the sales went up. **3a** F. A. STEEL One dead fish stinks a whole tank. **b** J. RULE They stank up rooms with their farts.

▸ **B** *noun*. **1** A foul, disgusting, or offensive smell; a stench. ME. ▸**b** A contemptible person. *slang*. E20.
2 A row, a fuss; a furore. *colloq.* E19.
3 In *pl.* Natural science, esp. chemistry, as a subject studied in school or (formerly) university. *slang*. M19.

> **1** OUIDA So much stink of oil and sickly smell of silkworms. J. C. OATES The frank, undisguised stinks of the lavatory. **2** L. SANDERS [She] commanded a world press. She could raise a tremendous stink if she chose to do so. *Skiing* If your ski school .. organises classes which are larger than 12 .. kick up a stink. **3** *Times* Everyone who did .. elementary 'stinks' at school remembers the name of Bunsen and his burner.

Phrases: **like stink** *colloq.* furiously, intensely, extremely hard or fast.
Comb.: **stink beetle** = *stink-bug* below; **stink-bird** any of various birds with a strong odour, as (in Guyana) the hoatzin, (in Australia) a warbler of the genus *Sericornis*; **stinkblaar** [Dutch *blaar* leaf] *S. Afr.* the thorn-apple, *Datura stramonium*; **stink bomb** a small hand-held missile releasing an unpleasant smell on impact; **stink-bug** an insect which emits an unpleasant smell; *spec.* a pentatomid shield bug, which ejects a strong-smelling liquid if attacked; **stink-cat** *S. Afr.* the zorilla or muishond, *Ictonyx striatus*; **stink gland** in various animals, a gland producing a fetid secretion; **stinkhorn (fungus)** any of various gasteromycetous fungi, esp. *Phallus impudicus*, in which the gleba emits a powerful stench; **stinkstone** MINERALOGY a kind of stone, esp. a bituminous limestone, which gives out a fetid odour when rubbed or broken; **stinkweed** any of several plants having a disagreeable smell; *esp.* (*a*) the wall rocket, *Diplotaxis muralis*; (*b*) *US* the thorn-apple, *Datura stramonium*; **stinkwood** any of various trees having wood which gives off a disagreeable smell, esp. (*S. Afr.*) *Ocotea bullata*, of the laurel family (more fully ***black stinkwood***), (*Austral.*) *Zieria arborescens*, of the rue family, (*NZ*) *Coprosma foetidissima*, of the madder family; the wood of these trees.
■ **stinkeroo**, **-aroo** *noun* (*slang*, orig. *US*) (*a*) a thing, esp. a performance, of a very low standard; (*b*) a furore, a row: M20.

stinkard /ˈstɪŋkəd/ *noun*. L16.
[from prec. + -ARD.]
1 A smelly or despicable person. L16.
2 Any of various animals of the weasel family with a strong smell; *esp.* the teledu. L18.
3 A petrel, a fulmar. *Nautical slang*. M19.

stinker /ˈstɪŋkə/ *noun*. Chiefly *slang*. E17.
[from STINK *verb* + -ER^{1}.]
1 a A smelly or despicable person. Freq. *joc.*. E17. ▸**b** A thing with an offensive smell. M19.
2 A heavy blow. *rare*. E19.
3 A petrel, a fulmar. L19.
4 *fig.* **a** A letter, review, etc., expressing strong disapproval. E20. ▸**b** A repugnant or objectionable thing; *spec.* a difficult task or problem. E20.

†**stinkibus** *noun*. *slang*. E18–L19.
[from STINK *noun* + Latin *-ibus* dat. pl. ending.]
Bad liquor, *esp.* adulterated spirits.

stinking /ˈstɪŋkɪŋ/ *adjective & adverb*. OE.
[from STINK *verb* + -ING^{2}.]
▸ **A** *adjective*. **1** That smells foul or offensive. OE. ▸**b** Of a smell: foul, offensive. M16.
2 *fig.* Disgusting, contemptible. Now *rare*. ME.
3 Extremely or disgustingly rich or drunk. Also, oversupplied *with* something, esp. money. *colloq.* L19.
Special collocations: **stinking badger** = TELEDU. **stinking bird** = *stink-bird* s.v. STINK *noun & verb*. **stinking bug** = *stink-bug* s.v. STINK *noun & verb*. **stinking camomile** a mayweed with a fetid smell, *Anthemis cotula*. **stinking cedar** a gymnospermous tree of Florida, *Torreya taxifolia*, of the yew family, with fetid leaves, branches, and wood. **stinking fish** (*a*) a worthless or rotten thing; ***cry stinking fish***, disparage one's own efforts, products, etc.; (*b*) in Ghana, fish preserved in salt. **stinking gum** *Austral.* a eucalyptus, *Eucalyptus tereticornis*, whose leaves have a strong unpleasant smell. **stinking hellebore** a European hellebore, *Helleborus foetidus*, with purple-tipped greenish apetalous flowers. **stinking iris** the gladdon, *Iris foetidissima*. **stinking mayweed** = *stinking camomile* above. **stinking Roger** any of various foul-smelling plants; *esp.* (*a*) *dial.* a figwort, *Scrophularia nodosa*; (*b*) *Austral.* a N. American marigold, *Tagetes minuta*, occurring as a weed. **stinking smut** bunt, a fungoid disease of wheat, so named because of the smell of rotten fish given off by the spore masses. **stinking weed** a senna of the south-eastern US and the W. Indies, *Cassia occidentalis*. **stinking Willie** *Scot. & NZ* ragwort, *Senecio jacobaea*. **stinking yew** = *stinking cedar* above.
▸ **B** *adverb*. †**1** So as to stink. *rare*. L16–M17.
2 ***stinking rich***, ***stinking drunk***, extremely or disgustingly rich or drunk. *colloq.* L16.
■ **stinkingly** *adverb* (*a*) in a stinking manner; (*b*) *colloq.* extremely: E16. **stinkingness** *noun* LME.

stinko /ˈstɪŋkəʊ/ *adjective & adverb*. *slang* (orig. *US*). E20.
[from STINK *verb* + -O.]
▸ **A** *adjective*. **1** Of a very low standard. E20.
2 Intoxicated; extremely drunk. E20.
▸ **B** *adverb*. ***stinko drunk***, extremely drunk. M20.

stink-pot /ˈstɪŋkpɒt/ *noun*. Also **stinkpot**. M17.
[from STINK *noun* + POT *noun*^{1}.]
1 A small missile emitting a suffocating smoke when thrown, used as a diversionary tactic in attacking and boarding a ship (*obsolete* exc. *Hist.*); a stink bomb. M17.
2 A bird with a strong smell, *esp.* a petrel. *Nautical slang*. M19.
3 A common musk turtle, *Sternotherus odoratus*, which is found in SE Canada and the eastern US, and emits a foul-smelling secretion when disturbed. Also ***stink-pot terrapin***, ***stink-pot turtle***. M19.
4 *slang*. **a** A contemptible or objectionable person or (*occas.*) thing. Freq. as a term of abuse. M19. ▸**b** A boat or vehicle which emits foul exhaust fumes. L20.

stinky /ˈstɪŋki/ *adjective*. Now *colloq.* LME.
[from STINK *noun* + -Y^{1}.]
= STINKING *adjective*.
¶ Not recorded between LME and M19.

stint /stɪnt/ *noun*^{1}. Also (long *rare*) **stent** /stɛnt/. ME.
[from the verb.]
▸ **I** The action of the verb.
†**1** (A) cessation of action or motion; a pause. ME–E17.
2 Orig., (a) limitation, (a) restriction. Now *spec.*, excessive restriction in the supply of necessities, comforts, etc.; the condition of being kept scantily supplied. L16.
†**3** An act of putting a mare to a stallion. Cf. STINT *verb* 14. *rare*. Only in M18.

> **2** J. G. HOLLAND His wife and children had money lavished on them without stint. E. R. PITMAN No need for stint where supplies were always at hand.

▸ **II 4** A natural, prescribed, or customary amount, quantity, portion, or allowance. *obsolete* exc. as below. LME.
5 A maximum number of cattle allotted to a given piece of pasture or common land or to a person having the right of common pasturage; a portion of land allotted for pasturing a limited number of livestock. LME.
6 An allotted quota of work; a definite task; a period of time spent on a particular job, a shift; *spec.* an amount of work (to be) done in a shift by a miner. E16.
†**7** A natural, prescribed, or customary limit of extent, duration, etc. E16–E18.
8 A beaver-dam. *Canad. dial.* L18.

> **4** SWIFT My stint [of wine] in company is a pint at noon and half .. at night. W. COWPER Wisdom beyond the common stint I mark In this our guest. A. YOUNG A child's stint .. for braiding nets .. is four-pence a day. **c** G. BERKELEY Their stint .. is an hour and half a day for painting. R. KIPLING Letting in the water for the evening stint at Robert's Mill. *Times Lit. Suppl.* Handing over to his successor .. at the end of a five-and-a-half-year stint.

■ **stintless** *adjective* (*a*) (of grief, suffering, etc.) unable to be assuaged; (*b*) unstinting: L16. **stinty** *adjective* (*rare*) meagre, niggardly M19.

stint /stɪnt/ *noun*^{2}. ME.
[Origin unkn.]
Any of several small sandpipers, chiefly of the genus *Calidris*; *esp.* (*a*) the dunlin; (*b*) the sanderling.

stint /stɪnt/ *verb*. Also (long *obsolete* exc. *dial.*) **stent** /stɛnt/.
[Old English *styntan*; in some senses prob. infl. by corresp. Old Norse verb meaning 'shorten'. Ult. from Germanic. Cf. STUNT *verb*^{1}.]
▸ **I** †**1** *verb trans.* Make blunt or dull. Only in OE.
▸ **II** Stop, shorten.
2 *verb intrans.* Of a person: cease (an) action; desist. Also foll. by *to do*, †*of*. Now *arch. & dial.* ME. ▸†**b** Of a process, condition, activity, etc.: abate, come to an end. ME–L17.
3 *verb intrans.* Cease moving; pause in a journey. Now *arch. rare*. ME. ▸†**b** Abstain from moving, stand still; remain in a place, stay. ME–L15. ▸†**c** Of a stream or blood: cease flowing. LME–E17.
†**4** *verb trans.* **a** Cause (a person) to cease (an) action or desist. Also foll. by *of*. ME–E19. ▸**b** Put an end to, stop, (an event, phenomenon, state of affairs, etc.). ME–M18. ▸**c** Diminish, nullify, (a feeling, power, etc.). LME–M17.
5 *verb trans.* Cause (an animal, a person) to come to a halt; stop the flow of (a fluid, esp. blood). Long *obsolete* exc. *dial.* ME.
6 *verb trans.* Leave off, discontinue, (one's own action; †*doing*); hold in check, restrain, (oneself, one's action, etc.). Now *arch. & dial.* ME.
7 *verb trans.* Check the growth of, stunt. Also, force (a plant) *into* bloom by restricting the supply of nourishment. M18.

> **2** SHELLEY Would neither stint nor stick Our flesh from off our bones to pick. **4** MILTON Strength .. To stint th' enemy. **b** C. NESS Strife is easier stirred than stinted. **c** W. GOUGE Where faith hath failed, the divine power hath been stinted.

▸ **III** Limit, prescribe.
8 a *verb trans.* Set bounds to; limit in extent or scope; confine to certain limits. Now *rare*. E16. ▸†**b** *verb intrans.* Of a piece of land: have a boundary (*at* or bordering *upon*). *rare*. E17–M18.
9 *verb trans.* Limit (the pasturage of common land) to a certain number of livestock; assign a limited right of pasturage to (a person). E16.
†**10** *verb trans.* Prescribe (a specific action, amount, place, time, etc.). E16–M17.
11 *verb trans.* Restrict (a person) *to* or to a certain action, quantity, share, allowance, etc. M16.
12 a *verb trans.* Be niggardly towards (a person, esp. oneself); supply with a niggardly or inadequate amount (*of*). E18. ▸**b** *verb trans.* Limit (a supply) unduly; be sparing, mean, or grudging with (food, money, effort, etc.). M19. ▸**c** *verb intrans.* Be mean or sparing, economize, go short. M19.
13 *verb trans.* Allot a quota of work to (a person) as a stint. (Cf. STINT *noun*^{1} 6.) *dial.* L18.
14 *verb trans.* In *pass.* Of a mare: be served (by a stallion). E19.

> **8a** J. GAY Stint not to truth the flow of wit. A. W. KINGLAKE The law of nations does not stint the right of executing justice. **11** LD MACAULAY Stinted himself to one bottle at a meal. **12a** A. B. JAMESON Parents who stinted themselves of necessary things. W. S. CHURCHILL Her Majesty was so stinted by Parliament that she was not able to pay me even a living wage. **b** C. MACKENZIE Joseph .. had stinted nothing to make it a memorable occasion. **c** R. FRAME The family had never stinted in its hospitality to her. M. ROBINSON The proprietor chose to stint on wages.

■ **stinter** *noun* LME.

stintage /ˈstɪntɪdʒ/ *noun*. M17.
[from STINT *noun*^{1} or *verb* + -AGE.]
1 = STINTING *noun* 2. M17.
2 The allotment of stints. M17.

stinted /ˈstɪntɪd/ *adjective*. E16.
[from STINT *verb* + -ED^{1}.]
†**1 a** Fixed or limited by authority or decree; appointed, set. E16–L18. ▸**b** *spec.* Of a liturgy, prayer, etc.: prescribed in set form by ecclesiastical authority. L16–E18.
2 Limited, scanty. E17.
3 Of pasture: divided into or subject to rights of pasturage; limited to the pasturing of a specific number of livestock. L17.
4 Of a plant or animal: stunted, undersized. M18.
5 Of a mare or she-ass: in foal. M19.
¶ Earlier in UNSTINTED.
■ **stintedly** *adverb* M19.

stinting /ˈstɪntɪŋ/ *noun*. ME.
[from STINT *verb* + -ING^{1}.]
1 The action of STINT *verb*. ME.
2 A piece of common land set apart for use by a particular person. ME.

stipe /stʌɪp/ *noun*[1]. **L18.**
[French from Latin STIPES.]
BOTANY. A stalk; *esp.* (*a*) the stalk which supports the pileus of a basidiomycetous fungus; (*b*) the petiole of a fern blade; (*c*) in certain algae, the part joining the lamina to the holdfast.

stipe /stʌɪp/ *noun*[2]. *slang.* **M19.**
[Abbreviation of STIPENDIARY.]
1 A stipendiary magistrate. **M19.**
2 A stipendiary racing steward. Chiefly *Austral.* **E20.**

stipel /ˈstʌɪp(ə)l/ *noun.* Also in Latin form **stipella** /stɪˈpɛlə/, pl. **-llae** /-liː/. **E19.**
[French *stipelle* from mod. Latin *stipella* dim. of STIPULA.]
BOTANY. A small stipule at the base of a leaflet in a compound leaf.
■ **stipellate** /stɪˈpɛlət/ *adjective* having stipels **E19.**

stipend /ˈstʌɪpɛnd/ *noun.* **LME.**
[Old French *stipend(i)e* or Latin *stipendium*, from *stips*, *stip-* payment, wages, alms + *pendere* weigh, pay.]
1 A soldier's pay. Now *rare* or *obsolete.* **LME.**
2 A salary or fixed regular sum paid for the services of a teacher, public official, or (esp.) a minister of religion. **LME.** ▸**b** Any fixed regular payment; *spec.* (*a*) a pension; (*b*) an allowance. **M16.**
†**3** A fee; wages. **E16–M19.**

📖 **2** N. FARAH He would become a clerk in a government office and bring back a monthly stipend. M. LANE The perpetual curacy . . carried a stipend of £180 per annum.

■ **stipended** *adjective* (*rare*) receiving a stipend **E17.** **stipendless** *adjective* **L17.**

stipendiary /stʌɪˈpɛndjəri, stɪ-/ *noun & adjective.* **LME.**
[Latin *stipendiarius*, from *stipendium* STIPEND: see -ARY[1].]
▸ **A** *noun.* A recipient of a stipend; *spec.* (*a*) a salaried minister of religion; †(*b*) a mercenary; (*c*) = ***stipendiary magistrate*** below. **LME.**
▸ **B** *adjective.* **1** Receiving a stipend; working for pay (as opp. to voluntarily). **M16.**
2 Pertaining to or of the nature of a stipend. **M17.**
Special collocations: **stipendiary magistrate** a paid professional magistrate with functions similar to those of a Justice of the Peace. **stipendiary steward** *Austral.* a paid steward controlling the running of horse-races etc.
■ Also †**stipendary** *noun & adjective* **LME–M17.**

†**stipendiate** *verb trans.* **M17–M19.**
[Latin *stipendiat-* pa. ppl stem of *stipendiari* be in receipt of pay, from *stipendium* STIPEND: see -ATE[3].]
Pay a stipend to.

stiper /ˈstʌɪpə/ *noun. rare.* Long *obsolete* exc. *dial.*
[Old English *stipere* = Low German, Middle Dutch, Middle High German *stiper*, Flemish *stijper*.]
A prop, a support.

stipes /ˈstʌɪpiːz/ *noun.* Pl. **stipites** /ˈstɪpɪtiːz/. **M18.**
[Latin = log, post, tree-trunk.]
1 *BOTANY.* = STIPE *noun*[1]. **M18.**
2 *ZOOLOGY.* A part or organ resembling a stalk; *esp.* the second joint of the maxilla of an insect. **E19.**

stipitate /ˈstɪpɪtət/ *adjective.* **L18.**
[mod. Latin *stipitatus*, from Latin *stipit-*, STIPES: see -ATE[2].]
BOTANY & ZOOLOGY. Having a stipe or (short) stalk.

stipites *noun* pl. of STIPES.

stipple /ˈstɪp(ə)l/ *noun.* **M17.**
[In sense 1 from Dutch *stippel* dim. of *stip* point; in sense 2 from the verb.]
1 In *pl.* Dots or small spots used in or produced by stippling. **M17.**
2 The process, technique, or effect of stippling; stippled work. Also, an engraving produced by stippling. **M19.**

📖 **1** C. HAYES The effect can be achieved with streaks . . stipples or . . any combination of marks. **2** M. SENDAK These pictures combine Parrish's then favourite techniques, wash, line, and stipple. *transf.*: W. GOLDING The sun was making a stipple of bright spots over the undergrowth. *attrib.*: ***stipple engraving***, ***stipple pattern***, etc.

stipple /ˈstɪp(ə)l/ *verb trans.* **M18.**
[Dutch *stippelen* frequentative of *stippen* to prick or speckle, from *stip* point: see -LE[3].]
1 Paint, draw, engrave, (an illustration, surface, etc.) with dots, small spots, or flecks instead of lines; paint *in* or apply dots, spots, etc., of (pigment, colour, etc.). Now also, produce a roughened texture on (paint, cement, a surface, etc.). **M18.**
2 *transf.* Of a natural process etc.: produce spots, flecks, etc., on (a surface). **L18.**

📖 **2** A. LURIE The shadows of high clouds . . stippling the ground with . . patches of light.

■ **stippled** *adjective* (*a*) that has been stippled; (*b*) having a dotted, spotted, or flecked appearance: **E19.** **stippler** *noun* a person who or thing which stipples something, *esp.* a brush for stippling **L19.** **stippling** *noun* (*a*) the action of the verb; (*b*) a stippled design, work, or appearance: **E19.**

stipula /ˈstɪpjʊlə/ *noun.* Now *rare* or *obsolete.* Pl. **-lae** /-liː/, **-las.** **M18.**
[mod. Latin use of Latin = straw, STUBBLE *noun.*]
BOTANY. = STIPULE.

stipular /ˈstɪpjʊlə/ *adjective.* **L18.**
[from STIPULA + -AR[1].]
BOTANY. Of, pertaining to, or having a stipule or stipules; situated on, near, or in place of a stipule.

stipulate /ˈstɪpjʊlət/ *adjective.* **L18.**
[from STIPULA + -ATE[2].]
BOTANY. Having a stipule or stipules.

stipulate /ˈstɪpjʊleɪt/ *verb.* **E17.**
[Latin *stipulat-* pa. ppl stem of *stipulari*, perh. from *stipula* straw (from the custom of breaking a straw to confirm a promise): see -ATE[3]. Cf. STUBBLE.]
1 *verb intrans.* Make a contract, bargain, or covenant (*with* a person); *spec.* in *ROMAN LAW*, make an oral contract for the undertaking of one's demand, in the form of question and answer legally required. **E17.**
2 a *verb trans.* Specify or demand, esp. as an essential part or condition of an agreement, contract, offer, etc. Freq. as ***stipulated*** *ppl adjective.* **M17.** ▸**b** *verb intrans.* Make an explicit demand *for* something as a condition of agreement. **L18.**
3 †**a** *verb intrans.* Stand surety or bail (*for* a person). *rare.* **L17–E19.** ▸**b** *verb trans.* Promise or guarantee (*to do*, *that*, †a thing). Now *rare.* **M18.**

📖 **2a** R. ELLMANN Both stipulated that no biography be written of them. A. WEST Rules that stipulated what might or might not be done. M. DIBDIN A will stipulating that his estate was to be divided equally between the two sons. ANNE STEVENSON Sylvia looked at two unfurnished flats . . but the landlord had stipulated no children. **b** J. AUSTEN He did not stipulate for any particular sum.

stipulation /stɪpjʊˈleɪʃ(ə)n/ *noun.* **M16.**
[Latin *stipulatio(n-)*, formed as prec.: see -ATION.]
†**1** An undertaking to do something. **M16–E18.** ▸**b** *LAW.* A contract, an agreement, a treaty. *obsolete* exc. as in sense 2 below. **M17.**
2 a *ROMAN LAW.* (The making of) an oral contract for the undertaking of one's demand, in the legally required form. Cf. STIPULATE *verb* 1. **E17.** ▸**b** (A requirement or condition of) an agreement between opposing parties or their counsels relative to the course of a judicial proceeding. *US.* **E19.**
3 *MARITIME LAW.* A promise or guarantee that an undertaking will be honoured. *rare.* **M17.**
4 The action or an act of stipulating a term or condition of a contract or agreement; a stipulated term or condition, esp. of a contract or agreement. **M18.**

📖 **4** E. WILSON He . . made a stipulation in his will that his wife should not be obliged to seal his coffin. Y. MENUHIN I made one stipulation, namely that I should record the music first.

stipulative /ˈstɪpjʊlətɪv/ *adjective.* **M20.**
[from STIPULATE *verb*: see -ATIVE.]
That makes a stipulation.
stipulative definition *LOGIC* specifying the sense in which a word, phrase, etc., is to be used.

stipulator /ˈstɪpjʊleɪtə/ *noun.* **E17.**
[Latin, formed as STIPULATE *verb*: see -OR.]
1 *ROMAN LAW.* The person who asks the question in a stipulation. Cf. STIPULATE *verb* 1. **E17.**
†**2** A person who makes a formal promise or pledge on behalf of another. **E17–E18.**
■ **stipulatory** *adjective* (now chiefly *ROMAN LAW*) of the nature of or characterized by stipulation **M17.**

stipule /ˈstɪpjuːl/ *noun.* **L18.**
[(French from) Latin STIPULA: see -ULE.]
BOTANY. A small leaflike appendage of a leaf, usu. borne in pairs at the base of the petiole.
■ **stipuled** *adjective* having (large) stipules **L18.**

stipulode /ˈstɪpjʊləʊd/ *noun.* **L19.**
[from prec. + -ODE[1].]
BOTANY. In a charophyte, a one-celled organ resembling a stipule and subtending the branchlets.

stir /stəː/ *noun*[1]. Also (*Scot. & north.*) **steer** /stɪə/. **LME.**
[from STIR *verb.*]
1 A slight or momentary movement; a brief interruption or disturbance of a state of calm or stillness. **LME.**
2 Commotion, tumult; general excitement; fuss; (vigorous) activity, bustle; *esp.* an instance of this. Formerly also (in *pl.*), public disturbance, riot, insurrection. **LME.**
3 *fig.* Stimulation of feeling or thought; emotion; intellectual activity; an instance of this. **M16.**
4 An act of stirring something with a spoon or other implement. **E19.**

📖 **1** J. HILTON There was hardly any stir of wind, in contrast to the . . gales that had raged the night before. **2** S. CLARKE Stirs or rebellions against the Empire. C. THIRLWALL The stir of preparation immediately began. P. P. READ His provocative sermons denouncing capitalism had caused quite a stir. **3** KEATS They could not in the selfsame mansion dwell Without some stir of heart. **4** J. BETJEMAN He gives his Ovaltine a stir.

stir /stəː/ *noun*[2]. *Scot. colloq.* **L18.**
[Alt. of SIR *noun.*]
As a form of respectful or polite address: sir.

stir /stəː/ *noun*[3]. *slang.* **M19.**
[Origin uncertain: perh. from Romany *sturbin* jail.]
(A) prison. Freq. in ***in stir.***
Comb.: **stir-crazy** *adjective & noun* (a person who is) mentally deranged from long imprisonment.

stir /stəː/ *verb.* Infl. **-rr-.**
[Old English *styrian* corresp. to Old Saxon *farsturian* subvert (Middle Low German *vorsturen*), Middle High German *stürn* stir, poke (German *stören*), Middle Swedish *styr(i)a*, Norwegian *styrje* make a disturbance, from Germanic.]
▸ **I** *verb trans.* **1** Move, set in motion; *esp.* cause to make a slight or momentary movement; disturb, move gently to and fro. **OE.** ▸†**b** Utter, cause (a voice or sound) to be heard. Also, make (a gesture). **OE–E17.** ▸**c** Move (a thing) from the normal place or position; shift, displace. Usu. in neg. contexts. Now *rare* or *obsolete.* **OE.** ▸**d** Move (a limb etc.), esp. slightly. Usu. in neg. contexts. **ME.** ▸†**e** Brandish; wield (a weapon). **ME–E17.** ▸†**f** Cause to move along or away; drive, convey. **ME–L16.** ▸**g** Rouse or disturb with a push or prod. **L16.**
2 *refl.* Move or walk about; take exercise; move from one's place. Now *rare* or *obsolete* exc. as passing into senses 9 and 12. **OE.**
3 Move or agitate with an implement, device, etc.; *spec.* (*a*) move a spoon or other instrument round and round in (a liquid, a soft mass, etc.) so as to mix the ingredients or constituents; (*b*) poke (a fire) so as to encourage burning; (*c*) (now *Scot.*) plough or turn up (earth); *spec.* replough, cross-plough. **OE.**
4 *fig.* Disturb, trouble; put into tumult or confusion. *obsolete* exc. *Scot. & dial.* **OE.**
5 †**a** Of a food, medicine, etc.: act as a stimulant to, stimulate physically. **OE–L17.** ▸**b** Rouse from rest or inaction; excite to activity. **OE.**
6 Move to increased action; urge, incite, instigate. Formerly also, prompt, (try to) persuade; exhort, entreat. **OE.**
7 Excite or arouse (passion); prompt or evoke (anger, affection, suspicion, a memory, etc.); arouse feeling or emotion in, affect (strongly), move. **OE.** ▸†**b** Instigate or set in train (unrest, commotion, etc.). **OE–M17.** ▸**c** Provoke, annoy; tease. *Austral. colloq.* **L20.**
8 Bring into notice or debate; raise or moot (a subject or question). Now *rare.* **OE.**
9 *refl.* Rouse oneself to action or from a lethargic state; begin to act briskly; busy oneself *to do* something. Formerly also, fight valiantly. **ME.**

📖 **1** G. VIDAL A faint breeze stirred the dust. **c** B. FRANKLIN Laying heavy burdens on men's shoulders, which they themselves would not stir. **d** SIR W. SCOTT Thy companion had been slain by thy side, . . without thy stirring a finger in his aid. **2** F. FULLER The more a Man stirs himself, the more Animal Spirits are made in the Brain. **3** S. LEACOCK I . . stirred the fire into a blaze. G. VIDAL Enid stirred the martini with her forefinger. **5b** T. S. ELIOT April is the cruellest month . . stirring Dull roots with spring rain. **6** G. F. KENNAN It was only the Socialists . . who could stir the war-weary . . army to a new military effort. **7** H. ROTH He had been strangely stirred by . . Sternowitz's short narrative. J. WAIN Still calm, still not stirred to any damaging or ennobling depths. ANNE STEVENSON Her eventful life . . could not have failed to stir Sylvia's imagination. *New Yorker* A hammering excitement that no other university has ever stirred in me. **9** K. CROSSLEY-HOLLAND Time your companions stirred themselves. Tell them to get up and dress.

▸ **II** *verb intrans.* †**10** Be capable of movement; be (continuously) in motion. Also, move or pass from one place to another. **OE–M17.**
11 Begin to move; make a slight movement, move to and fro; move slightly (usu. in neg. contexts). Also, show signs of life or consciousness. **OE.** ▸**b** Leave, go out of a building or (esp.) one's home. Usu. in neg. contexts. Freq. foll. by *abroad*, †*forth*, *out of.* **L15.** ▸**c** (Of a plant) show signs of growth (*rare*); *fig.* (of an idea, an intellectual movement, etc.) begin to become apparent, show outward signs of activity or development. **M19.**
12 Of emotion, feeling, etc.: be roused or excited. **OE.**
13 Be astir; get up; be out of bed, be up and about. **ME.** ▸**b** Esp. of news: be in circulation, be current. Now *rare.* **LME.** ▸**c** Happen, take place; be happening or afoot. **E16.**
14 Move briskly; be on the move, be busy or active. Also (*fig.*), be active or occupied *about* something; instigate action (foll. by *in*). **ME.** ▸**b** Make a commotion or tumult; rise in revolt or insurrection. Long *rare* or *obsolete.*

ME. ▸**c** Cause trouble; be a source of irritation, make a nuisance of oneself. *colloq.* (chiefly *Austral.*). M20.

> 🕮 **10** G. HERBERT While rocks stand, And rivers stirre. **11** E. MITTELHOLZER At length Ramgolall stirred, for the pale finger of dawn had touched his sleeping brain. J. CAREY A world in which you can hardly stir without wounding someone. **b** P. AUSTER He does not even contemplate stirring from his room. **13** A. RANSOME People were stirring in the camp. **c** R. DAVIES Nothing much was stirring in the outdoor carnival line till mid-May. **14** SIR W. SCOTT Friends in parliament, capable of stirring in so weighty an affair. THACKERAY Her husband stirred and bustled about.

Phrases, & with adverbs in specialized senses: ***stir a finger***: see FINGER *noun*. **stir in** mix (an added ingredient) with a substance by stirring. **stir it** *colloq.* cause trouble; upset a settled or harmonious state of affairs. ***stir one's stumps***: see STUMP *noun*[1]. ***stir the possum***: see POSSUM *noun*. **stir up** (*a*) set in motion, agitate; mix together thoroughly by stirring; (*b*) rouse to action or emotion; rouse from apathy; incite (revolt, trouble, etc.); †(*c*) rouse from sleep or rest; (*d*) excite; induce; stimulate (feeling or emotion).

stirabout /ˈstəːrəbaʊt/ *noun*. L17.
[from STIR *verb* + ABOUT *adverb*.]
1 a Porridge made by stirring oatmeal in boiling water or milk. Orig. *Anglo-Irish*. L17. ▸**b** A dish consisting of oatmeal fried in dripping. Chiefly *dial.* E19.
2 *fig.* A bustle; a muddle; a busy bustling person. *colloq.* M19.

stire /stʌɪə/ *noun*. LME.
[Origin unkn.]
An old variety of cider apple.

stir-fry /ˈstəːfrʌɪ/ *verb & noun*. M20.
[from STIR *verb* + FRY *verb*.]
▸**A** *verb trans.* Fry (meat, vegetables, etc.) rapidly on a high heat, while stirring and tossing them. M20.
▸**B** *noun.* A dish consisting of stir-fried meat, vegetables, etc. L20.

†**stiria** *noun*. Pl. **-iae**. M17–E18.
[Latin = icicle.]
A concretion resembling an icicle.
■ †**stiriated** *adjective* formed into striiae M17–E18.

stirk /stəːk/ *noun*. Chiefly *Scot. & dial.*
[Old English *stirc*, *styr(i)c*, perh. from *stēor* STEER *noun*[1] + *-oc*, *-uc* -OCK. Cf. Middle Low German, Middle Dutch *sterke* young cow, Middle Dutch *stierken* bull calf.]
1 A young bullock or heifer, usually between one and two years old. OE.
2 A foolish person. L16.

stirless /ˈstəːlɪs/ *adjective*. Chiefly *literary*. E19.
[from STIR *noun*[1], *verb* + -LESS.]
Not stirring, motionless.

Stirling /ˈstəːlɪŋ/ *noun*[1]. M19.
[The Revd Robert *Stirling* (1790–1878), Scottish minister and engineer.]
1 In full ***Stirling engine***. Orig., an external-combustion air engine invented by Stirling. Now usu., a machine used to provide power or refrigeration, operating on a closed cycle in which a working fluid is cyclically compressed and expanded at different temperatures. M19.
2 ***Stirling cycle***, the thermodynamic cycle on which an ideal Stirling engine would operate, in which a fluid undergoes isothermal expansion, cooling at constant volume by giving up heat to a regenerator, isothermal compression, and warming at constant volume by gaining heat from the regenerator. L19.

Stirling /ˈstəːlɪŋ/ *noun*[2]. M20.
[James *Stirling* (1692–1770), Scottish mathematician.]
MATH. Used *attrib.* and in *possess.* to designate concepts in number theory developed by Stirling.
Stirling approximation, **Stirling formula**, **Stirling's approximation**, **Stirling's formula** either of two functions of an integer *n* which are approximations for factorial *n* when *n* is large, n^n/e^n and (more accurately) $\sqrt{(2\pi n)}n^n/e^n$. **Stirling number**, **Stirling's number** an integer belonging to either of two arrays used in combinatorics, (*a*) the number of ways of arranging the integers 1 to *m* in *n* disjoint non-empty ordered sets, the first element of each ordered set being the least; (*b*) the number of ways of partitioning the integers 1 to *m* into *n* disjoint non-empty sets.

stirp /stəːp/ *noun*. E16.
[formed as STIRPS.]
1 The stock of a family; a line of descent; a race, a clan; the descendants of a common ancestor. Also, pedigree, lineage. Now *arch. rare*. E16.
†**2** A scion, a member of a family. L16–E17.
†**3** *GENETICS.* The genic component of a gamete or a fertilized ovum. L19–E20.

> 🕮 **1** H. D. THOREAU The last of that stirp, sole survivor of that family.

stirpes *noun* pl. of STIRPS.

stirpiculture /ˈstəːpɪkʌltʃə/ *noun*. *obsolete* exc. *Hist.* L19.
[formed as STIRPS + -CULTURE.]
The breeding of distinct pure strains or stocks; *esp.* human eugenics.

stirpital /ˈstəːpɪt(ə)l/ *adjective*. *rare*. L19.
[Irreg. formed as next + -AL[1].]
LAW. Pertaining to division *per stirpes*.

stirps /stəːps/ *noun*. Pl. **stirpes** /ˈstəːpiːz/. L17.
[Latin = stock, stem.]
1 *LAW.* A branch of a family; the person who with his or her descendants forms a branch of a family. Freq. in PER STIRPES. L17.
2 *BIOLOGY.* Lineage, stock; *spec.* in *BOTANY*, a permanent variety. Now *rare*. M19.

stirrer /ˈstəːrə/ *noun*. LME.
[from STIR *verb* + -ER[1].]
1 A person who or thing which excites or provokes something, as unrest, passion, etc., or incites a person to something. Freq. foll. by *up*. LME. ▸†**b** A person who makes a commotion or raises a tumult. LME–M17. ▸**c** A person who stirs up trouble or discontent; an agitator, a troublemaker. *colloq.* M20.
2 An implement or machine for stirring a liquid etc. LME.
3 a A person or animal that moves briskly; a busy or active person. Long *rare* or *obsolete*. LME. ▸**b** A person who moves about or is astir. Freq. in ***early stirrer***, a person who is up and about early. M16.

> 🕮 **1** *Academy* Goethe was undoubtedly . . a tireless stirrer-up of ideas. **c** S. ELDRED-GRIGG She'd always been a stirrer in the family. **2** *attrib.*: *Ideal Home* A stirrer fan situated in the roof of the oven.

stirring /ˈstəːrɪŋ/ *verbal noun*. OE.
[from STIR *verb* + -ING[1].]
The action of STIR *verb*; an instance of this.

> 🕮 *Sunday Times* A reflection of the deeper stirrings in Polish society. J. M. COETZEE Listening to the stirring of the children.

stirring /ˈstəːrɪŋ/ *adjective*. OE.
[from STIR *verb* + -ING[2].]
1 Moving, esp. slightly; that is in motion; moving about or along. OE.
2 That excites or incites; rousing, stimulating; moving; thrilling. LME.
3 Moving briskly, active; actively occupied, busy. LME. ▸**b** Characterized by or full of bustle or activity. E17.

> 🕮 **1** KEATS A lawn besprinkled o'er With flowers, and stirring shades. **2** *Times Lit. Suppl.* Plenty of blood and action . . . Stirring stuff. **3** LD MACAULAY No man could be a stirring and thriving politician who was not prepared to change.

■ **stirringly** *adverb* LME.

stirrup /ˈstɪrəp/ *noun*.
[Old English *stigrāp* = Old Saxon *stigerēp*, Middle Dutch *steegereep*, Old High German *stegareif* (German *Stegreif*), Old Norse *stigreip*, from Germanic base of STY *verb*[1], ROPE *noun*[1].]
1 Either of a pair of supports for a rider's foot, consisting of a usu. metal loop with a flat base and a leather strap attaching this loop to each side of a saddle. Also, the metal loop of such a support only; = ***stirrup-iron*** below. OE.
2 A thing shaped like a stirrup; *spec.* a U-shaped clamp or support. ME.
3 Any of various kinds of footrest or looped strap analogous to a stirrup; *spec.* (*a*) in a crossbow, a footrest used to steady and brace the bow while it is being bent and loaded; (*b*) a device used by a shoemaker to keep the last steady on the knee; (*c*) a kind of footless stocking with a strap passing underneath the foot; such a strap; a similar strap attached to stretch trousers; (*d*) either of a pair of supports used to hold the legs of a female patient raised and apart during a gynaecological examination, labour, etc. LME.
4 *NAUTICAL.* **a** A metal band or plate used to secure a keel to a ship's hull. LME. ▸**b** Any of several short ropes hanging from the yards of a square-rigged sailing ship, the lower end of the rope having a thimble through which passes a footrope or horse, used when working on the sails. L15.
5 *ANATOMY.* = STAPES. E17.
6 In reinforced concrete construction, each of the vertical or diagonal members which bind together the upper and lower reinforcement of a beam etc. E20.

Phrases: **hold the stirrup** (*a*) help a person to mount a horse by holding the stirrup steady, esp. as a manifestation of homage or reverence; (*b*) *fig.* be subservient. **lose one's stirrups** let one's feet accidentally slip out of the stirrups.
Comb.: **stirrup-bar** (*a*) each of the bars on a saddle-tree to which a stirrup-strap is attached; (*b*) the bar of a stirrup, on which the foot rests; **stirrup-bone** = sense 5 above; **stirrup-cup** (*a*) a glass of wine etc. offered to a person (orig. on horseback) about to depart; (*b*) the drinking-vessel used for this; **stirrup-iron** the metal loop of a stirrup; **stirrup-leather** the strap attaching a stirrup to a saddle; **stirrup pants** stretch trousers with a strap passing underneath the foot; **stirrup-pump** a portable hand-operated water pump with a foot-plate resembling a stirrup, used to extinguish small fires with water drawn from a bucket; **stirrup-strap** = *stirrup-leather* above; **stirrup-vase** *ARCHAEOLOGY* a false-necked amphora with a square-cut handle on either side of the false spout.

■ **stirrupless** *adjective* (*rare*) LME.

stirrup /ˈstɪrəp/ *verb trans.* E17.
[from the noun.]
1 Provide (as) with a stirrup or stirrups. Chiefly as ***stirruped*** *ppl adjective*. E17.
2 Flog with a stirrup-leather or with a shoemaker's stirrup. *arch. slang*. M18.
3 *NAUTICAL.* Attach stirrups or ropes to. *rare*. M18.

stir-up /ˈstəːrʌp/ *noun & adjective*. E19.
[from ***stir up*** s.v. STIR *verb*.]
▸**A** *noun*. The action or an act of stirring up something or someone; the state of being stirred up; agitation, commotion. E19.
▸**B** *attrib.* or as *adjective*. **1** ***Stir-up Sunday***, the Sunday before Advent Sunday (so called from the opening words of the Collect for the day). *colloq.* E19.
2 Having the quality of stirring up someone; rousing. *rare*. L19.

stishovite /ˈstɪʃəvʌɪt/ *noun*. M20.
[from S. M. *Stishov*, 20th-cent. Russian chemist + -ITE[1].]
MINERALOGY. A dense tetragonal polymorph of silica, formed at very high pressure and found in meteorite craters.

stitch /stɪtʃ/ *noun*[1].
[Old English *stiċe* = Old Frisian *steke*, Old Saxon *stiki* prick, stab, Old High German *stih* (German *Stich*) prick, sting, stitch, Gothic *stiks* point, from Germanic, from base of STICK *verb*[1].]
▸**I** †**1** A prick, puncture, or stab inflicted by a pointed implement. Only in OE.
2 A sharp sudden localized pain, like that produced by the thrust of a pointed weapon. Now *spec.*, an acutely painful cramp in the side of the body often resulting from running or vigorous exercise. OE. ▸**b** In *pl.* Fits of laughter. Chiefly in ***in stitches***. *colloq.* M20.
†**3** *fig.* A grudge, a dislike, a ground for complaint. Chiefly in ***have a stitch against***, ***take a stitch against***. L16–L17.

> 🕮 **2** I. WATSON We ran all the rest of the way; and I arrived with a stitch in my side. **b** B. CHATWIN Two clowns . . keep everyone in stitches.

▸**II 4 a** A single pass of a threaded needle in and out of a fabric which is being sewn; the thread or loop left in the fabric between two successive needle holes as a result of this action. ME. ▸**b** *MEDICINE.* A single pass of a threaded needle through the edges of a wound or incision to join them together; the length or loop of thread or other material fastened in the skin or flesh as a result of this action. Usu. in *pl.* LME. ▸**c** A single complete movement of the needle or other implement used in knitting, crochet, embroidery, etc.; the portion of the work produced by such a movement. L16. ▸**d** A slight or single action, stroke of work of any kind. Usu. in neg. contexts. Now *arch. rare*. L16.
5 A thread or loop as a basic constituent of a sewn or woven fabric; the least piece of fabric or item of clothing. L15.
6 A particular method of sewing, knitting, crocheting, embroidery, etc.; the design or pattern of work thus produced. M16.
7 A tailor. *joc.* L17.
8 *BOOKBINDING.* A fastening of leaves, esp. those of pamphlets, with thread or wire drawn through a hole previously pierced. *obsolete* exc. *Hist.* M19.

> 🕮 **4a** *Proverb*: a stitch in time saves nine. THACKERAY She had not . . advanced many stitches in the darning of that table-cloth. **b** R. RENDELL He . . put half a dozen stitches in the wound. **c** V. GLENDINNING Emmeline picked up a few stitches in the matted knitting. **d** T. MIDDLETON I'll not do a stitch of service for you. **5** A. HOLLINGHURST No one here wears a stitch of clothing. **6** ***back-stitch***, ***chain stitch***, ***cross-stitch***, ***moss-stitch***, ***running stitch***, etc.

Phrases: **a good stitch** *dial.* a considerable distance (in walking). **drop a stitch** let a stitch fall from the end of a knitting-needle, crochet hook, etc. **every stitch** (*a*) all the clothes one is wearing; (*b*) *NAUTICAL* every available piece of sail. ***set a stitch***: see SET *verb*[1].
Comb.: **stitchbird** a small honey-eater of New Zealand, *Notiomystis cincta*, which has a clicking call resembling the word 'stitch'; **stitch weld** *noun & verb* (*a*) *noun* a weld produced by stitch welding; (*b*) *verb trans.* subject to stitch welding; **stitch welder** a machine that performs stitch welding; **stitch welding** a form of spot welding in which a series of overlapping spot welds is produced automatically by machine; **stitch-work** embroidery; tapestry; **stitchwort** [from its reputed ability to relieve a stitch or sudden pain in the side] (*a*) (more fully ***greater stitchwort***) a spring-flowering hedge plant, *Stellaria holostea*, of the pink family, with starry white flowers and opposite lanceolate leaves; (*b*) (with specifying word) any of several other plants of this genus.
■ **stitchless** *adjective* (*a*) without stitches; (*b*) without a stitch of clothing, naked: E20.

stitch /stɪtʃ/ *noun*[2]. Now *Scot. & dial.* L15.
[Prob. orig. identical with prec.]
1 A ridge or balk of land; *esp.* a strip of ploughed land between two water-furrows. Also, a narrow ridge in which potatoes etc. are grown. L15.

†**2** The depth to which a ploughshare is driven in making a furrow. E–M17.

stitch /stɪtʃ/ *noun*³. Now *dial.* E17.
[Origin unkn.]
A shock of grain consisting of a number of sheaves placed upright and supporting each other, usu. in a field.

stitch /stɪtʃ/ *verb*¹. ME.
[from STITCH *noun*¹.]
1 *verb trans.* †**a** Stab, pierce; *transf.* afflict with a stitch or sharp sudden pain. ME–E17. ▸**b** Make (a hole) by piercing. *rare.* E16.
2 *verb trans.* Fasten together or join (pieces of fabric etc.) with a stitch or (usu.) a continuous line or series of stitches; make or mend (a garment) in this way. Usu. foll. by *together, up*. ME.
3 *verb trans.* Decorate with stitches; embroider. E16.
4 *verb trans.* BOOKBINDING. Fasten together (a number of sheets or sections) by passing a thread or wire through all the sheets at once. Cf. SEW *verb*¹ 1e. M16.
5 *verb trans.* **a** Fasten or attach (something) by sewing. Foll. by *to, in, on*, etc. M16. ▸**b** Enclose *in* or put *into* a cover or receptacle secured by stitching. Also foll. by *up*. M19.
6 *verb trans.* MEDICINE. Join together the edges of (a wound or incision) by (repeatedly) passing a threaded needle through the flesh and fastening off the length or loop of thread etc.; secure with a suture. Also foll. by *up*. L16.
7 *verb intrans.* Make stitches; work with a needle and thread; sew. L17.

> **2** H. ALLEN Clothes . . stitched with . . exquisite needle-work. *fig.*: *Screen International* Funding . . is currently being stitched together from a banking consortium. **3** R. BAGOT Its button-holes stitched with red. **5b** MRS ALEXANDER A thousand pounds' worth stitched in my belt. **7** M. KEANE Violet stitched away . . at her tapestry.

Comb., & with adverbs in specialized senses: **stitchdown (shoe)** a shoe or boot on which the lower edge of the upper is turned outward and stitched on to the sole; **stitch up** (*a*) *slang* cause (a person) to be charged with or convicted for a crime, esp. by informing or manufacturing evidence; cheat; (*b*) *slang* consolidate, finalize, or secure (a deal, the outcome of a set of circumstances, etc.) to one's advantage; (see also senses 2, 5b, 6 above); **stitch-up** *slang* (*a*) an act of incriminating a person for a crime; (*b*) an act of securing the outcome of a deal etc. to one's advantage.
■ **stitcher** *noun* (*a*) a person who stitches or sews something, esp. as an occupation; (*b*) a tool or machine used for stitching: L16. **stitchery** *noun* needlework E17.

stitch /stɪtʃ/ *verb*² *trans.* Long *dial.* L17.
[from STITCH *noun*³.]
Set up sheaves of grain in stitches or shocks.

stitch /stɪtʃ/ *verb*³ *trans.* Chiefly *Scot. & dial.* L18.
[from STITCH *noun*².]
Turn up (soil) in ridges in order to cover or protect the roots of potatoes etc. Also, plough (land) *up* deeply.

stitchel /ˈstɪtʃ(ə)l/ *noun*¹. *obsolete* exc. *dial.* M17.
[Perh. rel. to next.]
A nuisance, a pest.

stitchel /ˈstɪtʃ(ə)l/ *adjective & noun*². *local.* Now *rare* or *obsolete.* L18.
[Origin uncertain: cf. STICKLE *adjective.*]
(Designating) a kind of short bristly hair in the fleece of certain breeds of sheep.

stitching /ˈstɪtʃɪŋ/ *noun.* E16.
[from STITCH *verb*¹ + -ING¹.]
1 The action of STITCH *verb*¹. E16.
†**2** The feeling of a sharp sudden pain. M–L16.
3 Stitches collectively; a series of stitches. M16.
4 Sewing thread. *rare.* E17.

> **1** P. PARISH A local anaesthetic given . . for the stitching of a minor injury. **3** M. KEANE Gloves . . made of chamois leather, white with black stitching.

stith /stɪθ/ *noun. obsolete* exc. *north.* ME.
[from (the same root as) STITHY.]
= STITHY *noun* 1.

stith /stʌɪθ/ *adjective & adverb. obsolete* exc. *Scot.*
[Old English *stīþ* = Old Frisian *stith*, Old Norse *stinnr* (Middle Swedish *stinder*), from Germanic.]
▸ **A** *adjective.* **1** (Of a thing) not bending or giving easily, inflexible, unyielding; (of a person) steadfast, stubborn. OE. ▸†**b** Of a place of defence or confinement: strong, stout; formidable. OE–LME.
2 †**a** Of the neck: stiff. Only in OE. ▸**b** Rigid in death. *Scot.* M18.
†**3** Hard, stern, or cruel towards people or things. OE–ME.
4 Intense in degree or quality; not mild or weak; violent; severe; strong. Now only of the weather, a storm, etc. OE.
†**5** Stalwart, valiant, mighty. Chiefly *poet.* ME–L15.
▸ **B** *adverb.* Strongly, firmly, violently; harshly, severely. Now only in *stith-driven*, (of snow etc.) driven with force or severity. OE.

stithy /ˈstɪði/ *noun & verb.* Now chiefly *arch.* or *poet.* ME.
[Old Norse *steði*, from Germanic base also of STAND *verb*: infl. by assoc. with SMITHY. Cf. STITH *noun.*]
▸ **A** *noun.* **1** An anvil. ME.
†**2** ANATOMY. The incus of the ear. *rare.* L16–E17.
3 A forge, a smithy. E17.
†**4** A disease of horses and cattle. E17–E18.
▸†**B** *verb trans.* Forge, shape by heating and hammering. LME–E17.

†**stitling** *noun. rare.* LME–E19.
[Alt. of STICKLING.]
A stickleback.

stive /stʌɪv/ *noun*¹. L18.
[Dutch †*stuive* rel. to *stuiven* rise as dust.]
Dust; *esp.* the floating dust of flour produced during grinding.

†**stive** *noun*² see STEEVE *noun*¹.

stive /stʌɪv/ *verb*¹ *trans.* Now chiefly *Scot.* ME.
[formed as STEEVE *verb*².]
Compress and stow (cargo) in a ship's hold. Also *transf.*, pack (a commodity etc.) tightly; crowd (a room, a space, etc.) with things or people. Also foll. by *up*.

stive /stʌɪv/ *verb*². Now *rare.* LME.
[App. alt. of STEW *verb* after Old French *estuver.*]
†**1** *verb trans.* = STEW *verb* 1. *rare.* Only in LME.
2 *verb intrans.* Remain in a stifling atmosphere; suffocate. Cf. STEW *verb* 3d. L16.
3 *verb trans.* Shut up in a close hot place; stifle, suffocate. Freq. foll. by *up*. Cf. STEW *verb* 3a. E18.
■ **stivy** *adjective* stuffy M19.

stiver /ˈstʌɪvə/ *noun.* LME.
[Middle & mod. Dutch *stuiver*, Middle Low German *stüver*, prob. rel. to STUB *noun.*]
1 *Hist.* A small coin (orig. silver, later nickel) of the Netherlands equal to one-twentieth of a guilder. LME.
2 A coin of small value; a small amount of money; *transf.* the smallest quantity or amount. E17.

> **2** *Blackwood's Magazine* They didn't care a stiver if my head was blown off.

stiver /ˈstɪvə/ *verb. dial.* M18.
[from STIFF *adjective* + -ER⁵.]
1 *verb intrans.* (Esp. of the hair) stand stiff, bristle, stand on end; *fig.* become angry. M18.
2 *verb trans.* Make (hair) bristle or stand on end. Also foll. by *up*. L19.

St Kilda /s(ə)nt ˈkɪldə/ *noun.* L19.
[An island in the Outer Hebrides, now uninhabited.]
Used *attrib.* to designate rodents and birds found only on St Kilda.
St Kilda field mouse = *St Kilda wood mouse* below. **St Kilda house mouse**, **St Kilda mouse** a large house mouse of a local race with a pale belly, now extinct. **St Kilda wood mouse** a large wood mouse of a local race with a buff belly. **St Kilda wren** a large wren of a local race greyer and paler than the typical form.
■ **St Kildan** *noun* (*Hist.*) a native or inhabitant of St Kilda M18.

St Louis encephalitis /s(ə)nt ˈluːɪ(s) ɛnˌkɛfəˈlʌɪtɪs, -ˌsɛf-/ *noun phr.* M20.
[from *St Louis*, a town in Missouri, USA.]
MEDICINE. A viral encephalitis which can be severe, transmitted by mosquitoes. Also called ***encephalitis C***.

St Lucian /s(ə)nt ˈluːʃ(ə)n/ *noun & adjective.* M19.
[from *St Lucia* (see below) + -AN.]
▸ **A** *noun.* A native or inhabitant of St Lucia, an island in the Caribbean. M19.
▸ **B** *adjective.* Of or pertaining to St Lucia. M20.

STM *abbreviation.*
1 Scanning tunnelling microscope, microscopy.
2 Short-term memory.

stoa /ˈstəʊə/ *noun.* Pl. **stoas**, **stoai** /ˈstəʊʌɪ/. E17.
[Greek.]
1 ***the Stoa***, the great hall in Athens in which the philosopher Zeno lectured, and from which his followers were called Stoics; the Stoic school of philosophy. Also called ***the Porch***, ***the Portico***. E17.
2 A portico, a roofed colonnade. L18.

stoach /stəʊtʃ/ *verb trans. & intrans. dial.* M18.
[Origin unkn.]
Esp. of an animal: trample (wet ground) into holes.

stoai *noun pl.* see STOA.

stoat /stəʊt/ *noun.* LME.
[Origin unkn.]
1 A carnivorous mammal of the weasel family, *Mustela erminea*, native to Eurasian and N. American tundra and forest, and having a brown and white (or in winter, an all-white) coat with a black tip to the tail. Also (esp. when in its winter coat) called ***ermine***. LME.
2 *fig.* A treacherous person. Also, a sexually aggressive man, a lecher. M19.

stoat /stəʊt/ *verb trans. rare.* L19.
[Origin unkn.]
In tailoring, sew (cloth) with an invisible stitch. Chiefly as ***stoated*** *ppl adjective.*

stob /stɒb/ *noun.* Now chiefly *Scot. & dial.* ME.
[Var. of STUB *noun.*]
1 A stick, a twig broken off. ME.
2 Orig., a stump, a part remaining after mutilation. Now only (*Scot.*), the remainder or remnant of a rainbow. LME.
3 A stake, a post, *esp.* one used for fencing (now *Scot. & US*); a gibbet. L15.
4 A short thick nail. *obsolete* exc. *Scot.* L15.
5 A thorn; a prickle; a splinter. M17.
6 A thatch-peg. E18.
7 A saddlers' awl. L19.
Comb.: **stob-mill** a windmill pivoted on a central post; **stob-thatch** roofing consisting of broom or brushwood laid across the rafters.
¶ Recorded LOE in place-name.

stoccado /stɒˈkɑːdəʊ/ *noun. arch.* Pl. **-os**. L16.
[Refash. of Italian *stoccata* from *stocco* point of a sword, dagger, from Germanic: see -ADO. Cf. STOCK *noun*².]
A thrust or stab with a pointed weapon.

stochastic /stəˈkastɪk/ *adjective.* M17.
[Greek *stokhastikos*, from *stokhazesthai* aim at a mark, guess, from *stokhos* an aim, a guess: see -IC.]
1 Pertaining to conjecture. Long *rare* or *obsolete.* M17.
2 Randomly determined; that follows some random probability distribution or pattern, so that its behaviour may be analysed statistically but not predicted precisely. M20. ▸**b** MUSIC. Designating music in which details within an overall sound structure are determined stochastically by composer or computer. M20.
■ **stochastically** *adverb* L17. **stochasˈticity** *noun* the property of being stochastic L20.

stocious /ˈstəʊʃəs/ *adjective. slang* (chiefly *Anglo-Irish*). Also **-tious**. M20.
[Origin unkn.]
Drunk, intoxicated.

stock /stɒk/ *noun*¹ & *adjective.*
[Old English *stoc(c)* = Old Frisian *stokk*, Old Saxon, Middle & mod. Dutch *stok* (German *Stock* stick), Old Norse *stokkr* trunk, block, log, from Germanic.]
▸ **A** *noun.* **I** A trunk, a stem.
1 A tree-trunk deprived of its branches; a tree stump. *arch. rare.* OE. ▸**b** A log, a block of wood. Now *rare* or *obsolete* exc. *Scot.* OE. ▸**c** An idol, a graven image. *arch. derog.* OE. ▸**d** A type of what is lifeless, motionless, or without consciousness; *esp.* a senseless or stupid person. ME.
2 The trunk or woody stem of a living tree or shrub (as opp. to the root and branches); *esp.* one into which a graft is inserted. ME. ▸†**b** The trunk or torso of the human body. LME–L16. ▸**c** The hardened stalk of a plant, esp. a brassica. Chiefly *Scot.* E17. ▸**d** BOTANY. A rhizome. M19.
3 *fig.* The source of a line of descent, the progenitor of a family or people; (a line of) descent, the descendants of a common ancestor; a family (of human beings, animals, plants, or languages); ancestry, an ancestral type. ME. ▸**b** A kind, a species. *obsolete* exc. *dial.* LME. ▸†**c** Pedigree; a genealogy, a genealogical tree. M16–M17. ▸†**d** An archetype; a source of something. E17–M18.

> **3** C. DARWIN In the case of strongly marked races . . there is . . strong evidence that all are descended from a single wild stock. E. A. FREEMAN One of Swegen's . . sons might well become the stock of a new dynasty. W. W. FOWLER When a stock or tribe . . took possession of a district. N. PODHORETZ American Jews of East European immigrant stock.

▸ **II** A post, a supporting structure.
4 †**a** A post, a stake. OE–L17. ▸**b** A pillar or block supporting a smith's anvil. ME. ▸**c** The main upright part of anything; *spec.* the vertical beam of a cross. Long *rare.* LME.
5 *Hist.* In *pl.* (treated as *pl.* or *sing.*) & (long *rare*) *sing.* A device for punishment, usu. consisting of an adjustable framework mounted between posts, with holes for trapping the ankles and occas. also the wrists, in which an offender was confined and exposed to public assault and ridicule. Cf. PILLORY *noun.* ME. ▸**b** *transf.* In *pl.* Any of various devices in which limbs were confined; *spec.* (*a*) a pillory; (*b*) *joc.* tight boots. *obsolete* exc. *Hist.* LME. ▸**c** A frame in which to confine an animal, esp. a horse, for veterinary attention or shoeing. M19.
6 A hollow receptacle; *spec.* †(*a*) an alms-box; †(*b*) a basin, *esp.* a stoup; (*c*) the wooden trough or box in a fulling-mill in which the cloth is beaten; (*d*) (orig. *Scot.*) any of the wooden sockets fixed in holes in the bag of a set of bagpipes to receive the pipes and chanter. LME.
7 In *pl.* The supports for a ship or boat in process of construction. LME.
8 The block or table on which a butcher or fishmonger cuts or displays goods. Chiefly *Scot.* Long *rare* or *obsolete.* LME.

9 A gun-carriage. **LME.**

10 The outer rail of a bedstead; the side of a bed away from the wall. Long *obsolete* exc. *Scot.* **E16.**

11 A ledge at the back or side of a fireplace, for keeping a kettle or pot warm. *dial.* **L16.**

12 A board at the bottom of a brick mould (also ***stock-board***). Now also *ellipt.* = ***stock-brick*** below. **L17.**

13 A stand or frame supporting a spinning-wheel or churn. *rare. obsolete* exc. *dial.* **L17.**

> 📖 **5** SHAKES. *Merry W.* But that my admirable dexterity of wit . . deliver'd me, the knave constable had set me i' th' stocks . . for a Witch.

▶ **III** (Part of) a tool, instrument, etc.

14 *NAUTICAL.* The crossbar of an anchor. **ME.**

15 The butt of a musket, rifle, etc. **LME.**

16 The block of wood from which a bell is hung. **L15.**

†**17** A saddle-tree. **L15–M18.**

18 The hub of a wheel. **L16.**

19 The part of a plough to which the share is attached. *rare.* Long *obsolete* exc. *dial.* **L16.**

20 A handle, as of a tool, whip, fishing-rod, etc. **L17.**

21 A tool or a part of an implement or machine that holds or supports a working (usu. revolving) part; *spec.* (***a***) = **BRACE** *noun*¹ 3; (***b***) = ***headstock*** (a) s.v. **HEAD** *noun & adjective*; (***c***) a tailstock. **L18.**

22 The shorter and thicker of the two pieces of a T-square. **E19.**

▶ **IV** Money, assets, a store.

23 a A fund, (a sum of) money for a particular purpose, as (***a***) a sum used or available for investment in a commercial enterprise; †(***b***) an endowment for a son; (***c***) the capital of a business, company, corporation, etc. Now *rare* or *obsolete* exc. as in sense b below. **LME.** ▸**b** Capital raised by a business, company, corporation, etc., through the issue and subscription of shares; shares in such capital; shares in some commodity, industry, etc., collectively; a kind of stock, a part into which a company's capital is divided (freq. in ***stocks and shares***). Also, money lent to a government at fixed interest; the right to receive such interest. **L17.** ▸**c** *fig.* Reputation, esteem; popularity. **M20.**

24 A store of (a specified kind of) goods available and on hand for sale, distribution, etc.; a quantity of anything accumulated for future use; a store to be drawn on as occasion requires. **LME.** ▸**b** *MINING.* Mined or quarried material of workable size. **E18.**

25 The equipment and animals used by a farm etc.; the raw materials, equipment, vehicles, etc., used by a firm, esp. an industrial concern; *spec.* (***a***) livestock; (***b***) rolling-stock. **E16.**

†**26 a** An estate or other property producing income; a person's total property. **M16–L18.** ▸**b** The total wealth of a nation. **M17–E19.**

†**27** In double entry bookkeeping, the heading of the ledger account summarizing the assets and liabilities of a trader, firm, etc. **L16–M19.**

28 Liquid made by boiling meat, vegetables, or fish, kept for use as a foundation for soup, gravy, sauce, etc. **M18.**

29 Material used in a manufacturing process; raw material. **L19.** ▸**b** *spec.* = ***film stock*** s.v. **FILM** *noun.* **L19.**

> 📖 **23b** *Times* Furness stock did not move on the announcement of an interim dividend. *Sunday Times* How many stocks does one need . . in a portfolio? *attrib.*: *Listener* The ads . . suggest . . a computer to take care of your stock portfolio. ***common stock, debenture stock, growth stock, joint stock,*** etc. **c** CLIVE JAMES She had . . enough cachet to raise my stock at the Algonquin. **24** M. PATTISON We have not cared to keep on hand a larger stock than we could dispose of. W. GASS They were unloading all their old stock, clearing their warehouses. J. FRAME Renée's contribution to the . . business was her help with the stock. **25** C. G. SELIGMAN Cattle are . . most valued . . and the attainment of 1,000 head of stock is marked by a special ceremony. *Modern Railways* The stock to form the 08.35 runs from Wimbledon. *Farmers Weekly (Durban)* Bush area is . . suitable for small stock such as goats. **28** A. PRICE The hare—in a fine brown stock, with lots of onions.

▶ **V** Other uses.

30 A stocking. *obsolete* exc. *dial. & Hist.* **LME.**

31 Any plant of the cruciferous genus *Matthiola* or one or two related genera; *spec.* a biennial or perennial cruciferous garden flower, *Matthiola incana*, with flowers in racemes. **M16.**

32 A swarm of bees. **M16.**

33 In certain card-games, the undealt cards of the pack, left on the table to be drawn from according to the rules of the game. Also (occas.), the set of cards used in a particular game. **L16.**

34 The portion of a tally given to a person making a payment to the Exchequer. Long *obsolete* exc. *Hist.* **E17.**

35 A cow's udder. *obsolete* exc. *dial.* **E17.**

36 A band of usu. stiff close-fitting material worn around the neck, formerly by men generally, and now, by both sexes, in horse-riding. Also, a piece of black material worn on the chest under a clerical collar. **L17.**

37 A rabbit-burrow. *obsolete* exc. *dial.* **M18.**

38 *THEATRICAL.* A stock company; repertory. Chiefly *US.* **E20.**

39 *ellipt.* = ***stock-car*** (b) below. *US.* **M20.**

> 📖 **31** ***Brompton stock, night-scented stock, sea-stock, Virginia stock,*** etc. **36** T. KENEALLY The black silk of his clerical stock was worn at the collar.

Phrases: ***film stock***: see **FILM** *noun.* **in stock** on the premises of a shop, warehouse, etc., and available for immediate sale or distribution. ***laughing-stock***: see **LAUGHING** *verbal noun.* ***lock, stock, and barrel***: see **LOCK** *noun*². **on the stocks** under construction, in preparation. **out of stock** not immediately available for sale etc. ***rolling-stock***: see **ROLLING** *adjective.* **stock and station** *Austral. & NZ* designating a firm or agent dealing in farm products and supplies; ***stock, lock, and barrel***: see **LOCK** *noun*². **take stock** (***a***) *COMMERCE* make an examination and inventory of one's stock; (***b***) review and assess one's position, situation, etc. **take stock in** concern oneself with, attach importance to. **take stock of** (***a***) make a review or assessment of (a situation etc.); (***b***) *colloq.* scrutinize (a person). ***tap stock***: see **TAP** *noun*¹ 1c. †**upon the stock of** on the basis of. ***upper-stock***: see **UPPER** *adjective* 3b. ***white stock***: see **WHITE** *adjective.*

▶ **B** *attrib.* or as *adjective.* **1** Kept regularly in stock for sale, loan, etc. **E17.** ▸**b** Of a medicinal or chemical preparation: kept ready for use. Of a container: holding such a preparation. **M19.**

2 *THEATRICAL.* Of or pertaining to repertory or a stock company. Now chiefly *US.* **E18.**

3 *fig.* Of a theme, phrase, response, etc.: readily available for use; commonly used, constantly appearing or recurring; commonplace, hackneyed; automatic and superficial; conventional. **M18.**

> 📖 **1** *Heritage Outlook* Many books . . are illustrated . . with stock shots from picture libraries. ***stock line, stock model, stock size,*** etc. **3** W. S. MAUGHAM The characters . . are the stock figures of Victorian fiction. P. BAILEY 'It's worse than a cat being strangled,' was my mother's stock response to . . music.

Comb. & special collocations: **stock-blind** *adjective* totally blind; ***stock-board***: see sense A.12 above. **stock-book**: for keeping records of goods acquired, in stock, and disposed of; **stock bowler** *CRICKET* a reliable but unspectacular bowler; **stock-boy**: (***a***) *Austral.* employed to look after livestock; (***b***) *N. Amer.* employed by a business firm to look after stock; **stockbreeder** a farmer who raises livestock; **stock-brick** a hard solid brick pressed in a mould; **stock-car** (***a***) *N. Amer.* a railway truck for transporting livestock; (***b***) (orig. *US*) a car with the basic chassis of a commercially produced vehicle, extensively modified and esp. strengthened for a form of racing in which collisions often occur; **stock-card** (now *rare* or *obsolete*) a large wool-card fastened to a tree-trunk or other support; **stock certificate** *COMMERCE* (***a***) a document issued by the Treasury, entitling the holder to a certain amount of a particular government stock; (***b***) *US* a certificate of share ownership; **stock character** a fictional (esp. dramatic) character representing a type in a conventional way; **stock company** (chiefly *US*) (***a***) a company the capital of which is represented by stock; (***b***) *THEATRICAL* a repertory company performing mainly at a particular theatre; **stock control** the regulation of the acquisition of stocks of goods, components, etc., in accordance with requirements; **stock cube**: of concentrated dehydrated meat, vegetable, or fish stock for use in cooking; **stock culture** an uncontaminated culture of a micro-organism maintained continuously as a source of experimental material; **stock duck** *Scot.* [repr. a different word of Scandinavian origin] a mallard; **stock exchange** (also with cap. initials) (***a***) (the site of) a building or market where stocks and shares are traded; (***b***) the dealers working in a stock market; (***c***) *the* level of transactions or level of prices in a stock market; **stock-father** *arch.* the progenitor of a family or people; **stock-frost** *local* ground-ice; ***stock-gillyflower***: see **GILLYFLOWER** 2; **stockhorse** *Austral. & NZ* a stockman's horse; **stock-hut** *Austral.* a stockman's hut; **stock-in-trade** (***a***) goods kept on sale by a dealer, shopkeeper, etc.; (***b***) *collect.* the everyday requisites or equipment of a trade, profession, etc.; (***c***) *fig.* a ready supply of characteristic phrases, attitudes, etc.; **stockjobber** (***a***) = **JOBBER** 3; (***b***) *US* an unscrupulous dealer in stocks; **stockjobbery** *rare* the business of a stockjobber, stockjobbing; **stockjobbing** *adjective & noun* (***a***) (engaged in) the business of a stockjobber; (***b***) *derog.* (involved in) speculative dealing in stocks and shares; **stockkeeper** (***a***) (chiefly *Austral. & NZ*) a person who keeps or looks after livestock, esp. cattle; (***b***) a person in charge of the stock of a warehouse etc.; **stock knife** (***a***) a knife for cutting wood, esp. for shaping the soles of clogs; (***b***) a stockman's knife; **stocklist** a regular publication stating a dealer's stock of goods with current prices etc.; **stock-lock**: enclosed in a wooden case, usu. fitted on an outer door; **stockman** (***a***) (orig. *Austral.*) a man employed to look after cattle or other livestock; (***b***) a farmer who raises livestock; **stockmanship** the art of raising or looking after livestock; **stock market** (***a***) = ***stock exchange*** above; (***b***) a market for trade in livestock; **stock option** = ***share option*** s.v. **SHARE** *noun*²; **stock-out** an occurrence of being out of stock of an item wanted by a customer; **stockpot**: for cooking stock for soups etc; **stock-proof** *adjective* (*Austral. & NZ*) (of a fence) effective in preventing livestock from straying; **stock-purse** a fund for the common purposes of a group of people; **stock rail** *RAILWAYS* each of the outer fixed rails at a set of points; **stock-rider** *Austral. & NZ*: employed to ride after cattle on an unfenced station; **stockroom** a room for storing goods held in stock; **stock-route** *Austral.* a right of way for livestock travelling over occupied land; **stock-size** *adjective* designating or pertaining to a person who wears ready-made clothes of a size normally kept in stock; **stock split, stock splitting** *US* the division of a stock into an increased number of shares; **stock-still** *adverb & pred. adjective* completely motionless; **stocktake** an instance of stocktaking; **stocktaker** a person employed in stocktaking; **stocktaking** (***a***) (an instance of) the process of making an examination and inventory of the stock in a shop, warehouse, etc.; (***b***) *fig.*: the action or an act of reviewing and assessing one's position, resources, etc.; **stock unit** *Austral. & NZ* a hypothetical unit of feed requirement calculated as the amount needed to feed one 55 kg ewe rearing a single lamb for a year. **stock-whip** *Austral. & NZ*: for driving cattle.

■ **stockless** *adjective* (***a***) (of a gun or esp. an anchor) without a stock; (***b***) (of a farm etc.) without livestock: **L19.**

†**stock** *noun*². **E16.**

[Aphet. from Old & mod. French *estoc*, from †*estoquier* stab, from Low German *stoken*. Cf. **STUG.**]

1 A thrusting sword. Only in **16.**

2 *FENCING.* A thrust with a pointed weapon. **L16–E17.**

stock /stɒk/ *noun*³. **L19.**

[German, lit. 'stick'.]

1 *MINING.* A vertical cylindrical body of ore. *rare.* **L19.**

2 *GEOLOGY.* A discordant intrusion of igneous rock having a roughly oval cross-section and steep sides, smaller than a batholith. **L19.**

stock /stɒk/ *verb*¹. **ME.**

[from **STOCK** *noun*¹.]

▶ **I** †**1** *verb trans.* Imprison in the stocks. **ME–L17.**

2 *verb trans.* Pull *up* by the roots, uproot, dig *up*, (a tree, stump, weeds, etc.); fell (a tree) by digging round and cutting its roots. **LME.** ▸**b** *transf.* Pull up (stones etc.); break or loosen (the surface of the ground) with a pick. Usu. foll. by *up.* **E19.**

†**3** *verb trans.* Strengthen (hose or stockings) with a patch or patches. **LME–L17.**

4 *verb trans.* Fix (a bell) to its stock; fit (a gun etc.) with a stock. **LME.**

5 *verb trans.* Supply, provide, or fill with stock; *spec.* (***a***) put livestock on (a farm, land, etc.); (***b***) fill (a pond, river, etc.) with fish; (***c***) supply goods, equipment, etc., to (a shop); (***d***) fill (a shelf, rack, container, etc.) with items, commodities, etc. Freq. foll. by *with.* **LME.**

6 *verb trans.* **a** Lay up or *up* in store. Now *rare* or *obsolete* exc. as in sense b. **E18.** ▸**b** Keep (an item or commodity) in stock for sale etc. **L19.**

7 *verb intrans.* Provide stock; lay in or obtain a stock or supply. Freq. foll. by *up.* **M19.**

> 📖 **5** J. GALSWORTHY He . . began methodically stocking his cigar-case from a bundle. N. CHOMSKY Its . . reading room is well stocked with the latest newspapers. W. BOYD Ornamental fishponds . . stocked with . . carp. *fig.*: F. SPALDING Stocking her mind with an unorthodox jumble of ideas. **6b** *She* Perrier water seems to be the favourite drink, although we do stock champagne. **7** *Times* Housewives stocked up against the shortage. **stock up on** obtain or renew a supply of (a commodity etc.).

▶ **II 8** *verb trans.* In *pass.* Of a female animal: be impregnated. **L15.**

9 *verb intrans.* Of corn, grass, etc.: send out shoots, sprout. *obsolete* exc. *Scot.* **L16.**

10 *verb trans.* Stunt, check the growth of, (a plant or animal). Chiefly as ***stocked*** *ppl adjective. dial.* **E17.**

11 *verb trans.* Refrain from milking (a cow being shown at market). *obsolete* exc. *dial.* **L17.**

†**12** *verb trans.* Invest, lay *out*, (money). Chiefly *Scot.* **L17–M19.**

†**13** *verb trans.* Harden (stone) by exposure to the weather. *local.* **E18–M19.**

14 *verb intrans.* Of a limb etc.: stiffen. *Scot.* **E19.**

15 *verb trans.* Arrange or shuffle (playing-cards) fraudulently. **M19.**

stock /stɒk/ *verb*² *trans. obsolete* exc. *dial.* **E17.**

[from **STOCK** *noun*².]

†**1** Strike with a thrust of a pointed weapon. *rare.* Only in **E17.**

2 Of a bird: peck (at); root *up* with the beak. Cf. **STOCK** *verb*¹ 2. **M17.**

stockade /stɒˈkeɪd/ *noun & verb.* **E17.**

[Aphet. from French †*estocade*, alt. of †*estacade*, from Spanish *estacada*, from *estaca*, from Proto-Romance from Germanic base of **STAKE** *noun*¹: see **-ADE.**]

▶ **A** *noun.* **1** A line or enclosure of upright stakes, piles, or posts, erected for defensive purposes; *spec.* (*FORTIFICATION*) a usu. wooden barricade with loopholes to fire from. **E17.**

2 a A cattle-pen. **M19.** ▸**b** A prison, *esp.* a military one. Orig. & chiefly *N. Amer.* **M19.** ▸**c** A row of piles serving as a breakwater or protecting an embankment. **L19.**

▶ **B** *verb trans.* Protect or fortify with a stockade. **M18.**

†**stockado** *noun & verb.* Pl. **-oes. L16.**

[Alt. of **STACCADO** as if from **STOCK** *noun*¹: cf. prec.]

▶ **A** *noun.* = **STOCKADE** *noun* 1. **L16–E19.**

▶ **B** *verb trans.* = **STOCKADE** *verb.* **M17–M18.**

stockbroker /ˈstɒkbrəʊkə/ *noun.* **E18.**

[from **STOCK** *noun*¹ + **BROKER.**]

A broker who, for a commission, buys and sells securities on behalf of clients; *spec.* a member of a stock exchange dealing in stocks and shares. Now also (in Britain), a broker-dealer.

Comb.: **stockbroker belt** an affluent residential area, esp. in the Home Counties of England, associated with stockbrokers and business people; **Stockbroker's Tudor, Stockbroker**

Tudor *colloq.* a style of mock-Tudor architecture associated with a stockbroker belt.

■ **stockbrokerage** *noun* the business of a stockbroker **M19**. **stockbroking** *noun* stockbrokerage (usu. *attrib.*) **L18**.

stock dove /ˈstɒk dʌv/ *noun phr.* **ME**.

[from STOCK *noun*[1] + DOVE *noun*, prob. so named as nesting in trees (as distinct from *rock-dove* s.v. ROCK *noun*[1] 5). Cf. Flemish †*stockduive*, German *Stocktaube*.]

A wild pigeon, *Columba oenas*, of Europe, N. Africa, and central Asia, smaller than the woodpigeon and grey without white markings.

stocked /stɒkt/ *adjective.* **LME**.

[from STOCK *verb*[1], *noun*[1]: see -ED[1], -ED[2].]

That has been stocked; provided with or possessing a stock or store, having a handle. Freq. with specifying word.

poorly stocked, *well-stocked*, etc.

stocker /ˈstɒkə/ *noun.* **LME**.

[from STOCK *verb*[1], *noun*[1] + -ER[1].]

†**1** A piece of wood used in building; a pole. Only in **LME**.

2 A person who makes or fits gun-stocks. **M17**.

3 A person employed to fell or uproot trees. *local.* **L17**.

4 An animal, esp. a young steer or heifer, destined for butchering but kept until matured or fattened. *N. Amer.* **L19**.

5 A person employed to look after stock held in a warehouse, garage, etc. Chiefly *US.* **E20**.

6 A stock-car; a stock-car racer. *US colloq.* **L20**.

7 A component or vehicle as regularly manufactured and held in stock (as opp. to customized). *US colloq.* **L20**.

¶ Recorded earlier in **ME** as a surname.

stockfish /ˈstɒkfɪʃ/ *noun.* Pl. **-es** /-ɪz/, (usu.) same. **ME**.

[In sense 1 from Middle & mod. Low German, Middle Dutch *stokvisch*, of unkn. origin; in sense 2 Afrikaans, from Dutch *stokvis* stockfish, hake.]

1 (A) cod or other gadoid fish cured by being split open and dried in the open air without salt. **ME**.

2 The South African hake, *Merluccius capensis*, a large edible marine fish. *S. Afr.* **E19**.

📖 **1** DICKENS Old John sat, mute as a stockfish.

stockholder /ˈstɒkhəʊldə/ *noun.* **M18**.

[from STOCK *noun*[1] + HOLDER *noun*[1].]

1 COMMERCE. An owner of stock or stocks in a company etc. Now also, a shareholder. **M18**.

2 An owner of (esp. large) herds of cattle or flocks of sheep. Now *Austral.* **E19**.

■ **stockholding** *adjective* & *noun* (*a*) (of, pertaining to, or engaged in) the business of a stockholder; (*b*) (of, pertaining to, or engaged in) the practice of holding goods etc. in stock: **M19**.

Stockholm /ˈstɒkhəʊm/ *noun.* **M19**.

[The capital of Sweden.]

1 ***Stockholm tar***, a kind of tar prepared from resinous pinewood and used in shipbuilding, skin ointments, etc. **M19**.

2 ***Stockholm syndrome***, a sense of trust or affection felt by a hostage or victim towards a captor (orig. with ref. to a bank robbery in Stockholm). **L20**.

Stockholmer /ˈstɒkhəʊmə/ *noun.* **M20**.

[formed as prec. + -ER[1].]

A native or inhabitant of Stockholm.

stockinet /stɒkɪˈnɛt/ *noun* & *adjective.* Also **-ette**. **L18**.

[Prob. alt. of *stocking-net*, simulating a dim.: see -ET[1], -ETTE, STOCKING *noun*[2].]

▶**A** *noun.* **1** A kind of elastic knitted fabric for making clothes, esp. underwear. **L18**.

2 A garment made of such fabric. **M19**.

▶**B** *attrib.* or as *adjective.* Made of or of the nature of stockinet. **E19**.

stocking /ˈstɒkɪŋ/ *noun*[1]. **ME**.

[from STOCK *verb*[1] + -ING[1].]

1 The action of STOCK *verb*[1]. **ME**.

2 The parts forming the stock of a gun. **M16**.

3 *Hist.* (An instance of) detention in the stocks. **M16**.

4 The equipment and livestock (as opp. to the crops) of a farm. **M18**.

1 ***set stocking***: see SET *adjective*.

stocking /ˈstɒkɪŋ/ *noun*[2] & *verb.* **L16**.

[from STOCK *noun*[1], *verb*[1]: see -ING[1].]

▶**A** *noun.* **1** A close-fitting knitted or woven garment covering the foot and part or all of the leg. Now chiefly *spec.*, a woman's usu. semi-transparent or diaphanous leg-covering (esp. of silk or nylon) reaching to the thigh; (esp. *US*) a sock. **L16**. ▸**b** A Christmas stocking. **M19**. ▸**c** A stocking used for storing money; a store of money. **L19**.

2 A garment or surgical appliance resembling a stocking; a cylindrical bandage for the leg, *esp.* (in full ***elastic stocking***) a covering of elastic webbing worn as a remedial support, esp. for a leg affected with varicose veins. **L17**.

3 A part (esp. the lower part) of an animal's leg coloured differently from the rest of the leg and the body; *esp.* a white portion on a horse's leg, extending up to the knee or hock. **E19**.

📖 **1** *Harper's Magazine* He stands over seven feet in his stockings. *Daily Telegraph* A . . Kiss-a-Gram girl . . in a see-through bra, black knickers and fishnet stockings.

Phrases etc.: ***body-stocking***: see BODY *noun*. ***Christmas stocking***: see CHRISTMAS *noun*. ***shoes and stockings***: see SHOE *noun*. ***silk stocking***: see SILK *noun* & *adjective*.

Attrib. & comb.: In the senses 'knitted using stocking-stitch, made of stockinet', as ***stocking cloth***, ***stocking material***, ***stocking-web***, etc. Special combs., as **stocking cap** a knitted woollen hat with a long tapered end which hangs down; **stocking filler** a small gift suitable for putting in a Christmas stocking; **stocking-foot** the part of a stocking which covers the foot, esp. as a place for storing money (***in one's stocking feet***, wearing only stockings or socks on one's feet, without shoes, esp. when being measured); **stocking-frame** *Hist.* an early form of knitting-machine; **stocking mask** a nylon stocking pulled over the face to disguise the features, used esp. by criminals; **stocking-masked** *adjective* wearing a stocking mask; **stocking-net** plain knitting done orig. on a stocking-frame (cf. STOCKINET); **stocking-stitch** KNITTING a stitch of alternate rows of plain and purl, making an even pattern; **stocking stuffer** *N. Amer.* = ***stocking filler*** above; **stocking tights** = TIGHT *noun* 1b; **stocking-weaver** *Hist.*: using a stocking-frame; **stocking-yarn** thread used in making hosiery.

▶**B** *verb trans.* Provide with stockings. **M18**.

■ **stockinged** *adjective* (*a*) wearing a stocking or stockings; (*b*) (of the foot) having a stocking or sock but no shoe on (***in one's stockinged feet*** = ***in one's stocking feet*** above): **E17**. **stockinger** *noun* (*Hist.*) a stocking-weaver **M18**. **stockingless** *adjective* **M18**.

stockish /ˈstɒkɪʃ/ *adjective.* **L16**.

[from STOCK *noun*[1] + -ISH[1].]

Resembling a block of wood; *esp.* (of a person) excessively dull or stupid.

■ **stockishly** *adverb* **M19**. **stockishness** *noun* **M19**.

stockist /ˈstɒkɪst/ *noun.* **E20**.

[formed as prec. + -IST.]

A dealer who stocks goods of a particular type for sale.

stockpile /ˈstɒkpʌɪl/ *noun* & *verb.* Orig. *US.* **L19**.

[from STOCK *noun*[1] + PILE *noun*[3].]

▶**A** *noun.* **1** A pile of coal or ore accumulated at the surface after being mined. **L19**.

2 An accumulated reserve of goods, materials, munitions, weapons, etc., available for use during a shortage, emergency, etc. **M20**.

📖 **2** *Daily Telegraph* The threat . . was increasing . . with the mounting nuclear stockpiles. *Listener* Most European countries keep a 2 months' stockpile of oil.

▶**B** *verb trans.* & *intrans.* Accumulate a stockpile of (goods, materials, weapons, etc.). **E20**.

📖 G. MARKSTEIN She . . stock-piled the pills . . until she had collected a fatal dose. *Country Life* Inflation would mean ever-advancing prices so wine merchants . . started to stockpile.

■ **stockpiler** *noun* **M20**.

stockwork /ˈstɒkwəːk/ *noun.* **E19**.

[German *Stockwerk*.]

MINING. A deposit (esp. of tin) in which the ore is distributed through a large mass of rock.

stocky /ˈstɒki/ *adjective.* **LME**.

[from STOCK *noun*[1] + -Y[1].]

†**1** Made of a piece of wood, wooden. *rare.* Only in **LME**.

2 Of a plant: of stout and sturdy growth; not unduly slender or spindly. **E17**. ▸**b** Of a root: woody, as opp. to fibrous. **E20**.

3 Of a person, animal, etc.: of stout and sturdy build; short and thickset. **L17**.

4 Headstrong, intractable; impudent; boisterous. *dial.* **M19**.

■ **stockily** *adverb* **L19**. **stockiness** *noun* **L19**.

stød /stəːd/ *noun.* **M20**.

[Danish, lit. 'push, jolt'.]

LINGUISTICS. A glottal stop or catch.

stodge /stɒdʒ/ *noun.* **E19**.

[from the verb.]

1 Thick tenacious mud or soil. Chiefly *dial.* **E19**.

2 Food of a semi-solid consistency, *esp.* stiff starchy food; *spec.* heavy and usu. fattening food (often with little nutritional value). *colloq.* **M19**.

3 A hard effort; an unfulfilling occupation. *colloq.* **M19**.

4 a Gorging with food. Also, a heavy solid meal. *colloq.* **L19**. ▸**b** Food of any kind. *slang.* **L19**.

5 Dull, heavy, or platitudinous writings, notions, etc. *colloq.* **E20**.

6 = STODGER. *colloq. rare.* **E20**.

📖 **2** L. DEIGHTON You're putting on a lot of weight. It's all that stodge you eat. *Times* Puddings are in the . . tradition of English stodge.

stodge /stɒdʒ/ *verb.* **L17**.

[Phonetically symbolic, after *stuff* and *podge*. Cf. STOG *verb*[1].]

▶**I** *verb trans.* **1 a** Fill quite full, stuff to stretching point. Now *dial.* **L17**. ▸**b** Gorge (oneself, one's stomach) with food. *colloq.* **M19**. ▸**c** *fig.* Repel by excess, glut. Also foll. by *off*. *colloq.* **L19**.

2 Mix in a thick mass. *dial.* **E19**.

3 a In *pass.* Be stuck in the mud, be bogged (down). *dial.* & *colloq.* **L19**. ▸**b** Trudge through (mud). *rare.* **E20**.

▶**II** *verb intrans.* **4** Walk or trudge through mud or slush; walk ponderously with short heavy steps. *dial.* & *colloq.* **M19**.

5 Work steadily *at* something heavy or tedious. *colloq.* **E20**.

6 Gorge oneself with food. *colloq.* **E20**.

Comb.: **stodge-full** *adjective* (*dial.* & *colloq.*) full to distension or repletion.

stodger /ˈstɒdʒə/ *noun. colloq.* (now *rare*). **E20**.

[from STODGY + -ER[1].]

A stodgy person; a person who is lacking in spirit or liveliness.

stodgy /ˈstɒdʒi/ *adjective.* **E19**.

[from STODGE *noun*, *verb* + -Y[1].]

1 a Of a thick semi-solid consistency. **E19**. ▸**b** Of (esp. starchy) food: thick, glutinous. **M19**. ▸**c** Of food, a meal, etc.: heavy, solid, difficult to finish, overfilling. **L19**.

2 Of a person: bulky in figure (and stiff and clumsy). Also *occas.*, (of a thing) bulky, distended. Now *rare.* **M19**.

3 *fig.* Dull, heavy; lacking interest, freshness, or brightness; stiff, turgid, ponderous. *colloq.* **L19**.

📖 **1b** J. B. PRIESTLEY It's not very nice. The crust's too thick and stodgy. **3** C. SAGAN Such ideas are stodgy in their unimaginativeness. *Company* Retailers . . whose stodgy conservatism is out of tune with the market.

■ **stodgily** *adverb* **E20**. **stodginess** *noun* **L19**.

stoechas /ˈstiːkas/ *noun.* **M16**.

[Latin from Greek *stoikhas*. Cf. STICKADOVE.]

French lavender, *Lavandula stoechas*.

stoechiology *noun* var. of STOICHEIOLOGY.

stoep /stuːp/ *noun. S. Afr.* **L18**.

[Afrikaans from Dutch, rel. to STEP *noun*[1]. Cf. STOOP *noun*[3].]

A raised platform or veranda running along the front and sometimes round the sides of a house.

Comb.: **stoep-room** a room accessible mainly from a stoep; **stoepsitter** a person who habitually sits idly on the stoep of a house.

stog /stɒg/ *verb*[1]. Infl. **-gg-**. **E19**.

[Perh. symbolic, after *stick*, *bog*, etc. Cf. STODGE *verb*.]

1 *verb intrans.* Walk clumsily or heavily; plod *on*. Chiefly *Scot.* **E19**.

2 *verb trans.* In *pass.* Be stuck in mud, a bog, etc.; be bogged down (*lit.* & *fig.*). *dial.* & *colloq.* **M19**.

stog *verb*[2] & *noun* var. of STUG *verb* & *noun*.

stogie /ˈstəʊgi/ *noun.* Also †**stoga**, **stogy**. **M19**.

[from *Conestoga*, Pennsylvania (app. by assoc. with drivers of Conestoga wagons: see CONESTOGA 2).]

1 A rough heavy kind of boot or shoe. *US.* **M19**.

2 A long slender roughly made cigar. *N. Amer.* **M19**.

Stoic /ˈstəʊɪk/ *noun* & *adjective.* **LME**.

[Latin *stoicus*, from Greek *stōikos*, formed as STOA: see -IC.]

▶**A** *noun.* **1** A member of the ancient Greek school of philosophy founded by Zeno (fl. *c* 300 BC) and characterized by its austere ethical doctrines. **LME**.

2 (Usu. **s-**.) A person who practises repression of emotion, indifference to pleasure and pain, and patient endurance in adversity. **L16**.

▶**B** *adjective.* **1** (Usu. **s-**.) = STOICAL 2. **L16**.

2 Of or belonging to the school of the Stoics or its system of philosophy. **E17**.

stoical /ˈstəʊɪk(ə)l/ *adjective.* **LME**.

[formed as prec. + -AL[1].]

1 Of or belonging to the Stoics; characteristic of the Stoic philosophy. **LME**.

2 Of disposition, behaviour, etc.: characterized by indifference to pleasure and pain. Of a person: resembling a Stoic; practising repression of emotion, indifference to pleasure and pain, and patient endurance in adversity. **L16**.

📖 **2** B. MONTGOMERY I used to praise the Russian . . people for their stoical endurance of many hardships.

■ **stoicalness** *noun* **E18**.

stoically /ˈstəʊɪk(ə)li/ *adverb.* **E17**.

[from STOIC, STOICAL: see -ICALLY.]

1 (Usu. **S-**.) In the manner of a Stoic; in accordance with Stoic philosophy. Now *rare.* **E17**.

2 In a stoical manner; with indifference or fortitude. **E19**.

stoicheiology /stɔɪkʌɪˈɒlədʒi/ *noun.* Now *rare* or *obsolete.* Also **stoechio-** /stiːkɪˈɒ-/. **M19**.

[formed as next, after German *Stöchiologie*: see -LOGY.]

A branch of logic or of physiology which deals with the elementary principles of the subject.

stoichiometrical /ˌstɔɪkɪəˈmɛtrɪk(ə)l/ *adjective.* Also **stoicheio-**; **stoicho-** /stɔɪkə-/. **M19**.

[from next + -ICAL.]

CHEMISTRY. Of or pertaining to stoichiometry; (of a chemical formula) in which the numbers of atoms are simple integers determined by valency; (of quantities of reactants) present or involved in the simple integral ratios prescribed by an equation or formula.

▪ **stoichiometric** *adjective* = STOICHIOMETRICAL L19. **stoichiometrically** *adverb* M20.

stoichiometry /stɔɪkɪˈɒmɪtri/ *noun.* Also **stoicheio-**, **stoichometry** /stɔɪˈkɒmɪtri/. E19.
[from Greek *stoikheion* element + -METRY, after German *Stöchiometrie*.]
CHEMISTRY. (The determination or measurement of) the fixed, usu. rational numerical relationship between the quantities of elements or other substances participating in a reaction or constituting a compound.

†Stoician *noun.* LME–E19.
[French *stoicien* from Latin *stoicus* STOIC: see -IAN.]
= STOIC *noun* 1.

stoicise *verb* var. of STOICIZE.

Stoicism /ˈstəʊɪsɪz(ə)m/ *noun.* E17.
[from STOIC + -ISM.]
1 The philosophy of the Stoics. E17.
2 (Usu. **s-**.) Stoical attitude or behaviour; repression of emotion, fortitude, resignation. M17.

stoicize /ˈstəʊɪsʌɪz/ *verb trans. rare.* Also **-ise**. E18.
[from STOIC + -IZE.]
Make stoical.

stoit /stɔɪt, stɔːt/ *verb intrans. Scot. & dial.* E18.
[Origin uncertain: perh. from Germanic base of Old Norse *stauta* beat, strike (Icelandic = stutter, stumble), rel. to Dutch *stuiten* rebound. Cf. STOT *verb*.]
1 Rebound, bounce; move unsteadily, lurch. Also foll. by *about, along*. Chiefly *Scot.* E18.
2 Of a fish: leap above the surface of the water. E19.

stoiter /ˈstɔɪtə, ˈstɔːtə/ *verb intrans. Scot. & north.* E18.
[Frequentative of prec.]
Swerve or lurch in walking; stagger, totter.

stoke *noun* see STOKES *noun*[1].

stoke /stəʊk/ *verb.* M17.
[Back-form. from STOKER.]
1 *verb trans.* Feed and stir up (a fire, furnace, boiler, etc.) to maintain or increase the heat produced. Freq. foll. by *up*. M17. ▸**b** *fig.* Encourage, incite, fuel. Freq. foll. by *up*. M19. ▸**c** Excite, thrill, elate. *slang* (orig. SURFING). M20.
2 a *verb trans.* Feed (oneself or another) as if stoking a furnace; shovel (food) into one's mouth steadily and continuously. L19. ▸**b** *verb intrans.* Eat, esp. voraciously. Freq. foll. by *up*. L19.

> 🕮 **1** J. COX The only way to get the woodstove cranking . . was to stoke it every half hour. **b** N. HERMAN Anxieties can stoke an incipient paranoia.

Comb.: **stokehold** (*a*) a compartment containing the boilers of a steamship, where the stokers tend the furnaces; (*b*) a hold in which coal is stored. **stoke-hole** [orig. translating Dutch *stookgat*] (*a*) the space in front of a furnace where the stokers stand to tend the fires; (*b*) an aperture through which a fire is fed and tended; (*c*) the opening to a hold in which fuel is stored.

▪ **stoked** *ppl adjective* (*a*) that is stoked up or *up*; (*b*) *slang* excited, pleased; hooked *on*: E20.

stoker /ˈstəʊkə/ *noun.* M17.
[Dutch, from *stoken* feed (a furnace), Middle Low German, Middle Dutch *stoken* push, poke, from base also of STICK *verb*[1]: see -ER[1].]
1 A person who feeds and tends a furnace; (more fully ***mechanical stoker***) a machine which automatically feeds fuel into a furnace. M17.
2 In *pl.* Smuts and cinders which escape through the funnel of a steam engine. Chiefly *Nautical slang*. Now *rare*. L19.

Stokes /stəʊks/ *noun*[1]. In sense 2 **s-**. L19.
[Sir George *Stokes* (1819–1903), Irish-born physicist and mathematician.]
PHYSICS. **I** *attrib.* **1** Used *attrib.* and in *possess.* to designate concepts and phenomena discovered by Stokes or arising out of his work, esp. regarding sedimentation. L19.
1 Stokes' formula = *Stokes' law* (b) below. **Stokes' law** (*a*) the principle (not always true) that in fluorescence the wavelength of the emitted radiation is longer than that of the radiation causing it; (*b*) the principle that the resisting force on a spherical particle moving through a fluid is equal to $6\pi\eta Vr$ (where η is the viscosity of the fluid, *V* the speed of the particle, and *r* its radius), and its limiting rate of fall equal to $2gr^2\rho/9\eta$ (where *g* is the acceleration due to gravity and ρ the difference in density between the particle and the fluid). **Stokes' line**, **Stokes' shift**: pertaining to or exhibiting spectral emission at a lower frequency than the incident radiation. **Stokes' theorem**: that the surface integral of the curl of the function over any surface bounded by a closed path is equal to the line integral of a vector function round that path.
▸**II** Pl. same. Also (*rare*) as *sing.* **stoke** /stəʊk/.
2 The unit of kinematic viscosity in the cgs system, equal to 1 cm^2/s. M20.

Stokes /stəʊks/ *noun*[2]. E20.
[Sir Wilfrid *Stokes* (1860–1927), English engineer.]
In full ***Stokes trench mortar***, ***Stokes mortar***. A type of light muzzle-loading mortar.

Stokes–Adams /stəʊksˈadəmz/ *noun.* E20.
[William *Stokes* (1804–78) and Robert *Adams* (1791–1875), Irish physicians.]
MEDICINE. Used *attrib.* to designate occasional transient cessation of the pulse and loss of consciousness, esp. caused by heart-block.
Stokes–Adams attack, ***Stokes–Adams disease***, ***Stokes–Adams syndrome***.

Stokes' aster /stəʊks ˈastə/ *noun phr.* Also **Stokes's aster** /ˈstəʊksɪz/. L19.
[Jonathan *Stokes* (1755–1831), English physician and botanist.]
A plant related to the asters, *Stokesia laevis*, with blue or lilac flowers, native to the south-eastern US and grown for ornament.

STOL /stɒl/ *abbreviation.*
AERONAUTICS. Short take-off and landing.

stola /ˈstəʊlə/ *noun.* Pl. **-lae** /-liː/, **-las**. E18.
[Latin *stola*, Greek *stolē*: see next.]
CLASSICAL HISTORY. A long robe worn by Greek and Roman women.

stole /stəʊl/ *noun*[1].
[Old English *stole* fem., *stol* neut., from Latin *stola* from Greek *stolē* equipment, array, clothing, garment, from base of *stellein* to place or array.]
1 A long robe. Now *poet.* or *Hist.* OE. ▸**b** An ecclesiastical gown, a surplice. *rare.* E19.
2 ECCLESIASTICAL. A vestment consisting of a narrow strip of silk or linen, worn over the shoulders (by deacons over the left shoulder only) and hanging down to the knee or lower. OE. ▸**b** An embroidered strip of linen hanging down in front of an altar. *rare.* E16.
3 A woman's long scarf or shawl, worn loosely over the shoulders. L19.
Comb.: **stole-fees** (esp. ROMAN CATHOLIC CHURCH) = SURPLICE *fees*.

stole /stəʊl/ *noun*[2]. LME.
[Var. of STOOL *noun* (in sense 'commode, privy').]
Hist. In full ***groom of the stole***. A high officer of a royal household ranking next below the vice-chamberlain.

stole /stəʊl/ *noun*[3]. Now *rare* or *obsolete*. E19.
[Irreg. from Latin STOLO. Cf. STOOL *noun* 8e.]
BOTANY. = STOLON 1.

stole /stəʊl/ *ppl adjective.* Now *dial. & non-standard.* LME.
[Strong pa. pple of STEAL *verb*.]
= STOLEN *ppl adjective*.

stole *verb* see STEAL *verb*.

stoled /stəʊld/ *adjective.* M16.
[from STOLE *noun*[1] + -ED[2].]
Wearing a stole; *rare* (of an altar) covered with a stole or stoles.

stolen /ˈstəʊlən/ *ppl adjective.* ME.
[pa. pple of STEAL *verb*.]
1 Obtained by theft. ME.
2 Accomplished or enjoyed by stealth, secret. ME. ▸**b** Of a hen's nest: made in a concealed place. M19.
3 Of time: obtained by contrivance. L16.
4 Of a crop: interpolated in a rotation of crops. M19.
5 SPORT. (Of a run, score, etc.) made surreptitiously or by taking advantage of distractions etc.; *spec.* in BASEBALL, (of a base) gained while the pitcher is delivering the ball. L19.

> 🕮 **1** R. A. FREEMAN The police . . caught him . . with all the stolen property in his possession. **2** J. HAYWARD Stolen embraces . . prov'd to be ever the best.

▪ **stolen-wise** *adverb* (now *arch. rare*) stealthily E19.

stolen *verb pa. pple*: see STEAL *verb*.

Stolichnaya /stəˈliːtʃnʌɪə/ *noun.* M20.
[Russian, lit. 'of the capital, metropolitan'.]
(Proprietary name for) a variety of Russian vodka.

stolid /ˈstɒlɪd/ *adjective.* L16.
[French †*stolide* or Latin *stolidus*, perh. rel. to *stultus* foolish: see -ID[1].]
Dull and impassive; not easily excited or moved; lacking or concealing emotion, animation, etc.

> 🕮 *Athenaeum* A stolid seriousness which its inventors never can have intended. A. SETON A stolid child who seldom smiled.

¶ Rare before 19.
▪ **stolidly** *adverb* M19. **stolidness** *noun* E18.

stolidity /stəˈlɪdɪti/ *noun.* L16.
[French †*stolidité* or Latin *stoliditas*, from *stolidus*: see prec., -ITY.]
The attribute of being stolid; dull impassiveness.

stollen /ˈstɒlən, ˈʃtɒ-/ *noun.* E20.
[German.]
A rich fruit loaf, often with nuts added.

stolo /ˈstəʊləʊ/ *noun.* Now *rare* or *obsolete*. Pl. **stolones** /stəˈləʊniːz/. E18.
[Latin: see next.]
1 BOTANY. = STOLON 1. E18.
2 ZOOLOGY. In full ***stolo prolifer***. = STOLON 2. L19.

stolon /ˈstəʊlɒn/ *noun.* E17.
[Latin *stolo(n-)* shoot, scion.]
1 BOTANY. Orig., a sucker. Now, a long horizontal side-stem of a plant that roots at the tip to form a new plant. Cf. RUNNER 12a. E17.
2 ZOOLOGY. A branched structure connecting parts of a compound organism such as a coral; in some organisms, a stalk from which new individuals are budded. M19.
▪ **stolonate** *adjective* (chiefly ZOOLOGY) bearing stolons; developed from a stolon: L19. **stoˈlonial** *adjective* (chiefly ZOOLOGY) of, pertaining to, or of the nature of a stolon E20. **stoˈlonic** *adjective* = STOLONIAL M20. **stoloˈniferous** *adjective* (chiefly BOTANY) producing stolons, spreading or reproducing by means of stolons L18. **stoloniˈzation** *noun* (ZOOLOGY) the formation of stolons, esp. by certain ascidians during reproduction E20.

stolones *noun* pl. of STOLO.

stolovaya /stoˈlovaja, stəˈlɒvʌɪə/ *noun.* M20.
[Russian.]
In Russia, a canteen, a cafeteria.

stolport /ˈstɒlpɔːt/ *noun.* Also **STOLport**. M20.
[from *STOL* s.v. S, S + PORT *noun*[1].]
An airport for aircraft which need only a short runway for take-off and landing.

Stolypin /stəˈliːpɪn/ *noun.* E20.
[Pyotr Arkadyevich *Stolypin* (1862–1911), Russian conservative statesman.]
1 ***Stolypin's necktie***, a hangman's noose. *slang.* Now *Hist.* E20.
2 Chiefly *Hist.* In full ***Stolypin car***. A type of railway carriage for the transport of prisoners, introduced after the Russian Revolution of 1905. L20.

stoma /ˈstəʊmə/ *noun.* Pl. **stomata** /ˈstəʊmətə/, (in sense 3 usu.) **-mas**. L17.
[mod. Latin from Greek *stoma*, *stomat-* mouth.]
1 ANATOMY & ZOOLOGY. Any of various small openings or pores in an animal body; *spec.* an opening resembling a mouth in various invertebrates. L17.
2 BOTANY. Any of the minute pores in the epidermis of the leaf or stem of a plant, forming a slit of variable width between two specialized cells (guard-cells), which allows movement of gases in and out of the intercellular spaces. Also, the whole pore with its associated guard-cells. M19.
3 MEDICINE. An artificial opening made into a hollow organ, esp. one on the surface of the body leading to the gut or trachea. M20.
3 attrib.: ***stoma patient***, ***stoma therapy***, etc.
▪ **stomal** *adjective* (chiefly MEDICINE) of or pertaining to a stoma or stomas M20.

stomach /ˈstʌmək/ *noun.* ME.
[Old French *stomaque*, (also mod.) *estomac* from Latin *stomachus* from Greek *stomakhos* throat, gullet, mouth of an organ, (later) stomach, from *stoma* mouth.]
1 The internal organ or cavity in which food is received and (initial) digestion occurs, being in humans a pear-shaped enlargement of the alimentary canal in the upper left abdomen, linking the oesophagus to the small intestine; each of a series of such organs in various animals (e.g. in ruminants, the rumen, reticulum, omasum, and abomasum). ME. ▸**b** *loosely.* The organs of digestion; the power or faculty of digestion. LME. ▸**c** The seat or location of hunger, nausea, gluttony, discomfort from overeating, unpleasant sensations (esp. of fear), etc. LME. ▸†**d** The throat, the oesophagus. *rare.* LME–M17.
2 The lower front part of the body, the belly, the abdomen. Formerly also, the chest. Also *spec.*, a protuberant belly. LME.
3 a Appetite, relish for food. Now only foll. by *for*. LME. ▸**b** *fig.* Liking, inclination, readiness (for an undertaking, conflict, danger, etc.). Now usu. foll. by *for, to do*. LME.
†**4** = STOMACHER *noun*[1] 2. Also, a chest-covering for a horse. *Scot.* L15–M16.
5 The inward seat of emotion, feelings, or secret thoughts. Now *rare* exc. as passing into sense 1c. L15.
6 Temper, disposition, attitude (esp. towards a person); *occas.* friendliness. Long *literary*, with qualifying adjectives, as *bold, high, proud, malicious*, etc. L15.
†**7 a** Pride, obstinacy. E16–M18. ▸**b** Spirit, courage, valour. E16–M17. ▸**c** Malice, ill will; vexation, pique. M16–E19.
8 BREWING. The odour of the vapour produced during fermentation. M19.

> 🕮 **1c** J. T. STORY I fell headlong with that sickening feeling in the stomach. **2** W. HORWOOD His stomach had a pleasing roundness and his face was cheerful. P. FUSSELL Troops crawling on their stomachs through the malarial jungles. **3b** G. F. KENNAN People had no further stomach for war.

Phrases: ***butterflies in the stomach***: see BUTTERFLY 3. ***have eyes bigger than one's stomach***: see EYE *noun*. ***honey stomach***: see HONEY *noun*. **lie on the stomach** = *sit heavy on the stomach* s.v. SIT *verb*. MUSCULAR ***stomach***. **on an empty stomach** after a period without food. **on a full stomach** soon after a large meal. ***pit of the stomach***: see PIT *noun*[1]. ***sick at the stomach***, ***sick to the stomach***: see SICK *adjective*. ***sit heavy on the stomach***: see SIT *verb*. **stick in one's stomach**, **stick in the stomach** make a lasting (esp. painful) impression on the mind. ***strong stomach***: see STRONG *adjective*. ***sucking stomach***: see SUCKING *adjective*. ***upset stomach*** = ***stomach upset*** below.

Comb.: **stomach-ache** pain in the stomach or abdominal region; **stomach-achey** *adjective* (*colloq.*) causing or having stomach-ache; **stomach muscle** (*a*) a muscle in the front wall of the abdomen; (*b*) a smooth muscle of the gastric wall; **stomach-pump** a kind of pump or syringe for forcing liquid etc. into or out of the stomach via a tube in the mouth; **stomach-tooth** a lower canine milk tooth, where eruption is associated with stomach upsets in infants; **stomach-tube** a tube introduced into the stomach through the gullet esp. for cleansing or emptying it; **stomach upset** a temporary slight disorder of the digestive system; **stomach-worm** any of various nematodes infesting the gut of mammals, esp. *Haemonchus contortus* of the abomasum of sheep.

■ **stomachal** *adjective* (now *rare*) gastric, stomachic LME. **stomachless** *adjective* E17.

stomach /ˈstʌmək/ *verb*. E16.
[Orig. from French *s'estomaquer* be offended, Latin *stomachari* be resentful, be angry with, from *stomachus* (see prec.); later from the noun.]
†**1** *verb trans.* Be offended at, resent. E16–E19.
†**2** *verb intrans.* Take offence, feel resentment. M16–E18.
†**3** *verb trans.* Inspire with resentment, fury, or courage; incite. Only in M16.
†**4** *verb trans.* Excite the indignation of, offend, vex. L16–L17.
5 *verb trans.* **a** Endure, put up with, tolerate. L17. ▸**b** Find sufficiently palatable to swallow; eat or drink without nausea or vomiting. E19.
6 *verb trans.* Turn the stomach of, nauseate. *rare*. L18.

> 🕮 **5a** B. CASTLE He just could not stomach the bureaucracy and the ideological starvation there. **b** R. RENDELL He couldn't stomach the lemonade and strawberry pop.

stomached /ˈstʌməkt/ *adjective*. M16.
[from STOMACH *noun*, *verb*: see -ED[2], -ED[1].]
1 Having a stomach (of a specified kind or condition). M16.
†**2** Offended; incited, encouraged. L16–E18.
1 *large-stomached*, *weak-stomached*, etc.

stomacher /ˈstʌməkə/ *noun*[1]. LME.
[Prob. aphet. from Old French (perh. Anglo-Norman) *estomachier*, from *estomac* STOMACH *noun*: see -ER[2].]
1 Orig., an ornamental V- or U-shaped piece of stiff material worn (chiefly in the 15th and 16th cents.) under a man's doublet to cover the chest and stomach. Later, a kind of warm waistcoat. *obsolete* exc. *Hist.* LME. ▸†**b** A warm poultice, piece of chain-mail, etc., for the chest. *rare*. LME–L17.
2 An ornamental triangular panel filling the open front of a woman's dress, covering the breast and pit of the stomach and often jewelled or embroidered. Also (more fully ***stomacher brooch***), an ornament worn on the front of a bodice. M16.

stomacher /ˈstʌməkə/ *noun*[2]. E19.
[from STOMACH *noun* + -ER[1].]
A blow to the stomach.

stomachful /ˈstʌməkfʊl, -f(ə)l/ *noun*. M19.
[from STOMACH *noun* + -FUL.]
As much as will fill one's stomach.

†**stomachful** *adjective*. E17.
[formed as prec.]
1 Obstinate, self-willed. E17–E19.
2 Resentful, angry. E17–M18.
3 Spirited, courageous. E17–E19.
■ †**stomachfully** *adverb* E17–M18. †**stomachfulness** *noun* E17–M18.

stomachic /stəˈmakɪk/ *adjective & noun*. M17.
[French *stomachique* or Latin *stomachicus* from Greek *stomakhikos*, from *stomakhos* STOMACH *noun*: see -IC.]
▶ **A** *adjective*. **1** Of or pertaining to the stomach; gastric. M17.
†**2** Caused or affected by a disorder of the stomach. *rare*. M17–L19.
3 Good for the stomach. M17.
▶ **B** *noun*. A stomachic medicine. M18.
■ **stomachical** *adjective & noun* (now *rare* or *obsolete*) (*a*) *adjective* = STOMACHIC *adjective* 1, 3; †(*b*) *noun*= STOMACHIC *noun*: E17. **stomachically** *adverb* (*rare*) as regards the stomach; by, or by reason of, a disorder of the stomach: L17.

†**stomachous** *adjective*. M16.
[Latin *stomachosus*, from *stomachus* STOMACH *noun*: see -OUS.]
1 Spirited, courageous. *rare*. Only in M16.
2 Resentful, bitter. L16–M17.

> 🕮 **2** SPENSER Who . . with sterne lookes, and stomachous disdaine, Gaue signes of grudge and discontentment vaine.

stomachy /ˈstʌməki/ *adjective*. E19.
[from STOMACH *noun* + -Y[1].]
1 Ready to take offence, irritable. *dial.* E19.
2 High-spirited. *dial.* L19.
3 Big-bellied, paunchy. *colloq.* L19.
4 Of the voice or a vocal sound: deeply resonant, as if produced in the stomach. *colloq.* M20.

stomapod /ˈstɒməpɒd/ *adjective & noun*. Now *rare* or *obsolete*. M19.
[mod. Latin *Stomapoda* noun pl., irreg. from Greek *stoma* mouth + *pod-*, *pous* foot.]
ZOOLOGY. = STOMATOPOD.

stomata *noun pl.* see STOMA.

stomatal /ˈstəʊmət(ə)l, ˈstɒ-/ *adjective*. M19.
[from mod. Latin *stomat-*, STOMA + -AL[1].]
BOTANY & ZOOLOGY. Of or pertaining to a stoma or stomata; of the nature of a stoma; having stomata, stomatous.

stomate /ˈstəʊmət/ *noun*. M19.
[App. an English sing. for the pl. *stomata*: see STOMA.]
BOTANY. = STOMA 2.

stomatic /stəˈmatɪk/ *adjective & noun*. M17.
[Late Latin *stomaticus* adjective, *-cum* noun, from Greek *stomatikos*, *-on*, from *stomat-*, *stoma* mouth: see -IC.]
▶ **A** *adjective*. **1** Of a medicine: good for diseases of the mouth. Now *rare* or *obsolete*. M17.
2 BOTANY & ZOOLOGY. = STOMATAL. M19.
▶†**B** *noun*. A stomatic medicine. M17–M19.

stomatiferous /stəʊməˈtɪf(ə)rəs, stɒ-/ *adjective*. M19.
[from mod. Latin *stomat-*, STOMA + -FEROUS.]
BOTANY. Bearing stomata.

stomatitis /stəʊməˈtʌɪtɪs, stɒ-/ *noun*. M19.
[mod. Latin, from *stomat-*, STOMA: see -ITIS.]
MEDICINE. Inflammation of the mucous membrane of the mouth.
■ **stomatitic** /-ˈtɪtɪk/ *adjective* of, pertaining to, or affected with stomatitis E20.

stomato- /ˈstəʊmətəʊ, ˈstɒ-, stəˈmatəʊ/ *combining form*.
[from mod. Latin or Greek *stomat-*, *stoma* mouth: see -O-.]
Chiefly ZOOLOGY & MEDICINE. Forming nouns and adjectives in the sense 'of or relating to the mouth, a stoma, or a structure resembling a mouth'.
■ **stomatoˈdaeum**, **-deum** *noun* (EMBRYOLOGY & ZOOLOGY) = STOMODAEUM L19. **stomatoˈgastric** *adjective* pertaining to or connected with the mouth and stomach; *spec.* designating a system of visceral nerves in invertebrates: M19. **stomatoˈlogical** *adjective* relating to stomatology E20. **stomaˈtologist** *noun* a specialist in stomatology E20. **stomaˈtology** *noun* the branch of medicine that deals with diseases of the mouth L19. **stomatoplasty** *noun* (MEDICINE, *rare*) plastic surgery of the mouth M19. **stomatoporoid** *adjective* (ZOOLOGY & PALAEONTOLOGY) of, resembling, or characteristic of a branching colonial bryozoan of the genus *Stomatopora* L19.

stomatopod /stəˈmatəpɒd/ *adjective & noun*. L19.
[mod. Latin *Stomatopoda* (see below): see STOMATO-, STOMAPOD.]
ZOOLOGY. ▶**A** *adjective*. Of, characteristic of, or belonging to the order Stomatopoda (Hoplocarida) of malacostracan crustaceans, including the mantis shrimps. L19.
▶ **B** *noun*. A stomatopod crustacean, a mantis shrimp. L19.

stomatous /ˈstɒmətəs/ *adjective*. *rare*. L19.
[from mod. Latin *stomat-*, STOMA + -OUS.]
BOTANY & ZOOLOGY. Having stomata; stomatiferous.
■ Also **stomatose** *adjective* E20.

stomia *noun*[1], *noun*[2] see STOMION, STOMIUM.

stomion /ˈstɒmɪɒn/ *noun*. Pl. **-mia** /-mɪə/. M20.
[Greek, dim. of *stoma* mouth.]
GREEK ANTIQUITIES. A doorway forming the entrance to an ancient tomb.

stomium /ˈstəʊmɪəm/ *noun*. Pl. **stomia** /ˈstəʊmɪə/, **-miums**. E20.
[mod. Latin formed as prec.]
BOTANY. In a fern, the part of the wall of the sporangium which ruptures to release the spores.

stomochord /ˈstəʊməkɔːd/ *noun*. L19.
[from Greek *stoma* mouth + CHORD *noun*[2], after *notochord*.]
ZOOLOGY. The notochord of an enteropneust.

stomodaeum /stəʊməˈdiːəm/ *noun*. Also **-deum**. L19.
[mod. Latin, irreg. from Greek *stoma* mouth + *hodaios* that is in or on the road.]
EMBRYOLOGY & ZOOLOGY. The anterior portion of the gut immediately inside the mouth, which is lined with ectodermal rather than endodermal cells; the foregut. Cf. PROCTODAEUM.
■ **stomodaeal** *adjective* of or pertaining to a stomodaeum L19.

stomp /stɒmp/ *noun*. E20.
[from the verb.]
1 Chiefly JAZZ. ▸**a** A lively dance, usu. involving heavy stamping; a tune or song suitable for such a dance; stomping rhythm. E20. ▸**b** A heavy stamping step to the beat of such a dance. E20.
2 A party characterized by lively dancing to popular music; *spec.* (*US*) = ***rent party*** s.v. RENT *noun*[1]. E20.
3 A heavy tramping gait or walk. L20.
Comb.: **stomp dance** a ceremonial N. American Indian dance characterized by heavy stamping steps; **stomp ground** a place where Indian stomp dances are traditionally performed.
■ **stompy** *adjective* (chiefly JAZZ) playing with or having a lively stamping rhythm, stomping M20.

stomp /stɒmp/ *verb*. Orig. *US dial.* E19.
[Var. of STAMP *verb*.]
1 *verb intrans.* **a** = STAMP *verb* 2a. Freq. foll. by *on*. E19. ▸**b** = STAMP *verb* 2C. E20. ▸**c** = STAMP *verb* 2b. E20.
2 *verb trans.* **a** = STAMP *verb* 3a. E20. ▸**b** Stamp or trample on (a person etc.); *gen.* beat up, beat in a fight etc. Chiefly *US*. M20. ▸**c** Stamp *out*, eradicate. M20. ▸**d** Beat *out* (a rhythm) with one's foot. L20. ▸**e** Trudge between (a series of places); tramp around (an area). L20.
3 Chiefly JAZZ. ▸**a** *verb trans.* Perform (a dance) to a lively stamping rhythm. E20. ▸**b** *verb trans. & intrans.* Foll. by *off*: beat (a tempo) with one's foot as a signal to a jazz band to start to play; signal to (a band) in this way. Now chiefly *Hist.* E20. ▸**c** *verb intrans.* Dance or play a stomp. E20.

> 🕮 **1a** C. MCCULLERS He took down his records of German lieder . . and stomped on them. *fig.*: *Observer* They stomped all over Newport County . . winning 3–1. **b** S. BOOTH This audience stomped for fifteen minutes. **c** M. GORDON I would stomp into the bathroom, bad-tempered. **2a** M. C. SMITH The host's carload entered, stomping snow off their boots. **stomp one's feet** stamp one's feet. **e** C. HOPE He tirelessly stomped the country.

■ **stomping** *verbal noun* the action of the verb; ***stomping ground*** = STAMPING-*ground*: E19.

stomper /ˈstɒmpə/ *noun*. L19.
[from prec. + -ER[1].]
1 A shoe, a boot; *spec.* a large heavy shoe. Usu. in *pl. N. Amer. slang*. L19.
2 Chiefly JAZZ. A person who performs a stomp. Also, a lively stomping tune or song. E20.
1 ***waffle stomper***: see WAFFLE *noun*[1].

stompie /ˈstɒmpi/ *noun*. *S. Afr. colloq.* M20.
[Afrikaans, dim. of *stomp* STUMP *noun*[1]: see -IE.]
A cigarette butt; a partially smoked cigarette, *esp.* one stubbed out and kept for relighting later.

stompneus /ˈstɒmpnəːs/ *noun*. *S. Afr.* E18.
[Dutch = blunt nose.]
Any of several edible sparid fishes found off the coast of southern Africa, *esp.* the red and silver *Chrysoblephus gibbiceps* (more fully ***red stompneus***) and the silvery *Rhabdosargus globiceps* (more fully ***white stompneus***). Also called ***stumpnose***.

-stomy /stəmi/ *suffix*.
[from Greek *stoma* mouth, opening + -Y[3]: cf. -TOMY.]
MEDICINE. Forming nouns denoting surgical operations in which (*a*) an opening is made into the internal organ denoted by the preceding element, as ***colostomy***, ***ileostomy***, etc., or (*b*) a permanent connection is made between the internal organs indicated, as ***gastro-duodenostomy***, ***gastro-enterostomy***, etc.

stone /stəʊn/ *noun*, *adjective*, & *adverb*.
[Old English *stān* = Old Frisian, Old Saxon *stēn* (Dutch *steen*), Old & mod. High German *stein*, Old Norse *steinn*, Gothic *stains*, from Germanic.]
▶ **A** *noun*. Pl. **-s**, (in sense 12, also) same.
1 A piece of rock or hard mineral substance (other than metal) of a small or moderate size. OE. ▸†**b** A rock, a cliff, a crag; a mass of rock; rocky ground. OE–L17. ▸**c** A meteorite, now *esp.* one containing a high proportion of silicates or other non-metals. E17. ▸**d** Grey colour; a shade of yellowish or brownish grey. M19.
2 A piece of rock or mineral substance (other than metal) of a definite form and size, usually artificially shaped, and used for some special purpose, as for building, for paving, or in the form of a block, slab, or pillar set up as a memorial, a boundary-mark, etc., to convey information, or for some ceremonial purpose, as an altar, a monument, etc. OE. ▸**b** *spec.* A gravestone, a tombstone. ME. ▸**c** A stone or pebble used as a missile, being thrown with the hand or from a sling or, formerly, shot from a firearm. ME. ▸**d** A heavy stone thrown by an athlete, now usually replaced by an iron ball or shot. Now *rare*. ME. ▸**e** A flat slab or tablet of stone for grinding something on, or for smoothing or flattening something; *spec.* in PRINTING, (*a*) a slab of stone used for lithography; (*b*) a large flat table or sheet, now usu. of metal, on which pages of type are made up. LME. ▸**f** A shaped piece of stone for grinding or sharpening something, as a grindstone, millstone, or whetstone. L16. ▸**g** A curling-stone. E19. ▸**h** A round piece or counter, orig. of stone, used in various board games, esp. the Japanese game of go. M19.
3 A jewel, a gem, a precious stone; *spec.* a diamond; *Austral. & NZ* (an) opal, opal-bearing material. OE.
4 a A lump of metallic ore. Now *rare* or *obsolete*. OE. ▸†**b** A lodestone. LME–M17.
5 a MEDICINE. A hard abnormal concretion in the body, esp. in the kidney, the urinary bladder, or the gall bladder; the material of this. Also, a condition caused by the formation of such a concretion; lithiasis. OE. ▸**b** A hard natural formation in an animal. E17.
6 The hard compact material of which stones and rocks consist; hard mineral substance other than metal. ME. ▸**b** A particular kind of rock or hard mineral matter;

spec. in BUILDING, (*a*) limestone, (*b*) sandstone. LME. ▸**c** = *PHILOSOPHER'S stone*. Now *rare*. LME.

7 a As a type of motionlessness or fixity, or formerly of stability or constancy. Cf. ROCK *noun*[1] 2b. ME. ▸**b** As a type of hardness or of insensibility, stupidity, cruelty, deadness, or lack of feeling. Formerly also, a silent person; a stupid person, a blockhead. ME.

8 In *pl.* Testicles. Now chiefly *slang* or *dial.* ME.

9 The stony endocarp of a drupe, enclosing the seed or kernel. Also, a hard seed or pip in any pulpy fruit, as a grape-pip. ME.

†**10** A vessel of stone or stoneware; a stone jar, basin, etc. Cf. STEAN. LME–E18.

11 A hailstone. LME.

12 A unit of weight, varying at different periods and for different commodities, but usually equal to 14 pounds (approx. 6.35 kg) and used esp. in expressing the weight of a person or a large animal. Also occas., a piece of metal of this weight, used in weighing or as a standard. Also ***stone-weight***. LME.

13 GAMES. A domino. M19.

🕮 **1a** H. D. THOREAU I . . sat down on a stone at the foot of the telegraph-pole. M. E. BRADDON The shallow streamlet came tumbling picturesquely over gray stones. P. SAYER I . . dislodged a stone with my foot. Underneath was a toad. *Proverb*: A rolling stone gathers no moss. **2** ***coping-stone, cornerstone, foundation-stone, hoarstone, milestone, paving-stone, standing stone, staddle stone, stepping-stone***, etc. **b** S. PLATH The old part of the graveyard . . , with its worn, flat stones. **c** L. T. C. ROLT Hissing and booing accompanied by showers of stones. **e** L. HEREN There was no place more exciting than the stone just before edition time. **3** D. H. LAWRENCE He sent her a little necklace of rough stones, amethyst and opal and brilliants and garnet. **5a** E. H. FENWICK A stone impacted low down in the ureter. ***chalk-stone, gallstone, kidney-stone***, etc. **6** D. MADDEN A dead knight and his lady carved in stone. **b** F. HOYLE Some stones such as Shap granite are unique to particular surface outcrops. ***Bath stone, ironstone, limestone, moonstone, mudstone, pipe-stone, Portland stone, pudding-stone, pumice stone, ragstone, sandstone, sarsen stone, soapstone***, etc. **7b** DICKENS The widow's lamentations . . would have pierced a heart of stone. **9** A. MASON He chewed the last olive, spat out the stone, . . and sat back contentedly. **12** *Times* He has the best part of a stone in weight to lose before he reaches his fastest.

Phrases: **a stone's throw** the distance that a stone can be thrown by the hand; a short or moderate distance. **cast a stone (at)**, **cast stones (at)** make an attack (on), bring an accusation (against), make aspersions (on a person's character etc.). **cast the first stone** [with allus. to *John* 8:7] be the first to make an accusation (esp. though guilty oneself). ***get blood out of a stone***, ***get blood from a stone***: see BLOOD *noun*. ***kill two birds with one stone***: see BIRD *noun*. **leave no stone unturned** try every available possibility. ***philosophers' stone***: see PHILOSOPHER. ***rolling stone***: see ROLLING *adjective*. **throw a stone (at)**, **throw stones (at)** = *cast a stone (at)* above. **throw the first stone** = *cast the first stone* above. ***white stone***: see WHITE *adjective*.

▸**B** *attrib.* or as *adjective*. **1** Consisting of stone; made of or built of stone; of or pertaining to stone or stones. OE. ▸**b** Made of stoneware; contained in stoneware bottles. OE.

†**2** Of a male domestic animal: not castrated. Chiefly in ***stone-horse***. M16–M19.

3 Of the colour of stone; grey; of a yellowish or brownish grey. M19.

4 Complete, utter; excellent. *slang*. E20.

5 = STONED 5. *US slang*. *rare*. M20.

🕮 **1** SIR W. SCOTT The sword . . rolled on the stone floor with a heavy clash. **b** E. HAYWOOD Always keep your pickles in stone jars. **4** D. A. DYE He was stuck with a stone lunatic.

▸**C** *adverb*. With following adjective: as a stone, like a stone (with intensive force), as ***stone-blind, stone-cold, stone-dead, stone-deaf, stone-hard, stone-still***, etc. Now also (*slang*) as gen. intensifier: completely, utterly, as ***stone crazy, stone drunk, stone motherless broke***, etc. ME.

stone-broke *adjective* (*slang*) = *stony-broke* s.v. STONY *adjective*; **stone-cold sober** completely sober.

Comb. & special collocations: **Stone Age** ARCHAEOLOGY the prehistoric period characterized by the predominance of stone weapons and tools; **stone-age** *adjective* of, pertaining to, characteristic of, or resembling (that of) the Stone Age; *fig.* primitive, outmoded; **stone axe** (*a*) *Hist.* a two-edged axe used for cutting stone; (*b*) ARCHAEOLOGY an axe made of stone; **stone-bark** BOTANY bark consisting chiefly of hardened and thickened cells (cf. *stone-cell* below); **stone-bass** †(*a*) a W. Indian fish of the genus *Pagrus*; (*b*) a large spiny yellow-brown serranid fish of the central Atlantic, *Polyprion americanus*, often found around driftwood and floating wreckage (also called ***wreckfish***); **stone-blue** *noun & adjective* (*a*) *noun* a compound of indigo with starch or whiting, esp. for use in laundry; the blue colour of this; (*b*) *adjective* of the colour of stone-blue; **stone-boat** (*a*) (long *rare*) a boat for transporting stones; (*b*) *N. Amer.* a flat-bottomed sled used for transporting stones and other heavy objects; **stone-bow** (*a*) an arch of stone (long *obsolete* exc. as name of a gate of the city of Lincoln); (*b*) (now *rare*) a kind of light crossbow or catapult used for shooting stones or pellets; **stone-brake** the parsley fern, *Cryptogramma crispa*; **stone bramble** a freq. thornless bramble of rocky woods, *Rubus saxatilis*, with bright red fruit; **stone-brash** a subsoil consisting of loose broken stone; **stonebreak** (now *rare* or *obsolete*) = SAXIFRAGE 1; **stonebuck** = STEINBOCK 1; **stone canal** ZOOLOGY in echinoderms, a canal, usually having calcareous walls, leading from the madreporite to the main vessel of the water-vascular system; **stone-cast** (now *rare*) = *a stone's throw* above; **stonecat** a N. American freshwater catfish, *Noturus flavus*; **stone-cell** BOTANY a short, much-pitted, strongly lignified type of sclereid, occurring esp. in seed-coats and in the flesh of the pear; **stone-china** a kind of white stoneware resembling porcelain; **stone circle** ARCHAEOLOGY = CIRCLE *noun* 8; **stone-coal** †(*a*) mineral coal as distinguished from charcoal; (*b*) a hard variety of coal, *esp.* anthracite; **stone-colour** = sense A.1d above; **stone-coloured** *adjective* = sense B.3 above; **stone-coral** = *stony coral* s.v. STONY *adjective*; **stone-crab** (*a*) any of various crabs, *esp.* the edible *Menippe mercenaria* of Caribbean and adjoining coasts; (*b*) *US local* = HELLGRAMMITE; **stone-craft** the art or skill of working in stone; sculpture; **stone cream** a traditional sweet resembling blancmange made with arrowroot and served cold on a layer of jam; **stone-crusher** a machine for crushing or grinding stone; **stone curlew** any bird of the family Burhinidae of mottled brown and grey waders, esp. *Burhinus oedicnemus*, which inhabits esp. stony open country and has a cry similar to the curlew's; also called ***thick-knee***; **stonecutter** a person who or machine which cuts, shapes, or carves stone for building or for ornamental or other purposes; ***stonecutter's disease***, lung disease caused by inhaling fine stone-dust; **stone-delf** (now *dial.*) a stone-quarry; **stone-dresser** a person who or machine which dresses or shapes stone for building; **stone-dust** *noun & verb* (*a*) *noun* dust or powder made of particles of broken stone; (*b*) *verb trans.* subject to stone-dusting; **stone-dusting** the introduction of stone-dust to the air in a mine to make the coal-dust less combustible; **stone-dyke** a dyke of stone, a stone fence or embankment; **stone face** *colloq.* (a person having) a face which reveals no emotions; a poker-faced person; **stone-fall** a fall of meteorites, or of loose stones on a mountain slope; **stone-field** an expanse of ground covered with large stones; *spec.* = FELSENMEER; **stonefish** any of various fishes typically found under stones; *esp.* the highly venomous scorpaenid *Synanceia verrucosa*, a bottom-dwelling fish of tropical seas, resembling a small rock and bearing poison glands at the base of the erect dorsal spines; **stone frigate** *Naval slang* a naval shore establishment or barracks; formerly *spec.* a naval prison; **stone-fruit** a fruit having the seed or kernel surrounded by a stone within the pulp; a drupe; **stone garland** PHYSICAL GEOGRAPHY a low bank or terrace of large stones occurring on a steep slope and curved downwards so as to resemble a garland or necklace; **stone-getter** a workman who gets stone from a quarry, a quarryman; **stone-ginger** *noun & adjective* (*slang*) (*a*) *noun* a certainty, a sure thing; (*b*) *adjective* certain; **stoneground** *adjective* (esp. of flour) ground by means of millstones (rather than metal rollers); **stone guard** an attachment serving to prevent stones entering the air-intake system of an engine; a similar device protecting any part of a vehicle, esp. the windscreen; **stone-heading** MINING a heading driven through stone or rock; **Stone Indian** = ASSINIBOINE *noun* 1, 2 (cf. STONEY *noun*[2]); **stone-jug** (*a*) a jug made of stoneware; (*b*) see JUG *noun*[2] 3; **stone-lily** a fossil crinoid; **stone line** GEOLOGY a layer of isolated stones between subsoil and underlying rock; the line of stones as this which appears in a section through the soil; **stone loach** a loach, *Noemacheilus barbatulus*, of clear rivers and lakes; **stoneman** a man who works in or with stone; PRINTING a compositor; **stone marten** (the fur of) a S. Eurasian marten, *Martes foina*, which is brown with a white throat; also called ***beech marten***; **stone-mint** the American dittany, *Cunila origanoides*; **stone net** PHYSICAL GEOGRAPHY a network of stone rings or polygons; **stone parsley** a pinnate-leaved umbelliferous hedge plant, *Sison amomum*; **stone pavement** PHYSICAL GEOGRAPHY an area of ground covered with large flattish stones; **stone pine** (*a*) a Mediterranean pine tree, *Pinus pinea*, with edible seeds (also called ***parasol pine, umbrella pine***); (*b*) (with specifying word) any of several related pines; ***Swiss stone pine***, a pine of central European mountains, *Pinus cembra*, sometimes grown for timber or turpentine (also called ***arolla***); **stone-pit** a pit from which stones are dug, a quarry; **stone-plover** any of various plovers and other small game-birds esp. of stony shores; **stone polygon** PHYSICAL GEOGRAPHY a naturally occurring arrangement of stones in the rough shape of an open polygon; **stone ring** (*a*) PHYSICAL GEOGRAPHY a natural circle of stones on the ground, similar to a stone polygon; (*b*) ARCHAEOLOGY a stone circle; **stone river** a dense linear accumulation of rocks and large stones occurring along a valley bottom or down a slope; *esp.* any of several such in the Falkland Islands; **stoneroller** any of several N. American minnows of the genus *Campostoma*, found in clear brooks and streams; **stone-root** the horse-balm, *Collinsonia canadensis*; **stone run** = *stone river* above; **stone-saw** a saw, usually without teeth, for cutting stone for building etc.; **stone-shot** a stone or stones used as missiles, esp. as shot for cannon; **stone stripe** PHYSICAL GEOGRAPHY any of several evenly spaced bands of coarse rock debris separated by finer material occurring on slopes in cold environments; **stonewash**, **stonewashed** *adjectives* (of a garment or fabric, esp. denim) washed with abrasives to produce a worn or faded appearance; ***stone-weight***: see sense A.12 above; **stonewort** a charophyte (orig., one of the genus *Chara*, from the calcareous deposits on the stem); **stone-yard** a yard in which stone-breaking or stone-cutting is done.

▪ **stoneless** *adjective* having or containing no stone LME. **stonelike** *adjective* resembling (that of) stone or a stone. E17.

stone /stəʊn/ *verb*. ME.

[from the noun.]

1 *verb trans.* Throw stones at, pelt with stones; *esp.* put to death by pelting with stones. ME.

†**2** *verb trans.* Clear or free (ground) from stones. L15–M17.

†**3** *verb trans.* Turn into stone, make hard like stone, petrify. Chiefly *fig.* E17–M19.

4 *verb trans.* Provide or fit with stones; pave or build up with stone or stones. Also, cover or shut *up* with stones. E17.

5 *verb trans.* Take the stones out of (fruit). M17.

6 *verb trans.* Rub or polish with a stone; sharpen on a whetstone; scour and smooth (leather) with a stone. L17.

7 *verb intrans.* Of a fruit: form a stone in the process of growth. M19.

8 a *verb intrans.* Become intoxicated with drink or drugs, esp. (foll. by *out*) to the point of unconsciousness. *slang* (chiefly *US*). M20. ▸**b** *verb trans.* Intoxicate; make ecstatic. See also STONED. *slang* (orig. *US*). M20.

🕮 **1** A. MASON The guilty man was accordingly stoned. C. PHILLIPS Some boys were stoning the guava trees for fruit. *Sun* A police van hit a lamp post after it was stoned by 30 youths.

Phrases: **stone me** expr. astonishment, disbelief, etc. ***stone the crows***: see CROW *noun*[1] 1.

stonechat /ˈstəʊntʃat/ *noun*. L18.

[from STONE *noun* + CHAT *noun*[3].]

A small migratory chat, *Saxicola torquata*, which has an orange breast and dark head and inhabits heath and open country in Eurasia and Africa. Also (locally or with specifying word), any of several related birds.

stonecrop /ˈstəʊnkrɒp/ *noun*.

[Old English *stāncrop*, from STONE *noun* + 2nd elem. of unkn. origin.]

Any of several small sedums of walls and dry stony ground, *esp.* (more fully ***biting stonecrop***) *Sedum acre*, a small mosslike plant with bright yellow flowers and fleshy pungent-tasting leaves. Also (with specifying word) any other plant of the genus *Sedum* or allied genera (family Crassulaceae).

stoned /stəʊnd/ *adjective*. ME.

[from STONE *noun, verb*: see -ED[1], -ED[2].]

1 a Paved or covered with stones. *rare*. ME. ▸†**b** Built of stone; fortified with stone. Only in LME.

†**2** Of a male domestic animal (esp. a horse): having testicles, not castrated. LME–L17.

†**3** Of fruit: having a stone or stones. E16–E18.

4 Of fruit: having the stone or stones removed. E18.

5 Drunk, extremely intoxicated. Also, in a state of drug-induced euphoria, incapacitated or stimulated by drugs, drugged. (Foll. by *on* an intoxicant.) Also foll. by *out*. *slang* (orig. *US*). M20.

stonefly /ˈstəʊnflʌɪ/ *noun*. LME.

[from STONE *noun* + FLY *noun*[1].]

A member of the order Plecoptera of hemimetabolous insects whose larvae are typically found under stones in streams; *spec.* in ANGLING, (an artificial fly imitating) *Perla bicaudata*.

Stonehenge /stəʊnˈhɛn(d)ʒ/ *noun*. LOE.

[from STONE *noun* + 2nd elem. prob. derived from HANG *verb*. Cf. HENGE *noun*[1].]

A large megalithic monument on Salisbury Plain in Wiltshire, England, including several concentric stone circles of various ages; a similar structure elsewhere.

stonemason /ˈstəʊnmeɪs(ə)n/ *noun*. M18.

[from STONE *noun* + MASON *noun*.]

= MASON *noun* 1.

▪ **stonemasonry** *noun* the art or skill of a stonemason; work executed by a stonemason: E19.

stonen /ˈstəʊnən/ *adjective*. Long *rare* exc. *dial.*

[Old English *stænen* = Old Frisian *steinen*, Old High German, Middle High German *steinen*, Gothic *staineins*, from Germanic base of STONE *noun*: see -EN[4].]

Made of stone.

stoner /ˈstəʊnə/ *noun*[1]. ME.

[from STONE *verb* + -ER[1].]

A person who stones a thing or person, esp. so as to kill; a device for removing stones from fruit etc.

stoner /ˈstəʊnə/ *noun*[2]. LME.

[from STONE *noun* + -ER[1].]

†**1** A jeweller. Only in LME.

2 With qualifying numeral: a person who or thing which weighs a specified number of stones. M19.

Stonesfield slate /ˌstəʊnzfiːld ˈsleɪt/ *noun phr.* M19.

[from a village in Oxfordshire.]

GEOLOGY. A stratum of thin-bedded limestone and calcareous sandstone forming part of the Oolite series in western England; a slab of this stone used for roofing.

stonewall /ˈstəʊnwɔːl, stəʊnˈwɔːl/ *verb*. L19.

[from *stone wall* (STONE *noun* + WALL *noun*[1]), as the type of an immovable barrier.]

1 *verb intrans.* CRICKET. Block balls persistently, play solely on the defensive. L19.

2 a *verb intrans.* Obstruct (esp. parliamentary) business by lengthy speeches, evasive answers, etc.; practise obstruction, refuse to give clear answers. Orig. *Austral.* L19. ▸**b** *verb trans.* Obstruct (business, an organization), block (an enquiry, request, etc.), obstruct or refuse to answer (a person etc.). Also, dismiss (a subject) by evasion or obstruction. Orig. *Austral.* L19.

📖 **2a** T. CLANCY Oh, sure, we can . . talk to them, but they'll stonewall for a while and then what? **b** I. WELSH Whitworth's gonna bullshit us, stonewall us, ignore us, until we just shut up abaht it. *Advocate* She has also stonewalled queries about her love life.

■ **stonewaller** *noun* a person who stonewalls L19.

stoneware /ˈstəʊnwɛː/ *noun*. L17.
[from STONE *noun* + WARE *noun*².]
A kind of dense, impermeable, usu. opaque pottery, made from clay containing a high proportion of silica and partly vitrified during firing.
Nottingham stoneware, ***Rhenish stoneware***, etc.

stonework /ˈstəʊnwəːk/ *noun*. OE.
[from STONE *noun* + WORK *noun*. Cf. Old Saxon *stēnwerk*.]
1 Work built or made of stone, masonry; the parts of a building etc. made of stone. OE.
2 The process of working in stone, esp. in building; the work or art of a mason. L18.
■ **stoneworker** *noun* a worker in stone, *esp*. a mason L19.

stoney /ˈstəʊni/ *noun*¹. Chiefly *dial*. M19.
[from *stoney* var. of STONY *adjective* or from STONE *noun* + -Y⁶.]
A child's coloured marble made of stone or a similar material.

Stoney /ˈstəʊni/ *noun*². Chiefly *Canad*. E20.
[from STONE *noun* + -Y¹.]
= ASSINIBOINE *noun* 1. Cf. ***Stone Indian*** s.v. STONE *noun, adjective, & adverb*. Also ***Stoney Indian***.

stoney *adjective* var. of STONY *adjective*.

stonify /ˈstəʊnɪfʌɪ/ *verb trans. & intrans. rare*. E17.
[from STONE *noun* or STONY *adjective* + -FY.]
Turn into stone, petrify.

†stonish *verb trans*. LME–E17.
[Aphet. from ASTONISH.]
= ASTONISH 1, 3.

stonk /stɒŋk/ *noun & verb*. In sense A.1 also **stunk** /stʌŋk/. M19.
[Perh. imit.]
▶ **A** *noun*. **1** A game of marbles; a coloured marble; a stake in a game of marbles. *Scot. & north*. Now *rare*. M19.
2 A concentrated artillery bombardment. *Military slang*. M20.
▶ **B** *verb trans*. Bombard with concentrated artillery fire. *Military slang*. M20.
■ **stonking** *adjective* (*slang*) (as an intensifier) powerful, exciting, formidable, considerable L20.

stonker /ˈstɒŋkə/ *noun*. *slang*. L20.
[from STONK *noun & verb* + -ER¹.]
Something which is very large or impressive of its kind.

stonker /ˈstɒŋkə/ *verb trans. slang* (chiefly *Austral. & NZ*). E20.
[from prec. + -ER⁵.]
Put out of action; kill; outwit.
■ **stonkered** *adjective* (very) drunk, (very) tired E20.

stony /ˈstəʊni/ *adjective*. OE.
[from STONE *noun* + -Y¹.]
1 a Esp. of land: rocky, having the character of stone or rock. Now chiefly *poet*. OE. ▸**b** Full of stones; containing many stones or pebbles. LME. ▸**†c** Of a fruit: having a stone, having many pips or seeds. L16–L18.
2 *fig*. **a** Esp. of the heart: unfeeling, insensitive, hardened, obdurate. ME. ▸**b** Of fear, grief, silence, etc.: cold and harsh, grim, unrelenting. L16. ▸**c** Rigid, fixed, motionless, expressionless. M17.
3 a Made or consisting of stone. Now chiefly *poet*. LME. ▸**b** Consisting of stones; (of a blow) inflicted by a stone. Chiefly *poet*. Now *rare* or *obsolete*. L16. ▸**c** Of a meteorite or meteoritic material: consisting mostly of silicates and other non-metals. E19.
4 a Resembling stone in consistency; hard like stone; very hard. LME. ▸**b** Of a quality (as hardness or colour): like that of stone. M16.
5 Of or pertaining to stone or stones. *rare*. M19.
6 = ***stony-broke*** below. *slang*. L19.
1a fall on stony ground *fig*. (of a suggestion etc.) be ignored, be unproductive.
Comb. & special collocations: **stony-broke** *adjective* (*colloq*.) penniless, ruined, out of money (cf. STONE *adverb*); **stony coral** a coral which secretes a calcium carbonate skeleton, a scleractinian coral; **stony-hearted** *adjective* having a stony heart, cruel, unfeeling, merciless; **stony-iron** *noun & adjective* (designating) a meteorite which contains appreciable quantities of both stony material and iron.
■ **stonily** *adverb* M19. **stoniness** *noun* LME.

†stony *verb trans*. ME.
[Aphet. from ASTONY (prob. sometimes confused with STUN *verb*).]
1 Stupefy with noise or shock; confound, amaze. Also, stupefy with a blow, stun. ME–L17.
2 Cause loss of feeling or function in (a body or a limb); benumb, deaden. LME–L17.

stood *verb pa. t. & pple* of STAND *verb*.

stooge /stuːdʒ/ *noun & verb*. *colloq*. (orig. *US*). E20.
[Origin unkn.]
▶ **A** *noun*. **1** A stage hand; a person who acts as a butt or foil, esp. for a comedian; a straight man; a conjuror's assistant. E20.
2 A newcomer, a novice; *spec*. (*Criminals' slang*) a first offender. M20.
3 An assistant, *esp*. one undertaking mundane or unpleasant tasks; an unquestioningly loyal or obsequious subordinate; a compliant person; a puppet, a tool. M20.
4 An airforce patrol or mission flown without expectation of encountering the enemy. *Military slang*. M20.

📖 **3** M. SPARK I thought she was running a gang, but now . . I think she may be their stooge.

▶ **B** *verb intrans*. **1** Act as a stooge. Usu. foll. by *for*. M20.
2 Of an aircraft: cruise (*Military slang*). Also (*gen*.), drift, move aimlessly. Usu. foll. by *about, along, around*. M20.

📖 **1** D. GIFFORD His . . accent . . became popular through his stooging for comedians.

stook /stʊk/ *noun*¹ & *verb*. ME.
[from or corresp. to Middle Low German *stūke*. Sense 3 is perh. a different word.]
▶ **A** *noun*. **1** = SHOCK *noun*¹ 1. ME. ▸**b** *transf*. A pile, a mass. M19.
2 A bundle of straw. *dial*. L16.
3 A pillar of coal left to support the roof of a mine. Cf. STOOP *noun*¹ 4. E19.

📖 **1** *Sunday Dispatch* Stooks of corn and . . hay have been swept into rivers.

▶ **B** *verb trans. & intrans*. Arrange (sheaves) in stooks. L16.

📖 *Daily Telegraph* Stooked corn standing up out of . . flooded fields.

■ **stooker** *noun* M17.

stook /stʊk/ *noun*². *arch. slang*. M19.
[Perh. from German *Stück* piece.]
A pocket handkerchief.

stookie /ˈstʊki/ *noun*. *Scot. & north*. L18.
[Alt. of STUCCO *noun*.]
1 Plaster of Paris; plaster; a plaster cast. L18.
2 A plaster statue, a wax figure or dummy. Also (*transf*.), a slow-witted person, a blockhead. E19.

stool /stuːl/ *noun*.
[Old English *stōl* = Old Frisian, Old Saxon *stōl*, Old High German *stuol* (Dutch *stoel*, German *Stuhl*), Old Norse *stóll*, Gothic *stōls* throne, from Germanic base of STAND *verb*: see -LE¹.]
1 †a A seat or chair for one person; *esp*. a chair of authority, state, or office, as a royal or episcopal throne; *fig*. a place or position of authority, state, etc. OE–E19. ▸**b** A seat, as a ducking-stool, used to punish offenders. *obsolete* exc. *Hist*. ME. ▸**†c** A seat by a grave or tomb. LME–M16. ▸**†d** A church pew. L16–E17. ▸**e** In W. Africa: a chief's throne; chiefdom. E19.
2 a A low short bench on which to rest the foot, to step, or to kneel; a footstool. ME. ▸**b** A seat without arms or a back, usu. for one person and consisting of a piece of wood for a seat set on three or four legs or a single central pedestal. LME. ▸**c** A high seat of this kind used esp. by an office clerk for writing at a high desk; *fig*. a situation as clerk in an office. *arch*. M19.
3 †a A seat enclosing a chamber-pot; a close-stool, a commode. Also, a privy, a lavatory. LME–L18. ▸**b** The action or an act of evacuating the bowels or discharging faeces. M16. ▸**c** Faeces; a discharge of faecal matter. Usu. in *pl*. L16.
†4 A frame or support used in embroidery or tapestry. LME–M16.
5 A supporting base or stand forming a raised platform. LME.
†6 (The head or top of) a mushroom. Cf. TOADSTOOL *noun*. *rare*. LME–M18.
7 A bench, a counter, a table, a trestle. *Scot., north., & Canad. dial*. E16.
8 a The stump of a tree; the head of the stump, from which new shoots spring. L16. ▸**b** A stump of a tree felled or headed to produce coppice-wood, saplings, etc.; the base of a plant cut down to produce shoots or branches for layering. Also, a set or group of these. E18. ▸**c** A cluster of stems or foliage springing from a single stump, root, or grain. E18. ▸**d** The underground root containing the latent buds in perennial plants which produce new stems or foliage each year. L18. ▸**e** BOTANY. [By confusion with STOLE *noun*³.] A stolon. E19.
9 ARCHITECTURE. The sill of a window. Now *US*. M17.
10 A section of a vein of ore in a mine ahead of the miner working it. Now *rare* or *obsolete*. M17.
11 A brick-moulder's shed or workshop; the gang of workers employed in one shed. Also, a moulder's bench. L17.
12 NAUTICAL. **a** A minor channel abaft the main channels to which the backstays of a ship are fastened. E18. ▸**b** The lowest transom of a ship's stern-frame. L18.
13 a A decoy-bird (orig. a pigeon fixed to a stool), *esp*. one used in wildfowling; a perch on which a decoy-bird is placed. *US*. E19. ▸**b** In full ***stool-pigeon***. A person acting as a decoy, esp. for criminals. Also, a police informer. Orig. *US*. E20.
14 In *pl*. In oyster farming, material spread on the seabed for oyster spawn to cling to. *US*. M19.
1b stool of REPENTANCE. 2b *bar-stool, camp-stool, piano-stool*, etc. **fall between two stools** *fig*. incur failure through vacillation between two different courses of action, or through not coming clearly within two relevant spheres of interest or responsibility. **3a groom of the stool** *Hist*. = STOLE *noun*².
Comb.: **stoolball** (*a*) a team game resembling cricket, now played chiefly by children, in which a hard ball is bowled underarm at a wicket defended by a player with a bat; (*b*) *rare* a ball used in this game; ***stool-pigeon***: see sense 13b above.
■ **stooled** *adjective* (*rare*) provided with or having a stool or stools E20.

stool /stuːl/ *verb*. M16.
[from prec.]
1 *verb intrans*. Evacuate the bowels; discharge faeces. *rare*. M16.
2 *verb trans*. Put or set (a person) on a stool; *spec*. †(*a*) condemn (a person) to the stool of repentance; (*b*) in W. Africa: enthrone (a new chief). *rare*. L17.
3 a *verb intrans*. (Of a plant) produce new shoots or stems from a stool or root; (of corn, grass, etc.) produce lateral shoots giving a cluster of stems or foliage. Also foll. by *out*. L18. ▸**b** *verb trans*. Cut back (a plant) to or near ground level in order to induce new growth. E20.
4 *verb trans*. Work (a vein of ore in a mine). *rare*. E19.
5 a *verb trans*. Entice (wildfowl) by means of a decoy-bird. M19. ▸**b** *verb intrans*. Of a bird: come to or be enticed by a decoy. *US*. L19. ▸**c** *verb intrans*. Act as a stool-pigeon; inform *on* (a person). *colloq*. (chiefly *N. Amer*.). E20.

stoolie /ˈstuːli/ *noun*. *N. Amer. slang*. E20.
[from ***stool-pigeon*** s.v. STOOL *noun* + -IE.]
A police informer, a stool-pigeon.

stooling /ˈstuːlɪŋ/ *noun*. M16.
[from STOOL *verb* + -ING¹.]
1 The framework supporting a mill. Cf. STOOL *noun* 5. M16.
2 The action or process of evacuating the bowels. Also, the matter evacuated. L16.
3 The action of producing young shoots or stems from a stool or root; the forming of a cluster of stems of corn etc. from lateral shoots. M19.

stoop /stuːp/ *noun*¹. Now *Scot. & dial*. ME.
[from Old Norse *stólpi*.]
1 A post, a pillar. ME.
2 A pillar of coal supporting the roof of a mine. Cf. STOOK *noun*¹ 3. M16.
3 *fig*. A person who or thing which supports or sustains something or someone. *Scot*. L16.
†4 The pillory. *slang*. L18–E19.

stoop /stuːp/ *noun*². L16.
[from STOOP *verb*¹.]
1 An act of stooping; a bending of the body forwards; a bow. L16. ▸**b** *fig*. An instance of condescending behaviour; a voluntary descent from a position regarded as superior. M17.
2 The action of descending from a height; *spec*. the swoop of a bird of prey on its quarry, the descent of a falcon to the lure. L16.
3 †a Descent or declivity of a mountain; a downward slope or incline. E17–E18. ▸**b** A waterfall. *dial. rare*. M19.
4 A stooping posture. E18.

📖 **1** T. CHALMERS A passage often narrow . . requiring a very low stoop. †**give the stoop** bow; *fig*. yield, give way. **b** DRYDEN Can any Loyal Subject see With Patience such a Stoop from Sovereignty? **4** B. NEIL Something . . anguished about the stoop of his . . shoulders.

stoop /stuːp/ *noun*³. *N. Amer*. M18.
[Dutch STOEP.]
A small raised platform at the entrance door of a house; a set of steps approaching this; a small porch or veranda.
Comb.: **stoop ball** a ball game resembling baseball, in which the ball is thrown against a stoop or building rather than to a batter.

stoop *noun*⁴ see STOUP.

stoop /stuːp/ *verb*¹.
[Old English *stūpian* = Middle Dutch *stūpen*, Old Norse *stúpa*, from Germanic base rel. to STEEP *adjective*.]
1 *verb intrans*. **a** Of a person: lower the body by bending the trunk or the head and shoulders forward, sometimes bending the knee at the same time. Freq. foll. by *down, over*. OE. ▸**b** Of the head or shoulders: bend forward, become bowed. LME. ▸**c** Of a dog, esp. a hound: put the nose to the ground to pick up a scent. E16. ▸**†d** Of a quadruped: crouch. L16–E17.

2 *verb intrans.* Of a thing: incline from the perpendicular; bend down; slope; tilt over. OE.

3 *verb intrans.* Carry one's head and shoulders bent or the trunk inclined forwards; *esp.* adopt this posture habitually or permanently. ME.

4 *verb trans.* Cause to bend or bow down, bring to the ground; *fig.* humiliate, subdue. Now chiefly as ***stooped*** *ppl adjective.* ME.

5 *verb intrans. fig.* ▸**a** Bow to superior power or authority; humble oneself, show obedience. Usu. foll. by *to*, *under*. Now *rare*. ME. ▸**b** Condescend *to* an inferior; deign to adopt a position, course of action, etc., regarded as beneath oneself. L16. ▸†**c** Submit *to* something onerous. E–M17. ▸**d** Degrade oneself; descend or lower oneself *to* some conduct, esp. of an unworthy or morally reprehensible nature. M18.

†**6** *verb trans.* **a** Let down, lower; *esp.* (NAUTICAL & MILITARY) lower (a sail or ensign). M16–L17. ▸**b** Of a bird etc.: direct (its flight) downwards. *rare*. Only in E19.

7 *verb intrans.* †**a** Be lowered in amount or degree. L16–E17. ▸**b** Descend from a height. Now *arch.* or *poet.* E17.

8 a *verb intrans.* (Of a bird of prey) descend swiftly on the quarry, swoop (foll. by *at*, *on*); (of a falcon) descend to the lure. L16. ▸†**b** *verb trans.* Of a bird of prey: swoop on (the quarry). L16–E17.

9 *verb trans.* **a** *fig.* Condescend to apply (one's thoughts etc.) to something unworthy. Now *rare*. L16. ▸**b** Bend (the head, body, etc.) forwards and downwards; bend (one's ear) toward. M17.

10 *verb trans.* Tilt (a cask) so as to allow the contents to flow out. Now *dial.* M17.

11 *verb trans.* Train (a dog, esp. a hound) to put the nose to the ground to pick up a scent. L18.

> 📖 **1a** J. STEINBECK He stooped over and tied it around the . . dog's neck. **2** SHAKES. *Ven. & Ad.* The grass stoops not, she treads on it so light. **3** P. H. JOHNSON He had begun to stoop slightly, as if his height worried him. **4** *Blackwood's Magazine* The wretched impolicy which stoops Government to the rabble. **5a** E. YOUNG Thrace by conquest stoops to Macedon. **b** GOLDSMITH If you can stoop to an alliance with a family so poor. **d** L. KENNEDY I was greatly shocked that a woman of her achievements . . should stoop to . . shabby fibbing. **9a** J. COLLIER I'm sorry the Author should stoop his Wit thus Low. **b** G. P. R. JAMES Stooping his head to prevent . . branches striking him in the face.

Comb.: **stoop crop** *N. Amer.* a crop whose cultivation requires stoop labour; **stoop labour** *N. Amer.* agricultural labour performed in a stooping or squatting position; **stoop tag** *N. Amer.* = ***squat tag*** s.v. SQUAT *verb*.

■ **stooper** *noun* (*a*) (now *dial.*) a wedge for stooping or tilting a cask; (*b*) a person who stoops or bends down; a person with a stooping posture: L18. **stooping** *verbal noun* the action of the verb; an instance of this: LME. **stoopingly** *adverb* in a stooping manner; with the head or body bent or bowed down: M16.

stoop /stuːp/ *verb*² *trans.* *obsolete* exc. *Scot.* M17.
[from STOOP *noun*¹.]
Mark out with pillars or posts.

stoop and roop /stuːp (ə)nd ˈruːp/ *adverbial phr.* *Scot. & north.* E18.
[Origin unkn.]
Completely, entirely.

stoop-gallant /ˈstuːpgal(ə)nt/ *noun.* Now *arch.* or *Hist.* M16.
[from STOOP *verb*¹ + GALLANT *noun* = French *trousse-galant*.]
A disease, an illness, an affliction; orig. *spec.* the sweating sickness prevalent in England in the 15th and 16th cents.

stoopid /ˈstuːpɪd/ *adjective & noun.* *non-standard* or *joc.* M19.
[Repr. a pronunc.]
(A person who is) stupid.

stoopy /ˈstuːpi/ *adjective.* *rare.* E20.
[from STOOP *noun*² or *verb*¹ + -Y¹.]
Having a stoop.

stoor *noun* see STOUR *noun*.

stooshie /ˈstʊʃi/ *noun.* Also **stushie**. *Scot. colloq.* E19.
[Origin unkn.]
A disturbance, row, or fracas.

stooth /stuːθ/ *noun.* Chiefly *dial.* ME.
[Prob. var. of STUD *noun*¹.]
1 A post, an upright lath. Now only *spec.*, an upright batten in a lath and plaster wall or partition. ME.
†**2** A stud, a knob. LME–L15.

stoothe /stuːð/ *verb trans.* Chiefly *Scot. & dial.* LME.
[from prec.]
†**1** Decorate with studs or knobs. LME–M16.
2 Provide (a wall) with the framework on which lath and plaster is fixed; make or cover (a wall or partition) with lath and plaster. L15.
■ **stoothing** *noun* (*a*) the action of the verb; (*b*) a wall or partition of lath and plaster: L18.

stop /stɒp/ *noun*¹. Now *dial.*
[Old English *stoppa* = Old Saxon *stoppo*, from Germanic. Cf. STOUP.]
1 A pail, a bucket. OE.
†**2** = STOUP 3. LME–M16.
†**3** A pitcher, a flagon, a tankard. *Scot.* L15–L17.

stop /stɒp/ *noun*². LME.
[from the verb.]
▸ **I 1** The action or an act of impeding, obstructing, or checking the progress or activity of something; the state of being impeded or checked; an obstruction of progress or activity. LME. ▸**b** FENCING. The action of checking an opponent's attack by making a simultaneous attack in which the opponent runs on to one's sword-point. Cf. ***stop-thrust*** below. L15. ▸†**c** A sudden check in a horse's charge or gallop. Only in L16. ▸**d** A police officer's stopping of a suspect for questioning. M20.

2 A cessation, a pause, the ending of an activity, process, etc. L15. ▸**b** A pause or breaking-off in a person's speech or conversation. M16.

3 The action of filling or closing up a gap or aperture. L16.

4 a A halt in a journey; a standstill, a cessation of progress or forward movement. L16. ▸**b** A stay of considerable duration; a stay at a place, esp. during the course of a journey. M17. ▸**c** A place at which a halt is made; a designated stopping-place for a bus, train, etc. L19.

5 A block or obstruction caused by traffic congestion; a traffic jam. Now *rare*. E17.

6 An order stopping payment, esp. of a lost or stolen cheque, credit card, etc.; a veto or prohibition *against* a claim; a refusal to pass tokens as currency. M17.

> 📖 **1** THACKERAY If people only made prudent marriages, what a stop to population there would be! **2** SHAKES. *1 Hen. IV* And time . . Must have a stop. **b** DICKENS The smiling . . look of Florence brings him to a dead stop. **4a** P. MARSHALL He brought the car to a jolting stop. **b** G. DALY Chester, their first stop on a honeymoon tour. **5** STEELE There was a Stop of Coaches attending Company coming out of the Cathedral. **6** *Which?* The . . Bank will put a stop on your card when you tell them it's lost.

▸ **II 7** A thing which fills or stops a gap or aperture; a plug. LME.

8 a A thing which arrests or impedes progress or activity; an impediment, an obstacle. Now *rare* or *obsolete*. E16. ▸†**b** A thing which finishes something or brings something to an end. L16–E17. ▸†**c** CRICKET. = ***longstop*** s.v. LONG *adjective*¹. L18–M19. ▸**d** BOXING. A guard or attack preventing an opponent's blow from reaching its mark. E19. ▸**e** In Newmarket and similar games, a card which stops the run of a sequence; in *pl.*, the game of Newmarket. E19. ▸**f** During a shoot, a person posted in a particular place in order to keep game which has been started within range. L19. ▸**g** BRIDGE. A card that can reasonably be counted on, in conjunction with other cards in the same suit, to take a trick in that suit. E20.

9 a A part of a mechanism (as a pin, a bolt, or a block of wood) used to check the motion or thrust of something, keep another part in place, or determine the position of something. E16. ▸**b** A device preventing a watch from being overwound. L17. ▸**c** CARPENTRY. Each of the pieces of wood nailed on the frame of a door forming a rebate against which the door shuts. M19. ▸**d** A bookbinder's small circular tool used instead of mitring to stop a fillet when it intersects at right angles (*rare*). Also, the ending of a rule where it crosses another line. L19. ▸**e** LACE-MAKING. A junction of the different sets of warp-threads, taken as a basis for measurement in jacquard weaving. L19.

10 †**a** A weir or dam across a river; a sluice, a floodgate. L16–E19. ▸**b** A blind alley in a maze. M17.

11 ARCHITECTURE. The projection, often decorated, against which a chamfer, string-course, hood-moulding, etc., terminates. E19.

12 NAUTICAL. **a** A small line used as a lashing, esp. for a furled sail. M19. ▸**b** A projection on the upper part of a mast. M19.

13 OPTICS & PHOTOGRAPHY. A plate or diaphragm with a central hole used to cut off marginal rays of light round a lens, or to reduce the effective diameter of the lens of a camera or enlarger. Also, a unit of change of relative aperture (or exposure or film speed), a reduction of one stop being equivalent to a halving of the value. M19.

> 📖 **8a** SHAKES. *L.L.L.* These be the stops that hinder study quite.

▸ **III** MUSIC. **14 a** In an organ, a graduated set of pipes producing tones of the same character, operated by handles or drawstops, and used to vary tone colour, simulate the sounds of other instruments, etc. Also more fully ***organ-stop***. L15. ▸**b** The handle or knob by which air is admitted or excluded from a set of organ-pipes; a drawstop. L16. ▸**c** In a harpsichord, a mechanism with a similar purpose to an organ-stop, by which the position of a jack is altered so as to vary tone etc. M18.

15 a The closing of a finger-hole or aperture in the air passage of a wind instrument so as to alter the pitch; a metal key used for this purpose. Also, the hole or aperture thus closed. L15. ▸**b** An act of pressing the finger on a string of a stringed instrument so as to raise the pitch of its tone. Also, the part of the string (sometimes marked by frets on the instrument) where pressure is applied in order to produce a required note. M16.

> 📖 **14a** J. RUSKIN Accompanying flourishes . . on the trumpet stop.

▸ **IV 16 a** A punctuation mark, esp. a full stop; a character used in cryptography to represent a punctuation mark. L16. ▸**b** PROSODY. A break in verse as read aloud which is required by the sense (as opp. to ***pause***, a break required by the metre). M19. ▸**c** In a telegram, a full stop. Also = PERIOD *noun* 9c. M20.

17 PHONETICS. **a** The complete closure of the orinasal passages in articulating a plosive consonant. M17. ▸**b** More fully ***stop consonant***. Any of a class of consonants the formation of which is effected by first closing the vocal tract and then releasing the breath abruptly, as /p/, /b/, /d/, /t/, etc. L19.

> 📖 **16a** M. EDGEWORTH The corrector . . scarcely had occasion to alter a word . . or a stop.

▸ **V 18** A hole in the ground in which a female rabbit keeps her litter for safety. L17.

19 The indentation in the middle of a dog's face between the forehead and the nose. M19.

Phrases: †**at a stop** at a standstill; taken aback. ***full stop***: see FULL *adjective*. **give a stop to** check the progress of. †**make a stop of**, †**make stop of** = ***put a stop to*** below. **pull out all the stops** make every possible effort. **put a stop to** arrest the progress of; bring to an end, abolish. ***short stop***: see SHORT *adjective*. ***solo stop***: see SOLO *adjective*. ***speaking stop***: see SPEAKING *ppl adjective*. **stop of the exchequer** *Hist.* the suspension of payment of the Government debt to the London goldsmiths in 1672. ***T-stop***: see T, T. ***tremolo stop***: see TREMOLO *noun* 2a. ***wage stop***: see WAGE *noun*. **with all the stops out** exerting oneself fully; making every effort.

Comb.: (See also combs. of the verb.) **stop band** ELECTRONICS a band of frequencies which are highly attenuated by a filter; **stop bath** PHOTOGRAPHY a bath for stopping the action of a preceding bath (esp. development) by neutralizing any of its chemical still present; **stop bead** a bead or narrow moulding on the inner edge of a sash-window preventing the inner sash from swinging into the room; **stop bit** TELECOMMUNICATIONS (in asynchronous data transfers) a bit which indicates the end of a character or string or of the whole transmission; **stop-block** †(*a*) a block of wood indicating the position of a fire hydrant; (*b*) a buffer at the end of a railway line; **stop-butt** a slope or bank constructed behind the targets at a rifle range to stop bullets; **stop button** a button which is pressed to stop the action of a machine; **stop chords** JAZZ chords played on the first beat of every bar or every other bar, as the only accompaniment to a solo; **stop chorus** JAZZ a solo accompanied by stop chords; ***stop consonant***: see sense 17b above; **stop-cylinder** a printing machine in which the cylinder is stopped to permit the return of the reciprocating carriage; **stop-dog** = ***stop-hound*** below; **stop-drill** a drill with a shoulder or collar limiting the depth of penetration; **stop-gate** (*a*) a gate by which the water in one section of a canal can be shut off from the next in case of damage to the bank; (*b*) a stop-valve; **stop-handle** = ***stop-knob*** below; **stop-hound** a foxhound trained to hunt slowly and to stop at a signal from the huntsman; **stop-knob** the knob or handle which is pulled out to open a particular stop in an organ; **stop lamp** a light on the rear of a vehicle, which is automatically illuminated when the brakes are applied; **stop light** (*a*) = ***stop lamp*** above; (*b*) a red traffic light; **stop list** (*a*) a list of people etc. deprived of particular rights, privileges, or services; *spec.* a list of people with whom members of an association are forbidden to do business; (*b*) a list of prohibited books; (*c*) a list of words automatically omitted from a computer-generated concordance or index; **stop-lock** a lock with a short rise or fall, constructed at a canal junction to prevent the free passage of water between the two canals; **stop log** a log or plank, or a beam or plate of concrete or steel, fitting between vertical grooves in walls or piers to close a water channel; **stop-net** (*a*) a net fixed or cast across a river or tidal channel to intercept fish; (*b*) in CRICKET etc., a net to stop the ball; **stop-netting** = ***stop-net*** (b) above; **stop-order** (*a*) an order issued by the Court of Chancery to stay payment of funds in the custody of the Court; (*b*) an order directing a broker to buy or sell stock at a specified price, in order to limit loss; **stop-ridge** ARCHAEOLOGY a ridge on a celt, pipe, etc. which prevents one part from slipping too far over another; **stop-seine** a seine-net which is lifted at once into the fishing boat with the catch enclosed; **stop sign** a sign indicating that traffic should stop; *N. Amer.* a red traffic light; **stop signal** a signal indicating that a train should stop; **stop-thrust** FENCING a thrust delivered at one's opponent at the moment when he or she advances for attack (cf. sense 1b above); **stop time** JAZZ a stop chorus; a series of stop chords; **stop-valve**: closing a pipe against the passage of liquid; **stop volley** esp. in TENNIS, a checked volley, played close to the net, dropping the ball dead on the other side; **stopway** an area at the end of an airfield runway in which an aircraft can be stopped after an interrupted take-off; **stop word** a word on a stop list that is automatically omitted from or treated less fully in a computer-generated concordance or index.

■ **stopless** *adjective* without a stop or stops; *spec.* †(*a*) *rare* unceasing; (*b*) (of an organ-pipe) having no stops; (*c*) without punctuation: M17.

stop /stɒp/ *verb.* Infl. **-pp-**. Pa. t. & pple **stopped**, †**stopt**.
[Old English (*for*)*stoppian*, corresp. to Old Frisian *stoppia*, Middle Low German *stoppen*, Old High German *stopfōn* (German *stopfen*), from West Germanic, from late Latin *stuppare* to stuff.]
▸ **I 1** *verb trans.* Block or obstruct (the external opening of the eyes, ears, etc.) (*lit. & fig.*). Now chiefly in ***stop one's ears***, ***stop a person's mouth*** below. OE.

2 *verb trans.* Make (a road, channel, etc.) impassable by blocking up or obstructing its passage or outlet; close (a road) to public access. Freq. foll. by *up*. ME.
†**3** *verb trans.* Staunch the bleeding of, bind up, (a wound). ME–E17.
†**4** *verb trans.* Shut up in a place; keep *in*. ME–L17.
5 *verb trans.* †**a** Stuff (the inside of a bird, fruit, etc.) preparatory to cooking; pad (a garment, cushion, etc.). ME–E17. ▸**b** Pack tightly, cram (a receptacle with something). *obsolete* exc. *Scot.* LME. ▸**c** Plug (the feet of a horse) with something as a dressing. Now *rare* or *obsolete*. L16.
6 a *verb trans.* Block or close up (an entrance, aperture, vent, etc.). ME. ▸**b** *verb trans.* Act as a block to, choke up. Also (in *pass.*), be choked up *with* (dirt etc.). Now usu. foll. by *up*. E16. ▸**c** *verb trans.* Block the mouth of (a fox's earth) prior to a hunt. Also, block up the earths in (a particular district). M16. ▸†**d** *verb intrans.* Become choked up. L16–L18. ▸**e** *verb trans.* MUSIC. Close (a finger-hole or aperture of a wind instrument) so as to alter the pitch and produce a particular note. M19.
7 *verb trans.* **a** Fill up, repair, (a leak, hole, crack, etc.); fill in fissures or holes in (a surface to be painted, covered with a wash, etc.). Also foll. by *up*. ME. ▸**b** Plug (the seams of a boat) with oakum or other caulking material. Formerly also, caulk (a ship). M16. ▸**c** Plug the cavity of (a decayed tooth) with a filling or stopping. L16.
8 *verb trans.* **a** Close (a vessel or receptacle) by blocking the mouth with a plug, stopper, etc.; close (the mouth of a vessel). Also, shut up (something) *in* a stoppered vessel. Also foll. by *down*, *up*. LME. ▸**b** Plug the upper end of (an organ-pipe) giving a note an octave lower. L17.
9 *verb trans.* **a** Close up, obstruct, (a duct or passage in the body); block the passage or passages of (a bodily organ). Also foll. by *up*. LME. ▸†**b** In *pass.* Of a person: be afflicted with an obstruction or blockage of the bodily passages or organs. LME–L16. ▸†**c** Make constipated. M16–M18.
10 *verb trans.* **a** Thrust or push (a thing) *in* or *into* a receptacle or place. Chiefly *Scot.* LME. ▸**b** Thrust in the point or end of (a thing), insert; put in (a plant). *Scot.* & *north.* M18.
†**11** *verb trans.* Mend (a garment); repair (cloth, metal-work) with an inferior material. L15–M17.
12 *verb trans.* Tamp (tobacco) in a pipe. *rare.* M19.

> 📖 **2** *Society* The . . carriage stopping the way. **4** SHAKES. *Com. Err.* Stop in your wind sir. **6a** SHAKES. *A.Y.L.* Stop that, 'twill fly . . out at the chimney. **7a** W. R. H. TROWBRIDGE It would cost . . a lot to stop the leaks in a seven-acre roof. **8a** J. TYNDALL A tube . . stopped watertight will answer for this experiment.

▸ **II 13** *verb trans.* **a** Prevent or stem the passage of; dam or block the channel of (running water etc.); keep *out* or exclude (light, the weather, etc.). LME. ▸**b** Staunch (bleeding, blood). L16.
14 *verb trans.* **a** Check or impede the onward movement of; bring to a standstill or state of rest; cause to halt on a journey. Also, prevent the departure of. LME. ▸**b** FENCING & BOXING etc. Check (an opponent, a stroke, a blow, etc.) with a counter movement or stroke; counter (a blow etc.). E18. ▸**c** Shoot or bring down (game, a bird). Also, (of a bullet or wound) arrest the rush of (a charging enemy or wild animal) with rifle-fire. M19. ▸**d** BOXING. Defeat (an opponent) by a knockout. Orig. *US.* L19. ▸**e** Be hit by (a bullet). Freq. in ***stop one***, be hit or killed. *colloq.* (orig. MILITARY). E20. ▸**f** Drink. Chiefly in ***stop one***, take a drink. *Austral. slang.* E20. ▸**g** RACING. Check (a horse) in order to stay out of the running; pull, rein in. M20.
15 *verb trans.* **a** Withhold or deduct (a sum of money) in paying wages or repaying a debt, in order to cover rent, special clothing, etc. LME. ▸**b** Withhold (goods) as security or in lieu of payment. M18.
16 *verb trans.* **a** Cause (a person) to desist from or pause in a course of action or conduct. Freq. foll. by *from*, *in*. LME. ▸**b** Hold (a thing) in check; cause (a thing) to cease action. LME. ▸**c** Cause (a person) to break off from speaking or pause in a conversation. M16.
17 *verb trans.* **a** Restrain or prevent (a person) from an intended action. Also foll. by *from*. LME. ▸†**b** LAW. Bar, preclude; = ESTOP 2. M16–E18. ▸**c** Stay or suspend (proceedings); prevent (a decree etc.) from taking effect. L17. ▸**d** Of a camera: give a still picture of (a moving object). M20.
†**18** *verb trans.* Hamper or impede the course or progress of (affairs, a project, etc.); hinder (a person). LME–E18.
19 *verb trans.* **a** Put an end to (a movement, activity, course of events). LME. ▸**b** Prevent the onset of. M16.
20 *verb trans.* MUSIC. Obtain the required pitch from (a string of a violin etc.) by pressing a finger down at the appropriate point; produce (a note, sound) by this means. L15.
21 *verb trans.* **a** Discontinue (an action, a sequence of actions, work, etc.). E16. ▸**b** Put an end to the issue or supply of (an allowance etc.). M19.
22 †**a** *verb intrans.* REAL TENNIS. Mark or record the chases. *rare.* Only in M16. ▸†**b** *verb intrans.* CRICKET. Of a fielder: field the ball; (more fully ***stop behind***) act as longstop. M18–M19. ▸**c** *verb trans.* REAL TENNIS. Keep (the ball) from entering the dedans, winning-gallery, or grille. Now *rare.* E19. ▸**d** *verb trans.* CRICKET. Of a batsman: play (a ball) defensively, without attempting to hit it away. M19.
23 *verb trans.* Cause (a machine or piece of mechanism) to cease operation. M16.
24 *verb trans.* Intercept and detain (goods, post, etc.) in transit. E17.
25 *verb trans.* NAUTICAL. ▸**a** Bring (a ship) to anchor by gradually checking the cable. Chiefly in ***stop the cable***, prevent the cable running out too fast. E17. ▸**b** Make fast (a cable etc.). L18.
26 *verb trans.* HORTICULTURE. Pinch out the head of (a plant); remove (a shoot or a portion of it) by pinching. L17.
27 *verb trans.* Instruct a bank to withhold payment on (a cheque etc.). E18.
28 *verb trans.* ARCHITECTURE. Cause (a rib, chamfer, moulding, etc.) to terminate in a specified form or position. M19.
29 *verb trans.* PHONETICS. Check the flow of (the breath) to form a stop consonant. M19.
30 BRIDGE. Be able to prevent opponents from taking all the tricks in (a suit). E20.

> 📖 **13a** GIBBON The course of the river was stopped . . , and the waters were confined. **14a** J. CONRAD The gale had freshened . . stopping the traffic on the river. **c** W. LENNOX At the . . [pigeon-shooting] handicap Moncrieff stopped a bird at seventy-five yards. **15** *Spectator* Sixpence a day stopped out of his money. **16a** E. M. FORSTER You have stopped me from brooding. **b** G. VILLIERS Hold, stop your murd'ring hands. **c** F. E. GRETTON 'Yes, my lord; but—' Garrow stopped him short. **17a** M. KENNEDY Make an entrance if you like. I'm not stopping you. **19a** C. P. SNOW Briers stopped the jollity with a hard voice. **21a** G. VIDAL Wishing the man would . . stop asking questions. R. RENDELL It was . . too early . . to stop work.

▸ **III 31** *verb intrans.* (Of a thing) cease from motion or action; (of a process) cease activity; come to an end; (of a machine, clock, etc.) cease working. E16.
32 *verb intrans.* **a** Cease from forward movement, come to a standstill or point of rest; *spec.* (of a horse) check, pull up. M16. ▸**b** Pause on the or one's way (*to do* something). E18.
33 *verb intrans.* **a** Leave off or pause momentarily in an activity; pause in speech; break off a conversation. L16. ▸**b** In *imper.* Halt! Wait a moment! L16. ▸**c** BRIDGE. Refrain from increasing one's bid beyond a specified level. Freq. foll. by *in*. M20.
34 *verb intrans.* **a** Desist in a course of action or from something one is accustomed to do. L17. ▸**b** Foll. by *at*: hesitate, hold back. Freq. in ***stop at nothing*** below. L17. ▸**c** Set a limit on one's activity or behaviour *at* a certain point; refrain from exceeding a certain degree or extent. M18.
35 *verb intrans.* Make a halt on a journey; (of a bus, train, etc.) halt at a designated place to pick up and set down passengers. M18.
36 *verb intrans.* (Of something immaterial) have its limit of operation at a specified point; (of a series, something material) come to an end. Freq. foll. by *at*. M18.
37 *verb intrans.* **a** Stay as a visitor, resident, or guest. L18. ▸**b** Remain (*for* a meal etc., *at* home); prolong one's stay in a place, stay on. E19.

> 📖 **31** P. G. WODEHOUSE His watch . . seemed to have stopped. **32a** G. VIDAL They stopped at the second floor. **b** J. RUSKIN Everybody stopped as they passed, to look at his cart. **33b** O. WILDE 'Stop!' cried Virginia, stamping her foot. **34a** E. CALDWELL When I get started . . , I don't want to stop. **b** J. STEINBECK There is no crime he will stop at. **35** G. GREENE The train stopped at Watford. **36** R. CHALLONER The severities exercised against catholics did not stop here. **37a** V. WOOLF Come and stop with us in September. **b** *Motor Cycle News* Stop for the last six races.

▸ **IV 38** *verb trans.* Provide with stops or punctuation marks, punctuate. L18.
39 *verb trans.* & *intrans.* PROSODY. Conclude or divide (a line of spoken verse) with a stop or break. Cf. STOP *noun*[2] 16b. M19.

Phrases, & with adverbs & prepositions in specialized senses: ***stop a gap***: see GAP *noun*. ***stop a packet***: see PACKET *noun* 3. †**stop a person's eyes** cover a person's eyes. ***stop a person's mouth***: see MOUTH *noun*. †**stop a person's sight** cover a person's eyes. †**stop a person's way** stand in a person's way (*lit.* & *fig.*), bar a person's passage. ***stop at nothing***: see NOTHING *pronoun* & *noun*. ***stop behind***: see sense 22c above. **stop by** (orig. *N. Amer.*) (*a*) pay a brief visit; (*b*) call at, visit (a place). **stop dead** (cause to) come to an abrupt halt; (cause to) cease or leave off abruptly. **stop down** PHOTOGRAPHY reduce the aperture of (a lens) with a diaphragm. **stop in** *US* pay a brief visit, drop in. ***stop off***: see ***stop over*** below. **stop on** continue in one place or employment. ***stop one***: see senses 14e, f above. **stop one's ears** (*a*) block one's ears, esp. with the hands or fingers, to avoid hearing; (*b*) *fig.* make oneself deaf to something, refuse to listen, close one's mind against arguments, etc. †**stop one's nose**, †**stop one's nostrils** block the nose to avoid an unpleasant smell etc. **stop out** (*a*) stay out late; (*b*) *N. Amer.* interrupt one's studies at college for a time in order to pursue some other activity; (*c*) ETCHING cover (parts of a plate) to prevent the acid from taking effect. **stop off**, **stop over** (orig. *US*) make a halt, break one's journey (*at* a place). **stop payment** (*a*) declare oneself unable to meet one's financial obligations; (*b*) instruct a bank to withhold payment on a cheque etc. **stop short** = ***stop dead*** above. ***stop short at***, ***stop short of***: see SHORT *adverb*. **stop the breath of** (now *rare* or *obsolete*) prevent the breathing of, suffocate, choke; cause to die. ***stop the cable***: see sense 25 above. **stop the press** suspend the operation of printing, esp. so as to insert late news. **stop the show** (orig. *US*) cause an interruption of a performance by provoking prolonged applause or laughter, or requests for encores (cf. ***show-stopper*** s.v. SHOW *noun*[1]). **stop the tide** NAUTICAL prevent a ship being carried with the tide. **stop thief!** a cry for help to arrest a running thief. **stop up** stay up instead of going to bed. ***stop your gab***: see GAB *noun*[2]. ***when the kissing has to stop***: see KISSING *verbal noun*.

Comb.: (See also combs. of STOP *noun*[2].) Esp. with ref. to the technique of stopping a cine camera between frames so as to create special effects, esp. animation, as ***stop-action***, ***stop-frame***, ***stop-shot***, etc. Special combs., as **stop-and-frisk**, **stop-and-search** *adjectives* of or pertaining to the stopping and searching of suspects by the police; **stop-and-start** *adjective* alternately stopping and starting; **stop-loss** *adjective* (of an order to sell stock etc.) intended to save further loss than has been already incurred by falling prices; **stop-me-and-buy-one** *noun* & *adjective* (of or pertaining to) a travelling vendor, *esp.* one selling ice-creams; **stop-motion** a device for automatically stopping a machine or engine when something has gone wrong; **stop-off** (*a*) an act of stopping off or halting for a visit; (*b*) a place where one stops off; **stop-out** (*a*) *colloq.* a person who stays out late; (*b*) *N. Amer.* a student who interrupts his or her studies for a time in order to pursue some other activity; an interruption of studies for this purpose; **stopover** (*a*) an act of stopping over or breaking one's journey; (*b*) a place where one stops over; **stop press** *noun* & *adjective* (of or pertaining to) late news inserted in a newspaper after printing has begun; (designating) a column in a newspaper reserved for this; **stop-start** *adjective* = ***stop-and-start*** above; **stop-tap** the time at which drinks cease to be served in a public house; **stop-water** NAUTICAL (*a*) a thing fixed or towed overboard to reduce a ship's speed; (*b*) a plug or other device for making a joint watertight.

■ **stoppa'bility** *noun* (*rare*) lack of resistance to stoppage L19. **stoppable** *adjective* able to be stopped or prevented (earlier in UNSTOPPABLE *adjective*) M20.

stop-and-go /stɒp (ə)nd ˈɡəʊ/ *adjective.* E20.
[from prec. + AND *conjunction*[1] + GO *verb*.]
= STOP-GO *adjective*.

stopbank /ˈstɒpbaŋk/ *noun.* *Austral.* & *NZ.* M20.
[from STOP *noun*[2] + BANK *noun*[1].]
A levee, an embankment built to prevent a river from overflowing its banks.

stopcock /ˈstɒpkɒk/ *noun.* L16.
[from STOP *noun*[2] or *verb* + COCK *noun*[1].]
An externally operated valve for regulating the flow of a liquid or gas through a pipe etc.

stope /stəʊp/ *noun* & *verb.* M18.
[App. rel. to STEP *noun*[1].]
MINING. ▸**A** *noun.* †**1** A step or notch in the side of a pit, or in an upright beam, to receive the end of a stemple or crosspiece. M18–M19.
2 A steplike working in the side of a pit. M18.
▸ **B** *verb trans.* & *intrans.* **1** Cut or excavate (mineral ground) in stopes or layer after layer; extract (ore) by this process. Also foll. by *out*. L18.
2 GEOLOGY. Of magma: make (its way) by detaching and absorbing blocks of the surrounding rock. Freq. as ***stoping*** *verbal noun*. E20.
■ **stoper** *noun* a person who stopes ore etc. L19.

stopgap /ˈstɒpɡap/ *noun* & *verb.* M16.
[from STOP *verb* + GAP *noun*.]
▸ **A** *noun.* †**1** An argument in defence of some point attacked. Only in M16.
2 A thing that temporarily supplies a need; a substitute. Also, a person who temporarily occupies a post or vacancy until a permanent appointment can be made. L17.
3 An utterance, often with no inherent significance, intended to fill up a gap or an awkward pause in conversation or discourse. E18.

> 📖 **2** E. BLISHEN There were suddenly absentees on the staff—I was needed as a stopgap. *attrib.*: *Flight International* The plan is a stop-gap measure to tide the company over.

▸ **B** *verb intrans.* Infl. **-pp-**. Act as a stopgap or substitute; fill a post or vacancy temporarily. M20.

stop-go /stɒpˈɡəʊ/ *adjective* & *noun.* E20.
[from STOP *verb* + GO *verb*.]
▸ **A** *adjective.* **1** Of a sign or light: indicating alternately that traffic should stop or proceed. E20.
2 Alternately stopping and going, or acting and not acting. M20.
3 ECONOMICS. Of, pertaining to, or designating a policy of alternately restricting demand to contain inflation, and expanding credit to stimulate demand and reduce unemployment. M20.

> 📖 **2** *Green Magazine* Taxis operating in stop-go urban environments.

▸ **B** *noun.* ECONOMICS. A stop-go policy; the economic cycle resulting from this. M20.

stoppage /ˈstɒpɪdʒ/ *noun*. LME.
[from STOP *verb* + -AGE.]
1 Deduction from payments; a sum stopped or deducted from a person's wages. LME.
2 a Obstruction of a road, stream, etc. Formerly also, an obstacle, something that obstructs. M16. ▸**b** A traffic jam. E18.
3 An obstructed condition of a bodily organ; a blockage of a duct or passage in the body. L16.
4 Interception and detention of goods in transit. E17.
5 The action of stopping something or causing something to cease; ending or discontinuance of supply. M17.
6 a Cessation of movement or activity; a stop or halt in a journey. L18. ▸**b** A cessation or interruption of work owing to disagreement between employer and employees; a strike. E20.
7 The action of stopping payment or of declaring oneself unable to meet one's financial obligations. E19.

📖 **1** LD MACAULAY She should receive her income regularly and without stoppages. **3** M. UNDERWOOD The Snuffles, or stoppage of the nose. **5** P. FUSSELL Frequent narrative stoppage, overall clumsiness. **6b** ***token stoppage***: see TOKEN *noun & adjective*. **7** *Law Times* Several companies, the stoppage of one of which . . has ruined a number of persons.

Stoppardian /stɒˈpɑːdɪən/ *adjective*. L20.
[from *Stoppard* (see below) + -IAN.]
Of, pertaining to, or characteristic of the plays of the British dramatist Tom Stoppard (b. 1937).

stopper /ˈstɒpə/ *noun & verb*. L15.
[from STOP *verb* + -ER[1].]
▶**A** *noun*. **1** A person who stops something; *spec.* †(*a*) a person who obstructs or blocks up something; (*b*) a person who causes something to halt or cease; (*c*) CRICKET a wicket-keeper; (*d*) FOOTBALL a player whose function is to block attacks on goal from the middle of the field. L15. ▸**b** BASEBALL. A pitching ace; *spec.* (*a*) a starting pitcher depended on to win a game or reverse a losing streak; (*b*) a relief pitcher who prevents the opposing team from scoring highly. M20.
2 A thing that stops up a hole or passage; *spec.* (*a*) a plug for closing the neck of a bottle, the end of a tube, etc., usu. with an integral knob serving as a handle (cf. STOPPLE *noun* 1); (*b*) a substance used to fill up cracks or holes on a surface, esp. prior to painting; (*c*) a small plug for compressing tobacco in the bowl of a pipe. L16.
3 NAUTICAL. A rope or clamp for checking and holding a rope cable, anchor chain, etc. E17.
4 A thing that causes something to halt or cease; *spec.* (*a*) a device or mechanism for stopping machinery; (*b*) the after part of a rowlock; (*c*) BRIDGE. = STOP *noun*[2] 8g; (*d*) *colloq.* a thing which attracts and holds the attention; something striking or impressive. E19.
5 Any of several trees of the genus *Eugenia*, of the myrtle family, natives of Florida and the W. Indies which are used medicinally to stop loose bowels; esp. *E. axillaris* (more fully ***white stopper***), *E. confusa* (more fully ***red stopper***), and *E. foetida* (more fully ***gurgeon stopper***). L19.
6 A stopping train. *colloq.* M20.

📖 **2** D. PROFUMO A large hip-flask . . with a round stopper. **4** *Mountain Biker* Hydrostop brakes are among the best stoppers. **put a stopper on** (*a*) put an end to (something); (*b*) keep (a person) quiet; stifle (debate etc.). ***CONVERSATION-stopper***.

▶**B** *verb trans.* **1** NAUTICAL. Secure (a cable) with a stopper. M18.
2 Fit or provide with a stopper; close or plug (a bottle etc.) with a stopper. E19. ▸**b** METALLURGY. Close (a mould for an ingot) with a metal plate, a mass of sand, etc. (Foll. by *down*.) L19.
3 Put an end to; stop. E19.
■ **stopperless** *adjective* M19.

stopping /ˈstɒpɪŋ/ *noun*. LME.
[from STOP *verb* + -ING[1].]
▶**I 1** The action of STOP *verb*. LME.
†**2** = STOPPAGE 3. LME–L18.
3 The placing of stops, punctuation. E18.
▶**II 4** A thing inserted to stop or plug a hole, crevice, or passage; *spec.* (*a*) a filling for stopping a decayed tooth; (*b*) a substance used to stop holes etc. on a surface to be painted; (*c*) *rare* a pad saturated with grease inserted within a horseshoe so as to keep the horse's foot moist. LME.
5 †**a** A dam, an embankment. Only in L16. ▸**b** A partition or wall in a ventilation passage of a mine for controlling or directing the flow of air. E18.
Attrib. & comb.: In the senses 'bringing to a stop or halt', as ***stopping effect***, ***stopping power***, etc., 'coming to a standstill, halting', as ***stopping distance***, ***stopping-point***, etc., 'filling holes or crevices', as ***stopping-knife***, ***stopping-tool***, etc. Special combs., as **stopping-ground** ETCHING (now *rare*) a mixture used to cover the parts of a plate to prevent the acid from taking effect; **stopping house** *Canad.* a boarding-house; a house offering accommodation to travellers; **stopping mixture** ETCHING (now *rare*) a substance used as a stopping-ground; **stopping-place** (*a*) a place at which a person or thing stops; (*b*) CANAD. HISTORY a stopping house; a settlement where groups of travellers customarily stop for food and lodging; **stopping rule** STATISTICS any rule in sequential testing or sampling for deciding when an investigation should be terminated, in view of the trends in the results obtained; **stopping station** any of the stations at which an express train stops.

stopping /ˈstɒpɪŋ/ *ppl adjective*. LME.
[from STOP *verb* + -ING[2].]
†**1** Esp. of food: tending to cause constipation. LME–M17.
2 That stops. E16.
Special collocations: **stopping train** a train which stops at some or all intermediate stations on a particular line.

stopple /ˈstɒp(ə)l/ *noun & verb*. ME.
[Partly from STOP *verb* + -EL[1], -LE[1]; partly aphet. from ESTOPPEL.]
▶**A** *noun*. **1** A stopper, a bung, a plug (generally replaced by STOPPER). ME. ▸**b** MUSIC. The plug of a stopped organ-pipe. Now *rare* or *obsolete*. L18. ▸**c** An earplug. *US*. M20.
†**2** The action of stopping; a stoppage, a prohibition. L16–M17.
▶**B** *verb trans.* Put a stopple on; close with a stopple. L18.

stoppo /ˈstɒpəʊ/ *noun*. Pl. **-os**. M20.
[from STOP *noun*[2] or *verb* + -O.]
1 A rest or break from work. *slang*. M20.
2 An escape, a getaway. Esp. in ***take stoppo***, make a rapid escape in order to avoid detection. *Criminals' slang*. M20.
2 attrib.: ***stoppo car***, ***stoppo driver***, etc.

†**stopt** *verb pa. t. & pple*: see STOP *verb*.

stopwatch /ˈstɒpwɒtʃ/ *noun & verb*. Also **stop-watch**. M18.
[from STOP *verb* + WATCH *noun*.]
▶**A** *noun*. A watch with a mechanism for instantly starting or stopping at will so as to record elapsed time, chiefly used for accurately timing races. M18.
▶**B** *verb trans.* Time with a stopwatch. L20.

stop-work /ˈstɒpwəːk/ *noun & adjective*. M19.
[from STOP *verb* + WORK *noun*.]
▶**A** *noun*. = STOP *noun*[2] 9b. M19.
▶**B** *adjective*. **1** Designating a meeting requiring employees to attend in company time. *Austral. & NZ*. E20.
2 Designating an order requiring work to stop. *N. Amer.* L20.

storable /ˈstɔːrəb(ə)l/ *adjective*. M19.
[from STORE *verb* + -ABLE.]
Able to be stored.
■ **storaˈbility** *noun* L20.

storage /ˈstɔːrɪdʒ/ *noun*. E17.
[from STORE *verb* + -AGE.]
1 Capacity or space for storing. E17.
2 A place where something is stored. L18.
3 Rent paid for the use of a store, esp. a warehouse. L18.
4 The action of storing or laying up a thing or things in reserve; the condition or fact of being stored. E19.
5 *spec.* **a** ELECTRICITY. The conversion of electrical energy into chemical or other energy from which electricity may be generated again. L19. ▸**b** COMPUTING. The retention of data and instructions in a device from which they can be retrieved as needed; the part of a memory or other device in which data are stored. E20.
Phrases: ***cold storage***: see COLD *adjective*. ***night storage heater***: see NIGHT *noun*. ***pumped storage***: see PUMPED *adjective*[2] 1. ***thermal storage***: see THERMAL *adjective*. ***working storage***: see WORKING *noun*.
Comb.: **storage battery**, **storage cell** a secondary battery, cell, in which electrical energy is stored; **storage heater** a heating apparatus which functions by means of stored heat; *esp.* an electric heater which accumulates heat outside peak hours for later release; **storage heating** heating by means of storage heaters; **storage life** the length of time for which an item liable to deterioration remains fit for use during storage; shelf life; **storage location** COMPUTING a place in a storage device capable of storing one unit of data and usu. specifiable by an address; **storage ring** PHYSICS an approximately circular accelerator in which particles can be effectively stored by being made to circulate continuously at high energy; **storage unit** (*a*) a domestic cupboard or container, esp. one of a set, or one designed to accommodate an electrical appliance etc.; (*b*) a unit in which data is stored in a computer; **storage wall** a partition wall consisting of cupboards, often designed to be opened from either side.

storax /ˈstɔːraks/ *noun*. LME.
[Latin from Greek var. of *sturax* STYRAX.]
1 Any of several fragrant resinous exudations: orig. (more fully ***gum storax***), resin from the styrax tree, much prized by the ancients; now chiefly (more fully ***liquid storax***), liquidambar. LME.
2 = STYRAX 2. L17.

store /stɔː/ *noun, adjective, & adverb*. ME.
[Aphet. from Old French *estor*, from *estorer* STORE *verb*.]
▶**A** *noun*. **1 a** That with which a household, camp, etc., is stocked; food, clothing, etc., collected for future use. Now *rare*. ME. ▸**b** In *pl.* Articles as food, clothing, arms, etc., accumulated so as to be available for a particular purpose (orig. esp. for the equipment and maintenance of an army, a ship, etc.); *Aeronautics slang* guns, bombs, etc. carried on an aircraft. M17.
2 a A place where stores are kept, a warehouse, a storehouse. ME. ▸**b** COMPUTING. = MEMORY *noun* 1C. M19.
3 Storage, reserve, keeping. Now *rare* exc. in ***in store***, ***in store for*** below. ME.
4 A person's possessions; accumulated goods or money. Now *rare*. ME.
†**5** Livestock. In later use chiefly in ***young store***, ***old store***. ME–L17.
†**6** A body of people. LME–M16.
7 Value, worth. Now only in ***set store by***, ***set great store by***, ***set little store by***, etc. below. LME.
8 Sufficient or abundant supply (*of* something needed); plenty, abundance (of food etc.). Now *rare*. L15.
9 a A quantity of something kept available for future use; a reserve, a deposit, a stock. L15. ▸**b** In *pl.* Stocks, reserves; treasures, accumulated resources. E16.
10 A sheep, steer, cow, or pig acquired or kept for fattening. Also, an animal kept for breeding or as part of the ordinary stock of a farm. E17.
11 A place where goods are kept for sale; *esp.* a large shop dealing in a great variety of articles; a retail outlet, a chain of retail outlets; *gen.* (*N. Amer. & Austral.*) a shop of any size. E18.

📖 **1a** SHELLEY The garrison of Patras Has store but for ten days. **4** DRYDEN Increase thy Wealth, and double all thy Store. **8** M. ARNOLD Oft thou hast given them store Of flowers. **9a** P. S. BUCK His wretched store of a few dried beans and a bowlful of corn. G. DALY The outbursts used up her small store of strength. **10** ***store bullock***, ***store cattle***, ***store cow***, ***store lamb***, ***store sheep***, ***store stock***, etc. **11** M. MEYER A general store which sold practically everything. ***chain store***, ***cooperative store***, ***department store***, etc.; ***store buyer***, ***store detective***, etc.

Phrases: ***FIVE-and-ten cent store***. **good store**, **great store** *arch. & poet.* abundance. ***immediate access store***: see IMMEDIATE *adjective*. **in good store**, **in great store** *arch. & poet.* in abundance. **in store** in reserve, laid up for future use. **in store for** (of future events or conditions) awaiting, prepared for (a person). **keep store** *N. Amer.* own or manage a shop. ***MONOPRIX store***. ***multiple store***: see MULTIPLE *adjective*. ***NAVAL stores***. **set store by**, **set great store by**, **set little store by**, etc., regard as of (great, little, etc.) worth or value. ***small stores***: see SMALL *adjective*. **the Stores** *colloq.* (now *rare*) a large department store, orig. and esp. one run by a cooperative society.
Comb.: **store-bought**, (*US dial.*) **store-boughten** *adjectives* bought (esp. ready-made) from a store, not home-made; **store church** *N. Amer.* a church set up in a (vacant) shop; **store-farm** (chiefly *Scot.*) a farm on which animals are reared, a stock farm; **storehouse** a building in which goods are stored; *transf. & fig.* a store or treasury from which something may be obtained in plenty, an abundant store (*of*); **storekeeper** a person who has charge of a store or stores; a person who superintends the receipt and issue of stores; *N. Amer. & Austral.* a shopkeeper; **storeman** a storekeeper, esp. in the army; *N. Amer. & Austral.* a person who keeps or serves in a store, a shopkeeper; **store pay** *N. Amer.* (now *rare*) payment made in goods rather than cash; **storeroom** (*a*) a room set apart for the storing of goods or supplies, esp. those of a ship or household; (*b*) *rare* storage space; **storeship** a ship employed to carry military or naval stores; **storesman** = ***storeman*** above; **store-wide** *adjective* operating or applying throughout the whole of a store.
▶**B** *adjective (pred. & postpositive) & adverb*. In plenty, abundant(ly). Also ***good store***, ***great store***. Now *arch. & dial.* M16.

store /stɔː/ *verb*. ME.
[Aphet. from Old French *estorer* from Latin *instaurare* renew, repair, RESTORE *verb*.]
▶**I** *verb trans.* **1** Supply, stock (a person, place, etc.) *with* (or †*of*) something. ME.
2 Provide for the continuance or improvement of (a stock, a breed). *obsolete* exc. in ***store the kin*** below. ME.
†**3** Restore (what is ruined or weakened). Only in ME.
4 Keep in store for future use; collect and keep in reserve; form a store, stock, or supply of; accumulate, hoard. (Foll. by *up*, *away*.) ME. ▸**b** COMPUTING. Retain (data or instructions) in some physical form that enables subsequent retrieval; transfer *into* a store or storage location. E20.
5 Of a receptacle or storage device: hold, keep, contain, have storage for. E20.

📖 **1** J. RUSSELL The lakes are stored with pike, perch, . . and trout. **2 store the kin** *Scot.* (of a person) continue to live, perpetuate the family. **4** J. RHYS I must return . . to see my furniture . . stored properly. DAY LEWIS Apples which had been stored . . through the winter. P. ACKROYD All these things he stored up in his memory. D. PROFUMO She picked the uneaten food off the plates and stored it away. **b** *New Scientist* One optical disc can store up to 200 million bytes of information.

▶**II** *verb intrans.* **6** Accumulate or acquire stores; gather things into a store. *rare*. E19.
Comb.: **store-and-forward** *attrib. adjective* (TELECOMMUNICATIONS) designating or pertaining to a data network in which messages are routed to one or more intermediate stations where they may be stored before being forwarded to their destinations.

storefront /ˈstɔːfrʌnt/ *noun.* Chiefly *N. Amer.* L19.
[from STORE *noun* + FRONT *noun*.]
1 The side of a shop facing the street; (a building with) a shop window. L19.
2 A room or rooms at the front of shop premises, esp. as used for some other purpose, as a small business, a centre for religious worship or proselytizing, etc. L20.
2 attrib.: ***storefront church***, ***storefront cinema***, ***storefront law office***, ***storefront mission***, ***storefront temple***, etc.

storer /ˈstɔːrə/ *noun.* ME.
[from STORE *verb* + -ER[1].]
1 A person who or thing which stores something or keeps something in store. ME.
2 A thing, esp. a young tree, kept to replenish a stock. Now *rare* or *obsolete*. M16.

storey /ˈstɔːri/ *noun.* Also (earlier) **story**. Pl. **-reys**, **-ries**. LME.
[Aphet. from Anglo-Latin *(h)istoria* spec. use of Latin *historia* HISTORY *noun*, STORY *noun*[1]; perh. orig. a tier of painted windows.]
1 Each of the stages or portions one above the other of which a building consists; a room or set of rooms on one floor or level. LME.
2 Each of a number of tiers or rows (of columns, windows, panels, etc.) arranged horizontally one above another. LME.
3 A thing compared to a storey of a building; each of a series of stages or divisions lying horizontally one over the other; *spec.* a layer within the canopy of a forest. E17.

> **1** N. SHUTE The top floor of a seven storey building. C. WILSON A strange house, whose upper storey was furnished in rococo style. **3** K. TYNAN Many good plays . . are built in two storeys—a ground floor of realism and a first floor of symbolism.

Phrases & comb.: **first storey** orig., the storey next above the ground floor; now usu. (orig. *US*), the ground floor. ***second storey***: see SECOND *adjective*. **storey box** each of a series of boxes (for keeping bees) arranged one over the other. ***sunk storey***: see SUNK *adjective* 2. ***sunken storey***: see SUNKEN *adjective* 3. **upper storey** *joc.* the head as the seat of the mind or intellect.

storeyed /ˈstɔːrɪd/ *adjective.* Also (earlier) **storied**. E17.
[from prec. + -ED[2].]
Divided into storeys, having (a specified number of) storeys.
one-storeyed, ***two-storeyed***, ***three-storeyed***, etc.

storge /ˈstɔːɡi/ *noun.* M17.
[Greek *storgē* rel. to *stergein* to love.]
Natural affection, *esp.* that of parents for their offspring.

storial /ˈstɔːrɪəl/ *adjective.* LME.
[Aphet. from late Latin *historialis*, from Latin *historia* HISTORY *noun*.]
Pertaining to or of the nature of history.
¶ Not recorded between L16 and M20.

storiate /ˈstɔːrɪeɪt/ *verb trans.* L19.
[Back-form. from STORIATION: see -ATE[3]. Cf. next.]
Decorate with storiation.

storiated /ˈstɔːrɪeɪtɪd/ *adjective.* L19.
[from (the same root as) prec.: see -ED[1]. Cf. HISTORIATED.]
Decorated with storiation.

storiation /stɔːrɪˈeɪʃ(ə)n/ *noun.* L19.
[from STORY *verb* + -ATION. Cf. STORIATE, STORIATED.]
Decoration with artistic designs representing historical, legendary, or emblematic subjects.

storied /ˈstɔːrɪd/ *adjective*[1]. LME.
[from STORY *noun*[1], *verb* + -ED[2], -ED[1], after medieval Latin *historiatus*, Old French *(h)istorié*.]
1 Ornamented with scenes from history or legend in sculpture, painting, or other art; inscribed with a memorial record. LME.
2 Celebrated in or associated with legend, history, or stories; legendary, fabled. Chiefly *literary* exc. *N. Amer.* E18.

storied *adjective*[2] see STOREYED.

storier /ˈstɔːrɪə/ *noun.* ME.
[In sense 1 aphet. from Old French *historieur*, from *historier* HISTORY *verb*; in sense 2 from STORY *verb* + -ER[1].]
†**1** A chronicler, a historian. ME–M17.
2 A storyteller. E19.

stories *noun*[1] pl. of STORY *noun*[1].

stories *noun*[2] *pl.* see STOREY.

storiette /stɔːrɪˈɛt/ *noun.* Also **storyette**. L19.
[from STORY *noun*[1] + -ETTE. Cf. NOVELETTE.]
A very short story.

storify /ˈstɔːrɪfʌɪ/ *verb*[1] *trans.* E17.
[from STORY *noun*[1] + -FY.]
Represent or recount as or in a story, make into a story.

storify /ˈstɔːrɪfʌɪ/ *verb*[2] *trans.* E19.
[from STOREY + -FY.]
Arrange (beehives) in storeys or stacks.

storiology /stɔːrɪˈɒlədʒi/ *noun. rare.* M19.
[from STORY *noun*[1] + -OLOGY.]
The branch of knowledge that deals with the origin and development of popular tales and legends.
■ **storioˈlogical** *adjective* L19. **storiologist** *noun* M19.

stork /stɔːk/ *noun.*
[Old English *storc* = Old Saxon (Dutch) *stork*, Old High German *stor(a)h* (German *Storch*), Old Norse *storkr*, from Germanic, prob. rel. to base of STARK *adjective* (with ref. to the birds' rigid stance).]
1 Any of various large wading or terrestrial birds chiefly of the family Ciconiidae, having long legs and a long stout bill; *esp.* the Eurasian white stork, *Ciconia ciconia*, which stands over three feet high, has brilliant white plumage with black wing-tips and red legs and bill, and nests on tall trees, buildings, etc. Also *fig.*, this bird as the bringer of newly born babies. OE.
2 The bird or its flesh as an article of food. Long *rare* or *obsolete*. LME.
3 Any of several varieties of domestic pigeon typically having white plumage with black wing-tips. Also ***stork pigeon***. M19.

> **1** T. HERBERT Upon many of these Mosques the Storks have pyld their nests. *Listener* Her eldest daughter . . is aware that the stork did not bring her. ***adjutant stork***, ***black stork***, ***jabiru stork***, ***marabou stork***, ***saddlebill stork***, ***shoe-billed stork***, etc. ***King Stork***: see KING *noun*.

Comb.: **stork's-bill** any of various small plants constituting the genus *Erodium*, of the cranesbill family, characterized by long-beaked fruits, pink or purplish flowers, and usu. pinnate or pinnately lobed leaves; esp. *E. cicutarium* (more fully ***common stork's-bill***), of sandy ground, and *E. moschatum* (more fully ***musk stork's-bill***), formerly grown for its faint musky smell.
■ **storkish** *adjective* of, pertaining to, or resembling a stork; like that of a stork: L16. **storkling** *noun* a young stork E19.

stork /stɔːk/ *verb trans. US slang.* M20.
[from the noun, with ref. to the bird as the mythical bringer of newly born babies.]
Make pregnant.

storken /ˈstɔːk(ə)n/ *verb intrans. Scot. & north.* LME.
[Old Norse *storkna* coagulate, corresp. to Old High German *kistorchanēn* become rigid, Gothic *gastaurknan* dry up, from Germanic base of STARK *adjective*.]
1 Become sturdy, thrive, gain strength. LME.
2 Esp. of blood or melted fat: stiffen with cold, congeal. L16.

storm /stɔːm/ *noun.*
[Old English *storm* = Old Saxon (Dutch) *storm*, Old & mod. High German *sturm*, Old Norse *stormr*, from Germanic, prob. from base repr. also by STIR *verb*.]
1 A violent disturbance of the atmosphere, taking the form of high winds, often with heavy falls of rain, hail, or snow, thunder and lightning, rough conditions with high foaming waves at sea, and clouds of sand or dust in arid regions. Occas., a heavy fall of rain, hail, or snow, a violent outbreak of thunder and lightning, unaccompanied by strong wind. Also in ASTRONOMY, a violent disturbance of the atmosphere of a star or planet. OE. ▸**b** *spec.* A snowstorm. Also, a quantity of fallen snow. *Scot.* L17. ▸**c** A wind of a particular degree of violence; *spec.* one classed as force 10 or 11 on the Beaufort scale (between a gale and a hurricane), having an average velocity of 48–63 knots (55–72 miles per hour) or, in some classifications, of 56–63 knots (64–72 miles per hour). E19. ▸**d** A period of hard weather with frost and snow. *Scot. & N. Amer.* L19. ▸**e** In *pl.* Storm windows. *N. Amer.* M20.
2 A heavy discharge or downfall (of missiles, blows, etc.). OE.
3 *fig.* **a** A violent disturbance of affairs, whether political, social, or domestic; tumult. OE. ▸**b** A sudden rush (of sound, tears, etc.); a violent outburst (of protest, censure, ridicule, etc.); a passionate expression of feeling; a vigorous or vehement dispute. LME. ▸**c** Commotion or disturbance of mind; a mass of powerful thoughts or feelings. M16.
4 MEDICINE. A paroxysm, a violent attack (of pain, disease, etc.). Usu. with specifying word, as ***asthmatic storm***, ***rheumatic storm***. M16.
5 MILITARY. [from the verb.] A violent assault on a fortified position. M17.

> **1** W. CATHER A storm had come up . . , bringing . . torrents of rain. P. SAYER As . . winter deepened the storms became very rough. ***dust-storm***, ***hailstorm***, ***rainstorm***, ***sandstorm***, ***snowstorm***, ***thunderstorm***. **3b** J. HIGGINS The orchestra stood . . and there was a storm of applause.

Phrases: ***any port in a storm***: see PORT *noun*[1]. **buy up a storm**, **cook up a storm**, etc., *N. Amer. colloq.* buy, cook, etc., (esp. a lot of) things with great enthusiasm and energy. ***electric storm***: see ELECTRIC *adjective*. **go down a storm** *colloq.* be received, esp. by an audience, with great enthusiasm. ***magnetic storm***: see MAGNETIC *adjective*. **storm and stress** = STURM UND DRANG. **storm in a teacup** a great excitement about a trivial matter. **take by storm** take possession of by a sudden attack; *fig.* achieve sudden and overwhelming success with or in.

Comb.: **storm apron** *US* a waterproof sheet used to cover the front of an open carriage in wet weather; **storm-area** the area over which a storm spreads itself; **storm-beach** an expanse of sand or gravel thrown up on the coast by storms; **storm-bird** = STORM PETREL; **stormbound** *adjective* prevented by storms from leaving port or continuing a voyage; **storm cellar** (chiefly *US*) a cellar or dugout made as a shelter from storms; **storm centre** the comparatively calm central area of a cyclonic storm; *fig.* the central point around which a storm of controversy, trouble, etc., rages; **storm choke** a safety valve installed in an oil-well pipe below the ocean surface to stop excess oil flow in the event of damage at the wellhead; **storm cloud** a dark heavy cloud which drops rain or threatens to do so; **storm coat** (chiefly *US*) a waterproof coat or heavy overcoat for use in stormy weather; **storm cock** the mistle thrush (from its continuing to sing in stormy weather); **storm-collar** a high coat-collar that can be turned up and fastened; **storm cone** = CONE *noun* 9; **storm cuff** a tight-fitting cuff inside the end of a sleeve which prevents rain or wind from getting in; **storm door** (orig. *US*) an outer or supplementary door for protection in bad weather; **storm drain** a drain built to carry away excess water in times of heavy rain; **storm-drum** = DRUM *noun*[1] 11; **storm-finch** = STORM PETREL; **storm-flap** a piece of material designed to protect an opening or fastening from the effects of rain, as on a tent, coat, etc.; **storm-glass** a hermetically sealed tube containing a solution supposed to change in appearance on the approach of a storm; **storm-god**, **storm-goddess** a deity supposed to rule the storms; **storm-jib** NAUTICAL a small heavy jib used in a high wind; **storm lantern** (orig. *US*) = ***hurricane-lamp*** s.v. HURRICANE *noun*; **storm-light** (***a***) the lurid light seen in a stormy sky; (***b***) = CORPOSANT; **storm-porch** a porch for the protection of an outer door from storms; **stormproof** *adjective* (***a***) impervious to storm; protected from or affording protection from stormy weather; (***b***) proof against storming or assault; **storm-sail** NAUTICAL a sail of heavy canvas and reduced dimensions used in stormy weather; **storm sewer** *N. Amer.* = ***storm drain*** above; **storm shutter** an outside window-shutter for use in stormy weather; **storm-signal** a visible signal (as a lamp, flag, etc.) which gives warning of the approach (and direction) of a storm; *fig.* an indication of an imminent outburst of emotion or conflict; **storm-stayed**, †**-staid**, **storm-stead** *adjectives* (chiefly *Scot.*) prevented by bad weather from making or continuing a journey; **storm surge** a rising of the sea in a region as a result of the wind and atmospheric pressure changes associated with a storm; **storm-system** the group of low-pressure areas revolving round a centre of lowest pressure which constitute a cyclonic storm; **storm track** the path traversed by the centre of a cyclonic storm, or of successive storms; **storm-warning** (***a***) a warning or indication of the approach of a storm; (***b***) = ***storm-signal*** above; **storm-water** an abnormal amount of surface water resulting from a heavy fall of rain or snow; **storm-wave** a wave associated with a storm, *esp.* an abnormally heavy wave caused by storm surge; **storm wind** the wind which accompanies a storm; *spec.* = sense 1c above; **storm window** (***a***) (chiefly *N. Amer.*) a detachable outer window put up in winter as insulation and to protect an inner one from the effects of storms; (***b***) (chiefly *Scot.*) a dormer window.
■ **stormless** *adjective* free from storms L15.

storm /stɔːm/ *verb.* LME.
[from the noun; not continuous with Old English *styrman*.]
1 *verb intrans.* Of the wind, the sea, the weather: be tempestuous or stormy, rage. Long *rare*. LME. ▸**b** *impers.* in ***it storms***, ***it is storming*** etc., it is blowing a gale; it is raining, snowing, etc., heavily. Long *US*. M16.
2 *verb trans.* In *pass.* Be exposed to severe weather; suffer severely from cold. Now *dial.* LME.
3 *verb intrans.* Complain with rough and violent language; rage. Foll. by *at*, *against* (a grievance or person). M16. ▸**b** *verb trans.* Say, utter, violently or angrily; put into some state by storming. M19.
4 *verb trans.* Make stormy; *fig.* trouble, vex, disturb. L16.
5 *verb trans.* MILITARY. Make a vigorous assault on (a fortified position); take or attempt to take by storm or assault. Also *gen.*, (attempt to) overwhelm or enter by force. M17.
6 *verb intrans.* Rush to an assault or attack; *gen.* rush violently or overwhelmingly. Foll. by adverb. M17.

> **1b** M. F. MAURY It is now snowing and storming furiously. **3** D. M. THOMAS She stormed at headwaiters to find us a table. **b** V. WOOLF 'What's the use of going now?' he had stormed. **5** *Armed Forces* They stormed a guerrilla fortress. *fig.*: *Blackwood's Magazine* Storming the citadels of . . bureaucracy. **6** *Daily Mirror* Two goals down . . , they stormed back for a 2–2 draw. J. TROLLOPE She . . stormed down to the flat . . and confronted him.

■ **stormable** *adjective* able to be taken by storm M17. **stormer** *noun* (***a***) a person who storms or rages; (***b***) a person who takes a place etc. by storm; (***c***) *slang* a thing of surpassing size, vigour, or excellence: E17. **storming** *adjective* (***a***) that storms; (***b***) *slang* (chiefly SPORT) displaying outstanding vigour, speed, or skill; (***c***) *slang* excellent, fantastic: M16.

stormful /ˈstɔːmfʊl, -f(ə)l/ *adjective.* M16.
[from STORM *noun* + -FUL.]
Subject to or having many storms; tempestuous, stormy (*lit. & fig.*).
■ **stormfully** *adverb* stormily M19.

Stormont /ˈstɔːmɒnt, -m(ə)nt/ *noun.* M20.
[A suburb of Belfast, location of Stormont Castle.]
1 The administration presided over by the Secretary of State for Northern Ireland, housed at Stormont Castle. M20.
2 The Northern Ireland parliament which met at the Parliament House in the grounds of Stormont Castle from 1920 until its suspension in 1972. M20.

storm petrel /ˈstɔːm pɛtr(ə)l/ *noun phr.* **L18.**
[from STORM *noun* + PETREL.]

1 A very small European sea bird of the open ocean, *Hydrobates pelagicus*, having blackish plumage with a white rump (also ***British storm petrel***). Also (with specifying word), any of various other petrels of the family Hydrobatidae. **L18.**

2 A person who delights in conflict, or whose appearance on the scene heralds trouble. **M19.**

1 ***Leach's storm petrel***, ***Wilson's storm petrel***, etc.

storm troop /ˈstɔːm truːp/ *noun phr.* **E20.**
[translating German *Sturmtruppen* pl.]

1 In *pl.* ▸**a** = ***shock troops*** s.v. SHOCK *noun*[2]. **E20.** ▸**b** *spec.* (*Hist.*) The troops of the Nazi political militia (*Sturmabteilung*). **E20.**

2 A branch or detachment of storm troops. *rare.* **M20.**

■ **storm-troop** *verb intrans.* behave in an aggressive manner like storm troops **M20.** **storm trooper** *noun* (**a**) *Hist.* a member of the Nazi political militia; (**b**) a member of a group of shock troops; a militant activist, a member of a group of vigilantes: **M20.**

stormy /ˈstɔːmi/ *adjective.* **ME.**
[from STORM *noun* + -Y[1].]

1 (Of the weather, sky, sea, etc.) disturbed or affected by a storm or tempest; wild, rough, tempestuous; (of a place or region) subject to storms. **ME.**

2 (Of a person, an expression, etc.) angry, angry-looking; (of an event, period, etc.) full of or characterized by violent or emotional outbursts. **ME.**

3 Associated or connected with storms; indicative or symbolic of storms. *poet.* **M16.**

1 MILTON Beyond the stormy Hebrides. *Manchester Examiner* An Atlantic steamer . . ploughing . . across stormy oceans. **2** INA TAYLOR Stepchildren, with whom she had . . a stormy relationship. *Times* The Central Committee postponed a final assessment . . after a stormy debate.

Special collocations: **stormy petrel** = STORM PETREL.
■ **stormily** *adverb* **LME.** **storminess** *noun* **L16.**

stornello /stɔːˈnɛləʊ/ *noun.* Pl. **-lli** /-li/. **L19.**
[Italian.]

A short popular Italian lyric, usually improvised; a poem in a metre derived from this form.

Storting /ˈstɔːtɪŋ/ *noun.* **M19.**
[Norwegian, from *stor* great + *ting* assembly: cf. THING *noun*[2].]

The Norwegian parliament.

story /ˈstɔːri/ *noun*[1]. Pl. **-ies.** **ME.**
[Aphet. from Anglo-Norman *estorie* (Old French *estoire*, mod. *histoire*) from Latin *historia* HISTORY *noun*.]

1 A true narrative, or one presumed to be true, relating to important events and famous people of the past; a historical account or anecdote. **ME.**

†**2** A historical work, a book of history. **ME–M18.**

†**3** Historical writing or records in general; history as a branch of knowledge, or as opp. to fiction. Also, the events recorded by historians. **ME–M18.**

†**4** A painting or sculpture representing a historical subject; any work of pictorial or sculptural art containing figures. **ME–L17.**

5 a A recital or account of events that have or are alleged to have happened; a series of events that are or might be narrated. **LME.** ▸**b** With *possess.*: a person's account of his or her experiences or the events of his or her life. **E17.** ▸**c** An indication of past events or present circumstances as revealed or discovered in a work of visual art, a person's appearance, etc.; a discernible theme or meaning. Also, a coherent account or set of facts resulting from (esp. scientific) investigation. **E17.** ▸**d** With *possess.* or *of*: (the series of events in) the development or past existence of a person, thing, country, institution, etc., considered as narrated or as a subject for narration. **L17.**

6 A narrative of real or (usu.) fictitious events, designed for the entertainment of the hearer or reader; a series of traditional or imaginary incidents forming the matter of such a narrative; a tale, an anecdote; a (short) work of fiction. **LME.** ▸†**b** A subject of stories; a target of amusement. **E17–M18.** ▸**c** A mere tale, an account with no basis in fact. **M17.** ▸**d** Without article: traditional, poetic, or romantic legend or history. **L18.**

7 An allegation, a statement, an account, a piece of gossip; a particular person's representation of the facts of a matter. **E17.**

8 *euphem.* A lie. Also (now only *Black English*), a storyteller, a liar. *colloq.* **L17.**

9 A succession of significant incidents, the plot or story-line (of a novel, poem, drama, etc.). **E18.**

10 A narrative or descriptive article in a newspaper or magazine; material or a subject which is or can be made suitable for such an article, a piece of news. Orig. *US.* **L19.**

11 The commercial prospects or circumstances of a particular company. *colloq.* **L20.**

1 DAY LEWIS He would act the biblical stories on which he was commenting. **3** DRYDEN The destruction being so swift . . as nothing can parallel in Story. **5a** M. E. BRADDON He told the story of George's disappearance. **b** *New Yorker* Willa had sold her story to Universal Pictures. **c** *Scientific American* Examination of the lunar samples . . began to reveal a different story. **d** E. SNOW No more confused an epic, than the story of Red China. **6** *Woman* A well-written and compelling story that . . you'll enjoy. **b** SHAKES. *Meas. for M.* Sir, make me not your story. **7** G. DALY When Howell died . . , the story went round that he had been found . . with his throat cut. P. D. JAMES His story is that the affair was over. **9** D. COOK Sundry bursts of patriotic oratory . . help the story in no way. **10** J. MANN The news media . . got on to the story very quickly. **11** *New York Times* Profitable companies with solid stories.

Phrases: ***a likely story***: see LIKELY *adjective* 1. **another story** a different thing altogether, a matter requiring or meriting separate treatment. **as the story goes**, **the story goes** (as) it is reported. CONTINUED ***story***. ***cut a long story short***: see SHORT *adjective*. FAIRY ***story***. ***just-so story***: see JUST *adverb*. ***long short story***: see LONG *adjective*[1]. ***old story***: see OLD *adjective*. SHAGGY-***dog story***. ***short story***: see SHORT *adjective*. **tell its own story** = ***tell its own tale*** s.v. TALE *noun*. **the same story**, **the same old story** a repetition of a familiar occurrence, situation, or excuse, the predictable course of events. ***the story goes***: see ***as the story goes*** above. **the story of my life**, **the story of his life**, etc., *colloq.* an event, statement, or situation that supposedly epitomizes one's, a person's, life or experience. **the whole story** the full account of the matter, all that there is to be said. **what is the story on** —? tell me (all) about —?

Comb.: **storyboard** *noun & verb* (**a**) *noun* a large surface on which is displayed a series of rough drawings representing sample shots, outlining the plot of a film, television advertisement, etc.; (**b**) *verb trans.* plan by means of a storyboard; **story-book** *noun & adjective* (**a**) *noun* a book containing stories, esp. children's stories; (**b**) *attrib. adjective* unreal, romantic, conforming to the conventions of a story, esp. one with a happy ending; **story editor** an editor who advises on the content and form of film or television scripts; **story-line** (an outline of) the principal stages by which a story (esp. a film script) unfolds, a plot.

■ **storyless** *adjective* not containing or having a story or stories **M19.**

story *noun*[2] see STOREY.

story /ˈstɔːri/ *verb trans.* Now *rare* exc. *poet.* **LME.**
[from STORY *noun*[1].]

1 Orig., record historically, relate the history of. Later, tell as a story, tell the story of. **LME.**

2 Decorate with paintings or sculpture; represent in painting or sculpture. **LME.**

storyette *noun* var. of STORIETTE.

storyteller /ˈstɔːrɪtɛlə/ *noun.* **E18.**
[from STORY *noun*[1] + TELLER *noun*[1].]

1 A person who tells a story or stories; a person who tells anecdotes; a writer of stories. **E18.**

2 A liar. *colloq.* **M18.**

■ **storytelling** *noun & adjective* (**a**) *noun* the activity of telling stories; an instance of this; (**b**) *adjective* that tells stories or a story; *colloq.* lying: **E18.**

stoss /stɒs, *foreign* ʃtoːs/ *adjective.* **L19.**
[German = thrust, push.]

GEOLOGY. Designating the side of an object that faces a flow of ice or water.

stoss-side, ***stoss slope***, etc.

stot /stɒt/ *noun*[1].
[Old English *stot(t)* perh. cogn. with Old Norse *stútr* bull. Cf. Anglo-Latin *stottus* steer, *stotta* heifer.]

▸ **I** †**1** A horse. **OE–LME.**

2 A young bull, *esp.* a steer. *north.* **ME.**

3 A heifer. *north. rare.* **L17.**

▸ **II** *transf.* †**4** A woman, *esp.* a coarse or lewd one. **LME–L15.**

5 A stupid, clumsy person. *Scot. & dial.* **L19.**

stot /stɒt/ *noun*[2]. Chiefly *Scot.* **E16.**
[Rel. to the verb.]

1 The action of rebounding; a rebound. **E16.**

2 A leap or spring, esp. in dancing; the swing or rhythm of a tune. **L16.**

stot /stɒt/ *verb intrans.* Infl. **-tt-.** **E16.**
[Origin unkn. Cf. STOIT.]

1 Rebound, bounce (*from*, *off*); fall or hit with a bounce (*on*, *against*); jump, start, spring. *Scot. & north.* **E16.**

2 Move with a jumping or springing step, bound along, bounce up and down; stagger, lurch, move unsteadily. Now also *spec.*, (of an animal) make short high jumps, esp. as a defensive or warning action (typical esp. of some antelopes). **E19.**

■ **stotter** *noun* (**a**) a ball or other object that bounces or rebounds; (**b**) *slang* a very attractive girl: **L19.**

stotin /stɒˈtiːn/ *noun.* **L20.**
[Slovene, from *sto* hundred.]

A monetary unit of Slovenia, equal to one-hundredth of a tolar.

stotinka /stɒˈtɪŋkə/ *noun.* Pl. **-ki** /-ki/. **L19.**
[Bulgarian = hundredth.]

A monetary unit of Bulgaria, equal to one-hundredth of a lev. Usu. in *pl.*

stotty /ˈstɒti/ *noun. north.* Also **-ttie.** **L20.**
[Origin unkn.]

In full ***stotty cake***. A kind of coarse bread originally made in NE England from spare scraps of white dough; a soft roll made from this.

stoun /stuːn/ *verb trans.* Long *obsolete* exc. *Scot. & north.* **ME.**
[Aphet. from Old French *estoner* ASTONE. Cf. STUN *verb*, STOUND *verb*[2].]

Stun, stupefy; astound.

stound /staʊnd, stuːnd/ *noun*[1] *& verb*[1]. *obsolete* exc. *Scot. & dial.*
[Old English *stund* = Old Frisian *stunde*, Old Saxon *stunda* (Dutch *stond*), Old High German *stunta* (German *Stunde* hour), Old Norse *stund*, from Germanic.]

▸ **A** *noun.* **1** A (short) time, a while; a moment. Formerly also *spec.* (**a**) a time to act, an opportune moment; (**b**) a hard, testing, or painful time. **OE.**

2 A sharp pain, a pang; a shock; a thrill (of delight). **ME.** ▸**b** Roar, violent noise. **E17.**

▸ **B** *verb.* †**1** *verb intrans.* Remain, stay. Only in **ME.**

2 *verb intrans. & (now rare or obsolete) trans.* (Cause to) ache, smart, throb, etc. *Scot. & north.* **L15.**

■ **stounding** *ppl adjective* (*north.*) smarting, acutely painful **M19.**

stound /staʊnd, stuːnd/ *noun*[2]. *obsolete* exc. *Scot. & dial.* **M16.**
[App. from next.]

A state of stupefaction or amazement.

stound /staʊnd, stuːnd/ *verb*[2] *trans. obsolete* exc. *Scot. & dial.* **ME.**
[Aphet. from ASTOUND *verb*.]

Stun; stupefy, bewilder.

stoup /stuːp/ *noun.* Also (esp. in sense 2) **stoop.** **ME.**
[Old Norse *staup* = Old English *stēap*, Middle Low German *stōp*, Middle & mod. Dutch *stoop*, Old High German *stouf* (German dial. *Stauf*), from Germanic base rel. to Old English *stoppa*, Old Saxon *stoppo* pail, from West Germanic. Cf. STEEP *verb*[1], STOP *noun*[1].]

1 A pail, a bucket. Formerly also, a large jar or small cask for holding liquids. *obsolete* exc. *Scot.* **ME.**

2 A drinking-vessel; *spec.* a beaker, a flagon, a tankard. Also (freq. with defining word), such a vessel as a measure of capacity. Now *arch.* exc. *Scot. & north.* **LME.**

3 A vessel for holy water, *esp.* a stone basin set in or against a wall, at or near the entrance of a church. **LME.**

2 *Milton Keynes Express* Those travellers who may . . have stopped for a stoop of ale. ***pint stoup***, ***quart stoup***.

■ **stoupful** *noun* (*arch.*) as much as a stoup of ale etc. will hold **L16.**

stour /stʊə/ *noun.* Also (*dial.*) **stoor**, †**stowre.** **ME.**
[Anglo-Norman *estur*, Old French *esto(u)r* = Italian *stormo*, from Germanic base also of STORM *noun*; in branch II perh. a different word.]

▸ **I 1** An armed combat, a fight; (a) conflict, (a) struggle. *obsolete* exc. *arch. & Scot.* **ME.**

2 Tumult, uproar; commotion. Now *Scot. & dial.* **LME.** ▸**b** A storm; *esp.* a driving storm. *Scot. & north.* **E19.**

†**3** A time of turmoil, stress, or adversity. **LME–E19.**

▸ **II 4** Flying dust raised by rapid movement, the wind, etc; a deposit of dust; deposited dust. Chiefly *Scot. & north.* **LME.**

†**5** A cloud of spray. *Scot. rare.* **E16–E19.**

Phrases: **like stour** *Scot.* very swiftly or vigorously. **kick up a stour** *Scot.* make a fuss.

■ **stoury** *adjective* (*Scot.*) dusty, full of flying dust **L18.**

stour /stʊə/ *adjective & adverb. obsolete* exc. *Scot.* Also **sture.**
[Late Old English *stōr* from Old Norse *stórr* (Swedish, Danish *stor*) big, great, prob. ult. from base also of STAND *verb*; perh. also partly rel. to Middle Low German *stūr*, Middle Dutch *stuur*, *stūre* rough, wild, furious: cf. STEER *adjective*.]

▸ **A** *adjective.* †**1 a** Of a natural agency: violent, fierce. **LOE–LME.** ▸**b** (Of a fight) fiercely contested; (of conditions) causing great pain or hardship, severe. Only in **ME.** ▸**c** Of a sound: great in volume, loud. **LME–E16.**

†**2 a** Great in number, numerous. Only in **ME.** ▸**b** Of an object: great in size, mass, or bulk. **ME–L17.**

3 Of a person or animal: strong, sturdy, stalwart. **ME.** ▸†**b** Of bearing, behaviour, speech, etc.: valiant; resolute; reckless. **LME–M16.**

4 Of a person, looks, etc.: stiff, unbending; stern, surly. **ME.**

5 Coarse in texture, rough; stiff. **LME.** ▸**b** *spec.* Of a voice: harsh. **L18.**

▸ **B** *adverb.* Esp. of wind blowing: violently, fiercely. **ME.**

■ **stourly** *adverb* †(**a**) *rare* greatly; (**b**) *Scot.* fiercely; stoutly, vigorously: **ME.** **stourness** *noun* (*obsolete* exc. *Scot.*) **LME.**

stoush /staʊʃ/ *verb & noun. Austral. & NZ slang.* **L19.**
[Origin unkn.]

▸ **A** *verb trans.* Thrash, hit, fight; attack verbally. **L19.**

▸ **B** *noun.* Fighting; a brawl, a fight; a thrashing. **L19.**

stout /staʊt/ *noun*[1]. *obsolete* exc. *dial.*
[Late Old English *stūt*, of unknown origin.]

A gadfly, a horsefly; a gnat.

stout /staʊt/ *noun*[2]. **L17.**
[Prob. ellipt. for *stout ale* or *stout beer*: see next.]

Orig., any strong beer. Now *spec.*, a strong dark beer brewed with roasted malt or barley.

stout /staʊt/ *adjective, verb, & adverb.* ME.
[Anglo-Norman, Old French (dial.) *stout* (Old French *estout*), from West Germanic (cf. Old Frisian *stult*, Middle Low German *stolt*, Middle & mod. Dutch *stout*, Old & mod. High German *stolz* proud), perh. rel. to STILT *noun*.]
▶ **A** *adjective.* **I** †**1 a** Proud, haughty, arrogant. ME–M19. ▸**b** Stately, magnificent, splendid. Only in ME.
†**2** Fierce, furious; formidable, menacing. ME–E17.
3 Of a person: valiant, brave; dauntless and vigorous, esp. in conflict, resistance, etc. ME. ▸**b** Of courage, the heart, etc.: unwavering, steadfast. E16. ▸**c** Of resistance, an assault, etc.: vigorous. L16. ▸†**d** Of a person, effo[rt], etc.: energetic. E17–E18.
4 †**a** Obstinate, intractable, stubborn, rebellious. LME–M19. ▸**b** Of an utterance, attitude, words, etc.: resolute, defiant. *arch.* LME. ▸**c** Of a person: resolute, determined; unyielding, uncompromising. M16.

> 🕮 **1a** SHAKES. *2 Hen. VI* As stout and proud as he were lord of all. **3** T. FULLER That Stout Prelate who when the Scots invaded England . . utterly routed . . them. J. LOCKE Some Men by . . their Constitutions are Stout, others Timorous. S. KAYE-SMITH Wipe your eyes, and be a stout gal. **b** T. H. WHITE He had a stout heart, and did not want to give in. **4a** J. H. NEWMAN Resistance from his old stout will and hardened heart.

▶ **II 5 a** Strong in body; of powerful build; sturdy. *obsolete* exc. *US dial.* ME. ▸**b** Robust in health, resilient. *obsolete* exc. *Scot.* L17. ▸**c** Of a fox or horse: having endurance or stamina. E18.
6 Of a building, tree, ship, machine, etc.: strong, solid, sturdy; able to withstand wear, rough weather, etc. ME.
7 a Of a wind: strong. *obsolete* exc. *Scot.* LME. ▸†**b** Of a sound: loud, harsh. LME–M16.
8 Of a plant or its parts: strong in growth. L16.
†**9** Of an alcoholic drink, esp. ale or beer: having body. Cf. STOUT *noun*². L17–E19.
10 Of a material object or substance: rather thick; of considerable thickness or solidity. M18.
11 Of a person: inclined to corpulence; *euphem.* fat. E19. ▸**b** Of (a part of) an animal: thick, massive. M19.

> 🕮 **10** H. MCMURTRIE The web . . is formed of such stout materials that it will arrest small Birds. D. MADDEN Catherine keeps a diary, stout as a ledger. **11** L. STRACHEY She . . was stout but . . with the plumpness of a vigorous matron. R. RENDELL A large stout woman, puffily overweight.

Special collocations: **stout fellow** *arch. colloq.* (*a*) a dependable man; (*b*) *interjection* expr. approval of what a man has done. **stout party** *joc.* a fat person; esp. in ***collapse of stout party***, a catch-phrase reporting the reaction of a pompous or overbearing person to a crushing reply. ***stout trencherman***: see TRENCHERMAN 1.
▶ **B** *verb trans.* (with *it*) & †*intrans.* Be defiant; act defiantly or stubbornly. *obsolete* exc. in ***stout it out*** (now *rare*), persist defiantly under pressure; brazen it out. ME.
▶ **C** *adverb.* = STOUTLY. Now *rare.* ME.
■ **stouten** *verb trans.* & *intrans.* make or grow stout M19. **stoutish** *adjective* M19. **stoutness** *noun* LME.

stout-hearted /staʊtˈhɑːtɪd/ *adjective.* M16.
[from STOUT *adjective* + HEART *noun* + -ED².]
Brave, courageous, dauntless. Formerly also, stubborn, intractable.
■ **stout-heartedly** *adverb* L19. **stout-heartedness** *noun* L17.

stoutly /ˈstaʊtli/ *adverb.* ME.
[from STOUT *adjective* + -LY².]
1 Bravely, valiantly; manfully. ME.
2 Resolutely, determinedly, uncompromisingly. ME. ▸†**b** Stubbornly, obstinately. L16–M17.
†**3** Vigorously, energetically; lustily. ME–E19.
†**4** Proudly, haughtily, arrogantly, defiantly. LME–M17.
5 Orig., splendidly, ornately. Later, strongly, massively, solidly. LME.

stove /stəʊv/ *noun & verb*¹. LME.
[Middle Low German, Middle Dutch *stove* (Dutch *stoof* foot-warmer) = Old High German *stuba* (German *Stube* living-room), rel. to Old English *stofa* bathroom, from Germanic base perh. also rel. to STEW *noun*¹, *verb*. Cf. STOW *noun*³.]
▶ **A** *noun.* †**1** (A room for) a hot-air bath; a sweating-room. LME–M18.
†**2** Esp. in northern Europe, a sitting-room or bedroom heated with a furnace. M16–E18.
3 An apparatus (usu. enclosed) burning fuel or electricity to produce or provide heat; *esp.* (*a*) a furnace, a kiln; (*b*) (the hob of) a cooker, an oven. Also, any of various containers heated for a particular purpose. M16. ▸**b** The grate of a fireplace. M18.
4 A hothouse for plants. L17.

> 🕮 **3** L. GRANT-ADAMSON Something boiled over and she darted to the stove. G. SAYER Open fires and paraffin stoves were the only source of heat. ***everything but the kitchen stove***: see KITCHEN *noun & adjective*. ***pot-belly stove***: see POT-BELLY 3.

Comb.: **stove-enamel** a vitreous enamel (*a*) sufficiently heat-resistant for use on the surfaces of stoves; (*b*) hardened by heating in a stove after application; **stove-grate** (*a*) = sense 3b above; (*b*) the grid or bars in a stove on which fuel rests; **stove lifter** *N. Amer.* a curved piece of iron for lifting a stove-lid.
▶ **B** *verb trans.* †**1** Subject to a hot-air bath. Only in LME.
2 Put, raise, or force (plants) in a hothouse. E17.
†**3** Keep (a person or animal) in a hot room. E17–M19.
4 a Dry in a stove; *spec.* (NAUTICAL) dry (ropes) thus in preparation for tarring. E17. ▸**b** Use heat to fuse a coating to (an object). M20.
5 Stew (meat or vegetables). *obsolete* exc. *Scot. & north.* M17.
6 Fumigate or disinfect (cloth, wool, etc.) with sulphur or other fumes. E19.
7 Burn away (a tree stump). *Austral.* L19.
■ **stoveless** *adjective* L19.

stove /stəʊv/ *ppl adjective.* M19.
[pa. pple of STAVE *verb*.]
1 Chiefly NAUTICAL. That has been stove in. Also ***stove-in***. M19.
2 ***stove-up***, exhausted, run down. *N. Amer. slang.* E20.

stove /stəʊv/ *verb*² *trans.* E19.
[formed as prec.]
= STAVE *verb* 3.

stove *verb*³ *pa. t. & pple*: see STAVE *verb*.

stoven /ˈstʌv(ə)n/ *noun. obsolete* exc. *dial.*
[Old English *stofn* = Old Norse *stofn*.]
A stem or trunk of a tree. Also, a sapling, a shoot from the stump of a tree.

stoven /ˈstəʊv(ə)n/ *ppl adjective.* M19.
[Irreg. pa. pple of STAVE *verb*: see -EN⁶.]
= STOVE *ppl adjective* 1.

stove-pipe /ˈstəʊvpʌɪp/ *noun & adjective.* L17.
[from STOVE *noun* + PIPE *noun*¹.]
▶ **A 1** Any of the pipes conveying hot air in a stove or hot-house. L17.
2 A pipe conducting smoke and gases from a stove to a chimney, funnel, etc. M19.
3 *colloq.* **a** A man's tall cylindrical (usu. silk) hat. Also ***stove-pipe hat***. Orig. *US.* M19. ▸**b** In *pl.* Trousers. Now usu. *spec.*, narrow tight-fitting trousers. M19. ▸**c** *US MILITARY.* A portable trench mortar. E20.
▶ **B** *attrib.* or as *adjective.* Designating narrow tight-fitting trousers. M20.

stover /ˈstəʊvə/ *noun*¹. Now chiefly *dial.* ME.
[Aphet. from Anglo-Norman *estover*: see ESTOVERS.]
†**1** The provision of food needed for a journey or a stay. Only in ME.
2 †**a** Winter food for cattle. M16–L17. ▸**b** *spec.* Hay made from clover; broken straw etc. from the threshing-floor; stubble. Also (*US*), cornstalks used as fodder. M17.

stover /ˈstəʊvə/ *noun*². L16.
[from STOVE *verb*¹ + -ER¹.]
A person who stoves cloth, wool, etc.

†**stover** *verb intrans. rare.* M17–L18.
[Perh. from STOVER *noun*¹.]
Stand up or up like stubble; bristle (*up*).

stovies /ˈstəʊviz/ *noun pl. Scot. & north.* L19.
[from STOVE *verb*¹ 5 + -IE.]
A dish of potatoes stewed in a pot.

stow /stəʊ/ *noun*¹.
[Old English *stōw* = Old Frisian *stō* from Germanic base also of STAND *verb*.]
1 A place; *esp.* a geographical location. Long *obsolete* exc. in place-names. OE.
2 A hurdle for penning sheep. *dial.* M19.
1 ***Stow-on-the-Wold***, ***Chepstow***, etc.

stow /stəʊ/ *noun*². Long *rare* or *obsolete* exc. in comb. M16.
[Origin unkn.]
MINING. = STOWCE *noun*.
Comb.: **stow-blade** either of two upright pieces of wood connected at the top with the sole-trees of a stowce.

stow /stəʊ/ *noun*³. Also (earlier) †**stowe**. L16.
[Var. of STOVE *noun*.]
†**1** A stove; *spec.* (*a*) a hot-air bath; (*b*) a heated room; (*c*) a hothouse for plants. L16–M18.
2 In tin plate making, a raised structure containing the furnace. M19.

stow /stəʊ/ *verb*¹. LME.
[Aphet. from BESTOW; in sense 5 perh. infl. by Dutch *stouwen*.]
1 *verb trans.* Place, lodge, find room or accommodation for, (a person). LME. ▸†**b** Arrest, imprison. LME–E17.
†**2** *verb trans.* Spend, invest, (money); apply (money or goods) to a particular purpose. Cf. BESTOW *verb* 1b. LME–M18.
3 *verb trans.* **a** Place (an object) in a container, under cover, etc., for storage, convenient access, etc.; pack (belongings, equipment, etc.). LME. ▸**b** Fill, pack, (a container or vehicle), esp. with things compactly arranged. E18.
4 *slang.* †**a** *verb intrans.* Stop speaking, be quiet. Usu. in *imper.* M16–E19. ▸**b** *verb trans.* Desist or abstain from. L17.
5 *verb trans.* NAUTICAL. ▸**a** Place, arrange, or store (cargo, provisions, equipment, etc.) in proper order on a ship. M16. ▸**b** Fasten down (people) under the hatches. E17. ▸**c** Furl (a sail). M17. ▸**d** Put cargo in (the hold etc.); load, fit up, (a ship). L17.
6 Foll. by *away*: ▸**a** *verb trans.* Remove and store until required; hide away; put out of the way or out of sight. Also (*joc.*), eat up (food). L18. ▸**b** *verb intrans.* Be or become a stowaway. L19.

> 🕮 **1** SHAKES. *Oth.* O thou foul thief, where hast thou stow'd my daughter? W. ROBERTSON Beatrix Ruthven was . . stowed in a chamber prepared for her by the queen's direction. R. INGALLS She opened the car door and stowed him in the back. **3a** J. GLASSCO When everything was stowed we . . needed three taxis to take us to the station. N. LOWNDES Marina . . stowed the bread and potatoes . . into a cupboard. D. PROFUMO They watched the rest of the party . . stowing their rods and tackle with meticulous care. **b** R. G. CUMMING The morning was spent in stowing the waggons. ***solid stowing***: see SOLID *adjective & adverb*. **4b** *Punch* Thought is dreary, Reflection is slow. Stow thinking. P. ANGADI 'Stow that yelping,' he shouted at Jessie. **stow it!** (*a*) be quiet!; (*b*) stop it! **5a** SHELLEY Stow the eatables in the aft locker. **6a** A. HIGGINS She . . stowed away her town clothes in the wardrobe.

Comb.: **stow-board** MINING: where debris or other rubbish is put; **stow-master** a person in charge of stowing a boat.
■ **stowable** *adjective* E17.

stow /stəʊ/ *verb*² *trans. obsolete* exc. *Scot. & dial.* E16.
[Origin unkn.]
Crop, cut close; *esp.* (*a*) crop the ears of (a sheep); (*b*) lop off the branches of (a tree) or the leaves of (a plant).
■ **stowing** *noun* (*rare*) (*a*) the action of the verb; †(*b*) *Scot.* (in *pl.*) leaves taken for food from young greens: E17.

stowage /ˈstəʊɪdʒ/ *noun.* LME.
[from STOW *verb*¹ + -AGE.]
1 The action of stowing cargo, goods, etc.; an instance of this. LME. ▸**b** The way in which a ship's cargo is stowed. M18.
2 Room or space for stowing anything; the capacity of a warehouse, ship's hold, etc. M16. ▸**b** Capacity for food. *joc.* M17.
3 The condition or process of being stowed; the goods etc. with which a vessel is (to be) stowed. E17.
4 A place in which something is stowed. M17.

> 🕮 **1** R. H. DANA The mate . . has the charge of the stowage . . and delivery of the cargo. **2** attrib.: ***stowage capacity***, ***stowage room***, ***stowage space***, etc. **b** SIR W. SCOTT I have still some stowage left for beef and bannocks.

stowaway /ˈstəʊəweɪ/ *noun.* M19.
[from *stow away*: see STOW *verb*¹.]
1 A person hiding in a ship, aeroplane, etc., to get free passage or make an escape. M19.
2 A place where things may be stowed. E20.

stow-ball /ˈstəʊbɔːl/ *noun.* Long *obsolete* exc. *Hist.* M17.
[Origin unkn.]
An outdoor ball game similar to golf, common in the 16th and 17th cents.

stow-boat /ˈstəʊbəʊt/ *noun. local.* L16.
[Perh. alt. of ***stall boat*** s.v. STALL *noun*¹, infl. by STOW *verb*¹.]
A kind of boat used in fishing for sprats.
■ **stow-boating** *noun* fishing for sprats in a stow-boat M19.

stowce /stəʊs/ *noun & verb.* M17.
[Origin unkn.]
MINING. ▶**A** *noun sing.* & in *pl.* A kind of windlass for drawing up ore; a model of this, serving to mark or secure legal right of possession of a mining tract. M17.
▶ **B** *verb trans.* Mark (a tract) with a stowce. M17.

†**stowe** *noun* see STOW *noun*³.

stower /ˈstaʊə/ *noun*¹. *obsolete* exc. *dial.* ME.
[Old Norse *staurr*.]
1 A stake or post used in building. ME.
2 Each of the upright staves or bars in the side of a cart or wagon. LME.
3 A rung of a ladder. L15.
4 A punt-pole. L18.

stower /ˈstəʊə/ *noun*². M18.
[from STOW *verb*¹ + -ER¹.]
A person who stows a ship, cargo, tackle, etc.

stow-net /ˈstəʊnɛt/ *noun.* L19.
[Prob. from STALL *noun*¹ + NET *noun*¹.]
A kind of net used in fishing for sprats.

†**stowre** *noun* var. of STOUR *noun*.

STP *abbreviation.*
1 Latin *Sanctae Theologiae Professor* Professor of Sacred Theology.
2 [Prob. with allus. to scientifically treated petroleum, an oil additive.] 2,5-dimethoxy-4-methylamphetamine, a synthetic hallucinogen.
3 SCIENCE. Standard temperature and pressure.

str. *abbreviation.*
1 Strait.
2 Stroke (of an oar).

strabism /ˈstreɪbɪz(ə)m/ *noun*. Now *rare*. M17.
[Anglicized from STRABISMUS.]
= STRABISMUS.

strabismal /strəˈbɪzm(ə)l/ *adjective*. L19.
[formed as next + -AL¹.]
= next.
■ **strabismally** *adverb* squintingly L19.

strabismic /strəˈbɪzmɪk/ *adjective*. M19.
[from STRABISMUS + -IC.]
Chiefly MEDICINE. Of, pertaining to, or having strabismus.
■ **strabismical** *adjective* having strabismus M19.

strabismometer /streɪbɪzˈmɒmɪtə/ *noun*. M19.
[from next + -OMETER.]
OPHTHALMOLOGY. An instrument for measuring the degree of strabismus.
■ **strabismometry** *noun* measurement of the degree of strabismus L19.

strabismus /strəˈbɪzməs/ *noun*. L17.
[mod. Latin from Greek *strabismos*, from *strabizein* to squint, from *strabos* squinting.]
1 MEDICINE. A disorder of the eye-muscles resulting in an inability to direct the gaze of both eyes to the same object simultaneously; squinting, a squint. L17.
2 *fig.* Perversity of intellectual perception. M19.

stracchino /straˈkiːnəʊ/ *noun*. M19.
[Italian.]
In full ***stracchino cheese***. A variety of soft cheese made in the north of Italy.

stracciatella /stratʃəˈtɛlə/ *noun*. M20.
[Italian.]
An Italian soup made with stock, eggs, and cheese.

Stracheyan /ˈstreɪtʃɪən/ *adjective*. E20.
[from *Strachey* (see below) + -AN.]
Of, pertaining to, or characteristic of the English biographer and critic Giles Lytton Strachey (1880–1932), or his writing.

stract /strakt/ *adjective*. *obsolete* exc. *dial.* L16.
[Aphet. from DISTRACT *ppl adjective*.]
Deranged; out of one's mind; insane.

Strad /strad/ *noun*. *colloq.* L19.
[Abbreviation.]
= STRADIVARIUS.

straddle /ˈstrad(ə)l/ *noun*. E17.
[from the verb.]
1 The action or an act of straddling. E17. ▸**b** The distance between the feet or legs of a person straddling. M19. ▸**c** ATHLETICS & GYMNASTICS. A movement, *spec.* a style of high jump, in which the legs are held wide apart. M20.
2 A thing which straddles or is straddled; *spec.* †(*a*) *rare* a cart, sledge, or similar form of transport; (*b*) = SADDLE *noun* 1b. L17.
3 An attempt to take an equivocal or non-committal position with regard to a question, esp. politically. *US colloq.* M19.
4 POKER. A doubling of an opening stake by a player. M19.
5 STOCK EXCHANGE. An option giving the holder the right of either calling for or delivering a commodity at a stated price. L19.
6 Each of the vertical timbers by which the different sets are supported in a mine shaft. *US.* L19.
7 A grouping of discharged shots, bombs, etc., falling short of and over a specified target. E20.
Comb.: **straddle-bob** *dial.* a black beetle, *esp.* a scarab; **straddle-bug** (*a*) *US & dial.* a long-legged beetle, *esp.* the dung-beetle *Canthon laevis*; (*b*) *US colloq.* a person who takes up an equivocal or non-committal position with regard to a question, esp. politically; **straddle carrier** a vehicle for manoeuvring large loads by straddling and lifting them beneath its chassis; **straddle harvester**, **straddle machine** an agricultural device which straddles rows of bushes or plants to facilitate fruit-picking; **straddle milling** the milling of two parallel faces of a workpiece simultaneously by means of a pair of cutters on a single shaft.

straddle /ˈstrad(ə)l/ *verb*. M16.
[Alt. of STRIDDLE *verb*.]
1 *verb intrans.* Stand or sit with the legs wide apart. M16. ▸**b** Of the legs: be wide apart. M17. ▸**c** Stand or stride *across* or *over*; sit astride *on* or *across*. L17.
2 *verb trans.* Part (the legs) widely in standing or walking. Also foll. by *out*. M16.
3 *verb intrans.* Walk with the legs wide apart; *dial.* swagger, strut. E19.
4 *verb trans.* Sit, stand, or walk with one leg on either side of (a thing); stride over; bestride. E19. ▸**b** Discharge shots, bombs, etc., so that they fall short of and over (a target); (of discharged shots, bombs, etc.) fall short of and over (a specified target). E20.
5 *verb trans. & intrans.* Occupy or take up an equivocal or non-committal position with regard to (a question) esp. politically. *US colloq.* M19.
6 *verb trans.* POKER. Double (an opening stake). M19.

📖 **2** B. BAINBRIDGE He straddled his feet wider apart. **4** P. LIVELY He pulled out a chair and straddled it, .. elbows on the back. *transf.*: *Scottish World* Stirling straddles the great divide between the Highlands and the Lowlands.

Phrases: **straddle the market** *US colloq.* simultaneously have large holdings of one commodity while having sold or not possessing large holdings of another.
■ **straddler** *noun* M19.

straddle /ˈstrad(ə)l/ *adverb*. E19.
[from the noun Cf. ASTRADDLE.]
Astraddle, astride (*of*).

📖 J. MASEFIELD Molly Wolvesey riding straddle.

stradiot /ˈstradɪɒt/ *noun*. M16.
[Italian *stradiotto* from Greek *stratiōtēs* soldier: see -OT².]
Hist. A member of a class of light cavalry, originally raised in Greece and Albania, serving as mercenaries in the 16th and 17th cents.

Stradivarius /stradɪˈvɛːrɪəs/ *noun*. M19.
[Latinized form of *Stradivari* (see below).]
A violin or other stringed instrument made by Antonio Stradivari of Cremona (*c* 1644–1737) or any of his pupils.

strafe /strɑːf, streɪf/ *verb & noun*. *colloq.* (orig. MILITARY). E20.
[from German *Gott strafe England* 'may God punish England', catch-phrase in Germany during the 1914–18 war.]
▶ **A** *verb trans.* **1** Punish; damage; attack fiercely; *fig.* reprimand severely. E20.
2 *spec.* Attack from low-flying aircraft with bombs, machine-gun fire, etc.; bombard, harass with gunfire. E20.

📖 **2** J. G. BALLARD RAF fighters strafed an ammunition train.

▶ **B** *noun*. An act of strafing; an instance of being strafed; *fig.* a severe reprimand. E20.

📖 *Guardian* The subject of the strafe was the standard of food.

■ **strafer** *noun* E20. **strafing** *noun* the action or an act of strafing; an instance of this; *fig.* a severe reprimand: E20.

Straffordian /straˈfɔːdɪən/ *noun*. M17.
[from *Strafford* (see below) + -IAN.]
Hist. Any of the fifty-nine members of the House of Commons who in 1641 voted against the bill impeaching the English statesman Thomas Wentworth, Earl of Strafford (1593–1641). Usu. in *pl.*

straggle /ˈstrag(ə)l/ *noun*. LME.
[from the verb.]
†**1** Straggling order or condition. Only in ***at straggle***, ***at the straggle***, ***to straggle***, ***to the straggle***. *Scot.* LME–M16.
2 A body or group of straggling people or things; an irregular or straggling growth of something. M19.

📖 **2** P. L. FERMOR Gypsy hovels appeared and a straggle of kilns and sheds. L. ERDRICH Her .. hair poked in straggles round her ears.

straggle /ˈstrag(ə)l/ *verb*. LME.
[Perh. alt. of frequentative of STRAKE *verb*¹: see -LE³.]
1 *verb intrans.* Wander, roam (*about*, *away*, etc.); *spec.* stray away from or trail behind a main body, esp. on a line of march. Also NAUTICAL (now *Hist.*), be absent from one's ship without leave, overstay one's leave. LME. ▸**b** Be arranged in a dispersed or sporadic fashion; lack or lose regularity and compactness of design; have an irregular winding course. Also foll. by *away*, *along*, *over*, etc. E17. ▸**c** (Of a plant, branch, etc.) grow irregularly or loosely; grow long and loose; (of hair) grow or spread in thin lank untidy strands. L17.
2 *verb trans.* Cause to straggle; *spec.* †(*a*) scatter, disperse; (*b*) (in *pass.*) be arranged stragglingly. Chiefly as ***straggled*** *ppl adjective*. L16.

📖 **1** *Quarterly Review* They sickened or straggled or frankly deserted. P. LIVELY The mourners straggled out into the road. **b** N. HAWTHORNE The road .. straggled onwards into the .. forest. ANNE STEVENSON Heptonstall straggles along a steep slope near the top of a hill. **c** BROWNING How these tall .. geraniums straggle! A. SILLITOE Her hair straggled untidily over the pillow.

Comb.: **straggle-brained** *adjective* crazy, mentally confused.
■ **straggling** /ˈstraglɪŋ/ *verbal noun* (*a*) the action of the verb; (*b*) *spec.* in NUCLEAR PHYSICS, the spread of the energies, ranges, etc., of charged particles about a mean value as a result of collisions during passage through matter: L16. **stragglingly** *adverb* in a straggling manner L16. **straggly** *adjective* characterized by straggling, tending to straggle M19.

straggler /ˈstraglə/ *noun*. M16.
[from prec. + -ER¹.]
1 A person who straggles; *spec.* (*a*) a person who strays away from or trails behind a main body, esp. on a line of march; (*b*) NAUTICAL (now *Hist.*) a member of a ship's company who is absent from his ship without leave or who overstays his leave. M16. ▸**b** An animal that strays from its habitat or companions; *spec.* (*a*) a migratory bird found outside its usual range; (*b*) *Austral. & NZ* a stray domestic animal, esp. a sheep. M16.
2 A thing that grows stragglingly; *spec.* (*a*) a plant etc. growing singly or apart from others of its kind; (*b*) a plant, branch, etc., growing irregularly or loosely. M16.

straif /streɪf/ *noun*. *obsolete* exc. *dial.* LME.
[Alt. of STRAY *noun* after *waif*.]
A stray animal or thing. Chiefly in ***waifs and straifs***.

straight /streɪt/ *noun*¹. Also †**strait**. LME.
[from STRAIGHT *adjective*¹ & *adverb*¹.]
†**1** ***upon straight***, upright, erect. Only in LME.
2 Straight direction or position. Chiefly in ***on the straight***, ***out of straight*** below. *arch.* M17. ▸**b** *The* truth. Chiefly in ***get at the straight***, ***get the straight***, ***hear the straight***. *US colloq.* M19.
3 A straight form or position; a level. M17. ▸**b** GEOMETRY. A straight line. *rare*. L19.
4 A straight part of something, esp. a racecourse. M19.
5 a In poker etc., a series of five cards forming a sequence but not all of the same suit. M19. ▸**b** SHOOTING. A perfect score, with every shot fired making a hit. E20.
6 a (A drink of) neat or very strong spirits, esp. whisky. *colloq.* (orig. *US*). M19. ▸**b** A cigarette, *esp.* one containing tobacco as opp. to marijuana. *slang*. M20.
7 a = ***straight man*** s.v. STRAIGHT *adjective*¹ & *adverb*¹. M20. ▸**b** A person who conforms to social conventions, *spec.* (*a*) a heterosexual; (*b*) a person who does not take hallucinogenic or narcotic drugs. *slang* (orig. *US*). M20.
8 A shoe designed to be worn on either foot. M20.
Phrases: ***home straight***: see HOME *noun & adjective*. **inside straight** in poker etc., four cards which will form a straight if a fifth card of a particular value is added. **on the straight** (*a*) along a straight line; (*b*) parallel with the side, not diagonally; (*c*) *slang* behaving reputably. **out of straight** deviating from the required straight form or position; out of true; awry. ***upon straight***: see sense 1 above.
¶ Early forms show confusion with *strait*.

†**straight** *noun*² var. of STRAIT *noun*¹.

straight /streɪt/ *adjective*¹ & *adverb*¹. Also †**strait**. ME.
[Obsolete pa. pple & ppl adjective of STRETCH *verb*. Cf. DISTRAUGHT *adjective*.]
▶ **A** *adjective*. **1** Extending uniformly in one direction; not curving, bending, or angular. ME. ▸**b** Of a person, back, etc.: having an erect posture, not bowed or stooping. LME. ▸**c** Of a limb etc.: held with the joint not flexed. LME. ▸**d** Of hair: not curly or waved. M18.
2 Of a road, course, etc.: direct, undeviating; leading directly to a specified destination; not circuitous. LME. ▸**b** Of a look: bold, steady. LME. ▸**c** Of a stroke, throw, etc.: aimed precisely. M19. ▸**d** Of a statement, comment, etc.: outspoken, unreserved; candid, not evasive. *colloq.* L19. ▸**e** Designating or pertaining to a tennis match where the winner has not conceded a set (freq. in ***win in straight sets***); *gen.* (orig. *US*) consecutive, in unbroken sequence. L19. ▸**f** RACING. Designating a bet which backs a horse etc. to win. E20. ▸**g** Straightforward, simple, uncomplicated. M20.
†**3** Of a mountain: steep. *Scot.* LME–L18.
4 a Orig., trustworthy, honest. Later (*colloq.*), law-abiding, not dishonest or criminal. LME. ▸**b** Well-behaved, steady (freq. in ***keep a person straight*** (a) below); *spec.* (of a woman) virtuous, chaste. Now chiefly *arch.* M19. ▸**c** Conforming to perceived standards, conventional, socially acceptable. Also *spec.*, (*a*) heterosexual; (*b*) not characterized by unconventional sexual practices; (*c*) not addicted to or intoxicated by hallucinogenic drugs; sober, abstinent. *slang* (orig. *US*). M20.
5 Not oblique; not deviating from the vertical or the horizontal. L16. ▸**b** CRICKET. Of the bat: held so as not to incline to either side. M19.
6 a With nothing owing, settled, balanced; free from debt or obligation. *colloq.* E17. ▸**b** In proper order, not disturbed or disarranged. M19.
7 a Unmixed, unadulterated, undiluted; *spec.* (of spirits) neat. Orig. *US.* M19. ▸**b** Designating poker, whist, etc., in an unmodified form of the game. M19. ▸**c** Designating or pertaining to jazz characterized by adherence to a score or set orchestration. E20.
8 Of music, drama, literature, etc.: serious as opp. to popular or comic; employing the conventional techniques of its art form. L19.
9 Intoxicated by narcotic or hallucinogenic drugs; high. *US slang.* M20.

📖 **1** J. CONRAD This broad curve in the straight seaboard. TOLKIEN The trail is straight, and turns neither right nor left. **b** TENNYSON A daughter .. Straight, but as lissome as a hazel wand. **c** W. FAULKNER Lying flat .. with .. his arms straight beside him. **2** GEO. ELIOT Hetty .. asked the straightest road northward. **b** G. B. SHAW She takes his hand .. with a frank, straight look into his eyes. **c** *Saturday Review* A straight hit made directly from the shoulder. **d** I. MURDOCH Subtle people .. can see too much ever to give a straight answer. **e** *Daily Telegraph* He should have won in straight sets. *Listener* Company earnings .. reflected their 16th straight annual gain. **f** *Daily Sketch* It .. can be used either for straight or place betting. **g** *Times* The tapes all emerged as inferior in straight comparisons. *Money & Family Wealth* A straight majority of borrowers must approve the change. **4a** R. V. JONES He was far too straight to engage in anything . . not entirely above board. **c** *Sunday Express* Some . . are camp but they know you're straight. **5** DICKENS In its whole constitution it had not a straight floor. OED I don't think that picture is quite straight. **6a** *Listener* After the war we made a huge effort to get straight by austerity and stringent controls. **b** H. MORTEN The . . patients lay quiet . . ; everything was straight for the night. **7a** *Decanter* Connoisseurs choose to drink this Scotch straight, with ice. **8** A. UPFIELD I write . . straight novels, not these beastly thrillers. V. GLENDINNING Edith . . loved music halls, which she preferred to the straight theatre.

Phrases: **get something straight** *colloq.* make something clear, reach an understanding about something. **go straight** *colloq.* (*a*) begin to live honestly or honourably; *spec.* desist from criminal activities, reform; (*b*) begin to conform to social conventions; *spec.* give up the use of hallucinogenic or narcotic drugs, (of a homosexual) adopt a heterosexual way of life. **keep a person straight** (*a*) (now chiefly *arch.*) ensure that a person is well-behaved and steady; (*b*) keep a person informed. ***put the record straight***: see RECORD *noun*. ***royal straight (flush)***: see ROYAL *adjective*. ***set the record straight***: see RECORD *noun*. **straight and narrow** *adjective & noun phr.* (*a*) *adjective* (of a way, course, etc.) strictly in accordance with law and morality; (*b*) *noun the* course of morally correct behaviour.

► **B** *adverb*. **1** In a straight course or direction; directly to or from a place or to a mark or object; without deviating; not circuitously or obliquely; by the shortest way (freq. foll. by *on*). Also, all the way, continuously to the end; right *across*, *through*, etc. ME. ▸†**b** Directly (opposite), due (east etc.). E16–E19. ▸**c** In a straight line, not crookedly. M16.

2 Immediately, without delay. *arch.* LME.

3 In an erect posture, upright. LME.

4 Honestly, honourably. Chiefly in ***go straight*** below. M19.

5 a Without adulteration, admixture, or dilution. *colloq.* (orig. *US*). M19. ▸**b** In a straightforward or simple manner; without embellishment or affectation; seriously, according to the conventional techniques of a specified art form. *colloq.* (orig. *US*). M20.

6 Frankly, outspokenly. Also (*colloq.*), really, certainly, definitely. L19.

7 Consecutively, in a row. *N. Amer. colloq.* M20.

🕮 **1** J. BUCHAN Whenever she saw me she would make straight for me. I. MURDOCH She shone the . . torch straight into my face. P. INCHBALD It's getting . . late . . . Oughtn't we to go straight there. **b** G. B. BELZONI The tomb faces the north-east, and the direction of the whole runs straight south-west. **c** SWIFT I cannot write straighter in bed, so you must be content. *Hair Styling* Long hair shimmers when it's cut straight all around. **2** COLERIDGE The boat came close . . . And straight a sound was heard. LD MACAULAY The bridge must straight go down. **3** R. LEHMANN I was . . standing up straight. **5a** *This Week Magazine* She . . still drinks her liquor straight. **6** D. H. LAWRENCE I'm awfully sorry, I am, straight. M. SPARK I told him straight what I feel. **7** H. ROBBINS People are getting tired of the same show for three weeks straight.

Phrases: **play it straight**, **play straight** (*a*) act (a part) seriously without affectation or 'hamming'; (*b*) play jazz etc. according to a score or set orchestration rather than by improvising. **straight away** at once, immediately. ***straight from the shoulder***: see SHOULDER *noun*. **straight off** *colloq.* immediately, at once, without deliberation or preparation. **think straight** *colloq.* think clearly or logically.

Comb. & special collocations: **straight-A** *adjective* (*N. Amer.*) designating a student with straight A's; **straight-ahead** *adjective* simple, straightforward; *spec.* (orig. *US*) (of popular music) unembellished, unadorned; **straight angle** †(*a*) a right angle; (*b*) an angle of 180 degrees; **straight arch** an arch having radiating joints but a straight intrados and extrados line; **straight-arm** *adjective, noun, & verb* (*a*) *adjective* with the arm unflexed, straight-armed; (*b*) *noun* (orig. AMER. FOOTBALL) an act of warding off an opponent or removing an obstacle with the arm unflexed; (*c*) *verb trans.* (orig. AMER. FOOTBALL) ward off (an opponent) or remove (an obstacle) with the arm unflexed; **straight-armed** *adjective* having a straight arm; with the arm unflexed; **straight arrow** *N. Amer. slang* an honest or genuine person; **straight A's** *N. Amer.* uniform top grades; **straight-backed** *adjective* having a straight back, not bowed or stooping; **straight-bred** *adjective* descended from one breed only, not crossbred; **straight chain** CHEMISTRY a chain of atoms (usu. of carbon) that is neither branched nor formed into a ring; (freq. *attrib.* with hyphen); **straight-cut** *adjective* (*a*) cut on straight lines; (*b*) *slang* honest, respectable; (*c*) (of tobacco etc.) with the leaves cut lengthwise into long strands; **straight drive** CRICKET a drive in which the ball is hit back down the pitch towards or past the bowler; **straight-drive** *verb trans.* (CRICKET) hit (the ball) in a straight drive; **straight driver** CRICKET a batsman who straight-drives the ball; **straight-edge** (*a*) a bar with one edge accurately straight, used for testing; (*b*) (more fully ***straight-edge razor***) = ***straight razor*** below; **straight eight** (a motor vehicle having) an internal-combustion engine with eight cylinders in line; **straight eye** the ability to see whether an object is placed straight; **straight face** an intentionally expressionless face, esp. avoiding a smile though amused; **straight-faced** *adjective* having a straight face, solemn; **straight-facedly** *adverb* in a straight-faced manner; **straightfacedness** the state or quality of being straight-faced; **straight fight** a direct contest between two candidates; ***straight flush***: see FLUSH *noun*³; **straight forth** (now *arch. rare*) (*a*) directly in front or onwards; (*b*) immediately, at once; **straight goods** *US slang* (*a*) the truth; (*b*) an honest person; **straight-grain** BOOKBINDING morocco damped and worked to produce a grain in parallel straight lines; **straight-grained** *adjective* (BOOKBINDING) (of morocco) damped and worked to produce a grain in parallel straight lines; **straight-haired** *adjective* having straight hair, *spec.* leiotrichous; **straight job** *US slang* a single-unit truck, having the body built directly on to the chassis; **straight leg** *US Military slang* a member of the non-flying personnel; **straight-line** *adjective* (*a*) that follows a straight line, undeviating; *fig.* direct, uncomplicated; (*b*) of or pertaining to a method of depreciation allocating a given percentage of the cost of an asset each year for a fixed period; **straight-lined** *adjective* composed of or containing straight lines; having the form of a straight line; rectilinear; **straight man** a performer who provides lines or cues for a comedian to react to, a stooge, a feed; **straight muscle** *spec.* (now *rare*) the rectus muscle of the eye; **straight mute** a simple cone-shaped mute for a trumpet or trombone; **straight-necked** *adjective* having a straight neck; *spec.* (of a hunted animal, esp. a fox) running with outstretched neck or in a straight line; **straight-out** *adjective & noun* (*colloq.*, chiefly *US*) (*a*) *adjective* unrestrained, completely (esp. politically) committed to a course of action; straightforward, unqualified, genuine; (*b*) *noun* a straight-out supporter, an uncompromising partisan; **straight peen** a type of hammer having the peen in line with the handle; †**straight-pight** *adjective* (*rare*, Shakes.) having a tall and erect figure; **straight razor** a razor with a long blade that folds into its handle for storage, a cutthroat razor; **straight-run** *adjective* (OIL INDUSTRY) (of a petroleum fraction) produced by distillation without cracking or other chemical alteration of the original hydrocarbons; **straight shooter** *slang* (chiefly *N. Amer.*) an honest person; **straight six** (a motor vehicle having) an internal-combustion engine with six cylinders in line; **straight stitch** a single short separate embroidery stitch; **straight talk** *colloq.* a piece of plain speaking; **straight time** (orig. & chiefly *US*) payment for work carried out within normal or regular hours; **straight-time** *adjective* (orig. & chiefly *US*) of or pertaining to straight time; **straight ticket** the list of a party's official candidates (chiefly in ***vote the straight ticket***); ***straight tip***: see TIP *noun*⁶; **straight up** *adverb* (*N. Amer. colloq.*) (*a*) truthfully, honestly; (*b*) without admixture or dilution; **straight-up** *adjective* (*a*) perpendicular; (*b*) *colloq.* exact, complete; true, trustworthy; (*c*) *N. Amer. colloq.* unmixed, undiluted; **straight-up-and-down** *adjective* (*a*) simple, presenting no difficulties; (*b*) candid, straightforward; ***straight wire***: see WIRE *noun*.

¶ Early forms show confusion with *strait*.

■ **straightish** *adjective* somewhat straight, fairly straight L18. **straightly** *adverb* (*a*) in a straight manner; in a straight line; directly; (*b*) (*poet. & dial.*, *rare*) immediately, at once: LME. **straightness** *noun* E16.

†**straight** *adjective*² & *adverb*² var. of STRAIT *adjective*¹ & *adverb*¹.

straight /streɪt/ *verb trans.* Now chiefly *Scot.* LME.
[from STRAIGHT *adjective*¹.]
1 Stretch (*out*); extend. LME.
2 Make straight, straighten. Also, lay out (a corpse). M16.

straightaway /streɪtəˈweɪ/ *adverb, adjective, & noun.* M17.
[from STRAIGHT *adverb*¹ + AWAY *adverb*.]
► **A** *adverb*. (Also as two words.) Immediately, at once, without deliberation or preparation. M17.

🕮 M. E. ATKINS He would send . . a van straightaway and tow her car in.

► **B** *adjective*. Of a course etc.: straight, direct. Chiefly *US*. L19.

► **C** *noun*. A straight course in rowing or sailing. Also, a straight section esp. of a road or racecourse. Chiefly *N. Amer.* L19.

straighten /ˈstreɪt(ə)n/ *verb*¹. Also †**straiten**. M16.
[from STRAIGHT *adjective*¹ + -EN⁵.]
1 *verb trans.* Make straight. Also foll. by *out*. M16.
2 *verb trans. fig.* Unravel, disentangle, clarify; *colloq.* make a situation clear to (a person). Now only foll. by *out*. L16.
3 *verb trans.* Put in order, tidy up. Also (*slang*), repay money to (a person). M19.
4 *verb intrans.* **a** Become straight. Also foll. by *out*. L19. ▸**b** Stand *up*. L19.
5 *verb intrans.* **a** Settle *up* an account or debt with a person. *colloq.* E20. ▸**b** Foll. by *up*: adopt an honest course of life; reform. *slang* (orig. *US*). E20.
6 *verb trans.* Bribe, corrupt. Also foll. by *out*. *slang* (orig. *US*). E20.

🕮 **1** J. DICKEY The . . arrow was badly bent, and I straightened it. P. MARSHALL He examined . . her chemically straightened hair. **2** H. C. BEECHING Moral questions that I should like to hear straightened out. W. STYRON You're confusing me. Straighten me out. **4a** R. KIPLING Dick's shoulders straightened again.

■ **straightener** *noun* E17.

†**straighten** *verb*² var. of STRAITEN *verb*¹.

straightforward /streɪtˈfɔːwəd/ *adjective & adverb.* E19.
[from STRAIGHT *adverb*¹ + FORWARD *adverb*.]
► **A** *adjective*. **1** Proceeding or directed straight forward; without circumlocution or digression; undeviating. E19.
2 Purposeful, unwavering, single-minded. Now *esp.*, frank, honest, outspoken. E19.
3 Presenting a clear course; free from difficulties; uncomplicated, simple. M19.

🕮 **1** N. HAWTHORNE Its peculiar expression eludes a straightforward glance. B. JOWETT Of . . benevolent actions we can give a straightforward account. **2** R. C. TRENCH Serving with a straightforward and downright obedience . . God. T. S. ELIOT Excuse my bluntness: I am a rough straightforward Englishman. **3** R. FRAME Summer-wear was straightforward: a . . cotton shift and espadrilles. *Which?* A fairly straightforward installation job should cost . . £20.

► **B** *adverb*. Directly in front or onwards; in direct order. Now *rare*. E19.

🕮 J. F. W. HERSCHEL To walk uprightly and straight-forward on firm ground.

■ **straightforwardly** *adverb* M19. **straightforwardness** *noun* E19.

†**straight-lace** *verb*, **straight-laced** *adjective* see STRAIT-LACE *verb*, STRAIT-LACED.

straightwards /ˈstreɪtwədz/ *adverb*. Long *obsolete* exc. *dial. rare*. M17.
[from STRAIGHT *adverb*¹ + -WARDS.]
In a straight direction.

straightway /ˈstreɪtweɪ/ *adverb*. *arch.* LME.
[Orig. two words, from STRAIGHT *adjective*¹ + WAY *noun*.]
†**1** By a direct course, straight from or to a place. LME–L16.
2 Immediately; without delay; at once. E16.

🕮 **2** E. B. BROWNING Straightway everybody followed my good example.

straightways /ˈstreɪtweɪz/ *adverb*. Now *rare* or *obsolete*. E16.
[Orig. two words, formed as prec. + -WAYS.]
1 = STRAIGHTWAY 2. E16.
†**2** In a straight line. Only in L18.

straightwise /ˈstreɪtwʌɪz/ *adverb*. *rare*. L16.
[formed as prec. + -WISE.]
= STRAIGHTWAY 2.

straik /streɪk/ *noun*¹. *Scot. & north.* M16.
[from (the same root as) STRAIK *verb*¹.]
1 A levelled measure of corn etc. Freq. in ***by straik***. Cf. STRICK *noun* 2. M16.
2 A piece of wood coated with sand or emery, used for sharpening a scythe. E18.
3 The required quantity of malt for a brewing. Also, the liquor prepared from this. Now *rare*. E19.

straik *noun*² see STRAKE *noun*.

straik /streɪk/ *verb*¹ *trans. Scot.* L16.
[Prob. var. of STROKE *verb*¹.]
Level (corn etc.) in a measure. Cf. STRICK *verb* 1.

straik *verb*² see STRAKE *verb*¹.

strain /streɪn/ *noun*¹.
[Old English (Northumbrian) *strīon* aphet. from *ġestrēon* = Old Saxon, Old High German *gistriuni* rel. to Old English *(ġe)strēonan*, *(ge)strienan* gain, get, beget = Old High German *(gi)striunen*, from Germanic, rel. to Latin *strues* pile, heap, *struere* pile up, build. Cf. STRIND *noun*.]
†**1** Gain, acquisition; treasure. OE–ME.
†**2** Begetting, generation. Only in ME.
†**3** A speck, spot, or thread found in an egg (esp. representing, or thought to represent, the embryo). ME–M18.
4 Offspring, progeny. Now *arch. rare*. ME.
5 Pedigree, lineage, ancestry, descent. *arch.* ME.
6 a The descendants of a common ancestor; a race, a stock, a line. ME. ▸**b** A specified line of ancestry; a genealogical admixture of a specified kind. M19.
7 a A tendency, quality, or feature of a person's character or constitution perceived as being hereditary; an admixture of a specified quality in a person's character. L16. ▸**b** Character or constitution perceived as being hereditary. E17.
8 A kind or class of person or thing having some attribute in common. Now *rare*. L16.
9 A breed or stock of animals, plants, etc.; a variety developed by breeding; a distinct (natural or cultured) variety of a micro-organism. E17.

🕮 **4** P. J. BAILEY The starry strain of spirit, thence we are. **5** T. HEYWOOD Epaphus . . To Phaeton objects, that he was bred Of mortall straine. **6a** M. PRIOR The long Heroes of the Gallic Strain. **b** G. J. WHYTE-MELVILLE The strain of Greek blood . . tempered his Roman courage, with the pliancy, essential to conspiracy. *Pall Mall Gazette* These animals are . . better if dashed with a strain of the bloodhound. **7a** J. O'HARA The suicide strain had skipped one generation to come out in the next. A. S. BYATT Single-mindedness was another strain in the Potter character. **b** J. TILLOTSON Infirmities and diseases, which being propagated, spoil the Strain of a Nation. **8** R. W. EMERSON A genius of so fine a strain. **9** R. CARSON Insects . . developing strains resistant to chemicals. J. RABAN To cross-breed cattle and develop new strains of maize. **Strain 19** a strain of the bacterium *Brucella abortus* used as a vaccine against brucellosis in horses and cattle.

strain /streɪn/ *noun*². LME.
[from STRAIN *verb*¹.]
►†**I 1** A utensil or device for straining, a strainer. LME–M17.
► **II** †**2** Constraint, bondage. Also, compulsion. E16–M17.

3 An injury caused by straining a muscle etc. M16.
4 An extension to an extreme degree of a quality, activity, etc.; a stretch. Now *rare*. L16. ▸†**b** Chiefly *LAW*. A strained construction or interpretation. L16–M18.
5 a A strong muscular effort. Formerly *spec.*, an effort to vomit, a retching. L16. ▸**b** Extreme or excessive effort; a straining *at* or *after* an objective. Formerly also, laboured or affected speech or thought. L17.
6 Force tending to pull things apart, move a thing against resistance, or alter a thing in shape; the condition of a body or a particle subjected to such force or pressure; *spec.* in *techn.* use, the proportional deformation produced in a body by the application of stress. Also *loosely*, load, stress. E17.
7 †**a** In *pl.* Trials, hardships. Only in E17. ▸**b** Pressure or exigency that makes severe demands on one's strength, endurance, or resources or that puts at risk a feeling, relation, or condition. M19. ▸**c** An expense or financial liability incurred by an insurance office which is not covered by reserves accumulated from the relevant policies. E20.

> 📖 **3** W. TREVOR Hoovering brings on the strain in her back. **4** SWIFT To Break an.. Officer only for Blasphemy, was.. a very high strain of absolute Power. **5a** W. F. BUTLER Row, .. row away... Bend to the strain, men! **b** J. MORLEY They move without conscious.. strain after virtue. **6** J. S. FOSTER Since the cantilever at this point is neither stretched nor compressed there is no strain in it. **7b** E. JOHNSON Both feared his health would break down under the strain of foreign travel. P. ROAZEN It caused a permanent strain on their marriage.

▸ **III 8 a** Orig., a passage of the Bible. Later, a passage or extract of a song or poem. M16. ▸**b** A stream or flow of impassioned or uncontrolled language. Now *rare* or *obsolete*. M17.
9 *MUSIC*. A definite section of a piece of music. L16. ▸**b** A musical sequence of sounds; a melody, a tune. L16.
10 Style or manner of expression; a tone or tendency in speech or writing. E17.

> 📖 **8a** J. MARTINEAU Who, having the strains of David, would pore over Leviticus? **b** STEELE Addresses came.. with foolish Strains of Obedience without Reserve. **9b** BARONESS ORCZY The dainty strains of the minuet. **10** J. BRUCE Observe the strain and character of that wonderful reply. B. WEBB A curious strain of contempt underlying his pleasant banter.

▸†**IV 11** The track of a deer. E–M17.

Phrases etc.: **at full strain**, **at strain** straining, using the utmost effort. **take the strain** assume a burden, take a responsibility.
Comb.: **strain ageing** *METALLURGY* the cold working of iron and steel followed by ageing, either at room temperature or at temperatures up to the recrystallization temperature; the resultant increase in hardness and decrease in ductility; **strain energy** (*a*) *MECHANICS* energy stored in an elastic body under loading; (*b*) *CHEMISTRY* the excess heat of formation of a cyclic molecule over the value calculated from corresponding bonds in non-cyclic molecules; **strain gauge** *ENGINEERING* a device for indicating the strain of a material or structure at the point of attachment; **strain-harden** *verb intrans.* undergo strain hardening (freq. as ***strain-hardened*** *ppl adjective*); **strain hardening** *METALLURGY* increase in strength and hardness and decrease in ductility of a metal as a result of strain ageing; **strainmeter** *ENGINEERING* = ***strain gauge*** above; **strain rosette** *ENGINEERING* = ROSETTE *noun* 1(e); **strain-slip cleavage** *GEOLOGY* a rock structure characterized by parallel, closely-spaced shear planes with microscopic transverse folds between them.
■ **strainful** *adjective* (*rare*) causing or filled with strain; stressful: M20.

strain /streɪn/ *verb*[1]. ME.
[Old French *estrei(g)n-* stem of *estreindre* (mod. *étreindre*) from Latin *stringere* draw tight, bind tightly.]
▸ **I 1** *verb trans.* †**a** Bind fast; confine in bonds. ME–M16. ▸**b** Fasten or attach firmly *to*. Long *rare* or *obsolete*. LME.
†**2** *verb trans.* Control, restrain. ME–L16.
3 *verb trans.* Clasp tightly in one's arms (now only *to* oneself, one's heart, etc.). LME.
4 †**a** *verb intrans. & trans.* Esp. of a hawk: seize (prey) in the claws. LME–L16. ▸**b** *verb trans.* Clasp tightly in the hand; *spec.* †(*a*) press or squeeze (another's hand or fingers, a person by the hand), esp. in affection or farewell; (*b*) *rare* clasp (one's own hands) forcibly; (*c*) *arch.* grip or grasp tightly (a weapon etc.). E16.
5 *verb trans.* Orig., hurt by physical pressure; pinch. Later *spec.*, constrict painfully (as) with a binding cord. LME.
†**6** *verb trans.* **a** Compress, contract, or diminish in bulk or volume. Also, draw (the brows) *together*. LME–M16. ▸**b** *refl.* Squeeze oneself through a constricted space. Only in 17.
†**7** *verb trans.* Press hard on, afflict, distress. LME–M18.
†**8** *verb trans.* Force, press, or constrain (*to, to do*). LME–E17. ▸**b** Urge or insist on (a thing). LME–E17.
†**9** *verb trans.* Extract (liquor or juice) by pressure; squeeze *out*; *fig.* extort (money, a confession, etc.). L15–E19.

> 📖 **1b** C. MERIVALE The bonds which strained them to the conquerors. **2** T. PHAER You gave me might these stormy winds to strain. **3** SHAKES. *Hen. VIII* Our king has all the Indies in his arms.. when he strains that lady. D. H. LAWRENCE 'Sure?' she whispered, straining him to her. **4b** SIR W. SCOTT Straining the curtal-axe in his gripe. J. S. WINTER 'Mrs Ferrers,' cried Lassie, straining her.. hands together... 'Tell me the whole truth.' **5** TENNYSON The wounding cords that bind and strain The heart. **6b** MARVELL Practising.. To strain themselves through Heavens Gate. **7** T. BOSTON Being strained with this message I laid it before the Lord. **8** R. KNOLLES The enemie,.. strained by necessitie, .. will prey vpon your countries. **b** SHAKES. *Oth.* Note if your lady strain his entertainment With any strong or vehement importunity. **9** SHAKES. *Merch. V.* The quality of mercy is not strain'd: It droppeth as the gentle rain from heaven. POPE The Bard.. strains, from hard-bound brains, eight lines a year.

▸ **II 10** *verb trans.* Extend with some effort; subject to tension, stretch; *spec.* (*a*) tie or fasten (bonds etc.) tightly; †(*b*) stretch and hold extended (a person's body or limbs) on a cross, rack, etc., as torture or punishment; (*c*) extend and make taut (a line, wire, etc.), stretch (material) *on* a frame, *over* a surface, etc.; (*d*) tighten up (a string of a musical instrument) to raise the pitch. LME.
11 *verb trans. fig.* ▸**a** Distort the meaning or sense of (words, a decree, etc.). LME. ▸**b** Transgress the strict requirements of (one's conscience), violate the spirit of (one's oath). L16. ▸†**c** Apply or use (a thing) beyond its province. L16–M17. ▸**d** Force (prerogative, power, etc.) beyond its legitimate extent or scope. E17. ▸†**e** Raise to an extreme degree. Only in 17. ▸**f** Orig., make severe demands on the resources of (a person). Later, make severe or excessive demands on (one's resources, credit, friendship, etc.). E17. ▸†**g** Insist on unduly, be excessively punctilious about. M17–E18. ▸**h** Bring (a person, situation, etc.) to a state of extreme tension. M17.
12 *verb trans.* Stretch (one's sinews, nerves, muscles) beyond the normal degree (as) through intense exertion; force to extreme effort, exert to the utmost (one's limbs, powers, etc.). LME. ▸**b** *verb intrans.* Of the eye or ear: try to make out an indistinct sight or sound. Chiefly *poet.* M19.
13 a *verb trans.* Injure (a limb, muscle, tendon, etc., oneself) by stretching or overexertion; sprain. E17. ▸**b** *verb trans.* Impair or put at risk the strength of (a material thing) by excessive tension or disruptive force. M18. ▸**c** *verb trans.* *PHYSICS & ENGINEERING.* Subject to strain, distort by loading. M19. ▸**d** *verb intrans.* *ENGINEERING.* Be subjected to strain, be distorted. M19.

> 📖 **10** DRYDEN Beware To strain his Fetters with a stricter Care. *Law Times* The barbed wire fence.. was strained to posts.. 6ft. high. **11a** LD MACAULAY Defective laws should be altered.., and not strained by the tribunals. *Times* Kallir .. says that these painters were 'not professional artists', but this is surely straining words. **d** W. S. CHURCHILL The King .. strained all expedients to the limits. **e** DRYDEN She strains her Malice more. **f** E. LONGFORD French finances were so dangerously strained that he was planning.. loans. **h** MILTON Matters now are strain'd Up to the highth. C. LAMB While he held you in converse, you felt strained to the height. **12** M. ELPHINSTONE This.. exercise only operates on the arms.., but the others strain every muscle in the frame. E. BOWEN Straining her eyes over her work. **b** R. C. HUTCHINSON My ears were straining for the return of the planes. **13a** Z. TOMIN The professor had strained his back. **b** SMOLLETT The coach was so hard strained, that one of the irons which connect the frame snapped.

▸ **III 14** *verb trans.* Pass (liquid) through a porous or perforated medium, esp. a sieve or similar device, which keeps back solid matter; free (solid matter) from liquid by this process; purify or refine by filtration. LME. ▸**b** Remove (liquid) by filtration, drain off. Also foll. by *from, out, off*. E16.
15 *verb intrans.* Filter; trickle; *rare* (of a stream) flow. L16.

> 📖 **14** *Green Cuisine* Strain the yoghurt through a J-cloth. **b** T. BRUGIS Straine all the.. water from them through a .. Cloth. **15** BACON Sea water.. Straying through the Sandes, leaueth the Saltnesse. J. BUCHAN The river.. strains in mazy channels and backwaters.

▸ **IV 16** *verb refl.* Exert oneself physically, esp. so as to be in danger of injury. Now *rare* or *obsolete* exc. as passing into sense 12. LME.
17 a *verb intrans.* Make violent and continuous physical effort; exert oneself to the utmost. Also foll. by *forward, together*. LME. ▸**b** *verb intrans.* Of a deer: run at full speed, gallop. Now *rare*. L16. ▸†**c** *verb trans.* Direct (one's steps) hastily; make (one's way) with effort. L16–M18. ▸**d** *verb intrans.* Pull forcibly (*at* a rope etc.). L18.
18 *verb intrans.* Use one's utmost endeavours; strive vigorously. Also foll. by *to do, after, for*. L16.
19 *verb intrans.* **a** Make an effort to defecate. M17. ▸†**b** Retch, heave, make an effort to vomit. L17–E18.

> 📖 **16** R. BROME Use this whistle for me, I dare not straine my selfe to winde it. **17a** R. BRAUTIGAN The first-grader strained around, trying to read what was written on his back. *transf.*: T. S. ELIOT Words strain, Crack and sometimes break. **b** SIR W. SCOTT Nor farther might the quarry.. strain. **d** B. CHATWIN A.. spaniel was panting and straining at its leash. **18** R. GRAVES Straining in memory, I can find No cause why you should weep. F. TOMLIN Jean Cocteau's straining after effect.

▸†**V 20** *verb trans.* Use (the voice) in song; play on (an instrument). Also, utter (words, notes, etc.) in song. L16–M17. ▸**b** *verb intrans.* Sing. *rare*. Only in E17.

> 📖 **20** SHAKES. *Rom. & Jul.* The lark.. sings so out of tune, Straining harsh discords. E. FAIRFAX The priests.. With sacred hymnes their holy voices straine.

Phrases etc.: **strain a point** *arch.* exceed customary or permitted limits in one's course of action. **strain at** make a difficulty of accepting; scruple at; see also sense 17d above. **strain at a gnat** [with allus. to *Matthew* 23:24, where sense is properly 'strain a liquid if it contains even a gnat'] be unduly fussy or scrupulous about something of little importance. ***strain at the leash***: see LEASH *noun*. ***strain every nerve***: see NERVE *noun* 1a. **strain up** force up to a higher scale of estimation.
■ **strainable** *adjective* (*rare*) L15.

strain /streɪn/ *verb*[2]. *obsolete* exc. *dial.* LME.
[Aphet. from DISTRAIN.]
LAW. †**1** *verb trans.* = DISTRAIN 1, 3. LME–L17.
2 *verb intrans.* = DISTRAIN 2. E16.

strained /streɪnd/ *adjective*. LME.
[from STRAIN *verb*[1] + -ED[1].]
That has been strained; *spec.* (*a*) produced under compulsion or by deliberate effort; artificial, forced, not spontaneous or natural; (*b*) showing signs of nervous tension; (*c*) distorted from the natural meaning or intention; laboured, far-fetched; (*d*) subjected to a dangerous degree of tension, brought to breaking-point (*lit. & fig.*).

> 📖 G. GREENE The strained good humour, the jest with dry lips, went on and on. M. FRAYN She sat pale and strained, her eyes cast down, saying nothing. V. GLENDINNING The atmosphere.. in Miss Fry's study was strained.

■ **strainedly** *adverb* L16. **strainedness** *noun* M17.

strainer /ˈstreɪnə/ *noun*. ME.
[formed as prec. + -ER[1].]
1 A person who or thing which strains; *spec.* a utensil or device for straining, filtering, or sifting; a filter, a sieve, etc.; any natural structure or process performing a similar function. ME.
2 A device for stretching or tightening. E16.
3 = ***straining-post*** s.v. STRAINING *noun*. *Austral. & NZ*. L19.
Comb.: **strainer arch**: placed across an aisle, nave, etc., to prevent the walls leaning inwards; **strainer post** (chiefly *Austral. & NZ*) = ***straining-post*** s.v. STRAINING *noun*.

straining /ˈstreɪnɪŋ/ *noun*. LME.
[from STRAIN *verb*[1] + -ING[1].]
1 The action or an act of straining; the fact of being strained. LME.
2 A substance strained or extracted by straining; *esp.* a strained liquid. L16.
Comb.: **straining-frame** a frame on which paper, canvas, etc. is stretched; **straining-post** a post from which wire fencing is stretched tight.

straining /ˈstreɪnɪŋ/ *adjective*. LME.
[formed as prec. + -ING[2].]
†**1** Astringent, styptic. *rare*. LME–M16.
2 That strains. M16.
■ **strainingly** *adverb* L15.

strainless /ˈstreɪnlɪs/ *adjective*. E20.
[from STRAIN *noun*[2] + -LESS.]
Produced without strain; free from strain.
■ **strainlessly** *adverb* E20.

strainometer /streɪˈnɒmɪtə/ *noun*. E20.
[from STRAIN *noun*[2] + -OMETER.]
= ***strain gauge*** s.v. STRAIN *noun*[2].

straint /streɪnt/ *noun*. *rare*. M16.
[Aphet. from Old French *estrainte*, *estreinte* (mod. *étreinte*), from *estreindre* STRAIN *verb*[1].]
Application of force or pressure.

strait /streɪt/ *noun*[1]. Also †**straight**. ME.
[formed as STRAIT *adjective*[1] & *adverb*[1].]
1 A time of great need or of awkward, difficult, or distressing circumstances, a difficulty, a fix (now usu. in *pl.*). Also (now *rare* or *obsolete*), a dilemma, a difficult choice. ME. ▸**b** *gen.* Privation, hardship. M19.
2 *sing.* & †in *pl.* A narrow confined place, space, or way. Formerly also *sing.*, a narrow lane, alley, or passage. Now *rare* or *obsolete*. LME. ▸**b** *spec.* A narrow passage in the body. *arch.* M16.
3 *sing.* & (usu.) in *pl.* A narrow passage of water connecting two seas or large bodies of water. Now chiefly in proper names. LME.
4 †**a** A narrow pass or gorge between mountains; a defile, a ravine. LME–L18. ▸**b** A narrow stretch of a river; in *pl.*, narrows. Now *rare* or *obsolete*. LME. ▸**c** A narrow strip of land with water on each side, an isthmus. Now *poet.* *rare*. M16.
†**5** In *pl.* Cloth of single width. LME–E18.
6 A tile about half the usual breadth, for a gable end. E18.

> 📖 **1** J. F. HENDRY The Rilkes were in dire financial straits. G. DALY There was always room at Cheyne Walk for a fellow artist in straits. **3** ***Davis Strait***, ***Straits of Gibraltar***, ***Straits of Malacca***, etc.

Phrases & comb.: **Straits-born** *adjective* born in the former Straits Settlements. **Straits Chinese** a person of Chinese origin born in the former Straits Settlements. †**straits of time** pressure or insufficiency of time. **Straits Settlements** *Hist.* the British possessions in the Malay peninsula. **up the Straits** *Nautical slang* in the Mediterranean.
¶ Early forms show confusion with *straight*.

†**strait** *noun*[2] var. of STRAIGHT *noun*[1].

strait /streɪt/ *adjective*[1] & *adverb*[1]. Also †**straight**. ME.
[Aphet. from Old French *estreit* (adjective) tight, close, narrow, (noun) narrow place, strait of the sea, distress, from Latin *strictus* STRICT. Cf. STRESS *noun*.]
▶ **A** *adjective*. **I 1** Of limited spatial capacity; cramped, confined. *arch.* ME.
2 Of a passageway etc.: so restricted in scope as to make transit difficult. Now chiefly *fig.*, esp. in ***strait and narrow*** below. *arch.* ME.
3 Tightly joined or fitted; *spec.* (*a*) (of a garment) tight-fitting; †(*b*) (of bonds, a knot) tightly fastened; †(*c*) (*rare*, Spenser) (of an embrace) close; †(*d*) (of muscles etc.) tense, not lax. *obsolete* exc. *Scot.* & *dial.* ME.
†**4** Of limited breadth or width; narrow. LME–E16.

📖 **1** J. A. FROUDE The . . pasture grounds were too strait for the numbers crowded into them. **2** SIR W. SCOTT If the stairs be too strait to admit his fat carcass. LD MACAULAY That road was . . so strait that a handful of resolute men might have defended it. **strait and narrow** *the* conventional, limited course or way of life. **3** L. STERNE His blue and gold had become so miserably too strait for him.

▶ **II** †**5** Rigorous, severe; involving hardship or privation; strictly regulated. ME–M17.
6 Orig., exacting in one's actions or dealings, stern, strict. Later *spec.*, strict or scrupulous in morality or religious observance. *arch.* ME.
7 Stringent, strictly worded or enforced, allowing no evasion. Formerly also *spec.*, (of a legal instrument) peremptory. *arch.* ME.
8 Of imprisonment etc.: close, strict. Formerly also, (of an action, proceeding, etc.) strictly conducted. Now *rare*. ME.

📖 **5** S. PURCHAS They . . containe their bodies in strait chastitie. **6** SHAKES. *Timon* Five talents is his debt; His means most short, his creditors most strait. J. PRIESTLEY Educated . . in very straitest principles of reputed orthodoxy. **7** TENNYSON Then the King . . Bound them by so strait vows to his own self. **8** CARLYLE Back to thy Arrestment, . . or indeed to strait confinement.

▶ **III** †**9** Strictly specified, exact, precise; *esp.* (of an account) exactly rendered. ME–M17.
†**10** Stingy, close, selfish. ME–M18.
11 †**a** Of means, circumstances, etc.: limited so as to cause hardship or inconvenience; inadequate. LME–L18. ▸**b** Of a person: in want *of*, straitened *for*. *obsolete* exc. *Scot.* & *dial.* M17.
12 Of a word etc.: limited in application or meaning. *obsolete* exc. *dial.* LME.
13 Of friendship etc.: close, intimate. Now *rare*. E16.

📖 **9** S. HIERON The word Create: in strait speaking, it betokeneth the making of a thing of nought. **10** SHAKES. *John* I beg cold comfort; and you are so strait . . that you deny me that. L. STERNE A sordid wretch, whose strait heart is open to no man's affliction. **11a** J. LOGAN Money is hard to be got out of the Treasury these strait times. **13** H. ROGERS Or any similar strait alliance . . of religion and morality.

Special collocations & comb.: **strait waistcoat** a strait-jacket. **strait-waistcoat** *verb trans.* confine in a strait-jacket.
▶ **B** *adverb*. **1** Tightly. *obsolete* exc. *dial.* ME.
†**2** In careful keeping, securely; in close confinement or strict custody. ME–E17.
3 Severely, oppressively; so as to cause hardship. Now *rare*. ME.
†**4** With rigorous exactness; strictly, exactly, precisely. ME–L16.
5 Graspingly, stingily, avariciously. *obsolete* exc. *dial.* ME.
†**6** In a crowded condition; with adequate space. LME–M16.
¶ Early forms show confusion with *straight*.
■ **straitly** *adverb* (*arch.*) in a strait manner; strictly, severely: ME. **straitness** *noun* (*arch.*) the state of being strait; an instance of this; strictness, severity; (a) hardship, (a) privation: ME.

†**strait** *adjective*[2] & *adverb*[2] var. of STRAIGHT *adjective*[1] & *adverb*[1].

strait /streɪt/ *verb*. Long *obsolete* exc. *Scot.* ME.
[from STRAIT *adjective*[1].]
†**1** *verb trans.* Confine in or force into a narrow space, hem in. ME–M17.
2 *verb trans.* Cause to become narrow, make narrow; reduce in size. Usu. in *pass.* LME.
†**3** *verb trans. fig.* Press severely on; subject to hardship; (in *pass.*) be hard put to it, be at a loss. LME–M17.
4 *verb trans.* Tighten, make taut or more secure. *rare*. LME.
5 *verb trans.* Restrict in freedom of action; constrain. L15–M17.
†**6** *verb trans.* Keep poorly supplied, stint. E16–M17.
7 *verb trans.* Limit in amount or degree; impute limitation to. M16–M17.

straiten /ˈstreɪt(ə)n/ *verb*[1]. Also †**straighten**. E16.
[from STRAIT *adjective*[1] + -EN[5].]
1 *verb trans.* †**a** Deprive partially *of* (a possession or privilege). E16–M17. ▸**b** Reduce or restrict the freedom, power, or privileges of (a person). *arch.* L16.
2 *verb trans.* Make narrow; *esp.* narrow or contract (a passage, road, stream, etc.). *arch.* M16. ▸†**b** Close the ranks of (an army). *rare*. L16–E17.
3 *verb trans.* Confine in or force into a narrow space; hem in closely. Also foll. by *in*. Now *rare*. L16.
4 *verb intrans.* Become narrow. *arch.* E17.
5 *verb trans.* Reduce to straits; subject to privation, hardship, or distress. E17. ▸**b** Inconvenience by shortage of something specified (freq. foll. by *for*). Usu. in *pass.* *arch.* E17. ▸**c** *spec.* Make short of money, impoverish. L17.
†**6** *verb trans.* Hamper, impede in action. E17–E18.
7 *verb trans.* Tighten (a knot, bonds, etc.). *obsolete* exc. *Scot.* M17.
8 *verb trans.* Restrict in range, scope, or amount. M17.

📖 **1a** J. HOWELL The King is streightned of that liberty he formerly had. **b** J. MARTINEAU Our spirit . . is so straitened by the bands of sin . . that there is no freedom. **2** J. AUSTEN The passage was straitened by tables. J. M. GOOD The throat is rough and straightened from the second day of the eruption. **3** MILTON To dwell In narrow circuit strait'nd by a Foe. A. P. STANLEY The small tribe of Dan, already straitened between the mountains and the sea. **4** G. J. CAYLEY The valley . . began to straiten . . to so narrow a gorge. **5** W. H. PRESCOTT The viceroy . . endeavoured to straiten the garrison there by desolating the surrounding country. R. ADAMS He was a vagabond in a strange country, . . straitened by need. **b** D. HUME The garrison, being straightened for provisions, were obliged to capitulate. **7** POPE Morality . . Gasps, as they straiten at each end the cord. **8** A. W. KINGLAKE The conquest of the shores of the Bosphorus . . would straiten . . England's authority in the world.

Phrases: **straiten a person's quarters** (chiefly MILITARY) reduce the area occupied by a person.
■ **straitened** *ppl adjective* that has been straitened; *spec.* (of circumstances) characterized by hardship or poverty: E17.

†**straiten** *verb*[2] var. of STRAIGHTEN *verb*[1].

strait-jacket /ˈstreɪtdʒakɪt/ *noun* & *verb*. E19.
[from STRAIT *adjective*[1] + JACKET *noun*.]
▶ **A** *noun*. A strong garment for the upper body, usu. having long sleeves, for confining the arms of a violent prisoner, mental patient, etc.; *fig.* a severe restriction. E19.

📖 *attrib.*: R. GODDEN I did write poems but always in some strait-jacket form: sonnets, rondels, triolets.

▶ **B** *verb trans.* Confine in a strait-jacket; *fig.* severely restrict. Usu. in *pass.* M19.

📖 G. B. SHAW The dramatist is so strait-jacketed in theories of conduct.

strait-lace /streɪt ˈleɪs/ *verb trans.* & *intrans.* Also (earlier) †**straight-**. M17.
[Back-form. from next.]
Fasten (a garment etc.) with a lace or laces. Freq. as ***strait-lacing*** *verbal noun*.

strait-laced /streɪt ˈleɪst/ *adjective*. Also (earlier) †**straight-**. M16.
[from STRAIT *adverb*[1] + LACED *adjective*.]
1 †**a** Limited or restricted in range or scope; *spec.* (of a person) uncommunicative, unsympathetic; obstinate, grudging. M16–L17. ▸**b** Of a person etc.: excessively rigid or scrupulous in matters of conduct; severely virtuous; prudish. M16.
2 †**a** Wearing a tightly laced bodice or other garment. E17–E18. ▸**b** Of a bodice etc.: tightly laced. Now *rare* or *obsolete*. M19.
■ **straitlacedness** *noun* L19.

strake /streɪk/ *noun*. Also (*Scot.*) **straik**. ME.
[Anglo-Latin *stracus*, *straca*, prob. from Germanic base of STRETCH *verb*. Cf. STRECK, STREEK.]
1 A section of the iron rim of a wheel; a strip of iron fixed along or across the edge of a wheel (cf. TIRE *noun*[2]). Also, a strip of iron attached to the left side of a plough. ME.
2 A stripe or streak of different colour from the rest of the surface of which it forms part; a ray or streak of light. Now *Scot.* & *dial.* LME.
3 NAUTICAL. Each of the continuous lines of planking or plates of uniform breadth in the side of a vessel, extending from stem to stern. Also, the breadth of a plank as a unit of vertical measurement in a ship's side. LME.
4 A strip or narrow tract of land or water. Now only *Scot.* E16. ▸**b** A stretch of ground travelled over. Also, length of stride; speed in travelling, pace. Now only *Scot.* M16.
5 A swath (of mown grass); a wisp (of straw). L16.
6 A wheel-rut, a furrow. *rare*. Now *Scot.* E17.
7 *sing.* & in †*pl.* MINING. A shallow pit (usu. lined with boards) or a wooden trough or sluice used for washing or concentrating ore. M18.
8 A protruding ridge on a chimney or similar structure to prevent oscillation in the wind; a similar attachment on an aircraft, vehicle, etc., for this purpose or generally to improve aerodynamic stability. Cf. SPOILER 3. M20.
■ **straky** *adjective* (now *dial.*) streaky M17.

strake /streɪk/ *verb*[1]. Also (*Scot.*) **straik**. ME.
[from (Germanic base of) STRAKE *noun*.]
▶ **I 1** *verb intrans.* Move, go, proceed. Now *rare* or *obsolete*. ME.
2 *verb intrans.* Extend, stretch. Chiefly *dial.* L16.
▶ **II 3** *verb trans.* Mark with lines, streak. Chiefly *dial.* Cf. STROKE *verb*[2] 1. Chiefly *dial.* M16.
4 *verb intrans.* Become streaky. *rare*. E20.
▶ **III 5** *verb trans.* MINING. Wash or concentrate (ore) in a strake. L18.

strake *verb*[2] see STROKE *verb*[1].

straked /streɪkt/ *adjective*[1]. Now *rare*. ME.
[from STRAKE *verb*[1] + -ED[1].]
Streaked, striped.

straked /streɪkt/ *adjective*[2]. L16.
[from STRAKE *noun* + -ED[2].]
Of a wheel: fitted with strakes.

stram /stram/ *verb intrans.* *dial.* & *US colloq.* Now *rare* or *obsolete*. Infl. **-mm-**. L18.
[Origin unkn.]
Stretch out the limbs; walk with a flourish.

stramash /strəˈmaʃ/ *verb* & *noun*. Chiefly *Scot.* & *north*. L18.
[App. imit.: cf. SMASH *verb*[1].]
▶ **A** *verb trans.* Smash. L18.
▶ **B** *noun*. **1** An uproar, a state of noise and confusion; a row. E19.
2 A state of ruin, a smash. E19.

†**stramazon** *noun*. L16–E19.
[Italian *stramazzone* (French *estramaçon*) a knock-down blow, from *stramazzare* knock (a person) down, from *stramazzo* straw mattress, straw scattered on the floor from *strame* from Latin *stramen* straw.]
FENCING. A high vertical downward cut.

strambotto /stramˈbɒtto, stramˈbɒtəʊ/ *noun*. Pl. ***-tti*** /-(t)ti/. E20.
[Italian.]
An Italian verse form of eight lines, common esp. in the 15th and 16th cents. and freq. set to music.

stramin /ˈstramɪn/ *noun*. E20.
[Maker's name in Danish.]
A kind of coarse sacking formerly used for making plankton nets.

stramineous /strəˈmɪnɪəs/ *adjective*. E17.
[from Latin *stramineus*, from *stramen* straw: see -OUS.]
1 Consisting of or relating to straw; *fig.* valueless. E17.
2 Chiefly BOTANY. Straw-coloured; dull pale yellow. M19.

strammel /ˈstram(ə)l/ *noun*. Orig. *slang*. Now only *Scot.* Also (earlier) †**stru-**. M16.
[Perh. ult. from French *estramer* spread with straw or rushes, from Latin *stramen* straw.]
1 Straw. M16.
†**2** Hair. E18–L19.

stramonium /strəˈməʊnɪəm/ *noun*. M17.
[mod. Latin *stram(m)onium*, perh. rel. to Russian *durman*.]
1 The thorn-apple, *Datura stramonium*. M17.
2 An alkaloid prepared from this plant, related to atropine. E19.

strand /strand/ *noun*[1].
[Old English *strand* = Middle Low German *strant*, *strand* (whence Dutch, German *Strand*), Old Norse *strǫnd*, of unkn. origin.]
1 The land bordering a sea, lake, or (formerly) a river; a coast, a shore, a beach; *esp.* the part of a shore which lies between the tidemarks or (ECOLOGY) just above the high-water mark. Exc. *techn.* now *arch.* & *dial.* OE.
†**2** A quay, wharf, or landing-place by the side of navigable water. ME–M19.
3 ***the Strand***, a street in London, the buildings along which originally ran down to the shore of the River Thames between London and Westminster. ME.
4 A region, a land, *esp.* a foreign country. Chiefly *poet.* LME.

📖 **1** B. MOORE A cove where curraghs were drawn up on the strand.

Comb.: **strandflat** a very wide rocky platform, close to sea level, that extends along much of the Norwegian coastline between cliffs and the sea; a part of this; **strand-line** a line marking the position of a former shoreline from which the sea (or a lake) has since receded; **strand-wolf** *S. Afr.* the striped hyena.

strand /strand/ *noun*[2]. Chiefly *Scot.* & *north*. Now *rare*. ME.
[Origin unkn.]
1 A stream, a brook, a rivulet; a stream of liquid. Formerly also (*poet.*), a body of water, the sea. ME.
2 A channel, a gutter. *Scot.* M16.

strand /strand/ *noun*[3]. **L15.**
[Origin unkn.]
1 Each of the strings or yarns which, when twisted together or laid, form a rope, cord, line, fibre, cable, etc. **L15.** ▸**b** Each of the lengths of twisted wire used to form an electric cable or similar conductor. **M19.**
2 Each of the threads or strips in a woven or plaited material; a thread or strip drawn from such material. **E19.**
3 Any long narrow esp. flexible piece of material; *esp.* (***a***) a string of beads, pearls, etc.; the material on which they are strung; (***b***) a tress or thin lock of hair; (***c***) a thread or filament in an animal or plant structure; (***d***) a single linear polymer of a long-chain molecule, esp. DNA. **E19.**
4 a *fig.* A single theme, line of reasoning, etc., within a more complex whole. **E19.** ▸**b** *BROADCASTING.* A regular series of programmes with a common theme, style, or format. **L20.**

📖 **1** E. WILSON The . . wool . . comes in three strands which can be easily separated. **3** P. GALLICO Three strands of pearls were wound about her throat. S. RADLEY Alison pushed a strand of damp hair out of her eyes. *Practical Gardening* The fungal strands penetrate the roots of the tree. **4a** I. MURDOCH I am simply trying to hold on to the strands of . . quite a complicated argument.

strand /strand/ *verb*[1]. **E17.**
[from STRAND *noun*[1].]
1 *verb trans.* **a** Drive or wash aground on a shore or bank; leave aground (esp. by the ebbing of the tide); beach, ground. Freq. in *pass.* **E17.** ▸**b** *fig.* Abandon in an isolated or inaccessible position; leave (behind), esp. by withdrawing a means of access or transport. Usu. in *pass.* **M19.**
2 *verb intrans.* Run aground. **L17.**

📖 **1** G. GREENE The water went down too quickly and one of them was stranded. **b** *Listener* Holidaymakers . . are stranded all night in their cars at Dover because of a seamen's strike. **2** *Ships Monthly* She stranded off a desolate stretch of the African coast.

■ **stranding** *verbal noun*[1] the action of washing ashore, running aground, etc.; an instance of this: **E19.**

strand /strand/ *verb*[2]. **L18.**
[from STRAND *noun*[3].]
1 a *verb intrans.* Of a rope: break one or more of its strands. **L18.** ▸**b** *verb trans.* Break one or more of the strands of (a rope). Usu. in *pass.* **M19.**
2 *verb trans.* Form (a rope, wire, etc.) by twisting strands together. **L19.**
3 *verb trans.* Insert a strand or filament into; fix a strand or thread across. **L19.**
■ **stranding** *verbal noun*[2] (***a***) the action of the verb, esp. in rope-making; (***b***) the process of cutting furs or leather in diagonal strips and resewing in a longer narrower shape: **E19.**

†**strandage** *noun.* **ME–E18.**
[from STRAND *noun*[1] + -AGE.]
A charge or toll levied on fish or other commodities landed on a strand.

stranded /ˈstrandɪd/ *ppl adjective*[1]. **E18.**
[from STRAND *verb*[1] + -ED[1].]
1 That has been driven or washed ashore; that has run or been left aground. **E18.**
2 *fig.* Abandoned in an isolated or inaccessible position; left (behind) in difficulties, esp. by the withdrawal or failure of a means of access or transport. **M19.**

stranded /ˈstrandɪd/ *ppl adjective*[2]. **E19.**
[from STRAND *verb*[2], *noun*[3]: see -ED[1], -ED[2].]
1 Of a rope: having one or more strands broken. **E19.**
2 Composed of (a specified number of) strands. **L19.**
3 Of a fur garment: made of skins cut into diagonal strips and resewn. **M20.**
2 ***double-stranded***, ***three-stranded***, etc. ***single-stranded***: see SINGLE *adjective*.

Strandlooper /ˈstrandluːpə, *foreign* ˈstrantlʊəpər/ *noun.* Also **-loper**, **s-**. **M18.**
[Afrikaans *strandloper*, from Dutch *strand* seashore, STRAND *noun*[1] + *lo(o)per* walker, runner.]
1 Any of various birds of sandy (esp. coastal) regions of southern Africa, *esp.* a sand plover. *S. Afr.* **M18.**
2 A member of a people, related to the Bushmen and Nama, who lived on the southern shores of southern Africa from prehistoric times until the last millennium. Also, a member of a people, possibly the same, still living on the Namibian coast. *S. Afr.* **M19.**
3 *ARCHAEOLOGY.* Usu. in *pl.* A member of any prehistoric people who were nomadic about coastal areas or inland shores. **M20.**
4 A beachcomber. *colloq.* **M20.**
■ **strandlooping** *adjective & noun* (*ARCHAEOLOGY*) wandering about coastal areas or lake shores **M20.**

Strandveld /ˈstrandvɛlt, -ntf-/ *noun. S. Afr.* **L19.**
[Afrikaans, from Dutch *strand* (see prec.) + VELD. Cf. SANDVELD.]
The Strandveld, a strip of flat land along the southernmost coast of Africa.

strange /streɪn(d)ʒ/ *adjective & adverb.* **ME.**
[Aphet. from Old French *estrange* (mod. *étrange*) from Latin *extraneus*: see EXTRANEOUS. Cf. ESTRANGE.]
► **A** *adjective.* †**1** Of or belonging to another country; originating or situated outside one's own land, foreign, alien. **ME–M18.**
2 Of a person etc.: belonging to some other place or neighbourhood; unknown to the locality specified or implied. **ME.**
3 Belonging to others; not of one's own kin or family. Long *obsolete* exc. *dial.* **ME.**
4 Unknown, unfamiliar; not known or experienced before. (Foll. by *to.*) **ME.**
5 Unusual, abnormal, now esp., to a degree that excites wonder or astonishment; remarkable, extraordinary, queer, surprising, peculiar, unaccountable. **ME.**
6 Of a person: unfriendly; shy; distant or cold in demeanour; not affable, familiar, encouraging, or compliant. *arch. & dial.* **ME.**
†**7** Introduced from outside, not originating where it is found; *MEDICINE* = FOREIGN *adjective* 8. **LME–L17.**
8 Exceptionally great (in degree, intensity, amount, etc.), extreme. *obsolete* exc. as passing into sense 5. **LME.**
9 Of a person: unfamiliar or unacquainted with something (specified or implied); fresh or unaccustomed *to*. **M16.**
10 *PARTICLE PHYSICS.* Of, designating, or containing any of the class of subatomic particles that have a non-zero strangeness value (orig. so called as having unexpectedly long lifetimes); designating a quark flavour associated with a charge of −⅓ (symbol *s*). **M20.**

📖 **1** M. PARKER To the reader, both English and strange. **2** SWIFT A strange Dog happens to pass through a Flesh-Market. **4** C. S. FORESTER Everything was strange to him in the darkness. INA TAYLOR It was very brave . . to stay on alone in a strange country. A. STEVENS All young animals . . possess a . . wariness of anything strange. **5** C. DARWIN Successive males . . perform strange antics before the females. J. M. BARRIE It is strange that one so common should attract one so fastidious. U. LE GUIN Others thought him strange, unlike them. *New Scientist* Centaurs, dragons, unicorns, virgins, . . and other strange and wondrous beings. **10** ***strange matter***, ***strange quark***, etc.

Phrases: **feel strange** (***a***) feel slightly unwell; (***b***) be uncomfortable or ill at ease. **make strange** (now *dial. & N. Amer.*) make difficulties, refuse to assent or comply, be reluctant or uncooperative; be distant or unfriendly, affect coyness or ignorance, affect or feel surprise, dislike, or indignation. **strange to say** it is surprising or unusual (that).
Special collocations: **strange attractor** *MATH.* (an equation or fractal set representing) a complex pattern of non-repetitive behaviour typical of certain dynamic systems involving feedback or sensitive dependence on initial conditions (also called ***chaotic attractor***). **strange woman** *arch.* a prostitute; *the* class of prostitutes collectively.

► **B** *adverb.* **1** In a peculiar, surprising, or unusual manner; strangely. Now *dial.* or *colloq.* **M16.**
2 Very, extremely. Now *dial.* **M17.**

strange /streɪn(d)ʒ/ *verb.* Now *Scot. & dial.* **LME.**
[Aphet. from Old French *estrangier* ESTRANGE.]
†**1** *verb trans.* Estrange; remove, keep apart, or estrange *from*. Also, make strange or different. **LME–E18.**
†**2** *verb intrans.* Be removed or become alienated *from*; become strange or changed. Only in **LME.**
3 *verb intrans. & trans.* Be surprised, wonder at or *at*. **M17.**

Strangelove /ˈstreɪn(d)ʒlʌv/ *noun.* **L20.**
[formed as DR STRANGELOVE.]
= DR STRANGELOVE.
■ **Strange'lovean**, **-ian** *adjective* characteristic of a Dr Strangelove **L20.**

strangely /ˈstreɪn(d)ʒli/ *adverb.* **LME.**
[from STRANGE *adjective* + -LY[2].]
†**1** In an unfriendly or unfavourable manner; with cold or distant bearing. **LME–E18.**
2 In an uncommon or exceptional degree; very greatly, extremely. *obsolete* exc. as passing into sense 3. **LME.**
3 In an unusual or exceptional manner, esp. so as to excite wonder or astonishment; surprisingly, unaccountably, oddly. **LME.**

📖 **3** C. PHILLIPS Venice looked strangely distant and eerie. *Sun* Customs officers spotted him walking strangely.

strangeness /ˈstreɪn(d)ʒnɪs/ *noun.* **LME.**
[from STRANGE *adjective* + -NESS.]
1 The quality of being strange, unfamiliar, unusual, or extraordinary. **LME.** ▸**b** A strange circumstance, object, event, etc. Formerly also, strange matter, strange stuff. **M16.**
†**2** Absence of friendly feeling or relations; discouraging or uncomplying attitude towards others; coldness, aloofness. **LME–M18.**
3 *PARTICLE PHYSICS.* A property of matter manifested in certain hadrons, now attributed to a strange quark and represented by a quantum number S, which is conserved in strong but not weak interactions; the flavour of the strange quark. **M20.**

stranger /ˈstreɪn(d)ʒə/ *noun & adjective.* **ME.**
[Aphet. from Old French *estrang(i)er* (mod. *étranger*), from Latin *extraneus*: see STRANGE *adjective*, -ER[2].]
► **A** *noun.* †**1** An unusual verse form. Only in **ME.**
2 A person who belongs to another country, a foreigner; *esp.*, a person who lives in or comes to a country to which he or she is a foreigner; an alien. Now *rare* exc. as passing into senses 3, 5. **LME.** ▸†**b** A thing that comes from abroad; *esp.* an exotic plant. **L16–M18.**
3 A person who is not a native of a country, town, or place; a newcomer, a person who is not (yet) acquainted with a place or is not (yet) well known. **LME.** ▸†**b** In parochial registers: a person not belonging to the parish. Only in **16.**
4 a A guest, a visitor, a person who is not a member of the household. Now passing into sense 5. **LME.** ▸**b** A thing popularly imagined to forebode the coming of an unexpected visitor, as a floating tea leaf in a cup, an excrescence on the wick of a candle, a piece of soot flapping on the bar of a grate, or a moth flying towards one. Chiefly *dial.* **L18.**
5 a An unknown person; a person whom one has not seen before. Also, a person with whom one is not (yet) well acquainted, a person who is not, or is no longer, a friend. Freq. in ***a perfect stranger***, ***a total stranger***, ***an utter stranger***. (Foll. by *to.*) **LME.** ▸**b** A person whose visits have long ceased; an infrequent visitor. **M16.** ▸**c** In full ***little stranger***. A newborn or expected child. *joc.* **L17.** ▸**d** As a form of address: a person whose name is unknown, or (*joc.*) who has not been seen for some time. *colloq.* (orig. *US dial.*). **E19.** ▸**e** An animal which has strayed from a neighbouring flock or herd. *Austral. & NZ.* **M19.**
6 a A non-member of a society. Now *rare.* **LME.** ▸**b** In the Houses of Parliament and other courts and parliaments, a person who is not a member or official and may be present only on sufferance. **E18.**
7 †**a** A person who has no share in (some privilege or business). Foll. by *of*, *from*. **L15–E17.** ▸**b** *LAW.* A person who is not privy or party *to* an act or action (opp. ***privy***). Also, a person not standing towards another in some implied relation. **M16.**
8 An alien thing; a thing that has no place in a class, a thing's nature, a person's character or thoughts, etc. Foll. by *to*. Now *rare.* **E17.**
9 a Any of several uncommon moths; *esp.* the small noctuid *Lacanobia blenna*, of coastal regions in Continental Europe. **M19.** ▸**b** An Australasian fish similar to a wrasse, *Haletta semifasciata* (family Odacidae), which is blue with gold stripes. Also called ***rock whiting***, ***blue rock whiting***. *Austral.* **L19.**

📖 **2** E. A. FREEMAN In a generation or two the stranger ceased to be a stranger. **3** F. HERBERT The stranger might think nothing could live or grow in the open here. **4a** I. MURDOCH Jack did not like strangers in the house, so there was no regular charwoman. **5a** A. EDEN A great number of people, many of them strangers, for some came from distant parts of the estate. **b** A. UPFIELD Hello, Mr. Muir! You're quite a stranger.

Phrases: **be a stranger to** (***a***) be unaware or ignorant of; (***b***) be unaccustomed to or unacquainted with, have no experience of. **make a stranger of** treat with ceremony, not as one of the family (usu. with neg.). **spy strangers** in Parliamentary use, formally demand the exclusion of non-members from the House by the conventional formula 'I spy strangers'.

► **B** *attrib.* or as *adjective.* That is a stranger; of, or pertaining to strangers; foreign, alien. Chiefly *poet.* **LME.**
■ **strangerhood** *noun* = STRANGERSHIP **M19.** **strangership** *noun* the condition or fact of being a stranger **E19.**

stranger /ˈstreɪn(d)ʒə/ *verb trans. rare.* **E17.**
[from the noun.]
†**1** Make a stranger of; alienate. (Shakes.) Only in **E17.**
2 Make strange. **M19.**

📖 **1** SHAKES. *Lear* Dower'd with our curse, and stranger'd with our oath.

strangle /ˈstraŋg(ə)l/ *noun.* **LME.**
[from the verb.]
†**1** The action of strangling; strangulation. **LME–M17.**
†**2** = STRANGLES. **L16–E17.**
3 = STRANGLEHOLD 1. **L19.**

strangle /ˈstraŋg(ə)l/ *verb.* **ME.**
[Aphet. from Old French *estrangler* (mod. *étrangler*) from Latin *strangulare* from Greek *straggalan* rel. to *straggalē* halter, cogn. with *straggos* twisted.]
1 *verb trans.* **a** Kill by external compression of the throat or windpipe, esp. by means of a rope or the hands passed tightly round the neck. **ME.** ▸**b** Constrict painfully (the neck or throat). **LME.**
2 *verb trans.* Kill by stopping the breath; smother, suffocate, choke. Now *rare.* **ME.** ▸†**b** Kill by poison etc.; *rare* kill by the sword. **LME–E17.**
3 *verb intrans.* Be choked or suffocated; be strangled. **ME.**
4 *verb trans.* **a** Hinder the growth of (a plant) by crowding or entwining it; impede the action of (an internal

bodily organ) by compression; *fig.* suppress (a laugh, a gasp, a yawn). Formerly also, stifle or quench (a fire, heat). **LME.** ▸**b** *fig.* Prevent the growth or rise of; hamper or destroy by excessive restrictions; suppress. **LME.**

> **1a** P. D. JAMES Out there somewhere is a mass murderer who enjoys strangling women. **b** JOYCE A . . muffler strangling his unshaven neck. **3** R. DAHL She dropped . . soapflakes into his open mouth . . . Would he strangle? **4a** *National Geographic* Rata . . strangles the tree to which it attaches itself. U. LE GUIN She laughed her loud, cheerful laugh, quickly strangling it so as not to wake the baby. **b** J. H. ROSE The exclusive privileges retained by the Dutch . . almost strangled the trade of Antwerp.

Comb.: **strangle-weed** any of several kinds of dodder (genus *Cuscuta*).

▪ **strangled** *ppl adjective* that has been strangled, choked, or suppressed; uttered (as if) from a constricted throat: **LME.**

stranglehold /ˈstraŋɡ(ə)lhəʊld/ *noun.* **L19.**
[from STRANGLE *noun, verb* + HOLD *noun*¹.]
1 *WRESTLING.* A hold which stops the opponent's breath. **L19.**
2 *fig.* Complete and exclusive control (over a person, situation, etc.). (Foll. by *on.*) **E20.**

strangler /ˈstraŋɡlə/ *noun.* **LME.**
[from STRANGLE *verb* + -ER¹.]
1 A person who or thing which strangles someone or something. **LME.**
2 *spec.* **a** *BOTANY.* An epiphytic plant, esp. in a tropical rainforest, which smothers its host tree with twining branches or aerial roots. **L19.** ▸**b** = CHOKE *noun*² 7. **E20.**
Comb.: **strangler tree** *US* any of several trees of the genus *Clusia* (family Guttiferae), which grow as parasites on other trees.

strangles /ˈstraŋɡ(ə)lz/ *noun.* **E17.**
[Pl. of STRANGLE *noun*: see -S¹.]
A disease in horses and related animals, characterized by inflamed swellings in the throat. Now *spec.* an infectious streptococcal fever, esp. affecting the respiratory tract.

strangulate /ˈstraŋɡjʊleɪt/ *verb trans.* **M17.**
[Latin *strangulat-* pa. ppl stem of *strangulare* STRANGLE *verb*: see -ATE³.]
†**1** Choke, stifle, suffocate. Only in **M17.**
2 *MEDICINE.* Constrict or compress (an organ, duct, hernia, etc.) so as to prevent circulation or the passage of fluid; remove (a growth) by constricting it with a ligature. **L18.**
3 = STRANGLE *verb* 1a. *rare.* **E19.**
4 Choke (a plant); prevent the flow of sap in (a tree). **M19.**

strangulated /ˈstraŋɡjʊleɪtɪd/ *ppl adjective.* **L18.**
[from prec. + -ED¹.]
1 *MEDICINE.* Of a vessel, an intestine, etc.: congested by constriction and the lack of circulation. **L18.**
2 (Of a voice, speech, etc.) sounding as though the speaker's throat is constricted; (of prose etc.) cramped or forced in style. **M20.**
1 strangulated hernia a hernia so constricted at its neck that circulation or passage of fluids in the protruded part is impaired or prevented.

strangulation /straŋɡjʊˈleɪʃ(ə)n/ *noun.* **M16.**
[Latin *strangulatio(n-)*, formed as STRANGULATE: see -ATION.]
1 The action or process of stopping respiration by compression of the air passage, esp. by a forcible compression of the windpipe; the condition of being so strangled. **M16.**
2 *MEDICINE.* Constriction so as to stop circulation or the passage of fluids, esp. as a complication of hernia. **M18.**
3 Chiefly *BIOLOGY.* A strangulated part; a constriction. *rare.* **E19.**
4 Excessive constriction of a channel or passage. **L19.**

strangullion /straŋˈɡʌljən/ *noun.* Now *rare* or *obsolete.* **LME.**
[Old French *(e)stranguillon* (mod. *étranguillon*) from Italian *stranguglione*, from Latin *strangulare* STRANGLE *verb*.]
A disease, esp. in horses, characterized by inflammation and swelling of the glands of the throat.

strangury /ˈstraŋɡjʊri/ *noun.* **LME.**
[Latin *stranguria* from Greek *straggouria*, from *stragg-*, *stragx* drop squeezed out + *ouron* urine: see -Y³.]
MEDICINE. A condition characterized by pain in the urethra and a strong desire to urinate, caused by irritation of the bladder or by some invasive cancers.
▪ **stran'gurious** *adjective* (*rare*) of, pertaining to, characteristic of, or affected with strangury **M18.**

strap /strap/ *noun.* **L16.**
[Dial. form of STROP *noun*.]
†**1** A snare for birds. **L16–E17.**
2 A piece of timber serving to fasten two objects together, or to support the roof of a mine. Now *rare* or *obsolete.* **L16.**
3 *NAUTICAL.* = STROP *noun* 2. **E17.**
4 A fixed loop or band of leather, cloth, etc., to be grasped by the hand or arm, as used to draw on a boot, to steady oneself in a moving vehicle, etc. **E17.** ▸**b** A short band attached to the bottom of each leg of a pair of trousers, that passes from side to side under the foot or the boot. Usu. in *pl.* **M19.**
5 a A narrow band of iron or other metal used in the form of a plate, loop, or ring to fasten a thing in position, hold together timbers or parts of machinery, etc. **E17.** ▸**b** A narrow flattened projection on a metal article for screwing down to a wooden surface or for slipping under a metal plate; *esp.* each of the leaves of a strap-hinge. **M19.**
6 A narrow strip of leather, cloth, or other material, freq. fitted with a buckle, esp. as used to fasten or secure something. **L17.** ▸**b** A leather band or thong used for flogging; (usu. with *the*) the application of this as a punishment. **E18.**
7 *MEDICINE.* A band of material used to hold in place a broken or dislocated limb etc.; a strip of adhesive plaster used to hold together the edges of a wound, fasten on a dressing, etc. **E18.**
8 A razor-strop. *obsolete* exc. *dial.* **M18.**
9 *MECHANICS.* An endless band or belt by which motion is transmitted between two wheels, pulleys, etc. **L18.**
10 Credit, trust. Freq. in ***on strap***, ***on the strap***. *slang.* **E19.**
11 As a term of abuse: an impudent woman or girl. *Anglo-Irish.* **M19.**
12 An energetic spell of work. *colloq. rare.* **M19.**
13 *JOURNALISM.* In full ***strap-line***. A subsidiary heading or caption, *esp.* one printed above a headline. **M20.**

> **6** F. KING The children wore identical white shoes, with straps across the instep. P. FARMER Undoing his straps, she lugs the baby out of the pushchair. ***chin-strap***, ***shoulder-strap***, ***watch-strap***, etc. **b** A. S. NEILL As a young teacher, I used the strap vigorously.

Comb.: **strap-bolt** *noun & verb* (*a*) *noun* a bolt with a flattened end for riveting or screwing down to a surface; (*b*) *verb trans.* fasten *down* with a strap-bolt; **strap brake** a brake consisting of a friction strap applied to a cylindrical bearing surface; **strap-end** (chiefly *ARCHAEOLOGY*) a metal fastening on the end of a strap; **strap-fork** a device with prongs for guiding the driving-belt of a machine from one pulley to another; **strap-game** (*obsolete* exc. *Hist.*) a cheating game; (also called ***fast and loose***); **strap handle** a handle on a ceramic jug, ewer, etc., made from a flattened piece of clay formed into a loop; **strap-handled** *adjective* having strap handles; **strap-hang** *verb intrans.* (*colloq.*) be a straphanger in a railway carriage etc.; **straphanger** *colloq.* a passenger compelled to stand and hold on by a strap in a crowded bus, railway carriage, etc.; *gen.* a person who commutes to work by public transport; **strap hinge** (*a*) a hinge with long leaves or flaps for screwing down to a surface; (*b*) a hinge with one leaf lengthened for insertion into an iron plate; **strap iron** (chiefly *US*) iron in the form of long narrow strips, esp. used as binding plates; **strap-laid** *adjective* (of a rope) made in a flat form by binding together two or more hawser-laid ropes; ***strap-line***: see sense 13 above; **strap-rail** *US* a flat railway rail laid on a continuous longitudinal sleeper; **strap railroad**, **strap railway**, **strap road** *US* a railway line constructed with strap-rails; **strap-shaped** *adjective* long, narrow, and parallel-sided; *BOTANY* (of a floret in a composite flower) ligulate; **strap shoe** a shoe fastened by means of a strap across the instep; **strapwork** ornamentation in the form of narrow flat bands or fillets of metal, wood, embroidery, etc., folded and interlaced; **strapwort** a small annual plant of SW England and much of western Eurasia, *Corrigiola litoralis*, of the pink family, with strap-shaped leaves and tiny white flowers.
▪ **strapless** *adjective* not having a strap or straps; *spec.* (of a woman's dress) without shoulder-straps: **M19.** **straplike** *adjective* resembling (that of) a strap **M19.**

strap /strap/ *verb.* Infl. **-pp-**. **E18.**
[from the noun.]
▶**I** *verb trans.* **1** Provide with a strap; fasten, bind, or secure with a strap or straps. (Foll. by *on*, *up*, *together*, etc.) **E18.** ▸**b** *MEDICINE.* Apply straps of adhesive plaster to (a wound, swollen joint, etc.); fasten (dressing) *on* with tape or plaster; (foll. by *up*) dress and bandage (a wound, a wounded person). **M19.**
2 Beat with a strap or leather thong. **M18.**
3 Sharpen (a razor or knife), esp. with a strap or strop; strop. Now chiefly *US.* **L18.**
4 Groom (a horse). **M19.**
5 Give credit for (goods); buy (goods) on credit. *dial.* & *slang.* **M19.**

> **1** J. WINTERSON Two hairy arms lifted me up and strapped me on to a cold trolley. K. ISHIGURO Setsuko was strapping up his sandals.

▶**II** *verb intrans.* **6** Work closely and energetically (*at* a task); buckle down *to* one's work. Also foll. by *away*. *slang.* **E19.**
7 Of a person: be bound and hanged. *Scot. rare.* **E19.**
8 Be fastened by a strap. **E20.**
Phrases: **strap in**, **strap oneself in**, **strap oneself up**, **strap up** fasten one's safety belt.
Comb.: **strap-down** *adjective* (*ASTRONAUTICS*) designating an inertial guidance system in which the gyroscopes are fixed to the vehicle rather than mounted in gimbals; **strap-on** *adjective* & *noun* (*a*) *adjective* that can be attached by a strap or straps; *spec.* in *ASTRONAUTICS*, designating a booster rocket mounted on the outside of the main rocket so as to be jettisonable; (*b*) *noun* a strap-on booster.

St Raphaël /sɛ̃ rafaɛl/ *noun.* **L19.**
[See below.]
An aperitif wine from St Raphaël, a town in the department of Var in SE France.

strapontin /strapɔ̃tɛ̃/ *noun.* Pl. pronounced same. **E20.**
[French.]
A tip-up seat, usu. additional to the ordinary seating in a theatre, taxi, etc., esp. in France.

strappado /strəˈpɑːdəʊ, stra-, -ˈeɪdəʊ/ *noun.* Pl. **-os.** **M16.**
[French *(e)strapade* from Italian *strappata* from *strappare* snatch: see -ADO.]
Hist. **1** A form of punishment or torture in which the victim was secured to a rope, usu. with the hands tied behind the back, made to fall from a height almost to the ground, then stopped with a jerk; an application of this; the instrument used. **M16.**
†**2** [By confusion with STRAP *noun* 6b.] A beating, a flogging. **M17–M18.**

strapped /strapt/ *adjective.* **L18.**
[from STRAP *noun* + -ED².]
1 a Provided with a strap, bound or fastened with a strap or straps. **L18.** ▸**b** Trimmed with straps; *spec.* (of a seam etc.) strengthened by overlaying with a strip of stronger material. **L19.**
2 Subject to a shortage (esp. of money). Now freq. foll. by *for*. *colloq.* (orig. *US*). **M19.**

> **2** E. WHARTON 'Fact is . . I'm a little mite strapped just this month.' T. D. RHONE When you are a bit strapped for cash, check with me.

strapper /ˈstrapə/ *noun.* **L17.**
[from STRAP *verb* + -ER¹. In sense 1 from STRAPPING *adjective*.]
1 A tall robust person, esp. a woman. *colloq.* **L17.**
2 A person who straps or grooms horses. Now chiefly *Austral.* **E19.**
3 A worker who provides or secures a thing with straps. **L19.**
4 An apprentice, a learner, a junior. Cf. UNDERSTRAPPER. *slang.* **L20.**

strapping /ˈstrapɪŋ/ *noun.* **E19.**
[from STRAP *verb* + -ING¹.]
1 The action of STRAP *verb*; an instance of this. **E19.**
2 a *MEDICINE.* Adhesive plaster for binding up wounds. **E19.** ▸**b** Iron straps or bands for strengthening woodwork etc. **M19.** ▸**c** Leather straps for harness, machinery, etc. **L19.** ▸**d** *DRESSMAKING.* Trimming composed of narrow bands. **L19.**

strapping /ˈstrapɪŋ/ *adjective* (usu. *attrib.*). **M17.**
[from STRAP *verb* + -ING².]
1 Orig., (of a young woman) full of activity, vigorous, lusty. Now, (of a person of either sex, a racehorse, etc.) strongly and stoutly built, robust, sturdy. **M17.**
2 Big, whopping. *colloq. rare.* **E19.**

> **1** M. R. MITFORD A stout strapping country wench. *Times* They . . are the finest-looking men you want to see; all well-built, strapping fellows.

strapple /ˈstrap(ə)l/ *noun & verb.* Long *obsolete* exc. *dial.* **OE.**
[Origin unkn.]
▶†**A** *noun.* A band wrapped round the lower leg. **OE–L15.**
▶**B** *verb trans.* †**1** Provide with strapples. Only in **E17.**
2 Entangle, bind with cords or straps. **E17.**

strappy /ˈstrapi/ *adjective.* **L20.**
[from STRAP *noun* + -Y¹.]
Of footwear or clothes: having (esp. prominent) straps.

Strasbourg /ˈstrazbəːɡ, -bʊəɡ/ *noun.* Also **-burg.** **L19.**
[The principal town of Alsace in NE France.]
1 Used *attrib.* in the names of things associated with Strasbourg. **L19.**
2 The European Parliament, established in 1958, based in the premises of the Council of Europe at Strasbourg. Also, the European Court of Human Rights. **L20.**
1 Strasbourg pâté pâté de foie gras, formerly esp. as made into Strasbourg pie. **Strasbourg pie** goose liver pâté enclosed in pastry. **Strasbourg turpentine**: obtained from the silver fir, *Abies alba*.

Strasbourgeois /strazburʒwa/ *adjective & noun.* **L20.**
[French, from prec. + *-ois* -ESE.]
▶**A** *adjective.* Of, belonging to, or characteristic of Strasbourg. **L20.**
▶**B** *noun.* Pl. same. A native or inhabitant of Strasbourg. **L20.**

Strasburg *noun* var. of STRASBOURG.

strass /stras/ *noun*¹. **E19.**
[German, from Josef *Strasser* (fl. 18th cent.), the inventor.]
A dense form of glass used to make imitation jewellery; paste.

strass /stras/ *noun*². **E20.**
[French *strasse* threads of waste raw silk.]
A kind of waxed straw with a silky appearance, used for dress trimmings etc.

strata *noun pl.* see STRATUM.

stratagem /ˈstratədʒəm/ *noun*. L15.
[French *stratagème* from Latin *strategema* from Greek *stratēgēma*, from *stratēgein* be a general, from *stratēgos* STRATEGUS.]
1 A military ploy, a piece of strategy, *esp.* an artifice or trick designed to outwit or surprise the enemy. L15. ▸**b** *gen.* Military artifice. L16.
2 An artifice, a trick, a device or scheme for gaining an advantage. L16. ▸**b** Skill in devising expedients; cunning. L16.
†**3** A bloody or violent deed. L16–E17.
■ **strategeˈmatical** *adjective* (*arch. rare*) = STRATAGEMICAL E17. **strataˈgemical** *adjective* (long *rare*) of, concerned with, or of the nature of (a) stratagem L16. **strataˈgemically** *adverb* (*rare*) E17.

stratal /ˈstrɑːt(ə)l, ˈstreɪ-/ *adjective*. L19.
[from STRATUM + -AL¹.]
Of, pertaining to, or involving a stratum or strata.

stratege *noun* see STRATEGUS.

strategetic /stratɪˈdʒɛtɪk/ *adjective*. Now *rare* or *obsolete*. M19.
[Greek *stratēgētikos*, from *stratēgein*: see STRATAGEM, -IC.]
= STRATEGIC *adjective* 1.
■ Also **strategetical** *adjective* E19.

strategian /strəˈtiːdʒɪən/ *noun*. *rare*. E17.
[formed as STRATEGY + -AN, -IAN.]
†**1** = STRATEGY 1a. Only in E17.
2 = STRATEGIST. E20.

strategic /strəˈtiːdʒɪk/ *adjective & noun*. E19.
[French *stratégique* from Greek *stratēgikos*, from *stratēgos* STRATEGUS: see -IC.]
▸**A** *adjective*. **1** Of or pertaining to strategy; useful or important with regard to strategy. Also *gen.*, concerned with or involving careful planning towards an advantage; *loosely* important. E19.
2 Of, pertaining to, or designating (nuclear) weapons, aircraft, or bombing intended to destroy the economic and industrial installations, communications facilities, etc., of an enemy country. Cf. TACTICAL 1b, c. M20.
3 (Of a material, an installation, a facility) essential to a country for fighting a war; of or pertaining to such materials etc. M20.
Special collocations: **Strategic Defense Initiative** a projected US defence system against intercontinental missiles, using orbiting satellites armed with lasers, missiles, etc. (abbreviation ***SDI***; also called ***Star Wars***).
▸**B** *noun*. In *pl.* & (*rare*) *sing.* The strategic art, strategy. Cf. TACTICS 1. M19.

strategical /strəˈtiːdʒɪk(ə)l/ *adjective*. M19.
[formed as prec.: see -ICAL.]
= STRATEGIC *adjective* 1.

strategically /strəˈtiːdʒɪk(ə)li/ *adverb*. E19.
[from STRATEGIC, STRATEGICAL: see -ALLY.]
In a strategic or calculated manner; as regards strategy, according to the principles of strategy.

strategise *verb* var. of STRATEGIZE.

strategist /ˈstratɪdʒɪst/ *noun*. M19.
[French *stratégiste*, from *stratégie* STRATEGY: see -IST.]
A person who exercises or is skilled in strategy.

strategize /ˈstratɪdʒʌɪz/ *verb intrans*. *US*. Also **-ise**. M20.
[from STRATEGY + -IZE.]
Formulate a strategy or strategies; plan a course of action. Freq. as ***strategizing*** *verbal noun*.

strategus /strəˈtiːɡəs/ *noun*. Pl. **-gi** /-ɡʌɪ/. Also in Greek form **-gos** /-ɡɒs/, pl. **-goi** /-ɡɔɪ/, and (*rare*) Anglicized as **stratege** /ˈstratiːdʒ/. M17.
[Latin from Greek *stratēgos*, from *stratos* army + *-ag-*, *agein* to lead.]
GREEK HISTORY. A commander-in-chief, general, or chief magistrate at Athens and in the Achaean league.

strategy /ˈstratɪdʒi/ *noun*. L17.
[French *stratégie* from Greek *stratēgia* office or command of a general, generalship, from *stratēgos*: see prec.]
1 GREEK HISTORY. †**a** A government or province ruled by a strategus. *rare*. Only in L17. ▸**b** The office of a strategus. *rare*. M19.
2 The art of a commander-in-chief; the planning and direction of the larger military movements and overall operations of a campaign. Cf. TACTICS 1. E19. ▸**b** An instance or variety of this. M19. ▸**c** The art or skill of careful planning towards an advantage or a desired end; an instance of this, a stratagem. M19. ▸**d** In game theory, business theory, etc., a plan for successful action based on the rationality and interdependence of the moves of opposing or competing participants. M20.

Stratfordian /stratˈfɔːdɪən/ *noun & adjective*. E19.
[from *Stratford*-upon-Avon (see below) + -IAN.]
▸**A** *noun*. **1** A native or inhabitant of Stratford-upon-Avon, a town in Warwickshire, birthplace of William Shakespeare. E19.
2 A supporter of the Stratfordian view of Shakespeare's plays (see sense B. below). Also called ***Shakespearian***. E20.
▸**B** *adjective*. Designating or pertaining to the view that Shakespeare did write the plays generally attributed to him. E20.

strath /straθ/ *noun*. *Scot.* M16.
[Gaelic *s(t)rath* = Old Irish *srath* (mod. *sraith*).]
A broad river valley bounded by hills or high ground. Formerly also, a stretch of flat land by the waterside.

strathspey /straθˈspeɪ/ *noun*. Also **S-**. M18.
[from *Strathspey* the valley of the River Spey in Scotland.]
A dance, orig. for two, now for four dancers in a set, resembling the reel, but slower. Also, the music or tune (usually in 4/4 time) used to accompany this dance. Also †***strathspey minuet***, †***strathspey reel***.

straticulate /strəˈtɪkjʊlət/ *adjective*. L19.
[from STRATUM, after *reticulate*, *vermiculate*, etc.: see -ULE, -ATE².]
GEOLOGY & MINERALOGY. Arranged in thin layers.
■ **straticuˈlation** *noun* arrangement in thin layers L19.

stratification /ˌstratɪfɪˈkeɪʃ(ə)n/ *noun*. E17.
[French, from *stratifier* STRATIFY: see -FICATION.]
1 †**a** The action of laying something down in layers, esp. (in tanning, chemistry, etc.) in alternating layers of two materials intended to act one on the other. E17–L19. ▸**b** The placing of seeds close together in moist sand, peat, etc., esp. in layers, to preserve them or promote germination. E20.
2 The formation, by a natural process, of strata or layers one above the other; *spec.* the formation of strata in the earth's crust by successive deposits of sediment; the fact or state of existing in the form of strata, stratified condition; the manner in which a thing, esp. a part of the earth's crust, is stratified. Also, a layer or stratum so produced. L18. ▸**b** ELECTRICITY. The striated appearance assumed by an electric discharge passing through a highly rarefied gas; each of the striations. Now *rare* or *obsolete*. M19. ▸**c** SOCIOLOGY. The formation and establishment of social or cultural levels resulting from differences in occupation and political, ethnic, or economic influence. M19. ▸**d** BIOLOGY & MEDICINE. The thickening of a tissue, calculus, etc., by the deposition or growth of successive thin layers. L19. ▸**e** The existence in a lake or other body of water of two or more distinct layers differing in temperature, density, etc. L19. ▸**f** Production of a stratified charge in the cylinder of an internal-combustion engine. E20.
3 STATISTICS. The (usu. notional) division of a population into distinct groups from each of which a proportion of an overall sample may be taken. E20.
2c ***social stratification***: see SOCIAL *adjective*.

stratificational /ˌstratɪfɪˈkeɪʃ(ə)n(ə)l/ *adjective*. M20.
[from prec. + -AL¹.]
1 LINGUISTICS. Of, pertaining to, or designating a theory in which language is viewed or analysed in terms of a series of strata or structural layers, each with its own rules of formation and related to each other. M20.
2 Of or pertaining to social or cultural strata. M20.
1 ***stratificational grammar***, ***stratificational linguistics***, ***stratificational theory***, etc.
■ **stratificationalism** *noun* (adherence to) the theory that language comprises several structural layers M20. **stratificationalist** *noun* an adherent of stratificationalism M20.

stratified /ˈstratɪfʌɪd/ *ppl adjective*. L18.
[from STRATIFY + -ED¹.]
1 Arranged in strata or layers; exhibiting stratification. L18.
2 STATISTICS. Employing or obtained by means of the technique of stratification. E20.
Special collocations: **stratified charge** in an internal-combustion engine, a rich mixture for ignition in each cycle followed by a lean one for combustion, usu. achieved by having a side chamber in each cylinder into which the mixture for ignition is introduced (freq. *attrib.* with hyphen).

stratiform /ˈstratɪfɔːm/ *adjective*¹. E19.
[French *stratiforme*: see STRATUM, -FORM.]
= STRATIFIED 1. Also *esp.*, (of a mineral deposit) formed parallel to the bedding planes of the surrounding rock.

stratiform /ˈstratɪfɔːm/ *adjective*². M19.
[from STRATUS + -I- + -FORM.]
METEOROLOGY. Of cloud etc.: developed in a predominantly horizontal direction.

stratify /ˈstratɪfʌɪ/ *verb*. M17.
[French *stratifier*: see STRATUM, -FY.]
1 *verb trans.* **a** Arrange in alternate layers. M17. ▸†**b** In *pass.* Be placed in alternate layers *with* something else. L18–E19. ▸**c** Preserve or promote the germination of (seeds) by stratification. E20.
2 *verb trans.* **a** GEOLOGY. Of a natural agency: deposit (rocks, sediments, etc.) in strata or beds; form strata in. Usu. in *pass.* L18. ▸**b** *gen.* Arrange in strata or layers. Freq. in *pass.* M19.
3 *verb intrans.* Assume the form of strata; become stratified. M19.
4 *verb trans. & intrans.* STATISTICS. Subdivide (a population) into groups in order to take a stratified sample. M20.

stratigraphy /strəˈtɪɡrəfi/ *noun*. M19.
[from STRATUM + -I- + -GRAPHY.]
The branch of geology that deals with the order and relative position of the strata of the earth's crust; the stratigraphical features (of a country etc.), the order and relative position of strata. Also, (the analysis of) the relative position of things, esp. archaeological artefacts, occurring in layers or strata.
■ **stratigrapher** *noun* an expert in stratigraphy, a person who maps or delineates strata L19. **stratiˈgraphic** *adjective* of or pertaining to stratigraphy or the analysis of stratification L19. **stratiˈgraphical** *adjective* (now chiefly ARCHAEOLOGY) = STRATIGRAPHIC E19. **stratiˈgraphically** *adverb* in a stratigraphic respect, with regard to stratigraphy M19. **stratigraphist** *noun* (*rare*) = STRATIGRAPHER L19.

stratiote /ˈstratɪəʊt/ *noun*. *rare*. M17.
[Greek *stratiōtēs*, from *stratia* army.]
GREEK HISTORY. A soldier.

strato- /ˈstratəʊ, ˈstrɑːtəʊ, ˈstreɪtəʊ/ *combining form*.
[In sense 1 from STRATUS; in sense 2 from STRATUM: see -O-.]
1 METEOROLOGY. Forming names of types of cloud in which the stratus form is present as an element modifying one of the other forms.
2 Of or pertaining to layers or (geological) strata. M20. ▸**b** [back-form. from STRATO(SPHERE.] Travelling in or suitable for travel in the stratosphere, as ***stratojet***, ***stratonaut***, ***stratoplane***, ***stratosuit***, etc. (freq. *hyperbol.* in proprietary terms). M20.
■ **stratoˈcirrus** *noun*, pl. **-rri** /-rʌɪ, -riː/, METEOROLOGY, *rare* a cloud or cloud-type resembling cirrostratus but more compact L20. **stratoˈcumulus** *noun*, pl. **-li** /-lʌɪ, -liː/, METEOROLOGY a cloud or cloud-type consisting of a low horizontal layer of clumped or broken grey cloud (also called ***cumulostratus***) L19. **stratotype** *noun* (GEOLOGY) a particular group of strata chosen as defining a named stratigraphic unit or boundary M20. **stratovolˈcano** *noun* (GEOLOGY) a volcano built up of alternate layers of lava and ash M20.

stratocracy /strəˈtɒkrəsi/ *noun*. M17.
[from Greek *stratos* army + -CRACY.]
Government or political control by the army; military rule.
■ **ˈstratocrat** *noun* a military ruler L19. **stratoˈcratic** *adjective* pertaining to stratocracy M19.

stratopause /ˈstratəʊpɔːz/ *noun*. M20.
[from STRATO(SPHERE after *tropopause*.]
METEOROLOGY. The upper limit of the stratosphere, separating it from the mesosphere.

stratose /ˈstreɪtəʊs/ *adjective*. L19.
[from STRATUM + -OSE¹.]
BOTANY. Stratified; arranged in distinct layers.

stratosphere /ˈstratəsfɪə/ *noun*. E20.
[from STRATUM + -O- + -SPHERE.]
†**1** GEOLOGY. [German *Stratosphäre*.] The part of the earth's crust dominated by stratified rocks. *rare*. Only in E20.
2 METEOROLOGY. The region of the atmosphere extending above the troposphere to a height of about 50 km (30 miles), in which in the lower part there is little temperature variation with height, and in the higher part the temperature increases with height. Formerly, the lower part of this region, up to a height of about 20 km (12 miles). E20.
3 OCEANOGRAPHY. The bottom layer of the ocean, in which there is little temperature variation with depth. M20.
4 *fig.* An upper region, esp. in a hierarchy; a high, or the highest, plane, level, or rank. M20.

stratospheric /stratəˈsfɛrɪk/ *adjective*. E20.
[from prec. + -IC.]
1 Of or pertaining to the stratosphere; occurring or performed in the stratosphere. E20.
2 *fig.* Extremely high, from a very elevated point of view, rarefied; *esp.* (of cost) astronomical. M20.
■ **stratospherical** *adjective* = STRATOSPHERIC M20. **stratospherically** *adverb* to a stratospheric degree, astronomically M20.

Stratovision /ˈstratəʊvɪʒ(ə)n/ *noun*. *US*. M20.
[from STRATO- + TELE)VISION.]
TELEVISION. (Proprietary name for) a system whereby television programmes are broadcast to a wide area by retransmission from a circling aircraft.

stratum /ˈstrɑːtəm, ˈstreɪtəm/ *noun*. Pl. **strata** /ˈstrɑːtə, ˈstreɪtə/ (also (*non-standard*) used as sing. with pl. **stratas**). L16.
[mod. Latin use of Latin *stratum* lit. 'something spread or laid down', neut. pa. pple of *sternere* lay or throw down. Cf. STREET *noun*.]
1 *gen.* A quantity of a substance or material spread over a nearly horizontal surface to a more or less uniform thickness; a layer, a coat; *esp.* each of two or more parallel layers or coats successively superposed one upon another. L16.
2 A bed of sedimentary rock, usually consisting of a series of layers of the same kind representing continuous periods of deposition. L17.
3 ANATOMY & BIOLOGY. Each of a number of layers composing an animal or plant tissue or structure (freq. with mod.

Latin specifying word). Also *ECOLOGY*, a layer of vegetation in a plant community. **M18.**

4 A region of the atmosphere, of the sea, or of a quantity of fluid, assumed for purposes of calculation to be bounded by horizontal planes. **L18.**

5 *fig.* **a** A portion of a body of institutions, a set of traditions, an artist's work, etc., originating from one historical period, or representing one stage of development or level of analysis. **E19.** ▸**b** (Part of a population belonging to) a particular level or grade in social status, education, etc. **M19.**

6 *STATISTICS.* Each of the groups into which a population is divided in the technique of stratified sampling. **E20.**

> 🕮 **1** R. G. COLLINGWOOD An archaeologist finds a stratum of earth and stones and mortar, mixed with potsherds and coins. **2** N. CALDER Strata of every geologic period from the Precambrian to the Quaternary. **4** *REVERSING* **stratum.** **5a** R. ALTER The Hebrew Bible . . in all likelihood exploits prebiblical strata . . of an indigenous Hebrew literature. **b** L. STEPHEN The habit of reading spread to a lower social stratum.

Comb.: **strata-bound** *adjective* (*GEOLOGY*) confined to a single stratum or group of strata; **strata title** *Austral. & NZ* the freehold of or title to one or more storeys of a building.

stratum corneum /ˌstrɑːtəm ˈkɔːnɪəm/ *noun phr.* **M19.**
[Latin = horny layer.]
ANATOMY. The harder outermost layer of the epidermis of the skin, consisting of dead cells which have become keratinized.

stratus /ˈstrɑːtəs, ˈstreɪtəs/ *noun.* **E19.**
[mod. Latin from Latin *stratus* pa. pple of *sternere*: see **STRATUM.**]
METEOROLOGY. (A cloud-type consisting of) a broad usu. low sheet of cloud of nearly uniform thickness.

straught /strɔːt/ *adjective.* Long *arch. rare.* **E16.**
[Aphet. from **DISTRAUGHT** *adjective.*]
Distraught, out of one's wits.

†**straught** *verb pa. t. & pple*: see **STRETCH** *verb.*

Straussian /ˈstraʊsɪən/ *adjective & noun.* **E20.**
[from family name *Strauss* (see below) + **-IAN.**]
▸**A** *adjective.* **1** Of, pertaining to, or characteristic of the music of the German composer Richard Strauss (1864–1949). **E20.**
2 Of, pertaining to, or characteristic of the music of the Viennese Strauss family, a family of composers of whom Johann Strauss the younger (1825–99) was the foremost. **M20.**
▸**B** *noun.* An interpreter, student, or admirer of Richard Strauss or his music. **M20.**

stravaig /strəˈveɪɡ/ *verb.* Orig. & chiefly *Scot., Anglo-Irish, & north.* Also **-vage, -vague.** **L18.**
[Prob. aphet. from **EXTRAVAGE.**]
1 *verb intrans.* Wander about aimlessly. **L18.**
2 *verb trans.* Wander along (a road). **M20.**
■ **stravaiger** *noun* **M18.**

Stravinskian /strəˈvɪnskɪən/ *adjective & noun.* **E20.**
[from *Stravinsky* (see below) + **-IAN.**]
▸**A** *adjective.* Of, pertaining to, or characteristic of the Russian-born composer Igor Fyodorovich Stravinsky (1882–1971) or his music. **E20.**
▸**B** *noun.* An interpreter, student, or admirer of Stravinsky or his music. **E20.**
■ **Stravinskyite** *noun* = **STRAVINSKIAN** *noun* **E20.**

straw /strɔː/ *noun & adjective.*
[Old English *strēaw* = Old Frisian *strē*, Old Saxon, Old High German *strō* (Dutch *stroo*, German *Stroh*), Old Norse *strá*, from Germanic base rel. to **STREW** *verb.*]
▸**A** *noun.* **I** Cereal stems collectively.
1 The stems or stalks of certain cereals, chiefly wheat, barley, oats, and rye, esp. when dry and separated by threshing, used as thatch, as litter and fodder for cattle, filling for bedding, and plaited or woven as material for hats, baskets, etc. **OE.** ▸**b** The colour of straw, a pale brownish yellow. Also more fully ***straw colour***. **L16.**
2 a The stalks of various other plants, esp. peas and buckwheat. **ME.** ▸**b** (Esp. dried) pine needles. Also ***pine straw***. *US.* **M19.**
3 A material for hats, baskets, matting, etc., made from the plaited or woven stems of wheat or other cereal plants; a variety of this material; an imitation of this material made from paper etc. **M18.**

> 🕮 **1** *Pall Mall Gazette* The lofts over the stable were used as a storing place for hay and straw.

▸**II** A single stem of a cereal etc.
4 A tiny piece of straw or chaff. Now *rare* or *obsolete.* **OE.**
5 A stem of any cereal plant, esp. when dry and separated from the grain; a piece of such a stem. **ME.** ▸**b** = **OAT** *noun* 3. *rare. poet.* **L16.** ▸†**c** *BOTANY.* The culm of a grass. **L18–M19.** ▸**d** A hollow tube (orig. of straw or glass, now usu. paper or plastic) through which a drink is sucked. **M19.**
6 a As a type of a thing of trifling value or importance, esp. in ***not care a straw***, ***not care two straws***, etc., and similar phrs. **ME.** ▸**b** A trifle, a trivial matter. **L17.**
7 Any of various things shaped like a straw, as (*a*) a stick insect; (*b*) a long slender needle; (*c*) a plastic phial in which bull semen is stored for artificial insemination. **M18.**

> 🕮 **5d** J. RUSKIN I . . saw the Bishop of Oxford taught . . to drink sherry-cobbler through a straw. **6a** M. DICKENS You don't care two straws for people's happiness.

▸**III** †**8** [(Low) German *Stroh*, Dutch *stroo*.] A straw basket or other container used for certain goods, esp. glassware imported to America from Germany and the Netherlands; an equivalent unit of weight or quantity. *rare.* **L15–E19.**
9 *ellipt.* A straw hat. **E19.**

> 🕮 **9** R. B. PARKER He wore his summer straw with the big blue band.

Phrases: **catch at a straw**, **catch at straws** resort in desperation to any utterly inadequate expedient, like a person drowning. ***cheese straw***: see **CHEESE** *noun*[1]. **clutch at a straw**, **clutch a straw**, **clutch at straws**, **clutch straws** = ***catch at a straw*** above. **draw straws** (*a*) = ***gather straws*** below; (*b*) draw a lot or lots; ***draw the short straw*** be chosen by lot or by chance, esp. for some disagreeable task. **gather straws** (of the eyes) be sleepy. **grasp at a straw**, **grasp a straw**, **grasp at straws**, **grasp straws** = ***catch at a straw*** above. **have straws in one's hair** & vars. be insane, eccentric, or distracted. **in the straw** (now *arch. & dial.*) in childbed. ***long straw***: see **LONG** *adjective*[1]. **make bricks without straw** [with allus. to *Exodus* 5] perform a task without provision of the necessary materials or means. **man of straw** (*a*) a person or thing compared to a straw image, a counterfeit, a sham; (*b*) an imaginary adversary invented in order to be triumphantly confuted; (*c*) a person of no substance, *esp.* a person who undertakes financial responsibility without the means of discharging it; (*d*) a fictitious or irresponsible person fraudulently put forward as a surety or as a party in an action. ***pad in the straw***: see **PAD** *noun*[1] 1. ***pedal straw***: see **PEDAL** *noun*[2]. ***potato straw***: see **POTATO** *noun.* **straw in the wind** a small but significant indicator of the (future) course of events. **the final straw (that breaks the camel's back)**, **the last straw (that breaks the camel's back)** a slight addition to a burden or difficulty that makes it finally unbearable. See also **BEDSTRAW**, **JACKSTRAW.**

▸**B** *attrib.* or as *adjective.* **1** Made of straw. **LME.**
2 Of the pale brownish-yellow colour of straw. Also more fully ***straw-coloured***. **L16.**

Comb. & special collocations: **straw ballot** = ***straw vote*** below; **straw basher** *slang* a straw hat, a boater; **straw-blond**, **straw-blonde** *adjective & noun* (*a*) *adjective* (of hair) of a pale yellowish-blond colour; (*b*) *noun* (a person with) hair of this colour; **strawboard** (a piece of) coarse millboard made orig. from straw pulp, used for making boxes, book-covers, etc.; **straw boss** (orig. *US*) a subordinate or assistant foreman; **strawboy** each of a group of men in straw masks who traditionally invade wedding celebrations in parts of Ireland; **straw braid** = ***straw plait*** below; **straw-breadth** (now *rare*) the breadth of a straw; *fig.* a small distance, a hair's breadth; **strawchopper** a machine for chopping up straw; ***straw colour***: see sense A.1b above; ***straw-coloured***: see sense B.2 above; **straw-death** *arch.* a natural death in one's bed; **straw-dry** *adjective* as dry as straw, very dry; **strawflower** *N. Amer.* any of various kinds of everlasting, *esp.* the Australian *Helichrysum bracteatum* and plants of the genus *Helipterum*; **straw hat** (*a*) a hat made of plaited or woven straw; (*b*) *US* a theatre operating during the summer only and presenting various productions or companies (freq. *attrib.*, usu. with hyphen); **straw-hatter** *US* (a play presented in) a straw-hat theatre; **strawline** a light rope used to pull a heavier one into position, esp. in logging; **straw man** (*a*) a figure of a man made of straw; (*b*) = ***man of straw*** above; **strawneck** an Australian ibis, *Threskiornis spinicollis*, having a tuft of long coarse yellowish feathers on the neck and breast; **straw-necked ibis** = ***strawneck*** above; **straw-needle** a long thin needle, *esp.* one used for sewing together straw braids; **straw paper**: made from bleached and pulped straw; **straw plait** a plait or braid made of straw, used for making straw hats etc.; **straw poll** = ***straw vote*** below; **straw potatoes** very thinly cut potato chips, potato straws; **straw ring** a ring of plaited straw used to support a round-bottomed container in an upright position; **straw's breadth** = ***straw-breadth*** above; **straw-splitting** *verbal noun & ppl adjective* = ***hair-splitting*** s.v. **HAIR** *noun*; **straw tick** *US* a straw-filled mattress; **straw vote** (orig. *US*) an unofficial or rough vote taken to indicate the relative strength of opposing candidates or issues; **straw wine** [French *vin de paille*] a rich dessert wine made chiefly in the Jura region from grapes dried or partly dried in the sun on straw mats or wire frames; **straw-work** decoration done in plaited straw; **straw-worm** †(*a*) *ANGLING* a kind of caddis-fly larva; (*b*) *US* = **JOINTWORM** 2; **straw yard** (*a*) a yard littered with straw, in which horses and cattle are wintered, or in which hens are allowed to roam; (*b*) *slang* (now *rare* or *obsolete*) a night shelter for the homeless; (*c*) *colloq.* (now *rare*) a (man's) straw hat; **straw-yellow** *noun & adjective* (*a*) *noun* = sense A.1b above; (*b*) *adjective* = sense B.2 above.
■ **strawed** *adjective* (*rare*) provided or covered with straw **L19.** **strawish** *adjective* (*rare*) resembling straw **M16.** **strawless** *adjective* made without straw, containing no straw (chiefly *fig.*: cf. ***make bricks without straw*** above) **L17.**

straw /strɔː/ *verb.* Now *arch. & dial.* Pa. t. **strawed**; pa. pple **strawed**, (*rare*) **strawn** /strɔːn/. **ME.**
[Differentiated repr. of **STREW** *verb.*]
1 *verb trans. & intrans.* Scatter (rushes, straw, seed, flowers, etc.) on the ground or floor, or on the surface of something. **ME.**
2 *verb trans.* Cover (the ground, a floor, etc.) with something loosely scattered, as rushes, straw, flowers, etc. Now *rare* or *obsolete.* **ME.**
3 *verb trans.* Be strewn or spread on. **L16.**

> 🕮 **1** AV *Matt.* 25:24 Reaping where thou hast not sowen, & gathering where thou hast not strawed.

strawberry /ˈstrɔːb(ə)ri/ *noun & adjective.* **OE.**
[from **STRAW** *noun* + **BERRY** *noun*[1]: the reason for the name is obscure.]
▸**A** *noun.* **1** The edible fruit of any plant of the genus *Fragaria* (see sense 2), consisting of a much enlarged pulpy usu. scarlet receptacle studded with small yellow achenes; *esp.* the large succulent fruit of *F.* × *ananassa*, the kind commonly cultivated. **OE.**
2 Any of the plants constituting the genus *Fragaria*, of the rose family, which are characterized by having trifoliate leaves in a basal rosette, five-petalled white flowers, and long trailing runners; esp. *F. vesca* (more fully ***wild strawberry***), a small-fruited plant of woods and shady banks in Europe and temperate N. America. **OE.**
3 A representation of the fruit as an ornament. **E16.**
4 = ***strawberry red*** below. **L17.**
5 A variety of beadlet (sea) anemone having a crimson body with green spots. **M19.**
6 Any of various things resembling a strawberry in shape or colour, as (*a*) an emery bag in the shape of a strawberry; (*b*) *N. Amer. colloq.* a sore or bruise, *esp.* one caused by friction with the ground; (*c*) a nose having the colour of a strawberry, esp. as the result of heavy drinking. **E20.**

2 alpine strawberry a form of the wild strawberry grown for its fruit, which is borne over a long period. **barren strawberry** a kind of wild cinquefoil, *Potentilla sterilis*, resembling the wild strawberry in flower but lacking the characteristic fruit. ***hautboy strawberry***: see **HAUTBOY** 2.

▸**B** *attrib.* or as *adjective.* Of or resembling the colour of a strawberry, deep pinkish-red. **L17.**

Comb. & special collocations: **strawberry bass** *US* the black crappie, *Pomoxis nigromaculatus*; **strawberry birthmark** = ***strawberry mark*** below; **strawberry blite** a kind of goosefoot, *Chenopodium capitatum*, with red berry-like fruits, sometimes grown as a pot-herb; **strawberry blond**, **strawberry blonde** *adjective & noun* (*a*) *adjective* (of the hair) light reddish-blond in colour; (of a person) having light reddish-blond hair; (*b*) *noun* (a person, esp. a woman, with) hair of this colour; **strawberry bush** an American spindle tree, *Euonymus americanus*; **strawberry clover** a clover of clayey soils, *Trifolium fragiferum*, which in fruit develops a dense globose head resembling a strawberry, with inflated calyces; **strawberry colour** = ***strawberry red*** below; **strawberry dish** a round shallow dish of silver of a kind made in England in the 17th and 18th cents.; **strawberry geranium** a saxifrage grown for ornament, *Saxifraga stolonifera*, with round or heart-shaped leaves and stolons like those of the strawberry; **strawberry guava** a Brazilian guava, *Psidium littorale* var. *longipes*, with sweet purplish-red fruits resembling the strawberry in flavour; **Strawberry Hill (Gothic)** *ARCHITECTURE* [from the name of a house in Twickenham rebuilt in this style between 1750 and 1770 by Horace Walpole] an early phase of the Gothic revival preceding that of the 19th cent. (freq. *attrib.*); **strawberry leaf** (*a*) the leaf of the strawberry plant; formerly also, the plant itself; (*b*) (*sing.* & in *pl.*) *colloq.* (the rank of) a marquess, earl, or (esp.) duke [with allus. to the row of stylized strawberry leaves around the coronets of such peers]; **strawberry mark** a soft red birthmark, freq. not persistent in later life; **strawberry perch** *US* = ***strawberry bass*** above; **strawberry pot** a large garden pot with pockets in its sides, orig. designed to contain growing strawberry plants; **strawberry red** the deep pinkish-red colour of a strawberry; ***strawberry roan***: see **ROAN** *noun*[2]; **strawberry shrub** Carolina allspice, *Calycanthus floridus*; **strawberry spinach** = ***strawberry blite*** above; **strawberry tomato** a N. American ground cherry, *Physalis pruinosa*, grown for its edible berries; the fruit of such a plant; **strawberry tree** a chiefly Mediterranean evergreen tree of the heath family, *Arbutus unedo*, with orange-red fruits resembling strawberries, in the British Isles native only in Ireland; **strawberry weevil** a small black and white beetle, *Anthonomus signatus*, of eastern N. America, which lays its eggs in strawberry buds, so that no fruit is formed.

strawen /ˈstrɔːən/ *adjective. arch.* **LME.**
[from **STRAW** *noun* + **-EN**[4].]
Made of straw.

strawn *verb pa. pple*: see **STRAW** *verb.*

strawy /ˈstrɔːi/ *adjective.* **M16.**
[from **STRAW** *noun* + **-Y**[1].]
1 Consisting of or full of straw. **M16.**
2 Made with straw; filled, thatched, or covered with straw. **M16.**
3 *fig.* Light, worthless, or flammable as straw. **L16.**
4 Resembling straw in texture, colour, etc. **M17.**

stray /streɪ/ *noun.* **ME.**
[Anglo-Norman *strey*, aphet. from *astrey* adjective used as noun; partly from **STRAY** *verb*[2].]
1 An animal that has strayed or wandered away from its flock, home, or owner; *LAW* = **ESTRAY** *noun* 1. **ME.** ▸†**b** A vagrant, a trespasser; a person who has run away from service or employment. **M16–M18.** ▸**c** *fig.* A person who has gone astray in conduct, belief, purpose, etc. Now *rare* or *obsolete.* **E17.** ▸**d** A homeless, friendless person; an ownerless dog or cat. **M17.** ▸**e** A thing that has wandered or become separated from its usual or proper place, or from a main body; a detached fragment, an isolated specimen. **L18.**

2 The action of straying or wandering; an instance of this. Long *rare*. ME.
3 The right of allowing cattle to stray and feed on common land. *north*. M18. ▸**b** A piece of unenclosed land on which there is a common right of pasture; a common. L19.
4 *ELECTRICITY & TELECOMMUNICATIONS*. In *pl*. Atmospherics, static, noise. E20.
Phrases: ***waifs and strays***: see WAIF *noun*[1] 1a, 2.

stray /streɪ/ *adjective*. LME.
[Partly aphet. from ASTRAY *adjective*; partly attrib. use of the noun.]
1 Of an animal: that has wandered free from confinement or control; that has become separated from a herd, flock, etc.; that is or has become homeless or ownerless. LME.
2 Separated from others of the same kind; situated or occurring away from the usual or proper place or course; out of place, loose; isolated, wandering, occasional. L18.

📖 **1** R. C. HUTCHINSON A stray cat miaowing for a saucer of milk. **2** A. N. WILSON His stray moments of . . happiness. A. TYLER She looked through the bureau for a stray comb. G. GREENE Some stray rifle shots and once what sounded like . . a grenade.

Special collocations & comb.: **stray field** *PHYSICS & ENGINEERING* part of an electromagnetic field which extends beyond the area of its intended effect and may interfere with other components. **stray-line** *NAUTICAL* a submerged or floating line fixed at one end; a length of line by which something is lowered into the sea; orig. *spec*. the part of a log-line left unmarked so that measurement starts only when the log is clear of the wake.

stray /streɪ/ *verb*[1] *trans*. Long *obsolete* exc. *dial*.
[Old English *strēgan* = Gothic *straujan*, from Germanic base also of STREW *verb*.]
= STREW *verb*.

stray /streɪ/ *verb*[2]. ME.
[Aphet. from Anglo-Norman, Old French *estraier*, *estrayer*: see ASTRAY.]
1 *verb intrans*. Escape from confinement or control, wander away from a place, move or extend outside some definite area; become lost or separated from others; *euphem*. be stolen. (Foll. by *from, into, away, off*, etc.) ME.
2 *verb intrans*. Wander from the direct way, deviate. Chiefly *fig*., wander from the path of rectitude, err; wander or deviate in conduct, belief, purpose, etc. LME. ▸†**b** *verb trans*. Lead astray, distract. M–L16.
3 *verb intrans*. Wander up and down free from control, roam about. (Foll. by *about, along, in, through*, etc.) LME. ▸**b** Of a stream: meander. *poet*. Now *rare*. L16. ▸**c** Of the eyes, the fingers, a person's thoughts, wishes, etc.: wander idly, pass casually from one thing to another. M17.
4 *verb trans*. Wander in, over, or through (a place). Also, cause (the eye) to wander (over something). *poet. rare*. E17.

📖 **1** J. H. BURTON The town had strayed beyond the wall built round it. K. GRAHAME He's always straying off and getting lost. E. WAUGH Strands of barbed wire . . strayed across the ground. **2** GOLDSMITH I ask pardon, I am straying from the question. **3** R. MACAULAY We . . strayed among deep woods and ravines. **c** BROWNING His fingers . . were ever straying As if impatient to be playing Upon this pipe. G. VIDAL My eyes continually strayed back to my brother. **4** A. MACLAGAN How oft . . ha'e I strayed The mountain's heather crest.

■ **strayaway** *noun* (*poet., rare*) an animal that strays away E19. **strayed** *ppl adjective* that has gone astray (*lit. & fig.*) E16. **strayer** *noun* LME.

strayling /ˈstreɪlɪŋ/ *noun*. *rare*. M19.
[from STRAY *adjective* or *verb*[2] + -LING[1].]
A stray thing or person.

streak /striːk/ *noun*. Also †**strike**.
[Old English *strica* corresp. in sense and vowel-grade to Old Frisian *strike*, Middle Low German, Middle Dutch *strēke* (Dutch *streek*), Old & mod. High German *strich*, Gothic *striks*, from Germanic base of STRIKE *verb*. Cf. STROKE *noun*[1], *verb*[1].]
†**1** A line, a mark, a stroke, esp. as used in writing or as a unit of measurement. OE–M18.
2 A long thin usu. irregular line or band of contrasting colour; *spec*. a distinctive mark on an animal's coat, bird's plumage, etc. OE. ▸**b** *MINERALOGY*. A line of coloured powder produced by scratching a mineral or fossil, or rubbing it on a hard surface. L18. ▸**c** Chiefly *BIOLOGY*. A linear mark, a striation; a narrow tract of tissue. M19. ▸**d** A strand or strands of (usu. tinted) hair of a contrasting, esp. lighter, colour. Cf. HIGHLIGHT *noun* 3. M20.
3 a A faint line of light in darkness, esp. at dawn. L16. ▸**b** A flash of lightning, fire, etc. L18. ▸**c** A rapid move; (a journey made at) a fast rate. *slang*. M19. ▸**d** [from STREAK *verb*[2] 3c.] An act of running naked or topless in a public place as a stunt. *colloq*. (orig. *US*). L20.
4 a A strain or element of some contrasting or unexpected quality, esp. in a person's character. M17. ▸**b** A temporary run, esp. of luck; a spell, a series. M19.
5 *MINING*. A horizontal stratum of coal; a stratum or vein of ore. Cf. STRIKE *noun*[1] 6. L17.
6 a A long narrow strip of land, water, etc.; a line of colour representing a distant object in a landscape. E18. ▸**b** A tall thin person. *colloq*. M20.
7 Any of several moths having a streak of colour in their wings, esp. the geometrid *Chesias legatella*. E18.
8 *MICROBIOLOGY*. A light scratch made with the point of a needle covered with bacteria on the surface of a solid culture medium etc. L19.
9 Any of various virus diseases of plants marked by discoloured stripes (symptoms of necrosis) along the stem and veins. Also ***streak disease***. M20.

📖 **2** *Which?* Rain . . can degrade picture quality . . causing black or white streaks. **d** M. CHABON The new auburn streaks in her hair. **3a** E. FIGES A faint streak of rose flushed the sky. **b** D. M. THOMAS A streak of . . lightning flashed vertically to the lake. **4a** N. SHERRY Nearly twenty-one years old, Greene still retained a boyish streak. **b** *Golf* I have streaks where I hit the woods well but the irons badly. *Tennis* Navratilova extended her Championship streak to six consecutive titles. *World Soccer* Their lengthy unbeaten streak (15 games) has ended.

Phrases: **a losing streak**, **a winning streak** a series of losses or wins; freq. in ***on a losing streak***, ***on a winning streak***, experiencing such a series. ***blue streak***: see BLUE *adjective*. ***hairstreak***: see HAIR *noun*. **like a streak**, **like streaks** as fast as lightning. ***primitive streak***: see PRIMITIVE *adjective*. ***yellow streak***: see YELLOW *adjective*.
Comb.: **streak camera** (*a*) a camera which uses streak photography; (*b*) an electron-optical analogue of this allowing the resolution of events of the order of a picosecond duration, used esp. in high-speed spectroscopy; **streak culture** a bacterial culture initiated with a streak (see sense 8 above); ***streak disease***: see sense 9 above; **streak photograph**: taken by streak photography; **streak photography**: in which film is automatically and rapidly moved past the open shutter of a camera; **streak plate** (*a*) *MICROBIOLOGY* (a vessel containing) a streak culture; (*b*) *MINERALOGY* a small tablet of unglazed porcelain on which minerals may be rubbed to show the colour of the streak.

streak /striːk/ *verb*[1] *trans*. *obsolete* exc. *dial*. LME.
[Perh. from Old Norse *strjúka* stroke, rub, wipe. Cf. STRIKE *verb*, STROKE *verb*[1].]
1 Stroke; rub; clean or smooth by rubbing. Also, rub or smear *with*. LME.
2 Make level, flat, or even; lay evenly. LME.
¶ Recorded earlier in ME as a surname.

streak /striːk/ *verb*[2]. LME.
[from STREAK *noun*.]
†**1** *verb trans*. Cancel or score out by drawing a line or lines across. Cf. STRIKE *verb* 36a. LME–L16.
2 *verb trans*. **a** Mark with contrasting lines or bands; form streaks on or in. L16. ▸**b** Tint (the hair) with streaks. M20.
3 a *verb intrans*. [Orig. var. of STREEK 2.] Move very rapidly; rush at full speed. Also foll. by *off, out, up*, etc. M18. ▸**b** *verb trans*. Cause to move very rapidly. E20. ▸**c** *verb intrans*. Run naked or topless in a public place as a stunt. *colloq*. (orig. *US*). L20.
4 *verb intrans*. Of lightning: shoot out in a streak. M19.
5 *verb intrans*. Form streaks; become streaked or streaky. L19.
6 *verb trans*. *MICROBIOLOGY*. Draw (an infected needle etc.) over the surface of a solid culture medium to initiate a culture of varied density; inoculate (a medium) in this way. Also, transfer (a specimen) in this way. E20.

📖 **2a** J. MCCRAE The coming dawn that streaks the sky. P. ACKROYD The windows of the arcades and shops were streaked with dirty water. **b** P. ACKROYD She . . decided to streak her hair with blonde highlights. **3a** J. M. COETZEE A huge Alsatian streaking out to attack him. *Today's Golfer* He streaked away from the field . . to win by . . seven strokes. **5** D. JOHNSON The black mascara streaked down her face.

■ **streaker** *noun* (*colloq*.) a person who runs naked or topless in a public place as a stunt L20.

streak *verb*[3] var. of STREEK.

streaked /striːkt/ *adjective*. L16.
[from STREAK *verb*[2] + -ED[1].]
1 Marked with streaks; striped, striate. L16. ▸**b** Of meat, esp. bacon: streaky. L17.
2 Confused, upset, ashamed, disturbed. *US*. E19.

streaking /ˈstriːkɪŋ/ *noun*. L17.
[from STREAK *verb*[2] + -ING[1].]
1 The action of STREAK *verb*[2]. Also, a series or arrangement of streaks. L17.
2 A condition in a television picture in which small streaks of colour trail from the edges of other colours. M20.

streaky /ˈstriːki/ *adjective & noun*. L17.
[from STREAK *noun* + -Y[1].]
▶ **A** *adjective*. **1** Of the nature of a streak or streaks; occurring in or consisting of streaks. L17.
2 a Marked with streaks; streaked. M18. ▸**b** Of meat, esp. bacon: having lean and fat in alternate streaks. M19.
3 Irritable, ill-tempered; confused, upset. Cf. STREAKED 2. *US*. M19.
4 Changeable, variable, uncertain. *colloq*. L19.

📖 **2a** B. W. ALDISS His hair . . was a streaky white and grey. **4** *Daily News* The wind . . was streaky, and did not hit the boats at the same time.

▶ **B** *noun*. Streaky bacon. M20.
■ **streakily** *adverb* L19. **streakiness** *noun* M18.

streale /striːl/ *noun*. Long *obsolete* exc. *dial*.
[Old English *stræl* corresp. to Old Saxon *strāla*, Middle Dutch *strael*, *strāle* (Dutch *straal*), Old High German *strāla*, Middle High German *strāl(e)* (German *Strahl*), from Germanic.]
An arrow.

stream /striːm/ *noun*.
[Old English *strēam* = Old Frisian *strām*, Old Saxon *strōm*, Old High German *stroum* (Dutch *stroom*, German *Strom*), Old Norse *straumr*, from Germanic, from Indo-European base also of Greek *rhein* to flow, *rheuma* stream.]
1 a A course of water flowing continuously along a bed on the earth; *esp*. a small river. OE. ▸**b** Used as a type of pure drinking-water. *poet*. ME. ▸**c** In *pl*. The waters of a river. *poet*. E16.
2 The flow or current of a river; a current in the sea (cf. ***Gulf Stream*** s.v. GULF *noun*). Also, the central strongest part of such a current. OE.
†**3** *sing*. & in *pl*. Water, sea. OE–E17.
4 a *sing*. & in *pl*. A flow or current of a liquid issuing from a source, orifice, or vessel; *hyperbol*. a great effusion of blood or tears. OE. ▸**b** A current or flow of air, gas, or electricity. E18.
5 *transf. & fig*. **a** A continuous flow of words or time; a continuous series of events, influences, etc.; an outflow or influx of something. OE. ▸**b** An unbroken mass of people or things moving constantly in the same direction. E17. ▸**c** The prevailing direction of opinion or fashion. E17. ▸**d** *EDUCATION*. A division of pupils in one school year according to perceived ability; a group of pupils in such a division. Cf. TRACK *noun* 2e. M20. ▸**e** *COMPUTING*. A continuous flow of data or instructions; a channel for such a flow. M20.
†**6** A ray or beam of light; the tail of a comet. LME–L17.
†**7** A streamer, a pennant. LME–E17.
8 In a polar ice-field, a continuous ridge formed of pieces of ice and following the direction of the current. E19.

📖 **1a** J. HAWKES True highland with . . peaty streams and swift rivers. J. C. OATES The river is a wide dark featureless stream. **2** *Practical Boat Owner* A . . tide can be carried . . past Land's End before the stream sets to the north. **4a** G. P. R. JAMES From the . . arm of the knight, a stream of blood was . . beginning to flow. M. VERNEY Wine and ale . . flowed in streams. **b** W. T. BRANDE A stream of sulphuretted hydrogen gas is passed through it. **5a** J. CARY Shrieking . . a stream of encouragement and abuse. G. SAYER He produced a stream of stories. **b** T. DREISER Swiftly moving streams of traffic. A. C. AMOR Hunt . . scarcely knew how to cater for the endless stream of visitors.

Phrases: **against the stream** against the tide or current; *fig*. against the majority, the prevailing view, external pressures, etc. **in the stream** *NAUTICAL* (of a vessel) lying offshore. ***jet stream***: see JET *noun*[2] 3c. **on stream** (of a factory etc.) in operation. ***row against the stream***: see ROW *verb*[1]. **stream of consciousness**, **stream of thought** (*a*) *PSYCHOLOGY* an individual's thoughts and conscious reactions to external events perceived as a continuous flow (cf. ***thought-stream*** s.v. THOUGHT *noun*[1]); *loosely* an uncontrolled train of thought or association; (*b*) a method of narration which depicts events through such a flow in the mind of a character; an instance of this. ***third stream***: see THIRD *adjective & noun*. ***transpiration stream***: see TRANSPIRATION. **with the stream** with the tide or current; *fig*. with the majority, the prevailing view, external pressures, etc.; ***go with the stream***, do as others do.
Comb.: **stream-anchor** *NAUTICAL* an anchor intermediate in size between the bower and the kedge, esp. used for warping; **stream-flow** (orig. *US*) flow of water in streams and rivers; the rate or amount of this; **stream function** *PHYSICS* a mathematical function of position defined so that lines along which it has a constant value are the streamlines of a flow or the lines of force of a field; **streamside** *noun & adjective* (of or pertaining to) the side of a stream or streams; **stream-tide** a spring tide; **stream-tin** tin, or its ore cassiterite, found as pebbles in streams or alluvial beds; **stream-way** (*a*) the main current of a river; (*b*) the shallow bed of a stream, a watercourse; **stream-work(s)** *MINING* the washing of detrital deposits in order to obtain any metal, esp. tin ore, which they contain; a place where this is done.
■ **streamless** *adjective* M19. **streamlet** *noun* a small stream, a brook, a rivulet M16.

stream /striːm/ *verb*. ME.
[from prec.]
▶ **I** *verb intrans*. **1** Flow in or as in a stream; run or be carried in a full and continuous current. Also foll. by *down, into, out*, etc. ME.
2 Exude liquid in a continuous stream; run or overflow with moisture. LME.
3 a Of a luminous body: emit a continuous stream of beams or rays of light. Of a meteor, comet, etc.: emit a (widening) trail of light as it moves. LME. ▸**b** Be suffused *with* (radiant light). M19.
4 Of a flag, the hair, etc.: wave or float in the wind. M16.

5 a Of people or animals: move together continuously in an unbroken mass; flock. Freq. foll. by *down, in, out,* etc. **M18.** ▸**b** Go with a rush. *rare.* **M19.**

> 1 S. JOHNSON The torrents streamed into the plain. M. SARTON They had laughed . . till tears streamed down their cheeks. D. PLANTE Small blossoms from the trees streamed through the air. JOAN SMITH Moonlight streamed in from an uncurtained window. **2** B. JOWETT He was streaming with perspiration. **4** S. RADLEY Poles had been hoisted aloft, and from them streamed ribbons and flags. J. F. HENDRY Tolstoy strode along . . , his hair streaming in the wind. **5a** R. INGALLS They stood to one side to let the others stream past. D. LESSING The delegates were . . streaming out to . . their coaches.

▶ **II** *verb trans.* **6** Suffuse *with* flowing moisture. **ME.**

7 a Cause to flow; pour forth or emit (a liquid, rays of light, etc.) in a stream. Also foll. by *down, over,* etc. **LME.** ▸**b** Of a river or fountain: run with or have its stream composed of (blood, etc.). **E17.**

8 Cause (a flag) to float outwards or wave in the wind. Now *rare.* **L16.**

9 *MINING.* Wash (a detrital deposit) with a stream of water, in order to expose any ore in the detritus. **L18.**

10 *EDUCATION.* In a school, divide (pupils) into streams according to perceived ability; place (a pupil) in a stream. Also (esp. as ***streamed*** *ppl adjective*), organize (a school) according to this system. **M20.**

> **6** G. PINCKARD From . . only moderate exercise, I am . . streamed with perspiration. **7a** C. R. MARKHAM The moon streamed its floods of light over the forest.

Phrases: **stream the buoy** *NAUTICAL* throw the anchor-buoy overboard before casting anchor. ***stream the log***: see LOG *noun*[1].

streamer /ˈstriːmə/ *noun.* **ME.**
[from prec. + -ER[1].]
1 A flag streaming or waving in the air; *spec.* a long narrow flag or pennant. **ME.**
2 †**a** A luminous celestial object emitting a continuous stream of light. **LME–M17.** ▸**b** A long thin part of the tail of a comet. Formerly also, the entire tail of a comet. **E17.** ▸**c** A ray from the sun; *esp.* (in *pl.*) the sun's corona as seen in a solar eclipse. **L17.** ▸**d** In *pl.* The Aurora Borealis. **M18.** ▸**e** A thin line of luminosity extending from an electrode in a gas when the potential difference is too small to produce a spark or arc; a similar feature extending from a cloud or an object on the ground prior to a stroke of lightning along the same path. **E20.**
3 *transf.* A long narrow thing that hangs, flows, or waves; *spec.* †(**a**) a decoration on a pie or cake; (**b**) a long flowing ribbon, feather, etc., on an item of dress, esp. a hat; (**c**) a long narrow strip of coloured paper used as a festive decoration or rolled up in a coil which unwinds when thrown; (**d**) a long loose feather which stands out from the rest of a bird's plumage; (**e**) a banner headline; (**f**) *ANGLING* (chiefly *US*) a fly with feathers attached, resembling a small fish; the feathers so used. **LME.**
4 *MINING.* A person who washes detrital deposits for the ore they contain. **E17.**
5 A geometrid moth, *Anticlea derivata.* **L18.**
6 *EDUCATION.* [from STREAM *noun* 5d.] A school pupil belonging to or suitable for a specified stream in a school. Freq. in ***C-streamer***, a pupil of little academic ability. **M20.**
7 *COMPUTING.* A tape drive from which data can be transferred in bulk while the tape is in motion, used mainly for backup storage. Also ***tape streamer***. **L20.**

> **1** W. COWPER Hoist the sail, and let the streamers float Upon the wanton breezes. **3** GEO. ELIOT The orange-coloured ribbons and streamers of the . . Tory candidate. R. W. CHAMBERS Long streamers of clouds . . swept low on the western sky. E. L. RICE The room was gay, with streamers of coloured paper. K. O'HARA I was . . in an apron . . and a cap with streamers.

Comb.: **streamer weed** a freshwater plant with long fronds that stream and wave in the current; *esp.* water crowfoot.

streamer /ˈstriːmə/ *verb trans.* **E19.**
[from prec.]
Provide or fill with streamers.

streaming /ˈstriːmɪŋ/ *noun.* **LME.**
[from STREAM *verb* + -ING[1].]
The action of STREAM *verb*; *spec.* (**a**) *MINING* the washing of detrital deposits in order to obtain any ore which they contain; (**b**) *EDUCATION* the practice of dividing pupils in a school into streams; (**c**) *BIOLOGY* a flowing motion of the cytoplasm in a cell; (**d**) *COMPUTING* a high speed mode of tape transport in which the stopping tape overruns the gap between blocks and must be backed up for the next start; (**e**) *COMPUTING* a method of relaying data, esp. video and audio material, over the Internet or other network as a steady continuous stream. Also, an instance of this.

streaming /ˈstriːmɪŋ/ *ppl adjective.* **ME.**
[from STREAM *verb* + -ING[2].]
That streams; *spec.* (**a**) that flows or overflows; (**b**) that waves or issues in a stream.
streaming cold: accompanied by copious running of the nose and eyes.
■ **streamingly** *adverb* **L15.**

streamline /ˈstriːmlʌɪn/ *noun & adjective.* **M19.**
[from STREAM *noun* + LINE *noun*[2].]
▶ **A** *noun.* **1** *HYDRODYNAMICS & AERODYNAMICS.* Orig., a line whose direction is that of the motion of particles in a fluid. Now, a line the tangent of which at any point has the same direction as the flow of a fluid at that point (equivalent in the case of steady flow to the direction of motion of particles). **M19.**
2 A contour of a body coincident with a streamline of flow round it; *loosely* a smooth outline designed to minimize drag or resistance to motion. **E20.**
▶ **B** *attrib.* or as *adjective.* **1** Of fluid flow: free of turbulence, laminar. **L19.**
2 = STREAMLINED. **E20.**

streamline /ˈstriːmlʌɪn/ *verb trans.* **E20.**
[from prec. or back-form. from next.]
Design or redesign with a form which presents least resistance to a flow of air, water, etc.; give a smooth tapered form to. Also, simplify, reduce, esp. in order to make more efficient or better organized. Chiefly as STREAMLINED *ppl adjective*, STREAMLINING *noun.*

> *International Business Week* He streamlined the business, consolidating . . 23 banks into one.

■ **streamliner** *noun* (**a**) a streamlined thing, *esp.* a streamlined train; (**b**) a person who streamlines something: **M20.**

streamlined /ˈstriːmlʌɪnd/ *ppl adjective.* **E20.**
[from STREAMLINE *noun* or *verb* + -ED[1], -ED[2].]
1 Having a form designed to reduce resistance to a flow of air, water, etc.; having a smooth slender form. **E20.**
2 Having a simplified and more efficient structure or organization. **M20.**

streamlining /ˈstriːmlʌɪnɪŋ/ *noun.* **E20.**
[from STREAMLINE *verb* + -ING[1].]
Streamlined shape or structure; the action or result of giving this to something.

> *Discovery* To diminish air-resistance by the streamlining of both engine and train. *Daily Telegraph* Railway streamlining to be speeded.

streamy /ˈstriːmi/ *adjective.* **L15.**
[from STREAM *noun* + -Y[1].]
1 Full of or having many streams. **L15.**
2 Flowing in or as in a stream. **L16.**
3 Resembling, of the nature of, or issuing in a stream. **E17.**

streck /ˈstrɛk/ *adverb & adjective. obsolete* exc. *dial.* **ME.**
[Ult. from Germanic base of STRETCH *verb*. Cf. STRAKE *noun*, *verb*[1], STREEK.]
▶ **A** *adverb.* In a straight course, directly; immediately. **ME.**
▶ **B** *adjective.* Straight. **LME.**

streek /striːk/ *verb.* Now *Scot.* & *dial.* Also **streak**. **ME.**
[Ult. from Germanic base of STRETCH *verb*. Cf. STRAKE *noun*, *verb*[1], STRECK.]
1 *verb trans.* & *intrans.* = STRETCH *verb.* **ME.**
2 *verb intrans.* Go quickly; rush at full speed. Also foll. by *away, off,* etc. Now regarded as part of STREAK *verb*[2] 3a. **ME.**
3 *verb trans.* & *intrans.* Put (an implement, esp. a plough) into action. **L15.**

streel /striːl/ *noun*[1]. Chiefly *Anglo-Irish.* **M19.**
[Irish *s(t)raoill(e)* untidy or awkward person: cf. next, Irish *straille* wench, untidy girl.]
A disreputable untidy woman; a slut.
■ **streelish** *adjective* **L20.**

streel /striːl/ *verb & noun*[2]. Chiefly *Anglo-Irish.* **E19.**
[Cf. Irish *straoillim* trail, drag along on the ground.]
▶ **A** *verb intrans.* Trail on the ground; float at length. Also, (of a person) stroll, wander aimlessly. **E19.**
▶ **B** *noun.* A straggling procession of people. **L19.**

street /striːt/ *noun.*
[Old English *strǣt* = Old Frisian *strēte*, Old Saxon *strāta*, Old High German *strāz(z)a* (Dutch *straat*, German *Strasse*), from West Germanic from late Latin *strata* use as noun (sc. *via* way) of fem. pa. pple of Latin *sternere* throw or lay down. Cf. STRATUM.]
1 a A paved road, a highway. Now only in proper names of certain ancient (chiefly Roman) roads. **OE.** ▸†**b** *loosely.* A road, a way, a path. **OE–M16.**
2 A public road in a city, town, or village usu. running between two lines of houses or other buildings; such a road along with the pavements and buildings on either side. Freq. (with cap. initial) in proper names (abbreviation *St.*). **OE.** ▸**b** The people who live or work in, or regularly use, a particular street. **LME.** ▸**c** *transf.* A passage between continuous lines of people or things. **LME.**
3 a *PHYSICS.* More fully ***vortex street***. An arrangement of vortices in two parallel lines with clockwise rotation in one and anticlockwise rotation in the other. **E20.** ▸**b** *METEOROLOGY.* = ***cloud street*** s.v. CLOUD *noun.* **M20.**

> **2** L. HELLMAN He . . had bought a street of slum houses. H. DAVID The . . Tavern . . stands on the corner of Charlotte Street and Windmill Street. *Sunday Express* A narrow cobbled street lined with . . souvenir shops. ***Bow Street, Carnaby Street, Downing Street, high street, main street***, etc. **b** *Chambers's Journal* A mystery . . which the whole street had tried . . fathoming.

Phrases: **by a street** by a wide margin. ***cloud street***: see CLOUD *noun.* **down one's street** *colloq.* suited to one's taste or ability, ***right down one's street***, completely so. ***Easy Street***: see EASY *adjective.* **in the street(s)** out of doors, esp. in a town or city; in the public area outside the buildings in a street. ***mean streets***: see MEAN *adjective*[1]. **not in the same street as**, **not in the same street with** far behind in a race etc., far inferior to. **not the length of a street** no great interval. **on the street** (**a**) *N. Amer. slang* outside prison, at liberty; (**b**) *slang* (of drug acquisition) by illicit dealing; (**c**) out of work, unemployed; (**d**) = ***in the street(s)*** above. **on the streets** (**a**) homeless; (**b**) living by prostitution; (**c**) = ***in the street(s)*** above. **play both sides of the street** (chiefly *US*) ally oneself with both sides, behave inconsistently and opportunistically. ***Queer Street***: see QUEER *adjective & noun.* ***right down one's street***: see ***down one's street*** above. ***Short Street***: see SHORT *adjective.* **streets ahead (of)**, **streets better (than)** far ahead (of) in a race etc., far superior (to). **take to the streets** gather outdoors in a town in order to protest etc. ***the man in the street, the man on the street***: see MAN *noun.* **the street** (**a**) a particular street in which financial or other business is conducted or based; this business; those who conduct it; *spec.* (***the Street***) = WALL STREET, = ***Fleet Street*** s.v. FLEET *noun*[2]; (**b**) the money market after the Stock Exchange closes; (**c**) the realm of ordinary people, esp. as a source of popular political support or of fashionable urban subculture; (**d**) *US slang* the world outside prison or other confinement, freedom. ***two-way street***: see TWO-WAY *adjective* 4b. **up one's street** *colloq.* = ***down one's street*** above. ***up street***: see UP *preposition*[2]. ***vortex street***: see sense 3a above. ***walk the streets***: see WALK *verb*[1]. ***woman of the streets***: see WOMAN *noun.*

Comb.: **street arab**: see ARAB *noun* 3; **street boy** a homeless boy who lives chiefly in the streets; **streetcar** (**a**) *N. Amer.* a tramcar; (**b**) *Military slang* a shell; **street chemist** *US colloq.* a person who makes and deals in esp. illegal drugs; **street child** a homeless child who lives chiefly in the streets; **street cred** *noun & adjective* (*slang*) [abbreviation] (**a**) *noun* = ***street credibility*** below; (**b**) *adjective* = ***street credible*** below; **street credibility** *slang* popularity with or acceptability to people involved in fashionable street culture; (apparent) familiarity with current fashions, social issues, etc.; **street credible** *adjective* (*slang*) possessing street credibility; **street cries** the cries of hawkers in the street; **street culture** the outlook, values, lifestyle, etc., of (esp. young) people living in an urban environment, regarded as a fashionable subculture; **street dog** an ownerless dog living in the streets; **street door** the main outer door of a house or other building which opens on to the street; **street drug** an illegal drug sold on the streets; **street fight** an instance of street fighting; **street fighting**: conducted in the streets, esp. on a large scale for political or revolutionary ends; **street floor** *US* = ***ground floor*** s.v. GROUND *noun*; **street furniture** postboxes, road signs, litter bins, and other objects placed in the street for public use; **street girl** (**a**) a homeless girl who lives chiefly in the streets; (**b**) a prostitute; **street-grid** an arrangement of streets crossing at right angles to each other; **street hockey** *N. Amer.* a variety of hockey played on the street; **street jewellery** painted enamel advertising plates regarded as collectors' items; **street-keeper** a parish or district official appointed to keep order in the streets; **street kid** *colloq.* = ***street child*** above; **street lamp** a lamp or light, esp. on a lamp-post, that illuminates a road etc.; a lamppost supporting such a lamp. **street-legal** *adjective* (of a vehicle) legally roadworthy; **street level** (**a**) ground-floor level; (**b**) *fig.* the level of direct contact with the public, grass roots level; the level of operating esp. illegally on the streets; **street-light** †(**a**) a window opening on the street; (**b**) a street lamp; **streetman** *US slang* a petty criminal who operates on the streets esp. as a pickpocket or drug peddler; **street name** *US* the name of a stock-broking firm, bank, or dealer in which stock is held on behalf of a purchaser; **street-orderly** (now *rare*) a person who sweeps the streets; a scavenger; **street people** (chiefly *N. Amer.*) (**a**) homeless people who live on the streets; (**b**) people involved in petty urban crime, *esp.* illicit drug dealers; **street person** *N. Amer.* a vagrant who lives on the streets; **street-porter** *Hist.* a porter who lifts or carries heavy packages in the street; **street price** (**a**) a price obtained or quoted in dealings after the Stock Exchange closes; (**b**) the selling price of an illegal drug; **streetproof** *verb trans.* (*N. Amer.*) train (children) to be wary of dangers outside the home or school, esp. from drug dealers, child molesters, etc.; †**street-raking** *adjective* (*Scot.*) roaming the streets; **street rod** a hot rod suitable for use in the streets; **streetscape** a view or prospect provided by the design of a city street or streets; **street-smart** *adjective* (*N. Amer. slang*) = ***streetwise*** (b) below; **street smarts** *N. Amer. slang* shrewd awareness of how to survive in an urban society or environment; common sense; **street style** (a) style or fashion inspired by fashionable street culture; **street-sweeper** a person who or machine which sweeps the streets; **street-to-street** *adjective* (of fighting) taking place in the streets; **street tree** a tree planted at the edge of a street; **street urchin** a mischievous little street boy; **street value** the estimated selling price of an illegal drug; **street village** a long narrow village formed of buildings along either side of a main street; **streetwalker** a person who walks in the street, *spec.* a prostitute who solicits in the street; **street warden** (**a**) an air-raid warden assigned to a particular street or streets; (**b**) a warden appointed to watch for certain social problems in a particular street or streets; **streetway** (now only *poet.*) a paved road or highway, the part of a street meant for vehicles; **streetwise** *adjective* (*slang*, orig. *N. Amer.*) (**a**) familiar with fashionable street culture; (**b**) cunning in the ways of modern urban life; **street worker** (orig. *N. Amer.*) a social worker who works with juvenile delinquents.
■ **streetful** *noun* as much or as many as a street will hold **M19.** **streetlet** *noun* a small street **M16.** **streetward** *adverb & adjective* (**a**) *adverb* towards the street; (**b**) *adjective* facing or opening on to

the street: L16. **streety** *adjective* (*rare*) of, pertaining to, or characteristic of the streets M19.

street /striːt/ *verb trans.* M16.
[from prec.]
Provide with streets, lay out in streets.

Strega /ˈstreɪɡə/ *noun.* E20.
[Italian = witch.]
(Proprietary name for) a kind of orange-flavoured Italian liqueur.

streiml /ˈʃtreɪm(ə)l/ *noun.* Also ***sh-***, ***-mel***. Pl. ***-s***, ***-ach*** /-ɑːx/. E20.
[Yiddish, from Middle High German *streimel* stripe, strip.]
A round broad-brimmed hat edged with fur, worn by some Hasidic Jews.

strelitz /ˈstrɛlɪts/ *noun.* E17.
[Russian *strelets* archer, from *strelyat'* shoot, from *strela* arrow.]
RUSSIAN HISTORY. A soldier in a body of infantry raised by the Tsar Ivan the Terrible (1533–84) and abolished by Peter the Great (1672–1725).

strelitzia /strəˈlɪtsɪə/ *noun.* L18.
[from Charlotte of Mecklenburg-*Strelitz* (1744–1818), queen of George III + -IA[1].]
Any of several southern African plants constituting the genus *Strelitzia*, of the banana family, which have showy irregular flowers, two of the petals being united to form a long projecting tongue; *esp.* the bird-of-paradise flower, *S. reginae*, with orange and dark blue flowers, grown in hothouses.

strene /striːn/ *verb. obsolete* exc. *north.*
[Old English (*ge*)*strienan*: see STRAIN *noun*[1].]
†**1** *verb trans.* Beget or procreate (offspring). Also, gain, acquire. OE–LME.
2 *verb intrans. & trans.* Of dogs etc.: copulate (with). E18.

strengite /ˈstrɛŋʌɪt/ *noun.* L19.
[from J. A. *Streng* (1830–97), German mineralogist + -ITE[1].]
MINERALOGY. Hydrous ferric phosphate, occurring in incrustations of pinkish orthorhombic crystals and forming a series with variscite.

strength /strɛŋθ, strɛŋkθ/ *noun.*
[Old English *strengþu* = Old High German *strengida* from Germanic base also of STRONG *adjective*: see -TH[1].]
▶ **I** The quality or condition of being strong.
1 a Physical power; ability to exert muscular force. OE. ▸**b** Bodily vigour or efficiency in general, esp. as opp. to the weakness of illness, age, etc. OE. ▸**c** Power, whether mental, physical, or due to external resources, to act effectively; efficiency or vigour of mind or body. OE.
2 Capacity for moral effort or endurance; firmness of mind, purpose, etc. OE.
†**3** Superior power exerted for conquest, compulsion, etc.; force, violence. OE–LME.
4 Military power, esp. in numbers, equipment, or resources. OE. ▸**b** Defensive power of a fortification, fortified place, etc. LME.
5 Capacity in a thing to produce an effect; operative power. OE. ▸**b** *CARDS.* Effectiveness of a hand or player due to the cards held; the condition of being strong *in* a specified suit. M19.
6 Intensity of a force, physical condition, or feeling; potency or intensity of a drug, liquor, or active ingredient. ME.
7 The demonstrative force or weight of something, esp. evidence, an argument, etc. Formerly also, the force or import of a document. ME.
†**8** Legal authority or validity. LME–L17.
9 Power to sustain force without breaking or yielding. LME. ▸**b** *spec.* (*COMMERCE*) Firmness of prices, absence of lowering tendency. L19.
10 Firmness or richness of soil. L16.
11 Energy or vigour of literary or artistic creation; forcefulness of delineation, expression, etc. L17.

> 📖 **1a** M. DAS He wished he had the strength of a giant. **b** R. RENDELL His cuts and bruises were nearly healed, his strength returning. G. DALY The outbursts used up her small store of strength. **c** H. P. LIDDON His strength lay in accurate verbal scholarship. **2** J. H. NEWMAN Men who make such sacrifices . . evidence much strength of character. H. KUSHNER God . . can supply us with the strength we need. **4b** JOHN MORGAN Some Place of Strength, wherein to fortify himself. **5** SHAKES. *Mids. N. D.* Thy threats have no more strength than her weak prayers. *attrib.*: *Which?* Ready-made reading glasses have equal strength lenses. **6** R. V. JONES Weak signals on the expected wavelength . . increased in strength. N. HERMAN They spoke of currents and their treacherous strength. *Green Magazine* Cot deaths . . linked to the strength of surrounding electromagnetic fields. *Intercity Magazine* An ale's strength is measured by its Original Gravity. **8** *Law Times* The litigant should . . learn something of the strength of his opponent's case. **9** *Engineer* An all-welded . . frame for greater structural strength. **11** *Edinburgh Review* Dr Rennel's . . sermon . . is admirable for its strength of language. G. LEES The . . embodiment of swing, of sheer surging musical strength.

▶ **II** A strong thing.
12 A source of power or strength; a person or thing giving strength or support. Also, an attribute making for strength of character. OE.
†**13** A power, a faculty; an active property. OE–E16.
†**14** A feat of physical strength; an act requiring physical power. ME–L16.
15 a A stronghold, a fortress. Now *Hist.* (chiefly *Scot.*). ME. ▸†**b** A defensive work, a fortification. Also, a secure or defensive position. LME–E18.
†**16 a** *collect.* Troops, forces. ME–E18. ▸**b** A body of soldiers; a force. L15–E17.
17 The strongest part of something, esp. of a tide or current. E16.
18 a *MILITARY* etc. The number of people on the muster-roll of an army, regiment, etc.; the body of people enrolled; the number of ships in a navy or fleet. E17. ▸**b** *gen.* The number of people present or available. Also, a full complement. E17.

> 📖 **12** W. H. PRESCOTT The strength of his army lay in his Spanish veterans. **18a** B. MONTGOMERY Rifle platoons . . were under strength and the reinforcement situation was bad. C. RYAN Some companies had lost . . 50 per cent of their strength. **b** P. V. WHITE Voss called his men and divided his strength into several parts.

Phrases: **from strength** from a strong position. **from strength to strength** with ever-increasing success. **give me strength**: expr. exasperation. **in strength** in large numbers. **on the strength** (*MILITARY* etc.) on a muster-roll; (of an army marriage) officially approved and recognized. **on the strength of** encouraged by, relying on, on the basis of. ***OUTGROW one's strength.*** **strength through joy** [German *Kraft durch Freude*, a movement founded in Germany by the National Socialist Party in 1933] the promotion of physical and cultural recreational activities among working people. ***tensile strength***: see TENSILE 2. **the strength of** (*a*) the point or meaning of, the essence of; (*b*) ***that's about the strength of it***, that is what it amounts to; (*c*) ***get the strength of***, understand. ***tower of strength***: see TOWER *noun*[1]. ***wet strength***: see WET *adjective*.
■ **strengthful** *adjective* full of or characterized by strength LME. **strengthless** *adjective* without strength ME. **strengthlessly** *adverb* (*rare*) L19. **strengthlessness** *noun* M17.

strengthen /ˈstrɛŋθ(ə)n, -ŋkθ(ə)n/ *verb.* LME.
[from prec. + -EN[5].]
1 *verb trans.* Give moral support, courage, or confidence to; encourage, hearten. LME.
2 *verb trans.* Give defensive strength to, fortify; increase the fortifications of. LME.
3 *verb trans.* Give physical strength to, make stronger or more robust; reinforce. L16.
4 *verb trans.* Augment, intensify; *spec.* increase the strength or force of (reasons, a case, etc.), esp. by additional evidence. L16.
5 *verb intrans.* Become strong or stronger; grow in strength or intensity. E17.

> 📖 **1** D. MADDEN It strengthened her resolve to go to the convent. A. STEVENS Dreams can support and strengthen the ego. **3** W. BUCHAN Wine . . taken in moderation . . strengthens the stomach. *Times* The directors . . deemed it advisable to strengthen the insurance fund. *Down East* Heavy beams . . strengthened by wooden, angle supports. **4** *Spectator* I have . . drawn up some additional Arguments to strengthen the Opinion . . delivered. A. TROLLOPE The . . brilliancy of her white dress . . strengthened by the colour beneath it. C. P. SNOW His fellow feeling had strengthened mine. R. G. MYERS The . . initiatives should strengthen educational research. **5** *New Zealand Herald* The share market strengthened again on the . . Stock Exchange yesterday.

Phrases: **strengthen a person's hand(s)** enable or encourage a person to act with greater effect or vigour.
■ **strengthener** *noun* L16. **strengthening** *noun* (*a*) the action of the verb; an instance of this; (*b*) a thing that strengthens, supporting material, bracing; a source of strength: M16.

strengthily /ˈstrɛŋθɪli, -ŋkθ-/ *adverb. rare.* LME.
[from next + -LY[2].]
Strongly.

strengthy /ˈstrɛŋθi, -ŋkθi/ *adjective.* Chiefly *Scot. & north.* ME.
[from STRENGTH *noun* + -Y[1].]
†**1** Strong, mighty, powerful; difficult to overthrow. ME–L16.
2 Physically or muscularly strong. Now chiefly *dial.* LME.

strenkle *verb* var. of STRINKLE.

strenuity /strɪˈnjuːɪti/ *noun.* Now *rare.* LME.
[Latin *strenuitas*, from *strenuus*: see next, -ITY.]
The quality of being strenuous, strenuousness.

strenuous /ˈstrɛnjʊəs/ *adjective.* E17.
[from Latin *strenuus* brisk, active, valiant + -OUS.]
1 Of a person or a person's disposition: energetic, valiant, vigorously or unremittingly active. Also (now *rare*), zealous, earnest. E17. ▸**b** Of a voice or other sound: powerful, loud. *arch.* L17.
2 (Of action or effort) vigorous, energetic; requiring considerable sustained activity; (of a condition, period, etc.) characterized by considerable exertion. L17.

> 📖 **1** LD MACAULAY Those studies which form strenuous and sagacious men. **2** CARLYLE On this *Tragedy of Strafford* . . he expended many strenuous months. J. DUNN She enjoyed long strenuous walks . . across country.

■ **strenuˈosity** *noun* strenuousness L19. **strenuously** *adverb* LME. **strenuousness** *noun* M17.

strep /strɛp/ *noun. colloq.* E20.
[Abbreviation.]
1 Streptococcus; a streptococcal infection. E20.
2 = STREPTOMYCIN. M20.
Comb.: **strep throat** *N. Amer.* an acute sore throat with fever caused by streptococcal infection.

strepent /ˈstrɛp(ə)nt/ *adjective.* Now *rare* or *obsolete.* M18.
[Latin *strepent-* pres. ppl stem of *strepere*: see STREPITOUS, -ENT.]
Noisy.

†**streperous** *adjective.* M17–E19.
[from medieval Latin *streperus*, from Latin *strepere*: see STREPITOUS, -OUS.]
Noisy, harsh-sounding.

strephosymbolia /ˌstrɛfəʊsɪmˈbəʊlɪə/ *noun.* E20.
[from Greek *strephein* turn, twist + *symbolon* symbol + -IA[1].]
PSYCHOLOGY. Reversed perception of letters or words, esp. as a component of dyslexia.

strepie /ˈstriːpi, ˈstrɪəpi/ *noun. S. Afr.* E20.
[Afrikaans, from *streep* stripe + -IE.]
= ***bamboo-fish*** s.v. BAMBOO *noun*.

strepitant /ˈstrɛpɪt(ə)nt/ *adjective.* M19.
[Latin *strepitant-* pres. ppl stem of *strepitare* frequentative of *strepere* make a noise: see -ANT[1].]
Making a loud usu. harsh noise; noisy.
■ **strepiˈtation** *noun* (*rare*) a repeated harsh clattering noise E20.

strepitoso /strɛpɪˈtəʊzəʊ/ *adverb, adjective, & noun.* E19.
[Italian, lit. 'noisy, loud'.]
MUSIC. ▶**A** *adverb & adjective.* A direction: spirited(ly), boisterous(ly). E19.
▶ **B** *noun.* Pl. **-si** /-si/, **-sos**. A spirited or boisterous piece or passage. M20.

strepitous /ˈstrɛpɪtəs/ *adjective.* L17.
[from Latin *strepitus* noise, clatter, from *strepere* make a noise: see -OUS.]
Now chiefly *MUSIC.* Noisy, boisterous; accompanied by much noise.

> 📖 *Punch* Full orchestra, reinforced by gongs . . and sirens, brings the work to a . . strepitous conclusion.

strepsipterous /strɛpˈsɪpt(ə)rəs/ *adjective.* E19.
[from mod. Latin *Strepsiptera* (see below), from Greek *strepsi-* combining form of *strephein* twist + *pteron* wing: see -OUS.]
ENTOMOLOGY. Belonging or pertaining to the order Strepsiptera of minute holometabolous insects, the larvae and adult females of which are endoparasites of other insects, esp. bees, wasps, and plant-bugs. Cf. STYLOPS.
■ **strepsipteran** *adjective & noun* (*a*) *adjective* = STREPSIPTEROUS; (*b*) *noun* an insect of the order Strepsiptera, a stylops: M19.

strepsirhine /ˈstrɛpsɪrʌɪn/ *noun & adjective.* M19.
[from mod. Latin *Strepsirhini*, from Greek *strepsi-* (see prec.) + *rhin-*, *rhis* nose: see -INE[1].]
ZOOLOGY. ▶**A** *noun.* A strepsirhine primate. M19.
▶ **B** *adjective.* Designating any mammal having nostrils of a curved shape; *spec.* of, relating to, or designating a primate of the infraorder Strepsirhini (as in lemurs and lorises). L19.

strepto- /ˈstrɛptəʊ/ *combining form.* Before a vowel also **strept-**. L19.
[Greek, combining form of *streptos* twisted, from *strephein* turn, twist.]
Chiefly *SCIENCE.* Twisted; having the form of a twisted chain. Also, associated with or derived from streptococci or streptomycetes.
■ **streptoˈdornase** *noun* [from deoxyribonuclease] *MEDICINE* an enzyme produced by some streptococci and capable of dissolving pus and fibrinous exudates M20. **strepˈtolysin** *noun* (*MEDICINE*) a haemolytic toxin produced by certain streptococci E20. **streptovaricin** /-ˈvarɪsɪn/ *noun* (*PHARMACOLOGY*) each of a group of related antibiotics produced by the bacterium *Streptomyces spectabilis* M20. **streptozotocin** /-ˈzɒtəsɪn/ *noun* (*PHARMACOLOGY*) an antibiotic obtained from *Streptomyces achromogenes* that damages insulin-producing cells and is used to induce diabetes in laboratory animals M20.

streptocarpus /strɛptəˈkɑːpəs/ *noun.* E19.
[mod. Latin (see below), from STREPTO- + Greek *karpos* fruit.]
Any of various esp. southern African plants constituting the genus *Streptocarpus* (family Gesneriaceae), which are characterized by funnel-shaped violet, pink, etc., flowers and spirally twisted fruits and include several species grown for ornament. Also called ***Cape primrose***.

streptococcus /strɛptəˈkɒkəs/ *noun.* Pl. **-cocci** /-ˈkɒk(s)ʌɪ, -kˈɒk(s)iː/. L19.
[mod. Latin, from Greek *streptos* twisted (taken as 'twisted chain') + COCCUS.]
MEDICINE & BACTERIOLOGY. A non-motile Gram-positive spherical bacterium of the widespread genus *Streptococcus*,

usually occurring in chains, and including the agents of souring of milk and dental decay, and haemolytic pathogens causing various infections (including scarlet fever and pneumonia). Cf. STREP 1.

■ **streptococcal** *adjective* pertaining to or produced by streptococci L19. **streptococcic** /-kɒk(s)ɪk/ *adjective* (*rare*) = STREPTOCOCCAL E20.

streptokinase /strɛptə'kʌɪneɪz/ *noun.* M20.
[from STREPTO(COCCUS + KINASE.]
MEDICINE. An enzyme produced by haemolytic streptococci which activates plasminogen to form plasmin and is given intravenously to dissolve intravascular blood clots, or orally to reduce inflammation.

streptomycete /strɛptə'mʌɪsiːt/ *noun.* Pl. **-mycetes** /-'mʌɪsiːts, -mʌɪ'siːtiːz/. M20.
[Anglicized sing. of mod. Latin *Streptomyces* (see below), formed as STREPTO- + Greek *mukēs* fungus.]
BACTERIOLOGY. A filamentous actinomycete of the genus *Streptomyces*, members of which form chains of spores, and occur chiefly in soil as aerobic saprophytes resembling moulds.

streptomycin /strɛptə'mʌɪsɪn/ *noun.* M20.
[from prec. + -IN¹.]
PHARMACOLOGY. An antibiotic produced by the soil bacterium *Streptomyces griseus*, which was the first drug to be successful against tuberculosis but is now chiefly used with other drugs because of its toxic effects.

streptosolen /strɛptə'səʊlən/ *noun.* M20.
[mod. Latin (see below), from STREPTO- + Greek *sōlēn* pipe.]
An ornamental climbing shrub of the nightshade family, *Streptosolen jamesonii*, which is native to Colombia and Ecuador and bears clusters of orange flowers.

Streptothrix /'strɛptə(ʊ)θrɪks/ *noun.* Pl. **-thrices** /-'θrʌɪsiːz/. L19.
[mod. Latin (see below), formed as STREPTO- + Greek *thrix* hair.]
BACTERIOLOGY. A bacterium of the former genus *Streptothrix* (now included in *Actinomyces*), growing in interlacing masses of branching filaments.

■ **streptothricosis** /ˌstrɛptəʊθrɪ'kəʊsɪs/ *noun,* pl. **-coses** /-'kəʊsiːz/, *VETERINARY MEDICINE* a usu. chronic, sometimes fatal disease caused by actinomycetes, producing scabs on the skin of cows and other farm animals, esp. in the wet season in tropical regions E20. **streptothricin** /-'θrɪsɪn, -'θrʌɪsɪn/ *noun* (*BIOCHEMISTRY*) each of a group of related antibiotic but toxic compounds produced by the soil bacterium *Actinomyces lavendulae* M20.

Strepyan /'strɛpɪən/ *adjective.* Now *rare.* E20.
[French *Strépyien*, from *Strépy* in Belgium: see -AN.]
ARCHAEOLOGY. Designating or pertaining to a palaeolithic industry of Europe supposed to have existed before the Chellean.

stress /strɛs/ *noun.* ME.
[Aphet. from DISTRESS *noun* or partly from Old French *estrece*, *estresse* narrowness, straitness, oppression, ult. from Latin *strictus* STRICT: cf. STRAIT *adjective*¹ & *adverb*¹.]
▶ **I** †**1** Hardship, adversity, affliction. ME–E18.
†**2** Force, pressure, or violence against a person for the purpose of compulsion or extortion. ME–L17.
3 a Pressure, tension, etc., exerted on an object; the strain *of* a load or weight. Now *rare* exc. as in sense b below. ME. ▸**b** Orig., a force acting on or within a body or structure and tending to deform it (i.e. cause strain). Now usu., the intensity of this, the force per unit area. M19. ▸**c** Physical strain on a bodily organ. M19.
4 a The overpowering pressure *of* an adverse force or influence. E16. ▸**b** A state of affairs involving or characterized by strained effort, demand on physical or mental energy. Now *spec.* a condition or adverse circumstance that disturbs, or is likely to disturb, the normal physiological or psychological functioning of an individual; such conditions collectively; the resulting state of disturbance or distress. M17. ▸**c** A pressing demand. E19.
†**5** Dependence on a basis of argument, evidence, etc.; burden of proof; (degree of) reliance. Also, the weightiest or most important part or point (of a business, question, etc.); effectiveness (of a poem, statement, etc.). M17–L18.
6 Strained exertion, strong effort. Now *rare* or *obsolete.* L17.
7 Special significance, importance, or emphasis. M18.
8 Relative prominence or force of utterance, esp. as characterizing a particular syllable or syllables of a word, line of verse, etc., or particular words of a sentence. Also, a rhythmical or metrical pattern of accentuation; an accent, *esp.* the principal one in a word. M18.

🕮 **3b** ***principal stress***: see PRINCIPAL *adjective.* ***proof stress***: see PROOF *noun.* ***residual stress***: see RESIDUAL *adjective* 2d. ***Reynolds stress***: see REYNOLDS 2. **4a** J. R. GREEN The stress of poverty may have been the cause. M. HEWLETT Pious virgins, under stress of these things, swoon. **storm and stress** = STURM UND DRANG. **b** C. G. LANG Into the very midst of toil and stress a deep sense of joy. B. VINE In very moments of stress . . I always talk aloud to myself. G. DALY Her facial tic returned under stress. *Times Educ. Suppl.* Saturating seven-year-olds with . . tests . . creates stresses and strains within the classroom. **c** R. K. NARAYAN When the stress for cash became acute. **5** DEFOE I always put a great deal of stress upon his judgment. J. WESLEY The stress of the argument lies on this very point. **6** J. LOCKE They must not be put to a stress beyond their strength. **7** J. N. ISBISTER Psychoanalysis . . puts great stress on the importance of early infantile relationships. ***lay stress on***: see LAY *verb*¹. **8** ***strong stress***: see STRONG *adjective.*

▶ **II 9** *LAW.* = DISTRESS *noun* 3, 4. Long *obsolete* exc. *dial.* LME.

Comb.: **stress analysis** *ENGINEERING* analysis of the stresses within a mechanical structure in relation to its function; **stress analyst** *ENGINEERING* an expert in stress analysis; **stress-breaker** *DENTISTRY* a device attached to or built into a partial denture to reduce the occlusive forces borne by the teeth and underlying tissue; **stress-breaking** *adjective* (*DENTISTRY*) acting as a stress-breaker; **stress concentration** *ENGINEERING* (*a*) a local increase in the stress inside an object; (*b*) a stress raiser; **stress contour** *PHONETICS* a sequence of varying levels of stress within an utterance; **stress corrosion** *METALLURGY* the development of cracks as a result of the combined effects of stress and corrosion; **stress diagram** *MECHANICS* a diagram that represents graphically the stresses in a framed structure; **stress-dilatancy** *PHYSICS*: resulting from applied stress; **stress disease**: resulting from continual exposure to stress; **stress fracture** *MEDICINE* a fracture of a bone caused by the repeated application of a high load; **stress-free** *adjective* pertaining to or possessing freedom from mechanical or biological stress; **stress grade** an estimate of the strength of timber by stress-grading; **stress-grade** *verb trans.* grade (timber) by strength on the basis of the number and distribution of knots and other visible defects; **stress-group** *PHONETICS* a group of syllables forming a rhythmic unit with one primary stress; **stress incontinence** *MEDICINE* a condition (found chiefly in women) in which escape of urine occurs when the intra-abdominal pressure increases suddenly, as in coughing or lifting; **stress mark** (*a*) *PHONETICS* a symbol or diacritical mark indicating that a syllable is stressed; (*b*) *PHOTOGRAPHY* a mark (esp. a black line) on a print caused by friction or pressure on the film surface; **stress mineral** *GEOLOGY* a mineral whose formation in metamorphic rocks is thought to be dependent on shearing stress; **stress-neutral** *adjective* (*LINGUISTICS*) designating a suffix which does not affect the placement of stress in a word; **stress phoneme** *PHONETICS*: which is contrastive only in virtue of a distinctive degree of stress; **stress raiser** *ENGINEERING* a feature in the shape or composition of an object that causes a local increase in stress; **stress relaxation** *ENGINEERING* a decrease of stress in a material when the associated deformation is kept constant; **stress relief** *METALLURGY* the reduction of residual stress in a material by thermal treatment; **stress-relieve** *verb trans.* (*METALLURGY*) subject to stress relief (freq. as ***stress-relieved*** *ppl adjective*, ***stress-relieving*** *verbal noun*); **stress-strain** *adjective* (*ENGINEERING*) pertaining to or depicting the relation between mechanical stress and the strain it produces; **stress test** *MEDICINE* a test of cardiovascular fitness made by monitoring the heart rate and electrocardiogram during exercise; **stress-timed** *adjective* (*PHONETICS*) designating or pertaining to a language in which primary stresses occur at roughly equal intervals, irrespective of the number of unstressed syllables in between (opp. ***syllable-timed***).

■ **stressful** *adjective* causing or tending to cause stress or mental fatigue; full of or subject to stress or strain: M19. **stressfully** *adverb* L19. **stressfulness** *noun* L20. **stressless** *adjective* (chiefly *PHONETICS*) having no stress, unstressed L19.

stress /strɛs/ *verb*¹ *trans.* ME.
[Orig. aphet. from Old French *estrecier*, ult. from Latin *strictus* (see prec.); later senses from the noun.]
†**1** Compel or constrain (a person); restrict the liberty of, confine, (a person). ME–M16.
2 Subject to (freq. financial) hardship; afflict, trouble, oppress. Now *rare.* M16.
3 Subject to mechanical, physical, physiological, or psychological stress or strain; overwork, fatigue. M16.
4 Lay stress on, emphasize, (a word, phrase, fact, idea, etc.); *spec.* place a stress accent on (a syllable). M19.

🕮 **3** *Country Life* Transfer to a new environment stresses the calves. *Road Racing & Training* Stressing your body this way . . will improve your use of oxygen. *Engineering* Be sure that bolts are correctly stressed. *Times* We don't have to stress the boat or the crew. **4** R. BRIDGES It saved the monotony of a pentameter to stress the penultimate. G. LORD 'I want it done very, very neatly,' she stressed. R. FRASER At pains to stress the wild . . nature of the inhabitants. L. GORDON Eliot's play stresses that Becket's sainthood was not achieved without struggle.

■ **stressa'bility** *noun* (*LINGUISTICS*) the quality of being stressable M20. **stressable** *adjective* (*LINGUISTICS*) able to be stressed M20.

stress /strɛs/ *verb*² *trans. obsolete* exc. *dial.* LME.
[Aphet. from DISTRESS *verb.*]
Distrain.

stressed /strɛst/ *adjective.* M16.
[from STRESS *verb*¹ + -ED¹.]
1 That has been stressed; affected by or showing signs of stress or strain. M16.
2 *spec.* Marked or to be pronounced with a stress; emphasized. L19.
3 *ENGINEERING.* Subjected to mechanical stress; *spec.* prestressed. M20.

🕮 **1** D. JUDD The nursing staff felt . . stressed by the demands. *Maclean's Magazine* As the natural environment grows more stressed. **2** A. C. CLARK Rhythm . . depends upon . . stressed and unstressed syllables.

Comb. & special collocations: **stressed out** *adjective* (*colloq.*) (of a person) debilitated or exhausted as a result of stress; **stressed skin** an outer covering of an aircraft or other structure that bears a significant part of the stresses and contributes to the overall strength and stiffness.

stressman /'strɛsmən/ *noun.* Pl. **-men.** M20.
[from STRESS *noun* + MAN *noun.*]
ENGINEERING. = ***stress analyst*** s.v. STRESS *noun.*

stressor /'strɛsə/ *noun.* M20.
[from STRESS *verb*¹ + -OR.]
A single condition or agent that constitutes a stress for an organism.

stretch /strɛtʃ/ *noun & adjective.* M16.
[from the verb.]
▶ **A** *noun.* **1** Orig. (chiefly *Scot.*), an act overstepping the bounds of one's authority, the law, fairness, etc.; a deviation from custom or precedent. Now, any act or instance of extending the scope or application of something beyond its proper or normal limits; *spec.* (*a*) an unwarranted exercise *of* power or prerogative; (*b*) an extraordinary exercise *of* the imagination. Also, an exaggeration. M16.
2 a Amount of forcible extension or dilatation. E17. ▸**b** The action or an act of stretching a limb or limbs; extension of the limbs; *spec.* (*a*) an act of drawing up the body and extending the arms, as in tiredness or (*BASEBALL*) preparing to pitch; (*b*) a walk taken for exercise. L17. ▸**c** The fact or condition of being stretched. Now chiefly *fig.*, a state of physical or mental tension; (now *rare*) exhausting effort, mental strain. L17. ▸**d** Stretchability. L19. ▸**e** (Planned allowance for) modification of an aircraft design, esp. by lengthening the fuselage; *colloq.* an aircraft or motor vehicle modified so as to have an extended seating or storage capacity (usu. *attrib.*). M20.
3 Orig., length. Later, a continuous length or distance or expanse; a continuous portion of a journey, road, river, etc.; *spec.* (*a*) *NAUTICAL* a continuous sail or distance covered on one tack; (*b*) *LINGUISTICS* a definable extent of text or speech. M17. ▸**b** A continuous journey or march. Now *colloq.* L17.
4 A continuous period of or *of* time; an uninterrupted spell of work, service, activity, rest, etc. L17. ▸**b** *spec.* A term of hard labour; a year spent in prison. Now usu., a period of imprisonment, a prison sentence. *colloq.* E19.
5 A straight on a racetrack, *esp.* the home straight; *transf.* & *fig.* the concluding stage of a race, contest, event, project, etc. Orig. & chiefly *N. Amer.* M19.

🕮 **1** W. BLACKSTONE Distinguish between the arbitrary stretch, and the legal exertion, of prerogative. *Practical Wireless* Voltages which cannot, by any stretch of the imagination, be called lethal. **2b** C. M. YONGE He gave a yawn and a stretch. M. LOWRY Muscular hawkers lifted aloft, in one sinewy stretch of the forearm, heavy trays. M. M. KAYE The small brisk chimes made him start . . because, subconsciously, his nerves were on the stretch. **c** D. JOHNSON The string . . is kept at its stretch by means of a . . stick. **e** *New York Times* This big Mercedes stretch pulls up with them sittin' in the back. ***stretch jet***, ***stretch limousine***, etc. **3** R. H. DANA Two long stretches . . brought us into the roads. P. P. READ Returning with him to sit in his compartment for the last stretch of the journey. J. BARNES The scenery along this stretch of the Seine reminded him of Norfolk. *South African Panorama* Great stretches of inhospitable . . Kalahari. **4** R. SUTCLIFF He had long empty stretches of time on his hands. J. BARZUN The family lived first in Albany; then, for an unexampled stretch of seven years, in New York. **b** A. WILSON She had it in her power to send him to jail for quite a long stretch. **5** D. HAMMETT A horse . . coming down the stretch with a nose lead.

Phrases: **at a stretch** (*a*) without intermission, in one continuous period; (*b*) with much effort. **at full stretch** to capacity; working as hard or fast as possible. **at one stretch** = *at a stretch* above. ***home stretch***: see HOME *adjective.* ***two-way stretch***: see TWO-WAY *adjective* 2.

Comb. (partly from the verb): **stretch forming** the shaping of sheet metal under tension by the pressure of a punch; **stretch mark** a linear mark on the skin (esp. of the abdomen) when it has been distended by pregnancy or obesity (usu. in *pl.*); †**stretch-mouthed** *adjective* (*rare*, Shakes.) wide-mouthed; **stretchneck** *arch.* a pillory; **stretch receptor** *PHYSIOLOGY* a sensory receptor that responds to the stretching of tissue; **stretch reflex** *PHYSIOLOGY* a reflex contraction of a muscle in response to its being stretched; **stretch spinning** a spinning process during which the filaments are stretched.

▶ **B** *attrib.* or as *adjective.* Of a (usu. synthetic) fibre or fabric: elastic, capable of stretching; (of a garment) made of such fabric, esp. so as to fit closely. M20.

stretch /strɛtʃ/ *verb.* Pa. t. & pple †**straight**, †**straught**, **stretched**. See also STRAIGHT *adjective*¹.
[Old English *streccan* = Old Frisian *strekka*, Middle Low German, Middle Dutch *strecken* (Dutch *strekken*), Old & mod. High German *strecken*, from West Germanic. Cf. DISTRAUGHT *adjective*, STRAKE *noun*, STRECK, STREEK.]
▶ **I 1** *verb trans.* Prostrate (oneself, one's body); extend (one's limbs) in a reclining position. Also foll. by *out.* OE. ▸†**b** *verb trans.* Spread out on the ground; make (a bed) of straw etc. OE–L15. ▸**c** *verb trans.* Lay (a person) flat; *dial.* lay out (a corpse). Also (*slang*), kill, murder. ME. ▸†**d** *verb intrans.* Fall to the ground; lie *down* at full length. *rare.* LME–E19.

2 *verb trans.* **a** Extend (the arms) laterally; (of a bird) expand (the wings), esp. for flight. **ME.** ▸**b** Of a tree: grow (branches) to spread over a (specified) distance. **LME.**
3 *verb intrans. & refl.* Straighten to one's full height or length, esp. from a stooping, cramped, or relaxed position; straighten one's body and extend one's arms (and legs) to tighten the muscles after being relaxed (as in sleeping). **ME.**

📖 **1** K. A. PORTER He . . stretched himself in the nearest deck-chair. E. BOWEN He looked forward to stretching out his limbs—cramped by last night in the train. **c** W. H. PRESCOTT The struggle lasted . . till both of Pizarro's pages were stretched by his side. **2a** A. CHRISTIE Laid down her . . tools and stretched her arms widely. **3** SIR W. SCOTT Yawning and stretching himself like one whose slumbers had been broken. R. FRAME I would stretch up and touch the ceilings with my fingertips.

▸**II 4 a** *verb trans.* Put out or extend (a hand, arm, leg, etc.). Freq. foll. by *forward, forth, out.* **OE.** ▸**b** *verb intrans.* Orig., (of an arm) be extended. Later, extend one's arm or hand, reach *for* something. **ME.**
5 *verb trans.* †**a** Direct (one's hope, trust, etc.) towards someone or something; extend (relief) to a person. **OE–E18.** ▸**b** Hold out, hand, or reach (an object). *arch. rare.* **LME.**

📖 **4a** W. C. L. MARTIN The animal staggers . . its flanks heave, the head is stretched out. P. D. JAMES She stretched out her hand to click on the bedside light. *fig.*: A. CRAIG Pollarded trees . . stretched mutilated hands to the sky. **b** N. MOSLEY Children crowded in . . stretching immediately for food. **5b** LYTTON Said Gawaine, as he stretched his platter, 'I'll first the pie discuss.'

▸**III** †**6** *verb trans.* Direct (one's course). Only in **ME.**
7 *verb intrans.* Make one's way, esp. rapidly or with effort. **ME.**
8 *verb intrans.* NAUTICAL. Sail continuously in one direction. Also foll. by *away, off,* etc. **L17.**

📖 **7** DRYDEN Cormorants forsake the Sea, And stretching to the Covert wing their way. SIR W. SCOTT Stretch onward in thy fleet career! **8** F. MARRYAT They were stretching off the land.

▸**IV 9** *verb trans.* Place (an object) so as to reach from one point to another or across a space. Now chiefly *spec.*, extend (something flexible) from one point to another or across a space, by drawing it out to more or less the full length or width. **ME.** ▸†**b** Pitch (a tent). Also foll. by *out.* **LME–L16.**
10 *verb intrans.* Have a specified extent in space; extend or be continuous to a certain point or over a certain (now esp. large) distance or area; (long *rare* or *obsolete*) extend or run in a specified direction. **ME.** ▸**b** Have extent in time; endure, last. *rare.* **E17.**
†**11** *verb intrans. fig.* Have a specified capacity; be adequate for a specified purpose; have a specified extent or range of action or application. **ME–M17.**
†**12** *verb intrans.* Tend, be serviceable (*to*). **LME–E17.**

📖 **9** SIR W. SCOTT The veil which interested persons had stretched betwixt us. **10** DRYDEN A Tract of Land . . Along the Tyber, stretching to the West. J. HILTON The whole cultivated area stretched for perhaps a dozen miles. R. MACAULAY The Trojan plain stretching level to the sea.

▸**V 13** *verb trans.* Orig., fasten (a person) to a cross to execute by crucifixion. Later (now *Hist.*), exert a pull on (a person, a person's limbs), esp. as torture or punishment; rack. Also foll. by *out.* **ME.**
14 a *verb intrans. & refl.* Strain, press forward, use effort. Also foll. by *on. arch.* **ME.** ▸†**b** *verb trans.* Strain, exert to the utmost, (one's powers). **E–M17.**
15 *verb trans.* Make taut; make (a rope, piece of cloth, etc.) straight or even by pulling at the ends. Also, straighten (hair). **LME.** ▸**b** *verb intrans.* Become taut. **M19.**
16 a *verb trans.* Execute (a person) by hanging. *arch.* **L16.** ▸†**b** *verb intrans.* Of a person: be hanged. **L16–L17.**

📖 **13** SHAKES. *Meas. for M.* The Duke dare no more stretch this finger of mine than he Dare rack his own. **15** *New York Times* Huge white plastic tents stretched on steel frames. *Independent* Some of the canvases . . were stored, rolled up, . . and had to be stretched by exhibitions staff.

▸**VI 17** *verb trans.* **a** Lengthen or widen (a material thing) by force; pull out to greater length or width; enlarge in girth or capacity by internal pressure. Freq. foll. by *out.* **LME.** ▸**b** Open wide (the eyes, mouth, etc.). **L16.**
18 *verb intrans.* Be or admit of being lengthened or widened by force without breaking; *fig.* (foll. by *out*) last for a longer period of time, be prolonged. **L15.** ▸**b** JAZZ. Play in a relaxed improvisatory manner, esp. in a solo. Foll. by *out.* **M20.**
19 *verb trans. transf. & fig.* ▸**a** Enlarge or amplify beyond proper or natural limits; extend unduly the scope or application of (a law, rule, etc.) or the meaning of (a word); cause to last for a longer period of time, prolong, (usu. foll. by *out*). **M16.** ▸**b** *verb intrans. & trans.* Exaggerate. *colloq.* **L17.** ▸**c** Eke out (food), esp. to serve a greater number of people than originally intended. Also foll. by *out. colloq.* **L19.** ▸**d** ENGINEERING. Increase the capability or power of (an engine etc.). **M20.** ▸**e** *verb trans.* Cause (a person) to make the maximum use of his or her talents or abilities. **M20.**

📖 **17a** *Scientific American* Stretch a block of material and its girth contracts. **18** B. TAYLOR The thread won't stretch forever! . . It might be broken. **19** C. P. SNOW Here I was stretching the truth. A. PRICE Stretch those laws . . . But break—never! **b** SWIFT Not worth forty pounds, so I stretched a little when I said a thousand. R. STOUT Everyone in Washington is connected . . with Watergate. That's stretching it, but not much. **c** H. MACINNES Worrying how far she could stretch the beef stew. **e** D. DEVINE I hear good reports of your work . . however, we're not stretching you enough. *Times* Could ensure . . that the curriculum suited and stretched all children.

Phrases: †**stretch a halter** be hanged. **stretch a point** agree to something not normally allowed. ***stretch one's legs***: see LEG *noun*. ***stretch one's wings***: see WING *noun*. **stretch the neck of** *arch.* = sense 16a above. ***stretch the rules***: see RULE *noun*. **stretch to the oar**, **stretch to the stroke** *arch.* exert one's strength in rowing.
Comb.: (See also combs. of the noun) **stretch-out** (chiefly *N. Amer.*) (*a*) the practice of requiring workers to do extra work for little or no extra pay; (*b*) an economizing measure by which production is scheduled to proceed more slowly than originally planned.
■ **stretcha'bility** *noun* ability to be stretched **M20.** **stretchable** *adjective* able to be stretched **LME.**

stretcher /ˈstrɛtʃə/ *noun & verb.* **ME.**
[from STRETCH *verb* + -ER[1].]
▸**A** *noun.* **I 1** A person who stretches; *spec.* one employed to stretch cloth. **ME.**
2 An instrument or appliance for expanding fabric, making it taut, etc.; *spec.* a wooden frame on which an artist's canvas is spread and drawn taut ready for painting. **M16.**
3 A thing laid lengthways; *esp.* a brick or stone laid with its long side along the face of the wall. Cf. HEADER *noun* 2. **L17.**
4 A bar, rod, etc., serving as a brace or support; *spec.* (*a*) a crosspiece between the legs of a chair; (*b*) a board in a rowing-boat against which the feet of the rower are pressed; (*c*) a stick for keeping a fishing net expanded; (*d*) any of the extensible rods joining the ribs and the sliding sleeve of an umbrella. **L18.**
5 A framework of two poles with canvas or other material between, carried by two people and used for the emergency transport of a sick, injured, or dead person in a lying position. **M19.** ▸**b** A folding bed or bedstead; a camp-bed. Orig. & chiefly *Austral.* **M19.**

📖 **5** V. BRITTAIN I was carried off the boat on a stretcher, and pushed into one of the ambulances.

▸**II** †**6** A toe of a hawk or falcon. **L15–L17.**
7 An exaggeration; a lie. *arch. slang.* **L17.**
8 ANGLING. A tail-fly. **E19.**

📖 **7** J. K. JEROME The customary stretchers about the wonderful things we had done.

Comb.: **stretcher-bearer** a person who helps to carry a stretcher, esp. in a war or at a major accident; **stretcher bond** BRICKLAYING: in which only stretchers (and not headers) are used; **stretcher case** an injured or sick person needing conveyance on a stretcher; **stretcher fly** = sense 8 above; **stretcher-party** (chiefly MILITARY) a group of stretcher-bearers; **stretcher strain** METALLURGY a furrow on the surface of a metal produced by local deformation.
▸**B** *verb trans.* Carry (*off*) or convey (a sick or injured person) on a stretcher. **L20.**

stretching /ˈstrɛtʃɪŋ/ *verbal noun.* **LME.**
[from STRETCH *verb* + -ING[1].]
The action of STRETCH *verb*; an instance of this. Also foll. by *forth, out.*
Comb.: **stretching-board**: on which a corpse is laid out before being placed in a coffin; **stretching-bond** BRICKLAYING = ***stretcher bond*** s.v. STRETCHER *noun*; **stretching-course** BRICKLAYING: consisting wholly of stretchers; **stretching-iron** a flat metal plate used in smoothing or finishing leather.

stretching /ˈstrɛtʃɪŋ/ *ppl adjective.* **M16.**
[formed as prec. + -ING[2].]
That stretches.
stretching beam a tie-beam or brace used in building.

stretchy /ˈstrɛtʃi/ *adjective.* **M19.**
[from STRETCH *verb* + -Y[1].]
Able or inclined to stretch; elastic.
■ **stretchiness** *noun* **M20.**

stretta /ˈstrɛtə/ *noun.* Pl. **-tte** /-ti/, **-ttas.** **L19.**
[Italian, fem. of STRETTO.]
MUSIC. A final passage played at a (gradually) faster tempo.

stretto /ˈstrɛtəʊ/ *adverb & noun.* **M18.**
[Italian, lit. 'narrow'.]
MUSIC. ▸**A** *adverb.* A direction: with gradually increasing speed (esp. with ref. to a final passage). **M18.**
▸**B** *noun.* Pl. **-tti** /-ti/, **-ttos.** A fugal device in which the subject entries follow closely in succession, each subject overlapping with the next. Also, = STRETTA. **M19.**
stretto maestrale /mʌɪˈstrɑːli/ a stretto of a fugue played in canon.

streusel /ˈstrɔɪz(ə)l, ˈstruːz(ə)l/ *noun.* Chiefly *N. Amer.* **E20.**
[German, from *streuen* to sprinkle.]
(A cake or pastry with) a crumbly topping or filling made from fat, flour, cinnamon, and sugar. Freq. *attrib.*

strew /struː/ *noun.* **M16.**
[from the verb.]
A number of things strewn over a surface or scattered about. Usu. foll. by *of.*

📖 *Daily Telegraph* The wayside rubbish dump and the strew of 'unreturnable' bottles.

strew /struː/ *verb trans.* Pa. pple **strewn** /struːn/, **strewed.** Also (*arch.*) **strow** /strəʊ/; pa. pple **strowed**, (*arch.*) **strown** /strəʊn/.
[Old English *stre(o)wian* corresp. to Old Frisian *strēwa*, Old Saxon *strōian*, Old High German *strewen* (Dutch *strooien*, German *streuen*), Old Norse *strá*, ult. from Indo-European base repr. by Latin *sternere*. Cf. STRAW *noun & adjective, verb.*]
1 Spread loosely or scatter on the ground, a floor, or some other surface; sprinkle (something granulated or powdery) over a surface. Freq. foll. by *about, around, on, over.* **OE.**
2 Cover or spread (a surface) with or *with* loosely scattered or sprinkled things or material. Also foll. by *over.* Usu. in *pass.* **ME.**
3 a Level to the ground; lay low, throw down. Also foll. by *down.* Chiefly *poet.* **LME.** ▸**b** Calm (waves or a storm). *poet.* **L16.**
4 Be spread or scattered on (a surface). **E16.**

📖 **1** B. PYM On the table were strewn the bills. E. DAVID Arrange the fennel halves . . . Strew breadcrumbs over them. M. LEITCH Every drawer was turned out, and everything in it strewn on the floor. *fig.*: TENNYSON Heaven bursts her starry floors And strows her lights below. **2** H. KELLER The ground was strewn with the . . leaves of autumn. *Nature* The seafloor around the pillars is strewn by rubble. *fig.*: MILTON All our Law and Story strew'd With Hymns. **strewn field** GEOLOGY a region of the earth's surface over which tektites of a similar age are found. **4** K. MANSFIELD Scraps of newspaper . . and fruit skins strowed the pavement.

■ **strewage** *noun* strewn things or material **E20.** **strewer** *noun* **L16.** **strewing** *noun* (*a*) the action of the verb; †(*b*) (a layer or bed of) strewn things; *esp.* (in *pl.*), flowers, leaves, etc., strewn on a grave: **OE.** **strewment** *noun* (*arch.*) something strewn or for strewing; in *pl.*, flowers etc. strewn on a grave: **E17**

'strewth /struːθ/ *interjection. colloq.* Also **'struth, str-.** **L19.**
[from 'S- + TRUTH *noun*.]
God's truth!: an oath or forcible exclamation.

stria /ˈstrʌɪə/ *noun.* Pl. **striae** /ˈstrʌɪiː/. **M16.**
[Latin = furrow, grooving. Cf. STRIOLA.]
1 ARCHITECTURE. A fillet between the flutes of a column, pilaster, etc. **M16.**
2 a Chiefly SCIENCE. A small groove, channel, or ridge; a narrow streak, stripe, or band of distinctive colour, structure, or texture; *esp.* each of two or more. **L17.** ▸**b** MEDICINE. A purple streak on the skin appearing in certain fevers; a stretch mark (freq. with mod. Latin specifying word). **M19.** ▸**c** GLASS-MAKING. An imperfection in the form of a streak or band. Now *rare.* **M19.** ▸**d** ELECTRICITY. Each of the alternate bright and dark bands observed in Geissler tubes during an electric discharge. **M19.**
Phrases: **stria albicans** /ˈalbɪkanz/, pl. **-cantes** /-ˈkantiːz/, [= being white] MEDICINE a former stretch mark that has become pale and silvery following delivery. **stria atrophica** /əˈtrɒfɪkə/, pl. **-cae** /-kiː/ [=atrophic] MEDICINE a stretch mark. **stria gravidarum** /gravɪˈdɑːrəm/ [= of a pregnant woman] MEDICINE a stretch mark on the abdomen of a pregnant woman, usu. darker than the surrounding skin.
■ **striaeform** *adjective* having the form or structure of striae **E19.**

striata *noun* pl. of STRIATUM.

striate /ˈstrʌɪeɪt/ *adjective.* **L17.**
[Latin *striatus* pa. pple of *striare*, formed as STRIA: see -ATE[2].]
1 BOTANY, ZOOLOGY, & GEOLOGY. Marked with striae; having longitudinal lines, streaks, furrows, or ridges. **L17.**
2 ANATOMY. Of or pertaining to the corpus striatum. **L19.**

striate /strʌɪˈeɪt/ *verb trans.* **E18.**
[formed as prec.: see -ATE[3].]
Mark or score with striae; furrow, streak.

striated /strʌɪˈeɪtɪd/ *adjective.* **M17.**
[from (the same root as) STRIATE *adjective* + -ED[1].]
1 a Chiefly BIOLOGY & GEOLOGY. = STRIATE *adjective.* **M17.** ▸**b** Of an electric discharge: exhibiting striae. **M19.**
2 ARCHITECTURE. Channelled, grooved. **E18.**
3 Constituting striae. **M19.**
1 striated muscle ANATOMY muscle composed of regularly ordered fibres divided by transverse bands into striations, forming most of the body's musculature and usu. under voluntary control; also called ***skeletal muscle, striped muscle, voluntary muscle.***

striation /strʌɪˈeɪʃ(ə)n/ *noun*. M19.
[from STRIATE *verb*: see -ATION.]
1 Striated condition or appearance. M19.
2 Chiefly SCIENCE. Each of a set of striae; a streak, a band; *spec.* in GEOLOGY a groove or scratch cut in a rock surface by rock fragments embedded in a moving glacier. M19.

striatonigral /strʌɪˌeɪtə(ʊ)ˈnʌɪgr(ə)l/ *adjective*. L20.
[from CORPUS) *striatum* + -O- + SUBSTANTIA) *nigra* + -AL[1].]
ANATOMY. Connecting the corpus striatum and the substantia nigra.

striatum /strʌɪˈeɪtəm/ *noun*. Pl. **-ta** /-tə/. L19.
[mod. Latin, neut. of Latin *striatus* STRIATE *adjective*.]
ANATOMY. = CORPUS *striatum*; *spec.* the neostriatum.
■ **striatal** *adjective* E20.

striature /ˈstrʌɪətʃʊə/ *noun*. Now *rare* or *obsolete*. E18.
[Latin *striatura*, formed as STRIATE *adjective*: see -URE.]
Disposition of striae; striation.

†**strich** *noun*. *rare*. M–L16.
[Prob. from SCRITCH-*owl* after Latin *strix*.]
The screech owl or barn owl.

SPENSER The ruefull Strich, still waiting on the bere.

strick /strɪk/ *noun* & *verb*. LME.
[from weak grade of base of STRIKE *verb*.]
► **A** *noun*. **1** A bundle of broken hemp, flax, etc., for heckling or dressing ready for spinning. LME.
2 A dry measure of capacity for corn, coal, etc.; a vessel holding this measure. Cf. STRAIK *noun*[1] 1, STRIKE *noun*[1] 4. Now *Scot.* & *dial.* LME.
3 = STRIKE *noun*[1] 3. Cf. STRICKLE *noun* 1. Now *dial.* LME.
► **B** *verb trans.* **1** Strike off (grain) level with the brim of a measuring vessel. LME.
2 Prepare (hemp, flax, etc.) for heckling; heckle (hemp, flax, etc.). E19.

stricken /ˈstrɪk(ə)n/ *adjective*. L15.
[pa. pple of STRIKE *verb*.]
1 Of a measure: having its contents levelled with the brim of the measuring vessel; level, not heaped. L15.
2 Esp. of a deer: wounded in a hunt. E16.
3 Struck with a blow. Also, (of a sound or note) produced by striking a blow. M16.
4 Afflicted with grief, despair, etc.; affected by or overcome with illness; overwhelmed with misfortune, fear, etc.; (of a person's face) showing great distress. Freq. as 2nd elem. of comb. L18.

3 R. LOWELL The stricken . . gong made sounds like steam banging through pipes. **4** W. HORWOOD Appalled, hurt, stricken more in heart and mind than body. *New Yorker* She looked stricken as she saw the paint being absorbed by the rug. ***horror-stricken***, ***panic-stricken***, etc.

Special collocations: **stricken field** (chiefly *literary*) a joined engagement between armed forces or combatants; a pitched battle. **stricken hour** *arch.* a full hour as indicated by the striking of the clock.
¶ See also ***stricken in years***, ***stricken in age*** s.v. STRIKE *verb*.
■ **strickenly** *adverb* L19.

stricken *verb pa. pple*: see STRIKE *verb*.

strickle /ˈstrɪk(ə)l/ *noun* & *verb*.
[Old English *stricel* rel. to STRIKE *verb*.]
► **A** *noun*. **1** A straight piece of wood with which surplus grain is struck off level with the brim of a measure. Also (*rare*), the amount so measured. Cf. STRIKE *noun*[1] 3. OE. ▸**b** Any of various implements used for levelling a substance in casting or moulding. L17.
2 A tool used to whet a scythe. Also, a mechanical grinder. M17.
► **B** *verb trans.* FOUNDING. Strike (the superfluous sand) *off* with a strickle in moulding; shape (a core) or form (a mould) by means of a strickle. L19.

strict /strɪkt/ *adjective* & *adverb*. LME.
[Latin *strictus* pa. pple of *stringere* draw tight. Cf. STRAIT *adjective*[1] & *adverb*[1], STRINGENT.]
► **A** *adjective*. **I** *lit.* **1** Restricted as to space or extent. Now *rare* or *obsolete*. LME.
†**2** Drawn or pressed tightly together; tight, close. Also (*rare*), stretched taut. L15–M19.
3 †**a** Of a muscle etc.: tense; not slack or relaxed. L16–M18. ▸**b** Of a frost: keen, hard. *rare*. L19.
4 Stiffly and narrowly erect. *obsolete* exc. BOTANY. L16.
► **II** *fig.* †**5** Restricted or limited in amount, meaning, application, etc. L16–M18.
6 Rigorously established or implemented; *spec.* (**a**) (of a law, ordinance, etc.) stringently framed or executed, allowing no refusal or evasion; (**b**) (of an inquiry, investigation, etc.) carried out with unremitting attention to detail, relentless; (**c**) (of authority, discipline, etc.) admitting no leniency, severe; (**d**) (of custody, confinement, etc.) involving severe restriction of space or freedom of movement. L16.
7 Of a quality, condition, etc.: maintained without deviation or abatement; absolute, entire, complete; (of truth, accuracy, etc.) exactly answerable to fact or reality. L16.
8 Esp. of a person: severe, not lax or indulgent; rigorous in upholding standards of conscience and morality. L16.
9 Close; *spec.* (**a**) intimate; (**b**) (of a resemblance, correspondence, etc.) matching, exactly fitting. Now *rare* or *obsolete*. E17.
10 Accurately determined or defined; exact, precise, not vague or loose. M17.
11 Characterized by rigid conformity to rules or postulates; undeviating in adherence to specified principles or practice. M17.

5 T. GRANGER The predicate is more strict in signification then the subiect. **6** DICKENS Mrs. Squeers . . instituted a stricter search after the spoon. A. THWAITE He had to make a strict time-table and not allow himself any time off. **7** H. JAMES There being no strict, no absolute measure of it. J. K. JEROME I wish this book to be a strict record of fact, unmarred by exaggeration. **8** F. HARRISON Pitt . . was the statesman who finally established strict honour in the public service. G. GORER Those who think that . . modern parents are not strict enough. **9** STEELE There never was a more strict friendship than between those Gentlemen. **10** MILTON It shall be still in strictest measure. EDWARD WHITE Important words . . to be always taken in their strictest . . definition. **11** J. HERRIOT As a strict methodist he didn't drink or indulge in worldly pleasures. G. VIDAL She dislikes the strict conventions of our traditional art.

Special collocations: ***strict Communion***: see COMMUNION 5. **strict construction** LAW a literal interpretation of a statute by a court. **strict counterpoint**: see COUNTERPOINT *noun*[1] 1. **strict implication** LOGIC a relationship holding between propositions in which it is impossible for the antecedent to be true and the consequent false. **strict liability** LAW liability which does not depend on actual negligence or intent to harm. **strict settlement** LAW a settlement of land, intended to preserve descent in the eldest male line, by which each prospective heir on attaining his majority voluntarily relinquishes his power of disentailment. **strict tempo** MUSIC a strict and regular rhythm, esp. in music for ballroom dancing.
► **B** *adverb*. Strictly. *rare*. E18.

strictarian /strɪkˈtɛːrɪən/ *noun* & *adjective*. *rare*. M19.
[from STRICT *adjective* + -ARIAN.]
► **A** *noun*. A person holding rigidly conformist views. M19.
► **B** *adjective*. Characteristic of strictarians or their views. E20.

stricti juris /strɪktʌɪ ˈdʒʊərɪs, strɪktɪ ˈjʊərɪs/ *adverbial phr.* L17.
[Latin, lit. 'of strict law'.]
LAW. Strictly according to the law, *esp.* according to law as opp. to equity.

striction /ˈstrɪkʃ(ə)n/ *noun*. *rare*. L19.
[Latin *strictio(n-)*, from *strict-*: see STRICTURE *noun*[1], -ION.]
The action of constricting something.
curve of striction, **line of striction** GEOMETRY in a skew surface, the line that cuts each generator in that point of it that is nearest to the succeeding generator.

strictly /ˈstrɪk(t)li/ *adverb*. LME.
[from STRICT *adjective* + -LY[2].]
1 In a strict manner; rigorously, exactly; *spec.* with the use of words in their strict sense, precisely, (freq. in ***strictly speaking***). LME.
2 Definitely; exclusively. *colloq.* (chiefly *N. Amer.*). M20.

1 E. BOWEN Strictly, she was massive rather than fat. L. GORDON Mr Ramsay's thinking is strictly compartmentalised. **2** ***strictly for the birds***: see BIRD *noun*.

strictness /ˈstrɪk(t)nɪs/ *noun*. L16.
[formed as prec. + -NESS.]
The quality or condition of being strict; rigorousness, exactness; an instance of this.
in strictness (of speech) *arch.* taken or understood strictly; according to a strict conception, definition, or interpretation.

stricto sensu /strɪktəʊ ˈsɛnsuː/ *adverbial* & *adjectival phr.* M20.
[Latin = in the restricted sense.]
= SENSU STRICTO.

stricture /ˈstrɪktʃə/ *noun*[1] & *verb*. LME.
[Latin *strictura*, from *strict-* pa. ppl stem of *stringere* draw tight, touch lightly: see -URE.]
► **A** *noun*. **I 1 a** MEDICINE. A narrowing of a canal, duct, or passage, esp. of the urethra, oesophagus, or intestine. LME. ▸**b** PHONETICS. Partial or complete closure of the air passage in the production of speech sounds. M20.
2 The action of restricting, binding, or tightly enclosing something; tight closure; restriction; an instance of this. *lit.* & *fig.* LME.

2 J. BUCHAN The snow . . under the stricture of the frost was as dry and powdery as sand. E. S. PERSON Love . . liberates him from the strictures of self.

►†**II 3** A spark, a flash of light. *lit.* & *fig.* Only in 17.
► **III 4** Orig., an incidental remark or comment. Now, an adverse criticism or censorious remark. Usu. in *pl.* M17.
†**5** A touch, a slight trace. Only in L17.

4 V. WOOLF My writing . . he praises sufficiently to give his strictures a good deal of force.

► **B** *verb trans.* Criticize, censure. *rare*. M19.

†**stricture** *noun*[2]. *rare* (Shakes.). Only in E17.
[from STRICT *adjective* + -URE.]
Strictness.

strid /strɪd/ *noun*. E19.
[App. from STRIDE *noun*.]
A narrow gorge or chasm.

stridden *verb* pa. pple: see STRIDE *verb*.

striddle /ˈstrɪd(ə)l/ *noun*. *Scot.* & *dial.* E18.
[from the verb.]
A stride.

striddle /ˈstrɪd(ə)l/ *verb intrans.* Long *obsolete* exc. *Scot.* & *dial.* M16.
[Back-form. from next. Cf. STRADDLE *verb*.]
1 Stand with the legs wide apart; straddle. M16.
2 Stride. L18.

striddling /ˈstrɪdlɪŋ/ *adverb*. Long *obsolete* exc. *dial.* Also **-ings** /-ɪŋz/. LME.
[from weak grade of base of STRIDE *noun* or *verb* + -LING[2].]
Astride.

stride /strʌɪd/ *noun*.
[Old English *stride*, from weak grade of base of STRIDE *verb*; later directly from STRIDE *verb*.]
1 a The distance covered by a single long step; this as a unit of length. Freq. in ***lengthen one's stride***, ***shorten one's stride*** below. OE. ▸**b** A single long step in walking; an act of striding. ME. ▸**c** Progress. Usu. in *pl.* Chiefly in ***make strides***, ***take strides***, make advances, make progress; ***make great strides***, ***take great strides***, make significant advances, make good progress. E17.
2 Divergence of the legs when stretched apart laterally, as astride a gap etc.; the distance between the feet when the legs are parted in this manner. L16.
3 a An act of forward movement, esp. by a horse, completed when the feet are returned to their initial relative positions; the distance covered by such a movement. E17. ▸**b** A horse's regular or uniform movement in a race; a settled rate of progress. L19.
4 A person's gait as determined by the length of stride. L17. ▸**b** A distance travelled at a striding pace. *rare*. M19.
5 Fit or cut of a garment, esp. a pair of trousers, to accommodate the wearer's length of step. E19. ▸**b** In *pl.* Trousers. *slang*. L19.
6 JAZZ. A style of piano-playing, emphasizing beat and swing, in which the left hand alternately plays single bass notes on the downbeat and chords an octave higher on the upbeat. Also ***stride piano***. M20.

1a lengthen one's stride walk faster by taking longer steps. **shorten one's stride** walk slower by taking shorter steps. **b** R. FRAME Madame . . walked downhill with long, confident strides. ***a spit and a stride***: see SPIT *noun*[2]. **2** C. COTTON The Current's not so wide To put a Maid to an indecent stride. **3a take in one's stride** (**a**) clear (an obstacle) without changing pace to jump; (**b**) *fig.* deal with (a matter) without interrupting one's course of action; handle smoothly or with aplomb. **b get into one's stride** reach a settled or steady rate of progress or level of performance. **put a person off his or her stride**, **put a person out of his or her stride**, **throw a person off his or her stride**, **throw a person out of his or her stride** unsettle, disconcert. **4** POPE Her voice theatrically loud, And masculine her stride. **6** attrib.: ***stride accent***, ***stride bass***, ***stride tempo***, etc.

stride /strʌɪd/ *verb*. Pa. t. **strode** /strəʊd/; pa. pple **stridden** /ˈstrɪd(ə)n/, (*colloq.*) **strode**.
[Old English *stridan* (cf. *bestridan* BESTRIDE) = Middle & mod. Low German *striden* set the legs wide apart, prob. ult. from Germanic.]
1 *verb intrans.* Orig., stand or walk with the legs wide apart. Now only, (of an arch, bridge, etc.) span *over*, extend *across*. OE.
2 *verb intrans.* **a** Walk with long firm steps; step out decisively, vigorously, or hurriedly. Freq. foll. by *away*, *out*, etc. ME. ▸†**b** Tread. *rare* (Spenser). Only in L16.
3 *verb intrans.* **a** Take a long step; pass *over* or *across* an obstacle with a long step or by lifting the feet. ME. ▸†**b** Mount *on* a horse. ME–L15.
4 *verb trans.* Bestride (esp. a horse). ME.
5 *verb trans.* Step over or cross with a stride. L16.
6 *verb trans.* Walk about or along (a street etc.) with long firm steps. L16.
7 *verb intrans.* JAZZ. Play stride piano (see STRIDE *noun* 6). Chiefly as ***striding*** *ppl adjective*. M20.

1 SPENSER The gate was open, but therein did wait A sturdy villein, striding stiffe and bold. R. CUMBERLAND The bridge . . proudly strides with half a dozen lofty arches over a stream. **2a** R. COBB Edward . . striding out importantly like a Foreign Minister walking towards the film cameras. **3a** W. BRERETON The lowest of these hedges higher than any man can stride over. **4** SHELLEY The tempest is his steed, he strides the air. **5** J. CLARE A hedge to clamber or a brook to stride. **6** *Blackwood's Magazine* The brave ghosts who stride these fields . . are Englishmen.

Comb.: **stride level** a spirit-level supported at both ends so as to straddle over intervening projections.
■ **strider** *noun* (**a**) a person who strides; (**b**) *US* = ***pond-skater*** s.v. POND *noun*: M19. **stridingly** *adverb* in a striding manner M16.

stridency /ˈstrʌɪd(ə)nsi/ *noun*. **M19**.
[from STRIDENT + -ENCY.]
The quality of being strident.
 F. TOMLIN Her letters were of mounting stridency.
■ Also **stridence** *noun* (*rare*) **L19**.

strident /ˈstrʌɪd(ə)nt/ *adjective & noun*. **M17**.
[Latin *strident-* pres. ppl stem of *stridere* creak: see -ENT.]
▶ **A** *adjective*. **1** Making a harsh, grating, or creaking noise; loud and harsh, shrill. **M17**.
2 *PHONETICS*. Of a consonant, or the articulation of a consonantal sound: characterized by friction that is comparatively turbulent. **M20**.
 1 P. D. JAMES The telephone rang, sounding unnaturally strident in the quiet room. *transf.*: *Independent* Congress will now come under strident pressure . . for an amendment.
▶ **B** *noun*. A strident consonant. **M20**.
■ **stridently** *adverb* **M19**.

stridor /ˈstrʌɪdə/ *noun*. **M17**.
[Latin, from *stridere*: see prec., -OR.]
1 A harsh loud sound, a harsh or shrill grating or creaking noise. **M17**.
2 *MEDICINE*. A harsh vibrating noise when breathing in, caused by tracheal or laryngeal obstruction. **L19**.

stridulate /ˈstrɪdjʊleɪt/ *verb intrans*. **M19**.
[French *striduler*, from Latin *stridulus*: see next, -ATE[3].]
Make a harsh, grating, or shrill noise; *spec*. (of an insect etc.) produce sound by rubbing a part of the body against another.
■ **stridulant** *adjective* (*rare*) = STRIDULOUS **M19**. **striduˈlation** *noun* the action of stridulating; the stridulous noise produced by certain insects etc.: **M19**. **stridulator** *noun* an insect etc. that stridulates; the organ of an insect etc. that produces stridulation: **L19**. **stridulatory** /ˈstrɪdjʊlət(ə)ri, strɪdjʊˈleɪt(ə)ri/ *adjective* pertaining to, causing, or caused by stridulation; capable of stridulating: **M19**. **stridulent** *adjective* = STRIDULOUS **L19**.

stridulous /ˈstrɪdjʊləs/ *adjective*. **E17**.
[from Latin *stridulus* creaking, hissing, from *stridere*: see STRIDENT, -ULOUS.]
1 Emitting or producing a harsh or shrill grating sound; (of a sound) harsh, shrill, grating. **E17**.
2 *MEDICINE*. Pertaining to or affected with stridor. **E19**.
 1 G. A. LAWRENCE That . . stridulous young person, who . . screams when she talks, and squalls when she sings.
■ **stridulously** *adverb* **M19**. **stridulousness** *noun* **E18**.

strife /strʌɪf/ *noun*. Also †**strive**. **ME**.
[Aphet. from Old French *estrif* rel. to *estriver* STRIVE *verb*.]
1 The action or an act of contending or striving in opposition; a state of antagonism, enmity, or discord; (a) conflict, (a) dispute. **ME**. ▸†**b** Toil, pain, distress. *poet. rare*. **ME–M16**. ▸**c** A subject of contention. Now *rare* or *obsolete*. **M16**. ▸**d** Trouble, disgrace, difficulties. Freq. in *in strife*. *Austral. colloq*. **M20**.
2 Endeavour; strong effort. *rare*. **ME**.
3 Competition, emulation; a struggle or contest of emulation between rivals. Now *arch. rare*. **L15**.
 1 W. S. CHURCHILL Religious debate was earnest . . but . . civil strife for the sake of religion was a thing of the past. *Times* Standard Chartered Bank . . a significant presence in the strife-torn republic. **d** D. HEWETT If he hadn't sent . . the dough you'd really be in strife. **2** SHAKES. *All's Well* Which we will pay With strife to please you, day exceeding day. **3** SHAKES. *Ven. & Ad.* His art with nature's workmanship at strife, As if the dead the living should exceed.
Phrases: †**have strife**, †**hold strife** contend, quarrel, (*with*). *trouble and strife*: see TROUBLE *noun*.
■ **strifeful** *adjective* **LME**. **strifeless** *adjective* **E17**.

striffen /ˈstrɪf(ə)n/ *noun*. *Scot., N. Ir., & US local*. **E17**.
[Origin unkn.]
A thin membranous film; a thin skin or membrane.

strift /strɪft/ *noun*. Long *arch. rare*. **LME**.
[from STRIVE *verb* after *drift*, *thrift*, etc.]
The action or an act of striving; contention, strife.

strig /strɪg/ *noun & verb*. **M16**.
[Origin unkn.]
▶ **A** *noun*. **1** A stalk, a stem; *esp*. (*a*) the pedicel of a currant; (*b*) the stem of a hop cone. **M16**.
2 A long thin part attached to various implements or tools. **E18**.
▶ **B** *verb trans*. Infl. **-gg-**. Remove the strig or stalk from (currants etc.). **L19**.

striga /ˈstrʌɪgə/ *noun*. Pl. **-gae** /-dʒiː/. **M18**.
[Latin = row, strip.]
1 *BOTANY*. Orig., a row of stiff bristles. Now, a stiff adpressed bristle or bristle-like scale (usu. in *pl*.). *rare*. **M18**.
2 *ENTOMOLOGY*. A narrow transverse line or groove. Usu. in *pl*. **E19**.
■ **strigate** *adjective* (*rare*) *ENTOMOLOGY* having strigae **L19**. **striˈgated** *adjective* (*rare*) having a channelled or grooved surface **E18**.

striges /ˈstrʌɪdʒiːz/ *noun pl*. **M16**.
[Latin (Vitruvius); perh. misreading of *striae*, *strigae*.]
ARCHITECTURE. The fillets of a fluted column.

striggle /ˈstrɪg(ə)l/ *noun*. *rare. colloq*. **E20**.
[Perh. from STR(AGGLE *verb* + W)IGGLE *noun*.]
A wavy line; a squiggle.

strigil /ˈstrɪdʒɪl/ *noun*. **L16**.
[Latin *strigilis*, from base of *stringere* graze, touch lightly: see -IL.]
1 *CLASSICAL ANTIQUITIES*. An instrument with a curved blade, used to scrape sweat and dirt from the skin in a hot-air bath or after exercise; a scraper. **L16**.
2 *ENTOMOLOGY*. Any of various comblike structures used for stridulating, grasping, or cleaning. **L19**.

strigillate /ˈstrɪdʒɪleɪt/ *verb intrans*. **M20**.
[formed as prec.: see -ATE[3].]
ENTOMOLOGY. = STRIDULATE.

†**strigment** *noun*. *rare*. **M17–M18**.
[Latin *strigmentum*, from *stringere*: see STRIGIL, -MENT.]
The dirt and sweat scraped off the skin with a strigil.

strigose /ˈstrʌɪgəʊs/ *adjective*. **L18**.
[mod. Latin *strigosus*, from Latin STRIGA: see -OSE[1].]
1 *BOTANY*. Hispid, usu. with stiff adpressed hairs; (of a hair) stiff and adpressed. **L18**.
2 *ENTOMOLOGY*. Finely grooved or furrowed. **L18**.
■ Also **strigous** *adjective* (*rare*) **L18**.

strikable /ˈstrʌɪkəb(ə)l/ *adjective*. **E20**.
[from STRIKE *verb* + -ABLE.]
Able to be struck; that may cause an industrial strike.

strike /strʌɪk/ *noun*[1]. **ME**.
[from STRIKE *verb*. Cf. STREAK *noun*.]
†**1** A distance. Only in **ME**.
2 a *Hist*. A unit of dry capacity usu. equal to a bushel, but occas. equal to either half a bushel or two or four bushels. Also, a measuring vessel containing this quantity. Cf. STROKE *noun*[1] 7. **LME**. ▸†**b** The unit proportion of malt in ale or beer. **E17–E19**.
3 A straight piece of wood with which surplus grain is struck off level with the brim of a measure; *gen*. any similar instrument used to level a surface by striking off superfluous material. Cf. STRICK *noun* 3, STRICKLE *noun* 1. **LME**. ▸**b** More fully ***strike measure***. Measurement by means of a strike to ensure that a heaped vessel is exactly full; levelled measure. **L17**.
4 A bundle or hank of flax, hemp, etc.; = STRICK *noun* 2. **LME**.
5 a An act of striking a blow; a sudden attack; *spec*. a sudden military attack, esp. from the air, concentrated on selected targets. **LME**. ▸**b** The striking of a clock or bell. **L19**.
6 *MINING & GEOLOGY*. The horizontal course or compass direction of a surface, bedding plane, etc. Cf. STREAK *noun* 5. **E19**.
7 a An organized refusal to work on the part of a body of employees as a protest, esp. in order to try and obtain some concession from an employer. Cf. STRIKE *verb* 14. **E19**. ▸**b** *transf*. A concerted refusal to participate in some other expected activity esp. in order to register a protest or try to obtain some concession. **L19**.
8 *ANGLING*. **a** A jerk by which an angler secures a hooked fish. **M19**. ▸**b** A large catch of fish. **L19**.
9 A sudden find; a sudden success; *spec*. the discovery of oil etc. when drilling or a rich vein of ore when mining. **M19**.
10 a In ninepins and tenpins, the knocking down of all the pins with the first bowl. **M19**. ▸**b** *CRICKET*. The right of a batsman to receive the next ball. **L19**. ▸**c** *AMER. FOOTBALL*. A forward pass straight to a receiver. **M20**.
11 a *BASEBALL*. An act of striking at a pitched ball; a failure to do this properly, by which a batter incurs a penalty (three of which put him or her out); any act by a batter incurring the same penalty. **M19**. ▸**b** *fig*. A thing to one's discredit, a black mark. Chiefly *N. Amer*. **M20**.
12 An attempt to obtain or the obtaining of money by threat or blackmail. *US*. **L19**.
13 An impression made with a die or punch; *spec*. (*PRINTING*) a matrix for casting type, usually unfinished. **L19**. ▸**b** The impression left on a postage stamp by a hand stamp; a postmark applied by hand. **M20**.
14 (An) infestation of a sheep or cow with flies whose larvae burrow into the skin. **M20**.
 5a *CU Amiga* Rather than the usual dog fighting, F19 goes for the silent strike. ***first strike***, ***guerrilla strike***, ***pre-emptive strike***, ***second strike***, etc. **6** C. EMBLETON This trench . . cut obliquely across the strike of the strata. **7a** E. YOUNG-BRUEHL Because of the rail strikes, only Ernst and Oliver could attend the funeral. ***general strike***, ***lightning strike***, ***outlaw strike***, ***unofficial strike***, ***wildcat strike***, etc. *attrib*.: *Times Educ. Suppl*. Two of the unions are preparing for strike action to support their claim. **on strike** taking part in an organized refusal to work. **b** ***hunger strike***, ***rent strike***, etc. **9** *Listener* Britain's first big strike of natural gas on land. **11a** R. J. CONLEY The fifth batter . . after two strikes and one ball, hit a high fly. **b** *Listener* One of the main strikes against . . Heath was that he did not 'come over' on the box. ***three strikes (and you're out)***: see THREE.
Comb.: **strikebound** *adjective* immobilized by a strike; **strikebreak** *verb intrans*. work in place of others who are on strike (cf. BREAK *verb* 4e); **strikebreaker** a person who strikebreaks; **strike force** (*a*) a military force equipped to deliver a sudden attack; (*b*) a police unit organized for rapid and effective action against crime; ***strike-measure***: see sense 3b above; **strike pay** a periodical payment made by a trade union to a striker; **strike price** *FINANCE* (*a*) the price fixed by the seller of a security after receiving bids in a tender offer, typically for a sale of gilt-edged securities or a new stock market issue; (*b*) the price at which a put or call option can be exercised; **strike-slip** *GEOLOGY* in a fault, the component of the slip in a horizontal direction, parallel to the strike; ***strike-slip fault***, a fault in which displacement is predominantly parallel to the strike; **strike zone** *BASEBALL* an imaginary rectangle 17 inches wide, extending from the armpits to the knees of a batter, within which a strike must be thrown.

†**strike** *noun*[2] var. of STREAK *noun*.

strike /strʌɪk/ *verb*. Pa. t. **struck** /strʌk/; pa. pple †**striked**, **struck**, (*arch*. exc. *LAW & US*) **stricken** /ˈstrɪk(ə)n/, (*obsolete* exc. *Scot. & north*.) **strucken** /ˈstrʌk(ə)n/. See also STRIKED *ppl adjective*, STRICKEN *adjective*, STRUCK *ppl adjective*.
[Old English *strīcan* = Old Frisian *strīka*, Middle Low German *strīken*, Middle Dutch *strijken*, Old High German *strīhhan* (German *streichen*), from Germanic base of STREAK *noun*. Cf. STRICK, STRICKLE, STROKE *noun*[1], *verb*[1].]
▶ **I 1** *verb intrans*. †**a** Of a thing, esp. a stream of liquid: make its way; flow. **OE–LME**. ▸**b** Of a person: make one's way, proceed, go. Later usu. foll. by *forward*, *over*, etc. *arch*. **ME**.
2 *verb intrans*. **a** Of a boundary, path, mountain-range, etc.: take a certain course or direction. **LME**. ▸**b** Of a person, road, stream, etc.: proceed in a new direction; turn in a journey or course. Foll. by adverbs or prepositions. **L16**.
 1b M. GEE Impatient, she strikes straight down the steps to the . . promenade. **2b** T. HARDY He left the plateau and struck downwards across some fields. J. BALDWIN He struck out on a steep path.
▶ **II** Stroke, rub lightly, smooth, level.
3 *verb trans*. Go over lightly with an instrument, the hand, etc.; stroke, smooth; make level. Also foll. by *down*, *out*, *over*. Now *dial*. **OE**. ▸**b** Gently rub or stroke (a diseased part) in order to try to heal it. *obsolete* exc. *dial*. **LME**.
†**4** *verb trans*. Smear (a substance) on a surface; spread (a quantity of a surface) *with* or *over with* a substance. **LME–L18**.
5 *verb trans*. Make (a quantity of grain etc.) level with the brim of a measure with a strike or strickle; level the contents of (a measure) in this way. **LME**.
6 *verb trans*. Make (a brick or tile) by moulding. Formerly also, mould (wax, a candle, etc.). **L15**.
7 *verb trans*. *BRICKLAYING*. Level up (a joint) with mortar; spread (mortar) along a joint. **M17**. ▸**b** Trim superfluous mortar or grout from (tiling). **L17**.
8 *verb trans*. *TANNING*. Smooth and stretch (a skin). Also foll. by *out*. **M18**.
9 *verb trans*. *CARPENTRY*. Fashion (a moulding) with a plane. **M19**.
▶ **III** Lower or take down, esp. out of use.
10 *NAUTICAL*. **a** *verb trans. & intrans*. Lower (a sail, flag, etc.), esp. in salute or surrender. **ME**. ▸**b** *verb trans*. Lower (something) into the hold with a rope and tackle (usu. foll. by *down*). Also, hoist *out* from the hold and lower to the dock. **M17**.
11 *verb trans*. Discharge (a load); empty (a vessel). **E17**.
12 *verb trans*. *SHIPBUILDING*. Cause (a vessel) to slide *down* or *off* the slipway or cradle. **M17**.
13 *verb trans*. **a** *BUILDING*. Remove (scaffolding or other support) from a building etc. **L17**. ▸**b** Take down (a tent) for removal; take down the tents of (an encampment). **E18**. ▸**c** Unfix, put out of use, dismantle (esp. theatrical scenery). **L18**.
14 a *verb intrans*. (Of an employee) refuse to continue work; *esp*. (of a body of employees) cease working as an organized protest, usu. in order to try and obtain some concession. Cf. STRIKE *noun*[1] 7. **M18**. ▸**b** *verb trans*. Stop (work) as a strike. *arch*. **E19**. ▸**c** *verb trans*. Order or undertake such action against (a firm); order (a body of employees) to undertake such action. Now chiefly *N. Amer*. **L19**.
 10a P. THOMAS Both Ships struck their Yards and Top masts. W. FALCONER All foreign vessels strike to an English man of war in . . British seas. **b** W. C. RUSSELL He had struck the long gun forward down below. **13b** J. MCPHEE In the morning . . we strike the tents, pack the gear, and move on. *Outdoor Action* It took ages to strike camp. **c** *Illustrated London News* The first innings only was completed . . when the wickets were struck. *Listener* The minute we finish this evening, they'll start striking the set. **14a** A. PATON They're threatening to strike . . in the Mines for ten shillings a day. **c** *New York Times* Photoengravers voted . . to strike The New York Times.
▶ **IV** Impinge upon.
15 a *verb intrans*. (Of a moving body) come into collision or forcible contact with something; *spec*. (of a ship) collide with a rock etc., run aground; foll. by *on*, *upon*, *against*. Formerly also foll. by *together*: (of two or more moving bodies) collide. **ME**. ▸**b** *verb trans*. Come into for-

cible contact or collision with; *spec.* (of a ship) collide with (a rock etc.), run upon (the ground). M16.

16 *verb trans.* Of a beam or ray of light or heat: fall on, catch, touch. LME. **▸b** *verb intrans.* Of light: fall *on* or *upon.* M17.

17 *slang.* **†a** *verb trans. & intrans.* Steal (goods); rob (a person). M16–L17. **▸b** *verb trans.* Make a sudden demand on (a person) *for* a loan etc. M18. **▸c** *verb trans.* Induce (a person) to pay money by threat or blackmail. *US.* M19.

18 *verb trans. & intrans.* with *(up)on.* Of a sound, report, etc.: be heard by, reach, (the ear). L16.

19 a *verb trans.* Make an impression on, come to the attention of; impress, catch (one's eye, attention, or fancy, etc.). Also *spec.* (now *colloq.*), catch the admiration or affection of (a member of the opposite sex); *esp.* in *pass.*, be favourably impressed *by* or *with* (a person, idea, etc.), be keen *on.* L16. **▸b** *verb intrans.* Make an impression, catch the attention. (Foll. by *on.*) E18.

20 *verb trans.* Of a thought, an idea: come into the mind of, occur to, (a person). Freq. *impers.* in ***it strikes, it struck,*** etc. E17.

21 *verb trans.* **a** Come upon, reach, come to. L18. **▸b** Come across or encounter unexpectedly; find (the object of a search). Chiefly *US.* M19. **▸c** Discover (oil, ore, etc.) by drilling, mining, etc. M19.

> 🕮 **15b** I. MURDOCH He falls forward . . on the ground, his forehead strikes the floor. P. BARKER The . . woman's fist shot out and struck Elaine full in the mouth. *fig.*: POPE Shouts confus'dly rise, And bass, and treble voices strike the skies. **16** J. UPDIKE Golden sun strikes some buildings while others wait in shadow. **19a** C. JOHNSTON Staring at her, in such a way, as struck her notice. J. GALSWORTHY The extraordinary unreasonableness of her disaffection struck him with increased force. A. MACLEAN The entire film world . . strikes me as being crazy. **20** M. LEITCH It hadn't struck him that she wouldn't be wearing anything underneath. **21a** R. BOLDREWOOD They struck the river within a day's ride of Rainbar. **b** A. S. NEILL You . . are the most cocky people I have yet struck. **c** *Manchester Examiner* A seam of coal 6ft. thick has been struck. *fig.*: *Private Eye* As the athletes took the last hurdle it was obvious that Britain was going to strike gold.

▸ V Deal a blow, hit.

22 *verb trans.* Deal (a person, an animal) a blow; hit forcibly with the hand or a weapon. Also with double obj.: deal (a person etc.) a blow. ME. **▸b** *verb intrans.* Deal or aim a blow (*at*). E16.

23 *verb trans.* Hit (a material, an object) with an implement, esp. one designed for the purpose. Also with cognate obj.: hit (a stroke, a blow). ME. **▸b** *verb intrans.* Make a stroke with a hammer or other implement. ME. **▸c** *verb trans.* Deliver a blow with (the hand or something held in the hand), bang or slap (the fist or hand), stamp (the foot), *on, upon, against.* Cf. sense 47 below. M16.

24 *verb trans. & intrans.* Beat or sound (a drum etc.), esp. in order to summon recruits or as a signal to march; sound (an alarm) on a drum. Usu. foll. by *up. obsolete* exc. *Hist.* ME. **▸b** *verb intrans.* Of the pulse or heart: beat, throb. *rare.* L16.

25 a *verb trans.* Pierce, stab, or cut with a sharp or penetrating weapon, esp. so as to kill or wound. Formerly also, drive or thrust (a pointed tool, weapon, etc.) *in, into, through.* Now *rare.* ME. **▸b** *verb trans.* Remove or separate (*from*) with a cut or slash. Now usu. foll. by *off.* ME. **▸c** *verb trans. fig.* Of a feeling, etc.: pierce (a person) *to* the heart or quick. LME. **▸d** *verb trans. & intrans.* ANGLING. Secure a hook in the mouth of (a fish) by jerking the tackle; (of a hook or rod) secure (a fish) in this way. L16. **▸†e** *verb trans.* Broach (a cask). *rare.* E17–E18.

26 *verb intrans.* **a** Deliver a cut or thrust with a sharp weapon. (Foll. by *at.*) ME. **▸b** *fig.* Aim at the overthrow or defeat of a person etc. Usu. foll. by *at.* LME.

27 *verb trans.* Hit with a missile, shot, etc.; (of a shot etc.) hit (a person or thing). Now *rare.* LME.

28 a *verb trans.* Fight (a battle) (chiefly *Scot.*); attack (an enemy). LME. **▸b** *verb intrans.* Take up weapons, fight (*for*). L16. **▸c** *verb intrans. & trans.* with cognate obj. Make an attack; deliver (an offensive blow). E17. **▸d** *verb intrans.* Perform an aggressive or injurious action. M20.

29 *verb trans. & intrans.* Wound, attack, or aim a blow (at) with the horns, tusks, claws, or other natural weapon. Now chiefly *spec.*, (of a snake or other venomous animal) wound (a person) with its fangs or sting. Formerly also, (of a basilisk) kill or injure (a person) with its glance; (of a bird of prey) dart at and seize (prey). LME.

30 *verb trans.* Remove or drive (a thing) with or as with a blow of an implement or the hand. Usu. foll. by adverb or preposition. Cf. ***strike down*** below. Now *rare.* LME.

31 *verb trans.* Stamp or impress with or *with* a device; *spec.* (*a*) make (a coin) by stamping, coin (money); (*b*) print (*off*) from type, an engraving, etc. LME. **▸b** CINEMATOGRAPHY. Make (another print) *from* a motion picture film. L20.

32 a *verb trans.* Produce (fire, a spark, etc.) by rubbing two things together, or by rubbing one thing off another. Now *spec.*, light (a match) by friction; ELECTRICITY bring (an arc) into being. LME. **▸b** *verb intrans.* Orig., (of an electric charge), pass as a spark. Later, (of an electric discharge) come into being; (of a discharge tube) begin to discharge electricity. (Of an arc lamp) begin to form an arc. Also, (of a match) admit of being lit by friction; be lit. L18.

33 a *verb intrans. & trans.* Of a clock etc.: indicate (the time) with a chime or stroke, esp. one caused by a clapper or hammer hitting a bell or other sounding mechanism; make (one or more chimes or strokes). Cf. STROKE *noun*[1] 5. LME. **▸b** *verb intrans.* Of the time: be indicated in this way. LME. **▸c** *verb intrans. gen.* Of a piece of mechanism: make a stroke, hit or beat something. E17. **▸d** *verb trans.* Cause (a clock etc.) to sound the time; cause (a bell) to sound. L17.

34 a *verb trans. & intrans.* with *on, upon.* Tap, rap, knock. LME. **▸b** *verb trans.* Touch (a string, a key) so as to produce a musical note; play on (an instrument). Also, produce (music, a sound, a note) in this way. Cf. ***strike up*** (a) below. M16.

> 🕮 **22** *Examiner* [He] struck the boy a violent blow. J. STEINBECK He struck her in the face with his clenched fist. **b** T. WILLIAMS She . . strikes at him with the bottle. **23** R. CRAWLEY A ball struck moderately hard will traverse the table three or four times. **c** SIR W. SCOTT Striking his hand against the table, as if impatient of the long unbroken silence. **25a** J. G. LOCKHART The maid-servant . . struck her mistress to death with a coal-axe. J. MOYNAHAN Cock robins stricken by the hunting arrows of lady archers. **b** *Examiner* The soldier . . struck the head from the body. **c** D. EDEN The . . uncertainty in Aunt Annabel's voice would have struck her to the heart. **26a** LD MACAULAY Herminius struck at Seius, And clove him to the teeth. **b** *Saturday Review* The Revolution . . began to strike at Church and King. **28b** S. WALPOLE Austria . . was too timid to strike. **c** F. MARRYAT To strike one blow for the King, come what will. **30** N. BILLINGSLEY Then were his teeth struck out. **31** B. T. BRADFORD From this master print he intended to strike two more. *Scottish World* The Canadian Government . . have struck a silver dollar. **b** *Daily Telegraph* Selznick's film . . is reissued on a new . . print struck from the old negative. **32a** *transf.*: A. GISSING His words struck kindred sparks within herself. **b** R. WEST The matches are wet, they won't strike. J. BRAINE I heard a match strike and smelled cigar smoke. **33a** E. WAUGH As he reached the station it struck eleven. H. E. BATES The church clock . . striking hollow quarters. J. GARDNER The clock began striking, a whir of gears, then twelve . . tinny notes. **b** E. INCHBALD I will sit up 'till twelve strikes. **34b** POPE But hark! he strikes the golden lyre! G. VIDAL Someone struck a chord on the grand piano.

▸ VI Mark with a line or lines.

35 *verb trans.* Make or cut (a tally). Long *rare.* LME.

36 *verb trans.* **a** Cancel or score out or delete by or as by a stroke of a pen. (Foll. by *from, off, out (of)*, etc.) Now chiefly LAW. LME. **▸b** LAW. Form (a jury) by allowing each side to cancel the same number of people from the list of nominees. Also, form (a committee), make (a new register of voters). E18.

†37 *verb trans.* Mark (a surface) with a line or lines. (Foll. by *out, through.*) M16–M17.

38 *verb trans. & intrans.* AGRICULTURE. Mark off (land, a ridge) by ploughing once up and down the area; make (furrows) in this way. L16.

39 *verb trans.* Draw (a straight line), esp. by mechanical means; draw (a circle or arc) with compasses. E17.

> 🕮 **36a** HOR. WALPOLE Vernon is struck off the list of admirals. *Federal Reporter* The testimony given by the witness . . is . . stricken out of this case. *Times* The ruling was on a bid . . to have . . Rayner's writ and claims struck out. P. CORNWELL I think we'd be wise to strike this conversation . . go on as if it never happened. **b** *Toronto Sun* He struck a committee which . . recommended she be rehired.

▸ VII Happen suddenly by non-human agency.

40 *verb trans.* Of lightning, a thunderbolt: descend violently on and blast (a person or thing). Freq. in *pass.* Also foll. by *down.* LME. **▸b** Of a god: visit with lightning, esp. as a punishment. L16. **▸c** Of a storm, earthquake, etc.: descend on, befall. L16.

41 *verb trans.* Bring suffering, sickness, or death on (a person etc.) as if with a blow; afflict suddenly and unexpectedly, esp. as a punishment. Also foll. by *down.* LME. **▸b** Of a disease etc.: attack or afflict suddenly; make infirm, bring *down*, lay low. Usu. in *pass.* M16.

42 *verb trans.* **a** Cause (a person) to be overwhelmed or seized *with* terror, amazement, grief, or some other feeling. Formerly also, cause to suddenly feel grief, anger, etc., (foll. by *into, to*). LME. **▸b** Cause (a feeling, etc.) to be felt suddenly. (Foll. by *into.*) L16. **▸c** Prostrate mentally; shock, depress. *obsolete* exc. in ***strike all of a heap.*** L16.

43 *verb trans.* Deprive suddenly of life or one of the faculties as if by a blow (usu. with adjective compl.); in *pass.*, become suddenly *blind, dumb*, etc. M16. **▸b** *hyperbol.* With adjective compl.: make temporarily dumb, senseless, etc., with fear, amazement, etc.; shock, stun. M16. **▸c** Turn as by enchantment *into*; in *pass.* (*colloq.*), bewitched, enchanted. E17.

> 🕮 **40** E. MITTELHOLZER A coconut palm . . had been struck by lightning. P. DALLY Two young women . . had been struck and killed during that storm. **41b** R. H. HUTTON The climate struck him down, and he died at Teheran. J. BUCHAN Peter . . at school was stricken with appendicitis. **42a** SIR W. SCOTT He was struck with shame at having given way to such a paroxysm. **b** B. JOWETT His appearance will strike terror into his enemies. **43** J. HELLER It's as though I'm paralysed and struck dumb. **b** G. CUPPLES Well, strike me lucky . . if the whole affair warn't a complete trap! G. DURRELL This monstrous understatement struck me speechless.

▸ VIII Make a sudden movement.

44 *verb intrans.* Move quickly, dart, shoot. LME. **▸b** Start suddenly *into* (a song, tune); thrust oneself suddenly or vigorously *into* (a quarrel, debate, activity). E19.

45 *verb intrans.* **a** Of light: pierce or break *through.* M16. **▸b** Of cold, damp, etc.: go *through*, penetrate *to* or in a specified way. M16.

46 *verb trans.* Cause to penetrate, impart (life, warmth, dampness), *to, into, through.* E17.

47 *verb trans.* Thrust (the hand etc.) with a sudden movement; impel as with a blow. Cf. sense 23c above. E17.

48 *verb intrans. & (rare) trans.* with cognate obj. Make (a stroke) with the limbs in swimming or with an oar in rowing. Also foll. by *forward, out.* M17.

49 a *verb trans.* Of a plant, cutting, etc.: send down or put forth (a root or roots); cause (a cutting etc.) to root. M17. **▸b** *verb intrans.* (Of a plant, cutting, etc.) put forth roots; (of a root) penetrate the soil. Also foll. by *in, down.* L17. **▸c** *verb intrans. transf.* Of an oyster: attach itself to an object. L19.

50 a *verb trans.* Change the colour of (a substance) by chemical action (*into* another colour); produce or assume (a specified colour) by this means. M17. **▸b** *verb trans.* Cause (a colour, dye) to take or sink in. M18. **▸c** *verb intrans.* Of a dye: sink in; spread, run. L18.

51 a *verb intrans.* Of a horse: put down the forefeet *short, close*, etc. L17. **▸b** *verb trans. & intrans.* with *into.* Of a horse: alter its pace into (a faster movement). E19.

52 *verb trans.* Impregnate (fish etc.) with salt in curing. L18.

> 🕮 **44b** F. M. PEARD Atherton . . struck into the conversation again. **45b** RIDER HAGGARD The . . damp of the place struck to his marrow. S. MIDDLETON The air struck sharp as he stepped briskly. **46** CONAN DOYLE His voice . . struck a chill into the girl's heart. **47** *Temple Bar* He struck a quick hand through a . . bundle of papers. **48** S. TYTLER He . . struck out, and swam for a few yards. **49a** *Garden News* Best results are obtained from striking them in a propagator. **b** *Weekly Times (Melbourne)* Small . . conifers will strike from cuttings.

▸ IX Settle, agree.

53 *verb trans.* Settle, arrange the terms of, agree on (a treaty, covenant, agreement, etc.). Esp. in ***strike a bargain*** s.v. BARGAIN *noun* 2. Cf. ***strike hands, strike up*** (b) below. LME.

54 *verb trans.* Balance (an account etc.); arrive at (a figure, loss, or profit) by balancing an account. M16.

55 Determine, estimate, (an average, a mean). E18.

Phrases: **stricken in years**, **†stricken in age** *arch.* advanced in years, enfeebled by age. ***strike a balance***: see BALANCE *noun.* ***strike a bargain***: see BARGAIN *noun* 2. ***strike a blow***: see BLOW *noun*[1] 1. ***strike a chord***: see CHORD *noun*[2] 4. ***strike a docket***: see DOCKET *noun* 1c. ***strike a false note***: see NOTE *noun*[2]. **strike a light** produce a flame by friction; also as *interjection*, expr. amazement, alarm, etc. **strike a line** take a course or direction. ***strike all of a heap***: see HEAP *noun.* **strike an attitude** take up a particular body posture. ***strike a path*** = ***strike a line*** above. ***strike at the root of, strike at the roots of***: see ROOT *noun*[1]. ***strike for tall timber, strike for the tall timber***: see TALL *adjective.* **strike ground** NAUTICAL reach the bottom of the sea etc. with a sounding line. **strike hands** *arch.* (of two parties to an agreement) touch or clasp hands to seal an agreement; seal an agreement *with* (another). **strike it rich** find a rich mineral deposit; find a source of abundance; find success. **strike lucky** have a lucky success. **strike me blind** *Nautical slang* boiled rice. ***strike me pink!***: see PINK *adjective*[2]. ***strike off the rolls***: see ROLL *noun*[1]. ***strike oil***: see OIL *noun.* **strike one's colours** lower one's flags, esp. in salute or surrender. ***strike one's flag***: see FLAG *noun*[4]. ***strike root***: see ROOT *noun*[1]. **strike short** miss the mark. **strike soundings** = ***strike ground*** above. ***strike the beam***: see BEAM *noun.* ***strike the first blow***: see BLOW *noun*[1] 1. ***strike the right note***: see NOTE *noun*[2]. ***strike while the iron is hot***: see IRON *noun.* **strike wide** miss the mark. **†struck in years** = ***stricken in years*** above.

With adverbs in specialized senses: **strike back** (*a*) retaliate; (*b*) (of a gas-burner) burn from an internal point before the gas has become mixed with air. **strike down** (*a*) fell (a person or animal) to the ground with a blow; (*b*) bring low, afflict; (*c*) (of the sun) beat down oppressively; (*d*) (chiefly *N. Amer.*) hold or regard as invalid; overturn (a ruling) in a higher court. **strike home** (*a*) deal an effective blow; (*b*) (of words etc.) have an intended and usu. powerful effect. **strike in** †(*a*) join *with* (a person or party) as a co-worker, confederate, etc.; be in agreement *with* (an opinion, project, etc.); (*b*) (of a disease or pathological condition) attack the interior of the body from the surface; (*c*) intervene in an affair, quarrel, etc.; (see also senses 3, 10b, 12, 40, 41 above). **strike off** (*a*) cancel by or as by a stroke of a pen; remove from a list or record; *spec.* in *pass.*, (of a doctor, solicitor, etc.) be removed from the register of those qualified to practise, be no longer able to practise, as a result of misconduct etc.; (*b*) produce (a copy of a document etc.) quickly or effortlessly; (see also senses 12, 25b, 31, 36a above). **strike out** (*a*) cancel or erase by or as by a stroke of a pen; remove from a record, text, list, etc.; (*b*) produce or elicit as by a blow or stroke; produce by a stroke of invention; (*c*) represent in a working drawing or plan; sketch rapidly; (*d*) open up or carve out for oneself (a path, course, career, etc.); (*e*) go energetically; (*f*) hit out violently, lay about oneself; (*g*) in various games, play the ball so as to put it or oneself out; *spec.* in BASEBALL, put (a batter) out by means of three strikes; (see also senses 3, 8, 10b, 36a, 37, 48 above). **strike up** (*a*) *verb phr. trans. & intrans.* begin to play or sing (a piece of music, a song) (cf. sense 34b above); (*b*) *verb phr. trans.* conclude, make and seal, (an agreement, bargain, etc.); (*c*) *verb phr. trans.* start up esp. casually (a friendship, conversation, etc.) *with* another; †(*d*) *verb phr. trans.* cause (heat, light) to spring up or be emitted; (*e*) *verb phr. intrans.* rise up quickly, spring up; (*f*) *verb phr. trans.* (in *pass.*) *US* be bewildered; be taken *with* or keen *on* (esp. a member of the opposite sex); (see also sense 24 above).

Comb.: **strike-back** *adjective* designating the capacity of nuclear forces to retaliate after an attack; **strike-out** BASEBALL an out called when a batter has made three strikes; **strike-over** *US* the typing of a character on a spot formerly occupied by another character; **strike through** PRINTING the penetration of printing ink through to the other side of the paper.

striked /strʌɪkt/ *ppl adjective.* Now *rare.* L16.
[from prec. + -ED[1].]
Of a measure of grain etc.: levelled with a strike or strickle. Opp. ***heaped***.

†striked *verb* pa. pple: see STRIKE *verb.*

striker /ˈstrʌɪkə/ *noun.* LME.
[from STRIKE *verb* + -ER[1].]
▸ **I** A person who strikes.
†**1 a** A person who roams as a vagrant. Only in LME. ▸**b** A hired ruffian. Formerly also, a footpad. L16.
2 A person who strikes a blow or blows, esp. with a weapon or other object. Also, an animal which strikes a blow or blows. L16.
3 A person whose occupation involves striking; *spec.* (*a*) a maker of bricks or tiles; (*b*) a person who spears fish; (*c*) a person who wields a sledgehammer in metalworking; (*d*) TANNING a person who smooths and stretches skins. L16.
4 In various games: a player who is to hit, or whose turn it is to hit, the ball; *spec.* (FOOTBALL & HOCKEY) an attacking player positioned well forward whose main role is to score goals. Also (RUGBY FOOTBALL) = HOOKER *noun*[1] 3. L17.
5 An employee who is on strike. M19.
6 *US.* **a** MILITARY. An officer's batman or servant. M19. ▸**b** An apprentice, an assistant, esp. on a steamboat. L19.

> **2** G. A. HENTY Before the whip could again fall .. Vincent .. wrested it from the hands of the striker. **4** *Sunday Mail (Glasgow)* The striker .. sidestepped a tackle and neatly shot low. **5** *New Yorker* The strikers returned to work after ten days. ***hunger striker, rent striker***, etc.

▸ **II** A thing that strikes or is used for striking.
7 = STRICKLE *noun* 1. L15.
8 A thing which comes into sudden contact with another thing or person; *spec.* (*a*) a weapon, a missile; (*b*) a steel or flint for making sparks etc. M17.
9 A clock or watch which strikes. Chiefly with qualifying adjective. L18. ▸**b** That part of a bell, clock, etc., which strikes. L19.
10 A device striking the primer in a gun. E19.
11 A preparation for striking or fixing a dye. L19.

> **9** G. MUSGRAVE A large .. eight-day clock, the loudest striker I ever heard.

Comb.: **striker-plate** = *striking-plate* s.v. STRIKING *verbal noun.*
¶ Recorded earlier in ME in surnames.

striking /ˈstrʌɪkɪŋ/ *verbal noun.* LME.
[formed as prec. + -ING[1].]
The action of STRIKE *verb*; an instance of this.
Comb.: **striking-circle** HOCKEY an elongated semicircle in front of the goal, from within which the ball must be hit in order to score; **striking distance** the distance within which one is near enough to hit or achieve something; **striking force** (*a*) the force with which a projectile strikes; (*b*) a military body ready to attack at short notice; **striking-line** a harpoon line; **striking-plate** a metal plate against which the end of a spring-lock bolt strikes, when the door or lid is being closed; **striking platform** ARCHAEOLOGY a flat area on a core of flint or stone on which a blow is struck to detach a flake; the part of a flake so detached that preserves a part of this area; **striking price** STOCK EXCHANGE the price at which a purchase or sale may be effected; ***striking-tache***: see TACHE *noun*[3] 1.

striking /ˈstrʌɪkɪŋ/ *ppl adjective.* E17.
[from STRIKE *verb* + -ING[2].]
That strikes; *spec.* (*a*) (of a clock etc.) that strikes or chimes to indicate the time; (*b*) that strikes the attention; impressive, remarkable; (*c*) (of an employee) that is on strike.

> A. LURIE She was very striking then, beautiful really. *Garden* It .. provides a striking contrast to the purple summer foliage of a nearby sumach.

■ **strikingly** *adverb* M18. **strikingness** *noun* E19.

Strimmer /ˈstrɪmə/ *noun.* Also **s-**. L20.
[Prob. blend of STRING *noun* and TRIMMER.]
(Proprietary name for) a usu. electrically powered grass trimmer having a nylon cutting cord which rotates rapidly on a spindle.

strim-stram /ˈstrɪmstram/ *noun.* Long *obsolete* exc. *dial.* E18.
[Imit. Cf. STRUMSTRUM.]
A crude or decrepit guitar or similar instrument.

strind /strɪnd/ *noun.* Long *obsolete* exc. *Scot.*
[Old English (Anglian) *strȳnd* etc., from (*ge*)*strīenan*: see STRAIN *noun*[1].]
Generation, descent, lineage; a race, a breed, a stock; offspring, progeny; an inherited quality; individual nature or character; = STRAIN *noun*[1] 4–7, 9.

Strindbergian /strɪndˈbəːgɪən/ *adjective.* E20.
[from *Strindberg* (see below) + -IAN.]
Of, pertaining to, or characteristic of the Swedish dramatist Johan August Strindberg (1849–1912), or his works.

Strine /strʌɪn/ *adjective & noun. colloq.* M20.
[Repr. an alleged Australian pronunc. of 'Australian'.]
▸ **A** *adjective.* Australian. M20.
▸ **B** *noun.* **1** An Australian. M20.
2 English as spoken by (esp. uneducated) Australians; a comic transliteration of Australian speech (e.g. *Emma Chissitt?* = how much is it?). M20.

string /strɪŋ/ *noun & adjective.*
[Old English *streng* = Middle Low German *strenge*, Middle Dutch *strenc*, *stranc*, Old High German *stranc* (German *Strang*), Old Norse *strengr*, from Germanic base of STRONG *adjective.*]
▸ **A** *noun.* **I 1** *gen.* A line made of twisted strands, a cord, a rope, a cable. Formerly also *joc.*, the hangman's rope. Also, a whip. *obsolete* exc. *dial.* OE.
2 (A piece of) thin line made of twisted threads of spun cotton, hemp, etc., fibre, used esp. for tying or holding things together, pulling, etc.; (a) thin cord, (a) stout thread; twine. OE. ▸**b** A thin cord used as a snare. *rare.* ME. ▸**c** A fishing-line. Now *slang.* L16. ▸**d** A thread on which beads, pearls, etc., are strung. E17. ▸**e** A kind of confidence trick. *US slang.* M19. ▸**f** The usual natural colour of string, light greyish brown. E20.
3 A length of catgut, nylon, wire, or other material (fitted to a musical instrument) which produces a musical sound when made to vibrate. OE. ▸**b** In *pl.* Stringed instruments. Now *spec.*, such instruments played with a bow (violins, violas, cellos, double basses); the section of an orchestra playing such instruments. ME.
4 A bowstring. OE. ▸**b** *fig.* With ordinal numeral: an alternative resource available if another should fail, an alternative, something held in reserve; a reserve selection for a sporting team etc.; each of a number of alternative players or teams in order of selection or seniority. Orig. & chiefly with *second* (see ***second string*** below). M17.
5 a A length of line by which a person or an animal is led or dragged along; a leash. Freq. *fig.* ME. ▸**b** A cord for moving or controlling a puppet. Freq. *fig.* M19. ▸**c** *fig.* A limitation, condition, or restriction attached to something. Freq. in ***no strings (attached)***. Orig. *US.* L19.
6 A piece of cord, tape, ribbon, etc., used (freq. in a pair) for tying up or fastening an article of clothing, for securing a hat or bonnet by being tied under the chin, for binding the hair, for closing a bag or purse, etc. ME. ▸†**b** In *pl.* The ties of a book. L16–M17.
†**7** A cord or ribbon worn as a decoration; the ribbon of a knightly order. M17–E19.
8 Orig., the cord or chain wound on the barrel of a watch. Later (*obsolete* exc. as in sense 2 above), a cord or chain for carrying a watch. M17.

> **1** R. H. BARHAM To see a man swing At the end of a string. **2** J. ROSSNER She cut the string on Dawn's package. A. CROSS Reading glasses .. attached to a string around her neck. A. S. BYATT He pulled a string and the bathroom heater fizzed into .. action. *fig.*: BEVERLEY CLEARY Her hair whipped around her face in wet strings. **3** N. HINTON A new set of strings for the guitar. *fig.*: S. RICHARDSON The dear man makes me spring to his arms whenever he touches this string. **b** E. HEATH I .. listened to the strings playing Mozart's *Eine Kleine Nachtmusik*. *Jazz Journal International* I would like to do an album with strings and .. voices. **4** AV *Ps.* 11:2 They make ready their arrow vpon the string. **b** *Squash World* Wiltshire looked assured of success when the third and fifth strings emerged victorious. **5a** S. RICHARDSON They govern me as a child in strings.

▸ **II 9** A very narrow elongated piece of animal or plant tissue; a ligament, tendon, nerve, or other fibre; a tough piece of fibre in meat or other food, as a tough piece connecting the two halves of a bean-pod etc.; *dial.* a tendril, a runner. OE.
10 a A ray, a line; GEOMETRY a chord. Also, a wire, a rail. *rare. obsolete* exc. as below. ME. ▸**b** BILLIARDS etc. The baulk-line. *US.* M19.
11 MINING. A thin vein of ore etc.; a ramification of a lode. E17.
†**12** = STRINGHALT. *rare.* M17–E19.
13 = *stringboard* below. E18.
14 NAUTICAL. A strake of planking on the inside of a ship immediately below the gunwale. E18.
15 A line of fencing. *US.* L18.
16 = *string-course* below. E19.
17 ***string of tide***, a strong tidal current in a narrow channel. *Shetland.* M19.
18 a PARTICLE PHYSICS. A hypothetical subatomic object consisting of a spinning massless one-dimensional entity with dynamic properties like those of a flexible elastic string. L20. ▸**b** In full ***cosmic string***. An inhomogeneity in the structure of space–time having the form of an extensive or looped threadlike concentration of energy, hypothesized to be formed in the phase transitions of the early universe. L20.
▸ **III 19** A thread or line with a number of things on it; *esp.* a number of beads, pearls, etc., strung on a thread; a number of fish strung on a thread passed through the gills; a number of things linked together in a line. (Foll. by *of.*) L15. ▸**b** BILLIARDS etc. A number of beads etc. on a wire for keeping a player's score; the number of points scored. *US.* Now *rare* or *obsolete.* M19.
20 †a A set of people; a band, a faction. L16–L17. ▸**b** A set of horses, draught animals, or (formerly) slaves; *esp.* the horses belonging to a particular racing yard or jumping stable. M18. ▸**c** A group of prostitutes working for the same person. *US slang.* E20.
21 A number of animals driven in single file tied one to the other; a number of animals, vehicles, or persons following one behind the other. L17.
22 A number of things in a line; a row, a chain, a range. L17. ▸**b** OIL INDUSTRY. Orig. (more fully ***string of tools***), the drilling bit and weights that occupy the hole in drilling. Now, the entire drilling assembly in the hole (more fully ***drill string***, ***drilling string***); the coupled lengths of pipe or casing in the hole. L19. ▸**c** MATH. & COMPUTING etc. A sequence of symbols or linguistic elements in a definite order. M20. ▸**d** COMPUTING. A linear sequence of records or data. M20.
23 A continuous series or succession of words, incidents, characters, etc.; (usu. *derog.*) a continuous stream of utterance. Usu. foll. by *of.* E18. ▸**b** The thread of or *of* a narrative. *rare.* M19. ▸**c** A continuous series of successes or failures; a continuous sequence of games, turns at play, etc. Chiefly *N. Amer.* L19.

> **19** D. M. THOMAS Women carried strings of onions round their necks. R. FRAME She stood straightening her strings of blue beads. **21** S. E. WHITE The train consisted of a string of freight cars. P. MATTHIESSEN A herder leads his strings of shaggy ponies. A. BRINK A constant string of .. boy-friends. **22** T. TRYON The string of six cabins .. spread out along the linepath. **23** E. PEACOCK The fox sang a string of doggerel. D. WELCH A whole string of embarrassing questions. N. MONSARRAT He had a string of names—John Standish Surtees Prendergast Vereker. *Horticulture Week* The computer carries out a string of orders.

Phrases etc.: ***cosmic string***: see sense 18b above. ***drill string***, ***drilling string***: see sense 22b above. ***eyestrings***: see EYE *noun.* **first string** a person or thing regarded as a first choice or most important resource. **harp on one string**, **harp on the same string**, etc., dwell tediously on one, the same, etc., subject. **have in a string**, **have on a string** *fig.* have under control, be able to do what one likes with. **have two strings to one's bow**, **have many strings to one's bow**, etc., have two, many, etc., alternative resources. ***heart-strings***: see HEART *noun.* ***oil string***: see OIL *noun.* **pull strings** *fig.* exert influence privately. **pull the strings** *fig.* control the course of affairs, be the hidden operator in what is ostensibly done by another. **second string (to one's bow)** an alternative resource in case another fails; an alternative, a reserve; a person or thing regarded as a second choice. ***silver string***: see SILVER *noun & adjective.* **string and sealing-wax** (the type of) simple or unpretentious scientific equipment (freq. *attrib.*). **string of the tongue** the fraenum of the tongue. ***string of tide***: see sense 17 above. ***string of tools***: see sense 22b above. ***sympathetic strings***: see SYMPATHETIC *adjective.* ***terminal string***: see TERMINAL *adjective.*

Comb.: **string art**: of making pictures by winding yarn round nails driven into a surface; **string bass** (the player of) a double-bass; **string bean** (*a*) any of various beans eaten in their unripe fibrous pods, *esp.* the French bean and runner bean; (*b*) *colloq.* a tall thin person; **string bed** = CHARPOY; **stringboard** a supporting timber or skirting in which the ends of the steps in a staircase are set; **string-coloured** *adjective* of the usual natural colour of string, light greyish brown; **string cot** = CHARPOY; **string-course** a course or band of masonry or bricks projecting slightly from the general surface of a wall; **string figure** a figure made by passing string round the fingers of both hands, a cat's cradle; **string galvanometer**: utilizing a fine conducting fibre, for measuring rapidly-fluctuating currents; **string-line** = sense 10b above; **string man** = STRINGER 5; **string-piece** a long horizontal member holding together and supporting the framework of a bridge, pier, or other structure, a stringer; **string-puller** a person who exerts influence esp. behind the scenes; **string-pulling** the exertion of influence esp. behind the scenes; ***string telephone***: see TELEPHONE *noun* 1; **string theory** a cosmological theory based on the hypothetical existence of cosmic strings; **string tie** a very narrow necktie, usu. worn in a bow.
▸ **B** *attrib.* or as *adjective.* **1** (Of a musician) that plays a stringed instrument; consisting of strings or string

players; (of an instrument) stringed; (of music) played by or written for strings. L15.

2 Made or consisting of string; *spec.* (of a garment etc.) woven or knitted from stringlike material with a very open mesh. E18.

3 String-coloured. M20.

> **1** *string orchestra, string quartet*, etc. **2** P. LIVELY The string bag of shopping. *Listener* Don your string vest and boxer shorts.

■ **stringful** *noun* as many as can be strung on a string; *fig.* a long series *of*: E17. **stringless** *adjective* L16. **stringlike** *adjective* resembling (that of) string L19.

string /strɪŋ/ *verb.* Pa. t. & pple **strung** /strʌŋ/, (earlier, now *rare*) **stringed**. LME.
[from the noun.]

▶ **I** *verb trans.* **1** Draw up, arrange, or extend in a line or row; distribute widely at intervals. Freq. foll. by *out*. LME.

2 Provide or fit with a string or strings; attach a string or strings to; *spec.* prepare (a bow) for shooting an arrow by positioning the string so that it can be drawn tight; *poet.* tune (a stringed instrument). LME. ▸**b** Provide with or *with* nerves or sinews etc. Usu. in *pass.* M17.

3 Remove the (natural) string or strings from; *esp.* remove the strings from (beans). Orig. *spec.*, prepare (a lamprey) for eating. E16.

4 *fig.* Make tense, brace, invigorate, or sensitize (the nerves or sinews, the mind, etc.); freq. foll. by *up*. Also, bring to a specified condition of tension etc. Usu. in *pass.* L16.

5 Bind, tie, or fasten with a string or strings. E17.

6 Thread (beads etc.) on or as on a string; make (a necklace) in this way; join *together* on or as on a string. Also, hang or suspend by a connecting string (freq. foll. by *up*). E17. ▸**b** *fig.* Put (esp. words, ideas, etc.) together in a connected sequence. E17.

7 Kill by hanging. Usu. foll. by *up*. *colloq.* E18.

8 Deceive, hoax. *slang* (now chiefly *N. Amer.*). E19.

9 Provide, equip, or adorn *with* something suspended or slung. M19.

10 Extend or stretch from one point to another. Also foll. by *out*. M19.

> **1** CONAN DOYLE Ten thousand men, strung over a large extent of country. S. CHITTY His children . . followed strung out behind him like a row of ducklings. **2** SHAKES. *Two Gent.* Orpheus' lute was strung with poets' sinews. J. HURDIS He tipt his arrow, strung his bow. **b** *fig.*: DRYDEN Their Language is not strung with Sinews like our English. **3** A. LEE Busy in the kitchen, perhaps . . stringing beans. **4** DRYDEN Toil strung the Nerves and purifi'd the Blood. R. M. BALLANTYNE A . . British tar . . whose nerves were tightly strung and used to danger. *HIGHLY strung*. **5** J. PUDNEY A diagram showing how parcels were to be stringed. **6** M. DE LA ROCHE Ernest, stringing afresh a necklet of enormous . . beads. *fig.*: ARTHUR LYONS Small, exclusive communities . . strung like . . pearls along the highway. **b** *Rolling Stone* Baez seems content to simply string verses. O. KEEPNEWS I have been able to string together some sensible observations. **9** M. GALLANT A . . tennis court strung with Christmas lights. **10** S. E. WHITE Stringing booms across the river—obstructing navigation.

▶ **II** *verb intrans.* **11 a** Be hanged. Also foll. by *up*. *Scot.* E18. ▸**b** Hang like a string *from*. L19.

12 Move or progress in a string or disconnected line. (Foll. by *out, off*, etc.) E19.

13 *BILLIARDS* etc. Determine the order of play by striking the cue-ball from baulk to rebound off the top cushion, first stroke going to the player whose ball comes to rest nearer the bottom cushion. E19.

14 Of a viscous substance: form into strings, become stringy. M19.

15 Work as a stringer in journalism. M20.

> **12** W. D. LIGHTHALL The pedestrians are already stringing off along the road. S. TROTT They strung out in a line across the street.

With adverbs in specialized senses: **string along** *colloq.* deceive, fool; *esp.* keep (a person) in a state of misplaced confidence by encouragement or apparent compliance. **string along with** *colloq.* keep company with; agree or go along with, usu. unenthusiastically. **string out** *colloq.* prolong, esp. unduly; cause to last as long as possible.

stringed /strɪŋd/ *adjective.* ME.
[from STRING *noun* + -ED².]
Having a string or strings; having strings of a specified number or type; *spec.* (of a musical instrument) producing sound by means of vibrating strings. Also, (of music) produced by strings or stringed instruments.

stringed *verb pa. t. & pple*: see STRING *verb*.

stringendo /strɪnˈdʒɛndəʊ/ *adverb, adjective, & noun.* M19.
[Italian, pres. pple of *stringere* press, squeeze, bind together, from Latin: see next.]
MUSIC. ▶**A** *adverb & adjective.* A direction: with increasing speed and excitement. M19.
▶**B** *noun.* Pl. **-dos, -di** /-diː/. An increase of speed and excitement; a passage (to be) played with such an increase. M20.

stringent /ˈstrɪn(d)ʒ(ə)nt/ *adjective.* E17.
[Latin *stringent-* pres. ppl stem of *stringere* bind: see -ENT. Cf. STRICT *adjective*.]

1 Astringent, styptic. Long *rare*. E17.

2 Of reasoning: compelling, convincing. M17.

3 That draws or binds tight; tightly enfolding or compressing. *rare*. M18.

4 Of a regulation, procedure, requirement, condition, obligation, etc.: rigorous, strict; requiring exact performance, leaving no loophole or discretion, hard to comply with. M19.

5 Of a money market: tight. L19.

> **4** H. GREEN The need for stringent economy. *Which?* Defrosting frozen food is one of the most stringent tests of a microwave oven's performance. S. ROSENBERG Rigid labor laws were enforced and even more stringent ones were to follow.

■ **stringency** *noun* the quality of being stringent M19. **stringently** *adverb* M17. **stringentness** *noun* E18.

stringer /ˈstrɪŋə/ *noun.* ME.
[from STRING *noun* or *verb* + -ER¹.]

1 a A worker who makes strings for bows. *obsolete* exc. *Hist.* ME. ▸**b** A person who threads pearls etc. on a string. *rare*. E19. ▸**c** A worker who fits a piano or other musical instrument with strings. M19.

2 A person who strings words etc. together. L18.

3 A long horizontal structural member in a framework, e.g. of a bridge, aircraft, etc.; a longitudinal member that strengthens a structure. M19. ▸**b** *SHIPBUILDING.* An inside strake of planking or plating supporting the ends of the beams. M19. ▸**c** A longitudinal railway sleeper. *US.* M19. ▸**d** A stringboard. L19.

4 a *MINING.* A narrow mineral vein traversing a mass of different material. L19. ▸**b** *METALLURGY.* A microscopic inclusion of impurity in a metal, elongated parallel to the direction of working. M20.

5 A journalist or reporter not on the regular staff of a newspaper or organization, *esp.* one retained on a part-time basis to report on events in a particular place. M20.

stringhalt /ˈstrɪŋhɔːlt/ *noun.* E16.
[from STRING *noun* + HALT *adjective* or *noun*¹. Cf. SPRINGHALT.]
A spasmodic lifting of a horse's hind leg, caused by abnormal muscular contractions.
■ **stringhalted** *adjective* affected with stringhalt L17.

stringing /ˈstrɪŋɪŋ/ *noun.* L16.
[from STRING *verb* + -ING¹.]

1 a *sing.* & †in *pl.* Strings collectively; (chiefly *Scot.*) ornamentation of lace or tape. L16. ▸**b** Inlaid lines in cabinet-work. E19. ▸**c** Material for the stringboard of a staircase, or for string-courses on a building. M19.

2 The action of STRING *verb*. E17.

stringy /ˈstrɪŋi/ *adjective.* M17.
[from STRING *noun* + -Y¹.]

1 Resembling string or fibre; consisting of stringlike pieces; *esp.* (of food) fibrous and tough; (of hair) hanging in thin strands. M17.

2 Of a viscous liquid: containing or forming glutinous threadlike masses, ropy. L17.

3 Of a sound or voice: thin in tone. E19.

4 Esp. of a person: thin, wiry, sinewy. M19.

> **1** *Forbes* Older rabbits with tough, stringy meat. I. MURDOCH Long straight greasy dark hair, sometimes plaited, sometimes stringy. **stringy-bark** *Austral.* (*a*) (the bark or wood of) any of various eucalypts, e.g. *Eucalyptus obliqua* and *E. muellerana*, having bark which splits into long tough fibres; (*b*) *colloq.* an inhabitant of the outback, an uncouth backwoodsman. **4** S. RAVEN A tall stringy, left-handed bowler. *Muscle Mag International* At a stringy 175 pounds, he still possessed speed and . . strength.

■ **stringily** *adverb* so as to be stringy, so as to resemble string M20. **stringiness** *noun* L17.

strinkle /ˈstrɪŋk(ə)l/ *verb trans. obsolete* exc. *Scot. & dial.* Also **strenkle** /ˈstrɛŋk(ə)l/. ME.
[Prob. var. of SPRINKLE *verb*.]
Sprinkle, scatter, strew (*with, on*, etc.)
■ **strinkling** *noun* (*a*) the action of the verb; (*b*) a small quantity sprinkled, a scattering: ME.

strio- /ˈstrʌɪəʊ/ *combining form* of STRIA, STRIATUM: see -O-.
■ **strioˈnigral** *adjective* (*ANATOMY*) (of a nerve fibre) running from the corpus striatum to the substantia nigra E20. **strioˈpallidal** *adjective* (*ANATOMY*) (of a nerve fibre) running from the neostriatum to the globus pallidus M20. **strioˈscopic** *adjective* of or pertaining to strioscopy L20. **striˈoscopy** *noun* electron microscopy using a hollow conical beam of particles, giving a bright image on a dark field M20.

striola /ˈstrʌɪəʊlə/ *noun.* Pl. **-lae** /-liː/. E20.
[mod. Latin, dim. of STRIA.]
ZOOLOGY & BOTANY. A small stria.

striolate /ˈstrʌɪələt/ *adjective.* M19.
[mod. Latin *striolatus*, formed as prec.: see -ATE².]
ZOOLOGY & BOTANY. Marked with small striae.
■ Also **striolated** *adjective* M19.

strip /strɪp/ *noun*¹. LME.
[from or cogn. with Middle & mod. Low German *strippe* strap, thong, prob. rel. to STRIPE *noun*¹, *noun*².]

1 A long narrow piece of or *of* some material (orig. cloth or paper), of approximately uniform breadth. LME. ▸†**b** An ornamental article worn about the neck and upper body, chiefly by women. L16–M17. ▸**c** A narrow flat bar of iron, steel, etc.; metal in this form. Also, an ingot ready for rolling into plates. L19. ▸**d** *ellipt.* A fluorescent strip light. L20.

2 A long narrow tract of or *of* territory, land, etc.; a long narrow portion of a surface. E19. ▸**b** An area of ground where aircraft can take off and land, an airfield. Also, a track used for motor racing etc. M20. ▸**c** A main street, esp. one leading out of a town, lined with shops, shopping malls, restaurants, bars, filling-stations, etc. Freq. with *the* and cap. initial; orig., *spec.* Sunset Strip in Hollywood. *colloq.* (chiefly *N. Amer.*). M20. ▸**d** *CRICKET.* The band of ground between the wickets. *colloq.* L20.

3 a *PHILATELY.* A row of unseparated postage stamps joined horizontally or vertically. E20. ▸**b** A sequence of cartoons telling a comic or serial story. Freq. in ***comic strip*** s.v. COMIC *adjective*. E20. ▸**c** *BROADCASTING.* A series broadcast at the same time each weekday. M20.

> **1** W. GOLDING A corridor of concrete with a strip of coconut matting down the centre. ANTHONY HUXLEY Flexible garage doors composed of metal strips. M. HOCKING The bird-table . . well provided with nuts and strips of fat. R. RENDELL Leonora started ripping up the tablecloth, tearing it into strips. ***Möbius strip***. **tear a person off a strip**, **tear a strip off a person** *colloq.* (orig. *Military slang*) angrily rebuke a person. ***test strip***: see TEST *noun*¹. **2** W. BLACK This road is bordered by a strip of common. ***Cherokee Strip***, ***Gaza Strip***, etc. ***median strip***: see MEDIAN *noun*² 4. **b** ***airstrip***, ***landing strip***, etc. **c** *Guardian* Bangkok has its own strip . . miles of girlie bars . . and soul food snack bars. **3b** D. POWELL A curious impression of being in a Buck Rogers strip . . gazing into another planet.

Comb.: **strip cartoon** = sense 3b above; **strip-chart** a long paper roll on which a recording pen traces changes of a measured quantity as the paper moves past the pen at a constant rate; **strip cropping** (*a*) *US* cultivation in which different crops are sown in alternate strips to prevent soil erosion; (*b*) the practice of growing crops in strips; **strip cultivation** (*a*) = ***strip farming*** below; (*b*) *ARCHAEOLOGY* the use of strip lynchets in farming; **strip development** *US* = ***ribbon development*** s.v. RIBBON *noun*; **strip farming** *Hist.* land cultivation in which the land was divided up into long narrow strips worked by different peasant-farmers; **strip-graze** *verb trans.* subject (land) to strip-grazing; **strip-grazing** *AGRICULTURE* farm management in which strips of land are alternately grazed and kept empty; rotational grazing; **strip light** a lighting device of linear form providing diffused lighting; now *spec.*, a tubular fluorescent lamp; **strip lighting** illumination by strip light(s); strip lights collectively; **stripline** *ELECTRICITY* a microstrip; **strip-loin** *N. Amer.* a particular cut of loin of beef; **strip lynchet** *ARCHAEOLOGY* a long narrow cultivation terrace; **strip mall** *N. Amer.* a (usu. small) shopping mall on a main street leading out of a town; **strip map** a long narrow map showing the course of a road or other route and the places adjacent; **strip mill** a rolling-mill for producing metal strip; **strip-mine** *verb trans.* obtain or work by strip-mining; **strip-mining**: in which surface material is removed in successive parallel strips to expose the mineral, the spoil from each new strip being placed in the previously excavated one; **strip steak** *US* a long steak cut from loin of beef.

■ **striplet** *noun* (*rare*) a small strip M19.

strip /strɪp/ *noun*². Long *obsolete* exc. *US.* E16.
[Aphet. from Anglo-Norman *estrepe*, from *estreper*: see ESTREPEMENT.]
LAW. = ESTREPEMENT.

strip /strɪp/ *noun*³. M19.
[from STRIP *verb*¹.]

1 In *pl.* Tobacco-leaf with the stalk and midrib removed. M19.

2 The action or an instance of taking off one's clothes, *esp.* (a performance of) striptease. E20.

3 The distinctive clothing worn by the members of a sports team when playing. L20.

strip /strɪp/ *verb*¹. Infl. **-pp-**. Pa. t. & pple **stripped**, (*arch.*) **stript**. ME.
[Corresp. to Middle Dutch *stroopen* (Dutch *stropen*), Old High German *stroufen* (German *streifen*), from West Germanic. Prob. already in Old English: cf. BESTRIP.]

▶ **I 1** *verb trans.* Remove the clothing from; unclothe, undress, make naked; divest or deprive of or *of* clothing (to a specified extent). ME. ▸**b** *verb intrans.* Take off one's clothes, undress oneself (to a specified extent); take off one's ordinary clothing in preparation for exercise, a sport, etc.; *spec.* (*colloq.*) perform a striptease, act as a stripper. Also foll. by *off*. L17. ▸†**c** *verb trans.* Discharge (a servant, orig. a liveried servant). *rare*. M18–M19.

2 *verb trans.* Deprive of possessions, an attribute, title, office, etc. Foll. by *of*, †*out of*, †*from*. ME.

3 *verb trans.* Remove the covering from (a thing); *esp.* remove the bark of (a tree). (Foll. by *of*.) ME. ▸**b** Remove bedclothes and linen from (a bed). L19. ▸**c** Pluck the old hair from (a dog). M20.

†**4** *verb trans.* Skin (an animal). ME–L18.

5 *verb trans.* Remove the foliage or fruit from (a branch, tree, etc.). (Foll. by *of.*) **E17.**

6 *verb trans.* Empty, make bare, or clear out (a place, room, etc.). (Foll. by *of* contents, ornaments, etc.) **E17.** ▸**b** Unpack or unload (a container, lorry, etc.). *slang.* **M20.**

7 *verb trans.* Take away the accessories, equipment, or fittings of; take apart, dismantle, esp. prior to repair, inspection, etc. Freq. foll. by *down.* **L17.**

📖 **1** M. PRIOR The Nymph . . Stript her self naked to the skin. BYRON An old man . . Stript to his waistcoat. T. SEATON The mutineers were stripped of their uniforms. SLOAN WILSON Tom . . had stripped the bodies of the warm clothes. D. DUNNETT The maid . . was . . stripping Mrs Sheridan down to the waist. **b** BUNYAN If thou intendest to win, thou must Strip, thou must lay aside every Weight. J. D. MACDONALD I'm working a place, . . singing and . . stripping some, but not down to raw. J. F. HENDRY He had to strip and put on school uniform. P. D. JAMES She stripped naked, put on . . a bikini. **strip well** look impressive when naked, have a good body. **2** W. H. DIXON The cardinal stripped him of his deanery. E. M. FORSTER Margaret saw Death stripped of any false romance. R. COBB I have endeavoured to strip the narrative of all superfluities. M. DAS They . . soon stripped him of all his money. **5** W. ELLIS The Rook . . will strip a Walnut Tree in a little time. I. WALLACE Autumn . . had already stripped the . . trees of their green foliage. **6** C. LAMB His . . shelves are . . stript of his favourite old authors. P. MARSHALL She . . began stripping the hangers of . . clothes. M. GARDINER A big, bare . . room, stripped of all but essentials. *New Yorker* Stripping a summer house bare during the winter is a speciality of . . burglars. **7** W. GREENER To strip a muzzle-loader, first remove the lock. *Country Life* Small fragments of . . damask were found when the chair was stripped down.

▶ **II 8** *verb trans.* Remove or take off (clothes, a garment, trappings, covers, a disguise, etc.). (Foll. by *off, away.*) **ME.**

9 *verb trans.* Take as plunder, take away (*from*). **ME.**

10 *verb trans.* Pull, tear, or peel off (an adhering covering of skin, bark, paper, etc.); pull off (leaves or fruit) from a tree, branch, etc.; remove (paint, varnish, etc.) from a surface etc., esp. with a solvent. (Foll. by *off, away.*) **LME.** ▸**b** *verb intrans.* Peel or become detached (easily). **L19.**

11 *verb trans.* Roll up (a sleeve). Usu. foll. by *up. arch.* **L16.**

12 *verb trans.* Clear off (vegetation); harvest (a crop). Chiefly *US & Austral.* **M19.**

📖 **8** A. CARY She stript from her finger the shining ring. J. R. GREEN Picture after picture strips the veil from the corruption of the mediæval church. R. W. CHAMBERS She stripped off her gloves. E. WALLACE He paused to strip his overcoat and take off his . . hat. F. SPALDING The Surrealists stripped away conventional logic. **9** R. GRAVES The risk of having your whole fortune stripped from you . . on a charge of treason. **10** H. GLASSE Take . . stalks of angelica . . , strip off the skins. T. MCGUANE The hawk was hooded over its prey, stripping meat from the breast.

▶ **III** *techn.* **13** *verb trans.* Remove the stalks or veins from (a leaf, *spec.* a tobacco-leaf). **L15.**

14 *verb trans.* MINING. Wash (ore) in order to separate metal. **L17.**

15 *verb trans.* Tear the thread from (a screw, bolt, etc.) or the teeth from (a gearwheel etc.); remove or damage (the thread, teeth) in this way. **M19.** ▸**b** *verb intrans.* (Of a screw etc.) lose its thread; (of a gearwheel etc.) lose its teeth; (of a bullet) issue from a rifled gun without spin owing to a loss of surface. **M19.**

16 *verb trans.* Smooth (a metal surface) by filing etc.; smooth the surface of by filing etc. **M19.**

17 *verb trans.* Remove (colour) from dyed material before re-dyeing; remove colour from (dyed material) before re-dyeing. **L19.**

18 *verb trans.* Remove electro-plated metal from (an article) by electrolysis. **L19.**

19 *verb trans.* **a** OIL INDUSTRY. Fractionate; extract or recover by fractionation. **E20.** ▸**b** CHEMISTRY. Extract or recover (a solute) *from* a solvent. **M20.**

20 *verb trans.* PHYSICS. Deprive (an atom, ion, etc.) *of* an electron or other particle; remove (an electron or other particle) *from* an atom, ion, etc. **M20.**

21 *verb trans.* PRINTING. Insert or assemble (a piece of film) with others for printing down on a plate. Usu. foll. by *in.* **M20.**

22 *verb trans.* COMMERCE. ▸**a** Sell off (the assets of a company) for profit. Cf. ASSET-*stripping.* **L20.** ▸**b** Foll. by *out*: eliminate (an item) from a statement of accounts for the purpose of comparison etc. **L20.**

Comb.: **strip cell** a bare cell in which a prisoner is subjected to sensory or physical deprivation; **strip club**: at which striptease performances take place; **strip-down** the process of stripping an engine etc. down; dismantling, disassembly; **strip-jack-naked** = *beggar-my-neighbour* s.v. BEGGAR *verb* 1; **strip joint** *slang* = *strip club* above; **strip-poker** a form of poker in which a losing player sheds a garment as a penalty or forfeit; **strip-search** *noun & verb* (*a*) *noun* a search of a prisoner etc. which involves removing all of his or her clothing; (*b*) *verb trans.* search (a person) in this way.

■ **strippable** *adjective* (*a*) (of a coating) able to be stripped off or removed; (*b*) able to be strip-mined: **M20.**

†**strip** *verb*². Infl. **-pp-**. **LME.**
[Ult. from Germanic base of STRIPE *noun*².]
1 *verb intrans.* Move or pass swiftly. **LME–E17.**
2 *verb trans.* Outstrip. **M16–L18.**

strip /strɪp/ *verb*³ *trans.* Infl. **-pp-**. **E17.**
[Cogn. with STRIPE *noun*¹. Cf. Western Flemish *strippen.* Cf. STRIPE *verb*³.]
1 Extract (milk) from a cow's udder; milk (a cow). Now *spec.*, extract the last drops of milk from (a cow). **E17.**
2 Pull and squeeze with an action resembling milking; *spec.* press out the ripe roe or milt from (a fish). **L19.**
3 ANGLING. Draw *in* (a line or fish) with the hand. **L20.**
Comb.: **strip cup** a cup with a strainer for collecting and inspecting a sample of milk from a cow.

strip /strɪp/ *verb*⁴ *trans.* Infl. **-pp-**. **L19.**
[from STRIP *noun*¹.]
1 Cut into strips. **L19.**
2 BROADCASTING. Broadcast (a series etc.) every weekday at the same time. **L20.**

stripagram /ˈstrɪpəgram/ *noun.* Also **stripo-**, **stripper-**, & other vars. **L20.**
[from STRIP *verb*¹ or *noun*³ + *-a-* + -GRAM. Cf. STRIPPER *noun*¹.]
A novelty telegram or greetings message sent through a commercial agency, delivered by a person (usu. a young woman) who performs a striptease for the recipient.

stripe /strʌɪp/ *noun*¹. **LME.**
[Origin uncertain: ult. cogn. with next. Cf. STRIP *noun*¹.]
1 A mark left by a lash etc.; a weal. *rare.* **LME.**
2 A blow or stroke, esp. (now only) with a whip, lash, cane, etc. *arch.* **L15.**

📖 **2** SPENSER With one stripe Her Lions clawes he . . away did wipe. *fig.*: T. T. LYNCH Each passing day . . may give a stripe, a smile, a counsel, a reproach.

stripe /strʌɪp/ *noun*². **LME.**
[Perh. back-form. from STRIPED: ult. rel. to Middle Low German, Middle Dutch *stripe* = Middle High German *strīfe* (German *Streifen*), from Germanic. Cf. prec., STRIP *noun*¹.]
1 A relatively long and narrow portion of a fabric, surface, etc., differing in appearance from the adjacent parts, often one of several similar parallel bands. **LME.** ▸**b** In *pl.* Prison uniform (patterned with stripes). *US slang.* **L19.** ▸**c** In full ***magnetic stripe***. A narrow strip of magnetic material along the edge of film, on which sound may be recorded. **M20.**
2 A striped fabric. **M18.**
3 GEOLOGY. A narrow band or stratum of rock. **L18.**
4 A strip, a shred; a narrow piece. **L18.**
5 A narrow strip of material sewn on a garment of different colour; *esp.* (*colloq.*) a chevron or similar mark of rank, good conduct, etc., on the sleeve of a uniform. **E19.**
6 A strip of land; a band of ice. **E19.**
7 A shade or variety of political, religious, etc., belief; *gen.* a sort, a class, a type. Orig. & chiefly *N. Amer.* **M19.**

📖 **1** I. COLEGATE His shirt had big blue stripes. *New York Times* Newer . . looms . . produce a raised stripe in taffeta. *Guardian* The natterjack . . distinguished . . by a yellow stripe. **Old Stripes, Stripes** *colloq.* (a name for) a tiger. ***Stars and Stripes***: see STAR *noun*¹ & *adjective.* **5** S. L. ELLIOTT Cops him . . at the pictures when he's supposed to be on guard and takes his stripes off him. R. B. PARKER A fatigue jacket with a staff sergeant's stripes. ***ship a stripe***: see SHIP *verb* 11. **7** *Newsweek* Egyptians of all political stripes were growing . . restive. J. MAY Fleet line officers of the most impressive stripe.

stripe /strʌɪp/ *verb*¹ *trans.* Now *rare.* **LME.**
[from (the same root as) STRIPE *noun*¹.]
Beat, whip, esp. as a punishment.

stripe /strʌɪp/ *verb*² *trans.* **LME.**
[from (the same root as) STRIPE *noun*².]
1 Ornament or mark with stripes. (Foll. by *with.*) **LME.**
2 Divide (land) into strips or plots. *Anglo-Irish.* **L19.**
3 Apply a magnetic stripe to (film). **M20.**
■ **striping** *noun* (*a*) the action of the verb; (*b*) a stripe or series of stripes of colour: **L15.**

stripe /strʌɪp/ *verb*³ *trans.* Long only *Scot. & north.* **L17.**
[Var. of STRIP *verb*³.]
Draw (esp. a blade) *through, over*, etc.

striped /strʌɪpt/ *adjective.* **LME.**
[Perh. of Low Dutch origin (cf. Dutch *strijpt*, Middle Low German *striped*); later from STRIPE *verb*² or *noun*²: see -ED¹, -ED².]
1 Marked with a stripe or stripes, having a band or bands of colour, streaked. **LME.**
2 Of film: having a magnetic stripe. **L20.**
1 ***blue-striped, green-striped, red-striped***, etc.
Special collocations: **striped bass** a large bass of N. American coastal waters, *Roccus saxatilis*, with dark horizontal stripes along the upper sides. ***striped hyena***: see HYENA 1a. ***striped*** KARANTEEN. **striped maple** a N. American maple, *Acer pensylvanicum*, having green bark striped with white. **striped mouse** any of various African mice of the genera *Lemniscomys* and *Rhabdomys*, with a striped back. **striped muscle** = ***striated muscle*** s.v. STRIATED 1. **striped pants** *colloq.* = ***striped trousers*** below. **striped possum** any of various possums of the genus *Dactylopsila*, native to New Guinea and Australia; *esp.* the black and white *D. trivirgata.* ***striped*** SKAAPSTEKER. **striped squill** = PUSCHKINIA. **striped squirrel** a chipmunk or similar striped rodent. ***striped*** SURMULLET. **striped trousers** trousers with a pattern of narrow vertical stripes, esp. as supposedly characteristic of civil servants and businessmen. **striped tuna** = ***skipjack tuna*** s.v. SKIPJACK 3.

striper /ˈstrʌɪpə/ *noun. colloq.* **E20.**
[from STRIPE *noun*² + -ER¹.]
1 With specifying numeral: a member of the navy, army, etc., whose uniform carries a number of stripes denoting rank. **E20.**
2 = STRIPED ***bass***. *N. Amer.* **M20.**
1 **one-striper** a lance-corporal. **three-striper** a sergeant. **two-striper** (*a*) a naval lieutenant; (*b*) a corporal.

stripey *adjective & noun* see STRIPY.

stripling /ˈstrɪplɪŋ/ *noun & adjective.* **ME.**
[Prob. from STRIP *noun*¹ + -LING¹.]
▶ **A** *noun.* A youth not yet fully grown; a lad. **ME.**

📖 *transf.*: DRYDEN I'm but a Stripling in the Trade of War.

▶ **B** *attrib.* or as *adjective.* That is a stripling; of or pertaining to a stripling or striplings; youthful. **M16.**

📖 M. ARNOLD Crossing the stripling Thames at Bab-lock-hithe.

stripogram *noun* var. of STRIPAGRAM.

stripped /strɪpt/ *ppl adjective.* **L16.**
[from STRIP *verb*¹ + -ED¹.]
1 That has been stripped. **L16.**
2 *spec.* Of wood (esp. pine) used for furniture etc.: that has had the paint or varnish removed so as to reveal the natural grain and colour. **M20.**
Comb.: **stripped-down** *adjective* (*a*) (of a motor vehicle etc.) that has had all superfluous or extraneous parts removed; *fig.* reduced to essentials, bare, lean; (*b*) disassembled, dismantled.

stripper /ˈstrɪpə/ *noun*¹. **L16.**
[from STRIP *verb*¹ + -ER¹.]
1 A person who strips something or someone; *esp.* a person who strips off some article or product. **L16.** ▸**b** A performer of striptease. **M20.**
2 a A machine or appliance for stripping something; a vessel etc. in which stripping is done. **M19.** ▸**b** A chemical agent used for stripping off a dye, paint, varnish, etc. **E20.**
3 In *pl.* High cards cut slightly wedge-shaped for the purposes of cheating. *slang.* **M19.**

📖 **1** H. LAWSON Bits of bark . . left by a party of strippers. J. AIKEN A stripper or a fluff-picker . . [in] a carpet factory. **b** A. MUNRO On Thursday nights they have a male stripper. **2** *Practical Householder* A wallpaper stripper . . can be hired. **b** ***paint-stripper***: see PAINT *noun.*

stripper /ˈstrɪpə/ *noun*². **M19.**
[from STRIP *verb*³ + -ER¹.]
1 A cow no longer giving much milk. *dial.* **M19.**
2 OIL INDUSTRY. In full ***stripper well***. An oil well in which production has dwindled to very little. **M20.**

strippergram *noun* var. of STRIPAGRAM.

strippeuse /strɪˈpəːz/ *noun. joc.* **M20.**
[from STRIPPER *noun*¹ after *danseuse* etc.]
A female striptease performer.

stripping /ˈstrɪpɪŋ/ *noun*¹. **ME.**
[from STRIP *verb*¹ + -ING¹.]
1 The action of STRIP *verb*¹; an instance of this. **ME.**
2 A thing stripped off or taken off in a thin layer. Usu. in *pl.* **E17.**
Comb.: **stripping film** photographic film having an emulsion layer which can be separated intact from its support after exposure.

stripping /ˈstrɪpɪŋ/ *noun*². **L18.**
[from STRIP *verb*³ + -ING¹.]
1 In *pl.* The last milk drawn from a cow. Also called ***strokings***. **L18.**
2 The action of STRIP *verb*³. **L19.**

strippy /ˈstrɪpi/ *adjective.* **E19.**
[from STRIP *noun*¹ + -Y¹.]
Of the nature of a strip, made up of strips.

stript *verb pa. t. & pple*: see STRIP *verb*¹.

striptease /ˈstrɪptiːz/ *noun.* **M20.**
[from STRIP *verb*¹ + TEASE *verb.*]
A kind of entertainment in which a (usu. female) performer undresses gradually before an audience, usu. to music; an instance of this.
attrib.: ***striptease act, striptease artist, striptease club***, etc.
■ **stripteaser** *noun* a performer of striptease **M20.** **stripteasing** *noun* the performance of striptease **M20.**

stripy /ˈstrʌɪpi/ *adjective & noun.* Also (the usual form as noun) **-ey**. **E16.**
[from STRIPE *noun*² + -Y¹.]
▶ **A** *adjective.* Having many stripes, striped; suggesting stripes or bands of colour. **E16.**

📖 L. ELLMANN I dressed my baby in stripy outfits. M. WARNER The snails were . . greyish-brown, with stripey markings.

▶ **B** *noun.* **1** Any of various striped marine fish. *Austral.* **E20.**

2 (A name for) a long-service able seaman (with good conduct stripes). *Nautical slang.* M20.

■ **stripiness** *noun* M20.

stritch /strɪtʃ/ *noun.* M20.
[Origin unkn.]
A musical instrument resembling a straightened alto saxophone.

†**strive** *noun* var. of STRIFE.

strive /strʌɪv/ *verb intrans.* Pa. t. **strove** /strəʊv/, **strived**; pa. pple **striven** /ˈstrɪv(ə)n/, **strived**. ME.
[Aphet. from Old French *estriver* rel. to *estrif* STRIFE.]
1 Be in a state of mutual hostility; quarrel, wrangle. Now *rare* or *obsolete.* ME.
2 Engage in violent conflict, struggle, (*with* or *against* an opponent, *for* a thing); *fig.* contend resolutely *with* or *against* natural forces, difficulties, etc. ME. ▸†**b** Contend in arms. ME–E18. ▸**c** Of things: be mutually opposed in action; come into conflict *with.* LME.
†**3** Argue, dispute, (*that, who,* etc.). ME–E17.
†**4** Contend in rivalry; compete, vie. (Foll. by *with.*) ME–E18.
5 Make strenuous efforts (*to do*). ME. ▸**b** Aim *for* or seek *after* a thing with strenuous efforts. ME.
6 Make one's way with effort. L16.

📖 **1** SIR W. SCOTT They say you cannot live in Rome and strive with the Pope. **2** DRYDEN For two Pretenders oft for Empire strive. S. AUSTIN Old . . enemies with whom they had so long striven. H. SPENCER The thing I desperately strove against . . did me immense good. **3** R. HAKLUYT They had strouen together who should haue him to his house. **4** DRYDEN The Rival Chariots in the Race shall strive. **5** H. ROTH She . . swallowed, striving desperately to calm herself. E. ROOSEVELT Many things . . showed how hard we must strive if we are to maintain our position. **b** L. W. MEYNELL She . . achieved the smart effect which some women strive after laboriously, but in vain. P. ZWEIG A stubborn craftsman who knew the effect he strove for. **6** W. B. CARPENTER Ever striving upwards, so as . . to reach . . a still loftier elevation.

■ **striver** *noun* LME. **striving** *noun* the action of the verb; an instance of this: ME. **strivingly** *adverb* in a striving manner LME.

†**stroak** *verb* var. of STROKE *verb*[1].

stroam /strəʊm/ *verb intrans. obsolete* exc. *dial.* Also **strome**. L18.
[Perh. after *stroll* and *roam.*]
Walk with long strides. Also, wander about idly.

strobe /strəʊb/ *adjective & noun.* M20.
[Abbreviation of STROBOSCOPIC.]
▶ **A** *adjective.* = STROBOSCOPIC. M20.
Special collocations & comb.: **strobe disc** a disc with alternate light and dark sectors of equal size for checking the speed of rotation of a thing, appearing stationary only when this speed is related in a definite way to the frequency of the illumination. **strobe lamp**, **strobe light** (*a*) an electric light that can be made to flash on and off rapidly and automatically; (*b*) *US* an electronic flash for a camera. **strobe-lighted**, **strobe-lit** *adjectives* illuminated by strobe lights. **strobe pulse** a rapidly repeated brief pulse of electromagnetic radiation or electrical current used as a reference in a recurrent phenomenon of longer period.
▶ **B** *noun.* **1** = ***strobe disc*** above. M20.
2 = ***strobe pulse*** above. M20.
3 = ***strobe light*** above. M20.

strobe /strəʊb/ *verb.* M20.
[from prec.]
1 *verb trans.* ELECTRONICS. Gate (GATE *verb*[1] 2) by means of a strobe pulse. M20.
2 *verb intrans.* Of a strobe light: flash on and off in rapid succession. Also, in CINEMATOGRAPHY & TELEVISION, exhibit or give rise to strobing (see below). M20.
■ **strobing** *verbal noun* (*a*) the action of the verb; (*b*) CINEMATOGRAPHY jerkiness in what should be a smooth movement on the screen; TELEVISION an irregular movement and loss of continuity sometimes seen in lines and stripes in a television picture: M20.

strobic /ˈstrəʊbɪk/ *adjective. rare.* L19.
[Greek *strobikos*, from *strobos* a twisting or whirling round: see -IC.]
That has, or appears to have, a spinning motion.

strobila /strəˈbʌɪlə/ *noun.* Pl. **-lae** /-liː/. M19.
[mod. Latin from Greek *strobilē* plug of lint twisted into the shape of a fir cone. Cf. STROBILUS.]
ZOOLOGY. **1** A stack of immature larval jellyfish (ephyrae) formed on a scyphistoma by budding. M19.
2 The segmented body of a tapeworm, consisting of a chain of proglottids. M19.
■ **strobiˈlation**, **ˌstrobiliˈzation** *nouns* the formation of strobilae L19.

strobilanthes /strəʊbɪˈlanθiːz/ *noun.* Pl. same. M19.
[mod. Latin (see below), from STROBILUS + Greek *anthos* flower, with ref. to the shape of the young inflorescence.]
Any of various herbaceous plants and shrubs constituting the genus *Strobilanthes*, of the acanthus family, native to tropical Asia, bearing clusters of blue or white tubular flowers.

strobile /ˈstrəʊbʌɪl/ *noun.* L18.
[French (in sense 1), or Anglicized from STROBILUS, STROBILA.]
1 BOTANY. = STROBILUS 1. L18.
2 ZOOLOGY. = STROBILA 2. Now *rare.* M19.

strobili *noun* pl. of STROBILUS.

strobiloid /ˈstrəʊbɪlɔɪd/ *adjective.* M19.
[from STROBILA, STROBILUS + -OID.]
ZOOLOGY & BOTANY. Resembling or of the nature of a strobila or strobilus.

strobilus /ˈstrəʊbɪləs/ *noun.* Pl. **-li** /-lʌɪ, -liː/. M18.
[Late Latin from Greek *strobilos* anything twisted up, a fir cone, etc.]
1 BOTANY. A fir cone or similar fruit; an inflorescence made up of imbricated scales, e.g. that of the hop. M18. ▸**b** In certain cryptogams (e.g. clubmosses and horsetails): an aggregation of sporophylls resembling a fir cone. L19.
2 ZOOLOGY. = STROBILA 2. *rare.* L19.
■ **strobiˈlaceous** *adjective* relating to or resembling a strobilus E19. **stroˈbiliform** *adjective* shaped like a strobilus M19.

strobo- /ˈstrəʊbəʊ/ *combining form* of STROBOSCOPE: see -O-.
■ **strobotorch** *noun* a light source designed to give very brief flashes of light at a known rate M20. **strobotron** *noun* a gas-filled cold-cathode discharge tube used as a strobotorch, the flashing rate being determined by the frequency of the voltage applied to a control grid M20.

stroboscope /ˈstrəʊbəskəʊp/ *noun.* M19.
[from Greek *strobos* a twisting or whirling round + -SCOPE.]
1 *Hist.* A scientific toy which produced the illusion of motion by a series of pictures viewed through the openings of a revolving disc. M19.
2 An instrument for observing the successive phases of a periodic motion by means of a strobe light flashing at an appropriate frequency. L19.
■ **stroboˈscopic**, **stroboˈscopical** *adjectives* relating to or of the nature of the stroboscope; involving rapid flashes of light: M19. **stroboˈscopically** *adverb* M19. **stroˈboscopy** *noun* the use of stroboscopic techniques or apparatus; stroboscopic effects: M20.

stroddle /ˈstrɒd(ə)l/ *verb trans. & intrans.* Now *dial.* E17.
[Var.]
= STRADDLE *verb.*

strode *verb pa. t. & pple*: see STRIDE *verb.*

stroganoff /ˈstrɒɡənɒf/ *noun.* M20.
[French, from Count Pavel Aleksandrovich *Stroganov* (1772–1817), Russian diplomat.]
In full ***beef stroganoff***, ***boeuf stroganoff***. A dish of strips of beef cooked in a sauce containing sour cream.

Stroh violin /ˌstrəʊ vʌɪəˈlɪn/ *noun phr.* E20.
[Augustus *Stroh* (1828–1914), German-born acoustic engineer, who invented the instrument, and his son Charles *Stroh*, who manufactured it.]
A type of violin having a metal diaphragm and horn attachment, formerly used for gramophone recording.

stroil /strɔɪl/ *noun. dial.* M18.
[Origin unkn.]
Any of several weeds with long creeping root-stocks, *esp.* couch grass, *Elytrigia repens.*

stroke /strəʊk/ *noun*[1]. ME.
[from ablaut var. of STRIKE *verb*: prob. already in Old English. Cf. STREAK *noun.*]
1 An act of striking with the hand, a weapon, etc.; a blow given or received. ME. ▸†**b** The mark left by a blow; a bruise, a wound, a cut. LME–E18. ▸†**c** A shot from a bow, gun, etc. Also, point of impact. LME–E18. ▸**d** In various games: an act of (successfully) striking the ball, a hit; *esp.* in GOLF, an act of hitting (at) the ball with a club, as a unit of scoring. M18.
2 *fig.* A damaging blow to a condition of things, a person's health, an institution, etc.; a calamitous event; a destructive action, *spec.* an act of divine chastisement or vengeance. ME. ▸**b** MEDICINE. A sudden attack of weakness, numbness, or hemiplegia (paralysis of one side of the body) caused by cerebral haemorrhage or ischaemia. Also called ***apoplexy***. Orig. more fully ***stroke of apoplexy***, ***stroke of paralysis***, ***apoplectic stroke***, ***paralytic stroke***, etc. L16. ▸**c** A hostile attack. L17–L18.
3 a A destructive discharge of lightning. Formerly also, a crash of thunder. ME. ▸**b** Incidence of light, moving particles, etc. Formerly also, shock, forcible impact. Now *rare.* M16.
†**4** Coinage, imprint of coin. *Scot.* LME–E17.
5 The striking of a clock; the sound produced by this. Cf. STRIKE *verb* 33a. LME.
†**6** A slice of meat. *rare.* Only in 16.
7 *Hist.* A measure of capacity, = STRIKE *noun*[1] 2a. M16.
†**8** An act or manner of striking or playing on a stringed instrument; a tune. M16–L18.
9 A pulsation, a beat (of the heart or pulse). M16.
10 a In negative context: a minimum amount of work. Chiefly in ***not do a stroke (of work)***. M16. ▸**b** A considerable amount of or *of* work, business, or trade. E18.
11 A linear mark made by the moving point of a pen, pencil, etc., esp. as a component line of a written character. M16. ▸**b** (A spoken representation of) a written or printed oblique line or solidus, esp. (*colloq.*) used in indicating alternatives. Also in LOGIC = SHEFFER'S STROKE. L19.
12 A movement of beating time; beat, metrical ictus. Now *rare* or *obsolete.* L16.
13 a Any of a series of combined movements of the arms and legs used by a swimmer to propel himself or herself through the water; style of executing such movements. L16. ▸**b** A single movement of the legs in walking or running, of the wings in flying, etc. E17. ▸**c** A single complete movement in either direction of a piston-rod or other piece of machinery having reciprocating motion. Also, the amplitude or length of such a movement. M18.
14 ROWING. **a** A single pull of the oar; style of rowing, esp. with ref. to the length or frequency of the pulls. L16. ▸**b** The member of a rowing crew who sits nearest to the stern of the boat and whose 'stroke' sets the time for the others; the position occupied by this rower. E19.
15 a A vigorous attempt to attain some object; a measure adopted for some purpose. Freq. in ***stroke of policy***. L16. ▸**b** In a game: an effective move or combination. M18.
16 A single movement of the pen, brush, knife, etc., in writing, painting, engraving, etc. M17. ▸†**b** Manner of handling the pencil, graver, etc. M17–E18.
17 †**a** Lineament, the line of a person's face etc.; *fig.* a characteristic trait. M17. ▸**b** *fig.* A felicitous or characteristic expression or thought in literary composition. M17.
18 a A feat, an achievement; a signal display of or *of* art, genius, wit, etc. L17. ▸**b** An unexpected piece *of* luck or misfortune. M19.
19 AGRICULTURE. An act of harrowing. M18.
20 BASKET-MAKING. A single movement analogous to a stitch in sewing or knitting; the result of this. E20.

📖 **1** C. ISHERWOOD You . . couldn't cut a man's head off with one stroke. R. JARRELL The cook . . beat her . . dough with steady strokes. B. EMECHETA Pa . . would probably cane her . . , just a few strokes. **d** *Evening Post (Nottingham)* They finished two strokes ahead of . . Terry Pale and Dave Stockton in the 72-hole tournament. ***push-stroke***, ***split stroke***, ***stab stroke***, etc. **2** HOR. WALPOLE The . . death of his royal protector was a dreadful stroke . . to Petitot. G. RAWLINSON The stroke of calamity fell on him. **3b** J. TYNDALL The . . ridges . . meet the direct stroke of the solar rays. **5** F. C. BURNAND Straining my ears to catch the . . first stroke of the hour. **10a** R. LEHMANN I never did a stroke at school or Oxford. **b** THACKERAY A trade doing a stroke of so many hogsheads a week. **11** B. MALAMUD Handwriting full of . . thick black strokes. **b** S. T. HAYMON We still haven't a clue . . why . . our murderer–stroke–murderers made the . . choice they did. **13a** J. BUCHAN He found deep water, and in two strokes was in grip of the tide. ***backstroke***, ***breast-stroke***, ***trudgen stroke***, etc. **c** *Airgun World* Weihrauch uprated the power of their HW 50s by lengthening the stroke. **15a** C. MERIVALE This stroke of policy was not unsuccessful. **16** MRS ALEXANDER The money . . can be handed over to you with the stroke of a pen. E. WELTY A . . bit of slatey stone, given shape by many little strokes from a penknife. **17b** G. O. TREVELYAN Reconstructing a paragraph for the sake of one happy stroke or apt illustration. **18a** G. B. SHAW I couldnt have done a smarter stroke of electioneering. D. HEWETT Sittin' there smilin' as if she was doin' a great stroke. **b** J. WAIN It was a stroke of bad luck for you to be born with a well-to-do father. L. KENNEDY I had a stroke of luck; an introduction to David Cecil.

Phrases: ***apoplectic stroke***: see sense 2b above. **a stroke above** *colloq.* a cut above, superior to. **at a stroke**, **at one stroke** with a single blow; *fig.* all at once. †**bear a stroke**, **bear a great stroke** = ***have a stroke*** below. †**bear the stroke** = ***have the stroke*** below. ***exhaust stroke***: see EXHAUST *noun* 1. ***finishing stroke***: see FINISHING *ppl adjective.* **have a good stroke** (now *north.*) have a hearty appetite. †**have a stroke**, †**have a great stroke**, etc., have an influential or controlling share in an enterprise or action. †**have the stroke** prevail, have authority. †**keep stroke** keep time, esp. in rowing. ***leader stroke***: see LEADER 20. ***long stroke***: see LONG *adjective*[2]. **off one's stroke** *colloq.* not performing as well as usual; ***put a person off his or her stroke***, distract, disconcert, or disturb a person. **on the stroke** punctually. **on the stroke of one** etc., when the clock is about to strike one o'clock etc. ***paralytic stroke***: see sense 2b above. **pull a stroke** *slang* play a dirty trick. ***put a person off his or her stroke***: see ***off one's stroke*** above. ***stretch to the stroke***: see STRETCH *verb.* ***stroke of apoplexy***, ***stroke of paralysis***: see sense 2b above. ***stroke of policy***: see sense 15a above. **stroke of State** a coup d'état. ***winning stroke***: see WINNING *ppl adjective* 2. †**without stroke (of sword)** without fighting.

Comb.: **stroke-haul** *noun & verb* (*a*) *noun* a fish-poacher's apparatus formed of three hooks joined back to back, and weighted with lead; (*b*) *verb trans. & intrans.* poach (fish) by such means; **stroke-maker** (CRICKET) a batsman who plays attractive, attacking strokes; **stroke-oar** (*a*) the oar nearest the stern of a rowing boat; (*b*) the rower who handles this (= sense 14b above); **stroke-oarsman** = ***stroke-oar*** (b) above; **strokeplay** (*a*) CRICKET the playing of attractive, attacking strokes; (*b*) GOLF = ***medal-play*** s.v. MEDAL *noun*; **stroke-side** the side of a rowing boat on which the stroke-oarsman sits; **strokesman** = ***stroke-oar*** (b) above; **stroke-stitch** NEEDLEWORK = ***straight stitch*** s.v. STRAIGHT *adjective*[1] & *adverb*[1].

■ **strokeless** *adjective* CRICKET unable to play strokes freely, esp. owing to the style of bowling M20. **stroker** *noun*[1] *(a) rare* a person who makes strokes in certain games, esp. polo; *(b)* (a motor vehicle with) an engine adapted to give high power and speed by grinding the crankshaft throws off centre in order to increase piston displacement: L19.

stroke /strəʊk/ *noun*[2]. M17.
[from STROKE *verb*[1].]
1 A stroking movement of the hand; an act of stroking, esp. as a form of caress. M17.
2 An act of copulation or masturbation. *slang. rare.* L18.
3 A comforting gesture of approval or congratulation; a flattering or friendly remark etc., esp. made to help or manipulate another. Chiefly *N. Amer. colloq.* M20.

> **1** DRYDEN His white man'd Steeds . . He chear'd to Courage with a gentle Stroke. H. E. BATES She gave her hair a long . . stroke with the brush. **2** H. GREEN It ended in a smashing stroke, he'd had both girls in the same bed.

Comb.: **stroke book** a pornographic book.

stroke /strəʊk/ *noun*[3]. *obsolete* exc. *dial.* L17.
[Alt. of STRAKE *noun.*]
= STRAKE *noun* 1.

stroke /strəʊk/ *verb*[1] *trans.* Also (*Scot.*) **strake** /streɪk/, †**stroak**.
[Old English *strācian* = Middle Low German, Middle Dutch *strēken* (Dutch *streeken*), Old High German *streihhon* (German *streichen*), from Germanic ablaut var. of base of STRIKE *verb*. Cf. STREAK *noun*.]
1 Pass one's hand etc. gently along the surface of (a person's hair, an animal's fur, etc.), esp. as a form of caress; (with adverbial extension) bring into a specified position by this action. OE. ▸**b** *fig.* Orig., soothe, flatter, (a person); treat indulgently. Now chiefly, reassure (a child etc.) by approval or congratulation; manipulate (a person) by means of flattery, persuasion, etc. Now chiefly *US colloq.*, esp. in political contexts. E16. ▸**c** Play (a plucked or keyboard instrument) with a light or gentle touch. M20.
†**2** Plight (one's troth). *rare.* LME–L18.
3 Orig., rub or smear (a thing) with a substance. Later (*obsolete* exc. *Scot. & north.*), smear (a thing) over a surface. Now only, brush (a thing) gently over a surface. LME.
4 Draw (a cutting instrument) along a surface for the purpose of sharpening. *arch.* L15.
5 Milk (a cow); *esp.* draw the last milk from (a cow) by squeezing the teat. Now *dial.* M16.
6 Work (stone) to create a fluted surface. M19.
7 NEEDLEWORK. Arrange (small gathers) in regular order and close succession by drawing the point of a blunt needle from the top of each gather downwards. L19.
8 SPORT. Hit or kick (a ball) smoothly and deliberately; score (a run etc.) in this manner. M20.

> **1** T. GRAY She . . strok'd down her band. H. ROTH David's mother stroked her shoulders soothingly. T. HEGGEN The Doctor stroked his moustache thoughtfully. *Raritan* Jacqueline with one slow lean arm began to stroke the dog. **b** *Time* Carter . . stroked the Jerusalem government by promising that the U.S. would never . . impose a Middle East settlement. T. CLANCY This American had a great deal of money, and was therefore worthy of stroking. **3** P. BARKER Audrey was . . stroking mascara onto her upper lashes.

Phrases: **stroke a person the wrong way**, **stroke a person's hair the wrong way** *fig.* ruffle a person's feelings.
■ **strokable** *adjective* suitable for stroking, able to be stroked L20. **stroker** *noun*[2] a person who strokes someone or something; *spec.* (chiefly *Hist.*) a person who cures diseases by stroking a part of the body: LME. **stroking** *noun (a)* the action of the verb; *(b)* (in *pl.*) the last milk drawn from a cow (also called *strippings*): LME.

stroke /strəʊk/ *verb*[2]. L16.
[from STROKE *noun*[1].]
▶ **I 1** *verb trans.* Mark with streaks or vertical lines, esp. strokes of the pen, pencil, etc. Cf. STRAKE *verb*[1] 3. *rare.* L16.
2 *verb trans.* Draw the horizontal line across the upright of (the letter t); cross. L19.
3 *verb trans.* Foll. by *out*, *through*: cancel by drawing a line or lines across; cross out. L19.
▶ **II 4** *verb trans.* **a** Row stroke in (a boat); act as stroke to (a crew). M19. ▸**b** Of an oarsman or crew: row at (a certain number of strokes per minute). E20.
5 *verb intrans.* Execute swimming strokes. M20.
6 *verb trans.* Strike or depress (a key or keys on a keyboard); perform keystrokes at (a keyboard). M20.

stroky /'strəʊki/ *adjective. rare.* M19.
[from STROKE *noun*[1] + -Y[1].]
Consisting of, of the nature of, strokes (of a pen).

stroll /strəʊl/ *noun.* E17.
[from (the same root as) the verb.]
1 = STROLLER 1. *obsolete* exc. *US* (*rare*). E17.
2 A leisurely walk, a saunter. Freq. in ***take a stroll***. L18. ▸**b** *fig.* Something achieved without due effort, a walkover; *spec.* in BASEBALL, a base on balls. *colloq.* (orig. *US*). E20.

stroll /strəʊl/ *verb.* E17.
[Prob. from German *strollen*, *strolchen* wander as a vagrant, from *Strolch* vagabond, of unkn. origin.]
†**1** *verb intrans.* Roam from place to place without any fixed abode. (Later in STROLLING *ppl adjective*.) E17–M18.
2 *verb intrans.* **a** Walk in a casual or leisurely fashion, as inclination directs; *loosely* take a walk. L17. ▸**b** *fig.* Proceed easily and without effort to a desired result, esp. in a sporting or other contest; *spec.* (*US*) in BASEBALL, secure a base on balls. E20.
3 *verb trans.* Walk in a leisurely fashion along (a path) or about (a place). Now chiefly *US.* L17.

> **2** G. F. BRADBY Youths strolling past their headmaster with insolent unconcern. E. FIGES They strolled round the pond together. **b** J. SNOW Lancashire strolled to victory by six wickets. **3** M. MOORCOCK Elegant ladies and gentlemen strolled the promenade.

■ **strolling** *ppl adjective* wandering, itinerant; esp. in ***strolling actor***, ***strolling player***, an actor who travels about giving performances in temporary buildings or hired rooms: E17.

stroller /'strəʊlə/ *noun.* E17.
[from prec. + -ER[1].]
1 A person who goes from place to place: *(a)* a strolling player; *(b)* (now chiefly *Scot.*) an itinerant beggar or pedlar. E17.
2 A person who walks at leisure, a saunterer; a casual traveller. M19.
3 A child's pushchair, *esp.* a collapsible buggy. Chiefly *US.* E20.
4 a A casual shoe. Usu. in *pl.* M20. ▸**b** A man's semi-formal jacket, typically cut-away and with tails. *US.* L20.

stroma /'strəʊmə/ *noun.* Pl. **-mas**, **-mata** /-mətə/. M19.
[mod. Latin use of late Latin = bed-covering, from Greek *strōma* anything spread or laid out for lying or sitting on, from base of *strōnnunai* spread.]
1 a ANATOMY. The supportive tissue of an epithelial organ, tumour, etc., consisting of connective tissues, blood-vessels, etc. M19. ▸**b** The spongy framework of protein fibres in a red blood cell. L19.
2 BOTANY. **a** A cushion-like mass of fungal tissue, having spore-bearing structures either embedded in it or on its surface. M19. ▸**b** The matrix of a chloroplast, in which the grana are embedded. E20.
■ **stromal** *adjective* (ANATOMY) of, pertaining to, or of the character of the stroma or supporting tissue of an organ M19.

stromateoid /strə(ʊ)'matɪɔɪd/ *noun & adjective.* L19.
[from mod. Latin *Stromateus* genus name, from Greek *strōmateus* a patchwork bed-cover, from STROMA: see -OID.]
▶ **A** *noun.* A fish of the family Stromateidae, which comprises the butterfishes. Also, any fish of the suborder Stromateioidei, which includes this family. L19.
▶ **B** *adjective.* Of, pertaining to, or resembling fishes of this family or suborder. L19.
■ **stromateid** *noun & adjective (a) noun* a fish of the family Stromateidae; *(b) adjective* of or pertaining to this family: M20.

stromatic /strə(ʊ)'matɪk/ *adjective.* L19.
[from mod. Latin *stromat-* STROMA + -IC.]
MYCOLOGY. Of the nature of or resembling a stroma.

stromatolite /strə(ʊ)'matəlʌɪt/ *noun.* M20.
[from next: see -LITE.]
A laminated calcareous mounded structure built up of layers of blue-green algae etc. and trapped sedimentary material; *esp.* in GEOLOGY, a fossilized structure of this kind from the early Precambrian.
■ **stromato'litic** *adjective* of the nature of or pertaining to stromatolites M20.

stromatolith /'strəʊmətəʊlɪθ/ *noun.* E20.
[from mod. Latin *stromat-* STROMA + -O- + -LITH.]
GEOLOGY. **1** A laminated rock structure with a complex interleaving of igneous and sedimentary components. Now *rare.* E20.
2 = STROMATOLITE. E20.
■ **stromato'lithic** *adjective* of the nature of or pertaining to a stromatolith E20.

stromatoporoid /strəʊmə'tɒpərɔɪd/ *noun & adjective.* L19.
[from mod. Latin *Stromatopora* genus name, from *stromat-* STROMA + -O- + *-pora* after *madrepora* MADREPORE: see -OID.]
PALAEONTOLOGY. ▶ **A** *noun.* Any of an extinct group of sessile coral-like marine organisms of uncertain affinity, which built up calcareous masses composed of laminae and pillars and occurred from the Cambrian to the Cretaceous. L19.
▶ **B** *adjective.* Pertaining to or characteristic of this group. L19.

stromatous /'strəʊmətəs/ *adjective.* L19.
[from mod. Latin *stromat-* STROMA + -OUS.]
MEDICINE. Of or pertaining to stroma.

stromb /strɒm/ *noun.* M19.
[Anglicized from STROMBUS.]
(The shell of) any of various marine gastropods of the family Strombidae, *esp.* a conch of the genus *Strombus.*
■ **stromboid** /'strɒmbɔɪd/ *adjective & noun (a) adjective* of, pertaining to, or resembling a stromb; *(b) noun* a stromb: M19.

Strombolian /strɒm'bəʊlɪən/ *adjective.* L19.
[from *Stromboli*, an active volcano forming one of the Lipari Islands, Italy + -AN.]
Pertaining to or characteristic of Stromboli; *spec.* in GEOLOGY, designating volcanic activity in which there are repeated or continuous eruptions of moderate force with the ejection of gases and lava bombs.

strombus /'strɒmbəs/ *noun.* E17.
[Latin = spiral shell from Greek *strombos* anything spirally twisted.]
(The shell of) any of various marine gastropods of the family Strombidae; a conch. Now chiefly as mod. Latin genus name. Cf. STROMB.

strome *verb* var. of STROAM.

stromeyerite /'strəʊmʌɪərʌɪt/ *noun.* M19.
[from Friedrich *Strohmeyer* (1776–1835), German chemist + -ITE[1].]
MINERALOGY. An orthorhombic sulphide of silver and copper, of a dark steel-grey colour with a blue tarnish.

strong /strɒŋ/ *adjective & noun.*
[Old English *strong*, *strang* = Old Saxon, Old Frisian *strang*, Middle Dutch *stranc*, Old Norse *strangr*, from Germanic, from a base whose mutated form is repr. in Old English (*rare*) *strenge* severe, Middle Low German, Middle Dutch *strenge* (Dutch *streng*), Old Saxon, Old High German *strengi* (German *streng*): see STRING *noun.* Cf. STRENGTH.]
▶ **A** *adjective.* **1 a** Of a living being, the body or limbs: physically powerful; able to exert great muscular force. OE. ▸**b** Physically vigorous or robust; hale, healthy; *spec.* restored to normal health and vigour after illness. Also, (of the nerves, brain, etc.) robust, resistant to weakness or infirmity. ME. ▸**c** Of an action: performed with muscular strength. LME. ▸**d** Of a runner, swimmer, pace, etc.: showing great staying power; that does not flag. M19.
2 a Having great moral power of endurance or effort; firm in will or purpose; brave, courageous, resolute. OE. ▸**b** Of a look, voice, etc.: indicative of strength of character. E19.
3 a Of an individual, a body, etc.: having control or authority over others; powerful, dominant. OE. ▸**b** Having great financial resources, rich. E17.
4 Eminently able or qualified to succeed in something; skilled *in*. Also, (of a quality, attribute, etc.) held to a high degree. OE.
5 a Of great or superior fighting power; (of an offensive etc.) conducted with a powerful fighting force. OE. ▸**b** Of an individual or a team: powerful or formidable as an opponent. LME. ▸**c** Powerful to the extent of a (preceding) specified number; *gen.* (of a body or gathering) having a (preceding) specified number. L16. ▸**d** *transf.* Of a body, party, etc.: numerous. Also, abundantly supplied with people or things of a specified kind. (Foll. by *in*.) E17.
6 a Of a fortress, town, military position, etc.: having powerful defences; difficult to take or invade. Cf. ***stronghold*** below. OE. ▸**b** Of a place of confinement or a secure container, as a cell, safe, etc.: difficult to escape from or break into. Cf. ***strongbox***, ***strongroom*** below. ME.
7 Of a material thing: capable of supporting strain or withstanding force; not easily broken, torn, injured, or forced out of shape; solid, stout; *spec.* *(a)* (of soil) firm, compact; rich; *(b)* (of food) solid, hard to digest; *(c)* (of hair or wool) thick-fibred, coarse; *(d)* MINING (of a vein) thick, massive. OE.
8 Severe, oppressive; *spec.* *(a)* (of a law, punishment, etc.) hard to bear, harsh, rigorous; *(b)* (of a disease, convulsion, etc.) severe, violent; *(c)* (of a crime etc.) gross, flagrant; (of a criminal) flagrantly guilty; *(d) colloq.* (of a charge) high, stiff; *(e)* (of a course of action, a measure) extreme, drastic. OE.
9 Of a current of air, water, etc.: having considerable force of movement. Of an electrical current: having a high rate of flow of charge. OE.
10 a (Of light, shadow, colour, etc.) vivid, intense; (of fire, heat, etc.) vigorous, intense; (of a voice or sound) loud, firm. OE. ▸**b** (Of feeling, conviction, belief, etc.) intense, fervid; uncompromising; (of a person) firmly convinced, decided in opinion; *colloq.* laying great stress on something (foll. by *for*, *on*). ME. ▸**c** Of the pulse or respiration: firm, forceful. LME. ▸**d** (Of a hold) firm, tenacious; (of effort, movement, pressure, etc.) forcible. L17.
11 a Of a drug, poison, chemical reagent, etc.: powerful in operative effect. OE. ▸**b** Of a lens: having great magnifying power. L19. ▸**c** PHYSICS. Of a field: having a high strength, exerting great force on particles, charges, etc. E20. ▸**d** PHYSICS. Designating the strongest of the known kinds of force between particles, which acts between nucleons and other hadrons when closer than about 10^{-13} cm (so binding protons in a nucleus despite the repulsion due to their charge), and which conserves strangeness, parity, and isospin. M20.
12 a Of a solution, a drink, etc.: containing a high proportion of an essential (esp. dissolved) substance; concentrated; *spec.* in CHEMISTRY, (of an acid or alkali) fully dissociated in aqueous solution into anions and cations. OE. ▸**b** Of a semi-liquid substance: stiff, viscid, concen-

trated. L17. ▸**c** Of flour: made with more glutinous wheat so as to rise more, be more absorbent, etc. M19.

13 Affecting the sense of taste or smell in a high degree; powerful in flavour, odour, or taste; pungent. OE.

14 a Of a motive, impulse, temptation, etc.: powerful; hard to resist. ME. ▸**b** Of an argument, evidence, proof, etc.: powerfully convincing, solid, irrefutable. ME. ▸**c** Of a sanction etc.: having legal force, effectual. Formerly also, (of a document) valid. LME. ▸**d** Of a case: well-supported by evidence or precedent. L17.

15 a (Of the mind or mental faculties) powerful; (of the memory) tenacious, retentive. LME. ▸**b** Of a mental impression: definite, distinct. L17.

16 a Of a resemblance or contrast: obvious, marked, significant. LME. ▸**b** (Of a line) broad, thick; (of an outline) bold. M18. ▸**c** Of an accent: broad, pronounced. E19. ▸**d** PHOTOGRAPHY. Of a negative: having marked contrast of light and shade; dense. L19.

17 Of language, an expression, a word: emphatic; immoderate, unrestrained. Also, (of a protest etc.) strongly worded, unrestrained. L17.

18 Of literary or other artistic work: vivid or forceful in style or execution. M18.

19 Of a syllable or musical beat: stressed, accented. L18.

20 GRAMMAR. **a** Of a Germanic noun or adjective: belonging to a declension in which the original Germanic stem ended other than in *n*. M19. ▸**b** Of a Germanic verb: forming the past tense and past participle by means of a change of vowel in the stem rather than by the addition of a suffix. Also occas. used to designate a particular verb-type in a non-Germanic language. M19.

21 CARDS. Of a player) holding commanding cards (*in* a specified suit); (of a hand or suit) composed of commanding cards. M19.

22 COMMERCE. Of prices, a market, etc.: holding steadily high or rising; not fluctuating or depressed. L19.

23 MATH. Of an entity or concept: implying more than others of its kind; defined by more conditions. M20.

🕮 **1a** THOMAS HUGHES He is as strong as a horse. W. LEWIS A strong girl with muscles like a blacksmith's. **b** L. DURRELL An exciting . . game, a test of strong nerves and speed. A. DAVIES How can I be ill when I feel so strong? **c** BYRON I burst my chain with one strong bound. **2a** SHAKES. *Rom. & Jul.* Be strong and prosperous In this resolve. **3a** F. E. PAGET The Church . . , strong in the aid antiquity, tradition, and apostolicity. J. HALPERIN In any human relationship there is a strong and a weak partner. **4** THACKERAY I am not very strong in spelling. *Times* A self-starter with strong interpersonal skills. **5a** W. S. CHURCHILL A strong cavalry force, which gathered strength as it marched. **c** M. L. KING A demonstration fifty thousand strong. **d** H. H. COLE The . . Museum . . is specially strong in arms and textile fabrics. **6a** F. P. VERNEY The king's position on the high ground was extremely strong. **7** J. C. LOUDON A strong clayey soil . . covered with a healthy vegetation. *Essentials* The strong re-usable grip-top. *fig.*: SHELLEY How strong the chains are which our spirit bind. **8** *Southern Star (Eire)* That's a strong sentence, Justice. **9** M. ROBERTS The tide was under her stronger and stronger, every minute. *Reader's Digest* The strong trade winds . . produce an active monsoon. **10a** R. BAGOT Her voice rang out clear and strong. D. LESSING Seeing him black . . against the strong light from the windows behind. P. BARKER The heat would be strong enough to . . burn her skin. **b** R. HOGGART Working-class people have a strong sense of being members of a group. P. H. JOHNSON It was not a matter . . on which he had any strong feelings. G. KEILLOR They are all strong for the Union here. **d** G. GROVE The second octave is produced by a stronger pressure of wind. *fig.*: SIR W. SCOTT His friend's . . finery had taken a strong hold of his imagination. **11a** SIR W. SCOTT I hate him like strong poison. **12a** O. MANNING A good strong pot of tea. M. KRAMER A deeply coloured, strong red wine. ***strong enough to trot a mouse on***: see TROT *verb*. **strong of** greatly impregnated or flavoured with. **13** A. SILLITOE His mother and father breathed a strong smell of ale. E. FEINSTEIN Cigarettes . . she preferred . . strong and masculine. **14a** *Daily Mirror* A strong possibility of industrial action. *Village Voice* A strong need to . . have a deep . . relationship with a significant other. **b** *Guardian* There is . . strong evidence that myalgic encephalomyelitis is a physical disorder. **15a** LD MACAULAY He loved with the whole energy of his strong mind. **b** P. WARUNG The circumstances . . are still strong in my recollection. **16a** I. L. BIRD A very strong resemblance between their dialects and pure Malayan. **b** R. MACNEIL Cards bearing . . good wishes in a strong black copperplate. **c** CONAN DOYLE 'I come,' he shouted . . , with a strong Breton accent. **d** *Hot Shoe International* The standard of the print was . . high, with a . . strong crisp contrast. **17** J. CONRAD I wasn't able to find words strong enough to express my . . mind. *New Scientist* Particular groups . . called, despite Klein's strong objections, Kleinian groups. **18** *Architects' Journal* A strong, abstract classical image. *Journal of Musicology* Rhythmically enlivened antiphonal singing gives way . . to a strong cadence. **19** W. D. WHITNEY The Germanic languages are all characterized by a . . strong accentual stress. T. HELMORE Expansions of the melodies . . on the stronger accents of the poetry. **22** *Correspondent* A strong economy . . made banks increasingly eager to lend.

Special collocations & comb.: **strong arm** (*a*) strength, power; ***strong arm of the law***, the police; (*b*) ***the strong arm***, physical force or violence; (*c*) a person who uses or is employed to use physical violence; a thug; a bouncer. **strong-arm** *adjective & verb* (*a*) *adjective* physically powerful; (of a criminal) using violence; (of an action, policy, etc.) involving or characterized by physical force or violence, heavy-handed, oppressive; (*b*) *verb trans. & intrans.* treat or behave violently or aggressively. **strong-back** (*a*) *W. Indies* any of various plants, e.g. the tree *Bourreria ovata*, of the borage family, believed to strengthen the back and used to make medicinal infusions; (*b*) NAUTICAL a beam placed across the davits, to which a ship's boat is secured at sea; a beam used to secure a hatch or to lift cables clear of the windlass. **strongbox** a strongly made small chest or safe for holding valuables. **strong card** (*a*) a card with which one can win; (*b*) *colloq.* a particular advantage or forte. **strong-docked** *adjective* (*rare*) well built around the buttocks. **strong drink** alcohol, *esp.* spirits; an alcoholic drink. **strong eye** *NZ* the ability, in a sheepdog, to control sheep; a sheepdog with this ability. **strong-eyed** *adjective* (chiefly *NZ*) (of a sheepdog) good at controlling sheep. **strong grade** PHILOLOGY the stressed ablaut-form. **strong hand** (now *rare*) the use of force or superior strength. **strong-handed** *adjective* (*rare*) (*a*) NAUTICAL (of a ship) well-manned; (of a captain) in charge of a well-manned ship; (*b*) forceful, imperious. **strong head** a high tolerance for alcoholic drink. **strongheaded** *adjective* head-strong. **strongheadedness** obstinacy. **stronghold** (*a*) a strongly fortified place of defence; a secure refuge; (*b*) a centre of support for a cause etc. **strong house** a fortified house, a castle. **strong interaction** PHYSICS interaction at short distances between subatomic particles mediated by the strong force (see sense 11d above). **strong joint** *US slang* a corrupt gambling house or game. ***strong language***: see LANGUAGE *noun*[1]. **strong man** (*a*) a man of great physical strength, *esp.* (usu. *strongman*) one who performs feats of strength professionally; (*b*) a dominating man; a man who exercises effective or absolute control. **strong-man's-weed** *W. Indies* the plant *Petiveria alliacea* (family Phytolaccaceae), used medicinally for its stimulating and sudorific properties. **strong meat** [with allus. to *Hebrew* 5:12] a doctrine or action acceptable only to a prepared or vigorous mind. **strong-minded** *adjective* (*a*) having determination; (*b*) (now *rare*) (of a woman) having or affecting supposedly masculine characteristics; feminist. **strong-mindedness** determination. **strong point** (*a*) a thing at which one excels, one's forte; (*b*) a specially fortified defensive position; (*c*) a fitting in an aircraft to which a parachutist's static line is connected. **strongroom** a secure room for keeping people or things in custody, *esp.* one in a bank etc. designed to protect valuables against fire and theft. **strong safety** AMER. FOOTBALL a defensive back positioned opposite the strong side which usually covers the tight end. ***strong silent type***: see SILENT *adjective*. **strong stomach** a stomach not easily affected by nausea. **strong stress** PROSODY accentuation which falls on syllables separated by a varying number of unstressed syllables, characteristic of certain poetic traditions, as Old English alliterative verse. **strong suit** (*a*) CARDS a suit in which one can take tricks; (*b*) *colloq.* something at which one excels. **strong water** †(*a*) = AQUA FORTIS; (*b*) *arch.* alcoholic liquor (now only in *pl.*). **strong woman** a woman who publicly performs feats of strength. **strong wood(s)** *Canad.* a region of thick afforestation (freq. *attrib.*).

▶ **B** *absol.* as *noun*. **1** A strong person. Usu. *collect. pl.*, *the* class of strong people. OE.

2 ***the strong of***, = ***the*** STRENGTH ***of***. *Austral. slang*. E20.

■ **strongfully** *adverb* (*arch.*) in a very strong or resolute manner LME. **strongish** *adjective* somewhat strong L18. **strongness** *noun* (long *rare*) the quality of being strong, strength LME.

strong /strɒŋ/ *verb*. *rare*. OE.
[from STRONG *adjective*.]

†**1** *verb intrans.* Become strong. OE–ME.

2 *verb trans.* Make strong, strengthen. Now *spec.* (*a*) cause to smell strong; (*b*) (with *it*) exaggerate, overdo something. Long *obsolete* exc. *colloq.* or *US dial.* OE.

strong /strɒŋ/ *adverb*.
[Old English *strange*, *stronge*: cf. STRONG *adjective*.]

= STRONGLY. Now chiefly in phrs. below.

come it strong: see COME *verb*. **come on strong** behave aggressively or assertively; perform or contest successfully. **come out strong** make a big display or impression; declare or express oneself vigorously. **going strong** continuing action vigorously; enjoying good health or success. ***go it strong***: see GO *verb*. ***pitch it strong***: see PITCH *verb*[2].

strongers /ˈstrɒŋəz/ *noun*. *Nautical slang*. E20.
[from STRONG *adjective* + -ER[6].]

Soogee-moogee.

strongly /ˈstrɒŋli/ *adverb*. OE.
[from STRONG *adjective* + -LY[2].]

1 In a strong manner; *spec.* (*a*) powerfully, forcibly; (*b*) so as to resist attack or displacement, firmly, securely; (*c*) violently, vehemently; (*d*) resolutely; emphatically. OE. ▸**b** PHYSICS. By means of the strong interaction. M20.

2 In a strong degree, to a strong extent. LME.

🕮 **1** W. H. PRESCOTT By this triumph . . Mary was seated more strongly . . on the throne. F. SWINNERTON I strongly advise you not to use drugs. L. NKOSI I received . . a strongly worded letter warning of . . expulsion. R. RENDELL He was . . strongly built but not fat. **2** A. GEIKIE Sea-water is always strongly salt to the taste. H. JAMES His apartment smelt strongly of . . liquor. A. BRINK The sun was beginning to come through quite strongly.

strongyle /ˈstrɒndʒʌɪl/ *noun*[1]. M19.
[mod. Latin *Strongylus* (see below) from Greek *stroggulos* round.]

A nematode worm of the genus *Strongylus* or the family Strongylidae, including several common disease-producing parasites of various animals and birds. Also ***strongyle worm***.

strongyle /ˈstrɒndʒɪl/ *noun*[2]. L19.
[Greek *stroggulē* fem. of *stroggulos* round.]

ZOOLOGY. A type of rod-shaped sponge spicule rounded at both ends.

strongyloid /ˈstrɒndʒɪlɔɪd/ *adjective & noun*. L19.
[from STRONGYLE *noun*[1] + -OID.]

ZOOLOGY. ▶**A** *adjective*. Resembling a strongyle; now *esp.* of the genus *Strongyloides*. L19.

▶ **B** *noun*. A strongyloid worm. L19.

strongyloides /strɒndʒɪˈlɔɪdiːz/ *noun*. Pl. same. Also **S-**. E20.
[mod. Latin (see below), from *Strongylus* STRONGYLE *noun*[1]: see -OID.]

MEDICINE & VETERINARY MEDICINE. A nematode worm of the genus *Strongyloides*. Also = STRONGYLOIDIASIS.

strongyloidiasis /ˌstrɒndʒɪlɔɪˈdʌɪəsɪs/ *noun*. Pl. **-ases** /-əsiːz/. M20.
[from prec. + -IASIS.]

MEDICINE & VETERINARY MEDICINE. (A disease caused by) infection with nematode worms of the genus *Strongyloides*, esp. *Strongyloides stercoralis*, a threadworm infesting the human and canine gut in tropical and subtropical regions, causing diarrhoea.

■ Also **strongyloiˈdosis** *noun*, pl. **-doses** /-ˈdəʊsiːz/, E20.

strongylosis /strɒndʒɪˈləʊsɪs/ *noun*. Pl. **-loses** /-ˈləʊsiːz/. L19.
[from STRONGYLE *noun*[1] + -OSIS.]

VETERINARY MEDICINE. (A disease caused by) infection with strongyles (nematode worms). Cf. STRONGYLE *noun*[1].

strontia /ˈstrɒnʃ(ɪ)ə/ *noun*. E19.
[from next: see -IA[1].]

CHEMISTRY. Strontium monoxide, a white basic solid.

strontia water an aqueous solution of strontium hydroxide (not now in techn. use).

strontian /ˈstrɒnʃ(ə)n/ *noun*. *obsolete* in *techn.* use. L18.
[A parish in the Scottish Highland Region (formerly Argyllshire) where the mineral was discovered in lead mines.]

Orig. = STRONTIANITE. Also *loosely*, strontia, strontium. Also more fully †***strontian earth***, †***strontian mineral***, †***strontian spar***.

Comb.: **strontian yellow** a yellow pigment produced by adding potassium chromate to a solution of a strontium salt.

strontian /ˈstrɒntɪən/ *adjective*. M20.
[from STRONTIUM + -AN.]

MINERALOGY. Having a constituent element partly replaced by strontium.

strontianite /ˈstrɒnʃ(ə)nʌɪt/ *noun*. L18.
[from STRONTIAN *noun* + -ITE[1].]

MINERALOGY. Native strontium carbonate, crystallizing in the orthorhombic system as pale greenish, yellowish, or white crystals, found esp. in veins.

†**strontic** *adjective*. Only in L19.
[from STRONTIUM + -IC.]

CHEMISTRY. In names of compounds: of strontium.

¶ Superseded by attrib. use of the noun.

†**strontites** *noun*. L18–M19.
[from STRONTIAN *noun* + *-ites* after *barytes*, assim. to -ITE[1].]

= STRONTIA.

■ †**strontitic** *adjective* L18–E19.

strontium /ˈstrɒntɪəm, ˈstrɒnʃ(ɪ)əm/ *noun*. E19.
[from STRONTIA + -IUM.]

A soft silvery-white metallic chemical element, atomic no. 38, which is one of the alkaline earth group, whose salts impart a red colour to flame. (Symbol Sr.)

Comb.: **strontium-90** a radioactive strontium isotope of mass 90 which is a product of the fission of uranium-235, harmful through being incorporated into plant and animal tissue in place of calcium, and sometimes used in radiotherapy.

strool /struːl/ *noun*. *Scot.* M19.
[Prob. from Gaelic: cf. Gaelic *sruth* stream, *srùlach* having many streams.]

A stream of water or other liquid.

strop /strɒp/ *noun*[1] & *verb*. LME.
[Middle & mod. Low German, Middle & mod. Dutch = Old English *strop* (which did not survive), Old High German *strupf* (German *Strüpfe* fem., also (Naut.) *Strop*), from West Germanic from Latin *struppus*, *stroppus*, prob. from Greek *strophos*: cf. STROPHE.]

▶ **A** *noun*. †**1** A band, a thong; a loop or noose of leather etc. LME–M18.

2 Chiefly NAUTICAL. A ring or band of leather, spliced rope, or iron used as a fastening or as a purchase for tackle. Cf. STRAP *noun* 3. LME.

3 A narrow band of metal. Long *obsolete* exc. *Scot. dial.* L16.

4 A device, esp. a strip of leather or leather-covered wood, used for sharpening a razor. E18.

▶ **B** *verb trans*. Infl. **-pp-**.

1 Sharpen or smooth with or on a strop. Cf. STRAP *verb* 3. M19.

2 NAUTICAL. Provide (a block) with a strop. M19.

strop /strɒp/ *noun*². *colloq.* L20.
[Back-form. from STROPPY.]
A bad mood; a fit of temper.

> L. FERRARI And Bianca [is] in a strop cos she's brought the wrong bikini.

strophae *noun* pl. of STROPHE.

strophanthidin /strə(ʊ)ˈfanθɪdɪn/ *noun*. L19.
[from next with inserted *-id-* (cf. -IDINE).]
PHARMACOLOGY. A toxic steroidal aglycone, prepared by hydrolysis of strophanthin-K and used as a cardiac stimulant.

strophanthin /strə(ʊ)ˈfanθɪn/ *noun*. L19.
[from mod. Latin *Strophanthus* (see below, next) + -IN¹.]
PHARMACOLOGY. Any of several toxic polycyclic glycosides obtained from certain trees of the African genera *Strophanthus* and *Acokanthera* (family Apocynaceae) and used as cardiac stimulants.
G-strophanthin = OUABAIN.

strophanthus /strə(ʊ)ˈfanθəs/ *noun*. L19.
[mod. Latin, from Greek *strophos* twisted cord + *anthos* flower, with ref. to the long segments of the corolla.]
Any of various climbing tropical shrubs constituting the genus *Strophanthus* (family Apocynaceae), the seeds of several of which (esp. *S. gratus* and *S. kombe*) have been used in Africa to make arrow poisons and are sources of the drug strophanthin. Also (now *rare*), the drug obtained from such a plant.

strophe /ˈstrəʊfi/ *noun*. Pl. **-phes** /-fɪz/, **-phae** /-fiː/. E17.
[Greek *strophē* (whence late Latin *stropha*) lit. 'turning', from *stroph-* ablaut var. of base of *strephein* to turn.]
Orig., a movement from right to left in Greek choruses and dances, answered by an antistrophe; the lines of choral song recited during this movement. Also (*PROSODY*), a metrically structured section of a usu. Greek choral ode or lyric verse, the structure of which is repeated in an antistrophe. More widely, a group of lines forming a section of a lyric poem.
■ **strophic** *adjective* (**a**) *PROSODY* pertaining to or consisting of strophes; belonging to the strophe as distinguished from the antistrophe; (**b**) (of a song) in which each verse is sung to the same tune; ***strophic variations***, a style of 17th-cent. Italian vocal music in which the melody varies in each stanza while the bass remains the same: M19. **strophical** *adjective* (*PROSODY*, *rare*) = STROPHIC (a) L19.

strophiole /ˈstrɒfɪəʊl/ *noun*. M19.
[mod. Latin *strophiolum*, from Latin dim. of *strophium* chaplet from Greek *strophion*, from *stroph-*: see prec.]
BOTANY. An excrescence like an aril on the funicle of certain seeds. Also, a caruncle.
■ **strophiolate** *adjective* having a strophiole E19.

strophulus /ˈstrɒfjʊləs/ *noun*. Now *rare* or *obsolete*. E19.
[mod. Latin, app. alt. of medieval Latin *scrophulus* from Latin SCROFULA.]
MEDICINE. A rash on the skin of an infant.

stroppy /ˈstrɒpi/ *adjective*. *colloq.* M20.
[Perh. abbreviation of OBSTREPEROUS with altered vowel. Cf. Swedish *stroppig* stuck-up, pompous.]
Bad-tempered, rebellious, awkward to deal with.

> L. GRIFFITHS This . . gas man, once stroppy . . and bolshie, is now fawning.

■ **stroppiness** *noun* M20.

stroud /straʊd/ *noun*. L17.
[Perh. from *Stroud*, a town in Gloucestershire.]
1 A blanket manufactured for barter or sale in trading with N. American Indians. Also ***stroud blanket***. *obsolete* exc. *Hist.* L17.
2 The coarse woollen material of which such blankets were made. M18.

Strouhal number /ˈstraʊəl nʌmbə, ˈstruːəl/ *noun phr.* M20.
[from Čeněk (or Vincent) *Strouhal* (1850–1922), Czech scientist.]
MECHANICS. A dimensionless quantity used in the analysis of the vibrations of a body in a moving fluid, defined as *vd/u* (or *u/vd*) where *u* is the fluid velocity, *v* the frequency of vibration, and *d* the effective diameter of the body.

stroup /struːp/ *noun*. *obsolete* exc. *Scot. & dial.* ME.
[Old Norse *str(j)úpe* = Middle & mod. Swedish *strupe*, Danish *strube* throat.]
1 The throat; the gullet, the windpipe. ME.
2 The spout of a pump, kettle, teapot, etc. Chiefly *Scot.* E16.

†**strout** *verb* var. of STRUT *verb*¹.

strouter /ˈstraʊtə/ *noun*. *Canad. dial.* L19.
[Perh. rel. to STRUT *noun*²: see -ER¹.]
A heavy post used to support and strengthen the end of a fishing stage or wharf.

strove *verb pa. t.*: see STRIVE *verb*.

strow, **strowed**, **strown** *verbs* see STREW *verb*.

Strowger /ˈstraʊgə/ *adjective*. E20.
[Almon B. *Strowger* (1839–1902), US undertaker.]
TELEPHONY. Designating a telephone exchange switching system invented by Strowger in 1891, involving successive step-by-step switches.

strown *verb pa. pple*: see STREW *verb*.

stroy /strɔɪ/ *verb trans. obsolete* or *dial.* ME.
[Aphet. from DESTROY.]
Destroy.

struck /strʌk/ *ppl adjective & noun*. E17.
[pa. pple of STRIKE *verb*.]
▶ **A** *ppl adjective*. Subjected to or affected by the action of STRIKE *verb*; *spec.* (**a**) subjected to a blow or stroke; (**b**) (of a jury) formed by striking off the same number of nominees from each side (cf. STRIKE *verb* 36b); (**c**) (of a measure) levelled with a strickle; (**d**) (chiefly *US*) pertaining to or affected by an industrial strike. E17.

> A. J. ELLIS Differences in the . . tone of struck strings. *Time* Roosevelt threatened to call out the armed forces to reopen struck mines. **struck joint** *BUILDING*: in which the mortar between two courses of bricks slopes inwards flush with one course but below the other.

▶ **B** *noun*. An acute infection of sheep by type C *Clostridium welchii*, causing sudden convulsive death after few symptoms. E20.
¶ See also ***struck in years*** s.v. STRIKE *verb*.

struck *verb pa. t. & pple*, **strucken** *verb pa. pple*: see STRIKE *verb*.

structural /ˈstrʌktʃ(ə)r(ə)l/ *adjective*. M19.
[from STRUCTURE *noun* + -AL¹.]
1 a Of or pertaining to building or construction; *spec.* (of a material) intended for construction. M19. ▸**b** Of or pertaining to the structure of a building etc. as distinguished from its decoration or fittings. L19.
2 a *BIOLOGY & MEDICINE.* Of or pertaining to the structure of an organism, organ, cell, etc., esp. with regard to mechanical properties or form rather than function. M19. ▸**b** *GEOLOGY.* Of or pertaining to the structure of the earth's crust, or of a rock, a formation, etc. M19. ▸**c** *CHEMISTRY.* Of or pertaining to the arrangement of atoms in molecules. M19. ▸**d** *BIOLOGY.* Of a gene: that specifies the amino acid sequence of a polypeptide. M20.
3 Of or pertaining to the arrangement and mutual relation of the parts of any complex whole. L19.
4 Of, pertaining to, or connected with the analysis of social, mental, or linguistic organization; *spec.* involving or pertaining to the formal laws and relations which make up the structure of a system, as distinguished from function or phenomenon. L19.

> **1b** *Times* Small stately home in . . excellent structural condition. **4** R. JAKOBSON The structural laws which underlie language. *British Journal of Sociology* In Islam . . there was the structural limit represented by tribalism.

Special collocations & comb.: **structural ambiguity** *LINGUISTICS* (an) ambiguity involving the grammatical relationships in a sentence etc. **structural analysis** *PSYCHOLOGY & LINGUISTICS* analysis of a system in terms of its components and their relationship to one another. **structural engineer** an expert in structural engineering. **structural engineering** the branch of civil engineering that deals with large modern buildings and similar structures. **structural formula** *CHEMISTRY* a plane schematic representation of the structure of a molecule using dots or lines to indicate the position and nature of the bonds between constituent atoms. **structural-functional** *adjective* (of analysis, a theory, etc.) that takes account of both structure and function. **structural grammar** a system of grammatical analysis in which units and classes are defined by their functional relations within the formal structure of the language. ***structural isomerism***: see ISOMERISM 1. **structural linguist** an expert in or student of structural linguistics. **structural linguistics** the branch of linguistics that deals with language as a system of interrelated elements without reference to their historical development. **structural load**: the load inherent in a structure itself, not imposed. **structural psychology** the branch of psychology that deals with the arrangement and composition of mental states and conscious experiences. **structural semantics** the branch of linguistics that deals with the sense relations that may be established between words and groups of words. **structural steel** strong mild steel in shapes suited to construction work. **structural unemployment** unemployment resulting from industrial reorganization due to technological change etc., rather than from fluctuations in supply and demand.
■ **structuˈrality** *noun* (*rare*) structural quality or character L19. **structurally** *adverb* M19.

structuralise *verb* var. of STRUCTURALIZE.

structuralism /ˈstrʌktʃ(ə)r(ə)lɪz(ə)m/ *noun*. E20.
[from prec. + -ISM.]
1 *PSYCHOLOGY.* A method, connected esp. with the American psychologist E. B. Titchener (1867–1927), of investigating the structure of consciousness through the introspective analysis of simple forms of sensation, thought, images, etc. E20.
2 Any theory or method which deals with the structures of and interrelations among the elements of a system, regarding these as more significant than the elements themselves; any theory concerned with analysing the surface structures of a system in terms of its underlying structure; *spec.* (**a**) *LINGUISTICS* any theory in which language is viewed as a system of interrelated elements at various levels, esp. after the work of Ferdinand de Saussure (see SAUSSUREAN); (**b**) *ANTHROPOLOGY & SOCIOLOGY* any theory or method of analysis which deals with the structure or form of human society and social relationships, *esp.* (after the work of the French anthropologist Claude Lévi-Strauss (b. 1908)) one concerned with the network of communication and thought underlying all human social behaviour; (**c**) a method of critical textual analysis which regards a text as a structure independent of its author or reader and considers how its structural relationships convey its meaning. M20.

> **2** *Scientific American* Structuralism recognizes that information about the world enters the mind . . as highly abstract structures. *Modern Painters* His disavowal of structuralism and semiotics which transpose pictorial . . into linguistic meaning. R. ALTER Todorov, in an essay . . that reflects French Structuralism . . , proposes four different meanings for the term 'verisimilitude.'

structuralist /ˈstrʌktʃ(ə)r(ə)lɪst/ *noun & adjective*. E20.
[from STRUCTURAL + -IST.]
▶ **A** *noun*. An advocate or adherent of structuralism or a structural analytic approach. E20.

> *Modern Painters* Structuralists, deconstructionists . . who cling dogmatically to anti-historicist assumptions.

▶ **B** *attrib.* or as *adjective*. Of or pertaining to structuralism or a structural analytic approach. E20.
■ **structuraˈlistic** *adjective* M20.

structuralize /ˈstrʌktʃ(ə)r(ə)lʌɪz/ *verb trans.* Also **-ise**. M20.
[formed as prec. + -IZE.]
Structure, give structure to. Also, apply structural theories or analysis to.
■ **structuraliˈzation** *noun* M20.

structurate /ˈstrʌktʃəreɪt/ *verb trans. rare*. M20.
[from STRUCTURE *noun* + -ATE³.]
= prec.

structuration /strʌktʃəˈreɪʃ(ə)n/ *noun*. E20.
[from STRUCTURE *verb* + -ATION.]
The condition or process of organization in a structural form.

structure /ˈstrʌktʃə/ *noun*. LME.
[Old & mod. French, or Latin *structura*, from *struct-* pa. ppl stem of *struere* build: see -URE.]
1 The action, practice, or process of building or construction. Now *rare* or *obsolete*. LME.
2 The arrangement and mutual relation of the constituent parts of a whole; composition, make-up, form. L16.
3 A thing which is built or constructed; a building, an edifice. More widely, any framework or fabric of assembled material parts. E17. ▸**b** Manner of building or construction; the way in which an edifice, machine, implement, etc., is constructed. M17. ▸**c** Buildings collectively. *rare*. L17.
4 An organized body, a combination of mutually connected and dependent parts, a component part or organ in an organism. M19.

> **2** J. D. WATSON The three-dimensional structures of proteins. *Horse & Rider* A seminar on structure and movement in the horse. V. GLENDINNING With the job she lost the comfortable structure of her days. *Apollo* Decorative . . paintings of vibrant chromatic structure. *Metals & Materials* The course structure consists of a foundation set of modules. ***career structure***, ***deep structure***, ***flow structure***, ***logical structure***, ***pillow structure***, ***surface structure***, etc. **3** W. COWPER This moveable structure of shelves. SLOAN WILSON A tall Victorian structure with a tower. *Architects' Journal* A fabric structure covers the central concourse. **4** C. DARWIN Any structure highly perfected for any particular habit, as the wings of a bird for flight.

Comb.: **structure-function** *adjective* pertaining to both structure and function; **structure plan** a plan drawn up by a local planning authority for the use of a prescribed area of land; **structure planning** the preparation of a structure plan.
■ **structureless** *adjective* lacking organic structure M19. **structuriˈzation** *noun* the process of giving a structure to something or of arranging material into an organized pattern M20. **structurize** *verb trans.* give a structure to, organize structurally M20.

structure /ˈstrʌktʃə/ *verb trans.* L17.
[from the noun.]
1 Build or form into a structure; give structure to. More widely, construct, organize. (*rare* before 20.) L17.
2 Place in or integrate into a structure. M20.
3 Present or manipulate (a situation etc.) so as to elicit a desired response or effect. M20.

> **2** J. A. C. BROWN Aggressiveness . . has become structured into his basic personality.

structured /ˈstrʌktʃəd/ *ppl adjective.* L19.
[from prec. + -ED[1].]
1 That has structure or organization; organized, formal. L19.
2 a Organized or arranged so as to elicit a desired response or effect. M20. ▸**b** *COMPUTING.* Of a program: organized in a logical way to facilitate debugging and modification; *spec.* composed of linked modules each with an entry point and an exit point, so that the program may be read straight through. M20.

> 📖 **1** *Listener* Societies have defined and structured rule systems of reward and punishment.

▪ **structuredness** *noun* M20.

structurism /ˈstrʌktʃərɪz(ə)m/ *noun.* M20.
[formed as next + -ISM.]
The artistic theory or practice of a structurist.

structurist /ˈstrʌktʃ(ə)rɪst/ *noun & adjective.* M19.
[from STRUCTURE *noun* + -IST.]
▸ **A** *noun.* **1** A builder. *rare.* M19.
2 An artist whose work emphasizes underlying structural forms and processes in nature; *esp.* the US artist Charles Biederman (b. 1906). M20.
▸ **B** *attrib.* or as *adjective.* Of or pertaining to structurists or structurism. M20.

strudel /ˈstruːd(ə)l, ˈʃtruː-/ *noun.* L19.
[German, lit. 'eddy, whirlpool'.]
A confection of thin layers of flaky pastry rolled up round a usu. fruit filling and baked.
strudel dough, strudel pastry, apple strudel: see APPLE *noun.*

struggle /ˈstrʌg(ə)l/ *noun.* L17.
[from the verb.]
1 An act or spell of struggling; a continued effort to resist force or free oneself from constraint; a strong effort under difficulties. L17. ▸**b** *spec.* A strong effort to continue breathing, as under suffocating conditions or when dying. L18.
2 *gen.* Contention, determined effort or resistance. E18.

> 📖 **1** P. P. READ Exhausted by the struggle between ecstasy and remorse. H. S. STREAN Arguments and power struggles with my boss. *Spin* A struggle ensued and a . . trooper was shot. **b** G. BATTISCOMBE He . . died quietly without a struggle. **2** MERLE COLLINS The black struggle in the United States. *Modern Painters* Struggle and labour have long been considered . . part of the creative process.

Phrases: **the struggle for existence**, **the struggle for life** (*a*) the relation between coexisting organisms or species which must compete for restricted resources necessary to survival; (*b*) the competition between people seeking a livelihood; (*c*) *gen.* a continued resistance to influences threatening destruction or extinction.

Comb.: **struggle-for-lifer** *slang* a person who has a struggle to live; **struggle meeting** in Communist China, a meeting at which those who have aroused official or public disfavour are criticized or denounced.

struggle /ˈstrʌg(ə)l/ *verb.* LME.
[Frequentative from base of unkn. origin, perh. symbolic: see -LE[3]. Doubtfully connected with Old Norse *strúgr* ill will, contention, or with Dutch *struikelen*, German *straucheln* stumble.]
1 *verb intrans.* Contend (*with*) in a close physical grapple; make violent or forceful bodily movements in order to resist force or escape from constraint. LME.
2 *verb intrans. fig.* Contend resolutely or strenuously, esp. with a superior opponent; make violent efforts to get free from domination, oppression, etc. (Foll. by *with, against, for.*) LME.
3 *verb intrans.* Make great efforts under difficulties; contend resolutely *with*, strive *to do*. L16.
4 *verb trans.* Bring *out* or *into* or cause to happen by striving or contending. Now *rare.* M17.
5 *verb intrans.* Manage or make one's way with difficulty *along, into, through, up*, etc. L17.

> 📖 **1** J. T. STORY They were policemen and Maria was struggling with them as they dragged her over. **2** SIR W. SCOTT My father . . sits at home struggling with his grief. M. BERGMANN Freud is a pleasure to read except when . . struggling against himself. M. DIBDIN Hints of spring struggled against the wintry dusk. **3** L. ELLMANN We struggle to communicate with him. *Woman* Amy struggled to carry on but . . came near to fainting. **5** P. KAVANAGH He fell . . but struggled to his feet quickly. B. BAINBRIDGE While his wife . . slept he . . struggled into his clothes. **struggle on** carry on with difficulty.

▪ **struggler** *noun* a person who struggles M16. **struggling** *ppl adjective* that struggles; now *esp.* that has difficulty making a living: L16. **strugglingly** *adverb* L16.

Struldbrug /ˈstrʌldbrʌg/ *noun. derog.* Also **-gg**. E18.
[Any of those inhabitants of the kingdom of Luggnagg in Swift's *Gulliver's Travels*, who were incapable of dying, but after the age of eighty continued to exist in a state of miserable decrepitude, regarded as legally dead, and receiving a small pittance from the State.]
A person incapacitated by age or infirmity, *esp.* one who has become a charge on the able members of society.

> 📖 *Times* The Opposition . . select this quavering old Struldbrugg . . to challenge Mrs Thatcher's Conservatism.

strum /strʌm/ *noun*[1]. LME.
[Origin unkn.]
1 *BREWING.* A wickerwork structure placed over the bung-hole of a mash-tub to prevent the grains and hops passing through when the liquor is drawn off. *obsolete* exc. *dial.* LME.
2 A perforated metal structure placed round the suction-pipe of a pump to prevent clogging by foreign matter. Also ***strum-box, strum-plate***. M19.

strum /strʌm/ *noun*[2]. *arch. slang.* L17.
[Abbreviation.]
= STRUMPET *noun.*

strum /strʌm/ *noun*[3]. L18.
[from (the same root as) the verb. Cf. earlier STRUMSTRUM.]
The action of STRUM *verb*; an instance of this.

strum /strʌm/ *verb.* Infl. **-mm-**. L18.
[Imit. Cf. earlier THRUM *verb*[3], STRUMSTRUM.]
1 *verb trans.* Play on (a keyboard or plucked stringed instrument), esp. carelessly or unskilfully; produce (notes, a tune, etc.) by such playing (also foll. by *out, over*). Also, play (a guitar, banjo, etc.) by sweeping the thumb or a plectrum up or down the strings. L18.
2 *verb intrans.* Play esp. carelessly or unskilfully on a keyboard or plucked stringed instrument. Also, play a guitar, banjo, etc., by sweeping the thumb or a plectrum up or down the strings. Also foll. by *away, on*. L18.

> 📖 **1** DAY LEWIS Strumming out on the piano the few simple hymn-tunes he had taught himself. I. ANSTRUTHER Some talked, a few sang, others strummed the grand piano. **2** I. MURDOCH A guitar on which she had strummed a while but never learnt to play.

▪ **strummer** *noun* L18.

struma /ˈstruːmə/ *noun.* Pl. **-mae** /-miː/. M16.
[mod. Latin from Latin = scrofulous swelling.]
1 *MEDICINE.* Orig., scrofula, a scrofulous swelling. Now, (a) swelling of the thyroid gland, (a) goitre. M16.
2 *BOTANY.* A similar swelling in a plant, as at the junction of the petiole and the leaf-blade and at the base of the capsule in certain mosses. M19.
1 struma lymphomatosa /lɪmˌfəʊməˈtəʊsə/ [mod. Latin = lymphomatous] = *HASHIMOTO's disease*.
▪ **struˈmatic** *adjective* (*rare*) suffering from struma M17. **strumatous** *adjective* (*rare*) = STRUMATIC L19. **struˈmitis** *noun* (*MEDICINE*) inflammation of a goitrous thyroid gland L19.

†strummel *noun* see STRAMMEL *noun*.

strumose /ˈstruːməs, -məʊs/ *adjective.* LME.
[from Latin *strumosus*: see STRUMA, -OSE[1].]
†1 = STRUMOUS 1. *rare.* Only in LME.
2 *BOTANY.* Having a struma or swelling. M19.

strumous /ˈstruːməs/ *adjective.* L16.
[formed as prec.: see -OUS.]
1 Affected with or tending to suffer from struma (usu. in sense of scrofula). Now *rare.* L16.
2 Of the nature of or caused by struma. Now *rare* or *obsolete.* L16.
3 *ZOOLOGY.* Having a natural protuberance on some part of the body. *rare.* E19.

strumpet /ˈstrʌmpɪt/ *noun, adjective, & verb. arch.* ME.
[Origin unkn.]
▸ **A** *noun.* An unchaste woman, a prostitute. ME.
▸ **B** *attrib.* or as *adjective.* That is a strumpet. L16.
▸ **C** *verb.* **†1** *verb trans.* Make into a strumpet. L16–L17.
†2 *verb trans.* Publicly denounce (reputation, virtue, etc.) as befitting a strumpet. L16–M17.
3 *verb intrans. & trans.* (with *it*). Of a man: consort with strumpets. Chiefly as ***strumpeting*** *verbal noun*. Long *rare.* E17.
▪ **strumpeˈtocracy** *noun* (*joc. & derog.*) government by strumpets E19.

†strumple *noun. rare.* L16–L19.
[from alt. of STUMP *noun*[1] + -LE[1], perh. infl. by STRUNT *noun*.]
The fleshy stem of a horse's tail.

†strumstrum *noun. rare.* L17–E18.
[Imit. redupl. Cf. STRUM *noun*[3], *verb*, STRIM-STRAM.]
A stringed instrument, esp. of a simple type.

strung /strʌŋ/ *ppl adjective.* L17.
[pa. pple of STRING *verb*.]
1 *gen.* That has been strung. L17.
2 As 2nd elem. of comb.: in a state of nervous tension of a specified kind. M19.
2 ***finely strung, high-strung, highly strung***.
Comb.: **strung-out** (*a*) spread out in a straggling line; extended, continuing in a long series; (*b*) *slang* (orig. & chiefly *N. Amer.*) weak or ill, esp. as a result of drug addiction; addicted to or intoxicated by drugs; **strung-up** *colloq.* (of a person) in a state of extreme nervous tension.

strung *verb* pa. t.: see STRING *verb*.

strunt /strʌnt/ *noun.* Now *Scot. & north.* E17.
[from dial. word rel. to STUNT *adjective*.]
The fleshy part of the tail of an animal, esp. of a horse, occas. of a bird. Also, the whole tail.

strunt /strʌnt/ *verb intrans. Scot.* L18.
[Prob. var. of STRUT *verb*[1]. Cf. Norwegian *strunta* walk stiffly, be stiff in manner.]
Move with a self-important air.

†struse *noun.* E18–M19.
[Perh. from Russian *struzhok* dim. of *strug* a kind of large boat.]
A flat-bottomed boat used for the transport of goods on Russian waterways.

strut /strʌt/ *noun*[1]. Long *obsolete* exc. *dial. rare.* ME.
[Old High German, Middle High German *strūz* (German dial. *Strauss*) from Germanic base perh. orig. meaning 'stand out, project, protrude': cf. STRUT *verb*[1], Norwegian *strutt* obstinate resistance.]
Strife, contention; a quarrel, a wrangle.

strut /strʌt/ *noun*[2]. L16.
[Prob. formed as next.]
A bar, rod, etc., designed to resist pressure or thrust in a framework; e.g. a diagonal timber acting as a brace to support a principal rafter.

strut /strʌt/ *noun*[3]. E17.
[from STRUT *verb*[1]. Cf. prec.]
1 A strutting walk; a stiff, self-important gait. E17.
2 A type of slow and complicated dance or dance step. M20.

> 📖 **1** *fig.*: *New York Review of Books* The rise of the imperial brag and strut that led to the Spanish–American War.

strut /strʌt/ *noun*[4]. L19.
[from STRUT *verb*[2].]
The action of STRUT *verb*[2]; deflection, e.g. of the spoke of a wheel, from the perpendicular.

†strut *adjective.* L16–E19.
[from next.]
So full as to be swollen or distended.

strut /strʌt/ *verb*[1]. Infl. **-tt-**. Also **†strout**. OE.
[Prob. formed as STRUT *noun*[1].]
†1 a *verb intrans.* Protrude stiffly from a surface or body; stick *out* or *up*. OE–E19. ▸**b** *verb trans.* Protrude, thrust forth, stick *out*. L16–L17.
†2 a *verb intrans.* Bulge, swell; protrude through being full or swollen. Freq. foll. by *out*. ME–M19. ▸**b** *verb trans.* Distend, cause to swell or bulge; cause to protrude through being full or swollen. Also, stuff or cram (*with*). M16–M18.
†3 *verb intrans.* Contend, strive, quarrel, bluster. Only in ME.
4 *verb intrans. & trans.* (*refl.* & with *it*). Behave arrogantly, boastfully, or vainly; exult, swagger, show off. *obsolete* exc. passing into *fig.* of sense 5. LME.
5 *verb intrans. & trans.* (with *it*). Walk with an exaggeratedly stiff step, holding the head erect. Freq. foll. by *about, off*, etc. E16. ▸**b** *verb trans.* Orig. (*rare*), (with adverbial obj.) strut for (a specified period). Later, (with cognate obj.) execute (a specified movement, esp. a step) by strutting; (with direct obj.) walk on or over (a floor, stage, etc.) with a strut. E17. ▸**c** *verb intrans.* Dance the strut (STRUT *noun*[3] 2). L20.
†6 a *verb refl.* Stand stiffly erect. *rare.* Only in L16. ▸**b** *verb intrans.* Raise oneself to or stand erect at one's full height. E17–E19.

> 📖 **1a** S. FOOTE A tulip strutting up like a magistrate's mace. W. IRVING A promontory, which strutted forth boldly into the waves. **b** S. COLVIL Wild-Boars strouting out their bristles. **2a** A. BEHN Lord how he's swoln? see how his Stomach struts. **b** R. HERRICK Let Thy servant . . sweat, To strut thy barnes with sheafs of Wheat. **4** R. COTGRAVE He swaggers, brags, or strouts it mightily. **5a** DICKENS Plump pigeons . . strutting on the eaves. V. NABOKOV All she wanted . . was to be . . a strutting and prancing baton twirler. L. GARFIELD He put on a confident . . air. He strutted importantly about. **b** SHAKES. *Macb.* A poor player, That struts and frets his hour upon the stage. HENRY FIELDING Strange monsters . . which, under the name of lords and ladies, strut the stage. **6b** J. BARLOW Taurus would shrink, Hemodia strut no more.

Phrases: **strut one's stuff** *N. Amer.* display one's ability.
▪ **strutter** *noun* ME. **struttingly** *adverb* in a strutting manner LME.

strut /strʌt/ *verb*[2]. Infl. **-tt-**. E19.
[from STRUT *noun*[2].]
1 *verb trans.* Brace or support by a strut or struts; hold in place or strengthen by an upright, diagonal, or transverse support. E19.
2 *verb intrans.* Be fixed diagonally or slantwise; be bent so as to form a sharp turn or angle. M19.
▪ **strutting** *noun* (*a*) the action of the verb (earliest as 1st elem. of comb.); (*b*) struts collectively: M18.

struthioid /ˈstruːθɪɔɪd/ *adjective & noun. rare.* L19.
[from mod. Latin *Struthio* genus name (see OSTRICH) + -OID.]
Chiefly *PALAEONTOLOGY*. ▸**A** *adjective.* Ostrich-like. L19.
▸ **B** *noun.* An ostrich-like bird. L19.

struthious /ˈstruːθɪəs/ *adjective.* L18.
[formed as prec. + -OUS.]
ZOOLOGY. Of or pertaining to the ostrich, *Struthio camelus*, or the order Struthioniformes; resembling an ostrich (*lit.* & *fig.*).

struthonian /stru:ˈθəʊnɪən/ *noun & adjective. joc.* M20.
[Irreg. from Latin *struthio(n-)* ostrich (with ref. to the former belief that ostriches bury their heads in the sand when pursued) + -IAN.]
▶ **A** *noun.* An ostrich-like person, *spec.* one who ignores unwelcome facts. M20.
▶ **B** *adjective.* Of or pertaining to a struthonian. M20.

Struwwelpeter /ˈstru:əlpi:tə, *foreign* ˈʃtrʊvəl,pe:tər/ *attrib. adjective.* E20.
[German *Struwwelpeter* shock-headed Peter (see below).]
Of, pertaining to, or resembling a character in a German children's book of the same name by Heinrich Hoffmann (1809–94), with long unkempt hair and extremely long fingernails.

strychnia /ˈstrɪknɪə/ *noun.* Now *rare.* E19.
[formed as next + -IA[1].]
CHEMISTRY. = next.

strychnine /ˈstrɪkni:n, -nɪn/ *noun & verb.* E19.
[French, formed as next + -INE[5].]
▶ **A** *noun.* A highly toxic alkaloid obtained chiefly from the seeds of plants of the genus *Strychnos*, esp. nux vomica, which causes contraction of the spine and respiratory paralysis and is used in experimental physiology as a stimulant. E19.
▶ **B** *verb trans.* Poison with strychnine. M19.
■ **strychnic** *adjective* pertaining to strychnine M19. **strychniniˈzation** *noun* (PHYSIOLOGY) the application of strychnine L19. **strychninize** *verb trans.* (PHYSIOLOGY) apply strychnine to M20. **strychnism** *noun* (MEDICINE) (the condition induced by) strychnine poisoning M19.

strychnos /ˈstrɪknɒs/ *noun.* M19.
[mod. Latin (see below), use as a genus name of Latin = a kind of nightshade, from Greek *strukhnos*.]
Any of various tropical trees, shrubs, and lianas constituting the genus *Strychnos* (family Loganiaceae), which includes nux vomica, *S. nux-vomica*, Ignatius's bean, *S. ignatii*, and other poisonous species.

stryddag /ˈstreɪtdax/ *noun. S. Afr.* Pl. **-dae** /-dɑ:ə/. M20.
[Afrikaans, lit. 'struggle day, day of battle'.]
In South Africa, a political (esp. Afrikaner) party rally.

Sts *abbreviation.*
Saints.

St Trinian's /s(ə)nt ˈtrɪnɪənz/ *noun.* M20.
[A girls' school invented in 1941 by the cartoonist Ronald Searle (b. 1920).]
Used **attrib.** with allus. to the characteristic style of hoydenish behaviour, school uniform, etc., of the girls in the cartoons, books, and films depicting St Trinian's.

Stuart /ˈstju:ət/ *adjective.* E19.
[from the House of *Stuart* (see below).]
Of or pertaining to the House of Stuart, the dynasty holding the sovereignty of Scotland from the accession in 1371 of Robert II, one of the hereditary stewards of Scotland, and of Britain from the accession in 1603 of James VI of Scotland to the English throne as James I, until the death of Anne in 1714; *spec.* of, designating, or pertaining to a style of architecture, clothing, furniture, etc., characteristic of the period between 1603 and the deposition of James II in 1688.

stub /stʌb/ *noun.*
[Old English *stub(b)* = Middle Low German, Middle Dutch *stubbe*, Old Norse *stubbr, stubbi*; partly also from Old English *styb* (which coalesced with the other form), from Germanic.]
1 The stump of a tree, shrub, etc., left after felling or cutting. Formerly also, a dead tree left standing. OE. ▸**b** A short piece of a broken branch remaining on a stem. ME. ▸†**c** The part of a tree-trunk close to the ground. M16–M17.
2 *sing.* & (usu.) in *pl.* Stubble. Now *dial.* ME.
3 A short thick nail; *spec.* a worn horseshoe nail, esp. (in *pl.*) as used with other similar material for making stub-iron. Also ***stub-nail***. LME.
4 A thing that is or appears to be stunted, worn down, or cut short, a stump; *spec.* (*a*) the broken or worn-down remnant of a more or less cylindrical object; *esp.* the butt or stump of a cigar or cigarette; (*b*) a rudimentary tail, horn, etc.; (*c*) a short thick piece of wood; (*d*) a short length of wire used in flower-arranging (also ***stub wire***). LME.
5 A sharp bit of wood; a splinter, thorn. Now *dial.* LME.
6 MECHANICS. A stud, a projection; *spec.* a stationary stud in a lock acting as a detent for the tumblers when their slots are in engagement with it. M16.
7 The counterfoil of a cheque, receipt, etc. Orig. *N. Amer.* L19.
8 AERONAUTICS (now *Hist.*). A short projection from the hull of an aeroplane or seaplane, aiding lateral stability; a stub wing. Also, an aircraft exhaust. M20.
9 FINANCE. An option entitling an investor selling a holding in a leveraged buyout to purchase ordinary shares at a specified future date. Also (more fully ***stub equity***), the equity remaining to shareholders during such a buyout; the quoted price of this. Orig. *US.* L20.

> 🕮 **1** SPENSER Old stockes and stubs of trees. **2** J. CLARE Ill it suits thee in the stubs to glean. **4** E. LISLE There will remain a little stub at the end of the twig. T. C. WOLFE A stub of pencil gripped between his fingers. J. CLAVELL The stub of the foremast that the storm had carried away jutted nastily. **7** J. THURBER He was careful to fill out cheque-book stubs.

Comb.: **stub-axle** an axle supporting only one wheel of a pair; **stub-bred** *adjective* (HUNTING) (of a fox) having its lair in undergrowth etc. instead of underground; **stub-end** (*a*) the butt end of a connecting-rod, weapon, etc.; (*b*) *US* the unconnected end of a stub track (also ***stub-end track***); (*c*) a cigarette stub; ***stub equity***: see sense 9 above; **stub-feather** any of the short unfledged feathers left on a fowl etc. after plucking; **stub-iron** a kind of iron orig. made from worn horseshoe nails and similar material; **stub-mortise**: going only part of the way through a piece of timber etc.; ***stub-nail***: see sense 3 above; **stub-pen** †(*a*) a worn quill pen; (*b*) a broad-nibbed pen; **stub station** *US* a railway station at which the tracks terminate; **stub-switch** *US* a switch on a railway track allowing the points to be lined up with the leads; **stub-tail** a short and thick or broad tail; **stub-tenon**: going only part of the way through; a piece of timber etc. **stub track** *US* a railway track, usu. at a terminus, connected to another at one end only; **stub wing** AERONAUTICS (*a*) a very short wing or similar structure (cf. sense 8 above); (*b*) the part of an aircraft's wing immediately next to the fuselage; ***stub wire***: see sense 4(d) above.

stub /stʌb/ *verb.* Infl. **-bb-**. LME.
[from the noun.]
1 *verb trans.* Grub up (tree stumps, trees, etc.) by the roots. Usu. foll. by *up*. LME.
2 *verb trans.* Clear (land) of tree stumps, trees, etc., by uprooting. Usu. foll. by *up*. LME.
3 *verb trans.* Cut down (a tree etc.) close to the root. Now *rare.* L16.
4 *verb trans.* Reduce to a stub or stump, esp. by wear. *rare.* L16.
5 *verb trans.* Cause (a horse) to be injured by the stub of a tree, shrub, etc. L17.
6 *verb trans.* Crush or pulverize (marl, stones, etc.) for spreading over land, a road, etc.; fill up the ruts in (a road) with crushed stones etc. Long *rare.* M18.
7 *verb trans.* Strike (one's toe) against something, esp. painfully. Orig. *US.* M19.
8 *verb trans.* Remove the stub-feathers from (a fowl) in plucking. L19.
9 *verb trans.* Extinguish (a cigar or cigarette) by pressing the lighted end against a hard object. Usu. foll. by *out*. E20.

> 🕮 **1** A. JESSOPP He . . stubbed up a hedge which had been the boundary. **2** L. STERNE We shall have a terrible piece of work . . in stubbing the Oxmoor. **7** ANNE STEVENSON He stubbed his little toe on a chest of drawers. By evening his foot had turned black. **9** A. LEE Henri stubbed out his cigarette on a crust of bread.

■ **stubber** *noun* ME.

stubbard /ˈstʌbəd/ *noun. dial.* M18.
[Perh. a surname.]
An old, early-ripening variety of apple. Also ***stubbard apple***.

stubbed /stʌbd/ *adjective.* E16.
[from STUB *noun*, *verb*: see -ED[2], -ED[1].]
1 Short and thick, stumpy. *obsolete* exc. *dial.* E16.
2 That has been stubbed, that has been made into a stub; *spec.* (*a*) (of a tree etc.) cut down to a stump; (*b*) worn down through usage, blunted; (*c*) (orig. *US*) (of a toe) that has been struck against something, esp. painfully. L16.
3 Orig., (of land) cleared of stubs. Later, (of land) having many stubs, covered with stubs. *rare.* L16.
Comb.: **stubbed-out** (of a cigar or cigarette) extinguished by being pressed against a hard object.

stubble /ˈstʌb(ə)l/ *noun & verb.* ME.
[Anglo-Norman *stuble*, Old French *estuble* (mod. *éteule*) from Latin *stup(u)la* from STIPULA. Cf. STIPULATE *verb*.]
▶ **A** *noun.* **1** *collect. sing.* & (now *rare*) in *pl.* The cut stalks of wheat or other grain left in the ground after reaping. ME. ▸**b** *sing.* A short bristly growth of unshaven hair on a cheek or chin; close-cropped hair on the head or chin. L16.
2 The straw of wheat or other grain gathered after harvesting. LME.
3 = ***stubble-field*** below. Usu. in *pl.* L18.

> 🕮 **1** W. SOMERVILLE The gay Pack In the rough bristly Stubbles range unblam'd. T. H. WHITE The wheat stood in stooks of eight among the tall stubble. **b** P. V. WHITE Nicks where the razor had sought out stubble in the early furrows of his face.

Comb.: **stubble-burning** the clearing of stubble from land by burning; **stubble-fed** *adjective* (of poultry etc.) fed on the stubble left in a reaped field; **stubble-field** a reaped field that has not been ploughed; **stubble-fire** a fire of stubble, *esp.* one caused by stubble-burning; **stubble-goose** a goose fattened for the table on stubble; **stubble-jumper** (*slang*, chiefly *Canad.*) a prairie farmer; **stubble-quail** a brown, black, and white quail, *Coturnix pectoralis*, of southern Australia; **stubble-rig** *Scot.* (*a*) a stubble-field; (*b*) the reaper who takes the lead.
▶ **B** *verb trans.* Remove stubble from. L15.
†**stubble it!**, †**stubble your whids!** hold your tongue!
■ **stubbled** *adjective* †(*a*) *rare* (of a goose) fattened on stubble; (*b*) covered with stubble, stubbly: LME. **stubbly** *adjective* (*a*) covered with stubble; (*b*) resembling stubble; *esp.* (of hair) short and bristly: LME.

stubborn /ˈstʌbən/ *adjective & verb.* ME.
[Origin unkn.]
▶ **A** *adjective.* **1** Orig., untameable, implacable, ruthless, fierce. Later, tenacious or persistent in refusing to obey or comply; unyielding, inflexible, obstinate; *esp.* unreasonably obstinate. ME.
2 Of a thing: refractory to treatment, intractable; *spec.* (*a*) of soil, metal, etc., difficult to work; (*b*) (now *rare*) hard, stiff, rigid. L15.

> 🕮 **1** S. BELLOW You . . call me mulish. As if you weren't twice as stubborn. *Blackwood's Magazine* If they met with stubborn resistance they would have to wait for us. **2** T. GRAY Their furrow oft the stubborn glebe has broke. H. M. STANLEY The bow is of stubborn hard brown wood.

▶ **B** *verb trans.* Make stubborn. *poet.* E19.
■ **stubbornly** *adverb* LME. **stubbornness** /-n-n-/ *noun* LME.

Stubbsian /ˈstʌbzɪən/ *adjective.* M20.
[from *Stubbs* (see below) + -IAN.]
1 Of, pertaining to, or characteristic of the English painter George Stubbs (1724–1806) or his work. M20.
2 Of, pertaining to, or characteristic of the historian William Stubbs (1825–1901), Bishop of Oxford, or his views. L20.

stubby /ˈstʌbi/ *noun. Austral. slang.* M20.
[from the adjective.]
1 A short squat beer-bottle, *esp.* one with a capacity of 375 ml; the contents of such a bottle. M20.
2 In *pl.* (Also **S-**.) (Proprietary name for) brief men's shorts. L20.

stubby /ˈstʌbi/ *adjective.* ME.
[from STUB *noun* + -Y[1].]
1 Having many stubs, stubbly; *spec.* (*a*) (of ground) covered with stubble; (*b*) (of the hair, a beard) composed of short, stiff bristles. ME.
2 Of the nature of or like a stub; short and thick or broad; short and blunt as a result of wear. L16.

> 🕮 **2** A. TYLER In Evie's stubby hands, the frills seemed fussy and out of place. J. LE CARRÉ A stubby little door, thickly panelled.

■ **stubbiness** *noun* M19.

Stube /ˈʃtu:bə/ *noun.* Pl. **-ben** /-bən/. M20.
[German = room.]
= BIERSTUBE.

stuc /stʌk/ *noun.* Also †**stuck**. M17.
[French, formed as STUCCO.]
†**1** = STUCCO *noun* 1a. M17–L18.
2 = STUCCO *noun* 1b. M20.

stuccador /ˈstʌkədɔ:/ *noun.* Also **-dore**. M20.
[Irreg. from Italian *stuccatore* formed as next. Cf. Spanish *estucador*.]
A stuccoer.

stucco /ˈstʌkəʊ/ *noun & verb.* L16.
[Italian, ult. from Germanic.]
▶ **A** *noun.* Pl. **-oes**.
1 a A fine plaster, esp. made from gypsum and pulverized marble, for covering walls, ceilings, etc., and making cornices and other architectural decorations. L16. ▸**b** A coarse plaster or calcareous cement esp. for covering a rough exterior surface to give the appearance of stone. M18. ▸**c** Plaster of Paris. M19.
2 a The process of ornamenting walls, ceilings, etc. with stucco; work or ornamentation produced by this process. L17. ▸**b** A building plastered with stucco. L20.
▶ **B** *verb trans.* Coat or ornament with stucco. E18.
■ **stuccoer** *noun* a worker in stucco E19. **stuccoist** /ˈstʌkəʊɪst/ *noun* a stuccoer M20.

†**stuck** *noun*[1]. *rare.* L16–E17.
[Perh. var. of STOCK *noun*[2].]
A sword. Later *spec.* in FENCING, a thrust, a lunge.

†**stuck** *noun*[2] var. of STUC.

stuck /stʌk/ *adjective.* E18.
[pa. pple of STICK *verb*[1].]
1 Of an animal, esp. a pig: stabbed by a spear, knife, etc.; butchered by having its throat cut. E18.
2 Of a moulding: shaped by a moulding-plane rather than by hand. M19.
3 Unable to move or go further (*lit.* & *fig.*); *spec.* wedged in. L19.
4 Attached or sealed (as) by adhesive. Freq. in comb., as ***stuck-down***, ***stuck-on***, etc. E20.

> 🕮 **1** R. BARNARD You yelled like a stuck pig. ***bleed like a stuck pig***: see PIG *noun*[1]. **3** J. AIKEN It keeps coming back again—like a stuck gramophone record. A. T. ELLIS I've nearly gone mad stuck on Crewe platform for an hour. ***be stuck for***: see STICK *verb*[1]. **4** D. FRANCIS I took an envelope out of my . . pocket. 'I want to read it.' . . 'Go ahead. It isn't stuck'. ***be stuck on***: see STICK *verb*[1]. ***get stuck in***, ***get stuck into***: see STICK *verb*[1].

■ **stuckness** *noun* M20.

stuck *verb pa. t. & pa. pple*: see STICK *verb*[1].

stuck-up /stʌk'ʌp/ *adjective. colloq.* E19.
[from STUCK *adjective* + UP *adverb*[2].]
Affectedly superior, pretentious, snobbish.

D. MADDEN Stuck-up baggage . . . You're better off without her for a friend.

■ **stuck'uppishness** *noun* M19.

stud /stʌd/ *noun*[1].
[Old English *studu*, *stuþu* = Middle High German *stud*, Old Norse *stoð* rel. to German *stützen* to prop, support.]
▶ **I 1** Orig., a wooden post of any kind, an upright prop or support. Later, any of the smaller uprights between the principle posts of a timber-framed wall. Now, any of the parallel, upright members in a timber- or metal-framed wall to which plasterboard or other cladding is fixed. OE.
2 *fig.* A person acting as a prop or support. Long *obsolete* exc. *dial.* LME.
3 Orig., the stem or trunk of a shrub, tree, etc. Later, a short branch. *rare.* L16.
4 The height of a room from floor to ceiling. Orig. & chiefly *US*. M19.
1b *mud and stud*: see MUD *noun*[1].
▶ **II 5** Orig. *spec.*, an ornamental round knob of metal or amber on a girdle, bridle, etc. Later, a boss, nail-head, etc., projecting from a surface, esp. for decoration or protection. LME. ▶**b** ARCHITECTURE. A carved disc, *esp.* one used as an ornament in Norman architecture. L17. ▶**c** Any of a series of small devices protruding slightly above the surface of a road as a marker etc.; *spec.* = CAT'S-EYE 4. M20. ▶**d** In full *ear-stud*. A small usu. round ornament worn on the lobe of the ear. M20. ▶**e** Any of a number of metal pieces set into the tyre of a motor vehicle to improve roadholding in slippery conditions. *N. Amer.* M20.
6 A projecting part in a mechanism; *spec.* (*a*) a lug or projecting socket to receive the end of an axle, pin, etc.; (*b*) a short rod or pin fixed in or projecting from something, and serving as a support, axis, or stop; (*c*) (chiefly *Hist.*) any of a number of spirally placed protuberances on the surface of a projectile to be fired from a rifled gun, giving the shot rotatory movement from the grooving of the gun. L17.
7 A fastener consisting of two buttons joined with a shank for use esp. with two buttonholes in a shirt-front. L18.
8 A rivet or crosspiece in each link of a chain-cable. M19.
Comb.: **stud-bolt** a cylindrical bolt, threaded at both ends, one end to be screwed into a hole in a casting etc., the other end passing through a hole in a cover-plate and secured by a nut; **stud-box** a cylindrical tool for inserting stud-bolts, having at the lower end a tapped hole and at the upper end a square shank operated by a spanner; **stud-fish** *US* either of two killifishes, the northern *Fundulus catenatus* and the southern *F. stellifer*; **stud-partition** a partition constructed of studs (sense 1 above); **stud-wall** a wall built of lath and plaster; **stud welding** a method of welding in which an arc is struck between a stud and the base metal, producing a pool of molten metal into which the stud is driven to form a weld; **stud-work** building in lath and plaster.

stud /stʌd/ *noun*[2] & *adjective*.
[Old English *stōd* corresp. to Middle Low German *stōt*, Old High German *stuot* (German *Stute* mare), Old Norse *stóð*, from Germanic base also of STAND *verb*. Cf. STEED.]
▶ **A** *noun*. **1** A place where horses are kept for breeding; the horses kept in such a place. OE. ▶†**b** A herd of horses, esp. mares, kept for breeding. ME–E17. ▶†**c** A breed or race of horses. ME–M16.
†**2** Horses collectively. Only in ME.
3 †**a** = *stud-mare* below. *Scot. rare.* L15–L16. ▶**b** = *stud-horse* (a) below. *N. Amer.* E19. ▶**c** = *stud poker* below. Chiefly *US*. M20.
4 Orig., the horses bred by and belonging to one person. Later, a number of horses (esp. racehorses or hunters) belonging to one owner. M17. ▶**b** A collection of animals of a particular kind, esp. dogs, belonging to one person. L18.
5 a A man noted for his sexual prowess. *colloq.* L19. ▶**b** A man, a fellow, *esp.* a well-informed one; a youth. *US Black slang.* E20.

3c L. ALTHER Caroline . . won at seven-card stud. **4b** *transf.*: R. KIPLING A Frenchman . . road racing . . and running a stud of six cars. **5a** S. RUSHDIE A notorious seducer; a ladies'-man; . . in short, a stud.

Phrases: **at stud** (of a stallion) available for breeding on payment of a fee. **stand at stud** (of a stallion) be available for breeding.
▶ **B** *attrib.* or as *adjective*. Of, pertaining to, or characteristic of a stud; *spec.* (*colloq.*) displaying a masculine sexual character. Also (chiefly *US slang*), fine, excellent. OE.
Comb. & special collocations: **stud-book** a book giving the pedigree of thoroughbred horses or other animals (esp. dogs) of pure stock; *transf. & fig.* a catalogue of aristocratic pedigree; **stud-farm** a place where horses are bred; **stud-groom** the head groom attached to a stud; **stud-horse** (*a*) a stallion kept for breeding; (*b*) = *stud poker* below; **stud-house** (*a*) a building for the accommodation of a stud; (*b*) (with cap. initials) the official residence of the Master of the Horse at Hampton Court; **stud-mare** a mare kept for breeding purposes, a brood-mare; **stud poker** a form of poker with betting after the dealing of successive rounds of cards face up.

■ **studded** *adjective* (*US*) (of a room) having a great or small vertical dimension (as 2nd elem. of comb., as *high-studded*, *low-studded*): L18.

stud /stʌd/ *verb trans.* Infl. **-dd-**. LME.
[from STUD *noun*[1].]
1 Provide with studs; *spec.* (*a*) supply or build with upright timbers; (*b*) set with bosses, nail-heads, etc., projecting from a surface, esp. for decoration or protection. Freq. as *studded ppl adjective*. LME.
2 Set at (esp. frequent) intervals in or over (a surface). Freq. as *studded ppl adjective*. M17.
3 Insert or place (a number of things) at (esp. frequent) intervals over a surface. Chiefly as *studded ppl adjective*. M19.

1 D. BOGARDE An ivory leopard . . studded all about with lumps of amber like a rich fruit cake. **2** A. J. TOYNBEE The south-west bank . . is studded with a series of port-cities. E. BOWEN Antlers and ironwork . . studded the walls.

studding /'stʌdɪŋ/ *noun*. LME.
[from prec. + -ING[1].]
1 The studs and adjoining members of a timber- or metal-framed wall. LME.
2 That with which a surface is studded. M19.
3 The height of a room from floor to ceiling; = STUD *noun*[1] 4. *US*. L19.

studding-sail /'stʌns(ə)l, 'stʌdɪŋseɪl/ *noun*. M16.
[Origin of 1st elem. uncertain: perh. from Middle Low German, Middle Dutch *stötinge*, from *stöten* thrust (Dutch *stooten*) cogn. with Old Saxon *stōtan*, Old High German *stōzzan* (German *stossen*), Gothic *stautan*.]
A sail set on a small extra yard and boom beyond the leech of a square sail in light winds. Also called *stunsail*.

studdle /'stʌd(ə)l/ *noun*.
[Old English *stodl* = Old Norse *stuðill* prop, rel. to STUD *noun*[1].]
1 An upright post. Long *obsolete* exc. *dial.* in *gen.* sense. OE.
2 *spec.* †**a** Any of the uprights of a loom. OE–E17. ▶**b** A prop or support in a mine. M18.

student /'stju:d(ə)nt/ *noun*[1]. LME.
[Latin *student-* pres. ppl stem of *studere*: see STUDY *verb*, -ENT.]
1 A person engaged in or fond of study. Also foll. by *of*, *in*, or preceded by specifying word. LME.
2 a A person following a course of study and instruction at a university, college, etc. Also foll. by *of*, *in*, or preceded by specifying word. LME. ▶**b** A school pupil. Orig. *US*. E20. ▶**c** An inexperienced user of illegal drugs; *spec.* a person taking small or occasional doses. *US slang*. M20.
3 a *spec.* A fellow of Christ Church, Oxford. M17. ▶**b** A person receiving a stipend from a college or other institution or from a special fund, esp. for a fixed period. E19.

1 A. CHRISTIE Events after dinner were not without their amusing side to a student of human nature. **2a** *Technology* Mechanical engineering students at Hendon Technical College. C. HEILBRUN Students at Somerville College, Oxford. *mature student*: see MATURE *adjective*. *perpetual student*: see PERPETUAL *adjective*.

Attrib. & comb.: In the senses 'that is a student', as *student nurse*, 'of or pertaining to a student or students', as *student grant*, *student hostel*, *student power*, etc. Special combs., as **student card**: issued to a member of a student body, and usu. entitling the holder to certain privileges; **student lamp**, **student's lamp** (*a*) (now *Hist.*) an Argand lamp with an automatically-controlled oil-flow; (*b*) a type of reading lamp with a light source of adjustable height; **student teacher** a student of a university or training college teaching in a school for a certain period as part of the qualification for a teaching certificate; **student-teacher** *adjective* designating the relation between students and their teacher or teachers; **student-teachership** the position of a student teacher.

■ **stu'dental** *adjective* (*rare*) of, pertaining to, or characteristic of a student or students M17. **studentess** *noun* (*rare*) a female student M19. **studenthood** *noun* the state or condition of being a student E20. **studentish** *adjective* somewhat resembling or characteristic of a student or students M20. **studentless** *adjective* without a student or students, having no students L19. **student-like** *adjective* resembling (that of) a student or students M19. **studentry** *noun* (*rare*) students collectively; a body of students: M19. **studentship** *noun* (*a*) an appointment to receive a stipend as a student from a college or other institution or from a special fund, esp. for a fixed period; (*b*) the condition or fact of being a student: L18. **studenty** *adjective* (*colloq.*) relating to or characteristic of a student or students; full of students: M20.

Student /'stju:d(ə)nt/ *noun*[2]. E20.
[Pseudonym of William Sealy Gosset (1876–1937), English brewery employee.]
STATISTICS. Used *attrib.* and in *possess.* to designate statistical concepts devised by Student.
Student distribution, **Student's distribution**, **Student's t-distribution**, **Student t-distribution** [*t* arbitrary] a statistical distribution which is that of a fraction whose numerator is drawn from a normal distribution with a mean of zero and whose denominator is the root mean square of *k* terms drawn from the same normal distribution (where *k* is the number of degrees of freedom). **Student's test**, **Student's t test** a test for statistical significance that uses tables of Student's distribution.

studentize /'stju:d(ə)ntʌɪz/ *verb trans.* Also **-ise**. M20.
[from prec. + -IZE.]
STATISTICS. Subject (data) to a standardization process intended to eliminate effects of an unknown parameter, esp. by division throughout by the estimated standard deviation. Chiefly as *studentized ppl adjective*.
■ **studenti'zation** *noun* M20.

studia *noun* pl. of STUDIUM.

studied /'stʌdɪd/ *adjective*. L15.
[from STUDY *verb* + -ED[1].]
1 Resulting from or characterized by deliberate effort or intention; produced or acquired by study or careful thought or planning; deliberate, intentional. L15.
2 Of a person: learned, skilled, or practised (*in* a subject). L15. ▶**b** Prepared (*for* or *to do* something) by study or thought. Now *rare* or *obsolete*. M16.

1 A. N. WILSON 'All right,' he said, with studied casualness. C. HOPE The invitation was so studied that one felt she had . . read it in a book. **2** P. HEYLIN So well was he studied in the Art. *Munsey's Magazine* The knowledge of a traveled and a studied man.

¶ Earlier in UNSTUDIED.
■ **studiedly** *adverb* M17. **studiedness** *noun* M17.

studio /'stju:dɪəʊ/ *noun*. Pl. **-os**. E19.
[Italian from Latin *studium*: see STUDY *noun*.]
1 The workroom of a sculptor, painter, photographer, etc. E19.
2 a A room in which a cinema film is made; *sing.* & (usu.) in *pl.*, a film-making complex with auxiliary buildings. Also, a film company. E20. ▶**b** A room in a broadcasting station etc. for recording or making transmissions; *sing.* & in *pl.*, the premises containing such a room or rooms. E20. ▶**c** A room for recording and editing music etc. E20.
3 = *studio flat* below. Orig. *US*. M20.
Comb.: **studio apartment** *N. Amer.* = *studio flat* below; **studio couch** a couch able to be converted into a bed; **studio flat** (*a*) a flat containing a room suitable as an artist's studio; (*b*) a one-roomed flat; **studio party** (*a*) an informal party held in an artist's studio; (*b*) a social gathering at a film studio; **studio portrait** a posed photograph, as taken in a photographer's studio; **studio potter** a potter (esp. a member of a small group) working in a studio producing hand-thrown pottery; **studio theatre** (an) experimental theatre.

studiolo /studi'ɔ:lo/ *noun*. Pl. **-li** /-li/. E20.
[Italian = small study.]
In Italy: a private study hung with paintings.

studious /'stju:dɪəs/ *adjective*. ME.
[Latin *studiosus*, from *studium* STUDY *noun*: see -IOUS.]
1 Assiduous in study; devoted to the acquisition of learning. ME. ▶**b** Of, pertaining to, or concerned with learning or study; (of a place) suited to study. E16.
2 Carefully attentive; taking care *to do* or *in doing* something; painstaking, zealous; anxiously desirous *of* (*doing*). LME. ▶**b** Planned with care; studied, deliberate. M18.

1 P. H. JOHNSON The concentration of a studious schoolgirl at her homework. **b** D. BREWSTER Persons of studious habits . . much occupied with the operations of their own minds. M. ARNOLD Wander'd from the studious walls To learn strange arts. **2** MILTON Studious they appere Of arts that polish Life. F. W. FARRAR In carrying out his policy Agrippa paid studious court to the Jews. **b** F. POLLOCK Dissent . . indicated with seemingly studious obscurity.

■ **studiously** *adverb* ME. **studiousness** *noun* M16.

Studite /'stju:dʌɪt/ *noun & adjective*. L17.
[medieval Latin *Studita* (ecclesiastical Greek *Stouditēs*) from *Studium* (*Stoudion*), from *Studius* (*Stoudios*) (see below) + -ITE[1].]
▶ **A** *noun*. A member of the monastic order founded by Studius in the 5th cent. AD at Constantinople, esp. as reformed by St Theodore at the end of the 8th cent. L17.
▶ **B** *attrib.* or as *adjective*. Of or pertaining to the Studites or their order. E20.

studium /'stju:dɪəm/ *noun*. Pl. **-ia** /-ɪə/. E17.
[Latin: see STUDY *noun*.]
Hist. = STUDY *noun* 4. Also = *studium generale* below.
studium generale /dʒɛnə'reɪli, -'rɑ:li/, pl. **-ia -lia** /-lɪə/, [neut. sing. of *generalis* GENERAL *adjective*] in the Middle Ages, a university attended by scholars from outside as well as within its own locality.

studmuffin /'stʌdmʌfɪn/ *noun. slang* (orig. *US*). L20.
[from STUD *noun*[2] + MUFFIN.]
A sexually attractive young man.

study /'stʌdi/ *noun*. ME.
[Aphet. from Old French *estudie* (mod. *étude*) from Latin *studium* zeal, affection, painstaking application. Cf. ÉTUDE.]
1 The action of studying; the devotion of time and attention to acquiring information or knowledge, esp. *of* a specified subject. ME. ▶**b** Orig., a particular branch of knowledge. Later (in *pl.*), a person's pursuit of academic knowledge. L15.
2 †**a** A state of perplexity or anxious thought; an uncertainty as to the wisdom of a course of action.

ME–L17. ▸**b** A state of deep thought, reverie, or abstraction. *obsolete* exc. in ***brown study*** s.v. BROWN *adjective*. ME. ▸**c** THEATRICAL. The action of memorizing a role; a person who memorizes a role. Freq. in ***be a quick study, be a slow study***, etc. L16.

3 A room for reading, writing, etc. ME. ▸†**b** A room or cupboard for books etc. Also, the books in such a room or cupboard; a private library. M16–M18.

†**4** A seat of learning; *spec.* a university. LME–L17.

†**5** Affection, friendliness; sympathy; pleasure or interest felt in something. LME–L17.

†**6** An employment, an occupation, a pursuit. LME–E17.

7 Thought directed to the accomplishment of a particular purpose; studied or deliberate effort or contrivance. Also, the object or aim of a person's interest, attention, or care. LME.

8 a That which is studied; the particular object of a person's pursuit of knowledge. M16. ▸**b** A thing deserving or requiring to be closely observed or investigated. M18.

9 a An artistic production executed for practice or as a preparation for future work; *esp.* a careful preliminary sketch for (a detail of) a picture. Also, a drawing, painting, etc., intended to bring out the characteristics of the object represented. M18. ▸**b** An essay, book, etc., devoted to the detailed consideration of a specified subject. M19.

10 MUSIC. = ÉTUDE. L19.

📖 **1** POPE The Man, who, stretch'd in Isis' calm retreat, To books and study gives sev'n years complete. *Times* Attempts to broaden the syllabus by including the study of atheism. **b** M. COREN Belloc decided to go up to Oxford and continue his studies. **2a** R. MEEKE At first in a study what to do, at last I promised. **3** P. MORTIMER Jake has a study downstairs, he used to work there a lot. **b** G. WHELER He . . hath a good Study of Manuscripts. **7** H. P. BROUGHAM The acquisition of a fortune is the study of all. SIR W. SCOTT It was his study to sooth this . . female by blandishments. **8a** POPE Be Homer's works your study and delight. **b** E. K. KANE Studies of colour that would have rewarded an artist. A. TYLER Ira's face was a study as he approached the car. **9a** S. CHITTY Portraits . . executed straight on to the canvas without preliminary studies. **b** R. FRASER There have . . been innumerable studies of Charlotte Brontë.

Phrases: ***advanced studies***: see ADVANCED 2. ***brown study***: see BROWN *adjective*. ***business studies***. **make a study of** study, observe carefully. ***social studies***: see SOCIAL *adjective*.

Comb.: **study circle**, **study group** a group meeting regularly to discuss a particular topic of study; **study hall** *US* the period of time in a school routine set aside for the preparation of school work.

study /ˈstʌdi/ *verb*. ME.

[Aphet. from Old French *estudier* (mod. *étudier*) from medieval Latin *studiare* (from Latin *studium* STUDY *noun*) for Latin *studere* be zealous, apply oneself, study.]

▸ **I** *verb intrans.* **1** Apply the mind to acquiring knowledge, esp. devoting time and effort to this end. ME. ▸**b** Be a student at a university, college, etc.; work as a student *under* the direction of a specified teacher. LME. ▸**c** Foll. by *up*: make a close study of a particular subject (freq. foll. by *on* the subject specified). *US colloq.* M20.

2 Think hard; meditate (*about, on*, etc.); reflect, try to remember or decide. Now *dial.* & *US colloq.* ME. ▸†**b** Be in doubt, be perplexed; consider anxiously. LME–L16. ▸†**c** Search *for* (*lit.* & *fig.*). M16–M18.

3 Try deliberately *to do*. *arch.* ME.

†**4 a** Employ one's thought or effort *in*. LME–L15. ▸**b** Concentrate one's efforts in a particular direction (freq. foll. by *to*); be anxious *for*; set one's mind *on*. LME–E17.

📖 **1** P. FRANCIS To Athens flies; Intensely studies with the Learn'd and Wise. **b** W. F. BUCKLEY She had . . studied under Clara Schumann. **2** MALCOLM X I studied about if I just *should* happen to say something to her—what would her position be? **c** S. RICHARDSON She must have studied for an expedient. **3** W. WOTTON He study'd to do as much Mischief as he could.

▸ **II** *verb trans.* †**5** Ponder, meditate on. Also (*rare*), cause to ponder; perplex. ME–M17. ▸**b** Deliberate or consider *how, why, what*, etc. ME–L18.

6 Apply the mind to acquiring knowledge of (a subject), esp. by the devotion of time and effort. LME. ▸**b** Be a student of (a specified subject) at a university, college, etc., esp. *under* the direction of a particular teacher. M16. ▸**c** Foll. by *up*: study (a subject) hastily. *colloq.* L19.

7 Examine in detail, try to understand or become minutely acquainted with; *spec.* (**a**) read (a book, text, etc.) with close attention; (**b**) scrutinize or look closely at (a visible object); (**c**) THEATRICAL memorize (a role). LME.

8 Plan, devise; think *out*. Now *rare*. M16.

9 Aim at or try to achieve (a specified quality). E17.

10 Exercise thought and deliberation in (an action, composition, etc.). M17.

11 Pay regard to, take notice of; *colloq.* consider the comfort or feelings of. M18.

📖 **5b** SHAKES. *Rich. II* I have been studying how I may compare This prison . . unto the world. **6** H. JAMES I don't know German; I should like to study it. **b** A. LEE I left to study French literature in Lausanne. **7** THACKERAY Studying . . ancient and modern orators with great assiduity. K. ISHIGURO Mariko went on studying her hands. S. BELLOW Meteorologists . . studying world air currents. **8** JONSON I will still study some revenge past this! **9** MILTON Nothing lovelier . . In woman, then to studie houshold good. OED He seems to have studied brevity rather than lucidity. **10** H. B. STOWE The arrangement of every leaf had carefully been studied. **11** S. HAYWARD Where a person . . is continually studying our advantage. *Spectator* A sensitive child who must be studied.

■ **studiable** *adjective* able or fit to be studied M19. **studier** *noun* (long *rare*) (**a**) a student (*of*, †*in*); (**b**) a person striving after or pursuing an object or end (foll. by †*for, of*): LME.

stufa /ˈstuːfə/ *noun*. *rare*. Orig. Anglicized as †**stufe**. M16.

[Italian, formed as next.]

1 A hot-air bath; = STOVE *noun* 1. M16.

2 A jet of volcanic steam. M19.

stufato /stʊˈfɑːtəʊ/ *noun*. *rare*. Pl. **-os**. Also (earlier) †**-ta**. L18.

[Italian, from *stufare* to stew. Cf. STIFADO.]

A meat stew.

†**stufe** *noun* see STUFA.

stuff /stʌf/ *noun*. ME.

[Aphet. from Old French *estoffe* (mod. *étoffe*) material, furniture, provision, perh. from *estoffer*: see next.]

1 †**a** Quilted material worn under chain-mail; this material serving in place of armour. Later, defensive armour. *poet.* ME–M16. ▸†**b** A body of soldiers; a garrison; an auxiliary force, reinforcement. LME–L15. ▸†**c** Military matériel; an army's stores or supplies; munitions of war. LME–L15. ▸†**d** Baggage, luggage (orig. *spec.* of a soldier or an army). LME–M17. ▸**e** Stock or provision of food. Also, corn or grain as a growing crop or in its harvested state. *obsolete* exc. *Scot.* LME. ▸**f** Movable property; household goods or furniture. Freq. in ***stuff of household***. *obsolete* exc. in HOUSEHOLD ***stuff***. LME. ▸†**g** The furnishing proper to a place or thing; accoutrements. LME–L17. ▸†**h** A pie-filling; stuffing. LME–L16. ▸**i** Goods for sale; stock-in-trade. *obsolete* exc. *north.* M16.

2 a Material for making garments; woven cloth of any kind; a particular kind of material; *spec.* a woollen fabric without a pile or nap. ME. ▸**b** The material for the gown worn by a junior counsel; *rare*. = ***stuff gown*** (b) below. L19.

3 a Material to work with or on; substance in an unworked state prior to being shaped, spun, etc. Now *rare* or *obsolete*. LME. ▸**b** Building materials collectively. Long *rare*. LME.

4 a The matter or substance of a literary work, as distinguished from the form. Now *rare*. LME. ▸**b** What a person is perceived to be made of; a person's capabilities or inward character. Also, solid qualities of intellect or character; capacity for endurance; the makings of future attainment or excellence. M16. ▸**c** The substance or matter of which a thing is formed or consists. L16.

5 a Literary or artistic output or material; literary or artistic compositions collectively. Now *rare* exc. as passing into sense 8 and (*colloq.*) journalists' and professional writers' copy. LME. ▸**b** A person considered as a substance or piece of matter. Chiefly with specifying word. Now *rare* exc. in ***hot stuff, bit of stuff*** below. L16. ▸†**c** Matter of thought. *rare* (Shakes.). Only in E17. ▸**d** A particular field of knowledge or expertise in an activity. Chiefly in ***know one's stuff*** s.v. KNOW *verb*. E20.

6 a Matter or a substance of any kind; matter not needing a specific designation, or where no specific designation exists. L15. ▸**b** An article of food or drink. Esp. in ***good stuff, the stuff*** (*colloq.*), whisky; ***the hard stuff*** (*colloq.*), strong alcohol. L16. ▸**c** Medicine, esp. in liquid form. Also ***doctor's stuff*** (see DOCTOR *noun*). Now *colloq.* or *derog.* E17. ▸**d** Garden or farm produce. L17. ▸**e** *spec.* A particular commercial or industrial commodity produced or dealt in. E18. ▸**f** Drugs, narcotics. Freq. in ***on the stuff***, addicted to drugs, on drugs. *slang* (orig. *US*). E20. ▸**g** Any collection of things or belongings which one is unable or unwilling to particularize. Also, business. *colloq.* E20.

7 Any of various kinds of material whose use is specific to certain trades or industries; *spec.* (**a**) CARPENTRY timber (freq. with specifying word); (**b**) PAPER-MAKING paper pulp; (**c**) MINING ore-bearing material; rock, earth, etc. containing metal or precious stones. M16.

8 Worthless ideas, writing, etc.; nonsense, rubbish; valueless matter, trash. Also as *interjection* expr. derision and in ***stuff and nonsense*** below. L16.

9 Money, cash (usu. with *the*). Also, stolen goods. *slang*. L18.

10 In various sports, the spin or work given to a ball in order to make it vary its course; the type of control which effects this. *N. Amer.* E20.

📖 **2a** J. UPDIKE The sumptuous wealth of stuffs—long dresses, velvet hangings. **3a** DONNE In all the Potters house, is there . . better stuffe then clay? **4a** MARVELL Having scarce stuffe enough for a letter. **b** R. K. NARAYAN He was of the stuff disciples are made of. L. MCMURTRY Jake ain't got the stuff to stand up to Call. **c** R. RENDELL What folly all this was, the stuff of nightmares and fantasies. **5a** R. LASSELS Some old painting, . . pitiful stuff. **6a** F. MORYSON Their boots . . shine with blacking stuffe. **b** D. PROFUMO Campbell was . . a devil for the hard stuff. **e** *Economist* Imported coal is unlikely to be as dear as British Coal's stuff. **g** M. KEANE A lot for Maman to do . . , hours of grown up stuff. I. MURDOCH I've had our stuff packed up . . ready to leave. **8** COLERIDGE Your art diplomatic is stuff:—no . . great man would negociate . . upon any such shallow principles.

Phrases: — **and stuff** *colloq.* — and other such useless or uninteresting matters. ***be made of sterner stuff***: see STERN *adjective*. ***bit of stuff***: see BIT *noun*² 6. ***doctor's stuff***: see DOCTOR *noun*. **do one's stuff** *colloq.* do what is required or expected of one; perform one's role. ***good stuff***: see sense 6b above. ***hot stuff***: see HOT *adjective*. †**in stuff** as regards the matter or substance. ***kitchen stuff***: see KITCHEN *noun, adjective, & verb*. ***know one's stuff***: see KNOW *verb*. **not give a stuff** *Austral.* & *NZ* (chiefly *slang*) not care the slightest amount. ***on the stuff***: see sense 6f above. ***rough stuff***: see ROUGH *adjective*. ***split stuff***: see SPLIT *adjective*. ***strut one's stuff***: see STRUT *verb*¹. **stuff and nonsense** rubbish; don't be ridiculous. ***stuff of household***: see sense 1f above. **that's the stuff**, **that's the stuff to give them**, **that's the stuff to give the troops** *colloq.* that is what is particularly appropriate to the situation, that is what is required. ***the hard stuff***: see sense 6b above. ***tough stuff***: see TOUGH *adjective*. ***white stuff***: see WHITE *adjective*.

Attrib. & comb.: In the senses 'made of stuff or woollen cloth', as ***stuff coat, stuff frock, stuff shawl***, etc., 'of or pertaining to the manufacture or sale of stuff or woollen cloth', as ***stuff-manufacturer, stuff-seller, stuff trade***, etc. Special combs., as **stuff gown** (**a**) a gown worn by a junior counsel who has not taken silk; (**b**) a junior counsel; **stuffover** *adjective & noun* (**a**) *adjective* (of a chair etc.) upholstered by having the material drawn over the frame of a fixed seat and secured beneath; (**b**) *noun* a stuffover seat.

■ **stuffless** *adjective* (*rare*) lacking in stuff or substance; insubstantial: L19.

stuff /stʌf/ *verb*¹. ME.

[Aphet. from Old French *estoffer* (mod. *étoffer*) equip, furnish, from Greek *stuphein* draw together, contract, rel. to *stupeion* oakum, Latin *stuppa*.]

1 *verb trans.* Orig. *spec.*, draw (knights) *together* in a tight formation. Later *gen.*, cram (a person) in a confined space; crowd (a number of people) *together*. ME.

†**2** *verb trans.* **a** Equip (a fortified town, a stronghold, an army, etc.) with men, arms, and stores; garrison (a town). ME–L17. ▸**b** Provide (troops) with support; reinforce; support, aid (a war). ME–M16.

†**3** *verb trans.* Supply (a person) with arms, provisions, money, etc. (foll. by *of, with*). Also, arm and equip (a soldier). ME–M17.

†**4** *verb trans.* **a** Equip or provide (a place) with goods, stock, inhabitants; stock with provisions or stores. LME–E17. ▸**b** Store (goods) in a receptacle or place; keep (animals) in a place. M16–E17.

†**5** *verb trans.* Give a lining to (a garment etc.). LME–L16.

6 *verb trans.* **a** Fill or line with material as a padding; distend or expand with padding; *esp.* fill (a cushion etc.) with stuffing to provide comfortable support. Also foll. by *out, up*. LME. ▸†**b** Of material: serve as padding or stuffing for. E16–E17. ▸†**c** Distend or expand as if by padding. L16–L17.

7 *verb trans.* Fill (poultry, hollowed vegetables, rolled meat, etc.) with a savoury or sweet mixture as a stuffing, esp. prior to cooking. Freq. as STUFFED *ppl adjective* 5. LME.

8 *verb trans.* **a** Pack (a receptacle) tightly, cram full; (foll. by *out*) fill (a receptacle) so full as to make it bulge. Freq. as STUFFED *ppl adjective* 1. LME. ▸**b** Crowd or cram (a vehicle, a room) *with* people. L16. ▸**c** Place fraudulent votes in (a ballot-box). *N. Amer.* M19. ▸**d** Pack or load (a freight container). *slang*. M20.

9 a *verb trans.* Fill (esp. oneself, one's stomach) to repletion with food. LME. ▸**b** *verb intrans.* Gorge oneself with food. E18. ▸**c** *verb trans.* Eat (food) greedily. Also foll. by *down*. M18.

10 *verb trans.* Orig., (of a bodily humour) clog, choke up (the body, its organs, etc.). Now, of catarrh etc.: block, cause stuffiness in (the head or nose). Now chiefly as STUFFED *ppl adjective* 4. LME.

11 *verb trans.* Fill out the skin of (an animal, bird, etc.) with material so as to resemble the living creature; *esp.* fill the skin of (an animal or bird) with materials as part of a taxidermic process to preserve it and restore it to its original form. M16.

12 *verb trans. fig.* ▸**a** Fill or pack (a literary text, speech, etc.) *with* facts, lies, protestations, etc.; fill (a person, a person's head or mind) *with* ideas, feelings, etc. M16. ▸**b** Hoax, cheat, (a person). *arch. slang*. M19.

13 a *verb trans.* Block up (an aperture, a cavity, etc.) by thrusting something tightly in; plug; fill up (a joint); fill (a tooth); *rare* fill in the inside of (a wall) with concrete or rubble. Also, (of a substance) fill *up* so as to block (an aperture). L16. ▸**b** Force or thrust (a thing) tightly into a receptacle or cavity; push, esp. clumsily or hastily. Freq. foll. by *in, into.* L16.

14 *verb trans.* **a** Dispose of as unwanted. Freq. in imprecations or expressions of contempt. *slang.* M20. ▸**b** Of a man: copulate with. *coarse slang.* M20.

📖 **1** J. LANGHORNE A number of people stuffed together . . in small huts. **6a** F. W. FARRAR Chewing in his agony the tow with which his mattress was stuffed. **7** E. DAVID A . . chicken, stuffed with its own liver. **8a** A. J. CRONIN A . . jacket, the side pockets stuffed to bursting point with pipe, handkerchief, an apple. **9a** *Homes & Gardens* We stuff ourselves silly on oysters, lobster, ham . . and mince pies. **c** S. ROE Estella stuffs cake. She forces it inside her. **12a** TENNYSON I . . stuff'd the boy with fears. F. HARRISON A book stuffed with curious facts. **13a** J. GILMOUR Stuffing the mouth of the hole with his white bonnet. **b** B. BAINBRIDGE He stuffed the letter into a drawer. **14a stuff it!** expr. rejection or disdain.

Comb.: **stuffbag**, **stuff sack** a bag, used esp. in camping, into which a sleeping bag, clothing, etc., can be stuffed or packed for ease of carrying or when not in use.

stuff /stʌf/ *verb*² *intrans. slang.* E20.
[Prob. back-form. from STUFFY *adjective*.]
Confine oneself in a stuffy atmosphere; remain cooped up indoors, esp. lazily or idly.

stuffage /ˈstʌfɪdʒ/ *noun.* M17.
[from STUFF *noun*, *verb*¹ + -AGE.]
1 The action of stuffing or filling something full; the material with which something is stuffed. M17.
†**2** Stuffiness (of the nose). Only in M18.

stuffed /stʌft/ *ppl adjective.* LME.
[from STUFF *verb*¹ + -ED¹.]
1 Orig., well stocked or equipped. Later, (of a receptacle) filled full, crammed. LME. ▸†**b** *fig.* Full, complete. *rare* (Shakes.). Only in E17.
2 Of a garment, cushion, etc.: filled out with padding. LME.
3 Of (the skin of) an animal, bird, etc.: filled with material so as to preserve it and resemble the original form of the living creature. L16.
4 Of the head, nose, etc.: blocked up, clogged, obstructed, esp. with catarrh etc. Freq. foll. by *up.* L16.
5 Of poultry, meat, vegetables, etc.: filled with a stuffing mixture, esp. prior to cooking. E18.

Special collocations & phrases: **get stuffed** *slang* go away! stop bothering me! rubbish! **stuffed monkey** a type of biscuit or cake made with almonds. **stuffed olive** a stoned (usu. green) olive filled with pimento. **stuffed owl** [ult. from Wordsworth] used *attrib.* with ref. to poetry which treats trivial or inconsequential subjects in a grandiose manner. **stuffed pepper** a dish of green or red pepper de-seeded and filled with tomatoes, rice, meat, etc., prior to cooking. **stuffed shirt** *colloq.* (orig. *US*) a person who is pompous and conservative, but usu. ineffectual. **stuffed vine leaves** an eastern (esp. Greek or Turkish) dish consisting of vine leaves wrapped round a savoury mixture of rice, onion, etc., prior to cooking.

stuffer /ˈstʌfə/ *noun.* E17.
[from STUFF *verb*¹ + -ER¹.]
1 A person who stuffs or fills something; a person whose occupation it is to stuff dead animals, upholstery, etc. E17.
2 A machine or implement used for stuffing. L19.
3 An advertising leaflet or similar material enclosed with other literature, esp. when sent by post. M20.
4 A person who smuggles drugs through Customs by concealing them in a bodily passage such as the anus or the vagina. *slang* (chiefly *US*). L20.

stuffing /ˈstʌfɪŋ/ *noun.* LME.
[from STUFF *verb*¹ + -ING¹.]
1 The action or result of STUFF *verb*¹; *esp.* (**a**) filling or cramming a thing or oneself with something; (**b**) blockage or obstruction of the throat, nose, etc., by catarrh; the sensation produced by this; (**c**) *N. Amer.* the placing of fraudulent votes into a ballot-box. LME.
2 a The material or padding used to stuff cushions, upholstery, etc. M16. ▸**b** A savoury or sweet mixture used to stuff poultry, rolled meat, vegetables, etc., esp. prior to cooking. M16. ▸**c** *fig.* Something perceived as or acting as filling or padding, *esp.* superfluous material intended to lengthen a book etc. M16.

📖 **1** SIR W. SCOTT Cowled gentry, that think of nothing but quaffing and stuffing! *Time* Defeated . . , he fought to prove ballot stuffing by the boss. **2a** J. P. DONLEAVY Armchairs distorted with lumps of stuffing and poking springs.

Phrases: **beat the stuffing out of**, **knock the stuffing out of** *colloq.* reduce to a state of weakness or feebleness; take the vigour or self-esteem out of. **put stuffing into** *colloq.* impart vigour or substance to; restore the self-confidence of. **take the stuffing out of** = *beat the stuffing out of* above.

Comb.: **stuffing-box** a chamber packed with fluid-tight elastic material, placed up against and around the hole through which a piston-rod or shaft passes, in order to prevent leakage.

stuffy /ˈstʌfi/ *adjective.* M16.
[from STUFF *noun* + -Y¹.]
†**1** Full of stuff or substance (*lit.* & *fig.*). M16–M17.
2 a Dull; lacking in freshness or interest. E19. ▸**b** (Of a room) poorly-ventilated, lacking fresh air; (of the atmosphere, weather, etc.) close, oppressive. Also, (of a person) habitually living in poorly-ventilated conditions. M19.
3 Angry, sulky. *US colloq.* E19.
4 Of a person, a person's nose, etc.: affected with a feeling of blockage or obstruction. M19.
5 Prim, conventional, strait-laced, pompous; boring. L19.

📖 **2a** MRS H. WARD Listening to a stuffy debate in the Senate. **b** M. DAS The compartment, which had no fans, became stuffy. **4** E. BOWEN She threw her cigarette out . . —to smoke more than one after breakfast made her feel stuffy. **5** B. BETTELHEIM Rejecting what we considered the stuffy bourgeois prejudices about sex.

■ **stuffily** *adverb* in a stuffy manner; *fig.* in a manner that lacks freshness or interest: L19. **stuffiness** *noun* the quality of being stuffy; *spec.* (**a**) the condition of lacking ventilation or fresh air; (**b**) a state or feeling of blockage and obstruction in the throat or nose; (**c**) *fig.* a conventional, pompous, or strait-laced attitude: E17.

stug /stʌg/ *verb & noun. Scot.* Also **stog** /stɒg/. L16.
[Origin uncertain: perh. alt. of STOCK *noun*².]
▶ **A** *verb trans.* Infl. **-gg-**. Stab, pierce with a pointed weapon or tool. L16.
▶ **B** *noun.* **1** A stab, a thrust; a prick, a puncture. L16.
2 CURLING. A chance shot which reaches its mark. E19.

stuggy /ˈstʌgi/ *adjective. Scot. & dial.* M19.
[Origin unkn.]
Stocky, thickset; sturdy.

Stuka /ˈstuːkə, ˈʃ-/ *noun & verb.* M20.
[Abbreviation of German *Sturzkampfflugzeug* dive-bomber.]
▶ **A** *noun.* A type of German dive-bomber (the Junkers Ju 87), esp. as used in the war of 1939–45. M20.

📖 *attrib.*: A. MACLEAN Banshee shrieking as the Stuka pilots switched on their sirens.

▶ **B** *verb trans.* In *pass.* Be attacked by a Stuka or Stukas. M20.

stukach /stuˈkatʃ/ *noun. slang.* Pl. **-i** /-i/. M20.
[Russian.]
Esp. in the former Soviet Union: an informer, a stool-pigeon.

stull /stʌl/ *noun*¹. *obsolete* exc. *dial.* ME.
[Origin uncertain: cf. German dial. *Stollen* slice of bread.]
A large piece or hunk of something edible.

stull /stʌl/ *noun*². L18.
[Perh. from German *Stollen* support, prop. Cf. next.]
A platform or framework of timber in a mine covered with boards to support miners whilst working or to carry ore or rubbish. Also, a framework of boards to protect miners from falling debris.

stulm /stʌlm/ *noun.* L17.
[Perh. from German *Stolln*, *Stollen*. Cf. prec.]
An adit or level in a mine.

stultification /ˌstʌltɪfɪˈkeɪʃ(ə)n/ *noun.* M19.
[from STULTIFY: see -FICATION.]
The action of stultifying someone or something; the state of being stultified; an instance of this.

stultificatory /ˌstʌltɪfɪˈkeɪt(ə)ri/ *adjective.* M20.
[from prec.: see -ORY².]
Stultifying.

stultify /ˈstʌltɪfʌɪ/ *verb trans.* M18.
[Late Latin *stultificare*, from Latin *stultus* foolish, fool: see -FY.]
1 LAW. Allege or prove to be insane or of unsound mind, esp. in order to evade some responsibility. Chiefly *refl.* M18.
2 Cause to be or appear foolish, ridiculous, or absurdly inconsistent; reduce to foolishness or absurdity. E19.
3 Make useless, ineffective, or futile, esp. as a result of tedious routine; deprive of freedom of action or originality; frustrate, stifle, enervate, neutralize, negate. M19.

📖 **2** C. KINGSLEY I, to stultify my book for the sake of popularity, money! **3** *Economist* Curiosity and originality are stultified.

■ **stultifier** *noun* M19. **stultifying** *ppl adjective* that stultifies someone or something; frustrating, stifling, enervating: E19. **stultifyingly** *adverb* M20.

stultiloquence /stʌlˈtɪləkwəns/ *noun.* E18.
[Latin *stultiloquentia*, from *stultiloquus*, from *stultus* foolish + *loquus* that speaks: see -ENCE.]
Foolish or senseless talk, babble, nonsense.
■ **stultiloquent** *adjective* (*rare*) talking foolishly M19.

stultiloquy /stʌlˈtɪləkwi/ *noun. rare.* M17.
[Latin *stultiloquium*, from *stultiloquus*: see prec.]
An instance of speaking foolishly, a foolish babbling.

stum /stʌm/ *noun.* M17.
[Dutch *stom* use as noun of *stom* dumb.]
1 Unfermented or partly fermented grape juice, must; *esp.* must in which the fermentation has been prevented or checked by fumigation with sulphur. M17. ▸**b** Must as used for renewing the fermentation of flat wines. Now *rare* or *obsolete.* L17.
2 Flat wine renewed by the addition of stum. Now *rare* or *obsolete.* M17.

📖 **1b** *fig.*: DRYDEN Thy bellowing Renegado Priests, That . . with thy Stumm ferment their fainting Cause.

stum /stʌm/ *verb trans.* Infl. **-mm-**. M17.
[Dutch *stommen*, formed as prec.]
1 Renew the fermentation of (wine) by adding stum. M17.
2 Fumigate (a cask) with burning sulphur, in order to prevent the contained liquor from fermenting; prevent or check the fermentation of (new wine) by fumigation in a cask. L18.

📖 **1** *fig.*: J. OLDHAM The poor Drunkard, when Wine stums his brains.

stuma *noun* see STUMER.

stumble /ˈstʌmb(ə)l/ *verb & noun.* ME.
[from Old Norse word repr. by Norwegian, Danish dial. *stumle*, Swedish dial. *stumla*, parallel to synon. *stumra*, from Germanic base also of STAMMER *verb*.]
▶ **A** *verb.* **1** *verb intrans.* Lurch forward or have a partial fall as a result of missing one's footing, catching one's foot on an obstacle, etc. Also foll. by *at, over.* ME. ▸**b** Knock or jostle *against* involuntarily. LME. ▸**c** Of a thing: strike unexpectedly *on. rare.* E18.
2 *verb intrans. fig.* ▸**a** Lapse or falter morally. Now *rare.* ME. ▸**b** Make a slip in speech or action; blunder through inadvertence or unpreparedness. *obsolete* exc. as passing into sense 4b. LME. ▸**c** Take offence; meet with a stumbling-block or obstacle to belief. Usu. foll. by *at.* E16. ▸**d** Foll. by *(up)on, (in)to, across*: find or encounter by chance and unexpectedly; come across. M16.
3 *verb trans.* †**a** Cause to trip up, bring to the ground, overthrow, (*lit.* & *fig.*). ME–M17. ▸**b** Puzzle, perplex; give pause or offence to. Now *rare.* E17. ▸†**c** Shake (a resolve, an opinion). E–L17.
4 *verb intrans.* Walk unsteadily and with frequent stumbles. Freq. foll. by *along, around.* ME. ▸**b** *fig.* Act in a blundering or hesitating manner; *esp.* make a mistake or repeated mistakes in speaking. LME.

📖 **1** E. WAUGH Cables over which they stumbled painfully. S. CHITTY The ground was rough and several times she stumbled into holes. **stumble at the threshold**, **stumble on the threshold** (chiefly *fig.*) fail or meet with a setback or obstacle at the beginning of an enterprise. **b** J. M. COETZEE A young sentry stumbles against me. **2a** THACKERAY They sinned and stumbled . . with debt, with drink. **c** N. BACON In case the Prelacy for England should stumble at the Supremacy of Rome. **d** T. MALLON Pepys's knack for stumbling upon psychological truths. N. HERMAN The fishing village we had stumbled upon. **3b** W. G. COLLINGWOOD The proud possessor of a cut-and-dry creed will be stumbled by this new milestone. **4** G. KEILLOR Dad . . stumbles around and breaks things. **b** *Precision Marketing* The Post Office . . continues to stumble from one . . disaster to another. B. A. MASON The announcer seemed shocked. He stumbled over his words.

Comb.: **stumbling-block** (**a**) *rare* a physical obstacle; (**b**) an instance of moral faltering or stumbling; (**c**) an obstacle to belief, understanding, etc.; a circumstance giving rise to difficulty, hindering progress, or impeding the implementation of something.

▶ **B** *noun.* The action or an act of stumbling; a partial fall; a blunder, a slip. M16.

📖 *Scotsman* The significant stumble made by the right hon. gentleman in his reply. ELLIS PETERS They followed . . Roscelin going before . . to prevent a possible stumble.

■ **stumbler** *noun* a person who or thing which stumbles; *esp.* a horse that is prone to stumbling: ME. **stumblingly** *adverb* in a stumbling manner L16. **stumbly** *adjective* (*rare*) (**a**) prone to stumbling; (**b**) apt to cause stumbling: L19.

stumblebum /ˈstʌmb(ə)lbʌm/ *noun. colloq.* (chiefly *US*). M20.
[from STUMBLE *verb* + BUM *noun*².]
A worthless, clumsy, or inept person; a tramp; a drunkard.

📖 *fig.* (*attrib.*): B. WOLFE It made its slapstick stumblebum way back and forth.

stumer /ˈstjuːmə/ *noun. slang.* In sense 3 also **stuma**. L19.
[Origin unkn.]
1 a A forged or worthless cheque; a counterfeit banknote or coin. Also, a fraud, a sham. L19. ▸**b** A person who has lost all his or her money, esp. as a result of gambling etc. Freq. in ***come a stumer*** below. *Austral.* Now *rare* or *obsolete.* L19.
2 A worthless person or thing; a failure. L19.
3 A state of anger, agitation, or worry. Chiefly *Austral.* M20.

📖 **1a** *Listener* The . . lead in The Times . . was a stumer—that NATO headquarters was moving. *attrib.*: L. LAMB The man who gave you a stumer cheque. **b come a stumer** be ruined; crash financially, esp. after losing a bet. **2** P. G. WODEHOUSE The agony of having put his . . all on a stumer that hadn't finished.

stumm *adjective & verb* var. of SHTOOM.

stummer /ˈstʌmə/ *verb intrans. obsolete* exc. *dial.* ME.
[from Old Norse *stumra*: see STUMBLE.]
Stumble (*lit.* & *fig.*).

stummick /ˈstʌmɪk/ *noun. non-standard.* L19.
[Repr. a pronunc.]
The stomach.

stump /stʌmp/ *noun*[1]. ME.
[Middle Low German *stump*, *stumpe*, Middle & mod. Dutch *stomp* = Old High German, German *Stumpf*.]
1 a The part remaining when a limb or other part of the body is amputated or severed. ME. ▸**b** A leg. *joc.* Chiefly in ***stir one's stumps*** below. LME. ▸**c** A limb or member that is rudimentary or has the appearance of being amputated or mutilated. M16. ▸**d** A wooden leg. Now *rare*. L17.
2 a The projecting portion of the trunk of a felled or fallen tree that remains fixed in the ground; a standing tree-trunk from which the upper part and the branches have been cut or broken off. LME. ▸**b** The base of a growing tree. Chiefly in ***buy on the stump*** below. L19.
3 a The part of a broken tooth left in the gum. LME. ▸**b** A thing (e.g. a pencil or a candle) that has been worn down or reduced to a small part of its original length. E16. ▸**c** A docked tail. M16. ▸**d** NAUTICAL. The lower portion of a mast when the upper part has been broken off or shot away. Also = ***stump mast*** below. E18. ▸**e** The remains of a haystack of which most has been cut away. *dial.* L18. ▸**f** The remaining portion of a leaf cut out of a book; the counterfoil or stub of a cheque. L19.
†**4** A broken-off end of something. Also, a splinter. *rare.* LME–E17.
5 A stake. Chiefly in ***pull up one's stumps*** below. M16.
6 a In *pl.* & (*rare*) *sing.* Stubble, esp. of hair cut close to the skin. L16. ▸**b** The stalk of a plant (esp. cabbage) when the leaves are removed. E19.
7 A stupid person, a blockhead; a short stocky person. Now chiefly *Scot.* L16.
8 A stringed instrument of the lute family, probably of a similar type to the cittern. *obsolete* exc. *Hist.* E17.
9 †**a** A peak, a summit. Only in M17. ▸**b** A post, a short pillar not supporting anything. Also, a pillar of coal in a mine with a passageway on either side. L17.
10 Orig., the stump of a tree used as a stand or platform for a speaker to address a meeting. Now, a place or an occasion of political speech-making or campaigning. Freq. in ***go on the stump*** below. Orig. *US.* E18.
11 CRICKET. **a** Each of the three (formerly two) uprights which, with the bails laid on the top of them, form a wicket. M18. ▸**b** An act of stumping a batsman out. Also ***stump-out***. M19. ▸**c** In *pl.* Close of play, when stumps are drawn. Chiefly *Austral.* M20.
12 Money. *arch. slang.* E19.
13 In full ***stump bed***, ***stump bedstead***. A bedstead without posts. E19.
14 A projecting stud in a lock or hinge. E19.
15 An animal or creature of a stumpy shape or with a stumpy tail; *esp.* (*dial.*) a stoat. M19.

> 📖 **1a** B. ENGLAND Their finger-nails went, shredded and torn away, to leave their fingers bleeding stumps. **c** P. P. CARPENTER The eyes are on stumps at the base of the tentacles. **2a** I. MURDOCH Stumps declared where . . elms had once stood. **3b** *fig.*: J. RABAN People . . dwindled . . to rudimentary stumps of identity. **10** J. CARROLL On the stump he was magnificent, striking great poses.

Phrases: **black stump** (*Austral.*) the last outpost of civilization; ***beyond the black stump***, in the back of beyond. **buy on the stump** buy (timber) before it has been cut. **draw stumps**, **draw the stumps** CRICKET pull up the stumps, as a sign of the discontinuance of play or of the termination of a match or game. **fight to the stumps** *fig.* fight on to the bitter end. **go on the stump** go about the country making political speeches; campaign as a political candidate or in support of a cause. **pull up one's stumps** †(*a*) break camp, resume a march; (*b*) leave one's home, job, or settled existence. **stir one's stumps** (*a*) move briskly, become busy or active; †(*b*) do one's duty zealously. **stump and rump** *Scot.* & *dial.* totally, completely. **up a stump** *colloq.* (chiefly *US*) perplexed, in difficulties. **wear to the stumps** (now *rare*) wear out, wear down completely (chiefly *fig.*).

Attrib. & comb.: In the senses 'of or pertaining to the stump of a tree', as ***stump fence***, ***stump land***, ***stump wood***, etc., 'of or pertaining to political speech-making or campaigning', as ***stump-orator***, ***stump speaker***, ***stump speech***, etc. Special combs., as ***stump bed***, ***stump bedstead***: see sense 13 above; **stump cricket** = SNOB *noun*[2]; **stump embroidery** = ***stump work*** below; **stump-end** (*a*) the end of the stump of a tail; (*b*) the remnant of a cheque-book containing the counterfoils or stubs; **stump-grubber** a machine used to excavate the stumps of trees after felling; **stump-grubbing** the excavation of tree stumps by manual or mechanical means; **stump-jump** *adjective* & *noun* (*Austral.*) (designating) a kind of plough by which land can be ploughed without clearing it of tree stumps; **stump jumper** *US colloq.* a person from a rural area, a hillbilly; **stump-machine** *US* = ***stump grubber*** above; **stump mast** NAUTICAL a lower mast without a top or platform near the head; **stump plant** a cutting consisting of a short cut-back stem and roots which may or may not be pruned; **stump water** *US* the rainwater which collects in the stumps of hollow trees, associated esp. with folk remedies and charms; **stump word** a word formed by abbreviating a single longer one, usu. to a single opening syllable or the minimum necessary for understanding; **stump-work** *noun* & *adjective* (made of) a type of raised embroidery popular between the 15th and 17th cents. and characterized by elaborate designs padded with wool or hair.
■ **stumpish** *adjective* of the nature or character of a stump E17.

stump /stʌmp/ *noun*[2]. L18.
[Prob. from French *estompe*, Dutch *stomp* (see prec.), infl. by prec.]
A short tapered rod or cylinder with a blunt point at each end usu. of rubber or of tightly rolled paper or soft leather, used for softening the edges of a pencil or crayon drawing or to blend the lines of shading so as to produce a uniform tint. Also called ***tortillon***.

stump /stʌmp/ *noun*[3]. L18.
[from STUMP *verb*[1].]
1 A heavy tread or gait, as of a person who is lame or has a wooden leg. L18.
2 A dare, a challenge to undertake something difficult or dangerous. *US colloq.* M19.

> 📖 **1** S. FOOTE I hear his stump on the stairs.

stump /stʌmp/ *adjective*. L16.
[Partly from attrib. use of STUMP *noun*[1]; perh. partly from Dutch, Low German *stomp*.]
1 Of a limb: mutilated, amputated; malformed. L16.
2 Worn down to a stump. *rare.* E17.
Special collocations & comb.: **stump-foot** (a person with) a club foot. **stump leg**: without a foot or with a club foot. **stumpnose** *S. Afr.* = STOMPNEUS. **stump-tail** (*a*) a stump-tailed dog; (*b*) *Austral.* a stump-tailed lizard (skink), *Trachydosaurus rugosus*. **stump-tailed** *adjective* having a very short tail.

stump /stʌmp/ *verb*[1]. ME.
[from STUMP *noun*[1].]
†**1** *verb intrans.* Stumble over an obstacle. Also, walk stumblingly. ME–E17.
2 *verb trans.* Reduce to a stump; truncate, mutilate. Also (now chiefly *Scot.*), stunt, dwarf. L16.
3 a *verb intrans.* & (*rare*) *trans.* Walk heavily, clumsily, or noisily along (a street etc.), as if with a wooden leg. Freq. foll. by *up*, *off*, *along*, etc. E17. ▸**b** *verb intrans.* & *trans.* (with *it*). Go on foot; be off, go away. *slang.* E19. ▸**c** *verb intrans.* Strike the floor with a staff etc. in walking. *rare.* L19.
†**4** *verb intrans.* & *trans.* Brag (about), boast (of). *rare.* E–L18.
5 *verb trans.* CRICKET. Esp. of a wicket-keeper: put (a batsman) out by dislodging a bail or knocking down a stump with the ball held in the hand, while the batsman is out of the crease. Also foll. by *out*. M18.
6 *verb trans.* Challenge or dare (a person) to undertake something difficult or dangerous. *US colloq.* M18.
7 *verb trans.* Dig up (a tree etc.) by the roots. Chiefly *US* & *Austral.* L18.
8 *verb trans.* Remove the stumps from (land). L18.
9 *verb intrans.* & *trans.* Pay up (money). E19.
10 *verb trans.* Make penniless; in *pass.*, be completely penniless. *slang.* E19.
11 *verb trans.* **a** Stub (a toe) against something. *US colloq.* E19. ▸**b** Stub out (a cigarette). Freq. foll. by *out*. E20.
12 *verb trans.* Cause to be at a loss; confront with an insuperable difficulty; baffle, puzzle. Freq. as ***stumped*** *ppl adjective*. Orig. *US.* E19.
13 *verb intrans.* & *trans.* (freq. with *it*). Travel over (a district) making speeches esp. for an election campaign; give a political address to (a meeting etc.). Chiefly *US.* M19.

> 📖 **2** M. S. GATTY The mortuary crosses were cut down, or stumped, in our churchyards. **3a** P. LIVELY She stumped up the path . . like a tough little pony. **12** C. BEDE That beastly Euclid altogether stumps me. *Successful Slimming* You're stumped for inspiration before you've even started. J. K. ROWLING *Powdered root of what to an infusion of what?* Harry glanced at Ron, who looked as stumped as he was. **13** W. GOLDING He stumped the country for the Labour Party. *Time* Taylor . . has been stumping for Dalton.

With adverbs in specialized senses: **stump up** (*a*) *verb phr. trans.* dig up (a tree etc.) by the roots; (*b*) *verb phr. trans.* wear out or exhaust (esp. a horse) by excessive strain; (*c*) *verb phr. trans.* & *intrans.* (*colloq.*) pay, come forward with, (money required).
■ **stumping** *verbal noun* the action of the verb; an instance of this: E19.

stump /stʌmp/ *verb*[2] *trans.* E19.
[from STUMP *noun*[2], after French *estomper*.]
Soften the edges of (a drawing) or blend (a line) with a stump or blunted shading stick.

stump /stʌmp/ *adverb*. L17.
[from STUMP *verb*[1].]
With a stump or a heavy tread. Usu. redupl.

> 📖 G. BORROW She heard . . a horse coming stump, stump, up to the door.

stumpage /ˈstʌmpɪdʒ/ *noun. N. Amer.* M19.
[from STUMP *noun*[1] + -AGE.]
1 The price paid for standing timber. Also, a tax charged in parts of the United States for the privilege of cutting timber on State lands. M19.
2 Standing timber considered with reference to its quantity or marketable value. M19.

stumper /ˈstʌmpə/ *noun*. M18.
[from STUMP *verb*[1] + -ER[1].]
1 CRICKET. A wicket-keeper. M18.
2 A person employed or skilled in stumping trees. *rare.* E19.
3 A question, a problem, etc., that stumps or puzzles one. E19.
4 A stump speaker. *US.* M19.
5 A device, attached to a tractor or similar vehicle, for uprooting tree stumps; a stump-grubber. M20.

stumpie /ˈstʌmpi/ *noun. Scot.* L18.
[from STUMP *noun*[1] + -IE.]
1 The stump of a quill pen. *joc.* L18.
2 A person with a stumpy or stocky figure. Also, a small child. E19.

stumpy /ˈstʌmpi/ *noun*. E19.
[from STUMP *noun*[1] + -Y[6].]
1 Money. *arch. slang.* E19.
2 A spritsail barge. L19.

stumpy /ˈstʌmpi/ *adjective*. E17.
[from STUMP *noun*[1] + -Y[1].]
1 Like a stump; short and thick, stocky. Formerly also, (of grass, stubble, etc.) full of stumps or short hard stalks. E17.
2 Of ground: full of tree stumps. *US.* L17.
3 Worn down to a stump. L18.

> 📖 **1** A. J. C. HARE The stumpy spire of the church could be seen. P. G. WODEHOUSE Men who are stumpy and about twenty pounds overweight. **3** W. HENRY 'Company!' groaned Doc, gritting his stumpy teeth.

■ **stumpily** *adverb* L19. **stumpiness** *noun* L19.

stun /stʌn/ *verb* & *noun*. ME.
[Aphet. from Old French *estoner* (mod. *étonner*) ASTONE.]
▶ **A** *verb*. Infl. **-nn-**.
1 *verb trans.* Render unconscious or unable to move by a blow, a fall, etc.; knock senseless. ME.
2 *verb trans.* Daze or astound due to something shocking, unbelievable or unexpected; amaze. ME.
3 *verb trans.* Of a sound: stupefy, bewilder; deafen temporarily. E17.
4 a *verb trans.* Strike or loosen the surface of (stone etc.) so as to cause splintering or exfoliation. Also, scratch or tear (a surface) in sawing. L17. ▸**b** *verb intrans.* Of stone etc.: exfoliate, peel off in splinters or thin layers. M19.

> 📖 **1** R. GRAVES Soldiers had waylaid Postumus . . , stunned him with a sandbag . . , and carried him off. **2** M. GARDINER I read of Louis' death. I was stunned. **3** *Quarterly Review* The ear is stunned by the . . roar of the Falls.

Comb.: **stun gas** a gas that incapacitates by causing temporary confusion and disorientation; **stun grenade** a grenade that stuns through its sound and flash without causing serious injury; **stun gun** a gun which stuns through an electric shock, ultrasound, etc., without causing serious injury.
▶ **B** *noun*. **1** The act of stunning or dazing someone; a stunning effect; the condition of being stunned. E18.
2 A flaw on the surface of a piece of stone. *rare.* M19.

> 📖 **1** J. RUSKIN In the first stun of our astonishment.

■ **stunned** *ppl adjective* (*a*) that has been stunned; dazed; astounded, bewildered; (*b*) *Austral.* & *NZ slang* drunk (cf. STUNG *ppl adjective* 2): M18.

Stundist /ˈstʊndɪst, ˈʃtʊn-/ *noun* & *adjective*. L19.
[Russian *shtundist* from German *Stunde* hour (said to be used by the German settlers as the name for their religious meetings): see -IST.]
▶ **A** *noun*. A member of a large Evangelical sect which arose among the peasantry of South Russia about 1860, as a result of contact with German Protestant settlers, and in opposition to the doctrine and authority of the Russian Orthodox Church. L19.
▶ **B** *attrib.* or as *adjective*. Of or pertaining to the Stundists or their doctrine or practices. L19.
■ **Stundism** *noun* (*rare*) the doctrine or practices of the Stundists L19.

stung /stʌŋ/ *ppl adjective*. ME.
[pa. pple of STING *verb*.]
1 Wounded or hurt by a sting (*lit.* & *fig.*). ME.
2 Drunk. Cf. STUNNED (b). *Austral. slang.* E20.

stung *verb pa. t.* & *pple*: see STING *verb*.

stunk *noun* see STONK.

stunk *verb pa. t.* & *pple*: see STINK *verb*.

stunkard /ˈstʌŋkəd/ *adjective. Scot.* M17.
[Origin unkn.]
Sulky, sullen.

stunner /ˈstʌnə/ *noun*. E19.
[from STUN *verb* + -ER[1].]
1 A thing that stuns or dazes someone or something; an amazing or astounding thing. E19.
2 A person or thing of extraordinary attractiveness or excellence; *esp.* a very attractive woman or girl. Cf. KNOCKER 3. *colloq.* M19.

📖 **1** *Fortune* A stunner when unions . . show solidarity with the boss. **2** ALBERT SMITH Watch the girl, Sir Frederick. Isn't she a stunner?

stunning /ˈstʌnɪŋ/ *verbal noun.* ME.
[from STUN *verb* + -ING¹.]
The action of STUN *verb*; the state of being stunned; *spec.* exfoliation or peeling away of a thin layer of stone.

stunning /ˈstʌnɪŋ/ *adjective.* M17.
[from STUN *verb* + -ING².]
1 That stuns someone; dazing, astounding; stupefying, deafening. M17.
2 Excellent, splendid; extremely attractive or impressive. *colloq.* M19.

📖 **1** D. DUNNETT A hurricane can punish one area badly . . . The noise is stunning. **2** *Boardroom* It . . has a stunning river view.

■ **stunningly** *adverb* E19.

stunpoll /ˈstʌnpəʊl/ *noun. dial.* L18.
[Perh. from STONE *noun* + POLL *noun*¹.]
A dolt, a blockhead.

stunsail /ˈstʌns(ə)l/ *noun.* Also **stuns'l.** M18.
[Contr.]
NAUTICAL. = STUDDING-SAIL.

stunt /stʌnt/ *noun*¹. E18.
[from STUNT *verb*¹.]
1 A person who or animal which has been hindered from attaining full growth or development. E18.
2 A check on growth. Also, a state of arrested growth or development. L18.
3 A fit of sulkiness or obstinacy. Chiefly in ***take stunt***, ***take the stunt***, become sulky or obstinate. *dial.* M19.
■ **stunty** *adjective* (*a*) stunted in growth, short in stature; (*b*) *dial.* sulky, obstinate; curt, blunt: E19.

stunt /stʌnt/ *noun*². L19.
[Origin unkn.; first used in US college slang.]
1 An act notable or impressive on account of the skill, strength, daring, etc., required to perform it, an exciting or dangerous feat or trick, an exploit; a theatrical turn; a daring aerobatic manoeuvre; a prescribed item or event in an athletic competition or display. Also, something intended to gain an effect or win an advantage; *spec.* (*a*) *Military slang* an attack or advance; (*b*) an advertising or promotional gimmick, a device, event, etc., designed to attract attention or publicity. L19.
2 A stint, a task, an exercise. Orig. *US.* L19.
3 *gen.* An act; a display of pretended feeling or emotion, a pretence. E20.

📖 **1** C. A. LINDBERGH We did a few stunts over the fair-grounds to get everyone's attention. *Sunday Times* His bisexuality . . was attracting sensational publicity. How much . . was simply a stunt? N. MAILER Houdini had pulled his favourite stunt of escaping from a sealed casket underwater. **2** G. H. LORIMER A twelve-hour stunt of making all the beds you've mussed. **3** M. FORSTER Paula doing her Florence Nightingale stunt.

Comb.: **stunt man**, **stunt woman**: employed to perform dangerous feats, esp. as a stand-in for a film actor.
■ **stunty** *adjective* having the character of a stunt; attention-seeking; gimmicky: L20.

stunt /stʌnt/ *adjective. obsolete* exc. *dial.* OE.
[Corresp. to Middle High German *stunz*, Old Norse *stuttr* short, from Germanic: perh. from base of STUMP *noun*¹.]
†**1** Foolish, stupid. OE–ME.
2 Obstinate, stubborn; rudely or angrily curt or blunt. ME.
3 Stunted in growth; stumpy, short and thick. L18.
4 Of a turn, bend, etc.: abrupt. *rare.* M19.
Comb.: **stunt-head** the vertical timbered end of a trench which has been excavated for the purpose of laying a sewer or a water main.
■ **stuntness** *noun* †(*a*) foolishness, stupidity; (*b*) *rare* abrupt brevity: OE.

stunt /stʌnt/ *verb*¹. L16.
[from prec. Cf. STINT *verb*.]
†**1** *verb trans.* Irritate, provoke to anger. Also, bring to an abrupt halt; nonplus. L16–M17.
2 *verb trans.* Check the growth or development of; dwarf; cramp. M17.
†**3** *verb intrans.* Become arrested in growth. Only in 18.
4 *verb intrans.* Become sullen or sulky. *dial.* L19.

📖 **2** J. M. COETZEE Trees . . were puny, stunted by the wind. *fig.*: M. MEYER Passionate women stunted and inhibited by the conventions of their time.

stunt /stʌnt/ *verb*². E20.
[from STUNT *noun*².]
1 *verb intrans.* Perform stunts, esp. aerobatics or other daring manoeuvres. E20.
2 *verb trans.* Use (an aeroplane etc.) for the performance of stunts. E20.

📖 **1** *Standard* They need to learn to . . stunt on BMX bikes for a new play. **2** C. A. LINDBERGH You can't stunt 'em . . no rolls or loops.

■ **stunter** *noun* E20.

stunted /ˈstʌntɪd/ *ppl adjective.* M17.
[from STUNT *verb*¹ + -ED¹.]
1 Checked in growth or development; dwarf; (of growth) checked, arrested. M17.
2 Of a thing: truncated, shortened; disproportionately short. Formerly also, worn down. E18.

📖 **1** B. BAINBRIDGE A stunted rambling rose that never bloomed. *fig.*: H. KUSHNER Without . . spiritual nourishment, our souls remain stunted and undeveloped.

■ **stuntedly** *adverb* E20. **stuntedness** *noun* M18.

stupa /ˈstuːpə/ *noun.* L19.
[Sanskrit *stūpa*. Cf. TOPE *noun*³.]
A round usu. domed structure erected as a Buddhist shrine.

stupe /stjuːp/ *noun*¹ & *verb.* LME.
[Latin *stup(p)a* tow from Greek *stup(p)ē*.]
▶**A** *noun.* A piece of tow, flannel, lint, etc., moistened with hot medicated liquid as a fomentation. LME.
▶**B** *verb trans.* †**1** Moisten (lint etc.) in hot liquid to form a stupe. *rare.* Only in M16.
2 Treat with a stupe. L17.

stupe /stjuːp/ *noun*². *colloq.* (now chiefly *dial.*). M18.
[Abbreviation of STUPID.]
A stupid person, a fool.

stupefacient /stjuːpɪˈfeɪʃ(ə)nt/ *adjective.* Long *rare.* M17.
[Latin *stupefacient-* pres. ppl stem of *stupefacere* STUPEFY: see -FACIENT.]
Chiefly *MEDICINE.* Stupefying, producing stupor.

stupefaction /stjuːpɪˈfakʃ(ə)n/ *noun.* LME.
[French *stupéfaction* from medieval Latin *stupefactio(n-)*, from Latin *stupefacere* STUPEFY: see -FACTION.]
The state of being stupefied; numbness, torpor, insensibility; overwhelming consternation; astonishment.

📖 DICKENS The pupils . . fell into a state of waking stupefaction. P. PEARCE He stood dumbfounded. He was roused from his stupefaction by the chill. C. HARMAN An abcess on the brain . . left him subject to comas and stupefaction.

stupefactive /stjuːpɪˈfaktɪv/ *adjective & noun.* Now *rare* or *obsolete.* LME.
[French *stupéfactif*, *-ive* or medieval Latin *stupefactivus*, formed as prec.: see -IVE.]
MEDICINE. ▶**A** *adjective.* Having the property of producing stupor or insensibility. LME.
▶†**B** *noun.* A stupefactive medicine. LME–M17.

stupefy /ˈstjuːpɪfʌɪ/ *verb.* Also (now *rare*) **-pify.** LME.
[French *stupéfier* from Latin *stupefacere* from *stupere*: see STUPID, -FY.]
1 *verb trans.* **a** Make stupid, torpid, or insensible; numb, deaden. LME. ▸**b** Stun with amazement, fear, etc.; astound. L16.
2 *verb intrans.* Become stupid, torpid, or insensible. Now *rare* or *obsolete.* E17.

📖 **1** M. O. W. OLIPHANT Anxiety stupefied instead of quickening his senses. P. G. WODEHOUSE The temptation to stupefy himself with drink was almost irresistible.

■ **stupefied** *adjective* that has been stupefied; in a state of stupefaction: M17. **stupefier** *noun* (now *rare*) a thing, esp. a medicine, that causes stupor L17. **stupefyingly** *adverb* in a manner or to an extent that stupefies a person M20.

stupendous /stjuːˈpɛndəs/ *adjective.* Also (earlier) †**-dious** /-dɪəs/. M16.
[Latin *stupendus* gerundive of *stupere*: see STUPID, -OUS. Cf. *horrendous*, *tremendous*.]
Amazing, astounding; remarkable; enormous; *colloq.* excellent, most pleasing, very considerable or substantial.

📖 E. DOWSON The most stupendous cold which has ever occurred to me. H. JAMES I had to make . . the most stupendous effort not to cry.

■ †**stupend** *adjective* = STUPENDOUS E17–M19. **stupendously** *adverb* M17. **stupendousness** *noun* M17.

stupent /ˈstjuːp(ə)nt/ *adjective. literary.* M19.
[Latin *stupent-* pres. ppl stem of *stupere*: see STUPID, -ENT.]
Stupefied.

stupeous /ˈstjuːpɪəs/ *adjective.* E19.
[from Latin *stup(p)eus* made of tow, from *stup(p)a* STUPE *noun*¹: see -OUS.]
ZOOLOGY & BOTANY. Having or covered with matted or tufted hairs or filaments.

stupid /ˈstjuːpɪd/ *adjective & noun.* M16.
[French *stupide* or Latin *stupidus*, from *stupere* be annoyed (at), be stunned or numbed: see -ID¹.]
▶**A** *adjective.* **1** Of a person: unintelligent, slow-witted; obtuse, foolish. M16. ▸**b** Of a quality, action, idea, etc.: silly, indicating folly or lack of understanding; typical of a stupid person. E17.
2 Having one's faculties dulled; stupefied; stunned, esp. with surprise, grief, etc. M16. ▸**b** Apathetic; indifferent, insensitive; characterized by stupor or insensibility, lethargic. Now *rare.* E17.
†**3** Of an inanimate object: incapable of or lacking sensation or consciousness. E17–M18.
4 Uninteresting, tiresome, boring. Also as a general term of disparagement. Now chiefly *colloq.* L18.
5 Obstinate, stubborn. *north.* L18.

📖 **1** JAS. HOGG 'What a stupid idiot I was!' exclaimed Wat. A. MACRAE Bob . . was not stupid where his own interests were concerned. **b** S. PATRICK Let us not . . persist in such a stupid error. L. DEIGHTON It was stupid to drink strong coffee so late at night. **2** SHAKES. *Wint. T.* Is not your father incapable Of reasonable affairs? Is he not stupid with age . . ? TENNYSON Enid could not say one tender word She felt so . . stupid at the heart. **b** POPE No tear had pow'r to flow, Fix'd in a stupid lethargy of woe. **4** E. O'NEILL You . . with your college education . . always reading your stupid books instead of working.

▶**B** *noun.* A stupid person. *colloq.* E18.
■ **stupidish** *adjective* E19. **stupidly** *adverb* (*a*) unintelligently, foolishly, in a manner indicative of stupidity; (*b*) (now *rare*) in a stupor; †(*c*) *rare* as a result of stupefaction: E17. **stupidness** *noun* (*rare*) E17.

stupidity /stjuːˈpɪdɪti/ *noun.* M16.
[French *stupidité* or Latin *stupiditas*, from *stupidus*: see prec., -ITY.]
1 The quality of being slow-witted, foolish, or unintelligent. Formerly also, apathy, indifference; numbness, stupor; the condition of having one's faculties dulled. M16.
2 A stupid idea, action, etc. M17.
3 Obstinacy. *north.* L19.

📖 **2** D. ROWE All the stupidities which prevent us from being ourselves.

stupify *verb* see STUPEFY.

stupor /ˈstjuːpə/ *noun.* LME.
[Latin, from *stupere*: see STUPID, -OR.]
1 A state of insensibility or unconsciousness; *spec.* in *MEDICINE*, a condition of near-unconsciousness characterized by great reduction in mental activity and responsiveness. LME.
2 **a** Admiring wonder, amazement. LME. ▸**b** A dazed, stunned, or torpid state of mind. L17.

📖 **1** LD MACAULAY James sank into a stupor which indicated the near approach of death. INA TAYLOR Men sprawled out in a drunken stupor. **b** P. G. WODEHOUSE Kirk awoke from the stupor which had gripped him.

Phrases: **stupor mundi** /stjuːpɔː ˈmʊndʌɪ, ˈmʊndiː/ [Latin = wonder of the world] an object of admiring bewilderment and wonder.

stuporous /ˈstjuːp(ə)rəs/ *adjective.* L19.
[medieval Latin *stuporosus*: see STUPOR, -OUS.]
Affected with or characterized by stupor.
■ Also **stuporose** /ˈstjuːpərəʊs/ *adjective* L19.

stupose /ˈstjuːpəʊs/ *adjective.* M19.
[formed as STUPE *noun*¹ & *verb* + -OSE¹.]
BOTANY. = STUPEOUS.

sturb /stəːb/ *verb trans. obsolete* exc. *US dial.* ME.
[Aphet. from DISTURB *verb*.]
Disturb, trouble, upset.
¶ Unrecorded between LME and L19.

sturdy /ˈstəːdi/ *adjective & noun.* ME.
[Aphet. from Old French *est(o)urdi*, stunned, dazed, reckless, violent (mod. *étourdi* thoughtless), ult. from Latin *ex-* EX-¹ + *turdus* thrush (taken as a type of drunkenness).]
▶**A** *adjective.* **I** †**1** **a** Impetuously brave; recklessly violent; ferocious, ruthless, cruel. ME–L17. ▸**b** Of a battle, blow, storm, etc.: furious, fierce, violent. LME–M17.
†**2** Of conduct, appearance, etc.: stern, harsh; surly. ME–E17.
†**3** Intractable, refractory; obstinate; rebellious, disobedient. ME–L18.
4 Of a material thing: tough, hard-wearing; strongly built, stout. LME. ▸**b** Of a plant: hardy. L17.
5 Of a person or animal: strong in physique, solidly built; physically robust. LME. ▸**b** *transf.* Of health, a movement, etc.: characterized by or displaying physical vigour or strength. L17.
6 *fig.* Uncompromising, blunt; stalwart, intellectually robust; determined, resolute, vigorous. L18.

📖 **4** DICKENS A violent gust of wind . . seemed to shake even that sturdy house. W. C. BRYANT Hasten thou And bring a sturdy javelin from the tent. **b** J. C. OATES Delicate Japanese trees . . were replaced by sturdier North American trees. **5** J. RATHBONE Curtis needed a strong and sturdy mount for he was above six feet. **b** A. P. STANLEY All were struck by the sturdy health . . of his frame. **6** J. R. GREEN The sturdy good sense of the man shook off the pedantry. G. GREENE A Tory country gentleman who . . had sturdy independent views on politics.

▶**II** **7** Giddy; *spec.* (of sheep) affected with the disease sturdy. Now *dial.* LME.
Special collocations: **sturdy beggar** (now *arch.* or *Hist.*) an able-bodied beggar or vagabond, *esp.* a violent one.
▶**B** *noun.* **1** A sturdy person. *rare.* L15.
2 A fatal infection causing loss of balance in domestic animals, esp. sheep; gid. L16.

■ **sturdied** *adjective* (of sheep or cattle) afflicted with sturdy E19. **sturdily** *adverb* LME. **sturdiness** *noun* LME.

sture *adjective & adverb* var. of STOUR *adjective & adverb*.

sturgeon /ˈstəːdʒ(ə)n/ *noun*. ME.
[Anglo-Norman from Old & mod. French *esturgeon*, from Proto-Romance form (repr. by medieval Latin *sturio*) of Germanic base of Old English *styrġa*, Middle Low German, Middle Dutch *störe* (Dutch *steur*), Old High German *sturjo* (German *Stör*), Old Norse *styrja*.]
1 A member of the family Acipenseridae of large anatomically primitive (chondrostean) bony fishes having an elongated, almost cylindrical body with longitudinal rows of bony scutes and a tapering blunt-ended snout, found in rivers and coastal waters of the north temperate zone and valued as food and as the source of caviar and isinglass. Freq. with specifying word indicating a particular species. ME.
2 *Canad.* In full ***sturgeon head***, ***sturgeon boat***, ***sturgeon scow***. A large broad flat boat with blunt ends resembling a sturgeon's snout, orig. propelled by poles and used to carry freight on rivers in the Canadian North-West. Now *Hist.* L19.
1 ***great sturgeon***, ***Russian sturgeon***, ***shovelnose sturgeon***, etc.

Sturge–Weber /stəːdʒˈwɛbə/ *noun*. M20.
[from W. A. *Sturge* (1850–1919) and F. P. *Weber* (1863–1962), English physicians.]
MEDICINE. ***Sturge–Weber syndrome***, ***Sturge–Weber disease***, a congenital malformation of blood-vessels of the brain also producing a port-wine naevus on the face and usually resulting in fits and mental handicap.

sturine /ˈstjʊəriːn, -ɪn/ *noun*. L19.
[German *Sturin*, from medieval Latin *sturio(n-)* sturgeon (used as mod. Latin specfic name): see -INE⁵.]
BIOCHEMISTRY. A protamine isolated from the testicles of sturgeons and other fish.

sturks *noun* var. of STERKS.

Sturmabteilung /ˈʃtʊrmapˌtaɪlʊŋ/ *noun*. E20.
[German, lit. 'storm division'.]
Hist. A Nazi paramilitary force active in Germany from 1921 to 1934. Abbreviation ***SA***. Cf. STORM TROOP 1b.

Sturmbannführer /ˈʃtʊrmbanˌfyːrər/ *noun*. M20.
[German = battalion leader.]
Hist. An officer in the Nazi *Schutzstaffel* or SS.

Sturmer /ˈstəːmə/ *noun*. M19.
[A village on the Essex–Suffolk border, where it was first raised.]
More fully ***Sturmer pippin***. A late-ripening variety of eating apple with a yellowish-green skin, sometimes slightly russeted, and yellowish flesh.

Sturm und Drang /ʃtʊrm ʊnt ˈdraŋ/ *noun phr*. M19.
[German, lit. 'storm and stress', title of a 1776 play by Friedrich Maximilian Klinger (1752–1831).]
(The period of) a radical movement in German literature in the late 1770s characterized by the violent expression of emotion and the rejection of neoclassical literary norms; *transf.* (a period of) emotion, stress, or turbulence.

sturnoid /ˈstəːnɔɪd/ *adjective*. L19.
[from Latin *sturnus* starling (used as mod. Latin genus name) + -OID.]
ORNITHOLOGY. Resembling the starlings in form or characteristics.

sturt /stəːt/ *noun & verb*. Chiefly *Scot*. LME.
[Metath. alt. of STRUT *noun*¹.]
▸ **A** *noun*. **1** Strife; violent quarrelling or behaviour. LME.
†**2** A state of mental disquiet or distress. E16–E18.
▸ **B** *verb*. †**1** *verb intrans*. Make trouble. Only in LME.
2 a *verb trans*. Attack, molest, disturb; *refl*. trouble or rouse oneself. *Scot*. E16. ▸**b** *verb intrans*. Be startled. *Scot*. L18.

Sturt's desert pea /ˌstəːts dɛzət ˈpiː/ *noun phr*. Also **Sturt pea** /stəːt/. M19.
[Charles *Sturt* (1795–1869), Austral. explorer, who first collected it.]
The clianthus of desert regions of western Australia, *Clianthus formosus*, which bears bright flowers blotched with black at the base of the standard.

stushie *noun* var. of STOOSHIE.

stuss /stʌs, stʌʃ/ *noun*. *US*. E20.
[Yiddish *shtos*, perh. from German *Stoss* push, stack.]
CARDS. A form of faro.

stut /stʌt/ *verb intrans*. *obsolete* exc. *dial*. Infl. **-tt-**. LME.
[Rel. to Germanic base of Middle Low German *stöten*, Old High German *stozan* (German *stossen*) strike against.]
Stutter.

stutter /ˈstʌtə/ *noun*¹. *obsolete* exc. *dial*. E16.
[from prec. + -ER¹.]
= STUTTERER.

stutter /ˈstʌtə/ *verb & noun*². L16.
[Frequentative of STUT: see -ER⁵. Cf. Middle & mod. Low German *stötern*, Dutch *stotteren*, German *stottern*.]
▸ **A** *verb*. **1** *verb intrans*. Talk with continued involuntary repetition of sounds or syllables, esp. initial consonants; stammer. L16.
2 *verb trans*. Say or utter with a stutter. Freq. foll. by *out*. M17.

1 F. M. FORD I muttered, I stuttered—I don't know how I got the words out. *fig*.: L. CODY Selwyn's stuttering typewriter was silent.

▸ **B** *noun*. An act or habit of stuttering. M19.
■ **stutterer** *noun* L16. **stutteringly** *adverb* in a stuttering manner, with a stutter M16.

sty /stʌɪ/ *noun*¹. Long *obsolete* exc. *north*.
[Old English *stīġ* = Old High German *stīga*, Middle Low German, Middle Dutch *stīge* from Germanic base also of STY *verb*¹.]
A narrow or steep path.

sty /stʌɪ/ *noun*². Also (now *rare*) **stye**.
[Old English *sti-* (in comb.) perh. identical with *stiġ* hall (see STEWARD *noun*), from Germanic, of which a parallel formation is repr. in Middle Low German *stege*, Middle Dutch *swijnstije*, Old Norse *stía* pen, fold.]
1 An enclosure where pigs are kept; a pigsty. OE.
2 *transf. & fig*. A filthy or squalid room or dwelling; a den of vice, a place of debauchery. LME.

sty /stʌɪ/ *noun*³. Also **stye**. E17.
[Back-form. from STYANY.]
An inflamed swelling on the eyelid, caused by bacterial infection of a gland at the base of an eyelash. Also called ***hordeolum***.

†**sty** *verb*¹. Also **stye**.
[Old English *stīgan* corresp. to Old Frisian *stīga*, Old Saxon, Old High German *stīgan* (Dutch *stijgen*, German *steigen*), Old Norse *stíga*, Gothic *steigan*, from Germanic from Indo-European stem meaning 'advance, go, rise', repr. also in Greek *steikhein*, *stikhos* STICH, *stoikhos* row. Cf. STILE *noun*¹.]
1 *verb intrans*. Ascend; rise or climb (*up*) to a higher level. OE–M17. ▸**b** *verb trans*. Ascend or climb (a hill etc.). OE–LME.
2 *verb intrans*. Go *down*, descend. OE–ME.

1 SPENSER The beast . . Thought with his winges to stye above the ground.

sty /stʌɪ/ *verb*². Also (now *rare*) **stye**.
[Late Old English *stiġian*: cf. Old High German *stīgōn*, Old Norse *stía*. See STY *noun*².]
1 *verb trans*. Pen *up* or confine (a pig or pigs) in a sty. LOE. ▸**b** *transf*. Pen *up* or confine (a person) as in a sty. E17.
2 *verb intrans*. Live as if in a sty. M18.

styan /ˈstʌɪən/ *noun*. *obsolete* exc. *dial*.
[Old English *stīgend* lit. 'riser', use as noun of pres. pple of *stīgan*: see STY *verb*¹.]
= STY *noun*³.

styany /ˈstʌɪəni/ *noun*. *obsolete* exc. *dial*. LME.
[from prec. + EYE *noun*.]
= STY *noun*³.

styca /ˈstʌɪkə/ *noun*. L17.
[Based on Old English (Northumbrian) *stycas* pl. of Old English *styċċe* piece (of money).]
Hist. A small silver or copper coin used in Anglo-Saxon Northumbria.

stye *noun*¹ see STY *noun*².

stye *noun*² var. of STY *noun*³.

†**stye** *verb*¹ var. of STY *verb*¹.

stye *verb*² see STY *verb*².

Stygian /ˈstɪdʒɪən/ *adjective*. M16.
[from Latin *Stygius* from Greek *Stugios*, from *Stux* STYX: see -IAN.]
1 a CLASSICAL MYTHOLOGY. Of or pertaining to the River Styx or (*gen*.) the underworld. M16. ▸**b** Of an oath: such as one dreads breaking; inviolable. *literary*. E17.
2 Characteristic of or resembling (the region of) the Styx; *spec*. (*a*) black, gloomy, indistinct; (*b*) infernal, hellish. *literary*. E17.

2 A. WILSON Why you . . should wish to plunge yourself in Stygian gloom, I cannot imagine.

stylagalmatic /stʌɪlagalˈmatɪk/ *adjective*. *rare*. E19.
[from Greek *stulos* column + *agalmat-*, *agalma* image: see -IC.]
ARCHITECTURE. Having or supported by figures serving as columns.

style /stʌɪl/ *noun & verb*. Also †**stile**. ME.
[Old & mod. French from Latin *stilus*, infl. in spelling by assoc. with Greek *stulos* column. Cf. STYLUS.]
▸ **A** *noun*. **I 1** An ancient implement for writing on wax etc., having a pointed end for incising characters and a flat broad end for erasures and smoothing the writing surface. ME. ▸**b** A sharp instrument or point for engraving, tracing, etc. M17. ▸**c** MEDICINE. A blunt-pointed probe. M17.
2 A pointer, pin, etc., for indicating a time, position, etc.; *esp*. the gnomon of a sundial. M16.
3 BOTANY. A narrowed freq. elongated projection of the ovary, bearing the stigma. L17.
4 ENTOMOLOGY. **a** A short unjointed abdominal appendage. E19. ▸**b** A terminal bristle on the antenna of a dipteran fly. E19.
5 ZOOLOGY. A small slender pointed process or part; a stylet. M19.

1 *Times Lit. Suppl.* Incised with metal styles in the polished plaster.

▸ **II** †**6 a** A written work; a literary or (occas.) oral composition. ME–L16. ▸**b** An inscription, a legend. E16–L17.
7 A legal, official, or honorific title; the recognized or correct designation for a person or thing. Also (long *rare*), an appropriate descriptive epithet. ME.
8 a The characteristic manner of literary expression of a particular writer, school, period, etc. ME. ▸**b** (Features pertaining to) the form and mode of expression of a text, as opp. to what is said or expressed. ME. ▸**c** A manner of speaking or conversing. M16. ▸**d** A recognized way of expressing dates using either of two dating methods (***New Style***, ***Old Style***) current in the Christian world since the introduction of the Gregorian calendar in 1582. L16.
9 a SCOTS LAW. The authorized form for drawing up a deed or instrument. L15. ▸**b** *gen*. Legal technicality of language or construction. Esp. in ***words of style***. M18.
†**10** A phrase, formula, etc., expressing a particular idea or thought. L16–M18.

7 W. PENN Which excellent Principles . . do worthily deserve . . the Stile of Divinity. M. ARNOLD I have always been shy of assuming the honourable style of Professor. **8b** B. JOWETT The Parmenides in point of style is one of the best . . Platonic writings. **10** T. WATSON *Be it enacted*, is the Royal Style.

▸ **III 11 a** A mode or manner of living or behaving; a person's bearing or demeanour. (*rare* before L18.) ME. ▸**b** A particular or characteristic way, form, or technique of making or producing a thing, esp. a work of art; a way of executing a task; a manner of performance. E18. ▸**c** A type, kind, or sort, esp. with ref. to appearance or form; *spec*. (***a***) a distinctive type of architecture; (***b***) a particular make, shape, or pattern of clothing or other goods; (***c***) a hairstyle. L18. ▸**d** = ***house style*** s.v. HOUSE *noun*¹ *& adjective*. L19.
12 A customary (esp. legal) procedure or way of doing something. *obsolete* exc. as in sense 11 above. LME.
13 a Elegance, refinement, or excellence of manner, expression, form, or performance. L16. ▸**b** Fashionableness, attractiveness, or flamboyance of appearance, bearing, etc. E19.

11a H. B. STOWE Some very homely women . . have a style that amounts to something like beauty. A. WESKER Got a country house? We can entertain in grand style! **b** C. EASTON Jacqueline found Tortelier's style of teaching . . exciting. **c** E. JENNINGS They slip on to the bus, hair piled up high. New styles each month. G. CLARE She only wore . . dresses of 'Edwardian' style. R. GODDEN The houses were built in Palladian style. **12** J. STRYPE An act against the custom and common style of the Court. **13a** *Daily Telegraph* The quintessence of style . . a compound of elegance, authority and wit. **b** N. P. WILLIS A plain . . city, with little or no pretensions to style. ALBERT SMITH An evident wish to throw a little style into their costume.

Phrases: ***cramp a person's style***: see CRAMP *verb*. **go out of style** go out of fashion. **in style** splendidly, showily, fashionably. ***New Style***: see NEW *adjective*. ***Old Style***: see OLD *adjective*. ***robe de style***: see ROBE *noun*¹. ***Winchester style***: see WINCHESTER 1.
Comb.: **style analysis** analysis of the characteristic style of an artist, writer, composer, period, etc., esp. as a basis for the attribution of a particular work; **style-book** (***a***) SCOTS LAW a book containing styles of deeds etc.; (***b***) a manual of house style; **style critic** an expert in style analysis; **style-setter** a person who or thing which starts or establishes a fashion; **style sheet** (***a***) a manual detailing the house style of a particular printing house, publication, etc.; (***b***) COMPUTING a type of template file consisting of font and layout settings to give a standardized look to certain documents.
▸ **B** *verb trans*. †**1** Name or address with an honorific title. *Scot*. E–M16.
2 Designate in a specified way. M16.
3 Use a style or styles to draw or trace (a design). M19.
4 Design, arrange, make, etc., in a particular (esp. fashionable) style. M20.

2 BURKE Liberty was found, under Monarchies stiled absolute. W. H. AUDEN So long as he can style himself the master.

■ **stylar** /ˈstʌɪlə/ (***a***) (*rare*) of or pertaining to a style or pointer, esp. (formerly) that of a sundial; (***b***) BOTANY of or pertaining to the style or styles of a flower: E17. **stylary** /ˈstʌɪləri/ *adjective* (*rare*, ZOOLOGY) of or pertaining to a style or stylet L19. **styleless** /-l-l-/ *adjective* devoid of style L18. **stylelessness** *noun* M20.

-style /stʌɪl/ *suffix*.
Forming adjectives & adverbs from adjectives & nouns with the sense '(in a manner) resembling or characteristic of (something that is) —', as ***Japanese-style***, ***peasant-style***, ***regency-style***, etc.

styler /ˈstʌɪlə/ *noun*. M20.
[from STYLE *verb* + -ER¹.]
1 = STYLIST 2b. Only as 2nd elem. of comb., as ***hair-styler***. *rare*. M20.
2 A device for styling hair. L20.

stylet /ˈstʌɪlɪt/ *noun*. L17.
[French, from Italian STILETTO.]
1 *MEDICINE*. A slender probe. Also, a wire run through a catheter or cannula in order to stiffen it or to clear it. L17.
2 †**a** *BOTANY*. = STYLE *noun* 3. Only in E18. ▶**b** *ZOOLOGY & ENTOMOLOGY*. = STYLE *noun* 4, 5; *esp*. (**a**) the dorsal part of the shaft of a bee's sting; (**b**) a piercing insect mouthpart. M19.
3 A pointed marking instrument; *spec*. a kind of pencil for the use of the blind. E19.
4 A stiletto, a dagger. E19.

styli *noun pl*. see STYLUS.

stylidium /stʌɪˈlɪdɪəm/ *noun*. E19.
[mod. Latin (see below), from Greek *stulos* column + -*idion* dim. suffix.]
Any of various chiefly Australian plants with tubular corollas constituting the genus *Stylidium* (family Stylidiaceae), the stamens of which unite with the style to form a column which springs up when touched. Also called ***trigger-plant***.

styliferous /stʌɪˈlɪf(ə)rəs/ *adjective*. E19.
[from STYLE *noun* + -FEROUS.]
BOTANY & ZOOLOGY. Bearing a style or styles.

styliform /ˈstʌɪlɪfɔːm/ *adjective*. L16.
[formed as prec. + -I- + -FORM.]
Chiefly *SCIENCE*. Shaped like a stylus; slender and elongated.

styling /ˈstʌɪlɪŋ/ *noun*. M19.
[from STYLE *verb* + -ING[1].]
1 Decorative patterning traced by a style. Cf. STYLE *verb* 3. *rare*. M19.
2 The action or result of making or arranging something in a (fashionable) style. Cf. STYLE *verb* 4. E20.

stylise *verb* var. of STYLIZE.

stylish /ˈstʌɪlɪʃ/ *adjective*. Orig. †**stilish**. L18.
[from STYLE *noun* + -ISH[1].]
Fashionable, chic; elegant; having style.

📖 L. M. MONTGOMERY I'm so glad you made my new dresses longer . . . flounces are so stylish this fall.

■ **stylishly** *adverb* L19. **stylishness** *noun* L18.

stylism /ˈstʌɪlɪz(ə)m/ *noun*. E20.
[from STYLE *noun* + -ISM.]
A stylistic device or effect; emphasis on style.

stylist /ˈstʌɪlɪst/ *noun*. L18.
[from STYLE *noun* + -IST, after German *Stilist*.]
1 a A person noted for or aspiring to good literary or rhetorical style. L18. ▶**b** *transf*. A sports player or musician who performs with style. L19.
2 a A person employed by a firm to create, coordinate, or promote new styles or designs, esp. of clothes or cars. Orig. *N. Amer*. E20. ▶**b** *ellipt*. A hairstylist. Orig. *N. Amer*. M20.

stylistic /stʌɪˈlɪstɪk/ *adjective & noun*. M19.
[from STYLE *noun* + -IST + -IC, after German *stilistisch* adjective, *Stilistik* noun.]
▶**A** *adjective*. Of or pertaining to (esp. literary or artistic) style. M19.
▶**B** *noun*. In *pl*. (treated as *sing*.) & *sing*. The branch of knowledge that deals with literary or linguistic style. M19.
■ **stylistically** *adverb* with regard to (esp. literary or artistic) style. L19. **stylistician** /-ˈstɪʃ(ə)n/ *noun* an expert in or student of stylistics M20.

stylite /ˈstʌɪlʌɪt/ *noun & adjective*. M17.
[ecclesiastical Greek *stulitēs*, from Greek *stulos* column: see -ITE[1].]
ECCLESIASTICAL HISTORY. ▶**A** *noun*. Also (*rare*) in Greek form **stylites** /stʌɪˈlʌɪtiːz/. An ascetic living on top of a pillar. M17.
▶**B** *adjective*. Designating or characteristic of a stylite. L19.
■ **stylitic** /stʌɪˈlɪtɪk/ *adjective* (characteristic) of a stylite M19. **stylitism** /stʌɪˈlɪtɪz(ə)m/ *noun* the stilitic way of life M19.

stylize /ˈstʌɪlʌɪz/ *verb trans*. Also **-ise**. L19.
[from STYLE *noun* + -IZE, after German *stilisieren*.]
Represent in a conventional non-realistic style; conventionalize. Chiefly as ***stylized*** *ppl adjective*.

📖 A. SETON She knew nothing of the stylized game of courtly love.

■ **styliˈzation** *noun* the action or result of stylizing something M20.

stylo /ˈstʌɪləʊ/ *noun*[1]. Pl. **-os**. L19.
[Abbreviation.]
= STYLOGRAPH 2.

stylo /ˈstʌɪləʊ/ *noun*[2]. *colloq*. Pl. **-os**. M20.
[Abbreviation of mod. Latin genus name (see below).]
A trifoliate leguminous plant, *Stylosanthes sundaica*, grown as a fodder plant in Australia and other tropical regions. Chiefly in ***TOWNSVILLE stylo***.

stylo- /ˈstʌɪləʊ/ *combining form*.
[from STYLOID: see -O-.]
Connected with the styloid and —, as ***stylomandibular***.

stylobata /stʌɪˈlɒbətə/ *noun*. Now *rare* or *obsolete*. Pl. **-tae** /-tiː/. M16.
[Latin: see next.]
ARCHITECTURE. = next.

stylobate /ˈstʌɪləbeɪt/ *noun*. L17.
[from Latin *stylobata* from Greek *stulobatēs*, from *stulos* column + -*batēs* base, from *bainein* to walk.]
ARCHITECTURE. A continuous base supporting a row of columns. Cf. STEREOBATE.

stylograph /ˈstʌɪləgrɑːf/ *noun*. M19.
[formed as STYLUS + -GRAPH.]
†**1** A sketch, drawing, etc., made with a style. *rare*. Only in M19.
2 A stylographic pen. L19.

stylographic /stʌɪləˈgrafɪk/ *adjective*. E19.
[formed as prec. + -GRAPHIC.]
Pertaining to stylography.
stylographic pen a kind of fountain-pen having a fine perforated tube as a writing-point instead of a split nib.

stylography /stʌɪˈlɒgrəfi/ *noun*. M19.
[formed as prec. + -GRAPHY.]
A method of writing, drawing, etc., with a style.

stylohyal /stʌɪləʊˈhʌɪəl/ *adjective & noun*. M19.
[formed as next + -AL[1].]
ANATOMY & ZOOLOGY. (Designating) one of the bones of the hyoid arch, in humans forming the styloid process of the temporal bone.

stylohyoid /stʌɪləʊˈhʌɪɔɪd/ *adjective & noun*. M19.
[from next + -O- + HYOID.]
ANATOMY. ▶**A** *adjective*. Of or pertaining to the stylohyal and the hyoid bone; *spec*. designating a muscle or a nerve connecting or associated with these. M19.
▶**B** *noun*. A muscle connecting the styloid process and the hyoid bone. M19.

styloid /ˈstʌɪlɔɪd/ *adjective*. E17.
[mod. Latin *styloides* from Greek *stuloeidēs* like a style, from *stulos* column: see -OID.]
ANATOMY & ZOOLOGY. Resembling a style in shape; styliform; *esp*. designating or pertaining to any of several slender pointed processes of bone, *spec*. that which projects from the base of the temporal bone.

stylolite /ˈstʌɪləlʌɪt/ *noun*. M19.
[from Greek *stulos* column + -LITE.]
GEOLOGY. A surface or seam within a limestone or (occas.) sandstone, characterized by irregular interlocking pegs and sockets around 1 cm in depth and a concentration of insoluble substances. Also, a grooved peg forming part of such a seam.
■ **styloˈlitic** *adjective* M19.

stylometric /stʌɪləˈmɛtrɪk/ *adjective*. M20.
[from STYLE *noun* + -O- + -METRIC.]
Of or pertaining to stylometry.

stylometrics /stʌɪləˈmɛtrɪks/ *noun*. M20.
[from prec.: see -ICS.]
= STYLOMETRY.

stylometry /stʌɪˈlɒmɪtri/ *noun*. M20.
[formed as prec. + -METRY.]
The statistical analysis of stylistic features of (esp. literary or philosophical) texts.
■ **stylometrist** *noun* a practitioner of stylometry M20.

stylophone /ˈstʌɪləfəʊn/ *noun*. Also **S-**. M20.
[from STYLE *noun* + -O- + -PHONE. Cf. XYLOPHONE.]
A miniature electronic musical instrument producing a distinctive buzzing sound when a stylus is drawn along its metal keyboard.

stylopized /ˈstʌɪləpʌɪzd/ *adjective*. Also **-ised**. M19.
[from STYLOPS: see -IZE, -ED[1].]
ENTOMOLOGY. Of a bee or other insect: infested with a stylops.
■ **stylopiˈzation** *noun* the state of being or becoming stylopized L19.

stylopodium /stʌɪləˈpəʊdɪəm/ *noun*. Pl. **-ia** /-ɪə/. Also Anglicized as **stylopod** /ˈstʌɪləpɒd/. M19.
[mod. Latin, from Greek *stulos* column + PODIUM.]
BOTANY. The enlarged base of the style in an umbelliferous plant.

stylops /ˈstʌɪlɒps/ *noun*. Pl. same, **-es**. L19.
[mod. Latin (see below), from Greek *stulos* column + *ōps* eye, face.]
ENTOMOLOGY. A strepsipterous insect; *spec*. one of the large genus *Stylops*.

stylostatistics /ˌstʌɪləʊstəˈtɪstɪks/ *noun*. M20.
[from STYLE *noun* + -O- + STATISTICS.]
= STYLOMETRY.

stylus /ˈstʌɪləs/ *noun*. Pl. **-li** /-lʌɪ, -liː/, **-luses**. E18.
[Erron. spelling of Latin *stilus*: see STYLE.]
1 *BOTANY*. = STYLE *noun* 3. Now *rare*. E18.
2 = STYLE *noun* 1. E19.
3 *ZOOLOGY*. = STYLE *noun* 5. M19.
4 a A tracing-point used to produce a written record in a chart recorder, telegraph receiver, etc. L19. ▶**b** A hard (esp. diamond or sapphire) point following a groove in a record and transmitting the recorded sound for reproduction; a similar point used to make such a groove when producing a record; a needle. L19.

styme /stʌɪm/ *noun*. Chiefly *Scot. & north*. Also **stime**. ME.
[Origin unkn.]
1 ***not see a styme***, be unable to see at all. ME.
2 A glimpse; the least bit, amount, or glimmer (*of* anything). L18.

stymie /ˈstʌɪmi/ *noun & verb*. Also **-y**, **sti(e)my**. M19.
[Origin uncertain: cf. prec.]
▶**A** *noun*. Orig. in *GOLF*, a situation on a green in which the path of a putt to the hole is obstructed by an opponent's ball; the ball thus forming an obstruction. Now chiefly *fig*., a difficult or frustrating situation; an obstruction. M19.
▶**B** *verb trans*. Pres. pple & verbal noun **stymieing**, **-mying**.
1 *GOLF*. Prevent an opponent from putting directly at the hole with a stymie; obstruct (an opponent's ball) thus. Now *rare*. M19.
2 *fig*. Obstruct, frustrate, thwart, (a person, project, etc.). Freq. as ***stymied*** *ppl adjective*. M19.

📖 **1** *Scotsman* Worthington was stimied and in trying to loft, knocked . . Williamson's ball into the hole. **2** *Listener* His efforts . . are stymied by a bizarre complication.

Stymphalian /stɪmˈfeɪlɪən/ *adjective*. M17.
[from Latin *Stymphalius*, from *Stymphalus* or -*um* (see below) from Greek *Stumphalos*: see -IAN.]
GREEK MYTHOLOGY. Of or belonging to Stymphalus, a district in Arcadia; *spec*. designating a kind of harmful bird which infested Stymphalus, destroyed by Hercules as the fifth of his twelve labours.

styptic /ˈstɪptɪk/ *adjective & noun*. LME.
[Latin *stypticus* from Greek *stuptikos*, from *stuphein* to contract: see -IC.]
▶**A** *adjective*. **1** Causing contraction of organs or tissue; harsh, acid, or raw to the palate. Now usu., astringent (*lit. & fig*.). LME.
2 Of a medicine, drug, etc.: that checks bleeding. LME.
2 styptic pencil a stick of styptic substance used to stem the bleeding of small cuts.
▶**B** *noun*. A substance which promotes contraction of tissue; an astringent; now *spec*. a substance which checks bleeding, a haemostatic drug etc. LME.
■ **styptical** *adjective* (now *rare* or *obsolete*) = STYPTIC *adjective* E16. **stypˈticity** *noun* styptic quality, astringency LME. **stypticness** *noun* (now *rare*) = STYPTICITY LME.

Stypven /ˈstɪpv(ə)n/ *noun*. Also **s-**. M20.
[from STYP(TIC + VEN(OM *noun*.]
MEDICINE. The dried and purified venom of Russell's viper, used in solution as a local haemostatic and coagulant.
Comb.: **Stypven time** coagulation time measured when Stypven is added as a coagulant.
¶ Proprietary name in the US.

styrax /ˈstʌɪraks/ *noun*. M16.
[Latin from Greek *sturax*. Cf. STORAX.]
1 The aromatic gum storax. M16.
2 More fully ***styrax tree***. The tree yielding this gum, *Styrax officinalis* (family Styracaceae), a Mediterranean tree with pendulous white flowers. Also, any of various other trees of this genus. L16.

styrene /ˈstʌɪriːn/ *noun*. L19.
[from STYROL + -ENE.]
CHEMISTRY. **1** A colourless toxic aromatic liquid hydrocarbon, $C_6H_5{\cdot}CH{=}CH_2$, obtained orig. from the storax tree and now as a petroleum by-product, easily polymerized and used in making plastics etc. L19.
2 = POLYSTYRENE. M20.

Styrian /ˈstɪrɪən/ *noun & adjective*. E17.
[from *Styria* (see below) from German *Steier(mark*: see -AN.]
▶**A** *noun*. A native or inhabitant of Styria, a province of Austria, formerly a duchy of the Austrian Empire. E17.
▶**B** *adjective*. Of or pertaining to Styria. E19.

Styrofoam /ˈstʌɪrəfəʊm/ *noun*. Chiefly *N. Amer*. Also **s-**. M20.
[from POLY)STYR(ENE + -O- + FOAM *noun*.]
A variety of expanded polystyrene. Freq. *attrib*.
¶ Proprietary name in the US.

styrol /ˈstʌɪrɒl/ *noun*. Now *rare* or *obsolete*. M19.
[from STYRAX + -OL.]
CHEMISTRY. = STYRENE 1.
■ Also **styrolene** *noun* L19.

styrone /ˈstʌɪrəʊn/ *noun.* M19.
[from STYRAX + -ONE.]
CHEMISTRY. Cinnamyl alcohol, a crystalline substance used as an antiseptic and bleach.

styryl /ˈstʌɪrʌɪl, -rɪl/ *noun.* M19.
[formed as prec. + -YL.]
CHEMISTRY. = CINNAMYL. Usu. in *comb.*

Styx /stɪks/ *noun.* LME.
[Latin from Greek *stux*, *stug-* rel. to *stugein* to hate, *stugnos* hateful, gloomy.]
CLASSICAL MYTHOLOGY. A dark gloomy river in Hades, over which Charon ferried the souls of the dead. Also *fig.* (*literary*), an evil gloomy place.

SU *abbreviation.*
PHYSICS. Special unitary (*sc.* group), with following numeral denoting the number of rows and of columns in the matrices that can be used to represent it, as *SU*(3) (cf. SPECIAL *adjective* 7).

suabe flute /ˈswɑːbə fluːt, ˈsweɪb/ *noun phr.* M19.
[from Italian *suabe* from German *Schwabe* SWABIAN + FLUTE *noun*[1].]
MUSIC. An organ flute-stop.

suable /ˈsuːəb(ə)l, ˈsjuː-/ *adjective.* Now chiefly *US.* E17.
[from SUE + -ABLE.]
Liable to be sued; legally subject to civil process.
■ **suaˈbility** *noun* (*US*) L18.

suade /sweɪd/ *verb trans. & intrans.* Now *rare* or *obsolete.* M16.
[Partly from Latin *suadere* advise, recommend; partly aphet. from PERSUADE.]
Persuade.

suaeda /ˈsweɪdə, suːˈiːdə, sjuːˈiːdə/ *noun.* E20.
[mod. Latin (see below), from Arab. *suwayda*.]
Any of various fleshy maritime plants constituting the genus *Suaeda*, of the goosefoot family; sea-blite.

†Suani *noun* see SVAN.

suan-pan /ˈswanpan/ *noun.* M18.
[Chinese *suànpan*, lit. 'reckoning board'.]
An abacus.

suant /ˈsuːənt/ *noun.* Long *obsolete* exc. *dial.* E17.
[Perh. rel. to SEWIN.]
A flounder; a plaice.

suant /ˈsjuːənt/ *adjective & adverb.* Now *dial.* LME.
[Anglo-Norman *sua(u)nt*, Old French *suiant*, *sivant* pres. pple of *sivre* (mod. *suivre*) follow from Proto-Romance alt. of Latin *sequi*: see -ANT[1].]
▶ **A** *adjective.* †**1** Following, ensuing. Only in LME.
2 Appropriate, suitable; even, smooth, regular; pleasing, agreeable. LME.
▶ **B** *adverb.* = SUANTLY. L18.
■ **suantly** *adverb* regularly, evenly, smoothly M16.

suasible /ˈsweɪsɪb(ə)l/ *adjective. rare.* L16.
[Late Latin *suasibilis*, from Latin *suas-*: see next, -IBLE.]
Able to be persuaded, esp. easily.

suasion /ˈsweɪʒ(ə)n/ *noun.* Now *formal.* LME.
[Old French, or Latin *suasio(n-)*, from *suas-* pa. ppl stem of *suadere*: see PERSUADE.]
Persuasion; an instance of this.

📖 G. DALY He would have been powerless to resist their moral suasion.

suasive /ˈsweɪsɪv/ *adjective & noun.* Now *formal.* E17.
[Var. of SUASORY by suffix-substitution: see -IVE.]
▶ **A** *adjective.* Having or exercising the power of persuasion; (foll. by *of*) exhorting or urging to. E17.
▶ **B** *noun.* A persuasive speech, motive, or influence. L17.
■ **suasively** *adverb* M19. **suasiveness** *noun* E18.

suasory /ˈsweɪs(ə)ri/ *adjective & noun. Now rare.* L16.
[Latin *suasorius*, from *suas-*: see SUASION, -ORY[2].]
▶ **A** *adjective.* Tending to persuade; persuasive. L16.
▶†**B** *noun.* = SUASIVE *noun.* E–M17.

suave /swɑːv/ *adjective.* LME.
[Old & mod. French, or Latin *suavis* sweet, agreeable (see SWEET *adjective*).]
†**1** Gracious, kindly. Chiefly *Scot.* LME–M16.
2 Pleasing, agreeable. *arch.* LME.
3 (Of a person (esp. a man), manner, etc.) blandly or superficially polite, smooth, sophisticated; (of wine etc.) bland, smooth. M19.

📖 **2** D. M. MULOCK To break the suave harmony of things. **3** P. G. WODEHOUSE A sleek, suave, unpleasant youth. H. INNES He had a soft purring voice that was a shade better than suave.

■ **suavely** *adverb* M19. **suaveness** *noun* E20.

suaveolent /sweɪˈviːələnt/ *adjective. rare.* M17.
[Latin *suaveolent-*, *-ens*, from *suave* adverbial neut. of *suavis* SUAVE + *olent-* pres. ppl stem of *olere* smell: see -ENT.]
Sweet-smelling.

suaviloquence /swɑːˈvɪləkwəns/ *noun. rare.* M17.
[Latin *suaviloquentia*, from *suaviloquens*, from *suavis* SUAVE + *-loquens* speaking, from *loqui* speak: see -ENCE.]
Pleasing or agreeable speech or manner of speaking.

suavity /ˈswɑːvɪti/ *noun.* LME.
[Partly from Latin *suavitas* (from *suavis* SUAVE); partly from French *suavité*: see -ITY.]
†**1** Pleasantness or agreeableness of taste, smell, sound, manner, etc. LME–E19.
2 The quality or condition of being suave in manner; *rare*, a suave action. E19.

sub /sʌb/ *noun & verb. colloq.* L17.
[Abbreviation.]
▶ **A** *noun.* **1** A subordinate; a person employed in a subordinate or secondary position, as a subeditor, subrector, etc. L17.
2 MILITARY. A subaltern. M18.
3 A subscription. E19.
4 A substitute. M19.
5 Subsistence; an advance or loan against expected income. M19.
6 = SUBMARINE *noun* 2. E20.
7 = SUBMARINE *noun* 2b. *N. Amer. colloq.* M20.
▶ **B** *verb.* Infl. **-bb-**.
†**1** *verb trans.* Subsoil-plough. Only in L18.
2 *verb intrans.* Act as a substitute (*for* a person). Chiefly *N. Amer.* M19.
3 *verb trans.* Lend or receive (a sum) as an advance against expected income; lend such a sum to (a person). L19.
4 *verb trans. & intrans.* Subedit. L19.
5 *verb trans.* In the manufacture of photographic film: coat with a substratum of gelatin etc. M20.
■ **subbing** *noun* (*a*) *gen.* the action of the verb, a result of this; (*b*) a substratum of gelatin etc. on a photographic film (cf. SUB *verb* 5): L18.

sub- /sʌb, *unstressed* səb/ *prefix.*
[from or after Latin, from *sub* preposition, = under, close to, up to, towards. In Latin *sub-* was reduced to *su-* before *sp-* and usu. assim. before *c, f, g, m, p, r*; a by-form *subs-* was normally reduced to *sus-* before *c, p, t*.]
▶ **I** As a living prefix.
1 Denoting a lower spatial position, as ***subdominant***, ***subsoil***, ***subterranean***; *spec.* (ANATOMY, BOTANY, & ZOOLOGY) denoting occurrence under, beneath, or (occas.) behind the part denoted by the 2nd elem., as ***subaxillary***, ***subcutaneous***, ***submucosa***.
2 Denoting inferior rank or importance, secondary or subordinate nature, or smaller size, as ***subcontinent***, ***subdean***, ***subheading***. ▸**b** Denoting a division or secondary part of a whole, as ***subculture***, ***subsection***, ***subset***. ▸**c** Prefixed to verbs to denote subordinate manner or capacity, as ***subserve***.
3 Prefixed to verbs to denote secondary or further action, as ***subcontract***, ***subdivide***, ***sublet***, and to related nouns, as ***sub-carrier***, ***subcontract***, ***subfeu***.
4 MATH. Prefixed to adjectives expressing ratio, to denote a ratio the opposite of that expressed by the 2nd elem., as ***subduple***, ***submultiple***.
5 Prefixed to adjectives and nouns with the senses 'next below (in space or time)', 'near or close (to)', as ***subnormal***, ***substandard***.
6 Prefixed to nouns, adjectives and derived adverbs, and (rarely) verbs, esp. in BOTANY & ZOOLOGY etc., with the senses 'somewhat', as ***subacid***, ***subacute***, 'nearly, approximately', as ***subcylindrical***, *subglabrous*, 'partial(ly)', as ***subaquatic***, ***subdelirium***.
7 CHEMISTRY. In names of compounds, denoting a relatively small or smaller than normal proportion of a component, esp. due to low oxidation state, as ***suboxide***, or (as in basic salts) the presence of another component, as ***subacetate***. Not now in formal nomenclature.
▶ **II** In words adopted or derived from Latin.
8 Prefixed to nouns, adjectives, and verbs with the sense 'secret(ly), covert(ly)', as ***suborn***, ***subreption***.
9 Prefixed to nouns and verbs with the senses 'from below, up, away', as ***subtract***, ***subvert***, 'so as to support', as ***subsidy***, ***subsist***, ***subvention***, 'so as to include', as ***subsume***.
10 Prefixed to verbs and their derivs. with the sense 'in place of another', as ***subrogate***, ***substitute***.
11 Prefixed to verbs with the sense 'in addition', as ***subjoin***.
¶ Opp. SUPER-. Freq. also treated as opp. SUPRA- (cf. INFRA-).
■ **subabˈdominal** *adjective* below the abdomen M19. **subaˈcuminate** *adjective* (BOTANY & ZOOLOGY) somewhat acuminate E19. **subadoˈlescent** *adjective & noun* = PREADOLESCENT *adjective & noun* M20. **subadult** /sʌbˈadʌlt, sʌbəˈdʌlt/ *adjective & noun* (*a*) *adjective* not fully adult; (*b*) *noun* a subadult animal: E20. **subˈagency** *noun* a subordinate agency; *spec.* (*US*) a subordinate government agency M19. **subˈagent** *noun* a subordinate agent E19. **sub-ˈalmoner** *noun* a subordinate almoner, one of the officials of the Royal Almonry M17. **subˈangular** *adjective* somewhat angular L18. **subanˈtarctic** *adjective* pertaining to or situated in the region immediately north of the Antarctic Circle L19. **subˈapical** *adjective* (BOTANY & ZOOLOGY) beneath or near the apex M19. **subapoˈstolic** *adjective* (ECCLESIASTICAL HISTORY) of, pertaining to, or characteristic of the period immediately following that of the Apostles L19. **subaˈquatic** *adjective* (*a*) = SUBAQUEOUS 1; (*b*) ZOOLOGY & BOTANY partly aquatic: L18. **subaˈrachnoid** *adjective & noun* (ANATOMY & MEDICINE) (designating or occurring in) the fluid-filled space around the brain between the arachnoid membrane and the pia mater M19. **sub-arch** *noun* (ARCHITECTURE) each of two or more subordinate arches grouped under a main arch M19. **subˈarcuate** *adjective* (BOTANY & ZOOLOGY) somewhat arcuate or bowed E19. **subˈarcuated** *adjective* (*a*) ZOOLOGY (*rare*) = SUBARCUATE; (*b*) ARCHITECTURE (of a window etc.) having two or more sub-arches: L18. **subarcuˈation** *noun* (ARCHITECTURE) the construction of two or more sub-arches; the system of arches so constructed: M19. **sub-assembly** *noun* a unit assembled separately but designed to be incorporated with other such units into a larger manufactured product E20. **subˈastral** *adjective* (*rare*) = SUBCELESTIAL M18. **subaˈstringent** *adjective & noun* (*a*) *adjective* somewhat astringent; (*b*) *noun* a subastringent substance: L17. **Sub-Atˈlantic** *adjective & noun* (designating or pertaining to) a relatively cool, wet climatic period in Europe following the Sub-Boreal and still current L19. **subatmosˈpheric** *adjective* (of pressure etc.) lower than that of the atmosphere at sea level M20. **subˈaudible** *adjective* (*a*) not loud enough to be audible; (*b*) (of a sound, a frequency) lower than the lowest audible, subsonic: M19. **subaˈxillary** *adjective* (*a*) ZOOLOGY (*rare*) = AXILLARY; (*b*) BOTANY beneath the axil: M18. **sub-ˈbasal** *adjective* situated near or below the base of a part or organ M19. **sub-base** *noun* (*a*) ARCHITECTURE the lowest part of a base which is divided horizontally; (*b*) a base placed under a machine etc. to raise it higher from the ground; (*c*) a secondary base; (*d*) a layer of coarse aggregate below the base of a road: E19. **sub-ˈbasement** *noun* a storey below a basement L19. **sub-biˈtuminous** *adjective* (GEOLOGY) (of coal) of inferior quality to bituminous, intermediate between this and lignite E20. **Sub-ˈBoreal** *adjective & noun* (designating or pertaining to) a cool, relatively dry climatic period in Europe following the Atlantic and preceding the Sub-Atlantic L19. **sub-ˈbottom** *adjective* of or pertaining to what is underneath the seabed M20. **sub-branch** *verb & noun* (*a*) *verb intrans.* divide into secondary or subordinate branches; (*b*) *noun* a secondary or subordinate branch: L17. **sub-breed** *noun* a variety of a breed, a secondary breed M19. **sub-brigaˈdier** *noun* (MILITARY HISTORY) an officer in the Horse Guards with the rank of a cornet L17. **sub-ˈcalibre** *adjective* (*a*) (of a projectile) smaller in calibre than the gun from which it is fired, and discharged from a secondary tube set inside the main barrel; (*b*) of, pertaining to, or used in the firing of such projectiles: L19. **sub-carrier** *noun* (TELECOMMUNICATIONS) a carrier wave used to modulate another carrier M20. **subcartiˈlaginous** *adjective* partly or incompletely cartilaginous M16. **subˈcaudal** *adjective & noun* (ZOOLOGY) (*a*) *adjective* situated under or near the tail; (*b*) *noun* a subcaudal part; *esp.* a subcaudal plate in a snake: L18. **subˈcellarer** *noun* (chiefly *Hist.*) a subordinate cellarer in a convent or monastery L15. **subˈcellular** *adjective* (BIOLOGY) smaller than a cell, situated or occurring within a cell or cells M20. **subˈcentral** *adjective* (*a*) nearly central; near the centre; close below the centre; (*b*) ANATOMY beneath a centrum: E19. **subˈcentrally** *adverb* (*a*) near the centre; (*b*) ANATOMY beneath a centrum: L19. †**subˈcitrine** *adjective* of a yellowish or greenish-yellow colour LME–E18. **subclaˈvicular** *adjective* (ANATOMY & SURGERY) situated, occurring, or performed below or beneath the clavicle M17. **subclimax** *noun* (ECOLOGY) the stage in an ecological succession preceding the climax, or at which a community is prevented by climatic or other factors from reaching the natural climax E20. **subˈclinical** *adjective* (MEDICINE) not giving rise to any observable symptoms M20. **subcoˈllector** *noun* (*Hist.*) an assistant collector of taxes etc. L15. **subcoˈmmissioner** *noun* an assistant commissioner E17. **subˈcompact** *adjective & noun* (*N. Amer.*) (designating) a car smaller than a compact car M20. **subˈconical** *adjective* approximately conical, slightly conical L18. **subˈconstable** *noun* (*Hist.*) a subordinate or assistant constable, esp. in the Royal Irish Constabulary E16. **subˈcool** *verb trans.* = SUPERCOOL *verb* 1 (freq. as ***subcooled*** *ppl adjective*, ***subcooling*** *verbal noun*) M20. **subˈcordate** *adjective* (BOTANY & ZOOLOGY) approximately cordate L18. **subˈcortical** *adjective* pertaining to or situated in the region underlying a cortex, esp. the cortex of the brain or the bark of a tree E19. **subˈcostal** *adjective* (*a*) ANATOMY situated below or on the underside of a rib, or beneath the ribs; (*b*) ENTOMOLOGY situated behind or near the costal vein of an insect's wing: E19. **subˈcranial** *adjective* beneath or below the cranium L19. **subcycle** *noun* a cycle which forms part of a larger cycle M20. **sub-deb** *noun* (*US colloq.*, now *rare*) = SUB-DÉBUTANTE E20. **sub-débutante** *noun* (*US*, now *rare*) a girl soon to come out as a social débutante; *loosely* a girl in her mid-teens: M20. **subˈdelegate** *noun* a person acting as a representative of or deputy for a delegate M16. **subˈdelegate** *verb trans.* (*a*) transmit (power) to a subdelegate; †(*b*) appoint (a person) to act as a subdelegate: E16. **subdelegation** *noun* the action of subdelegating a thing or person E17. **subdenomination** *noun* a subordinate denomination, category, or division M17. **subdialect** *noun* a subordinate dialect, a division of a dialect M17. **subdiaˈlectal** *adjective* of or pertaining to a subdialect M20. **subdiˈrectory** *noun* (COMPUTING) a directory below another directory in a hierarchy L20. **subdistrict** *noun* a division or subdivision of a district E19. **subˈdorsal** *adjective* (ZOOLOGY) situated near the back or upper surface M19. **subˈdural** *adjective* (ANATOMY & MEDICINE) situated or occurring between the dura mater and the arachnoid membrane L19. **subdwarf** *adjective & noun* (ASTRONOMY) (designating) a star which when plotted on the Hertzsprung–Russell diagram lies just below the main sequence, being less luminous than dwarf stars of the same temperature M20. **sub-ecoˈnomic** *adjective* not justifiable on purely economic grounds M20. **sub-element** *noun* a subordinate or secondary element M19. **sub-eleˈmentary** *adjective* (*a*) *rare* not quite elementary; (*b*) at a level or scale lower than elementary: E17. **subenˈtire** *adjective* (BOTANY) almost lacking indentations L19. **subˈequal** *adjective* (BOTANY & ZOOLOGY) nearly equal L18. **subˈequally** *adverb* (BOTANY & ZOOLOGY) nearly equally L19. **sub-era** *noun* (GEOLOGY) a period which is a subdivision of an era, used esp. with ref. to the Tertiary and Quaternary divisions of the Cenozoic M20. **subfactor** *noun* a secondary or subordinate factor E18. **sub-floor** *noun* a floor serving as a base for another floor L19. **subform** *noun* a subordinate or secondary form, a variety M20. **subˈfossil** *adjective & noun* (*a*) *adjective* partly fossilized; (*b*) *noun* a partly fossilized thing: M19. **subfraction** *noun* a fraction of a fraction; each of the portions into which a fraction may be divided: E17. **subfractioˈnation** *noun* (BIOCHEMISTRY) the process of separating a fraction into further components

M20. **sub-frame** *noun* (*a*) a frame for the attachment of a window or door-frame, or of panelling; (*b*) the frame on which the coachwork of a vehicle is built: E20. **subgiant** *noun* (ASTRONOMY) a star which when plotted on the Hertzsprung–Russell diagram lies between the main sequence and the giants, being less luminous than a giant of the same spectral type M20. **subˈglabrous** *adjective* (BOTANY & ZOOLOGY) almost glabrous M19. **subˈglacial** *adjective* existing or occurring under ice (esp. that of a glacier) E20. **subˈglacially** *adverb* under an ice sheet or glacier E20. **subglobose** /sʌbˈɡləʊbəʊs, sʌbɡləʊˈbəʊs/ *adjective* (BOTANY & ZOOLOGY) somewhat globose, almost spherical M18. **subˈglobular** *adjective* almost globular or spherical L18. **subˈgovernor** *noun* an official immediately below a governor in rank L17. **subgrade** *noun* (*a*) ENGINEERING the layer, natural or constructed, lying immediately below the foundations of a road or railway line; (*b*) a subsidiary or subordinate grade: L19. **subgrain** *noun* a small grain contained within another grain in a metal or mineral M20. **subharˈmonic** *noun & adjective* (*a*) *noun* an oscillation with a frequency equal to an integral submultiple of another frequency; (*b*) *adjective* designating or involving a subharmonic: E20. **subˈhedral** *adjective* (CRYSTALLOGRAPHY) having partially developed faces or incompletely bounded planes E20. **subiˈmago** *noun* (ENTOMOLOGY) in mayflies, a stage in the life cycle immediately preceding the imago M19. **subinˈcise** *verb trans.* perform subincision on E20. **subinˈcision** *noun* the practice of cutting an opening in the urethra on the underside of the penis, esp. as an initiatory rite L19. **subinˈhibitory** *adjective* (of a dose of a drug, chemical, etc.) enough to hinder but not prevent microbial growth M20. **subˈintellect** *verb trans.* (*rare*) supply mentally, understand L17. **subinteˈllection** *noun* (*rare*) the action of subintellecting something E17. **subˈintrant** *adjective & noun* (MEDICINE, now *rare*) (designating or characterizing) a fever etc. in which paroxysms occur so frequently as to overlap in time L17. **subintroˈduce** *verb trans.* introduce secretly or subtly M17. **subinvoˈluted** *adjective* (MEDICINE) (of an organ) exhibiting subinvolution L19. **subinvoˈlution** *noun* (MEDICINE) incomplete involution of an organ, esp. of the uterus after parturition M19. **subˈirrigate** *verb trans. & intrans.* subject (an area of land) to subirrigation E20. **subirriˈgation** *noun* the irrigation of land from beneath the surface, esp. by underground channels or pipes L19. **subkingdom** *noun* (*a*) BIOLOGY a taxonomic grouping ranking next below a kingdom; (*b*) a minor or subordinate kingdom: E19. **sublaˈcustrine** *adjective* lying or deposited at the bottom of a lake M19. **sublanguage** *noun* a specialized language or jargon associated with a specific group or context M20. **subˈlateral** *adjective* almost lateral, situated near the side E19. **sublattice** *noun* (PHYSICS & MATH.) a lattice whose points represent all those members of a fuller lattice having some property not possessed by the other members M20. **sub-ˈlethal** *adjective* having an effect (only just) less than lethal; *spec.* in GENETICS = SEMI-LETHAL *adjective*: L19. **subˈlethally** *adverb* in a sub-lethal manner M20. **sublevel** *noun* (PHYSICS) each of a group of energy levels of an atom or nucleus which coincide under a coarse approximation or when some factor (as a magnetic field) is removed M20. **sublexemic** /sʌblɛkˈsiːmɪk/ *adjective* (LINGUISTICS) below the level of a lexeme; not fully lexemic: M20. **sub-lieuˈtenancy** *noun* the position or rank of a sub-lieutenant M19. **sub-lieuˈtenant** *noun* a naval or (formerly) army officer ranking next below a lieutenant E18. **subˈlinear** *adjective* (*a*) (chiefly BOTANY & ZOOLOGY) nearly linear; (*b*) below a written or printed line: L18. **subˈlingual** *adjective* (*a*) MEDICINE (of a medicine etc.) that is placed under the tongue to be slowly dissolved; (*b*) ANATOMY situated under the tongue or on the underside of the tongue; *spec.* designating or pertaining to either of two small salivary glands on either side of the floor of the mouth: M17. **subˈlingually** *adverb* under the tongue M20. **sub-linˈguistic** *adjective* (*a*) not fully linguistic; at a level below that of language; (*b*) of or pertaining to a sublanguage: M20. **subˈliteral** *adjective* (of a diacritic) written or printed below a character M20. **subˈlittoral** *adjective & noun* (*a*) *adjective* lying near or just below the seashore; *spec.* in ECOLOGY, designating or pertaining to the biogeographic zone normally taken to extend from the line of mean low tide to the edge of the continental shelf; (*b*) *noun* the sublittoral zone: M19. **subˈlittorally** *adverb* in sublittoral regions M20. **subˈluminal** *adjective* pertaining to or having a speed less than that of light M20. **subˈluminous** *adjective* dim; *spec.* in ASTRONOMY, of less luminosity than the normal: M19. **subluxate** /sʌbˈlʌkseɪt/ *verb trans.* (MEDICINE) partially dislocate (chiefly as **subluxated** *ppl adjective*) L19. **subluxation** /sʌblʌkˈseɪʃ(ə)n/ *noun* (MEDICINE) (a) partial dislocation L17. **sub-maˈchine-gun** *noun* a hand-held lightweight machine-gun E20. **subman** *noun* (freq. *derog.*) a man of inferior development or ability; a brutal or stupid man: E20. **submanˈdibular** *adjective* (ANATOMY) situated beneath the jaw or mandible; *spec.* designating or pertaining to either of two salivary glands situated below the parotid glands: L19. **subˈmarshal** *noun* (*Hist.*) a deputy or under-marshal L16. **subˈmaster** *noun* a subordinate or assistant master in a school etc.; an assistant headmaster: LME. **submaxillary** /sʌbmakˈsɪləri/ *adjective* = SUBMANDIBULAR L18. **subˈmediant** *noun & adjective* (MUSIC) (designating) the sixth note of the diatonic scale of any key E19. **subˈmental** *adjective* (ANATOMY) situated beneath the chin or under the edge of the lower jaw M19. **submenu** *noun* (COMPUTING) a subsidiary menu displayed to indicate a range of options available under a general heading listed in a menu L20. **subˈmicron** *adjective* of a size or scale smaller than a micron M20. **subˈmillimetre** *adjective* less than a millimetre in size or length; pertaining to electromagnetic waves of such a length: M20. **subˈminiature** *adjective* smaller than miniature; very much reduced in size: M20. **sub,miniaturiˈzation** *noun* the development or use of subminiature devices, esp. in electronics M20. **subˈmodifier** *noun* (GRAMMAR) an adverb used in front of an adjective or another adverb to modify its meaning (for example *very* in *very cold* or *unusually* in *an unusually large house*) L20. **subˈmontane** *adjective* (*a*) (of a tunnel etc.) passing under or through mountains; (*b*) situated in the foothills or lower slopes of a mountain range: E19. **submuˈcosa** *noun* (ANATOMY) the layer of areolar connective tissue lying beneath a mucous membrane L19. **submuˈcosal** *adjective* (ANATOMY) of or pertaining to the submucosa E20. **subˈmucous** *adjective* (*a*) somewhat mucous; (*b*) ANATOMY & MEDICINE situated, occurring, or introduced beneath a mucous membrane; of or pertaining to the submucosa: L17. **submuˈnition** *noun* (chiefly *US*) a small short-range guided missile (usu. in *pl.*) L20. **subnetwork** *noun* (chiefly COMPUTING) a part of a larger network M20. **subocˈcipital** *adjective* (ANATOMY & MEDICINE) (*a*) situated under the occiput or below the occipital bone; (*b*) under or in the lowest part of the occipital lobe of the brain: M18. **subˈoctave** *noun* (MUSIC) the octave below a given note M17. **sub-ˈofficer** *noun* a subordinate officer E17. **suboˈpercular** *adjective & noun* (ZOOLOGY) (designating or pertaining to) the suboperculum M19. **suboˈperculum** *noun*, pl. **-la**, ZOOLOGY a bone situated below the operculum in the gill-cover of a fish M19. **subˈoptimal** *adjective* less than the optimal; not of the best sort or quality: E20. **suborˈbicular** *adjective* (chiefly BOTANY) almost orbicular M18. **subˈordinary** *noun* (HERALDRY) a subordinate ordinary L18. **subˈoval** *adjective* somewhat or almost oval M18. **subˈovate** *adjective* somewhat or almost ovate M18. **subˈoxic** *adjective* low in oxygen, almost or partly anoxic L20. **subˈparallel** *adjective* (chiefly GEOLOGY) almost parallel M19. **subpassage** /ˈsʌbpasɪdʒ, sʌbpaˈsɑːʒ/ *noun & verb* (BIOLOGY & MEDICINE) (*a*) *noun* the passage of a strain of micro-organisms cultivated in one animal through another, esp. to increase the virulence; (*b*) *verb trans.* subject to subpassage: M20. **subˈpatent** *adjective* (of a parasite or parasitic infection) present but not detectable; of or pertaining to such an infection: E20. **subˈpectoral** *adjective* (*rare*) beneath or within the chest or breast M19. **subˈpetiolar** *adjective* (BOTANY) situated under the petiole, as the buds of the plane tree L19. **subˈpetiolate** *adjective* (BOTANY) having a very short petiole M19. **subphonemic** /sʌbfə(ʊ)ˈniːmɪk/ *adjective* (LINGUISTICS) (of a difference of sound) that does not distinguish phonemes, not fully phonemic M20. **sub-plot** *noun* a subordinate plot in a play, novel, etc. E20. **subˈpolar** *adjective* (*a*) near to the polar regions, subarctic or subantarctic; (*b*) ASTRONOMY & SURVEYING beneath the north or south celestial: E19. **subpopuˈlation** *noun* (*a*) *rare* a population living underground; (*b*) a population forming part of a larger population, or derived from some other population: L19. **sub-preˈceptor** *noun* (*obsolete* exc. *Hist.*) an assistant preceptor or instructor L17. **subˈprincipal** *noun* a vice-principal of a university etc. (chiefly *Scot.*); MUSIC an open diapason sub-bass: M16. **subˈprior** *noun* an assistant or deputy prior ME. **subˈprioress** *noun* an assistant or deputy prioress LME. **subprogram** *noun* (COMPUTING) = SUBROUTINE M20. **subˈramose** *adjective* (BOTANY & ZOOLOGY) having a few lateral branches L18. **sub-range** *noun* (*a*) a subsidiary range (of mountains); (*b*) a range of values or conditions within a larger range: M19. **subˈrational** *adjective* below or less than (that which is) rational M19. **subregion** *noun* a division or subdivision of a region M19. **subˈregional** *adjective* of or pertaining to a subregion L19. **sub-rent** *verb trans.* rent (property) from a person who rents from someone else M19. **subring** *noun* (MATH.) a subset of a ring that is itself a ring with respect to the two binary operations of the set M20. **subroˈtund** *adjective* (chiefly BOTANY) almost orbicular, rounded M18. **sub-Saˈharan** *adjective* in or from the part of Africa south of the Sahara desert M20. **subsalt** *noun* (CHEMISTRY, now *rare* or *obsolete*) a basic salt E19. **subsample** *noun & verb* (*a*) *noun* a sample drawn from a larger sample; (*b*) *verb trans.* & *intrans.* take a subsample (of): E20. **subsatellite** *noun* (ASTRONAUTICS) a satellite of a satellite; *spec.* a small artificial satellite released from another satellite or spacecraft: L19. **subˈscapular** *adjective* (ANATOMY) below or on the undersurface of the scapula M19. **subsea** *adjective & adverb* (chiefly OIL INDUSTRY) (situated or occurring) beneath the surface of the sea E20. **subˈsemitone** *noun* (MUSIC) the leading note of a scale L18. **subˈsensible** *adjective* below or deeper than the range of the senses M19. **subˈsensual** *adjective* = SUBSENSIBLE L19. **subˈsensuous** *adjective* = SUBSENSIBLE M19. **subˈserous** *adjective* (ANATOMY & MEDICINE) designating, pertaining to, or affecting the tissue directly beneath a serous membrane M19. **subˈserrate** *adjective* (BOTANY) obscurely serrate L18. **subˈsessile** *adjective* (ZOOLOGY & BOTANY) not quite sessile; having only a very short stalk: M18. **sub-shell** *noun* (PHYSICS) in an electron shell, the complete set of orbitals that can be occupied by electrons of identical azimuthal quantum number *l*: M20. **subˈsocial** *adjective* (ZOOLOGY) living gregariously but without a fixed social organization E20. **subˈsolar** *adjective* †(*a*) *rare* exposed to the sun; (*b*) METEOROLOGY & ASTRONOMY directly underneath the sun, having the sun in the zenith: M17. **subˈsolidus** *adjective* (GEOLOGY) existing or occurring in conditions corresponding to a point in a phase diagram below a solidus, i.e. when the system is wholly solid M20. **sub-song** *noun* the part of a bird's song that is softer and less well-defined and significant than its characteristic series of notes E20. **subˈspinous** *adjective* (*a*) ZOOLOGY & BOTANY somewhat spinous; (*b*) MEDICINE *rare* under the spine of the scapula: E19. **substage** *noun* (*a*) GEOLOGY a subdivision of a stage; (*b*) an apparatus fixed beneath the ordinary stage of a compound microscope to support mirrors and other accessories: M19. **subˈstellar** *adjective* (*a*) NAVIGATION & ASTRONOMY designating a point on the earth's surface at which a particular star is vertically overhead; (*b*) ASTRONOMY much smaller than a typical star: E20. **substorm** *noun* (METEOROLOGY) a disturbance of the earth's magnetic field restricted to certain, usu. polar, latitudes and typically manifested as an aurora and related phenomena L19. **subˈstratosphere** *noun* the upper part of the troposphere, immediately below the stratosphere M19. **subsystem** *noun* a self-contained system within a larger system L19. **subˈtabulate** *verb trans.* (MATH.) expand (a mathematical table) by systematic interpolation; evaluate (a tabulated function) for a set of values of the argument in between the tabulated ones: M20. **subtabuˈlation** *noun* (MATH.) the process of subtabulating something E20. **subtack** *noun* (SCOTS LAW) a tack or lease granted by a superior to an inferior tenant E17. **subˈtacksman** *noun* (SCOTS LAW) a person who holds a subordinate tack at the hands of a tacksman E17. **subˈtalar** *adjective* (ANATOMY) designating or pertaining to (*a*) the joint in the foot, below the ankle, between the calcaneum (heel-bone) and the talus; (*b*) the posterior of the two articulations in this joint: M20. **subˈtangent** *noun* (MATH.) (the length of) the section of the *x*-axis lying between the points of intersection with a tangent to a curve and with a perpendicular drawn from the point of contact of the tangent E18. **sub-ˈteen** *noun & adjective* (orig. *US*) = PRE-TEEN M20. **sub-ˈteenager** *noun* = PRE-TEENAGER M20. **subˈtenure** *noun* the holding of land by a lease from a superior tenant M19. **subteˈrete** *adjective* (BOTANY) more or less terete M19. **subˈtertian** *adjective* (MEDICINE) designating or pertaining to a severe form of malaria caused by the sporozoan *Plasmodium falciparum* with a recurrence of fever every 36 to 48 hours E20. **subtest** *noun* a test which is subsidiary to or forms part of a main test, esp. (PSYCHOLOGY) in aptitude assessment M20. **subˈthalamic** *adjective* (ANATOMY) situated below the thalamus L19. **subˈthalamus** *noun*, pl. **-mi**, ANATOMY a region at the base of the fore-brain below the thalamus and next to the substantia nigra, concerned with motor functions E20. **subˈtidal** *adjective* (ECOLOGY) situated or occurring below the low tidemark M20. **subtone** *noun* a subordinate tone; an undertone: L19. **subˈtonic** *noun* (MUSIC) the note a semitone below the upper tonic of a scale; the leading note: M19. **subˈtreasurer** *noun* an assistant or deputy treasurer M16. **subˈtreasury** *noun* (*a*) a subordinate or branch treasury; (*b*) *US* the organization by which the separate safe keeping of the public funds is entrusted to specially appointed officers; any of the branches of the Treasury established in certain cities of the States for the receipt and safe keeping of public monies: M19. **subtriˈangular** *adjective* (chiefly ZOOLOGY & BOTANY) approximately triangular L18. **subˈtribal** *adjective* pertaining to a subtribe L19. **subtribe** *noun* a subdivision of a tribe M19. **subˈtriple** *adjective* (MATH., now *rare* or *obsolete*) that is one third of a quantity or number, of or in proportion of 1 to 3: M17. **subˈtriplicate** *adjective* (MATH., now *rare* or *obsolete*) of or in the ratio of the cube roots of two given quantities M17. **subˈtruncate** *adjective* (BOTANY & ZOOLOGY) almost truncate E19. **subtype** *noun & verb* (*a*) *noun* a subordinate type; a type included in a more general type; *spec.* a subdivision of a type of micro-organism; (*b*) *verb trans.* assign to a subtype: M19. **subˈtypical** *adjective* (*a*) of the character of a subtype; (*b*) not quite typical: M19. **subumˈbrella** *noun* (ZOOLOGY) the internal ventral or oral disc of a hydrozoan; the concave muscular lower layer of the umbrella of a jellyfish: L19. **subumˈbrellar** *adjective* (ZOOLOGY) beneath the umbrella; of or pertaining to the subumbrella: L19. **sub-ˈunderwrite** *verb trans.* (ECONOMICS) underwrite part of a liability underwritten by another M20. **sub-ˈunderwriter** *noun* (ECONOMICS) a person who underwrites part of a liability underwritten by another M20. **subˈungual** *adjective* (MEDICINE) under a fingernail or toenail M19. **subunit** *noun* a part of a unit; a distinct, freq. separable component; *esp.* (BIOCHEMISTRY) each of two or more polypeptide chains contained in a protein: M20. **subvariety** *noun* a subordinate or minor variety, esp. of a domestic animal or cultivated plant E19. **subˈvassal** *noun* (chiefly *Scot.*, now *Hist.*) an undervassal; a vassal of a vassal: L15. **subˈvassalage** *noun* (chiefly *Scot.*, now *Hist.*) the condition of being a subvassal; a property held by a subvassal: L18. **subˈvertebral** *adjective* (ANATOMY) situated below a vertebra or the vertebral column M19. **subˈvertical** *adjective* (*a*) below a vertex; (*b*) nearly vertical: L19. **subˈvital** *adjective* (*a*) GENETICS (of a gene) causing the death of a significant proportion of the individuals carrying it, but not as many as a semi-lethal gene; (*b*) BIOLOGY having some of the characteristics of living systems: M20. **subˈvocal** *adjective* (PHILOSOPHY) designating an unarticulated level of speech comparable to thought M20. **subvocaliˈzation** *noun* articulation with the lips or other speech organs silently or with barely audible sound, esp. while reading M20. **subˈvocalize** *verb trans.* & *intrans.* utter or form (words) by subvocalization M20. **subˈvocalizer** *noun* a person who subvocalizes M20. **subwarden** *noun* a deputy warden M17. **subwoofer** *noun* a loudspeaker component designed to reproduce only extremely low bass frequencies L20. **subˈzero** *adjective* (esp. of temperature) lower than zero M20. **subzone** *noun* (GEOLOGY) a subdivision of a zone L19.

suba /ˈʃuːbə/ *noun.* Pl. **-s**, same. E20.
[Hungarian.]
A long sheepskin cloak traditionally worn by Hungarian shepherds.

subacid /sʌbˈasɪd/ *adjective & noun.* M17.
[Latin *subacidus*, formed as SUB- + ACID *adjective*.]
▶ **A** *adjective.* Somewhat acid (*lit.* & *fig.*). M17.
▶ **B** *noun.* **1** Subacid quality or flavour. L18.
2 A subacid substance. E19.
■ **subaˈcidity** *noun* the quality or condition of being subacid M19.

†**subact** *verb trans.* Pa. pple **subact**, **subacted**. LME.
[Latin *subact-* pa. ppl stem of *subigere*, formed as SUB- + *agere* bring.]
1 Bring under control or into subjection; subdue. LME–L17.
2 Work up, mix, as in cultivating the ground, kneading dough, etc. E17–E19.
■ †**subaction** *noun* E17–E19.

subacute /sʌbəˈkjuːt/ *adjective.* M18.
[from SUB- 6 + ACUTE *adjective*.]
1 (Of an angle) moderately acute; pointed but not sharply so. M18.
2 MEDICINE. Developing faster than a chronic condition but not becoming acute. M19.
3 Of feelings etc.: not quite acute. M19.
■ **subacutely** *adverb* M19.

subadar /suːbəˈdɑː/ *noun. Anglo-Indian.* Also **subahdar**. L17.
[Persian & Urdu *ṣūba(h)dār*, formed as SUBAH + Persian *-dār* holding, holder.]
Hist. **1** The governor of a subah. L17.
2 The senior Indian officer in a sepoy regiment. M18.
■ **subadary** *noun* (*rare*) [Persian & Urdu *ṣūba(h)dārī*] = SUBAHSHIP M18.

subaerial /sʌbˈɛːrɪəl/ *adjective.* M19.
[from SUB- 1 + AERIAL *adjective*.]
Chiefly GEOLOGY & PHYSICAL GEOGRAPHY. Existing, occurring, or formed, in the open air or on the earth's surface, not under water or underground.
■ **subaerially** *adverb* L19.

For other words beginning with *sub-* see the main alphabetic sequence of entries

subah /ˈsuːbɑː/ *noun. Anglo-Indian* (now *Hist.*). Also **sou-**. **M18.**
[Persian & Urdu *ṣūba(h)* lit. 'collection or number of sirkars', from Arab. = heap, pile, collection.]
Hist. **1** A province of the Mughal Empire. **M18.**
2 = SUBADAR. **M18.**
■ **subahship** *noun* (**a**) = SUBAH 1; (**b**) the office of governor of a subah: **M18.**

subahdar *noun* var. of SUBADAR.

subalpine /sʌbˈalpʌɪn/ *adjective.* Also **sub-Alpine**. **M17.**
[Latin *subalpinus*, formed as SUB- + ALPINE *adjective.*]
1 Of or pertaining to the area at the foot of the Alps. **M17.**
2 Partly alpine in character or formation; *spec.* pertaining to or characteristic of higher mountain slopes below the tree line. **M19.**

subaltern /ˈsʌb(ə)lt(ə)n/ *adjective & noun.* **L16.**
[Late Latin *subalternus*, formed as SUB- + ALTERN.]
▶ **A** *adjective.* **1** Subordinate, inferior; *spec.* (of a military officer) of junior rank. **L16.** ▶**b** *SCOTS LAW* (now *Hist.*). (Of a vassal) holding land etc. of another's vassal; (of land) held by a vassal from another's vassal. **M17.**
2 a *LOGIC.* Of a proposition: particular, not universal. **L16.** ▶†**b** Designating a genus that is at the same time a species of a higher genus. **M17–M19.**
†**3** Succeeding in turn. *rare.* **E17–M18.**
▶ **B** *noun.* **1** A person or (formerly) a thing of inferior rank or status. **E17.**
2 *MILITARY.* An officer below the rank of captain, *spec.* a second lieutenant. **L17.**
3 *LOGIC.* A subaltern proposition. **L17.**
■ **subalternity** *noun* the quality or condition of being subordinate **E17.**

subalternate /sʌbɔːlˈtəːnət, -ɒl-/ *adjective & noun.* **LME.**
[Late Latin *subalternatus* pa. pple of *subalternare* to subordinate: see -ATE².]
▶ **A** *adjective.* †**1** Subordinate, inferior. **LME–L19.**
†**2** *LOGIC.* = SUBALTERN *adjective* 2b. **L16–M17.**
3 *BOTANY & ZOOLOGY.* Alternate, but tending to become opposite. **E19.**
▶ **B** *noun. LOGIC.* A particular proposition. **E19.**

subalternation /ˌsʌbɔːltəˈneɪʃ(ə)n, -ɒl-/ *noun.* **L16.**
[medieval Latin *subalternatio(n-)*, from *subalternat-* pa. ppl stem of *subalternare*: see prec., -ATION.]
†**1** Subordination. Only in **L16.**
†**2** Succession by turn. Only in **E17.**
3 *LOGIC.* The relation between a universal and a particular of the same quality; the opposition between propositions alike in quality but differing in quantity. **M17.**

sub-aqua /sʌbˈakwə/ *adjective.* **M20.**
[from SUB- 1 + Latin *aqua* water.]
Of or pertaining to underwater swimming or diving involving the use of an aqualung.

subaqueous /sʌbˈeɪkwɪəs/ *adjective.* **L17.**
[from SUB- 1 + AQUEOUS.]
1 Existing, made, occurring, etc., under water. **L17.**
2 Reflected (as) in deep water. *poet.* **L18.**
3 *fig.* Lacking real substance or strength. **M20.**
■ **subaquean** *adjective* (*rare*) = SUBAQUEOUS 1 **L18.**

subarctic /sʌbˈɑːktɪk/ *adjective & noun.* Also **sub-Arctic**. **M19.**
[from SUB- 5, 6 + ARCTIC.]
▶ **A** *adjective.* Nearly Arctic; pertaining to or characteristic of the region immediately south of the Arctic Circle; characterized by plants typical of this region. **M19.**
▶ **B** *noun.* The subarctic region. Also, the period of glacial recession in Europe characterized by subarctic plants. **M19.**

Subarian /suːbəˈriːən/ *noun & adjective.* **E20.**
[from Akkadian *Subar(tu* Assyria + -IAN.]
▶ **A** *noun.* **1** A member of an ancient people of northern Mesopotamia. **E20.**
2 The language (written in cuneiform) of this people. **E20.**
▶ **B** *adjective.* Of or pertaining to the Subarians or their language. **E20.**

subarrhation /sʌbəˈreɪʃ(ə)n/ *noun.* Now *rare.* **E17.**
[Latin *subarrhatio(n-)*, from *subarrhat-* pa. ppl stem of *subarrhare* pay earnest money, formed as SUB- + ARRHA: see -ATION.]
Hist. An ancient form of betrothal in which pledges of money, rings, etc., were given by the man to the woman.

subashi /suːˈbaʃə/ *noun.* **L16.**
[Turkish *subaşı*, from *su* army + *baş* head, chief.]
Hist. A Turkish official in command of a district or village.

subatomic /sʌbəˈtɒmɪk/ *adjective.* **E20.**
[from SUB- 2, 2b + ATOMIC.]
PHYSICS. Occurring in the atom; smaller than an atom. Also, dealing with or involving particles, forces, or phenomena on this scale.
subatomic level, subatomic particle, subatomic physics, etc.
■ **sub-ˈatom** *noun* (now *rare* or *obsolete*) a constituent part of an atom, a subatomic particle **L19.**

subaudition /sʌbɔːˈdɪʃ(ə)n/ *noun.* **M17.**
[Late Latin *subauditio(n-)*, from *subaudit-* pa. ppl stem of *subaudire* supply mentally, formed as SUB- + *audire* hear, after Greek *upakouein*.]
†**1** Hearing a little. *rare.* Only in **M17.**
2 Chiefly *GRAMMAR.* The action of mentally supplying something that is not expressed; implied or understood meaning. **L18.**

subauditur /sʌbɔːˈdʌɪtə/ *noun.* Now *rare.* **E19.**
[from Latin = 'it is understood', 3rd person sing. pres. indic. pass. of *subaudire*: see prec.]
= SUBAUDITION 2. Cf. SUBINTELLIGITUR.

subbie /ˈsʌbi/ *noun & verb. slang* (chiefly *Austral.*). Also **subby**. **L20.**
[from SUB(CONTRACTOR + -IE.]
▶ **A** *noun.* A subcontractor. **L20.**
▶ **B** *verb.* **1** *verb intrans.* Work as a subcontractor. **L20.**
2 *verb trans.* Subcontract (work). **L20.**

subbotnik /suːˈbɒtnɪk/ *noun.* Pl. **-i** /-i/, **-s**. **E20.**
[Russian, from *subbota* Saturday: see -NIK.]
In countries of the former USSR, the practice or an act of working voluntarily on a Saturday, for the benefit of the national economy.

Subbuteo /sʌˈbjuːtɪəʊ/ *noun.* **M20.**
[Punningly from mod. Latin *subbuteo*, specific name of the hobby, from SUB- + Latin *buteo* falcon (translating Greek *hupotriokhes* kind of hawk traditionally assoc. with the hobby).]
(Proprietary name for) a table-top version of football or other field game.

subby *noun & verb* var. of SUBBIE.

subcategory /ˈsʌbkatɪg(ə)ri/ *noun.* **E20.**
[from SUB- 2b + CATEGORY.]
A secondary or subordinate category; a subsection of a category.
■ **subcategoriˈzation** *noun* the action or an act of subcategorizing something **M20.** **subcategorize** *verb trans.* divide into subcategories **M20.**

subcelestial /sʌbsɪˈlɛstɪəl/ *adjective & noun.* **M16.**
[from late Latin *subcelestis*, formed as SUB- + Latin *caelestis* CELESTIAL: see -IAL.]
▶ **A** *adjective.* Situated or existing beneath heaven; *esp.* earthly, mundane. **M16.**
▶ **B** *noun.* A subcelestial being. **M17.**

subception /sʌbˈsɛpʃ(ə)n/ *noun.* **M20.**
[Blend of SUBLIMINAL and PERCEPTION.]
PSYCHOLOGY. Perception of stimuli not consciously apprehended.

subchanter /ˈsʌbtʃɑːntə/ *noun.* **E16.**
[from SUB- 2 + CHANTER, after medieval Latin *subcantor*, *-centor*. Cf. SUCCENTOR.]
Orig., a precentor's deputy, a succentor. Now, a vicar choral who assists in chanting the litany.
■ †**subchantress** *noun*: only in **LME.**

sub-cheese /sʌbˈtʃiːz/ *noun. Military slang* (orig. *Anglo-Indian*). **L19.**
[from Hindi *sab chīz*, from *sab* all + Persian & Urdu *chīz* thing (cf. CHEESE *noun*²).]
The lot; everything. Freq. in ***the whole sub-cheese***.

subchelate /sʌbˈkiːleɪt/ *adjective.* **M19.**
[from SUB- 2, 6 + CHELATE *adjective.*]
ZOOLOGY. Having a subchela. Also *occas.*, imperfectly chelate.
■ **subchela** *noun*, pl. **-lae**, a pincer-like claw in some crustaceans, in which the last limb segment is folded back against the previous one **L19.**

subclass /ˈsʌbklɑːs/ *noun.* **E19.**
[from SUB- 2b + CLASS *noun.*]
A subordinate or secondary class; *spec.* in *TAXONOMY*, a category or taxon ranking next below a class.

subclause /ˈsʌbklɔːz/ *noun.* Also **sub-clause**. **L19.**
[from SUB- 2, 2b + CLAUSE.]
1 Chiefly *LAW.* A subsidiary section of a clause. **L19.**
2 *GRAMMAR.* A subordinate clause. **M20.**

subclavian /sʌbˈkleɪvɪən/ *adjective & noun.* **M17.**
[from mod. Latin *subclavius*, formed as SUB- + *clavis* key (see CLAVICLE): see -AN.]
ANATOMY. ▶ **A** *adjective.* Lying or extending under the clavicle; *spec.* designating or pertaining to either of two main arteries serving the neck and arms, the left arising from the aortic arch and the right from the innominate artery. **M17.**
▶ **B** *noun.* A subclavian vessel, nerve, or muscle. **E18.**

subclavius /sʌbˈkleɪvɪəs/ *noun.* **E18.**
[mod. Latin: see prec.]
ANATOMY. In full ***subclavius muscle***. A small muscle extending from the first rib to the clavicle.

subcommittee /ˈsʌbkəmɪti/ *noun.* **E17.**
[from SUB- 2b + COMMITTEE.]
A committee formed (partly) from and responsible to a main committee, esp. for a special purpose.

For other words beginning with *sub-* see the entry for **sub-**

subconscious /sʌbˈkɒnʃəs/ *adjective & noun.* **M19.**
[from SUB- 5, 6 + CONSCIOUS.]
▶ **A** *adjective.* **1** *PSYCHOLOGY.* Of or pertaining to, existing in, the part of the mind which influences actions etc. without one's (full) awareness. **M19.**
2 Partly or imperfectly aware. **M19.**

> **1** J. MARQUAND I always had a subconscious sense of something dangerous impending. M. BISHOP The manifestations of a subconscious effort to heal himself.

▶ **B** *noun. PSYCHOLOGY.* The part of the mind which influences actions etc. without one's (full) awareness. **L19.**
■ **subconsciously** *adverb* **E19.** **subconsciousness** *noun* (**a**) partial or imperfect consciousness (*of*); (**b**) = SUBCONSCIOUS *noun*: **E19.**

subcontinent /sʌbˈkɒntɪnənt/ *noun.* **M19.**
[from SUB- 2 + CONTINENT *noun.*]
A large land mass smaller than a continent; a large section of a continent having a certain geographical or political identity or independence, *spec.* that including India, Pakistan, Bangladesh, and Sri Lanka.
■ **subcontiˈnental** *adjective* **L19.**

subcontract /sʌbˈkɒntrakt/ *noun.* **E19.**
[from SUB- 3 + CONTRACT *noun*¹.]
A contract for carrying out (a part of) a previous contract, *esp.* one to supply materials, labour, etc.

subcontract /sʌbkənˈtrakt/ *verb.* **E17.**
[from SUB- 3 + CONTRACT *verb.*]
†**1** *verb trans.* (in *pass.*). Be betrothed for the second time. *rare* (Shakes.). Only in **E17.**
2 *verb intrans.* Make or carry out a subcontract. **M19.**
3 *verb trans.* Employ a person, firm, etc. to do (work) as part of a larger contract or project. **L19.**
■ **subcontractor** *noun* **M19.**

subcontrary /sʌbˈkɒntrəri/ *adjective & noun.* **L16.**
[Late Latin *subcontrarius* translating late Greek *upenantios*, formed as SUB- + CONTRARY *adjective.*]
▶ **A** *adjective.* **1** *LOGIC.* Of a proposition: that is subaltern to a contrary proposition. **L16.**
2 Somewhat or partially contrary. **E17.**
3 *GEOMETRY.* Of or pertaining to two similar triangles having a common angle at the vertex but with the bases not parallel, so that the basal angles are equal but on opposite sides. Now *rare* or *obsolete.* **E18.**
▶ **B** *noun.* **1** *LOGIC.* A subcontrary proposition. **L17.**
2 *GEOMETRY.* A subcontrary section of a cone. Now *rare* or *obsolete.* **M19.**
■ **subcontrariety** /ˌsʌbkɒntrəˈrʌɪəti/ *noun* (*LOGIC*) the relation existing between subcontrary propositions **L17.** **subcontrarily** *adverb* (*rare*) **L16.**

subcritical /sʌbˈkrɪtɪk(ə)l/ *adjective.* **M20.**
[from SUB- 1, 5 + CRITICAL.]
Below a critical level, value, threshold, etc.; *spec.* (**a**) *METALLURGY* (at) less than the critical temperature above which ferrite changes into austenite; (**b**) *FLUID MECHANICS* (of a flow of fluid) slower than the speed at which waves travel in the fluid; (**c**) *NUCLEAR PHYSICS* containing or involving less than the critical mass.

subculture /ˈsʌbkʌltʃə/ *noun & verb.* **L19.**
[from SUB- 2, 3 + CULTURE *noun*, *verb.*]
▶ **A** *noun.* **1** *BIOLOGY & MEDICINE.* A culture of micro-organisms started from another culture; the process of starting a culture in this way. **L19.**
2 A cultural group or class within a larger culture, *esp.* one having beliefs, interests, customs, etc., at variance with those of the larger culture. **M20.**

> **2** L. GOULD Her London assignment . . with the newest darlings of the rock subculture.

▶ **B** *verb trans. BIOLOGY & MEDICINE.* Produce a subculture of. **L19.**
■ **subˈcultural** *adjective* (**a**) of or pertaining to a subculture; (**b**) that is inferior to or below the general cultural level: **M20.**

subcutaneous /sʌbkjuːˈteɪnɪəs/ *adjective.* **M17.**
[from SUB- 1 + CUTANEOUS *adjective.*]
1 Situated just under the skin; (of a parasite) living under the skin. **M17.**
2 Involving or pertaining to the injection of a medicine immediately beneath the skin; hypodermic. **M17.**
■ **subcutaneously** *adverb* under the skin, hypodermically **L19.**

subdeacon /sʌbˈdiːk(ə)n/ *noun.* **ME.**
[Anglo-Norman, Old French *sudekne*, *so-*, or ecclesiastical Latin *subdiaconus*, formed as SUB- + DEACON *noun.*]
In some Christian Churches, a minister of an order next below that of deacon; a cleric or lay clerk acting as assistant to a deacon at the Eucharist.
■ **subdeaconate** *noun* = SUBDIACONATE **L19.** **subdeaconship** *noun* = SUBDIACONATE **E17.** **subdeaconry** *noun* = SUBDIACONATE **M16.**

subdean /ˈsʌbdiːn/ *noun.* **LME.**
[Repr. an Anglo-Norman word = Old French *sou(z)deien*, from *sou(s)*, *sub-* SUB- + *deien* DEAN *noun*¹, after medieval Latin *subdecanus*.]
An official who ranks immediately below a dean or acts as a deputy for a dean.

■ **subdeanery** *noun* the office, position, or residence of a subdean L16.

subdiaconal /sʌbdʌɪˈakən(ə)l/ *adjective.* M19.
[medieval Latin *subdiaconalis*, from ecclesiastical Latin *subdiaconus* SUBDEACON: see -AL[1].]
Of or pertaining to a subdeacon.

subdiaconate /sʌbdʌɪˈakənət/ *noun.* E18.
[Late Latin *subdiaconatus* from ecclesiastical Latin *subdiaconus* SUBDEACON: see -ATE[1].]
The office or rank of subdeacon.

sub dio /sʌb ˈdiːəʊ/ *adverbial phr.* E17.
[Latin, lit. 'under the open sky'.]
In the open air.

subdisjunctive /sʌbdɪsˈdʒʌŋktɪv/ *adjective & noun.* M17.
[Late Latin *subdisjunctivus*, formed as SUB- + DISJUNCTIVE.]
GRAMMAR & LOGIC. ▶**A** *adjective.* Partly disjunctive. M17.
▶**B** *noun.* A subdisjunctive proposition or word. M17.

subdistinction /sʌbdɪˈstɪŋkʃ(ə)n/ *noun.* L16.
[In branch I from SUB- 2 + DISTINCTION; in branch II from late Latin *subdistinctio(n-)* from *subdistinct-* pa. ppl stem of *subdistinguere* insert a comma, formed as SUB- + *distinguere* DISTINGUISH: see -ION.]
▶**I 1** A subordinate distinction. L16.
†**2** A subdivision, a subspecies. E–M18.
▶†**II 3** A comma; a semicolon. M17–E19.

†**subdistinguish** *verb trans.* E17–L18.
[from SUB- 3 + DISTINGUISH, after late Latin *subdistinguere*: see prec.]
Distinguish into subordinate kinds, classes, species, etc.

subdivide /sʌbdɪˈvʌɪd/ *verb trans. & intrans.* LME.
[Late Latin *subdividere* formed as SUB- + DIVIDE *verb*.]
Divide again after a first division; break up into subdivisions; *loosely* divide.

Observer Architecture subdivided into a proliferation of styles.

■ **subdividable** *adjective* (*rare*) = SUBDIVISIBLE L17. **subdivider** *noun* (*a*) a person who subdivides something; (*b*) *spec.* a person who subdivides an area of land into a number of estates; a settler on or developer of such an area of land: L19. **subdividingly** *adverb* in subdivisions M19. **subdivisible** *adjective* able to be subdivided M19.

subdivision /ˈsʌbdɪvɪʒ(ə)n, sʌbdɪˈvɪʒ(ə)n/ *noun.* LME.
[Late Latin *subdivisio(n-)*, formed as SUB- + DIVISION *noun*.]
1 Each of the parts into which a division is or may be divided; a secondary or subordinate division. LME. ▶**b** MILITARY. Half of a division, company, etc. E17. ▶**c** An area of land subdivided into plots for the erection of houses; a housing estate. *N. Amer. & Austral.* M19.
2 The action or process of subdividing; the fact of being subdivided; an instance of this. (Foll. by *of*.) LME.

1 W. S. CHURCHILL The hundreds, subdivisions of the shire, were created. **c** *New Yorker* I longed for the suburbs—their open-skied subdivisions.

■ **subdiˈvisional** *adjective* of or pertaining to (a) subdivision; of the nature of subdivision; consisting of a subdivision: M17. **subdiˈvisive** *adjective* (*rare*) resulting from subdivision M19.

subdolous /ˈsʌbdələs/ *adjective.* Now *rare.* L16.
[from Latin *subdolus* (formed as SUB- + *dolus* cunning) + -OUS.]
Crafty, cunning, sly.
■ **subdolously** *adverb* L17. **subdolousness** *noun* M17.

subdominant /sʌbˈdɒmɪnənt/ *noun*[1]. L18.
[from SUB- 1 + DOMINANT *noun*.]
MUSIC. The note next below the dominant of a scale; the fourth note of the diatonic scale of a key.

subdominant /sʌbˈdɒmɪnənt/ *adjective & noun*[2]. E19.
[from SUB- 5 + DOMINANT.]
▶**A** *adjective.* Less than dominant, not quite dominant. Chiefly ECOLOGY, designating a plant which is prevalent in a community without being the dominant species. E19.
▶**B** *noun.* ECOLOGY. A subdominant species. M20.

subduable /səbˈdjuːəb(ə)l/ *adjective. rare.* E17.
[from SUBDUE + -ABLE.]
Able to be subdued.

subdual /səbˈdjuːəl/ *noun.* L17.
[formed as prec. + -AL[1].]
The action or an act of subduing a thing or person; the state of being subdued; subjection.

†**subduce** *verb trans.* LME.
[Latin *subducere*: see next.]
1 Remove, take away, withdraw; abstract; *refl.* retire *from* society, allegiance, etc., secede. LME–M18.
2 MATH. Subtract. L16–L17.

subduct /səbˈdʌkt/ *verb.* L16.
[Latin *subduct-* pa. ppl stem of *subducere*, formed as SUB- + *ducere* lead, bring.]
1 a *verb trans.* Take away (a quantity) *from*, subtract or deduct *from*; remove from position, withdraw from use, consideration, influence, etc. Now *rare.* L16. ▶†**b** *verb intrans.* Take something away *from.* M17–L18. ▶**c** *verb trans.* Take away or remove surreptitiously or fraudulently. Now *rare.* M18.
2 *verb trans.* Draw up, lift. Now *rare.* M19.
3 *verb trans. & intrans.* GEOLOGY. Move sideways and downwards underneath a neighbouring lithospheric plate. L20.

subduction /səbˈdʌkʃ(ə)n/ *noun.* LME.
[Latin *subductio(n-)*, formed as prec.: see -ION.]
1 Subtraction, deduction; withdrawal, removal; an instance of this. Now *rare.* LME. ▶†**b** Surreptitious or secret withdrawal. M17–E18.
2 The action of subduing, the fact of being subdued; subjection. (Foll. by *to*.) Now *rare.* L17.
3 GEOLOGY. The sideways and downward movement of the edge of a lithospheric plate into the mantle beneath a neighbouring plate. L20.
Comb.: **subduction zone** GEOLOGY a strip along which subduction is occurring.

subdue /səbˈdjuː/ *verb trans.* LME.
[from Anglo-Norman word = Old French *so(u)duire*, *suduire* deceive, seduce from Latin *subducere* withdraw, evacuate (see SUBDUCE) with sense derived from *subditus* pa. pple of *subdere* conquer, subdue, formed as SUB- + *dere* put.]
1 Conquer and bring into subjection (an army, people, or country) with military force. (Formerly foll. by *to*, *unto*, *under* a conqueror.) LME. ▶**b** Overcome or overpower (a person) by physical strength or violence. L16.
2 Bring (a person etc.) under one's control by intimidation, persuasion, etc.; quieten or make submissive thus; check, repress, (an emotion etc.). (Foll. by *to* a controller or control.) LME. ▶†**b** Bring or reduce *to* a low state. L15–E17. ▶†**c** Achieve, attain, (a purpose). *rare.* Only in L16.
3 Bring (land) under cultivation or to accessibility. M16.
4 MEDICINE. Reduce, allay, (a symptom etc.). Now *rare* or *obsolete.* E17.
5 Reduce the intensity, force, or vividness of (sound, colour, light, etc.), make less prominent. E19.

1 GIBBON The Samaritans were finally subdued by the regular forces of the East. **2** J. GALSWORTHY Soames made a tour of the room, to subdue his rising anger. R. FRASER To subdue them by punishment. **be subdued to what one works in** become reduced in capacity or ability to the standard of one's material. **5** G. GREENE Able to subdue her voice to a husky whisper.

■ **subduement** *noun* (*rare*) = SUBDUAL E17. **subduer** *noun* E16. **subduingly** *adverb* in a subduing manner, so as to subdue M19.

subdued /səbˈdjuːd/ *adjective.* L16.
[from prec. + -ED[1].]
That has been subdued; reduced in or lacking intensity, force, or vividness; understated, restrained; soft, quiet.

I. MURDOCH Millie had been of late . . more subdued, less boisterous. *San Diego* The subdued . . surroundings of this elegant French restaurant soothe patrons. *L.A. Style* Simple dressing—understated yet strong clothes in subdued colors.

■ **subduedly** *adverb* M19. **subduedness** *noun* E19.

subduple /sʌbˈdjuːp(ə)l, ˈsʌbdjuːp(ə)l/ *adjective.* Long *rare.* E17.
[from SUB- 4 + DUPLE.]
MATH. That is half of a quantity or number; of or in a proportion of one to two.

subduplicate /sʌbˈdjuːplɪkət/ *adjective.* M17.
[from SUB- 4 + DUPLICATE *adjective*.]
MATH. **1** Of or in the ratio of the square roots of two specified quantities. M17.
2 [By confusion.] = SUBDUPLE. M17.

subedit /sʌbˈɛdɪt/ *verb trans.* M19.
[Back-form. from next.]
Edit (a newspaper, book, etc.) under the supervision of a chief editor; prepare (copy) for printing, carry out final editing on (a text). Freq. as ***subediting*** *verbal noun.*

R. KIPLING Sub-editing, which meant eternal cuttings-down of unwieldy contributions.

subeditor /sʌbˈɛdɪtə/ *noun.* M19.
[from SUB- 2, 3 + EDITOR.]
An assistant editor; a person who subedits a text.
■ **subediˈtorial** *adjective* of or pertaining to a subeditor or subeditorship M19. **subeditorship** *noun* the position of subeditor M19.

suber /ˈsjuːbə/ *noun. arch.* E19.
[Latin = cork, cork-oak.]
CHEMISTRY & MEDICINE. Cork.

suberect /sʌbɪˈrɛkt/ *adjective.* E19.
[SUB- 6 + ERECT *adjective*.]
BOTANY & ZOOLOGY. Almost erect; not fully upright.

subereous /sjuːˈbɪərɪəs/ *adjective. rare.* E19.
[from late Latin *subereus*: see SUBER, -EOUS.]
Corky, suberose.

suberic /sjuːˈbɛrɪk/ *adjective.* L18.
[from SUBER + -IC.]
CHEMISTRY. ***suberic acid***, a solid dibasic acid, $HOOC(CH_2)_6COOH$, used in chemical syntheses; octanedioic acid.
■ **ˈsuberane** *noun* a liquid cyclic hydrocarbon C_7H_{14}, cycloheptane L19. **ˈsuberate** *noun* a salt or ester of suberic acid E19. **ˈsuberone** *noun* a mint-scented liquid cyclic ketone, $(CH_2)_6C{=}O$; cycloheptanone: M19.

suberification /sjuːˌbɛrɪfɪˈkeɪʃ(ə)n/ *noun.* L19.
[from SUBER + -I- + -FICATION.]
BOTANY. = SUBERIZATION.

suberin /ˈsjuːb(ə)rɪn/ *noun.* M19.
[from SUBER + -IN[1].]
BOTANY. An inert impermeable waxy polyester of fatty acids found in the cell walls of corky tissues.

suberize /ˈsjuːb(ə)rʌɪz/ *verb trans.* Also **-ise.** L19.
[from SUBER + -IZE.]
BOTANY. Impregnate the wall of (a plant cell) with suberin. Usu. in *pass.*
■ **suberiˈzation** *noun* the action of suberizing a plant cell L19.

suberose /ˈsjuːb(ə)rəʊs/ *adjective.* M19.
[from SUBER + -OSE[1].]
BOTANY. Having the appearance of cork; like cork in form or texture.
■ Also **suberous** /ˈsjuːb(ə)rəs/ *adjective* L17.

subfamily /ˈsʌbfamɪli, -m(ə)l-/ *noun.* M19.
[from SUB- 2b + FAMILY.]
1 TAXONOMY. A taxonomic grouping ranking next below a family. Also *gen.*, a subdivision of a family in classification (e.g. in linguistics). M19.
2 A subdivision of a human family, esp. consisting of a person living with a spouse or child within a larger primary family group. M20.

subfeu /ˈsʌbfjuː/ *noun & verb.* L17.
[from SUB- 3 + FEU *noun & verb*.]
SCOTS LAW. ▶**A** *noun.* An estate or fief granted by a vassal to a subvassal, a subinfeudation. L17.
▶**B** *verb trans.* = SUBINFEUD 1. M18.

subfeudation /sʌbfjuːˈdeɪʃ(ə)n/ *noun.* L17.
[from SUB- 3 + Latin *feudat-* (see FEUDATORY) + -ATION.]
LAW (chiefly *Scot.*). = SUBINFEUDATION 1.

subfeudatory /sʌbˈfjuːdət(ə)ri/ *noun.* M19.
[from SUB- 3 + FEUDATORY.]
A person holding a fief from a feudatory.

subfief /ˈsʌbfiːf/ *noun & verb.* M19.
[from SUB- 3 + FIEF.]
▶**A** *noun.* An estate or fief held from an intermediary instead of the original granter; *spec.* (*Hist.*) in Germany, a minor State subject to a more important State rather than directly to the Crown. M19.
▶**B** *verb trans.* Grant as a subfief. E20.

subfusc /ˈsʌbfʌsk, sʌbˈfʌsk/ *noun & adjective.* Also (now *rare*) **-fusk.** E18.
[Latin *subfuscus*, formed as SUB- + FUSK.]
▶**A** *noun.* Dark or dusky colour, gloom. Also, formal academic dress (dark in colour) as worn at some universities. E18.

J. CAREY At Oxford you wear subfusc for exams.

▶**B** *adjective.* Dark, dusky, dull; gloomy, sombre, subdued. M18.

P. FLEMING A kind of stringy, dowdy pheasant with subfusc plumage. *Punch* With such an unexhilarating cast-list you'd expect a muted, subfusc drama.

■ **subˈfuscous** *adjective* (*rare*) = SUBFUSC *adjective* M18.

subgenera *noun* pl. of SUBGENUS.

subgeneric /sʌbdʒɪˈnɛrɪk/ *adjective.* M19.
[from next after *genus generic*.]
Of or pertaining to a subgenus; constituting or typifying a subgenus.
■ **subgenerically** *adverb* so as to form a subgenus M19.

subgenus /ˈsʌbdʒɛnəs, -dʒiː-/ *noun.* Pl. **subgenera** /-dʒɛn(ə)rə, -dʒiː-/. E19.
[from SUB- 2b + GENUS.]
A subordinate genus; TAXONOMY a taxonomic grouping ranking next below a genus.

subgroup /ˈsʌbgruːp/ *noun & verb.* M19.
[from SUB- 2b + GROUP *noun*.]
▶**A** *noun.* **1** A subordinate group; a subdivision of a group. M19.
2 MATH. A series of operations forming part of a larger group. More widely, any group all of whose elements are elements of a larger group. L19.
2 *Sylow subgroup.*
▶**B** *verb trans.* Divide or classify into subgroups. E20.
■ **subgrouping** *noun* a subsidiary grouping or subgroup; the action of dividing or classifying into subsidiary groupings or subgroups: M20.

subgum /ˈsʌbgʌm/ *noun.* Also **sub gum**; **sup gum** /ˈsʌp/. E20.
[Chinese (Cantonese) *shâp kâm*, from *shâp* mixed + *kâm* brocade.]
A Chinese dish of mixed vegetables, as water chestnuts, mushrooms, bean sprouts, etc.

For other words beginning with *sub-* see the entry for **sub-**

subhead /ˈsʌbhɛd/ *noun & verb.* L16.
[from SUB- 2 + HEAD *noun*.]
▶ **A** *noun.* **1** An official next in rank to the head of an organization etc., a deputy head L16.
2 A subordinate division in a classification of a subject. L17.
3 A subordinate heading or title in a newspaper, book, chapter, etc. L19.
▶ **B** *verb trans.* Supply or provide with a subhead. M20.

subheading /ˈsʌbhɛdɪŋ/ *noun.* L19.
[from SUB- 2 + HEADING.]
= SUBHEAD 2, 3.

subhuman /sʌbˈhjuːmən/ *adjective & noun.* L18.
[from SUB- 5, 6 + HUMAN.]
▶ **A** *adjective.* Not quite human, less than human; of a lower order of being than the human; *fig.* debased, savage, bestial. Also, (of a primate) closely related to humans. L18.
▶ **B** *noun.* A subhuman person or creature. M20.
■ **subhuˈmanity** *noun* the quality of being subhuman; *rare* subhumans collectively: E20. **subhumanly** *adverb* E20.

subiculum /sjuːˈbɪkjʊləm/ *noun.* Pl. **-la** /-lə/. M19.
[mod. Latin, prob. var. of *subucula* undertunic.]
BOTANY. In certain fungi, a cobwebby or downy growth of mycelium under a fruiting body.

subinfeoff /sʌbɪnˈfiːf, -ˈfɛf/ *verb trans.* E17.
[from SUB- + *infeoff* var. of ENFEOFF.]
Hist. = next.

subinfeud /sʌbɪnˈfjuːd/ *verb trans.* E19.
[Back-form. from next.]
Hist. **1** Grant (an estate) by subinfeudation. E19.
2 Give (a person) possession *of* an estate by subinfeudation. M19.

subinfeudation /ˌsʌbɪnfjuːˈdeɪʃ(ə)n/ *noun.* M18.
[medieval Latin *subinfeudatio(n-)*, formed as SUB- + INFEUDATION.]
LAW (now *Scot.*).
1 The practice of a holder of lands by feudal tenure granting an estate to another, to be held in a similar way; the relation or tenure so established. M18.
2 An instance of this; an estate or fief created by this process. M18.
■ **subinfeudate** *verb trans.* = SUBINFEUD 1 M19. **subinfeudatory** *noun* a subvassal holding lands by subinfeudation L19.

subintelligitur /ˌsʌbɪntɛˈlɪdʒɪtə/ *noun.* M17.
[Latin = it is understood by implication, 3rd person sing. pres. indic. pass. of *subintelligere*, formed as SUB- + *intelligere* var. of *intellego*: see INTELLIGENT.]
An unexpressed or implied addition to a statement etc. Cf. SUBAUDITUR.

subitaneous /sʌbɪˈteɪnɪəs/ *adjective.* M17.
[Latin *subitaneus* sudden, from *subit-* pa. ppl stem of *subire* come or go stealthily, formed as SUB- + *ire* go: see -OUS.]
1 Sudden, hasty, unexpected; hastily produced or constructed. Now *rare.* M17.
2 *BIOLOGY.* Of the egg of a small aquatic invertebrate: hatching soon after it is laid. M20.

†**subite** *adjective.* L15–E18.
[Old French *subit*, fem. *subite*, or directly from Latin *subit-*: see prec.]
Sudden, hasty.

subitize /ˈsʌbɪtʌɪz/ *verb intrans. & trans.* Also **-ise.** M20.
[from Latin *subit-* (see SUBITANEOUS) + -IZE.]
PSYCHOLOGY. Apprehend immediately without counting (the number of items in a small sample).

subito /ˈsuːbɪtəʊ/ *adverb.* E18.
[Italian.]
MUSIC. A direction: suddenly, quickly.

subjacent /səbˈdʒeɪs(ə)nt/ *adjective.* L16.
[Latin *subjacent-* pres. ppl stem of *subjacere*, formed as SUB- + *jacere* lie down: see -ENT.]
1 Situated (immediately) underneath or below; underlying. L16.
2 Lying or situated at a lower level, at or near the base of a mountain etc. M17.
3 Taking place underneath or below. *rare.* M19.
■ **subjacency** *noun* the quality or state of being subjacent L19. **subjacently** *adverb* L19.

subject /ˈsʌbdʒɪkt/ *noun.* ME.
[Old French *sug(i)et* (mod. *sujet*), from Latin *subject-* pa. ppl stem of *subicere*, formed as SUB- + *jacere* throw, cast.]
▶ **I** †**1** A person bound to another by an obligation of allegiance, service, or tribute; *spec.* a feudal tenant or vassal. ME–L17. ▸**b** A person under the spiritual guidance of a priest or pastor or owing allegiance to a religious superior. ME–M16.
2 A person owing allegiance to and under the protection of a monarch or government; a person (other than the monarch) living under a monarchy; a member of a (freq. specified) State. (Foll. by *of*.) ME. ▸**b** A person etc. under the control of or owing obedience to another. (Foll. by *of*.) ME. ▸†**c** The people of a realm collectively. *rare* (Shakes.). Only in E17.
3 *LAW.* A thing over which a right is exercised; *Scot.* a piece of property. E18.

> 🕮 **2** *Times* Many . . Lebanese residing in Egypt became French subjects. E. LONGFORD His Majesty replied that he could not possibly sit down with a subject. A. BURGESS I am a subject of the British Crown. You can't put me under arrest. **b** G. CRABBE Tyrants . . have no feeling for their subject's pain.

▶ **II** †**4** The substance of which a thing consists or from which it is made. LME–L18.
5 *PHILOSOPHY.* **a** The central substance or core of a thing as opp. to its attributes. LME. ▸†**b** A thing having real independent existence. *rare* (Shakes.). Only in E17. ▸**c** More fully ***conscious subject***, ***thinking subject***. A thinking or cognizing entity or agent; the conscious mind; the self, the ego, esp. as opp. to anything external to the mind. L17.
6 *LOGIC.* **a** The thing about which a judgement is made. M16. ▸**b** The term or part of a proposition about which the predicate is affirmed or denied. E17.
7 *GRAMMAR.* A noun or noun-equivalent about which a sentence is predicated and (esp.) with which the verb agrees; the grammatical element typically denoting the actor in a predication. M17.

> 🕮 **7** C. P. MASON In the sentence 'Time flies', *time* is called the subject, and *flies* the predicate.

▶ **III 8** The matter or theme dealt with by an art or science; a topic of discussion, consideration, or investigation; an area of activity; a department or field of study. (Foll. by *of*.) LME. ▸**b** The theme *of* a literary composition etc.; what a book, film, etc., is about. L16. ▸**c** A figure, incident, type of scene, etc., represented by an artist; a representation of a person, scene, etc., in an artwork. E17. ▸**d** A particular department of art or science studied or taught. M19.
9 A thing or person giving rise to specified feeling, action, etc.; a ground, a motive, a cause. (Foll. by *for, of*.) L16.
10 A person or thing towards whom or which action, thought, or feeling is directed; an object of attention, treatment, thought, etc. (Foll. by *of*.) L16. ▸†**b** A person or a thing vulnerable *to* something injurious. Only in L16. ▸**c** A person or thing under consideration or in use; a person of specified character or tendencies; *spec.* (**a**) a person etc. suffering from or being treated for an ailment, undergoing experimentation, etc.; (**b**) *MEDICINE* a dead body as used for dissection. E18.
11 *MUSIC.* The theme or principal phrase of a composition or movement; the exposition or primary motif of a fugue. M18.

> 🕮 **8** L. ELLMANN She instantly moved on to the subject of men. M. BERGMANN Few subjects have evoked as much controversy as the differences between men and women. **b** T. MITCHELL All . . subjects dramatized by Euripides. **c** J. ROSENBERG Landscape . . one of the most popular subjects in Dutch art. K. CLARK Vast pictures of subjects from Homer and Plutarch. **d** M. DRABBLE French was her subject . . in school. **9** H. E. MANNING This text has been the subject of endless controversy. **10** J. PRIESTLEY Power cannot mean anything without a subject. P. P. READ The subjects of their conjecture were all in the room. **c** *Scientific American* Tens of thousands of subjects, monitored for dietary compliance. *Brain* Subject . . is a right-handed, 8-yr-old boy.

Phrases: **change the subject** introduce another theme for conversation, esp. to avoid causing offence, revealing a secret, etc. ***logical subject***: see LOGICAL *adjective.* **on the subject of** concerning, about.

Comb.: **subject catalogue** a catalogue, esp. in a library, arranged according to the subjects treated; **subject-heading** in an index or catalogue, a heading under which references to a subject are collected; **subject-object** *PHILOSOPHY* the object immediately present to the mind in cognition, as opp. to the real object; in Fichtean philosophy, the ego; ***subject superior***: see SUPERIOR *noun* 1C; **subject-term** *LOGIC* = sense 6b above.

■ **subjecthood** *noun* the state or condition of being a subject E20. **subjectless** *adjective* E19. **subjectship** *noun* M19.

subject /ˈsʌbdʒɪkt/ *adjective & adverb.* ME.
[Old French *suget*, *subject* (mod. *sujet*), from Latin *subject-*: see prec.]
▶ **A** *adjective.* **I 1** Owing obedience *to* a sovereign, government, colonizing power, etc.; under the rule or domination of another country, group, etc., in subjection. ME. ▸**b** Foll. by *to*: bound by a law or jurisdiction. LME.
2 Foll. by *to*: under the control or influence of, subordinate to. ME. ▸**b** Under obligation or bound *to*. *rare.* L16.
†**3** Submissive, obedient. LME–E17.
4 Prone or liable *to* or (formerly) *to do*; vulnerable, exposed, or susceptible *to* some (esp. harmful) occurrence, condition, etc. LME. ▸**b** In the book trade, liable to discount. *slang.* E20.
†**5** Apprehensible or perceptible *to* a faculty or sense; sensitive *to*. L16–M17.
6 Foll. by *to*: dependent or conditional upon, resting on the assumption of. M19.

> 🕮 **1** M. HOWITT The freest of all the states . . became subject to a despot. T. B. BOTTOMORE Perpetual conflict between the ruling class and the subject class. **2** G. BURNET The military power ought always to be subject to the civil. D. H. LAWRENCE She must relinquish herself into his hands and be subject to him. **4** P. PUSEY The field is subject to floods. L. ELLMANN All time tables are subject to alteration . . without notice. HARPER LEE She was subject to prolonged bouts of depression. **6** H. JAMES This transfer would be now wholly subject to Miss Brigstock's approval. *Which?* Felling of trees is subject to licensing by the Forestry Commission.

▶ **II 7 a** = SUBJACENT 2. *arch.* LME. ▸†**b** = SUBJACENT 1. L16–M17.
▶ **B** *adverb.* Foll. by *to*: conditionally upon, with the assumption of. M19.

> 🕮 *Field* Artichokes . . can provide a very useful long-term cover crop, subject to maintenance.

subject /səbˈdʒɛkt/ *verb.* LME.
[Old & mod. French *subjecter*, or Latin *subjectare* frequentative of *subicere*, *subject-*: see prec.]
1 *verb trans.* Make (a person, country, etc.) subject *to* a rule, jurisdiction, or (*arch.*) a conquering or sovereign power; (now *rare*) subjugate, subdue. LME.
2 *verb trans.* Make submissive or dependent; subordinate *to*. LME.
†**3** *verb intrans.* Be or become subject, submit *to*. LME–E18.
4 *verb trans.* Foll. by *to*: expose or make liable to; cause to experience or undergo, submit to specified treatment. Freq. in *pass.* M16.
5 *verb trans.* Place under or in a lower position; make subjacent *to*. Chiefly as ***subjected** ppl adjective. arch.* L16.
6 *verb trans.* †**a** *PHILOSOPHY.* In *pass.* Be attributed *to*, inhere *in* a subject. Only in 17. ▸**b** *LOGIC.* Make the subject of a proposition. E17.

> 🕮 **1** J. HELLER The city had been subjected to Macedonian rule, first by Philip, then by Alexander. **2** SIR W. SCOTT Unwilling to subject himself to . . polite society. **4** MAX-MÜLLER People began to subject the principal historical religions to a critical analysis. SCOTT FITZGERALD They were subjected . . to a careful scrutiny by the head waiter. H. MACMILLAN The Aden Protectorate was subjected to frequent minor attacks.

■ **subjectaˈbility** *noun* the condition of being subjectable; the degree to which something is subjectable: E20. **subjectable** *adjective* (*rare*) able to be subjected *to* LME. **subjectedly** *adverb* in a subjected or submissive manner M19. **subjectedness** *noun* L17. **subjectible** *adjective* (*rare*) = SUBJECTABLE E19.

subjectify /səbˈdʒɛktɪfʌɪ/ *verb trans.* M19.
[from SUBJECT *noun* + -I- + -FY.]
Identify with a subject, make subjective, interpret in subjective terms.
■ **subjectifiˈcation** *noun* the action of making or being made subjective L19.

subjectile /səbˈdʒɛktʌɪl/ *noun & adjective. rare.* M19.
[formed as prec. + -ILE.]
ART. ▶ **A** *noun.* A material on which a painting or engraving is made. M19.
▶ **B** *adjective.* Of a material: adapted to receive a painting etc. L19.

subjection /səbˈdʒɛkʃ(ə)n/ *noun.* ME.
[Old & mod. French, or Latin *subjectio(n-)*, from *subject-*: see SUBJECT *noun*, -ION.]
1 The action, state, or fact of dominating or subjugating; domination, control, subjugation. *arch.* ME.
2 The action, fact, or state of being subject; subordination. (Foll. by *to*.) LME.
†**3** Submission, obedience, homage. LME–L17.
4 a Legal or contractual obligation or liability. Now *rare.* LME. ▸†**b** A duty, task, or obligation, *esp.* an onerous one. L16–E18.
†**5 a** The subjects of a ruler collectively, a people. E16–M17. ▸**b** (The obligations surrounding) the condition of a subject. L16–M17.
†**6** *RHETORIC.* An answer added by a speaker to a question just asked; the figure involving this; an additional statement, a corollary. M16–M18.
7 The condition of being subject, exposed, or liable *to* something; exposure, liability. L16.
8 *LOGIC.* The act of supplying a subject to a predicate. L19.

> 🕮 **1** SPENSER They should all rise generally into rebellion, and cast away the English subjection. **2** J. YEATS The patriotic spirit . . lost its force in a common subjection to Rome. **5b** SHAKES. *Cymb.* He's true and shall perform All parts of his subjection loyally.

■ **subjectional** *adjective* (*rare*) involving or based on subjection E17.

subjective /səbˈdʒɛktɪv/ *adjective & noun.* LME.
[Latin *subjectivus*, from *subject-*: see SUBJECT *noun*, -IVE.]
▶ **A** *adjective.* †**1** Of, pertaining to, or characteristic of a political subject; submissive, obedient. LME–E18.
2 Of or pertaining to the real or inherent qualities of a thing or person; inherent; real, essential. Earliest in SUBJECTIVELY. Now *rare.* LME.

For other words beginning with *sub-* see the entry for **sub-**

3 *PHILOSOPHY.* Of or pertaining to the thinking subject; proceeding from or taking place within the individual consciousness or perception, originating in the mind; belonging to the conscious life. **E18.**

4 Of, pertaining to, or proceeding from an individual's thoughts, views, etc., derived from or expressing a person's individuality or idiosyncrasy; not impartial or literal; personal, individual. **M18.** ▸**b** Of a person etc.: tending to lay stress on one's own feelings or opinions; given to brooding, excessively introspective or moody. **M19.** ▸**c** Existing in the mind only; illusory, fanciful. **M19.** ▸**d** *PHYSIOLOGY.* Arising from internal causes; esp. (of a sensation) arising in the sense-organs or the brain, not representing an external stimulus. **M19.**

5 *GRAMMAR.* Of, pertaining to, or constituting the subject of a sentence or verb; *spec.* (of a word or case) constructed as or appropriate to a subject. **M19.**

> **3** G. PHELPS An . . analysis of love, seen . . as a purely subjective creation of the imagination. **4** *Discovery* Noise is a subjective phenomenon and cannot be directly measured. WILLY RUSSELL Criticism is never subjective and should not be confused with partisan interpretation. **5 subjective case** the nominative case.

▸**B** *noun.* That which is subjective; a subjective fact or thing; *GRAMMAR* (a word or form in) the subjective case. **E19.**

¶ Cf. OBJECTIVE.

■ **subjectively** *adverb* **LME.** **subjectiveness** *noun* **M19.**

subjectivise *verb* var. of SUBJECTIVIZE.

subjectivism /səbˈdʒɛktɪvɪz(ə)m/ *noun.* **M19.**
[from prec. + -ISM.]
PHILOSOPHY. The doctrine that knowledge, perception, morality, etc., is merely subjective and relative and that there is no objective truth; a theory or method based exclusively on subjective facts; the quality or condition of being subjective.

■ **subjectivist** *noun & adjective* (*a*) *noun* an adherent or advocate of subjectivism; (*b*) *adjective* of, pertaining to, or characterized by subjectivists or subjectivism: **L19.** **subjectivistic** *adjective* = SUBJECTIVIST *adjective* **L19.**

subjectivity /sʌbdʒɛkˈtɪvɪti/ *noun.* **E19.**
[formed as prec. + -ITY.]
The quality or character of being subjective, *esp.* the ability or tendency to present or view facts in the light of personal or individual feelings or opinions.

> C. LAMBERT His later works are a warning of the dangers of too great subjectivity on the part of the composer. D. JUDD The scientist attempts to be objective, while a psychoanalytic view of infants would include some reliance on a particular kind of subjectivity.

subjectivize /səbˈdʒɛktɪvʌɪz/ *verb trans.* Also **-ise.** **M19.**
[formed as prec. + -IZE.]
Make subjective.

subject-matter /ˈsʌbjɪk(t)matə/ *noun.* Also **subject matter.** **M16.**
[from SUBJECT *adjective* + MATTER *noun*, var. of earlier *matter subject* s.v. MATTER *noun*. Later interpreted as from MATTER *noun*.]
1 a The matter out of which a thing is formed, raw material used in an art, process, etc. **M16.** ▸†**b** The ground, basis, or source *of* something. Only in **17.**
2 The subject or theme of a book, speech, etc., a topic. **L16.**
3 The substance of a book, speech, etc., as opp. to ***form*** or ***style***. **M17.**
4 Matter treated in writing, discussion, a lawsuit, etc.; that dealt with by a science or branch of study; material expressed in a book, artwork, etc. **M17.**

> **3** J. BARZUN Dewey's effect on schooling was to dethrone subject-matter and replace it by techniques **4** A. H. SAYCE Articulate speech itself, the subject-matter of philology. C. HARMAN Occasionally, she turned to autobiographical subject-matter for her stories. *Field* The archetypal subject-matter of impressionist painting is landscape.

subjee /sʌbˈdʒiː/ *noun.* **E19.**
[Persian & Urdu *sabzī*, Urdu. *sabjī* greenness from Persian & Urdu *sabz* green.]
The leaves and seed capsules of the cannabis plant, *Cannabis sativa* subsp. *indica*, used for making bhang; a drink made from an infusion of bhang.

subjoin /səbˈdʒɔɪn/ *verb trans.* **L16.**
[French †*subjoindre* from Latin *subjungere*, formed as SUB- + *jungere*: see JOIN *verb*.]
1 Add or attach (a note, illustration, observation, etc.) at the end of a piece of speech or writing; append at the bottom of a page. **L16.**
2 Place in immediate juxtaposition; add as a related or subordinate element. **M17.**

> **1** C. THIRLWALL He subjoins, as a reason, the comparatively late age of Homer and Hesiod. JOHN BAXTER We subjoin from a catalogue a list of prices.

■ **subjoinder** *noun* (*rare*) a subjoined remark, note, etc. **M19.**

sub judice /sʌb ˈdʒuːdɪsi, sʊb ˈjuːdɪkeɪ/ *adjectival phr.* **E17.**
[Latin, lit. 'under a judge'.]
LAW. Under the consideration of a judge or court and therefore prohibited from public discussion elsewhere.

subjugable /ˈsʌbdʒʊɡəb(ə)l/ *adjective. rare.* **L19.**
[from Latin *subjugare* SUBJUGATE + -ABLE.]
Able to be subjugated.

subjugal /sʌbˈdʒuːɡ(ə)l/ *adjective. rare.* **L15.**
[Late Latin *subjugalis*, formed as SUB- + *jugum* yoke: see -AL¹.]
†**1** Under domination, subordinate. Only in **L15.**
†**2** *MUSIC.* Plagal. Only in **E17.**
3 Of a draught animal: accustomed to the yoke. **L19.**

subjugate /ˈsʌbdʒʊɡeɪt/ *verb trans.* Pa. pple **-ated**, (*arch.*) **-ate.** **LME.**
[Latin *subjugat-* pa. ppl stem of *subjugare*, formed as SUB- + *jugum* yoke: see -ATE³.]
1 Bring (a country, people, etc.) into subjection, vanquish, subdue. **LME.**
2 Bring under domination or control; make subservient or dependent. (Foll. by *to*.) **L16.**

> **1** H. PHILLIPS Their intention of making America a desert if they could not subjugate it. **2** F. TEMPLE Many species of animals perish as man fills and subjugates the globe. P. ACKROYD A . . man, whose . . imaginative gifts had been subjugated to the demands of duty.

■ **subjuˈgation** *noun* the action of subjugating, the condition of being subjugated, subjection; reduction to a state of subservience or dependence: **E17.** **subjugator** *noun* a person who or thing which subjugates a country etc., a conqueror **M19.**

subjunct /ˈsʌbjʌŋkt/ *noun.* **E20.**
[from Latin *subjunctus* pa. pple of *subjungere*, formed as SUB- + *jungere* join.]
GRAMMAR. An adverb or prepositional phrase used in a role that does not form part of the basic clause structure, for example *kindly* in *he kindly offered to help*.

subjunction /səbˈdʒʌŋkʃ(ə)n/ *noun.* Now *rare.* **M17.**
[Late Latin *subjunctio(n-)*, from Latin *subjunct-*: see next, -ION.]
The action of subjoining or appending a note etc.; the condition of being subjoined.

subjunctive /səbˈdʒʌŋktɪv/ *adjective & noun.* **M16.**
[French *subjonctif*, *-ive* or late Latin *subjunctivus*, from Latin *subjunct-* pa. ppl stem of *subjungere* SUBJOIN: see -IVE.]
▸**A** *adjective.* **1** *GRAMMAR.* Designating the mood of a verb of which the essential function is to state a relation wished, thought of, etc., by the speaker between the subject and predicate (as opp. to a relation of objective fact), freq. occurring in a subjoined or subordinate clause, as *if I were you*, *God help you*, *be that as it may*. Also, (of a statement etc.) having the verb in the subjunctive mood. **M16.**
2 Characteristic of what is expressed by the subjunctive mood; contingent, hypothetical. **M19.**
▸**B** *noun. GRAMMAR.* (An instance of) the subjunctive mood; a verb in the subjunctive mood. **E17.**

■ **subjunctively** *adverb* in the subjunctive mood, as a subjunctive **M17.** **subjuncˈtivity** *noun* the property or quality of being subjunctive; *spec.* the degree of realism or probability of a literary work: **L20.**

sublapsarian /sʌblapˈsɛːrɪən/ *noun & adjective.* **M17.**
[from mod. Latin *sublapsarius*, formed as SUB- + LAPSE *noun*: see -ARIAN.]
THEOLOGY. ▸**A** *noun.* = INFRALAPSARIAN *noun.* **M17.**
▸**B** *adjective.* = INFRALAPSARIAN *adjective.* **M17.**

■ **sublapsarianism** *noun* **M19.**

sublate /səˈbleɪt/ *verb trans.* **M16.**
[Latin *sublat-*, formed as SUB- + *lat-* pa. ppl stem of *tollere* take away.]
†**1** Remove, take away. **M16–M17.**
2 *LOGIC.* Deny, contradict, disaffirm. Opp. POSIT *verb* 2. **M19.**
3 *PHILOSOPHY.* In Hegelian philosophy, resolve (opposites) *into* a higher unity. **M19.**

sublation /səˈbleɪʃ(ə)n/ *noun.* **M16.**
[Latin *sublatio(n-)*, formed as prec.: see -ATION.]
†**1** A precipitate suspended in a liquid, esp. urine. **M–L16.**
2 *LOGIC & PHILOSOPHY.* The action or an act of sublating something. **E17.**

sublease /*as noun* ˈsʌbliːs, *as verb* sʌbˈliːs/ *noun & verb.* Also **sub-lease.** **E19.**
[from SUB- 3 + LEASE *noun*³, *verb*³.]
▸**A** *noun.* A lease of a property by a tenant to a subtenant. **E19.**
▸**B** *verb trans.* Lease (property) to a subtenant. **E19.**

■ **sub-lessee** *noun* the holder of a sublease **L19.** **sub-lessor** *noun* the granter of a sublease **L19.**

sublet /sʌbˈlɛt, *as noun* ˈsʌblɛt/ *verb & noun.* **M18.**
[from SUB- 3 + LET *verb*¹, *noun*².]
▸**A** *verb trans.* Infl. **-tt-**; pa. t. & pple **-let.** Sublease (property). Also, subcontract (work etc.). **M18.**
▸**B** *noun.* **1** = SUBLEASE *noun.* **E20.**
2 A subleased property. *colloq.* **M20.**

■ **sublettable** *adjective* **M19.** **subletter** *noun* **M19.**

For other words beginning with *sub-* see the entry for **sub-**

†**sublevation** *noun.* **M16.**
[Latin *sublevatio(n-)*, from *sublevat-* pa. ppl stem of *sublevare*, formed as SUB- + *levare* raise, lift: see -ATION.]
1 (A point of) elevation. **M16–E18.**
2 A rising, a revolt. Only in **17.**

sublimate /ˈsʌblɪmeɪt, -mət/ *noun.* **M16.**
[Latin *sublimatum* use as noun of neut. pa. pple of *sublimare*: see SUBLIME *verb*, -ATE¹.]
Chiefly *CHEMISTRY.* **1** More fully ***corrosive sublimate***, ***mercury sublimate***. Mercuric chloride, $HgCl_2$, a white crystalline powder which is a strong acrid poison and antiseptic. **M16.**
2 A solid product of sublimation. **E17.** ▸**b** *fig.* A refined or concentrated product. **L17.**

sublimate /ˈsʌblɪmeɪt/ *verb.* Pa. pple & ppl adjective **-ated**, (earlier) †**-ate.** **LME.**
[Latin *sublimat-* pa. ppl stem of *sublimare* SUBLIME *verb*: see -ATE³.]
†**1** *verb trans.* = SUBLIME *verb* 2a. **LME–M17.**
2 a *verb trans.* = SUBLIME *verb* 1a. **L15.** ▸**b** *verb intrans.* = SUBLIME *verb* 1b. *rare.* **M19.**
3 *verb trans.* = SUBLIME *verb* 3. **L16.**
4 *verb trans. & intrans.* = SUBLIME *verb* 4. **E17.**
5 *verb trans.* Refine away to non-existence. (Foll. by *into*.) **M19.**
6 *verb trans. & intrans. PSYCHOANALYSIS.* Refine or direct (instinctual energy, esp. that of the sexual impulse), so that it is manifested in acceptable ways. **E20.**

> **6** R. MACNEIL Gladys is sublimating her lust for the minister by polishing the candlesticks on the altar.

sublimation /sʌblɪˈmeɪʃ(ə)n/ *noun.* **LME.**
[Old & mod. French, or medieval Latin *sublimatio(n-)*, formed as SUBLIMATE *verb*: see -ATION.]
1 The action or process of subliming or converting a solid substance by heating directly into a vapour which resolidifies on cooling; the state of being so vaporized. Also, the action or process of changing physical state from the solid to the gaseous phase, or vice versa, without passing through the liquid phase. **LME.** ▸**b** A solid deposited by sublimation; a sublimate. **M17.** ▸**c** *GEOLOGY.* A process by which minerals vaporized deep in the earth are deposited nearer the surface. **E19.**
†**2** = SUBLATION 1. **M16–E17.**
3 The action or an act of elevating something or making something sublime; (a) transmutation into something higher or purer; (a) refinement. **E17.** ▸**b** An elated or ecstatic state of mind. **E19.** ▸**c** *PSYCHOANALYSIS.* The transformation of an instinctual drive, esp. the sexual impulse, so that it manifests in a socially acceptable way. **E20.**
4 The purest or most concentrated form of some quality, attribute, etc.; the height or extremity *of* something. **L17.** ▸**b** *PSYCHOANALYSIS.* The result of the refinement or transmutation of sexual or instinctual energy. **E20.**

> **1** *Scientific American* Atmospheric ice crystals form by direct sublimation from the air that is supersaturated with water. **3** T. HARPER This supernatural sublimation of man's nature. **4** T. HARDY That . . sublimation of all dismal sounds, the bark of a fox.

■ **sublimational** *adjective* of or pertaining to sublimation **M20.**

sublimator /ˈsʌblɪmeɪtə/ *noun. rare.* **M18.**
[medieval Latin = vaporizer, formed as SUBLIMATE *verb*: see -OR.]
A thing which sublimates something; *spec.* a part of a vacuum device which adsorbs gas on to a solid.

sublimatory /ˈsʌblɪmeɪt(ə)ri/ *adjective.* **E17.**
[formed as prec. + -ORY².]
†**1** *CHEMISTRY.* Suitable for subliming; used in sublimation. **E–M17.**
2 *PSYCHOANALYSIS.* Pertaining to sublimation of instinctual energy or of the sexual drive. **M20.**

sublime /səˈblʌɪm/ *adjective & noun.* **L16.**
[Latin *sublimis*, *-us*, formed as SUB- + an element variously identified with *limen* threshold or *limus* oblique.]
▸**A** *adjective.* **1** Dignified or lofty in bearing; aloof; haughty, proud. Chiefly *poet.* **L16.** ▸†**b** Exalted in feeling, elated. *rare* (Milton). **M–L17.**
2 Of language, style, etc.: elevated, grand; (of a writer, writing) characterized by this style. **L16.**
3 Situated or rising high up; (of a building etc.) towering. *arch. & poet.* **E17.** ▸**b** Of high rank or status; exalted. *arch.* **E18.** ▸**c** *ANATOMY.* Of a muscle: superficial. *rare.* **M19.**
4 Of a person, emotion, idea, etc.: of the most exalted, grand, or noble character; of high intellectual, moral, or spiritual level. Also (freq. *iron.*), of the most extreme kind; outstanding, supreme. **M17.** ▸**b** Refined; of the finest quality. **M17.**
5 Of nature, art, etc.: producing an overwhelming sense of awe, reverence, or high emotion, by reason of great beauty, vastness, or grandeur. **L17.**

> **1** MILTON His . . Eye sublime declar'd Absolute rule. **2** G. SAYER Of all poets he thought Dante the most sublime. **3b *the Sublime* PORTE.** **4** O. MANNING He smiled with sublime self assurance. A. THWAITE My purposes are . . sublime, and beautiful.

▶**B** *noun.* **1** (Usu. with *the*.) That which is sublime, esp. in nature and art. Formerly also, a sublime part, property, or feature. **L17.**
2 The height or acme *of* something. Now *rare* or *obsolete*. **E19.**

> 📖 **1** *Highlife* These tours . . tend to be a mix of the sublime and the ridiculous. *Times Lit. Suppl.* Massive landscapes . . suit the Romantic craving for the sublime.

■ **sublimely** *adverb* †(*a*) at or to a height; (*b*) in a sublime or exalted manner: **L16.** **sublimeness** *noun* **M17.** **sublimize** *verb trans.* make sublime, sublimate **E19.**

sublime /səˈblʌɪm/ *verb.* **LME.**
[Old & mod. French *sublimer*, or Latin *sublimare* lift up, elevate, formed as prec.]
1 a *verb trans.* Subject (a substance) to the action of heat to convert it into a vapour which on cooling is deposited in solid form; cause (a substance) to be given off or deposited by sublimation; extract by or as by sublimation. **LME.** ▸**b** *verb intrans.* Of a substance: pass from the solid to the gaseous state without liquefaction. Also, solidify from a vapour. **E17.**
2 *verb trans.* †**a** Exalt (a person); raise to high office or status. **M16–M17.** ▸**b** Raise or set up high; cause to rise. Freq. in *pass.* Chiefly *poet.* **M17.**
3 *verb trans.* Raise or refine to a high degree of purity or excellence; make (esp. morally or spiritually) sublime. Also foll. by *into*, *to*. **E17.**
4 *verb trans. & intrans.* Transmute (a thing) into something higher, nobler, or more excellent. (Foll. by *into*.) **M17.**

> 📖 **3** T. HARDY Bob's countenance was sublimed . . like that of a priest just come from the . . temple. **4** J. R. LOWELL F., whom whiskey sublimed into a poet.

■ **sub'limable** *adjective* (now *rare*) **M17.** **sublimifi'cation** *noun* the action of making or fact of being made sublime **L18.** **sublimified** *adjective* made sublime **L19.**

subliminal /səˈblɪmɪn(ə)l/ *adjective & noun.* **L19.**
[from SUB- 1 + Latin *limin-*, *limen* threshold + -AL¹, orig. translating German *unter der Schwelle* (*des Bewusstseins*) below the threshold (of consciousness).]
▶**A** *adjective.* **1** Below a threshold or lower limit; *spec.* below the threshold of sensation or consciousness; (of a state) supposed to exist but not strong enough to be recognized. **L19.**
2 Pertaining to or involving the unconscious influence of messages or other stimuli projected just below the threshold of awareness. **M20.**

> 📖 **1** N. SYMINGTON In a dream the subliminal cues . . not registered in waking life are often picked up. **2** *Audio Visual* Images hurtling on and off the screen in a poor imitation of subliminal advertising.

▶**B** *noun.* That which is subliminal; the subliminal self; a subliminal message. **E20.**
■ **subliminally** *adverb* **L19.**

sublimity /səˈblɪmɪti/ *noun.* **LME.**
[Latin *sublimitas*, formed as SUBLIME *adjective*: see -ITY.]
1 *gen.* The state or quality of being sublime; excellence or grandeur of character, action, style, etc. **LME.** ▸**b** (Also **S-**.) (A designation of) high position or status; *spec.* the title of the Sublime Porte. *arch.* **LME.**
2 A sublime person or thing; a sublime feature or quality. **M17.**
3 A high degree or standard; the height *of* something. **M17.**
4 The emotional state produced by the perception or contemplation of the sublime. Also, the quality in art or nature producing this. **L18.**

> 📖 **1b** BYRON In the Dardanelles, Waiting for his Sublimity's firman. **2** MILTON Knowledge and vertue . . such abstracted sublimities. **3** C. LAMB Such a sublimity of malice. **4** E. NORTH The scenery is full of charm . . and at times sublimity.

Sub.-Lt. *abbreviation.*
Sub-Lieutenant.

sublunar /sʌbˈluːnə/ *adjective & noun.* **E17.**
[Late Latin *sublunaris*, formed as SUB- + LUNAR.]
▶**A** *adjective.* **1** = SUBLUNARY *adjective.* Now *rare*. **E17.**
2 NAVIGATION & ASTRONOMY. Designating a point on the earth's surface which lies on a line joining the centre of the moon and the centre of the earth (i.e., at which the moon is vertically overhead). **M20.**
▶†**B** *noun.* = SUBLUNARY *noun.* Only in **17.**

sublunary /sʌbˈluːn(ə)ri/ *adjective & noun.* **L16.**
[formed as prec.: see -ARY². Cf. SUPERLUNARY, TRANSLUNARY.]
▶**A** *adjective.* **1** Of or pertaining to this world; earthly, terrestrial. **L16.** ▸**b** Of or pertaining to worldly affairs; material; temporal. **M17.**
2 Existing or situated beneath the moon; within the moon's orbit; subject to the moon's influence. **E17.** ▸†**b** Inferior, subordinate. **E–M17.**

> 📖 **1** T. HARDY Climbing higher . . and cutting himself off . . from all intercourse with the sublunary world. **b** A. WEST Mother's accounts . . are expressive of her states of feeling rather than descriptions of actual sublunary occurrences. **2** D. CUPITT Beyond the atmosphere . . a . . sphere, filling out the rest of the sublunary realm.

▶**B** *noun.* †**1** A sublunary person or thing. Usu. in *pl.* **M17–M18.**
2 That which is sublunary. **M20.**

> 📖 **2** C. S. LEWIS Aristotle's Nature . . covers only the sublunary.

submarginal /sʌbˈmɑːdʒɪn(ə)l/ *adjective & noun.* **E19.**
[from SUB- 1, 5 + MARGINAL.]
▶**A** *adjective.* **1** Situated near the margin of a body or organ; ENTOMOLOGY (of a cell or vein in an insect's wing) lying behind a marginal cell. **E19.**
2 Not fulfilling minimum requirements or criteria; *esp.* (ECONOMICS) not financially profitable. **M20.**

> 📖 **2** *Business Week* Losing the great profits on foreign crude, we can't afford submarginal operations.

▶**B** *noun.* A submarginal thing. **L19.**

submarine /ˈsʌbməriːn, sʌbməˈriːn/ *adjective, noun, & verb.* **M17.**
[from SUB- 1 + MARINE.]
▶**A** *adjective.* **1** Existing or occurring under the surface of the sea. **M17.**
2 Done, used, or intended for use under the surface of the sea. **M17.** ▸**b** *spec.* Of or pertaining to a submarine or submarines (see sense B.2 below). **L19.**

> 📖 **1** A. HARDY Perhaps . . submarine earthquake disturbances altered the sea-floor. N. CALDER A range of submarine mountains which runs out into the Atlantic. **2b** ***submarine commander, submarine crew, submarine fleet*** etc.

▶**B** *noun.* **1** A submarine animal or plant. Now *rare*. **E18.**
2 A vessel, esp. a warship, capable of operating under water and usu. equipped with torpedoes, missiles, and a periscope. **L19.** ▸**b** *transf.* = HOAGIE. *colloq.* (chiefly *N. Amer.*). **M20.**

> 📖 **2** *Ships Monthly* The Royal Navy's newest submarine, HMS Trenchant. ***Trident submarine***: see TRIDENT *noun* 4.

Special collocations & comb.: **submarine canyon** a narrow steep-sided trench eroded in a continental slope by underwater currents. **submarine chaser** MILITARY a small boat equipped for military operations against submarines. **submarine mine** an explosive charge laid beneath the surface of the sea, intended to explode on impact with an enemy vessel etc. **submarine net** a net laid beneath the surface of the sea to prevent the passage of submarines. **submarine sandwich** *colloq.* (chiefly *N. Amer.*) = sense B.2b above.

▶**C** *verb.* **1** *verb intrans.* Travel in or operate a submarine; *fig.* move as if a submarine; plunge or be propelled forward. **E20.**
2 *verb trans.* Attack (as) by submarine; *US slang* sabotage. Also, carry or send by submarine. **E20.**
3 *verb intrans. & trans.* AMER. FOOTBALL. Dive low and collide with (an opposing player). **M20.**

> 📖 **2** *American Banker* We are not about to sit back and be submarined and sabotaged. **3** *Washington Post* Donnelly . . writhes in agony after being submarined by Penn player while making layup.

■ **submariner** /sʌbˈmarɪnə/ *noun* a member of a submarine crew **E20.**

submerge /səbˈməːdʒ/ *verb trans.* **E17.**
[Latin *submergere*, formed as SUB- + MERGE.]
Cover over or sink (as) in water; immerse, flood; *fig.* inundate with work, problems, etc. Freq. in *pass.*

> 📖 R. K. NARAYAN The fast-drying lake bed . . was showing up an old temple which had been submerged. H. KISSINGER Planning for his trip to Peking . . soon submerged other considerations.

■ **submergement** *noun* submersion **E19.** **submergible** *adjective* = SUBMERSIBLE *adjective* (earlier in INSUBMERGIBLE) **L19.**

submerged /səbˈməːdʒd/ *ppl adjective.* **L18.**
[from prec. + -ED¹.]
Sunk or covered over (as) under water; immersed, inundated; *spec.* (*a*) BOTANY growing entirely under water; (*b*) (of a submarine etc.) operating below the surface of water.

> 📖 A. C. CLARKE They sank . . beneath the summit of the submerged mountain. R. FRASER The . . gregarious side of his nature slowly became submerged; he withdrew into himself. **submerged-arc welding** ENGINEERING a method of arc welding with a bare metal electrode in which both arc and electrode tip are covered in a loose flux powder fed to the welding area. **submerged tenth** the supposed fraction of the population permanently living in poverty.

submergence /səbˈməːdʒ(ə)ns/ *noun.* **M19.**
[from SUBMERGE *verb* + -ENCE.]
1 The state or condition of being submerged or covered with water; *esp.* the covering of an area of land with water or glacier ice. **M19.**
2 *fig.* The state or condition of being plunged in thought; the process or result of sinking into obscurity. **L19.**

submerse /səbˈməːs/ *verb trans.* **LME.**
[Latin *submers-* pa. ppl stem of *submergere* SUBMERGE.]
= SUBMERGE 1. Chiefly as ***submersed*** *ppl adjective.*

submersible /səbˈməːsɪb(ə)l/ *adjective & noun.* **M19.**
[from prec. + -IBLE, prob. after French *submersible*.]
▶**A** *adjective.* That may be submerged; *esp.* (of a vessel) capable of operating under water for short periods. **M19.**
▶**B** *noun.* A submersible vessel; a small submarine, *esp.* one used in underwater exploration, drilling, etc. **E20.**
■ **submersi'bility** *noun* **E20.**

submersion /səbˈməːʃ(ə)n/ *noun.* **LME.**
[Late Latin *submersio(n-)*, formed as SUBMERSE: see -ION.]
The action or an act of submerging something; the state or condition of being submerged; immersion; inundation.

submicroscopic /ˌsʌbmʌɪkrəˈskɒpɪk/ *adjective.* **E20.**
[from SUB- 2 + MICROSCOPIC *adjective*.]
Too small to be seen even with a microscope.
■ **submicroscopical** *adjective* = SUBMICROSCOPIC **M20.** **submicroscopically** *adverb* **M20.**

subminister /ˈsʌbmɪnɪstə/ *noun.* Now *rare* or *obsolete*. **M16.**
[from SUB- 2 + MINISTER *noun*.]
A subordinate or deputy minister.

subminister /sʌbˈmɪnɪstə/ *verb.* Now *rare* or *obsolete*. **E17.**
[from Latin *subministrare*, formed as SUB- + *ministrare* MINISTER *verb*.]
1 *verb trans.* Supply, furnish, esp. secretly. **E17.**
†**2** *verb intrans.* Minister *to* (*lit.* & *fig.*). Only in **17.**

submiss /sʌbˈmɪs/ *adjective. arch.* **L16.**
[Latin *submissus* pa. pple of *submittere* SUBMIT.]
1 = SUBMISSIVE. **L16.**
†**2** Of the voice etc.: low, subdued. **E17–L18.**
■ **submissly** *adverb* **L16.**

submissible /sʌbˈmɪsɪb(ə)l/ *adjective.* Now chiefly *US*. **M19.**
[Latin *submiss-* pa. ppl stem of *submittere* SUBMIT + -IBLE.]
Able to be submitted; now *esp.* (LAW) able to be submitted as judicial evidence.

submission /səbˈmɪʃ(ə)n/ *noun.* **LME.**
[Old & mod. French, or Latin *submissio(n-)*, formed as SUBMISS *adjective*: see -ION.]
1 a LAW. Agreement to abide by a decision or to obey an authority; reference to the decision or judgement of a (third) party, *esp.* reference of a matter *to* arbitration; an instance of this. Also (SCOTS LAW), a contract by which parties in a dispute agree to submit to arbitration; a document embodying this. **LME.** ▸**b** LAW. A proposition or argument submitted by counsel to a judge or jury. **E20.** ▸**c** The action or an act of submitting a matter *to* a higher authority for decision or consideration; a thing so submitted, an application, a proposal. **E20.**
2 The state or condition of being submissive or obedient; deferential conduct, attitude, or bearing; humility. *arch.* **LME.** ▸**b** In *pl.* Acts of deference or homage. *arch.* **E17.**
3 The action or an act of submitting or yielding to authority, another person, etc.; the condition of having so submitted; *spec.* (WRESTLING) the surrender of a competitor yielding to a hold. **L15.**
†**4** Admission, confession. *rare* (Shakes.). Only in **L16.**

> 📖 **1a** J. ERSKINE The day within which the arbiters are to decide is left blank in the submission. J. L. ESPOSITO The occasion for the . . secession from the main body of the community was Ali's submission to arbitration in his struggle. **b** R. C. A. WHITE The defendant's solicitor can make a submission of no case to answer. **c** E. BRIDGES It will not be possible to make any . . submission to Ministers before the recess. *Times* The submission of . . tenders by a number of British firms. **2** SHAKES. *1 Hen. VI* I . . in submission will attend on her. CLARENDON He had not that . . submission and reverence for the Queen as might have been expected. **3** F. HERBERT Don't waste the population, merely drive them into utter submission. J. WAINWRIGHT Her . . appearance was one of complete submission to circumstances over which she had no control.

■ **submissionist** *noun* an advocate of submission, esp. in political or national affairs **E19.**

submissive /səbˈmɪsɪv/ *adjective.* **L16.**
[from SUBMISSION, after *remission*, *remissive*, etc.]
Of a person, action, etc.: characterized by or displaying submission; yielding to power or authority; humble, obedient. Also foll. by *to*.

> 📖 M. FRENCH The long print skirts the women wore, their . . unmade-up faces, all suggesting a . . submissive role. M. HOCKING Janet became . . submissive and suffered Stephanie to put her to bed.

■ **submissively** *adverb* **L16.** **submissiveness** *noun* **E17.**

submit /səbˈmɪt/ *verb.* Infl. **-tt-**. **LME.**
[Latin *submittere*, formed as SUB- + *mittere* send, put.]
▶**I 1** *verb refl. & intrans.* Place oneself under a certain control or authority; become subject or surrender oneself to another. Freq. foll. by *to*, †*under*, †*unto*. **LME.** ▸**b** Cease resistance; yield, surrender; be submissive. **LME.**

For other words beginning with *sub-* see the entry for **sub-**

2 *verb refl. & intrans.* Surrender oneself *to* judgement, criticism, etc.; consent to undergo a certain treatment or abide by a certain condition, limitation, etc. Formerly also, consent or condescend *to do*. LME.
†**3** *verb refl.* Subject or expose oneself *to* danger etc. L15–E17.

📖 **1** M. ESSLIN He silently submits to the killer's raised knife. A. STEVENS Under no circumstances will he submit to an alien rule he cannot understand. **b** W. S. CHURCHILL To weaken the enemy and make him submit. **2** ISAIAH BERLIN We should . . submit with due humility to unavoidable necessity.

▶ **II 4** *verb trans.* Place under a certain control or authority; make subject or subordinate; cause to yield. Usu. foll. by *to*. Now *rare*. LME.
5 *verb trans.* Subject to a certain condition, treatment, operation, or process. Usu. foll. by *to*. LME.
6 *verb trans.* Refer or present to another for judgement, consideration, or approval. M16. ▸**b** *verb intrans. & trans.* SCOTS LAW. Refer (a disputed matter) to arbitration. L18.
7 *verb trans.* Esp. in LAW. Put forward as a contention or proposition; urge or represent, esp. deferentially. E19.

📖 **5** O. W. HOLMES Though I am not . . an editor, I know something of the trials to which they are submitted. P. P. READ The charge . . that we are afraid to submit the tenets of our faith to . . scrutiny. **6** A. C. AMOR He twice submitted drawings, only to be met with . . rejection. **7** P. HILL I submit we cannot chance a divided enquiry.

▶ **III 8** *verb trans.* Let or lay down; lower, sink; *spec.* place (one's neck) under the yoke or the axe. Chiefly *literary*. Now *rare* or *obsolete*. M16.
■ **submittable** *adjective* (chiefly *US*) = SUBMISSIBLE M20. **submittal** *noun* (*US*) a submitted report etc., a submission L19. **submitter** *noun* a person who submits; SCOTS LAW a person who makes a submission: E17.

sub modo /sʌb 'məʊdəʊ/ *adverbial phr.* E17.
[Latin, lit. 'under the way or manner'.]
LAW. Under certain conditions, with a qualification.

submultiple /sʌb'mʌltɪp(ə)l/ *adjective & noun.* Now *rare*. L17.
[Late Latin *submultiplus*, formed as SUB- + *multiplus* MULTIPLE.]
▶ **A** *adjective.* Designating or involving a submultiple. L17.
▶ **B** *noun.* A number of which another number is an exact multiple; an integral factor. M18.

subnascent /sʌb'neɪs(ə)nt/ *adjective.* L17.
[Latin *subnascent-* pres. ppl stem of *subnasci*, formed as SUB- + NASCENT.]
Growing underneath or up from beneath.

†**subnect** *verb trans.* L16–E18.
[Latin *subnectere*, formed as SUB- + *nectere* bind.]
Subjoin.

subnormal /sʌb'nɔːm(ə)l/ *noun.* E18.
[In sense 1 from mod. Latin *subnormalis* (*linea*), formed as SUB- + NORMAL; in sense 2 directly from the adjective.]
1 GEOMETRY. The part of the *x*-axis between the points of interception of a normal to a curve and perpendicular from the same point on the curve. E18.
2 EDUCATION & PSYCHOLOGY. A person who is below normal in academic or general ability. E20.

subnormal /sʌb'nɔːm(ə)l/ *adjective.* L19.
[from SUB- 5 + NORMAL *adjective*.]
1 Less than normal, below the normal. L19.
2 EDUCATION & PSYCHOLOGY. Of a level of intelligence and general ability which is below a given standard of normality. E20.
2 EDUCATIONALLY ***subnormal***.

subnormality /sʌbnɔː'malɪti/ *noun.* L19.
[from prec. + -ITY.]
The condition of being subnormal (*spec.* mentally subnormal).

subnuclear /sʌb'njuːklɪə/ *adjective.* M20.
[from SUB- 2, 2b + NUCLEAR *adjective*.]
PHYSICS. Smaller than or occurring in an atomic nucleus. Also, pertaining to or involving particles or phenomena on this scale.

subocular /sʌb'ɒkjʊlə/ *adjective.* E19.
[from SUB- + OCULAR.]
ANATOMY & ZOOLOGY. = SUBORBITAL *adjective* 1.

subodorate /sʌb'əʊd(ə)reɪt/ *verb trans. rare.* E17.
[Latin *subodorat-* pa. ppl stem of *subodorari*, formed as SUB- + *odorari* smell, inhale, from *odor* ODOUR: see -ATE³.]
Smell out; discover.

suborbital /sʌb'ɔːbɪt(ə)l/ *adjective & noun.* E19.
[from SUB- 1, 6 + ORBITAL.]
▶ **A** *adjective.* **1** ANATOMY & ZOOLOGY. Situated below (the orbit of) the eye; infraorbital, subocular. E19.
2 ASTRONAUTICS. Designating or having a trajectory that does not make a complete orbit of a planet. M20.
▶ **B** *noun.* ANATOMY & ZOOLOGY. A suborbital bone, cartilage, scale, etc. M19.

suborder /'sʌbɔːdə/ *noun.* E19.
[from SUB- 2b + ORDER *noun*.]
1 BIOLOGY. A taxonomic grouping ranking next below order. E19.
2 ARCHITECTURE. A secondary series of mouldings. *rare*. L19.

subordinacy /sə'bɔːdɪnəsi/ *noun.* E17.
[from SUBORDINATE *adjective* + -ACY.]
The state or condition of being subordinate; subordination.

subordinal /sʌb'ɔːdɪn(ə)l/ *adjective.* L19.
[from SUBORDER, after *order*, *ordinal*.]
BIOLOGY. Of, pertaining to, or of the rank of a suborder.

subordinate /sə'bɔːdɪnət/ *adjective, adverb, & noun.* LME.
[medieval Latin *subordinatus* pa. pple of *subordinare*: see next, -ATE², -ATE¹.]
▶ **A** *adjective.* **1** Of a person, position, etc.: of inferior rank; dependent upon the authority or power of another. Freq. foll. by *to*. LME.
2 Of a thing: dependent on or subservient to a chief or principal thing of the same kind. Freq. foll. by *to*. L16.
†**3** Submissive. *rare*. L16–L18.
4 Of inferior importance; secondary, minor. M17.
5 Lying underneath; underlying. Now *rare* or *obsolete*. M17.

📖 **1** E. LONGFORD Lord Cardigan's . . behaviour towards his subordinate officers was notorious. J. ROSSNER George had to content himself with a subordinate position. **2** W. H. PRESCOTT The subordinate part . . he was compelled to play. **subordinate clause** a clause serving as an adjective, adverb, or noun in a main sentence because of its position or a preceding conjunction. **subordinate legislation** LAW that part of the law which is enacted under delegated powers, as statutory instruments.

▶†**B** *adverb.* In subordination or secondary *to*. M17–E19.
▶ **C** *noun.* A subordinate person or thing; *esp.* a person working under another's control or orders. M17.

📖 P. V. WHITE The leader looked at his subordinates.

■ **subordinately** *adverb* M17. **subordinateness** *noun* (*rare*) M17.

subordinate /sə'bɔːdɪneɪt/ *verb trans.* L16.
[medieval Latin *subordinat-* pa. ppl stem of *subordinare*, formed as SUB- + *ordinare* ORDAIN: see -ATE³.]
1 Bring into a subordinate position; make dependent or subservient. Usu. foll. by *to*. L16.
2 Make inferior or secondary; consider as of less importance or value. Usu. foll. by *to*. E17.
3 ARCHITECTURE. Arrange (arches) in orders. L19.

📖 **1** J. P. STERN Life cannot be defined: to define it would be to subordinate it to reason. **2** B. MAGEE We have to subordinate . . our . . instinctual desires. N. F. DIXON Co-operation meant subordinating self-interest to the common goal.

Phrases: **subordinated debt**, **subordinated loan**, etc. COMMERCE: having a low priority for repayment. **subordinating conjunction** GRAMMAR: that joins a subordinate to a main clause.
■ **subordinative** *adjective* involving or characterized by subordination; GRAMMAR containing a subordinate clause or clauses: M17. **subordinator** *noun* (GRAMMAR) = ***subordinating conjunction*** s.v. SUBORDINATE *verb* M20.

subordination /səbɔːdɪ'neɪʃ(ə)n/ *noun.* LME.
[French, or medieval Latin *subordinatio(n-)*, formed as SUBORDINATE *verb*: see -ATION.]
1 Arrangement by rank or degree. Formerly also, (a rank in) a graded series. Now *rare* or *obsolete*. LME.
2 The action of subordinating oneself, a person or thing *to* another; the state or condition of being subordinate; submission, subjection. Opp. SUPERORDINATION 2. L16. ▸**b** GRAMMAR. The dependence of one clause or other unit on another. M19.
3 ARCHITECTURE. The action or fact of arranging arches in orders. L19.

subordinationism /səˌbɔːdɪ'neɪʃ(ə)nɪz(ə)m/ *noun.* M19.
[from prec. + -ISM.]
THEOLOGY. The doctrine that the second and third persons of the Trinity are inferior to the first.
■ **subordinationist** *noun & adjective* (*a*) *noun* a believer in subordinationism; (*b*) *adjective* of or pertaining to subordinationism or subordinationists: L19.

suborn /sə'bɔːn/ *verb trans.* M16.
[Latin *subornare*, formed as SUB- + *ornare* equip.]
1 Induce or procure to commit an unlawful act by bribery or other means; *esp.* bribe or induce to give false testimony or commit perjury. Freq. foll. by *to*. M16. ▸**b** Procure the performance of (an unlawful act) by bribery etc.; procure (evidence) by bribery or other unlawful means. E19.
†**2** Provide or procure, esp. secretly or stealthily. M16–E18.
†**3** Furnish, equip, adorn. L16–L17.
†**4** Introduce or put forward, esp. with a sinister motive. Only in 17.

📖 **1** D. L. SAYERS Am I supposed to have suborned my cook and parlourmaid to be my accomplices? *fig.*: P. D. JAMES Beauty suborns the critical faculty.

■ **subornation** /sʌbɔː'neɪʃ(ə)n/ *noun* the action or an act of suborning a person or thing; *spec.* (more fully ***subornation of perjury***) the action or an act of producing a witness on oath to commit perjury E16. **subornative** *adjective* (*rare*) of or pertaining to subornation E19. **suborned** *ppl adjective* unlawfully procured; obtained by bribery or corrupt means: M16. **suborner** *noun* L16.

suboscine /sʌb'ɒsʌɪn/ *adjective.* M20.
[from SUB- + OSCINE *adjective*.]
ORNITHOLOGY. Of, relating to, or denoting birds of the suborder Deutero-Oscines, which includes all passerine birds other than songbirds. Cf. OSCINE *adjective*.

subpoena /səb'piːnə, sə'piːnə/ *noun & verb.* LME.
[Latin *sub poena* under penalty, the first words on the writ.]
LAW. ▶**A** *noun.* A writ issued by a court or other authorized body requiring the attendance of a person at a stated time and place, subject to penalty for non-compliance. Also more fully ***writ of subpoena***, & in Latin phrs. below. LME.

📖 N. MAILER It was very hard . . to get a respond to a subpoena if he lived out of the state. **subpoena ad testificandum** /ad tɛstɪfɪ'kandəm/ [= in order to testify] a subpoena requiring a person's attendance at a court of law for the purpose of giving evidence. ***subpoena* DUCES TECUM**.

▶ **B** *verb trans.* Serve a subpoena on. Freq. in *pass.* M17.

📖 R. COBB The prosecution were certain to try to *subpoena* me as a witness. A. MACRAE My lawyer can arrange for you to be subpoenaed if you have trouble getting off work.

sub-prefect /'sʌbpriːfɛkt/ *noun.* M19.
[from SUB- 2 + PREFECT, after French *sous-préfet*.]
An assistant or deputy prefect; *spec.* an administrative officer of a department of France subordinate to the prefect.
■ **sub'prefecture** *noun* the office or position of a sub-prefect; the area administered by a sub-prefect: M19.

subreption /səb'rɛpʃ(ə)n/ *noun.* E17.
[Latin *subreptio(n-)*, from *subrept-* pa. ppl stem of *subripere*, formed as SUB- + *rapere* snatch: see -ION. Cf. SURREPTION *noun*¹.]
1 The action of obtaining something by surprise or misrepresentation; an attempt to do this; *spec.* in ECCLESIASTICAL & SCOTS LAW, the obtaining of a dispensation, gift, etc., by suppression of the truth. Cf. OBREPTION. E17.
2 A fallacious or deceptive argument, comment, etc.; a misrepresentation. Also, an inference drawn from this. M19.

subreptitious /sʌbrɛp'tɪʃəs/ *adjective.* E17.
[Latin *subreptitius*, *-icius*, from *subrept-*: see prec., -ITIOUS¹. Cf. SURREPTITIOUS.]
1 Characterized by subreption; obtained by subreption. E17.
2 Clandestine, secret; surreptitious. *rare*. M17.
■ **subreptitiously** *adverb* E17.

subreptive /səb'rɛptɪv/ *adjective. rare.* E17.
[Late Latin *subreptivus*, formed as prec.: see -IVE.]
= SUBREPTITIOUS 2.

subrision /sə'brɪʒ(ə)n/ *noun. literary. rare.* M17.
[from Latin *subris-* pa. ppl stem of *subridere*, formed as SUB- + *ridere* laugh, + -ION.]
The action or an act of smiling.
■ **subrisive** *adjective* smiling, playful M19.

subrogate /'sʌbrəgeɪt/ *verb trans.* LME.
[Latin *subrogat-* pa. ppl stem of *subrogare*, formed as SUB- + *rogare* ask, offer for election: see -ATE³. Cf. SURROGATE *verb*.]
1 *gen.* †**a** Elect or appoint in office as a substitute. LME–E18. ▸**b** Substitute (a thing) for another. Long *rare* or *obsolete*. M16.
2 LAW. Substitute (a person) *for* another in respect of a right or claim; cause to succeed *to* the rights of another. E19.

subrogation /sʌbrə'geɪʃ(ə)n/ *noun.* LME.
[Late & medieval Latin *subrogatio(n-)*, formed as prec.: see -ATION.]
†**1** *gen.* Substitution. LME–L17.
2 LAW. The substitution of one party for another in respect of a right or claim. E18.

sub rosa /sʌb 'rəʊzə/ *adjectival & adverbial phr.* M17.
[Latin, lit. 'under the rose' (as an emblem of secrecy).]
Of communication, consultation, etc.: (given, told, etc.) in secrecy or confidence.

subroutine /'sʌbruːtiːn/ *noun.* M20.
[from SUB- 2 + ROUTINE *noun*.]
COMPUTING. A subsidiary routine or set of instructions which performs a particular function and may be used any number of times during the running of a longer program without its being written out each time. Also called ***subprogram***.

subscribe /səb'skrʌɪb/ *verb.* LME.
[Latin *subscribere*, formed as SUB- + *scribere* write.]
1 *verb trans.* Write or sign (one's name) on a document etc., esp. at the foot as a witness or consenting party; *refl.* (with compl.) sign oneself as. Now *rare*. LME. ▸**b** Write or inscribe (a character, sentence, etc.) below or at the conclusion of something. Now *rare*. L16. ▸†**c** Write down the

For other words beginning with *sub-* see the entry for **sub-**

name of (a person) as being registered *for* a specified contribution. *rare* (Shakes.). Only in **L16**.

2 a *verb trans.* Write one's name at the foot of, sign, (a document etc.); show support for or attest by signing. **LME.** ▸**b** *verb intrans.* Write one's signature, esp. in support or as a witness. (Foll. by *to*.) **M16**.

†**3** *verb trans.* Agree to; support, sanction, concur in. **M16–L18.**

4 *verb intrans.* Foll. by *to*: express or feel agreement with an idea, proposal, etc.; hold as an opinion, assent to; (now *rare* or *obsolete*) agree or be a party to, countenance, collude in. **M16.**

5 *verb intrans.* Submit, yield, or defer *to*. Now *rare* or *obsolete*. **L16.**

6 a *verb intrans.* Foll. by *to*: admit or concede the force, validity, or truth of. Now *rare* or *obsolete*. **L16.** ▸†**b** *verb trans. & intrans.* Admit to (inferiority or error). *rare* (Shakes.). Only in **L16.** ▸†**c** *verb intrans.* Foll. by *to*: make acknowledgement or admission of. *rare* (Shakes.). Only in **E17.**

†**7** *verb intrans.* Foll. by *for*: make an undertaking on behalf of, vouch or answer for. *rare* (Shakes.). **L16–E17.**

†**8** *verb trans.* Sign away, yield up. *rare* (Shakes.). Only in **E17.**

9 a *verb trans.* Contribute or promise (a specified amount) *to* or *for* a fund, project, charity, etc., esp. regularly; pay or guarantee (money) *for* an issue of shares. **M17.** ▸**b** *verb intrans.* Undertake to contribute money *to* a fund, society, party, etc.; enter one's name on a list of contributors *to* a charity. Also, apply *for* or undertake to pay *for* shares; (foll. by *to*, *for*) arrange to receive a periodical etc. regularly. **M17.**

10 *BOOKSELLING.* †**a** *verb trans.* Issue (a book) to subscribers. Only in **E18.** ▸**b** *verb trans. & intrans.* (with *for*). Of a bookseller: agree before publication to take (a certain number of copies). **M19.** ▸**c** *verb trans.* Of a publisher etc.: offer (a book) to the retail trade. **E20.**

> 📖 **1** A. RADCLIFFE Vivaldi was ordered to subscribe his name and quality to the depositions. J. GALSWORTHY He could not tell how to subscribe himself, and only put 'Mark Lennan'. **2a** GIBBON The emperor was persuaded to subscribe the condemnation of . . Gallus. W. CRUISE He subscribed the will as a witness. ***subscribing witness***: see **WITNESS** *noun* 4. **4** B. W. ALDISS We subscribe to the idea that it is wrong to murder. A. STORR Freud did not subscribe to the belief in mediums. **9b** THACKERAY He . . subscribed handsomely to . . charities. INA TAYLOR He kept himself up to date by subscribing to numerous publications. **10c** *Bookseller* Your OUP traveller is subscribing the new Concise Oxford now.

■ **subscribable** *adjective* able to be subscribed **E19.**

subscriber /səbˈskraɪbə/ *noun.* **L16.**
[from prec. + **-ER**[1].]

1 A person subscribing or affixing a signature *to* a document etc.; a person adhering or assenting *to* an idea etc. **L16.**

2 A contributor *to* a project, fund, etc., a person subscribing *to* a periodical, *for* a share issue, etc. **L17.** ▸**b** A person paying a regular sum for the hire of a telephone etc. line. **L19.**

> 📖 **2** V. GLENDINNING He was a subscriber . . to *The Freewoman*.

Comb.: **subscriber trunk dialling** a service enabling subscribers to make trunk calls by direct dialling without the assistance of an operator; abbreviation ***STD***.

■ **subscribership** *noun* (*rare*) **E19.**

subscript /ˈsʌbskrɪpt/ *noun, adjective, & verb.* **E18.**
[Latin *subscript-* pa. ppl stem of *subscribere* **SUBSCRIBE.**]

▸ **A** *noun.* **1** That which is written underneath; a passage, note, etc. at the bottom or end of a document etc.; a signature. **E18.**

2 a A character, number, or symbol written or printed below (and usu. to the right of) a letter, number, etc., or below the line. **E20.** ▸**b** *COMPUTING.* A symbol (notionally written as a subscript but in practice usually not) used in a program, alone or with others, to specify one of the elements of an array. **M20.**

▸ **B** *adjective.* Written or printed underneath, esp. below the line; of or pertaining to a subscript; *spec.* in *MATH.* etc., (of a symbol) written below and usu. to the right of another symbol. **L19.**

iota subscript: see **IOTA** 1.

▸ **C** *verb.* **1** *verb trans.* Provide or label with a subscript; write as a subscript. **M20.**

2 *verb intrans.* Use or write a subscript. **M20.**

¶ Cf. SUPERSCRIPT.

■ **subscripted** *adjective* having a subscript, provided *with* a subscript; *spec.* in *COMPUTING*, specified out of an array by a subscript or subscripts: **M20.**

subscription /səbˈskrɪpʃ(ə)n/ *noun.* **LME.**
[Latin *subscriptio(n-)*, formed as prec.: see **-ION.**]

1 A piece of writing at the end of a document, book, etc.; something written or inscribed below a line, picture, etc. **LME.**

2 A signed name, a signature. **LME.**

3 The action or an act of affixing a signature; the signing *of* one's name or *of* a document. **L15.**

4 A signed declaration or statement; a rescript signed by a Roman emperor. *obsolete* exc. *Hist.* **L16.**

5 a A declaration of assent *to* articles of religion etc. **L16.** ▸†**b** Assent, approval; an instance of this. **L16–M17.** ▸†**c** Submission, allegiance. *rare* (Shakes.). Only in **E17.**

6 The action or an act of subscribing money to a fund, for a share issue, etc.; the raising of money for a certain object by collecting contributions. Formerly also, a scheme for raising money in this way. **M17.**

7 A contribution of money subscribed; *spec.* (**a**) a fee for the membership of a society etc., usu. to be paid regularly; membership of a society etc. maintained by the payment of such a fee; (**b**) payment for (usu.) a specified number of issues of a periodical etc.; an agreement to take and pay for such periodicals. **L17.** ▸**b** A sum of money subscribed by several people; a fund, a collection. Now *US.* **M18.**

8 *BOOKSELLING.* **a** The offering of a discount to those ordering and partially paying for a book before publication. Freq. in ***by subscription***. **E18.** ▸**b** The offering of a book by a publisher etc. to the retail trade; the taking up by the retail trade of a book thus offered. **L19.** ▸**c** The house-to-house sale of books by canvassers. *US.* **L19.**

Attrib. & comb.: In the sense 'supported by subscription, maintained or provided by subscribers, open to subscribers', as ***subscription library***, ***subscription room***, ***subscription school***, etc. Special combs., as **subscription book** (**a**) a book containing names of subscribers with the amounts of their subscriptions; (**b**) *US* a book sold from house to house by canvassers; **subscription concert** each of a series of concerts for which tickets are sold in advance; **subscription price** (**a**) the usu. discounted price at which a book is offered before publication to those ordering copies; (**b**) the usu. discounted price at which a periodical is supplied to subscribers; †**subscription receipt** a receipt for a share or shares taken up in a loan or commercial undertaking (cf. **SCRIP** *noun*[3]); **subscription television**, **subscription TV** *N. Amer.* a television service providing programmes for subscribers only.

■ **subscriptionless** *adjective* **L19.** **subscriptive** *adjective* (*rare*) pertaining to (a) subscription **M18.**

subsecive /ˈsʌbsɪsɪv/ *adjective.* Now *rare* or *obsolete.* **E17.**
[Latin *subsecivus* cut off and left remaining, formed as **SUB-** + *secare* cut: see **-IVE.**]

Remaining over, spare. Chiefly in ***subsecive hours***.

subsection /ˈsʌbsɛkʃ(ə)n/ *noun.* **E17.**
[from **SUB-** 2b + **SECTION** *noun.*]

A division of a section (esp. of a document, book, etc.).

■ **subsectioned** *adjective* divided into subsections **E19.**

subsellium /səbˈsɛlɪəm/ *noun.* Pl. **-llia** /-lɪə/. **E18.**
[Latin, formed as **SUB-** + *sella* seat.]

1 *ROMAN ANTIQUITIES.* A seat in an amphitheatre. **E18.**

2 *ECCLESIASTICAL.* = **MISERICORD** 4. **E19.**

■ **subsella** *noun*, pl. **-llae** /-liː/, = **SUBSELLIUM** 2 **M19.**

subsequence /ˈsʌbsɪkw(ə)ns/ *noun*[1]. **L15.**
[from **SUBSEQUENT** + **-ENCE.**]

1 That which is subsequent; a subsequent event, a sequel, a consequence. **L15.**

2 The condition or fact of being subsequent. **M17.**

subsequence /ˈsʌbsiːkw(ə)ns/ *noun*[2]. **E20.**
[from **SUB-** 2b + **SEQUENCE** *noun.*]

A sequence contained in or forming part of another sequence; *spec.* in *MATH.*, one derived from a sequence by the omission of a number of terms.

subsequent /ˈsʌbsɪkw(ə)nt/ *adjective & noun.* **LME.**
[Old & mod. French *subséquent* or Latin *subsequent-* pres. ppl stem of *subsequi*, formed as **SUB-** + *sequi* follow: see **-ENT.**]

▸ **A** *adjective.* **1** Following a specified thing in order or succession. **LME.**

2 Following a specified event etc. in time, esp. as a consequence. (Foll. by *to*.) **E16.** ▸**b** *PHYSICAL GEOGRAPHY.* Of a stream, valley, etc.: having a course or character corresponding to the resistance to erosion of the underlying rock, and so frequently following the strike of the strata. Cf. **CONSEQUENT** *adjective* 5, **OBSEQUENT** *adjective* 1. **L19.**

> 📖 **1** SIR W. SCOTT More of this in a subsequent chapter. **2** J. BUTLER Events contemporary with the miracles . . or subsequent to them. J. MARSH The residential building boom and subsequent railway construction. **subsequent to** after, following.

▸ **B** *noun.* †**1** A person or thing following or coming after another. **E17–E19.**

2 *PHYSICAL GEOGRAPHY.* A subsequent stream. **L19.**

subsequential /sʌbsɪˈkwɛnʃ(ə)l/ *adjective.* **L17.**
[from **SUBSEQUENT** *adjective* after *consequential.*]

Subsequent.

■ **subsequentially** *adverb* **L17.**

subsequently /ˈsʌbsɪkw(ə)ntli/ *adverb.* **E17.**
[formed as prec. + **-LY**[2].]

At a subsequent or later time. (Foll. by *to*.)

> 📖 C. DARWIN The large quadrupeds lived subsequently to that period. A. STEVENS A nervous breakdown from which he subsequently recovered.

subsere /ˈsʌbsɪə/ *noun.* **E20.**
[from **SUB-** 2 + **SERE** *noun*[2].]

ECOLOGY. A secondary sere. Cf. **PRISERE.**

subserve /səbˈsəːv/ *verb.* **LME.**
[Latin *subservire*, formed as **SUB-** + **SERVE** *verb*[1].]

†**1** *verb intrans.* Be of service *to*. *rare.* Only in **LME.**

2 *verb intrans.* **a** Be subservient *to*. **E17.** ▸**b** Act in a subordinate position. *rare.* **L17.**

3 *verb trans.* Serve as a means of furthering (a purpose, action, etc.), be instrumental in assisting or promoting. **M17.**

> 📖 **3** R. G. COLLINGWOOD The doctrine that art must not subserve any utilitarian end.

subserviate /səbˈsəːvɪeɪt/ *verb trans.* **L19.**
[Irreg. from **SUBSERVIENT** + **-ATE**[3].]

Make subservient or subordinate.

subservience /səbˈsəːvɪəns/ *noun.* **L17.**
[from next: see **-ENCE.**]

1 The condition or quality of serving as a means *to* an end. **L17.**

2 The condition of being subordinate or subject *to* another. Now usu. *spec.*, servile behaviour or attitude, submissiveness, obsequiousness. **E18.**

> 📖 **2** COLERIDGE The subservience . . of . . animal courage to intellect. M. LANE She was . . forced into a position of childlike subservience.

■ Also **subserviency** *noun* **M17.**

subservient /səbˈsəːvɪənt/ *adjective & noun.* **M17.**
[Latin *subservient-* pres. ppl stem of *subservire*: see **SUBSERVE**, **-ENT.**]

▸ **A** *adjective.* **1** Serving as a means to an end, instrumental. (Foll. by *to*.) **M17.**

2 Subordinate, subject, (*to*). **M17.**

3 Slavishly submissive, servile, obsequious. **L18.**

> 📖 **3** C. TOMALIN Grotesquely humble and subservient, she falls in with every whim of Maata's.

▸ **B** *noun.* A subservient person or thing. *rare.* **M19.**

■ **subserviently** *adverb* **L17.**

subset /ˈsʌbsɛt/ *noun.* **E20.**
[from **SUB-** 2, 2b + **SET** *noun*[2].]

A subordinate set, a part of a set, a set all the elements of which are contained in another set.

subshrub /ˈsʌbʃrʌb/ *noun.* **M19.**
[from **SUB-** 2, 6 + **SHRUB** *noun*[1], translating mod. Latin *suffrutex* (see **SUFFRUTICOSE**).]

BOTANY. A dwarf shrub; *spec.* one woody only at the base.

■ **subshrubby** *adjective* resembling a subshrub **M19.**

subside /səbˈsʌɪd/ *verb.* **M17.**
[Latin *subsidere*, formed as **SUB-** + *sidere* sit down.]

†**1** *verb trans.* Cause to sink in. *rare.* Only in **M17.**

2 *verb intrans.* **a** Of suspended matter etc.: sink down, fall to the bottom, precipitate. **L17.** ▸**b** Sink to a low, lower, or normal level, esp. in water or the ground; (of a valley) form a depression; (of a swelling etc.) be reduced so as to become flat; (of ground etc.) cave in or give way as the result of disturbance etc. **E18.** ▸**c** Of a person: sink down *into* or *on to* a sitting, lying, etc., position or place. Freq. *joc.* **L19.**

3 *verb intrans.* Abate, become calm or tranquil, cease from agitation; die down, fade away; fall *into* a state of quiet or of less intensity. **L17.**

4 *verb intrans.* Of a person: fall *into* an inactive or less active or efficient state; cease from activity, *esp.* lapse into silence. **E18.**

5 *verb intrans.* Be merged *in*; pass *into*. *rare.* **L18.**

> 📖 **2b** A. MOOREHEAD As the water subsides it leaves a great debris of uprooted timber. A. LURIE The lump on his head is subsiding. **c** W. MCILVANNEY The . . man made as if to get up again and then subsided. **3** R. L. STEVENSON 'One more cheer for Cap'n Smollett,' cried Long John, when the first had subsided. L. STRACHEY Public frenzy subsided as quickly as it had arisen. R. DAHL The shock . . of her death had begun to subside. **4b** *Daily News* Being told he must keep quiet . . he subsided. R. CHURCH I said nothing and subsided into my inner darkness.

■ **subsiding** *noun* the action of the verb, subsidence **L17.**

subsidence /səbˈsʌɪd(ə)ns, ˈsʌbsɪd(ə)ns/ *noun.* **M17.**
[Latin *subsidentia* sediment, from *subsidere* **SUBSIDE**: see **-ENCE.**]

1 A sediment, a precipitate. Now *rare* or *obsolete*. **M17.**

2 a The settling of matter suspended in a fluid etc. to the bottom, formation of sediment, precipitation. Now *rare.* **M17.** ▸**b** The sinking of liquid, ground, a structure, etc., to a low, lower, or normal level; now freq. *spec.* (orig. *GEOLOGY*) the gradual caving in or settling down of a piece of ground due to disturbance etc.; an instance of this. **M17.** ▸**c** A fall in rhythm or accent. **E19.**

3 The action or an act of sinking *into* inactivity, calm, or quiet; (a) fall in intensity. **M18.**

> 📖 **2b** *Which?* Coal seams worked near the surface cause the severest subsidence. **3** DICKENS A decided subsidence of her animosity.

■ Also **subsidency** *noun* (now *rare*) **M17.**

For other words beginning with *sub-* see the entry for **sub-**

subsidia *noun* pl. of SUBSIDIUM.

subsidiarity /səbsɪdɪˈarɪti/ *noun.* M20.
[from next + -ITY, translating German *Subsidiarität.*]
The quality of being subsidiary; *spec.* the principle that a central authority should have a subsidiary function, performing only those tasks which cannot be performed effectively at a more immediate or local level.

> *Economist* The diversity of a larger Community reinforces the need for the EC's principle of 'subsidiarity'.

subsidiary /səbˈsɪdɪəri/ *adjective & noun.* M16.
[Latin *subsidiarius*, formed as next: see -ARY[1].]
▶ **A** *adjective.* **1** Serving to help, assist, or supplement, auxiliary, supplementary (foll. by *to*). Also, subordinate, secondary. M16. ▸**b** Of a stream or valley: tributary. M19.
2 †**a** Consisting of a subsidy or subsidies. E–M17. ▸**b** Depending on or maintained by subsidies; *spec.* (of troops), paid for by subsidy, hired by a foreign power. M18.

> **1** H. J. LASKI The central problem is . . political, and all other questions are subsidiary to it. G. PHELPS *The Golden Ass* . . contains a number of subsidiary tales. R. V. JONES Radar was only a subsidiary target instead of being the main one. **subsidiary cells** BOTANY any of certain special epidermal cells (morphologically distinct from ordinary epidermal cells) surrounding the guard-cells of a stoma. **subsidiary company**: controlled by a holding company. **subsidiary goal** POLO (the driving of the ball into) a space to the side of each goalpost.

▶ **B** *noun.* †**1 a** The levy of a subsidy. *rare.* Only in L16. ▸**b** A subsidized State. Only in M18.
2 A subsidiary thing or person; an accessory, an auxiliary; an assistant; *spec.* (**a**) MUSIC a theme of inferior importance, subordinate to the first or second subject; (**b**) a subsidiary company; (**c**) POLO a subsidiary goal. E17.

> **2** *Daily Telegraph* A wholly-owned subsidiary of Imperial Chemical Industries.

■ **subsidiarily** *adverb* E17.

subsidise *verb* var. of SUBSIDIZE.

subsidium /səbˈsɪdɪəm/ *noun.* Pl. **-dia** /-dɪə/. M17.
[Latin: see SUBSIDY.]
A help, an aid, a subsidy.

subsidize /ˈsʌbsɪdʌɪz/ *verb trans.* Also **-ise**. L18.
[from next + -IZE.]
1 Pay money to secure the services of (mercenary or foreign troops); provide (a country or leader) with a subsidy to secure military assistance or neutrality. L18.
2 Support (an organization, activity, person, etc.) by grants of money. Also, reduce the cost of (a commodity or service) by subsidy. E19.

> **2** *Observer* They cannot apply for the Government-subsidised housing . . unless they have their families with them. P. ACKROYD His family were unlikely to subsidize further adventures. P. MAILLOUX He . . quietly subsidized many of the poor farmers by buying extra provisions for them.

■ **subsidiˈzation** *noun* E20. **subsidizer** *noun* L19.

subsidy /ˈsʌbsɪdi/ *noun.* LME.
[Anglo-Norman *subsidie* = Old & mod. French *subside* from Latin *subsidium* reserve of troops, support, assistance, rel. to *subsidere*, formed as SUB- + *sedere* SIT *verb.*]
1 Help, aid, assistance; an instance of this. *arch.* LME.
2 *Hist.* A grant by parliament to the sovereign for State needs; a tax levied or exaction made on a particular occasion. LME.
3 A grant or contribution of money; *spec.* (**a**) one paid by one State to another to assist in war, encourage neutrality, or repay military aid; (**b**) one granted by the State or a public body etc. to keep down the price of a commodity, service, etc.; (**c**) one awarded to a charity, arts group, etc., held to be in the public interest. Also, the giving of such a grant. LME.

> **3** D. CAUTE Talking of . . auction prices, farm subsidies. *Guardian* Publications must now exist without subsidy.

†**subsign** *verb trans.* L16–E18.
[Latin *subsignare*, formed as SUB- + *signare* SIGN *verb.*]
Sign one's name on or under, attest *with* one's signature or mark. Also, sign, affix, (one's name or seal).
■ †**subsignation** *noun* (a) signature; affixing of a seal: L16–E18.

sub silentio /sʌb sɪˈlɛntɪəʊ, -ʃɪəʊ/ *adverbial phr.* E17.
[Latin, lit. 'under silence'.]
In silence, without remark.

subsist /səbˈsɪst/ *noun.* M19.
[Abbreviation of SUBSISTENCE.]
= SUB *noun* 5. Also ***subsist money***.

subsist /səbˈsɪst/ *verb.* M16.
[Latin *subsistere* stand still or firm, cease, formed as SUB- + *sistere* stand.]
▶ **I 1** *verb intrans.* Of a material or (now usu.) immaterial thing: exist, have a real existence; remain in being, continue to exist, last. M16. ▸†**b** Continue in a condition or position; remain as a specified thing. E–M17.
2 *verb intrans.* Foll. by *in*: consist or reside in, be attributable to. M17.
†**3** *verb intrans.* **a** Of a person or material object: be or live in a certain place or state. M17–E19. ▸**b** Stay alive, survive. Only in 18.
†**4** Make a stand, stand firm, hold out. M17–E18.
†**5** Cease, stop at a certain point. M17–E18.

> **1** SHELLEY The central arch . . yet subsists. GLADSTONE He found that tradition subsisting among them.

▶ **II 6** *verb trans.* Provide sustenance for, support or maintain (esp. troops) with provisions or funds. Now *rare.* E17.
7 *verb intrans.* & (now *rare*) *refl.* Maintain or support oneself; keep oneself alive; live *on* food or money or *by* an occupation. M17.

> **7** C. DARWIN Ducks subsist by sifting the mud and water. L. URIS The settlers were subsisting on potato peelings and olives. K. TYNAN He . . subsisted on . . less than a pound a week.

subsistence /səbˈsɪst(ə)ns/ *noun.* LME.
[Late Latin *subsistentia*, formed as SUBSISTENT: see -ENCE.]
1 Substantial, real, or independent existence. LME.
†**2** THEOLOGY. = HYPOSTASIS 1. M16–E18.
†**3** A state or mode of existence. L16–L17.
4 A thing having substantial or real existence. E17.
†**5** The condition or quality of inhering or residing *in* something. E–M17.
6 Continued existence, continuance. Now *rare.* E17.
7 The action or condition of subsisting or of supporting life, the provision of food etc. Now *rare* exc. in ***means of subsistence***. M17. ▸**b** The upkeep or support *of* an army. M18.
8 (A) means of supporting life; (a) livelihood. Now *spec.*, a bare or minimal level of existence; an income providing this. M17. ▸†**b** Food supply, provisions. L17–L18. ▸**c** In full ***subsistence money***. Money allowed for maintenance; *spec.* an advance paid on wages due. L17.

> **7** S. SMILES Finding the door to promotion or even to subsistence closed against him. *Law Times* The court will not reduce the defendant to beggary by selling his only means of subsistence. *World Archaeology* Aborigines there base their subsistence on thirty-eight edible species of plants and forty-seven species of animals. **8** M. ROBINSON The wages of workers could not exceed subsistence.

Comb.: **subsistence allowance** = *subsistence money* below; **subsistence crop**: cultivated primarily for subsistence (opp. *cash crop*); **subsistence diet** the minimum amount of food needed to keep a person healthy; **subsistence farmer** a person engaged in subsistence farming; **subsistence farming**: serving only to support the farmer's household directly without producing a significant surplus for trade; **subsistence level** a standard of living providing only the bare necessities of life; *subsistence money*: see sense 8c above; **subsistence stores** US stores required to keep an army in food etc.; **subsistence wage**: providing only a minimal standard of living.

†**subsistency** *noun.* L16.
[formed as prec.: see -ENCY.]
1 THEOLOGY. = SUBSISTENCE 2. L16–E18.
2 = SUBSISTENCE 6. Only in E17.
3 = SUBSISTENCE 4. M17–M18.
4 = SUBSISTENCE 3. M–L17.

subsistent /səbˈsɪst(ə)nt/ *adjective & noun.* Now *rare* or *obsolete.* M16.
[Latin *subsistent-* pres. ppl stem of *subsistere* SUBSIST *verb*: see -ENT.]
▶ **A** *adjective.* †**1** Of a quality etc.: inherent or residing *in*. M16–L17.
2 Existing substantially or really. E17.
†**3** Continuing in existence, lasting. Only in E17.
4 Existing at a specified or implied time. M19.
▶ **B** *noun.* †**1** A subordinate, an inferior. Only in L16.
2 A person who or thing which subsists or exists. M17.
†**3** THEOLOGY. = SUBSISTENCE 2. L17–E19.

subsistential /sʌbsɪˈstɛnʃ(ə)l/ *adjective.* E17.
[formed as SUBSISTENCE + -AL[1].]
Pertaining to subsistence; *spec.* (THEOLOGY) = HYPOSTATIC 1.

subsizar /sʌbˈsʌɪzə/ *noun.* L16.
[from SUB- 2 + SIZAR.]
At Cambridge University, an undergraduate receiving financial assistance from his or her college and ranking below a sizar.
■ **subsizarship** *noun* L16.

subsoil /ˈsʌbsɔɪl/ *noun & verb.* L18.
[from SUB- 1 + SOIL *noun*[1].]
▶ **A** *noun.* The stratum of soil lying immediately under the surface soil. L18.
▶ **B** *verb trans.* Plough so as to cut into the subsoil; use a subsoil plough on. M19.

Comb.: **subsoil plough** *noun & verb* (**a**) *noun* a kind of plough with no mould-board, used in ploughed furrows to loosen the soil at some depth below the surface without turning it up; (**b**) *verb trans.* use a subsoil plough on.
¶ Cf. ***topsoil*** s.v. TOP *noun*[1] *& adjective.*
■ **subsoiler** *noun* a tool for loosening the subsoil, a subsoil plough M19.

subsonic /sʌbˈsɒnɪk/ *adjective & noun.* M20.
[from SUB- 5 + SONIC.]
▶ **A** *adjective.* **1** Pertaining to, capable of, or designating speeds less than that of sound. M20.
2 = INFRASONIC. M20.
▶ **B** *noun ellipt.* An aircraft not made to travel faster than sound. L20.
■ **subsonically** *adverb* M20.

subsp. *abbreviation.*
BIOLOGY. Subspecies.

subspace /ˈsʌbspeɪs/ *noun.* M20.
[from SUB- 1, 2 + SPACE *noun.*]
1 MATH. A space that is wholly contained in another space, or whose points or elements are all in another space. M20.
2 SCIENCE FICTION. = HYPERSPACE 2. M20.

sub specie aeternitatis /sʌb ˈspiːʃiː ɪˌtəːnɪˈtɑːtɪs/ *adverbial phr.* L19.
[Latin, lit. 'under the aspect of eternity'.]
Viewed in relation to the eternal; in a universal perspective.

subspecies /ˈsʌbspiːʃiːz/ *noun.* Pl. same. L17.
[from SUB- 2b + SPECIES.]
Chiefly TAXONOMY. A morphologically distinct subdivision of a species, *esp.* one geographically or ecologically (though not usually genetically) isolated from other such subdivisions; a race. Cf. VARIETY 6b.
■ **subspeciˈation** *noun* the evolutionary development of (a) subspecies M20. **subspeˈcific** *adjective* of, pertaining to, or of the nature of a subspecies L19. **subspeˈcifically** *adverb* L19.

sub specie temporis /sʌb ˌspiːʃiː tɛmˈpɔːrɪs/ *adverbial phr.* L19.
[Latin, lit. 'under the aspect of time'.]
Viewed in relation to time rather than eternity.

substance /ˈsʌbst(ə)ns/ *noun.* ME.
[Old & mod. French from Latin *substantia* being, essence, material property (rendering Greek *hupostasis* HYPOSTASIS, *ousia* ESSENCE *noun*), from *substant-* pres. ppl stem of *substare*, formed as SUB- + *stare* stand: see -ANCE.]
1 The essential nature or part of a thing etc., essence; *spec.* in THEOLOGY, the essential nature of God, in respect of which the three persons of the Trinity are one. ME.
2 That of which a physical thing consists; the essential (esp. solid) material forming a thing. Formerly *spec.*, the (esp. fleshy or muscular) matter or tissue composing an animal body or part. ME.
3 PHILOSOPHY. **a** A being subsisting by itself; a separate or distinct thing; a thing, a being. ME. ▸**b** The essential nature underlying phenomena, which is subject to modifications; the permanent substratum of things; that in which properties or attributes inhere. LME.
†**4** An underlying thing; a basis, a foundation; a ground, a cause. LME–L16.
5 A particular kind of matter, *esp.* one of a definite chemical composition. LME. ▸**b** *spec.* An intoxicating, stimulating, or narcotic chemical or drug, *esp.* an illegal one. Chiefly *N. Amer.* L20.
6 The theme or subject of an artwork, argument, etc., esp. as opp. to form or expression; the gist or essential meaning of an account, matter, etc. LME.
†**7** The vital part *of* something. LME–E17.
†**8** Amount, quantity, mass, (*of*). LME–L16.
†**9** The greater number or part, the majority, the bulk, (*of*). LME–M16.
†**10** A supply or provision *of*; maintenance, subsistence. LME–M16.
11 Means, wealth and possessions. LME. ▸†**b** An amount of wealth, a fortune; in *pl.*, riches. LME–M18.
12 a Substantial or solid quality in a thing; solidity, substantiality; seriousness or steadiness of a person's character. LME. ▸**b** A solid or real thing; reality. Freq. contrasted with ***shadow***. L16.
13 The consistency *of* a fluid. Now *rare.* LME.
14 A piece or mass of a particular kind of matter; a body of a specified composition or texture. Now *rare.* L16.

> **1** BURKE Bigots . . who hate sects . . more than they love the substance of religion. J. CARTWRIGHT Trends that are the substance of journalism. **2** W. S. LANDOR Give a countryman a plough of silver and he will plough with it all the season and never know its substance. D. J. CUNNINGHAM Longitudinally directed fibres . . embedded in its substance. **5** M. FARADAY A cloth or some other soft substance. H. E. ROSCOE On heating . . a substance called napthol . . is formed. K. A. PORTER A plate of some greasy substance. **6** J. BRYCE The penalty of greatness that its form should outlive its substance. W. GERHARDIE I forget the substance of the conversation. E. R. TUFTE Draw attention to the sense and substance of the data. **11** THACKERAY Reported to be a man of some substance. P. G. WODEHOUSE Men who waste their substance on wine, women, and song. **12a** N. HAWTHORNE Neither rulers nor people had any . . moral substance. W. LEWIS The significance . . sank in and took substance in her consciousness. *Embroidery* The fabric needs more substance.

Phrases & comb.: **controlled substance**: see CONTROL *verb* 2a. **in substance** (*a*) in reality; (*b*) in essentials, generally, apart from details. *NISSL substance*. *ROLANDO substance*. **substance abuse** (chiefly *N. Amer.*) use of (esp. illegal) intoxicating, stimulating, or narcotic chemicals or drugs. **substance abuser** (chiefly *N. Amer.*) a user of (esp. illegal) intoxicating, stimulating, or narcotic chemicals or drugs. **substance P** BIOCHEMISTRY an undecapeptide thought to be involved in the synaptic transmission of nerve impulses, esp. pain impulses. *sum and substance*: see SUM *noun*.

■ **substanced** *adjective* (*rare*) †(*a*) provided with wealth; (*b*) of a specified kind of substance; (*c*) made into a substance, made substantial: E17. **substanceless** *adjective* without substance, unsubstantial E19.

substandard /sʌbˈstandəd/ *adjective*. E20.
[from SUB- 5 + STANDARD *adjective*.]
1 Of less than the required or normal quality or size; of a lower standard than required, inferior. E20.
2 Of language: not conforming to standard usage; non-standard. M20.
3 CINEMATOGRAPHY. Of film: less than 35 mm wide; *spec.* 16 mm wide. M20.

📖 **1** *Guardian* A certain amount of substandard accommodation.

substant /ˈsʌbst(ə)nt/ *noun & adjective*. *rare*. L16.
[Latin *substant-*: see SUBSTANCE, -ANT[1].]
▶†**A** *noun*. A subsisting thing. Only in L16.
▶ **B** *adjective*. **1** Subsistent. M17.
2 Underlying. L19.

substantia /səbˈstanʃ(ɪ)ə/ *noun*. M19.
[Latin: see SUBSTANCE.]
ANATOMY. A distinct substance forming a part of a structure or tissue. Only in mod. Latin phrs.
substantia gelatinosa of Rolando /dʒɛlatɪˈnəʊsə/ [= gelatinous] = *ROLANDO substance*. **substantia nigra** /ˈnʌɪɡrə/ [= black] a curved layer of grey matter on each side of the midbrain, separating the tegmentum from the crus cerebri.

substantial /səbˈstanʃ(ə)l/ *adjective & noun*. ME.
[Old & mod. French *substantiel* or Christian Latin *substantialis* (rendering Greek *hupostatikos* HYPOSTATIC), from *substantia*: see SUBSTANCE, -AL[1].]
▶ **A** *adjective*. **I 1** Of solid material or structure, stout, solid; (of food or a meal) ample and nourishing, large and heavy. ME.
†**2** Of a person etc.: sturdy, strong, burly. LME–M17.
3 Of ample or considerable amount or size; sizeable, fairly large. LME.
4 Having solid worth or value, of real significance; solid; weighty; important, worthwhile. LME.
†**5** Of an act, measure, etc.: having force or effect, effective, thorough. LME–L17.
6 Possessing property and wealth, well-to-do, wealthy; of social standing or influence. LME.

📖 **1** E. GLASGOW So substantial that it took two men to push it. L. BLUE Have a substantial meal before the fast begins. I. MURDOCH Jack had put on weight . . . He seemed . . more substantial. **3** W. S. CHURCHILL A substantial section of the population. *Times* A substantial increase in consumer expenditure. *Sunday Times* The control and motivation of a substantial work force. **4** W. COWPER Foolish man . . quits . . Substantial happiness for transient joy. W. WILSON Sheffield was a sound and substantial scholar. *Lancet* His . . background . . enabled him to make a substantial contribution. **6** C. V. WEDGWOOD A Court chosen . . to represent the most . . substantial elements in the country.

▶ **II 7** Existing as a substance, having a real existence, subsisting by itself. LME.
8 a PHILOSOPHY. Of, pertaining to, or inherent in substance. LME. ▸**b** Of or pertaining to the substance or matter of a thing, esp. a body or organ. Now *rare*. E17.
9 Pertaining to or deriving from the essence of a thing. Now *rare* or *obsolete*. LME.
10 a Constituting or involving an essential point or feature; essential, material. LME. ▸**b** That is such in the main; real or true for the most part. L18.
11 Having substance; not imaginary, real; consisting of solid matter, corporeal. L16.

📖 **10b** W. PALEY The substantial truth of the narration. **11** R. ELLMANN Spirits are shadowy . . human beings substantial.

▶ **B** *noun*. In *pl.*
1 The things belonging to or constituting the substance; the essential parts or elements, the essentials. Now *rare*. LME.
2 Substantial or solid things. *rare*. M17.
3 The substantial or solid parts of a meal. *rare*. M18.
■ **substantialism** *noun* (PHILOSOPHY) the doctrine that substantial or unchanging realities underlie all phenomena L19. **substantialist** *noun & adjective* (*a*) *noun* = FLACIAN *noun*; PHILOSOPHY a holder of the doctrine of substantialism; (*b*) *adjective* of or pertaining to substantialism: M17. **substantialize** *verb trans. & intrans.* make or become substantial; invest with or acquire substance or actual existence: E19.

substantiality /səbstanʃɪˈalɪti/ *noun*. L15.
[Late Latin *substantialitas*, from *substantialis*: see prec., -ITY.]
1 The quality or state of being substantial; existence as a substance, substantial or real existence. L15.
2 Soundness, genuineness; solidity of position or status. M17.
3 Solidity or firmness of a structure etc. L18.
4 In *pl.* = SUBSTANTIAL *noun* 3. E19.

substantially /səbˈstanʃ(ə)li/ *adverb*. LME.
[from SUBSTANTIAL *adjective* + -LY[2].]
1 In substance; as a substantial thing or being. LME. ▸**b** Essentially, intrinsically. M17. ▸**c** Actually, really. E19.
†**2** In a sound or solid manner; effectively, thoroughly, soundly. LME–E18.
3 Solidly, strongly. LME.
†**4** With substantial or ample comfort. M17–E19.
5 In essentials, to all intents and purposes, in the main. L18.

📖 **5** W. D. WHITNEY It has maintained its own institutions . . substantially unchanged.

substantialness /səbˈstanʃ(ə)lnɪs/ *noun*. M16.
[formed as prec. + -NESS.]
The condition or quality of being substantial; solidity, soundness.

substantiate /səbˈstanʃɪeɪt/ *verb trans*. M17.
[medieval Latin *substantiat-* pa. ppl stem of *substantiare* give essence or substance to, from Latin *substantia* SUBSTANCE: see -ATE[3].]
1 Give substance or substantial existence to, make real or substantial. M17.
2 Give solidity to, make firm, strengthen. L18.
3 Give substantial form to, embody. L18.
4 Prove the truth of (a charge, claim, etc.); demonstrate or verify by evidence; give good grounds for. E19.

📖 **4** J. REED The . . Government found itself unable to substantiate its accusations. A. N. WILSON Writings . . quoted at great length to substantiate his point of view.

■ **substantiˈation** *noun* (*a*) *rare* embodiment; (*b*) the action of giving substance or solidity; (*c*) the action of substantiating or proving a statement etc.: M18. **substantiative** *adjective* serving to substantiate something E19. **substantiator** *noun* a person who substantiates something E20.

†**substantious** *adjective*. Chiefly *Scot*. L15.
[Old French *substantieux* from medieval Latin *substantiosus*, from *substantia* SUBSTANCE: see -IOUS.]
1 = SUBSTANTIAL *adjective* 4. L15–M19.
2 = SUBSTANTIAL *adjective* 1. E–M16.
3 = SUBSTANTIAL *adjective* 6. E16–M17.
4 = SUBSTANTIAL *adjective* 3. M16–M17.
■ †**substantiously** *adverb* E16–E17.

substantival /sʌbst(ə)nˈtʌɪv(ə)l/ *adjective*. M19.
[from next + -AL[1].]
1 GRAMMAR. Of, pertaining to, or consisting of a substantive or substantives. M19.
2 Existing substantially. L19.
■ **substantivally** *adverb* in a substantival manner; GRAMMAR as a substantive: L19.

substantive /səbˈstantɪv, ˈsʌbst(ə)ntɪv/ *adjective, noun, & verb*. LME.
[Old & mod. French *substantif*, *-ive* or late Latin *substantivus*, from *substantia* SUBSTANCE: see -IVE.]
▶ **A** *adjective*. **1** Having a separate and independent existence; not dependent on or subsidiary to another, independent, self-sufficient. LME. ▸**b** Of a dye: not needing a mordant. L18. ▸**c** MILITARY. Of an appointment, rank, etc.: permanent, not acting or temporary. M19.
2 GRAMMAR. **a** Designating a substance. Chiefly in ***noun substantive***, = SUBSTANTIVE *noun*. LME. ▸**b** Expressing existence. Chiefly in ***substantive verb***, †***verb substantive***, the verb 'to be'. L15. ▸**c** Of the nature of, equivalent to, or used as a noun or substantive; substantival. M17.
3 a Of law: relating to rights and duties as opp. to forms of procedure. Cf. ADJECTIVE *adjective* 3. L18. ▸**b** Belonging to the substance or essential nature of a thing; essential. M19.
4 Having a firm or solid basis; important, significant; of substantial extent or amount, considerable. E19.
5 Existing as a substance, having actual existence, real. M19.

📖 **1** M. GEE The cab was a substantive world and had no connection with ours. **4** GLADSTONE The only substantive doubt . . is about remaining in parliament. *Times* Volumes of substantive essays ranging the world of learning. **5** *Saturday Review* Prester John . . had a substantive original among the Mongols.

▶ **B** *noun*. A noun; a noun-equivalent. LME.
▶†**C** *verb trans*. = SUBSTANTIVIZE. *rare*. L17–E19.
■ **substantively** *adverb* in a substantive way; *esp.* in GRAMMAR, as a substantive or noun: M16. **substantiveness** *noun* M19. **subˈstantivism** *noun* the doctrine or theory of the substantivists L20. **subˈstantivist** *noun & adjective* (*a*) *noun* an advocate of a method of analysis based on experience and observation, an empiricist; *spec.* in ANTHROPOLOGY, an opponent of the application of formal economic theories to the study of primitive economies; (*b*) *adjective* of or pertaining to substantivism: M20. **substanˈtivity** *noun* substantiality L19.

substantivize /ˈsʌbst(ə)ntɪvʌɪz/ *verb trans*. Also **-ise**. M19.
[from prec. + -IZE.]
GRAMMAR. Make (a word etc.) into a noun or substantive.
■ **substantiviˈzation** *noun* E20.

substation /ˈsʌbsteɪʃ(ə)n/ *noun*. L19.
[from SUB- 2 + STATION *noun*.]
1 A building, establishment, etc., subordinate to a principal station or office. L19.
2 A station at which electrical current is switched, transformed, or converted, intermediate between a generating station and a low-tension distribution network. E20.

substituend /sʌbˈstɪtjʊənd/ *noun*. M20.
[Latin *substituendus* gerundive of *substituere* SUBSTITUTE *verb*: see -END.]
A thing that can be put in the place of another.

substituent /səbˈstɪtjʊənt/ *noun*. L19.
[from Latin *substituent-* pres. ppl stem of *substituere* SUBSTITUTE *verb*: see -ENT.]
CHEMISTRY. An atom or group of atoms taking the place of another atom or group in a compound, esp. replacing hydrogen in an organic compound.

substitute /ˈsʌbstɪtjuːt/ *noun*. LME.
[Latin *substitutus*, *-um* use as noun of masc. and neut. of pa. pple of *substituere* SUBSTITUTE *verb*.]
1 A person exercising deputed authority; a deputy, a delegate. LME.
2 A thing which is used or stands in place of something else. Usu. foll. by *for*. L16. ▸**b** GRAMMAR. A word, e.g. a pronoun, that can stand in the place of another. E19. ▸**c** A man-made foodstuff or other substance used as an alternative for a natural substance. M19.
3 LAW. A person nominated in remainder. L17.
4 a MILITARY (now *Hist.*). A person who for a remuneration does military service in place of a conscript. L18. ▸**b** SPORT. A player who replaces another after a match has begun. M19. ▸**c** *gen.* Any person who acts or is employed in place of another. M19.
5 A person who or thing which becomes the object of love (or some other emotion) deprived of its natural outlet. M20.

📖 **1** †**by substitute** (*rare*, Shakes.) by proxy.
2 M. BERGMANN Infatuation is customarily seen as . . a fake substitute for love. M. SEYMOUR A London park offers no substitute for a country walk. **c** M. MARRIN A sandwich . . made of white pre-sliced bread . . with some unidentifiable butter substitute. **4b** *Western Mail (Cardiff)* Carmichael, recalled from the substitutes' bench when Pender was injured. **c** G. STEIN Sometimes she taught . . in a coloured school as substitute for some teacher. **5** K. GIBBONS She wanted me around as a substitute for my daddy. *attrib.*: K. VONNEGUT I didn't want her to go on trying to be my substitute mother.

substitute /ˈsʌbstɪtjuːt/ *pa. pple & ppl adjective*. Chiefly & now only *Scot*. LME.
[Latin *substitutus* pa. pple of *substituere* SUBSTITUTE *verb*.]
†**1** *pa. pple*. Substituted. LME–L17.
2 *ppl adjective*. Substituted for or taking the place of another person; (of an official) appointed or acting as a deputy. Freq. *postpositive*. LME.
2 ***sheriff substitute***: see SHERIFF 1.

substitute /ˈsʌbstɪtjuːt/ *verb*. LME.
[Latin *substitut-* pa. ppl stem of *substituere*, formed as SUB- + *statuere* set up. See also SUBSTITUTE *adjective*.]
†**1** *verb trans*. **a** Appoint (a person) *to* an office as a deputy or delegate; set up as a ruler or official in the place *of* another. LME–M19. ▸**b** Depute, delegate. L16–E18.
2 *verb trans*. LAW. Nominate in remainder. M16.
3 *verb trans*. Put (a person or thing) in place of another. (Foll. by *for*, †*to*.) L16.
4 *verb trans*. Put in the place of, replace by a substitute (foll. by *by*, *with*). Freq. in *pass.* L17.
5 *verb intrans*. Act as a substitute (*for*). L19.

📖 **3** E. LONGFORD The Duke crossed out the entry and substituted the name of a veteran. *Times* The Egyptians adopted the rebus principle—a pictorial way of substituting pictures for words. **4** *Daily Telegraph* Nicholas has been substituted twice in Arsenal's last three games. **5** *New Yorker* I was substituting for a . . teacher on maternity leave.

■ **substitutaˈbility** *noun* ability to be substituted E20. **substitutable** *adjective* able to be substituted E19. **substituted** *ppl adjective* put in place of another; created or introduced by substitution; *esp.* in CHEMISTRY, having one or more substituents: M19. **substituter** *noun* a person who replaces another; a person who substitutes one thing for another: E17. **substitutory** *adjective* serving as a substitute L19.

substitution /sʌbstɪˈtjuːʃ(ə)n/ *noun*. LME.
[Late Latin *substitutio(n-)*, formed as prec.: see -ION.]
†**1** The appointment of a deputy or successor; deputation, delegation. LME–M18.
2 LAW. The designation of a person to succeed as heir on the failure of a person previously named. L16.
3 The putting of one person or thing in place of another; the taking of another's place, the exchanging

For other words beginning with *sub-* see the entry for **sub-**

of places; replacement. (Foll. by *for* the person or thing replaced, *by* the replacing person or thing.) E17.

4 MATH. **a** The replacement of one algebraic quantity by another of equal value but differently expressed. E18. ▸**b** The operation of passing from a simple serial arrangement to any other permutation of *n* variables. E18.

5 THEOLOGY. The replacing of one sacrificial victim with another; *esp.* Christ's suffering of punishment vicariously for humankind. M19.

6 CHEMISTRY. The replacement of an element or radical in a compound by another; the replacement of one atom or group of atoms in a molecule by another. M19.

7 BIOLOGY. The replacement of one organ, or function of an organ, by another. L19.

8 LINGUISTICS. A sound change consisting in the replacement of one phoneme by another. Also, the operation, in linguistic analysis, of replacing one unit with another in a given context. L19.

9 The dishonest replacement of one article of sale by another; the passing off of one manufacturer's goods for another's. E20.

Comb.: **substitution cipher**: in which the letters of the plain text are replaced by different ones; **substitution group** MATH. = PERMUTATION **group**.

substitutional /sʌbstɪˈtjuːʃ(ə)n(ə)l/ *adjective*. L18.
[from prec. + -AL¹.]
1 THEOLOGY. Of, pertaining to, or based on the principle of sacrificial substitution. L18.
2 Involving a substitution; constituting or forming a substitute. E19. ▸**b** METALLURGY. Of an alloy: involving the substitution at certain lattice sites of atoms of the minor component for those of the major. M20.
2b substitutional site a lattice site at which atomic substitution occurs.
■ **substitutionally** *adverb* L19.

substitutionary /sʌbstɪˈtjuːʃ(ə)n(ə)ri/ *adjective*. M19.
[formed as prec. + -ARY¹.]
= prec.

substitutive /ˈsʌbstɪtjuːtɪv/ *adjective*. E17.
[Partly from Latin *substitutivus*, formed as SUBSTITUTE *verb*, partly directly from SUBSTITUTE *verb*: see -IVE.]
†**1** Belonging to, characteristic of, or involving the appointment of a substitute or deputy. E–M17.
2 Taking the place of something else. M17.
3 LOGIC. = CONDITIONAL *adjective* 2. Now *rare* or *obsolete*. M17.
4 THEOLOGY. Involving a theory of sacrificial substitution. M19.
5 LAW. Dependent on a legal substitution or designation of heirs in remainder. M19.
■ **substitutively** *adverb* (*rare*) vicariously L19. **substituˈtivity** *noun* (LOGIC) the capacity of terms to function as logically equivalent substitutes for one another M20.

substract /səbˈstrakt/ *verb*. Now *non-standard*. M16.
[Late Latin *substract-* pa. ppl stem of *substrahere* alt. (after *abstrahere* ABSTRACT *verb*) of *subtrahere* SUBTRACT.]
†**1** *verb trans.* Withdraw; withhold *from*. M16–E18.
2 *verb trans.* Take (one number or quantity) away *from* another; subtract, deduct. L16.
■ **substraction** *noun* = SUBTRACTION L16. †**substractor** *noun* (*rare*, Shakes.) a slanderer: only in E17.

substrata *noun* pl. of SUBSTRATUM.

substratal /səbˈstreɪt(ə)l/ *adjective*. M19.
[from next or SUBSTRATUM: see -AL¹.]
Underlying; fundamental.

substrate /ˈsʌbstreɪt/ *noun*. E19.
[Anglicized from SUBSTRATUM.]
1 = SUBSTRATUM 1, 2. E19.
2 BIOCHEMISTRY. The substance on which an enzyme acts. E20.
3 BIOLOGY. The surface or material on which any particular organism occurs or grows. E20.
4 CHEMISTRY etc. Any underlying bulk phase, layer, etc., on which a substance, esp. a thin film, is deposited. M20.

substrate /ˈsʌbstreɪt/ *adjective*. Now *rare*. L17.
[Latin *substratus* pa. pple of *substernere*: see SUBSTRATUM.]
Underlying, fundamental; forming a substratum.
■ Also **substrative** /səbˈstreɪtɪv/ *adjective* E19.

†**substrate** *verb trans.* L16.
[Latin *substrat-* pa. ppl stem of *substernere*: see SUBSTRATUM.]
1 Form a substratum to. Only in L16.
2 In *pass.* Be situated underneath, be underlying; form a substratum. L16–E18.

substration /səbˈstreɪʃ(ə)n/ *noun*. M17.
[Late Latin *substratio(n-)*, formed as prec.: see -ATION.]
†**1** The prostration before the bishop of the third order of penitents (the prostrators) in the early Church. Also, the place where these penitents knelt. M17–E18.
2 A hypothesis. *rare*. M19.

substratum /sʌbˈstrɑːtəm, -ˈstreɪtəm/ *noun*. Pl. **-ta** /-tə/, (*rare*) **-tums**. M17.
[mod. Latin use as noun of neut. pa. pple of Latin *substernere*, formed as SUB- + *sternere*: see STRATUM.]
1 METAPHYSICS. That which is regarded as supporting attributes or accidents; the substance in which qualities inhere. M17.
2 An underlying layer or substance; the basis or foundation of a structure, condition, activity, etc. M17.
3 An underlayer of soil or earth; *esp.* in BIOLOGY, = SUBSTRATE *noun* 3. M18.
4 LINGUISTICS. Elements or features of a language identified as being relics of, or due to the influence of, an earlier extinct language. Cf. ADSTRATUM, SUPERSTRATUM 2. E20.

> 📖 **2** R. HEILBRONER If we look more deeply I think we can find a substratum of common problems. *Nature* Anatomical information . . forms an excellent substratum on which to build future experiments.

Comb.: **substratum language**: containing substratum (see sense 4 above); **substratum theory**: that attributes linguistic change to the influence of a substratum language.

substruct /səbˈstrʌkt/ *verb trans. rare*. M19.
[Latin *substruct-* pa. ppl stem of *substruere*, formed as SUB- + *struere* build, erect.]
Construct beneath; lay as a foundation.

substruction /səbˈstrʌkʃ(ə)n/ *noun*. E17.
[French, or Latin *substructio(n-)*, formed as prec.: see -ION.]
1 ARCHITECTURE. The substructure of a building etc. E17.
2 A basis, a foundation. M18.

substructure /ˈsʌbstrʌktʃə/ *noun*. E18.
[from SUB- 1 + STRUCTURE *noun*.]
An underlying or supporting structure.
■ **substructural** *adjective* of the nature of a substructure M19. **substructured** *adjective* having a substructure M20.

substylar /ˈsʌbstʌɪlə/ *noun & adjective*. Now *rare*. M17.
[from next + -AR¹, after French *soustylaire*.]
▸†**A** *noun*. = next. Only in M17.
▸**B** *adjective*. Designating a substyle. Chiefly in ***substylar line***. M17.

substyle /ˈsʌbstʌɪl/ *noun*. Now *rare*. Also †**-ile**. L16.
[from SUB- 1 + STYLE *noun*.]
The line on which the style or gnomon of a sundial stands.

†**subsult** *verb intrans. rare*. E17–E18.
[Latin *subsultare* frequentative of *subsilire*: see SUBSULTUS.]
Hop, jump about.

subsultory /səbˈsʌlt(ə)ri/ *adjective*. M17.
[from prec. + -ORY².]
Making or moving by sudden leaps or starts.
■ Also **subsultive** *adjective* (*rare*) M18.

subsultus /səbˈsʌltəs/ *noun*. E19.
[mod. Latin, from Latin *subsult-* pa. ppl stem of *subsilire*, formed as SUB- + *salire* leap.]
MEDICINE. Convulsive or twitching movement.

subsume /səbˈsjuːm/ *verb*. M16.
[medieval Latin *subsumere*, formed as SUB- + *sumere* take.]
†**1** *verb trans.* Put or give (a statement, instance, etc.) under another; subjoin, add. M16–M17.
2 LOGIC. **a** *verb intrans.* State a minor premiss or proposition. L16. ▸**b** *verb trans.* State as a minor proposition or concept *under* another. L17.
†**3** *verb trans.* Assume; infer. M–L17.
†**4** *verb trans.* Summarize. Only in L17.
5 *verb trans.* Include (an idea, instance, term, etc.) *under* another or *in* a rule, class, category, etc.; take up (*into*), absorb. E19.

> 📖 **5** B. RUSSELL Our generalisation has been subsumed under a wider generalisation. G. GORER It would be possible to subsume these three points into one more general statement.

■ **subsumable** *adjective* L19.

subsumption /səbˈsʌm(p)ʃ(ə)n/ *noun*. M17.
[medieval Latin *subsumptio(n-)*, from *subsumpt-* pa. ppl stem of *subsumere*: see prec., -ION.]
1 LOGIC. A proposition subsumed under another; a minor premiss. M17. ▸**b** SCOTS LAW (now *Hist.*). An account of an alleged crime. More fully ***subsumption of the libel***. M17.
2 The action or an act of subsuming something; the bringing of a concept etc. *under* a general term or a wider concept; the instancing of a case *under* a rule, category, etc. M17.

> 📖 **2** *Creative Camera* The complete subsumption of creative photography under the rubric of pictorialism.

subsumptive /səbˈsʌm(p)tɪv/ *adjective*. *rare*. E19.
[from prec., after *assumption*, *assumptive*, etc.]
Involving subsumption.

subsurface /ˈsʌbsəːfɪs/ *noun & adjective*. L18.
[from SUB- 1 + SURFACE *noun*.]
▸**A** *noun*. That which lies immediately below the surface; *spec.* subsoil. L18.
▸**B** *adjective*. Existing, lying, or operating under the surface of earth, water, etc. L19.

subtenant /sʌbˈtɛnənt/ *noun*. LME.
[from SUB- 3 + TENANT *noun*.]
A person who leases a property from a tenant; an undertenant.
■ **subtenancy** *noun* the status, right, or holding of a subtenant M19.

subtend /sʌbˈtɛnd/ *verb trans.* L16.
[Latin *subtendere*, formed as SUB- + *tendere* stretch.]
1 GEOMETRY. Stretch or extend under; *esp.* (of a line, dimension of an object, etc.) be opposite (a given angle), form (an angle) *at* a particular point by the meeting of lines projected from the extremities; (of a chord, angle, etc.) be opposite (a given arc), have bounding lines or points that meet or coincide with those of (a line or arc). L16.
†**2** In *pass.* Of an angle, a side of a figure: be extended *under*, be opposite *to*. L16–M17.
3 Chiefly BOTANY. Extend under, so as to support or enfold. L19.

> 📖 **1** W. WOLLASTON The same line . . at different distances subtends different angles at the eye.

subtense /səbˈtɛns/ *noun*. E17.
[from mod. Latin *subtensa* (sc. *linea* line) fem. pa. pple of *subtendere* SUBTEND.]
GEOMETRY. A subtending line; *esp.* the chord of an arc. Also, the angle subtended by a line at a point.
Comb.: **subtense method** SURVEYING a method of tacheometry in which the angle at the instrument is variable and the distance base is either constant or specially measured.

subter- /ˈsʌbtə/ *prefix*. M17.
[Latin *subter* (adverb & preposition) below, underneath.]
Forming compounds with the senses 'below, beneath, lower than', as ***subteraqueous***, ***subterhuman***, ***subternatural***, ***subterpose***, etc.; 'secretly', as ***subterfuge*** etc.

subterfuge /ˈsʌbtəfjuːdʒ/ *noun*. L16.
[French, or late Latin *subterfugium*, from Latin *subterfugere* escape secretly, formed as SUBTER- + *fugere* flee.]
1 A statement or action resorted to in order to avoid blame or defeat, justify an argument, etc.; a means of escape; an evasion, an excuse. L16.
†**2** A place to which a person escapes; a retreat, a refuge. E17–M19.
†**3** A thing which provides concealment; a cloak. M17–M18.

> 📖 **1** S. BRETT I hated all the subterfuges, I hated lying to you. N. SAHGAL He came home one night, with no attempt at subterfuge, . . at three a.m.

†**subterfuge** *verb*. *rare*. M17.
[from the noun.]
1 *verb intrans.* Employ a subterfuge or subterfuges; be evasive. M17–E19.
2 *verb trans.* Escape, evade, get out of. Only in M17.

subterranean /sʌbtəˈreɪnɪən/ *adjective & noun*. E17.
[from Latin *subterraneus*, formed as SUB- + *terra* earth: see -AN, -EAN. Cf. SUPERTERRANEAN.]
▸**A** *adjective*. **1** Existing or living below the surface of the earth; formed or constructed underground; operating or performed underground. E17. ▸**b** Growing underground (opp. ***aerial***). M19.
2 Existing under the earth; belonging to the underworld; infernal. E17.
3 Existing or working out of sight or in the dark; secret, concealed. M17.

> 📖 **1** J. RABAN Drilling . . under the desert to reach subterranean springs. **3** *Spectator* The dubious perimeter of subterranean society in San Francisco.

Special collocations: **subterranean clover** a European clover, *Trifolium subterraneum* (naturalized as a weed in pastures in Australia), whose fruiting heads bury themselves in the ground.
▸**B** *noun*. **1** A person who lives underground; a cave-dweller. E17.
2 An underground cave or dwelling. L18.
3 An inhabitant of the underworld, an infernal being. *rare*. M19.
■ **ˈsubterrane** *adjective & noun* (now *rare*) (**a**) *adjective* = SUBTERRANEAN *adjective*; (**b**) *noun* = SUBTERRANEAN *noun* 2: E17. †**subterraneal** *adjective* = SUBTERRANEAN *adjective* L16–E19. **subterraneanly** *adverb* in a subterranean manner, under the ground L19. **subterraˈneity** *noun* (now *rare* or *obsolete*) the condition of being subterranean; a place or thing found underground: L17. **subterraneous** *adjective* (now *rare*) = SUBTERRANEAN *adjective* E17. **subterraneously** *adverb* in a subterranean manner; secretly; in the dark; below the surface of the ground: E19. **subterraneousness** *noun* (*rare*) the quality of being subterranean E18. **subteˈrranity** *noun* (now *rare* or *obsolete*) = SUBTERRANEITY M17.

subterrene /sʌbtəˈriːn/ *adjective & noun*. E17.
[Latin *subterrenus*, formed as SUB- + TERRENE.]
▸**A** *adjective*. = SUBTERRANEAN *adjective* 1, 2. E17.
▸**B** *noun*. An underground cave or dwelling; *the* underworld. M19.

For other words beginning with *sub-* see the entry for **sub-**

subterrestrial /sʌbtəˈrɛstrɪəl/ *adjective & noun.* Now *rare.* E17.
[from SUB- 1 + TERRESTRIAL.]
▶ **A** *adjective.* **1** = SUBTERRANEAN *adjective* 1. E17.
†**2** = SUBTERRANEAN *adjective* 2. E17–E18.
▶ **B** *noun.* A creature living underground. E19.

subtext /ˈsʌbtɛkst/ *noun.* E18.
[from SUB- 1 + TEXT *noun.*]
†**1** Text appearing below other text on a page. Only in E18.
2 An underlying often distinct theme in a piece of writing, conversation, etc. M20.

📖 **2** *Notes & Queries* It will . . be difficult to read a Howells novel without looking for a sexual subtext. P. FUSSELL Many magazine ads indicate considerable skill in projecting a subtext as well as the obvious message.

■ **sub'textual** *adjective* of or pertaining to a subtext; underlying, implicit: M20.

Subtiaba /suːbtɪˈɑːbə/ *noun & adjective.* L19.
[San Juan Bautista de *Subtiaba*, a village in Nicaragua.]
▶ **A** *noun.* Pl. **-s**, same.
1 A member of an American Indian people of western Nicaragua. L19.
2 The Tlapanec language of this people (no longer spoken). E20.
▶ **B** *attrib.* or as *adjective.* Of or pertaining to the Subtiabas or their language. M20.

subtile *adjective* see SUBTLE.

subtilely *adverb* see SUBTLY.

subtilin /ˈsʌbtɪlɪn/ *noun.* M20.
[from mod. Latin *subtilis* subtle, used as specific epithet of *Bacillus subtilis*, orig. identified with *B. amyloliquefaciens* (see below): see -IN[1].]
BIOCHEMISTRY & PHARMACOLOGY. Any of a group of polypeptides of differing antibiotic activity derived from the bacterium *Bacillus amyloliquefaciens*, the most potent of which are used against Gram-positive bacteria and certain pathogenic fungi. Freq. with specifying letter, as ***subtilin A, subtilin B***, etc.

subtilisation *noun* var. of SUBTILIZATION.

subtilise *verb* var. of SUBTILIZE.

subtilisin /sʌbˈtɪlɪsɪn/ *noun.* M20.
[formed as prec.]
BIOCHEMISTRY. Any of a group of extracellular proteases derived from strains of the bacterium *Bacillus amyloliquefaciens.*

subtility /sʌbˈtɪlɪti/ *noun.* Long *arch.* LME.
[Old French *soutilité, subtilité* from Latin *subtilitas* SUBTLETY.]
= SUBTLETY 1, 2.

subtilization /ˌsʌtɪlʌɪˈzeɪʃ(ə)n/ *noun.* Also **-isation.** E17.
[French *subtilisation* or medieval Latin *subtilizatio(n-)*, from *subtilizare*: see next, -ATION.]
The action of SUBTILIZE; an instance or result of this.

📖 W. TAYLOR Saint John of Damascus . . introduced to Europe the oriental subtilizations about points of faith.

subtilize /ˈsʌtɪlʌɪz/ *verb.* Also **-ise.** L16.
[French *subtiliser* or medieval Latin *subtilizare*, from Latin *subtilis* SUBTLE: see -IZE.]
1 *verb trans.* Make subtle; now *esp.*, introduce subtleties or nice distinctions into; argue subtly on. L16. ▸**b** *verb trans.* Exalt, elevate, refine. (Foll. by *into.*) M17.
2 *verb intrans.* Make subtle distinctions; argue or reason in a subtle manner. (Foll. by *about, on, upon.*) L16.
■ **subtilism** *noun* (*rare*) (a) subtle doctrine E19. †**subtilizer** *noun* (*rare*) a person who makes subtle distinctions or reasons subtly E17–M18.

subtilly *adverb* see SUBTLY.

subtilty *noun* see SUBTLETY.

subtitle /ˈsʌbtʌɪt(ə)l/ *noun & verb.* E19.
[In senses A.3, B.2 from SUB- 1, in other senses from SUB- 2: see TITLE *noun, verb.*]
▶ **A** *noun.* **1** A secondary or additional title of a literary work. E19.
2 A repetition of the chief words of the full title of a book at the top of the first page of text. Also, a half-title. L19.
3 *CINEMATOGRAPHY & TELEVISION.* A printed line or lines at the bottom of a film etc., esp. translating or transcribing the dialogue. Freq. in *pl.* E20.
▶ **B** *verb trans.* **1** Provide (a book etc.) with a specified subtitle. L19.
2 *CINEMATOGRAPHY & TELEVISION.* Provide (a film or programme) with subtitles. M20.
■ **subtitler** *noun* M20.

subtle /ˈsʌt(ə)l/ *adjective.* Also (long *arch.*) **subtile.** ME.
[Old French *sutil, so(u)til* from Latin *subtilis.* See also SUTTLE *adjective.*]
1 Not easily grasped, understood, or perceived; now *esp.*, so delicate or precise as to elude observation or analysis. Formerly also, intricate, abstruse. ME. ▸**b** Working secretly, taking effect imperceptibly; insidious. E17.
2 (Of a person) skilful, expert, dexterous; (of a thing) ingenious, cleverly designed, skilfully contrived. *arch.* ME.
3 Penetrating, perceptive, acute; capable of making fine distinctions. ME.
4 Crafty, cunning; insidiously sly, deceitful. Long *rare* or *obsolete.* ME. ▸†**b** Of ground: tricky. E–M17.
5 Of thin consistency, not dense, rarefied; (of a smell, colour, etc.) pervasive or elusive by reason of tenuity, faint, delicate. LME. ▸**b** Of fine or delicate texture or composition. *arch.* LME.
6 Not thick or broad; thin, slender. Long *rare* or *obsolete.* LME.
†**7** Consisting of fine particles, finely powdered; (of particles) fine, minute. LME–L18.

📖 **1** A. BAIN Many inconsistencies are too subtle for the detection of an ordinary mind. P. GALLICO A change had gradually taken place in Hannah . . subtle but unmistakable. J. HERBERT She smiled . . that subtle mocking in her eyes. **b** A. G. GARDINER Tobacco, that subtle narcotic that gives the illusion of the flight of time. **2** D. MORRIS It takes a subtle, sensitised hand to feel for food in the water. **3** LD MACAULAY Subtle speculations touching the Divine attributes. **4b** SHAKES. *Coriol.* Like to a bowl upon a subtle ground, I have tumbled past the throw.

■ **subtleness** *noun* LME. **subtlist** *noun* (*rare*) a person who uses subtlety M19.

subtlety /ˈsʌt(ə)lti/ *noun.* Also (long *arch.*) **subtilty.** ME.
[Old French *s(o)utilté* from Latin *subtilitas*, from *subtilis*: see prec., -TY[1]. Cf. SUBTILTY.]
1 The quality or state of being subtle. ME.
2 An instance of this. Now *esp.*, a subtle argument; a fine distinction. LME.
3 *Hist.* An ornamental table decoration, usu. made of sugar and sometimes eaten. LME.

📖 **1** R. DAVIES The vice of the literary mind is excessive subtlety. A. S. BYATT Sea food, . . with sauces whose subtlety required and defied analysis. **2** MILTON A mystery indeed in their Sophistic Subtilties, but in Scripture a plain Doctrin. A. TAYLOR Gesture, . . eye contact and other subtleties of body language.

subtly /ˈsʌtli/ *adverb.* Also (long *arch.*) **subtilely, -tilly** /ˈsʌt(ə)li/. LME.
[from French *subtil* SUBTLE + -LY[2].]
In a subtle manner.

📖 D. HARTLEY Matter and motion, however subtly divided, or reasoned upon, yield nothing more than matter and motion still. *Antique Collector* The candles are electric, their light subtly enhanced by fibre optic tubes. *Independent* The subtly smoky flavour.

subtopia /sʌbˈtəʊpɪə/ *noun. derog.* M20.
[Blend of SUBURB and UTOPIA: cf. SUBURBIA.]
Suburbia regarded as an ideal place; *gen.* an area of unsightly and sprawling suburban development.
■ **subtopian** *adjective & noun* (*a*) *adjective* of, pertaining to, or characteristic of subtopia; (*b*) *noun* a resident of subtopia: M20. **subtopianize** *verb trans.* make (an area etc.) subtopian M20.

subtotal /ˈsʌbtəʊt(ə)l/ *noun & verb.* E20.
[from SUB- 2b + TOTAL *noun, verb.*]
▶ **A** *noun.* An intermediate total; the total of one part of a group of numbers to be added. E20.
▶ **B** *verb trans.* Infl. **-ll-**, ***-l-**. Add (numbers) so as to obtain a subtotal; obtain a subtotal from the contents of (a register etc.). M20.

subtotal /sʌbˈtəʊt(ə)l/ *adjective.* E20.
[from SUB- 6 + TOTAL *adjective.*]
SURGERY. Involving the removal of only part of an organ or tissue.

📖 ANNE STEVENSON Mrs Plath was . . to undergo a subtotal gastrectomy.

subtract /səbˈtrakt/ *verb.* M16.
[Latin *subtract-* pa. ppl stem of *subtrahere*, formed as SUB- + *trahere* draw.]
1 *verb trans.* Withdraw or withhold (a thing from a person's use or enjoyment). *arch.* M16.
2 *verb trans.* Remove *from* a place or position. Now only *refl.* M16.
3 a *verb trans.* Take away (one number *from* another); deduct (a portion etc.). M16. ▸**b** *verb intrans.* Perform the arithmetical process of subtraction. M17.

📖 **3a** B. CHATWIN Add a moustache, subtract a moustache: nothing would alter his . . nondescript appearance. R. FRAME A happy frame of mind subtracted ten . . years from her.

■ **subtracter** *noun* (*rare*) †(*a*) = SUBTRAHEND; (*b*) = SUBTRACTOR (a); (*c*) = SUBTRACTOR (b): E19. **subtractor** *noun* (*a*) *rare* a person who or thing which subtracts; (*b*) *ELECTRONICS* a circuit or device that produces an output dependent on the difference of two inputs or of multiples of them: M18.

For other words beginning with *sub-* see the entry for **sub-**

subtraction /səbˈtrakʃ(ə)n/ *noun.* LME.
[Late Latin *subtractio(n-)*, formed as prec.: see -ION.]
†**1** Withdrawal or removal from a place. Only in LME.
2 The withdrawal or withholding *of* something necessary or useful; an instance of this. *arch.* LME. ▸**b** *LAW.* The withdrawal or withholding of a right or privilege to which a person is lawfully entitled. M17.
3 The taking away of one number *from* another; deduction or removal of a portion etc.; lessening of a quantity by an amount equal to a second quantity; an instance of this. LME.

subtractive /səbˈtraktɪv/ *adjective & noun.* LME.
[from SUBTRACT + -IVE.]
▶ **A** *adjective.* **1** Of, pertaining to, or involving removal, subtraction, deduction, or decrease; (of a mathematical quantity) that is to be subtracted; negative, having a minus sign. LME.
2 *spec.* Of or pertaining to the reproduction of colours by filtering out different parts of the spectrum. E20.
▶ **B** *noun.* A thing that is subtracted or deducted from another; *spec.* (*LINGUISTICS*) a subtractive morph or morpheme. M20.

subtrahend /ˈsʌbtrəhɛnd/ *noun.* L17.
[Latin *subtrahendus* (sc. *numerus* number) gerundive of *subtrahere* SUBTRACT: see -END.]
MATH. A quantity or number to be subtracted from another (the minuend); *transf.* a sum of money to be deducted.

subtrist /sʌbˈtrɪst/ *adjective. rare* (Scott). E19.
[Latin *subtristis*, formed as SUB- + *tristis* sad.]
Somewhat sad.

subtropic /sʌbˈtrɒpɪk/ *adjective & noun.* L19.
[from SUB- 5, 6 + TROPIC *noun & adjective*[1].]
▶ **A** *adjective.* = SUBTROPICAL. L19.
▶ **B** *noun.* In *pl.* The regions adjacent to or bordering on the tropics. L19.

subtropical /sʌbˈtrɒpɪk(ə)l/ *adjective.* M19.
[formed as prec. + TROPICAL.]
1 Bordering on the tropics. M19.
2 Characteristic of regions bordering on the tropics; (of a climate, character, etc.) between temperate and tropical; almost tropical. M19.

subucula /səˈbjuːkjʊlə/ *noun.* Pl. **-lae** /-liː/, **-las.** OE.
[Latin, dim. formed as SUB- + stem of *induere* put on: see -CULE.]
Hist. An undertunic; *spec.* one worn beneath an alb by a priest in Anglo-Saxon England.

Subud /sʊˈbʊd/ *noun.* M20.
[Acronym, from Javanese *susila budhi dharma* interpreted as humanitarian action + life-force + devotion to God, from Sanskrit *suśīla* good disposition + *buddhi* understanding + *dharma* religious duty.]
A system of exercises by which the individual seeks to approach a state of perfection through divine power; a movement (founded in 1947 and led by the Javanese mystic Pak Muhammad Subuh) based on this system.

subulate /ˈsjuːbjʊlət/ *adjective.* M18.
[from Latin *subula* awl + -ATE[2].]
BOTANY & ZOOLOGY. Awl-shaped; slender and tapering to a point.
■ Also **subulated** *adjective* (*rare*) M18.

subungulate /sʌbˈʌŋgjʊlət, -leɪt/ *noun.* L19
[from SUB- + UNGULATE.]
ZOOLOGY. A mammal of a diverse group that comprises the elephants, hyraxes, sirenians, and perhaps the aardvark, and probably evolved from primitive ungulates.

suburb /ˈsʌbəːb/ *noun.* ME.
[Old & mod. French *suburbe*, pl. *-s* or Latin *suburbium*, pl. *-ia*, formed as SUB- + *urbs* city.]
1 *sing.* & in *pl.* (formerly treated as *sing.*). A district, esp. a residential area, lying (orig.) immediately outside or (now) within the boundaries of a town or city. ME.
2 Usu. in *pl.* The parts about the border of any place, time, etc.; the outskirts, the confines (*of* something). ME.

📖 **1** E. CALDWELL A quiet residential suburb . . several miles from . . Melbourne. A. N. WILSON Driving out of the beleaguered city into the suburbs. *attrib.*: *Century Magazine* The houses grow up . . higher—villas—suburb houses. ***outer suburb***: see OUTER *adjective.* **2** R. LYND Into the pavilion or some other part of the suburbs of the ground. B. PATTEN In the suburbs of the heart what you love and hate must mingle.

suburban /səˈbəːb(ə)n/ *noun & adjective.* ME.
[Latin *suburbanus*, formed as prec.: see -AN.]
▶ **A** *noun.* †**1** In *pl.* Suburbs. *rare.* Only in ME.
2 A resident in a suburb or the suburbs. LME.
▶ **B** *adjective.* **1** Of or belonging to a suburb or the suburbs of a town; living, situated, or carried on in the suburbs. E17.
2 Having characteristics regarded as typical of residents or life in the suburbs of a city; *esp.* (*derog.*) provincial, narrow-minded, uncultured, naive. E19.
3 = SUBURBICARIAN. *rare.* M19.

2 J. TROLLOPE Elizabeth despised Ann's houseproudness as deeply suburban.

¶ As noun in isolated use before M19.

■ **suburbanism** *noun* the characteristics of suburban life; a suburban peculiarity: L19. **suburbanite** *noun* a resident in the suburbs L19. **subur'banity** *noun* the condition of being suburban; a suburban feature: M19. **suburbani'zation** *noun* the action of suburbanizing or the condition of being suburbanized; an instance of this: E20. **suburbanize** *verb trans.* make (a district) suburban L19. **suburbanly** *adverb* M19.

suburbia /səˈbəːbɪə/ *noun.* Freq. *derog.* Also **S-**. L19.
[from SUBURB + -IA[1].]
The suburbs (orig. esp. of London); the residents or their way of life in the suburbs of a city.

Courier-Mail (Brisbane) Life in suburbia—a progression from mortgage to death.

†suburbial *adjective. rare.* E17–M19.
[from Latin *suburbium* SUBURB: see -AL[1].]
= SUBURBAN *adjective*.

†suburbian *adjective & noun.* E17–E19.
[formed as prec.: see -AN.]
(A) suburban.

suburbican /səˈbəːbɪk(ə)n/ *adjective.* M17.
[Alt.]
= next.

suburbicarian /səbəːbɪˈkɛːrɪən/ *adjective.* M17.
[from late Latin *suburbicarius*, from Latin *suburbium* SUBURB after *urbicarius* URBICARY: see -ARIAN.]
Designating any of the dioceses (now six in number) around Rome, or their churches etc., which are subject to the jurisdiction of the Pope and whose bishops form the body of cardinal bishops.
■ Also **su'burbicary** *adjective* M17.

subvent /səbˈvɛnt/ *verb trans.* E17.
[Latin *subvent-* pa. ppl stem of *subvenire*: see SUBVENTION.]
1 Come to the help of. *rare.* E17.
2 = SUBVENTION *verb.* E20.

†subventaneous *adjective.* M17–M18.
[from mod. Latin *subventaneus*, formed as SUB- + *ventum* wind: see -ANEOUS.]
(Of conception in an animal) supposedly caused by the wind; *esp.* (of an egg) infertile; *fig.* unproductive, vain. Cf. ***wind-egg*** s.v. WIND *noun*[1].

subvention /səbˈvɛnʃ(ə)n/ *noun & verb.* LME.
[Old & mod. French from late Latin *subventio(n-)*, from Latin *subvent-* pa. ppl stem of *subvenire* come to the help of, formed as SUB- + *venire* come: see -ION.]
▶ **A** *noun.* **1** A subsidy levied by the State. *obsolete* exc. *Hist.* LME.
2 The provision of help or relief; an instance of this. Now *rare.* LME.
3 A grant of money for the support of an object, institution, or person; now *esp.* a grant from a government or some other authority in support of a public enterprise. M19.
4 The granting of financial aid for the support of an undertaking. M19.

3 A. CROSS Universities had funds . . to provide subventions for worthy . . books. **4** H. EVANS They were talking to Associated, because the costs . . were . . £60,000: they needed subvention.

▶ **B** *verb trans.* Support or assist by the payment of a subvention. M19.
■ **subventionary** *adjective* of the nature of a subvention M19. **subventionize** *verb trans.* (*rare*) = SUBVENTION *verb* L19.

sub verbo /sʌbˈvəːbəʊ, sʊbˈwəːbəʊ/ *adverbial phr.* E20.
[Latin.]
= SUB VOCE. Abbreviation ***s.v.***

subverse /səbˈvəːs/ *verb trans. rare.* L16.
[Latin *subvers-* pa. ppl stem of *subvertere* SUBVERT.]
Subvert, upset.
■ **subversal** *noun* subversion L19.

subversion /səbˈvəːʃ(ə)n/ *noun.* LME.
[Old & mod. French, or late Latin *subversio(n-)*, formed as prec.: see -ION.]
The action or practice of subverting (esp. a political regime); an instance or result of this.

J. BARTH Our government's role in the subversion of Chilean democracy. G. STEINER These critical subversions of the positivist scheme. *Independent* Four . . students are to go on trial . . on charges of subversion.

■ **subversionary** *adjective* (*rare*) = SUBVERSIVE *adjective* M19. **subversionist** *noun* = SUBVERSIVE *noun* M20.

subversive /səbˈvəːsɪv/ *adjective & noun.* M17.
[medieval Latin *subversivus*, formed as prec.: see -IVE.]
▶ **A** *adjective.* Tending to subvert (esp. a political regime); seeking subversion. Also foll. by *of*, *to.* M17.

P. ACKROYD *Little Dorrit* is a subversive text. It is . . anti-capitalist . . , anti-authoritarian. P. MAILLOUX Exiled . . for teaching theological doctrines considered subversive.

▶ **B** *noun.* A subversive person; *esp.* a person seeking to overthrow a political regime, a revolutionary. L19.

Atlantic We felt as though we were members of the underground, violent subversives.

■ **subversively** *adverb* L20. **subversiveness** *noun* M20.

subvert /səbˈvəːt/ *verb trans.* LME.
[Old French *subvertir* or Latin *subvertere*, formed as SUB- + *vertere* turn.]
†**1** Demolish, raze to the ground (a city, stronghold, etc.). LME–L18. ▶**b** Upset, overturn (an object). M16–E18.
2 Undermine the character, loyalty, or faith of (a person); corrupt, pervert. Now *rare.* LME.
3 Disturb or overthrow (a system, condition, principle, etc.); attempt to achieve, esp. by covert action, the weakening or destruction of (a country, government, political regime, etc.). LME.

1 P. HOLLAND When those more ancient Churches were subverted, Aldred . . erected another. **b** EVELYN The tempest of wind . . which subverted . . huge trees. **3** WORDSWORTH Our active powers . . become Strong to subvert our noxious qualities. H. HALLAM Nothing so much strengthens any government as an unsuccessful endeavour to subvert it. *Scientific American* Toxins may subvert the immune system's battle plans. *Pen International* A spell in prison for attempting to subvert the state.

■ **subverter** *noun* L15. **subvertible** *adjective* (*rare*) able to be subverted E19.

sub voce /sʌb ˈvəʊsi, ˈvəʊtʃi, sʌb ˈwəʊkeɪ/ *adverbial phr.* M19.
[Latin.]
As a direction in a text: under the word or heading given. Abbreviation ***s.v.*** Cf. SUB VERBO.

subway /ˈsʌbweɪ/ *noun & verb.* E19.
[from SUB- 1 + WAY *noun*.]
▶ **A** *noun.* **1 a** An underground passage for conveying water pipes, gas pipes, telegraph wires, etc. E19. ▶**b** A tunnel beneath a road, river, railway, etc., for the use of pedestrians or vehicles. M19.
2 An underground railway. Chiefly *N. Amer.* L19.
Comb.: **subway alumni** *US slang* city-dwelling supporters of a college football team who are not graduates of the college; **subway series** *N. Amer. colloq.* a series of games between two teams in the same city.
▶ **B** *verb intrans.* Travel by subway or underground railway. *N. Amer. colloq.* E20.

succade /sʌˈkeɪd/ *noun.* Also †**-ate**. LME.
[Anglo-Norman *sukade*, Old Northern French *succade* (also *chuc(c)ade*), of unkn. origin: see -ADE.]
Fruit preserved in sugar, either candied or in syrup; in *pl.*, sweets of candied fruit or vegetable products.

succah /ˈsʊkə/ *noun.* L19.
[Hebrew *sukkāh* lit. 'hut'.]
Any of the booths in which a practising Jew spends part of the feast of Tabernacles. Cf. SUCCOTH.

†succate *noun* var. of SUCCADE.

†succatoon *noun. rare.* E18–E19.
[Origin unkn.]
A type of dyed cotton cloth.

succedanea *noun pl.* see SUCCEDANEUM.

†succedaneous *adjective.* M17–E19.
[Latin *succedaneus*, from *succedere* come close after: see SUCCEED, -ANEOUS.]
Taking the place of something else; acting as a substitute. Also (*rare*), supplementary. (Foll. by *to*.)

succedaneum /sʌksɪˈdeɪnɪəm/ *noun.* Pl. **-ea** /-ɪə/, **-eums**. E17.
[mod. Latin, neut. sing. of Latin *succedaneus*: see prec.]
1 A thing which takes the place of another; a substitute; *spec.* a medicine or drug substituted for another. (Foll. by *for*, *of*, †*to*.) E17.
†**2** A remedy, a cure. M–L18.
¶ See also CAPUT SUCCEDANEUM.

succedent /səkˈsiːd(ə)nt/ *adjective & noun.* Now *rare.* LME.
[Latin *succedent-* pres. ppl stem of *succedere* SUCCEED: see -ENT.]
▶ **A** *adjective.* **1** Following, succeeding; subsequent *to.* LME.
2 ASTROLOGY. Designating or pertaining to each of the four mundane houses (the 2nd, 5th, 8th, and 11th of the twelve divisions of the heavens) next anticlockwise from the angles (ANGLE *noun*[3] 3). Cf. CADENT *adjective* 1. L16.
▶ **B** *noun.* †**1** A thing that follows another. LME–E17.
2 ASTROLOGY. A succedent house. *obsolete* exc. *Hist.* LME.

succeed /səkˈsiːd/ *verb.* LME.
[Old & mod. French *succéder* or Latin *succedere* go under or up, come close after, go near, go on well, formed as SUB- + *cedere* go.]
▶ **I 1 a** *verb intrans.* Come next after and take the place of another by descent, election, or appointment; (freq. foll. by *to*) be the immediate successor in an office, position, etc.; inherit an estate, title, etc. LME. ▶†**b** Of an estate etc.: descend in succession; pass by inheritance *to.* Chiefly *Scot.* M16–E17.
2 *verb intrans.* Come next in an order of individual persons or things; follow on. (Foll. by *to*.) LME.
3 *verb intrans.* Follow or come *after* in the course of time or the sequence of events; take place or come into being subsequently (*to*). LME. ▶†**b** *verb intrans.* Follow as a consequence *of*; ensue, result (*from*). M16–E18. ▶**c** Come to pass, take place; happen *to.* M16–M17.
†**4** *verb intrans.* Be continued, go on. L15–E17.
†**5** *verb trans.* Follow, walk after. L15–L18.
6 *verb trans.* Come next after and take the place of (another) by descent, election, or appointment; be the immediate successor to (a person) in an office, position, etc.; inherit an estate, title, etc., from. E16. ▶†**b** Follow by imitating or reproducing the manners or appearance of. L16–E17.
7 *verb trans.* Come after or follow (another) in the course of time or the sequence of events; take place or come into being subsequently to. E16.

1 J. BUCHAN Gerard . . succeeded to great wealth. JOHN BROOKE George I was fifty-three when he succeeded to the throne. **2** A. DOBSON To make you read The pages that to this succeed. **6** G. L. HARDING Herod the Great was succeeded by Herod the Tetrarch. **b** SHAKES. *All's Well* Succeed thy father In manners, as in shape. **7** M. KEANE In the hour succeeding luncheon, the library was full. L. DURRELL Bursts of self-confidence were succeeded by depressions.

▶ **II** With ref. to success.
8 *verb intrans.* **a** Have the desired outcome, have a favourable result, turn out successfully. LME. ▶**b** Of a plant: grow well, thrive. E19.
9 *verb intrans.* Achieve a desired end; be successful in an endeavour (freq. foll. by *in*); manage to do something; prosper. E16.
†**10** *verb intrans.* Have a specified outcome, achieve a specified end; (with qualifying adverb) turn out or manage well, badly, etc. M16–L17.
†**11** *verb trans.* Give success to; prosper, further. E17–M19.

8 J. A. FROUDE No reason why an attempt . . might not succeed. **9** E. J. HOWARD He wanted to evade dinner . . and succeeded with . . ease. K. VONNEGUT He said no woman could succeed in the arts. P. USTINOV I succeeded in staying awake. *Proverb*: If at first you don't succeed, try, try again.

▶†**III 12** *verb intrans.* Come near *to*, approach. L16–L17.
■ **succeeder** *noun* (*a*) (now *rare*) a successor; (*b*) a successful person: LME. **succeeding** *ppl adjective* (*a*) following in a line of rulers or heirs, in the course of time or events, in immediate succession, etc.; subsequent; †(*b*) successful; †(*c*) ASTROLOGY = SUCCEDENT *adjective* 2; †(*d*) following one after another, successive, consecutive: M16.

succent /səkˈsɛnt/ *verb.* E17.
[Latin *succent-* pa. ppl stem of *succinere*: see next.]
†**1** *verb intrans.* Sing a bass. Only in E17.
2 Sing the second part of (a verse etc.). L19.

succentor /səkˈsɛntə/ *noun.* E17.
[Late Latin, from Latin *succinere* sing to, accompany, chime in, agree, formed as SUB- + *canere* sing: see -OR. Cf. SUBCHANTER.]
†**1** An abettor. *rare.* Only in E17.
2 Orig., a person who takes up the singing to lead a choir or congregation after the precentor. Now, a precentor's deputy in some cathedrals. M17.
■ **succentorship** *noun* the position or office of a succentor L17.

succenturiate /sʌksɛnˈtjʊərɪət/ *adjective. rare.* M17.
[Latin *succenturiatus* pa. pple of *succenturiare* receive as a recruit, formed as SUB- + *centuria* CENTURY: see -ATE[2].]
†**1** Substituted. Only in M17.
2 ANATOMY & ZOOLOGY. Accessory, subsidiary. M19.

succès /syksɛ/ *noun.* Pl. same. M19.
[French = success.]
1 ***succès d'estime*** /dɛstim/ [= of opinion or regard], a critical as opp. to a popular or commercial success. M19.
2 ***succès de scandale*** /də skɑ̃dal/, success due to notoriety or scandalous character. L19.
3 ***succès fou*** /fu/ [= mad], a success marked by wild enthusiasm. L19.

success /səkˈsɛs/ *noun.* M16.
[Latin *successus*, from *success-* pa. ppl stem of *succedere* SUCCEED.]
†**1** Succession; an instance of this. M16–L17.
2 †**a** The outcome or upshot of an event, affair, etc.; a result. M16–M18. ▶**b** An event. *rare.* L16. ▶†**c** The result of an experiment; the effect of a medicine. E17–M18.
3 A person's fortune in a particular situation; good or bad luck. Freq. with specifying word. *arch.* M16.
4 a The achievement of an endeavour; the attainment of a desired end; prosperity. Also, an instance of this; a successful undertaking or achievement. L16. ▶**b** A successful person or occasion. L19.

3 ***good success, ill success***, etc. **4a** I. WALLACE Peace was probable and . . the President had achieved a real success. *attrib.*: C. PRIEST The clinic claimed a success rate of 100 per cent. **b** J. CARTWRIGHT Magda's brother . . was . . a success with women. P. P. READ The late hour . . suggested that her party had been a success. **5** SPENSER All the sonnes of these fine brethren raynd By dew successe.

Comb.: **success story** *colloq.* a successful venture, achievement, etc.; *spec.* a person's rise from poverty to wealth etc.
■ **successless** *adjective* (now *rare*) unsuccessful L16. **successlessly** *adverb* M17. **successlessness** *noun* M17.

For other words beginning with *sub-* see the entry for **sub-**

†successantly *adverb. rare* (Shakes.). Only in **L16**.
[Arbitrary formation from Latin *success-* (see prec.) + -ANT[1] + -LY[2].]
In succession.

successful /səkˈsɛsfʊl, -f(ə)l/ *adjective.* **L16**.
[from SUCCESS + -FUL.]
Having or resulting in success; prosperous; *spec.* (of a person) attaining wealth or status.
■ **successfully** *adverb* **L16**. **successfulness** *noun* **M17**.

succession /səkˈsɛʃ(ə)n/ *noun.* **ME**.
[Old & mod. French, or Latin *successio(n-)*, from *success-*: see SUCCESS, -ION.]
▶ **I 1** The legal transmission of an estate, throne, etc., from one person to another. **ME**. ▶**†b** That to which a person succeeds as heir; an inheritance. *rare.* **LME–M18**.
2 The process by which one person succeeds another in the occupation of an estate, throne, etc.; the fact of succeeding according to custom or law *to* the rights and liabilities of a predecessor; *the* conditions under which this is done. **LME**. ▶**b** The action of succeeding to the episcopate by receiving lawfully transmitted authority by ordination. **M16**. ▶**c** *The* line or order of succession by inheritance. **E18**.
3 A person's right or privilege to succeed another in the occupation of an estate, throne, etc. **LME**.

> 📖 **1** MONMOUTH So long as the Earl of Warwick lived, he was not certaine of the Kingdoms succession. **2** SWIFT The security of the protestant succession in the house of Hanover. W. BLACKSTONE The power of the laws in regulating the succession to property. W. H. DIXON She stood in order of succession to the duchy. **3** DRYDEN What people is so void of common sense, To vote succession from a native prince. SIR W. SCOTT Endangering both his succession and his life.

▶ **II †4** *collect.* Successors, heirs, or descendants collectively; progeny, issue. **ME–L17**.
†5 a A generation of people; in *pl.*, future generations. **LME–E18**. ▶**b** Posterity. **E17–E18**.
6 a A series of persons or things in sequence; a continued line *of* sovereigns, heirs, etc. **L16**. ▶**†b** The followers of a school of thought collectively. Only in **17**.
7 A set of persons or things following in the place of others. **M17**.

> 📖 **6a** B. W. ALDISS Lucy . . the last of Joseph's long succession of girl-friends. R. FRAME After a succession of . . slow train journeys.

▶ **III** *techn.* **8 a** The action of a person or thing following or taking the place of another; the passing from one act or state to another; an instance of this. **LME**. ▶**†b** The action of following another in a course of conduct. *rare* (Shakes.). Only in **E17**.
9 ASTRONOMY. The ordered sequence of signs of the zodiac. Now *rare.* **L17**.
10 MUSIC. The order in which the notes of a melody proceed. Also = SEQUENCE *noun* 4b. **M18**.
11 MILITARY. A gradation of an army according to the dates of commissions. **M18**.
12 AGRICULTURE. **a** The rotation of crops. **L18**. ▶**b** The continuous cultivation of a crop throughout a season by successive sowings or plantings. **M19**.
13 GEOLOGY. **a** The continued sequence in a definite order of fossil species, types, etc., esp. as representing continuous descent of forms modified by evolution. **M19**. ▶**b** A group of strata whose order represents a single chronological sequence. **M20**.
14 ECOLOGY. A sequence of ecological changes in an area whereby one group of plant or animal species successively gives way to another, culminating in a climax community. **M19**.
Phrases: ***apostolic succession***: see APOSTOLIC *adjective* 1. **by succession** according to the customary or legal principle by which one person succeeds another in an inheritance, office, etc. **in succession** one after another in regular sequence. ***primary succession***: see PRIMARY *adjective*. ***quick succession***: see QUICK *adjective & adverb*. ***secondary succession***: see SECONDARY *adjective*.
Comb.: **succession house** HORTICULTURE any of a series of forcing-houses having regularly graded temperatures into which plants are moved in succession; **succession powder** *Hist.* a poison supposed to have been made of lead acetate; **Succession State** a State resulting from the overthrow or partition of a previous State.
■ **successional** *adjective* (*a*) pertaining to, characterized by, or involving the succession of an estate, throne, etc.; passing by succession; (*b*) following one after another, occurring in succession; (*c*) of or pertaining to horticultural or ecological succession: **E17**. **successionally** *adverb* (*rare*) by succession **M19**. **successionist** *noun* (*rare*) a person who maintains the validity or necessity of a succession; *esp.* an upholder of the doctrine of the apostolic succession: **M19**. **successionless** *adjective* without succession; having no successors: **E17**.

successive /səkˈsɛsɪv/ *adjective.* **LME**.
[medieval Latin *successivus*, from Latin *success-*: see SUCCESS, -IVE.]
▶ **I 1 a** Coming one after another in an uninterrupted sequence; following one another in order, consecutive. **LME**. ▶**b** Following another of the same kind in a regular sequence or series. **L16**.
2 Characterized by or involving sequential succession; brought about in succeeding stages. **L17**.

> 📖 **1a** A. STORR For six successive years, Freud was first in his class at school. **b** *Daily Telegraph* Radio Uganda . . remained silent for the second successive day.

▶**†II 3** Hereditary; descending or transmitted by succession or inheritance; succeeding by inheritance. Also, next in order of succession. **L16–E18**.
▶**†III 4** Successful. **L16–M17**.
■ **successiveness** *noun* **L17**. **succeˈssivity** *noun* (*rare*) **M19**.

successively /səkˈsɛsɪvli/ *adverb.* **LME**.
[from prec. + -LY[2].]
1 By successive stages of increase or decrease. Formerly also, by degrees, eventually. Now *rare.* **LME**. ▶**†b** Continuously, without interruption. **M16–L18**.
2 In succession; in turn. **LME**.
†3 By succession or inheritance. **LME–E18**.
†4 Successfully, favourably. **L16–L17**.

> 📖 **2** V. BROME Henderson was successively a patient, . . a colleague and a friend.

successor /səkˈsɛsə/ *noun.* **ME**.
[Old French *successour* (mod. *successeur*) from Latin *successor*, from *success-*: see SUCCESS, -OR.]
A person who or thing which succeeds another in an office, function, or position.

> 📖 *Japan Times* Members started . . looking for a successor to Prime Minister Noboru Takeshita. ***singular successor***: see SINGULAR *adjective*.

Comb.: **Successor State** = ***Succession State*** s.v. SUCCESSION.
■ **successorship** *noun* the condition or position of successor; succession: **E17**.

succi *noun* pl. of SUCCUS.

succinate /ˈsʌksɪneɪt/ *noun.* **L18**.
[from SUCCINIC + -ATE[1].]
CHEMISTRY. A salt or ester of succinic acid.

succinct /səkˈsɪŋkt/ *adjective.* **LME**.
[Latin *succinctus* pa. pple of *succingere*, formed as SUB- + *cingere* gird.]
▶ **I 1** Surrounded, encircled. *arch.* **LME**.
2 *spec.* Encircled with a belt or girdle; confined (as) by a girdle. *arch.* **E17**.
▶ **II 3** Expressed in few words; brief, concise; characterized by verbal brevity and conciseness; terse. **E17**.
4 Of a garment: not full; close-fitting. *arch.* **E18**.
5 Of short duration, brief, curt. *arch.* **L18**.
■ **succinctly** *adverb* in a succinct manner; with brevity, concisely: **L15**. **succinctness** *noun* **E17**.

succinctory /sʌkˈsɪŋkt(ə)ri/ *noun.* Also in Latin form **succinctorium** /sʌksɪŋˈtɔːrɪəm/, pl. **-ia** /-ɪə/. **L16**.
[Late Latin *succinctorium*, formed as SUB- + *cinctorium* girdle: see -ORY[1].]
ECCLESIASTICAL. A Eucharistic vestment worn by the Pope, consisting of a strip embroidered with an Agnus Dei, suspended from the girdle.

succinea /səkˈsɪnɪə/ *noun.* Pl. **-eae** /-iːiː/, **-eas**. **M19**.
[mod. Latin (see below), from fem. of *succineus*, from *succinum* amber.]
ZOOLOGY. Any gastropod mollusc of the genus *Succinea*, having a transparent amber-coloured spiral shell. Chiefly as mod. Latin genus name.

succinic /səkˈsɪnɪk/ *adjective.* **L18**.
[from Latin *succinum* amber + -IC.]
CHEMISTRY. ***succinic acid***, a dibasic organic acid, $HOOC(CH_2)_2COOH$, important as an intermediate in glucose metabolism, and orig. obtained by dry distillation of amber; butanedioic acid.

succinimide /sʌkˈsɪnɪmʌɪd/ *noun.* **M19**.
[from SUCCINIC + IMIDE.]
CHEMISTRY. A solid derivative of succinic acid whose molecule contains a five-membered ring including a nitrogen atom between two carbonyl groups; 2,5-diketopyrrolidine.

succinite /ˈsʌksɪnʌɪt/ *noun.* **E19**.
[from Latin *succinum* + -ITE[1].]
MINERALOGY. **1** An amber-coloured grossular garnet. **E19**.
2 Amber, esp. from the Baltic region. **M19**.

succinum /ˈsʌksɪnəm/ *noun.* **M16**.
[Latin.]
Amber.

succinyl /ˈsʌksɪnɪl, -ʌɪl/ *noun.* **M19**.
[from SUCCINIC + -YL.]
CHEMISTRY. The radical of succinic acid. Usu. in *comb.*
■ **succinylˈcholine** *noun* (PHARMACOLOGY) a basic compound formed by esterification of succinic acid with choline; used as a short-acting muscle relaxant and local anaesthetic (also called ***suxamethonium***) **M20**.

succor *noun, verb* see SUCCOUR *noun, verb.*

succorance /ˈsʌk(ə)r(ə)ns/ *noun.* **M20**.
[from SUCCOUR *noun*: see -ANCE.]
PSYCHOLOGY. The need for help, sympathy, and affection as a psychogenic force.
■ **succorant** *adjective* relating to succorance **M20**.

succory /ˈsʌk(ə)ri/ *noun.* **M16**.
[Alt. of French †*cicorée* (see CHICORY), after Middle Low German *suckerie*, Middle Dutch *sūkerie* (Dutch *suiker*).]
1 The plant chicory, *Cichorium intybus*, esp. in its wild form. Also, the leaves and roots of this plant used medicinally and as food. **M16**.
2 With specifying word: any of various composites, chiefly allied to the chicory. **M16**.
2 gum succory *US* a European wild lettuce, *Chondrilla juncea*, naturalized as a weed. **lamb succory** (chiefly *US*) = ***swine's succory*** below. **swine's succory** a small erect plant, *Arnoseris minima*, related to nipplewort, found esp. in sandy cornfields.

succotash /ˈsʌkətaʃ/ *noun.* **M18**.
[Narragansett *msiquatash* (pl.): cf. SQUASH *noun*[2].]
A dish of N. American Indian origin, usu. consisting of green maize and beans boiled together.

Succoth /sʊˈkəʊt, ˈsʌkəθ/ *noun.* **L19**.
[Hebrew *sukkōt* pl. of *sukkāh*: see SUCCAH.]
A Jewish autumn harvest and thanksgiving festival commemorating the sheltering of the Israelites in the wilderness. Also called ***feast of Tabernacles***.

succour /ˈsʌkə/ *noun.* Also ***-or**. **ME**.
[Old French *sucurs*, *socours* (mod. *secours*) from medieval Latin *succursus*, from Latin *succurs-* pa. ppl stem of *succurrere*: see the verb.]
1 Aid, help, assistance, esp. in time of need. **ME**.
2 A person who or thing which helps; a means of assistance; an aid. *arch.* **ME**. ▶**†b** *spec.* A financial grant, a subsidy. **E17–M18**.
3 Military assistance; *esp.* auxiliary forces, reinforcements. *arch.* **ME**.
4 Shelter, protection; a place of shelter, a refuge. *obsolete* exc. *dial.* **ME**.

> 📖 **1** F. W. FARRAR Paul's first impulse was to fly to the succour of his Roman brethren.

■ **succourless** *adjective* helpless; destitute: **LME**.

succour /ˈsʌkə/ *verb trans.* Also ***-or**. **ME**.
[Old French (i) *socorre*, (ii) *suc(c)ourir* (mod. *secourir*) from Latin *succurrere*, formed as SUB- + *currere* run.]
1 Help, assist, aid (esp. a person in need or danger). **ME**.
2 Provide with military assistance; bring reinforcements to; *spec.* relieve (a besieged place). *arch.* **ME**.
3 Shelter, protect. Now *dial.* **ME**.
4 Relieve, remedy (a condition of hardship, pain, etc.). Now *rare.* **LME**.
5 NAUTICAL. Strengthen, make firm. **L17**.

> 📖 **1** M. FORSTER When any of us was sick . . the rest rushed to succour them. G. GREENE Cut off from the secure life that had succoured him.

■ **succourable** *adjective* (*arch.*) providing assistance, helpful **LME**. **succourer** *noun* (*rare*) a person who or thing which aids or assists **LME**.

succous /ˈsʌkəs/ *adjective.* *rare.* **L17**.
[Latin *succosus*, from *succus* juice: see -OUS.]
Containing juice or sap; juicy.

succuba /ˈsʌkjʊbə/ *noun.* Pl. **-bae** /-biː/. Also (*rare*) **succube** /ˈsʌkjuːb/. **L16**.
[Late Latin = prostitute, from *succubare*, formed as SUB- + *cubare* lie.]
= SUCCUBUS.

succubi *noun* pl. of SUCCUBUS.

succubous /ˈsʌkjʊbəs/ *adjective.* **M19**.
[from late Latin *succubare* (see SUCCUBA) + -OUS.]
BOTANY. (Of a leaf, esp. in a foliose liverwort) obliquely inserted on the stem so that the upper margin is overlapped and covered by the lower margin of the leaf above; (of a plant) having its leaves so arranged. Opp. INCUBOUS.

succubus /ˈsʌkjʊbəs/ *noun.* Pl. **-bi** /-bʌɪ/. **LME**.
[medieval Latin, masc. form (with fem. meaning) corresp. to SUCCUBA, after INCUBUS.]
1 A demon in female form supposed to have sexual intercourse with sleeping men. **LME**. ▶**b** *gen.* A demon, an evil spirit. **E17**.
2 A prostitute, a whore. *arch. derog.* **E17**.

> 📖 **1** S. J. PERELMAN This is a hyperthyroid dame who fastens on ya like a succubus.

succulent /ˈsʌkjʊlənt/ *adjective & noun.* **E17**.
[Latin *succulentus*, from *succus* juice: see -LENT, -ULENT.]
▶ **A** *adjective.* **1** Full of juice, juicy; (of a plant, esp. a xerophyte) having thick fleshy leaves and/or stems adapted to storing water. **E17**.
2 Rich in content; interesting, stimulating; excellent. **E17**.

> 📖 **1** J. COX Blackberry roots . . send up their succulent thorny shoots. E. SEGAL A . . succulent cut of London broil, waiting to be carved. **2** GEO. ELIOT Succulent themes of converse or meditation.

▶ **B** *noun.* BOTANY. A succulent plant. **E19**.

■ **succulence**, **succulency** *nouns* the quality or condition of being succulent; juiciness: E17. **succulently** *adverb* L19.

succumb /səˈkʌm/ *verb*. L15.
[Old & mod. French *succomber* or Latin *succumbere*, formed as SUB- + *-cumbere* lie (see CUMBENT).]
†**1** *verb trans.* Bring down, bring low, overwhelm. L15–M16.
†**2** *verb intrans.* Fail in a cause; *spec.* fail in a lawsuit, usu. for lack of proof. *Scot.* M16–E18.
3 *verb intrans.* Sink under pressure; give way *to* force, authority, emotion, etc.; be overcome. E17. ▸**b** *spec.* Be overcome by the effect of a disease, wound, operation, etc.; die. M19.

📖 **3** D. HALBERSTAM Resisted Klauber's offers for a long time, but . . finally succumbed. P. ANGADI She succumbed to her deep need. **b** I. D. YALOM His father succumbed to the same type of lymphoma.

■ **succumber** *noun* (*rare*) M19.

succumbency /səˈkʌmb(ə)nsi/ *noun*. Now *rare*. M17.
[from next: see -ENCY.]
The action or an act of giving way or yielding; (a) submission.

†**succumbent** *adjective & noun*. *rare*. M17.
[Latin *succumbent-* pres. ppl stem of *succumbere*: see SUCCUMB, -ENT.]
▸ **A** *adjective*. **1** Subject or submissive *to*. Only in M17.
2 Underlying. Only in M17.
3 Succumbing. Only in E19.
▸ **B** *noun*. A person who kneels in a place of worship. Only in M17.

succursal /səˈkəːs(ə)l/ *adjective & noun*. M19.
[French *succursale*, from medieval Latin *succursus*: see SUCCOUR *noun*, -AL¹.]
▸ **A** *adjective*. Esp. of a religious establishment: subsidiary. M19.
▸ **B** *noun*. Also in French form **succursale** /səˈkəːsɑːl/. A subsidiary (esp. religious) establishment; a branch institution, business, etc. M19.

succus /ˈsʌkəs/ *noun*. Pl. **succi** /ˈsʌk(s)ʌɪ, ˈsʌk(s)iː/. L18.
[Latin.]
A juice; a fluid secretion in an animal or plant.
succus entericus /ɛnˈtɛrɪkəs/ intestinal digestive juice.

†**succussation** *noun*. M17–L18.
[medieval Latin *succussatio(n-)*, from Latin *succussat-* pa. ppl stem of *succussare* frequentative of *succutere*: see next, -ATION.]
Shaking up, violent shaking; jolting, trotting; an instance of this.

succussion /səˈkʌʃ(ə)n/ *noun*. E17.
[Latin *succussio(n-)*, from *succuss-* pa. ppl stem of *succutere*, formed as SUB- + *quatere* shake: see -ION.]
1 The action or an act of shaking something, esp. with violence; the condition of being shaken. E17.
2 *spec.* in MEDICINE. A method of diagnosis which consists in shaking the body to detect splashing sounds indicating the presence of fluid and air, esp. in pneumothorax; an instance of this; the sound produced. M18.
3 HOMOEOPATHY. The vigorous shaking of a preparation of a medicine. Cf. POTENTIZE. M19.
■ **succuss** /səˈkʌs/ *verb trans.* subject to succussion M19. **succussive** *adjective* (*rare*) characterized by a shaking motion M18.

such /sʌtʃ/ *demonstr. adjective* (in mod. usage also classed as a *determiner*), *adverb, & pronoun*. Also (now *dial.*) **sich** /sɪtʃ/.
[Old English *swilć, swelć, swylć* = Old Frisian *sâl(i)k*, Old Saxon *sulīk*, Old High German *solīh* (Dutch *zulk*, German *solch*), Old Norse *slíkr*, Gothic *swaleiks*, ult. from Germanic base of SO *adverb* etc., ALIKE *adjective* etc. Cf. ILK *adjective*¹ & *pronoun*¹, WHICH.]
▸ **A** *demonstr. adjective*. **I 1** Of the kind, degree, or category previously specified or implied contextually. Preceding the noun & any indef. article (*arch.*, also with indef. article omitted), or pred. OE.
2 Of the same kind or degree as something previously specified or implied contextually; of that kind; similar. *arch.* exc. with preceding numeral or indef. adjective (determiner), *any, no, many*, etc. OE.
3 *pred.* Of the character previously specified by a preceding adjective, so. (Used to avoid repetition.) *arch.* OE.

📖 **1** T. HARDY His wife, who seemed accustomed to such remarks. N. O. BROWN Such is the demonic energy with which Swift pursues his vision. I. MURDOCH She needed him, unless the horror should now place her beyond such needs. C. P. SNOW Such a passion was very rare. **2** M. BERESFORD One such district is the plain of Lancashire. *American Speech* The notes . . include references to some such studies. **3** DRYDEN A heroic poem, truly such. C. KINGSLEY Thought himself as good as his brother (though he was not such).

▸ **II 4** Of the kind, degree, category being or about to be specified. Preceding a noun & any indef. article and foll. by *as*, or in *such as . . such*. OE.
5 Having a specified or implied quality to an intense degree; so great, splendid, marvellous, etc. Freq. with consequence expr. (now only with *that* or *as to do* or *be*). ME.

📖 **4** G. BURNET The electress . . was forced to submit to such terms as were imposed on her. M. ELPHINSTONE Barbarity such as his was unexampled among princes. SIR W. SCOTT Such prisoners from whom he was desirous of extorting . . information. MRS ALEXANDER Deering could not endure the companionship of such a man as Vincent. M. DICKENS Such jobs as he did . . barely kept him in drink. I. MCEWAN Metallic sounds such as cutlery makes. **5** R. CURZON Cool and delicious, and there were such quantities of them. *Law Times* Allowing . . property to fall into such a state of disrepair that it was impossible to let. A. BIERCE He . . had borne himself with such gallantry as to attract the attention of . . officers. J. B. PRIESTLEY You never told us it was such a show place. I. MCEWAN Agreements . . enabled them to move through so many topics with such patience. J. C. OATES Fairchild's finger span is such that . . he can grip a basketball in his . . hand.

▸ **III 6** Of a particular kind, degree, or category not requiring to be or not being specified. Freq. in ***such-and-such*** below. LME.

📖 **6** E. A. FREEMAN The form always is that the King grants the bishopric or abbacy to such a person.

▸ **B** *adverb*. To a specified or implied extent; to the extent *that*; in such a manner *that*; so (*that*). OE.

📖 T. HARDY She had won such high opinion from a stranger. J. STEINBECK It would not have been good to eat such fine things openly. G. VIDAL Such a simple statement invited a straight question. M. PUZO It was because I had such few friends. H. SECOMBE It had been such a long time. *Review of English Studies* Herbert carefully structures his poems such that their . . ambiguities . . duplicate the opacity of the world in general.

▸ **C** *pronoun*. **1** The person(s) or thing(s) specified or implied contextually; *spec.* the aforesaid thing or things; it, they, them; that, those. OE.
2 A person or thing of the same kind previously specified or (with *as* or other rel. pronoun) about to be specified. OE.

📖 **1** R. SUTCLIFF Such of the group who had no business there melted away. T. MALLON Clichés get to be such . . by being true. E. GELLNER The theory of knowledge, or what I hold to be such. K. VONNEGUT My wife . . my second such, died two years ago. **2** R. MACAULAY The tea-shops were crowded with the continuous eating of such as Mavis. T. HARDY A plain soldier . . and we know what women think of such.

Phrases (of adjective, adverb, & pronoun): **and such** similar people or things. ***as such***: see AS *adverb* etc. **in such a wise, in such wise** *arch.* in such a manner, so. **no such thing** nothing of the kind. ***no such luck***: see LUCK *noun*. ***other such***: see OTHER *adjective* etc. **such-and-such** *adjective & pronoun* (**a**) *adjective* of a particular kind but not needing to be specified (***such-and-such a person***, someone, so-and-so); (**b**) *pronoun* a person or thing of this kind. ***such another***: see ANOTHER 1. **such a one** (**a**) such a person or thing (*as*); (**b**) *arch.* some person or thing unspecified. **such as** for example; (see also senses 4, 5a, b, 6 above). **such as it is, such as they are**, etc., despite its, their, etc., shortcomings. **until such time as, until such time that** until the time when.
■ **suchness** *noun* (**a**) (now chiefly PHILOSOPHY) the condition or quality of being such; quality; (**b**) BUDDHISM = TATHATA: OE. **suchwise** *adverb* (*arch. rare*) [from ***in such wise*** above] in such a manner LME.

suchlike /ˈsʌtʃlʌɪk/ *adjective & pronoun*. Also **such-like**. LME.
[from SUCH *adjective* + LIKE *adjective*. Cf. WHAT-LIKE.]
▸ **A** *adjective*. Of such a kind as that or (esp.) those specified previously or (rarely, with *as*) about to be specified; of a similar kind. LME.

📖 J. BRAINE Loaded weapons and such-like dangerous objects.

▸ **B** *pronoun*. People or things or (*rare*) a person or thing of a similar kind. Chiefly in ***and suchlike, or suchlike*** LME.

📖 *New Scientist* Prime numbers, perfect squares, cubes and suchlike.

suck /sʌk/ *noun*. ME.
[from the verb.]
1 a The action or an act of sucking milk from the breast; the milk sucked at one time. ME. ▸**b** An act of applying suction to something (as a pipe, wound, etc.) with the mouth. M18. ▸**c** An act of fellatio. *coarse slang*. L19.
†**2** Milk sucked or to be sucked from the breast. L16–M17.
3 A small draught of liquid; a drink, a sup, (*of*). E17.
4 The drawing of air by suction. M17.
5 The sucking action or sound of a whirlpool etc. L18.
†**6** A breast-pocket. *Criminals' slang*. E19–E20.
7 A deception; a disappointing event or result. *arch. slang*. M19.
8 A sweet; sweets collectively. *arch. colloq.* M19.
9 a A sycophant; a person, esp. a schoolchild, who curries favour. *slang*. L19. ▸**b** A worthless or contemptible person. Cf. SOOK *noun*¹. *Canad. slang*. L20.
10 In *pl.* As *interjection*. Expr. disappointment, or amusement or derision at another's discomfiture. *colloq.* E20.

📖 **1a** *fig.*: J. MCGAHERN His life has been one long suck on the tit of society. **at suck** engaged in sucking. ***give suck***: see SUCK *verb*. **b** L. STERNE I saw the cut, gave it [my finger] a suck. **5** J. O'FAOLAIN Reeds . . moved in rhythm to the suck of the waters. **9a** JOYCE You are McGlade's suck. **b** M. PIERCY Robin is a suck and a wimp. **10** J. LYMINGTON 'Sucks to you!' she said . . tossing her head so her pigtails swung.

suck /sʌk/ *verb*.
[Old English *sūcan* strong verb (cf. SOAK *verb*), becoming weak in Middle English, corresp. to Latin *sugere*, Old & mod. Irish *súigim*, from Indo-European base of imit. origin, of which a parallel base is repr. in Old English, Old Saxon *sūgan*, Middle Low German, Middle Dutch *sūgen* (Dutch *zuigen*), Old High German *sūgan* (German *saugen*), Old Norse *súga*.]
▸ **I** *verb trans.* **1** Draw (liquid, esp. milk from the breast, or another substance) into the mouth by contracting the muscles of the lips etc. to make a partial vacuum. OE.
2 Draw liquid or some other substance from (a fruit, an egg, etc.) by means of such action; *spec.* (of a baby or young animal) draw milk from (the breast, a teat, its mother). Also (long *obsolete* exc. *Scot.*), suckle (a baby or young animal). OE. ▸**b** Apply the lips and mouth to and perform such action on (an object). E18. ▸**c** Perform cunnilingus or esp. fellatio on. *coarse slang*. L19.
3 a Draw or drain (moisture, goodness, etc.) *from* or *out of* a thing. Formerly also (foll. by *from, of*), draw or use up (money or wealth) from a source. ME. ▸**b** Draw the moisture, goodness, etc., from; extract information, money, etc., from; drain *of*. LME. ▸**c** Derive (knowledge, comfort, etc.) (usu. foll. by *from* or *out of*). Also, take in or *in* along *with*. M16.
4 Draw in so as to engulf or drown (usu. foll. by *down, in*); *esp.* (*fig.*) draw *into* a course of action etc. E16.
5 Bring into a specified condition by sucking. M16.
†**6** Inhale (air, smoke, etc.). L16–E18.
7 Draw in some direction, esp. by producing a vacuum. Usu. foll. by adverb or preposition. L16.
8 Work (a pump) dry. Cf. sense 11 below. *rare*. M18.

📖 **1** G. GREENE They were sucking orangeade through straws. MOLLIE HARRIS From . . summer flowers we would suck honey. G. SWIFT A tiny baby sucking his mother's milk. **2** THACKERAY A . . languid nobleman . . sucking oranges. R. FRAME She . . sucked a twist of barley sugar. **b** W. LEWIS They sat . . sucking their old pipes. A. MACRAE Willowdene . . placidly sucked her thumb. **3** TENNYSON She . . sees a great black cloud . . suck the blinding splendour from the sand. **b** R. W. EMERSON The land sucked of its nourishment, by a small class of legitimates. **c** R. R. MARETT Conditions that enable us to suck strength . . out of the . . environment. **4** *Times* Half a dozen MPs have . . been sucked into this inquiry. P. FARMER She cannot forget the sadness . . , no matter how she lets herself be sucked in by other things. **5** SHAKES. *Ant. & Cl.* Dost thou not see the baby at my breast That sucks the nurse asleep? **6** POPE Some [spirits] . . suck the mist in grosser air below. **7** E. BLISHEN I caught sight of machinery; paper was being sucked through it. R. SILVERBERG Ferguson sucked his breath in deep and hard. *fig.*: *Times* Exports are starting to fall off, while more imports are being sucked in.

▸ **II** *verb intrans.* **9** Of a baby or young animal: draw milk from the breast or teat. Freq. foll. by *at*, †*of*, †*on*. OE.
10 Apply the lips and mouth to and perform a sucking action on an object, esp. to draw out liquid; *gen.* draw by suction, make a sucking action or sound. Freq. foll. by *at*. ME. ▸**b** Perform cunnilingus or esp. fellatio. *coarse slang*. E20.
11 Of a pump: draw air instead of water, as a result of a fault or of exhausting the water. E17.
12 Be disgraceful or repellent. *slang* (chiefly *N. Amer.*). L20.

📖 **9** F. CHURCHILL A child should not be weaned before nine months, nor suck after twelve. H. S. STREAN A baby sucking at his mother's breast. **10** R. JARRELL She was walking on a lonely shore. Sand sucked at her bare feet. J. C. OATES Sucking at her cigarette out of stubbornness. *Today* Employees gasping for a drag or sucking miserably on a Biro. **12** A. LURIE In their opinion modern London sucks.

Phrases etc.: **give suck** *arch.* [*suck* is now usu. regarded as a noun] give milk from the breast or teat, suckle. ***suck an orange***: see ORANGE *noun*. **suck dry** extract all the liquid out of; *fig.* exhaust of all resources. **suck-it-and-see** *adjective* (*colloq.*) (of a method etc.) experimental. **suck the blood of** *fig.* exhaust the financial, emotional, etc., resources of. **suck the hind teat, suck the hind tit** *slang* (chiefly *US*) be inferior, have no priority. ***suck the monkey***: see MONKEY *noun*. ***teach one's GRANDMOTHER to suck eggs***.
With adverbs in specialized senses: **suck around** *slang* (chiefly *US*) go about behaving sycophantically. **suck in** (**a**) absorb; (**b**) *arch. slang* cheat, deceive; (see also senses 3c, 4 above). **suck off** *coarse slang* cause (a person) to experience an orgasm by cunnilingus or esp. fellatio. **suck up** (**a**) absorb; (**b**) *colloq.* behave obsequiously (*to*), esp. for one's own advantage.
Comb.: **suck-bottle** (**a**) a baby's feeding-bottle; (**b**) *arch. slang* a tippler; **suck-egg** *noun & adjective* (**a**) *noun* an animal reputed to suck eggs, as a weasel or cuckoo; *fig.* an avaricious person; (**b**) *adjective* that sucks eggs; *US dial.* mean, contemptible; **suck-fish** = SUCKER *noun* 10; **suck-hole** *noun & verb* (**a**) *noun* (*US dial.*) a whirlpool, a pond; (**b**) *verb intrans. & noun* (*Canad. & Austral. coarse slang*) (behave like) a sycophant; **suck-teeth** *W. Indies* an act of sucking the teeth audibly to indicate annoyance, scorn, etc.; **suck-up** *N. Amer. colloq.* a person who behaves obsequiously, esp. for their own advantage.

■ **suckable** *adjective* (*rare*) (esp. of a food) that can be sucked M19.

sucken /ˈsʌk(ə)n/ *noun & adjective.* LME.
[Var. of SOKEN.]
SCOTS LAW (now *Hist.*).
▶ **A** *noun.* **1** The obligation of tenants within a district astricted to a mill. LME.
2 The lands astricted to a mill; *transf.* the area of a bailiff's jurisdiction or of a business's coverage. Cf. THIRL *noun*². L17.
▶ **B** *adjective.* Astricted *to* a mill. *rare.* M18.
■ **suckener** *noun* a tenant of a sucken M18. **suckening** *noun* the astriction of tenants to a mill M17.

sucker /ˈsʌkə/ *noun.* LME.
[from SUCK *verb* + -ER¹.]
▶ **I 1 a** A young animal (now chiefly *spec.* a pig or whale) not yet weaned. Formerly also, an unweaned child. LME. ▸**b** A person who is gullible or easily deceived; (foll. by *for*) a person who is very susceptible to or cannot resist a specified thing. *colloq.* (orig. *N. Amer.*). E19. ▸**c** *gen.* An object or thing (as specified by the context). *colloq.* (chiefly *US*). L20.
2 A person who or thing which (supposedly) sucks with the mouth. Freq. in local animal names. LME.
3 A person who lives at the expense of another; a sponger, a parasite. Now *US.* E16.
4 a A shoot thrown out from the base of a tree or plant; *spec.* one arising from the root below ground level, freq. at some distance from the stem. Also, a side-shoot from an axillary bud, as in tomato plants or maize. L16. ▸**b** *BOTANY.* = HAUSTORIUM. M19.
5 a The piston of a suction pump; the plunger of a syringe. E17. ▸**b** A pipe or tube through which something is drawn by suction; *local* a hood over a fireplace. M18. ▸**c** An air-hole fitted with a valve; a valve for regulating the flow of air. L18.
6 *ZOOLOGY.* An organ for absorbing nourishment by suction; *esp.* the proboscis of an insect. Also, an animal with such an organ. L17.
7 a Any of various chiefly N. American freshwater cypriniform fishes of the family Catastomidae, which have a conformation of the lips which suggests that they feed by suction. Cf. sense 10 below. *N. Amer.* M18. ▸**b** (A nickname for) a native or inhabitant of the State of Illinois. *US.* M19.
8 *GOLF.* A ball embedded in mud etc. which can be lifted without penalty. M20.

📖 **1a** *attrib.*: *Stock & Land (Melbourne)* The . . draft of sucker lambs sold before Christmas. **b** S. BELLOW For centuries love has made suckers of us. M. ATWOOD I fumble in my purse, find a ten, . . paying her off. I'm a sucker. *Opera Now* I'm a sucker for everything connected with Mozart. *attrib.*: G. NAYLOR You think I got this old . . by taking sucker bets? ***play for a sucker***: see PLAY *verb.* **2** ***bloodsucker, goatsucker, honeysucker***, etc. **4a** *Amateur Gardening* Remove any suckers growing away from the row. *fig.*: A. P. STANLEY A living sucker from the mother country.

▶ **II 9** A flat or concave animal or plant organ or a similar artificial device of rubber etc., used to adhere to a surface by means of suction and atmospheric pressure. L17. ▸**b** *spec.* A toy consisting of a leather suction pad with a string attached at the centre. *rare.* L17.
10 A fish having a suctorial disc for adhering to surfaces; *esp.* (*a*) a clingfish; (*b*) a lumpsucker; (*c*) a sea-snail; (*d*) a remora. Also, a lamprey, which has a round sucking mouth. Cf. sense 7a above. M18.

📖 **9** W. GOLDING Roots clung to the rock with suckers more difficult to remove than limpets. A. HARDY The lamprey attaches itself with its sucker to the skin of some large fish. *Baby* Rubber bath mats . . have . . suckers which attach firmly to the bath.

▶ **III 11** A sweet. Now chiefly *spec.* (*N. Amer.*), a lollipop. *colloq.* E19.
Comb.: **sucker-bashing** *Austral. colloq.* the cutting off of new growth from under the line where a tree has been ringbarked; **sucker-cup** any of the suctorial discs on the tentacles of a cephalopod; **sucker-disc** = sense 9 above; **sucker-fish** = senses 7a, 10 above; **sucker-foot** any of the tube-feet of an echinoderm; **sucker punch** an unexpected punch or blow; **sucker-up** *colloq.* a sycophant.
¶ Recorded earlier in ME as a surname.
■ **suckered** *adjective* (of an organ) provided with suckers M19.

sucker /ˈsʌkə/ *verb.* M17.
[from the noun.]
1 *verb trans.* Remove suckers from a plant. M17.
2 *verb intrans.* Of a plant: produce suckers. E19.
3 *verb trans.* Cheat, trick. *slang* (chiefly *N. Amer.*). M20.

suckerel /ˈsʌk(ə)r(ə)l/ *noun.* Long *rare* or *obsolete.* LME.
[from SUCK *verb* + -REL.]
A suckling; *esp.* an unweaned foal.

sucket /ˈsʌkɪt/ *noun.* Now *arch.* or *Hist.* L15.
[Alt. of *succate* var. of SUCCADE after SUCK *verb*: see -ET¹.]
= SUCCADE.
Comb.: **sucket fork**, **sucket spoon** a utensil for eating fruit, having a two-pronged fork at one end and a spoon at the other.

sucking /ˈsʌkɪŋ/ *noun.* LME.
[from SUCK *verb* + -ING¹.]
1 The action of SUCK *verb*; an instance of this. LME.
2 In *pl.* What is obtained by suction. *rare.* LME.
Comb.: **sucking-cushion** *ANATOMY* a lobulated mass of fat occupying the space in the cheek between the masseter and the external surface of the buccinator; **sucking-disc** = SUCKER *noun* 9; **sucking-pad** = *sucking-cushion* above; **sucking reflex** the instinct to suck possessed by young mammals; **sucking response** the action of sucking in a young mammal as a response to a stimulus; **sucking-up** *colloq.* sycophancy.

sucking /ˈsʌkɪŋ/ *adjective.* LOE.
[from SUCK *verb* + -ING².]
1 Of a child or young animal: not yet weaned. LOE. ▸**b** Of a bird: unfledged. Now chiefly in ***sucking dove***. L16. ▸**c** *fig.* Not fully developed; budding. M17.
2 *gen.* That sucks. E16.

📖 **1** AV *Isa.* 49:15 Can a woman forget her sucking child? **b** SHAKES. *Mids. N. D.* I will roar you as gently as any sucking dove. **c** F. MARRYAT He looks like a sucking Nelson. **2** B. CAPES A nightmare race over sucking quicksands.

Special collocations & comb.: **sucking-fish** any fish having a suctorial disc; *esp.* a remora (cf. SUCKER *noun* 10). ***sucking louse***: see LOUSE *noun* 1. **sucking stomach** *ENTOMOLOGY* (now *rare*) the expandable crop of a sucking insect.

suckle /ˈsʌk(ə)l/ *noun*¹. LME.
[Prob. abbreviation of HONEYSUCKLE: cf. SUCKLING *noun*².]
†**1** *sing.* & in *pl.* Clover. Also called ***lamb-suckle***. LME–E18.
2 Honeysuckle, *Lonicera periclymenum*. *poet. & dial.* E19.

suckle /ˈsʌk(ə)l/ *noun*². *rare.* L16.
[from the verb.]
†**1** A suckling. Only in L16.
†**2** A teat. Only in M17.
3 A suckling-house for lambs. *local.* E19.

suckle /ˈsʌk(ə)l/ *verb.* LME.
[Prob. back-form. from SUCKLING *noun*¹.]
1 *verb trans.* Feed (a child or young animal) from the breast or teat. LME. ▸**b** *fig.* Nourish; bring up, rear. M17.
2 *verb trans.* Cause to feed from the breast or teat; put to suck. Now *rare.* E16.
3 a *verb intrans.* Suck at the breast or teat. Also foll. by *on*. L17. ▸**b** *verb trans.* Suck milk from (the breast or teat). L20.

📖 **1** J. HERRIOT A large sow . . suckling a litter of . . twelve piglets. J. GATHORNE-HARDY Children of the poor had a better chance of survival because their own mothers suckled them. **b** P. CAREY Harry Joy was suckled on stories in . . the little weatherboard house. **2** W. MARSHALL Suckling calves after . . ten weeks old, is bad management. **3a** *Scientific American* Kittens . . develop a preference for the nipple on which they suckle during the first and second day. S. KITZINGER The baby suckles . . in . . her arms.

Comb.: **suckling-house** a building or room in which young calves or lambs are reared.

suckler /ˈsʌklə/ *noun.* L15.
[from prec. + -ER¹.]
1 An unweaned animal, esp. a calf. L15.
2 A person who rears young calves or lambs. *local.* E17. ▸**b** An animal that suckles its young. *rare.* M19.
3 In *sing.* & (usu.) *pl.* Flowering clover. Cf. SUCKLING *noun*² 1. *Scot. & north.* E18.
4 = SUCKER *noun* 4a. *dial.* L18.

suckling /ˈsʌklɪŋ/ *noun*¹. ME.
[from SUCK *verb* + -LING¹, prob. after Middle Dutch *sügeling* (Dutch *zuigeling*).]
An unweaned child or animal, esp. a calf.
single suckling: see SINGLE *adjective & adverb.*

suckling /ˈsʌklɪŋ/ *noun*². LME.
[App. from SUCKLE *noun*¹.]
1 Clover, *spec.* white clover, *Trifolium repens*. Chiefly *dial.* LME.
2 Honeysuckle, *Lonicera periclymenum*. *obsolete* exc. *dial.* M17.
1 yellow suckling lesser trefoil, *Trifolium dubium*, a dwarf yellow-flowered clover.

suckling /ˈsʌklɪŋ/ *ppl adjective.* L17.
[from SUCKLE *verb* + -ING².]
That suckles; *esp.* (of a child or young animal) not yet weaned.

sucky /ˈsʌki/ *adjective.* M20.
[from SUCK *verb* + -Y¹.]
1 Of a blow or wound: painful, severe. *Scot. dial. & colloq.* (now *rare*). M20.
2 Of an object etc.: that is or may be sucked, suckable. Also *fig.*, sickly sweet, sentimental, mawkish; obsequious, ingratiating. *colloq.* L20.
3 Of a baby: given to (excessive) sucking or suckling. *colloq.* L20.
4 Contemptible; unpleasant, disagreeable. *slang* (chiefly *N. Amer.*). L20.

📖 **4** *Independent* He mustn't do anything that's too nerdy, too sucky.

sucralfate /ˈsuːkr(ə)lfeɪt, ˈsjuː-/ *noun.* M20.
[from SUCR(OSE + AL(UMINIUM + *sul*)*fate* var. of SULPHATE.]
PHARMACOLOGY. A complex of aluminium and sulphated sucrose used in the treatment of gastric and duodenal ulcers.

sucrase /ˈsuːkreɪz, ˈsjuː-/ *noun.* E20.
[from SUCROSE + -ASE.]
BIOCHEMISTRY. = INVERTASE.

sucre /ˈsuːkreɪ/ *noun.* L19.
[from Antonio José de *Sucre* (1795–1830), S. Amer. popular leader.]
The basic monetary unit of Ecuador, equal to 100 centavos.

sucrier /ˈsuːkriːeɪ, *foreign* sykrie (*pl. same*)/ *noun.* M19.
[French, from *sucre* SUGAR *noun & adjective.*]
A sugar bowl, usu. made of porcelain and with a cover.

sucrose /ˈsuːkrəʊz, ˈsjuː-, -əʊs/ *noun.* M19.
[from French *sucre* SUGAR *noun & adjective* + -OSE².]
CHEMISTRY. †**1** = SACCHAROSE 1. M–L19.
2 A white crystalline disaccharide, $C_{12}H_{22}O_{11}$, composed of a glucose and a fructose unit, which is widely used in the form of household sugar, occurs in most plants, and is derived commercially from sugar cane and sugar beet. Cf. DEXTROSE, LAEVULOSE. M19.
Comb.: **sucrose density gradient**, **sucrose gradient** *BIOCHEMISTRY* a gradient of sucrose concentration used in the centrifugation of biological material to assist the separation of component substances according to density; **sucrose phosphate** *BIOCHEMISTRY* any of the esters that can be formed between sucrose and phosphoric acid; **sucrose phosphorylase** *BIOCHEMISTRY* a bacterial enzyme which catalyses the breakdown of sucrose, ultimately producing glucose-1-phosphate and fructose.

suction /ˈsʌkʃ(ə)n/ *noun.* E17.
[Late Latin *suctio(n-)*, from Latin *suct-* pa. ppl stem of *sugere*: see SUCK *verb*, -TION.]
1 The action or an act of sucking with the mouth. E17. ▸†**b** *transf.* The craving of appetite. E–M17. ▸**c** The drinking of alcoholic liquor. *arch. slang.* E19.
2 The production of a partial vacuum by the removal of air etc. in order to force in fluid etc. or procure adhesion; the force produced by this process. M17.
3 *ellipt.* A suction pump. L19.
Attrib. & comb.: Esp. in the sense 'designating a device or process which uses suction', as ***suction fan***, ***suction plate***, ***suction tube***, etc. Special combs., as **suction box**, **suction chamber** a chamber in a pump into which the liquid is conveyed by the suction pipe; **suction dredge**: using a suction pump to bring up soft material from the bed of a river etc.; **suction dredger**: carrying a suction dredge; **suction dredging** the use of a suction dredge; **suction gas** the town gas produced by a suction plant; **suction lift** *MECHANICS* the height to which a liquid can be drawn up a pipe by suction; **suction pipe** the pipe leading from the bottom of a suction pump; **suction plant** a form of gas producer in which the blast is induced by suction (see PRODUCER 4); **suction pressure** *BOTANY* the power of a cell to absorb water, defined as the difference between the osmotic pressure of the cell sap and the inward pressure of the cell wall; **suction pump** a pump for drawing liquid through a pipe into a chamber emptied by a piston; **suction stop** = CLICK *noun*¹ 3; **suction stroke** in an internal-combustion engine, a piston stroke in which fresh mixture is drawn into the cylinder; **suction valve** a non-return valve in a suction pump, steam engine, etc., which prevents incoming water etc. escaping under gravity or pressure.
■ **suctional** *adjective* (*rare*) of or pertaining to suction; having a power of suction: L19.

suctorial /sʌkˈtɔːrɪəl/ *adjective.* M19.
[from mod. Latin *suctorius*, from Latin *suct-*: see prec., -IAL.]
ZOOLOGY. Adapted for sucking, as the mouthparts of some insects; having organs adapted for sucking; involving or characterized by suction.
■ Also **suctorious** *adjective* (now *rare* or *obsolete*) E19.

suctorian /sʌkˈtɔːrɪən/ *noun & adjective.* M19.
[formed as prec.: see -IAN.]
▶ **A** *noun.* Orig., a cyclostome fish. Now, a ciliate protozoan of the aberrant subclass Suctoria, the members of which are sessile and stalked, and feed by means of suctorial tentacles. M19.
▶ **B** *adjective.* Of, pertaining to, or characteristic of a suctorial animal, esp. a ciliate of the subclass Suctoria. E20.

sucupira /sʊkəˈpɪərə/ *noun.* E20.
[Portuguese from Tupi *seui'pira*.]
A dark brown hardwood obtained from various leguminous trees of tropical S. America, *Sweetia fruticosa* and species of the genera *Bowdichia* and *Diplotropis*. Also, a tree from which this wood is obtained.

sud /sʌd/ *noun.* M16.
[Prob. from Middle Low German, Middle Dutch *sudde*, Middle Dutch *sudse* marsh, bog. Early mod. German has *Seifensod* soapsuds: cf. Middle High German *sōt* dishwater. Base prob. Germanic weak grade of SEETHE *verb.*]
†**1** In *pl.* Dregs; filth, muck. M16–M17.
2 a In *pl.* Froth which collects on the top of soapy water in which things are washed; lather, foam. Also, soapy water for washing. M16. ▸**b** A soap solution. *rare.* M19.
†**3** In *pl.* Flood-water; the water of the fens; water mixed with drift-sand and mud. L16–M19.

4 In *pl.* Beer. *slang* (orig. & chiefly *N. Amer.*). E20.

📖 **2a** P. THEROUX No women doing laundry, though their suds remained in the shallows. R. PILCHER Mrs Plackett was at the sink, elbow-deep in suds.

Phrases: **in the suds** (*a*) *slang* (now *rare*) in difficulties, in embarrassment; (*b*) *dial.* sulking, depressed; (*c*) being washed, in the wash.

▪ **sudser** *noun* (*US slang*) a soap opera M20. **sudsy** *adjective* (orig. *US*) consisting of, full of, or characterized by suds; soapy, frothy: M19.

sudamen /ˈsuːdəmɪn, ˈsjuː-/ *noun.* Pl. **sudamina** /-ˈdamɪnə/. L16.
[mod. Latin, from *sudare* to sweat.]
MEDICINE. A minute whitish vesicle or blister caused by sweat collecting in the upper layers of the skin after copious perspiration, esp. in certain fevers or after sunburn. Usu. in *pl.*

Sudan /suːˈdɑːn, -ˈdan, sʊ-/ *noun & adjective.* M19.
[The region in Africa lying between the Sahara and the equatorial region, now also a republic in NE Africa.]
▶ **A** *noun.* = SUDANESE *noun. rare.* M19.
▶ **B** *adjective.* **1** = SUDANESE *adjective.* L19.
2 CHEMISTRY. Designating various azo and diazo dyes (each distinguished by a roman numeral or a letter) mostly derived from 2-hydroxynaphthalene and anthraquinone, used as industrial dyes and biological stains, and available in various shades of orange and red to black. L19.
1 Sudan grass a Sudanese sorghum, *Sorghum sudanense*, cultivated for fodder in dry regions of the US.
▪ **sudano'philia** *noun* (MEDICINE) a condition in which cells containing particular fatty or lipid structures can be stained with a Sudan dye E20. **sudano'philic** *adjective* (MEDICINE) capable of taking up Sudan stains M20. **Sudani'zation** *noun* the action or process of making Sudanese in character, *spec.* at the time of Sudanese independence in 1956 L19.

Sudanese /suːdəˈniːz/ *adjective & noun.* L19.
[formed as prec. + -ESE 1.]
▶ **A** *noun.* Pl. same. A native or inhabitant of Sudan. L19.
▶ **B** *adjective.* Of or pertaining to Sudan. L19.

Sudanic /suːˈdanɪk, sʊ-/ *adjective & noun.* E20.
[formed as SUDAN + -IC.]
▶ **A** *adjective.* = SUDANESE *adjective*; *spec.* pertaining to or designating a language group comprising those languages spoken in central, northern, and eastern Africa which do not belong to the Bantu or Hamitic groups. E20.
▶ **B** *noun.* (Any of) the group of Sudanic languages. E20.

Sudano- /suːˈdɑːnəʊ, sʊ-/ *combining form.* M20.
[formed as SUDAN: see -O-.]
Forming nouns and adjectives in sense 'Sudanese and —', as ***Sudano-Guinean***.

sudarium /suːˈdɛːrɪəm, sjuː-/ *noun.* Pl. **-ria** /-rɪə/. E17.
[Latin, from *sudor* sweat. Cf. next.]
1 A cloth for wiping the face. E17.
2 = VERONICA 2. E17.
3 = SUDATORIUM. M19.

sudary /ˈsuːdəri, ˈsjuː-/ *noun. arch.* ME.
[formed as prec.: see -ARY[1].]
1 A sudarium, *esp.* one venerated as a relic of a saint. ME.
2 Orig. (CHRISTIAN CHURCH), the cloth which was wound around Jesus' head in the tomb. Later, a shroud. ME.
3 ECCLESIASTICAL. A ceremonial cloth of linen or silk, often fringed; *esp.* a humeral veil. LME.

sudation /suːˈdeɪʃ(ə)n, sjuː-/ *noun.* Now *rare.* L16.
[Latin *sudatio(n-)*, from *sudat-*: see SUDATORY, -ATION.]
The action of sweating.

sudatorium /suːdəˈtɔːrɪəm, ˈsjuː-/ *noun.* Pl. **-ria** /-rɪə/. M18.
[Latin, neut. sing. of *sudatorius*: see next, -ORIUM.]
Chiefly ROMAN ANTIQUITIES. A room in which hot-air or steam baths are taken to produce sweating.

sudatory /ˈsuːdət(ə)ri, ˈsjuː-/ *noun & adjective.* LME.
[Latin *sudatorius*, from *sudat-* pa. ppl stem of *sudare* to sweat: see -ORY[1], -ORY[2].]
▶ **A** *noun.* †**1** A medicinal drink which causes sweating. Only in LME.
2 = SUDATORIUM. E17.
▶ **B** *adjective.* Producing, accompanied by, or connected with sweating. L16.

sudd /sʌd/ *noun.* L19.
[Arab. = obstruction, dam, from *sadda* obstruct, block, congest.]
1 An area of floating vegetation which impedes navigation on the White Nile. L19.
2 *transf.* A temporary dam across a river. L19.

sudden /ˈsʌd(ə)n/ *adjective, adverb, & noun.* ME.
[Anglo-Norman *sodein*, *sud-*, Old & mod. French *soudain*, from late Latin *subitanus* alt. of Latin *subitaneus*, from *subitus* sudden.]
▶ **A** *adjective.* **1** Happening or coming without warning; unexpected, unforeseen; abrupt, hasty. ME. ▸**b** Of a turning etc.: abrupt, sharp. LME. ▸**c** Of an object: appearing or discovered unexpectedly. Now *arch. & poet.* LME.
2 Acting or done without forethought; impetuous, rash. *arch.* ME.
3 Done or taking place without delay; speedy; immediate; *poet.* producing an immediate result. *obsolete* exc. in ***sudden death*** below. ME. ▸†**b** (Of a person) quick to act; (of mental faculties) quick, sharp. L16–M18. ▸†**c** Of the eye: glancing quickly. L16–M17.
†**4** Happening soon; shortly to come or to be. LME–M18.
†**5** Brief, momentary. LME–L16.
†**6** Done, performed, etc., on the spur of the moment; impromptu. M16–M18.
7 Made, provided, or formed in a short time. *arch.* L16.

📖 **1** J. BUCHAN The sudden appearance made me start. A. THWAITE On a sudden impulse, he locked a master in a classroom. S. HOOD With a sudden switch of subject she enquired what had taken him to Perpignan. R. ALTER A fashionable London fop caught by the sudden downpour. **c** *Which?* Sudden, grey rocks jut from cropped grass. **2** SIR W. SCOTT Neither provoke me to be sudden by any unfit reply. **3** J. CLEVELAND He acquaints the Citizens with the Kings Peril . . and requests their sudden assistance. A. C. SWINBURNE Hast not thou One shaft of all thy sudden seven? **7** SHAKES. *Hen. V* Never was such a sudden scholar made.

Special collocations: **sudden death** (*a*) SPORT a means of deciding the winner of a tied game or match, consisting of an extra game, hole played, etc., or an extra period of play ending with the first to score; (*b*) an unexpected or quick death; (*c*) *US slang* a potent alcoholic drink. **sudden infant death (syndrome)** the phenomenon of sudden and unexpected deaths of apparently healthy infants (abbreviation *SIDS*) (cf. ***cot-death*** s.v. COT *noun*[4]).
▶ **B** *adverb.* Suddenly. Chiefly & now only *poet.* LME.
▶ **C** *noun.* **1** ***all of a sudden***, ***of a sudden***, (*arch.*) ***on a sudden***, †***at a sudden***, suddenly, unexpectedly. M16.
†**2** A sudden need, danger, etc.; an emergency. M16–E18.
▪ **suddenly** *adverb* ME. **suddenness** /-n-n-/ *noun* LME.

suddenty /ˈsʌd(ə)nti/ *noun.* Chiefly *Scot. obsolete* exc. *dial.* LME.
[Old French *sodeineté* (mod. *soudaineté*), from *sodein* SUDDEN: see -TY[1].]
1 Suddenness, unexpectedness; ***all on a suddenty***, ***in a suddenty***, ***in suddenty***, ***of (a) suddenty***, ***upon (a) suddenty***, suddenly, unexpectedly (cf. SUDDEN *noun* 1). LME.
2 SCOTS LAW. A sudden outburst of rage. Chiefly in ***on a suddenty***, ***on suddenty***, ***upon (a) suddenty***, without premeditation. LME.

Sudder /ˈsʌdə/ *adjective & noun.* *Indian subcontinent.* L18.
[Persian & Urdu = Arab. *sadr* foremost or highest part of a thing, chief place or seat, chest, breast, used in comb. with adjectival sense.]
▶ **A** *adjective.* Of a government department or official: chief, supreme. L18.
▶ **B** *noun. The* highest judicial court. Now *rare.* M19.

Sudeten /sʊˈdeɪt(ə)n/ *adjective & noun.* M20.
[See below.]
▶ **A** *adjective.* Of, pertaining to, or designating the predominantly German-speaking area in the vicinity of the Sudeten mountains (the Sudetenland) in NE Bohemia and Moravia, which was annexed by Germany from 1938 to 1945 and is now part of the Czech Republic. Freq. in ***Sudeten German***. M20.
▶ **B** *noun.* A native or inhabitant of the Sudetenland; a Sudeten German. M20.
▪ **Sudetic** *adjective* (now *rare*) of or pertaining to the Sudeten region E20.

sudoral /ˈsuːd(ə)r(ə)l, sjuː-/ *adjective.* Now *rare.* L19.
[from Latin *sudor* sweat + -AL[1].]
MEDICINE. Of or pertaining to sweating; *esp.* characterized by a disturbance of the function of sweating.

sudoresis /suːdəˈriːsɪs, sjuː-/ *noun.* Now *rare.* M19.
[mod. Latin, from Latin *sudor* sweat + *-esis* as in DIAPHORESIS.]
Sweating, diaphoresis; *spec.* in MEDICINE, profuse sweating.

sudoriferous /suːdəˈrɪf(ə)rəs, sjuː-/ *adjective.* L16.
[from late Latin *sudorifer* (from Latin *sudor* sweat) + -OUS: see -FEROUS.]
1 = SUDORIFIC *adjective* 1. Now *rare* or *obsolete.* L16.
2 Secreting or conveying sweat, as ***sudoriferous canal***, ***sudoriferous gland***, etc. E18.

sudorific /suːdəˈrɪfɪk, sjuː-/ *adjective & noun.* E17.
[mod. Latin *sudorificus*, formed as prec.: see -FIC.]
▶ **A** *adjective.* **1** Promoting or causing perspiration; diaphoretic. E17.
2 = SUDORIFEROUS 2. E18.
3 Consisting of sweat. Now *rare* or *obsolete.* E19.
▶ **B** *noun.* A diaphoretic. M17.

sudoriparous /suːdəˈrɪp(ə)rəs, sjuː-/ *adjective.* M19.
[from Latin *sudor* sweat + -I- + -PAROUS.]
PHYSIOLOGY. Secreting sweat; pertaining to the secretion of sweat or to the sweat glands.

sudorous /ˈsuːd(ə)rəs, ˈsjuː-/ *adjective.* Long *rare* or *obsolete.* M17.
[Latin *sudorus* or medieval Latin *sudorosus*, from Latin *sudor* sweat: see -OUS.]
Sweaty.

Sudra /ˈsuːdrə/ *noun.* M17.
[Sanskrit *śūdra*.]
A member of the lowest of the four main Hindu castes.

suds /sʌdz/ *verb.* M19.
[from pl. of SUD: see -S[1].]
1 *verb trans.* Lather, cover with soapsuds; wash in soapy water. M19.
2 *verb intrans.* Form suds. *US.* L19.
▪ **sudsable** *adjective* capable of forming soapsuds; (of a garment) washable in soapy water: M20.

sue /suː, sjuː/ *verb.* ME.
[Anglo-Norman *suer*, *siwer*, *sure*, *suir(e*, from pres. stem *siu-*, *sieu-*, *seu-* of Old French *sivre* (mod. *suivre*), from Proto-Romance alt. of Latin *sequi* follow.]
▶ **I** *verb trans.* †**1** Follow (a person or thing in motion, or a track, path, etc.). ME–L16.
†**2** Go in pursuit of; chase, pursue. ME–L19.
†**3** Follow (a person) as an attendant, companion, or adherent; accompany, attend on. ME–E16.
†**4** Take as a guide, leader, or example; follow as a disciple or imitator. ME–E16.
†**5** Comply with or obey (a person's will, a set of rules, etc.), follow (advice, an inclination, etc.). ME–M18.
†**6** Adopt or put into practice (a belief, way of life, occupation, etc.); engage in or occupy oneself with (a pursuit). ME–L18.
†**7** Carry out (an action); pursue (a subject). Also, follow up (an achievement). ME–L16.
8 a Institute a suit for, make a legal claim to; *gen.* petition or appeal for, seek to obtain or *to do.* Now *rare.* ME. ▸**b** *spec.* Apply before a court for the grant of (a writ or other legal process). Also, put in suit, enforce (a legal process). Freq. foll. by *out.* ME.
9 Court, be a suitor to (a woman). *arch.* ME.
†**10** Come after, succeed (in time); follow as a result. LME–M16.
†**11** Take (legal action); institute (a legal process); plead (a cause). LME–L16.
12 Institute legal proceedings against (a person); prosecute in a court of law; bring a civil action against. Also ***sue at law***. Freq. foll. by *for.* LME.
13 Petition, appeal to. *rare.* E16.

📖 **8b** H. HALLAM A party detained without any warrant must sue out his habeas corpus at common law. **12** W. LIPPMANN A workman who was injured could sue the master for damages. I. D. YALOM She sued the hospital for negligence in her husband's death.

▶ **II** *verb intrans.* †**14** Continue, proceed, go on. Only in ME.
†**15** Follow a person or thing in motion; follow as an attendant or adherent; go in chase or pursuit. Freq. foll. by *after*, *upon*, etc. ME–M16.
†**16** Do service or homage. Chiefly in ***serve and sue*** below. ME–L16.
†**17** Follow in time or in a succession or sequence; result, ensue. ME–M17.
18 Take legal action; institute legal proceedings; bring a suit (*for* something claimed). ME.
19 Make an appeal or plea *to* a person *for* a person or a thing; plead, entreat. LME.
†**20** Move, go, esp. quickly; sally *forth* or *out.* LME–E16.
21 Be a suitor to or *to* a woman. *arch.* L16.

📖 **18** R. LINDNER She's suing for a divorce. **19** P. GALLICO Like a lover . . suing for favour. P. GOODMAN A man . . cannot waste his life learning to sue to an ignorant electorate. **21** SHAKES. *L.L.L.* I love, I sue, I seek a wife.

Phrases: †**serve and sue** *verb phr. intrans. & trans.* attend and give personal service to (a lord etc.).
▪ **suer** *noun* †(*a*) a follower, a pursuer; (*b*) a person who sues or petitions, *esp.* a plaintiff: LME.

suede /sweɪd/ *noun & adjective.* Also **suède**. M17.
[French (*gants de*) *Suède* (gloves of) Sweden.]
▶ **A** *noun.* Leather, orig. esp. kidskin, with the flesh side rubbed to make a velvety nap; a shoe or other article made of this. M17.
Comb.: **suede brush**: used to brush suede; **suede cloth** = SUEDETTE; **suede-footed** *adjective* = ***suede-shoed*** below; **suedehead** a person, esp. a youth, similar to a skinhead but generally characterized by slightly longer hair and smarter clothes; **suede shoe** a shoe made with a suede upper; **suede-shoed** *adjective* wearing suede shoes.
▶ **B** *attrib.* or as *adjective.* Made of suede. M17.
▪ **sueded** *adjective* (esp. of leather) rubbed on the flesh side to make a velvety nap M20. **sue'dene** *noun & adjective* = SUEDETTE M20. **sue'dette** *noun & adjective* (made of) a woven fabric resembling suede, usu. with a velvety nap E20. **sue'dine** *noun & adjective* = SUEDETTE E20.

suerte /ˈswerte/ *noun.* M19.
[Spanish, lit. 'chance, fate, luck'.]
BULLFIGHTING. An action or pass performed by a bullfighter; each of the three stages of a bullfight (also called ***tercio***).

Suess /suːs/ *noun.* M20.
[Hans E. *Suess* (1909–93), Austrian-born US chemist.]
Used *attrib.* to designate certain phenomena in radiocarbon dating.

Suess effect the reduction in the proportion of carbon-14 in the atmosphere and in plants during the 20th cent. as a result of the increased burning of fossil fuels, which lack that isotope. **Suess wiggle** each of a series of relatively short-term irregularities in the calibration curve obtained for radiocarbon dating by dendrochronology.

suet /ˈsuːɪt, ˈsjuːɪt/ *noun.* ME.
[Ult. from Anglo-Norman *su(e, seu,* Old French *seu, siu, sif* (mod. *suif*) from Latin *sebum* tallow, suet, grease.]
1 The solid white fat round the loins and kidneys of certain animals, esp. cattle and sheep, used to make dough etc. in cooking or melted down to form tallow. ME.
†**2** HUNTING. The fat of deer. LME–L17.
Comb.: **suet-brained** *adjective* (*colloq.*) stupid; **suet crust** heavy pastry made with suet, esp. used for meat or fruit puddings; **suet face**: of a pale complexionless appearance; **suet-faced** *adjective* having a suet face; **suet-headed** *adjective* (*colloq.*) stupid; **suet pudding**: made of flour and suet and usu. boiled or steamed.
■ **suety** *adjective* (*a*) of the nature of or resembling suet; (*b*) full of or made with suet: M18.

Suevian /ˈswiːvɪən/ *noun & adjective.* M16.
[Latin *Suevus, Suebus*: see -IAN. Cf. SWABIAN.]
Hist. ▶**A** *noun.* A member of a confederation of ancient Germanic tribes which inhabited large territories in central Europe east of the Rhine. M16.
▶**B** *adjective.* Of or pertaining to these tribes. L16.
■ **Sueve** *noun* = SUEVIAN *noun* E20. **Suevic** *adjective* = SUEVIAN *adjective* L18.

suevite /ˈsweɪvʌɪt/ *noun.* M20.
[from Latin *Suevia, Suebia* (see SWABIAN *adjective*) + -ITE[1].]
PETROGRAPHY. A welded braccia in a glass matrix found associated with meteorite impact craters, similar to a tuff but showing signs of impact metamorphism.

suey pow /ˈsuːɪ paʊ/ *noun phr. US slang.* E20.
[Origin unkn.]
A cloth used to clean an opium bowl.

Suez group /ˈsuːɪz gruːp/ *noun phr.* M20.
[An Egyptian port at the head of the Red Sea.]
A group of Conservative MPs who opposed the withdrawal of British troops from the Suez Canal Zone in 1954 (now *Hist.*); *transf.* any group advocating the presence of British troops in the Middle or Far East.

†**suff** *noun.* L16–L17.
[Origin unkn. Cf. SURF.]
The inrush *of* the sea towards the shore.

suffect /səˈfɛkt/ *adjective & noun.* M19.
[Latin *suffectus* pa. pple of *sufficere* substitute: see SUFFICE.]
ROMAN ANTIQUITIES. ▶**A** *adjective.* Designating (the office of) an additional consul or consuls elected, as under the Empire, during the official year. Freq. *postpositive.* M19.
▶**B** *noun.* A consul suffect. E20.

†**suffection** *noun.* E17–E18.
[Late Latin *suffectio(n-)* noun of action from Latin *sufficere*: see SUFFICE.]
Substitution.

suffer /ˈsʌfə/ *verb.* ME.
[Anglo-Norman *suffrir, soeffrir, -er,* Old French *so(f)frir* (mod. *souffrir*) from Proto-Romance alt. of Latin *sufferre,* formed as SUB- + *ferre* bear.]
▶**I** Undergo.
1 a *verb trans.* Have (something harmful or painful) inflicted or imposed on one; submit to (pain, punishment, death, etc.); undergo, experience, be subjected to, (esp. something unpleasant or painful). ME. ▶**b** *verb intrans.* Be in pain or distress; undergo pain, punishment, death, etc. (Foll. by *from* a disease etc.) ME.
†**2** *verb intrans.* Hold out, wait patiently; be long-suffering. ME–M16.
3 *verb intrans.* Be the object of an action, be acted on, be passive. Now *rare.* LME.
4 *verb trans.* Endure the stress or painfulness of; bear, stand. *obsolete* exc. *dial.* LME.
5 *verb trans.* Inflict pain on. *obsolete* exc. *dial.* L15.
6 *verb intrans.* **a** Be put to death as a punishment, be executed; *spec.* undergo martyrdom. Now *arch.* or *literary.* M16. ▶†**b** Be killed or destroyed. *rare* (Shakes.). Only in E17.
7 *verb intrans.* Sustain damage or loss; be injured or impaired; be at fault. (Foll. by *from, under.*) L16.

> 🕮 **1a** SLOAN WILSON The man . . landed wrong and suffered a compound fracture of the right thigh. *Scotsman* Less fortunate concerns . . have suffered a setback. M. FRAYN The discomfiture Fiddlingchild would certainly suffer when he found out exactly what . . Anna was feeling. A. CROSS She had chosen to die rather than suffer recurring cancer. **b** A. MILLER How can I bring you from a rich country to suffer in a poor country? G. VIDAL I suffer from a most painful form of gout. **7** F. R. WILSON The edifice suffered in the civil wars. R. G. COLLINGWOOD My health was beginning to suffer from . . overwork. N. FARAH Your language suffers from lack of originality.

▶**II** Tolerate.
8 *verb trans.* Endure the existence, presence, or activity of; put up with, tolerate. Also foll. by *to do.* ME.
9 *verb intrans. & refl.* Allow oneself *to be* treated in a certain way; submit or consent *to be* or *do* something. *arch.* ME.
10 *verb trans.* Allow or permit (a person) *to do* something. Formerly also, allow (a person) to have (a thing). *arch.* ME.
†**11** *verb intrans.* Allow a certain thing to be done. ME–E17.

> 🕮 **8** S. BECKETT He suffered her to dress him. **suffer fools (gladly)** tolerate incompetence or foolishness (usu. in neg. contexts).

■ **sufferer** *noun* (*a*) a person who suffers pain, hardship, etc. (freq. foll. by *from*); †(*b*) a person who permits something to be done; (*c*) a person who is killed or executed, now *spec.* a martyr; (*d*) (now *rare*) a patient: LME.

sufferable /ˈsʌf(ə)rəb(ə)l/ *adjective.* ME.
[Anglo-Norman *suffrable,* Old French *so(u)ffrable,* from *suffrir, sof(f)rir*: see prec., -ABLE.]
†**1** Patient, long-suffering. ME–E17.
2 Able to be endured; bearable, tolerable. Also, tolerably good. ME.
†**3** Allowable, permissible. LME–M17.
4 Accompanied by suffering; painful. *rare.* Long *obsolete* exc. *dial.* M16.
■ **sufferably** *adverb* (*rare*) †(*a*) patiently; †(*b*) painfully; (*c*) tolerably: LME.

sufferance /ˈsʌf(ə)r(ə)ns/ *noun.* ME.
[Anglo-Norman, Old French *suffraunce, soffrance* (mod. *souffrance* suffering) from late Latin *sufferentia,* from Latin *sufferre*: see SUFFER, -ANCE.]
▶**I 1** Patient endurance, long-suffering. *arch.* ME.
2 = SUFFERING *noun* 2. *arch.* ME.
3 = SUFFERING *noun* 3. *arch.* LME.
4 Capacity to endure pain, hardship, etc.; endurance. M16.
1 *long sufferance*: see LONG *adjective*[1].
▶**II 5** Consent, acquiescence, permission; toleration, indulgence. Now *rare* exc. in ***on sufferance*** below. ME. ▶**b** *Hist.* Orig. *gen.*, an instance of permission being given, a licence. Later *spec.*, a licence to ship or discharge cargoes at specified ports. Also ***bill of sufferance.*** M16.
†**6** Suspension, delay; respite. E16–M18.
7 LAW. The condition of the holder of an estate who continues to hold it after the title has ceased without the express permission of the owner. Esp. in ***estate at sufferance, tenant at sufferance.*** L16.
5 on sufferance, upon sufferance by virtue of a tacit assent but without express permission; with toleration implied by lack of either consent or objection.
Comb.: **sufferance quay, sufferance wharf** *Hist.* a quay or wharf at which cargo could be shipped or landed under a sufferance (see sense 5b above).

suffering /ˈsʌf(ə)rɪŋ/ *noun.* ME.
[from SUFFER + -ING[1].]
†**1** = SUFFERANCE *noun* 1. Only in ME.
2 The bearing or undergoing of pain, hardship, etc. ME.
3 A painful condition; (a) pain or hardship suffered. Freq. in *pl.* LME. ▶**b** In *pl.* In the Society of Friends, the hardships of people distrained on for tithes etc. Now chiefly in ***Meeting for Sufferings***, an organization for investigating and relieving these. M17.
†**4** Permission; tolerance. LME–M17.

suffering /ˈsʌf(ə)rɪŋ/ *ppl adjective.* ME.
[formed as prec. + -ING[2].]
†**1** Patient, long-suffering; submissive. ME–L17.
†**2** Passive. *rare.* LME–L18.
3 Of a person, character, condition, etc.: that suffers pain, hardship, etc. L16.
3 suffering cats! & vars.: expr. surprise or annoyance.
■ **sufferingly** *adverb* (*rare*) ME.

suffete /ˈsʌfiːt/ *noun.* E17.
[Latin *suffes, suffet-,* var. of *sufes,* of Phoenician origin (cf. Hebrew *šōpēṭ* judge).]
ANTIQUITIES. Any of the supreme executive magistrates of the ancient republic of Carthage.

suffibulum /səˈfɪbjʊləm/ *noun.* Pl. **-la** /-lə/. M18.
[Latin, formed as SUB- + *fibula* brooch.]
ROMAN ANTIQUITIES. A rectangular veil, white with a purple border, worn by vestal virgins when attending at sacrifices.

suffice /səˈfʌɪs/ *verb.* ME.
[Old French *suffis-* pres. stem of *suffire,* from Latin *sufficere,* formed as SUB- + *facere* make, do.]
1 *verb intrans.* Be enough or adequate for a purpose (foll. by *for,* †*to, to do*). Also *impers.* in ***it will suffice that, it will suffices to do,*** etc. ME.
†**2** *verb intrans.* Have the necessary capacity or resources for doing something; be competent or able *to do* something. ME–E19.
†**3** *verb intrans.* Of a quality or condition: provide adequate means or opportunity; allow a certain thing to be done. LME–L15.
4 *verb trans.* Be enough for; meet the desires or needs of (a person); satisfy. Also *impers.* with *it.* (Formerly foll. by *of* the thing that satisfies.) LME. ▶**b** In *pass.* Be satisfied or content. *arch.* LME. ▶†**c** *refl.* Satisfy oneself. L15–E17.
†**5** *verb trans.* **a** Provide enough food for, satisfy the appetite of. Also, satisfy (the appetite). Usu. in *pass.* LME–L18. ▶**b** Satisfy (a desire, need, emotion, etc.). M16–M18.
†**6** *verb trans.* **a** Make sufficient provision for; supply *with.* LME–E18. ▶**b** Supply or provide (a product etc.). E17–E18.

> 🕮 **1** E. WAUGH Wages which . . barely sufficed for the necessaries of his household. G. F. KENNAN It will suffice . . to recall the highlights of the talks. D. LESSING This period of less than a week sufficed to start rumours. **suffice it to say** — I will say no more than —. **4** U. LE GUIN He never realized that imagination does not suffice some people.

■ **sufficer** *noun* (*rare*) a satisfier E20. **sufficingly** *adverb* (*rare*) so as to suffice E19.

sufficience /səˈfɪʃ(ə)ns/ *noun. arch.* LME.
[Old French, or late Latin *sufficientia,* from Latin *sufficient-*: see SUFFICIENT, -ENCE.]
1 The quality or condition of being enough; sufficient supply, means, or resources. LME.
†**2** Ability; competence. Also, a capable or competent person. LME–L17.
†**3** Satisfaction of one's needs; sustenance. LME–E17.
†**4** = SELF-SUFFICIENCY. LME–M17.

sufficiency /səˈfɪʃ(ə)nsi/ *noun.* L15.
[Late Latin *sufficientia*: see prec., -ENCY.]
1 †**a** Sufficient means or wealth; ability to meet financial obligations. L15–M18. ▶**b** A sufficient supply; an adequate income. E17. ▶**c** Adequate provision of food or physical comfort. L18.
2 The condition or quality of being sufficient for a purpose; adequacy. M16.
3 A sufficient quantity (*of* something); enough. M16.
4 Adequate ability or qualification to do something; competence. *arch.* M16. ▶†**b** An instance of this; a qualification; an accomplishment. L16–E18.
5 Excessive self-confidence; arrogance, conceit. *arch.* M17.

sufficient /səˈfɪʃ(ə)nt/ *adjective, noun, & adverb.* ME.
[Old French, or Latin *sufficient-* pres. ppl stem of *sufficere* SUFFICE: see -ENT.]
▶**A** *adjective.* **1 a** LAW. Of a document, security, etc.: legally satisfactory. ME. ▶**b** PHILOSOPHY. Adequate to satisfy an argument, situation, etc., satisfactory. Esp. in ***sufficient condition, sufficient reason.*** M17.
2 Adequate (esp. in quantity or extent) for a certain purpose; enough (*for* a person or thing, *to do* something). Also (*rare* exc. in allus. to *Matthew* 6:34) foll. by *to, unto.* LME. ▶**b** Achieving an object; effective. *rare.* M19.
†**3** Possessing talent or ability; competent, capable. (Foll. by *for* or *to* (a function), *to do* something.) LME–E19.
†**4** Of a person: having an adequate income; wealthy, well-to-do; qualified by means or status for an office. LME–L18.
5 Of a thing: of adequate quality; of a good standard, in good condition; substantial, solid. *obsolete* exc. *Scot.* LME.
6 More fully ***sufficient for oneself, sufficient unto oneself.*** = SELF-SUFFICIENT 1. *arch.* LME.
†**7** = SELF-SUFFICIENT 2. E17–E18.

> 🕮 **2** AV *Matt.* 6:34 Sufficient unto the day is the evil thereof. D. H. LAWRENCE Sufficient unto the moment is the appearance of reality. W. S. CHURCHILL The royal revenues were not sufficient to support the cost of the campaign. R. WEST A peasant of sufficient intelligence and enterprise could become a landowner.

Special collocations & phrases: ***sufficient for oneself***: see sense 6 above. ***not sufficient***: see NOT *adverb.* ***sufficient grace***: see GRACE *noun.* **sufficient statistic** a statistic containing all the information in the observations it is based on that is relevant to the estimate being made. ***sufficient unto oneself***: see sense 6 above.
▶**B** *noun.* †**1** The quality or condition of being sufficient; sufficiency. LME–E17.
2 A sufficient quantity or supply; sufficient means; enough. L15.
▶†**C** *adverb.* = SUFFICIENTLY. LME–E19.
■ **sufficiently** *adverb* in a sufficient manner; adequately, satisfactorily, enough: LME.

suffisance /səˈfiːs(ə)ns, *foreign* syfizɑ̃ːs/ *noun.* LME.
[Old & mod. French, from *suffisant* pres. pple of *suffire*: see SUFFICE, -ANCE.]
†**1** (A) sufficient supply or quantity; enough. LME–M17.
†**2** Ample means, wealth. LME–L16.
†**3** Ability; competence. LME–E17.
†**4** Satisfaction, contentment; a source of this. LME–L16.
5 Excessive self-confidence; arrogance, conceit. L18.

suffix /ˈsʌfɪks/ *noun.* L18.
[mod. Latin *suffixum* use as noun of neut. of *suffixus* pa. pple of Latin *suffigere,* formed as SUB- + *figere* FIX *verb.*]
1 GRAMMAR. An element placed at the end of a word or stem to form a derivative or as an inflection (e.g. ***-ed, -est, -ing, -ly, -ness***). L18.
2 MATH. An inferior index written to the right of a symbol, a subscript. M19.

■ **suffixal** *adjective* pertaining to or of the nature of a suffix L19. **suffixual** *adjective* = SUFFIXAL E20.

suffix /ˈsʌfɪks, səˈfɪks/ *verb trans.* E17.
[Partly from Latin *suffixus* (see prec.), partly from the noun.]
Chiefly as ***suffixed ppl adjective.***
1 Fix or place under; subjoin. E17.
2 Add as a suffix. L18.
■ **suffixˈation** *noun* the use of suffixes in grammar L19.

suffixoid /ˈsʌfɪksɔɪd/ *noun.* M20.
[Italian *suffissoido*: cf. SUFFIX *noun*. See -OID.]
GRAMMAR. A word-final element which resembles a suffix but is unproductive as a word-forming unit.

sufflaminate /səˈflamɪneɪt/ *verb trans.* Now *rare.* M17.
[Latin *sufflaminat-* pa. ppl stem of *sufflaminare*, from *sufflamen* bar, brake, drag-chain: see -ATE[3].]
Put an obstacle in the way of, obstruct.

sufflate /səˈfleɪt/ *verb trans.* Long *rare* or *obsolete.* E17.
[Latin *sufflat-* pa. ppl stem of *sufflare*, formed as SUB- + *flare* to blow: see -ATE[3].]
Blow up; inflate.

†**sufflation** *noun.* L16–E19.
[Latin *sufflatio(n-)*, formed as prec.: see -ATION.]
The action or an act of blowing; inflation; expiration. Also, inspiration by the Holy Spirit.

†**suffle** *verb intrans. & trans.* E17–L18.
[App. from French *souffler* from Latin *sufflare*: see SUFFLATE.]
Blow (up).

suffling /ˈsʌf(ə)lɪŋ/ *verbal noun. rare.* E20.
[from prec. + -ING[1].]
A sound as of blowing or heavy breathing.

sufflue /sʌˈfluː/ *noun.* M16.
[Origin unkn.]
HERALDRY. A charge resembling a clarion.

†**suffocate** *ppl adjective.* LME.
[Latin *suffocatus* pa. pple of *suffocare*: see next, -ATE[2].]
1 Suffocated by deprivation of air. LME–M17.
2 Smothered, overwhelmed. L15–E17.

> 2 SHAKES. *Tr. & Cr.* This chaos, when degree is suffocate, Follows the choking.

suffocate /ˈsʌfəkeɪt/ *verb.* L15.
[Latin *suffocat-* pa. ppl stem of *suffocare*, formed as SUB- + *fauces* throat: see -ATE[3].]
1 *verb trans.* Kill (a person or animal) by stopping the supply of air through the lungs or other respiratory organs. L15.
2 *verb trans.* Destroy as if by the exclusion of air; *fig.* smother, overwhelm. E16.
3 *verb trans.* Impede breathing in (a person); stifle, choke. L16.
4 *verb intrans.* Become stifled or choked; feel breathless. Also, die through lack of air. E18.

> 1 M. SPUFFORD She . . had put a pillow over his face, intending to suffocate him. 2 G. DALY He lived in terror that his all-consuming love would suffocate her. 3 J. LONDON His heart was pounding the blood into his throat and suffocating him. 4 A. STEVENS He suffered from psychosomatic attacks of choking, during which he feared he would suffocate.

■ **suffocating** *ppl adjective* (*a*) causing suffocation, stifling; (*b*) accompanied by or undergoing suffocation: E17. **suffocatingly** *adverb* so as to cause suffocation E19. **suffocative** *adjective* (now *rare*) causing suffocation; accompanied by suffocation: E17.

suffocation /sʌfəˈkeɪʃ(ə)n/ *noun.* LME.
[Latin *suffocatio(n-)*, formed as prec.: see -ATION.]
1 The action or an instance of suffocating; the condition of being suffocated. LME.
†**2** MEDICINE. In full ***suffocation of the womb*** & vars. Hysteria. LME–E18.

Suffolk /ˈsʌfək/ *noun.* M16.
[A county in SE England, forming part of East Anglia.]
1 Used *attrib.* to designate things found in, originating from, or characteristic of Suffolk, as ***Suffolk cheese, Suffolk cow, Suffolk ham, Suffolk pig***, etc. M16.
2 *ellipt.* A Suffolk cow, pig, or sheep; a Suffolk Punch. M19.

1 ***South Suffolk***: see SOUTH. **Suffolk bang** *Nautical slang* an inferior hard cheese. **Suffolk latch** a latch with a thumb-operated pivoted catch which lifts the latch when depressed. ***Suffolk Punch***: see PUNCH *noun*[4] 2. **Suffolk sheep** (an animal of) a black-faced hornless breed of sheep distinguished by a short fleece, large size, and lean meat.
■ **Suffolker** *noun* a native or inhabitant of Suffolk M19.

suffragan /ˈsʌfrəg(ə)n/ *noun & adjective.* LME.
[Anglo-Norman, Old French, repr. medieval Latin *suffraganeus*, from Latin *suffragium*: see SUFFRAGE, -AN.]
▶**A** *noun.* **1** More fully ***bishop suffragan, suffragan bishop.*** ▸**a** A bishop in relation to his archbishop or metropolitan by whom he may be summoned to attend synods and give his suffrage. LME. ▸**b** An assistant or subsidiary bishop, performing episcopal functions in a certain diocese but having no jurisdiction; in the Church of England, a bishop appointed to assist a diocesan bishop in a particular part of a diocese. LME.
†**2** A coadjutor, an assistant; a deputy, a representative. L15–M18.
▶**B** *adjective.* Of a see or diocese: subordinate *to* or to a metropolitan or archiepiscopal see. E18.
■ **suffraganal** *adjective* (*rare*) pertaining to a suffragan bishop L19. **suffraganate** *noun* the seat of a suffragan bishop L19. **suffraˈganean** *adjective* (*rare*) designating or pertaining to a suffragan E18. **suffraˈganeous** *adjective* (*rare*) = SUFFRAGANEAN E20. **suffraganship** *noun* the office or status of a suffragan M16.

†**suffragate** *verb.* E17.
[Latin *suffragat-* pa. ppl stem of *suffragari*, from *suffragium*: see next, -ATE[3].]
1 *verb trans.* Delegate, appoint. Only in E17.
2 *verb intrans.* Testify, bear witness *to*. Only in 17.
3 *verb intrans.* Vote (*for*); assent. M17–M19.

suffrage /ˈsʌfrɪdʒ/ *noun & verb.* LME.
[Latin *suffragium*, partly through Old & mod. French *suffrage*.]
▶**A** *noun.* **1** *sing.* & in *pl.* Prayers, *esp.* intercessory prayers; *spec.* prayers for the souls of the departed (esp. in ***do suffrage***). *arch.* LME. ▸**b** In *pl.* & (*rare*) *sing.* Liturgical intercessory petitions; *esp.* in the *Book of Common Prayer*, (*a*) the intercessory petitions pronounced by the priest in the Litany; (*b*) a series of petitions or versicles pronounced by the priest with the responses of the congregation. M16.
†**2** Help, support, assistance. Also, a person who helps. LME–E17.
3 A vote given by a member of a body, State, or society, in assent to a proposal or in favour of the election of a person; *gen.* a vote in support of or opinion in favour of some person or thing. M16. ▸**b** A marked paper or other object used to indicate a vote given. *rare.* M16.
4 Approval, sanction, consent. Formerly also, an instance of this, an expression of approval. *arch.* L16.
5 The collective opinion or vote of a body of people; *transf.* consensus of opinion, common or general consent. L16.
†**6** The support or assurance of evidence or testimony in favour of something. E17–E18.
7 The casting of a vote; election by voting. M17.
8 The right of voting in elections as a member of a particular group, citizen of a State, etc. Freq. with specifying word. Orig. *US.* L18.

> 5 R. NIEBUHR The suffrage of the governed determines the policy of the state. 8 *Arkansas Historical Quarterly* The Democrats adopted resolutions opposing negro suffrage. ***adult suffrage, female suffrage, universal suffrage, women's suffrage***, etc.

▶†**B** *verb.* **1** *verb intrans.* Vote *for* or *against*; agree *with*, give support *to*. E–M17.
2 *verb trans.* Elect by vote; give support to, side with. M17–M19.
■ †**suffrager** *noun* (*rare*) a voter E17–E18.

suffragette /sʌfrəˈdʒɛt/ *noun.* E20.
[from prec. + -ETTE, after SUFFRAGIST.]
Hist. A female supporter of the cause of women's political enfranchisement, *esp.* one working through organized (often militant) protest in Britain in the early 20th cent.
■ **suffragettism** *noun* the activity of the suffragettes E20.

suffragi /sʊˈfrɑːgi/ *noun.* E20.
[Egyptian *suffragī* from Turkish *sofracı*, from Arab. *sufra* food, dining-table + Turkish -*cı* agent-suff.]
A waiter, a butler.

suffragist /ˈsʌfrədʒɪst/ *noun.* E19.
[from SUFFRAGE + -IST.]
An advocate of the extension of the political franchise, esp. to women.
■ **suffragism** *noun* the advocacy of an extension of the suffrage, esp. to women L19. **suffraˈgistic** *adjective* pertaining to suffragism E20. **suffraˈgistically** *adverb* E20.

suffrago /səˈfreɪgəʊ/ *noun.* Now *rare* or *obsolete.* M19.
[Latin.]
ZOOLOGY. The hock of a quadruped; the tarsal joint of a bird.

suffrutescent /sʌfruːˈtɛs(ə)nt/ *adjective.* E19.
[formed as SUB- + FRUTESCENT.]
BOTANY. Somewhat suffruticose.

suffrutex /ˈsʌfrʊtɛks, səˈfruːt-/ *noun.* Now *rare.* Pl. **suffrutices** /səˈfruːtɪsiːz/. M16.
[mod. Latin, formed as SUB- + FRUTEX.]
BOTANY. A plant woody at the base but herbaceous above; a subshrub.

suffruticose /səˈfruːtɪkəʊs/ *adjective.* L18.
[mod. Latin *suffruticosus*, formed as *suffrutic-* SUFFRUTEX: see -OSE[1].]
BOTANY. Having the character of a subshrub; woody at the base but herbaceous above.

suffumigate /səˈfjuːmɪgeɪt/ *verb trans. rare.* LME.
[Latin *suffumigat-* pa. ppl stem of *suffumigare*, formed as SUB- + *fumigare* FUMIGATE.]
Fumigate from below.

suffumigation /səfjuːmɪˈgeɪʃ(ə)n/ *noun.* Now *arch.* or *Hist.* LME.
[Late Latin *suffumigatio(n-)*, formed as prec.: see -ATION.]
sing. & (usu.) in *pl.* Fumes, vapours, *esp.* ones generated by burning herbs, incense, etc., used for therapeutic effect or in religious rites; a substance used for this purpose. Also, the action of suffumigating something; an instance of this.

suffuse /səˈfjuːz/ *verb trans.* L16.
[Latin *suffus-* pa. ppl stem of *suffundere*, formed as SUB- + *fundere* pour.]
1 Of moisture, colour, etc.: spread over from within, flood through. Also (*transf.*), cover or fill (*with*). Freq. in *pass.* L16.
2 Pour (a liquid) over a surface. M18.

> 1 H. JAMES Her eyes . . had suddenly been suffused with tears. M. SARTON Laura . . saw the blush of pleasure suffuse Harriet's round face. P. LIVELY The evening sunlight . . suffused the whole place with a golden glow. M. ATWOOD When we . . pray, I feel suffused with goodness.

■ **suffusive** *adjective* tending to spread, cover, or fill L19.

suffusion /səˈfjuːʒ(ə)n/ *noun.* LME.
[Latin *suffusio(n-)*, formed as prec.: see -ION.]
1 MEDICINE. Extravasation; the spreading of a fluid through the body, an organ, etc.; the fluid so spread. Formerly also *spec.*, a cataract. Now *rare* exc. as in sense 3. LME.
2 The action of suffusing a surface with fluid, moisture, colour, etc.; the condition of being suffused or overspread. Also, an instance of this. E17.
3 A colouring spread over a surface, esp. the skin; *spec.* a flush of colour in the face, a blush. E18.

Sufi /ˈsuːfi/ *noun.* M17.
[Arab. *ṣūfī* lit. 'woollen', from *ṣūf* wool (from the rough woollen garment associated with ascetics).]
A member of any of various spiritual orders within Islam characterized by asceticism and mysticism.
■ **Sufic** *adjective* pertaining to the Sufis or their mystical system L19. **Sufiism** *noun* = SUFISM E19. **Sufism** *noun* the mystical system of the Sufis M19.

sufuria /sʊfʊˈrɪə/ *noun.* E20.
[Kiswahili, from *sufuri* from Arab. *ṣufrī* cauldron from *ṣufr* copper, brass.]
In E. Africa: a large metal cooking pot.

sug /sʌg/ *verb intrans. & trans.* Infl. **-gg-**. L20.
[Acronym, from sell under guise.]
Attempt to sell (to) under the guise of conducting market research.

sugan *noun* see SUGGAN.

sugar /ˈʃʊgə/ *noun & adjective.* ME.
[Old French *çukre*, *sukere* (mod. *sucre*) from Italian *zucchero*, prob. from medieval Latin *succarum*, SACCHARUM from Arab. *sukkar* from Persian *shakar* from Prakrit *śakara* from Sanskrit *śarkarā*.]
▶**A** *noun.* **1** A sweet crystalline substance obtained from various plants, esp. the sugar cane and sugar beet, used in cookery, confectionery, brewing, etc.; sucrose. Freq. with specifying words. ME. ▸**b** In *pl.* Kinds of sugar. L16. ▸†**c** = ***sugar cane*** below. L16–E19. ▸**d** A lump or teaspoonful of sugar, esp. as used to sweeten tea, coffee, etc. *colloq.* M20.
2 *transf.* & *fig.* **a** A pleasant thing used to reconcile a person to what is unpalatable (with allus. to sugar encasing a bitter-tasting pill); sweet words, flattery. ME. ▸**b** Money. Also ***sugar and honey***. *slang.* M19. ▸**c** A term of endearment: dear, darling. *colloq.* (chiefly *US*). E20. ▸**d** As *interjection.* A *euphem.* substitute for 'bugger' or 'shit' Cf. SUGAR *verb* 5. *slang.* E20. ▸**e** A narcotic drug; *spec.* (*a*) heroin; (*b*) LSD (taken on a lump of sugar). *slang.* M20.
3 CHEMISTRY. **a** Any of various inorganic compounds resembling sugar in form or taste. Usu. in *comb.* Now chiefly *Hist.* M17. ▸**b** Any of a class of simple carbohydrates composed of one or more monosaccharide units, which are soluble in water, usu. optically active, freq. sweet to the taste, and directly or indirectly fermentable, as sucrose, glucose, lactose, etc.; a saccharide. E19.

1 ***barley sugar, beet sugar, brown sugar, cane-sugar, caster sugar, demerara sugar, granulated sugar, icing sugar, loaf sugar, lump sugar, raw sugar, refined sugar, white sugar***, etc. **3b** ***fruit sugar, grape sugar, invert sugar, malt sugar, milk sugar, wood sugar***, etc.

Phrases: †**acid of sugar** oxalic acid. ***not made of sugar or salt***: see SALT *noun*[1]. **sugar of lead** (now *rare*) lead acetate. †**sugar of milk** lactose.

Comb.: **sugar-almond** a sweet consisting of an almond coated with hardened sugar; **sugar-apple** (the sweet edible fruit of) any of several W. Indian trees of the family Annonaceae, esp. the sweetsop, *Annona squamosa*; ***sugar aquatint***: see ***sugar lift aquatint*** below; **sugar-bag** (*a*) a bag or sack for sugar, *esp.* one made of coarse thick specially coloured paper or (*Austral.* & *NZ*) of fine sacking; (*b*) *Austral.* (the honey in) a wild bees' nest; **sugar-baker** *Hist.* a sugar-refiner; **sugar-baking** *Hist.* sugar-refining; **sugar bean** a French bean of a reddish mottled variety widely eaten in S. Africa; **sugar beet** a cultivar of the beet, *Beta vulgaris*, grown for the high sugar content of its root; **sugar-berry** any of various N. American species of the genus *Celtis*, spec. (the sweet edible fruit of) the hackberry, *Celtis occidentalis*; **sugar-box** *Hist.* a sugar bowl; **sugar-bush** (*a*) a plantation of sugar maples; (*b*) *S. Afr.* [translating Afrikaans *suikerbos*] any of several kinds of protea, esp. *Protea mellifera*, with copious nectar formerly used for syrup; (*c*) *US* an evergreen sumac, *Rhus ovata*, of the south-western US, bearing yellow flowers followed by dark red berries; **sugar-camp** *N. Amer.* a place in a maple forest or plantation where the sap is collected and boiled for sugar; **sugar cane** a grass, *Saccharum officinarum*, resembling bamboo, extensively cultivated in the tropics etc. for the sugar extracted from its stems; **sugar-coat** *verb trans.* make palatable or superficially attractive (chiefly as ***sugar-coated*** *ppl adjective*); **sugarcraft** the art of creating confectionery or cake decorations from sugar paste; **sugar daddy** *slang* a man who lavishes gifts on a much younger woman; **sugar-fungus** MYCOLOGY a kind of fungus which attacks decaying matter but can only utilize simple organic substances such as sugars; **sugar glider** a flying phalanger, *Petaurus breviceps*, which feeds on nectar, insects, etc., and is found commonly in parts of Australia and New Guinea; **sugar-grass** *Austral.* a sweetish fodder grass, *Eulalia fulva*; **sugar-gum** any of several Australian eucalypts, esp. *Eucalyptus cladocalyx*, with sweetish foliage relished by stock; **sugar-house** a sugar factory (***sugar-house molasses***, a low-grade molasses produced in sugar factories, now chiefly used in medicines etc.); **sugar kelp** a large brown seaweed, *Lactaria saccharina*, with a long crinkly blade-like frond and young stems that are edible; **sugar lift aquatint**, **sugar aquatint** a method of etching in which dark areas are drawn on a copper plate with a solution of black water-based ink and sugar; **sugar-maple** a N. American maple, *Acer saccharum*, one of the main sources of maple syrup and maple sugar (***sugar maple borer***, a wood-boring longhorn beetle, *Glycobius speciosus*, that is very destructive to maples in N. America); **sugar-mite** †(*a*) = ***silverfish*** (b) s.v. SILVER *noun & adjective*; (*b*) any mite that infects sugar etc., esp. *Glycyphagus domesticus*; **sugar nippers** (*a*) a tool for cutting loaf sugar into lumps; (*b*) a pair of sugar-tongs; **sugar-orchard** *N. Amer.* = ***sugar-bush*** (a) above; **sugar palm** a Malaysian and Indonesian palm, *Arenga saccharifera*, the sap of which is boiled to produce sugar; **sugar-paper** coarse paper like that used for making sugar-bags; ***sugar pea***: see ***sugar snap pea*** below; **sugar-pine** a tall graceful pine tree, *Pinus lambertiana*, of the south-western US, the heartwood of which exudes a sweet substance resembling sugar; **sugar-plum** *arch.* a small round or oval sweet of flavoured boiled sugar; *fig.* something very pleasing, esp. given as a sop or bribe; **sugar rag** *US* = ***sugar-teat*** below; **sugar sack** (*a*) fine sacking for making bags for sugar; (*b*) a bag made of this; **sugar sand** *N. Amer.* a fine sand raised by the sap of the maple tree, producing gritty sediment in maple syrup unless removed; **sugar snap pea**, **sugar pea** a type of mange-tout; **sugar snow** *N. Amer.* a snowfall in the maple sugar season, resulting in a longer run of sap; **sugar soap** an alkaline compound for removing paint or cleaning paintwork; **sugar-sops** (*obsolete* exc. *Scot.*) steeped slices of bread sweetened with sugar; **sugar squirrel** = ***sugar glider*** above; **sugar stick** a stick of boiled sugar; **sugar-teat**, **sugar-tit** (now chiefly *Hist.*) a small amount of moist sugar tied up in a cloth to form a nipple shape, used to pacify a baby; **sugar-tongs** small metal tongs with claws or spoons at the ends, for serving cube or lump sugar; **sugar-tree** *N. Amer.* = ***sugar maple*** above; **sugar trough** *US* a trough used for collecting maple sap; **sugar vase** a tall sugar-container for use at table; **sugar-weather** *Canad.* spring weather, characterized by cold nights and warm days, that starts the sap running in maple trees; **sugar-works** a sugar factory.

▸†**B** *adjective.* Sugary, sweet. LME–E19.

▪ **sugarish** *adjective* (*rare*) sugary, sweet LME. **sugarless** *adjective* L18.

sugar /ˈʃʊɡə/ *verb.* LME.
[from the noun.]
1 *verb trans.* Make more agreeable or palatable. Also foll. by *over.* LME. ▸**b** Flatter. Also foll. by *up.* E20.
2 *verb trans.* Coat, sprinkle, or sweeten with sugar. M16. ▸**b** *verb trans. & intrans.* ENTOMOLOGY. Spread a mixture of sugar, treacle, beer, etc., on (a tree-trunk etc.) in order to catch moths. Chiefly as ***sugaring*** *verbal noun.* M19.
3 *verb intrans.* Boil down maple sap until it thickens into syrup, or further until it crystallizes into sugar. Usu. foll. by *off. N. Amer.* L18.
4 *verb intrans.* Shirk while pretending to row hard. *Univ. slang.* L19.
5 *verb trans.* [Cf. SUGAR *noun* 2d.] *euphem.* Damn, curse, confound. Usu. in *pass. slang.* L19.

> 🕮 **1** ***sugar the pill***: see PILL *noun*[3] 1b. **2** L. GRANT-ADAMSON Coffee came. Joseph sugared his, took a sip.

▪ **sugaring** *noun* (*a*) the action of the verb; an instance of this; (*b*) sugary or sweet matter; sweetening; (*c*) a method of removing unwanted body hair by applying a mixture of lemon juice, sugar, and water to the skin and then peeling it off: E17.

sugarallie /ʃʊɡəˈrali/ *noun. Scot. colloq.* Also **-rollie** /-ˈrɒli/. E19.
[Alt. of blend of SUGAR *noun* and LIQUORICE.]
Liquorice.

sugarbird /ˈʃʊɡəbəːd/ *noun.* L17.
[from SUGAR *noun* + BIRD *noun.*]
†**1** A canary. Only in L17.
2 Either of two southern African passerines of the genus *Promerops* (family Promeropidae), which have very long tails, long curved bills, and feed on insects and nectar. L18.
3 Any of various other passerines that feed on nectar; *esp.* (*a*) = ***bananaquit*** s.v. BANANA; (*b*) = ***honeycreeper*** (b) s.v. HONEY *noun*; (*c*) *S. Afr.* = SUNBIRD 1b. L18.

sugar-candy /ʃʊɡəˈkandi/ *noun & adjective.* LME.
[Old French *sucre candi* from Arab. *sukkar* SUGAR *noun* + *kandī* candied, from *kand* candy from Persian from Sanskrit *khaṇḍa* piece, fragment, from *khaṇḍ-* break.]
▸**A** *noun.* **1** Sugar clarified and crystallized by repeated boiling and slow evaporation. LME.
2 *fig.* Something sweet, pleasant, or delicious. L16.
▸**B** *adjective.* Sugary, sweet. L16.
▪ **sugar-candied** *adjective* coated with sugar L16. **sugar-candyish** *adjective* resembling sugar-candy M19.

sugared /ˈʃʊɡəd/ *adjective.* LME.
[from SUGAR *noun*, *verb*: see -ED[2], -ED[1].]
1 Containing, coated, or sweetened with sugar. LME.
2 *fig.* †**a** Sweet-tasting, delicious; (of sound) sweet, dulcet; (of the tongue, mouth, etc.) producing sweet sounds or eloquent words. LME–M17. ▸**b** Superficially attractive, deceptively alluring; (of words, meaning, etc.) made more pleasant or welcome. LME.

> 🕮 **1** DICKENS Bonbons made of sugared nuts and almonds. P. SAYER On it were blue cups containing sugared tea. **2b** A. W. KINGLAKE The cheap sugared words are quickly forgotten.

sugar loaf /ˈʃʊɡə ləʊf/ *noun phr.* LME.
[from SUGAR *noun* + LOAF *noun*[1].]
1 A moulded conical mass of hard refined sugar. LME.
2 *transf.* A thing having the shape of a sugar loaf; *spec.* (*a*) *Hist.* (in full ***sugar-loaf hat***) a conical hat, pointed, rounded or flat at the top, worn during various periods until the early 19th cent.; (*b*) a high conical hill or mountain (also more fully ***sugar-loaf hill***, ***sugar-loaf mountain***). L16.
▪ **sugar-loafed** *adjective* shaped like a sugar loaf E18.

sugarollie *noun* var. of SUGARALLIE.

sugary /ˈʃʊɡ(ə)ri/ *noun.* L17.
[Irreg. from SUGAR *noun*: see -ERY.]
Orig. *gen.*, a place where sugar is manufactured. Now only *spec.* (*N. Amer.*), a place where maple-juice is collected and boiled for making sugar.

sugary /ˈʃʊɡ(ə)ri/ *adjective.* L16.
[from SUGAR *noun* + -Y[1].]
1 Full of or containing sugar; resembling (that of) sugar; sweet. L16.
2 *fig.* Excessively sweet or sentimental; falsely sweet or pleasant. L16.

> 🕮 **1** R. INGALLS She'd never liked sugary foods much. J. L. WATEN We left the town shrouded in a white, sugary mist. **2** CARLYLE The Dragon herself is all civility and sugary smiles. *New Yorker* Lanford Wilson's play . . is synthetic and sugary.

▪ **sugariness** *noun* M19.

suggan /ˈsʌɡ(ə)n, ˈsuːɡ(ə)n/ *noun.* Also (esp. in sense 2) **soogan**, **sugan** /ˈsuːɡ(ə)n/. L17.
[Irish *súgán.*]
1 A straw rope; a basic type of saddle, *esp.* one made from straw. *Anglo-Irish.* L17.
2 A thick blanket or padded quilt suitable for camping out. *N. Amer.* E20.

suggest /səˈdʒɛst/ *verb trans.* E16.
[Latin *suggest-* pa. ppl stem of *suggerere*, formed as SUB- + *gerere* bear, carry. Cf. earlier SUGGESTER.]
1 Introduce to the mind as an object of thought, an idea for (orig. esp. evil) action, etc.; propose (a theory, course of action, option, etc., *that, doing*). (Foll. by *to* a person.) E16. ▸**b** *refl.* Of an idea etc.: come into the mind. M18. ▸**c** Inspire, prompt the execution of. M19. ▸**d** Utter as a suggestion. M19.
†**2** Prompt (a person) to evil; tempt *to* or *to do* something. L16–M17. ▸**b** Insinuate into (a person's mind) the false idea *that*. Only in 17.
3 Call up the thought of (a thing) by association with something else; evoke. M17.
4 Make known indirectly; hint at, intimate; imply, give the impression, (*that*). L17.
5 LAW. Put forward in a suggestion (SUGGESTION 4). E18.

> 🕮 **1** SHAKES. *Ven. & Ad.* Jealousy . . Gives false alarms, suggesteth mutiny. I. MURDOCH As soon as Finn suggested this idea it seemed . . an irresistible one. R. P. GRAVES Housman suggested returning to Chablis for dinner. K. VONNEGUT They suggested to my parents that . . I should pursue a career as an artist. *absol.*: F. QUARLES The devil may suggest, compel he cannot. **b** F. A. PALEY The danger of approaching the crater in an eruption . . suggested itself. **c** L. STEPHEN The success of the Iliad naturally suggested an attempt upon the Odyssey. **d** J. BARTH 'Let's go see the show-boat' . . I suggested to Jeannine. **3** W. PLOMER His gait/ suggests a peahen walking on hot bricks. E. H. GOMBRICH The artist cannot copy a sunlit lawn, but he can suggest it. G. VIDAL It seemed to suggest his dream to him. **4** J. B. PRIESTLEY She made a . . movement that suggested she was ready . . to walk on again. I. MURDOCH The way Sadie had referred to it suggested that it had not yet been copied. G. VIDAL He suggested a bow without actually executing it.

▪ **suggestable** *adjective* (*rare*) = SUGGESTIBLE 2 M19.

suggesta *noun pl.* see SUGGESTUM.

suggester /səˈdʒɛstə/ *noun.* LME.
[from SUGGEST + -ER[1].]
†**1** A person who brought a false charge against another. LME–M17.
2 A person who suggests something. L17.

suggestible /səˈdʒɛstɪb(ə)l/ *adjective.* L19.
[formed as prec. + -IBLE.]
1 Able to be influenced by (hypnotic or other) suggestion; easily swayed. L19.
2 Able to be suggested. E20.
▪ **suggestiˈbility** *noun* L19.

suggestio falsi /səˌdʒɛstɪəʊ ˈfalsʌɪ/ *noun phr.* Pl. **suggestiones falsi** /səˌdʒɛstɪəʊniːz/. E19.
[mod. Latin, lit. 'suggestion of what is false'.]
A misrepresentation of the truth whereby something incorrect is implied to be true. Cf. SUPPRESSIO VERI.

suggestion /səˈdʒɛstʃ(ə)n/ *noun.* ME.
[Old & mod. French from Latin *suggestio(n-)*, formed as SUGGEST: see -TION.]
†**1** (An) incitement to evil. ME–M17.
2 The action of proposing a theory, course of action, etc.; an instance of this, a theory, plan, etc., suggested, a proposal. LME. ▸**b** PSYCHOLOGY. The introduction of a belief or impulse into the mind of a subject by words, gestures, etc.; the belief or impulse thus suggested. L19.
†**3** The action of making a false or suborned statement or supplying false information; an instance of this, a false charge. Freq. in ***false suggestion***. LME–L16.
4 LAW. An information given without an oath having been sworn; an entry of a fact on the record. L15.
5 The action or process of calling up the thought of a thing by association with something else. E17.
6 A slight trace, a hint, (*of* something). M19.
▪ **suggestionize** *verb trans.* (*rare*) influence or treat by hypnotic suggestion L19.

suggestiones falsi *noun phr.* pl. of SUGGESTIO FALSI.

suggestive /səˈdʒɛstɪv/ *adjective.* M17.
[from SUGGEST + -IVE.]
1 Calculated to suggest something; conveying a suggestion; evocative. (Foll. by *of.*) M17. ▸**b** *spec.* Tending to suggest something lewd or indecent. L19.
2 Of a plan etc.: that comes to mind. E19.
3 Of or pertaining to hypnotic suggestion. E20.
▪ **suggestively** *adverb* M19. **suggestiveness** *noun* M19. **suggesˈtivity** *noun* (*rare*) M19.

suggestor /səˈdʒɛstə/ *noun.* L16.
[from SUGGEST + -OR.]
1 = SUGGESTER. Now *rare* or *obsolete.* L16.
2 *spec.* An employee who submits a suggestion for improving working methods, productivity, etc. *US.* M20.

suggestum /səˈdʒɛstəm/ *noun.* Pl. **-tums**, **-ta** /-tə/. E18.
[Latin, formed as SUGGEST.]
Chiefly ROMAN ANTIQUITIES. A platform, a stage.

sugi /ˈsuːɡi/ *noun.* E18.
[Japanese.]
The Japanese cedar, *Cryptomeria japonica*.

sugillate /ˈsuːdʒɪleɪt, ˈsjuː-, ˈsʌdʒ-/ *verb trans.* Now *rare* or *obsolete.* E17.
[Latin *sugillat-* pa. ppl stem of *sugillare*: see -ATE[3].]
1 Orig., beat black and blue. Later *spec.* in MEDICINE (as ***sugillated*** *ppl adjective*), mark with sugillations, bruise. E17.
†**2** *fig.* Defame, revile. *rare.* Only in M17.

sugillation /suːdʒɪˈleɪʃ(ə)n, sjuː-, sʌdʒ-/ *noun.* Now *rare* or *obsolete.* L16.
[Latin *sugillatio(n-)*, formed as prec.: see -ATION.]
†**1** The action of SUGILLATE (*lit. & fig.*). L16–L17.
2 MEDICINE. A bruise; a mark resembling a bruise; an ecchymosis. M17.

suh /sʌ/ *noun.* L19.
[Repr. a pronunc.]
In representations of US Southern and black speech: sir.

Sui /sweɪ/ *adjective & noun.* M18.
[Chinese *Suí*]
(Designating or pertaining to) a dynasty ruling in China in the 6th and the 7th cents.

suiboku /ˈsuːɪbəʊkuː/ *noun.* E20.
[Japanese, lit. 'liquid ink', from *sui* water + *boku* ink stick.]
A style of Japanese painting, using black ink on a white surface and characterized by bold brush-work and subtle tones.

suicidal /suːɪˈsʌɪd(ə)l, sjuː-/ *adjective.* L18.
[from next + -AL[1].]
1 Self-destructive; fatally or disastrously rash. L18.
2 Of, pertaining to, or involving suicide; (of a person) inclined to commit suicide. M19.
▪ **suiciˈdality** *noun* the quality or condition of being suicidal M20. **suicidally** *adverb* M19.

suicide /ˈsuːɪsʌɪd, ˈsjuː-/ *noun*. M17.
[In sense 1 from mod. Latin *suicidium*, in sense 2 from mod. Latin *suicida*, both from Latin *sui* of oneself: see -CIDE.]
1 The action or an act of intentionally killing oneself. M17. ▸**b** *fig*. Action destructive to one's own interests etc. L18.
2 A person who commits suicide. Also, a person who attempts to commit suicide. M18.

🕮 **1** J. BARTH To contemplate suicide . . and . . resolve to destroy myself. J. D. SUTHERLAND His bitterness gave rise to thoughts of suicide. **commit suicide** [from suicide formerly being a crime], kill oneself intentionally. **b** S. BRETT To bring in a play by an unknown author *without any star names* is commercial suicide. **2** G. SWIFT Suicides often appear relaxed and calm before taking their lives.

Attrib. & comb.: In the sense 'designating, pertaining to, or taking part in a highly dangerous or suicidal military operation', as ***suicide mission***, ***suicide squad***, etc. Special combs., as **suicide blond**, **suicide blonde** *slang* a woman with hair dyed blond; **suicide clause** a clause in a life insurance policy which releases the insurer from liability if the insured commits suicide within a specified period; **suicide pact** an agreement between two or more people to commit suicide together; **suicide squeeze** BASEBALL the action of a runner on third base in running for home as the ball is pitched.
■ **suicidism** *noun* (*rare*) the practice of suicide E19. **suici'dologist** *noun* an expert in or student of suicidology M20. **suici'dology** *noun* the branch of science that deals with suicide and its prevention M20.

suicide /ˈsuːɪsʌɪd, ˈsjuː-/ *verb*. M19.
[from the noun.]
1 *verb intrans. & refl.* Commit suicide. M19.
2 *verb trans. euphem.* Kill. L19.

†suicism *noun*. M17.
[In sense 1 from Latin *sui* of oneself + -*c*- + -ISM; in sense 2 from SUI(CIDE *noun* + -ISM.]
1 Selfishness. Only in M17.
2 Suicide. M–L18.

suid /ˈsuːɪd, ˈsjuː-/ *noun & adjective*. M20.
[mod. Latin *Suidae* (see below), from Latin *sus* pig: see -ID³.]
ZOOLOGY. ▶**A** *noun*. An even-toed ungulate of the family Suidae, which comprises the pigs. M20.
▶**B** *adjective*. Of, pertaining to, or designating this family. L20.

sui generis /suːʌɪ ˈdʒɛn(ə)rɪs, suːiː; sjuː-/ *adjectival phr.* L18.
[Latin.]
Of its own kind; peculiar, unique.

sui juris /suːʌɪ ˈdʒʊərɪs, suːɪ-, sjuː-/ *adjectival phr.* E17.
[Latin, lit. 'of one's own right'.]
LAW. **1** ROMAN HISTORY. Of the status of a person who was not subject to paternal authority. E17.
2 Of full age and capacity. L17.

suikerbos /ˈsʌɪkəbɒs, *foreign* ˈsœikərbɔs/ *noun*. *S. Afr.* Also **-bossie** /-bɒsi, *foreign* -bɔsi/. E19.
[Afrikaans, from *suiker* SUGAR *noun* + *bos(ch)* BUSH *noun*¹.]
= ***sugar-bush*** (b) s.v. SUGAR *noun*.

sui-mate /ˈsuːʌɪˌmeɪt, ˈsuːiː-, ˈsjuː-/ *noun*. Now *rare*. M19.
[from Latin *sui* of oneself + MATE *noun*¹.]
CHESS. = SELFMATE.

suint /swɪnt/ *noun*. Now *rare*. L18.
[French (earlier †*suing*), from *suer* to sweat.]
The natural greasy substance found in the wool of sheep, consisting of fatty matter combined with potassium salts.

suisse /sɥis, swiːs/ *noun*. Pl. pronounced same. M19.
[French = Swiss.]
1 The porter of a large house; the beadle of a French church. M19.
2 *ellipt*. = ***petit suisse*** s.v. PETIT *adjective*². L19.

suit /suːt, sjuːt/ *noun*. ME.
[Anglo-Norman *siute*, Old French *si(e)ute* (mod. *suite*), from Proto-Romance fem. pa. pple (used as noun) of alt. of Latin *sequi*. Cf. SUE.]
▶**I** FEUDAL LAW. **1 a** Attendance by a tenant at the court of his lord, esp. as an obligation of tenure. Formerly also, a due paid in lieu of this. Also ***suit of court***. ME. ▸**b** Attendance of a person at the sheriff's court or at the court leet. Also ***suit real***, ***suit royal***, ***suit regal***, (*Scot.*) ***common suit***. LME. ▸**c** An instance of such attendance. LME.
2 = SUCKEN *noun* 1. LME.
▶**II** Pursuit; prosecution, legal process.
3 a A process instituted in a court of law for the recovery or protection of a right or a claim or the redress of a wrong; a lawsuit. Also ***suit at law***, ***suit in law***. ME. ▸**b** The action of suing in a court of law; legal prosecution. Formerly also, litigation. L15.
†**4** Pursuit, chase. Also foll. by *of*. ME–M18. ▸**b** That which is pursued; a quarry. L16–M17.
†**5** The prosecution *of* a cause. Also, the action of suing for a writ. LME–E17.
6 (A) petition, (a) supplication, (an) entreaty; *esp*. one made to a person in authority. Now *poet*. LME. ▸†**b** *transf.* Earnest search for or endeavour to obtain something. M16–E17.
7 The courting of a woman; (a) courtship. L16.

🕮 **3a** H. EVANS She was keen to file suit in the United States. E. SEGAL He's been an expert witness in . . medical malpractice suits. **7** M. M. KAYE His suit had been rejected . . on the score of his youth.

▶**III** Livery; style; sort.
†**8** A livery, a uniform; a matching material or uniform. ME–M17.
†**9** A pattern, a style of workmanship or design, *esp*. a matching one. LME–E16.
†**10** Kind, sort, class. M16–M17.
▶**IV** Following, company.
11 A group of followers; a train, a retinue; *spec*. the witnesses of a plaintiff in a lawsuit. *arch*. ME.
†**12** Offspring, *spec*. that of a villein. Only in ME.
▶**V** Set, series.
13 a A number of things of the same kind intended to be used together or forming a definite set, as a set *of* crockery, cutlery, etc., a suite *of* rooms. *arch*. exc. as in sense 13b below. LME. ▸**b** The complete set *of* sails required for a ship or for a set of spars. E17. ▸**c** A head of hair. *US*. M19.
14 a Orig., a set of outer clothes intended to be worn together at the same time. Now *spec*. a man's jacket and trousers (and sometimes also a waistcoat) of the same material; a similar set of clothes for a woman, often having a skirt instead of trousers. LME. ▸**b** A set of church vestments of the same colour and material. LME. ▸**c** A complete set of pieces of armour for covering the whole body. Chiefly in ***suit of armour***. E19. ▸**d** A set of clothes to be worn on a particular occasion or for a particular activity. Usu. with specifying word. L19. ▸**e** A person who wears a suit at work; *esp*. a business executive. *slang*. L20.
15 Each of the four sets (distinguished by their marks, esp. as spades, clubs, hearts, or diamonds) into which a pack of playing-cards is divided; a player's (esp. strong) holding in one such set at one time; one of these sets as proposed trumps in bridge, freq. as opp. to no trumps (freq. *attrib*.). E16.

🕮 **14a** B. W. ALDISS Farrer was . . given to tweed suits and heavy lace-up shoes. A. BROOKNER Emmy, dressed in a brown suit with a long skirt. ***Eton suit***, ***Norfolk suit***, ***sack suit***, etc. **d** ***evening suit***, ***play-suit***, ***pressure suit***, ***swimsuit***, ***wet suit***, etc.

▶**VI** Sequence.
†**16** A succession, a sequence. *rare*. LME–E17.
Phrases: †**at suit** engaged in litigation. ***common suit***: see sense 1b above. **follow suit** (*a*) play a card of the same suit as the leading card; (*b*) *fig*. do the same thing as another person. †**go to suit** go to law. **in suit** (*a*) (of a matter) in dispute; †(*b*) engaged in a lawsuit; being prosecuted. **in suit with** *arch*. in agreement or harmony with. ***long suit***: see LONG *adjective*¹. ***major suit***: see MAJOR *adjective*. ***minor suit***: see MINOR *adjective & noun*. **of a suit with** *arch*. of a piece with. ***short suit***: see SHORT *adjective*. ***strong suit***: see STRONG *adjective*. ***suit at law***, ***suit in law***: see sense 3a above. ***suit of court***: see sense 1a above. ***suit of dittos***: see DITTO *noun* 3. ***suit real***, ***suit regal***, ***suit royal***: see sense 1b above. See also ZOOT SUIT.
Comb.: **suit bag** (*a*) a protective covering for a suit which is not being worn; (*b*) a travelling bag for carrying a suit; **suit-hold** FEUDAL LAW tenure by suit and service to a superior; **suit length** a piece of material of the right size for making into a suit; **suit-roll** *Hist*. the roll of people bound to attend at a court; **suit-service** FEUDAL LAW service rendered by attendance at a lord's court; **suit-weight** *adjective* designating a fabric of an appropriate thickness for making up into suits.
■ **suited** *adjective* wearing a suit or clothing of a specified kind L16. **suiter** *noun* a travelling bag for carrying (a specified number of) suits M20. **suitlike** *adjective* †(*a*) suitable; (*b*) resembling (that of) a suit: L16.

suit /suːt, sjuːt/ *verb*. LME.
[from the noun.]
†**1** *verb intrans*. FEUDAL LAW. Attend the court of a superior lord. LME–M16.
†**2** *verb intrans*. Sue to a person *for* something. E16–E18.
†**3** *verb trans*. Sue for in a court of law (*Scot*.); bring a lawsuit against, sue. M16–E18.
†**4 a** *verb trans*. Seek to obtain; court, seek *in marriage*. Chiefly *Scot*. M16–M17. ▸**b** *verb intrans*. Pay court *to* a woman. L16–M18.
†**5** *verb trans*. Arrange in a set or series; sort out. M16–L17.
6 a *verb trans*. Provide with a suit of clothes; clothe, dress. Usu. in *pass*. *arch*. L16. ▸**b** *verb trans*. Foll. by *up*: provide with clothing designed for a particular activity. *US*. M20. ▸**c** *verb intrans*. Dress oneself *up* in clothing designed for a particular activity. M20.
†**7** *verb trans*. Match. *rare*. L16–L18.
8 *verb trans*. Make appropriate or agreeable; adapt, accommodate, make suitable. Usu. foll. by *to*. Freq. in *pass*. L16.
9 *verb trans*. Be agreeable or convenient to. L16.
10 *verb trans*. **a** Be suitable for, meet the requirements of. E17. ▸**b** Be good for, be favourable to the condition or esp. health of. E19. ▸**c** Go well with (a person's figure, features, character, etc.); become. E19.
11 *verb intrans*. Be suitable, fitting, or convenient; go well. Orig. usu. foll. by *with*. E17.
12 *verb trans*. Provide (*with*). Usu. in *pass*. *arch*. E17.

🕮 **6b** *Daily Telegraph* Only when everyone is suited up is the order given to tackle a disorderly crowd. **8** D. PARKER Mrs. Whittaker's dress was always studiously suited to its occasion. B. BETTELHEIM Subjecting prisoners to conditions specially suited to the purpose. **9** S. KAUFFMANN Let's have dinner together . . tomorrow or Wednesday, whichever suits you best. A. HIGGINS The main street was . . deserted. This suited her, for she disliked being stared at. U. HOLDEN Army life suited him. **10a** R. GRAVES She quoted from Homer, but with alterations to suit the context. R. COBB She could put on the charm . . when it suited her purpose. A. DILLARD The Bellingham airport was a . . clearing in a forest . . ; its runways suited small planes. **b** J. BUCHAN The . . autumn air did not suit my health. E. WAUGH I've never regretted coming away. The climate suits me. **c** R. LAWLER Not to my taste, but it suits you. M. MITCHELL Jenny's not sure these tight jeans really suit her. **11** SIR W. SCOTT His walking-dress . . had so much of a military character as suited . . with his having such a weapon. M. COREN They did not return to any permanent home. Gilbert had yet to find one which would suit.

Phrases: ***suit one's book***: see BOOK *noun*. **suit oneself** (*a*) *colloq*. do as one likes; (*b*) find something that satisfies one. **suit the action to the word** carry out what has been stated, esp. a promise or a threat, at once.
■ **suiting** *noun* (*a*) the action of the verb; (*b*) cloth used for making suits; a suit: M16.

suitable /ˈsuːtəb(ə)l, ˈsjuːt-/ *adjective & adverb*. M16.
[from prec. + -ABLE, after *agreeable*.]
▶**A** *adjective*. †**1** = SUABLE. *rare*. Only in M16.
†**2** Of furniture, dress, features, etc.: agreeing in shape, colour, pattern, etc.; matching. (Foll. by *to*, *with*.) L16–E18.
†**3** Of actions, qualities, etc.: agreeing in nature, condition, or action; corresponding; analogous. (Foll. by *to*, *with*.) L16–M18.
4 That is fitted for or appropriate to a purpose, occasion, person's character, etc. (Foll. by *for*, *to*.) E17.

🕮 **4** I. MURDOCH George . . is scouting around for a suitable post. BEVERLEY CLEARY They could . . go to a movie if her parents could find one suitable. M. KEANE Her . . hat would have been as suitable for a race-meeting . . as for a funeral.

▶**B** *adverb*. Suitably. *arch*. L16.
■ **suita'bility** *noun* L17. **suitableness** *noun* (*a*) the quality or condition of being suitable; (*b*) (now *rare*) an example of this: L16. **suitably** *adverb* L16.

suitcase /ˈsuːtkeɪs, ˈsjuːt-/ *noun*. E20.
[from SUIT *noun* + CASE *noun*².]
A usu. oblong travelling case for carrying clothes etc., with a handle and a flat hinged lid.
live out of a suitcase: see LIVE *verb*.
■ **suitcaseful** *noun* as much as a suitcase will hold E20.

suite /swiːt/ *noun*. L17.
[French: see SUIT *noun*.]
1 A set of people in attendance; a retinue. L17.
2 A succession, a series; a set of things belonging together. E18.
3 *spec*. **a** A set of rooms in a hotel etc. for use by one person or group of people. E18. ▸**b** MUSIC. Orig., a set or series of lessons etc. Later, a set of instrumental compositions, in dance style, to be played in succession; a set of selected pieces from an opera, ballet, etc., arranged to be played as one instrumental work. M18. ▸**c** A set of furniture, esp. a sofa and armchairs, of the same design. E19. ▸**d** GEOLOGY. A group of associated minerals, rocks, or fossils, esp. from the same place; an associated sequence of strata etc. that is repeated at different localities. M19.
4 A sequel. *rare*. L18.

🕮 **1** J. REED The Minister-President . . strode out with his suite of officers. F. HERBERT The Padishah Emperor . . came . . into the audience chamber followed by his suite. **2** P. V. PRICE Although it is wise to have . . something finer for special occasions, suites of glasses are quite unnecessary. *Photography* This film is . . part of a suite of four. **3a** R. P. JHABVALA A suite in one of the more famous London hotels. S. J. LEONARDI Each Oxford man occupied a suite. **c** J. TROLLOPE The . . sitting room which Nicholas remembered for its three-piece suite. **d** ***ophiolite association suite***.

¶ See also EN SUITE, TOUT DE SUITE.

suitor /ˈsuːtə, ˈsjuːtə/ *noun & verb*. ME.
[Anglo-Norman *seutor*, *suitour*, *sut(i)er*, *-or* from Latin *secutor* follower (with assim. to *suite* SUIT *noun*), from *secut-* pa. ppl stem of *sequi*: see SUE, -OR.]
▶**A** *noun*. †**1** A frequenter *of* a place. *rare*. Only in ME.
†**2** A member of a retinue or suite; an adherent, a follower. LME–M19.
3 FEUDAL LAW. A person who owed suit (SUIT *noun* 1a) to a court and acted as an assessor. LME.
4 A person who sues or petitions. *arch*. LME.
5 A petitioner or plaintiff in a lawsuit. LME.
6 A man seeking to marry a particular woman; a wooer. L16. ▸**b** A prospective buyer of a business or corporation, a maker of a takeover bid. L20.

►**B** *verb trans. & intrans.* Court, be a suitor (of). Now *dial.* M17.

■ **suitorship** *noun* the state or condition of being a suitor L18. **suitress** *noun* (*rare*) a female suitor E18.

suity /ˈsuːti, ˈsjuːti/ *adjective. rare.* E17.
[from SUIT *noun, verb* + -Y¹.]
1 Appropriate, suitable. Long *obsolete* exc. *dial.* E17.
2 Of hounds: matching those of a pack. M19.

†**suivante** *noun.* L17–E19.
[French, fem. of pres. pple of *suivre* follow.]
A personal maid.

Suk /suːk/ *noun*¹ *& adjective.* E20.
[Local name.]
►**A** *noun.* Pl. same, **-s**.
1 A member of an E. African people inhabiting an area on the Uganda–Kenya border. E20.
2 The Nilotic language of the Suk. E20.
►**B** *attrib.* or as *adjective.* Of or pertaining to the Suk or their language. M20.

suk *noun*² var. of SOUK *noun*¹.

suke *noun & interjection* var. of SOOK *noun*² *& interjection.*

sukebind /ˈsuːkbʌɪnd, ˈsjuː-/ *noun.* M20.
[Invented by Stella Gibbons in her book *Cold Comfort Farm* (1932). Cf. BIND *noun* 2a, b.]
An imaginary plant associated with superstition, fertility, and intense rustic passions.

sukey /ˈsuːki/ *noun. dial. & colloq.* E19.
[Dim. of the female forename *Susan*, occurring in the second verse of the nursery rhyme 'Polly put the kettle on' (known from M19).]
A kettle.

sukh *noun* var. of SOUK *noun*¹.

sukiya /sʊˈkiːjə/ *noun.* E20.
[Japanese, lit. 'room of fantasy, room of refined taste'.]
1 A room in which the tea ceremony is held, a tea-house. E20.
2 ARCHITECTURE. A style of Japanese architecture inspired by a certain type of tea-house, characterized by functionality of design and the use of wood and other natural materials. Freq. *attrib.* M20.

sukiyaki /sʊkɪˈjaki, -ˈjɑːki/ *noun.* E20.
[Japanese.]
A Japanese dish consisting of thin slices of beef fried with vegetables in sugar, stock, and soy sauce.

Sukuma /sʊˈkuːmə, -ˈkjuː-/ *noun & adjective.* M20.
[Bantu.]
►**A** *noun.* Pl. same, **-s**, (earlier) **Wasukuma**.
1 A member of a Bantu-speaking people of west central Tanzania. M20.
2 The language of this people. M20.
►**B** *attrib.* or as *adjective.* Of or pertaining to the Sukuma or their language. M20.

sul /sʊl/ *preposition.* M19.
[Italian.]
MUSIC. On, over. Only in phrs.
sul PONTICELLO. *sul* TASTO.

sulcus /ˈsʌlkəs/ *noun.* Pl. **-ci** /-sʌɪ/. M17.
[Latin = furrow, trench, ditch, wrinkle.]
1 A groove made with an engraving tool; a trench, a hollow. *rare.* M17.
2 ANATOMY. A groove or furrow in a body, organ, or tissue, *esp.* one between two convolutions of the brain. M18.
2 *sulcus of* ROLANDO.

■ **sulcal** *adjective* of or pertaining to a sulcus L19. **sulcate** *adjective* [Latin *sulcatus*] BOTANY & ZOOLOGY marked with parallel grooves M18. **sulcated** *adjective* (BOTANY & ZOOLOGY) sulcate L17. **sulcato-** *combining form* [-O-] BOTANY & ZOOLOGY sulcate and —: M19. **sulciform** /ˈsʌlsɪfɔːm/ *adjective* (ANATOMY & ZOOLOGY) having the form of a sulcus E19. **sulculus** *noun*, pl. **-li**, BOTANY & ZOOLOGY a small groove M19.

sulf- *combining form*, **sulfa** *noun*, etc.: see SULPH- etc.

sulfhemoglobin *noun*, **sulfhydric** *adjective*, **sulfhydryl** *noun* see SULPHAEMOGLOBIN, SULPHYDRIC, SULPHYDRYL.

sulfide *noun & verb*, **sulfinic** *adjective*, **sulfur** *noun*, etc.: see SULPHIDE etc.

sulham /ˈsʊlhɑːm/ *noun.* L18.
[Moroccan Arab. *selhām*, prob. from Berber.]
An Arab hooded cloak.

sulindac /sʌˈlɪndak/ *noun.* L20.
[from SUL(PH- + IND(ENE + AC(ETIC.]
PHARMACOLOGY. A non-steroidal analgesic and anti-inflammatory drug used to treat arthritis and other musculoskeletal disorders.

suling /ˈsʊlɪŋ/ *noun.* OE.
[Prob. from a verb rel. to *sulh* SULLOW: see -ING¹.]
Hist. A measure of land in Kent corresponding to the hide and the carucate of other counties.

Suliote /ˈs(j)uːlɪəʊt/ *noun & adjective.* Also **-ot**, **Soul-**. E19.
[Greek *Souliōtēs*, from *Suli*: see below, -OTE.]
►**A** *noun.* A native or inhabitant of the Suli mountains in Epirus, of mixed Greek and Albanian origin. E19.
►**B** *adjective.* Of or pertaining to the Suliotes. E19.

sulk /sʌlk/ *verb & noun.* L18.
[Perh. back-form. from SULKY *adjective*².]
►**A** *verb intrans.* **1** Keep aloof from others in moody silence; indulge in sullen ill humour; be sulky. L18.
2 *transf. & fig.* Move or respond sluggishly or inadequately; (of a fish) remain in hiding and motionless when hooked; (of a fire) not burn properly. L19.
►**B** *noun.* **1** A fit of sulking; the action of sulking. L18.
2 In *pl.* A state of ill humour or resentment marked by obstinate silence or aloofness from company. Freq. in ***the sulks***, esp. ***in the sulks***. L18.

📖 **1** F. WELDON Miss Martin . . following the death of her father, was in a sulk. **2** R. SUTCLIFF His sulks were forgotten, and he looked almost gay.

■ **sulker** *noun* L19.

†**sulke** *adjective. rare.* Only in M17.
[Origin uncertain: perh. repr. the base of Old English *āseolcan* become sluggish.]
Hard to sell.
¶ Perh. the source of SULKY *adjective*².

sulky /ˈsʌlki/ *noun & adjective*¹. M18.
[from next.]
►**A** *noun.* A light two-wheeled horse-drawn vehicle for one person; now *esp.*, one used in harness-racing; *Austral.* any light horse-drawn vehicle. M18.
►**B** *attrib.* or as *adjective.* Designating agricultural implements with a seat for the driver. *US.* M19.

sulky /ˈsʌlki/ *adjective*². M18.
[Perh. from SULKE + -Y¹.]
1 Silently and obstinately ill-humoured; sullen, morose; (of actions, attributes, etc.) indicative of such a mood. M18.
2 (Of the weather etc.) gloomy, dismal; sluggish, slow to respond; (of an animal, esp. a fish) that sulks. E19.

📖 **1** K. A. PORTER A tall boy with . . a sulky mouth. R. WEST Madge had fallen into one of her sulky silences.

■ **sulkily** *adverb* L18. **sulkiness** *noun* M18.

sull /sʌl/ *verb intrans. US.* M19.
[Back-form. from SULLEN *adjective*.]
Of an animal: refuse to go on. Of a person: become sullen, sulk.

sulla /ˈsʌlə/ *noun.* L18.
[Spanish.]
The French honeysuckle, *Hedysarum coronarium*.

sullage /ˈsʌlɪdʒ/ *noun.* Also **-iage** /-ɪɪdʒ/. M16.
[Perh. from Anglo-Norman *suillage*, formed as SOIL *verb*¹: see -AGE. The form *sulliage* is infl. by SULLY *verb*.]
1 Filth, refuse, *esp.* that carried off by drains; sewage; *fig.* defilement, pollution. M16.
2 Silt washed down and deposited by a stream or flood. L17.

Sullan /ˈsʌlən/ *adjective & noun.* M19.
[from *Sulla* (see below) + -AN.]
ROMAN HISTORY. ►**A** *adjective.* Of or pertaining to the Roman general and dictator Sulla (*c* 138–78 BC) or his party, or the laws and political reforms instituted by him. M19.
►**B** *noun.* A follower or adherent of Sulla. M19.

sullen /ˈsʌlən/ *adjective, noun, & adverb.* LME.
[Anglo-Norman *sulein, solain, -ein*, from *sol* = Old French *soule* SOLE *adjective & adverb*.]
►**A** *adjective.* †**1** Single, sole. LME–L15. ►**b** Strange, unusual; unique. LME–L15.
†**2** Solitary, alone; spent or done in solitude; done in secret. LME–M16.
3 Averse to company, disinclined to be sociable; characterized by gloomy ill humour; morose, resentful; (of actions, attributes, etc.) indicative of such a mood. LME.
►**b** *transf.* Of animals and inanimate things: refractory, stubborn. L16. ►†**c** *fig.* Baleful, malignant. L17–E18.
†**4** Solemn, serious. L16–E18.
5 Of immaterial things: dismal, melancholy; *poet.* of a deep, dull, or mournful tone. L16.
6 Of a dull colour; of gloomy or dismal aspect. L16.
7 Of water etc.: flowing sluggishly. *poet.* E17.

📖 **3** J. WAINWRIGHT In the car . . there had been long, almost sullen silences. **5** C. KINGSLEY An afternoon of sullen Autumn rain. **6** TOLKIEN The fire faded to sullen embers.

►**B** *noun.* †**1** A solitary person; a sullen person. Only in LME.
2 In *pl.* & (*rare*) *sing.* A state of gloomy ill humour; sullenness, sulks; depression. Chiefly in ***the sullens***. *arch.* L16.
►**C** *adverb.* Sullenly. *rare.* E18.

■ **sullenly** *adverb* L16. **sullenness** /-n-n-/ *noun* LME.

sullen /ˈsʌlən/ *verb trans. rare.* E17.
[from prec.]
Make sullen or sluggish.

sulliage *noun* var. of SULLAGE.

Sullivan principles /ˈsʌlɪv(ə)n ˌprɪnsɪp(ə)lz/ *noun phr. pl.* L20.
[Leon H. *Sullivan* (1923–2001), US businessman and minister.]
A set of principles concerning the employment of personnel in South Africa by US companies, formulated to counter racial discrimination.

sullow /ˈsʌləʊ/ *noun.* Chiefly *dial.*
[Old English *sulh* ult. rel. to Latin *sulcus* furrow.]
A plough.

sully /ˈsʌli/ *verb & noun.* L16.
[Perh. from French *souiller* SOIL *verb*¹.]
►**A** *verb.* **1** *verb trans.* **a** Spoil the purity of; taint, defile; disgrace. L16. ►**b** Make dirty, soil; pollute. E17.
†**2** *verb intrans.* Become soiled or tarnished. L16–L17.

📖 **1** M. LANE The Burney name . . had been sullied by a scrape which sent . . Charles down from Oxford. **b** U. HOLDEN No ball games . . must sully the grass.

Phrases: **sullied white** dirty white.

►†**B** *noun.* An act of sullying or polluting something (*lit. & fig.*); a stain, a blemish. E17–M18.

sulph- /sʌlf/ *combining form.* Also (*US & CHEMISTRY*) **sulf-**.
[Alt. of SULPHO-, SULPHA- used before a vowel or *h*.]
1 CHEMISTRY. = SULPHO-.
2 PHARMACOLOGY. = SULPHA-.

■ **sulphamate** *noun* (CHEMISTRY) a salt or ester of sulphamic acid M19. **sulˈphamic** *adjective* (CHEMISTRY): ***sulphamic acid***, a strong crystalline acid, $HOSO_2NH_2$, used esp. in cleaning agents; a substituted organic derivative of this: M19. **sulphamide** *noun* (CHEMISTRY) the compound $SO_2(NH_2)_2$ M19. **sulphane** *noun* (CHEMISTRY) a hydride of sulphur M20. **sulphaˈnilamide** *noun* (PHARMACOLOGY) the amide, $C_6H_8N_2O_2S$, of sulphanilic acid, a bacteriostatic compound that is the parent compound of the sulphonamides; a substituted derivative of this compound: M20. **sulphaˈnilic** *adjective* (CHEMISTRY): ***sulphanilic acid***, a crystalline acid, $(H_2N)C_6H_4SO_3HOH$, used in making dyes and other chemicals: M19. **sulphˈarsenide** *noun* (MINERALOGY) a salt containing both sulphide and arsenide ions L19. **sulphiˈsoxazole** *noun* [ISO- + OX- + AZOLE] PHARMACOLOGY a sulphonamide, $C_{11}H_{13}N_3O_3S$, used in the treatment of urinary tract infections; also called ***sulphafurazole***: M20. **sulˈphonium** *noun* [-ONIUM] a hypothetical cation, H_3S^+; a compound in which one or more of the hydrogen atoms in this cation is replaced by an organic radical: L19. **sulˈphoxide** *noun* (CHEMISTRY) any organic compound containing the group ·SO· joined to two carbon atoms L19.

sulpha /ˈsʌlfə/ *noun.* Also ***sulfa**. M20.
[formed as next.]
PHARMACOLOGY. In full ***sulpha drug***. A drug derived from sulphanilamide.

sulpha- /ˈsʌlfə/ *combining form.* Also ***sulfa-** (see note below).
[Abbreviation of SULPHA(NILAMIDE.]
PHARMACOLOGY. Forming nouns denoting drugs derived from sulphanilamide.
¶ The form *sulfa-* is usual in the US, and is also used in certain internationally approved drug names.

■ **sulfaˈmerizine** *noun* a sulphonamide, $C_{11}H_{12}N_4O_2S$, now used mainly in Sulphatriad M20. **sulfaquiˈnoxaline** *noun* a sulphonamide derivative of quinoxaline that is used as a coccidiostat in the treatment of caecal coccidiosis in poultry M20. **sulphaˈdiazine** *noun* a sulphonamide, $C_{10}H_{10}N_4O_2S$, used to treat meningococcal meningitis M20. **sulphaˈdimidine** *noun* [DI-² + PYRI)MIDINE] a sulphonamide, $C_{12}H_{14}N_4O_2S$, used to treat urinary tract infections; (a proprietary name for the drug is SULPHAMEZATHINE): M20. **sulphaˈfurazole** *noun* [FURAN + AZOLE] = SULPHISOXAZOLE M20. **sulphaˈmethazine** *noun* [METH- + AZINE] = SULPHADIMIDINE M20. **sulphameˈthoxazole** *noun* [METH- + OX- + AZOLE] a sulphonamide, $C_{10}H_{11}N_3O_3S$, used to treat respiratory and urinary tract infections, and as a component of the preparation co-trimoxazole M20. **Sulphaˈmezathine** *noun* (proprietary name for) sulphadimidine (sulphamethazine) M20. **sulphaˈpyridine** *noun* a sulphonamide, $C_{11}H_{11}N_3O_2S$, used to treat some forms of dermatitis M20. **sulphaˈsalazine** *noun* [SAL(ICYL + AZINE] a sulphonamide, $C_{18}H_{14}N_4O_5S$, used to treat ulcerative colitis and Crohn's disease M20. **sulphaˈthiazole** *noun* a sulphonamide, $C_9H_9N_3O_2S_2$, used in the topical treatment of vaginal infections M20. **Sulphaˈtriad** *noun* (proprietary name for) a mixed sulphonamide drug containing sulphadiazine, sulfamerizine, and sulphathiazole, used to treat acute infections M20.

sulphaemoglobin /ˌsʌlfhiːməˈgləʊbɪn/ *noun.* Also ***sulfhemo-**. L19.
[from SULPH- + HAEMOGLOBIN.]
BIOCHEMISTRY & MEDICINE. A sulphur-containing compound produced by the reaction of haemoglobin with soluble sulphides or sulphides absorbed from the gut, and giving rise to the greenish discoloration found in putrefying cadavers.

■ **sulphaemoglobiˈnaemia** *noun* the presence of sulphaemoglobin in the blood, e.g. as a result of assimilation of the sulphur group from a sulphonamide drug E20.

sulphate /ˈsʌlfeɪt/ *noun & verb.* Also (*US & CHEMISTRY*) **sulf-**. L18.
[French *sulfate*, from Latin SULPHUR: see -ATE¹.]
►**A** *noun.* A salt or (more fully ***sulphate ester***) an ester of sulphuric acid. L18.
Comb.: **sulphate ion** the ion SO_4^{2-}; **sulphate process** a method of making a tough brown paper by digesting wood chips with sodium hydroxide and sodium sulphate to form the pulp; **sulphate-reducing** *adjective* (BIOLOGY) (of a process or micro-

organism) bringing about the reduction of sulphate ions to sulphur; *spec.* designating certain bacteria which do this as part of their respiratory metabolism.

▶ **B** *verb.* **1** *verb intrans.* Become combined with sulphur or sulphuric acid; acquire a coating of sulphates. Chiefly as ***sulphating*** *verbal noun.* **L19.**

2 *verb trans.* **a** Form a deposit of sulphates on. *rare.* **L19.** ▸**b** Add sulphate ions to; convert into a sulphate. **E20.**

■ **sulphatase** *noun* (BIOCHEMISTRY) an enzyme which catalyses the hydrolysis of sulphate esters **E20.** **sulphated** *adjective* combined with sulphur or sulphuric acid; containing sulphates; *spec.* (of a lead-acid battery) having a deposit of lead sulphate on its plates: **E19.** **sulphatide** *noun* (BIOCHEMISTRY) any lipid that is a sulphate ester of a cerebroside **L19.** **sul'phation** *noun* conversion into a sulphate; incorporation of a sulphate ion into a molecule: **E20.**

sulphazin /ˈsʌlfəzɪn/ *noun.* Also ***sulf-**. **L20.**
[Russian *sul'fazin.*]
A suspension of sulphur in peach oil administered under the former Soviet authorities to induce fever.

sulphide /ˈsʌlfʌɪd/ *noun & verb.* Also (US & CHEMISTRY) **sulf-**. **M19.**
[from SULPHUR + -IDE.]
▶ **A** *noun.* **1** A compound of sulphur with one other element; *spec.* = THIO-ETHER. **M19.**
2 A cameo embedded in clear glass. **M20.**
▶ **B** *verb trans.* Convert into or impregnate with a sulphide. **M20.**
■ **sulphi'dation** *noun* impregnation with a sulphide **E20.** **sulphidic** /-ˈfɪdɪk/ *adjective* (CHEMISTRY) of or containing sulphides **E20.**

sulphinic /sʌlˈfɪnɪk/ *adjective.* Also (US & CHEMISTRY) **sulf-**. **L19.**
[from SULPH- + -INE[5] + -IC.]
sulphinic acid, any acid containing the group $\cdot SO_2H$.
■ **'sulphinate** *noun* a salt or ester of sulphinic acid **L19.** **'sulphinyl** *noun* the thionyl group, esp. in an organic compound **E20.**

sulphinpyrazone /sʌlfɪnˈpɪrəzəʊn/ *noun.* Also ***sulf-**. **M20.**
[from SULPHINIC + PYRAZ(OLE + -ONE.]
PHARMACOLOGY. A drug, $C_{23}H_{20}N_2O_3S$, which promotes the excretion of urates and is used to treat chronic gout.

sulphite /ˈsʌlfʌɪt/ *noun.* Also (US & CHEMISTRY) **sulf-**. **L18.**
[French *sulfite* arbitrary alt. of *sulfate* sulphate: see -ITE[1].]
A salt or ester of sulphurous acid.

sulpho- /ˈsʌlfəʊ/ *combining form.* Also (US & CHEMISTRY) **sulfo-**.
[from SULPHUR: see -O-.]
Sulphur; *spec.* (CHEMISTRY) forming nouns denoting compounds that contain sulphur, esp. as the sulphonyl group or in place of oxygen etc. (in this latter sense now superseded extensively by THIO-).
■ **sulpho-acid** *noun* (CHEMISTRY) an acid containing (esp. hexavalent) sulphur; *esp.* sulphonic acid: **M19.** **sulphobromo'phthalein** *noun* (PHARMACOLOGY) a dye derived from phenolphthalein, used in testing liver function **M20.** **sulpho'cyanate** *noun* (CHEMISTRY) = THIOCYANATE **M19.** **sulphocy'anic** *adjective* (CHEMISTRY) = THIOCYANIC **E19.** **sulpholipid** *noun* (BIOCHEMISTRY) a lipid whose structures terminate with a sulphonic acid group **M20.** **sulphosalt** *noun* orig. (CHEMISTRY), a salt of a sulpho-acid; now (MINERALOGY), any of a group of mostly rare minerals containing sulphur or selenium and two (or more) metallic elements: **M19.**

sulphonal /ˈsʌlfənal/ *noun.* Also ***sulf-**. **L19.**
[from SULPHONE + -AL[2].]
PHARMACOLOGY. A sulphonated derivative of methane, $(C_2H_5SO_2)_2CH(CH_3)_2$, formerly used as a hypnotic.

sulphonamide /sʌlˈfɒnəmʌɪd/ *noun.* Also (US & CHEMISTRY) **sulf-**. **L19.**
[from SULPHONE + AMIDE.]
CHEMISTRY & PHARMACOLOGY. An organic amide of a sulphonic acid, characterized by the group $\cdot SO_2N=$; *spec.* any of the drugs derived from sulphanilamide.

sulphonate /ˈsʌlfəneɪt/ *noun.* Also (US & CHEMISTRY) **sulf-**. **L19.**
[from SULPHONIC + -ATE[1].]
A salt or ester of sulphonic acid.

sulphonate /ˈsʌlf(ə)neɪt/ *verb trans.* Also (US & CHEMISTRY) **sulf-**. **L19.**
[from prec.: see -ATE[3].]
Convert into a sulphonate, e.g. by the action of sulphuric acid; introduce a sulphonic acid group into (a compound or molecule).
■ **sulpho'nation** *noun* **L19.**

sulphone /ˈsʌlfəʊn/ *noun.* Also (US & CHEMISTRY) **sulf-**. **L19.**
[German *Sulfon*, from *Sulfur* sulphur: see -ONE.]
Any chemical compound containing the group $\cdot SO_2\cdot$ joined to two hydrocarbon radicals.
■ **'sulphonyl** *noun* the divalent radical $\cdot SO_2\cdot$, derived from the sulphonic acid group **E20.** **sulphonylate** *verb trans.* introduce a sulphonyl group into **L20.** **sulphony'lation** *noun* conversion into a sulphonyl **M20.** ˌ**sulphonylu'rea** *noun* any of a group of compounds containing the group $\cdot SO_2NHCONH\cdot$, some of which are hypoglycaemic drugs used to treat diabetes **M20.**

sulphonic /sʌlˈfɒnɪk/ *adjective.* Also (US & CHEMISTRY) **sulf-**. **L19.**
[formed as prec. + -IC.]
sulphonic acid, any organic acid containing the group $\cdot SO_2OH$.

sulphur /ˈsʌlfə/ *noun & verb.* Also (US & CHEMISTRY) **sulfur**. **ME.**
[Anglo-Norman *sulf(e)re*, Old French *soufre* from Latin *sulfur*, *-phur*, *-pur*, perh. rel. to the Germanic word repr. by Old English *swef(e)l*.]
▶ **A** *noun.* **1 a** A pale yellow non-metallic chemical element, atomic no. 16, which occurs in crystalline and amorphous forms and in minerals as sulphides and sulphates, and was formerly believed to be present in hell-fire and lightning. Cf. BRIMSTONE 1. (Symbol S.) **ME.** ▸**b** ALCHEMY. One of the elementary principles of which all substances were supposed to be compounded. **LME.**
†**2** A compound of sulphur, *esp.* a sulphide. **L15–M19.**
†**3** Thunder, lightning; a discharge of gunpowder. Only in **E17.**
4 †**a** In *pl.* Deposits of native sulphur. **L17–L18.** ▸**b** A mineral containing or supposed to contain sulphur. **L18.**
5 An impression of a seal etc. taken in a mixture of sulphur and wax. **E19.**
6 Any of numerous yellow butterflies of the family Pieridae. Also ***sulphur butterfly***. **M19.**
7 Pungent language. *colloq.* **L19.**
8 A pale greenish-yellow colour. **E20.**
Phrases: **flowers of sulphur** amorphous sulphur in a fine powder, obtained by sublimation and used as a fungicide and insecticide. ***liver of sulphur***: see LIVER *noun*[1]. ***milk of sulphur***: see MILK *noun*. ***vegetable sulphur***: see VEGETABLE *adjective & noun*.
Comb.: †**sulphur acid** a sulphide of an electronegative metal such as arsenic; **sulphur bacterium** BIOLOGY: which derives its energy from the oxidation of sulphur or inorganic compounds of sulphur; **sulphur bath** †(*a*) a sulphur spring; (*b*) a bath to which flowers of sulphur have been added, formerly used to treat skin diseases; **sulphur-bottom (whale)** = ***blue whale*** s.v. BLUE *adjective*; ***sulphur butterfly***: see sense 6 above; **sulphur candle**: burnt to produce sulphur dioxide for fumigation; **sulphur-crested cockatoo** a white cockatoo with a yellow crest, *Cacatua galerita*, native to Australia; **sulphur cycle** ECOLOGY the cycle of changes whereby sulphur compounds are interconverted between sulphates and hydrogen sulphide in the air and sulphates, sulphides, and sulphur in organisms and the soil; **sulphur dioxide** a colourless pungent gas formed by burning sulphur in air and used as a food preservative; **sulphur match** *Hist.* a match tipped with sulphur; **sulphur print** METALLURGY a print on photographic bromide paper showing the distribution of sulphides in a steel surface with which it has been placed in contact; **sulphur shower** (the occurrence of) a deposit of yellow pollen in a pine forest; **sulphur spring** a spring whose water contains sulphur or sulphurous gases; **sulphur-tree** a hardwooded tree, *Morinda lucida*, found in west central Africa and used for building purposes; **sulphur tuft** a toadstool, *Hypholoma fasciculare*, with a yellow cap tinged with brown; **sulphur vivum** /ˈvʌɪvəm/ [Latin, neut. of *vivus* living] native or virgin sulphur; sulphur in a fused, partly purified form. **sulphurweed**, **sulphurwort** the plant hog's fennel, *Peucedanum officinale*, the resinous juice of whose root has a sulphurous smell; **sulphur-yellow** *noun & adjective* (of) the pale yellow colour characteristic of sulphur.
▶ **B** *verb trans.* Treat with sulphur; *esp.* fumigate with burning sulphur to bleach, disinfect, etc.; sprinkle (a plant) with flowers of sulphur; put (wine) into casks that have been fumigated with sulphur. **L16.**
■ **sulphured** *adjective* (*a*) full of sulphur; sulphurous; (*b*) that has been treated with sulphur: **E17.**

sulphurate /ˈsʌlfjʊreɪt/ *verb trans.* Also (US & CHEMISTRY) **sulf-**. **E17.**
[Orig. as pa. ppl adjective *sulphurated*, from Latin *sulphuratus*, formed as SULPHUR: see -ED[1].]
†**1** As ***sulphurated*** *ppl adjective.* Pertaining to brimstone or hell; satanic. Only in **E17.**
2 = SULPHURIZE. Chiefly as ***sulphurated*** *ppl adjective.* **M18.**
■ **sulphu'ration** *noun* (now *rare*) †(*a*) an act of anointing with sulphur; (*b*) the action of sulphurating something: **E18.** **sulphurator** *noun* an apparatus for sulphurating plants **M19.**

sulphureo- /sʌlˈfjʊərɪəʊ/ *combining form.* Also (US & CHEMISTRY) **sulf-**. **L17.**
[from Latin *sulphureus*: see next, -O-.]
Sulphureous and —.

sulphureous /sʌlˈfjʊərɪəs/ *adjective.* Also (US & CHEMISTRY) **sulf-**. **E16.**
[from Latin *sulphureus*, from *sulphur*: see SULPHUR, -EOUS.]
1 = SULPHUROUS 1. **E16.**
2 = SULPHUROUS 2. **M16.**
3 = SULPHUROUS 3. **M17.**
4 = SULPHUROUS 5. Also, of the bluish colour of the flame with which sulphur burns. **M17.**
†**5** CHEMISTRY. = SULPHUROUS 4. **E18–E19.**
■ **sulphureously** *adverb* **E20.** **sulphureousness** *noun* **L17.**

sulphuret /ˈsʌlfjʊret/ *noun. arch.* Also ***sulf-**. **L18.**
[from SULPHUR + -URET.]
CHEMISTRY. A sulphide.
■ **sulphuretted** *adjective* chemically combined with sulphur; containing dissolved sulphur; ***sulphuretted hydrogen***, the gas hydrogen sulphide: **E19.**

sulphuretum /sʌlfəˈriːtəm/ *noun.* Also ***sulf-**. Pl. **-ta** /-tə/. **E20.**
[from SULPHUR + -ETUM.]
ECOLOGY. An ecological community of organisms (mainly sulphur bacteria) which metabolizes sulphur compounds in a subcycle of the larger environmental sulphur cycle.

sulphuric /sʌlˈfjʊərɪk/ *adjective.* Also (US & CHEMISTRY) **sulf-**. **L18.**
[French *sulfurique*, from Latin SULPHUR: see -IC.]
1 ***sulphuric acid***, a highly corrosive dense oily acid, H_2SO_4, that is a strong protonating and oxidizing agent and is much used in the chemical industry, usu. in aqueous solution. **L18.** ▸**b** Of, pertaining to, or derived from sulphuric acid. **E19.**
†**2** Consisting of or containing sulphur. *rare.* **L18–E19.**
1 anhydrous sulphuric acid sulphur trioxide. **fuming sulphuric acid** a solution of sulphur trioxide in sulphuric acid. **German sulphuric acid** = ***fuming sulphuric acid*** above.

†**sulphurious** *adjective.* **L15–E18.**
[from Old French *sulphurieux*, from Latin SULPHUR + *-ieux* -IOUS.]
= SULPHUREOUS, SULPHUROUS.

sulphurise *verb* var. of SULPHURIZE.

sulphurity /sʌlˈfjʊərɪti/ *noun. rare.* Also ***sulf-**. **M17.**
[from SULPHUR + -ITY.]
The condition of being sulphurous.

sulphurize /ˈsʌlfjʊrʌɪz/ *verb trans.* Also **-ise**, (US & CHEMISTRY) **sulf-**. **L18.**
[French *sulfuriser*, from Latin SULPHUR: see -IZE.]
1 Cause to combine chemically with sulphur. **L18.**
2 Treat or dress with sulphur; vulcanize (rubber). **M19.**
3 Fumigate with burning sulphur. **M19.**
■ **sulphuri'zation** *noun* **L19.**

sulphurous /ˈsʌlf(ə)rəs/, *in Chemistry* sʌlˈfjʊərəs/ *adjective.* Also (US & CHEMISTRY) **sulf-**. **LME.**
[from Latin *sulphurosus* or from SULPHUR: see -OUS.]
1 Of or pertaining to sulphur; containing or consisting of sulphur. **LME.**
2 Produced by or emanating from sulphur; (esp. of smoke, smells, etc.) suggestive of burning sulphur. **E17.** ▸**b** Of thunder or lightning (*poet.*); thundery, sultry. **E17.**
3 Of hell; pertaining to or dealing with hell-fire. **E17.** ▸**b** *fig.* Ardent, fiery; heated; blasphemous, profane. **E17.**
4 CHEMISTRY. Designating compounds in which sulphur is present in a larger proportion than in sulphuric compounds; containing tetravalent sulphur; derived from sulphurous acid. **L18.**
5 Of the yellow colour of sulphur. **M19.**

📖 **2b** *She* The river . . lay still under a sulphurous sky. **3** SOUTHEY Like Satan rising from the sulphurous flood. **b** *Listener* Relations between the South Vietnamese and the US were sulphurous. **4 sulphurous acid** a weak acid with the notional formula H_2SO_3, known only in solution and as salts (sulphites). **sulphurous anhydride**, **sulphurous oxide** = ***sulphur dioxide*** s.v. SULPHUR *noun*.

■ **sulphurously** *adverb* **L19.** **sulphurousness** *noun* **L17.**

sulphury /ˈsʌlfəri/ *adjective.* Also (US & CHEMISTRY) **sulf-**. **LME.**
[from SULPHUR + -Y[1].]
= SULPHUROUS.

sulphuryl /ˈsʌlfjʊrʌɪl, -rɪl/ *noun.* Also (US & CHEMISTRY) **sulf-**. **M19.**
[from SULPHUR + -YL.]
The divalent radical $:SO_2$. Usu. in *comb.*

sulphydric /sʌlfˈ(h)ʌɪdrɪk/ *adjective.* Now *rare* or *obsolete.* Also ***sulfhy-**. **M19.**
[from SULPH- + HYDRIC *adjective*[1].]
CHEMISTRY. ***sulphydric acid***, = HYDROGEN **sulphide** (a).
■ **sulphydrate** *noun* = HYDROSULPHIDE **M19.**

sulphydryl /sʌlfˈ(h)ʌɪdrʌɪl, -rɪl/ *noun.* Also (US & CHEMISTRY) **sulfhy-**. **E20.**
[from prec. + -YL.]
= THIOL 1. Usu. in *comb.*

Sulpician /sʌlˈpɪʃɪən, -ʃ(ə)n/ *noun & adjective.* **L18.**
[French *sulpicien*, from *Sulpice*: see below, -IAN.]
ECCLESIASTICAL. ▶**A** *noun.* A member of a congregation of secular priests founded in 1642 by a priest of St Sulpice, Paris, mainly for the training of candidates for holy orders. **L18.**
▶ **B** *adjective.* Of, pertaining to, or belonging to this congregation. **L19.**

sulpiride /ˈsʌlpɪrʌɪd/ *noun.* **L20.**
[French, prob. from *sul(f-* SULPH- + *pir* alt. of PYR(O- + -IDE.]
PHARMACOLOGY. An anti-emetic and neuroleptic drug used to treat some psychiatric conditions.

sultan /ˈsʌlt(ə)n/ *noun.* **M16.**
[French, or medieval Latin *sultanus*, from Arab. *sulṭān* power, ruler.]
1 The monarch or chief ruler of a Muslim country; *spec.* (*Hist.*, **S-**) that of Turkey. Formerly also, a prince, a high official. Cf. SOLDAN. **M16.** ▸**b** An absolute ruler; a despot, a tyrant. **M17.**

2 Orig. more fully ***sultan's flower***. A plant of the Near East, *Centaurea moschata*, which is grown for its sweet-scented purple, pink, white, or yellow flowers. Now usu. ***sweet sultan***. M17.

3 A small white-crested variety of domestic fowl, originally brought from Turkey. M19.

Comb.: **sultan pink**, **sultan red** a rich dull pink or red; ***sultan's flower***: see sense 2 above.

■ **sultanate** *noun* a country subject to a sultan; the period of rule of a sultan or sultans; the position or office of sultan: E19. **sulta'nesque** *adjective* characteristic of a sultan M19. **sulta'ness** *noun* (now *rare*) = SULTANA 1 E17. **sul'tanic** *adjective* of, belonging to, or characteristic of a sultan; despotic, tyrannical: E19. **sultanism** *noun* rule like that of a sultan; absolute government; despotism, tyranny: E19. **sultanry** *noun* (*rare*) the position or office of sultan E17. **sultanship** *noun* (*a*) *rare* the position or office of sultan; (*b*) (with possess. adjective, as ***your sultanship*** etc.) a mock title of respect given to a despot or tyrant: E17. †**sultany** *noun* [Arab. *sulṭānī* (adjective) imperial, (noun) sultanate] (*a*) = SULTANIN; (*b*) = SULTANATE: E17–M19.

sultana /sʌl'tɑːnə, *in sense 5 also* s(ə)l-/ *noun*. L16.
[Italian, fem. of *sultano* sultan.]
1 A wife or concubine of a sultan; the queen mother or any other woman of a sultan's family. L16.
2 A mistress, a concubine. E18.
3 A Turkish warship. *obsolete* exc. *Hist.* E18.
4 Any of various gallinules, *esp.* the purple gallinule. Now *rare*. M19.
5 A kind of small seedless raisin used in puddings, cakes, etc. Also ***sultana raisin***. M19.
6 The plant busy Lizzie, *Impatiens walleriana*. M20.
Comb.: **sultana grape** the white seedless grape from which sultanas are made; **sultana mother** the mother of a reigning sultan; **sultana queen** the favourite concubine of a sultan; a favourite mistress; ***sultana raisin***: see sense 5 above.

†**sultane** *noun*. E17.
[French, fem. of *sultan* SULTAN.]
1 = SULTANIN. E17–E18.
2 = SULTANA 1. M–L17.
3 A rich gown trimmed with buttons and loops, fashionable in the late 17th and the 18th cents. L17–L19.
4 = SULTANA 3. L17–E18.

†**sultanin** *noun*. E17–M18.
[Italian *sultanino* or French *sultanin* from Arab. *sulṭānī* SULTANY.]
A former Turkish gold coin.

sultanize /'sʌlt(ə)naɪz/ *verb*. *rare*. Also **-ise**. L18.
[from SULTAN + -IZE.]
1 *verb intrans.* Rule as a sultan or despot. L18.
2 *verb trans.* Make sultan-like or despotic. E19.

†**sulter** *verb intrans.* L16–L17.
[Perh. rel. to SWELTER.]
Swelter.

sultry /'sʌltri/ *adjective*. L16.
[from prec.: see -Y¹.]
1 Of weather, the air, etc.: oppressively hot and humid; (of places, seasons of the year, etc.) characterized by such weather. L16. ▸**b** Of the sun etc.: producing oppressive heat. *poet.* L17.
2 Associated with oppressive heat; hot with toil; hot with anger or lust. Chiefly *poet.* M17.
3 Titillating, salacious; erotic, sensual; lascivious; (of language) profane, coarse. *colloq.* L19.
4 Of a situation: uncomfortable, dangerous. *colloq.* L19.

> 📖 **1** N. MONSARRAT The streets were sultry and airless under the encroaching sun. P. LIVELY It turned hot. A sullen . . July gave way to sultry August. **3** *L.A. Style* A full line of sultry stretch dresses. **4** CONAN DOYLE I shall make it pretty sultry for you . . at Woking.

■ **sultrily** *adverb* M19. **sultriness** *noun* the quality or condition of being sultry; sultry heat: M17.

Sulu /'suːluː/ *noun*¹ & *adjective*. E19.
[Samal *suluh* current.]
▶ **A** *noun*. Pl. same.
1 A member of either of the Muslim peoples inhabiting the Sulu archipelago in the Philippines; a Sama or Tau Sug. E19.
2 The language of either of these peoples. L19.
▶ **B** *adjective*. Of or pertaining to either of these peoples or their language. E20.

sulu /'suːluː/ *noun*². M19.
[Fijian.]
In Fiji: a length of cotton or other light fabric wrapped about the body as a sarong; a type of sarong worn from the waist by men and full-length by women; a similar fashion garment worn by women.

sum /sʌm/ *noun*. ME.
[Old French *summe*, (also mod.) *somme* from Latin *summa* main thing, substance, sum total, use as noun (sc. *res* thing, *pars* part) of fem. of *summus* highest. Cf. SUMMIT.]
1 A quantity of money (or precious metal etc.); a quantity of money *of* a specified amount. ME. ▸†**b** A quantity *of* goods regarded as worth so much. LME–L19. ▸†**c** A number or body *of* people; a host, a band. LME–E17.
2 a The ultimate end or goal; the highest attainable point. *arch.* ME. ▸†**b** A conclusion, an upshot. LME–L17.
†**3 a** A treatise, a manual; = SUMMA 3. ME–M18. ▸**b** The gist of something; a summary. LME–M19.
4 a The totality or aggregate of something immaterial. ME. ▸**b** A total number of enumerable things, *obsolete* exc. as passing into sense 5. LME.
5 A quantity resulting from the addition of two or more quantities. Formerly also, a result of multiplication, a product. Also = ***logical sum*** s.v. LOGICAL *adjective*. LME. ▸**b** A series of numbers to be added up. L16. ▸**c** An arithmetical problem in the solution of which some particular rule is applied; such a problem worked out; in *pl.* (*colloq.*) arithmetic, esp. as a school subject; numerical calculations. E19.
†**6** A number; an integer. LME–E18.

> 📖 **1** M. BEERBOHM They . . hope to raise the sum of £500. F. KING He pressed on me a sum far in excess of what I had spent. S. ROSENBERG His statues of Lenin . . and other great ones brought in large sums of money. **4a** LD MACAULAY Public events had produced an immense sum of misery. **b** GOLDSMITH The sum of my miseries is made up. **5b** SYD. SMITH An expert arithmetician adds up the longest sum with . . unerring precision. **c** DICKENS Sums in simple interest. *Evening Post (Nottingham)* Was the Board wrong to raise people's hopes before they had 'done their sums'?

Phrases: ***capital sum***: see CAPITAL *adjective* & *noun*². **gross sum** (now *rare* or *obsolete*) an overall total. **in sum** (*a*) (expressed) in a few words, briefly (now *rare*); in brief, in short, to sum up; †(*b*) all together, as a whole. ***logical sum***: see LOGICAL *adjective*. ***lump sum***: see LUMP *noun*¹. ***partial sum***: see PARTIAL *adjective*. **sum and substance** the essence of a thing; the gist of a matter. **the sum of things** [Latin *summa rerum*: see SUMMA *noun*] (*a*) the highest public interest, the public good; (*b*) the totality of being, the universe. **total sum**, **whole sum** = SUM TOTAL.

Comb.: **sum check** COMPUTING a check on the accuracy of a group of digits, in which they are added or otherwise manipulated and the result compared with a previously computed figure (which may accompany the group as a check digit or checksum).

sum /sʌm/ *verb*. Infl. **-mm-**. ME.
[Old & mod. French *sommer* or medieval Latin *summare* add, reckon up, from Latin *summa* SUM *noun*.]
1 a *verb trans.* Find the sum of, add. Also foll. by *up*. ME. ▸**b** *verb intrans.* & †*trans.* in *pass.* Amount *to*. LME. ▸**c** *verb trans.* Count; reckon *up*. L16. ▸**d** *verb intrans.* Do sums in arithmetic. E19.
†**2** *verb trans.* Bring to completion or perfection; consummate. Also foll. by *up*. L16–M17.
3 *verb trans.* Collect into or embrace in a small compass. Also foll. by *up*. Usu. in *pass.* E17.
4 *verb trans.* Give the substance of in a few words; summarize; (of a statement, principle, condition, etc.) express the essential features of, epitomize. Usu. foll. by *up*. E17.

> 📖 **1a** *Nature* He summed data of six previous studies. **3** LEIGH HUNT In that last blow his strength must have been summ'd. **4** C. BARKER From these fragments we may . . sum up . . Benedictine life.

With adverbs in specialized senses: **sum up** (*a*) *verb phr. trans.* & *intrans.* (LAW) (of a judge in a trial, or of counsel concluding his or her case) recapitulate (the evidence) to the jury before they retire to consider their verdict, giving an exposition of points of law when necessary; (*b*) *verb phr. trans.* form an estimate of the character of (a person); summarize the qualities of (a person); (see also senses above).

■ **summa'bility** *noun* the property of being summable E20. **summable** *adjective* M17.

sumac /'s(j)uːmak, 'ʃuː-/ *noun* & *verb*. Also **-ch**. ME.
[Old & mod. French, or medieval Latin *sumac(h)*, from Arab. *summāḳ*.]
▶ **A** *noun*. **1** A preparation of the dried and chopped leaves and shoots of plants of the genus *Rhus* (see sense 2), used in tanning and dyeing, and formerly as an astringent. ME.
2 Any of various shrubs and small trees of the genus *Rhus* (family Anacardiaceae); *spec.* the southern European *R. coriaria*, the chief source of the material used in tanning (see sense 1). M16.
Phrases: ***poison sumac***: see POISON *noun*, *adjective*, & *adverb*. ***stag-horn sumac***: see STAG-HORN 2a. ***varnish sumac***: see VARNISH *noun*. ***velvet sumac***: see VELVET *noun* & *adjective*. ***Venetian sumac***: see VENETIAN *adjective*.
▶ **B** *verb trans.* Tan with sumac. M19.

Sumatra /sʊ'mɑːtrə/ *noun* & *adjective*. E18.
[See sense B. below.]
▶ **A** *noun*. **1** (Also **s-**.) A violent squall in the Straits of Malacca and the Malay peninsula, blowing from the direction of Sumatra. E18.
2 A variety of tobacco plant yielding a light-coloured leaf. E20.
▶ **B** *adjective*. Designating things found in or obtained from Sumatra, a large island of the Malay archipelago that is now part of Indonesia. E19.

Sumatran /sʊ'mɑːtrən/ *adjective* & *noun*. E17.
[from *Sumatra* (see prec.) + -AN.]
▶ **A** *noun*. A native or inhabitant of Sumatra; the Sumatran language. E17.
▶ **B** *adjective*. Of or pertaining to Sumatra, its inhabitants, or their language; indigenous to Sumatra. L18.
Sumatran hare, **Sumatran rabbit** a striped short-eared rabbit, *Nesolagus netscheri*, of Sumatran forests. **Sumatran rhinoceros** a hairy rhinoceros, *Dicerorhinus sumatrensis*, of the forests of Sumatra and adjacent islands.

sumbitch /'sʌmbɪtʃ/ *noun*. *US slang*. L20.
[Contr.]
= ***son of a bitch*** s.v. SON *noun*¹.

sumbul /'sʌmbʌl, 'sʊmbʊl/ *noun*. L18.
[French from Arab. *sunbul*.]
The dried root of any of certain plants used or formerly used medicinally, esp. spikenard, *Nardostachys grandiflora*, and a kind of giant fennel, *Ferula sumbul*.

sumen /'s(j)uːmɛn/ *noun*. Now *rare* or *obsolete*. LME.
[Latin, from *sugere* suck.]
Orig. (ANATOMY), the hypogastrium; *transf.* the fat or rich portion of something. Later, a sow's udder.

Sumerian /sʊ'mɪərɪən, sjuː-/ *adjective* & *noun*. L19.
[French *sumérien*, from *Sumer*: see below, -IAN.]
▶ **A** *adjective*. Of or pertaining to Sumer, a district in SE Mesopotamia (present-day southern Iraq) which with Akkad formed Babylonia; designating the Sumerians or their language. L19.
▶ **B** *noun*. **1** The language of the non-Semitic inhabitants of Sumer in the third millennium BC, known from cuneiform inscriptions and now the oldest known written language. L19.
2 A non-Semitic native or inhabitant of Sumer. L19.
■ **Sumero-** *combining form* [-O-] Sumerian; Sumerian and —: L19. **Sumerogram** *noun* a character or group of characters representing a Sumerian word, used in written Hittite (Akkadian etc.) as a substitute for the equivalent (longer) word in that language M20. **Sume'rologist** *noun* an expert in or student of Sumerology M20. **Sume'rology** *noun* the branch of knowledge that deals with the Sumerian language and antiquities L19.

sumi /'suːmi/ *noun*. E20.
[Japanese = ink, blacking.]
A carbon-based pigment used for painting and writing.
Comb.: **sumi-e** /'suːmɪeɪ/ [*e* painting] Japanese ink painting; *collect.* sumi pictures.

sumi-gaeshi /ˌsuːmɪgaɪ'ɛʃi, ˌsuːmɪgə'eɪʃi/ *noun*. M20.
[Japanese, lit. 'corner throw', from *sumi* corner + *kaeshi* overturning.]
JUDO. A move in which a person falls to the mat and throws his or her opponent over the left shoulder.

sumless /'sʌmlɪs/ *adjective*. Chiefly *poet.* L16.
[from SUM *noun* or *verb* + -LESS.]
Without number, uncountable; incalculable.

summa /'sʊmə, 'sʌmə/ *noun* & *adverb*. LME.
[Latin: see SUM *noun*.]
▶ **A** *noun*. Pl. **-mmae** /-miː/, †**-mma(e)s**.
†**1** A sum total. LME–L18.
†**2** The quantity or number *of* something. L15–E16.
3 A treatise, a manual; a compendium of knowledge; = SUM *noun* 3a. E18.
4 A degree *summa cum laude*. L20.
Phrases: ***summa totalis*** /təʊ'tɑːlɪs, təʊ'teɪlɪs/ a sum total (cf. sense 1 above). ***summa summarum*** /sʊ'mɑːrəm, sʌ'mɛːrəm/ the grand total; *fig.* the ultimate result. ***summa rerum*** /'rɛːrəm, 'rɪərəm/ = ***the sum of things*** (a) s.v. SUM *noun*.
▶ **B** *adverb*. In sum, in short. Long *rare*. M16.

summa bona *noun phr.* pl. of SUMMUM BONUM.

summa cum laude /sʌmə kʌm 'lɔːdiː, sʊmə kʊm 'laʊdeɪ/ *adverbial* & *adjectival phr.* Chiefly *N. Amer.* L19.
[Latin, lit. 'with the highest praise'.]
With or of highest distinction; *spec.* (of a degree, diploma, etc.) of the highest standard. Cf. CUM *laude*, MAGNA CUM LAUDE.

summae *noun pl.* see SUMMA.

summage /'sʌmɪdʒ/ *noun*. Long *obsolete* exc. *Hist.* LME.
[medieval Latin *summagium* from Old French *somage*, from late Latin *sagma*: see SUMMER *noun*², -AGE.]
A toll payable for carriage on horseback.

summa genera *noun phr.* pl. of SUMMUM GENUS.

summand /'sʌmand/ *noun*. M19.
[medieval Latin *summandus* (sc. *numerus*) gerundive of *summare* SUM *verb*: see -AND.]
MATH. A quantity to be added to another.

summar /'sʌmə/ *adjective*. *Scot.* Chiefly LAW. M16.
[French *sommaire*, with assim. to its source, Latin *summarius*: see SUMMARY *adjective*.]
= SUMMARY *adjective*.
■ †**summarly** *adverb* summarily M16–E18.

summarily /'sʌm(ə)rɪli/ *adverb*. E16.
[from SUMMARY *adjective* + -LY².]
1 In few words, compendiously, briefly. E16. ▸†**b** *ellipt.* To put it shortly, in sum. L16–M17.
2 By summary legal procedure. M16.
3 Without formality or delay; without hesitation. E17.

summarize /ˈsʌməraɪz/ *verb trans.* Also **-ise**. L19.
[from next + -IZE.]
Make or be a summary of; sum up; state succinctly.
■ **summarizable** *adjective* L20. **summariˈzation** *noun* the action or process of summarizing something; a summary: M19. **summarizer** *noun* L19.

summary /ˈsʌm(ə)ri/ *noun*. E16.
[Latin *summarium*, from *summa*: see SUM *noun*, -ARY¹.]
A summary account or statement; an abridgement.

📖 J. T. STORY I had . . given him a summary of what I had discovered.

Comb.: **summary punch** a card punch that automatically punches the results obtained by a tabulator from a number of other cards.
■ **summarist** *noun* a person who compiles a summary L19.

summary /ˈsʌm(ə)ri/ *adjective*. LME.
[medieval Latin *summarius*, formed as prec.]
1 Containing the chief points of a matter; dispensing with unnecessary detail; compendious. Also, characterized by conciseness and brevity. LME. ▸†**b** General, not detailed. E16–E18. ▸**c** *LAW*. Of legal proceedings: carried out rapidly by the omission of certain formalities. Opp. ***plenary***. (Earlier in SUMMARILY 2.) M18.
†**2** Consisting of or relating to addition or a sum. *rare*. L16–E19.
†**3** Highest; supreme. *rare*. L16–M18.
4 Performed or effected by a short method; done without delay. (Earlier in SUMMARILY 3.) E18.

📖 **1** *British Journal of Sociology* I will merely outline my position . . in the most summary of fashions. **c** ***summary conviction***: see CONVICTION 1. **summary jurisdiction** authority to use summary proceedings, *spec.* that of a judge or magistrate to try a case without a jury. **summary offence** an offence that can only be tried summarily (opp. ***indictable offence***). **4** DICKENS He cleared the table by the summary process of tilting everything upon it into the fire-place.

■ **summariness** *noun* E19.

summat /ˈsʌmət/ *pronoun, noun, & adverb*. *dial. & non-standard*. M18.
[Repr. a pronunc.]
Somewhat.

summate /sʌˈmeɪt/ *verb*. E20.
[Back-form. from SUMMATION *noun*².]
1 *verb trans. & intrans.* Add together, combine; *spec.* in *PHYSIOLOGY* (of nerve impulses etc.) act cumulatively. E20.
2 *verb trans.* Summarize. M20.
■ **summator** *noun* a thing that performs summation M20.

†**summation** *noun*¹. L15–M19.
[Old French *som(m)acion*, from *sommer* summon: see -ATION.]
A summons.
¶ Rare after L15.

summation /sʌˈmeɪʃ(ə)n/ *noun*². M18.
[from SUM *noun* + -ATION. Cf. Old & mod. French *sommation*.]
1 The process of finding the sum of a series (*MATH.*); the adding up of numbers or other quantities; aggregation; an addition. M18.
2 An aggregate, a sum total; a resultant, a product. M19.
3 The process or effect by which repeated or multiple nerve impulses can produce a response that each impulse alone would fail to produce (*PHYSIOLOGY*); cumulative action or effect. L19.
4 A summary, a summing-up; *US LAW* a counsel's (or, formerly, a judge's) closing speech at the end of the giving of evidence. L19.

📖 **1** R. BRIDGES Happiness . . is not composable of any summation of particular pleasures. **2** L. GORDON *Little Gidding* had to be the summation of the preceding poems. *Nature* The spectrum is the summation of 696 12-min spectra. **4** *Scientific American* The . . book is . . a sober-sided summation of the decade past.

Comb.: **summation check** *COMPUTING* = *sum check* s.v. SUM *noun*; **summation tone** a combination tone whose frequency is the sum of the frequencies of the two contributing tones.
■ **summational** *adjective* produced by summation L19. ˈ**summative** *adjective* involving summation; additive, cumulative: L19. ˈ**summatively** *adverb* M20.

summed /sʌmd/ *adjective*. LME.
[In sense 1 from Old & mod. French *sommé* pa. pple of *sommer*; in sense 2 from SUM *verb*: see -ED¹.]
1 (Of a hawk) having the feathers fully grown; formerly also, (of a stag) having a full complement of antlers. Of plumage or (formerly) antlers: fully developed. Also ***full summed***. LME.
2 That has been summed (*up*). E17.

summer /ˈsʌmə/ *noun*¹.
[Old English *sumor* corresp. to Old Frisian *sumur*, Old Saxon, Old High German *sumar* (Dutch *zomer*, German *Sommer*), Old Norse *sumar*, from Germanic; rel. to Sanskrit *samā* year, Avestan *ham-* summer.]
1 The second and warmest season of the year, between spring and autumn: in the northern hemisphere freq. regarded as comprising June, July, and August, or (*ASTRONOMY*) reckoned from the summer solstice to the autumnal equinox; in the southern hemisphere corresponding to the northern winter (December to February). OE. ▸**b** *transf.* Summer weather; a season resembling summer; summery or warm weather. ME.
2 In *pl.* A specified number of years, esp. of a person's age. Chiefly *poet.* LME.
3 The mature stage of life; the height *of* achievement, powers, etc. M16.

📖 **1** E. WAUGH The dry sounds of summer, the frog-voices, the . . cicadas. V. S. PRITCHETT The summers at Melikhovo were delectable. **summer and winter**, **winter and summer** all the year round. ***Russian spring–summer encephalitis***. ***snow-in-summer***: see SNOW *noun*¹. **b** ***Indian summer***: see INDIAN *adjective*. ***St Luke's summer***, ***St Martin's summer***: see SAINT *noun & adjective*. **2** J. BETJEMAN I am thirty summers older. **3** J. BURROUGHS The red aborigine . . had his summer of fulness and contentment.

Attrib. & comb.: in the sense 'characteristic of, suitable for, or used or occurring in summer', (of plants and animals) 'active or flourishing in summer', (of fruits) 'ripening in summer', 'ripening early', (of crops) 'ripening in the summer of the year of their planting', as ***summer apple***, ***summer clothes***, ***summer cottage***, ***summer fly***, ***summer fruit***, ***summer garden***, ***summer holiday***, ***summer resort***, ***summer tourist***, ***summer wheat***, etc. Special combs., as **summer bird** (*a*) a bird that appears in summer, a summer migrant; (*b*) (with allus. to the cuckoo) a cuckold; **summer boarder** *US* a person who lives at a boarding-house in the country in summer; **summer camp** (orig. & chiefly *US*) a camp providing recreational and sporting facilities during the summer holiday period, usu. for children; **summer cholera** = *CHOLERA* ***infantum***; **summer cloud**: such as is seen on a summer's day, *esp.* a fleeting cloud; **summer complaint** = *CHOLERA* ***infantum***; **summer country** *NZ* high farmland only suitable for use in summer; **summer cypress** a pyramidal shrub of the goosefoot family, *Bassia scoparia*, grown for its ornamental feathery foliage (cf. ***burning bush*** (a) s.v. BURNING *ppl adjective*); **summer-day** = ***summer's day*** below; **summer diarrhoea** = *CHOLERA* ***infantum***; **summer-dream** a pleasant or happy dream; **summer duck** *N. Amer.* the wood duck, *Aix sponsa*; **summer egg** a thin-shelled egg that develops rapidly, produced (usu. parthenogenetically) in spring and summer by various freshwater invertebrates (usu. in *pl.*); **summer-fallow** *verb, noun, & adjective* (*a*) *verb trans. & intrans.* lay (land) fallow during the summer; (*b*) *noun* a lying or laying fallow during the summer; land that lies fallow in summer; (*c*) *adjective* lying fallow in summer; **summer-field**: with a summer crop; **summer grape**, a N. American wild grape, *Vitis aestivalis*; **summer-heat** the heat of summer; *spec.* an arbitrary summer temperature marked on a thermometer; **summer-herring** (*a*) a herring taken in summer; (*b*) *US* any of several fishes related to the herring, *esp.* the blueback herring, *Alosa aestivalis*; **summer-house** (*a*) (now *rare*) a summer residence in the country; (*b*) a light usu. simple building in a garden or park, used for sitting in during fine weather; ***summer*** HYACINTH; **summer kitchen** *N. Amer.* an extra kitchen adjoining or separate from a house, used for cooking in hot weather; **summer-land** (*a*) *dial.* a summer-fallow; (*b*) a land where it is always summer; *SPIRITUALISM* the intermediate state of the departed; **summer lightning** sheet lightning without audible thunder, the result of a distant storm; **summer lodge** *Canad.* = TUPIK; **summer-long** *adverb & adjective*, (lasting) throughout the summer; **summer master** *CANADIAN HISTORY* a person in charge of a trading post for the summer only; **summer mastitis** a severe inflammation of the udder in dry cows and pre-calving heifers, usu. associated with the bacterium *Corynebacterium pyogenes*; **summer-prune** *verb trans. & intrans.* [back-form.] prune during the growing season; **summer pruning** the selective cutting back of branches of trees or shrubs during the growing season; **summer pudding**: composed of bread or sponge soaked in puréed fruit (freq. raspberries and redcurrants); **summer red-bird** = ***summer tanager*** below; ***summer resident***: see RESIDENT *noun* 1b; **summer sausage** *N. Amer.* a dried or smoked sausage which can be made in winter and kept until summer; ***summer savory***: see SAVORY *noun*¹; **summer school** a school or course of education held in the summer, esp. at a university during the long vacation; †**summer's cloud** = ***summer cloud*** above; **summer's day** (*a*) a day in summer; (*b*) ***in a summer's day***, ***in some summer's day***, some day or other, one of these days; **summer season** (*a*) the season of summer; (*b*) a period in summer for which people are employed in connection with seasonal or holiday entertainment, trade, etc.; **summer snipe** the common sandpiper, *Actitis hypoleucos*; ***summer snowflake***: see SNOWFLAKE 3; **summer solstice** the occasion of the longest day in the year, when the sun reaches its greatest altitude north of the equator, on approx. 21 June (or in the southern hemisphere, south of the equator, on approx. 21 December); ***summer squash***: see SQUASH *noun*²; **summer stock** *N. Amer.* theatrical productions by a repertory company organized for the summer season, esp. at holiday resorts; **summer tanager** a tanager, *Piranga rubra*, the adult male of which is rosy red, and which is a common summer visitor in parts of the US; **summer teal** the garganey; **summer-tide** (now chiefly *poet.*) = SUMMERTIME *noun* 1; **summer-tilth** *dial.* (the cultivation of) fallow land; **summer-weight** *adjective* (of clothes) light, suitable for wear in summer; **summer wood** = ***late wood*** s.v. LATE *adjective*; ***summer yellowbird***: see YELLOW *adjective*.
■ **summeriness** *noun* (*rare*) summery character or quality M19. **summerish** *adjective* somewhat summer-like E18. **summerize** *verb* (*a*) *verb intrans.* (*rare*) spend the summer; (*b*) *verb trans.* (*US colloq.*) prepare (something) for summer: L18. **summerless** *adjective* having no summer; not summery: L19. **summer-like** *adjective* resembling (that of) summer M16. **summers** *adverb* (*N. Amer.*) during the summer; each summer: E20. **summerward(s)** *adverb* towards summer L19. **summery** *adjective* resembling or pertaining to summer; characteristic of or appropriate to summer; summer-like: L15.

summer /ˈsʌmə/ *noun*². ME.
[Anglo-Norman *sumer*, *somer*, Old French *somier* (mod. *sommier*) from Proto-Romance from late Latin *sagmarius* from *sagma* from Greek *sagma* pack-saddle.]
1 †**a** *gen.* A main beam in a structure. *Scot.* ME–E18. ▸**b** A horizontal bearing beam in a building; *spec.* the main beam supporting the girders or joists of a floor or (occas.) the rafters of a roof. Also ***summer-beam***, ***summer tree***. Cf. BREASTSUMMER. LME.
2 Any bar, rail, or support; *spec.* (*a*) (in *pl.*) a framework of stout bars fitted with cross rails or staves, added to a cart or wagon to increase its capacity; (*b*) a beam in the body of a cart or wagon; (*c*) *Scot.* a support laid across a kiln on which grain is spread for drying; (*d*) *TANNING* a horse or block on which skins are pared, scraped, or worked smooth. E16.
■ **summering** *noun* (*ARCHITECTURE*) (*a*) *collect.* the beds of the stones or bricks of an arch considered with ref. to their direction; (*b*) the radial direction of the joints of an arch; (*c*) the degree of curvature of an arch: E18.

summer /ˈsʌmə/ *noun*³. E17.
[from SUM *verb* + -ER¹.]
1 A person who sums or adds; (*colloq. & dial.*) an arithmetician. Esp. in ***summer-up***. E17.
2 *ELECTRONICS*. A circuit or device that produces an output dependent on the sum of two or more inputs or of multiples of them. M20.

summer /ˈsʌmə/ *verb*. LME.
[from SUMMER *noun*¹.]
1 *verb intrans.* Spend the summer, stay during the summer in a specified place; (of cattle, etc.) be pastured in summer. LME.
2 *verb trans.* Keep or maintain during the summer; *esp.* provide summer pasture for (cattle etc.). L16.
3 *verb refl. & intrans.* Sun oneself, bask. Chiefly *fig.* M19.
4 *verb trans.* Make summery, balmy, or genial. M19.

📖 **1** *New Yorker* He didn't live in Branson, but he used to summer here.

Phrases: **summer and winter**, **winter and summer** (*a*) *verb phr. trans.* (chiefly *Scot.*) maintain relations with constantly; know intimately; remain loyal to; (*b*) *verb phr. intrans.* spend the whole year (in a place); (*c*) *verb phr. intrans. & trans.* (*Scot.*) consider or discuss (a matter) at great length.

summerly /ˈsʌməli/ *adjective*. LOE.
[from SUMMER *noun*¹ + -LY¹.]
†**1** Of or pertaining to summer; taking place in summer. LOE–L18.
2 Having the qualities of summer; summer-like, summery. LOE.

summerly /ˈsʌməli/ *adverb*. *rare*. E17.
[from SUMMER *noun*¹ + -LY².]
In a manner or condition appropriate to summer.

summersault *noun & verb* var. of SOMERSAULT.

summertime /ˈsʌmətʌɪm/ *noun*. Also (esp. in sense 2) **summer time**. LME.
[from SUMMER *noun*¹ + TIME *noun*.]
1 The season or period of summer. LME.
2 The standard time adopted in some countries during the summer months, usu. for daylight saving; *spec.* (more fully ***British Summer Time***) in Britain, the standard time adopted between March and October, one hour ahead of Greenwich Mean Time. E20.

📖 **1** *attrib.*: *Black World* The ensemble worked as summertime actors.

summing /ˈsʌmɪŋ/ *noun*. LME.
[from SUM *verb*, *noun* + -ING¹.]
1 The calculation of a total amount. LME.
2 Chiefly as ***summing-up***: ▸**a** The summarizing of a matter; a summary account or statement, a conclusion. M16. ▸**b** A judge's address to a jury, reviewing and commenting on the evidence of the case before them. L18.
3 The action of working out arithmetical problems. E19.

📖 **2a** H. CARPENTER He judged people ruthlessly. 'Nice stupid man' was a frequent summing-up. **b** C. HARMAN After the summing-up . . the jury was absent for an hour and a half.

summing /ˈsʌmɪŋ/ *ppl adjective*. M19.
[from SUM *verb* + -ING².]
1 That sums or sums up; summarizing. M19.
2 *ELECTRONICS*. That performs summation; producing an output dependent on the sum of the inputs. M20.

Summist /ˈsʌmɪst/ *noun*. M16.
[medieval Latin *summista*, from *summa* SUM *noun* + *-ista* -IST.]
1 The author of a summa of religious doctrine etc., e.g. Thomas Aquinas, author of *Summa theologiae*, *Summa contra gentiles*; *gen.*, a medieval scholastic writer. M16.
†**2** An epitomizer, an abridger; *transf.* an epitome, a summary. E17–M18.

summit /ˈsʌmɪt/ *noun & verb.* LME.
[Old French *som(m)ete*, also *somet*, *sumet* (mod. *sommet*), from *som*, *sum* from Latin *summum* neut. sing. of *summus* (see SUM *noun*). Spelling assim. to next.]
▶ **A** *noun.* **1** The top or head of something; the vertex, the apex. Now *esp.* the highest point or ridge of a mountain; a peak. LME.
2 *fig.* **a** The highest point of power, success, etc.; the acme, the peak. E18. ▸**b** The highest level, *spec.* with ref. to politics and international relations; *ellipt.* a summit conference, meeting, etc. (see below). M20.

1 A. T. ELLIS The road levelled . . before beginning its ascent to the hill's summit. **2b** *Japan Times* The first summit between China and the Soviet Union in 30 years.

Comb.: **summit conference**, **summit meeting**: between heads of government to discuss international matters; **summit level** (*a*) the highest level reached by a canal, railway, etc.; (*b*) a level place in a railway or stretch of water in a canal, with descending planes on either side; ***summit meeting***: see ***summit conference*** above.
▶ **B** *verb intrans.* Take part in summit meetings. L20.
■ **summiˈteer** *noun* a participant in a summit meeting M20. **summiˈteering** *noun* participation in a summit meeting M20. **summitless** *adjective* having no summit M19. **summitry** *noun* the practice of holding summit meetings M20.

†summity *noun.* LME.
[Old & mod. French *sommité* from late Latin *summitas* from *summus*: see SUM *noun*, -ITY.]
1 = SUMMIT *noun* 1. LME–E18.
2 a = SUMMIT *noun* 2a. L16–M19. ▸**b** A person or thing at the head of a group, line, series, etc. Only in 17.

†summon *noun.* ME–E19.
[from the verb.]
= SUMMONS *noun.*

summon /ˈsʌmən/ *verb trans.* ME.
[Anglo-Norman, Old French *sumun-*, *sumon-*, *somon-* pres. stem of *somondre*, (also mod.) *semondre*, from popular Latin, from Latin *summonere*, formed as SUB- + *monere* warn.]
1 Call together (individuals, an assembly) by authority for action or deliberation; convene. Formerly also foll. by *up*. ME. ▸**b** Call (a peer) to parliament by writ of summons; *transf.* call to a peerage. LME.
2 Order to appear at a certain place, esp. to appear before a court or judge to answer a charge or give evidence; issue a summons against. ME.
3 Request the presence of; bid (a person) to approach by calling, ringing a bell, etc.; call to go in a specified direction. LME.
4 Call upon (a person) *to do* something. LME.
†5 Give warning or notice of, proclaim. LME–E17.
6 Bring (one's ability, courage, energy, etc.) into action; call *up*, gather *up*; muster. L16. ▸**b** *refl.* Pull oneself together. *rare* (Scott). E19.
7 Call *into* existence; call forth. M18.

1 W. S. CHURCHILL Parliament was . . summoned in the King's name. **2** B. JOWETT A witness who will not come of himself may be summoned. P. P. READ After Andrew had returned to his cell, he was summoned to the office of the Prior. **3** E. MANNIN Making agitated signs to summon a waiter. A. LEE Mama . . and I were summoned to the hospital because Daddy had stopped breathing. *transf.*: M. AMIS His cumbrous passage summons me from sleep. **5** SHAKES. *Wint. T.* Prepare you, lords; Summon a session. **6** P. P. READ Francis drank more whisky to summon up the strength to talk to people.

■ **summonable** *adjective* able or liable to be summoned E18.

summoner /ˈsʌm(ə)nə/ *noun.* ME.
[Anglo-Norman *somenour*, *sum-* = Old French *somoneor*, *sem-* (mod. *semonneur*) from Anglo-Latin *summonitor*, *-or-*, from Latin *summonere* SUMMON *verb*: see -ER².]
1 a A petty officer with the duty of summoning people to appear in court. Now *Hist.* ME. ▸**b** *gen.* A person who or thing which summons another to a place. L16.
2 A person who takes out a summons. *rare.* M19.

summons /ˈsʌm(ə)nz/ *noun.* ME.
[Old French *somonce*, *sumunse* (mod. *semonce*) from Proto-Gallo-Romance alt. of Latin *summonita* use as noun of fem. pa. pple of *summonere* SUMMON *verb*: cf. prec.]
1 An authoritative call to attend on some occasion. ME. ▸**b** *spec.* A call by writ to bishops, earls, barons, etc., to attend the national council or parliament. Also, the call to a peerage. ME.
2 A call by authority to appear before a court or judicial officer; the writ by which such a call is made. ME. ▸**b** SCOTS LAW. A writ issued by the Court of Session under the royal signet, or, if in a sheriff court, in the name of the sheriff. E17. ▸**c** In judges' chambers, the means by which one party brings the other before a judge to settle details in a suit. Now chiefly in ***summons for directions***. E19.
3 *gen.* An urgent call or command (*to do* something); a summoning sound, knock, etc. M16.
4 MILITARY. An act of summoning a place to surrender. E17.

3 SAKI Lancelot entered in response to a . . friendly summons to 'come in'.

summons /ˈsʌm(ə)nz/ *verb trans.* M17.
[from the noun.]
1 = SUMMON *verb* 1, 3, 4. Now *rare.* M17.
2 Call before a court, judge, or magistrate; take out a summons against. L18.
■ **summonsable** *adjective* liable to a summons, actionable L19.

summulist /ˈsʌmjʊlɪst/ *noun.* M17.
[medieval Latin *summulista* from *summula* dim. of *summa* SUM *noun*: see -IST.]
A writer of a brief treatise of a science; an abridger.

summum bonum /sʊməm ˈbɒnəm, sʌməm ˈbəʊnəm/ *noun phr.* Pl. ***summa bona*** /sʊmə ˈbɒnə, sʌmə ˈbəʊnə/. M16.
[Latin = highest good.]
The chief or a supreme good; *spec.* (ETHICS) the highest good as the end or determining principle in an ethical system.

summum genus /sʊməm ˈdʒɛnəs, sʌməm ˈdʒiːnəs/ *noun phr.* Pl. ***summa genera*** /sʊmə ˈdʒɛn(ə)rə, sʌmə/. L16.
[Latin = highest kind.]
The highest or most comprehensive class in a classification; *spec.* (LOGIC) a genus not considered as a species of a higher genus.

summum jus /sʊməm ˈjuːs, sʌməm ˈdʒʌs/ *noun phr.* L16.
[Latin = highest law.]
The utmost rigour of the law, extreme severity.

sumner /ˈsʌmnə/ *noun*¹. LME.
[Anglo-Norman *sum(e)nour*, from *sumen-*, *sumon-*: see -ER². Cf. SUMMON *verb*.]
Now only in the Isle of Man: a person employed to summon people to appear in court; *esp.* a summoning officer in an ecclesiastical court.

Sumner /ˈsʌmnə/ *noun*². M19.
[Thomas H. *Sumner* (1807–76), US shipmaster.]
Used ***attrib.*** and in ***possess.*** with ref. to a method devised by Sumner of finding an observer's position, using an approx. value of latitude or longitude based on dead reckoning in conjunction with an astronomical observation to calculate a position line.

sumo /ˈsuːməʊ/ *noun.* Pl. **-os**, same. L19.
[Japanese *sūmō*.]
A Japanese form of heavyweight wrestling in which a wrestler wins a bout by forcing his opponent outside a circle or making him touch the ground with any part of the body except the soles of the feet. Also, a sumo wrestler.
sumo wrestler, ***sumo wrestling***, etc.

sumotori /suːməʊˈtɔːri/ *noun.* L20.
[Japanese *sūmotori*, formed as prec. + TORI *noun*¹.]
A sumo wrestler.

sump /sʌmp/ *noun & verb.* ME.
[Middle & mod. Low German, Middle Dutch, or (in sense 2a) corresp. to German *Sumpf* rel. to SWAMP *noun*.]
▶ **A** *noun.* **1** A marsh, a swamp; (now *dial.*) a dirty pool or puddle. ME.
2 a MINING. A pit or well sunk at the bottom of an engine shaft to collect superfluous water from the mine. Also (usu. *dial.*), a drift, a small underground shaft. M17. ▸**b** Any pit, well, or hole used for collecting water or other fluid; *spec.* a cesspool. L17. ▸**c** An underground passage or chamber in which water collects, *esp.* one which is flooded. M20.
3 A depression in the bottom of the crankcase of an internal-combustion engine, which serves as a reservoir of lubricating oil. E20.
Comb.: **sump guard** a cowling for protecting the sump of a motor vehicle from perforation on poor roads; **sump-hole** = senses 2a, b above.
▶ **B** *verb intrans.* Dig a sump or small shaft. E18.

sumph /sʌmf/ *noun. Scot. & north.* E18.
[Origin unkn.]
A stupid fellow; a simpleton, a blockhead. Also, a surly or sullen person.
■ **sumphish** *adjective* stupid; sullen E18. **sumphishly** *adverb* E19. **sumphishness** *noun* M19.

sumph /sʌmf/ *verb intrans. Scot.* L17.
[Cf. prec.]
Orig., be stupid; later, be sullen, sulk.

sumpitan /ˈsʌmpɪtən/ *noun.* M17.
[Malay *sumpitan* from *sumpit* shooting with a blowpipe.]
In Malaysia and Indonesia, a blowpipe made from a hollowed cane and used for shooting poisoned arrows.

sump'n /ˈsʌmp(ə)n/ *noun. non-standard* (chiefly *US*). L19.
[Repr. a pronunc.]
= SOMETHING.

sumpsimus /ˈsʌm(p)sɪməs/ *noun.* M16.
[Latin, 1st person pl. perf. indic. of *sumere* take: see MUMPSIMUS.]
A correct expression taking the place of an incorrect but popular one.

sumpter /ˈsʌm(p)tə/ *noun & adjective. arch.* ME.
[Old French *som(m)etier* from Proto-Romance from late Latin *sagma*, *sagmat-*: see SUMMER *noun*², -ER². Cf. SEAM *noun*².]
▶ **A** *noun.* **†1** The driver of a packhorse. ME–E17.
2 A packhorse; a beast of burden. L16.
3 A pack, a saddle-bag. Now *rare.* L16.
▶ **B** *attrib.* or as ***adjective*** (freq. hyphenated).
†1 Designating a driver of a packhorse. LME–E18.
2 Designating an animal used for carrying a pack. LME.
3 Designating anything covering or carried by such an animal. M16.

sumption /ˈsʌm(p)ʃ(ə)n/ *noun.* LME.
[Latin *sumptio(n-)*, from *sumpt-* pa. ppl stem of *sumere* take: see -ION.]
†1 The reception of the sacrament or of Christ in the sacrament. LME–M17.
2 Orig., the taking of a thing as true without proof; an assumption, a premiss. Now only, the major premiss of a syllogism. L16.

sumptuary /ˈsʌm(p)tjʊəri/ *adjective & noun.* E17.
[Latin *sumptuarius*, from *sumptus* expenditure, expense, from *sumpt-*: see prec., -ARY¹.]
▶ **A** *adjective.* Pertaining to or regulating expenditure. Esp. in ***sumptuary law***. E17.
▶**†B** *noun.* A person responsible for expenditure. *rare.* Only in L18.

sumptuous /ˈsʌm(p)tjʊəs/ *adjective.* LME.
[Old & mod. French *sumptueux* from Latin *sumptuosus*, from *sumptus*: see prec., -OUS.]
†1 Of a charge, expense, etc.: involving a great outlay of money. LME–E17. ▸**b** Expensive to practise or maintain. Chiefly *Scot.* M16–M17.
2 Costly and magnificent in construction, decoration, etc.; lavish, extravagant, luxuriously elegant. L15. ▸**b** Of a natural object: splendid or magnificent in appearance. L16.
†3 Of a person: extravagant in expenditure, way of life, etc. M16–L18.

2 E. WAUGH Loyola College gave a large, sumptuous . . buffet supper for me. O. MANNING Edwina was dressed for some . . more sumptuous occasion. M. SCAMMELL A sumptuous estate with a luxurious house and an elaborate park.

■ **sumptuˈosity** *noun* (*a*) lavishness, extravagance, luxuriousness; (*b*) an instance of this, a sumptuous thing: M16. **sumptuously** *adverb* in a sumptuous manner; extravagantly, magnificently: L15. **sumptuousness** *noun* E16.

sumpy /ˈsʌmpi/ *adjective. dial.* E19.
[from SUMP + -Y¹.]
Boggy, swampy.

sum total /sʌm ˈtəʊt(ə)l/ *noun phr.* Pl. **sum totals**, **sums total**. LME.
[translating medieval Latin *summa totalis*: see SUM *noun*, TOTAL *adjective*.]
1 The aggregate of all the items in an account; the total amount. LME.
2 *gen.* The aggregate or totality *of*. M17.
■ **sum-totalize** *verb trans. & intrans.* reckon or state the sum total (of), sum up M19.

sum-up /ˈsʌmʌp/ *noun.* L19.
[from phr. *sum up*: see SUM *verb*.]
A summing-up, a summary.

sun /sʌn/ *noun*¹.
[Old English *sunne* (fem.) = Old Frisian *sunne*, Old Saxon, Old High German *sunna* (Dutch *zon*, German *Sonne*), Old Norse (poet.) *sunna*, Gothic *sunnō*, beside Old English *sunna* (masc.), Old High German, Old Saxon *sunno*, from Germanic word from Indo-European word rel. to Greek *hēlios*, Latin *sol*, Old English *sōl*, Old Norse *sól*.]
1 The large bright spherical object which is seen to pass across the sky each day from east to west, and which is the chief source of natural light and heat on earth, being in astronomical terms a star around which the earth revolves once in a year. OE. ▸**b** A luminary; *esp.* a star in the universe, whether orbited by planets or not. LME.
2 *fig.* A person or thing regarded as a representative or source of glory, radiance, inspiration, etc. Chiefly *poet.* OE.
3 The direct rays of the sun, sunlight, sunshine; warmth or light received from the sun. OE.
4 The sun as visible (freq. with ref. to the place reached in its daily cycle) at a particular time or place. Also (chiefly *poet.*), a climate as determined by the sun. LME.
5 a Sunrise or sunset as determining the period of a day. Freq. in ***between sun and sun***, ***from sun and sun***. *arch.* LME. ▸**b** A day. *poet.* or *rhet.* E17. ▸**c** A year. *poet.* M18.
6 = PARHELION 1. LME.
7 A representation of or object resembling the sun, esp. as surrounded by rays; HERALDRY an image of the sun with (freq. alternate straight and wavy) rays and usu. a human face (also ***sun in his splendour***, ***sun in splendour***). LME. ▸**b** A kind of circular firework. M18.

†**8** In HERALDRY, the tincture or in the fanciful blazon of arms of sovereign princes. In ALCHEMY, the metal gold. LME–M17.

> **1** HOBBES Yclad in Armour shining like the Sun. J. SILK The possible collision of a comet with the sun. **b** MILTON Other Suns perhaps With thir attendant Moons thou wilt descrie. **2** SIR W. SCOTT When the sun of my prosperity began to arise. **3** N. COWARD Mad dogs and Englishmen go out in the midday sun. J. FRAME Happy lolling around in the sun all year. S. MILLER The sun was streaming in and dust motes swam . . in the hot light. **4** BYRON With just enough of life to see My last of suns go down on me. E. WAUGH A breeze . . blowing from the heat of the setting sun. M. HOCKING The sun had come out . . fine and warm.

Phrases: **against the sun** (chiefly NAUTICAL) against the direction of the sun's apparent diurnal movement; from right to left, from west to east, anticlockwise. **beneath the sun** = *under the sun* below. **have been in the sun**, **have the sun in one's eyes** *slang* be drunk. ***land of the midnight sun***: see LAND *noun*[1]. ***land of the rising sun***: see LAND *noun*[1]. ***make hay while the sun shines***: see HAY *noun*[1]. ***mean sun***: see MEAN *adjective*[2]. ***MIDNIGHT sun***. **one's sun is set** the time of one's prosperity, success, etc., is over. **on which the sun never sets** (of an empire, orig. the Spanish and later the British) worldwide. **place in the sun** one's share of good fortune, prosperity, etc.; a favourable situation or position, prominence. ***raisins of the sun***: see RAISIN. **rise with the sun** get up out of bed very early. **rising sun** *poet.* the east. **setting sun** *poet.* the west. **shoot the sun** NAUTICAL = *take the sun* below. ***sun in his splendour***, ***sun in splendour***: see sense 7 above. **take the sun** NAUTICAL ascertain the altitude of the sun with a sextant in order to fix the latitude. **under the sun** on earth, in the world, in existence. ***when the sun is over the YARD-ARM***. **with the sun** (chiefly NAUTICAL) in the direction of the sun's apparent diurnal movement; from left to right; from east to west, clockwise.

Attrib. & comb.: In the sense 'serving for protection against the sun, used to keep sunlight off', as ***sun awning***, ***sun canopy***, etc.; 'giving maximum access to the sun, used or worn for sunbathing', as ***sun balcony***, ***sun porch***, ***sun top***, etc. Special combs., as **sun-and-planet gear**, **sun-and-planet wheels** a form of epicyclic gear consisting of a central wheel around which one or more outer wheels travel; **sun arc** CINEMATOGRAPHY an arc lamp used to simulate sunlight in film production; **sunbake** *verb intrans.* (*Austral.*) sunbathe (freq. as ***sunbaking*** *verbal noun*); **sun-baked** *adjective* dried, hardened, or baked by exposure to the sun; **sun-bath** a period of exposing the body to the sun, orig. as a method of medical treatment; **sunbathe** *verb & noun* (*a*) *verb intrans.* lie or bask in the sun, esp. to tan the body; (*b*) *noun* an act or spell of sunbathing; **sun-bathed** *adjective* bathed in sunshine; **sunbather** a sunbathing person; **sun bear** (*a*) a small bear, *Helarctos malayanus*, of SE Asia, having short dark fur with pale markings on the muzzle and breast; (*b*) *rare* the Himalayan black bear, *Selenarctos thibetanus*; **sunbed** (*a*) a lightweight, usu. folding, bed or couch used for sunbathing etc.; (*b*) a bed for lying on under a sun-lamp; **sunbelt** a strip of territory receiving a high amount of sunshine, *esp.* (usu. **S-**) the zone consisting of the most southerly states of the US, extending from California to the Carolinas; **sun bittern** a S. American bird of forest streams, *Eurypyga helias*, with strongly patterned brown and white plumage, sole member of the family Eurypygidae; **sun-blind** a window awning; **sunblock** a cream or lotion rubbed on to protect the skin from sunlight and prevent sunburn; **sun-bonnet** a light bonnet covering the neck and shading the face from the sun, esp. for children; **sunbow** (chiefly *poet.*) an arch of prismatic colours like a rainbow, formed by refraction of sunlight in spray or vapour; **sunbreak** (*a*) a burst of sunshine; (*b*) sunrise; (*c*) = BRISE-SOLEIL; **sun-bright** *adjective* (chiefly *poet.*) (*a*) bright as the sun, very bright; (*b*) bright with sunshine; **sun club** a club or resort for sunbathers or naturists; **sun compass** a navigational device for finding true north from the observed direction of the sun; **sun-crack** GEOLOGY a crack produced by the heat of the sun during the consolidation of a rock; **sun-cream** = SUNTAN *cream*; **sun-cure** *noun & verb* (*a*) *noun* a period of rest or treatment involving exposure to the sun's rays; (*b*) *verb trans.* cure or preserve (food) by exposure to the sun; **sun-dance** a dance, accompanied by rites of self-torture, practised in honour of the sun by certain N. American Indian peoples; **sun-deck** (*a*) the upper deck of a steamer; (*b*) *N. Amer.* a terrace or balcony situated so as to catch the sun; **sundial** an instrument or structure showing the time of day by the shadow of a pointer cast by the sun on a disc or dial marked to indicate the hours; **sun-disc** the disc of the sun; a usu. winged image of this emblematic of the sun-god; **sun-dog** = PARHELION; **sun-drenched** *adjective* illuminated by sunshine; having (typically) very sunny weather; **sun-dress** a sleeveless dress with a low neck and back, worn in sunny weather; **sundrops** any day-flowering plant of the genus *Oenothera* (see OENOTHERA); esp. *O. fruticosa* (cf. ***EVENING primrose***); **sunfall** (chiefly *poet.* & *rhet.*) sunset; **sunfast** *adjective* (*US*, of dye) not subject to fading by sunlight; **sun filter** = *sunscreen* (b) below; **sun furnace** = *solar furnace* s.v. SOLAR *adjective*[1]; **sungazer** a large girdle-tailed lizard, *Cordylus giganteus*, which is covered with large spiny scales and is found in southern Africa; **sun gear** = *sun wheel* (a) below; **sungem** a brilliantly coloured Brazilian hummingbird, *Heliactin cornuta*, having tufts of feathers on the sides of the head (also ***horned sungem***); **sunglass** (*a*) a lens for concentrating the rays of the sun, a burning-glass; (*b*) in *pl.*, spectacles with tinted lenses for protecting the eyes from sunlight or glare, dark glasses; **sun-god**, **sun-goddess** the sun worshipped or personified as a god or goddess; a god or goddess identified or specially associated with the sun; **sun-grazer** ASTRONOMY a comet whose orbit passes close to the sun; **sun-grazing** *adjective* that is a sun-grazer; **sungrebe** a finfoot; *esp.* the S. American *Heliornis fulica*; **Sun Gun** CINEMATOGRAPHY (proprietary name for) a portable incandescent lamp; **sun-hat** a usu. broad-brimmed hat worn to protect the head from the sun; **sun-helmet** a helmet of cork etc. formerly worn by white people in the tropics; **Sun King** an epithet of Louis XIV of France; **sun-kissed** *adjective* warmed, browned, or affected by the sun; **sun-lamp** (*a*) an electric lamp emitting radiation similar to that of sunlight; now *esp.* one producing ultraviolet light to give an artificial suntan, for therapy, etc.; (*b*) CINEMATOGRAPHY a large lamp with a parabolic reflector, used in film-making; **sun lotion** = *SUNTAN lotion*; **sun lounge** (*a*) a room with large windows to admit the maximum amount of sunlight; (*b*) *US* = *sunbed* (a) above; **sun-lounger** = *sunbed* (a) above; **sun-oil** = *SUNTAN oil*; **sun-painting** (chiefly *Hist.*) a sun-print; sun-printing; **sun parlour** *US* = *sun lounge* (a) above; **sun-perch** = SUNFISH *noun* 1; **sun-picture** (chiefly *Hist.*) a photograph; **sun plant** a purslane of tropical S. America, *Portulaca grandiflora*, grown for its large brightly coloured flowers; **sun-print** *noun & verb* (PHOTOGRAPHY, chiefly *Hist.*) (*a*) *noun* a print made from a negative by means of sunlight; (*b*) *verb trans. & intrans.* make a sun-print (of); **sun-ray** (*a*) (chiefly *poet.* & *rhet.*) a ray of sunlight, a sunbeam; (*b*) an artificial ultraviolet ray used for medical or cosmetic treatment (esp. in ***sun-ray lamp***); (*c*) ***sun-ray pleating***, ***sun-ray pleats***, widening pleats radiating out from a skirt's waistband; **sun-roof** (*a*) a sliding or hinged panel or a covered opening in the roof of a car, able to be opened to admit sunlight; (*b*) a part of a house roof suitable for sunbathing; **sun-rose** (chiefly HORTICULTURE) = HELIANTHEMUM (cf. ***rock rose*** (a) s.v. ROCK *noun*[1]); **sun-scald** [SCALD *noun*[2]] (*a*) damage to plant tissue, esp. bark or fruit, caused by exposure to excessive sunlight; (*b*) a patch of bright sunlight on the surface of water; **sun-scorch** = *sun-scald* above; **sun-scorpion** = SOLIFUGID; **sunscreen** (*a*) a screen giving protection against the sun; (*b*) a cream or lotion rubbed on to screen the skin from ultraviolet rays and prevent sunburn; **sun-seeker** (*a*) ASTRONAUTICS a photoelectric device used in satellites and spacecraft which maintains its orientation with respect to the sun and is used for navigation and to direct instruments; (*b*) a person seeking a sunny place in which to holiday or live; **sunshade** (*a*) an awning; (*b*) a parasol; (*c*) a hood or visor fixed on a hat etc. to keep the sun from the face; a broad-brimmed hat; (*d*) in *pl.* sunglasses; **sun-shaft** a shaft of sunlight, a sunbeam; **sun sign** ASTROLOGY a person's birth-sign; **sunspace** *N. Amer.* a room or area in a building having a glass roof and walls and intended to maximize the power of the sun's rays; **sunspecs** *colloq.* sunglasses; **sun-spider** = SOLIFUGID; **sun-spring** *arch.* sunrise; **sun spurge** a European spurge, *Euphorbia helioscopia*, common as a weed, having umbels subtended by yellow-tinged obovate leaves; **sun squirrel** any of various African squirrels of the genus *Heliosciurus*, that typically have a ringed tail and are noted for basking in the sun, which often causes bleaching of the fur; **sunstar** a starfish having numerous rays, esp. one of the genus *Solaster*; **sun-stricken** *adjective* [after *sunstroke*] affected with sunstroke; **sunstroke** sudden acute illness with collapse or prostration caused by the excessive heat of the sun; **sunstruck** *adjective* [after *sunstroke*] affected with sunstroke; **sun-suit** a light playsuit worn for sunbathing etc., freq. by children; **suntrap** a place or area sheltered from the wind and suitable for catching sunshine; **sun visor** a projecting shield on a cap or a fixed or hinged screen at the top of a vehicle windscreen, to shade the eyes from bright sunshine; **sun wheel** (*a*) the central wheel in a sun-and-planet gear; (*b*) a wheel-like figure with radiating arms or spokes, symbolic of the sun. See also SUNDEW, SUNFLOWER.

■ **sunlet** *noun* a little sun M19. **sunlike** *adjective* resembling (that of) the sun; characteristic of the sun, *esp.* very bright or resplendent: L16.

sun /sʊn/ *noun*[2]. Pl. ***sun***. E18.

[Japanese.]

A Japanese unit of length, equal to approx. 3.03 cm, 1.19 inch.

sun /sʌn/ *verb*. Infl. **-nn-**. ME.

[from SUN *noun*[1].]

1 *verb trans.* Place in or expose to the sun; warm or dry in sunshine. ME. ▸**b** Catch (salmon) by dazzling with reflected sunlight and spearing. Freq. as ***sunning*** *verbal noun*. M19.

2 *verb intrans.* & *refl.* Lie or bask in the sun; sunbathe. E16.

3 *verb intrans.* Shine as or like the sun. *rare*. E17.

4 *verb trans.* Shine on or light up as or like the sun. Chiefly *poet.* M17.

> **1** LYTTON The peacock . . was sunning his gay plumage. **2** S. ROE Black girls sunned themselves darker. E. WELTY The cook's cat, was sunning on a post. B. CHATWIN A man in his underpants sunned himself on the grass.

Sun. *abbreviation*.

Sunday.

sunbeam /ˈsʌnbiːm/ *noun*.

[Old English *sun(n)bēam*, *sunne-bēam* formed as SUN *noun*[1] + BEAM *noun*.]

1 A beam or ray of sunlight. OE. ▸**b** A person, esp. a woman or girl, who is a cheering or enlivening influence. Cf. ***little ray of sunshine*** s.v. RAY *noun*[1]. L19.

2 [Orig. translating a Brazilian word.] A radiant-coloured hummingbird. Now *spec.* one of the genus *Aglaeactis* of western S. America. E17.

> **1** B. CHATWIN The sunbeams, falling through sycamores, lit up spirals of midges.

■ †**sunbeamed** *adjective* (*rare*, Shakes.) = SUNBEAMY: only in L16. **sunbeamy** *adjective* bright as a sunbeam; genial: M19.

sunbird /ˈsʌnbəːd/ *noun*. In sense 2 usu. **sun-bird**. L18.

[from SUN *noun*[1] + BIRD *noun*.]

1 †**a** = DARTER 4. Only in L18. ▸**b** A member of the family Nectariniidae of small passerine birds that feeds on nectar, the males of which often have brilliant iridescent plumage, found in tropical and subtropical regions of the Old World. E19. ▸**c** = ***sun bittern*** s.v. SUN *noun*[1]. E19. ▸**d** A sun-grebe; = ***finfoot*** s.v. FIN *noun*[1]. L19.

2 (Usu. with hyphen.) A bird sacred to the sun or connected with sun-worship; the sun imagined as a bird. L19.

sunburn /ˈsʌnbəːn/ *verb & noun*. LME.

[from SUN *noun*[1] + BURN *verb*. Earliest as pa. pple.]

▶ **A** *verb*. Infl. as BURN *verb*; pa. t. & pple usu. **-burned**, **-burnt** /-bəːnt/.

1 *verb trans.* Burn or inflame (esp. the skin or body) by overexposure to the sun; affect with sunburn; tan, brown, or bake through exposure to the sun. Freq. as ***sunburnt***, ***sunburned*** *ppl adjectives*. LME.

2 *verb intrans.* Become inflamed, browned, or tanned by (excessive) exposure to the sun; be affected by sunburn. M19.

> **1** S. CLOETE The Englishmen were sunburnt, red as lobsters. **2** L. DEIGHTON A clear complexion that sunburnt easily.

▶ **B** *noun*. **1** The condition of being sunburnt; inflammation or tanning of the skin caused by (excessive) exposure to the sun; the brown colour or tan thus produced. M17.

2 In plants: = ***sun-scald*** s.v. SUN *noun*[1]. Also, development of chlorophyll in potatoes exposed to light. M19.

> **1** *Country Living* Ultraviolet B rays . . which cause tanning, sunburn, and, potentially, skin cancers.

sunburst /ˈsʌnbəːst/ *noun*. E19.

[from SUN *noun*[1] + BURST *noun*.]

1 A burst of sunlight; a sudden shining of the sun from behind a cloud. E19.

2 A thing constructed so as to imitate the sun with its rays, *spec.* an ornament or brooch, firework, a photographic filter. E20.

sunck /sʌŋk/ *noun*. L17.

[Algonquian *sonksq*, analysed as if containing *squaw*.]

The female chief of a N. American Indian people. Also ***sunck squaw***.

sundae /ˈsʌndeɪ, -di/ *noun*. Orig. *US*. L19.

[App. alt. of *Sunday*, with ref. either to a use of leftover ice-cream unable to be sold on a Sunday or to the dish being served only on this day.]

A dish of ice-cream topped or mixed with fruit, nuts, syrup, whipped cream, etc. Freq. with specifying word.

Sundanese /sʌndəˈniːz/ *adjective & noun*. L19.

[from Sundanese *Sunda* the western part of the island of Java + -ESE.]

▶ **A** *adjective*. Designating or pertaining to a mainly Muslim people of western Java, or their language. L19.

▶ **B** *noun*. Pl. same. A member of the Sundanese people; the Austronesian language of this people. L19.

sundang /ˈsʊndaŋ/ *noun*. E20.

[Malay.]

A Malaysian heavy two-edged sword.

Sunday /ˈsʌndeɪ, -di/ *noun, adverb, adjective, & verb*.

[Old English *sunnandæg* (Northumbrian *sunnadæg*) = Old Frisian *sunnandei*, Old Saxon *sunnundag* (Dutch *zondag*), Old High German *sunnuntag* (German *Sonntag*), Old Norse *sunnudagr*, from Germanic translation of Latin *dies solis* = late Greek *hēmera hēliou* day of the sun.]

▶ **A** *noun*. **1** The first day of the week, a Christian holiday and day of worship; the Christian Sabbath, the Lord's day. OE.

2 *ellipt.* **a** In *pl.* Sunday clothes. E20. ▸**b** A Sunday newspaper. Usu. in *pl.* M20.

1 ***Advent Sunday***, ***continental Sunday***, ***Easter Sunday***, ***Palm Sunday***, ***Passion Sunday***, ***stir-up Sunday***, etc. ***MONTH of Sundays***. ***one's Sunday best***: see BEST *adjective, noun, & adverb*. ***week of Sundays***: see WEEK *noun*.

▶ **B** *adverb*. On Sunday. Now *colloq.* ME.

▶ **C** *attrib.* or as *adjective*. Of Sunday; characteristic of Sunday; taking place on Sunday(s). LME.

▶ **D** *verb intrans.* Spend Sunday. Chiefly *US*. L19.

Special collocations & comb.: **Sunday child** = *Sunday's child* below. **Sunday closing** the closing on Sundays of shops (except for the sale of certain commodities), public houses, etc. ***Sunday dinner***: see ***Sunday lunch*** below. **Sunday driver** a person who drives chiefly at weekends, esp. slowly or unskilfully. **Sunday face** (*a*) (orig. *Scot.*) a sanctimonious expression; (*b*) *Anglo-Irish* a festive countenance. **Sunday-go-to-meeting** *adjective* = ***go-to-meeting*** s.v. GO *verb*. **Sunday joint** a roasted joint of meat traditionally served for Sunday lunch. **Sunday letter** = ***dominical letter*** s.v. DOMINICAL *adjective* 2. **Sunday lunch**: traditionally large and featuring roast meat. **Sunday observance** the keeping of Sunday as a day of rest and worship. **Sunday painter** an amateur painter, *esp.* one with little training. **Sunday punch** *US slang* a knockout blow or punch. **Sunday's child** a child born on Sunday, traditionally greatly blessed or favoured. **Sunday school** a school for the instruction of children on Sundays, now *spec.* in religion but orig. also in general subjects; (also as a type of wholesomeness, sanctimoniousness, or strict morality). **Sunday supplement** an illustrated section issued with a Sunday newspaper, freq. characterized as portraying voguish living.

■ **Sundayed** *adjective* = SUNDAYFIED L19. **Sundayfied** *adjective* appropriate to or reminiscent of Sunday, in Sunday clothes M19. **Sundayish** *adjective* reminiscent of or resembling Sunday L18. **Sundays** *adverb* (now *colloq.*) on Sundays, each Sunday ME.

sunder /ˈsʌndə/ *adjective & adverb.*
[Old English *sundor-* = Old Saxon *sundar-*, Old High German *suntar-*, *sunder-*. A.2 & B. from ASUNDER.]
▶ **A** *adjective.* †**1 a** Separate, peculiar, private. Only in comb. OE–LME. ▶**b** Various, sundry. Only in ME.
2 *in sunder*, asunder. Now *arch.* or *literary.* ME.
▶ **B** *adverb.* Asunder. *rare.* Long *Scot.* ME.

sunder /ˈsʌndə/ *verb.* Now *arch.* or *literary.*
[Late Old English *sundrian* (beside *syndrian*) for earlier *ā-*, *ge-*, *on-*, *tōsundrian* corresp. to Old High German *sunt(a)rōn*, *sund(e)rōn* (German *sondern*), Old Norse *sundra*.]
1 *verb trans.* Dissolve connection between two or more people or things; separate or part *from*. LOE. ▶†**b** Separate in thought, distinguish. ME–M16. ▶†**c** Dissolve, put an end to, (a state or condition). ME–M16. ▶**d** Separate by an intervening space or barrier; keep apart *from*. Usu. in *pass.* E17.
2 *verb trans.* Divide into two or more parts; split, break up, cleave. ME.
3 *verb intrans.* Become separated or severed *from*; (esp. of a couple or group) part, become estranged. ME.
4 *verb intrans.* Break or split apart or in pieces. LME.

📖 **1** J. FORD Twelue monthes we haue been sundred, but . . neuer more will part. W. S. CHURCHILL This issue of Catholic Emancipation . . had sundered Canning . . from Wellington and Peel. **2** W. F. BUCKLEY The German people . . were sundered by a consortium of powers. D. HOGAN No observer was sure which of the pair had sundered the relationship. **3** T. HOOD So brave Leander sunders from his bride. **4** *Times* That alliance has now sundered.

■ **sunderable** *adjective* able to be sundered, separable L19. **sunderance** *noun* (*rare*) severance, separation LME. **sunderer** *noun* L19. **sunderment** *noun* (*rare*) = SUNDERANCE E19.

Sunderland /ˈsʌndələnd/ *noun.* L19.
[See below.]
Used *attrib.* to designate things, esp. pottery, made in or associated with Sunderland, a town in Tyne and Wear; *spec.* (*a*) a type of coarse cream-coloured ware, usu. decorated with a pink lustre and transfers; (*b*) a type of coarse brown earthenware.

sundew /ˈsʌndjuː/ *noun.* L16.
[translating Dutch †*sondauw*, †*sundauw* = German *Sonnentau*, translating Latin ROS SOLIS (app. with ref. to the glistening gland-tipped hairs): cf. SUN *noun*[1], DEW *noun*.]
Any of various small insectivorous bog plants constituting the genus *Drosera* (family Droseraceae) having leaves covered with glandular hairs which secrete a sticky juice; esp. *D. rotundifolia* (more fully ***round-leaved sundew***).

sundown /ˈsʌndaʊn/ *noun.* E17.
[Perh. shortening of †*sun go down*.]
1 Sunset. E17.
2 A hat with a wide brim. *US.* L19.
Comb.: **sundown doctor**, **sundown lawyer** (*US colloq.*) a doctor, lawyer, practising outside normal working hours or in addition to his or her principal occupation.

sundowner /ˈsʌndaʊnə/ *noun.* M19.
[from prec. + -ER[1].]
1 A tramp, orig. *esp.* one habitually arriving at a sheep station etc. about sundown (under the pretence of seeking work) so as to obtain food and shelter. *Austral. & NZ colloq.* M19.
2 = SUNDOWN 2. *US colloq.* L19.
3 An alcoholic drink taken at sunset. Also, an evening drinks party. *colloq.* E20.

sundri /ˈsʊndri/ *noun.* M19.
[Sanskrit *sundarī*.]
In the Indian subcontinent: any of several trees of the genus *Heritiera* (family Sterculiaceae), esp. *H. fomes* and *H. littoralis*, which abound in the Ganges delta and yield a tough durable wood.

sun-dried /ˈsʌndrʌɪd/ *adjective.* E17.
[from SUN *noun*[1] + DRIED *ppl adjective*.]
Dried by exposure to the sun, esp. as opp. to artificial heat.

sundry /ˈsʌndri/ *adjective, adverb, pronoun, & noun.*
[Old English *syndrig*, corresp. to Middle Low German *sunder(i)ch*, Old High German *sunt(a)ric*: see -Y[1], SUNDER *verb*.]
▶ **A** *adjective.* **1** Having an existence or position apart; separate, distinct. *obsolete* exc. *dial.* OE.
†**2** Distinct or different for each respectively, individually assigned or possessed. OE–M18.
3 Of various kinds, miscellaneous; various, several. ME.
4 †**a** Different, other, (foll. by *from*); diverse, manifold. ME–M17. ▶†**b** Consisting of different elements, of mixed composition. *rare* (Shakes.). L16–E17. ▶**c** Consisting of miscellaneous items. L18.

📖 **3** A. R. HOPE Disturbing the placid repast of sundry forlorn cows. L. EDEL The three characters arrive in London after sundry minor adventures.

▶ **B** *adverb. obsolete* exc. *Scot.*
1 Separately, apart; severally, individually. OE.
2 In or to pieces, asunder. M16.
▶ **C** *pronoun.* A number *of*, several *of*. L16.

📖 W. D. WHITNEY Sundry of the modern European languages. ***all and sundry***: see ALL *pronoun* 4.

▶ **D** *noun.* In *pl.*
1 Small miscellaneous articles; *esp.* small items lumped together in an account etc. as not needing individual mention. M18.
2 CRICKET. Extras. Chiefly *Austral.* M19.

📖 **1** *Skin Diver* A drugstore that offers a wide variety of magazines, newspapers and sundries.

■ †**sundrily** *adverb* OE–L16. **sundriness** *noun* (now *rare* or *obsolete*) diversity, variety LME.

sun-dry /ˈsʌndrʌɪ/ *verb trans. & intrans.* L17.
[Back-form. from SUN-DRIED.]
Dry in the sun.

sunfish /ˈsʌnfɪʃ/ *noun.* Pl. **-es**, (usu.) same. E17.
[from SUN *noun*[1] + FISH *noun*[1].]
1 Any of various fishes of rounded form or brilliant appearance, or that are supposed to bask in the sun; *spec.* (*a*) any large fish of the family Molidae (order Plectognathi or Tetraodontiformes), having a circular body with long anal and dorsal fins and virtually no tail, esp. *Mola mola* of temperate and tropical seas; (*b*) any of various small deep-bodied freshwater fishes of the percoid family Centrarchidae, abundant in N. America; (*c*) a basking shark; (*d*) = OPAH; (*e*) a moonfish of the carangid genus *Selene*. E17.
†**2** A starfish with numerous rays. Only in L17.
3 The action or an act of sunfishing by a horse. *US slang.* E20.

sunfish /ˈsʌnfɪʃ/ *verb intrans. US slang.* L19.
[from the noun.]
Of a horse: buck by lowering each shoulder in turn, perform a sunfish.
■ **sunfisher** *noun* E20.

sunflower /ˈsʌnflaʊə/ *noun.* M16.
[from SUN *noun*[1] + FLOWER *noun*, translating mod. Latin *flos solis*.]
1 Any of several plants whose flowers turn towards the sun; *spec.* †(*a*) *rare* the heliotrope, *Heliotropium europaeum*; (*b*) (a flowering stem of) any of various N. American plants constituting the genus *Helianthus*, of the composite family, having conspicuous yellow-rayed flower-heads suggesting a representation of the sun; esp. *H. annuus*, a tall-growing plant commonly cultivated for its very large showy flowers and oily seeds. M16. ▶**b** Any of various yellow-rayed plants of the composite family resembling a helianthus. Usu. with specifying word. M18.
2 Any of various plants whose flowers open only in sunshine or in daylight: *esp.* †(*a*) (usu. ***little sunflower***, ***small sunflower***) the rock rose, *Helianthemum nummularium*; (*b*) *dial.* the scarlet pimpernel, *Anagallis arvensis*. L17.
Comb.: **Sunflower State** *US* the State of Kansas, of which the sunflower is the State flower.

Sung *noun & adjective* var. of SONG *noun*[2] *& adjective*.

sung *verb pa. t. & pple*: see SING *verb*[1].

sunga /ˈsʌŋɡə/ *noun.* Also ***sanga*** /ˈsaŋɡə/. M19.
[Local name.]
A bridge made of beams, used in the Himalayas.

†**Sungai** *noun & adjective* var. of SONGHAI.

sungates /ˈsʌngeɪtz/ *adverb.* Long *arch.* exc. *Scot.* L16.
[from SUN *noun*[1] + *gates* genit. of GATE *noun*[2].]
= SUNWAYS.

suni /ˈsuːni/ *noun.* L19.
[Bantu.]
A dwarf antelope of southern Africa, *Neotragus moschatus*.

sunk /sʌŋk/ *noun. Scot. & north.* E16.
[Origin unkn.]
1 A seat of turf. E16.
2 In *pl. & sing.* A straw pad used as a cushion or saddle. Cf. SOD *noun*[1] 2. L18.
3 A bank; a dyke. E19.

sunk /sʌŋk/ *ppl adjective.* LME.
[pa. pple of SINK *verb*: cf. SUNKEN *adjective*. Now generally restricted in adjectival use to senses implying deliberate human agency.]
1 = SUNKEN *adjective* 2. Now *rare.* LME.
2 = SUNKEN *adjective* 3. M17.
3 a Lowered in character, status, value, etc.; depraved, degenerate; (of the spirits) depressed, low. Now *rare* or *obsolete.* L17. ▶**b** In a hopeless position, in trouble, in a mess. *colloq.* (freq. *hyperbol.*). E20.
4 = SUNKEN *adjective* 1. L18.

📖 **2 sunk fence** a fence formed by or running along the bottom of a ditch. **sunk garden** = ***sunken garden*** s.v. SUNKEN *adjective* 3. **sunk storey** = ***sunken storey*** s.v. SUNKEN *adjective* 3. **3b** P. G. WODEHOUSE If the fuzz search my room, I'm sunk.

sunk *verb pa. t. & pple*: see SINK *verb*.

sunken /ˈsʌŋk(ə)n/ *adjective.* LME.
[pa. pple of SINK *verb*: see -EN[6]. Cf. SUNK *adjective*.]
1 That has sunk in water; beneath the surface of water etc., submerged. LME.
2 Of the eyes, cheeks, etc.: abnormally depressed or hollow; fallen in. E17.
3 Placed on a lower level than the surrounding area, recessed. M17.
4 That has sunk below the usual or general level; subsided, depressed, drooping; (of the sun) gone down below the horizon. E19.

📖 **1** J. CONRAD The treachery of sunken rocks. *Which?* Raising a sunken ship from the sea bed. **2** J. ROSSNER Large, dark, mournful eyes and sunken cheeks. **3** M. HOCKING A sunken lane which twisted down, wooded hills rising steeply to one side. **sunken fence** = ***sunk fence*** s.v. SUNK *adjective* 2. **sunken garden** (a part of) a garden recessed below the surrounding area or garden. **sunken storey** a storey below ground level, a basement. **4** A. N. WILSON His spirits seemed sunken and depressed.

sunken *verb pa. pple*: see SINK *verb*.

sunker /ˈsʌŋkə/ *noun. Canad. dial.* L19.
[from SUNK + -ER[1].]
A submerged rock.

sunket /ˈsʌŋkɪt/ *adverb & noun. Scot. & north.* L17.
[Prob. alt. of SOMEWHAT.]
▶† **A** *adverb.* To some extent, somewhat. L17–L18.
▶ **B** *noun.* Usu. in *pl.*
1 Something, *esp.* something to eat. E18.
2 A dainty, a titbit. E18.

sunless /ˈsʌnlɪs/ *adjective.* L16.
[from SUN *noun*[1] + -LESS.]
Without the sun or a sun; not lit by the sun's rays, dark or dull through absence of sunlight.

📖 S. HARVESTER Dull dusty sunless offices in the chaotic rabbit-warren of officialdom.

■ **sunlessness** *noun* M19.

sunlight /ˈsʌnlʌɪt/ *noun.* ME.
[from SUN *noun*[1] + LIGHT *noun*.]
The light of the sun; this as visible at a particular time or place; a patch or area lit by the sun.

📖 D. MADDEN The sunlight streamed through the chapel's high windows.

sunlight /ˈsʌnlʌɪt/ *adjective. poet. rare.* E19.
[from SUN *noun*[1] + LIGHT *adjective*[2], or from prec. after *starlight*.]
= SUNLIT.

sun-lighted /ˈsʌnlʌɪtɪd/ *ppl adjective.* L18.
[from SUN *noun*[1] + *lighted* pa. pple of LIGHT *verb*[2]: see -ED[1].]
= SUNLIT.

sunlighting /ˈsʌnlʌɪtɪŋ/ *noun.* M20.
[from SUNLIGHT *noun* + -ING[1].]
1 The illumination of a building etc. by sunlight. M20.
2 The action of doing daytime work in addition to one's usual night-time job. Cf. MOONLIGHT *verb* 3. L20.

sunlit /ˈsʌnlɪt/ *ppl adjective.* E19.
[from SUN *noun*[1] + LIT *adjective*.]
Lighted or illuminated by the sun.

📖 R. WEST Alice . . had gone out of the dark drawing-room into the sunlit garden.

sunly /ˈsʌnli/ *adjective. rare.* OE.
[from SUN *noun*[1] + -LY[1].]
Of, pertaining to, or resembling the sun, solar.

sunn /sʌn/ *noun.* L18.
[Hindi, Urdu *san* from Sanskrit *śana* hempen.]
A leguminous shrub, *Crotalaria juncea*, with long narrow leaves and bright yellow flowers, widely cultivated in southern Asia for its fibre; the fibre of this plant used for cordage, sacking, etc.

Sunna /ˈsʊnə, ˈsʌnə/ *noun.* Also **-ah**. E18.
[Arab. = custom, normative rule.]
The body of traditional customs attributed to Muhammad and accepted (together with the Koran) as authoritative by Muslims. Cf. SUNNI, SUNNITE.

Sunni /ˈsʊni, ˈsʌni/ *noun & adjective.* L16.
[Arab. = lawful, formed as prec.]
▶ **A** *noun.* Pl. same, **-s**. The majority religious group of Muslims, commonly described as orthodox and differing from the Shia in their understanding of the Sunna and in their rejection of the claim of Ali, Muhammad's son-in-law and the fourth caliph, to be the first true successor of the Prophet. Also, a member of this group, a Sunnite. L16.
▶ **B** *attrib.* or as *adjective.* Of, pertaining to, or designating the Sunni or their religion. E19.
■ **Sunnism** *noun* the doctrines or principles of Sunni L19. **Sunnite** *noun & adjective* = SUNNI E18.

sunnies /ˈsʌnɪz/ *noun pl. Austral. colloq.* L20.
[Abbreviation.]
Sunglasses.

sunnud *noun* var. of SANAD.

sunny /ˈsʌni/ *adjective*. ME.
[from SUN *noun*[1] + -Y[1].]
1 Of weather, a day, etc.: characterized by or full of sunshine, bright with sunlight. ME. **2** Exposed to sunlight, lit or warmed by the sun. M16. **3** Of a person, temperament, expression, etc.: bright and cheerful, good-natured, radiant. M16. **4** Of, produced by, or resembling the sun; (of hair) bright yellow, golden. L16.

> **1** H. KEMELMAN A lovely sunny day with a blue sky and picture-book clouds. **2** OUIDA This little gay room was certainly brighter and sunnier. **3** F. W. FARRAR The unquestioning truthfulness of a sunny nature.

Phrases & special collocations: **Sunny Jim** [from an energetic character used to advertise a brand of breakfast cereal] (*a*) a cheerful or good-natured person; (*b*) = ***Sonny Jim*** s.v. SONNY. **sunny side** (*a*) the side of a street, house, etc., tending to get more sun; (*b*) the more cheerful aspect of circumstances etc.; (*c*) ***on the sunny side of***, on the right side of (i.e. less than) an age; (*d*) ***sunny side up***, (of an egg) fried on one side only.
■ **sunnily** *adverb* in a sunny manner; chiefly *fig.*, brightly, cheerfully: M19. **sunniness** *noun* E17.

sunrise /ˈsʌnrʌɪz/ *noun*. LME.
[App. from clauses such as *before the sun rise*, where *rise* is a verb in the subjunct. Cf. SUNSET, SUNSHINE.]
The rising of the sun at daybreak; the time of this; the coloured or illuminated sky associated with sunrise; the direction of sunrise, the east.
Comb.: **sunrise industry** a new and expanding industry, esp. in electronics, computers, or telecommunications, regarded as signalling prosperity.
■ Also **sunrising** *noun* (*arch.*) ME.

sunset /ˈsʌnsɛt/ *noun & verb*. LME.
[App. from SUN *noun*[1] + SET *noun*[1], but perh. partly (like SUNRISE) from a subjunct. clause such as *before the sun set*.]
▶ **A** *noun*. **1** The setting of the sun at the end of the day; the time of this; the coloured or illuminated sky associated with sunset; the direction of sunset, the west. LME. **2** *fig.* The end or declining period of a time of prosperity, a person's life, etc. E17.

> **1** H. B. STOWE One of those intensely golden sunsets which kindles the . . horizon into one blaze of glory. **go off into the sunset**, **ride off into the sunset**, **sail off into the sunset** [from a conventional closing scene of many films] (freq. *iron.*) achieve a happy ending. **2** J. R. ILLINGWORTH The gloom that darkens, or the hope that glorifies the sunset of our days.

Comb.: **sunset home** (chiefly *US*) an old people's home; **sunset industry** an old and declining (esp. heavy) industry; **sunset law**, **sunset legislation** N. AMER. POLITICS: whereby a government agency or programme is automatically terminated at the end of a fixed period unless formally renewed; **sunset shell** a burrowing bivalve mollusc of the genus *Gari*, with a long oval shell which (in some kinds) is pinkish with ray-like markings.
▶ **B** *verb*. Infl. **-tt-**.
1 *verb intrans.* Decline, sink. *rare*. M20. **2** *verb trans.* N. AMER. POLITICS. Subject to or terminate by means of sunset legislation. L20.
■ **sunsetting** *noun* (*arch.*) = SUNSET *noun* 1 LME. **sunsetty** *adjective* suggestive of sunset M19.

sunshine /ˈsʌnʃʌɪn/ *noun, adjective, & verb*. ME.
[Prob. of a similar origin to SUNRISE & SUNSET, but cf. Old Frisian *sunnaskin*, Middle & mod. Low German *sunnenschīn*.]
▶ **A** *noun*. **1** The light of the sun, direct sunlight uninterrupted by cloud; a patch or area lit by the sun. Also, fine weather. ME. ▶†**b** A burst or spell of sunshine. E17–M18. **2** *fig.* **a** A source of happiness or prosperity. Freq. as a familiar form of address. Cf. ***ray of sunshine*** s.v. RAY *noun*[1]. L16. ▶**b** A favourable or gracious influence; a condition or atmosphere of happiness or prosperity. L16. ▶**c** Happiness, cheerfulness, joy; sunny disposition, brightness of expression. E18.

> **1** H. JAMES The purifying sunshine, which lay in generous patches upon the floor. I. MURDOCH The morning sunshine brightened the room. **2a** M. GEE Look, Sunshine, I'm a busy man. **b** E. A. FREEMAN To bask in the sunshine of the court. **c** D. M. MULOCK He thawed into . . enthusiasm beneath the sunshine of her influence.

Comb.: **sunshine law** *US*: making the official meetings and records of certain government agencies accessible to the public; **sunshine roof** = *sun-roof* (a) s.v. SUN *noun*[1]; **Sunshine State** (*a*) *US* any of the States of New Mexico, South Dakota, California, and Florida; (*b*) *Austral.* the State of Queensland; **sunshine-yellow** (of) a bright shade of yellow.
▶ **B** *attrib.* or as *adjective*. Now *rare*.
1 Full of or characterized by sunshine, sunny; *fig.* cheerful, happy, prosperous. L16. **2** Remaining faithful or consistent only in prosperity; fair-weather. L18.
▶ **C** *verb intrans.* Shine as or like the sun. *rare*. E17.
■ **sunshineless** *adjective* dull, gloomy M19.

sunshining /ˈsʌnʃʌɪnɪŋ/ *adjective*. Now *rare*. E17.
[from SUNSHINE *noun* + -ING[2].]
= SUNSHINY.

†**sun-shining** *noun*. *rare*. ME–M19.
[from SUN *noun*[1] + *shining* verbal noun of SHINE *verb*: see -ING[1].]
= SUNSHINE *noun*.

sunshiny /ˈsʌnʃʌɪni/ *adjective*. L16.
[from SUNSHINE *noun* + -Y[1].]
= SUNNY.

sunspot /ˈsʌnspɒt/ *noun*. E19.
[from SUN *noun*[1] + SPOT *noun*.]
1 A spot or mark on the skin caused by exposure to the sun. E19. **2** ASTRONOMY. A spot or patch on the surface of the sun, appearing dark by contrast with the surrounding areas, and consisting of a cool region in the photosphere associated with local concentration of magnetic flux lines. M19. **3** CINEMATOGRAPHY. A powerful arc lamp used to simulate sunlight in colour cinematography; = ***sun arc*** s.v. SUN *noun*[1]. M20. **4** A place that enjoys plentiful sunshine. L20.
Comb.: **sunspot cycle** the recurring increase and decrease in the number of sunspots, with a period averaging just over 11 years.

sunstone /ˈsʌnstəʊn/ *noun*. Also (esp. in sense 4) **sun-stone**. LME.
[from SUN *noun*[1] + STONE *noun*.]
†**1** [translating Latin *solis gemma*.] A white stone which throws out rays like the sun. Only in LME. **2** MINERALOGY. **a** Any of several varieties of feldspar showing red or golden reflections from minute embedded crystals of mica, iron oxide, etc. L17. ▶**b** = CAT'S-EYE 1. L18. **3** Amber (from the Greek myth that the Heliades or daughters of the sun, when changed into trees, wept amber). Chiefly *poet.* M19. **4** A stone sacred to the sun or connected with sun-worship. M19. **5** [translating Old Norse *sólarsteinn*.] A stone of uncertain properties, said in medieval Icelandic sources to enable location of the sun in an overcast sky. Chiefly *Hist.* L19.

sunt /sʌnt/ *noun*. E19.
[Arab. *sant*.]
In N. Africa and the Middle East: an acacia, *Acacia nilotica*, whose pods yield tannin; the wood of this tree. Cf. BABUL.

suntan /ˈsʌntan/ *verb & noun*. E19.
[from SUN *noun*[1] + TAN *noun*[1], *verb*.]
▶ **A** *verb intrans. & trans.* Infl. **-nn-**. Tan or brown (the skin or body) by exposure to the sun, esp. through sunbathing. Freq. as ***suntanned*** *ppl adjective*. E19.

> M. TWAIN That swarthy suntanned skin of his.

▶ **B** *noun*. **1** Tanning or browning of the skin caused by exposure to the sun, esp. through sunbathing; a tan thus obtained. E20. **2** In *pl.* Lightweight tan-coloured summer uniform worn by military personnel; trousers forming part of this uniform; casual trousers resembling these. *US*. M20.

> **1** N. SHERRY Working . . in the . . sun trying to get a suntan.

Comb.: **suntan cream**, **suntan lotion**, **suntan oil**: to protect the skin from sunburn and promote suntanning.

sun-up /ˈsʌnʌp/ *noun*. Chiefly *N. Amer.* E18.
[from SUN *noun*[1] + UP *adverb*[1], after *sundown*.]
Sunrise. Freq. in ***from sun-up to sundown***.

sunward /ˈsʌnwəd/ *noun, adverb & adjective*. M16.
[from SUN *noun*[1] + -WARD.]
▶ **A** *noun*. The direction of the sun. M16.
▶ **B** *adverb*. Towards the sun, in the direction of the sun. E18.
▶ **C** *adjective*. Moving or facing in the direction of the sun. M18.
■ Also **sunwards** *noun & adverb* L16.

sunways /ˈsʌnweɪz/ *adverb*. Also (*rare*) **-way**. M17.
[from SUN *noun*[1] + -WAYS.]
In the direction of the apparent daily movement of the sun; left to right, from east to west, clockwise.

sunwise /ˈsʌnwʌɪz/ *adverb & adjective*. M19.
[formed as prec. + -WISE.]
▶ **A** *adverb* = prec. M19.
▶ **B** *adjective*. Moving or facing sunwise. L19.

sunyata /ˈʃuːnjətɑː, s-/ *noun*. E20.
[Sanskrit *śūnyatā* emptiness, from *śūnya* empty, void.]
BUDDHISM. The doctrine that phenomena are devoid of an immutable or determinate intrinsic nature, often regarded as a means of gaining an intuition of ultimate reality.

Sun Yat-sen /sʌn jatˈsɛn/ *noun phr.* M20.
[Chinese (Cantonese) *Suen Yât Sin*, (Mandarin) *Sun Yixian*, name adopted by Sun Wen (1866–1925), founder in 1911 of the Republic of China.]
Used ***attrib.*** to designate a Chinese style of jacket or suit based on Western designs.

Sun Yat-senism /sʌn jatˈsɛnɪz(ə)m/ *noun phr.* E20.
[formed as prec. + -ISM.]
The political principles of Sun Yat-sen, concerned primarily with Chinese nationalism and democracy and the people's livelihood.

sup /sʌp/ *noun*[1].
[Old English *sūpa*: cf. SIP *verb*, SOUP *noun*.]
1 A small quantity of liquid such as can be taken into the mouth at one time; a mouthful, a sip. OE. **2** (Alcoholic) drink. *dial.* E19.
Phrases: **a bit and a sup**, **a bite and a sup**, **bit and sup**, **bite and sup** (now *arch. & dial.*) a little food and drink. **a good sup** *dial.* a fair amount, a considerable quantity, (of liquid).

sup /sʌp/ *noun*[2]. Also **sup.** (point). L19.
[Abbreviation.]
= SUPP.
colour sup, ***lit. sup.***, etc.

sup /sʌp/ *noun*[3]. M20.
[Abbreviation.]
MATH. Supremum (of).

sup /sʌp/ *verb*[1]. Infl. **-pp-**.
[Old English *sūpan* = Middle Low German *sūpen*, Old High German *sūfan* (Dutch *zuipen*, German *saufen* drink, booze), Old Norse *súpa* from Germanic strong verb.]
1 *verb trans. & intrans.* Take (liquid) into the mouth in small quantities; take (liquid food) with a spoon. Now chiefly *Scot. & north.* OE. ▶**b** *verb trans.* Drink, swallow, esp. by mouthfuls or spoonfuls. Foll. by *up*, *off*, †*out*, †*in*. LME. †**2** *verb trans.* Swallow up, consume; absorb, take in. Usu. foll. by *up* (or *in*). OE–M17. **3** *verb trans. fig.* Have experience of. Now chiefly in ***sup sorrow***. OE.

> **1** A. ALVAREZ The old man supped his pint.

With adverbs in specialized senses: †**sup out** eject, expel.

sup /sʌp/ *verb*[2]. Infl. **-pp-**. ME.
[Old French *super*, *soper* (mod. *souper*), from Germanic base also of SUP *verb*[1].]
1 *verb intrans.* Eat one's supper; take supper. (Foll. by *on*, *off*, (†*of*, *with*) the food.) ME. ▶**b** *verb trans.* Make a supper of. Also with cognate obj. *rare*. LME. **2** *verb trans.* Give the last feed of the day to (a hawk, horse, or hound). Also foll. by *up*. L16. †**3** *verb trans.* Of food: provide a supper for. *rare*. L16–M17. **4** *verb trans.* Entertain at supper. E17.

> **1** K. AMIS Hubert had taken care to sup well that evening. *Proverb*: Who sups with the devil will need a long spoon.

sup. *abbreviation*.
Supplement.

supari /suːˈpɑːriː/ *noun*. M17.
[Hindi *supārī*.]
In the Indian subcontinent: the areca palm; its seed, the betel-nut.

supawn /sʌˈpɔːn/ *noun*. *US*. M18.
[Dutch *sappaen* from Algonquian.]
A kind of porridge made from maize flour boiled in water.

supe /suːp, sjuːp/ *noun & verb*. *slang*. E19.
[Abbreviation.]
▶ **A** *noun*. A supernumerary; a superintendent. E19.
▶ **B** *verb intrans.* Act as a supernumerary in a theatre. L19.

supellectile /suːpəˈlɛktʌɪl, -tɪl/ *noun & adjective*. Now *rare* or *obsolete*. L16.
[Late Latin *supellectilis*, prob. formed as SUPER- + *lectus* couch, bed: see -ILE.]
▶ **A** *noun*. Furniture (*lit. & fig.*); apparatus, equipment. L16.
▶ **B** *adjective*. Pertaining to or of the nature of household furniture; *transf.* ornamental. E17.

supellex /suːˈpɛlɛks/ *noun*. *rare*. M16.
[Latin.]
Household furniture; the equipment for an experiment or operation.

super /ˈsuːpə, ˈsjuː-/ *noun*[1]. *colloq.* In sense 6 also **souper** /ˈsuːpə/. E17.
[In branch I from Latin *in super* on the top, over and above, from *in* in + *super* over, above. In branch II repr. SUPER- in various words beginning thus.]
▶†**I 1** A balance remaining; a debt outstanding. E–M17.
▶ **II 2** †**a** = SUPERSALT. Only in E19. ▶**b** = SUPERPHOSPHATE 2. E20. **3** A supernumerary; *spec.* = EXTRA *noun* 2. M19. **4** = SUPERHIVE; a box containing a certain number of sections of honey. M19. **5** = SUPERINTENDENT *noun* 2. M19. **6** A watch. *Criminals' slang*. M19. **7** = SUPERFINE *noun*. L19. **8** *Hist.* (**S-**.) The hydrogen bomb. M20. **9** CINEMATOGRAPHY & TELEVISION. Superimposition. M20. **10** High-octane petrol. *colloq.* M20. **11** Superannuation, pension. *Austral. & NZ*. L20.

11 J. FRAME All the retired old blokes . . lining up for their super every second Tuesday.

super /'su:pə, 'sju:-/ *noun*[2]. *US*. E20.
[Origin unkn.]
= MULL *noun*[4].

super /'su:pə, 'sju:-/ *adjective. colloq.* M19.
[Abbreviation of various adjectives beginning with SUPER-.]
1 = SUPERFICIAL *adjective* 1b. Orig. usu. *postpositive*. M19.
2 = SUPERFINE *adjective* 4. M19.
3 Very good or pleasant, excellent, splendid. Also as *interjection*. L19.

1 *Architectural Review* The entire area of 300 yards super was completed in under a week. **3** R. CROMPTON 'Wizard,' said William. 'Super,' said Ginger. K. MOORE She's going to give me the grandfather clock . . . I think it's super of her.

Special collocations & comb.: **Super Bowl** AMER. FOOTBALL (proprietary name for) the main championship game played annually between the champions of the National Football Conference and the American Football Conference. **super-de-luxe** *adjective* exceptionally good; excellent, splendid. **Super Tuesday** US POLITICS a primary election that takes place on the same day in several States.

super /'su:pə, 'sju:-/ *verb*[1]. *slang*. L19.
[Partly from SUPER *noun*[1], partly from verbs beginning with SUPER-.]
1 *verb intrans.* Appear in a play or film as an extra. L19.
2 *verb trans.* Remove (a pupil) from a school or class on account of age. Usu. in *pass. School slang*. E20.
3 *verb trans.* CINEMATOGRAPHY & TELEVISION. Superimpose (a caption etc.) on a film. M20.

super /'su:pə, 'sju:-/ *verb*[2] *trans. US*. E20.
[from SUPER *noun*[2].]
Back (a book) with mull.

super- /'su:pə, 'sju:-/ *prefix*.
[from or after Latin, from *super* adverb & preposition, above, on the top (of), beyond, besides, in addition. Cf. Sanskrit *upari-*, Greek *huper-* HYPER-, Old English *ofer-* OVER-.]
1 Denoting a higher spatial position, as ***superincumbent***, ***superpose***, ***superstructure***; *spec.* (ANATOMY & BIOLOGY) denoting occurrence above the part denoted by the 2nd elem., as ***supertemporal***.
2 Denoting superior rank or importance, or greater size, quantity, etc., as ***superpower***, ***supertanker***. ▸**b** Denoting a higher or more inclusive category or kind, as ***supercluster***, ***supergroup***. ▸**c** MUSIC. Forming nouns denoting a note next above another note, as ***supertonic***. ▸**d** MATH. = HYPER- 3C.
3 Denoting a high, unusual, or excessive degree of a quality, as ***superheat*** (verb & noun), ***supersubtle***, ***superweak***. ▸**b** CHEMISTRY. Denoting the presence of an element or group in the highest or (formerly) a particularly high proportion, as ***superoxide***, ***superphosphate***.
4 Denoting addition, supplementation, or repetition, as ***supercalendar***, ***superinfection***.
5 Redupl. to express (***a***) intensification of meaning; (***b***) a further increase in rank or degree, as ***super-supercluster***.
¶ Opp. SUB-. Freq. also treated as opp. INFRA- (cf. SUPRA-).
■ **super-a'chiever** *noun* a person who achieves extraordinary success at work L20. **superadia'batic** *adjective* (METEOROLOGY) designating or involving a lapse rate greater than that of dry air when it rises and expands adiabatically, or a temperature gradient in any fluid greater than that of an adiabatic expansion of the fluid during upward motion E20. **super'aerial** *adjective* situated above the atmosphere M17. **superaerody'namic** *adjective* of or pertaining to superaerodynamics or the phenomena with which it is concerned M20. **superaerody'namics** *noun* the branch of physics that deals with motion of and in a gas so rarefied that it has to be treated as a collection of individual particles rather than a continuous fluid M20. **super'affluence** *noun* extreme abundance M17. **supera'llowed** *adjective* (NUCLEAR PHYSICS) (of a beta decay) having an exceptionally high probability of occurrence M20. **superalloy** *noun* (METALLURGY) an alloy capable of withstanding high temperatures, high stresses, and often highly oxidizing atmospheres M20. **super'ambient** *adjective* situated around and above L17. **super'aqueous** *adjective* situated above water L19. **super'audible** *adjective* †(***a***) *rare* very loud; (***b***) (now *rare*) ultrasonic: E20. **super'average** *adjective* that exceeds the average M20. **superbike** *noun* (***a***) a motorcycle with a nominal engine capacity of 750 cc or more; (***b***) a de luxe (often expensive) model of bicycle: L20. **superbitch** *noun* (*slang*) an extremely unpleasant or malicious woman L20. **superbomb** *noun* (*Hist.*) (***a***) a fission bomb; (***b***) a fusion or hydrogen bomb: M20. **superbrain** *noun* (a person with) a brain with extraordinary powers E20. **superbug** *noun* (*colloq.*) (***a***) a genetically engineered bacterium; (***b***) a bacterium that has become resistant to antibiotics; (***c***) an insect that is difficult to control or eradicate, esp. because it has become immune to insecticides: L20. **super-'calender** *verb trans.* subject (paper) to additional calendering, so as to produce an extra smooth finish L19. **supercar** *noun* a high-performance sports car E20. **supercarrier** *noun* a very large aircraft carrier M20. **super'cautious** *adjective* extremely or excessively cautious M20. **super'cavitate** *verb intrans.* induce or undergo supercavitation M20. **supercavi'tation** *noun* cavitation (usu. deliberately enhanced) in which large air cavities form behind the blades of a propeller M20. **supercity** *noun* a very large city; a very highly developed city: M20. **super'civilized** *adjective* extremely or excessively civilized M19. **superco'llider** *noun* (PHYSICS) a collider in which superconducting magnets are used to accelerate particles to tens of teravolts L20. **supercolossal** *adjective* (*US colloq.*) very large, very good, stupendous M20. **supercomputer** *noun* an exceptionally powerful computer, capable of dealing with complex problems M20. **super'conscious** *adjective* transcending human or normal consciousness L19. **super'consciously** *adverb* in a superconscious manner L20. **super'consciousness** *noun* the state of being superconscious L19. **supercon'tract** *verb intrans.* & *trans.* (cause to) undergo supercontraction M20. **super-con'traction** *noun* the contraction of a hair or fibre to less than its original length after treatment with heat or chemicals M20. **supercrat** *noun* (*N. Amer.*) a powerful bureaucrat L20. **super'crescent** *adjective* growing over or on the top of something M17. **supercross** *noun* an indoor form of moto-cross L20. **supercurrent** *noun* (PHYSICS) an electric current flowing without dissipating energy, as in a superconductor M20. **super'dominant** *noun* & *adjective* (MUSIC) = SUBMEDIANT M19. **super-'Dreadnought** *noun* a battleship with an armament of big guns superior to that of the Dreadnoughts E20. **super'eloquent** *adjective* extremely eloquent L16. **superen'cipher** *verb trans.* encipher (a text etc.) after it has already been enciphered once L20. **superen'cipherment** *noun* the action of superenciphering something M20. **superex'change** *noun* (PHYSICS) an exchange force that acts between the electrons of two cations through those of an intervening anion, as in some antiferromagnetic materials M20. **super-'extra** *adjective* (esp. of bookbinding) of the very best quality M19. **superfamily** *noun* (BIOLOGY) a taxonomic grouping ranking next above family L19. **super'fatted** *adjective* (***a***) (of soap) containing more fat than can combine with the alkali; (***b***) *slang* (of a person) overweight, fat: L19. **superfecun'dation** *noun* (MEDICINE) = SUPERFETATION M19. **superfemale** *noun* (BIOLOGY) a female with a higher ratio of X chromosomes to autosomes than normal females E20. **superfix** *noun* [after *prefix*, *suffix*, etc.] PHONETICS a sequence of stress or other suprasegmental phonemes which is treated as a grammatical element M20. **superflow** *noun* (PHYSICS) flow of a superfluid M20. **superfluo'rescence** *noun* (PHYSICS) (***a***) the cooperative emission of radiation by a system of atoms as a result of fluoresence and the spontaneous correlation of excited atomic states; (***b***) superradiance: M20. **superfly** *adjective & noun* (US *slang*) (***a***) *adjective* (esp. of a narcotic drug) excellent, the best; (***b***) *noun* = PUSHER 1C: L20. **Superfund** *noun* (US) a government fund set up to finance the cleaning of sites polluted by toxic waste, in cases where the polluter is not known or no longer exists L20. **superga'lactic** *adjective* (ASTRONOMY) of or pertaining to a supergalaxy L20. **supergalaxy** *noun* (ASTRONOMY) a supercluster M20. **super'glottal** *adjective* situated or occurring above the glottis L19. **superglue** *noun* an exceptionally strong adhesive, such as cyanoacrylate L20. **supergrass** *noun* (*colloq.*) a police informer who informs on a large number of individuals or whose information is of exceptional value L20. **super'gravity** *noun* (PHYSICS) (a theory of) gravity as described or predicted by a supersymmetric quantum field theory L20. **supergrid** *noun* a distribution grid serving a larger area than other grids or incorporating other grids M20. **super'heavyweight** *noun & adjective* (of) a weight above heavyweight in boxing and other sports (in amateur boxing, above 91 kg); (designating) a boxer etc. of this weight: L20. **superhive** *noun* a removable upper compartment of a beehive M19. **superim'pending** *adjective* situated above or overhead E18. **superindi'vidual** *adjective & noun* (of or pertaining to) that which is above or greater than the individual E20. **superindi'vidualist** *adjective* (*rare*) = SUPERINDIVIDUAL *adjective* M20. **superin'due** *verb trans.* put on as a garment, esp. over another L17. †**superinstitute** *noun* appointment of a person to a benefice held by another M17–M18. **superinte'llectual** *adjective* that is beyond the scope of the intellect; that is more than intellectual: M17. **superin'telligent** *adjective* (***a***) beyond the range of intelligence; (***b***) very highly intelligent: M20. **superin'vest** *verb trans.* clothe as with an outer garment E17. **superi'onic** *adjective* (PHYSICS) having a high ionic electrical conductivity L20. **superla'ryngeal** *adjective* situated or occurring above the larynx E20. **superlattice** *noun* (***a***) METALLURGY an extensive arrangement of some of the atoms in a solid solution coexisting with the disorder of the remaining atoms (also called ***superstructure***); (***b***) METALLURGY a solid solution possessing this; (***c***) PHYSICS a small-scale periodicity in the composition of a semiconductor: M20. **superloo** *noun* (*colloq.*) a public convenience which offers a high standard of facilities and cleanliness M20. **super'luminal** *adjective* [Latin *lumin-*, *lumen* light] having or designating a speed greater than that of light M20. **super'luminally** *adverb* faster than light L20. **superma'jority** *noun* a number that is much more than half of a total, esp. in a vote L20. **supermale** *noun* (BIOLOGY) a male in which the ratio of X chromosomes to autosomes is lower than in normal males, or the ratio of Y chromosomes to autosomes is higher E20. **superma'rine** *adjective* occurring or performed above or on the surface of the sea E19. **super'massive** *adjective* (ASTRONOMY) having a mass many (i.e. typically between 10^6 and 10^9) times that of the sun M20. **supermind** *noun* (***a***) (a person with) an exceptional mind; (***b***) a collective or extended mind composed of several individual minds: E20. **supermini** *noun* (***a***) (COMPUTING) a mini supercomputer; (***b***) a type of small car with a relatively powerful engine: L20. **supermodel** *noun* a successful fashion model who has reached the status of a celebrity L20. **super'mullion** *noun* a mullion in the tracery of the upper part of a window M19. **super'mullioned** *adjective* having supermullions M19. **super'multiplet** *noun* (PHYSICS) (***a***) a group of transitions in an atom between spectral terms of different multiplicity, all involving the same change in the orbital quantum number *l* of an electron; (***b***) a multiplet comprising particles of different hypercharge as well as those of different charge: E20. **super'national** *adjective* = SUPRANATIONAL L19. **super'nationalism** *noun* = SUPRANATIONALISM E20. **super'normal** *adjective* exceeding that which is normal; extraordinary, exceptional: M19. **supernor'mality** *noun* the state or quality of being supernormal or exceptional; an instance of this: E20. **super'normally** *adverb* in a supernormal manner, to a supernormal degree L19. **super'numerous** *adjective* (long *rare* or *obsolete*) excessive in number, too numerous M17. **superoc'cipital** *adjective & noun* (now *rare*) = SUPRAOCCIPITAL *adjective & noun* M19. **super'octave** *noun* (MUSIC) an organ-stop sounding two octaves higher than the ordinary pitch L19. **super'orbital** *adjective* (***a***) (ANATOMY & ZOOLOGY, now *rare*) = SUPRAORBITAL; (***b***) ASTRONAUTICS designating or having a trajectory that goes beyond the orbit of a planet: M19. **super'ordinary** *adjective* beyond or superior to the ordinary, extraordinary M17. **superor'ganic** *adjective* (SOCIOLOGY) above the level of the organism; *esp.* designating (the evolution of) social and cultural phenomena which transcend the individuals in society M19. **superorganism** *noun* an organism composed of many independent organisms L19. **super'ovulate** *verb trans. & intrans.* (PHYSIOLOGY) (cause to) produce abnormally large numbers of ova at a single ovulation, esp. for animal breeding M20. **superovu'lation** *noun* (PHYSIOLOGY) production of abnormally many ova at once E20. **super'oxide** *noun* orig., the compound of oxygen with another element which contains the greatest possible proportion of oxygen; now, (a compound containing) the anion O_2^-; cf. PEROXIDE 1: M19. **super'oxygenate** *verb trans.* cause to have a high or excessive proportion of oxygen L18. **superparasite** *noun* (BIOLOGY) = HYPERPARASITE L19. **super'personal** *adjective* transcending the limits of what is personal M19. **super'physical** *adjective* = HYPERPHYSICAL E17. †**superplant** *noun* a plant growing on another plant; an epiphyte: E17–E19. **superplastic** *adjective & noun* (METALLURGY) (of, pertaining to, or designating) a metal capable of extreme plastic extension under load M20. **super'plastically** *adverb* in a superplastic manner M20. **superplas'ticity** *noun* the state or quality of being superplastic M20. **superpur'gation** *noun* extreme or excessive purging of the bowels M18. **super-race** *noun* a race of individuals with exceptional physical or intellectual qualities E20. **super-rat** *noun* a rat that is resistant to the action of the usual rat poisons L20. **super'rational** *adjective* above or beyond the scope of reason; higher than what is rational: L17. **super-re'fined** *adjective* extremely refined; highly refined: M18. **super-royal** *adjective* (***a***) *rare* higher than royal in rank; (***b***) (of paper) of the size next above royal: E17. †**supersalt** *noun* (CHEMISTRY) a salt containing an excess of the acid over the base, an acid salt E–M19. **super'scalar** *adjective* (COMPUTING) designating or relating to a microprocessor architecture which enables the execution of more than one instruction per clock cycle L20. **super'sensible** *adjective & noun* (that which is) above or beyond perception by the senses L18. **super'sensitive** *adjective* extremely or excessively sensitive M19. **supersensi'tivity** *noun* extreme or excessive sensitivity; PHYSIOLOGY an increased sensitivity of a tissue or organ to stimuli, as shown by a longer or increased response, a reduced threshold, or increased susceptibility: M20. **super'sensory** *adjective* (*rare*) extrasensory L19. **super'sensuous** *adjective* = SUPERSENSUAL 1 E19. **super'serviceable** *adjective* officious, unduly or excessively fawning E17. **superset** *noun* (MATH. & LINGUISTICS etc.) a set which includes another set or sets M20. **super'sexual** *adjective* (***a***) beyond or transcending sexuality; (***b***) having strong sexual desires: L19. **supersign** *noun* (***a***) a diacritical mark written or printed above a letter; (***b***) a combination of letters, figures, etc., forming a unit: M20. **supersound** *noun* sound which is too intense to be endured, or of too high a frequency to be perceived M20. **superspecies** *noun* (BIOLOGY) a monophyletic group of largely allopatric species which are closely related but too distinct to be regarded as subspecies of one species M19. **superstate** *noun* a dominant political community, *esp.* one formed from an alliance or union of several nations; *spec.* a superpower: E20. **superstore** *noun* a large store selling a variety of goods and typically situated away from a town's main shopping area M20. **superstring** *noun* (PHYSICS) an elementary particle in superstring theory; ***superstring theory***, a (version of) string theory that incorporates supersymmetry: L20. **supersy'mmetric** *adjective* (PHYSICS) possessing or pertaining to supersymmetry L20. **super'symmetry** *noun* (PHYSICS) a very general type of mathematical symmetry which relates fermions and bosons L20. **supertanker** *noun* a ship that is a very large tanker E20. **supertax** *noun* a higher rate of tax on incomes above a certain level, *esp.* (*Hist.*) that levied in Britain between 1909 and 1929 (succeeded by surtax) E20. **supertechno'logical** *adjective* (***a***) involving or using highly advanced technology; (***b***) beyond or superseding the technological: M20. **super'temporal** *adjective*[1] & *noun*[1] (***a***) *adjective* that is above time, transcending time; (***b***) *noun* a supertemporal thing: L17. **super'temporal** *adjective*[2] & *noun*[2] (now *rare*) = SUPRATEMPORAL *adjective*[1] & *noun* M19. **superun'leaded** *adjective & noun* (of or denoting) unleaded petrol with a higher octane rating than that of regular unleaded petrol, achieved by the addition of aromatic hydrocarbons L20. **supervoltage** *noun* a higher than usual voltage; *spec.* a voltage in excess of 200 kV in X-ray therapy: M20. **super'weak** *adjective* (PARTICLE PHYSICS) pertaining to or designating a proposed interaction several orders of magnitude weaker than the weak interaction which would not be invariant under charge conjugation and space inversion jointly L20. **super'worldly** *adjective* that is beyond what is attainable in this world L18.

superable /'su:p(ə)rəb(ə)l, 'sju:-/ *adjective*. E17.
[Latin *superabilis*, from *superare* overcome: see -ABLE. Cf. INSUPERABLE.]
Able to be overcome; surmountable.
■ **supera'bility** *noun* L19.

superabound /su:p(ə)rə'baʊnd, sju:-/ *verb intrans*. LME.
[ecclesiastical Latin *superabundare*, formed as SUPER- + *abundare* ABOUND.]
1 [With allus. to *Romans* 5:20.] Be more abundant than something else. LME.
2 Abound excessively; be very, or too, abundant. (Foll. by *in*, *with*.) E16.

1 F. W. FARRAR If grace superabounds over sin, why should we not continue in sin? **2** *Nature* Our world today superabounds with fact.

superabundant /suːp(ə)rəˈbʌnd(ə)nt, sjuː-/ *adjective.* LME.
[Late Latin *superabundant-* pres. ppl stem of *superabundare* SUPERABOUND: see -ANT[1].]
1 Abounding above measure; exceedingly plentiful. Now *rare.* LME.
2 Abounding above what is appropriate or desirable; exceeding the normal amount; too abundant. M16.
■ **superabundance** *noun* (*a*) the quality of being superabundant; the fact of superabounding; (*b*) a superabundant quantity or amount; a surplus: LME. **superabundancy** *noun* (now *rare*) (a) superabundance E17. **superabundantly** *adverb* LME.

superacid /ˈsuːpərasɪd, ˈsjuː-/ *adjective & noun.* E19.
[from SUPER- + ACID *adjective, noun.*]
▶ **A** *adjective.* †**1** CHEMISTRY. ***superacid salt***, = ***acid salt*** s.v. ACID *adjective* 2. E–M19.
2 Excessively or extremely acid. E20.
3 CHEMISTRY. Of, pertaining to, or of the nature of a superacid. E20.
▶ **B** *noun.* CHEMISTRY. A solution of a strong acid in a very acidic (usu. non-aqueous) solution, which is an extremely effective protonating agent. Also, an acid stronger than some standard acid. M20.
■ **superaˈcidity** *noun* E20.

superadd /suːpərˈad, sjuː-/ *verb.* LME.
[Latin *superaddere*, formed as SUPER- + ADD *verb.*]
1 *verb trans.* Add over and above; add to what has been added; *spec.* add as a further statement, mention in addition. LME.
2 *verb intrans.* Make a further addition *to.* M17.
■ **superaˈddition** *noun* (*a*) the action or an act of superadding; further addition; (*b*) a superadded thing: E17. **superaˈdditional** *adjective* of the nature of a superaddition M17.

superaltar /ˈsuːpərɔːltə, -rɒl-, sjuː-/ *noun.* ME.
[medieval Latin *superaltare*, formed as SUPER- + late Latin *altar(e)* altar.]
ECCLESIASTICAL. **1** A portable stone slab consecrated for use on an unconsecrated altar etc. ME.
2 A structure erected above and behind an altar; a reredos; a gradine. M19.

superannuate /suːpəˈranjʊət, sjuː-/ *adjective & noun.* Now *rare.* M17.
[formed as SUPERANNUATED.]
▶ **A** *adjective.* = SUPERANNUATED. M17.
▶ **B** *noun.* A superannuated person. E19.

superannuate /suːpəˈranjʊeɪt, sjuː-/ *verb.* M17.
[Back-form. from next: see -ATE[3].]
1 *verb trans.* (Of time) make antiquated or obsolete; dismiss or discard as antiquated or out-of-date. M17.
2 *verb trans.* Discharge from a post on account of age; *esp.* cause to retire on a pension, pension off. L17. ▸**b** Make (a post) pensionable; make pensionable the post of (an employee). L19.
3 *verb intrans. & trans.* (in *pass.*). Become too old for a post; reach the age at which one leaves a school, retires from work, etc. E19.

> **1** T. S. ELIOT This change . . does not superannuate either Shakespeare, or Homer.

■ **supeˈrannuable** *adjective* (of a post or salary) that entitles the holder to a pension M20.

superannuated /suːpəˈranjʊeɪtɪd, sjuː-/ *pa. pple & ppl adjective.* M17.
[medieval Latin *superannuatus*, formed as SUPER- + *annus* year, with assim. to Latin *annuus* ANNUAL: see -ATE[2], -ED[1].]
1 Disqualified or incapacitated by age; old and infirm. Formerly also, too old *to do* a thing; (foll. by *from*) incapable of by reason of age. M17.
2 Of a thing: worn out; antiquated, obsolete. M17. ▸**b** That has lasted a very long time; very old. *rare.* M17.
3 Discharged from a post with a pension after reaching a certain age. M18.

> **1** M. BISHOP The superannuated hippie in the soft-drink jersey.

superannuation /ˌsuːpəranjʊˈeɪʃ(ə)n, ˌsjuː-/ *noun.* M17.
[from SUPERANNUATE *verb*: see -ATION.]
1 †**a** The condition of being antiquated or obsolete. M17–M19. ▸**b** The condition of being old and infirm; impairment of the faculties by old age. Now *rare.* M18.
2 The action of superannuating an employee; a pension paid to a retired person; (in full ***superannuation contribution***) a regular payment made towards a person's future pension. E18. ▸**b** At certain public schools, the attainment of the specified age at which a pupil is required to leave. M19.

> **2** *Australian Financial Review* The unions also want to see superannuation extended into industries where coverage is low.

■ **superaˈnnuitant** *noun* a person in receipt of superannuation M19.

superate /ˈsuːpəreɪt, ˈsjuː-/ *verb trans. rare.* L16.
[Latin *superat-* pa. ppl stem of *superare*, formed as SUPER-: see -ATE[3].]
†**1** Rise above. Only in L16.
†**2** Surpass, exceed. L16–M17.
3 Overcome; get over. L16.

superb /suːˈpəːb, sjuː-/ *adjective.* M16.
[(Old & mod. French *superbe* from) Latin *superbus* proud, superior, distinguished.]
1 (Of a building, monument, etc.) of noble and magnificent proportions or aspect; grandly and sumptuously equipped or decorated; (of conditions, language, etc.) grand, stately, majestic. M16.
2 Of a person: proud, haughty. Now *rare.* M17.
3 Very fine, excellent. E18.
4 In names of birds and plants, with allus. to exceptionally bright coloration. M18.

> **3** J. BUCHAN Its back view was superb, covering the Cherwell valley. J. THURBER He was honestly frightened, or else he was a superb actor. **4** ***superb starling, superb sunbird, superb warbler***, etc.

■ **superbly** *adverb* M18. **superbness** *noun* L17.

†**superbious** *adjective. rare.* E16.
[from Old French *superbieus* or medieval Latin *superbiosus*, from Latin *superbia* pride, formed as prec.: see -IOUS.]
1 Proud, overbearing, insolent. E16–L17.
2 Stately, grand. L16–E18.

superbity /suːˈpəːbɪti, sjuː-/ *noun.* M16.
[from SUPERB + -ITY.]
Pride, arrogance.
¶ Obsolete after M17; revived after E20.

†**superbous** *adjective. rare.* L16–E18.
[Latin *superbus*: see SUPERB, -OUS.]
= SUPERBIOUS.

supercargo /suːpəˈkɑːgəʊ, sjuː-/ *noun.* Pl. **-oes**, ***-os**. L17.
[Alt. of SUPRACARGO after SUPER-.]
A representative of the ship's owner on board a merchant ship, responsible for overseeing the cargo and its sale. Formerly also, an agent who superintended a company's business abroad. Now chiefly *Hist.*
■ **supercargoship** *noun* the position or occupation of supercargo E19.

supercede *verb* see SUPERSEDE.

supercelestial /ˌsuːpəsɪˈlɛstɪəl, ˌsjuː-/ *adjective.* LME.
[from late Latin *supercaelestis* (= Greek *huperouranios*), formed as SUPER- + *caelestis*: see CELESTIAL.]
1 Situated or existing above the firmament. LME.
2 Of a nature or character higher than celestial. M16.

supercharge /ˈsuːpətʃɑːdʒ, ˈsjuː-/ *verb trans.* E20.
[from SUPER- 3 + CHARGE *verb.*]
Increase the pressure of the fuel-air mixture in (an internal-combustion engine).
■ **supercharger** *noun* a compressor that increases the pressure of the fuel-air mixture supplied to the cylinders of an internal-combustion engine, fitted to increase its efficiency E20.

super-charge /ˈsuːpətʃɑːdʒ, ˈsjuː-/ *noun.* In sense 2 usu. **supercharge**. M18.
[from SUPER- 1, 3 + CHARGE *noun.*]
1 HERALDRY. A charge borne over another charge. *rare.* M18.
2 An explosive charge of higher than usual pressure in the cylinders of an internal-combustion engine; increased pressure of the charge. E20.

supercharged /*in sense 1* suːpəˈtʃɑːdʒd, sjuː-; *in sense 2* ˈsuːpətʃɑːdʒd, ˈsjuː-/ *pa. pple & ppl adjective.* L19.
[from SUPER- 3 + *charged* pa. pple of CHARGE *verb.*]
1 Filled or imbued to excess; *esp.* highly charged with emotion. L19.
2 (Of the fuel-air mixture in an internal-combustion engine) increased in pressure by mechanical means; (of a vehicle or its engine) equipped with a supercharger. E20.

supercherie /sypɛrʃəri/ *noun.* Orig. Anglicized as †***superchery***. L16.
[French from Italian *soperchieria*, from *soperchio* superfluous, excessive.]
†**1** An attack made on a person at a disadvantage; (a piece of) foul play. L16–M17.
2 Trickery, deceit. M17.

supercilia *noun* pl. of SUPERCILIUM.

superciliary /suːpəˈsɪlɪəri, sjuː-/ *adjective & noun.* M18.
[from SUPERCILIUM + -ARY[1].]
ANATOMY & ZOOLOGY. ▶**A** *adjective.* Of or pertaining to the eyebrow or the region of the eyebrow; situated over the eye; having a marking over the eye. M18.
▶ **B** *noun.* A superciliary ridge or marking. M19.

supercilious /suːpəˈsɪlɪəs, sjuː-/ *adjective.* E16.
[from Latin *superciliosus*, formed as SUPERCILIUM: see -OUS.]
1 Haughtily contemptuous in character or demeanour; having or expressing an air of contemptuous indifference or superiority. (Earliest in SUPERCILIOUSLY.) E16.
†**2** Dictatorial, overbearing; censorious. L16–L18.
†**3** ZOOLOGY. In names of animals: distinguished by a conspicuous stripe, prominence, etc., over the eye. L18–E19.
■ **superciliously** *adverb* E16. **superciliousness** *noun* M17.

For other words beginning with *super-* see the entry for **super-**

supercilium /suːpəˈsɪlɪəm, sjuː-/ *noun.* Pl. **-ia** /-ɪə/. LME.
[Latin = eyebrow, ridge, summit, formed as SUPER- + CILIUM.]
1 ANATOMY. Orig., the eyebrow. Later, the lip of a bony cavity, esp. of the acetabulum. Long *rare* or *obsolete.* LME.
2 ARCHITECTURE. **a** A fillet above and below the scotia of an Attic base. Formerly also, a narrow fillet above the cymatium of a cornice. M16. ▸**b** The lintel of a doorframe. E19.
3 ZOOLOGY. A superciliary streak or marking. E19.

supercluster /ˈsuːpəklʌstə, ˈsjuː-/ *noun.* M20.
[from SUPER- 2b + CLUSTER *noun.*]
A cluster of objects that are themselves clusters; *esp.* (ASTRONOMY) a cluster of galactic clusters.
■ **superclustering** *noun* the formation or occurrence of superclusters M20.

supercoil /ˈsuːpəkɔɪl, ˈsjuː-/ *noun & verb.* M20.
[from SUPER- 2b + COIL *noun*[2].]
BIOCHEMISTRY. ▶**A** *noun.* A coiled coil; *spec.* a DNA superhelix. M20.
▶ **B** *verb trans. & intrans.* Make into or become a supercoil. M20.

superconductivity /ˌsuːpəkɒndʌkˈtɪvɪti, ˌsjuː-/ *noun.* E20.
[from SUPER- 3 + CONDUCTIVITY.]
PHYSICS. The property of having zero electrical resistivity, as exhibited by some substances at very low temperatures.
■ **superconˈduct** *verb intrans.* conduct electricity without any resistance M20. **superconˈducting** *ppl adjective* possessing no electrical resistance; (of a device) employing a substance in this state: E20. **superconˈduction** *noun* = SUPERCONDUCTIVITY; conduction of electricity without resistance: M20. **superconˈductive** *adjective* = SUPERCONDUCTING E20. **superconˈductor** *noun* a substance that becomes superconducting at sufficiently low temperatures; such a substance in the superconducting state: E20.

supercontinent /ˈsuːpəˌkɒntɪnənt, ˈsjuː-/ *noun.* M20.
[from SUPER- 2 + CONTINENT *noun.*]
GEOLOGY. Each of the large land masses that are thought to have existed in the geological past and to have divided to form the present continents.

supercool /ˈsuːpəkuːl, suːpəˈkuːl, ˈsjuː-/ *adjective. colloq.* L20.
[from SUPER- 3 + COOL *adjective.*]
Very cool, relaxed, or good.

supercool /suːpəˈkuːl, sjuː-/ *verb.* L19.
[from SUPER- 3 + COOL *verb.*]
1 *verb trans.* Cool (a liquid) to below its freezing point without solidification or without the occurrence of crystallization; cool to below the temperature of a phase transition without the change of phase occurring. L19.
2 *verb intrans.* Undergo supercooling. M20.

supercooled /suːpəˈkuːld, sjuː-/ *ppl adjective.* L19.
[from SUPER- 3 + *cooled* pa. pple of COOL *verb.*]
Liquid though below the freezing point. Also, apparently solid, but formed from a liquid without a definite change of phase and having (on the atomic scale) the disorder characteristic of a liquid.

> J. C. RICH Glass is . . a supercooled liquid, because the material has no definite melting point.

supercritical /suːpəˈkrɪtɪk(ə)l, sjuː-/ *adjective.* E17.
[from SUPER- 3 + CRITICAL.]
1 Highly critical. E17.
2 SCIENCE. Of, pertaining to, or designating a fluid at a temperature and pressure greater than its critical temperature and pressure. M20.
3 SCIENCE. Of a flow of fluid: faster than the speed at which waves travel in the fluid. Of an aerofoil: giving rise to such a flow over its surface when its speed relative to the bulk fluid is subcritical, but in such a way that flow separation is largely avoided. M20.
4 NUCLEAR PHYSICS. Containing or being more than the critical mass. M20.
■ ˌ**supercritiˈcality** *noun* supercritical state M20.

super-duper /suːpəˈduːpə, sjuː-/ *adjective. colloq.* (orig. *US*). M20.
[Redupl. extension of SUPER *adjective.*]
Exceptionally good; excellent, splendid.

superego /suːpərˈiːgəʊ, -ˈɛgəʊ, sjuː-/ *noun.* Pl. **-os**. E20.
[from SUPER- 2 + EGO.]
PSYCHOANALYSIS. In Freudian theory: the part of the mind which internalizes parental and social prohibitions or ideals early in life and imposes them as a censor on the wishes of the ego; the agent of self-criticism.

superelevation /ˌsuːpərɛlɪˈveɪʃ(ə)n, ˌsjuː-/ *noun.* M17.
[from SUPER- 1, 2 + ELEVATION.]
†**1** Elevation to a higher rank. *rare.* Only in M17.
2 The height of the outer edge of a curve on a railway or road above the inner; the difference in height between the two edges. L19.
■ **superˈelevate** *verb trans.* elevate above or higher; bank (a curve in a road etc.) E20. **superˈelevated** *adjective* characterized by superelevation, banked E20.

supereminent /suːpər'ɛmɪnənt, sjuː-/ *adjective*. M16.
[Latin *supereminent-* pres. ppl stem of *supereminere* rise above, formed as SUPER- + *eminere*: see EMINENT.]
1 Supremely or specially high. Now *rare*. M16.
2 Above others in rank or status. L16.
3 Distinguished *above* others in character or attainment; conspicuous *for* some quality; (of a quality etc.) specially remarkable, noteworthy above that of others. L16.

📖 **3** E. A. POE A fantastic bow-knot of super-eminent dimensions.

■ **supereminence** *noun* the quality or fact of being supereminent E17. **supereminency** *noun* (now *rare* or *obsolete*) supereminence L16. **supereminently** *adverb* E17.

supererogation /ˌsuːpərɛrə'geɪʃ(ə)n, ˌsjuː-/ *noun*. E16.
[Late Latin *supererogatio(n-)*, from *supererogat-* pa. ppl stem of *supererogare*, formed as SUPER- + *erogare* pay out, from *e-* E- + *rogare* ask: see -ATION.]
The performance of more than duty or circumstances require; doing more than is needed; *spec.* (ROMAN CATHOLIC CHURCH) the performance of good works beyond what God commands or requires, as constituting a store of merit which the Church may dispense to others to make up for their deficiencies. Freq. in ***work of supererogation***.
■ **supererogant** /suːpər'ɛrəgənt, sjuː-/ *adjective* (*rare*) supererogatory M18. **supe'rerogate** *verb* (**a**) *verb intrans.* (now *rare* or *obsolete*) do more than is commanded or required; †(**b**) *verb trans.* (*rare*) spend or give in addition; perform as a work of supererogation: L16. **supe'rerogator** *noun* (*rare*) a person who performs works of supererogation L17. **supere'rogatorily** *adverb* beyond the requirements of the case, superfluously M19. **supererogatory** /suːpərɛ'rɒgət(ə)ri, sjuː-/ *adjective* characterized by or having the nature of supererogation; superfluous: L16.

superessential /suːpərɪ'sɛnʃ(ə)l, sjuː-/ *adjective*. LME.
[Late Latin *superessentialis*, formed as SUPER- + ESSENTIAL.]
That is above essence or being; transcending all that exists.
■ **super'essence** *noun* that which is superessential L17. **superessentially** *adverb* in a manner or mode that transcends all being L18.

superessive /suːpər'ɛsɪv, sjuː-/ *noun*. E20.
[from Latin *superesse* be higher than, formed as SUPER- + *esse* be: see -IVE.]
GRAMMAR. A case or relation which expresses position above or on top of; a word, form, etc., in this case.

superette /suːpə'rɛt, sjuː-/ *noun*. Chiefly *US*. M20.
[from SUPER(MARKET + -ETTE.]
A small supermarket.

superexalt /suːpərɪg'zɔːlt, -rɛg-, sjuː-/ *verb trans.* E17.
[ecclesiastical Latin *superexaltare*, formed as SUPER- + EXALT *verb*.]
1 Raise to a higher or the highest rank; exalt supremely. E17.
2 Extol exceedingly. *rare*. E17.
■ **superexal'tation** *noun* E17.

superexcel /suːpərɪk'sɛl, -rɛk-, sjuː-/ *verb trans. & intrans.* Now *rare*. Infl. **-ll-**. LME.
[medieval Latin *superexcellere*, formed as SUPER- + EXCEL.]
Excel highly or supremely.

superexcellent /suːpər'ɛks(ə)lənt, sjuː-/ *adjective*. M16.
[Late Latin *superexcellent-*, *-ens*, formed as SUPER- + *excellent-*: see EXCELLENT.]
Excellent to a high degree; very or supremely excellent.
■ **superexcellence** *noun* the quality or condition of being superexcellent LME. **superexcellency** *noun* (now *rare*) superexcellence L16. **superexcellently** *adverb* L17.

superfecta /suːpə'fɛktə, sjuː-/ *noun*. *US*. L20.
[from SUPER- 2 after *perfecta*.]
A method of betting in which the better must pick the first four finishers of a race in the correct order.

superfetation /ˌsuːpəfiː'teɪʃ(ə)n, ˌsjuː-/ *noun*. E17.
[French *superfétation* or mod. Latin *superfetatio(n-)*, from *superfetare* conceive by superfetation, formed as SUPER- + FOETUS: see -ATION.]
1 A second conception occurring during pregnancy; the formation of a second foetus in a uterus already pregnant. E17. ▸**b** BOTANY. In early use, a process supposed to be analogous to superfetation in animals, e.g. the growth of a parasite, an excessive production of ears of corn. In mod. use, the fertilization of the same ovule by two different kinds of pollen. E17.
2 *fig.* Additional or superabundant production or occurrence; the growth or accretion of one thing on another; an instance of this; an accretion, an excrescence. E17.

†superfice *noun*. LME–E19.
[(Old French from) Latin SUPERFICIES.]
= SUPERFICIES 1, 2a, 3b.

superficial /suːpə'fɪʃ(ə)l, sjuː-/ *adjective & noun*. LME.
[Late Latin *superficialis*, formed as SUPERFICIES: see -AL¹.]
▸ **A** *adjective*. **1** Of or pertaining to the surface; existing or occurring at or on the surface, not deep; constituting the surface or outermost part; MEDICINE situated or occurring on the skin or immediately beneath it; situated near the surface of the body; GEOLOGY situated at the surface of the earth and independent of underlying rock. LME. ▸**b** Of or pertaining to area or two dimensions. LME.
†**2** MATH. Of a number: having two prime factors. LME.
3 Not involving a profound or serious issue; insignificant. LME.
4 Lacking depth or thoroughness, cursory; not profound, shallow; (of a person) having no depth of character or knowledge. LME.
5 Outward, readily apparent; only apparent, not real or genuine. M16.

📖 **1** J. ABERNETHY The superficial veins appear remarkably large. A. BRINK The marks on the flanks . . are superficial scratches only. **b superficial foot**, **superficial metre**, etc. (an area of) a square foot, metre, etc. **3** A. HOLLINGHURST I kept the conversation short and superficial. **4** E. WHARTON Her relation with her aunt was as superficial as that of . . lodgers who pass on the stairs. CONAN DOYLE There had been a superficial search of his room. R. G. COLLINGWOOD The differences between them were not superficial but went down to essentials. **5** BURKE There is a superficial appearance of equity in this tax. *Psychology Today* The students characterized physics problems by superficial features.

▸ **B** *absol.* as *noun*. **1** ***the superficial***, that which is superficial; those who are superficial. L16.
2 In *pl.* Superficial characteristics or qualities. M19.
■ **superficialism** *noun* superficiality M19. **superficialist** *noun* a person whose knowledge, observation, or treatment is superficial M17. **superfici'ality** *noun* the quality or fact of being superficial; *esp.* lack of depth or thoroughness; shallowness of character: M16. **superficialize** *verb* †(**a**) *verb trans.* make a surface of (paint), apply paint to; (**b**) *verb intrans.* do something superficially; (**c**) *verb trans.* give a superficial character to: L16. **superficialness** *noun* superficiality E17.

superficially /suːpə'fɪʃ(ə)li, sjuː-/ *adverb*. LME.
[from prec. + -LY².]
1 Not profoundly or thoroughly. LME.
2 On or at the surface; ANATOMY just beneath the surface. LME.
3 As to outward appearance or form; externally, on the surface. L16.

📖 **1** S. SPENDER I know quite a lot of things superficially but nothing really well. **3** B. PYM We were, superficially at any rate, a very unlikely pair.

†superficiary *adjective*. E17–E18.
[Late Latin *superficiarius* situated on another person's land, formed as SUPERFICIES: see -ARY¹.]
= SUPERFICIAL *adjective* 1, 4.

†superficie *noun*. LME–E18.
[formed as next.]
= next.

superficies /suːpə'fɪʃiːz, sjuː-/ *noun*. Pl. same. M16.
[Latin, formed as SUPER- + *facies* (see FACE *noun*).]
1 GEOMETRY. A magnitude of two dimensions, having only length and breadth; a surface. M16.
2 a The outer surface of an object. L16. ▸**b** A surface layer. Now *rare*. E17.
3 †a A thing likened to a surface; the outward form or aspect. L16–L18. ▸**b** The outward appearance as distinct from the real nature. L16.
4 Superficial area or extent. M17.
5 ROMAN LAW. A structure in or on the surface of a piece of land which is so closely connected with it as to form part of it; a right possessed by a person over such a structure on someone else's land. M19.

📖 **3b** *Listener* The superficies of the work's style and expression are . . inadequate guides.

superfine /'suːpəfʌɪn, suːpə'fʌɪn, sjuː-/ *adjective & noun*. LME.
[from SUPER- 3 + FINE *adjective*.]
▸ **A** *adjective*. †**1** Exceedingly subtle. *rare*. Only in LME.
2 Excessively refined, fastidious, or elegant. L16.
3 Consisting of very fine particles or very thin threads; (of a file) having very fine teeth. M17.
4 COMMERCE. Extremely fine in quality; of the very best kind; (of liquid) the purest or clearest. L17.
5 Superlatively fine or excellent. M19.

📖 **2** H. JAMES She . . used language at times a trifle superfine. **3** *Practical Wireless* Remove the silk by using superfine abrasive paper.

▸ **B** *noun*. In *pl.* Goods of superfine quality. E19.
■ **superfinely** *adverb* L17. **superfineness** *noun* (*rare*) L16.

superfluent /suː'pɜːflʊənt, sjuː-/ *adjective*. *rare*. LME.
[Latin *superfluent-* pres. ppl stem of *superfluere*: see SUPERFLUOUS, -ENT.]
1 Superfluous; superabundant. LME.
2 Flowing or floating above. *arch.* LME.
■ **superfluence** *noun* (*arch.*) superabundance L15.

superfluid /*as noun* 'suːpəfluːɪd, 'sjuː-, *as adjective* suːpə'fluːɪd, sjuː-/ *noun & adjective*. M20.
[from SUPER- 3 + FLUID *adjective & noun*.]
PHYSICS. ▸ **A** *noun*. A fluid that exhibits superfluidity. M20.
▸ **B** *adjective*. Exhibiting or pertaining to superfluidity. M20.

superfluidity /suːpəfluː'ɪdɪti, ˌsjuː-/ *noun*. M20.
[from SUPER- 3 + FLUIDITY.]
PHYSICS. The property of flowing without viscosity or friction which is exhibited by isotopes of liquid helium below certain temperatures; an analogous property of other collections of particles (as the electrons in a superconductor) that exhibit quantum effects on a macroscopic scale.

superfluity /suːpə'fluːɪti, sjuː-/ *noun*. LME.
[Old & mod. French *superfluité* from late Latin *superfluitas*, formed as next: see -ITY.]
1 The state or quality of being superfluous; excessiveness; superabundance; excess. LME.
2 A superfluous person or thing. LME.
†**3** (An instance of) extravagant or immoderate behaviour. LME–E19.

📖 **1** S. T. WARNER He chokes from superfluity of breath. **2** H. ADAMS Nature regards the female as the essential, the male as the superfluity of her world.

superfluous /suː'pɜːflʊəs, sjuː-/ *adjective & noun*. LME.
[Latin *superfluus*, from *superfluere*, formed as SUPER- + *fluere* flow: see -OUS.]
▸ **A** *adjective*. **1** Exceeding what is sufficient; extravagant; superabundant. Also foll. by *of*, †*in*. LME.
2 Not needed or required; redundant, uncalled-for; unnecessary (also foll. by *to do*). Also, (of a person) doing more than is required. LME. ▸†**b** Ineffective, unprofitable; vain. *rare*. M16–M17.
†**3 a** Exceeding propriety or the norm; immoderate, inordinate. LME–E17. ▸**b** MUSIC. = AUGMENTED 2. M18–M19.

📖 **1** C. M. YONGE He has not an ounce of superfluous flesh. R. MACAULAY She had been, like . . very young writers, superfluous of phrase, redundant. **2** E. POUND Use no superfluous word, no adjective which does not reveal something. N. CHOMSKY Reporters have told us the same thing so often that it is almost superfluous to quote. B. VINE Now her needs had changed, I was superfluous.

▸ **B** *absol.* as *noun*. ***the superfluous***, that which is superfluous; superfluous people as a class. *rare*. M19.
■ **superfluously** *adverb* E16. **superfluousness** *noun* M16.

superflux /'suːpəflʌks, 'sjuː-/ *noun*. E17.
[from SUPER- 3 + FLUX *noun*.]
1 (A) superfluity, (a) superabundance. E17.
2 An excessive flow; an overflow. M18.

superfrontal /'suːpəfrʌnt(ə)l, 'sjuː-/ *noun*. M19.
[medieval Latin *superfrontale*, formed as SUPER- + *frontale* FRONTAL *noun*.]
ECCLESIASTICAL. **1** An ornamental cloth placed over an altar, hanging a few inches over the frontal. M19.
2 = DOSSAL 2. L19.

superfuse /suːpə'fjuːz, sjuː-/ *verb trans.* M17.
[Latin *superfus-* pa. ppl stem of *superfundere*, formed as SUPER- + *fundere* FUSE *verb*¹.]
1 Pour over or *on*. Now *rare* in *gen.* sense. M17. ▸**b** PHYSIOLOGY. Subject (tissue) to, or employ (fluid) in, the technique of superfusion. Also, (of a liquid) flow over the surface of (tissue) in a thin layer. M20.
2 Sprinkle *with*. *rare*. M17.
3 = SUPERCOOL *verb* 1. *rare*. E20.
■ **superfusate** *noun* (PHYSIOLOGY) a solution which has been used in superfusion L20.

superfusion /suːpə'fjuːʒ(ə)n, sjuː-/ *noun*. M17.
[Late Latin *superfusio(n-)*, formed as prec.: see -ION.]
1 The action or process of pouring liquid over something. M17. ▸**b** PHYSIOLOGY. The technique of running a stream of liquid over the surface of a piece of suspended tissue, keeping it viable and allowing observation of the interchange of substances. M20.
2 The process of supercooling; the state of being supercooled. *rare*. M19.

supergene /'suːpədʒiːn, 'sjuː-/ *noun*. M20.
[from SUPER- 2 + GENE.]
GENETICS. A group of closely linked genes, freq. having related functions.

supergene /'suːpədʒiːn, 'sjuː-/ *adjective*. E20.
[from SUPER- 1 + -GENE.]
MINERALOGY. Involving enrichment or deposition by a downward-moving solution; (of an ore or mineral) so enriched or deposited.

supergiant /'suːpədʒʌɪənt, 'sjuː-/ *noun & adjective*. E20.
[from SUPER- 2 + GIANT.]
▸ **A** *noun*. **1** A very large star that is even brighter than a giant, often despite being relatively cool. E20.
2 A supergiant galaxy. L20.
▸ **B** *adjective*. **1** ASTRONOMY. **a** Of a star: that is a supergiant. M20. ▸**b** Of a galaxy: in the brightest of five luminosity classes. M20.
2 *gen.* Extremely large. L20.

For other words beginning with *super-* see the entry for **super-**

supergroup /ˈsuːpəgruːp, ˈsjuː-/ *noun.* M20.
[from SUPER- 2, 2b + GROUP *noun*.]
1 A group comprising several related groups. M20.
2 A rock music group formed by star musicians from different groups; an exceptionally talented or successful rock group. L20.

superheat /suːpəˈhiːt, sjuː-/ *verb & noun.* M19.
[from SUPER- 3 + HEAT *noun, verb*.]
▶ **A** *verb trans.* Heat to a very high temperature; *esp.* raise the normal temperature of (steam); more widely, heat (a substance) above the temperature of a phase transition without the change of phase occurring. M19.
▶ **B** *noun.* The state of being superheated; the excess of temperature of a vapour above its temperature of saturation. L19.
■ **superheater** *noun* an apparatus for superheating steam M19.

superheated /suːpəˈhiːtɪd, sjuː-/ *ppl adjective.* M19.
[formed as prec. + HEATED.]
1 Of steam or vapour: heated above its temperature of saturation. Also more widely, heated above the temperature of a phase transition without the change of phase occurring. M19.
2 *gen.* Excessively heated or hot. M19.

superheavy /suːpəˈhɛvi, sjuː-/ *adjective & noun.* M20.
[from SUPER- 3 + HEAVY *adjective & noun*.]
▶ **A** *adjective.* **1** *gen.* Extremely heavy, heavier than the normal. M20.
2 NUCLEAR PHYSICS. Of, pertaining to, or designating an element with an atomic mass or atomic number greater than those of the naturally occurring elements, esp. one belonging to a group above atomic no. 110 having proton/neutron ratios which in theory confer relatively long half-lives. M20.
▶ **B** *noun.* A superheavy element. *colloq.* L20.

superhelix /ˈsuːpəhiːlɪks, ˈsjuː-/ *noun.* Pl. **-lices** /-lɪsiːz/, **-lixes**. M20.
[from SUPER- 2b + HELIX.]
BIOCHEMISTRY. A helix formed from a helix, a coiled coil, esp. as a structure assumed by protein or DNA helices. Cf. SUPERCOIL *noun*.
■ **superˈhelical** *adjective* pertaining to or consisting of a superhelix M20. **superˈhelically** *adverb* L20. **superheˈlicity** *noun* the state of being superhelical L20.

superhet /ˈsuːpəhɛt, ˈsjuː-/ *noun. colloq.* E20.
[Abbreviation.]
= SUPERHETERODYNE *noun*.

superheterodyne /suːpəˈhɛt(ə)rədʌɪn, sjuː-/ *adjective & noun.* E20.
[from SUPER(SONIC *adjective* + HETERODYNE *adjective, noun*.]
ELECTRICAL ENGINEERING. ▶**A** *adjective.* Employing or involving a method of radio and television reception in which the receiver produces a tunable signal which is combined with the incoming signal to produce a predetermined, often ultrasonic, intermediate frequency, on which most of the amplification is performed. E20.
▶ **B** *noun.* A superheterodyne receiver. E20.

superhighway /ˈsuːpəˌhʌɪweɪ, ˈsjuː-/ *noun.* E20.
[from SUPER- + HIGHWAY.]
1 A broad main road for fast traffic; an expressway. *N. Amer.* E20.
2 COMPUTING. More fully ***information superhighway***. An extensive electronic network such as the Internet, used for the rapid transfer of information such as sound, video, and graphics in digital form. L20.

superhuman /suːpəˈhjuːmən, sjuː-/ *adjective & noun.* M17.
[Late Latin *superhumanus*, formed as SUPER- + *humanus* HUMAN.]
▶ **A** *adjective.* **1** Higher than (that of) a human. M17.
2 Beyond normal human capability, stature, etc. E19.

> 🕮 **1** P. P. READ The one article of Christian belief which confirms him as a superhuman being is his resurrection. **2** G. DURRELL We had, after superhuman efforts, got them to eat avocado pears.

▶ **B** *noun.* That which is superhuman; a superhuman being. L19.

> 🕮 G. B. SHAW Beware of the pursuit of the Superhuman: it leads to . . contempt for the Human.

■ **superhuˈmanity** *noun* the quality, condition, or fact of being superhuman L18. **superhumanize** *verb trans.* make or represent as superhuman M19. **superhumanly** *adverb* M19. **superhumanness** /-n-n-/ *noun* (*rare*) E20.

superhumeral /suːpəˈhjuːm(ə)r(ə)l, sjuː-/ *noun.* E17.
[Late Latin *superhumerale*, formed as SUPER- + *humeralis* HUMERAL.]
ECCLESIASTICAL. A vestment worn over the shoulders, as an ephod, amice, or pallium.

†**superial** *adjective.* LME–E18.
[medieval Latin adjective from Latin *superus* (see SUPERIOR) or *superius* (adverb) higher.]
Superior.

superimpose /suːp(ə)rɪmˈpəʊz, sjuː-/ *verb.* L18.
[from SUPER- 1 + IMPOSE *verb*, after next.]
1 *verb trans.* Place or lay (one thing) over another; *fig.* cause to follow on and exist side by side with something else. Usu. foll. by *on, over, upon*. L18. ▸**b** Place in a superior rank or position to others. M19.
2 *verb intrans.* Of two figures, sets of results, etc.: admit of being brought into coincidence; have corresponding values, variations, etc. L20.

> 🕮 **1** G. VIDAL Lozenges of light superimposed . . designs upon the tiled floor. J. LE CARRÉ It's a rotten system. It's superimposed on tribalism.

■ **superimposable** *adjective* E20.

superimposition /ˌsuːpərɪmpəˈzɪʃ(ə)n, ˌsjuː-/ *noun.* L17.
[from SUPER- 1 + IMPOSITION, after Latin *superimponere*: see IMPONE.]
1 The action or process of superimposing one thing on another; the state or fact of being superimposed. L17.
2 CINEMATOGRAPHY. An image created by superimposing two or more separate images. M20.

superincumbent /suːp(ə)rɪnˈkʌmbənt, sjuː-/ *adjective.* M17.
[from SUPER- 1 + INCUMBENT *adjective*.]
1 Lying or resting on something else; overlying. M17.
2 Suspended above; overhanging. Chiefly *literary*. E19.
3 Of pressure: exerted from above. M19.

> 🕮 **3** *fig.*: A. H. CLOUGH A tyrannous sense of superincumbent oppression.

superinduce /suːp(ə)rɪnˈdjuːs, sjuː-/ *verb trans.* M16.
[Latin *superinducere* cover over, in late Latin bring in, add, formed as SUPER- + INDUCE.]
1 Introduce or acquire in addition to or so as to displace another person or thing; *spec.* †(*a*) take (a second spouse); (*b*) *arch.* appoint (a person) over another in office. Also foll. by *on, upon*. M16.
2 Produce; bring about, induce (esp. an additional disease). Also foll. by *on*. E17.
3 Cover *with*; deposit *over* or *upon*. M17.

> 🕮 **1** M. HEWLETT Upon such a crisis . . Mary Beaton superinduced . . her aunt. **2** J. ADDAMS The tuberculosis superinduced . . by the inadequate rooms. **3** C. VANCOUVER A black peaty stratum, superinduced with . . red bog.

■ **superinducement** *noun* = next M17.

superinduction /suːp(ə)rɪnˈdʌkʃ(ə)n, sjuː-/ *noun.* E17.
[Late Latin *superinductio(n-)*, from *superinduct-* pa. ppl stem of *superinducere*: see prec., -ION.]
1 The action or an act of superinducing a person or thing. E17.
2 A superinduced thing; an extraneous addition. M18.

superinfection /suːp(ə)rɪnˈfɛkʃ(ə)n, sjuː-/ *noun.* E20.
[from SUPER- 4 + INFECTION.]
1 MEDICINE. (An) infection occurring after or on top of an earlier infection, esp. following treatment with broad-spectrum antibiotics. E20.
2 MICROBIOLOGY. The further infection (esp. by a virus) of cells already infected with a similar agent. E20.
■ **superinfect** *verb trans.* cause (an infected cell) to be further infected *with* an organism of a similar kind; (of a bacterium or virus) infect (an already infected cell): M20.

superintend /suːp(ə)rɪnˈtɛnd, sjuː-/ *verb.* E17.
[ecclesiastical Latin *superintendere* translating Greek *episkopein*, formed as SUPER- + INTEND.]
1 *verb trans.* Be responsible for the arrangement or management of (an institution, activity, etc.); oversee, supervise. E17.
2 *verb intrans.* Exercise supervision over an activity, person, etc.; act as overseer. M17.

> 🕮 **1** CONAN DOYLE A . . governess superintended the education of two . . children. **2** J. K. JEROME I want to . . superintend . . and tell him what to do.

■ **superintender** *noun* (*rare*) L18.

superintendence /suːp(ə)rɪnˈtɛnd(ə)ns, sjuː-/ *noun.* L16.
[formed as next: see -ENCE.]
†**1** A body of superintendents of the Church of Scotland. *rare*. Only in L16.
2 = SUPERINTENDENCY 1. E17.

superintendency /suːp(ə)rɪnˈtɛnd(ə)nsi, sjuː-/ *noun.* L16.
[medieval Latin *superintendentia*, formed as next: see -ENCY.]
1 The office or position of a superintendent; (the exercise of) the authority or right of superintending. L16.
2 A district etc. presided over by a superintendent. M18.

superintendent /suːp(ə)rɪnˈtɛnd(ə)nt, sjuː-/ *noun & adjective.* M16.
[ecclesiastical Latin *superintendent-* pres. ppl stem of *superintendere* SUPERINTEND: see -ENT.]
▶ **A** *noun.* **1** CHRISTIAN CHURCH. **a** = BISHOP *noun* 1. *obsolete* exc. *Hist.* M16. ▸**b** A chief or presiding minister in a non-episcopal Church; *spec.* (*a*) a Lutheran minister presiding over churches and pastors of a particular district; (*b*) *Hist.* (in the Church of Scotland) a minister supervising the administration of the Church in a particular district; (*c*) (in the Methodist Church) an itinerant minister, *esp.* the presiding minister of a circuit. M16.
2 *gen.* A person who superintends; an overseer; *esp.* the director or manager of a business or institution. L16. ▸**b** The chief administrative official of a district; a governor. M18. ▸**c** A police officer next above the rank of inspector; *US* the head of a police department. M19.
Comb.: **superintendent-general** an official having control over several superintendents.
▶ **B** *adjective.* Superintending, overseeing; holding the position of a superintendent. L16.
■ **superintendentship** *noun* †(*a*) (*rare, joc.*) a title for an Anglican bishop; (*b*) the office or position of a superintendent: M16.

superior /suːˈpɪərɪə, sjuː-/ *adjective, noun, & adverb.* LME.
[Old French *superiour* (mod. *supérieur*) from Latin *superior* compar. of *superus* that is above, from SUPER-: see -IOR.]
▶ **A** *adjective.* **1** On a higher physical level; situated above; upper. Formerly also, heavenly, celestial. LME. ▸**b** ASTRONOMY. Of a planet: having its orbit outside that of the earth (as Mars, Jupiter, etc.). L16. ▸**c** TYPOGRAPHY. Of a letter, figure, or symbol: written or printed above the line. L17. ▸**d** ANATOMY & BIOLOGY. Designating a part or organ situated above another (esp. of the same kind), or in a relatively high position. M18.
2 Higher in degree, rank, quality, importance, authority, etc. (foll. by *to*); greater or more numerous. Also, of a higher or more refined nature or character, supernatural, superhuman. LME.
3 Earlier; former. Long *rare* or *obsolete*. M16.
4 Foll. by *to*: above yielding to or being influenced by; unaffected by. M17. ▸**b** Having or displaying a high opinion of oneself; supercilious. M19.
5 Of high or above average quality etc. L18.

> 🕮 **1** E. BISHOP From our superior vantage point, we can clearly see a . . dugout. **2** R. G. COLLINGWOOD In the later nineteenth century the artist walked among us as a superior being. L. DEIGHTON You are my superior officer, Major Stinnes. *UnixWorld* The photo CD image . . is far superior to that provided by digital cameras. **4** M. O. W. OLIPHANT Strangely superior to her surroundings. **b** M. AMIS I didn't much like his superior tone. I. MURDOCH He was always so superior, everywhere the king.

Special collocations & phrases: **Father Superior** (the title of) the head of a monastery. ***Lady Superior***: see LADY *noun & adjective*. **Mother Superior** (the title of) the head of a convent or nunnery. ***superior conjunction***: see CONJUNCTION 2. **superior court** LAW any of the higher courts within a legal system whose decisions have weight as precedents. **superior numbers** more people; greater (esp. military) force or strength. **superior ovary** BOTANY: positioned above the calyx.
▶ **B** *noun.* **1** A person of superior rank or status; *esp.* a superior officer or official. LME. ▸**b** The head of a religious community or order. L15. ▸**c** *Hist.* A person granting tenure of a feudal fee to another. M16.
2 A person or (occas.) a thing of superior quality, character, etc. Also, a person's elder. M17.
3 TYPOGRAPHY. A superior letter, figure, or symbol, usu. smaller than the text characters; a superscript. E18.

> 🕮 **1** K. ISHIGURO To work for an incompetent superior can be a demoralizing experience. **c subject superior** a superior who holds as subject of a sovereign. **2** DICKENS I am very little your superior in years. B. JOWETT No one is the superior of . . Socrates in argument.

▶ **C** *adverb.* **1** In or to a higher position. *poet.* E18.
2 In a superior or supercilious manner. *literary*. E18.
■ **superiorly** *adverb* in a superior place, degree, or manner M16. **superiorship** *noun* (*a*) *rare* superiority; (*b*) the position or office of superior: E18.

superioress /suːˈpɪərɪərɪs, sjuː-/ *noun.* L17.
[from SUPERIOR *noun* + -ESS[1].]
A female superior; the head of a convent or nunnery.

superiority /suːˌpɪərɪˈɒrɪti, sjuː-/ *noun.* LME.
[Old & mod. French *supériorité* or medieval Latin *superioritas*, from Latin SUPERIOR: see -ITY.]
1 The quality or condition of being superior; higher rank, position, or state. Also, an instance of this. LME.
2 †**a** In *pl.* Superior authorities. M16–E18. ▸**b** The position or office of feudal superior. L16.
Comb.: **superiority complex** PSYCHOANALYSIS an attitude of superiority which conceals actual feelings of inferiority and failure; *colloq.* an exaggerated feeling of personal superiority.

superius /suːˈpɪərɪəs, sjuː-/ *noun.* L18.
[Latin, use as noun of SUPERIOR.]
EARLY MUSIC. The highest voice part in choral music; the cantus.

superjacent /suːpəˈdʒeɪs(ə)nt, sjuː-/ *adjective.* L16.
[Latin *superjacent-* pres. ppl stem of *superjacere*, formed as SUPER- + *jacere* lie down: see -ENT.]
Lying above or upon; overlying, superincumbent.

superlapsarian /suːpəlapˈsɛːrɪən, sjuː-/ *noun & adjective.* *rare*. M17.
[from SUPER- + Latin *lapsus* LAPSE *noun* + -ARIAN. Cf. SUPRALAPSARIAN.]
THEOLOGY. ▶**A** *noun.* = SUPRALAPSARIAN *noun*. M17.
▶ **B** *adjective.* = SUPRALAPSARIAN *adjective*. E19.

For other words beginning with *super-* see the entry for **super-**

superlative /suːˈpəːlətɪv, sjuː-/ *adjective & noun*. LME.
[Old & mod. French *superlative*, *-tif*, from late Latin *superlativus*, from Latin *superlatus* (use as pa. pple of *superferre*), formed as SUPER- + *lat-* pa. ppl stem of *tollere* take away: see -IVE.]
▶ **A** *adjective*. **1** GRAMMAR. Designating the highest or a very high degree of a quality or attribute; designating a form of an adjective or adverb expressing this (with inflection, as English -EST[1]; with modifier, as English *most*; with a word from a different root, as English *best* etc.). Cf. ***comparative***, ***positive***. LME. ▸**b** Exaggerative, hyperbolical. L16.
2 Of the highest quality or degree; supereminent, supreme. LME.

2 N. SHUTE A great designer, and a superlative engineer. **superlative surprise** CAMPANOLOGY an especially complicated method of change-ringing.

▶ **B** *noun*. **1** GRAMMAR. The superlative degree; a superlative form etc. of an adjective or adverb. M16. ▸**b** *transf.* An exaggerated or hyperbolical expression; exaggerated language or phraseology. Usu. in *pl.* L16.
2 The highest or utmost degree *of* something; the height, the acme. L16.
3 A person or thing surpassing all others of a kind; a supreme example of something. E17.

1b *Motorway Express* It is a splendid car worthy of superlatives.

■ **superlatively** *adverb* L16. **superlativeness** *noun* E18.

†superlucrate *verb trans. rare*. M–L17.
[Late Latin *superlucrat-* pa. ppl stem of *superlucrari*, formed as SUPER- + *lucrari*, from *lucrum* LUCRE: see -ATE[3].]
Make a profit of (a certain amount).
■ **†superlucration** *noun* profit, gain L17–M18.

superlunar /suːpəˈluːnə, sjuː-/ *adjective*. M18.
[formed as next, after *sublunar*.]
= next.

superlunary /suːpəˈluːnəri, sjuː-/ *adjective*. E17.
[medieval Latin *superlunaris*, formed as SUPER- + *luna* moon: see -ARY[2]. Cf. SUBLUNARY, SUPRALUNARY.]
Situated or originating above or beyond the moon; celestial; *fig.* extravagant, fantastic.

superman /ˈsuːpəman, ˈsjuː-/ *noun*. Pl. **-men**. E20.
[from SUPER- 2 + MAN *noun*, translation by G. B. Shaw of German *Übermensch*.]
An ideal superior man of the future, orig. described by Nietzsche (esp. in PHILOSOPHY); *loosely* a man of extraordinary power or ability.
■ **supermanhood** *noun* the condition or character of a superman E20. **supermanliness** *noun* the character or qualities of a superman E20. **supermanly** *adjective* characteristic of or appropriate to a superman E20.

supermarket /ˈsuːpəmɑːkɪt, ˈsjuː-/ *noun*. M20.
[from SUPER- 2 + MARKET *noun*.]
A large self-service store, freq. one of a chain, selling a wide range of foods, household goods, etc.
Comb.: **supermarket cart** (*US*), **supermarket trolley** a wire basket on wheels pushed around a supermarket by a customer collecting goods for purchase.
■ **supermarkeˈteer** *noun* a person or company involved in a supermarket business M20. **supermarketing** *noun* the retailing of goods through supermarkets; the business of managing a supermarket: M20.

supermart /ˈsuːpəmɑːt, ˈsjuː-/ *noun*. M20.
[from SUPER- 2 + MART *noun*[1].]
= prec.

supermen *noun* pl. of SUPERMAN.

supermundane /suːpəˈmʌndeɪn, sjuː-/ *adjective*. L17.
[medieval Latin *supermundanus*, formed as SUPER- + *mundus*: see MUNDANE. See also SUPRAMUNDANE.]
Of or pertaining to the region above the earth; above or superior to worldly affairs; *fig.* ideal, fantastic.
■ Also **superˈmundal** *adjective* (*arch. rare*) L16.

†supern *adjective*. L15.
[Old French *superne*, or Latin *supernus*, from *super* above, over.]
1 = SUPERNAL *adjective* 1. L15–M16.
2 = SUPERNAL *adjective* 2b. *rare*. Only in E18.

supernaculum /suːpəˈnakjʊləm, sjuː-/ *adverb & noun*. L16.
[mod. Latin, repr. German *auf den Nagel (trinken)* (drink) on to the nail.]
▶ **A** *adverb*. To the last drop; to the bottom of the glass (with ref. to the practice of upturning an emptied glass on the left thumbnail). L16.
▶ **B** *noun*. Pl. **-la** /-lə/.
1 A high quality wine etc.; *transf.* an excellent type or example of anything. E18.
2 A deep draught of a drink; a full glass or portion of something. E19.
■ **supernacular** *adjective* of high quality, excellent M19.

supernal /suːˈpəːn(ə)l, sjuː-/ *adjective & noun*. LME.
[Old French, or medieval Latin *supernalis*, from Latin *supernus*, formed as SUPER-: see -AL[1].]
▶ **A** *adjective*. **1** Of, in, or pertaining to heaven; = CELESTIAL *adjective* 1. LME.
2 Of, in, or pertaining to the sky; CELESTIAL *adjective* 2. *arch.* E16. ▸**b** *gen.* On or at the top; upper. *rare*. L16.
3 Of high rank; elevated, exalted. M16.
4 Exceptionally good or great; supreme. E19.

1 *New Yorker* The Kabbalistic image of a supernal man/woman larger than the universe. **2** J. AGEE As if the whole . . sky were one mild supernal breath.

▶ **B** *noun*. An inhabitant of heaven. *rare*. M18.
■ **supernally** *adverb* †(*a*) at or towards the top; (*b*) supremely, exceedingly: L16.

supernatant /suːpəˈneɪt(ə)nt, sjuː-/ *adjective & noun*. M17.
[Latin *supernatant-* pres. ppl stem of *supernatare*, formed as SUPER- + *natare* (see NATANT).]
▶ **A** *adjective*. **1** Of a fluid: lying above a solid residue which has been separated out by precipitation, centrifugation, etc., or (occas.) floating on the surface of a denser fluid. M17.
2 Of a part of a ship etc.: above the surface of the water. L17.
▶ **B** *noun*. A supernatant fluid. E20.

supernate /ˈsuːpəneɪt, ˈsjuː-/ *noun*. M20.
[from prec. after *filtrate*, *precipitate*, etc.]
= SUPERNATANT *noun*.

supernatural /suːpəˈnatʃ(ə)r(ə)l, sjuː-/ *adjective & noun*. LME.
[medieval Latin *supernaturalis*, formed as SUPER- + NATURAL *adjective & adverb*: see -AL[1].]
▶ **A** *adjective*. **1** That transcends or is above nature; of or pertaining to a supposed force or system above the laws of nature. LME.
2 Beyond the natural or ordinary; unnaturally or extraordinarily great. *arch.* M16.

1 R. A. KNOX Our Lord's coming . . must be regarded as . . an invasion of the natural by the supernatural world. P. FARMER I'd never . . looked for supernatural revelations.

▶ **B** *noun*. **1** In *pl.* Supernatural things. Now *rare*. L16.
2 A supernatural being. E18.
3 ***the supernatural***, that which is supernatural; supernatural forces, effects, etc. M19.

3 G. GORER Belief in the occult or supernatural.

■ **supernaturalism** *noun* (*a*) = SUPERNATURALNESS; (*b*) (a theory or doctrine asserting) belief in the supernatural: L18. **supernaturalist** *noun & adjective* (*a*) *noun* a believer in the supernatural; (*b*) *adjective* = SUPERNATURALISTIC: M17. **supernaturaˈlistic** *adjective* of, pertaining to, or holding belief in the supernatural M19. **supernatuˈrality** *noun* (*a*) = SUPERNATURALNESS; (*b*) a supernatural thing: M17. **supernaturaliˈzation** *noun* the action of making something supernatural; the fact of becoming supernatural: M20. **supernaturalize** *verb trans.* make or regard as supernatural M17. **supernaturally** *adverb* LME. **supernaturalness** *noun* supernatural character or quality M18.

supernature /ˈsuːpəneɪtʃə, ˈsjuː-/ *noun*. M19.
[from SUPER- 1 + NATURE *noun*, after *supernatural*.]
The realm or system of the supernatural.

supernova /suːpəˈnəʊvə, sjuː-/ *noun*. Pl. **-vae** /-viː/, **-vas**. M20.
[from SUPER- 2 + NOVA.]
ASTRONOMY. A star whose brightness increases suddenly like a nova but to a very much greater degree, as a result of an explosion that disperses most of its material.

supernumerary /suːpəˈnjuːm(ə)r(ə)ri, sjuː-/ *adjective & noun*. E17.
[Late Latin *supernumerarius* applied to soldiers added to a legion after it is complete, from *super numerum*: see SUPER-, -ARY[1].]
▶ **A** *adjective*. **1** In excess of the usual, proper, or prescribed number; additional, extra; now *esp.* (*a*) (of an official or employee) engaged only in case of need or emergency; (*b*) (of an actor) having a non-speaking or non-singing part on stage. E17.
2 Beyond the necessary number. Now *rare* or *obsolete*. M17.

1 *Nursing Times* I am doing a degree course in nursing and am . . supernumerary when I am in the wards.

▶ **B** *noun*. **1** A supernumerary person or thing; an extra; *esp.* a supernumerary official or employee. M17. ▸**b** A supernumerary actor or performer. M18. ▸**c** MILITARY. An additional officer attached to a body of troops for some special purpose. L18.
2 A retired Wesleyan minister. L18.
3 A supernumerary structure, esp. an extra tooth; *spec.* in GENETICS, a chromosome which may be absent from normal organisms of either sex, having little or no effect on phenotype and occurring irregularly. E20.

1b *Expression!* You feel like a supernumerary from Cavalleria Rusticana.

superordinate /suːpərˈɔːdɪnət, sjuː-/ *adjective, noun, & verb*. E17.
[from SUPER- 2 + ORDINATE *adjective & noun, verb*, after *subordinate*.]
▶ **A** *adjective*. Superior in relation to others; higher in rank or order. Freq. foll. by *to*. E17.
▶ **B** *noun*. A superordinate person or thing; a superior; *spec.* (LINGUISTICS) a word whose meaning implies or includes that of another (cf. HYPONYM 2). E19.
▶ **C** *verb trans*. Place in a superior position *to*. *rare*. M19.

superordination /ˌsuːpərɔːdɪˈneɪʃ(ə)n, ˌsjuː-/ *noun*. M17.
[Late (eccl.) Latin *superordinatio(n-)* choice of a bishop's successor, from *superordinat-* pa. ppl stem of *superordinare*, formed as SUPER- + *ordinare* ORDINATE *verb*.]
1 Ordination of a successor by the holder of an ecclesiastical office. *rare*. M17.
2 The action or an act of superordinating one thing to another; the state or condition of being superordinate. Opp. SUBORDINATION 2. M19.

†superparticular *adjective & noun*. M16–M19.
[Late Latin *superparticularis*, formed as SUPER- + PARTICULAR.]
MATH. & MUSIC. ▶**A** *adjective*. Designating a ratio of the value $(n + 1) : n$, as $\frac{3}{2}$, $\frac{5}{4}$, etc., or (more fully ***multiple superparticular***) of the value $(xn + 1) : n$, as $2\frac{1}{2}$ $(\frac{5}{2})$, $3\frac{1}{3}$ $(\frac{10}{3})$, etc. M16–M19.
▶ **B** *noun*. A ratio of this type. L16–L17.

superphosphate /suːpəˈfɒsfeɪt, sjuː-/ *noun*. L18.
[from SUPER- 3b + PHOSPHATE *noun*.]
1 CHEMISTRY. An acid phosphate; a phosphate derived from phosphoric acid by replacement of some of the hydrogen atoms. L18.
2 A chemical fertilizer containing calcium hydrogen phosphate and calcium sulphate, prepared by treating powdered phosphate rock with sulphuric acid. Also ***superphosphate of lime***. M19.
2 *serpentine superphosphate*: see SERPENTINE *noun*.

†superplus *noun*. Chiefly *Scot*. LME–E19.
[medieval Latin, formed as SUPER- + PLUS.]
= SURPLUS *noun*.

superpose /suːpəˈpəʊz, sjuː-/ *verb trans*. E19.
[French *superposer*, from *super-* SUPER- + *poser* POSE *verb*[1], after Latin *superponere*: cf. next.]
Chiefly as ***superposed*** *ppl adjective*.
1 Place above or on something else; superimpose. E19.
2 PHYSICS etc. Bring into the same position so as wholly or partially to coincide; cause (two motions, waves, etc.) to occur together in the same space without destroying one another. M19. ▸**b** MATH. Transfer (one magnitude) ideally to the space occupied by another, esp. so as to show that they coincide. L19.
■ **superposable** *adjective* L19.

superposition /suːpəpəˈzɪʃ(ə)n, sjuː-/ *noun*. M17.
[French, or late Latin *superpositio(n-)*, formed as SUPER- + *positio(n-)* POSITION *noun*.]
1 MATH. The action of ideally transferring one figure into the position occupied by another, esp. so as to show that they coincide. M17. ▸**b** PHYSICS etc. The action of causing two or more sets of physical conditions or phenomena (as waves, motions) to coincide, esp. as independent influences on a system. M19.
2 GEOLOGY. The deposition of one stratum upon another, or the condition of being so deposited. L18.
3 *gen.* The action of superposing something; the condition of being superposed. Also, an instance of this. M19.

superpower /ˈsuːpəpaʊə, ˈsjuː-/ *noun*. E20.
[from SUPER- 2 + POWER *noun*.]
1 Electrical power produced and distributed efficiently by the interconnection of existing local systems. Orig. & chiefly *US* (now *Hist.*). E20.
2 *gen.* Exceptional or extraordinary power of some kind. E20.
3 A nation or State with extreme or dominant power and influence in world politics; *spec.* the United States of America and (formerly) the Union of Soviet Socialist Republics. M20.

superradiant /suːpəˈreɪdɪənt, sjuː-/ *adjective*. M20.
[from SUPER- 3 + RADIANT *adjective*.]
PHYSICS. Involving or exhibiting superradiance.
■ **superradiance** *noun* the spontaneous emission of coherent radiation by a system of atoms, esp. when the coherence is due to the initial correlation of the atoms by an external macroscopic polarization M20. **superradiantly** *adverb* L20.

super-real /suːpəˈrɪəl, sjuː-/ *adjective*. M20.
[from SUPER- 2 + REAL *adjective*[2].]
= SURREAL.
■ **super-realism** *noun* M20. **super-realist** *noun* M20. **super-reaˈlistic** *adjective* E20. **super-reˈality** *noun* M20.

superregeneration /ˌsuːpəriːdʒɛnəˈreɪʃ(ə)n, sjuː-/ *noun*. E20.
[from SUPER- 4 + REGENERATION.]
ELECTRONICS. Regenerative amplification in which self-oscillation is prevented by repeated quenching of the signal at an ultrasonic frequency.
■ **superreˈgenerative** *adjective* employing or characterized by superregeneration E20.

supersaturate /suːpəˈsatjʊreɪt, -tʃəreɪt, sjuː-/ *verb trans.* L18.
[from SUPER- 3 + SATURATE *verb*.]
Saturate to excess; *CHEMISTRY* add more of some substance to (a given substance) than is sufficient to saturate it. Usu. in *pass.* (foll. by *with*).
■ **supersaturated** *ppl adjective* saturated to excess; having more of some (specified or implied) substance added than is sufficient for saturation: L18. **ˌsupersatuˈration** *noun* the action of supersaturating something; the condition or state of being supersaturated: L18.

superscribe /suːpəˈskrʌɪb, ˈsuːpəskrʌɪb, sjuː-/ *verb trans.* L15.
[Latin *superscribere*, formed as SUPER- + *scribere* write.]
1 Write (a name or other inscription) at the top or on the outside of a document etc. L15.
2 Write a name, inscription, etc., at the top or on the outside of; inscribe (*with*); *spec.* address (a letter) *to* a person. L16.
3 Write (one letter etc.) above another or above the line of writing. L18.

> 🕮 **1** HENRY FIELDING His Name . . is erased, and yours superscribed. *Times* The Signature was superscribed by the royal sign manual. **2** STEELE He received a Message . . superscribed *With Speed*. A. GRAY A letter . . superscribed to the correspondence page of a . . woman's magazine.

superscript /ˈsuːpəskrɪpt, ˈsjuː-/ *noun & adjective.* L16.
[Latin *superscriptus* pa. pple of *superscribere* SUPERSCRIBE. Cf. SCRIPT *noun*¹.]
► **A** *noun.* †**1** The address on a letter. *rare* (Shakes.). Only in L16.
2 A character or symbol written or printed above a letter or above the line of writing, usu. smaller than the text characters and used as a reference mark and in mathematical equations. E20.
► **B** *adjective.* Written or printed above a letter or above the line of writing; *esp.* (of a character or symbol) written or printed above and usu. to the right of another. L19.
¶ Cf. SUBSCRIPT.
■ **superscripted** *adjective* (*a*) = SUPERSCRIPT *adjective*; (*b*) provided with superscript characters: M20. **superscripting** *noun* the action of providing or printing a superscript or superscripts; the use of superscripts, esp. in electronic text-handling: L20.

superscription /suːpəˈskrɪpʃ(ə)n, sjuː-/ *noun.* LME.
[Late Latin *superscriptio(n-)*, from Latin *superscript-* pa. ppl stem of *superscribere* SUPERSCRIBE: see -ION.]
A superscribed piece of writing, signature, etc.; *spec.* (*a*) (long *arch.*) the address on a letter; (*b*) the heading of a document.

supersede /suːpəˈsiːd, ˈsjuː-/ *verb.* Also (earlier) **-cede**. L15.
[Old French *supercéder*, later *-séder*, from Latin *supersedere* (in medieval Latin freq. *-cedere*) set above, be superior to, refrain from, omit, formed as SUPER- + *sedere* sit.]
1 *verb trans.* Postpone, defer, put off. Now only in *LAW*. *Scot.* L15. ▸†**b** *verb intrans.* Defer action; delay, hesitate. *Scot.* M16–M17.
†**2** *verb trans.* Desist from; discontinue (a procedure etc.). E16–M18. ▸**b** *verb intrans.* Desist, forbear, refrain. Usu. foll. by *from*, *to do*. L16–M19. ▸**c** *verb trans. LAW.* Stop, stay, (a proceeding etc.). M17–M19.
†**3** *verb trans.* Omit to mention; refrain from mentioning. L16–L17.
†**4** *verb trans.* Render superfluous or unnecessary. M17–L18.
5 *verb trans.* Make ineffective or void; annul; override. Now *rare* or *obsolete.* M17.
6 *verb trans.* Take the place of; succeed and supplant *in* some respect; in *pass.*, be replaced *by* something regarded as superior. M17.
7 *verb trans.* Adopt or appoint a person or thing in place of (also foll. by *by*, *with*); promote another over the head of; in *pass.*, be removed from a position or office to make way for another. E18.

> 🕮 **6** DICKENS Mrs Wickam . . superseded Mrs. Richards as the nurse of little Paul. V. WOOLF The tractor had . . superseded the plough. *Times* The original wooden structure was destroyed when it was superceded by stone. **7** D. GARNETT He had been superseded in authority.

■ **supersedable** *adjective* L18. **superseder** *noun* L18. **supersedure** *noun* (chiefly *US*) = SUPERSESSION L18.

supersedeas /suːpəˈsiːdɪas, sjuː-/ *noun.* LME.
[Latin, lit. 'you shall desist', included in the wording of the writ.]
1 *LAW.* A writ commanding the stay of legal proceedings or suspending the powers of an officer. Also ***writ of supersedeas***. LME.
†**2** *fig.* A thing which stops or stays an action etc.; a check. M16–M18.

supersedere /suːpəsɪˈdɪəri/ *noun.* M16.
[Latin: see SUPERSEDE.]
SCOTS LAW. A judicial order granting a debtor protection against diligence (see DILIGENCE *noun*¹ 4). Also, a creditors' agreement to postpone action against a debtor temporarily.

supersensual /suːpəˈsɛnsjʊəl, -ˈsɛnʃʊəl, sjuː-/ *adjective.* L17.
[from SUPER- 2, 3 + SENSUAL.]
1 Above or beyond the perception of the senses; transcending the senses; spiritual. L17.
2 Extremely sensual. M19.
■ **supersensually** *adverb* L17.

supersession /suːpəˈsɛʃ(ə)n, sjuː-/ *noun.* M17.
[Latin *supersessio(n-)*, formed as next: see -ION.]
The action or an act of superseding; the condition of being superseded.

supersessive /suːpəˈsɛsɪv, sjuː-/ *adjective.* E19.
[from Latin *supersess-* pa. ppl stem of *supersedere* SUPERSEDE + -IVE.]
Foll. by *of*: superseding; displacing.

supersonic /suːpəˈsɒnɪk, sjuː-/ *adjective & noun.* E20.
[from SUPER- 2 + SONIC.]
► **A** *adjective.* **1** Ultrasonic. E20.
2 Involving, pertaining to, or designating speeds greater than (*spec.* up to five times) the speed of sound; (of aircraft) able to fly at such speeds. Cf. HYPERSONIC 2. M20.
3 Very fast. Also, excellent, wonderful, thrilling. *colloq.* M20.
► **B** *noun.* An aircraft designed to fly at speeds greater than that of sound. M20.
■ **supersonically** *adverb* M20. **supersonics** *noun* (*a*) (now *rare*) ultrasonics; (*b*) the branch of science and technology that deals with supersonic flight: E20.

superspace /ˈsuːpəspeɪs, ˈsjuː-/ *noun.* L20.
[from SUPER- 2 + SPACE *noun*.]
PHYSICS. A concept of space–time in which points are defined by more than four coordinates; a space of infinitely many dimensions postulated to contain actual space–time and all possible spaces.

superstar /ˈsuːpəstɑː, ˈsjuː-/ *noun.* E20.
[from SUPER- 2 + STAR *noun*¹.]
An exceptionally famous or successful actor, musician, sportsman or sportswoman, etc.; *transf.* an outstanding performer in any area.

> 🕮 S. MORLEY He . . wanted to be a working actor rather than a superstar. *Daily Star* Soccer superstar Bryan Robson has been invited.

■ **superstardom** *noun* L20.

superstition /suːpəˈstɪʃ(ə)n, sjuː-/ *noun.* ME.
[Old & mod. French, or Latin *superstitio(n-)*, from *superstare* stand on or over, formed as SUPER- + *stare* stand: see -ION.]
1 Irrational awe or fear of the unknown etc.; belief in a religion considered false or pagan; religious belief or practice founded on fear or ignorance; credulity regarding religion or the supernatural; an instance of this, a practice, belief, etc., based on such fear or ignorance. ME.
2 An irrational religious system; a religion regarded as false or pagan; a ceremony or observance of such a religion. Now *rare* or *obsolete.* E16.
3 *gen.* Widely held but irrational or unfounded belief; a common but unjustifiable idea of the effects or nature of a thing etc. L18.

> 🕮 **1** G. CHARLES Jimmy had a . . meaningless superstition . . about not shaking hands across doorways. C. FRANCIS Myth and superstition have always surrounded the sea. M. MOORCOCK The capital was rotten with superstition. Charm-sellers, occultists . . flourished. **3** H. SPENCER Of the political superstitions, . . none is so universally diffused as the notion that majorities are omnipotent. *Daily Telegraph* The cruel superstition that a human hydrophobic can legally be smothered.

■ **superstitional** *adjective* (now *rare*) characterized by superstition, superstitious L17. **superstitionist** *noun* (now *rare*) a superstitious person M17. **superstitionless** *adjective* L19.

superstitious /suːpəˈstɪʃəs, sjuː-/ *adjective.* LME.
[Old & mod. French *superstitieux* or Latin *superstitiosus*, from *superstitio(n-)*: see prec., -IOUS.]
1 Of the nature of, involving, or characterized by superstition. LME.
2 †**a** Magical; having or credited with supernatural power. LME–M17. ▸**b** Used in or regarded with superstition. Now *rare* or *obsolete.* M16.
†**3** Extraordinary; excessive; superfluous. LME–M17.
4 Subject to or influenced by superstition, believing or practising superstitions. E16. ▸†**b** Excessively or extravagantly devoted. L16–E18.
†**5** Extremely careful or particular; fastidious, punctilious. M16–E19.

> 🕮 **1** C. KINGSLEY The superstitious terror with which that meteor-shower would have been regarded in old times. **4** P. CAREY He did not think himself a superstitious man, but this 'coincidence' unnerved him. B. VINE Hollies, holy trees, that the superstitious farmer was afraid to cut.

■ **superstitiously** *adverb* M16. **superstitiousness** *noun* E16.

superstrata *noun* pl. of SUPERSTRATUM.

superstrate /ˈsuːpəstreɪt, ˈsjuː-/ *noun.* L20.
[from next after *substrate*.]
LINGUISTICS. = SUPERSTRATUM 2.

superstratum /suːpəˈstrɑːtəm, -ˈstreɪtəm, sjuː-/ *noun.* Pl. **-ta** /-tə/. E19.
[mod. Latin, use as noun of neut. sing. of pa. pple of Latin *supersternere* spread over: see SUPER-, STRATUM.]
1 A stratum or layer deposited over or on something; an overlying or superficial stratum. Cf. SUBSTRATUM 2. E19.
2 *LINGUISTICS.* A language responsible for linguistic change (esp. in vocabulary) in another on which it is imposed and over which it is temporarily dominant. Cf. SUBSTRATUM 4. M20.

superstruct /suːpəˈstrʌkt, sjuː-/ *verb trans.* Now *rare* or *obsolete.* M17.
[Latin *superstruct-* pa. ppl stem of *superstruere*, formed as SUPER- + *struere* build.]
Build on something else, construct on a foundation, erect as a superstructure, (*lit.* & *fig.*).

> 🕮 S. JOHNSON Those . . on whose approbation his esteem of himself was superstructed.

†**superstruction** *noun.* E17.
[mod. Latin, noun of action from Latin *superstruere*: see prec., -ION.]
1 A superstructure. Only in 17.
2 The action of building on something. *rare.* Only in M19.

superstructive /suːpəˈstrʌktɪv, sjuː-/ *noun & adjective.* Now *rare.* E17.
[formed as SUPERSTRUCT + -IVE.]
►†**A** *noun.* Something belonging to or constituting a superstructure. E–M17.
► **B** *adjective.* Belonging to or constituting a superstructure. M17.
■ **superstructor** *noun* a builder of a superstructure M18. **superstructory** *adjective* = SUPERSTRUCTIVE *adjective* M17.

superstructure /ˈsuːpəstrʌktʃə, ˈsjuː-/ *noun.* M17.
[from SUPER- 1 + STRUCTURE *noun*.]
1 The part of a building above the foundations; a material structure resting on something else, *spec.* the constructions above the upper deck of a ship. M17. ▸**b** *GEOLOGY.* A relatively shallow overlying layer of an orogenic belt that is unaffected by plutonic activity or metamorphism. M20. ▸**c** *BIOCHEMISTRY.* The higher-order structure of a protein or enzyme molecule which is superimposed on the sequence of amino acids or nucleotide bases. M20.
2 A concept or idea built or founded on something else. M17. ▸**b** In Marxist theory, the institutions and culture considered to result from or reflect the economic system underlying a society. E20.
3 *METALLURGY.* = SUPERLATTICE (a). M20.
■ **superstructural** *adjective* pertaining to or constituting a superstructure L19.

supersubstantial /suːpəsəbˈstanʃ(ə)l, sjuː-/ *adjective.* M16.
[ecclesiastical Latin *supersubstantialis*, formed as SUPER- + *substantia* SUBSTANCE: see -AL¹.]
CHRISTIAN THEOLOGY. That transcends substance; *spec.* (*a*) [translating Greek *epiousios*] (of the bread in the Eucharist) above or transcending material substance, spiritual; (*b*) (of God) above or transcending all substance or being, superessential.
■ **supersubstantiˈality** *noun* (*rare*) E17. **supersubstantially** *adverb* (*rare*) LME. **supersubstantiate** *verb trans.* (*rare*) make supersubstantial E17.

supersubtle /suːpəˈsʌt(ə)l, sjuː-/ *adjective.* Also **-subtile**. L16.
[from SUPER- 3 + SUBTLE.]
Extremely or excessively subtle, oversubtle.
■ **supersubtilize** *verb trans.* make oversubtle L19. **supersubtlety** *noun* excessive subtlety M19.

super-superlative /suːpəsuːˈpəːlətɪv, sjuː-/ *adjective & noun.* *rare.* E17.
[from SUPER- 2 + SUPERLATIVE.]
► **A** *adjective.* More than superlative, of the very highest quality or degree. E17.
► **B** *noun.* A super-superlative thing, a degree beyond the superlative. E19.
■ **super-superlatively** *adverb* M17.

superterranean /suːpətəˈreɪnɪən, sjuː-/ *adjective & noun.* L17.
[from SUPER- 1 + TERRANEAN, after *subterranean*.]
► **A** *adjective.* Existing or living on or above the surface of the earth. L17.
► **B** *noun.* A dweller above ground or on the earth. L17.
¶ Opp. *subterranean*.
■ **superterraneous** *adjective* = SUPERTERRANEAN *adjective* L17.

superterrene /suːpətəˈriːn, sjuː-/ *adjective.* E18.
[from SUPER- 1 + TERRENE *adjective*, after *subterrene*. Cf. late Latin *superterrenus*.]
1 = SUPERTERRANEAN *adjective.* E18.
2 = next. M18.

For other words beginning with *super-* see the entry for **super-**

superterrestrial /suːpətəˈrestrɪəl, sjuː-/ *adjective*. E18.
[from SUPER- 1 + TERRESTRIAL *adjective*.]
Existing in or belonging to a region above the earth, celestial.

supertonic /suːpəˈtɒnɪk, sjuː-/ *noun*. E19.
[from SUPER- 2C + TONIC *noun*.]
MUSIC. The note above the tonic, the second note of the diatonic scale of any key.

supertunic /suːpəˈtjuːnɪk, sjuː-/ *noun*. E17.
[medieval Latin *supertunica*, formed as SUPER- + TUNIC.]
ANTIQUITIES. An outer tunic; *spec.* the vestment worn over the dalmatic by a sovereign at his or her coronation.

supervacaneous /suːpəvəˈkeɪnɪəs, sjuː-/ *adjective*. Now *rare* or *obsolete*. M16.
[Latin *supervacaneus*, formed as SUPER- + *vacare* be empty or void: see -EOUS.]
Unnecessarily added to what is essential; superfluous, redundant.
■ **supervacaneously** *adverb* M17. **supervacaneousness** *noun* M18.

†**supervacuous** *adjective*. E17–L18.
[Latin *supervacuus*, formed as SUPER- + VACUOUS.]
= prec.

supervene /suːpəˈviːn, sjuː-/ *verb*. M17.
[Latin *supervenire*, formed as SUPER- + *venire* come.]
1 *verb intrans.* Of a condition, incident, etc.: occur as a change, interruption, or addition; come directly or shortly after as a consequence or in contrast; follow closely on. (Foll. by *on*, *upon*, (rare) *to*.) M17.
†**2** *verb trans.* Supervene on (a condition, occurrence, etc.); *rare* supersede. E18–E19.

📖 **1** *Daily News* Typhus supervening on a gunshot wound. E. JONES Next morning a harder mood supervened.

■ **supervener** *noun* (*rare*) M17.

supervenient /suːpəˈviːnɪənt, sjuː-/ *adjective*. L16.
[Latin *supervenient-* pres. ppl stem of *supervenire*: see prec., -ENT.]
Supervening, coming after, occurring subsequently. (Foll. by *to*.)
■ **supervenience** *noun* (*rare*) = next M17.

supervention /suːpəˈvɛnʃ(ə)n, sjuː-/ *noun*. M17.
[Late Latin *superventio(n-)*, from *supervent-* pa. ppl stem of *supervenire*: see SUPERVENE, -ION. In later use partly directly from SUPERVENE.]
The action or fact of supervening; subsequent occurrence.

supervisal /suːpəˈvʌɪz(ə)l, sjuː-/ *noun*. Now *rare*. M17.
[from next + -AL¹.]
Supervision.

supervise /ˈsuːpəvʌɪz, ˈsjuː-/ *verb & noun*. L15.
[medieval Latin *supervis-* pa. ppl stem of *supervidere*, formed as SUPER- + Latin *videre* see.]
▶ **A** *verb trans.* †**1** Look over, survey, inspect; read through, peruse. L15–E18. ▸**b** *spec.* Read through for correction, revise. M17–M18.
2 Superintend the execution or performance of (a task, operation, etc.); oversee the actions or work of (a person); *spec.* act as an academic supervisor to. L16.

📖 **2** W. S. CHURCHILL He had supervised the day-to-day administration of the country. D. F. GALOUYE Radcliff . . supervised a pair of attendants as they positioned the . . camera.

▶†**B** *noun*. Inspection, perusal. *rare* (Shakes.). Only in E17.
■ **supervi'see** *noun* a person being supervised, *spec.* by the police or by an academic tutor L19.

supervision /suːpəˈvɪʒ(ə)n, sjuː-/ *noun*. M17.
[medieval Latin *supervisio(n-)*, formed as prec.: see -ION.]
The action or function of supervising a person, task, etc.; management, direction, superintendence. Now also *spec.*, the overseeing of a student or his or her work by a tutor; a tutorial.

📖 J. S. NORTHCOTE The artists . . worked under ecclesiastical supervision. *Which?* Don't let children play near a swimming pool . . without supervision.

Comb.: **supervision order** a court order placing a child or young person under the supervision of a local authority or a probation officer in cases of delinquency etc.

supervisor /ˈsuːpəvʌɪzə, ˈsjuː-/ *noun*. LME.
[medieval Latin, formed as SUPERVISE: see -OR.]
1 A person who supervises a person, task, etc.; a manager, a superintendent. Now also *spec.*, a tutor overseeing a student (esp. a postgraduate) or his or her work. LME. ▸†**b** = OVERSEER *noun* 1. LME–M18. ▸**c** Orig., an inspector of highways. Now (*US*), a railway track inspector. M16.
†**2** An onlooker, a spectator, an observer. *rare* (Shakes.). Only in E17.
3 A person reading over a text etc., esp. in order to make corrections; a reviser. Now *rare* or *obsolete*. E17.
4 *COMPUTING*. A program (usu. part of an operating system) that controls the execution of other programs and the allocation of resources. Also, an operating system. M20.
■ **supervisorship** *noun* the office or function of a supervisor; a body of supervisors: L15.

supervisory /ˈsuːpəvʌɪz(ə)ri, ˈsjuː-/ *adjective*. M19.
[from SUPERVISE *verb* + -ORY².]
Of or pertaining to supervision, having the function of supervising a person, task, etc.

†**supervive** *verb*. M16.
[Late Latin *supervivere*, formed as SUPER- + Latin *vivere* to live.]
1 *verb intrans.* Remain alive, survive. M16–L17.
2 *verb trans.* Outlive. L16–E18.

superwoman /ˈsuːpəwʊmən, ˈsjuː-/ *noun*. Pl. **-women** /-wɪmɪn/. E20.
[from SUPER- 2 + WOMAN *noun*.]
A woman of exceptional strength or ability; a woman who successfully combines roles as career woman, wife, and mother.

sup gum *noun phr.* var. of SUBGUM.

supinate /ˈsuːpɪneɪt, ˈsjuː-/ *verb*. M19.
[Back-form. from next.]
1 *verb trans.* Render supine; put (a hand, a forelimb) into the supine position; turn (the palm) upwards. Also, turn (the leg) outwards. Opp. PRONATE *verb* 1. M19.
2 *verb intrans.* Of a limb, esp. (in running) the foot: undergo supination. Of a person: turn the foot inward (while running etc.) to take the weight on the outside edge. Opp. PRONATE *verb* 2. E20.

supination /suːpɪˈneɪʃ(ə)n, sjuː-/ *noun*. M17.
[Latin *supinatio(n-)*, from *supinat-* pa. ppl stem of *supinare*, from *supinus*: see SUPINE *adjective*, -ATION. Cf. PRONATION.]
The action of supinating; the position or condition of being supinated. Opp. PRONATION.

supinator /ˈsuːpɪneɪtə, ˈsjuː-/ *noun*. E17.
[mod. Latin, formed as prec.: see -OR.]
ANATOMY. A muscle that effects or assists in supination; *spec.* either of two muscles of the forelimb. Opp. PRONATOR.

supine /ˈsuːpʌɪn, ˈsjuː-/ *noun*. LME.
[Late Latin *supinum* use as noun of neut. sing. of Latin *supinus*: see next.]
GRAMMAR. A Latin verbal noun used in the accusative case in *-um* with verbs of motion or in the ablative in *-u*, esp. to express purpose.

supine /ˈsuːpʌɪn, ˈsjuː-/ *adjective*. LME.
[Latin *supinus*, from base of *super* above, *superus* higher: see -INE¹.]
1 Facing upwards; lying face upwards or on the back; *spec.* (of the hand or forelimb) with the palm upwards and the radius and ulna parallel. Later also *loosely*, lying flat. LME.
2 *fig.* Morally or mentally inactive; inert, indolent; passive. E17.

📖 **1** SIR T. BROWNE They buried their dead on their backs, or in a supine position. R. CHURCH I lay supine in the grasses . . staring up vertically. **2** SHELLEY The supine slaves Of blind authority. *Field* The supine way we English have of letting things slide.

■ **supinely** *adverb* in a supine position or manner (chiefly *fig.*) E17. **supineness** *noun* (*a*) supine behaviour or state of mind, inertness; (*b*) *rare* supine position or posture: E17. †**supinity** *noun* = SUPINENESS M16–M18.

supp /sʌp/ *noun*. *colloq.* Also **supp.** (point). M20.
[Abbreviation.]
A supplement to a newspaper or periodical. Chiefly in ***colour supp***.

suppable /ˈsʌpəb(ə)l/ *adjective*. *rare*. Now chiefly *Scot.* L15.
[from SUP *verb*¹ + -ABLE.]
Able to be supped.

suppedanea *noun* pl. of SUPPEDANEUM.

†**suppedaneous** *adjective*. *rare*. M17–E18.
[from late Latin *suppedaneus*: see next, -ANEOUS.]
Placed under or supporting the feet; functioning as a footstool, pedestal, etc.

suppedaneum /sʌpɪˈdeɪnɪəm/ *noun*. Pl. **-nea** /-nɪə/. M19.
[Late Latin = footstool, use as noun of neut. of *suppedaneus* under the feet, formed as SUB- + Latin *ped-*, *pes* foot.]
Hist. A support for the feet of a crucified person, projecting from the vertical shaft of the cross.

suppeditate /sʌˈpɛdɪteɪt/ *verb trans.* Long *rare* or *obsolete*. M16.
[Latin *suppeditat-* pa. ppl stem of *suppeditare*: see -ATE³.]
Provide, supply.
■ **suppedi'tation** *noun* the action of supplying something; supply: E17.

supper /ˈsʌpə/ *noun*¹ & *verb*. ME.
[Old French *soper*, *super* (mod. *souper*) use as noun of *soper* SUP *verb*²: see -ER⁴.]
▶ **A** *noun*. The last meal of the day; an evening meal, *esp.* a light or informal one; a snack taken late in the evening; a social etc. occasion featuring such a meal; the time at which such a meal is taken. ME.

📖 G. GREENE He took Beatrice out to supper at a fish restaurant. *Lydney (Glos.) Observer* We had a cider and cheese supper. ***bump supper***: see BUMP *noun*¹. ***fish supper***: see FISH *noun*¹. ***Last Supper***: see LAST *adjective*. ***sing for one's supper***: see SING *verb*¹. ***the Lord's Supper***: see LORD *noun*.

Comb.: **supper club** a restaurant or nightclub serving suppers and usu. providing entertainment; **supper dance**: during or after which supper is served; **supper-time**: when supper is (customarily) taken.

▶ **B** *verb*. **1** *verb trans.* Give supper to, provide with supper; entertain at supper. E17. ▸**b** Give the evening feed to and bed down for the night (a horse, cow, etc.). Also foll. by *up*. Chiefly *Scot.* & *north.* E19.
2 *verb intrans.* Take one's supper; sup. L17.
■ **suppering** *noun* (*a*) the action of the verb; (*b*) *Scot.* & *north.* the evening feeding of cattle etc. (also foll. by *up*); the food given: M18. **supperless** *adjective* E16.

supper /ˈsʌpə/ *noun*². E16.
[from SUP *verb*¹ + -ER¹.]
A person who sups or sips something. Freq. with specifying word.

supping /ˈsʌpɪŋ/ *noun*. LME.
[from SUP *verb*¹ + -ING¹.]
1 The action of SUP *verb*¹; drinking by spoonfuls or mouthfuls. Formerly also, an instance of this, a sup. LME.
2 In *pl.* & *sing.* Food that can be supped; liquid food, broth. Now *dial.* LME.

supplant /səˈplɑːnt/ *verb trans.* ME.
[Old & mod. French *supplanter* or Latin *supplantare* trip up, overthrow, formed as SUB- + *planta* sole of the foot.]
†**1** Trip up, cause to stumble or fall by tripping. *rare*. ME–M17.
†**2** *fig.* Cause the downfall of, bring low, overthrow; confound or frustrate (a plan etc.). ME–L18.
3 Dispossess and take the place of (a person), esp. by treacherous or underhand means (formerly foll. by *from*, *of*); take the place of, supersede, replace, (a thing). ME. ▸**b** Remove from a position, get rid of, oust. Now *rare*. L16.
†**4** Uproot (a plant etc.), root out (*lit.* & *fig.*). L16–M17.

📖 **3** R. GRAVES She became the virtual head of our family, supplanting my mother. A. BLOND The book will be supplanted by . . the microchip.

■ **supplan'tation** *noun* LME. **supplanter** *noun* ME.

supple /ˈsʊp(ə)l/ *noun*. *Scot.* & *north.* M17.
[App. var. of SWIPPLE assim. to next.]
1 = SWIPPLE. M17.
2 A cudgel. E19.

supple /ˈsʌp(ə)l/ *adjective* & *verb*. ME.
[Old & mod. French *souple* from Proto-Romance from Latin *supplic-*, *supplex* submissive, suppliant, formed as SUB- + *plicare* fold, bend.]
▶ **A** *adjective*. **1** Easily bent or folded without breaking or cracking, pliant, flexible; (of a person, the body, etc.) capable of bending easily and gracefully, lithe; (of movement etc.) characterized by graceful flexibility. ME.
2 *fig.* Yielding readily to persuasion or influence, compliant. (Foll. by *to*.) ME. ▸**b** Of the mind etc.: adaptable, elastic. L18.
3 Artfully or servilely submissive or obsequious, ingratiatingly accommodating. E17.
4 Clever, cunning. *Scot.* E18.

📖 **1** S. COLVIN In spite of her build, she was supple . . in all her movements. MOLLIE HARRIS Willow sticks . . did not become brittle but remained supple. A. S. BYATT Her . . kid gloves were supple.

▶ **B** *verb*. **1 a** *verb trans.* Make supple, pliant, or flexible; (long *arch.*) make submissive or compliant, mollify. ME. ▸**b** *verb intrans.* Become supple or flexible; (long *arch.*) be submissive or compliant (*to*). *rare*. LME.
†**2** *verb trans.* Soothe (a wound, swelling, etc.) by applying a dressing, ointment, etc.; anoint with oil etc. LME–L17.
†**3** *verb trans.* Reduce the hardness of, soften. M16–E18.

📖 **1a** J. R. LOWELL To supple and to train the faculties. J. BUCHAN Hard new boots not yet suppled by use.

supplejack /ˈsʌp(ə)ldʒak/ *noun*. L17.
[from SUPPLE *adjective* + JACK *noun*¹.]
1 a Any of various chiefly tropical climbing or twining shrubs with tough flexible stems, e.g. (in the W. Indies) *Paullinia barbadensis* and other plants of the family Sapindaceae, (in the southern US) *Berchemia scandens*, of the buckthorn family, (in Australasia) *Ventilago viminalis*, of the buckthorn family, and *Ripogonum scandens*, of the lily family. L17. ▸**b** The stem of any of these plants as a material. E19.
2 A tough pliant walking-stick or cane made of the stem of such a plant. M18.
3 A toy representing the human figure, with limbs manipulated by a string. *US*. Now *rare* or *obsolete*. L18.

supplely *adverb* var. of SUPPLY *adverb*.

supplement /ˈsʌplɪm(ə)nt/ *noun*. LME.
[Latin *supplementum*, from *supplere* SUPPLY *verb*¹: see -MENT.]
1 A thing or part added to remedy a deficiency; an addition; an auxiliary item or means; (MEDICINE) a nutrient or vitamin given to remedy a dietary deficiency. LME. ▸**b** A part added to a book, periodical, document, etc., to provide further information; *spec.* a separate section, esp. a magazine with coloured illustrations, issued with a newspaper or periodical. E16. ▸**c** MATH. The angle which when added to a given angle makes 180 degrees. L16. ▸**d** A surcharge payable for an additional service or facility. E20.
†**2** The action of supplying something needed; the remedying *of* a deficiency or shortcoming. L15–M17.
†**3** The action of supplying or providing something; a thing supplied; supply, provision. M16–M17. ▸**b** The reinforcement of troops; a reinforcement. M16–M17.

📖 **1** B. VINE Some vitamin supplement she took. **b** F. WELDON He put down his paper. He was reading the city supplement. ***colour supplement***: see COLOUR *noun*. ***SUNDAY supplement***. **d** R. FRASER Pushed her into a first class carriage and paid the supplement.

supplement /ˈsʌplɪmɛnt/ *verb trans.* E19.
[from the noun.]
Provide a supplement for, remedy a deficiency in, add to with a supplement; add as a supplementary statement or remark. Freq. foll. by *by, with*.

📖 G. GISSING He . . supplemented his meal with . . grapes. K. M. E. MURRAY Spare time in which to supplement his income by literary work.

■ **supplemenˈtation** *noun* the action of supplementing something; an instance of this, a supplementary addition: M19. **supplementer** *noun* M17.

supplemental /sʌplɪˈmɛnt(ə)l/ *adjective & noun.* E17.
[formed as prec. + -AL¹.]
▶ **A** *adjective.* = SUPPLEMENTARY *adjective.* Foll. by *to, of.* Now chiefly *US.* E17.
supplemental chord MATH. either of two chords which join any point on a circle to the two end-points of any diameter.
▶ **B** *noun.* A supplementary fact etc. *rare.* L17.
■ **supplementally** *adverb* M18.

supplementary /sʌplɪˈmɛnt(ə)ri/ *adjective & noun.* M17.
[formed as prec. + -ARY¹.]
▶ **A** *adjective.* Of the nature of, forming, or serving as a supplement; additional, auxiliary. (Foll. by *to.*) M17.

📖 M. WESLEY There were so many travellers . . that . . there was a supplementary boat. **supplementary angle** MATH. either of two angles whose sum is 180°. **supplementary arc** MATH. either of two arcs which together form a semicircle and connect the end-points of two supplemental chords. **supplementary benefit** *Hist.* a system allowing people on low incomes to claim State benefit, according to their circumstances (now replaced by ***income support***). **supplementary examination**: allowing failed students a second attempt to pass. **supplementary lens** PHOTOGRAPHY a simple lens which can be attached to a camera lens to enable it to focus more closely.

▶ **B** *noun.* A supplementary person or thing; *spec.* (in parliamentary question time) a question supplementary to those tabled in advance. E19.
■ **supplementarily** *adverb* as a supplement M19. **supplemenˈtarity** *noun* (*rare*) the condition or quality of being supplementary L20.

suppleness /ˈsʌp(ə)lnɪs/ *noun.* L16.
[from SUPPLE *adjective* + -NESS.]
The quality or condition of being supple.

†**supplete** *verb trans. rare.* Only in M17.
[Latin *supplet-*: see next.]
Supplement.

suppletion /səˈpliːʃ(ə)n/ *noun.* ME.
[Old French from medieval Latin *suppletio(n-)*, from Latin *supplet-* pa. ppl stem of *supplere* SUPPLY *verb*¹: see -ION.]
†**1** The action or an act of supplementing something, supplementation. *rare.* ME–L15.
2 LINGUISTICS. The replacement of a form in a grammatical paradigm by one derived from a different root (e.g. English *went* as the pa. t. of *go*). M20.

suppletive /səˈpliːtɪv/ *adjective & noun.* M17.
[from prec. + -IVE.]
▶ **A** *adjective.* **1** Remedying a deficiency, supplementary. *rare.* M17.
2 LINGUISTICS. Displaying suppletion. E20.
▶ **B** *noun.* LINGUISTICS. A suppletive form. M20.
■ †**suppletively** *adverb*: only in M17.

suppletory /ˈsʌplɪt(ə)ri/ *adjective & noun.* E17.
[formed as prec. + -ORY¹, -ORY².]
▶ **A** *adjective.* Remedying a deficiency, supplementary. Foll. by *to, of.* Now *rare.* E17.
▶†**B** *noun.* A supplement. M17–E18.
■ †**suppletorily** *adverb* as a supplement: only in E17.

Supplex /ˈsʌplɛks/ *noun.* L20.
[Prob. from SUPPL(E *adjective* + *-ex* (as in SPANDEX, LUREX, etc.).]
(Proprietary name for) a synthetic stretchable fabric which is permeable to air and water vapour, used in sports and outdoor clothing.

suppliable /səˈplʌɪəb(ə)l/ *adjective. rare.* M17.
[from SUPPLY *verb*¹ + -ABLE.]
Able to be supplied.

supplial /səˈplʌɪəl/ *noun.* Now *rare* or *obsolete.* M18.
[formed as prec. + -AL¹.]
The action of supplying something.

suppliance /səˈplʌɪəns/ *noun*¹. Now *rare.* L16.
[formed as prec. + -ANCE.]
Supply.

suppliance /ˈsʌplɪəns/ *noun*². *rare. poet.* E17.
[from SUPPLIANT *adjective*¹ + -ANCE.]
The action of a suppliant, supplication.
■ **suppliancy** *noun* the condition of a suppliant M19.

suppliant /ˈsʌplɪənt/ *noun & adjective*¹. LME.
[Old & mod. French, pres. pple of *supplier* from Latin *supplicare* SUPPLICATE: see -ANT¹.]
▶ **A** *noun.* A person who supplicates, a supplicant. LME.
▶ **B** *adjective.* Supplicating, humbly petitioning; expressing or involving supplication. L16.

📖 W. C. BRYANT Stretched forth their suppliant hands To Pallas.

■ **suppliantly** *adverb* M16.

†**suppliant** *adjective*². *rare* (Shakes.). Only in E17.
[from SUPPLY *verb*¹ + -ANT¹.]
Supplementary.

supplicant /ˈsʌplɪk(ə)nt/ *noun & adjective.* L16.
[Latin *supplicant-* pres. ppl stem of *supplicare* SUPPLICATE: see -ANT¹.]
▶ **A** *noun.* **1** A person who supplicates, a suppliant. L16.
2 *spec.* A person supplicating for a degree. M17.
▶ **B** *adjective.* = SUPPLIANT *adjective*¹. L16.
■ **supplicantly** *adverb* M19.

supplicat /ˈsʌplɪkat/ *noun.* M17.
[Latin = he or she supplicates.]
A supplication, a petition. Now only *spec.* (at certain English universities), a formal petition for a degree or for incorporation.

supplicate /ˈsʌplɪkeɪt/ *verb.* LME.
[Latin *supplicat-* pa. ppl stem of *supplicare*, formed as SUB- + *placere* propitiate: see -ATE³.]
1 *verb intrans.* Beg or entreat humbly, submit a formal petition. (Foll. by *to, for, that, to do.*) LME.
2 *verb trans.* Beseech, entreat, (a person, *to do*); petition formally or beg humbly for (a thing). M17.
3 *verb intrans. spec.* At Oxford University, present a formal petition for a degree or for incorporation. (Foll. by *for, to be.*) L17.
■ **supplicatingly** *adverb* in a supplicating manner M19.

supplication /sʌplɪˈkeɪʃ(ə)n/ *noun.* LME.
[Old & mod. French from Latin *supplicatio(n-)*, formed as prec.: see -ATION.]
1 The action or an act of supplicating; (a) humble petition or entreaty; (*obsolete* exc. *Hist.*) a written or formal petition. LME. ▸**b** At Oxford University, a formal petition for a degree or for incorporation. L17.
2 (A) humble prayer to God; ROMAN HISTORY a religious ceremony celebrating an important public event, esp. a victory. LME.

supplicator /ˈsʌplɪkeɪtə/ *noun.* M17.
[Late Latin, formed as SUPPLICATE: see -OR.]
A person who supplicates; a suppliant, a petitioner.

supplicatory /ˈsʌplɪkət(ə)ri, -ˈkeɪt(ə)ri/ *adjective.* LME.
[medieval Latin *supplicatorius*, formed as SUPPLICATE: see -ORY².]
1 Expressing, consisting of, or containing supplication. LME.
2 Of a person: suppliant, supplicating. *rare.* L19.

supplicavit /sʌplɪˈkeɪvɪt/ *noun.* LME.
[Latin = he or she has supplicated, 3 sing. perf. indic. of *supplicare* SUPPLICATE (from the first word of the writ).]
LAW (now *Hist.*). A writ requiring a person or persons to keep the peace.

supplice /ˈsʌplɪs/ *noun. rare.* E16.
[Orig. from Latin *supplicium*, from *supplic-*, *supplex* SUPPLE *adjective*; later from French.]
Punishment; torture.

supplier /səˈplʌɪə/ *noun.* L15.
[from SUPPLY *verb*¹ + -ER¹.]
†**1** A person taking the place of another, a substitute. Only in L15.
†**2** A helper, a supporter; an assistant. E16–M17.
3 A person who makes up a deficiency. *rare.* E17.
4 A person who or thing which supplies or provides something; *spec.* a person or establishment supplying articles commercially, a purveyor. E17.

📖 **4** M. KINGSLEY Van Huytemers and Peters are the two great suppliers of . . gin. *Which?* Only one UK milk supplier—the Milk Marketing Board.

supply /səˈplʌɪ/ *noun.* LME.
[from SUPPLY *verb*¹.]
▶ **I** The action of supplying something.
1 Assistance, support, relief. Long *Scot.* LME.
2 The action or an act of making up for a deficiency or fulfilling a want or need. E16.
3 The action or an act of providing something needed or wanted; the substitution of a thing or person for another. (Foll. by *of.*) L16. ▸**b** The action of filling a temporary vacancy, esp. as a member of the clergy or a teacher. Freq. in ***on supply***, acting in such a capacity. L16.
4 The provision of a person etc. with necessary or wanted things. (Foll. by *of.*) L18.

📖 **3** J. LEES-MILNE To work on . . the supply of stores to the . . forces in Egypt. **4** C. COLLINGWOOD Everything that relates to the supply of the Fleet.

▶ **II** A thing supplied; a means of supplying something.
†**5** *sing.* & in *pl.* Reinforcements of troops etc. LME–E18.
6 A person, esp. a member of the clergy or a teacher, filling a temporary vacancy or acting as a substitute for another; *spec.* = ***supply teacher*** below. M16.
†**7** **a** A supplement or appendix *to* a literary work. L16–M17. ▸**b** *gen.* A supplementary or additional thing, a supplement. E17–M18.
8 A quantity or amount of something supplied, a stock or store of something provided or obtainable. (Foll. by *of.*) L16. ▸**b** A system by which such a store (of water, gas, blood, etc.) is made available at a distance; a network by which something is conveyed to a site. Chiefly as 2nd elem. of comb. L19.
9 In *pl.* & (now *rare* exc. *attrib.*) *sing.* Provisions, equipment, or (formerly) funds for an army, expedition, etc. E17.
10 *sing.* & in *pl.* A sum of money granted by a national legislature for expenses of government not provided for by revenue. E17.
11 ECONOMICS. The amount of any commodity actually produced and available for purchase. Correl. to ***demand***. L18.

📖 **8** F. FITZGERALD The great . . jars held a year's supply of rice. N. HERMAN A plentiful supply of flats at negligible rents. H. CARPENTER Endless supplies of *marrons glacés*. **in short supply** available only in limited quantity, scarce. **b** *Nature* Most internal organs have a double nerve supply. *Daily Telegraph* To connect a studio flat to the water supply or public sewer. **9** B. JOWETT The invaders remained until their supplies were exhausted. *transf.*: G. ADAIR They had brought supplies: sandwiches and hard-boiled eggs. **11** J. M. KEYNES Prices are governed by . . supply and demand.

Attrib. & comb.: In the sense 'in charge of, carrying, or providing a supply or supplies, as for an army etc.', as ***supply base***, ***supply depot***, ***supply line***, ***supply officer***, ***supply store***, etc. Special combs., as **supply chain** the sequence of processes involved in the production and distribution of a commodity; **supply day**: on which the House of Commons debates an Opposition motion criticizing the Government's proposed expenditure; **supply-driven** *adjective* (ECONOMICS) caused or effected by factors on the side of supply; **supply drop** the dropping of supplies by parachute; **supply house** (*a*) *US* a commercial establishment selling supplies; (*b*) *Canad.* a hut, tent, etc., used as a storehouse; **supply-led** *adjective* (ECONOMICS) determined by factors on the side of supply; **supply-side** *adjective* (ECONOMICS) pertaining to the supply side of the economy; *spec.* designating a policy of low taxation and other incentives to produce goods and invest; **supply-teach** *verb intrans.* work as a supply teacher; **supply teacher** a teacher supplied by the education authority to fill a temporary vacancy; a person regularly employed in this way.

supply /səˈplʌɪ/ *verb*¹. LME.
[Old French *so(u)pleer*, *soup(p)leier*, *-oier*, *supplier* (mod. *suppléer*) from Latin *supplere* fill up, make good, complete, formed as SUB- + *plere* fill.]
†**1** *verb trans.* Help, assist; relieve; support, maintain. LME–E18.
†**2** *verb trans.* Provide with troops; reinforce. LME–E19.
†**3** *verb trans.* **a** Make up (a whole) by adding something; fill *up*, complete. LME–L16. ▸†**b** Add to, supplement. LME–M18.
4 *verb trans.* Make up or compensate for (a deficiency, loss, etc.); fulfil or satisfy (a need or want). LME.
5 **a** *verb trans.* Fill or occupy (a vacancy, place, etc.), esp. as a substitute. LME. ▸†**b** *verb trans.* Fulfil or perform (an office or function), esp. as a substitute. LME–M18. ▸**c** *verb trans.* Take the place of, act as substitute for, replace. Now *rare* or *obsolete.* E17. ▸**d** *verb trans.* & *intrans.* Of a member of the clergy etc.: occupy (a church etc.) as a substitute or temporarily; act as supply or substitute (for). E18.
6 *verb trans.* Provide or make available (something needed or wanted); furnish for use or consumption, esp.

commercially; yield, afford; add (something missing). LME.

7 *verb trans.* Provide with a thing needed or wanted (foll. by *with*); stock with provisions, provide with regular supplies, esp. commercially. E16. ▸**b** Provide with an occupant or contents, fill. *poet.* E17. ▸**c** ANATOMY & PHYSIOLOGY. Of a nerve, blood-vessel, etc.: provide with blood, nervous control, etc. (a part, organ, or foetus). M19.

> **4** H. L. MENCKEN In order to supply the deficiencies. **5a** LD MACAULAY She died; and her place was supplied by a German princess. ***supply the stead of***: see STEAD noun. **6** DRYDEN He . . left somewhat for the Imagination of his Readers to supply. I. MURDOCH To come painting with her, she would supply the materials. *Bookseller* We supply everything from cashpoints to window fittings. **7** W. S. JEVONS China supplies us with vast quantities of tea. J. AGEE These two . . had supplied themselves against possible hunger. L. DURRELL Clea . . supplies him with tobacco.

■ †**supplyment** *noun* (*rare*, Shakes.) (*a*) the act of supplying something; (*b*) a thing supplied: L16–E17.

†**supply** *verb*² *trans. & intrans.* M16–E18.
[Alt. by assim. to SUPPLY *verb*¹ or after *apply*.]
= SUPPLE *verb*.

supply /ˈsʌpli/ *adverb*. Also **supplely** /ˈsʌp(ə)lli/. E17.
[from SUPPLE *adjective* + -LY².]
In a supple manner, with suppleness.

support /səˈpɔːt/ *noun*. LME.
[from the verb.]
▸ **I** The action of supporting.

1 a The action of preventing a person from giving way or of backing-up a person or group; assistance, backing. Also, an instance of this. LME. ▸**b** Spiritual help; mental comfort. E16. ▸**c** Corroboration or substantiation (*of* a statement, principle, etc.); advocacy (*of* a proposal, motion, etc.). Chiefly in ***in support of***. L18. ▸**d** MILITARY. The action of supporting other troops. E19. ▸**e** The provision of services enabling something to fulfil its function or to remain operational. M20.

†**2** The bearing or defraying of a charge or expense. LME–L17.

3 a The action of holding up, keeping from falling, or bearing the weight of something; the condition of being so supported. M17. ▸**b** SCOTS LAW. The resting of the whole or part of a building or of a beam on the property of the servient tenement. L17.

4 a The action of keeping a person, animal, or thing from failing or perishing; *esp.* supply *of* a living being with what is necessary for subsistence; preservation. L17. ▸**b** The action of contributing to the success of or maintaining the value of something. E20.

> **1a** V. BRITTAIN Proclaimed enthusiastic . . support for the League of Nations. C. WILSON He . . needed support against his self-doubt. **b** M. SEYMOUR In her grief, she turned to him for support. ***moral support***: see MORAL *adjective*. **d in support** acting as a second line. **e** F. FITZGERALD Troops with their air and artillery support. **3a** G. HUNTINGTON Put her hand for support against the trunk of a tree. **4b** *Financial Times* French authorities giving support to the franc to steady its rate of decline.

▸ **II** A person who or thing which supports.

5 a A person who or thing which upholds or sustains an institution, condition, etc.; a supporter, a prop, a stay. LME. ▸**b** MILITARY. In *pl.* A supporting body of troops; the second line in a battle. M19. ▸**c** A supporting actor or film (cf. SUPPORT *verb* 9b). Also *ellipt.*, a support band. L19. ▸**d** COMPUTING. Software or peripherals available for use with a particular computer. L20.

6 a Orig., food, provisions. Later more widely, means of livelihood or subsistence; supply of necessities for living, maintenance. L16. ▸**b** A person who or thing which provides a means of livelihood or maintains a person or community. M18.

7 A thing which holds up or sustains the weight of something, or on which something rests; *spec.* in MEDICINE, an appliance or item of clothing worn to hold in place a weak or injured part of the body; a truss. L16. ▸**b** The substance or material on which a picture is painted. L19.

8 MATH. The smallest closed set of elements outside which a given function or mapping is zero. M20.

> **5a** L. STRACHEY She was not only his own solitary support; she was the one prop of the State. **c** *New Musical Express* The Prayer Boat . . have been confirmed as support on tour with The Pogues. **6b** N. ALGREN A working mother . . sole support of . . a growing family. **7** A. RANSOME Built supports to keep the . . cage off the ground. M. MARRIN Thick cushions formed a support for my back.

Attrib. & comb.: in the sense 'providing or acting as a support', as ***support equipment***, ***support service***, ***support staff***, etc. Special combs., as **support band** = ***support group*** (a) below; **support buying** the purchase of a commodity, a currency, or stocks and shares, in order to make the price higher than it would otherwise have been; **support cost** the financial cost of supporting something; *spec.* the cost of supporting the armed services; **support group** (*a*) a group of musicians taking a subordinate part in a concert; (*b*) a group of people giving support to a charitable or political organization; **support line** MILITARY the second line of troops in a battle; a trench occupied by such troops; **support price** a minimum price guaranteed to a farmer for agricultural produce and maintained by subsidy etc.; **support stockings**, **support tights**: reinforced with elastic yarn to support the muscles and veins of the legs; **support trench** MILITARY forming part of a line of strong points in the rear of the strong points of the firing-line.

■ **supportless** *adjective* †(*a*) (*rare*) intolerable; (*b*) lacking support, unsupported: M17.

support /səˈpɔːt/ *verb trans.* ME.
[Old & mod. French *supporter* from Latin *supportare*, formed as SUB- + *portare* carry.]

1 a Endure without opposition or resistance; bear with, put up with, tolerate. ME. ▸†**b** Undergo, endure, esp. with courage or determination; bear up against. E17–E19.

2 a Uphold or maintain the validity or authority of (a thing); give assistance in (a course of action). ME. ▸**b** Strengthen the position of (a person or community) by one's assistance or backing; uphold the rights, opinion, or status of; stand by, back up. LME. ▸**c** Provide authority for or corroboration of (a statement etc.); bear out, substantiate. M18. ▸**d** Second, speak in favour of (a proposition or proponent); maintain, argue the truth of (an opinion etc.). M18.

3 a Provide for the maintenance of, help to finance; bear the expense of, pay for. LME. ▸**b** LAW. Of an estate: provide for (a remainder). L17.

4 a Provide food or sustenance for; supply with necessities for living or growing. LME. ▸**b** Sustain (the vital functions); keep up the strength of (a person). E18.

5 a Hold, prop up; keep from falling or sinking. LME. ▸**b** HERALDRY. In *pass.* Be flanked by supporters. M16. ▸†**c** Take (a person) on one's arm. E17–E19. ▸**d** Sustain (a particular weight). E18.

6 a Maintain unimpaired, preserve from decay or depreciation. E16. ▸**b** Maintain in existence or in operation; keep up, keep going. M18. ▸**c** Preserve from failure, contribute to the success of (an undertaking). Also, maintain or keep up (a price). L18. ▸**d** COMPUTING. Of a computer, operating system, etc.: allow the use or operation of (a program, language, device, etc.). L20.

7 †**a** HERALDRY. In *pass.* Of a charge, esp. an animal: be superimposed on another charge. M16–E18. ▸**b** Constitute the foundation of (a structure); sustain in position above, hold up from below. E17.

8 Keep (a person, his or her mind, etc.) from failing or giving way; give confidence or strength to; encourage. E17.

9 a Occupy a position by the side of (a person) in order to give assistance or encouragement; assist by one's presence or attendance. E17. ▸**b** Give assistance to in a battle, esp. by a second line of troops; act with, take a part secondary to (a principal actor, group, etc.); assist as a subordinate in a contest, performance, etc. Freq. as ***supporting*** *ppl adjective*. M19. ▸**c** SPORT. Be a supporter or follower of (a team etc.). M20.

10 Sustain (a character) in a dramatic performance; *gen.* act or play (a part), maintain (a certain behaviour). E18.

> **1a** E. LANGLEY The thought was not to be supported without bitter tears. **2a** D. CAUTE I just came to support the demonstration. **b** E. ROOSEVELT Franklin and I had long supported Governor Smith politically. M. PUZO The Don offered to support Hagen in any undertaking. **c** G. SAYER Historical facts do not support the pacifist position. **3a** *Nature* This work was supported by the Cancer Research Campaign. **4a** J. SUTHERLAND The Wards with three children . . to support were feeling the financial pinch. *Country Walking* Lime-rich rocks support grass rather than heather. *refl.*: R. HOLMES I supported myself with freelance journalism. **b** D. H. LAWRENCE For . . years Miss Frost supported the heart-stricken, nervous invalid. **5a** J. G. COZZENS Supporting the pad against his palm, he started to write. G. GREENE He stumbled . . but the boy caught his elbow and supported him. D. PARKER An octagonal tray supporting a decanter of brandy. *refl.*: A. MACLEAN With her arms stretched out to support herself. **6b** J. CARTWRIGHT A town which was supported almost entirely by Scandinavian aid. **c** *Times* Bid speculation . . supported Grindlay Holdings, up 14p to 210p. **7b** M. GIROUARD Arches which support the first-floor balcony. **8** I. MURDOCH He had failed to . . support and console him. **9** W. S. CHURCHILL Finding no Federal troops . . to support him. *Auckland Metro* They supported the Stevie Wonder concert. **b** *Punch* Appeared in the early Python episodes in supporting roles. **supporting film** a less important film in a cinema programme.

■ **supportative** *adjective* (*rare*) = SUPPORTIVE *adjective* L20. **supportingly** *adverb* so as to provide support L19. †**supportment** *noun* the action or fact of providing support E17–M18.

supportable /səˈpɔːtəb(ə)l/ *adjective*. LME.
[from prec. + -ABLE.]
1 Bearable, tolerable, endurable. LME.
2 Able to be maintained, confirmed, or made good; defensible. LME.
†**3** Providing support or assistance. *rare*. Only in M16.
4 Able to be held up or sustained physically. *rare*. M19.

■ **supportaˈbility** *noun* M19. **supportably** *adverb* M19.

†**supportance** *noun*. L15.
[formed as prec. + -ANCE.]
1 = SUPPORT *noun* 1a, b. L15–M17.
2 Maintenance, sustenance. L16–M19.
3 The action of supporting, propping, or holding up. L16–E19.
4 A thing which provides a support. L16–M19.

supportasse /səˈpɔːtas/ *noun*. L16.
[Obscure formation on SUPPORT *verb*.]
Hist. A wire frame for supporting a large ruff.

†**supportation** *noun*. LME.
[Old French, from late Latin *supportatio(n-)*, from Latin *supportat-* pa. ppl stem of *supportare* SUPPORT *verb*: see -ATION.]
1 = SUPPORT *noun* 1a, b. LME–L17.
2 Bearing *of* expense. LME–M18.
3 The relief or maintenance *of* a person, building, institution, etc. by a supply of funds. LME–E18.
4 = SUPPORT *noun* 4a. L15–L17.
5 Endurance. E16–M18.
6 = SUPPORT *noun* 3a. L16–M18.

supporter /səˈpɔːtə/ *noun*. LME.
[from SUPPORT *verb* + -ER¹.]

1 a A person who sides with, backs up, or assists a particular person, cause, etc. LME. ▸**b** MILITARY. A force that supports another, as in a second line. L18.

2 a = SUPPORT *noun* 7. LME. ▸**b** A leg. Now only *joc.* E17. ▸†**c** BOTANY. Each of the divisions of the calyx, regarded as supporting the flower; a sepal. E17–E18. ▸**d** A jockstrap. L19.

3 a A person who keeps someone or something from failing, giving way, or perishing; a sustainer, a preserver. L15. ▸**b** CHEMISTRY. A substance that maintains some process, esp. combustion. *rare*. E19.

4 HERALDRY. A figure of an animal, human, etc., beside the shield and holding it; either of two such figures, on either side of the shield. M16.

5 a A person who attends another to give physical or moral support; an attendant, as in a procession. L16. ▸**b** A person who supports or follows a particular sport or sporting team. E20.

> **1a** C. TOMALIN She was . . an ardent supporter of the suffragette movement. **5a** ELLIS PETERS Between his two supporters he was hauled upright. **b** M. MEYER I was a fervent Surrey supporter.

■ **supportress** *noun* (now *rare*) a female supporter E17.

supportive /səˈpɔːtɪv/ *adjective*. L16.
[formed as prec. + -IVE.]
Providing support; encouraging; MEDICINE (of treatment) intended to improve general condition rather than directly influence a disease.

■ **supportively** *adverb* L20. **supportiveness** *noun* M20.

supposal /səˈpəʊz(ə)l/ *noun*. LME.
[Old French *sup(p)osail(l)e*, from *sup(p)oser* SUPPOSE *verb*: see -AL¹.]
1 The action of supposing; supposition, conjecture. Now *esp.*, an instance of this; a hypothesis, an assumption. LME.
†**2** A statement, an allegation. LME–M17.
†**3** A notion, an opinion. L16–E17.
†**4** A suggestion, a proposal. E–M18.

> **3** SHAKES. *Haml.* Holding a weak supposal of our worth, Or thinking . . Our state to be disjoint.

suppose /səˈpəʊz/ *noun*. M16.
[from the verb.]
1 An act of supposing; a supposition, a hypothesis, a conjecture. M16. ▸†**b** Supposition. L16–E18.
†**2** A belief, a notion. L16–M17.
†**3** Purpose, intention. L16–E17.
†**4** (An) expectation. Only in E17.

> **4** SHAKES. *Tr. & Cr.* We come short of our suppose so far, That . . yet Troy walls stand.

suppose /səˈpəʊz/ *verb trans.* ME.
[Old & mod. French *supposer* based on Latin *supponere* (see SUPPOSITION) but re-formed on Latin pa. pple *suppositus* and Old & mod. French *poser*: see POSE *verb*¹.]

†**1 a** Hold as an opinion; believe as a fact; think or be certain *that*. *obsolete* exc. *Scot. & dial.* ME. ▸**b** Foll. by *to do*: believe that one does (a thing). L15–L17.

†**2** Expect (a thing, *that*, *to do*). ME–M18.

3 Assume as a basis of argument; frame as a hypothesis; put as an imaginary case, posit. (Foll. by *that*.) ME.

4 a In *imper.* or as pres. pple with word or clause or parenthetically: used to introduce a hypothetical case or an example, later also a suggestion or proposal. ME. ▸**b** In *imper.* If; *esp.*, even if, although. *Scot.* LME.

†**5 a** Attribute (something) *to* a person. *rare*. LME–E17. ▸**b** Have in mind; think of, conceive, imagine; *spec.* suspect. LME–M18.

†**6** Form an idea of, imagine; guess. LME–L18.

7 a Lay down as true, take for granted. LME. ▸**b** Presume the existence or presence of. L17.

†**8** State, allege, esp. formally in an indictment. LME–M17.
9 Of a condition, fact, etc.: involve as a basis; require as a condition; imply, presuppose, signify. LME.
†**10** Feign, pretend; occas., forge. M16–L17.
11 a Assume as possible or true, esp. in default of knowledge; infer hypothetically; be inclined to think *that*. L16. ▸**b** Expect, intend, require; have as a duty, be obliged. Usu. in *pass.* Foll. by *to be, to do.* L17.
†**12** Substitute by artifice or fraud. E17–M18.
†**13** Put or place under something; append. *rare.* E17–L18.

4a T. HARDY As we are going . . suppose we . . call upon him? W. E. NORRIS My objections—supposing I have any—wouldn't give you a sleepless night. **11a** H. JAMES Do you suppose me so stupid as to quarrel with you? V. WOOLF Women . . usually boring her, she supposed . . girls would be worse. W. GOLDING Warships are . . slower . . than most people suppose. **I suppose (so)**: expr. hesitant agreement. **b** SLOAN WILSON They had been supposed to land in a field . . but it hadn't been like that. E. ROOSEVELT Government is supposed to serve the good of the people.

■ **supposable** *adjective* that may be supposed or assumed; presumable, imaginable: M17. **supposably** *adverb* (chiefly *US*) as may be supposed; presumably: M19. **supposer** *noun* (*rare*) a person who supposes or assumes something L16. **supposing** *noun* (*a*) the action of the verb; (*b*) an assumption, an opinion expressed: LME.

supposed /səˈpəʊzd/ *adjective.* L15.
[from prec. + -ED¹.]
1 Believed or thought to exist or to be a specified person or thing; assumed; hypothetical. L15.
†**2** Orig. *gen.*, feigned, pretended, counterfeit. Later *spec.* (of a child), not a genuine heir, illegitimate. M16–L18.
†**3** MUSIC. Designating a note added below the notes of a chord, or an upper note of a chord when used instead of the fundamental bass. L18–M19.
¶ Cf. earlier UNSUPPOSED *adverb*.
■ **supposedly** /səˈpəʊzɪdli/ *adverb* by supposition; as is supposed: E17.

supposita *noun* pl. of SUPPOSITUM.

suppositio materialis /sʌpəˌzɪʃɪəʊ mətɪərɪˈeɪlɪs, -ˈɑːlɪs/ *noun phr.* M19.
[medieval Latin.]
LOGIC. Use of a word or phrase simply as an example within a statement, without its normal semantic function.

supposition /sʌpəˈzɪʃ(ə)n/ *noun.* LME.
[Old & mod. French, or late Latin *suppositio(n-)* (translating Greek *hupothesis* HYPOTHESIS), from *supposit-* pa. ppl stem of *supponere* place under, substitute: see SUB-, POSITION *noun*.]
†**1** SCHOLASTIC LOGIC. **a** A thing held to be true and taken as the basis of an argument. LME–L16. ▸**b** Any of the different meanings of a term. L16–L17.
†**2** Fraudulent substitution of another thing or person in place of the genuine one; *spec.* insertion of a spurious writing, a forgery. M16–L18.
3 The action of assuming or (*esp.*) that which is assumed as a basis of an argument or a premiss from which a conclusion is drawn. L16.
4 An idea that something is true; a hypothetical inference; an uncertain or mistaken belief. L16. ▸†**b** *loosely.* A notion, a fancy; imagination; occas., suspicion, expectation. L16–L18.
†**5** MUSIC. The introduction of discordant passing notes. Also, the addition of a note below a chord, or the transference of an upper note of a chord to the bass, as in an inversion. E18–M19.

3 A. STORR Selecting . . evidence which supported his suppositions. **4** M. MEYER The mistaken supposition that I could speak German. †**in supposition** (*rare*, Shakes.) uncertain, doubtful.

■ **suppositional** *adjective* of the nature of, involving, or based on supposition; hypothetical, assumed: M17. **suppositionary** *adjective* (*rare*) = SUPPOSITIONAL E19.

suppositious /sʌpəˈzɪʃəs/ *adjective.* E17.
[Partly shortened from next, partly directly from prec.: see -ITIOUS².]
1 = SUPPOSITITIOUS 1, 2. Now *rare* or *obsolete.* E17.
2 Involving or based on supposition; hypothetical, assumed. L17.
■ **suppositiously** *adverb* spuriously; hypothetically: L17.

supposititious /səpɒzɪˈtɪʃəs/ *adjective.* E17.
[Latin *supposititius*, *-icius*, from *supposit-*: see SUPPOSITION, -ITIOUS¹.]
1 Fraudulently substituted for the genuine thing or person; spurious, counterfeit, false. E17. ▸**b** *spec.* Of a child: set up to displace the real heir or successor; occas., illegitimate. E17.
†**2** Pretended or imagined to exist; feigned, fictitious; imaginary. E17–L18.
3 = SUPPOSITIOUS *adjective* 2. L17.
■ **supposititiously** *adverb* E17. **supposititiousness** *noun* M17.

suppositive /səˈpɒzɪtɪv/ *adjective.* LME.
[Late Latin *suppositivus* (translating Greek *hupothetikos* HYPOTHETIC), from *supposit-*: see SUPPOSITION, -IVE.]
†**1** Placed under or below. Only in LME.
2 Of the nature of, implying, or based on supposition; suppositional. LME.

suppository /səˈpɒzɪt(ə)ri/ *noun.* LME.
[medieval Latin *suppositorium* use as noun of neut. sing. of late Latin *suppositorius* placed underneath, from *supposit-*: see SUPPOSITION, -ORY¹.]
A conical or cylindrical pellet designed to be inserted into the rectum or vagina to melt and release a medicament or serve as a lubricant.

suppository /səˈpɒzɪt(ə)ri/ *adjective.* L16.
[In sense 1 attrib. use of the noun; in sense 2 var. of SUPPOSITIVE by suffix-substitution.]
†**1** Used as or pertaining to a suppository. L16–E17.
2 = SUPPOSITIONAL. Now *rare.* M17.

suppositum /səˈpɒzɪtəm/ *noun.* Pl. ***-ta*** /-tə/. M17.
[medieval Latin, use as noun of neut. sing. of *suppositus* pa. pple of *supponere*: see SUPPOSITION.]
1 METAPHYSICS. A being that subsists by itself, an individual thing or person; occas., a being in relation to its attributes. Long *rare* or *obsolete.* M17.
2 LOGIC. An assumption. M19.

suppost /səˈpəʊst/ *noun. obsolete* exc. *Hist.* L15.
[Old French *suppost* (mod. *suppôt*) from medieval Latin *suppositus* (noun) subordinate, from Latin *suppositus*: see prec.]
1 A subordinate; a supporter, a follower. L15.
2 A member of a university. *Scot.* M16.

suppress /səˈprɛs/ *verb trans.* LME.
[Latin *suppress-* pa. ppl stem of *supprimere*, formed as SUB- + *premere* PRESS *verb*¹.]
1 a Cause (an activity etc.) to cease; put a stop to; *spec.* quell (a rebellion). LME. ▸†**b** Put down by force; overwhelm, subdue. LME–L18. ▸**c** Cause (a person, community, etc.) to become powerless or inactive. L15. ▸**d** Withhold or withdraw (a book etc.) from publication; prohibit the circulation of. M16.
2 Prevent (a feeling, reaction, etc.) from being expressed or displayed; restrain, stifle, subdue. E16.
3 Keep secret; refrain from disclosing or mentioning (information etc.). M16.
†**4 a** Press down; press or weigh on; *fig.* bear heavily on, weigh down. M16–M17. ▸**b** Rape. *rare* (Spenser). Only in L16.
5 Hinder from passage; stop the flow of (blood etc.). L16.
6 a Prevent or inhibit (an action or phenomenon); *esp.* eliminate or reduce (electrical interference or unwanted frequencies). E20. ▸**b** Fit with a suppressor. M20.

1a C. HILL The revolt was suppressed . . by Cromwell. **d** A. BRIGGS Despite . . efforts to suppress Wycliffe's Bible, over a hundred copies survived. **2** C. JACKSON Too difficult to suppress the . . gasp that gave her away. C. MUNGOSHI He suppressed an impulse to whistle. A. STORR Depressives tend to suppress their own opinions. J. DAWSON Ambrose suppressed a yawn. **3** R. L. STEVENSON Sternly . . suppressed all reference to his escape.

■ **suppressal** *noun* (*rare*) = SUPPRESSION *noun* 2 M17. **suppresser** *noun* (*rare*) = SUPPRESSOR L19. **suppressiˈbility** *noun* ability to be suppressed L20. **suppressible** *adjective* able to be suppressed (earlier in INSUPPRESSIBLE, UNSUPPRESSIBLE) M19. **suppressive** *adjective* having the quality or effect of suppressing someone or something, causing suppression (earlier in INSUPPRESSIVE) L18. **suppressively** *adverb* M19.

suppressant /səˈprɛs(ə)nt/ *noun.* M20.
[from prec. + -ANT¹.]
A thing which suppresses or restrains someone or something; *spec.* (in full ***appetite suppressant***) a substance or drug which suppresses appetite.

suppressed /səˈprɛst/ *adjective.* E17.
[formed as prec. + -ED¹.]
1 *gen.* That has been suppressed. E17.
2 BOTANY. Of a part normally present: absent, not developed. M19.
3 FORESTRY. Of a small tree: growing beneath the canopy of larger trees and receiving no direct light. L19.
4 Fitted with an interference suppressor. M20.
Special collocations: **suppressed carrier** TELECOMMUNICATIONS a carrier wave which is not transmitted with the signal, but is reintroduced in the receiving apparatus (usu. *attrib.*).
■ **suppressedly** /-sɪdli/ *adverb* in a suppressed tone M19.

suppression /səˈprɛʃ(ə)n/ *noun.* LME.
[Latin *suppressio(n-)*, from *suppress-*: see SUPPRESS, -ION.]
†**1** Impression, effect. Only in LME.
2 The action of suppressing an activity, person, community, etc., as by power or authority. L15. ▸**b** *spec.* Withdrawal from publication; prohibition of the circulation of a book etc. L17.
3 MEDICINE. Stoppage or reduction (of a discharge or secretion). M16.
4 The action of keeping something secret; refusal to disclose information etc. E18.
5 The action of stifling a feeling, reaction, etc. E18.
6 BOTANY. Absence or non-development of some part or organ normally present. M19.
7 a PSYCHOLOGY. The restraint or repression of an idea, activity, or reaction by something more powerful. L19. ▸**b** PSYCHOANALYSIS. The action or result of conscious inhibition of unacceptable memories, impulses, or desires. E20.
8 ELECTRICITY. Prevention of electrical interference. M20.
9 The lowering of normal stress levels in verse; an instance of this. M20.

suppressio veri /səˌprɛʃɪəʊ ˈvɪərʌɪ/ *noun phr.* Pl. **suppressiones veri** /səprɛʃɪˌəʊniːz/. M18.
[mod. Latin, lit. 'suppression of what is true'.]
A misrepresentation of the truth by concealing facts which ought to be made known. Cf. SUGGESTIO FALSI.

suppressor /səˈprɛsə/ *noun.* M16.
[from SUPPRESS + -OR.]
1 A person who or thing which suppresses someone or something. M16. ▸**b** *spec.* A device fitted to a machine or part to prevent it from causing electrical interference. M20.
2 GENETICS. A gene in whose presence the effects of some other gene are not expressed. Also ***suppressor gene***. E20.
3 ELECTRONICS. = ***suppressor grid*** below. M20.
Comb.: **suppressor cell** IMMUNOLOGY a thymus-dependent lymphocyte which can suppress the stimulation of antibody production in lymphocytes in the presence of antigens; ***suppressor gene***: see sense 2 above; **suppressor grid** ELECTRONICS in a thermionic valve, a coarse grid situated between the electrodes so as to stop secondary electrons emitted by the anode from reaching the screen grid; **suppressor T cell** = ***suppressor cell*** above.

†**supprise** *verb trans.* Chiefly *Scot.* LME–L18.
[Anglo-Norman, Old French *supris(e* var. of *sourpris(e)*, *sur-*, *sous-* pa. pple of *surprendre* SURPRISE *verb*.]
Surprise, esp. with violence.

suppurate /ˈsʌpjʊreɪt/ *verb.* LME.
[Latin *suppurat-* pa. ppl stem of *suppurare*, formed as SUB- + *pur-*, *pus* PUS: see -ATE³.]
†**1** *verb trans.* Cause (a sore, tumour, etc.) to form pus. LME–L18.
2 *verb intrans.* Form pus; become converted into and discharge pus. M17.

suppuration /sʌpjʊˈreɪʃ(ə)n/ *noun.* LME.
[Old & mod. French, or Latin *suppuratio(n-)*, formed as prec.: see -ATION.]
The process or condition of suppurating; the formation or discharge of pus; pus that is discharged.

suppurative /ˈsʌpjʊrətɪv/ *adjective & noun.* LME.
[Old & mod. French *suppuratif*, *-ive*, formed as prec.: see -ATIVE.]
▸ **A** *adjective.* **1** Of a drug etc.: having the property of promoting suppuration. Now *rare* or *obsolete.* LME.
2 Of inflammation or infection: attended or characterized by suppuration. L18.
▸ **B** *noun.* A drug etc. which promotes suppuration. Now *rare* or *obsolete.* LME.

†**supputation** *noun.* LME–E19.
[Latin *supputatio(n-)*, from *supputat-* pa. ppl stem of *supputare* count up, formed as SUB- + *putare* reckon.]
The action or an act of calculating or computing; a system of reckoning; *transf.* estimation, reckoning.
■ †**suppute** *verb trans.* calculate, reckon LME–E18.

supra /ˈsuːprə, ˈsjuː-/ *adverb, adjective, & preposition.* E16.
[Latin: see next.]
▸ **A** *adverb.* **1** Earlier in a book or article; = ABOVE *adverb* 2. Cf. UT SUPRA. E16.
†**2** In addition, besides; = ABOVE *adverb* 5. L16–L18.
▸†**B** *adjective.* Additional, extra. L16–L18.
▸ **C** *preposition.* ***supra protest*** [Italian *sopra protesto* lit. 'upon protest'], designating an acceptance of an originally protested bill given in order to preserve honour. E19.

supra- /ˈsuːprə, ˈsjuː-/ *prefix.*
[from or after Latin, from *supra* adverb & preposition (rel. to *super* over) above, beyond, in addition (to), before in time: see SUPER-.]
1 Forming adjectives and nouns with the senses 'over, above, higher than (in situation or position)'; 'on, upon' (***suprarenal***), 'of or pertaining to the upper part of' (***supramaxillary***).
2 Forming adjectives and nouns with the sense 'higher in quality, amount, or degree; superior; beyond, more than' (***supranational***).
3 Forming adjectives, nouns, and (rarely) verbs with the sense 'very highly, extremely, in the highest degree' (***suprasensual***).
4 Forming nouns and adjectives expressing or involving addition or repetition (***supradecompound***).
¶ Opp. INFRA-. Freq. treated as opp. SUB- (cf. SUPER-).
■ **supra-aˈxillary** *adjective* (of a branch or bud) arising above an axil L19. **suprachiasmatic** /-kʌɪəzˈmatɪk/ *adjective* (ANATOMY) situated above the optic chiasma; *spec.* designating a nucleus located in the periventricular zone of the hypothalamus: M20. **supraˈchorioid** *noun & adjective* (now *rare*) ANATOMY = SUPRACHOROID L19. **supraˈchoroid** *noun & adjective* (ANATOMY) (designating) a layer or lamina of loose cellular tissue lying between the choroid and the sclera M20. **suprachoˈroidal** *adjective* (ANATOMY) situated above

the choroid; *spec.* designating the space between the choroid and the sclera: L19. **supra'ciliary** *adjective & noun* (now *rare*) ANATOMY & ZOOLOGY = SUPERCILIARY E19. **supracla'vicular** *adjective* (ANATOMY) situated above the clavicle M19. **supraconduc'tivity** *noun* (now *rare*) = SUPERCONDUCTIVITY M20. **supra'condylar** *adjective* (ANATOMY & MEDICINE) situated or occurring above a condyle or condyles of the humerus, femur, etc. L19. **supra'crustal** *adjective & noun* (GEOLOGY) (a stratum, formation, etc.) lying above the basement rocks of the crust M20. **suprade'compound** *adjective* (BOTANY) triply or more than triply compound M18. **supra'facial** *adjective* (CHEMISTRY) (of a reaction) involving the formation of two new bonds on the same face of a molecule M20. **suprafix** *noun* (PHONETICS) = SUPERFIX M20. **supra'glacial** *adjective* (of melt water etc.) present on the surface of a glacier L19. **supra'human** *adjective* = SUPERHUMAN M18. **supra'lethal** *adjective* exceeding what is lethal M20. **supra'liminal** *adjective* (PSYCHOLOGY) above the threshold of sensation or consciousness; belonging to consciousness: L19. **supra'lineal** *adjective* (*rare*) = SUPRALINEAR L19. **supra'linear** *adjective* that appears or is written above the line M20. **supra'littoral** *adjective & noun* (ECOLOGY) (designating) a zone of the seashore extending from mean high water to the limit of the influence of sea spray or the start of land vegetation E20. **supra'lunar** *adjective* = SUPERLUNARY E18. **supra'lunary** *adjective* = SUPERLUNARY M17. **suprama'xillary** *adjective* (ANATOMY) situated in the upper jaw M19. **supra'maximal** *adjective* (PHYSIOLOGY) greater than what is required to produce the maximum response E20. **supreme'atal** *adjective* (ANATOMY) situated above the acoustic meatus L19. **supramo'lecular** *adjective* (chiefly BIOCHEMISTRY) composed of many molecules; higher in organization than a molecule: E20. **supra'nuclear** *adjective* (ANATOMY & MEDICINE) situated or occurring above a nucleus of the central nervous system L19. **supraoc'cipital** *adjective & noun* (ANATOMY & ZOOLOGY) (*a*) *adjective* situated at the upper part of the occiput or back of the head; (*b*) *noun* a bone at the back of the skull which is fused to the occipital in higher vertebrates: M19. **supra'optic** *adjective* (ANATOMY) situated above the optic chiasma; *spec.* designating a nucleus located in the lateral zone of the hypothalamus: E20. **supra,opticohypo'physial** *adjective* (ANATOMY) designating a tract of nerve fibres in the brain running from the supraoptic nucleus to the hypophysis M20. **supraorbital** *adjective* (ANATOMY & ZOOLOGY) situated above the orbit of the eye E19. **supra'personal** *adjective* = SUPERPERSONAL E20. **supra'pubic** *adjective* (ANATOMY & MEDICINE) situated or occurring above the pubis M19. **suprare'lational** *adjective* of a postulated being or power that transcends or includes all that is relational E20. **supra'scapula** *noun*, pl. **-lae**, ZOOLOGY a bone or cartilage in the upper or anterior part of the scapular arch or pectoral girdle in lower vertebrates M19. **supra'scapular** *adjective* (ANATOMY & ZOOLOGY) located above or upon the scapula; of, pertaining to, or connected with the suprascapula: E19. **suprascript** *adjective* written above L19. **supra'sellar** *adjective* (ANATOMY & MEDICINE) situated or occurring above the sella turcica M20. **supra'sensible** *adjective & noun* = SUPERSENSIBLE M19. **supra'sensual** *adjective* = SUPERSENSUAL M19. **supra'sensuous** *adjective* = SUPERSENSUAL 1 M19. **supraspecies** *noun* (BIOLOGY) = SUPERSPECIES M20. **supraspe'cific** *adjective* above the rank of a species M20. **supra'spinal** *adjective* (ANATOMY) (*a*) situated above the spine of the scapula; (*b*) = SUPRASPINOUS (b): M18. **supraspinatus** /-spʌɪˈneɪtəs/ *noun* (ANATOMY) a muscle arising from the supraspinal fossa of the scapula, serving to raise and abduct the arm M18. **supra'spinous** *adjective* (ANATOMY) (*a*) = SUPRASPINAL (a); (*b*) situated above or upon the spinous processes of the vertebrae: E19. **supra'sterol** *noun* (BIOCHEMISTRY) either of two biologically inactive isomers of calciferol produced by prolonged ultraviolet irradiation M20. **supra'temporal** *adjective*[1] *& noun* (ZOOLOGY) (*a*) *adjective* situated in the upper part of the temples or temporal region; *spec.* pertaining to or designating a bone in the skull of early reptiles; (*b*) *noun* a supratemporal bone, scale, etc.: M19. **supra'temporal** *adjective*[2] = SUPERTEMPORAL *adjective*[1] L19. **suprate'rrestrial** *adjective* = SUPERTERRESTRIAL L19. **supra'thermal** *adjective* (PHYSICS) having greater energy than that associated with thermal excitations M20. **supra-'threshold** *adjective* (PHYSIOLOGY) exceeding the threshold required for the perception of a stimulus M20. **supra'tidal** *adjective* designating that portion of a tidal flat which lies above the mean high water for spring tides; supralittoral: L20. **suprava'ginal** *adjective* (ANATOMY & MEDICINE) (*a*) situated above or outside a sheath or sheathing membrane; (*b*) situated or performed above the vagina: L19. **supraven'tricular** *adjective* (ANATOMY & MEDICINE) situated or occurring above a ventricle of the heart M19. **supra'vital** *adjective* (HISTOLOGY) (of a stain or the process of staining) involving living tissue, esp. blood, outside the body E20.

†supracargo *noun*. Pl. **-oes**. M17–M19.
[Spanish *sobrecargo*, from *sobre* over + *cargo* CARGO *noun*.]
= SUPERCARGO.

supralapsarian /suːprəlapˈsɛːrɪən, sjuː-/ *noun & adjective*. Also **S-**. M17.
[from mod. Latin *supralapsarius*, formed as SUPRA- + Latin *lapsus* fall, LAPSE *noun*: see -ARIAN. Cf. INFRALAPSARIAN, SUPERLAPSARIAN.]
THEOLOGY. ▶**A** *noun*. A Calvinist holding the view that God's election of only some to everlasting life was part of the divine plan prior to the Creation and the Fall. M17.
▶**B** *adjective*. Of or pertaining to the supralapsarians or their doctrine. M17.
■ **supralapsarianism** *noun* the doctrine of the supralapsarians L18.

supramundane /suːprəˈmʌndeɪn, sjuː-/ *adjective*. M17.
[Var. of SUPERMUNDANE: see SUPRA-.]
= SUPERMUNDANE.

supranational /suːprəˈnaʃ(ə)n(ə)l, sjuː-/ *adjective*. E20.
[from SUPRA- + NATIONAL *adjective*.]
Having power or influence that overrides or transcends national boundaries, governments, or institutions.
■ **supranationalism** *noun* E20. **supranatio'nality** *noun* M20.

supranatural /suːprəˈnatʃ(ə)r(ə)l, sjuː-/ *adjective & noun*. *rare*. M19.
[from SUPRA- + NATURAL *adjective*.]
= SUPERNATURAL.
■ **supranaturalism** *noun* M19. **supranaturalist** *noun* M19. **,supranatura'listic** *adjective* M19.

suprarenal /suːprəˈriːn(ə)l, sjuː-/ *adjective & noun*. E19.
[from SUPRA- + RENAL.]
ANATOMY. ▶**A** *adjective*. Situated above the kidney; *spec.* pertaining to or designating the adrenals and their associated blood-vessels etc. E19.
▶**B** *noun*. A suprarenal gland, blood-vessel, etc. M19.
■ **supra'renalin**, **supra'renin** *nouns* (now *rare*) = ADRENALIN E20.

suprasegmental /suːprəsɛgˈmɛnt(ə)l, sjuː-/ *adjective & noun*. M20.
[from SUPRA- + SEGMENTAL.]
LINGUISTICS. (Designating) a feature or features of a sound or sequences of sounds other than those constituting the consonantal and vocalic segments, as stress and intonation in English.
■ **suprasegmentally** *adverb* in terms of suprasegmental features M20.

suprema *noun* pl. of SUPREMUM.

supremacist /suːˈprɛməsɪst, sjuː-/ *noun & adjective*. M20.
[from SUPREMACY + -IST.]
▶**A** *noun*. A person who believes in the supremacy of a particular (specified) racial, social, etc., group. M20. ***White supremacist***: see WHITE *adjective*.
▶**B** *adjective*. Pertaining to or believing in such supremacy. M20.
■ **supremacism** *noun* the doctrine of supremacists (***White supremacism***: see WHITE *adjective*) M20.

supremacy /suːˈprɛməsi, sjuː-/ *noun*. M16.
[from SUPREME + -ACY, after PRIMACY.]
1 The state or condition of being supreme in authority, rank, or power; position of supreme authority or power. M16.
2 The position of being supreme in achievement, character, or estimation. L16.

> 🕮 **1** C. THIRLWALL The steps by which Sparta rose to a supremacy above . . the Dorian states. *Toronto Star* To invade, he had to have air supremacy over the English coast. **Act of Supremacy** ENGLISH HISTORY an act securing ecclesiastical supremacy to the Crown and excluding the authority of the Pope. ***White supremacy***: see WHITE *adjective*.

Suprematism /suːˈprɛmətɪz(ə)m, sjuː-/ *noun*. M20.
[Russian *suprematizm*.]
An orig. Russian artistic movement or style characterized by the use of geometrical shapes and a narrow range of colours.

suprematist /suːˈprɛmətɪst, sjuː-/ *noun & adjective*. L19.
[Partly alt. from (the same root as) SUPREMACIST, partly from prec.: see -IST.]
▶**A** *noun*. **1** = SUPREMACIST. *rare*. L19.
2 (**S-**.) An adherent or practitioner of Suprematism. M20.
▶**B** *adjective*. (**S-**.) Of, pertaining to, or characteristic of Suprematism. M20.

supreme /suːˈpriːm, sjuː-/ *adjective & noun*. L15.
[Latin *supremus* superl. of *superus* that is above, from *super* above: see SUPER-.]
▶**A** *adjective*. **1** Highest, loftiest, topmost. Now *poet.* L15.
2 Highest in authority, rank, or power. L15.
3 Of the highest quality, degree, or amount; greatest. L16. ▶**b** Of a point in time: most important, critical. L19.
4 Last, final; pertaining to death. *arch.* E17.

> 🕮 **1** LD MACAULAY Day set on Cambria's hills supreme. **2** D. FRASER General MacArthur was appointed to the S. Command of the 'South West Pacific'. **Supreme Court** the highest judicial court in a State etc.; (***Supreme Court of Judicature***: see JUDICATURE 1). **Supreme Soviet** the national legislature of the former USSR or of one of its constituent republics. ***the Supreme Being***: see BEING *noun*. **3** M. GIROUARD The garden had become the supreme symbol of the good life in the country. G. BATTISCOMBE Religion was to Frances . . a matter of supreme importance. *Review of English Studies* Mid-eighteenth century imitators . . saw Spenser primarily as a supreme moral allegorist. **the supreme sacrifice** the laying down of one's life for one's country etc.

▶**B** *noun*. **†1** A person having supreme authority, rank, or power. M16–E19.
2 THEOLOGY. ***the Supreme***, God. E18.
3 An example of the highest degree *of* something. M18.
4 [Anglicized from next.] A rich cream sauce (also ***supreme sauce***); a dish of esp. chicken breasts cooked in this. Also, a chicken breast. M20.
■ **supremely** *adverb* L15. **supremeness** *noun* M19.

suprême /syprɛm (*pl. same*), suːˈprɛm/ *noun*. E19.
[French, formed as prec.]
= SUPREME *noun* 4.

supremity /suːˈprɛmɪti, sjuː-/ *noun*. Now *rare*. M16.
[Late Latin *supremitas*, formed as SUPREME: see -ITY.]
= SUPREMACY.

supremo /suːˈpriːməʊ, suːˈpreɪməʊ, sjuː-/ *noun*. Pl. **-os**. M20.
[from Spanish (*generalísimo*) *supremo* supreme general.]
1 A supreme leader or ruler. M20.
2 *transf.* A person in overall charge of something. M20.

> 🕮 **2** *Observer* A new supremo for the inner cities . . should be nominated.

supremum /suːˈpriːməm, sjuː-/ *noun*. Pl. **suprema** /-ˈpriːmə/. M20.
[Latin = highest part, use as noun of neut. of *supremus* highest.]
MATH. The smallest number that is greater than or equal to each of a given set of real numbers; an analogous quantity for a subset of any other ordered set. Opp. ***infimum***.

Supt. *abbreviation*.
Superintendent.

suq *noun* var. of SOUK *noun*[1].

sur- /sɜː/ *prefix*.
[French (earlier *so(u)r-*) formed as SUPER-.]
Used in words adopted from French and rarely as a productive English prefix, in senses of SUPER-, as ***surcharge***, ***surcoat***, ***surname***, ***surpass***, ***survive***.
■ **†suraddition** *noun* (*rare*, Shakes.) an additional name or title: only in E17. **sur'anal** *adjective & noun* (ZOOLOGY) (*a*) *adjective* (situated) above the anus; (*b*) *noun* a suranal plate etc.: E20. **†surbed** *verb trans.* set (a block of stone) edgeways L17–M18. **sur'human** *adjective* (*literary*) = SUPERHUMAN *adjective* M20.

sura /sʊˈrɑː/ *noun*[1]. L16.
[Sanskrit *surā* alcoholic liquor, wine, *surākara* coconut palm.]
Hist. A drink made from the fermented sap of various species of palm; toddy.

sura /ˈsʊərə/ *noun*[2]. Also (earlier) **†assura**. E17.
[Arab. *sūra*, (with def. article) *as-sūra*, prob. from Syriac *ṣūrṭā* scripture.]
Any of the sections of the Koran.

sura /ˈsʊərə/ *noun*[3]. L18.
[Sanskrit.]
= DEVA.

surah /ˈsʊərə, ˈsjʊərə/ *noun & adjective*. L19.
[Repr. French pronunc. of SURAT.]
(Of) a soft twilled silk fabric.

surai /sʊˈrʌɪ/ *noun*. Also **surahi**, (earlier) **serai** /səˈrʌɪ/, & other vars. L17.
[Persian & Urdu *ṣurāhī*, from Arab., from *ṣurāhiya* pure wine.]
In the Indian subcontinent, a long-necked earthenware or metal flagon.

sural /ˈsʊər(ə)l, ˈsjʊər(ə)l/ *adjective*. E17.
[mod. Latin *suralis*, from *sura* calf of the leg: see -AL[1].]
ANATOMY. Of or pertaining to the calf of the leg. Esp. in ***sural artery***, ***sural nerve***, ***sural vein***.

suramin /ˈsʊərəmɪn/ *noun*. M20.
[Origin unkn.]
PHARMACOLOGY. A complex symmetric urea used to treat trypanosomiasis, onchocerciasis, and filariasis. Also ***suramin sodium***.

surance /ˈʃʊər(ə)ns/ *noun*. Long *arch.* & *dial.* ME.
[Old French, formed as SURE *adjective & adverb* after ASSURANCE: see -ANCE.]
= ASSURANCE 1, 3.

Surat /sʊˈrat, ˈsʊərat, sj-/ *noun & adjective*. E17.
[A port and district in Gujarat, India.]
(Designating) a kind of coarse, usu. uncoloured, cotton made in Surat; (designating) an article made from this.

surbahar /ˈsʊəbəhɑː/ *noun*. L19.
[Bengali *surbāhār*.]
A mellow-toned Indian stringed instrument, a bass sitar.

surbase /ˈsɜːbeɪs/ *noun*. L17.
[from SUR- + BASE *noun*[1].]
ARCHITECTURE. **1** A border or moulding immediately above the lower panelling of a wainscoted room. L17.
2 A cornice above the dado of a pedestal, podium, etc. E19.

surbased /sɜːˈbeɪst/ *adjective*. M18.
[French *surbaissé*, formed as SUR- + *baissé* lowered: see -ED[1].]
ARCHITECTURE. ***surbased arch***, an arch whose rise is less than half the span.

†surbate *noun*. L16–E18.
[from the verb.]
Soreness of the hoofs or feet caused by excessive walking.

†surbate *verb*. Pa. pple & ppl adjective. **-ated**, (*rare*) **-ate**. LME.
[Old French *surbatu* pa. pple of *surbatre*, formed as SUR-, BATTER *verb*[1].]
1 *verb trans.* Make (the hoofs or feet) sore with excessive walking; make (an animal or person) footsore. Chiefly as ***surbated*** *ppl adjective*. LME–L19.

2 *verb intrans.* Become footsore. L16–E18.

surcease /səːˈsiːs/ *noun.* Now chiefly *US.* L16.
[from the verb.]
The action or an act of bringing something to an end; the action of or an act of coming to an end; (a) cessation; *esp.* (a) temporary cessation, (a) respite.

> 📖 *Nature* 'Natural', in terms of food, means a blessed surcease from hyperactivity in children. A. DILLARD Sculptured forms piled overhead, one into another without surcease.

surcease /səːˈsiːs/ *verb. arch.* LME.
[Old French *sursis*, fem. *-sise* pa. pple of *surseoir* refrain, delay, suspend from Latin *supersedere* SUPERSEDE. At an early date assim. to CEASE *verb*.]
1 *verb intrans.* Leave off, stop, (finally or temporarily); cease. (Foll. by *from*, †*of*, *to do*.) LME. ▸†**b** *transf.* Forbear *to do*. M16–E17.
2 *verb intrans.* Come to an end; cease. LME.
3 *verb trans.* Leave off or discontinue (an action etc.). Also, refrain from. LME.
†**4** *verb trans.* Put a stop to, discontinue; cause to cease. LME–L17.
†**5** *verb trans.* Put off, defer. *rare.* M16–L17.

surcharge /ˈsəːtʃɑːdʒ/ *noun.* L15.
[from the verb.]
1 An additional or excessive load or burden; overloading. L15.
2 An esp. excessive or additional sum of money to be paid; *spec.* a charge made by assessors as a penalty for false returns of taxable property. M16. ▸**b** The showing of an omission in an account for which credit should have been given; a statement showing this. L17. ▸**c** An amount in an official account not passed by the auditor and having to be refunded by the person responsible. L19.
3 LAW. [translating medieval Latin *superoneratio*.] The overstocking of a common or forest. *obsolete* exc. *Hist.* M16.
4 An additional mark printed on a postage stamp, *esp.* one changing the face value. L19.
5 CIVIL ENGINEERING. A load placed upon uncompacted material to compress it. Also, the part of a load above the top of a retaining wall. L19.

surcharge /ˈsəːtʃɑːdʒ, səːˈtʃɑːdʒ/ *verb trans.* LME.
[Old French *surcharger*, formed as SUR-, CHARGE *verb*.]
1 Exact a surcharge from (a person); exact (a sum) as a surcharge. LME. ▸**b** Show an omission in (an account). M18.
2 LAW. Stock (a common or forest) with more cattle than is allowed or is sustainable by the pasture. *obsolete* exc. *Hist.* LME.
3 Oppress or overwhelm *with* an emotion etc.; burden excessively. M16. ▸**b** In *pass.* Have an excess of inhabitants, inmates, etc. L16.
4 Put an additional or excessive burden or weight upon; overload. L16. ▸**b** Fill to excess; saturate with a solution etc. E17.
†**5** Make an overwhelming attack on. *rare.* Only in L16.
6 Print an additional mark on (a postage stamp), esp. to change the face value. L19.
■ **surcharger** *noun* M16.

surcingle /ˈsəːsɪŋɡ(ə)l/ *noun.* ME.
[Old French *s(o)urcengle*, formed as SUR-, CINGLE.]
1 A girth for a horse or other animal; *esp.* one for keeping a blanket, pack, saddle, etc., in place. ME.
2 A belt worn with a cassock. Now *rare.* L17.

surcoat /ˈsəːkəʊt/ *noun.* ME.
[Old French *s(o)urcot(e)*, formed as SUR-, COAT *noun*.]
1 Orig. (now *Hist.*), an outer coat, usu. of rich material; *spec.* a loose robe worn over armour. Now, a short loose sleeveless garment worn as part of the insignia of an order of knighthood. ME.
2 An undershirt, a vest. *Scot.* M18.

surculus /ˈsəːkjʊləs/ *noun.* Now *rare* or *obsolete*. Pl. **-li** /-lʌɪ, -liː/. L18.
[Latin = young branch, shoot.]
BOTANY. A basal shoot or sucker, esp. of a rose.
■ **surculose** *adjective* (*rare*) producing shoots or suckers M19.

surd /səːd/ *adjective & noun.* M16.
[Latin *surdus* deaf, silent, mute, (of sound etc.) dull, indistinct. Sense 1 ult. from translation of Greek *alogos* not expressible, irrational, through Arab. *jidr aṣamm* lit. 'deaf root'.]
▸ **A** *adjective.* **1** MATH. Of a number or quantity (esp. a root): not expressible by an ordinary (finite) fraction; = IRRATIONAL *adjective* 1. M16.
2 *fig.* Irrational, stupid. E17.
†**3** Deaf. *rare.* L17–E19.
4 PHONETICS. Of a sound: voiceless. M18.
5 GRAMMAR. [mistranslating Arab. *aṣamm* solid, deaf.] Designating a triliteral Arabic verb in which the second and third letters of the root are the same. L18.
▸ **B** *noun.* **1** MATH. An irrational or surd number or quantity. M16.
2 PHONETICS. A surd sound. L18.

surd /səːd/ *verb trans. rare.* E17.
[formed as prec.]
Deaden the sound of (as) with a mute.

†**surdesolid** *noun & adjective.* M16–E18.
[mod. Latin *surdesolidus*, app. from *surde* irrationally + *solidus* solid.]
MATH. = SURSOLID.

surdity /ˈsəːdɪti/ *noun.* Now *rare* or *obsolete*. L16.
[French *surdité* or Latin *surditas*, formed as SURD *adjective & noun*: see -ITY.]
Deafness.

sure /ʃʊə, ʃɔː/ *adjective & adverb.* ME.
[Old French *sur(e)*, earlier *seür(e)* (mod. *sûr*) from Latin *securus* SECURE *adjective*.]
▸ **A** *adjective.* **I** Safe, secure.
†**1** Not exposed to danger or risk. ME–M17. ▸**b** Foll. by *for* or *from doing*: safe from doing, certain not to do. L16–M17.
†**2** Of a place, receptacle, etc.: affording protection or safety. ME–M17.
†**3** In safe custody, safe in one's possession or keeping; unable or unlikely to do harm or cause disturbance. LME–E18.
▸ **II** Trustworthy, firm, steadfast.
4 **a** That can be depended or relied on; trustworthy, reliable. Now *arch. & dial.* ME. ▸**b** Steady, steadfast, unfaltering. LME.
5 Of an object, esp. weaponry or armour: not liable to break or give way, sound. *arch.* ME.
6 Firmly established; stable; steadfast. Now only of immaterial things. *arch.* ME. ▸†**b** Of a possession etc.: that may be counted on to be received or held. LME–L17.
†**7** Engaged to be married, betrothed. Also, married. L15–M17. ▸**b** Bound by allegiance or devotion *to* a person or party. M16–E18.

> 📖 **4a** R. L. STEVENSON Loaded pistols were served out to all the sure men. **b** K. LINES Sure of eye . . and very quick on his feet. CLIVE JAMES To make it convincing as fiction would take a sure touch with language. **6** DRYDEN Th' immortal Line in sure Succession reigns.

▸ **III** Subjectively certain.
8 Certain in mind; having no doubt; assured, confident; convinced. (Foll. by *of*, *that*; formerly also (cf. sense 9 below) *to do*, *to be*.) ME.

> 📖 **8** H. MARTINEAU You might have been sure that I should remember you. G. GREENE It seemed to him . . a file had been shifted, but he couldn't be sure. S. BELLOW Come along to the doctor so I can be sure you weren't hurt. E. J. HOWARD She was not sure whether he was teasing her. A. LURIE He has suspected that she does not like him, and now he is sure of it. M. AMIS Perhaps it's *my* amber jewel—I'm not sure.

▸ **IV** Objectively certain.
9 Certain to come or happen; inevitable; certain to be, get, have, etc. (Foll. by *of*; (cf. sense 8 above) *to do*.) ME. ▸**b** Established as a truth or fact; not to be doubted. Now *rare.* L15.
10 (Of a method) unfailing, reliable; (of a sign) infallible. M16.

> 📖 **9** GOLDSMITH They who had . . fortunes were . . sure of getting good husbands. E. H. SEARS Confusion is the pretty sure result. P. FUSSELL Enemy agents within whose hearing the Americans were sure to blab. **10** B. VINE A window on the most fashionable shopping street . . is a sure sign of wealth. *Modern Maturity* One sure way to double-check . . is to pay close attention.

Phrases etc.: ***a sure find***: see FIND *noun*. **be sure that** take care that, ensure that. **be sure and —**, **be sure to —** take care to —, do not fail to —. **for sure** *colloq.* without doubt. **make sure** (*a*) (foll. by *of*) ensure the existence or happening of; (*b*) (usu. foll. by *of*, *that*) confirm or establish as a truth or fact, be certain; (*c*) *arch.* be convinced *that*. **sure card** a thing or person that will ensure success. ***sure find***: see FIND *noun*. **sure-fire** *adjective* (*colloq.*) certain to succeed. **sure-footed** *adjective* treading safely or firmly, not liable to slip or stumble; *fig.* not liable to make a mistake. **sure-footedly** *adverb* in a sure-footed manner. **sure-footedness** the quality of being sure-footed. **sure of oneself** self-confident. **sure thing** *colloq.* a certainty; as *interjection* (chiefly *N. Amer.*), certainly!, yes, indeed! **to be sure** (*a*) it is admitted, undeniably; (*b*) it must be admitted, indeed.
▸ **B** *adverb.* †**1** Completely, fully. Only in ME.
†**2** Securely, safely. LME–M17.
3 Certainly. Now *colloq.* LME.

> 📖 **3** M. CALLAGHAN Oh, come on . . . Sure you want to come. I can tell you want to come. A. LURIE Parts of it were pretty sure In a phony way. *Photography* Many companies sure are spending a lot of money.

Phrases: ***as sure as DEATH***. ***as sure as eggs is eggs***: see EGG *noun*. ***as sure as fate***: see FATE *noun*. ***sure enough***: see ENOUGH *adverb* 2.
■ **sureness** *noun* the quality or condition of being sure; *esp.* certainty, confidence, unerringness: LME.

sure /ʃʊə, ʃɔː/ *verb trans. obsolete* exc. *dial.* LME.
[Aphet. from ASSURE.]
†**1** = ASSURE 4. LME–M16.
†**2** = ASSURE 1. Only in LME.
†**3** Bind by a promise; plight one's troth; in *pass.*, be betrothed. LME–L16.
4 Make (a person) sure or certain; = ASSURE 3. LME.

surely /ˈʃʊəli, ˈʃɔːli/ *adverb.* ME.
[from SURE *adjective* + -LY[2].]
1 Without danger or risk; securely, safely. *arch.* ME. ▸†**b** With security of obligation or loyalty; steadfastly. LME–E17.
2 With certainty, assurance, or confidence. *arch.* LME.
3 So as to be certain to achieve or reach a result or end; inevitably. Now chiefly in ***slowly but surely***. LME.
4 **a** Certainly, assuredly, undoubtedly; indeed. LME. ▸**b** *esp.* Used to express a strong belief in the statement qualified, based on experience, or probability, or right, esp. in the face of imaginary or possible dissent. L16.

> 📖 **1** DRYDEN Thus surely bound, yet . . The slipp'ry God will try to loose his hold. **2** KEATS Knowing surely she could never win his . . heart. **3** J. R. GREEN Feudalism tottered slowly but surely to its grave. **4a** A. TYLER I surely do appreciate this. **b** T. HARDY Listen, surely there was a knock at the door? N. COWARD You have time for a little coffee surely? O. MANNING Surely they could have found her something better!

Sûreté /syrte/ *noun.* L19.
[French: see next.]
In full ***Sûreté nationale*** /nasjɔnal/. The French police department of criminal investigation.

surety /ˈʃʊərɪti, ˈʃʊəti/ *noun & verb.* ME.
[Old French *s(e)urté* (mod. *sûreté*) from Latin *securitas* SECURITY: see -TY[1].]
▸ **A** *noun.* **I** Means of being sure.
1 = SECURITY 5. *arch.* ME.
2 An assurance, a guarantee. Now *rare.* LME.
3 A person who undertakes responsibility for another's performance of an undertaking, as the payment of a debt, appearance in court, etc. LME. ▸**b** A sponsor at baptism. *arch.* M16.
▸ **II** Condition of being sure; something that is sure.
†**4** Safety; a safeguard. ME–E17. ▸**b** Security of contract, right, or possession. LME–M16.
5 Unerringness, sureness. *rare.* LME. ▸†**b** Trustworthiness, reliability. *rare.* L15–L16.
6 **a** Freedom from care or anxiety; assuredness, confidence. Long *rare.* LME. ▸**b** Certain knowledge. *arch.* E16.
7 †**a** Certainty of an end or result aimed at; certainty of a fact. LME–E17. ▸**b** A certainty, a fact. Chiefly in ***for a surety***, ***of a surety***, for certain. *arch.* LME.
Phrases: ***for a surety***, ***of a surety***: see sense 7b above. **stand surety** become a surety (*for*). **surety of peace**, **surety of the peace** *Hist.* a bond entered into for the maintenance of peace between parties.
▸†**B** *verb trans.* Be surety for. *rare* (Shakes.). Only in E17.
■ **suretyship** *noun* the position or function of a person who acts as a surety M16.

surf /səːf/ *noun & verb.* L17.
[Perh. alt. of SUFF with assim. to SURGE *noun*.]
▸ **A** *noun.* **1** The swell of the sea which breaks upon a shore, esp. a shallow shore; an instance of this. L17.
2 The mass or line of foam produced by this. M18.
3 A spell of surfing or of swimming in the surf. M20.
Comb.: **surf-and-turf** (chiefly *N. Amer.*) a dish containing both seafood and meat, typically shellfish and steak; **surfbird** a small, plover-like bird, *Aphriza virgata*, found on the Pacific coast of America; **surfboard** *noun & verb* (*a*) *noun* a long narrow board used in surfing; (*b*) *verb intrans.* surf; **surf-boat**: of buoyant build suitable for use in surf; **surf-bum** *slang* a surfing enthusiast who frequents beaches suitable for surfing; **surf-casting** fishing by casting a line into the sea from the shore; **surf-clam** a large clam of the family Mactridae found on the coasts of N. America; **surf-coot** = *surf scoter* below; **surf day**: marked by rough surf along the shore; **surf-duck** = *surf scoter* below; **surf-fish** *noun & verb* (*a*) *noun* any of various fishes of the Pacific coast of N. America; (*b*) *verb intrans.* fish by surf-casting; **surf-grass** any of several submerged marine flowering plants constituting the genus *Phyllospadix* (family Zosteraceae), of the northern Pacific, having thickened edible rootstocks; **surf music** a style of popular music originating in the US in the early 1960s and characterized by high harmony vocals and freq. by lyrics relating to surfing; **surf-perch** any of numerous fishes of the family Embiotocidae, found chiefly in coastal waters of the N. Pacific; also called ***sea-perch***; **surf-ride** *verb intrans.* surf; **surf-riding** the sport of surfing; **surf scoter** a N. American sea-duck, *Melanitta perspicillata*.
▸ **B** *verb.* **1** *verb intrans.* Form surf. *rare.* M19.
2 *verb intrans.* Ride on the crest of a wave towards the shore by standing on a surfboard. E20.
3 *verb trans.* **a** Ride (a boat) on the surf. M20. ▸**b** Surf at (a specified place). M20. ▸**c** *transf.* Ride illicitly on the roof or outside of (a train). *slang.* L20.
4 *verb trans.* Of a computer user: move from site to site on (the Internet). L20.
■ **surfable** *adjective* (of a wave) suitable for surfing M20. **surfing** *noun* the action of the verb; *esp.* the sport of riding on a wave on a surfboard: M20. **surfy** *adjective* having much surf; consisting of or resembling surf: M18.

surface /ˈsəːfɪs/ *noun & adjective.* E17.
[French, formed as SUR-, FACE *noun* after Latin SUPERFICIES.]
▸ **A** *noun.* **1** The outermost limiting part of a material body, immediately adjacent to empty space or to another body; each of a number of such limiting parts.

E17. ▸**b** The area of such a limiting part. M17. ▸**c** *fig.* The outward aspect of something, what is apparent on casual viewing or consideration. Freq. in ***on the surface***, = SUPERFICIALLY 3. E18.

2 *spec.* The upper layer or top of the ground (*MINING*), as distinct from underground workings and shafts; the top of a body of liquid. E17.

3 An extent or area of material considered as a medium. E17.

4 *GEOMETRY.* A magnitude or continuous extent having only two dimensions (length and breadth, without thickness), whether plane or curved, finite or infinite. M17. ▸**b** *AERONAUTICS.* An aerofoil, considered as generating intended effects superficially. M19.

📖 **1** A. MOOREHEAD The gold . . was lying there on the surface of the ground. *Listener* Poor roads—bad surfaces, dangerous bends. D. PROFUMO Gazing out . . at the bay, its surface webbed with light. **b** J. NICHOLSON To find the Surface of a Cylindrical Ring. **c** M. L. KING Beneath the surface . . there was a ground swell of discontent. B. BETTELHEIM To understand a man, we must search for what lies behind the surface. ***scratch the surface***: see SCRATCH *verb*. **2** J. MARQUAND He . . stirred at the champagne . . watching the bubbles rush up to the surface. INA TAYLOR The coal was so near to the surface it made the land of little use. **3 surface of revolution** a surface generated by the rotation of a line or plane figure about an axis. ***4 specific surface***: see SPECIFIC *adjective*.

▸**B** *attrib.* or as *adjective*. **1** Of or pertaining to the surface of something; *spec.* (*a*) of, pertaining to, employed in work on, the surface of the earth as opp. to underground; (*b*) transported by sea or overland as opp. to by air. L17.

2 Superficial. E19.

📖 **1** *Times* Miners' demands include pensions . . at 55 for surface workers. **2** S. PLATH I gathered all my news . . into a . . bitter heap, though I received it with surface gladness.

Special collocations & comb.: **surface-active** *adjective* (*PHYSICAL CHEMISTRY*) (of a substance) able to affect the wetting or surface tension properties of a liquid, acting as a surfactant. **surface blow** *ENGINEERING* a device for blowing off the surface water and scum in a steam boiler. **surface blow-off** the process of removing scum in this way. **surface casing** *OIL INDUSTRY* the length of casing in a borehole which is nearest the surface. **surface chemistry** the branch of chemistry that deals with the processes occurring at the boundaries between different phases. **surface-coated** *adjective* (of paper or cardboard) having a specially finished surface. **surface-colour** colour exhibited, in the case of certain substances, by the light reflected from the surface. **surface condensation** condensation of steam by a surface-condenser. **surface-condenser**: in a steam engine which condenses exhaust-steam by contact with cold metallic surfaces. **surface couching** *EMBROIDERY*: in which the couched thread is held flat on the surface of the fabric by stitches looped over it. **surface-crossing** a level crossing on a railway. **surface effect** an effect associated with or only encountered near a surface; freq. *attrib.*, esp. designating an air-cushion vehicle (hovercraft) in which the cushion is sealed by rigid side-walls and flexible seals fore and aft. **surface film** (*a*) a thin layer or coating on the surface of something, *esp.* one of oil or moisture; (*b*) the apparent membrane on the surface of water or other liquid caused by surface tension. **surface integral** *MATH.* an integral taken over the whole area of a surface. **surface mail** the conveyance of mail by land or sea as opp. to by air; the mail so conveyed. **surfaceman** (*a*) a miner who works above ground; (*b*) a railway worker who repairs the roadbed. **surface-mount** *adjective* (of an electronic component) having leads that are designed to be soldered on the side of a circuit board that the body of the component is mounted on. **surface noise** background noise or hissing heard in playing a gramophone record, caused by imperfections in the grooves. **surface paper** photographic or printing paper with a special surface on one side. **surface-plate** (*a*) an iron plate fixed to the upper surface of a rail on a railway; (*b*) an iron plate for testing the accuracy of a flat surface; (*c*) *PRINTING* a lithographic plate having a sensitized coating on which the image is formed. **surface-printed** *adjective*: by means of surface printing. **surface printing** printing from a plane surface. **surface-rib** *ARCHITECTURE*: applied to the surface of a vault merely for ornament. **surface-road** *US* a railway on the surface of the ground as opp. to one elevated or underground. **surface speed** the speed of which a submarine is capable when moving on the surface. **surface structure** *LINGUISTICS* in transformational grammar, the representation of grammatical or syntactic elements determining the form of a phrase or sentence (opp. ***deep structure***). **surface tension** *PHYSICS* the tension of the surface of a liquid caused by the attraction of the particles in the surface layer by the bulk liquid. **surface-to-air** *adjective* (of a missile) designed to be launched from the ground or at sea and directed at a target in the air. **surface-to-surface** *adjective* (of a missile) designed to be launched from the ground or at sea and directed to a target elsewhere on the earth's surface. **surface water** (*a*) water that collects on the surface of the ground; (*b*) the top layer of a body of water. **surface wave** a wave of displacement propagated along the surface of a solid or a liquid; (*RADIO* etc.) a ground wave that passes from a transmitter to a receiver along the earth's surface, partly in the ground and partly just above it.

■ **surfaceless** *adjective* having no surface or surface covering M20. **surfacely** *adverb* (*rare*) superficially L19. **surfacy** *adjective* superficial L19.

surface /ˈsəːfɪs/ *verb*. L18.
[from the noun.]

1 *verb trans.* Give the required surface to; *esp.* make smooth or even; cover the surface of (*with*). L18.

2 *verb trans.* **a** Bring or raise to the surface. L19. ▸**b** *fig.* Make known or visible; bring to (public) notice. *US colloq.* M20.

3 *verb intrans.* **a** Rise to the surface. L19. ▸**b** Become known or visible; come to (public) notice. M20. ▸**c** Become fully conscious or alert; wake up. *colloq.* M20.

📖 **1** *Practical Woodworking* I surfaced . . hard and softwoods at differing depths of cut. M. MEYER Roads . . were usually surfaced with cobblestones. **2** *New York Times* Another Times reporter surfaced one of the stories. **3a** J. FANE His smooth . . face and . . head were reminiscent of a seal surfacing in the sea. **b** J. WAINWRIGHT At . . home they allowed their feelings to surface a little more. V. GLENDINNING A fantasy that surfaced in times of . . depression. **c** D. PROFUMO James drifted to sleep, but . . surfaced suddenly from . . his dream.

■ **surfacer** *noun* (*a*) *rare* a person who smooths a surface; (*b*) a woodworking machine for cutting and planing wooden boards; (*c*) a paint used to smooth an uneven surface before applying another coat: L18. **surfacing** *noun* (*a*) the action of the verb; (*b*) the coating with which a body (*spec.* a road) is surfaced; (*c*) *Austral.* mining for gold etc. by washing the surface deposit; the deposit so treated: M19.

surfaced /ˈsəːfɪst/ *adjective*. M17.
[from SURFACE *noun*, *verb*: see -ED², -ED¹.]

1 Having a surface of a specified kind. M17.

2 Provided with a special surface or surfaces; esp. (of paper) treated on one side to receive a sharp printed impression. L19.

3 Of a submarine: at sea but not submerged. M20.

surfactant /səˈfakt(ə)nt/ *noun*. M20.
[from SURF(ACE *noun* + ACT(IVE + -ANT¹.]
CHEMISTRY. A surface-active agent, a substance which affects, esp. reduces, the surface tension of a liquid containing it.

surfeit /ˈsəːfɪt/ *noun*. ME.
[Old French *sur-*, *sorfe(i)t* from Proto-Romance (cf. late Latin *superficiens* excessive, Old French *sorfaisant* immoderate), formed as SUPER- + *facere* do, act.]

1 Excess, superfluity; an excessive amount *of* something. ME.

2 Excessive indulgence, formerly esp. in eating or drinking; gluttony, excess. ME. ▸**b** An excessive indulgence, *esp.* one in food or drink which overfills the stomach and produces discomfort. LME. ▸†**c** An excessive amount eaten. LME–E18.

3 A disease caused (or thought to be caused) by excessive eating or drinking; sickness, fever, or discomfort arising from intemperance. E16.

4 An aversion arising from excess; nausea, satiety. M17.

5 *MINING.* = ***choke-damp*** s.v. CHOKE *verb*. E18.

📖 **1** F. WELDON Mary's fault . . was a surfeit of certainty. A. LEE Mama had provided a surfeit of vegetables. **4 to a surfeit**, **to surfeit** to excess, *ad nauseam*.

Comb.: †**surfeit-water** a medicinal drink to ease indigestion.

surfeit /ˈsəːfɪt/ *adjective*. *arch.* E16.
[App. contr. of SURFEITED.]

1 Excessive; immoderate, intemperate. *Scot.* E16.

2 Satiated, surfeited. L17.

surfeit /ˈsəːfɪt/ *verb*. LME.
[from the noun.]

1 a *verb trans.* & *intrans.* Feed (a person) to excess or satiety; (of food) sicken (a person), usu. as a result of excess. LME. ▸**b** *verb trans.* *gen.* Fill or supply to excess; oppress or nauseate with overabundance of something. L16.

2 *verb intrans.* Eat or drink to excess; feast greedily. (Foll. by †*of*, *on*.) LME. ▸**b** *gen.* Indulge in anything to excess; take one's fill, revel. Now *rare* or *obsolete*. L16.

3 *verb intrans.* Suffer the effects of overindulgence in eating or drinking; become sick as a result of eating too much (formerly also from eating bad food). L16. ▸**b** *gen.* Suffer from overabundance; become nauseated by excess of something; grow sick *of*. Now *rare*. E17.

■ **surfeited** *ppl adjective* (*a*) fed or filled to excess; oppressed or nauseated by excess; (*b*) (*obsolete* exc. *dial.*) affected with the disease surfeit; unwell: L16. **surfeiter** *noun* a person who surfeits, *esp.* a glutton LME.

surfer /ˈsəːfə/ *noun*. E20.
[from SURF *noun* or *verb* + -ER¹.]

1 A person who swims in or rides on surf; *esp.* a person who rides a surfboard. E20.

2 A person who surfs the Internet, esp. a regular or enthusiastic user. L20.

surficial /səˈfɪʃ(ə)l/ *adjective*. L19.
[from SURFACE *noun* after *superficial*.]
GEOLOGY. Of or pertaining to the surface of the earth.

■ **surficially** *adverb* on the surface (esp. of the earth) L19.

surfie /ˈsəːfi/ *noun*. *slang* (chiefly *Austral.*). M20.
[from SURF *noun* + -IE.]
A surf-riding enthusiast, *esp.* a young male surfer.

For other words beginning with *sur-* see the entry for **sur-**

surfuse /səːˈfjuːz/ *verb trans.* & *intrans.* L19.
[from SUR- + FUSE *verb*¹.]
PHYSICS. Supercool. Chiefly as ***surfused*** *ppl adjective*.

■ **surfusion** *noun* supercooling L19.

surge /səːdʒ/ *noun*. L15.
[Old French *sourgeon* (mod. *surgeon*) or its base *sourge-*: see next. In sense 3 directly from the verb.]

†**1 a** A fountain, a stream. L15–M16. ▸**b** The source of a river or other stretch of water. Only in 16.

2 a A sudden or impetuous onset of a feeling, process, etc.; an agitated movement, a wave of change. Also (*spec.*), a rapid increase in price, activity, etc., esp. over a short period; a large but brief rise in pressure, voltage in an electric circuit, etc. E16. ▸**b** A high rolling swell of water, esp. on the sea; a large or violent wave. Also, such waves collectively; the rising or driving swell of the sea. Chiefly *poet.* or *rhet.* M16.

3 *NAUTICAL.* **a** The part of a capstan or windlass on which the rope surges. M17. ▸**b** The slipping back of a rope or chain wound round a capstan etc.; *gen.* a sudden jerk or strain. M18. ▸**c** A rhythmic motion forward and aft that is additional to any steady speed of the ship. M20.

📖 **2a** B. ENGLAND Ansell felt an immense surge of relief. J. A. MICHENER Some travellers, a trickle at first and then a surge. M. GIROUARD The surge in property . . values since the war. **b** W. DE LA MARE The solemn surge Of strange and lonely seas.

Comb.: **surge chamber**, **surge tank** *CIVIL ENGINEERING* a chamber connected by a T-junction to a water pipe so as to absorb surges of pressure by filling and drops in pressure by emptying; **surge voltage** *ELECTRICITY* the peak voltage produced in a transmission line by an electrical surge.

■ **surgeful** *adjective* (*poet.*, *rare*) full of surges or billows E17. **surgeless** *adjective* (*rare*) L16. **surgy** *adjective* full of or characteristic of surges; billowy, tempestuous: L16.

surge /səːdʒ/ *verb*. E16.
[Old French *sourge-* stem of *sourdre* or *sorgir* (mod. *surgir*) from Catalan *sorgir* anchor, *surgir* land from Latin *surgere* rise.]

1 *verb intrans.* Orig., come to anchor; later, rise and fall or toss on the waves. E16.

†**2** *verb intrans.* Rise, ascend; *esp.* (of a river, spring, etc.) rise or issue from its source or from underground. M16–M17.

3 *verb intrans.* Of the sea, a river, etc.: rise in great waves; swell or heave with great force. M16. ▸**b** *transf.* Move forcefully and violently or in large numbers; show a large, sudden, usu. brief increase in magnitude, power, speed, etc. M19. ▸**c** Of a feeling, activity, etc.: increase suddenly and rapidly; change violently. Freq. foll. by *up*. M19.

4 *verb trans.* Cause to move in swelling waves or billows; drive in waves. E17.

5 *NAUTICAL.* **a** *verb intrans.* (Of a rope or chain round a capstan etc.) slip back accidentally; (of a wheel) slip round without moving onwards. E17. ▸**b** *verb trans.* Let go or slacken suddenly (a rope round a capstan etc.). M18. ▸**c** *verb intrans.* Of a ship: sweep, pull, or jerk in a certain direction. M19.

📖 **3** C. MCKAY Waters surging down the mountain passes. **b** J. BUCHAN The crowd surged past me on the pavements. P. MARSHALL The big car surged forward like an animal gathering speed. **c** R. MACAULAY Grief, anger, jealousy surged up together in Pamela's throat. *Times* The London stockmarket surged to its highest level.

surgent /ˈsəːdʒ(ə)nt/ *adjective*. L16.
[Latin *surgent-* pres. ppl stem of *surgere* rise: see -ENT.]

1 Rising or swelling in waves, or as a flood or spring; surging (*lit.* & *fig.*). L16.

2 *PSYCHOLOGY.* A personality type characterized by cheerfulness and responsiveness. M20.

■ **surgency** *noun* (*PSYCHOLOGY*) the attribute possessed by the surgent personality M20.

surgeon /ˈsəːdʒ(ə)n/ *noun* & *verb*. ME.
[Anglo-Norman *surgien*, also *sirogen*, *cyrogen*, *sur(r)igien*, contr. of Old French *serurgien*, *cir-* (mod. *chirurgien*), ult. from Latin *chirurgia* surgery from Greek *kheirourgia*, from *kheir* hand + *ergon* work. Cf. CHIRURGEON.]

▸**A** *noun*. **1** A medical practitioner who practises surgery; a specialist in medical operations; *spec.* one with a legal qualification to practise. Formerly also more widely, a doctor. ME. ▸**b** A medical officer in the army, navy, or air force. L16.

2 a = ***surgeon-bird*** below. M19. ▸**b** = ***surgeonfish*** below. L19.

1 dental surgeon: see DENTAL *adjective*. ***plastic surgeon***: see PLASTIC *adjective* 1b. ***tree surgeon***: see TREE *noun*. ***veterinary surgeon***: see VETERINARY *adjective*.

Comb.: **surgeon-bird** = JACANA; **surgeonfish** any herbivorous tropical marine fish of the family Acanthuridae, having sharp movable spines on each side of the tail; **Surgeon General** *US* the senior medical officer of the Bureau of Public Health or similar State authority; **surgeon's knot** a reef knot with one or more extra turns in the first half-knot.

▸**B** *verb trans.* Cure as by surgery. ME.

■ **surgeoncy** *noun* (*arch.*) = SURGEONSHIP L18. **surgeoness** *noun* (*rare*) a female surgeon E18. **surgeonship** *noun* the office or position of a surgeon E19.

surgery /ˈsəːdʒ(ə)ri/ *noun*. ME.
[Old French *surgerie* contr. of *serurgerie*, *cir-*, from *serurgien*, *cir-*: see prec., -ERY. Cf. CHIRURGERY.]
1 The branch of medical practice which treats injuries, deformities, and other bodily disorders by physical operation or manipulation; surgical treatment, a surgical operation. ME.
2 A place where a doctor (esp. a general practitioner) or dentist sees and treats patients; the regular session at which a doctor or dentist receives patients for consultation in this place. M19.
3 A (usu. regular) session at which a Member of Parliament, local councillor, etc., is available to be consulted locally by his or her constituents; a room or office in which this takes place. M20. ▸**b** A similar occasion when free advice is provided by a lawyer, accountant, etc. L20.
4 *MATH*. The topological alteration of manifolds by conceptually removing a neighbourhood and replacing it by another having the same boundary; an instance of this. M20.

> **1** *Maledicta* The operating room, with .. a crucial surgery about to begin. *fig.*: *Winning* This year's course has undergone .. drastic surgery involving a reduction in duration. ***conservative surgery***: see CONSERVATIVE *adjective*. ***plastic surgery***: see PLASTIC *adjective* 1b. ***tree surgery***: see TREE *noun*. **2** *attrib.*: P. AUDEMARS These are surgery hours ... I have patients waiting.

surgical /ˈsəːdʒɪk(ə)l/ *adjective & noun*. L18.
[French *cirurgical* from Old French *cirurgien*: see SURGEON, -ICAL. Alt. after SURGEON, SURGERY.]
▶ **A** *adjective*. **1 a** Pertaining to, dealing with, or used in surgery. L18. ▸**b** *MEDICINE*. Arising as a complication of surgical treatment. M19. ▸**c** Of a garment: worn to correct or relieve an illness or deformity. L19.
2 Designating swift and precise military attack, esp. from the air. Orig. *US*. M20.

> **1a** T. MCGUANE He was wearing his surgical gown and hat. **surgical spirit** methylated spirit used in surgery for cleansing etc. **c** *British Medical Journal* Surgical shoes are commonly prescribed by orthopaedic surgeons. **2** *Annual Register* Israel used a surgical air strike to obliterate the PLO headquarters.

▶ **B** *noun*. Orig., a surgical operation; now, a surgical case or ward. *colloq.* E19.
■ **surgically** *adverb* by the application of, or in relation to, surgical treatment E19.

Surgicenter /ˈsəːdʒɪsentə/ *noun*. *US*. M20.
[from SURGI(CAL + CENTRE *noun*.]
(Proprietary name for) a surgical unit where minor operations are performed on out-patients.

surging /ˈsəːdʒɪŋ/ *verbal noun*. L16.
[from SURGE *verb* + -ING[1].]
1 The action of SURGE *verb*; *esp.* impetuous movement of the sea, rising or swelling of great waves. L16.
2 *NAUTICAL*. The action of suddenly slackening a rope or chain round a capstan etc. M19.
3 *ELECTRICITY*. The occurrence of surges in a current; a surge. E20.
4 *MECHANICS*. An increased action in a valve spring of an internal-combustion engine when the operating frequency of the valve coincides with the natural frequency of oscillation. M20.

suricate /ˈs(j)ʊərɪkeɪt/ *noun*. L18.
[French, of African origin.]
= ***grey meerkat*** (a) s.v. MEERKAT.

surimono /sʊərɪˈməʊnəʊ/ *noun*. Pl. same. L19.
[Japanese, from *suri* printing + *mono* thing.]
A print; *spec.* a small Japanese colour print used to convey greetings or to mark a special occasion.

Suriname /sʊərɪˈnam, sjʊə-/ *noun*. Also **-nam**. L17.
[A country in S. America, formerly called Dutch Guiana.]
Used *attrib.* to designate animals, plants, products, etc., found in or associated with Suriname.
Suriname cherry an American evergreen tropical shrub or small tree, *Eugenia uniflora*, of the myrtle family, grown as a hedge plant in the tropics; the edible red fruit of this plant, used in jellies and sherbets. **Suriname poison** a tropical American leguminous plant, *Tephrosia toxicaria*, used to stupefy fish; the poison derived from the leaves of this plant. ***Suriname QUASSIA***. **Suriname toad** any of several large aquatic S. American toads of the family Pipidae, having broad flat bodies and feet, and, in the female, pits in the back in which the eggs develop; *esp.* the common *Pipa pipa*.
■ **Surinamer** *noun* a native or inhabitant of Suriname M20.

Surinamese /ˌsʊərɪnaˈmiːz, ˌsjʊə-/ *adjective & noun*. M20.
[formed as prec. + -ESE.]
▶ **A** *adjective*. Of or pertaining to Suriname or its people. M20.
▶ **B** *noun*. Pl. same. A native or inhabitant of Suriname. L20.

†**surintendent** *noun*. M17–E18.
[French *surintendant*: see SUR-, INTENDANT.]
A superintendent.

surjection /səːˈdʒɛkʃ(ə)n/ *noun*. M20.
[from SUR- after *injection*.]
MATH. An onto mapping.
■ **surjective** *adjective* that is a surjection M20.

surly /ˈsəːli/ *adverb & adjective*. Also †**sirly**. LME.
[from SIR *noun* + -LY[1]: alt. in 16.]
▶† **A** *adverb*. In a lordly, imperious, or arrogant manner. LME–L17.

> SHAKES. *Jul. Caes.* I met a lion, Who glaz'd upon me, and went surly by.

▶ **B** *adjective*. †**1** Lordly; masterful, imperious; haughty, arrogant, supercilious. M16–E18.
2 Bad-tempered and unfriendly, morose, churlish. L16. ▸**b** *fig.* (Of soil etc.) refractory, intractable; (of weather etc.) rough and gloomy, threatening and dismal. M17.

> **2** J. BUCHAN His eye expressed a surly contempt. R. M. BRAMSON Tell surly salespeople that their demeanor is offensive. **b** R. CAMPBELL Across the swamp the surly day goes down.

Comb.: †**surly-borne** *adjective* (*rare*, Shakes.) haughty in bearing or demeanour.
■ **surlily** *adverb* E17. **surliness** *noun* L16.

Surlyn /ˈsəːlɪn/ *noun*. M20.
[Origin unkn.]
(Proprietary name for) a tough synthetic thermoplastic polymer used esp. to cover golf balls.

surma /ˈsʊəmə/ *noun*. Also **soorma**. E19.
[Urdu & Persian.]
A black powder consisting of lead sulphide or antimony sulphide, used by women of the Indian subcontinent for staining the eyebrows and eyelids.

surmaster /ˈsəːmaːstə/ *noun*. E16.
[Alt. of medieval Latin *submagister*, formed as SUB- + *magister* MASTER *noun*[1].]
The second master at St Paul's School, London.

surmise /səˈmʌɪz, ˈsəːmʌɪz/ *noun*. LME.
[Anglo-Norman, Old French, from *surmettre*: see next.]
†**1** A formal allegation or statement of information (*LAW*); *spec.* (*ECCLESIASTICAL LAW*) the allegation in the libel. Also, an allegation, a charge, *esp.* a false or unfounded one. LME–E18.
2 An idea that something may be true, but formed without proof or certainty; (a) conjecture, (a) suspicion; inference. E16. ▸†**b** A slight trace or suspicion *of* something. L16–M19.
†**3** The formation of an idea in the mind; conception, imagination. L16–M17.

> **2** M. GARDINER Ben's surmise was correct and Harry had indeed joined the Communist Party. **3** SHAKES. *Lucr.* From the feeling of her own grief brought By deep surmise of others' detriment.

surmise /səˈmʌɪz/ *verb*. LME.
[Anglo-Norman, Old French *surmis*, *-ise* pa. pple of *surmettre* accuse from late Latin *supermittere* (in medieval Latin accuse), formed as SUPER- + *mittere* put.]
†**1** *verb trans.* Make a charge or allegation of, accuse a person of (a crime etc.); *spec.* (*LAW*) submit as a charge, allege formally. (Foll. by *against*, *on*, *upon* a person.) LME–E17.
†**2** *verb trans.* Plan, contrive (*to do* something), esp. falsely or maliciously. E16–M17.
†**3** *verb trans.* Suppose, imagine (*that* a thing is so); expect. E16–E18. ▸**b** Form an idea of, conceive. L16–E17.
4 *verb trans. & intrans.* Form an idea or suspect that or *that* something may be true, but without proof or certainty; infer (something) conjecturally, guess. L16.

> **3b** *absol.*: SHAKES. *Haml.* I have a daughter .. Who .. Hath given me this. Now gather, and surmise. **4** W. S. MAUGHAM The French, for reasons which could only be surmised, were .. prepared to support him. T. S. ELIOT The question has to do, as you surmised, with Mr Simpkins. E. REVELEY Margery .. surmised that very soon they would be leaving.

■ **surmisable** *adjective* E19. **surmisal** *noun* (now *rare*) = SURMISE *noun* M17. **surmiser** *noun* †(*a*) a person who makes (esp. ill-founded) allegations or charges against someone; (*b*) a person who makes a surmise or conjecture: E16.

surmount /səˈmaʊnt/ *verb*. LME.
[Old & mod. French *surmonter*: see SUR-, SUPER-, MOUNT *verb*.]
†**1** *verb trans.* **a** Surpass in quality, achievement, etc.: excel, be superior to. LME–M17. ▸**b** Surpass in amount or size: exceed, be greater than, go beyond; transcend. LME–L18.
†**2** *verb intrans.* **a** Be superior, excel. LME–L17. ▸**b** Be greater or more numerous; predominate. M16–E17.
3 *verb trans.* Prevail over, get the better of, overcome (a person etc.); rise superior to, get over (a difficulty etc.). LME.
4 *verb trans.* Mount or rise above; reach above, be higher than. Now *rare*. LME.
†**5** *verb intrans.* Mount, rise (above something); extend in height. LME–M16. ▸**b** Amount *to*. M16–M17. ▸**c** Result from addition; be produced *from* something. L16–M17.
6 *verb trans.* Mount, get on top of; *esp.* climb across, get over. Also, extend across. M16.
7 *verb trans.* Be situated above (orig. in *HERALDRY*); stand or rest on top of; top, crown. Chiefly as ***surmounted*** *ppl adjective*. E17.

> **3** J. AIKEN Rachel is unable .. to surmount her speech impediment. **6** A. G. GARDINER We had taken nearly six hours to surmount the pass. **7** G. SANTAYANA A ruddy face, surmounted by a .. bowler hat. A. HOLLINGHURST Framed photographs surmounted a mahogany writing-desk.

■ **surmountable** *adjective* LME. **surmounted** *ppl adjective* (*ARCHITECTURE*) designating an arch or vault whose rise is greater than half the span E18.

surmullet /səːˈmʌlɪt/ *noun*. Pl. same, **-s**. L17.
[French *surmulet*, from Old French *sor* (mod. *saur*) red, of unkn. origin, + MULLET *noun*[1].]
Any of several edible red mullet, esp. (more fully ***striped surmullet***) *Mullus surmuletus*, which is red with three long yellow stripes, and (more fully ***plain surmullet***) *M. barbatus*.

surnai /ˈsʊənʌɪ/ *noun*. E20.
[Urdu *surnā*, *surnāe* = Persian *surnā*, *surnāy*.]
An oriental variety of oboe.

surname /ˈsəːneɪm/ *noun & verb*. Also (long *arch.*) **sirename** /ˈsʌɪərəneɪm/. ME.
[Anglo-Norman *surnoun* = Old & mod. French *surnom*, formed as SUR- + *noun* NAME *noun* (cf. NOUN), after medieval Latin *super-*, *supranomen*.]
▶ **A** *noun*. **1** A name, title, or epithet added to a person's name or names, *esp.* one indicating his or her birthplace or some characteristic or achievement. *arch.* ME. ▸†**b** A second or alternative name or title given to a person, place, building, etc. LME–M17.
2 The name which a person has in common with the other members of his or her family, as opp. to the Christian or given name; a family name. LME. ▸**b** A nickname, an appellation; *spec.* = COGNOMEN 2. Long *rare*. LME.
▶ **B** *verb trans.* Usu. in *pass.*
1 Give a specified surname to; call (a person) by his or her surname or family name. LME.
2 Give an additional name, title, or epithet to (a person). M16.
†**3** Call by an additional name; attach another appellation to; *gen.* designate, entitle. M16–L17.

surnap /ˈsəːnap/ *noun*. *obsolete* exc. *Hist.* LME.
[Anglo-Norman, Old French *sur-*, *sournap(p)e*, formed as SUR- + *nape* tablecloth.]
A towel or napkin provided at table for use when washing the hands.

surnominal /səːˈnɒmɪn(ə)l/ *adjective*. L19.
[from SURNAME *noun*, after *name*, *nominal*.]
Of or pertaining to surnames.

surpass /səˈpaːs/ *verb trans*. M16.
[French *surpasser*, formed as SUR- + *passer* PASS *verb*.]
1 Outdo (another) in degree or quality; do more or better than; be greater than, exceed; be superior to. M16.
2 Go beyond, overstep (a limit, certain period of time, etc.); pass over. *arch.* L16.
3 Be beyond the range, reach, or capacity of; be too much or too great for; transcend. L16.
4 a Extend above or beyond. Now *rare*. E17. ▸†**b** Rise or mount above; surmount. M17–M18.

> **1** W. S. CHURCHILL In quickness of mind the Queen was surpassed by few of her contemporaries. G. VIDAL Gallus continued to surpass me at all games. **surpass oneself** do even better than what one has previously achieved. **3** M. COREN The friendship .. surpasses most schoolboy affections.

■ **surpassable** *adjective* E17. **surpasser** *noun* a person who surpasses another E19.

surpassing /səˈpaːsɪŋ/ *ppl adjective & adverb*. L16.
[from prec. + -ING[2].]
▶ **A** *ppl adjective*. That surpasses what is ordinary; of a very high degree; pre-eminent, matchless. L16.
▶ **B** *adverb*. = SURPASSINGLY. *obsolete* exc. *poet.* L16.
■ **surpassingly** *adverb* in the highest degree; exceedingly: M17.

†**surpeach** *noun*. M18–M19.
[Urdu & Persian *sarpeč*.]
An ornament of gold, silver, or jewels, on a turban.

sur place /syr plas/ *adverbial phr*. E20.
[French.]
1 At the place in question; on the spot. E20.
2 *BALLET*. Without leaving the place where one has been standing. M20.

surplice /ˈsəːplɪs/ *noun*. ME.
[Anglo-Norman *surplis*, Old French *sourpelis* (mod. *surplis*) from medieval Latin *superpellicium*, *-eum* (sc. *vestimentum* garment) use as noun of neut. of adjective formed as SUPER- + *pellicia* fur garment (see PILCH *noun*, PELISSE).]
1 A loose white linen vestment with wide sleeves, reaching to the knees or feet and worn usu. over a cassock by clergy and choristers at church services. ME.

For other words beginning with *sur-* see the entry for **sur-**

2 *transf.* Any of various long loose or flowing garments. ME.

Comb.: **surplice fees**: received by an incumbent for the performance of marriages, funerals, and other ministerial offices.

■ **surpliced** *adjective* wearing a surplice M18.

surplus /ˈsəːpləs/ *noun, adjective, & verb.* LME.
[Anglo-Norman, Old French *so(u)rplus* (mod. *surplus*) from medieval Latin *superplus*, formed as SUPER- + *plus* more.]
▶ **A** *noun.* **1** What remains in excess of what is needed or already used; an amount left over; *spec.* an excess of income or assets over expenditure or liabilities. LME. ▸**b** *POLITICS.* In some systems of election: votes transferred from a candidate who has attained the quota necessary for election to another who has not. E20.
2 What remains to make up a whole; the remainder, the rest. Now *rare* or *obsolete.* LME.

📖 **1** A. BEVAN Backward communities where the agricultural population is able to produce only small surpluses.

▶ **B** *attrib.* or as *adjective.* **1** More than is needed or used; excess. LME.
2 *surplus value* (*ECONOMICS*), that part of the value of the results of human labour which accrues beyond the amount needed to reproduce the initial labour power; *gen.* the excess of income over expenditure. E19.
3 Of a shop or goods: (selling goods) surplus to (usu. military) requirements. M20.

📖 **1** R. MITCHISON The surplus population of the rural areas had to move to towns. M. FORSTER Taking care to allow the surplus ink to drip off her pen. **surplus to** more than is needed for. **3** G. JACKSON Some old surplus army blankets.

▶ **C** *verb trans.* Infl. **-s-**, ***-ss-**. Dispose of as surplus to requirements. Also foll. by *out*. Usu. in *pass.* *US Military slang.* M20.

surplusage /ˈsəːpləsɪdʒ/ *noun.* LME.
[medieval Latin *surplusagium* (also *super-*), from *surplus*: see prec., -AGE.]
1 = SURPLUS *noun* 1, 2. LME.
2 An excess of words, unnecessary words; *spec.* in *LAW*, an unnecessary word, clause, or statement in an indictment or plea. E16.

†**surpoose** *noun.* L17–E19.
[Urdu *sarpoš* = Persian *sarpūš* veil, from *sar* head + *pūš* covering.]
A cover of a (silver) vessel.

surprise /səˈprʌɪz/ *noun.* LME.
[Old & mod. French *surpris(e* use as noun of pa. pple of *surprendre*: see the verb.]
1 a *MILITARY.* The action or an act of attacking or seizing a place unexpectedly or without warning; sudden unexpected attack on or capture of a place, a body of troops, etc. LME. ▸**b** *gen.* The action or an act of coming upon a person unawares; a sudden attack. Now *rare* exc. in *take by surprise*, take unawares, shock by being unexpected. L16. ▸†**c** An attack of an illness; a sudden flood *of* an emotion. L17–E18.
2 A thing that takes a person by surprise; an unexpected occurrence; anything astonishing. L16. ▸**b** *spec.* A fancy dish, present, etc., designed to take a person by surprise. E18.
3 The emotion aroused by something unexpected; mild astonishment or amazement. Formerly also, alarm or terror caused by a sudden attack, disaster, etc. E17.
4 *CAMPANOLOGY.* A complex method of change-ringing. L19.

📖 **1a** *attrib.*: *Ottawa Journal* Government troops . . crushed Pancho Banderas . . in a surprise attack. **b** M. DICKENS She took Virginia by surprise by arriving . . in a taxi. **2** N. FARAH It is a delightful surprise to see you here. **surprise, surprise!** (freq. *iron.*) expr. or suggesting surprise. **b** F. O'CONNOR A Lime-Cherry Surprise, a special that day for ten cents. **3** P. FARMER He started in surprise and swung round to find me standing just behind him. K. VONNEGUT Much to my surprise, Father began to blossom as an artist. **4** *superlative surprise*: see SUPERLATIVE *adjective* 2.

Comb.: **surprise packet** a sealed packet with contents designed to give a surprise, sold at a low price (freq. *fig.*); **surprise-party** (*a*) a body of troops for an unexpected attack; (*b*) a celebration organized as a surprise for a friend by a group who meet at the friend's house without invitation, bringing food and drink.

surprise /səˈprʌɪz/ *verb.* L15.
[Old & mod. French *surpris(e* pa. pple of *surprendre* from medieval Latin *superprehendere*, formed as SUPER- + Latin *prehendere*: see PREHEND. Cf. earlier SURPRISED.]
†**1** *verb trans.* **a** Of an emotion, illness, etc.: affect suddenly or unexpectedly. Usu. in *pass.* L15–E18. ▸**b** Overcome, overpower (the mind, the will, the heart); captivate. L15–L17.
2 *verb trans.* **a** Attack suddenly and without warning, catch unprepared; *MILITARY* make an unexpected assault on (a place, a body of troops, etc.). E16. ▸†**b** Take possession of by force; take prisoner; capture, seize. L16–L18.
3 *verb trans.* Come upon (a person) unawares; catch in the act; *fig.* discover (something) suddenly, detect. L16.
4 *verb trans.* †**a** Implicate or ensnare (a person) by a sudden proposal or disclosure. M17–E18. ▸**b** Lead unawares, betray *into* doing something unintended. L17.
5 a *verb trans.* Affect with the characteristic emotion caused by something unexpected; arouse surprise or shock in (a person). Formerly also, alarm, terrify, amaze. L17. ▸**b** *verb intrans.* Be taken by surprise; be shocked. M20.

📖 **2a** T. MCGUANE His father had bought a . . radio for the trip, so they would not be surprised by weather. **3** CONAN DOYLE He surprised my secret, and has presumed . . upon his power of provoking a scandal. A. HIGGINS He had surprised her naked in the bathroom. **5a** M. MARRIN It surprised me . . how much people are prepared to pay for important paintings. *absol.*: W. COWPER The turns are quick, the polish'd points surprise.

■ **surprisable** *adjective* able to be surprised; liable to surprise or unexpected attack: M17. **surprisal** *noun* (now *rare* or *obsolete*) the action of surprising; the state of being surprised; something that surprises: L16. **surpriser** *noun* †(*a*) a capturer of a place, a body of troops, etc.; (*b*) a person who or thing which surprises someone: L16. **surprising** *adjective* †(*a*) admirable; (*b*) causing surprise by its unexpectedness: L16. **surprisingly** *adverb* M17. **surprisingness** *noun* L17.

surprised /səˈprʌɪzd/ *adjective.* LME.
[from (the same root as) prec. + -ED¹.]
1 Affected or characterized by surprise; startled, shocked; scandalized *at* a person. LME.
2 Attacked or come upon unexpectedly; captured by sudden attack; taken unawares. L16.

📖 **1** C. S. FORESTER That was wanton extravagance . . I'm surprised at you. G. DALY Usually shy, she was surprised to find herself almost garrulous. **you'd be surprised** *colloq.* the facts are not as you would think.

■ **surprisedly** /-zɪdli/ *adverb* L17. **surprisedness** /-zɪdnɪs/ *noun* L17.

surquidry /ˈsəːkwɪdri/ *noun.* Long *arch.* Also **-quedry**. ME.
[Old French *s(o)urcuiderie*, from *s(o)urcuidier*, formed as SUR- + *cuidier* think: see -RY.]
1 Arrogance, haughty pride, presumption. ME.
2 Excess (esp. of indulgence), surfeit. L16.
■ Also **surquidy** *noun* LME.

surra /ˈsuːrə, ˈsʌrə/ *noun.* L19.
[Marathi *sūr* from Sanskrit *svara* sound, tone (from sound cut off in the throat).]
A disease of horses, camels, and other domestic animals, chiefly in Asia and NE Africa, caused by the protozoan parasite *Trypanosoma evansi*, transmitted by tabanid flies, and usually fatal.

surreal /səˈrɪəl/ *adjective.* M20.
[Back-form. from next.]
Having the qualities of surrealist art; bizarre, dreamlike.
■ **surreˈality** *noun* M20. **surreally** *adverb* M20.

surrealism /səˈrɪəlɪz(ə)m/ *noun.* E20.
[French *surréalisme*: see SUR-, REALISM.]
A 20th-cent. movement in art and literature seeking to express the subconscious mind by various techniques including the irrational juxtaposition of images, the creation of mysterious symbols, and automatism; art or literature produced by or reminiscent of this movement.
■ **surrealist** *adjective & noun* (*a*) *adjective* of, pertaining to, or characteristic of surrealism; (*b*) *noun* an adherent of surrealism: E20. **surreaˈlistic** *adjective* characteristic or suggestive of surrealism M20. **surreaˈlistically** *adverb* M20.

surrebutter /sʌrɪˈbʌtə/ *noun.* L16.
[from SUR- + REBUTTER, after *surrejoinder*.]
LAW. An answer made by a plaintiff to a defendant's rebutter; *transf.* a further rejoinder.
■ **surrebut** *verb intrans.* (infl. **-tt-**) reply to a rebutter E18. **surrebuttal** *noun* = SURREBUTTER L19.

†**surreined** *ppl adjective. rare.* L16–E17.
[Prob. from SUR- + REIN *verb* + -ED¹.]
Of a horse: overridden, overworked.

📖 SHAKES. *Hen. V* A drench for sur-rein'd jades.

surrejoin /sʌrɪˈdʒɔɪn/ *verb intrans.* L16.
[Back-form. from next, after *rejoin*.]
LAW. Of a plaintiff: answer a defendant's rejoinder; make a surrejoinder.

surrejoinder /sʌrɪˈdʒɔɪndə/ *noun.* M16.
[from SUR- + REJOINDER.]
LAW. An answer made by a plaintiff to a defendant's rejoinder; *gen.* an answer to a rejoinder or reply.

surrender /səˈrɛndə/ *noun.* LME.
[Anglo-Norman, use as noun of inf. = Old French *surrendre*: see the verb, -ER⁴.]
1 *LAW.* **a** The giving up of an estate to a person who has it in reversion, so as to merge it in a larger estate; the giving up of a lease before its expiry; *spec.* the yielding up of a tenancy in a copyhold estate to the lord of a manor. Also *transf.*, a deed by which such surrender is made. LME. ▸**b** The giving up of letters patent granting an estate or office; *Hist.* the yielding up of tithes in Scotland to the Crown. LME. ▸**c** The giving up of property by a bankrupt to his or her creditors. Also, a bankrupt's appearance in the bankruptcy court for examination. M18. ▸**d** The abandonment of an insurance policy by the party assured on receiving in return a part of the premiums. L19.
2 The giving up of something into the possession or power of another who has or asserts a claim to it; *spec.* (*MILITARY*) submission of a town, territory, etc., to an enemy. Also more widely, resignation, abandonment. LME.

📖 **2** H. ROBBINS Her voice was filled with surrender to his . . assertiveness.

Comb.: **surrender value** the amount payable to a person who surrenders a life-insurance policy.
■ Also **surrendry** *noun* (now *rare*) M16.

surrender /səˈrɛndə/ *verb.* LME.
[Anglo-Norman, = Old French *surrendre*, formed as SUR- + *rendre* RENDER *verb*.]
1 *LAW.* **a** *verb trans.* Give up (an estate) to a person who has it in reversion; *spec.* (*Hist.*) give up (a copyhold estate) to the lord of a manor. LME. ▸**b** *verb trans.* Give up (letters patent, tithes) into the hands of the sovereign. L15. ▸**c** *verb refl. & intrans.* Of a bankrupt: appear in the bankruptcy court for examination. E18. ▸**d** *verb trans. & intrans.* (Of a person acting as bail) produce (the prisoner) in court at the appointed time; (of a prisoner on bail) appear in court at the appointed time. M18.
2 *verb trans.* Give up (something) into the possession or power of another who has or asserts a claim to it; yield on demand or compulsion *to* a person; *spec.* (*MILITARY*) give up (a town, territory, etc.) to an enemy. Also more widely, resign, abandon, relinquish possession of. E16.
3 *verb intrans. & refl.* **a** Give oneself up into the power of another, esp. as a prisoner; *spec.* (*MILITARY*) submit to or *to* an enemy. M16. ▸**b** *fig.* Give oneself up to some influence, course of action, etc.; abandon oneself entirely *to*. E18.

📖 **1d surrender to one's bail, surrender to bail** appear in a court of law after release on bail. **2** *Social History of Medicine* As a result of the war, Finland was surrendered to Russia. G. BOYCOTT Having surrendered all our local currency . . we had no money to buy food. S. BELLOW She . . surrendered all property rights in the settlement. **3a** W. S. CHURCHILL I . . surrendered myself a prisoner of war. B. W. ALDISS Following the fall of Mussolini, Italy surrendered unconditionally. **b** W. S. CHURCHILL The Colonial Office surrendered to the pressure of events. J. FRAME Surrendering to . . tiredness she fell asleep.

■ **surrendeˈree** *noun* (*LAW*) a person to whom an estate etc. is surrendered M17. **surrenderor** *noun* (*LAW*) a person who surrenders an estate etc. to another L17.

Surrentine /sʌˈrɛntʌɪn/ *adjective.* E17.
[Latin *Surrentinus*, from *Surrentum* (see below): see -INE¹.]
Of or pertaining to Surrentum, an ancient maritime town (now Sorrento) in Campania, Italy, famous for its wine.

surreption /səˈrɛpʃ(ə)n/ *noun*¹. LME.
[Latin *surreptio(n-)*, from *surrept-* pa. ppl stem of *surripere* seize secretly, (Vulgate) make false suggestions, formed as SUB- + *rapere* seize: see -TION. Cf. SUBREPTION.]
†**1** Suppression of the truth for the purpose of obtaining something; the action of obtaining something in this way; *gen.* fraudulent misrepresentation, underhand activity. LME–E18.
2 The action of seizing something by stealth; stealing, theft. Earliest in *by surreption*, by stealth, stealthily. Now *rare* or *obsolete.* LME.

†**surreption** *noun*². E16–E18.
[medieval Latin *surreptio(n-)* (= late Latin *subreptio(n-)* a creeping in: cf. also medieval Latin *surreptare* creep in stealthily), formed as SUB- + *rept-* pa. ppl stem of *repere* creep: see -TION.]
An unperceived creeping of insidious thoughts into a person's mind; the sudden onset of sinful thoughts or behaviour. Also, a lapse due to this.

surreptitious /sʌrəpˈtɪʃəs/ *adjective.* LME.
[Latin *surreptitius*, *-icius*, from *surrept-*: see SURREPTION *noun*¹, -ITIOUS¹. Cf. SUBREPTITIOUS.]
1 Obtained by suppression of the truth or by fraudulent misrepresentation. LME.
2 (Of a piece of writing) spurious, forged; (of an edition of a book) issued without authority, pirated. E17.
3 a Acting stealthily or secretly; crafty, sly. E17. ▸**b** Obtained, done, etc., by stealth or in secret; underhand, clandestine. M17.

📖 **3b** R. K. NARAYAN We had surreptitious drinks too, although there was prohibition. *Woman* Rosie took a surreptitious peep at Mark.

■ **surreptitiously** *adverb* L16. **surreptitiousness** *noun* (*rare*) E20.

Surrey /ˈsʌri/ *noun*¹. L19.
[A county in southern England.]
1 *Hist.* ***Surrey cart***, a type of light horse-drawn cart with open seats. L19.

For other words beginning with *sur-* see the entry for **sur-**

2 *Surrey chicken, Surrey fowl*, a fowl specially fattened before being killed and prepared for cooking. L19.

surrey /ˈsʌri/ *noun*². L19.
[from *Surrey cart* (see prec.), from which the carriage was adapted.]
Chiefly *Hist.* An American light four-wheeled carriage with two seats facing forwards.

surrogata *noun* pl. of SURROGATUM.

surrogate /ˈsʌrəgət/ *noun & adjective*. E17.
[Latin *surrogatus* pa. pple of *surrogare*: see the verb, -ATE¹.]
▶ **A** *noun*. **1** A person appointed by authority to act in place of another; a deputy. E17. ▸**b** The deputy of an ecclesiastical judge, of a bishop or bishop's chancellor, *esp.* one who grants licences to marry without banns. E17. ▸**c** *Hist.* In the former British colonies, a person appointed to act as judge in the vice-admiralty court in place of a regular judge; in New York and some other States, a judge having jurisdiction over the probate of wills and settlement of estates. E19.
2 A person or thing taking the place of another; a substitute (*for*, *of* something else). Also as 2nd elem. of comb. M17. ▸**b** *spec.* A surrogate partner in sex therapy. L20.
3 = ***surrogate mother*** (b) below. L20.

📖 **2** *Times Lit. Suppl.* Psychologists who condemn hunting as a surrogate for sexual intercourse. ***God-surrogate***, ***mother-surrogate***, etc.

▶ **B** *adjective*. That is a surrogate; taking the place of or standing for something else; representative. M17.

📖 *Raritan* Western cigarettes serve . . as a . . surrogate currency. **surrogate baby** a baby borne by a surrogate mother. **surrogate mother** (*a*) a person or animal acting the role of mother; (*b*) a woman who bears a child on behalf of another woman, either from her own egg fertilized by the other woman's partner or from the implantation in her womb of a fertilized egg from the other woman.

■ **surrogacy** *noun* (*a*) *rare* the office of a surrogate; (*b*) surrogate motherhood: E19.

surrogate /ˈsʌrəgeɪt/ *verb trans.* Now *rare*. M16.
[Latin *surrogat-* pa. ppl stem of *surrogare* var. of *subrogare* put in another's place: see SUBROGATE.]
= SUBROGATE 1.

surrogation /sʌrəˈgeɪʃ(ə)n/ *noun*. Now *rare*. M16.
[Late Latin *surrogatio(n-)*, formed as prec.: see -ATION.]
1 The appointment of a person to some office in place of another. M16.
2 *gen.* Substitution. M17.

surrogatum /sʌrəˈgeɪtəm/ *noun*. Pl. ***-ta*** /-tə/. M18.
[Latin, neut. sing. of *surrogatus*: see SURROGATE *noun & adjective*.]
SCOTS LAW. A thing put in the place of another; a substitute.

surround /səˈraʊnd/ *noun*. E19.
[from the verb.]
1 An act of surrounding a person or thing; *spec.* (orig. & chiefly *US*) a method of hunting wild animals by surrounding them and driving them into a place from which they cannot escape. E19.
2 A border, an edging, as of linoleum or felt round a carpet. L19.
3 The area around a place or thing; the vicinity, the surroundings, the environment. E20.

📖 **2** B. VINE A small photograph in a golden oval surround.

surround /səˈraʊnd/ *verb trans.* LME.
[Anglo-Norman *sur(o)under*, Old French *s(o)uronder* from late Latin *superundare*, formed as SUPER- + *undare* rise in waves, from *unda* wave.]
1 Overflow, inundate, flood, submerge. *obsolete* exc. *dial.* LME.
2 Place a thing or things on all sides of or all round; enclose *with* something. Also, stand or be situated around; extend round, encircle; edge. E17. ▸**b** MILITARY. Enclose (a place or a body of troops) on all sides so as to cut off communication or retreat; invest. M17.
†**3** Go or travel around; make a circuit of, *esp.* circumnavigate. M17–E19.

📖 **2** E. L. DOCTOROW She stood surrounded by colleagues and admirers. B. HEAD A wide porch . . surrounded the whole house. *fig.*: G. DALY If her husband had surrounded her with love and trust, Georgie might have been . . more relaxed. A. TAYLOR There is still a conspiracy of silence surrounding death.

Comb.: **surround sound** a system of stereophony involving three or more speakers surrounding the listener so as to give a more realistic effect.
■ **surrounder** *noun* L17.

surrounding /səˈraʊndɪŋ/ *noun*. LME.
[from prec. + -ING¹.]
†**1** Overflowing, inundation. LME–L16.
2 The action or fact of surrounding or encompassing someone or something. L18.
3 In *pl.* Those things which surround or are in the vicinity of a person or thing; the conditions affecting a person or thing; environment. M19.
4 *sing.* & in *pl.* A number of people standing around; a body of attendants; an entourage. L19.

📖 **3** R. FRY The artist is . . constantly observant of his surroundings.

surrounding /səˈraʊndɪŋ/ *ppl adjective*. M17.
[formed as prec. + -ING².]
That surrounds a person or thing; encompassing, encircling.

surroyal /ˈsəːrɔɪəl/ *noun*. LME.
[from SUR- + ROYAL *noun*.]
An upper or terminal branch of a stag's antler.

†**sursolid** *noun & adjective*. M16.
[App. alt. of mod. Latin *surdesolidus* (see SURDESOLID), assim. to SUR-.]
MATH. ▶ **A** *noun*. The fifth power of a number or quantity. Also, an equation of the fifth (or a higher, esp. odd) degree. M16–E19.
▶ **B** *adjective*. Of the fifth degree; that is a fifth power or root; involving the fifth (or occas. a higher) power of a quantity. M16–E18.

sursum- /ˈsəːsəm/ *combining form*.
[from Latin *sursum*.]
OPHTHALMOLOGY. Upwards.
■ **sursumˈduction** *noun* (the degree of) vertical movement upwards of one eye alone L19. **sursumˈvergence** *noun* (the degree of) simultaneous movement of one eye upwards and the other downwards L19. **sursumˈversion** *noun* the parallel upward movement of both eyes L19.

Sursum corda /səːs(ə)m ˈkɔːdə/ *noun phr.* M16.
[Latin, from *sursum* upwards + *corda* pl. of *cor* heart.]
CHRISTIAN CHURCH. In Latin Eucharistic liturgies, the words addressed by the celebrant to the congregation at the beginning of the Eucharistic Prayer; in English rites, the corresponding versicle, 'Lift up your hearts'.

surtax /ˈsəːtaks/ *noun & verb*. L19.
[French *surtaxe*, formed as SUR- + *taxe* tax.]
▶ **A** *noun*. An additional tax on something already taxed; *spec.* (*Hist.*) income tax at a higher rate charged on personal incomes above a certain level (succeeding supertax in the UK and abolished in 1973). L19.
▶ **B** *verb trans.* Tax additionally, charge with surtax. E20.

surtitle /ˈsəːtʌɪt(ə)l/ *noun & verb*. L20.
[from SUR- + TITLE *noun*.]
▶ **A** *noun*. A short piece of text projected on a screen above the stage during the performance of an opera, esp. to translate the libretto as it is sung or spoken. L20.
▶ **B** *verb trans.* Provide with surtitles. L20.
¶ Proprietary name in Canada and (in *pl.*) in the US.

surtout /ˈsəːtuː, səːˈtuː(t)/ *noun*. L17.
[French, from *sur* above + *tout* everything.]
1 A man's overcoat. L17. ▸†**b** *fig.* An outer covering or layer. M–L18.
†**2** A woman's hood with a mantle. L17–L18.

surturbrand /ˈsəːtəbrand/ *noun*. M18.
[German from Icelandic *surtarbrandur*, from Old Norse *Surtar* genit. of *Surtr* (rel. to *svartr* SWART) a mythical fire-bearing giant + *brandr* BRAND *noun*.]
Lignite as occurring in Iceland.

surucucu /suːˌruːkuːˈkuː/ *noun*. E17.
[Portuguese & Spanish from Tupi-Guarani *surucucú*.]
= ***bushmaster*** s.v. BUSH *noun*¹.

surveil /səˈveɪl/ *verb trans.* Infl. **-ll-**. M20.
[Back-form. from next.]
Subject to surveillance, keep a watch on.

surveillance /səːˈveɪl(ə)ns, səˈveɪəns/ *noun*. E19.
[French, from *surveiller*: see next, -ANCE.]
1 Watch or guard kept over a person or thing, esp. one under suspicion; spying. E19.
2 Supervision for the purpose of direction or control, superintendence. E19.

📖 **1** B. BAINBRIDGE If Meyer consorted with criminals then his house was bound to be under surveillance. **2** T. HARDY Trotting the length and breadth of . . two thousand acres in a cheerful spirit of surveillance.

surveillant /səːˈveɪl(ə)nt/ *noun & adjective*. Also (fem.) ***surveillante*** /syrvɛjɑ̃ːt, səːveɪˈjɑːnt/. E19.
[French, (use as noun of) pres. pple of *surveiller* watch over, formed as SUR- + *veiller* keep watch from Latin *vigilare*: see -ANT¹.]
▶ **A** *noun*. **1** A person who exercises surveillance. E19.
2 A teacher on non-teaching duty. M19.
▶ **B** *adjective*. Exercising surveillance. M19.

†**survene** *verb intrans. & trans.* M17–E18.
[Alt. of SUPERVENE by substitution of SUR-.]
= SUPERVENE.

survey /ˈsəːveɪ/ *noun*. L15.
[from the verb.]
†**1** Oversight, supervision, superintendence. L15–M17.
2 The action or an act of surveying something; (an) examination, (an) inspection; a comprehensive look; an appraising look. M16. ▸**b** A written statement embodying the result of an inspection etc. E17. ▸**c** A view, a prospect, a scene. L17.
3 A comprehensive discussion, description, or mental view of something. M16.
4 The process or (formerly) the art of surveying land; a map, plan, or description so obtained; a body of people or a department engaged in such work. E17.
5 A systematic collection and analysis of data relating to the opinions, habits, etc., of a population or the statistics of a thing, usu. taken from a representative sample; a poll. E20.

📖 **2** M. KEANE 'You're looking better' . . she gave him a kind survey. *Social History of Medicine* Van Wiggen provides a survey of . . changes in legislation between 1865 and 1940. **b** E. A. FREEMAN The value of the Domesday Survey cannot be overstated. **3** *Times* A survey of . . damage done on English oyster beds . . has just been concluded. **4** ***Ordnance Survey***: see ORDNANCE. ***SEISMIC survey***. ***TRIGONOMETRICAL survey***. **5** *Holiday Which?* In our survey of flights within the UK, we compared the airlines with each other. ***social survey***: see SOCIAL *adjective*.

Comb.: **survey course** *N. Amer.* an introductory academic course which gives a broad overview (esp. historical) of one subject.

survey /səˈveɪ/ *verb trans.* LME.
[Anglo-Norman *surveier*, *-veir*, from pres. stem *so(u)rvey-* of Old French *so(u)rveeir* from medieval Latin *supervidere*, formed as SUPER- + Latin *videre* see.]
1 Examine and ascertain the condition, situation, or value of; *spec.* examine the condition of (a building) on behalf of a prospective buyer or mortgagee. Also, have oversight of, supervise. LME.
2 Look at from a commanding position; take a comprehensive view of; consider as a whole. LME. ▸†**b** Observe, perceive, see. *rare*. L16–E17.
3 Determine by measurements the boundaries, extent, and situation of (land, a property, etc.) so as to construct a map, plan, or detailed description. M16.
4 Look carefully or appraisingly at; examine, scrutinize. Formerly also, explore (a country). L16.
5 Carry out a systematic investigation of (opinions, habits, etc.). M20.

📖 **2** G. SWIFT The history teacher . . surveys the outstretched view. B. CHATWIN He surveyed the sparkling . . plates, the salt-cellar, the cutlery. E. YOUNG-BRUEHL Freud's address . . carefully surveyed current . . psychoanalytic technique. **3** L. T. C. ROLT To survey the course of a projected canal. **4** E. TEMPLETON She . . surveyed herself in the mirror.

■ **surveyable** *adjective* (*rare*) M17. **surveyal** *noun* (*rare*) the action of surveying L17.

surveyance /səˈveɪəns/ *noun*. *rare*. LME.
[from SURVEY *verb* + -ANCE.]
Survey; oversight; inspection.
¶ Obsolete after L16; revived M19.

surveyor /səˈveɪə/ *noun*. LME.
[Anglo-Norman, Old French *sorve(i)our*, *sur-*, formed as SURVEY *verb*: see -OR.]
1 A supervisor, an overseer; *spec.* (*Hist.*) (the title of) an official in various government and municipal departments. LME. ▸†**b** An officer of the royal or other great household who superintended the preparation and serving of food. LME–E17. ▸†**c** A steward or manager of an estate. L15–L18.
2 Orig., a person who designed buildings and oversaw their construction. Now (in full ***quantity surveyor***), a person who estimates the quantities of labour and materials required for building and engineering work. LME.
3 A person who surveys land or buildings, esp. professionally. M16. ▸**b** = GEOMETER 3. L17.
4 a A person who looks at something; a beholder. *rare*. M16. ▸**b** A person who takes a mental view of something. E17.
5 DENTISTRY. An instrument used to survey the casts of teeth, esp. to determine parallelism between surfaces on different teeth. E20.

1 ***borough surveyor***, ***forest surveyor***, ***surveyor of highways***, ***surveyor of taxes***, etc.
Comb.: **surveyor-general**, pl. **surveyors-general**, **surveyor-generals**, a principal surveyor; a person with general oversight of a department, activity, etc.; *spec.* (*a*) (*Hist.*) a chief supervisor in certain departments of the British Government; (*b*) *US* a government officer who supervises the surveys of public lands.
■ **surveyorship** *noun* the position or office of surveyor L15.

surview /səˈvjuː, *as noun also* ˈsəː-/ *noun & verb*. LME.
[Anglo-Norman, Old French *surveue*, formed as SURVEY *verb*.]
▶ **A** *noun*. †**1** Inspection. LME–L15.
†**2** Supervision. Only in LME.
3 A comprehensive or detailed view of something, esp. in the mind; the action of taking such a view. L16.
▶ **B** *verb trans.* = SURVEY *verb* 2. Also, command a view of, overlook; see. *arch.* M16.

survivable /səˈvʌɪvəb(ə)l/ *adjective*. L19.
[formed as next + -ABLE.]
1 Capable of surviving. L19.
2 Able to be survived; not fatal. M20.

■ **surviva'bility** *noun* ability to survive, esp. a military attack E19.

survival /sə'vʌɪv(ə)l/ *noun.* L16.
[from SURVIVE *verb* + -AL¹.]
1 The action or fact of continuing to live after some event. L16. ▸**b** Continuance after the end or cessation of something else or after some event; continued existence; *spec.* continuance of a custom, observance, etc., after the disappearance of the circumstances in which it originated. E19. ▸**c** The practice of surviving or coping with harsh or warlike conditions, as an outdoor activity. Usu. *attrib.* L20.
2 A thing that continues to exist after the cessation of something else, or of other things of the kind; a surviving remnant; *spec.* a surviving custom, observance, etc. E18.

📖 **1** A. N. WILSON The hospital seemed to think his chances of survival were fifty-fifty. **b** *Times Educ. Suppl.* Such a scheme would . . make a school's survival dependent on its ability to attract enough pupils. **2** W. HAGGARD The man was a sort of dinosaur, a survival from another age.

Phrases: **survival of the fittest** BIOLOGY the continued existence of organisms which are best adapted to their environment, with the extinction of others, as a concept in the Darwinian theory of evolution (cf. ***natural selection*** s.v. NATURAL *adjective*).
Comb.: **survival bag** a large plastic bag used by climbers as a protection against exposure; **survival curve** a graph showing how the number of survivors varies with the size of a radiation dose or with the length of time after a dose; a graph showing the proportion of a population living after any given age; **survival kit** a pack of emergency rations etc., esp. as carried by servicemen; **survival value** (*a*) BIOLOGY the property of a character that makes the individuals possessing it more likely to survive and reproduce; (*b*) the ability to survive.

survivalism /sə'vʌɪv(ə)lɪz(ə)m/ *noun.* L19.
[from prec. + -ISM.]
1 ANTHROPOLOGY. The view that the evolution of a culture can be reconstructed from surviving customs, observances, etc. *rare.* L19.
2 A policy of trying to ensure one's own survival or that of one's social or national group. M20.
3 The pursuit or hobby of practising outdoor survival skills. L20.

survivalist /sə'vʌɪv(ə)lɪst/ *noun.* L19.
[formed as prec. + -IST.]
1 ANTHROPOLOGY. An adherent of survivalism. L19.
2 A person who succeeds in surviving; a person who makes a policy of aiming to survive. E20.
3 A person who practises survivalism as a pursuit or hobby; a person who trains in the use of combat equipment for survival. L20.

survivance /sə'vʌɪv(ə)ns/ *noun.* E17.
[French, formed as next: see -ANCE.]
1 Survival. Now *rare.* E17.
2 The succession to an estate, office, etc., of a survivor nominated before the death of the previous holder; the right of such succession in case of survival. L17.
■ Also †**survivancy** *noun* M17–M18.

survivant /sə'vʌɪv(ə)nt/ *adjective. rare.* M16.
[French, pres. pple of *survivre*: see next, -ANT¹.]
Surviving.

survive /sə'vʌɪv/ *verb.* LME.
[Anglo-Norman (& mod. French) *survivre*, Old French *sourvivre*, from Latin *supervivere*, formed as SUPER- + *vivere* live.]
1 *verb trans.* Continue to live or exist after; outlive, outlast; remain alive or well in spite of (a danger, accident, etc.). LME.
2 *verb intrans.* Continue to live or exist after some event (expressed or implied); be still alive or existent. L15. ▸**b** LAW. Of an estate etc.: pass *to* the survivor or survivors of two or more joint tenants or people with a joint interest. M17.

📖 **1** R. CAMPBELL I have never heard of anyone surviving the bite of a black mamba. A. FRASER The queen bore . . nine children . . of whom six survived infancy. **2** G. VIDAL The patient gasped, but survived. J. G. FARRELL It was necessary to summon the Major . . her only surviving relative. R. FRASER None of Mr Brontë's letters to his wife has survived.

■ **surviver** *noun* (now *rare* or *obsolete*) = SURVIVOR E17.

survivor /sə'vʌɪvə/ *noun.* E16.
[from prec. + -OR.]
1 LAW. A person who outlives others sharing a joint interest; *spec.* a joint tenant who inherits the estate on the death of the other joint tenant. E16.
2 *gen.* A person who or thing which survives; *esp.* a person remaining alive after an event in which others die. L16.
3 A person who has the knack of surviving afflictions unscathed or overcoming difficulties. *colloq.* L20.

📖 **2** R. GRAVES No news came . . about this massacre because there were no survivors. V. S. PRITCHETT As shepherds, they are the last survivors of a nomadic culture. **3** *Sun* Madonna . . was a survivor, determined to claw her way out of poverty.

survivorship /sə'vʌɪvəʃɪp/ *noun.* E17.
[from prec. + -SHIP.]
1 LAW. A right depending on survival; *spec.* the right of the survivor of people with a joint interest to take the whole on the death of the others; the right of future succession, in the event of survival, to a position not yet vacant. E17.
2 The state or condition of being a survivor; survival. L17.
3 The probability of surviving to a given age; the proportion of a population that does this. M20.

📖 **1** M. W. FREER He offered the government of Burgundy, with the survivorship for his son. **2** G. GROTE The Epikureans denied . . the survivorship of soul over body. **3** *Nature* Estimated costs of producing inbred young, expressed as a proportionate decrease in survivorship.

Comb.: **survivorship curve**: showing the proportion of a population surviving at different ages.

surwan /'sɔːwɑːn/ *noun.* E19.
[Urdu & Persian *sārwān*, from *sār* camel + *-wān* keeper.]
In the Indian subcontinent: a camel-driver.

sus *noun, adjective, & adverb, verb* vars. of SUSS *noun, adjective, & adverb, verb.*

Sus. *abbreviation.*
Susanna (Apocrypha).

susceptance /sə'sɛpt(ə)ns/ *noun.* L19.
[from SUSCEPTIBLE + -ANCE.]
ELECTRICITY. The imaginary part of the admittance, as opp. to the real part or conductance.

susceptibility /səsɛptɪ'bɪlɪti/ *noun.* M17.
[from next + -ITY.]
1 The quality or condition of being susceptible; capacity to undergo or be affected by something. (Foll. by *to* or (now *rare*) *of*.) M17.
2 In *pl.* Capacities of emotion, esp. such as may be hurt or offended; a person's sensitive feelings. M18.
3 PHYSICS. More fully ***magnetic susceptibility***. The capacity of a substance for being magnetized, as measured by the ratio of magnetization to magnetic field strength. L19.

📖 **1** J. HALPERIN Hardy's lifelong susceptibility to women. **2** W. M. CLARKE Dickens was conscious of the susceptibilities of his readers.

susceptible /sə'sɛptɪb(ə)l/ *adjective & noun.* E17.
[Late Latin *susceptibilis*, from Latin *suscept-* pa. ppl stem of *suscipere* take up, formed as SUB- + *capere* take: see -IBLE.]
▸**A** *adjective.* **1** Foll. by *of*: capable of undergoing (an action or process); allowing, admitting of; capable of taking (an attribute or quality); (esp. of the mind, feelings, etc.) capable of conceiving or feeling. E17. ▸†**b** Capable *of* an action, capable *of doing*. E–M19.
2 Foll. by *to* or (now *rare*) *of*: able to be affected by (an influence, disease, etc.); readily affected by; liable or vulnerable to. M17.
3 Without preposition: readily affected by feeling; impressionable, sensitive; capable of or likely to respond or react; MEDICINE capable of getting a disease, deficient in defences against a disease. E18.

📖 **1** GOLDSMITH No qualities . . are more susceptible of a finer polish than these. E. WILSON Everything mankind has . . done is susceptible of being explained in those terms. W. MARCH The charges they had brought . . were susceptible of more than one interpretation. **2** H. READ She was . . more susceptible than a normal person to extremes of heat and cold. S. BEDFORD He, being susceptible to beauty . . , fell in love with her. **3** *Discovery* The person, himself immune, . . is capable of infecting . . more susceptible persons.

▸**B** *noun.* MEDICINE. A person capable of contracting a disease or deficient in defences against one. E20.
■ **susceptibleness** *noun* susceptibility M17. **susceptibly** *adverb* L18.

susception /sə'sɛpʃ(ə)n/ *noun.* LME.
[Late Latin *susceptio(n-)*, from *suscept-*: see prec., -TION.]
†**1** The action of taking something up or taking something upon oneself; assumption, reception, acceptance, undertaking. (Foll. by *of*.) LME–M18.
2 The action or capacity of taking something into the mind; a thing so taken in. *rare.* M18.

susceptive /sə'sɛptɪv/ *adjective.* LME.
[Late Latin *susceptivus*, from Latin *suscept-*: see SUSCEPTIBLE, -IVE.]
Having the quality of taking or receiving, receptive; *esp.* impressionable; susceptible *of*.

📖 J. MORLEY The nature that is susceptive of passion. A. POWELL Persons . . rarely noticed they were being teased unless possessing susceptive antennae.

■ **susceptiveness** *noun* L19. **suscep'tivity** *noun* E18.

†**susceptor** *noun.* M17.
[Late Latin = a person who undertakes something, (in medieval Latin) godfather, from Latin *suscept-*: see SUSCEPTIBLE, -OR.]
1 A godfather or sponsor at baptism. M17–M18.
2 A supporter, a maintainer. *rare.* M–L17.

For other words beginning with *sur-* see the entry for **sur-**

suscipient /sə'sɪpɪənt/ *noun & adjective.* Now *rare* or *obsolete.* E17.
[Latin *suscipient-* pres. ppl stem of *suscipere*: see SUSCEPTIBLE, -ENT.]
▸**A** *noun.* A recipient, esp. of a sacrament. E17.
▸**B** *adjective.* Receiving, recipient; receptive. M17.

suscitate /'sʌsɪteɪt/ *verb trans.* Now *rare.* E16.
[Latin *suscitat-* pa. ppl stem of *suscitare*, formed as SUB- + *citare* set in rapid motion: see CITE, -ATE³.]
1 Stir up, excite; raise (a person) out of inactivity. E16.
†**2** Call into being or activity. M16–L19.
†**3** Give life or activity to; animate. M17–M19.
■ **susci'tation** *noun* M17.

sushi /'suːʃi, 'sʊʃi/ *noun.* L19.
[Japanese.]
A Japanese dish consisting of balls or rolls of cold boiled rice flavoured with vinegar and mixed with raw fish or other ingredients.

Susian /'suːzɪən/ *adjective & noun.* M16.
[Latin *Susianus*, Greek *Sousianē* (fem.), from Greek (*ta*) *Sousa* Susa (cf. Old Persian *Šuš*): see -IAN.]
Hist. ▸**A** *adjective.* Of or pertaining to the ancient country of Susiana (modern Khuzestan in western Iran) or its capital Susa (Shushan); of or pertaining to the Elamite language. M16.
▸**B** *noun.* A native or inhabitant of Susiana or Susa; the Elamite language. E19.
■ Also **Susi'anian** *adjective & noun* M19.

Susie-Q /'suːzɪ kjuː/ *noun.* M20.
[Origin unkn.]
A modern dance of black origin; the step characteristic of this dance.

suslik *noun* var. of SOUSLIK.

suspect /sə'spɛkt/ *noun*¹. *arch.* LME.
[Latin *suspectus* action of looking up, high regard, (in medieval Latin) suspicion, formed as SUSPECT *verb.*]
1 The action or an act of suspecting; the condition of being suspected; (a) suspicion. (Foll. by *of* the evil etc. suspected. Formerly foll. by *in*, *of*, or *to* the person or thing of which it is suspected.) LME.
†**2** Expectation; *esp.* apprehensive expectation. LME–E17.
1 †**have in suspect**, †**hold in suspect** be suspicious of, suspect.

suspect /'sʌspɛkt/ *adjective & noun*². ME.
[Old & mod. French, or Latin *suspectus* pa. pple of *suspicere* SUSPECT *verb.*]
▸**A** *adjective.* Suspected; regarded with suspicion or distrust; deserving suspicion, not sound or trustworthy. (Foll. by *of* the evil etc. suspected.) ME.

📖 W. C. WILLIAMS His praise of music and . . interest in it . . were to me always suspect. P. CAREY The skin glistened like a suspect apple which had been waxed. †**have suspect**, †**hold suspect** be suspicious of, suspect.

▸**B** *noun.* A person suspected of an offence, evil intention, etc.; a person of questionable character, *esp.* one under surveillance as such. L16.
¶ Obsolete as adjective after E18 and as noun after E17, until revived in E19 after French use of the word for 'a person suspected of hostility or indifference to the Revolution'.

suspect /sə'spɛkt/ *verb.* LME.
[Latin *suspect-* pa. ppl stem of *suspicere* look up, admire, suspect, formed as SUB- + *specere* look.]
1 *verb trans.* Imagine something evil, wrong, or undesirable in (a person or thing) on little or no evidence; believe to be guilty with insufficient proof or knowledge; be suspicious of, doubt the innocence of. (Foll. by *to be*; *of*, †*with*, or †*for* the evil etc. suspected. Formerly also foll. by obj. & compl.) LME.
†**2** *verb trans.* Expect; *esp.* expect with dread or apprehension. E16–L18.
3 *verb trans.* Imagine (something) to be possible or likely; have an impression of the existence or presence of; believe tentatively (*that*). M16.
4 *verb intrans.* Imagine something, esp. some evil, as possible or likely; have or feel suspicion. L16.
†**5** *verb trans.* Regard, take note of; respect. L16–M18.

📖 **1** SHAKES. *Wint. T.* Lest she suspect . . Her children not her husband's. V. WOOLF She suspected him of nameless atrocities. C. BAX The eighteenth century suspected all poetry, romance . . and enthusiasm. **3** COLERIDGE The plan . . would, I suspect, startle an unfamiliarised conscience. I. MURDOCH I suspect he's a bit frightened of his sister. G. GREENE There must have been a leak . . and they suspect a double agent.

■ **suspectable** *adjective* that can or should be suspected; open to suspicion: M18. **suspecter** *noun* E17. **suspector** *noun* E19.

suspected /sə'spɛktɪd/ *ppl adjective.* LME.
[from prec. + -ED¹.]
†**1** Given to suspecting, suspicious. Only in LME.
2 That one suspects of something evil or wrong; regarded with suspicion; imagined to be guilty or faulty. M16.
3 That one suspects to exist or to be such; imagined to be possible or likely. E18.

4 ***the suspected***, a noctuid moth, *Parastichtis suspecta*, of Europe and northern Asia. E20.

📖 **2** *Times* The search and detention of suspected ships. **3** *Which?* A suspected gas leak.

suspectful /səˈspɛktfʊl, -f(ə)l/ *adjective*. Now *rare* or *obsolete*. L16.
[from SUSPECT *noun*¹ + -FUL.]
1 Full of suspicion; mistrustful. L16.
†**2** Exciting or deserving suspicion. *rare*. E–M17.

†**suspection** *noun*. ME–E18.
[Old French, or medieval Latin *suspectio(n-)*, from Latin *suspect-*, formed as SUSPECT *verb*: see -TION.]
= SUSPICION *noun*.

†**suspectless** *adjective*. L16.
[from SUSPECT *noun*¹ + -LESS.]
1 Having no suspicion; unsuspecting. L16–M18.
2 Not liable to suspicion; unsuspected. E–M17.

suspectuous /səˈspɛktjʊəs/ *adjective*. *rare*. M17.
[formed as SUSPECT *noun*¹ + -UOUS.]
Full of suspicion, mistrustful.

suspend /səˈspɛnd/ *verb*. ME.
[Old & mod. French *suspendre* or Latin *suspendere*, formed as SUB- + *pendere* hang.]
▶ **I** With ref. to cessation.
1 *verb trans.* Debar, esp. temporarily, from a function, position, activity, or privilege. (Foll. by *from*, †*of*.) ME.
2 *verb trans.* Put a stop to, esp. temporarily; bring to a (temporary) stop; put in abeyance; make temporarily inactive. Usu. in *pass.*, without implication of a definite agent. ME. ▸†**b** *verb trans.* Put a stop to the use of (a place of worship), esp. temporarily; profane. LME–M16. ▸**c** *verb trans.* Cease from the execution or performance of; desist from, esp. temporarily. E17. ▸**d** *verb intrans.* Cease temporarily. *rare*. M17.
3 *verb trans.* Defer (execution of a sentence) pending discussion in the Court of Session or the High Court of Justiciary (*SCOTS LAW*). Formerly also *gen.*, defer, postpone; (of an event etc.) delay the accomplishment of. L15. ▸†**b** *verb trans.* Defer dealing with; pass over for the time being; disregard. L16–M18. ▸**c** *verb intrans.* *SCOTS LAW*. Present a bill of suspension, seek deferment of the execution of a sentence. M17.
4 *verb trans.* Keep (one's judgement) undetermined; refrain from forming (an opinion) or giving (assent) decisively. M16. ▸†**b** *verb intrans.* Suspend one's judgement, be in doubt. L16–M18. ▸†**c** *verb trans.* Doubt; apprehend, suspect. L16–L17.
5 *verb trans.* †**a** Keep in a state of mental attention; hold the attention of. M16–E19. ▸**b** Keep in suspense, uncertainty, or indecision. Now *rare*. E17.
6 *verb trans.* *MUSIC*. Prolong (a note of a chord) into a following chord, usually so as to produce a temporary discord. M19.

📖 **1** G. BATTISCOMBE Pusey had been suspended from preaching. **2** H. MACMILLAN The Speaker was forced to suspend the sitting for half-an-hour. **suspend payment** (of a company) cease meeting its financial obligations owing to insolvency or insufficient liquid funds. **c** GEO. ELIOT An old woman . . for the moment had suspended her wail to listen. **4** *Burlington Magazine* Concerning Cotes's portrait-group . . one may suspend judgement. **suspend disbelief** refrain from being sceptical; enter into the world of an invented story.

▶ **II** With ref. to hanging.
7 a *verb trans.* = HANG *verb* 1, 4. LME. ▸†**b** *verb intrans.* = HANG *verb* 8. L16–L17.
8 *verb trans.* **a** Cause to be dependent; in *pass.*, depend. Foll. by *on*. Now *rare*. E17. ▸†**b** Regard as dependent, make (a thing) depend, *on*. M17–L18.
9 *verb trans.* **a** Cause to remain in an elevated position without attachment. M17. ▸**b** Hold, or cause to be held, in suspension; (of a fluid) contain in the form of particles dispersed throughout its substance. M18.

📖 **7a** G. VIDAL A grey chandelier was suspended from the centre of the ceiling.

■ **suspendible** *adjective* (*rare*) able or liable to be suspended L17.

suspended /səˈspɛndɪd/ *ppl adjective* & *noun*. M16.
[from prec. + -ED¹.]
▶ **A** *ppl adjective*. That has been suspended; temporarily stopped; hanging; held in suspension. M16.
suspended animation cessation of several vital functions without death. **suspended ceiling**: with a space between it and the floor above from which it hangs. **suspended participle** = *dangling participle* s.v. DANGLING. **suspended sentence** *LAW* a sentence which is imposed but remains unenforced as long as the offender commits no further offence within a specified period.
▶ **B** *ellipt.* as *noun*. A suspended sentence. *slang*. L20.

suspender /səˈspɛndə/ *noun*. E16.
[formed as prec. + -ER¹.]
1 A person who or thing which suspends something; *SCOTS LAW* a person who presents a bill of suspension. E16.
2 a In *pl.* A pair of braces. *N. Amer.* E19. ▸**b** A device that can be fastened to the top of a stocking or sock to hold it up. L19.
3 An apparatus or natural structure which supports something suspended. M19.
Comb.: **suspender belt** a woman's undergarment consisting of a belt and elastic suspenders to which the tops of the stockings are fastened.

†**suspensation** *noun*. *rare*. L16–L18.
[medieval Latin *suspensatio(n-)*, from *suspensare* suspend, from Latin *suspens-*: see SUSPENSION, -ATION.]
= SUSPENSION.

suspense /səˈspɛns/ *noun*. LME.
[Anglo-Norman, Old French *suspens(e)* abeyance, delay, from medieval Latin *suspensum*, *suspensa* use as noun of neut. & fem. of Latin *suspensus* pa. pple of *suspendere* SUSPEND.]
1 a Temporary cessation, suspension. *obsolete* exc. *LAW*, esp. in ***in suspense***. LME. ▸†**b** Deferment, delay. LME–E19.
2 A state of uncertainty (and usually anxiety) about an awaited outcome, decision, etc.; the condition of waiting, esp. of being kept waiting, for such an outcome etc. Also, uncertainty what to do, indecision. Freq. in ***keep in suspense***, ***hold in suspense***. LME. ▸**b** A quality in a work of fiction that arouses excited expectation about the outcome, culprit, etc., in the mind of a reader, viewer, etc. M20.
3 The condition of being doubtful or undecided, as an attribute of something. E16. ▸†**b** Doubt as to a person's character or conduct. Only in L16.
4 The state of being undetermined or undecided; the action of suspending one's judgement. M16.
5 Suspension of a note of a chord. *rare*. M18.

📖 **2** G. DALY Keeping her in suspense about his intentions. **b** attrib.: ***suspense novel***, ***suspense story***, etc. **3** J. AUSTEN Such events are very interesting; but the suspense of them cannot last long.

Comb.: **suspense account** *BOOKKEEPING* an account in which items are entered temporarily before allocation to the correct or final account.
■ **suspenseful** *adjective* full of suspense; *esp.* arousing suspense in the mind of a reader etc.: M17.

suspense /səˈspɛns/ *adjective*. Now *rare* or *obsolete*. LME.
[(Old French from) Latin *suspensus*: see prec.]
†**1** Attentive. LME–L16.
2 In suspense; awaiting an outcome, decision, etc. LME.
3 Hanging, suspended. LME.
†**4** Cautious, deliberate. E16–L17.
†**5** Held back, restrained. *rare* (Milton). Only in M17.

suspension /səˈspɛnʃ(ə)n/ *noun*. LME.
[Old & mod. French, or Latin *suspensio(n-)*, from *suspens-* pa. ppl stem of *suspendere* SUSPEND: see -ION.]
1 The action of suspending something; the condition of being suspended; *esp.* temporary cessation or prevention; *MUSIC* the prolongation of a note of a chord into a following chord. LME. ▸**b** The state of being kept in suspense; uncertainty, suspense. Now *rare* or *obsolete*. M17.
2 a A support on which something is hung. M19. ▸**b** Attachment so as to allow movement about the point of attachment; the means by which a vehicle is supported on its axles. L19.
3 *PALAEOGRAPHY*. An abbreviation of a word by its first letter or letters accompanied by a special symbol; a word abbreviated in this way. L19.
4 A mixture in which small particles are distributed throughout a less dense liquid (or gas). E20.

📖 **1** C. HAMPTON The suspension of all political rights and banning of all political parties. **bill of suspension** *SCOTS LAW* a formal petition for execution of a sentence to be suspended. **4** P. PARISH Children can be given syrups and sweetened suspensions of drugs. **in suspension** distributed as small particles in a fluid.

Comb.: **suspension bridge** a bridge in which the roadway or railway is suspended from cables attached to and extending between supports; **suspension dot** = *suspension point* below; **suspension-feeder** a bottom-dwelling aquatic animal which feeds on organisms that occur in suspension in the water; **suspension point** each of a series of dots used to indicate an omission or interval in a printed text.

suspensive /səˈspɛnsɪv/ *adjective*. L15.
[Old & mod. French *suspensif*, *-ive* or medieval Latin *suspensivus*, from *suspens-*: see SUSPENSION, -IVE.]
†**1** Sustained. Only in L15.
†**2** Liable to be suspended. M16–L18.
3 Having the power or effect of deferring or temporarily stopping the operation of something; involving such action; *spec.* (*LAW*) designating a condition or obligation whose operation is suspended until some event occurs. E17.
4 Indecisive; undecided in mind; of, pertaining to, or in a state of suspense; (of a word, phrase, etc.) expressing or indicating suspense. E17.
■ **suspensively** *adverb* L15. **suspensiveness** *noun* E19.

suspensoid /səˈspɛnsɔɪd/ *noun*. E20.
[from SUSPENSION + -OID.]
PHYSICAL CHEMISTRY. A lyophobic colloid.

suspensor /səˈspɛnsə/ *noun*. M18.
[mod. Latin, from Latin *suspens-*: see SUSPENSION, -OR.]
†**1** A kind of catheter. Only in M18.
2 *BOTANY*. In spermatophytes and certain pteridophytes, the chain of cells which anchors the embryo in the embryo sac and pushes it down into the developing endosperm. M19.

suspensorium /sʌspɛnˈsɔːrɪəm/ *noun*. Pl. **-ria** /-rɪə/. M18.
[mod. Latin use of medieval Latin *suspensorium*: see next, -IUM.]
1 A suspensory bandage, sling, etc. Now *rare* or *obsolete*. M18.
2 The bone, or group of bones, cartilages, etc., by which the lower jaw is suspended from the skull in non-mammalian vertebrates. M19.

suspensory /səˈspɛns(ə)ri/ *adjective* & *noun*. LME.
[French †*suspensoire* (now *-oir*) from medieval Latin *suspensorium* stalk, from Latin *suspens-*: see SUSPENSION, -ORY¹.]
▶ **A** *adjective*. **1** Having the function of supporting something suspended; *spec.* (***a***) designating a ligament, muscle, etc., by which a part of the body is suspended or anchored; (***b***) designating a bandage, sling, etc., in which a diseased or injured part is suspended for support. LME.
†**2** Marked by or indicating mental suspense; doubtful. Only in 17.
3 = SUSPENSIVE 3. L19.
▶ **B** *noun*. †**1** A suspended weight used for traction. Only in LME.
2 A suspensory ligament, bandage, etc. L17.
■ **suspenˈsorial** *adjective* (*ANATOMY*) suspensory L19.

sus per coll *abbreviation*.
Hist. Latin *Suspendatur per collum* let him or her be hanged by the neck (in a record of a capital sentence).

suspicable /ˈsʌspɪkəb(ə)l/ *adjective*. Now *rare* or *obsolete*. E17.
[Late Latin *suspicabilis*, from Latin *suspicari* to suspect, formed as SUB- + *spic-* as in *suspicere* SUSPECT *verb*: see -ABLE.]
1 Open to suspicion. E17.
2 Appearing probable or likely. M17.

suspicion /səˈspɪʃ(ə)n/ *noun*. ME.
[Anglo-Norman *suspeciun* var. of Old French *sospeçon* (mod. *soupçon*) from medieval Latin *suspectio(n-)*; assim. to Old French *suspicion* from Latin *suspicio(n-)*, from *suspicere* SUSPECT *verb*: see -ION.]
1 The action of suspecting a person or thing; the feeling or thought of a person who suspects; an instance of this. (Foll. by *of* the person or the evil etc. suspected.) ME. ▸†**b** A suspicious circumstance. L16–L17.
2 Expectation, esp. of evil. *obsolete* exc. as passing into other senses. ME.
3 Imagination *of* something (not necessarily evil) as possible or likely; a faint belief *that* something is the case; a notion, an inkling. LME.
4 A slight indication or trace, a very small amount, (*of* something). E19.

📖 **1** G. MACDONALD A minute description of my . . person such as would . . clear me from any suspicion of vanity. A. STORR He suffered breakdown in which paranoid suspicions were the main feature. *Los Angeles* Police arrested him on suspicion of shoplifting. **3** J. W. KRUTCH The suspicion that gasoline fumes are a major cause of lung cancer. **4** K. MANSFIELD Hair . . with just the slightest suspicion of a crisp curl.

Phrases: **above suspicion** too obviously good or worthy to be suspected. †**bear suspicion**, †**have suspicion** entertain a suspicion. †**in suspicion** (*a*) suspecting; (*b*) suspected. †**of suspicion** that is (to be) suspected, suspicious. †**out of suspicion** beyond doubt. **take suspicion** = *bear suspicion* above. **under suspicion** suspected.
■ **suspicionless** *adjective* having no suspicion, unsuspecting M17.

suspicion /səˈspɪʃ(ə)n/ *verb trans.* & *intrans.* *dial.* & *colloq.* M17.
[from the noun.]
Suspect.
¶ Rare before M19.

suspicious /səˈspɪʃəs/ *adjective*. ME.
[Anglo-Norman, Old French *suspecious*, *suspicious* from Latin *suspiciosus*, from *suspicio*: see SUSPICION *noun*, -OUS.]
1 Inviting suspicion; that is or should be an object of suspicion; of questionable character or condition. (Formerly foll. by *that*, *of*.) ME.
2 Full of or feeling suspicion; disposed to suspect; mistrustful. (Foll. by *of*, †*that*.) LME.
3 Expressing, indicating, or characterized by suspicion. L15.

📖 **1** H. BANNERMAN The milk was so suspicious we had to open a tin of preserved milk. S. RADLEY If you hear any suspicious noises . . dial 999. **2** J. BUCHAN He has always been a little suspicious of foreigners.

■ **suspiciously** *adverb* (*a*) with suspicion; (*b*) so as to arouse suspicion: LME. **suspiciousness** *noun* L15.

†**suspiral** *noun*. LME.
[Old French *s(o)uspirail* (mod. *soupirail*) from medieval Latin *suspiraculum*, from *suspirare* SUSPIRE + *-culum* instr. suffix (see -CLE).]
1 A vent. LME–M16.
2 A pipe or passage for leading water into a conduit. LME–M16.
3 A settling tank, a cesspool. LME–L16.

suspiration /sʌspəˈreɪʃ(ə)n/ *noun*. Now *rare*. L15.
[Latin *suspiratio(n-)*, from *suspirat-* pa. ppl stem of *suspirare* SUSPIRE: see -ATION.]
1 Sighing; a sigh. L15.
2 (Deep) breathing; breath; a (deep) breath. E17.

suspire /səˈspʌɪə/ *verb*. Now chiefly *poet*. LME.
[Latin *suspirare*, formed as SUB- + *spirare* breathe.]
1 *verb intrans*. Sigh. Chiefly *fig.*, long *for*, yearn *after*. LME.
2 *verb trans*. Utter with a sigh. Also, breathe out. M16.
3 *verb intrans*. Breathe. L16.

suspirious /səˈspɪrɪəs/ *adjective*. M17.
[Latin *suspiriosus*, from *suspirium* a sigh, from *suspirare* SUSPIRE: see -OUS.]
1 Breathing painfully or with difficulty. Now *rare* or *obsolete*. M17.
2 Full of sighs, sighing. M18.

Susquehannock /sʌskwəˈhanək/ *noun* & *adjective*. Also **-hanna** /-ˈhanə/. E17.
[Algonquian.]
Hist. = CONESTOGA 1.

suss /sʌs/ *noun*, *adjective*, & *adverb*. *slang*. Also **sus**. M20.
[Abbreviation of SUSPICION *noun*. In sense 3 from the verb.]
▶ **A** *noun*. **1** Suspicion of having committed a crime; suspicious behaviour, *esp.* loitering. Freq. in ***on suss***. M20.
2 A suspected person, a police suspect. M20.
3 Know-how, *savoir faire*. L20.

📖 **1** F. FORSYTH You were in his section at the time he came under suss.

Comb.: **suss law** *Hist.* the law (in force 1824–1981) under which a person could be arrested on suspicion of having committed a crime.
▶ **B** *adjective*. Suspicious, suspect; of questionable provenance. M20.
▶ **C** *adverb*. Suspiciously. M20.

suss /sʌs/ *verb trans*. *slang*. Also **sus**. Infl. **-ss-**. M20.
[Abbreviation of SUSPECT *verb*.]
1 Suspect; *spec.* suspect (a person) of a crime. M20.
2 Imagine as likely; feel, surmise, (*that*); realize, grasp. M20.
3 Work or figure out; investigate, discover the truth about. Freq. foll. by *out*. M20.

📖 **2** T. BARLING You can bet . . they're coming at us from an angle we haven't sussed. *Blitz* You'll have sussed by now that there are two things going on. **3** P. LIVELY I'll go down and suss out the kitchen.

sussed /sʌst/ *adjective*. *colloq.* L20.
[from SUSS *verb* + -ED¹.]
In the know, well-informed.

Sussex /ˈsʌsɪks/ *noun*. E18.
[A county in SE England.]
1 Used ***attrib.*** to designate things produced, found in, originating from, or associated with Sussex. E18.
2 *ellipt.* A Sussex cow; a Sussex spaniel; a Sussex fowl. E20.
1 Sussex cow, **Sussex ox**, etc. a breed of red lowland beef cattle whose oxen were formerly used for draught; a cow etc. of this breed. **Sussex fowl** a breed of heavy domestic fowl; a fowl of this breed. **Sussex marble** a marble occurring in the Wealden clay of Sussex and Kent, formerly much used for pillars in churches. ***Sussex ox***: see ***Sussex cow*** above. **Sussex spaniel** a breed of long-coated, stocky, golden-brown spaniel; a dog of this breed. **2 *Light Sussex***: see LIGHT *adjective*² 2.

sussy /ˈsʌsi/ *adjective*. *slang*. M20.
[Abbreviation: see -Y¹.]
Suspicious; suspected.

sustain /səˈsteɪn/ *noun*. M17.
[from the verb.]
†**1** (A means of) sustenance. *rare*. M17–E18.
2 MUSIC. The effect or result of sustaining a note, esp. electronically. L20.

sustain /səˈsteɪn/ *verb*. ME.
[Anglo-Norman *sustein-*, Old French *so(u)stein-* tonic stem of *so(u)stenir* (mod. *soutenir*) from Latin *sustinere*, formed as SUB- + *tenere* hold, keep.]
1 *verb trans*. †**a** Support the efforts, conduct, or cause of (a person); support (a cause or course of action). ME–M18. ▸**b** Support the argument, maintain, *that*. Now *rare*. LME. ▸**c** Support as valid, correct, or just. LME. ▸**d** Be adequate as a ground or basis for; substantiate, corroborate. E19.
2 *verb trans*. Keep (a person, the mind, spirit, etc.) from failing or giving way. ME.
3 *verb trans*. Cause to continue in a certain state; maintain at the proper level or standard. ME.
4 *verb trans*. Maintain or keep going continuously (an action or process); carry on (a conflict or contest); *spec.* prolong (a musical note). ME.
5 *verb trans*. Support life in; provide for the life or needs of; (of food) give nourishment to. ME. ▸**b** Support (life). LME. ▸†**c** Supply (a person's need). *rare* (Shakes.). Only in E17.
6 *verb trans*. Provide for the upkeep of (an institution, estate, etc.). ME.
7 *verb trans*. Endure without failing or giving way; withstand. ME. ▸†**b** *verb intrans*. Bear up, hold out. LME–L16. ▸†**c** *verb trans*. Bear *to do*, tolerate that something should be done. Usu. in neg. and interrog. contexts. LME–E18.
8 *verb trans*. Undergo or experience (something); *esp.* suffer (an injury or loss). LME. ▸**b** Bear (a financial burden). *arch.* LME. ▸**c** Represent (a part or character); play the part of. M16.
9 *verb trans*. Support, bear the weight of, esp. for a long period. LME. ▸**b** Withstand (a weight or pressure). LME. ▸†**c** *verb trans*. & *intrans*. Hold (something) upright or in position. LME–E18.

📖 **2** P. G. WODEHOUSE The excitement which had sustained him . . had begun to ebb. J. BRAINE There was something to sustain me over the next four weeks. **3** G. S. HAIGHT Next to Lewes, John Blackwood did most to . . sustain George Eliot's genius. *News of the World* Goalkeeper Allan Ross sustained his side's dwindling hopes with saves. T. BENN Coal . . an industry which had sustained our manufacturing economy since the industrial revolution. **4** K. AMIS She played a slow arpeggio, sustaining it with the pedal. A. T. ELLIS She wondered how long Charles could sustain this conversation. J. SUTHERLAND This story opens with . . briskness . . and sustains a rattling pace thereafter. **5** J. TROLLOPE Ianthe bought . . a fudge bar . . to sustain her. P. MAILLOUX Tramping the roads . . sustaining himself entirely by begging. **7** A. R. WALLACE Each species [of plant] can sustain a certain amount of heat and cold. I. MURDOCH Antonia would not have sustained such a steady gaze for so long. **8** R. L. STEVENSON Labouring mankind had . . sustained a prolonged . . series of defeats. S. RADLEY Bell sustained multiple injuries. *Japan Times* They sustained burns and bruises. **9** L. SIMPSON These houses built of wood sustain Colossal snows.

■ **sustainer** *noun* (*a*) a person who or thing which sustains, upholds, or maintains something; (*b*) a supporting structure; (*c*) ASTRONAUTICS an auxiliary engine to maintain motion after boosters have ceased to operate: LME. **sustainment** *noun* (*a*) *arch.* = SUSTENANCE 1, 2; (*b*) the action of sustaining: LME.

sustainable /səˈsteɪnəb(ə)l/ *adjective*. E17.
[from prec. + -ABLE.]
†**1** Supportable, bearable. *rare*. Only in E17.
2 Able to be upheld or defended. M19.
3 Able to be maintained at a certain rate or level. M20. ▸**b** *spec.* Of economic activity, development, agriculture, etc.: not leading to depletion of resources or degradation of the environment. L20.

📖 **2** *North American Review* Religion may be morally useful without being intellectually sustainable. **3** P. GOUREVITCH Museveni . . sought a middle ground on which to build the foundations for a sustainable democratic order. **b** *Coloradoan* Sustainable development for . . the Brazilian rain forest would be harvesting plants and native roots . . and learning how to keep growing them. N. HUDSON Shifting cultivation . . can be damaging or sustainable according to how it is carried out.

■ **sustainaˈbility** *noun* L20. **sustainably** *adverb* L20.

sustained /səˈsteɪnd/ *ppl adjective*. L18.
[from prec. + -ED¹.]
That has been sustained; *esp.* maintained continuously or without flagging over a long period.
Special collocations & comb.: **sustained-release** *adjective* (PHARMACOLOGY) designating a preparation that releases a substance slowly or intermittently into the bloodstream so as to maintain a steady concentration, esp. administered orally in a capsule containing numerous tiny pellets with different coatings. **sustained yield** the quantity of a crop that can be periodically harvested without long-term depletion.
¶ Earlier in UNSUSTAINED.
■ **sustainedly** *adverb* M19.

sustaining /səˈsteɪnɪŋ/ *ppl adjective*. LME.
[from SUSTAIN *verb* + -ING².]
That sustains something.
sustaining pedal MUSIC (*a*) a piano pedal (usu. the right-hand one) that sustains the notes by keeping all the dampers raised when the keys are released (also called ***damper pedal***, ***loud pedal***); (*b*) a third (middle) pedal on some pianos that sustains only those notes played just before its depression. **sustaining programme** *US* a radio or television programme without a commercial sponsor.
■ **sustainingly** *adverb* M17.

sustenance /ˈsʌst(ə)nəns, -tɪn-/ *noun*. ME.
[Anglo-Norman *sustenaunce*, Old French *so(u)stenance* (mod. *soutenance*), from *so(u)stenir*: see SUSTAIN *verb*, -ANCE.]
1 A means of subsistence; a livelihood. ME.
2 Means of sustaining life; food; nourishment. ME. ▸†**b** A kind or a quantity of food. LME–L17.
3 The action of sustaining life with food or funds; the fact or state of being so sustained. Passing into senses 1, 2. LME.
†**4** Endurance. LME–L17.
†**5** The action of supporting or upholding something. LME–M19.
6 A means or source of support. LME.

📖 **1** W. IRVING The fur trade . . gave early sustenance . . to the great Canadian provinces. **2** I. COLEGATE For our daily sustenance . . the fruits of field and orchard. *fig.*: S. ROSENBERG Sustenance of our spirit we often derived from the theater. **3** J. YEATS Spaces . . covered with food-grasses and other plants, for the sustenance of the inhabitants.

sustenant /ˈsʌst(ə)nənt, -tɪn-/ *adjective*. *rare*. L19.
[from SUSTENANCE + -ANT¹.]
Sustaining. Foll. by *of*, *to*.

sustentacula *noun* pl. of SUSTENTACULUM.

sustentacular /sʌstɛnˈtakjʊlə/ *adjective*. L19.
[from next + -AR¹.]
ANATOMY & ZOOLOGY. Of tissue: forming a support, supporting.

sustentaculum /sʌstɛnˈtakjʊləm/ *noun*. Pl. **-la** /-lə/. M19.
[mod. Latin, formed as next: see -CULE.]
ANATOMY & ZOOLOGY. A supporting part or organ. Chiefly in mod. Latin phrs.

sustentate /ˈsʌstənteɪt/ *verb trans*. Now *arch.* *rare*. M16.
[Latin *sustentat-* pa. ppl stem of *sustentare* frequentative of *sustinere*: see SUSTAIN *verb*, -ATE³.]
Sustain.

sustentation /sʌstənˈteɪʃ(ə)n/ *noun*. LME.
[Old & mod. French, or Latin *sustentatio(n-)*, formed as prec. + -ATION.]
†**1** The action of bearing or enduring something, endurance. LME–M17.
2 Upkeep or maintenance of an institution, building, etc. LME.
3 The preservation *of* a condition or state; maintenance of something at a certain level. LME. ▸**b** The action of keeping something from failing or giving way. Formerly also, a means of doing this. Now *rare*. L15.
4 The provision of or *of* a person with a livelihood or means of living. Formerly also, a livelihood. LME.
5 The action of sustaining the life *of* something; the provision of the means of sustenance; PHYSIOLOGY the action of the vital processes that sustain life. LME. ▸**b** That which sustains life; sustenance, food. Now *rare*. LME.
6 a The action of supporting or holding something up; the condition of being so supported. Formerly also, a support. Now *rare*. LME. ▸**b** AERONAUTICS. The action or condition of being aerodynamically supported, either by the lift from a moving aerofoil or by an air-cushion. E20.

sustentative /ˈsʌstənteɪtɪv, səˈstɛntətɪv/ *adjective*. M17.
[In sense 1 from medieval Latin *sustentativus*, formed as SUSTENTATE; in sense 2 from prec.: see -IVE.]
1 Having the quality of sustaining. Long *rare*. M17.
2 PHYSIOLOGY. Pertaining to sustentation. L19.
■ Also **sustentive** *adjective* (*rare*) LME.

sustention /səˈstɛnʃ(ə)n/ *noun*. M19.
[from SUSTAIN *verb* after *detain*, *detention*, etc.]
1 The action of sustaining a condition, feeling, etc.; the prolongation of a musical note. M19.
2 The quality of being sustained in argument. L19.

Susu /ˈsuːsuː/ *noun*¹ & *adjective*. L18.
[Susu.]
▶ **A** *noun*. Pl. same. A member of a Mande people inhabiting NW Sierra Leone and the southern coast of Guinea in W. Africa; the language of this people. L18.
▶ **B** *adjective*. Of or pertaining to this people or their language. L18.

susu /ˈsuːsuː/ *noun*². E19.
[Oriya *śuśo*, Bengali *susuk*, from Sanskrit *śiṃśuka*.]
The river dolphin of the Ganges and Brahmaputra rivers, *Platanista gangetica*.

susuhunan /ˌsʌsuːhuːˈnɑːn/ *noun*. E19.
[Indonesian.]
Hist. (The title of) the ruler of Surakarta and of Mataram in Java.

susumber /səˈsʌmbə/ *noun*. *W. Indies*. Also **-ba**. E19.
[Perh. from Ewe *súsume* or Twi *nsúsũaa* an edible plant + Twi *mbá* young plants.]
A prickly nightshade, *Solanum torvum*, the berries of which are eaten as a relish with salt fish. Also called ***turkey-berry***.

susurr /sjuːˈsəː, suː-/ *verb intrans*. *rare* (now *literary*). E16.
[Latin *susurrare*: see next.]
= SUSURRATE.
■ **susurrant** *adjective* whispering, rustling L18.

susurrate /ˈsjuːsʌreɪt, ˈsuː-/ *verb intrans*. *rare* (chiefly *literary*). E17.
[Latin *susurrat-* pa. ppl stem of *susurrare*, from *susurrus* whisper: see -ATE³.]
Whisper; *esp.* make a whispering sound, rustle.

susurration /sjuːsʌˈreɪʃ(ə)n, suː-/ *noun*. LME.
[Late Latin *susurratio(n-)*, formed as prec.: see -ATION.]
1 Whispering; *rare* a whisper. Formerly *spec.*, malicious whispering. Now *rare*. LME.
2 *transf.* A whispering sound, a rustle. Now *literary*. M17.
📖 2 B. MASON The sea . . expiring in long susurrations on the shingle. A. T. ELLIS The susurration of something being unsheathed.

susurrus /sjuːˈsʌrəs, suː-/ *noun*. *literary*. LME.
[Latin = a whisper, humming, muttering, of imit. origin.]
†1 Malicious whispering. Only in LME.
2 A low soft whispering or rustling sound. E19.
📖 2 J. A. BAKER Plover fretted the horizon with the dark susurrus of their wings.
▪ **susurrous** *adjective* (*rare*) of the nature of a whisper; characterized by or full of whispering sounds: M19.

Sutherland table /ˈsʌðələnd ˌteɪb(ə)l/ *noun phr*. L19.
[from Harriet Elizabeth Leveson-Gower, Duchess of *Sutherland* (1806–68).]
A gateleg table with rectangular leaves.

sutile /ˈsjuːtɪl, -ʌɪl/ *adjective*. *rare*. L17.
[Latin *sutilis*, from *sut-* pa. ppl stem of *suere* SEW *verb*[1]: see -ILE.]
Made by sewing.

sutler /ˈsʌtlə/ *noun*. L16.
[Dutch †*soeteler* (mod. *zoetelaar*; Middle Low German *suteler, sudeler*), from †*soetelen* befoul, perform menial duties, follow a low trade, from Germanic base also of SUD.]
Hist. 1 A person who followed an army and sold provisions etc. to the soldiers. L16.
†2 Any person who sold provisions. Only in 18.
▪ **sutleress** *noun* (*rare*) a female sutler M18. **sutlership** *noun* (*rare*) the position or occupation of a sutler M19. **sutlery** *noun* (*a*) the occupation of a sutler; (*b*) a sutler's shop: E17.

sutra /ˈsuːtrə/ *noun*. E19.
[Sanskrit *sūtra* thread, string, rule.]
1 In Sanskrit literature, a rule or aphorism, or a set of these, on grammar, or Hindu law or philosophy, expressed with maximum brevity. E19.
2 A Buddhist scripture, usually doctrinal in content. Also, the Jain scriptures. L19.

suttee /sʌˈtiː, ˈsʌti/ *noun*. Also **sati**. L18.
[Sanskrit *satī* faithful wife, fem. of *sat* good.]
Chiefly *Hist.* 1 A Hindu widow who immolates herself on her husband's funeral pyre. L18.
2 The immolation of a Hindu widow in this way. E19.
▪ **sutteeism** *noun* the practice of suttee M19.

suttinly /ˈsʌtɪnli/ *adverb*. *Black English* & (chiefly *US*) *dial.* L19.
[Repr. a pronunc.]
Certainly.

†**suttle** *adjective*. L16–E19.
[Var. of SUBTLE.]
COMMERCE. Of a weight: from which tare or tret has been deducted.

suttle /ˈsʌt(ə)l/ *verb intrans*. *obsolete* exc. *Hist.* M17.
[Dutch †*soetelen*: see SUTLER.]
Carry on the business of a sutler. Chiefly as ***suttling*** *verbal noun*.
Comb.: **suttling-house**: where food and drink are supplied, esp. to soldiers.

suture /ˈsuːtʃə/ *noun & verb*. LME.
[French, or Latin *sutura*, from *sut-* pa. ppl stem of *suere* SEW *verb*[1]: see -URE.]
▶ **A** *noun*. **1** *MEDICINE.* The surgical joining of the edges of a wound or incision by stitching; (a length of) thread or wire used for this; a stitch made with this. LME. ▸**b** *gen.* Sewing, stitching; a stitch, a seam. Chiefly *fig.* E17.
2 *ANATOMY.* †**a** = RAPHE 1. LME–E18. ▸**b** The junction of two bones forming an immovable articulation; the line of such junction; *esp.* each of the serrated borders between the bones of the skull. L16.
3 *BOTANY, ZOOLOGY, & ANATOMY.* The junction, or (more freq.) the line of junction, of contiguous parts, as the line between adjacent whorls, chambers, or valves of a shell, the seam where the carpels of a pericarp join, etc. M17.
4 *GEOLOGY.* The (line of) junction formed by the collision of two lithospheric plates. L20.
2 ***coronal suture***, ***sagittal suture***, ***transverse suture***.
▶ **B** *verb trans.* **1** Secure with a suture; stitch up (a wound or incision). L18.
2 *GEOLOGY.* Join (lithospheric plates) by means of a suture. (Foll. by *together*.) L20.
▪ **sutural** *adjective* of, pertaining to, or situated in a suture E19. **suturally** *adverb* by means of or in the manner of a suture or sutures M19. **sutuˈration** *noun* (*MEDICINE*, now *rare* or *obsolete*) surgical stitching L19.

SUV *abbreviation*.
Sport utility vehicle.

suxamethonium /sʌksəmɪˈθəʊnɪəm/ *noun*. M20.
[from *sux-* repr. the sound of *succi* in SUCCINYL + *-a-* + METHONIUM.]
PHARMACOLOGY. = SUCCINYLCHOLINE.

suzerain /ˈsuːzəreɪn/ *noun & adjective*. Also fem. (*rare*) **-raine**. E19.
[French, Old French *suserain*, prob. from *sus* above, up (from Latin *su(r)sum* upward), after *souverain* SOVEREIGN.]
▶ **A** *noun*. **1** A feudal overlord. E19.
2 A sovereign or State having some control over another State that is internally autonomous. M19.
▶ **B** *attrib.* or as *adjective*. Of a ruler or State: holding the position of suzerain. M19.

suzerainty /ˈsuːzərenti/ *noun*. LME.
[In sense 1 from Old French *suserenete* from *suserain* (see prec.), in sense 2 from prec.: see -TY[1].]
†1 Supremacy. Only in LME.
2 The position, rank, or power of a suzerain. E19.

Suzuki /sʊˈzuːki/ *adjective*. M20.
[Shin'ichi *Suzuki* (see below).]
Designating, pertaining to, or using a method of teaching the violin (esp. to young children) developed by Shin'ichi Suzuki (1898–1998), Japanese educationalist and violin teacher, and characterized by exercises involving large groups and parental participation.

suzuribako /səzʊrɪˈbɑːkəʊ/ *noun*. Pl. same. M20.
[Japanese, from *suzuri* slab for ink + *hako* box.]
A box, often of finely-wrought lacquer-work, for holding Japanese writing implements.

SV *abbreviation*.
MEDICINE. Simian virus.
SV 40 a papovavirus which is capable of causing tumours in animals and animal tissue cultures.

s.v. *abbreviation*.
1 Side valve.
2 [Latin] *sub verbo, sub voce* under the word or heading given.

Svan /svɑːn/ *noun & adjective*. E17.
[Russian.]
▶ **A** *noun*. Orig. in Latin pl. form †**Suani**. Pl. **-s**, same. A member of a people living in western Georgia; the language of this people. E17.
▶ **B** *adjective*. = SVANETIAN *adjective*. M20.
▪ **Svanian** *adjective* = SVANETIAN *adjective* M20.

Svanetian /svɑːˈniːʃ(ə)n/ *adjective & noun*. M19.
[from Russian *Svanet(iya* (formed as SVAN) + -IAN.]
▶ **A** *adjective*. Of or pertaining to the Svans or their language. M19.
▶ **B** *noun*. = SVAN *noun*. M19.

svara /ˈswʌrə, sv-/ *noun*. L18.
[Sanskrit, lit. 'sound, tone'.]
In Indian music: a note of a musical scale.

svarabhakti /swʌrəˈbʌkti, sv-/ *noun*. L19.
[Sanskrit, from *svara* sound, vowel + *bhakti* separation.]
PHILOLOGY. The development of a vowel between two consonants, esp. in loanwords. Freq. *attrib.* in ***svarabhakti vowel***.
▪ **svarabhaktic** *adjective* L19.

Svarga *noun* var. of SWARGA.

svarita /ˈswʌrɪtə, sv-/ *noun*. E20.
[Sanskrit.]
The tone following the accented syllable of a word in Vedic Sanskrit. Cf. ANUDATTA, UDATTA.

SVD *abbreviation*.
Swine vesicular disease.

Svedberg /ˈsvɛdbəːɡ/ *noun*. M20.
[Theodor S. *Svedberg* (1884–1971), Swedish chemist.]
BIOCHEMISTRY. A unit of time equal to 10^{-13} second used in expressing sedimentation coefficients. (Symbol S.) Also ***Svedberg unit***.

svelte /svɛlt/ *adjective*. E19.
[French from Italian *svelto*.]
1 Slender, willowy. E19.
2 *transf.* Elegant, graceful. E20.
📖 1 B. T. BRADFORD Don't call me dumpling. I'm very *svelte* these days. A. BURGESS Svelte dark-haired sirens rather than big-boned Brünnhildes. 2 N. MARSH Is our svelte hired limousine at the door? R. FRAME Her svelte international friends.

Svengali /svɛŋˈɡɑːli/ *noun*. E20.
[A character in George du Maurier's novel *Trilby*.]
A person who exercises a controlling or mesmeric influence on another, esp. for a sinister purpose.

Sverdrup /ˈsvəːdrʊp/ *noun*. M20.
[H. U. *Sverdrup* (1888–1957), Norwegian oceanographer.]
A unit of flow equal to one million cubic metres per second. Also ***Sverdrup unit***.

Svetambara /ʃweˈtʌmbərə, ʃv-/ *noun*. E19.
[Sanskrit *Śvetāmbara* lit. 'white-clad'.]
A member of one of the two principal sects of Jainism, characterized by ascetic practices and, in the case of monks and nuns, the wearing of white clothing. Cf. DIGAMBARA.

SVGA *abbreviation*.
COMPUTING. Super video graphics array, a high-resolution standard for monitors and screens.

S-VHS *abbreviation*.
Super video home system.

s.vv. *abbreviation*.
[Latin.]
Sub verbis under the words or headings given.

SW *abbreviation*.
South-west(ern).

swab /swɒb/ *noun*[1]. M17.
[from the verb.]
1 **a** *NAUTICAL.* A mop for cleaning and drying decks. M17. ▸**b** Any mass or pad of absorbent material used for cleaning, mopping up, or applying esp. medication to a surface; *spec.* (*a*) an absorbent pad used in surgery; (*b*) a wad of absorbent material fixed to the end of a rod and used to collect a specimen of a secretion for pathological examination; (*c*) a specimen so collected. L18. ▸**c** A naval officer's epaulette; a naval officer. *slang* (now *rare* or *obsolete*). L18. ▸**d** A cylindrical brush for cleaning out the bore of a firearm; a soft brush for wetting the mould in founding. M19. ▸**e** *OIL INDUSTRY.* A plunger with a valve, used to raise fluid in a well and induce a flow. E20.
2 Orig. = SWABBER *noun*[1] 1. Now (*slang*) as a term of mild abuse: a loutish person. L17.

swab /swɒb/ *noun*[2]. Now *dial.* L17.
[Perh. same word as prec.]
= SWABBER *noun*[2].

swab /swɒb/ *verb*. Infl. **-bb-**. M17.
[Back-form. from SWABBER *noun*[1].]
†1 *verb intrans.* Behave in a loutish manner. *rare*. Only in M17.
2 *verb trans.* Apply a swab to; clean or wipe with a swab; take a specimen from (a person) with a swab. E18.
3 *verb trans.* Mop *up* (as) with a swab. M18.
4 *OIL INDUSTRY.* Put a swab into (an oil-well) in order to induce a flow. E20.
📖 2 A. P. HERBERT Jane took the stick-mop and . . swabbed all the stern part of the barge. D. WELCH The nurse lifted up my arm, swabbed a little place with cotton wool. *Independent* Everybody will be swabbed and their medical history recorded. 3 B. CHATWIN Cleaning women were swabbing up the mess from a banquet.

swabber /ˈswɒbə/ *noun*[1]. L16.
[Early mod. Dutch *zwabber*, ult. from Germanic base meaning 'sway', 'splash in water', repr. also in Middle & mod. Low German *swabben* splash, sway, slap, Norwegian *svabba* splash, wade, Low German *swabber* (German *Schwabber*) a mop, a swab, Dutch *zwabberen* to mop.]
1 *Hist.* A member of a ship's crew whose task was to swab the decks etc. L16. ▸**b** *transf.* Any person cleaning up with a mop. *rare*. E18.
2 As a term of mild abuse: a loutish person. Cf. SWAB *noun*[1] 2. Now *rare* or *obsolete*. E17.
3 A mop; *spec.* one for cleaning ovens. E17.

swabber /ˈswɒbə/ *noun*[2]. *obsolete* exc. *Hist.* L17.
[Perh. same word as prec.]
In *pl.*, a variety of whist in which the holder of the ace of hearts, the jack of clubs, or the ace or two of trumps, was entitled to part of the stakes; *sing.* any of these cards so used in this game.

swabbie /ˈswɒbi/ *noun*. *US Nautical slang*. Also **-y**. M20.
[from SWAB *noun*[1] + -IE.]
A (low-ranking) member of the navy. Cf. SWAB *noun*[1], SWABBER *noun*[1].

Swabian /ˈsweɪbɪən/ *noun & adjective*. E17.
[from *Swabia* (see below), earlier *Suabia* Latinized form of German *Schwaben* + -AN.]
▶ **A** *noun*. **1** A native or inhabitant of Swabia, a region and former duchy in SW Germany; the German dialect used in Swabia. E17.
2 A variety of pigeon. M19.
▶ **B** *adjective*. Of or pertaining to Swabia or the Swabians. L17.

swack /swak/ *noun, verb, & interjection*. *Scot.* LME.
[Imit. Cf. *thwack, whack*.]
▶ **A** *noun*. A smart heavy blow; a whack. Also, a dash, a rush. LME.
▶ **B** *verb*. **1** *verb trans.* Fling, dash. LME.
2 *verb intrans.* Strike heavily. LME.
3 *verb intrans.* Drink in large mouthfuls, gulp. *rare*. L18.
▶ **C** *interjection*. Expr. the sound of a smart heavy blow. L17.

swack /swak/ *adjective*. *Scot.* M18.
[App. from Flemish *zwack*.]
Supple; nimble; smart.

swacked /swakt/ *adjective*. *US slang*. M20.
[from SWACK *verb* + -ED[1].]
Drunk, intoxicated.

swad /swɒd/ *noun*¹. Long *arch. & dial.* **M16.**
[Perh. of Scandinavian origin: cf. Norwegian dial. *svadde* big stout man.]
1 A country bumpkin; a loutish or clumsy person. **M16.**
2 A soldier. **E18.**

swad /swɒd/ *noun*². *US & dial.* **E19.**
[Origin unkn.]
A thick mass or clump, a large amount, (*of* something).

swaddle /ˈswɒd(ə)l/ *noun.* Also (*obsolete* exc. *dial.*) **sweddle** /ˈswɛd(ə)l/. **OE.**
[from **SWATHE** *verb* + **-LE**¹.]
1 A length of bandage in which to swaddle an infant. Now *US*. **OE.**
2 *gen.* A bandage. *arch.* **OE.**

swaddle /ˈswɒd(ə)l/ *verb trans.* Also (*obsolete* exc. *dial.*) **sweddle** /ˈswɛd(ə)l/. **ME.**
[from **SWATHE** *verb* + **-LE**³.]
1 Wrap (a newborn child) in lengths of bandage to restrict movement; wrap in swaddling-clothes. **ME.** ▸**b** *fig.* Restrain the action of. **E19.**
2 Wrap bandages round; swathe or envelop with garments or wrappings. Usu. foll. by *in*, *with*. **E16.**
†**3** Beat soundly. *colloq.* **M16–E19.**

📖 **1** E. H. ERIKSON The ancient Russian extreme insists that the baby be swaddled up to the neck. **b** *Church Times* Her impatience with swaddled and routine thinking. **2** P. CAREY He rolled over, swaddling himself in his sheet.

swaddler /ˈswɒdlə/ *noun. slang* (chiefly *Anglo-Irish*). *derog.* **M18.**
[from prec. + **-ER**¹, prob. after the frequent references in sermons to the infant Jesus in swaddling-clothes.]
Orig., (a nickname for) a Methodist, esp. a preacher. Now, (a nickname for) any Protestant.

swaddling /ˈswɒdlɪŋ/ *noun.* **ME.**
[from **SWADDLE** *verb* + **-ING**¹.]
1 The action of **SWADDLE** *verb.* **ME.**
2 In *pl.* & (*rare*) *sing.* = ***swaddling-clothes*** below; *sing.* a bandage. **E17.**
†**3** [from **SWADDLER.**] Methodism; conduct supposedly characteristic of Methodists. *slang. derog.* **M–L18.**
Comb.: **swaddling-band(s)** (*arch.*), **swaddling-clothes** narrow lengths of bandage formerly wrapped round a newborn child to restrict movement; *fig.* early influences restraining freedom of action or thought.

swaddling /ˈswadlɪŋ/ *adjective. slang. derog.* **M18.**
[from **SWADDLER**: see **-ING**².]
Methodist; Protestant; canting.

swaddy /ˈswɒdi/ *noun. arch. slang.* **E19.**
[from **SWAD** *noun*¹ + **-Y**⁶.]
A soldier.

Swadeshi /swəˈdeɪʃi/ *noun & adjective.* **E20.**
[Hindi *svadeśī* from Sanskrit *svadeśīya* of one's own country, from *sva* own + *deśa* country.]
INDIAN HISTORY. (Designating or pertaining to) an Indian nationalist movement advocating the use of home-produced materials in industry and the boycott of foreign goods.

swadge /swɒdʒ/ *noun. colloq.* **M20.**
[Prob. blend of **SWAD** *noun*² and **WODGE.** Cf. **SWATCH** *noun*¹.]
A chunk, a mass.

swag /swag/ *noun & adjective.* **ME.**
[Prob. from the verb (though earlier).]
▸ **A** *noun.* †**1** A bulging bag. Cf. senses 6, 7 below. Only in **ME.**
†**2** A large blustering man. **L16–M18.**
3 (A) swaying or lurching movement. Now chiefly *Scot. & dial.* **M17.**
4 *local.* **a** A heavy fall or drop. **L17.** ▸**b** Subsidence; a sunken area of ground which collects water. **M19.**
5 A shop; a person who runs a shop selling trashy goods. *arch. slang.* **L17.**
6 A bundle of personal belongings carried by a traveller (*spec.* in the Australian bush), a tramp, or a miner. Now *Austral. & NZ.* **E18.**
7 The stolen goods carried off by a thief or burglar; *gen.* illicit gains. *slang.* **L18.**
8 An ornamental festoon of flowers, foliage, or fruit; a carved or moulded representation of this; a curtain or drapery fastened so as to hang like this. **L18.**
9 A great quantity *of* something (now chiefly *Austral. & NZ slang*); *dial.* a large draught of liquor. **E19.**

📖 **6** C. BARRETT With a light swag slung across my back, I set out. **7** U. SINCLAIR The 'swag' . . a gold watch . . a silver pencil. **8** A. CARTER The curtains swished open, gathering in swags at each side of a small stage. A. S. BYATT A high moulded ceiling, bulging with swags of . . roses and . . plaster apples. A. LEE A tunnel hung with swags of Virginia creeper. **9** D. HEWETT Collecting a swag of empty milk bottles under his arm. *Dressage Review* The young rider, with a swag of horses to choose from.

▸ **B** *attrib.* or as *adjective.* (Of goods) trifling, trashy; (of a shop or trader) selling such goods. *slang.* **E19.**

Comb.: **swag lamp**, **swag light** *N. Amer.* an overhead light externally wired so that the flex hangs in a loop across the ceiling; **swagman** (*a*) a man who sells trashy goods; (*b*) *Austral. & NZ* a man who travels with a swag; **swagsman** = *swagman* (b).
■ **swaggie** *noun* (*Austral. colloq.*) = ***swagman*** (b) **L19.**

swag /swag/ *verb.* Infl. **-gg-**. **E16.**
[Prob. of Scandinavian origin: cf. Norwegian dial. *svag(g)a* sway. Cf. prec.]
1 *verb trans.* Cause to sway or sag. **E16.** ▸**b** Arrange in swags; decorate with swags. Chiefly as ***swagged*** *ppl adjective.* **M20.**
2 *verb intrans.* Move heavily from side to side or up and down; sway. **M16.**
3 *verb intrans.* Hang (*down*) loosely or heavily; sag. **E17.**
4 Chiefly *Austral. & NZ.* ▸**a** *verb intrans. & trans.* (with *it*). Carry one's belongings in a swag; travel (*up* a region) with a swag. **M19.** ▸**b** *verb trans.* Pack up and carry (one's belongings) in a swag; travel (the country) with a swag. **M19.**
5 *verb trans. Criminals' slang.* ▸†**a** Steal. **M–L19.** ▸**b** Push or take roughly. **M19.**
Comb.: **swag-bellied** *adjective* (*arch.*) having a pendulous stomach; **swag belly** *arch.* (a person with) a pendulous stomach.

swage /sweɪdʒ/ *noun.* See also **SWEDGE** *noun.* **LME.**
[Old French *souage*, *-aige*, (also mod.) *suage*, of unkn. origin.]
1 An ornamental moulding or mount on a candlestick, basin, etc. Now *rare.* **LME.** ▸**b** A circular or semicircular depression, *spec.* on an anvil. **L17.**
2 †**a** A carpenter's gauge. Only in **L17.** ▸**b** A tool for bending cold metal or moulding potter's clay; a die or stamp for shaping wrought iron etc. by hammering or pressure. **L18.**

swage /sweɪdʒ/ *verb*¹ *trans. & intrans.* Now *arch. & dial.* **ME.**
[Partly from Anglo-Norman *suag(i)er*, *swag(i)er* from Proto-Romance verb, from Latin *suavis* sweet, partly aphet. from **ASSUAGE.**]
= **ASSUAGE.**

swage /sweɪdʒ/ *verb*² *trans.* **L17.**
[from **SWAGE** *noun.* Cf. **SWEDGE** *verb.*]
†**1** Ornament with a swage or moulding. Only in **L17.**
2 Shape or bend with a swage. **M19.**
■ **swager** *noun* (now *rare*) **L19.**

swaged /sweɪdʒd/ *adjective.* **LME.**
[from **SWAGE** *noun*, *verb*²: see **-ED**², **-ED**¹.]
†**1** Having a swage or ornamental moulding. **LME–M16.**
2 Shaped with a swage. **M19.**

swagger /ˈswagə/ *noun*¹. **E18.**
[from the verb.]
1 The action or an act of swaggering; swaggering behaviour; a swaggering gait or manner. **E18.**
2 *ellipt.* = ***swagger coat*** s.v. **SWAGGER** *verb. colloq.* **E20.**

📖 **1** E. WAUGH I sail to-morrow for East Africa . . William added with some swagger. J. CAREW He . . walked with a swagger that made him look ridiculous. H. CARPENTER Pound . . had a lot of Hemingway's swagger. He liked to imply that women flocked after him.

■ **swaggery** *adjective* (*a*) characterized by or displaying swagger, swaggering; (*b*) (of clothing) cut in a loose style: **L19.**

swagger /ˈswagə/ *noun*². **M17.**
[from **SWAG** *noun*, *verb*: see **-ER**¹.]
†**1** A person who causes a thing to sway. Only in **M17.**
2 A person carrying a swag, a tramp. *Austral. & NZ.* **M19.**

swagger /ˈswagə/ *adjective. colloq.* **L19.**
[from the verb.]
Smart, fashionable.

📖 G. MILLAR A swagger note-case in crocodile leather, edged with silver. K. AMIS I'll take you somewhere swagger.

swagger /ˈswagə/ *verb.* **E16.**
[App. from **SWAG** *verb* + **-ER**⁵.]
1 *verb intrans.* Sway; stagger. Now chiefly *dial.* **E16.**
2 *verb intrans.* Behave arrogantly; have an air of superiority, or a domineering manner; *esp.* walk arrogantly or self-importantly. **E16.**
3 *verb intrans.* Talk blusteringly; hector. Now only, talk boastfully, brag. **E16.** ▸**b** *verb trans.* Influence or force by blustering language; talk *into* or *out of* by hectoring. Now *rare* or *obsolete.* **E17.**

📖 **2** E. BOWEN He patted his breast pocket with complacency and swaggered off in the direction of the High Street. R. K. NARAYAN They would all swagger about . . as if they owned the place. **3** H. JAMES I don't want to swagger, but I suppose I'm rather versatile.

Comb.: **swagger cane** a short cane carried by a military officer; **swagger coat** a three-quarter-length coat cut with a loose flare from the shoulders; **swagger stick** = ***swagger cane*** above.
■ **swaggerer** *noun* **L16.** **swaggeringly** *adverb* in a swaggering manner, with a swagger **E17.**

Swahili /swəˈhiːli, swɑː-/ *noun & adjective.* In sense A.1 also (sing.) **Mswahili** /(ə)m-/, (pl.) **Waswahili** /wɑː-/. **E19.**
[Kiswahili, lit. 'pertaining to the coasts', from Arab. *sawāḥil* pl. of *sāḥil* coast.]
▸ **A** *noun.* Pl. same.
1 A member of a Bantu-speaking people inhabiting the E. African coast and adjacent islands. **E19.**
2 = **KISWAHILI.** **M19.**
▸ **B** *adjective.* Of or pertaining to the Waswahili or Kiswahili. **M19.**
■ **Swahilize** *verb trans.* (*rare*) make Swahili in character, form, habit, etc. **L19.**

swain /sweɪn/ *noun.* **LOE.**
[Old Norse *sveinn* boy, servant, attendant = Old English *swān* swineherd, Middle Low German *swēn*, Old High German *swein* (German dial. *Schwein*), from Germanic. Cf. **BOATSWAIN, COXSWAIN.**]
†**1** A young man attending a knight; a man of low rank. **LOE–L16.**
†**2** A male servant or attendant. **ME–E17.**
†**3** A (young) man; a boy. **ME–M17.**
4 A country labourer, *esp.* a shepherd; a rustic. *arch.* **L16.**
5 A country gallant; *gen.* a lover, a suitor. Chiefly *poet.* **L16.**
6 *Hist.* A freeholder in a forest. *rare.* **E17.**

📖 **5** B. BRYSON My wife had brought me here as her young swain one Sunday afternoon many years before.

■ **swainish** *adjective* resembling or characteristic of (that of) a swain **M17.**

swainmote *noun* var. of **SWANIMOTE.**

Swainson /ˈsweɪns(ə)n/ *noun.* **M19.**
[William *Swainson* (1789–1855), English naturalist.]
Used in *possess.* in the names of birds.
Swainson's hawk a dark-coloured narrow-winged buzzard, *Buteo swainsoni*, of western N. America. **Swainson's thrush** an olive-backed thrush, *Catharus ustulatus*, of western and northern N. America. **Swainson's warbler** a brown and white warbler, *Limnothlypis swainsonii*, of swamp regions in south-eastern N. America.

SWAK *abbreviation.*
Sealed with a kiss. Cf. SWALK.

Swakara /ˈswakərə/ *noun & adjective.* **M20.**
[from South West Africa (former name of Namibia, where the lamb is bred) + **KARA(KUL.)**]
(Designating or made of) the skin of a type of karakul lamb.

swale /sweɪl/ *noun*¹. *dial.* **LME.**
[Prob. of Scandinavian origin: cf. Old Norse *svalr* cool.]
Shade; a shady place. Also, the cold.

swale /sweɪl/ *noun*². *local.* **E16.**
[Origin unkn.]
A hollow low place; *spec.* (*a*) (chiefly *US*) a moist or marshy depression in a tract of land; (*b*) *US* a hollow between adjacent sand-ridges.

swale /sweɪl/ *verb*¹ *intrans.* **E19.**
[Prob. frequentative of **SWAY** *verb*: see **-LE**³.]
Move or sway up and down or from side to side.

swale *verb*² & *noun*³ var. of **SWEAL** *verb & noun.*

Swaledale /ˈsweɪldeɪl/ *noun.* **E20.**
[A region of North Yorkshire, England.]
(An animal of) a breed of small hardy long-woolled sheep first developed in Swaledale; the coarse wool produced by these sheep.

SWALK *abbreviation.*
Sealed with a loving kiss. Cf. SWAK.

swallo /ˈswɒləʊ/ *noun.* Pl. same. **L18.**
[Malay *suala.*]
= **BÊCHE-DE-MER** 1.

swallow /ˈswɒləʊ/ *noun*¹.
[Old English *swealwe* = Old Saxon *swala*, Old High German *swal(a)wa* (Dutch *zwaluw*, German *Schwalbe*), Old Norse *svala*, from Germanic.]
1 A streamlined, fast-flying, migratory songbird, *Hirundo rustica* (family Hirundinidae), which has mainly dark blue plumage, long pointed wings, and a long forked tail, and is popularly regarded as a harbinger of summer. Also (*N. Amer.*) ***barn swallow.*** **OE.** ▸**b** (Usu. with specifying word.) Any of various birds that resemble the swallow in some way but are unrelated to it; *esp.* (formerly) a swift. **LME.** ▸**c** (With specifying word.) Any of various other birds of the genus *Hirundo* or family Hirundinidae, *esp.* those with long tails. **E19.** ▸**d** A variety of domestic pigeon whose style of flight resembles that of a swallow. **M19.**
†**2** = ***flying fish*** (a) s.v. **FLYING** *ppl adjective.* Only in **M17.**
3 *ellipt.* = ***swallow dive*** below. **E20.**
4 Chiefly *Hist.* A female KGB agent who seduces men for the purposes of espionage. *slang.* **L20.**

📖 **1** *Proverb*: One swallow does not make a summer. **b** ***owl-swallow, sea-swallow, water-swallow, wood-swallow***, etc. **c** ***cliff swallow, rough-winged swallow, tree swallow***, etc.

Comb.: **swallow dive** a forward dive with the arms extended sideways until close to the water; **swallow-dive** *verb intrans.* perform a swallow dive; **swallow fork** (chiefly *US*) a forked cut on the ear used to mark cattle or sheep; **swallow-fork** *verb trans.* (chiefly *US*) cut a swallow fork in (the ear); **swallow-kite** a swallow-tailed kite; **swallow pigeon** = sense 1d above;

swallow prominent either of two Eurasian prominent moths of the genus *Pheosia*, having whitish wings with two dark streaks on the forewing; **swallow's-nest** (*a*) the nest of a swallow (***swallow's-nest fly***, a hippoboscid fly that infests swallows' nests; ***swallow's nest soup***, bird's-nest soup); (*b*) *transf.* anything lodged at a height, *esp.* a battery of guns; **swallow-tick** a tick which infests swallows; **swallow-winged** *adjective* shaped like a swallow's wings; (of a ship) having sails so shaped. See also SWALLOWTAIL.

■ **swallow-like** *adjective* resembling (that of) a swallow L16.

swallow /ˈswɒləʊ/ *noun*².

[Late Old English (*ge*)*swelg*, -*lh* gulf, abyss, corresp. to Middle Low German *swelch* (also *swalh*) throat, whirlpool, Old Norse *svelgr* whirlpool, from Germanic base also of next.]

1 A deep hole or opening in the earth; an abyss. Now only *spec.* as SWALLOW-HOLE. LOE.

2 A depth of water; a gulf, a whirlpool. *arch.* LOE.

3 The passage through which food and drink are swallowed; the gullet. *arch.* ME. ▸**b** Capacity for swallowing, appetite (*lit.* & *fig.*). *arch.* ME.

†**4** The function of swallowing; the sense of taste; *transf.* a taste. *rare.* ME–E19.

5 An act of swallowing; a gulp. E19. ▸**b** A quantity (esp. of liquid) swallowed at once. M19.

6 *NAUTICAL.* The space between the sheave and the shell in a pulley-block, through which the rope runs. M19.

📖 **3b** HENRY FIELDING Methus . . measures the honesty . . of mankind by a capaciousness of their swallow. **5** M. SARTON Jo took a swallow of coffee and put the cup down. J. HIGGINS White . . emptied the glass in one long swallow.

swallow /ˈswɒləʊ/ *verb*.

[Old English *swelgan* = Old Saxon (*far*)*swelgan*, Old High German *swel*(*a*)*han* (Dutch *zwelgen*, German *schwelgen*), Old Norse *svelga*, from Germanic strong verb from base also of prec.]

1 a *verb trans.* Take (food etc.) into the stomach through the throat and gullet. Also *gen.* (now *poet.*), eat, drink. Also foll. by *down*, *in*, *up*. OE. ▸**b** *verb intrans.* Take food etc. into the stomach through the throat and gullet; perform the muscular movement of the oesophagus required to do this. LME.

2 *verb trans.* Of a thing: cause (something) to disappear in its interior or depths; engulf. Freq. foll. by *up*. ME.

3 *verb trans.* **a** Destroy, consume, cause to vanish. Freq. foll. by *up*. ME. ▸**b** Incorporate; absorb; engross, occupy wholly. Now only foll. by *up*. ME. ▸**c** Eagerly take in the sense of, listen avidly to. *arch.* LME. ▸**d** Appropriate (a territory etc.); annex. Usu. foll. by *up*. M17. ▸**e** Foll. by *up*: traverse (a distance) rapidly. (Cf. DEVOUR 5.) L19.

4 *verb trans.* Accept without opposition or protest; submit to, accept meekly (an insult, injury, etc). L16.

5 *verb trans.* Believe unquestioningly. L16.

6 *verb trans.* Retract, recant. L16.

7 *verb trans.* Refrain from expressing (a feeling); refrain from uttering; repress. M17.

8 *verb trans.* Pronounce indistinctly, slur. L18.

📖 **1a** J. G. COZZENS He swallowed it in three gulps. E. MITTELHOLZER They made him swallow . . the tablets. M. LAVIN He swallowed down the last of his coffee. P. QUILLIN Gas can be caused by . . swallowing air with the food. **b** R. L. STEVENSON He kept swallowing as if he felt . . a lump in the throat. J. STEINBECK Lennie stopped chewing and swallowed. M. KEANE Professional . . tasters . . practically gargling wines before either swallowing or spitting. **2** G. GREENE The muskeg, the swamps deep enough to swallow whole trains. B. EMECHETA Thick forests seemed . . about to swallow them up. G. NAYLOR You could almost be swallowed up in the red cushions on those seats. *Times* The beloved machine has 'swallowed' your card. **3a** G. STEIN He swallowed all Anna's savings fixing up this house. J. P. HENNESSY Any profit the . . farmland might make would be swallowed up by Lord Northwick. D. MAY Every moment swallowed up and forgotten. **b** R. KIPLING He fell to work . . and was swallowed up in the . . joy of creation. P. MAILLOUX Franz's interest in socialism . . was . . swallowed up by his terrible anxiety. **d** F. E. GRETTON The hamlet of Horn, now swallowed up in the Park. **4** *Banker* CSFB had to swallow over $15 million of losses. *Business* Passengers . . might find our statement . . that British Rail is 'quite good' difficult to swallow. **5** P. G. WODEHOUSE Mrs. Gedge . . had swallowed his story, hook, line, and sinker. H. L. MENCKEN They swallowed . . imbecilities against all the known evidence. **7** SCOTT FITZGERALD Mr. Wolfsheim swallowed a new sentence he was starting and lapsed into . . abstraction. A. F. LOEWENSTEIN She'd done her best to swallow her anger and be nice to Ruth. M. WARNER I must swallow my pride, and overcome my fear.

Phrases: ***swallow a camel***: see CAMEL 1. **swallow bobby** *Austral. slang* make a false affidavit, customs declaration, etc. ***have swallowed the dictionary***: see DICTIONARY 1a.

■ **swallowable** *adjective* E19. **swallower** *noun* (*a*) a person who or thing which swallows; (*b*) *spec.* a deep-sea fish of the family Chiasmodontidae having an immensely distensible stomach which enables it to swallow fishes larger than itself, esp. (more fully ***black swallower***) *Chiasmodon niger* of the Atlantic: OE.

swallow-hole /ˈswɒləʊhəʊl/ *noun*. M17.

[from SWALLOW *noun*², *verb* + HOLE *noun*¹.]

An opening or cavity (esp. in a limestone formation) through which a stream disappears underground.

swallowtail /ˈswɒləʊteɪl/ *noun*. M16.

[from SWALLOW *noun*¹ + TAIL *noun*¹.]

1 An object shaped like a swallow's tail; *spec.* (*a*) a broad or barbed arrowhead; (*b*) = DOVETAIL *noun* 1, 2; (*c*) *FORTIFICATION* an outwork having two projections with a re-entrant angle between them; (*d*) the cleft two-pointed end of a flag or pennon; (*e*) *colloq.* a tailcoat. M16.

2 In full ***swallowtail willow***. The white willow, *Salix alba*. E17.

3 Any of various animals having a forked tail, esp. (*a*) any of various butterflies of the family Papilionidae having an elongated outgrowth on each hindwing, *esp.* the European *Papilio machaon*; (*b*) either of two marine fishes, *Trachinotus russelli* (family Carangidae) of the tropical Indo-Pacific, and *Trachichthodes lineatus* (family Trachichthyidae) of Australian waters; (*c*) a swallow-tailed kite. L17.

4 A tail like that of a swallow. E18.

swallow-tailed /ˈswɒləʊteɪld/ *adjective*. L17.

[from prec. + -ED².]

Having a swallowtail; (having a part) in the form of a swallow's tail.

swallow-tailed butterfly = SWALLOWTAIL 3(a). **swallow-tailed moth** a moth having an elongated outgrowth on each hindwing, esp. the pale-coloured geometrid *Ourapteryx sambucaria*. **swallow-tailed duck** the long-tailed duck, *Clangula hyemalis*. **swallow-tailed flycatcher** = ***scissor-tail*** s.v. SCISSORS *noun pl.* **swallow-tailed kite** a fork-tailed American kite, *Elanoides forficatus*.

swallowwort /ˈswɒləʊwəːt/ *noun*. M16.

[from SWALLOW *noun*¹ + WORT *noun*¹.]

1 Any of various European plants constituting the genus *Vincetoxicum* (family Asclepiadaceae), the follicles of which suggest a swallow with outspread wings; esp. (more fully ***white swallowwort***) *V. hirundinaria*, with whitish flowers, and (more fully ***black swallowwort***) *V. nigrum*, with dark purple flowers. M16.

2 The greater celandine, *Chelidonium majus*, reputedly used by swallows to restore their sight. L16.

swam *verb pa. t.* of SWIM *verb*.

swami /ˈswɑːmi/ *noun*. Also **-my**. L18.

[Sanskrit *svāmin*, nom. *svāmī*, master, prince.]

1 A Hindu image or temple. L18.

2 A male Hindu religious teacher. E20.

Comb.: **swami-house** a Hindu temple or shrine; **swami jewellery**: ornamented with figures of Hindu deities.

swamp /swɒmp/ *noun*. E17.

[Prob. ult. from Germanic base meaning 'sponge' or 'fungus'.]

A tract of low-lying ground in which water collects; a piece of waterlogged ground; a marsh, a bog. Orig. (in the N. American colonies), a tract of rich soil with a growth of vegetation but too moist for cultivation.

Comb.: **swamp angel** *US* a native or inhabitant of a swampy or remote region; **swamp apple** an edible leaf-gall on any of several N. American azaleas, esp. the swamp honeysuckle, *Rhododendron viscosum*; any of the plants supporting this gall; **swamp buggy** *N. Amer.* a vehicle used in swampy regions; **swamp cabbage** the skunk cabbage *Lysichiton americanus*; ***swamp cypress***: see CYPRESS *noun*¹ 1b; **swamp deer** an endangered deer, *Cervus duvaucelli*, which is found in the swamps and grassy plains of India and Nepal; also called ***barasingha***; **swamp fever** (*a*) malaria; (*b*) a contagious viral disease of horses, causing anaemia, emaciation, and usually death; **swamp fire** *Canad.* methane burning in a swampy area; a will-o'-the-wisp; **swamp gas** = ***marsh gas*** s.v. MARSH *noun*¹; **swamp hare** = ***swamp rabbit*** below; **swamphen** any of several rails, esp. (more fully ***purple swamphen***) the purple gallinule, *Porphyrio porphyrio*; **swamp honeysuckle** an azalea with pink or white flowers, *Rhododendron viscosum*, found in swamps in the eastern US; **swamp hook** *N. Amer.* a large hook used in swamping logs; **swampland** land consisting of swamps, swampy country; **swamp laurel** the sweet bay *Magnolia virginiana*; **swamp lily** any of several usu. lily-like N. American plants of swampy places, e.g. the atamasco lily, *Zephyranthes atamasco*, and the lizard's tail, *Saururus cernuus*; **swamp mahogany** a rough-barked coastal eucalyptus, *Eucalyptus robusta*, of eastern Australia; **swamp-oak** (*a*) *N. Amer.* any of several species of oak growing in swamps, e.g. (more fully ***swamp white oak***) *Quercus bicolor*; (*b*) *Austral.* any of various trees of the genus *Casuarina* (see CASUARINA) and the related genus *Allocasuarina*; **swamp ore** = ***bog iron (ore)*** s.v. BOG *noun*¹; **swamp pheasant** = ***PHEASANT coucal***; **swamp-pink** any of several pink-flowered N. American plants of swampy habitats, esp. *Helonias bullata*, of the lily family; **swamp plough** *NZ* a plough with a large mould-board, for use on heavy soils; ***swamp privet***: see PRIVET 2; **swamp quail** the brown quail, *Synoicus ypsilophorus*, of Australasia; **swamp rabbit** either of two dark brown rabbits of the genus *Sylvilagus* that are found on marshy ground in the south-eastern US, esp. *S. aquaticus*; **swamp rat** any of several African rodents, esp. of the genera *Otomys* and *Malacomys*, that frequent dense vegetation on swampy ground; **swamp robin** the towhee *Pipilo erythrophthalmus*, of N. America; **swamp rock** rock music associated with the southern US; ***swamp sassafras***: see SASSAFRAS 2; **swamp snake** a venomous olive-coloured snake, *Hemiaspis signata*, living in marshy and wet country on the east coast of Australia; **swamp sparrow** (*a*) *N. Amer.* a song sparrow, *Melospiza georgiana*, which is common in the US and Canada; (*b*) *NZ* = ***fern-bird*** s.v. FERN *noun*; **swamp wallaby** a large wallaby, *Wallabia bicolor*, which is found in moist thickets and open forest in eastern Australia; **swamp warbler** (*a*) *N. Amer.* any of several warblers of the family Parulidae, as the prothonotary warbler, *Protonotaria citrea*; (*b*) any of several African warblers of the family Sylviidae, esp. *Acrocephalus gracilirostris*, and (more fully ***yellow swamp warbler***) *Chloropeta gracilirostris*; ***swamp white oak***: see ***swamp-oak*** (a) above.

■ **swampish** *adjective* = SWAMPY E18.

swamp /swɒmp/ *adjective*. *Scot.* & *north.* LME.

[Perh. rel. to prec.]

Sunken, flattened; thin, lean.

swamp /swɒmp/ *verb*. M17.

[from the noun.]

1 *verb trans.* Bog down, entangle, or lose in a swamp. Usu. in *pass.* or *refl.* *N. Amer.* Now *rare* or *obsolete*. M17.

2 *verb trans.* Submerge in, inundate or soak with, water etc. Usu. in *pass.* L18.

3 *verb intrans.* Become swamped or submerged; fill with water and sink. L18.

4 *verb trans.* Clear (a road) for lumberers in a forest by felling trees, removing undergrowth, etc. Also, haul (logs) *out* to the skidways. *N. Amer.* L18.

5 *verb trans.* **a** Inundate with a large number of things; flood, overwhelm. E19. ▸**b** Ruin financially. Now *rare*. M19.

6 *verb intrans.* Work as a cattle-driver's assistant. Also, travel as a swamper (sense 3). *Austral. slang.* L19.

📖 **2** M. ROBINSON Their quarters were swamped in excrement. **5** J. M. COETZEE The shops are swamped with customers. M. DIBDIN A rush of helpless love swamped her. *Daily Star* He was being swamped by job offers.

swamper /ˈswɒmpə/ *noun*. L18.

[from SWAMP *noun* or *verb* + -ER¹.]

1 A native or inhabitant of a swampy region. *US*. L18.

2 a A worker who clears a road for lumberers in a forest. *N. Amer.* M19. ▸**b** An assistant to a cattle- or horse-driver. *slang* (orig. *US*). L19. ▸**c** An assistant to a lorry-driver. *N. Amer. slang.* E20. ▸**d** A man-of-all-work in a liquor saloon. Also, an assistant to a cook. *US*. E20.

3 A person who travels on foot but has baggage carried on a wagon; a person who obtains a lift. *Austral. slang.* L19.

swampy /ˈswɒmpi/ *adjective*. M17.

[from SWAMP *noun* + -Y¹.]

1 Of the nature of a swamp; marshy, boggy. M17.

2 Of or pertaining to a swamp; found in or coming from a swamp. L18.

■ **swampiness** *noun* M18.

swamy *noun* var. of SWAMI.

swan /swɒn/ *noun*.

[Old English *swan* = Old Saxon, Old High German *swan* (German *Schwan*), Old Norse *svanr* from Germanic, repr. also by Middle Low German, Middle Dutch *swane* (Dutch *zwaan*), Old High German *swana* (German dial. *Schwane*).]

1 Any of several large web-footed swimming birds constituting the genera *Cygnus* and *Coscoroba* (family Anatidae), characterized by a long and gracefully curved neck, with all-white plumage and black feet (in the northern-hemisphere forms). OE. ▸**b** A figure of a swan, as in heraldry. LME. ▸**c** (Usu. **S-**.) *The* constellation Cygnus. M16.

2 a An immaculate or faultless person; an excellent thing. ME. ▸**b** A singer; a bard, a poet (with allus. to the myth that the swan sings before its death). Chiefly with specifying word designating a river. *literary.* E17.

3 An apparently aimless journey; an excursion made for reconnaissance or for pleasure. *slang* (orig. *MILITARY*). M20.

1 ***Bewick's swan, mute swan, whooper swan***, etc.

Phrases: ***black swan***: see BLACK *adjective*. **the Swan of Avon** Shakespeare. ***turn geese into swans***: see GOOSE *noun*.

Comb.: **swan animalcule** any of various ciliate protozoans of the genus *Lacrymaria* and related genera, which have a long flexible and extensible anterior prolongation; **swan dive** *N. Amer.* a swallow dive; **swan-drop** (*a*) the knob on a swan's bill; (*b*) = ***swan-shot*** below; **swan flower** = ***swan plant*** below; **swan goose** a large long-necked goose, *Anser cygnoides*, which breeds in NE Asia; **swanherd** a person who tends swans; an official having charge of swans; **swan-hopper** = ***swan-upper*** below; **swan-hopping** = ***swan-upping*** below; **swan-maiden** [after German *Schwanenjungfrau*] *GERMANIC MYTHOLOGY* a maiden having the power of transforming herself into a swan by means of a robe of swan's feathers or of a magic ring or chain; **swan-mark** an official mark of ownership cut on the beak of a swan in swan-upping; **swan-marking** the operation of marking swans, swan-upping; **swan mussel** a large European freshwater mussel, *Anodonta cygnea*, which is found in ponds and slow-moving rivers; **swan plant** any of various tropical epiphytic orchids constituting the genus *Cycnoches*, having flowers with a long curved column; **swan's egg** a small oval variety of pear; **swan-shot** large shot used for shooting swans or in angling as a weight; **swansong** (*a*) a song like that fabled to be sung by a dying swan; (*b*) the last work or performance of a writer, artist, etc., before death or retirement; *gen.* any final action or effort; **swan-upper** an official who takes up and marks swans; **swan-upping** the practice of annually taking up and marking swans (esp. on the River Thames) with nicks on the beak in token of being owned by the Crown or some corporation; **swan-white** *adjective* (*poet.*) as white as a swan, snow-white.

■ **swanlike** *adjective* resembling (that of) a swan L16.

swan /swɒn/ *verb*[1] *trans. & intrans.* (*1 sing. pres. indic.*). *US slang.* **L18.**
[Prob. repr. English dial. pronunc. of 'shall warrant'; later taken as euphem. substitute for **SWEAR** *verb.* Cf. **SWANNY** *verb.*]
Declare, be bound, swear. Only in ***I swan.***

swan /swɒn/ *verb*[2]. Infl. **-nn-**. **L19.**
[from the noun.]
1 *verb intrans. & trans.* (with *it*). Swim like a swan. **L19.**
2 *verb intrans.* Orig. *spec.* (of an armoured vehicle), move about freely; now usu. (*gen.*), travel casually or aimlessly for pleasure; *derog.* go with a superior air. Freq. foll. by *about, around, off. slang* (orig. *Military*). **M20.**

2 *Sunday Express* She will jet in for the launch and then swan off. G. SWIFT Here he is . . swanning around in a hired Mercedes.

Swanee /ˈswɒni/ *noun.* **E20.**
[Var. of *Suwanee* a river in Georgia and Florida.]
1 ***Swanee whistle***, a small woodwind instrument with a slide-plunger to vary the pitch, chiefly used as a toy. **E20.**
2 ***down the Swanee, up the Swanee***, ruined, wasted; in trouble or difficulty; bankrupt. *slang.* **L20.**

swang /swaŋ/ *noun.* Chiefly *north.* **L17.**
[Perh. ult. rel. to **SWAMP** *noun.*]
A low-lying piece of ground liable to flooding; a bog, a swamp.

swang /swaŋ/ *verb*[1] *intrans. obsolete* exc. *dial.* **LME.**
[App. from Germanic base of **SWING** *verb.*]
Sway or swing to and fro.

swang *verb*[2] *pa. t.*: see **SWING** *verb.*

swanimote /ˈswɒnɪməʊt/ *noun. obsolete* exc. *Hist.* Also **swainmote** /ˈsweɪnməʊt/. **ME.**
[Repr. Old English word meaning 'meeting of swineherds', from *swān* swineherd (see **SWAIN**) + **GEMOT**.]
A forest assembly held three times a year in accordance with the Forest Charter of 1217, prob. orig. to organize the periodic pasturing and clearance of certain animals in the forest at various times of year.

swank /swaŋk/ *adjective*[1]. *Scot.* **L18.**
[App. from Middle Low German *swank*, Middle Dutch *swanc* flexible, supple, slender = Middle High German *swanc* (German *schwank*) from stem of Old English *swancor* pliant, supple, agile.]
Agile, active, nimble.

swank /swaŋk/ *verb, noun, & adjective*[2]. *colloq.* (orig. *dial.*). **E19.**
[Origin unkn.]
▶**A** *verb intrans.* **1** Behave or speak ostentatiously, swagger, boast; *gen.* make pretence. **E19.**
2 Work hard, swot. **L19.**

1 V. S. PRITCHETT A nondescript moneyed merchant who swanks about, giving orders to everyone.

▶**B** *noun.* **1** Ostentatious behaviour or talk; swagger; pretence. **M19.**
2 = **SWANKER**. **E20.**

1 R. CROMPTON Wot they want wiv such big 'ouses? Swank! That's all it is.

▶**C** *adjective.* Esp. of a building: stylish, expensive, luxurious. Chiefly *US.* **E20.**
■ **swanker** *noun* a person who swanks **M19.**

swankey *noun* var. of **SWANKY** *noun*[2].

swankie *noun & adjective* var. of **SWANKY** *noun*[1] *& adjective*[1].

swanking /ˈswaŋkɪŋ/ *noun & adjective.* **E16.**
[Cf. **SWANK** *adjective*[1], **SWANKY** *noun*[1] *& adjective*[1].]
▶**A** *noun.* A fine strapping fellow. Long *arch.* **E16.**
▶**B** *adjective.* Strong and active, stout, strapping. **E18.**

swankpot /ˈswaŋkpɒt/ *noun. slang.* **E20.**
[from **SWANK** *noun* + **POT** *noun*[1].]
An ostentatious or boastful person.

swanky /ˈswaŋki/ *noun*[1] *& adjective*[1]. *Scot. & north.* Also **-kie**. **E16.**
[Rel. to **SWANK** *adjective*[1], **SWANKING**.]
▶**A** *noun.* A smart, active, strapping young fellow. **E16.**
▶**B** *adjective.* Agile, active, strapping. **M19.**

swanky /ˈswaŋki/ *noun*[2]. *dial.* Also **-key**. **M19.**
[Perh. rel. to **SWANKY** *adjective*[1] with connotation 'thin, poor'.]
Weak beer or other liquor.

swanky /ˈswaŋki/ *adjective*[2]. *slang.* **M19.**
[from **SWANK** *noun or verb* + **-Y**[1].]
1 Of a person: swaggering; pretentious; boastful. **M19.**
2 Esp. of a building: imposing, stylish, posh. **M20.**

2 N. HORNBY We stand on the doorstep of their house (nothing swanky, a three-bedroomed terraced in Kensal Green). J. COE I bet she got herself all tarted up just so she could go . . to a swanky restaurant.

■ **swankily** *adverb* **E20.** **swankiness** *noun* **E20.**

Swanndri /ˈswɒndrʌɪ/ *noun. NZ.* **L20.**
[Alt. of **SWAN** *noun* + **DRY** *adjective.*]
(Proprietary name for) a type of all-weather woollen jacket.

swan-neck /ˈswɒnnɛk/ *noun & adjective.* **L17.**
[from **SWAN** *noun* + **NECK** *noun*[1]. Cf. German *Schwanenhals*, Swedish *svanhals*, also Middle High German *swanhals* narrow sickle.]
▶**A** *noun.* **1** Any of various structural parts or devices having a curved cylindrical form like a swan's neck. **L17.**
2 A neck like that of a swan; a long slender neck. **M19.**
▶**B** *attrib.* or as *adjective.* Of a curved form like a swan's neck. **M19.**
swan-neck deformity MEDICINE a deformity seen in fingers affected by rheumatoid arthritis, in which the interphalangeal joints are extended or flexed.
■ **swan-necked** *adjective* (*a*) having a long slender neck; (*b*) having a curved cylindrical form like a swan's neck: **E18.**

swanner /ˈswɒnə/ *noun.* **E16.**
[Partly reduced form of ***swanherd*** s.v. **SWAN** *noun*, partly from Middle Dutch *swanier* swan-warden: see **-ER**[1].]
A swanherd.

swannery /ˈswɒnəri/ *noun.* **L16.**
[formed as prec.: see **-ERY**.]
†**1** The keeping of swans. Only in **L16.**
2 A place where swans are kept and reared. **M18.**

swannie /ˈswɒni/ *noun. NZ colloq.* **L20.**
[Abbreviation: see **-IE**.]
= **SWANNDRI**.

swanny /ˈswɒni/ *adjective.* **M16.**
[from **SWAN** *noun* + **-Y**[1].]
1 Full of swans, having many swans. **M16.**
2 Of, pertaining to, or resembling (that of) a swan. **L16.**

swanny /ˈswɒni/ *verb trans. & intrans.* (*1 sing. pres. indic.*). *US slang.* **M19.**
[Prob. repr. English dial. pronunc. of 'shall warrant ye'. Cf. **SWAN** *verb*[1].]
= **SWAN** *verb*[1].

Swan River /swɒn ˈrɪvə/ *noun phr.* **M19.**
[A river of Western Australia.]
Used *attrib.* to designate things found in or associated with the Swan River.
Swan River daisy an annual Australian plant of the composite family, *Brachycome iberidifolia*, with pinnate leaves and blue, violet, or white daisy-like flowers.

swansdown /ˈswɒnzdaʊn/ *noun & adjective.* Also **swan's-down**. **E17.**
[from **SWAN** *noun* + **-'S**[1] + **DOWN** *noun*[2].]
▶**A** *noun.* **1** The fine down of a swan, used for trimmings, powder-puffs, etc. **E17.**
2 a A soft thick compact fabric of wool with a little silk or cotton. **E19.** ▶**b** A strong cotton fabric with a soft nap on one side; = ***cotton flannel*** s.v. **COTTON** *noun*[1]. **E19.**
▶**B** *attrib.* or as *adjective.* Made of swansdown. **L18.**

Swansea /ˈswɒnzi/ *noun & adjective.* **M19.**
[A city in S. Wales.]
(Designating) pottery and porcelain made at the Cambrian Pottery in Swansea from 1764 to 1870.

swanskin /ˈswɒnskɪn/ *noun & adjective.* **E17.**
[from **SWAN** *noun* + **SKIN** *noun.*]
▶**A** *noun.* **1** The skin of a swan (with the feathers on); *transf.* a soft or delicate skin. **E17.**
2 A fine thick type of flannel. Also, a blanket used by printers and engravers for absorbing and equalizing pressure. **L17.**
▶**B** *attrib.* or as *adjective.* Made or consisting of swanskin. **E17.**

SWANU /ˈswɑːnuː/ *abbreviation.*
South West African National Union.

swap /swɒp/ *noun.* Also **swop**. **LME.**
[from the verb.]
▶**I 1** An act of striking someone or something; a stroke, a blow. *obsolete* exc. *Scot. & dial.* **LME.**
▶**II 2** An act of exchanging something; an exchange. Also, a thing exchanged. *colloq.* **L16.**
3 FINANCE. In foreign exchange operations: an exchange of an amount of money at different rates. Also more widely, an arrangement between the central banks of two countries for stand-by credit to facilitate the exchange of each other's currency. Usu. *attrib.* **M20.**

2 H. KISSINGER A . . Jordan–Israel arrangement involving a swap of Gaza for West Bank territories. *Times* Heart swap hospitals hoping for more aid. **get the swap, have the swap** *slang* be dismissed from employment.

Comb.: **swapfile** COMPUTING a file on a hard disk used to provide space for programs which have been transferred from the processor's memory; **swap fund** US STOCK EXCHANGE a fund which investors enter by exchanging securities directly for shares in the fund, obtaining a diversified portfolio without selling stock, and thereby avoiding liability for capital gains tax on the sale of these securities; **swap-meet** (orig. *US*) a gathering at which enthusiasts discuss, exchange, or trade items of common interest; **swap shop** *colloq.* an agency for putting people with articles to exchange or trade in touch with one another.

swap /swɒp/ *verb.* Also **swop**. Infl. **-pp-**. **ME.**
[Prob. imit. of a smart resounding blow: cf. German dial. *Schwappe* in same sense, *schwappen* make a clapping or splashing noise.]
▶**I 1** *verb trans.* Move (something) quickly or briskly, esp. so as to hit something else; fling, throw forcibly; *refl.* sit *down* with force, plump oneself *down*. Long *arch.* exc. *Scot.* **ME.**
2 a *verb trans.* Strike, hit; cut, chop. Later only foll. by *off*. Long *arch.* exc. *Scot.* **LME.** ▶**b** *verb intrans.* Strike a person or thing; deal a blow or blows. Now *rare* or *obsolete.* **LME.**
3 a *verb intrans.* Move with haste or violence, esp. so as to hit something; sink or fall *down* suddenly; rush, fling oneself somewhere. Now *rare* or *obsolete.* **LME.** ▶**b** *verb intrans. & trans.* (with *it*). Flap or beat up and down. **E16.** ▶**c** *verb trans.* Pounce on, seize. **E18.**
4 *verb trans.* Drink quickly, toss off; eat up, devour. Foll. by *down, off, up*. Long *obsolete* exc. *Scot.* **E16.**
▶**II** †**5 a** *verb intrans.* Strike hands in token of an agreement or bargain. *rare.* Only in **LME.** ▶**b** *verb trans.* Strike (a bargain). Also foll. by *up*. **L16–L17.**
6 Chiefly *colloq.* ▶**a** *verb trans.* Give in exchange *for* something else; exchange (a thing) *with* another person; barter; change. Also foll. by *away, off.* **L16.** ▶**b** *verb intrans.* Make an exchange (*with* someone). **L18.**
7 *slang.* **a** *verb trans.* Dismiss from employment. **M19.** ▶**b** *verb trans.* Foll. by *off*: cheat, take in. Orig. *US.* **M19.** ▶**c** *verb intrans.* Change one's clothes. *rare.* **E20.**

6a J. CAREW We swapped stories about the doctor and Indra. G. BOYCOTT They brought in Malcolm Marshall for Roberts, swapping one . . fast bowler for another. *She* Few of us could imagine permanently swapping gender. *Times Lit. Suppl.* He even swapped pulpits with a local rabbi. ***swap horses in midstream***: see **HORSE** *noun.* **b** *Sun* He and his first wife used to have swapping parties.

Comb.: **swap-hook** (chiefly *dial.*) a reaping-hook for cutting crops close to the ground.
■ **swapper** *noun* (*a*) *colloq.* a person who swaps or exchanges something; (*b*) *slang & dial.* something very big; *spec.* a huge lie: **L17.** **swapping** *adjective* †(*a*) striking; flapping; (*b*) *dial.* swooping, pouncing; (*c*) *colloq.* very big, whopping: **LME.**

swap /swɒp/ *adverb.* Now only *Scot. & dial.* Also **swop**. **L17.**
[from the verb.]
At a blow; with sudden violence; suddenly and forcibly.

SWAPO /ˈswɑːpəʊ/ *abbreviation.*
South West African People's Organization.

swaption /ˈswɒpʃ(ə)n/ *noun.* **L20.**
[Blend of **SWAP** *noun* and **OPTION**.]
FINANCE. An option giving the right but not the obligation to engage in a swap.

Swaraj /swəˈrɑːdʒ/ *noun.* **E20.**
[Hindi *svarāj* from Sanskrit *svarājya*, from *sva* own + *rājya* rule.]
Hist. Self-government or independence for India; agitation in favour of this.
■ **Swarajist** *noun & adjective* (a person) advocating self-rule for India **E20.**

sward /swɔːd/ *noun & verb.*
[Old English *sweard* (beside *swearþ*: see **SWARTH** *noun*[1]), corresp. to Old Frisian, Middle Low German, Middle Dutch *swarde* hairy skin, Middle High German *swarte* (German *Schwarte* bacon rind, crust), Old Norse *svǫrðr* skin (of the head), walrus hide: ult. origin unkn.]
▶**A** *noun.* **1** The skin of the body; *esp.* (now *dial.*) the rind of pork or bacon. **OE.**
2 The surface or upper layer of soil usu. covered with grass or other herbage; a stretch of grassy turf. Orig. chiefly in ***sward of the earth, sward of the ground***, etc. **LME.**
Comb.: **sward-cutter** an implement for cutting a tough sward in preparation for ploughing.
▶**B** *verb.* **1** *verb intrans.* Form a sward; become covered with grassy turf. **E17.**
2 *verb trans.* Cover with a sward. Usu. in *pass.* **E17.**
■ **swarded** *adjective* covered with a sward or grassy turf; turfed: **E16.** **swardy** *adjective* covered with sward, swarded, turfy **M17.**

swarf /swɑːf/ *noun*[1] *& verb. Scot. & north.* **L15.**
[Rel. to Old Norse *svarfa* upset.]
▶**A** *noun.* A swoon, a fainting-fit; a state of insensibility, a stupor. **L15.**
▶**B** *verb.* **1** *verb intrans.* Faint, swoon. **E16.**
2 *verb trans.* Cause to faint; stupefy. **E19.**

swarf /swɔːf, swɑːf/ *noun*[2]. Also **swarth** /swɔːθ/. **M16.**
[Repr. Old English *geswearf, gesweorf, geswyrf* filings (cf. **SWERVE** *verb*), or from Old Norse *svarf* file-dust.]
1 Wet or greasy grit abraded from a grindstone or axle by friction during use; *gen.* any fine waste produced by a machining operation, esp. in the form of strips or ribbons; filings of metal etc. **M16.**
2 The material cut out of a gramophone record as the groove is made. **M20.**

Swarga /ˈswɑːgə/ *noun.* Also **Svarga** /ˈsvɑːgə/. **M18.**
[Sanskrit *svarga.*]
HINDUISM. Heaven, paradise; *spec.* the heaven presided over by Indra, where virtuous souls reside before reincarnation.

swarm /swɔːm/ *noun.*
[Old English *swearm* = Old Saxon, Middle Low German *swarm*, Old High German *swar(a)m* (German *Schwarm*), Old Norse *svarmr* from Germanic, prob. rel. to base of Sanskrit *svarati* it sounds, Latin **SUSURRUS**.]

1 A large number of honeybees which gather about the hive and leave *en masse* with a newly fertilized queen to establish a fresh colony; a compact mass or cluster of such bees. Also, a large gathering of winged ants or termites (about the nest), in which numerous queens are fertilized. OE. ▸**b** *transf.* A body of people who leave their home and travel elsewhere to found a new colony or community. M17.

2 A large or dense group of people, animals, or things; a crowd, a multitude; *esp.* a large or dense group of flying insects. LME. ▸**b** ASTRONOMY. A large number of asteroids, meteors, etc., occurring together in space. L19. ▸**c** ECOLOGY. = ***hybrid swarm*** s.v. HYBRID *adjective*. E20. ▸**d** A series of similar-sized earthquakes occurring together within a small area. M20.

🕮 **2** J. S. HUXLEY A swarm of daffodils, like those Wordsworth immortalized. A. BRINK A swarm of brown women and children were chasing birds.

Comb.: **swarm cell** BIOLOGY (*a*) a flagellated amoeboid cell produced by a myxomycete, lacking a cell wall and capable of encysting; (*b*) = ZOOSPORE; **swarm-spore** BIOLOGY = ZOOSPORE.

swarm /swɔːm/ *verb*¹. LME.
[from the noun.]
1 *verb intrans.* Of honeybees: gather in large numbers about the hive and leave *en masse* with a newly fertilized queen to establish a fresh colony. Of winged ants and termites: gather in large numbers about the nest, with the fertilization of numerous queens. LME. ▸**b** *transf.* Of a body of people: leave to found a new colony or community. E17. ▸**c** BIOLOGY. Of zoospores etc.: escape from the parent organism in a swarm, with characteristic movement; move or swim about in a swarm. M19.
2 *verb intrans.* Come together in a swarm or dense crowd; collect or congregate thickly; throng. Also, move along in a crowd. LME.
3 *verb intrans.* Occur or exist in swarms; crowd in large numbers. LME.
4 *verb intrans.* Of a place etc.: be crowded, contain large numbers of people or things. Now only foll. by *with*. L15.
5 *verb trans.* Fill with a swarm; crowd (a place) densely. Usu. in *pass.* M16.
6 *verb trans.* Produce a swarm of. *rare.* M19.

🕮 **2** V. WOOLF Women . . swarming in and out of shops. G. HUNTINGTON Children . . swarming about and screaming at . . play. **4** E. SEGAL Vanderbilt Hall swarmed with gaily chattering students. **5** *Today* Foot-in-the-door salesmen swarming devastated Towyn in North Wales.

swarm /swɔːm/ *verb*² *intrans.* & *trans.* M16.
[Origin unkn.]
Climb *up* (a pole, tree, etc.) by clasping with the arms and legs alternately; climb (a steep ascent) clinging with hands and knees.

swarmer /ˈswɔːmə/ *noun*¹. M19.
[from SWARM *verb*¹ + -ER¹.]
1 Any of a number that swarm; one of a swarm (as of insects); *spec.* (BIOLOGY) = ***swarm cell*** s.v. SWARM *noun*; (BACTERIOLOGY) = ***swarmer cell*** below. M19.
2 A beehive adapted for swarming, or from which a swarm is sent out. M19.
Comb.: **swarmer cell** BACTERIOLOGY a flagellated motile cell produced by certain species of stalked bacteria and slime moulds.

†**swarmer** *noun*². M–L18.
[German *Schwärmer* or Dutch *zwermer*, from German *schwärmen*, Dutch *zwermen* rove, stray.]
A firework, *esp.* a small rocket or serpent.

swarri *noun* var. of SAOUARI.

swarry /ˈswɒri/ *noun. joc.* M19.
[Repr. a pronunc.]
= SOIRÉE.

swart /swɔːt/ *adjective* & *noun.* Now only *dial., poet., & rhet.* See also SWARTH *adjective* & *noun*⁴.
[Old English *sweart* = Old Frisian, Old Saxon *swart*, Old High German *swarz* (Dutch *zwart*, German *schwarz*), Old Norse *svartr*, Gothic *swarts*, from Germanic.]
▸**A** *adjective.* **1** Dark in colour; black, blackish; *spec.* dark-complexioned, dusky, swarthy. OE. ▸†**b** Of the face or body: livid through suffering or emotion. LME–L16. ▸**c** Of the sun, or some other celestial object regarded as hot: producing a swarthy complexion. M17. ▸**d** Dressed in black. L17.
2 Wicked, iniquitous; baleful, malignant. OE.
▸†**B** *noun.* A person of swarthy complexion. *rare.* LME–M19.
▪ **swartish** *adjective* (*obsolete* exc. *dial.*) somewhat dark or swarthy LME. **swartness** *noun* swarthiness, duskiness LOE.

swart gevaar /swart xəˈfaːr/ *noun phr.* S. AFR. HISTORY. M20.
[Afrikaans, lit. 'black peril', from Dutch *zwart* black + *gevaar* danger.]
The threat to the Western way of life and white supremacy in South Africa believed by some to be posed by black people.

swarth /swɔːθ/ *noun*¹. Also **swath**.
[Old English *swearþ* var. of *sweard* SWARD.]
1 Skin, rind; *transf.* the surface or outside of something. Now *dial.* OE.
2 Green turf, grassland. Also ***green swarth***. Now only *Scot. & dial.* LME.

swarth /swɔːθ/ *noun*². Now *dial.* M16.
[Unexpl. alt. of SWATH *noun*¹.]
1 = SWATH *noun*¹ 3. M16.
2 = SWATH *noun*¹ 4a, b. E17.

swarth *noun*³ var. of SWARF *noun*².

swarth /swɔːθ/ *adjective* & *noun*⁴. E16.
[Var. of SWART.]
▸**A** *adjective.* Dusky, swarthy, black. E16.
▸**B** *noun.* Swarthiness; dusky complexion or colour. *rare.* M17.

swarth /swɔːθ/ *verb*¹ *trans.* & *intrans.* Now *dial.* E17.
[from SWARTH *noun*¹.]
= SWARD *verb*.

swarth /swɔːð/ *verb*² *trans.* M19.
[from SWARTH *adjective.*]
Make swarthy, darken.

swarthy /ˈswɔːði/ *adjective.* L16.
[Unexpl. alt. of SWARTY.]
1 Of a dark hue; black, blackish; *spec.* dark-complexioned, dusky. L16.
2 Malignant, dismal. M17.
▪ **swarthily** *adverb* with a swarthy colour M18. **swarthiness** *noun* L16.

swartrutter /ˈsvaːtrʌtə/ *noun. obsolete* exc. *Hist.* M16.
[Early mod. Dutch: see SWART *adjective*, RUTTER *noun*¹.]
Any of a class of irregular troopers, with black dress and armour and blackened faces, who infested the Netherlands in the 16th and 17th cents.

swartwitpens /swartˈvɪtpens/ *noun. S. African* Pl. same. M19.
[Afrikaans, from *swart* black + *wit* white + *pens* belly.]
= ***sable antelope*** s.v. SABLE *adjective*¹ 2.

swarty /ˈswɔːti/ *adjective.* Now *rare* or *obsolete.* L16.
[from SWART *adjective* + -Y¹.]
= SWARTHY.

swartzite /ˈswɔːtsʌɪt/ *noun.* M20.
[from Charles K. *Swartz* (1861–1949), US geologist + -ITE¹.]
MINERALOGY. A hydrated calcium magnesium uranyl carbonate, $CaMgUO_2(CO_3)_3 \cdot 12H_2O$, occurring as green monoclinic crystals.

swarve /swɔːv/ *verb*¹ *trans. local.* L15.
[Origin unkn.]
Choke with sediment; silt *up*. Usu. in *pass.*

†**swarve** *verb*². M16–L19.
[Origin unkn.]
= SWARM *verb*².

swash /swɒʃ/ *noun*¹ & *adverb.* E16.
[Imit.]
▸**A** *noun.* **I 1** Pigswill; wet refuse or filth. E16. ▸**b** *fig.* Worthless stuff, nonsense. *slang.* L19.
2 A body of water moving forcibly or dashing against something. L17.
3 = SWATCH *noun*³. Chiefly *US.* L17.
4 A heavy blow; the sound of this. E18.
5 a The action of water dashing or washing against the side of a cliff, ship, etc., or of waves against each other; the sound accompanying this. M19. ▸**b** The rush of seawater up the beach after the breaking of a wave. E20.
6 A waterlogged condition of land; ground under water. M19.
▸**II 7** A swaggerer; a swashbuckler; (now *Scot.*) an ostentatious person. M16.
8 Swagger; swashbuckling. L16.
Comb.: **swash mark** a mark on the sand of a beach left by the swash of waves; **swashplate** ENGINEERING a disc mounted obliquely on the end of a revolving shaft, which imparts a reciprocating motion to a rod parallel to the axis of the shaft; also called ***wobble plate***. **swash way** = *swatchway* s.v. SWATCH *noun*³.
▸**B** *adverb.* With a crash. M16.

swash /swɒʃ/ *noun*². *Scot. obsolete* exc. *Hist.* M16.
[Origin unkn.]
A drum; a trumpet.

swash /swɒʃ/ *adjective* & *noun*³. L17.
[Origin unkn.]
▸**A** *adjective.* **1** Inclined obliquely. L17.
2 PRINTING. Designating characters, usually cursive capitals, having flourished strokes. L17.
▸**B** *noun.* PRINTING. An extended ornamental flourish on a cursive (esp. capital) letter. L17.
Comb.: **swash-work**: in which the cuttings or mouldings traced round a cylinder are inclined to the axis.

swash /swɒʃ/ *verb.* M16.
[Imit.]
1 *verb intrans.* Make a noise as of swords clashing or of a sword beating on a shield; fence with swords; lash *out*. Also, behave ostentatiously, swagger. M16.
2 *verb trans.* Dash or throw violently; slash, beat. L16.
3 *verb intrans.* Move violently about; rush to and fro. L16.
4 *verb trans.* Splash (water) about; dash water on, souse with liquid; (of water) splash against. L16.
5 *verb intrans.* Of water or an object in water: make a splashing sound; splash *about*. L18.

swashbuckler /ˈswɒʃbʌklə/ *noun.* M16.
[from prec. + BUCKLER *noun.*]
1 A swaggering bully or ruffian; a noisy boaster. M16.
2 A book, film, or other work portraying swashbuckling characters. L20.
▪ **swashbucklering** *adjective* = SWASHBUCKLING *adjective* L19.

swashbuckling /ˈswɒʃbʌklɪŋ/ *adjective* & *noun.* L17.
[from prec.: see -ING².]
▸**A** *adjective.* Acting like, or characteristic of the conduct of, a swashbuckler; noisily swaggering, blustering; ostentatiously daring. L17.
▸**B** *noun.* Conduct characteristic of a swashbuckler; noisy swaggering. L19.
▪ **swashbuckle** *verb intrans.* [back-form.] swagger noisily, act like a blustering ruffian L19.

swasher /ˈswɒʃə/ *noun.* L16.
[from SWASH *verb* + -ER¹.]
A swashbuckler; a blustering braggart or ruffian; *Scot.* a swaggerer, a showy person.

swashing /ˈswɒʃɪŋ/ *ppl adjective.* M16.
[formed as prec. + -ING².]
1 Characterized by ostentation, or by showy or blustering behaviour; swaggering; swashbuckling; dashing. M16.
2 FENCING. Designating a particular stroke in fencing, perh. the stramazon; (of a weapon) slashing with great force. *obsolete* exc. *Hist.* E17.
3 Of water etc.: dashing and splashing. E17.

🕮 **2** SHAKES. *Rom. & Jul.* Gregory, remember thy swashing blow.

▪ **swashingly** *adverb* swaggeringly; in a swashbuckling style: M17.

swashy /ˈswɒʃi/ *adjective.* L18.
[from SWASH *noun*¹ or *verb* + -Y¹.]
Sloppy, watery; *fig.* wishy-washy.

swastika /ˈswɒstɪkə/ *noun.* L19.
[Sanskrit *svastika*, from *svasti* well-being, luck, from *su* good + *asti* being.]
1 An ancient symbol in the form of a cross with equal arms with a limb of the same length projecting at right angles from the end of each arm, all in the same direction and (usu.) clockwise. L19.
2 This symbol (with clockwise projecting limbs) used as the emblem of the German and other Nazi parties; = HAKENKREUZ. Also, a flag bearing this emblem. M20.
¶ Formerly pronounced /ˈswastɪkə/.
▪ **swastikaed** *adjective* decorated with or wearing a swastika, esp. as a badge of Nazism M20.

swat /swɒt/ *noun*¹. L18.
[from SWAT *verb*².]
A smart or violent blow. Also, a heavy fall.

🕮 *Listener* In a single swat, one . . blast once flattened 252 oil derricks.

Swat /swɒt/ *noun*² & *adjective.* Now *rare* or *obsolete.* L19.
[A district in the Malakand Division of North-west Frontier Province, Pakistan.]
= SWATI.

swat *noun*³ & *verb*¹ var. of SWOT.

swat /swɒt/ *verb*². Infl. **-tt-**. E17.
[North. & US alt. of SQUAT *verb.*]
1 *verb intrans.* Sit down, squat. *north.* E17.
2 a *verb trans.* Hit with a smart slap or a violent blow; dash. Now (*esp.*) crush (a fly etc.) with a blow. L18. ▸**b** *verb intrans.* Direct a blow or blows; hit *at* or *against*. E19.

🕮 **2b** J. DIDION The woman swatted listlessly at flies.

Swatantra /swəˈtantrə/ *noun.* M20.
[Sanskrit *svatantra* independent.]
INDIAN HISTORY. In full ***Swatantra party***. A liberal conservative political party (the Freedom Party) in the Republic of India from 1959 to 1972.

swatch /swɒtʃ/ *noun*¹. Orig. *Scot. & north.* E16.
[Origin unkn. Cf. SWADGE.]
†**1** Orig., a counterfoil. Later, a tally fixed to a piece of cloth before it is dyed. *north.* E16–L19.
2 A sample piece of cloth or other material. Also, a collection of samples bound together, a swatch-book. M17.
3 A sample, a specimen; *transf.* a portion, a patch. L17.

🕮 **3** R. BANKS The sky clear as black glass, with belts and swatches of stars all over.

Comb.: **swatch-book** a book of samples, esp. of fabrics.

swatch /swɒtʃ/ *noun*². Long *arch.* L16.
[App. irreg. var. of SWATH *noun*¹.]
A row of corn or grass cut.

swatch /swɒtʃ/ *noun*³. *local*. E17.
[Origin uncertain: in local English use chiefly in eastern counties.]
A passage or channel of water lying between sandbanks or between a sandbank and the shore.
Comb.: **swatchway** a channel across a bank or between shoals.

swatchel /ˈswɒtʃ(ə)l/ *noun*. *slang*. See also SWAZZLE. M19.
[Perh. from German *schwätzeln* frequentative of *schwatzen* chatter, tattle.]
Punch in a Punch-and-Judy show. Also, a swazzle. Freq. *attrib.*

swatching /ˈswɒtʃɪŋ/ *noun*. Now chiefly *Canad. dial.* L19.
[Origin unkn.]
A method of catching seals that come to the surface of open water in an ice-field.

swath /swɔːθ, swɒθ/ *noun*¹. Also (earlier esp. *north.*) **swathe** /sweɪð/.
[Old English *swæþ*, *swaþu*, corresp. to Old Frisian *swethe*, Middle Low German *swat*, *swade* (Dutch *zwad*, *zwade*), Middle High German *swade* (German *Schwade*). Cf. SWATCH *noun*².]
†**1** Track, trace. OE–ME.
2 a A measure of the width of a strip of grassland, perh. orig. reckoned by the breadth of one sweep of the mower's scythe. *local*. ME. ▸**b** The space covered by a sweep of the scythe; the width of grass or corn so cut. ME. ▸**c** A stroke of the scythe in reaping. *rare*. M17.
3 a A row or line of grass, corn, etc., as it falls or lies when mown or reaped; *collect.* a crop mown and lying on the ground. ME. ▸**b** Growing grass or corn ready for mowing or reaping. L16.
4 *transf.* & *fig.* **a** A broad strip or long extent of something. E17. ▸**b** A thing falling in a row or stream; *esp.* a line of troops mown down in battle. M19.

> 🕮 **4a** *Times Lit. Suppl.* Owing the United States Government a swath of back-taxes. **b** A. I. SHAND The dead lying in swathes as they had fallen.

Phrases: **cut a swath**, **cut a wide swath** *US slang* make a pompous display, swagger; cut a dash.
Comb.: **swath-board** a slanting board attached to the cutter of a mowing-machine, designed to force the cut grass etc. into a narrower swath; **swath-turner** a machine used for turning over swaths of hay.
■ **swather** *noun* a device on the front of a mowing-machine for raising uncut fallen grain and marking the line between cut and uncut grain L19.

swath *noun*² var. of SWARTH *noun*¹.

†**swath-band** *noun*. Also **swathe-band**. ME.
[from stem of SWATHE *verb* + BAND *noun*¹.]
1 In *pl.* Swaddling-clothes. ME–M17.
2 A bandage, a binder. M16–L17.

swathe /sweɪð/ *noun*¹. OE.
[Rel. to the verb.]
1 A band of linen, woollen, or other material in which something is enveloped; a wrapping. OE. ▸†**b** *sing.* & in *pl.* An infant's swaddling-clothes. M16–L18. ▸**c** A surgical bandage. Now *rare*. E17.
2 *transf.* A natural formation constituting a wrapping; an object covering something, as a cloud. E17.

> 🕮 **1** JULIA HAMILTON Chandeliers hung motionless in muslin swathes. *fig.*: *Spectator* Tied up helplessly in tight swathes of ignorance. **2** *Holiday Which?* Swathes of heather and bracken . . grooved by green valleys.

swathe *noun*² see SWATH *noun*¹.

swathe /sweɪð/ *verb trans.*
[Late Old English *swaþian*, of unkn. origin. Rel. to SWATHE *noun*¹.]
1 Envelop in a swathe or swathes; wrap up, bandage. LOE. ▸**b** Wrap (a bandage etc.) round something. M17.
2 Envelop or surround as with a wrapping; enclose, enfold. E17.

> 🕮 **1** J. GALSWORTHY Bilson brought champagne, a bottle swathed around the neck with white. **2** M. FORSTER The city was swathed in fog.

■ **swathing** *noun* (*a*) the action of the verb; (*b*) a wrapping; a bandage; ***swathing-bands***, ***swathing-clothes***, swaddling-clothes: LME.

†**swathe-band** *noun* var. of SWATH-BAND.

Swati /ˈswɒti/ *noun* & *adjective*. E19.
[from SWAT *noun*² & *adjective* + -I².]
▸**A** *noun*. A member of a people inhabiting the district of Swat in Pakistan. E19.
▸**B** *adjective*. Of or pertaining to this people. E20.

Swatow /ˈswɑːtaʊ, ˈswɒ-/ *noun*. E20.
[A port (now Shantou) in the province of Guangdong, China.]
Used *attrib.* to designate a type of porcelain produced in the Ming dynasty.

swats /swɒts/ *noun*. *Scot.* E16.
[Repr. Old English *swatan* beer.]
Newly brewed weak beer or ale.

SWAT team /ˈswɒt tiːm/ *noun phr.* L20.
[Acronym from Special Weapons And Tactics.]
In the US: a team assembled from an elite corps of police marksmen who specialize in high-risk tasks such as hostage rescue; *transf.* any team of specialists brought in to solve a difficult or urgent problem.

> 🕮 *Times* A SWAT team of hairdressers, make-up artists, and body waxers homes in on Bullock in an aircraft hangar.

swatter /ˈswɒtə/ *noun*. E20.
[from SWAT *verb*² + -ER¹.]
An instrument for swatting flies. Also, a person who swats flies.

swatter /ˈswatə/ *verb*. Long *Scot.* & *north.* LME.
[Imit.: cf. SQUATTER *verb*. See -ER⁵.]
†**1** *verb intrans.* Of liquid: run in a trickle, trickle *out*. Only in LME.
†**2** *verb intrans.* Move flounderingly. Only in LME.
3 *verb intrans.* Flutter and splash excitedly in water; splash water about. E16.
4 *verb trans.* Fritter *away* (time, money, etc.). L17.

swattle /ˈswat(ə)l/ *verb*. *north.* L17.
[Rel. to SWATTER *verb*: see -LE³.]
1 *verb intrans.* Make a splashing noise in or with water. L17. ▸**b** *verb intrans.* & *refl.* Tipple or guzzle drink. L18.
2 *verb trans.* Waste, squander; fritter *away*. L17.

swaver /ˈsweɪvə/ *verb intrans.* *Scot.* & *north.* LME.
[Perh. from Scandinavian stem *sveif-*: see -ER⁵. Cf. Old Norse *sveifla* swing (Norwegian dial. *sveivla* fan, waft).]
Stagger, totter.

sway /sweɪ/ *noun*. LME.
[from the verb.]
▸**I** The action of SWAY *verb*.
†**1** The motion of a rotating body. LME–E17.
2 The impetus or momentum of a body etc. in motion. Now *rare*. LME. ▸**b** A turn, a veer. *Scot.* E19.
3 Prevailing, overpowering, or controlling influence. E16.
†**4** Force or pressure bearing on an object. M16–L18.
†**5** Bias in a certain direction. L16–E19.
6 Power, authority, rule; government; a position of authority or power. L16.
7 Carriage, deportment. Now *rare* or *obsolete*. M18.
8 (A) movement backwards and forwards or from side to side. M19. ▸**b** NAUTICAL. A rhythmic linear motion of a vessel from side to side (as distinguished from the rotatory motion of a roll). M20.

> 🕮 **3** E. H. GOMBRICH No historian of art will be inclined to underrate the sway of style. J. MCDOUGALL Infants under the sway of hunger. E. YOUNG-BRUEHL Martha held sway over all matters domestic. *San Diego* Ivan managed to . . hold sway by joining forces with the church. *fig.*: B. RUBENS He tried again to beat his hand . . but . . he had lost sway over his body.

▸**II** Denoting an object.
†**9** The pole of a cart. *Scot.* Only in M16.
10 A lever, a crowbar. *dial.* M16.
11 A small pliable twig or rod, *esp.* one used in thatching. *dial.* M17.
12 A flat iron rod suspended in a chimney, on which to hang pots etc. *Scot.* & *north.* E19.

sway /sweɪ/ *verb*. ME.
[Origin uncertain: corresp. in form to Old Norse *sveigja* bend, give way, but corresp. in meaning to Dutch *zwaaien* swing, wave, walk totteringly, Low German *swājen* move to and fro (as) with the wind.]
†**1** *verb intrans.* Go, move; *esp.* go *down*, fall (*lit.* & *fig.*). ME–M16.
2 *verb intrans.* Move slowly and rhythmically backwards and forwards or from side to side as if on a pivot. LME. ▸**b** *fig.* Vacillate. *rare*. M16.
3 *verb trans.* Cause to move slowly and rhythmically backwards and forwards or from side to side as if on a pivot. M16. ▸**b** *fig.* Cause to vacillate. L16.
4 †**a** *verb intrans.* Be diverted in judgement or opinion (*from*); incline (*towards* a party etc.). M16–M17. ▸**b** *verb trans.* Divert (thoughts, feelings, etc.); divert *from* a course of action. Formerly also, induce *to do*. L16.
5 a *verb intrans.* Rule, govern. M16. ▸†**b** *fig.* Have a preponderating influence, prevail. L16–M18.
6 *verb trans.* **a** Rule, govern. Chiefly *poet.* L16. ▸**b** *fig.* Control or direct (a person, conduct, etc.); *esp.* influence or affect the decision etc. of (a person). L16.
7 *verb intrans.* Bend or move to one side or downwards, as a result of excess weight or pressure; lean, swerve. Now only (passing into sense 2), lean unsteadily *towards*. L16. ▸†**b** Move in a certain direction. L16–M17. ▸**c** Move *against* in a hostile manner. *rare*. L16.
8 *verb trans.* Cause to lean or hang down on one side as a result of excess weight; *dial.* weigh or press down; cause to swerve. Now *rare*. L16. ▸†**b** Strain (a horse) in the back; strain (the back of a horse). Cf. earlier SWAYED. *rare*. E–M17.
9 *verb trans.* Wield as an emblem of sovereignty or authority. Chiefly in ***sway the sceptre***, rule. *arch.* L16. ▸**b** *transf.* Wield (an instrument). *poet.* L16.
10 *verb trans.* & *intrans.* Swing. Now *dial.* L16.
11 *verb trans.* (foll. by *up*) & *intrans.* (with *away*). NAUTICAL. Hoist or raise (esp. a yard or topmast). M18.

> 🕮 **2** V. BRITTAIN The long . . grass . . swaying in the wind. D. WELCH My head reeled and I swayed a little. A. LEE Above it, swaying on a string, hung a stuffed white dove. **3** J. STEINBECK The wind blows . . and sways the pines. M. ATWOOD Girls who walk along . . swaying their little hips. **4a** SHAKES. *Hen. V* He seems indifferent; Or rather swaying more upon our part. **b** J. R. GREEN No . . love or hate swayed him from his course. **6b** B. MALAMUD Swaying a jury to render a judgement. C. JACKSON He was . . adamant . . and could not be swayed by dollars. A. T. ELLIS Betty . . was easily swayed by argument. **7** SHAKES. *3 Hen. VI* Sways . . this way, like a mighty sea Forc'd by the tide. V. GLENDINNING Leafy climbing plants . . swayed towards her.

Comb.: **sway-bar** (*a*) *Hist.* a circular piece of wood at the front of a carriage, sliding on the coupling poles when the carriage is turning; (*b*) (chiefly *N. Amer.*) a bar attached to the suspension of a motor vehicle, designed to reduce rolling when cornering; **sway-brace** *noun* & *verb* (*a*) *noun* a diagonal brace on a bridge designed to prevent swaying; (*b*) *verb trans.* strengthen with a sway-brace.
■ **swayable** *adjective* able to be influenced (earlier in UNSWAYABLE) M17. **swayer** *noun* L16. **swayingly** *adverb* with a swaying motion M19.

swayamvara /swəˈjʌmvərə/ *noun*. M19.
[Sanskrit *svayamvara* one's own choice.]
A Hindu ceremony in which a woman chooses her husband from amongst several contenders; a symbolic representation of this, preceding an arranged marriage.

sway-back /ˈsweɪbak/ *noun* & *adjective*. L19.
[Back-form. from next.]
▸**A** *noun*. **1** An inward curvature of the spine or back, esp. as caused by strain or old age; the condition characterized by this, lordosis; an animal, esp. a horse, having this condition. L19.
2 VETERINARY MEDICINE. A copper deficiency syndrome affecting the nervous system of young lambs, causing paralysis. Also called ***renguerra***. M20.
▸**B** *adjective*. Having a sway-back; *fig.* concave, having a concave part. L19.

sway-backed /ˈsweɪbakt/ *adjective*. L17.
[Of Scandinavian origin: cf. Danish †*sveibaget*, *sveirygget*, Swedish dial. *svegryggad*. Cf. next.]
Having a sway-back; *fig.* concave, having a concave part.

> 🕮 H. MACINNES The stone steps made sway-backed by centuries of . . feet.

swayed /sweɪd/ *adjective*. L16.
[from SWAY *verb* + -ED¹.]
Of a horse: sway-backed.

Swazi /ˈswɑːzi/ *noun* & *adjective*. L19.
[Nguni *Mswati*, a former king of this people.]
▸**A** *noun*. Pl. **-s**, same. A member of a Bantu (predominantly Nguni) people inhabiting Swaziland and parts of eastern Transvaal in South Africa; the language of this people, forming part of the Nguni language group. L19.
▸**B** *adjective*. Of or pertaining to this people or their language. L19.

swazzle /ˈswɒz(ə)l/ *noun*. M20.
[Var. of SWATCHEL.]
A device for producing the characteristic squeaky buzzing voice of Punch in a Punch-and-Judy show, consisting of two convex metal pieces with a length of cloth stretched between them, bound together and inserted into the back of the mouth.

SWB *abbreviation*.
Short wheelbase.

sweal /swiːl/ *verb* & *noun*. Now *dial.* Also **swale** /sweɪl/.
[Old English *swǣlan* weak trans., (rel. to) Old English *swelan* strong intrans. = Middle & mod. Low German *swelen* singe, make hay, etc., Old Norse *svæla* smoke out, from Germanic base perh. also of SWELT.]
▸**A** *verb*. **1** *verb trans.* Burn; set fire to; singe, scorch. OE. ▸**b** Cause (grass etc.) to dry or wither. L18.
2 *verb intrans.* Burn, blaze; be scorched; be burning hot. ME.
3 *verb intrans.* Of a candle or wax: melt *away*; gutter; *fig.* waste away. M17.
4 *verb trans.* Melt *away*; *fig.* waste *away*. M17.
▸**B** *noun*. A blaze; a flame; the guttering of a candle. L18.

swear /swɛː/ *noun*. Now *colloq.* M17.
[from the verb.]
1 A formal or solemn oath. M17.
2 A profane oath, a swear-word. Also, a bout of swearing. L19.

swear /swɛː/ *verb*. Pa. t. **swore** /swɔː/; pa. pple **sworn** /swɔːn/.
[Old English *swerian* = Old Frisian *swaria*, *swera*, Old Saxon *swerian*, Old High German *swer(i)en* (Dutch *zweren*, German *schwören*), Old Norse *sverja*, from Germanic strong verb from base repr. also by Old Norse *svar*, *svara* answer (noun & verb), ANSWER *noun*.]
▸**I 1 a** *verb intrans.* Appeal to a god or other sacred person or thing in confirmation of the truth of a solemn declar-

ation or statement. Now usu. foll. by *by*, *on*, *upon*. **OE.** ▸†**b** *verb trans.* Appeal to (a god etc.) in confirmation of the truth of a solemn declaration or statement. **ME–E17.**

2 a *verb trans. & intrans.* Promise solemnly or on oath (*that*, *to do*). Also. with direct speech as obj. **OE.** ▸**b** *verb trans.* Promise or undertake on oath to observe or perform (something). **ME.**

3 *verb trans.* Declare or affirm solemnly the truth or sincerity of (something) (usu. foll. by *that*, *to be*); *colloq.* declare or affirm emphatically, insist, (*that*, *to be*). **OE.** ▸**b** *verb intrans.* Give evidence on oath (*against* a person). Now *rare*. **OE.** ▸**c** *verb trans.* Value on oath *at* so much. **M19.**

4 *verb trans.* Take or utter (an oath); say as an oath or expletive. **OE.**

5 *verb intrans.* Use a profane or indecent word or phrase in anger or as an expletive; use such language habitually. Also foll. by *at*. **ME.** ▸**b** *transf.* Of an animal: utter a harsh sound or succession of such sounds (as if) to express anger. *colloq.* **L17.** ▸**c** *fig.* Of a colour etc.: fail to harmonize, clash. Foll. by *at*, (*rare*) *with*. *colloq.* **L18.**

6 *verb trans.* **a** Bring into a specified condition by taking an oath or using profane or indecent language. **L16.** ▸**b** Ascribe to a person in a sworn statement. Foll. by *on*, *to*, *upon*. **M18.**

> 🕮 **1a** T. Hearne I should be forced to quit, if I did not swear. Gibbon They had sworn, by the sacred head of the emperor. Tennyson And on the book . . Miriam swore. **b** Shakes. *Lear* Now, by Apollo, King, Thou swear'st thy gods in vain. **2a** A. Carnegie Having . . sworn months previously that they would not work. W. Holtby 'I'll larn her,' swore he to himself. W. S. Churchill Cranmer swore to obey the Pope with the usual oath. D. Madden Swear that when I'm dying . . you won't stay and watch. **b** Shakes. *1 Hen. VI* Then swear allegiance to his Majesty. **3** W. Cruise Every . . affidavit . . shall be sworn before a person duly authorized. N. Coward I'm sorry, darling, I swear I didn't mean it. L. Bruce I would fill out a report form, swearing that I had tried to find work that week. W. Sheed Tate swore to me that this had never happened . . before. R. Rendell Could have sworn the old man . . gave him the ghost of a wink. **4** W. Cowper He . . mumbling, swears A bible-oath to be whate'er they please. G. Vidal Swore fierce oaths under his breath. R. Bage Damnation! swore my Lord. **5** V. Woolf Her face was expressive of furious rage, and . . she swore in Spanish. D. Bagley 'Jesus!' he said reverently and with no intention to swear. A. Price He told me to do my *effing* duty—and David only swears like that when he intends to. **6a** D. W. Jerrold Because . . your shirt wanted a button, you . . almost swear the roof off the house.

▸ **II** With personal object.

7 *verb trans.* Cause to take an oath; bind (a person) by an oath (*to* a person, course of action, etc., (*arch.*) *to do*). Now chiefly in ***swear to secrecy***, ***swear to silence***. **OE.**

8 *verb trans. spec.* Admit to a (specified) function or office by administering a formal oath. Now usu. foll. by *in*. **OE.**

> 🕮 **7** Shakes. *Temp.* I'll swear myself thy subject. A. Bell Sydney swore his father to secrecy. J. B. Hilton 'A pity you had to blurt this out to Emily.' . . 'I swore her to silence.' **8** D. Acheson The Chief Justice then swore in the President. H. Bascom He was sworn in as a Corporal and will carry that rank.

With adverbs & prepositions in specialized senses: **swear by** — *colloq.* have or express great confidence in; (see also sense 1a above). †**swear down** (*a*) silence by swearing; (*b*) call down by swearing. †**swear for** — answer for under oath. **swear off** *colloq.* (chiefly *N. Amer.*) promise to abstain from (esp. alcoholic drink). **swear out** †(*a*) abjure; (*b*) *US* obtain the issue of (a warrant for arrest) by making a charge on oath. **swear to** — (*a*) (now *rare*) promise solemnly to undertake (an action); (*b*) (usu. in neg. contexts) express assurance of the truth of (a statement).

Phrases & comb.: ***hard swearing***: see HARD *adjective, adverb, & noun*. ***swear blind***: see BLIND *adverb*. ***swear like a trooper***: see TROOPER 1. ***swear pink***: see PINK *adjective*². **swear-word** a profane or indecent word, *esp.* one uttered as an expletive.

■ **swearer** *noun* **ME.**

sweat /swɛt/ *noun.* Also (earlier) †**swote**.

[Old English *swāt* = Old Frisian, Old Saxon *swēt* (Dutch *zweet*), Old High German *sweiz* (German *Schweiss*), from Germanic from Indo-European base repr. also by Latin *sudor*; alt. in Middle English after next.]

▸ **I 1** Watery fluid excreted through the pores of the skin, esp. as a response to excessive heat, exertion, or nervousness. **OE.**

2 A condition or fit of sweating. **ME.** ▸**b** A fit of sweating caused for a medicinal purpose; a training run, *esp.* one given to a horse as before a race. Formerly also, a medicine for inducing sweating, a diaphoretic. **LME.** ▸†**c** Sweating-sickness. **L15–M17.**

3 *transf.* Something resembling sweat; moisture exuded from or deposited on a surface. **LME.**

4 An industrial process involving the exudation, evaporation, or deposit of moisture. **L16.**

5 A gambling game played with three dice and a cloth marked with figures. *US.* **M19.**

6 In *pl.* A sweatshirt; sweat pants; a sweatsuit. *colloq.* (orig. *US*). **M20.**

> 🕮 **1** W. Golding The heat hit him . . and sweat streamed down his face. S. Trott Finishing a run, sweat running down his torso. **2** P. Bowles Awoke in a sweat with the hot . . sun pouring over her. A. Cohen Arnold . . had broken out in a sweat. **3** M. Twain Solid limestone that was dewy with a cold sweat.

▸ **II** *fig.* **7** Hard work, toil, effort; *esp.* a laborious task or undertaking. Now *colloq.* **OE.**

8 A state of anxiety. *colloq.* **E18.**

> 🕮 **7** W. S. Maugham Those critical works of mine were an awful sweat. *Target Gun* Helping to run the meeting was a bit of a sweat. **8** J. Gardner Thought I'd save you the sweat of wondering who was doing what to whom.

▸†**III 9** Blood; *spec.* the lifeblood. **OE–E16.**

Phrases: ***bloody sweat***: see BLOODY *adjective & adverb*. **by the sweat of one's brow** by one's own hard work. **cold sweat** sweat(ing) due to nervousness rather than to heat or exertion. **no sweat** *colloq.* no trouble; no need to worry. ***old sweat***: see OLD *adjective*.

Comb.: **sweat-band** a band of absorbent material lining a hat or worn round the head or wrist to soak up sweat; **sweat-bath** a steam or hot-air bath; **sweat-bee** any of various small solitary bees of the families Halictidae and Andrenidae, which may drink sweat from the skin; **sweat-box** (*a*) *slang* a narrow prison cell; (*b*) a box in which hides etc. are sweated; (*c*) *transf.* a heated compartment in which sweating is induced with the aim of weight loss; **sweat cooling** ENGINEERING a form of cooling in which the coolant is passed through a porous wall and evenly distributed over the surface, which is cooled by its evaporation; **sweat equity** *US slang* an interest in a property earned by a tenant in return for labour towards upkeep or renovation; **sweat fly** a common woodland fly, *Hydrotaea irritans*, which sips the sweat of humans and livestock; **sweat gland** ANATOMY each of the numerous minute coiled tubular glands just beneath the skin which secrete sweat; **sweat-hog** *US slang* a difficult student singled out for special instruction; **sweat-house** (*a*) a hut etc. in which steam or hot-air baths are taken; *spec.* a sweat lodge; (*b*) a building in which hides etc. are sweated; **sweat lodge** a sweat-house, made esp. with natural materials and used (orig. by N. American Indians) for ritual purification; **sweat pants** (chiefly *N. Amer.*) loose thick knitted trousers worn as leisurewear or by athletes before or after exercise; **sweat-pore** ANATOMY each of the pores of the skin through which sweat glands secrete sweat; **sweat-rag** *colloq.* a cloth used for wiping off sweat; **sweat rug**: put on a horse after exercise; **sweatshirt** a loose long-sleeved thick cotton shirt, worn as leisurewear or by athletes before or after exercise; **sweatshop** a workshop where sweated labour is used; **sweatsuit**: consisting of a sweatshirt and sweat pants.

¶ Variant form *swote* obsolete after **M16**; form *sweat* recorded from **ME.**

■ **sweatful** *adjective* (chiefly *poet.*) (of work) inducing or accompanied by sweat, laborious, distressing **E17.** **sweatless** *adjective* (*rare*) without sweat; *fig.* indolent, idle: **E17.**

sweat /swɛt/ *verb.* Pa. t. **sweated**, (now *US & dial.*) **sweat**; pa. pple **sweated**, †**sweat**.

[Old English *swǣtan* = Middle Low German, Middle Dutch *swēten* (Dutch *zweeten*), Old High German *sweizzen* roast (German *schweissen* weld, fuse), from Germanic verb from base of prec.]

▸ **I 1** *verb intrans.* Excrete sweat through the pores of the skin. **OE.**

2 *verb trans.* Exude through the pores of the skin, as or like sweat. **OE.** ▸**b** *fig.* Get rid of (as) by sweating. Also foll. by *away*, *out*. **OE.** ▸**c** Foll. by *off*: remove or lose (weight etc.) by strenuous exercise. **L19.**

3 *verb trans.* Cause to sweat; *spec.* give (a horse) a run for exercise. **L16.** ▸**b** Interrogate (a prisoner etc.) closely; extort a confession from (a prisoner) by torture or close interrogation. *slang.* **M18.**

4 *verb trans.* Soak or stain with sweat. Now chiefly *N. Amer.* **L16.**

> 🕮 **1** G. Vidal Though the room was not hot, I was sweating nervously. **2b** J. Snow I . . sweated the drink . . out of my system. J. M. Coetzee You must sweat the fever out. **sweat blood** (*a*) exert oneself to the utmost; (*b*) be extremely anxious. ***sweat one's guts out***: see GUT *noun*. **c** T. O'Brien Sweat off the fat rolls, turn lean. **3** W. van T. Clark Cold as it was, the climb had sweated him.

▸ **II** *fig.* **5** *verb intrans.* Work hard, toil, labour. Freq. foll. by *to do*. **OE.** ▸**b** *verb trans.* Exact hard work from; *spec.* (chiefly as SWEATED) employ (labour, workers) at very low wages for long hours under poor conditions. **E19.**

6 a *verb intrans. & trans.* (with *it*). Suffer anxiety or distress. Now *colloq.* **LME.** ▸**b** *verb trans.* Foll. by *out*: await or endure anxiously. *colloq.* **L19.** ▸**c** *verb intrans.* Foll. by *on*: await (an event or person) anxiously. *slang* (chiefly *Austral.*). **E20.**

7 *verb trans.* **a** Work hard to get, make, or produce. (Foll. by *out*.) **L16.** ▸**b** NAUTICAL Set or hoist (a sail etc.) taut, so as to increase speed. **L19.**

8 *verb intrans.* Undergo severe punishment or suffering. Freq. in ***sweat for it***, suffer the penalty. Now *rare* or *obsolete*. **E17.**

> 🕮 **5** *Ink* The administrative side is sweating to make this . . happen. *Golf World* Players who . . sweated long and hard . . to secure a spot among the lower reaches. **6a** J. Wainwright Put Barker in the dock and . . you could have made him sweat. D. Mamet Don't sweat it, George . . . You've nothing to hide. **b** D. Fletcher I had no intention of telling Hugo . . . Let him sweat that one out. **7** Byron Sweating plays so middling, bad were better.

▸ **III** *transf.* **9** *verb intrans.* Exude or condense moisture in the form of drops on a surface, *spec.* as part of a manufacturing process. **OE.** ▸**b** *verb trans.* Cause to exude moisture in this way; *spec.* (*a*) subject (hides or tobacco) to fermentation in manufacturing; (*b*) heat (meat, vegetables, etc.) in a pan with fat or water, in order to extract the juices. **L17.** ▸**c** *verb trans.* METALLURGY. Subject (metal) to partial melting, esp. to fasten or join by solder without a soldering iron. **L19.**

10 *verb trans.* Exude (moisture etc.) in drops like sweat. **LME.**

11 *verb intrans.* Ooze *out* like sweat. **LME.**

12 *verb trans.* Lighten (a gold coin) by friction or attrition. *rare.* **L18.**

13 *verb trans.* Deprive or rob of something; rob (a vessel) of some of its contents. *arch. slang.* **E19.**

> 🕮 **9** *Homes & Gardens* Lay the fish . . in the pan . . and let them sweat in their own juices. *Amateur Gardening* Fruit . . put into store . . starts to sweat. **b** J. Grigson Sweat the onion . . in a little olive oil.

■ **sweatingly** *adverb* (*rare*) †(*a*) as in the form of sweat; (*b*) so as to cause sweating: **L16.**

sweated /ˈswɛtɪd/ *ppl adjective.* **M17.**

[from prec. + -ED¹.]

1 That has been sweated. **M17.**

2 *spec.* (Of labour etc.) employed at very low wages for long hours under poor conditions; (of goods) produced under such conditions of employment. **L19.**

sweater /ˈswɛtə/ *noun.* **LME.**

[from SWEAT *verb* + -ER¹.]

1 A person who sweats; *spec.* a person who employs workers at low wages under poor conditions. **LME.**

2 A medicine that induces sweating; a diaphoretic. *rare.* **L17.**

3 †**a** In *pl.* Clothes worn during exercise by a person or a horse in order to induce profuse sweating. **E–M19.** ▸**b** Orig., a woollen vest or jersey worn during exercise in order to help weight loss, later also worn before or after exercise for warmth. Now chiefly, any jersey or pullover, esp. a heavy woollen one, worn for warmth as an informal garment. **L19.**

4 A laborious task or occupation. *arch. colloq.* **M19.**

Comb.: **sweater girl** *N. Amer. colloq.* a young woman who wears tight-fitting sweaters; **sweater-shirt** (*a*) *US* a knitted garment that may be worn as a sweater or as a shirt; (*b*) = ***sweatshirt*** s.v. SWEAT *noun*.

■ **sweatered** *adjective* wearing a sweater **E20.**

sweating /ˈswɛtɪŋ/ *verbal noun.* **ME.**

[from SWEAT *verb* + -ING¹.]

The action of SWEAT *verb*; an instance of this.

Comb.: **sweating-house** = ***sweat-house*** (a) s.v. SWEAT *noun*; **sweating pen** *Austral.* a pen in which sheep are kept (formerly, to sweat so as to soften the wool) before shearing; **sweating-room** (*a*) a room in which steam or hot-air baths are taken; (*b*) a room in which cheeses are placed to remove excess moisture; **sweating-sickness** a fever characterized by profuse sweating and freq. fatal (now chiefly *Hist.* with ref. to epidemics of various diseases in England in the 15th and 16th cents.); ***sweating-tub***: see TUB *noun*¹ 1b.

sweaty /ˈswɛti/ *adjective.* **LME.**

[from SWEAT *noun* + -Y¹.]

1 Causing sweat by being excessively hot or laborious. **LME.** ▸**b** Severe, demanding. *colloq.* **E20.**

2 Moist, stained, or odorous with sweat. **E16.** ▸**b** *transf.* Full of or exuding moisture like sweat. **E17.**

3 Of or consisting of sweat. **M18.**

■ **sweatily** *adverb* **E19.** **sweatiness** *noun* **L17.**

sweddle *noun, verb* see SWADDLE *noun, verb*.

Swede /swiːd/ *noun & adjective.* In sense A.2 now **s-**. **E17.**

[Middle Low German, Middle Dutch *Swēde* (Dutch *Zweed*) prob. from Old Norse *Svíþjóð* people of the Swedes, Sweden, from *Svíar* Swedes + *þjóð* people.]

▸ **A** *noun.* **1** A native or inhabitant of Sweden, a country occupying the eastern part of the Scandinavian peninsula. **E17.**

2 The purple- or yellow-skinned, usu. yellow-fleshed, root (i.e. the swollen hypocotyl and stem-base) of a variety of rape, *Brassica napus* var. *napobrassica*, which resembles a turnip but is larger, with a rigid neck, and which is used as a vegetable and as cattle-food; the plant from which this is obtained. Also called ***rutabaga***. **E19.**

Comb.: **Swede-basher** *slang* a farmworker; a rustic; **Swede turnip** = sense 2 above.

▸ **B** *adjective.* = SWEDISH *adjective*. Chiefly *Canad.* **M20.**

Swede saw a type of saw with a bowlike tubular frame and many cutting teeth.

Swedenborgian /swiːd(ə)nˈbɔːdʒɪən, -gɪən/ *noun & adjective.* **L18.**

[from *Swedenborg* (see below) + -IAN.]

▸ **A** *noun.* A follower or adherent of the Swedish philosopher Emanuel Swedenborg (1688–1772) or his religious teachings. **L18.**

▶ **B** *adjective.* Of or pertaining to Swedenborg, his teachings, or his followers. E19.
■ **Swedenborgianism** *noun* E19.

swedge /swɛdʒ/ *noun & verb.* M17.
[Var.]
▶ **A** *noun.* A smith's tool used in making horseshoes; = SWAGE *noun* 2b. M17.
▶ **B** *verb trans.* = SWAGE *verb*[2]. M19.

Swedish /ˈswiːdɪʃ/ *noun & adjective.* E17.
[from *Sweden* or SWEDE *noun*: see -ISH[1].]
▶ **A** *noun.* The North Germanic language of Sweden. E17.
▶ **B** *adjective.* Of or pertaining to Sweden in Scandinavia, its people, or its language. M17.
Swedish drill, **Swedish exercises**, **Swedish gymnastics** a system of therapeutic muscular exercises. **Swedish ivy** a southern African evergreen labiate plant, *Plectranthus oertendahlii*, grown as a house-plant. **Swedish massage** a system of massage first devised in Sweden. **Swedish masseur**, (fem.) **Swedish masseuse** a person who provides Swedish massage (professionally). **Swedish modern** = *Danish modern* s.v. DANISH *adjective*. **Swedish nightingale** the thrush nightingale, *Luscinia luscinia*; (occas.) the redwing, *Turdus iliacus*. **Swedish turnip** = SWEDE *noun* 2. **Swedish** VALLHUND. **Swedish whitebeam** a small Scandinavian tree, *Sorbus intermedia*, resembling the whitebeam but with lobed leaves.

swee /swiː/ *noun. S. Afr.* M19.
[Imit.: cf. Afrikaans *swie*.]
In full ***swee waxbill***. A waxbill, *Estrilda melanotis*, of tropical Africa, which has greenish plumage with a bright red rump. Also called ***yellow-bellied waxbill***.

Sweeney /ˈswiːni/ *noun. slang.* M20.
[from *Sweeney* Todd, a fictitious barber who murdered his customers, in a play by George Dibdin Pitt (1799–1855).]
1 A member or *the* members of a police flying squad. *rhyming slang.* M20.
2 (A nickname for) a barber. M20.

sweeny /ˈswiːni/ *noun. US.* Also **swinny** /ˈswɪni/. E19.
[Prob. from German dial. *Schweine* emaciation, atrophy.]
Atrophy of the shoulder-muscles in the horse.
■ **sweenied** *adjective* suffering from sweeny M19.

sweep /swiːp/ *noun.* L15.
[from the verb. Cf. SWIPE *noun*.]
▶ **I** An apparatus that sweeps or has a sweeping motion.
†**1** A broom, a mop. *rare.* Only in L15.
2 A long pole mounted as a lever for raising buckets of water from a well; *gen.* any lever. M16. ▸**b** A long oar used to propel a ship, barge, etc. when becalmed, or to assist in steering. L18.
3 A ballista. Long *obsolete* exc. HERALDRY. L16.
4 A sail of a windmill. M17.
5 An instrument for drawing curves with a large radius, a beam-compass. Also, a profile cutter. L17.
6 A length of cable used in mine-laying etc. for sweeping the bottom of the sea. L18.
7 FOUNDING. A movable templet used in moulding with loam. M19.
▶ **II** An act of sweeping.
8 a An act of clearing up or away. Now only in ***make a clean sweep*** below. M16. ▸**b** Victory in all the games in a contest etc. by one team or competitor, or the winning of all the places in a single event (chiefly *N. Amer.*). Also, (in the game of cassino) the removal of all the cards on the board by pairing or combining them; (in whist) the winning of all the tricks in a hand. E19. ▸**c** An act of passing over an area in order to capture or destroy the occupants of it, *spec.* a sortie by an aircraft. M19.
9 A continuous and rapid or forceful movement (also foll. by adverb); *fig.* an action or process regarded as such a movement. E17. ▸**b** A forcibly moving body of water. E19.
10 A movement describing a continuous curve or a more or less circular path. L17. ▸**b** ELECTRONICS. A steady movement across the screen of a cathode-ray tube of the spot produced by the electron beam; the moving spot itself, the line it generates. E20. ▸**c** ELECTRONICS. A steady, usu. repeated, change in the magnitude or frequency of a voltage or other quantity between definite limits. M20.
11 An act of wielding a tool or weapon, swinging an arm, etc., so as to describe a circle or arc. E18. ▸**b** CRICKET. An attacking stroke made on the front foot from a half-kneeling position, in which the bat is brought across the body to hit the ball square or backward of square on the leg side. L19.
12 A survey of an area (esp. of the night sky) made by moving an instrument or the direction of gaze in an arc or circle, or by fixing it while an observed object moves in this way. L18. ▸**b** A comprehensive search, *spec.* for electronic listening or recording devices. *colloq.* M20. ▸**c** In *pl.* exc. *attrib.* A regular survey of the relative popularity ratings of local television stations, carried out to determine advertising rates; a period during which such a survey is done. *US.* L20.
13 An act of sweeping with a broom. Also foll. by adverb. E19.
14 The action or an act of something brushing or passing along or over a surface; the sound of this. E19.

9 A. MARSH-CALDWELL The noiseless sweep by of the large white owl. CARLYLE The first sweep of royal fury being past. U. SINCLAIR The wind had full sweep. **10** S. CRANE The sweep of the Allies . . around the French right. M. WESLEY A heron flapping its way with lazy sweeps. **11** R. MACAULAY It . . made bold sweeps with the brush. J. M. COETZEE With great sweeps he was gesturing from horizon to horizon. **12** A. MACLEAN Smith made a swift 360° sweep of his horizon. **14** GEO. ELIOT The faint sweep of woollen garments.

▶ **III** A curve or curved object.
15 a SHIPBUILDING. A curved line used in a plan to indicate the shape of the timbers; the curve of a ship's timbers. *obsolete* exc. *Hist.* E17. ▸**b** ARCHITECTURE. The continuously curved part of an arch; any curved section of masonry in a building. L17. ▸**c** *gen.* A curved or flowing line or form; a curve. E18. ▸**d** A curved drive leading to a house. L18.

15a *New Scientist* 17th-century hulls were generated by . . circular arcs, known as sweeps. **c** SIR W. SCOTT The . . downward sweep of his long-descending beard. *Country Life* Incorporating such . . details as sweep, surface scars and knots when describing softwoods.

▶ **IV** Range, extent.
16 The reach or range of movement of a thing, esp. in a circular or curving course. L17.
17 A wide (esp. curving) stretch or expanse of land, water, etc. M18. ▸**b** A series *of* buildings. Formerly also, a suite (*of* rooms). M18.
18 The range or scope of something abstract. L18.
19 AERONAUTICS. = ***sweepback*** s.v. SWEEP *verb*. E20.

16 G. L. CRAIK From the minutest disclosures of the microscope to beyond the farthest sweep of the telescope. **17** M. AYRTON The large window . . gives me a panorama of the sweep of the bay. T. O'BRIEN Looking out over the sweeps of land. **18** M. CONEY Her vendetta was beginning to look small against the sweep of Time and events.

▶ **V** Something swept up.
†**20** The crop of hay raised from a meadow. *rare.* Only in L17.
21 *sing.* & in *pl.* Gold and silver dust swept up from jewellers' workshops etc. L18. ▸**b** *gen.* Anything which is swept up, in, or along. M19.
22 = SWEEPSTAKE 3. *colloq.* M19.
▶ **VI** A person who or thing which sweeps.
23 A person whose business is to remove soot from chimneys. Earliest in ***CHIMNEY-sweep***. E18. ▸**b** A disreputable person. *dial. & arch. slang.* M19.
24 Any of several scaly-finned Australasian marine fishes of the genus *Scorpis* or the family Scorpidae. M19.
Phrases: **at one sweep**, **at a sweep** with a single blow or stroke. ***Irish Sweep***: see IRISH *adjective*. **make a clean sweep (of)** (*a*) abolish or get rid of (something) completely; (*b*) win all the prizes in (a contest etc.). **the Sweeps** (a nickname for) the Rifle Brigade.

sweep /swiːp/ *verb.* Pa. t. & pple **swept** /swɛpt/. Also (earlier) †**swope**, pa. t. freq. †**swoped**, pa. pple †**swopen**.
[Old English *swāpan* (pa. t. *swēop*) = Old Frisian *swēpa*, Old High German *sweifan* set in circular motion, wind (German *schweifen* sweep in a curve, rove), Old Norse *sveipa*, from Germanic. Cf. SWIPE *verb*.]
▶ **I 1** *verb trans.* Remove (as) with a broom or brush by repeated friction upon a surface. Foll. by *away*, *off*, etc. OE. ▸**b** CURLING. = SOOP 2. E19.
2 *verb trans.* Drive together or into a place or collect up (as) with a broom. Freq. foll. by *up*. ME. ▸**b** Gather up in one action. Chiefly in ***sweep the stakes*** (cf. earlier SWEEPSTAKE). L16. ▸**c** Win every award, event, or place in (a contest). *N. Amer.* M20.
3 a *verb trans.* Cut *down* or *off* with a vigorous swinging stroke. Now *rare.* LME. ▸**b** *verb trans. & intrans.* CRICKET. Hit (the ball) with a sweep. E20.
4 *verb trans.* **a** Remove forcibly or as at one blow from a position, rank, etc.; abolish swiftly. Usu. foll. by *away*. M16. ▸**b** Drive or carry away or along with force and speed; *fig.* (usu. in *pass.*) affect powerfully. Foll. by *along*, *away*, *from*, *off*. L16.
5 *verb trans.* Move or remove with a forcible continuous action; *esp.* push *aside*, *away*, *back*, etc.; *fig.* dismiss or dispose of curtly or lightly, brush *aside*. L16.
6 *verb trans.* **a** Carry or trail along in a stately manner. *rare.* L16. ▸**b** Move or draw over and in contact with a surface. E19.
7 *verb intrans. & trans.* Propel (a barge etc.) with sweeps. L18.
8 *verb trans.* Move *round* with speed and force, or over a wide extent. M19.

1 R. BAGOT Spider-webs . . which we have swept away. **2** T. WILLIAMS They rush to the poker table and sweep up their winnings. R. ROBINSON Sweeping the broken glass into the gutter. **b** DRYDEN Ames-Ace, that swept my Stakes away. **3** SIR W. SCOTT I would rather you swept my head off with your long sword. **4a** *European Investor* To sweep away the former dominance of the Treasury. **b** J. BUCHAN Barbara and Mary . . swept the child off with them. H. CARPENTER Other beach houses having been swept away . . in a storm. L. WHISTLER She was . . likely . . in the first excitement of his ardour, to be swept away. P. MAILLOUX Swept along by the truth of his own fancies. **5** A. J. WILSON She impatiently swept off the snowy lemon leaves. S. E. WHITE Miss Bishop turned to the piano, sweeping aside her . . draperies as she sat. M. DAS He . . swept his . . hair back from his forehead.

▶ **II 9** *verb trans.* Pass a broom or brush over the surface of (something) so as to remove small loose particles; clean (as) with a broom or brush. Also foll. by *down*, *out*, *up*, or with *clean* as compl. OE. ▸**b** *verb intrans.* Clean a floor, room, etc., in this way. OE. ▸**c** *verb trans. fig.* Examine (a building, telephone line, etc.) for electronic listening or recording devices. *colloq.* M20.
10 *verb trans.* Pass over the surface of (something) in the manner of a broom; move over and in contact with; brush; *poet.* produce music from (strings, a stringed instrument), produce (music) from a stringed instrument. E16. ▸**b** *verb trans. & intrans.* (with *for*). Drag (a river-bed etc.) in search of something submerged. M17. ▸**c** ENTOMOLOGY. Drag a net over the surface of (foliage etc.) to catch insects. E19.
†**11** *verb trans.* Wipe. M16–M17.
12 *verb trans.* Move swiftly and evenly over or along the surface of; *esp.* (*fig.*) affect swiftly and widely, *spec.* achieve widespread popularity throughout. L16.
13 *verb trans.* Clear *of* something by vigorous or violent action. E17.
14 *verb trans.* Direct the eyes or an optical instrument to every part of (an area) in succession; survey or view the whole extent of; direct (one's gaze or eyes) at something in this way. M18.
15 *verb trans.* Chiefly MILITARY. ▸**a** Of artillery: have within range. M18. ▸**b** Range over (an area of sea or land), esp. to destroy, ravage, or capture. L18.

9 A. HIGGINS Imogen swept the desk clear with the heel of her hand. C. MUNGOSHI Zakeo loved . . sweeping out the room. B. CHATWIN He chopped wood, swept the street and the synagogue, and acted as watchdog. **b** J. G. FARRELL Sweeping rather indiscriminately with . . twigs as a broom. **10** R. CAMPBELL The branches . . descended to sweep the ground. K. MOORE The girl wore a red velvet dress that swept the floor. **12** W. CATHER A quick pink swept over her face. D. BOGARDE She felt a sense of despair sweep her. *New York Review of Books* His . . children died in the epidemics then sweeping Russia. **13** C. THIRLWALL The country was completely swept of every thing valuable. **14** A. C. CLARKE Loren swept his eye across the audience. *Out of Town* Sweep the sea with a pair of binoculars. **15a** *Times* An area swept by machine-gun . . fire. **b** R. COLLIER A few day and night fighters, sweeping the raiders' normal routes.

▶ **III 16** *verb intrans.* Move with a strong or swift even motion; move rapidly along over a surface or area, esp. with violence or destructive effect. Usu. foll. by adverb. OE.
17 *verb intrans.* Move or walk in a stately manner; move along majestically. LME. ▸**b** Trail *along* or *after*. M17.
18 *verb trans.* Trace, mark out, (a line, esp. a wide curve, or an area). M17.
19 *verb intrans.* Move continuously in a long stretch or over a wide extent, esp. in a curve. E18.
20 *verb intrans.* Esp. of a geographical feature: extend continuously over a long or wide stretch. L18.
21 *verb trans.* Perform (esp. a curtsy) with an expansive movement; take *off* (one's hat) with such a movement. M19.
22 *verb trans.* FOUNDING. Form (a mould) with a sweep. L19.

16 H. ROTH Icy horror swept up and down his spine. E. MANNIN Occasionally a car swept past them, obliterating everything in dense clouds of white dust. R. INGALLS The official swept forward towards a door at the far end of the hall. P. DALLY Hurricanes . . swept in from the Atlantic. M. FORSTER Piedmontese troops were said to be sweeping south. **17** A. TROLLOPE Having so spoken, she swept out of the room. **19** SCOTT FITZGERALD The boat . . was sweeping in an immense . . circle of spray. **20** R. WARNER Meadows gently swept downwards to the river. A. BURGESS The veranda . . swept, in a huge curve, round the entire flat.

Phrases: **sweep a person off his or her feet** (usu. in *pass.*) affect a person with powerful emotion, esp. love. **sweep a thing under the carpet**, **sweep a thing under the rug** *fig.* seek to conceal a thing in the hope that others will overlook or forget it. **sweep the board** (*a*) win all the money in a gambling game; (*b*) win all possible prizes etc.
Comb.: **sweepback** AERONAUTICS the degree to which an aircraft wing is angled backwards with respect to the fuselage; the property of a wing of being so angled; **sweep-chimney** (*obsolete* exc. *dial.*) a chimney-sweep; **sweep-forward** AERONAUTICS the degree to which an aircraft wing is angled forwards with respect to the fuselage; the property of a wing of being so angled; **sweep hand**

= *sweep second-hand* below; **sweep-net** a large fishing net enclosing a wide area; **sweep second-hand** a second-hand on a clock or watch, mounted on the same arbor as the other hands; **sweep-wire** a submerged wire towed over a minefield by a minesweeper.

■ **sweepage** *noun* (now *rare*) (*a*) matter, esp. refuse, that is swept up; (*b*) grass etc. that is mown in a field: E17.

sweep /swi:p/ *adverb*. L17.
[from the verb.]
With a sweeping movement.

sweeper /ˈswi:pə/ *noun*. LME.
[from SWEEP *verb* + -ER[1].]
†1 A broom for sweeping out an oven. LME–L16.
2 A person who sweeps, or who cleans something by sweeping. Also foll. by *of*. LME.
3 A person who or a vessel which sweeps for something under water; *spec.* a minesweeper. L18.
4 A machine for sweeping a floor, carpet, road, etc. M19. ▸**b** (A person operating) an electronic device for detecting listening or recording apparatus. *colloq.* M20.
5 A tree growing close to and overhanging a stream. Also, a drifting tree. *N. Amer.* L19.
6 CRICKET. A batsman who sweeps. M20.
7 SOCCER & HOCKEY. A defending player positioned close to the goalkeeper and playing across the width of the field. M20.
8 ELECTRONICS. A circuit or device which causes a regular sweep of a cathode-ray beam. *colloq.* M20.
9 In motorcycle or bicycle racing: a bend or turn negotiated with a controlled sideways skid of the rear wheel; such a skid. *slang.* L20.

sweeping /ˈswi:pɪŋ/ *noun*. LME.
[from SWEEP *verb* + -ING[1].]
1 The action of SWEEP *verb*. LME.
2 In *pl.* & †*sing.* Something swept up, esp. dust or refuse. LME. ▸**b** *fig.* In *pl.* The lowest or most contemptible people *of* a place, society, etc. L16.

sweeping /ˈswi:pɪŋ/ *adjective*. L16.
[from SWEEP *verb* + -ING[2].]
1 That sweeps. L16.
2 *fig.* Having a wide scope; wide in range or effect; involving generalization, taking no account of particular cases or exceptions. L18.

> 2 *Times* The state of emergency . . gives sweeping powers of arrest. *Independent* I make this sweeping assertion on the basis of . . experience.

■ **sweepingly** *adverb* E19. **sweepingness** *noun* M19.

sweepstake /ˈswi:psteɪk/ *noun*. Also **-stakes** /-steɪks/. L15.
[from SWEEP *verb* + STAKE *noun*[2].]
†1 A person who takes the whole of the stakes in a gambling game; *fig.* a person who takes or appropriates everything. L15–L17.
†2 The action of sweeping or clearing everything away, total removal. Chiefly in *make sweepstake*. L15–M17.
3 A race (esp. a horse-race) or contest in which the competitors' stakes are taken by the winner or winners as a prize; the prize or prizes offered in such a race; *transf.* a betting transaction or a lottery in which the participants' stakes are given to the winner. L18.
3 *Irish Sweepstake*: see IRISH *adjective*.

sweepy /ˈswi:pi/ *adjective*. Chiefly *poet.* L17.
[from SWEEP *noun* or *verb* + -Y[1].]
Characterized by sweeping movement or form.

sweer /swɪə, swə:/ *adjective*. *Scot. & north.*
[Old English *swǣr(e)*, *swār* = Old Frisian *swēre*, Old Saxon *swār*, Middle Low German *swēr*, *swār*, Middle Dutch *swær*, *swāre* (Dutch *zwaar*), Old High German *suāri*, *suār* (German *schwer*), Old Norse *svárr*, Gothic *swērs*, from Germanic.]
†1 Grievous, oppressive. OE–ME.
†2 Oppressed in mind, grieved, sad. OE–LME.
3 Disinclined for effort; indolent, lazy. OE.
4 Reluctant, unwilling, disinclined, (*to do*). ME.
■ **sweerness** *noun* (*a*) indolence, laziness; (*b*) unwillingness, disinclination: OE. **sweert** *adjective* (*Scot.*) = SWEER 3, 4 E19.

sweet /swi:t/ *noun*. ME.
[from the adjective.]
1 **a** That which is sweet to the taste; something having a sweet taste. Chiefly *poet.* ME. ▸**b** A sweet food or drink. LME. ▸**c** In *pl.* Syrup added to wine or other liquor to sweeten and improve its flavour; wine etc. thus sweetened. L17. ▸**d** *spec.* A sweet dish forming a course of a meal; such a course; (a) pudding, (a) dessert. Orig. usu. in *pl.* M19. ▸**e** A small piece of confectionery, esp. in lozenge or drop form, made of sugar with flavouring, chocolate, etc. Cf. earlier SWEETIE, SWEETMEAT. M19. ▸**f** In *pl.* Drugs, *esp.* amphetamines. *US slang.* M20.
2 A beloved person; darling, sweetheart. Freq. as a form of address. ME.
3 Sweetness of taste, sweet taste. *rare.* ME.
4 That which is pleasant to the mind or feelings, the pleasant part *of* something; (a) pleasure, (a) delight. Now freq. in *pl.* ME.
5 **a** Sweetness of smell, fragrance. In *pl.*, sweet scents or perfumes. *poet.* LME. ▸**b** In *pl.* Substances having a sweet smell; fragrant flowers or herbs. Now *rare.* E17.
6 **a** A sweet sound. *poet. rare.* L16. ▸**b** In *pl.* A woman's breasts. *poet.* E19.

> 1d J. BETJEMAN Is trifle sufficient for sweet? **e** *boiled sweet*: see BOILED *adjective*. 2 F. L. BARCLAY Why, what is the matter, Sweet? 4 G. VILLIERS To waste the sweets of life, so quickly gone.

Comb.: **sweetshop** a (usu. small) shop selling sweets as its main item; **sweet trolley**: for carrying a selection of cold sweet dishes offered in a restaurant.

sweet /swi:t/ *adjective & adverb*.
[Old English *swēte* = Old Frisian *swēte*, Old Saxon *swōti* (Dutch *zoet*), Old High German *s(w)uozi* (German *süss*), Old Norse *sœtr*, from Germanic from Indo-European word repr. by Sanskrit *svādu*, Greek *hēdus*, Latin *suavis*.]
▶ **A** *adjective*. 1 Pleasing to the sense of taste; *spec.* having or designating the pleasant flavour characteristic of sugar, honey, and many ripe fruits. Opp. *bitter*, *sour*. OE.
2 Having or designating a pleasant smell, as of roses or perfume; fragrant. OE. ▸†**b** *spec.* Perfumed, scented. L16–M17.
3 Of food etc.: fresh, wholesome; not acidic through fermentation; not stale or rotten; (of butter) fresh and unsalted. OE. ▸**b** Formerly (CHEMISTRY etc.), free from corrosive salt, acid, etc. Now (of petroleum, coal, etc.), free from sulphur compounds, *esp.* hydrogen sulphide or alkyl mercaptans. Opp. *sour*. M17.
4 Having, producing, or designating a pleasant sound; melodious, harmonious. OE. ▸**b** Of or designating music (esp. jazz) played at a steady tempo without improvisation. Orig. & chiefly *US*. E20.
5 Pleasing in general; gratifying, agreeable, delightful; attractive or lovely in appearance. Now chiefly *literary*. OE. ▸**b** Pretty, charming; endearing, attractive. *colloq.* L18. ▸**c** As an intensive in phrases meaning 'nothing at all', as *sweet nothing*, *sweet* FANNY ADAMS. *slang.* E20.
6 Dearly loved or prized, precious; beloved, dear. Freq. as an affectionate or (*arch.*) respectful form of address. OE. ▸**b** One's own; particular, individual, pet. Chiefly *iron.* Freq. in *one's (own) sweet life*, *one's (own) sweet self*, *one's (own) sweet time*, *one's (own) sweet way*, etc. E17.
7 Of a person, action, mood, etc.: good-natured, affectionate, amiable; kind, obliging, thoughtful. OE.
8 **a** Of weather etc.: warm, mild. Of land, soil, etc.: rich, fertile. LME. ▸†**b** ART. Delicate, soft. Cf. SWEETEN 5b. Only in M17. ▸**c** Easily managed or dealt with; working, moving, or performed easily or smoothly. L17.
9 Fine, in order, ready. Freq. in *she's sweet*, all is well. *Austral. slang.* L19.

> 1 T. THOMSON A sweet taste, not unlike that of liquorice. I. MCEWAN No sweet things to eat or drink, no chocolate, no lemonade. 2 DICKENS The rich, sweet smell of the hayricks. H. KELLER The air is sweet with the perfume of jasmines, heliotropes and roses. 3 R. BROOKE Is the water sweet and cool . . above the pool? 5 M. E. BRADDON Sweeter to you to help others than to be happy yourself. S. TROTT Life! I thought. How sweet it is! **b** *Punch* Do look at this sweet little monkey on the organ! I. MCEWAN Caroline said: 'Isn't it sweet when men are shy?' 6 SHAKES. *1 Hen. VI* Thy life to me is sweet. TENNYSON My own sweet Alice, we must die. M. TWAIN Go to thy rest, sweet sir. **b** H. MACINNES Katie has complicated everything in her own sweet way. 7 SCOTT FITZGERALD Be sweet to your mother at Xmas. E. J. HOWARD It was sweet of you to take them all. 8c *Times* The engine is . . more responsive and sweet than its predecessor.

Phrases: **be sweet on** *colloq.* †(*a*) behave affectionately or gallantly towards; (*b*) be enamoured of or infatuated with. **keep a person sweet** keep a person well-disposed towards oneself, esp. by deference or bribery. *make sweet music*: see MUSIC *noun*. *she's sweet*: see sense 9 above. *short and sweet*: see SHORT *adjective*. *sweet as a nut*: see NUT *noun*.
▶ **B** *adverb*. Sweetly. ME.
Special collocations & comb.: **Sweet Adeline** /ˈadɪlʌɪn/ *noun & verb* (*US*) [title of a popular close harmony song] (*a*) *noun pl.* a group or organization of female barber-shop singers; (*b*) *verb intrans.* (of women) sing in barber-shop style. **sweet Alice** *dial. & colloq.* sweet alyssum, *Lobularia maritima*. *sweet alison*, *sweet alyssum*: see ALYSSUM 2. **sweet-and-sour** *adjective & noun* (*a*) = *sour-sweet* s.v. SOUR *adjective*; (*b*) (food, a dish) cooked in a sauce containing sugar and vinegar or lemon etc. **sweetback (man)** *US slang* a male lover, a ladies' man; a pimp. **sweet-bag** *Hist.* a small bag or sachet filled with a scented or aromatic substance, used for perfuming the air, clothes, etc. *sweet basil*: see BASIL *noun*[1] 1. **sweet bay** (*a*) the bay tree, *Laurus nobilis*; (*b*) a magnolia with aromatic leaves, *Magnolia virginiana*, of swamps in the US. **sweetbread** the thymus gland (or, rarely, the pancreas) of an animal, esp. as used for food. **sweet bread** †(*a*) unleavened bread; (*b*) (chiefly *Scot. & dial.*) (a) sweet-tasting cake or pastry; (*c*) *Canad. dial.* bread containing molasses and raisins prepared esp. at Christmas. *sweet-brier*: see BRIER *noun*[1] 1. **sweet broom** *W. Indies* a tropical weed of the figwort family, *Scoparia dulcis*. **sweet butter** a type of unsalted butter made from fresh pasteurized cream. *sweet calamus*: see CALAMUS 2. *sweet cassava*: see CASSAVA 1. **sweet cherry** a type of cherry eaten as dessert, the fruit of *Prunus avium*; the tall tree which bears this fruit. *sweet chestnut*: see CHESTNUT *noun* 1a. *sweet* CICELY. **sweet clover** any of various melilots. **sweet coltsfoot** the winter heliotrope, *Petasites fragrans*. **sweetcorn** a kind of maize with kernels having a high sugar content; these kernels, eaten as a vegetable when young. *sweet cumin*: see CUMIN 2. **sweet dreams** *interjection* (to a person going to bed) sleep well! **sweet-eyed** *adjective* having attractive eyes. *sweet* FENNEL. **sweet fern** *US* a shrub of the bog myrtle family, *Comptonia peregrina*, having fragrant fernlike leaves. **sweet flag** a waterside plant, *Acorus calamus*, of the arum family, which has leaves like those of an iris and an aromatic root used medicinally, as a flavouring, and formerly to strew floors. *sweet gale*: see GALE *noun*[1]. *sweet galingale*: see GALINGALE 2. **sweet-grass** (*a*) any of various grasses or other plants relished by cattle for their sweet succulent foliage; *spec.* any of various marsh grasses constituting the genus *Glyceria*; (*b*) *N. Amer.* any of several fragrant grasses, esp. holy grass, *Hierochloe odorata*, used in basket-making. **sweet gum** a N. American tree, *Liquidambar styraciflua*, of the witch-hazel family, yielding a resinous gum. **sweet Jesus** *interjection* expr. surprise, exasperation, dismay, etc. **sweet John** *arch.* a narrow-leaved variety of sweet william, *Dianthus barbatus*. **sweetleaf** a tree of the southern US, *Symplocos tinctoria* (family Symplocaceae), having sweet-flavoured leaves eaten by horses and cattle. **sweet lemon** any of several trees related to the lemon but with less acid fruit, *esp.* sweet lime. **sweet life** = DOLCE VITA. *sweet lime*: see LIME *noun*[3] 1b. **sweetlip (emperor)** a popular sporting and food fish, *Lethrinus chrysostomus* (family Lethrinidae), which has dark vertical bands and red fins, and is found on the Great Barrier Reef. **sweetlips** any of several brightly coloured grunts which are found on coral reefs etc. in the Indo-Pacific (usu. with specifying word). **sweet mamma** *US slang* a female lover. **sweet man** *US slang* = *sweetback (man)* above. *sweet* MARJORAM. **sweetmart** (now *dial.*) the pine marten. *sweet maudlin*: see MAUDLIN *noun* 2. **sweetmeal** sweetened wholemeal; a biscuit made from this. **sweet milk** fresh milk as opp. to skimmed milk or buttermilk. **sweetmouth** *verb trans.* (*slang*) flatter. †**sweet mouth** = *sweet tooth* below. **sweet-mouthed** *adjective* †(*a*) sweet-toothed; (*b*) speaking sweetly (usu. iron.). **sweet music** light instrumental music of a popular or conventional character; (*make sweet music*: see MUSIC *noun*). **sweet Nancy** *dial.* the pheasant's eye narcissus, *Narcissus poeticus*, esp. the double variety. **sweet nothings** *colloq.* sentimental endearments. **sweet olive** an evergreen shrub or tree of eastern Asia, *Osmanthus fragrans*, of the olive family, grown for its fragrant white flowers. *sweet orange*: see ORANGE *noun* 1. **sweet papa** *US slang* = *sweetback (man)* above. **sweet pea** an annual climbing leguminous plant, *Lathyrus odoratus*, a native of Sicily and S. Italy, cultivated for its showy sweet-scented flowers of many colours; also, the scent of this flower, esp. as used in cosmetics etc. *sweet pepper*: see PEPPER *noun*. *sweet pinesap*: see *pinesap* s.v. PINE *noun*[2]. *sweet potato*: see POTATO *noun* 1. *sweet rocket*: see ROCKET *noun*[2] 3. **sweet scabious** (*a*) a southern European scabious, *Scabiosa atropurpurea*, grown for its dark purple, lilac, white, etc., flowers; (*b*) *US* a kind of fleabane, *Erigeron annuus*. **sweet-scented** *adjective* sweet-smelling, fragrant (*sweet-scented vernal grass*: see VERNAL *adjective* 1b). **sweet sedge** = *sweet flag* above. *sweet seventeen*: see *sweet sixteen* below. **sweet singer** (*a*) a religious poet; (*b*) a popular, esp. sentimental, writer or singer; (*c*) *Hist.* (more fully *sweet singer of Israel*, app. with ref. to 2 *Samuel* 23:1) a member of a sect or sects flourishing in the late 17th cent. **sweet sixteen**, **sweet seventeen** (now chiefly *joc.*): regarded as the characteristic age of girlish beauty. *sweet sorghum*: see SORGHUM 1b. **sweet-sour** *adjective & noun* = *sweet-and-sour* (a) above. **sweet spot** the point on a bat, club, racket, etc., at which it makes most effective contact with the ball. **sweetstuff** †(*a*) *euphem.* gin; (*b*) sweets, confectionery, cakes, etc., collectively. *sweet sultan*: see SULTAN 2. **sweet talk** *colloq.* endearments, flattery, esp. when persuasive or insincere. **sweet-talk** *verb trans. & intrans.* (*colloq.*) flatter in order to persuade, talk persuasively or flatteringly (to). **sweet-throated**, **sweet-tongued** *adjectives* having a sweet voice. **sweet tooth** a taste or liking for sweet-tasting things. **sweet-toothed** *adjective* having a sweet tooth. **sweet-veld** *S. Afr.* an area of land providing good nutritious grazing; the vegetation of such an area. *sweet vernal grass*: see VERNAL *adjective* 1b. *sweet violet*: see VIOLET *noun* 1. **sweet water** †(*a*) a sweet-smelling liquid preparation, a liquid perfume or scent; (*b*) fresh water; (*c*) a variety of white grape of especially sweet flavour. **sweet-water** *adjective* living in or consisting of fresh water. **sweet william** a garden pink, *Dianthus barbatus*, with dense cymes of fragrant red, pink, white, or mottled flowers; *sweet-william catchfly*, a garden campion, *Silene armeria*, with a similar inflorescence. **sweet wine**: having a sweet taste (opp. *dry wine*). **sweetwood** (the timber of) any of various W. Indian or tropical American trees and shrubs, chiefly of the laurel family; *sweetwood bark*, cascarilla bark. **sweet wort** BREWING a sweet-flavoured wort; *esp.* the infusion of malt before the hops are added. **sweet yarrow** a yellow-flowered plant, *Achillea ageratum*, of SW Europe.
■ **sweetful** *adjective* (long *dial.*) full of sweetness L16. **sweetish** *adjective* somewhat or slightly sweet L16. **sweetishness** *noun* M18.

sweet /swi:t/ *verb trans.* OE.
[from the adjective.]
1 Make sweet, sweeten, (*lit.* & *fig.*). Now *rare.* OE.
2 Give pleasure to, delight, gratify. *obsolete* exc. *W. Indies.* ME.

sweeten /ˈswi:t(ə)n/ *verb*. LME.
[from SWEET *adjective* + -EN[5].]
1 *verb trans.* Make sweet or sweeter in taste; *esp.* add sugar, honey, etc., to (food or drink). LME. ▸**b** Make sweet or sweeter in smell. Also, make fresh or wholesome, purify. L16. ▸**c** Make sweet or sweeter in sound. L16.
2 *verb trans.* Make (a person, mood, etc.) amenable or pleasant. M16. ▸**b** Relieve, comfort, soothe, (a person etc.). Also, mollify, appease. Now *rare* or *obsolete.* M17.
3 *verb trans.* Make (a thing) pleasant or agreeable. Also, make less unpleasant or painful, alleviate, mitigate. L16. ▸**b** Make less offensive or objectionable. Now *rare* or *obsolete.* M17.

4 *verb trans.* Persuade by flattery or gifts; cajole; bribe. Also foll. by *up*. Now *slang & dial.* L16.

5 *verb trans.* **a** Make pliable; cause to work smoothly or easily. E17. ▸**b** ART. Blur, soften, (a tint, line, etc.). L17. ▸**c** Make (soil) mellow and fertile. M18. ▸**d** Neutralize (an acid) by means of an alkali. *rare.* L19. ▸**e** OIL INDUSTRY. Free (petroleum products) from sulphur or sulphur compounds. E20.

6 *verb intrans.* Become sweet or sweeter. E17.

7 *verb intrans.* **a** CARDS. Increase the stakes. L19. ▸**b** Bid at an auction merely in order to raise the price. *slang.* L19. ▸**c** FINANCE. Increase the collateral of a loan by adding further securities. L19.

> 🕮 **1** M. STOTT Mugs of cocoa sweetened with condensed milk. ***sweeten the pill***: see PILL *noun*[3] 1b. **b** D. MADDEN The air, sweetened with the scent of flowers, blew through . . the rooms. **3** J. H. NEWMAN Hope of future good . . sweetens all suffering. M. E. BRADDON The home ties . . which sweeten other lives were unknown to her.

■ **sweetening** *noun* the action of the verb; an instance of this; something which sweetens; something imparting a sweet flavour; ***long sweetening***: see LONG *adjective*[1]; ***short sweetening***: see SHORT *adjective*: L16.

sweetener /ˈswiːt(ə)nə/ *noun.* L16.
[from prec. + -ER[1].]

1 A thing making something sweet to the taste etc.; something giving food, drink, etc., a sweet flavour; *spec.* (a capsule etc. of) any of various low-calorie sugar substitutes. L16. ▸†**b** An alkali etc. used to neutralize acidity; a thing which renders soil richer and less acidic. L17–L18. ▸**c** ART. A brush used for softening lines etc. Cf. SWEETEN 5b. M19.

2 A thing or person that makes something (more) pleasant, agreeable, or tolerable; something pleasing, gratifying, or comforting. M17. ▸**b** Esp. in politics, business, etc.: a means of persuasion, an inducement for a deal etc., a bribe; a concession, an appeasement. *colloq.* M18.

3 a A decoy, a cheat, a sharper. *slang.* Long *rare* or *obsolete.* L17. ▸**b** A person bidding at an auction merely in order to raise the price. *slang.* E19.

> 🕮 **1** S. DOWELL Sugar . . began to displace honey as a sweetener for food. W. MCILVANNEY The cup containing instant coffee and one sweetener. **2** R. BLAIR Friendship! . . Sweetener of life.

sweetheart /ˈswiːthɑːt/ *noun & verb.* Orig. two words. ME.
[from SWEET *adjective* + HEART *noun*.]

▶ **A** *noun.* **1** A beloved or lovable person; a person with whom one is in love; darling, dear. Freq. as a friendly, intimate, ironic, or contemptuous form of address. ME. ▸†**b** An illicit or clandestine lover; a mistress. L16–L18. ▸**c** Anything especially good of its kind. *N. Amer. colloq.* M20.

2 Any of various things likened to a heart or sweetheart; *spec.* (*a*) a heart-shaped cake or tart; (*b*) a bur, thorny spray, or other part of a plant which attaches itself to a person's clothes; in *pl.*, a plant bearing such burs etc., e.g. cleavers, *Galium aparine*; (*c*) *colloq. & dial.* a tame rabbit. M18.

3 More fully ***sweetheart rose***. Any of several roses having small pink, white, or yellow flowers particularly attractive as buds, esp. a type of dwarf polyantha. *N. Amer.* E20.

> 🕮 **1** H. ROBBINS 'You don't have to be afraid any more, sweetheart'. H. L. KLAWANS They had . . been childhood sweethearts, gone to the same college, married.

Attrib. & comb.: In the sense 'pertaining to or designating an industrial agreement reached privately by employers and trade unions for their own interests', as ***sweetheart agreement***, ***sweetheart deal***, ***sweetheart union***, etc. Special combs., as **sweetheart neck**, **sweetheart neckline** a neckline on a dress, blouse, etc., shaped like the top of a heart; **sweetheart plant** either of two tropical American climbing plants with heart-shaped leaves, *Philodendron cordatum* and *P. scandens*, of the arum family, grown as house-plants; ***sweetheart rose***: see sense 3 above.

▶ **B** *verb trans. & intrans.* Be a sweetheart (of), behave amorously (to), court. E18.

■ **sweethearter** *noun* M19.

sweetie /ˈswiːti/ *noun. colloq.* Also **-ty**. L17.
[from SWEET *adjective*, *noun* + -IE.]

1 A sweet, an item of confectionery. Also, sweet food generally. Orig. *Scot.* L17.

2 (A) sweetheart; a lovable person. Also ***sweetie-pie***. Orig. *US.* L18.

3 A green-skinned hybrid variety of grapefruit, noted for its sweet taste. L20.

> 🕮 **2** M. MARRIN No, sorry, sweetie, I didn't mean it.

sweetikin /ˈswiːtɪkɪn/ *noun. colloq.* Also **-kins** /-kɪnz/. L16.
[formed as prec. + -KIN: see -S[4].]
= SWEETIE 2.

sweeting /ˈswiːtɪŋ/ *noun.* ME.
[from SWEET *adjective*, *noun* + -ING[3].]

1 (A) sweetheart, a beloved person; darling. Chiefly as a form of address. *arch.* ME.

2 A sweet-flavoured variety of apple. M16.

2 Tolman sweeting, ***Tolman's sweeting***: see TOLMAN.

sweetling /ˈswiːtlɪŋ/ *noun. rare.* M17.
[formed as prec. + -LING[1].]

1 = SWEETING 1. *arch.* M17.

2 A small sweet thing. M19.

sweetly /ˈswiːtli/ *adverb.* OE.
[from SWEET *adjective* + -LY[2].]

In a sweet manner, with sweetness; so as to be pleasing to the mind or senses; fragrantly; melodiously; kindly; delightfully; efficiently.

> 🕮 W. M. PRAED She . . sang as sweetly as a caged canary. C. BRONTË I fell sweetly asleep. C. WESTON The secretary smiled sweetly . . 'I'll do that, Mr. Farr.'

sweetmeat /ˈswiːtmiːt/ *noun.* Now *arch. & literary.*
[Old English *swētmettas*, *swōtmettas* delicacies, from SWEET *adjective* + MEAT *noun*.]

A sweet; an item of confectionery or sweet food, as a small fancy cake or pastry, a preserved or candied fruit, a sugared nut, etc.; such food collectively.

sweetness /ˈswiːtnɪs/ *noun.* OE.
[formed as prec. + -NESS.]

1 The quality of being sweet; pleasantness to the mind or senses; fragrance, melodiousness, charm. OE.

2 A sweet thing; a sweet-tasting substance, *spec.* (*Canad.*) molasses; *rare* a sweet sound or tone. OE.

†**3** Excessive fondness for sweet things. *rare.* LME–E17.

> 🕮 **1** T. GRAY Full many a flower is born to . . waste its sweetness on the desert air. A. BAIN The sweetness of . . fruit is known to arise from sugar. R. GODDEN His little girl . . a tot of nauseating sweetness. I. COLEGATE A Handel flute sonata, played with plangent sweetness. **sweetness and light** (now freq. *iron.*) extreme mildness and reason, now esp. when uncharacteristic.

sweetsop /ˈswiːtsɒp/ *noun.* L17.
[from SWEET *adjective* + SOP *noun*[1].]

The sweet fruit of a widely cultivated tropical American tree, *Annona squamosa*, allied to the soursop; the tree bearing this fruit. Also called ***sugar-apple***.

sweety *noun* var. of SWEETIE.

swell /swɛl/ *noun, adjective, & adverb.* ME.
[Sense A.1 prob. repr. Old English *geswell*; other senses from the verb.]

▶ **A** *noun.* †**1** A swelling due to disease etc. Only in ME.

2 The rising or heaving of the sea etc. in long rolling waves that do not break, as after a storm; such a wave or waves collectively; *spec.* long-period wave movement persisting after the wind causing it has dropped, or due to a distant storm. Cf. SEA 5d. E16. ▸**b** The rising of a river above its ordinary level. Now *rare* or *obsolete.* M18.

3 The condition of being swollen, distended, or increased in bulk; an instance of this; swelling or protuberant form. Also, a protuberance, a bulge. M17. ▸**b** *fig.* Increase in amount. Now *rare* or *obsolete.* M18.

4 a The swelling or welling up of a feeling, emotion, etc.; an instance of this. Now *rare* or *obsolete.* E18. ▸**b** Arrogant, pompous, or pretentious manner or behaviour; (an instance of) swagger. Freq. in ***cut a swell***, cut a dash, swagger. Now *rare* or *obsolete.* E18. ▸†**c** Turgid or inflated language. M18–M19.

5 A gradually and evenly rising hill or upland, a piece of rising ground. Also (GEOLOGY), a submarine rise; a dome. M18.

6 Gradual increase of sound, esp. music, in volume or fullness; an instance of this, a rising burst *of* music etc.; *spec.* in MUSIC, (a mark denoting) a crescendo followed by a diminuendo. M18. ▸**b** MUSIC. A mechanism for producing a crescendo or diminuendo in an organ, harmonium, etc., consisting of a shutter, lid, or (now usu.) series of slats operated by a pedal or lever. L18.

7 A fashionable or stylish person, a dandy; a person of wealth or good social position; *transf.* a person of distinguished achievements, a person who is very clever or good *at* something. *arch. colloq.* L18.

> 🕮 **2** D. BAGLEY The oily swells . . surged in from the mouth of the bay. G. SANTAYANA The ship was rolling slightly . . in the long placid swell. **3** JOHN HOLLAND The irregular swells and hollows on the surface of a casting. **4a** W. COWPER The swell of pity, not to be confin'd Within the scanty limits of the mind. **5** J. BUCHAN A swell of moorland which crowned a . . plateau. **6** H. CAINE The soar and swell of the psalm filled the room. G. K. CHESTERTON Through the night came . . a strong swell of human voices. **b** ***Venetian swell***: see VENETIAN *adjective*. **7** M. EDGAR A grand little lad was young Albert, All dressed in his best; quite a swell.

Comb.: **swell-box** MUSIC a box enclosing organ-pipes, fitted with a shutter, slats, etc., as part of a swell (sense 6b); **swell-organ** MUSIC the section of an organ with its pipes enclosed in a swell-box.

▶ **B** *adjective.* †**1** Proud, arrogant. Only in LME.

2 Orig. (*arch.*), of or pertaining to wealth or social distinction; stylish, fashionable, smart. Now also (chiefly *N. Amer.*) *loosely*, excellent, fine, splendid; most pleasant, kind, or effective. *colloq.* E19.

> 🕮 **2** P. G. WODEHOUSE A country-house party with a lot of swell people. D. HAMMETT 'She's full of gas and ready to go.' 'Swell'. C. PORTER What a swell party this is. R. BANKS She could apologize, and everything would be swell. **swell mob** *slang* (*obsolete* exc. *Hist.*) a class of pickpockets who assumed the dress and manners of wealthy people to escape detection; ***swell-mobsman***, a member of the swell mob.

▶ **C** *adverb.* In a splendid manner, very well, excellently. *colloq.* (now chiefly *N. Amer.*). M19.

■ **swelldom** *noun* (*arch. colloq.*) people of fashion and social distinction collectively, the world of swells M19. **swellish** *adjective* (*arch. colloq.*) characteristic of or suitable for a swell or fashionable person, stylish, dandified E19. **swellishness** *noun* (*arch. colloq.*) M19. **swellism** *noun* (*arch. colloq.*) the character, style, or practice of a swell or fashionable person M19.

swell /swɛl/ *verb.* Pa. t. **swelled**, †**swole**; pa. pple **swollen** /ˈswəʊlən/, **swelled**.
[Old English *swellan* = Old High German *swellan* (German *schwellen*), Old Norse *svella*, from Germanic.]

1 *verb intrans. & trans.* Increase in size or bulk, as from internal pressure due to growth, absorption, inflation, etc.; (cause to) become distended or filled out, rise or raise above the surrounding level, *spec.* (of part of the body) as a result of disease or injury. (Foll. by *out*, *up*.) Freq. as SWOLLEN *ppl adjective*, SWELLED *ppl adjective*. OE. ▸**b** (Cause to) be distended or protuberant in form, appear to swell thus. L17.

2 a *verb trans.* Affect with an emotion, as pride, vanity, joy, etc.; puff up, inflate. Foll. by *with*. Freq. as **SWOLLEN** *ppl adjective*. ME. ▸**b** *verb intrans.* Of an emotion etc.: grow and expand in the mind. Of a person, the heart, etc.: be affected or filled *with* a welling emotion; feel full of pride, joy, vanity, etc. ME.

3 a *verb intrans.* Behave proudly, arrogantly, or overbearingly, be puffed up. *obsolete* exc. as passing into sense 3b. ME. ▸**b** *verb intrans. & trans.* (with *it*). [Infl. by SWELL *noun*.] Behave pompously or pretentiously, swagger. L18.

4 a *verb intrans.* Of water etc.: rise above the ordinary level, well *up*, rise in waves. ME. ▸**b** *verb trans.* Cause (water etc.) to rise above the ordinary level; whip up into waves. E17.

5 *verb intrans.* Now only of an immaterial thing: become greater in amount, degree, intensity, etc.; expand; *spec.* (of sound, esp. music) become gradually louder or fuller, (of a musical instrument) emit a swelling note or sound, (foll. by *up*, *out*). LME.

6 *verb trans.* Make greater in amount, degree, or intensity; increase, add to. E17. ▸**b** Raise in status etc.; exalt. Now *rare* or *obsolete.* E17. ▸**c** Utter or sound with increasing volume or intensity. *rare.* L18.

> 🕮 **1** DICKENS The Major . . swelling every already swollen vein in his head. A. HENFREY A substance softening or swelling up in water. E. LANGLEY His rounded belly made his white shirt . . swell out. **b** R. RENDELL A . . wall behind which meadows swelled. **2b** THACKERAY Becky's soul swelled with pride and delight at these honours. LD MACAULAY The spirit of Englishmen . . swelled up high and strong against injustice. **4a** *Daily Telegraph* Heights of foam which swell up as high as the rail of the bulwarks. **b** T. PRINGLE A very heavy rain . . swells the river to an unfordable size. **5** A. RADCLIFFE The . . organ and the choral sounds swelled into full and solemn harmony. *Times* The ranks of the unemployed are . . daily swelling. H. ROTH A low hum . . had now swollen to a roar. R. BERTHOUD The class had swelled to some twenty students. **6** A. J. WILSON The property . . swelled my estate to very unusual proportions. *Daily Chronicle* Dates, figs, medlars and mangos swell the number of fruits.

swell- /swɛl/ *combining form.*
[Repr. SWELL *noun*, *verb*.]
That swells.

■ **swellfish** *noun* a puffer fish M19. **swell-front** *noun* (*US*) a curved front of a house; a house having such a front: M19. **swell-head** *noun* (*colloq.*) = SWELLED *head* M19. **swell-headed** *adjective* (*colloq.*) conceited E19. **swell-shark** *noun* any of several small sharks of the genus *Cephaloscyllium*, which inflate the body by swallowing air when brought to the surface; esp. *C. ventriosum*, which is found off the coast of California L19.

swelled /swɛld/ *ppl adjective.* L16.
[from SWELL *verb* + -ED[1]. Less common in adjectival use than SWOLLEN *adjective*.]

That has swelled, swollen.

swelled head *colloq.* inordinate conceit, excessive pride or vanity; a person affected with this.

swelling /ˈswɛlɪŋ/ *noun.* OE.
[from SWELL *verb* + -ING[1].]

1 A swollen, distended, or protuberant part of something; a protuberance; *spec.* a part of the body enlarged as a result of disease or injury. OE.

2 The process or an instance of swelling, becoming distended or rising in intensity etc.; the condition of having become swollen; distension, dilatation, expansion; *spec.* enlargement of part of the body as a result of disease or injury. ME.

3 a A swelling wave, tide, or flood. *arch.* LME. ▸**b** The rising of water above the ordinary level; the swell of the sea; the rise of the tide. *arch.* M16.

4 Inflation by pride, vanity, etc.; proud or arrogant behaviour or feeling, swagger. *arch.* LME.

📖 **1** P. MAILLOUX Regular spraying of his larynx . . began to reduce the swelling. **2** S. JOHNSON To repress the swellings of vain hope. C. EASTON Glandular fever . . causes swelling of the lymph glands and spleen.

swelling /ˈswɛlɪŋ/ *adjective.* OE.
[from SWELL *verb* + -ING[2].]
1 That swells; becoming distended or filled out; rising in intensity etc. OE.
2 Of water: rising above the normal level, rising in waves. Chiefly *poet.* M16.
3 Of style or language: grand, magnificent, majestic; usu. *derog.*, inflated, bombastic, turgid. L16.
4 Becoming greater in amount, increasing, growing; *loosely* great in amount, full, abundant. E17.

📖 **1** W. SHENSTONE The wind propitious fill'd The swelling sails. S. JOHNSON Milk pressed from the swelling udder. M. DAS The swelling veins on the speaker's throat glistened with sweat. **4** P. MARSHALL Those passing near . . were being pressed . . by the swelling numbers behind them.

■ **swellingly** *adverb* M17.

swelp me /swɛlp ˈmiː/ *interjection. arch.* L19.
[Contr.]
= *so help me (God)* s.v. HELP *verb* 1.

swelt /swɛlt/ *verb.* Now *dial.*
[Old English *sweltan* = Old Saxon *sweltan*, Old High German *swelzan*, Old Norse *svelta*, Gothic *swiltan*, from Germanic stem perh. repr. also by SWEAL.]
1 a *verb intrans.* Die, perish. OE. ▸†**b** *verb trans.* Cause to perish. Only in ME.
2 *verb intrans.* Be overcome with strong emotion, a fit of sickness, etc.; faint, swoon. ME.
3 a *verb intrans.* Be overpowered or oppressed with heat, swelter. LME. ▸**b** *verb trans.* Oppress or overwhelm with heat. LME. ▸†**c** *verb intrans.* Burn or rage as with fever. Only in L16.

swelter /ˈswɛltə/ *verb & noun.* ME.
[from base of prec. + -ER[5].]
▸ **A** *verb.* **1** *verb intrans.* Of a person, place, weather, etc.: be oppressed by or become faint with heat, be uncomfortably hot; sweat profusely. ME.
2 *verb trans.* Oppress with heat, cause to sweat or become faint with heat. Usu. in *pass.* L16.
†**3** *verb intrans. & trans.* (in *pass.*). Be bathed *in* liquid, welter, wallow. L16–M19.
4 *verb trans. & intrans.* Exude or sweat (venom) as if by heat. (Chiefly with allus. to Shakes.) E17.

📖 **1** M. FORSTER The city sweltered in a heat haze. E. SEGAL Summer came and Barney . . sweltered in his doorman's uniform. **2** JOHN NEAL I was half sweltered to death, under a great pile o' blankets. **4** SHAKES. *Macb.* Toad that under cold stone . . Swelt'red venom sleeping got.

▸ **B** *noun.* A sweltering condition, sweltering weather. M19.
do a swelter *slang* (now *rare*) perspire.

sweltering /ˈswɛlt(ə)rɪŋ/ *adjective.* L16.
[from prec. + -ING[2].]
That swelters; uncomfortably or oppressively hot; (of heat etc.) oppressive, intense.

📖 R. L. STEVENSON The heat was sweltering, and the men grumbled . . over their work. A. BURGESS It was a sweltering summer in the Italian lowlands.

■ **swelteringly** *adverb* in a sweltering manner, so as to cause sweltering, (*swelteringly hot*, oppressively hot) L19.

sweltry /ˈswɛltri/ *adjective.* Now chiefly *arch. & dial.* Also **sweltery** /ˈswɛlt(ə)ri/. L16.
[formed as prec. + -Y[1].]
Oppressively hot, sweltering, sultry; oppressed with heat.

swelty /ˈswɛlti/ *adjective.* Now *dial.* LME.
[from SWELT + -Y[1].]
†**1** About to faint. Only in LME.
2 Sweltering, sultry. L16.

†**swenge** *verb* var. of SWINGE *verb*[1].

†**swepe** *noun & verb.* Long *Scot.*
[Old English *swipu*, *swipe* = Old Norse *svipa* from Germanic.]
▸ **A** *noun.* A whip, a lash. OE–E19.
▸ **B** *verb trans.* Strike with a whip, lash. ME–E20.

swept /swɛpt/ *adjective.* M16.
[pa. pple of SWEEP *verb*.]
1 That has been swept. Also foll. by adverb. M16.
2 ELECTRONICS. Of (the frequency of) a signal: increased (or decreased) through a range of values, usu. rapidly and repeatedly. M20.
Special collocations & comb.: **swept-back** *adjective* (AERONAUTICS) designating a wing having its leading edge angled backwards. **swept-up** (of hair) brushed or combed up towards the top of the head. **swept valley** BUILDING a valley made from tapering tiles or slates. **swept volume** MECHANICS the volume through which a piston or plunger moves as it makes a stroke. **swept wing** AERONAUTICS a swept-back wing. **swept-wing** *adjective & noun* (AERONAUTICS) (designating) an aircraft with swept-back wings.

swept *verb pa. t. & pple* of SWEEP *verb*.

swerve /swəːv/ *verb & noun.*
[Old English *sweorfan* = Old Frisian *swerva* creep, Middle Dutch *swerven* stray, Old High German *swerban* move quickly back and forth, Old Norse *sverfa* file, Gothic *(af)swairban* wipe (away).]
▸ **A** *verb.* †**1** *verb trans.* File, scour. Only in OE.
†**2** *verb intrans.* Depart, leave. *rare.* OE–LME.
3 *verb intrans.* Turn aside; deviate from a direct course; glance. Also foll. by *from, into, off*, etc. OE. ▸**b** Turn or bend in a specified direction, esp. abruptly. Also foll. by *to*. L16. ▸**c** CRICKET & BASEBALL. (Of a ball) deflect in the air as a result of a spinning action on delivery; (of a bowler or pitcher) deliver a ball with this action. L19.
4 *verb intrans. fig.* Change one's opinion or course of action; abandon one cause etc. in favour of another (usu. foll. by *from, to*). Formerly also, desert or be disloyal to a person (foll. by *from*). LME. ▸†**b** Err or stray morally; transgress. L16–E17.
5 *verb trans.* Cause to turn aside or change direction. LME.
†**6** *verb intrans.* Sway, reel, totter. Chiefly *poet.* L15–E19.
7 *verb intrans.* Rove, stray, wander. Now *dial.* M16.
†**8** *verb intrans.* = SWARM *verb*[2]. *poet.* Only in 17.

📖 **3** E. L. DOCTOROW The car came past his house . . and swerved into the telephone pole. L. ELLMANN Fran had to swerve to avoid touching him. **b** D. H. LAWRENCE The hills swerved inland, to meet the sheer . . sides of dry mountains. P. ACKROYD The light, glancing through a bell-jar, swerved upwards. **4** P. ACKROYD I never swerved from my ideal. **5** E. ALBEE He swerved the car, to avoid a porcupine.

▸ **B** *noun.* The action or an act of swerving; a deviation or divergence from a course etc.; a swerving movement. M18.

📖 R. S. THOMAS His grass-green eye Missed neither swoop nor swerve of the hawk's wing.

■ **swerveless** *adjective* (*literary*) unswerving, unwavering M19. **swerver** *noun* (*a*) a person who or thing which swerves, formerly *spec.*, a transgressor; (*b*) CRICKET & BASEBALL a swerving delivery; a bowler or pitcher who swerves: L16.

sweven /ˈswɛv(ə)n/ *noun.* Long *arch.*
[Old English *swef(e)n*, = Old Saxon *sweƀan*, Old Norse *svefn*, from Germanic; rel. to Greek *hupnos*, Latin *somnus* sleep.]
1 A dream; a vision. OE.
†**2** Sleep. *rare.* OE–M17.

SWF *abbreviation.*
Single white female.

SWG *abbreviation.*
Standard wire gauge.

swidden /ˈswɪd(ə)n/ *verb & noun.* Orig. *dial.* L18.
[Var. of SWITHEN.]
▸ **A** *verb trans.* Singe, scorch; AGRICULTURE clear (land) by slashing and burning vegetation. L18.
▸ **B** *noun.* AGRICULTURE. An area of land cleared for cultivation by slashing and burning vegetation. Also, the method of clearing land by this means. M19.

Swiderian /swɪˈdɪərɪən/ *adjective & noun.* M20.
[French *swidérien*, German *swiderien*, from *Swidry* a site of this type near Warsaw: see -AN.]
ARCHAEOLOGY. (Of, pertaining to, or designating) a final palaeolithic culture in Poland and neighbouring countries.

swift /swɪft/ *noun.* M16.
[from the adjective.]
▸ **I 1 a** A newt. Long *obsolete* exc. *dial.* M16. ▸**b** Any of several swift-running small lizards, as the N. American fence-lizard, *Sceloporus undulatus*. M17.
2 Any of numerous birds comprising the family Apodidae, which have long curved wings and forked tails and feed on insects caught in rapid flight; *esp.* the common swift, *Apus apus*, a black bird with a screaming call which is a summer visitor to Britain and Europe. M17. ▸**b** A domestic pigeon of any of several long-winged fancy breeds. Also **swift pigeon**. L19.
3 Any of several long-winged moths of the genus *Hepialus* or the family Hepialidae. Also **swift moth**. E19.
2 *chimney swift*: see CHIMNEY *noun*. *palm swift*: see PALM *noun*[1]. *SPINE-tailed swift*. *tree swift*: see TREE *noun*.
▸ **II 4** A light usu. adjustable reel for holding a skein of silk, wool, etc. M16. ▸**b** A cylinder in a wool-carding machine. M19.

swift /swɪft/ *adjective, adverb, & verb*[1].
[Old English *swift*, from Germanic base of SWIVE.]
▸ **A** *adjective.* **1** Moving or capable of moving at great speed; (of an action) performed at high speed; quick, rapid. OE.
2 Coming or performed without delay; prompt, speedy. OE. ▸**b** Of a person: quick to adopt a specified course or action. Usu. foll. by *to (do)*. ME.
3 Of short duration; brief. Chiefly *poet.* ME.

📖 **1** J. F. LEHMANN The horses dropped from their swift trot to an amble. J. FRAME The time was . . so swift that it seemed to flow beyond his range of being. **2** *Irish Press* The need for a 'swift clearance' of the rubbish . . mounting on the city's streets. **b** A. HELPS Let us not be swift to imagine that lies are never of any service. **3** SHELLEY Swift summer into the Autumn flowed.

Comb. & special collocations: **swift-foot** *adjective & noun* (*a*) *adjective* = *swift-footed* below; (*b*) *noun* a fast-moving person or animal; **swift-footed** *adjective* running or moving swiftly; **swift fox** a small fox, *Vulpes velox*, of N. American prairies; **swift-winged** *adjective* flying swiftly, rapid in flight.
▸ **B** *adverb.* Swiftly. *arch.* exc. in comb. LME.

📖 J. BUCHAN Streams which ran swift and . . very clear. J. A. BISHOP Swift-snapping windshield wipers and dimmed headlights.

▸ **C** *verb intrans.* Move swiftly; hasten. *rare.* E17.
■ **swiftly** *adverb* in a swift manner, quickly; with swift movement or action: OE. **swiftness** *noun* OE. **swifty** *adjective* (*rare*, chiefly *poet.*) swift LME.

swift /swɪft/ *verb*[2] *trans.* L15.
[Prob. of Scandinavian or Low German origin, from base repr. by Old Norse *svipta* reef (sails), *sviptingar* reefing-ropes, Dutch *zwichten* take in (sails), *zwichtlings*, *zwichtlijnen*, cat-harpings, and ult. rel. to SWIFT *adjective*. Cf. SWIFTER.]
NAUTICAL. Tighten or make fast with a rope or swifter drawn taut.

swiften /ˈswɪft(ə)n/ *verb. rare.* E17.
[from SWIFT *adjective* + -EN[5].]
†**1** *verb trans.* Make swift; hasten. E–M17.
2 *verb intrans.* Become swift; move swiftly; hasten, hurry. *literary.* M19.

swifter /ˈswɪftə/ *noun & verb.* E17.
[Rel. to SWIFT *verb*[2].]
▸ **A** *noun.* **1** NAUTICAL. A rope drawn taut to tighten or make fast rigging etc.; *spec.* the forward shroud supporting the lower mast of a ship. E17.
2 A cable used to secure a raft of logs. *N. Amer.* L19.
▸ **B** *verb trans.* NAUTICAL. = SWIFT *verb*[2]. L18.

Swiftian /ˈswɪftɪən/ *adjective.* M18.
[from *Swift* (see below) + -IAN.]
Of, pertaining to, or characteristic of the Irish satirist Jonathan Swift (1667–1745) or his works.
■ **Swiftianism** *noun* a piece of writing, an expression, etc., in the style characteristic of Swift M19.

swiftie /ˈswɪfti/ *noun.* M20.
[from SWIFT *adjective* + -IE.]
1 A person who moves or acts swiftly. *colloq.* M20.
2 An act of deception; a trick. *Austral. slang.* M20.

swiftlet /ˈswɪftlɪt/ *noun.* L19.
[from SWIFT *noun*[1] + -LET.]
Any of various small swifts constituting the genera *Collocalia* and *Aerodramus*, of eastern Asia and Australasia, typically gregarious, nesting in caves and able to echolocate, and building nests largely of saliva (some used for bird's-nest soup). Occas. also, a young or small swift.

swig /swɪɡ/ *noun*[1] *& verb*[1]. M16.
[Origin unkn.]
▸ **A** *noun.* **1** Drink, esp. alcoholic liquor. Now *dial. & slang.* M16.
2 A deep swallow or draught of a drink, esp. of alcoholic liquor. *colloq.* E17.

📖 **2** B. PYM Taking a swig of brandy out of a small flask.

▸ **B** *verb. colloq.* Infl. **-gg-**.
1 *verb intrans.* Drink in deep draughts; drink eagerly or copiously. Also foll. by *at*. M17.
2 *verb trans.* Drink (esp. alcoholic liquor) in deep draughts; drink from (a bottle etc.) in this manner. Also foll. by *down*. L17.

📖 **1** C. P. SNOW Steen swigged at his glass of whisky. *Times* He . . swigged from a bottle of water. **2** E. DAVID Anisette is not a liqueur . . to swig down in quantity. P. MULDOON Swigging a quart of whiskey.

■ **swigger** *noun* (*colloq.*, chiefly *US*) a habitual or heavy drinker, esp. of alcohol M20.

swig /swɪɡ/ *verb*[2] *& noun*[2]. M17.
[Perh. rel. to SWAG *verb* with general sense 'cause to sway about, pull'.]
▸ **A** *verb.* Infl. **-gg-**.
1 *verb trans.* Castrate (a ram) by tying the scrotum. Now *rare* or *obsolete.* M17.
2 *verb trans. & intrans.* NAUTICAL. Pull on and tighten (a rope) attached at one end to a fixed and the other to a movable object. Usu. foll. by *on*. L18.
3 *verb intrans.* Sway (*about*); waver. Chiefly *Scot.* E19.
▸ **B** *noun.* NAUTICAL.
1 A tackle with ropes etc. not parallel. E19.
2 The action or an act of swigging on a rope. M19.

swiggle /ˈswɪɡ(ə)l/ *verb. rare.* L17.
[App. frequentative of prec: see -LE[3].]
†**1** *verb trans.* Sprinkle. Only in L17.
2 *verb intrans. & trans.* Wriggle. M19.
3 *verb trans.* Shake or splash (liquid etc.) about. *dial.* M19.

swigman /ˈswɪɡmən/ *noun. slang.* Long *rare* or *obsolete.* Pl. **-men.** M16.
[Origin unkn.]
A pedlar.

swill /swɪl/ *verb & noun.*
[Old English *swillan*, *swilian*, with no certain cognates.]
▶ **A** *verb.* **1** *verb trans.* Wash or rinse *out* (a container or cavity); now *esp.* cleanse by pouring water freely over or through (a surface etc.) (also foll. by *down*). Formerly also (*gen.*), wash, soak. OE. ▸**b** Stir around in (a container of) liquid; move or shake (liquid) around in a container or cavity. L16. ▸**c** Wash *away*, etc., with liquid, esp. water. Also, pour (liquid) freely down. L16.
2 *verb intrans. & trans.* Drink (esp. alcohol) greedily or to excess. E16.
3 *verb trans.* Supply with an abundance or excess of drink; fill *with* drink. M16.
4 *verb intrans.* Move or splash about, as liquid shaken in a container; flow freely or forcibly *over* a surface. M17.

📖 **1** CONAN DOYLE The top step swilled down and the other ones dry. S. MIDDLETON He took the cup to the kitchen, swilled it clean . . and returned. **b** B. BAINBRIDGE What a noise Lionel made swilling water round his mouth. **c** *Lancashire Life* He . . swilled off the pit grime. **2** P. V. WHITE Brendan Boyle, swilling the rum . . from an ugly, iron pannikin. **3** GEO. ELIOT Something they love better than swilling themselves with ale. **4** L. GRANT-ADAMSON Water swilled over the harbour road.

▶ **B** *noun.* **1** Liquid or partly liquid food, chiefly kitchen refuse, used for pig-food, pigswill; *fig.* worthless matter, rubbish. M16. ▸**b** A liquid mess, a slop; unappetizing or sloppy food. M17.
2 Copious or heavy drinking; alcoholic liquor, esp. when taken in excess. Also (*colloq.*), a bout of hasty drinking in a public house etc. immediately before closing time (only in ***six o'clock swill*** etc. below). E17.

📖 **1** A. S. BYATT Circe, dismissing the swine to their swill. *Washington Journalism Review* A lot of reporters thought the interviews were just a bunch of swill. **2** *attrib.*: *Independent* No room for tables and chairs in the swill hour.

Phrases: **six o'clock swill**, **ten o'clock swill**, etc., *colloq.* the customary bout of hasty drinking in a public house etc. immediately before closing-time.
Comb.: **swill-tub** a container for pigswill.
■ **swiller** *noun* †(*a*) *rare* a scullion; (*b*) a heavy drinker: L15. **swilling** *noun* (*a*) the action of the verb; †(*b*) (usu. in *pl.*) = SWILL *noun* 1; (*c*) in *pl.*, dirty liquid (as) produced by washing out a container etc.; (*d*) inferior liquor: OE.

swim /swɪm/ *noun.* M16.
[from the verb.]
†**1** The clear part of a liquid floating above a sediment; supernatant. M16–L17.
2 a A swimming movement; *esp.* a smooth gliding of the body. L16. ▸**b** A swimming or dizzy sensation. *colloq.* & *dial.* E19.
†**3** The swim-bladder of a fish. M17–M19.
4 An act or instance of swimming in water. M18. ▸**b** A popular dance of the 1960s with movements resembling swimming. M20.
5 a A deep pool in a river etc. frequented by fish. E19. ▸**b** An extent of water of sufficient depth for swimming. L19.
6 An enterprise; a scheme. *slang.* M19.
7 Either of the overhanging blunt ends of a barge; the overhanging portion of the stern of a shallow-water craft. M19.

📖 **2a** KEATS The moon . . Above a cloud . . with a gradual swim Coming into the blue. **4** D. HOGAN Ward had taken a bus to the sea so he could have a swim. **5b** *Caves & Caving* The canal then became a swim.

Phrases: **in the swim** involved in or acquainted with current affairs or events. **in the swim with** in company with, in league with. **out of the swim** not involved in or acquainted with current affairs or events.
Attrib. & comb.: Designating garments worn while swimming, as ***swim-cap***, ***swim-trunks***, ***swimwear***. Special combs., as **swim-bladder** a gas-filled sac in the body of a bony fish by which buoyancy is maintained and controlled; **swimdress** *US* = ***swimsuit*** below; **swim-feeder** in coarse fishing, a short perforated tube for the gradual release of maggots; **swim-fin** = FLIPPER *noun* 1b; **swimgloat** the enjoyment of brief social success without consequent corruption; **swim-hole** = *SWIMMING hole*; **swim-pool** = ***swimming pool*** s.v. SWIMMING; **swimsuit** a woman's or girl's garment worn for swimming; **swimsuited** *adjective* wearing a swimsuit.

swim /swɪm/ *verb.* Infl. **-mm-**. Pa. t. **swam** /swam/; pa. pple **swum** /swʌm/.
[Old English *swimman* = Old Saxon, Old High German *swimman* (Dutch *zwemmen*, German *schwimmen*), Old Norse *svim(m)a*, from Germanic.]
▶ **I** *verb intrans.* **1** Propel the body through water while afloat by working the limbs or (of a fish) the fins and tail. OE.
2 Float on or at the surface of a liquid; be supported on or in water or other liquid. OE. ▸**b** Of a ship etc.: move or float on water. Long *rare.* OE.
3 Of liquid: move freely over a surface; flow. Usu. foll. by *over.* LME.
4 Be covered or immersed in a liquid; *fig.* be full of or flooded with an emotion etc. Foll. by *in*, *with.* LME.
5 (Appear to) move easily or quickly as if through water; glide along, around, etc. M16. ▸**b** Appear to undulate, reel, or whirl before the eyes. L17.
6 Be affected with dizziness; have a giddy sensation. E18. ▸**b** Of the eyes: be troubled or blurred. E19.

📖 **1** P. MARSHALL You could see the bugs swimming around in it. A. LAMBERT I swam with a . . breast-stroke . . cleaving the water with my hands. **2** J. STEINBECK Meat juice bubbled up . . and a stick of . . celery swam like a fish. **4** C. MUNGOSHI Cigarette ends and ash swimming in dark . . puddles of beer. **5** R. L. STEVENSON She . . swam across the floor as though she scorned the drudgery of walking. M. SARTON Images of Lawrie's birthday swam up into her consciousness. **b** D. PROFUMO The flat print swam under his stare. **6** V. GLENDINNING Leo's head swam. Voices in six languages assaulted his brain.

▶ **II** *verb trans.* **7** Traverse (a stretch of water) or cover (a distance etc.) by swimming. Also, perform (a stroke or movement) in swimming. OE.
8 a Convey or propel by swimming. E17. ▸**b** Cause to swim or move through water; *spec.* drive (an animal) to swim across a river etc. M17.
9 Cause to float; buoy up; *spec.* (*Hist.*) test (a person) suspected of witchcraft by immersion in water to establish his or her ability to float. M17. ▸**b** Provide sufficient depth for (a thing) to swim or float. L18.

📖 **7** N. TINBERGEN The chicks dive . . and swim considerable distances under water. **8a** N. SHAVE Be able to swim them to safety if necessary. **b** J. BUCHAN We would . . swim our horses over the estuary . . at high-tide. **9** W. S. CHURCHILL The Navy would swim the ship in accordance with the . . wishes of the Air Ministry.

Phrases: ***sink or swim***: see SINK *verb.* **swim against the tide** act against prevailing opinion or tendency. **swim fair** (of a plough) go steadily. **swimming crab** any of various coastal crabs of the genus *Liocarcinus*, which have the rear legs modified as paddles for swimming; ***velvet swimming crab***: see VELVET *noun & adjective.* **swim with the tide** act in conformity with prevailing opinion or tendency.
■ **swimathon** *noun* a long-distance swimming race; a marathon swimming event: M20. **swimmable** *adjective* M19. **swimmingly** *adverb* (*a*) with easy unimpeded progress, smoothly; (*b*) with a gliding movement: E17. **swimmingness** *noun* (*rare*) a misty or moist appearance of the eyes E18. **swimmist** *noun* (*rare*) a habitual or professional swimmer L19. **swimmy** *adjective* †(*a*) *rare* graceful, elegant; (*b*) inclined to dizziness; (*c*) (of the eyes) watery, tearful; (of a sound) indistinct because of reverberation: E19.

swimmer /ˈswɪmə/ *noun.* LME.
[from SWIM *verb* + -ER[1].]
1 A person or animal that swims in the water, *esp.* one of a specified proficiency. LME.
2 An animal or bird that (habitually) swims, or whose structure is adapted for swimming. LME.
3 A swimming organ of an animal; *esp.* a swimmeret, (now *dial.*) the swim-bladder of a fish. L16.
4 A thing which floats on the surface of liquid; *spec.* an angler's float. E17.
5 †*sing.* & in *pl.* A swimming costume; swimming trunks. *colloq.* (chiefly *Austral.*). E20.

📖 **1** P. D. JAMES She won't drown. She's a strong swimmer. **swimmer's itch** *MEDICINE* a painful skin eruption caused by penetration by the cercaria of blood flukes, esp. *Schistosoma mansoni*, during swimming. ***synchronized swimmer***: see SYNCHRONIZE *verb.* **5** *Courier-Mail (Brisbane)* If I go swimming on the main beach, I would wear swimmers.

swimmeret /ˈswɪmərɛt/ *noun.* M19.
[from prec. + -ET[1].]
In crustaceans, an abdominal limb or appendage adapted for swimming, a pleopod. Also, a similar organ in some aquatic insect larvae.

swimming /ˈswɪmɪŋ/ *noun.* LME.
[from SWIM *verb* + -ING[1].]
1 The action of SWIM *verb*; an instance of this. LME.
2 A state of dizziness or giddiness; vertigo. M16.
1 ***synchronized swimming***: see SYNCHRONIZE *verb.*
Attrib. & comb.: Designating garments worn when swimming, as ***swimming costume***, ***swimming trunks***, etc. Special combs., as **swimming-bath** = ***swimming pool*** below; **swimming-bell** a bell-shaped or dome-shaped organ by contraction of which an animal (esp. a coelenterate) propels itself through the water; **swimming-bladder** = ***swim-bladder*** s.v. SWIM *noun*; **swimming hole** (chiefly *N. Amer., Austral., & NZ*) a bathing place in a stream or river; **swimming pool** an indoor or outdoor pool built for swimming in.

Swinburnian /swɪnˈbəːnɪən/ *adjective.* M19.
[from *Swinburne* (see below) + -IAN.]
Of, pertaining to, or characteristic of the English poet Algernon Charles Swinburne (1837–1909) or his work.
■ **Swinburnianism** *noun* (an) imitation of Swinburne in poetic style, subject matter, etc. M20.

swindle /ˈswɪnd(ə)l/ *verb & noun.* L18.
[Back-form. from next.]
▶ **A** *verb.* **1** *verb intrans.* Practise fraud; deceive or cheat for purposes of gain. L18.
2 *verb trans.* Cheat; defraud *out of* money, possessions, etc. Also, bring into a specified condition by cheating. E19.
3 *verb trans.* Obtain by fraud. Now *rare* or *obsolete.* E19.

📖 **1** C. ACHEBE Accusing the outgoing Government of all kinds of swindling and corruption. **2** *San Diego* Move into the antique trade by swindling an old man out of an antique . . table. **3** *Daily Telegraph* After an investigation . . he owned up to swindling the larger sum.

▶ **B** *noun.* **1** An act of swindling; a fraudulent transaction or scheme. M19.
2 A specious or false representation; a pretence. *colloq.* M19.

📖 **1** T. BERGER The daily swindles perpetrated . . on the defenseless seekers of apartments. **2** T. G. BOWLES The Mediterranean is a mere swindle. It is . . not a sea, but a miserable puddle. *Reader's Digest* Blunt . . declared Post-Impressionist paintings: 'Either a bad joke or a swindle'.

Comb.: **swindle sheet** *slang* (chiefly *US*) an expense account; *joc.* a logbook, a time sheet.

swindler /ˈswɪndlə/ *noun.* L18.
[German *Schwindler* giddy-minded person, extravagant projector, cheat, from *schwindeln* be giddy, act thoughtlessly or extravagantly, swindle.]
A person who practises fraud or deceit for purposes of gain; a cheat.

📖 E. TEMPLETON He had fallen victim to swindlers, when investing large sums of money.

■ **swindlery** *noun* the practice of a swindler; swindling: M19.

swine /swʌɪn/ *noun.* Pl. same, in sense 2 also **-s.**
[Old English *swīn* = Old Frisian, Old Saxon, Old High German, *swīn* (Dutch *zwijn*, German *Schwein*), Old Norse *svín*, Gothic *swein*, from Germanic use as noun of adjective; from Indo-European base, repr. also by Latin *sus* (*suis*), Greek *hus.* Cf. -INE[1].]
1 An animal of the pig kind; an adult pig, a hog. Now chiefly *dial., literary, & techn.* exc. in comb. OE.
2 *fig.* A lascivious or coarse person; now *esp.* as a gen. term of abuse for a person, esp. a man. ME. ▸**b** An awkward or unpleasant task, experience, etc. *colloq.* M20.

📖 **1** ***cast pearls before swine***: see PEARL *noun*[1] 2. **2** S. MILLIGAN The cowardly swines have run away. **b** H. MACINNES This car's . . a swine to drive at slow speeds. **a swine of a** — an awkward or unpleasant —.

Comb.: **swine-back** (*a*) (an animal having) a markedly convex or arched back; (*b*) = HOGBACK 2; **swine-backed** *adjective* having a convexly curved surface or outline; **swine-chopped** *adjective* (of a dog) having the lower jaw projecting in front of the upper one; **swine-cote** *arch. & dial.* a pigsty; **swine-cress** either of two small cruciferous weeds with warty fruits, *Coronopus squamatus* and (more fully ***lesser swine-cress***) *C. didymus*; †**swine-drunk** *adjective* extremely drunk; **swine erysipelas** an infectious, sometimes fatal, fever of pigs caused by the bacterium *Erysipelothrix rhusiopathiae*; **swine fever** an infectious viral disease of pigs involving fever, diarrhoea, internal haemorrhage, and debility; ***African swine fever***, an acute or chronic viral disease of pigs, chiefly in sub-Saharan Africa, transmitted by ticks; **swine flu** = ***swine influenza*** below; **swine-head** *poet.* a swinish or self-indulgent person; **swineherd** a keeper of a herd of pigs; **swineherdship** *rare* the position of a swineherd; **swine-hull** *dial.* a pigsty; **swine influenza** an infectious virus disease of pigs, esp. young ones, characterized by fever, coughing, and difficulty in breathing; influenza in humans caused by the same or a closely related virus; **swine-pox** †(*a*) chickenpox; (*b*) an infectious pustular virus disease of pigs; **swine's cress** = ***swine-cress*** above; **swine's feather** *MILITARY HISTORY* a pointed stake fixed in the ground or carried in a musket rest, as a weapon of defence against cavalry; **swine's grass** (now *Scot.*) knotgrass, *Polygonum aviculare*; **swine's grease** (now *dial.*) pig fat, lard; **swine-sty** (now *dial.*) a pigsty; ***swine's succory***: see SUCCORY 2; **swine vesicular disease** an infectious virus disease of pigs (similar to foot-and-mouth disease) characterized by mild fever and blisters round the mouth and feet.
■ **swinehood** *noun* the condition of a swine E19. **swinely** *adjective* (*rare*) swinish LME. **swinery** *noun* (*a*) a pigsty, a piggery; (*b*) a swinish condition; swine collectively: L18.

swing /swɪŋ/ *noun*[1]. OE.
[In sense 1 app. repr. Old English *geswing*; in other senses from SWING *verb.*]
▶ **I** Abstract senses.
†**1** A stroke with a weapon. OE–LME.
†**2** Impulse; inclination. M16–E18.
3 Steady or vigorous pace or progress of an event, action, period of time, etc. L16. ▸**b** A swift tour involving a number of stops; *spec.* a political campaign tour. *N. Amer.* M19. ▸**c** A break during a period of work; a shift system incorporating such breaks. *US slang.* E20.
4 Freedom of action, free scope. L16.
5 A forceful movement of propulsion or momentum (as) of an object swung or flung. *arch.* L16.
6 A movement to and fro, (as) of an object from above, or an object turning on a fixed centre or axis; the curve traced in this way, the amount or extent of this. L16. ▸**b** A discernible movement in general opinion away from one position towards another, *spec.* a change in the

relative distribution of popular support for political parties. L19. ▸**c** *CRICKET.* A curving deviation of a ball from a straight line of flight on delivery. E20. ▸**d** *ELECTRICITY.* An increase or decrease in the magnitude of a current or voltage; the difference between its greatest and smallest values. E20. ▸**e** *BRIDGE.* The difference between the total scores of two teams of two pairs playing the same deal at two tables. M20.

7 The action or an act of brandishing or waving about a weapon or other body; a movement describing a curve; *colloq.* a blow or punch delivered with such a movement. M17.

8 a A steady flowing rhythm characterizing a piece of verse. E19. ▸**b** Jazz or dance music with an easy flowing rhythm, *esp.* that played by big bands in the 1930s and 1940s; the rhythmic feeling or drive of this music. L19.

🕮 **3** E. LANGLEY Picking would be in full swing in a week's time. J. HARVEY He resumed his work; but disjointedly . . with no sort of swing. B. PYM She found the firework party in full swing. **4** S. E. WHITE A kindly girl, whose parents gave her free swing. **5** DRYDEN And rising as he threw, With its full swing the fatal Weapon flew. **6** S. JOHNSON One was detected by his gait, and another by the swing of his arms. *Practical Woodworking* Check the snugness of fit and the swing of the door. **b** *City Limits* The most interesting thing . . in fashion recently has been the swing away from utility. *Private Investor* Trade . . has shown a pronounced swing . . in the direction of Europe. ***mood swing***: see MOOD *noun*¹. **7** *Golf Monthly* Unless the basics are right in the swing, there isn't much chance that you'll hit the ball. *Daily Telegraph* Hand injuries caused to people taking swings at opponents in brawls.

▶**II 9** A seat suspended from above on ropes or rods, on or in which a person may sit and swing to and fro. L17.

10 The rope or chain attached to the tongue of a wagon, along which the draught animals between the leaders and the wheelers are attached. M19.

11 The group of outriders who keep a moving herd of cattle in order. *US.* E20.

Phrases: **go with a swing** (of a party or other event) be lively or successful. **in full swing** at the height of activity. **swings and roundabouts** [from phr. *you lose on the swings what you make on the roundabouts*] a state of affairs in which different actions result in no eventual gain or loss.

Comb.: **swingometer** *colloq.* [from SWING *noun*¹ after *barometer* etc.] a device consisting of a dial with a movable pointer, used to demonstrate the effect of a political swing on an election; **swing man** (*a*) an outrider in a swing; (*b*) a jazz musician who plays swing music; (*c*) *US slang* a versatile sports player who can play effectively in different positions; (*d*) *slang* a drug pedlar; **swing set** a frame for children to play on, including one or more swings.

Swing /swɪŋ/ *noun*². M19.

[Captain *Swing*: see below.]

Hist. Used *attrib.* to designate acts of intimidation practised against English farmers and landowners between 1830–1, involving threatening letters signed by a fictitious Captain Swing and the burning of agricultural property.

swing /swɪŋ/ *verb.* Pa. t. **swung** /swʌŋ/, (now chiefly *Scot. & north.*) **swang** /swaŋ/; pa. pple **swung**.

[Old English *swingan* = Old Frisian *swinga*, Middle & mod. Low German *swingen*, Old High German *swingan* (German *schwingen* brandish etc.), from Germanic base parallel to that of SWINK.]

†**1** *verb trans.* Whip or beat (a person); strike with a weapon or the hand. OE–LME. ▸**b** *verb trans. COOKERY.* Beat (an egg etc.). OE–L15. ▸**c** *verb intrans.* Strike a blow *with*; come *together* with blows. ME–L15.

†**2** *verb intrans.* Move or go with rapid violence, rush. OE–L16. ▸**b** *verb trans.* Carry, drive, or throw with force. ME–L16.

3 a *verb trans.* Orig., draw *out* (a sword) with a vigorous movement, brandish, wave *about.* Later passing into senses 6, 9b, wield (an implement); bring down (something held or grasped) with a curving or rotatory movement. LME. ▸**b** *verb trans. & intrans.* Throw (a punch). L19.

4 a *verb trans.* Hang or suspend so as to be free to sway; (*rare*) execute by hanging. E16. ▸**b** *verb intrans.* Hang or be suspended so as to be free to sway; *colloq.* be executed by hanging. M16.

5 *verb intrans.* Move freely to and fro as an object suspended from a support above. M16. ▸**b** Of a person: move to and fro through the air on a suspended rope or a swing (SWING *noun*¹ 9). M17. ▸**c** (Of a bell) peal; (of a sound) ring *out.* M17. ▸**d** *fig.* Waver, vacillate; change from one mood or opinion to the opposite. M19.

6 *verb trans.* Cause to move freely to and fro. M16. ▸**b** *verb trans.* Cause (a person) to move back and forth on a swing (SWING *noun*¹ 9), suspended rope, etc. E17. ▸**c** *verb trans.* Of a bell: sound (a peal). E19. ▸**d** *verb trans.* Lift and transport (something suspended), esp. from point to point. M19. ▸**e** *verb refl. & intrans.* Hoist (oneself) up or transport from point to point by grasping a support above and leaping. L19.

7 *verb intrans.* Move to and fro or from side to side as if suspended; sway. E17.

8 *verb intrans.* Turn in alternate directions, or in either direction, (as if) on an axis or pivot. Also foll. by adverb. M18. ▸**b** Go along or round in a curve or with a sweeping motion; wheel. E19. ▸**c** *CRICKET.* Of a bowled ball: follow a curving course. E20. ▸**d** *ASTRONAUTICS.* Of a spacecraft: pass *by* a planet etc., using its gravitational field to change course. M20.

9 *verb trans.* Cause to turn in alternate directions, or in either direction, (as if) on an axis or pivot; *spec.* (*NAUTICAL*) turn (a ship) to all compass points in succession, in order to ascertain the deviation of its magnetic compass; turn or cause to face in another direction. M18. ▸**b** Cause to move in a curve. E19. ▸**c** Turn a starting-handle in order to start (a motor vehicle, its engine). *colloq.* E20. ▸**d** *CRICKET.* Of a bowler: cause (a ball) to follow a curving course. M20.

10 *verb intrans.* Go or walk with a (vigorously) swaying step. M19.

11 *verb trans.* **a** Direct; control (*US*); have a decisive influence on (esp. voting). L19. ▸**b** Bring about; contrive, manage. Freq. with *it. colloq.* M20.

12 *verb trans. MECHANICS.* Fix (the work) on the centre or centres in a lathe; (of a lathe) be able to admit (a specified diameter of work). L19.

13 a *verb intrans. & trans.* (with *it*). Play jazz music with swing. E20. ▸**b** *verb trans.* Play (a tune) with swing. M20.

14 *verb intrans.* **a** Enjoy oneself, have fun, esp. in an unconstrained manner; be lively or fashionable; be up to date. *slang.* M20. ▸**b** Be promiscuous; *spec.* advocate or engage in group sex or swapping sexual partners. *slang.* M20. ▸**c** Of a party: be lively or successful. *colloq.* L20.

🕮 **3** MILTON Go baffl'd coward, lest I . . swing thee in the Air. B. HARTE Each swung a lasso. J. BUCHAN The forest settler who swung an axe all day. **4a** B. MACDONALD Our hammock . . was swung between two . . apple trees. **b** E. JONG What Satisfaction . . to hear the Snap of her . . Neck and see her swing at Tyburn. **5** J. STEINBECK His arms did not swing at his sides, but hung loosely. H. WILLIAMSON The skirt did not swing as she turned round . . the pleats followed sluggishly. A. TYLER The keys were still swinging from the ignition. **b** E. WAUGH A chandelier that one of his young ladies had tried to swing on. **d** A. PRICE Alternate bouts of rage and triumph as the argument swung this way and that. D. PROFUMO His attention swung between one wave of conversation and another. **6** E. BOWEN Gerald walked across the lawn . . swinging his racquet. P. FARMER Teenagers . . sat along a wall swinging their legs. **e** P. FARMER The monkey swung down from the trees. G. NAYLOR He swung himself down the ladder. ELLIS PETERS Hugh . . swung himself into the high saddle. **7** J. ARBUTHNOT If the Coach swung but the least to one side, she used to shriek. E. B. BROWNING Dodona's oak swang lonely Henceforth, to the tempest only. **8** C. S. FORESTER Her stern was swinging in to bump against the *Santa Barbara's* bow. G. VIDAL She let the door swing creakily shut. G. LORD She swung round to see if something was behind her. **b** A. RANSOME The bus swung out of the station yard. L. SPALDING The river here swings across a valley. **9** T. HEGGEN Sam swung the telescope around to have a look. A. MACLEAN He swung the heavy iron door to. **b** G. GREENE It . . swung the machete in a wide arc. C. MACKENZIE He swung the car round . . in front of the school. **10** R. S. SURTEES He . . swung into the hall with a noisy flourish. **11a** J. BARTH Anything could happen to swing one more vote our way. J. WILCOX You got a few bucks you can swing this way? **b** P. BARRY Isn't that a pretty big order to swing at this late date? S. BELLOW He said, 'That depends', implying that he might be able to swing it.

Phrases: ***no room to swing a cat in***, ***not room to swing a cat in***: see ROOM *noun*¹. **swing around the circle** *US* make a political tour of a constituency. **swing both ways** *slang* have sexual partners of both sexes. **swing Douglas**, **swing Kelly** *Austral. slang* wield an axe. **swing the gate** *Austral. & NZ slang* be a fast and expert shearer. ***swing the lead***: see LEAD *noun*¹.

Comb.: **swing-back** (*a*) an act of swinging back; *fig.* reaction against something, a reversion to a previous state; (*b*) a style of coat cut to swing as the wearer moves; **swingball** (proprietary name for) a game of table-skittles in which a suspended ball is thrown to hit the skittles on the return pass; **swing-boat** a boat-shaped swing at a fair etc.; **swing bowler** *CRICKET*: who swings the ball; **swing bowling** *CRICKET*: involving swinging the ball; **swing-bridge** that can be turned on a pivot (either at one end or in the centre) to allow the passage of ships; **swing-by** *noun & adjective* (*ASTRONAUTICS*) (designating a space flight including) a change of course made by using the gravitational field of a planet etc.; **swing-chair** a rocking-chair; **swing-coat**: cut so as to swing when the wearer moves; **swing-door**: constructed so as to open in either direction and to swing shut when released; **swing-gate** a gate constructed so as to swing shut when released; *spec.* (*Austral.*) a gate which while opening one way for sheep or cattle to pass, closes off another; **swing-glass** = *swing mirror* below; **swing hand** *BRIDGE* a hand which proves to be decisive in the overall result of a rubber or match; **swing mirror**: fixed on pivots so that the angle may be altered; **swing needle** a sewing-machine needle which can move sideways to sew zigzag or patterned stitches; **swing-over** a change-over; **swing pass** *AMER. FOOTBALL* a short pass to a back running to the outside; **swing room** *US* a room in which employees may relax while temporarily off duty; **swing-rope** (*a*) *NAUTICAL* a small rope by which a boat swings; (*b*) a rope for a swing; **swing-round** *fig.* a striking change or reversal; **swing-shift** *US* a work shift from afternoon to late evening; **swing-tail** †(*a*) a long tail that swings about; (*b*) *AERONAUTICS* a hinged rear section of an aircraft fuselage which can be swung to one side for loading large items of cargo; **swing-ticket** a tag carrying information on price, size, material, etc., attached to the article by a string; **swing-tool**: which fixes the work on the centre of a lathe; **swing-tree** = *swingletree* (b) s.v. SWINGLE *noun*¹; **swing vote**, **swing voter** *US*: having a decisive influence on the result of a poll; **swing-wheel** the escape-wheel of a clock, which drives the pendulum; the balance-wheel of a watch; **swing wing** an aircraft wing that can move from a right-angled to a swept-back position.

swinge /swɪn(d)ʒ/ *noun. obsolete exc. dial.* M16.

[Rel. to next.]

†**1** Power, authority, influence; sway. M16–M17.

†**2** Freedom of action, free scope = SWING *noun*¹ 4. M16–L17.

†**3** Impulse; inclination. M16–E19.

†**4** Impetus, momentum; a forceful sweeping or whirling movement. L16–L17.

5 A stroke, a swinging blow. E17.

6 A leash for a dog. M17.

swinge /swɪn(d)ʒ/ *verb*¹. Also (earlier) †**swenge**. Pres. pple & verbal noun **swingeing**.

[Old English *swengan*, from Germanic verb repr. in Gothic *afswaggidai* be in doubt. See also SWINGEING *adjective & adverb*.]

†**1** *verb trans.* Shake, shatter. OE–LME.

†**2** *verb intrans.* Move violently, dash (*at*). OE–LME.

3 *verb trans.* Beat, thrash, flog. Now *arch. & dial.* ME. ▸†**b** *fig.* Chastise. M16–E18.

†**4** *verb trans.* Smite, dash, fling. Only in ME.

†**5** *verb trans.* Drink *up* or *off*. *slang.* E16–M17.

†**6** *verb trans.* Whirl round, spin. M16–L17.

†**7** *verb trans.* Brandish, flourish; lash (the tail). L16–E17.

8 *verb trans.* Cut down with a scythe. *dial.* L16.

Comb.: **swinge-buckler** *arch.* = SWASHBUCKLER.

swinge /swɪn(d)ʒ/ *verb*² *trans.* Now *dial. & US.* Pres. pple & verbal noun **swingeing**. L16.

[Prob. alt. of SINGE *verb*, infl. by SWEAL.]

Singe, scorch.

swingeing /ˈswɪn(d)ʒɪŋ/ *adjective & adverb.* M16.

[In sense A.1 after SWINGE *noun*; in other senses from SWINGE *verb*¹ + -ING².]

▶**A** *adjective.* †**1** Powerful, authoritative. Only in M16.

2 Very great in size, amount, or effect; huge, far-reaching, esp. in severity. L16.

🕮 **2** B. CASTLE He introduced swingeing increases in taxation. *Wine* They needed . . a bit of sweetness to balance their swingeing acidity.

▶**B** *adverb.* Hugely, immensely. L17.

▪ **swingeingly** *adverb* hugely, immensely L17.

swinger /ˈswɪŋə/ *noun*¹. M16.

[from SWING *verb* + -ER¹.]

1 A person who or thing which swings. M16. ▸**b** A gramophone record with an eccentric spindle-hole. M20.

2 *spec.* A lively fashionable person; a person who is promiscuous or advocates or engages in group sex or swapping of sexual partners. *slang.* M20.

swinger /ˈswɪn(d)ʒə/ *noun*². L16.

[from SWINGE *verb*¹ + -ER¹.]

†**1** A vigorous or forceful person. L16–L17.

2 a A forceful or effective thing; *esp.* a very big thing. *colloq.* Now *rare.* L16. ▸†**b** *spec.* A great lie. L17–L18. ▸**c** A heavy blow. M19.

swinging /ˈswɪŋɪŋ/ *adjective.* M16.

[from SWING *verb* + -ING².]

1 That swings. M16.

2 Of gait, melody, etc.: vigorously rhythmical. E19.

3 Fine, splendid, excellent. *colloq.* M20.

1 swinging boom *NAUTICAL* a boom swung or suspended over the ship's side, used to stretch the foot of a lower studding-sail, and (when at anchor) for a boat to ride by. **swinging-bridge** = *swing-bridge* s.v. SWING *verb.*

▪ **swingingly** *adverb* with a swinging movement L19.

swingle /ˈswɪŋg(ə)l/ *noun*¹. ME.

[Middle Dutch *swinghel* from base of SWING *verb* + -LE¹.]

1 A wooden instrument for beating and scraping flax or hemp so as to remove any woody or coarse parts. ME.

2 The swipple of a flail. *local.* LME. ▸**b** Chiefly *Hist.* A weapon resembling a flail. E19.

3 A crank. *dial.* L17.

Comb.: **swingle-bar** = *swingletree* (b) below; **swingle-hand**, **swingle-staff** = sense 1 above; **swingletree** (*a*) (*obsolete exc. dial.*) a board used in dressing flax or hemp with a swingle; (*b*) a cross-bar pivoted at the middle, to which the traces are fastened in a cart, plough, etc.; (*c*) *dial.* = sense 2 above.

swingle /ˈswɪŋg(ə)l/ *noun*². *N. Amer. slang.* M20.

[Blend of SWINGING *adjective* and SINGLE *noun.*]

A lively socially active single person, *spec.* one in search of a sexual partner.

swingle /ˈswɪŋ(ə)l/ *verb*¹ *trans. & intrans.* ME.

[from SWINGLE *noun*¹.]

Beat and scrape (flax or hemp) with a swingle.

swingle /ˈswɪŋ(ə)l/ *verb*². LME.

[Frequentative of SWING *verb*: see -LE³.]

†**1** *verb trans.* Swing or flourish about. Only in LME.

2 *verb intrans.* Swing; hang. *dial.* M18.

swingster /ˈswɪŋstə/ *noun. slang.* M20.
[from SWING *noun*[1] + -STER.]
A musician who plays jazz with swing.

swing-swang /ˈswɪŋswaŋ/ *noun.* L17.
[Redupl. of SWING *verb*.]
A swinging to and fro; a reciprocating movement.

swingy /ˈswɪŋi/ *adjective. colloq.* M20.
[from SWING *noun*[1] + -Y[1].]
1 Of music: having an easy flowing rhythm. M20.
2 Of a garment, esp. a skirt or dress: cut as to swing as the wearer moves. M20.
3 Of gait: characterized by a swinging movement. M20.

Swinhoe /ˈswɪnhəʊ/ *noun.* M19.
[Robert *Swinhoe* (1836–77), English diplomat and ornithologist.]
Used in *possess.* to designate Asian birds described by Swinhoe.
Swinhoe's pheasant a pheasant, *Lophura swinhoii*, which has striking plumage in shades of blue, green, white, etc., and is confined to the highlands of Taiwan.

swinish /ˈswʌɪnɪʃ/ *adjective.* ME.
[from SWINE *noun* + -ISH[1].]
1 Having the character of a pig; characteristic of a pig; coarse, gross; unpleasant. ME.
2 Resembling (that of) a pig in appearance. L16.
3 That is a pig; consisting of pigs; *rare* pertaining to a pig or pigs. L16.

> **1** P. BARRY I *was* sort of swinish to him. R. H. MORRIESON Taking refuge from disgrace in swinish slumber.
> **2** E. R. EDDISON Gabriel with little swinish eyes watched him eagerly.

■ **swinishly** *adverb* M16. **swinishness** *noun* L16.

swink /swɪŋk/ *verb & noun.*
[Old English *swincan* from base parallel to that of *swingan* SWING *verb*.]
▶ **A** *verb.* Pa. t. & pple **swinked**, (*arch.*) **swinkt**.
1 *verb intrans.* Labour, toil, work hard. Now *arch.* & *dial.* OE.
2 *verb trans.* Labour or work at (a task); set (a person) to work, overwork. Now only as ***swinked*** *ppl adjective*, wearied with toil. *arch.* ME.
3 *verb trans.* & *intrans.* Drink. *obsolete* exc. *Scot. dial.* M16.
▶ **B** *noun.* †**1** Trouble, affliction. *rare.* OE–LME.
2 Labour, toil. Now *arch.* & *dial.* ME.
■ **swinker** *noun* (*arch.*) a toiler, a labourer ME.

swinny *noun* var. of SWEENY.

swipe /swʌɪp/ *noun.* E17.
[Prob. var. of SWEEP *noun*. Partly from the verb.]
▶ **I 1** = SWEEP *noun* 2, 3. *local.* E17.
▶ **II 2** A stroke or blow made with a full swing of the arm. *colloq.* M18. ▶**b** A swath of corn. *dial.* M19. ▶**c** A streak, a stripe. L19. ▶**d** An electronic device for reading information magnetically encoded on a card, usu. incorporating a slot through which the card is passed. L20.
3 *sing.* & (earlier, now *arch.*) in *pl.* (treated as *sing.*). Weak or poor quality beer. *slang* (now chiefly *Austral.*). L18.

> **2** G. DURRELL She . . . leapt at the bars . . and took a swipe at my face. K. AMIS The batsman skipped out to meet the ball and gave a great swipe at it. *fig.*: W. KAY He also took a swipe at the condescension of the upper classes. **c** *New Yorker* The white, wool felt cloche with a swipe of veiling.

▶ **III 4** A groom, a stableboy. *US slang.* E20.
5 An objectionable person; such people collectively. *slang.* E20.
Comb.: **swipe card** an identity card, credit card, etc., with magnetically encoded information which can be read when the card is passed through an electronic device.

swipe /swʌɪp/ *verb.* L18.
[Prob. var. of SWEEP *verb*. Cf. prec.]
1 *verb trans.* & *intrans.* Swallow (a drink) in one gulp. *dial.* & *slang.* L18.
2 *verb intrans.* Strike or attempt to strike *at* with a full swing of the arm. E19. ▶**b** *verb trans.* Strike with a swinging blow. M19. ▶**c** *verb trans.* Pass (an identity card, credit card, etc.) through an electronic device which reads magnetically encoded information. L20.
3 *verb intrans.* & *trans.* = SWEEP *verb* 10b. L19.
4 *verb trans.* Steal. *slang* (orig. *US*). L19.

> **2** J. DIDION Swiping at a mosquito with his free hand. **b** J. B. MORTON The exasperated man swiped the psychologist full in the face. **4** T. ROETHKE That beautiful Greek anthology you sent me some student swiped.

■ **swiper** *noun* M19.

swipey /ˈswʌɪpi/ *adjective. arch. slang.* E19.
[from SWIPE *noun*, *verb* + -Y[1].]
Drunk; tipsy.

swipper /ˈswɪpə/ *adjective.*
[Old English (*ge*)*swipor* = Old High German *swephar*, *swepfar* rel. to SWEEP *verb*.]
†**1** Crafty, cunning. Only in OE.
2 Quick, nimble. Now *dial.* LME.

swipple /ˈswɪp(ə)l/ *noun.* LME.
[Prob. orig. from SWEEP *verb* + -LE[1]. Cf. SUPPLE *noun*.]
The part of a flail that strikes the grain in threshing. Cf. SUPPLE *noun* 1.

swire /swʌɪə/ *noun.*
[Old English *swēora*, *swīora* corresp. to Old Norse *svíri* neck, beak of a ship, (also in place-names), from Germanic.]
†**1** The neck. OE–L16.
2 A hollow near the summit of a mountain or hill; a gentle depression between two hills. Now chiefly in place-names. OE.

swirl /swəːl/ *noun.* Orig. *Scot.* LME.
[Perh. of Low Dutch origin (cf. Dutch *zwirrelen* whirl), prob. frequentative formation on imit. base repr. also by Middle Low German *swirren*, German *schwirren*, Danish *svirre* whirl.]
1 An eddy, a whirlpool; a whirling body of water, air, dust, etc. LME.
2 A whirling motion. L18. ▶**b** ENGINEERING. A circular motion imparted to the mixture entering the cylinder of an internal-combustion engine. E20.
3 A twist, a curl, esp. as an ornament or as part of a pattern or design. L18.

> **1** R. LEHMANN The rooks flew up in a swirl from the furrows. J. THURBER Leaving in its wake a furious swirl of foam upon the surface. U. HOLDEN The fog came in swirls.
> **2** S. E. WHITE His guide brought the canoe with a swirl of the paddle. J. CHEEVER The vindictive swirl of a blizzard.
> **3** M. ATWOOD He paints very swiftly, in . . frenzied loops and swirls. *Grocer* Leicester cheese with a swirl of full fat soft cheese.

Comb.: **swirl skirt**: cut in the form of a circle or with many gores, so as to swirl when the wearer walks.
■ **swirly** *adjective* (*a*) having a twisted or curled form; (*b*) moving with a whirling motion: L18.

swirl /swəːl/ *verb.* Orig. *Scot.* LME.
[from (the same root as) the noun.]
1 *verb intrans.* Move or be carried along with a whirling motion. LME.
2 *verb trans.* Carry along or cause to move with a whirling motion. E16 ▶**b** Give a twisted form to; twist or wind round in a curl. E20.
3 *verb intrans.* (Of the head) swim; (of a person) be giddy. E19.

> **1** D. M. THOMAS Floods swirled around us and we huddled close. M. WESLEY The aromatic smoke swirled up. B. VINE When she got up her skirt swirled. *fig.*: P. P. READ Embarrassment, disgust, confusion, all swirled around his mind. **2** W. T. WATTS-DUNTON Continents of cloud were . . swirled from peak to peak. W. SOYINKA Swirling his drink round and round his glass. **b** *New Scientist* A tall ripening crop has been swirled and flattened in a circular shape.

swish /swɪʃ/ *noun*[1]. Also redupl. **swish-swish**. E19.
[Imit.]
1 A hissing sound, as of a slender object moved rapidly through the air or an object moving swiftly in contact with water; a rustling sound, as made by silk; movement accompanied by such a sound. E19.
2 A splash *of* water on a surface. *arch.* M19.
3 A cane or birch for flogging; a stroke with this. Also, a cane etc. for keeping off flies. M19.
4 An effeminate male homosexual. *US slang.* M20.
5 CRICKET. A rapid or careless attacking stroke. *colloq.* M20.

> **1** R. L. STEVENSON The swish of the sea against the bows. A. LURIE Vanishing with a swish of her dress. K. VONNEGUT The swish of tires in the gravel driveway.

swish /swɪʃ/ *noun*[2]. M19.
[Origin unkn.]
A type of mortar used in building in W. Africa.

swish /swɪʃ/ *adjective. colloq.* L19.
[Prob. from SWISH *noun*[1].]
Smart, elegant, fashionable.

> *Daily Telegraph* Jonathan King takes off . . to visit a swish ski resort for the rich and famous. *Independent* Top people were gathered in a swish country house hotel.

swish /swɪʃ/ *verb.* M18.
[Imit.]
1 *verb intrans.* & *trans.* (Cause to) move with a swinging motion, esp. so as to make a swish or a hissing or rustling sound; (cause to) make such a sound. M18.
2 *verb trans.* Flog (esp. a schoolboy). *arch.* M19.

> **1** A. BURGESS The windscreen wipers swished softly. S. MIDDLETON Cars swished along the road. R. INGALLS She dropped . . margarine into the spaghetti and swished it around. P. L. FERMOR The horses . . swished their tails. D. PROFUMO He swished the fly-line on to the water.

swish /swɪʃ/ *interjection & adverb.* Also redupl. **swish-swish**. M19.
[Imit.]
▶ **A** *interjection.* Expr. a swish or a hissing or rustling sound. M19.
▶ **B** *adverb.* With a swish. L19.

swish-swash /ˈswɪʃswɒʃ/ *noun & adverb.* M16.
[Redupl. of SWISH *noun*[1]. Cf. WISH-WASH.]
▶ **A** *noun.* A weak or poor quality drink. Now *rare.* M16.
▶ **B** *adverb.* With an alternate or repeated swishing movement. M19.

swish-swish *noun, interjection & adverb* see SWISH *noun*[1], *interjection & adverb*.

swishy /ˈswɪʃi/ *adjective.* E19.
[from SWISH *noun*[1], *verb* + -Y[1].]
1 Characterized by swishing. E19.
2 Effeminate. *slang.* M20.

Swiss /swɪs/ *noun & adjective.* E16.
[French *Suisse* from Middle High German *Swiz* Switzerland (German *Schweiz*). Cf. SWITZER.]
▶ **A** *noun.* Pl. same, †**-es**.
1 A native or inhabitant of Switzerland, a country in central Europe. E16.
2 A dialect of German, French, or Italian used in Switzerland. *rare.* M19.
3 = ***Swiss muslin*** below. L19.
4 A tournament played according to the Swiss system (see sense B.2 below). M20.
▶ **B** *adjective.* **1** Of, pertaining to, associated with, or characteristic of the Swiss or Switzerland. M16.
2 Designating a system of organizing (esp. bridge or chess) tournaments, in which after the first round each player or team is matched against an opponent with a similar score, but no two opponents may meet more than once. M20.
Special collocations & comb.: **Swiss Army knife** a penknife incorporating several blades and other tools such as scissors and screwdrivers. **Swiss bank** a bank in Switzerland at which clients' anonymity and security are preserved by a system of numbered accounts. **Swiss banker**: who works in a Swiss bank. ***Swiss*** CHARD. **Swiss cheese** *noun & adjectival phr.* (*a*) *noun phr.* cheese from Switzerland, freq. characterized by large holes; (*b*) *adjectival phr.* characteristic of Swiss cheese, characterized by large holes or spaces; ***Swiss cheese plant***, an evergreen Central American climbing plant, *Monstera deliciosa*, of the arum family, grown as a house-plant for its large ovate perforated leaves. **Swiss cottage** a chalet. **Swiss cream** a type of trifle. **Swiss darning** a technique in which coloured stitches are sewn on to knitted garments to make patterns or motifs that seem to have been knitted. **Swiss file** a small fine-cut file. **Swiss-German** *adjective & noun* (*a*) *adjective* of or pertaining to Schweizerdeutsch or the part of Switzerland where this is spoken; (*b*) *noun* a native or inhabitant of the part of Switzerland where Schweizerdeutsch is spoken (cf. ***German-Swiss*** s.v. GERMAN *noun*[1] & *adjective*[1]). **Swiss guard** *sing.* & in *pl.* Swiss mercenaries employed as a special guard, formerly by sovereigns of France etc., now only at the Vatican. **Swiss muslin** a thin crisp plain-weave muslin, freq. ornamented with dots or figures. **Swiss roll** a cylindrical cake with a spiral cross-section made from a flat piece of sponge cake spread with jam etc. and rolled up. **Swiss steak** *N. Amer.* a dish of (usu. less tender) steak that has been floured, pounded, and cooked by braising with vegetables; a cut of meat suitable for cooking in this way. ***Swiss stone pine***: see ***stone pine*** s.v. STONE *noun*.
■ †**Swisser** *noun* a Swiss person M16–M18. **Swissess** *noun* (*rare*) a Swiss woman or girl L18.

switch /swɪtʃ/ *noun.* L16.
[In branch I prob. from Low German: cf. Hanoverian dial. *swutsche* var. of Low German *swukse* long thin stick (cf. *zwuksen* bend up and down, make a swishing noise); in branch II from the verb.]
▶ **I 1** A thin tapering riding-whip. L16.
2 A thin flexible shoot cut from a tree. E17.
3 A movable rail or pair of rails forming a junction at which trains etc. are diverted from one line to another; *spec.* = POINT *noun*[1] 15g. Also, such a junction. L18. ▶**b** COMPUTING. A program instruction that selects one or other of a number of possible branches, as determined by the value of a variable. M20. ▶**c** FINANCE. A computer system which manages the transfer of funds between point-of-sale terminals and financial institutions; *spec.* (**S-**) an EFTPOS system in the UK. Also, the transfer of funds by such a system. L20.
4 A device for making and breaking a connection in an electric circuit. M19.
5 A long tress of hair; esp. one of false or detached hair tied at one end and used in hairdressing to supplement the natural growth of hair. L19.
6 A stag having horns without branches. E20.

> **1** J. AUSTEN To cut off the heads of some nettles . . with his switch. ***ride switch and spur***: see SPUR *noun*[1].
> **2** J. BALDWIN Their mother would . . cut a switch from a tree and beat him. **3** J. DOS PASSOS He let a freight train get past a switch. K. KESEY A simple job on the railroad . . out in the sticks on a lonely switch. **asleep at the switch** *N. Amer. colloq.* negligent of or oblivious to one's responsibility, off guard.
> **4** U. HOLDEN A bedside lamp with a switch hanging from a . . flex. B. VINE Turning on lights as she pressed the switch. ***knife switch***, ***oil switch***, ***pressel switch***, ***rotary switch***, ***throw-over switch***, etc. ***throw the switch***: see THROW *verb*.
> **5** P. V. WHITE Rose . . brushed Laura's hair, holding it in one long switch. W. KENNEDY Josie . . lost a lot of her hair. She wears a switch.

▶ **II 7** A sharp stroke or blow with a cane, whip, etc. E19.
8 A change from one state, course, etc., to another; a transfer; a deviation. E20. ▶**b** BRIDGE. A change of suit

either in bidding or in play. E20. ▸**c** An exchange; *spec.* a substitution involving deception. *colloq.* M20.

> 📖 **8** *Economist* Cultivation of wheat in new areas would make possible a switch to industrial crops. S. HOOD With a sudden switch of subject she enquired what had taken him to Perpignan.

Comb.: **switch-blade (knife)** a pocket knife with a blade on a spring, released by pressing a button etc. on the handle; **switch cane** a large bamboo, *Arundinaria gigantea* subsp. *tecta*, of the south-east US; **switch deal** ECONOMICS a deal involving purchase and resale, or sale and repurchase, of a commodity in order to profit by differential values of currency, or one involving repurchase or resale through a third party; **switch dealer** ECONOMICS a person who makes switch deals; **switch dealing** ECONOMICS the practice of making switch deals; **switch dollar** ECONOMICS a unit of any non-sterling currency comprising the proceeds from the sale of foreign securities, used to invest in other foreign securities; **switch-engine** a locomotive used for shunting; **switchgear** the switching equipment used in the generation and transmission of electric power; **switch gene** GENETICS a gene whose different alleles determine the expression of alternative groups of other genes during development; **switch-girl** *Austral.* a female switchboard operator; **switch-grass** a tall rhizomatous N. American panic-grass, *Panicum virgatum*, which forms large clumps; **switch-hitter** *N. Amer.* (*a*) BASEBALL an ambidextrous batter; (*b*) *slang* a bisexual; **switch-hitting** *adjective* (of a baseball batter) ambidextrous; **switch hook** the hook or support of a telephone which operates the circuit switch when the receiver is removed from it; **switch-horn** a stag's horn without branches; a stag with such horns; **switch-knife** = *switch-blade (knife)* above; **switch-lamp**, **switch-lantern**, (*US*) **switch-light** a lamp or lantern fixed on a railway switch to indicate which track is open; **switchman** a railway worker operating a switch, a pointsman; **switch mechanism** GENETICS the mechanism by which a switch gene operates; **switch-plant** BOTANY a plant with few leaves but having green branches resembling switches which perform the function of leaves; **switch-reference** LINGUISTICS the use in some languages of different forms of 3rd person pronouns to refer to different people in the discourse; **switch selling** a sales technique whereby cheap or non-existent goods are placed on offer on favourable terms to entice the consumer into buying similar but more expensive items; **switch tail** a long flowing tail (esp. of a horse) that can be swished about; **switch-tender** a person in charge of a set of switches on a railway; **switch-tower** *US* a signal-box; **switchyard** *US* (*a*) the part of a railway yard taken up by points, and in which trains are made up; (*b*) an enclosed area of a power system containing the switchgear.

■ **switchy** *adjective* (*rare*) resembling a switch or slender rod; moving or bending like a switch: E19.

switch /swɪtʃ/ *verb.* E17.
[from the noun.]

1 *verb trans.* Strike or beat (as) with a switch; drive *along*, *into*, etc., (as) with a switch. E17.
2 *verb trans.* Cut off the switches or projecting twigs from (a tree, hedge, etc.). Now *Scot.* E19.
3 *verb trans.* Flourish like a switch; lash; move with a jerk or jerks; ANGLING cast (a line) in this way. M19.
4 Chiefly *US.* ▸**a** *verb trans.* Divert (a train etc.) on to another line by means of a switch. M19. ▸**b** *verb intrans.* Of a train etc.: be diverted in this way. Of a railway line: branch *off* at a switch. M19.
5 *fig.* **a** *verb trans.* Turn *off*, divert. Chiefly *US.* M19. ▸**b** *verb trans.* Exchange (items), esp. with intent to deceive; reverse the positions of. L19. ▸**c** *verb intrans.* Change or transfer (*from*) one thing *to* another; alter (to another), change position, subject, etc.; *spec.* (BRIDGE) change *to* another suit in bidding or in play. E20. ▸**d** *verb trans.* Change from one to another of (similar things); transfer, alter. E20.
6 **a** *verb trans. & intrans.* Cause (an electrical device) to start or stop operating by means of a switch, turn on or off (usu. foll. by *on*, *off*). L19. ▸**b** *verb trans.* Change the state of (a device having two states). M20. ▸**c** *verb intrans.* Of a device having two states: pass from one state to the other. Of its state: change. M20. ▸**d** *verb intrans.* Foll. by *over*: change over to another state by means of a switch; *esp.* change the channel of a radio or television set. M20. ▸**e** *verb trans.* Foll. by *through*: direct (a telephone link) through a subsidiary receiver by means of a switch. L20.
7 *fig.* **a** *verb trans. & intrans.* Foll. by *on*, *off*: start or stop performing an action as if by means of a switch; display or cease to display (a quality or emotion). E20. ▸**b** *verb intrans.* Foll. by *off*: cease to pay attention. E20.

> 📖 **1** SIR W. SCOTT Nelly switched her little fish-cart downwards to St. Ronan's Well. R. M. BALLANTYNE We heard him switching his boots as he passed along the street. **3** J. KOSINSKI The horse switched its tail. **5b** F. WELDON Praxis managed to switch envelopes so that an empty one was dispatched instead. **c** A. ALI Was called to the Bar then switched over to solicitor. W. ABISH Didn't expect to find you driving the bus, said Franz. I switched with another driver, said Hagen. D. LEAVITT His declared major was history, but he was thinking of switching to English. **d** *New Yorker* Enid was prone to switching lanes if the road was empty. C. EASTON For laughs . . the performers all switched instruments. **6a** B. PYM Rhoda switched on a bar of the electric fire. *Listener* Many viewers may have missed it by switching off in fatigue. P. CAMPBELL The lad . . switched off the machinery. A. TYLER I'd come home and switch on the TV. **7a** A. MACRAE When his charm was switched off Bob could be extremely difficult. *Pharmaceutical Journal* Cytotoxic drugs . . 'switch on' in cells with low oxygen levels. **b** D. LODGE They switch off, they daydream. M. COREN Gilbert's ability to ignore the . . panic . . and simply switch off.

Phrases: **I'll be switched!** *N. Amer. colloq.* expr. exasperation, denial, or surprise. **switch in**, **switch out** bring into, or take out of, a circuit by operating a switch.

Comb.: **switch-around** the switching of one thing for another, an exchange, a reversal; **switchfoot**, pl. **-s**, SURFING a surfer who can surf with either foot forward on the board; **switch-off** the switching off of an electrical power supply or device, by means of a switch; **switch-on** the switching on of an electrical power supply or device; **switch-over** a switch from one course etc. to another, a change-over.

■ **switchable** *adjective* able to be switched or changed over M20. **switcher** *noun* M19.

switchback /ˈswɪtʃbak/ *noun & verb.* M19.
[from SWITCH *verb* + BACK *adverb*.]

▶ **A** *noun.* Orig., a form of railway used on steep slopes, consisting of zigzag lines connected by switches, at each of which the train is reversed in direction. Now, a railway consisting of alternate sharp ascents and descents, each ascent of the train being partly or wholly effected by the momentum of its previous descent; *esp.* such a railway at a fair etc.; *transf.* a road with alternate sharp ascents and descents. Freq. *attrib.* M19.
▶ **B** *verb intrans.* Take a zigzag course like a switchback. E20.

switchboard /ˈswɪtʃbɔːd/ *noun.* L19.
[from SWITCH *noun* + BOARD *noun*.]

An apparatus for controlling, and for making connections between, various electric circuits; *spec.* in TELEPHONY, an installation for the manual control of telephone connections.

multiple switchboard: see MULTIPLE *adjective*.

switched /swɪtʃt/ *adjective.* M18.
[from SWITCH *noun*, *verb*: see -ED[1], -ED[2].]

†**1** Of a horse: having a switch tail. Only in M18.
2 Of cream: whipped. Of an egg: beaten. *rare.* E20.
3 Of an electrical device: turned *on* or *off* by a switch. M20.
4 Having a switch; obtained by switching; subjected to switching. M20.

3 switched-on (*a*) *colloq.* aware of what is considered fashionable and up to date; (*b*) *slang* excited; under the influence of drugs.

switchel /ˈswɪtʃ(ə)l/ *noun. N. Amer.* L18.
[Origin unkn.: cf. SWIZZLE *noun*[1].]

1 A drink made of molasses and water, sometimes flavoured with vinegar, ginger, or rum. L18.
2 (A drink of) tea, esp. amongst fishermen and sealers. *dial.* L19.

switcheroo /swɪtʃəˈruː/ *noun. colloq.* (chiefly *N. Amer.*). M20.
[from SWITCH *noun* + -EROO.]

An unexpected exchange or change of position, behaviour, etc.

switching /ˈswɪtʃɪŋ/ *verbal noun.* E17.
[from SWITCH *verb* + -ING[1].]

1 The action of SWITCH *verb*; an instance of this. E17.
2 STOCK EXCHANGE. The purchase (or sale) of one stock, and the sale (or purchase) of another stock, at a stipulated price difference. M20.

Comb.: **switching yard** = *switchyard* (a) s.v. SWITCH *noun*.

swith /swɪθ/ *adverb.* Now *Scot. & dial.*
[Old English *swīþe* = Old Saxon *swīþo*, Old Frisian *swīthe*, *swīde*, Old High German, Middle High German *swinde* (German *geschwind*), from Germanic adjective repr. by Old English *swīþ* strong: ult. origin unkn.]

†**1** Strongly, forcibly; extremely, excessively. OE–LME.
2 At a rapid rate, very quickly, swiftly. ME.
3 Without delay, instantly, immediately, at once. ME.

> 📖 **3** R. BURNS Kings and nations—swith, awa!

swithen /ˈswɪð(ə)n/ *verb trans. & intrans. obsolete* exc. *dial.* See also SWIDDEN. E17.
[Old Norse *sviðna* be singed, rel. to *sviða* roasting, burning, singeing. Cf. SWITHER *verb*[2].]

Burn, scorch.

swither /ˈswɪðə/ *verb*[1] *& noun. Scot. & dial.* E16.
[Origin unkn.]

▶ **A** *verb intrans.* Be or become uncertain; be perplexed or undecided; hesitate. E16.
▶ **B** *noun.* **1** A state of perplexity, indecision, or hesitation; doubt, uncertainty. E18.
2 A state of agitation or excitement; a flurry, a fluster. M18.

swither /ˈswɪðə/ *verb*[2] *trans. & intrans. Scot. & dial.* M19.
[Old Norse *sviðra* burn, singe, rel. to *sviðna*: see SWITHEN.]

= SWITHEN.

Switzer /ˈswɪtsə/ *noun & adjective. arch.* M16.
[Middle High German *Switzer*, *Schwytzer*, (German *Schweizer*), from *Swiz*: see SWISS.]

▶ **A** *noun.* **1** = SWISS *noun* 1. M16.
2 In *pl.* Swiss guards. M16.
▶ **B** *adjective.* = SWISS *adjective*. L16.

■ **Switzeress** *noun* a Swiss female E18.

swive /swʌɪv/ *verb.*
[Old English *swīfan* = Old Frisian *swīva* be uncertain, Old Norse *svífa* rove, ramble, Old High German *swebēn*, Middle High German *sweben* (German *schweben*) hover, from Germanic from Indo-European. Cf. SWIFT *adjective*.]

†**1** Move in a course, sweep. Only in OE.
2 *verb trans. & intrans.* Copulate (with). Now *literary & joc.* ME.

■ **swiver** *noun* a person who swives; a person given to sexual indulgence: LME.

swivel /ˈswɪv(ə)l/ *noun.* ME.
[from weak grade of prec.: see -EL[1].]

1 A fastening or coupling device enabling an object fastened to it to turn freely on it or one part to revolve without turning another. ME. ▸**b** *spec.* A pivoted rest for a gun, esp. on the gunwale of a boat, enabling it to turn horizontally in any direction. L17.
2 In full ***swivel-gun***. A gun or cannon mounted on a pivoted rest so as to turn horizontally in any direction. E18.
3 A small shuttle used in ribbon-weaving etc. Also ***swivel shuttle***. L19.

> 📖 **1** N. GORDIMER He . . tried the aerial at every angle its swivel allowed.

Comb.: **swivel-bridge** a swing-bridge; **swivel chair** a chair the seat of which turns horizontally on a pivot; **swivel eye** *colloq.* a squinting eye; an eye that rolls in its socket; **swivel-eyed** *adjective* squint-eyed, squinting; ***swivel-gun***: see sense 2 above; **swivel hips** a trampolining exercise consisting of a seat drop followed by a half-twist into another seat drop; **swivel-hook**: fastened to something by means of a swivel; ***swivel shuttle***: see sense 3 above.

swivel /ˈswɪv(ə)l/ *verb*[1]. Infl. **-ll-**, ***-l-**. L18.
[from the noun.]

1 *verb trans. & intrans.* Turn on or as on a swivel; rotate. L18.
2 *verb trans.* Provide or fit with a swivel; fasten *to* by means of a swivel. L19.

> 📖 **1** G. SWIFT My interviewer swivelled his chair round. F. FORSYTH Two cameras on the . . wall swivelled to follow them.

swivel /ˈswɪv(ə)l/ *verb*[2] *intrans. & trans. US dial.* Infl. **-ll-**, ***-l-**. L19.
[Alt. of SHRIVEL *verb*.]

Shrivel (*up*).

swivet /ˈswɪvɪt/ *noun. dial.* (chiefly *US*). L19.
[Origin unkn.]

A state of agitation; a fluster, a panic. Also, a hurry. Freq. in ***in a swivet***.

swizz /swɪz/ *noun. slang.* Also **swiz**. E20.
[Abbreviation of SWIZZLE *noun*[2].]

A disappointment; something unfair; a swindle.

> 📖 N. BAWDEN 'What a swizz,' John said in a . . grumbling tone, secretly rather relieved that this was all there was. *Smash Hits* It's very mediocre entertainment, a bit of a swizz at £9.99.

swizzle /ˈswɪz(ə)l/ *noun*[1]. *colloq.* E19.
[Origin unkn.: cf. SWITCHEL.]

A mixed alcoholic drink, *esp.* an unshaken cocktail containing rum or brandy.

Comb.: **swizzle-stick**: used for stirring and frothing or flattening drinks; ***swizzle-stick tree***, a small aromatic evergreen tree, *Quararibea turbinata* (family Bombacaceae), of tropical America.

swizzle /ˈswɪz(ə)l/ *noun*[2]. *slang.* E20.
[Prob. alt. of SWINDLE *noun*.]

= SWIZZ.

swizzle /ˈswɪz(ə)l/ *verb. colloq. & dial.* M19.
[from SWIZZLE *noun*[1].]

1 *verb intrans.* Drink to excess, swig, tipple. M19.
2 *verb trans.* Stir with a swizzle-stick. M19.

■ **swizzled** *adjective* intoxicated, drunk M19. **swizzler** *noun* (now *rare*) (*a*) a drunkard; (*b*) a swindler: L19.

SWM *abbreviation.*

Single white male.

Swoe /swəʊ/ *noun.* Also **s-**. M20.
[Perh. blend of SWUNG *ppl adjective* and HOE *noun*[2].]

(Proprietary name for) a hoe with an angled trapezoidal blade which can be used in two directions.

†**swole** *verb pa. t.*: see SWELL *verb*.

swollen /ˈswəʊlən/ *adjective.* Also (*arch.*) **swoln** /swəʊln/. ME.
[pa. pple of SWELL *verb*.]

1 **a** Increased in bulk, as by internal pressure; distended, filled out, bulging, protuberant; *esp.* enlarged or distended as a result of disease. ME. ▸**b** Of a body of water: risen above the ordinary level; brimming, welling up. E17. ▸**c** Increased in amount or degree. M17.
2 *fig.* **a** (Of a feeling or mental state) causing a sense of enlargement, inflated; (of a person) affected with such a

feeling, *esp.* inflated with pride, puffed up. LME. ▸**b** Of language: turgid, inflated, bombastic. E17.

> **1a** J. CAREW Children with limbs like twigs, and swollen bellies wandered listlessly .. down the .. road. T. TRYON A badly swollen eye. **b** L. NKOSI The river is swollen and turbulent. **c** *What Mortgage* The demand for mortgages has decreased .. due to swollen house prices.

Special collocations & comb.: **swollen head** *colloq.* (*a*) (a person suffering from) excessive pride; (*b*) a hangover. **swollen-headed** *adjective* (*colloq.*) having a swollen head. **swollen shoot** a fatal virus disease of cocoa trees, spread by mealy bugs and distinguished by swelling of the young shoots.
■ **swollenness** /-n-n-/ *noun* (*rare*) L19.

swollen *verb pa. pple*: see SWELL *verb*.

swoln *ppl adjective* see SWOLLEN *adjective*.

swoof /swʊf/ *verb & noun. Scot.* L16.
[Var. of SOUGH *noun*¹, *verb*¹.]
= SOUGH *verb*¹, *noun*¹.

swoon /swuːn/ *noun.* ME.
[Orig. in phr. *in swoon, on swoon* alt. of ASWOON.]
1 The action of swooning or the condition of a person who has swooned; syncope. Orig. & esp. in ***fall in swoon***. *arch.* ME. ▸**b** A fainting-fit. LME.
†**2** A deep or sound sleep. *rare* (Spenser). Only in L16.

swoon /swuːn/ *verb intrans.* ME.
[Back-form. from SWOONING or from SWOWN.]
1 Fall into a fainting-fit; faint. Also, enter a state of rapture or ecstasy. ME.
2 Sink *into* or *to* a less active condition or a state of rest. E19.

> **1** M. FORSTER The snowy crags of the Alps almost made her swoon with fright. *fig.*: LONGFELLOW All the landscape seems to swoon In the happy afternoon.

■ **swooned** *adjective* in a swoon LME. **swooningly** *adverb* in a swooning manner L15.

swooner /ˈswuːnə/ *noun.* E20.
[from SWOON *verb* + -ER¹.]
1 A person who swoons or faints, or pretends to do so. E20.
2 A person who sings in a manner resembling crooning. *US.* M20.

swooning /ˈswuːnɪŋ/ *noun.* ME.
[from SWOWN + -ING¹.]
1 Fainting, syncope. ME.
2 A swoon; a fainting-fit. ME.

swoony /ˈswuːni/ *adjective.* E20.
[from SWOON *noun* or *verb* + -Y¹.]
1 Inclined to swoon. E20.
2 Inducing a swoon; *transf.* distractingly attractive, delightful. *colloq.* M20.

swoop /swuːp/ *noun.* M16.
[from the verb.]
†**1** A blow, a stroke. M16–E18.
2 The action of swooping down; *esp.* the sudden pouncing of a bird of prey from a height on its quarry. E17. ▸**b** A sudden descent on a place etc., as by a body of troops; a surprise attack, a raid. E19.

> **2** R. S. THOMAS His grass-green eye Missed neither swoop nor swerve of the hawk's wing. **b** *Times* Police swoop breaks up Polish peace meeting. **at one swoop, at one fell swoop, in one swoop, in one fell swoop** at one sudden descent; at a single blow, in one go.

swoop /swuːp/ *verb.* M16.
[Perh. dial. devel. of Old English *swāpan* SWEEP *verb*.]
†**1** *verb intrans.* Move in a stately manner, as with trailing garments; sweep along. M16–E17.
2 *verb trans.* Remove forcibly with a sweeping motion; scoop *up*, sweep *away*. E17.
3 *verb trans.* Seize with a sweeping movement; pounce on. Now *rare.* M17.
4 *verb intrans.* Come down suddenly *on* or *upon* a place etc., esp. with the intention of capture; make a sudden attack or raid. L18.
5 *verb intrans.* Of a bird etc.: make a rapid sweeping descent through the air, esp. *on* or *upon* prey. M19.

> **2** *New Yorker* He .. swoops the boy up, and runs back across the field. **4** *Times* Dutch police swooped at dawn on a flat in .. Amsterdam. *transf.*: P. D. JAMES The wind .. renewed its strength and came swooping down on her. **5** M. CONEY A night-hunting owl swooped low .. snatching some squealing rodent from the grass.

■ **swooper** *noun* M19. **swooping** *ppl adjective* †(*a*) sweeping or trailing along the ground; (*b*) descending with a rapid sweeping movement; (*c*) (of a surface) sloping steeply: L16.

†**swoopstake** *noun & adverb.* Only in E17.
[Alt. of SWEEPSTAKE after SWOOP *verb*.]
▸ **A** *noun.* = SWEEPSTAKE 2. Only in E17.
▸ **B** *adverb.* By sweeping all the stakes at once; indiscriminately. Only in E17.

> SHAKES. *Haml.* That, swoopstake, you will draw both friend and foe, Winner and loser?

swoose /swuːs/ *noun.* E20.
[Blend of SWAN *noun* and GOOSE *noun*.]
The hybrid offspring of a swan and a goose.

swoosh /swuːʃ, swʊʃ/ *verb, noun, & adverb.* M19.
[Imit.]
▸ **A** *verb intrans.* Make the noise of a sudden rush of liquid, air, etc.; move with this noise. M19.

> A. F. LOEWENSTEIN Some ducks circled, preparing for a landing, then swooshing down in perfect formation.

▸ **B** *noun.* Such a noise or movement. L19.
▸ **C** *adverb.* With or as with a swoosh. E20.
■ **swooshy** *adjective* (*colloq.*) characterized by or making a swoosh M20.

swop *noun, verb, adverb* vars. of SWAP *noun, verb, adverb*.

†**swope** *verb* see SWEEP *verb*.

sword /sɔːd/ *noun.*
[Old English *sweord, swurd, swyrd* = Old Frisian, Old Saxon *swerd*, Old High German *swert* (German *Schwert*), Old Norse *sverð*, from Germanic, of uncertain origin.]
1 A weapon for cutting and thrusting, consisting of a hilt with a cross-guard and a long straight or curved blade with a sharp point, later often worn on ceremonial occasions as a symbol of honour or authority. OE.
2 A thing that wounds or kills; a cause of death or destruction; anything viewed as a weapon of attack. OE.
3 The use of swords in warfare etc.; *transf.* slaughter, warfare; military force. Also, the military profession, the army. OE.
4 The sword regarded as a symbol of penal justice; the authority of a ruler or magistrate to punish offenders; *gen.* power of government, authority, jurisdiction. Also, the office of an executive governor or magistrate. LME.
5 a Any of various mechanical devices in the form of a flat wooden blade or bar. M16. ▸**b** The sharp projecting jawbone of a swordfish. M17. ▸**c** A swordlike ray or flash of light. M19.
6 In *pl.* One of the four suits in packs of playing-cards in Italy, Spain, and Spanish-speaking countries, and in tarot. E19.

> **2** SHAKES. *Macb.* This avarice .. hath been the sword of our slain kings. **4** *English Historical Review* Richemont .. had been offered the sword of constable of France.

Phrases: **at swords' points** in a state of open hostility. ***Damocles' sword, Damocles's sword***: see DAMOCLES. ***draw one's sword against***: see DRAW *verb*. ***measure swords***: see MEASURE *verb*. **put to the sword** kill, esp. in war; *fig.* overcome, quash. ***sword of Damocles***. **Sword of State** a sword borne before the sovereign on State occasions. ***short sword***: see SHORT *adjective*. ***the edge of the sword***: see EDGE *noun*. ***Toledo sword***. ***unsheathe the sword***: see UNSHEATHE *verb*. ***without stroke of sword***: see STROKE *noun*¹.
Comb.: **sword-and-buckler** *adjective* armed with or using a sword and buckler; **sword-and-sorcery** a genre of fiction characterized by heroic adventures and elements of fantasy; **sword-arm** the arm with which the sword is wielded, the right arm; *rhet.* military power or action; **sword-bayonet**: which may be used as a sword; **sword-bean** any of several tropical beans with long flat pods, esp. the jack bean, *Canavalia gladiata*, and the closely allied *C. ensiformis*; **sword-belt**: by which a sword in its scabbard is suspended; **swordbill** (more fully ***sword-billed hummingbird***) a S. American hummingbird, *Ensifera ensifera*, which has a very long bill; **sword-cane** a hollow cane or walking-stick containing a steel blade which may be drawn out and used as a sword; **sword-case**: used to hold a sword; later also, a receptacle at the back of a carriage for swords, sticks, etc.; **sword-cut** a cutting stroke dealt with the edge of a sword; **sword-cutler**: who makes sword-blades or swords; **sword dance**, **sword dancing**: in which the performers brandish swords or step about swords laid on the ground; **sword dancer** a performer of a sword dance; ***sword dancing***: see ***sword dance*** above; **sword-fern** any of several ferns with long narrow fronds, esp. the N. American *Polystichum munitum* and the tropical *Nephrolepis exaltata*; **sword grass** (*a*) any of various plants with long, narrow, esp. sharp-edged leaves, e.g. reed canary-grass, *Phalaris arundinacea*, and (*Austral.*) the cutting grass, *Gahnia psittacorum*; (*b*) any of several noctuid moths of the genera *Agrotis* and *Xylena*, with streaked brown or grey forewings; *esp.* the Eurasian *X. exsoleta*; **sword-hand** the hand with which a sword is wielded, the right hand; **sword-in-hand** *adjective* armed with a sword; *fig.* militant; **sword knot** a ribbon or tassel tied to the hilt of a sword orig. for fastening it to the wrist; **sword-law** government by military force; martial law; **sword lily** a gladiolus (genus *Gladiolus*); **sword-mat** NAUTICAL a piece of matting used to protect parts of the rigging etc., so called from the wooden blade with which the fabric is beaten close in weaving; **sword-proof** *adjective* capable of resisting the stroke of a sword; **sword-rattling** *adjective* that threatens military action; aggressive, pugnacious; **sword-sedge** an Australian sedge, *Lepidosperma gladiatum*, valuable as a sand-binder; **sword-side** the male line of descent; **sword-smith** a sword-cutler; **swordstick** = ***sword-cane*** above; **sword-swallower** a person who entertains for money by swallowing or pretending to swallow swords; **swordtail** a small Central American freshwater fish, *Xiphophorus helleri* (family Poeciliidae), which has a prolonged lower edge to the tail and is popular as an aquarium fish; **sword-work** = SWORDPLAY 1.
■ **swordless** *adjective* LME. **swordlike** *adjective* resembling (that of) a sword. L16.

sword /sɔːd/ *verb trans. rare.* E17.
[from the noun.]
1 Equip or arm with a sword. Chiefly as SWORDED 1. E17.
2 Thrust like a sword. E19.
3 Strike, slash, or kill with a sword. M19.

sword-bearer /ˈsɔːdbɛːrə/ *noun.* LME.
[from SWORD *noun* + BEARER.]
1 An official who carries a sword of State before a person of rank on ceremonial occasions. LME. ▸**b** *gen.* Any person who carries or wears a sword. M16.
2 A ruler or magistrate having authority to punish offenders. M17.
3 *Hist.* One of an order of knights in Poland, founded in 1204. M17.

sworded /ˈsɔːdɪd/ *adjective.* OE.
[from SWORD *noun* + -ED².]
1 Equipped or armed with a sword. OE.
2 Having some part resembling a sword. L17.

sworder /ˈsɔːdə/ *noun.* M16.
[formed as prec. + -ER¹, after Latin *gladiator*.]
1 = SWORD-BEARER 3. M16.
2 A person who fights or kills another with a sword; a gladiator. L16.
3 A person skilled in the use of the sword; a swordsman. E19.

swordfish /ˈsɔːdfɪʃ/ *noun.* Pl. **-es** /-ɪz/, (usu.) same. LME.
[from SWORD *noun* + FISH *noun*¹.]
1 A large marine game-fish, *Xiphias gladius* (family Xiphiidae), which has the upper jaw prolonged into a swordlike extension and is found in all tropical and warm-temperate seas; the flesh of this used as food. LME.
2 (Usu. **S-**.) *The* constellation Dorado. L18.
■ **swordfishing** *noun* fishing for swordfish L19.

swording /ˈsɔːdɪŋ/ *adjective.* Now *arch. rare.* E17.
[App. from SWORD *noun* + -ING²: cf. SWORDER.]
Martial, warlike.

†**swordman** *noun* see SWORDSMAN.

swordplay /ˈsɔːdpleɪ/ *noun.* OE.
[from SWORD *noun* + PLAY *noun*.]
1 Orig., a fight, a battle. Later, the action of wielding a sword briskly; the art or practice of fencing. OE.
2 Spirited or skilful controversy or debate. M19.
3 A kind of sword dance. *rare.* L19.
■ **swordplayer** *noun* (now *rare*) a person skilled in swordplay; a gladiator; a fencer: LME.

swordsman /ˈsɔːdzmən/ *noun.* Also (earlier) †**swordman**. Pl. **-men**. LME.
[from SWORD *noun* + -'S¹ + MAN *noun*.]
1 A man who uses, or is skilled in the use of, a sword; *spec.* a skilled fencer. LME. ▸**b** A soldier armed with a sword. LME.
2 A warrior, a fighter, a soldier. E17.
■ **swordsmanship** *noun* M19.

swore *verb pa. t.* of SWEAR *verb*.

sworn /swɔːn/ *adjective.* ME.
[pa. pple of SWEAR *verb*.]
1 Bound by or as by an oath; designating that which a person has vowed to be. Later also more widely, thoroughly devoted to some course of action; resolute, out-and-out, inveterate. ME.
2 Appointed or admitted with a formal oath to some office or function. LME.
3 Affirmed or promised by an oath; confirmed by swearing. E19.

> **1** *Observer* The .. soldier-politician of the Christian Phalange Party .. a sworn enemy of the Left-Muslim Alliance. W. HORWOOD Much experience in these matters for one who is a sworn celibate. **sworn brother** a close or devoted friend or companion. **sworn man** †(*a*) = SIDESMAN 1; (*b*) a man bound by oath to the performance of a duty or office, a vassal, a henchman. ***sworn to secrecy***: see SECRECY 1.

sworn *verb pa. pple* of SWEAR *verb*.

swot /swɒt/ *noun & verb. slang.* Also **swat**. M19.
[Var. of SWEAT *noun*.]
▸ **A** *noun.* **1** Work or study at school or college (orig. *spec.* in mathematics); *gen.* labour, toil. M19.
2 A person who studies hard. M19.
▸ **B** *verb.* Infl. **-tt-**.
1 *verb intrans.* Work hard at one's studies; bone *up*. M19.
2 *verb trans.* Study (a subject) hard or hurriedly; learn, mug *up*. E20.
■ **swotter** *noun* = SWOT *noun* 2 E20.

SWOT analysis /swɒt əˈnalɪsɪs/ *noun phr.* L20.
[Acronym from Strengths, Weaknesses, Opportunities, Threats.]
A study undertaken by an organization to identify its internal strengths and weaknesses, as well as its external opportunities and threats.

†**swote** *noun* see SWEAT *noun*.

swound /swaʊnd/ *noun & verb.* Now *arch. & dial.* LME.
[Later form of SWOON *noun* with parasitic *d*.]
▶ **A** *noun.* A fainting-fit, a swoon. LME.
▶ **B** *verb intrans.* Swoon, faint. M16.

†**swown** *adjective* (orig. & chiefly *pred.*). Only in ME.
[Aphet. from Old English *geswōgen* pa. pple of stem of *ā-, oferswōgan* suffocate, choke (with weeds).]
Fainting, in a swoon.
¶ Perh. the source of SWOON *verb*.

SWP *abbreviation.*
Socialist Workers' Party.

SWR *abbreviation.*
Standing-wave ratio.

swum *verb pa. pple* of SWIM *verb*.

swung /swʌŋ/ *ppl adjective.* LME.
[pa. pple of SWING *verb*.]
†**1** COOKERY. Beaten up. Only in LME.
2 Having been swung, oscillated, suspended, etc. E19.
Special collocations: **swung dash** a curved dash ~, used in dictionaries to stand for the headword of an entry or for a specified part of it.

swung *verb pa. t. & pple* of SWING *verb*.

swy /swʌɪ/ *noun. Austral. slang.* E20.
[German *zwei* two.]
1 Two; *spec.* a two-shilling coin or a two-year prison sentence. E20.
2 The game of two-up. M20.
Comb.: **swy game** a game of two-up; **swy school** a group of people gathered to play two-up.

SY *abbreviation.*
Steam yacht.

-sy /si/ *suffix.*
Var. of -Y⁶; used as hypocoristic dim. suffix added to: (i) proper names, as ***Betsy***, ***Patsy***, etc. (also in the form ***-cy***, as ***Nancy***); (ii) common nouns, as ***mopsy***, ***petsy***, ***popsy***. Also (freq. *derog.* or *joc.*), forming adjectives, as ***artsy-fartsy***, ***booksy***, ***folksy***, ***itsy-bitsy***, etc.

syagush /ˈsjɑːguːʃ/ *noun.* Now *rare* or *obsolete.* Also ***syah-gush***. E18.
[Persian & Urdu *siyāh-goš* black-eared.]
= CARACAL.

sybarite /ˈsɪbərʌɪt/ *noun & adjective.* Also **S-**. M16.
[Latin *Sybarita* from Greek *Subaritēs*, from *Subaris* Sybaris (see below): see -ITE¹.]
▶ **A** *noun.* A native or inhabitant of Sybaris, an ancient Greek city of southern Italy, traditionally noted for the indulgence and luxury of its way of life; *transf.* a person who is self-indulgent or devoted to sensuous luxury or pleasure; a sensualist. M16.
📖 G. DALY A sybarite .. Millais slept in most mornings.
▶ **B** *adjective.* = SYBARITIC. L16.
■ **sybaritish** *adjective* sybaritic M17. **sybaritism** *noun* sybaritic habits or practices; devotion to luxury, sensuousness: M19.

sybaritic /sɪbəˈrɪtɪk/ *adjective.* E17.
[Latin *Sybariticus* from Greek *Subaritikos*, from *Subaris*: see prec., -IC.]
1 Characterized by or devoted to excessive self-indulgence or luxury; sensuously luxurious. E17.
2 (**S-**.) Of or pertaining to the ancient city of Sybaris (see prec.) or its inhabitants. L18.
📖 **1** *Times* A sybaritic day .. taking treatments ranging from aromatherapy to .. osteopathy.
■ **sybaritical** *adjective* (now *rare*) = SYBARITIC E17. **sybaritically** *adverb* M19.

sybow /ˈsʌɪbəʊ/ *noun. Scot.* L16.
[formed as CIBOULE.]
Orig. = CIBOULE. Now, a spring onion.

sycamine /ˈsɪkəmɪn, -ʌɪn/ *noun. rare.* E16.
[Greek *sukaminon* (fig-)mulberry, from Hebrew *šiqmāh*, with assim. to Greek *sukon* fig.]
The black mulberry, *Morus nigra*.
¶ Chiefly in biblical translations.

sycamore /ˈsɪkəmɔː/ *noun.* Also (esp. & now only in sense 1) **sycomore**. ME.
[Old French *sic(h)amor* (mod. *sycomore*) from Latin *sycomorus* from Greek *sukomoros*, from *sukon* fig + *moron* mulberry.]
1 (Now usu. **syco-**.) A fig tree, *Ficus sycomorus*, common in Egypt, Syria, etc., having leaves resembling those of the mulberry. ME.
2 A large Eurasian maple, *Acer pseudoplatanus*, with pendulous racemes and five-lobed leaves, introduced to Britain as an ornamental tree and now naturalized; the wood of this tree. L16.
3 a In N. America, (the wood of) any of several kinds of plane tree (genus *Platanus*), *esp.* the buttonwood, *P. occidentalis*. E18. ▸**b** In Australia, (the wood of) any of several rainforest trees, *esp.* (more fully ***satin sycamore***) *Ceratopetalum succirubrum*, of the family Cunoniaceae, and (more fully ***silver sycamore***) *Cryptocarya glaucescens*, of the laurel family. L19.
4 A European noctuid moth, *Acronicta aceris*, which has mottled grey forewings and larvae that feed on sycamore etc. M19.
Comb.: **sycamore-fig** = sense 1 above; the fruit of this tree; **sycamore maple** = sense 2 above; **sycamore moth** = sense 4 above; **sycamore tree** any of the trees called ***sycamore*** (see above); **sycamore tussock moth** = sense 4 above.

syce /sʌɪs/ *noun.* Also **sais**. M17.
[Persian & Urdu *sā'is* from Arab.]
In parts of Africa and Asia, and esp. in the Indian subcontinent: a groom, a servant who attends to horses, drives carriages, etc.; a chauffeur. Also, an attendant following on foot a mounted rider or a carriage.

sycee /sʌɪˈsiː/ *noun.* E18.
[Repr. Cantonese pronunc. of Chinese (Mandarin) *xì sī* lit. 'fine silk' (because the silver, if pure, can be drawn out into fine threads).]
In China, fine uncoined silver in the form of lumps of various sizes, usually stamped with a banker's or assayer's seal, formerly used as a medium of exchange. Also ***sycee silver***.

sycomore *noun* see SYCAMORE.

sycon /ˈsʌɪkɒn/ *noun.* M19.
[Greek *sukon* fig (in sense 2 through mod. Latin genus name).]
†**1** BOTANY. = SYCONIUM. Only in M19.
2 ZOOLOGY. A grade of sponge structure of the syconoid type; a stage in sponge development characterized by this structure; a sponge of this type or stage. Cf. ASCON, LEUCON. L19.
■ **syconoid** *adjective & noun* (ZOOLOGY) (*a*) *adjective* of, pertaining to, or designating sponges showing some folding of the body wall, with choanocytes only lining radial canals; (*b*) *noun* a sponge of this type: E20.

syconium /sʌɪˈkəʊnɪəm/ *noun.* Pl. **-nia** /-nɪə/. M19.
[mod. Latin, from Greek *sukon* fig.]
BOTANY. A multiple fruit developed from numerous flowers embedded in a fleshy receptacle, as in the fig.
■ Also **syconus** *noun* M19.

sycophancy /ˈsɪkəf(ə)nsi, -fansi/ *noun.* E17.
[Latin *sycophantia* from Greek *sukophantia*, from *sukophantēs* SYCOPHANT: see -CY.]
1 *Hist.* In ancient Athens, the practice or occupation of an informer; slanderous accusation, the spreading of malicious reports. E17.
2 Servile or abject flattery; obsequiousness; the character or quality of a servile or abject flatterer. M17.
📖 **2** G. LEES Sycophancy, the abject acclamation and supine worship that surrounded him.

sycophant /ˈsɪkəfant/ *noun, adjective, & verb.* M16.
[French *sycophante* or Latin *sycophanta* from Greek *sukophantēs*, from *sukon* fig + base of *phainein* show, of unkn. origin (association with informing against the illegal exportation of figs from ancient Athens, recorded by Plutarch, cannot be substantiated).]
▶ **A** *noun.* **1** Orig., an informer, *spec.* a person in ancient Athens who informed against lawbreakers. Formerly also, a slanderous accuser, a traducer. *obsolete* exc. GREEK HISTORY. M16.
2 A servile or abject flatterer; an obsequious person, a toady. L16.
†**3** An impostor, a deceiver. L16–E18.
📖 **1** B. GOOGE The poisened lips of slandrous sicophants. **2** J. PORTER Dover, sycophant and snob that he was, smarmily agreed.
▶ **B** *attrib.* or as *adjective.* Sycophantic. L16.
▶ **C** *verb. rare.*
1 *verb trans.* Flatter in a servile manner; slander, spread malicious reports about. M17.
2 *verb intrans.* = SYCOPHANTIZE (a). M17.
■ **sycophantish** *adjective* somewhat like a sycophant; obsequious: E19. **sycophantize** *verb intrans.* (*rare*) (*a*) act as a sycophant; deal in servile or abject flattery; †(*b*) utter slanderous accusations; spread malicious reports: E17. **sycophantly** *adverb* (*rare*) L17. †**sycophantry** *noun* = SYCOPHANCY L17–E18.

sycophantic /sɪkəˈfantɪk/ *adjective.* L17.
[Greek *sukophantikos*, from *sukophantēs*: see prec., -IC.]
Of, pertaining to, or characteristic of, a sycophant; *esp.* servilely flattering; obsequious. Formerly also, slanderous.
📖 R. WEST A sycophantic oration in praise of the Emperor.
■ †**sycophantical** *adjective* = SYCOPHANTIC M16–E18. **sycophantically** *adverb* M17.

sycosis /sʌɪˈkəʊsɪs/ *noun.* Pl. **-coses** /-ˈkəʊsiːz/. L16.
[mod. Latin from Greek *sukōsis*, from *sukon* fig: see -OSIS.]
MEDICINE. †**1** Any of various ulcers etc. on the skin, resembling a fig. L16–E19.
2 A severe and purulent inflammation of the hair follicles due to bacterial infection, esp. in the beard area (more fully ***sycosis barbae*** /ˈbɑːbiː/ [Latin = of the beard]). E19.

Sydenham's chorea /ˌsɪd(ə)nəmz kɒˈrɪə/ *noun phr.* L19.
[Thomas *Sydenham* (1624–89), English physician.]
MEDICINE. A disorder of childhood or pregnancy that is a neurological form of rheumatic fever, affecting motor activities and characterized by involuntary movements. Also called ***St Vitus's dance***.

Sydney /ˈsɪdni/ *noun.* L19.
[See below.]
▶ **I 1** Used *attrib.* to designate things from or associated with Sydney, the capital of New South Wales, Australia, or the area surrounding it. L19.
Sydney bluegum a tall smooth-barked eucalyptus, *Eucalyptus saligna*, of damp areas. **Sydney-side** *noun & adjective* (of or pertaining to) Sydney and its surrounding area. **Sydneysider** a native or inhabitant of Sydney or of New South Wales, Australia. ***Sydney golden wattle***: see GOLDEN *adjective*.
▶ **II 2** ***Sydney or the bush***, all or nothing. *Austral. colloq.* E20.

syed *noun* var. of SAYYID.

syenite /ˈsʌɪənʌɪt/ *noun.* L18.
[from Latin *syenites* (*lapis*), (stone of) *Syene*, from Greek *Suēnē* Aswan, Egypt: see -ITE¹.]
GEOLOGY. A coarse-grained igneous rock, allied to granite, composed mainly of alkali feldspar, with hornblende, other ferromagnesian minerals, and accessory oxides.
■ **syenitic** /-ˈnɪtɪk/ *adjective* containing or composed of syenite; having the character of syenite: L18.

syenodiorite /sʌɪənəʊˈdʌɪərʌɪt/ *noun.* E20.
[from SYEN(ITE + -O- + DIORITE.]
GEOLOGY. = MONZONITE.

syke *noun* var. of SIKE *noun*¹.

†**syke** *verb* var. of SIKE *verb*.

Sykes's monkey /ˈsʌɪksɪz ˌmʌŋki/ *noun phr.* Also **Sykes' monkey**. M19.
[from William Henry *Sykes* (1790–1872), English soldier and naturalist.]
A diademed monkey (*Cercopithecus mitis*) of an E. African race having a chestnut saddle and white ruff.

syl- /sɪl/ *prefix.*
assim. form of SYM- before *l*.

Sylheti /sɪlˈheti/ *noun & adjective.* Also **-tti**. M19.
[from *Sylhet* (see below) + -I².]
▶ **A** *noun.* Pl. same, **-s**.
1 A native or inhabitant of Sylhet, a city in north-eastern Bangladesh, or the region surrounding it. M19.
2 The dialect of Bengali spoken in this region. E20.
▶ **B** *adjective.* Of or pertaining to the Sylheti or their dialect. L20.

syllab /ˈsɪləb/ *noun. obsolete* exc. *Scot. & dial.* Also **syllabe**. LME.
[Old French *sillabe*: see SYLLABLE *noun*.]
= SYLLABLE *noun*.

syllabarium /sɪləˈbɛːrɪəm/ *noun. rare.* Pl. **-ria** /-rɪə/. M19.
[mod. Latin: see next.]
A syllabary.

syllabary /ˈsɪləb(ə)ri/ *noun.* L16.
[mod. Latin *syllabarium*, from Latin *syllaba* SYLLABLE *noun* + *-arium* -ARY¹, after *abecedarium* ABECEDARY.]
Orig. (*rare*) a collector of words. Later, a list or system of characters representing syllables and (in some languages or stages of writing) serving the purpose of an alphabet.

syllabatim /sɪləˈbeɪtɪm/ *adverb. rare.* E17.
[Latin, from *syllaba* SYLLABLE *noun*, after *literatim*, *verbatim*.]
By syllables; syllable by syllable.

syllabation /sɪləˈbeɪʃ(ə)n/ *noun. rare.* M19.
[from Latin *syllaba* SYLLABLE *noun* + -ATION.]
Syllabification.

syllabe *noun* var. of SYLLAB.

syllabi *noun pl.* see SYLLABUS.

syllabic /sɪˈlabɪk/ *adjective & noun.* E18.
[French *syllabique* or late Latin *syllabicus* from Greek *sullabikos*, from *sullabē* SYLLABLE *noun*: see -IC.]
▶ **A** *adjective.* **1 a** Of a unit of sound: forming or constituting a syllable. E18. ▸**b** Of or pertaining to a syllable or syllables. M18. ▸**c** (Of a symbol or character) representing a syllable; (of writing or a writing-system) consisting of symbols or characters representing syllables. E19. ▸**d** Of verse or metre: based on or determined by the number of syllables in a line etc. E20.
2 a Of a style of singing, esp. plainsong: in which each syllable is sung to one note (i.e. with no slurs or runs). L18. ▸**b** Pronounced syllable by syllable; articulated with distinct separation of syllables. L19.
📖 **1b** T. R. LOUNSBURY Impart to the line syllabic regularity. **c** P. LE P. RENOUF Egyptian phonetic signs have syllabic values. **d** A. F. SCOTT The determining feature of syllabic verse is the number of syllables in the line. **2b** S. J. DUNCAN His English was careful, select, syllabic.
▶ **B** *ellipt.* as *noun.* **1** A syllabic symbol; a symbol or character representing a syllable. L19.
2 A syllabic sound; a unit of sound capable by itself of forming a syllable, or constituting the essential element of a syllable. L19.

3 A word or phrase pronounced syllable by syllable. *rare*. L19.

4 In *pl.* Syllabic verse. M20.

4 *Times Lit. Suppl.* The line in .. neo-Miltonic syllabics is fundamentally of twelve syllables.

■ †**syllabical** *adjective* = SYLLABIC *adjective* M16–E19. **syllabically** *adverb* in a syllabic manner; (*a*) syllable by syllable; as a separate syllable; †(*b*) syllable for syllable; in every detail; (*c*) in relation to a syllable or syllables; by syllabic symbols or characters: E17. **syllabicness** *noun* (*rare*) = SYLLABICITY L19.

syllabicate /sɪˈlabɪkeɪt/ *verb trans.* M17.
[Back-form. from next.]
Syllabify.

syllabication /sɪˌlabɪˈkeɪʃ(ə)n/ *noun.* L15.
[medieval Latin *syllabicatio(n-)*, from *syllabicat-* pa. ppl stem of *syllabicare*, from Latin *syllaba* SYLLABLE *noun*: see -ATION.]
Syllabification.

syllabicity /sɪləˈbɪsɪti/ *noun.* M20.
[from SYLLABIC *adjective* + -ITY.]
The quality of being syllabic; syllabicness.

syllabification /sɪˌlabɪfɪˈkeɪʃ(ə)n/ *noun.* M19.
[from Latin *syllaba* SYLLABLE *noun*: see -FICATION.]
Formation of syllables; the action or an act or method of dividing words into syllables; articulation by syllables.

G. BATTISCOMBE He admired Christina's voice .. especially .. her 'clear-cut method of syllabification'.

syllabify /sɪˈlabɪfʌɪ/ *verb trans.* & *intrans.* E20.
[Back-form. from prec.]
Form or divide (a word) into syllables; articulate (a word) by syllables; syllabicate.

syllabise *verb* var. of SYLLABIZE.

syllabism /ˈsɪləbɪz(ə)m/ *noun.* L19.
[from Latin *syllaba* SYLLABLE *noun* + -ISM.]
The use of syllabic characters. Also, syllabification.

syllabize /ˈsɪləbʌɪz/ *verb trans.* Also **-ise**. L16.
[medieval Latin *syllabizare* from Greek *sullabizein*, from *sullabē* SYLLABLE *noun*: see -IZE.]
Form or divide (a word) into syllables; articulate (a word) with distinct separation of syllables; syllabify.
■ **syllabiˈzation** *noun* syllabification E20.

syllable /ˈsɪləb(ə)l/ *noun.* LME.
[Anglo-Norman *sillable*, alt. of Old French *sillabe* (mod. *syllabe*) from Latin *syllaba* from Greek *sullabē*, from *sullambanein* collect, put, or bring together, formed as SYN- + *lambanein* take.]

1 a A unit of pronunciation uttered without interruption, forming the whole or part of a word and comprising a sound of greater sonority (vowel or vowel-equivalent) with or without one or more sounds of less sonority (consonants or consonant-equivalents) before or after. Also, a symbol, character, or set of characters, representing a corresponding element of written language. LME. ▸**b** A word of one syllable. Now *rare*. LME.

2 a The least amount of speech or writing; the least mention or trace *of* something. Freq. in neg. contexts. LME. ▸†**b** In *pl.* Minute details of language or statement; exact or precise words. L16–E17.

1a D. PROFUMO 'Catholics,' confided Alec, pronouncing the word with three syllables. **in words of one syllable** in simple language; expressed plainly or bluntly. ***syllable-count***, ***syllable-stress***, etc. CLOSED ***syllable***. ***open syllable***: see OPEN *adjective*. **b** J. B. PRIESTLEY 'His wife!' .. The .. woman let loose these two syllables. **2a** J. R. GREEN Dante is mentioned but once .. without a syllable of comment.

Comb.: **syllable-timed** *adjective* of or having a rhythm in which syllables occur at roughly equivalent time intervals, as opp. to ***stress-timed***.

syllable /ˈsɪləb(ə)l/ *verb trans.* L15.
[from prec.]
†**1** Arrange in syllables. Only in L15.

2 Utter or express in (or as in) syllables or articulate speech; pronounce syllable by syllable; articulate distinctly. M17. ▸**b** Read (something) syllable by syllable; read with close attention; spell out. *rare*. E18. ▸**c** Represent by syllables. *rare*. L19.

2a V. WOOLF Their tongues join .. in syllabling the sharp-cut words.

syllabled /ˈsɪləb(ə)ld/ *adjective.* L16.
[from SYLLABLE *noun*, *verb*: see -ED[2], -ED[1].]
1 Having a specified number of syllables (freq. as 2nd elem. of comb.). L16.

2 That has been syllabled or uttered in syllables. M19.

syllabub /ˈsɪləbʌb/ *noun.* Also **sill-**. M16.
[Origin unkn.]
1 Orig., a drink made of milk mixed with wine, cider, rum, etc. and often sweetened, spiced, and served warm. Later, a cold dessert made of milk or cream (usu. mixed with white wine), flavoured, sweetened, and whipped to a thick but light consistency. M16.

2 *fig.* Something frothy and insubstantial; *esp.* empty or lightweight writing or discourse. E18.

1 attrib.: ***syllabub glass***, ***syllabub pot***, etc. **2** J. WESLEY Greek books (compared with which .. the English are whipped Syllabub).

syllabus /ˈsɪləbəs/ *noun.* Pl. **-buses** /-bəsɪz/, **-bi** /-bʌɪ/. M17.
[mod. Latin, orig. a misreading of Latin *sittybas* accus. pl. of *sittyba* from Greek *sittuba* title-slip, label.]
1 a A concise statement or table of the headings of a discourse, the subjects of a series of lectures, etc.; a list of contents; an abstract, a summary. M17. ▸**b** A statement or outline of the subjects covered by a course of teaching; a programme of study. Also, a statement of the requirements for a particular examination. L19.

2 ROMAN CATHOLIC CHURCH. (**S-**.) A summary statement of points decided by papal decree regarding heretical doctrines or practices; *spec.* that annexed to the encyclical *Quanta cura* of Pope Pius IX, 8 December 1864. L19.

1a J. M. GOOD Preached .. with nothing more than a syllabus of his discourse before him. **b** F. DHONDY A play by Shakespeare .. on our syllabus.

syllepsis /sɪˈlɛpsɪs/ *noun.* Pl. **syllepses** /-iːz/. LME.
[Late Latin from Greek *sullēpsis* taking together, formed as SYN- + *lēpsis* taking.]
GRAMMAR & RHETORIC. A figure of speech in which a word, or a particular form or inflection of a word, is made to cover two or more functions in the same sentence whilst agreeing grammatically with only one (e.g. a sing. verb serving as predicate to two subjects, sing. and pl.), or is made to apply to two words in different senses (e.g. literal and metaphorical). Cf. ZEUGMA.

sylleptic /sɪˈlɛptɪk/ *adjective.* M19.
[Greek *sullēptikos*, from *sullēpsis*: see prec., -IC.]
Pertaining to, of the nature of, or involving syllepsis.
■ **sylleptical** *adjective* = SYLLEPTIC M19. **sylleptically** *adverb* E19.

syllid /ˈsɪlɪd/ *noun* & *adjective.* E20.
[mod. Latin *Syllidae* (see below), from *Syllis* genus name: see -ID[3].]
▶ **A** *noun.* Any of several small errant polychaete worms of the family Syllidae, which have three tentacles on the head and are found on rocky shores. E20.
▶ **B** *adjective.* Of, pertaining to, or designating this family. E20.

sylloge /ˈsɪlədʒi/ *noun. rare.* L17.
[Greek *sullogē*, from *sullegein* collect.]
A collection; a summary.

syllogise *verb* var. of SYLLOGIZE.

syllogism /ˈsɪlədʒɪz(ə)m/ *noun.* LME.
[Old French *sil(l)ogisme*, earlier *sillogime* (mod. *syllogisme*) or Latin *syllogismus* from Greek *sullogismos*, from *sullogizesthai* intensive of *logizesthai* reckon, compute, conclude, from *logos* reasoning, discourse: see SYN-, LOGOS, -ISM.]
1 LOGIC. A form of reasoning in which a conclusion is deduced from two given or assumed propositions called the premisses, which contain a common or middle term that is absent from the conclusion (e.g. *All As are Bs, all Bs are Cs, therefore all As are Cs*). LME. ▸**b** *transf.* A form or process of reasoning or something regarded as such; *esp.* one which is specious or subtle. Also, an artifice, a trick. Freq. *joc.* or *iron.* LME.

2 The form of syllogistic reasoning, reasoning in that form; the form of reasoning from generals to particulars. Also, deduction or mediate inference (as distinguished from induction or immediate inference). L16.

1 ***horned syllogism***: see HORNED *adjective*. **b** F. W. FARRAR Took refuge in what St. Chrysostom calls 'the syllogism of violence'.

syllogist /ˈsɪlədʒɪst/ *noun.* L18.
[from prec. or SYLLOGIZE: see -IST.]
A person who reasons by syllogisms; a person versed in syllogism.

syllogistic /sɪləˈdʒɪstɪk/ *adjective.* LME.
[Latin *syllogisticus* from Greek *sullogistikos*, from *sullogizesthai*: see SYLLOGISM, -IC.]
Of, pertaining to, or consisting of a syllogism or syllogisms.
■ **syllogistical** *adjective* (now *rare*) †(*a*) = SYLLOGISTIC; (*b*) inclined or prone to reasoning by syllogisms; dealing in syllogisms: E16. **syllogistically** *adverb* (*a*) in a syllogistic manner; (*b*) *gen.* with logical formality or precision, according to logical rules: L16.

syllogize /ˈsɪlədʒʌɪz/ *verb.* Also **-ise**. LME.
[Old French *sil(l)ogiser* or late Latin *syllogizare*, from Greek *sullogizesthai*: see SYLLOGISM, -IZE.]
1 *verb intrans.* Use syllogisms; reason, esp. syllogistically. LME.

2 *verb trans.* Reason (a person) *out of* a condition by syllogizing. *rare*. E18. ▸**b** Deduce (a fact, conclusion, etc.) by syllogism. M19.

1 F. HARRISON He does not syllogize about the origin of things. **2** SOUTHEY Syllogize himself out of all hopes of an hereafter.

■ **syllogiˈzation** *noun* (*rare*) M17. **syllogizer** *noun* L16.

Sylow /ˈsiːlɒf/ *noun.* L19.
[Peter Ludwig *Sylow* (1832–1918), Norwegian mathematician.]
MATH. Used *attrib.* and in *possess.* to designate concepts in group theory propounded by Sylow.
Sylow's theorem each of three theorems concerning the relationship of groups and Sylow subgroups. **Sylow subgroup** a subgroup whose order is the largest power of the prime *p* which divides the order of the group.

sylph /sɪlf/ *noun.* M17.
[mod. Latin pl. *sylphes*, *sylphi*, German pl. *Sylphen*: perh. based on Latin *sylvestris* of the woods + *nympha* nymph.]
1 a Any of a race of elemental beings or spirits of the air (orig. in the system of Paracelsus). M17. ▸**b** A slender graceful woman or girl. M19.

2 Each of three hummingbirds of the genera *Neolesbia* and *Aglaiocercus*, which have long forked tails. M19.

1b A. BURGESS Heavy in build .. Frieda .. was no sylph.

■ **sylphish** *adjective* pertaining to or characteristic of a sylph; sylphlike: M18. **sylphlike** *adjective* resembling (that of) a sylph; slender, graceful: E19. **sylphy** *adjective* = SYLPHISH M19.

sylphid /ˈsɪlfɪd/ *noun* & *adjective.* L17.
[French *sylphide*, from *sylphe* SYLPH: see -ID[2].]
▶ **A** *noun.* A young or small sylph. L17.
▶ **B** *attrib.* or as *adjective.* Sylphish, sylphlike. L18.

Sylphon /ˈsɪlfɒn/ *noun.* E20.
[Invented word.]
(Proprietary name for) a concertina-like metal bellows used in valves, seals, etc.
¶ Proprietary name in the US.

sylva /ˈsɪlvə/ *noun.* Also **silva**. Pl. **-vae** /-viː/, **-vas**. M17.
[Latin *silva* a wood, woodland (misspelt *sylva* after synon. Greek *hulē* wood: see HYLE). In sense 2, after the title (*Silvae*) of Statius's collection of occasional poems.]
1 A treatise on forest trees; (a descriptive catalogue of) the trees of a particular region. Cf. FLORA 2. M17.

†**2** A collection of pieces, esp. of poems. Also (*rare*), a thesaurus of words or phrases. M17–L18.

†**sylvage** *noun. rare.* ME–L18.
[formed as prec. + -AGE.]
Woody growth, wooded or wild country.

sylvan /ˈsɪlv(ə)n/ *noun* & *adjective.* Also **silvan**. M16.
[French *sylvain*, †*silvain* or Latin *Silvanus* woodland god, from *silva*: see SYLVA, -AN.]
▶ **A** *noun.* A native or inhabitant of a wood or forest; *spec.* (*a*) CLASSICAL MYTHOLOGY an imaginary being believed to haunt woods or groves; a spirit of the woods; (*b*) a person living in a wood, or in a woodland region; a forester; (*c*) a creature, esp. a bird, living in or frequenting the woods; (*d*) *rare* a woodland tree, shrub, etc. Chiefly *arch.* & *poet.* M16.
▶ **B** *adjective.* **1** Of, pertaining to, situated in, or characteristic of, a wood or woods. L16.

2 Consisting of or formed by woods or trees. Chiefly *poet.* L16.

3 Having or characterized by woods or trees; wooded. E17.

2 SHELLEY The pillared stems Of the dark sylvan temple. **3** D. ARKELL In such sylvan surroundings, he must have felt himself .. still in the country. D. M. THOMAS To think of himself .. living in sylvan seclusion.

■ **sylvanity** /-ˈvanɪti/ *noun* sylvan quality or character M19. **sylvanly** *adverb* E19. **sylvanry** *noun* sylvan scenery E19.

Sylvaner /sɪlˈvɑːnə/ *noun.* E20.
[German.]
1 A variety of vine first developed in German-speaking districts, the dominant form bearing white grapes; a vine or grape of this variety. E20.

2 A white wine made from these grapes. M20.

sylvanite /ˈsɪlvənʌɪt/ *noun.* L18.
[from *Tran)sylvan(ia* a region of Romania + -ITE[1]. Cf. *sylvanium* (German *Sylvan*), old name for tellurium.]
MINERALOGY. †**1** Native tellurium, usu. with impurities. L18–E19.

2 A monoclinic telluride of gold and silver that occurs as silver or yellow crystals or masses with metallic lustre. M19.

sylvatic /sɪlˈvatɪk/ *adjective.* Also **silv-**, †**selv-**. M17.
[Latin *silvaticus*, formed as SYLVA: see -ATIC.]
1 Belonging to or found in woods; of the nature of a wood or woodland; sylvan. Formerly also, rustic, boorish. *rare*. M17.

2 VETERINARY MEDICINE. Designating certain diseases (as rabies, plague, etc.) when contracted by wild animals, and the pathogens causing them. M20.

†**sylvester** *noun*[1]. M17.
[In sense 1 formed as SYLVESTER *adjective*; in sense 2 from Latin *silvestre* (sc. *granum*), neut. of *silvestris* SYLVESTER *adjective*.]
1 A spirit of the woods (in the system of Paracelsus). Only in M17.

2 An inferior kind of cochineal dye (supposed, like the true cochineal, to be derived from the seed of a plant). L17–E18.

Sylvester /sɪlˈvɛstə/ *noun*². M19.
[Saint *Sylvester* (d. 335) Bishop of Rome from 314 to 335.]
St Sylvester's day, 31 December.
Comb.: **Sylvester-eve**, **Sylvester-night** New Year's Eve.

sylvester /sɪlˈvɛstə/ *adjective*. *rare*. Also **sil-**. L16.
[Latin *silvester* (*syl-*), *-tris*, formed as SYLVA.]
= SYLVESTRIAN *adjective*¹.

sylvestral /sɪlˈvɛstr(ə)l/ *adjective*. M19.
[formed as prec. + -AL¹.]
BOTANY. Of a plant: growing typically in woods or bushy places.

sylvestrene /sɪlˈvɛstriːn/ *noun*. L19.
[from mod. Latin *sylvestris* specific epithet of *Pinus sylvestris*, the Scots pine, formed as next: see -ENE.]
CHEMISTRY. A liquid monocyclic terpene, $C_{10}H_{16}$, which is a by-product of pine oil extraction.

sylvestrian /sɪlˈvɛstrɪən/ *adjective*¹. Also **sil-**. M17.
[from Latin *silvestris*, formed as SYLVA: see -IAN.]
Belonging to or found in woods; sylvan, rustic.

Sylvestrian /sɪlˈvɛstrɪən/ *adjective*² & *noun*. L19.
[from *Sylvester* (see below) + -IAN.]
ECCLESIASTICAL HISTORY. ▶**A** *adjective*. Designating or belonging to an order of Benedictines founded in 1231 by Sylvester Gozzolini (d. 1267). L19.
▶**B** *noun*. A member of this order L19.
■ Also †**Sylvestrin(e)** *adjective & noun* L17–M18.

Sylvian /ˈsɪlvɪən/ *adjective*. Also **S-**. M19.
[from SYLVIUS: see -IAN.]
ANATOMY. Designating certain structures in the brain, esp. a large diagonal fissure on the lateral surface of the brain, which separates off the temporal lobe. Cf. SYLVIUS.

sylviculture *noun*, **sylvicultural** *adjective*, etc., vars. of SILVICULTURE etc.

sylvinite /ˈsɪlvɪnʌɪt/ *noun*. L19.
[from SYLVINE + -ITE¹.]
A mixture of the minerals sylvite and halite which is mined as an ore of potash.

sylvite /ˈsɪlvʌɪt/ *noun*. M19.
[from mod. Latin (*sal digestivus*) *Sylvii* old name of this salt, from SYLVIUS: see -ITE¹.]
MINERALOGY. Native potassium chloride, a colourless or white salt that crystallizes in the cubic system and is used extensively as a fertilizer.
■ Also **sylvine** /-iːn/ *noun* M19.

Sylvius /ˈsɪlvɪəs/ *noun*. E19.
[François de la Boë *Sylvius* (1614–72), Flemish anatomist.]
ANATOMY. Used with *of* to designate certain structures in the brain, esp. the Sylvian fissure.

sym- /sɪm/ *prefix*.
[Repr. Greek *sum-*, assim. form of *sun-* SYN-.]
Assim. form of SYN- before *b*, *m*, *p*.
■ **symˈblepharon** *noun* [Greek *blepharon* eyelid] adhesion of the eyelid to the eyeball E19. **symˈpatric** *adjective* [Greek *patra* fatherland] BIOLOGY (of species, speciation, etc.) occurring in the same area; overlapping in distribution: E20. **symˈpatrically** *adverb* (BIOLOGY) by means of sympatric speciation; without physical isolation: M20. **sympatry** *noun* (BIOLOGY) sympatric speciation; the occurrence of sympatric forms: E20. **symˈpelmous** *adjective* [Greek *pelma* sole of the foot] ORNITHOLOGY having the tendons of the deep flexors of the toes united before separating to the digits L19. **symˈpetalous** *adjective* (BOTANY) = GAMOPETALOUS L19. **symˈphalangism** *noun* (ANATOMY) a congenital malformation in which the phalanges of a digit are fused end to end E20. **symport** *noun* [after TRANSPORT *noun*] BIOCHEMISTRY flow of two substances through a membrane in the same direction at a rate which is increased by a cooperative effect M20.

symbiont /ˈsɪmbɪɒnt, -bʌɪ-/ *noun*. L19.
[from SYM- + Greek *biount-* pres. ppl stem of *bioun* live, from *bios* life.]
BIOLOGY. Either of two organisms living in symbiosis.

symbiosis /sɪmbɪˈəʊsɪs, -bʌɪ-/ *noun*. Pl. **-oses** /-ˈəʊsiːz/. E17.
[mod. Latin from Greek *sumbiōsis* a living together, from *sumbioun* live together, from *sumbios* (adjective) living together, (noun) companion, partner, formed as SYM- + *bios* life: see -OSIS.]
1 Living together, communal living. *rare*. E17.
2 BIOLOGY. An interaction between two dissimilar organisms living in close physical association; *esp*. one in which each benefits the other. Cf. COMMENSALISM, HELOTISM, MUTUALISM. L19.
3 *transf. & fig*. A relationship or association of mutual advantage between people, organizations, etc. E20.
■ **ˈsymbiose** *verb intrans*. (BIOLOGY) live as a symbiont M20. **ˈsymbiote** *noun* (BIOLOGY) (*a*) a combination of two symbiotic organisms; (*b*) = SYMBIONT: L19. **symbiˈotic** *adjective* (*a*) BIOLOGY associated or living in symbiosis; pertaining to or involving symbiosis; (*b*) *transf. & fig*. mutually advantageous: L19. **symbiˈotically** *adverb* L19.

symbiotrophic /ˌsɪmbʌɪəˈtrəʊfɪk, -ˈtrɒfɪk; -bɪə-/ *adjective*. E20.
[from prec. + -TROPHIC.]
ECOLOGY. Obtaining nourishment through symbiosis.

symbol /ˈsɪmb(ə)l/ *noun*¹ & *verb*. LME.
[Latin *symbolum* from Greek *sumbolon* mark, token, watchword, outward sign, formed as SYM- + base of *bolē*, *bolos* a throw. Cf. next.]
▶**A** *noun*. **1 a** CHRISTIAN THEOLOGY. A formal authoritative statement or summary of Christian doctrine; a creed or confession of faith, *spec*. the Apostles' Creed. LME. ▶†**b** A brief statement; a motto, a maxim. L16–M18.
2 a A thing conventionally regarded as representing, typifying, or recalling something else by possessing analogous qualities or by association in fact or thought; *esp*. a material object representing an abstract concept or quality. Freq. foll. by *of*. L16. ▶**b** An object representing something sacred; *spec*. (ECCLESIASTICAL) either of the elements in the Eucharist, as representing the body and blood of Christ. L17. ▶**c** Symbolism. *rare*. M19. ▶**d** NUMISMATICS. A small device on a coin, additional to and usu. independent of the principal device. L19.
3 A written mark, a line, a dot, or a configuration of these, used as a conventional representation of a sound, word, object, process, function, etc., *spec*. of a chemical element or a mathematical quantity. E17.

> 🕮 **1a** H. M. LUCKOCK The Western Bishops, who alone adhered to the Nicene Symbol in its integrity. **2a** K. CLARK In his work clouds . . became symbols of destruction. H. KUSHNER The wedding ring . . is a symbol of intimacy and loyalty. ***incomplete symbol***: see INCOMPLETE *adjective*. **c** *Listener* A readable book provided you ignore . . Fowler's seeking after symbol. **3** ***terminal symbol***: see TERMINAL *adjective*.

▶**B** *verb trans*. Infl. **-ll-**, ***-l-**. Symbolize (something). M19.
■ **symbolled** *adjective* (*rare*) (*a*) represented by a symbol; symbolized; (*b*) decorated with symbols: E19. **symbolling** *noun* (*US*) (*a*) the action of the verb; (*b*) the use of symbols in human communication; (*c*) a thing that symbolizes something: M19.

†**symbol** *noun*². E17–E19.
[Latin *symbola* from Greek *sumbolē*, from *sumballein* put together, formed as SYM- + *ballein* throw. Cf. prec.]
A contribution, esp. to a feast; a share, a portion. Cf. SHOT *noun*¹ 15a.

symbolatry /sɪmˈbɒlətri/ *noun*. *rare*. L19.
[Contr.]
= SYMBOLOLATRY.

symbolic /sɪmˈbɒlɪk/ *adjective* & *noun*. M17.
[French *symbolique* or late Latin *symbolicus* from Greek *sumbolikos*, from *sumbolon*: see SYMBOL *noun*¹, -IC. As noun chiefly after German *Symbolik*, French *symbolique*.]
▶**A** *adjective*. **1** Pertaining to or characterized by the use of written symbols to represent whole words as opp. to individual sounds. M17.
2 Expressed, represented, or conveyed by means of symbols or symbolism; involving or depending on representation by a symbol or symbols; using symbols or symbolism. L17.
3 Of the nature or character of a symbol; constituting or serving as a symbol; also foll. by *of*. Also *spec*., (of a sequence of sounds) expressing or suggesting a semantic feature or attribute other than sound (cf. ONOMATOPOEIA), as manner or speed of movement etc.; (of word formation, a word) involving such sound sequences. L17.
4 CHRISTIAN THEOLOGY. Pertaining to or of the nature of a formal creed or confession of faith. *rare*. M19.

> 🕮 **2** R. C. TRENCH An allegorical, or more truly a symbolic, meaning underlying the literal. **3** J. FULLER Pilgrimage is a symbolic act . . the outward sign of an inward direction.

Special collocations: **symbolic address** COMPUTING an address consisting of a symbol chosen by the programmer. **symbolic delivery** LAW (*a*) = ***symbolical delivery*** s.v. SYMBOLICAL 2; (*b*) delivery of goods in which the seller delivers to the buyer a document of title to the goods or other means of control over them, rather than the goods themselves. **symbolic interaction** SOCIOLOGY the sharing and use of common symbols, as language or gestures performing a linguistic function, in human communication. **symbolic interactionism** SOCIOLOGY the view of social behaviour that emphasizes linguistic or gestural communication, esp. the role of language in the formation of the child as a social being. **symbolic logic**: that uses a special notation of symbols to represent propositions etc.; mathematical logic.
▶**B** *noun*. †**1** In *pl*. (treated as *sing*.). The use of written symbols, as in mathematics. *rare*. Only in M17.
2 In *pl*. (treated as *sing*.) & (*rare*) *sing*. The branch of knowledge that deals with symbols; *spec*. (*a*) the branch of theology that deals with creeds and confessions of faith; (*b*) the branch of anthropology that deals with symbols and symbolic rites and ceremonies. *rare*. M19.

symbolical /sɪmˈbɒlɪk(ə)l/ *adjective*. E17.
[from late Latin *symbolicus*: see prec., -ICAL.]
1 = SYMBOLIC *adjective* 3. E17.
2 = SYMBOLIC *adjective* 2. E17.
3 = SYMBOLIC *adjective* 1. M17.
4 = SYMBOLIC *adjective* 4. M18.

2 symbolical delivery, **symbolical possession** SCOTS LAW (now *Hist*.) a form of sasine in which the transfer of heritable property is recognized by the delivery of symbolic objects, as earth and stone to represent lands etc. **4 symbolical books** *spec*. the authentic documents (the Confession of Augsburg etc.) constituting the Lutheran confession of faith.
■ **symbolicalness** *noun* (*rare*) M17.

symbolically /sɪmˈbɒlɪk(ə)li/ *adverb*. E17.
[from prec., SYMBOLIC + -LY².]
1 In a symbolic manner; by means of symbols or symbolism. E17.
2 By, or in relation to, written or mathematical symbols or characters. M19.

symbolisation *noun*, **symbolise** *verb* vars. of SYMBOLIZATION, SYMBOLIZE.

symbolism /ˈsɪmbəlɪz(ə)m/ *noun*. L16.
[from SYMBOL *noun*¹ + -ISM, partly after French *symbolisme*.]
1 a The use of symbols to represent concepts or qualities; the practice of assigning a symbolic character to objects or acts. Also, symbols collectively or in general. L16. ▶**b** A symbolic meaning attributed to natural objects or facts. M19. ▶**c** The use of symbols in literature or art; *spec*. (*a*) a school or style of painting, originating in France in the late 19th century, in which the non-naturalistic use of colour and form was employed to represent or evoke ideas or emotional states; (*b*) an analogous movement or style in poetry, in which indirect suggestion rather than direct expression was employed to represent or evoke ideas or emotions. M19.
†**2** Correspondence in nature or quality. Cf. SYMBOLIZATION 1a. *rare*. E–M18.
3 The use, or a system, of written symbols or characters. *rare*. M19.
4 = SYMBOLIC *noun* 2. *rare*. M19.

> 🕮 **1a** A. KOESTLER The geometrical symbolism of the Zodiac. **b** *Interview* I love the idea, the symbolism, of the frog—long life and fertility.

symbolist /ˈsɪmbəlɪst/ *noun* & *adjective*. L16.
[from SYMBOL *noun*¹ + -IST; in sense 2c after French *symboliste*.]
▶**A** *noun*. **1** ECCLESIASTICAL HISTORY. A person who holds that the elements in the Eucharist are mere symbols of the body and blood of Christ. *obsolete* exc. *Hist*. L16.
2 a A person who uses symbols or practises symbolism. E19. ▶**b** An adherent or practitioner of symbolism in art or literature. L19.
3 A person versed in the study or interpretation of symbols or symbolism. M19.
▶**B** *attrib*. or as *adjective*. Of or pertaining to artistic or literary symbolism or symbolists. L19.

> 🕮 T. EAGLETON The symbolist preoccupation with poetry as music.

■ **symboˈlistic**, **symboˈlistical** *adjectives* pertaining to or characteristic of a symbolist, esp. in art or literature; pertaining to or characterized by symbolism: M19. **symboˈlistically** *adverb* E20.

symbolization /ˌsɪmbəlʌɪˈzeɪʃ(ə)n/ *noun*. Also **-isation**. E17.
[French *symbolisation*, †*-ization*, formed as next: see -ATION.]
1 †**a** The fact of corresponding in nature or quality. Cf. SYMBOLISM 2. Only in 17. ▶**b** The action of conforming in (esp. religious) tenets or practice; conformity (*with*). Now *rare* or *obsolete*. M17.
2 The action of representing something by a symbol or symbols; a thing representing something; a symbol; symbolism. Formerly also, the action of making something symbolic. E17. ▶**b** *spec*. Representation by written symbols; a set of written symbols or characters. M19.

> 🕮 **2** E. H. SEARS The grand and beautiful . . are not the symbolization of spiritual qualities. *Nature* This is followed by . . a section on weather symbolisation and a photographic index.

symbolize /ˈsɪmbəlʌɪz/ *verb*. Also **-ise**. L16.
[French *symboliser*, †*-izer*, formed as SYMBOL *noun*¹ + -IZE.]
†**1** *verb intrans*. Correspond (*with*); be similar in nature or quality. L16–E19. ▶**b** *verb trans. & intrans*. Mix or combine (elements or substances, esp. those of similar qualities). L16–M17.
2 *verb intrans*. Agree in (esp. religious) tenets or practice; hold similar opinions or principles; conform. Now *rare* or *obsolete*. E17.
3 a *verb trans. & intrans*. Represent (something) by a symbol or symbols. E17. ▶**b** *verb trans*. Be a symbol of; represent as a symbol. E17.
4 Make into or treat as a symbol; regard as symbolic. *rare*. M17.
5 *verb trans*. Formulate or express in a creed or confession of faith. Cf. SYMBOL *noun*¹ 1. *rare*. L19.

> 🕮 **1** T. JACKSON Happie is that Land . . where ciuill pollicie and spirituall wisedome . . doe rightly symbolize. **2** A. W. HADDAN Those who profess to be Churchmen, but in this particular symbolize with . . Nonconformists. **3b** E. ROOSEVELT The dove of peace symbolizes the efforts of the Soviet Union to protect the people from . . war. C. SAGAN The raised and empty right hand symbolizes that no weapon is being carried.

■ **symbolizer** *noun* (*rare*) **E17.**

symbolo-fideism /sɪmbələʊˈfʌɪdiːɪz(ə)m/ *noun. rare.* **E20.**
[from SYMBOL *noun*[1] + -O- + FIDEISM. Cf. French *symbolo-fidéisme*.]
The doctrine that symbols are of the essence of religious dogma, and that the attitude of faith has priority over intellectual belief.
■ **symbolo-fideist** *noun* an adherent or supporter of symbolo-fideism **M20.**

symbolography /sɪmbəˈlɒgrəfi/ *noun.* **M17.**
[from SYMBOL *noun*[1] + -OGRAPHY.]
†**1** The representation of things by symbols. Only in **M17.**
2 The writing of symbols or symbolic characters; such characters collectively; symbolic writing. **M19.**

symbology /sɪmˈbɒlədʒi/ *noun.* **M19.**
[Irreg. from SYMBOL *noun*[1] + -LOGY.]
The branch of knowledge that deals with the use of symbols; *gen.* the use of symbols, symbolism; symbols collectively.

> *Broadcast* The coding and symbology to which the viewer is accustomed in his . . media experience.

■ **symboˈlogical** *adjective* **M19.**

symbololatry /sɪmbəˈlɒlətri/ *noun. rare.* **E19.**
[from SYMBOL *noun*[1] + -O- + -LATRY.]
Worship of or excessive veneration for symbols.

symmachy /ˈsɪməki/ *noun. rare.* **E17.**
[Greek *summakhia* alliance in war, from *summakhos* (adjective) fighting together or in alliance, (noun) an ally, formed as SYM- + *makhē* fight.]
Hist. An alliance made in wartime against a common enemy.

symmelia /sɪˈmiːlɪə/ *noun.* **E20.**
[from SYM- + Greek *melos* limb: see -IA[1].]
MEDICINE & ZOOLOGY. A congenital malformation in which a pair of the limbs, esp. the lower limbs, are united. Cf. SYMPODIA *noun*[1].
■ **symmelian** *adjective & noun* (a person or animal) characterized by symmelia **L19.**

symmetallic /sɪmɪˈtalɪk/ *adjective.* **L19.**
[from SYM- + METALLIC, after *bimetallic*.]
ECONOMICS. Using two metals, esp. a standard of currency based on stabilizing the price of a reserve monetary unit that corresponds to a fixed combination of gold and silver, rather than stabilizing the price of either metal separately.
■ **symˈmetallism** *noun* the symmetallic system or standard of currency **L19.** **symˈmetallist** *noun & adjective* (*a*) *noun* an advocate or supporter of symmetallism; (*b*) *adjective* of or favouring symmetallism: **L19.**

symmetral /ˈsɪmɪtr(ə)l/ *adjective.* **M17.**
[from medieval Latin *symmetrus* commensurable from Greek *summetros*, formed as SYM- + *metron* measure: see -AL[1].]
†**1** Agreeing in measurement, commensurate. *rare.* Only in **M17.**
†**2** *CHRISTIAN THEOLOGY.* Of the early Christian Church: commensurate with the divine idea or pattern; agreeing with the Word of God. **M–L17.**
3 Chiefly *CRYSTALLOGRAPHY.* Related to or determining symmetry. Now *rare.* **L19.**

symmetric /sɪˈmɛtrɪk/ *adjective.* **L18.**
[from SYMMETRY + -IC.]
= SYMMETRICAL.
symmetric determinant *MATH.* a determinant in which the constituents in each row are the same respectively, and in the same order, as those in the corresponding column, and which is therefore symmetrical about its principal diagonal. **symmetric difference** *MATH. & LOGIC* the class of elements belonging to one or other, but not to both, of two sets. **symmetric group** *MATH. & LOGIC* the group of all the permutations of a set of unlike entities.

symmetrical /sɪˈmɛtrɪk(ə)l/ *adjective.* **M18.**
[from SYMMETRY + -ICAL, after *geometrical*.]
1 Having the parts or elements regularly and harmoniously arranged; regular in form; correctly proportioned, well-balanced. **M18.**
2 Possessing symmetry; having similar or corresponding parts repeated on each side of a contained plane or around an axis; (of parts or organs) repeated on each side of a plane or around an axis; *MEDICINE* (of a disease) affecting such corresponding parts, or both sides of the body, simultaneously. **L18.** ▸**b** Designating a mathematical expression, function, or equation whose value and sign are not altered by interchanging the values of any two of the variables or unknown quantities; *PHYSICS* designating a state represented by such a wave function; *LOGIC* (of a binary relation) such that when two or more terms for which it is true are interchanged, it remains true. **E19.**
3 *BOTANY.* Of a flower: having the same number of parts in each whorl; isomerous. **M19.**

> **1** J. RUSKIN The symmetrical clauses of Pope's logical metre. **2** M. GIROUARD A garden front . . completely symmetrical except for the off-centre cupola. **b symmetrical determinant** *MATH.* = *SYMMETRIC* **determinant**. **symmetrical difference** *MATH. & LOGIC* = *SYMMETRIC* **difference**.

■ **symmetriˈcality** *noun* (*rare*) symmetricalness **L19.** **symmetrically** *adverb* in a symmetrical manner; so as to be symmetrical: **L16.** **symmetricalness** *noun* †(*a*) *CHRISTIAN THEOLOGY* the quality or fact of being commensurate with the divine pattern; (*b*) the quality or fact of being symmetrical; symmetry: **L17.**

symmetrize /ˈsɪmɪtrʌɪz/ *verb.* Also **-ise.** **M18.**
[French *symétriser*, or directly from SYMMETRY + -IZE.]
1 *verb intrans.* Be symmetrical, correspond symmetrically, *with. rare.* **M18.**
2 *verb trans.* Make symmetrical; give symmetry to. **L18.**

> **2** *Contemporary Review* Incident . . narrative . . eloquence,—all perfectly symmetrized with incomparable artistic skill.

■ **symmetriˈzation** *noun* **M19.**

symmetrodont /sɪˈmɛtrədɒnt/ *noun & adjective.* **M20.**
[mod. Latin *Symmetrodonta* (see below), from Latin *symmetria* SYMMETRY + -ODONT.]
PALAEONTOLOGY. ▸**A** *noun.* Any of several primitive fossil mammals of the extinct order Symmetrodonta, characterized by teeth with three cusps in a symmetrical triangle, and known from the Upper Jurassic and Lower Cretaceous of N. America, Europe, and eastern Asia. **M20.**
▸**B** *adjective.* Of or pertaining to an animal of this order. **M20.**

symmetrophobia /ˌsɪmɪtrəˈfəʊbɪə/ *noun.* **E19.**
[from next + -O- + -PHOBIA.]
Irrational fear or avoidance of symmetry, as evidenced or supposed to be evidenced in Egyptian temples, Japanese art, etc.

symmetry /ˈsɪmɪtri/ *noun.* **M16.**
[French †*symmétrie* (now *symétrie*) or Latin *symmetria* from Greek *summetria*, from *summetros*, formed as SYM- + *metron* measure: see -METRY.]
1 Proportion; relative measurement and arrangement of parts. *obsolete* exc. as passing into sense 2. **M16.**
2 Correct or pleasing proportion of the parts of a thing; harmony of parts with each other and the whole; a regular or balanced arrangement and relation of parts. Also, beauty resulting from this. **L16.** ▸†**b** A person's or animal's (well-proportioned) figure or form. **E17.** ▸**c** Agreement, congruity, *with* something. Now *rare* or *obsolete.* **E17.**
3 Correspondence, *spec.* exact correspondence, in relative position, size, and shape of the parts of something with respect to a central point or one or more dividing lines or planes; a structure exhibiting this; *PHYSICS & MATH.* a property by which something is effectively unchanged by a particular operation; an operation or set of operations that leaves something effectively unchanged; *PHYSICS* a property that is conserved. **L16.** ▸**b** *MATH. & LOGIC.* The fact of an expression or function being symmetrical. **L19.**
4 *BOTANY.* Equality of the number of parts in each whorl of a flower. **M19.**

> **2** Y. MENUHIN I had above me two elder beings and below me two younger, a symmetry of love to frame me. P. DE MAN The specular symmetry of the two texts . . involves the entire system with flawless consistency. **3** M. MITCHELL The white house reared its perfect symmetry before her, tall of columns, wide of veranda. ***axis of symmetry, bilateral symmetry, mirror symmetry, plane of symmetry, trigonal symmetry***, etc.

Comb.: **symmetry-breaking** *adjective & noun* (*PHYSICS*) (causing) the absence of manifest symmetry in a situation despite its presence in the laws of nature underlying it; **symmetry group** *MATH.* a group whose elements are all the symmetry operations of a particular entity; **symmetry operation** *PHYSICS* an operation or transformation that leaves something effectively unchanged.

symmory /ˈsɪməri/ *noun.* **M19.**
[Greek *summoria*, from *summoros* sharing (sc. the burden of taxation), formed as SYM- + *mor-* portion, share: see -Y[3].]
GREEK HISTORY. Each of the sections or fellowships, graded according to wealth, into which the citizens of Athens and other cities were divided for purposes of taxation.

sympathectomy /sɪmpəˈθɛktəmi/ *noun.* **E20.**
[from SYMPATH(ETIC + -ECTOMY.]
Surgical excision of a sympathetic ganglion or other part of the sympathetic system; an instance of this.
■ **sympathectomized** *adjective* that has undergone sympathectomy **E20.**

sympathetic /sɪmpəˈθɛtɪk/ *adjective & noun.* **M17.**
[from SYMPATHY after *pathetic*: see -IC.]
▸**A** *adjective.* **1 a** Of, pertaining to, or resulting from sympathy or an affinity, correspondence, or paranormal influence. Now chiefly *Hist.* exc. in ***sympathetic magic*** below. **M17.** ▸**b** *PHYSIOLOGY* etc. Designating a condition, action, or disorder induced in a person, organ, or part by a similar or corresponding one in another. Now chiefly in ***sympathetic ophthalmia*** below. **E18.** ▸**c** *ANATOMY & PHYSIOLOGY.* Of, pertaining to, or designating one of the major divisions of the autonomic nervous system, consisting of a double chain of ganglia along the spinal column supplying the internal organs, intestines, blood-vessels, etc., and governing their function by reflex action in balance with the parasympathetic system. **M18.** ▸**d** Of, pertaining to, or designating sounds arising from vibrations induced in an object by sound waves from another. **M19.**
2 a In accordance or harmonious agreement; according with one's temperament or inclinations, congenial. Now chiefly as passing into sense 3. **L17.** ▸**b** Tending to evoke sympathy. Also, pleasant, likeable. Cf. SYMPATHIQUE. **E20.**
3 a Of, characterized by, or expressive of sympathy or mutuality of feeling. **L17.** ▸**b** (Capable of) feeling sympathy; sharing, responsive to, or affected by the feelings of another or others; compassionate; (foll. by *to*) inclined to favour, give support to, or approve. **E18.**

> **2a** WORDSWORTH Now o'er the soothed accordant heart we feel A sympathetic twilight slowly steal. **b** H. W. FOWLER Macbeth . . is not made sympathetic, however adequately his crime may be explained. A. EDEN It was not a sympathetic house . . the furnishing and pictures were ugly. **3a** SCOTT FITZGERALD He considered he was very fair to Russia—he had no desire to make anything but a sympathetic picture. A. SILLITOE She made sympathetic noises, unable to get upset about it. **b** *Times* Known to be sympathetic to the Baath, or Socialist Party. P. DALLY He was a sympathetic listener.

Special collocations: **sympathetic ink** = *INVISIBLE* **ink**. **sympathetic magic** a type of magic, based on the belief of affinity between things or actions, that seeks to achieve an effect by performing an associated action or using an associated thing. **sympathetic nerve** *ANATOMY* a nerve of the sympathetic system. **sympathetic ophthalmia** *MEDICINE* autoimmune disease of one eye following damage to the other. **sympathetic strike**: by workers in support of the action of strikers in another union, industry, etc. **sympathetic strings** *MUSIC* strings on an instrument (as a sitar) which are not played but vibrate (and thereby sound a note) in sympathetic resonance with the note of a string which has been played near them.
▸**B** *noun.* **1** *ANATOMY.* A sympathetic nerve; the sympathetic system. **E19.**
2 A person affected by a sympathetic pain or injury. Also, a sympathetic person, a sympathizer. *rare.* **L19.**
■ **sympathetical** *adjective* (*arch.*) = *SYMPATHETIC* *adjective* **M17.** **sympathetically** *adverb* **E17.** **sympatheticoˈtonia** *noun* (*PHYSIOLOGY*) = SYMPATHICOTONIA **E20.** **sympatheticoˈtonic** *adjective & noun* (*PHYSIOLOGY*) = SYMPATHICOTONIC **E20.** **sympatheticoˈtonus** *noun* (*PHYSIOLOGY*) = SYMPATHICOTONIA **E20.**

sympathic /sɪmˈpaθɪk/ *adjective.* Now *rare.* **M17.**
[French SYMPATHIQUE, from *sympathie*: see SYMPATHY, -IC.]
1 = SYMPATHETIC *adjective* 1a, 1b, 2. **M17.**
2 *ANATOMY.* = SYMPATHETIC *adjective* 1c. **E19.**
■ Also †**sympathical** *adjective* **L16–M17.**

sympathico- /sɪmˈpaθɪkəʊ/ *combining form.*
[from SYMPATH(ET)IC: see -O-.]
MEDICINE & PHYSIOLOGY. = SYMPATHO-.

sympathicotonia /sɪmˌpaθɪkəˈtəʊnɪə/ *noun.* **M20.**
[from prec. + Greek *tonos* TONE *noun* + -IA[1].]
PHYSIOLOGY. The state or condition in which there is increased influence of the sympathetic nervous system and heightened sensitivity to adrenalin. Cf. VAGOTONIA.
■ **sympathicoˈtonic** *adjective & noun* (*a*) *adjective* displaying or promoting sympathicotonia; (*b*) *noun* a sympathicotonic person: **M20.** **sympathiˈcotony** *noun* = SYMPATHICOTONIA **L20.**

sympathicotropic /sɪmˌpaθɪkəˈtrəʊpɪk, -ˈtrɒpɪk/ *adjective.* **E20.**
[from SYMPATHICO- + -TROPIC.]
PHARMACOLOGY. Possessing an affinity for the sympathetic nervous system.

sympathique /sɛ̃patik/ *adjective.* **M19.**
[French.]
Of a thing, a place, etc.: agreeable, to one's taste, suitable. Of a person: likeable, in tune with or responsive to one's personality or moods. Cf. SYMPATHETIC *adjective* 2b.

sympathisch /zymˈpaːtɪʃ/ *adjective.* **E20.**
[German.]
= SYMPATHIQUE.

sympathize /ˈsɪmpəθʌɪz/ *verb.* Also **-ise.** **L16.**
[French *sympathiser*, from *sympathie* SYMPATHY: see -IZE.]
1 *verb intrans.* Suffer with or like another; be affected in consequence of something else being affected; respond sympathetically to some influence. Cf. SYMPATHY 1. Foll. by *with.* **L16.**
2 *verb intrans.* †**a** Have an affinity; agree in qualities; be alike; (foll. by *with*) resemble. Cf. SYMPATHY 2. **L16–M17.** ▸**b** Agree, be in harmony or accord; harmonize. Foll. by *with.* **E17.**
†**3** *verb trans.* Correspond to, match. **L16–E17.** ▸**b** Represent or express by something corresponding or fitting; apprehend by analogy. **L16–M17.** ▸**c** Make up or compound of corresponding parts or elements. **L16–E17.**
4 *verb intrans.* Feel sympathy; share, be affected by, or responsive to the feelings, condition, or experience of another or others; feel pity or compassion for another's suffering or grief. Freq. foll. by *with.* **E17.** ▸**b** Express sympathy, esp. for another's suffering or grief; condole *with* a person. **M18.** ▸**c** Agree with or be inclined to approve of

an opinion; share an opinion or aim *with* a person or party; be inclined to favour or give support to a cause etc. (usu. foll. by *with*). E19.

> 2a SHAKES. *Hen. V* The men do sympathise with the mastiffs in robustious and rough coming on. **b** F. L. WRIGHT Textures and patterns that sympathize in their own design . . with the design of the particular house they occupy. **3** SHAKES. *Lucr.* True sorrow then is feelingly suffic'd When with like semblance it is sympathiz'd. **4** LYNDON B. JOHNSON I sympathized with the . . Prime Minister in the heavy burdens she had assumed. **c** *National Review (US)* Men who had sympathized with the Allied cause.

■ **sympathizer** *noun* a person who or thing which sympathizes; *esp.* a person inclined to favour or give support to a party, cause, etc. E19.

sympatho- /ˈsɪmpəθəʊ/ *combining form.*
[from SYMPATH(ETIC: see -O-.]
Forming nouns and adjectives in sense 'of or pertaining to the sympathetic nervous system'.
■ **sympatho-aˈdrenal** *adjective* (PHYSIOLOGY) pertaining to or involving the sympathetic nervous system and the medulla of the adrenal gland, and their activity M20. **sympathoblast** *noun* (MEDICINE) a small relatively undifferentiated cell formed in the early development of nerve tissue which develops into a sympathetic neurone M20. **sympathoblasˈtoma** *noun*, pl. **-mas**, **-mata** /-mətə/, MEDICINE a malignant tumour composed chiefly of sympathoblasts M20. **sympathoˈgonia** *noun pl.* [Greek *gonos* offspring, begetting] MEDICINE undifferentiated embryonic cells of the sympathetic nervous system which give rise to sympathoblasts M20. **sympathogoniˈoma** *noun*, pl. **-mas**, **-mata** /-mətə/, MEDICINE a malignant tumour composed chiefly of sympathogonia M20. **sympathoˈlytic** *adjective* (MEDICINE) annulling or opposing the transmission of nerve impulses in the sympathetic system M20. **sympathomiˈmetic** *adjective & noun* (PHARMACOLOGY) (*a*) *adjective* producing physiological effects characteristic of the sympathetic nervous system by promoting the stimulation of sympathetic nerves; (*b*) *noun* a substance which does this: E20. **sympathotropic** /-ˈtrəʊpɪk, -ˈtrɒpɪk/ *adjective* (PHARMACOLOGY) = SYMPATHICOTROPIC M20.

sympathy /ˈsɪmpəθi/ *noun.* L16.
[Latin *sympathia* (whence French *sympathie*) from Greek *sumpatheia*, from *sumpathēs* having a fellow-feeling, formed as SYM- + base of PATHOS: see -Y³.]
1 a An affinity or correspondence between particular subjects enabling the same influence to affect each subject similarly or each subject to affect or influence the other, esp. in a paranormal way. Now chiefly *Hist.* or as passing into other senses. L16. ▸**b** PHYSIOLOGY & MEDICINE. A relation between two organs or parts (or between two people) such that a disorder or condition of the one induces a corresponding condition in the other. Now *rare*. E17.
2 Agreement, accord; *esp.* agreement in qualities; correspondence. *obsolete* exc. as passing into sense 3a. L16.
3 a Concordance or harmony of inclinations or temperament, making people congenial to one another; mutuality or community of feeling. L16. ▸**b** The quality or state of being affected by the suffering or grief of another; a feeling or expression of compassion or condolence. Freq. foll. by *for*, *with*. E17. ▸**c** *gen.* The quality or state of being affected with a feeling similar or corresponding to that of another; the fact or capacity of sharing or being responsive to the feelings or condition of another or others; an instance of this. Freq. foll. by *with*. M17. ▸**d** *sing.* & in *pl.* A favourable attitude towards a party, cause, etc.; inclination to favour or support; agreement with or approval of an opinion, aim, etc. Freq. foll. by *with*. E19.

> 1a W. G. BLACK That doctrine of sympathy which accompanies all remedies by association. **2** SHAKES. *Oth.* There should be . . sympathy in years, manners and beauties. **3a** G. TINDALL There had always been a lot of understanding and sympathy between them. **b** R. CONGREVE Our sympathies to the unborn generations which . . shall follow us. J. FRAME I'm writing to express my sympathy with you in your loss of a brother. ***tea and sympathy***: see TEA *noun* 1. **c** P. FUSSELL His . . complex comic sympathy for poor middle-class Evans. **d** M. MEYER He disinherited Raymond and his sister because of their left-wing sympathies.

Phrases: **in sympathy** (*a*) having or expressing or resulting from sympathy (*with* another); (*b*) by way of sympathetic action; *spec.* (of a commodity price) rising or falling in response to another commodity's price movement or to an event or circumstance affecting the market.
Comb.: **sympathy card** a printed card expressing condolence on a bereavement; **sympathy strike** = ***sympathetic strike*** s.v. SYMPATHETIC *adjective*; **sympathy striker** a person taking part in a sympathetic strike.
■ **sympathist** *noun* (*rare*) a person who sympathizes, a sympathizer E19.

symphilism /ˈsɪmfɪlɪz(ə)m/ *noun.* E20.
[from SYM- + -PHIL + -ISM.]
ZOOLOGY. A cooperative symbiosis between ants or termites and certain other arthropods which they feed and tend, and which usu. yield a substance or render a service in return.
■ **symphile** *noun* an insect or other arthropod that lives with ants etc. in a relationship of symphilism E20. **symˈphilic** *adjective* pertaining to or designating a symphile E20. **symphilous** *adjective* = SYMPHILIC E20. **symphily** *noun* = SYMPHILISM L19.

symphonic /sɪmˈfɒnɪk/ *adjective.* M19.
[from SYMPHONY + -IC, after *harmonic*.]
1 a Involving similarity of sound, esp. in Welsh prosody. *rare*. M19. ▸**b** Having the same pronunciation; = HOMOPHONOUS 2. *rare*. L19.
2 Harmonious. *rare*. M19.
3 MUSIC. Of, pertaining to, or having the form or character of a symphony. M19.

> 3 *Classic CD* Pesek welds these six works into a symphonic whole. *fig.*: *Sunday Telegraph* His symphonic novel is not for the faint-hearted. **symphonic ballet** a ballet choreographed to the music of a symphony, with an emphasis on pattern rather than narrative. **symphonic jazz** (*a*) jazz influenced by the form and instrumentation of classical music; (*b*) classical music scored and performed in jazz style. **symphonic poem** [translating German *symphonische Dichtung*] an extended orchestral composition, usu. in one movement and freer in form than a symphony, on a descriptive or rhapsodic theme.

■ **symphonically** *adverb* M19.

symphonie *noun* see SYMPHONY.

symphonious /sɪmˈfəʊnɪəs/ *adjective. literary.* M17.
[from Latin *symphonia* SYMPHONY + -OUS, after *harmonious*.]
1 Full of or characterized by symphony or harmony of sounds; *fig.* concordant; agreeing harmoniously *with*. M17.
2 Sounding together or in combination. *rare*. E19.

> 1 MILTON The sound Symphonious of ten thousand Harpes. R. L. STEVENSON The shadows . . and the silence made a symphonious accompaniment about our walk.

■ **symphoniously** *adverb* M18.

symphonise *verb* var. of SYMPHONIZE.

symphonism /ˈsɪmf(ə)nɪz(ə)m/ *noun.* M20.
[from SYMPHON(Y + -ISM.]
Music of a symphonic kind; symphonies collectively.

symphonist /ˈsɪmf(ə)nɪst/ *noun.* M17.
[from next or from SYMPHONY + -IST.]
†**1** A chorister whose singing is in tune and in time. *rare*. Only in M17.
2 Orig., an orchestral performer playing in a symphony or musical interlude to a vocal composition. Now (*rare*), a member of a symphony orchestra. M18.
3 A composer of orchestral symphonies. L18.

symphonize /ˈsɪmf(ə)nʌɪz/ *verb.* Also **-ise**. L15.
[medieval Latin *symphonizare* (from Latin *symphonia* SYMPHONY), or directly from SYMPHONY: see -IZE.]
1 *verb intrans.* Sing, play, or sound together, in combination or in harmony. Now *rare*. L15.
†**2** *verb intrans.* Agree, be in accordance, harmonize, *with*. M17–E18.
†**3 a** *verb trans.* Accompany musically. *rare*. Only in E19. ▸**b** *verb intrans.* Play a symphony. *rare*. Only in M19.
4 *verb trans.* Give the character or style of a symphony to (a piece of music), make symphonic. M20.

> 1 DE QUINCEY His . . wolfish howl . . may have symphonized with the ear-shattering trumpet.

symphony /ˈsɪmf(ə)ni/ *noun.* In sense 1 also **-ie**. ME.
[Old French †*simphonie* (mod. *sym-*) from Latin *symphonia* instrumental harmony, voices in concert, musical instrument from Greek *sumphōnia*, from *sumphōnos* harmonious, formed as SYM-: see -PHONY.]
1 Any of various medieval or Renaissance musical instruments, as a dulcimer, virginal, etc. ME.
2 The quality, esp. of music, of having a harmonious sound. *obsolete* exc. *Hist.* LME.
3 Agreement, accord, concord. L16.
4 a Music in parts for an ensemble of voices or instruments, or both; concerted music; a performance or strain of such music. Chiefly *poet.* & *rhet.* L16. ▸**b** *fig.* A combination or collection of utterances or sounds comparable to concerted music; a harmoniously pleasing arrangement or juxtaposition of colours. L16.
5 MUSIC. **a** An instrumental passage at the beginning or in the middle of a vocal composition, such as a cantata or madrigal, similar to a ritornello, although not usu. repeated as a refrain throughout. Also, a short interlude for orchestra alone between the movements of a large-scale vocal work. Formerly also, a more extended instrumental piece, often in three movements, forming the overture to an opera. M17. ▸**b** An elaborate composition, usu. for full orchestra, in three or more movements, and similar in form to a sonata, but usually of grander dimensions and broader style. L18. ▸**c** *ellipt.* = ***symphony orchestra*** below. E20.

> 2 DISRAELI Stanzas . . resonant with subtle symphony. **3** CARLYLE Their domestic symphony was subject to furious flaws. **4a** A. RADCLIFFE To join in the choral symphonies of the nuns. **b** W. J. LOCKE She sat as hostess . . at the table, a symphony in . . gold and black. **5b** D. C. PEATTIE Listening to a Sibelius symphony rolling out. *attrib.*: A. H. COMPTON Seeking a little relaxation at a symphony concert.

Comb.: **symphony orchestra** a large orchestra suitable for playing symphonies etc.

For other words beginning with *sym-* see the entry for **sym-**

symphylan /sɪmˈfʌɪlən/ *adjective & noun.* L19.
[from mod. Latin *symphyla* (see below), formed as SYM- + Greek *phulē*, *phulon* tribe, race: see -AN.]
ZOOLOGY. ▸**A** *adjective.* Of or pertaining to the small myriapod class Symphyla, whose members resemble small whitish centipedes but lack eyes and poison claws, and show some affinities with insects. L19.
▸**B** *noun.* A myriapod of this class. M20.
■ Also **symphylid** *adjective & noun* M20.

symphysis /ˈsɪmfɪsɪs/ *noun.* Pl. **-physes** /-fɪsiːz/. L16.
[mod. Latin from Greek *sumphusis* growing together (esp. of bones), formed as SYM- + *phusis* growth.]
1 ANATOMY & ZOOLOGY. The union of two bones or skeletal elements by fusion of the bone or by cartilaginous connection; the part, or line of junction, where this occurs or occurred, esp. where two similar bones on opposite sides of the body are united in the median line, as that of the pubic bones. L16.
2 The union or fusion of other separate parts, either surgically or naturally. Now *rare*. L19.
1 symphysis mandibulae /manˈdɪbjʊliː/ [Latin = of the jaw], **symphysis menti** /ˈmɛnti/ [Latin = of the chin] ANATOMY the line of union of the two halves of the lower jaw. **symphysis pubis** /ˈpjuːbɪs/ ANATOMY the cartilaginous mass connecting the two pubic bones.
■ **symphyseal**, **symphysial** /-ˈfɪzɪəl/ *adjectives* of or pertaining to a symphysis; situated at or forming a symphysis: M19. **symphysiˈotomy** *noun* (MEDICINE) (an instance of) a surgical operation to cut through the symphysis pubis to facilitate delivery M19.

sympiesometer /ˌsɪmpɪɪˈsɒmɪtə/ *noun.* Now *rare* or *obsolete*. E19.
[Irreg. from Greek *sumpiesis* compression, from *sumpiezein* compress, formed as SYM- + *piezein* to press: see -OMETER.]
A barometer in which there is gas above the column of liquid in the tube, so that the pressure of the atmosphere acts against the pressure of both the liquid and the gas, a thermometer being attached for correction of the readings.

symplasm /ˈsɪmplaz(ə)m/ *noun.* E20.
[from SYM- + PLASM.]
1 BACTERIOLOGY. A group of bacterial cells that have coalesced into one amorphous mass. Now *rare* or *obsolete*. E20.
2 BOTANY. (The cytoplasm of) a symplast. M20.
■ **symˈplasmic** *adjective* E20.

symplasma /sɪmˈplazmə/ *noun.* Pl. **-mata** /-mətə/. E20.
[from SYM- + PLASMA.]
MEDICINE. A mass of cell nuclei and cytoplasm regarded as formed by the breaking down of the cell walls of the outer layer of the placenta.

symplasmatic /sɪmplazˈmatɪk/ *adjective.* E20.
[from SYMPLASM, SYMPLASMA after *plasma*, *plasmatic*.]
1 MEDICINE. Of or pertaining to a symplasma. E20.
2 BOTANY. Of or pertaining to a symplasm. L20.

symplast /ˈsɪmplast, -plɑːst/ *noun.* L19.
[German *Symplast*.]
†**1** BIOLOGY. = SYNCYTIUM. L19–E20.
2 BOTANY. A continuous network of interconnected plant cell protoplasts. M20.
■ **symplastic** *adjective* of or pertaining to a symplast or symplasm; ***symplastic growth***, growth of adjacent plant cells at an equal rate without disruption of plasmodesmata: E20.

symplectic /sɪmˈplɛktɪk/ *adjective & noun.* In sense A.2 also **-plek-**. M19.
[from Greek *sumplektikos*, formed as SYM- + *plekein* twine, plait, weave: see -IC.]
▸**A** *adjective.* **1** ZOOLOGY. Designating a bone of the suspensorium in the skull of fishes, between the hyomandibular and the quadrate bones. M19.
2 PETROGRAPHY. Of a rock or its texture: exhibiting an intimate intergrowth of two different minerals, esp. one where one mineral has a vermicular habit within the other as a result of secondary action. E20.
3 MATH. Involving, pertaining to, or designating the group of linear transformations (and their matrix equivalents) under which a given non-degenerate skew-symmetric bilinear form is invariant; (in Hamiltonian mechanics) designating such forms acting on manifolds and vector spaces. M20.
▸**B** *noun.* ZOOLOGY. The symplectic bone. L19.
■ **symplectically** *adverb* (MATH.) M20. **symplectite** *noun* (PETROGRAPHY) a symplectic intergrowth; a rock with symplectic texture: E20.

symploce /ˈsɪmpləsi/ *noun.* M16.
[Late Latin from Greek *sumplokē* an interweaving, formed as SYM- + *plekein*: see prec.]
RHETORIC. The repetition of one word or phrase at the beginning, and of another at the end, of successive clauses or sentences; a combination of anaphora and epistrophe.

sympodia /sɪmˈpəʊdɪə/ *noun*¹. M19.
[from Greek *sumpod-*, *sumpous* with the feet together + -IA¹.]
MEDICINE & ZOOLOGY. A congenital malformation in which the legs or lower extremities are united. Cf. SYMMELIA.

sympodia *noun*² pl. of SYMPODIUM.

sympodial /sɪmˈpəʊdɪəl/ *adjective*. L19.
[In sense 1 from next; in sense 2 from SYMPODIA *noun*¹: see -IAL.]
1 *BOTANY*. Pertaining to, of the nature of, or producing a sympodium. L19.
2 *ANATOMY & ZOOLOGY*. Affected with sympodia; having the lower extremities united. E20.
■ **sympodially** *adverb* (*BOTANY*) in the manner of a sympodium L19.

sympodium /sɪmˈpəʊdɪəm/ *noun*. Pl. **-dia** /-dɪə/. M19.
[mod. Latin, formed as SYM- + Greek *pod-*, *pous* foot: see -IUM.]
BOTANY. An apparent axis formed by successive lateral growth, each year's terminal bud dying at the end of the season. Cf. MONOPODIUM 2.

symposia *noun* pl. of SYMPOSIUM.

symposiac /sɪmˈpəʊzɪak/ *noun & adjective*. L16.
[Latin *symposiacus* (adjective), *symposiaca* (noun pl.) or Greek *sumposiakos* adjective, from *sumposion* SYMPOSIUM: see -AC.]
▶ **A** *noun*. †**1** = SYMPOSIAST 1. *rare*. Only in L16.
2 A convivial meeting or conversation; an account of this; a symposium. Now *rare*. E17.
▶ **B** *adjective*. Of, pertaining to, or suitable for a symposium; of the nature of a symposium; convivial. M17.

symposial /sɪmˈpəʊzɪəl/ *adjective*. L18.
[from SYMPOSIUM + -AL¹.]
= SYMPOSIAC *adjective*.

symposiarch /sɪmˈpəʊzɪɑːk/ *noun*. E17.
[Greek *sumposiarkhos*, from *sumposion* SYMPOSIUM + *-arkhos* -ARCH.]
The master, director, or president of a symposium; the leader of a convivial gathering.

symposiast /sɪmˈpəʊzɪast/ *noun*. M17.
[from Greek *sumposiazein* drink together (from *sumposion* SYMPOSIUM), on Greek analogies: cf. *enthusiast*.]
1 Orig. (*rare*), a symposiarch. Now, a member of a drinking-party; a banqueter. M17.
2 A participant in a symposium or conference. L19.

> 🕮 **2** *Verbatim* What the symposiasts . . discussed were criteria for assessing a dictionary.

symposiastic /sɪm,pəʊzɪˈastɪk/ *adjective*. *rare*. M17.
[medieval Greek *sumposiastikos*, formed as prec.: see -IC.]
= SYMPOSIAC *adjective*.

symposium /sɪmˈpəʊzɪəm/ *noun*. Pl. **-ia** /-ɪə/, **-iums**. L16.
[Latin from Greek *sumposion*, from *sumpotēs* fellow-drinker, formed as SYM- + *potēs* drinker.]
1 A drinking-party; a convivial meeting, *esp*. (*Hist*.) one held by the ancient Greeks for drinking, conversation, philosophical discussion, etc.; *Hist*. an account of such a meeting or the conversation at it. L16.
2 a A meeting or conference for the discussion of a particular subject; a collection of opinions delivered or a series of articles contributed at such a meeting or conference. L18. ▸**b** A collection of essays or papers on various aspects of a particular subject by a number of contributors. L19.

> 🕮 **1** CHESTERFIELD Your Symposium [is] intended more to promote conversation than drinking. **2a** *Marketing* A one-day symposium for people involved . . in marketing and product development. **b** R. HEILBRONER Writing in a symposium on behavior, . . Wilson presents the following 'optimistic' estimate.

sympotical /sɪmˈpɒtɪk(ə)l/ *adjective*. *rare*. E19.
[from late Latin *sympoticus* or Greek *sumpotikos*, from *sumpotēs*: see SYMPOSIUM, -ICAL.]
= SYMPOSIAC *adjective*.
■ Also **sympotic** *adjective* L20.

symptom /ˈsɪm(p)təm/ *noun*. LME.
[medieval Latin *synthoma* from late Latin *symptoma* from Greek *sumptōma* chance, accident, mischance, from *sumpiptein* fall upon, happen to, formed as SYM- + *piptein* to fall.]
1 *MEDICINE*. A physical or mental phenomenon, circumstance, or change of condition arising from and accompanying a disorder and constituting evidence of it; a characteristic sign *of* a particular disease. Now *spec*. a subjective indication perceptible to the patient, as opp. to an objective one (cf. SIGN *noun* 6c). LME.
2 a *gen*. A phenomenon or circumstance accompanying a condition, feeling, etc., and serving as evidence of it; a sign or indication of the existence *of* something. E17. ▸**b** In neg. contexts: a slight or the least sign *of* something; a trace, a vestige. E18.

> 🕮 **2a** H. CARPENTER His playing of the fool was a symptom . . of pessimism. *Gamut* These incidents are symptoms of contemporary . . society's deep-seated insecurity. **b** HOR. WALPOLE Europe could scarce amass the symptom of a fleet.

Comb.: **symptom complex**, **symptom group** *MEDICINE* a set of symptoms occurring together and characterizing or constituting a particular disease.
■ **symptomless** *adjective* L19. **symptoˈmology** *noun* = SYMPTOMATOLOGY M19.

symptomatic /sɪm(p)təˈmatɪk/ *adjective & noun*. L17.
[French *symptomatique* or late Latin *symptomaticus*, from *symptoma* SYMPTOM: see -IC.]
▶ **A** *adjective*. **1** *MEDICINE*. **a** Occurring as a consequence of some other disease; secondary; not idiopathic. Now *rare* or *obsolete*. L17. ▸**b** Of the nature of or constituting a symptom of a particular disease. E18. ▸**c** Of a patient: displaying the symptom or symptoms of a particular disease. M20.
2 Pertaining to or concerned with symptoms. M18.
3 *gen*. That is a symptom or sign of something; serving as a symptom or sign of a condition, quality, etc.; characteristic and indicative *of*. M18.

> 🕮 **1a** HENRY FIELDING If this fever should prove more than symptomatic, it would be impossible to save him. **3** E. H. GOMBRICH Changes in fashion . . are often symptomatic of social change. S. MILLER She'd grown . . and that great surge in height seemed symptomatic to her of the distance she'd traveled from them.

▶ **B** *noun*. In *pl*. = SYMPTOMATOLOGY. *rare*. M18.
■ **symptomatical** *adjective* (now *rare* or *obsolete*) = SYMPTOMATIC *adjective* L16. **symptomatically** *adverb* E17.

symptomatize /ˈsɪm(p)təmətʌɪz/ *verb trans*. Also **-ise**. L18.
[from Greek *sumptōmat-*, *sumptōma* SYMPTOM + -IZE.]
Be a symptom of; characterize or indicate as a symptom.

symptomatology /sɪm(p)təməˈtɒlədʒi/ *noun*. L18.
[formed as prec. + -OLOGY.]
MEDICINE. The symptoms of a disease collectively; the branch of medicine that deals with the study and classification of symptoms; a discourse or treatise on symptoms.
■ ˌ**symptomatoˈlogical** *adjective* M19. ˌ**symptomatoˈlogically** *adverb* L19. **symptomatologist** *noun* M19.

symptomize /ˈsɪm(p)təmʌɪz/ *verb trans*. Also **-ise**. L19.
[from SYMPTOM + -IZE.]
= SYMPTOMATIZE.

sympto-thermal /sɪmptəˈθɜːm(ə)l/ *adjective*. M20.
[from SYMPTOM + THERMAL.]
Designating a contraceptive method based on the monitoring of a woman's body temperature and of physical symptoms related to ovulation.

syn- /sɪn/ *prefix*. In sense 2 also as attrib. adjective **syn**.
[from or after Latin from Greek *sun-*, from *sun* with; in Latin reduced to *sy-* before *st*, *z* and assim. to *syl-* before *l*, SYM- before *b*, *m*, *p*, and *sys-* before *s*. In sense 3 from SYNTHETIC *adjective*.]
1 Together, similarly, alike.
2 *CHEMISTRY*. (Usu. italicized.) Designating geometrical isomers of organic compounds containing C=N or N=N in which the principal atoms or groups attached to the doubly bonded atoms are on the same side of the plane of the double bond (opp. ***anti-***).
3 Denoting synthetic products.
■ **syˈnalgia** *noun* (*MEDICINE*) referred pain L19. **synanˈthropic** *adjective* (*BIOLOGY*) living in a habitat made or altered by humans M20. **syˈnapomorphy** *noun* (*BIOLOGY*) the possession by two organisms of a characteristic (not necessarily the same in each) that is derived from one characteristic in an organism from which they both evolved; such a derived characteristic: M20. **synaposeˈmatic** *adjective* (*BIOLOGY*) of or having similar warning coloration etc. L19. **syncrude** *noun & adjective* (designating or pertaining to) a synthetic product made from coal in imitation of crude oil L20. **syncyaˈnosis** *noun*, pl. **-noses** /-ˈnəʊsiːz/, *BOTANY* an endosymbiotic relationship between a unicellular blue-green alga and another organism; such an alga: M20. **synˈdiploidy** *noun* (*GENETICS*) doubling of the chromosome number in gametes by fusion of daughter cell nuclei M20. **syˈnechthran** *noun* [Greek *ekhthros* hostile] *ZOOLOGY* an insect living with ants or other social insects but treated as unwelcome E20. **synform** *noun* (*GEOLOGY*) a fold that is concave upwards, irrespective of the chronological sequence of the strata (opp. ***antiform***) M20. **synfuel** *noun* (a) fuel made from coal, oil shale, etc., as a substitute for a petroleum product L20. **syngas** *noun* a mixture of carbon monoxide and hydrogen, esp. when produced from coal L20. **syngen** *noun* (*BIOLOGY*) a group of organisms capable of interbreeding; *spec*. in *MICROBIOLOGY*, a genetically isolated subdivision in some protozoan species comprising individuals of compatible mating types: M20. **synjet** *noun* jet fuel derived from syncrude L20. **synˈkaryon** *noun*, pl. **-ya** /-ɪə/, [see KARYO-] *BIOLOGY* (a cell having) a pair of nuclei, or a nucleus produced by the fusion of two nuclei E20. **synkineˈmatic** *adjective* (*GEOLOGY*) = SYNTECTONIC M20. **synkiˈnesis** *noun* (*PHYSIOLOGY*) associated movement, *esp*. reflex muscular coordination L19. **synkiˈnetic** *adjective* (*PHYSIOLOGY*) of or pertaining to synkinesis E20. **synˈnema** *noun*, pl. **-mata** /-mətə/, [-NEMA] *MYCOLOGY* the elongated fruiting body of some fungi, consisting of columns of conidiophores E20. **synˈneusis** *noun* [Greek *neusis* swimming] *GEOLOGY* the clustering together of crystals of a mineral in a rock E20. **synoekete** /sɪˈniːkiːt/ *noun* [Greek *sunoiketēs* housemate] *ENTOMOLOGY* an insect living with ants or other social insects without provoking a hostile or a favourable reaction E20. **synoil** *noun* synthetic oil L20. **synoroˈgenic** *adjective* (*GEOLOGY*) formed or occurring during a period of orogenesis M20. **synroc** *noun* [ROC(K *noun*¹] any of various synthetic crystalline materials made chiefly of oxides of metals and metalloids and devised to contain radioactive waste in stable solid solution deep underground L20. **synˈsacral** *adjective* (*ZOOLOGY*) pertaining to the synsacrum E20. **synˈsacrum** *noun* (*ZOOLOGY*) an elongated composite sacrum containing a number of fused vertebrae, present in birds and some extinct reptiles E20. **synsediˈmentary** *adjective* (*GEOLOGY*) formed or occurring at the time of deposition of (the) sediment M20. **synseˈmantic** *adjective* (of a word or phrase) having no meaning outside a context; syncategorematic: E20. **synˈsepalous** *adjective* (*BOTANY*) = GAMOSEPALOUS M19. **syntecˈtonic** *adjective* (*GEOLOGY*) formed or occurring during a period of tectonic activity M20. **syntecˈtonically** *adverb* (*GEOLOGY*) during a period of tectonic activity M20. **synˈtenic** *adjective* [Greek *tainia* band, ribbon] *GENETICS* (of genes) occurring on the same chromosome L20. **synteny** *noun* (*GENETICS*) syntenic condition L20.

synaeresis /sɪˈnɪərɪsɪs/ *noun*. Also ***syner-**. L16.
[Late Latin from Greek *sunairesis*, from *sun-* SYN- + *hairesis*, from *hairein* take.]
1 *GRAMMAR & PROSODY*. Contraction of two or more syllables into one, esp. of two vowels into a diphthong or a simple vowel. Opp. ***diaeresis***. L16.
2 The contraction of a gel accompanied by the separating out of liquid; *MEDICINE* the contraction of a blood clot into a firm seal. M19.

synaesthesia /sɪnɪsˈθiːzɪə/ *noun*. Also ***synes-**. Pl. **-iae** /-ɪiː/. L19.
[from SYN- after *anaesthesia*.]
1 *PSYCHOLOGY*. The production of a mental sense-impression relating to one sense by the stimulation of another sense, as in coloured hearing. Also, a sensation produced in one part of the body by stimulation of another part. L19.
2 The use of metaphors in which terms relating to one kind of sense-impression are used to describe sense-impressions of other kinds. M20.
3 *LINGUISTICS*. **a** The expression of more than one kind of sense-impression by the same word. M20. ▸**b** The transfer of the meaning of a word from one kind of sensory experience to another. M20. ▸**c** = PHONAESTHESIA. L20.

synaesthesis /sɪnɪsˈθiːsɪs/ *noun*. Also ***synes-**. L19.
[from SYN- + AESTHESIS.]
1 The total mental activity of a non-rational animal. *rare*. L19.
2 In aesthetic theory, the balancing of different appetencies to produce harmony and equilibrium. E20.

synaesthetic /sɪnɪsˈθɛtɪk/ *adjective & noun*. Also ***synes-**. E20.
[In senses A.1, B from SYNAESTHESIA after *anaesthetic*. In sense A.2 from SYNAESTHESIS after *aesthetic*.]
▶ **A** *adjective*. **1** Of, pertaining to, or exhibiting synaesthesia. E20.
2 Of or pertaining to synaesthesis. E20.
▶ **B** *noun*. A synaesthetic person. M20.
■ **synaesthetically** *adverb* E20.

synagog *noun* see SYNAGOGUE.

synagogal /sɪnəˈgɒg(ə)l/ *adjective*. L17.
[from next + -AL¹.]
Of, pertaining to, or characteristic of a (or the) synagogue.
■ Also **synagogical** /-ˈgɒdʒ-, -ˈgɒg-/ *adjective* E17.

synagogue /ˈsɪnəgɒg/ *noun*. Also ***-gog**. ME.
[Old French *sinagoge* (mod. *synagogue*) from late Latin *synagoga* from Greek *sunagōgē* meeting, assembly, (Septuagint) synagogue, from *sunagein* bring together, assemble, from *sun-* SYN- + *agein* lead, bring.]
1 The regular assembly of Jews for religious observance and instruction; public Jewish worship. ME.
2 The body of all Jews; a community of Jews locally organized into a society for religious worship etc.; the office-holders of such a community. Also, the Jewish religion, Judaism. ME.
3 A building or place of meeting for Jewish worship and religious instruction. ME. ▸†**b** *gen*. A place of worship, a temple. Freq. *derog*. LME–M17.
4 An assembly. Chiefly in biblical use. Long *arch*. ME.
5 An assembly *of* the wicked or heretical. *derog*. *obsolete* exc. in ***synagogue of Satan***. M16.

> 🕮 **1** J. L. WATEN After synagogue and lunch, . . Auntie Fanny read to us from . . the Bible. **2 the Great Synagogue** *Hist*. a Jewish council of 120 members, said to have been founded and presided over by Ezra after the return from the Babylonian captivity.

synalepha *noun* see SYNALOEPHA.

synallagmatic /sɪnəlagˈmatɪk/ *adjective*. L18.
[Greek *sunallagmatikos*, from *sunallagma* covenant, contract, from *sunallassein*, from *sun-* SYN- + *allassein* to exchange: see -IC.]
Of a contract, treaty, etc.: imposing mutual obligations, reciprocally binding.

synaloepha /sɪnəˈliːfə/ *noun*. Also **-phe** /-fi/, ***-leph-**. M16.
[Late Latin from Greek *sunaloiphē*, from *sunaleiphein* smear or melt together, from *sun-* SYN- + *aleiphein* anoint.]
GRAMMAR & PROSODY. Contraction of two syllables into one; *esp*. (in verse) the obscuration of a vowel at the end of a word when the next word begins with a vowel.

synangium /sɪˈnandʒɪəm/ *noun*. Pl. **-ia** /-ɪə/. L19.
[mod. Latin, formed as SYN- + Greek *aggeion* vessel: see -IUM.]
BOTANY. A compound structure formed by the fusion of groups of sporangia (in certain tropical ferns) or groups of pollen-sacs (in certain cycads).
▪ **synangic** *adjective* E20.

synanthous /sɪˈnanθəs/ *adjective*. M19.
[from SYN- + Greek *anthos* flower + -OUS.]
BOTANY. **1** Of a plant: in which the leaves expand at the same time as the flowers. M19.
2 Exhibiting synanthy. E20.
▪ **synanthic** *adjective* exhibiting synanthy M19. **synanthy** *noun* abnormal fusion of two or more flowers M19.

synaphea /sɪnəˈfiːə/ *noun*. E19.
[Greek *sunapheia* connection, from *sunaphēs* connected, united, from *sun-* SYN- + *haptein* fasten, fix.]
CLASSICAL PROSODY. Maintenance of the same rhythm throughout, esp. in anapaestic verse.

synapse /ˈsʌɪnaps, ˈsɪn-/ *noun*. L19.
[Anglicized from SYNAPSIS.]
ANATOMY. A junction between two nerve cells or their threadlike extremities, consisting of a minute gap between two specialized regions of the cell surface, across which an impulse passes by diffusion of a neurotransmitter. Also *loosely*, any junction between excitable cells by which an impulse may pass.

synapse /ˈsʌɪnaps, ˈsɪn-/ *verb intrans*. E20.
[In sense 1 from SYNAPSE *noun*; in sense 2 from SYNAPSIS.]
1 ANATOMY. Of a nerve cell or axon: form a synapse. E20.
2 GENETICS. Of chromosomes or genes: undergo synapsis. Chiefly as ***synapsed ppl adjective***. M20.

synapses *noun* pl. of SYNAPSE *noun*, SYNAPSIS.

synapsid /sʌɪˈnapsɪd, sɪˈnap-/ *adjective & noun*. E20.
[from mod. Latin *Synapsida* (see below), formed as SYN- + Greek (*h*)*apsid-*, (*h*)*apsis* arch: see -ID[3].]
▶ **A** *adjective*. Of or pertaining to the subclass Synapsida of extinct reptiles (considered close relatives of mammals) having a single temporal opening on each side of the skull, which were abundant in the late Permian and early Triassic and included pelycosaurs, therapsids, and cynodonts. E20.
▶ **B** *noun*. A reptile of the subclass Synapsida. Also called ***mammal-like reptile***. E20.

synapsis /sɪˈnapsɪs/ *noun*. Pl. **synapses** /sɪˈnapsiːz/. M17.
[mod. Latin from Greek *sunapsis* connection, junction, from *sun-* SYN- + *hapsis* joining, from *haptein* join.]
1 *gen*. Connection. *rare*. M17.
2 BIOLOGY. The fusion of paired chromosomes during meiosis. L19.
3 ANATOMY. = SYNAPSE *noun*. Now *rare* or *obsolete*. L19.

synaptic /sɪˈnaptɪk, sʌɪ-/ *adjective*. L19.
[In sense 1 from SYNAPSIS, in sense 2 from SYNAPSE *noun*, after Greek *sunaptikos* (cf. *ellipse*, *ellipsis*, *elliptic*): see -IC.]
1 BIOLOGY. Of or pertaining to meiotic synapsis. L19.
2 ANATOMY. Of or pertaining to a synapse or synapses between nerve cells. E20.
▪ **synaptically** *adverb* by means of synapses, with regard to synapses E20.

synapticula /sɪnapˈtɪkjʊlə/ *noun*. Pl. **-lae** /-liː/. Also **-lum** /-ləm/, pl. **-la** /-lə/. M19.
[from Greek *sunaptikos* connective + *-cula* dim. suffix: see -CULE.]
ZOOLOGY. A connecting bar, as running transversely between the septa of some corals, the gills of some protochordates, etc.
▪ **synapticular** *adjective* of or pertaining to synapticulae L19. **synapticulate** *adjective* having synapticulae L19.

synapto- /sɪˈnaptəʊ, sʌɪ-/ *combining form*.
[from SYNAPSE *noun*, SYNAPSIS: see -O-.]
PHYSIOLOGY & BIOLOGY. Forming nouns and corresp. adjectives connected with (*a*) synapses of nerve cells; (*b*) synapsis of chromosomes.
▪ **synaptoˈgenesis** *noun* the formation of synapses between nerve cells M20. **synapˈtology** *noun* the branch of biology that deals with the structure and operation of synapses M20. **synaptoˈnemal** *adjective* (CYTOLOGY): ***synaptonemal complex***, a set of several parallel threads seen adjacent to and coaxial with pairing chromosomes in meiosis M20. **synaptoˈsomal** *adjective* of or pertaining to a synaptosome or synaptosomes L20. **synaptosome** *noun* a presynaptic nerve ending which, when isolated, seals up to form an intact sac M20.

synarchy /ˈsɪnɑːki/ *noun*. *rare*. M18.
[Greek *sunarkhia*, from *sunarkhein* rule jointly, formed as SYN- + -ARCHY.]
Joint rule; participation in government.

synarthrosis /sɪnɑːˈθrəʊsɪs/ *noun*. Pl. **-throses** /-ˈθrəʊsiːz/. L16.
[Greek *sunarthrōsis*, from *sun-* SYN- + *arthrōsis* ARTHROSIS.]
ANATOMY. (An) articulation in which the bones are firmly and immovably fixed together, as in the sutures of the skull and the sockets of the teeth.
▪ **synarthrodial** *adjective* M19.

synastry /sɪˈnastri/ *noun*. M17.
[Late Latin *synastria* from Greek *sunastria*, from *sun-* SYN- + *astr-*, *astēr* star: see -Y[3].]
ASTROLOGY. Comparison of two horoscopes; conformity or compatibility so discovered.

synaxarion /sɪnakˈsarɪən/ *noun*. Also in Latin form **-ium** /-ɪəm/. Pl. **-ia**. M19.
[ecclesiastical Greek *sunaxarion*, from *sunaxis* SYNAXIS.]
An account of the life of a saint, read at the morning office in some Orthodox and other Eastern Churches; a collection of such accounts.
▪ **syˈnaxarist** *noun* the compiler of a synaxarion E20.

synaxis /sɪˈnaksɪs/ *noun*. Pl. **synaxes** /sɪˈnaksiːz/. E17.
[ecclesiastical Latin from ecclesiastical Greek *sunaxis*, from *sunagein* gather together.]
CHRISTIAN CHURCH. Orig. (now chiefly *Hist.*), a meeting for worship, esp. for the Eucharist. Now usu. *spec.*, the service of readings, psalms, etc., which forms the first part of a eucharistic liturgy.

sync /sɪŋk/ *noun & verb*. *colloq*. Also **synch**. E20.
[Abbreviation.]
▶ **A** *noun*. Synchronism; synchronization; *fig.* conformity, agreement, harmony with one's surroundings. E20.
📖 M. MUGGERIDGE The sync frequently went awry, with the words . . and the movements of the singer's lips not tallying.
▶ **B** *verb trans*. Synchronize. M20.
Phrases etc.: **in sync** according or agreeing well (*with*). ***lip-sync***: see LIP *noun*. **out of sync** not according or agreeing well (*with*).

syncarpous /sɪnˈkɑːpəs/ *adjective*. M19.
[from SYN- + Greek *karpos* fruit + -OUS.]
BOTANY. Of a gynoecium: having united carpels. Opp. APOCARPOUS.
▪ **syncarpy** *noun* (*a*) syncarpous condition; (*b*) abnormal fusion of two or more fruits: M19.

syncategorematic /sɪnˌkatɪɡ(ə)rɪˈmatɪk/ *adjective*. E19.
[(medieval Latin *syncategorematicus* from) Greek *sugkatēgorēmatikos*, from *sugkatēgorēma*, from *sugkatēgorein* predicate jointly: see -IC.]
Of a word: having no meaning by itself, but only in conjunction with one or more other words or concepts. Opp. ***categorematic***.
▪ **syncategorematical** *adjective* (*rare*) M17. **syncategorematically** *adverb* (*rare*) E17.

syncellus /sɪnˈsɛləs/ *noun*. Now *rare*. Pl. **-lli** /-liː/. E18.
[Late Latin, lit. 'cell-mate', later, domestic chaplain, from Byzantine Greek *sugkellos*, from *sun-* SYN- + Latin *cella* cell.]
ECCLESIASTICAL HISTORY. Orig., an ecclesiastic who lived with a prelate; *esp.* the domestic chaplain of an Orthodox metropolitan or patriarch. Later, a dignitary who was associated with a prelate and succeeded to his office.

synch *noun & verb* var. of SYNC.

synchondrosis /sɪŋkɒnˈdrəʊsɪs/ *noun*. Pl. **-droses** /-ˈdrəʊsiːz/. L16.
[mod. Latin from late Greek *sugkhondrōsis*, from *sun-* SYN- + *khondros* cartilage: see -OSIS.]
ANATOMY & ZOOLOGY. The junction of two bones by cartilage; a joint, sometimes slightly movable, in which this occurs; *spec.* (in full ***sacro-iliac synchondrosis***) the articulation of the sacrum with the ilium.
▪ **synchondrosial** *adjective* of, pertaining to, or constituting a synchondrosis M19. **synchondrosially** *adverb* in the manner of a synchondrosis E20.

synchro /ˈsɪŋkrəʊ/ *noun*. Pl. **-os**. M20.
[Abbreviation of SYNCHRONIZE, SYNCHRONOUS.]
1 A synchronizing device; *spec.* = SELSYN. M20.
2 Synchronized swimming. *colloq*. M20.
1 ***synchro receiver***, ***synchro transmitter***, etc.

synchro- /ˈsɪŋkrəʊ/ *combining form*.
[formed as prec.: see -O-.]
Synchronous, synchronized.
▪ **synchroˈcyclotron** *noun* (PHYSICS) a cyclotron in which greater energies are achieved by decreasing the frequency of the accelerating electric field as the particles gain energy, to allow for their relativistic increase in mass M20. **synchroflash** *noun* (PHOTOGRAPHY) a flash whose operation is synchronized with the opening of the shutter M20. **synchroscope** *noun* (*a*) ELECTRICAL ENGINEERING an instrument for indicating any difference in frequency or phase between two alternating voltages; (*b*) ELECTRONICS an oscilloscope adapted to display only one cycle of a waveform regardless of its frequency: E20. **synchro-swim**, **synchro-swimming** *nouns* synchronized swimming L20.

synchromesh /ˈsɪŋkrəmɛʃ/ *noun*. E20.
[from SYNCHRO- + MESH *noun & verb*.]
A mechanism that facilitates gear-changing in a motor vehicle by automatically causing gearwheels to rotate in synchronism before they engage.

Synchromism /ˈsɪŋkrəmɪz(ə)m/ *noun*. E20.
[from SYN- + Greek *khrōma* colour + -ISM.]
ART. A movement resembling Orphism, initiated by the American painters Stanton Macdonald-Wright (1890–1973) and Morgan Russell (1886–1953), with emphasis on the abstract use of colour.
▪ **Synchromist** *noun & adjective* (*a*) *noun* a practitioner or adherent of Synchromism; (*b*) *adjective* of or pertaining to Synchromists or Synchromism: E20. **Synchromy** *noun* an abstract painting of a type characteristic of Synchromism E20.

synchronal /ˈsɪŋkrən(ə)l/ *adjective & noun*. Now *rare* or *obsolete*. M17.
[formed as SYNCHRONOUS + -AL[1].]
▶ **A** *adjective*. = SYNCHRONOUS 1, 2. (Foll. by *to*.) M17.
▶†**B** *noun*. A simultaneous event. M–L17.

synchroneity /sɪŋkrəˈniːɪti, -ˈneɪɪti/ *noun*. E20.
[from SYNCHRONOUS + *-eity*, after *simultaneity* etc.]
Chiefly GEOLOGY. = SYNCHRONISM 1.

synchronic /sɪnˈkrɒnɪk/ *adjective*. M19.
[formed as SYNCHRONOUS + -IC. In sense 2 after French *synchronique*.]
1 = SYNCHRONOUS 1, 2. M19.
2 Concerned with or pertaining to the state of a language, culture, etc., at one particular time, past or present, without regard to historical development. Opp. ***diachronic***. E20.
📖 **2** E. E. EVANS-PRITCHARD Social anthropologists generally study synchronic problems while historians study diachronic problems.
▪ **synchronical** *adjective* (now *rare*) = SYNCHRONIC M17. **synchronically** *adverb* in a synchronic manner; *spec.* with regard to a particular time rather than to historical development: M18.

synchronicity /sɪŋkrəˈnɪsɪti/ *noun*. M20.
[from SYNCHRONIC + -ITY.]
The simultaneous occurrence of events which appear meaningfully related but have no discoverable causal connection; *loosely* synchrony, simultaneity.

synchronise *verb*, **synchroniser** *noun*, etc., vars. of SYNCHRONIZE etc.

synchronism /ˈsɪŋkrənɪz(ə)m/ *noun*. L16.
[Greek *sugkhronismos*, from *sugkhronos* SYNCHRONOUS: see -ISM.]
1 Coincidence or concurrence at the same point in time; contemporary existence or occurrence. Also, an instance of this, a coincidence in time. L16.
2 A statement or argument that two or more events etc. are synchronous; a historical account or table which treats comtemporaneous but separate events in conjunction; a synchronological description. L16. ▸**b** Agreement in relation to the time of events described. *rare*. E17. ▸**c** Consistency in historical detail, as in architecture. M19. ▸**d** Representation of events of different times together, as in the same picture. M19.
3 The fact of keeping time; the fact of proceeding or successively recurring at the same rate and exactly together; coincidence of period, as of two sets of movements, vibrations, or alternations of electric current. M19.
▪ **synchronist** *noun* (*rare*) a person living at the same time as another, a contemporary E18.

synchronistic /sɪŋkrəˈnɪstɪk/ *adjective*. L17.
[from prec. + -ISTIC.]
1 Of, pertaining to, or exhibiting synchronism; involving synchronism, synchronous, simultaneous. L17.
2 LINGUISTICS. = SYNCHRONIC *adjective* 2. M20.
3 Pertaining to or having the quality of synchronicity. M20.
▪ **synchronistical** *adjective* (now *rare* or *obsolete*) = SYNCHRONISTIC 1 E17. **synchronistically** *adverb* (*a*) in accordance with synchronism, synchronically; (*b*) synchronously: L17.

synchronize /ˈsɪŋkrənʌɪz/ *verb*. Also **-ise**. E17.
[from SYNCHRONISM + -IZE.]
1 a *verb intrans*. Occur at the same time; coincide in point of time; be contemporary or simultaneous. (Foll. by *with*.) E17. ▸**b** *verb trans*. Cause to be or represent as synchronous; ascertain or set forth the correspondence in date of (events etc.). E19.
2 a *verb intrans*. Occur at the same successive instants of time; keep time *with*; (of two sets of movements etc.) go at the same rate, have coincident periods, etc.; proceed exactly together; (of clocks etc.) indicate the same time as each other. M19. ▸**b** *verb trans*. Cause to go at the same rate; *esp.* cause (a clock etc.) to indicate the same time as another; cause (a device) to operate simultaneously or in synchronization *with* another; cause (two or more devices) to operate in this way. L19. ▸**c** *verb intrans*. Operate in synchrony with another device etc. M20.
3 *verb trans*. *gen*. Combine, coordinate. L20.
📖 **1a** H. J. LASKI His effective government will synchronize with the commencement of his reign. **2** *Midnight Zoo* Bremmer noticed how the mouth failed to synchronize with the words. **b** H. BARNES Electronic flash-lighting . . is . . employed, the camera mechanism being synchronized to the flash. B. BAINBRIDGE We ought to work out some sort of signal and synchronize watches. **3** *Time* Both media synchronize national interests with multinational scope.
Phrases: **synchronized swimmer** a performer of synchronized swimming. **synchronized swimming** a form of swimming in which participants make coordinated leg and arm movements in time to music.
▪ **synchroniˈzation** *noun* the action of synchronizing E19.

For other words beginning with *syn-* see the entry for **syn-**

synchronizer /ˈsɪŋkrənʌɪzə/ *noun*. Also **-iser**. L19.
[from SYNCHRONIZE *verb* + -ER¹.]
A person or thing which synchronizes; *spec.* (*a*) a device for synchronizing clocks, photographic or sound apparatus, etc.; (*b*) an apparatus for keeping two electric motors at the same speed, or for indicating the difference of their speeds.

📖 *New Scientist* The light-dark cycle is the major synchronizer of circadian, as well as seasonal rhythms.

synchronology /sɪŋkrəˈnɒlədʒi/ *noun*. M18.
[from SYN- + CHRONOLOGY.]
Comparative chronology; arrangement of events according to dates, those of the same date being placed or treated together.
■ **synchronoˈlogical** *adjective* pertaining to or constructed according to synchronology M19.

synchronous /ˈsɪŋkrənəs/ *adjective*. M17.
[from late Latin *synchronus* from Greek *sugkhronos*, from *sun-* SYN- + *khronos* time: see -OUS.]
1 Existing or happening at the same time; belonging to the same period of time; occurring at the same moment; contemporary; simultaneous. (Foll. by *with*.) M17. ▸**b** Relating to or treating of different events or things belonging to the same time or period. E19.
2 Recurring at the same successive instants of time; keeping time *with*; going at the same rate and exactly together; having coincident periods. L17. ▸**b** ELECTRICITY. Of a machine or motor: working in time with the alternations of current. L19. ▸**c** COMPUTING & TELECOMMUNICATIONS. Of apparatus or methods of working: making use of equally spaced pulses that govern the timing of operations. M20. ▸**d** Of a satellite: revolving round the parent planet at the same rate as the planet rotates. Of an orbit: such that a satellite in it is synchronous. M20.
3 LINGUISTICS. = SYNCHRONIC *adjective* 2. M20.

📖 **1** H. W. BATES The rainy season on the coasts is not synchronous with that of the uplands. **b synchronous curve** a curve which is the locus of the points reached at any instant by a number of particles descending from the same point down a family of curves under the action of gravity.

■ **synchronously** *adverb* L18.

synchrony /ˈsɪŋkrəni/ *noun*. M19.
[from Greek *sugkhronos*: see prec., -Y³.]
1 = SYNCHRONISM 1, 2. M19.
2 LINGUISTICS. Synchronic treatment or study. M20.

synchrotron /ˈsɪŋkrətrɒn/ *noun*. M20.
[from SYNCHRO- + -TRON.]
PHYSICS. An accelerator in which electrons or protons gain energy from an alternating electric field as they travel round a closed orbit in a magnetic field, the strength or frequency of the field being increased to keep the radius of the path constant as the particles gain mass relativistically.
Comb.: **synchrotron radiation** polarized radiation emitted by a charged particle as it spirals at high speed in a magnetic field.

synchysis /ˈsɪŋkɪsɪs/ *noun*. Pl. **-chyses** /-kɪsiːz/. L16.
[Late Latin from Greek *sugkhusis*, from *sugkhein* mingle, confuse, from *sun-* SYN- + *khein* pour.]
1 RHETORIC. A confused arrangement of words in a sentence, obscuring the meaning. L16.
2 MEDICINE. Softening of the vitreous humour of the eye. *rare*. L17.

syncitium *noun* var. of SYNCYTIUM.

Synclavier /sɪnˈklavɪə/ *noun*. Also **s-**. L20.
[from SYN(THESIZER + CLAVIER.]
A digital synthesizer operated by a keyboard.
¶ Proprietary name in the US.

synclinal /sɪnˈklʌɪn(ə)l, ˈsɪŋklɪn(ə)l/ *adjective*. M19.
[from SYN- + Greek *klinein* to lean, slope + -AL¹.]
1 GEOLOGY. Pertaining to or of the nature of a syncline. Opp. ***anticlinal***. M19.
2 Sloping towards each other. L19.
■ **synclinally** *adverb* M19.

syncline /ˈsɪŋklʌɪn/ *noun*. L19.
[formed as prec. after *incline*.]
GEOLOGY. A fold from whose axis the strata incline upwards on either side. Opp. ANTICLINE.
■ **syncliˈnorium** *noun*, pl. **-ria** /-rɪə/, a system of folds which has an overall synclinal form L19.

syncopal /ˈsɪŋkəp(ə)l/ *adjective*. L17.
[from SYNCOPE *noun* + -AL¹.]
MEDICINE. Pertaining to or of the nature of syncope or fainting.

syncopate /ˈsɪŋkəpeɪt/ *verb*. E17.
[Late Latin *syncopat-* pa. ppl stem of *syncopare* affect with syncope: see SYNCOPE *noun*, -ATE³.]
1 *verb trans.* Shorten (a word) by omitting one or more syllables or letters in the middle; in *pass.*, be formed or produced in this way. E17.
2 MUSIC. **a** *verb trans.* Mark (a note, passage, etc.) by syncopation. M17. ▸**b** *verb intrans.* Be marked by syncopation; beat out a syncopated rhythm. L18.

📖 **2a** *fig.*: I. HAY A nautical roll, syncopated by gout. **b** *Sunday Express* Her eager feet . . now syncopate to the beat of drums.

■ **syncopated** *ppl adjective* (*a*) that has been syncopated; characterized by syncopation; (*b*) playing or composing syncopated music: M17.

syncopation /sɪŋkəˈpeɪʃ(ə)n/ *noun*. M16.
[medieval Latin *syncopatio(n-)*, formed as prec.: see -ATION.]
1 GRAMMAR & PROSODY. = SYNCOPE *noun* 2. Also, alteration of normal stress to fit a poetic metre. M16.
2 MUSIC. The displacement of the beats or accents in a passage so that strong beats become weak or vice versa; the shifting of beat so produced; a syncopated rhythm. L16. ▸**b** Music characterized by a syncopated rhythm; *spec.* dance music influenced by ragtime. E20.

syncopator /ˈsɪŋkəpeɪtə/ *noun*. E20.
[from SYNCOPATE + -OR.]
A person who performs syncopated jazz music, usu. in a dance band. Usu. in *pl.* in the name of a band.

syncope /ˈsɪŋkəpi/ *noun*. LME.
[Late Latin from Greek *sugkopē*, from *sun-* SYN- + *kop-* stem of *koptein* strike, cut off.]
1 Fainting; temporary loss of consciousness caused by an insufficient flow of blood to the brain, freq. due to blood loss, shock, long standing, overheating, etc. Also occas., local loss of blood pressure in any part of the body. LME.
2 Shortening of a word by omission of one or more syllables or letters in the middle; a word so shortened. M16.
†**3** MUSIC. = SYNCOPATION 2. M17–L18.
4 *gen.* A cutting short of something; sudden cessation or interruption. *rare*. M17.

†**syncope** *verb*. *rare*. Pres. pple & verbal noun **syncopeing**. LME.
[Old French *syncoper* or late Latin *syncopare* SYNCOPATE.]
1 *verb trans.* Cut short, reduce; slur over (a word or syllable). Only in LME.
2 MUSIC. **a** *verb trans.* Syncopate. E–M18. ▸**b** *verb intrans.* Be syncopated. M18–E19.

syncopic /sɪnˈkɒpɪk/ *adjective*. *rare*. L19.
[from SYNCOPE *noun* + -IC.]
MEDICINE. = SYNCOPAL.

syncretic /sɪnˈkrɛtɪk, -ˈkriːtɪk/ *adjective*. M19.
[from SYNCRETISM + -IC.]
1 Characterized by syncretism; aiming at a union or reconciliation of diverse beliefs, conventions, or systems. M19.
2 PSYCHOLOGY. Pertaining to or characterized by the fusion of concepts or sensations. M20.

📖 **1** R. N. FRYE The primary inspiration . . is from Greece . . although the art may be described as syncretic. I. M. LEWIS Both religions co-exist in a loose syncretic relationship.

■ **syncretically** *adverb* E20.

syncretise *verb* var. of SYNCRETIZE.

syncretism /ˈsɪŋkrɪtɪz(ə)m/ *noun*. E17.
[mod. Latin *syncretismus* from Greek *sugkrētismos*, from *sugkrētizein* SYNCRETIZE: see -ISM.]
1 Attempted union or reconciliation of diverse or opposite tenets or practices, esp. in philosophy or religion; *spec.* the principles of the 17th-cent. German theologian George Calixtus, who aimed to harmonize the beliefs of Protestant sects and ultimately of all Christians. Freq. *derog.* E17.
2 LINGUISTICS. The merging of two or more inflectional forms or categories. E20.
3 PSYCHOLOGY. The process of fusing diverse ideas into a general inexact impression; an instance of this. E20.
■ **syncretist** *noun* a practitioner or advocate of syncretism or the reconciliation of diverse beliefs etc. M18. **syncretistic** *adjective* (*a*) of, pertaining to, or characteristic of syncretists or syncretism; (*b*) = SYNCRETIC *adjective* 2: E19. **syncretistical** *adjective* (*rare*) = SYNCRETISTIC M18.

syncretize /ˈsɪŋkrɪtʌɪz/ *verb*. Also **-ise**. L17.
[Greek *sugkrētizein* combine, as two parties against a third; ult. origin unkn.: see -IZE.]
†**1** *verb intrans.* Combine, agree, accord. Only in L17.
2 a *verb intrans.* Practise syncretism. L19. ▸**b** *verb trans.* Treat in a syncretistic manner. E20.
■ **syncretiˈzation** *noun* L20.

syncytium /sɪnˈsɪtɪəm/ *noun*. Also **-cit-**. Pl. **-tia** /-tɪə/. L19.
[from SYN- + Greek *kutos* receptacle, vessel: see -CYTE, -IUM.]
BIOLOGY. A single cell or cytoplasmic mass containing several nuclei, formed by fusion of cells or by division of nuclei; a tissue in which the cytoplasm of constituent cells is continuous; *spec.* in EMBRYOLOGY, a structure of this kind forming the outermost layer of the trophoblast.
■ **syncytial** *adjective* of the nature of or pertaining to a syncytium (***respiratory syncytium virus***: see RESPIRATORY *adjective*) L19.

For other words beginning with *syn-* see the entry for **syn-**

syndactyl /sɪnˈdaktɪl, -ʌɪl/ *adjective & noun*. Also **-yle**. M19.
[from SYN- + Greek *daktulos* finger.]
MEDICINE & ZOOLOGY. ▶**A** *adjective*. Having some or all of the fingers or toes wholly or partly united, naturally or as a malformation. M19.
▶**B** *noun*. A syndactyl animal. M19.
■ **syndactylism** *noun* = SYNDACTYLY L19. **syndactylous** *adjective* of or exhibiting syndactyly M19. **syndactyly** *noun* the condition of being syndactyl M19.

synderesis /sɪndɪˈriːsɪs/ *noun*. Also **synt-** /sɪnt-/. Pl. **-reses** /-ˈriːsiːz/. LME.
[medieval Latin (also *synteresis*) from Greek *suntērēsis* careful guarding or watching, from Greek *suntērein* guard, watch over, from *sun-* SYN- + *tērein* guard, keep.]
THEOLOGY. Conscience, esp. serving as a guide for conduct; innate moral sense. Also, that part of the soul which can unite with God.

syndesmo- /sɪnˈdɛsməʊ/ *combining form*. Before a vowel also **syndesm-**.
[from Greek *sundesmos* binding, ligament, from *sun-* SYN- + *desmos* bond, connection: see -O-.]
ANATOMY & MEDICINE. Of or pertaining to connective tissue, esp. ligaments.
■ **syndesˈmology** *noun* the branch of anatomy that deals with ligaments L18. **syndesmophyte** *noun* a bony outgrowth from an injured joint, *esp.* one between vertebrae leading to spinal rigidity M20. **syndesˈmosis** *noun*, pl. **-moses** /-ˈməʊsiːz/, (a joint characterized by) the joining of two bones immovably by a ligament L16. **syndesˈmotic** *adjective* of the nature of or pertaining to (a) syndesmosis L19.

syndetic /sɪnˈdɛtɪk/ *adjective*. E17.
[Greek *sundetikos*, from *sundein* bind together, from *sun-* SYN- + *dein* bind: see -IC.]
1 Serving to unite or connect; connective; GRAMMAR of or using conjunctions. E17.
2 In librarianship and data processing: designating or pertaining to a catalogue, index, etc., which uses cross-references to indicate links between entries. L19.

syndeton /ˈsɪndɪtən/ *noun*. M20.
[Back-form. from ASYNDETON, POLYSYNDETON.]
GRAMMAR. A construction in which the parts are joined by a connecting word or phrase.

syndic /ˈsɪndɪk/ *noun*. E17.
[French *syndic*, †*syndique* delegate, chief magistrate of Geneva from late Latin *syndicus* delegate of a corporation from Greek *sundikos* defendant's advocate, from *sun-* SYN- + base of *dikē* judgement, *deiknusthai* show: see -IC.]
1 A government officer, having different powers in different countries; an officer of law; a magistrate entrusted with civil affairs; *spec.* each of four chief magistrates of Geneva. E17.
2 A person deputed as a business agent for a corporation or a university; *spec.* in some universities, a member of a special committee of the senate. E17.
†**3** A censor of the actions of another. E–M17.
4 = ASSIGNEE 2. *rare*. E18.

syndical /ˈsɪndɪk(ə)l/ *adjective*. M19.
[French, from *syndic* SYNDIC: see -AL¹.]
Of or pertaining to syndicalism; organized in unions.
syndical chamber, **syndical union** [French *chambre syndicale*] a trade union.

syndicalism /ˈsɪndɪk(ə)lɪz(ə)m/ *noun*. E20.
[French *syndicalisme*, formed as prec.: see -ISM.]
Chiefly *Hist.* A movement aiming to transfer ownership of the means of production and distribution to unions of workers, esp. by means of a general strike.
■ **syndicalist** *noun & adjective* (*a*) *noun* an advocate of syndicalism; (*b*) *adjective* of or pertaining to syndicalists or syndicalism: E20. **syndicaˈlistic** *adjective* E20.

syndicat d'initiative /sēdika dinisjatiːv/ *noun phr*. Pl. ***syndicats d'initiative*** (pronounced same). E20.
[French.]
In France, a tourist information office.

syndicate /ˈsɪndɪkət/ *noun*. E17.
[French *syndicat* from medieval Latin *syndicatus*, from late Latin *syndicus*: see SYNDIC, -ATE¹.]
1 A council or body of syndics; *spec.* a university committee appointed for a specific duty. Also, a meeting of such a body. E17.
2 The office, status, or jurisdiction of a syndic. Now *rare* or *obsolete*. M17.
3 A group of business people who have agreed to cooperate in pursuing a scheme requiring large capital funds, esp. a scheme to control the market in a particular commodity; a group of people who pool their financial resources to buy or rent property, gamble, etc.; an association or agency supplying articles etc. simultaneously to a number of newspapers, periodicals, etc. M19. ▸**b** *spec.* A network of criminals controlling racketeering and other organized crime; *esp.* the American Mafia. Chiefly *N. Amer.* E20. ▸**c** Orig. MILITARY. Any of a number of sub-groups into which participants on a training course are divided, esp. for a particular assignment. E20.
■ **syndicaˈteer** *noun* a member of a (financial) syndicate E20.

syndicate /ˈsɪndɪkeɪt/ *verb trans.* E17.
[In sense 1 from medieval Latin *syndicat-* pa. ppl stem of medieval Latin *syndicare* subject to an enquiry; in senses 2, 3 from the noun: see -ATE[3].]
†**1** Judge, censure. E17–E19.
2 Control, manage, or effect by a syndicate; *esp.* publish simultaneously in a number of newspapers, periodicals, etc.; offer shares or a share in (a financial venture); *spec.* in HORSE-RACING, sell (a horse) to a syndicate. L19.
3 Combine into a syndicate. L19.
■ **syndiˈcation** *noun* †(*a*) *rare* the action of judging someone; (*b*) the formation of a syndicate; (*c*) publication or ownership by a syndicate: M17. **syndicator** *noun* †(*a*) *rare* a judge; (*b*) *US* a person who forms a syndicate: E17.

syndiotactic /ˌsɪndʌɪəˈtaktɪk/ *adjective.* Also **syndyo-**. M20.
[from Greek *sunduo* two together + *taktos* arranged, ordered + -IC.]
CHEMISTRY. Having or designating a polymeric structure in which the repeating units have alternating stereochemical configurations.
■ **syndiotactically** *adverb* M20. **syndiotacˈticity** *noun* M20.

syndrome /ˈsɪndrəʊm/ *noun.* M16.
[mod. Latin from Greek *sundromē*, from *sun-* SYN- + *drom-*, *dramein* run.]
1 MEDICINE. A group of symptoms or pathological signs which consistently occur together, esp. with an (originally) unknown cause; a condition characterized by such a set of associated symptoms. M16.
2 *gen.* †**a** A concurrence, a concourse; a set of concurrent things. Only in M17. ▸**b** A characteristic combination of opinions, behaviour, features, social factors, etc. Usu. with specifying word or phr. M20.

> **1** O. SACKS Parkinsonism was one of the first neurological syndromes to be recognized. ***Cushing's syndrome***, ***Down's syndrome***, ***Munchausen's syndrome***, ***postviral syndrome***, ***sick building syndrome***, etc. **2b** *New York Times* The 'Nimby' . . syndrome now makes it almost impossible to build or locate vital facilities. *Autocar* The material had developed 'bobbly sweater syndrome'. ***CHINA syndrome***. ***STOCKHOLM syndrome***.

■ **synˈdromic** *adjective* (*rare*) L19.

syndrum /ˈsɪndrəm, -drʌm/ *noun.* L20.
[from SYN(THESIZER + DRUM *noun*[1].]
A drum incorporating electronic amplification, alteration of pitch, etc.

syndyotactic *adjective* var. of SYNDIOTACTIC.

syne *verb & noun* var. of SIND.

syne /sʌɪn/ *adverb. Scot. & north.* ME.
[Contr. of SITHEN. Cf. SEN *preposition, conjunction, & adverb.*]
1 Immediately afterwards; then. Cf. SINCE *adverb* 1. ME.
2 At a later time, subsequently. Esp. in ***soon or syne***, sooner or later. LME.
3 = SINCE *adverb* 2. LME.
4 = SINCE *adverb* 3. L16.

synecdoche /sɪˈnɛkdəki/ *noun.* LME.
[Latin from Greek *sunekdokhē*, from *sunekdekhesthai* lit. 'take with something else', from *sun-* SYN- + *ekdekhesthai* take, take up.]
GRAMMAR & RHETORIC. A figure of speech in which a more inclusive term is used for a less inclusive one or vice versa, as a whole for a part or a part for a whole.

synecdochical /sɪnɛkˈdɒkɪk(ə)l/ *adjective.* L16.
[from prec. + -ICAL.]
1 GRAMMAR & RHETORIC. Involving or constituting synecdoche. L16.
2 ANTHROPOLOGY. Involving synecdochism. *rare.* L19.
■ **synecdochic** *adjective* = SYNECDOCHICAL L18. **synecdochically** *adverb* in a synecdochical manner, by synecdoche E17.

synecdochism /sɪˈnɛkdəkɪz(ə)m/ *noun.* M19.
[from SYNECDOCHE + -ISM.]
1 GRAMMAR & RHETORIC. Synecdochical style; the use of synecdoche. M19.
2 ANTHROPOLOGY. Belief or cultural practice in which a part of an object or person is taken as equivalent to or standing for the whole. *rare.* M19.

synechia /sɪˈniːkɪə/ *noun.* Pl. **-iae** /-iiː/. M19.
[Greek *sunekheia* continuity, from *sunekhēs* continuous, from *sun-* SYN- + *ekhein* have, hold: see -IA[1].]
MEDICINE. Adhesion of the iris to the cornea (more fully ***anterior synechia***) or to the capsule of the lens (more fully ***posterior synechia***).

synechism /ˈsɪnɪkɪz(ə)m/ *noun.* L19.
[from Greek *sunekhēs*: see prec., -ISM.]
PHILOSOPHY. The doctrine that continuity is one of the most important principles in scientific explanation.
■ **synechist** *noun* an adherent of synechism E20.

synecology /sɪnɪˈkɒlədʒi/ *noun.* E20.
[from SYN- + ECOLOGY.]
BIOLOGY. The branch of science that deals with whole communities and the interactions of the organisms in them. Cf. AUTECOLOGY.
■ **synecoˈlogical** *adjective* E20. **synecoˈlogically** *adverb* as regards synecology M20. **synecologist** *noun* M20.

synectic /sɪˈnɛktɪk/ *adjective.* L19.
[Late Latin *synecticus* from Greek *sunektikos*, from *sunekhein* hold together, from *sun-* SYN- + *ekhein* have, hold: see -IC.]
Of a cause: producing its effect directly, immediate. Formerly *spec.* in MEDICINE, (of a disease) producing symptoms by its very nature.
■ Also †**synectical** *adjective*: only in L17.

synectics /sɪˈnɛktɪks/ *noun.* Orig. *US.* Also **S-**. M20.
[from prec., perh. after *dialectics*: see -ICS.]
A method of problem-solving, esp. by groups, which seeks to utilize creative thinking and imaginative correlation.
¶ Proprietary name in the US.

synedrion /sɪˈnɛdrɪən/ *noun.* Chiefly *Hist.* Also **-drium** /-drɪəm/. Pl. **-dria** /-drɪə/. L16.
[(mod. Latin from) Greek *sunedrion*, from *sunedros* sitting with, from *sun-* SYN- + *hedra* seat.]
A judicial or representative assembly, a council, a congress; *spec.* the Jewish sanhedrin.
■ **synedrian** *noun & adjective* (*a*) *noun* a member of a synedrion; (*b*) *adjective* of or belonging to a synedrion: E17.

synenergy /sɪnˈɛnədʒi/ *noun. rare.* L17.
[from SYN- + ENERGY.]
= SYNERGY.

syneresis *noun* see SYNAERESIS.

synergetic /sɪnəˈdʒɛtɪk/ *adjective.* M19.
[Greek *sunergētikos* cooperative, from *sunergein*: see SYNERGY, -ETIC.]
= SYNERGISTIC *adjective* 2, 3.
■ **synergetical** *adjective* (*rare*) L17. **synergetically** *adverb* M20.

synergic /sɪˈnəːdʒɪk/ *adjective.* M19.
[from Greek *sunergos* working together, from *sunergein*: see SYNERGY, -IC.]
Pertaining to, exhibiting, or involving synergy; *esp.* in CHEMISTRY, of or pertaining to the mutual strengthening of sigma and pi bonds.
■ **synergically** *adverb* L19.

synergid /sɪˈnəːdʒɪd/ *noun.* Also in Latin form **-ida** /-ɪdə/, pl. **-idae** /-ɪdiː/. L19.
[mod. Latin *synergida*, from Greek *sunergein* cooperate: see -ID[2].]
BOTANY. Either of the two haploid nuclei which lie beside the egg cell at the apex of the embryo sac and are sometimes regarded as helping to direct the pollen-tube to the egg.

synergise *verb* var. of SYNERGIZE.

synergism /ˈsɪnədʒɪz(ə)m/ *noun.* M18.
[formed as SYNERGIC + -ISM.]
1 THEOLOGY. The doctrine that the human will cooperates with divine grace in the work of regeneration; such cooperation. M18.
2 Orig. (PHARMACOLOGY), the combined activity of two drugs, etc., when this is greater than the sum of the effects of each one separately. Now also *gen.*, = SYNERGY 2. E20.

synergist /ˈsɪnədʒɪst/ *noun.* M17.
[formed as SYNERGIC + -IST.]
1 THEOLOGY (chiefly *Hist.*). A person who holds the doctrine of synergism. M17.
2 MEDICINE. An agent (as a chemical substance or a muscle) that cooperates with or enhances the effect of another. L19.

synergistic /sɪnəˈdʒɪstɪk/ *adjective.* E19.
[formed as prec. + -IC.]
1 THEOLOGY (chiefly *Hist.*). Of or pertaining to synergism. E19.
2 Of a substance, agent, or factor: cooperating with or enhancing the effect of another; exhibiting synergism or synergy. L19.
3 *gen.* Cooperative, interacting, mutually reinforcing or stimulating. M20.

> **3** *Times* Mr Kent and Sir Hector . . have continued to stress the synergistic benefits of the merger.

■ **synergistical** *adjective* (now *rare*) = SYNERGISTIC 1 M17. **synergistically** *adverb* L19.

synergize /ˈsɪnədʒʌɪz/ *verb intrans.* Also **-ise**. E20.
[from SYNERGY + -IZE.]
Esp. of a biochemical agent or agents: act synergistically (*with*).

synergy /ˈsɪnədʒi/ *noun.* M17.
[mod. Latin *synergia* from Greek *sunergia*, from *sunergein* work together: see -Y[3].]
†**1** Cooperation. Only in M17.
2 Orig., combined or correlated action of a group of parts of the body (as motor neurones or muscles). Now also *gen.*, the production by two or more agents, substances, etc., of a combined effect greater than the sum of their separate effects (cf. SYNERGISM 2). M19.
3 Increased effectiveness, achievement, etc., produced by combined action, cooperation, etc. M20.

synesthesia *noun*, **synesthetic** *adjective*, etc., see SYNAESTHESIA etc.

For other words beginning with *syn-* see the entry for **syn-**

syngameon /sɪnˈgamɪən/ *noun.* E20.
[from SYNGAM(Y + -*e*- + -ON.]
GENETICS. A cluster of species and subspecies between the members of which natural hybridization occurs.

syngamy /ˈsɪŋgəmi/ *noun.* E20.
[from SYN- + -GAMY.]
BIOLOGY. **1** Free interbreeding between organisms. E20.
2 The fusion of two cells, or of their nuclei, in reproduction. E20.
■ **synˈgamic**, **syngamous** *adjectives* E20.

syngeneic /sɪndʒɪˈniːɪk, -ˈneɪɪk/ *adjective.* M20.
[from SYN- + Greek *genea* race, stock + -IC.]
IMMUNOLOGY. Genetically similar or identical and hence immunologically compatible; so closely related that transplantation does not provoke an immune response; = ISOGENEIC.

syngenesious /sɪndʒɪˈniːzɪəs/ *adjective.* M18.
[from mod. Latin *Syngenesia* (see below), formed as SYN- + Greek GENESIS + -*ia* -IA[1]: see -OUS.]
BOTANY. Of stamens: united by their anthers so as to form a tube. Formerly *spec.*, (of a plant) belonging to the Linnaean class Syngenesia, comprising plants with stamens united in this way and corresponding to the modern family Compositae.

syngenesis /sɪnˈdʒɛnɪsɪs/ *noun.* M19.
[from SYN- + -GENESIS.]
BIOLOGY. Sexual reproduction by combination of male and female elements.

syngenetic /sɪndʒɪˈnɛtɪk/ *adjective.* M19.
[from SYN- + -GENETIC.]
1 BIOLOGY. Of or pertaining to syngenesis. M19.
2 GEOLOGY. Designating or pertaining to a mineral deposit or formation produced at the same time as the enclosing or surrounding rock. E20.
■ **syngenetically** *adverb* M20.

syngnathid /ˈsɪŋgnəθɪd, sɪnˈgneɪθɪd/ *noun & adjective.* E20.
[mod. Latin *Syngnathidae* (see below), from *Syngnathus* genus name of a pipefish, formed as SYN- + Greek *gnathos* jaw: see -ID[3].]
ZOOLOGY. ▸**A** *noun.* A fish of the family Syngnathidae, characterized by jaws extended into a tubular snout, and including pipefishes and sea horses. E20.
▸**B** *adjective.* Of, pertaining to, or designating this family. M20.
■ **syngnathous** *adjective* (now *rare*) = SYNGNATHID *adjective* L19.

syngraph /ˈsɪŋgrɑːf/ *noun.* Now *rare.* M17.
[Latin *syngraphus* from Greek *sungraphos*, from *sungraphein* compose in writing, draw up, from *sun-* SYN- + *graphein* write.]
A written contract or bond signed by both or all the parties; a joint statement in writing.

synizesis /sɪnɪˈziːsɪs/ *noun.* Pl. **-zeses** /-ˈziːsiːz/. E19.
[Late Latin from Greek *sunizēsis*, from *sunizanein* sink down, collapse, from *sun-* SYN- + *hizanein* seat, sit, settle down, from *hizein* seat, sit.]
†**1** MEDICINE. Closure of the pupil of the eye. *rare.* Only in E19.
2 GRAMMAR & PROSODY. Synaeresis, esp. without the formation of a recognized diphthong. M19.
3 CYTOLOGY. A stage of meiosis in some species in which all the chromosomes contract together. E20.
■ **synizetic** *adjective* M20.

synochus /ˈsɪnəkəs/ *noun.* Also **-cha** /-kə/. E17.
[medieval Latin from Greek *sunokhos*, from *sun-* SYN- + *okh-* stem of *ekhein* have, after *sunekhein* hold together, continue.]
MEDICINE (chiefly *Hist.*). Continuous fever.
■ **synochal** *adjective* of or pertaining to synochus M16. **synochous** *adjective* synochal E19.

synod /ˈsɪnəd, -ɒd/ *noun.* LME.
[Late Latin *synodus* from Greek *sunodus* meeting, from *sun-* SYN- + *hodos* way, travel.]
1 ECCLESIASTICAL. An assembly of the clergy (and sometimes the laity) of a particular Church within a nation, province, district, diocese, etc., convened to discuss and decide church affairs; *spec.* in the Presbyterian system, an ecclesiastical court representing a number of presbyteries and subject to the General Assembly. Formerly also, a general council of the early Church. LME.
2 *gen.* An assembly, a convention, a council. L16.
†**3** ASTROLOGY. A conjunction of two planets etc. M–L17.

> **1** ***deanery synod***, ***diocesan synod***, ***legatine synod***, etc. **General Synod** the governing assembly of the Church of England since 1969, comprising three houses consisting respectively of bishops and elected representatives of non-episcopal clergy and laity.

synodal /ˈsɪnəd(ə)l/ *adjective & noun.* LME.
[Late Latin *synodalis*, from *synodus* SYNOD: see -AL[1].]
▸**A** *adjective.* **1** = SYNODICAL 1. LME.
2 = SYNODICAL 2. M16.
3 Of, pertaining to, or connected with a synod or an episcopal visitation (cf. sense B.2 below). Now *Hist.* L16.
▸**B** *noun.* **1** A synodal decision, constitution, or decree. Long *obsolete* exc. *Hist.* L15.
2 A payment made by the inferior clergy to a bishop, orig. on the occasion of a synod, later at an episcopal or archidiaconal visitation. M16.

†**3** A synod. Only in L16.
■ **synodally** *adverb* by the action or authority of a synod M17.

synodic /sɪˈnɒdɪk/ *adjective*. M17.
[Late Latin *synodicus* from late Greek *sunodikos*, from *sunodus* SYNOD: see -IC.]
1 *ECCLESIASTICAL*. Synodal, synodical. M17.
2 *ASTRONOMY*. Of or pertaining to conjunctions of stars, planets, etc.; *esp.* designating or pertaining to the period between successive conjunctions of two objects. M17.
2 synodic month the period of orbit of the moon, reckoned from its successive conjunctions with the sun (i.e. from new moon to new moon); a lunar month.

synodical /sɪˈnɒdɪk(ə)l/ *adjective*. M16.
[formed as prec.: see -ICAL.]
1 *ECCLESIASTICAL*. Enacted or made by or at a synod. M16.
2 *ECCLESIASTICAL*. Of the nature of a synod. M16.
3 *ASTRONOMY*. = SYNODIC 2. E17.

synodically /sɪˈnɒdɪk(ə)li/ *adverb*. E17.
[from SYNODICAL, SYNODIC: see -ICALLY.]
1 By the action or authority of a synod. E17.
2 In synod, as a synod. E17.

synodite /ˈsɪnədʌɪt/ *noun*. M17.
[In sense 1 from late Greek *sunoditēs*, from *sun-* SYN- + *hoditēs* traveller (from *hodos* journey). In sense 2 from late Latin *synodita*. In sense 3 from SYNOD + -ITE¹.]
†**1** A fellow-traveller. Only in M17.
2 A coenobite. *rare*. M19.
3 *Hist.* An adherent of a synod; *derog.* a Chalcedonian. *rare*. M19.

synodsman /ˈsɪnədzmən/ *noun*. Pl. **-men**. L17.
[from SYNOD + -'S¹ + MAN *noun*.]
1 Orig. (*Hist.*), a lay representative at a synod in a medieval diocese. Later, a sidesman. *rare*. L17.
2 In Anglican Churches, a member of a synod, esp. of the General Synod. L19.

synoecious /sɪˈniːʃəs/ *adjective*. Also *****synec-**. M19.
[from SYN- + *-oecious*, after *dioecious*, *monoecious*.]
BOTANY. Of a bryophyte: having antheridia and archegonia mixed together on the same branch.
■ Also **synoicous** /-ˈnɔɪkəs/ *adjective* M19.

synoecism /sɪˈniːsɪz(ə)m/ *noun*. L19.
[Greek *sunoikismos*, from *sunoikizein* cause to dwell with, unite under a capital city, from *sun-* SYN- + *oikizein* found as a colony, colonize, from *oikos* house: see -ISM.]
GREEK HISTORY. The union of several towns or villages into or under one capital city.
■ **synoecize** *verb trans.* unite into or under one capital city L19.

synonym /ˈsɪnənɪm/ *noun*. Also in Latin form †**synonymum** /sɪˈnɒnɪməm/, pl. **-nyma** /-nɪmə/. LME.
[Latin *synonymum* from Greek *sunōnumon* use as noun of neut. sing. of *sunōnumos* adjective, formed as SYN- + *onuma* name: see -NYM.]
1 A word or phrase having the same sense as another in the same language. Also, a word having the same general sense or denoting the same thing as another in the same language, but having a different emphasis or appropriate to a different context (as *serpent, snake*; *Greek, Hellene*; *happy, joyful*; *kill, slay*), or having a different range of other senses (as *ship, vessel*; *tube, pipe*). LME. ▸**b** The equivalent of a word in another language. L16.
2 A name, idea, expression, etc., which is suggestive of or strongly associated with another. M17.
3 *TAXONOMY*. A systematic name having the same, or nearly the same, application as another; *esp.* one which has been superseded. M17.
■ **syˈnonymist** *noun* a person who studies or makes a list of synonyms M18.

synonymic /sɪnəˈnɪmɪk/ *adjective & noun*. E19.
[from prec. + -IC.]
▸**A** *adjective*. Of, pertaining to, consisting of, or exhibiting synonyms. E19.
▸**B** *noun*. In *pl.* (treated as *sing.*) & †*sing.* The branch of grammar that deals with synonyms. M19.
■ **synonymical** *adjective* †(*a*) *rare* = SYNONYMOUS 1; (*b*) = SYNONYMIC *adjective*: M17. **synonymically** *adverb* as a synonym or synonyms L16.

synonymise *verb* var. of SYNONYMIZE.

synonymity /sɪnəˈnɪmɪti/ *noun*. L19.
[from SYNONYMOUS + -ITY.]
1 The quality or fact of being synonymous or having the same meaning; = SYNONYMY 4. L19.
2 *transf.* Identity of nature of things having different names. L19.

synonymize /sɪˈnɒnɪmʌɪz/ *verb*. Also **-ise**. L16.
[from SYNONYM + -IZE.]
1 *verb trans.* Give the synonyms of. *rare*. L16.
2 *verb intrans.* Be synonymous *with*. *rare*. E17.
3 *verb intrans.* Use synonyms; express the same meaning by different words. *rare*. E18.
4 *verb trans.* **a** Be synonymous with (a concept, phrase, etc.). M20. ▸**b** Regard (terms, concepts, etc.) as synonymous. L20.

synonymous /sɪˈnɒnɪməs/ *adjective*. E17.
[from medieval Latin *synonymus* from Greek *sunōnumos*: see SYNONYM, -OUS.]
1 Having the character of a synonym; equivalent in meaning; (of a word or phrase) denoting the same thing or idea as another. Also, (of things) of the same nature but denoted by different names. Freq. foll. by *with*, (now *rare*) *to*. E17. ▸**b** Synonymic. *rare*. E19.
2 Of a word, idea, etc.: suggestive of or associated with another. Freq. foll. by *with*. M17.
3 †**a** Of the same description; similar. L17. ▸**b** Having the same name; denoted by the same word; = HOMONYMOUS 2. Now *rare*. M18.

> 🕮 **1** R. NIEBUHR State and nation are not synonymous and . . states frequently incorporate several nationalities.
> **2** M. LANE The one whose name is synonymous with tyranny. B. CHATWIN Revolutionary freedom was synonymous with free love.

■ **synonymously** *adverb* by or as a synonym, with the same meaning M17. **synonymousness** *noun* M19.

†**synonymum** *noun* see SYNONYM.

synonymy /sɪˈnɒnɪmi/ *noun*. In sense 1 also (earlier) †**sinonima**. M16.
[Late Latin *synonymia* from Greek *sunōnumia*, from *sunōnumos*: see SYNONYM, -Y³.]
1 The use of synonyms or of words as synonyms; *spec.* a rhetorical figure in which synonyms are used for amplification. M16.
†**2** = SYNONYM 1. E17–L18.
3 A set of synonyms; synonyms collectively. L17.
4 The quality or fact of being synonymous; identity of meaning or application. L18.

synopsis /sɪˈnɒpsɪs/ *noun*. Pl. **synopses** /sɪˈnɒpsiːz/. E17.
[Late Latin from Greek *sunopsis*, from *sun-* SYN- + *opsis* view.]
1 A brief or condensed statement presenting an overall view of something; *esp.* a brief summary of the plot of a play, film, book, etc.; an outline. Also, an edition of the Gospels (usu. the first three) presented in parallel columns with similar passages adjacent to each other. E17.
2 A general view or prospect. *rare*. M19.
3 *ORTHODOX CHURCH*. A book of prayers for the use of the laity. M19.

> 🕮 **1** K. AMIS He was soon engaged on a synopsis and the drafting of a specimen chapter.

■ **synopsize** *verb trans.* make a synopsis of, epitomize L19.

synoptic /sɪˈnɒptɪk/ *adjective & noun*. E17.
[Greek *sunoptikos*, from *sunopsis*: see prec., -IC.]
▸**A** *adjective*. **1 a** Pertaining to or forming a synopsis; giving an overall view; *spec.* depicting or pertaining to weather conditions over a large area at the same time. E17. ▸**b** Of a mental act or faculty, conduct, etc.: pertaining to or involving a combined or comprehensive mental view of something. M19.
2 (Usu. **S-**.) Designating the first three Gospels, as giving a more or less similar account of events. Also, of or pertaining to these Gospels. M19.
▸**B** *noun*. Each of the Synoptic Gospels or their writers. Usu. in *pl.* M19.
■ **synoptical** *adjective* = SYNOPTIC 1, 2 M17. **synoptically** *adverb* in the way of a synopsis; so as to present a general view: M17. **synoptist** *noun* each of the writers of the Synoptic Gospels (usu. in *pl.*) M19.

synoptophore /sɪˈnɒptəfɔː/ *noun*. M20.
[from SYN- + OPTO- + -PHORE.]
OPHTHALMOLOGY. An instrument for measuring the deviations of the visual axes of eyes not properly coordinated for binocular vision.

synostosis /sɪnɒˈstəʊsɪs/ *noun*. Pl. **-stoses** /-ˈstəʊsiːz/. M19.
[from SYN- + Greek *osteon* bone + -OSIS.]
ANATOMY & MEDICINE. Union or fusion of adjacent bones by growth of bony substance (either normal or abnormal).
■ **synostose** /ˈsɪnəstəʊz/ *verb trans.* (usu. in *pass.*) & *intrans.* affect or be affected with synostosis L19. **synostotic** /-ˈstɒtɪk/ *adjective* pertaining to, characterized by, or affected with synostosis M19.

synovia /sʌɪˈnəʊvɪə, sɪ-/ *noun*. M17.
[mod. Latin *sinovia*, *synovia*, *sinophia*, prob. invented arbitrarily by Paracelsus for a nutritive body fluid and for gout.]
Synovial fluid. Formerly also, a discharge of this fluid from a damaged joint.

synovial /sʌɪˈnəʊvɪəl, sɪ-/ *adjective*. M18.
[from prec. + -AL¹.]
ANATOMY & MEDICINE. Designating, pertaining to, or involving the thick colourless lubricating fluid secreted inside joints and the sheaths of tendons.
synovial joint a freely movable joint lined with synovial membrane. **synovial membrane** a membrane of mesothelium and connective tissue which forms a capsule around a freely movable joint and secretes synovial fluid.
■ **synovectomy** /sʌɪnəˈvɛktəmi, sɪ-/ *noun* (*MEDICINE*) surgical excision of (part of) the synovial membrane of a joint, esp. the knee, or of a tendon sheath, esp. to relieve pain; an instance of this: E20. **synovially** *adverb* by a synovial joint L19. **synoˈvitis** *noun* (*MEDICINE*) inflammation of a synovial membrane M19.

syntactic /sɪnˈtaktɪk/ *adjective*. E19.
[Greek *suntaktikos*, from *suntassein*: see SYNTAX, SYNTAXY, -IC.]
1 Of or pertaining to syntax. E19.
2 *MINERALOGY & CHEMISTRY*. Exhibiting or characterized by syntaxy. M20.
2 syntactic foam a plastic foam made by introducing small hollow spheres into a liquid matrix which then solidifies.

syntactical /sɪnˈtaktɪk(ə)l/ *adjective*. L16.
[formed as prec.: see -ICAL.]
= SYNTACTIC 1.

syntactically /sɪnˈtaktɪk(ə)li/ *adverb*. E18.
[from SYNTACTIC, SYNTACTICAL: see -ICALLY.]
According to the rules of (grammatical or logical) syntax; as regards syntax.

syntactician /sɪntakˈtɪʃ(ə)n/ *noun*. L18.
[from SYNTACTIC + -IAN: see -ICIAN.]
†**1** (**S-**.) = SYNTAXIAN. *rare*. Only in L18.
2 An expert in or student of syntax. E20.

syntacticist /sɪnˈtaktɪsɪst/ *noun*. L19.
[formed as prec. + -IST.]
= SYNTACTICIAN 2.

syntactics /sɪnˈtaktɪks/ *noun*. *rare*. M20.
[from SYNTACTIC after *semantics*: see -ICS.]
LINGUISTICS. The branch of linguistics that deals with the formal relations of signs to each other.

syntagm /ˈsɪntam/ *noun*. E17.
[Anglicized from late Latin SYNTAGMA.]
†**1** = SYNTAGMA 1. Only in 17.
2 Chiefly *LINGUISTICS*. = SYNTAGMA 3. M20.

syntagma /sɪnˈtagmə/ *noun*. Pl. **-mata** /-mətə/, **-mas**. M17.
[Late Latin from Greek *suntagma*, from *suntassein*: see SYNTAXIS.]
1 An orderly collection of statements, propositions, etc.; a systematic treatise. *rare*. M17.
2 *ANCIENT HISTORY*. A division of the population of a country, or of a body of troops. *rare*. E19.
3 Chiefly *LINGUISTICS*. A syntactic unit comprising one or more (esp. linguistic) signs or elements. M20.
■ **syntagˈmatic** *adjective* (chiefly *LINGUISTICS*) of or pertaining to the syntactic or (*transf.*) any sequential relationship between elements or units M20. **syntagmatically** *adverb* M20.

syntax /ˈsɪntaks/ *noun*. L16.
[French *syntaxe* or late Latin *syntaxis* from Greek *suntaxis*, from *suntassein*, from *sun-* SYN- + *tassein* arrange.]
1 *LINGUISTICS*. **a** The order of words in which they convey meaning collectively by their connection and relation. Also, the established rules and usages of grammatical construction; the branch of grammar that deals with these. L16. ▸**b** *LOGIC & COMPUTING*. The order and arrangement of words or symbols forming a logical sentence; the rules by which elements in a formal system, programming language, etc., are combined. E20.
2 Orderly or systematic arrangement of parts or elements; a connected order or system of things. E17.
3 (Usu. **S-**.) (The name of) a class in a Roman Catholic school, college, or seminary, now only *spec.* the fifth class, immediately above Grammar and below Poetry, in certain Jesuit schools. E17.

> 🕮 **1a** *Mind* The syntax of the Aryan languages differs . . from that of non-inflectional languages. **b** ***logical syntax***: see LOGICAL *adjective*. **2** J. D. EVANS The decoration . . derives its general syntax . . from the repertoire of the preceding phases.

Comb.: **syntax language** *LOGIC & COMPUTING* the language used to refer to the syntactical forms of an object language; a metalanguage.
¶ Sense 2 became obsolete in L17 but was revived in M20.

syntaxeme /ˈsɪntaksiːm/ *noun*. *rare*. M20.
[from SYNTAX + -EME.]
LINGUISTICS. A unit of syntactic analysis, *esp.* one which cannot be further analysed into components.
■ **syntaˈxemic** *adjective* L20.

syntaxes *noun* pl. of SYNTAX, SYNTAXIS.

syntaxial /sɪnˈtaksɪəl/ *adjective*. M20.
[from SYNTAXY: see -IAL.]
CRYSTALLOGRAPHY. Of, pertaining to, or exhibiting syntaxy.
■ **syntaxially** *adverb* M20.

Syntaxian /sɪnˈtaksɪən/ *noun*. E18.
[from SYNTAX + -IAN.]
A member of the Syntax (see SYNTAX 3).

syntaxic /sɪnˈtaksɪk/ *adjective*. M20.
[from SYNTAXY, SYNTAXIS + -IC.]
1 *CRYSTALLOGRAPHY*. = SYNTAXIAL *adjective*. M20.
2 *PSYCHOLOGY*. Designating or pertaining to thought processes that are objective and open to corroboration. M20.

syntaxical /sɪnˈtaksɪk(ə)l/ *adjective*. *rare*. L16.
[from SYNTAX + -ICAL.]
= SYNTACTIC 1.

For other words beginning with *syn-* see the entry for **syn-**

syntaxis /sɪnˈtaksɪs/ *noun.* Pl. **-taxes** /-ˈtaksiːz/. M16.
[Late Latin: see SYNTAX.]
†**1** = SYNTAX 1a. M16–M18.
2 *GEOLOGY.* An arrangement of fold axes or mountain ranges converging towards a common point. E20.
3 *CRYSTALLOGRAPHY.* = SYNTAXY. M20.

syntaxy /ˈsɪntaksi/ *noun.* M20.
[French *syntaxie*, formed as SYNTAX: see -TAXY.]
CRYSTALLOGRAPHY. Ordered crystal growth or intergrowth in which the secondary material has the same orientation as the parent.

synteresis *noun* var. of SYNDERESIS.

syntexis /sɪnˈtɛksɪs/ *noun.* E20.
[Greek *suntēxis*, from *suntēkein* fuse together, from *sun-* SYN- + *tēkein* melt.]
GEOLOGY. The alteration of magma by the melting or assimilation of another rock.
■ **syntectic** *adjective* E20.

synth /sɪnθ/ *noun. colloq.* L20.
[Abbreviation.]
A musical synthesizer.

synthalin /ˈsɪnθəlɪn/ *noun.* E20.
[from SYNTH(ETIC *adjective* + *-a-* + INSU)LIN.]
PHARMACOLOGY. A synthetic toxic aliphatic diguanidine which has the hypoglycaemic effect of insulin when taken orally.

synthase /ˈsɪnθeɪz/ *noun.* M20.
[from SYNTH(ESIS + -ASE.]
BIOCHEMISTRY. An enzyme which catalyses the linking together of two molecules, esp. without the direct involvement of ATP. Cf. LIGASE, SYNTHETASE.

synthesis /ˈsɪnθɪsɪs/ *noun.* Pl. **-theses** /-θɪsiːz/. LME.
[Latin from Greek *sunthesis*, from *suntithenai*, from *sun-* SYN- + *tithenai* put, place.]
▶†**I 1** *GRAMMAR.* **a** Apposition. Only in LME. ▸**b** The construction of a sentence according to sense, in violation of strict syntax. E17–E18.
▶**II 2** *LOGIC & PHILOSOPHY.* **a** The action of proceeding in thought from causes to effects, or from laws or principles to their consequences. E17. ▸**b** In Kantian philosophy, the action of the understanding in combining and unifying isolated sense-data into a cognizable whole. E19. ▸**c** In Hegelian philosophy, the final stage of a dialectic progression in which an idea is proposed (thesis), then negated (antithesis), and finally transcended by a new idea that resolves the conflict between the first and its negation. Cf. ANTITHESIS 6, THESIS 2. L19.
3 *MEDICINE.* The joining of divided parts in surgery. Now *rare* or *obsolete.* E18.
4 a *CHEMISTRY.* Formation of a compound by combination of its elements or constituents; *esp.* artificial preparation of organic compounds by reactions rather than by extraction from natural products. Also, a method for producing a particular compound. M18. ▸**b** *PHYSICS.* Production of white or other compound light by combination of its constituent colours, or of a complex musical sound by combination of its component simple tones. M19.
5 *LINGUISTICS.* The tendency of a language to mark categories by inflections rather than by (groups of) distinct words. Also, the process of making compound and derivative words. M19.
6 *gen.* The action or an act of putting together parts or elements to make up a complex whole; the combination of immaterial or abstract things, or of elements into an ideal or abstract whole; the state of being so put together. Also, a complex whole made up of a number of united parts or elements. M19.

🕮 **4a** *Journal of Molecular Biology* Sequential enzyme sequences involved in the synthesis of essential metabolites. *Nature* Catalysts for the synthesis of industrially important . . polymers. ***Perkin synthesis, Perkin's synthesis***: see PERKIN 2.

▶**III 7** *ROMAN ANTIQUITIES.* A loose flowing robe worn at meals and festivities. E17.
Comb.: **synthesis gas** a gas used as a feedstock in the industrial synthesis of a chemical, *esp.* a mixture of hydrogen and carbon monoxide.
¶ In various senses contrasted with *analysis.*

synthesise *verb* var. of SYNTHESIZE.

synthesiser *noun* var. of SYNTHESIZER.

synthesist /ˈsɪnθɪsɪst/ *noun.* M19.
[from SYNTHESIZE + -IST.]
A person who uses a synthetic rather than an analytic method.

synthesize /ˈsɪnθɪsʌɪz/ *verb trans.* Also **-ise**. M19.
[from SYNTHESIS + -IZE.]
1 Make a synthesis of; put together or combine into a complex whole; make up by combination of parts or elements. M19.
2 *CHEMISTRY.* Produce (a compound, esp. an organic one) by synthesis. M19.

🕮 **1** J. BARNES An ability to synthesise the observations of others. **2** *Nature* Histamine is synthesized maximally in the hypothalamus. *Scientific American* Plutonium 239, synthesised from uranium 238 by the absorption of a neutron. *fig.*: K. AMIS He couldn't synthesize enough of the required righteous indignation.

synthesizer /ˈsɪnθɪsʌɪzə/ *noun.* Also **-iser**. M19.
[from prec. + -ER[1].]
1 A person who or thing which synthesizes something. M19.
2 Any of various types of instrument for generating and combining signals of different frequencies; *esp.* a computerized instrument, usu. with a keyboard, used to create a wide variety of musical sounds electronically. E20.
2 ***Moog synthesizer, speech synthesizer, voice synthesizer,*** etc.

synthespian /sɪnˈθɛspɪən/ *noun.* L20.
[Blend of SYNTHETIC and THESPIAN.]
A computer-generated actor, either as part of an animated film or appearing to interact with human actors.
¶ Proprietary name in the US.

synthetase /ˈsɪnθɪteɪz/ *noun.* M20.
[from SYNTHET(IC *adjective* + -ASE.]
BIOCHEMISTRY. An enzyme which catalyses a particular synthesis; *esp.* a ligase, a synthase.

synthetic /sɪnˈθɛtɪk/ *adjective & noun.* L17.
[French *synthétique* or mod. Latin *syntheticus* from Greek *sunthetikos*, from *sunthetos*, from *suntithenai*: see SYNTHESIS, -IC. Cf. next.]
▶**A** *adjective.* **1 a** *LOGIC & PHILOSOPHY.* Proceeding from causes or general principles to consequences or particular instances; deductive. L17. ▸**b** *KANTIAN PHILOSOPHY.* Pertaining to the synthesis of the manifold. Also, designating judgements which add to the subject attributes not directly implied in it. E19.
2 Of, pertaining to, involving, or using synthesis, or combination of parts into a whole; constructive. E18.
3 a *CHEMISTRY.* Pertaining to or involving chemical synthesis; (of an organic compound, a gem, etc.) produced by artificial synthesis, esp. in imitation of a natural substance; (of a fibre) manufactured from a chemically synthesized polymer. Also, made from synthetic materials rather than natural ones. M18. ▸**b** *fig.* Artificial, imitation, invented. M20. ▸**c** *AERONAUTICS.* Designating or pertaining to training, exercises, etc., simulating on the ground what is performed in the air. M20.
4 *LINGUISTICS.* Characterized by the marking of categories by inflections rather than by (groups of) distinct words. Also, pertaining to or characterized by the combination of simple words or elements into compound or derivative words. E19.
5 *BIOLOGY.* **a** Combining different, esp. generalized characters which in the later course of evolution are specialized in different organisms. *rare.* M19. ▸**b** Designating the Neo-Darwinian theory of evolution. M20.

🕮 **2** *Nature* Similarly unusual coordination numbers no longer present an important challenge to the synthetic chemist. **3a** A. TULL Natural and synthetic additives are used in foods. ***synthetic resin***: see RESIN *noun* 3.

▶**B** *noun.* A product obtained by artificial synthesis rather than from natural sources; *esp.* a synthetic fibre or fabric. Usu. in *pl.* M20.
¶ In various senses contrasted with *analytic.*

synthetical /sɪnˈθɛtɪk(ə)l/ *adjective.* E17.
[formed as prec.: see -ICAL.]
1 = SYNTHETIC 1a. E17. ▸**b** = SYNTHETIC 1b. L18.
2 = SYNTHETIC 3a. Now *rare.* M18.
3 = SYNTHETIC 2. L18.

synthetically /sɪnˈθɛtɪk(ə)li/ *adverb.* M18.
[from SYNTHETIC *adjective*, SYNTHETICAL: see -ICALLY.]
In a synthetic manner; by synthesis.

synthetise *verb* var. of SYNTHETIZE.

synthetist /ˈsɪnθɪtɪst/ *noun.* M19.
[from SYNTHETIC + -IST.]
= SYNTHESIST.

synthetize /ˈsɪnθɪtʌɪz/ *verb trans.* Also **-ise**. E19.
[Greek *sunthetizesthai*, from *sunthetos*: see SYNTHETIC, -IZE.]
= SYNTHESIZE.

synthon /ˈsɪnθɒn/ *noun.* M20.
[from SYNTHESIS + -ON.]
CHEMISTRY. A constituent part of a molecule to be synthesized which provides a convenient basis for a stage in the synthesis.

Syntocinon /sɪntə(ʊ)ˈsʌɪnɒn, sɪnˈtəʊsɪnɒn/ *noun.* M20.
[from SYN- + OXY)TOCIN + *-on.*]
PHARMACOLOGY. (Proprietary name for) a synthetic preparation of oxytocin.

syntonic /sɪnˈtɒnɪk/ *adjective.* L19.
[In sense 1 from SYN- + TONE *noun* + -IC. In sense 2 from SYNTONY + -IC.]
1 *ELECTRICITY.* Designating (a system of telegraphy using) electrical instruments which are accurately tuned or adjusted so that one responds only to signals of the frequency emitted by the other. L19.
2 *PSYCHIATRY.* Designating or exhibiting the responsive, lively type of temperament which is liable to manic-depressive psychosis. E20.
■ **ˈsyntone** *noun* (*PSYCHIATRY*) a person with a syntonic temperament M20. **syntonically** *adverb* E20.

syntony /ˈsɪntəni/ *noun.* In sense 2 also **-tonia** /-ˈtəʊnɪə/. L19.
[In sense 1 from SYNTONIC + -Y[3]. In sense 2 from German *Syntonie.*]
1 *ELECTRICITY.* The condition of being tuned to the same or corresponding frequencies. L19.
2 *PSYCHIATRY.* The state or condition of being syntonic. E20.
3 *fig.* Sympathy, close correspondence, a state of being attuned. M20.

🕮 **3** J. WAINWRIGHT There was a . . basic syntony which each felt for the other.

syntrophy /ˈsɪntrəfi/ *noun.* L19.
[from SYN- + -TROPHY.]
BIOLOGY. A relationship between individuals of two different species etc. (now usu., two bacterial strains) in which one or (usu.) both benefit nutritionally from the presence of the other.
■ **syntrophic** /-ˈtrəʊfɪk, -ˈtrɒfɪk/ *adjective* M20. **synˈtrophism** *noun* = SYNTROPHY M20.

syntype /ˈsɪntʌɪp/ *noun.* E20.
[from SYN- + -TYPE.]
TAXONOMY. Each of a set of specimens from which a species was originally described and named without the selection of a holotype.

synusia /sɪˈn(j)uːsɪə/ *noun.* Pl. **-iae** /-ɪiː/. Also **-ium** /-ɪəm/, pl. **-ia**. E20.
[Greek *sunousia* society, company, after German *Synusie.*]
ECOLOGY. A group of organisms (usu. plants) within a community which have similar life-forms and occupy approximately the same ecological niche.

syph /sɪf/ *noun. slang.* E20.
[Abbreviation.]
Syphilis. Freq. as ***the syph.***

syphilide /ˈsɪfɪlʌɪd/ *noun.* E19.
[French *syphilides* pl., formed as SYPHILIS + *-ide*: cf. -ID[2], PINTID.]
MEDICINE. A skin condition caused by syphilis, *esp.* a rash typical of the infectious second stage of the disease.

syphilis /ˈsɪfɪlɪs/ *noun.* E18.
[mod. Latin, orig. in *Syphilis, sive Morbus Gallicus*, title of a Latin poem (1530) by Girolamo Fracastoro (1483–1553), Veronese physician, from *Syphilus* a character in it, the supposed first sufferer of the disease.]
A chronic disease caused by the spirochaete *Treponema pallidum*, contracted chiefly by infection during sexual intercourse, but also congenitally by infection of a developing foetus, and rarely via wounds.
primary syphilis the first stage of syphilis, characterized by a chancre in the part infected. **secondary syphilis** the second stage of syphilis, affecting esp. the skin, lymph nodes, and mucous membranes. **tertiary syphilis** the third stage of syphilis, involving the spread of tumour-like lesions (gummas) throughout the body, freq. damaging the cardiovascular and central nervous systems. **quaternary syphilis** neurosyphilis.
■ **syphiliˈzation** *noun* inoculation or infection with syphilis M19. **syphilize** *verb trans.* (*MEDICINE*) (*a*) inoculate with the virus of syphilis, as a means of cure or prevention; (*b*) infect with syphilis: M19. **syphiloid** *adjective* resembling (that of) syphilis E19.

syphilitic /sɪfɪˈlɪtɪk/ *adjective & noun.* L18.
[mod. Latin *syphiliticus*, from SYPHILIS: see -ITIC.]
▶**A** *adjective.* Of, pertaining to, caused by, or affected with syphilis. L18.
▶**B** *noun.* A person affected with syphilis. L19.

syphilo- /ˈsɪfɪləʊ/ *combining form* of SYPHILIS: see -O-.
■ **syphiloˈderma** *noun*, pl. **-mata**, = SYPHILIDE M19. **syphiˈlology** *noun* the branch of medicine that deals with syphilis L19. **syphiloˈphobia** *noun* irrational or excessive fear of venereal disease, *spec.* syphilis M19.

syphiloma /sɪfɪˈləʊmə/ *noun.* Now *rare.* Pl. **-mata** /-mətə/, **-mas**. M19.
[from SYPHILIS + -OMA.]
MEDICINE. A syphilitic lesion; = GUMMA.

syphilosis /sɪfɪˈləʊsɪs/ *noun.* Pl. **-loses** /-ˈləʊsiːz/. L19.
[from SYPHILIS + -OSIS.]
MEDICINE. A syphilitic condition.

syphon *noun, verb* vars. of SIPHON *noun, verb.*

Syracusan /ˈsʌɪrəkjuːz(ə)n/ *noun & adjective.* L15.
[Latin *Syracusanus*, from *Syracusae* Syracuse (see below) from Greek *Surakousai*: see -AN.]
▶**A** *noun.* A native or inhabitant of Syracuse, a city in Sicily. L15.
▶**B** *adjective.* Of or pertaining to Syracuse or its inhabitants. L16.
■ Also †**Syracusian** *noun & adjective* L16–L18.

For other words beginning with *syn-* see the entry for **syn-**

Syrah /ˈsiːrə/ *noun.* Also **Sirrah**. L19.
[French: see SHIRAZ.]
= SHIRAZ 2, 3.

Syrette /sɪˈrɛt/ *noun.* M20.
[from SYRINGE + -ETTE.]
(Proprietary name for) a disposable injection unit comprising a collapsible tube with an attached hypodermic needle and a single dose of a drug (esp. morphine).

Syriac /ˈsɪrɪak/ *noun & adjective.* E17.
[Latin *Syriacus* from Greek *Suriakos*, from *Suria*: see next, -AC.]
▶ **A** *noun.* Orig., Aramaic. Later, western Aramaic, the Aramaic dialect of the Syrian Christians, now only in liturgical use. E17.
▶ **B** *adjective.* Of, pertaining to, or written in Syriac. E17.

Syriacism /ˈsɪrɪəsɪz(ə)m/ *noun.* M17.
[from prec. + -ISM.]
= SYRIASM.

Syrian /ˈsɪrɪən/ *adjective & noun.* LOE.
[Old French *sirien* (mod. *syrien*), from Latin *Syrius* from Greek *Surios*, from *Suria* Syria (see below).]
▶ **A** *adjective.* Of, pertaining to, or characteristic of (the inhabitants of) Syria, historically a region including present-day Lebanon, Israel, and Jordan, and parts of Iraq and Saudi Arabia, now a State. LOE.
▶ **B** *noun.* A native or inhabitant of ancient or modern Syria. LME.
■ **Syrianize** *verb trans.* give a Syrian character to L19.

Syriarch /ˈsɪrɪɑːk/ *noun.* M19.
[Late Latin *Syriarcha*, *-us* from Greek *Suriarkhēs*, from *Suria*: see prec., -ARCH.]
Hist. The director of public games in Syria under the Romans.

Syriasm /ˈsɪrɪaz(ə)m/ *noun.* L17.
[Irreg. contr. of SYRIACISM.]
A Syriac idiom or expression.

syringa /sɪˈrɪŋɡə/ *noun.* M17.
[mod. Latin, from Greek *surigg-*, *surigx* pipe, SYRINX, from the former use of the stems to make pipe-stems.]
A mock orange (genus *Philadelphus*), *esp.* the commonly grown *Philadelphus coronarius* and its hybrids; *BOTANY* a plant of the genus *Syringa*, a lilac.

syringe /sɪˈrɪn(d)ʒ, ˈsɪ-/ *noun & verb.* LME.
[medieval Latin *syringa*, formed as SYRINX.]
▶ **A** *noun.* **1** A small cylindrical instrument, typically consisting of a tube fitted with a nozzle and a piston or bulb, for drawing in a quantity of liquid and ejecting it forcibly in a stream, used in medicine esp. for injecting drugs, vaccines, etc., through a needle and cleansing wounds or body cavities. Now also, a similar instrument used for various purposes, as compressing air, squirting water over plants, etc. LME.
2 A natural structure or organ resembling a syringe, as in certain bugs. E19.
Comb.: **syringe passage** a technique for maintaining a strain of micro-organisms or parasitic protozoans by transferring them through generations of laboratory animals by inoculation with a syringe; **syringe-passage** *verb trans.* subject to syringe passage.
▶ **B** *verb trans.* **1** Treat with a syringe; spray liquid into (the passage of the ear, a wound) or on to (a plant) with a syringe. LME.
2 Inject (liquid) with a syringe. M17.
■ **syringeful** *noun* as much as a syringe will hold M18.

syringeal /sɪˈrɪn(d)ʒɪəl/ *adjective.* L19.
[from Latin *syring-*, SYRINX + -AL[1].]
ZOOLOGY. Of, pertaining to, or connected with the syrinx of a bird.

syringes *nouns* pls. of SYRINGE *noun*, SYRINX.

syringo- /sɪˈrɪŋɡəʊ/ *combining form.*
[from Latin *syring-*, *syrinx* or its source Greek *surigx*: see next, -O-.]
MEDICINE. Of or pertaining to a long cavity or fistula.
■ **syringoˈbulbia** *noun* [BULB *noun* + -IA[1]] the formation of an abnormal cavity in the medulla oblongata of the brain (usu. an extension of that of syringomyelia), resulting in loss of sensation and movement in the mouth and throat E20. **syringomyˈelia** *noun* [Greek *muelos* marrow] formation of an abnormal longitudinal cavity in the spinal cord; dilatation of the central canal of the spinal cord: L19.

syrinx /ˈsɪrɪŋks/ *noun.* Pl. **syrinxes**, **syringes** /sɪˈrɪndʒiːz/. E17.
[Latin from Greek *surigx*, *surigg-* pipe, tube, channel, fistula.]
1 A set of pan-pipes. E17.
2 *ARCHAEOLOGY.* A narrow gallery cut in rock, esp. in an ancient Egyptian tomb. Usu. in *pl.* L17.
3 *ZOOLOGY.* The organ of the voice in birds, situated at or near the junction of the trachea and bronchi. L19.

syrma /ˈsəːmə/ *noun.* M18.
[Latin from Greek *surma*, from *surein* drag or trail along.]
GREEK ANTIQUITIES. A long trailing garment worn by a tragic actor.

Syro- /ˈsʌɪrəʊ/ *combining form.*
[Greek *Suro-* combining form of *Suros* a Syrian: cf. SYRIAN.]
Forming adjectives and nouns with the sense 'Syrian and —', as ***Syro-Arabian***, ***Syro-Chaldaic***, etc.

syrop *noun* see SYRUP.

Syrophoenician /ˌsʌɪrəʊfəˈnɪʃ(ə)n, ˈniː-/ *noun & adjective.* M16.
[from Latin *Syrophoenix*, *-ic-* from Greek *Surophoinix*, *-ik-*: see SYRO-, PHOENICIAN.]
Hist. ▶ **A** *noun.* A native or inhabitant of Syrophoenicia, a Roman province including Phoenicia and the territories of Damascus and Palmyra. M16.
▶ **B** *adjective.* Of or pertaining to Syrophoenicia or its inhabitants. M19.

syrphid /ˈsəːfɪd/ *adjective & noun.* L19.
[mod. Latin *Syrphidae* (see below), from *Syrphus* genus name, from Greek *surphos* gnat: see -ID[3].]
ENTOMOLOGY. ▶ **A** *adjective.* Of, pertaining to, or designating the dipteran family Syrphidae, which includes the hoverflies. L19.
▶ **B** *noun.* A fly of this family, a hoverfly. M20.

syrtis /ˈsəːtɪs/ *noun. arch.* Pl. **-tes** /-tiːz/. Also **syrt**. E16.
[Latin from Greek *Surtis*, name of either of two large quicksands off the northern coast of Africa, from *surein* drag along, sweep away.]
A quicksand.

syrtos /ˈsɪətɒs/ *noun.* L19.
[mod. Greek from Greek *surtos* lit. 'drawn, led', pa. pple of *surein*: see prec.]
A Greek folk-dance in which the participants form a line or chain led by one person who intermittently breaks away to perform improvised steps.

syrup /ˈsɪrəp/ *noun & verb.* Also ***sirup**. As noun also (*arch.*) **syrop**. LME.
[Old & mod. French *sirop* or medieval Latin *siropus*, *sirupus*, ult. from Arab. *šarāb* wine, drink, fruit syrup: cf. SHRAB, SHERBET, SHRUB *noun*[2].]
▶ **A** *noun.* **1** A thick sweet liquid; *esp.* a concentrated solution of sugar in water, fruit juice, etc., used to contain a medicine or as a sweetener, preservative, or article of food. LME. ▸**b** *spec.* Condensed sugar cane juice; part of this remaining uncrystallized at various stages of refining. M16. ▸**c** *transf.* A liquid with the consistency of syrup. M19.
2 *fig.* Orig., a pleasant thing having therapeutic properties. Later, (a thing containing or imparting) sweetness or delight. Now *esp.*, excessive sweetness, cloying sentimentality. M16.

> 📖 **2** S. NICHOLSON O lend me thy insinuating power, Words steep'd in syrop of Ambrosia. *Spectator* Mr. Gurney's poems are almost all of them syrup.

Phrases: **golden syrup** a bright golden-yellow syrup drained off in the process of obtaining refined crystallized sugar. **syrup of figs** a laxative prepared from dried figs, usu. with senna and carminatives.
▶ **B** *verb trans.* **1** Make into or bring to the consistency of a syrup. *rare.* LME.
2 Cover with or immerse in syrup. E17.
†**3** Treat with medicinal syrup. L17–L18.
■ **syrupy** *adjective* (*a*) having the texture or consistency of syrup; (*b*) *fig.* excessively sweet or sentimental: E18.

sysop /ˈsɪsɒp/ *noun. slang.* L20.
[Abbreviation from *sys(tem op(erator*.]
A computer system operator.

syssitia /sɪˈsɪtɪə/ *noun.* M19.
[Greek *sussitia* pl. of *sussition* common meal, from *sun-* SYN- + *sitos* food: see -IA[2].]
GREEK ANTIQUITIES. Meals eaten together in public; the Spartan and Cretan custom of eating the main meal of the day at a public mess.

systaltic /sɪˈstaltɪk/ *adjective.* Now *rare.* L17.
[Late Latin *systalticus* from Greek *sustaltikos*, from *sun-* SYN- + *staltos* verbal adjective from *stal-* stem of *stellein* put, place.]
1 *PHYSIOLOGY.* Of the nature of contraction, esp. with alternate contraction and dilatation. L17.
†**2** Of ancient Greek music: causing sadness or tender emotion. L17–L18.

†**systasis** *noun.* Pl. **-ases**. E17.
[Greek *sustasis* composition, collection, union, from *sun-* SYN- + *sta-*: see next, STASIS.]
1 The action or result of setting or putting things together; combination, synthesis. E17–E18.
2 A political union or confederation. *rare.* Only in L18.

systatic /sɪˈstatɪk/ *adjective.* M17.
[medieval Latin or mod. Latin *systaticus* from Greek *sustatikos* astringent (in ecclesiastical Greek, commendatory), from *sun-* SYN- + *sta-*: see next, -IC.]
†**1** Of a method: involving synthesis, synthetic. *rare.* Only in M17.
2 *ECCLESIASTICAL HISTORY.* Of a letter: introductory, commendatory. E20.

system /ˈsɪstəm/ *noun.* E17.
[French *système* or late Latin *systema* from Greek *sustēma*, *sustēmatos*, from *sunistanai*, from *sun-* SYN- + *sta-* base of *histanai* set up.]
1 *gen.* A group or set of related or associated material or immaterial things forming a unity or complex whole; *spec.* (*arch.*) the universe. E17. ▸**b** *SCIENCE.* A group or set of objects naturally associated or of phenomena sharing a common cause. M19. ▸**c** A set of objects or appliances arranged or organized for some special purpose, as parts of a mechanism, components of an interdependent or interconnecting assembly or network, etc. M19.
2 A body of theory or practice pertaining to or prescribing a particular form of government, religion, philosophy, etc.; a comprehensive and methodically arranged conspectus of a subject. E17. ▸**b** *transf.* A comprehensive and methodical exposition of or treatise on a subject. *obsolete* exc. in titles of books. M17. ▸**c** With *the*. The established or prevailing political, economic, or social order, esp. regarded as oppressive. Also, any impersonal restrictive institution or organization. E19.
3 *MUSIC.* In ancient Greek music, a compound interval consisting of several degrees (opp. DIASTEM); a scale or series of notes extending through such an interval and serving as a basis for composition. Also, a set of staves connected by a brace in a score. E17.
4 An organized scheme or plan of action, *esp.* a complex or comprehensive one; an orderly or regular procedure or method; *spec.* (*a*) a formal or established scheme or method of classification, notation, etc.; (*b*) a consistent method of betting devised or used by a gambler. M17. ▸**b** Orderly arrangement or method; classification; orderliness. L17.
5 *PHYSICS.* A group of bodies moving about one another in space under a dynamical law, as the law of gravitation; *ASTRONOMY* a group of celestial objects connected by their mutual attractive forces, esp. moving in orbits about a centre. L17.
6 *BIOLOGY.* **a** A set of organs or parts in an animal or plant body which have the same or similar structure, or which together serve the same physiological function. M18. ▸**b** *The* whole body of an organism regarded as an organized whole; the sum of an organism's vital processes or functions. M18.
7 *GEOLOGY.* A major stratigraphic division, composed of a number of series and corresponding to a period in time; the rocks deposited during a specific period. E19.
8 *CRYSTALLOGRAPHY.* Each of the six (or seven) basic geometrically distinct ways in which different minerals crystallize, constituting the six (or seven) classes of crystalline forms. E19.
9 *GREEK PROSODY.* A group of connected verses or periods, esp. in anapaestic metres. M19.
10 *METALLURGY.* The set of the various phases that two or more given metals are capable of forming at different temperatures and pressures. Usu. with specifying word, as ***alloy system***. E20.
11 *LINGUISTICS.* A group of paradigmatically interrelated terms, units, or categories. M20.
12 *COMPUTING.* A group of related or interconnected hardware units or programs or both, esp. when dedicated to a single application; *spec.* = ***OPERATING system***. M20.

> 📖 **1** E. BANCROFT The blessings of Nature . . in . . our habitable system. J. PRIESTLEY The Greeks distributed their years into systems of four, calling them Olympiads. W. PALEY The universe itself is a system. **2** TENNYSON A dust of systems and of creeds. J. MARTINEAU Morality is not a system of truths, but a system of rules. B. JOWETT In the Hegelian system ideas supersede persons. **c** *Ottawa Journal* The deeply moving . . story of a young man who wouldn't surrender to the system. **4** *Times* The T.A. system of signalling invented by Admiral Tryon. J. SYMONS A racing system, something to do with backing second favourites. A. LOOS A new system she thought up of how to learn French. ***net system***, ***periodic system***, ***solid system***, ***tally system***, etc. **5** ***planetary system***, ***solar system***, etc. **6a** ***digestive system***, ***immune system***, ***lateral line system***, ***limbic system***, ***nervous system***, ***portal system***, ***pyramidal system***, ***reticular system***, etc.

Phrases: **all systems go** everything functioning correctly, ready to proceed. ***Continental System***: see CONTINENTAL *adjective*. ***decimal system***: see DECIMAL *adjective*. **get a thing out of one's system** *colloq.* rid oneself of a preoccupation or anxiety. ***mercantile system***: see MERCANTILE. ***public address system***: see PUBLIC *adjective & noun*. ***SEXUAL system***. ***social system***: see SOCIAL *adjective*.
Comb.: **system-building** (*a*) systematic thought, the process of building an intellectual system; (*b*) a method of construction using standardized prefabricated components; **system D** *slang* a (usu. unscrupulous) way of getting or keeping out of trouble, bluff; **system integrator** *COMPUTING* a company which markets commercial integrated software and hardware systems; **system operator** a person who operates procedures for the whole of a computer system; *spec.* the supervisor of an electronic bulletin board; **system program** *COMPUTING* a program forming part of an operating system; **systems analysis** the analysis of complex operations and processes, esp. as an aid to decision-making or the efficient implementation of a computer system; **systems analyst** a person engaged in systems analysis; **systems design** the matching of a computer system to the situation in which it is

to be used; **systems engineering** (*a*) the investigation of complex artificial systems in relation to the apparatus that is or might be involved in them; (*b*) the design and installation of computer systems; **systems integrator** = *system integrator* above; **system software** COMPUTING = *systems software* below; **systems program** = *system program* above; **systems software** COMPUTING system programs collectively.

■ **systemed** *adjective* (*rare*) systematized, systematic M18. **systemist** *noun* (*rare*) = SYSTEMATIST L18. **systemiˈzation** *noun* = SYSTEMATIZATION M19. **systemize** *verb trans.* = SYSTEMATIZE 1 L18. **systemizer** *noun* = SYSTEMATIZER L19. **systemless** *adjective* having no system; disordered, unsystematic, structureless: M19.

systematic /sɪstəˈmatɪk/ *noun & adjective.* M17.
[Late Latin *systematicus* from Greek *sustēmatikos*, from *sustēma* SYSTEM: see -IC. Cf. next.]

▶ **A** *noun.* **1** A systematician, a systematist. Long *rare* or *obsolete.* M17.

2 In *pl.* (treated as *sing.*). The branch of biology that deals with the interrelationships of different species and their classification; systematic zoology, botany, etc.; taxonomy. L19.

▶ **B** *adjective.* †**1** = SYSTEMATICAL 1b. *rare.* Only in L17.

2 a (Of a text, exposition, activity, etc.) arranged or conducted according to a system, plan, or organized method; (of a person) acting according to a system, regular and methodical, thorough. E18. ▸**b** Habitual, deliberate, premeditated; acting or carried out with malicious intent. E19.

3 BIOLOGY. Pertaining to, following, or seeking to construct a system or systems of classification; classificatory. L18.

4 CHEMISTRY. Of a chemical name or nomenclature: constructed from conventional formative elements in accordance with a set of rules so as to represent the detailed chemical structure of the compound etc. named. Cf. TRIVIAL *adjective* 6. M19.

5 = SYSTEMIC *adjective* 1b. *rare.* L19.

> 📖 **2** ISAIAH BERLIN No systematic attempt to discuss the problem of free will as such. J. HELLER Aristotle craved definition, explanation, systematic investigation, and proof, even in geometry. **b** L. STEPHEN Pope . . was a systematic appropriator . . of other men's thoughts. J. R. GREEN They turned religion into a systematic attack on English liberty.

Special collocations: **systematic ambiguity** LOGIC (a) variation in meaning of a term or expression, of a kind governed and explicable by a rule. **systematic desensitization** PSYCHIATRY a treatment for phobias in which the patient is exposed to progressively more anxiety-provoking stimuli and taught relaxation techniques. **systematic error** STATISTICS an error having a non-zero mean, so that its effect is not reduced when observations are averaged. **systematic theology** the branch of theology that deals with giving a coherent rationally ordered account of the body of religious doctrine.

■ **systematician** /-ˈtɪʃ(ə)n/ *noun* a person who constructs or adheres to a system L19. **systematicity** /-ˈtɪsɪti/ *noun* the quality of being systematic L20.

systematical /sɪstəˈmatɪk(ə)l/ *adjective.* Now *rare* or *obsolete.* M17.
[formed as prec.: see -ICAL.]

1 = SYSTEMATIC *adjective* 2a. M17. ▸**b** Abstract, theoretical, impractical. M18. ▸**c** = SYSTEMATIC *adjective* 2b. M18.

†**2** Of or pertaining to the system of the universe or the solar system; cosmic. L17–L18.

3 BIOLOGY. = SYSTEMATIC *adjective* 3. E19.

systematically /sɪstəˈmatɪk(ə)li/ *adverb.* M17.
[from prec., SYSTEMATIC: see -ICALLY.]
In a systematic manner.

systematize /ˈsɪstəmətʌɪz/ *verb.* Also **-ise**. M18.
[from Greek *sustēma*, *-mat-* SYSTEM + -IZE.]

1 *verb trans.* Arrange systematically; make systematic; devise a system for (a procedure, classification, etc.). M18.

2 *verb intrans.* Construct a system. L19.

■ **systematism** *noun* (*rare*) the practice of systematizing, esp. to excess M19. **systematist** /ˈsɪstəmətɪst, sɪˈstɛmətɪst/ *noun* a person who constructs or follows a system; *spec.* a biologist specializing in systematics, or (formerly) advocating a natural system of classification: E18. **systematiˈzation** *noun* (*a*) the action or process of systematizing; (*b*) a systematic arrangement, statement, etc.: E19. **systematizer** *noun* L18.

Système International /sistɛm ɛ̃tɛrnasjɔnal/ *noun phr.* M20.
[French.]
= ***International System of Units*** s.v. INTERNATIONAL *adjective.*

systemic /sɪˈstɛmɪk, -ˈstiːm-/ *adjective & noun.* E19.
[Irreg. from SYSTEM + -IC.]

▶ **A** *adjective.* **1 a** PHYSIOLOGY & MEDICINE. Of, pertaining to, or affecting the system or body as a whole; *esp.* designating the general circulation, as distinguished from the pulmonary circulation supplying the respiratory organs. E19. ▸**b** Pertaining to or affecting a particular system of bodily organs. L19. ▸**c** Of a herbicide, insecticide, or fungicide: entering the system of a plant or animal and freely transported within its tissues. M20.

2 *gen.* Of or pertaining to a system or systems; systematic. M19.

2 systemic grammar, **systemic linguistics** LINGUISTICS a method of analysis based on the conception of language as a network of systems determining the options from which speakers choose in accordance with their communicative goals.

▶ **B** *noun.* A systemic herbicide, insecticide, or fungicide. M20.

■ **systemically** *adverb* L19.

systoflex /ˈsɪstə(ʊ)flɛks/ *noun.* E20.
[from unkn. 1st elem. + FLEX *noun*[2].]
ELECTRICAL ENGINEERING. Flexible sleeving for insulating electric wires.

systole /ˈsɪst(ə)li/ *noun.* M16.
[Late Latin, from Greek *sustolē*, from *sustellein* contract.]

1 CLASSICAL PROSODY. The shortening of a vowel or syllable long by nature or position. Opp. DIASTOLE. M16.

2 PHYSIOLOGY. The phase of the heartbeat when the heart contracts and drives the blood outward. Also, any similar rhythmical contraction (formerly *esp.* that of the lungs in breathing). Opp. DIASTOLE. L16.

■ **syˈstolic** *adjective* L17.

systrophe /ˈsɪstrəfi/ *noun.* L19.
[from SYN- + Greek *strophē* turning.]
BIOLOGY. The clumping together of chloroplasts in a cell when exposed to bright light.

systyle /ˈsɪstʌɪl/ *noun & adjective.* E18.
[Latin *systylos* from Greek *sustulos*, from *sun-* SYN- + *stulos* column.]
ARCHITECTURE. (A building) having close intercolumniation such that the distance between the columns equals two diameters of a column.

syzygy /ˈsɪzɪdʒi/ *noun.* E17.
[Late Latin *syzygia* from Greek *suzugia* yoke, pair, copulation, conjunction, from *suzugos* yoked, paired, from *sun-* SYN- + stem of *zeugnunai* yoke.]

1 PROSODY. A combination of two different feet in one measure, a dipody. E17.

2 ASTRONOMY. †**a** = CONJUNCTION 2. M17–E18. ▸**b** Conjunction or opposition of two celestial objects; either of the points (in space or time) at which these take place, esp. in the case of the moon with the sun (new moon and full moon). Cf. QUADRATURE 3. E18.

3 A pair of connected or correlative things; *spec.* in GNOSTIC PHILOSOPHY, a pair of opposites or aeons. M19.

4 ZOOLOGY. **a** A suture or immovable union of two joints of a crinoid; the joints united in this way. L19. ▸**b** The conjunction of two organisms without loss of identity; in sporozoans, close attachment of pairs of gametocytes prior to fusion. L19.

■ **syˈzygial** *adjective* (ASTRONOMY & ZOOLOGY) pertaining to or of the nature of a syzygy or syzygies M19. **syˈzygium** *noun* (ZOOLOGY) = SYZYGY 4b L19.

Szechuan /sɛˈtʃwɑːn/ *adjective.* Also **Sichuan** /sɪˈtʃwɑːn/, **Szechwan**. M20.
[See below.]
Designating (food cooked in) the distinctively spicy style of cuisine originating in Szechuan, a province in SW China.

Szechuanese /sɛtʃwɑːˈniːz/ *noun & adjective.* Also **-chwa-**. E20.
[formed as prec. + -ESE.]

▶ **A** *noun.* Pl. same.

1 A native or inhabitant of Szechuan. E20.

2 The form of Chinese spoken in Szechuan. M20.

▶ **B** *attrib.* or as *adjective.* Of or pertaining to the Szechuanese or the form of Chinese spoken by them. E20.

Szechwan *adjective* var. of SZECHUAN.

Szechwanese *adjective & noun* var. of SZECHUANESE.

Szekel /ˈsɛk(ə)l/ *noun & adjective.* Also in German form **Szekler** /ˈsɛklə/. M19.
[Hungarian *Székely.*]

▶ **A** *noun.* A member of a Magyar people living in eastern Transylvania. M19.

▶ **B** *attrib.* or as *adjective.* Of or pertaining to this people. M19.

Sze Yap /siː ˈjap/ *noun & adjective.* M20.
[Chinese.]
(Designating or pertaining to) the form of Cantonese spoken in the south of Guangdong Province.

szlachta /ˈʃlaxta/ *noun.* L19.
[Polish.]
Hist. The aristocratic or landowning class in Poland before 1945.

Tt

T, t /tiː/.
The twentieth letter of the modern English alphabet and the nineteenth of the ancient Roman one, corresp. to Greek *tau*, Hebrew *taw*. The sound normally represented by the letter is a voiceless alveolar plosive consonant. In modern English T also has the sound /ʃ/ in the unstressed combinations *-tion*, *-tious*, *-tial*, *-tia*, *-tian*, *-tience*, *-tient*, after any letter except *s* (as in ***nation***, ***partial***, ***patience***, etc.), in which the /ʃ/ represents both the *t* and its following *i*. This pronunciation arises from a shift of the original Latin /t/ in these combinations to /ts/ then /s/, written *c* in French, but later in both French and English restored to *t* while still representing /s/ which, when combined with following *i* (pronounced as the semivowel /j/), became /ʃ/. After *s*, the original sound of T has remained, as in ***bestial***, ***Christian***, etc. More recently, T has developed the sound /tʃ/ when followed by *u* sounded /juː, jʊ, jʊə/ in the unstressed combinations *-tual*, *-tue*, *-tuous*, *-ture*, as in ***actual***, ***nature***, and *ti* after *s* has also sometimes become /tʃ/, as in ***question***. T is usually silent between *s* and syllabic *l* or *n*, as in ***castle***, ***fasten***, etc., between *s* and *m* in ***Christmas***, and between *f* and syllabic *n* in ***often***, ***soften***. (See also **TH**.) Pl. **tees**, **T's**, **Ts**. See also **TAU** *noun*[1], **TEE** *noun*[1].
▶ **I 1** The letter and its sound.
2 The shape of the letter. ▶**b** *ELECTRICITY.* (Cap. T.) A network of three impedances that can be represented diagrammatically as a T in which the stem and each arm is an impedance.
1 cross the t's = *dot the i's (and cross the t's)* s.v. **DOT** *verb*. **to a T** exactly, properly, to a nicety. **2 cross the T** *NAUTICAL* (of a fleet or ship) cross in front of an approaching (enemy) fleet or ship approximately at right angles, thus securing tactical advantages. **T account** *BOOKKEEPING* a standard form of ledger account with a T-shaped arrangement of lines on the page; a simplified version of this. **T-back** (*a*) a high-cut undergarment or swimming costume having only a thin strip of material passing between the buttocks; (*b*) a style of back on a bra or bikini top in which the shoulder straps meet a supporting lateral strap below the shoulder blades (forming an inverted T-shape). **T-bar** a metal bar with a T-shaped cross-section; a T-shaped fastening on a shoe (cf. ***T-strap*** below); *spec.* a type of ski-lift consisting of a series of T-shaped bars by which skiers are towed uphill. **T-bone (steak)** a beefsteak cut from the sirloin and containing a T-shaped bone. **T-connected** *adjective* (*ELECTRICITY*) connected to form a T-shaped network of impedances. **T-formation** *AMER. FOOTBALL* a T-shaped offensive formation of players. **T-junction** a T-shaped intersection (of pipes etc.); *spec.* a T-shaped road junction. **T-shaped** *adjective* having a shape or cross-section like the capital letter T; having a long straight central piece with a right-angled cross-piece at one end. **T-square** a T-shaped instrument for drawing parallel lines or right angles. **T-strap** a T-shaped instep strap on a shoe; a shoe with such a strap. **T-top** a car roof having removable panels; a car with such a roof. ***T totum***: see **TEETOTUM**.
▶ **II** Symbolical uses.
3 Used to denote serial order; applied e.g. to the twentieth (or often the nineteenth, either I or J being omitted) group or section, sheet of a book, etc. ▶**b** *ASTRONOMY.* ***T Tauri star*** /ˈtɔːrʌɪ/, any of a class of relatively young bright variable stars.
4 a *PHYSICS.* Used to denote the quantum number of isospin. ▶**b** *BACTERIOLOGY.* (Cap. T. With following numeral.) Used to denote certain strains of phages of the bacterium *Escherichia coli* much used experimentally; ***T-even***, designating the strains for which the numeral is even. ▶**c** Used to denote the time at which an event is scheduled to occur, esp. that at which a spacecraft is due to be launched. ▶**d** *BIOLOGY.* (Cap. T.) Designating lymphocytes that are derived from or have been processed by the thymus, which are responsible for cellular immune reactions.
5 *STATISTICS.* ***t test***, = ***Student's test*** s.v. **STUDENT** *noun*[2].
▶ **III 6** Abbrevs.: **T** = (*MUSIC*) tasto; taxed (officially stamped on a letter); (*MUSIC*) tempo; (*MUSIC*) tenor; (as *prefix*) tera-; (*PHYSICS*) tesla; thunder (in a ship's logbook); (*BIOLOGY*) thymine (in DNA sequences); (*PHYSICS*) time; (*LINGUISTICS*) transformational (as in ***T-rule***); (*PHOTOGRAPHY*) transmission (in ***T-stop***, a measured point on a scale of aperture values based on the actual light transmitted through a camera lens); treasury (in ***T-Bill***); tri- (in ***2,4,5-T***, 2,4,5-trichlorophenoxyacetic acid, $C_6H_2Cl_3{\cdot}O{\cdot}CH_2COOH$, a selective herbicide used esp. for controlling brushwood); (*PHYSICS & CHEMISTRY*) tritium; (*MUSIC*) tutti. **t.** = ton(s); tonne(s). **t** (*PHYSICS*) = top or truth (a quark flavour).

t' *preposition, adverb, & conjunction*: see **TO** *preposition, adverb, & conjunction*.

't *pers. pronoun* see **IT** *pers. pronoun*.

-t /t/ *suffix*[1] (not productive).
[Old English from Germanic, ult. of same origin as **-TH**[1].]
Forming abstract nouns from verbs after (orig.) velar, labial, or sibilant consonants, as ***draught***, ***drift***, ***haft***, ***might***, ***thirst***.

-t /t/ *suffix*[2] (not productive).
Later var. of **-TH**[1] after a fricative as in ***drought***, ***height***, ***sleight***, ***theft***.

-t /t/ *suffix*[3].
[Var. of **-ED**[1].]
Forming the pa. t. & pple of some weak verbs, esp. after a voiceless consonant other than /t/ (see **-ED**[1]), or as a contr. of *-ded*, *-ed* after *l*, *m*, *n*, *r* (as in ***girt***, ***sent***, ***spilt***). In some verbs existing as a parallel form to *-ed*, sometimes with difference of use, as ***leaned*** and ***leant***, ***roasted*** and ***roast***, ***spoiled*** and ***spoilt***.

TA *abbreviation*.
1 Teaching assistant, assistantship. *N. Amer.*
2 Territorial Army.
3 *PSYCHOLOGY.* Transactional analysis.

Ta *symbol*.
CHEMISTRY. Tantalum.

†**ta** *pronoun*[1] *& noun*[1], *pronoun*[2] *& noun*[2] see **THEE** *pronoun & noun*, **THOU** *pronoun & noun*[2].

ta /tɑː/ *interjection*. *colloq.* **L18.**
[Childish form of *thank you*.]
Thank you.

taaffeite /ˈtɑːfʌɪt/ *noun*. **M20.**
[from E. C. R. *Taaffe* (1898–1967), Bohemian-born Irish gemmologist + **-ITE**[1].]
MINERALOGY. A rare mauve gemstone, similar to spinel, which is a beryllium magnesium aluminate with a hexagonal crystal structure.

taaibos /ˈtʌɪbɒs/ *noun*. *S. Afr.* **E19.**
[Afrikaans, from Dutch *taai* tough + *bos* bush.]
Any of various shrubs or trees with tough branches and bark, *esp.* any of several shrubby sumacs (genus *Rhus*).

taal /tɑːl/ *noun*. *S. Afr.* Also **T-**. **L19.**
[Dutch = language, speech from Middle Dutch *tāle* = Old English *talu* **TALE** *noun*.]
the taal, Afrikaans.

TAB *abbreviation*. *Austral. & NZ.*
Totalizator Agency Board.

tab /tab/ *noun*[1]. **LME.**
[Origin uncertain; cf. **TAG** *noun*[1].]
1 a A small flap, loop, or strip attached to or projecting from an object, by which the object may be taken hold of, hung up, fastened, identified, etc. **LME.** ▶**b** A similar flap etc. serving as ornamentation on the edge or surface of a garment. **M19.** ▶**c** A pull-tab. **M20.**
2 *transf.* A small piece of something, as sod or turf. **E18.**
3 An ear. *dial. & slang.* **M19.**
4 An account, a check. Also (chiefly *N. Amer.*), a bill, a charge, a price. **L19.**
5 *MILITARY.* A coloured marking on the collar distinguishing a senior or staff officer. **E20.**
6 *AERONAUTICS.* A usu. hinged part of a control surface that modifies the action or response of the surface. **M20.**
7 A cigarette. *north. & slang.* **M20.**
8 A tablet, a pill, *esp.* one containing an illegal drug. *slang.* **M20.**

🕮 **1a** *Daily News* Strong leather tabs are . . fastened to the backs of the . . volumes. **4** M. AMIS I finished my wine and settled the tab. *New Yorker* Get this lady something to drink and put it on my tab. **keep a tab on**, **keep tabs on** *colloq.* (*a*) keep account of; (*b*) have under observation or in check. **pick up the tab** undertake to pay the bill. **8** *News of the World* I've got LSD for £5 a tab.

Comb.: **tab collar** a shirt collar whose points are fastened down.

tab /tab/ *noun*[2]. *slang.* **E20.**
[Abbreviation of **TABBY** *noun* 2.]
An elderly woman. Also (*Austral.*), a young woman or girl.

tab /tab/ *noun*[3]. *slang.* **E20.**
[Abbreviation of ***tableau curtain*** s.v. **TABLEAU**.]
THEATRICAL. A tableau curtain; a loop for suspending this.

tab /tab/ *noun*[4]. **E20.**
[Abbreviation.]
= **TABULATOR** 2.
Comb.: **tab key** a key on a typewriter or computer keyboard used to pre-set the movement of the carriage, cursor, etc.

TAB /tab/ *noun*[5]. **E20.**
[from typhoid + *A* + *B*.]
MEDICINE. A vaccine against typhoid and two forms of paratyphoid designated *A* and *B*.

tab /tab/ *verb*[1] *trans.* Infl. **-bb-**. **E19.**
[from **TAB** *noun*[1].]
1 Provide with a tab or tabs; ornament with tabs. Chiefly as ***tabbed*** *ppl adjective*. **E19.**
2 Identify, name; label. Also, watch, keep tabs on. *colloq.* (chiefly *US*). **E20.**

🕮 **2** M. PUZO He had Jordan tabbed as a . . gambler.

tab /tab/ *verb*[2] *intrans. Military slang.* Infl. **-bb-**. **L20.**
[Origin uncertain: perh. rel. to **TAB** *noun*[1].]
Esp. in the Parachute Regiment: = **YOMP** *verb*. Chiefly as ***tabbing*** *verbal noun*.

tabac /taˈbak/ *noun*[1] *& adjective*. **L19.**
[French = tobacco.]
(Of) a deep shade of brown, tobacco.

tabac /taba/ *noun*[2]. Pl. pronounced same. **E20.**
[French.]
In French-speaking countries: a tobacconist's shop.

tabacosis /tabəˈkəʊsɪs/ *noun*. Pl. **-coses** /-ˈkəʊsiːz/. **L19.**
[formed as **TABAC** *noun*[1] *& adjective* + **-OSIS**.]
MEDICINE. Lung disease caused by the inhalation of tobacco dust.

tabagie /tabaʒi/ *noun*. Pl. pronounced same. **E19.**
[French, irreg. from *tabac* tobacco.]
A group of smokers who meet together in the manner of a club.

tabanid /ˈtabənɪd, təˈbanɪd/ *adjective & noun*. **L19.**
[from Latin *tabanus* gadfly, horsefly (used as mod. Latin genus name) + **-ID**[3].]
▶ **A** *adjective*. Of, pertaining to, or designating the dipteran family Tabanidae, including horseflies and other large bloodsucking flies. **L19.**
▶ **B** *noun*. A fly of this family; a horsefly, a cleg. **L19.**

tabard /ˈtabəd, -ɑːd/ *noun*. **ME.**
[Old French *tabart* of unkn. origin.]
†**1** A coarse outer garment formerly worn by the common people or by monks and foot-soldiers. **ME.**
2 *Hist.* A short open surcoat worn by a knight over his armour and emblazoned with armorial bearings. **LME.**
3 a An official coat or jerkin worn by a herald and emblazoned with the arms of the sovereign. **L16.** ▶**b** A woman's or girl's sleeveless or short sleeved jerkin or loose overgarment. **E20.**

🕮 **3b** *Housewife* A beach tabard . . over a bikini. P. D. JAMES A dress . . topped with an elaborately patterned . . tabard.

■ **tabarded** *adjective* wearing a tabard **M19.**

tabardillo /tabɑːˈdɪl(j)əʊ, *foreign* tabarˈdiʎo/ *noun*. **E17.**
[Spanish.]
MEDICINE. A fever with a rash, common in Mexico and S. America. Now *spec.* an epidemic form of murine typhus found in Mexico.

tabaret /ˈtabərɪt/ *noun*. **L18.**
[Prob. from **TABBY** *noun & adjective*: cf. **TABINET**.]
A fabric of alternate satin and watered silk stripes used in upholstery.

Tabasco /təˈbaskəʊ/ *noun*. Also **t-**. Pl. **-os**. **L19.**
[A river and State of Mexico.]
More fully ***Tabasco pepper sauce***, ***Tabasco sauce***. (Proprietary name for) a very pungent sauce made from the pulp of the ripe fruit of *Capsicum frutescens*.

tabasheer /tabəˈʃɪə/ *noun*. Also **-shir**. **L16.**
[Portuguese *tabaxir* from Persian & Urdu *tabāšīr* ult. from Sanskrit *tvac* bark + *kṣīra* sap.]
A white siliceous concretion in the stems of bamboos, esp. *Bambusa arundinacea*, used medicinally in tropical Asia.

tabatière /tabatjɛːr/ *noun*. *rare*. Pl. pronounced same. **E19.**
[French, alt. of *tabaquière*, from *tabac* **TOBACCO**.]
A snuffbox.

tabbing /ˈtabɪŋ/ *verbal noun*. **M20.**
[from **TAB** *noun*[4] + **-ING**[1].]
The action or effect of using the tabulator on a typewriter or computer keyboard.

tabbouleh /təˈbuːleɪ/ *noun*. **M20.**
[Arab. *tabbūla*.]
A Syrian and Lebanese salad made with burghul, parsley, onion, mint, lemon juice, oil, and spices.

tabby /ˈtabi/ *noun & adjective.* L16.
[In senses A.1, B.1 from Old & mod. French *tabis*, †*atabis* (cf. medieval Latin *attabi*) from Arab. adjective *ʻattābī*, from *al-ʻAttābiyya* a quarter of Baghdad in which the fabric was manufactured. The connection of the other senses is unclear.]
► **A** *noun.* **1 a** A kind of silk taffeta, formerly striped, later with a uniform waved or watered finish. L16. ▸**b** A dress or gown made of tabby. Now *rare.* E18.
2 a An elderly spinster. Also, a spiteful or ill-natured female gossip. Chiefly *derog.* M18. ▸**b** A young woman or girl, *esp.* an attractive one. *slang.* E20.
3 = ***tabby cat*** below. L18.
4 (A) concrete made of lime, shells, gravel, and stones which dries very hard. L18.
5 ENTOMOLOGY. Any of several pyralid moths of the genera *Aglossa* and *Epizeuxis*, generally having the forewings greyish-brown, clouded with a darker colour. Usu. with qualifying word. E19.

📖 **1a** HOR. WALPOLE The Duke . . dressed in a pale blue watered tabby. **2a** SIR W. SCOTT Lady Penelope, or any other tabby of quality. **3** A. BURGESS A tabby dozed on top of a cardboard box. ***red tabby, silver tabby.***

► **B** *adjective.* **1** Made or consisting of the fabric tabby. M17.
2 Esp. of a cat: of a brownish, tawny, or grey colour, marked with darker parallel stripes or streaks; brindled. Also ***tabby-coloured***. Cf. ***tabby cat*** below. M17.

📖 **1** J. BUCHAN A parade of satin bodices and tabby petticoats. **2** *Daily News* A beautifully marked tabby tom. T. S. ELIOT Her coat is of the tabby kind, with tiger stripes.

Special collocations & comb.: **tabby cat** a domestic cat, *esp.* a female one (see also sense B.2 above). **tabby weave**, **tabby weaving** = ***plain weave***, ***plain weaving*** s.v. PLAIN *adjective*[1] & *adverb.*
■ **tabbyhood** *noun* (*derog.*, *rare*) the condition of being an elderly spinster L18.

tabby /ˈtabi/ *verb trans.* E18.
[from prec.]
1 Give a wavy appearance to (silk etc.) by calendering. E18.
2 Stripe or streak in parallel lines with darker markings. Chiefly as ***tabbied*** *ppl adjective.* M19.

📖 **2** G. W. THORNBURY Beautiful fish . . tabbied with dark veins.

tabella /təˈbɛlə/ *noun.* Pl. **-llae** /-liː/. L17.
[Latin = tablet.]
PHARMACOLOGY. = TABLET *noun* 3a.

tabellion /taˈbɛlɪən/ *noun.* LME.
[Latin *tabellio(n-)* notary, scrivener from *tabella* tablet, letter: see -ION.]
Hist. A scrivener, a subordinate notary; *esp.* in the Roman Empire and pre-revolutionary France, an official scribe with some of the functions of a notary.

taberdar /ˈtabədɑː/ *noun.* M17.
[from TABARD + -AR[3]: lit. 'one who wears a tabard'.]
Hist. A holder of any of certain scholarships of Queen's College, Oxford.

tabernacle /ˈtabənak(ə)l/ *noun.* ME.
[Old & mod. French, or Latin *tabernaculum* tent, booth, shed, dim. of *taberna* TAVERN: see -CLE.]
1 JEWISH HISTORY. A curtained tent used as a portable sanctuary for the Ark of the Covenant and other sacred furniture during the period of exodus when the Israelites lived in the wilderness. ME. ▸**b** JEWISH ANTIQUITIES. The Jewish Temple, as the place which continued the sacred functions and associations of the earlier tabernacle. LME.
2 *fig.* A dwelling-place, a place of abode; *spec.* (***a***) the dwelling-place of God; (***b***) the human body regarded as the temporary abode of the soul or of life. ME.
3 †**a** An ornate canopied structure, as a tomb or shrine. ME–L15. ▸**b** A canopied niche or recess for holding an image. LME. ▸**c** ECCLESIASTICAL. An ornamented receptacle for the pyx containing the consecrated host. LME.
4 Esp. in biblical use, a usu. portable temporary dwelling; a hut, a tent, a booth. LME.
5 a A temporary place of worship; *esp.* (*Hist.*) one used while the churches were rebuilt after the Great Fire of London in 1666. L17. ▸**b** A meeting-house or other Nonconformist place of worship. M18.
6 NAUTICAL. A socket or support for a mast hinged at its base so that it may be lowered to pass under bridges. L19.

📖 **2** R. HAKLUYT Seated a good league distant from his tabernacles. N. HAWTHORNE Fruits, milk, freshest butter, will make thy fleshy tabernacle youthful. **4** F. MORYSON The Army . . pitched their Tents or Tabernacles. **feast of Tabernacles** = SUCCOTH. **5a** A. EDGAR Not a tabernacle of canvas . . but a moveable pulpit made of wood. **6** M. CONEY Wind almost lifted the mast out of its tabernacle.

Comb.: **tabernacle-work** (***a***) ornamental carved work in a canopy over a niche, stall, or pulpit, or in a carved screen in a church; (***b***) architectural work in which tabernacles form the characteristic feature.
■ **tabernacled** *adjective* (*rare*) made with tabernacle-work, having a carved canopy LME.

tabernacle /ˈtabənak(ə)l/ *verb.* M17.
[medieval Latin *tabernaculare*, from Latin *tabernaculum*: see prec.]
1 *verb intrans.* Occupy a tabernacle, tent, or temporary dwelling; dwell for a limited time. Chiefly *fig.*, (of Christ) dwell among humankind; (of the Spirit of Christ) dwell within humankind. M17.
2 *verb trans.* Place in a tabernacle; enshrine. E19.

tabernacular /tabəˈnakjʊlə/ *adjective. rare.* L17.
[from Latin *tabernaculum*: see TABERNACLE *noun*, -AR[1].]
1 Of the style or character of an architectural tabernacle; constructed or decorated with openwork and tracery. L17.
2 Savouring of the language of a tabernacle or Nonconformist conventicle. *contempt.* M19.

tabes /ˈteɪbiːz/ *noun.* L16.
[Latin = wasting away.]
1 MEDICINE. Slow progressive emaciation of the body or its parts. Now *rare* exc. in mod. Latin names of particular conditions. L16.
2 Decay of trees or other plants caused by disease or injury. *rare.* M19.
1 tabes dorsalis /dɔːˈseɪlɪs/ [late Latin = DORSAL *adjective*] = ***locomotor*** ATAXIA. **tabes mesenterica** /mɛsɛnˈtɛrɪkə/ [mod. Latin] tuberculosis of the mesenteric lymph nodes.
■ **tabetic** /təˈbɛtɪk/ *adjective & noun* (***a***) *adjective* of, pertaining to, or affected with tabes (now usu. *spec.*, tabes dorsalis); (***b***) *noun* a person affected with tabes (dorsalis): M19.

tabescent /təˈbɛs(ə)nt/ *adjective.* L19.
[Latin *tabescent-* pres. ppl stem of *tabescere* begin to waste away, from *tabere* waste away: see -ENT.]
Wasting away.

tabi /ˈtɑːbi/ *noun.* Pl. same, **-s**. E17.
[Japanese.]
A thick-soled Japanese ankle sock with a separate stall for the big toe.

tabid /ˈtabɪd/ *adjective.* Now *rare.* M17.
[Latin *tabidus* wasting, from *tabere* waste, melt: see -ID[1].]
1 Orig. MEDICINE. Affected with tabes; wasted by disease; consumptive. M17.
2 Causing consumption or wasting. Formerly also, decomposed. M17.
3 Of the nature of tabes; characterized by wasting away. M18.

tabific /təˈbɪfɪk/ *adjective. rare.* M17.
[Latin *tabificus*, from TABES: see -FIC.]
Causing or characteristic of tabes; emaciating.

tabinet /ˈtabɪnɪt/ *noun.* L18.
[App. arbitrarily from TABBY *noun & adjective*: cf. TABARET.]
A watered fabric of silk and wool resembling poplin. (Chiefly associated with Ireland.)

tabl /tɑːb(ə)l/ *noun.* L19.
[Arab.: see ATABAL.]
In the Middle East and N. Africa: a drum usu. played with the hand.

tabla /ˈtʌblə, ˈtʌblɑː/ *noun.* M19.
[Persian & Urdu *tabla(h)*, Hindi *tablā* from Arab. *ṭabl*: see prec.]
A pair of small hand drums used in Indian music, one of which is larger than the other; the smaller of these drums.

tablature /ˈtablətʃə/ *noun.* L16.
[French, from Italian *tavolatura* a prick-song, from *tavolare* set to music.]
1 MUSIC. Musical notation, *esp.* of a kind that differs from ordinary staff notation (now chiefly *Hist.*); *spec.* a form of notation used esp. for the lute or (more recently) the guitar, in which lines denote the instrument's strings, and markings indicate fingering and other features; a similar notation for the flute and other wind instruments, in which lines denote the instrument's holes. L16.
2 A tabular formation bearing an inscription or design; a tablet. *arch.* E17.
3 †**a** A painting or picture. E–M18. ▸**b** *collect.* Work consisting of or resembling paintings or pictures. Now *rare.* E18. ▸**c** *fig.* A picture or representation formed by description or in the imagination. L18.

📖 **1** *Early Music* Our edition includes voice and tablature. *Dirty Linen* Three formats—a free . . guitar tablature booklet comes with each.

table /ˈteɪb(ə)l/ *noun.* OE.
[Latin *tabula* plank, tablet, list; in Middle English superseded by forms from Old & mod. French *table* from Latin: cf. TABLET *noun.*]
► **I** A flat slab or board, or object resembling this.
1 A flat and comparatively thin piece of wood, stone, metal, or other solid material; a board, plate, slab, or tablet, *esp.* one forming a surface used for a particular purpose. Now *rare.* OE.
2 *spec.* **a** A tablet bearing or intended to bear an inscription or device, as any of the stone tablets used for the Ten Commandments, a memorial tablet on a wall, or a notice-board. *arch.* OE. ▸†**b** A small portable tablet for writing on. ME–M17. ▸**c** CLASSICAL HISTORY. In *pl.* The tablets on which certain collections of ancient Greek and Roman laws were inscribed; *transf.* the laws themselves. E18.
3 †**a** In *pl.* Backgammon; any similar game. Also, the pieces used in backgammon. ME–E19. ▸**b** *sing.* & in *pl.* A board, esp. one consisting of two or more folding leaves, for backgammon, chess, or any similar game. Also (*sing.*), each of the folding leaves or (later) sections of such a board. LME.
4 ARCHITECTURE. **a** A horizontal projecting member, as a string-course or cornice. ME. ▸**b** A flat usu. rectangular vertical surface, sunk into or projecting beyond the surrounding surface; a panel. L17.
†**5** A board or other flat surface on which a picture is painted; the picture itself. LME–E18.
6 PALMISTRY. A quadrangular space between certain lines in the palm of the hand. LME.
7 ANATOMY. Either of the two dense bony layers of the skull separated by the diploe. LME.
8 A flat plate, board, etc., used with or forming part of a mechanism or apparatus; *spec.* (***a***) a flat metal plate for supporting something to be worked on; (***b***) the upper part of the soundboard in an organ, perforated with holes for admitting air to the pipes. LME.
9 a In full ***table diamond***. A diamond cut with a large flat upper (and sometimes lower) surface surrounded by smaller facets. L15. ▸**b** The flat surface of a table diamond or other gem. M18.
10 A flat elevated tract of land; a tableland, a plateau; a flat mountain-top. L16.
11 A large flat circular sheet of crown glass. L17. ▸**b** A crystal of flattened or short prismatic form. L18.
12 (Usu. **T-**.) *The* constellation Mensa. Also ***Table Mountain***. M19.

📖 **2a** G. P. R. JAMES The statue of Moses breaking the tables. **3b** *Daily Telegraph* The board . . is divided into four 'tables' of six points each. D. HOGAN Men shifted chess pieces on small tables. **8** E. H. KNIGHT The shaping-machine . . has two tables . . both of which are movable. V. AUSTIN All cutting with a chisel should be done on the table. **10** H. F. TOZER A valley . . filled . . by a level table of land.

► **II** A raised board at which people may sit.
13 A piece of furniture consisting of a raised flat top of wood, stone, or other solid material, supported usu. on one or more legs, and used to place things on for various purposes; *spec.* (***a***) one on which food is served, and at or around which people sit at a meal; (***b***) in a church, that on which the elements are placed at the Eucharist, esp. when the rite is not regarded as sacrificial (more fully ***the holy table***, ***the Lord's table***); (***c***) one on which a game, esp. a game of chance, is played; (***d***) one on which a surgeon operates or on which a body is laid for post-mortem examination; (***e***) one around which discussions or negotiations are held. ME.
14 *transf.* **a** A company of people at a table. *spec.* (***a***) a group seated at a table for dinner etc.; (***b***) an official body of people who transact business seated around a table (cf. BOARD *noun* 7). ME. ▸**b** Provision of food for meals; supply of food in a household etc., esp. as hospitality for a guest. LME. ▸**c** In a Presbyterian church, each dispensing of the sacrament. Now *rare.* E18. ▸**d** BRIDGE. The dummy hand. M20.

📖 **13** *Times* He cleared the table to go 6–3 ahead. *Daily Express* Bosses appealed to striking workers to resume negotiations . . . 'Come back to the table before more people die.' R. BANKS The long white table where refreshments were being set out. M. KRAMER Brought by waiters to the table one course at a time. ***bird table***, ***card-table***, ***coffee-table***, ***cold table***, ***Communion table***, ***dining-table***, ***dressing-table***, ***gateleg table***, ***high table***, ***occasional table***, ***operating-table***, ***picnic table***, ***side-table***, ***snooker-table***, ***toilet table***, ***top table***, ***trestle table***, ***writing table***, etc. **14a** *Holiday Which?* At 11 p.m., . . some tables are singing heart-rending tunes. **b** J. M. BRINNIN The Captain's Table . . tended . . to reflect his own personal tastes.

► **III** A tabulated arrangement or statement.
15 A systematic display of numbers, words, or items of any kind, in a definite and compact form, so as clearly to exhibit some set of facts or relations; *esp.* a display of information in columns and lines occupying a single defined area. LME. ▸†**b** = ***table of contents*** s.v. CONTENT *noun*[1] 1b. LME–E19. ▸**c** A list, written or recited, of multiplications of two factors, weights, measures, etc. Usu. in *pl.* Cf. MULTIPLICATION ***table***. L17. ▸**d** = ***league table*** s.v. LEAGUE *noun*[2]. M20. ▸**e** COMPUTING. A collection of data stored in memory as a series of records, each defined by a unique key stored with it. M20.

📖 **15** A. KOESTLER A work on trigonometry with extensive tables. *Which?* Telephones . . in coloured bands in the Table are recommended. ***log table***, ***periodic table***, ***timetable***, etc. **c** *Times Educ. Suppl.* Learning to use a calculator is an acceptable replacement for class chanting of tables. **d** *World Soccer* Everton suffered three league defeats and tumbled down the table.

Phrases: **at table** eating a meal at a table. **first table** the first of two divisions of the Decalogue, relating to religious duties. ***lay*** *all one's cards on the table*, *lay one's cards on the table*: see CARD *noun*² 1. **lay on the table** (*a*) leave or postpone for the present; postpone indefinitely; (*b*) present for immediate discussion. **lie on the table** be postponed, esp. indefinitely. *life-table*: see LIFE *noun*. **on the table** under consideration or discussion. †**pair of tables** a backgammon board (cf. sense 3 above). *Peutingerian table*. *plane-table*: see PLANE *adjective*. **pleasures of the table** good food and drink as a source of enjoyment. *Prutenic tables*: see PRUTENIC *adjective*. *put all one's cards on the table*, *put one's cards on the table*: see CARD *noun*² 1. *rotary table*: see ROTARY *adjective*. ROUND TABLE. *Rudolphine tables*. *sand-table*: see SAND *noun*. **second table** (*a*) the second of two divisions of the decalogue, relating to moral duties; (*b*) a servants' table at a meal, *spec.* the senior of two servants' tables. **the Twelve Tables** the set of laws drawn up in Rome in 451–450 BC, forming an important source of Roman jurisprudence. **turn the tables (on)** reverse one's relations (with), esp. by turning an inferior position into a superior one (orig. in backgammon). **under the table** *colloq.* drunk to the point of insensibility. **under-the-table** *adjective* (of a deal etc.) clandestine, hidden, kept secret.

Comb.: **table bell** *Hist.* a small handbell placed on a table for summoning attendants; **table-board** †(*a*) a board for backgammon or any similar game; (*b*) a board forming the top of a table; a table (*obsolete* exc. *dial.*); (*c*) *US* board consisting of meals without lodging; **table-book** (now *rare*) a small book for making notes or memoranda; **table-centre** an ornamental piece of embroidery, decorated work, etc., for the centre of a table; **table centrepiece** a decorative object, esp. one arrayed with flowers etc., placed at the centre of a table; **table-clock** a clock that may be placed on a table; **tablecloth** a cloth for covering a table, *esp.* one spread over the top of a table for a meal; **table-cover** a cloth used to cover a table, esp. permanently or when not in use for meals; **table-cut** *adjective* (of a diamond or other precious stone) cut in the form of a table (see sense 9 above); **table-decker** (now *rare*) an attendant, esp. in the royal household, who lays the table for meals; **table desk** (*a*) a desk with a broad, flat top; (*b*) a kind of folding writing-box that opens to provide a sloping desktop for use on a table; *table diamond*: see sense 9a above; **table game** a game played on a table or similar surface, usu. with balls, counters, or other pieces; **table-hop** *verb intrans.* (*colloq.* chiefly *N. Amer.*) socialize in a restaurant by going from table to table; **table jelly** (a preparation for) a flavoured jelly served as a dessert; **table knife** a knife used at a meal, esp. in eating a main course; **tableland** (*a*) an extensive elevated region of land with a generally level surface; a plateau; (*b*) elevated level ground; **table licence** a licence to serve alcoholic drinks only with meals; **table linen** linen for use at table, as tablecloths, napkins, etc.; **table-maid** a female domestic servant who lays the table and waits at meals; †**tableman** a piece used in a board game, esp. backgammon; **table manners** proper behaviour or deportment while eating at table; **table-mat** a mat laid on a table to protect it from hot dishes etc.; **table-money** (*a*) a special extra allowance of money made to higher officers in the army etc. for official hospitality; (*b*) a charge made in some clubs for the use of the dining-room; **tablemount** *Oceanography* = GUYOT; **table-mountain** (*a*) a flat-topped mountain; (*b*) see sense 12 above; **table-moving** = *table-turning* below; **table-music** music printed in parts, so that it may be performed by people seated at a table; *table napkin*: see NAPKIN 1; **Table Office** in the House of Commons, the office where the civil servants work who prepare the notice papers and the order book; **table-plan** a seating plan for those attending a formal meal; **table-plate** (*a*) articles of usu. silver or gold plate, for use at meals; (*b*) a plate from which food is eaten at table; **table-rapper** a person who practises table-rapping; **table-rapping** the production of raps or knocking sounds on a table without apparent physical means, ascribed by some to departed spirits, and used as a supposed means of communication with them; **table ruby** a ruby cut with a large flat upper surface surrounded by smaller facets (cf. sense 9a above); **table salt** powdered or easily powdered salt for use at table; **tablescape** a decorative arrangement of ornaments or other objects on a tabletop; **table-screen** (*a*) a trestle table in a woolshed; (*b*) a small Chinese porcelain tile designed to be placed vertically on a table to protect other items from sunlight; **table-service** (*a*) service or attendance at table; (*b*) a set of utensils for use at table, as a dinner service; **table-setting** (*a*) the act of setting or laying a table; (*b*) the cutlery etc. required to set a place at table; **table-shore** *Nautical* a low level shore; *table skittles*: see SKITTLE *noun* 1a; **tablespoon** a large spoon (larger than a dessertspoon) for serving food; also, a tablespoonful; **tablespoonful** the amount a tablespoon will hold (a recognized measure for culinary ingredients etc.); **table stakes** a method of controlling stakes at poker; **table-stone** a flat stone, *esp.* (*Archaeology*) one supported by two or more upright stones, the capping stone of a dolmen; **table talk** talk at table; miscellaneous informal conversation at meals; **table talker** *rare* a person who talks informally at table, *esp.* one who is skilled at this; **table tape** *Computing* a magnetic tape containing tabulated numerical information; **table tennis** an indoor game based on lawn tennis, played with small rubber- or plastic-covered bats and a ball bounced on a table divided by a net; ping-pong; **table-tilting**, **table-tipping** the tilting or tipping of a table by supposed spiritual agency; **table-tomb** a gravestone or tomb containing a burial-chest with a flat top like a table; **table-turner** a person who practises table-turning; **table-turning** the action of turning or moving a table without apparently adequate means, ascribed by some to spiritual agency; **tableware** dishes, plates, knives, forks, etc., for use at meals; **table-water** water, esp. bottled mineral water, suitable for drinking at table; **table wine** (an) ordinary wine suitable for drinking with a meal.

■ **tableful** *noun* the amount or number that a table will hold or accommodate; as many as can be seated at a table; as many or much as can fit on a table: M16. **tablewise** *adverb* in the manner or form of a table LME.

table /ˈteɪb(ə)l/ *verb*. LME.
[from the noun.]
1 *verb trans.* Enter in a table or list; tabulate. Now *rare*. LME.
2 a *verb trans.* Provide (a guest or customer) with food or hospitality at table; provide with daily meals, board. Now *rare*. LME. ▸**b** *verb intrans.* Have a meal, dine; eat habitually (*at* or *with*). Now *rare* or *obsolete*. M16.
3 *verb trans.* & †*intrans.* *Carpentry.* Join (timbers) firmly together by means of alternate flat oblong projections and recesses which interlock. L16.
4 *verb trans.* Picture, depict. Now *rare* or *obsolete*. E17.
5 *verb trans.* Place or lay on a table; *spec.* lay (an appeal, proposal, etc.) on a table for discussion or consideration; bring forward or submit for discussion. Also, postpone consideration of (a matter). Cf. *lay on the table* s.v. TABLE *noun*. E18.
6 *verb trans.* *Nautical.* Strengthen (a sail) with a broad hem. L18.

> **5** *Times* Lord Salisbury has tabled . . a motion for the appointment of a Select Committee. *Time Out* Tabling Parliamentary questions about the total cost.

tableau /ˈtabləʊ, *foreign* tablo/ *noun*. Pl. **-eaux** /-əʊz, *foreign* -o/. L17.
[French from Old French *tablel* dim. of *table* TABLE *noun*: see -EL².]
1 A picture; *fig.* a picturesque presentation or description. L17.
2 A table, a schedule; an official list. L18. ▸**b** *Math.* In full ***simplex tableau***. A table displaying the constraints in problems of the type soluble by the simplex method. M20.
3 a A group of people etc. forming a picturesque scene. E19. ▸**b** = ***tableau vivant*** below. E19. ▸**c** *Theatrical.* A motionless representation of the action at some (esp. critical) stage in a play; a stage direction for this. Also (*transf.*), the sudden creation of a striking or dramatic situation. M19.
4 *Cards.* The arrangement of the cards as laid out in a game of patience. L19.

> **1** *Apollo* One tableau showed the costumes that might have been worn to Madame Bovary's . . wedding. **3b** J. Baldwin We . . stood there as though we were posing for a tableau. **c** R. Lindner They faced each other, frozen in a tableau of mutual hatred. *Dance* A succession of tableaux and mock ballets.

Phrases: ***tableau vivant*** /tablo vivɑ̃, tabləʊ ˈviːvɒ̃/, pl. ***-x -s*** (pronounced same), [lit. 'living picture'] a silent and motionless representation of a character, scene, incident, etc., by a person or group of people; *transf.* a picturesque actual scene.
Comb.: **tableau curtain** *Theatrical* each of a pair of curtains drawn open by a diagonal cord.

tabled /ˈteɪb(ə)ld/ *adjective*. LME.
[from TABLE *noun*, *verb*: see -ED², -ED¹.]
Made in or into the form of a table or flat surface; shaped like a table.

table d'hôte /ˈtɑːb(ə)l dəʊt, *foreign* tablə doːt/ *noun phr.* E17.
[French = host's table.]
Orig., a common table for guests at a hotel or eating-house. Now usu., a meal at a hotel, restaurant, etc., consisting of a set menu at a fixed price.

tablement /ˈteɪb(ə)lm(ə)nt/ *noun*. ME.
[from TABLE *noun* + -MENT, after Latin *tabulamentum*.]
Architecture. = TABLE *noun* 4a. Also, a foundation, a basement.

tabler /ˈteɪblə/ *noun*¹. M16.
[from TABLE *noun*, *verb* + -ER¹.]
†**1** A player at backgammon. M–L16.
2 A person who regularly eats at another's table for payment. Now *rare* or *obsolete*. L16.
3 A person who tables a motion, resolution, etc. E20.
4 (**T-**.) A member of the Round Table association; a Round Tabler. M20.

†**tabler** *noun*² see TABLIER.

tablet /ˈtablɪt/ *noun*. ME.
[Old French *tablete* (mod. *tablette*) from Proto-Romance dim. of Latin *tabula* TABLE *noun*: see -ET¹. Cf. TABLETTE.]
1 a A small flat slab of stone, metal, or wood bearing or intended to bear an inscription, a carving, or a picture. ME. ▸**b** A smooth stiff sheet for writing on, usu. either of two or more linked together, formerly made of clay or wax-covered wood, latterly of ivory, cardboard, etc. ME. ▸**c** (A slab used as) a roofing or flooring tile. LME. ▸**d** Usu. with specifying word. A pad of paper. *N. Amer.* L19. ▸**e** A small metal disc used like a staff (see STAFF *noun*¹ 10) on a single-track railway. L19. ▸**f** A rigid card used in tablet-weaving. E20. ▸**g** *Computing.* A flat, usu. rectangular surface on which a stylus, one's finger, etc. may be moved in order to position a cursor on a VDU. M20.
†**2** A flat ornament of precious metal or jewellery, worn about the person. LME–E17.
3 a A small flat or compressed piece of some solid substance; *spec.* (*a*) a measured quantity of a medicine or drug, compressed into a solid flattish round or oval shape and designed to be swallowed whole; (*b*) a flat cake of soap. LME. ▸**b** A type of crumbly fudge (or formerly, hardbake) made in or suitable for cutting into tablets; a piece of this. Chiefly *Scot.* M18. ▸**c** A piece of compressed moulding material of standard size, shape, etc., ready for further processing. Cf. PREFORM *noun* 1. M20.
4 *Architecture.* = TABLE *noun* 4. L18.

> **1a** P. Mailloux A tablet in the . . Square . . commemorates the martyrdom. **votive tablet** (now *arch.* or *Hist.*) an inscribed panel formerly hung in a temple after deliverance from shipwreck, a dangerous illness, etc. **b** *Chambers's Journal* Nearly forty thousand inscribed tablets of baked clay. **d** T. McGuane Left me with a pencil and a lined tablet. **3a** *Which?* The tablets contain . . a bulking agent and dextrose. *Health Now* A pancreatin tablet after meals can help.

Comb.: **tablet paper** *US* notepaper from a writing-pad; **tablet-weaving** an early method of weaving, in which warp-threads are passed through holes in a number of parallel tablets, which are then rotated to form sheds.

tablet /ˈtablɪt/ *verb*. M19.
[from prec.]
1 *verb trans.* Provide with a tablet, *esp.* one bearing an inscription; affix a tablet to. M19.
2 *verb trans.* & *intrans.* Make (a medicine, drug, etc.) into a tablet. L19.

tabletop /ˈteɪb(ə)ltɒp/ *noun* & *adjective*. E19.
[from TABLE *noun* + TOP *noun*¹.]
▶ **A** *noun.* The top or upper surface of a table; a flat top of a hill, rock, etc. E19.
▶ **B** *adjective.* That takes place on or that can be placed or used on a tabletop; *spec.* designating or pertaining to photography of a subject which can be contained on a tabletop, esp. photography of a small-scale model which gives the illusion of a larger subject. E20.
■ **tabletopped** *adjective* having a flat top like a table M19.

tablette /ˈtablɛt, -ɪt/ *noun*. E18.
[French: see TABLET *noun*.]
1 = TABLET *noun* 1b. E18.
2 = TABLET *noun* 3a. E18.
3 *Architecture.* = TABLE *noun* 4. E18.

tablier /ˈtablɪeɪ; *foreign* tablje (*pl. same*)/ *noun*. In sense 1 also (earlier) †**-ler**. ME.
[Old & mod. French, ult. from Latin *tabula*: see TABLE *noun*, -ER².]
†**1** A backgammon board or chessboard. Also, backgammon. ME–L15.
2 *Hist.* A part of a woman's dress resembling an apron; the front of a skirt having the form of an apron. M19.
3 *Anthropology.* An extension of the labia minora characteristic of Khoisan women. L19.

tablina *noun* pl. of TABLINUM.

tabling /ˈteɪblɪŋ/ *noun*. LME.
[from TABLE *noun*, *verb* + -ING¹.]
1 The action of setting down or entering in a table; tabulation. Also, the action of laying a proposal etc. on the table. Now *rare*. LME.
2 *Architecture.* The making of a table or horizontal projecting member; such a member. LME.
†**3** The action of playing at tables (see TABLE *noun* 3a). M16–E17.
4 The action of providing or fact of being provided with meals; boarding, board. Now *rare* or *obsolete*. M16.
5 *Nautical.* A broad hem made at the edge of a sail to strengthen it. M18.
6 Tables collectively; accommodation of tables. L19.

tablinum /təˈblʌɪnəm/ *noun*. Pl. **-na** /-nə/. E19.
[Latin, from *tabula* TABLE *noun*.]
Roman Antiquities. An apartment or recess in an ancient Roman house, opening out of the atrium and containing the family archives, statues, etc.

tabloid /ˈtablɔɪd/ *noun*. L19.
[from TABLET *noun* + -OID, orig. proprietary name of a medicinal or pharmaceutical preparation sold in tablet form.]
1 A small (medicinal) tablet. Also *fig.*, anything in a compressed or concentrated form (freq. *attrib.*). L19.
2 A newspaper, usu. popular in style with easily assimilable news and features, bold headlines, large photographs, and pages half the size of those of the average broadsheet. E20.

> **1** Taffrail Morphia tabloids were served out . . to badly injured men. *Melody Maker* Playing . . 'Three Blind Mice' . . as a tabloid Hungarian Rhapsody. **2** V. Glendinning When he married . . a girl . . half his age, the tabloids made the most of it. ***tabloid journalism***, ***tabloid journalist***, ***tabloid newspaper***, ***tabloid press***.

■ **tabloiˈdese** *noun* the style of writing characteristic of tabloid newspapers L20. **tabloiˈdesque** *adjective* resembling a tabloid newspaper, esp. in the sensationalized reporting of news L20. **tabloidiˈzation** *noun* (*a*) compression of literature etc. into short and easily assimilated form; (*b*) change in style and content from the factual to the sensational, esp. in television news: M20.

tabnab /ˈtabnab/ *noun*. *Nautical slang*. M20.
[Origin unkn.]
A cake, a bun, a pastry; a savoury snack.

taboo /tə'buː/ *adjective & noun.* Also **tabu**, (chiefly *NZ*) **tapu** /'tɑːpuː/. L18.
[Tongan *tabu*.]
▶ **A** *adjective.* **1** Set apart for or consecrated to a special use or purpose; forbidden to general use or to a particular person or class of people; inviolable, sacred; forbidden, unlawful. Also, (of a person) prohibited from food or from certain actions. L18.
2 *transf. & fig.* Esp. of a word, topic, or activity: avoided or prohibited, esp. by social custom. E19.

> **2** *Times* In the bedroom it is allowed; in the bathroom it is taboo. *Mother & Baby* Ski-ing and hang-gliding are absolutely taboo during pregnancy.

▶ **B** *noun.* **1** The putting of a person or thing under temporary or permanent prohibition or interdict, esp. as a social custom; the fact or condition of being taboo; a customary prohibition or interdict. Also, the system or custom, esp. in certain societies, by which such prohibitions occur. L18.
2 *transf. & fig.* Prohibition or interdiction of the use or practice of anything; ostracism; *spec.* a prohibition of the use of certain words, topics, etc., esp. in social conversation. M19.

> **1** A. STORR A totem . . is protected by taboos which generally forbid . . even touching it. **2** A. STEVENS The repressive taboo which rendered all sexual experience unspeakable.

¶ Orig. a social practice of various Pacific islands, as New Zealand, Melanesia, Polynesia, etc.
■ **tabooism** *noun* a system of taboo L19.

taboo /tə'buː/ *verb trans.* Also **tabu**, (chiefly *NZ*) **tapu** /'tɑːpuː/. L18.
[from the noun.]
1 Put under a (literal) taboo. L18.
2 *transf. & fig.* **a** Forbid or debar by personal or social influence; put under a social ban; ostracize, boycott. L18. ▸**b** Give a sacred or privileged character to (a thing) and so restrict its use; forbid, prohibit (*to*). E19.

> **1** F. B. JEVONS On the day of a chief's decease work is tabooed. M. DIBDIN He had broken the rules of the tribe and had been tabooed. **2a** *Nature* Human sex play has a large, though tabooed, orogenital component. **b** J. R. LOWELL That sacred enclosure of respectability was tabooed to us.

taboot /tɑː'buːt/ *noun*¹. E17.
[from Arab. (Urdu & Persian) *tābūt* coffin, box, Ark of the Covenant, ult. from Egyptian.]
A box or coffin sacred to Muslims; *spec.* a box, representing the tomb of Husain, which is carried in procession through the streets during Muharram.

taboot /'tɑːbuːt/ *noun*². M19.
[Arab., abbreviation of *tābūt raf al-miyāh* lit. 'box for raising water', Archimedes screw: see prec.]
A form of water-wheel used in Egypt.

taboparesis /ˌteɪbəʊpə'riːsɪs/ *noun.* E20.
[from TABES + -O- + PARESIS.]
MEDICINE. A form of neurosyphilis combining features of tabes dorsalis and general paresis.
■ Also **tabopa'ralysis** *noun* E20.

tabor /'teɪbə/ *noun.* Also †**tabour**. ME.
[Old French *tabur, tabour*, beside *tanbor, tamb(o)ur*, app. of Oriental origin: cf. Persian *tabīra, tabūrāk* drum, perh. infl. by Arab. *tunbūr* a kind of lute or lyre.]
Hist. **1** A drum. Later *spec.*, a small drum, used esp. to accompany a pipe or trumpet; a tabret. ME.
2 A player on a tabor. *rare.* LME.

tabor /'teɪbə/ *verb intrans.* Now *rare.* Also †**tabour**. ME.
[from prec. or from Old French *taborer*.]
Play or beat on or as on a tabor; drum.
■ **taborer** *noun* (*obsolete* exc. *Hist.*) a person who plays a tabor; a drummer: ME.

†**taborin** *noun.* L15–L19.
[French (mod. *tambourin*), from Old French *tabour* TABOR *noun.*]
A small drum struck with one drumstick and used to accompany a flute which the same person plays with the other hand.

Taborite /'tabərʌɪt/ *noun.* M17.
[German *Taboriten* pl. from Czech *táborite* (sing. *táborita*), from *tábor* from Hungarian = camp, encampment, so called from their encampment on a craggy height, perh. also with allus. to Mount Tabor, the traditional site of Christ's transfiguration: see -ITE¹.]
Hist. A member of the extreme party of the Hussites.

tabot /ta'bɒt/ *noun.* L17.
[Geez: cf. TABOOT *noun*¹.]
A box, representing the Ark of the Covenant, which stands on the altar in an Ethiopian church.

†**tabour** *noun, verb* vars. of TABOR *noun, verb.*

tabouret /'tabərɛt, -reɪ/ *noun.* M17.
[French, dim. of *tabour*: see TABOR *noun*, -ET¹.]
1 A low backless seat or stool for one person. M17.
2 A small table, esp. one used as a stand for house-plants; a bedside table. *US.* E20.

tabret /'tabrɪt/ *noun.* LME.
[from TABOR *noun* + -ET¹.]
1 *Hist.* A small tabor; a timbrel. LME.
†**2** A performer on a tabret. LME–M17.

Tabriz /tə'briːz/ *adjective & noun.* E20.
[A city in NW Iran.]
(Designating) a carpet or rug made in Tabriz, the older styles of which often have a rich decorative medallion pattern.

tab show /'tab ʃəʊ/ *noun phr. US slang.* M20.
[from TAB(LOID + SHOW *noun*¹.]
A short version of a musical, *esp.* one performed by a travelling company.

tabu *adjective & noun, verb* var. of TABOO *adjective & noun, verb.*

tabula /'tabjʊlə/ *noun.* Pl. **-lae** /-liː/. M16.
[Latin: see TABLE *noun.*]
1 a *tabula rasa* /'rɑːzə/ [lit. 'scraped'], a tablet from which the writing has been erased, ready to be written on again; a blank tablet; *fig.* a clean slate; a mind having no innate ideas (as in some views of the human mind at birth). M16. ▸**b** An ancient writing-tablet; *transf.* a body of laws inscribed on a tablet. Cf. TABLE *noun* 2b, c, TABLET *noun* 1b. L19. ▸**c *tabula gratulatoria*** /ˌgratjʊlə'tɔːrɪə/ [late Latin, fem. of *gratulator* congratulatory], a list in a Festschrift of the people and institutions who have subscribed to the publication. M20.
2 *ANATOMY & ZOOLOGY.* A thin flat structure; *esp.* (**a**) = TABLE *noun* 7; (**b**) a horizontal septum in a coral. M19.

> **1a** *Nation* France had become a *Tabula rasa*, and everything had to be reorganized.

tabular /'tabjʊlə/ *adjective.* M17.
[Latin *tabularis*, from *tabula* TABLE *noun*: see -AR¹.]
1 Having the form of a table, tablet, or slab; broad and flat; consisting of, or tending to split into, pieces of this form; *spec.* (of a crystal etc.) of a short prismatic form with a broad flat base and top. M17.
2 a Of a number, quantity, etc.: entered in, or calculated by means of, a table or tables. E18. ▸**b** *PRINTING.* Of matter to be printed: organized in the form of a table. L18. ▸**c** Of the nature of or pertaining to a table, scheme, or systematic display; set down or arranged systematically, as in lines and columns. E19.

> **1** H. R. SCHOOLCRAFT At the head of the grave a tabular piece of cedar . . is set. J. D. DANA Levynite occurs in crystals, usually tabular. **tabular iceberg**, **tabular berg** a flat-topped iceberg which has broken away from an ice-shelf. **tabular spar** the mineral wollastonite. **2c** J. BENTHAM A set of systematic and tabular diagrams.

■ **tabularly** *adverb* M19.

tabulary /'tabjʊləri/ *noun.* M17.
[Latin *tabularium* record-office, archives, from *tabula* TABLE *noun*: see -ARY¹, -ARIUM.]
ROMAN ANTIQUITIES. A place where the public records were kept in ancient Rome or (later) elsewhere.

tabulary /'tabjʊləri/ *adjective.* Now *rare.* L16.
[formed as TABULAR: see -ARY².]
= TABULAR 2a, c.

tabulate /'tabjʊlət/ *adjective.* L16.
[Late Latin *tabulatus* pa. pple of *tabulare*: see next, -ATE².]
†**1** Formed of tables or panels; panelled. Only in L16.
2 Formed like a tablet; broad and flat, tabular. L16.
3 *ZOOLOGY.* Having horizontal septa or partitions, as certain fossil corals. M19.

tabulate /'tabjʊleɪt/ *verb trans.* E17.
[Late Latin *tabulat-* pa. ppl stem of *tabulare*, from Latin *tabula*: see TABLE *noun*, -ATE³.]
†**1** Enter on a roll. *Scot.* E17–M18.
2 Shape with a flat top or upper surface. Also, compose of thin parallel layers. Only as ***tabulated ppl adjective***. L17.
3 Put into tabular form; arrange or exhibit (facts or figures) in a table; draw up a table of. M18.

> **2** R. J. SULLIVAN The zoned or tabulated form of the onyx. **3** W. C. ROBERTS-AUSTIN The results, tabulated or plotted into curves.

tabulation /tabjʊ'leɪʃ(ə)n/ *noun.* M17.
[from prec.: see -ATION.]
1 The action or process of tabulating something; arrangement in the form of a table or systematic display. M17.
2 *ARCHITECTURE.* Division into successive levels by tables or horizontal members. L19.

tabulator /'tabjʊleɪtə/ *noun.* L19.
[formed as prec.: see -OR.]
1 A person who tabulates data etc.; one who draws up a table or scheme. L19.
2 A machine or device which tabulates data etc.; *spec.* a key on a typewriter or computer keyboard (formerly, a separate device on a typewriter) used to pre-set the movement of the carriage, cursor, etc., in tabular work, indentation, etc. Also (*COMPUTING*), a machine which produces lists, tables, or totals from a data-storage medium such as punched cards or tape. L19.

> **2** *Daily Telegraph* Silver Reed . . Typewriter . . with many features, including 8-position pre-set tabulator.

tabulatory /'tabjʊlət(ə)ri/ *adjective. rare.* E20.
[formed as TABULATE *verb* + -ORY².]
Relating to or consisting in tabulation.

tabule /'tabjuːl/ *noun.* L19.
[from Latin *tabula*: see TABLE *noun.*]
A medicine or drug prepared in a flattened form; a tablet.

Tabun /'tɑːbʊn/ *noun.* M20.
[German, of unkn. origin.]
An organophosphorus nerve gas developed in Germany in the 1930s.

tacamahac /'takəməhak/ *noun.* Also **tacamahaca** /takəmə'hɑːkə/. L16.
[Spanish †*tacamahaca* (now *tacamaca*) from Aztec *tecomahiyac*.]
1 Orig., the aromatic resin of the gumbo-limbo, *Bursera simaruba* (family Burseraceae), used for incense. In later use, any of various similar resins obtained from other W. Indian and S. American trees of the genus *Bursera* and the allied genus *Protium*, and from Indo-Malayan trees of the genus *Calophyllum* (family Guttiferae), etc., which were formerly used extensively in medicine. L16.
2 (The gum exuded from the buds of) any of the N. American balsam poplars, e.g. *Populus balsamifera*. M18.

tacan /'takən/ *noun.* M20.
[Acronym, from *tactical air navigation*.]
A navigational aid system for aircraft which measures bearing and distance from a ground beacon.

> *attrib.*: *Pilot* Instrument flying will be . . a challenge . . for those unaccustomed to making tacan approaches while juggling charts and joysticks.

tac-au-tac /'takəʊtak/ *noun.* E20.
[French, lit. 'clash for clash', from *tac* (imit.).]
FENCING. A parry combined with a riposte.

taccada /tə'kɑːdə, 'takədə/ *noun.* M19.
[Sinhalese *takkada*.]
The Indo-Pacific rice-paper plant, *Scaevola sericea*, the young stems of which have a pith used for making rice-paper, artificial flowers, etc.

tace /'teɪsi/ *verb intrans. (imper.).* Long *arch.* L16.
[Latin, imper. of *tacere*: see next.]
Be silent. Chiefly in ***tace is Latin for a candle*** (used as a veiled hint to a person to keep silent about something).

tacenda /tə'sɛndə/ *noun pl.* M19.
[Latin, pl. of *tacendum* use as noun of neut. gerundive of *tacere*: see next.]
Things to be passed over in silence; matters not to be mentioned or made public, *esp.* those of an embarrassing nature.

tacet /'teɪsɛt/ *adverb & noun.* E18.
[Latin = is silent, from *tacere* be silent.]
MUSIC. ▶**A** *adverb.* A direction: be silent for a time; pause. E18.
▶ **B** *noun.* A pause. L18.

Taceval /'takɪval/ *noun. Military slang.* L20.
[from TACTICAL *adjective* + EVALUATION *noun.* Cf. CASEVAC.]
The evaluation of tactical planning and deployment; *spec.* a NATO exercise designed to provide training in this.

tach /tak/ *noun*¹. *US colloq.* M20.
[Abbreviation.]
= TACHOMETER.

tach *noun*² var. of TACHE *noun*².

tache /tɑːʃ, taʃ/ *noun*¹. ME.
[Old French *teche*, (also mod.) *tache*, ult. from Frankish = a token.]
1 a A spot, a blotch, a blot. *obsolete* exc. *Scot.* ME. ▸**b** *MEDICINE.* A blemish on the skin, an organ, etc. Usu. with French specifying word. L19. ▸**c** *ART.* A dab or dash of colour. Cf. TACHISM. M20.
2 *fig.* †**a** A moral spot or blemish; a fault or vice; a bad quality or habit. ME–E17. ▸**b** An imputation of fault or disgrace; a stain or blot on one's character; a stigma. *Scot.* E17.
3 A distinctive mark, quality, or habit; a trait, a characteristic. *obsolete* exc. *dial.* LME.

> **1c** *Art & Design* Bright colour taches . . dispel the suggestions of a formal composition. **2b** M. NAPIER The only tache upon his military fame.

tache /tatʃ/ *noun*². Now *rare.* Also **tach**. LME.
[Old French *tache* fibula, clasp, a large nail: alt. of TACK *noun*¹.]
1 A device for fastening two parts together; a fibula, a buckle, a hook and eye, etc.; a hook from which an object is suspended. Cf. TACK *noun*¹ 1. *arch.* LME. ▸**b** A band or strap used for fastening. Cf. TACK *noun*¹ 3. *rare. obsolete* exc. *Scot.* E17. ▸**c** *fig.* A means of attachment, a link, a connecting bond. E18.
2 A rest for the shank of a punch or drill. Now *dial.* L17.

tache /tatʃ/ *noun*³. In sense 1 also **teache**. M17.
[French *tache, têche* plate of iron.]
1 In sugar-making, each pan of the series through which the juice of the sugar cane passes during the evaporation process; *esp.* the smallest and last of these pans (also ***striking-tache***). M17.
†**2** A flat iron pan in which tea leaves are dried. E18–E19.

tache /tatʃ, taʃ/ *verb*¹ *trans.* LME.
[Old French *tachier* (mod. *tacher*) stain, soil, formed as TACHE *noun*¹.]
1 Stain or taint, esp. morally, or with the imputation of guilt or disgraceful conduct; stigmatize. *obsolete* exc. *Scot.* LME.
2 Blemish, deface; mar or spoil slightly by handling or use; make the worse for wear. *Scot.* E18.

tache /tatʃ/ *verb*² *trans.* ME.
[Partly from TACHE *noun*², partly aphet. from ATTACH *verb*.]
1 Fasten, fix, secure (a person or thing). *obsolete* exc. *Scot. & dial.* ME.
†**2** = ATTACH *verb* 1, 4. LME–M17.

tacheometer /takɪˈɒmɪtə/ *noun*. L19.
[from Greek *takhe-* stem of *takhus* quick, swift, and *takhos* swiftness: see -OMETER.]
SURVEYING. A theodolite for the rapid location of points on a survey.
■ **tacheometric** /ˌtakɪəˈmɛtrɪk/ *adjective* pertaining to a tacheometer or tacheometry E20. **tacheometry** *noun* surveying by means of a tacheometer L19.

tachi /ˈtatʃi/ *noun*. M20.
[Japanese.]
A long, single-edged, samurai sword with a slightly curved blade, worn slung from the belt.

tachinid /ˈtakmɪd/ *noun & adjective*. L19.
[mod. Latin *Tachinidae* (see below), from *Tachina* genus name, from Greek *takhinē*, fem. of *takhinos* swift: see -ID³.]
ENTOMOLOGY. ▶**A** *noun.* Any of numerous small hairy flies constituting the family Tachinidae, the larvae of which are parasitic on other insects etc. L19.
▶**B** *adjective.* Of, pertaining to, or designating this family. E20.

tachism /ˈtaʃɪz(ə)m/ *noun*. Also ***tachisme*** /taʃism/. M20.
[French *tachisme*, from *tache* TACHE *noun*¹: see -ISM.]
A chiefly French style of painting, popular in the 1940s and 1950s, characterized by irregular dabs or splotches of colour and aiming to achieve a spontaneous and random effect so as to evoke subconscious emotions or states of mind.

tachist /ˈtaʃɪst/ *noun & adjective*. Also ***tachiste*** /taʃist/. L19.
[French *tachiste*, formed as prec. + *-iste* -IST.]
ART. ▶**A** *noun.* **1** *Hist.* A person painting in an impressionist or post-impressionist style, usu. by juxtaposing small patches of unmixed colour. Freq. *derog.* L19.
2 A practitioner of tachism. M20.
▶**B** *adjective.* Of or pertaining to tachism or its practitioners. M20.

tachistoscope /taˈkɪstəskəʊp/ *noun*. L19.
[from Greek *takhistos* swiftest + -SCOPE.]
An instrument which presents objects to the eye for a fraction of a second, e.g. to determine the amount of detail that can be apprehended by a single act of attention.
■ **tachistoˈscopic** *adjective* E20. **tachistoˈscopically** *adverb* E20.

tacho /ˈtakəʊ/ *noun*. *colloq.* Pl. **-os**. M20.
[Abbreviation.]
= TACHOMETER.

tacho-generator /ˌtakəʊˈdʒɛnəreɪtə/ *noun*. M20.
[from *TACHO(METER) generator*.]
An instrument that generates a voltage proportional to the rate of rotation of a shaft etc.

tachograph /ˈtakəgrɑːf/ *noun*. E20.
[from Greek *takhos* speed + -GRAPH.]
A device used in motor vehicles, esp. heavy goods vehicles and coaches, for automatically recording speed, travel time, and other information.

🕮 *attrib.*: *Truck & Driver* The company's tachograph records revealed that they had . . driven in excess of 75 mph.

tachometer /taˈkɒmɪtə/ *noun*. E19.
[from Greek *takhos* speed + -METER.]
1 An instrument for measuring the velocity of a machine; *esp.* one that indicates the speed of a vehicle engine in revolutions per minute. E19.
2 Any of various instruments for measuring the velocity of moving fluid, as water current, blood flow, etc. M19.
Comb.: **tachometer generator** = TACHO-GENERATOR.
■ **tachometry** *noun* the measurement of velocity; (the branch of science that deals with) the use of tachometers: L19. **tachoˈmetric** *adjective* of or pertaining to tachometry; employing a tachometer: M20.

ta chuan /tɑː ˈtʃwɑːn/ *noun phr.* L19.
[Chinese *dàzhuàn* (Wade–Giles *ta chuan*), from *dà* big + *zhuàn* seal character.]
In Chinese calligraphy, an early form of script used during the Chou dynasty.

tachy- /ˈtaki/ *combining form* of Greek *takhus* swift.
■ **tachyˈgenesis** *noun* (*ZOOLOGY*) acceleration in development by the shortening or suppression of embryonic or larval stages L19. **tachylite**, **-lyte** *noun* (*PETROGRAPHY*) a black volcanic glass formed by the cooling of basaltic magma M19. **tachymetaˈbolic** *adjective* (*ZOOLOGY*) of, pertaining to, or designating an animal exhibiting tachymetabolism; homoiothermic: L20. **tachymeˈtabolism** *noun* (*ZOOLOGY*) the high level of metabolism characteristic of warm-blooded vertebrates; homoiothermy: L20. **taˈchymeter** *noun* (*SURVEYING*) = TACHEOMETER M19. **tachyphyˈlaxis** *noun* (*PHARMACOLOGY*) a rapidly diminishing response to successive doses of a drug E20. **tachypnoea** /takɪpˈniːə/ *noun* (*MEDICINE*) abnormally rapid breathing L19. **tachypnoeic** /takɪpˈniːɪk/ *adjective* (*MEDICINE*) exhibiting tachypnoea M20. **tachyscope** *noun* (*obsolete* exc. *Hist.*) a kinetoscope in which a series of representations of an object are rapidly revolved so as to present the appearance of motion L19. **tachyˈsterol** *noun* (*BIOCHEMISTRY*) an oily isomer of ergosterol which forms calciferol when subjected to ultraviolet irradiation M20. **tachyˈzoite** *noun* (*MICROBIOLOGY*) a rapidly multiplying form of a toxoplasma L20.

tachycardia /takɪˈkɑːdɪə/ *noun*. L19.
[from prec. + Greek *kardia* heart.]
Chiefly *MEDICINE.* Abnormal rapidity of heart action.
■ **tachyˈcardiac** *noun & adjective* (*a*) *noun* a person subject to or affected with tachycardia; (*b*) *adjective* of or pertaining to tachycardia: L19.

tachygraph /ˈtakɪgrɑːf/ *noun*. E19.
[French *tachygraphe* from Greek *takhugraphos* swift writer: see TACHY-, -GRAPH.]
1 A person who practises tachygraphy; a shorthand writer, a stenographer, esp. in ancient Greece and Rome. E19.
2 A tachygraphic manuscript or writing. Also, a tachygraphic character or sign. L19.
■ **taˈchygrapher** *noun* a stenographer; = TACHYGRAPH 1: L19.

tachygraphic /takɪˈgrafɪk/ *adjective*. M18.
[French *tachygraphique*: see prec., -IC.]
Of or pertaining to the art of tachygraphy or rapid writing; *spec.* pertaining to cursive handwriting, or to writing (as the medieval writing of Greek and Latin) with many contractions, ligatures, and abbreviated forms.
■ Also **tachygraphical** *adjective* (*rare*) M18.

tachygraphy /taˈkɪgrəfi/ *noun*. M17.
[from Greek *takhus* swift + -GRAPHY.]
Stenography, shorthand; *spec.* cursive characters; Egyptian hieratic writing; the medieval writing of Greek and Latin with its many abbreviations and contractions.

tachykinin /takɪˈkʌɪnɪn/ *noun*. M20.
[from TACHY- + KININ, after *bradykinin*.]
BIOCHEMISTRY. Any of a class of kinins having a rapid stimulant effect on smooth muscle.

tachyon /ˈtakɪɒn/ *noun*. M20.
[from TACHY- + -ON.]
PARTICLE PHYSICS. A hypothetical particle that travels faster than light, having either a mass or an energy which must be imaginary.

tacit /ˈtasɪt/ *adjective*. E17.
[Latin *tacitus* pa. pple of *tacere* be silent.]
1 Unspoken; silent, emitting no sound; noiseless, wordless. E17. ▸**b** Saying nothing. Now *rare*. E17.
2 Implied without being openly expressed or stated; understood, inferred. M17.

🕮 **1** J. S. C. ABBOTT Those tacit prayers to which no language can give adequate expression. **2** D. H. LAWRENCE A natural, tacit understanding, a using of the same language. C. MACKENZIE By tacit consent the conversation was allowed to drift away . . to less controversial topics. ***tacit relocation***: see RELOCATION.

■ **tacitly** *adverb* M17. **tacitness** *noun* (*rare*) M17.

Tacitean /tasɪˈtiːən/ *adjective*. L19.
[from *Tacitus* (see below) + -EAN.]
Pertaining to or resembling the Roman historian Cornelius Tacitus (*c* 54–117), or resembling his weighty and sententious style.

🕮 *Listener* The lapidary, Tacitean phrases of . . [Cockburn's] *Memorials*.

taciturn /ˈtasɪtəːn/ *adjective*. L18.
[French *taciturne* or Latin *taciturnus*, from *tacitus* TACIT.]
Characterized by habitual silence or disinclination for conversation; reserved in speech; saying little; uncommunicative.

🕮 D. MURPHY As I am naturally taciturn . . maintaining silence . . did not dismay me. M. FORSTER Stuart is taciturn on that subject as on most.

■ **taciturnly** *adverb* M19.

taciturnity /tasɪˈtəːnɪti/ *noun*. LME.
[Old & mod. French *taciturnité* or Latin *taciturnitas*, from *taciturnus*: see prec., -ITY.]
1 Habitual silence or disinclination for conversation; reservedness in speech; a taciturn character or state. LME.
2 *SCOTS LAW.* The silence of a creditor with regard to a debt or obligation over a period short of that necessary for prescription, which can be pleaded in extinction of the debt etc. on the inference that the creditor has either abandoned the debt or has had it satisfied in some way. M18.

🕮 **1** M. COREN Taciturnity was not Gilbert's forte. He ached to tell people the . . news.

tack /tak/ *noun*¹. ME.
[Prob. from unrecorded var. of Old French *tache*: see TACHE *noun*². The relation with TACK *verb*¹ and with *attack, attach, detach* is uncertain.]
▶**I 1** A thing for fastening one thing to another, or fastening things together; a fibula, a buckle, a hook or stud fitting into an eye or loop, etc. *obsolete* exc. as passing into senses 2, 3. Cf. TACHE *noun*² 1. ME.
2 A small sharp-pointed nail, usu. with a flat and comparatively broad head, used esp. for fastening an object to something in a temporary manner, so as to allow for easy undoing; *N. Amer.* a drawing-pin. Also more fully ***tack-nail***. LME.
3 A strip or band used for fastening; *spec.* (*a*) a strip or band secured at each end to a wall for supporting plants; (*b*) a strip of lead soldered to a pipe at one end, with the other fastened to a wall or support. Cf. TACHE *noun*² 1b. M16.
4 Orig., an act of tacking or fastening together, esp. in a slight or temporary way. Now, a long stitch used in fastening seams etc., loosely or temporarily together preparatory to permanent sewing. Also (*Scot.*), a very slight fastening or tie, by which something is loosely held. E18.

🕮 **2** D. W. JERROLD Driving tin tacks into a baby's coffin. ***carpet-tack***, ***thumb-tack***, ***tin-tack***, etc.

▶**II 5 a** A hanging shelf or storage rack. *obsolete* exc *dial.* LME. ▸**b** Either of the handles of a scythe. *dial.* E19. ▸**c** A temporary prop or scaffold in a mine. *dial.* M19.
6 A thing attached as an addition or rider; a supplement, an appendix; *spec.* an extraneous clause appended to a financial bill in parliament in order to ensure the bill's passing. E18.

🕮 **6** W. MINTO The Lords refused to pass the Money Bill till the tack was withdrawn.

▶**III 7 a** Hold; holding quality; endurance, strength, substance. Now *Scot. & dial.* LME. ▸**b** Adhesive quality, stickiness; a sticky quality or condition in varnish, ink, etc. L19.

🕮 **7a** J. CARYL There was tack in it . . silver that had strength in it.

▶**IV 8** *NAUTICAL.* **a** A rope, wire, etc., used to secure the windward clews or corners of the lower square sails to a ship's side when sailing close-hauled to the wind; the rope, wire, etc., used to secure amidships the windward lower clew of a fore-and-aft sail. LME. ▸**b** The lower windward clew or corner of a sail, to which the tack or rope etc. is attached. M18.
9 a *NAUTICAL.* An act of tacking; the direction in which a sailing ship moves as determined by the position of its sails and regarded in terms of the wind direction; a temporary change of course in sailing made by turning the ship's head to the wind; one of a consecutive series of such movements to port and starboard alternately, tracing a zigzag course, and made by a ship in order to reach a point to windward. E17. ▸**b** *transf. & fig.* A zigzag course on land. L18.
10 *fig.* A course of action or policy, esp. one representing a change or divergence from a former or other course. L17.

🕮 **9a** J. CONRAD I . . put the ship round on the other tack. **10** S. KNIGHT A hostile . . expert on Freemasonry, changed tack and wrote . . conciliatory articles. P. FITZGERALD Perhaps I'm . . on the wrong tack in thinking there's anything mysterious about her.

Phrases: **bring the port tacks aboard** set the sails to, or sail with, the wind on the port side. **bring the starboard tacks aboard** set the sails to, or sail with, the wind on the starboard side. **bring the tacks aboard** haul the tacks or ropes into such a position as to trim the sails to the wind, set sail. ***get down to brass tacks***: see BRASS *noun & adjective*. **haul the tacks aboard** = ***bring the tacks aboard*** above. **have the port tacks aboard** = ***bring the port tacks aboard*** above. **have the starboard tacks aboard** = ***bring the starboard tacks aboard*** above. **on the port tack** (of a ship) with the wind on the port side. **on the starboard tack** (of a ship) with the wind on the starboard side.
Comb.: **tack coat** a thin coating of tar, asphalt, etc., used in road-making and applied to a surface before a road is laid to form an adhesive bond between the two; **tack-hammer** a light hammer

for driving tacks; **tack-nail** = sense 2 above; **tack rag** *N. Amer.* an impregnated cloth used for cleaning a surface prior to painting or varnishing; **tack weld** *verb & noun* (*a*) *verb trans.* join (materials) at intervals with provisional welds in order to hold them in position for subsequent work; (*b*) *noun* a weld of this type.

tack /tak/ *noun*[2]. Chiefly *Scot. & north.* ME.
[Prob. from Old Norse *tak* (beside *taka*) seizure, hold, bail, security, from *taka* TAKE *verb*.]
▸ **I** †**1** A customary payment levied by a ruler, feudal superior, etc. ME–L16.
2 Tenure or tenancy of land etc.; *esp.* leasehold tenure of a farm, mill, etc.; the period of tenure. Also, (*rare*), a leasehold tenement, a farm. *Scot. & north.* LME. ▸**b** A period *of* time, a spell *of* weather, etc. *Scot.* E18.
3 An agreement, a compact, a bargain. *Scot.* E18.
4 Hired pasturage for cattle. *dial.* E19.
▸ **II 5** A catch or haul of fish; = TAKE *noun* 1(f). *Scot. & north.* L16.
Comb.: **tack-duty** the rent payable on land held in leasehold; the rent paid by a tacksman; **tack-money** payment for pannage or pasture.

tack /tak/ *noun*[3]. *obsolete* exc. *dial.* LME.
[In sense 1, app. from var. of Old French *teche*: see TACHE *noun*[1]; sense 2 is perh. transf. from 1, but may be of different origin.]
†**1** A spot, a stain; a blemish. Cf. TACHE *noun*[1] 1, 2. LME–E17.
2 A taste or flavour (*of* something); *esp.* an unusual, strong, or unpleasant flavour. E17.

tack /tak/ *noun*[4]. L16.
[Origin unkn.]
Foodstuff (chiefly in ***hard tack***, ***soft tack***). Also (*gen.*), stuff, *esp.* something of little value or inferior quality. Cf. TACKLE *noun* 7.

> D. C. MURRAY I thought the canteen tack the nastiest stuff I had ever tasted.

†**tack** *noun*[5]. *rare.* L17–E19.
[Origin unkn.]
A billiard-cue.

tack /tak/ *noun*[6]. L18.
[Abbreviation of TACKLE *noun*.]
†**1** = TACKLE *noun* 1. *dial.* L18.
2 The saddle, bridle, etc., of a horse; = TACKLE *noun* 6. E20.
Comb.: **tack room** the room in a stables where the saddles, bridles, etc., are kept.

tack /tak/ *noun*[7]. *rare* (chiefly *dial.*). E19.
[Imit.]
A short sharp sound, *esp.* one resulting from a slap or blow.

tack /tak/ *noun*[8]. *US colloq.* M20.
[Abbreviation.]
= TACHOGRAPH, TACHOMETER.

tack /tak/ *noun*[9]. *colloq.* L20.
[Back-form. from TACKY *adjective*[1].]
Something tacky or cheap and seedy or vulgar; rubbish, junk.

tack /tak/ *verb*[1]. LME.
[Rel. to TACK *noun*[1]: see TACHE *verb*[2].]
▸ **I 1** *verb trans.* **a** Attach, fasten (a thing to another, or things together). *obsolete* exc. *dial.* & as passing into sense 2. LME. ▸†**b** *transf. & fig.* Attach. M16–L18. ▸†**c** Join (a couple) in marriage. *slang.* L17–E19.
2 *verb trans.* Attach in a temporary manner; *esp.* fasten with tacks or short nails, or stitch (seams etc.) loosely or temporarily together. LME.
†**3** *verb trans.* Connect or link by an intervening part. M17–M18.
4 *verb trans.* Join together (events, accounts, etc.) so as to produce or show a connected whole; *esp.* bring (disparate or unconnected parts etc.) into arbitrary association. L17.
5 *verb trans.* Add as a supplement; append, annex; *spec.* append (an extraneous clause) to a financial bill to ensure that the bill is passed. Also foll. by *on*. L17.
6 *verb trans.* LAW. Unite (a third or subsequent encumbrance) to the first, whereby it acquires priority over an intermediate mortgage. Now *Hist.* E18.

> **1** STEELE He . . tacked together the Skins of Goats. **b** W. GILPIN He who works without taste . . tacks one part to another as his . . fancy suggests. **2** *Blitz* I have a photograph . . tacked to my study wall. M. WESLEY Tacking a sleeve into the armhole of a . . dress. **3** HOR. WALPOLE They . . have tacked . . the wings to a house by a colonade. **4** G. S. HAIGHT She . . could tack together long quotations from books . . to make convincing reviews. **5** A. TYLER A tacked-on, gray frame addition gave it a ramshackle look. *Balance* Holiday insurance is an extra tacked onto the car recovery package—something of an afterthought.

▸ **II 7** *verb intrans.* NAUTICAL. ▸**a** Alter a sailing ship's course by turning the head to the wind and across it, so as to bring the wind on the opposite side of the vessel; go about in this way (also foll. by *about*). Hence (freq. of a ship), make a run or course obliquely against the wind; proceed by a series of such courses to port and starboard alternately, the net distance gained being to windward. Cf. GYBE *verb* 2a, WEAR *verb*[2]. M16. ▸**b** Of the wind: change its direction. *rare.* E18.
8 *verb intrans.* **a** *fig.* Change a course of action, a policy, or one's conduct. Also (*rare*), proceed by indirect methods. M17. ▸**b** *transf.* Follow a zigzag course on land. E18.
9 *verb trans.* Alter the course of (a ship) by turning the head to the wind (opp. WEAR *verb*[2]). Also, navigate (a ship) against the wind by a series of tacks. M17.

> **7a** I. WATSON We tacked against the prevailing wind. **8a** W. STUBBS He is not . . diverted, although he sometimes consents to tack. **b** K. ROBERTS He tacked from pub to pub.

■ **tacker** *noun* (*a*) a person (esp. in the early 18th cent.) who favoured the tacking of extraneous clauses to financial bills, in order to secure their passage through the House of Lords; (*b*) a person who tacks or fastens articles etc.; a machine for driving in tacks; (*c*) *dial. & Austral.* a small child, esp. a boy: E18.

tack /tak/ *verb*[2] *trans. obsolete* exc. *dial.* E17.
[from TACK *noun*[3].]
Taint; stain; *dial.* give a taste or a strong or unpleasant flavour to.

tack /tak/ *verb*[3] *trans.* Now *dial.* E18.
[Aphet. from ATTACK *verb*.]
Attack.

tack /tak/ *verb*[4] *trans. Scot. & dial.* M19.
[from TACK *noun*[2].]
1 Put *out* (cattle) to hired pasture; take (cattle) to pasture for hire. M19.
2 Take a lease of (a farm etc.). *Scot. rare.* L19.

tack /tak/ *verb*[5] *trans. & intrans.* M20.
[Abbreviation of TACKLE *verb*.]
Put a saddle and bridle on (a horse). Usu. foll. by *up*.

tacket /ˈtakɪt/ *noun & verb.* Now *Scot. & dial.* ME.
[from TACK *noun*[1] + -ET[1].]
▸ **A** *noun.* A nail. Later, a small nail, a tack; *esp.* (*Scot. & north.*) a hobnail used to stud the soles of shoes etc. ME.
▸ **B** *verb trans.* Stud (shoes etc.) with tackets. Chiefly as ***tacketed*** *ppl adjective.* M19.
■ **tackety** *adjective* (*Scot.*) (of a shoe) studded with tackets M19.

tackie *noun* var. of TAKKIE.

tackifier /ˈtakɪfʌɪə/ *noun.* M20.
[from TACKY *adjective*[2] + -FY + -ER[1].]
A substance that makes something sticky; an adhesive agent or ingredient.

tackily /ˈtakɪli/ *adverb*[1]. E20.
[from TACKY *adjective*[2] + -LY[2].]
In a slightly adhesive or sticky manner.

tackily /ˈtakɪli/ *adverb*[2]. *colloq.* M20.
[from TACKY *adjective*[1] + -LY[2].]
In a tasteless, cheap, or vulgar style; shabbily, dowdily.

tackiness /ˈtakɪnɪs/ *noun*[1]. L19.
[from TACKY *adjective*[2] + -NESS.]
The quality of being tacky or slightly adhesive.

tackiness /ˈtakɪnɪs/ *noun*[2]. *colloq.* L20.
[from TACKY *adjective*[1] + -NESS.]
The quality of being cheap, vulgar, or in poor taste.

tacking /ˈtakɪŋ/ *noun.* L17.
[from TACK *verb*[1] + -ING[1].]
The action of TACK *verb*[1]; *esp.* (*a*) NAUTICAL the action of making a tack or a series of tacks in a sailing vessel whilst beating to windward; (*b*) joining or fastening together, esp. in a slight or temporary manner. Also, something which is tacked or joined on; a series of long temporary stitches or tacks.

> C. FRANCIS Winds around Britain blow from the west or south-west, necessitating tacking (or zigzagging). attrib.: ***tacking-cotton***, ***tacking-thread***, etc.

Comb.: **tacking iron** PHOTOGRAPHY a tool used for attaching tissue etc. to a print or mount by the application of heat at chosen points.

tackle /ˈtak(ə)l, *in sense 2 also* ˈteɪk(ə)l/ *noun.* ME.
[Prob. from Middle & mod. Low German *takel* (whence also Dutch, German *Takel*, Swedish *tackel*), from *taken* = Middle Dutch *tacken* lay hold of: see -LE[1]. In sense 8 from TACKLE *verb*. See also TEAGLE.]
1 Apparatus, implements, appliances; equipment, gear, *esp.* that required for a particular task etc. ME.
2 a Orig., a ship's equipment, gear, or rigging. Later *spec.*, the running rigging and pulleys used in working the sails etc. ME. ▸**b** Cordage; a rope used for any purpose. E16.
†**3** Implements of war, weapons collectively; *esp.* arrows. Also, a weapon; an arrow. LME–L18.
4 Equipment for fishing; fishing-gear. LME.
5 a A mechanism consisting of a combination of ropes, pulley-blocks, hooks, etc. for raising or shifting heavy objects. Also ***block and tackle***. L15. ▸**b** In mining, a windlass for hoisting ore etc. Also, the apparatus of cages or buckets, with their chains and hooks, for raising ore or coal. L19.
6 The equipment of a horse; = TACK *noun*[6]. L17.
7 Foodstuff; food or drink; stuff. Cf. TACK *noun*[4]. *colloq.* M18.
8 a An act of tackling or intercepting, seizing, etc. a person, esp. in football and other sports. L19. ▸**b** AMER. FOOTBALL. The position outside the guard in the forward line; the player in this position. L19.

> **1** J. K. JEROME George wanted the shaving tackle. **8a** *Football Monthly* Butcher, in making his tackle, succeeded only in bringing him down. *Down East* As the . . horse tried to resume speed, our clerk made a flying tackle.

Phrases etc.: ***ground tackle***: see GROUND *noun*. ***jigger-tackle***: see JIGGER *noun*[1]. ***luff-tackle***: see LUFF *noun*[1] 5. ***relieving tackle***: see RELIEVE *verb*. **stand to one's tackle**, **stick to one's tackle** (now *rare*) stand one's ground, stand firm in one's resolve.
Comb.: **tackle-block** a pulley over which a rope runs; = BLOCK *noun* 3; **tackle-fall** a rope for applying force to the blocks of a tackle; **tackle-porter** = ***tackle-house porter*** s.v. TACKLE-HOUSE; **tackle-room** = ***tack room*** s.v. TACK *noun*[7].

tackle /ˈtak(ə)l/ *verb.* LME.
[from prec.]
1 *verb trans.* †**a** Equip (a ship) with tackle; provide with the necessary equipment. LME–L17. ▸**b** Handle or work (the tackle or rigging of a ship). Long *rare.* E16.
†**2** *verb trans.* Raise or hoist with tackle. *rare.* Only in E18.
3 *verb trans.* Harness (a horse). E18.
4 a *verb trans.* Grip, take hold of, grapple with; try to overcome, attack (a person or animal) physically. E19. ▸**b** *verb trans.* Enter into a discussion or argument with; approach or question on some subject. M19. ▸**c** *verb trans.* Try to deal with (a task, a difficulty, etc.); try to solve (a problem). M19. ▸**d** *verb intrans.* Set to; grapple *with* something. *rare* (chiefly *dial.*). M19. ▸**e** *verb trans.* Begin to eat, tuck into, fall on (food) with relish. L19.
5 *verb trans. & intrans.* In RUGBY & AMER. FOOTBALL, seize and stop (a player in possession of the ball). In FOOTBALL, intercept or obstruct (a player in possession of the ball) to cause him or her to lose possession. Also (in other sports), obstruct, challenge, or intercept (a player) so as to deprive him or her of the ball or other object of play. L19.

> **1a** T. NICOLLS The shyppe be . . tacled with sayle and ballast. **3** R. BOLDREWOOD I'll get a spare saddle and bridle, and will tackle him. **4a** M. MACHLIN Larry . . tackled him, throwing him down on the . . ground. **b** S. UNWIN Government Departments . . if tackled fearlessly when . . wrong, usually prove astonishingly timid. **c** A. BROOKNER His . . French interlude fell away . . as he tackled his English sentence. *Which?* Setting up task forces to tackle special problems in the area. **e** B. PYM Breakfast . . meant tackling a plate of bacon and eggs. **5** ***late tackling***: see LATE *adjective*.

■ **tackler** *noun* L17.

tackled /ˈtak(ə)ld/ *adjective.* M16.
[from TACKLE *noun*, *verb*: see -ED[2], -ED[1].]
1 Provided or equipped with a tackle or harness. Long *rare.* M16.
†**2** Made of tackle or ropes. *rare* (Shakes.). Only in L16.

tackle-house /ˈtak(ə)lhaʊs/ *noun.* Now *Hist.* M16.
[from TACKLE *noun* + HOUSE *noun*[1].]
A house or building in which porters employed in loading and unloading ships kept their tackle. Also, a house or building equipped with a tackle or pulley for hoisting heavy goods; a warehouse for loading and unloading merchandise carried by ships.
Comb.: **tackle-house porter** orig., a porter employed at a tackle-house; later (also = ***tackle-porter*** s.v. TACKLE *noun*), a porter authorized to act as such by one of the London Merchant Companies, as opp. to a ***ticket-porter*** who was licensed by the corporation (still a titular office in some London Merchant Companies).

tackling /ˈtaklɪŋ/ *noun.* ME.
[from TACKLE *verb* + -ING[1].]
†**1** The tackle or rigging of a ship. ME–M18.
2 Arms, weapons, etc. *obsolete* exc. in ***stand to one's tackling***, ***stick to one's tackling*** below. LME.
3 †**a** Gear, equipment, etc.; = TACKLE *noun* 1. M16–E19. ▸**b** = TACKLE *noun* 6. *obsolete* exc. *N. Amer.* M17.
†**4** = TACKLE *noun* 4. M16–M19.
5 The action of TACKLE *verb*; *esp.* the action of intercepting, seizing, etc., a player in various sports. L19.
2 stand to one's tackling, **stick to one's tackling** (now *rare*) stand one's ground; = ***stand to one's tackle*** s.v. TACKLE *noun*.
Comb.: **tackling bag** AMER. & RUGBY FOOTBALL a stuffed bag suspended and used for practice in tackling; **tackling dummy** AMER. FOOTBALL = ***tackling bag*** above.

tacksman /ˈtaksmən/ *noun. Scot.* Pl. **-men**. M16.
[from TACK *noun*[2] + -'S[1] + MAN *noun*.]
A person who holds a tack or lease of land, a farm, a mill, etc.; a leaseholder; *esp.* (in the Highlands) a middleman leasing a large piece of land which is then sublet for farming in smaller units.

tacky /ˈtaki/ *noun & adjective*[1]. E19. *colloq.*
[Origin unkn.]
▸ **A** *noun.* **1** A weak or feeble horse; a horse of inferior quality. *US.* E19.
2 A poor white person of the southern States from Virginia to Georgia. *US.* M19.

▸**B** *adjective.* Dowdy, shabby, seedy; showing poor taste or style, cheap, vulgar. Orig. *US.* M19.

📖 *New York Times* Marred by tacky Art Deco trim . . and its pink brick walls. *Rhythm* Keyboard players who . . use those new tacky Hammond . . sounds.

tacky /ˈtaki/ *adjective*². L18.
[from TACK *noun*¹ + -Y¹.]
Of paint, glue, varnish, etc.: slightly sticky or adhesive after application.

📖 I. WATSON The surface . . felt tacky, like paint which hadn't quite dried. *Truck & Driver* Tobacco smoke . . causes the red blood cells to get tacky and to stick to each other.

tacnode /ˈtaknəʊd/ *noun.* M19.
[from Latin *tactus* touch + NODE.]
GEOMETRY. = OSCULATION 2(b).

taco /ˈtɑːkəʊ, ˈtakəʊ/ *noun.* Pl. **-os.** M20.
[Mexican Spanish.]
A Mexican dish comprising a tortilla or cornmeal pancake rolled or folded and filled with various mixtures, such as seasoned mincemeat, chicken, beans, etc.

📖 *attrib.*: *New Yorker* In . . Oklahoma City suburbs . . there are two taco joints for every tree.

Comb.: **taco chip** a fried fragment of a taco, freq. flavoured with chilli etc. and eaten cold like a potato crisp.

Taconic /təˈkɒnɪk/ *adjective.* M19.
[*Taconic* Range of mountains in eastern New York State, USA.]
GEOLOGY. Of, pertaining to, or designating rocks, systems, etc., exemplified in the Taconic Range.
Taconic orogeny an episode of mountain building that affected eastern N. America in the Ordovician.

taconite /ˈtakənʌɪt/ *noun.* E20.
[from prec. + -ITE¹.]
GEOLOGY. A type of chert used as an iron ore in parts of N. America.

tacouba /təˈkuːbə/ *noun.* M20.
[Origin unkn.]
In Guyana, a tree which has fallen across a river forming a bridge or obstruction.

tacrine /ˈtakriːn/ *noun.* M20.
[from T(ETRA- + ACR(ID)INE.]
PHARMACOLOGY. In full ***tacrine hydrochloride***. A synthetic drug, 1,2,3,4-tetrahydroacridin-9-ylamine hydrochloride, $C_{13}H_{14}N_2 \cdot HCl$, that inhibits the breakdown of acetylcholine by cholinesterase and has been used to enhance neurological function in patients with Alzheimer's disease.

tacsonia /takˈsəʊnɪə/ *noun.* M19.
[mod. Latin (see below), from Quechua.]
Any of several W. Indian and Central American passion-flowers of the former genus *Tacsonia* (family Passifloraceae), now included in *Passiflora*.

tact /takt/ *noun.* E17.
[Old & mod. French, or Latin *tactus* touch, from *tact-* pa. ppl stem of *tangere* touch. In sense 3 directly from French.]
▸**I 1** *MUSIC.* = TACTUS. E17.
▸**II 2 a** The sense of touch; touch. Now *rare.* M17. ▸**b** *fig.* A keen faculty of perception or ability to make fine distinctions likened to the sense of touch. L18.
3 Delicate and sensitive appreciation of what is appropriate and proper in dealing with others, esp. so as to avoid giving offence; adroitness or judgement in dealing with others or handling difficult or delicate situations; the faculty of saying or doing the right thing at the appropriate time. E19.

📖 **2a** G. GROTE Percepta . . of tact, vision, hearing . . have each its special bodily organ. **b** COLERIDGE Have a better tact of what will offend . . readers. **3** P. DE MAN The tact with which such a potentially mischievous task should be carried out. R. RENDELL She seemed to have the tact . . to realise . . Burden wanted privacy.

Tactel /ˈtaktɛl/ *noun.* L20.
[Invented name: perh. infl. by TACTILE.]
(Proprietary name for) a polyamide textile fibre; fabric made from this fibre, often characterized by a soft, silky feel.

tactful /ˈtaktfʊl, -f(ə)l/ *adjective.* M19.
[from TACT + -FUL.]
Having or displaying tact; (of an action) inspired by tact.

📖 P. H. GIBBS A tactful man . . writes nothing likely to offend public opinion. M. GIROUARD The . . architect . . had a reputation for the tactful handling of old houses.

■ **tactfully** *adverb* L19. **tactfulness** *noun* E20.

tactic /ˈtaktɪk/ *noun.* M17.
[mod. Latin *tactica* from Greek *taktikē* (sc. *tekhnē* art), fem. of *taktikos* TACTIC *adjective*¹. In sense 1 from Greek *taktikos* (sc. *anēr* man).]
†**1** A tactician. Only in M17.
2 = TACTICS 1. M18. ▸**b** A tactical ploy, action or manoeuvre; an instance of military tactics. L18.
†**3** *MATH.* The branch of mathematics that deals with the manipulation of the order or arrangement of numbers. M–L19.

📖 **2b** B. MOORE To offer some delaying tactic, or . . a compromise. A. BROOKNER To offer . . sympathy was not . . an heroic tactic.

tactic /ˈtaktɪk/ *adjective*¹. E17.
[mod. Latin *tacticus* from Greek *taktikos* of arrangement or tactics, from *taktos* verbal adjective of *tassein* set in order: see -IC.]
1 = TACTICAL 1. Now *rare* or *obsolete.* E17.
2 Of or pertaining to arrangement or order. E19.
3 *LINGUISTICS.* Of or pertaining to (some level) of tactics. Cf. TACTICS 3. M20.

tactic /ˈtaktɪk/ *adjective*². *rare.* E17.
[from Latin *tact-* pa. ppl stem of *tangere* touch: see -IC.]
Of, belonging or relating to touch; tactile.

tactical /ˈtaktɪk(ə)l/ *adjective.* L16.
[from Greek *taktikos*: see TACTIC *adjective*¹, -AL¹.]
1 a Of or pertaining to military or naval tactics. L16. ▸**b** Of aircraft, bombing, etc.: employed in direct support of military or naval operations. Cf. STRATEGIC *adjective* 2. E20. ▸**c** Of nuclear weapons: intended for short-range use against an enemy's forces. Cf. STRATEGIC *adjective* 2. M20.
2 †**a** Relating to the construction of a sentence. *rare.* Only in L17. ▸**b** Of or relating to arrangement, *esp.* according to skilfully planned procedure or actions with a view to ends. L19. ▸**c** Of voting: involving the transfer of electoral allegiance, esp. with the intention of denying victory to the party one opposes where one's preferred candidate has little chance of success. L20.
3 Of a person, a person's actions, etc.: characterized by skilful tactics; adroit in planning or devising means to ends. L19.

📖 **2b** *Running* It was going to be a tactical race. *Sunday Times* Lowe's first . . tactical mistake was to announce the . . news in a letter. **c** *Economist* Labour's tactical voters . . switched to Liberal.

■ **tactically** *adverb* L19.

tactician /takˈtɪʃ(ə)n/ *noun.* L18.
[from TACTIC *noun* + -IAN.]
A person versed or skilled in military tactics; a person adroit or skilled in planning or devising means to ends.

📖 J. HELLER A clever tactician at office politics.

tacticity /takˈtɪsɪti/ *noun.* M20.
[from TACTIC *adjective*¹ + -ITY.]
CHEMISTRY. The stereochemical arrangement of the units in the main chain of a polymer.

tactics /ˈtaktɪks/ *noun pl.* (also treated as *sing.*). E17.
[Repr. mod. Latin *tactica* from Greek *ta taktika* neut. pl. of *taktikos*, from *taktos* ordered, arranged, from base of *tassein* set in order: see -ICS.]
1 The art of deploying military, air, or naval forces in order of battle, and of planning and executing military manoeuvres in actual contact with an enemy. Cf. STRATEGY 2. E17.
2 The plans and procedure adopted to carry out a scheme or achieve an end. Also, a skilful device or skilful devices. M17.
3 The branch of linguistics that deals with the relation and arrangement of linguistic units. M20.

📖 **1** E. A. FREEMAN Though the chiefs are Norman, the tactics are English. **2** D. HALBERSTAM His . . reflex was for tactics, he had an intuitive sense of the chessboard.

tactile /ˈtaktʌɪl/ *adjective & noun.* E17.
[Latin *tactilis*, from *tact-* pa. ppl stem of *tangere* touch: see -ILE.]
▸**A** *adjective.* **1** Perceptible to the touch; tangible. E17.
2 a Of or pertaining to touch; characterized or influenced by, or relating to, the sense of touch. Also, having the quality of being pleasing or interesting to the touch. L17. ▸**b** Of a bodily organ, receptor, etc.: having or providing the sense of touch. M18. ▸**c** *PSYCHOLOGY.* Of, pertaining to, or characterized by responses that involve tactile imagery; (of a person) responding to perceptions more readily in terms of tactile imagery than in auditory or visual terms. L19.

📖 **1** J. UPDIKE To be forgiven, by God: this notion . . was for me a tactile actuality. **2a** H. CARPENTER He seemed to have no tactile sense . . his fingers were . . unfeeling. *Woodworker* Works which appeal to the sense of touch . . are said to have a tactile quality. **tactile value** *ART* in painting, the illusion of tangibility or three-dimensionality in the representation of figures and objects; the attribute or impression of a tangible, three-dimensional quality.

▸**B** *noun. PSYCHOLOGY.* A tactile person. E20.
■ **tactilely** *adverb* M20. **tactility** /-ˈtɪlɪti/ *noun* the quality or condition of being tactile; *esp.* the quality of being pleasing or interesting to the touch: M17.

tactily /ˈtaktɪli/ *adverb. rare.* L19.
[Irreg. from TACT + -LY².]
= TACTFULLY *adverb.*

taction /ˈtakʃ(ə)n/ *noun.* E17.
[Latin *tactio(n-)*, from *tact-* pa. ppl stem of *tangere* touch: see -ION.]
The action of touching; contact.

tactless /ˈtaktlɪs/ *adjective.* M19.
[from TACT + -LESS.]
Having or showing no tact; lacking in adroitness or sensitivity when handling difficult or delicate situations.

📖 M. SENDAK I was tactless enough to mutter aloud at the desecration. *Independent* She then went on to make some rather tactless remarks about girls wanting to be hairdressers and childminders.

■ **tactlessly** *adverb* L19. **tactlessness** *noun* L19.

tactoid /ˈtaktɔɪd/ *noun.* E20.
[from Greek *taktos* ordered: see TACTIC *adjective*¹, -OID.]
PHYSICAL CHEMISTRY. A small anisotropic birefringent region in a dilute isotropic sol, consisting of an aggregate of parallel rodlike particles or macromolecules.
■ **tactosol** *noun* a sol containing tactoids E20.

tactor /ˈtaktə/ *noun.* Now *rare.* E19.
[from Latin *tact-* (see TACTILE) + -OR.]
ZOOLOGY. A touch receptor; a feeler.

tactual /ˈtaktjʊəl/ *adjective.* M17.
[from Latin *tactus* touch, from *tact-*: see TACTILE, -AL¹.]
Of or pertaining to touch; tactile; caused by touch.
■ **tactuality** /-ˈalɪti/ *noun* M19. **tactually** *adverb* M19.

tactus /ˈtaktəs/ *noun.* M18.
[Latin: see TACT.]
MUSIC. Beat; a principal accent or rhythmic unit, esp. in 15th- and 16th-century music.

tad /tad/ *noun. colloq.* (chiefly *N. Amer.*). M19.
[Origin unkn. Cf. SMIDGE, TIDGE.]
1 A mean person. Now *rare* or *obsolete.* M19.
2 A young or small child, esp. a boy. L19.
3 A small amount; (freq. used adverbially) *a* little, somewhat, slightly. M20.

📖 **3** *Q* A tad short overall on memorability.

ta-da /təˈdɑː/ *interjection.* Also **ta-dah** & other vars. M20.
[Imit. Cf. TARA *interjection*¹, TARANTARA.]
Repr. a fanfare; indicating an impressive entrance, a dramatic announcement.

taddy /ˈtadi/ *noun. Scot.* M19.
[*Taddy* & Co. of London, the manufacturers.]
A kind of snuff.

tadger *noun* var. of TODGER.

tadpole /ˈtadpəʊl/ *noun.* L15.
[formed as TOAD + POLL *noun*¹.]
1 The tailed aquatic larva of a frog, toad, or other amphibian, from the time it leaves the egg until it loses its gills or tail and acquires legs. L15.
2 *ZOOLOGY.* The tailed larva of a tunicate. L19.
Comb.: **tadpole-fish** a small tadpole-shaped fish, *Raniceps raninus*, of the cod family, found in the NE Atlantic.

Tadzhik *noun & adjective* var. of TAJIK.

tae-bo /ˈtʌɪbəʊ/ *noun.* L20.
[from Korean *tae* leg + *bo*, short for BOXING *noun*².]
An exercise system combining elements of aerobics and kick-boxing.
¶ *Tae-bo* is a proprietary name.

taedium vitae /tʌɪdɪəm ˈviːtʌɪ, tiːdɪəm ˈvʌɪtiː/ *noun phr.* M18.
[Latin, formed as TEDIUM + *vitae* genit. of *vita* life.]
Weariness of life; disgust with life; extreme ennui or inertia, often as a pathological state with a tendency to suicide.

tae kwon do /tʌɪ kwɒn ˈdəʊ, teɪ/ *noun phr.* M20.
[Korean, lit. 'art of hand and foot fighting'.]
A modern Korean system of unarmed combat developed chiefly in the mid 20th cent., combining elements of karate, ancient Korean martial art, and kung fu, differing from karate in its wide range of kicking techniques and its emphasis on different methods of breaking objects.

tael /teɪl/ *noun.* L16.
[Portuguese (pl. *taéis*) from Malay *tahil* weight.]
1 (The trade name for) a Chinese *liang*, a weight used in China and the East, orig. of varying amount but later fixed at about 38 grams (1⅓ oz.). L16.
2 a A money of account, orig. a tael (in weight) of standard silver, the value of which fluctuates with the price of the metal. L16. ▸**b** A Chinese gold coin based on the value of a tael of silver. E20.

taele *noun* var. of TJAELE.

taenia /ˈtiːnɪə/ *noun.* Also **tenia.** Pl. **-niae** /-nɪiː/, **-nias.** M16.
[Latin from Greek *tainia* band, fillet, ribbon.]
1 *ARCHITECTURE.* A fillet or band between a Doric architrave and frieze. M16.
2 *ZOOLOGY.* A tapeworm. Now only as mod. Latin genus name. E18.

3 *GREEK ANTIQUITIES.* A headband, ribbon, or fillet. M19.
4 *ANATOMY.* A ribbon-like structure. Usu. with specifying word. L19.

4 **taeniae coli** /ˈkəʊlʌɪ/ [Latin = of the colon] longitudinal ribbon-like muscles of the colon.
■ **taeniacide**, **-nicide** *noun* (*MEDICINE*) an agent that destroys tapeworms M19. **taeniafuge**, **-nifuge** *noun & adjective* (*MEDICINE*) (an agent) that expels tapeworms from the body M19. **taeniasis** /tiːˈnʌɪəsɪs/ *noun*, pl. **-ases** /-əsiːz/, *MEDICINE & ZOOLOGY* infestation with tapeworms, esp. of the genus *Taenia* L19. **taeniate** *adjective* ribbon-like; taenioid: M19. **taenioid** *adjective* ribbon-shaped; related to or resembling the tapeworms: M19.

taeniodont /ˈtiːnɪə(ʊ)dɒnt/ *noun.* M20.
[mod. Latin *Taeniodontia* (see below), from prec. + -ODONT.]
PALAEONTOLOGY. Any of several primitive herbivorous fossil mammals constituting the order Taeniodontia, known from the Palaeocene and Eocene of N. America and characterized by deep powerful jaws and short stout limbs.

taenite /ˈtiːnʌɪt/ *noun.* M19.
[from TAENIA + -ITE¹.]
MINERALOGY. †1 A variety of feldspar occurring as striped crystals. Only in M19.
2 A nickel-iron alloy occurring as lamellae and strips in meteorites. M19.

Tafelmusik /ˈtaːfəlmuˌziːk/ *noun.* L19.
[German, lit. 'table music'.]
1 Music so printed as to enable the same page to be read by two or more people seated on opposite sides of a table. L19.
2 Music intended to be performed at a banquet or a convivial meal, esp. popular in the 18th cent. L19.

Tafelwein /ˈtaːfəlvʌɪn/ *noun.* L20.
[German, lit. 'table wine'.]
Ordinary German wine of less than middle quality, suitable for drinking with a meal. Cf. ***table wine*** s.v. TABLE *noun*, *VIN **de table***.

Taff /taf/ *noun.* E20.
[Abbreviation.]
= TAFFY *noun*¹.

tafferel /ˈtaf(ə)r(ə)l/ *noun.* E17.
[Dutch *taffereel* panel, picture, dim. of *tafel* table.]
†1 A panel; *esp.* a carved panel. E–M17.
2 *NAUTICAL.* The upper part of the flat portion of a ship's stern above the transom, usually decorated with carvings etc. Later = TAFFRAIL. L17.

taffeta /ˈtafɪtə/ *noun & adjective.* Also (now *rare*) **-ty** /-ti/. LME.
[Old French *taffetas* or medieval Latin *taffata*, ult. from Persian *tāfta* use as noun of pa. pple of *tāftan* shine.]
▶ **A** *noun.* **1** Orig., a plain-weave glossy silk. Now, a fine lustrous silk or silk mixture esp. with a crisp texture. LME.
2 *fig.* Florid or bombastic language; = FUSTIAN *noun* 2. *rare.* E19.

📖 **1** R. GODDEN Doors are opened and there are voices, laughter, the rustle of silk and taffeta. *ARMOZEEN* ***taffeta.***

▶ **B** *adjective.* **1** Made of taffeta; of the nature of taffeta. M16.
2 *fig.* Florid, bombastic; overdressed. Also, dainty, fastidious. Now *dial.* L16.

📖 **2** T. MIDDLETON Can taffeta girls look plump without pampering?

Taffia /ˈtafɪə/ *noun. joc. colloq.* Also **Tafia**. L20.
[Blend of TAFFY *noun*¹ and MAFIA.]
Any supposed network of prominent or influential Welsh people, *esp.* one which is strongly nationalistic.

taffrail /ˈtafreɪl/ *noun.* E19.
[Alt. of TAFFEREL, with final syllable assim. to RAIL *noun*².]
NAUTICAL. The after rail at the stern of a ship.

Taffy /ˈtafi/ *noun*¹. *colloq.* Freq. considered *offensive.* M17.
[Repr. an ascribed Welsh pronunc. of male forename *Davy* or *David*, Welsh *Dafydd*.]
(A nickname for) a Welsh person, esp. a man.

taffy /ˈtafi/ *noun*². Now *Scot.*, *north.*, & *N. Amer.* E19.
[Earlier form of TOFFEE *noun*.]
1 A confection similar to toffee made from brown sugar or treacle, boiled with butter and pulled until glossy. Also, toffee. E19.
2 Crude or insincere flattery; blarney. *US slang.* L19.

📖 **1** H. HORWOOD Thinking of the buff-and-brown taffy . . that used to fill the departed glass jars. K. MILLETT Each wonderful swatch of hair like a chunk of taffy stretched. ***salt-water taffy***: see ***salt-water*** (c) s.v. SALT *noun*¹ *& adjective*¹. **2** *North American Review* Throw in a little trade-taffy about the Blessings of Civilization.

Comb.: **taffy apple** a toffee-apple; **taffy pull**, **taffy pulling** a social occasion on which young people meet to make taffy.

tafia /ˈtafɪə/ *noun*¹. *W. Indies.* M18.
[French from W. Indian creole, alt. of RATAFIA.]
A liquor resembling rum distilled from the lower grades of molasses, refuse brown sugar, etc.

Tafia *noun*² var. of TAFFIA.

tafone /taˈfəʊni/ *noun.* Pl. **-ni** /-ni/. M20.
[Corsican Italian *tafòne* hole, hollow.]
GEOLOGY. A shallow rounded cavity in rock produced by weathering. Usu. in *pl.*

taft /tɑːft/ *noun & verb.* L19.
[Origin unkn.]
▶ **A** *noun.* In plumbing, a widening-out of the end of a lead pipe into a broad thin flange. L19.
Comb.: **taft joint** a joint between two lead pipes, made by tafting the end of one pipe, shaping the other to fit into it, and soldering them.
▶ **B** *verb trans.* Expand and turn outwards at a sharp angle the end of (a lead pipe) so as to form a wide edge or fastening flange. L19.

tag /tag/ *noun*¹. LME.
[Origin unkn. Cf. DAG *noun*¹.]
▶ **I** **1** Orig., any of a number of narrow often pointed hanging sections of a slashed garment. Later, any hanging ragged or torn piece; an end or rag of ribbon etc. LME.
2 A metal or plastic point at the end of a lace, string, strap, etc., to facilitate insertion through an eyelet; an aglet. M16.
3 An ornamental pendant; a tassel, jewelled ribbon, shoulder-knot, etc. L16.
4 A catkin. Usu. in *pl. rare.* L16.
5 A small pendent piece or part attached more or less loosely to a main body; *spec.* (**a**) a matted lock of sheep's wool; a dag-lock; a twisted or matted lock of hair; (**b**) a shred of tissue. M17.
6 An extremity differentiated by colour etc.; *spec.* (**a**) the tailpiece of an angler's fly; (**b**) the tip of an animal's tail. L17.
7 A strip of parchment to which the pendent seal of a deed is attached. L17.
8 **a** A thing added to a text, speech, etc. for illustration or clarification; *spec.* (**a**) a brief and usually familiar quotation; a stock phrase; (**b**) the refrain or catch of a song or poem; (**c**) the last words of a speech in a play etc. E18. ▸**b** A musical phrase added to the end of a piece in composition or performance. E20. ▸**c** *LINGUISTICS.* An interrogative formula used to convert a statement into a question. M20.
9 Inflammation of the underside of the tail in sheep owing to diarrhoeal irritation. Also ***tag-sore***. Now *rare* or *obsolete.* M18.
10 A label attached by one end to an object, indicating ownership, origin, price, etc. Freq. with specifying word. Orig. *US.* M19. ▸**b** *ELECTRONICS.* A small metal projection to which a wire may be soldered or attached. E20. ▸**c** = ***licence plate*** s.v. LICENCE *noun.* Usu. in *pl. US colloq.* M20. ▸**d** *COMPUTING.* A character or set of characters appended to an item of data in order to identify it. M20. ▸**e** An epithet; a popular designation (*colloq.*). Also (*slang*, orig. *US*) the signature or identifying mark esp., elaborately decorative, of a graffiti artist. M20. ▸**f** The price of a commodity. Also, an account, a bill. M20. ▸**g** More fully ***electronic tag***. An electronic device attached to a person or thing for monitoring or surveillance. L20.

📖 **8a** L. STEPHEN Adding little moral tags . . to the end of his plays. J. CONRAD A Latin tag came into my head about the . . descent into the abyss. **10** ***dog-tag***, ***name-tag***, ***price tag***, etc.

▶ **II** **11** *collect.* In full ***tag and rag***. The rabble, the common people. *obsolete* exc. in ***ragtag and bobtail*** etc. s.v. BOBTAIL *noun* 3b. Cf. TAGRAG. M16.
12 A lower servant in a large establishment. Cf. PUG *noun*² 4. *arch. colloq.* M19.
13 A person following another as a detective or spy. *slang.* M20.

Comb.: **tag axle** *N. Amer.* a non-powered set of wheels on a truck etc., attached to support extra weight; **tagboard** (**a**) *US* a type of strong cardboard, used esp. for making luggage labels; (**b**) *ELECTRONICS* a board of insulating material containing two or more parallel lines of tags between which components can be mounted; **tag day** *N. Amer.* = ***flag-day*** s.v. FLAG *noun*⁴; **tag-end** the last part or remnant of something; **tag line** *US* a punch-line; **tag-lock** a matted lock of sheep's wool; a dag-lock; **tag-phrase** an automatically repeated or overused phrase; **tag question** *LINGUISTICS* a question converted from a statement by an appended interrogative formula; a formula so used; **tag sale** *US* a sale of miscellaneous second-hand items; **tag-sore** = sense 9 above; **tag strip** *ELECTRONICS* a strip of insulating material on which are mounted a line of tags; **tag-tail** (**a**) *ANGLING* = ***gilt-tail*** s.v. GILT *ppl adjective*; (**b**) *fig.* a hanger-on; **tag-worm** = ***tag-tail*** (a) above.
■ **taglet** *noun* (*rare*) a small tag: *spec.* a tendril; a catkin: L16.

tag /tag/ *noun*² *& adjective.* M18.
[Origin uncertain: perh. var. of TIG *noun*¹.]
▶ **A** *noun.* **1** A children's game in which one player pursues the others and the player who is caught in turn becomes the pursuer; also called ***tick***, ***tig***, ***touch***, ***touch-last***, etc. Also, the pursuer in this game. M18.
2 *BASEBALL.* The act of putting out a runner by a touch with the ball or with the (gloved) hand holding the ball. Also ***tag-out***. M20.
▶ **B** *attrib.* or as *adjective.* Of, pertaining to, or designating a form of wrestling between single alternating representatives of two teams. M20.
tag team a pair of wrestlers who fight as a team (see sense A. above); *transf.* two people completing a single task as a team.

tag *noun*³ var. of TEG.

tag /tag/ *verb*¹. Infl. **-gg-**. E17.
[from TAG *noun*¹.]
1 *verb trans.* Provide with a tag or tags, label; *spec.* (**a**) add a short written or spoken phrase, esp. a quotation or rhyme, to (a text); (**b**) attach an identifying label etc. to (an animal), esp. to enable a migratory pattern to be traced; (**c**) *BIOLOGY & CHEMISTRY.* = LABEL *verb* 2; (**d**) *COMPUTING* label (an item of data) in order to identify it for subsequent processing or retrieval; (**e**) *slang* (orig. *US*) decorate (a building etc.) with a graffiti tag or tags. E17.
2 *verb intrans.* Hang down, trail, dangle. Long *obsolete* exc. *Scot. rare.* E17.
3 *verb trans.* †**a** Fasten, stitch, or tack together; join. L17–E18. ▸**b** *spec.* Join or string together (verses or rhymes). E18.
4 *verb intrans.* Trail behind; follow closely. Freq. foll. by *after*, *along*, *(a)round*, *on. colloq.* L17. ▸**b** *verb trans.* Follow closely; *spec.* follow as a detective or spy. L19.
5 *verb trans.* Add, esp. as an afterthought; join or tack *on* (*to*). Chiefly *fig.* E18.
6 *verb trans.* Cut off tags from (sheep). E18.

📖 **1** *Nature* Anglers tagged 954 bass. P. D. JAMES The . . exhibits, packed and tagged, would be carried to the police car. *fig.*: *Blitz* The film began to be tagged 'the Brat Pack Western'. **3a** SWIFT Resistance, and the succession of the house of Hanover, the whig writers . . tag together. **b** J. R. LOWELL A pretty knack at tagging verses. **4** DAY LEWIS I would tag around with him, hardly understanding a word he said. **b** H. KURNITZ You're supposed to be tagging him for a credit bureau. **5** THACKERAY I have no other moral . . to tag to the present story.

Comb.: **tag-along** *adjective & noun* (*N. Amer. colloq.*) (**a**) *adjective* that is towed or trailed behind something else; (of a follower or companion) uninvited, unwelcome; (**b**) *noun* an uninvited or unwelcome follower or companion.
■ **taggable** *adjective* able to be tagged E20. **tagger** *noun*¹ (**a**) a person who or thing which tags something; *spec.* (*slang*, orig. *US*) a person who decorates a building etc. with a graffiti tag or tags; (**b**) a piece of very thin sheet iron, esp. coated with tin (usu. in *pl.*): M17.

tag /tag/ *verb*². Infl. **-gg-**. L19.
[from TAG *noun*².]
1 *verb trans.* Touch (a player) in a game of tag. L19. ▸**b** *BOXING.* Strike (an opponent). *slang* (orig. *US*). M20.
2 *BASEBALL & SOFTBALL.* **a** *verb trans.* Put out (a runner) by touching with the ball or with the (gloved) hand holding the ball. Also foll. by *out.* E20. ▸**b** *verb intrans.* Foll. by *up*: (of a runner) (return to and) touch base after a fly ball is caught. M20. ▸**c** *verb trans.* Make a hit or run off (a pitcher). M20.
■ **tagger** *noun*² the pursuer in a game of tag L19.

†**Tagala** *noun & adjective* see TAGALOG.

Tagalic /təˈgɑːlɪk/ *noun & adjective.* E19.
[formed as next: see -IC.]
▶ **A** *noun.* †**1** The Tagalog language. Only in E19.
2 An Austronesian language group to which Tagalog belongs. L20.
▶†**B** *adjective.* Of or pertaining to Tagalog. Only in E19.
■ †**Tagalian** *noun* (*rare*) = TAGALOG *noun*: only in E18.

Tagalog /təˈgɑːlɒg/ *noun & adjective.* Also (earlier) †**-la**. E19.
[Tagalog, from *tagá* native + *ilog* river.]
▶ **A** *noun.* Pl. **-s**, same. A member of a people living in the region of Manila and southern Luzon in the Philippines. Also, the Austronesian language of this people, an official language of the Republic of the Philippines. E19.
▶ **B** *adjective.* Of or pertaining to this people or their language. E19.

Tagamet /ˈtagəmɛt/ *noun.* L20.
[Arbitrary formation; *-met* prob. from *cimetidine*.]
PHARMACOLOGY. (Proprietary name for) the drug cimetidine.

tagetes /təˈdʒiːtiːz/ *noun.* L18.
[mod. Latin (see below), from *Tages* an Etruscan god.]
Any of various freq. yellow- or orange-flowered plants constituting the genus *Tagetes*, of the composite family, which are native to Central and S. America and include the French marigold, *T. patula*, and African marigold, *T. erecta*, both commonly grown for ornament.

taggant /ˈtag(ə)nt/ *noun.* L20.
[from TAG *verb*¹ + -ANT¹.]
A substance used for tagging or identification; *spec.* a distinctively coloured powder added to a particular batch of explosive during manufacture.

tagged /tagd/ *adjective.* LME.
[from TAG *noun*[1], *verb*[1]: see -ED[2], -ED[1].]
That has been tagged, provided with a tag or tags.

Prima A tagged fox moved 52 linear miles to a new territory. *DSNA Newsletter* It gives researchers the option of searching the tagged text.

taggeen /tə'gi:n/ *noun. Anglo-Irish.* L19.
[from Irish *taidhgín*, dim. of *Tadhg*: see TEAGUE, -EEN[2].]
A small cup or glass of spirits; a dram.

tagging /'tagɪŋ/ *noun.* LME.
[from TAG *noun*[1] or *verb*[1] + -ING[1].]
1 The action of TAG *verb*[1]; the action or process of providing with a tag or tags; *spec.* (*a*) the action or process of attaching an electronic tag to a person or thing for the purpose of monitoring or surveillance (also ***electronic tagging***); (*b*) *slang* (orig. *US*) the action or process of decorating a building etc. with graffiti tags. LME.
2 Tags, esp. (*slang*, orig. *US*) graffiti tags, collectively. L20.

Taghairm /'tɑ:g(ə)rəm/ *noun. Scot.* L18.
[Gaelic.]
Hist. A method of divination said to have been practised in the Scottish Highlands.

tagine /tə'ʒi:n, tə'dʒi:n/ *noun.* Also **tajine**. M20.
[Moroccan Arab. *ṭažin* from Arab. *ṭājin* frying pan.]
A N. African stew of spiced meat and vegetables prepared by slow cooking in a shallow earthenware cooking dish with a tall, conical lid.

Tagliacotian *adjective* var. of TALIACOTIAN.

tagliarini /taljə'ri:ni/ *noun.* M19.
[Italian *taglierini* pl., from *tagliare*: see next.]
Pasta made in very narrow strips; an Italian dish consisting largely of this and usu. a sauce.

tagliatelle /taljə'tɛli/ *noun.* L19.
[Italian, from *tagliare* to cut. Cf. prec.]
Pasta made in narrow strips; an Italian dish consisting largely of this and usu. a sauce.

taglioni /tɑ:l'jəʊni/ *noun. obsolete* exc. *Hist.* E19.
[Surname of an Italian family of dancers and choreographers in the 18th and 19th cents.]
A short braid-trimmed overcoat fashionable in the early 19th cent.

tagma /'tagmə/ *noun.* Pl. **tagmata** /-mətə/. L19.
[Greek = something arranged, from *tassein* set in order.]
†**1** BIOLOGY. Any of the aggregates of molecules supposed to make up a living structure. Only in L19.
2 ZOOLOGY. Each of the morphologically distinct regions, comprising several adjoining segments, into which the bodies of arthropods and some other segmented animals are divided. Usu. in *pl.* E20.
3 LINGUISTICS. A feature of grammatical arrangement or syntax; *esp.* in tagmemics, the smallest meaningful unit of grammatical substance (opp. ***tagmeme***). Now *rare.* M20.
■ **tag'mosis** *noun* (ZOOLOGY) the formation of tagmata E20.

tagmeme /'tagmi:m/ *noun.* M20.
[formed as prec. + -EME.]
LINGUISTICS. **1** The smallest meaningful unit of grammatical form. M20.
2 The correlate of a grammatical function and the class of items which can perform it. M20.

tagmemic /tag'mi:mɪk/ *adjective.* M20.
[from prec. + -IC.]
LINGUISTICS. Of or pertaining to tagmemes or tagmemics.

tagmemics /tag'mi:mɪks/ *noun pl.* (also treated as *sing.*). M20.
[formed as prec. + -ICS.]
LINGUISTICS. A mode of linguistic analysis based on identifying the function of each grammatical position in the sentence etc. and the class of words by which it can be filled.
■ **tagmemicist** *noun* a student or expert in tagmemics M20.

tagnicati /tanjɪ'kɑ:ti/ *noun.* E19.
[Spanish *tañicati* from Guarani.]
The white-lipped peccary, *Tayassu pecari*.

tagrag /'tagrag/ *adverb, noun, & adjective.* Orig. as two words. L16.
[from TAG *noun*[1] + RAG *noun*[1]. Cf. RAGTAG.]
▶†**A** *adverb.* All to rags and tatters. Also, one and all; in a mingled crowd or heap. L16–M18.
▶**B** *noun.* **1** *collect.* The rabble, the common people. Now chiefly in ***tagrag and bobtail*** below. E17. ▸**b** A member of the rabble; a low despicable person. Now *rare* or *obsolete.* M17.
2 A ragged tag or appendage. E19.
1 *tagrag and bobtail*: see BOBTAIL *noun* 3b.
▶**C** *adjective.* Orig., of or belonging to the rabble. Later, consisting of or dressed in rags and tatters, ragged. E17.
■ **tagraggery** *noun* a tagrag collection or assemblage; a mass of worthless odds and ends: M19.

tagua /'tagwə/ *noun.* M19.
[Spanish from Quechua *tawa*.]
An ivory palm, *Phytelephas macrocarpa*, of northern S. America.
Comb.: **tagua-nut** the ivory-nut, the fruit of this palm.

taguan /'tagwən/ *noun.* E19.
[App. a local name in the Philippines.]
Either of two giant flying squirrels of SE Asia, *Petaurista petaurista* and *P. philippensis*.

tahali /tɑ:hə'li:/ *noun. poet. rare.* M19.
[Spanish.]
A baldric.

taharah /taha'rɑ:/ *noun.* Pl. **-rot(h)** /-'rəʊt/. E19.
[Hebrew *ṭohŏrāh* purification, cleansing.]
In Jewish ritual, an act of washing a corpse before burial.

tahina /tɑ:'hi:nə/ *noun.* Also **tahini** /tɑ:'hi:ni/. M20.
[(mod. Greek *takhini* from) Arab. *ṭaḥīnā*, from *ṭaḥana* grind, crush, pulverize.]
A Middle Eastern paste or sauce made from sesame seeds.

Tahiti /tɑ:'hi:ti/ *noun.* M19.
[An island in the S. Pacific. Cf. earlier OTAHEITE.]
Used *attrib.* to denote things found in or obtained from Tahiti.
Tahiti arrowroot a starchy powder made from the tubers of the pia, *Tacca leontopetaloides*. **Tahiti chestnut** (the fruit of) the ivi, *Inocarpus fagifer*.

Tahitian /tɑ:'hi:ʃ(ə)n, tɑ:'hi:tɪən/ *noun & adjective.* E19.
[from *Tahiti* (see below) + -AN. Cf. earlier OTAHEITEAN.]
▶**A** *noun.* A native or inhabitant of Tahiti, an island in the S. Pacific. Also, the Polynesian language of Tahiti. E19.
▶**B** *adjective.* Of or pertaining to Tahiti, its inhabitants, or their language. E19.

tahr /tɑ:/ *noun.* Orig. (now *rare*) **tehr** /tɛ:/. M19.
[Local (Himalayan) name, perh. ult. same as THAR *noun*[1].]
A wild goat of the genus *Hemitragus*, found in mountainous regions of southern Asia and Arabia, esp. *H. jemlahicus* of the Himalayas, which has long brown fur and curved horns.

tahsil /tɑ:'si:l/ *noun.* M19.
[Persian & Urdu *taḥṣīl* from Arab. = collection, levying of taxes.]
In the Indian subcontinent, an administrative division comprising several villages, formerly *spec.*, for revenue administration.

tahsildar /tɑ:'si:ldɑ:/ *noun.* L18.
[formed as prec. + Persian *-dār* holding, holder.]
Formerly, the chief collector of revenue in a subdivision of a district in India. Now, the official in charge of a tahsil.

Tahunian /tɑ:'hu:nɪən/ *adjective.* M20.
[French *Tahounien*, from *Tahouneh* (see below): see -IAN.]
Of, pertaining to, or designating a neolithic industry of ancient Palestine represented by remains found at Tahouneh.

tai /tʌɪ/ *noun*[1]. E17.
[Japanese.]
A deep red-brown Pacific sea bream, *Pagrus major*, eaten as a delicacy in Japan.

Tai /tʌɪ/ *noun*[2] *& adjective.* L17.
[Var. of THAI.]
▶**A** *noun.* Pl. same.
1 A member of a group of peoples of SE Asia including the Thai. L17.
2 A Sino-Tibetan group of languages including Thai. M19.
▶**B** *adjective.* Of or pertaining to these peoples or their languages. M19.

taiaha /'tʌɪaha/ *noun. NZ.* M19.
[Maori.]
A long-handled Maori club with a sharp tip.

T'ai Chi /tʌɪ 'tʃi:/ *noun.* M18.
[Chinese *tàijí* (Wade–Giles *t'ai chi*), from *tài* extreme + *jí* limit.]
1 TAOISM & NEO-CONFUCIANISM. The ultimate point, constituting both source and limit, of the life-force. Also, the symbol representing this. M18.
2 In full ***T'ai Chi Ch'uan*** /'tʃwɑ:n/ [Chinese *quán* fist]. A Chinese martial art and system of callisthenics consisting of sequences of very slow controlled movements, believed to have been devised by a Taoist priest in the Song dynasty. M20.

Taig /teɪg/ *noun. slang* (considered *offensive*). L20.
[Var. of TEAGUE.]
In Northern Ireland, a Roman Catholic.

taiga /'tʌɪgə/ *noun.* L19.
[Russian *taiga* from Mongolian.]
The swampy coniferous forest of high northern latitudes, *esp.* that between the tundra and steppes of Siberia.

taiglach *noun pl.* var. of TEIGLACH.

taihoa /tʌɪ'həʊə/ *interjection. NZ.* M19.
[Maori.]
Wait a bit; by and by; presently.

taiko /'tʌɪkəʊ/ *noun.* Pl. same, **-os**. L19.
[Japanese.]
A Japanese drum; *spec.* any of a class of barrel-shaped drums.

tail /teɪl/ *noun*[1].
[Old English *tæg(e)l* = Middle Low German *tagel* twisted whip, rope's end, Old High German *zagal* animal's tail (German dial. *Zagel*, *Zāl*), Old Norse *tagl* horse's (or cow's) tail, Gothic *tagl* hair of the head, camel's hair, from Germanic.]
1 The hindmost part of an animal, esp. when prolonged beyond the rest of the body as a flexible appendage. Also, a representation of this. OE. ▸**b** *Hist.* A horse's tail as used in the Ottoman Empire as a symbol of a pasha's rank. E18.
2 A thing resembling an animal's tail in shape or position; *spec.* (*a*) the luminous trail of particles extending from the head of a comet; †(*b*) a germinating sprout of barley; (*c*) a twisted or braided tress of hair; a pigtail; (*d*) a stroke or loop, esp. as extending below the line, forming the lower portion of a written or printed letter or figure; (*e*) the stem of a note in music; (*f*) the rear part of an aeroplane, with the tailplane and rudder, or of a rocket; (*g*) MATH. an extremity of a curve, esp. that of a frequency distribution, approaching the horizontal axis of a graph; the part of a distribution that this represents; (*h*) any of the tenons in the shape of a reversed wedge in a dovetail joint. ME.
3 The lower or hanging part of a garment; *spec.* (*a*) (now *colloq.* & *dial.*) the train of a woman's dress; (*b*) the hanging part of the back of a coat; (*c*) the bottom or lower edge of a dress, skirt, etc., reaching (nearly) to the ground (usu. in *pl.*); (*d*) *colloq.* in *pl.*, a tailcoat; evening dress including this; (*e*) (*sing.* & in *pl.*) the back part of a shirt reaching below the waist. ME.
4 a The buttocks (freq. in ***work one's tail off*** below). Now chiefly *dial.* & *N. Amer. colloq.* ME. ▸**b** The external genitals, esp. of a woman. LME. ▸**c** Orig., a prostitute. Later, women collectively regarded as a means of male sexual gratification; sexual intercourse; (freq. in ***piece of tail*** s.v. PIECE *noun*). *coarse slang.* M19.
5 a A train or band of followers; a retinue. *arch.* ME. ▸**b** A person who secretly follows and watches another, esp. as a detective or a spy. Also, people in the act of following others collectively. *colloq.* (orig. *US*). E20.
6 The lower, hindmost, or final part of something; *spec.* (*a*) the rear end of an army (esp. comprising the non-combatant personnel), marching column, procession, etc. (cf. TOOTH *noun* 3c); (*b*) a terminal or concluding passage, the final part of a period of time, event, etc.; (*c*) the rear part of a cart, plough, or harrow; a plough-tail; (*d*) *obsolete* exc. *dial.* the stern of a ship; (*e*) the part of a mill-race below the wheel (more fully ***tail-race***); the lower end of a pool or stream; (*f*) the image on the reverse of a coin; (in *pl.*) this side turned upwards after a toss; (*g*) the spit or extremity of a reef or sandbank where it shelves; (*h*) the unexposed end of a brick or stone in a wall; the exposed end of a slate or tile in a roof; (*i*) the lower edge of a page or cover; †(*j*) a small evening party following a dinner or ball; (*k*) PHONETICS the syllable(s) following the nucleus in the same tone-group; (*l*) the rear part of a motor vehicle. LME.
7 *sing.* & in *pl.* The inferior or waste part of something; sediment, dregs; *spec.* poor quality corn, barley, etc., or flour made from this. M16.
†**8** = ***tail-ill*** below. L16–M18.
9 The inferior, least influential, or least skilful members of a specified group; *spec.* (*a*) CRICKET the weaker batsmen constituting the end of a batting order; (*b*) the poorer animals of a flock or herd. M17.

1 R. DAWKINS Tails of birds of paradise and peacocks. A. HARDY The long rat-like tail was quite . . robust. **2** *Nature* The region is part of the magnetic tail of the planet. D. G. PHILLIPS An incredibly greasy . . dangling tail of hair. **3** D. LEAVITT The wind was blowing the tails of his trenchcoat up. **6** *Practical Householder* A . . washer is slipped onto the tail of the taps. **9** *Cricketer* The tail folded up once he had square-cut . . hard to cover point.

Phrases: **be on a person's tail** follow or pursue a person closely, esp. as a detective or a spy. ***cat-o'-nine-tails***: see CAT *noun*[1] 6. **chase one's tail** make futile efforts; go round in circles. ***crag and tail***: see CRAG *noun*[1] 1. ***drake's tail***: see DRAKE *noun*[2]. ***flat-tail mullet***: see FLAT *adjective*. ***have a tiger by the tail***: see TIGER *noun*. ***heads I win, tails you lose***: see HEAD *noun*. ***like a dog with two tails***: see DOG *noun & adjective*. ***make head or tail of***: see HEAD *noun*. ***piece of tail***: see PIECE *noun*. ***put salt on the tail of***: see SALT *noun*[1]. ***sting in the tail***: see STING *noun*[2] 5. **tail of the eye** the outer corner of the eye. **the tail wags the dog** the less important or subsidiary factor dominates the situation; the proper roles are reversed. **turn tail** orig. FALCONRY (*a*) turn the back; (*b*) run away, take to flight. ***twist a person's tail***, ***twist the lion's tail***: see TWIST *verb*. **with one's tail between one's legs** *colloq.* in a state of dejection or humiliation. **with one's tail up** *colloq.* in good spirits, cheerful. **work one's tail off** *colloq.* work strenuously.

Comb.: **tail-area** STATISTICS an area under the curve of a frequency distribution lying between one end of the curve and any ordinate on the same side of the mode; **tail assembly** AERONAUTICS = EMPENNAGE; **tail-bandage** (*a*) a bandage divided into strips at the end; (*b*) a strip of material to protect a horse's tail from injury or dishevelment; **tail-bay** (*a*) the space between a girder and a wall; (*b*) the narrow area just below the lock in a canal lock, opening out into the lower stretch of water; **tail-block** (*a*) NAUTICAL a small single block with a short piece of rope attached; (*b*) = *tailstock* below; **tailboard** a hinged or removable flap at the rear end of a cart, lorry, etc.; **tail-bone** each of the caudal vertebrae in an animal; also, the coccyx; **tail boom** AERONAUTICS each of the main spars of the longitudinal framework carrying the tail of an aeroplane when not supported by the fuselage; **tailcoat** a man's long-skirted coat divided at the back into tails and cut away in front, worn on formal occasions; **tailcoated** *adjective* wearing a tailcoat; **tail comb** a comb with a tapering tail or handle used in styling to lift, divide, or curl the hair; **tail cone** AERONAUTICS the conical rear end of the fuselage of an aircraft; **tail covert** ORNITHOLOGY each of the smaller feathers covering the bases of the rectrices or quill-feathers of a bird's tail (usu. in *pl.*); **tail-dragger** AERONAUTICS an aeroplane that lands and taxies on a tail wheel or tail skid, its nose off the ground; **tail-drain**: for carrying off water from a field etc.; **tail fin** (*a*) the caudal fin of a fish; (*b*) AERONAUTICS a small projecting surface on the tail of an aircraft, esp. to ensure stability; (*c*) an upswept projection on the rear of a motor vehicle; **tail-flap** (*a*) the flattened tail of a crustacean; (*b*) AERONAUTICS an adjustable control surface on the tail of an aircraft; **tail-flower** any of various tropical American aroids constituting the genus *Anthurium*, so called from their spicate inflorescence that resembles a tail; **tail-fly** the fishing-fly at the end of a leader; also called *stretcher-fly*; **tail gas** gas produced in a refinery and not required for further processing; **tail-grape** any of various shrubs constituting the genus *Artabotrys* (family Annonaceae), of tropical Asia and Africa, which climb by means of the recurved hooks on their peduncles; **tail gunner** = *rear gunner* s.v. REAR *adjective*[1], *noun*, & *adverb*; **tail-head** the root of an animal's tail; **tail-heaviness** the state of being tail-heavy; **tail-heavy** *adjective* (of an aircraft etc.) having a tendency for the rear end to drop relative to the front; **tail-hound** any of the hounds at the back of a pack; **tail-ill** (now *rare* or *obsolete*) partial or complete paralysis in the hind limbs of a domestic animal; **tail-lamp**, **tail-light** a (usu. red) light at the rear of a train, motor vehicle, etc.; **tail parachute** AERONAUTICS a deceleration parachute attached to the tail of an aircraft; **tailpiece** (*a*) the final part of something; an appendage at the rear of something; (*b*) a small decoration or illustration at the end of a book, chapter, etc.; (*c*) a triangular piece of wood to which the lower ends of strings are fastened in some musical instruments; **tail-pin** MUSIC (*a*) a structure on a violin etc. to which the tailpiece is attached; (*b*) a metal spike on a cello etc. to support it at the correct height from the ground; **tailpipe** (*a*) the suction pipe of a pump; (*b*) (chiefly *N. Amer.*) a pipe to remove exhaust gases from the manifold of an aircraft engine; (*c*) *N. Amer.* the (rear section of the) exhaust-pipe of a motor vehicle; **tail-pipe** *verb trans.* (*arch. colloq.*) tie a tin can etc. to the tail of (a dog) to cause distress and fright; **tailplane** AERONAUTICS the horizontal stabilizing surface of the tail of an aircraft; **tail-pole** a lever or beam for turning a windmill to the wind; **tail-race** (*a*) see sense 6(e) above; (*b*) MINING a water channel for the removal of tailings; (*c*) the watercourse leading from the turbine of a power station, dam, etc.; **tail-rhyme** rhyme involving couplets, triplets, or stanzas, each with a tag or additional short line; **tail-rod** a continuation of a piston-rod, passing through the back cover of a cylinder, and serving to steady the piston and rod; **tail-rope** (chiefly *techn.*) a rope forming or attached to the lower, hindmost, or final part of something; NAUTICAL (now *N. Amer.*) = SHEET *noun*[2] 4; **tail rotor** AERONAUTICS an auxiliary rotor at the tail of a helicopter designed to counterbalance the torque of the main rotor; **tail-screw** the screw in a lathe moving the back centre tail-spindle to and fro; the tailpiece; **tail-shaft** the section of the shaft in a screw steamer nearest the propeller; **tail skid** AERONAUTICS a runner supporting an aircraft's tail when on the ground; **tail-slide** AERONAUTICS the backward movement of an aircraft from a vertical stalled position; **tailspin** *noun* & *verb* (*a*) *noun* a spin by an aircraft with the tail spiralling; *fig.* a state of chaos, panic, or loss of control; (*b*) *verb intrans.* perform or go into a tailspin; **tail-spindle** a spindle in the tailstock of a lathe; **tail-spine** ZOOLOGY a long spine projecting behind the body of a horseshoe crab like a tail; **tailstock** the adjustable fixing at the other end of a lathe from the main support or headstock; **tail-twisting** *fig.* harassment, malicious annoyance; **tail unit** AERONAUTICS = EMPENNAGE; **tail-valve** the air-pump valve in some forms of condenser; *spec.* a snifting valve; **tail-wag** sideways or up-and-down motion of the back end of a moving object, as a bullet, a vehicle trailer, etc.; **tail-walk** *verb intrans.* (of a fish) move over the surface of water by propulsion with the tail; **tail-walking** the action of tail-walking; **tail-water** the water in a mill-race below the wheel, or in a canal etc. below a lock; **tail wheel** a wheel supporting the tail of a vehicle, esp. of an aircraft on the ground; **tail wind** a wind blowing in the direction of travel of a vehicle or aircraft.

■ **tailless** /-l-l-/ *adjective* without a tail ME. **taillessness** *noun* L19. **tail-like** *adjective* resembling a tail M19. **tailward** *noun, adverb, & adjective* (*rare*) = TAILWARDS E20. **tailwards** *noun, adverb, & adjective* (*a*) *noun* (long *rare*) the direction towards the tail; (*b*) *adverb* towards or in the direction of the tail; (*c*) *adjective* directed or going tailwards: E17. **tailwise** *adverb* (*rare*) (*a*) with the tail foremost; backwards; (*b*) in the manner of a tail: M19.

tail /teɪl/ *noun*[2]. ME.

[Old & mod. French *taille*, from *taillier*: see TAIL *verb*[1].]

▶†**I 1** Shape, fashion, bodily form or appearance. *rare*. Only in ME.

▶†**II 2** A subsidy or tallage levied by a king or feudal lord; a tax. ME–M17.

3 A tally; a score, an account. ME–L17.

▶**III 4** LAW (now *Hist.*). The limitation of the succession of land or other property so that it cannot be bequeathed or sold but must pass to the holder's descendants, failing which it reverts to the donor or the donor's heirs or assigns. Chiefly in phrs. below. LME.

4 in tail under the limitation of tail. *tail female*: see *tail male* below. **tail general** limitation of the succession to legitimate descendants. **tail female**, **tail male** limitation of the succession to female or male descendants respectively. **tail special** limitation of the succession to a specified class of heirs.

tail /teɪl/ *adjective*. L15.

[Anglo-Norman *taile*, Old French *taillié* pa. pple of *taillier*: see TAIL *verb*[1].]

LAW (now *Hist.*). Of land or other property: settled in tail (see TAIL *noun*[2] 4). Usu. *postpositive*.

tail /teɪl/ *verb*[1]. ME.

[Old French *taillier* (mod. *tailler*), from Proto-Romance (medieval Latin *tailliare*), from Latin *talea* rod, twig, cutting.]

▶**I** †**1** *verb trans.* Cut up, cut to pieces, slaughter. Only in ME.

†**2** *verb trans.* Put into shape, trim, make ready. Only in ME.

†**3** *verb trans.* Cut, esp. to a certain size or shape; shape, fashion. LME–M16.

▶**II** †**4** *verb trans.* Decide or determine in a specified way; settle or arrange (a matter). ME–L15.

5 *verb trans.* LAW. Settle the succession of (land or other property) so that it cannot be bequeathed or sold but must pass to the donee's descendants or a designated class of such descendants. LME.

▶†**III 6** *verb trans.* Of a king or feudal lord: levy a subsidy or tallage on; tax. ME–L16.

▶†**IV 7** *verb trans.* Mark or record on a tally; charge (a person) with a debt. LME–M17.

8 *verb intrans.* Deal by tally, or on credit. E–L16.

9 *verb trans.* Tally or agree with; equal. Only in M17.

tail /teɪl/ *verb*[2]. E16.

[from TAIL *noun*[1].]

▶**I** *verb trans.* **1** Fasten to the back of something else; join (one thing on *to* another). E16.

2 Grasp or drag by the tail. M17.

3 Remove the tail from; *spec.* (*a*) remove the stalks from (fruit); (*b*) dock the tail of (a lamb). L18.

4 Have sexual intercourse with (a woman). *slang*. L18.

5 BUILDING. Insert the end of (a beam, stone, or brick) *into* a wall etc.; let in, dovetail. E19.

6 Be or put oneself at the end of (a procession etc.); terminate. M19.

7 a Follow, drive, or tend (sheep, cattle, or horses). *Austral. & NZ*. M19. ▸**b** Follow someone closely, *spec.* as a detective or spy. *colloq.* (orig. *US*). E20.

8 Provide with a tail. Cf. earlier TAILED *adjective* 1. L19.

> 📖 **1** J. SCOTT What is this but to tail one folly to another? **2** *stave and tail*: see STAVE *verb*. **3** *top and tail*: see TOP *verb*[1]. **6** *Fraser's Magazine* A male author heads and a male author tails the procession. **7b** M. PUZO They . . tailed the old man to his office.

▶**II** *verb intrans.* **9** Of a ship: run *aground* stern foremost. E18.

10 Of water or flames: move back against a prevailing current of water or air. L18.

11 Of a body of people or animals: move or proceed in a line; esp. lengthen out into a straggling line; drop behind, fall away. L18.

12 Of a ship etc.: be or be placed with the stern in a specified position relative to the wind, current, etc. M19.

13 BUILDING. Of a beam, stone, or brick: be inserted by the end *into* a wall etc., be let in, be dovetailed. M19.

14 Of a stream: flow or fall *into*. L19.

15 Of a fish: show its tail at the surface. L19.

With adverbs in specialized senses: **tail away** = *tail off* (a) below. **tail off** (*a*) fall behind or away in a straggling line; become fewer or slighter or smaller; end inconclusively; (*b*) (*colloq.*) go off, esp. in a specified direction; withdraw; (*c*) overtake (another competitor in a race etc.). **tail on** join on in the rear.

Comb.: **tail-off** *colloq.* a decline or gradual reduction, esp. in demand.

tail /teɪl/ *verb*[3] *trans.* L18.

[Var. of TILL *verb*[1].]

Set (a trap or snare); bait (a trap).

tailback /ˈteɪlbak/ *noun*. M20.

[In sense 1 from TAIL *noun*[1] + BACK *noun*[1]; in sense 2 from TAIL *verb*[2] + BACK *adverb*.]

1 AMER. FOOTBALL. The player stationed furthest from the forwards. M20.

2 A queue of stationary or slowly moving motor vehicles, esp. extending back from an obstruction. L20.

tailed /teɪld/ *adjective*. ME.

[from TAIL *noun*[1], *verb*[2]: see -ED[2], -ED[1].]

1 Having or provided with a tail or tails; ZOOLOGY & BOTANY = CAUDATE. Freq. as 2nd elem. of comb., as ***long-tailed***, ***white-tailed***, etc. ME.

2 That has been tailed. M16.

tail-end /teɪlˈɛnd, ˈteɪlɛnd/ *noun*. LME.

[from TAIL *noun*[1] + END *noun*.]

1 †**a** The buttocks. Only in LME. ▸**b** The lower, hindmost, or final part of something; the part opposite the head. M18.

2 The inferior or weaker part of something; *spec.* (*a*) CRICKET the weaker batsmen constituting the end of a batting order; (*b*) *rare* a quantity of inferior grain, flour, etc. L19.

Comb.: **tail-end Charlie** (*a*) a tail gunner; the last aircraft in a flying formation; (*b*) a tail-ender.

■ **tail-ender** *noun* (esp. in SPORT) a person at the tail-end of something L19.

tailer /ˈteɪlə/ *noun*. M19.

[from TAIL *verb*[2] + -ER[1].]

1 A person who tails something; *spec.* a follower, a hanger-on. Now *rare* or *obsolete*. M19.

2 ANGLING. **a** A fish that tails. L19. ▸**b** A device with a metal loop used for landing large fish by the tail. M20.

3 A person who follows, drives, or tends sheep or cattle. Also, a straggling animal. *Austral.* L19.

Comb.: **tailer-out** *Austral. & NZ* a person who guides timber coming off a saw.

taileron /ˈteɪlərɒn/ *noun*. M20.

[Blend of TAIL *noun*[1] and AILERON.]

AERONAUTICS. A horizontal control surface on an aircraft's tail which can function as both elevator and aileron.

tailgate /ˈteɪlgeɪt/ *noun & adjective*. M19.

[from TAIL *noun*[1] + GATE *noun*[1].]

▶**A** *noun*. **1** A tailboard. Also, the door at the back of an estate or hatchback car. Orig. *US*. M19.

2 A lower gate of a canal lock. L19.

▶**B** *attrib.* or as *adjective*. **1** Designating a style of jazz trombone playing characterized by improvisation in the manner of the early New Orleans musicians. M20.

2 Designating or pertaining to an informal meal served from the open tailgate of a parked car. *N. Amer.* L20.

tailgate /ˈteɪlgeɪt/ *verb intrans. & trans. colloq.* (orig. *US*). M20.

[from prec.]

Drive too close behind (another vehicle).

■ **tailgater** *noun* M20.

tailing /ˈteɪlɪŋ/ *noun*. M17.

[from TAIL *verb*[2] + -ING[1].]

1 The end or final part of something. *rare*. M17. ▸**b** *spec.* The part of a beam or projecting brick or stone embedded in a wall. M19.

2 The action of TAIL *verb*[1]. E18.

3 a Grain or flour of inferior quality. (Usu. in *pl.*) M18. ▸**b** In *pl.* The leavings or the residue of any product, esp. ore. M19.

tailism /ˈteɪlɪz(ə)m/ *noun*. M20.

[from TAIL *noun*[1] + -ISM.]

POLITICS. In Communist usage, the error of accommodating policy to the wishes of the masses rather than taking an active revolutionary role.

†**taillage** *noun* var. of TALLAGE *noun*.

taille /taːj, taːj/ *noun*. Pl. pronounced same. M16.

[French: see TAIL *noun*[2].]

1 In France, a tax levied on the common people. *obsolete* exc. *Hist.* M16.

2 Cut, shape, form; shape of the bust from the shoulders to the waist; figure, build. M17.

3 MUSIC (now *Hist.*). The register of a tenor or similar voice; an instrument of this register. M19.

taille-douce /tajdus/ *noun*. M17.

[French = soft cutting, formed as prec. + *douce* (see DOUCE *adjective*).]

Engraving on a metal plate with a graver or burin as opp. to a dry-point or etching needle.

tailleur /tajœːr/ *noun*. Pl. pronounced same. E20.

[French, formed as TAILLE + *-eur* -OR.]

A woman's tailor-made suit.

taillie *noun & verb* var. of TAILYE.

tailor /ˈteɪlə/ *noun*. ME.

[Anglo-Norman *taillour*, Old French *tailleur* cutter, from Proto-Romance base of TAIL *verb*[1]: see -OR.]

1 A person whose occupation is to make clothes; *esp.* one who makes men's outer clothes to measure. ME.

2 Any of various fishes, as the silverside, the bleak, the fall herring, and esp. (now chiefly *Austral.*) the bluefish, *Pomatomus saltatrix*. L17.

3 A crane-fly, a daddy-long-legs. L17.

Comb.: **tailor-bird** any of various Asiatic passerine birds, chiefly of the genus *Orthotomus*, which stitch together the edges of leaves with cotton, etc., to form a cavity for their nest; orig. *spec.* (more fully ***long-tailed tailor-bird***) *O. sutorius* of southern and eastern Asia; **tailor-fashion** *adverb* = TAILOR-WISE *adverb*; **tailor-herring** = *fall* HERRING; **tailor-made** *adjective & noun* (*a*) *adjective* (of clothing) made by a tailor; (of a cigarette) ready made as opp. to hand-rolled; *fig.* made or suited for a particular purpose, designed according to specific requirements; (*b*) *noun* a tailor-made garment; a tailor-made cigarette; **tailor-madeness** the state of being tailor-made; **tailor-make** *verb trans.* (orig. *US*) make or suit for a particular purpose; design according to specific requirements; **tailor's chair** a legless seat with back and knee rest for a person sitting tailor-wise; **tailor's chalk** hard chalk or soapstone used in tailoring etc. for marking fabric as a guide to fitting; **tailor's dummy** a lay figure on which to fit or display clothes; **tailor-shad** = *tailor-herring* above; **tailor's muscle** = SARTORIUS; **tailor's tack** a large stitch taken through two thicknesses of fabric and severed, leaving the ends of thread as a guide to fitting (usu. in *pl.*); **tailor's twist** a fine strong silk thread used by tailors.

■ **tailordom** *noun* (*a*) the condition or fact of being a tailor; (*b*) the domain of tailors; (*c*) *rare* tailoring: M19. **tailoress** *noun* a female tailor LME. **tailorism** *noun* (*a*) (an item of) tailor-made clothing; (*b*) *rare* behaviour or attitudes characteristic of tailors: M19. **tailorize** *verb* (*a*) *verb intrans.* work as a tailor; sit cross-legged in the traditional position of a tailor; (*b*) *verb trans.* treat as a tailor: E19. **tailorly** *adjective* of, pertaining to, or characteristic of a tailor M19. **tailorship** *noun* the function of performance of a tailor; tailoring: M19. **tailor-wise** *adverb* in a cross-legged position, the traditional attitude of a tailor seated at work L19. **tailory** *noun* (*a*) the skill or work of a tailor; (*b*) a tailor's workshop or establishment; (*c*) goods or wares sold by a tailor; tailor-made clothes collectively: LME.

tailor /ˈteɪlə/ *verb.* M17.
[from prec.]
1 *verb intrans.* Make clothes; *spec.* work as a tailor, be a tailor. M17.
2 *verb trans.* Make (esp. men's) outer clothes for (a person). Freq. as ***tailored*** *ppl adjective.* E19.
3 *verb trans.* Make (clothes) as a tailor. M19. ▸**b** *fig.* Design or alter (something) to suit a specific need. Orig. *US.* M20.
4 *verb trans.* Miss or wound (a bird) in shooting. *slang.* L19.

📖 **2** *Westminster Gazette* He wore a frock coat, and seemed faultlessly tailored. **3b** G. DALY To tailor her behaviour to fit different people and situations.

■ **tailorable** *adjective* able to be adapted L20. **tailored** *ppl adjective* that has been tailored; tailor-made; (of outer clothes) well cut and fitted: M19. **tailoring** *noun* (*a*) the action of the verb; (*b*) tailor-made clothing: M17.

tailye /ˈtɛlji, ˈtɛli/ *noun & verb. Scot.* Also **tailzie**, **taillie**. LME.
[Partly formed as TAIL *noun*[2], partly from Old French *taillíee*, *taillé*, *taillie* fem. of pa. pple of *taillier*: see TAIL *verb*[1].]
▶ **A** *noun.* **1** A cut piece; a cut or slice of meat. LME.
†**2** Arrangement, fixture. Only in LME.
3 SCOTS LAW. A legal disposition regulating the tenure and descent of an estate or title; an entail. LME.
†**4** An account, a reckoning. L15–E16.
▶ **B** *verb trans.* †**1** Determine, settle, appoint, arrange. Only in LME.
†**2** Keep account or tally of. L15–M16.
3 SCOTS LAW. Make a legal disposition regulating tenure and descent of (an estate or title); entail. M16.
†**4** Cut; cut to shape. Only in L16.

tainchel(l) *noun* var. of TINCHEL.

Taino /ˈtʌɪnəʊ/ *adjective & noun.* M19.
[Taino *taino* noble, lord.]
▶ **A** *adjective.* Pertaining to or designating an extinct Arawak people formerly inhabiting the Greater Antilles and the Bahamas. M19.
▶ **B** *noun.* Pl. **-os**, same. A member of the Taino people; the Arawak language of the Taino people. M20.

taint /teɪnt/ *noun.* LME.
[Partly aphet. from ATTAINT *noun*, partly Old French *teint*, *taint* from Latin *tinctus* and Old French *teinte* from late Latin *tincta* uses as noun of pa. pple of *tingere* TINGE *verb*.]
▶†**I 1** = ATTAINT *noun* 2. LME–E17.
2 = ATTAINT *noun* 3. E16–M19.
3 A conviction; *spec.* = ATTAINT *noun* 4. M16–E18.
▶ **II 4 a** A stain, a blemish; a spot or trace of some bad or undesirable quality. LME. ▸†**b** *spec.* A flaw or blemish in a hawk's plumage as a result of bad feeding. Only in L15. ▸**c** An unpleasant scent or smell. E20.
†**5** A worm, maggot, or other small invertebrate supposed to infect or poison livestock. Also ***taint-worm***. *arch.* L16.
6 A contaminating or corrupting influence; a cause or condition of corruption or decay; an infection. E17. ▸**b** A trace of latent disease. E17.

📖 **4a** SHAKES. *Twel. N.* I hate ingratitude more in a man Than . . any taint of vice. N. PODHORETZ Free of the taint of commercialism. **c** H. WILLIAMSON The taint most dreaded by the otters . . the scent of Deadlock, the . . hound. **6** H. MARTINEAU Health . . was affected by the taint the marsh gave to the atmosphere.

▶†**III 7** Colour, hue, tint; tinge; dye. M–L16.
■ **taintless** *adjective* (chiefly *poet.*) free from taint; without stain or blemish; immaculate, innocent: L16. **taintlessly** *adverb* M19. **taintlessness** *noun* E19.

taint /teɪnt/ *verb.* Pa. t. & pple **-ed**, (earlier) †**taint**. ME.
[Partly aphet. from ATTAINT *verb*, partly from Anglo-Norman *teinter*, from *teint* pa. pple of Old & mod. French *teindre* from Latin *tingere* TINGE *verb*.]
▶†**I 1** *verb trans.* = ATTAINT *verb* 2. ME–E18.
2 *verb trans.* = ATTAINT *verb* 4. Only in E17.
3 *verb trans.* = ATTAINT *verb* 3. Only in M18.
▶†**II 4** *verb trans.* Colour, dye, tinge. L15–E18.
5 *verb trans.* Apply tincture, balm, or ointment to (a wound etc.). L16–M17.
▶†**III 6** *verb trans.* Touch or hit, esp. in jousting. Also, break (a lance etc.), esp. in jousting. E16–E17.
▶ **IV 7 a** *verb trans.* Corrupt, contaminate. L16. ▸**b** *verb intrans.* Become corrupted or contaminated; (of meat) putrefy. E17. ▸**c** *verb trans. spec.* Drive *out* (rabbits) from a burrow by the introduction of an offensive smell. E20.
8 *verb trans.* Affect, esp. to a slight degree; imbue slightly *with* some bad or undesirable quality. L16.
†**9** *verb trans.* Cause detriment to; injure, impair; *spec.* sully or tarnish (a person's honour). L16–E18.
†**10 a** *verb trans.* Affect with weakness; cause to lose vigour or courage. *rare.* Only in E17. ▸**b** *verb intrans.* Lose vigour or courage; become weak or faint. *rare.* E–M17.

📖 **7a** MILTON The truth With superstitions and traditions taint. **b** T. MORTON Fish and Flesh . . will taint . . notwithstanding the use of Salt. **8** P. FARMER Making everything she said seem tainted by emotion. M. COREN Cynicism had not yet tainted the East Coast character. **9** SHAKES. *Twel. N.* Sure the man is tainted in's wits. **10b** SHAKES. *Macb.* Till Birnam wood remove to Dunsinane I cannot taint with fear.

tainted /ˈteɪntɪd/ *adjective.* L16.
[from TAINT *noun*, *verb*: see -ED[2], -ED[1].]
That has been tainted; affected by a taint.

📖 E. WILSON Families . . poisoned by ptomaine from tainted meat. M. FLANAGAN All money is tainted.

tainture /ˈteɪntʃə/ *noun.* Now *rare.* LME.
[Partly from Old French *tainture*, (also mod.) *teinture* from Latin *tinctura* dyeing, TINCTURE *noun*, partly aphet. from ATTAINTURE.]
▶ **I** †**1** Colour, shade. LME–L15.
2 Tainting, corruption or contamination, infection. L16.
▶†**II 3** Imputation of dishonour, attainture. Only in E17.

tai-otoshi /tʌɪəʊˈtɒʃi/ *noun.* M20.
[Japanese, from *tai* body + *otoshi* the act of dropping.]
JUDO. The major body drop throw.

taipan /ˈtʌɪpan/ *noun*[1]. M19.
[Chinese (Cantonese) *daaihbāan*.]
Orig., a foreign merchant or businessman in China. Now *esp.*, the head of a foreign business in China.

taipan /ˈtʌɪpan/ *noun*[2]. M20.
[Aboriginal.]
A large dark brown venomous elapid snake, *Oxyuranus scutellatus*, of northern Australia.

Taiping /ˈtʌɪpɪŋ/ *noun.* M19.
[Chinese *Taiping*, from *tai* great + *ping* peace.]
An adherent of a rebellion against the Manchu dynasty in southern China in 1850.

taipo /ˈtʌɪpəʊ/ *noun. NZ.* Pl. **-os**. M19.
[Origin unkn.]
1 An evil spirit. M19.
2 = WETA. E20.

Tairona /tʌɪˈrəʊnə/ *noun & adjective.* L19.
[Spanish.]
▶ **A** *noun.* Pl. **-s**, same. A member of an extinct Chibchan people of northern Colombia. L19.
▶ **B** *adjective.* Of or pertaining to the Taironas. L19.

tai-sabaki /tʌɪsəˈbaki/ *noun.* M20.
[Japanese, from *tai* body + *sabaki* turning.]
JUDO. Positioning of the body, esp. in preparation for a throw, by means of rotation.

taisch /tʌɪʃ/ *noun.* Also **taish**. L18.
[Gaelic *taibhse* from Old Irish *taidbse* phantasm. Cf. THIVISH.]
In Scottish folklore, the apparition of a living person who is about to die; *gen.* something perceived by second sight.

Taisho /ˈtʌɪʃəʊ/ *noun.* E20.
[Japanese, lit. 'great righteousness'.]
The period of rule of the Japanese emperor Yoshihito (1912–26).

tait /teɪt/ *noun. Austral.* L19.
[Aboriginal.]
= ***honey possum*** s.v. HONEY *noun.*

Taita /ˈtʌɪtə/ *noun & adjective.* L19.
[Bantu.]
▶ **A** *noun.* Pl. same.
1 A member of a people of southern Kenya. L19.
2 The Bantu language of this people. L19.
▶ **B** *adjective.* Of or pertaining to the Taita or their language. E20.

Taiwanese /tʌɪwəˈniːz/ *noun & adjective.* M20.
[from *Taiwan* (see below) + -ESE.]
▶ **A** *noun.* Pl. same. A native or inhabitant of Taiwan (formerly Formosa), a large island off the SE coast of China. Also, the Chinese dialect of Taiwan. M20.
▶ **B** *adjective.* Of or pertaining to Taiwan, the Taiwanese, or their dialect. M20.
¶ Cf. FORMOSAN.

taj /tɑːdʒ/ *noun.* M19.
[Persian *tāj* crown.]
1 *Hist.* A crown worn by an Indian prince of high rank. M19.
2 A tall conical cap worn by a dervish. L19.

Tajik /tɑːˈdʒiːk/ *noun & adjective.* Also **Tadzhik**. E19.
[Persian *tājik* a person who is neither an Arab nor a Turk, a Persian.]
▶ **A** *noun.* Pl. **-s**, same.
1 A member of a people of Iranian descent inhabiting Afghanistan and the Turkestan region of central Asia; now *spec.* a native or inhabitant of the Republic of Tajikistan. E19.
2 The Iranian language of this people. M20.
▶ **B** *adjective.* Of, pertaining to, or designating the Tajiks or their language. E20.

tajine *noun* var. of TAGINE.

taka /ˈtɑːkɑː/ *noun.* L20.
[Bengali *ṭākā* from Sanskrit *ṭaṅka*: see TANGA *noun*[1].]
The basic monetary unit of Bangladesh, equal to one hundred poisha.

takable /ˈteɪkəb(ə)l/ *adjective.* Also **takeable**. LME.
[from TAKE *verb* + -ABLE.]
†**1** Comprehensible, intelligible. Only in LME.
2 *gen.* Able to be taken; that may or can be taken. M17.

Taka-diastase /takəˈdʌɪəsteɪz/ *noun.* L19.
[from Jokichi *Takamine* (1854–1922), Japanese-born biochemist and industrialist + DIASTASE.]
PHARMACOLOGY. (Proprietary name for) an amylolytic preparation containing various enzymes, obtained by the treatment of rice or bran with the mould *Aspergillus oryzae*.

takahe /ˈtɑːkəhi, ˈtakəheɪ/ *noun.* M19.
[Maori.]
A rare giant flightless rail of New Zealand, *Porphyrio mantelli*, having a large pinkish-red bill and legs and iridescent blue-green plumage. Also called ***notornis***.

takamakie /ˌtɑːkəmɑːkɪˈjeɪ/ *noun.* Also **-kiye** & other vars. E20.
[Japanese.]
Decorative Japanese lacquer-work done in relief, esp. in gold.

take /teɪk/ *noun.* E16.
[from the verb.]
1 That which is taken; *spec.* (*a*) (long *obsolete* exc. *dial.*) = TACK *noun*[2] 2; (*b*) *dial.* land taken or leased; a holding; (*c*) money taken or received in payment or as the proceeds of a business or transaction; in *pl.*, takings, receipts; *US colloq.* personal income or earnings; (*d*) (*slang*, chiefly *US*) money acquired by theft or fraud; (*e*) *US colloq.* a percentage of a sum of money deducted for tax etc.; (*f*) the quantity of fish etc. caught at one time, a catch; (*g*) (PRINTING, *obsolete* exc. *Hist.*) a portion of copy given at one time to a compositor for setting; (*h*) (CINEMATOGRAPHY, orig. *US*) a scene or sequence of film photographed continuously at one time; ***take one***, ***take two***, etc., the first, second, etc., scene or sequence of such film; (*i*) (orig. *US*) a sound recording. E16.
2 The action or process, or an act, of taking; *spec.* †(*a*) *rare* a seizure; a spell in magic or witchcraft; enchantment; (*b*) *dial.* the action of taking or leasing land; (*c*) the action or process of catching fish etc.; (*d*) (CHESS etc.) the capture of a piece or pieces; (*e*) MEDICINE a successful inoculation with a vaccine; (*f*) AGRICULTURE successful germination and growth of seed; (*g*) MEDICINE an acceptance by the body of tissue foreign to the site or to the individual; (*h*) (orig. *US*) the action of making a sound recording. L17.
3 A crook, *esp.* a swindler or confidence trickster. *Austral. & NZ slang.* M20.

📖 **1** *Daily Telegraph* Small boats being used to ferry the takes of fish to the . . steamer. W. GOLDING Clouds and . . sun succeeded each other, like takes in a film. *Listener* An unprecedented sum but peanuts in terms of the movie's ultimate take. **2** *Times Lit. Suppl.* A good problem seldom commences with a check or take. *Nursing Times* Persistent negative nitrogen balance results in . . poor graft take.

Phrases: ***double take***: see DOUBLE *adjective & adverb.* **on the take** (*slang*, orig. *US*) taking bribes; able to be suborned.

take /teɪk/ *verb.* Pa. t. **took** /tʊk/; pa. pple **taken** /ˈteɪk(ə)n/. LOE.
[Old Norse *taka* = West Frisian *take*, East Frisian *tāken*, Middle Dutch *tāken* grasp, seize, catch, rel. by ablaut to Gothic *tēkan*, ult. origin unkn.]
▶ **I** †**1** *verb intrans. & trans.* Touch. Also foll. by *on.* LOE–ME.
▶ **II** Seize, grasp, catch.
2 *verb trans.* Get possession of, esp. by force; capture, make prisoner, arrest. LOE. ▸**b** Capture (a wild animal, bird, etc.); (of an animal, bird, etc.) seize or catch (prey). ME. ▸**c** Capture (an opponent's piece) in chess etc.; win (a trick) in a card-game. LME. ▸**d** CRICKET. Catch (the ball) after it strikes the bat and before it touches the ground; dismiss (a batsman) by this action; (of a bowler) dismiss a batsman from (a wicket), esp. by causing the ball to hit the stumps. M19.

3 *verb trans.* Lay hold of, grasp with the hand etc.; seize and hold. ME.
4 *verb trans.* Of a natural or supernatural agency: affect the condition of, esp. suddenly and adversely; in *pass.*, be suddenly and strongly affected by (freq. foll. by *with*). ME. ▸**b** *verb trans.* In *pass.* Have a seizure or sudden attack of illness, esp. with the loss of sensation or consciousness. Now *rare* or *obsolete* exc. *dial.* LME. ▸**c** *verb intrans.* Of fire: kindle, begin burning; catch hold. Now *rare.* E16. ▸**d** *verb intrans.* with compl. Reach a particular condition; *esp.* become *ill*, *sick*, etc. Now *colloq.* & *dial.* L17.
5 *verb trans.* Orig., rebuke. Later, check, pull up, interrupt. Long *obsolete* exc. in ***take up*** (o) below. ME.
6 *verb intrans.* (Of a projection) pierce and hold an object; (of an object) be pierced and held by a projection (*rare*). Also, (of part of a mechanism) engage with a corresponding part (usu. foll. by *into*). ME. ▸**b** *verb trans.* Of an instrument or tool: be applied to and act on (an object). M17.
7 *verb trans.* Strike or hit (a person) usu. *in*, *on*, *across*, *over*, etc., a part of the body; land (a blow etc.) on. Also with double obj. ME.
8 *verb intrans.* **a** Of a plant, seed, etc.: begin to grow; take root, strike, germinate. Also, (of tissue etc.) continue in a healthy state after being grafted or transplanted. LME. ▸**b** Of ice: form, esp. in a lake or river. *dial.* & *N. Amer.* E19.
9 *verb trans.* Come on suddenly (a person, esp. in a particular condition or situation); *fig.* catch or detect *in* wrongdoing. *arch.* exc. in ***take by surprise*** & similar phrases. M16. ▸**b** Extort money from, esp. by trickery, swindle, cheat. Freq. foll. by *for*. *slang.* E20. ▸**c** MOTOR RACING. Overtake (a competitor). L20.
10 a *verb trans.* Catch the fancy or affection of; captivate, delight, please. M16. ▸**b** *verb intrans.* Win favour, gain acceptance; *esp.* become popular. M17. ▸**c** *verb trans.* Attract and hold (a person's gaze or attention). M18.
11 *verb intrans.* Have an intended result; succeed, be effective, take effect. E17.

> 🕮 **2** A. LOVELL The Turks had taken two Castles in Hungary. J. WAIN They're not taking me alive. **b** *Hounds* The hare may not be taken on a Sunday in the North. **d** *Sunday Times* With the last ball . . Willis had Solkar taken at slip. *Wisden Cricket Monthly* Going to take a lot of wickets for the simple reason that he bowls straight. **3** G. GREENE He took her by the throat and shook her. I. MURDOCH Mor took her hand in his. **4** SHAKES. *Merry W.* He blasts the tree and takes the cattle. DRYDEN I am taken on the sudden with a grievous swimming in my Head. *Temple Bar* An intense weariness of life took him. **d** D. ROWE Bill's mother took ill and went into hospital. **6** J. NICHOLSON The next tooth of the pinion will take into the gap in . . the rack. E. K. KANE A floe, taking upon a tongue of ice . . began to swing . . like a pivot. **7** OED The ball took me an awful whack on the chest. P. G. WODEHOUSE My missile took the lad squarely on . . the nose. **8a** R. RENDELL The fuchsia cuttings had taken and were looking good. **9** AV *Ecclus* 36:26 A man . . lodgeth wheresoeuer the night taketh him. **b** S. BELLOW They make millions. They have smart lawyers . . I got taken. **c** *Motoring News* Al used his car's superior . . speed to take Michael . . then moved into the lead. **10a** H. JAMES She had been immensely taken . . with that idea of mine. **b** E. JOHNSON Lever's story, *A Day's Ride*, was not taking with the public. **c** P. G. WODEHOUSE Dolly Molloy unquestionably took the eye. She was a spectacular blonde. **11** T. CAMPBELL The treachery took: she waited wild. B. SCHULBERG She was married . . But it didn't take.

▸ **III** Bring into a specified position or relation.
12 *verb trans.* Transfer (an object) into one's hand or hold by one's own voluntary physical act. ME. ▸†**b** Put (a garment) *on* or *about* one. ME–E17.
13 *verb trans.* Put or receive voluntarily into one's body; eat, drink; swallow (food, drink, or medicine); inhale (snuff, tobacco smoke, etc.). ME. ▸**b** Expose oneself to (air, water, etc.) for one's physical benefit. Freq. in ***take the air*** s.v. AIR *noun*[1] 2b. LME.
14 *verb trans.* Bring or receive (a person) into a specified relation to oneself, as of service, protection, care, or companionship. ME. ▸**b** *spec.* Enter into marriage or cohabitation with (esp. a woman). Freq. in ***take in marriage***. ME. ▸**c** Have sexual intercourse with (esp. a woman). E20.
15 *verb trans.* Enter into possession or use of (a thing), esp. by one's own direct act; appropriate; *spec.* in LAW, enter into actual possession of (an estate etc.). ME. ▸**b** *verb intrans.* Enter into possession of a thing; *spec.* in LAW, enter into actual possession. ME. ▸**c** *verb trans.* Regularly receive, buy, or subscribe to (esp. a particular newspaper or periodical). L16. ▸**d** *verb trans.* Get the use of (esp. accommodation) by payment or formal agreement. E17.
16 *verb trans.* **a** Assume (a specified form, character, role, name, etc.). ME. ▸†**b** Adopt (a law or custom). ME–M16. ▸**c** Assume possession of (something symbolizing a particular function or occupation); adopt (a badge or emblem). ME.
17 *verb trans.* Make oneself responsible for (a duty etc.); commit oneself to the performance of (a function etc.) (freq. foll. by *on*, *on oneself*). Also, bind oneself by the terms of (an oath, vow, etc.). ME. ▸**b** *verb trans.* Assume the right, presume, or venture *to do*. Usu. foll. by *on* oneself etc. ME. ▸†**c** *verb intrans.* Assume authority or importance; assert oneself. Also, behave presumptuously or haughtily, put on airs. Usu. foll. by *on* oneself etc. LME–E18. ▸†**d** *verb trans.* Profess or claim *to do*; assume or presume *that*. Also, pretend *to do*. Usu. foll. by *on* oneself etc. L15–M17.
18 a *verb intrans.* Side *against* or (*rare*) show support *for* a person. ME. ▸**b** *verb trans.* Adopt as one's own (a part or side in a contest or controversy), ally oneself with (a side or party). LME.
19 *verb trans.* Undertake and perform (a specified function, service, etc.); *spec.* (**a**) perform (a part) in a play etc.; (**b**) answer (a telephone call). LME.
20 *verb trans.* Appropriate (credit etc.) where, or as if, due; assume (leave, permission, etc.) to have been granted. E16.
21 *verb trans.* GRAMMAR. Of a word, clause, or sentence: have or require (a particular inflection, case, mood, etc.) as part of the appropriate construction. E19.

> 🕮 **12** WORDSWORTH Lucy took The lantern in her hand. M. MARRIN He took my coat from me in the hall. **13** E. B. BROWNING The medical men have allowed him to take some chicken broth. JAN MORRIS I take my breakfast at George's Café. **14** *Scribner's Magazine* He would freely take them into his confidence. E. PEACOCK He took pupils to increase his income. **c** G. PALEY On Judy's bed he took her at once without a word. **15** W. CRUISE The question . . whether the heirs . . took any estate under this appointment. V. WOOLF Hurry, or the best seats'll be taken. **c** *Times*: *Mail* readers . . will . . be getting their news a day later than you who take *The Times*. **d** M. SINCLAIR The people who took Greffington Hall for the summer holidays. **16a** SIR W. SCOTT The mountain mist took form and limb. *Times* France cannot take the offensive. **c** W. BLACKSTONE King William . . did not take the crown by hereditary right or descent. **17** T. F. TOUT Grenville refused to take office without Fox. A. CHRISTIE Every day . . Greta was taking a bit more upon herself, giving orders. **18b** E. HAYWOOD To take the party, which would best become his honour and reputation. **19** M. LINSKILL Will you favour us by taking the tenor? D. CUSACK I'll take Sheila's class if you like. **20** G. GREENE I shall do the real work and it will be the ghosts who take the credit. **21** D. W. GOODWIN Causal sentences regularly take the Indicative.

▸ **IV** Select or use for a particular purpose.
22 *verb trans.* Pick out (an individual person or thing) from a group; select, choose. ME.
23 *verb trans.* Adopt or choose for a particular purpose or (foll. by *as*, *for*) in a particular capacity. Also, have recourse to or avail oneself of (a means or method); *spec.* (**a**) proceed to use as a means of transport, *esp.* mount (a horse) or board (a ship, train, etc.) for a journey (freq. foll. by *to* or *for* a destination); (**b**) use (a stick, belt, etc.) to administer a beating *to* a person; (**c**) make use of (an opportunity). ME.
24 *verb trans.* Achieve the shelter or protection afforded by (a place); reach, go to, or enter, esp. for refuge or safety. Freq. in ***take refuge***, ***take sanctuary***, & similar phrs. ME. ▸**b** Proceed to follow (a road, course, etc.). ME.
25 *verb trans.* Deal with or treat in a certain way, *spec.* (**a**) give instruction in (a subject) in a school, college, university, etc.; (**b**) select or use (a topic etc.) as an example; (**c**) tackle (a problem). Also, consider; reckon. ME. ▸**b** Confront, attack; overcome, defeat; kill. *colloq.* M20.
26 *verb trans.* Occupy or enter on the occupation of (a particular place or position). ME.
27 *verb trans.* Begin (esp. a story) again; resume. LME.
28 *verb trans.* Use, occupy, or consume (a specified amount of material, time, energy, etc.); *colloq.* require (a person or thing of specified capacity or ability) *to do*. LME. ▸**b** Of a person: require a particular size *in* shoes, clothing, etc., for a correct fit. L19.

> 🕮 **22** S. JOHNSON I'll take you five children from London, who shall cuff five Highland children. **23** *Examiner* That great genius is taken as the standard of perfection. D. FRASER Aboard an armoured trawler . . having taken ship at St. Nazaire. A. TYLER If I was to take a brush to it, my hair would spring straight out. **24** T. STEVENSON A harbour which may be easily taken and left in stormy weather. *Publishers Weekly* Two . . drivers get lost in Vietnam and take shelter in an abandoned supply depot. **b** T. MCGUANE He took a dirt road out past a . . field. *fig.*: H. HALLAM Elizabeth had taken her line as to the Court of Rome. **25** H. BRACKEN The Business is to take the Distemper in its first Stage. W. T. BRANDE Let us take a fresh-water lake as an example. **b** J. L. CARR Come on, Findlayson. Let's go take the bastards. **26** SHAKES. *Lear* Thou robed man of justice, take thy place. J. AGEE The prayer-desks were all taken; he knelt . . on the bare floor. **27** *absol.*: DRYDEN I must forsake This Task; for others afterwards to take. **28** *Daily Telegraph* If it takes three more years, we fight on. O. NASH Wondering how many bamboo shoots a day it takes to feed a baby Giant Panda.

▸ **V** Obtain from a source, derive.
29 *verb trans.* Obtain or derive (a thing) deliberately from a particular source; copy or borrow (an illustration, passage of text, etc.) from the work of another; base (a sculpture, picture, etc.) on a specified original. Now usu. foll. by *from*. ME. ▸**b** *spec.* Obtain (a product) from its natural source; *esp.* harvest (a crop). Now *rare*. L15.
30 *verb trans.* Derive (esp. a name, character, or attribute) from a particular source. Freq. foll. by *from*. ME.
31 *verb trans.* Get as a result or product by a particular process; *spec.* (**a**) obtain (information, evidence, etc.) or ascertain (a fact) by inquiry, questioning, or examination; carry out (an examination etc.) in order to ascertain a fact; (**b**) ascertain by measurement or scientific observation; make or perform (a measurement or observation); †(**c**) measure off (a length or distance). ME.
32 *verb trans.* Make a written or pictorial record of; *spec.* (**a**) (foll. by *down*) record (a speech etc.) in writing; (**b**) draw or delineate (a picture, likeness, etc.); paint etc. a picture of; (**c**) make (a photograph) with a camera; photograph (a person or thing). LME. ▸**b** *verb intrans.* Of a person or thing: be photographed with a specified degree of success. L19.

> 🕮 **29** H. H. GIBBS The Frontispiece . . is taken from Seymour's 'Compleat Gamester'. R. STRANGE Scriptural references have been taken from the Revised Standard Version. **30** LD MACAULAY No English title had ever before been taken from a . . battle . . within a foreign territory. **31** OED The weather was too cloudy to take any observations. A. N. WILSON Mrs Moore took my temperature and put me to bed. **32** M. D. CHALMERS Minutes of the meeting must be taken. G. CLARE This picture must have been taken in late spring.

▸ **VI** Receive, accept, exact.
33 *verb trans.* Receive or obtain (something given, bestowed, or administered); *spec.* be awarded (a degree) on fulfilling the required conditions. ME. ▸**b** Suffer, undergo, submit to. ME. ▸**c** Hear or be told (something). *arch.* ME. ▸**d** Receive instruction in (a subject); learn (a lesson); embark on (a course of study etc.). Freq. in ***take lessons***. L17.
34 *verb trans.* Receive (something offered willingly), not refuse or reject; accept. Freq. in ***take it or leave it*** & similar phrs. ME. ▸**b** Of a female animal: allow copulation with (a male). *rare*. L16. ▸**c** Of a fish: accept (the bait). M19.
35 *verb trans.* Receive or get (a specified sum) in payment. ME.
36 *verb trans.* Exact (satisfaction or reparation) for an offence; inflict (vengeance). Also (now *rare* or *obsolete*), exact or accept (a promise, oath, etc.); LAW administer or witness (an oath) (cf. sense 17 above). ME.
37 *verb trans.* Accept and act on (advice, a hint, warning, etc.); accept as true or correct; believe. Freq. in ***take it from me*** below. ME.
38 *verb trans.* React to or regard (esp. a piece of information or a new situation) in a specified way. ME. ▸**b** Accept without objection, opposition, or resentment; put up with, tolerate. L15.
39 *verb trans.* Become subject to the particular and esp. visible effects of; *spec.* (**a**) absorb or become impregnated with (moisture etc.), esp. damagingly; (**b**) contract (an illness, infection, etc.); (**c**) fall into (a fit or trance). ME. ▸**b** *verb intrans.* Become affected in a particular way; *spec.* (**a**) catch fire, kindle; (**b**) (of a river, lake, etc.) begin to freeze. L16. ▸**c** *verb trans.* Allow (water) to enter; (of a cavity, recess, etc., in a structure) receive (a corresponding part of another structure). L17.
40 *verb trans.* †**a** Include, comprise; contain. ME–M17. ▸**b** Of water: submerge (a person) *up to* or *over* a specified part of the body. Now *Scot.* M17.
41 *verb trans.* Indulge in or enjoy (recreation, rest, etc.). LME.
42 *verb trans.* Orig. (*rare*), wager (a particular stake) on something. Later, accept (a wager); accept a wager from (a person). LME.
43 *verb trans.* Approach and attempt to pass or succeed in passing (an obstruction); clear (a fence, ditch, etc.); mount (a slope), get round (a corner). L16.

> 🕮 **33** SIR W. SCOTT Knighthood he took of Douglas' sword. R. G. COLLINGWOOD I had taken my degree and begun to work as a teacher. **b** C. M. YONGE He professed himself ready to take his trial. H. GREEN Someone has . . taken a most awful fall. **c** MILTON Then take the worst in brief, Samson is dead. **34** DICKENS He can take no denial. **35** G. VIDAL I . . never took a penny from him. **36** T. FORREST To take satisfaction . . for the death of Fakymolano's brother. **37** C. M. YONGE Would that France had taken to itself the teaching! **38** E. M. FORSTER She did not take a disappointment as seriously as Miss Quested. J. CANNAN How well they were taking it. **b** CLIVE JAMES The thought of . . mechanisms . . travelling through the sky was almost too much to take. **39** T. HEARNE The Book hath taken wet, and the Letters . . are hardly visible. W. R. COOPER A granite . . capable of . . taking a high polish. **40b** SIR W. SCOTT Mountain torrents . . took the soldiers up to the knees. **41** E. HEATH I had mostly taken my holidays in Europe. **42** O. WISTER 'Bet you five dollars you can't find it.' 'Take you.' **43** E. BOWEN The taxi took the corners of the . . streets abruptly. *Skiing* Each boy takes the jump in turn, with varying degrees of grace.

▸ **VII** Receive mentally, apprehend.

44 *verb trans.* Begin to have or be affected by (a feeling or state of mind); experience or feel (pleasure, pride, etc.). ME. ▸**b** *verb intrans.* Conceive a fancy or liking for something. *rare.* E17.

45 *verb trans.* **a** Reach or make (a decision, resolution, etc.), form and retain (an estimate, view, etc.). ME. ▸**b** Conceive and exercise (courage, compassion, etc.). ME. ▸**c** Exert (notice, care, etc.); pay (attention). Now chiefly in ***take care***, ***take heed***, & other similar phrs. ME.

46 *verb trans.* Understand or apprehend (a person or thing) in a specified way; ***take it***, suppose or be of the opinion (*that*); consider or suppose (a person or thing) *to be* or *to do*. ME. ▸†**b** With adjectival compl. (without *to be*): understand as, suppose to be, consider as. ME–E18.

47 *verb trans.* **a** Orig., reckon or count as, include in the meaning of. Later (now *rare* or *obsolete*), understand to mean, interpret as. ME. ▸**b** Suppose, esp. wrongly, to be, consider as. Usu. foll. by *for*. LME.

48 *verb trans.* Grasp the meaning of, comprehend. LME.

49 *verb trans.* †**a** In *pass.* Be reputed or esteemed *well*, *honourably*, etc. Only in 16. ▸**b** Regard or esteem *as*. M16.

> 🕮 **44** *Observer* The palaeobotanists . . are . . taking a lively interest in London's boles. **45a** HENRY FIELDING Having taken a resolution to leave the Country. *Scotsman* Most other road-users take a stern view of the private motorist. **b** *Mirabella* I took courage in being a journalist on the alert . . for new trends. **c** R. BAGE I took no concern about any of them. **46** C. HARE I take it that we are still cut off from the outside world. I. MURDOCH I turned southward down what I took to be Shaftesbury Avenue. **b** MILTON They took themselves not bound by . . Religion to any former Covnant. **47a** J. HARINGTON Which word many . . simple hearers and readers take for a precious stone. **b** T. F. POWYS The hounds . . took him for a weasel. **48** D. L. SAYERS If you take my meaning. N. FREELING Bric-a-brac which looks good but isn't if you take me. **49a** COVERDALE *Judith* 16:21 Iudith was . . right honorably taken in all the londe of Israel. **b** A. BRIGGS The circulation of small coins has been taken as a sign of vigorous local trade.

▸ **VIII** Remove, lead, convey.

50 *verb trans.* Carry, convey, (a thing, esp. a gift) to a person; cause (a person or animal) to accompany one, conduct, escort; (of a vehicle) carry or convey (a person); (of a road etc.) lead (a person) *to* a specified place or in a specified direction. ME. ▸**b** *fig.* Induce (a person) to go, be the cause of (a person's going), esp. *to* a specified place. M19.

51 *verb trans.* Carry away, remove; extract; deprive or rid a person or thing of. Freq. foll. by *from*, *off*. ME. ▸**b** *verb trans.* Remove by death. ME. ▸**c** *verb trans.* Subtract, deduct, (*from*). LME. ▸**d** *verb intrans.* Foll. by *from*: detract from, lessen, diminish. E17. ▸**e** *verb intrans.* Foll. by adverb or adverbial phr.: be able or adapted to be removed, detached, etc. M17.

†**52** *verb trans.* Deliver, hand over; give; commit, entrust. (Foll. by *to* a person, or with indirect obj.) ME–M16.

53 *verb refl.* & *intrans.* Orig., commit oneself *to* the protection of God, Christ, etc. Later (*arch.*), have recourse *to* a specified means of protection or safety; apply oneself *to* a specified pursuit, action, or object. ME. ▸†**b** *verb intrans.* Foll. by *into*: give oneself up to a specified form of indulgence. *rare.* M18–M19.

54 *verb intrans.* & †*refl.* Begin *to do*, set oneself *to doing*, esp. as a habitual action. ME.

55 *verb intrans.* & *refl.* Make one's way, go, or proceed in a specified direction, esp. promptly. ME. ▸**b** *verb intrans.* Of a road, river, etc.: go or run in a specified direction. *obsolete exc. dial.* E17.

> 🕮 **50** OED Will this road take me to Abingdon? R. P. JHABVALA Olivia went to visit Mrs. Saunders. She took flowers . . for her. C. STORR She . . saw a bus which would take her most of the way home. **b** G. GREENE Your business must be very important to take you on such an uncomfortable journey. **51** V. WOOLF She couldn't take her eyes off her. J. STEINBECK He took a small oyster from the basket. M. ROBERTS Helen takes the tray . . from her mother. **b** E. O'NEILL It was God's will that he should be taken. **c** C. HUTTON 6–2 denotes that 2 is to be taken from 6. **d** *Temple Bar* It takes greatly from the pleasure. **52** N. UDALL Who tooke thee thys letter? **53** E. TOPSELL The Gyants . . took them to their heels. E. L. ARNOLD She would not eat . . and at last took her to crying. **b** CARLYLE Taking deeply into tobacco. **54** *Times* He took to cultivate his genius by reading. O. MANNING The girls took to meeting on Saturday evenings. **55** G. LORD She . . took herself out to the front verandah. **b** S. R. CROCKETT At this point the drove-road took over the Folds Hill.

▸ **IX** Make, do, perform.

†**56** *verb trans.* Arrange, agree on, or conclude (esp. a truce or an alliance). ME–M17.

57 *verb trans.* Perform, make, or do (an act, movement, etc.). LME.

58 *verb trans.* Raise or make (an objection, exception, distinction, etc.). M16.

> 🕮 **56** SHAKES. *Sonn.* Betwixt mine eye and heart a league is took. **57** I. MURDOCH I took a quick look back. F. O'CONNOR He took a trip to New York. **58** LD MACAULAY Between punishments and disabilities a distinction was taken. S. WILBERFORCE I know well the objections men can take.

Phrases: (A selection of cross-refs. only is included: see esp. other nouns.) **be taken ill** become ill, esp. suddenly. ***give and take***, ***give or take***: see GIVE *verb*. **have what it takes** *colloq.* possess the necessary attributes or qualities, esp. for success. **take a bath** immerse oneself in water for cleansing or therapy. ***take a bit of doing***: see BIT *noun*². ***take account of***: see ACCOUNT *noun* 4. ***take action***: see ACTION *noun*. ***take advice***. **take a fall** *US* (*a*) *slang* be arrested or convicted of a crime; (*b*) *colloq.* suffer a fall. ***take a grip on oneself***: see GRIP *noun*¹. ***take aim***: see AIM *noun*. **take a joke** be able to bear teasing or amusement at one's expense (chiefly in neg. contexts). **take alarm** accept and act on a warning of danger; become alarmed or roused to a sense of danger. **take a person out of himself or herself** distract a person's attention from his or her own concerns; amuse, divert or occupy a person. ***take a person's name in vain***: see VAIN *adjective*. ***take a seat***: see SEAT *noun*. ***take a wife***: see WIFE *noun*. ***take boat***: see BOAT *noun* 1. ***take breath***. ***take by storm***: see STORM *noun*. ***take charge***: see CHARGE *noun*. ***take farewell (of)***: see ***take one's farewell (of)*** below. ***take five***: see FIVE *noun* 1. ***take for granted***: see GRANT *verb*. ***take heart (of grace)***: see HEART *noun*. ***take hold***: see HOLD *noun*¹ 2. ***take in a reef***: see REEF *noun*¹ 1. ***take into account***: see ACCOUNT *noun*. **take it** †(*a*) affirm or asseverate *on* one's death, honour, etc.; (*b*) assume *that*; (*c*) *colloq.* endure a difficulty or hardship, esp. *well*, *badly*, etc. (freq. in ***be able to take it***, ***can't take it***); (*d*) ***take it easy***: see EASY *adverb*; (*e*) ***take it from me***, believe me, take my word for it; (*f*) ***take it from there***, take over or continue from the point or situation described; (*g*) ***take it in turns***: see TURN *noun*; (*h*) ***take it on oneself***, venture or presume (*to do*); (*i*) ***take it or leave it***: see sense 34 above. **take it out of a person** (*a*) exhaust the strength of a person; (*b*) exact satisfaction from or have revenge on a person. **take it out on a person** relieve one's anger or frustration by attacking or treating a person harshly. ***take its course***: see COURSE *noun*¹. ***take its toll***: see TOLL *noun*¹ 3. ***take leave of one's senses***: see LEAVE *noun*¹. ***take lessons***: see sense 33d above. ***take note***: see NOTE *noun*². ***take on board***: see BOARD *noun*. **take one's farewell (of)**, **take farewell (of)** *arch.* say goodbye (to), take one's leave (*of*). ***take one's medicine***: see MEDICINE *noun*¹. ***take one's time***: see TIME *noun*. ***take on trust***: see TRUST *noun*. ***take orders***: see ORDER *noun*. ***take possession***. ***take prisoner***. ***take refuge***: see REFUGE *noun*. ***take stock***: see STOCK *noun*¹. **take that!**: (*a*) accompanying the delivery of a blow; (*b*) emphasizing a foregoing statement. ***take the air***: see AIR *noun*¹ 2b. **take the biscuit**, **take the bun**, **take the cake** *colloq.* be extremely or especially amusing, annoying, outrageous, etc. ***take the count***: see COUNT *noun*¹ 1b. ***take the field***: see FIELD *noun*. ***take the Fifth (Amendment)***: see FIFTH *adjective*. ***take the helm***: see HELM *noun*². ***take the long view***: see VIEW *noun*. ***take the pledge***: see PLEDGE *noun*. ***take the rap***: see RAP *noun*¹. ***take the sacrament***: see SACRAMENT *noun*. ***take the salute***: see SALUTE *noun*¹. **take the stage** (of a performer) come on to the stage during or at the beginning of a performance; *fig.* come into public view or prominence. ***take the strain***: see STRAIN *noun*². ***take the sun***: see SUN *noun*¹. ***take the veil***: see VEIL *noun* 1. ***take the water***: see WATER *noun*. ***take the weight off (one's feet)***: see WEIGHT *noun*. ***take the wind out of a person's sails***: see WIND *noun*¹. **take things as they come** deal with events as they arise, without anticipating difficulties. ***take thought***: see THOUGHT *noun*¹. ***take to heart***: see HEART *noun*. ***take to task***: see TASK *noun*. ***take to the HEATHER***. ***take to wife***: see WIFE *noun*. ***take turns***: see TURN *noun*. ***take under one's wing***: see WING *noun*. ***take up the torch***: see TORCH *noun*. ***take us as you find us***: see FIND *verb*.

With adverbs in specialized senses: ***take aback***: see ABACK 3. **take about** act as an escort to. **take apart** (*a*) dismantle, take to pieces; search thoroughly; demolish, wreck; (*b*) *colloq.* beat or defeat soundly. **take away** (*a*) remove or carry elsewhere; subtract; (*b*) clear the table after a meal; (*c*) detract *from*; (*d*) buy (food) from a shop or restaurant for eating off the premises. **take back** (*a*) resume possession of; restore to an original position; (*b*) withdraw or retract (a statement); (*c*) carry (a person) back in thought to a past time; (*d*) PRINTING transfer (text) to the previous line or page; (*e*) (now *rare* or *obsolete exc. dial.*) go back, return. **take down** (*a*) lower; carry down; (*b*) dismantle (a structure); *spec.* fell (a tree); demolish (a house); distribute (type); (*c*) (of a male escort) lead (a woman) down to a formal dinner etc.; (*d*) humble, humiliate; (*e*) (now *Scot.* & *north.*) lessen, abate, reduce; (*f*) write down (spoken words); write down the spoken words of; *spec.* record a statement in a legislative assembly with a view to invoking disciplinary procedure; (*g*) *Austral. slang* cheat, trick, swindle. **take in** (*a*) draw or receive in (esp. air, moisture, etc.); absorb; swallow; inhale; (*b*) undertake (washing, sewing, etc.) to be done at home for pay; ***take in one another's washing***: see WASHING *noun* 3; (*c*) subscribe to and receive regularly a newspaper or periodical; (*d*) (of a male escort) lead in (a woman) to a formal dinner etc.; (*e*) receive or admit (a person) into an establishment as a patient, lodger, or guest, etc.; †(*f*) take (a person) prisoner, capture (a town); (*g*) reduce the size or extent of, contract; make (a garment) fit more closely; furl (a sail); (*h*) enclose (a piece of land); annex; (*i*) admit into a number or list, esp. of topics for consideration; comprise, embrace; *colloq.* include (a specified place) on one's itinerary; (*j*) receive into or grasp with the mind; comprehend, understand, realize; learn; (*k*) perceive in one view or at a glance; (*l*) believe or accept unquestioningly (freq. in ***take it all in***); (*m*) *colloq.* deceive, cheat, trick (usu. in *pass.*); (*n*) STOCK EXCHANGE receive contango on (stocks or shares); accept (stocks etc.) as security for a loan; (*o*) *slang* take into custody, arrest; †(*p*) ***take in with***, take the part or side of; (*q*) *N. Amer. dial.* (esp. of a school term) start, begin. **take off** (*a*) remove (a person or thing) from something; lift, pull, or cut off, detach, subtract, deduct; *spec.* remove (clothing) from the person; (*b*) *arch.* drink at one draught; drink off; (*c*) lead away summarily; *refl.*, take one's departure, be off; (*d*) *fig.* divert, distract, dissuade; (*e*) remove or withdraw from a specified position or function; dismiss; withdraw (a coach, train, etc.) from running; CRICKET remove and replace (a bowler) after a spell of bowling; (*f*) *arch.* remove by death, put to death, kill; (*g*) remove (something imposed), esp. so as to provide relief or respite; (*h*) remove or do away with (a quality, condition, etc.); alleviate the effect of; detract *from*; (*i*) make or obtain (an impression) from something; print off; draw a likeness of, portray; (*j*) *colloq.* imitate or copy; mimic, esp. in mockery; caricature, parody; (*k*) abate, grow less, decrease; (*l*) (chiefly *colloq.*) go or depart, esp. hastily; (*m*) make a start in jumping or leaping; launch a jump or leap; (*n*) AERONAUTICS (of a pilot, plane, etc.) perform the operations involved in beginning flight; become airborne; (of prices, costs, etc.) rise steeply or suddenly; (of a scheme, project, etc.) be launched (successfully), become popular; (*o*) *US dial.* absent oneself from work, school, etc. **take on** (*a*) bring (a person or thing) on to something, lift, pull, or place on, add; (*b*) assume (a form, quality, etc.); begin to perform (an action or function); (*c*) take (a person) into one's employment or on to one's staff; (*d*) undertake; begin to handle or deal with; (be willing to) tackle or meet (an opponent in sport, a fight, a debate, etc.); undertake the management of; (*e*) (now *colloq.* & *dial.*) be greatly agitated; show great distress; (*f*) *arch. rare* behave proudly or haughtily; presume; (*g*) take service or employment, engage oneself; enlist; (also foll. by *with*). **take out** (*a*) remove (a person or thing) from within a room, receptacle, enclosure, etc.; extract, draw out; (*b*) withdraw (a person or thing) from a number or set; leave out, omit; (*c*) lead out; *spec.* escort (a person) on an outing; (*d*) make (a copy) from an original; *esp.* extract (a passage) from a book etc.; (*e*) apply for and obtain (a licence, summons, etc.) in due form from the proper authority; (*f*) obtain, receive, or spend, the value of (a commodity) *in* a specified form; (*g*) *US* go away, make off, start out; (*h*) *slang* kill, murder; destroy or obliterate (a specific target); (*i*) *Austral.* & *NZ colloq.* accept as a punishment, reward, etc.; win; (*j*) BRIDGE remove (a partner or a partner's call) from a suit by bidding a different one or no trumps. **take over** (*a*) take by transfer from or in succession to another; assume control or ownership of (a thing, esp. a business concern) from or after another organization or individual; ***take over from***, relieve, take the place of, succeed; (*b*) carry or convey across, transport; (*c*) PRINTING transfer (text) to the following line or page. **take together** consider or reckon together or as a whole; reckon as a group or collection. ***take unawares***: see UNAWARES *adverb*. **take up** (*a*) (*arch.* in *gen.* sense) lift, raise, or pick up; *spec.* raise or lift from some settled position; pick up (a pen, a book, etc.) in order to write, read, etc.; allow (a passenger) to board a train, bus, etc.; (*b*) conduct, convey, or carry (a person or thing) to a higher place or position; bring (a horse, ox, etc.) from pasture into the stable or stall; (*c*) pull up or in, so as to tighten or shorten; shorten or tighten (a garment) by hemming, tucking, etc.; tie up or constrict (a vein or artery); (*d*) take into one's possession, possess oneself of; apply for or claim (a benefit, grant, etc.); (*e*) accept or pay (a bill of exchange); advance money on (a mortgage); subscribe for (stock, shares, etc.) on issue; (*f*) *Scot.* & *N. Amer.* make a collection of (money); †(*g*) obtain or get from some source; apprehend, perceive; deduce; contract; (*h*) (of wood, water, etc.) be receptive of a substance; absorb (a fluid); (*i*) ENGINEERING accept, absorb, or assimilate (by gearing etc.); (*j*) grasp with the mind; understand (*obsolete* exc. *Scot.*); appreciate (a point in a discussion, lecture, etc.); (*k*) accept (something offered, as a challenge or a bet); *colloq.* accept a challenge or a bet from (a person) (freq. in ***take a person up on***); (*l*) take (a person) into one's protection, patronage, etc.; adopt as a protégé; (*m*) capture, seize; FALCONRY bring under restraint (a young hawk at hack) for training; seize by legal authority, arrest, or apprehend (a person); (*n*) check oneself, stop short (now *rare* or *obsolete*); *US* (of a horse) check, (of a rider) rein in; (*o*) check (a person) in speaking; interrupt abruptly; rebuke or reprimand sharply or severely; †(*p*) oppose, encounter, or cope with (a person); (*q*) begin again (something left off or begun by another); resume; (*r*) *US* (esp. of a school term) commence, start; (*s*) become interested or engaged in (a pursuit); proceed to deal practically with (a matter, question, etc.); espouse or embrace (a cause); †(*t*) make up, settle, or arrange amicably (a dispute, quarrel, etc.); (*u*) proceed to occupy (a place or position); station or place oneself in; (*v*) take up one's quarters, lodge; (*w*) occupy (space, time, etc.) entirely or exclusively; use up or consume (labour or material); engage fully or engross (a person, one's attention, etc.), esp. *with* a specified topic; (usu. in *pass.*); (*x*) *US* (foll. by *for*) stand up for, take the part of, side with; (*y*) (foll. by *with*) associate or begin to keep company with; become friendly with, form a relationship with; *arch.* adopt or espouse (esp. as a settled practice); be satisfied with; content oneself with, tolerate.

With prepositions in specialized senses: **take after** resemble (esp. a parent or ancestor) in character, habits, appearance, etc. **take against** begin to dislike, esp. impulsively. **take to** (*a*) (*obsolete* exc. *dial.*) undertake; take charge of, undertake the care of; (*b*) have recourse to (esp. a specified means of conveyance); (*c*) repair or resort to (a place, region, etc.); *esp.* take refuge in; †(*d*) become attached to, become an adherent of; (*e*) devote or apply oneself to (a pursuit etc.); begin or fall into the practice or habit of; (*f*) adapt oneself *well*, *badly*, etc., to (a specified pursuit); (*g*) take a liking to, conceive an affection for; (*h*) *NZ slang* attack, esp. with the fists.

Comb.: **take-all** a disease of wheat and other cereals caused by the fungus *Ophiobolus graminis*, which produces foot-rot, yellowing, stunted growth, and death of young plants; **take-apart** *adjective* able to be taken to pieces and reassembled; **take-away** *noun* (*a*) GOLF the initial movement of the club at the beginning of a back-swing; (*b*) an establishment selling cooked food to be eaten off the premises; a meal etc. from such an establishment; **take-away** *adjective* that may be taken away; *spec.* of, designating, or pertaining to cooked food sold to be eaten away from the premises of sale; **take-charge** *adjective* (*colloq.*, orig. & chiefly *N. Amer.*) pertaining to or characterized by leadership or authority; **take-down** (*a*) an act of taking something down; (*b*) (a rifle with) the capacity to have the barrel and magazine detached from the stock; (*c*) *Austral. slang* a deceiver, a cheat, a thief; (*d*) a wrestling manoeuvre in which an opponent is swiftly brought to the mat from a standing position; (*e*) *colloq.* (chiefly *N. Amer.*) a police raid or arrest; **take-home** *adjective* (orig. *US*) able to be taken home; ***take-home pay***, the remainder of a person's earnings after the deduction of tax etc.; **take-in** *colloq.* a cheat, a deception; **take-it-or-leave-it** *adjective* & *noun* (*a*) *adjective* allowing acceptance or rejection; showing indifference; (*b*) *noun* (an instance of) take-it-or-leave-it behaviour; **take-leave** *adjective & noun (arch.)* (*a*) *adjective* of or pertaining to leave-taking; (*b*) *noun* (an act of) leave-taking; **take-with** *adjective (US colloq.)* that may be taken along with one; *spec.* of or pertaining to purchased goods to be taken by the customer rather than delivered by the vendor.

takeable *adjective* var. of TAKABLE.

Takelma /tə'kɛlmə/ *noun & adjective.* L19.
[Takelma, lit. 'those dwelling along the river'.]
▶ **A** *noun.* Pl. **-s**, same. A member of a Penutian people of SW Oregon. Also, the language of this people. L19.
▶ **B** *adjective.* Of or pertaining to the Takelmas or their language. E20.

taken *verb pa. pple* of TAKE *verb.*

take-off /'teɪkɒf/ *noun & adjective.* E19.
[from *take off* s.v. TAKE *verb.*]
▶ **A** *noun.* **1** A thing that detracts from something; a drawback. *arch.* E19.
2 An act of mimicking; a mimic; a caricature; a skit, a parody. *colloq.* M19.
3 a An act of springing from the ground in jumping or leaping; *transf.* a place or spot from which a jump or leap is launched. M19. ▸**b** AERONAUTICS. The action or an act of becoming airborne. E20.
4 CROQUET. A stroke made from contact with a croqueted ball in which the striker's ball moves further than the other. L19.
5 An act of starting off on a journey etc.; a departure. E20.
6 *spec.* in ECONOMICS. The beginning of (a new phase of accelerated or increased) growth or development. M20.

> 📖 **2** C. WITTKE Take-offs on theatrical stars . . often displayed rare powers of mimicry. *Listener* A take-off of Italian opera . . *The Beggars' Opera* is a parody of the pastoral mode. **3b** M. MEYER We played Scrabble . . while waiting for take-off at Heathrow. ***vertical take-off***: see VERTICAL *adjective.*

Phrases: ***power take-off***: see POWER *noun.*
▶ **B** *attrib.* or as *adjective.* **1** Of or pertaining to a take-off. L19.
2 Designating or pertaining to a (part of a) mechanism for taking something off or removing something. L19.
3 That may be taken off; designed to be readily put on and taken off. M20.

take-out /'teɪkaʊt/ *adjective & noun.* E20.
[from *take out* s.v. TAKE *verb.*]
▶ **A** *adjective.* **1** Designed or made to be taken out; *spec.* (*a*) of or pertaining to a mechanical device to be pulled or folded out as required; (*b*) designating or pertaining to take-away food. Orig. & chiefly *N. Amer.* E20.
2 BRIDGE. Designating a bid or call that takes the bidder's partner out. M20.
2 take-out double = INFORMATORY *double.*
▶ **B** *noun.* **1** BRIDGE. An act of taking out. E20.
2 A tax deducted from winnings on a horse-race. *US.* M20.
3 In BOWLS, an act of knocking an opponent's wood away from the jack; in CURLING, an act of striking an opponent's stone out of play. M20.
4 A pull-out article in a newspaper or journal printed without a break in successive columns or pages. *US.* M20.
5 = ***take-away*** *noun* (b) s.v. TAKE *verb. colloq.* (orig. & chiefly *N. Amer.*). M20.

takeover /'teɪkəʊvə/ *noun.* Orig. *US.* E20.
[from *take over* s.v. TAKE *verb.*]
1 An act of taking over; a thing which is taken over. E20.
2 A (usu. forcible) assumption of power or government; a military coup. M20.
3 ECONOMICS. The assumption of control or ownership of a business concern by another company, *esp.* the buying-out of one company by another. M20.
Comb.: **takeover bid** ECONOMICS an attempt or offer to gain a controlling interest sufficient to take over a business concern; **takeover bidder** ECONOMICS a person or organization making a takeover bid.

taker /'teɪkə/ *noun.* ME.
[from TAKE *verb* + -ER[1].]
1 A person who takes something; *spec.* †(*a*) *rare* a person who takes another into his or her protection; (*b*) *arch.* a person who captures or apprehends another; a captor; †(*c*) = PURVEYOR 3; (*d*) (now *rare* or *obsolete*) a robber, a thief, a pilferer; a plagiarist; (*e*) a person who takes a bet; a person who accepts an offer, suggestion, etc. ME.
2 A thing which takes something. Formerly *spec.* in *pl.*, nippers, claws. *rare.* E17.
Comb.: **taker-in** (*a*) a person who takes someone or something in; *spec.* a deceiver; (*b*) an apparatus or mechanism which takes in or receives something; **taker-off** (*a*) a person who takes someone or something off; *spec.* a mimic; (*b*) an apparatus or mechanism which takes something off; **taker-up** a person who or thing which takes up someone or something; *spec.* †(*a*) a person who takes another under his or her protection, a patron, a guardian; (*b*) (now *rare*) a purchaser or purveyor of commodities; (*c*) *rare* a receiver of money paid; (*d*) *rare* a person who takes possession of an estate.

take-up /'teɪkʌp/ *noun.* E19.
[from *take up* s.v. TAKE *verb.*]
1 A contrivance or device which takes something up; *spec.* (*a*) *rare* a tuck or gather in a garment; (*b*) the part of the mechanism in a loom or other machine by which the material already woven or treated is wound up; (*c*) CINEMATOGRAPHY an apparatus for gathering up film after exposure in a projector or camera; (*d*) = UPTAKE *noun* 2; (*e*) a device in a machine for tightening a rope, thread, etc. E19.
2 The action or process, or an act, of taking something up; *spec.* (*a*) the process in a loom or other machine of winding up the material already woven or treated; (*b*) *rare* the action of making a tuck or gather in a garment; (*c*) the acceptance of something offered; *esp.* the claiming of a State benefit (cf. UPTAKE *noun* 6); (*d*) STOCK EXCHANGE the action of paying in cash for stock originally bought on margin. M19.

takhaar /'takhɑː/ *noun. S. Afr. colloq.* (chiefly *derog.*). Pl. **-hare** /-hɑːriː/, **-haars.** L19.
[Afrikaans, from Dutch *tak* branch + *haar* hair.]
An unkempt, unsophisticated person, esp. from a rural area; a backvelder.

takht /tɑːkt/ *noun.* L20.
[Persian *taḵt.*]
In Eastern countries, a sofa, a bed.

takhtrawan /tɑːk'trɔːən/ *noun.* Now *rare.* Also **-trevan** /-'triːv(ə)n/. L18.
[Persian *taḵt-i-rawān* formed as prec. + *rawān* pres. pple of *raftan* proceed, travel.]
In Eastern countries, a litter, a sedan chair.

takin /'tɑːkɪn/ *noun.* M19.
[Local Tibeto-Burman name.]
A large shaggy horned ruminant, *Budorcas taxicolor*, of Tibet, Bhutan, and northern Myanmar (Burma), related to the musk ox.

taking /'teɪkɪŋ/ *noun.* ME.
[from TAKE *verb* + -ING[1].]
1 The action or process of TAKE *verb*; an instance of this. ME. ▸**b** A seizure or sudden attack of illness or pain (long *obsolete* exc. *dial.*). Formerly also, enchantment, esp. of a malign nature; malignant influence. M16.
2 That which is taken; *spec.* (*a*) prey, a catch, fish etc. caught at one time; (*b*) in *pl.*, proceeds, business receipts or earnings; (*c*) (PRINTING, *obsolete* exc. *Hist.*) a portion of copy given to a compositor for setting at one time, a take. ME.
3 a Condition, situation, plight. Only in ***in a taking***, ***in taking***, †***at a taking***, †***at taking***, freq. with specifying word. *obsolete* exc. *Scot.* E16. ▸**b** *spec.* A disturbed or agitated state of mind. Freq. in ***in a taking***. *arch.* L16.

> 📖 **1** G. BOYCOTT There had been a big score for the taking. *Daily Telegraph* The taking of aspirin by pregnant women. **2** B. RUBENS Half a day's takings in the shop . . would amount to something like fifteen pounds. **3b** ELLIS PETERS They must be in a taking at all these changes we're seeing.

taking /'teɪkɪŋ/ *adjective.* L15.
[formed as prec. + -ING[2].]
That takes; *spec.* (*a*) *rare* that seizes possession of something, rapacious; (*b*) that takes the fancy; captivating, charming, attractive; †(*c*) blighting, blasting, pernicious; (*d*) infectious, catching.

> 📖 M. PRIOR Phillis has such a taking way, She charms my very soul.

■ **takingly** *adverb* E17. **takingness** *noun* M17.

Taki-Taki /'tɑːkɪtɑːki/ *noun & adjective.* M20.
[App. alt. of TALKEE-TALKEE.]
(Of) an English-based creole language of Suriname. Also called ***Sranan***.

takkie /'taki/ *noun. S. Afr.* Also **tackie**. E20.
[Origin uncertain: perh. rel. to TACKY *adjective*[2].]
A rubber-soled canvas shoe; a plimsoll, a tennis shoe. Also, a track shoe with a rubber sole. Usu. in *pl.*

Takulli /tə'kʌli/ *noun pl.* E19.
[Carrier Indian *dakelne* pl. Carriers, Indians, lit. 'people who go by boat on the water'.]
The Carrier Indians of British Columbia.

takyr /'tɑːkɪə/ *noun.* Pl. **-s**, same. M19.
[Chagatai *takir.*]
In central Asia, a wide expanse of clay covered with water in spring and dry in summer.

tala /'tɑːlə/ *noun*[1]. Also **tal** /tɑːl/. L19.
[Sanskrit *tāla* hand-clapping, musical time.]
INDIAN MUSIC. Time, rhythm; any of a series of traditional metrical patterns.

tala /'tɑːlə/ *noun*[2]. Pl. same, **-s.** M20.
[Samoan *tālā.*]
The basic monetary unit of Western Samoa, equal to 100 sene.

Talaing /tə'lʌɪŋ/ *noun & adjective.* L18.
[Burmese.]
▶ **A** *noun.* Pl. **-s**, same. = MON *noun*[1]. L18.
▶ **B** *attrib.* or as *adjective.* = MON *adjective.* M19.

talak /tə'lɑːk/ *noun.* Also **talaq.** L18.
[Arab. *ṭalāq*, from *ṭalaqat, ṭaluqat* be repudiated.]
In Islamic law: divorce, esp. by the husband's verbal repudiation of his wife in the presence of witnesses.

talapoin /'taləpɔɪn/ *noun.* L16.
[French from Portuguese *talapão* from Mon *tala pōi* lit. 'lord of merit', used as a respectful title for a Buddhist monk.]
1 A Buddhist monk or religious teacher, *spec.* one from Pegu in Myanmar (Burma). L16.
2 ZOOLOGY. In full ***talapoin monkey***. A W. African monkey, *Miopithecus talapoin*, which is the smallest in the Old World. L18.

talaq *noun* var. of TALAK.

talar /'teɪlə/ *noun.* L16.
[Latin *talaris*, from *talus* ankle: see -AR[1].]
†**1** A winged sandal (see TALARIA). Only in L16.
2 Chiefly CLASSICAL ANTIQUITIES. A long robe reaching to the ankles. M18.

talaria /tə'lɛːrɪə/ *noun pl.* L16.
[Latin, neut. pl. of *talaris*: see prec., -IA[2].]
ROMAN MYTHOLOGY. Winged sandals or small wings attached to the ankles of some gods and goddesses, esp. Mercury.

talaric /tə'larɪk/ *adjective. rare.* M19.
[Irreg. from Latin *talaris* (see TALAR) + -IC.]
Of a robe etc.: reaching to the ankles.

talayot /tə'lɑːjɒt/ *noun.* L19.
[Catalan *talaiot* small watch-tower, from Hispano-Arab. *ṭāli'āt* pl. of *ṭāli'a* watch-tower.]
ARCHAEOLOGY. A Bronze Age stone tower characteristic of the Balearic Islands, usu. circular with a large central pillar supporting the roof. Cf. NURAGH.

talbot /'tɔːlbət/ *noun.* LME.
[Prob. from the English family name *Talbot* (see below).]
(An animal of) a large white or light-coloured breed of hound with long hanging ears, heavy jaws, and great powers of scent, formerly used for tracking and hunting; a representation of such a dog, esp. (HERALDRY) that in the badge and supporters of the Talbot family, Earls of Shrewsbury.

Talbot's law /'tɔːlbəts lɔː/ *noun phr.* E20.
[from William Henry Fox *Talbot* (1800–77), English photographer and polymath.]
OPTICS. The law that a flickering source of light, varying in either colour or intensity, will be perceived as a constant light source exhibiting the mean value of the varying quantity, provided that the frequency of flickering exceeds the flicker fusion frequency of the eye. Also more fully ***Talbot–Plateau law*** [Joseph Antoine Ferdinand *Plateau* (1801–83), Belgian physicist].

Talbotype /'tɔːlbətʌɪp/ *noun.* M19.
[from *Talbot* (see prec.) + TYPE *noun.*]
Hist. The calotype process, which was patented by Fox Talbot; a photograph produced by this.

talc /talk/ *noun.* Also †**talk.** L16.
[medieval Latin *talcum* from Arab. *talk* from Persian.]
1 a MINERALOGY. A monoclinic hydrated silicate of magnesium, occurring as white, grey, or pale green masses or translucent laminae that are very soft and have a greasy feel; a variety of this. Cf. STEATITE. L16. ▸**b** Talcum powder. M20.
2 Common mica, esp. in large transparent laminae. Now *rare.* E17.
1a †oil of talc a preparation formerly used as a cosmetic, believed to be obtained from talc. **2 *Muscovy talc***: see MUSCOVY 1.
Comb.: **talc light** a window made from mica rather than glass; **talc powder** = ***talcum powder*** s.v. TALCUM *noun*; **talc schist**, **talc slate** GEOLOGY a schistose rock consisting largely of talc; **talc window** = ***talc light*** above.
■ **talcose** *adjective* of, pertaining to, containing, or resembling talc L18. **talcous** *adjective* = TALCOSE E18.

talc /talk/ *verb trans.* Infl. **-ck-**, **-c-**. L19.
[from the noun.]
Treat with talc; coat (a photographic plate) with talc; dust (the skin) with talcum powder.

talcum /'talkəm/ *noun & verb.* M16.
[medieval Latin: see TALC *noun.*]
▶ **A** *noun.* = TALC *noun* 1a. Now chiefly (in full ***talcum powder***), a preparation of powdered talc, esp. perfumed or medicated for general cosmetic and toilet use. Formerly also, = TALC *noun* 2. M16.
▶ **B** *verb trans.* Treat with talcum powder. E20.

talcy /'talki/ *adjective.* L17.
[from TALC *noun* + -Y[1].]
1 Pertaining to, of the nature of, or consisting of talc. L17.
2 Full of or suggestive of talcum powder. *colloq.* L20.

tale /teɪl/ *noun*.
[Old English *talu* = Old Frisian *tale*, Old Saxon *tala* (Dutch *taal* speech), Old High German *zala* (German *Zahl* number), Old Norse *tala* tale, talk, number, from Germanic base of also TELL *verb*. Branch II prob. from Old Norse.]
▶ **I** †**1** The action of telling, relating, or saying something; discourse, conversation, talk. OE–L16.
2 A thing told; a report of (alleged) events; a statement. OE. ▸†**b** *The* subject of public gossip. *rare*. ME–L16. ▸**c** In *pl.* Things told so as to violate confidentiality or secrecy; idle or mischievous gossip. Freq. in ***tell tales***. ME.
3 A story or narrative, true or fictitious, told for interest or entertainment; a literary composition cast in narrative form. ME.
4 a A mere fiction, as opp. to a factual narrative; a false or baseless story. ME. ▸**b** A thing now existing only in story; a thing of the past. *rare*. L18.

🕮 **2** J. B. PRIESTLEY Mr. Oakroyd plunged into his tale, beginning with his adventures . . and ending with Leonard's letter. ALDOUS HUXLEY Bernard poured out the tale of his miseries. **c** SARA MAITLAND She knew that Clare had . . been telling tales; or at least complaining to her colleagues. **3** A. THWAITE Old countrymen Tell tales of hedgehogs sucking a cow dry. K. VONNEGUT Bluebeard is a fictitious character in a very old children's tale. **4a** B. HINES If Casper came to me with that tale, I'd . . say, 'That's a bit of a tall story.'

▶ **II 5** Numerical statement or reckoning; counting, numbering. *arch. & literary*. OE.
6 The number or amount (to be) made up; the complete sum or total. *arch. & literary*. ME.
†**7** An account of money or other commodity given and received. LME–E19.

🕮 **5** S. JOHNSON There were . . Lord Monboddo, and Sir Joshua, and ladies out of tale. **6** BURKE He will hardly be able to make up his tale of thirty millions of souls.

Phrases: ***a tale of a tub***: see TUB *noun*^{1}. **by tale** *arch. & literary* as determined by counting individual items as opp. to weighing or measuring the aggregate. ***fisherman's tale***: see FISHERMAN 1. †**give no tale of**, †**hold no tale of** regard as of no value. **in a tale**, **in the same tale** *arch.* in the same category; in agreement. **live to tell the tale** survive to recount an unpleasant experience. ***old wives' tale***: see OLD WIFE 1. ***tale of terror***: see TERROR *noun*. ***tale of woe***: see WOE *noun*. **tell a tale**, **tell its own tale** be significant or revealing. ***tell tales***: see sense 2c above. ***tell tales out of school***: see SCHOOL *noun*^{1}. ***TRAVELLER's tale***.
Comb.: **talebearer** a person who maliciously gossips or betrays confidences; **talebearing** the spreading of malicious gossip; **tale-piet** *Scot. & north.* a tell-tale; **taleteller** (*a*) a narrator; (*b*) a talebearer, a tell-tale; **tale-telling** *noun & adjective* = STORYTELLING.

tale /teɪl/ *verb*. Now *rare*.
[Old English *talian* = Old Saxon *talon* reckon, Old High German *zalōn* number, reckon (German *zahlen* pay), Old Norse *tala* speak, discourse, from Germanic: see prec.]
▶ **I** †**1** *verb trans.* Consider (a person or thing) to be. OE–LME.
2 *verb trans.* Count up; deal *out* by number. E17.
▶ **II** †**3** *verb trans.* Utter, tell, relate. ME–L16.
†**4** *verb intrans.* Talk, gossip; tell tales. ME–L15.

talea /ˈtɑːlɪə/ *noun*. Pl. **taleae** /ˈtɑːlɪiː/. M20.
[Latin, lit. 'stick, cutting'.]
MUSIC. A repeated rhythmic pattern in late medieval isorhythmic motets.

Taleban *noun pl.* var. of TALIBAN.

talegalla /talɪˈɡalə/ *noun*. M19.
[mod. Latin (see below), from Malagasy *talèva* + Latin *gallus* cock.]
ORNITHOLOGY. Any of several brush-turkeys of the genera *Talegalla* and *Alectura*, esp. *A. lathami*.

talent /ˈtalənt/ *noun*^{1}.
[Old English *talente*, *talentan* = Old High German *talenta* from Latin *talenta* pl. of *talentum* weight, sum of money, from Greek *talanton*. In branch II from Old French *talent* from Latin *talentum* in Proto-Romance sense 'disposition, inclination of mind'. In branch III a fig. use of sense 1b, with allus. to the parable of the talents (*Matthew* 25:14–30).]
▶ **I 1 a** *Hist.* An ancient unit of weight, varying at different times and in different places; *esp.* one used by the Athenians and Romans, equivalent to nearly 57 lb (26 kg). OE. ▸**b** *Hist.* Such a weight of silver or (less freq.) gold used to represent a sum of money (among the ancient Greeks and Romans, equal to 60 minas). OE. ▸†**c** *fig.* Treasure, wealth, abundance. LME–M17.
▶†**II** Inclination, disposition.
2 Inclination for something; wish, desire, appetite. ME–M16.
3 Disposition of mind or character; quality of flavour. *rare*. ME–E17.
4 Hostile or angry disposition; ill will, anger. Cf. MALTALENT. LME–L17.
5 The characteristic disposition of a person or animal. M17–L18.

🕮 **4** W. TEMPLE Several Writers shew their ill Talent to this Prince. **5** SWIFT The talent of human nature to run from one extreme to another.

▶ **III** Mental endowment; natural ability.
6 a A person's mental etc. ability, or a particular faculty, regarded as something divinely entrusted to him or her for use and improvement. LME. ▸**b** A special natural ability or aptitude for or *for* a given thing. Also (*rare*), a thing for which one has a natural ability. E17. ▸**c** *sing.* & in *pl.* Superior mental powers, skill, or ability. Freq., skill cultivated by effort, as opp. to ***genius***. E17.
7 People of talent or ability collectively (usu. with *the*). Also, a particular talented or able person. E19. ▸**b** *The* backers of horses, as opp. to the bookmakers. *arch. slang*. L19. ▸**c** The women (*occas.* men) of a particular locality collectively, regarded in terms of sexual promise or desirability. *colloq.* M20.

🕮 **6a** C. KINGSLEY Remember that your talents are a loan from God. **b** E. ROOSEVELT Pussie's musical talent kept her in touch with . . artistic people. B. TRAPIDO Jonathan read the German to the manner born because accents were a great talent with him. A. DAVIES She discovered a startling talent for catching rabbits. ***wild talent***: see WILD *adjective, noun, & adverb*. **c** SYD. SMITH A work in which great and extraordinary talent is evinced. H. JAMES He has talents by which he might distinguish himself. **7** *Spectator* The studio, with its presiding talent, Lee Strasberg. *Woman* Besides commissioning top authors . . we feel that it's only fair to give new talent a chance. *Rolling Stone* This . . club will feature the best new black talent. **Administration of All the Talents**, **All the Talents** *Hist., iron.* the Ministry of Lord Grenville, 1806–7. ***c local talent***: see LOCAL *adjective*.

Comb.: **talent scout** a person looking for talented performers, esp. in sport and entertainment; **talent show**: consisting of performances by promising entertainers, esp. ones seeking to enter show business professionally; **talent-spot** *verb trans.* recognize the sporting or show-business potential of (a person); **talent-spotter** = ***talent scout*** above.
▪ **talentless** *adjective* devoid of talent or ability M19.

†**talent** *noun*^{2} var. of TALON.

talent /ˈtalənt/ *verb trans. rare*. L15.
[from the noun.]
†**1** Fill with desire. Only in L15.
2 Endow with talent or talents. Usu. in *pass.* L15.

talented /ˈtaləntɪd/ *adjective*. LME.
[from TALENT *noun*^{1} + -ED^2.]
†**1** Naturally inclined or disposed *to* something. Only in LME.
2 Endowed with or possessing talent; gifted, accomplished. E19.

tales /ˈteɪliːz/ *noun*. L15.
[Latin, pl. of *talis* such, in *tales de circumstantibus* such of the bystanders, the first words of the writ.]
LAW. A supply of substitute jurors summoned from among those present in court where the original jury has become deficient in number by challenges, exemptions, etc.; the writ for summoning or act of supplying such substitutes. Freq. in ***pray a tales***, ***grant a tales***, ***award a tales***.
Comb.: **talesman** /ˈteɪliːzmən, ˈteɪlz-/ a member of the tales summoned to complete a jury.

†**talg** *noun* see TALLOW.

talha /ˈtalə/ *noun*. Also **talh** /tal/. M19.
[Arab. *ṭalḥa* (collect. pl. *ṭalḥ*).]
A small spiny acacia of NE Africa, *Acacia seyal*, the gum of which is used as a substitute for gum arabic. Also ***talha tree***.

tali *noun* pl. of TALUS *noun*^{1}.

Taliacotian /ˌtalɪəˈkəʊʃ(ə)n/ *adjective*. Also **t-**, **Taglia-** /ˌtaɡlɪə-/. M17.
[from *Taliacotius*, Latinized form of the name of Gasparo *Tagliacozzi* (1546–99), Italian surgeon: see -AN.]
MEDICINE. Pertaining to or described by Tagliacozzi; esp. in ***Taliacotian operation***, a plastic operation for restoration of the nose using a flap of tissue taken from the upper arm.

taliation /talɪˈeɪʃ(ə)n/ *noun*. *obsolete* exc. *Hist.* L16.
[App. extended form of TALION.]
(A) retaliation; *spec.* (LAW) = TALION.

Taliban /ˈtalɪban/ *noun pl.* Also **Taleban**. L20.
[Persian *ṭālibān*, pl. of *ṭālib* seeker, enquirer, student (so named because the movement reputedly began amongst Afghani students exiled in Pakistan).]
A fundamentalist Islamic movement, founded in 1994, which held power in much of Afghanistan 1996–2001.

talik /taˈlɪk/ *noun*^{1}. Also ***taliq***, ***taʼ-***. L18.
[Arab. *taʻlīḳ* lit. 'suspension, hanging together'.]
A Persian script developed between the 11th and 13th cents., characterized by an unusual method of attachment of letters one to another, and sharing certain stylistic features with *nastalik*.

talik /ˈtalɪk/ *noun*^{2}. M20.
[Russian, from *tayat'* melt.]
PHYSICAL GEOGRAPHY. An area of unfrozen ground surrounded by permafrost.

talio /ˈtalɪəʊ/ *noun*. E17.
[Latin: see next.]
(A) retaliation.

talion /ˈtalɪən/ *noun*. LME.
[Old & mod. French from Latin *talio(n-)*, from *talis* such, the like: see -ION.]
Retaliation; = LEX TALIONIS.
▪ **taliˈonic** *adjective* (*rare*) of or pertaining to the law of talion L19.

talipes /ˈtalɪpiːz/ *noun*. M19.
[mod. Latin, from Latin *talus* ankle + -I- + *pes* foot.]
MEDICINE. The condition of having a club-foot.
Comb.: **talipes equinovarus** [Latin *equinus* EQUINE, VARUS *noun*^{2}] the commonest variety of club-foot, in which the foot is twisted inwards and downwards so that the person walks on the outer edge of the tip; **talipes valgus** [Latin VALGUS] a form of club-foot in which the foot is turned outwards, so that the person walks on the inner edge of the foot; **talipes varus** [Latin VARUS *noun*^{2}] a form of club-foot in which the foot is turned inwards, so that the person walks on the outer edge of the foot.

talipot /ˈtalɪpɒt/ *noun*. L17.
[Malayalam *tālipat* from Sanskrit *tālīpatra*, from *tālī* fan palm + *patra* leaf.]
A very tall southern Indian fan palm, *Corypha umbraculifera*, with enormous leaves which are used as sunshades etc.

taliq, **taʼliq** *nouns* vars. of TALIK *noun*^{1}.

talisman /ˈtalɪzmən/ *noun*. Pl. **-mans**, **-men**. M17.
[French or Spanish (= Italian *talismano*), app. from medieval Greek *telesmon* alt. of late Greek *telesma* completion, performance, religious rite, consecrated object, from *telein* complete, perform (a rite), consecrate, from *telos* result, end.]
1 An object supposed to have occult or magic powers, *esp.* an inscribed stone or ring worn as an amulet to avert evil or bring good luck, health, etc. M17.
2 *fig.* A thing that acts as a charm or achieves remarkable results. L18.

🕮 **1** A. BURL A time of personal magic, everyone carrying talismen and charms. **2** A. LURIE Garments . . advertised . . as 'good investments', talismans that will give their wearer 'a sense of security'. *Vanity Fair* Ray . . strokes the Dalmatian's glistening coat as though it were a talisman of . . perpetual youth.

▪ **talisˈmanic** *adjective* of, pertaining to, or of the nature of a talisman L17. **talisˈmanical** *adjective* (now *rare*) = TALISMANIC M17. **talisˈmanically** *adverb* (*rare*) M19.

talk /tɔːk/ *noun*^{1}. LME.
[from the verb.]
1 a The action or practice of conversing; informal oral communication; discussion, conversation. LME. ▸**b** An instance of such talk; a conversation. M16. ▸**c** Orig., a public exchange of views, a conference. Now (in *pl.*), formal discussions or negotiations between representatives of different countries, conflicting parties, etc. M16. ▸**d** A powwow with or among N. American Indians; an oral message to or from such a meeting or group. *US* (*obsolete* exc. *Hist.*). E18.
2 a The action of addressing a person; a specified mode of speech or address; *derog.* empty words, verbiage. M16. ▸**b** An informal lecture or address. M19.
3 a Mention (*of* a subject); gossip; (a) rumour. M16. ▸**b** *The* subject of gossip, rumour, or topical conversation. E17.
4 A way of speaking; native language or dialect. L18.

🕮 **1a** L. URIS There was always talk and debate, a . . scandal to discuss. J. GROSS No advanced civilization without conversation: talk was not only enjoyable, it was liberating. **c** *Annual Register* The talks broke down . . when it became clear that no agreement was possible. **2a** *Modern Painters* Educators . . writing documents full of talk about transferable skills, . . and the rest. **b** *Wandsborough Borough News* The . . Committee will vote . . after hearing each of the short-listed candidates give a 10-minute talk. *Nature* There will be . . scientific talks by invited speakers. **3a** *Times* Talk is that . . BT shares are likely to command a premium of up to 20p. **b** LD MACAULAY Just when these letters were the talk of all London. **4** F. WARNER The soldiers Speak Latin, but Greek is the common talk.

Phrases & comb.: **big talk**, **tall talk** boastful or pretentious talk. ***chalk and talk***: see CHALK *noun*. ***jive talk***: see JIVE *noun* 3. ***small talk***: see SMALL *adjective*. ***straight talk***: see STRAIGHT *adjective*^{1}. ***sweet talk***: see SWEET *adjective & adverb*. **talk radio** a form of radio programme in which a presenter talks about topical issues and encourages listeners to ring in to air their opinions. **talk-shop** *colloq.* = ***talking-shop*** s.v. TALKING *verbal noun*. **talk show** = ***chat show*** s.v. CHAT *noun*^{2}. **talktime** the time during which a mobile telephone is in use to handle calls, esp. as a measure of the duration of the telephone's battery. **talkwriter** a computer that produces printed output corresponding to speech. ***tall talk***: see ***big talk*** above. **the talk of the town** the chief current topic of conversation.

talk *noun*^{2} see TALC *noun*.

talk /tɔːk/ *verb*. ME.
[from Germanic base of TALE *noun*, *verb* or TELL *verb* + frequentative suffix *-k*: cf. LURK *verb*.]
▶ **I** *verb intrans.* **1** Have or exercise the power of speech; communicate or exchange thoughts, feelings, information, etc., by speaking; have a discussion, converse, (*with* a person); speak, utter words, say things, (*to* a person). Also, (freq. *derog.*) chat or chatter idly or trivially. ME. ▸**b** *spec.* Gossip, esp. critically; spread rumour. M17.

▸**c** Say something to the point, esp. something a listener wants to hear. *colloq.* **M19.** ▸**d** Reveal or betray a secret; *spec.* disclose incriminating information. Also foll. by *to.* **E20.**
2 *transf.* **a** Communicate without speaking, as by writing, sign language, eye contact, etc. Also, be powerfully expressive; have influence. **E18.** ▸**b** Communicate by radio. Usu. foll. by *to, with.* **E20.**
3 Of an inanimate object: make sounds or noises resembling or suggesting speech. **L18.**

📖 **1** D. BARNES He felt that he could talk to her, tell her anything. C. P. SNOW I've always wanted to have the chance to talk with you. *fig.*: E. O'NEILL You understand, it was the liquor talking, if I said anything to wound you. **b** LD MACAULAY Difficult to prevent people talking, and . . loose reports were not to be regarded. H. ROBBINS You should be ashamed . . . People will talk. **c** M. HASTINGS 'Now you're talking.' Jukes said approvingly . . . 'That's the best bit of sense you've spoke today.' **d** W. GOLDING I won't talk I know nothing. **2a** *Financial Times* Visiting Poles . . should make a detour to the . . State to see how money talks and nominations can be bought. **3** V. S. REID He tells militiamen to make their muskets talk.

▸ **II** *verb trans.* **4** **a** Utter (words etc.); express in talk or speech. **ME.** ▸**b** Use as a spoken language; speak in (a particular language, dialect, etc.). **M19.**
5 Speak about, discuss, (a subject). Now also (*colloq.*), consider, have in mind, envisage, think in terms of. **LME.**
6 Bring or drive (a person) into a specified state by talking. **L16.**

📖 **4a** A. ADAMS I have written many things to you that . . I never could have talked. **5** G. GREENE 'Sympathies East or West?' 'We never talk politics.' *Washington Post* We're talking big money here. **6** SHAKES. *Much Ado* They would talk themselves mad. R. MACAULAY He . . used to talk one sick about how little scope he had.

Phrases, & with prepositions & adverbs in specialized senses: **hark who's talking!** *colloq.* = *look who's talking!* below. **know what one is talking about** be expert or authoritative. **look who's talking!** *colloq.* expr. indignation, amusement, etc., at a person equally open to a criticism he or she has made of another. **talk about** have as the subject of discussion; consider; deal with. **talk about** — (in *imper.*, freq. *iron.*) reinforcing or emphasizing as a clear or extreme example of (a thing). **talk a good game** *US colloq.* talk convincingly yet fail to act effectively. **talk a person's ear off** *N. Amer.* talk incessantly and wearyingly to (a person). **talk at** — (*a*) make remarks intended for but not directly addressed to (a particular person); (*b*) address (a person) in an insensitively impersonal manner. **talk away** (*a*) consume (time) in or by talking; (*b*) carry on talking, talk freely. **talk back** (*a*) reply defiantly, answer back; (*b*) respond on a two-way radio system. ***talk big***: see BIG *adverb.* **talk down** (*a*) talk condescendingly or patronizingly *to* (a person); (*b*) silence (a person) by talking more loudly or persistently; (*c*) denigrate, belittle; (*d*) depress the value of (shares, a currency, commodity, etc.) by tactical public statements; (*e*) enable (a pilot, aircraft, etc.) to land by radio instructions from the ground. **talking of** while we are discussing (a specified person, subject, etc.). **talk into** — persuade (a person) into (an action, concession, etc.). **talk nineteen to the dozen** talk incessantly or rapidly. **talk of** — (*a*) speak about, discuss, mention, (a person or thing); (*b*) express a somewhat vague intention of (doing something). **talk one's way in**, **talk one's way out** effect an entrance or exit by talking persuasively. **talk out** (*a*) block the progress of (a parliamentary bill) by prolonging discussion to the time of adjournment; (*b*) *talk out of*, dissuade from (an action, plan, etc.). ***talk out of turn***: see TURN *noun.* **talk over**, **talk round** gain agreement or compliance from (a person) by persuasive talking. **talk over** — speak so as to interrupt (another speaker etc.), esp. on a tape, broadcast, etc. ***talk poor-mouth***: see POOR *adjective.* ***talk round***: see *talk over* above. **talk shop** talk, esp. inopportunely or tediously, about one's occupation, business, etc. ***talk someone's language***: see LANGUAGE *noun*[1]. **talk tall** talk boastfully. ***talk the hind leg(s) off a*** DONKEY. ***talk the same language***: see LANGUAGE *noun*[1]. **talk through** discuss (a matter) thoroughly. **talk through** — (*a*) guide (a person) through a task, performance, etc., by continuous instruction, advice, etc.; (*b*) guide a person through (a task, performance, etc.) by continuous instruction, advice, etc.; (*c*) ***talk through one's hat*** (colloq.), talk foolishly, wildly, or ignorantly; bluff, exaggerate; (*d*) ***talk through the back of one's neck***, ***talk through one's neck***: see NECK *noun*[1]. **talk to** — (*a*) reprove, scold; (*b*) ***talk to oneself***, talk alone regardless of any hearers; (see also senses 1, 1d, 2b above). ***talk turkey***: see TURKEY *noun*[2]. **talk up** (*a*) talk strenuously in support of (a thing), discuss in favourable terms, praise, advocate; (*b*) stimulate interest in by (usu. exaggerated) praise. **you can talk** (*iron.*), **you can't talk** *colloq.*: rebuking a person as being equally open to a criticism he or she has made of another.

Comb.: **talkback** *adjective & noun* (*a*) *adjective* designating apparatus and facilities for two-way communication, esp. between a broadcasting studio and control room; (*b*) *noun* a talkback system; (*Austral. & NZ*) a phone-in; **talk-down** the action or process of talking down an aircraft or pilot; **talk-out** *colloq.* (*a*) an instance of talking out a parliamentary bill, a filibuster; (*b*) an exhaustive discussion.

▪ **talkable** *adjective* (*rare*) ready or disposed to converse, affable **L18.** **talkathon** *noun* [-ATHON] (*colloq.*, orig. *US*) an abnormally long or prolonged session of talk or discussion; *spec.* (*a*) a filibuster; (*b*) a lengthy talk show or broadcast political interview: **M20.** **talker** *noun* a talkative person, a speaker, a conversationalist **LME.**

talkative /ˈtɔːkətɪv/ *adjective.* **LME.**
[from TALK *verb* + -ATIVE.]
Fond of or given to talking; chatty, garrulous.

📖 *fig.*: STEELE Nothing is so talkative as misfortune.

▪ **talkatively** *adverb* **L16.** **talkativeness** *noun* **E17.**

talked /tɔːkt/ *ppl adjective.* **M19.**
[from TALK *verb* + -ED[1].]
1 ***talked-of***, familiarly or vaguely spoken about. **M19.**
2 ***talked-about***, discussed. Chiefly with qualifying adverb. **E20.**

📖 **2** J. D. WATSON The wine turned the conversation to the currently talked-about Cambridge popsies.

talkee-talkee /ˈtɔːkɪtɔːki/ *noun. colloq.* **E19.**
[Redupl. of TALK *noun*[1] + -EE[2].]
1 Any of various English-based pidgins or creoles, esp. in the W. Indies; *spec.* Taki-Taki. **E19.**
2 Talk; *esp.* small-talk, chatter, continuous prattling. *derog.* **E19.**

📖 **2** *attrib.*: T. H. HUXLEY The discourses are . . lessons and not talkee-talkee lectures.

talkfest /ˈtɔːkfɛst/ *noun. slang* (chiefly *N. Amer.*). **E20.**
[from TALK *noun*[1], *verb* + FEST.]
A session of lengthy discussion or conversation, a talkathon. Cf. GABFEST.

talkie /ˈtɔːki/ *noun. colloq.* (orig. *US*). **E20.**
[from TALK *verb* + -IE, after MOVIE.]
A cinema film with a synchronized vocal soundtrack. Cf. SILENT *adjective* 2d.

talk-in /ˈtɔːkɪn/ *noun.* **M20.**
[from TALK *verb*, *noun*[1] + -IN[2].]
1 A gathering or meeting for discussion, a conference; *spec.* a protest meeting at which a matter at issue is discussed. **M20.**
2 A (usually) live radio or television discussion, *esp.* one involving audience participation. **L20.**

talking /ˈtɔːkɪŋ/ *verbal noun.* **ME.**
[from TALK *verb* + -ING[1].]
The action of TALK *verb.* Also (now *rare* exc. in ***talking-to*** below), an instance of this.

📖 G. VIDAL Bob did most of the talking and Jim listened.

Comb.: **talking blues** a (freq. humorous) blues song in which the lyrics are more or less spoken rather than sung; **talking cure** psychotherapy which relies on verbal interaction, *esp.* psychoanalysis; **talking-point** a topic suitable for or inviting discussion or argument; **talking-shop** *derog.* a centre for idle and unconstructive talk; *spec.* an institution regarded as a place of argument rather than action; **talking-to** a reprimand, a reproof.

talking /ˈtɔːkɪŋ/ *ppl adjective.* **M16.**
[formed as prec. + -ING[2].]
That talks; having the power of speech; expressive; loquacious.
talking book (orig. *US*) a recorded reading of a book, esp. for the blind. **talking clock** = ***speaking clock*** s.v. SPEAKING *ppl adjective.* **talking drum** in W. Africa, each of a set of drums of different pitch which are beaten to transmit words in a tonal language. **talking film** = TALKIE. **talking head** *colloq.* (usu. in *pl.*) a television presenter, interviewer, etc., shown in close-up talking directly to the camera. **talking machine** (chiefly *US*): designed to imitate or reproduce human speech. **talking picture** = ***talking film*** above.

talky /ˈtɔːki/ *adjective. colloq.* **E19.**
[from TALK *noun*[1] + -Y[1].]
1 Full of conversation; talkative, loquacious. **E19.**
2 Of a play, book, etc.: wordy, long-winded; containing verbose or tedious dialogue. **M20.**
Comb.: **talky-talky** *adjective & noun* (*derog.*) (*a*) *adjective* full of (usu. trivial) talk; (*b*) *noun* trivial conversation; excessive talkativeness; **talky-talk** trivial conversation, talk for talking's sake.

tall /tɔːl/ *adjective & adverb.* **LME.**
[Repr. Old English *ge*)*tæl* swift, prompt = Old Frisian *tel*, Old Saxon *gital*, Old High German *gizal* quick.]
▸ **A** *adjective.* †**I 1** Prompt, ready, active. *rare* exc. in ***tall of hands***, ***tall of one's hands***, deft or skilful with one's hands, dexterous. **LME–M17.**
2 Comely, handsome; elegant, fine. **LME–M17.**
3 Good at fighting; strong in combat; doughty, bold, valiant. **LME–E19.**
4 Orig., able or eminent (*at* something). Later (*US slang*), good, excellent. **L16–M19.**

📖 **3** W. PRYNNE He like a tall fellow . . interdicted the King, with the whole Realme. **4** H. B. STOWE They . . make jist the tallest kind o' broth and knicknacks.

▸ **II 5** Of a person or animal: of great or more than average height. Of a thing: high, esp. relative to width; standing higher than the surrounding objects. Also, having a specified height. **M16.** ▸**b** Of more than average length measured from bottom to top. **E17.** ▸**c** Of a game-bird: high-flying. **E20.**
6 *fig.* †**a** Lofty, grand. **M17–E19.** ▸**b** Of language: pompous, pretentious. *colloq.* **L17.** ▸**c** Of a story or statement: exaggerated, extravagant, excessive; unlikely. **M19.** ▸**d** CRICKET. Of scoring: occurring at a high rate. *slang.* **M19.**

📖 **5** N. ROWE Yon tall Mountains That seem to reach the Clouds. CARLYLE Hohmann . . was so tall, you could not . . touch his bare crown with your hand. OED He is a little taller than his brother. *Independent* Figures, each a few inches tall, moulded in a wax-like substance. **b** SIR W. SCOTT A second edition . . a tall copy, as collectors say. **6a** I. WATTS The tall titles, insolent and proud. **c** C. MACKENZIE Do you believe that yarn . . ? It sounds . . a pretty tall story.

Special collocations & comb.: **tall drink**: served in a tall glass. **tall-grass** *adjective* (of a prairie etc.) characterized by certain tall moisture-favouring grasses (cf. ***short-grass*** s.v. SHORT *adjective*). **tall hat** a top hat. ***tall oat-grass***: see ***oat-grass*** s.v. OAT *noun.* **tall order** an exorbitant or unreasonable demand; a very difficult task. ***tall poppy (syndrome)***: see POPPY *noun* 1b. **tall ship** a high-masted sailing ship. ***tall talk***: see TALK *noun*[1]. **tall timber** *N. Amer.* uninhabited forest (***break for tall timber***, ***break for the tall timber***, ***strike for tall timber***, ***strike for the tall timber***, head for uninhabited forest, *fig.* run away, escape).

▸ **B** *adverb.* In a tall or extravagant manner; as if tall; elatedly, proudly. Chiefly in phrs. below. **M19.**
sit tall sit erect, with a straight back. ***talk tall***: see TALK *verb.* **walk tall** hold one's head high, have dignity, pride, or self-respect.

▪ **tallish** *adjective* inclining towards tallness, fairly tall **M18.** **tallness** *noun* **M16.**

tallage /ˈtalɪdʒ/ *noun.* Also †**taillage**, †**talliage**. **ME.**
[Old French *taillage*, from *taillier*: see TAIL *verb*[1], -AGE.]
Hist. Orig., a tax levied by Norman and early Plantagenet monarchs on the towns and demesne lands of the Crown. Later also, any of various levies or duties, *esp.* a tax levied on feudal dependants by their superiors.

tallage /ˈtalɪdʒ/ *verb trans.* **LME.**
[from prec.]
Hist. Impose tallage on; tax.

tallboy /ˈtɔːlbɔɪ/ *noun.* **L17.**
[from TALL + BOY *noun.*]
1 A tall-stemmed glass or goblet. Now *local.* **L17.**
2 A tall chest of drawers (often mounted on legs), usually in two sections, one standing on the other. **M18.**
3 A kind of tall chimney-pot. **L19.**

Tallensi /təˈlɛnsi/ *noun & adjective.* **E20.**
[Tallensi.]
▸ **A** *noun.* Pl. same. A member of an African people of northern Ghana; the Voltaic language of this people. **E20.**
▸ **B** *attrib.* or as *adjective.* Of or pertaining to the Tallensi. **M20.**

talliable /ˈtalɪəb(ə)l/ *adjective.* Long *obsolete* exc. *Hist.* **M16.**
[Old French *taillable*, from *taillier*, or from medieval Latin *talliabilis*: see TAIL *verb*[1], -ABLE.]
Subject to tallage, liable to be taxed.

†**talliage** *noun* var. of TALLAGE *noun.*

talliate /ˈtalɪeɪt/ *verb trans. rare.* **M18.**
[Latin *talliat-* pa. ppl stem of medieval Latin *talliare*: see TAIL *verb*[1], -ATE[3].]
Hist. = TALLAGE *verb.*

tallith /ˈtalɪθ/ *noun.* **E17.**
[Rabbinical Hebrew *tallit*, from biblical Hebrew *tillel* to cover.]
The shawl with fringed corners traditionally worn by male Jews at prayer.

tallow /ˈtaləʊ/ *noun & verb.* As noun also (earlier) †**talg**, †**talug**. **ME.**
[Middle Low German *talg*, *talch*, of unkn. origin.]
▸ **A** *noun.* **1** A hard fatty substance which is usu. obtained by rendering the suet of sheep or cattle, contains stearin, palmitin, and olein, and is used for making candles and soap, dressing leather, etc. **ME.** ▸**b** The fat or adipose tissue of an animal, *esp.* that which yields the above suet. Now *rare.* **LME.**
2 Any of various greases or greasy substances obtained from plants, minerals, etc. Now *rare.* **M18.**
3 In full ***tallow candle***. A candle made of tallow. **E19.**
2 mineral tallow = HATCHETTITE. **vegetable tallow** a vegetable fat used as tallow.
Comb.: ***tallow candle***: see sense 3 above; †**tallow-catch** (*rare*, Shakes.) a very fat person; **tallow-chandler** a maker or seller of tallow candles; **tallow-chandlery** the business or workplace of a tallow-chandler; **tallow-cut** *adjective* = ***tallow-topped*** below; **tallow-dip** a candle made by dipping a piece of string in melted tallow; **tallow-drop** a style of cutting precious stones so that at least one side is made smooth and convex (freq. *attrib.*); **tallow-face** (chiefly *derog.*) (*a*) (now *rare*) a pale, yellowish-white face; †(*b*) (*rare*, Shakes.) a person with such a face; **tallow-faced** *adjective* (of a person) having a pale, yellowish-white face; **tallow-nut** the mountain plum, *Ximenia americana*, whose fruit has an oily seed; **tallow shrub** the wax myrtle or bayberry, *Myrica cerifera*; **tallow-top** a precious stone cut in tallow-drop fashion; **tallow-topped** *adjective* (of a precious stone) cut in tallow-drop fashion; **tallow-tree** any of several trees yielding substances resembling tallow; *spec.* (*a*) (more fully ***Chinese tallow-tree***) a Chinese tree of the spurge family, *Sapium sebiferum*, cultivated for the fatty covering of its seeds; (*b*) a W. African tree, *Pentadesma butyracea* (family Guttiferae), whose seeds yield an edible fat; **tallow-wood** a large Australian eucalyptus, *Eucalyptus microcorys*, which yields a very hard greasy wood.

▶**B** *verb*. **1 a** *verb trans*. Smear or grease (formerly esp. the bottom of a ship) with tallow. LME. ▶†**b** *verb intrans*. Of (the bottom of) a ship: be greased with tallow. M17–E18. **2** *verb intrans*. Of a cow etc.: form, produce, or yield tallow. E18. ▶**b** *verb trans*. Cause (a cow etc.) to form or produce tallow; fatten. M18.

▪ **tallowed** *adjective* (*a*) that has been tallowed; †(*b*) (of a cow etc.) producing or containing much tallow: LME. **tallower** *noun* †(*a*) *rare* an animal which produces tallow; (*b*) a tallow-chandler: E19. **tallowish** *adjective* of the nature of or resembling tallow M16.

tallowy /ˈtaləʊi/ *adjective*. LME.
[from TALLOW *noun* + -Y¹.]
1 Having the nature or properties of tallow; *spec*. greasy. LME. **2** Of a cow etc.: having much tallow. *rare*. L15. **3** Resembling tallow in colour or complexion. M19.

tallwood *noun* var. of TALWOOD.

tally /ˈtali/ *noun*. LME.
[Anglo-Norman *tallie* = Anglo-Latin *tal(l)ia* from Latin *talea* cutting, rod, stick: cf. TAIL *noun*².]
1 *Hist*. A usu. squared wooden stick or rod, scored across with notches representing the amount of a debt or payment and then split lengthways across the notches into two halves (one retained by each party) the correspondence of which constituted legal proof of the debt etc.; *spec*. such a stick or rod given by the Exchequer as a receipt for a tax paid, a loan to the sovereign, etc. LME. ▶**b** Either of the corresponding halves of a thing; a corresponding thing or part; a duplicate, a counterpart. M17. **2** The record of an amount due, a number, etc.; an account. Also, a score, a reckoning, a total; *spec*. (*a*) BASEBALL a single run; (*b*) *Austral*. & *NZ* a total number of sheep shorn. L16. **3** A number, a group; *esp*. a particular number (now freq. five) taken as a group or unit to facilitate keeping a tally or counting. Later also, the last of a specified number forming such a group or unit. L17. ▶**b** A mark (orig. the notch of a tally) or set of marks representing a fixed quantity of things delivered, received, counted, etc. E18. ▶**c** A system of paying for goods by instalments, a tally being kept by the seller; credit. Freq. *attrib*. E19. **4** A tab, label, or ticket used for identification, as (*a*) one inscribed with the name, class, etc., of the plant or tree to which it is attached or adjacent; (*b*) a distinguishing mark identifying a consignment of or denoting a quantity of goods; (*c*) a miner's identification tag. E19.

> 🕮 **1** J. FRANCIS Tallies . . bundled up like . . faggots in the hands of brokers. **2** C. WALKER A Tally of every mans faults but his own hanging at his Girdle. *Liverpool Echo* Marksman Alex . . took his tally to nine goals from his last four games. V. S. NAIPAUL Add one more human being to the tally of human beings he had encountered. **3c** *tally-business*, *tally-master*, *tally-shop*, *tally-trade*.

Phrases: **live tally** *slang* cohabit (*with* a person) outside marriage. **on tally**, **on the tally** on credit, on the tally system.
Comb.: **tally-board**: on which an account, score, etc., is notched or chalked; **tally card** *US* a score-card; **tally clerk** (*a*) a person who keeps a tally of goods, esp. cargo loaded or unloaded in docks; (*b*) *US* a person who assists in counting and recording votes; **tallyman** (*a*) a person who sells goods on a tally system, esp. from door to door; (*b*) a person who keeps a tally of anything, a tally clerk; (*c*) *slang* a man cohabiting with a woman to whom he is not married; **tally sheet**: on which a tally is kept; **tally-stick**: used as or like a tally (see sense 1 above); **tally system** a system of selling goods on short-term credit or an instalment plan (cf. sense 3c above); **tallywoman** (*a*) a woman who sells goods on a tally system, esp. from door to door; (*b*) *slang* a woman cohabiting with a man to whom she is not married.

tally /ˈtali/ *verb*¹. LME.
[from the noun.]
1 a *verb trans*. Mark, set *down*, or enter (a number, amount, etc.) (as) on a tally; record, register. LME. ▶**b** *verb trans*. *spec*. Identify, count, and record (goods, esp. items in a ship's cargo). E19. ▶**c** *verb trans*. Mark or identify (goods etc.) (as) by a tally or identifying label etc. M19. ▶**d** *verb intrans*. & *trans*. SPORT. Score (a run, goal, etc.). Chiefly *N. Amer*. M19. **2** *verb trans*. Count (*up*), reckon; estimate. M16. †**3** *verb intrans*. Deal on tally or credit (*with* a person). *rare*. L16–E18. †**4** *verb trans*. Cause (things) to correspond or agree; match. E17–E19. **5** *verb intrans*. Agree, correspond; fit. E18.

> 🕮 **1d** *New York Times* The home players tallied only five times during the entire contest. *Billings (Montana) Gazette* The Angels tallied their fifth run in the third inning. **2** K. KESEY Tally what the gas comes to and send the bill to the hospital. *Guernsey Weekly Press* A few anxious moments as points were tallied. *Scientific American* The age of the skeleton is . . best tallied from the . . closing of the gaps in various bones. **4** T. JEFFERSON Peculiarly tallied in interests, by each wanting exactly what the other has to spare. **5** E. HEATH The description he produced tallied with my experience. WILBUR SMITH Eleven helicopters in the emplacements, which tallied with his own estimate.

▪ **tallying** *noun* (*a*) the action of the verb; (*b*) exact agreement: LME.

tally /ˈtali/ *verb*². Now *rare*. LME.
[Origin unkn.]
NAUTICAL. **1** *verb trans*. Haul taut (the fore or main lee sheets). LME. **2** *verb intrans*. Catch hold of a rope. Foll. by *on (to)*. M19.

tally-ho /talɪˈhəʊ/ *interjection*, *noun*, & *verb*. L18.
[App. alt. of French *taïaut*, of unkn. origin.]
▶**A** *interjection*. In HUNTING, signalling the sighting of a fox. L18.
▶**B** *noun*. Pl. **-hos**.
1 A cry of 'tally-ho!' L18. **2** *Hist*. Any of various fast horse-drawn coaches or coach services; *spec*. (*US*) a large four-in-hand. M19.
▶**C** *verb*. **1** *verb trans*. Signal the presence of (a fox) by a tally-ho; urge (hounds) with a tally-ho. E19. **2** *verb intrans*. Cry 'tally-ho'. E19.

†**talm** *verb* see TAWM.

talma /ˈtalmə/ *noun*. M19.
[François Joseph *Talma*, French tragedian (1763–1826).]
Hist. A kind of cape or cloak popular in the 19th cent.

Talmud Chacham /ˈtalmɪd ˈxɑːxəm, talˈmɪd xəˈxam/ *noun phr*. Pl. ***Talmide Chachamim*** /talmɪˈdeɪ xɑːxəˈmɪm, talˈmɪdeɪ xəˈxɑːmɪn/. M19.
[Hebrew, lit. 'disciple of a wise man'.]
JUDAISM. A learned person, *esp*. an expert in the Jewish law. Cf. HAHAM.

Talmud /ˈtalmʊd, -məd, talˈmʊd/ *noun*. M16.
[Post-biblical Hebrew *talmūḏ* instruction, from Hebrew *lāmaḏ* learn.]
Orig., the Gemara; either of the recensions of the Gemara, *esp*. the Babylonian one. Now chiefly, *the* body of Jewish law consisting of the Mishnah and the Gemara.
Comb.: **Talmud Torah** (*a*) the field of study that deals with the Jewish law; (*b*) (freq. *attrib*.) a communal school where children are instructed in Judaism.

▪ **Talˈmudic** *noun* & *adjective* †(*a*) *noun* = TALMUDIST; (*b*) *adjective* of, pertaining to, or characteristic of the Talmud: E17. **Talˈmudical** *adjective* Talmudic E17. **Talmudism** *noun* belief in or practice of the teaching of the Talmud E17. **Talmudist** *noun* (*a*) any of the authors of the Talmud; (*b*) a believer in the Talmud; an expert on or student of the Talmud: M16. **Talmuˈdistic** *adjective* (*rare*) Talmudic M17. **Talmuˈdistical** *adjective* (*rare*) Talmudic L16. **talmudiˈzation** *noun* the action of talmudizing something, the state of being talmudized E20. **talmudize** *verb trans*. make Talmudic, allegorize M19.

talo- /ˈteɪləʊ/ *combining form*. L19.
[from Latin *talus* ankle-bone: see -O-.]
ANATOMY. Forming adjectives designating the articulation of, or ligaments joining, the talus and other bones, as ***talocalcaneal***, ***talofibular***, ***talonavicular***.

talon /ˈtalən/ *noun*. Also †**talent**. ME.
[Old & mod. French from Proto-Romance, from Latin *talus* ankle-bone.]
1 A heel-like part or object, as (*a*) NAUTICAL (now *rare* or *obsolete*) the curved back of a ship's rudder; (*b*) ARCHITECTURE an ogee moulding; (*c*) the projection on the bolt of a lock against which the key presses; (*d*) ZOOLOGY a low projection on the posterior lingual corner of the tribosphenic upper molar tooth. ME. †**2** = HEEL *noun*¹ 1b. LME–M17. **3** A claw of an animal, esp. a bird or beast of prey. Usu. in *pl*. LME. ▶**b** A grasping human finger or hand. Usu. in *pl*. L16. **4** CARDS. The cards remaining after the hands have been dealt. M19. **5** COMMERCE. The last part of a dividend-coupon sheet, entitling the holder to a new sheet on presentation. M19.

> 🕮 **3** SWIFT A kite . . would have . . carried me away in his talons. *fig*.: H. BRODKEY His . . impatience to make Annetje walk, escape the talons of the drug. **b** SHAKES. *L.L.L*. If a talent be a claw, look how he claws him with a talent.

▪ **taloned** *adjective* E17. **talonid** /ˈtalənɪd, təˈlɒnɪd/ *noun* & *adjective* (ZOOLOGY) (of or pertaining to) the depressed posterior part of the tribosphenic lower molar tooth L19.

talook, **talooka** *nouns* vars. of TALUK.

talookdar *noun* var. of TALUKDAR.

talpa /ˈtalpə/ *noun*. Now *rare* or *obsolete*. LME.
[Latin = mole.]
MEDICINE. An encysted cranial tumour; a wen.

tal qual /tal ˈkwal/ *noun* & *adverbial phr*. *Canad*. *dial*. Also **talqual**. M18.
[Latin *tal(is qual(is* such as, of which sort or quality.]
(A catch or batch of fish) sold just as they come, i.e. without regard to differences of size or quality.

†**talug** *noun* see TALLOW.

taluk /ˈtɑːlʊk, tɑːˈluːk/ *noun*. Also **-look**, **-ka** /-kə/, **-luq**. L18.
[Persian, Urdu *taʿalluk* estate from Arab. (= dependence, attachment), from *taʿallaḳa* adhere, be attached or connected.]
In the Indian subcontinent: orig., a hereditary estate; now, an administrative district for taxation purposes, usu. comprising a number of villages, a collectorate.

talukdar /tɑːˈluːkdɑː/ *noun*. Also **-look-**, **-luq-**. L18.
[from prec. + Persian *-dār* holding, holder.]
In the Indian subcontinent: orig., the holder of a taluk; now, the official in charge of a taluk.

taluq, **taluqdar** *nouns* vars. of TALUK, TALUKDAR.

talus /ˈteɪləs/ *noun*¹. Pl. **tali** /ˈteɪlʌɪ/. L16.
[Latin.]
ANATOMY. A small bone in the foot, articulating with the tibia to form the ankle joint. Also called ***ankle-bone***, ***astragalus***.

talus /ˈteɪləs/ *noun*². Pl. **-uses**. M17.
[French, of unkn. origin.]
1 A slope; *spec*. (FORTIFICATION) the sloping side of a wall or earthwork. M17. **2** GEOLOGY. A scree slope, consisting of material which has fallen from the face of the cliff above. M19. ▶**b** *gen*. The slope of a mountain, hill, or iceberg. Now *rare*. M19.
Comb.: **talus cone** a cone-shaped mass of detritus in a cave etc., consisting of material which has fallen from (a hole in) the roof.

talweg *noun* var. of THALWEG.

talwood /ˈtalwʊd/ *noun*. *obsolete* exc. *Hist*. Also **-ll-**. ME.
[translating Old French *bois de tail*, from *tail* cutting, cut: see BUSH *noun*¹, TAIL *verb*¹.]
Wood for fuel, cut up usu. to a prescribed size.

TAM /tam/ *abbreviation*.
Television audience measurement.

tam /tam/ *noun*. L19.
[Abbreviation. Cf. TAMMY *noun*³.]
A tam-o'-shanter.

tamable *adjective* var. of TAMEABLE.

Tamagotchi /taməˈɡɒtʃi/ *noun*. L20.
[Japanese, from *tamago* egg + *uotchi* watch.]
(Proprietary name for) an electronic toy displaying a digital image of an animal, which has to be looked after and responded to by the 'owner' as if it were a pet.

tamale /təˈmɑːli/ *noun*. L17.
[Mexican Spanish *tamal*, pl. *tamales*, from Nahuatl *tamalli*.]
A Mexican dish of seasoned meat and maize flour steamed or baked in maize husks.

tamandua /təˈmand(j)ʊə/ *noun*. E17.
[Portuguese from Tupi *tamanduá*, from *ta* (contr. of *taly*) ant + *monduar* hunter.]
A New World anteater. Now *spec*., either of two small arboreal prehensile-tailed anteaters, *Tamandua mexicana* (more fully ***northern tamandua***) and *T. tetradactyla* (more fully ***southern tamandua***).

Tamang /taˈmaŋ/ *noun* & *adjective*. M20.
[Nepali from *rta-maṅ* (owner of) many horses.]
▶**A** *noun*. Pl. **-s**, same.
1 A member of a Buddhist people inhabiting mountainous parts of Nepal and Sikkim. M20. **2** The Tibeto-Burman language of this people. L20.
▶**B** *adjective*. Of or pertaining to this people or their language. M20.

tamanoir /ˈtamənwɑː/ *noun*. L18.
[French from Carib *tamanoà* from Tupi *tamanduá*: see TAMANDUA.]
The giant anteater or ant-bear, *Myrmecophaga tridactyla*.

tamanu /ˈtamənuː/ *noun*. M19.
[Tahitian.]
The tree *Calophyllum inophyllum* (family Guttiferae), of southern Asia etc., a source of tacamahac. Also ***tamanu tree***. Also called **poon**.

tamarack /ˈtamərak/ *noun*. E19.
[Canad. French *tamarac*, prob. from Algonquian.]
Any of several N. American coniferous trees, *esp*. the American larch or hackmatack, *Larix laricina*, and (also ***tamarack pine***) the lodgepole pine, *Pinus contorta* var. *latifolia*. Also, the timber of any of these trees.

tamarau /ˈtamərau/ *noun*. L19.
[Tagalog.]
A small black buffalo, *Bubalus mindorensis*, native to Mindoro in the Philippines.

tamari /təˈmɑːri/ *noun*. L20.
[Japanese.]
A Japanese variety of rich wheat-free soy sauce. Also ***tamari sauce***.

tamarillo /taməˈrɪləʊ/ *noun*. Orig. *NZ*. Pl. **-os**. M20.
[Invented word: cf. Spanish TOMATILLO.]
= ***tree tomato*** s.v. TREE *noun*.

tamarin /ˈtam(ə)rɪn/ *noun.* L18.
[French from Galibi.]
Any of numerous small neotropical monkeys with fine silky coats and long bushy tails which belong to the genera *Saguinus* and *Leontopithecus*, and together with the marmosets constitute the family Callitricidae.
lion tamarin, negro tamarin, etc.

tamarind /ˈtam(ə)rɪnd/ *noun.* LME.
[medieval Latin *tamarindus* from Arab. *tamr hindī* Indian date. Cf. Old French *tamarinde* (mod. *tamarin*).]
1 The fruit of the tree *Tamarindus indica* (see sense 2 below), a brown pod containing one to twelve seeds embedded in a soft brown sticky acid pulp, valued for its laxative qualities and also used to make chutney, cooling drinks, etc.; in *pl.*, the pulp of this fruit. LME.
2 The leguminous tree bearing this fruit, *Tamarindus indica*, with pinnate leaves and fragrant yellow red-streaked flowers, widely grown as a shade tree in tropical countries. Also ***tamarind tree***. E17.
3 Chiefly with specifying word: any of various trees which resemble the tamarind in some respect. M19.
3 Manila tamarind (the edible fruit of) a leguminous tree of Central America, *Pithecellobium dulce*. **native tamarind** *Austral.* the tree *Diploglottis australis* (family Sapindaceae); the fruit of this tree, blood-red inside with black seeds. **velvet tamarind** (the edible fruit of) a small leguminous tree of tropical W. Africa, *Dialium guineense*.
Comb.: **tamarind water** a cooling drink made from infused tamarinds.

tamarisk /ˈtam(ə)rɪsk/ *noun.* LME.
[Late Latin *tamariscus* var. of Latin *tamarix*, of unkn. origin.]
Any of various shrubs or small trees constituting the genus *Tamarix* (family Tamaricaceae), with slender feathery branches, minute scalelike leaves, and spikes of tiny pink flowers, growing in sandy places in southern Europe, western Asia, etc.; esp. *T. gallica*, freq. planted by the seashore in southern England etc. Also (in full ***German tamarisk***), the allied shrub *Myricaria germanica*, of river gravel in Continental Europe.

tamarugo /taməˈruːgəʊ/ *noun.* Pl. **-os**. L20.
[Chilean Spanish.]
A small evergreen leguminous tree, *Prosopis tamarugo*, native to the salt deserts of northern Chile, which can be used to provide fodder in arid regions.

tamasha /təˈmɑːʃə/ *noun.* Also (earlier) †**tom-**. E17.
[Persian & Urdu *tamāšā* (for *tamāšī*) walking about for amusement, entertainment, from Arab. *tamāšā* walk about together, from *mašā* walk.]
1 In the Indian subcontinent: an entertainment, a show, a spectacle, a public function. E17.
2 A fuss, a commotion. *colloq.* L19.

Tamashek /ˈtaməʃɛk/ *noun & adjective.* L19.
[Berber.]
(Designating or pertaining to) the Berber dialect of the Tuaregs.

tambala /tamˈbɑːlə/ *noun.* L20.
[Nyanja = cockerel.]
A monetary unit of Malawi, equal to one-hundredth of a kwacha.

tamber /ˈtambə/ *noun.* E20.
[Phonetic respelling.]
LINGUISTICS. = TIMBRE *noun*³.

tambo /ˈtambəʊ/ *noun*¹. Pl. **-os**. M19.
[Abbreviation.]
Chiefly *Hist.* The tambourine player in a troupe of black-face minstrels; a tambourine played by such a musician.

tambo /ˈtambəʊ/ *noun*². Pl. **-os**. M19.
[Spanish from Quechua *tampu*.]
A lodging house or roadside inn in the Andes, esp. in Peru.

tamboo-bamboo /tambuːˈbambuː/ *noun.* M20.
[from alt. of TAMBOUR *noun* + BAMBOO.]
A small W. Indian drum made of bamboo.

tambookie /tamˈbuːki/ *noun & adjective.* Also **-bouki** & other vars. L18.
[Afrikaans *tamboekie*, formed as TEMBU + *-kie* dim. suffix.]
▸†**A** *noun.* (**T-**.) = TEMBU *noun.* L18–E20.
▸**B** *adjective.* †**1** (**T-**.) = TEMBU *adjective.* Only in 19.
2 ***tambookie grass***, any of several tall coarse grasses of southern Africa, esp. of the genera *Cymbopogon* and *Hyparrhenia*, used for thatching. M19.

tamboritsa *noun* var. of TAMBURITZA.

tamboti /tamˈbuːti/ *noun. S. Afr.* Also **-botie**, **-buti** /-ˈbʊəti/, **tombotie** /tɒm-/. M19.
[Xhosa *um-Thombothi* lit. 'poison tree'.]
A deciduous tree of southern Africa, *Spirostachys africana*, of the spurge family with heavy scented wood and caustic sap (also ***tamboti tree***). Also, the timber of this tree (also ***tamboti wood***).

tambouki *noun & adjective* var. of TAMBOOKIE.

tambour /ˈtambʊə/ *noun.* L15.
[French: see TABOR *noun*.]
1 A drum; now *esp.* a small drum with a deep tone. L15.
2 ARCHITECTURE. **a** = BELL *noun*¹ 3C. E18. ▸**b** Any of the courses forming the shaft of a cylindrical column. E18. ▸**c** A lobby with a ceiling and folding doors serving to obviate draughts, esp. in a church porch. E18. ▸**d** A wall of circular plan, as one supporting a dome or surrounded by a colonnade. E19.
3 A projecting part of the main wall of a real tennis court on the hazard side, with a sloping end face. Also, a similar buttress or projection in some fives courts. E18.
4 a A circular frame formed of one hoop fitting inside another, in which fabric is held taut for embroidering. L18. ▸**b** Material embroidered or embroidery done using such a frame. Also = ***tambour-lace*** below. L18. ▸**c** A kind of fine gold or silver thread. M19.
5 MILITARY. A small redan defending an entrance or passage. M19.
6 MEDICINE. A stretched membrane forming part of an instrument for recording arterial pulsations, respiratory movements, etc., by slight changes in air pressure. L19.
7 A sliding flexible shutter or door on a desk, cabinet, etc., made of strips of wood attached to a backing of canvas. M20.
Comb.: **tambour desk**: having a tambour or flexible sliding door; **tambour-frame** = sense 4a above; **tambour hook** EMBROIDERY a small steel hook set in a handle, used in working with a tambour; **tambour-lace** lace consisting of needlework designs on machine-made net; **tambour-needle** EMBROIDERY = ***tambour hook*** above; **tambour-stitch** (*a*) a kind of loop-stitch used in working with a tambour; (*b*) a crochet stitch by which a pattern of intersecting ridges is produced.

tambour /ˈtambʊə/ *verb trans. & intrans.* M18.
[from the noun.]
Work or embroider using a tambour-frame. Freq. as ***tamboured*** *ppl adjective*, ***tambouring*** *verbal noun*.
■ **tambourer** *noun* E19.

tamboura /tamˈbʊərə/ *noun.* L16.
[Arab. *tanbūr*, Persian *tunbūra* from Persian *dunbara*, *dunba bara* lit. 'lamb's tail'.]
MUSIC. **1** A long-necked lute of the Near East and Balkans, with a pear-shaped body and a fretted neck. L16.
2 A long-necked fretless type of lute with a round body and usu. four wire strings, used to provide a drone accompaniment in Indian music. M19.

†**tambouret** *noun. rare.* M17.
[from TAMBOUR *noun* + -ET¹.]
1 = TABOURET 1. Only in M17.
2 A small drum. L18–M19.

tambourin /ˈtambərɪn/ *noun.* L18.
[French, dim. of TAMBOUR *noun*.]
1 A quick Provençal dance in duple time; a piece of music for this dance. L18.
2 A long narrow Provençal drum or tabor of a kind orig. used to accompany this dance. M19.

tambourine /tambəˈriːn/ *noun.* L16.
[French *tambourin*: see prec., -INE⁴.]
A musical instrument consisting of a hoop with a skin stretched over one side and pairs of small jingling discs in slots round the circumference, played by shaking, striking, or drawing the fingers across the skin.
Comb.: **tambourine dove** a black and white African dove, *Turtur tympanistria*, with a resonant call.
■ **tambourinist** *noun* a person who plays the tambourine M20.

tamburitza /tamˈbʊrɪtsə/ *noun.* Also **tamboritsa** /-ˈbɒr-/ & other vars. M20.
[Serbo-Croat.]
MUSIC. = TAMBOURA 1.

tambuti *noun* var. of TAMBOTI.

tame /teɪm/ *adjective.*
[Old English *tam* = Old Frisian, Middle & mod. Low German, Middle & mod. Dutch *tam*, Old High German *zam* (German *zahm*), Old Norse *tamr*, from Germanic from Indo-European base repr. also by Latin *domare*, Greek *daman* to tame, subdue.]
1 Of an animal (*occas.* a person): no longer wild, domestic, domesticated; having the disposition of a domesticated animal; accustomed to humans; not showing the natural shyness, fear, or fierceness of a wild animal; tractable, docile. OE. ▸†**b** Well known, familiar. *rare* (Shakes.). Only in E17.
2 (Of a plant) produced by cultivation, not wild; (of land) cultivated. Now *US*. LME.
3 Subdued as by taming; submissive; meek; servile. M16.
4 Lacking animation, force, or effectiveness; having no striking features; uninspiring; insipid, dull. E17.
5 Of a person: retained or available to act as needed or asked: on hand and amenable, cooperative, compliant (passing into sense 3). *colloq.* E18.

📖 **1** J. CONRAD Tame Indians coming miles to market. J. TROLLOPE He had kept a tame hare in a basket in his study. *Skin Diver* The fish are so tame you almost have to push them away from your facemask. **tame cat** *fig.* an unassertive person, one who is dominated by or subservient to another person or group. **2** A. FRY A big field of good tame hay. **3** LD MACAULAY The tribunal lately so insolent, became on a sudden strangely tame. G. M. TREVELYAN Mill . . preached the doctrine of revolt against the tame acceptance of conventional opinions. **4** R. C. HOARE On descending . . the scenery . . becomes tamer. W. H. AUDEN The rather tame conclusion That no man by himself has life's solution. A. LIVINGSTONE The dichotomy . . between wild spirit and tame domestic comfort. **5** A. CHRISTIE The tame psychiatrists who do jobs for us. J. MANN He listed the questions their tame members were to ask.

■ **tamely** *adverb* like a tame animal; submissively, quietly; without resistance; without spirit or animation: L16. **tameness** *noun* M16.

tame /teɪm/ *verb*¹.
[Old English *temman*, *temian*, from Germanic base of TAME *adjective*: superseded in Middle English by forms directly from the adjective.]
1 *verb trans.* Bring (a wild animal) under the control or into the service of humans; reclaim from the wild state, make tame, domesticate. OE. ▸†**b** Bring under or into cultivation. E17–M18.
2 *verb trans.* Overcome the wildness or fierceness of (a person, animal, or thing); control, subdue, curb; make tractable or docile. OE.
3 *verb trans.* Reduce the intensity of; temper, soften, mellow. L15.
4 *verb intrans.* Become tame; grow more tractable or docile. Also foll. by *down*. M17.

📖 **1** C. LYELL The lake-dwellers succeeded in taming that formidable brute. **2** MILTON This River-dragon tam'd at length submits To let his sojourners depart. N. GORDIMER His hair, still long, had been combed wet until tamed. R. FRASER Marriage to Maria helped tame a spirit that could flash out into unwise behaviour. *Time* The battle to tame inflation has been exasperating. **3** F. T. PALGRAVE Manhood's colours tamed to gray. H. CARPENTER She tries to tame her masculine aggression and to cultivate feminine self-control. **4** L. ADAMIC Now . . in power, the Radicals tamed down and changed their color. *New Yorker* The okapi tames readily.

Comb.: **tame-poison** the swallowwort *Vincetoxicum officinale* (family Asclepiadaceae), the root of which was formerly used as an antidote to poisons.
■ **tamer** *noun* M16.

tame /teɪm/ *verb*² *trans. obsolete* exc. *dial.* LME.
[Aphet. from ATTAME, ENTAME *verb*¹.]
1 Pierce, cut into; break or cut open for use. LME.
†**2** Injure, hurt. LME–L15.

tameable /ˈteɪməb(ə)l/ *adjective.* Also **tamable**. M16.
[from TAME *verb*¹ + -ABLE.]
Able to be tamed.
■ **tameaˈbility**, **tameableness** *nouns* E19.

tamein /təˈmeɪn/ *noun.* M19.
[Burmese.]
An ankle-length garment resembling a sarong worn (chiefly by women) in Myanmar (Burma).

tameless /ˈteɪmlɪs/ *adjective.* L16.
[from TAME *verb*¹ + -LESS.]
That has never been or cannot be tamed; untamed, untameable.
■ **tamelessness** *noun* E19.

tameletjie /taməˈlɛki, -tʃi/ *noun. S. Afr.* M19.
[Afrikaans, perh. from *tabletje* small cake.]
(A piece of) hard toffee often containing almonds or pine nuts. Now also, a sweet consisting of a roll of compressed and sweetened dried fruit (also more fully ***tameletjie-roll***).

Tamil /ˈtamɪl/ *adjective & noun.* Also (earlier) †**-ul**. M18.
[(Portuguese, Dutch *Tamul* from) Tamil *Tamil* = Prakrit *Damila*, *Davila*, Sanskrit *Dramiḍa*, *Draviḍa*. Cf. DRAVIDIAN.]
▸**A** *adjective.* Designating or pertaining to (the language of) a Dravidian people inhabiting the southern Indian subcontinent and parts of Sri Lanka. M18.
▸**B** *noun.* Pl. **-s**, same.
1 The Dravidian language of this people. L18.
2 A member of this people. M19.
■ **Taˈmilian** *adjective & noun* = TAMIL M19. †**Tamulian** *adjective & noun* = TAMIL M18–M19. †**Tamulic** *adjective* designating or pertaining to the Tamil language L18–L19.

tamine /taˈmiːn/ *noun & adjective. obsolete* exc. *Hist.* M16.
[Aphet. from French *étamine* STAMIN. Cf. TAMMY *noun*¹.]
(Made of) a thin woollen or worsted fabric.

†**tamis** *noun.* E17.
[French = medieval Latin *tamisium*, from West Germanic base of TEMSE *verb*. Cf. TAMMY *noun*².]
1 A sieve, a strainer. Also, a cloth used for straining liquids. E17–E19.
2 BOTANY. The anthers of a flower. M17–E18.

Tamla /ˈtamlə/ *noun & adjective.* **L20.**
[US record company. Cf. next.]
= MOTOWN.
¶ *Tamla* is a US proprietary name.

Tamla Motown /tamlə ˈməʊtaʊn/ *noun & adjectival phr.* **M20.**
[from prec. + MOTOWN.]
= MOTOWN.
¶ *Tamla/Motown* is a proprietary name.

Tammany /ˈtaməni/ *noun & adjective.* **M19.**
[*Tammany* Hall, the building housing the central organization of the Democratic Party in New York City.]
▶ **A** *noun.* In full ***Tammany Hall***. (The central organization of) the Democratic Party in New York (City), notorious for corruption in the 19th and early 20th cents. (now chiefly *Hist.*); *gen.* a corrupt political organization or group; corruption in municipal or regional politics. **M19.**
▶ **B** *attrib.* or as *adjective.* Pertaining to or characteristic of Tammany. **M19.**
■ **Tammanyism** *noun* the system or principles of Tammany; political corruption: **E20. Tammanyite** *noun* a person who adopts the methods and principles of Tammany, a supporter of Tammany **L19.**

tammar /ˈtamə/ *noun.* Also (earlier) †**dama**. **M19.**
[Aboriginal.]
A greyish-brown scrub wallaby, *Thylogale eugenii*, found in SW Australia. Also ***tammar wallaby***.

tammie norie /ˈtamɪ ˈnɒri/ *noun. Scot.* **E18.**
[from Scot. form of male forename *Tommy* + *norie* of unkn. origin.]
The puffin, *Fratercula arctica*.

Tammuz *noun* var. of THAMMUZ.

tammy /ˈtami/ *noun*[1] & *adjective.* **M17.**
[Prob. rel. to TAMINE.]
(Made of) a fine worsted cloth often with a glazed finish.

tammy /ˈtami/ *noun*[2]. Now *rare.* **M18.**
[App. from French TAMIS, assim. to prec.]
A strainer.

tammy /ˈtami/ *noun*[3]. **L19.**
[from TAM + -Y[6].]
A tam-o'-shanter.

tam-o'-shanter /taməˈʃantə/ *noun.* **M19.**
[*Tam o' Shanter*, (the hero of) a poem by Robert Burns (1790).]
A round woollen bonnet or cloth cap of Scottish origin fitting closely round the brows but large and full above. Also more fully ***tam-o'-shanter bonnet***, ***tam-o'-shanter cap***. Cf. TAM, TAMMY *noun*[3].

tamoxifen /təˈmɒksɪfɛn/ *noun.* **L20.**
[from (alt. of) T(RANS- + AM(INE + OXY- + PHEN(OL, elems. of the systematic name.]
PHARMACOLOGY. A non-steroidal drug which acts as an oestrogen antagonist and is used to treat breast cancer and infertility in women.

tamp /tamp/ *verb trans.* **E19.**
[Prob. back-form. from var. of TAMPION, taken as = *tamping*.]
1 MINING. Pack (a blast-hole) with clay, sand, etc., to concentrate the force of the explosion. Also, ram home (the charge) in a blast-hole. **E19.**
2 a Ram or pound down (earth, gravel, road material, ballast, etc.) usu. so as to produce a firm base or level surface. Also, pack round with earth etc. Also foll. by *down*. **L19.** ▶**b** Pack or consolidate tobacco in (a pipe etc.); pack down (tobacco) in a pipe etc. Also foll. by *down*. **E20.** ▶**c** Oppress or constrict as by ramming; subdue or contain by force. Also foll. by *down*. *US.* **M20.**

> 🕮 **2a** J. G. BALLARD Powers . . tamped the mixture down into the narrow channel. *Guardian* Tamp the earth to just the right firmness when planting out seedlings.

■ **tamping** *noun* (*a*) the action of the verb; (*b*) material used for packing into a blast-hole or for tamping down around something: **E19.**

tampan /ˈtampan/ *noun.* **M19.**
[Perh. from Setswana.]
A bloodsucking tick of the genus *Ornithodorus*, esp. *O. moubata*, the vector of African relapsing fever.

Tampax /ˈtampaks/ *noun.* **M20.**
[Arbitrary formation from TAMPON *noun*.]
(Proprietary name for) a sanitary tampon for women.

tamper /ˈtampə/ *noun.* **M19.**
[from TAMP + -ER[1].]
1 A person who or thing which tamps something; *esp.* a machine or device for tamping down earth, ballast, etc. **M19.**
2 A casing around a nuclear bomb which reflects neutrons and increases the efficiency of the explosive. **M20.**

tamper /ˈtampə/ *verb.* Also (earlier) †**temper**. **M16.**
[Alt. of TEMPER *verb*[1]. Branch II prob. represents the original use.]
▶**I 1** *verb intrans.* Busy oneself for some end, *esp.* machinate, scheme, plot (foll. by *in*, *for*, *with*, *to do*, etc.). Now only, (foll. by *with*) deal improperly with, exert a secret or corrupt influence on, *spec.* bribe. **M16.**
2 *verb intrans.* Foll. by *with*: meddle or interfere with so as to cause alteration or harm; make unauthorized changes in. **L16.** ▶†**b** *spec.* Meddle *with* medically. **M17–L18.**
3 *verb trans.* Bias, influence, corrupt; meddle with, alter improperly. Now chiefly as ***tampered*** *ppl adjective. rare.* **L17.**

> 🕮 **1** HOR. WALPOLE The queen dowager tampered in this plot. C. M. YONGE He was trafficking with her enemies and tampering with her friends. **2** V. WOOLF He was incapable of untruth; never tampered with a fact. M. GORDON He went over his collections . . convinced that someone had been tampering with them. B. CHATWIN The curator warned him not to tamper with the labels.

▶†**II 4** *verb intrans. & trans.* Work in or *in* (clay etc.); temper (clay). *rare.* **L16–M18.**
Comb.: **tamper-evident** *adjective* (of packaging etc.) designed to make obvious any improper interference with the contents; **tamper-proof** *adjective* proof against being tampered with; not readily susceptible to misuse; **tamper-resistant** *adjective* resistant to being tampered with.
■ **tamperer** *noun* **L16.**

tampico /ˈtampɪkəʊ/ *noun.* **L19.**
[Name of a port in eastern Mexico from which the fibre was exported.]
Any of various kinds of stiff fibre obtained from plants, including istle, *piassava*, and sisal. Also ***tampico fibre***, ***tampico hemp***.

tampion /ˈtampɪən/ *noun.* Also **tomp-** /ˈtɒmp-/. **LME.**
[French TAMPON.]
1 A plug, a bung, a stopper; *esp.* (*a*) a stopper for the muzzle of a gun; (*b*) a plug for the top of an organ-pipe. **LME.**
†**2** A wooden disc or cylinder made to act as a wad in a muzzle-loading gun. **LME–E19.**

tampon /ˈtampɒn/ *noun & verb.* **M19.**
[French, nasalized var. of Old & mod. French *tapon*, from Frankish: cogn. with TAP *noun*[1].]
▶ **A** *noun.* **1** A plug of soft material (to be) inserted into a wound, orifice, etc., to arrest bleeding, absorb secretions, etc.; *esp.* one for insertion into the vagina to absorb menstrual blood. **M19.**
2 A dabber or inking ball used to ink a plate in intaglio printing. **L19.**
▶ **B** *verb trans.* Plug with a tampon. **M19.**
■ **tamponage** *noun* = TAMPONADE 1 **E20.**

tamponade /tampəˈneɪd/ *noun.* **L19.**
[from prec. + -ADE.]
1 MEDICINE. The surgical use of a tampon or tampons. **L19.**
2 Compression of the heart by an excessive accumulation of blood or other fluid in the pericardial sac. Also ***cardiac tamponade***. **M20.**

tam quam *noun phr.* var. of TANQUAM.

tam-tam /ˈtamtam/ *noun.* **M19.**
[Perh. from Hindi *tam-tam* TOM-TOM *noun*.]
MUSIC. A large metal gong, *spec.* one of a Chinese kind which lacks a definite pitch.

†**Tamul** *adjective & noun* see TAMIL.

Tamworth /ˈtamwəθ/ *noun.* **M19.**
[A town in Staffordshire, England.]
(An animal of) a breed of long-bodied, usu. red or brown pig.

tan /tan/ *noun*[1] & *adjective.* **LME.**
[from the verb. Cf. Old & mod. French *tan*, medieval Latin *tannum*.]
▶ **A** *noun.* **1** Crushed bark of oak or other trees, used as a source of tannin for converting hides into leather, and (formerly) in powdered form as a styptic and astringent. **LME.** ▶**b** Spent bark from tanning, used as a covering for paths, rides, etc. Also ***spent tan***. **M18.** ▶**c** The astringent principle of tanning bark, tannin; liquor containing this. **E19.**
2 a A brown skin colour resulting from exposure to the sun or other source of ultraviolet light. Cf. SUNTAN. **M18.** ▶**b** A yellowish-brown colour. **L19.**
3 a A shoe, boot, or garment of a tan colour. Usu. in *pl.* **E20.** ▶**b** *Hist.* A member of the Black and Tans. Usu. in *pl.* **M20.**
1 *flowers of tan*: see FLOWER *noun* 11.
Comb.: **tanbark** = sense A.1, 1b above; **tan-bed** a hotbed made of spent tan; **tan-house**: a building in which tanning is done; **tan-pit** (*a*) a tan-vat; (*b*) a tan-bed; **tan-vat** a receptacle, tub, or pit containing the liquor in which hides are placed in tanning; **Tan war** *Hist.* the conflict between the Black and Tans and the Irish nationalist forces in 1921; **tan-yard** a place where tanning is carried on, a tannery.
▶ **B** *adjective.* Of a yellowish-brown colour. Also, bronzed, suntanned. **E16.**
■ **tannish** *adjective* somewhat tan, rather yellowish-brown **M20.**

tan /tan/ *noun*[2]. **M17.**
[Abbreviation.]
MATH. Tangent (of).

tan /tan/ *noun*[3]. Pl. same. **L19.**
[Japanese.]
1 A Japanese unit of area for arable land and forest, equal to approx. 0.1 hectare or a quarter of an acre. **L19.**
2 A Japanese measure of cloth, now usu. equivalent to about twelve metres in length and a third of a metre in width; a piece or roll of cloth of this size. **L19.**

tan /tan/ *noun*[4]. Pl. same, **-s**. **L19.**
[Chinese *dàn* (Wade–Giles *tan*).]
A female character in a Chinese opera.

tan /tan/ *verb.* Infl. **-nn-**. **LOE.**
[Prob. from medieval Latin *tannare*, perh. of Celtic origin; reinforced in Middle English from Old French *tan(n)er*.]
1 *verb trans.* Convert (skin, hide) into leather by soaking in a liquid containing tannic acid (orig. from bark) or other agents. **LOE.** ▶**b** Treat (fishing nets, sails, etc.) with a preservative. **E17.**
2 *verb trans.* Make (the face, skin, etc.) brown by exposure to ultraviolet light from the sun or other source; suntan; *gen.* cause to turn brown. **M16.** ▶**b** *verb intrans.* Become sunburnt or brown by exposure. **M16.**
3 *verb trans.* Thrash, beat. Orig. & freq. in ***tan a person's hide*** s.v. HIDE *noun*[1]. **M17.**
4 *verb trans.* Chiefly PHOTOGRAPHY. Harden chemically, esp. in a process involving light. **L19.**

> 🕮 **2** F. KING She grinned revealing small, wicked teeth tanned with nicotine. **b** R. LOWELL The passengers were tanning On the Mediterranean in deck-chairs. **3** E. WAUGH Behave, or I'll tan yer arses for yer. J. I. M. STEWART University professors don't tan their daughters.

■ **tannable** *adjective* able to be tanned **L19. tanning** *noun* the action of the verb; an instance of this, a thrashing, a beating: **L15.**

tana *noun* var. of THANA.

tanager /ˈtanədʒə/ *noun.* Orig. †**tangara**. **E17.**
[Tupi (whence also Portuguese) *tangará*: later refash. after mod. Latin *Tanagra* genus name, itself perh. infl. by next.]
Any of numerous often brightly coloured American passerine birds of the subfamily Thraupinae, related to the buntings.
scarlet tanager, ***summer tanager***, etc.

Tanagra /ˈtanəgrə/ *noun.* **L19.**
[A city of Boeotia in ancient Greece.]
Used *attrib.* to designate terracotta statuettes of the 5th to 3rd cents. BC found near Tanagra.

Tanaiste /ˈtɔːnɪʃtə/ *noun.* Also **Tá-**. **M20.**
[Irish *tánaiste*: see TANIST.]
The deputy prime minister of the Republic of Ireland.

Tanak /təˈnɑːk/ *noun.* Also ***Tenach*** & other vars. Pl. **-im** /-ɪm/. **M20.**
[Hebrew *tĕnak* acronym, from *tōrāh* law, *nĕbī'īm* prophets, *kĕtūbīm* hagiographa.]
The Hebrew Scriptures, comprising the three canonical divisions of the Law, the Prophets, and the Hagiographa or Writings.

tanalized /ˈtan(ə)lʌɪzd/ *adjective.* Also **-ised**. **M20.**
[from *Tanalith* proprietary name for a wood preservative + -IZE + -ED[1].]
Of timber: treated with a preservative.

T and A *abbreviation.*
1 Tits and ass. *US slang.*
2 Tonsillectomy and adenoidectomy; tonsils and adenoids.

tandava /ˈtɑːndəvə/ *noun.* **E20.**
[Sanskrit *tāṇḍava*.]
A vigorous and masculine Indian style of dancing, associated with Siva.

tandem /ˈtandəm/ *noun, adverb, adjective, & verb.* **L18.**
[Joc. use of Latin, = at length.]
▶ **A** *noun.* **1** (A vehicle drawn by) two horses or other animals harnessed one in front of the other. **L18.**
2 *gen.* An arrangement of two people or similar things working together. **M19.**
3 A bicycle or (less usu.) tricycle equipped with saddles and pedals for two riders one in front of the other. **L19.**
4 *in tandem*, arranged one behind the other; *fig.* together, in partnership. **M20.**

> 🕮 **1** *Horse International* Competitive classes for horse and pony teams, pairs, singles and tandems. **4** I. ASIMOV Two seats in tandem, each of which could hold three. E. J. HOWARD They drove in tandem with Villy leading.

▶ **B** *adverb.* As a tandem; one behind or after the other; together. **L18.**
▶ **C** *attrib.* or as *adjective.* **1** Of the nature of a tandem; involving or making use of two similar things one behind or after the other. **E19.**
2 Cooperative, joint, dual; involving two people, organizations, etc. **M20.**

1 LYTTON A light cart drawn by two swift horses in a tandem fashion. *Archaeology* A series of tandem camera exposures. **tandem axle** (designating or utilizing) an arrangement of two axles for supporting the rear of an articulated lorry or trailer. **tandem garage**: with space for two vehicles to be parked one behind the other. **2** *Times Lit. Suppl.* The tandem authors of this study merely add to the confusion. *Which?* Some airfields offer tandem jumps—you leave the plane . . strapped to an instructor.

▶ **D** *verb. rare.*
1 *verb intrans.* Drive or ride a tandem. E19.
2 *verb trans.* Arrange or work as a tandem. L19.
■ **tandemer**, **tandemist** *nouns* a rider of a tandem bicycle or tricycle L19. **tandemly** *adverb* (GENETICS) (with genes etc. joined) end to end M20.

tandoor /'tandʊə, tan'dʊə/ *noun.* Also (in sense 1 usu.) **tandour**; (earlier) †**ten-** & other vars. M17.
[Sense 1 from French *tandour* from Turkish *tandır* var. of Persian, Arab. *tannūr* oven, furnace; sense 2 from Urdu, *tandūr*, Persian *tanūr* ult. from Arab. *tannūr*. Cf. ATHANOR.]
1 A square table with a brazier under it, round which people sit for warmth in cold weather in Persia, Turkey, and adjacent countries. Now *rare.* M17.
2 A clay oven of a kind used orig. in northern India and Pakistan; a shop selling food cooked in such an oven. M19.

tandoori /tan'dʊəri/ *adjective & noun.* M20.
[Persian & Urdu, from *tandūr*: see prec.]
▶ **A** *adjective.* Designating, pertaining to, or using a style of Indian cooking based on the use of a tandoor. M20.
▶ **B** *noun.* Tandoori cooking or food; a tandoori dish. M20.

tandour *noun* see TANDOOR.

tanekaha /tɑːnɪ'kɑːhə/ *noun. NZ.* L19.
[Maori.]
A celery-top pine (genus *Phyllocladus*), esp. *P. trichomanoides*.

tang /taŋ/ *noun*[1]. ME.
[Old Norse *tange* point, spit of land, tang of a knife etc. (Norwegian, Danish *tange*, Swedish *tång(e)*). Cf. TWANG *noun*[2].]
1 a The tongue of a snake (formerly believed to be a stinging organ); the sting of an insect. *obsolete* exc. *dial.* ME. ▸**b** A sharp point or spike; the pin of a buckle; a prong, a tine. *dial.* L17. ▸**c** The tongue of a Jew's harp. *Scot.* L19.
2 A pointed projection on the blade of a knife, chisel, file, or other implement by which the blade is held firmly in the handle, stock, etc. Also, a projection from the barrel of a gun by which the barrel can be fixed to the stock. LME.
3 A penetrating taste, flavour, or smell; a slight taste, flavour, or smell *of* something; an aftertaste. Cf. TWANG *noun*[2] 1. LME.
4 *fig.* **a** A trace or smack of some quality, opinion, form of speech, etc. (Foll. by *of*.) L16. ▸**b** Distinctive or characteristic flavour or quality. M19.
5 A surgeonfish. M18.
6 TYPOGRAPHY. A piece of superfluous metal formed on a piece of type in casting. L19.

3 J. CLAVELL He smelled a tang to the breeze, part salt and part smoke. J. COX Cold and creamy with a light citrus tang. M. FLANAGAN Worcestershire sauce might lure out her old love of spice and tang. **4a** T. GRAY The language has a tang of Shakespear that suits an old fashioned fable. J. HAWKES In the air a faint but palpable tang of wildness. **b** *New Yorker* Extreme disproportion of length and width . . lends tang to his horizontal paintings.

tang /taŋ/ *noun*[2]. Chiefly *Scot.* M16.
[Of Scandinavian origin (cf. Old Norse (Icelandic) *þang*, Norwegian, Danish *tang*). Cf. TANGLE *noun*[1].]
Coarse seaweed, wrack.
black tang bladderwrack, *Fucus vesiculosus*.
Comb.: **tang-fish** a seal.

tang /taŋ/ *noun*[3]. E17.
[Imit.]
A strong ringing note produced by a bell, plucked string, etc. Also (perh. infl. by TANG *noun*[1]), a sound of a particular tone, esp. an inflection in speech, a twang.

BUNYAN Nor is there anything gives such a tang When by these Ropes these Ringers ring. H. ALLEN He spoke it with a slight Scotch tang and a softening of the vowels.

Tang /taŋ/ *noun*[4] *& adjective.* M17.
[Chinese *táng*.]
(Designating or pertaining to) a dynasty ruling in China from the 7th to the 10th cent.

tang /taŋ/ *verb*[1] *trans.* LME.
[from TANG *noun*[1].]
1 (Of an insect) sting; (of a snake) bite with poison. *obsolete* exc. *dial.* LME.
2 Provide (a tool etc.) with a tang. Freq. as ***tanged ppl adjective.*** M16.
3 Affect with a tang or (unpleasant) taste. L17.

tang /taŋ/ *verb*[2]. M16.
[Imit. Cf. TANG *noun*[2].]
1 *verb trans.* Strike (a bell etc.) so as to produce a sharp loud ringing note. M16.
2 *verb trans.* Utter with a tang or ringing tone. E17.
3 *verb intrans.* Emit a sharp and loud ringing or clanging sound; ring, clang. L17.
4 *verb trans.* Make a ringing or clanging noise near (swarming bees) so as to make them settle. Cf. TING *verb* 2. *dial.* M19.

2 SHAKES. *Twel. N.* Let thy tongue tang arguments of state. **3** W. S. CHURCHILL The steel sides of the truck tanged with a patter of bullets.

tanga /'taŋgə/ *noun*[1]. Also **tanka** /'taŋkə/ & other vars. L16.
[Partly from Portuguese from Sanskrit *ṭaṅka* a weight (whence also Persian *tanka*, *tanga*), prob. ult. from Turkic, partly also from Tibetan *tanka*, perh. from Sanskrit *ṭaṅka*: cf. TICAL.]
Any of various coins or moneys of account used in parts of the Indian subcontinent, Iran, Tibet, and elsewhere in central Asia.

tanga /'taŋgə/ *noun*[2]. E20.
[Portuguese, ult. of Bantu origin.]
1 ANTHROPOLOGY. A triangular loincloth or pubic covering worn by indigenous peoples in tropical America. E20.
2 A very brief bikini made of triangles of material connected by thin ties. L20.

Tanganyikan /taŋgə'njiːk(ə)n/ *adjective & noun. obsolete* exc. *Hist.* E20.
[from *Tanganyika* (see below) + -AN. Cf. TANZANIAN.]
▶ **A** *adjective.* Of or pertaining to Tanganyika, a territory in E. Africa now forming the continental part of the republic of Tanzania. E20.
▶ **B** *noun.* A native or inhabitant of Tanganyika. M20.

†**tangara** *noun* see TANAGER.

tangata /'taŋʌtə/ *noun.* Pl. same. M19.
[Maori.]
In Maori parlance: a person, a human being.
tangata whenua /'fɛnuːə/ [lit. 'people of the land'] local people.

tangelo /'tan(d)ʒələʊ/ *noun.* Pl. **-os**. E20.
[from TANG(ERINE + POM)ELO.]
A hybrid citrus fruit, a cross between a tangerine and a grapefruit or pomelo; the tree bearing this fruit.

tangena *noun* var. of TANGHIN.

tangent /'tan(d)ʒ(ə)nt/ *adjective & noun.* L16.
[Latin *tangent-* pres. ppl stem of *tangere* touch: see -ENT.]
▶ **A** *adjective.* **1** GEOMETRY. Of a line or surface: touching (but not normally intersecting) another line or surface; in contact; that is a tangent. L16. ▸**b** *gen.* Touching, contiguous. *rare.* M19.
2 *fig.* Divergent, erratic. *rare.* L18.

1 G. BERKELEY The earth, . . without flying off in a tangent line, constantly rolls about the sun. *Scientific American* The radiation is emitted tangent to these trajectories.

▶ **B** *noun.* **1** MATH. One of the three fundamental trigonometrical functions (cf. SECANT *noun* 1, SINE 2): orig., the length of a straight line normal to the radius drawn from one end of a circular arc and terminated by the secant drawn from the centre of curvature through the other end of the arc; now, the ratio of this line to the radius; (equivalently, as a function of an angle) the ratio of the side of a right-angled triangle opposite a given angle to the side opposite the other acute angle (the tangent of an obtuse angle being numerically equal to that of its supplement, but of opposite sign). Abbreviation TAN *noun*[2]. L16. ▸**b** GEOMETRY. A straight line touching a curve or curved surface, i.e. one meeting it at a point but not (ordinarily) intersecting it at that point; SURVEYING a line touching a curve at a point where the curve starts or finishes. M17.
2 MUSIC. An upright pin or wedge fixed at the back of the key of a clavichord, which strikes the string and makes it sound, and acts also as a bridge to determine the pitch of the note. L19.
1 hyperbolic tangent a hyperbolic function equal to the hyperbolic sine divided by the hyperbolic cosine. ***logarithmic tangent***. **b at a tangent**, **in a tangent**, **on a tangent** in a direction diverging from a previous course or direction; chiefly *fig.*, abruptly from one course of action, subject, thought, etc., to another.
Comb.: **tangent distance** SURVEYING the length of a tangent from the tangent point to its intersection with a tangent from the other end of the curve; **tangent galvanometer**: in which the tangent of the angle of deflection of the needle is proportional to the strength of the current passing through the coil; **tangent point** SURVEYING the point at which a curve starts or finishes; **tangent screw** a screw acting tangentially on a toothed circle or arc to enable delicate measurements or adjustments.
■ **tangency** *noun* the quality or condition of being tangent; a state of contact: E19. **tan'gental** *adjective* of, pertaining to, or of the nature of a tangent M19.

tangent /'tan(d)ʒ(ə)nt/ *verb intrans. literary.* E20.
[from the noun.]
Go away or fly off at a tangent; diverge from one's course.

tangential /tan'dʒɛnʃ(ə)l/ *adjective.* M17.
[from TANGENT *adjective & noun* + -IAL.]
1 Of, pertaining to, or of the nature of a tangent; acting, lying, etc., in the direction of or along a tangent. M17.
2 *fig.* **a** That merely touches a subject or matter; peripheral. E19. ▸**b** Going off at a tangent; erratic; divergent; digressive. M19.

2a *Guardian* He played only a *tangential role* in all this. *Nature* Reporting . . is seriously deficient in areas tangential to the main argument. **b** J. FANE John probably hid his shy sensitivity behind his tangential talk.

■ **tangenti'ality** *noun* L19. **tangentially** *adverb* M19.

tanger /'taŋə/ *noun.* L19.
[from TANG *verb*[1], *noun*[1] + -ER[1].]
1 A person who has a noticeable effect on others. Also, a deceitful person. L19.
2 A person who fits implements with a tang. E20.

tangerine /tan(d)ʒə'riːn/ *adjective & noun.* In senses A.1, B.1 **T-**. E18.
[from *Tanger*, *Tangier* (see below) + -INE[1].]
▶ **A** *adjective.* **1** Of or pertaining to Tangier, a seaport in Morocco on the Strait of Gibraltar. E18.
2 Of the colour tangerine; reddish-orange. E20.
▶ **B** *noun.* **1** A native or inhabitant of Tangier. M19.
2 A mandarin orange, *esp.* one with a deep reddish-orange peel; the tree bearing such a fruit, *Citrus reticulata*. M19.
3 A reddish-orange colour. L19.

tanghin /'taŋgɪn/ *noun.* Also **-guin**, **-gena** /-giːnə/, & other vars. L18.
[French from Malagasy *tangena*, *-gen'*.]
1 A poison formerly used in Madagascan trial by ordeal and obtained from the kernels of *Cerbera tanghin* (family Apocynaceae), a Madagascan shrub with large purplish fruit. L18.
2 The shrub yielding this poison. M19.

tangi /'taŋi/ *noun*[1] *& verb. NZ.* M19.
[Maori.]
▶ **A** *noun.* A ceremonial Maori funeral; a traditional funeral feast; a lamentation. M19.
▶ **B** *verb intrans.* (Formally) lament or mourn someone or something. M19.

tangi /'taŋgi/ *noun*[2]. E20.
[Persian & Urdu = narrowness, from *tang* narrow.]
A gorge or defile in NW Pakistan.

tangible /'tan(d)ʒɪb(ə)l/ *adjective & noun.* L16.
[French, or late Latin *tangibilis*, from Latin *tangere* touch: see -IBLE.]
▶ **A** *adjective.* **1** Able to be touched; discernible or perceptible by touch; having material form. L16.
2 *fig.* That can be grasped by the mind or dealt with as fact; definite, objective; substantial. E18.
3 Able to be affected emotionally. *rare.* E19.

1 LD MACAULAY Desire of having some visible and tangible object of adoration. C. D. E. FORTNUM A very early period . . known to us . . by the tangible memorials of primitive inhabitants. J. HERBERT The atmosphere was charged, the expectation almost tangible. **tangible assets**: physical and material assets which can be precisely valued or measured. **2** D. L. SAYERS Some tangible sort of reason, like money. *Raritan* No evidence that oaths affected behavior in any tangible way.

▶ **B** *noun.* A tangible thing; something material or objective. L19.
■ **tangi'bility** *noun* M17. **tangibleness** *noun* E18. **tangibly** *adverb* M19.

tangle /'taŋg(ə)l/ *noun*[1]. Chiefly *Scot.* M16.
[Prob. from Norwegian *tångel*, *tongul*, repr. Old Norse *þongull*: ult. rel. to TANG *noun*[2].]
Coarse seaweed; oarweed; *spec.* either of two species of seaweed with long feathery fronds, *Laminaria digitata* and *L. saccharina*, the young stalk and fronds of which are sometimes eaten. Also ***sea-tangle***, ***tangle-weed***.

tangle /'taŋg(ə)l/ *noun*[2]. E17.
[from the verb.]
1 A tangled condition; a tangled mass; a confused mass of intertwined threads, hairs, branches, etc.; a single long thread, line, etc., coiled or knotted confusingly; a snarl, a ravel. E17.
2 *transf.* & *fig.* A complicated and confused assemblage; a muddle, a jumble; an intricate system *of* routes, etc.; a confused network of opinions, facts, etc.; a confused or complicated state. M18.
3 Any of various plants having long, winding, tangled stalks, or of tangled growth. M19.
4 MEDICINE. A tangled mass of neurofibrils found in or around cells of the central nervous system esp. as a characteristic feature of Alzheimer's disease and other neurological disorders. E20.

📖 **1** OED This string is all in a tangle. J. M. COETZEE He freed three fenceposts from the tangle of broken fencing. U. HOLDEN The knobbly branches growing in a tangle. **2** J. BUCHAN The only man that can straighten out the tangle. J. CAREW His father . . left nothing but a tangle of debts. M. MARRIN To the north a tangle of motorways rises. **3 blue tangle(s)** *US* a kind of huckleberry, *Gaylussaca frondosa*. **red tangle** *dial.* a dodder, *Cuscuta epithymum*.

tangle /ˈtaŋg(ə)l/ *verb.* ME.
[Prob. of Scandinavian origin.]
1 *verb trans.* = ENTANGLE *verb* 2. ME.
2 *verb trans.* = ENTANGLE *verb* 1. Also, cover with intertwined vegetation etc. E16.
3 *verb trans.* Catch and hold fast (as) in a net or snare; entrap. E16.
4 *verb trans.* Intertwine in a confused mass; intertwine the parts or threads of in this way; make tangled. Freq. foll. by *up*. M16.
5 *verb intrans.* **a** Become involved in conflict or argument; fight, contend; get involved, associate. (Foll. by †*against, with, up with*.) Now *colloq.* (*rare* before 20). M16. ▸**b** Be or become entangled or intertwined. Also, have a tangled course, twist about confusedly. L16.

📖 **1** MILTON Tangl'd in the fold Of dire necessity. *Time* Hotels tangled in bankruptcy proceedings. **2** M. E. HERBERT Gardens . . tangled over with . . bright creepers. D. LEAVITT There were clothes and underwear tangled among the bedsheets. **3** *fig.*: TINDALE *Matt.* 22:15 The farises . . toke counsell howe they myght tangle him in his wordes. **4** LD MACAULAY He had cut the knot which the Congress had only twisted and tangled. G. VIDAL A sharp wind tangled her hair. **5a** D. HAMMETT While we're tangling, them bums will eat us up. L. GRIBBLE No better fun in the world than tangling with the Hun. *Listener* He . . tangles romantically with his producer's wife. **b** J. CAREW You could . . catch crabs where the mangrove roots tangled by the seashore. P. SCUPHAM The cockpit tangling on the shrouded hill. A. CARTER A kitten tangling up in a ball of wool.

Comb.: **tanglefoot** (chiefly *N. Amer.*) (*a*) *slang* intoxicating liquor; (*b*) *colloq.* material applied to a tree-trunk as a grease-band; **tangle-footed** *adjective* having tangled feet, stumbling; **tangle-leg(s)** (*a*) = *hobblebush* s.v. HOBBLE *noun*; (*b*) *slang* = *tanglefoot* (a) above.

■ **tangled** *ppl adjective* intertwined in a complicated and confused manner; matted, mixed up; *fig.* complicated, intricate: L16. **tanglement** *noun* the condition of being tangled; an instance of this; a tangle: M19. **tangler** *noun* (*rare*) E16. **tangling** *noun* (*a*) the action of the verb; (*b*) in *pl.*, something tangled: M16. **tanglingly** *adverb* in a tangling manner M19.

tangly /ˈtaŋgli/ *adjective*[1]. M18.
[from TANGLE *noun*[1] + -Y[1].]
Strewn with or consisting of tangle or seaweed.

tangly /ˈtaŋgli/ *adjective*[2]. E19.
[from TANGLE *noun*[2] + -Y[1].]
Full of tangles; tangled.

tango /ˈtaŋgəʊ/ *noun*[1] & *verb*. Pl. **-os**, (now *rare*) **-oes**. L19.
[Amer. Spanish, perh. of African origin.]
▸ **A** *noun*. **1** A kind of Spanish flamenco dance. L19.
2 A syncopated ballroom dance in 2/4 or 4/4 time, of S. American origin, characterized by slow gliding movements and abrupt pauses; a piece of music intended to accompany or in the rhythm of this dance. L19.
▸ **B** *verb intrans.* Dance a tango. E20.

📖 *Proverb*: It takes two to tango.

■ **tangoist** *noun* an exponent of the tango E20.

tango /ˈtaŋgəʊ/ *noun*[2] & *adjective*. E20.
[Abbreviation of TANGERINE, prob. infl. by prec.: see -O.]
(Of) a deep orange colour.

tangor /ˈtaŋgɔː, ˈtanɔː/ *noun*. M20.
[from TANG(ERINE + OR(ANGE *noun*.]
A natural hybrid citrus fruit, a cross between the tangerine and the sweet orange.

tangoreceptor /ˈtaŋgəʊrɪˌsɛptə/ *noun*. E20.
[from Latin *tangere* to touch + -O- + RECEPTOR.]
PHYSIOLOGY. A sensory receptor which responds to touch or pressure.

tangram /ˈtangram/ *noun*. M19.
[Origin unkn.]
A Chinese geometrical puzzle consisting of a square cut into seven pieces which can be combined to make various shapes.

tanguin *noun* var. of TANGHIN.

tangun /ˈtaŋgʌn/ *noun*. L18.
[Tibetan *rta-ṅan*.]
A pony from Tibet or Bhutan.

Tangut /ˈtaŋguːt/ *noun* & *adjective*. L16.
[App. from Mongolian, from Chinese *Dǎng Xiàng* (Wade–Giles *Tanghsiang*).]
Hist. ▸**A** *noun*. Pl. same, **-s**. A member of a Tibetan people who inhabited NW China and western Inner Mongolia, and formed an independent kingdom from the late 10th to the mid 13th cent.; the language of this people. L16.
▸ **B** *adjective*. Of or pertaining to this people or their language. L19.

tangy /ˈtaŋi/ *adjective*. L19.
[from TANG *noun*[1] + -Y[1].]
1 Having a sharp, distinct, or spicy taste or smell. L19.
2 Distinctive in style or content; *esp.* mildly sensational or scandalous, spicy. L19.

📖 **2** *Punch* Despite a twinkly fondness for waggish puns . . his style isn't exactly tangy. H. WOUK She knew a tangy tale or two about Madge.

■ **tangily** *adverb* M20. **tanginess** *noun* L20.

tanh /tanˈɛɪtʃ, θan/ *noun*. L19.
[from TAN *noun*[2] + *h* (for *hyperbolic*).]
MATH. Hyperbolic tangent (of).

tania *noun* var. of TANNIA.

tanist /ˈtanɪst/ *noun*. M16.
[Irish, Gaelic *tánaiste* lit. 'second in excellence, second in rank'. Cf. TANAISTE.]
Hist. The heir apparent to a Celtic chief, usu. the most vigorous adult of his kin, elected during the chief's lifetime.

■ **tanistry** *noun* the system of determining heirship by election of a tanist L16.

taniwha /ˈtanɪwɑː, *foreign* ˈtanifa/ *noun*. *NZ*. M19.
[Maori.]
A water monster of Maori legend.

tanjib /tanˈdʒiːb/ *noun*. E18.
[Persian, from *tan* body + *zīb* adornment.]
A fine kind of muslin made chiefly in Uttar Pradesh, India. Also, a lightweight plain-woven cotton fabric, esp. as produced in Britain for the Far East market.

tank /taŋk/ *noun*[1]. E17.
[Gujarati *tāṅkũ*, Marathi *tāṅkẽ* underground cistern, perh. also infl. by Portuguese *tangue* = Spanish *estanque*, French *étang* from Latin *stagnum* pond. In branch II, from use of *tank* as a code word for secrecy during manufacture in Britain in 1915.]
▸**I 1** In the Indian subcontinent, a pool or lake (usu. man-made) or a large cistern, used as a reservoir for storing water; *Austral.* & *US* a man-made reservoir. E17. ▸**b** A natural pool or pond. *dial.* & *US*. L17.
2 A (large) receptacle or storage chamber for liquid or gas; *spec.* (*a*) a fuel container in a motor vehicle, aircraft, etc.; (*b*) a receptacle with transparent sides in which to keep fish, an aquarium. L17.
3 *ellipt.* **a** A tank engine. E20. ▸**b** A tank top. L20.
4 A cell in a police station, jail, etc.; *esp.* one in which drunks are held. *US slang*. E20.

📖 **2** K. AMIS 'Low on petrol, Ivor?' 'No, I had a full tank when I picked you up.' ***fuel tank***, ***gas tank***, ***oil tank***, ***storage tank***, ***water tank***, etc. ***a tiger in one's tank***: see TIGER *noun*. ***deep tank***: see DEEP *adjective*. ***septic tank***: see SEPTIC *adjective*. **3a** ***pannier tank***, ***saddle tank***. **4** *Punisher* The only place you're going is the maximum security tank.

▸**II 5** An armoured military vehicle moving on a tracked carriage and mounted with one or more guns and occas. other weapons. E20.
6 In *pl.* *The* Royal Tank Corps of the British army. *slang*. M20.

📖 **5** D. LEAVITT Four foot eleven and built like a tank.

Comb.: **tank-buster** *slang* an aircraft or other device designed to combat tanks; **tank car** *N. Amer.* = *tank wagon* below; **tank circuit** *ELECTRONICS* a resonant circuit placed in the anode circuit of a valve oscillator in order to supply energy to an aerial for transmission; **tank engine** a railway engine which carries water and fuel receptacles on its own framing and not in a separate tender; **tank farm** an area of oil or gas storage tanks; **tank-farming** hydroponics; **tank killer** = *tank-buster* above; **tank locomotive** = *tank engine* above; **tank suit** *N. Amer.* a woman's one-piece swimming costume with a scooped neck; **tank top** a sleeveless close-fitting upper garment with round neck and deep armholes (similar to the top of a tank suit); **tank town** *US* a small unimportant town, orig. one at which trains stopped to take on water; **tank transporter** a wheeled vehicle for the transportation of a military tank; **tank trap** an obstacle intended to impede or prevent the progress of tanks; **tank wagon** a railway wagon carrying a tank for transporting liquid in bulk.

■ **tankful** *noun* as much as a tank will hold L19. **tankless** *adjective* L19.

tank /taŋk/ *noun*[2]. *rare*. L17.
[Hindi *ṭāk* from Sanskrit *ṭaṅka*: see TANGA *noun*[1].]
In the Indian subcontinent: a unit of weight esp. for pearls, varying in different locations.

tank /taŋk/ *noun*[3]. *slang*. M20.
[Prob. abbreviation of TANKARD.]
The amount held by a drinking-vessel; a drink, esp. of beer.

tank /taŋk/ *verb*. M19.
[from TANK *noun*[1].]
▸**I 1** *verb trans.* Immerse in a tank; duck. *dial.* M19.
2 *verb trans.* Put (liquid etc.) into a tank; store, keep, or treat in a tank. L19.
3 Chiefly foll. by *up*. ▸**a** *verb intrans.* & *refl.* Fill oneself with (alcoholic) drink, get drunk. *slang*. L19. ▸**b** *verb trans.* & *intrans.* Fill the tank of (a vehicle etc.) with fuel; refuel. *colloq.* M20.
4 *verb intrans.* *colloq.* (orig. *US*). ▸**a** *TENNIS*. Lose or fail to finish a match deliberately. L20. ▸**b** Fall rapidly in value, popularity, etc., be unsuccessful; (of shares etc.) crash. L20.

📖 **3a** J. MCCLURE He'd arrived half-tanked already. **b** *transf.*: ALDOUS HUXLEY A child tanked up with sugar or glucose is likely to get through a party without untoward incidents. **4b** *Independent* He ran up his holdings to almost $1m . . and then went on to lose almost everything when the . . stock tanked. *Arena* [The group's] first single tanked so badly that Capitol refused to make any videos for future singles.

▸**II 5** *verb intrans.* Make one's way (as) in a tank; go forcefully and rapidly; *fig.* (foll. by *over*) overwhelm or override a person. *colloq.* M20.
6 *verb trans.* Defeat convincingly, beat, thrash. *colloq.* L20.

📖 **5** A. THIRKELL He tanked right over her without so much as noticing her.

Tanka /ˈtaŋkə/ *noun*[1] & *adjective*. M19.
[Chinese (Cantonese) *taàn ka*, from *taàn* egg + *ka* family, people.]
▸ **A** *noun*. Pl. same, **-s**. Inhabitants of Guangzhou (Canton) and other places on the Chinese coast, living entirely on boats by which they earn their living. M19.
▸ **B** *adjective*. Pertaining to or designating these people. M19.

tanka /ˈtaŋkə/ *noun*[2]. Pl. same, **-s**. L19.
[Japanese, from *tan* short + *ka* song.]
A Japanese poem consisting of thirty-one syllables in five lines, the first and third lines having five and the others seven syllables. Also called ***uta***.

tanka /ˈtaŋkə/ *noun*[3]. E20.
[Tibetan *t'án-ka*, *t'án-ga* image, painting.]
A Tibetan religious scroll-painting on woven material, hung as a banner in temples and carried in processions.

tanka *noun*[4] var. of TANGA *noun*[1].

tankage /ˈtaŋkɪdʒ/ *noun*. M19.
[from TANK *noun*[1] + -AGE.]
1 Tanks collectively; a system of storage tanks; storage capacity in tanks; *spec.* the fuel capacity of an aircraft etc. M19.
2 The action or process of storing liquid in tanks; a fee charged for this. L19.
3 (A fertilizer or animal feed made from) the residue from tanks in which animal carcasses have been rendered. L19.

tankard /ˈtaŋkəd/ *noun*. ME.
[Origin uncertain: cf. Middle & mod. Dutch *tanckaert*, Anglo-Latin *tancardus*, *tank-*.]
†**1** A large open vessel like a tub, used for carrying liquid. Also, an amphora. ME–L17.
2 A drinking-vessel, orig. one made of wooden staves and hooped, now usu. a tall one-handled jug or mug, sometimes with a lid, used chiefly for drinking beer. Also, the contents of or an amount held in such a vessel. L15.
2 ***cool tankard***: see COOL *adjective*.

tanker /ˈtaŋkə/ *noun*. E20.
[from TANK *noun*[1] + -ER[1].]
▸**I 1** A ship fitted with tanks for transporting oil or other fluids in bulk. E20.
2 A road or rail vehicle with a container designed for transporting fluids in bulk. E20.
3 An aircraft used for carrying fuel in bulk, *esp.* one from which other aircraft can refuel in flight. M20.
▸**II 4** A soldier who fights or has fought in a tank. *Military slang*. E20.

tankette /taŋˈkɛt/ *noun*. Now *Hist.* E20.
[from TANK *noun*[1] + -ETTE.]
A small armoured vehicle for use by infantry.

tankini /taŋˈkiːni/ *noun*. L20.
[Blend of *tank top* (see TANK *noun*[1]) and BIKINI.]
A women's two-piece swimsuit combining a top half styled like a tank top with a bikini bottom.

tanky /ˈtaŋki/ *noun*. *slang*. E20.
[from TANK *noun*[1] + -Y[6].]
1 *NAUTICAL*. A petty officer in charge of a ship's fresh-water tanks and usu. also other stores; a navigating officer's assistant. E20.
2 *Hist.* A member of the (British) Communist Party who supported a policy of military intervention by the Soviet Union to preserve Communist regimes. L20.

tanling /ˈtanlɪŋ/ *noun*. *rare*. E17.
[from TAN *adjective* + -LING[1].]
A person who is tanned by the sun's rays; a person of dark skin.

tanna /ˈtɑːnə/ *noun*. Pl. **-im** /-ɪm/. E18.
[Aramaic = teacher, from *tnā* repeat, learn, cogn. with Hebrew *šānāh*.]
Jewish Hist. Any of the Jewish doctors of the law of the first two centuries AD whose opinions are recorded in the Mishnah and other writings.

■ **tannaitic** /tanerˈɪtɪk/ *adjective* of or pertaining to the tannaim E20.

tannage /ˈtanɪdʒ/ *noun*. M17.
[from TAN *verb* + -AGE, perh. partly from Old & mod. French.]
1 The process or occupation of tanning. M17.
2 A tannery. *Scot*. M18.
3 Tanned hide or skin. L18.

tannaim *noun* pl. of TANNA.

tannase /ˈtaneɪz/ *noun*. E20.
[from TANNIN + -ASE.]
BIOCHEMISTRY. An enzyme (found in plants) which hydrolyses ester linkages in tannins.

tannate /ˈtaneɪt/ *noun*. E19.
[from TANNIC + -ATE[1].]
CHEMISTRY. A salt or ester of a tannic acid.

tanned /tand/ *adjective*. LME.
[from TAN *verb* + -ED[1].]
1 a Made into leather; preserved by tanning. LME. ▸**b** Beaten, thrashed. *slang*. E20.
2 a That has been made brown, esp. by exposure to the sun; sunburnt. E16. ▸**b** Yellowish brown, tawny. E16.
3 Spread or covered with tan. L19.

tanner /ˈtanə/ *noun*[1]. OE.
[Partly from TAN *verb*, partly from Old French *tanere* from medieval Latin *tannator*: see -ER[1].]
1 A person whose occupation is the tanning of hides or skins. OE.
2 A lotion, cream, etc., designed to promote the formation of a suntan or to produce a similar tan artificially. M20.

tanner /ˈtanə/ *noun*[2]. *slang* (now *Hist.*). E19.
[Origin unkn.]
A sixpence.

tannery /ˈtan(ə)ri/ *noun*. LME.
[from TANNER *noun*[1] + -Y[3]: see -ERY. Cf. Old & mod. French *tannerie*.]
1 The process or occupation of tanning. LME.
2 A place or building where tanning is carried on. M18.

tannia /ˈtanɪə/ *noun*. Also **tania**, **tanya**. M18.
[Carib *taya*, Tupi *taya*, *taña*.]
An aroid plant, *Xanthosoma sagittifolium*, cultivated in Brazil, the W. Indies, W. Africa, etc., for its edible tubers; a tuber of this plant (usu. in *pl.*).

tannic /ˈtanɪk/ *adjective*. M19.
[French *tannique*, formed as TANNIN: see -IC.]
Of or derived from tan; chiefly in ***tannic acid*** (CHEMISTRY), = TANNIN. Also, containing tannin.

tannie /ˈtani/ *noun*. *S. Afr. colloq.* M20.
[Dim. of Afrikaans TANTE.]
1 As a form of address: auntie. M20.
2 A prim elderly woman. *derog.* M20.

tannin /ˈtanɪn/ *noun*. E19.
[French *tanin*, from *tan* TAN *noun*[1]: see -IN[1].]
CHEMISTRY. Any of a group of yellowish or brownish acidic astringent compounds related to gallic acid, which occur in galls, barks, and other plant tissues, and have the property of combining with animal hide and converting it into leather; such substances collectively.

Tannoy /ˈtanɔɪ/ *noun & verb*. Also **t-**. M20.
[from *tantalum alloy*.]
▸**A** *noun*. (Proprietary name for) a sound reproducing and amplifying apparatus used for public address systems; such a system. M20.

B. BAINBRIDGE The pilot announced over the Tannoy that they were flying across the Soviet border.

▸**B** *verb trans.* Transmit or announce over a Tannoy system. M20.
¶ Registered as a proprietary name for more general electrical use in 1928.

Tanoan /təˈnəʊən/ *noun & adjective*. L19.
[from Spanish *Tano* from Tewa *tʰáːnu*: see -AN.]
▸**A** *noun*. A language family comprising several Pueblo Indian languages. L19.
▸**B** *adjective*. Of or pertaining to this language family. E20.

tanquam /ˈtankwam/ *noun*. Also ***tam quam*** /tam ˈkwam/. M16.
[from Latin *tam .. quam* as .. as (beginning the clauses of the writ).]
LAW (now *Hist.*). = QUI TAM 1.

tanrec *noun* var. of TENREC.

tansu /ˈtansuː/ *noun*. Pl. same. L19.
[Japanese.]
A Japanese chest of drawers.

tansy /ˈtanzi/ *noun*. ME.
[Old French *tanesie* (mod. *tanaisie*), perh. aphet. from medieval Latin *athanasia* from Greek = immortality.]
1 An aromatic bitter-tasting herb of the composite family, *Tanacetum vulgare*, with pinnatisect leaves and terminal corymbs of yellow rayless button-like flowers, formerly widely used in medicine and cookery. ME. ▸**b** With specifying word: any of various plants resembling tansy in foliage, smell, etc. LME.
2 A cake, omelette, or other dish flavoured with juice of tansy, eaten esp. at Easter. Now chiefly *Hist.* LME.
1b wild tansy silverweed, *Potentilla anserina*. **2 †like a tansy** done etc. to perfection, completely satisfactory.

tant *noun* see TANTE.

tantadlin /tanˈtadlɪn/ *noun*. *obsolete* exc. *dial.* Also **-blin** /-blɪn/, **-flin** /-flɪn/. M17.
[Origin unkn.]
1 A tart or round piece of pastry. M17.
2 A turd. Orig. *slang*. M17.

tantalate /ˈtantəleɪt/ *noun*. M19.
[from TANTALIC + -ATE[1].]
CHEMISTRY. A salt containing oxyanions of tantalum.

Tantalean /tanˈteɪlɪən/ *adjective*. L17.
[from Latin *tantaleus*, formed as TANTALUS: see -AN, -EAN. Cf. next.]
Of or pertaining to Tantalus; like (that of) Tantalus.

Tantalian /tanˈteɪlɪən/ *adjective*[1]. E17.
[formed as TANTALUS + -IAN.]
= prec.

tantalian /tanˈteɪlɪən/ *adjective*[2]. M20.
[from TANTALUM + -IAN.]
MINERALOGY. Having a constituent element partly replaced by tantalum.

tantalic /tanˈtalɪk/ *adjective*. M19.
[from TANTALUM + -IC.]
CHEMISTRY. Of or containing tantalum, esp. in its pentavalent state.
tantalic acid a weakly acidic hydrated oxide of pentavalent tantalum precipitated from solutions of tantalates.

tantalise *verb* var. of TANTALIZE.

†Tantalism *noun*. *rare*. E17–E19.
[formed as TANTALUS + -ISM.]
Punishment or torment like that of Tantalus; tantalization.

tantalite /ˈtantəlʌɪt/ *noun*. E19.
[from TANTALUM + -ITE[1].]
MINERALOGY. An orthorhombic tantalate of ferrous iron, occurring as black lustrous crystals.

tantalize /ˈtantəlʌɪz/ *verb trans.* Also **-ise**. L16.
[formed as TANTALUS + -IZE.]
1 Torment, tease, or fascinate by the sight, promise, or expectation of something which is out of reach; raise and then disappoint the hopes of, keep in a state of frustrated expectancy. L16.
2 Work into an intricate, overelaborate, or artificial form. *rare*. E19.

1 J. TYNDALL The mirage .. which so tantalized the French soldiers in Egypt. J. C. POWYS No longer the .. playful .. girl, who delighted in tantalizing the senses of men. *absol.*: *Time* His life as self-styled genius and unrepentant poseur continues to tantalize.

■ **tantaliˈzation** *noun* M17. **tantalizer** *noun* L18. **tantalizing** *ppl adjective* exciting hopes or desires which are not or cannot be satisfied L17. **tantalizingly** *adverb* M19.

tantalum /ˈtantələm/ *noun*. E19.
[formed as next + *-um* after other metallic elements (usu. in -IUM), with ref. to the metal's failure to react with acids.]
A hard high-melting chemical element, atomic no. 73, belonging to the group of transition metals, which occurs in tantalite, columbite, and other minerals and is used esp. in hard or chemically resistant alloys. (Symbol Ta.)

tantalus /ˈtantələs/ *noun*. In sense 1 usu. **T-**. M18.
[Latin *Tantalus* from Greek *Tantalos* a mythical king of Phrygia condemned to stand up to his chin in water which receded whenever he tried to drink, and under branches of fruit which drew back whenever he tried to pick their fruit.]
1 A person likened to Tantalus; one never satisfied. *rare*. M18.
2 A stork of the genus *Mycteria* (formerly *Tantalus*); *spec.* the American wood ibis, *M. americana*. Now *rare*. E19.
3 A stand in which decanters can be locked up while remaining visible. L19.

tantamount /ˈtantəmaʊnt/ *adjective*. M17.
[from the verb and noun.]
Usu. *pred.* (with *to*, †*as*, †*with*): that amounts to as much, that comes to the same thing; of the same amount; equivalent.

JOHN BROOKE The accusation was tantamount to treason. D. ADAMS Listening to other people's phone messages was tantamount to opening their mail.

tantamount /ˈtantəmaʊnt/ *verb & noun*. Long *rare*. E17.
[Italian *tanto montare* amount to as much.]
▸**A** *verb intrans.* Foll. by *to*: amount to as much as, be equivalent to. E17.
▸**B** *noun*. An equivalent. M17.

tantara /tantəˈrɑː, tanˈtɑːrə/ *interjection & noun*. Also **tantarara** /tantərəˈrɑː/. M16.
[Imit.]
(Expr. the sound of) a flourish on a trumpet or similar instrument; a fanfare.

tant bien que mal /tɑ̃ bjɛ̃ kə mal/ *adverbial phr.* M18.
[French, lit. 'as well as badly'.]
With indifferent success; moderately well, after a fashion.

tante /tɑ̃ːt, tɑːnt; ˈtantə/ *noun*. Also (esp. as a title) **T-**; (*S. Afr.*, usu. preceding a name beginning with a vowel) **tant** /tɑːnt, tant/. E19.
[(German, Dutch (whence Afrikaans) from) French, contr. of †*ta ante*, from *ta* your + †*ante* AUNT.]
Esp. among those of French, German, or Afrikaans origin: an aunt; a mature or elderly woman (related or well known to the speaker or writer). Freq. as a title prefixed to a forename or as a form of address; *S. Afr.* a respectful form of address to an older or elderly woman.

tanti /ˈtantʌɪ/ *pred. adjective*. *arch.* L16.
[Latin = of so much, genit. of *tantum* neut. of *tantus* so great.]
Of so much value; worthwhile. Formerly also as *interjection*: so much *for* (that, him, her, etc.).

tantivy /tanˈtɪvi/ *adverb, noun, adjective, interjection, & verb*. M17.
[Prob. imit. of the sound of galloping horses. Later infl. by TANTARA: cf. TIVY.]
▸**A** *adverb*. At full gallop; swiftly; headlong. Now *rare* or *obsolete*. M17.
▸**B** *noun*. **1** A rapid gallop or ride; a headlong rush. *arch.* M17.
2 *Hist.* [from a contemporary caricature in which a number of High Church clergymen were represented as mounted on the Church of England and 'riding tantivy' to Rome.] A post-Restoration High Churchman or Tory, esp. in the reigns of Charles II and James II. L17.
3 A blast or flourish on a horn, esp. a post-horn or hunting horn. *arch.* L18.
▸**C** *attrib.* or as *adjective*. That rides very swiftly, rushing headlong, swift (*arch.*); *Hist.* designating or pertaining to the post-Restoration High Church or Tory party (see sense B.2 above). L17.
▸**D** *interjection*. Repr. the sound of galloping hoofs or feet, or the sound of a horn, esp. a post-horn or hunting horn. Cf. TIVY *interjection*. *arch.* L17.
▸†**E** *verb intrans.* Ride full tilt; hurry away. *rare*. L17–L18.

tant mieux /tɑ̃ mjø/ *interjection*. M18.
[French.]
So much the better. Cf. TANT PIS.

tanto /ˈtantəʊ/ *noun*. Pl. same, **-os**. L19.
[Japanese, from *tan* short, brief + *tō* sword.]
A Japanese short sword or dagger.

tanto /ˈtantəʊ/ *adverb*. L19.
[Italian from Latin *tantum* so much.]
MUSIC. So, so much. (Modifying adjectives from Italian.)

tantony /ˈtantəni/ *noun*. M16.
[Aphet. from *Saint Anthony*, formed as SAINT *noun & adjective* + ANTHONY.]
1 In full ***tantony bell***. A hand-bell; a small church bell. M16.
2 More fully ***tantony pig***. The smallest pig of a litter. Cf. ANTHONY. M17.

tant pis /tɑ̃ pi/ *interjection*. L18.
[French.]
So much the worse. Cf. TANT MIEUX.

tantra /ˈtantrə/ *noun*. Also **T-**. L18.
[Sanskrit = loom, warp, groundwork, system, doctrine.]
1 Any of a class of Hindu or Buddhist religious writings of the late medieval period, often of a magical, erotic, or mystical nature. L18.
2 Tantrism. M20.
■ **tantric** *adjective* of or pertaining to the tantras or tantrism E20. **tantrism** *noun* (adherence to) the doctrine or principles of the tantras L19. **tantrist** *noun* an adherent of tantrism L19.

tantrum /ˈtantrəm/ *noun*. E18.
[Origin unkn.]
An outburst of bad temper or petulance; *spec.* a fit of bad temper in a young child.

W. IRVING An author, who was always in a tantrum if interrupted. D. JUDD The child .. having temper tantrums and being excessively irritable.

Tantum ergo /tantəm ˈɜːɡəʊ/ *noun phr.* E18.
[Latin, first two words of the penultimate stanza *Tantum ergo sacramentum Veneremur cernui* 'Therefore we, before him bending, This great sacrament revere'.]
(A setting of) the last two stanzas of the hymn of St Thomas Aquinas *Pange lingua gloriosi Corporis mysterium* 'Now, my tongue, the mystery telling', sung esp. at the service of benediction.

tanya *noun* var. of TANNIA.

Tanzanian /tanzəˈniːən/ *noun & adjective.* M20.
[from *Tanzania* (see below) + -AN. Cf. TANGANYIKAN.]
▸ **A** *noun.* A native or inhabitant of the E. African republic of Tanzania, formed by the union of the republics of Tanganyika and Zanzibar. M20.
▸ **B** *adjective.* Of or pertaining to Tanzania. M20.

tanzanite /ˈtanzənʌɪt/ *noun.* M20.
[formed as prec. + -ITE[1].]
MINERALOGY. A blue or violet gem variety of zoisite, containing vanadium.

Tao /taʊ, ˈtɑːəʊ/ *noun.* Also **Dao** /daʊ, ˈdɑːəʊ/. M18.
[Chinese *dào* (Wade-Giles *tao*) way, path, right way (of life), reason.]
1 In TAOISM, the or *the* absolute being or principle underlying the universe; ultimate reality. M18. ▸**b** = TAOISM. M18.
2 Orig. & chiefly CONFUCIANISM. The way, method, or norm to be followed, esp. in conduct. M20.

Taoiseach /ˈtiːʃəx/ *noun.* M20.
[Irish, lit. 'chief, leader'. Cf. TOISECH.]
The Prime Minister of the Republic of Ireland.

Taoism /ˈtaʊɪz(ə)m, ˈtɑːəʊ-/ *noun.* Also **Dao-** /ˈdaʊ-, ˈdɑːəʊ-/. M19.
[from TAO + -ISM.]
A Chinese religious philosophy based on writings attributed to Laoze (*c* 605–530 BC), characteristically concerned with the achievement of harmony with nature and the Tao.
■ **Taoist** *noun & adjective* (*a*) *noun* an adherent of Taoism; (*b*) *adjective* of or pertaining to Taoism or the Taoists: M19. **Taoˈistic** *adjective* M19.

taonga /tɑːˈɒŋɡə/ *noun. NZ.* M19.
[Maori, = property, anything highly prized.]
In Maori culture: an object or natural resource which is highly prized.

Taos /taʊs, ˈtɑːɒs/ *adjective & noun.* M19.
[See below.]
▸ **A** *adjective.* Of or pertaining to the Pueblo Indian people living in Taos, a town in New Mexico, or their language. M19.
▸ **B** *noun.* Pl. same.
1 The Tiwa language of the Taos Indians. M20.
2 A Taos Indian. M20.

taotai /ˈtaʊtaɪ/ *noun.* M18.
[Chinese *dàotái* (Wade-Giles *tao-t'ai*), from *dào* way + *tái* (as noun) terrace, pavilion (freq. as 2nd elem. of title); (as adjective) dignified, exalted.]
Hist. (The title of) a provincial officer responsible for the civil and military affairs of a district in China.

Tao-te-Ching /taʊtiːˈtʃɪŋ/ *noun.* E20.
[Chinese, lit. 'the Book of the Way and its Power'. Cf. TAO.]
The central Taoist text, attributed to Laoze (*c* 605–530 BC), which defined the Tao and established the philosophical basis of Taoism. See TAOISM.

tao-tieh /ˈtaʊtjə/ *noun.* E20.
[Chinese *tāotiè*.]
A mythical fierce and voracious Chinese monster with a head but no body; a representation of this, found esp. on metalware of the Zhou period.

taovala /taʊvələ/ *noun.* M20.
[Tongan.]
In Tonga: a piece of fine matting worn ceremonially round the waist over a kilt.

tap /tap/ *noun*[1].
[Old English *tæppa* = Middle Low German, Middle Dutch *tappe* (Dutch *tap*), Old High German *zapho* (German *Zapfen*), Old Norse *tappi*, from Germanic.]
1 Orig., a peg or stopper for closing and opening the vent-hole in a cask, barrel, etc. Now also, a hollow or tubular structure through which liquid or gas from a pipe or vessel may be drawn, having a peg, valve, or other device for shutting off or regulating the flow; *spec.* one providing access to a supply of piped water for household etc. use. OE. ▸**b** ELECTRICAL ENGINEERING. = TAPPING *noun*[1] 2. E20. ▸**c** STOCK EXCHANGE. A government stock issued in large quantities over a period of time. Also ***tap stock***. M20.
2 The liquid drawn from a particular tap; *spec.* a particular kind or quality of drink etc. *colloq.* E17.
3 An object shaped like a slender tapering cylinder; *esp.* a tap root. M17.
4 MECHANICS. A tool used for cutting the thread of an internal screw, consisting of a male screw of hardened steel, grooved lengthways to form cutting edges. L17.
5 A taproom, a tap-house. *colloq.* E18.
6 a A device for listening secretly to or monitoring a telephone conversation. Cf. TAP *verb*[1] 6. E20. ▸**b** An act or instance of using such a device; a recording made in this way. M20.

> 🕮 **1** P. FITZGERALD Frank fetched him a glass of water from the tap at the sink. CONAN DOYLE By turning the outside tap the room could be flooded with gas. ***cold tap***, ***hot tap***, ***mixed tap***, etc. **3** C. MARSHALL The tap of the oak will make its way downward, in a direct line. **6b** W. GARNER He'd made a phone tap, and overheard a reference to an agent.

Phrases: **on tap** (*a*) ready to be drawn off by tap; (*b*) ready for immediate consumption or use (*lit. & fig.*); (*c*) *spec.* (STOCK EXCHANGE) (of a security) made readily available in large quantities. **on the tap** *slang* begging, asking for a loan.
Comb.: **tap-bolt** a threaded bolt for screwing into a part (as opp. to one that penetrates a part and receives a nut); **tap-borer** a tapering instrument for boring bung-holes or tap-holes; **tap-changer** ELECTRICAL ENGINEERING an apparatus for accomplishing tap-changing; **tap-changing** ELECTRICAL ENGINEERING the process of changing the connection to a transformer from one tap to another so as to vary the turns ratio and hence control the output voltage under a varying load; **tap-cinder** refuse produced in a puddling furnace; **tap-hole** (*a*) the hole in a cask, tub, etc., in which the tap is inserted; (*b*) a small opening in a furnace for molten metal etc. to run out; **tap-hose** (*obsolete* exc. *dial.*) a strainer placed over the tap-hole in a mash-tub, cask, etc., to prevent solid matter from passing into or through the tap; **tap-house** a place where beer drawn from the tap is sold in small quantities, *esp.* an alehouse; **tap-lash** (*obsolete* exc. *dial.*) (*a*) very weak or stale beer, dregs; (*b*) *derog.* a publican; **tap-rivet** *noun & verb* (*a*) *noun* = *tap-bolt* above; (*b*) *verb trans.* secure by tap-bolts; **taproom** a room in which alcoholic drinks are available on tap; ***tap stock***: see sense 1c above; **tap-tool** = sense 4 above; **tap water**: drawn through a tap, esp. from a piped supply for household use; **tap wrench**: for turning a tap-tool.
■ **taplet** *noun* (STOCK EXCHANGE) a limited issue of tap stock; an issue of stock rather smaller than a tap; cf. TRANCHETTE: L20.

tap /tap/ *noun*[2]. ME.
[from TAP *verb*[2].]
1 An act of tapping; a light but audible blow, a rap; the sound made by this. ME. ▸**b** Tap-dancing (*ellipt.*). Also, a piece of metal attached to the toe or heel of a tap shoe. M20. ▸**c** PHONETICS. (The speech sound produced by) a single rapid contact made by a flexible organ, such as the tip of the tongue, on a firmer surface, such as the alveolar ridge. M20. ▸**d** A shot fired from a gun, esp. in target-shooting. *slang.* L20.
2 A piece of leather for renewing the worn-down heel or sole of a boot or shoe. Also, (a piece of iron for shielding) the sole of a shoe. Cf. TAP *verb*[2] 3. *N. Amer. & dial.* L17.
3 In *pl.* (usu. treated as *sing.*). A military signal on a drum or bugle for lights in army quarters to be put out; a similar call sounded on the bugle at a military funeral; also = ***last post*** s.v. POST *noun*[6]. *US.* E19.
4 The slightest amount *of work*. Only in neg. contexts. *colloq.* L19.

> 🕮 **1** F. MARRYAT A sharp double tap at the street-door announced the post. **a tap on the wrist** a light reprimand. ***tip for tap***: see TIP *noun*[2]. **c** *Language* Individual closures of a trill are . . more rapid than the single closure of a tap.

Comb.: **tap-dance** *noun & verb* (*a*) *noun* a dance or form of display dancing characterized by rhythmic tapping of the toes and heels; (*b*) *verb intrans.* perform a tap-dance; **tap-dancer** a person who performs a tap-dance; **tap-in** BASKETBALL a goal scored by tapping the ball into the basket, usu. when following up an unsuccessful shot; **tap-kick** *noun & verb* (RUGBY FOOTBALL) (*a*) a light kick of the ball to restart play from a penalty and retain possession; (*b*) *verb trans.* give (a ball) a tap-kick; **tap pants** *US* a type of fashionable knickers; **tap penalty** RUGBY FOOTBALL: taken with a tap-kick; **tap shoe**: with a specially hardened sole or attached metal plates at toe and heel to make a tapping sound in tap-dancing; **tap-tap** a repeated tap, a series of taps.

tap /tap/ *verb*[1]. Infl. **-pp-**.
[Old English *tæppian* (= Middle & mod. Low German, Middle & mod. Dutch *tappen*, Middle & mod. High German *zapfen*), formed as TAP *noun*[1].]
1 *verb trans.* Provide (a cask etc.) with a tap. Cf. TAP *noun*[1] 1. OE.
2 a *verb trans.* Draw (alcoholic drink) from a tap; draw and sell (alcoholic drink) in small quantities. LME. ▸†**b** *verb trans.* Retail (any commodity). *Scot.* L15–E17. ▸**c** *verb intrans.* Act as a tapster. Long *rare* or *obsolete.* L16.
3 *verb trans.* Open up, pierce, or break into so as to extract the contents from; *spec.* ▸**a** draw liquor from (a cask, barrel, etc.); ▸**b** MEDICINE & VETERINARY MEDICINE pierce the body wall of (a person or animal) so as to draw off accumulated fluid; drain (a cavity) of accumulated fluid; ▸**c** cut into and draw sap from (a tree); ▸**d** *fig.* establish trade or communication with, obtain information, supplies, or resources from. Also foll by *into.* L16.
4 *verb trans.* Obtain (the contents of) a thing by tapping; draw off or let out (esp. liquid) from any source. L16.
5 *verb trans.* Provide (a hole, bolt, etc.) with a screw-thread; *spec.* cut a female screw-thread in. E19.
6 Connect a listening device to (a telephone, telegraph line, etc.) to listen to a call or transmission. M19.

> 🕮 **2a** T. H. WHITE In the cellars of the monasteries the butlers were tapping new and old ale. **3** C. BROWN Maple trees . . were being tapped for the sap to make maple syrup. C. FRANCIS Technology can now tap . . the sea's once inaccessible resources. ANTHONY SMITH Most of us do not tap the potential of our . . brain power. F. POPCORN Televised religion has tapped into an intimate connection with the public. **4** C. CHAPLIN He was dying of dropsy. They tapped sixteen quarts of liquid from his knee. ***tap a person's*** CLARET. **6** E. FAIRWEATHER She was frightened to talk . . because our phone is tapped.

tap /tap/ *verb*[2]. Infl. **-pp-**. ME.
[Old & mod. French *taper*, or imit.: cf. CLAP *verb*[1], FLAP *verb*, RAP *verb*[1].]
1 *verb trans.* **a** Strike lightly but distinctly (and usu. repeatedly). ME. ▸**b** Strike something lightly with (the foot, hand, etc.). LME. ▸**c** Arrest (a person). *slang.* M19.
2 *verb intrans.* Strike (usu. repeatedly) a light but distinct blow; make a sound thus; *esp.* knock lightly *on* or *at* a door etc. to attract attention. LME. ▸†**b** *spec.* Of a hare or rabbit: make a drumming noise with the feet. L16–E18. ▸**c** Sound, esp. as a signal. L19.
3 *verb trans. & intrans.* Add a thickness of leather to the sole or heel of (a boot or shoe). Cf. TAP *noun*[2] 2. *N. Amer. & dial.* M18.
4 *verb trans.* Designate or select (a person) for a task, honour, etc. *US colloq.* M20.

> 🕮 **1** H. CRANE Wiggling a pen or tapping a typewriter. B. PYM If she had been carrying a fan she would surely have tapped his arm with it. **tap out** send or produce (a signal, message, etc.) by a tap or series of taps. **tap up** rouse by tapping at the door. **b** T. DREISER She was . . tapping her gold slippers to the melody. **2** R. CHANDLER His fingers tapped gently on the . . table. J. SIMMS Her door was shut, so I tapped on it gently. **c** C. JOHNSON A bell would tap for a waiter to come.

tapa /ˈtapə/ *noun*[1]. Also **-pp-**, **kapa** /ˈkapə/. E19.
[Polynesian.]
A kind of unwoven cloth made from the bark of the paper mulberry, *Broussonetia papyrifera*.

tapa /ˈtapə/ *noun*[2]. Pl. pronounced /-s/. M20.
[Spanish, lit. 'cover, lid'.]
In a bar or café, esp. one providing Spanish food, a savoury snack to accompany a glass of wine etc. Usu. in *pl.*
Comb.: **tapas bar** a bar or café providing tapas.

tapaculo /tapəˈkjuːləʊ/ *noun.* Pl. **-os.** M19.
[Spanish, from *tapa* cover + *culo* rump.]
Any of several S. American ground-dwelling passerine birds of the family Rhinocryptidae, which are related to the antbirds and have generally dark plumage and a long tail which is often held upright.

tapadero /tapəˈdɛːrəʊ/ *noun.* Pl. **-os.** Also **-ra** /-rə/. M19.
[Spanish = cover, lid, stopper, from *tapar* stop up, cover.]
In the western US, a leather hood for the front of a stirrup, to hold and protect the foot esp. when riding through brush.

tapas /ˈtʌpəs, ˈtapas/ *noun.* Also (earlier) **tapasya** /təˈpʌsjə, -pas-/. E19.
[Sanskrit *tapas* lit. 'heat', *tapasyā*.]
HINDUISM & JAINISM. Religious austerity, ascetic practice.

tape /teɪp/ *noun & verb.*
[Old English *tæppa*, *tæppe*, perh. rel. to Old Frisian *tapia*, Middle Low German *teppen* pluck, tear.]
▸ **A** *noun.* **1** A narrow strip of woven material, esp. as used for tying or fastening; material woven into a strip of this kind. OE. ▸**b** More fully ***tape-measure***. A narrow strip of woven material or (now) strong flexible metal or plastic marked for measuring lengths, esp. as kept coiled in a case and released by a winch or spring; a case holding such a tape. E19. ▸**c** A strip of material stretched across a course or track, esp. to mark the finishing point in a race, or used to mark off an area or form a barrier. M19. ▸**d** A non-commissioned officer's chevron or similar mark of rank, good conduct, etc., on the sleeve of a uniform; a stripe. *Military slang.* M20.
2 Strong liquor, *esp.* gin. *arch. slang.* E18.
3 The paper strip or ribbon on which received messages are printed in a recording telegraph system, or on which data or instructions are represented by punched holes. Also, a length or reel of this. L19.
4 Long narrow flexible material (usu. coated plastic) whose magnetic properties enable it to be used as a recording medium for data or for audio or video material (also ***magnetic tape***); a length or reel of this; a recording on this. Also, a cassette containing such a tape. M20.
5 Paper, plastic, etc., in the form of a long narrow flexible strip coated with adhesive and used for fastening, sticking, masking, or insulating. Freq. with specifying word. M20.

📖 1 SIR W. SCOTT A bundle tied with tape, and sealed .. with black wax. **c breast the tape** reach the finishing-line, win a race. **on the tapes** at the very end of a race. 3 ***perforated tape, punched tape, ticker tape***, etc. 4 *New Yorker* Most thefts of computer tapes are probably not reported to the police. *Independent* Watching a tape of the assassination. **on tape** recorded on magnetic tape. **steel tape** *Hist.* magnetic tape made of thin steel, formerly used for sound recording. 5 ***adhesive tape, electrician's tape, insulating tape, masking tape, sticky tape***, etc.

Comb.: **tape cartridge** a tape cassette, esp. of a type using eight-track tape; **tape cassette** a cassette containing a magnetic tape; **tape deck** a platform with capstans for using magnetic tape, esp. one which can play back but not record; **tape-delay** the use of a tape recorder to introduce an interval between recording and playing back or transmitting; **tape drive** COMPUTING a tape transport or tape deck; **tape-grass** a submerged aquatic plant, *Vallisneria spiralis*, of the frogbit family, with narrow grasslike leaves; **tape guipure**: made with linen tape twisted and folded into a pattern and decoratively embroidered; **tape hiss** extraneous high-frequency background noise during the playing of a tape recording; **tape-line** a line of tape; *esp.* a tape-measure kept coiled in a case and released by means of a winch or spring; **tape machine** (*a*) an instrument for receiving and recording telegraph messages; (*b*) a machine for sizing cotton threads to be used in weaving; (*c*) a tape recorder; ***tape-measure***: see sense 1b above; **tape player** a machine for recording and playing back tapes; **tape punch** COMPUTING a device which punches holes in paper tape to record data in coded form; **tape reader** COMPUTING a device for reading information recorded on paper or magnetic tape; **tape record** *rare* a record or recording on tape; **tape-record** *verb trans.* record (sounds etc.) on magnetic tape; **tape recorder** an apparatus for recording and playing back sounds etc. on magnetic tape; **tape recording** (the making of) a recording on magnetic tape; **tape recordist** a person who makes tape recordings; **tape reproducer** a machine that plays or copies tapes but does not record them; **tapescript** (a transcript or text of) a tape recording of the spoken word; **tape-sizer** = TAPER *noun*[2] 1; ***tape streamer***: see STREAMER *noun* 7; **tape-tied** *adjective* (*a*) tied with tape; (*b*) *fig.* restricted by bureaucracy; **tape transport** a mechanism which controls the movement of recording tape past a stationary head; a tape deck.

▶ **B** *verb trans.* **1** Attach a tape to; fit with tapes; tie (*up*), fasten, seal or bind with tape; *spec.* (*a*) mark *off* (an area) with tape; (*b*) join the sections of (a book) with tape. Also, stick (*up*) or affix with adhesive tape. E17. ▶**b** Tie (*up*) or gag (a victim etc.) with adhesive tape. *slang.* M20.

2 Give *out* or use in a sparing or measured way. *Scot.* E18.

3 Measure with a tape-line; *spec.* (GUNNERY) get the range of (a position) by using a tape-line together with a range-finder. L19.

4 Measure (a specified length, width, etc.). L19.

5 Record on (magnetic) tape. M20.

📖 4 *Muscle Power* My chest had measured 46½ inches .. later it taped 50½! 5 T. BARR Hollywood studios that are used to tape TV shows. R. RENDELL Any objections if I record this interview? Tape it, I mean?

Phrases: **get taped**, **have taped** size up or fully understand (a person or thing).

¶ See also RED TAPE.

■ **tapeless** *adjective* E20. **tapism** *noun* (*rare*) = RED-TAPISM M19.

tapénade /tapenad/ *noun.* M20.
[French, from Provençal *tapeno*: see -ADE.]
A Provençal dish, usu. served as an hors d'oeuvre, made mainly from black olives, capers, and anchovies.

taper /ˈteɪpə/ *noun*[1], *adjective*, & *verb.*
[Old English *tapor*, *-er*, *-ur* from Latin *papyrus* PAPYRUS by dissimilation of *p-* to *t-*, with ref. to the use of the pith for a wick.]
▶ **A** *noun.* **1** Orig., any wax candle, *esp.* a votive candle. Now chiefly, a long wick coated with wax for conveying a flame, a slender candle. OE. ▶**b** *fig.* A thing represented as (usu. feebly) burning or giving light. OE.

2 An object that tapers towards one end or extremity, as a tapering tube; an object resembling a wax taper. (*rare* before 20.) L16.

3 Gradual diminution in width or thickness; continuous gradual decrease in one direction or along one dimension. L18.

📖 1 HENRY MILLER I would sit in the flickering light of the burning taper. b F. SKURRAY The new-born moon display'd Her feeble taper. 2 MORSE TAPER.

Comb.: **taper-lock**, (US proprietary) **Taper-Lock** MECHANICS a type of tapered bush inserted into a pulley, sprocket, etc., to enable it to be mounted rigidly on a shaft; **taper tap** MECHANICS a tap tapered lengthways for about two thirds of its length, used to begin the tapping of a screw thread.

▶ **B** *adjective.* Tapering towards one end or extremity (orig. the top); resembling a wax taper; slender, tapering. L15.

▶ **C** *verb.* **1** *verb intrans.* Shoot *up* or rise like a flame, spire, or pyramid; *fig.* rise continuously in honour, dignity, rank, etc. Now *rare* or *obsolete.* L16.

2 *verb intrans.* Diminish gradually in breadth or thickness towards one end; grow gradually smaller in one direction; *fig.* diminish gradually in intensity, amount, etc. Freq. foll. by *off*, *away*, *down.* E17.

3 *verb trans.* Reduce gradually and regularly in breadth or thickness in one direction; *fig.* reduce gradually in intensity, amount, etc. Freq. foll. by *off*, *down.* L17.

📖 2 C. THUBRON His voice tapered whispering away. *International Combat Arms* Annual production of Soviet fighters has tapered down from 950 .. to 650. 3 *Scientific American* Adrenocortical steroids .. can .. cause a relapse if they are tapered off too rapidly.

■ **tapered** *adjective* (*a*) made to taper, tapering; (*b*) lit by tapers, provided with tapers: M17. **taperer** *noun* the bearer of a taper in a religious ceremony LME. **taperingly** *adverb* in a tapering manner L19. **taperness** *noun* (*rare*) the condition of being taper M18. **taperwise** *adverb* in the manner of a taper; so as to taper towards one end: LME.

taper /ˈteɪpə/ *noun*[2]. L19.
[from TAPE *verb* + -ER[1].]
1 WEAVING. An operator of a tape machine. Also called ***tape-sizer***. L19.
2 A person who uses or deals with tape or tapes; *spec.* one who records or edits a tape. E20.

tapespond /ˈteɪpspɒnd/ *verb intrans.* M20.
[from TAPE *noun* + CORRE)SPOND.]
Correspond by means of tape-recorded spoken messages.

tapestry /ˈtapɪstri/ *noun.* Also †**tapissery**. LME.
[Old & mod. French *tapisserie*, from *tapissier* tapestry-worker or *tapisser* cover with carpet, from *tapis* carpet, TAPIS *noun*.]
1 A (piece of) thick textile fabric decorated with pictures or designs painted, embroidered, or (usu.) woven in colours, often hung on a wall. LME. ▶**b** (A piece of) embroidery, orig. as imitating this, usually done in wools on canvas. L19.
2 *fig.* A scene, phenomenon, or circumstance presenting rich colour or variety, intricacy of design, etc. L16.
3 In full ***tapestry needle***. A blunt needle with a large eye, used in tapestry-making and canvas embroidery. L19.

📖 1 A. GRAY Tapestries worked in .. gold thread hung from an elaborate cornice. 2 J. R. LOWELL Present and Past .. inseparably wrought Into the seamless tapestry of thought. *Great Outdoors* Varieties of heather that create the .. colourful Autumn tapestry.

Comb.: **tapestry beetle** a dermestid beetle, *Attagenus piceus*, whose larvae are destructive to tapestry, woollens, etc.; **tapestry moth** a relative of the clothes moths, *Trichophaga tapetzella*, that attacks coarser textiles; ***tapestry needle***: see sense 3 above; ***tapestry work*** = senses 1, 1b above; **tapestry-worker** a person engaged in tapestry work.

tapestry /ˈtapɪstri/ *verb trans.* E17.
[from prec.]
1 Cover, hang, or adorn (as) with tapestry. Chiefly as ***tapestried*** *ppl adjective.* E17.
2 Work or depict in tapestry. E19.

tapet /ˈtapɪt/ *noun.* Long *obsolete* exc. *Hist.* Also **-pit**. OE.
[Late Latin *tapetium* from Latin *tapete* carpet.]
A piece of decorated cloth resembling a tapestry, used as a hanging, table-cover, carpet, etc.

tapetal /təˈpiːt(ə)l/ *adjective.* L19.
[from TAPETUM + -AL[1].]
BOTANY. Of or pertaining to the tapetum.

tapette /tapɛt/ *noun* & *adjective.* M20.
[French slang = pederast, homosexual, from *taper* hit, tap + *-ette* -ETTE.]
▶ **A** *noun.* Pl. pronounced same. A passive male homosexual; an effeminate man. M20.
▶ **B** *adjective.* Of a man: effeminate; like a *tapette*. M20.

tapetum /təˈpiːtəm/ *noun.* E18.
[Late Latin, from Latin *tapete* carpet.]
1 ZOOLOGY. A reflective layer of the choroid in the eyes of many animals, causing them to shine in the dark. E18.
2 BOTANY. A layer of cells forming a nutrient tissue, which surrounds the pollen mother cells in the anthers of flowering plants or the spore mother cells in pteridophytes. L19.

tapeworm /ˈteɪpwəːm/ *noun.* M18.
[from TAPE *noun* + WORM *noun*.]
Any of various flatworms constituting the order Cestoda, the adults of which are long ribbon-shaped worms parasitic in the intestines of vertebrates, and consist of a small head or scolex and numerous egg-producing segments.

taphonomy /taˈfɒnəmi/ *noun.* M20.
[from Greek *taphos* grave + -O- + -NOMY.]
The branch of palaeontology that deals with the processes by which animal and plant remains become preserved as fossils.
■ **tapho'nomic** *adjective* of or pertaining to taphonomy L20. **tapho'nomical** *adjective* = TAPHONOMIC M20. **taphonomist** *noun* an expert in or student of taphonomy L20.

taphrogenesis /tafrə(ʊ)ˈdʒɛnɪsɪs/ *noun.* E20.
[from Greek *taphros* pit + -GENESIS.]
GEOLOGY. The formation of large-scale rift phenomena etc. by high-angle or block faulting, esp. as the result of tensional forces at plate boundaries.
■ **taphrogenic** *adjective* of or pertaining to taphrogenesis E20.

tapia /ˈtɑːpɪə/ *noun.* M18.
[Spanish = mud-wall.]
Clay or mud puddled, compressed, and dried, as a material for walls.

tapicer /ˈtapɪsə/ *noun.* Long *obsolete* exc. *Hist.* Also †**-isser**. ME.
[Anglo-Norman *tapicer*, Old French *tapicier* (mod. *tapissier*), formed as TAPIS *noun*: see -ER[2].]
A maker or weaver of figured cloth or tapestry.

tapioca /tapɪˈəʊkə/ *noun.* E18.
[Tupi-Guarani *tipioca*, from *tipi* residue, dregs + *ok*, *og* squeeze out.]
A starchy substance in hard white grains obtained from the roots of the cassava and used in food, esp. puddings.

tapir /ˈteɪpə, -ɪə/ *noun.* L18.
[Spanish or Portuguese, from Tupi *tapyra*.]
Each of four odd-toed ungulate mammals constituting the genus *Tapirus* and family Tapiridae, which have large rotund bodies, thick muscular necks, and a short flexible proboscis, and are found in the tropical rainforests of Central and S. America and SE Asia.
Brazilian tapir: see BRAZILIAN *adjective.* ***Malayan tapir***: see MALAYAN *adjective.*

tapis /ˈtapi/ *noun.* Pl. same. L15.
[Old French *tapiz* (also mod.) *tapis* from late Latin *tapetium* from Greek *tapētion* dim. of *tapēs*, *tapēt-* tapestry.]
A cloth, esp. of a decorated oriental fabric of a type exported to France in the 18th cent., worked with artistic designs in colours, used as a curtain, tablecloth, etc.; a tapestry.
on the tapis (of a subject) under discussion or consideration. ***tapis vert*** /tapi vɛːr/, pl. ***tapis verts*** (pronounced same), [= green] a long strip of grass, a grass walk.

†**tapis** *verb.* Also **-pp-**. ME.
[Old French *tapiss-* lengthened stem of *tapir* (mod. *se tapir*).]
1 *verb intrans.* Lie close to the ground; lie low, lurk, hide. ME–E19.
2 *verb trans.* Hide, conceal (esp. oneself). M17–M19.

†**tapisser**, †**tapissery** *nouns* vars. of TAPICER, TAPESTRY *nouns.*

tapit *noun* var. of TAPET.

Tapleyism /ˈtaplɪɪz(ə)m/ *noun.* M19.
[from Mark *Tapley* a character in Dickens's *Martin Chuzzlewit*.]
Optimism in the most hopeless circumstances.

tapotement /təˈpəʊtm(ə)nt/ *noun.* L19.
[French, from *tapoter* to tap: see -MENT.]
A percussive technique used in massage, consisting of hacking, clapping, and pounding actions.

tappa *noun* var. of TAPA *noun*[1].

tappable /ˈtapəb(ə)l/ *adjective.* E20.
[from TAP *verb*[1] + -ABLE.]
Esp. of a tree: able or ready to be tapped.

tappal /təˈpɔːl/ *noun.* L18.
[Origin unkn.]
In the Indian subcontinent: orig., the carrying of mail by relays of runners, a person delivering mail; now, the postal service, the mail; a delivery of mail.

tapped /tapt/ *adjective.* L17.
[from TAP *noun*[2], *verb*[2]: see -ED[2], -ED[1].]
That has been tapped, provided with a tap; *spec.* (*a*) PHONETICS pronounced with a tap; (*b*) RUGBY FOOTBALL (of a penalty) taken with a tap-kick.

tapper /ˈtapə/ *noun*[1]. LOE.
[from TAP *verb*[1] + -ER[1].]
1 = TAPSTER 1. Long *obsolete* exc. *dial.* LOE. ▶†**b** = TAPSTER 2. *Scot.* L15–E17.
2 A person who or thing which taps something. L19.
2 ***rubber-tapper, wire-tapper***, etc.

tapper /ˈtapə/ *noun*[2]. E19.
[from TAP *verb*[2] + -ER[1].]
A person who or thing which taps something; *spec.* (*a*) a hammer for striking a bell; (*b*) a telegraph key.

Tappertitian /tapəˈtɪʃ(ə)n/ *adjective. rare.* L19.
[from *Tappertit* (see below) + -IAN.]
Characteristic of or resembling Simon Tappertit, a conceited apprentice in Dickens's *Barnaby Rudge*.

tappet /ˈtapɪt/ *noun.* M18.
[App. from TAP *verb*[2] + -ET[1].]
A projecting arm or part in a machine, which intermittently makes contact with another part (esp. a cam) when the machine moves, so as to give or receive motion.

tappety-tap *interjection*, *adverb*, & *noun* var. of TAPPITY-TAPPITY.

tapping /ˈtapɪŋ/ *noun*[1]. LME.
[from TAP *verb*[1] + -ING[1].]
1 The action of TAP *verb*[1]. LME. ▶**b** The result of tapping; that which is drawn or runs from a tap. L16.
2 ELECTRICAL ENGINEERING. An intermediate connection made in a winding. E20.

1 *rubber-tapping*, *wire-tapping*, etc.
Comb.: **tapping-bar** a sharp-pointed crowbar for opening the tap-hole of a furnace; **tapping coil** ELECTRICAL ENGINEERING a coil which acts as a tapping; **tapping-hole** a tap-hole in a furnace.

tapping /ˈtapɪŋ/ *noun*². LME.
[from TAP *verb*² + -ING¹.]
The action of TAP *verb*²; an act or instance of this, a light distinct rap or knock.
Comb.: **tapping key** a button or lever operating a mechanical device for making or breaking an electric circuit, used in telegraphy etc.

†**tappis** *verb* var. of TAPIS *verb*.

tappity-tappity /ˌtapɪtɪˈtapɪti/ *interjection, adverb, & noun*. Also **tappety-tap** /ˈtapətɪˈtap/ & other vars. M20.
[Imit.]
▶ **A** *interjection & adverb*. Repr. a succession of tapping or pattering sounds; with a succession of such sounds. M20.
▶ **B** *noun*. A succession of tapping or pattering sounds. L20.

tap root /ˈtap ruːt/ *noun phr. & verb*. Also (esp. as verb) **tap-root**. E17.
[from TAP *noun*¹ + ROOT *noun*¹.]
▶ **A** *noun*. A straight tapering root, growing directly downwards and forming the centre from which subsidiary rootlets spring. E17.
▶ **B** *verb intrans*. Of a plant: send down a tap root. M18.
■ **tap-rooted** *adjective* having a tap root E18.

tapsalteerie *adverb* see TOPSY-TURVY *adverb*.

tapster /ˈtapstə/ *noun*.
[Old English *tæppestre* orig. fem. of TAPPER *noun*¹: see -STER.]
1 A person (orig. a woman) who draws and serves ale or other alcoholic drinks at an inn, bar, etc.; the keeper of a tavern. OE.
†**2** A person who sells by retail or in small quantities. Cf. TAPPER *noun*¹ 1b. LME–L16.
■ **tapstress** *noun* a female tapster L17.

tap-too *noun* see TATTOO *noun*¹.

tapu *adjective & noun, verb* see TABOO *adjective & noun, verb*.

tapul /ˈtapʊl/ *noun*. M16.
[Origin unkn.]
Hist. Part of a suit of armour; *spec.* the vertical central ridge of the breastplate.

taqueria /taːkəˈriːə/ *noun*. *US*. L20.
[Mexican Spanish, formed as TACO.]
A restaurant specializing in tacos.

taqueté /takte/ *adjective*. M20.
[French, from *taquet* wedge, peg.]
BALLET. Designating or pertaining to a style of point-work accentuated with quick precise short steps.

tar /tɑː/ *noun*¹.
[Old English *teru*, *teoru*, corresp. to Middle Low German *ter(e* (Low German *teer*, whence Dutch, German *Teer*), Middle Dutch *tar*, *ter(re*, Old Norse *tjara*, from Germanic, gen. held to be ult. rel. to TREE *noun*. In sense 2 perh. abbreviation of TARPAULIN *noun* 2.]
1 A very thick viscid black or dark-coloured flammable liquid obtained by the destructive distillation of wood, coal, or other organic substances, chemically a mixture of hydrocarbons with resins, alcohols, etc., having a heavy resinous or bituminous odour, and used for coating and preserving timber, cordage, etc.; any similar product produced e.g. by the burning of tobacco. OE. ▸**b** A person of mixed black (or Indian etc.) and white origin. Cf. TAR-BRUSH 2. *derog. & racially offensive*. L19. ▸**c** Tarmac, tarmacadam; a road surfaced with this. *colloq.* M20. ▸**d** Orig. (now *rare*), opium taken as an intoxicant or stimulant drug. Now, heroin, esp. in a potent black form (more fully ***black tar***). *US slang*. M20.
2 (A nickname for) a sailor. M17.
3 With qualifying word. Any of various natural substances resembling tar, as bitumen. M18.
1 beat the tar out of, **kick the tar out of**, **knock the tar out of** *US slang* beat severely, reduce to a state of helplessness. ***Stockholm tar***: see STOCKHOLM 1. **tar and feathers** US HISTORY the practice or an act of tarring and feathering someone. **2 *Jack tar***: see JACK *noun*¹ 3a. **3 *mineral tar***: see MINERAL *adjective*.
Comb.: **tar acid** any phenolic constituent of coal tar distillates that reacts with dilute sodium hydroxide to give water-soluble salts; **tar-baby** (*a*) in J. C. Harris's *Uncle Remus*, the doll smeared with tar, intended by Brer Fox to catch Brer Rabbit; *transf.* a difficult problem, a problem which is only aggravated by attempts to solve it; (*b*) (*derog. & racially offensive*) a black person (*US*); a Maori (*NZ*); **tar ball** a ball of crude oil found in or on the sea; **tar-barrel** a barrel containing or that has contained tar, esp. as used for making a bonfire; **tar base** any of numerous cyclic nitrogenous bases present in coal tar distillates; **tar-box** (*obsolete exc. Hist.*) a box formerly used by shepherds to hold tar as a salve for sheep; **tar-boy** *Austral. & NZ slang* an assistant in a shearing shed who puts tar or other disinfectants on the cuts suffered by sheep during shearing; **tarheel** *US colloq.* a native or inhabitant of North Carolina (tar being a principal product of that State); **tar kiln** a covered heap of wood or coal from which tar is obtained by burning; **tar-paper** *noun & adjective* (chiefly *N. Amer.*) (made of) paper impregnated with tar, often used as a building material; **tar-pavement**, **tar-paving** a form of surfacing for roads, pathways, etc., composed mainly of tarmacadam; **tar-pit** (*a*) a seepage of natural tar, *esp.* one in which animals have become trapped and their remains preserved; (*b*) *fig.* a complicated or difficult situation or problem; something in which one becomes bogged down; **tar-pot** (*a*) a pot containing or that has contained tar; (*b*) *joc.* a sailor (cf. sense 2 above); (*c*) (*derog. & racially offensive*) a black person (*US*); a Maori (*NZ*); **tar-sand** a deposit of sand impregnated with bitumen; **tar-water** an infusion of tar in cold water, formerly used as a medicine; **tar-weed** *US* any of various plants of the composite family of the genera *Madia*, *Hemizonia*, and *Grindelia*, so called from their viscidity and heavy scent; **tar-wood** resinous wood from which tar is obtained.
■ **tarrish** *adjective* (*rare*) (*a*) resembling tar in taste, consistency, etc.; (*b*) of or pertaining to sailors; nautical: L17.

tar /tɑː/ *noun*². L19.
[Persian & Urdu *tār* lit. 'string, wire'.]
In the Indian subcontinent: a telegram.

tar /tɑː/ *verb*¹. *arch.* Infl. **-rr-**.
[Old English *terġan* = Middle & mod. Dutch *tergen*, German *zergen*.]
1 *verb trans.* Irritate, annoy, provoke. Now *dial.* exc. in ***tar on***, incite, encourage to action. OE.
†**2** *verb intrans.* ***tar and tig***, ***tig and tar***, act forcefully or wantonly; use force and violence. *Scot.* LME–M16.

tar /tɑː/ *verb*² *trans.* Infl. **-rr-**. OE.
[from TAR *noun*¹.]
1 Coat or cover with tar. OE. ▸**b** Smear (a person's body) with tar. Chiefly in ***tar and feather*** (US HISTORY), smear with tar and then cover with feathers as a form of punishment or a sign of disgrace. M18.
2 *fig.* Mark or stain as with tar. Chiefly in ***tarred with the same brush***, ***tarred with the same stick***, having or marred by the same or similar faults or unpleasant qualities. E17.

📖 **2** S. UNWIN One blunder of one person . . was fully publicized and used to tar the entire . . organization.

■ **tarring** *verbal noun* the action of the verb; an instance of this: L15.

tara /ˈtɑːrə/ *noun*. M19.
[Perh. from Aboriginal.]
An Australasian bracken, *Pteridium esculentum*, with an edible root; the root of this fern.

tara /taˈrɑː/ *interjection*¹. L17.
[Imit. a fanfare. Cf. TARARA, TARATANTARA.]
Indicating an impressive entrance, a notable event, etc.

📖 *New Yorker* The hair, the dress, the makeup. Ta-ra! Transformed.

tara /təˈrɑː/ *interjection*². *colloq.* (chiefly *north.*). M20.
[Alt. of TA-TA.]
Goodbye.

tarada /təˈrɑːdə/ *noun*. M20.
[Arab. *tarrāda* swift war canoe, from *ṭarada* pursue, chase.]
A swift, graceful canoe used by the Marsh Arabs of Iraq.

taradiddle /ˈtarədɪd(ə)l/ *noun & verb*. *colloq.* Also **tarra-**. L18.
[Origin unkn. 2nd elem. perh. rel. to DIDDLE *verb*².]
▶ **A** *noun*. **1** A petty lie; a fib. L18.
2 Pretentious or empty talk; senseless activity; nonsense. L20.

📖 **2** M. GALLANT The letter was legal taradiddle and carried about as much weight.

▶ **B** *verb*. Now *rare*.
1 *verb intrans.* Tell fibs. E19.
2 *verb trans.* Impose on, or bring into some condition, by telling fibs. E19.

📖 **2** *Examiner* His enemies . . squibbed, and paragraphed, and taradiddled him to death.

■ **taradiddler** *noun* a petty liar L19.

Tarahumara /tarəhuːˈmɑːrə/ *noun & adjective*. L19.
[Spanish: origin unkn.]
▶ **A** *noun*. Pl. same.
1 A member of an Uto-Aztecan people of NW Mexico. L19.
2 The language of this people. L19.
▶ **B** *adjective*. Of or pertaining to this people or their language. E20.

taraire /təˈrʌɪriː/ *noun*. L19.
[Maori.]
A large New Zealand forest tree of the laurel family, *Beilschmiedia tarairi*, with white wood.

tarakihi /tarəˈkiːhi, tarəˈkiː/ *noun*. *NZ*. Also **tera-** /tɛrə-/. L19.
[Maori.]
A fish of the morwong group found off New Zealand coasts, *Cheilodactylus macropterus*, silver in colour with a black band behind the head and edible white flesh.

taramasalata /tarəməsəˈlɑːtə/ *noun*. Also **-mo-**. E20.
[mod. Greek *taramosalata*, from *taramas* preserved roe (from Turkish *tarama* a preparation of soft roe or red caviar) + *salata* salad.]
A fish pâté made from the roe of the grey mullet or from smoked cod's roe, mixed with garlic, lemon juice, olive oil, etc.

Taranaki gate /tarəˈnaki ˈɡeɪt/ *noun phr.* M20.
[from *Taranaki* a province in New Zealand + GATE *noun*¹.]
In New Zealand: a makeshift gate made of wire strands attached to upright battens.

Taranchi /təˈrɑːntʃi/ *noun & adjective*. Also **Taranji**. L19.
[Chagatai *Taranči* lit. 'farmer, labourer'.]
▶ **A** *noun*. Pl. **-s**, same.
1 A member of a people of mixed Turkoman and Iranian descent inhabiting the Ili basin region of Kazakhstan in central Asia. L19.
2 The Turkic language of this people. L20.
▶ **B** *adjective*. Of or pertaining to the Taranchis or their language. L19.

†**tarand** *noun*. Also **-dre**, **-dus**, & other vars. LME–M18.
[French *tarande*, †*-dre* from medieval Latin *tarandus*, Latin *tarandrus* (Pliny) a northern animal, app. the reindeer.]
A mythical creature said to have the power of changing colour to match its surroundings. Also, a reindeer.

Taranji *noun & adjective* var. of TARANCHI.

tarantass /tar(ə)nˈtas/ *noun*. M19.
[Russian *tarantas*.]
A springless four-wheeled Russian carriage on a long flexible wooden chassis.

tarantella /tar(ə)nˈtɛlə/ *noun*. Also **-telle** /-ˈtɛl/. L18.
[Italian, dim. of *Taranto* (Latin *Tarentum*), a town in southern Italy: popularly assoc. with *tarantola* TARANTULA. Cf. TARENTINE.]
1 A rapid whirling southern Italian dance popular since the 15th cent. L18.
2 A piece of music for such a dance or composed in its triplet rhythm, with abrupt transitions from the major to the minor. M19.

tarantism /ˈtar(ə)ntɪz(ə)m/ *noun*. M17.
[Italian *tarantismo*, from *Taranto*: see prec.]
A nervous condition characterized by an impulse to dance energetically, esp. (*Hist.*) as widespread in southern Italy from the 15th to 17th cents. and popularly associated (either as an effect or a cure) with the bite of the tarantula.

tarantula /təˈrantjʊlə/ *noun*. M16.
[medieval Latin from Old Italian *tarantola*, from *Taranto*: see TARANTELLA.]
1 A large black wolf-spider of southern Europe, *Lycosa tarentula*, whose slightly poisonous bite was formerly supposed to cause tarantism. M16. ▸**b** Any of various large, hairy, or poisonous spiders; *spec.* (orig. *US*) any large hairy tropical mygalomorph spider of the family Theraphosidae; *Austral.* a huntsman spider. L18.
2 The bite of the tarantula. Also = TARANTISM. Now *rare* or *obsolete*. L16.
3 [By confusion.] = TARANTELLA 1. *rare*. L17.
Comb.: **tarantula-hawk** any of several spider-hunting (pompilid) wasps of the genus *Pepsis*, of the SW United States; **tarantula-juice** *US slang* inferior whiskey.
■ **tarantular** *adjective* = TARANTULOUS M19. **tarantulate** *verb* (*a*) *verb intrans.* dance as if affected by tarantism; (*b*) *verb trans.* affect with tarantism: M18. **tarantulous** *adjective* of or pertaining to the tarantula (chiefly *fig.* with ref. to tarantism) L19.

Tarantulle /tar(ə)nˈtuːl/ *noun*. L19.
[Extension of TULLE.]
(Proprietary name for) a kind of cotton fabric.

tarara /təˈrɑːrə/ *interjection*. L19.
[Imit. a fanfare. Cf. TARA *interjection*¹, TARATANTARA.]
= TARATANTARA 1.

Tarascan /təˈraskən/ *noun & adjective*. E20.
[from Spanish *Tarasco* an American Indian lang. of SW Michoacán, Mexico + -AN.]
▶ **A** *noun*. Pl. **-s**, same.
1 A member of an American Indian people of the mountain area about Lake Pátzcuara in Michoacán, Mexico. E20.
2 The language of this people. E20.
▶ **B** *adjective*. Of or pertaining to the Tarascans or their language. E20.

tarata /təˈrɑːtə/ *noun*. *NZ*. M19.
[Maori.]
= ***lemonwood*** (a) s.v. LEMON *noun*¹.

taratantara /tɑːrəˈtant(ə)rə, -ˈtɑːrə/ *noun*. M16.
[Imit., after Latin & Italian. Cf. TARA *interjection*¹, TARARA.]
1 (Repr.) the sound of a trumpet or bugle; a fanfare. M16.
†**2** *fig.* Loud, extravagant, or pretentious talk. L16–L17.

📖 **1** *Listener* A troop of horses, moving in column to the taratantara of bugles.

taraxacum /təˈraksəkəm/ *noun*. E18.
[medieval Latin *altaraxacon* from Arab. & Persian *tarakšakūn*, *-kūk* dandelion, wild endive, ult. from Persian *talk* bitter + *čakūk* purslane.]

Any of the numerous plants constituting the genus *Taraxacum*, of the composite family, including dandelions. Also, a preparation of the dried root of the dandelion, formerly used as a tonic and diuretic.
■ **taraxacin** *noun* a bitter crystalline substance present in dandelions **M19.**

tarbagan /ˈtɑːbəg(ə)n/ *noun.* **E20.**
[Russian from Turkic: cf. Mongolian *tarbaqan*.]
A large marmot, *Marmota sibirica*, of the eastern and central Asian steppes; the fur of this animal.

tarboosh /tɑːˈbuːʃ/ *noun.* Also **tarbush**. **E18.**
[Egyptian Arab. *tarbūš* from Ottoman Turkish *terpōş*, Turkish *tarbuş* from Persian *sarpūš*, from *sar* head + *pūš* cover.]
A cap similar to a fez, usu. of red felt with a tassel at the top, worn by Muslim men either alone or as part of a turban.
■ **tarbooshed** *adjective* wearing a tarboosh **L19.**

tar-brush /ˈtɑːbrʌʃ/ *noun.* **E18.**
[from TAR *noun*[1] + BRUSH *noun*[2].]
1 A brush used for applying tar to something. **E18.**
2 Black (or Indian etc.) ancestry. Chiefly in ***a dash of the tar-brush***, ***a touch of the tar-brush***, a trace of black (or Indian etc.) ancestry. *derog. & racially offensive.* **L18.**

Tarbuck knot /ˈtɑːbʌk nɒt/ *noun phr.* **M20.**
[from Kenneth *Tarbuck*, Brit. mountaineer (b. 1914), who invented it.]
MOUNTAINEERING. An adjustable safety knot similar to a prusik knot, but which, when subjected to a sudden heavy load, yields for a very short distance and then locks solid.

tarbush *noun* var. of TARBOOSH.

†**tardation** *noun.* **E16–E18.**
[Late Latin *tardatio(n-)*, from *tardat-* pa. ppl stem of *tardare* delay: see -ATION.]
The action of delaying, delay; slackening of speed.

Tardenoisian /tɑːdɪˈnɔɪzɪən/ *adjective & noun.* **E20.**
[French *Tardenoisien*, from *Tardenois* (see below) + -IAN.]
ARCHAEOLOGY. (Of or pertaining to) a mesolithic culture using small flint implements, remains of which were first discovered at Fère-en-Tardenois, in the department of Aisne, NE France.

tardigrade /ˈtɑːdɪgreɪd/ *adjective & noun.* **E17.**
[French, or Latin *tardigradus* from *tardus* slow + -I- + *-gradus* walking.]
▶ **A** *adjective.* **1** Walking or moving slowly; slow-paced. Also (*fig.*), sluggish in thought or action, unprogressive. **E17.**
2 Of or pertaining to the suborder Tardigrada of edentate mammals, comprising the sloths. **L18.**
3 Of or pertaining to the phylum Tardigrada, which comprises minute animals with chitinous exoskeletons, stout bodies, and eight stubby legs that inhabit water films on mosses and other specialized aquatic habitats and can survive desiccation. **M19.**

> 📖 **1** *Sunday Correspondent* Bowls players . . devoted to this tardigrade sport.

▶ **B** *noun.* **1** A mammal of the suborder Tardigrada, a sloth. **E19.**
2 An animal of the phylum Tardigrada. Also called ***water bear***. **M19.**
■ **tarˈdigradous** *adjective* = TARDIGRADE *adjective* 1 **M17.**

Tardis /ˈtɑːdɪs/ *noun.* Also **t-**. **L20.**
[from *TARDIS* (said to be an acronym from Time And Relative Dimensions In Space), a time machine in the British TV science-fiction series *Doctor Who* (1963–), outwardly resembling a police telephone box.]
An object, building, etc., resembling Doctor Who's TARDIS, esp. in being (***a***) a time machine, or (***b***) larger on the inside than it appears from the outside.

> 📖 M. SAWYER Granny's house is big . . . But it's collapsed into itself, like a Tardis in reverse: she lives in just the sitting-room.

tardity /ˈtɑːdɪti/ *noun.* Now *rare.* **LME.**
[Old French *tardité* from Latin *tarditas*, from *tardus* slow: see -ITY.]
1 Slowness or sluggishness of movement or action. **LME.**
2 The fact or condition of being delayed or late; lateness. **L16.**

tardive /ˈtɑːdɪv/ *adjective.* **L15.**
[French *tardif*, *-ive*: see TARDY *adjective*.]
†**1** = TARDY *adjective* 1. **L15–E17.**
2 MEDICINE. Of a disease or condition: of late appearance or development. **E20.**
2 tardive dyskinesia a neurological disorder, usu. a late-developing side-effect of long-term antipsychotic drug therapy, characterized by involuntary movements of the face and jaw.
¶ In gen. sense superseded by TARDY *adjective*.

tardon *noun* var. of TARDYON.

tardy /ˈtɑːdi/ *adjective & adverb.* **M16.**
[Old & mod. French *tardif*, *-ive* from Proto-Romance, from Latin *tardus* slow: see -Y[7]. Superseded TARDIVE (cf. HASTY).]
▶ **A** *adjective.* **1** Slow in motion or action; making slow progress; slow or sluggish in nature. **M16.**
2 Acting, coming, or happening after the proper, expected, or desired time; delaying or delayed; reluctant (*to do*). **M17.** ▸**b** Late for a meeting, school, an appointment etc. *N. Amer.* **M17.**

> 📖 **1** J. SHUTE Montanus, in whose heresie Tertullian (though else a good man) was tardie. *Sunday Mail (Brisbane)* For once, there is . . regret that the service is not a tad more tardy. †**take tardy** overtake; come upon unprepared or unawares; find out, catch in a crime etc. **2** M. HOCKING She was old and a tardy spring mattered. **b** P. MAILLOUX He had been due at eight, but was characteristically tardy.

▶ **B** *adverb.* Behind time, late. Now only *arch.* in ***come tardy off***, fall short, be performed inadequately. **L16.**
■ **tardily** *adverb* **L16.** **tardiness** *noun* **E17.**

tardy /ˈtɑːdi/ *verb trans.* Long *rare.* **E17.**
[from the adjective.]
Make tardy; delay, slow down.

tardyon /ˈtɑːdɪɒn/ *noun.* Also **tardon** /ˈtɑːdɒn/. **M20.**
[from TARDY *adjective* + -ON.]
PHYSICS. A subatomic particle that travels at less than the speed of light.

tare /tɛː/ *noun*[1]. **ME.**
[Origin unkn.]
1 The seed of a vetch, usu. in ref. to its small size. **ME.**
2 a Any of various wild vetches; *esp.* either of two small-flowered kinds occurring as weeds in cornfields, *Vicia hirsuta* (in full ***hairy tare***) and *V. tetrasperma* (in full ***smooth tare***). **LME.** ▸**b** The common vetch, *Vicia sativa*, grown as fodder. Usu. in *pl.*, a crop of this plant. **L15.** ▸**c** A type of cereal bait used for fishing. **L20.**
3 In *pl.* In versions of the parable in *Matthew* 13:24–30 and allusions to it: an injurious weed resembling corn when young (probably darnel, *Lolium temulentum*). **LME.**

> 📖 **3** M. L. KING When the harvest is gleaned the evil tares will be separated from the good wheat.

tare /tɛː/ *noun*[2] *& verb*[1]. **LME.**
[French = waste in goods, deficiency, tare from medieval Latin *tara* from Arab. *tarḥ* that which is thrown away, from *taraha* reject, deduct, subtract.]
▶ **A** *noun.* **1** The weight of a wrapping, container, or receptacle in which goods are packed, which is deducted from the gross weight in order to ascertain the net weight; a deduction made from the gross weight to allow for this or (formerly) for any waste. Also (esp. as ***tare weight***), the weight of a motor vehicle, aircraft, etc., without its fuel or load. **LME.**
2 CHEMISTRY. The weight of a container in which a substance is weighed (deducted in ascertaining the weight of the substance). **L19.**

> 📖 **1** *Railway Magazine* Weight of each unit is approximately 39 tonnes tare with seats for 84 passengers. **tare and tret** the two deductions used in calculating the net weight of goods (cf. TRET); the arithmetical rule for calculating these.

▶ **B** *verb trans.* Ascertain, allow for, or indicate the tare of. **E19.**
■ **taring** *noun* (***a***) the calculation and deduction of the tare on goods; (***b***) deduction for defective goods: **E17.**

tare *verb*[2] *pa. t.*: see TEAR *verb*[1].

tarentaal /tar(ə)nˈtɑːl/ *noun. S. Afr.* **E19.**
[Afrikaans, perh. from Portuguese *Terra de Natal*.]
A guinea-fowl; *spec.* (***a***) the helmeted guinea-fowl, *Numida meleagris*; (***b***) the crested guinea-fowl, *Guttera edouardi*.

Tarentine /ˈtar(ə)ntʌɪn/ *adjective & noun.* **ME.**
[Latin *Tarentinus* of Tarentum (see below): see -INE[1]. Cf. TARANTELLA.]
Hist. ▶ **A** *adjective.* Of or pertaining to the ancient city of Tarentum (now Taranto) in southern Italy. **ME.**
▶ **B** *noun.* A native or inhabitant of Tarentum. **L16.**

tarentola /təˈrɛntələ/ *noun.* **L19.**
[mod. Latin from Italian dial. = salamander from Old Italian *tarantola*: see TARANTULA.]
= ***Moorish gecko*** s.v. MOORISH *adjective*[2] 1.

tarfa /tɑːˈfɑː/ *noun.* Also **-ah**. **M19.**
[Arab. *ṭarfā'*.]
A Middle Eastern tamarisk, *Tamarix mannifera*, associated with the formation of manna.

targa /ˈtɑːgə/ *adjective & noun.* **L20.**
[Italian = plate, shield. A model of Porsche motor car (introduced in 1965) with a detachable hood (see below), prob. after the *Targa Florio* (= Florio Shield), a motor time-trial held annually in Sicily.]
▶ **A** *adjective.* Designating a type of detachable roof hood or panelling on a convertible sports car, *esp.* one which when removed leaves a central roll-bar for passenger safety. **L20.**
▶ **B** *noun.* A car having this feature. **L20.**

targe /tɑːdʒ/ *noun.* Now *arch. & poet.*
[Old English *targa*, *targe* corresp. to Old Norse *targa* shield, Old High German *zarga*, Middle & mod. High German *zarge* edging, border, reinforced in Middle English from Old French.]
A shield; *spec.* a light shield or buckler, carried esp. by foot-soldiers and archers.

targe /tɑːdʒ/ *verb trans. Scot.* **L18.**
[Origin unkn.]
1 Question closely, cross-examine. **L18.**
2 Keep in strict order, watch over strictly. **E19.**
3 Reprimand, scold loudly; beat, thrash. **E19.**
■ **targer** *noun* a person who targes someone; *esp.* a scold: **E19.**

target /ˈtɑːgɪt/ *noun.* **LME.**
[Dim. of TARGE *noun*: see -ET[1].]
1 A light round shield or buckler; a small targe. *arch.* **LME.**
2 A thing resembling a shield in shape; *spec.* †(***a***) *Scot.* an ornament of precious metal, often jewelled, worn esp. in a head-dress; (***b***) a joint of lamb comprising the neck and breast; the fore-quarter without the shoulder; (***c***) *US* a disc-shaped indicating device on a railway track switch, actuated mechanically to indicate the switch's position. **E16.**
3 A circular or rectangular object, marked with concentric circles, fired or aimed at for shooting practice. Also, any object, person, or point, fired or aimed at (*lit. & fig.*); a place or object selected for military attack; the part of the body at which a boxer's or fencer's attack is directed. **M18.** ▸**b** A person who or thing which becomes the object of general abuse, criticism, scorn, etc. **M18.** ▸**c** A shooting match; the score made at such a match. Now *rare.* **E19.** ▸**d** PHYSICS. The object or material at which a beam of particles is directed, as in a cathode-ray tube or particle accelerator. **E20.** ▸**e** BIOLOGY & MEDICINE. A region in a cell or tissue which is especially sensitive to radiation. **M20.** ▸**f** An objective, *esp.* a minimum amount set in fund-raising; a result aimed at; something to be attained; a goal which one strives to achieve. **M20.** ▸**g** A person who is the object of a security or espionage operation, *esp.* one kept under surveillance as a suspected spy. Orig. *US.* **M20.**

> 📖 **3** R. V. JONES I had never shot a fox, a difficult target for a pistol. S. RADLEY A collection like this makes your house an obvious target for burglars. *New Scientist* A tiny missile . . that carries its own radar system to home in on a target. **b** E. SEGAL The targets of their wit were actually sitting in the theater as they were insulted. **f** R. BERTHOUD Henry had set himself a target of thirty sculptures a year. ***on target***: see ON *preposition*.

Attrib. & comb.: In the senses 'of or pertaining to shooting or shooting practice', as ***target pistol***, ***target-practice***, ***target-range***, ***target-rifle***, etc., 'designating an object of attack', as ***target area***, ***target-ship***, etc., 'designating a particular group at which a publication, advertising, propaganda, etc., is aimed', as ***target audience***, ***target group***, ***target population***, etc., 'by which a desired goal is specified', as ***target date***, ***target figure***, ***target output***, ***target price***, etc. Special combs., as **target cell** BIOLOGY & MEDICINE an abnormal form of red blood cell which appears as a dark ring surrounding a dark central spot, typical of certain kinds of anaemia; **target dialect** the variety of a language learned as a second dialect; **target indicator** an object, as a flare, dropped in order to illuminate or delimit a target for aerial bombing; **target language** (***a***) the language into which a text etc. is translated; (***b***) a foreign language which a person intends to learn or acquire; **target man** †(***a***) a man armed with a target or shield; (***b***) *US* a signal-man who operates signalling targets on a railway track; (***c***) (FOOTBALL & HOCKEY etc.) a forward used in central positions to whom other players direct long passes, (in football usu. to the forward's head); **target organ** BIOLOGY an organ which responds to a particular hormone or hormones; **target pin** ARCHERY a mark on a bow used like the sight on a gun; **target program** COMPUTING = ***object program*** s.v. OBJECT *noun*; **target-rich** *adjective* (MILITARY, orig. & chiefly *US*) having many sites regarded as potential targets for military or terrorist attack; **target theory** BIOLOGY & MEDICINE the theory proposing the existence of targets (sense 3e above); **target tissue** BIOLOGY a tissue which responds to a particular hormone or hormones; **target-tug** an aircraft for towing targets used in aerial shooting practice.

target /ˈtɑːgɪt/ *verb.* **E17.**
[from prec.]
†**1** *verb trans.* Protect (as) with a light round shield or buckler; shield. Only in **17.**
2 *verb trans.* Use (a person or thing) as a target; *spec.* (***a***) make (a person) the object of abuse, scorn, ridicule, etc.; (***b***) select or identify (a person, organization, etc.) as an object of attack, attention, etc.; (***c***) aim (esp.) a missile or nuclear weapon at (a place). **M19.**
3 *verb trans.* Signal the position of (a railway track switch etc.) by means of a target or indicating device. *US.* **L19.**
4 *verb trans.* Plan or schedule (something) to attain a desired goal or objective, esp. a financial one. **M20.**
5 *verb trans.* Aim (esp. a missile or nuclear weapon) at a place. Freq. foll. by *on*. **M20.**
6 *verb intrans.* Aim for a particular objective or result. Usu. foll. by *for*. **M20.**

7 *verb trans.* Aim so as to follow a designated course or fulfil a specific function or need (freq. foll. by *to do*); aim *at* a particular market. L20.

> 🕮 **2** S. Brill The airline industry was being targeted for a recruiting drive. *Bulletin (Sydney)* The IRA has generally targeted prominent political or military figures. *Times Educ. Suppl.* Streamlining programmes to target specific audiences. **4** *Daily Telegraph* Investment income . . is targeted to reach £1 million in two years. **5** *Observer* Enough warheads to target some on China as well. **7** *Marketing Week* The product . . has been targeted at the 18–24-year-old female drinker.

■ **targetable** *adjective* (*a*) (of a nuclear missile etc.) able to be aimed at a target; (*b*) (of a military installation, military equipment, etc.) that may be selected or identified as a target: M20.

targeted /ˈtɑːgɪtɪd/ *adjective.* M17.
[from TARGET *noun, verb*: see -ED², -ED¹.]
1 Provided with or having a light round shield or buckler, or with something resembling one. Long *rare*. M17.
2 Selected or identified as a target. M20.
3 Aimed, directed; given a target. M20.

> 🕮 **2** *Bookseller* You're guaranteed a large targeted audience of decision makers. *Broadcast* Molinare's targeted turnover for 1985 . . will . . be in the region of £8 million. **3** *Guardian* The development of new targeted degrees.

targeteer /tɑːgɪˈtɪə/ *noun. obsolete* exc. *Hist.* L16.
[Prob. from Italian *targhettiere*, from *targhetta* target: see -EER.]
A foot-soldier armed with a light round shield or buckler.

targetry /ˈtɑːgɪtri/ *noun.* L20.
[from TARGET *noun* + -RY.]
The practice of establishing or aiming at (esp. economic) targets. Freq. with specifying word.
monetary targetry etc.

Targui /tɑːˈgiː/ *noun.* E19.
[from Tamashek masc. sing. of TUAREG *noun.*]
A man of the Tuareg people.

Targum /ˈtɑːgəm, tɑːˈguːm/ *noun.* Pl. **-s**, **-im** /-ɪm/. Also **t-**. L16.
[(Hebrew from) Aramaic *targūm* interpretation, from *targēm* interpret: see DRAGOMAN. Cf. TRUCHMAN.]
Any of various ancient Aramaic translations, interpretations, or paraphrases of the Hebrew Scriptures, at first preserved by oral transmission, and committed to writing from about AD 100 onwards.
■ **Tarˈgumic** *adjective* of or pertaining to the Targums L19. **Targumist** *noun* (*a*) any of the translators and commentators who compiled the Targums; (*b*) an expert in the language and literature of the Targums: M17. **Targumize** *verb trans.* (*rare*) make a Targum of or on L17.

tariff /ˈtarɪf/ *noun & verb.* L16.
[French *tarif* from Italian *tariffa* from Turkish *tarife* from Arab. *taʿrīfa* from *ʿarrafa* notify, apprise.]
▶ **A** *noun.* †**1** An arithmetical table or statement; a table of multiplication, a ready reckoner, etc. L16–L18.
2 An official list or schedule giving the customs duties to be levied on particular classes of imports or exports; an item on such a list; the duty levied on an article or class of articles. Also, the complete system of such duties as established in any country. L16.
3 A table or scale of fixed charges made by a private or public business, as a list of prices for a hotel, a schedule of rates payable for a public utility, etc. Also, standard charges agreed between insurers etc. M18.
4 LAW. A scale of sentences and damages for crimes and injuries of different severities. L20.

> 🕮 **2** M. E. G. Duff The adoption of a free-trade tariff. *Car & Driver* The nasty import tariff that's levied on two-door sport-utility vehicles. attrib.: ***tariff barrier***, ***tariff duty***, ***tariff-treaty***, ***tariff war***, etc. **3** *Times* British Gas gave an undertaking not to increase domestic tariffs for 12 months. R. Hayman A cabdriver . . demanded three lire but refused to show them the tariff.

Comb.: **tariff-reform** (*a*) *gen.* the reform of a tariff, or of existing tariff conditions; (*b*) *Hist.* in the US, a reform in favour of reducing import duties, and generally moving away from protectionism; in Britain in the early 20th cent., a reform in favour of the extension of tariffs on imports, as opp. to free trade; **tariff-reformer** an advocate or supporter of tariff-reform; **tariff wall** a national trade barrier in the form of a tariff.
▶ **B** *verb.* †**1** *verb intrans.* Set tariffs, deal with tariffs. *rare*. Only in M18.
2 *verb trans.* Subject (goods) to a tariff or duty; fix the price of (something) according to a tariff. E19.

> 🕮 **2** *Westminster Review* The best Gascony wine . . tariffed in London . . at £13 the tun.

■ **tariffable** *adjective* able to be subjected to a tariff L19.

tariqa /taˈriːkə/ *noun.* E19.
[Arab. *ṭarīqa* manner, way, creed.]
The Sufi way or path of spiritual learning; Sufi doctrine.

tarkashi /tɑːˈkaʃiː/ *noun.* L19.
[Urdu & Persian *tār-kaśī* lit. 'wire-drawing'.]
Esp. in the Indian subcontinent: the craft of inlaying wood with brass wire; the artefacts so produced.

tarlatan /ˈtɑːlət(ə)n/ *noun & adjective.* E18.
[French *tarlatane*, dissimilated form of *tarnatane*, prob. of Indian origin.]
▶ **A** *noun.* A thin stiff open-weave muslin, used esp. for ball-dresses. Also, a dress made of this fabric. E18.
▶ **B** *attrib.* or as *adjective.* Made of tarlatan. M19.

> 🕮 R. West She wore . . full tarlatan skirts.

Tarmac /ˈtɑːmak/ *noun & verb.* Also (esp. as verb) **t-**. E20.
[Abbreviation.]
▶ **A** *noun.* (Proprietary name for) a kind of tarmacadam consisting of iron slag bound with tar and creosote; a surface made of tarmacadam. E20.
the Tarmac *colloq.* the runway at an airport etc.
▶ **B** *verb.* Infl. **-ck-**. Cover with tarmacadam; apply tarmacadam to. Freq. as ***tarmacked*** *ppl adjective.* M20.

tarmacadam /tɑːməˈkadəm/ *noun & verb.* L19.
[from TAR *noun*¹ + MACADAM.]
▶ **A** *noun.* A material for surfacing roads, consisting of broken stone or ironstone slag bound with tar alone, or of tar mixed with pitch or creosote. L19.
▶ **B** *verb trans.* Cover with tarmacadam, apply tarmacadam to. Chiefly as ***tarmacadamed*** *ppl adjective.* E20.

†**tarmaret** *noun* see TURMERIC.

tarn /tɑːn/ *noun.* Orig. *north.* ME.
[Old Norse *tjǫrn*, Swedish dial. *tjärn*, *tärn*, Norwegian *tjörn*, Danish *tjern*.]
A small mountain lake.

tarnal /ˈtɑːn(ə)l/ *adjective & adverb. slang* (chiefly *US*). L18.
[Aphet. dial. pronunc. of ETERNAL, DAMNATION: see next.]
Damned, infernal: used as an intensive expr. annoyance or contempt.

tarnation /tɑːˈneɪʃ(ə)n/ *noun, adjective, & adverb. slang* (chiefly *US*). L18.
[Alt. of DARNATION, DAMNATION: app. assoc. with prec.]
▶ **A** *noun.* = DAMNATION *noun* 3. L18.
▶ **B** *adjective.* Damned, damnable, infernal, execrable. L18.
▶ **C** *adverb.* Damnably, infernally, execrably. L18.

tarnhelm /ˈtɑːnhɛlm/ *noun.* L19.
[German, from *tarn-* stem of *tarnen* conceal + *Helm* HELM *noun*¹.]
In Wagner's opera *Der Ring des Nibelungen* (1853–74), a magic helmet ensuring the wearer's invisibility or enabling a change of appearance at will.

tarnish /ˈtɑːnɪʃ/ *verb & noun.* LME.
[French *terniss-* lengthened stem of *ternir*, from *terne* dark, dull: see -ISH². Cf. DERN *adjective*².]
▶ **A** *verb.* **1** *verb intrans.* Become dull, dim, or discoloured; (*esp.* of metal) lose lustre by surface oxidation etc. LME. ▸**b** *fig.* Esp. of a person's honour or reputation: become impaired, tainted, or sullied. L17.
2 *verb trans.* Dull or dim the lustre of, discolour. L16. ▸**b** *fig.* Impair, sully, or cast a slur on (esp. a person's honour or reputation). L17.

> 🕮 **1** T. H. Huxley Many metals rapidly . . tarnish when exposed to even the driest air. **b** Dryden Till thy fresh glories, which now shine so bright . . tarnish with our daily sight. **2** *New Scientist* Enough hydrogen sulphide gas to discolour housepaint and tarnish silverware. **b** *Independent* Football is our national game . . . Its image . . has been much tarnished.

Phrases: **tarnished plant-bug** either of two brownish mirid bugs, ***Lygus lineolaris*** (in N. America) and *L. rugulipennis* (in Europe), which are pests of numerous fruits, vegetables, and other crops.
▶ **B** *noun.* The fact of tarnishing or condition of being tarnished; loss of lustre, discoloration. Also, a stain, a blemish; a coating or film formed on an exposed surface of a mineral or metal. E18.

> 🕮 Dickens Effacing the old rust and tarnish on the money.

■ **tarnishable** *adjective* L19.

tarnowitzite /ˈtɑːnəvɪtsʌɪt/ *noun.* M19.
[from *Tarnowitz*, a town in Silesia (now Tarnowskie Góry, Poland) + -ITE¹.]
MINERALOGY. A variety of aragonite containing lead.

taro /ˈtɑːrəʊ, ˈtarəʊ/ *noun.* Pl. **-os**. M18.
[Polynesian name.]
A food-plant, *Colocasia esculenta*, of the arum family, cultivated in many varieties in the tropics for its starchy tubers or its succulent leaves. Cf. DASHEEN, EDDO.

taroc *noun* var. of TAROCK.

tarocchino /tarəˈkiːnəʊ/ *noun.* M19.
[Italian, from *tarocchi* (see next) + dim. suffix *-ino*.]
A modified form of tarot, played with a reduced number of cards. Also (*rare*) = TAROCCO 2.

tarocco /taˈrɒkəʊ/ *noun.* Pl. **-cchi** /-ki/. M18.
[Italian, of unkn. origin.]
Hist. **1** A tarot card. M18.
2 *sing.* & in *pl.* (treated as *sing.*). A card-game, usu. for 3 or 4 players, played with a traditional 78-card tarot pack. E19.

tarock /ˈtarək/ *noun.* Also **taroc**. E17.
[Italian *tarocchi* pl. of TAROCCO.]
1 A tarot card. *rare*. E17.
2 A card-game, usu. for 3 players and popular in Austria, Hungary, and Germany, played with a mixed pack of 54 cards, 32 of which are standard cards and 22 tarot cards. M18.

tarogato /ˈtarogato/ *noun.* Pl. **-os**. E20.
[Hungarian *tárogató*.]
A Hungarian woodwind instrument, with a conical bore, orig. a shawm, but later reconstructed with a single reed and fitted with keys and resembling a soprano saxophone, now a historical national instrument.

tarot /ˈtarəʊ/ *noun.* L16.
[French, formed as TAROCK.]
1 *sing.* & in *pl.* Any of various games played with a pack of tarot cards (see sense 2); *spec.* (*a*) = TAROCK 2; (*b*) = TAROCCO 2. L16.
2 Any of a pack of 78 playing-cards having five suits, the last of which is a set of permanent trumps, first used in Italy in the 15th cent. and now also used for fortune-telling. Also, any of the trump cards in such a pack. Also ***tarot card***. L19.

tarp /tɑːp/ *noun & verb. N. Amer. & Austral. colloq.* E20.
[Abbreviation.]
▶ **A** *noun.* (A) tarpaulin. E20.
▶ **B** *verb trans.* Cover with a tarpaulin. L20.

tarpan /ˈtɑːpan/ *noun.* M19.
[Kirghiz.]
ZOOLOGY. A greyish wild horse of eastern Europe and western Asia, extinct since 1919.

†**tarpaulian** *noun & adjective. rare.* M17.
[from next: see -IAN.]
▶ **A** *noun.* A sailor; = TARPAULIN *noun* 2a. M–L17.
▶ **B** *adjective.* Of or pertaining to a sailor or sailors; = TARPAULIN *adjective* 2. Only in E18.

tarpaulin /tɑːˈpɔːlɪn/ *noun, adjective, & verb.* E17.
[Prob. from TAR *noun*¹ + PALL *noun*¹ + -ING¹.]
▶ **A** *noun.* **1 a** A waterproof protective covering or sheet of heavy-duty treated cloth, esp. tarred canvas. Also, canvas or other cloth so tarred; other waterproofed protective cloth. E17. ▸**b** A sailor's tarred or oilskin hat. M19.
2 a *transf.* (A nickname for) a sailor, esp. an ordinary sailor. Now *arch. rare*. M17. ▸**b** *Hist.* A superior naval officer (captain etc.) as opp. to a military officer appointed to command a man-of-war. *rare*. L17.

> 🕮 **1a** M. Dibdin At the side of the house . . stood a large skip covered with a tarpaulin.

Comb.: **tarpaulin muster** (*a*) a collection or pooling of money among sailors; (*b*) *Austral.* a pooling of clothes, funds, etc. for common use.
▶ **B** *attrib.* or as *adjective.* **1** Made of tarpaulin. E17.
2 Of or pertaining to a sailor or sailors. Now *arch. rare*. M17.
▶ **C** *verb trans.* Cover with a tarpaulin. L19.

> 🕮 F. Anstey Some tarpaulined cattle-vans.

Tarpeian /tɑːˈpiːən/ *adjective.* E17.
[from Latin *Tarpeia*, legendary daughter of the commander of the citadel, which she betrayed to the Sabines, and who was said to be buried at the foot of the rock: see -IAN.]
ROMAN HISTORY. Designating a cliff on the Capitoline Hill in ancient Rome over which convicted traitors were hurled. Chiefly in ***Tarpeian rock***.

tarpon /ˈtɑːpɒn/ *noun.* L17.
[Prob. from Dutch *tarpoen*, perh. ult. from a Central American language.]
A large silvery game-fish with a bluish back, *Tarpon atlanticus*, of the tropical Atlantic. Also, a similar Indo-Pacific fish, *Megalops cyprinoides*.

Tarquinian /tɑːˈkwɪnɪən/ *adjective.* E17.
[from Latin *Tarquinius* (see below) + -AN.]
Of or pertaining to either of two semi-legendary kings of ancient Rome, Tarquinius Priscus (616–578 BC) and Tarquinius Superbus (534–510 BC), or the dynasty to which these kings belonged.

tarradiddle *noun & verb* var. of TARADIDDLE.

tarragon /ˈtarəg(ə)n/ *noun.* M16.
[Repr. medieval Latin *tragonia* and *tarchon*, perh. an Arab. deformation (*tarḵūn* through Persian *tarḵūn*) of Greek *drakōn* (assoc. with *drakontion* dragonwort).]
A kind of wormwood, *Artemisia dracunculus*, native to Russia and eastern Europe and grown as a herb; the aro-

matic leaves of this plant as used to flavour salads, soups, etc.
Comb.: **tarragon vinegar**: made by steeping the young shoots and leaves of tarragon in wine vinegar.

Tarragona /tarəˈɡəʊnə/ *noun.* L19.
[A town and province in NE Spain.]
Any of various sweet fortified red or white wines produced in the Tarragona region. Also ***Tarragona wine***.

tarras /ˈtarəs/ *noun.* E17.
[Dutch †*tarasse*, †*terras*, †*tiras* (now *tras*), ult. from Proto-Romance from Latin *terra* earth. Cf. TERRACE *noun*.]
A light-coloured tuff used esp. for making cement and mortar. Also called ***trass***.

†tarras *verb trans.* L15–E19.
[Orig. prob. from French *terracer*, *terrasser*, formed as TERRACE *noun*; later app. from prec.]
Cover or coat with plaster or (later) tarras.

tarriance /ˈtarɪəns/ *noun. arch.* LME.
[from TARRY *verb* + -ANCE.]
1 The action of tarrying; delay, procrastination. LME.
2 Temporary residence or sojourn in a place. Formerly also, waiting in expectation or *for* someone or something. M16.
> **1** T. HARDY Worn with tarriance I care for life no more. **2** T. HODGKIN During this tarriance at Rome . . Theodoric commenced . . draining the Pontine Marshes.

tarrier /ˈtarɪə/ *noun*[1]. *arch.* LME.
[from TARRY *verb* + -ER[1].]
1 A person who tarries or delays; a lingerer, a procrastinator. LME.
†2 A person who or thing which delays someone; a hinderer, a hindrance. *rare.* M16–E17.

tarrier /ˈtarɪə/ *noun*[2]. LME.
[Old French *tarere* (mod. *tarière*) from late Latin *taratrum*. Cf. Irish *tarathar*.]
Orig., a boring tool, an auger. Now, a tool for extracting a bung from a barrel.

tarrock /ˈtarək/ *noun.* Chiefly *Scot.* & *dial.* L17.
[Origin unkn.]
Any of various sea birds, *esp.* (in various localities) an Arctic tern, a kittiwake, a young common gull, a guillemot.

tarrow /ˈtarəʊ/ *verb intrans. Scot.* LME.
[App. by-form of TARRY *verb*. Cf. *harrow*, *harry*.]
Delay, hesitate, show reluctance.

tarry /ˈtari/ *noun.* LME.
[from TARRY *verb*.]
†1 The action of tarrying; delay, tarriance. LME–L18.
2 Temporary residence; a sojourn, a stay. Now chiefly *US*. LME.

tarry /ˈtɑːri/ *adjective.* LME.
[from TAR *noun*[1] + -Y[1].]
1 Consisting or composed of tar; resembling tar in taste, consistency, colour, etc. LME.
2 Covered, coated, or impregnated with tar; looking as if smeared with tar. L16.
> **1** M. MACHLIN Oil stays on the surface of the water long enough to get tarry. S. HOOD The headmaster sipped his thick tarry tea. **2** DICKENS Two or three tarry boys.

Comb.: **tarry-breeks** (orig. *Scot.*) (a nickname for) a sailor.
■ **tarriness** *noun* L19.

tarry /ˈtari/ *verb.* Now chiefly *arch.* & *literary.* ME.
[Origin uncertain: in earliest use identical in form with TAR *verb*[1] and Old French *tarier*, but the sense is against identity. Cf. TARROW.]
†1 *verb trans.* Delay, retard, defer (a thing, an action); protract, prolong. ME–L16.
†2 *verb trans.* Detain, keep back (a person or agent) for a time; keep waiting or in check; impede, hinder. ME–E17.
3 *verb intrans.* Delay or be tardy in beginning or doing anything, defer coming or going; wait before doing something, or in expectation of a person or event, or until something is done (freq. foll. by *till*, *for*, *to do*). ME.
4 *verb intrans.* Remain or reside temporarily, sojourn; stay (in a place). Also, remain or continue in a specified state or condition. Freq. foll. by *in*. ME.
5 *verb trans.* Wait for or in expectation of; expect. ME.
> **1** T. STOCKER Whiche Citie not meanyng to tarrie the siege. **2** A. GOLDING So many stops tary us and stay us back. **3** E. PEACOCK They had not long to tarry for the coming of their host. I. WALLACE He . . escaped . . to find Beecher, the valet, patiently tarrying in the hall. **4** J. BUCHAN Some Icelander who has tarried too long in Scotland. J. BALDWIN His mother required . . that he tarry no longer in sin. **5** H. H. MILMAN The Lord Mayor tarried the sermon, which lasted into the night.

■ **tarrying** *verbal noun* (*a*) the action of the verb; (*b*) *US HISTORY* a local courtship custom in which a couple lie with each other fully clothed in a blanket and talk and kiss: ME.

tarryhoot /tarɪˈhuːt/ *verb intrans.* Chiefly *US dial.* M20.
[Origin unkn.]
Go about with much noise and fuss; gallivant *around*. Chiefly as ***tarryhooting*** *verbal noun & ppl adjective.*

†tarrying-iron *noun* var. of TIRING-IRON.

tars /tɑːz/ *noun. obsolete* exc. *Hist.* Also **tarse**. ME.
[Old French *tarse*, medieval Latin (*pannus*) *Tarsicus* (cloth) of *Tarsus*: formerly held to be Tarsus in Cilicia, but prob. referring to Tarsia or Tharsia, app. Turkestan.]
A rich and expensive fabric of Oriental origin, used in 14th- and 15th-cent. Europe. Also ***cloth of tars***.

tars- *combining form* see TARSO-.

tarsal /ˈtɑːs(ə)l/ *adjective & noun.* E19.
[from TARSUS + -AL[1].]
▶ **A** *adjective.* **1** *ANATOMY* & *ZOOLOGY.* Of or pertaining to the tarsus of the ankle or foot. E19.
2 *ANATOMY.* Of or pertaining to the tarsi of the eyelids. M19.
▶ **B** *noun.* A tarsal bone, joint, etc. L19.

†tarse *noun*[1]. OE–M18.
[Old English *teors* = Old High German, Middle High German *zërs*, Middle Dutch *teers*, *teres*.]
The penis.

tarse *noun*[2] var. of TARS.

tar-seal /ˈtɑːsiːl/ *verb & noun. Austral.* & *NZ.* E20.
[from TAR *noun*[1] + SEAL *verb*[1].]
▶ **A** *verb trans.* Surface (a road etc.) with tarmacadam or tar. Chiefly as ***tar-sealed*** *ppl adjective.* E20.
▶ **B** *noun.* A road surface made with tarmacadam or tar; a road so surfaced. M20.

tarsi *noun* pl. of TARSUS.

tarsia /ˈtɑːsɪə/ *noun.* L17.
[Italian.]
= INTARSIA.

Tarsian /ˈtɑːsɪən/ *adjective & noun.* L19.
[from *Tarsus* (see below) + -IAN.]
▶ **A** *adjective.* Of or pertaining to Tarsus, a city in southern Turkey on the River Tarsus, the birthplace of St Paul. L19.
▶ **B** *noun.* A native or inhabitant of Tarsus. E20.

tarsier /ˈtɑːsɪə/ *noun.* L18.
[French, from *tarse* TARSUS (with ref. to the animal's long tarsal bones).]
ZOOLOGY. Any of several small arboreal nocturnal primates constituting the genus *Tarsius* and family Tarsiidae, of Sumatra, Borneo, Sulawesi, and the Philippines, having large eyes and feeding on insects and small vertebrates.

tarsioid /ˈtɑːsɪɔɪd/ *noun & adjective.* E20.
[from prec. + -OID.]
ZOOLOGY & *PALAEONTOLOGY.* ▶**A** *noun.* A primate, esp. a fossil, belonging to the group of which tarsiers are the living representatives. E20.
▶ **B** *adjective.* Resembling a tarsier; related to the tarsiers. E20.

tarsitis /tɑːˈsʌɪtɪs/ *noun.* L19.
[from TARSUS + -ITIS.]
MEDICINE. Inflammation of (the tarsus of) the eyelid.

Tarskian /ˈtɑːskɪən/ *adjective.* M20.
[from Alfred *Tarski* (1902–83), Polish-born US mathematician: see -IAN.]
PHILOSOPHY & *MATH.* Of or pertaining to Tarski or his work in semantics; *spec.* pertaining to or involving his formal definition of truth.

tarso- /ˈtɑːsəʊ/ *combining form.* Before a vowel also **tars-**.
[from TARSUS: see -O-.]
ANATOMY, *ZOOLOGY*, & *MEDICINE.* **1** Of, pertaining to, or connected with the tarsus (ankle or foot).
2 Of or pertaining to the tarsi of the eyelids.
■ **tarˈsalgia** *noun* pain in the tarsal region of the foot L19. **tarˈsectomy** *noun* (*a*) (an instance of) excision of one or more of the tarsal bones; (*b*) (an instance of) excision of a section of the tarsus of the eyelid: L19. **tarsoplasty** *noun* = BLEPHAROPLASTY L19. **tarsorrhaphy** *noun* [Greek *rhaphē* seam] temporary suturing of the eyelids to protect the cornea or to allow healing M19. **tarˈsotomy** *noun* (an instance of) cutting or removal of tarsal cartilage M19.

tarsometatarsal /ˌtɑːsəʊmɛtəˈtɑːs(ə)l/ *adjective & noun.* M19.
[from TARSO- + METATARSAL.]
ANATOMY & *ZOOLOGY.* ▶**A** *adjective.* Of, pertaining to, or connecting the tarsus and the metatarsus. Also, of or pertaining to a tarsometatarsus. M19.
▶ **B** *noun.* A tarsometatarsal bone, ligament, etc. M19.

tarsometatarsus /ˌtɑːsəʊmɛtəˈtɑːsəs/ *noun.* Pl. **-tarsi** /-ˈtɑːsʌɪ, -siː/. M19.
[from TARSO- + METATARSUS.]
ZOOLOGY. A long bone in the lower leg of birds and some reptiles, formed by fusion of tarsal and metatarsal structures.

tarsonemid /tɑːsəˈniːmɪd/ *adjective & noun.* E20.
[mod. Latin *Tarsonemidae* (see below), from *Tarsonemus* genus name, from TARSO- + Greek *nēma* thread: see -ID[3].]
▶ **A** *adjective.* Of, pertaining to, or designating the family Tarsonemidae of mites, which includes several important pests. E20.
▶ **B** *noun.* A mite of this family. M20.

tarsus /ˈtɑːsəs/ *noun.* Pl. **-si** /-sʌɪ, -siː/. LME.
[mod. Latin from Greek *tarsos* the flat part of the foot, the eyelid.]
1 *ANATOMY.* The skeleton of the posterior part of the foot, consisting of seven small bones arranged in two transverse series, including the talus or ankle-bone; *ZOOLOGY* the corresponding part in other tetrapod animals; (the part of the leg including) the tarsometatarsus of a bird or reptile. LME. ▸**b** *ZOOLOGY.* In insects and other arthropods, a series of small limb-segments forming the foot and articulating with the tibia. E19.
2 *ANATOMY.* The thin sheet of fibrous connective tissue which supports the edge of each eyelid. L17.

tart /tɑːt/ *noun*[1]. LME.
[Old French *tarte* = medieval Latin *tarta*, of uncertain origin.]
Orig., a baked dish consisting of a pastry crust containing and covering a filling such as meat, fish, cheese, etc.; a pie. Now *esp.*, (*a*) an open pastry case with a sweet or savoury filling; a quiche; (*b*) a pie with a fruit or sweet filling.
> R. GODDEN French strawberry tarts which we ate . . in a patisserie.

tart /tɑːt/ *noun*[2]. *slang.* M19.
[Prob. abbreviation of SWEETHEART *noun*.]
1 (Orig. a term of endearment for) a girl or woman (now chiefly *derog.*); *Austral.* & *NZ* a wife, a girlfriend. M19.
2 A prostitute; a promiscuous woman. L19.
3 A young favourite of an older boy or man (not necessarily a catamite). Also, a male prostitute. M20.
> **2** *Stage* The play is set in the . . apartment of a high class tart with some . . classy clients.

■ **tartish** *adjective*[1] (*colloq.*) tarty; showy or flashy in dress, manner, etc.: E20.

tart /tɑːt/ *adjective.* OE.
[Origin unkn. Cf. TEART.]
†1 Of pain, suffering, discipline, etc.: sharp, severe, grievous. OE–E17.
2 Sharp, sour, or acid in taste. Formerly also, biting, pungent. LME.
†3 Esp. of an edge, point, or weapon: keen, sharp. L15–E17.
4 *fig.* Of words, speech, a speaker: sharp or bitter in tone; cutting, caustic. E17.
> **1** SHAKES. *Lear* Another way The news is not so tart. **2** J. COX Ripe blackcurrants . . taste both sweet and tart. **4** LD MACAULAY Ill humour . . might . . impel him to give a tart answer.

¶ Sense 1 not recorded between OE and L16.
■ **tartish** *adjective*[2] somewhat tart, slightly sour or acid E18. **tartly** *adverb* in a tart manner; sharply; with sharpness of tone: OE. **tartness** *noun* OE.

tart /tɑːt/ *verb. colloq.* M20.
[from TART *noun*[2].]
1 *verb trans.* & *refl.* Foll. by *up*: dress or make (oneself, a person) up, esp. in a showy, provocative, or gaudy manner; *fig.* decorate or refurbish (a building etc.) in a gaudy, showy, or flashy way. M20.
2 *verb intrans.* **a** Be a womanizer; chase women. M20. ▸**b** (Esp. of a girl or woman) act like a tart or prostitute; behave promiscuously or provocatively; (of a person) behave in a showy or flashy manner, show off. Freq. foll. by (*a*)*round*, *about*. M20.
> **1** B. PYM Tarted-up seventeenth-century cottage with modern additions. A. LURIE She'd be damned if she was going to tart herself up to go to a . . restaurant. **2b** D. LESSING Kate . . tarting around the room in one of Georgie's dresses.

tartan /ˈtɑːt(ə)n/ *noun*[1] & *adjective.* Orig. *Scot.* L15.
[Perh. from Old French *tertaine* var. of TIRETAINE; perh. also infl. by TARTARIN *noun*.]
▶ **A** *noun.* **1 a** A kind of woollen cloth woven in stripes of various colours crossing at right angles so as to form a regular pattern and worn esp. by the Scottish Highlanders, each clan having a distinctive pattern. Also, a chequered pattern like that of tartan cloth, a tartan pattern on other fabric etc. Freq. with specifying word indicating (a pattern traditionally associated with) a particular clan. L15. ▸**b** *transf.* A person wearing tartan; a Highlander, a Scot; wearers of tartan collectively, the men of a Highland regiment. E19. ▸**c** A member of a Protestant youth gang in Northern Ireland, traditionally supporters of Glasgow Rangers Football Club. L20.
2 *ANGLING.* An artificial salmon-fly. M19.
3 (**T-**.) (Proprietary name for) a synthetic resin material used for surfacing running tracks, ramps, etc. M20.
> **1a** ***Balmoral tartan***, ***Frazer tartan***, ***Stewart tartan***, etc.

▶ **B** *adjective.* **1** Made of tartan cloth; having a chequered pattern like that of tartan. M16.
2 *transf.* & *fig.* Designating something pertaining to Scotland or the Scottish, or evoking Scottish national fervour. M20.

📖 1 W. TREVOR Lavinia was wearing a tartan skirt. 2 EDMUND WARD I'm no threat to your dreams of a tartan sunrise. **tartan tax** *colloq.* tax levied by a Scottish assembly after devolution, esp. when causing Scottish taxpayers to pay more than their English counterparts.

■ **tartanry** *noun* tartan things collectively, esp. worn or displayed as a mark of Scottish national fervour; Scottishness; Scottishry: L20.

tartan /ˈtɑːt(ə)n/ *noun*². Also **tartane**. E17.
[French *tartane* from Italian *tartana*, perh. ult. from Arab. *tarīda*. Cf. TARTANA *noun*¹.]
A small single-masted vessel with a large lateen sail and a foresail used in the Mediterranean.

tartan /ˈtɑːt(ə)n/ *verb trans.* E19.
[from TARTAN *noun*¹.]
Clothe or dress in tartan. Freq. as **tartaned** *ppl adjective.*

tartana /tɑːˈtɑːnə/ *noun*¹. L16.
[Italian: see TARTAN *noun*².]
= TARTAN *noun*².

tartana /tɑːˈtɑːnə/ *noun*². E19.
[Spanish.]
Chiefly *Hist.* A covered light carriage used in Spain, esp. in Valencia.

tartane *noun* var. of TARTAN *noun*².

tartar /ˈtɑːtə/ *noun*¹. LME.
[medieval Latin *tartarum* from medieval Greek *tartaron*, of unkn. origin.]
1 Potassium bitartrate (potassium hydrogen tartrate), a white crystalline substance present in grape juice and deposited in an impure reddish-brown form during the fermentation of wine. Also called ***argol***. LME. **2** A calcareous or other hard concretion or crust deposited by a liquid. Now *spec.* the hard calcified deposit or calculus which forms on the surface of the teeth. E17.
Phrases & comb.: ***cream of tartar***: see CREAM *noun*². †**oil of tartar** a saturated solution of potassium carbonate; **salt of tartar** (*obsolete* exc. *Hist.*) potassium carbonate. **tartar emetic** antimony potassium tartrate, a toxic compound used as a mordant and insecticide, and in medicine (though not now as an emetic). ***vitriolated tartar***: see VITRIOLATED 2.

Tartar /ˈtɑːtə/ *noun*² & *adjective*. LME.
[Old & mod. French *Tartare* or medieval Latin *Tartarus* (infl. by Latin TARTARUS), formed as TATAR (now the preferred ethnological term). Cf. TARTARE.]
▶ **A** *noun.* **1** Orig., a member of the combined forces of central Asian peoples, including Mongols and Turks, who under the leadership of Genghis Khan (1202–27) overran much of Asia and eastern Europe and later established a far-reaching and powerful empire in central Europe. Now = TATAR *noun* 1. LME. **2** †**a** A strolling vagabond, a thief, a beggar. *slang.* L16–L17. ▶**b** A person supposed to resemble a Tartar in disposition; a rough, violent-tempered, or irritable and intractable person. L16. **3** The language of the Tartars; = TATAR *noun* 2. M17.

📖 **2b** T. KENEALLY He got a bloody tartar for a wife.

Phrases: **catch a Tartar** encounter or get hold of a person who can neither be controlled nor got rid of; meet with a person who is unexpectedly more than one's match.
▶ **B** *adjective.* **1** Of or pertaining to the Tartars, their language, or the former land of Tartary. M18. **2** *fig.* Rough; violent-tempered; intractable. E19.
1 tartar sauce a sauce made of mayonnaise and chopped gherkins, capers, etc., usu. served with fish (cf. TARTARE ***sauce***, ***sauce*** TARTARE).
■ **Tartarly** *adjective* (*rare*) having the supposed qualities of a Tartar; rough and fierce: E19.

†**Tartar** *noun*³. E16–E17.
[French *Tartare* or Latin TARTARUS.]
= TARTARUS.

tartare /tɑːˈtɑː/ *adjective*. L19.
[French: see TARTAR *noun*² & *adjective*.]
Tartar. Only in phrs. below.
sauce tartare, **tartare sauce** = ***tartar sauce*** s.v. TARTAR *noun*² & *adjective*. STEAK ***tartare***.

Tartarean /tɑːˈtɛːrɪən/ *adjective*. E17.
[from Latin *Tartareus*, from TARTARUS: see -AN, -EAN.]
Of or belonging to Tartarus in Greek mythology; pertaining to hell or to purgatory; infernal; hellish.

📖 M. INNES This cellarage had .. been boarded over .. in the interest of housing some Tartarean electrical device.

tartareous /tɑːˈtɛːrɪəs/ *adjective*¹. E17.
[from TARTAR *noun*¹ + -EOUS.]
†**1** Of the nature of or characterized by a calcareous deposit or other concretion. Only in 17. †**2** CHEMISTRY. Of the nature of, containing, or derived from tartar. M17–E19. **3** BOTANY. Of a lichen: having a thick rough crumbling surface. E19.

†**Tartareous** *adjective*². E–M17.
[formed as TARTAREAN + -OUS.]
= TARTAREAN.

tartaret /ˈtɑːtərɪt/ *noun. rare.* L16.
[French †*tartaret*, *-ot*, app. so called because supposed to come from Tartary.]
In full ***tartaret falcon***. The Barbary falcon, *Falco pelegrinoides*.

Tartarian /tɑːˈtɛːrɪən/ *noun & adjective*. LME.
[from Old French *Tartarien* or (later) its source medieval Latin *Tartaria* TARTARY: see -IAN.]
▶ **A** *noun.* A Tartar. LME.
▶ **B** *adjective.* Of or pertaining to Tartary or the Tartars; = TARTAR *adjective* 1. Now chiefly in names of things of actual or supposed Tartar origin. LME.
Tartarian lamb = BAROMETZ. **Tartarian oats** a form of cultivated oat, *Avena orientalis*, in which the panicle droops to one side.

tartaric /tɑːˈtarɪk/ *adjective*¹. L18.
[French †*tartarique* from medieval Latin *tartarum* TARTAR *noun*¹: see -IC.]
CHEMISTRY. Of the nature of, related to, or derived from tartar. Now chiefly in ***tartaric acid***, a dicarboxylic acid, $CO_2H(CHOH)_2CO_2H$, the parent acid of tartrates, of which there are four optical isomers; *spec.* = ***DEXTROTARTARIC acid***.

Tartaric /tɑːˈtarɪk/ *adjective*². E19.
[from TARTAR *noun*² + -IC.]
= TARTAR *adjective* 1.

tartarin /ˈtɑːtərɪn/ *noun & adjective. obsolete* exc. *Hist.* Also **-ine**. ME.
[Old French, formed as TARTARY: see -INE¹.]
▶ **A** *noun.* A rich fabric, apparently of silk, imported from the East, prob. from China through Tartary. ME.
▶ **B** *adjective.* Made of tartarin. LME.

tartarize /ˈtɑːtərʌɪz/ *verb trans.* Now *rare* or *obsolete*. Also **-ise**. L17.
[from TARTAR *noun*¹ + -IZE.]
CHEMISTRY. **1** Treat or purify using cream of tartar or (formerly) salt of tartar. L17. **2** Cause to combine with tartaric acid to form a tartrate. L17.

†**tartarous** *adjective*. E17–E19.
[from TARTAR *noun*¹ + -OUS.]
Of, pertaining to, or designating a deposit or concretion; consisting of or resembling tartar; derived from tartar, tartaric.

Tartarus /ˈtɑːt(ə)rəs/ *noun*. M16.
[Latin from Greek *Tartaros*.]
1 GREEK MYTHOLOGY. An abyss below Hades where the Titans were confined; a place of punishment in Hades; *gen.* hell. M16. **2** A hellish or horrific place or situation. E19.

📖 **2** DE QUINCEY The dismal Tartarus of the kitchens.

Tartary /ˈtɑːtəri/ *noun*. LME.
[Old & mod. French *Tartarie* from medieval Latin *Tartaria* land of the Tartars.]
1 A region in Asia and eastern Europe, conquered by the Tartars under Genghis Khan in the 13th cent., extending east to the Pacific Ocean. LME. †**2** The region of Tartarus. L16–E17.

tarte /tart/ *noun.* Pl. pronounced same. M20.
[French = TART *noun*¹.]
A (French) fruit pie or tart.
tarte Tatin /tatɛ̃/ [*Tatin*, surname of sisters reported to have invented the dish in the mid-19th cent.], a type of upside-down apple tart consisting of pastry baked over slices of fruit arranged in caramelized sugar, the whole being turned out after cooking and served fruit side up.

tarten /ˈtɑːt(ə)n/ *verb trans. rare.* L19.
[from TART *adjective* + -EN⁵.]
1 Make tart or sharp. L19. **2** Affect with sharpness or acidity. E20.

tartine /tɑːˈtiːn/ *noun*. E19.
[French, from *tarte* TART *noun*¹.]
A slice of (usu. toasted) bread spread with butter or jam.

tartlet /ˈtɑːtlɪt/ *noun*. LME.
[Old & mod. French *tartelette* dim. of *tarte* TART *noun*¹; in sense 2, also infl. by TART *noun*²: see -LET.]
1 A small tart, usu. an individual open pastry case with a sweet or savoury filling. LME. **2** A young prostitute or tart. *colloq.* L19.

tartrate /ˈtɑːtreɪt/ *noun*. L18.
[French, from *tartre* TARTAR *noun*¹: see -ATE¹.]
CHEMISTRY. A salt or ester of tartaric acid.

tartrazine /ˈtɑːtrəziːn/ *noun*. L19.
[formed as TARTRATE + AZO- + -INE⁵.]
CHEMISTRY. A brilliant orange-yellow dye which is a complex sulphur-containing azo derivative of tartaric acid and is used to colour food, medicines, and cosmetics.

tartronic /tɑːˈtrɒnɪk/ *adjective*. M19.
[French *tartronique*, arbitrarily from TARTARIC.]
CHEMISTRY. ***tartronic acid***, a hydroxylated derivative, $HOCH(COOH)_2$, of malonic acid, used in chemical synthesis.
■ **ˈtartronate** *noun* a salt or ester of tartronic acid M19.

Tartuffe /tɑːˈtuːf/ *noun*. Also **-tufe**. L17.
[French, the principal character (a religious hypocrite) in the comedy *Tartuffe* by Molière (1664), app. from Italian *Tartufo*, a use of *tartufo* truffle, as a concealed object.]
A religious hypocrite; a hypocritical pretender to excellence of any kind.
■ **Tartufferie**, **-ery** *noun* Tartuffism; an instance of this: M19. **Tartuffism** *noun* the character or conduct of a Tartuffe; hypocrisy: L17. **Tartuffian** *adjective* pertaining to or characteristic of a Tartuffe; hypocritical, pretentious: L19.

tartufo /tɑːˈtuːfəʊ/ *noun.* Pl. **-fi** /-fi/, **-fos**. L17.
[Italian.]
A truffle; esp. in ***tartufi bianchi*** /ˈbjaŋki/, white truffles.

tarty /ˈtɑːti/ *adjective. colloq.* E20.
[from TART *noun*² + -Y¹.]
Resembling or suggestive of a tart or prostitute, promiscuous; provocative; cheap, showy, gaudy.

📖 *Catch* I don't like the top—it's dead tarty and cheap looking.

■ **tartily** *adverb* L20. **tartiness** *noun* L20.

tarve /tɑːv/ *noun. US. rare.* M19.
[Origin unkn.]
A turn; a bend, a curve.

Tarvia /ˈtɑːvɪə/ *noun*. Chiefly *N. Amer.* E20.
[from TAR *noun*¹ + Latin *via* road.]
(Proprietary name for) a road-surfacing and binding material made from tar.

tarwhine /ˈtɑːwʌɪn/ *noun*. L18.
[Aboriginal.]
An edible Australian bream, *Rhabdosargus sarba*.

Tarzan /ˈtɑːz(ə)n/ *noun*. E20.
[The hero, who is orphaned in Africa as a baby and reared by apes in the jungle, of a series of novels by the Amer. author Edgar Rice Burroughs (1875–1950).]
A man distinguished by physical strength or great agility; a man used to living in the jungle.
■ **Tarzaˈnesque** *adjective* M20.

Tas. *abbreviation.*
Tasmania.

Tasaday /təˈsɑːdʌɪ, ˈtasədʌɪ, -deɪ/ *noun & adjective*. L20.
[App. from Tasaday, from *tau* person + *sa* (place marker) + *dáya* inland.]
▶ **A** *noun.* Pl. same, **-s**. A member of a small group of people living on the Philippine island of Mindanao, formerly alleged to represent a long-isolated stone-age people discovered only in the 1960s. Also, the language of this group, an Austronesian dialect. L20.
▶ **B** *attrib.* or as *adjective.* Of or pertaining to the Tasaday or their language. L20.

tasajo /təˈsɑːhəʊ, *foreign* taˈsaxo/ *noun*. Chiefly *N. Amer.* L18.
[Spanish = slice of dried meat, of unkn. origin. See also TASSO.]
Buffalo meat cut into strips and dried in the sun.

tasca /ˈtaska/ *noun*. L20.
[Spanish & Portuguese.]
In Spain and Portugal: a tavern, a bar, *esp.* one serving food.

Taser /ˈteɪzə/ *noun*. Orig. & chiefly *US*. L20.
[from the initial letters of *Tom Swift's electric rifle* (a fictitious weapon) after LASER *noun*².]
A weapon firing barbs attached by wires to batteries to cause temporary paralysis.

tash /taʃ/ *noun. colloq.* L19.
[Abbreviation.]
= MOUSTACHE 1. Cf. TAZ.

Tashi Lama /ˈtaʃi ˌlɑːmə/ *noun phr.* L18.
[from the Tibetan Buddhist monastery *Tashi Lhunpo* + LAMA.]
A title of the Panchen Lama.

tashlik /taʃˈliːk/ *noun*. Also **-ch** /-x/. L19.
[Hebrew *tašlīk* thou shalt cast, from *hišlīk* to cast.]
A Jewish custom for New Year's Day, of reciting biblical verses indicative of sin and forgiveness by a river or sea into which crumbs are thrown as a symbol of casting away sins.

Tasian /ˈtɑːsɪən, ˈteɪʃ(ə)n/ *adjective & noun*. E20.
[from Deir *Tasa* (see below) + -IAN.]
ARCHAEOLOGY. ▶**A** *adjective.* Of, pertaining to, or designating a predynastic neolithic culture represented by remains found at Deir Tasa, a village in Upper Egypt. E20.
▶ **B** *noun.* (A person of) the Tasian culture. E20.

tasimeter /təˈsɪmɪtə/ *noun*. L19.
[from Greek *tasis* tension + -METER.]
An apparatus for measuring minute variations of temperature, length, etc. by means of changes in the electrical conductivity of carbon resulting from alterations of pressure caused by expansion and contraction.

task /tɑːsk/ *noun*. **ME.**
[Old Northern French *tasque* var. of Old French *tasche* (mod. *tâche*) from medieval Latin *tasca* alt. of *taxa*, from *taxare*: see TAX *verb*.]
1 A piece of work imposed on or undertaken by a person; *spec.* (**a**) (*obsolete* exc. *Hist.*) a fixed quantity of labour to be performed by a person; (**b**) the work allotted as a duty to a specified person; (**c**) (now *arch.* & *Scot.*) a lesson to be learned or prepared; (**d**) PSYCHOLOGY a piece of work or an exercise given to a subject in a psychological test or experiment (cf. AUFGABE). **ME.** ▸**b** *gen.* A thing that has to be done, *esp.* one involving labour or difficulty. **L16.**
†**2** A fixed payment to a king, lord, or feudal superior; an impost, a tax; a tribute. **LME–M18.**

🕮 **1** A. G. GARDINER When you are reading a thing as a task you need reasonable quiet. *Which Micro?* Your task . . is to pick up ten items of treasure. **b** J. A. FROUDE He had taken upon himself a task beyond the ordinary strength of man. O. SITWELL Fishermen had . . begun their unending task of patching their great lengths of slimy fish-net.

Phrases: **take to task** †(*a*) undertake as one's task or special piece of work; †(*b*) take (a person or thing) in hand, deal with; (*c*) call to account about a matter; rebuke, scold. †**under task** (*rare*, Milton) under the command of a taskmaster; by compulsion.
Comb.: **task force** (orig. *US*) an armed force organized for a special operation under a unified command; *transf.* a unit organized for a special task; **task group** a naval task force or subdivision of such a force; **task-work** (*a*) work paid for by the amount produced or work done; piece-work; (*b*) work, esp. involving labour or difficulty, performed as a task.

task /tɑːsk/ *verb trans.* **LME.**
[from the noun.]
†**1** Impose a tax on; tax; exact tribute from. **LME–M17.**
2 Compel (a person) to undertake a task; impose or assign a task on or to (a person). Also foll. by *to*, *with*, *to do*. **M16.**
3 Subject to severe burden, labour, or trial; make great demands on (abilities, resources, etc.); tax. **L16.** ▸**b** Chiefly NAUTICAL. Test the soundness of (timbers etc.). **E19.**
4 Orig., take to task; reprove, scold. Later, tax *with* wrongdoing etc. **L16.**
5 Give or portion *out* (work) as a task. *rare.* **M17.**

🕮 **1** CAXTON He shal taske . . your corn. **2** SHAKES. *L.L.L.* But now to task the tasker. *Defense Update International* The squadron was tasked with acclimatising the Buccaneer to RAF use. **3** W. IRVING He tasked his slender means to the utmost in educating him. **4** J. COOKE I call thee vp, and taske thee for thy slownesse.

tasker /ˈtɑːskə/ *noun*. Now *rare*. **LME.**
[from prec. + -ER[1].]
1 A thresher who is paid according to the amount produced. **LME.** ▸**b** *gen.* A person who works or is paid according to the amount produced or work done as opp. to the time taken; a piece-worker. Now *dial.* **E17.**
†**2** A person who assesses or regulates a rate or price for lodgings, goods, etc. **M16–E17.**
3 A person who imposes or sets a task; a taskmaster. **L16.**

taskmaster /ˈtɑːskmɑːstə/ *noun*. **M16.**
[from TASK *noun* + MASTER *noun*[1].]
A person whose job is to assign tasks and monitor performance; an overseer. Also *fig.*, a person who imposes a task or duty on another, esp. regularly or severely.

🕮 R. DAVIES Willard . . was the taskmaster, demanding the greatest skill I could achieve.

■ **taskmastership** *noun* the position or office of a taskmaster **E19.**

taskmistress /ˈtɑːskmɪstrɪs/ *noun*. **E17.**
[formed as prec. + MISTRESS *noun*.]
A female taskmaster.

Taslan /ˈtaslən/ *noun*. **M20.**
[Invented word.]
(Proprietary name for) a process for bulking or texturing synthetic yarns; a yarn subjected to this process.

taslet /ˈtaslɪt/ *noun*. *Scot. arch.* **E16.**
[from (the same root as) TASSE + -LET. Cf. TASSET.]
= TASSE. Usu. in *pl.*

TASM *abbreviation*.
Tactical air-to-surface missile.

Tasmanian /tazˈmeɪnɪən/ *adjective* & *noun*. **E19.**
[from *Tasmania* (see below), from Abel Janszoon *Tasman* (1603–59), Dutch explorer and discoverer of the island: see -IAN.]
▶ **A** *adjective*. Of or pertaining to Tasmania, a State of the Commonwealth of Australia consisting of one large and several smaller islands SE of the continent, or its inhabitants. **E19.**
Tasmanian cedar any of several Tasmanian coniferous trees constituting the genus *Athrotaxis*, allied to the cryptomerias. **Tasmanian devil** = DEVIL *noun* 5(c). **Tasmanian tiger**, **Tasmanian wolf** = THYLACINE.
▶ **B** *noun*. A native or inhabitant of Tasmania; formerly *spec.*, a member of the now extinct aboriginal people of Tasmania. **M19.**

Tasmanoid /ˈtazmənɔɪd/ *adjective*. **E20.**
[formed as TASMANIAN + -OID.]
Of, pertaining to, or resembling the extinct aboriginal people of Tasmania.

tass /tɑːs, tas/ *noun*[1]. Long *dial.* **ME.**
[Old & mod. French *tas* (masc.), *tasse* (fem.) from Frankish base also of Middle Dutch *tass*, Dutch *tas*. Cf. Anglo-Latin *tassa* haycock.]
A heap, a pile, a stack.

tass /tas/ *noun*[2]. Now chiefly *Scot.* **L15.**
[Old & mod. French *tasse* from Arab. *ṭās* cup from Persian *tašt* bowl.]
A cup, a small goblet; the contents of this. Also, a small drink of liquor.

Tass /tas/ *noun*[3]. **E20.**
[Russian acronym, from *Telegrafnoe agentstvo Sovetskogo Soyuza* Telegraphic Agency of the Soviet Union.]
The official news agency of the former USSR.

tasse /tas/ *noun*. *obsolete* exc. *Hist.* **LME.**
[Perh. from Old French = purse from Middle High German *tasche* pouch, pocket from Old High German *tasca* rel. to Old Saxon *dasga* pouch, Middle Dutch *tassche*, *tessche*, prob. ult. from medieval Latin *tasca*: see TASK *noun*.]
In a suit of armour, one of a series of articulated overlapping splints or plates forming a protective skirt for the thighs and the lower part of the trunk. Usu. in *pl.*

tassel /ˈtas(ə)l/ *noun*[1] & *verb*. **ME.**
[Old French *tas(s)el* clasp, of unkn. origin. Cf. Anglo-Latin *tassellus*, *-um* tassel, fringe.]
▶ **A** *noun*. †**1** A clasp or fibula for a cloak etc. Only in **ME.**
2 A decorative tuft or bunch of loose threads or thin cords hanging from a solid interwoven knob or knot of the same material. **ME.**
3 A thing resembling or suggesting a tassel; *spec.* †(*a*) *rare* a tuft; a fringe; (*b*) a pendent catkin, blossom, etc.; *esp.* (*N. Amer.*) the panicle of male (staminate) spikes at the top of a maize-plant. **E17.**
4 A piece of gold or silver plate fastened to an ecclesiastical vestment. *rare.* **M19.**

🕮 **2** A. LURIE A monogrammed shirt and Italian shoes with tassels. P. FITZGERALD Enough breeze . . to make the tassel at the end of the blind-cord tap against the window. **3** R. CAMPBELL Flowers with their scented tassels beat the wind.

Comb.: **tassel-bush** the silk-tassel bush *Garrya elliptica*; **tassel fish** the giant threadfin, *Eleutheronema tetradactylum*; **tassel-flower** (*a*) a tropical plant, *Emilia javanica*, of the composite family, grown for its tassel-shaped orange, scarlet, etc., flower-heads; (*b*) love-lies-bleeding, *Amaranthus caudatus*; **tassel-grass** = *tassel-weed* below; **tassel** HYACINTH; **tassel-pondweed** = *tassel-weed* below; **tassel-stitch** an embroidery stitch in which loops of thread are left and then cut to form a fringe; **tassel-weed** either of two plants of brackish water, *Ruppia cirrhosa* and *R. maritima* (family Ruppiaceae), with filiform leaves and spikes of inconspicuous flowers, the peduncles lengthening in fruit.
▶ **B** *verb*. Infl. **-ll-**, ***-l-**.
1 *verb trans.* Provide or decorate with a tassel or tassels. **LME.**
2 *verb intrans.* Of maize etc.: form tassels, flower, bloom. Also foll. by *out*. Chiefly *N. Amer.* **M18.**
■ **tasselled** *adjective* (*a*) provided or decorated with a tassel or tassels; (of a person) wearing a tassel or tassels; (*b*) formed into or resembling a tassel or tassels: **E17. tasseller** *noun* (*rare*) †(*a*) a maker of tassels; (*b*) a person who wears a tassel or tassels: **ME. tasselling** *noun* (*a*) the action of the verb; (*b*) tassels collectively: **L19. tasselly** *adjective* (*rare*) having many tassels **E17.**

tassel /ˈtas(ə)l/ *noun*[2]. Also **torsel** /ˈtɔːs(ə)l/. **M17.**
[Old French (mod. *tasseau*) from popular Latin blend of Latin *taxillus* small die and *tessella* small square piece of stone.]
ARCHITECTURE. A small piece of stone, wood, etc., supporting the end of a beam or joist.

tasset /ˈtasɪt/ *noun*. **M19.**
[French *tassette*, †*tasette* small pouch, protective steel plate for the thigh, from *tasse*: see TASSE, -ET[1]. Cf. TASLET.]
Chiefly *Hist.* = TASSE. Usu. in *pl.*

tassie /ˈtasi/ *noun*[1]. *Scot.* **E18.**
[from TASS *noun*[2] + -IE.]
A small cup.

Tassie /ˈtazi/ *noun*[2]. *Austral. slang.* **L19.**
[Abbreviation of TASMANIAN, *Tasmania*: see -IE. Cf. AUSSIE.]
Tasmania; a Tasmanian.

tasso /ˈtasəʊ/ *noun*. **M19.**
[Perh. from TASAJO: cf. Louisiana French *tasseau* jerked beef.]
= TASAJO.

tastable *adjective* var. of TASTEABLE.

taste /teɪst/ *noun*[1]. **ME.**
[Old French *tast*, from *taster* TASTE *verb*.]
▸†**I 1** The sense of touch; the action of touching, touch. Only in **ME.**
2 An attempt (*rare*). Also, an act of testing; a test, an examination. **ME–M17.**

🕮 **2** SHAKES. *Lear* He wrote this but as an essay or taste of my virtue.

▶ **II** †**3** The action of tasting, or perceiving a flavour with the tongue or other organ; the fact of being tasted. **ME–M18.**
4 a A small portion of food or drink to be tasted as a sample, a sip; *US slang* (an) alcoholic drink. **LME.** ▸**b** *fig.* A slight experience (*of*). **LME.**
5 The faculty or sense of perceiving the characteristic sensation produced in the tongue or other organ by contact with a substance, esp. a soluble one. **LME.**
6 a The sensation produced in the tongue or other organ by contact with a substance, esp. a soluble one; savour, sapidity; the characteristic sensation so produced by a specified substance. **LME.** ▸†**b** Odour, scent, smell. **LME–L15.**

🕮 **3** SHAKES. *Rom. & Jul.* The sweetest honey . . in the taste confounds the appetite. **4a** W. TREVOR A taste of sherry . . ? I have a nice sweet little sherry. **b** K. AMIS How do you like your first taste of teaching? **5** *Cornhill Magazine* Taste . . is not equally distributed over the whole surface of the tongue alike. **6** M. AMIS The taste of milk in my mouth. *fig.*: SHAKES. *Macb.* I have almost forgot the taste of fears.

▶ **III 7** Mental perception of quality; judgement, discriminative faculty. *obsolete* exc. as passing into sense 9. **ME.**
8 The fact or condition of liking or preferring something; an inclination, liking, or predilection *for*. **LME.** ▸†**b** Enjoyment, pleasure. (Foll. by *in*, *of*.) **E17–E18.**
9 The sense of what is appropriate, harmonious, or beautiful; aesthetic discernment in art, literature, fashion, etc. **LME.** ▸**b** Style or manner exhibiting aesthetic discernment, *esp.* that characteristic of a specified period or country; good or bad aesthetic quality (freq. with specifying word). **M18.**

🕮 **7** DRYDEN If . . they demand of me . . more than discretion in Commerce, and a taste in Confidence. **8** SWIFT Whoever hath a taste for true humour. A. WILSON Neither the elaborate whimsy nor the leer were to Sonia's taste. **9** G. M. TREVELYAN In the Eighteenth Century, taste had not yet been vitiated by too much machine production. D. L. SAYERS He has excellent taste in ties, . . socks, and things like that. **b** C. HARE Nothing . . could have been in worse taste than this observation. *Times* A pair of George III mahogany armchairs in the French taste.

Phrases: **a bad taste in the mouth**, **a bitter taste in the mouth**, etc., *colloq.* a lingering feeling of repugnance or disgust left behind by a distasteful or unpleasant experience. ACQUIRED *taste*. *a taste of one's own medicine*: see MEDICINE *noun*[1]. BURNT *taste*. **out of taste** (now *rare* or *obsolete*) not able to distinguish flavours.
Comb.: **taste-blind** *adjective* insensitive to taste; unable to taste a specified substance; **taste-blindness** the state or condition of being taste-blind; **taste bud**, **taste bulb** any of the groups of cells which provide the sense of taste in mammals, forming small swellings on the surface of the tongue; **taste-cup**, **taste-pit** ENTOMOLOGY an olfactory sensillum which consists of a minute pit in the body wall with a conical sensory peg in the centre; **taste-test** *verb trans.* test (a thing) by tasting, test the taste of (a thing).
■ **tastesome** *adjective* (*obsolete* exc. *Scot. rare*) pleasant to the taste, tasty **L16.**

taste /teɪst/ *noun*[2]. *US.* **L18.**
[Origin unkn.]
Narrow thin silk ribbon.

taste /teɪst/ *verb*. **ME.**
[Old French *taster* (mod. *tâter*) touch, feel, try, app. from Proto-Romance blend of Latin *tangere* touch and *gustare* taste.]
▶ **I** †**1** *verb trans.* Examine or explore by touch; feel; handle. **ME–M17.** ▸**b** *verb intrans.* Feel, touch; grope. **LME–L15.**
2 *verb trans.* †**a** Put to the proof; try, test; (*rare*) attempt *to do*. **ME–L17.** ▸**b** *spec.* Test the quality of (timber) by boring or chipping. Now *rare* or *obsolete*. **E18.**

🕮 **1** LD BERNERS The men of armes . . tasted the dyke with their speares. **2a** T. SHERLEY I thowght to tast her affectyon unto your lordship.

▶ **II 3 a** *verb trans.* & *intrans.* with *of*. Have experience or knowledge of; experience, feel; have a slight experience of. **ME.** ▸†**b** *verb trans.* Have sexual intercourse with. **E16–M18.**

🕮 **3a** J. H. BURTON Just returned from tasting the tender mercies of France as a galley-slave. I. MURDOCH I had tasted despair in the past. J. MAY Allowed to taste . . enough of your new powers to want a whole lot more. **b** SHAKES. *Cymb.* You have tasted her in bed.

▶ **III 4** *verb trans.* Sample or test the flavour or quality of (food etc.) by the sense of taste; put a small quantity of (food etc.) into the mouth in order to ascertain the flavour or quality, esp. of a specified commodity. Also foll. by *of*. **ME.** ▸**b** *verb trans.* *Hist.* Test (food or drink) by putting a small quantity into the mouth to detect poison. (Foll. by *to* the person on whose behalf this was done.) **L16.**
5 a *verb trans.* & *intrans.* with *of*. Eat or drink a small portion of (food or drink). **ME.** ▸**b** *verb intrans.* Drink a small quantity of alcohol. *Scot.* **E19.**

6 *verb trans.* Perceive by the sense of taste; perceive or experience the taste or flavour of; *transf.* (now *poet. & dial.*) perceive by some other sense, esp. smell. LME. ▸**b** *verb intrans.* Experience or distinguish a flavour; have or exercise the sense of taste. LME.

7 *verb intrans.* Have a taste or flavour of a specified or implied kind; produce a certain taste in the mouth; have a taste or flavour *of*. M16.

8 *verb trans.* Cause a pleasant taste in (the mouth etc.); *fig.* please, be agreeable to. Long *obsolete* exc. *Scot. & dial.* L16.

9 *verb trans.* Give a specified taste or flavour to; flavour. Long *rare*. L16.

10 *verb trans.* Like the taste of; *fig.* approve of, enjoy, take pleasure in. Now *arch. & dial.* E17.

🕮 **4** E. WAUGH The Colonel tasted the punch and pronounced it excellent. **b** C. V. WEDGWOOD Formally tasting what he ate and drank as a precaution against poison. **5a** M. MOORCOCK She tasted course after course, but was unable to eat very much. *fig.*: F. QUARLES Wisdom digests, what knowledge did but tast. **b** OED Do you never taste? **6** D. BAGLEY He licked his lips and tasted salt water. G. M. FRASER I've never tasted meat like that first buffalo-hump. *transf.*: KEATS I must taste the blossoms that unfold In its ripe warmth. **b** OED I have got a very bad cold, and can neither taste nor smell. **7** F. WELDON It tasted . . sour and rancid on the tongue. B. CHATWIN The cherry jam tasted of chemical preservative. *fig.*: A. H. CLOUGH The place, the air Tastes of the nearer north. **8** *fig.*: P. SIDNEY Bitter griefs tastes mee best, pain is my ease. **9** JONSON We will have a bunch of radish and salt to taste our wine. **10** GEO. ELIOT The work . . I am told is much tasted in a Cherokee translation.

Phrases: ***taste blood***: see BLOOD *noun*.

■ **tastingly** *adverb* (*rare*) in a tasting manner L16.

tasteable /ˈteɪstəb(ə)l/ *adjective*. Also **tastable**. LME.
[from TASTE *verb* + -ABLE.]
†**1** Capable of feeling or perceiving by the sense of touch. *rare*. Only in LME.
2 Able to be tasted. L16.
†**3** Pleasant to the taste; tasty. M17–L18.

tasted /ˈteɪstɪd/ *adjective*. *arch.* LME.
[from TASTE *noun*[1], *verb*: see -ED[2], -ED[1].]
1 That has been tasted; perceived by the taste. LME.
2 Having a specified taste or flavour. E17.
3 Having taste or critical discernment of a specified kind. E19.

tasteful /ˈteɪs(t)fʊl, -f(ə)l/ *adjective*. E17.
[from TASTE *noun*[1] + -FUL.]
1 Having an agreeable taste; palatable, tasty; *fig.* pleasing. Now *rare*. E17.
2 Having or showing good taste. M18.
■ **tastefully** *adverb* E17. **tastefulness** *noun* E18.

tasteless /ˈteɪs(t)lɪs/ *adjective*. L16.
[from TASTE *noun*[1] + -LESS.]
1 Lacking the sense of taste; unable to taste. Now *rare*. L16.
2 Without taste or flavour; insipid; *fig.* dull, uninteresting. E17.
3 Devoid of good taste; not having or showing good taste. L17.
■ **tastelessly** *adverb* M19. **tastelessness** *noun* E17.

taster /ˈteɪstə/ *noun*. LME.
[Orig. from Anglo-Norman *tastour* = Old French *tasteur*, from *taster* TASTE *verb*; later directly from TASTE *verb* + -ER[1].]
1 A person who tastes something; *spec.* a person whose business or employment is to test the flavour or quality of a commodity by tasting (freq. as 2nd elem. of comb.). LME. ▸**b** *Hist.* A person employed by another to taste his or her food and drink to detect poison. LME.
2 A device by which a small portion of food or drink is taken for tasting; *spec.* (*a*) a small shallow (esp. silver) cup for tasting wines; (*b*) an instrument for extracting a small portion from the interior of a cheese. LME.
3 A small portion of food or drink; a taste; *spec.* a portion of ice-cream served in a shallow glass. L18.
1 *tea-taster*, *wine-taster*, etc.

tastevin /tastəvɛ̃/ *noun*. Pl. pronounced same. M20.
[French *tastevin*, *tâte-vin* wine-taster.]
A small shallow (esp. silver) cup for tasting wines, of a type used in France. Also (**T-**), a member of a French order or guild of wine-tasters.

tasting /ˈteɪstɪŋ/ *noun*. ME.
[from TASTE *verb* + -ING[1].]
1 The action of TASTE *verb*; an instance of this. ME.
2 A small portion of food or drink taken to try the taste; a taste. Formerly also, one offered as a sacrifice. LME.
3 A gathering at which food or drink (esp. wine) is tasted and evaluated. Freq. as 2nd elem. of comb. M20.
3 *tea-tasting*, *wine-tasting*, etc.

tasto /ˈtastəʊ/ *noun*. Pl. **-os**. M18.
[Italian = touch, key.]
MUSIC. A key of a piano or other keyboard instrument; the finger-board of a stringed instrument.
sul tasto /sʊl/ [SUL]: directing that a stringed instrument is to be played with the bow over the finger-board. **tasto solo**: directing that the bass notes are to be played alone without any harmony.

tasty /ˈteɪsti/ *adjective*. Now *colloq. & dial.* E17.
[from TASTE *noun*[1] + -Y[1].]
1 Pleasing to the taste; appetizing, savoury; *fig.* pleasant, agreeable, attractive. E17.
2 Characterized by or displaying good taste; tasteful, elegant. Now *rare*. M18.
■ **tastily** *adverb* L18. **tastiness** *noun* L19.

tat /tat/ *noun*[1]. *slang*. L17.
[Origin unkn.]
1 A die, esp. a false or loaded one. Usu. in *pl.* L17.
2 In *pl.* Teeth; *esp.* false teeth. *slang* (chiefly *Austral.*). E20.

tat /tɑːt/ *noun*[2]. E19.
[Hindi *ṭāṭ*.]
1 Coarse canvas for sacking or cheap clothing made from jute or from bamboo strips. E19.
2 A tray or shelf of hessian or other coarse fabric on which green tea leaves are spread to dry. E20.

tat /tat/ *noun*[3]. M19.
[Abbreviation.]
= TATTOO *noun*[3].

tat /tat/ *noun*[4]. *colloq.* M19.
[Prob. back-form. from TATTY *adjective*[1].]
1 A rag. Also, a shabby person. M19.
2 Rubbish, junk, worthless goods; poorly-made or tasteless clothing. M20.

Tat /tɑːt/ *noun*[5]. Pl. **-s**, same. M19.
[Russian from Turkish *tat* alien.]
A member of a people perh. related to the Tajiks and living in Azerbaijan and Dagestan; the Iranian language of this people.

tat /tat/ *noun*[6]. L19.
[Origin unkn. Cf. TATTY *adjective*[1].]
A tangled or matted lock of hair.

tat /tat/ *noun*[7]. L20.
[from *trans-activating transcription*.]
GENETICS. A gene present in human immunodeficiency viruses, which produces proteins regulating the expression of other genes.
Comb.: **tat protein**: produced by this gene.

tat /tat/ *verb*[1] *trans.* Long *dial. rare*. Infl. **-tt-**. E17.
[Origin uncertain: perh. imit.]
Touch lightly, pat, tap.

tat /tat/ *verb*[2]. Infl. **-tt-**. L19.
[Back-form. from TATTING *noun*[1].]
1 *verb intrans.* Do tatting. L19.
2 *verb trans.* Make by tatting. E20.

tat /tat/ *verb*[3] *intrans. slang. rare*. Infl. **-tt-**. M19.
[from TAT *noun*[4]. Cf. TOT *verb*[3].]
Collect rags and items of refuse for profit.

ta-ta /tɑːˈtɑː, ˈtatɑː, taˈtɑː/ *interjection, noun, & adjective*. *nursery & colloq.* E19.
[Origin unkn.: cf. earlier DA-DA.]
▸**A** *interjection.* Goodbye. E19.
▸**B** *noun.* **1** A walk, an outing. L19.
2 A hat, bonnet, etc. E20.
▸**C** *attrib.* or as *adjective. LINGUISTICS.* Of, designating, or pertaining to the theory that language originated in an attempt to imitate the body's gestures with the vocal organs. M20.

tatami /təˈtɑːmi/ *noun*. E17.
[Japanese.]
1 A rush-covered straw mat forming the standard floor-covering in Japan. Also ***tatami mat***. E17.
2 A standard unit in room measurement in Japan, approx. 1.83 by 0.91 metres. E20.

Tatar /ˈtɑːtə/ *noun & adjective*. E17.
[Turkish name of a Tatar tribe. Cf. TARTAR *noun*[2] & *adjective*.]
▸**A** *noun.* **1** A member of a group of Turkic peoples probably originating in Manchuria and Mongolia and now found mainly in parts of Siberia, Crimea, the N. Caucasus, and districts along the River Volga. E17.
2 The Turkic language of these peoples. L19.
▸**B** *adjective.* Of or pertaining to the Tatars or their language. E19.

tate /teɪt/ *noun*. *Scot. & north.* E16.
[Perh. ult. of Scandinavian origin: cf. Old Norse *tæta* (*sundr*) tear (to shreds), Icelandic *tæta* tease, *tæta í sundur* tear to pieces, *tætla* rag, shred.]
1 A small tuft or lock of hair, wool, etc.; a small handful of grass, hay, or corn. E16.
2 A bit; a small piece; a particle or morsel of something. E18.

tater /ˈteɪtə/ *noun*. *colloq.* M18.
[Alt. Cf. TATIE, TATTIE.]
= POTATO *noun* 2.
Comb.: **tater-trap** *arch. slang* the mouth.

Tathagata /təˈtɑːɡətə, -ˈθɑː-/ *noun*. M19.
[Pali *Tathāgata*, from *tathā* in that manner, so + *gata* gone.]
(An honorific title of) a Buddha, *spec.* the Buddha Gautama; a person who has attained perfection.

tathata /tataˈtɑː, taθ-/ *noun*. M20.
[Pali *tathatā* true state of things, from *tathā* in that manner, so.]
BUDDHISM. The ultimate nature of all things, as expressed in phenomena but inexpressible in language.

Tatianist /ˈteɪʃ(ə)nɪst/ *noun*. M18.
[from *Tatian* (see below) + -IST.]
A follower of Tatian, a 2nd-cent. Christian apologist and Gnostic; an Encratite.
■ Earlier †**Tatian** *noun* L16–M17.

tatie /ˈteɪti/ *noun*. *colloq.* L18.
[Alt. Cf. TATER, TATTIE.]
= POTATO *noun* 2.

tâtonnement /tatɔnmɑ̃/ *noun*. Pl. pronounced same. M19.
[French, from *tâtonner* feel one's way, proceed cautiously: see -MENT.]
Experimentation, tentative procedure; an instance of this.

tatou *noun* var. of TATU.

tatpurusha /tatˈpʊrʊʃə/ *adjective & noun*. M19.
[Sanskrit *tat-puruṣa* lit. 'his servant'.]
GRAMMAR. (Designating) a compound in which a first nominal element qualifies, limits, or determines the second, the grammatical status of which as noun, adjective, or participle remains unchanged, e.g. English *guidebook*, *ocean-going*.

tatter /ˈtatə/ *noun*[1]. LME.
[Old Norse *tǫtrar* rags (Icelandic *tötur* a rag, *tötrar* rags, tatters, Norwegian dial. *totra*) rel. to Old English *tættec* rag.]
An irregularly torn piece, strip, or scrap hanging from a piece of cloth etc.; a scrap, a rag; in *pl.*, tattered or ragged clothing, rags.

🕮 J. POYER The . . material . . had cracked in places, and a long tatter trailed along one arm. *Daily Express* Filthy grey curtains hung in tatters at broken windows. **in tatters** *colloq.* (of a plan, argument, etc.) ruined, demolished. **tear to tatters** = *tear to shreds* s.v. SHRED *noun*.

■ **tattery** *adjective* full of tatters; tattered, ragged: M19.

tatter /ˈtatə/ *noun*[2]. *rare*. L19.
[from TAT *verb*[2] + -ER[1].]
A person who tats or does tatting.

tatter /ˈtatə/ *noun*[3]. *slang*. L19.
[from TAT *verb*[3] + -ER[1]. Cf. TOTTER *noun*[2].]
A refuse-gatherer, a rag-collector.

tatter /ˈtatə/ *verb*[1]. LME.
[App. back-form. from TATTERED *adjective*.]
1 *verb trans.* Make tattered; reduce to tatters. LME.
2 *verb intrans.* Be or become tattered. *rare*. L16.

🕮 **1** T. HOOD Shrieking for flesh to tear and tatter. **2** DYLAN THOMAS Our strips of stuff that tatter as we move.

tatter /ˈtatə/ *verb*[2] *intrans.* Long *obsolete* exc. *dial.* LME.
[Middle & mod. Dutch *tateren*: see TATTLE *verb*.]
Talk idly, chatter, tattle.

tatterdemalion /tatədɪˈmeɪljən/ *noun & adjective*. *arch.* Also **-mallion** /-ˈmaljən/. E17.
[from TATTER *noun*[1] or TATTERED *adjective*: ending unexpl.]
▸**A** *noun.* A person in ragged or tattered clothing; a ragamuffin. E17.
▸**B** *attrib.* or as *adjective.* Of, pertaining to, or characteristic of a tatterdemalion. E17.

tattered /ˈtatəd/ *adjective*. ME.
[Orig. from TATTER *noun*[1], later also from TATTER *verb*[1]: see -ED[2], -ED[1]. See also TOTTERED.]
1 Orig., dressed in clothing jagged or slashed for ornamentation. Later, having ragged or torn clothing. ME.
†**2** Having unkempt dishevelled hair; shaggy. Cf. TATTY *adjective*[1]. ME–E18.
†**3** Having long pointed projections; jagged. LME–E16.
4 Torn or rent so as to hang in tatters; ragged. M16.
†**5** Dilapidated, battered, shattered; (of troops) routed, disintegrated. L16–E19.

🕮 **1** *Nursery rhyme*: This is the man all tattered and torn. **4** QUILLER-COUCH A pile of dusty, tattered volumes. P. S. BUCK Their paper clothes were tattered and showed their clay bodies through the rents. **5** J. AUSTEN I do not like ruined, tattered cottages.

tattersall /ˈtatəs(ə)l/ *noun & adjective*. L19.
[Richard *Tattersall* (1724–95), English horseman and founder (in 1776) of a firm of horse auctioneers: from the traditional design of horse blankets.]
▸**A** *noun.* More fully ***tattersall check***. A fabric with a pattern of coloured lines forming squares like a tartan. L19.
▸**B** *attrib.* or as *adjective.* Made of tattersall. M20.

tattie /ˈtati/ *noun. colloq. & dial.* **L18.**
[Alt. Cf. TATER, TATIE.]
= POTATO *noun* 2. Also *fig.*, a stupid person.
Comb.: **tattie-bogle** *Scot.* a scarecrow; *fig.* a simpleton; **tattie-trap** *arch. slang* the mouth.

tatting /ˈtatɪŋ/ *noun*[1]. **M19.**
[Origin unkn.]
A kind of knotted lace made by hand with a small shuttle and used esp. for edging or trimming. Also, the action or process of making this.

tatting /ˈtatɪŋ/ *noun*[2]. **E20.**
[from TAT *verb*[3] + -ING[1].]
The action of TAT *verb*[3]; rag- or scrap-collecting as a livelihood.

tattle /ˈtat(ə)l/ *verb & noun.* **L15.**
[Middle Flemish *tatelen* parallel to Middle Flemish, Middle Dutch, Middle Low German *tateren*, of imit. origin: see -LE[3]. Cf. PRATTLE, TITTLE *verb*[1], TITTLE-TATTLE.]
▶ **A** *verb.* **†1** *verb intrans.* Speak hesitatingly, falter, stammer; (of a young child) utter meaningless sounds, prattle. **L15–E18.**
2 *verb intrans.* Talk idly or frivolously; chatter; chat, gossip; *spec.* talk indiscreetly, reveal secrets. **M16.**
3 *verb trans.* Utter (words) idly or frivolously; now *spec.* tell (tales), reveal (secrets). **L16.**
4 *verb trans.* Get or bring into a specified condition by tattling. *rare.* **M18.**

> 📖 **1** J. LYLY The babe shall now begin to tattle and call hir Mamma. **2** LYTTON She tattled on, first to one . . then to all. BETTY SMITH If he tattled, he knew he would be tortured . . by the one he reported. **3** SHAKES. *Tit. A.* Let the ladies tattle what they please. **4** S. JOHNSON Lest the hours . . should be tattled away without regard to literature.

▶ **B** *noun.* **1** Idle or frivolous talk; chatter, gossip. **E16.**
2 An outbreak of tattling; a chat, a gossip. Now *rare.* **L16.**

> 📖 **1** J. I. M. STEWART Not too good a show, if village tattle is to be believed. **2** W. M. PRAED Three dukes . . very nearly slain . . would have made a tattle For many a day.

■ **tattling** *verbal noun* the action of the verb, tale-telling; an instance of this: **L15. tattling** *ppl adjective* that tattles; tale-telling: **M16. tattlingly** *adverb* (*rare*) **M19.**

tattler /ˈtatlə/ *noun.* **M16.**
[from prec. + -ER[1].]
1 A person who tattles; *spec.* a tell-tale. **M16.**
2 A watch, *esp.* a striking watch, a repeater. *slang.* **L17.**
3 Either of two sandpipers constituting the genus *Heteroscelus*; esp. (more fully ***wandering tattler***) *H. incanus*, which is mainly grey with yellowish legs, and breeds in NW Canada. **M19.**

tattle-tale /ˈtat(ə)lteɪl/ *noun & adjective. colloq.* (orig. & chiefly *N. Amer.*). **L19.**
[formed as prec. + TALE *noun* after *tell-tale*.]
▶ **A** *noun.* **1** A person who reveals secrets, a tell-tale. **L19.**
2 A tachograph. **M20.**
▶ **B** *attrib.* or as *adjective.* That reveals secrets, tell-tale. **M20.**
Special collocations & comb.: **tattle-tale grey** *noun & adjective* (of) an off-white colour, (of) pale grey.

tattle-tale /ˈtat(ə)lteɪl/ *verb intrans. colloq.* (orig. & chiefly *N. Amer.*). **E20.**
[from prec.]
Reveal secrets, tell tales.

tattoo /təˈtuː, ta-/ *noun*[1]. Also (earlier) **tap-too** /tapˈtuː/. **M17.**
[Dutch *taptoe* lit. 'close the tap' (of the cask), from *tap* TAP *noun*[1] + *toe* = *doe toe* close.]
1 MILITARY. An evening drum or bugle signal recalling soldiers to their quarters. **M17.** ▸**b** A drum beat intended to raise an alarm, attract attention, etc. **L17.** ▸**c** A military entertainment consisting of an elaboration of the evening tattoo by extra music, marching, and the performance of exercises by troops. **M18.**
2 A rhythmic tapping or drumming; a continuous beating, thumping, or rapping. **M18.**

> 📖 **1b** N. HINTON He grabbed his drumsticks and beat a furious tattoo on the drums. **2 devil's tattoo** an idle tapping or drumming with the fingers on a surface as a sign of annoyance, impatience, boredom, etc.

tattoo /təˈtuː, ta-/ *noun*[2]. **L18.**
[Polynesian (Tahitian, Samoan, Tongan *ta-tau*, Marquesan *ta-tu*).]
The action or practice of tattooing the skin; a mark or design made by tattooing the skin.

tattoo /ˈtatuː/ *noun*[3]. **L18.**
[Hindi *taṭṭū*.]
In full ***tattoo horse***. A small horse or pony bred in the Indian subcontinent.

tattoo /təˈtuː, ta-/ *verb*[1]. *rare.* **L18.**
[from TATTOO *noun*[1].]
1 *verb trans.* Beat a tattoo on (a drum etc.). **L18.**
2 *verb intrans.* Beat a tattoo (*with*). **E19.**

tattoo /təˈtuː/ *verb*[2] *trans.* **M18.**
[from (the same root as) TATTOO *noun*[2].]
Make an indelible mark or pattern on the body of (a person etc.) by inserting a pigment or pigments into punctures in the skin. Also, make (an indelible mark or pattern) on the body of a person etc. in this way.

> 📖 A. TYLER An eagle tattooed on his forearm. *transf.*: LONGFELLOW Proof-sheets of Evangeline all tattooed with Folsom's remarks.

■ **tattooer** *noun* a person who practises tattooing **L18. tattooing** *noun* the action or practice of tattooing; the result of tattooing, a tattoo: **L18. tattooist** *noun* a tattooer, *esp.* one who practises tattooing as a profession **L19.**

tatty /ˈtati/ *noun.* **L18.**
[Hindi *taṭṭī* wicker frame.]
In the Indian subcontinent: a door- or window-screen consisting of matting of khus-khus-grass roots in a frame, hung and kept damp to cool and perfume the air.

tatty /ˈtati/ *adjective*[1]. *Scot.* **E16.**
[App. ult. rel. to Old English *tættec* rag (cf. TATTER *noun*[1]). Cf. TAT *noun*[4], *noun*[5], next.]
(Of hair) tangled, matted; (of a person etc.) having tangled or matted hair.

tatty /ˈtati/ *adjective*[2]. *colloq.* **M20.**
[from TAT *noun*[4] + -Y[1]. Cf. prec.]
Untidy, scruffy; shabby, worn, neglected. Also, of inferior quality, tawdry.

> 📖 R. COBB The Pantiles looked tatty and rather forlorn. A. GUINNESS I couldn't undertake to sell . . a very tatty edition of the complete works of Dickens.

■ **tattily** *adverb* **M20. tattiness** *noun* **M20.**

tatu /ˈtatuː/ *noun.* Now *rare.* Also **tatou**. **M16.**
[Portuguese *tatu* or French *tatou*, from Tupi *tatu*.]
An armadillo.

tau /tɔː, taʊ/ *noun*[1]. Also **†taw**. **ME.**
[Greek formed as TAW *noun*[2].]
1 The nineteenth (orig. the final) letter (Τ, τ) of the Greek alphabet, corresponding in form to the letter T. **ME.**
2 A T-shaped mark, sign, or object; *spec.* †(***a***) the sign of the cross as made with the hand; (***b***) (more fully ***tau cross***) a cross in which the transverse piece surmounts the upright piece (also called ***St Anthony's cross***); (***c***) = ANKH; (***d***) (more fully ***tau-staff***) a T-shaped pastoral staff. **ME.**
3 PARTICLE PHYSICS. Freq. written τ. ▸**a** A meson that decays into three pions, now identified as a kaon. Also ***tau meson***. **M20.** ▸**b** An unstable heavy charged lepton which has a spin of ½ and a mass of approx. 1780 MeV, and which decays into an electron or muon or into hadrons, with one or more neutrinos. Also ***tau lepton***, ***tau particle***. **L20.**

tau *noun*[2] see TAW *noun*[3].

taua /ˈtaʊa/ *noun.* **M19.**
[Maori.]
Chiefly *Hist.* A Maori army or war-party.

taubada /taʊˈbɑːdə/ *noun.* **L19.**
[Motu *tau-bada* important person.]
In New Guinea, a person in a position of authority (also as a respectful form of address).

Tauberian /taʊˈbɪərɪən/ *adjective.* **E20.**
[Alfred *Tauber* (1866–?1942), Slovak mathematician + -IAN.]
MATH. Designating theorems in which the behaviour in the limit of a series or function is deduced from a weaker limiting property together with some additional condition, esp. theorems in which convergence is deduced from summability.

Tauchnitz /ˈtaʊknɪts, ˈtaʊxnɪts/ *adjective & noun.* **M19.**
[See below.]
▶ **A** *adjective.* Of or pertaining to English language editions of British and American books published by the German publisher Christian Bernhard, Baron von Tauchnitz (1816–95). **M19.**
▶ **B** *noun.* A Tauchnitz book. **M19.**

taught /tɔːt/ *ppl adjective*[1]. **LME.**
[pa. pple of TEACH *verb*. Cf. earlier UNTAUGHT *adjective*.]
1 Of a person: orig., learned; later, instructed, trained, esp in a specified way. **LME.**
2 Of a subject etc.: conveyed by instruction. **E20.**
1 *ill-taught*, *well-taught*, etc.

†taught *adjective*[2] see TAUT *adjective*.

taught *verb pa. t. & pple* of TEACH *verb*.

tauhinu /taʊˈhɪnuː/ *noun. NZ.* Also (*colloq.*) **tawhine** /tɑːˈwɪni/. **M19.**
[Maori.]
An evergreen shrub, *Pomaderris phylicifolia*, of the buckthorn family, native to New Zealand and Australia, bearing downy leaves and small yellow flowers.

taula /ˈtaʊlə/ *noun.* **L19.**
[Catalan from Latin *tabula* table.]
ARCHAEOLOGY. A megalithic Bronze Age structure found on Minorca, consisting of two slabs forming a T-shaped column, freq. enclosed by a horseshoe-shaped wall.

taum *verb* see TAWM.

†taumaly *noun* var. of TOMALLEY.

taungya /ˈtaʊnjə/ *adjective & noun.* **L19.**
[Burmese, from *taung* hill + *ya* plot, field.]
▶ **A** *adjective.* Of, designating, or pertaining to a method of shifting cultivation practised in Myanmar (Burma) and a system of tropical forest management based on this. **L19.**
▶ **B** *noun.* A temporary hillside clearing for crop-growing. **E20.**

taunt /tɔːnt/ *noun.* **E16.**
[French *tant* (in *tant pour tant* so much for so much, tit for tat) from Latin *tantum* neut. of *tantus* so great.]
1 An insulting or provoking remark or speech; a thing said to anger or pain a person; a gibe, a jeer. Formerly also (*rare*), the object of such a remark or speech. **E16.**
†2 *taunt for taunt*, like for like, tit for tat, in reply or rejoinder. **M16–E17.**
†3 A smart or clever rejoinder, a jesting or witty quip. **M16–E17.**

> 📖 **1** P. BAILEY My cousins responded with taunts of 'Cowardy cowardy custard'.

Comb.: **taunt-song** a taunting song; *spec.* [translating Hebrew *māšāl*] any of various passages in the Bible expressing contempt and derision for a fallen tyrant.

taunt /tɔːnt/ *adjective.* **L15.**
[Origin uncertain: sense 2 prob. aphet. from ATAUNT.]
1 Orig., haughty; stuck-up. Later, saucy, pert. Long *obsolete* exc. *dial.* **L15.**
2 NAUTICAL. (Of a mast) excessively tall or lofty; (of a ship) having very tall masts and narrow sails. **E17.**

taunt /tɔːnt/ *verb.* **E16.**
[from the noun.]
1 †a *verb intrans. & trans.* Make a smart or effective rejoinder (to); exchange banter (with). Only in **16.** ▸**b** *verb trans.* Tease, pester, bother. *dial.* **E19.**
2 *verb trans.* Utter a taunt or taunts to (a person); reproach (a person) *with* something in a sarcastic, scornful, or insulting way. **M16.** ▸**b** *verb intrans.* Utter a taunt or taunts. *arch.* **M16.** ▸**c** *verb trans.* Utter or express (words, ideas) tauntingly. *rare.* **L19.**
3 *verb trans.* Persuade or provoke (a person) to a specified course with a taunt or taunts. **E19.**

> 📖 **2** V. BROME A bullying schoolmate . . who taunted him with his 'fancy' manners. D. ARKELL Verlaine was taunted and tormented until he could stand no more. **c** P. BARR 'Scaredy-cat!' Frank taunted.

■ **taunter** *noun* **M16. taunting** *noun* the action of the verb; an instance of this; a taunt: **M16. taunting** *adjective* that taunts a person **M16. tauntingly** *adverb* **E16. tauntingness** *noun* (*rare*) **E18.**

Taunton turkey /ˈtɔːntən ˈtəːki/ *noun. US.* **M19.**
[from *Taunton*, a town in Massachusetts, USA + TURKEY *noun*[2].]
= ALEWIFE 2.

tauon /ˈtaʊɒn, ˈtɔːɒn/ *noun.* **L20.**
[from TAU *noun*[1] + -ON.]
PARTICLE PHYSICS. = TAU *noun*[1] 3b.

taupata /ˈtaʊpətə/ *noun.* **M19.**
[Maori.]
A New Zealand evergreen shrub or small tree, *Coprosma repens*, of the madder family, with shiny leaves, small white flowers, and orange-red berries.

taupe /təʊp/ *noun & adjective.* **E20.**
[French from Latin *talpa* mole.]
(Of) a brownish shade of grey resembling the colour of moleskin.

Taurean /ˈtɔːrɪən/ *adjective & noun.* **M17.**
[from Latin *taureus*, from Latin *taurus* bull, Taurus: see -EAN.]
▶ **A** *adjective.* **1** (**t-**.) = TAURINE *adjective.* **M17.**
2 Of or pertaining to the sign Taurus; (characteristic of a person) born under Taurus. **E20.**
▶ **B** *noun.* A person born under the sign Taurus. **E20.**

taureau /ˈtɔːrəʊ/ *noun.* Pl. **-x** /-z/. **L18.**
[Canad. French from French *taureau* bull from Latin *taurus*.]
Hist. In Canada, a buffalo-hide bag for carrying pemmican; the pemmican carried in such a bag.

Taurian /ˈtɔːrɪən/ *adjective & noun.* **L19.**
[Irreg. from Latin *taurus* bull, Taurus: see -IAN.]
▶ **A** *adjective.* **1** (**t-**.) = TAURINE *adjective. rare.* **L19.**
2 = TAUREAN *adjective* 2. **E20.**
▶ **B** *noun.* = TAUREAN *noun.* **M20.**

tauric /ˈtɔːrɪk/ *adjective. rare.* **E19.**
[from Greek *tauros* or Latin *taurus* bull + -IC.]
= TAURINE *adjective.*

tauricide /ˈtɔːrɪsʌɪd/ *noun. rare.* M19.
[from Latin *taurus* bull + -I- + -CIDE.]
1 A person who kills a bull; *spec.* a matador. M19.
2 The killing of a bull. L19.

Taurid /ˈtɔːrɪd/ *noun & adjective.* L19.
[from TAURUS + -ID³.]
ASTRONOMY. (Designating) any of an annual shower of meteors which appear to radiate from the constellation Taurus in November.

tauriform /ˈtɔːrɪfɔːm/ *adjective.* E18.
[Latin *tauriformis*, from *taurus* bull: see -FORM.]
Having the form of a bull.

taurine /ˈtɔːriːn/ *noun*[1]. M19.
[from TAUR(OCHOLIC + -INE⁵.]
BIOCHEMISTRY. A sulphur-containing amino acid, $NH_2CH_2CH_2SO_3H$, important in fat metabolism but not essential in the human diet.

taurine /ˈtɔːrʌɪn/ *adjective & noun*[2]. E17.
[Latin *taurinus*, from *taurus* bull: see -INE¹.]
▶ **A** *adjective.* Of or pertaining to, or belonging to a bull; of the nature of or like a bull; bovine. E17.
▶ **B** *noun.* A taurine animal, a bull. *rare.* L19.

tauroboly /tɔːˈrɒbəli/ *noun.* Also (earlier) in Latin form **taurobolium** /tɔːrəˈbəʊlɪəm/, pl. **-lia** /-lɪə/. L15.
[Latin *taurobolium* from Greek *taurobolos*, from *tauros* bull + stem of *bolē* a cast, stroke, wound.]
GREEK ANTIQUITIES. The killing of a bull or bulls; *spec.* a sacrifice of a bull including a ritual bath in bulls' blood, in honour of the fertility and nature goddess Cybele; a representation of this.

taurocholic /tɔːrə(ʊ)ˈkɒlɪk/ *adjective.* M19.
[from Greek *tauros* bull + *kholē* bile + -IC: cf. CHOLIC.]
BIOCHEMISTRY. ***taurocholic acid***, an acid, $C_{26}H_{45}NO_7S$, formed by the combination of taurine with cholic acid and occurring in bile.
■ **taurocholate** /tɔːˈrɒkəleɪt/ *noun* a salt or ester of taurocholic acid M19.

taurodont /ˈtɔːrədɒnt/ *adjective.* E20.
[from Greek *tauros* bull + -ODONT.]
Of primate molar teeth: having large crowns and pulp cavities, and short roots.
■ **tauroˈdontism** *noun* the condition of having taurodont teeth E20.

tauromachy /tɔːˈrɒməki/ *noun. literary.* M19.
[Greek *tauromakhia*, from *tauros* bull: see -MACHY.]
A bullfight; the practice or custom of bullfighting.

Taurus /ˈtɔːrəs/ *noun.* OE.
[Latin *taurus* bull, Taurus.]
1 (The name of) a constellation of the northern hemisphere, lying on the ecliptic between Cetus and Orion; ASTROLOGY (the name of) the second zodiacal sign, usu. associated with the period 21 April to 20 May (see note s.v. ZODIAC); the Bull. OE. ▶**b** A person born under the sign Taurus; = TAUREAN *noun.* E20.
2 STOCK EXCHANGE. [Acronym, from *T*ransfer and *au*tomated *r*egistration of *u*ncertified *s*tock.] A computerized system for handling and recording share transactions on the London Stock Exchange. L20.

Tau Sug /tɔː ˈsʊg/ *noun & adjective.* E20.
[Tau Sug, from *tau* people + *sug* current. Cf. SULU.]
▶ **A** *noun.* Pl. same. A member of a Muslim people inhabiting the Sulu archipelago in the Philippines and originating in the Butuan area of north-east Mindanao; the Austronesian language of this people. E20.
▶ **B** *attrib.* or as *adjective.* Of or pertaining to this people or their language. E20.

taut /tɔːt/ *adjective.* Also (earlier) †**taught**. ME.
[Perh. alt. of var. of TOUGH *adjective.*]
1 Distended, full to distention. Long *obsolete* exc. *dial.* ME.
2 Of a rope, cord, etc.: drawn or pulled tight, tense, not slack. NAUTICAL. Of a sail: tightly drawn when tacking. E17. ▶**b** In good order or condition, trim. E19.

> 📖 **2** M. SINCLAIR Perceptible slackening of the taut muscles of his mouth. V. WOOLF My nerves are taut as fiddle strings. **b** *taut ship*: see SHIP *noun* 1.

■ **tautly** *adverb* L19. **tautness** *noun* L17.

taut /tɔːt/ *verb trans. & intrans. Scot.* L18.
[Origin uncertain: perh. rel. to TATTY *adjective*¹.]
Make or become tangled or matted.

taut- *combining form* see TAUTO-.

†**tautaug** *noun* var. of TAUTOG.

tauten /ˈtɔːt(ə)n/ *verb trans. & intrans.* E19.
[from TAUT *adjective* + -EN⁵.]
Make or become taut; tighten.

> 📖 C. MORGAN His faded shirt . . tautened by the forward drag of his arms.

tauto- /ˈtɔːtəʊ/ *combining form* of Greek *tauto* contr. of *to auto* the same. Before a vowel also **taut-**.
■ **tautochrone** *noun* MATH. (now *rare* or *obsolete*) the curve such that a particle moving on it from any point, under the action of gravity or other force, will reach a fixed point in the same time L18. **tautonym** *noun* (BOTANY & ZOOLOGY) a scientific name in which the same word is used for both genus and species E20. **tautoˈnymic** *adjective* (BOTANY & ZOOLOGY) pertaining to or constituting a tautonym L19. **tauˈtonymy** *noun* (BOTANY & ZOOLOGY) the use of tautonyms E20. **tautoˈousian** *adjective* (THEOLOGY, now *rare*) having absolutely the same essence L17. **tauˈtophony** *noun* repetition of the same sound M19. **tautosyˈllabic** *adjective* belonging to the same syllable L19. **tautoˈzonal** *adjective* (CRYSTALLOGRAPHY) belonging to or situated in the same zone L19.

tautog /tɔːˈtɒg/ *noun.* Also †**tautaug**. M17.
[Narragansett *tautauog*, pl. of *taut.*]
A labroid fish, *Tautoga onitis*, abundant on the Atlantic coast of N. America, and esteemed for food. Also called ***blackfish***, ***oyster-fish***.

†**tautologia** *noun* see TAUTOLOGY.

tautologic /tɔːtəˈlɒdʒɪk/ *adjective. rare.* E19.
[formed as next + -IC.]
Tautological.

tautological /tɔːtəˈlɒdʒɪk(ə)l/ *adjective.* E17.
[from TAUTOLOGY + -ICAL.]
1 Of, pertaining to, characterized by, or involving tautology. E17.
†**2** Repeating the same sound. *rare.* L17–E18.
■ **tautologically** *adverb* E17.

tautologize /tɔːˈtɒlədʒʌɪz/ *verb intrans.* Also **-ise**. E17.
[from TAUTOLOGY + -IZE, after *apology, apologize.*]
Use or practise tautology.

tautologous /tɔːˈtɒləgəs/ *adjective.* E18.
[from next + -OUS, after *analogy, analogous.*]
Tautological.
■ **tautologously** *adverb* M19.

tautology /tɔːˈtɒlədʒi/ *noun.* Also (earlier) in Latin form †**-logia**. M16.
[Late Latin *tautologia* from Greek, from *tautologos* repeating what has been said: see TAUTO-, -LOGY.]
1 The contextual repetition, orig. of the same word or phrase, now usu. of the same idea or statement in different words, esp. as a fault of style. M16.
2 An instance of this; a tautological phrase or expression. L16.
3 PHILOSOPHY. The absolute identification of cause and effect; an expression of this. *rare.* M17.
4 LOGIC. A compound proposition which is unconditionally true for all the truth-possibilities of its component propositions and by virtue of its logical form. E20. ▶**b** A proposition that is true by virtue of the meaning of its terms. M20.
■ **tautologism** *noun* (*rare*) the use or practice of tautology; an instance of this; *spec.* the combination of two synonymous words or syllables for semantic precision: E19. **tautologist** *noun* a person who uses or practises tautology E18.

tautomer /ˈtɔːtəmə/ *noun.* E20.
[from TAUTO- + ISOMER.]
CHEMISTRY. Each of two or more isomers of a compound which exist together as interconvertible forms in equilibrium, owing to the reversible migration of an atom or group within the molecule.
■ **tautoˈmeric** *adjective* L19. **tauˈtomerism** *noun* the fact or condition of being tautomeric L19. **tau,tomeriˈzation** *noun* the conversion of a compound into another tautomeric form M20. **tauˈtomerize** *verb intrans.* change into another tautomeric form M20.

tav *noun* var. of TAW *noun*³.

Tavastian /təˈvastɪən/ *noun & adjective.* E20.
[from *Tavast(ehus* Swedish name for Hämeenlinna, a town in the province of Häme, Finland + -IAN.]
▶ **A** *noun.* A member of a Finnic people inhabiting central Finland; the Finno-Ugric language of this people. E20.
▶ **B** *attrib.* or as *adjective.* Of or pertaining to this people or their language. M20.
■ **Tavastlander** /ˈtavəstlandə/ *noun* a Tavastian L19.

tave /teɪv/ *verb intrans.* Long *dial.* ME.
[App. ult. from Old Norse: cf. Norwegian dial. *tava* toil or struggle ineffectually, be exhausted.]
Strike out or struggle ineffectually; toil or labour with difficulty.

Tavel /təˈvɛl/ *noun.* L19.
[A commune in the department of Gard, France.]
A rosé wine produced at Tavel.

tavel *verb* var. of TEVEL.

tavelle /təˈvɛl/ *noun. rare.* Also †**-ell**. E16.
[French *tavelle* app. from Latin *tabella* tablet.]
†**1** The bobbin on which silk is wound for use in the shuttle. E16–E17.
2 A large drum or bobbin on which silk is wound off the cocoons. M19.

tavern /ˈtav(ə)n/ *noun & verb.* ME.
[Old & mod. French *taverne* from Latin *taberna* hut, tavern. In sense B.1 repr. medieval Latin *tabernare.*]
▶ **A** *noun.* **1** An inn, a public house. *arch.* ME.
†**2** A shop or workshop attached to or under a house; a cellar. Long *dial. rare.* E16–E20.
Comb.: **tavern-keeper** a person who manages and owns a tavern.
▶ **B** *verb. rare.* Chiefly as ***taverning*** *verbal noun.*
†**1** *verb trans.* Of a leaseholder or copyholder: subdivide (a holding), esp. by erecting a building and apportioning land to it. M–L16.
2 *verb intrans.* Frequent taverns. L16.
†**3** *verb intrans.* Keep a tavern, be a tavern-keeper. Only in L18.

taverna /təˈvɜːnə/ *noun.* E20.
[mod. Greek from Latin *taberna* TAVERN.]
A Greek restaurant.

taverner /ˈtav(ə)nə/ *noun. arch.* ME.
[Anglo-Norman = Old French *tavernier*, from *taverne*: see TAVERN, -ER².]
1 A tavern-keeper. ME.
†**2** A frequenter of taverns; a habitual drinker. ME–E17.

Tavgi /ˈtavgi/ *noun & adjective.* Pl. of noun same. L19.
[Russian.]
= NGANASAN *noun & adjective.*

TAVR *abbreviation.*
Hist. Territorial and Army Volunteer Reserve.

taw /tɔː/ *noun*[1]. *rare. obsolete* exc. *Scot.* M16.
[from TAW *verb.* Cf. TAWS.]
†**1** Tawed leather. Only in M16.
2 A thong, a whip, a lash. L18.

taw /tɔː/ *noun*[2]. Long *obsolete* exc. *Scot. rare.* E17.
[Origin unkn.]
A fibre of a root.

taw /taʊ/ *noun*[3]. Also **tav** /tɑːf/, (now *rare*) **tau**. M17.
[Hebrew *tāw*. Cf. TAU *noun*¹.]
The final letter of the Hebrew alphabet; the corresponding letter in any of various ancient Semitic alphabets.

taw /tɔː/ *noun*[4]. E18.
[Origin unkn.]
1 A large marble. Cf. TOLLEY. E18.
2 A game of marbles. E18.
3 The line from which a player shoots a marble in a game of marbles. M18.

†**taw** *noun*[5] var. of TAU *noun*¹.

taw /tɔː/ *verb trans.*
[Old English *tawian* rel. to Old Saxon *tōgean*, Middle Low German, Middle Dutch *touwen*, Old High German *zouwen*, Gothic *taujan*, from Germanic base meaning 'do, make, prepare'. Cf. TEW *verb*¹, TOOL *noun.*]
1 Make ready, prepare, or dress (raw material) for use or further treatment; *spec.* make (hide) into leather without tannin, esp. by steeping in a solution of alum and salt. OE.
†**2** Treat (a person) abusively or with contumely; torment; harass; outrage. OE–M16.
3 Whip, flog, or thrash (a person). *obsolete* exc. *Scot. & dial.* E17.
■ **tawer** *noun* LME.

tawa /ˈtɑːwə, ˈtaʊə/ *noun*[1]. M19.
[Maori.]
A tall New Zealand forest tree, *Beilschmiedia tawa*, of the laurel family, with fruit resembling damsons.

tawa /təˈwɑː/ *noun*[2]. M19.
[Hindi, Panjabi *tavā* frying-pan, griddle.]
A circular griddle used in the Indian subcontinent for cooking chapattis and other food.

tawdry /ˈtɔːdri/ *noun & adjective.* E17.
[Shortening of TAWDRY LACE.]
▶ **A** *noun.* †**1** = TAWDRY LACE. Only in E17.
2 Cheap and gaudy finery. L17.

> 📖 **2** S. SMILES A poor bedizened creature, clad in tawdry.

▶ **B** *adjective.* **1** Pertaining to or of the nature of cheap and gaudy finery; showy but worthless; *transf. & fig.* wearing cheap and gaudy finery; made or decorated in a showy but worthless style; trumpery; meretricious. L17.
†**2** Untidy; slovenly; ungraceful. *rare.* L17–E19.

> 📖 **1** M. MUGGERIDGE The glories of imperial power are threadbare and tawdry. P. D. JAMES Hilary Robarts's strong-coloured cotton looked tawdry.

■ **tawdrily** *adverb* M18. **tawdriness** *noun* L17.

†**tawdry lace** *noun phr.* M16–M18.
[Contr. of *St Audrey's lace*, from *St Audrey*, Etheldrida (d. 679), patron saint of Ely, in whose honour a fair was held + LACE *noun.*]
A silk cord or ribbon worn as a necklace in the 16th and early 17th cents.

¶ Cheap and gaudy finery was traditionally sold at St Audrey's fair.

tawhai /'tɑːfʌɪ, 'tɑːwʌɪ/ *noun. NZ.* L19.
[Maori.]
Any of several kinds of nothofagus.

tawhine *noun* see TAUHINU.

tawhiri /tɑː'fiːri, tɑː'wiːri/ *noun.* L19.
[Maori.]
A New Zealand pittosporum, *Pittosporum tenuifolium*, noted for its fragrant white blossoms.

tawie /'tɔːi/ *adjective. Scot.* L18.
[Prob. from TAW *verb* + -Y¹.]
Esp. of an animal: tractable, docile, easy to manage.

tawm /tɔːm/ *verb intrans.* Long *obsolete* exc. *dial.* Orig. †**talm**. Also (*dial.*) **taum**. ME.
[Rel. to Old Norse *talma* hinder, obstruct.]
Become exhausted; tire, faint.

tawn /tɔːn/ *verb, noun, & adjective. rare.* E18.
[App. alt. of TAN *verb*, infl. by TAWNY *adjective*.]
▶†**A** *verb trans.* Tan (the skin) by exposure; make brown or tawny. Only in E18.
▶**B** *noun.* A tan; a brown or tawny colour. M18.
▶**C** *adjective.* Tanned; of a brown or tawny colour. E20.

tawny /'tɔːni/ *adjective & noun.* ME.
[Anglo-Norman *tauné*, Old French *tané*, from *tan* TAN *noun*¹. Cf. TENNÉ.]
▶**A** *adjective.* Of an orange- or yellow-brown colour. Formerly also, of any of several shades of brown. ME.

📖 D. H. LAWRENCE Her suave, tawny neck was bare and bewitching.

▶**B** *noun.* †**1** Woollen cloth of a tawny colour. Also (*rare*), a garment made of such cloth. ME–L18.
2 Tawny colour; HERALDRY = TENNÉ. LME.
3 A black or dark-skinned person. Cf. ***tawny-moor*** below. *arch. derog.* M17.
4 = ***tawny port*** below. E20.

📖 **2** P. V. PRICE The deep aureole of light orange darkening to tawny.

Special collocations & comb.: **tawny eagle** a uniformly brown eagle, *Aquila rapax*, found in Africa and Asia. **tawny frogmouth** the most widespread frogmouth, *Podargus strigoides*, which is found throughout Australia. **tawny grisette** an edible mushroom, *Amanita fulva*, with an orange-brown cap, growing chiefly in birchwoods on peaty soil. †**tawny-moor** *derog.* = sense B.3 above. **tawny owl** a mottled brown owl, *Strix aluco*, found commonly throughout Eurasia and N. Africa, and characterized by its familiar hooting call; also called ***brown owl***. **tawny pipit** a large pale pipit, *Anthus campestris*, found in much of Europe, central Asia, and N. Africa. **tawny port** a port wine made from a blend of several vintages matured in wood.
▪ **tawniness** *noun* M16.

tawpie /'tɔːpi/ *noun & adjective. Scot.* Also **tawpy**. E18.
[Prob. from Old Norse. Cf. Norwegian *tåp*, Danish *tåbe* simpleton, Swedish *tåp* simpleton, *tåpig* foolish, simple-minded.]
▶**A** *noun.* A foolish, senseless, or thoughtless girl or woman. E18.
▶**B** *adjective.* Of a girl or woman: foolish, senseless, or thoughtless. Now *rare.* E18.

taws /tɔːz/ *noun & verb.* Chiefly *Scot.* Also **tawse**. E16.
[App. pl. of TAW *noun*¹, but recorded earlier.]
▶**A** *noun.* **1** A whip for driving a spinning-top; *esp.* one made of a thong. E16.
2 Chiefly *Hist.* A leather strap or thong divided at the end into narrow strips used as an instrument of corporal punishment. Treated as *sing.* or *pl.* L16.

📖 **2** S. HOOD The leather tawse came out of the headmaster's desk.

▶**B** *verb trans.* Beat with a taws. *rare.* L18.

tax /taks/ *noun.* ME.
[from the verb.]
1 A contribution to State revenue, compulsorily levied on people, businesses, property, income, commodities, transactions, etc. Freq. with specifying word. ME.
†**2** A task; a piece of work assigned to a person; a lesson. *rare.* LME–L17.
3 An oppressive or burdensome obligation or duty; a burden, a strain, a heavy demand. E17.
†**4** A charge, an accusation; censure. E–M17.

📖 **1** R. PILCHER All of this . . will be subject to duties and tax. *European Investor* A tax of 0.5 per cent on the net assets. ***corporation tax***, ***income tax***, ***inheritance tax***, ***poll tax***, ***property tax***, ***window tax***, etc.

Phrases: ***capital transfer tax***: see CAPITAL *adjective & noun*². ***direct tax***: see DIRECT *adjective*. INSPECTOR ***of taxes***. ***negative income tax***: see INCOME *noun*¹. SELECTIVE ***employment tax***. ***value added tax***: see VALUE *noun*.

Comb.: **tax allowance** a sum to be deducted from gross income in the calculation of taxable income; **tax avoidance** the arrangement of financial affairs to reduce tax liability within the law; **tax bite** *N. Amer. colloq.* an amount that one is compelled to pay as tax; **tax-book** a list of property subject to taxation, with the amount payable; **tax bracket** a range of incomes taxed at a given rate; **tax break** *colloq.* (orig. *US*) a tax advantage or concession allowed by government; **tax code** a code number assigned by tax authorities representing the tax-free part of an employee's income; **tax collector** an official who receives money due as taxes; **tax credit** a sum that can be offset against a tax liability; *spec.* one resulting in a payment to any person whose liability is less than this sum; ***tax-deductible***: see DEDUCTIBLE *adjective*; **tax deduction** a deduction that may be made from one's tax or taxable income; **tax disc** a circular label displayed in the window of a motor vehicle certifying payment of motor vehicle excise duty; **tax-dodger** *colloq.* a person who practises tax avoidance or tax evasion; **tax dollar** *N. Amer.* a dollar paid as tax; **tax-eater** (now chiefly *US*) a person supported from the public revenue; **tax-eating** *adjective* (chiefly *US*) of, pertaining to, or characteristic of a tax-eater; **tax-evader** a person who practises tax evasion; **tax evasion** the illegal non-payment or underpayment of income tax; **tax-exempt** *adjective & noun* (*a*) *adjective* free from a liability to be taxed; (*b*) *noun* a tax-exempt security; **tax exemption** freedom from a liability to be taxed; **tax exile** a person who lives in a country etc. chosen for its lower taxes on personal income; the state of living in a country etc. chosen for its lower taxes on personal income; **tax-free** *adjective* not liable to be taxed; **tax gatherer** *arch.* a collector of taxes; **tax haven** a country etc. where income tax is low; **tax holiday** *colloq.* a period of tax exemption or tax reduction, esp. one of fixed duration; **tax inspector** = INSPECTOR ***of taxes***; **tax-loss** a loss that can be offset against taxable profit earned elsewhere or in a different period; **taxman** an inspector or collector of taxes; *the* Board of Inland Revenue personified; **taxpayer** (*a*) a person who pays a tax or taxes; a person liable to taxation; (*b*) *US colloq.* a building just large enough to generate income sufficient for its expenses; any small building; **tax point** the date on which value added tax becomes chargeable in any particular transaction; **tax relief** remission of a proportion of income tax; **tax return** a declaration of income for taxation purposes; **tax shelter** a means of organizing business affairs to reduce tax liability; **tax-sheltered** *adjective* providing a tax shelter; **tax-taker** *arch.* a tax-collector; **tax threshold** the level of income at which tax begins to be payable; **tax year** a year as reckoned for taxation (in Britain reckoned from 6 April).
▪ **taxless** *adjective* free from taxes or taxation; untaxed: E17.

tax /taks/ *verb trans.* ME.
[Old & mod. French *taxer* from Latin *taxare* censure, charge, compute, perh. from Greek *tassein* order, fix.]
▶**I 1** Orig., estimate or determine the amount of (a fine, penalty, damages, etc.); assess. Now only in LAW, examine and assess (costs). ME.
2 Impose a tax on; subject to taxation (esp. *at* a specified rate). ME.
†**3** Ordain or prescribe (a course of action etc.); order (a person) *to* or *to do.* LME–E19.
4 *fig.* Burden; make heavy demands on; put a strain on. L17.
5 Set a fixed price for (an article); charge (a person) a fixed price. *US local.* M19.

📖 **1** W. BLACKSTONE Costs on both sides are taxed . . by the . . officer of the court. **taxing-master** an officer in a court of law who examines and assesses items in a solicitor's disputed bill of costs. **2** ADAM SMITH All the arable lands . . are taxed at a tenth of the rent. H. T. BUCKLE The right of the people to be taxed entirely by their representatives. **4** M. LEITCH You're a fool, and you're beginning to tax my patience. W. HORWOOD The problem had taxed the elders considerably.

▶**II** †**6** Enter in a list, register, enrol. *rare.* E–M16.
▶**III 7** Censure; charge or confront (a person) *with* wrongdoing etc. M16.
†**8** Call in question; challenge or dispute (a statement etc.). E17–L18.

📖 **7** DRYDEN You have justly taxed my long neglect. A. POWELL Taxing him with the offence.

▪ **taxative** *adjective* (*rare*) (*a*) of a limiting or defining nature; (*b*) having the function of taxing a person or thing; of or pertaining to taxation: L17.

taxa *noun* pl. of TAXON.

taxable /'taksəb(ə)l/ *adjective & noun.* L15.
[Anglo-Norman, Old French (Anglo-Latin *taxabilis*), formed as TAX *verb*; later directly from prec.: see -ABLE.]
▶**A** *adjective.* Able to be taxed; subject to a tax. L15.

📖 *Saturday Review* Consumers of taxable commodities had no reason to complain of Mr. Lowe's Budget.

▶**B** *noun.* A taxable person or thing. Orig. *US.* M17.
▪ **taxa'bility** *noun* E19. **taxableness** *noun* M19. **taxably** *adverb* E20.

taxaceous /tak'seɪʃəs/ *adjective.* M19.
[from mod. Latin *Taxaceae* (see below) from Latin *taxus* yew: see -ACEOUS.]
BOTANY. Of or pertaining to the Taxaceae or yew family, often included in the order Coniferales.

taxation /tak'seɪʃ(ə)n/ *noun.* ME.
[Anglo-Norman *taxacioun*, Old & mod. French *taxation* from Latin *taxatio(n-)*, from *taxare* TAX *verb*: see -ATION.]
1 The estimation or determination of the amount of a fine, penalty, damages, etc.; assessment. Now only in LAW, examination and assessment of costs. ME.
2 Orig., a tax imposed or levied. Later, the imposition or levying of taxes; the action of taxing a person or thing; the fact of being taxed. LME.
†**3** Accusation; censure, blame. L16–M17.
†**4** Enrolment, registration, census. *rare.* Only in L17.

📖 **1** *Daily Telegraph* Challenging the bill-taxation by a court official. **2** *New York Times* Immediate taxation to raise money. ***direct taxation***: see DIRECT *adjective*.

taxator /tak'seɪtə/ *noun.* LME.
[medieval Latin, from Latin *taxare* TAX *verb*: see -ATOR.]
1 A person who assesses a subsidy, impost, or tax; an assessor; a person who levies a tax. Now *Hist.* LME.
2 = TAXER 1b. *rare.* M19.

tax-cart /'takskɑːt/ *noun. obsolete* exc. *Hist.* L18.
[from TAX *noun* + CART *noun*.]
= TAXED ***cart***.

taxed /takst/ *ppl adjective.* L15.
[from TAX *verb* + -ED¹.]
That has been taxed; *spec.* (of a motor vehicle) having had excise duty paid for the current period.
taxed cart (*obsolete* exc. *Hist.*) a two-wheeled (orig. springless) one-horse open cart, used mainly for agricultural or trade purposes, on which excise duty was reduced or remitted. **taxed ward** SCOTS LAW (now *Hist.*) in land tenure, a wardship in which a fixed annual sum was paid to the superior in lieu of the whole profits.
¶ Earlier in UNTAXED.

taxe de séjour /taks də seʒuːr/ *noun phr.* Pl. ***taxes de séjour*** (pronounced same). E20.
[French, lit. 'tax of visit'.]
A tax imposed on visitors to spas or tourist resorts in France and French-speaking countries.

taxeme /'taksiːm/ *noun.* M20.
[from Greek *taxis* arrangement + -EME.]
LINGUISTICS. A unit of grammatical relationship, *esp.* one, such as word order or stress, that cannot be further analysed or lacks meaning by itself.
▪ **ta'xemic** *adjective* of or pertaining to taxemes, of the nature of a taxeme M20. **ta'xemics** *noun* the branch of linguistics that deals with taxemes M20.

taxer /'taksə/ *noun.* Also (the usual form in sense 2) **taxor**. LME.
[Anglo-Norman *taxour*, from *taxer* TAX *verb*: see -ER¹, -OR.]
1 †**a** A person who determines the amount of a tax; an assessor. LME–L17. ▸**b** *Hist.* A university officer (usu. either of two) who fixed the rents of students' lodgings. M16.
2 A person who levies a tax or taxes. E17.
†**3** A person who finds fault or censures. Only in E17.

taxes *nouns* pls. of TAX *noun*, TAXIS.

-taxes *suffix* pl. of -TAXIS.

taxes de séjour *noun phr.* pl. of TAXE DE SÉJOUR.

taxflation /taks'fleɪʃ(ə)n/ *noun. US.* L20.
[Blend of TAXATION and INFLATION.]
ECONOMICS. An increase in income tax payable by a person whose income is linked to the rate of inflation and who consequently moves to a higher tax bracket.

taxi /'taksi/ *noun & verb.* E20.
[Colloq. abbreviation of TAXIMETER. In sense 2 directly from the verb.]
▶**A** *noun.* **1** More fully ***taxi-cab***. A motor-car licensed to ply for hire and usu. fitted with a taximeter. E20. ▸**b** A (small) passenger aeroplane, a taxiplane; a taxi-boat. *colloq.* E20.
2 An act or spell of taxiing. M20.
3 A prison sentence of between five and fifteen years. *US slang.* M20.
Comb.: **taxi-boat** a boat that may be hired like a taxi; ***taxi-cab***: see sense A.1 above; **taxi dance** (orig. & chiefly *US*) a dance at which taxi dancers are available; **taxi dancer** (orig. *US*) a dance-partner available for hire; a professional dance-partner; **taxi-driver** the driver of a taxi; *colloq.* an aeroplane pilot; **taxi-girl** a young female taxi dancer; **taxiplane** a piloted light aeroplane available for public hire; ***taxi rank***: see RANK *noun* 1(c); **taxi-ride** a journey in a taxi; a short distance by car; **taxi service** a service providing transport by taxi; **taxi squad** AMER. FOOTBALL a group of players taking part in practices and available as reserves for the team; **taxi strip**, **taxi track**, **taxiway** a route along which aircraft can taxi when moving to or from a runway.
▶**B** *verb.* **1 a** *verb intrans.* Of an aircraft or pilot: move slowly along the ground or water under the machine's own power before take-off or after landing. E20. ▸**b** *verb trans.* Cause (an aircraft) to taxi. E20.
2 a *verb intrans.* Travel in a taxi. E20. ▸**b** *verb trans.* Convey in a taxi. L20.

taxiarch /'taksɪɑːk/ *noun.* E19.
[Greek *taxiarkhos* from *taxis* TAXIS: see -ARCH.]
GREEK HISTORY. The commander of a taxis of soldiers.

taxidermy /'taksɪdəːmi/ *noun.* E19.
[from Greek *taxis* arrangement + *derma* skin: see -Y³.]
The art of preparing, stuffing, and mounting the skins of animals with lifelike effect.
▪ **taxi'dermal** *adjective* of or pertaining to taxidermy L19. **taxi'dermic** *adjective* taxidermal M19. **taxidermist** *noun* a person who practises or is skilled in taxidermy E19.

taximeter /ˈtaksiːmiːtə/ *noun*. **L19.**
[French *taximètre*, from *taxe* tariff, tax + *-mètre* -METER.]
An automatic device fitted to a taxi, recording the distance travelled and the fare due.

taxine /ˈtaksiːn/ *noun*. **E20.**
[from Latin *taxus* yew + -INE⁵.]
CHEMISTRY. An alkaloid obtained from the leaves, shoots, and seeds of yew, and responsible for their poisonous properties.

taxinomy /takˈsɪnəmi/ *noun*. Now *rare* or *obsolete*. **M19.**
[formed as next + -NOMY.]
= TAXONOMY 1.

taxis /ˈtaksɪs/ *noun*. Pl. **taxes** /ˈtaksiːz/. **L16.**
[Greek = arrangement, from *tassein* arrange.]
†**1** *RHETORIC.* A figure of speech in which individual elements are systematically arranged. Only in **L16.**
†**2** *ARCHITECTURE.* Arrangement of the elements of a building in due proportion; ordonnance. Only in **E18.**
3 *MEDICINE.* (An instance of) a surgical operation to reposition a displaced part by means of traction. Now *rare* or *obsolete*. **M18.**
4 *GREEK HISTORY.* A company of soldiers, esp. foot-soldiers; a military division of varying size. **M19.**
5 *PHILOLOGY.* Order or arrangement of words. *rare*. **L19.**
6 *BIOLOGY.* The motion or orientation of an organism or part of one, related to the direction of a stimulus. Cf. TROPISM. **L19.**

-taxis /ˈtaksɪs/ *suffix*. Pl. **-taxes** /ˈtaksiːz/.
[from prec.]
BIOLOGY. Forming nouns with the senses (***a***) motion or orientation related to the direction of a stimulus, as ***chemotaxis***, ***geotaxis***, ***phototaxis***; (***b***) arrangement or order, as ***phyllotaxis***. Cf. -TAXY.

taxodium /takˈsəʊdɪəm/ *noun*. **M19.**
[mod. Latin (see below), from Greek *taxos*, Latin *taxus* yew: see -ODE¹.]
Either of two N. American coniferous trees constituting the genus *Taxodium*, the bald cypress, *T. distichum*, of the southern US, and *T. mucronatum*, of Mexico.

taxogen /ˈtaksədʒ(ə)n/ *noun*. **M20.**
[Irreg. from Greek TAXIS + -O- + -GEN.]
CHEMISTRY. The monomer in the chain of a telomer.

taxol /ˈtaksɒl/ *noun*. **M20.**
[from Latin *taxus* yew + -OL.]
PHARMACOLOGY. **1** *Hist.* A preparation for regulating the bowels. **M20.**
2 A compound obtained from the bark of certain yews, which inhibits the growth of some tumours. **L20.**
¶ A proprietary name.

taxon /ˈtaksɒn/ *noun*. Pl. **taxa** /ˈtaksə/. **E20.**
[Back-form. from TAXONOMY: see -ON.]
A taxonomic group of any rank, as species, family, class, etc.; an organism contained in such a group.

> 🕮 *Watsonia* Many infraspecific taxa [of *Trifolium repens*] have been described for wild populations.

taxonomic /taksəˈnɒmɪk/ *adjective*. **M19.**
[from next + -IC.]
1 Pertaining or relating to taxonomy or classification. **M19.**
2 *LINGUISTICS.* Involving or concerned with the identification and classification of the units into which languages are analysed. **M20.**
▪ **taxonomical** *adjective* (now *rare*) = TAXONOMIC **L19.** **taxonomically** *adverb* **L19.**

taxonomy /takˈsɒnəmi/ *noun*. **E19.**
[Irreg. from Greek TAXIS + -O- + -NOMY.]
1 Classification, esp. in relation to its general laws or principles; the branch of science, or of a particular science or subject, that deals with classification; *esp.* the systematic classification of living organisms. **E19.**
2 A classification *of* something. **M20.**
▪ **taxonomer** *noun* (now *rare*) = TAXONOMIST **L19.** **taxonomist** *noun* an expert in or student of taxonomy **L19.** **taxonomize** *verb trans.* classify taxonomically **L20.**

taxor *noun* see TAXER.

taxwax /ˈtakswaks/ *noun*. Long *obsolete* exc. *dial.* **E18.**
[Alt.]
= PAXWAX.

-taxy /taksi/ *suffix*.
[from Greek *-taxia*, TAXIS arrangement, order.]
Forming nouns with the sense 'arrangement or order', as ***epitaxy***, ***heterotaxy***, ***meiotaxy***. Cf. -TAXIS.

Tayacian /təˈjeɪʃ(ə)n/ *adjective & noun*. **M20.**
[French *Tayacien*, from *Tayac* (see below) + -IAN.]
ARCHAEOLOGY. (Designating) a stage of palaeolithic culture before the Mousterian period, characterized by flake tools, remains of which were first found at Tayac in the department of the Dordogne, SW France.

tayassu /tɑːjəˈsuː/ *noun*. Also **tayaçu**. **M17.**
[Tupi *tayaçu* lit. 'with large teeth'.]
The collared peccary, *Tayassu tajacu*. Now only as mod. Latin genus name.

tayberry /ˈteɪb(ə)ri/ *noun*. **L20.**
[from *Tay* a river in Scotland + BERRY *noun*¹.]
A dark purple soft fruit produced by crossing the raspberry and an American blackberry, introduced in Scotland in 1977; the plant bearing this fruit.

Taylor /ˈteɪlə/ *noun*. **E19.**
[Brook *Taylor* (1685–1731), English mathematician.]
MATH. **1** ***Taylor's theorem***, the theorem that the values of a function $f(x)$ can be approximated over any interval throughout which its first n derivatives exist by the first n terms of Taylor's series (with $h = x - a$) plus a remainder dependent on the nth derivative of $f(x)$. **E19.**
2 ***Taylor series***, ***Taylor's series***, an infinite series of the form $f(a) + hf'(a) + h^2f''(a)/2! + \dots + h^{n-1}f^{(n-1)}(a)/(n-1)! + \dots$, where $f^{(i)}(a)$ is the value of the ith derivative of a function $f(x)$ at $x = a$; an analogous series for a function of more than one variable. **M19.**

Taylorise *verb* var. of TAYLORIZE.

Taylorism /ˈteɪlərɪz(ə)m/ *noun*¹. **M19.**
[from N. W. *Taylor* (see below) + -ISM.]
The theological system of N. W. Taylor (1786–1858) of New Haven, Connecticut, a modified form of Calvinism.

Taylorism /ˈteɪlərɪz(ə)m/ *noun*². **E20.**
[from F. W. *Taylor* (see TAYLOR SYSTEM) + -ISM.]
The principles or practice of the Taylor system of management.

Taylorize /ˈteɪlərʌɪz/ *verb trans.* Also **-ise**. **M20.**
[formed as TAYLORISM *noun*² + -IZE.]
Introduce the Taylor system into (an organization etc.); manage (an organization etc.) in accordance with this system. Chiefly as ***Taylorized***, ***Taylorizing*** *ppl adjectives*.
▪ **Taylori'zation** *noun* **E20.**

Taylor system /ˈteɪlə sɪstəm/ *noun phr.* **E20.**
[F. W. *Taylor* (1856–1915), US engineer + SYSTEM.]
A system of scientific management and work efficiency expounded by Taylor.

tayra /ˈtʌɪrə/ *noun*. **M19.**
[Tupi *taira*.]
A large weasel, *Eira barbara*, which is related to the martens, has a glossy dark brown body with a paler head and neck, and is found in the forests etc. of Central and S. America.

Tay-Sachs /teɪˈsaks/ *noun*. **E20.**
[from Warren *Tay* (1843–1927), English ophthalmologist + Bernard *Sachs* (1858–1944), US neurologist.]
MEDICINE. Used ***attrib.*** with ref. to a fatal inherited metabolic disorder in which an enzyme deficiency causes accumulation of gangliosides in the brain etc., resulting in spasticity, dementia, and death in childhood.

taz /taz/ *noun*. *colloq.* **M20.**
[Abbreviation.]
= MOUSTACHE 1. Cf. TASH.

tazetta /təˈzɛtə/ *noun*. **M19.**
[mod. Latin (see below), specific epithet from Italian *tazzetta* little cup, formed as TAZZA: see -ET¹.]
A fragrant polyanthus narcissus, *Narcissus tazetta*, having white flowers with a yellow corona, native to the Mediterranean region; any of the numerous varieties developed from this plant.

tazia /təˈziːə/ *noun*. **E19.**
[Arab. *ta'ziya* consolation, mourning.]
1 A representation, often made of paper and elaborately decorated, of the tomb of Husain (grandson of Muhammad) carried in procession during Muharram. **E19.**
2 A play commemorating the suffering and death of Husain, performed esp. on the anniversary of the event each year. **L19.**

tazza /ˈtɑːtsə/ *noun*. Pl. **tazze** /ˈtɑːtsi/, **tazzas**. **E19.**
[Italian from Arab. *tasa*: see TASS *noun*².]
A shallow ornamental wine-cup or vase, *esp.* one mounted on a foot.

TB *abbreviation*.
1 Torpedo boat.
2 Treasury bill.
3 Tuberculosis; tubercle bacillus.

Tb *symbol*.
CHEMISTRY. Terbium.

TBD *abbreviation*.
Torpedo-boat destroyer.

TBS *abbreviation*.
1 Talk between ships (a short-wave radio apparatus used between ships).
2 Tight building syndrome.

tbs. *abbreviation*. Also **tbsp.**
Tablespoon(ful).

TBT *abbreviation*.
Tributyl tin.

Tc *symbol*.
CHEMISTRY. Technetium.

TCA *abbreviation*.
Trichloroacetic acid (a herbicide).

TCD *abbreviation*.
Trinity College, Dublin.

TCDD *abbreviation*.
Tetrachlorodibenzo(para)dioxin.

tch /tʃ/ *interjection, noun, & verb*. Freq. redupl. **L19.**
[Imit. of a click of the tongue against the teeth.]
▶**A** *interjection & noun*. (An exclamation) expr. irritation, annoyance, or impatience. **L19.**

> 🕮 *Daily Mirror* Tch! Of all the times to go down wi' flu!

▶**B** *verb intrans.* Say 'tch'. **L19.**

tcha /tʃɑː/ *interjection & noun*. Also **tchah**. **M19.**
[Imit.]
(An exclamation) expr. impatience or contempt.

> 🕮 M. MITCHELL He .. looked away with a 'Tchah!' of angry disgust.

Tchaikovskian /tʃʌɪˈkɒfskɪən/ *adjective & noun*. **M20.**
[from *Tchaikovsky* (see below) + -AN.]
▶**A** *adjective*. Of, pertaining to, or characteristic of the Russian composer, Pyotr Ilyich Tchaikovsky (1840–93) or his music. **M20.**
▶**B** *noun*. An admirer, student, or imitator of Tchaikovsky or his music. **M20.**

Tchambuli /tʃəmˈbuːli/ *noun & adjective*. **M20.**
[Papuan.]
▶**A** *noun*. Pl. same. A people inhabiting the Sepik river region of Papua New Guinea; the language of this people. **M20.**
▶**B** *attrib.* or as *adjective*. Of or pertaining to this people or their language. **M20.**

tchaush *noun* var. of CHIAUS *noun*¹.

Tchekhovian *adjective* var. of CHEKHOVIAN.

Tcheremiss *noun* var. of CHEREMISS.

†**tchernozem** *noun* var. of CHERNOZEM.

tchetvert /ˈtʃɛtvɛrt/ *noun*. **E19.**
[Russian *chetvert'* quarter.]
Hist. A Russian measure of capacity for grain etc. equal to about 8.6 kg.

tchick /tʃɪk/ *noun, interjection, & verb*. **E19.**
[Imit. of a click made by pressing part of the tongue against the palate and withdrawing it with suction.]
▶**A** *noun & interjection*. (A command) used to urge on a horse. **E19.**
▶**B** *verb intrans.* Say 'tchick'; make a sound resembling a 'tchick'. Also = TCH *verb*. **E19.**

tchin /tʃɪn/ *noun*. Also **chin**. **M19.**
[Russian *chin* rank.]
In Russia: rank; people of high rank.

tchinovnik *noun* var. of CHINOVNIK.

tchotchke *noun* var. of TSATSKE.

Tchuktchi *noun & adjective* var. of CHUKCHI.

TCP *abbreviation*.
1 *PHYSICS.* Time (reversal), charge (conjugation), and parity (conservation).
2 *COMPUTING.* Transmission control protocol.
3 *CHEMISTRY.* Tricresyl phosphate.
2 TCP/IP [proprietary name] transmission control protocol/Internet protocol, a standard for the connection of computer systems to the Internet.

TD *abbreviation*.
1 Irish *Teachta Dála*, a member of Dáil Éireann, the lower house of the Irish parliament.
2 Territorial Decoration (in the Territorial Army).
3 *AMER. FOOTBALL.* Touchdown.

TDE *abbreviation*.
2-dichlorethane, an organochlorine insecticide formerly used on fruit and vegetables.

t.d.s. *abbreviation*.
MEDICINE. Latin *Ter die sumendus* to be taken three times a day.

Te *symbol*.
CHEMISTRY. Tellurium.

te /tiː/ *noun*¹. Also **ti**. M19.
[Later form of SI.]
MUSIC. The seventh note of a scale in a movable-doh system; the note B in the fixed-doh system.

te /teɪ/ *noun*². L19.
[Chinese *dé* virtue (Wade–Giles *te*).]
In *TAOISM*, the essence of Tao inherent in all beings; in *CONFUCIANISM* and in extended use, moral virtue.

tea /tiː/ *noun*. M17.
[Prob. from Dutch *tee* (now *thee*) from Chinese (Min) *te*, (Mandarin) *chá* CHA.]
1 The dried leaves of the plant *Camellia sinensis* (see sense 2); the drink made by infusing these leaves in hot (boiling) water. Also (with specifying word), a particular variety or blend of such leaves. M17. ▸**b** A drink of tea. E20.
2 The plant from which tea is obtained, *Camellia sinensis* (family Theaceae), a shrub or tree with white flowers and oval evergreen leaves, long cultivated in China and now also in Japan, India, Kenya, and elsewhere. M17.
3 Usu. with specifying word. An infusion made in the same way as tea from the leaves, flowers, etc., of various other plants or from any other substance; a drink of such an infusion; (the leaves of) any of the plants from which such an infusion can be made. M17.
4 a Alcoholic liquor. *slang*. L17. ▸**b** Marijuana; *spec.* marijuana brewed in hot water to make a drink. *slang* (orig. *US*). M20.
5 A meal or social gathering at which tea is served. Now *esp.* (*a*) a light afternoon meal, usu. consisting of tea, cakes, sandwiches, etc. (also more fully ***afternoon tea***, ***five o'clock tea***); (*b*) (in parts of the UK, and in Australia and NZ) a main meal in the evening that usually includes a cooked dish, bread and butter, and tea (also more fully ***high tea***). M18.
6 *ellipt.* A tea rose. M19.

📖 **1** A. GHOSH His digestion was . . ruined by the hard-boiled tea . . drunk at roadside stalls. ***China tea***, ***green tea***, ***gunpowder tea***, ***Indian tea***, ***lapsang souchong tea***, etc. ***cup of tea***: see CUP *noun* 1. **not for all the tea in China** *colloq.* (orig. *Austral.*) not for anything, not at any price. **rich tea (biscuit)** a semi-sweet biscuit. ***Russian tea***: see RUSSIAN *adjective*. **tea and sympathy** *colloq.* hospitality and consolation offered to a distressed person. **3** ***beef tea***, ***camomile tea***, ***Jersey tea***, ***Labrador tea***, ***Mexican tea***, ***Oswego tea***, ***sassafras tea***, etc. **5** P. P. READ Gail had taken Lucy . . to tea with some friends. **take tea with** *slang* have dealings with, associate with; *esp.* deal with in a hostile manner. **6** ***hybrid tea***: see HYBRID *adjective*.

Attrib. & comb.: In the senses 'of, pertaining to, or dealing with tea as a commodity', as ***tea-broker***, ***tea-duty***, ***tea merchant***, ***tea trade***, etc., 'containing or intended to contain tea as a drink', as ***tea-bowl***, ***tea mug***, etc., 'of or pertaining to the tea plant or its cultivation', as ***tea district***, ***tea estate***, ***tea plantation***, etc. Special combs., as **tea bag** (*a*) *Canad.* a bag for carrying provisions; (*b*) a small perforated bag containing tea for infusion; **tea ball** (chiefly *N. Amer.*) a ball of wire or perforated metal to hold tea for infusion; **tea bar** a bar or café at which tea and other refreshments are sold; **teaberry** the checkerberry, *Gaultheria procumbens*, whose leaves can be used as a substitute for tea; the fruit of this plant; **tea-billy** *Austral. & NZ* a tin can used as a tea-kettle or teapot; **tea-box** (*a*) a box for containing tea; a tea chest; (*b*) *Canad.* (now *rare*) a box for carrying food and cooking utensils on an expedition; **tea boy** (*a*) *arch.* a manservant; (*b*) a youth (occas. a man) employed to make and serve tea, esp. in an office, factory, etc.; **tea-bread** (*a*) a usu. loaf-shaped cake containing dried fruit that has been soaked in tea before baking; (*b*) a kind of light or sweet bread for eating at tea; **tea break** a pause, usu. between periods of work, allowing for relaxation, the drinking of tea, etc.; **tea-brick** a brick or block of compressed tea leaves; ***tea caddy***: see CADDY *noun*¹ 1; **teacake** a small light flat cake consisting of a yeast dough and dried fruit, usu. eaten toasted and buttered; **tea-can** a metal can used for brewing or carrying tea; **tea-canister** (*a*) a tea caddy; (*b*) *slang* a brandy-flask; **tea cart** *US* a tea trolley; **tea ceremony** in Japan, an elaborate ritual, following precise rules, for preparing, serving, and drinking green tea, as an expression of Zen Buddhist philosophy; **tea chest** (*a*) (*obsolete* exc. *Hist.*) a tea caddy; (*b*) a light metal-lined wooden box in which tea is packed for transport; **tea-clipper** a clipper or fast sailing ship formerly employed in the tea trade; **tea cloth** (*a*) = ***tea towel*** below; (*b*) a small tablecloth used at afternoon tea; **tea cosy** (*a*) see COSY *noun* 1; (*b*) (in full ***tea-cosy hat***) a round knitted hat resembling a tea cosy; **tea dance** (*a*) an afternoon tea with dancing; (*b*) *Canad.* a social gathering held by Indians (so called because orig. the Hudson's Bay Company contributed tea etc. to such events); **tea-dance** *verb intrans.* attend or dance at a tea dance; move in the style of dancing associated with a tea dance (chiefly as ***tea dancing*** *verbal noun*); **tea-drinker** a person who drinks tea, esp. habitually or in large quantities; **tea-drinking** (*a*) the drinking of tea; †(*b*) a social gathering at which tea is provided; **tea-dust** *noun & adjective* (*a*) *noun* tea of inferior quality, often made from leaves broken in the course of production; (*b*) *adjective* designating a dark green or brownish (often speckled) glaze on Chinese pottery, esp. used on decorative ware; **tea fight** *joc. colloq.* a tea party; **tea garden** (*a*) a garden or open-air enclosure, where tea and other refreshments are served to the public; (*b*) a tea plantation; **tea girl** a girl employed to make and serve tea, esp. in an office, factory, etc.; **tea glass** a glass from which tea (esp. without milk) is drunk; **tea gown** a long loose-fitting dress, usu. made of fine fabric and lace-trimmed, worn at afternoon tea and popular in the late 19th and early 20th cents.; **tea green** a shade of greyish green resembling the colour of tea; **teahead** *slang* (orig. *US*) a habitual user of marijuana (cf. sense 4b above); **tea house** a refreshment-house, esp. in China or Japan, where tea is served; **tea infuser** = ***tea-maker*** (c) below; **tea interval** a break for afternoon tea or light refreshment, esp. during a cricket match; ***tea-kettle***: see KETTLE 1(a); **tea lady** a woman employed to make and serve tea, esp. in an office, factory, etc.; **tea machine**: for making or dispensing tea; **tea-maker** (*a*) a person who dries the leaves and prepares tea for the tea-trade; (*b*) a person who makes or infuses tea; (*c*) a vessel or device for infusing tea; (*d*) a machine incorporating a timer, and intended to be kept by the bedside, which can be pre-set to make tea automatically at a given time, esp. when one awakes; **teaman** (*a*) a merchant who deals in tea; (*b*) *US slang* a dealer or user of marijuana; **tea master** an expert in the proper conduct of the Japanese tea ceremony; **tea oil** an oil resembling olive oil, obtained from the seeds of the sasanqua and other species of *Camellia*, which is used for various purposes in China and Japan; **tea olive** = the sweet olive, *Osmanthus fragrans*; **tea pad** *US slang* a place where marijuana can be bought and smoked; **tea party** (*a*) a party at teatime; a social gathering at which tea and other light refreshments are served; (*b*) *slang* a gathering at which marijuana is smoked; **tea place** a teashop; **tea plant** (*a*) = sense 2 above; (*b*) any of various plants whose leaves can be infused like tea; (*c*) ***Duke of Argyll's tea plant*** = ***Duke of Argyll's tea-tree*** s.v. TEA-TREE 3; **tea-planter** a proprietor of a tea plantation; a cultivator of tea plants; **tea plate** a small shallow plate for use at afternoon tea; **tearoom** (*a*) a room or small café where tea is served; (*b*) *N. Amer. slang* a public lavatory used as a meeting-place by homosexuals; **tea-scented** *adjective* having a scent like that of tea; ***tea-scented rose***, a tea rose; **tea-scrub** in Australia and New Zealand, a scrub or thicket of tea-trees; **tea-seed oil** = ***tea oil*** above; **tea-service**, **teaset** a set of matching plates, cups, saucers, etc., often including a teapot, milk jug and sugar bowl, for serving tea; **tea-taster** a person whose business is to test the quality of samples of tea by tasting them; **tea-tent**: in which tea is served at an outdoor event; **tea-things** the articles comprising a teaset; the items of crockery etc. used at teatime; **teatime** the time in the afternoon or evening at which the meal called tea is customarily eaten or at which tea is drunk; **tea towel** a towel or cloth for drying washed crockery etc.; **tea tray**: on which a teaset is carried; **tea-treat** (chiefly in Cornwall) a publicly provided outdoor tea party for children, esp. of a Sunday-school; **tea trolley** a small wheeled trolley from which tea is served; **tea wagon** †(*a*) an East Indiaman used to carry cargoes of tea; (*b*) *US* = ***tea trolley*** above; **tea-ware** china etc. for serving tea, tea-things; **tea yellows** a disease of the tea plant, esp. in Africa, caused by sulphur deficiency and indicated by small, chlorotic leaves, and the eventual death of the bush.

¶ Orig., & still dial., pronounced /teɪ/.

■ **tealess** *adjective* without tea; not having had one's tea: E19.

tea /tiː/ *verb*. Pa. t. & pple **-'d**, **-ed**. E19.
[from the noun.]
1 *verb trans.* Give tea to; entertain to tea. E19.
2 *verb intrans.* Drink tea; eat the meal called tea, have one's tea. E19.

📖 **1** C. AMORY Mrs . . Fields . . was still teaing authors in her parlor in her eighties.

tea-board /ˈtiːbɔːd/ *noun*. Now *local*. M18.
[from TEA *noun* + BOARD *noun*.]
A tea-tray, *esp.* a wooden one.
■ **teaboardy** *adjective* (*arch. slang*) (of a picture) of a type found on tea-trays; superficially pleasant and slickly painted: L19.

teach /tiːtʃ/ *noun*. *colloq.* M20.
[Abbreviation. Cf. PREACH *noun*².]
A teacher.

teach /tiːtʃ/ *verb*. Pa. t. & pple **taught** /tɔːt/.
[Old English *tǣċan* (pa. t. *tǣhte*, Northumbrian *tāhte*) rel. to base also of TOKEN *noun*, from Germanic base meaning 'show', from Indo-European base repr. by Greek *deiknunai* show, *deigma* sample.]
▸ **I** †**1** *verb trans.* Show, present or offer to view. Only in OE.
†**2** *verb trans.* Show or point out (a thing, the way, etc.) to a person. OE–LME.
3 a *verb trans.* (orig. with dat. obj.). Show (a person) the way; direct, conduct, guide (*to*, *from* a place). Also, direct or refer (*to* something). Long *obsolete* exc. *dial.* OE. ▸**b** *verb intrans. NAUTICAL.* Of a line in marine architecture: point in a particular direction. M19.
4 *verb trans.* Show (a person) what is to be observed or done; ordain or decree (something). *obsolete* or passing into branch II. OE.
▸ **II 5** *verb trans.* Impart information about or the knowledge of (a subject or skill); give instruction, training, or lessons in (a subject etc.). OE. ▸**b** Impart information or knowledge to (a person); educate, train, or instruct (a person); give (a person) moral guidance. Also with double obj. OE.
6 *verb trans.* Enable (a person) *to do* something by instruction or training; show or explain to (a person) a fact or how to do something by instruction, lessons, etc. Usu. foll. by *that*, *to do*. OE. ▸**b** Induce (a person) by example or punishment to do or not to do something. Also (*colloq.*), make (a person) disinclined to do something. Usu. foll. by *to do*. ME.
7 *verb intrans.* Impart knowledge or information; act as a teacher; give instruction, lessons, or training. OE.

📖 **5** *Times Lit. Suppl.* Go on teaching *Heart of Darkness* with Achebe's essay as accompaniment. *New Scientist* The British Council is concentrating . . on retraining redundant teachers of Russian to teach English. **b** L. STEFFENS Chicago has something to teach every . . town in the country. C. P. SNOW He taught us algebra and geometry. D. EDEN One should be taught manners young. **6** W. CATHER Don't they . . teach you . . that you'd all be heathen Turks if it hadn't been for the Bohemians? A. GHOSH He taught Robi to climb the mango tree. *fig.*: T. HOOK James's lank hair . . was taught to curl gracefully. **b** *New Statesman* That'll teach you to spill my whisky. **7** *Green Magazine* Ready to teach . . at the touch of a button, ISM is based around . . musical marvels.

▸†**III 8** *verb trans.* = BETEACH. OE–L15.
Phrases: ***teach a person a lesson***: see LESSON *noun*. ***teach a person a thing or two***: see THING *noun*¹. ***teach one's GRANDMOTHER to suck eggs***. ***teach school***: see SCHOOL *noun*¹. †**teach to** train to; accustom to the use or practice of. **teach yourself** *adjective* (of a textbook, course of study, etc.) intended for use without the assistance of a teacher.

teachable /ˈtiːtʃəb(ə)l/ *adjective*. LME.
[from TEACH *verb* + -ABLE.]
1 Of a subject: that can be taught or imparted by instruction, training, etc. LME.
†**2** Capable of teaching something; instructive. L15–L17.
3 Of a person: able to be taught; apt at learning; receptive to instruction; tractable. L15.

📖 **3** C. KINGSLEY These old Greeks were teachable, and learnt from all the nations around. M. BURT The . . receivable, teachable quality in woman or in man.

■ **teachaˈbility** *noun* L19. **teachableness** *noun* L16. **teachably** *adverb* E19.

teache *noun* see TACHE *noun*³.

teacher /ˈtiːtʃə/ *noun*. ME.
[from TEACH *verb* + -ER¹.]
†**1** A thing which shows something or points something out; *spec.* the index finger. *rare*. Only in ME.
2 a A person who or thing which teaches or instructs; an instructor; *esp.* a person employed to teach in a school. ME. ▸**b** In the early Congregational churches of New England, one of several officers appointed to give religious instruction. *obsolete* exc. *Hist.* M17.

📖 **2a** C. PHILLIPS An English literature teacher decided to demonstrate his knowledge. *fig.*: WORDSWORTH His daily teachers had been woods and rills. attrib.: ***teacher appraisal***, ***teacher-librarian***, ***teacher-training***, ***teacher-tutor***, etc. ***ELEMENTARY teacher***. ***primary teacher***: see PRIMARY *adjective*. ***secondary teacher***: see SECONDARY *adjective*. ***supply teacher***: see SUPPLY *noun*.

Comb.: **teacher edition** an edition prepared especially for the use of teachers; **teachers' aide** an assistant employed to help the teaching staff of a school in a variety of ancillary and supervisory duties; **teacher's pet** the favourite pupil of a teacher (*lit.* & *fig.*).
■ **teacheress** *noun* (now *rare* or *obsolete*) a female teacher LME. **teacherly** *adjective* of, pertaining to, or characteristic of a teacher L17. **teachership** *noun* the office or function of a teacher M19.

teacherage /ˈtiːtʃərɪdʒ/ *noun*. *N. Amer.* E20.
[from prec. + -AGE, after *parsonage*, *vicarage*, etc.]
A house or lodgings provided for a teacher by a school.

teach-in /ˈtiːtʃɪn/ *noun*. Orig. *US*. M20.
[from TEACH *verb* + -IN².]
An informal debate on a matter of public, usu. political, interest, orig. between the staff and students of a university; a conference attended by members of a profession on topics of common concern. Also, an informal lecture or discussion for disseminating information.

📖 *Guardian* A college-wide teach-in on the main election issues.

teaching /ˈtiːtʃɪŋ/ *noun*. ME.
[from TEACH *verb* + -ING¹.]
1 The action of TEACH *verb*; the imparting of information or knowledge; the occupation, profession, or function of a teacher. ME.
2 That which is taught; a doctrine, an instruction, a precept. Freq. in *pl.* ME.

📖 **1** R. G. MYERS Research related to the . . science curriculum and the teaching of science. attrib.: ***teaching aid***, ***teaching post***, ***teaching strategy***, etc. ***initial teaching alphabet***: see INITIAL *adjective*. **2** *Omni* These 'masters' base their teachings on the sacred philosophies of the East.

Comb.: **teaching hospital** a hospital at which medical students are taught; **teaching machine** any of various devices for giving instruction according to a programme that reacts to pupils' responses.

teaching /ˈtiːtʃɪŋ/ *ppl adjective*. M17.
[from TEACH *verb* + -ING².]
That teaches, having the quality or function of teaching.
teaching fellow *US* a student at a graduate school who carries out teaching or laboratory duties in return for a stipend, free tuition, or other benefit.

teacup /ˈtiːkʌp/ *noun.* E18.
[from TEA *noun* + CUP *noun*.]
1 A cup from which tea is drunk, usu. with a single handle and with a matching saucer. Also, the arrangement of tea leaves left in a cup, the interpretation of which is a method of fortune-telling. E18.
2 As much as a teacup contains, a teacupful. M18.
1 *storm in a teacup*: see STORM *noun*.
Comb.: **teacup-and-saucer comedy** comedy of a mild, inoffensive, and respectable nature.
■ **teacupful** *noun* as much as a teacup will hold E18.

tea'd, **teaed** *verbs pa. t. & pple*: see TEA *verb*.

teaed /tiːd/ *adjective. US slang.* E20.
[from TEA *noun* + -ED[2].]
In a state of euphoria induced by alcohol or marijuana (see TEA *noun* 4). Usu. foll. by *up*.

teagle /ˈtiːg(ə)l/ *noun & verb.* Chiefly *north.* E19.
[Var. of TACKLE *noun, verb*.]
▶ **A** *noun.* **1** A mechanism for lifting, a hoist or tackle; *esp.* one used for moving goods from floor to floor of a warehouse etc. E19.
2 A string of baited fish-hooks used to trap birds. E20.
▶ **B** *verb trans.* **1** Hoist or lift (as) with a teagle or tackle. M19.
2 Catch with a teagle. E20.

Teague /teɪg, tiːg/ *noun. colloq.* See also TAIG. M17.
[Anglicized spelling of Irish name *Tadhg*.]
1 (A nickname for) an Irishman. Now *rare* or *obsolete*. M17.
2 = TAIG. L20.

teak /tiːk/ *noun & adjective.* L17.
[Portuguese *teca* from Tamil & Malayalam *tēkku*.]
▶ **A** *noun.* **1** More fully ***Indian teak***. A large tree of the verbena family, *Tectona grandis*, of India and SE Asia, with opposite egg-shaped leaves and panicles of white flowers; the timber of this tree, a dark heavy oily wood of great strength and durability. L17. ▸**b** The typical colour of this timber, a rich reddish-brown. M20.
2 Usu. with specifying word: any of various other trees producing strong or durable timber, or otherwise resembling Indian teak. L17.
2 African teak (the timber of) *Oldfieldia africana*, an African tree of the spurge family. **Australian teak** = FLINDOSA. **Nigerian teak**, **West African teak** (the timber of) the iroko *Chlorophora excelsa*.
▶ **B** *adjective.* Made of teak. E18.

teal /tiːl/ *noun.* Pl. **-s**, same. ME.
[Origin unkn.: rel. to Middle Low German *tēlink*, Middle Dutch *tēling*, *teiling* (Dutch *teling*).]
1 Any of several small dabbling ducks of the genus *Anas* and related genera; esp. *A. crecca* (also ***green-winged teal***), which breeds in Eurasia and N. America, the male of which has a chestnut head with a green stripe, and the N. American *A. discors* (in full ***blue-winged teal***), the male of which has a grey head with a white crescent. ME.
2 The flesh of a teal as food. LME.
3 A dark greenish-blue colour resembling the colour of the teal's head and wing patches. E20.
1 *falcated teal*, ***Laysan teal***, ***summer teal***, ***winter teal***, etc.
Comb.: **teal blue** (of) a dark greenish-blue colour.
■ **tealery** *noun* a place in which teals are kept and reared L19.

tea leaf /ˈtiː liːf/ *noun phr.* Pl. **tea leaves** /liːvz/. M18.
[from TEA *noun* + LEAF *noun*[1].]
1 A leaf of the tea plant, *esp.* (in *pl.*) dried leaves for making a drink of tea. Also (usu. in *pl.*), these leaves after infusion or as dregs, sometimes used for fortune-telling. M18.
2 A thief. *rhyming slang.* L19.

> 1 C. AIKEN I'm no old woman who squints in a cup of tea-leaves for a portent.

team /tiːm/ *noun.*
[Old English *tēam* = Old Frisian *tām* bridle, progeny, Old Saxon *tōm*, Old High German *zoum* (German *Zaum*), Old Norse *taumr* bridle, rein, from Germanic base = pull, draw, rel. to Latin *ducere*. Cf. TEEM *verb*[1].]
▶ **I 1** †**a** The bearing of children. OE–ME. ▸**b** A family or brood of young animals. Now *spec.* a litter of pigs, a brood of ducks. Long *dial.* OE.
†**2** Offspring, family, line of descendants; race, stock. Cf. ***bairn-team*** s.v. BAIRN. OE–LME.
▶ **II 3 a** Pl. after a numeral same. A set of draught animals; two or more oxen, horses, dogs, etc. in harness to pull together. OE. ▸**b** Part of the equipment used to harness draught animals to a plough, harrow, or cart. Now (*dial.*), a chain. ME. ▸**c** *transf.* The stock of horses (or other animals) belonging to one owner or stable. *dial. rare.* M17.
4 a A number of people associated in some joint action; *fig.* a group of people compared to a team of draught animals. Now *esp.*, a set of players forming one side in a game, match, or any team sport; a group of people collaborating in their professional work or in a particular enterprise or task. E16. ▸**b** *spec.* A gang. *slang* (chiefly *Criminals'*). M20.
5 a One animal or more in harness together with the vehicle being drawn; (now *dial.*) a horse and cart, a wagon with two horses. Also (*US local*) a cart or other vehicle to be drawn by one horse (***single team***) or two horses (***double team***). L16. ▸**b** A load drawn by a team. Now *rare* or *obsolete* exc. *US.* L18. ▸**c** *fig.* A person of superior ability; an outstandingly gifted or able person. Chiefly in ***a whole team (and the dog under the wagon)***. *US colloq.* M19.
6 A flock of wild ducks or other birds flying in line. L17.

> 3a C. THIRLWALL A thousand team of cattle conveyed the timber. 4a *Field* Furse and his team . . investigate . . cycles in the island's meteorology. *Highlife* To see the famous Washington Redskins football team in action. attrib.: ***team game***, ***team leader***, ***team manager***, ***team member***, ***team player***, ***team sport***, etc.

▶ **III** *ANGLO-SAXON LAW.* **7 a** In a suit for the recovery of allegedly stolen goods, the action or procedure by which the holder transferred or referred it back to a third person (generally the party from whom the goods were received) to defend the title to them. OE. ▸**b** The right or prerogative of jurisdiction in a suit of team, together with the fees and profits thence accruing; from the 11th cent. usually included in crown charters granting land to a lord etc. Freq. in ***toll and team***. ME.
Phrases: **in the team** *NAUTICAL* (of a number of ships) stationed in a line so as to blockade a port. ***toll and team***: see TOLL *noun*[1] 1.
Comb.: **team-boat** (chiefly *US*) a boat, *esp.* a ferry, drawn or propelled by horse-power; **team handball** a game played by two teams of seven players each on a rectangular court using a ball propelled only with the hands; **team-land** (*obsolete* exc. *Hist.*) = PLOUGH-LAND 1; **team-man** a member of a sporting team who cooperates (well or badly) with his colleagues; **team-mate** a fellow member of a team or group; **team ministry** a group of clergy of incumbent status who minister jointly to several parishes under the leadership of a rector or vicar; **team race**: won by the team whose members finish on aggregate in higher positions than their opponents; **team rector** a rector who leads a team ministry; **teamsman** = TEAMSTER 1; **team spirit** willingness to act as a member of a team or group rather than as an individual; **team-talk** a pep-talk addressed to a team, a discussion amongst a team; **team-teach** *verb intrans. & trans.* (of a teacher or teachers) teach (students) as (part of) a team working together; **team-teaching** teaching by a team of teachers working together; **team vicar** a vicar who leads a team ministry; **teamwork** (*a*) (now *rare*) work done with a team of animals; (*b*) the combined action of a team of players or a group of people, esp. when effective and efficient; cooperation.

team /tiːm/ *verb.* M16.
[from prec. branch II.]
1 a *verb trans.* Harness (animals) in a team. M16. ▸**b** *verb trans.* Convey or transport (goods etc.) by means of a team. Chiefly *N. Amer.* M19. ▸**c** *verb intrans.* Drive a team; work as a teamster. *N. Amer.* M19.
2 *verb intrans. & trans.* Join together (*with* or with another or others) (as) in a team; join in common action or cooperate (*with* or with another or others). Usu. foll. by *up*. M20. ▸**b** *verb trans.* Foll. by *with*: match or coordinate (clothes, colours, etc.). Usu. in *pass.* M20.

> 1a *Encycl. Brit.* The horses are teamed in pairs. **b** B. W. ALDISS A long black sledge teamed by the dogs. **c** L. I. WILDER Hauling lumber . . I had to team, to earn money. **2** *Times* We teamed up with Hotwork . . to develop new . . burners. *Flicks* Rock stars . . teaming for a re-make of 'Some Like It Hot'. **b** *TV Times* Tartans . . and stripes were teamed with colourful knits.

teamer /ˈtiːmə/ *noun.* L16.
[from TEAM *noun, verb*: see -ER[1].]
1 A person who drives a team of animals; a teamster. L16.
2 A member of a team; esp. a member of a specified sports team. M20.

> 2 *Evening Post (Nottingham)* First teamers Ken MacDonald and Graeme Fraser came back . . to help Corsairs defeat Nottingham University.

teamster /ˈtiːmstə/ *noun.* L18.
[from TEAM *noun* + -STER.]
1 The driver or owner of a team of animals; a teamer. L18.
2 A lorry-driver; a person whose occupation is truck-driving. *N. Amer.* E20.

teanel /ˈtiːn(ə)l/ *noun.* Now *north.*
[Old English *tǣnil*, *-el* = Middle High German *zeinel*; cf. Old High German *zeinnā*, *zeinā*, Middle High German *zeine* basket, Gothic *tainjō* wicker basket, Old English *tān*, Old High German *zein*, Old Norse *teinn* twig, osier-wand.]
A basket.

teapot /ˈtiːpɒt/ *noun & verb.* L17.
[from TEA *noun* + POT *noun*[1].]
▶ **A** *noun.* A pot with a lid, spout, and handle, in which tea is brewed and from which it is poured. L17.
Comb. & phrases: **teapot tempest**, **tempest in a teapot** *N. Amer.* = ***storm in a teacup*** s.v. STORM *noun*.
▶ **B** *verb trans.* Infl. **-tt-**. Present (a person) with a teapot, esp. in recognition of services rendered. *rare.* M19.

> C. BEDE Gentlemen . . return thanks for having been 'teapotted'.

■ **teapotful** *noun* as much as a teapot will hold L19.

teapoy /ˈtiːpɔɪ/ *noun.* E19.
[from Hindi *ti-* three + Urdu & Persian *pāī* foot: sense and spelling infl. by TEA *noun*.]
A small three-legged table or stand; *esp.* such a table with a receptacle for tea or a tea caddy.

tear /tɪə/ *noun*[1].
[Old English *tēar*, (Northumbrian) *tehher*, *taeher* = Old Frisian *tār*, Old High German *zah(h)ar* (German *Zähre*, orig. pl.), Old Norse *tár*, Gothic *tagr*, from Indo-European, repr. also by Old Latin *dacruma* (Latin *lacruma*, *-ima*), Greek *dakru*.]
1 a A drop of the clear watery fluid appearing in or flowing from the eye, as a result of emotion, physical irritation, pain, etc. Usu. in *pl.* OE. ▸**b** A tear as an expression of grief or sorrow. Usu. in *pl.* ME.
2 *transf. & fig.* A drop of liquid, *esp.* one welling up or falling spontaneously. Usu. in *pl.* OE.
3 *spec.* Any of various gums oozing from plants in tear-shaped or globular beads, which then become solid or resinous. Now usu. in *pl.* OE.
4 Anything resembling a tear in shape, *esp.* a decorative air cavity in glassware (cf. ***tear-drop*** (b) below). M19.

> 1b MILTON He must not flote upon his watry bear . . With-out the meed of som melodious tear. **2** S. BELLOW He punched at the door . . and waited, staring at its . . trickles and tears of enamel. **3** *Daily News* Tears of frankincense, the gum resin produced by an Indian tree. **4** D. LIVINGSTONE It occurs generally in tears or rounded lumps.

Phrases: ***crocodile tears***. **in tears** crying, shedding tears. ***Job's tears***: see JOB *noun*[3] 1. ***Pele's tears***: see PELE *noun*[1] 2. **St Lawrence's tears** *colloq.* the Perseids (so called because they appear about St Lawrence's day, 10 August). ***vale of tears***: see VALE *noun*[1] 2. ***valley of tears***: see VALLEY *noun*. ***water with one's tears***: see WATER *verb*. **without tears** (esp. of a method of learning) without difficulty; easily mastered.
Comb.: **tear bomb** a bomb containing tear-gas; **tear bottle** a bottle containing tears; *spec.* = LACHRYMATORY *noun* 1; **tear-drop** (*a*) a single tear; = sense 1 above; (*b*) a thing resembling a tear-drop in shape, *esp.* a decorative air cavity in glassware, a jewel, etc.; **tear-gas** *noun & verb* (*a*) *noun* a gas causing tears when inhaled, used in warfare or riot control to disable opponents or make crowds disperse; (*b*) *verb trans.* attack with tear-gas, drive *out of* a place with tear-gas; **tear-gland** a gland that secretes tears; **tear-jerk** *verb intrans.* evoke sadness or sympathy (freq. as ***tear-jerking*** *verbal noun & ppl adjective*); **tear-jerker** *colloq.* a sentimental film, song, story, etc., calculated to evoke sadness or sympathy; **tear-smoke** = ***tear-gas*** (a) above.
■ **tearlet** *noun* a little or tiny tear M19. **tearlike** *adjective* resembling (that of) a tear M16.

tear /tɛː/ *noun*[2] *& adjective.* Now *rare* or *obsolete.* LME.
[App. from Dutch or Low German: cf. Middle Dutch, Middle Flemish, Middle Low German, Low German *teer*, *tēr* contr. of *teeder*, *tēder* fine, thin, delicate, tender.]
▶ **A** *noun.* Something of the finest or best quality; *esp.* the finest fibre of flax or hemp. Formerly also, the finest flour. LME.
▶†**B** *adjective.* Esp. of flour and hemp: fine, delicate; of the best quality. LME–M16.

tear /tɛː/ *noun*[3]. E17.
[from TEAR *verb*[1].]
1 A torn part or place; a rent, a fissure. E17.
2 The action or an act of tearing or forcibly pulling apart; damage caused by tearing. Freq. in ***tear and wear***, ***wear and tear*** s.v. WEAR *noun*. M17.
3 a A rushing gallop or pace. Freq. in ***full tear***, full tilt, headlong. M19. ▸**b** A spree; a prolonged drinking-bout. *slang* (chiefly *N. Amer., Scot., & Austral.*). M19. ▸**c** A rage; a fit of temper or agitation. *colloq. & dial.* M19. ▸**d** *SPORT.* A successful run, a winning streak. Freq. in ***on a tear***. *US slang.* L20.

> 1 A. BRINK His pants were patched, never mind the tear in the seat. **3b** N. MAILER A drunken private on a whore-house tear.

Comb.: (See also combs. of TEAR *verb*[1].) **tear-fault** *GEOLOGY* = ***strike-slip fault*** s.v. STRIKE *noun*[1].

tear /tɛː/ *verb*[1]. Pa. t. **tore** /tɔː/, (*arch. & dial.*) **tare** /tɛː/. Pa. pple **torn** /tɔːn/, (*dial.*) **tore** /tɔː/.
[Old English *teran* = Old Saxon *terian*, Middle Low German, Middle & mod. Dutch *teren*, Old High German *zeran* (German *zehren*) destroy, consume, Gothic (*dis*)*tairan*, from Indo-European base repr. by Greek *derein* flay.]
▶ **I 1** *verb trans.* **a** Pull apart by force, pull to pieces, rip up. OE. ▸**b** Make (a hole etc.) by tearing. ME. ▸**c** Break (something hard or solid) by force or violent impact; shatter. Now *dial.* L16.
2 *verb trans.* Wound or injure (esp. part of the body) by violent tearing; lacerate. OE.
3 *verb trans. fig.* ▸**a** Violently disrupt or divide; split into parties or factions. OE. ▸**b** Sound loudly or piercingly in (the air, sky, etc.). L16. ▸**c** Wound, cause pain to (the heart, emotions, etc.); (foll. by *apart*, *up*) make distraught, distress, upset (a person). M17. ▸**d** *verb trans.* with *it*. Spoil a person's chances; dash a person's hopes; cause a problem. *colloq.* E20.

4 *verb trans.* Pull (one's hair) out or *out* in a frenzy of grief or anger. Now chiefly *fig.*, behave with desperation or extreme anger. OE.
5 *verb trans.* **a** Pull or wrench violently or with some force; pull *down*. Foll. by *away, down, off*, etc. ME. ▸**b** *fig.* Remove by force or violence; *refl.* make oneself leave, force oneself *away*. L16.
6 *verb intrans.* Make a tear or rent; pull violently; (foll. by *at*) pull at repeatedly in order to rip apart or lacerate. E16.
7 *verb intrans.* Undergo tearing; become torn; *dial.* split, snap, break. E16.

> **1a** J. AGEE The hogs . . scuffled over the snake, tore it apart. SLOAN WILSON He had torn the letter into small bits. **2** R. RAYNER My left knee ached. Three years ago I'd torn the cartilage. **3a** R. BUSH His first marriage was torn apart by an instinctive . . revulsion. *Pen International* A country constantly torn apart by the forces of history. **b** DRYDEN Her fellow Nymphs the Mountains tear With loud Laments. **c** M. FLANAGAN Find where the hate comes from. That's what tearing me up. P. LEWIS His domineering mother bickers with the . . father until the boy screams at them: 'You're tearing me apart!' **d** *New Yorker* 'That does rather tear it.' Lucy said. The detour would add fifteen miles. **5a** J. M. COETZEE Dogs . . tore out the throats of a dozen ewes. J. DISKI Great machines that . . tore vast tracts of forest down. **b** G. KENDALL Tearing his eyes away from it, he reached into his case. **6** M. GEE She snatched up the parcel and tore at it feebly. *fig.*: R. JAFFE Alexander's guilt began to tear at their relationship. **7** L. ELLMANN Jeremy grabbed the sleeve of my nightgown, which tore.

▸**II 8** *verb intrans.* Move with violence or impetuosity; dash; go or travel hurriedly or at speed. *colloq.* L16. ▸**b** *verb trans.* Make (*one's way*) thus. *colloq.* M19.
9 *verb intrans.* Complain violently; rave, rage, (*dial.*). Formerly also, rant and bluster. E17.

> **8** E. BOWEN A ferocious wind . . tore through the city. A. LURIE I was tearing along, doing near eighty I guess.

Phrases: **be torn between** have difficulty in choosing between (equal but conflicting desires, loyalties, etc.). †**tear a cat** play the part of a roistering hero, rant and bluster. **tear apart** (*a*) subject to rigorous criticism; (*b*) search (a place) thoroughly. ***tear a person off a strip, tear a strip off a person***: see STRIP *noun*¹ 1. **tear down** (*a*) *US colloq.* punish; criticize severely; (*b*) demolish. **tear into** (*a*) make an energetic or vigorous start on (an activity etc.); (*b*) attack verbally, reprimand severely. **tear it up** *US slang* approach something with abandon; *JAZZ* play unrestrainedly and with verve. ***tear limb from limb***: see LIMB *noun*¹. **tear off a bit, tear off a piece** *slang* (orig. *Austral.*) copulate with a woman. ***tear oneself away***: see sense 5b above. ***tear one's hair***: see sense 4 above. †**tear the cat** play the part of a roistering hero, rant and bluster. ***tear to shreds***: see SHRED *noun*.
Comb.: **tear-arse**, (*N. Amer.*) **-ass** *noun & verb* (*slang*) (*a*) *noun* a very active busy person; (*b*) *verb intrans.* drive recklessly, rush *around* wildly and rowdily; **tear-cat** *adjective & noun* (long *arch.*) (*a*) *adjective* swaggering, ranting, bombastic; (*b*) *noun* a bully, a swaggerer; **teardown** the complete dismantling of a piece of machinery, esp. an engine; **tear-off** *adjective & noun* (*a*) *adjective* adapted to be easily torn off; perforated; (*b*) *noun* a sheet or slip of paper so attached as to be easily torn off; **tear sheet** (chiefly *US*) a sheet torn from a publication (or, later, separately printed and unbound) to be sent to an advertiser whose advertisement appears on it as proof of insertion; any page which can be removed from a newspaper or magazine for use separately; *gen.* a tear-off sheet from a calendar etc.; **tear-thumb** any of several N. American persicarias with prickly stems and midribs, esp. *Persicaria sagittatum*; **tear-up** *slang* a spell of wild, destructive behaviour; a mêlée; *JAZZ* an unrestrained, rousing performance.
▪ **tearable** *adjective* able to be torn M19. **tearer** *noun* (*a*) a person who or thing which tears something; (*b*) a person who rushes along or about; (now *dial.*) a ranter, a swaggerer, a bully: M16. **tearing** *noun* (*a*) the action of the verb; an instance of this; †(*b*) a wound made by tearing the flesh; (*c*) a fragment torn off: LME.

tear /tɪə/ *verb*². Now *rare*. OE.
[from TEAR *noun*¹.]
1 a *verb intrans.* Shed tears, weep. *obsolete* exc. *Scot. & dial.* OE. ▸**b** Of the eyes: shed or emit tears. Now chiefly *N. Amer.* OE.
2 *verb trans.* Fill or sprinkle (as) with tears. Now *rare* or *obsolete*. E17.

> **1b** JAYNE PHILLIPS The fumes were still so strong our eyes teared.

tearaway /ˈtɛːrəweɪ/ *adjective & noun*. M19.
[from TEAR *verb*¹ + AWAY *adverb*.]
▸**A** *adjective.* Characterized by impetuous speed. Also, unruly, reckless. M19.

> *Guardian* The tearaway start of a novel published at 16.

▸**B** *noun.* An impetuous, unruly, or reckless young person or animal. Also, a hooligan, a ruffian, a petty criminal. L19.

> *People* He admits he was a bit of a tearaway at school.

tearful /ˈtɪəfʊl, -f(ə)l/ *adjective*. L16.
[from TEAR *noun*¹ + -FUL.]
1 Crying or inclined to cry; shedding tears. L16.
2 Causing or accompanied by tears; sad, melancholy. E17.

> **1** *Daily Express* A tearful Sarah . . told detectives . . how she was duped. **2** *News of the Week* We had a . . tearful reunion and we've been the best of friends since.

▪ **tearfully** *adverb* E19. **tearfulness** *noun* M19.

tearing /ˈtɛːrɪŋ/ *adjective & adverb*. E17.
[from TEAR *verb*¹ + -ING².]
▸**A** *adjective.* **1** That tears or rends; *esp.* (*fig.*) severely distressing, harrowing. Also, causing a sensation as of tearing or rending. E17.
2 Of a wind or storm: so violent as to tear things up or in pieces; raging. *rare.* M17.
3 a Violent or reckless in action or behaviour; impetuous, passionate; ranting, roistering; boisterous, exuberant. *colloq.* Now *rare.* M17. ▸**b** Impressive, splendid, grand. *slang.* Now *rare.* L17.
4 Moving with extreme or impetuous speed; rushing. M18.

> **1** G. LORD The tearing pain in her ankle eased. **3a** S. PEPYS There was . . much tearing company in the house. **4** A. MORICE Don't go. Not unless you're in a tearing hurry.

▸**B** *adverb.* Furiously. Chiefly in ***tearing mad***. *colloq. & dial.* L17.

tearless /ˈtɪəlɪs/ *adjective*. E17.
[from TEAR *noun*¹ + -LESS.]
Not shedding tears, not weeping.

> R. KENAN In her world she had been expected to be tearless, patient, comforting to other members of the family.

▪ **tearlessly** *adverb* M19. **tearlessness** *noun* E20.

tea rose /ˈtiː rəʊz/ *noun & adjectival phr.* M19.
[from TEA *noun* + ROSE *noun*.]
▸**A** *noun.* **1** A garden rose of a group derived from a Chinese hybrid rose, *Rosa × odorata*, the flowers of which are often pale yellow with a pink tinge and have a delicate scent supposed to resemble that of tea. M19.
2 The pale pinkish-yellow colour esp. associated with this rose. L19.
3 A perfume made from or named after this rose. L19.
▸**B** *adjective.* Usu. **tea-rose**. Of the colour of the tea rose, pale pinkish-yellow. E20.

teart /tiːət/ *adjective & noun*. M19.
[Dial. var. of TART *adjective*.]
▸**A** *adjective.* (Of grass, pasture, etc.) sour; containing an excess of molybdenum; causing scouring. M19.
▸**B** *noun.* **1** Teart quality in grass. L19.
2 = TEARTNESS. M20.
▪ **teartness** *noun* (*VETERINARY MEDICINE*) scouring in cattle resulting from grazing a teart pasture M20.

teary /ˈtɪəri/ *adjective*. LME.
[from TEAR *noun*¹ + -Y¹.]
1 Full of or suffused with tears; tearful, sad. Now *colloq.* LME.
2 Of the nature of or consisting of tears. *rare.* LME.

> **1** J. IRVING His . . eyes were teary and he could not see . . clearly. N. HORNBY His dad gave him a hug and got a bit teary. **2** H. CONSTABLE The shoare of that salt tearie sea.

tease /tiːz/ *noun*. L17.
[from next.]
1 The action or an instance of teasing. L17.
2 a A person fond of teasing; a person who takes pleasure in making fun of or bothering others in a playful or irritating way. *colloq.* M19. ▸**b** A woman regarded as provocatively refusing sexual intercourse. *colloq.* L20.

> **1** H. ACTON Interspersing my letters with Mark Twainish Americanism was one of my teases. **2a** E. M. FORSTER Vyse was a tease . . he took a malicious pleasure in thwarting people. **b** *Face* The insults are pitched at . . a 'little tease'.

tease /tiːz/ *verb.*
[Old English *tǣsan* = Middle & mod. Low German, Middle Dutch *tēzen* (Dutch *teezen*), Old High German *zeisan* (German dial. *zeisen*), from West Germanic. Cf. TOZE *verb*¹.]
1 *verb trans.* **a** Pull apart or pick (wool etc.) into separate fibres; comb or card (wool, flax, etc.) in preparation for spinning; open or separate *out* by pulling apart. OE. ▸**b** Comb (the surface of woven cloth) with teasels, drawing all the fibres in the same direction so as to raise a nap. M18. ▸**c** *HAIRDRESSING.* Back-comb (the hair) so as to give fullness and lift. Chiefly *N. Amer.* M20.
2 a *verb trans. & intrans.* Worry or irritate (a person or animal) by persisting in behaviour which is likely to annoy. Now *esp.*, make fun of or bother (a person or animal) persistently in a playful or irritating way. E17. ▸**b** Tempt or entice, esp. sexually, while refusing to satisfy the desire aroused. L19. ▸**c** *verb intrans.* Perform a striptease. *US colloq.* E20.
3 *verb trans.* Flog. *arch. slang.* E19.

> **1a** B. PYM Viola hesitated, teasing out the fringe of her . . stole. **b** A. PRATT Blankets . . made of goats'-wool, teased into a satiny surface. **c** E. JONG Women in mini-skirts and teased blond hair. **2a** E. WAUGH Was he teasing, or did he really mean I was like a film star? C. STEAD It . . was a pleasure to tease Louisa, for she fell into every trap.

Phrases: **tease out** *fig.* extract, obtain or ascertain, esp. by painstaking effort; unravel (the meaning or sense) of.
▪ **teasable** *adjective* (*rare*) able to be teased M19. **teasing** *verbal noun* the action of the verb; an instance of this: L16. **teasingly** *adverb* in a teasing manner M18.

teasel /ˈtiːz(ə)l/ *noun & verb*. Also **teazle**.
[Old English *tǣs(e)l* = Old High German *zeisala* (Middle High German *zeisel*), from West Germanic base also of TEASE *verb*: see -EL¹, -LE¹.]
▸**A** *noun.* **1** Any plant of the genus *Dipsacus* (family Dipsacaceae), the members of which have prickly stems and small lilac or white flowers packed in ovoid or cylindrical heads between spine-tipped bracts; *esp.* (more fully ***fuller's teasel***) *D. sativus*, which has stiff reflexed bracts and was formerly widely grown for fulling (see sense 2), and (more fully ***wild teasel***) *D. fullonum*, a similar wild plant with straight flexible bracts. OE.
2 The dried prickly flower-head of the fuller's teasel (see sense 1), used for teasing woven cloth so as to raise a nap. LME.
3 A device used as a substitute for teasels in the textile industry. M19.
Comb.: **teasel-bur, teasel-head** = sense 2 above.
▸**B** *verb trans.* Raise a nap on (cloth) (as) with teasels. M16.
▪ **teaseler** *noun* ME.

teaser /ˈtiːzə/ *noun*. LME.
[from TEASE *verb* + -ER¹.]
1 a A device or machine for teasing wool etc. LME. ▸**b** A person who teases wool etc. L15.
2 a A person who makes fun of or bothers others in a teasing way; a tease. M17. ▸**b** An inferior stallion or ram used to excite mares or ewes before serving by the stud animal. E19. ▸**c** = TEASE *noun* 2b. *colloq.* L19. ▸**d** A striptease act; a striptease artist. E20.
3 a A thing difficult to tackle or deal with, *esp.* a difficult question or task. *colloq.* M18. ▸**b** A flogging. *arch. slang.* M19. ▸**c** *CRICKET.* A ball that is difficult to play. M19. ▸**d** A knotted rope's end. *Nautical slang.* E20. ▸**e** *THEATRICAL.* An overhead border, curtain, etc., suspended across the inside of the proscenium arch so as to conceal the space above the stage from the audience. *US.* E20. ▸**f** *ANGLING.* An object (orig. live bait, now usu. brightly coloured wood or metal) trailed behind a boat to attract fish. E20. ▸**g** A small toy pipe with a coil of paper attached to one end which shoots out when the pipe is blown and then springs back. M20.
4 *ELECTRICAL ENGINEERING.* †**a** The shunt winding of a compound-wound dynamo or motor. Only in L19. ▸**b** The winding or transformer that is connected to the middle of the other transformer in a T-connected system. E20.
5 An introductory advertisement, *esp.* an excerpt or sample designed to stimulate interest or curiosity; a trailer for a film; the sequence preceding the credit titles in a television programme. Orig. & chiefly *US.* M20.

> **2a** *Fast Forward* The teaser only gets pay-off if you react. **c** J. GARDNER Sensual in a very obvious way. Herbert . . suspected she was a teaser with men. **3a** C. MACKENZIE The *Times* crossword was rather a teaser this morning. **5** T. CLANCY The news show . . would contain a teaser . . to make people watch it instead of their usual evening TV fare.

teashop /ˈtiːʃɒp/ *noun*. M18.
[from TEA *noun* + SHOP *noun*.]
A shop where dried tea is sold. Also, a café where tea and other light refreshments are served, a tearoom.
▪ **teashoppy** *adjective* characteristic of or resembling a teashop M20.

Teasmade /ˈtiːzmeɪd/ *noun*. M20.
[Perh. from phr. *tea's made*.]
(Proprietary name for) an automatic tea-maker.

> J. MORTIMER It's a Teasmade, Mother . . it'll wake you up and give you a cup of tea.

teaspoon /ˈtiːspuːn/ *noun*. L17.
[from TEA *noun* + SPOON *noun*.]
1 A small spoon used esp. for stirring tea or other drinks in a cup. L17.
2 A teaspoonful. L18.

> **2** E. DAVID A heaped teaspoon of tarragon leaves.

▪ **teaspoonful** *noun* as much as a teaspoon will hold; in medical prescriptions, recipes, etc. = 4 ml: E18.

teasy /ˈtiːzi/ *adjective*. *colloq. & dial.* M19.
[from TEASE *verb* + -Y¹.]
1 Bad-tempered, irritable, tetchy. M19.
2 Teasing, irritating. E20.

teat /tiːt/ *noun*. ME.
[Old French *tete* (mod. *tette*), prob. of Germanic origin, replacing earlier TIT *noun*³.]
1 The nipple of a mammary gland in female mammals (except monotremes), from which the milk is sucked by the young; any of the projections from the udder of a cow etc., through which the milk is discharged. Formerly also, the whole breast or udder. ME. ▸†**b** *fig.* A source of nourishment or supply. LME–L17.

2 *transf.* A thing resembling a nipple or teat, esp. a device of rubber etc. for sucking milk from a bottle. LME.

📖 **1** †**at the teat** (*rare*, Shakes.) at the breast. **suck the hind teat**: see SUCK *verb*. **b** DONNE God's mercies . . are teats of his graces. **2 dummy teat**: see DUMMY *noun & adjective*.

Comb.: **teat-cup** a device forming part of a milking machine and placed over a cow's teat during milking.
■ **teated** *adjective* (chiefly as 2nd elem. of comb.) having teats M17.

tea-table /ˈtiːteɪb(ə)l/ *noun & verb*. L17.
[from TEA *noun* + TABLE *noun*.]
▶ **A** *noun*. **1** A table on which tea is served, or on which tea-things are laid for a meal; a table laid for tea; a tea-table as the place of a social gathering for tea and conversation. L17. ▸**b** This as a special piece of furniture, usually small and of a light and elegant make. E18.
2 *transf.* The company assembled at tea. E18.

📖 **1** *attrib.*: H. SPENCER While ghost-stories . . enliven tea-table conversation. **2** E. K. KANE Explaining to the tea-table this evening's outfit.

▶ **B** *verb trans.* In literature, treat a dramatic event in a trivial or cosily domestic way. M20.

†**teather** *noun & verb* var. of TETHER.

tea-tree /ˈtiːtriː/ *noun*. M18.
[from TEA *noun* + TREE *noun*.]
1 = TEA *noun* 2. M18.
2 Any of various shrubs or trees whose leaves are, or were formerly, infused like tea: cf. TEA *noun* 3. L18. ▸**b** *spec.* In Australia, Tasmania, and New Zealand, any of various shrubs or trees of the myrtle family, chiefly of the genera *Leptospermum* and *Melaleuca* (including the manuka *L. scoparium*). Cf. TI-TREE. L18.
3 In full ***Duke of Argyll's tea-tree***. The box-thorn *Lycium barbarum*, reputedly confused by an 18th-cent. Duke of Argyll with a specimen of the tea plant, *Camellia sinensis*. M19.
2b white tea-tree the kanuka, *Leptospermum ericoides*.
Comb.: **tea-tree oil** a fragrant oil with antiseptic properties, obtained from an Australian tea-tree (esp. *Melaleuca alternifolia*) and used in soaps and other products.

†**teaz** *noun, verb* see TEE *noun*[2], *verb*.

teaze-tenon /ˈtiːztɛnən/ *noun*. E18.
[from unkn. 1st elem. + TENON *noun*[1].]
CARPENTRY. A structure at the top of a post with a double shoulder and a tenon from each for supporting two level pieces of timber crossing each other at right angles.

teazle *noun & verb* var. of TEASEL.

Tebele /təˈbiːli, -ˈbeɪli/ *noun & adjective*. L19.
[Sesotho (*lè*)*tèbèlè*: see NDEBELE.]
(Of) a South Eastern Bantu language.

Tebet /ˈtɛbɛt/ *noun*. Also †**Tebeth**, **Tevet** /ˈtɛvɛt/. LME.
[Hebrew *ṭēḇēṯ*.]
In the Jewish calendar, the fourth month of the civil and tenth of the religious year, usu. coinciding with parts of December and January.

Tebilized /ˈtiːbɪlʌɪzd/ *adjective*. M20.
[from Tootal Broadhurst Lee Company Ltd, the Manchester company which invented and patented the process (see below) + -IZE + -ED[1].]
Of cotton and other fabrics: made crease-resistant by impregnation with a synthetic resin.
¶ Proprietary name.

TEC *abbreviation*.
Training and Enterprise Council.

tec /tɛk/ *noun*[1]. *slang*. L19.
[Abbreviation.]
1 A detective. L19.
2 In full ***tec story***. A detective story. E20.

tec *noun*[2] see TECH.

tecbir *noun* var. of TEKBIR.

tech /tɛk/ *noun & adjective*. In sense A.1 also **tec**. E20.
[Abbreviation.]
▶ **A** *noun*. **1** A technical college or school; an institute of technology. *colloq.* E20.
2 = TECHNICIAN 3. M20.
3 = TECHNOLOGY 2a. Chiefly in ***high tech***, ***low tech***. L20.
▶ **B** *adjective*. = TECHNICAL *adjective*. *colloq.* M20.

techie /ˈtɛki/ *noun*. Also **techy**. M20.
[from TECH *noun* + -IE, -Y[6].]
1 A student at a technical college. *US College slang.* M20.
2 An expert in or enthusiast for (esp. computing) technology. *colloq.* L20.

technetium /tɛkˈniːʃɪəm/ *noun*. M20.
[mod. Latin, from Greek *tekhnētos* artificial, from *tekhnasthai* make by art, from *tekhnē*: see TECHNIC, -IUM.]
A radioactive chemical element of the transition series, atomic no. 43, which is a dense refractory metal produced in reactors as a fission product of uranium and by neutron irradiation of molybdenum 98, and is used as a tracer in scintigraphy etc.; symbol Tc. Cf. MASURIUM.

technetronic /tɛknɪˈtrɒnɪk/ *adjective*. M20.
[from Greek *tekhnē* (see next) + ELEC)TRONIC.]
Conditioned, determined, or shaped by advanced technology and electronic communications.

technic /ˈtɛknɪk/ *adjective & noun*. E17.
[Latin *technicus* from Greek *tekhnikos* of or pertaining to art, from *tekhnē* art, craft: see -IC.]
▶ **A** *adjective*. Of or pertaining to art or an art. Now *rare*. E17.
▶ **B** *noun*. **1** A technical term, expression, or detail; a technicality. Chiefly *US*. *rare*. E19.
2 *sing.* & in *pl.* (treated as *sing.* or *pl.*). Technical details or methods collectively; the technical side of a subject, *esp.* the formal or mechanical part of an art (cf. TECHNIQUE 1). M19.
3 The science or study of an art or arts, esp. of the mechanical arts or applied sciences; technology. Usu. in *pl.* M19.

📖 **2** J. MORLEY Accepted rules . . constitute the technics of poetry. J. R. LOWELL In the technic of this art, perfection can be reached only by long training.

technica /ˈtɛknɪkə/ *noun*. *rare*. L18.
[Latinized form of Greek *tekhnika* technical matters, use as noun of neut. pl. of *tekhnikos*: see prec.]
= TECHNIC *noun* 2.

technical /ˈtɛknɪk(ə)l/ *adjective & noun*. E17.
[formed as TECHNIC + -AL[1].]
▶ **A** *adjective*. **1** Of a person: having knowledge of or expertise in a particular art, science, or other subject. E17.
2 Pertaining to, involving, or characteristic of a particular art, science, profession, or occupation, or the applied arts and sciences generally. M17.
3 *transf.* Of a writer, textbook, etc.: using or dealing with terms that belong to a particular subject or field; requiring specialist knowledge to be understood; treating a subject in a specialist way. L18.
4 Officially or properly so called or regarded; that is such according to the particular terminology or from the particular viewpoint of an art, science, etc. M19.
5 Legally such; so regarded according to a strict legal interpretation. E20.
6 FINANCE. Pertaining to or designating a market in which prices are determined chiefly by internal factors. E20.

📖 **1** G. MILLERSON The technical director is in charge of the technical . . staff on the show. **2** L. HUDSON A problem of a purely technical nature: the structure of benzene. *Hippocrates* Callipygian—a technical term for 'having lovely buttocks'. *Scientific American* Yet 40 percent of ordinary dictionary words are technical. *UnixWorld* Keeping track of queries . . a major headache for the technical support staff. **3** *Guardian* A technical writer who can keep . . readers up-to-date . . in a fast-moving industry. *Times Educ. Suppl.* An ambitious . . technical encyclopaedia for the upper junior . . years. **5** P. G. WODEHOUSE You ought to have had the scoundrel arrested . . . It was a technical assault.

Special collocations: **technical college**, **technical school**: at which mechanical arts and applied sciences are taught. **technical difficulty** (esp. in LAW) a difficulty arising from a method of procedure. **technical drawing** the exact delineation of (planned or designed) objects. **technical foul** BASKETBALL: which does not involve contact between opponents. **technical hitch** an interruption or breakdown due to mechanical failure; *loosely* an unexpected obstacle or snag. **technical knockout** BOXING the ending of a fight by a referee on the grounds of one boxer's inability to continue, the opponent being declared the winner. ***technical school***: see ***technical college*** above. **technical sergeant** *US* a rank of non-commissioned officer in the US air force, above staff sergeant and below master sergeant.
▶ **B** *noun*. In *pl.* Technical terms or points; technicalities. L18.
■ **technicalism** *noun* (*rare*) technical style or treatment; addiction to technicalities: E19. **technicalist** *noun* (*rare*) a person versed in or addicted to technicalities E19. **technically** *adverb* M17. **technicalness** *noun* E19.

technicality /tɛknɪˈkalɪti/ *noun*. E19.
[from prec. + -ITY.]
1 Technical quality or character; the use of technical terms or methods. E19.
2 A technical point, term, or expression; something particularly belonging to an art or other subject referred to. Usu. in *pl.* E19.

📖 **2** A. J. AYER The Board . . was prevented from appealing on a legal technicality. P. CAREY We had never grasped the technicalities of the television sets.

technician /tɛkˈnɪʃ(ə)n/ *noun*. M19.
[from TECHNIC + -IAN.]
1 A person familiar with the technical terms or requirements of a particular subject. M19.
2 A person skilled in the technique or mechanical part of an art or craft. M19.
3 A person qualified in the practical application of a science or mechanical art; *spec.* a person employed to look after technical equipment and to carry out practical work in a laboratory etc. M20.

📖 **2** *Dancing Times* He is a virtuoso . . a stylist as well as an exceptional technician. **3** *Guardian* Hospital laboratory technicians . . will refuse to carry out tests. D. FRANCIS Two technicians . . were dismantling . . apparatus.

technicise *verb* var. of TECHNICIZE.

technicism /ˈtɛknɪsɪz(ə)m/ *noun*. L18.
[from TECHNIC, TECHNICAL + -ISM.]
1 A technical term or expression, a technicality. L18.
2 Technical quality or character. Also, a condition in which technical and scientific subjects are stressed. M20.

technicist /ˈtɛknɪsɪst/ *noun & adjective*. L19.
[formed as prec. + -IST.]
▶ **A** *noun*. A technician; a person with technical knowledge. L19.
▶ **B** *attrib.* or as *adjective*. Of or pertaining to technicism. M20.

technicity /tɛkˈnɪsɪti/ *noun*. M20.
[from TECHNIC, TECHNICISM + -ITY.]
Technical quality or character; the extent to which a people, culture, etc., has technical skills.

technicize /ˈtɛknɪsʌɪz/ *verb trans.* *rare*. Also **-ise**. E20.
[from TECHNIC, TECHNICAL + -IZE.]
Make technical; subject to a high degree of technicality.

technicology /tɛknɪˈkɒlədʒi/ *noun*. M19.
[from Greek *tekhnikos* TECHNIC + -OLOGY.]
= TECHNOLOGY 1.

Technicolor /ˈtɛknɪkʌlə/ *noun & adjective*. Also (in senses A.2, 3, & corresp. uses of the adjective) **t-**, **-our**. E20.
[from TECHNIC(AL + COLOUR *noun*.]
▶ **A** *noun*. **1** (Proprietary name for) any of various processes of colour cinematography, esp. using synchronized monochrome films and employing dye transfer and separation negatives. E20.
2 *transf.* & *fig.* Vivid colour characteristic of colour cinematography; artificial brilliance. *colloq.* M20.
3 PARTICLE PHYSICS. = HYPERCOLOUR. L20.
▶ **B** *attrib.* or as *adjective*. Filmed in Technicolor; vividly coloured; artificially bright. M20.

📖 *Broadcast* The Disney/Sky deal to launch a joint channel was announced in a technicolour fanfare. **technicolor yawn** *slang* an act of vomiting.

■ **technicolored** *adjective* M20.

technicum /ˈtɛknɪkəm/ *noun*. M20.
[Russian *tekhnikum* from mod. Latin *technicum* neut. sing. of Latin *technicus* TECHNIC.]
In countries of the former USSR, a technical college.

technification /ˌtɛknɪfɪˈkeɪʃ(ə)n/ *noun*. M20.
[from TECHNI(CAL + -FICATION.]
The adoption or imposition of technical methods.

technique /tɛkˈniːk/ *noun*. E19.
[French use as noun of adjective from Latin *technicus* TECHNIC.]
1 Manner of esp. artistic execution or performance in relation to mechanical or formal details; the mechanical or formal part of an art. Also, skill or ability in this area. E19. ▸**b** A skilful or efficient way of doing or achieving something; a knack, a trick. M20.
2 *spec.* Manner of performance or skill in sexual relations. E20.

📖 **1** G. GROVE A player may be perfect in technique, and yet have neither soul nor intelligence. G. DALY A fine craftsman whose technique was envied by other painters. **b** *Scientific American* A standard technique is to label fish . . by attaching colored beads. A. TAYLOR I practised . . relaxation techniques for riding the waves of fear. **2** V. SACKVILLE-WEST His technique could be faultless . . . He was very gentle with Teresa.

techno /ˈtɛknəʊ/ *adjective & noun*. L20.
[Abbreviation of TECHNOLOGICAL.]
▶ **A** *adjective*. Using technological means of enhancing the quality of performance, sound, etc. L20.
▶ **B** *noun*. A type of popular music characterized by the use of synthesized sounds and having a fast heavy dance beat. L20.

techno- /ˈtɛknəʊ/ *combining form*.
[Greek *tekhno-* combining form of *tekhnē* art, craft: see -O-.]
Forming words with the sense 'relating to an art or craft, or to an applied science; relating to or using technology'.
■ **technobabble** *noun* (*colloq.*) pretentious (pseudo-)technical jargon L20. **technocomplex** *noun* (ARCHAEOLOGY) a widely diffused group of cultures with many general factors in common but specific differences within these M20. **techno-ecoˈnomic** *adjective* relating to technology and economics M20. **techno-enˈvironment** *noun* an environment influenced or controlled by technology L20. **technofear** *noun* fear of using technological

equipment, esp. computers L20. **technofreak** *noun* an enthusiast for technology or for the technical complexities of a particular piece of equipment L20. **techno'graphic** *adjective* of or pertaining to technography L19. **tech'nography** *noun* the description of the development of the arts and sciences, forming a preliminary stage of technology L19. **tech'nonomy** *noun* the practical application of the principles of the arts and sciences, forming a final stage of technology L19. **technophile** *noun* a person who favours or enjoys technology L20. **technophobe** *noun* a person who fears technology M20. **techno'phobia** *noun* fear of technology, technofear M20. **techno'phobic** *adjective & noun* (*a*) *adjective* pertaining to or affected with technophobia; (*b*) *noun* a technophobe: L20. **techno-speak** *noun* technical language or jargon L20. **technostress** *noun* (psychosomatic illness caused by) stress from working with (esp. computer) technology L20. **technostressed** *adjective* affected by technostress L20. **technostructure** *noun* a group of technologists or technical experts that controls the workings of industry or government M20. **techno-thriller** *noun* a thriller whose plot centres on advanced technology, as computers, weapons, military vehicles, etc. L20.

technocracy /tɛkˈnɒkrəsi/ *noun.* E20.
[from TECHNO- + -CRACY.]
The control of society or industry by technical experts; a ruling body of such experts. Also, an instance of such control.

technocrat /ˈtɛknəkrat/ *noun.* M20.
[formed as prec. + -CRAT.]
An advocate of technocracy. Also, a member of a technocracy, a technologist exercising administrative power.
■ **techno'cratic** *adjective* M20. **techno'cratically** *adverb* M20.

technologic /tɛknəˈlɒdʒɪk/ *adjective. rare.* M19.
[formed as TECHNOLOGY + -IC.]
= next.

technological /tɛknəˈlɒdʒɪk(ə)l/ *adjective.* E17.
[formed as next + -ICAL.]
Pertaining or relating to technology; using technology; *spec.* (*a*) belonging to technical phraseology or methods; (*b*) resulting from developments in technology.

📖 *Atlantic* American technological arrogance—the attitude that if something is not invented here, it doesn't exist. *Woman* Technological miracles are now commonplace in many hospitals.

■ **technologically** *adverb* M19.

technology /tɛkˈnɒlədʒi/ *noun.* E17.
[Greek *tekhnologia* systematic treatment, from *tekhnē* art, craft: see -OLOGY.]
1 a The branch of knowledge that deals with the mechanical arts or applied sciences; a discourse or treatise on (one of) these subjects, orig. on an art or arts. E17. ▸**b** The terminology of a particular subject; technical nomenclature. M17.
2 a The mechanical arts or applied sciences collectively; the application of (any of) these. M19. ▸**b** A particular mechanical art or applied science. M20.

📖 **1a** *Times Educ. Suppl.* Curriculum advisers . . recommend . . English, maths, science, technology and a modern language. **2a** C. FRANCIS The . . triumph of early northern boat-building technology was the Viking ship. E. SEGAL Tiny . . premature infants, their lives wholly dependent on technology. ***high technology***: see HIGH *adjective, adverb, & noun.* INFORMATION ***technology***. ***new technology***: see NEW *adjective*. **b** *New York Times* Fiber-optics and other digital technologies.

Comb.: **technology assessment** the assessment of the effects on society of new technology; **technology park** = SCIENCE ***park***; **technology transfer** the transfer of new technology or advanced technological information from developed to under-developed countries.
■ **technologism** *noun* (*rare*) belief in the government of society according to technological principles M20. **technologist** *noun* (*a*) an expert in or student of technology; (*b*) *US* a laboratory technician: M19. **technologize** *verb trans. & intrans.* make or become technological M20.

techy *noun* var. of TECHIE.

techy *adjective* var. of TETCHY.

teckel /ˈtɛk(ə)l/ *noun.* L19.
[German.]
= DACHSHUND.

Tecla /ˈtɛklə/ *noun.* E20.
[Origin unkn.]
(Proprietary name for) a make of artificial pearl.

tecoma /tɪˈkəʊmə/ *noun.* M19.
[mod. Latin (see below), from Aztec *tecomaxochitl* chalice vine, with misapplication of name.]
Any of various trees and (freq. climbing) shrubs constituting the genus *Tecoma* (family Bignoniaceae), of tropical America, freq. grown for their showy trumpet-shaped chiefly yellow flowers; also called ***trumpet-flower***.

tectibranch /ˈtɛktɪbraŋk/ *noun & adjective.* M19.
[from mod. Latin *Tectibranchiata* (see below), from Latin *tectus* covered + Greek *bragkhia* gills.]
ZOOLOGY. ▸**A** *noun.* Any gastropod mollusc of the former division Tectibranchiata, comprising marine opisthobranchs in which the gills are more or less covered by the mantle, with small shells which are often concealed, and including the bubble-shells, sea hares, and many sea-slugs. M19.
▸**B** *adjective.* Of, pertaining to, or belonging to this division. L19.

tectiform /ˈtɛktɪfɔːm/ *adjective & noun.* M19.
[from Latin *tectum* roof + -I- + -FORM.]
▸**A** *adjective.* **1** ZOOLOGY. Roof-shaped; sloping down on each side from a median ridge. M19.
2 ARCHAEOLOGY. Designating a roof-shaped design or symbol found in palaeolithic cave-paintings and engravings. E20.
▸**B** *noun.* ARCHAEOLOGY. A tectiform design or symbol. E20.

tecto- /ˈtɛktəʊ/ *combining form* of Latin *tectum* roof: see -O-.
■ **tectoce'phalic** *adjective* (MEDICINE) = SCAPHOCEPHALIC *noun* L19. **tecto'cuticle** *noun* (ENTOMOLOGY) a cement layer which is sometimes present on the outer surface of the epicuticle M20. **tecto'spinal** *adjective* (ANATOMY) designating a group of nerve fibres which run from the tectum of the midbrain to the spinal cord E20.

tectogenesis /tɛktə(ʊ)ˈdʒɛnɪsɪs/ *noun.* M20.
[German *Tektogenese*, from Greek *tektōn*, *-on-*: see next, -GENESIS.]
GEOLOGY. The formation of the highly distorted rock structures characteristic of mountain ranges, as distinct from the formation of mountainous topography itself. Cf. OROGENESIS.
■ **'tectogene** *noun* a long, narrow belt of downwarping in the earth's crust, said to be an underlying feature of mountain ranges and oceanic trenches M20. **tectoge'netic** *adjective* = TECTOGENIC L20. **tecto'genic** *adjective* of, pertaining to, or involving tectogenesis M20.

tectonic /tɛkˈtɒnɪk/ *adjective.* M17.
[Late Latin *tectonicus* from Greek *tektonikos*, from *tekton-*, *-ōn* carpenter, builder: see -IC.]
1 Of or pertaining to building or construction. M17.
2 GEOLOGY. Pertaining to the actual structure of the crust of the earth (or of another planet or a moon), or to general changes affecting it. L19.
2 plate tectonic: see PLATE *noun*.
■ **tectonical** *adjective* (GEOLOGY) = TECTONIC M20. **tectonically** *adverb* M20. **'tectonism** *noun* (GEOLOGY) = DIASTROPHISM M20.

tectonics /tɛkˈtɒnɪks/ *noun.* M19.
[formed as prec.: see -S[1].]
1 The art and process of producing practical and aesthetically pleasing buildings or other constructions. M19.
2 GEOLOGY. The structural arrangement of rocks in the earth's crust (or on another planet or a moon); the branch of geology that deals with rock structures, esp. large-scale ones. L19.
2 plate tectonics: see PLATE *noun*.
■ **tectonician** /-ˈnɪʃ(ə)n/ *noun* (GEOLOGY) an expert in or student of tectonics M20.

tectonisation *noun* var. of TECTONIZATION.

tectonite /ˈtɛktənʌɪt/ *noun.* M20.
[from Greek *tektōn*: see TECTONIC, -ITE[1].]
GEOLOGY. A deformed rock whose fabric shows foliation or lineation resulting from differential movement during its formation.

tectonization /tɛktənʌɪˈzeɪʃ(ə)n/ *noun.* Also **-isation**. M20.
[from TECTONIC + -IZATION.]
GEOLOGY. Modification (of rocks etc.) by tectonic processes.
■ **'tectonize** *verb trans.* alter (rock etc.) by tectonic processes; chiefly as ***tectonized*** *ppl adjective.* M20.

tectono- /tɛkˈtɒnəʊ/ *combining form* of TECTONIC, TECTONICS, forming terms in GEOLOGY: see -O-.
■ **tectono'physical** *adjective* of or pertaining to tectonophysics M20. **tectono'physicist** *noun* an expert in or student of tectonophysics M20. **tectono'physics** *noun* the branch of geophysics that deals with the forces that cause movement and deformation in the earth's crust M20. **tec'tonosphere** *noun* = TECTOSPHERE E20. **tec,tonostrati'graphic** *adjective* of or pertaining to the correlation of rock formations with one another in terms of their connection with a tectonic event L20. **tectono'thermal** *adjective* involving both tectonism and geothermal activity L20.

tectorial /tɛkˈtɔːrɪəl/ *adjective.* L19.
[from Latin *tectorium* covering, a cover + -AL[1].]
ANATOMY. Covering like a roof.
tectorial membrane (*a*) a strong fibrous band connecting the occipital bone with the second and third cervical vertebrae; (*b*) (more fully ***tectorial membrane of the cochlear duct***) a delicate gelatinous mass resting on the organ of Corti in the inner ear, and connected with the hairs of the hair-cells.

tectosilicate /ˈtɛktə(ʊ),sɪlɪkeɪt/ *noun.* Also **tekto-**. M20.
[from Greek *tektonia* carpentry (taken as 'framework') + SILICATE.]
MINERALOGY. Any of a group of silicates in which the four oxygen atoms of each SiO_4 tetrahedron are shared with four neighbouring tetrahedra in a three-dimensional framework.

tectosphere /ˈtɛktə(ʊ)sfɪə/ *noun.* M20.
[from Greek *tektōn* (see TECTONIC) + -O- + -SPHERE.]
GEOLOGY. The part of the earth which moves in coherent sections during plate tectonic activity, being coterminous with the lithosphere under the oceans. Also called ***tectonosphere***. Cf. TEKTOSPHERE.
■ **tecto'spheric** *adjective* of or pertaining to the tectosphere L20.

tectrix /ˈtɛktrɪks/ *noun.* Pl. **tectrices** /ˈtɛktrɪsiːz/. L19.
[mod. Latin, from Latin *tect-* pa. ppl stem of *tegere* cover: see -TRIX.]
ORNITHOLOGY. = COVERT *noun* 6. Usu. in *pl.*

tectum /ˈtɛktəm/ *noun.* E20.
[Latin = roof.]
ANATOMY. **1** More fully ***tectum mesencephali*** /mɛsɛnˈsɛfəlʌɪ/. The roof of the midbrain, lying to the rear of the cerebral aqueduct. E20.
2 More fully ***optic tectum***, ***tectum opticum*** /ˈɒptɪkəm/. The part of the tectum mesencephali concerned with the functioning of the visual system. E20.
■ **tectal** *adjective* of or pertaining to the tectum mesencephali or the optic tectum E20.

Ted /tɛd/ *noun.* M20.
[Abbreviation.]
A Teddy boy.

ted /tɛd/ *verb trans.* Infl. **-dd-**. ME.
[Old Norse *teðja*, pa. t. *tadda* rel. to *tad* dung, *toddi* small piece (see TOD *noun*[2]), Old High German, German dial. *zetten* to spread.]
1 Spread out or strew and sometimes turn (new-mown grass, cut corn, or straw) on the ground to dry. ME.
2 *transf. & fig.* Scatter; dissipate. Now *rare*. M16.
3 Arrange, tidy (the hair, a room, etc.). *dial.* E19.

📖 **1** A. UTTLEY The haymakers . . tedding the grass with their forks.

†**tedder** *noun & verb* var. of TETHER.

teddy /ˈtɛdi/ *noun.* E20.
[Pet-form of certain male forenames, as *Theodore*, *Edward*. In senses 1, 2 perh. from *Theodore* Roosevelt: see next.]
1 = TEDDY BEAR 1. Freq. as a name for a teddy bear. E20.
2 = SAMMY *noun* 2. Now *rare* or *obsolete*. E20.
3 *sing.* & in *pl.* A woman's undergarment combining chemise and panties. Orig. *N. Amer.* E20.
4 = TEDDY BOY. M20.

📖 **3** *Chatelaine* A body-smoothing teddy with deep insets of lace.

teddy bear /ˈtɛdi bɛː/ *noun phr.* E20.
[from *Teddy* pet name of *Theodore* Roosevelt (1858–1919), US president 1901–9, famous as a bear-hunter, + BEAR *noun*[1].]
1 A stuffed toy bear, made esp. of a soft furry fabric. E20. ▸**b** *transf.* A person who resembles a teddy bear in appearance or in being cuddly or lovable. M20.
2 Usu. *attrib.* ▸**a** A fur-lined high-altitude flying suit. *US slang.* E20. ▸**b** A heavy or furry coat; *spec.* one of natural-coloured fabric with a pile like alpaca. E20. ▸**c** A fleecy fabric made of wool and mohair. M20.
3 = LAIR *noun*[3]. *Austral. rhyming slang.* M20.
4 = TEDDY 3. L20.

📖 **1** *Ladies Home Journal (US)* A worn . . teddy bear . . was my 'security blanket'. **teddy bears' picnic** [a song (c 1932) by Jimmy Kennedy and J. W. Bratton] an occasion of innocent enjoyment.

■ **teddy-bearish** *adjective* resembling a teddy bear L20.

Teddy boy /ˈtɛdi bɔɪ/ *noun phr. colloq.* M20.
[from *Teddy* pet-form of *Edward*, with ref. to the style of dress during the reign of Edward VII, King of Great Britain 1901–10, + BOY *noun*.]
A youth, esp. of the 1950s, affecting an Edwardian style of dress and appearance, usu. a long jacket and drainpipe trousers. More widely (*arch.*), any rowdy young man.

Teddy girl /ˈtɛdi ɡəːl/ *noun phr. colloq.* M20.
[formed as prec. + GIRL *noun*.]
A girl who associates with or behaves like a Teddy boy.

tedesco /teˈdesko/ *noun*[1] *& adjective.* Pl. **-schi** /-ski/. E19.
[Italian = German from medieval Latin *theodiscus*, ult. from Germanic base of DUTCH *adjective*. Cf. TUDESQUE.]
(An instance of) German influence in Italian art or literature; showing such influence.

Tedesco /tɛˈdɛskəʊ/ *noun*[2]. *colloq.* Also **Tu-** /tʊ-/. Pl. **-os**. L19.
[Ladino, from Spanish, Portuguese *tudesco* German: cf. prec.]
Among Sephardic Jews: an Ashkenazic Jew.

Te Deum /tiː ˈdiːəm, teɪ ˈdeɪəm/ *noun phr.* OE.
[Latin.]
1 An ancient Latin hymn of praise beginning *Te deum laudamus* 'We praise you, O God', sung as an expression of thanksgiving on special occasions, and sung or recited regularly at Roman Catholic matins and (in translation) at Anglican matins. OE.
2 A recital of this; any (public) expression of thanksgiving or exultation. L17.
3 A musical setting of this hymn. M19.

tedious /'ti:dɪəs/ *adjective.* LME.
[Old French *tedieus* or late Latin *taedioscus*, from Latin *taedium* TEDIUM: see -OUS, -IOUS.]
1 Long and tiresome; wearisome; *esp.* (of a speech or narrative, or a person delivering such) prolix so as to cause weariness or boredom. LME. ▸†**b** Long in time or extent. *joc. rare.* E–M17.
2 Irksome, troublesome, disagreeable, painful. Now chiefly *dial.* LME.
3 Late, dilatory, slow. *obsolete exc. dial.* L15.

📖 **1** A. N. WILSON The bishop's sermon had been . . the most tedious twenty minutes of the year. J. COX No gardener needs to be reminded that weeding is tedious work. P. P. READ A . . tedious woman who held forth at great length on any subject.

■ **tediously** *adverb* M16. **tediousness** *noun* LME.

tedium /'ti:dɪəm/ *noun.* M17.
[Latin *taedium* weariness, disgust, from *taedere* be wearisome.]
The state or quality of being tedious; wearisomeness, boredom.

tee /ti:/ *noun*[1]. L15.
[Repr. pronunc. of *T, t* as the letter's name.]
1 The letter T, t; the shape of the capital letter T; a T-shaped object. L15.
2 *ellipt.* A T-shirt. *N. Amer.* L20.

📖 **1** *attrib.: Engineering* Reinforced concrete tee beams. **to a tee** = *to a T* s.v. T, T 1.

tee /ti:/ *noun*[2]. Orig. *Scot.* Also (earlier) †**teaz**. L17.
[Origin unkn.]
GOLF. A cleared place from which a golf ball is struck at the beginning of play for each hole; a support on which a ball is placed to be struck, orig. a small heap of earth or sand, now usu. a small wooden or plastic peg with a concave top.

tee /ti:/ *noun*[3]. Orig. *Scot.* L18.
[Origin uncertain: perh. identical with TEE *noun*[1].]
A mark aimed at in curling, quoits, and similar games.

tee /ti:/ *noun*[4]. E19.
[Burmese *h'ti* umbrella.]
A conical metallic structure, usually hung with bells, surmounting the pagodas of Myanmar (Burma) and adjacent countries.

tee /ti:/ *verb trans.* Also (earlier) †**teaz**. Pa. t. & pple **teed**. L17.
[from TEE *noun*[2].]
GOLF. Place (a ball) on a tee ready to be struck.
With adverbs in specialized senses: **tee off** (*a*) *verb phr. intrans.* play a ball from a tee; *transf.* begin, start, esp. a game or performance; (*b*) *verb phr. trans.* (*fig.*, *N. Amer. slang*) anger, annoy, irritate (esp. as **teed off**); **tee up** *verb phr. trans. & intrans.* (*a*) place (a ball) on a tee ready to be struck; (*b*) *transf.* prepare, get ready, esp. to play.
Comb.: **teeing-ground** a small patch of ground from which a ball is teed off; **tee-off** the start of play in golf and (now also) other sports.

teedle /'ti:d(ə)l/ *verb trans. Scot. rare.* E19.
[Prob. imit. Cf. TOOTLE *verb.*]
Sing (a tune) without words; hum.

tee-hee /ti:'hi:/ *verb, interjection, & noun.* ME.
[Imit.]
▸ **A** *verb intrans.* Pa. t. & pple **-heed**. Utter 'tee-hee' in laughing; laugh lightly and usu. derisively; titter, giggle. ME.
▸ **B** *interjection.* Repr. a light usu. derisive laugh. LME.
▸ **C** *noun.* A laugh of this kind; a titter, a giggle. L16.

teem /ti:m/ *verb*[1].
[Old English (Anglian) *tēman*, (West Saxon) *tīeman*, from Germanic base of TEAM *noun.*]
†**1 a** *verb trans.* LAW. Refer (property) *to* a third person for evidence of ownership. Only in OE. ▸**b** *verb intrans.* Refer or appeal *to* for confirmation or testimony. OE–ME. ▸**c** *verb intrans.* Attach oneself (*to* a person) in loyalty or trust; turn *to*. Only in ME.
2 *verb trans.* Bring forth, give birth to, bear (offspring). *arch.* OE.
†**3** *verb intrans.* Bring forth young, bear offspring; be or become pregnant. OE–M17.
4 *verb intrans.* Be full of (as if ready to give birth); be prolific or abundant; be swarming or crowded with or *with*. L16.

📖 **4** M. MCCARTHY Overcrowded slums teeming with rickety children. A. BURGESS Beneficent nature teems all around us. J. FRAME The country is full of legends. Teeming with them.

Comb.: †**teeming-date** (*rare*, Shakes.) breeding-time, reproductive period.
■ **teemful** *adjective* prolific, productive, teeming M18.

teem /ti:m/ *verb*[2]. ME.
[Old Norse *tœma* to empty, from *tómr* TOOM *adjective.*]
1 *verb trans.* **a** Empty (a vessel etc.); remove the contents of; *spec.* drain the liquid from. Chiefly *dial. & techn.* ME. ▸**b** Empty out, pour out; *spec.* pour (molten steel) into an ingot mould. Chiefly *dial. & techn.* L15.
2 *verb intrans.* Of water etc.: pour, flow in a stream, flow copiously; (of rain) pour. Also foll. by *down*. E19.

📖 **2** JO GRIMOND The rain . . seemed to teem down incessantly.

Phrases: **teeming and lading** the falsifying of accounts by making up embezzled cash with funds received at a later date.
■ **teemer** *noun* a person who teems, empties, or unloads something M17.

teen /ti:n/ *noun*[1]. *arch.*
[Old English *tēona* = Old Frisian *tiona, tiuna*, Old Saxon *tiono*, and Old English *tēon* = Old Norse *tjón* rel. to Greek *duē* misfortune, misery, Sanskrit *dunoti*.]
†**1** Harm inflicted or suffered; injury, hurt, damage. OE–E17.
2 Irritation, annoyance; anger, rage; spite, malice. Formerly also, a cause of annoyance. *obsolete exc. Scot. & dial.* OE.
3 Affliction, suffering, woe. ME. ▸**b** Trouble or pains taken about something. LME.

teen /ti:n/ *noun*[2]. L16.
[from -TEEN.]
1 In *pl.* The numbers from thirteen to nineteen inclusive, whose names end in *-teen*, used esp. to denote years of a person's life (chiefly ***one's teens***), years of a century, or units of a scale of temperature. L16.
2 A person who is in his or her teens, a teenager. Freq. *attrib.* Now chiefly *N. Amer.* E19.

📖 **1** *Listener* In the teens and twenties of this century. J. FRAME She hadn't slept this way since her teens in a summer camp. **2** *Weekly World News (US)* A teen, confined in a mental hospital for killing his . . parents. *attrib.: Daily Star* A story in teen magazine My Guy.

■ **teener** *noun* (*US*) a teenager L19. **teenhood** *noun* the state of being in one's teens L19. **teenspeak** *noun* the language and way of speaking of teenagers L20.

†**teen** *adjective.* Chiefly *Scot. & north.* ME–E19.
[App. from TEEN *noun*[1].]
Angry, irritated, enraged.

teen /ti:n/ *verb*[1]. *obsolete exc. Scot. & dial.* OE.
[from TEEN *noun*[1].]
1 *verb trans.* **a** Irritate, anger, enrage. OE. ▸†**b** Injure, harm, hurt. ME–E17.
†**2 a** *verb trans.* Cause grief or sorrow to; distress. Only in ME. ▸**b** *verb intrans.* Be distressed, grieve. ME–E17.

teen *verb*[2] var. of TIND.

-teen /ti:n/ *suffix.*
[Old English *-tēne, -tӯne* = Old Frisian *-ten(e, -tīne*, Old Saxon *-tein*, Old High German *-zehan*, Gothic *-taihun* (Dutch *-tien*, German *-zehn*).]
An inflected form of TEN, added to the simple numerals from ***three*** to ***nine***, to form the names of those from ***thirteen*** to ***nineteen***.

teenage /'ti:neɪdʒ/ *adjective & noun.* As noun usu. **teen age**. E20.
[from TEEN *noun*[2] + AGE *noun.*]
▸ **A** *adjective.* **1** Designating a person in his or her teens. E20.
2 Pertaining to, suitable for, or characteristic of a person in his or her teens. M20.

📖 **1** *Modern Maturity* Fewer than half of teenage mothers finish high school. **2** C. PHILLIPS I had little writing experience beyond a handful of teenage stories. *Practical Health* Spots are undoubtedly the bane of teenage life.

▸ **B** *noun.* The period of a person's life from the ages of thirteen to nineteen inclusive, the teens; an age falling within these limits. M20.
■ **teenaged** *adjective* of teen age M20.

teenager /'ti:neɪdʒə/ *noun.* M20.
[from prec. + -ER[1].]
A person in his or her teens; *loosely* an adolescent.

📖 *Times Lit. Suppl.* Teenagers . . had not been invented in the 1880s. *Sphere* A feisty, outspoken, streetwise teenager growing up in Brooklyn.

■ **teenagery** *noun* the period or state of being a teenager M20.

teend *verb* var. of TIND.

teenful /'ti:nfʊl, -f(ə)l/ *adjective. obsolete exc. dial.*
[Old English *tēonful*, from TEEN *noun*[1] + -FUL.]
Troublesome, distressing; angry; spiteful; sorrowful.

teensy /'ti:nzi, -si/ *adjective. colloq.* (orig. *US dial.*). Also **-sie**. L19.
[Prob. from TEENY *adjective*[2] + -SY.]
= TEENY *adjective*[2].
Comb.: **teensy-weensy** *adjective* very tiny.

teenty /'ti:nti/ *adjective. US colloq.* M19.
[Alt. of TEENY *adjective*[2].]
Very tiny, delicately small.

teeny /'ti:ni/ *noun. colloq.* M20.
[from (the same root as) TEENY-BOPPER, infl. by TEENY *adjective*[2].]
= TEENY-BOPPER.

teeny /'ti:ni/ *adjective*[1]. *obsolete exc. dial.* L16.
[from TEEN *noun*[1] + -Y[1].]
Spiteful; irritable.

teeny /'ti:ni/ *adjective*[2]. *colloq.* E19.
[Var. of TINY.]
Tiny, very small.

📖 A. TYLER She had sat . . watching for the teeniest, briefest glimpse of Leroy.

Comb.: **teeny-tiny**, **teeny-weeny** *adjectives* very tiny.

teeny-bopper /'ti:nɪbɒpə/ *noun. colloq.* M20.
[from TEEN *noun*[2] or TEEN(AGER + -Y[6] + BOPPER. Also infl. by TEENY *adjective*[2].]
A young teenager or pre-teenager, *esp.* a female one who keenly follows the latest fashions in pop music, clothes, etc.

📖 *attrib.: Time* David Cassidy, 26, teeny-bopper heartthrob who sang his way to rock stardom.

■ **teenybop** *adjective* (*colloq.*) of, pertaining to, or consisting of teeny-boppers M20.

teepee *noun* var. of TEPEE.

Teepol /'ti:pɒl/ *noun.* M20.
[Prob. from TEE *noun*[1] + *p* (repr. initial letters of Technical Products, the original manufacturer) + -OL.]
(Proprietary name for) an alkyl sulphate industrial detergent obtained by reacting olefins with sulphuric acid and neutralizing the products.

teer /tɪə/ *verb trans.* Now *dial. & techn.* ME.
[Old & mod. French *terrer* plaster, daub, (mod.) cover with earth etc., from *terre* earth.]
1 Spread or cover with earth, clay, or plaster; construct (a wall etc.) with clay or cob. ME.
2 Spread (colour), esp. when printing. L18.
Comb.: **teer-boy** in calico printing, an attendant responsible for spreading fresh colour on a printer's pad.
■ **teerer** *noun* a teer-boy M19.

tees *noun pl.* see T, T.

teesoo /'ti:su:/ *noun.* Also **tisso**. E19.
[Hindi *ṭesū, kesū* from Sanskrit *kiṃśuka* dhak.]
In the Indian subcontinent: the flowers of the dhak tree, *Butea monosperma*; the orange dye obtained from these.

Teeswater /'ti:zwɔ:tə/ *noun.* L18.
[A district in County Durham, England.]
1 (An animal of) a breed of long-woolled sheep originating in the Tees valley. L18.
2 = ***shorthorn*** (a) s.v. SHORT *adjective.* E19.

teetar *noun* var. of TITAR.

teetee *noun* var. of TITI *noun*[3].

teeter /'ti:tə/ *noun. dial. & N. Amer.* M19.
[from next.]
1 A see-saw; a see-sawing motion; the pastime of playing see-saw. Also *fig.*, hesitation between two alternatives, vacillation. M19.
2 The spotted sandpiper, *Actitis macularia*. M19.

teeter /'ti:tə/ *verb.* M19.
[Var. of TITTER *verb*[2].]
1 *verb intrans.* **a** See-saw. *dial. & US.* M19. ▸**b** Move like a see-saw; sway, move or balance unsteadily; totter. M19.
2 *verb trans.* Move (anything) with a see-saw motion; tip up and down. *dial. & N. Amer.* L19.

📖 **1b** K. VONNEGUT She teetered on high-heeled . . shoes. *Parenting* They watched buildings . . teeter and collapse. *fig.:* A. CARTER Children teetering between tears and laughter. **teeter on the brink**, **teeter on the edge** be in imminent danger (of disaster etc.).

Comb.: **teeter-tail** = TEETER *noun* 2.
■ **teetery** *adjective* tottery, insecure; faint, unsteady E20.

teeter-totter /'ti:tətɒtə/ *verb & noun.* L19.
[Redupl. of TEETER *verb* or TOTTER *verb*. Cf. TITTER-TOTTER.]
▸ **A** *verb intrans.* = TEETER *verb* 1b. L19.
▸ **B** *noun.* A see-saw. Formerly also, the pastime of playing see-saw. *dial. & N. Amer.* E20.

teeth *noun* pl. of TOOTH *noun.*

teethe /ti:ð/ *verb.* LME.
[from *teeth* pl. of TOOTH *noun.*]
1 *verb intrans.* Develop or cut teeth. Now chiefly as TEETHING *verbal noun.* LME.
2 *verb trans.* Provide with teeth, set teeth in. Chiefly *dial.* L18.

📖 **1** E. TAYLOR Baby was teething and kept them awake at night.

■ **teether** *noun* a small object for an infant to bite on while teething; a teething ring: M20.

teething /'ti:ðɪŋ/ *verbal noun.* M18.
[from prec. + -ING[1].]
The action of TEETHE *verb*; the process of growing or cutting teeth, esp. milk teeth.
Comb.: **teething problems** = ***teething troubles*** below; **teething ring** a small ring or disc for an infant to bite on while

teething; **teething troubles** initial difficulties in an enterprise etc., regarded as temporary.

teethy /ˈtiːθi/ *adjective*[1]. Now *Scot. & north.* LME.
[Origin unkn. Cf. TEETY.]
Testy, peevish, crabbed.

teethy /ˈtiːθi/ *adjective*[2]. E19.
[formed as TEETHE + -Y[1].]
Well supplied with teeth.

teetotal /tiːˈtəʊt(ə)l/ *adjective, noun, & verb.* M19.
[Redupl. or extension of TOTAL *adjective*, app. first used by a working man, Richard Turner of Preston, in a speech in 1833 advocating total abstinence from all alcoholic liquor, as opp. to abstinence from spirits only.]
▶ **A** *adjective.* Of, pertaining to, characterized by, or advocating total abstinence from alcoholic drink. M19.

Guardian He himself had become a Muslim . . but he was not . . teetotal.

▶ **B** *absol.* as *noun.* Teetotalism; a society for the promotion of teetotalism. Also, a teetotaller. Now chiefly *dial.* M19.
▶ **C** *verb intrans.* Infl. **-ll-**, *****-l-**. Practise or advocate teetotalism. Chiefly as ***teetotalling*** *ppl adjective & verbal noun.* M19.

A. N. WILSON The happy peasants . . leading pure, teetotalling, non-smoking lives.

■ **teetotalish** *adjective* M19. **teetotalist** *noun* (now *rare*) a teetotaller M19.

teetotaler *noun* see TEETOTALLER.

teetotalism /tiːˈtəʊt(ə)lɪz(ə)m/ *noun.* M19.
[from TEETOTAL + -ISM.]
The principle or practice of total abstinence from alcoholic drink.

teetotaller /tiːˈtəʊt(ə)lə/ *noun.* Also *****-aler.** M19.
[formed as prec. + -ER[1].]
A person advocating or practising abstinence from alcoholic drink, esp. by pledge.

teetotally /tiːˈtəʊt(ə)li/ *adverb.* E19.
[Redupl. of TOTALLY. In sense 2 also from TEETOTAL + -LY[2].]
1 Totally, entirely, wholly. *dial. & US.* E19.
2 To a teetotal extent; in a teetotal manner; with total abstinence from alcoholic drink. M19.

1 A. J. DAWSON I'll be teetotally damned if that ain't the limit!

teetotum /tiːˈtəʊtəm/ *noun & verb.* Orig. †**T totum.** E18.
[T (standing for *totum*, and inscribed on one side of the toy) + Latin *totum* all, the whole (stakes).]
▶ **A** *noun.* **1** A small four-sided disk or die with an initial letter on each side, and a central spindle by which it may be spun like a small top, the uppermost letter, when it stops, determining whether the spinner has won or lost. Now also, any light top spun with the fingers. E18.
2 A game of chance played with this device. M18.
▶ **B** *verb intrans.* Spin like a teetotum, gyrate. M19.

teety /ˈtiːti/ *adjective.* Now *dial.* Also **tetty.** E17.
[Origin unkn. Cf. TEETHY *adjective*[1].]
Testy, peevish, fractious.

teevee /tiːˈviː/ *noun. informal.* M20.
[Repr. pronunc. of *TV*.]
(A) television.

teff /tɛf/ *noun.* L18.
[Amharic *tēf*.]
The principal cereal grass of Ethiopia, *Eragrostis tef*, grown elsewhere as a fodder plant.

tefillin /tiːˈfiliːn/ *noun pl.* E17.
[Aramaic *tēpillīn* prayers.]
Jewish phylacteries; the texts inscribed on these.

TEFL /ˈtɛf(ə)l/ *abbreviation.*
Teaching of English as a foreign language.

Teflon /ˈtɛflɒn/ *noun & adjective.* M20.
[from TE(TRA- + FL(UOR- + *-on* (cf. NYLON, RAYON *noun*[2]).]
▶ **A** *noun.* (Proprietary name for) polytetrafluoroethylene. M20.
Comb.: **Teflon-coated** *adjective* = sense B. below.
▶ **B** *attrib.* or as *adjective.* Coated with Teflon; *transf.* (of a politician) having an undamaged reputation, in spite of scandal or misjudgement, able to deflect criticism on to others, so that nothing sticks to oneself. M20.

†**tefterdar** *noun* var. of DEFTERDAR.

teg /tɛg/ *noun.* Also **tag** /tag/. E16.
[Origin uncertain: cf. Old Swedish *takka*, Swedish *tacka* ewe.]
†**1** A woman. *contempt.* Only in E16.
2 A (formerly only female) sheep in its second year, or from the time it is weaned until its first shearing; a yearling sheep. M16. ▸**b** The wool of a teg. Also ***teg wool.*** M19.
†**3** A female deer in its second year. M16–L18.

Tegean /tɛˈdʒiːən, ˈtɛdʒɪən/ *noun & adjective.* E18.
[from Greek, Latin *Tegea* Tegea: see below, -EAN.]
▶ **A** *noun.* A native or inhabitant of the ancient city of Tegea in Arcadia. E18.
▶ **B** *adjective.* Of or pertaining to Tegea or its inhabitants. M18.

Tegeate /ˈtɛdʒɪeɪt/ *noun & adjective. rare.* L16.
[Latin *Tegeates*, from *Tegea*: see prec., -ATE[2].]
= prec.

tegestology /tɛdʒɛˈstɒlədʒi/ *noun.* M20.
[Irreg. from Latin *teges, -etis* covering, mat, from *tegere* to cover + *-t-* + -OLOGY.]
The collecting of beer-mats.
■ **tegestologist** *noun* a collector of beer-mats M20.

tegmen /ˈtɛgmɛn/ *noun.* Pl. **-mina** /-mɪnə/. E19.
[Latin = covering, from *tegere* to cover.]
1 *ENTOMOLOGY.* A covering; *esp.* a sclerotized forewing serving to cover the hindwing in the orders Orthoptera, Dictyoptera, etc. Cf. ELYTRON. E19.
2 *ANATOMY.* A covering structure or roof; *esp.* (more fully ***tegmen tympani*** /ˈtɪmpənʌɪ/) a plate of thin bone forming the roof of the middle ear, a part of the temporal bone. L19.

tegmentum /tɛgˈmɛntəm/ *noun.* Pl. **-ta** /-tə/. M19.
[Latin, var. of *tegumentum* TEGUMENT.]
1 *BOTANY.* Any of the protective scales of a leaf-bud. M19.
2 *ANATOMY.* A covering; *spec.* the upper and dorsal portion of each of the cerebral peduncles, separated by the substantia nigra from the crura cerebri. L19.
■ **tegmental** *adjective* L19.

tegmina *noun* pl. of TEGMEN.

tegu /ˈtɛguː/ *noun.* M20.
[Abbreviation of mod. Latin *teguixin*: see next.]
Any of several large Central and S. American lizards of the family Teiidae; *esp.* (more fully ***common tegu***) *Tupinambis teguixin*, which feeds on small vertebrates etc.

teguexin /tɛˈgwɛksɪn/ *noun.* Now *rare* or *obsolete.* L19.
[Alt. of mod. Latin *teguixin* (specific name) from Aztec *tecoixin, tecouixin* lizard.]
= prec.

tegula /ˈtɛgjʊlə/ *noun.* Pl. **-lae** /-liː/. E19.
[Latin = tile, from *tegere* to cover.]
1 *ENTOMOLOGY.* A small scalelike sclerite covering the base of the forewing in the orders Lepidoptera, Hymenoptera, Diptera, etc. E19.
2 *ARCHAEOLOGY.* A flat roof-tile, used esp. in Roman roofs. Cf. IMBREX. L19.
■ **tegular** *adjective* pertaining to or resembling a tile or tegula; composed of or arranged like tiles: E19. **tegularly** *adverb* (*rare*) in the manner of tiles; overlapping like tiles: L18.

tegument /ˈtɛgjʊm(ə)nt/ *noun.* LME.
[Latin *tegumentum* covering, formed as TEGMEN: see -MENT.]
1 = INTEGUMENT 1. LME.
2 = INTEGUMENT 2. Now *rare* or *obsolete.* M17.
■ **teguˈmental** *adjective* of, pertaining to, or of the nature of a tegument; tegumentary: E19. **teguˈmentary** *adjective* constituting, or serving as, a tegument; pertaining to or occurring in the tegument: E19.

tehr *noun* see TAHR.

Tehrani /tɛˈ(h)rɑːni/ *noun & adjective.* M20.
[from *Tehran* (see below) + -I[2].]
▶ **A** *noun.* A native or inhabitant of Tehran, the capital of Iran. M20.
▶ **B** *adjective.* Of, pertaining to, or characteristic of the city of Tehran, or of its inhabitants. M20.

Tê-hua *adjective & noun* var. of DEHUA.

Tehuelche /tɛˈwɛltʃeɪ/ *noun.* Pl. same, **-s.** L18.
[Araucanian = southern abode.]
1 A member of a S. American Indian people inhabiting the Patagonian plain of southern Argentina; a Patagonian. L18.
2 The language of this people. L19.
■ **Tehuelchian** *adjective & noun* (**a**) *adjective* of or pertaining to the Tehuelche; (**b**) *noun* the language of the Tehuelche: E20.

Teian /ˈtiːən/ *adjective.* M17.
[Greek *tēios* of or from *Teōs* Teos (see below) + -IAN.]
Of or relating to Teos, an ancient Ionian city on the west coast of Asia Minor north of Ephesus.

teichoic /tʌɪˈkəʊɪk/ *adjective.* M20.
[from Greek *teikhos* wall + -IC.]
BIOCHEMISTRY. ***teichoic acid***, any of various polymers of ribitol or glycerol phosphate that are found in the walls of Gram-positive bacteria.

teichopsia /tʌɪˈkɒpsɪə/ *noun.* L19.
[from Greek *teikhos* town wall + *opsis* sight + -IA[1].]
MEDICINE. The seeing of shimmering lights, sometimes in the form of battlements and often accompanied by black spots in the field of vision, a frequent phenomenon at the start of migraine attacks. Also called ***fortification spectra.***

Te igitur /tiː ˈɪdʒɪtə/ *noun phr.* E19.
[Latin, lit. 'thee therefore', the opening words of the prayer.]
The first prayer in the canon of the Mass in the Roman and some other Latin liturgies; the liturgical book itself.

teiglach /ˈteɪgləx/ *noun pl.* Also **taig-** & other vars. E20.
[Yiddish *teiglekh* pl. of *teigl* dough pellet from *teig* dough ult. from Old High German *teic*: see DOUGH *noun*.]
A Jewish confection made of pellets of dough boiled in honey.

teil /tiːl/ *noun.* Now *rare* or *obsolete.* LME.
[Old French var. of *til* from Proto-Romance var. of Latin *tilia* linden tree.]
Any lime tree, esp. *Tilia* × *vulgaris*. Also, in biblical translations, a kind of terebinth tree, *Pistacia palaestina* (*rare*).

Teilhardian /teɪˈjɑːdɪən/ *adjective & noun.* M20.
[from Pierre *Teilhard* de Chardin (1881–1955), French scientist and theologian + -IAN.]
▶ **A** *adjective.* Of or pertaining to Teilhard de Chardin or his writings, which are noted for their attempt to synthesize science and the Christian faith. M20.
▶ **B** *noun.* An adherent or follower of Teilhard de Chardin. L20.

tein /ˈteɪɪn/ *noun.* Pl. same, **-s.** L20.
[Kazakh.]
A monetary unit of Kazakhstan, equal to one-hundredth of a tenge.

teind /tiːnd/ *noun & verb. Scot. & north.* ME.
[Var. of TENTH *noun*.]
▶ **A** *noun.* †**1** The tenth part; a tenth. ME–L15.
2 *spec.* A tithe paid (voluntarily or legally) to the Church; *spec.* (in Scotland) a land tax payable to the Established Church but transferred to the minister in whose parish the land lies. Now usu. in *pl.* ME.
3 *transf.* The payment or system of teinds. E19.
2 parsonage teinds: see PARSONAGE 3.
▶ **B** *verb.* Now *rare* or *obsolete.*
1 *verb intrans.* Pay teinds or tithes. LME.
2 *verb trans. & intrans.* Assess or take as a tithe. L15.

†**teise** *verb trans.* LME–E19.
[Origin unkn.]
Drive (esp. a hunted beast); chase; urge on (hounds, horses, etc.).
■ †**teiser** *noun* a person who or animal which rouses game for hunting LME–L18.

teistie *noun* var. of TYSTIE.

tej /tɛdʒ/ *noun.* M19.
[Prob. from Amharic.]
A kind of mead, the national drink of Ethiopia.

Tejano /təˈhɑːnəʊ/ *noun & adjective.* Pl. **-os.** E20.
[Amer. Spanish, alt. of *Texano* Texan.]
▶ **A** *noun.* **1** A native or inhabitant of Texas, *esp.* one of Mexican origin or ancestry; a Texan. E20.
2 A style of folk or popular music originating with the Mexican-American inhabitants of southern Texas and deriving elements from Mexican-Spanish vocal traditions and from Czech and German dance tunes and rhythms. L20.
▶ **B** *adjective.* Of, relating to, or characteristic of the Tejanos or their music. L20.

tekbir /ˈtɛkbɪə/ *noun.* Also **tec-.** E18.
[Arab. *tekbir*, colloq. pronunc. of *takbīr* magnify, proclaim the greatness of, from base also of *kabīr* great, *'akbar* greater, greatest.]
A cry of *Allāhu 'akbar* 'Allah is most great', uttered by Muslims.

tekke /ˈtɛkeɪ/ *noun*[1]. M17.
[Turkish *tekke*, Arab. *takiyya*, Persian *takya* place of repose, pillow, abode of a dervish or fakir, perh. ult. from Arab. *ittakā'a* lean on.]
A monastery of dervishes, esp. in Ottoman Turkey.

Tekke /ˈtɛkeɪ/ *noun*[2] *& adjective.* Also (earlier) †**Tuckeh.** E19.
[Turkic *Teke*.]
▶ **A** *noun.* A member of a Turkoman people inhabiting Turkmenistan in central Asia. E19.
▶ **B** *attrib.* or as *adjective.* **1** Designating a Turkoman of this people. E19.
2 Designating a short-piled predominantly red carpet or rug made by members of this people. Also ***Tekke Bokhara.*** E20.

teknonymy /tɛkˈnɒnɪmi/ *noun.* L19.
[from Greek *teknon* child + -NYM + -Y[3].]
The practice among certain peoples of naming a parent from his or her child.
■ **teknonymous** *adjective* practising teknonymy L19.

tekoteko /ˈtɛkəʊtɛkəʊ/ *noun. NZ.* Pl. same, **-os.** M19.
[Maori.]
A carved human figure, *esp.* one placed on a gable.

tektite /ˈtɛktʌɪt/ *noun.* E20.
[from Greek *tēktos* molten (from *tēkein* make molten): see -ITE[1].]
Any of numerous small black glassy objects that occur scattered over an area in several parts of the earth, and are thought to have been thrown up in molten form from meteorite impacts.
Comb.: **tektite field** = ***strewn field*** s.v. STREW *verb.*

tektosilicate *noun* var. of TECTOSILICATE.

tektosphere /ˈtɛktə(ʊ)sfɪə/ *noun.* Now *rare* or *obsolete.* E20.
[formed as TEKTITE + -O- + -SPHERE.]
GEOLOGY. = ASTHENOSPHERE. Cf. TECTOSPHERE.

tel- *combining form* see TELE-.

Tel. *abbreviation.*
1 Telegraph; telegraphic.
2 Telephone.

telaesthesia /tɛlɪsˈθiːzɪə/ *noun.* Also ***teles-**. L19.
[formed as TELE- + Greek *aisthēsis* perception: see -IA¹.]
Perception by paranormal means, independently of the recognized senses.
■ **telaesthetic** *adjective* (*rare*) having or pertaining to telaesthesia L19.

telamon /ˈtɛləmən, -məʊn/ *noun.* Pl. **telamones** /tɛləˈməʊniːz/. E17.
[Latin *telamones* (pl.) from Greek *telamōnes* pl. of *Telamōn* Telamon, a mythical hero.]
ARCHITECTURE. A male figure used as a pillar to support an entablature or other structure. Cf. CARYATID.

telangiectasis /tɛˌlandʒɪˈɛktəsɪs/ *noun.* Pl. **-ases** /-əsiːz/. Also **-ectasia** /-ɛkˈteɪzɪə/, pl. **-iae** /-ɪiː/. Formerly Anglicized as †**-ectasy**. M19.
[from Greek *telos* end + *aggeion* vessel + *ektasis* extension, dilatation.]
MEDICINE. (A condition characterized by) dilatation of the capillaries causing them to appear as small red or purple clusters, often spidery in appearance, on the skin or the surface of an organ.
■ **telangiectatic** /-ˈtatɪk/ *adjective* pertaining to or resulting from telangiectasis M19.

telautograph /tɛˈlɔːtəgrɑːf/ *noun.* Now *rare.* L19.
[from TELE- + AUTOGRAPH, after *telegraph*.]
A telegraphic apparatus by which the movements of a pen or pencil at the transmitting end are reproduced at the receiving end to generate a facsimile.
■ **telauto'graphic** *adjective* L19. **telau'tography** *noun* the use of a telautograph L19.

Tel Avivian /tɛl əˈviːvɪən, -ˈvɪv-/ *noun.* M20.
[from *Tel Aviv* (see below) + -IAN.]
A native or inhabitant of Tel Aviv, a city in Israel.

telco /ˈtɛlkəʊ/ *noun. colloq.* (orig. *US*). Pl. **-os**. L20.
[Abbreviation.]
A telecommunications company.

†**teld** *noun* see TILT *noun*¹.

tele /ˈtɛli/ *noun*¹. *colloq.* M20.
[Abbreviation.]
= TELEVISION. Cf. TELLY.

tele /ˈtɛli/ *noun*². M20.
[Greek *tēle* far (off).]
Psychic affinity between people separated by time or space.

tele /ˈtɛli/ *adjective. colloq.* L20.
[Abbreviation.]
= TELEPHOTOGRAPHIC *adjective*².

tele- /ˈtɛli/ *combining form.* Before a vowel occas. **tel-**.
[Greek *tēle-* combining form of *tēle* far (off).]
1 Forming words denoting or connected with instruments or appliances for, or methods of, operating or communicating over long distances.
2 *spec.* Forming chiefly nouns denoting or relating to (*a*) people, activities, or things connected with television (cf. TELE *noun*¹); (*b*) services obtained or transactions effected by telephone or computer link.
■ **tele-ad** *noun* an advertisement placed in a newspaper etc. by telephone L20. **telebanking** *noun* a method of effecting banking transactions at a distance by electronic means L20. **telebetting** *noun* a method of placing bets at a distance by electronic means L20. **telebroking** *noun* the transaction of stock market business at a distance by electronic means L20. **telecamera** *noun* (*a*) a telephotographic camera; (*b*) a television camera: E20. **telecast** *noun* & *verb* (orig. *US*) (*a*) *noun* broadcasting by television, a television broadcast; (*b*) *verb trans.* broadcast or transmit by television: M20. **telecaster** *noun* a person who broadcasts on television M20. **telecentre** *noun* a telecottage L20. **tele'centric** *adjective & noun* (*OPTICS*) (designating) a lens system of which the aperture or stop is at the principal focus E20. **telecine** *noun* (*a*) the broadcasting or transmission of (a) cinema film on television; (*b*) (an) apparatus for doing this; (*c*) a cinema film broadcast in this way: M20. **tele'cobalt** *noun* radioactive cobalt used as a radiation source in teletherapy M20. **telecom** *noun* (*colloq.*) (*a*) *sing.* & in *pl.*, telecommunications; (*b*) a telecommunications network: M20. **teleco'mmand** *noun* electronic remote control of machines L20. **teleco'mmute** *verb intrans.* work from home, communicating by telephone, telex, etc. L20. **teleco'mmuter** *noun* a person who telecommutes L20. **telecomputer** *noun* a computer with the ability to use telecommunications L20. **telecon** *noun* (*a*) *US MILITARY* a device for sending teletype messages by radio or underwater cable and (usually) displaying them on a screen; (*b*) = TELECONFERENCE: M20. **teleconference** *noun* a conference with participants in different locations linked by telecommunication devices M20. **tele'conferencing** *noun* the action of holding a teleconference L20. **teleconnection** *noun* (*GEOLOGY*) the correlation over long distances of varves or other deposits that can be used for dating purposes M20. **telecon'trol** *noun* = TELECOMMAND M20. **teleconverter** *noun* (*PHOTOGRAPHY*) a camera lens designed to be fitted in front of a standard lens to increase its effective focal length M20. **Telecopier** *noun* (US proprietary name for) a device which transmits and reproduces graphic material over a telephone line M20. **telecottage** *noun* [translating Swedish *telestuga*] a room or building, esp. in a rural area, containing computer equipment for the shared use of people living in the area L20. **telecurie'therapy** *noun* [CURIE] *MEDICINE* = TELETHERAPY M20. **telediag'nosis** *noun* (*MEDICINE*) the long-distance assessment of a patient's condition, using closed-circuit television, or by unconventional means M20. **te'lediphone** *noun* [*Ediphone*, proprietary name] a machine for recording speech from a telephone line or radio for subsequent transcription or broadcasting M20. **telefac'simile** *noun* facsimile transmission M20. **Telefax** *noun* (*a*) (proprietary name for) a system for sending and receiving messages by facsimile; (*b*) = TELEFACSIMILE: M20. **telefilm** *noun* a cinema film broadcast on television; (the medium producing) such films: M20. **tele'genic** *adjective* (orig. *US*) (*a*) (having an appearance or manner) that shows to advantage on television; (*b*) providing an interesting or attractive subject for television: M20. **teleg'nosis** *noun* = CLAIRVOYANCE 1 E20. **teleki'nesis** *noun* movement of a body at or to a distance by paranormal means L19. **teleki'netic** *adjective* of or pertaining to telekinesis L19. **telelens** *noun* (*PHOTOGRAPHY*) a telephotographic lens E20. **telemarket** *verb trans.* (orig. *US*) market (goods, services, etc.) by means of usu. unsolicited telephone calls to prospective customers L20. **tele'marketer** *noun* a practitioner of telemarketing L20. **tele'medicine** *noun* (*MEDICINE*) the remote diagnosis and treatment of patients using telecommunications technology L20. **telemeeting** *noun* = TELECONFERENCE L20. **telemessage** *noun* a message sent by telephone or telex and delivered in written form L20. **telemotor** *noun* a hydraulically-operated steering control used mainly in ships L19. **teleoperation** *noun* = TELECOMMAND L20. **tele'operator** *noun* a machine operated by remote control so as to imitate the movements of its operator M20. **teleplay** *noun* a play written or adapted for television; a screenplay for a television drama: M20. **telepoint** *noun* (*a*) a service enabling a user of a cordless telephone to connect it with the conventional telephone network; (*b*) a public place offering such a service: L20. **tele'politics** *noun* political activity conducted through television M20. **telepresence** *noun* the use of remote control and the feedback of sensory information to give a person the impression that he or she is at another location; a sensation of being elsewhere created in this way: L20. **teleprint** *verb trans.* send or print (a message etc.) by teleprinter L20. **teleprinter** *noun* a device for transmitting telegraph messages as they are keyed and printing messages received E20. **tele'processing** *noun* data processing involving terminals located at a distance from the processor M20. **teleprompt** *verb trans.* assist by means of a teleprompter M20. **teleprompter** *noun* (orig. *US*) an electronic device, placed close to a television or cinema camera but out of camera range, that slowly unrolls a speaker's script in order to prompt or assist him or her (cf. AUTOCUE) M20. **telepuppet** *noun* (*colloq.*) a telechiric device, *esp.* one used in space M20. **teleradi'ography** *noun* (*MEDICINE*) radiography in which the X-ray tube is placed at a distance from the plate so as to minimize distortion E20. **tele'radium** *noun* radium used as a radiation source in teletherapy M20. **telere'cord** *verb trans.* make a telerecording of (a programme) M20. **telerecording** *noun* (the action of making) a recording of a television programme during transmission; a recorded television broadcast: M20. **tele'robot** *noun* a robot which receives instructions or information through telecommunications L20. **telero'botic** *adjective* pertaining to or designating a machine operated by remote control using telecommunications L20. **telero'botically** *adverb* by means of a telerobot; as regards telerobotics: L20. **telero'botics** *noun* the branch of technology that deals with the development and use of telerobots L20. **teleroentge'nography** *noun* (*MEDICINE*, chiefly *US*) = TELERADIOGRAPHY E20. **telesales** *noun pl.* selling conducted or sales made by telephone L20. **telescreen** *noun* a television screen M20. **teleseism** *noun* a distant or remote earth tremor as recorded on a seismograph E20. **tele'seismic** *adjective* of or pertaining to teleseisms E20. **teleseme** *noun* (now *rare* or *obsolete*) an electric signalling apparatus used in hotels etc., fitted with an indicator which shows the article or service required L19. **teleshopper** *noun* a person who engages in teleshopping L20. **teleshopping** *noun* the ordering of goods from shops by telephone or by a direct computer link L20. **tele'software** *noun* (*COMPUTING*) software transmitted or broadcast for use by independent receiving terminals L20. **tele'spectroscope** *noun* a combination of a telescope and a spectroscope, for spectroscopic observations at great (esp. astronomical) distances L19. **tele'stereoscope** *noun* an optical instrument designed to allow stereo viewing of distant objects M19. **teleteaching** *noun* teaching at a distance by electronic means M20. **tele'therapy** *noun* (*MEDICINE*) radiotherapy using a source of radiation at a distance from the patient E20. **telether'mometer** *noun* a thermometer that indicates the temperature measured elsewhere L19. **telethon** *noun* (orig. *N. Amer.*) an exceptionally long television programme to raise money for a charity or cause M20. **teletyper** *noun* = TELEPRINTER E20. **tele'typesetter** *noun* an apparatus for the automatic casting and setting of type controlled by instructions recorded on perforated tape E20. **tele'typewriter** *noun* = TELEPRINTER E20. **teleview** *verb intrans.* (now *rare*) watch television M20. **televiewer** *noun* a person who watches television M20. **telework** *verb intrans.* = TELECOMMUTE L20. **teleworker** *noun* = TELECOMMUTER L20.

telecabine /ˌtɛlɪkaˈbiːn/ *noun.* Also **telecabin** /ˈtɛlɪkabɪn/. M20.
[French *télécabine*.]
A kind of ski-lift in which people are carried in enclosed cars; a car on such a ski-lift.

telechiric /tɛlɪˈkʌɪrɪk/ *adjective & noun.* M20.
[from TELE- + Greek *kheir* hand + -IC.]
▸ **A** *adjective.* Designating, pertaining to, or involving a manipulating device operated at a distance by a person who receives feedback from sensors in the device. M20.
▸ **B** *noun.* **1** In *pl.* The branch of technology that deals with telechiric devices. M20.
2 A telechiric device or system. M20.
■ **telechir** /ˈtɛlɪkɪə/ *noun* = TELECHIRIC *noun* 2 L20.

telecommunication /ˌtɛlɪkəmjuːnɪˈkeɪʃ(ə)n/ *noun.* M20.
[French *télécommunication*, formed as TELE-: cf. COMMUNICATION.]
(A mode of) communication over a distance, esp. by cable, telegraph, telephone, or broadcasting; (usu. in *pl.*, treated as *sing.*) the branch of technology that deals with such communication(s).

> 🕮 *attrib.*: *Engineering* The plan . . to put a telecommunications satellite into orbit round the earth.

teledu /ˈtɛlɪduː/ *noun.* E19.
[Javanese.]
Either of two burrowing mustelid carnivores of Java and Sumatra, *Mydaus javanensis* and *M. marchei*, which can eject a foul-smelling liquid in self-defence. Also called ***stinking badger***, ***stinkard***.

teleferic /tɛlɪˈfɛrɪk/ *noun.* Also ***téléphérique***, **-f-**, /teleferik (*pl. same*)/; **telepherique** /ˌtɛlɪfɛˈriːk/. E20.
[Italian *teleferica*, French *téléphérique*, from Greek *tēle-* TELE- + *pherein* carry: see -IC.]
A cableway.

telega /tɛˈleɪgə/ *noun.* Orig. †**telego**, pl. **-oes**. M16.
[Russian.]
A crude four-wheeled Russian cart without springs.

telegony /tɪˈlɛgəni/ *noun.* Now *rare.* L19.
[from TELE- + -GONY.]
BIOLOGY. The (hypothetical) influence of a previous sire seen in the progeny of a subsequent sire from the same dam.
■ **telegonic** /tɛlɪˈgɒnɪk/ *adjective* L19.

telegram /ˈtɛlɪgram/ *noun & verb.* M19.
[from TELE- + -GRAM, after next.]
▸ **A** *noun.* A message sent by telegraph, usually delivered in written form. M19.

> 🕮 M. DE LA ROCHE He wired you! Show me the telegram!

▸ **B** *verb trans. & intrans.* Infl. **-mm-**. Send a telegram (to); telegraph (a person, message, etc.). M19.

> 🕮 A. F. LOEWENSTEIN She'd telegrammed ahead accepting the offer. *Independent* The message he telegrammed to Rome.

■ **telegra'mmatic**, **tele'grammic** *adjectives* (*rare*) (*a*) of or pertaining to telegrams; (*b*) very concise: M19.

telegraph /ˈtɛlɪgrɑːf/ *noun & verb.* E18.
[French *télégraphe*: cf. TELE-, -GRAPH.]
▸ **A** *noun.* **1** Any of various signalling devices or systems (orig. a kind of semaphore) for transmitting messages to a distance; *esp.* one consisting of a transmitter and a receiver connected by a wire along which an electric current passes, the signals being made by making and breaking the circuit (also more fully ***electric telegraph***). Also in titles of newspapers. E18. ▸**b** A large board displaying scores, results, or other basic information at a cricket match, race meeting, etc., so as to be visible at a distance. Also ***telegraph board***. M19.
2 A telegram. *obsolete* exc. *US dial.* E19.
3 A scout, a spy; *spec.* (*Austral. slang*) one who warns bushrangers about the movements of police and pursuing troopers. E19.

> 🕮 **1** *attrib.*: ***telegraph boy***, ***telegraph clerk***, ***telegraph message***, ***telegraph wire***, etc. *fig.*: D. MACARTHUR News . . spread rapidly by the 'bamboo telegraph' through the Philippines. ***bush telegraph***: see BUSH *noun*¹. ***night telegraph letter***: see NIGHT *noun*.

Comb.: **telegraph blank** *US* a form with spaces for writing the words of a telegram to be dispatched; **telegraph board** = sense 1b above; **telegraph editor** *US* a newspaper journalist who edits news received by telegraph; **telegraph key** a small lever or other device for making and breaking the circuit of a telegraph; **telegraph plant** a leguminous plant of tropical Asia, *Codariocalyx motorius*, in which the leaflets move by jerks under the influence of warmth; **telegraph-pole** each of a series of poles for carrying a telegraph or telephone wire above the ground.

▸ **B** *verb.* **1 a** *verb intrans.* Signal by telegraph; send a telegram. E19. ▸**b** *verb trans.* Send or announce (a message, news, etc.) by telegraph; send a message to, summon, (a person) by telegraph or telegram. E19.
2 *fig.* **a** *verb intrans.* Signal (*to* a person). E19. ▸**b** *verb trans.* Convey (a signal, message, etc.) by signs; (now *rare* or *obsolete*) signal to (a person). E19.
3 *verb trans.* **a** *SPORT.* Initiate (a punch, throw, move, etc.) in a way that makes one's intention obvious. E20. ▸**b** *gen.* Give (esp. clumsily or prematurely) an advance indication of (an act, outcome, etc.). M20.

> 🕮 **1b** C. LYELL Out of town for two days, he was telegraphed back again. R. CAMPBELL Galloping post-haste to telegraph the news to the Durban Press. **2b** A. CHRISTIE Lucy's delicate eyebrows telegraphed . . an appeal.

■ **telegrapher** /ˈtɛlɪgrɑːfə, tɪˈlɛgrəfə/ *noun* (*a*) = TELEGRAPHIST; (*b*) a person who sends a telegraph message: L18. **telegra'phese** *noun* (*joc.* & *colloq.*) abbreviated language, (a) concise elliptical style L19. **telegraphist** /tɪˈlɛgrəfɪst, ˈtɛlɪgrɑːfɪst/ *noun* a person skilled or employed in telegraphy, a telegraph operator M19.

telegraphic /tɛlɪˈgrafɪk/ *adjective.* L18.
[from prec. + -IC.]
1 Of (the nature of), pertaining to, or resembling a telegraph; (transmitted) by telegraph. L18.
2 Of speech or style: abbreviated, elliptical; concise; *spec.* in PSYCHOLOGY, characteristic of infants at about two years of age in omitting inessential words. L19.

📖 **1** P. HOWARD The mutineers were not in telegraphic communication with Europe. **telegraphic address** an abbreviated or other registered address for use in telegrams. **2** R. KIPLING Telegraphic sentences, half nodded to their friends. ROGER BROWN Telegraphic speech is . . composed of contentive words . . and entirely lacking functors.

■ **telegraphically** *adverb* E19.

telegraphone /tɪˈlɛgrəfəʊn/ *noun. obsolete* exc. *Hist.* E20.
[Blend of TELEGRAPH and TELEPHONE.]
An obsolete form of telephone in which the spoken message was magnetically recorded on metal ribbon at the receiving end.

telegraphy /tɪˈlɛgrəfi/ *noun.* L18.
[from TELEGRAPH *noun* + -Y³.]
The art or science of constructing or using telegraphs; the working of a telegraph. Now also (*gen.*), the science or practice of constructing or using communication systems for reproducing information.
spark telegraphy: see SPARK *noun*¹. *wireless telegraphy*: see WIRELESS *adjective.*

Telegu *noun & adjective* var. of TELUGU.

teleguide /ˈtɛlɪgʌɪd/ *verb trans.* M20.
[French *téléguider*, formed as TELE-: see GUIDE *verb.*]
Guide or operate (a missile etc.) by remote control.
■ **teleguidance** *noun* the operation of a missile etc. by remote control M20.

teleiosis /tɛlʌɪˈəʊsɪs, tɛleɪ-/ *noun. rare.* L19.
[Greek *teleiōsis*, from *teleioun* to perfect or complete: see -OSIS.]
Perfection, completion.

telemark /ˈtɛlmɑːk/ *noun & verb.* E20.
[*Telemark*, an administrative district in southern Norway.]
SKIING. ▶**A** *noun.* A swing turn with one ski considerably advanced and the knee bent, employed to change direction or stop short. Freq. *attrib.* E20.
▶**B** *verb intrans.* Perform a telemark. E20.

telematics /tɛlɪˈmatɪks/ *noun.* L20.
[from TELE- + INFORMATICS.]
(The branch of information technology which deals with) the long-distance transmission of computerized information.
■ **telematic** *adjective* of or pertaining to telematics L20.

telemeter /ˈtɛlɪmiːtə, tɪˈlɛmɪtə/ *noun & verb.* M19.
[from TELE- + -METER.]
▶**A** *noun.* **1** Any of various instruments for measuring the distances of objects, esp. in surveying and military operations. Now *rare.* M19.
2 An electrical apparatus for recording the readings of an instrument at a distance; *esp.* an instrument for measuring a quantity at one place and transmitting the result to another place for display or recording. L19.
3 (Usu. **T-**.) (US proprietary name for) a system of pay-TV involving a coin-box attached to the television set. *US.* M20.
▶**B** *verb trans.* Measure (a quantity) and transmit the result to a distant point; transmit (a measurement or observation). (Foll. by *back.*) Freq. as ***telemetered*** *ppl adjective*, ***telemetering*** *verbal noun.* E20.
■ **teleˈmetric** *adjective* pertaining to, connected with, or serving as a telemeter L19. **teleˈmetrically** *adverb* by telemetry M20.

telemetry /tɪˈlɛmɪtri/ *noun.* L19.
[formed as prec. + -METRY.]
The process or practice of obtaining measurements and relaying them for recording or display to a point at a distance; the transmission of measurements by the apparatus making them. Also, apparatus used for this; information so transmitted.

telencephalon /tɛlɛnˈsɛf(ə)lɒn, -ˈkɛf-, tiːl-/ *noun.* L19.
[from TEL(E- + ENCEPHALON.]
ANATOMY. The anterior part of the forebrain, consisting, in the adult brain, of the cerebral hemispheres and the anterior parts of the hypothalamus and third ventricle. Cf. DIENCEPHALON.
■ ˌ**telenceˈphalic** *adjective* E20.

telenovela /ˌtɛlnəʊˈvɛlə, *foreign* ˌtelenoˈbela/ *noun.* L20.
[Spanish.]
In Latin America: a televised soap opera.

teleo- /ˈtɛlɪəʊ, ˈtiːlɪəʊ/ *combining form.*
[Greek, combining form of *teleos* complete, perfect, from *telos* end: see -O-. Cf. TELO-.]
Chiefly BOTANY & ZOOLOGY. Complete, perfect; (having some part) at a most advanced stage of development or evolution.
■ **teleosaur** *noun* (PALAEONTOLOGY) an extinct marine crocodile of the Triassic and Jurassic family Teleosauridae, having a slender snout and short front legs M19.

teleological /tɛlɪəˈlɒdʒɪk(ə)l, tiːl-/ *adjective.* L18.
[from next + -ICAL.]
Of, pertaining to, or involving teleology; relating or appealing to a goal, end, or final cause.

📖 D. CUPITT Teleological—that is . . explained in terms of the divinely appointed purpose. *Paragraph* With the liberal focus on the individual subject goes a teleological picture of his evolution. **teleological argument**: for the existence of God from the evidence of design in nature.

■ **teleologic** *adjective* (*rare*) = TELEOLOGICAL M19. **teleologically** *adverb* M19. **teleˈologism** *noun* (*rare*) belief in a teleological theory or doctrine L19. **teleˈologist** *noun* an exponent of or believer in teleology M19.

teleology /tɛlɪˈɒlədʒi, tiːl-/ *noun.* M18.
[mod. Latin *teleologia*, from Greek *telos* end + *-logia* -LOGY.]
Orig. (now *rare*), the branch of philosophy that deals with ends or final causes. Later, the belief that nature shows signs of divine or cosmic design or purpose. Now also, the belief or theory that certain phenomena or acts are to be explained in terms of purpose or intention; explanation in such terms; (evidence of) purposiveness in nature.

📖 E. JONES He never abandoned determinism for teleology. *Mind* No goal-directedness or teleology in the mechanisms of natural selection. *New Scientist* History, where some degree of teleology can be admitted, and biology, where it cannot.

teleonomy /tɛlɪˈɒnəmi/ *noun.* M20.
[formed as TELEOLOGY + -NOMY.]
BIOLOGY. The property of living systems of being organized towards the attainment of ends without true purposiveness.
■ **teleoˈnomic** *adjective* M20.

teleost /ˈtiːlɪɒst/ *noun & adjective.* M19.
[from TELEO- + Greek *osteon* bone.]
ZOOLOGY. ▶**A** *noun.* A fish of the subclass Teleostei, comprising fishes with a more or less completely ossified skeleton, including most of the familiar types of fish (and excluding rays, skates, sharks, sturgeons, garfishes, and lungfishes). M19.
▶**B** *adjective.* = TELEOSTEAN *adjective.* L19.
■ **teleˈostean** *adjective & noun* (*a*) *adjective* of, pertaining to, or characteristic of (fishes of) the subclass Teleostei; (*b*) *noun* = TELEOST *noun*: M19.

telepathy /tɪˈlɛpəθi/ *noun.* L19.
[from TELE- + -PATHY.]
The communication or perception of thoughts, feelings, etc., by (apparently) extrasensory means.
■ ˈ**telepath** *verb & noun* (*a*) *verb trans. & intrans.* communicate by telepathy; (*b*) *noun* a telepathic person, a believer in or expert on telepathy: L19. **telepaˈthetic** *adjective* (*rare*) = TELEPATHIC L19. **teleˈpathic** *adjective* pertaining to, or effected by, telepathy; (of a person) having the power of telepathy: L19. **teleˈpathically** *adverb* L19. **telepathize** *verb intrans. & trans.* communicate by telepathy E20.

telepherique, ***téléphérique*** *nouns* see TELEFERIC.

telephone /ˈtɛlɪfəʊn/ *noun & verb.* M19.
[from TELE- + -PHONE: cf. TELEPHONY.]
▶**A** *noun.* **1** Any of various devices for conveying sound to a distance, as (*a*) a system of telegraphic signalling using musical notes; (*b*) a kind of foghorn used on ships, railway trains, etc.; (*c*) a speaking-tube. *obsolete* exc. in ***string telephone***, a toy consisting of two stretched membranes, discs, etc., connected by a cord which, when stretched, transmits sound waves mechanically. M19.
2 An apparatus for transmitting speech or sound (or electronic information) in the form of an electrical signal passed along a wire or line between two instruments, as used in communication systems; an instrument forming part of this, now usu. a single unit consisting of or including a handset with a transmitting microphone, a receiving diaphragm, and a numbered dial or set of buttons by which connection can be made to another such instrument. Also (in full ***radio telephone***), a radio apparatus resembling this but operating by means of radio waves transmitted between the instruments. M19. ▶**b** *ellipt.* = ***telephone call*** below. M20.

📖 **2** E. SEGAL The telephone rang. Linc sighed . . and picked up the receiver. *attrib.*: ***telephone dial***, ***telephone extension***, ***telephone handset***, ***telephone line***, ***telephone message***, ***telephone receiver***, etc. **on the telephone** (*a*) having a telephone; (*b*) by means of or using the telephone.

Comb.: **telephone banking**: in which the customer conducts transactions by telephone, usu. by means of a computerized system using touch-tone dialling or voice-recognition technology (cf. ***telebanking*** s.v. TELE-); **telephone bill** a statement of charges for the use of a telephone; **telephone book** = ***telephone directory*** below; **telephone booth**, **telephone box** = ***phone booth*** s.v. PHONE *noun*²; **telephone call** a call made on a telephone; = CALL *noun* 9; **telephone directory**: alphabetically listing the names, addresses, and numbers of telephone subscribers, esp. in a particular locality; ***telephone exchange***: see EXCHANGE *noun* 3b; **telephone girl** a girl or woman employed at a switchboard to connect telephone calls; ***telephone kiosk***: see KIOSK 4; ***telephone number***: see NUMBER *noun* 4; **telephone pad**: for noting telephone messages etc.; **telephone pole**: supporting a telephone cable; **telephone poll**: conducted by interviews over the phone; **telephone set** the assembly of components, including transmitter, receiver, etc., which make up a telephone (the instrument); **telephone tag** *colloq.* the activity of continually trying to reach a person by telephone and failing because when either party rings the other is not there; **telephone tap** an instance of tapping a telephone (cf. TAP *verb*¹ 6).

▶**B** *verb.* **1 a** *verb intrans.* Speak to or send a message to a person by telephone; make a telephone call. L19. ▶**b** *verb trans.* Convey or send (news, a message, etc.) by telephone; ring up (a person or number). L19.
2 *verb trans.* Provide (a place) with telephones. *rare.* E20.

📖 **1a** D. COOPER He telephoned to Felicity, but there was no reply. **b** C. CONNOLLY I . . have had the porter telephone that I am asleep. E. MCBAIN Bert . . took the telephoned message. *fig.*: R. KIPLING I hear the hard trail telephone a far-off horse's feet.

■ **telephonable** *adjective* able to be reached or contacted by telephone E20. **telephoner** *noun* a person who telephones E20. **teleˈphonic** *adjective* of, pertaining to, of the nature of, or (sent) by means of a telephone M19. **telephonically** /-ˈfɒnɪk(ə)li/ *adverb* L19. **telephonist** /tɪˈlɛf(ə)nɪst/ *noun* an operator in a telephone exchange or at a switchboard L19. **telephonitis** /-ˈnʌɪtɪs/ *noun* (*joc.*) a compulsive desire to make telephone calls M20.

telephonograph /tɛlɪˈfəʊnəgrɑːf/ *noun. obsolete* exc. *Hist.* L19.
[Blend of TELEPHONE and PHONOGRAPH.]
An instrument, now obsolete, consisting of a combination of telephone and phonograph by which telephone messages could be recorded. Also, a telegraphone.
■ **telephonoˈgraphic** *adjective* L19.

telephony /tɪˈlɛf(ə)ni/ *noun.* M19.
[from French *télégraphie* + -PHONY; in sense 2 prob. from German *Telephonie.*]
†**1** A system of telegraphic signalling using musical sounds. Cf. TELEPHONE *noun* 1. Only in M19.
2 The art or science of making telephones; a system of telephones; the working or use of a telephone. L19.
2 RADIO-TELEPHONY. *wireless telephony*: see WIRELESS *adjective.*

telephote /ˈtɛlɪfəʊt/ *noun. obsolete* exc. *Hist.* L19.
[from TELE- + Greek *phōt-*, *phōs* light, after *telephone.*]
Any of various devices used or proposed for transmitting signals at a distance by means of light, or for the electrical transmission of pictures and visual images.
■ †**telephotic** *adjective*: only in L19.

telephoto /ˈtɛlɪfəʊtəʊ/ *noun*¹. Now *rare.* E20.
[from TELEPHOTO(GRAPHIC *adjective*¹. Cf. TELEPHOTE.]
A system for the transmission of pictures by telegraphy.

telephoto /ˈtɛlɪfəʊtəʊ/ *adjective & noun*². L19.
[Abbreviation of TELEPHOTOGRAPHIC *adjective*².]
▶**A** *adjective.* = TELEPHOTOGRAPHIC *adjective*². L19.
▶**B** *noun.* Pl. **-os**. A telephoto lens or camera. Also, a photograph taken with one. E20.

telephotographic /ˌtɛlɪfəʊtə(ʊ)ˈgrafɪk/ *adjective*¹. Now *rare.* L19.
[from TELEGRAPHIC with inserted *photo-* (from Greek *phōtos*, *phōs* light): cf. TELEPHOTE.]
Designating or pertaining to an apparatus for the electrical transmission of visual images; phototelegraphic.
■ **teleˈphotograph** *noun*¹ (an image produced by) a phototelegraphic instrument L19. **telephoˈtography** *noun*¹ the transmission of pictures by telegraphy, phototelegraphy L19.

telephotographic /ˌtɛlɪfəʊtə(ʊ)ˈgrafɪk/ *adjective*². L19.
[from TELE- + PHOTOGRAPHIC.]
Of or pertaining to the photographing of distant objects, within the field of sight but beyond the limits of distinct vision.
telephotographic lens a lens or combination of lenses with a narrower field of view than a standard lens, giving an enlarged image.
■ **teleˈphotograph** *noun*² & *verb* (*a*) *noun* a photograph of a distant object taken with a telephotographic lens; (*b*) *verb trans.* photograph with a telephotographic lens or camera: E20. **telephoˈtography** *noun*² the photographing of distant objects using a camera with a telephotographic lens L19.

teleport /ˈtɛlɪpɔːt/ *noun*¹. L20.
[from TELE- + PORT *noun*¹.]
(The name of) a centre providing interconnections between different forms of telecommunications, esp. one linking satellites to ground-based communications.

teleport /ˈtɛlɪpɔːt/ *verb & noun*². M20.
[Back-form from next.]
▶**A** *verb trans. & intrans.* In science fiction: transport or be transported across space and distance instantaneously, esp. by the use of advanced technology or psychic powers. M20.
▶**B** *noun.* An act of teleporting. L20.

teleportation /ˌtɛlɪpɔːˈteɪʃ(ə)n/ *noun.* M20.
[from TELE- + TRANS)PORTATION.]
1 = TELEKINESIS. M20.
2 In science fiction: instantaneous transportation across space or distance, esp. by advanced technology or psychic powers. M20.

For other words beginning with *tele-* see the entry for **tele-**

telescope /ˈtɛlɪskəʊp/ *noun*. M17.
[Italian *telescopio*, mod. Latin *telescopium*: see TELE-, -SCOPE.]
1 An optical instrument for making distant objects appear nearer and larger, containing an arrangement of lenses, or of curved mirrors and lenses, by which rays of light are collected and focused and the resulting image magnified. Also, an instrument or apparatus that serves the same purpose for other wavelengths of the electromagnetic spectrum, esp. in astronomy. M17.
2 (Usu. **T-**.) *The* constellation Telescopium. M19.
1 ***astronomical telescope***, ***Cassegrain telescope***, ***Galilean telescope***, ***guiding telescope***, ***Schmidt telescope***, ***terrestrial telescope***, etc. **hand-telescope** a small portable refracting telescope constructed from two or more tubes fixed end to end so that they can slide one into another for adjustment of focus or ease of carrying. ***radio telescope***: see RADIO *noun*. ***reflecting telescope***: see REFLECT *verb* 3. ***REFRACTING telescope***.
Comb.: **telescope-driver** a mechanism for moving an astronomical telescope to follow the apparent movement of a celestial object and so keep it in the field of view; **telescope-sight** = *TELESCOPIC sight*; **telescope word** (chiefly *US*) a portmanteau word.
■ **telescopist** /tɪˈlɛskəpɪst/ *noun* (now *rare*) a person (skilled in) using a telescope L19. **telescopy** /tɪˈlɛskəpi/ *noun* (*rare*) the art or practice of using or making telescopes M19.

telescope /ˈtɛlɪskəʊp/ *verb*. M18.
[from prec.]
†**1** *verb trans*. Watch the actions of (a person) from a distance as if with a telescope. *rare*. Only in M18.
2 *verb trans*. Make into or use as a telescope. M19.
3 a *verb trans*. Force (parts of a thing) one into another like the sliding tubes of a hand-telescope; crush and compress (a carriage, vehicle, etc.) lengthwise by the force of an impact; *fig*. combine, conflate, compress, condense. L19. ▸**b** *verb intrans*. (Have tubular parts designed to) be fitted together or collapse like the sections of a hand-telescope; (*lit*. & *fig*.) be telescoped. L19.

> 📖 **3a** *Times* A Pacific express train . . ran into a locomotive, completely telescoping the baggage wagons. *Expositor* Possible that St. John had . . 'telescoped' the two accounts together. E. PAUL Taxi No.1 was promptly telescoped by another. R. BUSH Women at the top of the stairs are telescoped into one . . who dominates the poem. **b** R. CAMPBELL Like trucks in railway smashes, back to front, they telescope, rebound . . and shunt. *Which?* An axial compression steering column . . telescopes if the front of the car is crumpled.

telescopic /tɛlɪˈskɒpɪk/ *adjective*. E18.
[formed as prec.: see -IC.]
1 (Of the nature) of, pertaining to, or made with a telescope. E18. ▸**b** Capable of viewing and magnifying distant objects, far-seeing, (*lit*. & *fig*.). E18.
2 Seen by means of a telescope; *spec*. (of a star etc.) visible only through a telescope. E18.
3 Consisting of concentric tubular parts designed to slide one within another. M19.

> 📖 **1** J. R. ILLINGWORTH Telescopic discovery of a star which mathematical calculations have already prophesied. *Observer* The . . long-distance telescopic camera. **telescopic rifle**: with a telescopic sight. **telescopic sight** a small telescope mounted as a sight on a firearm or surveying instrument. **b** R. W. EMERSON These Saxons . . have . . the telescopic appreciation of distant gain.

■ **telescopical** *adjective* (now *rare*) = TELESCOPIC M17. **telescopically** *adverb* in a telescopic manner, by means of a telescope M19.

Telescopium /tɛlɪˈskəʊpɪəm/ *noun*. E19.
[mod. Latin, from TELESCOPE *noun* + -IUM.]
(The name of) an inconspicuous constellation of the southern hemisphere, south of Sagittarius; the Telescope.

telesis /ˈtɛlɪsɪs/ *noun*. L19.
[mod. Latin, from Greek *telein* finish, complete, from *telos* end.]
Intelligent direction of effort towards achieving an end.

telesthesia *noun* see TELAESTHESIA.

telestic /tɛˈlɛstɪk/ *adjective*. *rare*. L17.
[Greek *telestikos*, from *telestēs* hierophant in the mysteries, from *telos* end: see -IC.]
ANTIQUITIES. Of or pertaining to religious mysteries; mystical.

telestich /tɛˈlɛstɪk, ˈtɛlɪs-/ *noun*. M17.
[Irreg. from Greek *telos*, *tele-* end + *stikhos* row, line of verse, after ACROSTIC.]
A short poem in which the successive final letters of the lines spell a word or words.

Teletex /ˈtɛlɪtɛks/ *noun*. L20.
[Prob. blend of TELEX and TEXT *noun*.]
(Proprietary name for) a kind of electronic text transmission system.

teletext /ˈtɛlɪtɛkst/ *noun*. L20.
[from TELE- + TEXT *noun* & *verb*.]
A system by which an adapted television set is able to show alphanumeric information selected from displays transmitted using the spare capacity of existing television channels. Cf. CEEFAX, ORACLE *noun* 9, VIDEOTEX.

Teletype /ˈtɛlɪtʌɪp/ *noun* & *verb*. Also **t-**. E20.
[from TELE- + TYPE(WRITER.]
▶ **A** *noun*. **1** (Proprietary name for) a type of teleprinter. E20.
2 A message received and printed by a teleprinter. M20.
▶ **B** *verb trans*. & *intrans*. Communicate by means of a Teletype or other teleprinter. E20.

teleutosorus /təˌljuːtəˈsɔːrəs/ *noun*. Pl. **-ri** /-rʌɪ, -riː/. E20.
[formed as next + SORUS.]
MYCOLOGY. = TELIUM.

teleutospore /tɛˈljuːtəspɔː/ *noun*. L19.
[from Greek *teleutē* completion, end (from *telos* end) + -O- + SPORE.]
MYCOLOGY. = TELIOSPORE.

televangelist /tɛlɪˈvan(d)ʒ(ə)lɪst/ *noun*. Orig. *US*. L20.
[Blend of TELEVISION and EVANGELIST.]
An evangelical preacher who appears regularly on television to promote beliefs and appeal for funds.
■ **televanˈgelical** *adjective* of or pertaining to televangelism L20. **televangelism** *noun* the use of television for evangelistic purposes L20.

televise /ˈtɛlɪvʌɪz/ *verb*. E20.
[Back-form. from next.]
1 *verb trans*. Transmit (a programme, scene, pictures, etc.) by television. E20.
2 *verb intrans*. **a** Be (well etc.) suited for television presentation. M20. ▸**b** Make a television broadcast. M20.

> 📖 **1** *Economist* The BBC's Panorama programme . . televised on July 18th. *Japan Times* A nationally televised news conference.

■ **televisable** *adjective* able to be televised, suitable for televising L20.

television /ˈtɛlɪvɪʒ(ə)n, tɛlɪˈvɪʒ(ə)n/ *noun*. E20.
[from TELE- + VISION *noun*.]
1 A system for reproducing on a screen visual images transmitted (usu. with sound) by radio signals; (now *rare*) the vision of distant objects obtained by such a system. E20.
2 The medium, art form, or occupation of broadcasting on television; (with specifying word) a particular television service or company. Now also, televised entertainment, the content of television programmes. E20.
3 A device with a screen for receiving television signals. Also more fully ***television set***. M20.

> 📖 **1** *Glasgow Herald* John L. Baird . . invented an apparatus which makes television possible. M. HOCKING We'll watch television. ***cable television***: see CABLE *noun* 3c. ***satellite television***: see SATELLITE *noun*. **2** N. WIENER Television . . as an independent industry. *Observer* It proved, as discussions on these emotive imponderabilia always do, highly absorbing television. *Private Eye* That ghastly woman with the teeth who's always on television. *attrib*.: ***television announcer***, ***television audience***, ***television camera***, ***television celebrity***, ***television commercial***, ***television journalist***, ***television personality***, ***television programme***, ***television series***, ***television studio***, ***television viewer***, etc. ***trial by television***: see TRIAL *noun*.

Comb.: **television camera tube** an electron tube of the kind used in television cameras for converting a visual image into an electrical signal; **television engineer**: who designs or maintains the mechanical and electrical equipment involved in the transmission and reception of television signals; **television evangelist** (orig. *US*) = TELEVANGELIST; **television licence** a licence, renewable annually on payment of a fee, to use a television set; **television network** a system of television stations; a television broadcasting organization or channel; **television satellite**: put into orbit round the earth to reflect back television signals; ***television set***: see sense 3 above; **television station** an organization transmitting television programmes; **television tube** (*a*) = ***picture tube*** S.V. PICTURE *noun*; (*b*) = ***television camera tube*** above; **television-wise** *adverb* (*rare*) in the manner of television; with regard to television.
¶ Freq. abbreviated to *TV*.
■ **televisionless** *adjective* (*rare*) M20.

televisionary /tɛlɪˈvɪʒ(ə)n(ə)ri/ *noun* & *adjective*. *joc*. E20.
[Blend of TELEVISION and VISIONARY.]
▶ **A** *noun*. **1** An enthusiast for television. E20.
2 A television celebrity. E20.
▶ **B** *adjective*. Pertaining to or induced by television. M20.

> 📖 *Times* If, in a televisionary trance, we are induced to buy some commodity.

televisor /ˈtɛlɪvʌɪzə/ *noun*. E20.
[formed as TELEVISE: see -OR.]
1 An apparatus for transmitting or receiving television pictures; *esp*. one designed and patented by John Logie Baird (1888–1946). *obsolete* exc. *Hist*. E20.
2 A television broadcaster. *rare*. M20.

televisual /tɛlɪˈvɪzjʊəl, -ˈvɪʒjʊəl/ *adjective*. M20.
[from TELEVISION, after VISUAL *adjective*.]
Of, pertaining to, characteristic of, or appearing on television; suitable for or effective on television.
■ **televisuˈality** *noun* (*rare*) L20. **televisually** *adverb* from a televisual standpoint; on or for television: M20.

telex /ˈtɛlɛks/ *noun* & *verb*. As noun also **T-**. M20.
[from TEL(EPRINTER + EX(CHANGE *noun*.]
▶ **A** *noun*. **1** An international system of telegraphy in which printed messages are transmitted and received by teleprinters using the public telecommunication lines; (an) apparatus used for this. M20.
2 A telexed message. L20.
▶ **B** *verb trans*. & *intrans*. Send (a message) or contact (a person, firm, etc.) by telex. M20.

telharmonium /tɛlhɑːˈməʊnɪəm/ *noun*. *obsolete* exc. *Hist*. E20.
[from TEL(EPHONE + HARMONIUM.]
A huge electrical musical instrument with a keyboard, invented by the American scientist Thaddeus Cahill (1867–1934) and intended to transmit music by telephone.

telia *noun* pl. of TELIUM.

telic /ˈtɛlɪk/ *adjective*. M19.
[Greek *telikos* final, from *telos* end: see -IC.]
1 GRAMMAR. Of a conjunction or clause: expressing purpose. M19.
2 Directed or tending to a definite end; purposive. L19.

Telinga /təˈlɪŋgə/ *noun*. Also †**-ll-**. L17.
[Tamil *teliṅkam*. Cf. TELUGU.]
1 = TELUGU *noun* 2. L17.
2 a = SEPOY. Now *Hist*. M18. ▸**b** A member of the Telugu people. E19.
Comb.: **Telinga potato** *Hist*. the edible tuber of an aroid plant, *Amorphophallus paeoniifolius*, formerly widely grown in the Indian subcontinent; the plant bearing such tubers.

teliospore /ˈtiːlɪə(ʊ)spɔː/ *noun*. E20.
[from next + -O- + SPORE.]
MYCOLOGY. In a rust or smut fungus: any of the usu. dark, two-celled spores formed at the end of the growing season, which overwinter and on germination in the following spring produce basidia. Cf. UREDINIOSPORE.

telium /ˈtiːlɪəm/ *noun*. Pl. **telia** /ˈtiːlɪə/. E20.
[from Greek *telos* end + -IUM.]
MYCOLOGY. A sorus in which teliospores develop.
■ **telial** *adjective* E20.

tell /tɛl/ *noun*[1]. Now *Scot*. & *dial*. M18.
[from TELL *verb*.]
1 A thing told; a tale, a statement, an account. M18.
2 A talk, a conversation, a gossip. M19.

tell /tɛl/ *noun*[2]. M19.
[Arab. *tall* hill, hillock.]
ARCHAEOLOGY. In the Middle East, a mound formed by the accumulated remains of ancient settlements.

tell /tɛl/ *verb*. Pa. t. & pple **told** /təʊld/, (*US dial*. & *Black English*) **tole** /təʊl/.
[Old English *tellan* = Old Frisian *talia*, *tella*, Old Saxon *tellian*, Middle & mod. Low German, Middle Dutch *tellen*, Old High German *zellen*, German *zählen* reckon, count (cf. *erzählen* recount, relate), Old Norse *telja*, from Germanic base also of TALE *noun*.]
▶ **I** †**1** *verb trans*. & (*rare*) *intrans*. Mention or name (a series of things or people) one after another in order; give a list (of). OE–LME.
2 *verb trans*. & *intrans*. with *of*, *about*. Give an account or narrative of (facts, actions, or events); narrate or relate (a tale or story). OE. ▸**b** *verb intrans*. Of a tale or story: be related with a particular effect; sound well etc. when told. *rare*. L16.
3 *verb trans*. & †*intrans*. Make known by speech or writing; communicate (information, facts, ideas, news, etc.); state, report; *arch*. declare formally or publicly; proclaim. ME. ▸**b** *verb intrans*. Give evidence or be an indication *of*. L18.
4 a *verb trans*. Utter (words); recite (a passage etc.); say. Now *Scot*. & *dial*. ME. ▸**b** *verb trans*. Express (thoughts etc.) in words; utter (specified words); say. ME. ▸**c** *verb intrans*. Talk, converse, gossip. Now *dial*. M17.
5 *verb trans*. **a** Inform (a person) of something; make aware, apprise, acquaint; instruct. (Foll. by *of*, *about*.) ME. ▸**b** Inform *on* a person to (another person). *colloq*. E20.
6 *verb trans*. Assert positively to or assure (a person). ME.
7 a *verb trans*. With *can* or *be able*: state; know; perceive, understand. Freq. in neg. & interrog. contexts. LME. ▸**b** Distinguish (esp. one thing *from* another), recognize. L17.
8 a *verb trans*. & *intrans*. Disclose or reveal (something secret or private); divulge (confidential information). LME. ▸**b** *verb trans*. Foretell, predict. Long only in ***tell a person's future*** etc., passing into sense 5a. LME.
9 *verb trans*. Order or direct (a person) *to do*; give an order or direction to. L16.

For other words beginning with *tele-* see the entry for **tele-**

📖 **2** TINDALE *Acts* 15:12 Barnabas and Paul . . tolde what signes and wondres God had shewed. G. CRABBE He told of bloody fights. G. GREENE He was telling another fishing story. **3** AV *2 Sam.* 1:20 Tell it not in Gath, publish it not in the streetes of Askelon. G. VIDAL A lot of news to tell his mother. E. FEINSTEIN I am told she is highly regarded as a research scientist. **b** J. BUCHAN There stood the car. . . with the dust on her which told of a long journey. **4a** H. BINNING You use to tell over some words in your prayers. **b** POPE Who dares think one thing, and another tell, My heart detests him. B. JOWETT Let me tell you the pleasure which I feel in hearing of your fame. **5** H. MACINNES 'Call the police.' 'It's done,' Tony told her. S. CHITTY They told her of lost fortunes. **6** THACKERAY I can tell you there is a great art in sub-editing a paper. **7a** S. JOHNSON Whether this short rustication has done me any good I cannot tell. J. FOWLES I always thought people could tell I lived on my own. **b** R. H. DANA They can be told by their . . dress, manner, and . . speech. G. GREENE Less capable . . of telling truth from falsehood. **8a** SHAKES. *Twel. N.* She never told her love. THACKERAY She told no more of her thoughts now than she had before. **9** B. MONTGOMERY He must do what he was told.

▶ **II 10** *verb trans.* Count (the members of a series or group); enumerate, reckon. Now chiefly *arch. & dial.* OE. ▶**b** *spec.* Count (voters, votes cast). E16.

11 a Reckon up or calculate the total amount or value of (money etc.). (Foll. by *out, over.*) *arch.* OE. ▶**b** *verb trans.* Count out (pieces of money) in payment; pay (money). Freq. foll. by *down, out, into a person's hand.* Now *arch., Scot., & dial.* ME. ▶**c** *verb intrans.* Be counted; amount *to*. Now *rare.* LME.

📖 **10** J. CLARE The shepherd had told all his sheep. **11a** N. P. WILLIS As a miser tells his gold. **b** W. RAYMOND Biddlecombe . . told the money out in gold.

▶ **III** †**12** *verb trans.* Account, consider, or estimate as being (something specified). OE–LME.

†**13** *verb intrans. & trans.* with cogn. *obj.* Make account *of*; have a specified estimate or opinion *of*. ME–L15.

14 *verb intrans.* Count for something; act or operate with effect; make an impression. Also, have weight or influence *in favour of* or *against*. L18.

📖 **14** G. A. BIRMINGHAM Your want of a proper education tells against you. M. COX The exertion of going up a hill tells on the legs.

Phrases: **all told** in all. **as far as one can tell** judging from the available information. **don't tell me (that)** — I find it hard to believe that—. ***do you mean to tell me that —?***: see MEAN *verb*[1]. *HEAR* ***tell***. **I'll tell you what** *colloq.*: used to call special attention in making a proposal etc. **I tell you** *colloq.*: used to emphasize a statement. **I tell you what** = *I'll tell you what* above. **it is told, it was told**, etc., the story or legend is, was, etc. (*how, that*, etc.). **it tells** a (specified or understood) book or other source tells (*how, that*, etc.). **I told you so** I warned you that this would happen, I said that this was the case. ***kiss and tell***: see KISS *verb*. ***live to tell the tale***: see TALE *noun*. ***not tell one's shirt***: see SHIRT *noun*. ***tell a lie***: see LIE *noun*[1]. ***tell apart***: see APART *adverb* 3. ***tell a person a thing or two***: see THING *noun*[1]. **tell a person goodbye, tell a person hello**, etc., (chiefly *US*) say goodbye, hello, etc., to a person. ***tell a person's fortune***: see FORTUNE *noun*. **tell a person what to do with** —, **tell a person where to put** — *colloq.*: expr. emphatic rejection. ***tell a person where to get off, tell a person where he or she gets off***: see GET *verb*. ***tell a tale***: see TALE *noun*. **tell away** = *tell out* (b) below. **tell it like it is** *colloq.* (orig. *US Black English*) relate the facts of a matter realistically or honestly, holding nothing back. ***tell its own tale***: see TALE *noun*. **tell me about it** *iron.* I know that only too well. 'You're telling me!' **tell me another** *colloq.*: expr. disbelief or incredulity. **tell off** (*a*) count off from the whole number or company; detach (esp. so many men for a particular duty); *gen.* assign to a particular task, position, etc.; (*b*) *colloq.* reprimand, scold. ***tell one's beads***: see BEAD *noun* 1. **tell out** (*a*) (long *arch. & dial.*) separate or exclude by counting; count out; (*b*) *Scot. dial.* drive away (pains etc.) by uttering incantations. ***tell tales***: see TALE *noun* 2c. ***tell tales out of school***: see SCHOOL *noun*[1]. ***tell that to the horse-marines***: see HORSE-MARINE 1. ***tell that to the marines***: see MARINE *noun* 2. **tell the time** determine the time from the face of a clock or watch. ***tell the truth***: see TRUTH *noun*. **tell the world** *colloq.* announce openly; assert emphatically. ***tell volumes***: see VOLUME *noun*. **there is no telling** it is impossible to know. ***truth to tell***: see TRUTH *noun*. ***to tell the truth***: see TRUTH *noun*. ***to tell tother from which***: see TOTHER *pronoun* 1. ***you don't mean to tell me that —?***: see MEAN *verb*[1]. **you're telling me** *colloq.* there is no need to tell me; I know that only too well.

Comb.: **tell-all** *adjective & noun* (of) a revelatory account disclosing esp. secret or confidential information; **tell-truth** (now *rare* or *obsolete*) a person who or thing which tells the truth; a truthful or candid person or writing.

■ **tellable** *adjective* able to be told or narrated; fit to be told; worth telling (earlier in UNTELLABLE): L15.

tellen *noun* see TELLIN.

teller /ˈtɛlə/ *noun*[1]. ME.
[from TELL *verb* + -ER[1].]
A person who or thing which tells something; *spec.* (*a*) a person employed to receive and pay out money in a bank; (*b*) *Hist.* each of four officers of the Exchequer responsible for the receipt and payment of moneys; (*c*) a person who counts voters or votes cast, esp. in a deliberative assembly; (*d*) a person who relates stories.

📖 G. BUTLER You're a teller of tales, young lady . . . Quite a Scheherazade.

Comb.: **teller machine** a machine which provides money or performs other banking services when a special card is inserted and a password is typed in; more fully ***automated teller machine, automatic teller machine***, abbreviation ***ATM***.

■ **tellership** *noun* the position or office of a teller M18.

teller *noun*[2] *& verb* see TILLER *noun*[3] *& verb*.

Teller mine /ˈtɛlə mʌɪn/ *noun phr.* M20.
[Anglicized form of German *Tellermine*, from *Teller* plate + *Mine* MINE *noun*.]
Chiefly *Hist.* A disc-shaped German anti-tank mine containing TNT, used in the war of 1939–45.

telligraph /ˈtɛlɪɡrɑːf/ *noun.* Now *rare.* Also (earlier) in Latin form †**-graphum**. L19.
[Anglo-Latin *telligraphum*, irreg. from Latin *tellus* land: see -I-, -GRAPH.]
Hist. = TERRIER *noun*[2].

tellin /ˈtɛlɪn/ *noun.* Also (earlier) **tellen** /ˈtɛlən/. E18.
[formed as next.]
A burrowing marine bivalve of the family Tellinidae, having unequal shell valves and long siphons.

tellina /tɛˈlʌɪnə/ *noun.* L17.
[Latin from Greek *tellinē* a kind of shellfish.]
A tellin, *esp.* one of the genus *Tellina*.
■ **tellinite** /ˈtɛlɪnʌɪt/ *noun* (GEOLOGY) a fossil tellin shell L18.

telling /ˈtɛlɪŋ/ *noun.* ME.
[from TELL *verb* + -ING[1].]
The action of TELL *verb*; an instance of this; (now *arch. & dial.*) an account, a description.

📖 S. T. FELSTEAD A story that is well worth the telling. ***lose nothing in the telling, not lose in the telling***: see LOSE *verb*. **that would be telling** *colloq.* that would be to divulge (esp. secret or confidential) information.

Comb.: **telling-off** *colloq.* a scolding, a reprimand.

telling /ˈtɛlɪŋ/ *adjective.* L16.
[from TELL *verb* + -ING[2].]
That tells. Chiefly *fig.*, effective, forcible, striking.

📖 F. TOMLIN Eliot's own letters contained . . telling points.

¶ Earlier in UNTELLING.
■ **tellingly** *adverb* M19.

†**Tellinga** *noun* var. of TELINGA.

tellograph /ˈtɛləɡrɑːf/ *noun.* Long *obsolete* exc. *Hist.* L18.
[Irreg. from Greek *tēle* TELE- + *lo(gos* word + -GRAPH.]
A signalling apparatus consisting of a number of posts, each carrying a pointer able to be turned into various positions to express different numbers, the combinations of which denoted letters or words according to a prearranged code.

tellow *noun & verb* see TILLER *noun*[3] *& verb.*

tell-tale /ˈtɛlteɪl/ *noun & adjective.* M16.
[from TELL *verb* + TALE *noun*.]
▶ **A** *noun.* **1** A person who or thing which reveals something not intended to be made known; *spec.* (*a*) a person who discloses (esp. discreditable) information about another's private affairs or behaviour, a tale-bearer, a tattler (also nursery & colloq., ***tell-tale-tit***); (*b*) a small hidden object placed so that its disturbance reveals any intrusion. M16. ▶**b** Any of various sandpipers whose loud alarm call scatters ducks and other game-birds, esp. (*US*) a yellowlegs. E19.

2 A device for the automatic monitoring or registering of a process etc.; an indicator, a gauge; *spec.* (*a*) BUILDING a piece of glass or clear plastic, often graduated, fixed over a crack in a building to reveal any further movement in the fabric; (*b*) a light on the dashboard of a motor vehicle showing when the direction indicator or main-beam lights are in use. E19.

▶ **B** *attrib.* or as *adjective.* That tells tales, that is a tell-tale. L16.

📖 D. BARLOW Careful examination will reveal the tell-tale nits attached to the hairs.

tellurate /ˈtɛljʊreɪt/ *noun.* E19.
[from TELLURIC *adjective*[1] + -ATE[1].]
CHEMISTRY. A salt or ester of a telluric acid.

†**telluret** *noun.* Only in M19.
[from TELLURIUM + -URET.]
CHEMISTRY. = TELLURIDE.
■ †**telluretted** *adjective* combined with tellurium; ***telluretted hydrogen***, the gaseous compound hydrogen telluride, TeH_2: E19–M20.

tellurian /tɛˈljʊərɪən/ *adjective & noun.* M19.
[from Latin *tellur-*, *tellus* earth + -IAN.]
▶ **A** *adjective.* Of or pertaining to the earth; earthly, terrestrial. M19.
▶ **B** *noun.* An inhabitant of the earth. M19.

telluric /tɛˈl(j)ʊərɪk/ *adjective*[1]. E19.
[from TELLURIUM + -IC.]
CHEMISTRY & MINERALOGY. Derived from or containing tellurium, esp. in the hexavalent state.
telluric acid any of several acids of tellurium other than tellurous acid, such as H_6TeO_6 and H_2TeO_4. **telluric ochre** = TELLURITE 1.

telluric /tɛˈl(j)ʊərɪk/ *adjective*[2]. M19.
[from Latin *tellur-*, *tellus* earth + -IC.]
Of or belonging to the earth, terrestrial; *spec.* (*a*) designating or pertaining to natural electric currents in the upper layers of the earth; (*b*) pertaining to or involved in the effect of atmospheric absorption on astronomical spectra. Also, of or pertaining to earth or the soil.

telluride /ˈtɛljʊrʌɪd/ *noun.* M19.
[from TELLURIUM + -IDE.]
CHEMISTRY. A compound of tellurium with a more electropositive element or (formerly) with a radical.

tellurion /tɛˈl(j)ʊərɪən/ *noun.* M19.
[from Latin *tellur-*, *tellus* earth + Greek neut. suffix *-ion*. Cf. TELLURIUM 2.]
A model resembling an orrery, designed to illustrate the effect of the earth's rotation, orbit about the sun, and tilted axis in producing day and night and the succession of the seasons (sometimes also showing the phases of the moon); *fig.* a thing which shows or records the passage of the seasons etc.

tellurism /ˈtɛljʊrɪz(ə)m/ *noun. obsolete* exc. *Hist.* M19.
[formed as prec. + -ISM.]
A theory which supposes the phenomena of mesmerism to arise from an all-pervasive magnetic influence.

tellurite /ˈtɛljʊrʌɪt/ *noun.* L18.
[from next + -ITE[1].]
1 MINERALOGY. Native tellurium oxide, occurring as minute whitish or yellow orthorhombic crystals. L18.
2 CHEMISTRY. A salt of tellurous acid; a salt of an anion containing tellurium in a low oxidation state. M19.

tellurium /tɛˈl(j)ʊərɪəm/ *noun.* E19.
[from Latin *tellur-*, *tellus* earth + -IUM (in sense 1 orig. after *uranium*).]
1 A rare chemical element, atomic no. 52, which is a silvery-white brittle metalloid resembling selenium in its properties, occurring esp. in gold and silver ores, and used in semiconductors. (Symbol Te.) E19.
2 = TELLURION. *rare.* E20.

Tellurometer /tɛljʊəˈrɒmɪtə/ *noun.* Also **t-**. M20.
[formed as prec.: see -OMETER.]
(Proprietary name for) an instrument for accurately measuring distances on land by sending a microwave signal to a distant station and timing the arrival of a return signal.

tellurous /ˈtɛljʊrəs/ *adjective.* M19.
[from TELLURIUM + -OUS, after *ferrous* etc.]
CHEMISTRY. Of or containing tellurium, esp. in a low oxidation state.
tellurous acid the acid H_2TeO_3, a white solid.

tellus /ˈtɛləs/ *noun.* LME.
[Roman goddess of the earth.]
The earth, esp. personified as a goddess.

telly /ˈtɛli/ *noun. colloq.* M20.
[Shortening of TELEVISION: see -Y[6]. Cf. TELE *noun*[1].]
1 Television. M20.
2 A television set. M20.
3 A television performance; a booking or session of filming for this. M20.

telmatology /tɛlməˈtɒlədʒi/ *noun.* E20.
[from Greek *telmat-*, *telma* bog + -OLOGY.]
The branch of ecology that deals with peatbogs.

telnet /ˈtɛlnɛt/ *noun & verb.* M20.
[from TEL(ECOMMUNICATION + NET(WORK *noun*.]
COMPUTING. ▶**A** *noun.* A protocol used in TCP/IP networks which allows the user of one computer to log in to another computer, esp. remotely via the Internet; a program that establishes such a connection; a link thus established. M20.
▶ **B** *verb intrans.* Infl. **-tt**. Log *in* or make a connection *to* a computer, esp. remotely via the Internet, using a telnet program. L20.
■ **telnettable** /ˈtɛlnɛtəb(ə)l, tɛlˈnɛt-/ *adjective* accessible over a network, esp. the Internet, by means of telnet L20.

telo- /ˈtiːləʊ, ˈtɛləʊ/ *combining form.*
[from Greek *telos* end: see -O-. Cf. TELEO-.]
Chiefly BIOLOGY. At or near an end; pertaining to a physical end of something, or to its completion.
■ **teloblast** *noun* each of a number of proliferating cells at one end of the embryo in segmented animals, as insects and annelids L19. **teloˈcentric** *adjective & noun* (CYTOLOGY) (*a*) *adjective* (of a chromosome) having the centromere at one end; (*b*) *noun* a telocentric chromosome: M20. **teloˈdendrion** *noun*, pl. **-dria**, each of the terminal branches into which the axon of a nerve cell divides L19. **teloˈdendron** *noun*, pl. **-dria**, = TELODENDRION M20. **teloˈlecithal** *adjective* (of an egg or egg cell) having a large yolk situated at or near one end L19. **telomere** *noun* (CYTOLOGY) a compound structure at the end of a chromosome in a eukaryote M20. **teloˈmeric** *adjective* (CYTOLOGY) pertaining to, associated with, or towards a telomere L20. **teloˈpeptide** *noun* (BIOCHEMISTRY) a peptide sequence at or near the end of a polypeptide molecule M20. **teloˈtaxis** *noun* (BIOLOGY) directional movement made by an animal to keep a particular source of stimulation acting on its sense receptor(s) M20.

telogen /ˈtɛlə(ʊ)dʒ(ə)n, ˈtiː-/ *noun.* M20.
[from prec. + -GEN.]
1 *BIOLOGY.* The stage in the life of a hair after growth has ceased. E20.
2 *CHEMISTRY.* A compound that causes termination of the chain in polymerization. M20.

teloi *noun* pl. of TELOS.

telome /ˈtiːləʊm/ *noun.* M20.
[from TELO- + -OME.]
BOTANY. Any of various structural units derived from terminal branches of stems and regarded as the precursors of leaves and other organs.

telomer /ˈtɛləmə, ˈtiː-/ *noun.* M20.
[from TELO- + -MER.]
CHEMISTRY. A polymer of low molecular weight consisting of a chain of a limited number of units terminated at each end by a radical from a telogen.
■ **telomeriˈzation** *noun* the formation of a telomer M20.

telophase /ˈtiːləfeɪz, ˈtɛ-/ *noun.* L19.
[from TELO- + PHASE *noun*.]
BIOLOGY. The final phase of mitosis and meiosis, following anaphase and preceding interphase, in which the chromatids or chromosomes are collected in nuclei at opposite ends of the cell; a cell at this stage.
■ **teloˈphasic** *adjective* E20.

telos /ˈtɛlɒs/ *noun.* Pl. **-loi** /-lɔɪ/. M16.
[Greek = end.]
1 = FINIS 1. *rare.* M16.
2 End, purpose, (an) ultimate object or aim. L19.
¶ Orig. in Greek characters.

telpher /ˈtɛlfə/ *adjective, verb, & noun.* L19.
[Syncopated from TELE- + -PHORE.]
▶**A** *adjective.* Of or relating to a system of telpherage. L19.
▶**B** *verb trans.* Transport (goods etc.) by telpherage. *rare.* L19.
▶**C** *noun.* A telpher unit or system. E20.

telpherage /ˈtɛlf(ə)rɪdʒ/ *noun.* L19.
[from (the same word as) prec. + -AGE.]
Transport effected by electricity; *spec.* a system for transporting goods etc. by electrically driven trucks or cable-cars.

tel quel /tɛl ˈkɛl/ *adjectival phr.* L19.
[French.]
Just as it is; without improvement or modification.

telson /ˈtɛls(ə)n/ *noun.* M19.
[Greek = limit.]
ZOOLOGY. The last segment of the abdomen, or an appendage to it, in crustaceans and arachnids, as the middle flipper of a lobster's tail fin, the tail-spine of a horseshoe crab, the sting of a scorpion.
■ **telsonic** /-ˈsɒnɪk/ *adjective* M20.

Teltag /ˈtɛltag/ *noun.* M20.
[Prob. from TELL *verb* + TAG *noun*[1].]
A label attached to manufactured goods giving information about size, weight, performance, etc.

Telugu /ˈtɛləguː/ *noun & adjective.* Also **Telegu.** L18.
[Kannada & Tamil. Cf. Telugu *telungu*.]
▶**A** *noun.* Pl. **-s**, same.
1 A member of a Dravidian people of SE India. L18.
2 The language of this people. L18.
▶**B** *attrib.* or as *adjective.* Of or pertaining to this people or their language. E19.

temazepam /təˈmeɪzɪpam, -ˈmazɪ-/ *noun.* L20.
[from *tem-* of unkn. origin, after *oxazepam*.]
PHARMACOLOGY. A tricyclic compound, $C_{16}H_{13}ClN_2O_2$, used as a tranquillizer and short-acting hypnotic.

tembe /ˈtɛmbeɪ/ *noun.* L19.
[Kiswahili.]
In E. Africa: a rectangular house with mud walls and a flat roof.

temblor /tɛmˈblɔː/ *noun. US.* L19.
[Amer. Spanish.]
An earthquake.

tembo /ˈtɛmbəʊ/ *noun.* M19.
[Kiswahili.]
In E. Africa: an alcoholic drink made esp. from coconut-palm sap; palm wine.

Tembu /ˈtɛmbuː/ *noun & adjective.* E19.
[Xhosa *umtembu*.]
▶**A** *noun.* Pl. **-s**, same. A member of a Xhosa-speaking people of SE South Africa. E19.
▶**B** *adjective.* Of or pertaining to this people. E20.

temenggong /tɛmɛŋˈgɒŋ/ *noun.* L18.
[Malay.]
Chiefly *Hist.* In any of several of the States of Malaya, a high-ranking official, usu. commanding the army and the police.

temenos /ˈtɛmənɒs/ *noun.* Pl. **-noi** /-nɔɪ/. E19.
[Greek, from stem of *temnein* cut off, sever.]
Chiefly *ARCHAEOLOGY.* A piece of ground surrounding or adjacent to a temple; a sacred enclosure or precinct.

temerarious /tɛməˈrɛːrɪəs/ *adjective.* Now *literary.* M16.
[from Latin *temerarius*, from *temere* blindly, rashly: see -ARIOUS.]
1 Characterized by temerity; reckless, rash. M16.
†**2** Acting or happening at random; fortuitous, casual, haphazard. M17–L18.
■ **temerariously** *adverb* M16. **temerariousness** *noun* E18.

temerity /tɪˈmɛrɪti/ *noun.* LME.
[Latin *temeritas*, from *temere*: see prec., -ITY.]
1 Excessive boldness; rashness, recklessness; an instance of this. LME.
†**2** Chance, fortuity. *rare.* Only in L17.

> 📖 **1** G. DALY If she had the temerity to return . . she would be a social outcast.

■ **temeritous** *adjective* (*rare*) L19.

temerous /ˈtɛm(ə)rəs/ *adjective.* Now *rare.* M16.
[from Latin *temere* blindly, rashly: see -OUS.]
Rash, foolhardy; = TEMERARIOUS 1.
■ **temerously** *adverb* LME. **temerousness** *noun* L16.

Temiar /ˈtɛmɪɑː/ *noun & adjective.* M20.
[Sakai.]
▶**A** *noun.* Pl. **-s**, same. A member of a Sakai people of the Malay peninsula; the Sakai dialect of this people. M20.
▶**B** *attrib.* or as *adjective.* Of or pertaining to this people or their dialect. M20.

temmoku /ˈtɛməʊkuː/ *noun.* Also **tenmo-** /ˈtɛnməʊ-/. L19.
[Japanese from Chinese *tiān mù* eye of heaven.]
A type of Chinese porcelain or stoneware with lustrous black or dark brown glaze; the glaze used on such porcelain or stoneware.

Temne /ˈtɛmni:/ *noun & adjective.* L18.
[Temne.]
▶**A** *noun.* Pl. **-s**, same.
1 A member of a people of Sierra Leone. L18.
2 The language of this people. E19.
▶**B** *attrib.* or as *adjective.* Of, pertaining to, or designating this people or their language. L18.

temnospondyl /tɛmnə(ʊ)ˈspɒndɪl/ *adjective & noun.* E20.
[mod. Latin *Temnospondyli* pl., an extinct order of amphibians, formed as next.]
▶**A** *adjective.* = TEMNOSPONDYLOUS. E20.
▶**B** *noun.* A temnospondylous amphibian. M20.

temnospondylous /tɛmnə(ʊ)ˈspɒndɪləs/ *adjective.* E20.
[from Greek *temnein* to cut + *spondulos* vertebra + -OUS.]
ZOOLOGY. Having vertebrae composed mainly of large intercentra.

témoignage /temwaɲaːʒ/ *noun.* M20.
[French, from *témoigner* bear witness: see -AGE.]
Testimony, witness; *esp.* testimony regarding the character or beliefs of a person.

temp /tɛmp/ *adjective, noun, & verb. colloq.* E20.
[Abbreviation of TEMPORARY.]
▶**A** *adjective.* Temporary. E20.
▶**B** *noun.* A temporary employee, esp. a secretary. M20.
▶**C** *verb intrans.* Work as a temporary employee, esp. a secretary. L20.

temp. /tɛmp/ *noun. colloq.* Pl. **temps.** (point). L19.
[Abbreviation.]
= TEMPERATURE 7.

temp. /tɛmp/ *preposition.* M17.
[Abbreviation of Latin *tempore*.]
In the time of.

Tempe /ˈtɛmpi:/ *noun. literary* (now *rare*). L16.
[A valley in Thessaly, Greece, traditionally noted for its beauty.]
A beautiful valley; a delightful rural spot.

tempeh /ˈtɛmpeɪ/ *noun.* M20.
[Indonesian *tempe*.]
An Indonesian dish made by deep-frying fermented soya beans.

temper /ˈtɛmpə/ *noun.* LME.
[from next.]
▶**I 1 a** The due or proportionate mixture or combination of elements or qualities; the condition or state resulting from this; proper or fit condition; an instance of this. Long *rare* or *obsolete.* LME. ▶**b** (A) proportionate arrangement of parts; *fig.* a middle course; a compromise. *arch.* E16.
†**2** = COMPLEXION *noun* 2. LME–M18.
3 The degree of hardness and elasticity or resiliency given to metal, esp. steel, by tempering. LME.
4 Actual state or attitude of the mind or feelings; inclination, mood. Freq. with specifying word. LME.
†**5** = TEMPERAMENT 4. L15–E18.
†**6** = TEMPERATURE 7a. M16–L19.
7 Mental balance or composure, esp. under provocation; calmness, equanimity, (now chiefly in ***keep one's temper***, ***lose one's temper***, ***out of temper***, below). L16.
†**8** Bodily habit, constitution, or condition. L16–E18.
9 = TEMPERAMENT 6. L16.
10 An angry state of mind; irritation, anger; a fit of this. E19.

> 📖 **1a** J. LYLY For the curing and keeping in temper of the body. **b** G. BURNET So strongly does the World love Extreams, and avoid a Temper. **2** J. MOXON Examine the Temper of your Stuff . . how the Plane will work upon it. **3** H. WILLIAMSON The steel had lost its temper, and crystallised after cooling. **4** LD MACAULAY The Commons . . in no temper to listen to such excuses. **5** ADDISON The Temper of their Climate . . relaxes the Fibers of their Bodies. **6** F. BRITTEN Sufficient heat . . to lower the temper of the hole. **7** S. SMILES A weakness . . was his want of temper; . . genius was sacrificed to . . irritability. **8** HENRY MORE The Hare, whose temper and . . body are plainly fitted . . for her Condition. **9** G. BORROW Educated for the Church, which, not suiting his temper, he had abandoned. **10** V. SACKVILLE-WEST Her temper would get the better of her. P. DALLY Prone to outbursts of temper when frustrated.

▶**II 11** †**a** Mortar, plaster. *rare.* Only in L16. ▶**b** In sugar-making, an alkaline solution serving to neutralize the acid in the raw cane-juice and clarify it. M17. ▶**c** *POTTERY.* A material added to clay to promote ductility. E20.

Phrases: **in a bad temper** in an angry mood. **in a good temper** in an amiable mood. **keep one's temper**, **lose one's temper** keep, lose, one's calmness or equanimity. **out of temper** (*a*) having lost one's calmness or equanimity; (*b*) in an angry mood. **show temper** display anger or irritation, be petulant.

Comb.: **temper-brittle** *adjective* exhibiting temper-brittleness; **temper-brittleness** *METALLURGY* notch-brittleness produced in certain steels when held in or cooled slowly through a certain temperature range; **temper-pin** *Scot.* (*a*) a wooden screw for adjusting the band of a spinning-wheel; †(*b*) *rare* a tuning-screw or peg of a violin etc.; (*c*) *fig.* temper, disposition; **temper-screw** a set-screw for adjustment; *esp.* a screw connection for automatically adjusting a boring-drill.

■ **temperish** *adjective* (*rare*) inclined to or exhibiting bad temper E20. **tempersome** *adjective* (*a*) (orig. *dial.*) having a quick temper; (*b*) *pseudo-arch.* displaying extreme conditions of weather: L19. **tempery** *adjective* (chiefly *dial.*) short-tempered E20.

temper /ˈtɛmpə/ *verb*[1] *trans.*
[Old English *temprian* (= Old Saxon *temperon*) from Latin *temperare* mingle, restrain oneself. The sense development was prob. infl. by Old French *temprer*, Old & mod. French *tremper*, (mod.) *tempérer* temper, moderate. Cf. TAMPER *verb*.]
▶**I 1** Bring (a thing) to a required condition or state by admixture of or combination with a specified ingredient; alloy or dilute in this way. Freq. foll. by *with*. *arch.* OE.
2 Modify, esp. by admixture of some other quality etc.; reduce to a degree or condition free from excess in either direction; moderate, mitigate. Freq. foll. by *with*, *by*. OE.
†**3** Bring into a required state of body or health; cure, heal, refresh. OE–E17.
4 Mix, mingle, or blend (ingredients, one ingredient *with* another) in the required proportions. *arch.* ME.
†**5** Make by due mixture or combination; concoct, compose, devise. LME–M17.
6 Bring into a required frame of mind; dispose favourably, persuade; mollify, pacify. *arch.* LME.

> 📖 **1** HENRY SMITH As wine is tempered with water, so let discretion temper zeale. **2** J. MOORE Our admiration of the Romans is tempered with horror. J. SIMMS Greed, in children, is tempered by a sense of justice. *Proverb*: God tempers the wind to the shorn lamb. **3** J. HOLLYBUSH He may drinke a litle wyne vpon it, to tempere hys mouth of the bitternesse. **4** J. S. BLACKIE If wisely you temper, and skilfully blend The hard-headed Scot with the quick-witted Grecian. **5** P. HOLLAND Certain dames . . boiled and tempered ranke poisons. **6** STEELE The Lady so well tempered and reconciled them . . that she forced them to join Hands.

▶**II 7** Conduct, manage; regulate; control, rule, govern. *obsolete* exc. *dial.* OE.
8 Restrain, esp. within due limits, check, curb. OE.
9 Adjust according to need or requirement; adapt, accommodate, make suitable. Foll. by *to*. Now *rare* or *obsolete*. LME.

> 📖 **7** POPE Supremest Jove Tempers the fates of human race above. **8** BYRON Since they are tumultuous, Let them be temper'd, yet not roughly. **9** MILTON They were indeed not temper'd to his temper.

▶**III 10** Bring (clay, mortar, etc.) to the required degree of malleability by the admixture of water etc. Formerly also, mix (esp. medicinal or culinary ingredients) with water etc. to bring to a required consistency. ME. ▶**b** *PAINTING.* Prepare (colours) for use by the admixture of oil etc. ME. ▶**c** Increase the pliability of (straw for corn-dolly making) by dampening it with water. M20.
11 a Tune, adjust the pitch of (a musical instrument). *obsolete* exc. as passing into sense c. ME. ▶**b** Bring into harmony, attune. Foll. by *to*. *arch.* LME. ▶**c** Tune (a piano etc.) so as to adjust intervals correctly. E18.
12 Bring (metal, esp. steel) to a required degree of hardness and elasticity or resiliency by heating, and then cooling in liquid, esp. cold water. LME. ▶**b** Toughen (hardened steel) by reheating and then cooling. Cf. ANNEAL *verb* 4. E20.
†**13** Steep or dissolve (a substance) in a liquid; *fig.* suffuse. L15–M17.
14 Set or adjust the share and other parts of (a plough) in the proper position for making the furrow of the required depth and width. Now *rare* or *obsolete.* E16.

15 Soften (iron, wax, etc.) by heating; melt. Long *obsolete* exc. *dial.* M16.

> 10 F. MORYSON Lime tempered, not with water, but with wine, incredibly durable. 12 J. T. BROCKETT Water in which smiths cool their iron and temper steel.

■ **temperer** *noun* L15.

†**temper** *verb*² see TAMPER *verb*.

tempera /'tɛmp(ə)rə/ *noun*. M19.
[Italian, in *pingere a tempera* paint in distemper.]
A method of painting using esp. an emulsion e.g. of pigment with egg, esp. as a fine art technique on canvas. Also, the emulsion etc. used in this method.

temperable /'tɛmp(ə)rəb(ə)l/ *adjective*. Now *rare*. LME.
[Orig. prob. from medieval Latin *temperabilis*, later from TEMPER *noun*, *verb*¹: see -ABLE.]
†1 = TEMPERATE *adjective* 1, 3a. LME–E17.
2 Able to be tempered. M19.

†**temperality** *noun*. *rare* (Shakes.). Only in L16.
[from TEMPER *noun* + -ALITY.]
= TEMPER *noun* 4.

temperament /'tɛmp(ə)rəm(ə)nt/ *noun & verb*. LME.
[Latin *temperamentum* due mixture, from *temperare* TEMPER *verb*¹: see -MENT.]
▶ **A** *noun*. **I** †1 The blending in due proportion of particular elements; the state or condition resulting from this. LME–L17.
†2 A mixture, *esp.* one having a specified consistency or composition. L15–L17.
3 *Hist.* = COMPLEXION *noun* 2. L15.
4 The condition of the weather or climate regarded as resulting from a combination of heat or cold, dryness or humidity; climate. *arch.* L16.
†5 = TEMPERATURE 7a. M17–L18.
6 Constitution or habit of mind, esp. as determined by physical constitution and affecting behaviour; natural disposition, personality. E19.

> 2 N. INGELO That the Soul is not a Temperament of Corporeal Humours is manifest. 3 J. WOODALL Let no man attribute to all salts one temperament. T. L. PEACOCK The gentleman was naturally of an atrabilarious temperament. 6 B. WEBB Holdane is hostile—by temperament and by training—to a militarist state. R. FRASER An attractive personality with a somewhat volatile temperament.

▶ **II** 7 Moderation; alleviation, mitigation; due regulation. *arch.* LME.
8 **a** A middle course or state between extremes of any kind; a medium, a mean. *arch.* E17. ▶**b** The action or an act of duly combining or adjusting different principles, claims, etc.; (an) adjustment, (a) compromise. *arch.* M17.
9 *MUSIC*. The adjustment of intervals in tuning a piano etc. so as to fit the scale for use in several or all keys; an instance of this. E18.

> 7 *Temple Bar* That a certain temperament of speed was ensured. 8a H. HALLAM A judicious temperament, which the reformers would have done well to adopt. b BURKE There is no medium,.. no temperament,.. no compromise with Jacobinism. 9 **equal temperament** an adjustment in which the 12 semitones are equal intervals.

▶ **B** *verb trans*. Provide with a temperament, esp. of a specified kind. *rare*. M19.

temperamental /tɛmp(ə)rə'mɛnt(ə)l/ *adjective*. M17.
[from prec. + -AL¹.]
1 Of or pertaining to the temperament; constitutional. M17.
2 (Of a person) liable to erratic or moody behaviour; (of a machine etc.) working erratically or unpredictably. E20.

> 1 J. MEYERS Lawrence, isolated and lonely in Cornwall, was pleased to form a friendship with his temperamental opposite. 2 *Omni* Anomalies in epileptics' brains cause groups of neurons.. to periodically misfire like temperamental spark plugs. JOANNE HARRIS Five years ago he had seemed the embodiment of the temperamental artist.. a doomed, damaged figure of romance.

■ **temperamentally** *adverb* M19.

temperance /'tɛmp(ə)r(ə)ns/ *noun & adjective*. ME.
[Anglo-Norman *temperaunce* from Latin *temperantia* moderation, from *temperant-* pres. ppl stem of *temperare* TEMPER *verb*¹: see -ANCE.]
▶ **A** *noun*. **I** 1 Rational self-restraint; the practice or habit of exercising self-control or moderation. ME.
2 *spec.* Moderation in eating and drinking; *esp.* total or partial abstinence from alcoholic drink; teetotalism. ME.

> 1 B. WHITELOCKE It pleased God to give me much patience and temperance to beare this.. ingratitude. H. E. MANNING Temperance is the excellence of the will in controlling the passion for pleasure. 2 M. MEYER After a period of complete temperance, her father began to drink absinthe.

▶†**II** 3 The action or fact of mixing or combining elements in due proportion, tempering, modification. Also, the state or condition resulting from this. LME–M17.

4 Moderate temperature; mildness of weather or climate; temperateness. LME–E17.
▶ **B** *attrib.* or as *adjective*. Advocating or concerned with abstinence from alcoholic drink. M19.

temperate /'tɛmp(ə)rət/ *adjective*. LME.
[from Latin *temperatus* pa. pple of *temperare* TEMPER *verb*¹: see -ATE².]
1 **a** Orig., not affected by passion or emotion, mild, forbearing. Later, not extreme, not strongly partisan; moderate, dispassionate. LME. ▶**b** Showing self-restraint and moderation in action or conduct; practising temperance. LME.
2 Not excessive in degree; moderate. LME.
3 *spec.* **a** Of a region or climate: characterized by mild temperature. LME. ▶**b** Of food: produced in, or suitable for production in, a moderate climate. M20.
4 Restricted in extent of authority; not absolute; limited; constitutional. *arch.* M16.
5 *MICROBIOLOGY*. Of a phage: able to exist as a prophage for a number of generations without causing lysis of the host cell; giving rise to lysogenic bacteria. M20.

> 1a SHAKES. *John* Peace, lady! pause, or be more temperate. E. BOWEN The temperate voice of the announcer paused for a moment. b W. BESANT A young man of strictly temperate habits should.. suddenly become a drunkard. 2 H. H. WILSON Extending Christianity.. must proceed from temperate and gradual proceedings. W. H. PRESCOTT At the temperate hour of nine, the bridal festivities closed. 3a C. LYELL Mild winters and less temperate summers. ***temperate zone*** either of two zones or belts of the earth's surface lying between the torrid and frigid zones; ***north temperate zone***, the zone or belt lying between the tropic of Cancer and the Arctic Circle; ***south temperate zone***, the zone or belt lying between the tropic of Capricorn and the Antarctic Circle. 4 ROBERT BURTON Whether Monarchies should be mixt, temperate, or absolute.

■ **temperately** *adverb* LME. **temperateness** *noun* LME.

†**temperate** *verb trans*. Pa. pple **-ated**, (orig.) **-ate**. LME–M19.
[Latin *temperat-* pa. ppl stem of *temperare* TEMPER *verb*¹: see -ATE³.]
Temper.

temperative /'tɛmp(ə)rətɪv/ *adjective*. Now *rare* or *obsolete*. LME.
[Late Latin *temperativus*, from Latin *temperat-* (see next) + -ATIVE.]
Having the quality of tempering something; tending to a temperate state.

temperature /'tɛmp(ə)rətʃə/ *noun*. LME.
[French *température* or Latin *temperatura*, from *temperat-* pa. ppl stem of *temperare* TEMPER *verb*¹: see -URE.]
†1 The fact or state of being tempered or mixed, esp. in due proportion; the state or condition resulting from this. LME–E19.
†2 The action or process of tempering or mixing elements, esp. in due proportion. M16–L17.
†3 **a** Moderation in action, speech, thought, etc.; freedom from excess or violence. M16–M17. ▶**b** A middle condition or position; a middle course, a compromise. L16–E18.
4 **a** *Hist.* = COMPLEXION *noun* 2. M16. ▶†**b** = TEMPERAMENT *noun* 6. L16–M18.
†5 A (temperate) condition of climate. M16–E18.
†6 = TEMPER *noun* 3. L16–M17.
7 **a** The state of a substance or body with regard to objective warmth or coldness, referred to a standard of comparison; *spec.* that quality or condition of a body which in degree varies directly with the amount of heat contained in the body; a particular degree of this, esp. as measurable according to a numerical scale using a thermometer or similar instrument. L17. ▶**b** A body temperature above the normal. Freq. in ***have a temperature***, ***run a temperature***. *colloq.* L19.

> 1 T. SECKER The Foundation of all.. is a proper Temperature of Fear and Love. 2 P. HOLLAND Made a temperature of brass and iron together. 3a C. NOBLE With that moderation and temperature as the late Protector.. has said and done. b J. HUGHES His Constitution is a just Temperature between Indolence.. and Violence. 4a S. JOHNSON No temperature so exactly regulated but that some humour is fatally predominant. b L. STERNE Any one may do a casual act of good-nature, but a continuation.. is a part of the temperature. 5 CAPT. J. SMITH The temperature of this Country doth agree well with English constitutions. 6 P. HOLLAND Our steele is of a more soft and gentle temperature than that of the Levant. 7a A. MACLEAN The inside temperature was still below freezing. F. SMYTH The temperature of the corpse.. removed to the laboratory, was 81°F. N. LAWSON Nothing can ruin food more easily than the wrong temperature. ***absolute temperature***: see ABSOLUTE *adjective* 10. *CRITICAL* ***temperature***. ***Debye temperature***: see DEBYE 1. ***effective temperature***: see EFFECTIVE *adjective* 5b. ***Kelvin temperature***: see KELVIN 1. ***potential temperature***: see POTENTIAL *adjective* 3. *SERIAL* ***temperatures***. ***theta temperature***: see THETA 2. *VIRTUAL* ***temperature***. b E. F. BENSON He has.. had a temperature for nearly a week.

Comb.: **temperature-chart** (*a*) a chart recording a temperature-curve; (*b*) a chart of a region indicating temperatures at different points, as by isotherms; **temperature coefficient** *PHYSICS* a coefficient expressing the relation between a change in a physical property and the change in temperature that causes it; **temperature-curve** a curve showing variations of temperature, esp. a person's body temperature, over a period of time; ***temperature inversion***: see INVERSION 10; **temperature-regulation** *BIOLOGY* = THERMOREGULATION; **temperature–salinity** the temperature and salinity of water, esp. considered in relation to depth (usu. *attrib.*).
■ **temperatured** *adjective* (*rare*) having temperature of a stated kind L19.

tempered /'tɛmpəd/ *adjective*. ME.
[from TEMPER *noun*, *verb*¹: see -ED², -ED¹.]
1 That has been tempered. ME.
2 Having a temper, esp. of a specified kind. Freq. as 2nd elem. of comb. ME.

> 1 DRYDEN The temper'd metals clash, and yield a silver sound. A. POWELL Uncertain what exactly he meant.. I gave a tempered reply. 2 ***bad-tempered***, ***good-tempered***, ***hot-tempered***, etc.

tempest /'tɛmpɪst/ *noun*. ME.
[Old French *tempest(e)* (mod. *tempête*) from Proto-Romance from Latin *tempestas* season, weather, storm from *tempus* time, season.]
1 A violent windy storm. ME. ▶**b** A thunderstorm. *dial.* & *US local*. M16.
2 *transf.* & *fig.* **a** A violent commotion or disturbance; a tumult; an agitation. ME. ▶†**b** Calamity, misfortune, trouble. ME–L15.
3 Orig., a crowded assembly. Later, a confused or tumultuous throng. M18.

> 1 DRYDEN A Station safe for Ships, when Tempests roar. A. P. STANLEY The whole air filled.. with a tempest of sand driving in your face like sleet. ***teapot tempest***, ***tempest in a teapot***: see TEAPOT *noun*. 2 *Daily Chronicle* This fine passage.. drew a tempest of cheering. F. HERBERT Paul took a deep breath, trying to still the tempest within him.

Comb.: **tempest-tossed** *adjective* (chiefly *poet.*) thrown violently about (as) by a tempest.

tempest /'tɛmpɪst/ *verb*. Now *rare*. LME.
[Old French *tempester*, formed as prec.]
1 *verb trans*. Affect (as) by a tempest (*lit.* & *fig.*). LME.
2 *verb intrans*. Of the wind etc.: be violently strong; rage, storm. Also *impers.* in ***it tempests***, ***it is tempesting***, etc. Now *arch.* & *dial.* L15.

tempestive /tɛm'pɛstɪv/ *adjective*. *arch.* E17.
[Latin *tempestivus* timely, from *tempestas* TEMPEST *noun*: see -IVE.]
1 Timely, seasonable. E17.
2 = TEMPESTUOUS 1. *rare*. M19.
■ **tempestively** *adverb* (*arch.*) E17.

tempestuous /tɛm'pɛstjʊəs/ *adjective*. LME.
[Late Latin *tempestuosus*, from *tempestas* TEMPEST *noun*: see -UOUS.]
1 Of, pertaining to, involving, or resembling a violent windy storm; very stormy. LME.
2 Characterized by a violent commotion or disturbance; (of a person etc.) turbulent, impetuous, passionate. LME.

> 1 M. SARTON A tempestuous night, high winds howling about the eaves. 2 R. WEST Augustine's tempestuous spirit could not bear this time of prudent waiting.

■ **tempestuously** *adverb* LME. **tempestuousness** *noun* M17.

tempête /tɛm'pɛt, *foreign* tɑ̃pɛt/ *noun*. L19.
[French: see TEMPEST *noun*.]
A country dance popular in England in the late 19th cent.; a piece of music for this dance.

tempi *noun pl.* see TEMPO *noun*¹.

tempietto /tɛmpɪ'ɛtəʊ/ *noun*. Pl. **-tti** /-ti/. L19.
[Italian, lit. 'little temple'.]
A small usu. circular building resembling a miniature temple.

Templar /'tɛmplə/ *noun*. Also (earlier) †**-er**. ME.
[Anglo-Norman *templer*, Old & mod. French *templier* from medieval Latin *templari(u)s* from Latin *templum* TEMPLE *noun*¹: see -AR².]
1 *Hist.* More fully ***Knight Templar***. A member of a military and religious order, orig. occupying a building on the site of Solomon's temple in Jerusalem, founded chiefly for the protection of pilgrims to the Holy Land, and suppressed in 1312. ME. ▶**b** In full ***Knight Templar***. A member of an American Masonic order. Usu. in *pl.* *US*. M19. ▶**c** In full ***Good Templar***. A member of an American temperance society organized on Masonic lines. Usu. in *pl.* *US*. M19.
2 A lawyer or law student with chambers in the Temple, London. L16.
■ **Templardom** *noun* (*rare*) the world of Templars, Templars collectively L19. **Templary** *noun* (*a*) = TEMPLAR *noun* 1; (*b*) (chiefly *Hist.*) Templars collectively; the system or organization of Templars: LME.

templar /'tɛmplə/ *adjective*. E18.
[Late Latin *templaris*, from *templum* TEMPLE *noun*¹: see -AR¹.]
Of, pertaining to, or characteristic of a temple.

template /ˈtɛmplɪt, -pleɪt/ *noun*. Also (earlier) **templet** /ˈtɛmplɪt/. L17.
[Prob. from TEMPLE *noun*[3] + -ET[1], alt. after *plate*.]
1 A timber or plate used to distribute the weight in a wall or under a beam etc. L17.
2 a A pattern or gauge, usu. a piece of thin board or metal plate, used as a guide in cutting or drilling metal, stone, wood, etc.; a flat card or plastic pattern used esp. for cutting cloth for patchwork. L17. ▸**b** OIL INDUSTRY. A frame anchored to the sea floor to which an offshore platform may be attached. L20.
3 Chiefly BIOLOGY. A substance whose atomic or molecular structure determines the manner in which other molecules are combined; *spec.* a molecule of nucleic acid that so acts to determine the sequence of assembly of nucleic acids or proteins. M20.

temple /ˈtɛmp(ə)l/ *noun*[1] & *verb*. OE.
[Latin *templum* open or consecrated space, reinforced in Middle English by Old French *temple*.]
▸**A** *noun*. **I 1** A building regarded primarily as the dwelling-place, or devoted to the worship, of a god or gods. OE. ▸**b** *Hist.* Each of three successive religious buildings of the Jews in Jerusalem. OE. ▸**c** A synagogue. Now chiefly *N. Amer.* L16.
2 Any place regarded as occupied by God, esp. a Christian's person or body. OE.
3 A building for public Christian worship; a (large) church; *esp.* a Protestant church in France and some French-speaking countries. LME.
4 The central place of Mormon worship. M19.

📖 **1** R. K. NARAYAN Even as a young girl I danced in our village temple. L. SPALDING Gathering stones for a temple so they could worship their own god.

▸**II 5** †**a** The headquarters of the Knights Templars, on the site of Solomon's temple in Jerusalem; the order or organization of the Templars. OE–M17. ▸**b** *Hist.* The place in Paris which formed the headquarters of the Templars in Europe. E17.
6 Either of two of the Inns of Court in London (more fully ***Inner Temple*** and ***Middle Temple***) standing on the site of the buildings once occupied by the Templars. LME.

Comb.: **temple block** a percussion instrument consisting of a hollow block of wood which is struck with a stick (usu. in *pl.*); **temple dancer** a professional dancing-girl in the service of a temple, esp. in Eastern countries; **Temple parliament** *rare* = PARLIAMENT *noun* 5b; **temple prostitute**, **temple prostitution**: in the service of a temple, esp. in Eastern countries.

▸**B** *verb*. **1** *verb trans.* Enclose (as) in a temple; devote a temple to. Chiefly *poet.* OE.
†**2** *verb intrans.* Reside or dwell as in a temple. Only in E18.
3 *verb trans.* Make or fashion into a temple. Chiefly *poet.* M19.
■ **templed** *adjective* (chiefly *poet.*) (*a*) that has been templed; (*b*) provided with a temple or temples: E17. **templeless** /-l-l-/ *adjective* LME. **templify** *verb trans.* (long *rare* or *obsolete*) make into or like a temple E17.

temple /ˈtɛmp(ə)l/ *noun*[2]. ME.
[Old French (mod. *tempe*) from Proto-Romance alt. of Latin *tempora* pl. of *tempus*.]
1 The flat part of either side of the head between the forehead and the ear. (Freq. in *pl.*) ME.
†**2** An ornament to be worn on the side of a woman's forehead. Only in LME.
3 Each of the side-pieces of a pair of spectacles. *US.* L19.

temple /ˈtɛmp(ə)l/ *noun*[3]. LME.
[French, perh. ult. identical with prec.]
1 A contrivance for keeping cloth stretched to a required width during weaving. Usu. in *pl.* LME.
2 In full ***temple mould***. = TEMPLATE 2a. *rare*. L17.

†**Templer** *noun* see TEMPLAR *noun*.

templet /ˈtɛmplɪt/ *noun*[1]. Also †**-ette**. M16.
[French *templette* dim. of *temple*: see TEMPLE *noun*[2], -ET[1]. Sense 2 prob. a different word.]
†**1** = TEMPLE *noun*[2] 2. Only in M16.
2 Each of the four-sided oblique facets of a brilliant. L19.

templet /ˈtɛmplɪt/ *noun*[2]. M19.
[from TEMPLE *noun*[3] + -ET[1], perh. through French.]
= TEMPLE *noun*[3] 1.

templet /ˈtɛmplɪt/ *noun*[3]. Chiefly *literary*. M19.
[from TEMPLE *noun*[1] + -ET[1].]
A small or miniature temple.

templet *noun*[4] see TEMPLATE.

†**templette** *noun* var. of TEMPLET *noun*[1].

tempo /ˈtɛmpəʊ/ *noun*[1]. Pl. **-pi** /-piː/, **-pos**. M17.
[Italian from Latin *tempus* time.]
1 The timing of an attack in fencing so that one's opponent is within reach. *rare*. M17.
2 MUSIC. Relative speed or rate of movement; pace; time; *spec.* the (esp. characteristic) speed at which music for a dance etc. is or should be played. L17.
3 The rate of motion or activity (*of* someone or something). L19.

📖 **2** *Music* A return to Verdi's original tempos. ***STRICT tempo***. **tempo giusto** /ˈdʒuːstəʊ/ [lit. 'strict time'] the speed at which a particular style of music is or should be played. ***tempo rubato***: see RUBATO *adjective*. **3** E. BAKER The rain slowed down to a steady, all-night tempo.

tempo /ˈtɛmpəʊ/ *noun*[2]. Also **ten-**. Pl. **-os**, same. M19.
[Japanese *tempō* from *Tempō* designation of the period of Japanese history 1830–44.]
Hist. An oval bronze coin of Japan with a square central hole, first minted in 1835 and current in the 19th cent.

temporal /ˈtɛmp(ə)r(ə)l/ *adjective*[1] & *noun*[1]. In sense B.2 also in Latin form **temporale** /tɛmpɒˈreɪliː, -ˈrɑːleɪ/. ME.
[Old & mod. French *temporel* or Latin *temporalis*, from *tempor-*, *tempus* time: see -AL[1]. In sense B.2 from ecclesiastical Latin *temporale* use as noun of neut. of *temporalis*.]
▸**A** *adjective*. **1** Of, pertaining to, or concerned with secular as opp. to sacred or religious matters, lay; (of law) civil or common as opp. to canonical; (of rule, government, etc.) civil as opp. to ecclesiastical. ME.
2 Lasting or existing only for a time; passing, temporary. Now *rare* exc. as passing into sense 3. LME.
3 Of or pertaining to a present life as distinguished from a future existence; concerning or involving material as opp. to spiritual interests; worldly, earthly. LME.
4 GRAMMAR. **a** Pertaining to or depending on the length of syllables. Now *rare*. L17. ▸**b** Of or pertaining to time. L18.
5 Of, pertaining to, or relating to time. L19.

📖 **1** W. PETTY The Government of Ireland is by the King, 21 Bishops . . and the Temporal Peers. **temporal power** the power of an ecclesiastic, esp. the Pope, in temporal matters. ***the Lords temporal***: see LORD *noun*. **2** J. SYLVESTER A temporall beauty of the lampfull skies. **3** J. PRIESTLEY The Jews . . expected . . a temporal prince. **5** A. WEIR A vast quantity of temporal and spatial experience.

▸**B** *noun*. **1 a** That which is temporal; in *pl.*, temporal things or matters. LME. ▸**b** Temporal power, a secular possession. Usu. in *pl.* = TEMPORALITY 1b. LME.
2 ECCLESIASTICAL. The part of the breviary and missal which contains the daily offices in the order of the ecclesiastical year. Cf. SANCTORALE. LME.
■ **temporalism** *noun* (*a*) secularism; concern with temporal matters or interests; (*b*) support for temporal power: L19. **temporalist** *noun* (*rare*) a supporter of temporal power M17. **temporalize** *verb trans.* (*rare*) make temporal E19. **temporally** *adverb* LME. **temporalness** *noun* (long *rare* or *obsolete*) E17.

temporal /ˈtɛmp(ə)r(ə)l/ *adjective*[2] & *noun*[2]. LME.
[from late Latin *temporalis*, from *tempora* the temples: see TEMPLE *noun*[2], -AL[1].]
ANATOMY. ▸**A** *adjective*. Of, pertaining to, or situated in the temples of the head. LME.
temporal bone either of two bones forming part of the side of the skull on each side and enclosing the middle and inner ear. **temporal lobe** the lowest lobe in each cerebral hemisphere of the brain.
▸**B** *noun*. A temporal artery, bone, lobe, etc.; (now *rare*) = TEMPORALIS. M16.

temporale /tɛmpəˈrɑːl/ *noun*[1]. M19.
[Spanish *temporal* storm, spell of rainy weather.]
A weather condition on the Pacific coast of Central America consisting of strong south-west winds bringing heavy rain.

temporale *noun*[2] see TEMPORAL *adjective*[1] & *noun*[1].

temporalis /tɛmpəˈreɪlɪs/ *noun*. L17.
[Late Latin: see TEMPORAL *noun*[2] & *adjective*[2].]
ANATOMY. A fan-shaped muscle which closes the lower jaw, arising from the side of the skull, passing behind the zygomatic arch, and inserted on the coronoid process. Also ***temporalis muscle***.

temporality /tɛmpəˈralɪti/ *noun*. LME.
[Late Latin *temporalitas*, from *temporalis* TEMPORAL *adjective*[1]: see -ITY. Cf. next.]
1 †**a** = TEMPORALTY 1. LME–E19. ▸**b** In *pl.* Secular possessions, *esp.* the secular properties and revenues of a religious foundation or of an ecclesiastic. LME.
†**2** = TEMPORALTY 2. LME–L17.
3 The quality or condition of being temporary. M17.

temporalty /ˈtɛmp(ə)r(ə)lti/ *noun*. LME.
[from TEMPORAL *adjective*[1] + -TY[1].]
1 Temporal matters; temporal authority. Now *rare* or *obsolete*. LME. ▸**b** = TEMPORALITY 1b. Now *rare* or *obsolete*. LME.
2 The laity. Formerly also, the condition or estate of a layman. *arch.* LME.

temporaneous /tɛmpəˈreɪnɪəs/ *adjective*. Now *rare* or *obsolete*. M17.
[from late Latin *temporaneus* timely, from Latin *tempor-*, *tempus* time: see -ANEOUS.]
Pertaining or relating to time, temporal. Formerly also, lasting only for a time, temporary.
■ **temporaneously** *adverb* E19. **temporaneousness** *noun* E18.

temporary /ˈtɛmp(ə)rəri/ *adjective* & *noun*. M16.
[Latin *temporarius*, from *tempor-*, *tempus* time: see -ARY[1].]
▸**A** *adjective*. **1 a** Lasting or meant to last for a limited time only; not permanent; made or arranged to supply a passing need. M16. ▸**b** Belonging or relating to a particular time or period; of passing interest, ephemeral. *obsolete* exc. as passing into sense 1a. L18. ▸**c** MILITARY. Designating or pertaining to a person commissioned for the duration of a war (esp. those of 1914–18 and 1939–45). E20.
†**2** = TEMPORAL *adjective*[1] 3. E17–M18.
†**3** METAPHYSICS. Occurring or existing in time, not from eternity. L17–E18.

📖 **1** P. FITZGERALD Hired, on a temporary basis . . , to look after the children. *Japan Times* The forces, housed in . . 120 temporary barracks at the castle. ***temporary CARTILAGE***. **temporary hardness** water hardness which is removed by boiling to precipitate bicarbonates. **temporary tooth** a deciduous tooth, a milk tooth. **c** ***temporary captain***, ***temporary rank***, etc. **2** J. HOWE In our temporary state, while we are under the measure of time.

▸**B** *noun*. †**1** In *pl.* Things belonging to this life, temporal goods. L16–M17.
2 †**a** A person whose religious life or devotion endures only for a time. E–M17. ▸†**b** A contemporary. Only in M17. ▸**c** A time-server, a temporizer. *rare*. E20.
3 A person employed or holding a post temporarily; *spec.* a secretary or clerical worker supplied by an agency to cover an absence or vacancy for a limited period. M19.
■ **temporarily** *adverb* L17. **temporariness** *noun* L17.

temporize /ˈtɛmpərʌɪz/ *verb intrans.* Also **-ise**. L16.
[French *temporiser* bide one's time from medieval Latin *temporizare* delay, from Latin *tempor-*, *tempus* time: see -IZE.]
1 Comply temporarily with the requirements of a particular time or occasion; avoid committing oneself so as to gain time, procrastinate; employ delaying tactics, esp. in dealing *with* a person or thing. L16.
2 Negotiate or discuss terms *with*; mediate *between*. *arch.* L16.

📖 **1** H. A. L. FISHER He . . tolerated polygamy and slavery . . and even temporized with the symbols of polytheism. L. DURRELL He was temporizing . . unwilling to commit himself. A. CARTER 'Not yet,' she temporized. **2** A. W. KINGLAKE This calm Mahometan . . strove to temporise as well as he could betwixt the angry Churches.

■ **tempoˈrization** *noun* M18. **temporizer** *noun* M16. **temporizingly** *adverb* in a temporizing manner M19.

temporo- /ˈtɛmpərəʊ/ *combining form*.
[from TEMPORAL *adjective*[2]: see -O-.]
ANATOMY. Of or pertaining to the temporal region or bone (and another region or bone).
■ **temporomanˈdibular** *adjective* of, pertaining to, or designating the hinge joint between the temporal bone and the lower jaw L19.

Tempranillo /tɛmprəˈniːl(j)əʊ/ *noun*. Pl. **-os**. L19.
[A village in northern Spain.]
A type of grape grown in Spain; red Rioja wine made from such grapes.

temps /tɑ̃/ *noun*. Pl. same. L19.
[French, lit. 'time'.]
BALLET. **1** A movement in which there is no transfer of weight from one foot to the other. L19.
2 A movement forming one part of a step. E20.

temps perdu /tɑ̃ pɛrdy/ *noun phr.* M20.
[French, lit. 'time lost'.]
The past, contemplated with nostalgia and a sense of irretrievability.

tempt /tɛm(p)t/ *verb trans.* ME.
[Old French *tempter* var. of Old & mod. French *tenter* from Latin *temptare* handle, test. In branch I also partly aphet. from ATTEMPT *verb*. Cf. TENT *verb*[2].]
▸**I 1** Make trial of, put to the test, try the quality, worth, or truth of, esp. in a way involving risk or danger. Long *rare* or *obsolete* exc. in ***tempt fate*** etc. below. ME. ▸†**b** = ATTEMPT *verb* 4b. *rare*. ME–L15. ▸**c** Put oneself at risk in or on, risk the dangers of. *arch.* LME.
†**2** = ATTEMPT *verb* 1. LME–M16. ▸**b** = ATTEMPT *verb* 2b. *rare*. E–M18.

📖 **1** AV *Gen.* 22:1 God did tempt Abraham. POPE Nor tempt the wrath of Heav'ns avenging Sire. **c** DRYDEN The first to lead the Way, to tempt the Flood.

▸**II 3** Try to attract, entice, or incite (a person) to do something, esp. a wrong or forbidden thing, through the promise or prospect of some pleasure or advantage. Also, be attractive to, allure; dispose, incline; induce, persuade. Also foll. by *to*, *to do*, *into doing*. ME.
4 In biblical translations: try to draw (a person) to make an erroneous statement. *arch.* LME.
5 Elicit, evoke, (*from*). L20.

📖 **3** G. GREENE He was tempted to lie but resisted. E. BOWEN What can I . . tempt you to? The *profiteroles* here are not always bad. N. WILLIAMS Henry had tried to tempt him into making a racist statement. **5** *Angler's Mail* It is . . a case of less feed and smaller hook baits to tempt bites.

Phrases: **be tempted to** be strongly disposed to. **tempt fate**, **tempt fortune**, **tempt Providence**, etc., risk provoking the adversity of fate, fortune, Providence, etc.

■ **tempta'bility** *noun* the state or condition of being temptable E19. **temptable** *adjective* able to be tempted; liable or open to temptation: LME. **temptableness** *noun* (*rare*) L17.

temptation /tɛm(p)'teɪʃ(ə)n/ *noun.* Also †**tent-**. ME.
[Old French *temptacion* var. of Old & mod. French *tentation* from Latin *temptatio(n-)*, from *temptat-* pa. ppl stem of *temptare*: see prec., -ATION.]
1 The action or process of tempting someone; the fact of being tempted; an instance of this. ME.
2 Tempting quality, enticingness. Long *rare* or *obsolete*. LME.
3 A thing that tempts someone; a cause or source of temptation. L16.
†**4** A severe or painful trial or experience; an affliction, a trial. L16–M17.

🕮 **1** E. M. FORSTER He did not want to read that letter—his temptations never lay in that direction. E. J. HOWARD He . . resisted the temptation to tease her. **The Temptation**: of Jesus in the wilderness by the Devil (with ref. to *Matthew* 4:1–11). **2** H. BROOKE The . . trees reached forth fruits of irresistible temptation. **3** J. A. FROUDE The command of a permanent military force was a temptation to ambition.

■ **temptational** *adjective* L19. **temptationless** *adjective* M17. **temptatious** *adjective* full of temptation; tempting, alluring: E17.

tempter /'tɛm(p)tə/ *noun.* LME.
[Old French *tempteur* from eccl. Latin *temptator*, from Latin *temptare*: see TEMPT *verb*, -ER².]
A person who or thing which tempts someone. **the Tempter** the Devil.

tempting /'tɛm(p)tɪŋ/ *verbal noun.* ME.
[from TEMPT *verb* + -ING¹.]
The action of TEMPT *verb*; an instance of this.

tempting /'tɛm(p)tɪŋ/ *adjective.* LME.
[from TEMPT *verb* + -ING².]
That tempts someone; attractive, inviting.

🕮 E. BOWEN To leave the house after dark . . was not tempting, for lamps . . were few and dim. W. HORWOOD Here and there the path branched up some tempting byway.

■ **temptingly** *adverb* L16. **temptingness** *noun* E19.

temptress /'tɛm(p)trɪs/ *noun.* L16.
[from (the same root as) TEMPTER + -ESS¹.]
A female tempter.

tempura /'tɛmpʊrə/ *noun.* E20.
[Japanese *tenpura*, prob. from Portuguese *tempêro* seasoning.]
A Japanese dish consisting of shellfish or whitefish and often vegetables, fried in batter.

tempus /'tɛmpəs/ *noun.* L19.
[Latin = time.]
MUSIC. In medieval mensurable music, the duration of the breve relative to that of the semibreve.

temse /tɛms, tɛmz/ *noun.* Long *dial.* LME.
[from next. Cf. Middle Low German *temes*, *temse*, Middle Dutch *temse* (Dutch *teems*), German dial. *Zims*.]
A sieve, *esp.* one used for sifting flour; a strainer.

temse /tɛms, tɛmz/ *verb trans.* Long *dial.*
[Old English *temesian*, from West Germanic, ult. origin unkn. Cf. Middle Low German *temesen*, Middle Dutch *temsen* (Dutch *teemsen*).]
Sift (esp. flour) through a sieve; strain.

temulency /'tɛmjʊlənsi/ *noun.* Now *rare.* E17.
[Latin *temulentia* drunkenness, formed as next: see -ENCY.]
Drunkenness, intoxication.
■ Also **temulence** *noun* (*rare*) E19.

temulent /'tɛmjʊlənt/ *adjective.* Now *rare.* E17.
[Latin *temulentus*, from base of *temetum* intoxicating drink after *vinolentus* from *vinum* wine.]
1 Drunken, intoxicated. E17.
2 Intoxicating. E19.
■ **temulently** *adverb* E17. **temulentness** *noun* E18.

temura /təmʊ'rɑː/ *noun.* Also **-ah**. E20.
[Hebrew *tĕmūrāh* exchange.]
A cabbalistic method of interpreting the Hebrew Scriptures by the systematic replacement of the letters of a word with other letters.

ten /tɛn/ *adjective & noun (cardinal numeral).*
[Old English (Anglian) *tēn(e*, (West Saxon) *tīen(e* = Old Frisian *tiān*, *tēne*, *tīne*, Old Saxon *tehan* (Dutch *tien*), Old High German *zehan* (German *zehn*), Old Norse *tíu*, Gothic *taihun*, from Germanic from Indo-European, whence also Latin *decem*, Greek *deka*, Sanskrit *daśa*.]
► **A** *adjective.* One more than nine (a cardinal numeral represented by 10 in arabic numerals, x, X in roman). OE.

🕮 J. CONRAD I was only ten years old. *New Yorker* The strikers returned to work after ten days. *Guardian* Ten people were arrested and three police officers injured. **ten feet tall** full of self-assurance or pride. ***Ten Words***: see WORD *noun*. ***the Ten Commandments***: see COMMANDMENT 2. ***the Ten Tribes***: see TRIBE *noun*. ***upper ten thousand***: see UPPER *adjective*.

► **B** *noun.* **1** Ten persons or things identified contextually, as parts or divisions, years of age, points, runs, etc., in a game, chances (in giving odds), minutes, inches, shillings (now *Hist.*), pence, etc. OE.
2 One more than nine as an abstract number; the symbol(s) or figure(s) representing this (10 in arabic numerals, x, X, in roman). OE. ▸**b** In *pl.* The digit second from the right of a whole number in decimal notation, representing a multiple of ten less than a hundred. M16.
3 A set of ten; a thing having a set of ten as an essential or distinguishing feature; *spec.* (**a**) a playing-card marked with ten pips or spots; (**b**) a ten-oared boat; (**c**) a ten-pound note, a ten-dollar bill. OE.
4 The time of day ten hours after midnight or midday (on a clock, watch, etc., indicated by the numeral ten displayed or pointed to). Also ***ten o'clock***. LME.
5 The tenth of a set or series with numbered members, the one designated ten, (usu. ***number ten***, or with specification, as ***book ten***, ***chapter ten***, etc.); a size etc. denoted by ten, a shoe, glove, garment, etc., of such a size (also ***size ten***). E16.
6 Each of a set of ten; *spec.* a candle of which ten constitute a pound in weight. E19.

🕮 **1** H. KEMELMAN I was divorced from his mother—he was ten at the time. J. LE CARRÉ The time was ten to eleven. ***nine times out of ten***: see NINE *adjective*. **ten to one** ten chances to one; odds of ten times the amount of a bet; very probably. **the Ten** (now *Hist.*) the group of countries forming the European Economic Community between 1981 and 1985 following the admission of Greece and until the withdrawal of Greenland. ***top ten***: see TOP *noun*¹ & *adjective*. ***upper ten***: see UPPER *adjective*. **2** W. GOLDING Investing tens of millions of dollars. **count ten**, **count up to ten** enumerate one to ten, esp. in order to check oneself from speaking impetuously. **3** T. MCGUANE The gulls came . . by the tens and twenties. J. ARCHER The young man drew a ten and asked for another card. *Which?* More than eight out of ten agreed that on-the-spot fines should be given. ***ten a penny***: see PENNY *noun*. **ten out of ten** ten marks or points out of ten; full marks. **4** THACKERAY It was ten o'clock when he woke up. ***ten o'clock swill***: see SWILL *noun*. **5** ***Number ten***: see NUMBER *noun*.

Comb.: Forming compound numerals with multiples of a hundred, as **210** (read ***two hundred and ten***, US also ***two hundred ten***), etc. With nouns + -ER¹ forming nouns with the sense 'something (identified contextually) being of or having ten —s', as **ten-seater**, **ten-wheeler**, etc. Special combs., as **ten-code** a code of signals (all beginning 'ten') orig. used in US police radio communication and later adopted by citizens' band radio operators; **ten-eighty**, **1080** [a laboratory serial number] sodium fluoroacetate used as a potent poison for rodents and other mammals; **ten-finger** a starfish with ten arms; **ten-foot** *adjective* measuring, or having, ten feet; ***would not touch with a ten-foot pole***: see POLE *noun*¹ 1; **ten-four**, **10-4** *interjection* in the ten-code, message received; *loosely*, expr. affirmation; **ten-gallon** *adjective* that can contain ten gallons; ***ten-gallon hat***, ***ten-gallon sombrero***, a high-crowned, wide-brimmed hat of a kind esp. worn by cowboys; **ten-gauge** *adjective* (of a bullet, shell, gun, etc.) having a calibre such that ten bullets etc. of matching size weigh one pound; **ten-inch** *adjective* measuring ten inches; *spec.* (*Hist.*) designating a gramophone record, usu. a seventy-eight, having this diameter; **ten-minute rule**, **ten-minutes rule** a rule of the House of Commons allowing brief discussion of a motion to introduce a bill, each speech being limited to ten minutes; **ten o'clock** (**a**) see sense B.4 above; (**b**) any of several plants whose flowers open late in the morning; *esp.* (*W. Indies*) a kind of purslane, *Portulaca grandiflora*; (**c**) a light meal taken at ten o'clock; **tenpence** (**a**) ten pence, esp. of the old British currency before decimalization; (**b**) (usu. two words) since 1968, a coin worth ten (new) pence; **tenpenny** *adjective & noun* (**a**) *adjective* worth or costing tenpence or ten (new) pence; ***tenpenny nail*** [orig. costing tenpence per hundred] a large nail; (**b**) *noun* a coin worth tenpence or ten (new) pence; **ten per center** *US Theatrical slang* a theatrical agent, esp. one who takes ten per cent commission; **tenpin** (**a**) in *pl.* (usu. treated as *sing.*), a game in which ten pins or skittles are set up and bowled at to be knocked down (also ***tenpin bowling***); (**b**) a pin or skittle used in this game (usu. in *pl.*); **ten-pointer** a stag having antlers with ten points; **ten-pound** *adjective* of or involving the amount or value of ten pounds; weighing ten pounds; **ten-pounder** (**a**) a thing weighing ten pounds; *spec.* (*N. Amer.*) either of two fishes of the genus *Elops*, related to the tarpon and found in the warmer parts of the Pacific and Atlantic; (**b**) a gun throwing a shot that weighs ten pounds; (**c**) a thing that is worth ten pounds; *spec.* a ten-pound note; **ten signal** *US* a signal that forms part of the ten-code; **ten-speed** a set of gears on a vehicle, esp. a bicycle, with ten different speeds (freq. *attrib.*); **ten-spot** *adjective & noun* (**a**) *adjective* having ten spots; (**b**) *noun* (*N. Amer.*) a ten-dollar bill; a playing-card with ten spots; **ten-strike** in the game of tenpins, a throw which bowls over all the pins; *fig.* a success (*US colloq.*); **ten tenth(s)** *adjective* complete, one hundred per cent; **ten-to-two** a position of the hands (esp. on the steering wheel of a car) or feet resembling that of the hands of a clock at ten minutes to two (freq. *attrib.*); **ten-twenty** = TWENTY *noun* 6; **ten-week stock** a form of Brompton stock, *Matthiola incana*, grown as an annual; **ten-year** *adjective* of ten years' duration or standing.

■ **tenfold** *adjective, noun, adverb, & verb* (**a**) *adjective* ten times as great or as numerous; *loosely* many times as great; having ten parts, divisions, elements, or units; (**b**) *noun* a tenfold amount; (**c**) *adverb* to ten times the number or quantity; (**d**) *verb trans.* increase tenfold: OE. **tenner** *noun* (*colloq.*) (**a**) a ten-pound note, a ten-dollar bill; (**b**) a period of ten years: M19.

tenable /'tɛnəb(ə)l/ *adjective.* L16.
[Old & mod. French, from *tenir* to hold: see -ABLE.]
1 Able to be maintained or defended against attack or objection; defensible. L16.
2 *gen.* Able to be held, retained, restrained, or kept in control. Now *rare*. E17.
3 Of an office, position, etc.: able to be occupied, possessed, or enjoyed. (Earlier in UNTENABLE 2.) M19.

🕮 **1** W. C. WILLIAMS I had to retreat to a more tenable position. **3** *Royal Air Force Journal* Scholarships in . . Engineering, tenable at University College, Southampton. A. J. AYER A Research Fellowship at Trinity, tenable for five years.

■ **tena'bility** *noun* tenableness (earlier in UNTENABILITY) M19. **tenableness** *noun* M17.

tenace /'tɛnəs/ *noun.* M17.
[French from Spanish *tenaza* lit. 'pincers, tongs'.]
WHIST & BRIDGE. A combination of two cards, one ranking next above, and the other next below, a card held by an opponent. Also, the holding of such cards.

Tenach *noun* var. of TANAK.

tenacious /tɪ'neɪʃəs/ *adjective.* E17.
[Latin *tenac-*, *tenax* holding fast (from *tenere* to hold) + -OUS: see -ACIOUS.]
1 a Holding together, strongly cohesive; not easily pulled apart or broken. E17. ▸**b** Adhesive; sticky. M17.
2 Holding or inclined to hold fast; clinging tightly. M17.
3 a Keeping a firm hold, retentive *of* something. M17. ▸**b** *fig.* Strongly retentive of or inclined to retain a principle, method, etc. Also (of memory), retentive. M17.
4 Persistent, resolute; stubborn. M17.
†**5** Persistently chary *of* or averse *to*. M18–E19.

🕮 **1b** W. COWPER Female feet, Too weak to struggle with tenacious clay. **2** T. CAMPBELL Old oaks . . Whose gnarled roots, tenacious and profound. **3b** P. G. WODEHOUSE When once an idea had entered Steve's head he was tenacious of it. **4** M. L. KING Racism is a tenacious evil, but . . not immutable. I. D. YALOM I was as tenacious as he and refused to be dissuaded.

■ **tenaciously** *adverb* M17. **tenaciousness** *noun* tenacity M17.

tenacity /tɪ'nasɪti/ *noun.* LME.
[Old & mod. French *ténacité* or Latin *tenacitas*, formed as prec.: see -ACITY.]
1 The quality of retaining what is held, physically or mentally; firmness of hold or purpose. LME.
2 Cohesiveness, toughness; viscosity; stickiness. M16.
†**3** Tendency to keep fast hold of money; miserliness, parsimony. L16–E18.

🕮 **1** P. USTINOV They defended it with the tenacity of animals. I. D. YALOM The tenacity of her love obsession, which had possessed her for eight years.

tenacle /'tɛnək(ə)l/ *noun.* Now *rare*. LME.
[Latin *tenaculum*: see next, -CLE.]
†**1** In *pl.* Forceps, pincers, nippers. LME–L16.
2 An organ by which a climbing plant attaches itself. Formerly, a stalk, a peduncle. L15.

tenaculum /tɪ'nakjʊləm/ *noun.* Pl. **-la** /-lə/. L17.
[Latin = holder, holding instrument, from *tenere* to hold.]
1 MEDICINE. A kind of surgical hook or forceps for picking up arteries etc. L17.
2 ZOOLOGY. Any of various organs or structures for support or attachment; ENTOMOLOGY = RETINACULUM 2b. L19.

tenaille /tɪ'neɪl/ *noun.* L16.
[Old & mod. French from Latin *tenacula* pl. of *tenaculum*: see prec.]
†**1** In *pl.* Pincers, forceps. L16–E18.
2 FORTIFICATION. A small low work, consisting of one or two re-entering angles, placed before the curtain between two bastions. L16.

tenaillon /tɪ'naljən/ *noun.* M19.
[French, from *tenaille*: see prec., -OON.]
FORTIFICATION. A work sometimes placed before each face of a ravelin, leaving the salient angle exposed.

tenancy /'tɛnənsi/ *noun.* LME.
[from next + -ANCY, repr. medieval Latin *tenantia*, *tenentia*.]
†**1** That which is held by a tenant; *spec.* (**a**) a holding; (**b**) a position or office. *rare*. LME–L17.
2 LAW. A holding or possession of lands or tenements by any right or title; *spec.* occupancy under a lease. Also, the state or condition of being a tenant; the duration or period of a tenure. L16.
3 Occupation of or residence in any place, position, or condition. L16.

🕮 **2** *Listener* The . . squatters were eventually given tenancy by the Greater London Council. M. BERLINS You become entitled to a 'statutory tenancy' . . with full security of tenure. C. HARMAN Sylvia and Valentine took up the tenancy.

Phrases etc.: ***joint-tenancy***: see JOINT *adjective*. ***several tenancy***: see SEVERAL *adjective* 7. **tenancy at will** a tenancy of unspecified duration, terminable by either side. **tenancy in common** a shared tenancy in which each holder has a distinct, separately transferable interest.

tenant /ˈtɛnənt/ *noun*. ME.
[Old & mod. French, use as noun of pres. pple of *tenir* to hold from Latin *tenere* to hold: see -ANT[1].]
1 *LAW*. A person who holds or possesses lands or tenements by any kind of right or title. ME.
2 A person who rents a piece of land, a house, etc., by lease for a set time. LME.
3 *transf*. & *fig*. A person who or thing which inhabits or occupies any place; an inhabitant, an occupant, a dweller. LME.

2 *Listener* Mrs Peggy Edwards, spokesperson for the local tenants' association. K. VONNEGUT A man .. had become a mere tenant in a building he used to own. **3** T. CAMPBELL The dim-eyed tenant of the dungeon gloom.

Phrases: ***joint-tenant***: see JOINT *adjective*. ***share tenant***: see SHARE *noun*[2]. ***sitting tenant***: see SITTING *ppl adjective* 4. ***STATUTORY tenant***. **tenant at will** a tenant who is such under a tenancy at will. ***tenant PARAVAIL***. **tenant to the praecipe** a tenant against whom a praecipe was brought, being one to whom an entailed estate had been granted so that it might be alienated by a recovery.
Comb.: **tenant farmer** a person who farms rented land; **tenant right** the rights or entitlements of a tenant; *spec*. the right of a tenant to continue a tenancy at the termination of the lease; **tenant-righter** *colloq*. an advocate or supporter of tenant right.
■ **tenantless** *adjective* L16. **tenantship** *noun* the condition or position of a tenant; tenancy, occupancy: L19.

tenant /ˈtɛnənt/ *verb*. M17.
[from prec.]
1 *verb trans*. Hold or occupy as a tenant, be the tenant of (land, a house, etc.). M17.
2 *verb intrans*. Reside, dwell, live *in*. *rare*. M17.

1 TENNYSON We bought the farm we tenanted before. *fig*.: R. BROUGHTON Alternate clouds and sunshine tenant the sky.

tenantable /ˈtɛnəntəb(ə)l/ *adjective*. M16.
[from TENANT *noun*, *verb* + -ABLE.]
Able to be tenanted or inhabited; fit for occupation.

tenantry /ˈtɛnəntri/ *noun*. LME.
[from TENANT *noun* + -RY.]
1 The state or condition of being a tenant; tenancy. LME.
2 Land let out to tenants; the profits of such land. LME. ▸†**b** Land, property, etc., held by a tenant under a landlord. LME–E17.
3 The body of tenants on an estate or estates. E17. ▸**b** *transf*. A set of occupants or inhabitants. L18.
4 *spec*. That part of a manor or estate occupied and farmed by tenants, as distinct from the owner's or landlord's demesne. L18.

tenas /ˈtɛnas/ *adjective*. *N. Amer. slang*. L19.
[Chinook Jargon from Nootka *t'an'a* child.]
Small.

Tenby daffodil /ˈtɛnbɪ ˈdafədɪl/ *noun phr*. L19.
[*Tenby*, a town in Dyfed, Wales.]
A small daffodil found near Tenby, *Narcissus obvallaris* (prob. a naturalized cultivar of *N. pseudonarcissus*), in which both corona and perianth segments are deep yellow.

Tencel /ˈtɛnsɛl/ *noun*. M20.
[Invented name.]
(Proprietary name for) a cellulosic fibre obtained from wood pulp using recyclable solvents; a fabric made from this.

tench /tɛn(t)ʃ/ *noun*[1]. ME.
[Old French *tenche* (mod. *tanche*) from late Latin *tinca*.]
A heavy-bodied Eurasian freshwater fish, *Tinca tinca*, of the carp family, which is found in still water; the flesh of this fish as food.

tench /tɛn(t)ʃ/ *noun*[2]. *slang*. M19.
[Abbreviation of DETENTION, PENITENTIARY.]
A place of detention, a penitentiary.

tend /tɛnd/ *noun*. *rare*. M17.
[from TEND *verb*[2].]
The action or fact of tending; aim, tendency.

tend /tɛnd/ *verb*[1]. ME.
[Aphet. from ATTEND, INTEND.]
†**1** *verb trans*. Turn one's ear to, listen to. Cf. ATTEND *verb* 1. ME–E19.
2 *verb intrans*. (with *to*, †*to do*, *unto*) & *trans*. Turn the mind, attention, or energies (to); apply oneself (to); = ATTEND *verb* 2. Now chiefly *dial*. & *US*. ME.
3 *verb trans*. Have as one's purpose, plan *to do* (something); = INTEND *verb* 11. *obsolete* exc. *Scot*. & *dial*. ME.
4 *verb trans*. & *intrans*. (with *on*, *upon*). Wait on as an attendant or servant; escort, follow, or accompany in order to give service or assistance; = ATTEND *verb* 4. Now *rare*. LME.
5 *verb trans*. & *intrans*. (with †*of*, *on*). Go to, be present at (a meeting, ceremony, etc.); = ATTEND *verb* 5. Now *dial*. & *US*. LME.
6 *verb trans*. Apply oneself to the care and service of; look after; have charge of; *spec*. (**a**) wait on and minister to (the sick); (**b**) cultivate (a plant etc.). Cf. ATTEND *verb* 6. L15.
7 **a** *verb trans*. Watch, watch for, wait for. *obsolete* exc. *dial*. E17. ▸†**b** *verb intrans*. Wait in expectation or readiness. Only in E17.

2 W. FAULKNER You got to wait a little while. Then I'll tend to you. **4** DEFOE I tend on them, to fetch things for them. **6** D. LESSING Herds of .. cattle he tended as a youngster. P. ROTH Visitors tending the graves .. weeding like patient gardeners. R. GODDEN She was tended until her death by her youngest daughter. **tend bar** *N. Amer*. serve drinks from a bar.

tend /tɛnd/ *verb*[2]. ME.
[Old & mod. French *tendre* from Latin *tendere* stretch.]
▶ **I 1** *verb intrans*. Direct a course, move or be inclined to move. (Foll. by *from*, *to*, *towards*.) ME.
2 *verb intrans*. *fig*. Be disposed to acquire or come finally to some quality, state, opinion, etc. Foll. by *to*, *towards*. LME.
3 *verb intrans*. Lead or conduce *to* some state, action, or result; *loosely* be apt or inclined to *or* to *do*. M16.
4 *NAUTICAL*. **a** *verb intrans*. Of a ship at anchor: swing round with the tide or wind. L18. ▸**b** *verb trans*. Turn (a ship at anchor) with the tide or wind. L18.

1 P. MATTHIESSEN The path tends west around small mountains. **2** *Atlantic* His poetry tending toward the Byronic. **3** G. VIDAL Such things tended to bore her. B. BETTELHEIM Children tend to dress .. and talk like TV characters they admire.

▶ **II 5** *verb intrans*. †**a** Extend or reach (*to*). *obsolete*. LME–E18. ▸**b** *MATH*. Foll. by *to*: (of a variable, series, function, etc.) approach a given quantity as a limit. L19.
6 *verb trans*. Offer, proffer; provide, supply. Long *obsolete* exc. *dial*. L15.
†**7** *verb trans*. & *intrans*. Relate or refer to or *to*; concern. L16–M17.
†**8** *verb trans*. Stretch, make taut; set (a trap etc.). M17–L18.

Tendai /ˈtɛndʌɪ/ *noun*. E18.
[Japanese from Chinese *Tiāntāi*, the mountain in Zhejiang (Chekiang) province, SE China where the doctrines of the sect were formulated.]
A Buddhist sect introduced into Japan from China by the monk Saichō (767–822), founded by Zhi Yi (515–97) and characterized by elaborate ritual, moral idealism, and philosophical eclecticism.

tendance /ˈtɛnd(ə)ns/ *noun*. *arch*. L16.
[Aphet. from ATTENDANCE or from TEND *verb*[1] + -ANCE.]
1 The action of attending to, or looking after, anything; tending, attention, care. L16.
2 The bestowal of personal attention and care; *esp*. ministration to the sick or weak. L16.
3 Attendants collectively; train, retinue. E17.

tendant /ˈtɛnd(ə)nt/ *adjective* & *noun*. *arch*. ME.
[Aphet. from ATTENDANT.]
▶ **A** *adjective*. Attending, giving attention or service, waiting (upon). ME.
▶ **B** *noun*. An attendant. L16.

tendence /ˈtɛnd(ə)ns/ *noun*. Now *rare*. LME.
[Old & mod. French *tendance* from medieval Latin *tendentia*: see next, -ENCE.]
= TENDENCY 1, 2.

tendency /ˈtɛnd(ə)nsi/ *noun*. E17.
[medieval Latin *tendentia*, from Latin *tendent-* pres. ppl stem of *tendere* TEND *verb*[2]: see -ENCY.]
1 The fact or quality of tending to something; a disposition, leaning, or inclination toward some purpose, object, result, etc. E17.
†**2** Movement toward or in the direction of something. M17–E18.
3 Drift or aim of a discourse; purpose of a story, novel, etc. M18.
4 *POLITICS*. A political association within a larger party or movement, esp. a left-wing group within a socialist party. E20.

1 ISAIAH BERLIN Suppressing any tendencies likely to lead to .. disorderly forms of life. G. VIDAL She had a tendency to become hysterical if she had to do anything unusual.

tendent /ˈtɛnd(ə)nt/ *adjective*. Now *rare*. ME.
[Old French, pres. pple of *tendre* TEND *verb*[2]: see -ENT.]
Tending, having a tendency (*to*, *towards*).
¶ Obsolete before 18, revived late in 19.

tendential /tɛnˈdɛnʃ(ə)l/ *adjective*. M19.
[from TENDENCY, after *presidency*, *presidential*, *residency*, *residential*, and similar pairs: see -ENT.]
Having or of the nature of a tendency; *spec*. tendentious.

tendentious /tɛnˈdɛnʃəs/ *adjective*. E20.
[formed as prec.: see -IOUS.]
Having an underlying purpose; (of writing etc.) composed with the intention of promoting a particular cause or viewpoint.

Listener A tendentious and jazzed-up version of part of the lecture which had appeared in the local .. press.

■ **tendentiously** *adverb* E20. **tendentiousness** *noun* E20.

tendenz /tɛnˈdɛnts/ *noun*. L19.
[German from English TENDENCE or French *tendance*.]
= TENDENCY 3.
Comb.: **tendenzroman** /tɛnˈdɛntsrəmɑːn/ [German *Roman* novel] a novel containing an unexpressed but definite purpose.

tender /ˈtɛndə/ *noun*[1]. LME.
[from TEND *verb*[1] + -ER[1], or aphet. from ATTENDER.]
1 A person who tends or waits on another; an attendant, a nurse. Also, an assistant to a skilled worker. *obsolete* exc. *dial*. LME.
2 A ship or boat used to attend a larger one, esp. to supply goods and provisions, convey orders, or carry passengers to and from shore. Also *spec*., a small naval vessel responsible to, and whose crew are appointed to, a larger parent vessel. L17.
3 A person who attends to or has charge of something, esp. a machine, business, etc. E19.
4 A truck attached to the rear of a steam locomotive to carry fuel, water, etc. E19.
5 A vehicle used by a fire brigade to transport hoses, ladders, or other equipment to a fire. Usu. with qualifying word, as ***fire tender***, ***hose tender***. L19.

2 M. RULE We got out to the excavation site .. in our twelve-man tender. **3** J. M. COETZEE All that remains is to be a tender of the soil. ***bartender***: see BAR *noun*[1].

tender /ˈtɛndə/ *noun*[2]. M16.
[from TENDER *verb*[2].]
1 *LAW*. A formal offer made by one party to another; *spec*. an offer of money etc. made to discharge a debt or liability. M16.
2 *gen*. An offer of anything for acceptance. L16.
3 *COMMERCE*. A written offer made by one party to another to supply goods or carry out work at set price or rate. Also, a method of issuing shares by which offers above a stated minimum price are invited. M17.
4 Money or other commodities that may be legally tendered or offered in payment; currency prescribed by law as that in which payment may be made. M18.

1 **plea of tender** a plea that the defendant has always been ready to satisfy the plaintiff's claim and now brings the amount into court. **3** L. T. C. ROLT Decided to invite tenders for the hull of the ship and her engines. **4** J. GILMOUR In Urga, brick tea and silver are the common tenders. ***legal tender***: see LEGAL *adjective*.

tender /ˈtɛndə/ *adjective* & *noun*[3]. ME.
[Old & mod. French *tendre* from Latin *tener* tender, delicate.]
▶ **A** *adjective*. **I** Soft, delicate.
1 Soft or delicate in texture or consistency; easily broken, cut, compressed, chewed, etc. Formerly also (*rare*), frail, slender. ME.
2 **a** Of delicate constitution; not strong or robust; unable to endure hardship, fatigue, etc. ME. ▸**b** Of an animal or plant: needing protection, easily injured by severe weather etc., not hardy. E17.
3 Having the weakness and delicacy of youth; immature. ME.
4 Of colour, light, or (*occas*.) sound: soft, subdued; not strong or glaring. E16.
5 Of a subject matter, topic, etc.: requiring tact or careful handling; delicate, ticklish. E17.

1 *Green Cuisine* Simmer for 40 minutes, or until the carrots are tender. *Essentials* Succulent cooked sausages and tender hams. **2b** *Which?* Take cuttings of tender types and keep in a cold frame over winter. **3** A. THWAITE A baptised believer of unusually tender years. R. CLAY I've felt the burden of my mother's worry all my tender young life. **4** K. ISHIGURO A tender light was falling across the foliage.

▶ **II** Gentle or sensitive towards or about others.
6 Of an action or instrument: not forcible or rough; acting or touching gently. ME.
7 **a** Of a person, a person's feelings, etc.: kind, loving, mild, affectionate. ME. ▸†**b** *transf*. That is the object of tender feeling; beloved, precious. LME–E17.
8 **a** Careful of the welfare or integrity *of*; solicitous *for*. Now *rare*. ME. ▸**b** Careful to avoid or prevent something; scrupulous, cautious. Foll. by *of*, *in*, †*to do*. Now *rare*. E17.
9 Sensitive to, or easily affected by, external physical forces or impressions; *esp*. sensitive to pain, easily hurt. LME. ▸**b** Of a ship: leaning or readily inclined to roll in response to the wind. E18.
10 Sensitive to emotional influences; impressionable, readily touched; easily offended or hurt. L16.

📖 **7a** G. GREENE Out of a long marriage she has remembered nothing tender, .. considerate. JULIA HAMILTON His tender concern made her .. aware of her own treachery. **8b** C. BURY Her heart should be tender of ridiculing their suffering. **9** A. TAYLOR Her skin was too tender to be touched. **10** H. P. BROUGHAM The form of words used, out of regard to tender consciences.

Phrases: **tender loving care** *colloq.* solicitous care and attention such as is given by nurses. **the tender passion** romantic love.

▶†**B** *absol.* as *noun.* Tender state, feeling, or regard. LME–E19.

Comb. & special collocations: **tender annual** an annual plant needing the protection of a greenhouse; **tender-conscienced** *adjective* having a tender conscience; scrupulous; **tender-dying** *adjective* (*rare*) dying young; **tender-eared** *adjective* having tender ears; *fig.* sensitive to blame or criticism; **tender-eyed** *adjective* (*a*) having gentle or weak eyes; †(*b*) fond, doting; **tender-footed** *adjective* having or moving (as) with tender feet; *fig.* cautious, timid, inexperienced; **tender-hearted** *adjective* having a tender heart; kind, compassionate; loving; **tender-heartedness** the quality or state of being tender-hearted; †**tender-hefted** *adjective* (*rare*, Shakes.) set in a delicate haft or bodily frame; womanly, gentle; **tender mercies** *iron.* attention, care, or treatment which is unlikely to be in the best interests of the recipient; **tender-minded** *adjective* having a tender mind; sensitive, idealistic; **tender-mindedness** the quality or state of being tender-minded; **tenderpad** [after TENDERFOOT 2] a recruit to the Cub Scout movement who has passed the enrolment test; **tender plant** *fig.* something needing careful nurture to survive and develop.

■ **tenderish** *adjective* (*rare*) somewhat tender L18. **tenderling** *noun* (*a*) (now *rare*) a delicate person or creature; *contempt.* an effeminate person; (*b*) a person of tender years, a young person: M16. **tenderly** *adverb* in a tender manner, with tenderness ME. **tenderness** *noun* (*a*) the quality or state of being tender; (*b*) an instance of this: ME.

tender /ˈtɛndə/ *verb*[1]. *arch.* & *dial.* LME.
[from TENDER *adjective*.]

†**1** *verb intrans.* Become tender; be affected with pity; soften. LME–M16.

2 *verb trans.* Make tender; *spec.* (*a*) make gentle or compassionate; (*b*) make delicate; (*c*) make (physically) tender or soft. LME.

3 *verb trans.* Feel or act tenderly towards; hold dear, care for, cherish. Formerly also, regard favourably, regard or treat with pity. LME.

📖 **2** M. K. RAWLINGS The meat .. had been coarse and stringy .. and it took long cooking to tender it.

■ **tenderer** *noun*[1] (*a*) a person who behaves with pity towards another; (*b*) a person or thing which makes something tender: L16.

tender /ˈtɛndə/ *verb*[2]. M16.
[Old & mod. French *tendre* from Latin *tendere* stretch, hold forth (cf. TEND *verb*[2]). For the unusual retention of the French inf. ending cf. RENDER *verb*.]

1 *verb trans.* **a** LAW. Formally offer or advance (a plea, an averment, evidence, etc.); *spec.* offer (money etc.) to discharge a debt or liability. M16. ▶†**b** Lay *down* (money) in payment. *rare.* Only in E17.

2 *verb trans. gen.* Present (anything) for approval or acceptance; offer, proffer. L16.

3 *verb intrans.* COMMERCE. Make a tender for a proposed contract to supply goods or carry out work. Usu. foll. by *for*. Cf. TENDER *noun*[2] 3. M19.

📖 **1b** *transf.*: SHAKES. *Meas. for M.* Had he twenty heads to tender down On twenty bloody blocks, he'd yield them up. **2** J. BUCHAN I wanted to pay her for the milk and tendered a sovereign. R. PARK My resignation was accepted almost before I'd tendered it. **tender an oath** *verb phr. trans.* & *intrans.* offer or present an oath (*to* a person); challenge (a person) to take an oath.

■ **tenderable** *adjective* (COMMERCE) that may be tendered; available on fulfilment of contract: M19. **tenderer** *noun*[2] a person who tenders or makes a formal offer, esp. for a proposed contract M17.

tenderfoot /ˈtɛndəfʊt/ *noun.* Pl. **-foots**, **-feet** /-fiːt/. M19.
[from TENDER *adjective* + FOOT *noun*.]

1 A newly arrived immigrant, orig. to the ranching and mining regions of the western US, unused to the hardships of pioneer life; a greenhorn. More widely, a raw inexperienced person. Chiefly *N. Amer.* M19.

2 A recruit to the Scout and Guide movements who has passed the enrolment tests. E20.

tenderize /ˈtɛndərʌɪz/ *verb trans.* Also **-ise**. M18.
[formed as prec. + -IZE.]

Make tender, *esp.* make (meat) tender by beating, slow cooking, etc.

■ **tenderizer** *noun* something used to make meat tender M20.

tenderloin /ˈtɛndəlɔɪn/ *noun.* E19.
[from TENDER *adjective* + LOIN.]

1 The most tender and juicy part of the loin of beef, pork, etc., taken from under the short ribs in the hind quarter; *US* the fillet or undercut of a sirloin. E19.

2 A district in a city (orig. New York) where vice and corruption are prominent. Also ***tenderloin district***. *US slang.* L19.

¶ In sense 2 app. with ref. to the bribes made to the police to persuade them to turn a blind eye.

tenderometer /tɛndəˈrɒmɪtə/ *noun.* M20.
[from TENDER *adjective* + -OMETER.]

An instrument for testing the tenderness of raw peas for picking, processing, etc.

tendido /tenˈdiðo/ *noun.* Pl. **-os** /-ɒs/. M19.
[Spanish, pa. pple of *tender* stretch.]

An open tier of seats above the *barrera* in a bullring.

tendines *noun* pl. of TENDO.

tendinitis /tɛndɪˈnʌɪtɪs/ *noun.* Also **tendo-**. E20.
[mod. Latin *tendin-*, *tendo* TENDON + -ITIS.]

MEDICINE. Inflammation of a tendon.

tendinous /ˈtɛndɪnəs/ *adjective.* M17.
[French *tendineux* from mod. Latin *tendo*, *tendin-* (cf. Italian *tendine*), which repl. *tendon-*, on the model of Latin words in *-do*, *-din-*: see TENDON, -OUS.]

Of the nature of a tendon; consisting of tendons.

tendo /ˈtɛndəʊ/ *noun.* Pl. **tendines** /ˈtɛndɪniːz/. L19.
[medieval or mod. Latin: see prec.]

ANATOMY. = TENDON 1. Chiefly in mod. Latin phrs.
tendo Achilles, **tendo calcaneus** /kalˈkeɪnɪəs/ = ***ACHILLES tendon***.

tendo- /ˈtɛndəʊ/ *combining form* of TENDON: see -O-. Cf. TENO-.
■ **tendo-synoˈvitis** *noun* = TENOSYNOVITIS L19.

tendon /ˈtɛndən/ *noun.* LME.
[French, or medieval Latin *tendo(n-)* (from Latin *tendere*: see TEND *verb*[2]) translating Greek *tenōn* sinew (whence late Latin *tenon*) use as noun of aorist pa. pple of *teinein* stretch.]

1 A band or cord of dense fibrous tissue which forms the termination of a muscle and by which its pull is transmitted to a bone etc.; a sinew. Cf. APONEUROSIS. LME.

2 ENTOMOLOGY. Any of various slender chitinous parts; *esp.* one to which muscles are attached for moving appendages. E19.

3 ENGINEERING. A steel rod or wire that is stretched while in liquid concrete so as to prestress it as it sets. M20.

1 *ACHILLES tendon.*

Comb.: **tendon organ**, **tendon spindle** a sensory spindle in a tendon.

■ **tendonous** *adjective* (now *rare*) = TENDINOUS L16.

tendonitis *noun* see TENDINITIS.

†**tendoor** *noun* see TANDOOR.

tendre /tɑ̃ːdr/ *noun.* Pl. pronounced same. L17.
[French, from *tendre* TENDER *adjective*.]

(A) tender feeling or regard; (a) fondness, (an) affection.

tendresse /tɑ̃drɛs/ *noun.* Pl. pronounced same. LME.
[French, formed as prec. Cf. -ESS[2].]

= prec.

tendril /ˈtɛndrɪl/ *noun* & *verb.* M16.
[Prob. alt. (after French dim. †*tendrillon*) of Old & mod. French *tendron* (earlier *tendrun*) tender part or shoot, cartilage = Italian *tenerume* shoots from Proto-Romance, from Latin *tener* TENDER *adjective*. Cf. next.]

▶ **A** *noun.* **1** A slender threadlike appendage of a plant (a modified branch, leaf, inflorescence, etc.), often growing in a spiral form, which stretches out and twines round any suitable support. M16.

2 a *transf.* Something resembling a plant tendril, *esp.* a slender curl or ringlet of hair. E17. ▶**b** *fig.* A part of a usu. immaterial thing which entwines itself pervasively or clings like a plant tendril. M19.

📖 **2a** *Scientific American* A long tendril of gas and stars. M. WESLEY Brian .. pushed tendrils of Susie's hair up under her cap. **b** R. SILVERBERG Tendrils of unreality began to invade her conscious mind.

▶ **B** *verb intrans.* Infl. **-ll-**, ***-l-**. Curl or progress like a tendril. *rare.* L19.

■ **tendrillar** *adjective* resembling a tendril or tendrils E20. **tendrilled** *adjective* having a tendril or tendrils; *transf.* curly, curling: E19. **tendrilly**, **tendrilous** *adjectives* full of tendrils; resembling a tendril: M19.

tendron /ˈtɛndrən/ *noun.* LME.
[Old & mod. French: see prec.]

1 A young tender shoot or sprout of a plant; a bud. Now *rare.* LME.

2 In *pl.* The cartilages of the ribs, esp. (in COOKERY) of a deer or calf. LME.

tendu /tɑ̃dy/ *adjective.* E20.
[French, pa. pple of *tendre* stretch.]

BALLET. Stretched out or held tautly.

-tene /tiːn/ *suffix.*
[Greek *tainia* band, ribbon.]

CYTOLOGY. Forming nouns denoting stages of the first meiotic division, as ***diplotene***, ***leptotene***, ***pachytene***, ***zygotene***.

Tenebrae /ˈtɛnɪbriː, -breɪ/ *noun.* M17.
[Latin = darkness.]

ECCLESIASTICAL HISTORY. The office of matins and lauds as formerly sung on the last three days of Holy Week, at which candles were successively extinguished in memory of the darkness during the crucifixion. Also, this office set to music.

†**tenebres** *noun.* ME.
[Old & mod. French *tenèbres* from Latin TENEBRAE.]

1 Darkness, obscurity. ME–M17.

2 = TENEBRAE. ME–E19.

tenebrescence /tɛnɪˈbrɛs(ə)ns/ *noun.* M20.
[from Latin *tenebrescens* pres. pple of *tenebrescere* grow dark, from TENEBRAE: see -ENCE.]

PHYSICS. The property of darkening, esp. reversibly, in response to incident radiation.

■ **tenebresce** *verb intrans.* darken reversibly in this way M20. **tenebrescent** *adjective* M20.

tenebrific /tɛnɪˈbrɪfɪk/ *adjective. arch.* L18.
[from Latin TENEBRAE: see -FIC.]

Causing or producing darkness; obscuring.

tenebrio /tɪˈnɛbrɪəʊ/ *noun.* Pl. **-os**. Also (earlier) †**tenebrion**. M17.
[Latin, from TENEBRAE.]

†**1** A person who lurks in the dark; a nocturnal prowler. Also, a night-spirit. *rare.* M17–M18.

2 ENTOMOLOGY. A tenebrionid; *spec.* a meal-beetle. Now only as mod. Latin genus name. M18.

tenebrionid /tɪˌnɛbrɪˈəʊnɪd/ *noun* & *adjective.* E20.
[mod. Latin *Tenebrionidae* (see below), from *Tenebrio* genus name, from prec.: see -ID[3].]

ENTOMOLOGY. ▶**A** *noun.* Any of various beetles constituting the family Tenebrionidae, most of which are dark-coloured nocturnal scavengers, found esp. in dry regions, and which include the cellar beetles, flour beetles, etc. Also called ***darkling beetle***. E20.

▶ **B** *adjective.* Of or pertaining to this family. E20.

tenebrious /tɪˈnɛbrɪəs/ *adjective.* L16.
[Alt. of TENEBROUS by substitution of -IOUS for -OUS.]

= TENEBROUS.

tenebrist /ˈtɛnəbrɪst/ *noun.* E20.
[formed as TENEBROSO: see -IST.]

= TENEBROSO *noun*.

■ **tenebrism** *noun* the style of the *tenebrosi* M20.

tenebrity /tɪˈnɛbrɪti/ *noun. rare.* L18.
[from Latin TENEBRAE: see -ITY.]

The quality of being dark; darkness.

tenebrose /ˈtɛnɪbrəʊs/ *adjective.* L15.
[Latin *tenebrosus*, formed as TENEBRAE: see -OSE[1].]

Dark; *fig.* gloomy, obscure.

tenebrosi *noun* pl. of TENEBROSO *noun*.

tenebrosity /tɛnɪˈbrɒsɪti/ *noun.* LME.
[Old & mod. French *ténébrosité* formed as TENEBROSE: see -ITY.]

Darkness, obscurity.

tenebroso /teneˈbroso/ *noun* & *adjective.* L19.
[Italian = dark from Latin *tenebrosus* TENEBROSE.]

▶ **A** *noun.* Pl. **-si** /-si/. A member of a group of early 17th-cent. Italian painters influenced by Caravaggio, whose work is characterized by dramatic contrasts of light and shade. L19.

▶ **B** *adjective.* Designating the style of this group of painters. L19.

tenebrous /ˈtɛnɪbrəs/ *adjective.* Chiefly *literary.* LME.
[Old French *tenebrus* (mod. *ténébreux*) from Latin *tenebrosus* TENEBROSE: see -OUS.]

Full of darkness, dark; *fig.* obscure, gloomy.

📖 J. BUCHAN Everything was drained of colour and frozen into a tenebrous monotony. S. HEANEY Aside from their tenebrous conversation, I sat learning my catechism.

■ **tenebrousness** *noun* (*rare*) darkness E18.

tenement /ˈtɛnəm(ə)nt/ *noun.* ME.
[Old French (mod. *tènement*) from medieval Latin *tenementum*, from Latin *tenere* to hold: see -MENT.]

†**1** LAW. The fact of holding as a possession; tenure. ME–M17.

2 LAW. Land or buildings held from a superior by any kind of tenure; a holding; *spec.* in *pl.*, property held by freehold. Cf. TENURE *noun* 2. ME.

3 a *gen.* A building or house used as a residence; a dwelling-place, an abode. LME. ▶**b** *transf.* & *fig.* Anything serving or regarded as an abode; *spec.* (*a*) the body as the abode of the soul; (*b*) the abode of an animal. L16.

4 *spec.* **a** In England, a part of a house or block of flats, as a flat or room, let out or occupied as a separate residence. L16. ▶**b** In Scotland & the US, a large house or multi-storey building constructed as or adapted into a number of separately owned or leased residences. Also ***tenement house***, ***tenement of houses***. Cf. HOUSE *noun*[1] 1b. L17.

📖 **2** *Times* The 40 .. *tenements* into which Sark is divided. **lands and tenements** lands and all other freehold interests. **3b** C. BRONTË That spirit—now struggling to quit its material tenement. **4a** G. GISSING On each story are two tenements. **b** K. CLARK The grim, narrow tenements of the Old Town of Edinburgh. *Times* Bernard Street consists of four-storey tenement blocks.

■ **teneˈmental** *adjective* of or pertaining to a tenement or tenements; leased to tenants: M18. **teneˈmentary** *adjective* (*a*) leased to tenants; (*b*) consisting of tenements: M17. **tenemented** *adjective* let in tenements or separate dwellings L19. **tenementer** *noun* (*Scot. rare*) the holder of a tenement; a leaseholder, a tenant: L16.

tenendas /tɪˈnɛndɑːs/ *noun.* L17.
[Latin, lit. 'to be held' accus. pl. fem. of gerundive of *tenere* to hold.]
SCOTS LAW (now *Hist.*). That part of a charter defining the tenure by which the lands granted were to be held.

tenendum /tɪˈnɛndəm/ *noun.* E17.
[Latin, lit. 'to be held' neut. gerundive of *tenere* to hold.]
LAW (now *Hist.* exc. *US*). That part of a deed defining the tenure by which the things granted are to be held. Cf. HABENDUM.

†tenent *noun.* M16–E18.
[from Latin *tenent-* pres. ppl stem of *tenere* to hold: see -ENT.]
= TENET.

tenent /ˈtɛnənt/ *adjective.* M19.
[from Latin *tenentem* holding, pres. pple of *tenere* to hold.]
ZOOLOGY. Of hairs on the feet of insects, spiders, etc.: used for holding or attachment.

tenente /teˈnente/ *noun.* E20.
[Italian, Portuguese. Cf. TENIENTE.]
A lieutenant (in Italy, Brazil, etc.).

teneral /ˈtɛn(ə)r(ə)l/ *adjective.* L19.
[from Latin *tener* TENDER *adjective* + -AL[1].]
ENTOMOLOGY. Of an adult insect: with a soft cuticle, as when it has recently emerged from the pupa.

Tenerife /tɛnəˈriːf/ *noun.* Also **-riffe**. L18.
[The largest of the Canary Islands.]
1 A white wine produced on Tenerife. L18.
2 Used *attrib.* to designate a kind of handmade lace from the Canary Islands. E20.

tenesmus /tɪˈnɛzməs/ *noun.* E16.
[medieval Latin from Latin *tenesmos* from Greek *tēnesmos*, *teinesmos* straining, from *teinein* stretch, strain.]
MEDICINE. A frequent, excessive, and painful desire to defecate, accompanied by straining, but with little or no production of faeces. Formerly also, a similar desire to urinate, strangury.

tenet /ˈtɛnɪt, ˈtiːnɛt/ *noun.* L16.
[Latin, lit. 'he holds' 3 pres. sing. of *tenere* to hold, superseding earlier TENENT *noun.*]
A doctrine, dogma, principle, or opinion, in religion, philosophy, politics, etc., held by a group or person. Also *loosely*, any opinion held.

> ISAIAH BERLIN He . . was convinced of the validity of his . . philosophical tenets. G. F. KENNAN The ideological tenets of Russian communism.

tenge /ˈtɛŋgeɪ/ *noun.* Pl. same, **-s**. L20.
[Kazakh & Turkmen, lit. 'coin, rouble'.]
1 The basic monetary unit of Kazakhstan, equal to 100 teins.
2 A monetary unit of Turkmenistan, equal to one-hundredth of a manat.

Tengmalm's owl /ˈtɛŋmalmz ˈaʊl/ *noun phr.* M19.
[from Peter *Tengmalm* (1754–1803), Swedish naturalist.]
A small owl, *Aegolius funereus*, of northern coniferous forests, resembling the little owl but with deeper facial discs edged with black.

tenia *noun* var. of TAENIA.

teniente /teˈnjente/ *noun.* L18.
[Spanish. Cf. TENENTE.]
A lieutenant (in Spain etc.).

tenko /ˈtɛŋkəʊ/ *noun.* Pl. **-os**. M20.
[Japanese.]
In a Japanese prison camp in the war of 1939–45: a muster parade or roll-call of prisoners.

tenmantale /ˈtɛnmənteɪl/ *noun. obsolete* exc. *Hist.* Also **-men-** & other vars. LOE.
[from TEN + MAN *noun* + TALE *noun* perh. after unattested Old English phr. with the sense 'a number of ten men'.]
1 In Yorkshire or perh. (more widely) the Danelaw, a tithing. Also, the system by which each member of a tithing was responsible for the others, a frank-pledge. LOE.
2 In the Danelaw, a land tax levied on a carucate; a carucage. LOE.

tenmoku *noun* var. of TEMMOKU.

Tenn. *abbreviation.*
Tennessee.

tennantite /ˈtɛnəntʌɪt/ *noun.* M19.
[from Smithson *Tennant* (1761–1815), English chemist + -ITE[1].]
MINERALOGY. A blackish-grey sulpharsenide of copper and iron that crystallizes in the cubic system and is an important ore of copper. Cf. FAHLERZ.

tenné /ˈtɛni/ *adjective & noun.* Also **tenny**. M16.
[French †*tenné* var. of Old French *tané* TAWNY.]
HERALDRY. (Of) a tawny colour; orange, orange-brown, bright chestnut.

Tennessean /tɛnəˈsiːən/ *noun & adjective.* E19.
[from next + -AN: see -EAN.]
▸ **A** *noun.* A native or inhabitant of Tennessee. E19.
▸ **B** *adjective.* Of, pertaining to, or characteristic of Tennessee. M19.

Tennessee /tɛnəˈsiː/ *noun.* L19.
[A State of the US.]
Used *attrib.* to designate things from Tennessee.
Tennessee marble a kind of marble found in Tennessee and freq. used in building and sculpture. **Tennessee walker**, **Tennessee walking horse** (an animal of) a lightly built breed of horse developed in Tennessee and distinguished by its specialized natural gait.

tennies /ˈtɛnɪz/ *noun pl. US colloq.* M20.
[from *tenn(is shoe)* s.v. TENNIS *noun* + -IE + -S[1].]
Tennis shoes.

tennis /ˈtɛnɪs/ *noun & verb.* LME.
[Prob. from Old French *tenez* imper. of *tenir* hold, take, presumably the server's call to an opponent used as the name of the game.]
▸ **A** *noun.* **1** More fully ***real tennis*** [REAL *adjective*[2]]. A game played on an enclosed rectangular court, later with a penthouse round three of its sides, in which a hard ball is driven to and fro across a net with a racket. LME.
2 A game for two or four players (now the most popular form of tennis) played with a soft ball and rackets on an open court with a net across the centre and a surface of smooth grass or hard gravel, cement, asphalt, etc.; (also, esp. in early use, more fully ***lawn tennis***). Also (with specifying word), any of various games resembling this, adapted for playing in a smaller space, on a table, etc. L19.
1 ***court tennis***, ***royal tennis***. **2** ***deck tennis***, ***short tennis***, ***table tennis***, etc.
Attrib. & comb.: In the sense 'used or worn in playing tennis', as ***tennis dress***, ***tennis shirt***, ***tennis shorts***, etc. Special combs., as **tennis arm**, **tennis elbow**, **tennis knee** a strained arm, elbow, or knee of a kind typically caused by playing tennis and involving tenosynovitis; **tennis-ball** (*a*) a ball used in playing (real or lawn) tennis; (*b*) *fig.* a thing or person that is tossed or bandied about like a tennis-ball; **tennis club** (the premises of) an association for playing tennis; **tennis-court** a court used in playing (real or lawn) tennis; ***tennis elbow***: see ***tennis arm*** above; **tennis-ground** a tennis-court or set of courts; ***tennis knee***: see ***tennis arm*** above; **tennis net** a net stretched across the centre of a (real or lawn) tennis-court, over which players strike the ball; **tennis-play** the game of real tennis; the playing of this; **tennis player** a person who plays tennis (now usu. lawn tennis, formerly real tennis); **tennis pro**, **tennis professional** a professional tennis player employed as an instructor and player at a tennis club, holiday resort, etc.; **tennis-racket** a racket used in playing (real or lawn) tennis; **tennis shoe** a light canvas or leather soft-soled shoe suitable for tennis or general casual wear.
▸ **B** *verb intrans.* **†1** Play real tennis. L15–L16.
2 Play lawn tennis. *rare.* L19.

tenny *adjective & noun* var. of TENNÉ.

Tennysonian /tɛnɪˈsəʊnɪən/ *adjective & noun.* M19.
[from *Tennyson* (see below) + -IAN.]
▸ **A** *adjective.* Of or pertaining to the English poet Alfred (Lord) Tennyson (1809–92), or his writings. M19.
▸ **B** *noun.* An admirer or student of Tennyson or his writings. M19.
■ **Tennysoniˈana** *noun pl.* [-ANA] publications or other items concerning or associated with Tennyson M19. **Tennysonianism** *noun* a characteristic trait or mannerism of Tennyson's style; an imitation of that style: M19. **Tennysonianly** *adverb* in a Tennysonian manner M20.

teno- /ˈtɛnəʊ, ˈtiːnəʊ/ *combining form.*
[from Greek *tenōn* tendon: see -O-.]
ANATOMY & MEDICINE. Forming words with the sense 'of or pertaining to a tendon'. Cf. TENDO-.
■ **teˈnorrhaphy** *noun* (an instance of) the surgical re-uniting of a severed tendon by suture L19. **tenosynoˈvitis** *noun* inflammation of a tendon sheath, causing pain and swelling L19. **teˈnotomy** *noun* (an instance of) the surgical division of a tendon M19. **teˈnotomize** *verb trans.* perform tenotomy upon (a tendon or muscle) L19.

tenon /ˈtɛnən/ *noun*[1] *& verb.* LME.
[French, from *tenir* to hold + *-on*: see -OON.]
▸ **A** *noun.* A projection on the end or side of a piece of wood or other material, made to fit into a corresponding cavity, esp. a mortise, in another piece. LME.
mortise and tenon, ***tenon and mortise***: see MORTISE *noun.*
Comb.: **tenon-saw** a fine saw for making tenons etc., with a thin blade and small teeth.
▸ **B** *verb.* **1** *verb trans.* Secure firmly, esp. by means of tenon and mortise. L16.
2 a *verb trans.* Cut as or fit with a tenon. L18. ▸**b** *verb intrans.* Fit in by or as by a tenon. L18.

> **1** H. STEPHENS The . . posts are . . tenoned into the sill.

■ **tenoner** *noun* a machine for forming tenons M20.

Tenon /ˈtɛnən/ *noun*[2]. M19.
[Jacques René *Tenon* (1724–1816), French anatomist.]
ANATOMY. Used in *possess.* and with *of* to designate structures described by Tenon.
Tenon's capsule the capsule of connective tissue that encloses the posterior part of the eyeball. **Tenon's space** the episcleral space between Tenon's capsule and the sclera.
■ **tenoˈnitis** *noun* inflammation of Tenon's capsule L19.

tenor /ˈtɛnə/ *noun*[1] *& adjective.* Also (now *rare*) **tenour**. ME.
[Anglo-Norman *tenur*, Old French *tenour* (mod. *teneur* course, import) from Latin *tenor* continuous course, substance, import of a law, etc., from *tenere* to hold: see -OR.]
▸ **A** *noun.* **I 1 a** The general sense or meaning which runs through a document, speech, etc.; substance, purport, drift. ME. ▸**b** LAW. An exact copy of a document, a transcript. Also, the actual wording of a document. LME. ▸**c** *Hist.* The value of a banknote or bill as stated on it. E18.
2 †a The action or fact of holding on or continuing; continuance, duration. LME–L17. ▸**b** Continuous progress; prevailing course or direction; *esp.* the prevailing course of a person's life or habits. LME. ▸**c** Habitual condition, prevailing state, esp. of a person's mind. Now *rare* or merged with sense 2b above. L16.
†3 Quality, nature; *esp.* quality of tone. M16–E18.
4 The subject to which a metaphor refers, as distinct from the literal meaning of the words used. Opp. ***vehicle***. M20.

> **1a** J. H. BURTON Countless papers, expressed in . . verbose and tedious tenor. A. BROOKNER The very tenor of the conversation excluded men. **2b** J. RATHBONE Little of note occurred to disturb the even tenor of our lives.

▸ **II 5** MUSIC. **a** The adult male voice intermediate between the bass and the counter-tenor or alto; a part written for or sung by such a voice. LME. ▸**b** A singer having such a voice; a person singing a tenor part. L15. ▸**c** An instrument, string, bell, etc., having such a part or compass. M16.

> **5a** J. NEEL The . . high tenor rose effortlessly above the Bach Choir's best efforts. **b** BYRON The tenor's voice is spoilt by affectation. **c** *Melody Maker* Dave Gelly . . blows jazz tenor with the New Jazz Orchestra.

▸ **B** *adjective.* Designating or pertaining to a voice, instrument, string, etc., of the pitch intermediate between bass and alto; intended for or suited to such a voice or instrument. E16.
tenor clarinet, ***tenor recorder***, ***tenor saxophone***, ***tenor violin***, etc. **tenor bell** the largest bell of a peal or set. **tenor clef**: placing middle C on the second highest line of the stave.

tenor /ˈtɛnə/ *noun*[2]. Now *dial.* L15.
[Alt.]
= TENON *noun*[1].

tenore /teˈnoːre/ *noun.* M18.
[Italian: cf. TENOR *noun*[1] *& adjective.*]
= TENOR *noun*[1] 5a, b.
PRIMO tenore. ***tenore di grazia*** /di ˈgratsja/ [= of grace] a light or lyric tenor. ***tenore robusto*** /roˈbusto/ [= strong, robust] a dramatic tenor.

tenorino /tɛnəˈriːnəʊ/ *noun.* Pl. **-ni** /-ni/. M19.
[Italian, dim. of TENORE.]
A high tenor.

tenorist /ˈtɛn(ə)rɪst/ *noun.* M19.
[French *ténoriste*, Italian *tenorista*, from TENORE: see -IST.]
A person who sings a tenor part or plays a tenor instrument, *spec.* a person who plays the tenor saxophone.

tenorite /ˈtɛnərʌɪt/ *noun.* M19.
[from Michelo *Tenore* (1781–1861), president of Naples Academy of Sciences + -ITE[1].]
MINERALOGY. A triclinic oxide of copper that occurs in minute iron-grey scales or black masses and is an ore of copper.

tenoroon /tɛnəˈruːn/ *noun.* M19.
[from TENOR *noun*[1] *& adjective* + -OON.]
MUSIC. **1** Chiefly *Hist.* A wooden reed-instrument intermediate in pitch between the oboe and the bassoon. M19.
2 A reed-stop in an organ, resembling the oboe stop; any stop having a similar range. M19.

tenour *noun & adjective* see TENOR *noun*[1] *& adjective.*

tenpo *noun* var. of TEMPO *noun*[2].

tenrec /ˈtɛnrɛk/ *noun.* Also **tan-** /ˈtan-/. L18.
[French *tanrec* from Malagasy *tàndraka*, *tràndraka*.]
Any of several insectivorous mammals constituting the family Tenrecidae, native chiefly to Madagascar and resembling shrews or hedgehogs; *esp.* the tailless and spiny *Tenrec ecaudatus* of Madagascar and the Comoro Islands.

TENS /tɛnz/ *abbreviation.*
MEDICINE. Transcutaneous electrical nerve stimulation, a system of pain-relief in which an electric current is applied to nerve fibres by means of electrodes attached to the skin.

tense /tɛns/ *noun*. ME.
[Old French *tens* (mod. *temps*) from Latin *tempus*.]
1 Time. *obsolete* exc. with allus. to 2 below. ME.
2 GRAMMAR. Any of the various (sets of) forms of a verb which distinguish temporal and associated features of a denoted action or state in relation to the time of utterance, writing, etc.; the quality of a verb by which it represents or distinguishes such features. Cf. ASPECT *noun* 9, MOOD *noun*^{2} 2. LME.

> 📖 **2** C. P. MASON The tenses of the English verb are made partly by inflection. *fig.*: SIR W. SCOTT You are . . jealous, in all the tenses and moods of that amiable passion? ***sequence of tenses***: see SEQUENCE *noun* 4.

■ **tensed** *adjective* (GRAMMAR) having a tense or tenses L20. **tenseless** *adjective* (GRAMMAR) having no tenses or distinctions of tense L19. **tenselessly** *adverb* (GRAMMAR) without regard to or distinctions of tense M20.

tense /tɛns/ *adjective & verb*. L17.
[Latin *tensus* pa. pple of *tendere* stretch.]
▶ **A** *adjective*. **1** Esp. of a cord, fibre, or membrane (drawn) tight, (stretched) taut. L17. ▸**b** *spec.* (PHONETICS) of a speech sound, esp. a close vowel: pronounced with enhanced tension in the vocal muscles. Cf. LAX *adjective* 5c. E20.
2 *fig.* In a state of, causing, or characterized by nervous strain or tension; excited, excitable; keenly sensitive. E19.

> 📖 **1** A. W. TOURGEE Every muscle as tense as those of the tiger waiting for his leap. D. H. LAWRENCE His brows were tense with . . irritation. **2** V. GLENDINNING She did nothing but wait, tense and expectant.

▶ **B** *verb*. **1** *verb trans.* Make tense; stretch tight. Earliest as ***tensed*** *ppl adjective*. L17.
2 *verb intrans.* Become tense. Also foll. by *up*. M20.

> 📖 **1** G. CASEY When his turn came he tensed himself to go through with it. M. LAVIN He found himself tensing the muscles of his face. J. MCGAHERN The tensed body of the boy as he holds out his hand for the cane. **2** J. O'FAOLAIN I won't say 'relax' . . that only makes people tense up. A. LAMBERT I . . take her hand, which tenses and then relaxes.

■ **tensely** *adverb* L18. **tenseness** *noun* E18. **tensify** *verb trans.* (*rare*) make tense M19.

tensegrity /tɛnˈsɛɡrɪti/ *noun*. M20.
[from *tens(ional int)egrity*.]
A stable three-dimensional structure consisting of members under tension that are contiguous and members under compression that are not; the characteristic property of such a structure.

tenser /ˈtɛnsə/ *noun*. LME.
[Anglo-Norman = Old French *tense* defence, protection, from *tenser* (= medieval Latin *tensare*) protect, exact payment for protection, of unkn. origin: see -ER^{2}.]
Hist. An inhabitant of a city or borough who was not a citizen or freeman, but paid a rate for permission to reside and trade; a denizen.

tensible /ˈtɛnsɪb(ə)l/ *adjective*. E17.
[Late Latin *tensibilis*, from *tens-*: see TENSION, -IBLE.]
= TENSILE 1.

tensile /ˈtɛnsʌɪl, -ɪl/ *adjective*. E17.
[medieval Latin *tensilis*, from *tens-*: see TENSION, -ILE.]
1 Able to be stretched or drawn out; ductile. E17.
2 Of or pertaining to tension; exercising or sustaining tension. M19.
2 tensile strength the maximum sustainable stress in a material under tension (elongation). **tensile test**: for determining the tensile strength of a sample of material (usu. metal).
■ **tensility** /-ˈsɪl-/ *noun* M17.

tensimeter /tɛnˈsɪmɪtə/ *noun*. E20.
[from TENS(ION + -IMETER.]
CHEMISTRY. A form of manometer for measuring and comparing vapour pressures.

tensiometer /tɛnsɪˈɒmɪtə/ *noun*. E20.
[from TENSIO(N + -METER.]
1 An instrument for measuring the surface tension of a liquid, or esp. the tension of soil moisture. E20.
2 An instrument for measuring tension in a stretched wire, beam, rope, etc. M20.
■ **tensioˈmetric** *adjective* M20. **tensiometry** *noun* M20.

tension /ˈtɛnʃ(ə)n/ *noun & verb*. M16.
[Old & mod. French, or from Latin *tensio(n-)*, from *tens-* pa. ppl stem of *tendere* stretch: see -ION.]
▶ **A** *noun*. **1** PHYSIOLOGY & MEDICINE. The condition, in any part of the body, of being stretched or strained; a sensation indicating or suggesting this; a feeling of tightness. M16.
2 PHYSICS etc. A strained condition of (the particles of) a body when subjected to forces acting in opposite directions away from each other, balanced by forces of cohesion; a force or group of forces tending to stretch an object, esp. as a measurable quantity. L17. ▸**b** Chiefly PHYSIOLOGY & SOIL SCIENCE. = PRESSURE *noun* 2. L17. ▸**c** The degree of tightness or looseness of the stitches in knitting or machine sewing. L19.
3 *fig.* Mental straining, (a state or source of) psychological or social strain; *spec.* (*a*) intense intellectual effort; (*b*) an intense sense of uncertainty or expectation, suppressed excitement; (*c*) a situation, esp. a volatile one, characterized by strained relations between people, communities, or nations; (*d*) PSYCHOLOGY (a state of) stress or conflict produced by anxiety, need, mental disequilibrium, etc. M18. ▸**b** The balance created by the interplay of conflicting or contrasting elements in a work of art, esp. a poem. M20.
4 ELECTRICITY. The stress along lines of force in a dielectric. Also, potential difference, electromotive force; chiefly in ***high tension***, ***low tension***, (usu. *attrib.*). L18.

> 📖 **2** J. E. GORDON Wood is three or four times as strong in tension as it is in compression. **3** *Woman's Illustrated* Do you enjoy making amusing remarks to relieve tension in a conversation? *Times* Mr. Crosland . . spoke of the . . underlying tensions in the country. W. STYRON I sensed a disturbing tension in the room. P. ROAZEN Wilhelm had relieved his tensions by smoking. **b** N. FRYE The harsh . . poem . . will show the tension and driving accented impetus of music.

Comb. & phrases: NERVOUS ***tension***; PREMENSTRUAL ***tension***; ***surface tension***: see SURFACE *noun & adjective*; **tension bar** a (metal) bar used to apply or resist a tensile force; **tension wood** = REACTION ***wood***; ***vapour tension***: see VAPOUR *noun*.
▶ **B** *verb trans.* Subject to tension; tighten, make taut. Chiefly as ***tensioned*** *ppl adjective*. L19.

> 📖 W. H. HODGSON It might . . have snapped, through my having tensioned it too highly.

■ **tensional** *adjective* of, pertaining to, of the nature of, or affected with tension M19. **tensionally** *adverb* by means of tension, as a result of tension M20. **tensionless** *adjective* E20.

tensioner /ˈtɛnʃ(ə)nə/ *noun*. M20.
[from prec. + -ER^{1}.]
A device for applying tension to cables, pipelines, etc.

tensity /ˈtɛnsɪti/ *noun*. M17.
[formed as TENSE *adjective* + -ITY.]
The quality or condition of being tense; a state of tension.

tensive /ˈtɛnsɪv/ *adjective*. E18.
[French *tensif*, *-ive*, formed as prec.: see -IVE.]
Causing tension; esp. (of pain) giving a sensation of tension or tightness.

tensometer /tɛnˈsɒmɪtə/ *noun*. M20.
[from TENS(ION + -OMETER.]
An apparatus for measuring tension or tensile strength. Cf. TENSIOMETER.

tenson /ˈtɛns(ə)n/ *noun*. M19.
[French = Provençal *tenso*.]
A contest in verse-making between troubadours; a poem or song composed for or sung in such a contest.

tensor /ˈtɛnsə, -sɔː/ *noun*. E18.
[mod. Latin, from Latin *tendere* stretch (in sense 2 after *vector*): see -OR.]
1 ANATOMY. A muscle that stretches or tightens some part. Also ***tensor muscle***. E18.
2 MATH. †**a** In quaternions, a quantity expressing the ratio in which the length of a vector is increased. M–L19. ▸**b** An abstract entity represented by an array of components that are functions of coordinates such that, under a transformation of coordinates, the new components are related to the transformation and to the original components in a definite way. E20.
Comb.: **tensor field** a field for which a tensor is defined at each point; **tensor force** a force between two bodies that has to be expressed as a tensor rather than a vector, *esp.* a non-central force between subatomic particles.
■ **tensorial** /-ˈsɔːrɪəl/ *adjective* M20.

tent /tɛnt/ *noun*^{1}. ME.
[Old & mod. French *tente*, ult. from Latin *tent-* pa. ppl stem of *tendere* stretch.]
1 A portable shelter or dwelling of canvas, cloth, etc., supported by a pole or poles, or a frame, and stretched and secured by ropes fastened to pegs driven into the ground; *spec.* = PAVILION *noun* 1. ME. ▸**b** *fig.* An abode, residence, or dwelling-place. *arch.* LME.
2 *transf.* Anything liked to or resembling a tent; *spec.* (*a*) PHOTOGRAPHY a curtained box serving as a portable darkroom; (*b*) the silken web of a tent-caterpillar; (*c*) = OXYGEN ***tent***; (*d*) in Trinidad, a venue (orig. a temporary structure erected at carnival time) for calypso dancing. L16.
3 A portable open-air pulpit for use when a congregation is too large for a church. *Scot.* L17.
1 attrib.: ***tent-cloth***, ***tent-frame***, ***tent-pole***, etc.
Comb.: **tent-bed** (*a*) a small low bed used (esp. for a patient) in a tent, a camp-bed; (*b*) a bed with an arched canopy and covered sides; **tent-caterpillar** the gregarious larva of any of several American lasiocampid moths, esp. of the genus *Malacosoma*, which spins a tentlike web of silk; **tent city** a very large collection of tents; **tent club**: organized for the sport of pigsticking; **tent coat**, **tent dress**: that is narrow at the shoulders and very wide at the hem; **tent-door** the entrance or opening of a tent; ***tent dress***: see ***tent coat*** above; **tent-fly** = FLY *noun*^{2} 5; **tent-maker** (*a*) a person who makes tents; (*b*) (a moth whose larva is) a tent-caterpillar; **tent-master** a person in charge of a camp or tent; **tent-peg** a peg which, when stuck in the ground, holds an attached cord of a tent taut; **tent-pegger** a competitor in tent-pegging; **tent-pegging** a sport in which a rider at full gallop tries to carry off on the point of a lance a tent-peg fixed in the ground; **tent ring** *Canad.* a ring of stones for holding down a tent, tepee, etc.; **tent-sack** a large weatherproof sack for emergency use by a stranded mountaineer; **tent show** a show, esp. a circus, put on in a tent; **tent-stake** *US* = ***tent-peg*** above; **tent town** a temporary settlement, as of gold-miners, refugees, etc.; **tent-trailer** (orig. and chiefly *N. Amer.*) a kind of trailer consisting of a wheeled frame with a collapsible tent cover attached; **tent village** a small encampment, a douar.
■ **tentage** *noun* tents collectively, tent accommodation E17. **tentless** *adjective* E19. **tentlike** *adjective* resembling (that of) a tent M19. **tentwise** *adverb* in the manner or shape of a tent M16.

tent /tɛnt/ *noun*^{2}. *obsolete* exc. *Scot.* & *north*. ME.
[Aphet. from ATTENT *noun* or ENTENT *noun*.]
1 Attention, heed; care. ME.
†**2** = ATTENT *noun* 1. Only in ME.
■ **tentful** *adjective* (*rare*) careful, attentive LME.

tent /tɛnt/ *noun*^{3}. LME.
[Old & mod. French *tente*, from *tenter*, from Latin *temptare* touch, feel, try: cf. TEMPT. Sense 3 may be a different word.]
†**1** A surgical probe. LME–L17.
2 MEDICINE. Orig., a roll or wad, usually of soft absorbent material, often medicated, used in cleaning wounds, absorbing discharges, or keeping wounds or natural orifices open. Now usu. *spec.*, a piece of dried material (esp. sponge or seaweed) shaped to fit an orifice (esp. that of the cervix) and designed to dilate it slowly by swelling with moisture. LME.
†**3** A paste which sets hard, used in setting precious stones. L16–M17.

tent /tɛnt/ *noun*^{4}. LME.
[Spanish *tinto* dark-coloured, from Latin *tinct-* pa. ppl stem of *tingere* dye, colour.]
A sweet deep-red wine of low alcoholic content, chiefly from Spain, used esp. as sacramental wine. Cf. TINTO.

†**tent** *noun*^{5}. M16.
[Prob. abbreviation of TENTER *noun*^{1}.]
A frame for stretching embroidery, tapestry, etc.

tent /tɛnt/ *verb*^{1}. *obsolete* exc. *Scot.* & *north*. ME.
[App. from TENT *noun*^{2}.]
1 *verb intrans. & trans.* Give heed or pay attention *to* or to. ME.
2 *verb trans.* Take charge or care of, look after. LME.
†**3** *verb trans.* Observe, watch. *Scot.* E18–L19.
†**4** *verb trans.* Beware. Usu. with obj. clause. *Scot.* M18–M19.
5 *verb intrans.* Take care to prevent or hinder (a person) *from* doing something. *north*. L18.
6 *verb intrans.* Watch for and scare away (birds); guard (corn, seed, etc.) from birds. *north*. M19.

tent /tɛnt/ *verb*^{2} *trans.* Long *obsolete* exc. *Scot.* ME.
[Old French *tenter*: see TEMPT.]
Tempt.

tent /tɛnt/ *verb*^{3} *trans. arch.* L16.
[App. from TENT *noun*^{3}.]
Chiefly MEDICINE. Treat with a tent; apply a tent to. Formerly also, probe.

tent /tɛnt/ *verb*^{4}. M16.
[from TENT *noun*^{1}.]
†**1** *verb trans.* Put up (a tent or canvas). *rare*. M16–M17.
2 *verb intrans.* **a** Dwell or reside temporarily; sojourn. E17. ▸**b** *spec.* Live in a tent; camp. M19.
3 *verb trans.* Cover or canopy as with a tent. M19.
4 *verb trans.* Accommodate or lodge in a tent. M19.
5 *verb trans.* Arrange in a shape suggesting a tent; *esp.* = STEEPLE *verb* 3. M20.

> 📖 **3** *Microwave Know-how* Keep the meat hot . . by tenting it loosely with foil. **5** D. LEAVITT He had been sitting quietly . . his hands tented over his temples.

tentability /tɛntəˈbɪlɪti/ *noun*. *rare*. M19.
[Late Latin (Vulgate) *tentare* tempt, whence medieval Latin *tentabilis*: see -BILITY.]
= TEMPTABILITY.

tentacle /ˈtɛntək(ə)l/ *noun*. M18.
[Anglicized from TENTACULUM.]
1 ZOOLOGY. A slender flexible limb or appendage in an animal, esp. an invertebrate, used for grasping, or bearing sense organs. M18.
2 *fig.* A strong insidious binding force; a channel for covert gathering of information, exercise of influence, etc. Usu. in *pl.* M19.
3 BOTANY. A long thin extension, a tendril, a feeler; a sensitive glandular hair, as in a sundew. L19.

> 📖 **1** D. NICHOLS The animal remained . . on the sea-bottom and searched the surrounding area with its tentacles. **2** J. LE CARRÉ His tentacles extended to every banking house in Europe. **3** C. MILNE Brambles have sent out their annual tentacles of growth.

■ **tentacled** *adjective* having tentacles M19.

tentacula *noun* pl. of TENTACULUM.

tentacular /tɛnˈtakjʊlə/ *adjective*. E19.
[formed as TENTACULUM + -AR^{1}.]
Pertaining to or of the nature of a tentacle or tentacles; *fig.* of widespread (esp. covert) influence.

tentaculate /tɛnˈtakjʊlət/ *adjective*. M19.
[formed as prec. + -ATE[2].]
ZOOLOGY. Having tentacles.
■ Also **tentaculated** *adjective* L18.

tentacule /ˈtɛntəkjuːl/ *noun*. *rare*. M19.
[formed as TENTACLE: see -CULE.]
= TENTACLE.

tentaculiferous /tɛnˌtakjʊˈlɪf(ə)rəs/ *adjective*. Now *rare*. M19.
[from TENTACULUM + -I- + -FEROUS.]
Of an animal or organ: bearing tentacles.

tentaculiform /tɛnˈtakʊlɪfɔːm/ *adjective*. Now *rare*. M19.
[formed as prec. + -I- + -FORM.]
ZOOLOGY. Resembling a tentacle; long, slender, and flexible.

tentaculite /tɛnˈtakjʊlʌɪt/ *noun*. M19.
[from mod. Latin *Tentaculites* genus name of a typical form: see TENTACULUM, -ITE[1].]
PALAEONTOLOGY. A fossil invertebrate of uncertain affinities, found in marine sediments of Ordovician to Devonian age and having a conical, usually ringed shell.

tentaculum /tɛnˈtakjʊləm/ *noun*. Now *rare*. Pl. **-la** /-lə/. M18.
[mod. Latin from Latin *tentare* = *temptare* feel, try: see TEMPT, -CULE.]
= TENTACLE 1.

tentamen /tɛnˈteɪmɛn/ *noun*. Now *rare* or *obsolete*. Pl. ***-tamina*** /-ˈtamɪnə/. L17.
[Latin, from *tentare*: see TENTATIVE, TEMPT *verb*.]
An attempt, a trial, an experiment.

†**tentation** *noun* var. of TEMPTATION.

tentative /ˈtɛntətɪv/ *adjective* & *noun*. L16.
[medieval Latin *tentativus*, from Latin *tentat-* pa. ppl stem of *tentare* var. of *temptare* try: see TEMPT *verb*, -IVE.]
▶**A** *adjective*. Of the nature of an experiment or trial, experimental; provisional; hesitant, uncertain. L16.

> SCOTT FITZGERALD He took a tentative step to see if the weakness had gone. G. BATTISCOMBE Guesswork can only produce tentative conclusions. J. DUNN Her tentative grasp of the facts . . undermined her confidence.

▶**B** *noun*. Something done as an experiment or trial; an essay, an attempt. Now *rare*. M17.
■ **tentatively** *adverb* L16. **tentativeness** *noun* M19.

tented /ˈtɛntɪd/ *adjective*. E17.
[from TENT *noun*[1], *verb*[4]: see -ED[2], -ED[1].]
1 a Of a place: covered with tents. E17. ▸**b** Of an encampment: consisting of tents. L19.
2 Formed or shaped like a tent. M18.
3 a Of a person: lodged in or provided with a tent. E19. ▸**b** Of an activity etc.: held or occurring in a tent. L19.
4 Of a vehicle: having a tentlike cover, covered with a tilt. L19.

tenter /ˈtɛntə/ *noun*[1] & *verb*. ME.
[medieval Latin *tentorium*, from Latin *tent-* pa. ppl stem of *tendere* stretch.]
▶**A** *noun*. **1** A framework on which milled or printed cloth is stretched so that it can dry without shrinking or losing shape. Cf. STENTER *noun* 2. ME.
†**2** = TENTERHOOK 1. L16–M19.
†**3** MEDICINE. A roll or wad of absorbent material. Cf. TENT *noun*[3] 2. Only in 17.
▶**B** *verb trans*. **1** Stretch (cloth) on a tenter or tenters. LME.
†**2** *fig*. Set on tenterhooks; hurt as by stretching; rack, torture, (the feelings etc.). E17–M18.

tenter /ˈtɛntə/ *noun*[2]. M19.
[from TENT *verb*[4] + -ER[1].]
1 A person who lives or stays in a tent. M19.
2 A person whose job is to erect and strike tents. M19.

tenterhook /ˈtɛntəhʊk/ *noun*. L15.
[from TENTER *noun*[1] + HOOK *noun*.]
1 Any of the hooks set in a close row along the upper and lower bar of a tenter to hold the edges of the cloth firm; a hooked or right-angled nail or spike. Later also (*transf*.), a hooked organ or part. Usu. in *pl*. L15.
2 *fig*. In *pl*. That on which something is stretched, strained, or distorted; a cause of suffering or painful suspense. M16.

> **2** DISRAELI Honest men . . sometimes strain truth on the tenter-hooks of fiction. **on tenterhooks** in a state of painful suspense or agitated expectancy.

tenth /tɛnθ/ *adjective* & *noun*.
[Old English *teogoþa*, *tēoþa*, repl. in Middle English by forms from TEN + -TH[2]: cf. TITHE *adjective* & *noun*, TEIND.]
▶**A** *adjective*. Next in order after the ninth, that is number ten in a series, (represented by 10th). OE.
tenth Muse: see MUSE *noun*[1]. **tenth part** *arch*. = sense B.3 below. **tenth wave** a very large wave (*lit*. & *fig*.).
▶**B** *noun*. **1** The tenth person or thing of a category, series, etc., identified contextually, as day of the month, (following a proper name) person, esp. monarch or pope, of the specified name, etc. OE.
2 MUSIC. An interval embracing ten consecutive notes in the diatonic scale; a note a tenth above another given note; a chord of two notes a tenth apart. LME.
3 Each of ten equal parts into which something is or may be divided, a fraction which when multiplied by ten gives one, (= ***tenth part*** above); *spec*. (*Hist*.) ten per cent of a person's or property's annual produce or profits, as an ecclesiastical tax, royal subsidy, etc. L15.

> **3** J. COWELL No man dischargeth well his conscience . . that paieth not duly the tenth of every Lamb. *Scientific American* A few tenths of a percentage point . . reflect an enormous . . achievement. *New Scientist* Doing two-thirds of the world's work and earning one-tenth of its income. SUBMERGED ***tenth***.

Comb.: Forming compound numerals with multiples of a hundred, as ***two-hundred-and-tenth*** (*210th*), etc. Special combs., as **tenth-rate** *adjective* of extremely poor quality, very inferior; **tenth-value** *adjective* designating a thickness of material that reduces the intensity of radiation passing through it by a factor of ten.
■ **tenthly** *adverb* in the tenth place LME.

tenth /tɛnθ/ *verb trans*. *rare*. L16.
[from prec.]
Decimate, tithe.

Tenthredo /tɛnˈθriːdəʊ/ *noun*. M17.
[Latinization of Greek *tenthrēdōn* a kind of wasp.]
ENTOMOLOGY. A sawfly. Now only as mod. Latin genus name.

†**tentigo** *noun*. E17–M19.
[Latin.]
Priapism, getting an erection; lecherousness.
■ †**tentiginous** *adjective* excited to lust, lecherous, lascivious E17–E18.

tenting /ˈtɛntɪŋ/ *noun*. M19.
[from TENT *verb*[4] or *noun*[1] + -ING[1].]
1 Staying in or as in a tent; camping. Also (with ref. to a circus etc.) touring with and performing in a tent. Freq. *attrib*. M19.
2 Material for tents. L19.

tenting /ˈtɛntɪŋ/ *adjective*[1]. *rare*. E19.
[from TENT *noun*[1] + -ING[2].]
Resembling a tent; converging like the sides of a tent.

tenting /ˈtɛntɪŋ/ *adjective*[2]. L19.
[from TENT *verb*[4] + -ING[1].]
Of a circus: touring with or performing in a tent.

tentive /ˈtɛntɪv/ *adjective*. Long *obsolete* exc. *dial*. LME.
[Old French *tentif*, *-ive*, or aphet. from INTENTIVE or (in later use) ATTENTIVE. Cf. TENTY.]
= ATTENTIVE.

tentorium /tɛnˈtɔːrɪəm/ *noun*. Pl. **-ria** /-rɪə/. M17.
[Latin = tent, from *tent-* pa. ppl stem of *tendere* stretch: see -ORIUM.]
†**1** A tentlike covering. *rare*. Only in M17.
2 ANATOMY. A fold of the dura mater forming a partition between the cerebrum and cerebellum. E19.
3 ZOOLOGY. An internal skeletal framework in the head of an insect. L19.
■ **tentorial** *adjective* M19.

tent-stitch /ˈtɛntstɪtʃ/ *noun*. M17.
[from unkn. 1st elem. + STITCH *noun*[1].]
In embroidery etc., (a pattern worked in) a series of parallel stitches arranged diagonally across the intersections of the threads; a stitch in such a series.

tentwort /ˈtɛntwəːt/ *noun*. Now *rare* or *obsolete*. M16.
[Prob. from TAINT *noun* + WORT *noun*[1].]
The wall rue, *Asplenium ruta-muraria*.

tenty /ˈtɛnti/ *adjective*. Long *obsolete* exc. *Scot*. LME.
[formed as TENTIVE. Cf. HASTY, TARDY *adjective*.]
Attentive, watchful; cautious, prudent.
■ **tentily** *adverb* (*rare*) LME.

tenue /təny/ *noun*. E19.
[French, use as noun of fem. pa. pple of *tenir* hold, keep.]
Deportment, bearing; propriety, manners.

> A. L. ROWSE It was not a questioning of morals, but of taste and *tenue*. GRANDE ***tenue***.

tenues *noun* pl. of TENUIS.

tenui- /ˈtɛnjʊɪ/ *combining form*.
[from Latin *tenuis*: see -I-.]
Chiefly BOTANY & ZOOLOGY. Slender, narrow, thin.
■ **tenuiˈfolious** *adjective* narrow-leaved M17. **tenuiˈrostral** *adjective* (of a bird) slender-billed M19.

tenuious /tɪˈnjuːɪəs/ *adjective*. Now *rare* or *obsolete*. L15.
[from Latin *tenuis* thin + -OUS. See also TENUOUS.]
= TENUOUS.

tenuis /ˈtɛnjʊɪs/ *noun*. Pl. **-ues** /-jʊiːz/. M17.
[from Latin = thin, slender, fine, translating Greek *psilon* bare, smooth, so applied to the consonants kappa, pi, and tau.]
PHONETICS. (A letter representing) a voiceless stop.

tenuity /tɪˈnjuːɪti/ *noun*. LME.
[Latin *tenuitas*, from *tenuis* thin: see -ITY.]
1 Thinness; *spec*. (***a***) slenderness; (***b***) the state of being dilute or rarefied. LME.
2 Meagreness; feebleness; poverty. M16.

> **1** S. JOHNSON The quick transition from the thickness of the forepart, to the tenuity—the thin part—behind. M. F. MAURY Air may be expanded to an indefinite degree of tenuity. H. JAMES The tenuity of the thread by which his future hung.

tenuous /ˈtɛnjʊəs/ *adjective*. L16.
[Irreg. from Latin *tenuis* + -OUS. Cf. TENUIOUS.]
1 Of low density; sparse; rarefied; insubstantial. L16.
2 Slender, thin, slim; small. M17.
3 *fig*. Insignificant; meagre, weak; vague. Also (of a distinction), oversubtle. E19.

> **1** *Observer* The image of the sun faintly reflected back from . . tenuous gas in space. **2** P. D. JAMES The wave retreated to leave its tenuous lip of foam.

■ **tenuously** *adverb* L19. **tenuousness** *noun* E20.

tenure /ˈtɛnjə/ *noun*. LME.
[Old French, from *tenir* to hold from Latin *tenere*: see -URE.]
1 LAW. The (form of) right or title by which, or conditions under which, land or buildings are held, esp. when not freehold. Cf. TENEMENT 1. LME.
2 A holding of land; = TENEMENT 2. Long *rare* or *obsolete*. LME.
3 The action or fact of holding anything; the possession of a position, power, or office; the duration or period of such possession, a term. L16. ▸**b** (Title to) authority *over* or control *of* a person or thing. L19. ▸**c** *spec*. Guaranteed permanent employment in a job (esp. as a lecturer or teacher) after a probationary period. M20.

> **1 military tenure**: see MILITARY *adjective*. ***tenure in capite***: see CAPITE. ***tenure in villeinage***: see VILLEINAGE 1. **3** D. FRASER Brooke's tenure of command at Stanmore only lasted thirteen months. **c** *Times Lit. Suppl*. The first book gets you tenure. *attrib*.: *Nature* The tenure system simply allows dead wood to remain in the university.

Comb.: **tenure track** (chiefly *N. Amer*.) an employment structure whereby the holder of a (usu. academic) post is guaranteed consideration for eventual tenure, usu. within a specified period.
■ **tenurial** /tɛˈnjʊərɪəl/ *adjective* of or pertaining to the tenure of land L19. **tenurially** *adverb* L19.

tenure /ˈtɛnjə/ *verb trans*. L20.
[Back-form. from next.]
Give (a person) a tenured post.

tenured /ˈtɛnjəd/ *adjective*. M20.
[from TENURE *noun* + -ED[2].]
(Of a post, esp. in a university or school) carrying a guarantee of permanent employment until retirement; (of a teacher, lecturer, etc.) having guaranteed tenure of office.

tenuto /təˈnuːtəʊ/ *adverb*, *adjective*, & *noun*. M18.
[Italian, pa. pple of *tenere* hold.]
MUSIC. ▶**A** *adverb* & *adjective*. A direction: giving the note its full time-value; sustained(ly). (Abbreviation ***ten.***) M18.
▶**B** *noun*. Pl. **-tos**, **-ti** /-ti/. A note or chord played tenuto. M20.

teocalli /tiːəˈkali/ *noun*. E17.
[Amer. Spanish from Nahuatl *teo:kalli*, from *teo:tl* god + *kalli* house.]
An ancient Mexican or Central American place of worship, usually consisting of a truncated pyramid surmounted by a temple.

Teochew /tiːəʊˈtʃuː/ *noun*. L19.
[Chinese dial. var. of putonghua place-name *Cháozhōu*.]
A member of a people of the Shantou district of Guangdong in southern China; the form of Chinese spoken by this people.

teonanacatl /ˌtiːənɑːnəˈkat(ə)l, tiːənəˈnakət(ə)l/ *noun*. L19.
[Nahuatl, from *teo:tl* god + *nanacatl* mushroom.]
Any of several hallucinogenic fungi, esp. *Psilocybe mexicana*, found in Central America.

teosinte /tiːəʊˈsɪnti/ *noun*. L19.
[French *téosinté* from Nahuatl *teocintli*, app. from *teo:tl* god + *cintli*, *centli* dried ear of maize.]
A Mexican grass grown as fodder, *Zea mexicana*, allied to maize but with several stems from the base.

tepa /ˈtiːpə/ *noun*. M20.
[from the initial letters of TRI-, ETHYLENE, PHOSPH-, and AMIDE, elems. of the systematic name.]
CHEMISTRY. An organophosphorus compound, $PO(N(CH_2)_2)_3$, used as an insect sterilant and formerly to treat cancer.

tepache /teˈpatʃe/ *noun*. E20.
[Mexican Spanish, from Nahuatl *tepiatl*.]
Any of several Mexican drinks of varying degrees of fermentation, typically made with pineapple, water, and brown sugar.

tepal /'tɛp(ə)l, 'tiːp(ə)l/ *noun.* **M19.**
[French *tépale*, blend of *sépale* SEPAL and *pétale* PETAL *noun*.]
BOTANY. A segment of a perianth in which the corolla and calyx are not differentiated.

tepary /'tɛpəri/ *noun.* **E20.**
[Origin unkn.]
In full ***tepary bean***. A legume native to the south-western US, *Phaseolus acutifolius*, cultivated in Mexico, Arizona, etc., for its drought-resistant qualities.

tepee /'tiːpiː/ *noun.* Also **teepee**, **tipi**. **M18.**
[Sioux *tʰipi* dwelling.]
A conical tent of the N. American Indians, made of skins, cloth, canvas, etc., stretched over a frame of poles fastened together at the top (cf. WIGWAM). Now also, a structure imitating or resembling such a tent.

tepefy /'tɛpɪfʌɪ/ *verb trans. & intrans.* Also **-ify**. **M17.**
[Latin *tepefacere* make tepid from *tepere* be lukewarm: see -FY.]
Make or become tepid.

tephigram /'tɛfɪgram/ *noun.* **E20.**
[from TEE *noun*[1] (*T* being a symbol for temperature) + PHI (ϕ being a symbol for entropy) + DIA)GRAM.]
METEOROLOGY. A diagram in which one axis represents temperature and another potential temperature (as a measure of entropy), used to represent the thermodynamic state of the atmosphere at different heights.

tephra /'tɛfrə/ *noun.* **M20.**
[Greek = ashes.]
GEOLOGY. Dust and rock fragments that have been ejected into the air by a volcanic eruption.

tephramancy /'tɛfrəmansi/ *noun.* **M17.**
[from Greek *tephra* ashes + -MANCY.]
Divination by means of ashes.

tephrite /'tɛfrʌɪt/ *noun.* **L19.**
[from Greek *tephros* ash-coloured (from *tephra* ashes) + -ITE[1].]
GEOLOGY. Any of a class of fine-grained basaltic extrusive igneous rocks containing calcic plagioclase, augite, and nepheline or leucite.
■ **tephritic** /-'frɪtɪk/ *adjective* **L19.**

tephritid /tɪ'frɪtɪd/ *adjective & noun.* **M20.**
[mod. Latin *Tephritidae* (see below), from *Tephritis* genus name, prob. from Greek *tephros* ash-coloured: see -ID[3].]
ENTOMOLOGY. ▶**A** *adjective.* Of, pertaining to, or designating the dipteran family Tephritidae (formerly Trypetidae) of large fruit flies and gall flies. **M20.**
▶ **B** *noun.* A fly of this family. **M20.**

tephrochronology /ˌtɛfrəʊkrə'nɒlədʒi/ *noun.* **M20.**
[from TEPHRA + -O- + CHRONOLOGY.]
The dating of volcanic eruptions and other events by studying layers of tephra.
■ **tephrochrono'logical** *adjective* **M20.**

tephroite /'tɛfrəʊʌɪt/ *noun.* **M19.**
[Irreg. formed as TEPHRITE.]
MINERALOGY. An orthorhombic manganese silicate of the olivine group which forms ashy grey or reddish crystalline masses.

tepid /'tɛpɪd/ *adjective.* **LME.**
[Latin *tepidus*, from *tepere* be warm.]
1 Esp. of a liquid: slightly warm; neither hot nor cold. **LME.**
2 *fig.* = LUKEWARM 2. **E16.**
📖 **2** E. WAUGH The smart set . . were tepid in their support.
■ **tepidity** /tɛ'pɪdɪti/ *noun* the quality or condition of being tepid **M17.** **tepidly** *adverb* **L17.** **tepidness** *noun* = TEPIDITY **E19.**

tepidarium /tɛpɪ'dɛːrɪəm/ *noun.* Pl. **-ria** /-rɪə/. **E19.**
[Latin, formed as prec.: see -ARIUM.]
In an ancient Roman bath, the warm room between the frigidarium and the caldarium. Also, a similar room in a Turkish bath.

tepify *verb* var. of TEPEFY.

†**tepor** *noun.* **M17–M18.**
[Latin, from *tepere* be warm.]
= TEPIDITY.

teporingo /tɛpɒ'rɪŋgəʊ/ *noun.* Pl. **-os**. **M20.**
[Mexican Spanish.]
= ***volcano rabbit*** s.v. VOLCANO *noun*.

teppan-yaki /'tɛpanjaki/ *noun.* **L20.**
[Japanese, from *teppan* steel plate + *yaki* fry, grill, roast.]
A Japanese dish of meat, fish, or both, fried with vegetables on a hot steel plate forming the centre of the dining-table.

tequila /tɛ'kiːlə/ *noun.* **M19.**
[Mexican Spanish, from the name of a town producing the drink.]
A Mexican spirit made by distilling the fermented sap of a maguey, *Agave americana*, or a related species; a drink of this. Cf. MESCAL.
Comb.: **tequila plant** the maguey from the sap of which tequila is made; **tequila sunrise** a cocktail containing tequila and grenadine.

Tequistlatec /tɛ'kɪstlətɛk/ *noun & adjective.* **L19.**
[A village where it is spoken.]
(Of) the language of an American Indian people of SE Oaxaca, Mexico.
■ Also **Tequistla'tecan** *noun & adjective* **L19.**

ter /tə/ *preposition, adverb, & conjunction. non-standard.* **M19.**
[Repr. a pronunc.]
= TO *preposition, adverb, & conjunction.*

ter- /təː/ *combining form.*
[Latin *ter* thrice.]
Thrice, three times; threefold; *esp.* in CHEMISTRY, having three atoms or radicals of a particular kind.
¶ Largely superseded by TRI-.
■ **termo'lecular** *adjective* involving three molecules **E20.** **ter'polymer** *noun* a polymer composed of three different monomers **M20.** **terpolymeri'zation** *noun* polymerization in which three different monomers form a terpolymer **M20.** **ter'valent** *adjective* = TRIVALENT **M19.**

tera- /'tɛrə/ *combining form.*
[from Greek *teras* monster.]
Used in names of units of measurement etc. to denote a factor of one millon million (10^{12}), as ***tera-electronvolt***, ***terahertz***, ***terasecond***, ***teravolt***, ***terawatt***; also (in COMPUTING) denoting the closely equivalent factor of 2^{40} (approx. 1.100×10^{12}), as ***terabit***, ***terabyte***. Abbreviation ***T***.

teraflop /'tɛrəflɒp/ *noun.* **L20.**
[from TERA- + acronym from *floating-point operations per second* (with *-s* taken as pl. suffix -S[1]).]
COMPUTING. A unit of computing speed equal to one million million (10^{12}) or 2^{40} floating-point operations per second.

teraglin /'tɛrəglɪn/ *noun.* Chiefly *Austral.* **L19.**
[Aboriginal.]
Either of two edible sciaenid fishes, the geelbek, *Atractoscion aequidens*, and (in full ***silver teraglin***) the jewfish, *Otolithes ruber*, both found in Australian waters.

terai /tə'rʌɪ/ *noun.* **L19.**
[A belt of marshy jungle lying between the southern foothills of the Himalayas and the plains, from Hindi *tarāī* marshy lowlands.]
In full ***terai hat***. A wide-brimmed felt hat with a double-layered crown and a vent, worn by travellers etc. in subtropical regions.

terakihi *noun* var. of TARAKIHI.

terap /tə'rap/ *noun.* **M19.**
[Malay.]
A Malaysian evergreen tree, *Artocarpus elasticus*, of the mulberry family, closely related to the breadfruit tree. Also, the large edible fruit of this tree; the fibrous bark of the tree, used to make string or cloth.

teraphim /'tɛrəfɪm/ *noun pl.* (also treated as *sing.*). **LME.**
[Late Latin (Vulgate) *theraphim* from (Septuagint) Greek *theraphin* (*Judges* 17:5) from Hebrew *tĕrāpīm* (Aramaic *-in*).]
Holy images or household gods revered and used for divination among the pre-exilic Hebrews; *sing.* an individual one of these.
■ Also **teraph** *noun*, pl. **-s** [back-form. after *seraph*] **E19.**

terato- /'tɛrətəʊ, tɛ'ratəʊ/ *combining form.*
[from Greek *terat-*, *teras* monster: see -O-.]
Of or pertaining to monsters or abnormal forms and congenital malformations.
■ **teratocarci'noma** *noun*, pl. **-mas**, **-mata** /-mətə/, MEDICINE a form of malignant teratoma occurring esp. in the testis **M20.**

teratogen /tɛ'ratədʒ(ə)n, 'tɛrətədʒ(ə)n/ *noun.* **M20.**
[from TERATO- + -GEN.]
MEDICINE. An agent or factor which causes malformation of a developing embryo.

teratogenesis /tɛrətə'dʒɛnɪsɪs/ *noun.* **E20.**
[formed as prec. + -GENESIS.]
BIOLOGY & MEDICINE. The production of congenital malformations.
■ **teratogenic** *adjective* pertaining to teratogenesis; acting as a teratogen: **L19.** **teratoge'nicity** *noun* teratogenic property **M20.**

teratoid /'tɛrətɔɪd/ *adjective.* **L19.**
[from TERATO- + -OID.]
BIOLOGY & MEDICINE. Resembling a monster; formed by abnormal development.

teratology /tɛrə'tɒlədʒi/ *noun.* **L17.**
[from TERATO- + -LOGY.]
1 A marvellous or incredible tale; a collection of such tales. Also, mythology relating to fantastic creatures, monsters, etc. **L17.**
2 The branch of medicine and of developmental biology which deals with congenital defects and abnormal formations. **M19.**
■ **terato'logical** *adjective* of or pertaining to teratology **M19.** **teratologist** *noun* a specialist in teratology **M19.**

teratoma /tɛrə'təʊmə/ *noun.* Pl. **-mas**, **-mata** /-mətə/. **L19.**
[from TERATO- + -OMA.]
MEDICINE. A tumour, esp. of the gonads, formed of cells of distinct heterogeneous tissues foreign to the site of the tumour and arising from an embryological abnormality.
■ **teratomatous** *adjective* of the nature of a teratoma **L19.**

terbium /'təːbɪəm/ *noun.* **M19.**
[from *Ytterby*, Sweden (cf. YTTERBIUM) + -IUM.]
A rare silvery metallic chemical element, atomic no. 65, that is a member of the lanthanide series. (Symbol Tb.)
■ **terbia** *noun* terbium oxide, Tb_2O_3 **E20.**

terbutaline /təː'bjuːtəliːn/ *noun.* **M20.**
[from TER- + BUT(YL (elems. of the systematic name) + *-aline* after ISOPRENALINE etc.]
PHARMACOLOGY. A sympathomimetic agent used esp. as a bronchodilator in the treatment of asthma.

terce /təːs/ *noun.* Also **tierce**. See also TIERCE *noun*[1]. **LME.**
[Old French *terce* var. of Old & mod. French *tierce* from Latin *tertia* use as noun of fem. of *tertius* THIRD *adjective*.]
▶**I 1** ECCLESIASTICAL. The third of the daytime canonical hours of prayer, appointed for the third hour of the day (about 9 a.m.); the office appointed for this hour. Formerly also, the part of the day between 9 a.m. and noon. **LME.**
2 SCOTS LAW (now *Hist.*). A third share of a dead man's heritable estate allowed to his widow for life. **L15.**
▶**II** See TIERCE *noun*[1].
■ **tercer** *noun* (SCOTS LAW, now *rare* or *obsolete*) a widow who has terce **L16.**

tercel *noun* var. of TIERCEL *noun*.

tercentenary /təːsɛn'tiːn(ə)ri, -'tɛn, təː'sɛntɪn(ə)ri/ *adjective & noun.* **M19.**
[from TER- + CENTENARY.]
▶**A** *adjective.* Of or pertaining to a period of three hundred years or a tercentenary; tercentennial. **M19.**
▶**B** *noun.* A duration of three hundred years; *esp.* (a celebration of) a three-hundredth anniversary. **M19.**

tercentennial /təːsɛn'tɛnɪəl/ *adjective & noun.* **L19.**
[from TER- + CENTENNIAL.]
= TERCENTENARY *adjective & noun*.

terceroon /təːsə'ruːn/ *noun. rare.* **M18.**
[from Spanish *tercero* a third person, from *tercio* third (being third in descent from a black person): see -OON.]
A person with one parent a white person and the other a mulatto; a quadroon.

tercet /'təːsɪt/ *noun.* **L16.**
[French from Italian *terzetto*, from *terzo* (from Latin *tertius* third) + *-etto* -ET[1].]
PROSODY. A set or group of three lines rhyming together, or bound by double or triple rhyme with the adjacent triplet or triplets; *spec.* (***a***) each of the triplets of terza rima; (***b***) either of two triplets forming the last six lines of a sonnet.

tercio /'təːsɪəʊ, 'təːʃɪəʊ, *foreign* 'terθio/ *noun.* Pl. **-os** /-əʊz, *foreign* -ɔs/. In sense 1 also †**tertio**. **L16.**
[Spanish *tercio*, Italian †*tertio*, *terzo*, Portuguese *têrço* a regiment, from Latin *tertium* a third.]
1 A regiment of Spanish (or, formerly, Italian) infantry, orig. of the 16th and 17th cents. Also *gen.*, a body of infantry forming a main division of an army. **L16.**
2 a BULLFIGHTING. Each of the three stages of a bullfight. Also called ***suerte***. **M20.** ▸**b** Each of the three concentric circular areas into which a bullring is considered to be divided. **M20.**

terebellid /tɛrə'bɛlɪd/ *noun & adjective.* **M20.**
[from *Terebellidae* (see below) from use as genus name of mod. Latin *terebella*, dim. of *terebra* borer: see -ID[3].]
ZOOLOGY. ▶**A** *noun.* A marine tube-dwelling polychaete worm of the family Terebellidae, feeding by means of a crown of slender tentacles. **M20.**
▶**B** *attrib.* or as *adjective*. Of, pertaining to, or designating this family. **M20.**

terebene /'tɛrəbiːn/ *noun.* Now *rare.* **M19.**
[from TEREB(INTH + -ENE.]
†**1** CHEMISTRY. = TERPENE. **M–L19.**
2 PHARMACOLOGY. A mixture of fragrant liquid terpenoids obtained by the action of sulphuric acid on turpentine and formerly used in medicated soaps, inhalants, etc. **L19.**

terebenthene /tɛrə'bɛnθiːn/ *noun.* Now *rare.* **M19.**
[French *térébenthène*, *térébenthine* formed as TEREBINTHINA: see -ENE.]
CHEMISTRY. The chief constituent of oil of turpentine, α-pinene.

terebic /tə'rɛbɪk/ *adjective.* **M19.**
[from TEREB(INTH + -IC.]
CHEMISTRY. ***terebic acid***, a cyclic ester and carboxylic acid, $C_7H_{10}O_4$, obtained by oxidation of turpentine.

For other words beginning with *ter-* see the main alphabetic sequence of entries

terebinth /ˈtɛrəbɪnθ/ *noun.* LME.
[Old French *t(h)erebinte* (mod. *térébinthe*), corresp. to Spanish, Italian *terebinto* or their source Latin *terebinthus* from Greek *terebinthos*, earlier *terbinthos*, *terminthos*, of alien origin.]
1 Either of two large Mediterranean shrubs of the genus *Pistacia* (family Anacardiaceae) with leaves like those of the ash, *P. terebinthus*, a former source of turpentine, and *P. palaestina*. Also ***terebinth tree***. LME.
†**2** The resin from *Pistacia terebinthus*: see TURPENTINE. L15–L17.

terebinthina /tɛrəbɪnˈθiːnə/ *noun.* Now *rare.* L17.
[medieval Latin *terebinthina (resina)* terebinthine resin: see next.]
Chiefly PHARMACOLOGY. Turpentine.

terebinthine /tɛrəˈbɪnθʌɪn, -iːn/ *noun & adjective.* E16.
[Latin *terebinthinus* (= Greek *terebinthinos*), from *terebinthus*: see TEREBINTH, -INE¹.]
▶†**A** *noun.* **1** The terebinth. Only in E16.
2 Turpentine. L16–E18.
▶**B** *adjective.* **1** Of, pertaining to, of the nature of, or related to the terebinth. M16.
2 Of, pertaining to, or consisting of turpentine; turpentinic, turpentiny. M17.
▪ **terebinthinate** *adjective & noun* (**a**) *adjective* terebinthine, terebinthinated; (**b**) *noun* a product or preparation of turpentine: L17. **terebinthinated** *adjective* (*rare*) impregnated with turpentine M17. **terebinthinous** *adjective* of, pertaining to, or resembling (that of) the terebinth M19.

terebra /ˈtɛrɪbrə/ *noun.* Pl. **-bras**, **-brae** /-briː/. E17.
[Latin = borer.]
†**1** An instrument for boring, esp. a surgical trephine. E17–L18.
2 ENTOMOLOGY. The modified ovipositor or sting of a female hymenopteran, esp. of one which pierces plant tissues to lay its eggs. E18.

terebrant /ˈtɛrɪbr(ə)nt/ *adjective.* E19.
[Latin *terebrant-* pres. ppl stem of *terebrare* bore, from *terebra* borer: see -ANT¹.]
Having the function of boring or piercing; (of a hymenopteran insect) having a boring ovipositor.

terebrate /ˈtɛrɪbrət/ *adjective. rare.* E20.
[formed as next: see -ATE².]
ENTOMOLOGY. = TEREBRANT.

terebrate /ˈtɛrɪbreɪt/ *verb trans. & intrans.* Now *rare.* E17.
[Latin *terebrat-* pa. ppl stem of *terebrare*: see TEREBRANT, -ATE³.]
1 Pierce, bore, perforate (something); penetrate (something) by boring. E17.
2 = BORE *verb²*. *joc.* M19.
▪ **tereˈbration** *noun* (now *rare* or *obsolete*) the action of boring or perforating, esp. in surgery, in cultivating fruit trees, etc. LME.

terebratulid /tɛrɪˈbratjʊlɪd/ *noun & adjective.* M20.
[from mod. Latin *Terebratulida(e)* (see below), from *Terebratula* genus name, from *terebrat-* pa. ppl stem of *terebrare* bore: see -ULE, -ID³.]
ZOOLOGY. ▶**A** *noun.* A member of the family Terebratulidae or the order Terebratulida of mainly fossil articulate brachiopods (lamp-shells) originating in the Devonian, having a short pedicle and a calcareous loop supporting the tentacles. M20.
▶**B** *adjective.* Of, pertaining to, or designating this family or order. M20.

teredo /təˈriːdəʊ/ *noun.* Pl. **-dos**, **-dines** /-dɪniːz/. LME.
[Latin from Greek *terēdōn*, from base of *teirein* rub hard, wear away, bore.]
ZOOLOGY. Orig., any wood-boring invertebrate animal. Now *spec.* a boring bivalve mollusc of the genus *Teredo* (see ***shipworm*** s.v. SHIP *noun*).

Terek /ˈtɛrɪk/ *noun.* L18.
[A river flowing into the Caspian Sea from the Caucasus, at whose mouth the bird is common during migration.]
In full ***Terek sandpiper***. An Old World sandpiper, *Xenus cinereus*, with a slightly recurved bill and pale brown and white plumage, which breeds in northern Eurasia and winters on southern coasts esp. around the Indian Ocean.

terem /ˈtɛrəm/ *noun.* L19.
[Russian, lit. 'tower'.]
Hist. In Russia, a separate and secluded chamber or apartment for women.

Terena /tɛˈreɪnə/ *noun & adjective.* Also **Tereno** /-nəʊ/. L19.
[Terena.]
▶**A** *noun.* Pl. same, **-s**.
1 A member of a people of the southern Mato Grosso in Brazil. L19.
2 The Arawakan language of this people. M20.
▶**B** *attrib.* or as *adjective.* Of or pertaining to the Terena or their language. E20.

Terentian /təˈrɛnʃ(ə)n/ *adjective.* L16.
[from Latin *Terentianus*, from *Terentius* Terence (see below): see -AN.]
Of, pertaining to, or in the style of the Roman dramatic poet Terence (Publius Terentius Afer, 190–159 BC).

terephthalic /tɛrəfˈθalɪk/ *adjective.* M19.
[from TEREBIC + PHTHALIC.]
CHEMISTRY. ***terephthalic acid***, the *para* isomer of phthalic acid, used esp. in the manufacture of plastics and other polymers.
▪ **terephthalamide** *noun* an amide of terephthalic acid M19. **terephthalate** *noun* a salt or ester of terephthalic acid M19.

teres /ˈtɛriːz/ *noun.* E18.
[mod. Latin from Latin: see TERETE.]
ANATOMY. Either of two muscles arising from the shoulder-blade and attached to the upper part of the humerus, one (in full ***teres major***) drawing the arm towards the body and rotating it inwards, the other (in full ***teres minor***) rotating it outwards.
Phrases: **pronator teres** a pronating muscle of the forearm, between the humerus and ulna, near the elbow, and the radius.

†**teresa** *noun.* L18–M19.
[Prob. from Empress Maria *Theresa* of Austria (1717–80).]
A light gauze scarf worn over the head by women in the 18th cent.

Teresian /təˈriːsɪən, -zɪən, -ʒ(ə)n/ *noun & adjective.* Also **Th-**. E17.
[from St *Teresa* of Avila (1515–82), Spanish Carmelite nun + -IAN.]
▶**A** *noun.* A member of a reformed order of Carmelite nuns and friars (Discalced Carmelites) founded by St Teresa of Avila. Also, a member of a religious society of Roman Catholic laywomen, named after St Teresa. E17.
▶**B** *adjective.* Of or pertaining to St Teresa or the order she founded. M19.

terete /təˈriːt/ *adjective.* E17.
[Latin *teret-*, *teres* rounded (off).]
Smooth and rounded; *spec.* in BOTANY & ZOOLOGY, cylindrical or slightly tapering, without substantial furrows or ridges.

tereu /tiːˈruː/ *noun.* Chiefly *poet.* L16.
[Latin, voc. of *Tereus*, in Greek mythol. the husband of Procne and raper of Philomela (who was changed into a nightingale: the nightingale's song being supposed to perpetuate her reproachful calls).]
Repr. the note supposed to be sung by a nightingale.

terga *noun* pl. of TERGUM.

Tergal /ˈtəːg(ə)l/ *noun.* M20.
[French, formed as TER(EPHTHALIC + GAL(LIC *adjective*¹. Cf. TERITAL.]
(Proprietary name for) a kind of polyester yarn; fabric made of this.

tergal /ˈtəːg(ə)l/ *adjective.* M19.
[from Latin *tergum* back + -AL¹.]
ZOOLOGY. Of or pertaining to the tergum; dorsal.

tergeminous /təːˈdʒɛmɪnəs/ *adjective. rare.* M17.
[from Latin *tergeminus* (poet. var. of TRIGEMINUS) born three at a birth + -OUS.]
Threefold, triple.

tergite /ˈtəːdʒʌɪt, -gʌɪt/ *noun.* L19.
[from TERGUM + -ITE¹.]
ZOOLOGY. A sclerite of a tergum of an arthropod; a section of the dorsal exoskeleton. Cf. PLEURITE, STERNITE.

tergiversate /ˈtəːdʒɪvəseɪt, -ˌvəːseɪt/ *verb intrans.* M17.
[Latin *tergiversat-* pa. ppl stem of *tergiversari* turn one's back, practise evasion, from *tergum* back + *vers-* pa. ppl stem of *vertere* turn: see -ATE³. Cf. TERGIVERSE.]
1 Change one's party or one's principles, turn renegade, apostatize; use subterfuge or evasion. Freq. as ***tergiversated*** *ppl adjective*, ***tergiversating*** *verbal noun & ppl adjective*. M17.
2 *lit.* Turn the back (for flight or retreat). *rare.* L19.
▪ **tergiversator** *noun* E18.

tergiversation /ˌtəːdʒɪvəˈseɪʃ(ə)n/ *noun.* L16.
[Latin *tergiversatio(n-)*, formed as prec.: see -ATION.]
1 The action of turning one's back on or forsaking something; desertion or abandonment of a cause, party, etc.; betrayal, apostasy. Also, an instance of this. Formerly also, refusal to obey. L16.
2 Turning from straightforward action or statement; shifting of stance, equivocation, prevarication. Also, an instance of this, an evasion, a subterfuge. L16.
†**3** *lit.* The turning of one's back, esp. in preparation for flight or retreat. Only in M17.

> 📖 **2** *New Yorker* The familiar tergiversations of city politicians.

▪ **tergiverˈsatory** *adjective* evasive, shifty, given to tergiversation L19.

tergiverse /ˈtəːdʒɪvəːs/ *verb. rare.* E17.
[Latin *tergiversari* TERGIVERSATE.]
†**1** *verb trans.* Turn backwards, reverse. Only in E17.
2 *verb intrans.* = TERGIVERSATE. L17.

tergum /ˈtəːgəm/ *noun.* Pl. **-ga** /-gə/. E19.
[Latin = back.]
ZOOLOGY. **1** A sclerotized region forming the dorsal part of each segment of the body of an arthropod. Cf. PLEURON, STERNUM 2. E19.
2 Either of the two upper plates of the shell of a cirripede. M19.

Terital /ˈtɛrɪt(ə)l/ *noun.* M20.
[Italian, formed as TERGAL *noun* + ITAL(IAN *adjective*.]
Any of various natural and synthetic (chiefly polyester) fibres; fabric or floor-covering made of this.
¶ Proprietary name in the US.

teriyaki /tɛrɪˈjɑːki/ *noun.* M20.
[Japanese, from *teri* gloss, lustre + *yaki* grill, fry, roast.]
A Japanese dish consisting of fish or meat marinated in soy sauce and grilled. Also (in full ***teriyaki sauce***), a mixture of soy sauce, sake, ginger, etc., used as a marinade or glaze.

term /təːm/ *noun.* ME.
[Old & mod. French *terme* from Latin TERMINUS.]
▶**I** A limit in space or time.
1 a That which limits the extent of something; a limit, an extremity, a physical boundary. Usu. in *pl.* Long *arch. rare.* ME. ▸**b** Extreme limit of duration; conclusion, termination. Now *rare.* ME. ▸**c** That to which movement or action is directed or tends; an object, an end, a goal. Formerly also occas., a starting-point, an origin. Now *rare* or *obsolete.* LME.
2 A definite point in time at which something is to be done, esp. at the beginning or end of a period; a set or appointed time or date, esp. for payment of money due. Now only *spec.* (chiefly *Scot.*), each of the days in the year fixed for payment of rent, wages, beginning and end of tenancy, etc.; a term-day, a quarter day. ME.
3 A portion of time having definite limits; the length of time for which something lasts or is intended to last; a period, esp. a set or appointed period of office, imprisonment, investment, etc.; duration, span of (remaining) life. ME.
4 ASTROLOGY. A part of a sign of the zodiac assigned to a particular planet. Now *rare* or *obsolete.* LME.
5 Each of the periods (usu. three or four in the year) appointed for the sitting of courts of law, or for instruction and study in a university or school. Also (freq. without article) = ***term-time*** below. LME. ▸†**b** The session of a court of law; the court in session. E16–M17.
6 LAW. In full ***term of years***, (*US*) ***term for years***. An estate or interest in land etc. for a certain period. LME.
7 †**a** In *pl.* The menstrual periods; *transf.* the menstrual discharge, menses. M16–E18. ▸**b** The completion of the period of pregnancy; the (normal) time of childbirth. Also ***full term***. M19.

> 📖 **1b** GIBBON He had now reached the term of his prosperity. **3** C. CAUSLEY Kos . . Where Hippocrates lived out his term. R. TRAVERS Ashe served five terms of six months imprisonment. E. SEGAL FDR was elected to an unprecedented fourth term. *Money Management* Investments with tax payable during the term produce lower returns. **5** ***Hilary term***, ***Michaelmas term***, ***Trinity term***; ***Easter term***, ***Lent term***, ***spring term***, ***summer term***, etc. **7b** G. BOURNE The approximate length of the baby at term is 50 cm. See also PRETERM.

▶**II** Limiting conditions.
8 a In *pl.* Conditions under which some action may be undertaken, a dispute settled, an agreement reached, etc.; stipulated requirements or limitations. ME. ▸**b** *spec.* Conditions with regard to payment for goods or services; payment offered, charges made. L17. ▸**c** A condition, a prerequisite *of* something. *rare.* L18.
†**9** *sing.* & (usu.) in *pl.* Condition, state; in weakened sense, relation, respect. LME–M17.
10 In *pl.* Standing, footing, mutual relation between two people or parties. Usu. in phrs with qualifying words, as ***on equal terms***, ***on good terms***, ***on terms of intimacy***, etc. (formerly with *in*). M16.

> 📖 **8a** A. WILSON Any sensible executors . . would have had the terms of Stokesay's will annulled long ago. G. BROWN Under the terms of my lease I wasn't allowed to sub-let. R. JENKINS Neither of the two was willing to accept the other's terms. **9** SHAKES. *Haml.* A sister driven into desp'rate terms. **10** E. JONES The two men remained on fairly friendly terms.

▶**III** An expression. [from Latin *terminus* orig. rendering Greek *horos* boundary, used in sense 13 below.]
11 a A word or phrase used in a definite or precise sense in some particular subject or discipline; a technical expression. LME. ▸**b** Any word or group of words expressing a notion or conception, or used in a particular context; an expression (*for* something). Usu. with qualifying adjective or phr. L15.
12 In *pl.* Words or expressions collectively (usu. of a specified kind); manner of expressing oneself, way of speaking. Usu. with qualifying adjective preceded by *in*. LME.
13 MATH. Either of the two quantities composing a ratio or a fraction; each of the quantities forming a series or progression; each of two or more quantities in an algebraical expression or equation, esp. connected by the

For other words beginning with *ter-* see the entry for **ter-**

signs of addition or subtraction. LME. ▸**b** *gen.* A member or item in a series. M19. ▸**c** *PHYSICS.* Each of a set of numbers corresponding to an atomic state, being proportional to the binding energy of a valence electron, such that lines in the spectrum of an atom have wave numbers given by the differences between two numbers in the set; an atomic state so represented. Also ***spectral term***. E20.

14 *LOGIC.* Each of the two elements (subject and predicate) of a proposition; each of the three elements combined in the premisses of a syllogism (***major term***, ***middle term***, ***minor term*** below). M16.

> 📖 **11a** E. L. MASCALL Scientific theories need . . technical terms . . whose definition . . is extremely complicated. **b** M. MEAD The animal world is drawn on . . for terms of abuse and . . love. ***term of endearment***, ***term of reproach***, etc. **12** J. WAIN You're telling me, in pretty unmistakable terms, to mind my own business.

▸ **IV 15** *ARCHITECTURE.* A pillar or pedestal, usu. squared and narrower at the foot, from which springs a statue or bust representing the head or upper part of the body; a terminal figure. Cf. HERM, TERMINUS 2b. E17.

16 *NAUTICAL.* In full ***term-piece***. A piece of carved work below the taffrail of a wooden ship. *obsolete* exc. *Hist.* M19.

Phrases: **absolute term** a term in an equation or formula which does not involve the variable or unknown quantity. *BUILDING-term*. **come to terms** agree on conditions; come to an agreement; *fig.* (foll. by *with*) reconcile oneself to, become reconciled with. *CONNOTATIVE term*. ***eat one's terms***: see EAT *verb*. **full term** (*a*) = sense 7b above; (*b*) an unabbreviated expression; (*c*) (usu. with cap. initials) the part of a university term during which lectures are given. ***in no uncertain terms***: see UNCERTAIN *adjective* 3b. **in terms** (*a*) *pred.* (now *rare*) engaged in arranging conditions, negotiating; (*b*) *adverbial* expressly, plainly; formerly also = ***on terms*** (a) below. **in terms of** in the mode of expression or thought belonging to (a subject or category); *loosely* as regards, with reference to; *MATH.* (of a series or expression) stated in terms involving some particular quantity. ***law term***: see LAW *noun*[1]. ***long-term***: see LONG *adjective*[1]. **lowest terms** *MATH.* the form of a fraction when the numerator and denominator are the least possible, i.e. have no common factor; *fig.* the simplest condition of anything. **major term** *LOGIC* the term which enters into the predicate of the conclusion of a syllogism. **make terms** agree on conditions, come to terms. **middle term** *LOGIC* a term common to both premisses of a syllogism. **minor term** *LOGIC* the term which forms the subject of the conclusion of a syllogism. **on one's own terms**, **on its own terms** in a manner dictated by the person or thing concerned. ***on speaking terms***: see SPEAKING *verbal noun*. **on terms** (*a*) *adverbial* on (certain) conditions; (*b*) *pred.* on friendly terms; on equal terms (esp. with regard to score at cricket etc.); (now *rare*) = ***in terms*** (a) above. ***proprietary term***: see PROPRIETARY *adjective* 2. ***short-term***: see SHORT *adjective*. **terms of reference** the points referred to an individual or group for decision or report; that which defines the scope of an inquiry. **terms of trade** the ratio between the prices paid for imports and those received for exports. **think in terms of** *colloq.* make (a particular consideration) the basis of one's attention, plans, etc.

Comb.: **term-catalogue** a catalogue of the books and other publications during a term or quarter; **term-day** a day appointed as a term (sense 2 above), esp. for payment of money due; *spec.* each of the Scottish quarter days, esp. Whitsunday and Martinmas day, on which tenancies and the engagement of servants customarily begin; **term paper** *N. Amer.* a student's essay or dissertation representative of the work done during a single term; ***term-piece***: see sense 16 above; **term-policy** an insurance policy issued for a definite term or period; **term symbol** *PHYSICS* a symbol of the type ^3P, denoting the values of *L* and *S* for a spectral term; **term-time** the part of the year which falls within an academic or legal term; **termwise** *adverb & adjective* (*MATH.*) (carried out) term by term, treating each term separately.

■ **termless** *adjective* (*a*) boundless, endless; (*b*) *rare* (*poet.*) indescribable; (*c*) *rare* without terms or conditions: M16.

term /tɜːm/ *verb trans.* LME.

[In sense 1 prob. from French †*termer* bring to an end; in senses 2, 3 from the noun.]

†**1** Bring to an end or conclusion; terminate. LME–L16.

2 Express or denote by a particular term or terms; name, call, denominate, designate. M16.

†**3** State, affirm. L16–M17.

> 📖 **2** P. ACKROYD Eliot's preoccupation with what he termed 'The Social Function of Poetry.'

termagant /ˈtɜːməg(ə)nt/ *noun & adjective.* ME.

[Old French *Tervagan*(*t* from Italian *Trivigante*, *-vag-*, explained as if from Latin TRI- + *vagant-*, pres. ppl stem of *vagari* wander: see -ANT[1].]

▸ **A** *noun.* **1** (**T-**.) A god imagined in medieval Christendom to be worshipped esp. by Muslims and represented in mystery plays as a violent overbearing personage. Long *arch.* ME.

2 A violent, boisterous, overbearing, or quarrelsome person; a blusterer, a bully. Now usu. *spec.*, a violent, overbearing, or quarrelsome woman. E16.

▸ **B** *attrib.* or as *adjective.* Having the character of a termagant. L16.

> 📖 C. STEAD Saul (who only in fishing found peace from his termagant wife).

■ **termagancy** *noun* termagant quality, violence of temper or disposition E18.

termer /ˈtɜːmə/ *noun. obsolete* exc. *Hist.* E16.

[from TERM *noun* + -ER[1].]

†**1** = TERMOR. E16–M17.

2 A person resorting to London during term, either for legal business, or for amusement etc. M16.

†**3** A person who holds office only for a term or limited period. Only in M17.

termes *noun* see TERMITE.

terminable /ˈtɜːmɪnəb(ə)l/ *adjective.* LME.

[from TERMINE *verb* + -ABLE.]

†**1** That may be determined or finally decided. Only in LME.

2 Able to be terminated; that may come or be brought to an end; limitable, finite, not lasting or perpetual. L16.

■ **termina'bility** *noun* L19. **terminableness** *noun* M19. **terminably** *adverb* L16.

terminal /ˈtɜːmɪn(ə)l/ *adjective & noun.* LME.

[Latin *terminalis*, from *terminus* end, boundary: see -AL[1].]

▸ **A** *adjective.* **1** Occurring at the end (in time); forming the last member of a series or succession; closing, final, ultimate. (*rare* before M19.) LME. ▸**b** *MEDICINE.* Of or pertaining to the final stage of a fatal disease, or a patient or patients with a disease in such a stage. L19. ▸**c** Ruinous, disastrous, very great; incurable, irreversible. *colloq.* L20.

†**2** *HERALDRY.* Of a coat of arms: differenced by a border. L15–L16.

3 a Pertaining to or marking a boundary. Now *rare.* M18. ▸**b** Designating a statue, figure, etc. terminating in and apparently springing from a pillar or pedestal, or the pillar or pedestal itself. Cf. TERM *noun* 15, TERMINUS 2b. M19.

4 Situated at or forming the end or extremity of something; *spec.* (*a*) *CRYSTALLOGRAPHY* designating the faces, edges, or angles of a crystal at the extremities of its longest axis; (*b*) *ZOOLOGY & ANATOMY* situated at or forming the (outer) end of a part or series of parts; (*c*) *BOTANY* (of a flower, inflorescence, etc.) growing at the end of a stem, branch, etc. (opp. ***axillary***). E19. ▸**b** Situated at the end of a railway line; forming or pertaining to a (railway) terminus. M19.

5 Belonging to or lasting for a term or definite period; *esp.* pertaining to a university or law term; occurring every term or at fixed terms; termly. E19.

6 *LOGIC.* Pertaining to a term. *rare.* L19.

> 📖 **1** *New Statesman* People . . speculated whether the Labour Party was not in the process of terminal disintegration. *New Yorker* I had eighty-seven days of terminal leave when the war was over. **b** *Times* She is in hospital with terminal cancer. **c** *Times* A bad case of terminal tiredness had lowered my resistance. **4** *Garden* Sweetly scented flowers . . conspicuous in dense terminal clusters.

Special collocations: **terminal ballistics** the branch of ballistics that deals with the impact of the projectile on the target. **terminal guidance**: of a missile immediately prior to detonation. **terminal juncture** *LINGUISTICS* a juncture that occurs at the end of a syntactic unit. **terminal market** *COMMERCE* a market that deals in futures. **terminal moraine** *GEOLOGY* a moraine at the lower end of a glacier. **terminal nosedive** *AERONAUTICS* a nosedive during which an aircraft reaches its terminal velocity. **terminal string** *LINGUISTICS* in transformational grammar, a string consisting wholly of terminal symbols. **terminal symbol** *LINGUISTICS* in transformational grammar, a symbol that cannot be further rewritten. **terminal velocity** the constant speed that a freely falling object eventually attains when the resistance of the medium prevents further acceleration.

▸ **B** *noun.* †**1** In *pl.* [Latin *Terminalia*.] An ancient Roman festival held annually in honour of the god Terminus. *rare.* Only in M17.

2 A part or structure situated at or forming the end, or an end, of something; *spec.* (*a*) *ELECTRICITY* each of the free ends of an open circuit (by connecting which the circuit is closed); a structure forming such an end, as each of the metal contacts of a battery etc.; (*b*) *PHYSIOLOGY* the structure at the end of a nerve fibre; (*c*) a carving or other ornament at the end of something, as a finial; (*d*) a device for entering data into a computer or receiving its output; *esp.* one that can be used by a person as a means of two-way communication with a computer. M19.

3 A final syllable, letter, or word; a termination. *rare.* M19.

4 a A station at the end of a railway line, a terminus; a place or town at which a railway line has a terminus. Also, a terminus for long-distance buses etc.; a departure and arrival building for air passengers at an airport. L19. ▸**b** In *pl.* Charges made by a railway company for the use of a terminus or other station, esp. for loading or unloading goods etc. Now *rare.* L19. ▸**c** An installation where oil is stored at the end of a pipeline or at a port of call for oil tankers. M20.

5 A terminal figure; = TERM *noun* 15, TERMINUS 2b. L19.

6 A person with a terminal illness. M20.

■ **terminally** *adverb* M17.

terminalia /tɜːmɪˈneɪlɪə/ *noun.* M19.

[mod. Latin (see below), from Latin *terminalis* TERMINAL *adjective* + -IA[2].]

Any of numerous evergreen tropical trees constituting the genus *Terminalia* (family Combretaceae), which have leaves freq. clustered at the end of branches and include the myrobalan, *T. bellirica* and *T. chebula*, and the Indian almond, *T. catappa*.

terminalization /ˌtɜːmɪn(ə)lʌɪˈzeɪʃ(ə)n/ *noun.* Also **-isation**. E20.

[from TERMINAL *adjective* + -IZATION.]

CYTOLOGY. The movement of a chiasma or chiasmata towards the end of a separating chromosome pair.

■ **terminalized** *adjective* (of a chiasma) that has undergone terminalization M20.

terminate /ˈtɜːmɪnət/ *ppl adjective.* LME.

[Latin *terminatus* pa. pple of *terminare*: see next, -ATE[2].]

Limited, bounded, ended, having a definite limit or termination. Now usu. *spec.*, (*a*) *MATH.* (of a decimal) not recurring or infinite; (*b*) *GRAMMAR* (*rare*) = TERMINATIVE *adjective* 4b.

terminate /ˈtɜːmɪneɪt/ *verb.* L16.

[Latin *terminat-* pa. ppl stem of *terminare* limit, end, from *terminus* end, boundary: see -ATE[3].]

▸ **I** *verb trans.* †**1** Determine; state definitely. Also, express in words. *rare.* L16–E18.

2 Direct (an action) to something as object or end. Foll. by *in*, *to*, *upon*. Now *rare* or *obsolete.* L16. ▸†**b** Of a thing: be the object of (an action). M17–E18.

3 Bring to an end, put an end to, cause to cease; finish, end (an action, condition, etc.). E17. ▸**b** Come at the end of, form the conclusion of. L18. ▸**c** End (a pregnancy) before term by artificial means. M20. ▸**d** Dismiss from employment. *N. Amer. colloq.* L20. ▸**e** Assassinate. *N. Amer. colloq.* L20.

†**4** Limit, restrict, confine *to* or *in*. Only in 17.

5 Bound or limit spatially; form the physical end or extremity of. Now usu. in *pass.* M17.

> 📖 **3** V. BRITTAIN Death had . . terminated the . . intimate correspondences. *Acorn User* The program may be terminated by typing 'QUIT'. **d** J. KRANTZ If you terminate her she'll be working for Ford . . tomorrow. ***e terminate with extreme prejudice***: see PREJUDICE *noun* 1.

▸ **II** *verb intrans.* **6** Come to an end, so as to extend no further; have its ultimate end (or beginning) *in* something. E17.

7 Come to an end (in space); *esp.* have its end or extremity at a specified place, or of a specified form; end *at*, *in*, or *with* something; (of a train or bus service, etc.) come to a terminus, go no further. M17. ▸**b** Of a word: end *in* (a specified letter, syllable, etc.). E19.

8 Be directed to something as object or end. *rare.* L17.

9 Come to an end (in time); end, cease, conclude. Also, issue, result *in* something. E18.

> 📖 **6** M. HALE All this vicissitude of things must terminate in a first cause. **7** J. BARTH The boulevard terminates in a circular roadway. **9** I. MURDOCH With this incident my relations with Sadie must terminate.

termination /tɜːmɪˈneɪʃ(ə)n/ *noun.* LME.

[Old French *termination*, *terminaison* or Latin *terminatio*(*n-*), formed as prec.: see -ATION.]

▸ **I** The action of terminating.

†**1** Determination, decision. LME–M17.

2 The action of putting an end to something or bringing something to a close. Formerly also, the action of limiting something spatially, bounding. E17. ▸**b** *CHEMISTRY & BIOCHEMISTRY.* The cessation of the building up of a polymer molecule. M20. ▸**c** Dismissal from employment. Chiefly *N. Amer.* M20. ▸**d** The ending of pregnancy before term by artificial means; *esp.* an induced abortion. M20. ▸**e** Assassination (*spec.* of an intelligence agent). L20.

▸ **II** The point or part in which anything ends.

3 End (in time), cessation, close, conclusion. Also, outcome, result. L15.

4 The final syllable, letter, or group of letters in a word; *spec.* in *GRAMMAR*, a final element affixed to a word or stem to express some relation or modification of sense; an (inflectional or derivative) ending, a suffix. M16.

5 A limit, a bound; an end, an extremity (of a material object or portion of space). M18.

■ **terminational** *adjective* (chiefly *GRAMMAR*) of, pertaining to, or forming a termination or terminations; closing, final: E19.

terminative /ˈtɜːmɪnətɪv/ *adjective.* LME.

[Old & mod. French *terminatif*, *-ive* or medieval Latin *terminativus*, formed as prec.: see -IVE.]

1 Forming a boundary, limit, or extremity of something. Now *rare* or *obsolete.* LME.

†**2 a** Constituting an end, final, ultimate; *esp.* constituting the ultimate object or end of some action. E17–E18. ▸**b** Directed to something as ultimate object. M–L17.

3 Bringing or coming to an end; finishing, concluding; conclusive; *MEDICINE* (of a condition) terminal (now *rare*). L17.

4 *GRAMMAR.* **a** Denoting destination or direction towards. Now *rare.* M19. ▸**b** Designating an aspect of a verb which denotes a completed action, or its completion. E20.

■ **terminatively** *adverb* L16.

terminator /ˈtəːmɪneɪtə/ *noun.* L18.
[In sense 1 mod. spec. use of late Latin *terminator*; in senses 2, 3 from TERMINATE *verb*, TERMINATION + -OR.]
1 *ASTRONOMY.* The line of separation between the illuminated and unilluminated parts of the visible disc of the moon or a planet. L18.
2 *gen.* A person or thing which terminates something. M19.
3 *BIOCHEMISTRY.* A sequence of polynucleotides that causes transcription to end, resulting in the release of the newly synthesized nucleic acid from the template molecule. M20.

terminatory /ˈtəːmɪnət(ə)ri/ *adjective. rare.* M18.
[from TERMINATE *verb* + -ORY².]
Forming the end or extremity; terminal.

†**termine** *verb trans.* ME.
[Old & mod. French *terminer* from Latin *terminare.*]
1 Determine, decide, settle. ME–E18.
2 State definitely; declare, affirm. LME–L15.
3 Set bounds to, define, outline; usu. in *pass.* be bounded. LME–E17.
4 Bring to an end; terminate, finish, conclude. LME–E17.

terminer /ˈtəːmɪnə/ *noun. obsolete* exc. *Hist.* LME.
[Anglo-Norman, use as noun of Old French *terminer*: see prec., -ER⁴.]
LAW. The final determining of a judge or court. Only in OYER ***and terminer***.

termini *noun* pl. of TERMINUS.

terminism /ˈtəːmɪnɪz(ə)m/ *noun.* L19.
[from Latin *terminus* end, limit, (in medieval Latin) term + -ISM.]
1 *PHILOSOPHY.* = NOMINALISM. L19.
2 *THEOLOGY.* The doctrine that God has appointed a definite term or limit in the life of each individual, after which the opportunity for salvation is lost. L19.
■ **terminist** *noun* an adherent of terminism E18. **termiˈnistic** *adjective* of or pertaining to terminism M19.

terminology /təːmɪˈnɒlədʒi/ *noun.* E19.
[German *Terminologie*, from Latin *terminus* in its medieval Latin sense 'term': see -LOGY.]
The system of terms belonging to any science or subject; technical terms collectively; nomenclature. Also, the branch of study that deals with the proper use of terms.
■ **terminoˈlogical** *adjective* pertaining to terminology; ***terminological inexactitude*** (euphem., joc.), (a) falsehood: E20. **terminoˈlogically** *adverb* as regards terminology M19. **terminologist** *noun* an expert in terminology L19.

terminus /ˈtəːmɪnəs/ *noun.* Pl. **-ni** /-nʌɪ/, **-nuses**. M16.
[Latin = end, limit, boundary.]
1 The point at which motion or action ends or to which it is directed, a goal, an end, a finishing-point. Also occas., the point from which motion or action starts; starting-point. Orig. & chiefly in Latin phrs. below. M16.
2 *ROMAN HISTORY.* **a** (**T-**.) The god presiding over boundaries or landmarks. E17. ▸**b** A statue or bust of the god Terminus, orig. used as a boundary-marker; any statue in the form of a term (see TERM *noun* 15); the pedestal of such a statue. M17.
3 A boundary, a limit. *rare.* L17.
4 a (The station at) the end of a railway line; the place at which a tramline, bus route, etc., ends. M19. ▸**b** *gen.* An end, an extremity; the point at which something comes to an end. M19.
Phrases: ***terminus ad quem*** /ad ˈkwɛm/ [end to which] the finishing-point of an argument, policy, period, etc. ***terminus ante quem*** /antɪ ˈkwɛm/ [end before which] the finishing-point of a period, the latest possible date for something. ***terminus a quo*** /ɑː ˈkwəʊ/ [end from which] the starting-point of an argument, policy, period, etc. ***terminus post quem*** /pəʊst ˈkwɛm/ [end after which] the starting-point of a period, the earliest possible date for something.

termite /ˈtəːmʌɪt/ *noun.* Also in Latin form **termes** /ˈtəːmiːz/ (now only as mod. Latin genus name). L18.
[Latin *termit-*, *termes* woodworm, alt. of earlier *tarmes* perh. by assim. to *terere* rub.]
1 A member of the order Isoptera of chiefly tropical insects which live in large nests in social groups with physically distinct castes of individual, and are very destructive to timber owing to their ability to digest wood. Also called ***white ant***. L18.
2 *fig.* A person who works relentlessly or esp. destructively. M20.
Comb.: **termite-hill**, **termite-mound** a roughly conical mound often of huge size constructed from cemented earth as a nest by termites, a termitarium.
■ **termiˈtarium** *noun*, pl. **-ria**, a termites' nest, esp. in the form of a mound M19. **termitary** /ˈtəːmɪt(ə)ri/ *noun* = TERMITARIUM E19. **termitic** /təˈmɪtɪk/ *adjective* (now *rare*) of, pertaining to, or formed by termites L19. **termiting** *noun* the extraction of termites for food, esp. by chimpanzees L20. **termiˈtologist** *noun* a person who studies termites M20. **termiˈtophagous** *adjective* feeding on termites L19. **termitophile** *noun* a termitophilous insect E20. **termiˈtophilous** *adjective* (of a beetle etc.) inhabiting the nests of termites L19.

termly /ˈtəːmli/ *adjective.* L16.
[from TERM *noun* + -LY¹.]
Occurring every term or at fixed terms; periodical. Now esp., occurring every academic term.

termly /ˈtəːmli/ *adverb.* LME.
[from TERM *noun* + -LY².]
Term by term; every term, or at fixed terms; periodically.

termon /ˈtəːmən/ *noun.* M16.
[Old Irish *termonn* (mod. Irish *tearmann*) from Latin TERMINUS.]
Hist. In Ireland, land belonging to a religious house and exempt from secular charges; church land. Also ***termon-land***.
■ **termoner** *noun* [Irish *tearmannach*] a tenant of church land M16.

termor /ˈtəːmə/ *noun.* ME.
[Anglo-Norman *termer*, from *terme* TERM *noun*: see -OR.]
LAW (now *Hist.*). A person who holds lands or tenements for a term of years, or for life. Cf. TERM *noun* 6.

tern /təːn/ *noun*¹. *rare.* LME.
[App. from French *terne*, from Latin *terni* three each.]
A set of three; a triplet; *spec.* †(***a***) a double three in dice playing; (***b***) in a lottery, three winning numbers drawn together; (***c***) in verse, a group of three stanzas.

tern /təːn/ *noun*². L17.
[Of Scandinavian origin: cf. Norwegian *terna*, Danish *terne*, Swedish *tärna*, from Old Norse *þerna*.]
Any of numerous birds of the family Sternidae, comprising mainly sea and coastal birds similar to gulls but with a slender body, pointed wings, and a forked tail (and the top of the head black in the most familiar kinds).
Arctic tern, common tern, fairy tern, Inca tern, marsh tern, roseate tern, Sandwich tern, sooty tern, etc.

terna /ˈtəːnə/ *noun.* L19.
[Latin *terna* (*nomina*) three (names) at once.]
ROMAN CATHOLIC CHURCH. A list of three names of candidates for office submitted to the Pope or other authority to choose from.

ternal /ˈtəːn(ə)l/ *adjective. rare.* L16.
[from medieval Latin *ternalis*, from *terni*: see TERNARY, -AL¹.]
Consisting of three; threefold, triple. Also, third (of each group of three).

ternar /ˈtəːnə/ *noun. obsolete* exc. *Hist.* L17.
[from late Latin *ternarius*: see next.]
A student of the third or lowest rank at a Scottish university, *spec.* St Andrews.

ternary /ˈtəːnəri/ *adjective & noun.* LME.
[Latin *ternarius*, from *terni* three at a time, three by three, from *ter* thrice: see -ARY¹.]
▶ **A** *adjective.* **1** Pertaining to or consisting of three things or parts; characterized by the number three; of or belonging to the third order or rank, tertiary; third in a series. LME.
2 *CHEMISTRY & MINERALOGY.* Pertaining to or consisting of three elements or constituents. E19.
3 *BOTANY.* Esp. of parts of a flower: arranged in threes around a common axis. M19.

📖 **1** W. H. HADOW The most primitive Ternary form consists of a melody in three clauses.

▶†**B** *noun.* A set or group of three; a trio; a multiple of three. Also (**T-**), the Holy Trinity. LME–L18.

ternate /ˈtəːneɪt/ *adjective.* M18.
[mod. Latin *ternatus*, in form pa. pple of medieval Latin *ternare* make threefold: see -ATE².]
Produced or arranged in threes; *spec.* in *BOTANY*, (***a***) (of a compound leaf) divided into three leaflets or equal parts; (***b***) (of leaves) arranged in whorls of three.
■ **ternately** *adverb* M19.

terne /təːn/ *noun.* M19.
[Prob. from French *terne* dull, tarnished.]
METALLURGY. **1** In full ***terne plate***. Thin sheet iron coated with an alloy of lead and tin; a sheet or plate of this. M19.
2 A lead-based alloy containing about 20 per cent tin and (often) some antimony. Also ***terne metal***. L19.

ternery /ˈtəːnəri/ *noun.* L19.
[from TERN *noun*² + -ERY.]
A place where terns breed; a colony of terns.

ternion /ˈtəːnɪən/ *noun.* L16.
[Latin *ternio(n-)*, ult. from *ter* thrice.]
A set of three things or people; a triad; *spec.* a quire of three sheets, each folded in two.

terotechnology /ˌtɛrətɛkˈnɒlədʒi, ˌtɪərə-/ *noun.* L20.
[from Greek *tērein* watch over, take care of + -O- + TECHNOLOGY.]
The branch of technology and engineering concerned with the installation, maintenance, and replacement of industrial plant and equipment and with related subjects and practices.
■ **terotechnoˈlogical** *adjective* L20. **terotechnologist** *noun* L20.

For other words beginning with *ter-* see the entry for **ter-**

terp /təːp/ *noun*¹. Pl. **-s**, **-en** /-ən/. M19.
[West Frisian from Old Frisian *therp*, umlaut var. of *thorp* village: cf. THORP.]
A man-made mound or hillock, the site of a prehistoric village, and still in many cases occupied by a village or church, orig. and esp. in parts of Friesland below sea level or liable to flooding.

terp /təːp/ *noun*², *adjective, & verb. slang.* M20.
[Abbreviation of TERPSICHORE, TERPSICHOREAN *adjective.*]
THEATRICAL. ▶**A** *noun.* A stage dancer, esp. a chorus girl. Also, a ballroom dancer. M20.
▶ **B** *attrib.* or as *adjective.* Dancing; pertaining to dancing. M20.
▶ **C** *verb intrans.* Dance. M20.

terpane /ˈtəːpeɪn/ *noun.* E20.
[from TERPENE + -ANE.]
CHEMISTRY. Any of a class of saturated hydrocarbons having the same carbon skeleton as the terpenes.

terpen *noun pl.* see TERP *noun*¹.

terpene /ˈtəːpiːn/ *noun.* L19.
[from German *Terpentin* TURPENTINE + -ENE.]
CHEMISTRY. Any of a class of volatile aromatic hydrocarbons with the formula $C_{10}H_{16}$ and typically of isoprenoid structure, many of which occur in essential plant oils, esp. of conifers and citrus trees. More widely, any terpenoid.
■ **terpeneless** *adjective* having no terpenes; *spec.* (of an essential oil) having had terpene components removed to prevent spoiling by oxidation: E20.

terpenoid /ˈtəːpɪnɔɪd/ *noun & adjective.* M20.
[from prec. + -OID.]
CHEMISTRY. ▶**A** *noun.* Any of a large class of organic compounds (including terpenes, diterpenes, sesquiterpenes, etc.) which have the formula $(C_5H_8)_n$ and molecules composed of linked isoprene units; a compound related to these in molecular structure. M20.
▶ **B** *adjective.* Of the nature of or pertaining to a terpenoid or terpenoids; related to terpenes. M20.

terpin /ˈtəːpɪn/ *noun.* M19.
[from TERPENE + -IN¹.]
CHEMISTRY. A saturated cyclic terpenoid, of which there are several isomers, known chiefly as a crystalline hydrate, $C_6H_{10}(CH_3)_3(OH)_2$, obtainable by acidification of α-pinene.
■ **terˈpineol** *noun* each of a group of isomeric terpenoid alcohols of the formula $C_{10}H_{17}OH$, having a scent of lilac and used in perfumery L19.

Terpsichore /təːpˈsɪk(ə)ri/ *noun.* E18.
[Greek *Terpsikhorē* the Muse of dancing, lit. 'dance-enjoying', from *terpein* delight + *khoros* dance, CHORUS *noun.*]
A (female) dancer. Also, the personification of the art of dancing.
■ **Terpsichorean** /ˌtəːpsɪkəˈriːən/ *adjective* of, pertaining to, or of the nature of dancing E19.

terr /təː/ *noun. slang.* L20.
[Abbreviation of TERRORIST *noun.*]
In Zimbabwe prior to independence and in South Africa, a guerrilla fighting to overthrow the white minority government.

terra /ˈtɛrə/ *noun.* Pl. **terrae** /ˈtɛriː, -ʌɪ/. E17.
[(Italian from) Latin, = earth.]
1 A medicinal or other earth, bole, etc. Usu. with specifying word. E17.
2 With specifying word: land, territory. E20.
3 (**T-**.) In science fiction, the planet Earth. M20.
1 terra alba /ˈalbə/ [Latin, fem. of *albus* white] any of various white earths, as pipeclay, kaolin, etc.; now *spec.* white pulverized gypsum used in the manufacture of paper, paint, etc. **terra ponderosa** /pɒndəˈrəʊzə, -sə/ [Latin, fem. of *ponderosus* heavy] barium sulphate, heavy spar. **terra rossa** /ˈrɒsə/ [Italian, fem. of *rosso* red] *SOIL SCIENCE* a reddish soil occurring on limestone in Mediterranean climates. **2 terra cognita** /kɒgˈniːtə/ [Latin, fem. of *cognitus* known] *fig.* familiar territory. **terra ignota** /ɪgˈnəʊtə/ [Latin, fem. of *ignotus* unknown] = TERRA INCOGNITA. **terra irredenta** /ɪrɪˈdɛntə/ [Italian: see IRREDENTIST] = IRREDENTA.

terrace /ˈtɛrəs/ *noun.* E16.
[Old French *terrace*, (also mod.) *-asse* rubble, platform, from Proto-Romance from Latin *terra* earth.]
1 Orig., an open gallery; a colonnade, a portico; a balcony. Later, a raised platform or balcony in a theatre, auditorium, etc. E16.
2 a A raised level, esp. paved area, adjoining a house etc. or in a garden, for walking or sitting; the levelled top of a natural slope or river-bank, esp. forming a series. L16. ▸**b** *MILITARY.* A raised earthwork, constructed by a besieging force as a place from which to launch an assault or gain a vantage point. *arch. rare.* L16. ▸**c** Chiefly *ARCHAEOLOGY.* = CULTIVATION ***terrace***. L18. ▸**d** A flight of wide shallow steps providing standing room for spectators at a sports (esp. a football) ground (usu. in *pl.*); any of these steps. Also (in *pl.*), *the* spectators occupying such a flight of steps. M20.
3 The flat roof of a house, esp. in warm climates, where the roof is used as a cool resting area. L16.

4 A naturally occurring formation of the earth's surface with a level top and sloping sides; *spec.* (*a*) a table-land; (*b*) GEOLOGY a horizontal shelf or bench on the side of a hill or on sloping ground, formed at the former margin of a river, sea, etc. L17.
5 A row of houses on a raised level, or along the top or face of a slope. Also, a row of houses built in one block and usu. of uniform style; the street on to which such a row of houses faces. M18. ▸**b** = ***terrace house*** below. L19.
6 A soft spot in marble, which is cleaned out and the cavity filled up with a paste. Cf. TERRACY. *rare.* L19.

📖 **1** *Guardian* The music sounds better in the top terrace . . than in the lower terraces. **2a** SIR W. SCOTT The garden . . was laid out in terraces, which descended rank by rank . . to a large brook. A. BRINK I took him to a café terrace and ordered two beers. **c** P. MATTHIESSEN The path follows a dike between the . . canal and the green terraces of rice. **d** *Match* Celebrating his goal with a . . rush to the fans on the terraces. **5** D. STOREY A few doors down the terrace lived Mr. Reagan.

Comb.: **terrace-cultivation** (chiefly ARCHAEOLOGY) cultivation of hillsides in terraces (sense 2c above); **terrace house** any of a row of usu. similar houses joined by party-walls.

terrace /ˈtɛrəs/ *verb trans.* E17.
[from the noun or French *terrasser*.]
Form into or provide with a terrace or terraces; construct in terrace form.

📖 *Westminster Gazette* The Kusi River . . brings down enormous quantities of silt, . . terracing the land. C. MILNE The slope had to be terraced into level areas supported by dry-stone walls.

terraced /ˈtɛrəst/ *adjective.* M17.
[from TERRACE *noun, verb*: see -ED², -ED¹.]
Formed into or provided with a terrace or terraces; constructed in terrace form.

📖 N. FARAH A terraced tea-shop with chairs arranged outside. **terraced house** = ***terrace house*** s.v. TERRACE *noun*. **terraced roof** = TERRACE *noun* 3.

terracette /tɛrəˈsɛt/ *noun.* E20.
[from TERRACE *noun* + -ETTE.]
PHYSICAL GEOGRAPHY. Any of a number of small parallel terraces on a steep hillside, usu. caused by the slippage of soil etc. Also called ***sheepwalk***.

terracing /ˈtɛrəsɪŋ/ *noun.* L18.
[from TERRACE *verb* + -ING¹.]
†**1** Walking or strolling on a terrace in a garden. *rare.* Only in L18.
2 The action of TERRACE *verb*; an instance of this. Also, a terraced structure or formation; a series or range of terraces; *spec.* = TERRACE *noun* 2d. E19.

📖 **2** CARLYLE The diggings and terracings of the Hill-side. *Glaswegian* The customers stood on the terracing, often without any cover.

terracotta /tɛrəˈkɒtə/ *noun & adjective.* E18.
[Italian *terra cotta* baked earth from Latin *terra cocta*.]
▸**A** *noun.* **1** Hard unglazed usu. brownish-red earthenware, used chiefly for decorative tiles and bricks and in modelling. E18. ▸**b** A statuette or figurine made of this substance. E19.
2 The typical brownish-red colour of this earthenware. L19.

📖 **1b** *Modern Painters* Photographs of my terracottas and my other student work.

▸**B** *attrib.* or as *adjective.* Of or pertaining to terracotta; made of terracotta; of the typical colour of terracotta, brownish red. M19.

📖 C. RAINE Two terracotta nipples like patches from a cycle kit.

terraculture /ˈtɛrəkʌltʃə/ *noun. rare.* M19.
[Irreg. from Latin *terra* earth + -CULTURE.]
Agriculture.

terracy /ˈtɛrəsi/ *adjective.* Long *rare* or *obsolete.* E18.
[from TERRACE *noun* + -Y¹.]
Of marble: containing terraces or soft spots. Cf. TERRACE *noun* 6.

terrae *noun* pl. of TERRA.

terrae filius /tɛriː ˈfɪlɪəs, tɛrʌɪ/ *noun phr.* Pl. ***terrae filii*** /ˈfɪlɪʌɪ, ˈfɪliː/. L16.
[Latin = a son of the earth, a man of unknown origin.]
1 A person of doubtful or obscure parentage. L16.
2 At Oxford University, an orator who made a humorous and satirical speech during the Act or public defence of candidates' theses. Cf. PREVARICATOR 2, TRIPOS 2a. *obsolete* exc. *Hist.* M17.

terra firma /tɛrə ˈfəːmə/ *noun phr.* E17.
[Latin = firm land.]
1 a The territories on the Italian mainland which were subject to the State of Venice. *obsolete* exc. *Hist.* E17. ▸†**b** The northern coastland of S. America (Colombia), as distinguished from the W. Indies. Also, the isthmus of Panama. *rare.* M18–E19.
†**2** A mainland or continent, as distinct from an island etc. M17–E18.
3 The land as distinguished from the sea; dry land; firm ground. L17.
†**4** Landed estate; land. *joc.* & *colloq.* L17–E18.

terraform /ˈtɛrəfɔːm/ *verb trans.* M20.
[from TERRA + FORM *verb*¹.]
Chiefly SCIENCE FICTION. Transform (a planet, environment, etc.) into something resembling the earth, esp. as regards suitability for human life.

terrage /ˈtɛrɪdʒ/ *noun. obsolete* exc. *Hist.* ME.
[Old French *terage*, from popular Latin *terraticum*, from Latin *terra* earth: see -AGE.]
LAW. A payment, a duty; *spec.* (*a*) a toll or duty paid by vessels for landing; (*b*) a duty paid for the site of a stall at a fair or market. Cf. GROUNDAGE, PICKAGE.

terraglia /tɛrˈɑːlɪə/ *noun.* M19.
[Italian = earthenware, china, from Latin *terra* earth.]
CERAMICS. An Italian cream-coloured earthenware, *esp.* that manufactured from 1728 at Nove, near Bassano, Italy, by G. B. Antonibon and his descendants.

terrain /tɛˈreɪn/ *noun & adjective.* In sense A.3 usu. **-ane**. E18.
[French from popular Latin var. of Latin *terrenum* use as noun of neut. of *terrenus* TERRENE.]
▸**A** *noun.* **1** Orig. (in HORSEMANSHIP), part of the training-ground in a riding-school. Later, position, standing-ground. E18.
2 a Ground, a tract of land, esp. with regard to its physical characteristics or their capacity for use by the military tactician in manoeuvres etc. Also, a region, a territory. M18. ▸**b** *fig.* A particular area of knowledge or subject matter; a sphere of influence or action. M19.
3 GEOLOGY. A fault-bounded area or region with a distinctive stratigraphy, structure, and geological history, which is different from those of adjacent areas. Now usu. *spec.*, a fragment of a tectonic plate, bounded by strike-slip faults. E19.

📖 **2a** J. BARNES Miss Logan . . struggled to keep up as the terrain grew more precipitous. P. D. JAMES A falling match, briefly illuminating the contours of a vast unexplored terrain. **b** P. BOWLES His discourse . . went into personal experiences. This terrain was more fertile. *American Ethnologist* It was into this . . meaningful terrain . . that the nonconformist evangelists entered in the 19th century.

Comb.: **terrain-following** *adjective* automatically responding to the changing height of the terrain; chiefly in ***terrain-following radar***, a radar system allowing rapid flight of an aircraft, missile, etc., close to the ground by constant adjustments of altitude.
▸**B** *adjective.* Of the earth, terrestrial. *rare.* L19.

terra incognita /ˌtɛrə ɪnˈkɒɡnɪtə, ɪnkɒɡˈniːtə/ *noun phr.* E17.
[Latin = unknown land.]
An unknown or unexplored territory, land, or region; *fig.* an unknown or unexplored area of study, knowledge, or experience. Freq. without article.

📖 A. BRIGGS The historical landscape . . looks at first like a *terra incognita*. *New Scientist* The largest region of geological terra incognita left on the global map.

terrain vague /tɛrɛ̃ vag/ *noun phr.* E20.
[French colloq., lit. 'waste ground'.]
Wasteland, no man's land; a grey area.

📖 *Sunday Times* Alastair Reid occupies a *terrain vague* between reportage and *belles lettres*.

Terra Japonica /ˌtɛrə dʒəˈpɒnɪkə/ *noun phr.* L17.
[mod. Latin = Japanese earth.]
= CATECHU.

terral /tɛˈrɑːl/ *noun.* M19.
[Spanish, from Latin *terra* land, earth.]
A land breeze blowing off the coast of Spain or S. America.

terramare /tɛrəˈmɑːri, -ˈmɛːri/ *noun.* Pl. **-mares**. Also in Italian form **-mara** /-ˈmɑːrə/, pl. **-mare** /-ˈmɑːreɪ/. M19.
[French, from Italian dial. *terramara* for *terra marna*, from *terra* earth + *marna* marl.]
An ammoniacal earthy deposit found in flat mounds in late neolithic lake-dwellings or settlements in the valley of the Po in Italy, and collected as a fertilizer. Also, a prehistoric dwelling or settlement of this kind (usu. in *pl.*).

📖 *attrib.*: L. MUMFORD It is doubtful if there is any direct connexion between the *terramare* settlements and the Roman towns.

Terramycin /tɛrəˈmʌɪsɪn/ *noun.* M20.
[from Latin *terra* earth + -MYCIN.]
PHARMACOLOGY. (Proprietary name for) oxytetracycline.

Terran /ˈtɛrən/ *adjective & noun.* M20.
[formed as prec. + -AN.]
▸**A** *adjective.* In science fiction, of or pertaining to the planet Earth or its inhabitants. M20.
▸**B** *noun.* In science fiction, an inhabitant of the planet Earth. M20.

terrane *noun* see TERRAIN *noun*.

terranean /tɛˈreɪnɪən/ *adjective & noun.* M17.
[formed as next: see -AN.]
▸**A** *adjective.* Pertaining to, or proceeding from, the earth. M17.
▸**B** *noun.* = TERRAN *noun. rare.* E20.

terraneous /tɛˈreɪnɪəs/ *adjective. rare.* E18.
[from Latin *terra* earth, after †*mediterraneous*, *subterraneous*: see -ANEOUS.]
1 Of or pertaining to the earth; terrestrial. E18.
2 BOTANY. Growing on land. L19.

terrapin /ˈtɛrəpɪn/ *noun*¹. E17.
[Alt. of an Eastern Algonquian word (cf. Eastern Abnaki *turepé* turtle): -*in* of unkn. origin.]
1 More fully ***diamondback terrapin***. A small edible turtle, *Malaclemys terrapin*, which is found in the brackish coastal marshes of the eastern US. E17. ▸**b** The flesh of this animal as food. M19.
2 Any of various small carnivorous aquatic and semi-aquatic turtles of the family Emydidae, most of which are found in freshwater in warmer areas; *esp.* (more fully ***European pond terrapin***) *Emys orbicularis*, which occurs in much of Europe except the NW, and adjacent areas. M19.
2 painted terrapin, ***stink-pot terrapin***, etc.

Terrapin /ˈtɛrəpɪn/ *noun*². Also **t-**. M20.
[Prob. use of prec.]
(Proprietary name for) a type of prefabricated one-storey building, designed for temporary use.

📖 *attrib.*: A. CLEEVES His classroom was one of two in a Terrapin hut.

terraqueous /tɛˈreɪkwɪəs/ *adjective.* M17.
[from Latin *terra* earth + AQUEOUS.]
1 Consisting of, or formed of, land and water. Chiefly in ***terraqueous globe***, the earth, the world. M17.
2 (Of a plant) living in land and water; (esp. of a journey) extending over land and water. *rare.* L17.

terrar /ˈtɛrə/ *noun. obsolete* exc. *Hist.* Also **terrer**. LME.
[medieval Latin *terrarius* use as noun of adjective = pertaining to land or lands.]
An officer of a religious house, originally bursar for the farms and manors belonging to the house, but whose duties by the 16th cent. were mainly connected with attending to visitors and strangers.

terrarium /tɛˈrɛːrɪəm/ *noun.* Pl. **-riums**, **-ria** /-rɪə/. L19.
[mod. Latin, from Latin *terra* earth, after AQUARIUM.]
1 A vivarium for land animals; *esp.* a glass case etc. in which small land animals are kept under observation. L19.
2 A sealed transparent globe or similar container in which plants are grown. M20.

terra rosa /tɛrə ˈrəʊzə/ *noun phr.* L19.
[Italian, lit. 'rose-coloured earth'.]
A light red pigment produced from iron oxide and used in oil and watercolour painting; the light red colour of this pigment, similar to Venetian red.

Terra Sienna /ˌtɛrə sɪˈɛnə/ *noun phr.* M18.
[Italian *terra di Siena* earth of Siena.]
= SIENNA 1.

terra sigillata /ˌtɛrə sɪdʒɪˈleɪtə/ *noun phr.* LME.
[medieval Latin = sealed earth.]
1 An astringent bole, of fatty consistency and reddish colour, orig. obtained from the Aegean island of Lemnos, formerly valued as a medicine and antidote. *obsolete* exc. *Hist.* LME.
†**2** Red pigment; ruddle. M16–E17.
3 ARCHAEOLOGY. A type of fine Roman earthenware, esp. Samian ware, made from this or a similar earth from the 1st cent. BC to the 3rd cent. AD in Gaul (also Italy and Germany), usu. red in colour and sometimes decorated with stamped figures or patterns. E20. ▸**b** A ware made in imitation of this, *esp.* a 17th-cent. glazed redware from Silesia and a kind of grey Maltese earthenware. M20.

terrasse /tɛras/ *noun.* Pl. pronounced same. L19.
[French: see TERRACE *noun*.]
In France etc.: a flat, paved area outside a building, esp. a café, where people sit to take refreshments.

terrazzo /təˈrɑːtsəʊ/ *noun.* Pl. **-os**. E20.
[Italian = terrace, balcony.]
A flooring-material made of chips of marble or granite set in concrete and polished to give a smooth surface.

📖 *attrib.*: B. MOORE A large room with terrazzo flooring.

†**terre** *noun. rare.* LME–E19.
[French from Latin *terra* earth.]
Land; a country estate.

For other words beginning with *ter-* see the entry for **ter-**

terre-à-terre /tɛratɛːr/ *adjectival & adverbial phr.* E18.
[French from Italian *terra a terra* level with the ground.]
BALLET. Of a step or manner of dancing: in which the feet remain on or close to the ground. Also *transf.*, without elevation of style; down-to-earth, realistic; pedestrian, unimaginative.

Time & Tide His friend and chief was, intellectually, very *terre-à-terre*.

terre cuite /tɛːr kɥit/ *noun phr.* M19.
[French, lit. 'baked (cooked) earth'.]
= TERRACOTTA 1.

†**terreity** *noun. rare.* E17–M18.
[from medieval Latin *terreitas*: see -ITY.]
The essential quality of earth; earthiness.

terrella /tə'rɛlə/ *noun.* E17.
[mod. Latin = little earth, dim. from Latin *terra* earth + -ELLA.]
†**1** A spherical magnet. E17–M19.
2 A little Earth; a small celestial or planetary body. Long *rare.* L17.

terrene /tɛ'riːn/ *adjective & noun.* ME.
[Anglo-Norman from Latin *terrenus*, from *terra* earth.]
▶ **A** *adjective.* **1** Of or pertaining to this world; earthly; worldly, secular, mundane, as opp. to heavenly, spiritual, etc.; = TERRESTRIAL *adjective* 1. ME.
2 Of the nature of earth; earthy. E17.
3 Occurring on or inhabiting dry land; = TERRESTRIAL *adjective* 4. M17.
4 Of or pertaining to the planet Earth; = TERRESTRIAL *adjective* 2. Long *rare* or *obsolete.* M17.

1 T. KEN Wash your own spirit clean From all concupiscence terrene. **2** *Punch* Peanut butter's glistening surface— . . its 'terrene unctuosity'.

▶ **B** *noun.* The earth, the world. Also, a land, a territory. Chiefly *literary.* M17.

MILTON A Province wide Tenfold the length of this terrene.

■ **terrenely** *adverb* (*rare*) †(*a*) as regards landed estate; territorially; (*b*) in a terrene or worldly manner; mundanely: L15. **terreneness** *noun* (now *rare* or *obsolete*) terrene quality; earthiness: M17.

terrenity /tɛ'rɛnɪti/ *noun. rare.* M17.
[formed as prec. + -ITY.]
The quality or condition of being earthy; earthy matter.
¶ Formerly obsolete (M17 only) but revived L20.

terreno /tɛ'reɪnəʊ/ *noun.* Long *rare* or *obsolete.* Pl. **-os.** M18.
[Italian (*piano*) *terreno*, from Latin *terrenum* use as noun of neut. of *terrenus* TERRENE.]
A ground floor. Also, a parlour.

†**terreous** *adjective.* M17–E19.
[from Latin *terreus* earthen, earthy, from *terra* earth: see -EOUS.]
Earthy; pertaining to earth or soil.

terre pisée /tɛːr pize/ *noun phr.* M20.
[French, lit. 'beaten earth'.]
= PISÉ *noun.*

terreplein /'tɛːpleɪn, *foreign* tɛrplɛ̃ (*pl. same*)/ *noun.* L16.
[French *terre-plein* from Italian *terrapieno*, from *terrapienare* fill with earth, from *terra* earth + *pieno* (from Latin *plenus*) full.]
1 Orig., a talus or sloping bank of earth behind a wall or rampart. Later, the surface of a rampart behind a parapet; *spec.* the level space on which guns are mounted, between the banquette and the inner talus. L16.
2 The level base (above, on, or below the natural surface of the ground) on which a battery of guns is mounted in field fortifications. Also, the natural surface of the ground around a fortification. M17.

terrer *noun* var. of TERRAR.

†**terrestreity** *noun* var. of TERRESTRITY.

terrestrial /tɪ'rɛstrɪəl/ *adjective & noun.* LME.
[from Latin *terrestris*, from *terra* earth: see -IAL.]
▶ **A** *adjective.* **1** Of or pertaining to this world, or earth as opp. to heaven; earthly; worldly; mundane. LME.
2 Of, pertaining to, or referring to the planet Earth. Freq. in ***terrestrial ball***, ***terrestrial globe***, the Earth. M16. ▸**b** Proceeding from, or belonging to, the solid earth or its soil; not atmospheric. *rare.* L16. ▸**c** Consisting of earth or soil. *joc. rare.* M19. ▸**d** ASTRONOMY. Designating planets which are similar in size or composition to the planet Earth, as Mercury, Venus, and Mars. L19. ▸**e** TELECOMMUNICATIONS. Pertaining to or designating broadcasting, data transmission, etc., which does not make use of satellites. M20.
†**3** Of or resembling earth; possessing earthlike properties or qualities; earthy. L16–M18.
4 a ZOOLOGY. Living on land as opp. to in water; air-breathing. Also, (of a bird or insect) not capable of flight, cursorial; (of a mammal) living on the ground, not arboreal. L16. ▸**b** BOTANY. Growing on land or in the soil. Opp. ***aquatic***, ***epiphytic***, etc. M19.
5 Of or pertaining to dry land. E17.

1 A. LIVINGSTONE Having to sacrifice great thoughts for the sake of terrestrial truth. *Gay Times* Peta Masters . . as the goddess whose terrestrial guise is as a . . *dyke fatale.* **2** *Kindred Spirit* This major terrestrial energy flow . . materialized into stone. **terrestrial telescope** a telescope used for observing terrestrial objects and giving an uninverted image (opp. ***astronomical telescope***). **5** A. ALISON Napoleon was . . advancing in his career of terrestrial empire.

▶ **B** *noun.* An inhabitant of the earth, *esp.* a human being, a mortal. Also (*rare*, Shakes.), a man of secular estate, a layman. L16.

New Statesman The space-craft known to terrestrials as 'Flying Saucers'.

■ **terrestri'ality** *noun* (ZOOLOGY & ANTHROPOLOGY) the state or condition of living primarily on the ground, usu. as opposed to in the trees; cf. ARBOREALITY: M20. **terrestrialize** *verb trans.* make terrestrial or earthly E19. **terrestrially** *adverb* E17.

†**terrestrious** *adjective.* E17.
[formed as prec. + -OUS.]
1 = TERRESTRIAL *adjective* 3. E17–M18.
2 = TERRESTRIAL *adjective* 5. M17–M19.

†**terrestrity** *noun.* Also **-eity.** LME–M18.
[medieval Latin *terrestritas*, *-treitas*, formed as TERRESTRIAL: see -ITY.]
(The quality or condition of containing) earthy matter, either residual or in suspension.

terret /'tɛrɪt/ *noun.* Also **-it.** See also TORRET. L15.
[Old French *toret*, *touret* dim. of *tour* TOUR *noun*: see -ET[1].]
1 Either of the two rings by which the leash is attached to the jesses of a hawk. Now *rare* or *obsolete.* L15.
2 A ring etc. by which an object can be attached to a chain. E16.
3 A ring on a dog's collar by which a string or lead can be attached. Long *rare.* M16.
4 Either of the rings or loops on a harness-pad or saddle, for the driving-reins to pass through. Also, any ring attached elsewhere to a harness for a similar purpose. E18.

terre-tenant /'tɛːtɛnənt/ *noun.* LME.
[Anglo-Norman *terre tenaunt* = holding land, from *terre* land + *tenaunt* TENANT *noun.*]
LAW (now *Hist.*). A person who has the actual possession of land; the occupant of land. Also, an owner in fee of land acquired from a judgement debtor.

terre-verte /tɛː'vɛːt/ *noun.* M17.
[French = green earth.]
A soft green earth of varying composition used as a pigment, *esp.* a variety of glauconite obtained from Italy, Cyprus, and France; the colour of this pigment, a soft greyish green.

terribilità /terribili'ta/ *noun.* Also **-biltà** /-bil'ta/. L19.
[Italian.]
1 ART. Awesomeness or emotional intensity of conception and execution in an artist or work of art; orig. a quality attributed to Michelangelo by his contemporaries. L19.
2 *gen.* Terrifying or awesome quality. M20.

2 *Times* The terribilità has long been drained from air travel.

terribility /tɛrɪ'bɪlɪti/ *noun. rare.* L15.
[French †*terribleté*, later also †*terribilité* from Latin *terribilitas*, from *terribilis*: see TERRIBLE, -ITY.]
Terribleness.

terribiltà *noun* var. of TERRIBILITÀ.

terrible /'tɛrɪb(ə)l/ *adjective, adverb, & noun.* LME.
[Old & mod. French from Latin *terribilis*, from *terrere* frighten: see -IBLE.]
▶ **A** *adjective.* **1** Causing or fit to cause terror; inspiring great fear or dread; appalling, frightful. LME.
2 a Causing a feeling similar to dread or awe; very violent, severe, or painful; *colloq.* very great or bad; excessive. L16. ▸**b** Of a person: outrageous; behaving in a shocking or outrageous manner. M19. ▸**c** Exceedingly incompetent; of shockingly poor performance or quality. E20.

1 I. MURDOCH Remembering . . the scene as . . something potent with the most terrible menace. M. AMIS She told me something so terrible, . . so annihilating that I can't remember a word. **2a** I. MURDOCH It's a terrible bore, but we *must* go and see Millie. J. NEEL There will be a terrible bang and the . . building will combust. **b** C. HAMPTON Men I fall in love with turn out to be such terrible people. **terrible infant** = ENFANT TERRIBLE. **terrible twins** *joc.* a pair of associates whose behaviour is troublesome or outrageous. **c** C. HARKNESS Men . . wearing . . terrible old plus-fours, scruffy jackets. *New Yorker* He didn't win . . very often—he was a terrible speller.

▶ **B** *adverb.* Exceedingly; = TERRIBLY 2a. Now chiefly *colloq.* & *US.* L15.

E. O'NEILL She was terrible old-fashioned.

▶ **C** *noun.* A terrible thing or being; something causing great fear or dread. Usu. in *pl.* E17.

J. STRUTHERS One has, between Grecian and Gothic story, generated a new race of terribles.

■ **terribleness** *noun* M16.

terribly /'tɛrɪbli/ *adverb.* LME.
[from prec. + -LY[2].]
1 In a terrible manner; so as to cause terror or dread; frightfully. LME.
2 a Very severely or painfully; *colloq.* exceedingly, extremely, very greatly. E17. ▸**b** In an exceedingly incompetent manner, very poorly. *colloq.* M20.

1 R. W. HAMILTON At death . . the consequences of guilt are often most terribly revealed. **2a** JILLY COOPER They used . . to be terribly rich. *Woman's Journal* She's a home person . . and terribly shy. **b** J. MITCHELL You can sing terribly and get away with it.

terricolous /tɛ'rɪkələs/ *adjective.* M19.
[from Latin *terricola* earth-dweller, from *terra* earth: see -I-, -COLOUS.]
1 ZOOLOGY. Living on the ground or in the soil; *spec.* of or pertaining to earthworms. M19.
2 BOTANY. Of a lichen: growing on soil (and not, e.g., on rocks or tree trunks). E20.
■ **terricole** /'tɛrɪkəʊl/ *adjective & noun* (*a*) *adjective* = TERRICOLOUS; (*b*) *noun* a terricolous animal; *esp.* an earthworm: L19. **terricoline** *adjective* (ZOOLOGY) = TERRICOLOUS L19.

terrier /'tɛrɪə/ *noun*[1] & *verb.* LME.
[Old French (*chien*) *terrier*, from medieval Latin *terrarius*, from Latin *terra* earth.]
▶ **A** *noun.* **1 a** (An animal of) any of various breeds of small active dog, originally trained to turn out foxes etc. from their earths, and divided into two classes, the short- or smooth-haired, and the long- or rough-haired. LME. ▸**b** *fig.* A tenacious, eager, or energetic person or animal. M16.
2 (**T-**.) A member of the Territorial Army. *colloq.* E20.

1a ***bull-terrier***, ***Jack Russell terrier***, ***Scottish terrier***, ***Sealyham terrier***, ***Yorkshire terrier***, etc. **b** *Daily Star* He was an apprentice with Watford—a gutsy midfield terrier.

Comb.: **terrier-man** HUNTING a man employed to be in charge of the terriers.

▶ **B** *verb.* **1** *verb intrans.* Burrow in the manner of a terrier. *rare.* M20.
2 *verb trans.* Make *one's way* like a terrier. *rare.* M20.

1 R. COLLIER Working with hand-shovels . . , Marotta and his crew began to terrier away.

¶ Recorded earlier in ME as a surname.

terrier /'tɛrɪə/ *noun*[2]. L15.
[Old French, use as noun of adjective, from medieval Latin *terrarius* (as in *liber terrarius*), *terrarium*, from Latin *terra* land.]
1 Orig., a register of landed property, including lists of vassals and tenants, and detailing their holdings, services, and rents; a rent-roll. Later, a book recording the site, boundaries, acreage, etc., of the lands belonging to a private person or corporation. Also, an inventory of property or goods. Now *Hist.* L15.
2 *transf.* & *fig.* A survey, a register. Now *rare.* M17.

1 *Antiquaries Journal* The diocese . . did not require informative terriers from its clergy.

terrific /tə'rɪfɪk/ *adjective.* M17.
[Latin *terrificus*, from *terrere* frighten: see -FIC.]
1 Causing terror, terrifying; terrible, frightful. M17.
2 a Very severe; of great size or intensity; excessive. *colloq.* E19. ▸**b** Excellent, exceedingly good, splendid. *colloq.* M20.

1 MILTON The Serpent . . with brazen Eyes And hairie Main terrific. **2a** J. BALDWIN It was a terrific scandal. If you were in Paris . . you certainly heard of it. **b** A. GARVE Perdita . . looked terrific in midnight-blue velvet.

■ **terrifically** *adverb* (*a*) in a terrifying manner; frightfully, appallingly; (*b*) *colloq.* excessively, exceedingly: E19. **terrificness** *noun* E18.

terrification /ˌtɛrɪfɪ'keɪʃ(ə)n/ *noun.* Chiefly *Scot.* E17.
[Latin *terrificatio(n-)*, from *terrificat-* pa. ppl stem of *terrificare*: see next, -ATION.]
1 The action of terrifying a person or animal; the condition of being terrified; consternation; a state of terror or alarm. E17.
2 A source of alarm or dismay; a troublesome person. *rare.* E19.

terrify /'tɛrɪfʌɪ/ *verb trans.* L16.
[Latin *terrificare*, from *terrificus*: see TERRIFIC, -FY.]
1 Make very afraid, fill with terror, frighten or alarm greatly; drive *from* or *out of* a place etc. by frightening; alarm or frighten *into* a course of action etc. L16.
2 Irritate, worry, harass, tease. Now *dial.* M17.
†**3** Make terrible or frightening. *rare* (Milton). Only in M17.

1 SIR W. SCOTT It may terrify her to death. P. ROAZEN The bullfight . . made a terrifying impression on him. A. WALKER She forced the whole story out of her . . inexperienced, terrified, and pale-as-ashes mother.

For other words beginning with *ter-* see the entry for **ter-**

■ **terrified** *adjective* that has been terrified; greatly frightened or alarmed (*at*, *by*, etc.): L16. **terrifier** *noun* a terrifying person or thing E17. **terrifyingly** *adverb* in a terrifying manner E19.

terrigenous /tɛˈrɪdʒɪnəs/ *adjective*. L17.
[from Latin *terrigenus* earth-born + -OUS.]
1 Esp. of an animal: produced from the earth; earth-born. *rare*. L17.
2 GEOLOGY. Land-derived; *esp.* designating a marine deposit consisting of material eroded from the land. L19.

terrine /təˈriːn/ *noun*. E18.
[French = large earthenware pot, fem. of Old French *terrin* earthen, from Latin *terra* earth: cf. TUREEN.]
1 Orig. = TUREEN. Now, an earthenware or similar fireproof vessel, *esp.* one in which a terrine or pâté is cooked or sold. E18.
2 Orig., a dish of meat, game, poultry, etc., stewed in a tureen or covered earthenware vessel. Now, a kind of pâté, usu. coarse-textured, cooked in and often served from a terrine or earthenware vessel. E18.

📖 **1** *House & Garden* Line the terrine with cling film. **2** *Great Hospitality* Terrine of venison, studded with goose liver . . and mango-filled morels.

territ *noun* var. of TERRET.

territoria *noun* pl. of TERRITORIUM.

territorial /tɛrɪˈtɔːrɪəl/ *adjective & noun*. In senses A.4, B. usu. **T-**. E17.
[Late Latin *territorialis*, from *territorium* TERRITORY: see -IAL.]
▶ **A** *adjective*. **1 a** Of or pertaining to a particular territory; limited to a district or locality; local. E17. ▸**b** SCOTS LAW. Of jurisdiction: extending over and restricted to a defined territory (see TERRITORY 1c). L18. ▸**c** In Scotland, of or pertaining to an ecclesiastical district, not a parish. Freq. in ***territorial church***, one organized to serve a particular district, esp. a poor and densely populated one, without regard to the existing parish boundaries. Now *rare*. E19.
2 a Of, belonging to, or relating to territory or land, or the territory under the jurisdiction of a State or ruler. M18. ▸**b** Of or pertaining to landed property. Now *rare*. L18. ▸**c** Owning or having landed property; landed. Now *rare*. M19. ▸**d** ZOOLOGY. Of or pertaining to the territory defended by an animal or animals; designating an animal or species that defends its territory. E20.
3 Of or belonging to any of the Territories of the United States or Canada. E19.
4 Of or pertaining to the Territorial Army. E20.

📖 **1a** *Architects' Journal* A territorial allowance . . will be paid or a car issued, as appropriate. **2a** P. CUTTING Videos . . explaining the geography and territorial disputes within the country. **c** R. CONGREVE The territorial and moneyed aristocracy . . is being brought daily into . . opposition to the people. **4** R. KIPLING We found the Territorial battalion undressin' in slow time.

Special collocations: **Territorial Army** in the UK, a volunteer force locally organized to provide a reserve of trained and disciplined manpower for use in an emergency (known as the *Territorial and Army Volunteer Reserve* 1967–79). **territorial imperative** ZOOLOGY the need to claim and defend a territory. **territorial limits** the limits of a State's territorial waters. **Territorial Regiments** the infantry regiments of the British army, each of which used to be associated in name, depot, etc., with a particular county or locality. **territorial waters** the area of sea under the jurisdiction of a State and within a stated distance of the shore (traditionally reckoned as three miles from low-water mark, but now extended by many States).
▶ **B** *noun*. A member of the Territorial Army; in *pl.*, the Territorial Army collectively. E17.

📖 J. COLVILLE The lack of training of our troops, most of whom . . are inexperienced territorials.

■ **territorially** *adverb* E19.

territorialise *verb* var. of TERRITORIALIZE.

territorialism /tɛrɪˈtɔːrɪəlɪz(ə)m/ *noun*. L19.
[from TERRITORIAL + -ISM. In sense 2, translating German *Territorialsystem*.]
1 A system giving predominance to the landed class; landlordism. L19.
2 *Hist.* A theory of Church government in which the civil power has supreme authority. L19.
3 In Scotland, the organization of church work on territorial lines (see TERRITORIAL *adjective* 1c). L19.
4 ZOOLOGY. = TERRITORIALITY 2. M20.
■ **territorialist** *noun* (*a*) a member or representative of the landed class; (*b*) *Hist.* a member of a Jewish organization, whose aim was to secure a separate territory for the Jews: M19.

territoriality /ˌtɛrɪtɔːrɪˈalɪti/ *noun*. L19.
[formed as prec. + -ITY.]
1 Territorial quality or condition; the position or status of being a territory. L19.
2 ZOOLOGY. A pattern of behaviour in which an animal or group of animals defends an area against others of the same species. M20.

territorialize /tɛrɪˈtɔːrɪəlʌɪz/ *verb trans*. Also **-ise**. E19.
[formed as prec. + -IZE.]
Make a territory of; place on a territorial basis; associate with or limit to a particular territory or district.

■ **territoriali'zation** *noun* L19.

Territorian /tɛrɪˈtɔːrɪən/ *noun*. L19.
[from TERRITORY + -AN.]
A native or inhabitant of the Northern Territory of Australia.

territorium /tɛrɪˈtɔːrɪəm/ *noun*. Pl. **-ria** /-rɪə/. E20.
[Latin: see next.]
ROMAN HISTORY. The district or area of land surrounding and within the boundaries of a Roman or provincial city and under its jurisdiction. Also, the districts surrounding States having dealings with Rome.

territory /ˈtɛrɪt(ə)ri/ *noun*. In sense 4 also **T-**. LME.
[Latin *territorium*, from *terra* land, after *dormitorium*, *praetorium*.]
1 †**a** The district or area of land surrounding a city or town and under its jurisdiction; *spec.* = TERRITORIUM. LME–M17. ▸**b** The extent of the land belonging to or under the jurisdiction of a ruler or State. LME. ▸**c** SCOTS LAW. The defined district over which a judge's jurisdiction extends and to which it is restricted. M18. ▸**d** ZOOLOGY. An area defended by an animal or group of animals against others of the same species. Cf. ***home range*** s.v. HOME *noun*. L18. ▸**e** An area defended by a team or player in a game. L19. ▸**f** The geographical area over which a goods-distributor or sales representative operates. Orig. *US*. E20.
2 A tract of land, a district of undefined boundaries; a region. E17.
3 *fig.* **a** An area of knowledge; a sphere of thought or action, a province. M17. ▸**b** ANATOMY. A tract or region of the body supplied by a specified blood-vessel etc. L19.
4 An organized division of a country (now esp. Canada and Australia) administered by a federal or external government, but not yet admitted to the full rights of a State. L18.

📖 **1b** B. BETTELHEIM A devastating defeat . . ; the last Italian territories were lost. ***capital territory***: see CAPITAL *adjective & noun*². ***federal territory***: see FEDERAL *adjective*. SCHEDULED **territory**. **2** *BBC Wildlife* Swampy territory in the . . Yucatan peninsula. **3a** M. HOCKING Life is an act of faith, . . a venture into uncharted territory. **come** or **go with the territory** be an essential or inescapable element (esp. an unwelcome one) of a role or situation. **4** R. J. CONLEY Liquor was illegal in Indian Territory, but everyone knew where to get it.

terroir /tɛːˈwɑː, *foreign* tɛrwaːr (*pl. same*)/ *noun*. L15.
[French, from medieval Latin *terratorium*, formed as TERRITORY.]
†**1** Territory; soil. L15–M17.
2 The complete natural environment in which a particular wine is produced, including factors such as the soil, topography, and climate. Also (in full ***goût de terroir*** /ˌɡuː də tɛrˈwɑː, *foreign* ɡu də tɛrwaːr/), the characteristic taste and flavour imparted to a wine by this environment. L20.

terror /ˈtɛrə/ *noun & verb*. LME.
[Old French *terrour* (mod. *terreur*) from Latin *terror*, from *terrere* frighten: see -OR.]
▶ **A** *noun*. **1** The state of being terrified or extremely frightened; intense fear or dread; an instance or feeling of this. LME.
2 The state or quality of being terrible or causing intense fear or dread; a thing or person that causes terror; something terrifying. Also, a literary genre concerned with the excitation of pleasurable feelings of fear by the depiction of violence, the supernatural, etc. (freq. in ***novel of terror***, ***tale of terror*** below). LME. ▸**b** A formidable or exasperating person; a troublesome person or thing, *esp.* a troublesome child. Also ***holy terror***. *joc.* & *colloq.* L19.
3 The use of organized repression or extreme intimidation; terrorism; *spec.* = ***the Terror*** below. E19.

📖 **1** L. HUDSON The terror in which she wakes, her pulse racing. G. DALY He lived in terror that his all-consuming love would . . force her to reject him. **2** R. W. EMERSON The terrors of the storm. C. S. FORESTER All his reading . . had warned him of the terrors of a lee shore. **b** A. MCCOWEN At school I was known as a terror and went looking for fights. **3** *Reader's Digest* The terror began with the cold-blooded massacre of students in Tiananmen Square.

Phrases: ***balance of terror***: see BALANCE *noun*. ***holy terror***: see sense 2b above. ***king of terrors***: see KING *noun*. **novel of terror** a tale of terror in novel form. ***Red Terror***: see RED *adjective*. **reign of terror** a period of remorseless repression or bloodshed during which the general community live in constant fear of death or violence. **tale of terror** a work of fiction in which violence, the supernatural, etc., are depicted so as to excite pleasurable feelings of fear in the reader. **the Terror** FRENCH HISTORY the period of the French Revolution from about March 1793 to July 1794, marked by extreme repression and bloodshed. ***White Terror***: see WHITE *adjective*.
Comb.: **terror-bombing** intensive and indiscriminate aerial bombing designed to frighten a country into surrender; **terror raid** a bombing raid of this nature; **terror-stricken**, **terror-struck** *adjectives* affected with terror, terrified.
▶ **B** *verb trans*. Strike with terror, terrify. *arch.* L16.
■ **terrorless** *adjective* lacking terror; not causing fear or dread: E19.

terrorise *verb* var. of TERRORIZE.

terrorism /ˈtɛrərɪz(ə)m/ *noun*. L18.
[French *terrorisme*, from Latin *terror*: see TERROR, -ISM.]
Terrorist principles and practices; the systematic employment of violence and intimidation to coerce a government or community, esp. into acceding to specific political demands; the fact of terrorizing or being terrorized.

📖 *New York Times* All attempts to destroy democracy by terrorism will fail. *Japan Times* Carvalho . . has been freed after almost five years in prison on terrorism charges. **reign of terrorism** *arch.* = ***the Terror*** s.v. TERROR *noun*.

terrorist /ˈtɛrərɪst/ *noun & adjective*. L18.
[French *terroriste*, from Latin *terror*: see TERROR, -IST.]
▶ **A** *noun*. **1 a** FRENCH HISTORY. In the French Revolution, an adherent or supporter of the Jacobins, who advocated and practised methods of partisan repression and bloodshed in the propagation of the principles of democracy and equality. L18. ▸**b** *gen.* A person who uses and favours violent and intimidating methods of coercing a government or community. M19.
2 A person who tries to awaken or spread a feeling of fear or alarm; an alarmist, a scaremonger. *derog.* Now *rare*. E19.

📖 **1a** P. HERVÉ Endeavouring to defend the king from the terrorists. **b** *Spectator* His war-time exploits as a terrorist in the Resistance. *Deccan Herald (Bangalore)* Terrorists made an abortive attempt to kill a securityman. **2** P. THOMPSON Pretended terrorists . . who affect to be alarmed for the condition of every white female.

▶ **B** *attrib.* or as *adjective*. Of, pertaining to, or characteristic of, terrorists or terrorism. E19.

📖 A. GHOSH He had been a member of one of the secret terrorist societies.

■ **terro'ristic** *adjective* characterized by or practising terrorism L19. **terro'ristically** *adverb* L20.

terrorize /ˈtɛrərʌɪz/ *verb*. Also **-ise**. E19.
[from TERROR + -IZE.]
1 *verb trans.* Fill or inspire with terror; *esp.* coerce by terror; use terrorism against. E19.
2 *verb intrans.* Foll. by *over*: govern, or maintain power, by terrorism; practise intimidation. *rare*. M19.

📖 **1** W. TREVOR Youths who'd been terrorising the neighbourhood. *Japan Times* Doctors . . camping . . in the wilderness terrorized by strange happenings.

■ **terrori'zation** *noun* L19. **terrorizer** *noun* L19.

terry /ˈtɛri/ *noun & adjective*. L18.
[Origin unkn.]
▶ **A** *noun*. A pile fabric with the loops uncut, now used esp. for towels; a baby's nappy made of terry towelling. Also, an uncut loop raised when weaving a pile fabric. L18.

📖 W. D. HOWELLS The furniture was in green terry.

▶ **B** *attrib.* or as *adjective*. Of or pertaining to terry; made of terry. M19.
terry towelling, (*US*) **terry cloth** an absorbent cotton or linen fabric used for making towels, babies' nappies, etc.

Terry Alt /tɛri ˈɔːlt/ *noun*. Also **Terryalt**. M19.
[Origin uncertain: perh. from *Terry Alts*, an innocent bystander suspected of a violent assault on a man.]
IRISH HISTORY. A member of a secret agrarian association active in western Ireland in the 1830s.

Tersanctus /təːˈsaŋktəs/ *noun*. M19.
[Latin, from *ter* thrice + *sanctus* holy.]
CHRISTIAN CHURCH. = SANCTUS 1, TRISAGION.

terse /təːs/ *adjective*. E17.
[Latin *tersus* pa. pple of *tergere* wipe, polish.]
†**1** Wiped, brushed; polished, burnished; sharp-cut; neat, spruce. E17–E19.
†**2** *fig.* Esp. of language: polite, polished, refined, cultured. E17–L18.
3 Of written matter, a writer, speech, etc.: neatly concise; compact and pithy in style or language; to the point. Also, (esp. of a person's manner or speech) brusque, curt, abrupt. L18.

📖 **2** J. EDWARDS Turned the whole Bible into pure, terse, elegant Latin. **3** H. WOUK She was almost uncivil, . . giving terse cool answers to questions. M. HUNTER This much one learns in writing for children—to be terse without losing the . . meaning.

■ **tersely** *adverb* L16. **terseness** *noun* L18.

tertia /ˈtəːʃə/ *noun*. M17.
[App. alt. of TERCIO.]
Hist. A division of infantry; a tercio; a regiment.

tertial /ˈtəːʃ(ə)l/ *noun & adjective*. M19.
[from Latin *tertius* third + -AL¹.]
ORNITHOLOGY. (Of or pertaining to) a tertiary feather.

tertian /ˈtəːʃ(ə)n/ *adjective & noun*. LME.
[Latin (*febris*) *tertiana*, from *tertius* third: see -AN.]
▶ **A** *adjective*. **1** MEDICINE. Designating a fever recurring every alternate (by inclusive reckoning every third) day;

For other words beginning with *ter-* see the entry for **ter-**

esp. in *tertian malaria*, *arch.* *tertian ague*, the commonest form of malaria due to infection by *Plasmodium vivax*. LME.

2 Third in order. Now only *spec.*, of or pertaining to the third year of an arts course in some Scottish universities (see sense B.3 below). L16.

3 MUSIC. Relating to the mean-tone temperament in which the major thirds are perfectly in tune. L19.

4 ROMAN CATHOLIC CHURCH. ***Tertian Father***, a Jesuit undergoing tertianship. L19.

▶ **B** *noun*. **1** MEDICINE. A tertian fever. LME.

2 A former unit of capacity for liquids, esp. wine or oil, equal to a third of a tun (70 imperial gallons, approx. 318 litres). Also, a large cask of this capacity; a puncheon. *obsolete* exc. *Hist.* LME.

3 In some Scottish universities (now only St Andrews), a third-year arts student. E19.

4 MUSIC. A mixture stop in an organ consisting of two ranks of open flue pipes usu. tuned a 17th and 19th above the fundamental. L19.

1 double tertian a fever in which there are two sets of peaks, each of them tertian.

tertianship /ˈtəːʃ(ə)nʃɪp/ *noun*. M19.
[from prec. + -SHIP.]
ROMAN CATHOLIC CHURCH. In the Jesuit order, a period of training in piety of the nature of a second novitiate undertaken one or two years before admission to final vows.

tertiary /ˈtəːʃ(ə)ri/ *noun & adjective*. M16.
[Latin *tertiarius* of the third part or rank, from *tertius* third: see -ARY¹.]

▶ **A** *noun*. **1** ROMAN CATHOLIC CHURCH. A member of the third order of a monastic body. M16.

2 GEOLOGY. †**a** A rock or deposit of later date than the Cretaceous. Usu. in *pl.* M–L19. ▸**b** (T-.) The period following the Mesozoic (or Secondary) era, which is a sub-era of the Cenozoic comprising the epochs from the Palaeocene to the Pliocene; the system of rocks dating from this time. L19.

3 ORNITHOLOGY. Orig., any of the innermost secondaries, when these are distinctive. Later, any of the feathers growing on the humerus, in cases where they function as remiges. Usu. in *pl.* M19.

4 Any of the colours resulting from a mixture of a primary and a secondary colour, as blue-green, mauve, etc. M19.

> 📖 **4** *Daily News* The most brilliant of positive colours as well as the quieter tertiaries.

▶ **B** *adjective*. **1** Of the third rank or importance; belonging to the third order, class, or category; third. M17. ▸**b** CHEMISTRY. (Of an organic compound) having the characteristic functional group located on a saturated carbon atom which is itself bonded to three other carbon atoms; designating, involving, or characterized by such an atom. Also, (of an amide, amine, or ammonium compound) derived from ammonia by replacement of three hydrogen atoms by organic radicals. M19. ▸**c** Designating the sector of the economy or workforce concerned with services, as transport, leisure, etc., rather than with the production of foodstuffs or raw materials, or with manufacturing. Freq. in ***tertiary industry*** below. M20.

2 GEOLOGY. †**a** Designating mountains of the most recent formation. Only in 19. ▸†**b** Designating or pertaining to a later date than the Cretaceous. Only in 19. ▸**c** (T-.) Designating or pertaining to the Tertiary (sense A.2b above). L19.

3 Of a colour: resulting from a mixture of a primary and a secondary colour. M19.

4 ORNITHOLOGY. Designating a feather that is a tertiary. M19.

5 MEDICINE. Of or pertaining to the third or late stage of a disease, esp. syphilis. L19.

6 ROMAN CATHOLIC CHURCH. Of or pertaining to the third order of a monastic body. L19.

> 📖 **1** *Sunday Times* A . . combination of secondary and tertiary causes . . led to his death.

Special collocations: **tertiary care** MEDICINE the most highly specialized medical care a patient can receive, as treatment by a consultant-based team in a major hospital. **tertiary college** a college at which tertiary education is provided. **tertiary education** education at the level next above that provided by secondary education and which may precede, include, or replace university, vocational, or professional training. **tertiary industry** (a) service industry; economic activity concerned with services rather than the production of raw material or with manufacturing. **tertiary recovery** the recovery of oil by advanced methods after conventional artificial means have ceased to be productive. **tertiary road** (orig. *US*) a road of a class lower than that of a secondary road; a minor or unsurfaced road. **tertiary structure** BIOCHEMISTRY the overall three-dimensional structure resulting from folding and covalent cross-linking of a protein or polynucleotide molecule. ***tertiary*** SYPHILIS. **tertiary treatment** a final treatment for sewage effluent to remove phosphates etc. before the water is discharged into rivers etc.

tertiate /ˈtəːʃɪeɪt/ *verb trans*. Long *rare*. E17.
[from late Latin *tertiat-* pa. ppl stem of *tertiare*, from *tertius* third: see -ATE³.]
1 Do (something) for the third time. Also, divide into three parts. E17.
†**2** Ascertain the strength of (a cannon) by measuring the thickness with calliper compasses in three places. L17–E19.
■ **terti'ation** *noun* division into three parts M17.

†**tertio** *noun* see TERCIO.

tertium comparationis /ˈtəːʃɪəm ˌkɒmpareɪʃɪˈəʊnɪs, ˈtəːtjəm ˌkɒmparɑːtɪˈəʊnɪs/ *noun phr.* E20.
[Latin = the third element in comparison.]
The factor which links or is the common ground between two elements in comparison.

tertium quid /ˌtəːʃɪəm ˈkwɪd, ˌtəːtjəm/ *noun phr.* E18.
[Late Latin translating Greek *triton ti* some third thing.]
Something indefinite or left undefined related in some way to two definite or known things, but distinct from both.

tertius /ˈtəːʃɪəs/ *adjective*. E19.
[Latin = third.]
Designating the youngest (in age or standing) of three people, esp. pupils, with the same surname. (Appended to a surname and used esp. in public schools.) Cf. PRIMUS *adjective* 2, SECUNDUS.

tertius gaudens /ˌtəːʃɪəs ˈgaʊdɛnz/ *noun phr.* L19.
[Latin, from *tertius* third + *gaudens* pres. pple of *gaudere* rejoice.]
A third party benefiting by the conflict or estrangement of two others.

> 📖 D. NEWSOME Better for them both to withdraw to allow the election of a *tertius gaudens*.

tertulia /terˈtulja/ *noun*. L18.
[Spanish.]
In Spain, an evening party, a soirée.

Tertullianism /təːˈtʌlɪənɪz(ə)m/ *noun*. E18.
[from *Tertullian* (see below), from Latin *Tertullianus*: see -ISM.]
The doctrine of the Christian writer Quintus Tertullian (*c* 160–*c* 220), a modification of Montanism; the rigid ascetic discipline connected with this.
■ **Tertullianist** *noun* an adherent or student of Tertullianism; *esp.* any of an early sect following this doctrine and discipline: E18.

teru-tero /ˈtɛruːˈterəʊ/ *noun*. Pl. **-os**. M19.
[Imit.]
A plover of northern S. America, *Vanellus cayanus*, which has spurred wings and a noisy cry.

†**terve** *verb trans. & intrans.* LME–M16.
[Corresp. to Old High German *zerben* (from Germanic verb meaning 'turn oneself over'), Old English *tearflian* roll over and over, wallow: prob. already in Old English. Cf. TOPSY-TURVY. See also OVERTERVE.]
Turn; turn upside down or over.

Tervueren /təˈvʊərən/ *noun*. M20.
[Flemish *Terveueren* (French *Tervuren*), a small town in Belgium east of Brussels.]
(An animal of) a breed of fawn-coloured rough-coated Belgian sheepdog, with dark pricked ears and a black muzzle.

Terylene /ˈterɪliːn/ *noun*. M20.
[from ***polyeth)ylene ter(ephthalate*** s.v. POLYETHYLENE, by inversion.]
(Proprietary name for) polyethylene terephthalate used as a textile fibre.

terza rima /tɛːtsə ˈriːmə/ *noun phr.* E19.
[Italian = third rhyme.]
PROSODY. A form of iambic verse of Italian origin, consisting of triplets in which the middle line of each triplet rhymes with the first and third of the next (*a b a*, *b c b*, *c d c*, etc.), as in Dante's *Divina Commedia*.

terzetto /tɛːtˈsetəʊ, təːt-/ *noun*. Pl. **-ttos**, **-tti** /-tiː/. E18.
[Italian: see TERCET.]
MUSIC. A vocal or (occas.) instrumental trio.

terzina /terˈtsina/ *noun*. *rare*. Pl. ***-ne*** /-ne/. M19.
[Italian = triplet.]
= TERCET.

teskere *noun* var. of TEZKERE.

TESL /ˈtɛs(ə)l/ *abbreviation*.
Teaching of English as a second language.

tesla /ˈtɛzlə/ *noun*. Also **T-**. Pl. **-s**, (in sense 2, also) same. L19.
[Nikola *Tesla* (1856–1943), Croatian-born US physicist.]
1 ***Tesla coil***, a type of induction coil invented by Tesla, employing a spark gap in place of an interruptor and capable of producing an intense high-frequency discharge. L19.
2 PHYSICS. (Usu. **t-**.) The SI unit of magnetic flux density, equal to one weber per square metre or 10,000 gauss. (Symbol T.) M20.

For other words beginning with *ter-* see the entry for **ter-**

Teso /ˈtɛsəʊ/ *noun & adjective*. Pl. of noun same. E20.
[Nilo-Hamitic name.]
(A member) of a Nilo-Hamitic people of central Uganda and western Kenya; (of) the Nilo-Hamitic language of this people.

TESOL /ˈtɛsɒl/ *abbreviation*.
Teaching (or teachers) of English to speakers of other languages.

TESSA /ˈtɛsə/ *abbreviation*.
Tax-exempt special savings account.

tessaract *noun* var. of TESSERACT.

tessaraglot /ˈtɛs(ə)rəglɒt/ *adjective*. *rare*. E18.
[from Greek *tessara-* combining form of *tessares* four + *glōtta* tongue.]
Of, in, or pertaining to four languages.

tesselate *adjective, verb*, **tesselated** *adjective*, **tesselation** *noun* vars. of TESSELLATE *adjective*, *verb* etc.

tessella /tɛˈsɛlə/ *noun*. *rare*. Pl. **-llae** /-liː/. L17.
[Latin, dim. of TESSERA.]
A small tessera.
■ **'tessellar** *adjective* of the nature or form of a tessella or tessellae M19.

tessellate /ˈtɛsələt/ *adjective*. Also **-elate**. E19.
[formed as next: see -ATE².]
= TESSELLATED.

tessellate /ˈtɛsəleɪt/ *verb*. Also **-elate**. L18.
[Late Latin *tessellat-* pa. ppl stem of *tessellare*, from TESSELLA: see -ATE³. Cf. next.]
1 *verb trans.* Make, combine, or fit into a mosaic (*lit. & fig.*); decorate with mosaics; make with tesserae. L18.
2 *verb trans. & intrans.* MATH. Cover (a plane surface) completely by the repeated use of (esp. identical) geometrical shapes, without gaps or overlapping; divide (a surface) *into* such a pattern of repeating shapes. Also, so fill or divide (a space or higher dimensional analogue). M20.

tessellated /ˈtɛsəleɪtɪd/ *adjective*. Also **-elated**. L17.
[(from Italian *tessellato* from) Latin *tessellatus*, formed as prec.: see -ATE², -ED¹.]
1 Consisting of or arranged in small cubes or squares; BOTANY & ZOOLOGY having colours or surface-divisions in regularly arranged squares or patches; chequered, reticulated. L17.
2 Of a floor, pavement, etc.: composed of small blocks of variously coloured material arranged in a pattern, ornamented with mosaic. E18.
3 Combined or arranged (as) in a mosaic. M19.

tessellation /tɛsəˈleɪʃ(ə)n/ *noun*. Also **-ela-**. M17.
[formed as TESSELLATE *verb*: see -ATION.]
1 An arrangement of shapes, colours, minute parts, etc., closely fitted together; *spec.* an arrangement of (esp. identical) polygons in a pattern without gaps or overlapping. M17.
2 The action or art of tessellating; the state of being tessellated. E19.

> 📖 **1** *fig.*: J. S. LE FANU The writings of the Apostolic Fathers are . . a tesselation of holy writ. **2** J. FORSYTH The work is not mosaic, for there is no tessellation.

tessera /ˈtɛs(ə)rə/ *noun*. Pl. **-rae** /-riː/. M17.
[Latin from Greek, neut. of *tesseres* var. of *tessares* four.]
1 a CLASSICAL ANTIQUITIES. A small quadrilateral tablet of wood, bone, etc., used as a token, tally, ticket, etc. M17. ▸**b** *fig.* A distinguishing sign or token; a watchword. M17.
2 A small square block of marble, glass, tile, etc., used in mosaic. L18.
3 ZOOLOGY. Each of the plates of an armadillo's carapace. E20.

> 📖 **1b** JOHN OWEN Making subjection to the pope . . the tessera and rule of all church communion. **2** *Times* The workmen had to learn to set the tesserae, one by one . . , into the cement.

■ **tesserate** /ˈtɛs(ə)rət/ *adjective* (*rare*) = TESSELLATED 2 E18.

tesseract /ˈtɛsərakt/ *noun*. Also **-ar-**. L19.
[from Greek *tesser(a-* combining form of *tesseres* (see prec.) + *akt(is* ray.]
MATH. A four-dimensional hypercube.

tesseral /ˈtɛs(ə)r(ə)l/ *adjective*. M19.
[from TESSERA: see -AL¹.]
1 Of, pertaining to, or resembling a tessera or tesserae; composed of tesserae. M19.
2 CRYSTALLOGRAPHY. Isometric, cubic. *rare*. M19.
3 MATH. Relating to the division of a spherical surface by two intersecting lines; ***tesseral harmonic***, a spherical surface harmonic which is the product of two factors depending respectively on latitude and longitude. L19.

tessitura /tɛsɪˈtʊərə/ *noun*. L19.
[Italian.]
MUSIC. The range within which most tones of a voice part or melody lie.

> 📖 K. AMIS Moving from top to bottom of the wide tessitura with no loss of tone.

tessular /ˈtɛsjʊlə/ *adjective.* Now *rare* or *obsolete.* L18.
[Irreg. from TESSERA + -ULE + -AR[1].]
CRYSTALLOGRAPHY. = TESSERAL 2.

test /tɛst/ *noun*[1]. LME.
[Old French (mod. *têt*), from Latin *testum*, *testu* var. of *testa* tile, earthen vessel, pot. Later treated as from TEST *verb*[2].]
1 Orig., a cupel used to treat gold or silver alloys or ore. Now, a cupel together with its iron frame, forming the movable hearth of a reverberatory furnace. LME.
2 *The* means of determining the existence or genuineness of anything; a critical examination or trial of a theory, a person's character, etc.; a standard for comparison or trial, a criterion. L16. ▸**b** A means of testing conformity in (esp. religious) belief; *spec.* (*Hist.*) an oath or declaration prescribed by any of the Test Acts. M17.
3 a CHEMISTRY etc. (An application of) a procedure for examining a substance under known conditions or with a specific reagent to determine its identity or the presence or absence of some constituent, activity, etc. Also, a substance by means of which this may be done. E19. ▸**b** (An application of) a procedure for determining the physical properties of a substance, material, etc., or the capabilities of a machine, etc., esp. to assess suitability for some purpose. Freq. as 2nd elem. of comb. L19. ▸**c** A procedure for assessing a person's aptitude, competence, skill, or knowledge, or for determining a person's mental or physiological condition; *spec.* (*a*) a set of problems in an academic subject to be solved without assistance, a relatively informal examination; (*b*) a driving test. Freq. as 2nd elem. of comb. E20.
4 *ellipt.* = *test match* below. E20.

> 2 B. MONTGOMERY His conclusions have stood the test of repeated re-examination. J. DUNN Some sort of metaphysical test of their fitness for life. **b** H. PAUL The belief in tests ought to be dead as the belief in witches. **3a** ***Millon's test, phosphatase test, Schiff test***, etc. **b** ***impact test, Izod test, Turing test***, etc. **c** E. H. CLEMENTS Mummy always drives. I haven't taken my test yet. J. ELLIOTT Doing her Anglo-Saxon grammar for a test tomorrow. E. SEGAL Painful tests he would undergo at the hands of . . Yale's senior neurologist. ***aptitude test, blood test, breath test, intelligence test, performance test, pregnancy test, screen test, tuberculin test***, etc. **4** attrib.: ***test batsman, test captain, test cricket, test team***, etc.

Phrases: ***alpha test***: see ALPHA 2b(f). ***blank test***: see BLANK *adjective.* ***means test***: see MEAN *noun*[1]. PATERNITY ***test***. **put to the test** try the character of (a person), cause to undergo testing. ***spot test***: see SPOT *noun, adjective, & adverb.* **stand the test of time, withstand the test of time** be or remain unchanged or unaffected by the passage of time.

Comb.: **Test Act** *Hist.* any of various statutes making eligibility for public office conditional on professing the established religion, *esp.* a 1673 act (repealed in 1828) requiring employees of the Crown to receive Anglican communion, acknowledge the monarch as head of the Church of England, and repudiate the doctrine of transubstantiation; **test ban** a ban on the testing of nuclear weapons; **test bed** (*a*) a piece of equipment for testing machines, esp. aircraft engines, before acceptance for general use; (*b*) *fig.* a testing-ground; **test card** (*a*) OPHTHALMOLOGY a large card printed with rows of letters of decreasing size, used in testing visual acuity (cf. SNELLEN); (*b*) TELEVISION a still picture transmitted outside normal programme hours to facilitate assessing the quality and position of the screen image; **test case** LAW an action brought to ascertain the law, thereby setting a precedent for other cases involving the same principle; **test chart** OPHTHALMOLOGY = *test card* (a) above; **test-cross** *noun & verb* (GENETICS) (*a*) *noun* a back cross between an individual whose genotype for a certain trait is unknown and one that is homozygous recessive for that trait, to determine the unknown genotype from that of the offspring; (*b*) *verb trans.* make the subject of a test-cross; **test drive** a drive taken to ascertain the qualities of a motor vehicle with a view to its regular use; **test-drive** *verb trans.* take a test drive in (a motor vehicle); **test-fire** *verb trans.* (orig. *US*) fire (a gun or missile) experimentally; **test flight**: for testing the performance of an aircraft etc.; **test-fly** *verb trans.* test the performance of (an aircraft etc.) in flight; **test-frame** the iron frame or basket in which a cupel is placed; **test-furnace** a reverberatory refining furnace, *esp.* one for treating silver-bearing alloys; **test-market** *verb & noun* (*a*) *verb trans.* (orig. *US*) put (a new product) on the market, usu. in a limited area, to assess consumers' response; (*b*) *noun* an area in which a product is test-marketed; **test match** (chiefly CRICKET & RUGBY FOOTBALL) an international match, *esp.* each of a series of matches between a touring team and the host country; **test meal** MEDICINE a standard meal given to stimulate secretion of digestive juices, which can then be extracted and tested; **test paper** (*a*) a paper impregnated with a chemical solution which changes colour in contact with certain other chemicals, and so acts as a test for the presence of the latter; (*b*) a paper set to test the knowledge etc. of a student, esp. one preparing for an examination; **test-piece** (*a*) a piece of anything as a sample for testing; (*b*) a piece of music (to be) performed by the contestants in a musical competition; **test pilot**: who test-flies an aircraft; **test-pilot** *verb trans.* = *test-fly* above; **test-pit** ARCHAEOLOGY a small preliminary excavation made to gain an idea of the contents or stratigraphy of a site; **test-retest** *adjective* (PSYCHOLOGY) of or designating a method by which a test is given to a subject on two occasions separated by a lapse of time; **test rig** ENGINEERING an apparatus used for assessing the performance of a piece of mechanical or electrical equipment; **test signal** a sequence of electrical impulses used for testing purposes in television broadcasting; **test specimen** a piece of metal etc. prepared for a mechanical test; **test strip** a strip of material used in testing; *esp.* in PHOTOGRAPHY, a strip of sensitized material, sections of which are exposed for different lengths of time to assess its response; **test well**: made in testing a site for oil.

test /tɛst/ *noun*[2]. *obsolete* exc. *Scot.* LME.
[App. from Latin *testis* witness: cf. ATTEST *noun.*]
†**1** A witness; evidence, witness borne. LME–M17.
†**2** = TESTE *noun.* E–M18.
3 = TESTAMENT 3. *Scot. rare.* L19.

test /tɛst/ *noun*[3]. LME.
[Latin *testa*: see TEST *noun*[1].]
†**1** A piece of earthenware, an earthenware vessel; a potsherd. LME–E17.
2 ZOOLOGY. The shell of certain invertebrates; the tough translucent outer layer of a tunicate. M19.

test /tɛst/ *verb*[1]. L15.
[Old French *tester* from Latin *testari* attest, make one's will, from *testis* witness; in sense 3 app. from TESTE.]
†**1** *verb trans.* Leave by will or testament, bequeath. *Scot. rare.* L15–E18.
2 *verb intrans.* Make a will, execute a testament. *obsolete* exc. *Scot.* L16.
3 *verb trans.* LAW (now *Hist.*). Date and sign the teste of (a writ etc.). E18.
4 *verb trans.* SCOTS LAW. Authenticate (a deed or written instrument) by a duly drawn-up clause signed by witnesses. M18.

test /tɛst/ *verb*[2]. E17.
[from TEST *noun*[1].]
1 *verb trans.* Subject (gold or silver) to a process of separation and refining in a test; assay. E17.
2 *verb trans.* Subject (a person, thing, theory, etc.) to a test; try (out); evaluate (a hypothesis etc.) by experiment or critical examination; put to the test; try the patience or endurance of (a person). E17. ▸**b** CHEMISTRY. Subject to a chemical test. Freq. foll. by *for* (a particular chemical). M19.
3 *verb intrans.* Undergo or take a test. Also (with noun, adjective, or adverbial compl.), achieve or receive a specified rating, result, score, etc., in a test. Orig. & chiefly *N. Amer.* M20.
4 *verb intrans.* Apply or carry out a test on a person or thing. Also foll. by *for.* M20.

> 2 D. LESSING One has to test everything one says and does against general standards. P. FITZGERALD Courage and endurance are useless if they are never tested. S. HOOD Reverend . . Murdoch . . tested the children on their knowledge of the Gospels. B. BETTELHEIM The . . discussion group on whom he used to test his new ideas. **test out** put (a theory etc.) to a practical test. **test the water** *fig.* make a preliminary or tentative exploration, ***tried and tested***: see TRIED *ppl adjective* 3. **3** T. MCGUANE A poor student who tested in the high percentiles. *Newsweek* Word that Magic Johnson had tested positive for HIV . . whipped round the country.

testa /ˈtɛstə/ *noun.* Pl. **testae** /ˈtɛstiː/. L18.
[Latin: see TEST *noun*[1].]
1 BOTANY. The protective outer covering of a seed; the seed-coat. L18.
†**2** ZOOLOGY. = TEST *noun*[3] 2. *rare.* Only in M19.

†**testable** *adjective*[1]. E17.
[Late Latin *testabilis*, from Latin *testari*: see TESTATE *noun & adjective*[1], -ABLE.]
1 LAW. Qualified to testify; able to make a will. E17–E18.
2 Devisable. L17–M18.

testable /ˈtɛstəb(ə)l/ *adjective*[2]. M17.
[from TEST *verb*[2] + -ABLE.]
†**1** Proving when tested to be of a specified kind. *rare.* Only in M17.
2 Able to be tested or tried; *spec.* (of a scientific hypothesis etc.) able to be empirically tested. M17.

> 2 B. MAGEE Scientific laws are testable in spite of being unprovable.

■ **testaˈbility** *noun* M20.

testacean /tɛˈsteɪʃ(ə)n/ *adjective & noun.* M19.
[formed as next + -AN.]
ZOOLOGY. ▸**A** *adjective.* Of an invertebrate animal (now esp. an amoeboid protozoan): having a shell. M19.
▸**B** *noun.* Orig., a shellfish, a mollusc. Now, any testacean animal, *esp.* a shelled amoeba. M19.

testaceous /tɛˈsteɪʃəs/ *adjective.* M17.
[Latin *testaceus*, formed as TEST *noun*[3]: see -ACEOUS.]
1 Having a shell, esp. a hard, calcareous, unarticulated shell. M17.
2 Of the nature of shells; consisting of a shell or shelly material. M17. ▸†**b** PHARMACOLOGY. Of a medicinal powder: prepared from the shells of animals. E18–M19.
3 Of a dull brownish-red colour like that of unglazed pottery, as a tile, a flower-pot, etc. L17.

testacy /ˈtɛstəsi/ *noun.* M19.
[from TESTATE *adjective*[1], after INTESTACY.]
LAW. The condition or fact of dying testate.

testae *noun* pl. of TESTA.

testament /ˈtɛstəm(ə)nt/ *noun.* ME.
[Latin *testamentum* will (in Christian Latin also translating Greek *diathēkē* covenant), from *testari* bear witness, make a will, from *testis* witness: see -MENT.]
1 = COVENANT *noun* 4. Long *arch.* ME.
2 (**T-**.) ▸**a** (The books of) either of the main divisions of the Christian Bible. ME. ▸**b** (A copy of) the New Testament. E16.
3 LAW. A formal declaration of a person's wishes as to the disposal of his or her property (formerly esp. personal property) after death; a will. Now *rare* or *obsolete* exc. in ***last will and testament***. Cf. WILL *noun*[1] 9. ME. ▸**b** *transf.* & *fig.* A (freq. spiritual) legacy, something bequeathed. ME.
4 A witness, a testimony; evidence, proof. Freq. foll. by *to.* LME.
5 SCOTS LAW. A document nominating an executor to administer personal or movable estate after the death of its owner. E16.

> 2 ***New Testament***: see NEW *adjective.* ***Old Testament***: see OLD *adjective.* **3b** J. GROSS *On Liberty* is a personal testament as well as a political tract. **4** *Which?* The company's success is . . a testament to good store design.

■ **testaˈmental** *adjective* pertaining to or of the nature of a testament E17.

testamentary /tɛstəˈmɛnt(ə)ri/ *adjective.* LME.
[Latin *testamentarius*, formed as prec.: see -ARY[1].]
1 Of, pertaining to, or of the nature of a will. LME.
2 Made or appointed by will. M16. ▸**b** Expressed or contained in a will. M18.
3 Of or pertaining to the Old or New Testament. M19.
■ **testamentarily** *adverb* (*rare*) in a testamentary manner, by will L18.

testamur /tɛˈsteɪmə, -ˈstɑːmʊə/ *noun.* M19.
[Latin, lit. 'we testify' (used in the document), from *testari*: see TESTATE *noun & adjective*[1].]
In a university, a certificate from the examiners declaring that a candidate has satisfied them. Later also *gen.*, any certificate.

testata *noun* pl. of TESTATUM.

testate /ˈtɛsteɪt/ *noun & adjective*[1]. LME.
[Latin *testatus* pa. pple of *testari* (also *-are*) bear witness, make one's will, attest: see -ATE[1], -ATE[2].]
LAW. ▸**A** *noun.* **1** A person who at death has left a valid will. LME.
†**2** A person who has given testimony; testimony, evidence. E–M17.
▸**B** *adjective.* **1** That has left a valid will at death. L15.
2 Settled by will. L18.

testate /ˈtɛsteɪt/ *adjective*[2]. M20.
[from TEST *noun*[3] + -ATE[2].]
= TESTACEAN *adjective.*

testate /ˈtɛsteɪt/ *verb intrans. rare.* E17.
[Latin *testat-* pa. ppl stem of *testari*: see TESTATE *noun & adjective*[1], -ATE[3].]
Bear witness, testify.

testation /tɛˈsteɪʃ(ə)n/ *noun.* M17.
[Latin *testatio(n-)*, formed as prec.: see -ATION.]
†**1** Attestation, testimony. Only in M17.
2 The disposal of property by will. M19.

testator /tɛˈsteɪtə/ *noun.* ME.
[Anglo-Norman *testatour* from Latin *testator*, from *testari*: see TESTATE *noun & adjective*[1], -OR.]
A person who makes a will, *esp.* one who has died leaving a will.

testatrix /tɛˈsteɪtrɪks/ *noun.* Pl. **-trices** /-trɪsiːz/, **-trixes**. L16.
[Late Latin, fem. of TESTATOR: see -TRIX.]
A female testator.

testatum /tɛˈsteɪtəm/ *noun.* Pl. **-ta** /-tə/. E17.
[Latin, use as noun of neut. of pa. pple of *testari*: see TESTATE *noun & adjective*[1].]
LAW. †**1** A writ formerly issued by a sheriff who had received a writ of capias, testifying that the defendant was not to be found within his jurisdiction. E17–M19.
2 The witnessing-clause of a deed. *rare.* M19.

teste /ˈtɛstiː, -steɪ/ *noun & preposition.* LME.
[Latin, abl. of *testis* witness, in the formula of authentication *teste meipso* lit. 'I myself being a witness'.]
▸**A** *noun.* LAW (now *Hist.*). Orig., the final clause in a royal writ naming the person who authenticates the monarch's seal. Later, the concluding part of any duly attested writ, giving the date and place of issue. LME.
▸**B** *preposition.* On the authority or testimony of (a specified person). M19.

> 2 *Listener* He tells us, *teste* Evelyn Waugh, of a Sitwellian habit of leaving Sitwell press cuttings . . in bowls.

testee /tɛˈstiː/ *noun.* M20.
[from TEST *verb*[2] + -EE[1].]
A person subjected to a test of any kind.

tester /ˈtɛstə/ *noun*¹. **LME.**
[medieval Latin *testerium*, *testrum*, *testura*, from Proto-Romance word meaning 'head', ult. from Latin *testa* tile.]
1 A canopy over a bed, esp. a four-poster bed. Formerly also, a structure at the head of a bed ascending to and (occas.) supporting the canopy. **LME.**
2 *transf.* A structure that covers or overhangs, as (*a*) a canopy carried over a dignitary; (*b*) the soundboard of a pulpit. **LME.**

tester /ˈtɛstə/ *noun*². *obsolete* exc. *Hist.* **M16.**
[App. alt. of **TESTON.**]
Orig., an English teston, *esp.* one of debased metal. Later (*slang*), a sixpence.

tester /ˈtɛstə/ *noun*³. **M17.**
[from **TEST** *verb*² or *noun*¹ + **-ER**¹.]
1 A person who or device which tests someone or something. **M17.**
2 *BIOLOGY.* A stock or strain of an organism used to investigate some genetic characteristic of another strain. **E20.**
3 A device dispensing a trial sample of a product, esp. a cosmetic or perfume. Orig. *US.* **L20.**

†**testern** *verb trans. rare* (Shakes.). Only in **L16.**
[from **TESTER** *noun*².]
Give a sixpence to, tip, (a person).

testes *noun* pl. of **TESTIS.**

testi *noun* pl. of **TESTO.**

testicle /ˈtɛstɪk(ə)l/ *noun.* **LME.**
[Latin *testiculus* dim. of **TESTIS**: see **-CLE.**]
1 Either of the two ellipsoidal glandular organs in male humans and other mammals which contain the sperm-producing cells and are usually enclosed in a scrotum. **LME.** ▸**b** Each of the testes or male gonads in non-mammalian animals. *rare.* **E18.**
†**2** The ovary in females. **LME–L17.**

testicular /tɛˈstɪkjʊlə/ *adjective.* **M17.**
[from prec. + **-AR**¹.]
1 Of, pertaining to, or functioning as a testicle or testis. **M17.**
2 Resembling a testicle or pair of testicles in form; testiculate. **M18.**
1 testicular feminization, **testicular feminizing** a familial condition produced in genetically male persons by the failure of tissue to respond to male sex hormones, resulting in a normal female anatomy but with testes in place of ovaries.

testiculate /tɛˈstɪkjʊlət/ *adjective.* **M18.**
[formed as prec. + **-ATE**².]
Esp. of the twin tubers of some orchids: shaped like a pair of testicles.
■ Also **testiculated** *adjective* (now *rare* or *obsolete*) **E18.**

†**testif** *adjective* see **TESTY.**

†**testificate** *noun.* Chiefly *Scot.* **L16.**
[Latin *testificatum* (that which is) testified, use as noun of neut. pa. pple of *testificari* **TESTIFY**: see **-ATE**¹.]
1 (A piece of) evidence, an indication. **L16–L19.**
2 A solemn written statement; a certificate; a testimonial. **E17–M19.**

testification /ˌtɛstɪfɪˈkeɪʃ(ə)n/ *noun.* Now *rare.* **LME.**
[Old French †*testificacion*, or Latin *testificatio(n-)*, from *testificat-* pa. ppl stem of *testificari* **TESTIFY**: see **-FICATION.**]
The action or an act of testifying; testimony, anything serving as evidence or proof.

†**testificator** *noun. rare.* **M18–M19.**
[Latin *testificat-*: see prec., **-OR.**]
A person who testifies.

testificatory /ˌtɛstɪfɪˈkeɪt(ə)ri/ *adjective.* **L16.**
[formed as prec.: see **-ORY**².]
Of such a kind as to testify or serve as evidence.

testify /ˈtɛstɪfʌɪ/ *verb.* **LME.**
[Latin *testificari* (later *-are*) bear witness, proclaim, from *testis* witness: see **-FY.**]
1 *verb trans.* Bear witness to, assert the truth of, serve as evidence or proof of, (a statement etc.); give or be evidence *that.* **LME.**
2 *verb intrans.* Bear witness; give testimony; serve as evidence. **LME.**
3 *verb trans. & intrans.* Profess openly, proclaim, declare, (a fact, belief, etc.); declare (a thing) solemnly. Freq. in biblical allusions. **LME.**
4 *verb trans.* Display, manifest, express, (a desire, emotion, etc.). **M16.**

> 🕮 **1** T. JEFFERSON The superlative wisdom of Socrates is testified by all antiquity. W. HANNA Manuscript volumes . . remain to testify his diligence. M. BERGMANN Russell's poem testifies that the capacity to fall in love is not extinguished in old age. **2** J. QUINCY Testified to me of the affection with which he was regarded. T. CAPOTE We'll get a new trial, and Perry will testify and tell the truth. P. ACKROYD Some of them testified against me . . in the dock. J. HALPERIN Four acquaintances . . testified to his good character. **3** P. STRANGFORD They testify their faith therein openly and aloud.

■ **testifier** *noun* a person who testifies **L16.**

testimonial /tɛstɪˈməʊnɪəl/ *adjective & noun.* **LME.**
[Old French *tesmoignal* (also mod.) *testimonial*, from *tesmoin* (mod. *témoin*) witness, or from late Latin *testimonialis*, from Latin *testimonium* **TESTIMONY** *noun*: see **-IAL.**]
▸ **A** *adjective.* **1** Of, pertaining to, or of the nature of testimony; serving as evidence. *arch.* **LME.**
2 Serving as a testimonial or token of esteem. **M19.**

> 🕮 **1** †**letter testimonial**, †**letters testimonial** a letter testifying to the bona fides of the bearer; credentials. **2** *Daily Express* A testimonial dinner was given to . . the millionaire American. **testimonial match** *SPORT* a match of which the proceeds go to a particular player or person being honoured.

▸ **B** *noun.* **1** Chiefly *LAW.* Anything serving as evidence, *esp.* oral or documentary testimony; a written attestation, an affidavit. Also, a certificate; *spec.* an official warrant or pass. *obsolete* exc. as in sense 2. **LME.**
2 A formal letter or other document testifying to a person's qualifications, character, or conduct; a recommendation of a person or thing, usu. in writing. **L16.**
3 A gift presented (usu. publicly) to a person as a mark of esteem, in acknowledgement of services, merit, etc.; a tribute. **M19.**

> 🕮 **2** W. RAEPER Monson was . . happy to write a testimonial for him to the theological college. J. HALPERIN Testimonials he had brought . . procured personal introductions to . . William Dean Howells. **3** attrib.: *Pall Mall Gazette* The testimonial craze . . is highly inconvenient to people of moderate means.

■ **testimonialize** *verb trans.* give a testimonial to (a person) **M19.**

testimonium /tɛstɪˈməʊnɪəm/ *noun.* **L17.**
[formed as next.]
1 A letter testifying to the piety and learning of a candidate for holy orders; a certificate of proficiency given by a university, college, etc. **L17.**
2 *LAW.* In full ***testimonium clause***. A concluding part of a document (usu. beginning 'In witness whereof') stating the manner of its execution. **E19.**

testimony /ˈtɛstɪməni/ *noun.* **ME.**
[Latin *testimonium*, from *testis* witness: see **-MONY.**]
1 Evidence, proof, *esp.* (*LAW*) evidence given in court, an oral or written statement under oath or affirmation. **ME.**
2 a *The* Mosaic law, *the* decalogue. **LME.** ▸**b** In *pl.* The precepts (of God). **M16.**
3 a (An) open acknowledgement or profession, esp. of religious faith or experience. *arch.* **M16.** ▸**b** An expression or declaration of disapproval; a protestation. *arch.* **L16.**
†**4** A written certificate, a testimonial. **L16–M17.**

> 🕮 **1** R. L. STEVENSON That she was married . . was sorely contradicted by the testimony of her appearance. J. BALDWIN He stated that he was not involved, and asked one of the boys to corroborate his testimony. J. THURBER Let us . . consider the testimony of three separate eyewitnesses. ***bear testimony***: see **BEAR** *verb*¹. ***2a Ark of Testimony***: see **ARK** 2. **3a** *Quest* Students have given testimonies to . . their faith in . . Christ. **seal one's testimony with blood**, **seal one's testimony with one's blood** be martyred for one's religious faith.

testimony /ˈtɛstɪməni/ *verb.* **ME.**
[Old Northern French *testimoiner* from medieval Latin *testimoniare*, formed as prec.]
†**1** *verb trans.* **a** Bear witness or testify to. Only in **ME.** ▸**b** Test or prove by evidence. *rare* (Shakes.). Only in **E17.**
2 *verb intrans.* Bear witness (*to*). Long *rare.* **LME.**

testing /ˈtɛstɪŋ/ *verbal noun*¹. **L17.**
[from **TEST** *verb*¹ + **-ING**¹.]
The action of **TEST** *verb*¹; *esp.* the making of a will.

testing /ˈtɛstɪŋ/ *verbal noun*². **L17.**
[from **TEST** *verb*² + **-ING**¹.]
The action of **TEST** *verb*².
Comb.: **testing-ground** an area used for demonstration and experiment (*lit. & fig.*); **testing station** *NZ* an establishment where motor vehicles are tested for roadworthiness.

testis /ˈtɛstɪs/ *noun.* Pl. **testes** /ˈtɛstiːz/. **E18.**
[Latin = witness (i.e. to virility).]
ANATOMY. **1** The primary male organ of reproduction (paired in humans and other vertebrates), in which sperm are produced; a testicle. **E18.** ▸†**b** The ovary in females. **E18–M19.**
2 In *pl.* The posterior pair of optic lobes at the base of the brain in mammals. *rare.* **L19.**
1 ***retractile testis***: see **RETRACTILE** *adjective*¹.

testo /ˈtɛsto/ *noun.* Pl. ***-ti*** /-ti/. **E18.**
[Italian from Latin *textus* **TEXT.**]
MUSIC. **1** The words of a song; the libretto of an opera; the text or theme of a composition. Cf. **TEXT** *noun* 6. **E18.**
2 The narrator in an oratorio or similar work. **M20.**

teston /ˈtɛst(ə)n/ *noun. obsolete* exc. *Hist.* Also **testoon** /tɛˈstuːn/. **M16.**
[Obsolete French, or from Italian †*testone* from *testa* head from Latin *testa* tile: see **-OON.**]
NUMISMATICS. **1** Orig., a silver coin struck at Milan by Galeazzo Maria Sforza (Duke of Milan 1468–76), bearing a portrait or head of the duke. Later, any of various similar or equivalent silver coins (with or without a portrait) used in Italy and France. **M16.**
2 An English coin, usu. of debased metal bearing a portrait of the monarch, originally worth a shilling but rapidly devalued. **M16.**
3 A Scottish silver coin weighing about 76 grains, originally bearing a portrait of Mary Stuart. **M16.**
4 A silver coin first coined by Manoel I of Portugal *c* 1500, originally weighing 122 grains (later less). Also, an obsolete Italian coin. **L16.**

testosterone /tɛˈstɒstərəʊn/ *noun.* **M20.**
[from **TESTIS** + **-O-** + **-STERONE.**]
BIOLOGY. A steroid hormone that stimulates the development of male secondary sexual characteristics, produced in the testes and, in very much smaller quantities, in the ovaries and adrenal cortex.
Comb.: **testosterone propionate** *PHARMACOLOGY* the propionic acid ester of testosterone, given parenterally as a longer-lasting alternative to testosterone.

†**testril** *noun. rare.* **E17–E20.**
[Dim. alt. of **TESTER** *noun*².]
A sixpence.

test-tube /ˈtɛsttjuːb/ *noun.* **M19.**
[from **TEST** *noun*¹ + **TUBE** *noun.*]
A cylindrical container of thin transparent glass, closed at one end, used in scientific laboratories etc. to hold small amounts of liquid.
Attrib. & comb.: Designating procedures and operations, esp. fertilization, carried out artificially or under laboratory conditions, and the results of such operations, as ***test-tube bull***, ***test-tube pregnancy***, etc.; **test-tube baby** (*a*) (now *rare*) a baby conceived by artificial insemination; (*b*) a baby that has developed from an ovum fertilized outside the mother's body; **test-tube cultivation**, **test-tube culture** the raising of bacteria in a nutrient medium contained in a test-tube.

testudinal /tɛˈstjuːdɪn(ə)l/ *adjective.* **E19.**
[Latin *testudin-*, *testudo* **TESTUDO**: see **-AL**¹.]
(Characteristic) of or shaped like a tortoise; vaulted, arched.

testudinate /tɛˈstjuːdɪnət/ *adjective. rare.* **M19.**
[formed as prec.: see **-ATE**².]
1 Shaped like a testudo; vaulted, arched. **M19.**
2 Of or pertaining to tortoises. **M19.**
■ **testudinated** *adjective* = **TESTUDINATE** 1 **E18.**

testudineous /tɛstjuːˈdɪnɪəs/ *adjective.* **M17.**
[Latin *testudineus*, from next: see **-EOUS.**]
Slow, dilatory.

testudo /tɛˈstjuːdəʊ, -ˈstuː-/ *noun.* Pl. **-dos**, **-dines** /-dɪniːz/. **LME.**
[Latin, from *testa* pot, shell, *testu* pot-lid.]
†**1** *MEDICINE.* An encysted cranial tumour. Long only in Dicts. **LME–M19.**
2 *ZOOLOGY.* A tortoise, *esp.* one of the genus *Testudo* including the common European species. Now chiefly as mod. Latin genus name. **LME.**
3 *Hist.* A movable screen with an arched roof, used to protect besieging troops; a protective screen formed by a body of troops in close array with overlapping shields usu. above their heads. **LME.**
4 *MUSIC HISTORY.* In antiquity, a kind of lyre. **E18.**

testy /ˈtɛsti/ *adjective.* Also (earlier) †**-tif.** **LME.**
[Anglo-Norman *testif*, from Old French *teste* (mod. *tête*) head from Latin *testa*: see **TEST** *noun*¹. Cf. **-IVE.**]
1 Orig., headstrong, impetuous, rash. Later, aggressive, contentious. Long *obsolete* exc. as passing into sense 2. **LME.**
2 Irritable; impatient of being thwarted; irascible, short-tempered; peevish, touchy. **E16.**

> 🕮 **2** SHAKES. *Jul. Caes.* Must I . . crouch Under your testy humour? *Spectator* Folks less intractable and testy than such prejudiced disputants.

■ **testily** *adverb* **M18.** **testiness** *noun* **M16.**

Tet /tɛt/ *noun.* **L19.**
[Vietnamese.]
The Vietnamese lunar New Year. Freq. *attrib.*

tetampan /tɛˈtampan/ *noun.* **E19.**
[Malay.]
In Western Malaysia, an ornate shoulder cloth worn by a royal servant.

tetanal /ˈtɛtən(ə)l/ *adjective. rare.* **M20.**
[formed as next + **-AL**¹.]
MEDICINE. Of, pertaining to, causing, or characteristic of tetanus (sense 1). Chiefly in ***tetanal toxin***, tetanus toxin.

tetanic /tɪˈtanɪk/ *adjective.* **E18.**
[Latin *tetanicus* from Greek *tetanikos*, from *tetanos*: see **TETANUS**, **-IC.**]
MEDICINE. Of, pertaining to, characterized by, or characteristic of tetanus or tetany; *esp.* designating tonic muscular contraction.
■ **tetanically** *adverb* **L19.**

tetanize /ˈtɛt(ə)nʌɪz/ *verb trans.* Also **-ise**. M19.
[from TETANUS + -IZE.]
PHYSIOLOGY. Produce tetanic contraction in. Chiefly as ***tetanized*** *ppl adjective*, ***tetanizing*** *verbal noun & ppl adjective*.
■ **tetaniˈzation** *noun* the production of tetanic contraction in a muscle L19.

tetano- /ˈtɛt(ə)nəʊ/ *combining form* of TETANUS: see -O-.
■ **tetanoˈlysin** *noun* a tetanus toxin which causes tissue destruction in an infected cut E20. **tetanoˈspasmin** *noun* a tetanus toxin which spreads along the nerves causing tetanic spasms and lockjaw E20.

tetanoid /ˈtɛt(ə)nɔɪd/ *adjective. rare.* M19.
[from TETANUS + -OID.]
MEDICINE. Of the nature of or resembling tetanus.

tetanus /ˈtɛt(ə)nəs/ *noun.* LME.
[Latin from Greek *tetanos* muscular spasm, from *teinein* stretch.]
1 MEDICINE. An acute infectious disease characterized by tonic rigidity and violent spasms of some or all of the voluntary muscles, caused by infection with the bacterium *Clostridium tetani*, usu. by contamination of a wound; lockjaw. LME.
2 PHYSIOLOGY. Tonic muscular contraction. L19.
Comb.: **tetanus toxin** a toxin produced by the tetanus bacillus; *spec.* tetanospasmin.

tetany /ˈtɛt(ə)ni/ *noun.* L19.
[French *tétanie* intermittent tetanus, from prec.: see -Y[3].]
MEDICINE. A condition characterized by intermittent muscular spasms, esp. in the face and extremities, caused chiefly by deficiency of free calcium in the blood plasma.

tetarteron /tɪˈtɑːt(ə)rən/ *noun.* E20.
[Greek *tetartēron* lit. 'measure of capacity', from *tetartos* fourth.]
NUMISMATICS. A Byzantine gold coin of the 10th & 11th cents.

tetarto- /tɪˈtɑːtəʊ/ *combining form.*
[from Greek *tetartos* fourth: see -O-.]
CRYSTALLOGRAPHY. Forming adjectives and related nouns with ref. to crystal forms having one fourth of the holohedral number of faces etc.
■ **tetartoˈhedral** *adjective* having a quarter of the number of faces as the holohedral class of the crystal system concerned M19. **tetartoˈhedrism** *noun* the property or quality of crystallizing in tetartohedral forms M19. **tetartoˈhedron** *noun*, pl. **-dra**, **-drons**, a tetartohedral crystal L19.

tetch /tɛtʃ/ *noun. obsolete* exc. *dial.* M17.
[Perh. back-form. from TETCHY.]
A fit of petulance or anger.

tetched /tɛtʃt/ *adjective. US dial. & colloq.* M20.
[Alt. of TOUCHED.]
Slightly insane, slightly impaired in intelligence.

tetchous /ˈtɛtʃəs/ *adjective. US dial.* L19.
[from next: see -OUS.]
= TETCHY 1.

tetchy /ˈtɛtʃi/ *adjective.* Also **techy**. L16.
[Prob. from var. of TACHE *noun*[1]: see -Y[1].]
1 Easily irritated, offended, or angered; testy, irritable; touchy. L16.
2 *fig.* Of land: difficult to work or manage. *dial.* M19.
📖 **1** M. HOCKING The solemnity . . had developed into a tetchy anxiety. K. LETTE Julian gave a tetchy sigh.
■ **tetchily** *adverb* M17. **tetchiness** *noun* E17.

tête /tɛt (*pl. same*), teɪt/ *noun. obsolete* exc. *Hist.* M18.
[French, lit. 'head'.]
A woman's hair or wig, worn high and elaborately ornamented in the fashion of the late 18th cent.

tête-à-tête /teɪtɑːˈteɪt, tɛtaˈtɛt/ *noun, adverb, adjective, & verb.* L17.
[French, lit. 'head to head'.]
▶ **A** *noun.* **1** A private conversation or interview, esp. between two people. L17.
2 An S-shaped sofa, enabling two people to sit face to face. M19.
▶ **B** *adverb.* Together in private; face to face. E18.
▶ **C** *attrib.* or as *adjective.* Private, confidential; involving or attended by only two people. E18.
▶ **D** *verb intrans.* Engage in private conversation (*with* another person). M19.

tête-bêche /tɛtbɛʃ; -ˈbɛʃ, teɪt-/ *noun & adjective.* Pl. of noun pronounced same. L19.
[French, from *tête* head + *bêche* (reduced from *béchevet*) lit. 'double bed-head'.]
PHILATELY. (A postage stamp) printed upside down relative to the next stamp in the same row or column.

tête de boeuf /tɛt də bœf/ *adjectival phr.* L19.
[French, lit. 'ox's head'.]
EMBROIDERY. Designating an embroidery stitch involving two slanting stitches in the form of a vee.

tête de cuvée /tɛt də kyve/ *noun phr.* Pl. **têtes de cuvées** (pronounced same). E20.
[French, lit. 'head of the vatful'.]
(Wine from) a vineyard producing the best wine in the locality of a village.

tête de mouton /tɛt də mutɔ̃/ *noun phr. obsolete* exc. *Hist.* Pl. **têtes de mouton** (pronounced same). M18.
[French, lit. 'sheep's head'.]
A woman's hairstyle with close frizzy curls.

tête de nègre /tɛt də nɛgr/ *adjectival phr.* E20.
[French, lit. 'Negro's head'.]
Of a dark brown colour approaching black.

tête de pont /tɛt də pɔ̃/ *noun phr.* Pl. **têtes de pont** (pronounced same). L18.
[French.]
A bridgehead.

tetel /ˈteɪt(ə)l, ˈtɛt(ə)l/ *noun.* Now *rare.* M19.
[Origin unkn.]
= TORA.

tête montée /tɛt mɔ̃te/ *adjectival & noun phr.* E19.
[French, lit. 'excited head'.]
▶ **A** *adjectival phr.* Overexcited, agitated, worked up. E19.
▶ **B** *noun phr.* An overexcited or agitated state of mind. M19.

têtes de cuvées *noun phr.* pl. of TÊTE DE CUVÉE.

têtes de mouton, **têtes de pont** *noun phrs.* pls. of TÊTE DE MOUTON, TÊTE DE PONT.

tether /ˈtɛðə/ *noun & verb.* Also †**teather**, †**tedder**. LME.
[Old Norse *tjóðr* corresp. to Middle Low German, Middle Dutch *tüder*, *tudder* (Dutch *tuier*), Old High German *zeotar* fore-pole, from Germanic base meaning 'fasten'.]
▶ **A** *noun.* **1** A rope or cord by which an animal is tied to a stake etc. and thereby restricted in movement or confined to the spot. LME. ▸**b** A rope used for some other purpose; *spec.* (*a*) a boat's tow rope; (*b*) a noose. Now *rare* or *obsolete.* E16.
2 *fig.* **a** The furthest extent of one's knowledge, authority, freedom of action, etc.; scope, limit. L16. ▸**b** A bond, a fetter. E17.
📖 **2a** N. BACON A large Teather, and greater privilege than ever the Crown had. **b** BYRON Weary of the matrimonial tether.
Phrases: **the end of one's tether** the extreme limit of one's patience, resources, abilities, etc. ***wallop in a tether***: see WALLOP *verb* 5.
▶ **B** *verb trans.* **1 a** Tie or confine with a tether. LME. ▸**b** *gen.* Fasten, make fast. M16.
2 *fig.* Bind by conditions or circumstances. LME.
📖 **1a** R. MACAULAY I took charge of the camel, and tethered it to its tree. **b** G. GREENE The watch was safely tethered by its silver chain . . to the mayor's waistcoat. **2** H. JAMES She would fain see me all my life tethered to the law.

Tethys /ˈtɛθɪs/ *noun.* L19.
[Latin from Greek *Tēthus* a sea-goddess, sister and wife of Oceanus.]
GEOLOGY. A large sea that lay between Laurasia and Gondwanaland during late Palaeozoic times. Also ***Tethys Ocean***, ***Tethys Sea***.
■ **Tethyan** *adjective* of or pertaining to Tethys L19.

Teton /ˈtiːtɒn, -t(ə)n/ *noun & adjective.* E19.
[Dakota *tʰítʰųwą* lit. 'dwellers on the prairie'.]
= LAKOTA.

tetr- *combining form* see TETRA-.

tetra /ˈtɛtrə/ *noun.* M20.
[Abbreviation of mod. Latin *Tetragonopterus* former genus name (lit. 'tetragonal finned').]
Any of various small, often brightly coloured tropical freshwater fishes of the characin family, freq. kept in aquaria.
NEON *tetra*.

tetra- /ˈtɛtrə/ *combining form.* Before a vowel also **tetr-**. M19.
[Greek, combining form of *tettares* four.]
Having four, fourfold.
■ **tetraalkyllead** /ˌtɛtraalkɪlˈlɛd/ *noun* a compound whose molecule consists of four alkyl radicals bonded to an atom of lead, as tetraethyl lead E20. **tetracene** *noun* (CHEMISTRY) = NAPHTHACENE M20. **tetraˈchloride** *noun* (CHEMISTRY) a compound of four atoms of chlorine with some other element or radical (***carbon tetrachloride***: see CARBON *noun*) M19. **tetraˌchlorodiˌbenzodiˈoxin** *noun* (CHEMISTRY) = TETRACHLORODIBENZOPARADIOXIN L20. **tetraˌchlorodiˌbenzoparadiˈoxin**, **-benzo-*p*-dioxin** *noun* (CHEMISTRY) a chlorinated tricyclic hydrocarbon, $C_{12}H_4O_2Cl_4$, which is a toxic by-product of the manufacture of 2,4,5-T (also called ***dioxin***, ***TCDD***) M20. **tetrachloroˈethane**, **-chlorethane** *noun* (CHEMISTRY) either of two isomeric compounds, $C_2H_2Cl_4$, that are dense colourless liquids; *spec.* the symmetrical isomer, which is used in solvents and is toxic: L19. **tetrachoric** /-ˈkɔːrɪk, -ˈkɒrɪk/ *adjective* (STATISTICS) designating or pertaining to a table in which data are divided into two according to either of two criteria, so having four subdivisions E20. **tetraˈchotomous** *adjective* having four branches, esp. all from the same point E19. **tetraˈchotomy** *noun* (a) division into four branches or members M19. **tetraˈcolon** *noun*, pl. **-la**, GREEK PROSODY a metrical period consisting of four cola E18. **tetracoral** *noun* (PALAEONTOLOGY) a fossil coral of the order Rugosa, a rugose coral L19. **tetraˈcyclic** *adjective* (*a*) BOTANY (of a flower) having the parts in four whorls; (*b*) CHEMISTRY containing four rings in the molecule: L19. **tetraˈdactyl** *adjective & noun* (*a*) *adjective* having four fingers, toes, or finger-like processes; (*b*) *noun* (*rare*) an animal, esp. a vertebrate, having four toes on each foot: M19. **tetraˈdactylous** *adjective* = TETRADACTYL *adjective* E19. **tetraˈdecane** *noun* (CHEMISTRY) any of a series of saturated hydrocarbons (alkanes) with the formula $C_{14}H_{30}$; *spec.* (also *n-tetradecane*) the unbranched isomer $CH_3(CH_2)_{12}CH_3$: L19. **tetraˈdecyl** *noun* (CHEMISTRY) the radical $C_{14}H_{29}$· derived from tetradecane M19. †**tetradiapason** *noun* (MUSIC) an interval of four octaves E18–E19. **tetradrachm** *noun* (ANTIQUITIES) an ancient Greek silver coin worth four drachms L16. **tetraˈdynamous** *adjective* (BOTANY) having six stamens in pairs, four of which are longer than the others (as in the family Cruciferae) E19. **tetraˈethyl** *adjective* (CHEMISTRY) having four ethyl groups in the molecule; ***lead tetraethyl***, ***tetraethyl lead***, a colourless oily toxic liquid, $Pb(C_2H_5)_4$, added to petrol as an antiknock agent: E20. **tetraethylaˈmmonium** *noun* (CHEMISTRY) the quaternary ion $(C_2H_5)_4N^+$, whose salts have been used as ganglion-blocking agents to treat hypertension M19. **tetrafluoroˈethylene** *noun* (CHEMISTRY) a dense colourless gas, $F_2C{=}CF_2$, which is polymerized to make plastics such as polytetrafluoroethylene M20. **tetragamy** /tɪˈtragəmi/ *noun* (*a*) a fourth marriage; (*b*) marriage with four women simultaneously: M19. **tetraglot** *adjective* speaking, written in, or composed in four languages L16. **tetragnath** *adjective & noun* (*a*) *adjective* (*rare*) having four jaws; (*b*) *noun* a spider of the small family Tetragnathidae, having prominent chelicerae: E17. **tetragram** *noun* a word of four letters; *spec.* the Tetragrammaton: M17. **teˈtragynous** *adjective* (BOTANY) having four pistils L19. **tetraˈhydrate** *noun* (CHEMISTRY) a hydrate containing four molecules of water in every molecule of the compound L19. **tetraˈhydric** *adjective* (CHEMISTRY) containing four hydroxyl groups in the molecule L19. **tetrahydroˈcannabinol** *noun* (CHEMISTRY) a derivative of cannabinol that is the active principle in cannabis and hashish M20. **tetrahydroˈfuran** *noun* (CHEMISTRY) a colourless liquid heterocyclic compound, C_4H_8O, used esp. as a solvent for plastics and as an intermediate in organic syntheses E20. **tetrahydroˈnaphthalene** *noun* (CHEMISTRY) a compound derived from naphthalene by the addition of four hydrogen atoms; *spec.* = TETRALIN: L19. †**tetralogue** *noun* (*rare*) (*a*) a conversation between four people or parties; (*b*) = TETRALOGY 1: M17–E19. **tetramer** *noun* (CHEMISTRY) a compound whose molecule is composed of four molecules of monomer E20. **tetraˈmeric** *adjective* (CHEMISTRY) of the nature of a tetramer, consisting of a tetramer or tetramers M20. **teˈtramerism** *noun* (BIOLOGY) the condition or character of being tetramerous L19. **teˌtrameriˈzation** *noun* (CHEMISTRY) the formation of a tetramer from smaller molecules L20. **teˈtramerous** *adjective* (BIOLOGY) having parts arranged in groups of four E19. **tetramorph** *noun* (ART) a composite figure combining the iconographical symbols of the four evangelists (cf. *Revelation* 4:6–8) M19. **tetraˈmorphic** *adjective* (*a*) BOTANY & ZOOLOGY occurring in four different forms; (*b*) of or pertaining to a tetramorph: L19. **teˈtrandrous** *adjective* (BOTANY) having four stamens E19. **tetraˈnucleotide** *noun* (BIOCHEMISTRY) an oligonucleotide containing four nucleotides; *spec.* (now *Hist.*) one composed of four different bases, formerly thought to constitute the nucleic acid molecule: E20. **tetrapaˈrental** *adjective & noun* (BIOLOGY) (an organism) produced by the fusion of two embryos L20. **tetrapaˈresis** *noun* (MEDICINE) muscular weakness of all four limbs L20. **tetrapaˈretic** *adjective* (MEDICINE) of, pertaining to, or affected by tetraparesis L20. **tetraˈpetalous** *adjective* (BOTANY) having four petals L17. **tetraˈphonic** *adjective* designating or pertaining to certain forms of quadraphonic recording and reproduction M20. **tetrapody** /tɪˈtrapədi/ *noun* (PROSODY) a line or group of four metrical feet M19. **tetrapolis** /tɪˈtrapəlɪs/ *noun* a district or State division consisting of four cities or towns M19. **tetraˈpolitan** *adjective* of or pertaining to four cities M19. **teˈtrapterous** *adjective* (of an insect, a fruit, etc.) having four wings or winglike appendages E19. **tetraˈpylon** *noun* a building or structure with four gates E20. **tetraˈpyrrole** *noun* (CHEMISTRY) a compound containing four pyrrole nuclei, esp. in the form of a ring (as in porphin) E20. **tetraˈquetrous** *adjective* [after TRIQUETROUS] BOTANY having four sharp angles L19. **tetraˈsepalous** *adjective* (BOTANY) having four sepals E19. **tetraˈspermous** *adjective* (BOTANY) having four seeds M18. **tetraspoˈrangium** *noun*, pl. **-gia**, BOTANY a sporangium producing or containing tetraspores L19. **tetraspore** *noun* (BOTANY) any of certain kinds of spore occurring in groups of four; *esp.* (in a red alga) each of the four spores produced by a tetrasporophyte, two of which produce male plants and two female: M19. **tetraˈsporophyte** *noun* (BOTANY) (in a red alga) the asexual diploid plant, resembling a gametophyte, which develops from a carpospore and gives rise to tetraspores E20. **tetrastoon** /tɪˈtrastəʊɒn/, pl. **-stoa** /-stəʊə/ *noun* [Greek, use as noun of neut. of *tetrastoos* having four porticoes: see STOA] ARCHITECTURE a courtyard with open colonnades on all four sides M19. **tetrastyle** *noun & adjective* (ARCHITECTURE) (a structure) having or consisting of four columns E18. **tetrateuch** *noun* the first four books of the Pentateuch E20. **tetraˈthionate** *noun* (CHEMISTRY) a salt of tetrathionic acid M19. **tetrathiˈonic** *adjective*: ***tetrathionic acid*** (CHEMISTRY), a colourless strongly acidic oxyacid of sulphur, $H_2S_4O_6$ M19. **tetraˈtomic** *adjective* (CHEMISTRY) †(*a*) = TETRAVALENT; (*b*) containing four atoms in the molecule: M19. **teˌtrazotiˈzation** *noun* (CHEMISTRY) the process of tetrazotizing a compound E20. **teˈtrazotize** *verb trans.* (CHEMISTRY) convert (a compound) into a form containing two diazo groups E20.

tetrabasic /tɛtrəˈbeɪsɪk/ *adjective.* M19.
[from TETRA- + BASIC *adjective*.]
CHEMISTRY. Of an acid: having four replaceable hydrogen atoms.

tetrabranchiate /tɛtrəˈbraŋkɪət/ *adjective & noun.* M19.
[mod. Latin *tetrabranchiata*, formed as TETRA- + Greek *bragkhia* gills: see -ATE[2].]
(Designating or pertaining to) a cephalopod having two pairs of gills, sometimes placed in a (mainly fossil) group

Tetrabranchiata including the ammonites and nautiloids.

tetracaine /ˈtɛtrəkeɪn/ *noun*. Chiefly *US*. **M20**.
[from TETRA- + -CAINE.]
PHARMACOLOGY. = AMETHOCAINE.

tetrachloroethylene /ˌtɛtrəklɔːrəʊˈɛθɪliːn/ *noun*. **E20**.
[from TETRA- + CHLORO-[1] + ETHYLENE.]
CHEMISTRY. An inert colourless liquid, $Cl_2C{=}CCl_2$, used as a dry-cleaning fluid and vermifuge. Also called ***perchloroethylene***.

tetrachord /ˈtɛtrəkɔːd/ *noun*. **E17**.
[In sense 1 from Greek *tetrakhordon*, formed as TETRA- + *khordē* string (see CORD *noun*[1]). In sense 2 from TETRA- + CHORD *noun*[1].]
MUSIC. **1** *Hist*. An ancient musical instrument with four strings. **E17**.
2 A scale, usu. of four notes, spanning an interval of a fourth; *spec*. in ancient Greek music, each of the basic sets of four notes spanning a fourth which were combined in pairs or groups of three or four to form scales, adjacent sets having a note in common or being separated by a tone. Formerly also, the interval of a fourth. **E17**.

tetracosactrin /ˌtɛtrəkɒˈsaktrɪn/ *noun*. **M20**.
[from *tetracos-* chem. prefix for '24' (from TETRA- + ICOS-) + A(DRENO)C(ORTICO)TR(OPH)IC + -IN[5].]
PHARMACOLOGY. A synthetic polypeptide consisting of the first 24 amino acids of corticotrophin, resembling it in action but lacking its antigenic property, and used in the long-term treatment of inflammatory and degenerative disorders.

tetractinellid /tɪˌtraktɪˈnɛlɪd/ *adjective & noun*. **L19**.
[from mod. Latin *Tetractinellida* (see below), from TETRA- + Greek *aktin-*, *aktis* ray + -ELLA: see -ID[3].]
ZOOLOGY. ▶**A** *adjective*. Of or pertaining to the order (or class) Tetractinellida of sponges having siliceous spicules with four points arranged tetrahedrally. **L19**.
▶**B** *noun*. A sponge of this group. **L19**.

tetractys /tɪˈtraktɪs/ *noun*. Also **-akt-**. **E17**.
[Greek *tetraktus*.]
A set of four; *spec*. in Pythagoreanism, the sum of the first four positive integers (= 10) regarded as the source of all things.

tetracycline /tɛtrəˈsʌɪkliːn/ *noun*. **M20**.
[from TETRACYCLIC + -INE[5].]
PHARMACOLOGY. A tetracyclic compound, $C_{22}H_{24}N_2O_8$, which is a broad-spectrum antibiotic. Also, any of several antibiotics structurally related to this compound, used to treat various kinds of infection.

tetrad /ˈtɛtrad/ *noun*. **M17**.
[Greek *tetrad-*, *tetras* a group of four, the number four: see -AD[1].]
1 A sum, group, or set of four. **M17**.
2 *CHEMISTRY*. Orig., a tetravalent element or group. Now, a tetrameric unit within a polymer. **M19**.
3 *BIOLOGY*. A group of four cells, spores, pollen-grains, etc. Also, a group of four homologous chromatids formed during meiotic division. **L19**.
4 A square block of four 1-kilometre squares within a 10-kilometre square, used as a unit in biological recording. **M20**.

📖 **1** A. STEVENS A tetrad of distinct elements—earth, air, fire and water.

■ **teˈtradic** *adjective* of, pertaining to, or of the nature of a tetrad; *spec*. (*CHEMISTRY*, now *rare* or *obsolete*) tetravalent **L18**. **Tetradite** *noun* (*ECCLESIASTICAL HISTORY*) a worshipper of a tetrad, *esp*. one who believes that there are four persons in the Godhead **E18**.

tetragon /ˈtɛtrəg(ə)n/ *noun*. **E17**.
[Late Latin *tetragonum* from Greek *tetragōnon* quadrangle, use as noun of *tetragōnos* quadrangular, formed as TETRA-: see -GON.]
1 *ASTROLOGY*. A quartile aspect. Now *rare* or *obsolete*. **E17**.
2 A plane figure with four straight sides and four angles. **M17**.
3 A quadrangular building, court, etc. **M17**.

tetragonal /tɪˈtrag(ə)n(ə)l/ *adjective*. **L16**.
[from prec. + -AL[1].]
1 Of or pertaining to a tetragon; having four angles; quadrangular. In *BOTANY & ZOOLOGY* also, quadrangular in cross-section. **L16**.
2 Belonging to or being a crystal system in which there are three mutually perpendicular crystallographic axes, two being equal and the third of a different length. **M19**.
■ **tetragonally** *adverb* in a tetragonal manner or form **L19**.

tetragonous /tɪˈtrag(ə)nəs/ *adjective*. **M18**.
[formed as prec. + -OUS.]
BOTANY. Quadrangular in cross-section.

Tetragrammaton /tɛtrəˈgramətɒn/ *noun*. Pl. **-ata** /-ətə/. **LME**.
[Greek, use as noun of neut. of *tetragrammatos* having four letters, formed as TETRA- + *grammatos*, *gramma* letter.]
The Hebrew name of God transliterated in four letters as YHWH or JHVH (see JEHOVAH), often regarded as ineffable and treated as a mysterious symbol of (the name of) God. Also (*gen*.), any (symbolic) word of four letters.

tetrahedra *noun* pl. of TETRAHEDRON.

tetrahedral /tɛtrəˈhiːdr(ə)l, -ˈhɛdr(ə)l/ *adjective*. **L18**.
[from late Greek *tetraedros* (see TETRAHEDRON) + -AL[1]. Cf. -HEDRAL.]
1 Of a prism, pyramid, etc.: having four sides or faces (in addition to the base or ends); bounded by four plane surfaces. **L18**.
2 Of, pertaining to, or having the form of a tetrahedron; having axes of symmetry corresponding to the vertices of a tetrahedron; *spec*. in *CRYSTALLOGRAPHY*, belonging to a division of the cubic system in which the regular tetrahedron is the characteristic form. **E19**.
Special collocations: **tetrahedral number** each of the series of integers 1, 4, 10, 20, . . . , the *n*th member of which is the sum of the first *n* triangular numbers.
■ **tetrahedrally** *adverb* in a tetrahedral manner or form **M19**. †**tetrahedric** *adjective* tetrahedral: only in **L19**.

tetrahedrite /tɛtrəˈhiːdrʌɪt, -ˈhɛdrʌɪt/ *noun*. **M19**.
[from (the same root as) next + -ITE[1].]
MINERALOGY. Native sulphide of antimony, iron, and copper, forming a series with tennantite and typically occurring as tetrahedral crystals. Cf. FAHLERZ.

tetrahedron /tɛtrəˈhiːdrən, -ˈhɛd-/ *noun*. Pl. **-dra** /-drə/, **-drons**. **L16**.
[Late Greek *tetraedron*, use as noun of neut. of *tetraedros* four-sided: see TETRA-, -HEDRON.]
A solid figure or object with four plane faces; a triangular pyramid; *esp*. (more fully ***regular tetrahedron***) one with four equal equilateral triangular faces.

tetrahexahedron /ˌtɛtrəhɛksəˈhiːdrən, -ˈhɛd-/ *noun*. Pl. **-dra** /-drə/, **-drons**. **E19**.
[from TETRA- + HEXAHEDRON.]
GEOMETRY & CRYSTALLOGRAPHY. A solid figure or object with twenty-four plane faces; *esp*. one formed by replacing each face of a cube with a square pyramid.

tetrakis- /ˈtɛtrəkɪs/ *prefix*.
[Greek *tetrakis* four times.]
Fourfold; *spec*. in *CHEMISTRY*, forming names of compounds containing four groups identically substituted or coordinated. Cf. BIS-, TRIS-.
■ **tetrakis-hexaˈhedron** *noun*, pl. **-dra**, **-drons**, = TETRAHEXAHEDRON **L19**.

tetraktys *noun* var. of TETRACTYS.

Tetralin /ˈtɛtrəlɪn/ *noun*. **E20**.
[from TETRA- + *-alin* after †*naphthalin* NAPHTHALENE.]
A colourless liquid cyclic hydrocarbon used as a solvent for other hydrocarbons, esp. in varnishes, lacquers, etc.; 1, 2, 3, 4-tetrahydronaphthalene.
¶ Proprietary name in the US.

tetralogy /tɪˈtralədʒi/ *noun*. **M17**.
[Greek *tetralogia*, formed as TETRA-: see -LOGY.]
1 A group of four related plays, speeches, operas, etc.; *spec*. (*GREEK ANTIQUITIES*) a series of four dramas, three tragic and one satyric, performed in Athens at the festival of Dionysus. **M17**.
2 *MEDICINE*. A set of four symptoms jointly characteristic of a disorder; *esp*. = ***FALLOT's tetralogy***. **E20**.

tetrameter /tɪˈtramɪtə/ *noun & adjective*. **E17**.
[Late Latin *tetrametrus* from Greek *tetrametros*, formed as TETRA- + *metron* measure.]
PROSODY. ▶**A** *noun*. A line of four metrical feet. **E17**.
▶**B** *attrib*. or as *adjective*. Consisting of a tetrameter or tetrameters. **L18**.

Tetra Pak /ˈtɛtrə pak/ *noun phr*. Also **Tetra pack** & as one word. **M20**.
[from TETRA- + PACK *noun*.]
(Proprietary name for) a kind of plasticized cardboard carton for packing milk and other drinks, folded from a single sheet into a box shape, orig. tetrahedral, now freq. rectangular.

tetraplegia /tɛtrəˈpliːdʒə/ *noun*. **E20**.
[from TETRA- + PARA)PLEGIA.]
MEDICINE. = QUADRIPLEGIA.
■ **tetraplegic** *adjective & noun* = QUADRIPLEGIC *adjective & noun* **E20**.

tetraploid /ˈtɛtrəplɔɪd/ *adjective & noun*. **E20**.
[from TETRA- + -PLOID.]
BIOLOGY. ▶**A** *adjective*. (Of a cell) containing four sets of chromosomes (i.e. the diploid complement twice over); (of an individual) composed of tetraploid cells. **E20**.
▶**B** *noun*. A tetraploid individual. **E20**.
■ **tetraploidy** *noun* tetraploid condition **E20**.

tetrapod /ˈtɛtrəpɒd/ *noun & adjective*. **E19**.
[mod. Latin *tetrapodus* from Greek *tetrapod-*, *tetrapous* four-footed, formed as TETRA- + *pod-*, *pous* foot.]
▶**A** *noun*. **1** A four-footed animal; *spec*. in *ZOOLOGY*, a member of the group Tetrapoda, which includes all vertebrates higher than fishes (i.e. amphibians, reptiles, birds, and mammals). **E19**.
2 An object with four legs or supports; *spec*. a spherical block of concrete with four tetrahedrally arranged conical projections, placed in the sea near a harbour etc. to break the force of strong waves. **M20**.
▶**B** *adjective*. Having four feet or four limbs; *spec*. (*ZOOLOGY*) of or pertaining to the Tetrapoda. **L19**.

tetrarch /ˈtɛtrɑːk/ *noun*. **OE**.
[Late Latin *tetrarcha*, classical Latin *tetrarches* from Greek *tetrarkhēs*: see TETRA-, -ARCH.]
1 *ROMAN HISTORY*. A ruler of any of four divisions of a country or province; a ruler subordinate to Rome, esp. in Syria. **OE**.
2 *transf*. Any ruler of one of four divisions, elements, etc.; any subordinate ruler. **E17**.
3 Each of four joint rulers, heads, etc. **M17**.
■ **tetrarchate** /ˈtɛtrəkeɪt/ *noun* the office or position of a tetrarch **M17**.

tetrarch /ˈtɛtrɑːk/ *adjective*. **L19**.
[from TETRA- + Greek *arkhē* beginning.]
BOTANY. Of a vascular bundle: having four strands of xylem, formed from four points of origin.

tetrarchic /tɪˈtrɑːkɪk/ *adjective*. **E19**.
[Greek *tetrarkhikos*, from *tetrarkhēs*: see TETRARCH *noun*, -IC.]
Of or pertaining to a tetrarch or tetrarchy.

tetrarchical /tɪˈtrɑːkɪk(ə)l/ *adjective*. **M17**.
[formed as prec. + -AL[1].]
†**1** Divided into tetrarchies. Only in **M17**.
2 = TETRARCHIC *adjective*. **M17**.

tetrarchy /ˈtɛtrɑːki/ *noun*. **LME**.
[Latin *tetrarchia* from Greek *tetrarkhia* from *tetrarkhēs* TETRARCH *noun*: see -Y[3].]
1 (An area under) the government or jurisdiction of a tetrarch. **LME**.
2 (A government of) four tetrarchs jointly; a country divided into four petty governments. **E17**.

tetrasome /ˈtɛtrəsəʊm/ *noun*. **E20**.
[from TETRA- + -SOME[3].]
BIOLOGY. (Each of) a set of four homologous chromosomes in a cell (two extra to the normal complement). Also, a tetrasomic individual.

tetrasomic /tɛtrəˈsəʊmɪk/ *adjective & noun*. **E20**.
[formed as prec. + -IC.]
CYTOLOGY. ▶**A** *adjective*. Of, pertaining to, or characterized by a tetrasome. **E20**.
▶**B** *noun*. A tetrasomic chromosome, cell, or individual. **M20**.
■ **ˈtetrasomy** *noun* tetrasomic condition **M20**.

tetrastich /ˈtɛtrəstɪk, tɪˈtras-/ *noun*. **L16**.
[Latin *tetrastichon* from Greek *tetrastikhon* use as noun of neut. of *tetrastikhos* containing four rows, formed as TETRA- + *stikhos* row, line of verse.]
PROSODY. A group (esp. a stanza) of four lines.
■ **tetraˈstichic** *adjective* (*rare*) pertaining to or of the nature of a tetrastich, consisting of tetrastichs **L19**.

tetrastichous /tɪˈtrastɪkəs/ *adjective*. **M19**.
[from mod. Latin *tetrastichus* from Greek *tetrastikhos* (see prec.) + -OUS.]
BOTANY. Esp. of a spike of grass: having four vertical rows.

tetrasyllable /ˈtɛtrəsɪləb(ə)l/ *noun*. **L16**.
[from TETRA- + SYLLABLE *noun*.]
A word of four syllables.
■ **tetrasyˈllabic** *adjective* having four syllables **L18**. **tetrasyˈllabical** *adjective* (*rare*) = TETRASYLLABIC **M17**.

tetrathlon /tɛˈtraθlɒn, -lən/ *noun*. **M20**.
[from TETRA- + Greek *athlon* contest, after PENTATHLON etc.]
An athletic or sporting contest in which competitors engage in four different events, esp. riding, shooting, swimming, and running.

tetravalent /tɛtrəˈveɪl(ə)nt/ *adjective*. **M19**.
[from TETRA- + -VALENT.]
CHEMISTRY. Having a valency of four.

tetrazole /ˈtɛtrəzəʊl/ *noun*. **L19**.
[from TETRA- + AZO- + -OLE[2].]
CHEMISTRY. An acidic crystalline compound whose molecule is a five-membered ring of one carbon and four nitrogen atoms, CH_2N_4.

tetrazolium /tɛtrəˈzəʊlɪəm/ *noun*. **L19**.
[from prec. + -IUM.]
CHEMISTRY. The cation or the radical derived from tetrazole; any of various derivatives of this, *esp*. the chloride of its triphenyl derivative, a dye used as a test for viability in biological material.

Tetrazzini /tɛtrəˈziːni/ *noun*. **E20**.
[The name of Luisa *Tetrazzini* (1871–1940), Italian operatic soprano.]
A type of pasta dish with a cream sauce and mushrooms, served esp. as an accompaniment to poultry. Also ***chicken Tetrazzini***.

For other words beginning with *tetra-* see the entry for **tetra-**

tetrevangelium /ˌtɛtrɛvanˈdʒɛlɪəm/ *noun.* Pl. **-lia** /-lɪə/. L19.
[formed as TETRA- + ecclesiastical Latin *evangelium* EVANGEL *noun*[1].]
A manuscript or book of the four gospels.

†**tetric** *adjective.* M16–E19.
[formed as next: see -IC.]
= next.

tetrical /ˈtɛtrɪk(ə)l/ *adjective. arch.* E16.
[from Latin *t(a)etricus* (formed as TETROUS): see -ICAL.]
Austere, severe, harsh, morose.

tetrobol /ˈtɛtrəbɒl/ *noun.* L17.
[Late Latin *tetrobolon* from Greek *tetrōbolon*, formed as TETRA- + *obolos* OBOL.]
A silver coin of ancient Greece worth four obols.

tetrode /ˈtɛtrəʊd/ *noun.* E20.
[from TETRA- + -ODE[2].]
ELECTRONICS. A thermionic valve having four electrodes.

tetrodon /ˈtɛtrədɒn/ *noun.* Also **-dont** /-dɒnt/. L18.
[mod. Latin (former) genus name (see below), from Greek *tetra-* TETRA- + -ODON.]
A puffer fish, *esp.* one of the genus *Tetraodon*.
■ **tetrodoˈtoxin** *noun* a poisonous substance found esp. in the ovaries of certain puffer fishes (family Tetraodontidae) which affects the action of nerve cells E20.

tetromino /tɛˈtrɒmɪnəʊ/ *noun.* Pl. **-oes**. M20.
[from TETR(A- + D)OMINO.]
Each of the five distinct planar shapes consisting of four identical squares joined by their edges.

tetrose /ˈtɛtrəʊz, -s/ *noun.* E20.
[from TETRA- + -OSE[2].]
CHEMISTRY. A monosaccharide with four carbon atoms in its molecule, e.g. erythrose.

tetrous /ˈtɛtrəs/ *adjective.* Now *rare.* M17.
[from Latin *taetr-*, *taeter* foul: see -OUS.]
Offensive, foul.

tetroxide /tɛˈtrɒksʌɪd/ *noun.* M19.
[from TETRA- + OXIDE.]
CHEMISTRY. Any oxide containing four atoms of oxygen in its molecule or empirical formula.

tetryl /ˈtɛtrɪl, -ʌɪl/ *noun.* M19.
[from TETRA- + -YL.]
CHEMISTRY. †**1** = BUTYL 1. M–L19.
2 A yellow crystalline explosive used esp. as a detonator and priming agent; tetranitromethylaniline, $(NO_2)_3C_6H_2N(CH_3)NO_2$. E20.

tetter /ˈtɛtə/ *noun & verb.*
[Old English *teter* cogn. with Sanskrit *dadru* skin disease; cf. Lithuanian *dēdervinė* tetter; repr. in Old High German *zittaroh*, German dial. *Zitteroch*, etc.]
► **A** *noun.* MEDICINE. Any of various skin diseases of humans, horses, etc., as ringworm, eczema, impetigo. Freq. with specifying word. Now *rare*. OE.
► **B** *verb. rare.*
†**1** *verb trans.* Affect (as) with a tetter. Only in E17.
2 *verb intrans.* Crack, disintegrate. E20.
Comb.: **tetter-berry** (now *dial.*) (the fruit of) the white bryony, *Bryonia dioica*, variously said to cure and to produce skin diseases; **tetterworm** (now *rare* or *obsolete*) tetter, *esp.* a form of ringworm; **tetterwort** (now *dial.*) the greater celandine, *Chelidonium majus*, reputed to cure skin diseases.
■ **tettered** *adjective* afflicted with tetter (chiefly *fig.*) E20. **tetterous** *adjective* (now *rare*) of, affected by, or resembling tetter E18. **tettery** *adjective* (now *rare* or *obsolete*) of the nature of tetter; tetterous: L17.

tettigoniid /tɛtɪˈgəʊnɪɪd/ *noun & adjective.* E20.
[mod. Latin *Tettigoniidae* (see below), from *Tettigonia* genus name, from next + *-onia*: see -ID[3].]
ENTOMOLOGY. ► **A** *noun.* Any of various orthopterous insects constituting the family Tettigoniidae, which stridulate by rubbing the forewings together and comprise the bush-crickets and katydids. Also called ***long-horned grasshopper***. E20.
► **B** *adjective.* Of, pertaining to, or designating this family. M20.

tettix /ˈtɛtɪks/ *noun.* L18.
[Greek.]
A cicada; *esp.* (in ancient and modern Greece) the southern European *Cicada orni*.
golden tettix GREEK HISTORY an ornament worn in the hair by Athenians before Solon's time, as an emblem of their being indigenous.

tetty *adjective* var. of TEETY.

tetur *noun* var. of TITAR.

teuchat *noun* var. of TEWHIT.

teuchter /ˈtjuxtə, ˈtʃu-/ *noun. Scot.* Freq. *derog.* M20.
[Origin unkn.]
A Highlander, *esp.* a Gaelic speaker or anyone from the North; a person regarded as uncouth or rustic.

teucrium /ˈtjuːkrɪəm/ *noun.* E17.
[mod. Latin (see below), from Greek *teukrion*.]
Any of numerous chiefly Mediterranean labiate herbs and shrubs constituting the genus *Teucrium*, which includes the wood sage, *T. scorodonia*, and wall germander, *T. chamaedrys*.

teuf-teuf /ˈtʌftʌf, tʌfˈtʌf/ *noun, interjection, & verb.* E20.
[French: imit. Cf. TUFF-TUFF.]
► **A** *noun & interjection.* (Repr.) a repeated sound of gases escaping from the exhaust of a combustion engine. E20.
► **B** *verb intrans.* Of a car etc.: move with or make this sound. E20.

Teut /tjuːt/ *noun. colloq.* M19.
[Abbreviation.]
= TEUTON.

Teut- *combining form* see TEUTO-.

Teut. *abbreviation.*
Teutonic.

teuthology /tjuːˈθɒlədʒi/ *noun.* L19.
[mod. Latin *teuthologia* irreg. from Greek *teuthis* cuttlefish, squid: see -OLOGY.]
The branch of zoology that deals with cephalopod molluscs.
■ **teuthologist** *noun* L19.

Teuto- /ˈtjuːtəʊ/ *combining form.* Before a vowel also **Teut-**.
[Irreg. from TEUTON, TEUTONIC + -O-.]
Forming nouns and adjectives with the sense 'Teutonic (and)' as ***Teut-Aryan***, ***Teuto-British***, ***Teuto-Celtic***, etc.
■ **Teutoˈmania** *noun* a craze or excessive liking for what is Teutonic or German M19. **Teutophil(e)** *noun & adjective* (a person who is) friendly towards Germany or fond of Germany and things German E20. **Teutophobe** *adjective & noun* (a person who is) affected with Teutophobia E20. **Teutoˈphobia** *noun* dread or dislike of Germany and things German E20.

Teuton /ˈtjuːt(ə)n/ *noun.* E18.
[Latin *Teutoni*, *Teutones* (pl.), from Indo-European base meaning 'people', 'country', 'land'.]
1 *Hist.* A member of a former northern European people inhabiting Jutland in the 4th cent. BC and combining with the Cimbrians in the 2nd cent. BC to devastate France and threaten the Roman republic, until heavily defeated by a Roman army. E18.
2 A member of a Teutonic nation; a member of any of the peoples speaking a Germanic language, *esp.* a German. M19.

Teutonic /tjuːˈtɒnɪk/ *adjective & noun.* E17.
[French *teutonique* from Latin *Teutonicus*, from *Teutones*: see prec., -IC.]
► **A** *adjective.* **1** *Hist.* Of or pertaining to the former northern European people known as the Teutons. E17.
2 Designating or pertaining to the Germanic branch of the Indo-European language family or the Germanic-speaking peoples. *arch.* E17. ▸**b** Of or pertaining to the Germans; German; displaying the characteristics attributed to Germans. M17.

📖 **2** J. R. MCCULLOCH The Normans, as well as the Saxons, were of Teutonic extraction. **b** *Sunday Times* German youths . . schooled in Teutonic ideals of discipline, courage, skill.

Special collocations: **Teutonic cross** HERALDRY a silver-rimmed elongated black cross, being the badge of the Teutonic Knights. **Teutonic Knights**, **Teutonic Order (of Knights)** a military and religious order of German knights, priests, etc., founded *c* 1191 as the Teutonic Knights of St Mary of Jerusalem for service during the Third Crusade, and which later conquered areas of Russia and the Baltic provinces; the Order was re-established as an honorary ecclesiastical institution in Austria in 1834 and reformed in 1929.
► **B** *noun.* **1** = GERMANIC *noun.* Formerly also *spec.*, the German language. *arch.* E17.
†**2** = TEUTON 2. *rare.* M–L17.
†**3** A Teutonic Knight. Usu. in *pl.* L17–L18.
■ **Teutonically** *adverb* in the manner of a Teuton or German; in characteristically German style: M19. **Teutonicism** /-sɪz(ə)m/ *noun* Teutonic or German quality; a Teutonic expression; a Teutonism: M19.

Teutonise *verb* var. of TEUTONIZE.

Teutonism /ˈtjuːt(ə)nɪz(ə)m/ *noun.* M19.
[from TEUTON + -ISM.]
1 Teutonic or Germanic character, type, quality, or spirit; attachment to German attitudes or ideas. M19.
2 An idiom or mode of expression peculiar to or characteristic of the Teutonic languages, esp. of German; a Germanism. L19.
■ **Teutonist** *noun* (*a*) a person versed in the history etc. of the Teutonic race or languages; (*b*) a person attached to Teutonic or German attitudes or ideas; a person whose writings have a Teutonic character or style: L19.

Teutonize /ˈtjuːt(ə)nʌɪz/ *verb.* Also **-ise**. M19.
[from TEUTON + -IZE.]
1 *verb trans.* Make Teutonic or German in character, style, etc. M19.
2 *verb intrans.* Adopt Teutonic or German characteristics; become Teutonic or German in style, habits, etc. *rare.* L19.

📖 **1** *Daily Telegraph* Hahn was accused . . of anglicising German education and teutonising the British variety.

■ **Teutoniˈzation** *noun* the action or process of Teutonizing L19.

TeV *abbreviation.*
Tera-electronvolt(s).

tevel /ˈtɛv(ə)l/ *verb. obsolete* exc. *Scot. & dial.* Also **tav-** /ˈtav-/. Infl. **-ll-**. ME.
[Origin unkn. Perh. different words.]
†**1** *verb intrans.* Talk, converse; discuss, argue. Only in ME.
†**2** *verb intrans.* Struggle, strive, contend; labour. Only in LME.
3 *verb intrans.* Behave in a disorderly or violent manner; rage. *Scot.* E19.
4 *verb trans.* Confuse, put into a disorderly state. *Scot.* E19.

Tevet *noun* var. of TEBET.

tevish *noun* var. of THIVISH.

tew /tjuː/ *noun*[1]. LME.
[from TEW *verb*[1].]
†**1** The tawing of leather. Only in LME.
†**2** Preparatory work; labour. Only in M17.
3 Constant work and bustling; a state of worry or excitement. *Scot., US, & dial.* E19.

tew /tjuː/ *noun*[2]. *obsolete* exc. *dial.* LME.
[Corresp. to West Frisian *tuch*, late Middle Dutch, mod. Dutch *tuig*, Middle Low German, Low German *tüch*, Middle High German *ziuc*, German *Zeug* apparatus, tools, utensils, tackle, etc.]
1 Fishing tackle; nets, fishing-lines, etc. LME–E17.
2 Implements, tools, necessary materials for work; gear. E17.

tew /tjuː/ *verb*[1]. ME.
[App. rel. to TAW *verb*.]
► **I 1** *verb trans.* = TAW *verb* 1. *obsolete* exc. *Scot., US, & dial.* ME.
2 *verb trans.* Work (something) into a proper consistency by beating etc.; temper (mortar). Now *dial.* LME.
†**3** *verb trans.* **a** Deal with; employ. Only in L15. ▸**b** Prepare or bring into a proper state or condition for some purpose. L16–E17.
4 *verb trans.* †**a** = TAW *verb* 2, 3. L16–L17. ▸**b** Toss about, turn over, (hay); crease, disarrange, (dress); pull about; vex. Also in *pass.*, be involved or mixed *up with*. *dial.* L19.
► **II 5** *verb intrans.* Work hard, exert oneself; bustle *about*. Now *Scot., US, & dial.* L18.
6 *verb trans.* Fatigue or tire (esp. oneself) with hard work. *Scot. & dial.* E19.

tew /tjuː/ *verb*[2] *trans. obsolete* exc. *north.* E17.
[App. from TOW *verb*[1].]
Haul, tow, (a ship, net, etc.); drag, pull, tug.

Tewa /ˈteɪwə/ *noun & adjective.* M19.
[Tewa *téwa* moccasins.]
► **A** *noun.* Pl. same, **-s**. A member of a Pueblo Indian people of the Rio Grande area in the south-western US; the Tanoan language of this people. M19.
► **B** *adjective.* Of or pertaining to the Tewa or their language. E20.

tewel /ˈtjuːəl/ *noun.* Now *dial.* Also **tuel**. LME.
[Old French *tuel*, *tuele* tube, pipe (mod. French *tuyau*) = Spanish, Portuguese, Provençal *tudel* tube, from Proto-Romance.]
†**1** A shaft or opening for the escape of smoke etc.; a chimney. Also, a conduit, a pipe. LME–E18.
2 The anus; the rectum, esp. of a horse. *obsolete* exc. *dial.* LME.
3 = TUYÈRE. L17.

tewhit /ˈtiː(h)wɪt, ˈtjuːɪt/ *noun. Scot. & north.* Also **tewit** /ˈtiːwɪt, ˈtjuːɪt/, (*Scot.*) **teuchat** /ˈtjuːxət/, & other vars. LME.
[Orig. imit.]
The lapwing. Cf. PEEWIT 1.

te-whit *noun & interjection* var. of TE-WIT.

tew-iron /ˈtjuːʌɪən/ *noun.* Now *rare.* LME.
[Repr. French TUYÈRE, assim. to TEW (EL *noun* and IRON *noun*.]
= TUYÈRE.

tewit *noun* var. of TEWHIT.

te-wit /ˈtɛwɪt, təˈwɪt/ *noun & interjection.* Also **te-whit**. E16.
[Imit.]
(Repr.) the cry of an owl or other bird.

tewly /ˈtjuːli/ *adjective.* Now *dial.* M16.
[Origin unkn.]
Weak, sickly, delicate; poorly, unwell.

TEWT /tjuːt/ *noun. Army slang.* M20.
[from tactical exercise without troops.]
An exercise used in the training of junior officers.

tewtaw /ˈtjuːtɔː/ *verb & noun. obsolete* exc. *dial.* E17.
[Origin unkn. Cf. TAW *verb*.]
► **A** *verb trans.* Beat or dress (hemp or flax). E17.
► **B** *noun.* An implement for breaking hemp or flax. M17.

Tex /tɛks/ *noun*¹. *US colloq.* E20.
[Abbreviation.]
(A nickname for) a Texan.

tex /tɛks/ *noun*². M20.
[Abbreviation of TEXTILE.]
A system of measuring the fineness of fibres and yarns, by the weight in grams of a length of 1000 metres.

Tex. *abbreviation.*
Texas.

Texan /ˈtɛks(ə)n/ *adjective & noun.* M19.
[from next + -AN.]
▸**A** *adjective.* Of or pertaining to the State of Texas. M19.
▸**B** *noun.* A native or inhabitant of Texas. M19.

Texas /ˈtɛksəs/ *noun.* In sense 1 also **t-**. M19.
[A large State in the south-western US.]
▸**I 1** The uppermost structure of a river-steamer, in which the officers' quarters are located. *US.* M19.
2 An elevated gallery in a grain-elevator. *US.* E20.
▸**II 3** Used *attrib.* to designate things from, found in, or associated with Texas. M19.
Texas armadillo the nine-banded armadillo, *Dasypus novemcinctus.* **Texas fever** VETERINARY MEDICINE bovine babesiosis; also called ***redwater fever.*** **Texas leaguer** BASEBALL (now *rare* or *obsolete*) a fly ball that falls to the ground between the infield and the outfield and results in a base hit. **Texas longhorn** (an animal of) a breed of cattle once common in Texas, distinguished by long horns and able to thrive in dry regions. **Texas Ranger** a member of the Texas State police force (formerly, of certain locally mustered regiments in the federal service during the Mexican War). **Texas Tower** [from its resemblance to a Texas oil rig] any of a chain of radar towers built along the eastern coast of the US.

Texel /ˈtɛks(ə)l/ *noun.* M20.
[An island in the West Frisian group off the northern coast of the Netherlands.]
(An animal of) a hardy, hornless breed of sheep with a heavy fleece originally developed on the island of Texel. Also ***Texel sheep***.

Texian /ˈtɛksɪən/ *adjective & noun.* Now *rare.* M19.
[from TEXAS + -IAN.]
= TEXAN.

Texican /ˈtɛksɪk(ə)n/ *noun & adjective.* M19.
[Blend of TEXAN and MEXICAN.]
▸**A** *noun.* A Texan; *spec.* a Texan of Mexican background. M19.
▸**B** *adjective.* = TEX-MEX *adjective.* L20.

Tex-Mex /tɛksˈmɛks/ *adjective & noun.* M20.
[from TEX(AN + MEX(ICAN.]
▸**A** *adjective.* Of or pertaining to the blend of Texan and Mexican language, culture, or cuisine existing or originating in (esp. southern) Texas. M20.

> 🕮 *Times* She wasn't eating sushi any more . . . She'd moved on to Tex-Mex cuisine.

▸**B** *noun.* The Texan variety of Mexican Spanish. Also, a Texan style of cooking characterized by the adaptation of Mexican ingredients and influences, as tacos, enchiladas, ground beef, etc., with a more moderate use of hot flavourings such as chilli. M20.

text /tɛkst/ *noun & verb.* LME.
[Old Northern French *tixte,* (also mod. French) *texte* from Latin *textus* tissue, style of literary work, (in medieval Latin) the Gospel, written character, from *text-* pa. ppl stem of *texere* weave.]
▸**A** *noun.* **1 a** The wording of something written or printed; the actual words, phrases, and sentences as written. LME. ▸**b** The wording adopted by an editor as the most faithful representation of the author's original work; a book or edition containing this. Also, any form in which a piece of writing exists or is current, as ***a good text, a corrupt text.*** M19. ▸**c** A textbook. L19. ▸**d** COMPUTING. Data in textual form, esp. as stored, processed, or displayed in a word processor or text editor. M20.
2 a The original words of an author or document, *spec.* (***a***) in the original language, as opp. to a translation; (***b***) in the original form and order, as opp. to a revision, paraphrase, or commentary. LME. ▸**b** The main body of a book or other printed work as distinct from notes, illustrations, appendices, etc. LME. ▸**c** LINGUISTICS. (A unit of) connected discourse whose function is communicative and which forms the object of analysis and description. M20.
3 a *spec.* The actual words and sentences of Holy Scripture; the Bible itself; a book of the Bible. Long *rare.* LME. ▸**b** A copy of the Scriptures, or of a book of the Scriptures; *spec.* a copy of the four Gospels. *obsolete* exc. *Hist.* LME.
4 a A short passage from the Scriptures, *esp.* one quoted as authoritative or illustrative of a point of belief or doctrine, used to point a moral, or chosen as the subject or starting-point of a sermon. LME. ▸**b** A short passage from a book or writer considered as authoritative. Also (now *rare*), a maxim, a proverb; *spec.* a maxim used as a copybook heading. LME. ▸**c** The theme or subject of a work or discussion; a statement used as a starting-point for a discussion etc. E17.
5 In full ***text-hand***. A fine large kind of handwriting, *esp.* the large and formal hand in which the text of a manuscript was written, as distinct from the smaller or more cursive hand used for the commentary etc. M16.
6 The words of a poem etc. set to music; = TESTO 1. L19.

> 🕮 **1a** A. FRASER The herald had difficulty in making out the exact text of the declaration of war. ***plain text***: see PLAIN *adjective*¹ *& adverb.* **b** F. H. A. SCRIVENER The vast importance of preserving a pure text of the sacred writers. **c** *Omnibus* One of our most important texts on the subjects . . directs our attention to the relations of concord and discord. **2a** H. KISSINGER *The People's Daily* printed the entire text of the President's speech. ***parallel text***: see PARALLEL *adjective.* **b** *Punch* The text is complemented by many attractive drawings. **c** R. ALTER Our minds identify grammatical forms . . with the same cultural reflexes . . that we use to decipher nonliterary texts. **4a** V. S. REID Pastor says his text comes from St. Paul's Epistle to the Ephesians. **c** SIR W. SCOTT Is it fit for a heretic . . to handle such a text as the Catholic clergy? **5** ***church text***: see CHURCH *noun.* ***round text***: see ROUND *adjective.*

Comb.: **text editor** COMPUTING a program for modifying text held in a computer or processor; a terminal or keyboard used for this; **text file** COMPUTING a file used to store data in textual form; the data so stored; ***text-hand***: see sense 5 above; **text-letter** (now *rare* or *obsolete*) a large or capital handwritten letter; **text linguistics** the linguistic study of texts or discourses as the natural domain of linguistic theory rather than sentences (see sense 2c above); **text-man** †(***a***) a person learned in scriptural texts and proficient in their apt citation; a textualist; (***b***) *rare* the author of a textbook; **text message** a short written message transmitted electronically to or from a mobile phone, or via the Internet; **text messaging** the sending of text messages; **text paper** a newspaper containing serious articles; a quality newspaper; **text-pen** a pen suitable for writing in text-hand; **textphone** a telephone developed for the use of the deaf, having a small screen and a keyboard with which one may type a message to be received by another textphone; **text-picture** an illustration occupying a space in the text of a book; **text processing** COMPUTING the manipulation of text, esp. the transformation of it from one format to another; word processing; **text processor** COMPUTING a program for text processing; a word processor; **text-writer** †(***a***) a professional writer of text-hand, before the introduction of printing; (***b***) an author of a legal textbook.

▸**B** *verb.* †**1** *verb intrans. & trans.* Cite a text or texts (at). M16–E17.
2 *verb trans.* Orig., write or print in text-hand or in capital or large letters. Now, set (a poem etc.) to music (see sense A.6 above). L16. ▸**b** *verb intrans.* Write in text-hand. Now *rare.* M17.
3 *verb trans.* Send a text message to. Also, send as a text message. L20.

> 🕮 **2** SHAKES. *Much Ado* And text underneath, 'Here dwells Benedick the married man.' **3** *Publican Newspaper* Customers will be invited to text a message . . if they want to take part. *Leicester Mercury* I texted my mother and my friends when I got my results.

■ **textless** *adjective* E20.

textbook /ˈtɛks(t)bʊk/ *noun & adjective.* M18.
[from TEXT *noun* + BOOK *noun.*]
▸**A** *noun.* †**1** A student's text of a classical work with sufficient space between the lines for an interpretation dictated by a master to be inserted. Only in M18.
2 A book used as a standard work for the study of a particular subject; *esp.* one written specially for this purpose. L18.
3 A book containing a selection of Scripture texts, arranged for daily use or easy reference. *rare.* M19.

> 🕮 **2** J. BRIGGS He was the author of several successful textbooks on arithmetic. *Holiday Which?* The town is like a superb, animated architectural textbook.

▸**B** *attrib.* or as *adjective.* Typical of a textbook or standard work; following the example of a textbook; exemplary; accurate; classic. Also (*derog.*), rigidly adhering to a stereotype; mechanical. Cf. COPYBOOK *adjective* 2. E20.

> 🕮 J. BERMAN Linton is a text-book example of a narcissistic personality disorder.

■ **textbookish** *adjective* E20.

textile /ˈtɛkstʌɪl/ *noun & adjective.* E17.
[Latin *textilis*, from *text-*: see TEXT, -ILE.]
▸**A** *noun.* **1** A woven fabric. Also, any kind of cloth; any of various materials, as a bonded fabric, which do not require weaving. E17.
2 Natural or synthetic fibres, filaments, or yarns, suitable for being spun and woven or manufactured into cloth etc. M17.
3 Among naturists: a person who is not a naturist, *spec.* a person who wears a swimming costume on the beach. *slang.* L20.

> 🕮 **1** *Smithsonian* Textiles . . unlikely to appear on a real person—metallic-looking weaves in pink and silver.

▸**B** *attrib.* or as *adjective.* **1** Woven; made of or resembling a textile; suitable for weaving or for manufacturing as a textile. M17.
2 Of or pertaining to weaving or textiles. M19.
3 Among naturists: not naturist, *spec.* (of a place etc.) prohibited to nudists. *slang.* L20.

> 🕮 **1** *Wall Street Journal* DuPont Co. announced it will close its textile rayon operation. **textile cone** a venomous Indo-Pacific cone-shell, *Conus textile,* which has a mottled pattern on the shell. **2** S. ELDRED-GRIGG Work . . on an assembly line in a textile mill.

textology /tɛkˈstɒlədʒi/ *noun.* L20.
[German *Textologie* from Russian *tekstologiya,* formed as TEXT: see -OLOGY.]
The branch of knowledge that deals with the evolution of texts, esp. through rewriting, editing, translation, and text production; textual classification.
■ **textoˈlogical** *adjective* L20.

textorial /tɛkˈstɔːrɪəl/ *adjective. rare.* L18.
[Latin *textor* weaver, *textorius* pertaining to weaving, from *text-*: see TEXT, -AL¹.]
Of or pertaining to weavers or weaving.

textual /ˈtɛkstjʊəl/ *adjective.* LME.
[medieval Latin *textualis,* from *textus*: see TEXT, -UAL.]
†**1** Of a person: well acquainted with texts or authors; well-read; exact in citing a text. LME–E17.
2 Of, concerning, or contained in a text. LME.
3 Based on, following, or conforming to the text of a work, esp. of the Scriptures. E17.

> 🕮 **2** *Review of English Studies* The . . degree of attention to textual accuracy is almost too fastidious. ***textual criticism***: see CRITICISM 2.

■ **textually** *adverb* (***a***) in or as regards the text; (***b***) in the actual words of the text; verbatim: E17.

textualism /ˈtɛkstjʊəlɪz(ə)m/ *noun.* E19.
[from prec. + -ISM.]
1 Strict adherence to a text, esp. that of the Scriptures; the principles or practice of a textualist. E19.
2 Textual criticism, esp. of the Bible. L19.
■ **textualist** *noun* (***a***) a person learned in the text of the Bible; (***b***) a person who adheres strictly to a text, esp. that of the Scriptures: E17.

textuality /tɛkstjʊˈalɪti/ *noun.* M19.
[formed as prec. + -ITY.]
1 = TEXTUALISM 1. M19.
2 The nature or quality of a text or discourse; the identifying quality of a text. L20.

> 🕮 **2** *Times Lit. Suppl.* Kenner's lead article . . views Joyce . . as a ceaseless experimenter with textuality itself.

textuary /ˈtɛkstjʊəri/ *adjective & noun.* E17.
[medieval Latin *textuarius,* from *textus*: see TEXT, -ARY¹.]
▸**A** *adjective.* †**1** That adheres strictly to the text of Scripture. *rare.* Only in E17.
2 Of or belonging to a text; textual. M17.
†**3** That ranks as a textbook; regarded as authoritative. M–L17.
▸**B** *noun.* A textualist; a textual critic or scholar. Also, a person able at citing texts, esp. from the Bible. E17.

†**textuist** *noun.* M17–E18.
[from Latin *textus*: see TEXT, -IST.]
A textual scholar; a textuary.

textura /tɛkˈstjʊərə/ *noun & adjective.* E20.
[German (also *Textur*) from Latin *textura* TEXTURE *noun.*]
(Designating or pertaining to) any of a group of typefaces first used in the earliest printed books, distinguished by narrow, angular letters and a strong vertical emphasis. Also, (designating or pertaining to) the formal manuscript hand on which these typefaces were based.

textural /ˈtɛkstʃ(ə)r(ə)l/ *adjective.* M19.
[from TEXTURE *noun* + -AL¹.]
Of or pertaining to texture or surface quality; characterized by texture, esp. in art, music, etc.
■ **texturally** *adverb* M19.

texture /ˈtɛkstʃə/ *noun & verb.* LME.
[Latin *textura* weaving, from *text-*: see TEXT, -URE.]
▸**A** *noun.* †**1** The process or art of weaving. LME–E18.
2 Any structure having the appearance or consistency of woven fabric; a tissue; a web; *arch.* a woven fabric; cloth. LME.
3 Constitution; distinctive nature or quality resulting from composition; mental disposition. Also (LITERARY CRITICISM), the quality of a piece of writing, esp. with regard to imagery, alliteration, rhythm, etc.; MUSIC the quality of sound created by the combination of the different elements of a work or passage. E17.
4 The tactile quality or appearance of a surface or substance; the physical or perceived structure and composition of the constituent parts or formative elements of something, as soil, rock, organic tissue, food, etc. M17.
5 The character, appearance, or tactile quality of a textile fabric as determined by its weave or arrangement of threads. L17.
6 ART. The representation of the tactile quality and nature of a surface. M19.

> 📖 2 BROWNING When the dyer dyes A texture. 3 J. MOYNAHAN The issues of life and death are fully worked into the very texture of events. *Gramophone* Schumann was not so expert in handling orchestral textures. *Times Lit. Suppl.* Meck propels the narrative through a variety of textures. ***open texture***: see OPEN *adjective.* 4 A. GEIKIE Gneiss is too various in its texture and the rate of its decomposition. A. J. CRONIN The skin was of a lovely texture, smooth and tender. *Health Shopper* Oatbran . . and honey toasted to give . . a light crunchy texture. 5 *Country Homes* A collection of Coir . . in Panama, Bouclé and Herringbone textures. 6 *Ashmolean* He . . exhibited a reduced version of this group in which the . . exquisite textures were even more remarkable.

Comb.: **texture brick** a roughened or rough-hewn brick.

▶ **B** *verb trans.* Make (as) by weaving (now *rare*); provide with a distinctive or characteristic texture. Chiefly as TEXTURED *adjective.* L17.

> 📖 *Hair* The hair was then textured on the crown and razored at the nape.

■ **textureless** *adjective* M19.

textured /ˈtɛkstʃəd/ *adjective.* L19.
[from prec.: see -ED[2], -ED[1].]
1 Of a (specified) texture; having a distinctive or characteristic texture; not smooth. L19.
2 Of vegetable protein food: given a texture resembling meat. Freq. in ***textured vegetable protein***. M20.

> 📖 1 *Which?* Paper with pieces of wood embedded in it to give a textured effect. *Bon Appetit* A light-textured, single-layer cake. *Country Homes* A photographer with a talent for rich textured still lifes. **textured yarn** a yarn which has been modified to give a special texture to the fabric.

texturing /ˈtɛkstʃərɪŋ/ *noun.* L19.
[formed as prec. + -ING[1].]
The representation of the texture of a surface in painting or engraving. Also, a textured quality, esp. in music; the process of giving a textured effect to yarn.

texturize /ˈtɛkstʃərʌɪz/ *verb trans.* Also **-ise.** M20.
[from TEXTURE *noun* + -IZE.]
Impart a particular texture to (esp. fabric or food). Chiefly as ***texturized*** *ppl adjective.*

textus /ˈtɛkstəs/ *noun.* Pl. same. M19.
[Latin, in medieval Latin sense: see TEXT.]
1 ***textus receptus*** /rɪˈsɛptəs/ [lit. 'received text'], a text accepted as authoritative; *spec.* (usu. with cap. initials) the received text of the Greek New Testament. M19.
2 = TEXT *noun* 3b. L19.

tezkere /ˈtɛzkərə/ *noun.* Also ***tes-***. E17.
[Turkish from Arab. *taḏkira* memorandum, record, note, pass.]
A Turkish official memorandum or certificate of any kind; a permit, a licence; *esp.* an internal passport.

TG *abbreviation.*
1 Thank God.
2 LINGUISTICS. Transformational-generative (grammar).

T-group /ˈtiːgruːp/ *noun.* M20.
[from T(RAINING + GROUP *noun*.]
PSYCHOLOGY. A group of people undergoing therapy or training in which they observe and seek to improve their own interpersonal relationships or communication skills.

TGV *abbreviation.*
French *Train à grande vitesse* (a type of high-speed French passenger train).

TGWU *abbreviation.*
Transport and General Workers' Union.

th.
A consonantal digraph representing the voiced and voiceless dental fricatives /ð/ and /θ/ in all words of Germanic origin, as (voiced) ***brother***, ***northern***, (voiceless) ***thick***, ***thumb***, /θ/ in words of Greek origin, as ***theist***, and /t/ in words from mod. French, as ***bibliothèque***. Old English largely represented /ð/ and /θ/ interchangeably with the letters thorn (þ) and eth (ð), *th* being borrowed from Latin in which it transliterated Greek theta. The digraph *th* superseded thorn and eth with the advent of printing.

Th *symbol.*
CHEMISTRY. Thorium.

Th. *abbreviation.*
Thursday.

-th /θ/ *suffix*[1].
[Sense 1 from or after Old English and Old Norse, ult. from Indo-European; sense 2 from or after Old English *-þu*, *-þo*, *-þ* from Germanic from Indo-European. See also -T[1], -T[2].]
1 Forming nouns from verbs denoting an action or process, as ***bath***, ***birth***, ***death***, ***oath***, ***growth***, ***stealth***.
2 Forming nouns of state from adjectives, as ***filth***, ***health***, ***length***, ***strength***, ***truth***, ***depth***, ***breadth***, ***wealth***.

-th /θ/ *suffix*[2]. Also **-eth**.
[Repr. Old English *-þa*, *-þe*, *-oþa*, *-oþe*, ult. from Indo-European, understood to be identical with one of the suffixes of the superlative degree.]
1 Forming ordinal and fractional numbers from all cardinal numerals from *four* onwards. The ordinals from ***twentieth*** to ***ninetieth*** are formed with ***-eth***. In compound numerals ***-th*** is added only to the last, as $1/1345$, the ***one thousand three hundred and forty-fifth*** part; in his ***one-and-twentieth*** year.
2 Denoting an unspecified ordinal numeral representing the name of an unspecified or fictitious regiment. *literary.*

-th *suffix*[3] var. of -ETH[1].

tha *pers. pronouns & nouns* see THEE *pers. pronoun & noun*, THOU *pers. pronoun & noun*[2].

thack /θak/ *noun.* Now *Scot. & dial.*
[Old English *þæc* = Middle Dutch *dac* (Dutch *dak*), Old & mod. High German *dach* roof, Old Norse *þak* roof, thatch, from Germanic base also of THATCH *verb*. Cf. THATCH *noun*.]
†1 The roof of a house or building. OE–E16.
2 = THATCH *noun* 1a. OE. ▶**b** The covering of straw with which the top of a haystack etc. is thatched. Freq. in ***thack and rape*** below. L18.
2b thack and rape the thatching of a haystack and the straw rope securing it.
Comb.: **thack-board** a wooden roofing-tile, a shingle; **thack house** a thatched house; **thack-stone** a thin flat stone used for roofing; **thack-tile** a roofing-tile.

thack /θak/ *verb*[1]. Now *Scot. & dial.* OE.
[from the noun. Cf. THATCH *verb*, THEEK.]
1 *verb intrans.* = THATCH *verb* 3b. OE.
2 *verb trans.* = THATCH *verb* 3a. ME.
■ **thacker**, **thackster** *nouns* a thatcher ME. **thacking** *noun* (*a*) the action of the verb; (*b*) material used for thatching, thatch: LME.

thack /θak/ *verb*[2]. Long *obsolete* exc. *dial.*
[Old English *þaccian*, app. imit. Cf. THWACK *verb*.]
†1 *verb trans.* Hit with the palm of the hand; pat, slap lightly. OE–LME.
†2 *verb trans.* Dab (an ointment) on; clap (something) *on* or *in* a place. OE–L16.
3 *verb trans.* Thwack, beat, flog. M19.

Thackerayan /ˈθakərɪən, θakəˈreɪən/ *adjective & noun.* M19.
[from *Thackeray* (see below) + -AN.]
▶**A** *adjective.* Of, pertaining to, or characteristic of the English novelist William Makepeace Thackeray (1811–63) or his works. M19.

> 📖 C. PETERS The story is Thackerayan in its delight in visual detail . . and deliberate anachronism.

▶**B** *noun.* An admirer or student of Thackeray or his writing. E20.
■ **Thackeray'ana** *noun pl.* publications or other items concerning or associated with Thackeray E20.

thaft *noun* var. of THOFT.

Thai /tʌɪ/ *noun & adjective.* E19.
[Thai = free.]
▶**A** *noun.* Pl. same, **-s**.
1 The Tai language of Thailand (formerly Siam), a country in SE Asia. E19.
2 A native or inhabitant of Thailand; a member of the people forming the largest ethnic group in Thailand and also inhabiting neighbouring regions. M19.
▶**B** *adjective.* Of or pertaining to Thailand, its inhabitants, or their language. E19.
Thai silk wild silk woven in Thailand according to traditional designs, often with bright colours. **Thai stick** a marijuana cigarette.
■ **Thailander** *noun* = THAI *noun* 2 M20.

thaive *noun* var. of THEAVE.

Thakali /təˈkɑːliː/ *noun & adjective.* E20.
[Thakali.]
▶**A** *noun.* Pl. **-s**, same.
1 A member of a Nepalese people of Mongolian origin. E20.
2 The Tibeto-Burman language of this people. L20.
▶**B** *attrib.* or as *adjective.* Of or pertaining to the Thakalis or their language. L20.

thakin /θəˈkɪn/ *noun.* Also **Th-**. E20.
[Burmese.]
1 In Myanmar (Burma), used as a term of respectful address to a man. E20.
2 *Hist.* A member of a nationalist movement that arose in Burma (Myanmar) during the 1930s. E20.

thakur /ˈtɑːkʊə/ *noun.* Also **Th-**. E19.
[Hindi *ṭhākur* lord from Sanskrit *ṭhakkura* chief, lord.]
In the Indian subcontinent, a chief or noble, esp. of the Rajputs. Freq. as a title and term of respectful address.

thalamencephalon /ˌθaləmɛnˈsɛfəlɒn, -ˈkɛf-/ *noun.* L19.
[from THALAM(O- + ENCEPHALON.]
ANATOMY. The part of the diencephalon that is concerned with the relaying of sensory information, comprising the epithalamus, thalamus, hypothalamus, and ventral thalamus.

thalami *noun* pl. of THALAMUS.

thalamic /θəˈlamɪk, ˈθaləmɪk/ *adjective.* M19.
[from THALAMUS + -IC.]
Chiefly ANATOMY. Of or pertaining to a thalamus.

thalamite /ˈθaləmʌɪt/ *noun. rare.* L19.
[Greek *thalamitēs*, from *thalamos* inner chamber, ship's hold.]
GREEK HISTORY. A rower in one of the tiers of a trireme, generally believed to be the lowest tier. Cf. THRANITE, ZYGITE.

thalamo- /ˈθaləməʊ/ *combining form* of THALAMUS: see -O-.
■ **thalamo'cortical** *adjective* designating sensory nerve fibres running from the thalamus to the cerebral cortex E20. **thalamo'striate** *adjective* designating a vein that collects blood from the thalamus and the corpus striatum E20. **thala'motomy** *noun* (MEDICINE) (an instance of) a surgical operation to destroy a specific part of the thalamus, used for the relief of pain or Parkinsonism and occas. to treat mental illness M20.

thalamus /ˈθaləməs/ *noun.* Pl. **-mi** /-mʌɪ, -miː/. L17.
[Latin from Greek *thalamos* inner chamber.]
1 ANATOMY. Orig., a part of the brain at which a nerve originates or appears to originate; *spec.* an optic thalamus. Now, either of two masses of grey matter lying between the cerebral hemispheres on either side of the third ventricle, which relay sensory information and act as a centre for pain perception. L17.
2 BOTANY. The receptacle of a flower. L17.
3 GREEK ANTIQUITIES. An inner or secret room; a women's apartment. M19.

thalassaemia /θaləˈsiːmɪə/ *noun.* Also ***-ssemia**. M20.
[from THALASS(O- (from its original discovery in Mediterranean countries) + Greek *haima* blood + -IA[1].]
MEDICINE. Any of a group of hereditary haemolytic blood diseases widespread in Mediterranean, African, and Asian countries, caused by the faulty synthesis of part of the haemoglobin molecule and leading to anaemia and other symptoms. Usu. with specifying word or prefixed Greek letter(s).
thalassaemia major the homozygous form of thalassaemia, which results in the severest symptoms; also called ***Cooley's anaemia***.
■ **thalassaemic** *noun* a person with thalassaemia L20.

thalassian /θəˈlasɪən/ *adjective & noun.* Now *rare.* M19.
[from Greek *thalassios* marine, from *thalassa* sea: see -AN.]
▶**A** *adjective.* Of or pertaining to the sea, marine; *spec.* in ZOOLOGY, designating or pertaining to marine turtles. M19.
▶**B** *noun.* ZOOLOGY. A marine turtle. M19.

thalassic /θəˈlasɪk/ *adjective.* M19.
[French *thalassique*, from Greek *thalassa* sea: see -IC.]
Of or pertaining to the sea, marine (freq. *poet.*); *spec.* (*a*) of or pertaining to deep sea waters; (*b*) (esp. of a civilization or culture) pertaining to or associated with inland seas.

thalasso- /θəˈlasəʊ/ *combining form* of Greek *thalassa* sea: see -O-.
■ **thalasso'graphic**, **thalasso'graphical** *adjectives* oceanographic L19. **thala'ssography** *noun* oceanography L19. **thalasso'phobia** *noun* irrational fear of the sea, or of wide uninterrupted vistas E19. **thalasso'therapy** *noun* the use of seawater as a therapeutic treatment L19.

thalassocracy /θaləˈsɒkrəsi/ *noun.* M19.
[Greek *thalassokratia*, from *thalassa* sea: see -CRACY.]
A nation's mastery at sea; a nation's sovereignty of large areas of the sea; a maritime empire.

> 📖 *Times Lit. Suppl.* What about the . . Cretan thalassocracy, whose catastrophic demise is . . incontrovertible?

thalassocrat /θəˈlasəkrat/ *noun.* M19.
[formed as prec.: see -CRAT.]
A person with mastery of the sea; a ruler of a maritime empire.

thale cress /ˈθeɪl krɛs/ *noun phr.* L18.
[from Johann *Thal* (1542–83), German physician + CRESS.]
A small white-flowered cruciferous plant, *Arabidopsis thaliana*, of walls and dry open ground.

thaler /ˈtɑːlə/ *noun.* L18.
[German (now *Taler*) DOLLAR.]
Hist. A German silver coin; a dollar (see DOLLAR 1).

thali /ˈtɑːli/ *noun*[1]. L19.
[Tamil *tāli*.]
A gold pendant that is hung round the bride's neck as part of a southern Indian wedding ceremony.

thali /ˈtɑːli/ *noun*[2]. M20.
[Hindi *thālī* from Sanskrit *sthālī*.]
A metal platter or flat dish on which Indian food is served; an Indian meal comprising a selection of assorted dishes, esp. served on such a platter.

thaliacean /θalɪˈeɪʃ(ə)n/ *adjective & noun.* L19.
[from mod. Latin *Thaliacea* (see below), from *Thalia* former genus name formed as next: see -AN.]
ZOOLOGY. ▶**A** *adjective.* Of, pertaining to, or designating a tunicate of the class Thaliacea, which comprises the salps. L19.
▶**B** *noun.* A salp. L19.

Thalian /θəˈlʌɪən/ *adjective. literary. rare.* M19.
[from Greek *Thaleia* (lit. 'blooming', from *thallein* to bloom), the Muse of comedy and pastoral poetry.]
Comic.

thalictrum /θəˈlɪktrəm/ *noun.* M17.
[mod. Latin (see below), use as genus name of Latin *thalictrum* from Greek *thaliktron*.]
Any of the various plants constituting the genus *Thalictrum*, of the buttercup family, *esp.* those grown for ornament; = ***meadow rue*** s.v. MEADOW *noun*.

thalidomide /θəˈlɪdəmʌɪd/ *noun.* M20.
[from PH)THAL(IC + IM)IDO- + I)MIDE, elems. of the systematic name.]
PHARMACOLOGY. A non-barbiturate sedative and hypnotic, $C_{13}H_{10}N_2O_4$, which was found to be teratogenic when taken early in pregnancy, sometimes causing malformation or absence of limbs in the foetus.
Comb.: **thalidomide baby**, **thalidomide child**, etc.: with a congenital abnormality due to the effects of thalidomide.

thallic /ˈθalɪk/ *adjective.* M19.
[from THALLIUM + -IC.]
CHEMISTRY. Of or containing thallium, esp. in the trivalent state.
thallic oxide thallium trioxide, Tl_2O_3, a brownish-black solid.

thalline /ˈθalʌɪn/ *adjective.* M19.
[from THALLUS + -INE[1].]
BOTANY. Of the margin of the apothecium of a lichen: having the structure and colour of the thallus.

thallium /ˈθalɪəm/ *noun.* M19.
[from Greek *thallos* green shoot (from *thallein* to bloom), from the vivid green line distinguishing its spectrum + -IUM.]
A rare bluish-white metallic chemical element, atomic no. 81, which is soft and malleable like lead, and forms toxic compounds which are used as poisons, in glass-making, and in electronics. (Symbol Tl.)
Comb.: **thallium glass** a variety of glass of great density and refracting power, which contains thallium instead of lead or potassium.

thalloid /ˈθalɔɪd/ *adjective.* M19.
[from THALLUS + -OID.]
BOTANY. Having the form of a thallus; *spec.* (of a liverwort) having the plant body not differentiated into stems and leaves (opp. ***foliose***).

thallophyte /ˈθaləfʌɪt/ *noun.* M19.
[from mod. Latin *Thallophyta* (pl.), formed as THALLUS: see -PHYTE.]
BOTANY. A plant or plantlike organism consisting of a thallus; *spec.* one belonging to the former class Thallophyta, comprising algae, fungi, lichens, and bacteria.
■ **thallophytic** /-ˈfɪtɪk/ *adjective* L19.

thallose /ˈθaləʊs/ *adjective.* E20.
[from THALLUS + -OSE[1].]
BOTANY. Of a liverwort: thalloid.

thallous /ˈθaləs/ *adjective.* L19.
[from THALLIUM + -OUS.]
CHEMISTRY. Of or containing thallium, esp. in its monovalent state.
thallous oxide thallium monoxide, Tl_2O, a black powder used in glass-making etc.
■ Also **thallious** /ˈθalɪəs/ *adjective* (now *rare*) M19.

thallus /ˈθaləs/ *noun.* Pl. **-lli** /-lʌɪ, -liː/. E19.
[Greek *thallos* green shoot, from *thallein* to bloom.]
BOTANY. A plant body (as in algae, fungi, lichens, and some liverworts) not differentiated into stem and leaves, lacking true roots or a vascular system, and freq. flattened and ribbon-like.

thalweg /ˈtɑːlvɛg, ˈθɑːlwɛg/ *noun.* Also **tal-**. M19.
[German, from *thal* (now *Tal*) valley + *Weg* way.]
PHYSICAL GEOGRAPHY. The line of fastest descent from any point on land; *esp.* one connecting the deepest points along a river channel or the lowest points along a valley floor.

thamin /θəˈmɪn/ *noun.* L19.
[Burmese.]
A reddish-brown deer, *Cervus eldii*, found in marshy country in SE Asia.

Thammuz /ˈtamʊz/ *noun.* Also **Tammuz**. M16.
[Hebrew *tammūz*.]
In the Jewish calendar, the tenth month of the civil and fourth of the religious year, usu. coinciding with parts of June and July.

Thamud /θəˈmuːd/ *noun pl.* L19.
[formed as next.]
An ancient people inhabiting NW Arabia between the 4th cent. BC and the 7th cent. AD.

Thamudic /θəˈmuːdɪk/ *adjective & noun.* E20.
[from Arab. *Tamūd* Thamud + -IC.]
▶ **A** *adjective.* Of or pertaining to the Thamud; *spec.* of, pertaining to, or designating an ancient language, allied to early Arabic and known only from graffiti inscriptions dating from the 5th to the 1st cents. BC discovered in northern and central Arabia. E20.
▶ **B** *noun.* The Thamudic language. M20.

Thamudite /ˈθamjʊdʌɪt/ *noun & adjective. rare.* M19.
[formed as prec.: see -ITE[1].]
▶ **A** *noun.* A member of the Thamud. M19.
▶ **B** *adjective.* Thamudic. L19.

†**than** *adverb, conjunction[1], noun, & adjective* var. of THEN *adverb* etc.

than /ðan, *unstressed* ð(ə)n/ *conjunction[2] & preposition.* Also †**then**.
[Old English *þanne, þonne, þænne*, also *þan, þon*; orig. the same word as THEN *adverb, conjunction[1]*, etc., from which it was not finally differentiated in form until the 18th cent.]
1 a *conjunction & preposition.* Introducing the second elem. in a statement of comparison. Foll. by noun, pers. pronoun, adjective, inf., clause, etc.; with pers. pronoun there may be ellipsis of the clause, the pers. pronoun being either subjective or objective depending on its relation to the unexpressed verb or (*informal*) always objective, *than* being treated as a preposition (as *I know you better than she (does); I know you better than (I know) her; I know you better than her (= than she does)).* OE. ▸**b** *conjunction.* Followed by *that* (*arch.*) or *to do* in a statement expressing hypothesis or consequence. E16.
2 *conjunction.* Introducing the second elem. in a statement of difference or expressing preference. Freq. preceded by *other, different* (see note s.v. DIFFERENT *adjective*). OE.
3 *conjunction.* †**a** With ellipsis of preceding comparative: rather than, more than. ME–M17. ▸**b** Except, besides, but, other than. *arch.* LME. ▸**c** Used after *hardly, scarcely*: when. M19.

1a HENRY FIELDING Sophia, than whom none was more capable of [etc.]. SIR W. SCOTT I . . could not be expected . . to be wiser than her. J. CONRAD It wasn't more than ten feet by twelve. R. MACAULAY I have done her less than justice. V. WOOLF I'm a great deal happier than I was at 28. INA TAYLOR A . . creature who looked far older than her fifty years. B. VINE A man a few years older than me. **b** AV *Isa.* 28:20 The bed is shorter, then that a man can stretch himselfe on it. V. WOOLF It's easier now to go on than to stop. **2** W. LEWIS One of the 'lower orders' dressed up . . like a toff cannot be otherwise than *odd*. C. HARMAN A . . preference for spectating rather than partaking in sports. *Atlanta* Amenities . . dramatically different than those offered . . 10 years ago. *Warsaw Voice* The Politburo's special envoy . . is none other than Igor Ligachev, Gorbachev's greatest rival. *Health Now* The common misconception that . . lambs etc. have no purpose . . other than to be eaten. **3a** J. TRAPP Job was . . tortured by his interpretations, then . . by his botches and ulcers. **b** J. RUSKIN There is nothing left for him than the blood that comes . . up to the horsebridles. **c** *Raritan* Scarcely has this law . . been formulated than it is breached.

thana /ˈtɑːnə/ *noun. Indian subcontinent.* Also **tana**. E19.
[Hindi *thānā* from Sanskrit *sthāna* place, station.]
1 A police station. Formerly also, a military station or fortified post. E19.
2 A political division of a district under the jurisdiction of a police station. M20.
■ **thanadar** /tɑːnəˈdɑː/ *noun* [Persian & Urdu *thānadār*, from *thānā(h)* from Hindi + *-dār* holding, holder] †(*a*) the commander of a military post; (*b*) the head officer of a police station: E19.

thanage /ˈθeɪnɪdʒ/ *noun. obsolete* exc. *Hist.* LME.
[Anglo-Norman (also *thaynage*), from THANE + -AGE.]
The tenure by which lands were held by a thane; the land held by a thane. Also, the rank, position, or jurisdiction of a thane.

thanato- /ˈθanətəʊ/ *combining form* of Greek *thanatos* death: see -O-. Before a vowel **thanat-**.
■ **thanatocoeˈnosis**, *-cen- noun, pl. **-noses** /-ˈnəʊsiːz/, PALAEONTOLOGY a group of fossils occurring in the same location but not necessarily representing a former biocoenosis M20. **thanatoid** *adjective* (*rare*) (*a*) MEDICINE resembling death; (*b*) ZOOLOGY deadly poisonous: M19. **thanatoˈphilia** *noun* undue or abnormal fascination with death L20. **thanatoˈphobia** *noun* irrational fear of death M19. **thanatoˈphoric** *adjective* (MEDICINE) lethal, deadly; *spec.* designating a fatal form of dwarfism: L20. **thanaˈtopsis** *noun* (*rare*) contemplation of death E19.

thanatology /θanəˈtɒlədʒi/ *noun.* M19.
[from prec. + -LOGY.]
The branch of science that deals with death, its causes and phenomena, and (now) with the effects of approaching death and the needs of the terminally ill and their families.
■ **thanatoˈlogical** *adjective* M19. **thanatologist** *noun* (*a*) an expert in or student of thanatology; (*b*) an undertaker: E20.

Thanatos /ˈθanətɒs/ *noun.* M20.
[Greek: see THANATO-.]
FREUDIAN PSYCHOLOGY. The urge for destruction or self-destruction. Cf. EROS 2.

thane /θeɪn/ *noun.*
[Old English *þeg(e)n* = Old Saxon *þegan* man, Old High German *degan* boy, servant, warrior, hero (German *Degen* warrior), Old Norse *þegn* freeman, liegeman, from Germanic, from Indo-European base repr. also by Greek *teknon* child, *tokeus* parent. See also THEGN.]
†**1** A servant, a minister, an attendant; *spec.* a disciple, esp. of Christ. OE–L16.
†**2** A military attendant, follower, or retainer; a soldier. Only in OE. ▸**b** A warrior, a brave man. Cf. EARL 1b. *poet.* OE–ME.
3 *Hist.* In the Old English constitution: a man who held lands from the king or other superior by military service, ranking below a hereditary nobleman or earl (EARL 1) and above an ordinary freeman or churl (CHURL 2). Cf. THEGN. OE.
4 SCOTTISH HISTORY. A man who held lands from the king and ranked with the son of an earl; the chief of a clan, who became one of the king's barons. LME. ▸**b** *transf.* A Scottish lord; (in allus. to Shakes. *Macb.*) a person abandoning loyalty to another in adversity. M18.
Comb.: **thane-land** land held by an English thane, or by military tenure; **thanewer** [Old English *þegnwer*] the wergeld of an English thane.
■ **thanedom** *noun* the position or rank of a thane; the domain or jurisdiction of a Scottish thane: LME. **thanehood** *noun* (*rare*) the condition or rank of a thane L19. **thaneship** *noun* the office or position of a thane OE.

thang /θaŋ/ *noun. slang* (chiefly *US*). M20.
[Repr. a southern US pronunc.]
= THING *noun[1]*.

thank /θaŋk/ *noun.*
[Old English *þanc* = Old Frisian *thank, thonk*, Old Saxon *þank*, Middle Dutch, Old High German *danc* (German, Dutch *dank*), Gothic *þagks*, from Germanic base also of THINK *verb[2]*.]
†**1** A thought. OE–ME.
†**2** Favourable thought or feeling, good will; grace, favour. OE–E17.
3 An expression of gratitude; an appreciative or grateful acknowledgement of a service or favour. Formerly also, the action of expressing gratitude. Long only in *pl.* exc. *poet.* & *joc.* OE.
†**4** Gratitude; appreciation felt towards a person for favour or services received. ME–L17.
5 In *pl.*, as a polite rejoinder: thank you. Freq. in ***thanks awfully***, ***thanks a lot***, ***thanks very much***, etc. L16.

3 SIR T. MORE Turning to god with lawde and thanke. A. CROSS Kate returned home to . . offer warm thanks for . . Western upholstery. A. ROBERTSON My colleagues . . deserve special thanks for their support. **5** E. SEGAL 'Sure you won't stay over?' . . 'No, no—thanks, but I've a load of studying.' *Sun* Thanks for being so patient.

Phrases: ***con thanks***: see CON *verb[1]* 3. ***get thank***: see ***have thank*** below. **give thanks** express gratitude, esp. to God; now *esp.*, say grace at a meal. †**have thank**, †**get thank** (*a*) be thanked; (*b*) be thought worthy of thanks, get the credit *for*, have the merit or honour *of* (something). **no thanks to**, **small thanks to** not by virtue of; not because of; despite. ***pick a thank***: see PICK *verb[1]*. ***return thanks***: see RETURN *verb*. ***small thanks to***: see ***no thanks to*** above. **thanks be** *interjection* (*colloq.*) thanks be to God; thank goodness. **thanks to** (*a*) thanks be given to, thanks are due to; (*b*) (freq. *iron.*) owing to, as the (good or bad) result of, in consequence of.
Comb.: **thank-offering** an offering or gift made (*spec.* to a god) by way of thanks or acknowledgement.

thank /θaŋk/ *verb.*
[Old English *þancian* = Old Saxon *þankon*, Old High German *dankōn* (Dutch, German *danken*), from Germanic base of prec.]
†**1** *verb intrans.* Give thanks (*to*). OE–M16.
2 *verb trans.* (orig. with dat. obj.). Give thanks to; express gratitude or acknowledgement to. (Foll. by *for*, †*of*.) OE.
3 *verb trans.* Return thanks or express one's gratitude for (something). Now *arch. rare.* LME.
4 *verb trans.* Give the thanks or credit *for* something to (a person); hold (a person etc.) responsible *for* something; (freq. *iron.*) blame. LME.

2 E. HALL The Frenche kyng . . thanked the kyng of Englande of his kynde offre. A. GILBERT Miss Alice wouldn't thank you for tying her into a chair. G. BATTISCOMBE Christina wrote thanking him for . . a Christmas present. *Which?* We'd like to thank all those who helped us. **3** BYRON Charles forgot To thank his tale. **4** D. L. SAYERS [She] has only herself to thank . . she's asking for trouble.

Phrases: **God be thanked** *arch.* = ***thank God*** (a) below. **I will thank you to do**, **we will thank you to do**, etc.: expr. a command or reproach. **thank God**, **thank goodness**, **thank heaven(s)**, etc. (*a*) expr. pious gratitude; (*b*) *colloq.* expr. relief or pleasure. ***thank one's lucky stars***, ***thank one's stars***: see STAR *noun[1]* & *adjective*. **thank you**: a polite formula acknowledging a gift, favour, or service, or an offer accepted or refused; also used to emphasize a preceding statement, esp. one implying refusal or denial.
■ **thanker** *noun* L16. **thanking** *verbal noun* (*arch.*) the action of the verb; an instance of this: OE.

thankee /ˈθaŋkiː/ *noun & interjection. colloq.* E19.
[Repr. pronunc. of *thank ye*.]
(A) thank you.

thankful /ˈθaŋkfʊl, -f(ə)l/ *adjective.* OE.
[from THANK *noun* + -FUL.]
1 Feeling thanks or appreciation; (of an action, words, etc.) expressive of thanks or appreciation; grateful; pleased, glad, relieved. OE.

†**2 a** Deserving thanks, gratitude, or credit; acceptable, agreeable. OE–E17. ▸**b** Of a payment: giving satisfaction, satisfactory. *Scot.* L15–L17.

> 🕮 **1** J. TROLLOPE The.. detritus people are thankful to leave behind when they move house. J. FANE A tiny minority of those who accepted her largesse were truly thankful for it. **thankful for small mercies** grateful for minor benefits or good fortune.

■ **thankfulness** *noun* E16.

thankfully /ˈθaŋkfʊli, -f(ə)li/ *adverb.* OE.
[from prec. + -LY[2].]
1 In a thankful manner; with thanks; gratefully. OE.
†**2** So as to please or satisfy; acceptably, pleasingly; satisfactorily. LME–L16.
3 (Modifying a sentence.) Let us be thankful (that); fortunately. (Considered *erron.* by some.) M20.

> 🕮 **1** DEFOE He accepted thankfully all my presents. H. SECOMBE The policeman sank thankfully into an armchair. **3** *Shooting Magazine* An alarming safety situation .. caused many a raised eyebrow but thankfully nothing worse.

thankless /ˈθaŋklɪs/ *adjective.* LME.
[from THANK *noun* + -LESS.]
1 Not feeling, actuated by, or expressing gratitude; ungrateful. LME.
2 Without thanks; unthanked. *rare.* LME.
3 Of a task etc.: not likely to win or receive thanks; deserving no thanks. L15.

> 🕮 **1** R. PILCHER When friends come a long way.. it seems pretty thankless to send them away without so much as a cup of tea. B. W. ALDISS The.. Queen.. had lain down her life for her thankless children. **3** A. BRIEN A characteristic Russian government job: prestigious, demanding, thankless and.. unpaid.

■ **thanklessly** *adverb* E17. **thanklessness** *noun* L16.

thanksgive /ˈθaŋksgɪv/ *verb trans. & intrans. rare.* Pa. t. **-gave** /-geɪv/; pa. pple **-given** /-gɪv(ə)n/. M17.
[Back-form. from THANKSGIVING.]
Give thanks (for).

thanksgiver /ˈθaŋksgɪvə/ *noun.* E17.
[formed as next + GIVER.]
A person who gives thanks.

thanksgiving /ˈθaŋksgɪvɪŋ, θaŋksˈgɪvɪŋ/ *noun.* M16.
[from THANK *noun* + -S[1] + GIVING.]
1 a The giving of thanks; the expression of thanks or gratitude, esp. to God. M16. ▸**b** A public celebration, marked with religious services, held as an expression of gratitude to God. Also, a day set apart for this purpose; *spec.* (**T-**) = ***Thanksgiving Day*** below. M17.
2 An act or expression of thanks; *esp.* a form of words used to give thanks to God. M16.

> 🕮 **1a** D. HOGAN Páid offered prayers in thanksgiving for his safe arrival. **b** E. HARDWICK Christmas is near.. a lighted tree has been in the hardware store since Thanksgiving. **2** LD MACAULAY The ministers selected from that liturgy .. prayers and thanksgivings. **General Thanksgiving** a form of thanksgiving in the *Book of Common Prayer* or the Alternative Service Book. ***sacrifice of praise and thanksgiving***: see SACRIFICE *noun.*

Comb.: **Thanksgiving Day** a national holiday, orig. set apart for feasting and thanksgiving to God, celebrated on the fourth Thursday in November in the US and on the second Monday in October in Canada.

thankworthy /ˈθaŋkwəːði/ *adjective.* LME.
[from THANK *noun* + -WORTHY.]
Worthy of thanks or appreciation; deserving gratitude or credit.

> 🕮 T. K. CHEYNE A faulty but at that time thankworthy book.

■ **thankworthily** *adverb* M16. **thankworthiness** *noun* M19.

thank-you /ˈθaŋkjuː/ *noun & adjective.* Also **thankyou**. L18.
[from *thank you* s.v. THANK *verb.*]
▸**A** *noun.* An instance of thanking someone; an utterance of 'thank you'; an action or gift as an expression of thanks. *colloq.* L18.

> 🕮 A. ROBERTSON A special thank you to colleagues.. who have helped in the preparation of this book. A. S. BYATT They had despatched their fervent thank-yous in January.

▸**B** *attrib.* or as *adjective.* Designating something written or done to convey thanks or gratitude. Freq. in ***thank-you letter, thank-you note.*** E20.

thank-you-ma'am *US colloq.* a hollow or ridge in a road, which causes people passing over it in a vehicle to nod the head involuntarily, as if in acknowledgement of a favour.

thapsia /ˈθapsɪə/ *noun.* LME.
[Latin from Greek, perh. from *Thapsos*, an Aegean island.]
Any of several large umbelliferous plants of the genus *Thapsia*, of the Mediterranean region; esp. *T. garganica.*

thar /θɑː/ *noun*[1]. M19.
[Nepali *thār*. Cf. TAHR.]
1 In the Himalayas: the serow (a goat antelope), *Capricornis sumatraensis*. Now *rare.* M19.
2 = TAHR. L19.

thar *adverb, conjunction, interjection, pronoun, & noun*[2] see THERE *adverb* etc.

tharm /θɑːm/ *noun. obsolete* exc. *dial.*
[Old English *þarm*, *þearm* = Old Frisian *therm*, Middle & mod. Dutch *darm*, Old & mod. High German *darm*, Old Norse *þarmr*, from Germanic, from Indo-European base meaning 'go through'.]
1 An intestine. Usu. in *pl.*, the bowels, the entrails. OE.
2 Material made from intestines; catgut, esp. for violin-strings; in *pl.*, violin-strings. L17.

that /ðat, *unstressed* ðət/ *pronoun, noun, conjunction, adjective* (in mod. usage also classed as a *determiner*), *& adverb.* Also (now only repr. dial. or affected pronunc.) **thet** /ðɛt/.
[Old English *þæt* nom. & accus. sing. neut. of the simple demonstr. pronoun & adjective *se, sēo, þæt*, from Germanic: cf. THE, THEN *conjunction*[1], THERE, THIS, THOSE.]
▸**A** *pronoun & noun.* Pl. THOSE, (formerly) THO *pronoun.*
▸**I** *demonstr. pronoun.* **1** The thing or (now usu. as subject of *be* in stating or asking who or what *that* (person) is) person indicated, mentioned, or understood. OE.
2 The fact, action, circumstance, opinion, etc., implied or contained in the previous (*occas.* following) statement. OE. ▸**b** The time or date marked by an event or action previously mentioned. ME.
3 a Preceded by *and*: used instead of repeating a word or phrase (esp. describing an event or course of action) in the previous clause. *arch.* OE. ▸**b** *emphatic.* Representing a word or phr. in the previous clause or sentence, freq. in expressing agreement or confirmation. (Usu. as obj. or compl., and freq. with inverted construction.) *colloq.* ME.
4 In opposition to ***this***: the other of two things, esp. the further or less immediate or obvious etc.; another unspecified thing of the same kind. Cf. sense C.3 below. OE. ▸**b** [A Latinism.] The former. Cf. THIS *pronoun* 3b. Now *rare* or *obsolete.* ME.
5 a As antecedent to a rel. pronoun or adverb expressed or understood: the thing, something, or (now only as in sense 1 above) the person, described or specified in some way, the one. ME. ▸**b** With following defining phr.: the thing described or specified in some way, the one. LME. ▸**c** With ellipsis of following relative pronoun or adverb: the thing which, the person who. Now only in emphatic use. L16.

> 🕮 **1** BROWNING 'Bless us,' cried the Mayor, 'what's that?' TENNYSON A sweet voice that. W. S. MAUGHAM Nice to have a young fellow like that around. V. WOOLF Beauty—isn't that enough? M. DUKE He laughed. 'That's my girl. That's better.' M. AMIS Why would you want to.. do a thing like that? **2** T. HARDY All three in one ship—think of that! J. RHYS This makes me rather sad. That's why I didn't write. I. MURDOCH That was marriage, thought Dora; to be enclosed in the aims of another. O. MANNING He'll be found guilty—that goes without saying. G. VIDAL I like handsome men, you know that! R. P. JHABVALA If God wants her to die here, that is what she will do. **b** T. JEFFERSON On the 24th, or within two or three days of that. W. S. MAUGHAM She read.. the gossip columns, after that the woman's pages. **3a** L. RITCHIE It was necessary.. to act, and that promptly. **b** T. HARDY 'Will you give me a lift home?' '*That* I will, darling.' S. WOODS 'It could mean a lot of work..' 'It could that', Gilbey agreed. **4** DRYDEN This is not fair; nor profitable that. *Listener* Motifs from this Tourangeau château or that. B. VINE When reproved, she had whined, tossing herself this way and that. **5a** OED That was our member who spoke first at the meeting. L. STEFFENS Another such conceit of our egotism is that which deplores our politics. D. BARNES In the heart of the lover will be traced.. that which he loves. **b** M. EDGEWORTH Turning from the history of meanness to that of enthusiasm. BROWNING That in the mortar—you call it a gum? T. HARDY The husband's business was that of a gunmaker. **c** R. W. EMERSON Every ship is a romantic object, except that we sail in. M. ARNOLD Who is that stands by the dying fire?

▸**II** *rel. pronoun.* **6** Introducing a clause defining or restricting the antecedent, esp. a clause essential to the identification of the antecedent (and thus completing its sense). Cf. WHICH *rel. pronoun* 4, WHO *rel. pronoun* 4. OE.
7 Introducing a clause describing or stating something additional about the antecedent (the sense of the main clause being complete without the rel. clause); which, who(m). Now usu. *informal* or *poet.* OE. ▸**b** In neg. contexts with verbs of knowing, learning, etc., introducing a statement qualifying the main clause: according to what, as far as. LME.
8 As subj. or obj. of the rel. clause, with ellipsis of the antecedent: what; the one or ones who. *arch.* OE.
9 a With ref. to time: on which, when. OE. ▸**b** From the time that; since. Now *non-standard. rare.* ME. ▸**c** *gen.* With imperfect rel. clause (with ellipsis of a preposition etc. suggested by the main clause): with (in, on, etc.) which. Now *non-standard.* LME.
10 Preceded by a descriptive noun or adjective, in a parenthetic exclamatory clause. *arch.* LME.
11 With a possess. adjective in the rel. clause corresponding to the antecedent: of which, of whom. *obsolete* exc. *dial.* LME.

> 🕮 **6** AV *Ps.* 65:2 O thou that hearest prayer. S. WARREN There's nothing.. that we need be afraid of. OED The play that you were talking about. J. BUCHAN The present.. no longer has the solidity that it had in youth. E. J. HOWARD People very seldom say all that they feel. **7** LD MACAULAY False Sextus That wrought the deed of shame. R. BRIDGES Lazy mists, that still Climb'd on the shadowy roots of every hill. **b** CARLYLE But Protestantism has not died yet, that I hear of! **8** AV *Exod.* 3:14 And God saide vnto Moses, I AM That I AM. K. DIGBY Of her ancestors there have been that have exalted and pulled down kings. W. MORRIS In peace eat that ye have. **9a** AV *Gen.* 2:17 In the day that thou eatest thereof, thou shalt surely die. M. EDGEWORTH The night that he went to the play. **b** S. BELLOW It's already three weeks that I took down the curtains. **c** SHAKES. *Merch. V.* Who riseth from a feast With that keen appetite that he sits down. G. W. DASENT If you will only see things in the light that we see them. **10** TINDALE *Rom.* 7:24 O wretched man that I am. **11** B. K. GREEN He had traded the horse that I had worked on his teeth.

▸**III** *noun.* Pl. **-s**.
12 A thing referred to as 'that'. Freq. opp. ***what***. M17.

> 🕮 R. HARRIES None of these thises and thats.. are the 'loved one.'

▸**B** *conjunction.* **1** Introducing a subord. clause expr. a statement or hypothesis. OE. ▸**b** Introducing a clause in apposition to or exemplifying the statement in the principal clause: in that, in the fact that. Long *arch.* OE. ▸**c** Introducing an exclamatory clause expr. sorrow, indignation, bewilderment, etc. (Now usu. with *should*.) OE.
2 Introducing a clause expr. a reason, cause, or basis of what is stated in the main clause. OE.
3 a Introducing a clause expr. purpose, aim, or intention: with simple subjunctive (*arch.*), or with *may, might, should*, (rarely) *shall*. OE. ▸**b** Introducing an exclamatory clause expr. desire or longing: with verb in (past) subjunctive. ME. ▸**c** Introducing a clause expr. a hypothetical desired result: with verb in subjunctive or its equivalent. E17.
4 Introducing a clause expr. a result or consequence (in fact or in supposition): with verb usually in indicative. Now usu. (exc. *arch.*) with antecedent *so* or *such*. OE.
5 In neg. constructions: but that, but. (Now expressed by *without doing* or *being*.) *arch.* OE.
6 Used redundantly with conjunctions, or with other words now also used as conjunctions. *arch.* OE.
7 Used as a substitute instead of repeating a previous conjunction. *arch.* ME.

> 🕮 **1** AV *Prov.* 19:2 That the soule be without knowledge, it is not good. W. COWPER We have borne The ruffling wind, scarce conscious that it blew. J. MORLEY Rousseau was persuaded that Madame d'Epinay was his betrayer. C. M. YONGE It was for his own supremacy that he fought. L. URIS Could it be that the *Exodus* was driven by mystic forces? V. GLENDINNING She agreed.. that it was too sultry.. for serious gardening. **b** AV *1 Kings* 8:18 Thou diddest well that it was in thine heart. **c** SHAKES. *Temp.* That a brother should Be so perfidious. SHELLEY Great God! that such a father should be mine! **2** LD MACAULAY I should be very sorry that it were known. G. DALY He was grateful that the relationship had evolved into something less stormy. M. KRAMER The greatness of rich, strong white wines.. is that they manage to be powerful yet graceful. **3a** A. J. CHRISTIE Christ.. had prayed that Peter's faith should not fail. A. S. J. TESSIMOND Losing battles Fought that the sons of sons may win. **b** W. COWPER Oh that those lips had language! G. W. DASENT I would give all my goods that it had never happened. **4** SHAKES. *Wint. T.* I'd shriek, that even your ears Should rift to hear me. W. COWPER Did famine or did plague prevail That so much death appears? H. CARPENTER A dormouse (who lived to be so old that its eyebrows turned white). *Guardian* Brands of soya yoghurt.. so unpalateable that they have ended up down the sink. **5** GOLDSMITH I never attempted to be impudent yet, that I was not taken down. **6** SHAKES. *Jul. Caes.* When that the poor have cried, Caesar hath wept. A. WRIGHT The reason is, cause that Ordinances are nothing without the Lord. **7** AV *Job* 31:38 If my land cry against me, or that the furrowes likewise thereof complaine.

▸**C** *demonstr. adjective.* Cf. THOSE, THO *adjective.*
1 As neut. sing. of the def. article: the. Long *obsolete* exc. in ***of that ilk*** (see ILK *pronoun*[1] 2), where not now perceived as distinct from sense 2. OE.
2 Indicating or identifying a person or thing either as being pointed out or as having just been mentioned, or (often interchangeable with *the* but usu. more emphatic) as being distinguished by a following rel. clause or phr. completing the description. LOE. ▸**b** Indicating a person or thing assumed to be known, or (esp. before a noun or noun phr. in apposition) believed to be such as is stated. Freq. (esp. before a person's name) implying censure, dislike, or scorn. ME. ▸**c** With pl. noun or numeral: those. Now only with plurals taken in a collective sense. ME.
3 In opposition to ***this***: designating the other of two things, esp. the further or less immediate or obvious,

etc.; designating another unspecified thing of the same kind. ME.

4 Of such kind or degree; such, so great. Foll. by *that* (conjunction), †*as. arch.* LME.

> **2** DRYDEN Like that bold Greek who did the East subdue. H. DAVY The root is that part of the vegetable which least impresses the eye. I. WALTON [This fish] was almost a yard broad, and twice that length. T. HOOK Sophy, put down that knife. S. T. WARNER That beach edged with tin huts. I. MURDOCH Why don't you like that sort of song? G. GORDON Was that virtuoso violinist with . . waxed moustaches still at Florian? **b** SPENSER Thy gay Sonne, that winged God of Loue. G. MEREDITH In that England of yours, women marry for wealth. A. CHRISTIE It's not that Jack again, is it? G. F. FIENNES B. W. and Jenkin Jones referred to each other as 'that man Ward' (or 'Jones'). **c** GOLDSMITH There's that ten guineas you were sending to the poor gentleman. M. E. BRADDON During that rainy six weeks. **3** SHAKES. *L.L.L.* You that way: we this way. E. A. FREEMAN The temporary . . superiority of this or that Bretwalda. R. JAFFE Would they like this Tudor house or that Spanish one? G. R. TURNER My schooled beliefs about the sanctity of this attitude or that convention. **4** L. OLIPHANT He blushed to that degree that I felt quite shy.

▶**D** *adverb.* **1** So much, so (freq. with dependent clause) (now *dial.*); *colloq.* (with neg.) very. LME.

2 To the extent, degree, or amount understood, specified, or indicated; (precisely) as — as that. E19.

> **1** J. B. PRIESTLEY I'm that bewildered today I hardly know what I'm saying. D. EDEN I'm that worried, I can't sleep. *Spare Rib* It's not that easy in a place like Sheffield. P. BAILEY He weighed a ton, . . he was that bloated. S. GRAY Poor Tannie Rita died. She wasn't that old, you know. **2** M. BRIDGMAN 'I . . recollect you that high'—holding her hand about six inches off the table. *Publishers Weekly* Estimated sale before Christmas: 250,000—if they can be printed that fast.

Phrases: **all that** all that sort of thing; that and everything of the kind; ***not so — as all that, not as — as all that***, not quite so —, not too —. **and all that** and so forth, et cetera; ***and all that jazz***: see JAZZ *noun* 3. **and that** *colloq.* = ***and all that*** above. **at that** *colloq.* moreover, into the bargain. ***for all that***: see ALL *pronoun & noun* 3. ***how's that?***: see HOW *adverb*. ***in order that***: see ORDER *noun*. **like that** of that kind or nature; in that manner; *colloq.* effortlessly, instantly; ***be like that***: see LIKE *adjective* etc. ***not all that***: see NOT *adverb*. ***not that***: see NOT *adverb*. ***now that***: see NOW *conjunction*. ***take that!***: see TAKE *verb*. **that her** —, **that my** —, etc. *arch.* that — of hers, mine, etc. **that is (to say)**: (*a*) introducing (or more rarely following) an explanation of a preceding word or words; (*b*) accompanying (usu. following) an explanatory limitation or condition of a preceding statement. ***that lot***: see LOT *noun*. **that once** *colloq.* on that one occasion. **that one** the particular thing or (*colloq.*, *derog.*) person indicated, specified, or understood. **that said**: introducing a concessive statement. ***that's it***: see IT *pers. pronoun*. **that's right** *colloq.*: expr. approval or assent. **that's that** *colloq.* there is no more to be said (or done), the matter is settled, closed, finished, etc. **that's what** *colloq.* (adding emphasis to a preceding statement) and that is the truth. ***that there***. **that was**: (*a*) added when a married woman is referred to by her maiden name; *occas.* when a deceased person is referred to; (*b*) added for emphasis after a statement beginning 'That was'. **that was that** *colloq.* there was no more to be said (or done), that was the end of the matter. ***this and that, this or that, this, that, and the other, this, that, or the other***: see THIS.

¶ As *rel. pronoun* and *conjunction* often omitted by ellipsis: I am monarch of all [that] I survey. We were sorry [that] you couldn't come.

■ **thatness** *noun* (PHILOSOPHY) the quality or condition of being 'that', i.e. of existing as a definite thing M17.

thataboy /ˈðatəbɔɪ/ *interjection. slang* (chiefly *US*). M20.
[formed as ATTABOY.]
= ATTABOY.

thataway /ˈðatəweɪ/ *adverb. colloq.* (orig. *US*). M19.
[from THAT *demonstr. adjective* + WAY *noun* with intrusive *a*.]
1 In that direction. Freq. *joc.*, with ref. to the route taken by the object of pursuit. M19.
2 In that manner; like that. L19.

thatch /θatʃ/ *noun*. LME.
[Alt. of THACK *noun* after next.]
1 a Material used in thatching, as straw, reeds, palm leaves, etc.; (a) roof-covering made of this. Formerly also, a roof-covering made of tiles or lead. Cf. earlier THACK *noun* 2. LME. ▸**b** A thatched house. L17.
2 a Tall coarse grass. *US*. E17. ▸**b** In the W. Indies, (the leaves of) any of several palms used for thatching, esp. *Thrinax parviflora* (more fully ***palmetto thatch***), *Coccothrinax argentea* (more fully ***silver thatch***), and *Sabal jamaicensis* (more fully ***bull thatch***). L17.
3 a A covering *of* something, esp. hair; the hair of the head. Also (*slang*), a woman's pubic hair. M17. ▸**b** A matted layer of plant debris, moss, etc., on a lawn; material forming such a layer. M20.

> **3a** K. ROBERTS His thatch of dark blond hair was . . unkempt.

Comb.: **thatch-palm** a palm whose leaves are used for thatching (cf. sense 2b above).

■ **thatchless** *adjective* having the thatch missing or destroyed L19. **thatchy** *adjective* having much thatch; resembling thatch: M19.

thatch /θatʃ/ *verb*.
[Old English *þeccan* = Old Frisian *thekka*, Old Saxon *þekkian*, Old High German *decchen* (Dutch *dekken*, German *decken*), Old Norse *þekja*, from Germanic base also of THACK *noun*: vowel later assim. to THACK *noun*, *verb*[1]. Cf. THEEK.]
†**1** *verb trans.* Cover. Only in OE.
2 *verb trans.* Serve as a covering or roof to. *rare*. OE.
3 a *verb trans.* Provide with a roof or covering of straw, reeds, palm leaves, etc., laid so as to give protection from the weather. Freq. in *pass*. LME. ▸**b** *verb intrans.* Act as a thatcher; make a thatched roof. LME.
4 *verb trans. fig.* Cover as with thatch. L16.

> **3a** T. PENNANT Many . . churches are thatched with heath. **4** R. W. EMERSON What if Trade . . thatch with towns the prairie broad.

■ **thatched** *ppl adjective* made of, covered, or roofed with thatch LME. **thatcher** *noun* a person who thatches roofs; *esp.* a person whose occupation is thatching: ME. **thatching** *noun* (*a*) the action of the verb; (*b*) = THATCH *noun* 1: LME.

Thatcherite /ˈθatʃərʌɪt/ *noun & adjective*. L20.
[from *Thatcher* (see below) + -ITE[1].]
▶**A** *noun.* An advocate or supporter of the views or policies of the British Conservative politician Margaret Hilda Thatcher (b. 1925), Prime Minister (1979–90). L20.
▶**B** *adjective.* Of, pertaining to, or characteristic of Margaret Thatcher or Thatcherism. L20.
■ **Thatcheˈresque** *adjective* characteristic of Margaret Thatcher or her policies L20. **Thatcherism** *noun* the political and economic policies advocated by Margaret Thatcher L20.

Thathanabaing /ˌθɑːðənɑːˈbʌɪŋ/ *noun*. M19.
[Burmese, from *thathana* teaching, instruction + *baing* possess.]
The chief Buddhist dignitary in Myanmar (Burma).

thaught *noun* var. of THOUGHT *noun*[2].

thaumatin /ˈθɔːmətɪn/ *noun*. L20.
[from mod. Latin *Thaumat(ococcus* (see below), formed as next + COCCUS: see -IN[1].]
BIOCHEMISTRY. A sweet-tasting protein isolated from the fruit of the African plant *Thaumatococcus daniellii* (family Marantaceae).

thaumato- /ˈθɔːmətəʊ/ *combining form* of Greek *thauma*, *-mat-* wonder, marvel: see -O-.
■ **thaumaˈtolatry** *noun* excessive reverence for the miraculous or marvellous E19. **thaumaˈtology** *noun* the description or study of miracles M19.

thaumatrope /ˈθɔːmətrəʊp/ *noun*. E19.
[formed as prec. + Greek *-tropos* turning.]
A zoetrope or similar device illustrating the persistence of visual impressions; *spec.* one consisting of a card or disc with different figures on the two sides, which appear to combine into one when the card or disc is rotated rapidly.
■ **thaumaˈtropical** *adjective* (*rare*) E19.

thaumaturge /ˈθɔːmətəːdʒ/ *noun*. Orig. †**-urg**. Also in Latin form **thaumaturgus** /θɔːməˈtəːɡəs/, pl. **-gi** /-ɡʌɪ/. E18.
[medieval Latin *thaumaturgus* from Greek *thaumatourgos*, formed as THAUMATO- + *-ergos* working: later assim. to French.]
A performer of miracles, a worker of wonders; a magician.
■ Also **thaumaturgist** *noun* E19.

thaumaturgic /θɔːməˈtəːdʒɪk/ *noun & adjective*. L16.
[formed as prec. + -IC.]
▶**A** *noun.* †**1** The art of making apparently magical devices. Only in L16.
2 In *pl.* Feats of magic, conjuring tricks. M18.
▶**B** *adjective.* **1** That works or can work miracles or wonders. L17.
2 Of, pertaining to, or involving thaumaturgy. E19.
■ **thaumaturgical** *adjective* = THAUMATURGIC *adjective* M17.

thaumaturgus *noun* see THAUMATURGE.

thaumaturgy /ˈθɔːmətəːdʒi/ *noun*. E18.
[Greek *thaumatourgia*, formed as THAUMATO- + *-ergos* working: see -Y[3].]
The performing of miracles or wonders; magic.

thaw /θɔː/ *noun*. Also (*obsolete* exc. *dial.*) **thow** /θaʊ/. LME.
[from the verb.]
1 The melting of ice and snow after a frost; an instance of this; a condition of the weather marked by the rise of temperature above the freezing point. LME.
2 A reduction in the coldness or formality of relations; an increase in friendliness or cordiality. Also, a relaxation of esp. political control or restriction; a lessening of harshness, a liberalization. M19.

> **1** J. CLAVELL We were trapped in the ice and had to wait for the thaw. P. FITZGERALD The splintering of ice in the first spring thaw. *fig.*: BUNYAN If the Sun of Righteousness will arise upon him, his frozen Heart shall feel a Thaw. ***silver thaw***: see SILVER *noun & adjective*. **2** *Times* The hopes and naivety of the post-Stalin thaw. *Modern Maturity* Glasnost and the . . thaw in the Cold War.

Comb.: **thaw-lake** a (seasonal) lake formed by melted snow or ice.

■ **thawy** *adjective* characterized by a thaw, esp. in the weather; of or pertaining to a thaw: E18.

thaw /θɔː/ *verb*. Also (*obsolete* exc. *dial.*) **thow** /θaʊ/. Pa. pple **-ed**, †**thawn**.
[Old English *þawian* = Middle Low German *döien*, Dutch *dooien*, Old High German *douwen*, from West Germanic.]
▶**I** *verb trans.* **1** Convert (a frozen substance, *esp.* ice or snow) to a liquid state. OE.
2 Free from the physical effect of frost; unfreeze (a frozen thing); make (a person etc.) warm again after being very cold. Also foll. by *out*. L16.
3 *fig.* Soften to sympathy or geniality; break down the coldness and reserve of; make less harsh or severe. L16.

> **1** SHAKES. *Merch. V.* Where Phoebus' fire scarce thaws the icicles. *fig.*: J. COX Energy to thaw the frozen lake of my ideas. **2** LYTTON After I was lodged, thawed, and fed, I fell . . asleep. W. GOLDMAN 'Hungry for anything special?' 'Thaw me out some chicken, maybe.' **3** S. RICHARDSON She is a charming girl, and may be thawed by kindness. *New York Times* Krushchev invited the columnist . . to a hunting lodge . . to discuss ways of thawing the cold war.

▶**II** *verb intrans.* **4** Esp. of ice or snow: pass from a frozen to a liquid or semi-liquid state, melt. ME.
5 *impers.* in ***it thaws, it is thawing***, etc., the local temperature is such that ice, snow, etc., begins to melt. ME.
6 Become unfrozen; become warm again after being very cold. Also foll. by *out*. L16.
7 *fig.* Become more sympathetic or genial; throw off coldness and reserve; become less harsh or severe, unbend. L16.

> **5** A. J. CRONIN It thawed and the roads turned to slush. **6** E. BOWEN His nose . . nipped by the wind, thawed painfully in the even warmth of the house. A. T. ELLIS Eric . . fondled the beef to ensure . . it had thawed properly. **7** R. POLLOK Pride of rank And office, thawed into paternal love. H. ROTH That brusque, cold manner of his had thawed a little. B. BAINBRIDGE Muriel might be a shade off-hand. But she'll thaw.

■ **thawer** *noun* (*rare*) a person who or thing which causes thawing M17. **thawing** *verbal noun* the action of the verb; an instance of this, a thaw: ME.

thawless /ˈθɔːlɪs/ *adjective. literary.* E19.
[from THAW *noun* or *verb* + -LESS.]
That does not thaw; that never thaws.

†**thawn** *verb pa. pple*: see THAW *verb*.

THC *abbreviation*.
Tetrahydrocannabinol.

THD *abbreviation*.
Total harmonic distortion.

the /*before a consonant* ðə; *before a vowel* ðɪ; *stressed* ðiː/ *adjective* (usu. called the *definite article*; in mod. usage also classed as a *determiner*) & *adverb*. Also (*poet.*) **th'**, (now as pseudo-arch. article) **ye** /jiː/.
[Old English *se* masc., *sēo*, *sīo* fem., *þæt* neut. (cf. THAT), ult. superseded by forms from late Old English (Northumbrian & N. Mercian) *þē* (orig. nom. masc.), corresp. to Old Frisian *thi*, *thiu*, *thet*, Old Saxon *se*, *þē*, *þie*, *þiu*, *þat* (Dutch *de*, *dat*), Old High German *der*, *diu*, *daz* (German *der*, *die*, *das*), Old Norse *sá*, *sú*, *þat*, Gothic *sa*, *sō*, *þata* (with suffix), from Germanic: ult. cogn. with Greek *ho*, *hē*, *to*, Sanskrit *sa*, *sā*, *tat*, Avestan *hō*, *hā*, *taṯ*. As adverb repr. Old English *þē*, *þȳ*, *þon*, instrumental case. Cf. THAT, TONE *pronoun & adjective*, TOTHER *pronoun & adjective*.]
▶**A** *adjective.* **I 1** Designating one or more persons or things already mentioned or known, particularized by context or circumstances, inherently unique, familiar, or otherwise sufficiently identified. OE. ▸**b** With proper names, esp. of rivers, mountain ranges, groups of islands, certain countries and regions, ships, buildings, works of art, etc. OE. ▸**c** With names of diseases, ailments, or afflictions. Now *colloq.* OE. ▸**d** With names of branches of learning, crafts, pursuits, etc. Now chiefly *dial.* ME. ▸**e** With names of languages. Without *language* now regarded as ellipt. LME. ▸**f** With verbal nouns. Now chiefly after *for*. LME.
2 Designating one or more persons or things particularized by a rel. clause, a phr. introduced by preposition or inf., an adjective, a pple, or a noun (*dial.* a noun characterizing a trade or occupation) in apposition. Also with an adjective used absol. OE.
3 With the effect of a possess. adjective: designating a part of the body, an article of dress, (*colloq.*) a relative or acquaintance, or occas. other attribute, of a person previously named, indicated, or understood. LOE.
4 With a weight, measure, or other unit, used in stating a rate: per, a; each. ME.
5 With a surname: designating the chief of an Irish or Scottish clan. M16.
6 Preceding the name of a woman, less commonly of a man. Cf. LA *adjective*. Chiefly *joc.* M18.
7 *emphatic*. Best known, best entitled to be called —; the well-known, the pre-eminent, the typical, the only (worth mentioning). L18.

📖 **1** EVELYN The Queene was . . in her . . riding habit. W. CONGREVE What's the matter now? BURKE Make the Revolution a parent of settlement, and not a nursery of future revolutions. TENNYSON As shines the moon in clouded skies. J. H. NEWMAN I will come and wake thee on the morrow. TOLKIEN In a hole in the ground there lived a hobbit. S. HOOD The gate squeaked at his entrance. *New Yorker* Gambling debts in the hundreds of thousands of dollars. **b** ***the Missouri, the Nile, the Severn; the Andes, the Drakensberg, the Hindu Kush; the Canary Islands, the Hebrides; the Argentine, the Gambia, the Lebanon, the Sudan, the Yemen; the Camargue, the Tyrol, the Sahara (Desert); the Bismarck; the Alhambra, the Savoy; the Albert Hall; the Mona Lisa; the Eroica; the Timaeus; the Flying Scotsman; the Matterhorn.*** **c** ***the flu, the measles, the pox; the creeps, the jitters.*** **d** SHAKES. *Tam. Shr.* The mathematics and the metaphysics fall to them. **e** SHAKES. *Merch. V.* You will . . swear that I have a poor pennyworth in the English. G. K. CHESTERTON 'Chivalrous' is not the French for 'horsy'. *Time* This new autobiography has been translated from the German by Ewald Osers. **f** *Athenaeum* The narrative loses nothing in the telling. A. BARON It's yours for the asking. **2** SHAKES. *Merch. V.* The man that hath no music in himself . . Is fit for treasons. MILTON The huntress Dian. SOUTHEY These vile taxes will take twenty pounds from me, at the least. T. GRAY The dark unfathom'd caves of ocean. *Mirror* The best . . of husbands. J. AUSTEN I shall not be the person to discourage him. E. GASKELL Th' longest lane will have a turning. FRANCIS THOMPSON That utterance . . Of the doomed Leonidas. R. BRIDGES The Oxford of 1850 was singularly unsympathetic. J. WAIN Caution was the one virtue he recognised. ***Alfred the Great, Richard the Third; Attila the Hun, Thomas the Tank Engine, William the Conqueror, Jones the Bread.*** **3** DICKENS To be hanged by the neck, till he was dead. TENNYSON Pale was the perfect face . . And the voice trembled. H. G. WELLS 'All's well with the Missus?' . . he asked. *Empire* She's banging the boss. **4** SOUTHEY They are very dear, ten reales the couple. *Which?* If you're paying by the mile, check . . the milometer. **5** ***The Chisholm, The Mackintosh, The O'Gorman Mahon.*** **6** P. G. WODEHOUSE The Bellinger . . had sung us a few songs. **7** BROWNING Saint Praxed's ever was the church for peace. TOLKIEN Am I right in guessing that you are *the* Glóin, one of the twelve companions? *New Yorker* Zutty Singleton was *the* drummer in Chicago.

► **II 8** Used preceding a (sing.) noun used generically or as the type of its class; (with a pl. noun) all those described as —. **OE.**

9 With an adjective used absol. (*arch.* with a ppl adjective used absol. and compl.): that which is —; those persons who or things which are —. **OE.**

📖 **8** DEFOE To act the rebel. LYTTON The pen is mightier than the sword. LD MACAULAY On the Sunday he goes perhaps to Church. TENNYSON As careful robins eye the delver's toil. D. J. ENRIGHT How clever they are, the Japanese. A. THWAITE A green mound, Its edges sheared by the plough. **9** TINDALE *John* 12:8 The povre all wayes shall ye have with you. SMOLLETT A nose inclining to the aquiline. BYRON Here ceased the swift their race. SHELLEY What a thing is Poverty Among the fallen on evil days.

► **B** *adverb.* **1** Preceding a compar. adjective or adverb, the two words forming an adverbial phrase as part of the predicate. **OE.**

2 ***the —er . . . the —er . . . , the more — . . . the more — . . .*** , (expr. proportional or equal variation of two things): by how much . . . by so much, in what degree . . . in that degree . . . **OE.**

📖 **1** W. COWPER Your fav'rite horse Will never look one hair the worse. J. RUSKIN If others do not follow their example,—the more fools they. M. KRAMER Some wines are the better for being exposed to air. ***all the*** (with compar.): see ALL *adverb* 6. ***none the*** (with compar.): see NONE *adverb* 1b. ***so much the*** (with compar.): see ***so much*** s.v. SO *adverb* etc. **2** N. SHUTE The more I thought about it the more inexplicable it seemed. *Honey* The general rule is the younger the better; there's a big demand for teenage models.

the- *combining form* see THEO-.

thé /te/ *noun.* Pl. pronounced same. **L18.**
[French = tea.]
A tea party; a light meal including tea. Now only in phrs.
thé complet /kɔ̃plɛ/, pl. **-s -s** (pronounced same), [lit. 'complete tea'] a light meal including tea and usu. bread and cake. ***thé dansant*** /dɑ̃sɑ̃/, pl. **-s -s** (pronounced same), [lit. 'dancing tea'] an afternoon entertainment at which there is dancing and tea is served.

theandric /θiːˈandrɪk/ *adjective.* **E17.**
[ecclesiastical Greek *theandrikos*, from *theandros* god-man, from *theos* god + *andr-*, *anēr* man: see -IC.]
At once human and divine; *esp.* (CHRISTIAN THEOLOGY) (of action) of the joint agency of human and divine natures in Christ. Cf. next.

theanthropic /θiːanˈθrɒpɪk/ *adjective.* **M17.**
[from ecclesiastical Greek *theanthrōpos* god-man, from *theos* god + *anthrōpos* man: see -IC.]
Pertaining to or of the nature of both god and man; at once human and divine; embodying deity in human form. Cf. prec.
■ **the'anthropy** *noun* (*rare*) theanthropic nature, theanthropism **M17.**

theanthropism /θiːˈanθrəpɪz(ə)m/ *noun.* **E19.**
[formed as prec. + -ISM.]
A doctrine of the union of divine and human natures; *esp.* (CHRISTIAN THEOLOGY) belief in the manifestation of God as man in Christ.
■ **theanthropist** *noun & adjective* (**a**) *noun* a believer in theanthropism; (**b**) *adjective* of or pertaining to theanthropists or theanthropism: **E19.**

thearchy /ˈθiːɑːki/ *noun.* **M17.**
[ecclesiastical Greek *thearkhia*, from *theos* god + *arkh(e)ia* government, rule: see -Y³.]
1 Rule or government by a god or gods; an instance of this. **M17.**
2 An order or system of gods. **M19.**
■ **the'archic** *adjective* **M19.**

theater *noun & adjective* see THEATRE.

Theatine /ˈθiːətʌɪn/ *noun & adjective.* **M16.**
[mod. Latin *Theatinus* adjective, from *Teate*, former name of Chieti, city in Italy (see below): see -INE¹.]
ROMAN CATHOLIC CHURCH. ► **A** *noun.* A member of a monastic order founded in 1524 by St Cajetan and John Peter Caraffa, Archbishop of Chieti, later Pope Paul IV. **M16.**
► **B** *adjective.* Of or pertaining to the Theatines. **L17.**

theatral /ˈθɪətr(ə)l/ *adjective.* Now *rare.* **L16.**
[Latin *theatralis*, from *theatrum*: see next, -AL¹.]
Theatrical; dramatic.

theatre /ˈθɪətə/ *noun & adjective.* Also ***theater**. **LME.**
[Old French *t(h)eatre* (mod. *théâtre*) or Latin *theatrum* from Greek *theatron*, from *theasthai* behold.]
► **A** *noun.* **1** A building or (esp. in antiquity) a place constructed in the open air, in which dramatic plays or other spectacles can be performed before an audience. **LME.** ▸**b** A natural bowl or hollow suggesting an ancient Greek or Roman theatre. **LME.**
2 a A stage or platform on which a play is acted. Long *obsolete* exc. *fig.* **LME.** ▸**b** A platform, dais, or raised stage, used for a public ceremony. *obsolete* exc. *Hist.* **M16.** ▸**c** The audience at a theatre. **E17.**
†**3** In titles: a book giving an overview of a subject; a manual, a treatise. **M16–E18.**
4 *fig.* A place or region where action takes place in public view; the scene or field of action; *esp.* (also ***theatre of war***) a particular region or each of the separate regions in which a war is fought. **L16.**
5 a More fully ***lecture theatre***. A room or building for lectures, scientific demonstrations, etc., with seats in tiers for an audience. **E17.** ▸**b** More fully ***operating theatre***. A room in a hospital specially designed for surgical operations, orig. one for the performance of operations in front of observers. **M17.** ▸**c** In full ***picture theatre***. A cinema. Now chiefly *N. Amer., Austral., & NZ.* **E20.**
6 Dramatic performance as an art, an institution, or a profession; the stage; the production and performance of plays; the drama of a particular time or place, or of a particular writer. (Freq. with *the*.) **M17.** ▸**b** Theatrical or dramatic entertainment (of a specified quality); action with the quality of drama or theatrical technique; dramatic effect, spectacle, outward show. **E20.**

📖 **1b** BYRON Girt by her theatre of hills. **2** *fig.*: D. BREWSTER A noble position on the theatre of public life. **4** C. LYELL The theatre of violent earthquakes. W. S. CHURCHILL Larger operations . . impend in the Middle East theatre. **6** F. FERGUSSON The attempt is made to draw the deductions, for Sophocles' theatre and dramaturgy, which the present view of *Oedipus* implies. B. BETTELHEIM I was so infatuated with the theater that . . I decided to study drama. **b** A. J. P. TAYLOR Austrian Baroque civilisation . . was theatre, not reality. *Listener* You have to admit . . the Old City is good theatre. *Landscape* This room is pure theatre—a triumph of scenographic architecture.

Phrases: ***dinner theatre***: see DINNER *noun*. ***idols of the theatre***: see IDOL *noun* 5b. ***lecture theatre***: see sense 5a above. ***little theatre***: see LITTLE *adjective*. ***living theatre***: see LIVING *ppl adjective*. ***national theatre***: see NATIONAL *adjective*. ***operating theatre***: see sense 5b above. ***patent theatre***: see PATENT *adjective* 2. ***picture theatre***: see sense 5c above. ***saloon theatre***: see SALOON 4b. **theatre-in-the-round** [*in the round* (b) s.v. ROUND *noun*¹] dramatic performance in the round. **Theatre of Cruelty** a non-verbal form of drama conceived by the French director Antonin Artaud (1896–1948) and intended to communicate a sense of pain, suffering, and evil through the portrayal of extreme physical violence. **Theatre of Fact** documentary drama. **Theatre of the Absurd** drama portraying the futility and anguish of human struggle in a senseless and inexplicable world; *transf.* absurd or ludicrous events. ***theatre of war***: see sense 4 above.

Comb.: **theatre club** a theatre for which tickets are sold only to members, esp. in order to circumvent censorship; **theatre-goer** a person who often attends theatres; **theatre-land** the district of a city in which most of the theatres are situated; **theatre-list**: of patients scheduled to undergo surgery; **theatre nurse** a hospital nurse qualified to assist in the operating theatre; **theatre organ** = *CINEMA organ*; **theatre party**: in which the guests, besides being entertained at dinner or supper, are taken to a theatre; **theatre seat** (**a**) a seat in a theatre; (**b**) a tip-up seat of a kind used in theatres; **theatre sister** a nurse supervising a nursing team in an operating theatre; **theatre workshop** a theatre company concerned esp. with experimental and unconventional theatrical productions.
► **B** *attrib.* or as *adjective.* Of or pertaining to a theatre of war; *esp.* designating nuclear weapons for use in a particular region, as opp. to intercontinental or strategic weapons. **L20.**
■ **theatreless** *adjective* **M19.**

theatric /θɪˈatrɪk/ *adjective.* **M17.**
[Late Latin *theatricus* from Greek *theatrikos*, from *theatron* THEATRE: see -IC.]
1 = THEATRICAL *adjective* 1a, 2, 3. **M17.**
2 Like a theatre or amphitheatre in shape or formation. **M18.**

theatrical /θɪˈatrɪk(ə)l/ *adjective & noun.* **M16.**
[formed as prec.: see -ICAL.]
► **A** *adjective.* **1 a** Of or pertaining to the theatre or stage; of or pertaining to actors or acting. **M16.** ▸†**b** = THEATRIC *adjective* 2. Only in **M18.**
2 Having the style of dramatic performance; extravagantly or irrelevantly histrionic; showy, spectacular. **L16.**
3 Simulated, artificial, assumed. **L17.**

📖 **2** C. ISHERWOOD Grete, who obviously wasn't hurt, at once set up a loud, theatrical wail. E. LONGFORD His smooth black hair and dark eyes and the occasional theatrical gesture made a dramatic impression. **3** LD MACAULAY How far the character in which he [Byron] exhibited himself was genuine, and how far theatrical.

► **B** *noun.* **1** In *pl.* The performance of stage plays, dramatic performances. Also *fig.*, the activity of a theatrical character; histrionics; show, spectacle; pretence. **L17.**
2 In *pl.* Matters pertaining to the stage and acting. Also, the theatrical column of a newspaper. **M18.**
3 A professional actor or actress. Usu. in *pl.* **M19.**

📖 **1** E. L. VOYNICH It's only the usual theatricals, because he's ashamed to face us. S. NASH Young men who had wasted their time on amateur theatricals. **3** N. STREATFEILD You could hardly see the walls for photographs; you know what theatricals are.

■ **theatricalism** *noun* theatrical behaviour, style, or character **M19.** **theatri'cality** *noun* (**a**) theatrical quality or character; theatricalism, theatricalness; an instance of this; (**b**) *rare* a theatrical person: **M19.** **theatricali'zation** *noun* the process of making something theatrical; dramatization: **L19.** **theatricalize** *verb* (**a**) *verb trans.* make theatrical; (**b**) *verb intrans.* (*colloq.*) act on the stage; visit the theatre: **L18.** **theatricalness** *noun* **E18.**

theatrically /θɪˈatrɪk(ə)li/ *adverb.* **M17.**
[from THEATRICAL, THEATRIC: see -ICALLY.]
In a theatrical manner.

theatrics /θɪˈatrɪks/ *noun pl.* **E19.**
[from THEATRIC *adjective* + -S¹.]
1 = THEATRICAL *noun* 2. **E19.**
2 = THEATRICAL *noun* 1. **E20.**

theatrize /ˈθɪətrʌɪz/ *verb. rare.* Also **-ise**. **L17.**
[Greek *theatrizein*, from *theatron* THEATRE: see -IZE.]
†**1** *verb trans.* Make a spectacle or show of. **L17–E18.**
2 *verb intrans.* Act theatrically, play a part. **M19.**
3 *verb trans.* Make theatrical; dramatize. **L19.**

theatro- /ˈθɪətrəʊ, θɪˈatrəʊ/ *combining form* of Greek *theatron* THEATRE: see -O-.
■ **theatrocracy** /θɪəˈtrɒkrəsi/ *noun* [Greek *theatrokratia*] the absolute power of the ancient Athenian democracy, as exhibited at their assemblies in the theatre **E19.** **the'atrophone** *noun* (*Hist.*) a telephone adapted and linked up to a theatre, enabling the subscriber to hear a performance of a play, opera, etc., remotely **L19.**

theatrum /teɪˈɑːtrəm/ *noun.* **M16.**
[Latin: see THEATRE.]
1 ***theatrum mundi*** /ˈmʌndʌɪ, ˈmʊndiː/ [lit. 'of the world'], the theatre thought of as a presentation of all aspects of human life. **M16.**
2 A theatre, a playhouse. **L18.**

theave /θiːv/ *noun. dial.* Also **thaive** /θeɪv/. **LME.**
[Origin unkn.]
A young ewe, usu. one between the first and second shearing.

Thebaic /θiːˈbeɪɪk/ *adjective.* In sense 2 also **t-**. **L17.**
[Latin *Thebaicus* from Greek *Thēbaikos*, from *Thēbai*, *Thēbē* Thebes (see below): see -IC. In sense 2 with ref. to Egypt as a major source of opium.]
1 Of or pertaining to the ancient Egyptian city of Thebes. Formerly *spec.*, designating the Sahidic version of the Bible. **L17.**
†**2** PHARMACOLOGY. Of or derived from opium. **M–L18.**
1 Thebaic marble, **Thebaic stone** syenite from Upper Egypt, used in ancient times for columns, vases, etc.

Thebaïd /ˈθiːbeɪɪd/ *noun.* **E18.**
[Greek *Thēbaid-*, *-bais*, Latin *Thebaid-*, *-bais*, from Greek *Thēbai* Thebes: see THEBAN, -ID².]
CLASSICAL HISTORY. **1** The heroic poem of Statius relating to Thebes in Boeotia. **E18.**

2 The territory belonging to the Egyptian or the Boeotian city of Thebes. **M19.**

thebaine /θɪˈbeɪiːn, eɪn, ˈθiːbəiːn/ *noun.* **M19.**
[from Greek *Thēbai* Thebes (cf. **THEBAIC**) + **-INE**⁵.]
CHEMISTRY. A toxic crystalline alkaloid, $C_{19}H_{21}NO_3$, extracted from opium.

Theban /ˈθiːb(ə)n/ *adjective & noun.* **LME.**
[Latin *Thebanus*, from *Thebae*, Greek *Thēbai* Thebes (see below): see **-AN.**]
▶**A** *adjective.* **1** Of or pertaining to Thebes, capital of ancient Boeotia in Greece. **LME.**
2 Of or pertaining to Thebes, ancient capital of Upper Egypt. Cf. **THEBAIC** *adjective.* **M17.**
▶**B** *noun.* A native or inhabitant of (Boeotian) Thebes, a Boeotian. **LME.**

thebe /ˈθeɪbeɪ/ *noun.* Pl. same. **L20.**
[Setswana = shield.]
A monetary unit of Botswana, equal to one-hundredth of a pula.

Thebesian /θɪˈbiːsɪən/ *adjective.* **L19.**
[from Adam Christian *Thebesius* (1686–1732), German anatomist + **-AN.**]
ANATOMY. Designating structures in the heart discovered or investigated by Thebesius.
Thebesian valve a valve at the point of entry of the cardiac vein into the right atrium. **Thebesian vein** any of a number of small veins bringing blood from the tissue of the heart into the right auricle.

theca /ˈθiːkə/ *noun.* Pl. **thecae** /ˈθiːsiː/. **E17.**
[Latin from Greek *thēkē* case.]
Chiefly *ANATOMY, ZOOLOGY, & BOTANY.* **1** A receptacle, a sheath, a cell; *esp.* one enclosing some organ, part, or structure, as (*a*) either of the lobes of an anther, each containing two pollen-sacs; (*b*) the loose sheath enclosing the spinal cord; (*c*) a cuplike or tubular structure containing a coral polyp. **E17.**
2 *ANATOMY.* In full ***theca folliculi*** /fəˈlɪkjʊlʌɪ/ [mod. Latin = of the follicle]. An envelope of hormonally active cells enclosing a tertiary (vesicular) or a mature (Graafian) ovarian follicle. **M19.**
Phrases & comb.: **theca cell tumour** *MEDICINE* an oestrogen-secreting ovarian tumour, sometimes malignant, consisting of cells like those of the theca folliculi; also called ***thecoma***. **theca externa** /ɛkˈstəːnə/ *ANATOMY* the outer fibrous layer of the theca folliculi. ***theca folliculi***: see sense 2 above. **theca interna** /ɪnˈtəːnə/ *ANATOMY* the inner vascular layer of the theca folliculi.
■ **thecal** *adjective* of, pertaining to, or of the nature of a theca **M19.** **thecate** *adjective* having a theca **L19.**

thecium /ˈθiːsɪəm/ *noun.* Pl. **-ia** /-ɪə/. **L19.**
[mod. Latin from Greek *thēkion* dim. of *thēkē* **THECA.**]
BOTANY. In a discomycetous fungus or lichen: the fertile part of the apothecium.

theco- /ˈθiːkəʊ/ *combining form* of **THECA**: see **-O-**.
■ **thecosome** *noun* (*ZOOLOGY*) a pteropod of the order Thecosomata, members of which have the body enclosed in a shell **L19.**

thecodont /ˈθiːkədɒnt/ *noun & adjective.* **M19.**
[mod. Latin *Thecodontia* (see below), formed as **THECO-** + **-ODONT.**]
PALAEONTOLOGY. ▶**A** *noun.* A member of the order Thecodontia of archosaurian reptiles with teeth fixed in sockets in the jawbone, known from fossil remains of the Triassic period. **M19.**
▶**B** *adjective.* Designating, of, or pertaining to this order of reptiles; characteristic of or resembling the thecodonts, esp. as regards dentition; *spec.* having teeth growing in sockets (as mammals and some reptiles). **M19.**
■ **thecodontian** /-ˈdɒntɪən/ *noun & adjective* (*a*) *noun* = **THECODONT** *noun*; (*b*) *adjective* of or pertaining to the order Thecodontia: **L20.**

thecoma /θɪˈkəʊmə/ *noun.* Pl. **-mas**, **-mata** /-mətə/. **M20.**
[from **THECO-** + **-OMA.**]
MEDICINE. = ***THECA cell tumour.***

thee /ðiː, *unstressed* ðɪ/ *pers. pronoun, 2 sing. objective (accus. & dat.), & noun.* Now *arch. & dial.* Also †**ta**, (*dial.*) **tha** /ðɑː, *unstressed* ðə/.
[Old English (i) accus. *þec, þeh*, (later) *þē* = Old Frisian *thi*, Old Saxon *þic, þī*, Old High German *dih* (German *dich*), Old Norse *þik*, Gothic *þuk*, (ii) dat *þē* = Old Frisian *thī*, Old Saxon *þī*, Old & mod. High German *dir*, Old Norse *þér*, Gothic *þus*, both from Germanic from Indo-European (base of accus. also repr. by Latin *te*, Greek *se*, (Doric) *te*). Cf. **THOU** *pers. pronoun & noun*².]
▶**A** *pronoun.* **1** Objective (direct & indirect) of **THOU** *pers. pronoun*: the person addressed by the speaker or writer, you. **OE.** ▸**b** Yourself. **OE.**
2 Subjective: = **THOU** *pers. pronoun* 1. Also with verb in 3rd person sing. (Formerly esp. in use in the Society of Friends.) Now *rare.* **ME.**

> 🕮 **1** SHELLEY Hail to thee, blithe Spirit! TENNYSON I have loved thee long. T. HARDY We've been out waiting to meet thee! **b** SHAKES. *Rich. III* Hie thee to hell . . Thou cacodemon. **2** B. RUSSELL What thee says about our marriage is very generous.

▶**B** *noun.* **1** A self; a person identical with the person addressed by the speaker or writer. **L16.**
2 The pronoun 'thee' as a word. Freq. in ***thees and thous***. **L17.**
¶ See note s.v. **THOU** *pers. pronoun & noun*².

thee /θiː/ *verb*¹ *intrans.* Long *obsolete* exc. *Scot.*
[Old English *þīon, þēon*, contr. of unrecorded verb cogn. with Old Saxon *thīhan*, Old High German *(gi)dīhan* (German *gedeihen*), Gothic *þeihan*, from Germanic.]
Thrive, prosper; grow, increase.

thee /ðiː/ *verb*² *trans. & intrans.* Pa. t. & pple **theed**, **thee'd**. **M17.**
[from the pronoun.]
Use the pronoun 'thee' (to); address (a person) as 'thee'. Freq. in ***thee and thou***.

theek /θiːk/ *verb trans. Scot. & north.* Also **theik** & other vars. **LME.**
[Var. of **THACK** *verb*¹.]
Roof (a building); cover (esp. a roof); *esp.* thatch.

theetsee *noun* var. of **THITSI**.

theft /θɛft/ *noun.*
[Old English (West Saxon) *þiefþ*, later *þȳfþ, þyft*, (non-West Saxon) *þēofþ, þēoft* = Old Frisian *thiūfthe, thiūfte*, Old Norse *þýfð, þýft*, from Germanic base of **THIEF**: see **-T**².]
1 The action of a thief; the action or practice of stealing; larceny; *spec.* (*LAW*) dishonest appropriation of another's property with intent to deprive him or her of it permanently. Also, an instance of this. **OE.**
2 That which has been stolen. Now *rare.* **OE.**
Comb.: **theft-boot**, **-bote** *Hist.* the taking of a payment from a thief (as a bribe or compensation) in order to secure him or her from prosecution.

theftuous /ˈθɛftjʊəs/ *adjective.* Orig. *Scot.* **LME.**
[from prec. + **WISE** *noun*¹: cf. **RIGHTEOUS.**]
1 Of the nature of theft. **LME.**
2 Of the nature of a thief; given to stealing. **M17.**
■ **theftuously** *adverb* (chiefly *Scot.*) **LME.**

thegn /θeɪn/ *noun.* **M19.**
[Mod. repr. of Old English *þeg(e)n* **THANE**, adopted in 19 as a spelling to distinguish the Old English use of *thane* from the Scottish use (see **THANE** 4) made familiar by Shakes.]
Hist. = **THANE** 3.
■ **thegnhood** *noun* the condition or position of a thegn; the order of thegns, thegns collectively: **M19.** **thegnly** *adjective* of, pertaining to, or becoming to a thegn **L19.** **thegnship** *noun* the office, function, or position of a thegn **L19.**

thegosis /θɪˈɡəʊsɪs/ *noun.* **L20.**
[from Greek *thēgos* sharp + **-OSIS.**]
ZOOLOGY. The action of grinding the teeth; the sharpening of teeth by means of this.

theik *verb* var. of **THEEK**.

theileria /θʌɪˈlɪərɪə/ *noun.* **E20.**
[mod. Latin (see below), from Sir Arnold *Theiler* (1867–1936), S. African zoologist: see **-IA**¹.]
VETERINARY MEDICINE. A piroplasm of the genus *Theileria*, which comprises tick-borne organisms some of which cause theileriasis.
■ **theileriasis** /θʌɪlɪəˈrʌɪəsɪs/ *noun*, pl. **-ases** /-əsiːz/, an acute, usu. fatal, feverish disease of cattle, sheep, etc., caused by a piroplasm of the genus *Theileria* or a related genus **M20.**

theine /ˈθiːiːn, ˈθiːɪn/ *noun.* **M19.**
[from mod. Latin *Thea* former genus name of the tea plant from Dutch *thee*, formed as **TEA** *noun*: see **-INE**⁵.]
CHEMISTRY. Caffeine; *esp.* that obtained from tea (orig. thought to be a different substance).

their /ðɛː/ *possess. pronoun & adjective* (in mod. usage also classed as a *determiner*), *3 pl.* **ME.**
[Old Norse *þeir(r)a* genit. pl. of *sá, sú, þat* **THE** *adjective*, **THAT**, also used as genit. pl. of 3 pers. pronoun. Cf. **THEIRN, THEIRS, THEM, THEY.**]
▶†**A** *pronoun.* = **THEIRS. ME–E17.**
▶**B** *adjective* (*attrib.*).
1 Of them; of themselves; which belongs or pertains to them(selves). **ME.** ▸**b** In titles (as ***Their Lordships***, ***Their Majesties***): that they are. **M16.**
2 In relation to a singular noun or pronoun of undetermined gender: his or her. (Considered *erron.* by some.) **ME.**
3 After a noun (esp. a personal name): substituting for the genit. inflection or possess. suffix **'s**. *arch.* **M16.**

> 🕮 **1** J. STEINBECK The fishermen . . shifted their oars. E. BOWEN Two girls in their twenties had been engaged. SCOTT FITZGERALD Imagine their objecting to us having champagne for breakfast. I. MURDOCH There was no question of their seeing Elizabeth. G. VIDAL Let the children find their own way. **2** *Oxford Times* A trustworthy . . person with the ability to work on their own initiative. **3** S. PEPYS The House of Lords their proceedings in petitioning the King.

theirn /ðɛːn/ *possess. pronoun. dial.* **M19.**
[from **THEIR** *pronoun* after *my* and *mine*, *thy* and *thine*, etc.]
= **THEIRS.**

theirs /ðɛːz/ *possess. pronoun & adjective.* **ME.**
[from **THEIR** *pronoun* + **-'S**¹. Cf. prec.]
▶**A** *pronoun.* **1** Their one(s); that or those belonging or pertaining to them. **ME.**
2 ***of theirs***, belonging or pertaining to them. **LME.**

> 🕮 **1** K. A. PORTER I wouldn't swap my kind of troubles for theirs. ***get theirs***: see **GET** *verb.* **2** *Society* An old acquaintance of theirs.

▶†**B** *adjective* (*attrib.*). = **THEIR** *adjective* 1 (esp. when followed by another possessive). *rare.* **ME–L18.**

theirselves /ðɛːˈsɛlvz/ *pronoun pl.* Now *dial. & non-standard.* Also **-self**. **ME.**
[from **THEIR** + **SELF** *noun*: see **-S**¹. Cf. **THEMSELVES.**]
= **THEMSELVES.**

> 🕮 J. HANSEN Everybody helps theirself at the dispensary.

theism /ˈθiːɪz(ə)m/ *noun*¹. **L17.**
[Greek *theos* god + **-ISM.**]
The doctrine or belief of theists; belief in the existence of God or gods (opp. ***atheism***); *spec.* belief in one God who created and intervenes in the universe. Cf. **DEISM.**

theism /ˈθiːɪz(ə)m/ *noun*². Now *rare.* **L19.**
[from mod. Latin *Thea* (see **THEINE**) + **-ISM.**]
MEDICINE. Caffeinism caused by excessive tea-drinking.

theist /ˈθiːɪst/ *noun.* **M17.**
[from Greek *theos* god + **-IST.**]
Orig., a person who believes in God or gods (opp. ***atheist***). Now, a person who believes in one God who created and intervenes in the universe. Cf. **DEIST.**
■ **the'istic** *adjective* (*a*) of or pertaining to theists or theism; (*b*) *rare* of or pertaining to God or gods: **L18.** **the'istical** *adjective* = **THEISTIC** (a) **L17.**

thekedar *noun* var. of **THIKADAR.**

thelemic /θɛˈliːmɪk/ *adjective.* **E20.**
[from Greek *thelēma* will + **-IC**: see next.]
That permits people to do as they wish.

thelemite /ˈθɛlɪmʌɪt/ *noun. rare.* **M17.**
[French from Greek *thelēma* will + **-ITE**¹, with ref. to the Abbey of Thélème in Rabelais, the only law of which was (in Old French) *fay ce que vouldras* do what thou wilt.]
A person who does what he or she wishes.

thelytoky /θiːˈlɪtəki, θiːlɪˈtəʊki/ *noun.* Also **thelyotoky** /θiːlɪˈɒtəki/. **L19.**
[from Greek *thēlutokos* bearing female children + **-Y**³.]
ZOOLOGY. Parthenogenesis in which unfertilized eggs give rise to females. Cf. **ARRHENOTOKY.**
■ **thelytokous** *adjective* **L19.**

them /ðɛm, *unstressed* ð(ə)m/ *pers. pronoun, 3 pl. objective (dat. & accus.) & demonstr. adjective.* **ME.**
[Old Norse *þeim* to those, to them, dat. pl. of *sá, sú, þat*, **THE** *demonstr. adjective*, **THAT**, pl. *þeir* **THEY.** Properly a dat. form used early as a direct obj.]
▶**A** *pronoun.* **1** Objective (direct & indirect) of **THEY** *pronoun*: the persons, animals, or things previously mentioned or implied or easily identified. **ME.** ▸**b** Themselves: direct (*arch.* exc. after prepositions) & indirect (*arch.* exc. *US dial.*) objective. **ME.**
2 Subjective: (now only *dial.* or *joc.*) those; (*colloq.*, esp. pred. after *be* & after *than, as*) they. **LME.**
3 In relation to a singular noun or pronoun of undetermined gender: him or her. (Considered *erron.* by some.) **M18.**

> 🕮 **1** G. GREENE They had always sounded plausible when he described them. I. MURDOCH She was invited with Paul to their houses but never got to know them well. E. BAKER Why should he give them what they wanted? W. S. MAUGHAM There was a photograph of the three of them. D. BARNES People were uneasy when she spoke to them. **them and us**, **us and them**: expr. a sense of division, lack of commonality, etc., within a group of people. **b** LD MACAULAY They then bethought them of a new expedient. **2** J. S. WINTER It was them told me about her. T. ALLBEURY No can do, friend. Them's my orders. J. MORTIMER Them as chooses to live in South Africa can take care of themselves. **3** I. MURDOCH If anybody rings up tell them I'm not available.

▶**B** *adjective.* Those. Now *dial. & non-standard.* **L16.**

> 🕮 D. L. SAYERS Shall I put them peas on?

thema /ˈθɛmə, ˈθiːmə/ *noun. rare.* Pl. **-mata** /-mətə/. **M16.**
[Latin: see **THEME.**]
†**1** The theme or subject of a declamation or discourse; a thesis. **M16–M18.**
2 *LINGUISTICS.* = **THEME** *noun* 4. **E17.**
3 *MUSIC.* = **THEME** *noun* 6. **E19.**

thematic /θɪˈmatɪk/ *adjective & noun.* **L17.**
[Greek *thematikos*, from *thema* **THEME**: see **-IC.**]
▶**A** *adjective.* **1** *gen.* Of or pertaining to a theme or themes. **L17.**
2 *MUSIC.* Of, pertaining to, or constituting melodic themes or subjects; pertaining to themes and their development. **M19.**
3 *LINGUISTICS.* **a** Of or pertaining to the theme or inflectional stem of a word; *spec.* (of a vowel) occurring between a stem and a suffix; (of a verb-form etc.) having such a vowel. **M19.** ▸**b** Of, pertaining to, or designating the theme of a sentence. **M20.**
4 *Hist.* Of or pertaining to the division of the Byzantine Empire into themes or provinces. **E20.**

📖 1 *Stamps* Subjects . . illustrated should appeal to many thematic collectors. *Scots Magazine* All the exhibits have been re-organised on thematic lines. **Thematic Apperception Test** PSYCHOLOGY a projective test designed to reveal a person's social drives or needs by the interpretations given to a series of ambiguous pictures. **2 thematic catalogue**: containing the opening themes or passages of musical pieces as well as their names and other details.

▶**B** *noun*. **1** That part of logic which deals with themes or subjects of thought. *rare*. L19.

2 LINGUISTICS. A thematic verb-form. M20.

3 In *pl.* (treated as *sing.* or *pl.*). A body of subjects or topics of discussion or study. L20.

📖 3 F. SPALDING In her late poems her earlier thematics are repeated.

■ **thematical** *adjective* = THEMATIC L19. **thematically** *adverb* L19.

thematize /ˈθiːmətʌɪz/ *verb trans.* Also **-ise**. M20.

[from Greek *themat-* stem of *thema* (see next) + -IZE.]

1 Make thematic; present or select as a theme. M20.

2 LINGUISTICS. **a** Convert (part of a sentence) into a theme. M20. ▸**b** Modify (a verb-form) by adding a thematic vowel. M20.

📖 1 D. LEAVITT What's thematized here is the endless battle between nature and art. **2a** *Word* English normally uses the passive voice, thematizing the grammatical object.

■ **themati'zation** *noun* M20.

theme /θiːm/ *noun & verb*. ME.

[Old French *tesme* from Latin *thema* (to which it was soon conformed in spelling) from Greek *thema* proposition, from *the-* base of *tithenai* place.]

▶**A** *noun*. **1 a** A subject on which a person speaks, writes, or thinks; a topic of discussion or composition. ME. ▸†**b** *transf.* A subject which provokes a person to act; a cause *of* or *for* action or feeling. L16–E19. ▸**c** LINGUISTICS. The part of a sentence which indicates what is being talked about and on which the rest of the sentence makes a statement, asks a question, etc. Opp. RHEME 2. Cf. TOPIC *noun* 3b. M20.

2 *spec.* The text of a sermon; a proposition to be discussed. *obsolete* exc. as in sense 1 above. LME–E17.

3 A written exercise on a given subject, *esp.* a school essay. Now *US*. M16.

4 LINGUISTICS. The inflectional stem of a word, consisting of the root with modification. M16.

5 ASTROLOGY. The disposition of the celestial objects at a given time, as at the moment of a person's birth. Cf. HOROSCOPE *noun*. M17.

6 MUSIC. The principal melody or plainsong in a contrapuntal piece; a prominent or frequently recurring melody or group of notes in a composition. Also, a simple tune on which variations are constructed. L17.

7 *Hist.* Each of the twenty-nine provinces into which the Byzantine Empire was divided. L18.

📖 **1a** E. M. FORSTER The themes he preferred were the decay of Islam and the brevity of love. M. MEYER These four plays, for all their differences, share one theme. **4** F. A. MARCH The variable final letters of a noun are its case-endings, the rest is its theme. **6** *Classic CD* A bold theme stated at the very beginning, driving the entire . . *Allegro*.

Comb.: **theme music**, **theme song**, **theme tune** (*a*) music, a song, or a tune which recurs in a film, musical, etc.; (*b*) a signature tune; **theme park** an amusement park organized round a unifying idea or group of ideas; **theme pub**, **theme restaurant** a pub or restaurant in which the decor, food and drink served, etc., is such as to suggest a particular foreign country, historical period, etc.; ***theme song***, ***theme tune***: see ***theme music*** above.

▶**B** *verb trans.* Provide with a theme or subject. Chiefly as ***themed*** *ppl adjective*. L16.

📖 *Daily Telegraph* Mr Braden has selected themed anthologies of transatlantic humour.

Themistian /θɪˈmɪstɪən/ *noun*. *rare*. L19.

[from *Themistius*, 6th-cent. founder of the sect and deacon of Alexandria + -AN.]

ECCLESIASTICAL HISTORY. A member of a Monophysite sect which attributed to Christ imperfect knowledge.

themselves /ð(ə)mˈsɛlvz/ *pronoun pl.* Also (earlier & now *rare*) **-self**, (*rare*) **-selfs** /-sɛlfs/. ME.

[from THEM *pronoun* + SELF *adjective* (but long interpreted as THEM *pronoun* + SELF *noun*: see -S[1]).]

▶**I** *emphatic*. **1** In apposition to a subjective or (rarely) objective pronoun or a noun: these particular people, animals, or things. ME.

2 (Not appositional.) ▸**a** Subjective: they themselves. Now *arch.* & *dial.* exc. *colloq.* after *be* & after *than*, *as*. LME. ▸**b** Objective: the people etc. in question themselves. LME.

📖 1 I. MURDOCH They were not themselves tempted by success. P. ACKROYD The offices themselves were grand.

▶**II** *refl.* **3** Refl. form (indirect, direct, & after prepositions) of THEY *pronoun*; (to, for, etc.) the people etc. in question themselves. ME.

4 In concord with a singular pronoun or noun of undetermined gender or where the meaning implies more than one: himself or herself. (Considered *erron.* by some.) LME.

📖 3 R. G. MYERS Researchers . . are often unsure of themselves. ELLIS PETERS They muffled themselves all in white to be invisible against the snow. *Lifestyle* Human guinea pigs who willingly subject themselves to a variety of tests. *New Scientist* Normal refrigerators turn themselves on and off to vary cooling. **4** G. W. DASENT Every one likes to keep it to themselves. A. T. ELLIS I think somebody should immediately address themself to this problem.

Phrases: **be themselves** (*a*) act in their normal unconstrained manner; (*b*) feel as well as they usually do (usu. in neg. contexts). **by themselves** on their own.

then /ðɛn/ *adverb*, *conjunction*[1], *noun*, & *adjective*. Also †**than**.

[Old English *þænne*, *þanne*, *þonne* = Old Frisian *thenne*, *thanne*, *than*, Old Saxon *þanna*, *þan*, Old High German *danne*, *denne* (Dutch *dan*, German *dann*), from demonstr. base also of THAT, THE: cf. THAN *conjunction*[2] & *preposition*.]

▶**A** *adverb*. **1 a** At that time or moment; at a specified time or moment in the past or future. Cf. NOW *adverb* 1. OE. ▸**b** *spec.* At the time defined by a relative or other clause; at the time spoken of or referred to. Cf. NOW *adverb* 4. ME.

2 a At the moment immediately following an action etc. just referred to; thereupon, directly after that. Also, indicating the action or occurrence next in order of time: next, after that, afterwards. Cf. FIRST *adverb* 2. OE. ▸**b** In the next place, next, esp. in a series or narrative; in addition, and also, besides. ME.

3 In that case; in those circumstances; when that happens. OE.

4 That being so; on that account; therefore, as may be inferred. OE.

📖 **1a** C. LAMB I hope . . to pay you a visit (if you are then at Bristol). G. GREENE He had caught what was then known as a social disease. J. KOSINSKI There was no TV then. C. HARMAN Sylvia cried only rarely, but she cried then. **b** F. SWINNERTON And then, when I was about twenty, I began to try my luck with editors. **2a** V. WOOLF Then we went to Gordon Square to fetch my umbrella. M. ROBERTS You give me your news and then I'll give you mine. G. DALY First she lost her temper, then he lost his. **b** D. C. PEATTIE Then there are the bird guides. **3** INA TAYLOR If she wrote any articles then . . she would be paid at the standard rate. **4** SIR W. SCOTT 'Ha!' said the Countess, hastily; 'that rumour then is true.' R. LEHMANN Aren't I in love with him after all then?

▶†**B** *conjunction*. At the time that; when. OE–LME.

▶**C** *noun*. That time or moment; *the* past; (esp. after prepositions) the time spoken of or referred to. (Earliest after prepositions.) Cf. NOW *noun* 1. ME.

📖 *Listener* The rakes' progresses leading from the happy then to the guilt-ridden now. C. PHILLIPS Until then the tension will not slacken.

▶**D** *adjective*. That or who was such at the time in question. M16.

📖 *Times* Working on the scripts with his then wife. *Nature* He accepted a peerage from the then Prime Minister.

Phrases: **but then** but, that being so; but on the other hand. **by then (that)** (now *arch.* & *dial.*) by the time (that). ***every now and then***: see EVERY *adjective* 1. ***now and then***: see NOW *adverb*. ***now then***: see NOW *adverb* 5. **then and there** or **there and then** at that precise time and place; immediately and on the spot. ***well then***: see WELL *interjection*. ***what then?***: see WHAT.

Comb.: **thenabouts** *adverb* about that time; **then-a-days** *adverb* (*rare*) in those days, at that (past) time; **then-clause** the apodosis in a conditional sentence;

†**then** *conjunction*[2] & *preposition* var. of THAN *conjunction*[2] & *preposition*.

thenar /ˈθiːnə/ *adjective & noun*. M17.

[Greek = palm of the hand, sole of the foot.]

ANATOMY. ▶**A** *adjective*. Designating the ball of the thumb and the muscle that constitutes this. Chiefly in ***thenar eminence***, ***thenar muscle***. M17.

▶**B** *noun*. The thenar eminence or muscle; PALMISTRY a line that crosses the thenar eminence. Now *rare*. M17.

■ **thenal** *adjective* (now *rare*) of, pertaining to, or designating the palmar aspect of the forearm E19.

thenardite /θɛˈnɑːdʌɪt, tɛ-/ *noun*. M19.

[from *Thénard* (see next) + -ITE[1].]

MINERALOGY. Anhydrous sodium sulphate, an orthorhombic mineral that occurs as white to brownish translucent crystals in evaporated salt lakes.

Thénard's blue /ˈteɪnɑːz ˈbluː/ *noun phr.* M19.

[from Baron Louis-Jacques *Thénard* (1777–1857), French chemist + -'S[1] + BLUE *noun*.]

= ***cobalt blue*** s.v. COBALT *noun* 2.

thence /ðɛns/ *adverb & pronoun*. Now chiefly *arch.* & *literary*. ME.

[from THENNE + -S[3]. The spelling *-ce* is phonetic, to retain the unvoiced sound denoted in the earlier spelling by *-s*. Cf. HENCE, WHENCE.]

▶**A** *adverb*. **1** From that place; from there. ME.

2 At a place distant or away from there; distant; absent. Now *rare*. ME.

3 From that time or date; thenceforth. LME.

4 From that, as a source or cause; for that reason. M17.

📖 1 T. HARDY They were shown into the house-steward's room and ushered thence along a . . passage. **3** J. K. JEROME The English boy plays till he is fifteen, and works thence till twenty.

▶**B** *pronoun*. ***from thence***, from that place or time; from that source or cause; for that reason. ME.

📖 BOLINGBROKE From thence down to the present day.

Comb.: **thenceafter** *rare* after that time, thereafter; **thencefrom** *adverb* (*arch.*) = THENCE *adverb*.

thenceforth /ðɛnsˈfɔːθ, ˈðɛnsfɔːθ/ *adverb & pronoun*. LME.

[from prec. + FORTH *adverb*.]

Also ***from thenceforth***.

1 From that time onward. LME.

2 From that place or point onward. *rare*. LME.

thenceforward /ðɛnsˈfɔːwəd/ *adverb*. Also †**-s**. LME.

[formed as prec. + FORWARD *adverb*.]

= THENCEFORTH.

†**thenne** *adverb*. OE–LME.

[Old English *þanone*, *þanon* = Old Frisian *thana*, Old Saxon *þanana*, Old High German *danana*, *danan* (Dutch *dan*, German *dannen*), from West Germanic.]

= THENCE *adverb*.

¶ The 1st elem. of THENCE *adverb*.

theo- /ˈθiːəʊ/ *combining form*. Before a vowel **the-**.

[Greek from *theos* god: see -O-.]

Of or pertaining to God or gods.

■ **theo'centric** *adjective* centring or centred in God; having God as its centre: L19. **theo'centricism** *noun* (*rare*) = THEOCENTRISM E20. **theocen'tricity** *noun* = THEOCENTRISM M20. **theo'centrism** *noun* theocentric doctrine or belief M20. **theodidact** *noun* & *adjective* (a person) taught by God E18. **the'olatry** *noun* the worship of God or gods E19. **theo'mania** *noun* religious mania; *spec.* a mental illness in which the patient believes himself or herself to be a god or to be possessed by one: M19. **theo'maniac** *noun* a person affected with theomania M19. **the'onomy** *noun* (*rare*) government by God L19. **the'ophagous** *adjective* of, pertaining to, or marked by theophagy L19. **the'ophagy** *noun* (*a*) the 'eating' of God in the Eucharist; (*b*) ANTHROPOLOGY the eating of a meal at which it is believed that a god is ingested with the consecrated food: L19. **theo'phobia** *noun* irrational fear of God; dread of divine anger; *rare* aversion to or hatred of God: L19. **theo'phoric** *adjective* = THEOPHOROUS L19. **the'ophorous** *adjective* [Greek *theophoros*, from *pherein* to bear] bearing or containing the name of a god E20. **theo'politics** *noun* (*rare*) politics based on the law of God M18.

theobroma /θɪəˈbrəʊmə/ *noun*. M18.

[mod. Latin, lit. 'food of the gods', formed as THEO- + Greek *brōma* food.]

Any of various small tropical American trees of the genus *Theobroma* (family Sterculiaceae); esp. *Theobroma cacao*, whose seeds (cacao) are the source of cocoa and chocolate.

■ **theobromine** *noun* (CHEMISTRY) a bitter volatile alkaloid, $C_7H_8N_4O_2$, which is found esp. in cocoa and chocolate products and resembles caffeine in its effects M19.

theocracy /θɪˈɒkrəsi/ *noun*. E17.

[Greek *theokratia*, formed as THEO-: see -CRACY.]

A form of government by God or a god either directly or through a priestly order etc.; *loosely* a system of government by a sacerdotal order, claiming a divine commission. Also, a State so governed; *spec.* (**T-**.) the commonwealth of Israel from Moses and the Exodus to the election of Saul as king.

📖 R. HEILBRONER The virtual deification of Mao has made China very nearly a personal theocracy.

theocrasia /θɪəˈkreɪzɪə/ *noun*. E20.

[formed as next.]

= THEOCRASY 1.

theocrasy /ˈθiːəkreɪsi, θɪˈɒkrəsi/ *noun*. E19.

[Greek *theokrasia* a mingling with God, formed as THEO- + *krasis* mingling: see -Y[3].]

1 MYTHOLOGY. The mingling of several gods into one personality. Also, a mixture of the worship of different deities. E19.

2 The union of the soul with God through contemplation (among Neoplatonists etc.). M19.

theocrat /ˈθiːəkrat/ *noun*. E19.

[from next: see -CRAT.]

1 A person who rules in a theocracy as the representative of God or a god; a divine or deified ruler. E19.

2 A believer in or advocate of theocracy. M19.

📖 1 *Observer* The Ayatollah gathered at his bedside . . the 15 most powerful theocrats within the regime.

theocratic /θɪəˈkratɪk/ *adjective*. M18.

[formed as THEOCRACY + -IC, after *aristocratic* etc.]

Of, pertaining to, or of the nature of theocracy.

■ **theocratical** *adjective* L17. **theocratically** *adverb* E19.

Theocritean /ˌθɪɒkrɪˈtiːən/ *adjective*. M19.

[Latin *Theocritus* from Greek *Theokritos* Theocritus: see below.]

Of, pertaining to, or characteristic of Theocritus, a Greek poet of Sicily of the 3rd cent. BC, or his writings, esp. his pastoral poetry; pastoral, idyllic.

theodicaea /ˌθiɒdɪˈsiːə/ *noun. rare.* M19.
[App. irreg. Latinization of French *théodicée*: see next.]
= next.

theodicy /θɪˈɒdɪsi/ *noun.* L18.
[French *théodicée* title of a work by Leibniz, from Greek *theos* god + *dikē* justice: see -Y³.]
The vindication of divine providence in relation to the existence of evil; an instance of this; a doctrine etc. in support of this (cf. OPTIMISM 1).

EDWARD WHITE Their theodicy is based on the belief that out of . . evil God will bring . . good.

■ **theodiˈcean** *noun & adjective* (*a*) *noun* (*rare*) a person who presents or maintains a theodicy; (*b*) *adjective* of, pertaining to, or of the nature of a theodicy: L19.

theodolite /θɪˈɒdəlʌɪt/ *noun.* L16.
[mod. Latin *theodelitus*, ult. origin unkn. See -ITE².]
SURVEYING. Orig., an instrument for measuring horizontal angles, consisting of a horizontal graduated circle and an alidade. Now, a tripod-mounted telescopic instrument for measuring both horizontal and vertical angles.
■ **theodoˈlitic** *adjective* (*rare*) M19.

Theodosian /θɪəˈdəʊsɪən/ *adjective & noun.* M18.
[from *Theodosius* (see below) + -AN.]
ECCLESIASTICAL HISTORY. ▸**A** *adjective.* Of or pertaining to the Roman emperor Theodosius II (AD 408–50). Also, of or pertaining to the Roman emperor Theodosius I (d. AD 395), who tried to ban paganism and make orthodox Christianity the State religion. M18.
Theodosian Code a collection of laws, including those banning paganism and penalizing heresy, made under Theodosius II.
▸**B** *noun.* **1** A follower of the 6th-cent. Alexandrian rhetorician Theodosius, who in AD 535 became leader of a division of the Monophysites. L18.
2 A member of a sect founded by the 16th-cent. Russian monk Theodosius. M19.

Theodotian /θɪəˈdəʊʃɪən/ *noun.* M19.
[from *Theodotus* (see below) + -IAN.]
ECCLESIASTICAL HISTORY. A follower of the Byzantine tanner Theodotus (fl. AD 190), who taught the doctrine of the Monarchians.

theogony /θɪˈɒɡəni/ *noun.* E17.
[Greek *theogonia* generation or birth of the gods, formed as THEO- + -GONY.]
The generation or genealogy of the gods in a particular religion or culture; *spec.* an account or the study of this.
■ **theoˈgonic** *adjective* of, pertaining to, or of the nature of theogony M19. **theoˈgonical** *adjective* = THEOGONIC E18. **theogonist** *noun* a student of or expert in theogony L17.

theolog *noun* see THEOLOGUE.

theologal /θɪˈɒləɡ(ə)l/ *adjective & noun. rare.* L15.
[Old & mod. French *théologal* from Latin *theologus* (see THEOLOGER) + -AL¹.]
▸†**A** *adjective.* ***theologal virtue*** = ***theological virtue*** s.v. THEOLOGICAL *adjective* 1. L15–E17.
▸**B** *noun.* ROMAN CATHOLIC CHURCH. A lecturer in theology and scripture attached to a cathedral or collegiate church. M17.

theologaster /ˌθiɒləˈɡastə/ *noun.* E17.
[mod. Latin, from *theologus*: see THEOLOGER, -ASTER.]
A shallow or inferior theologian; a pretender in theology.

theologate /θɪˈɒləɡət/ *noun.* L19.
[mod. Latin *theologatus*, from classical Latin *theologus*: see next, -ATE¹.]
ROMAN CATHOLIC CHURCH. A theological college or seminary.

theologer /θɪˈɒlədʒə/ *noun.* Now *rare.* L16.
[ecclesiastical Latin use of classical Latin *theologus* theologian from Greek *theologos*, or from THEOLOGY + -ER¹: see -LOGER.]
1 An expert in or student of a monotheistic religion. L16.
2 An expert in or student of a polytheistic religion. E17.

theologian /θɪəˈləʊdʒɪən/ *noun.* L15.
[Old & mod. French *théologien*, from *théologie* or Latin *theologia* THEOLOGY: see -IAN.]
1 An expert in or student of theology; *spec.* a person who studies or makes a profession of esp. Christian theology; a divine. L15.
2 A person who holds to a usu. rigid set of theoretical principles. Cf. THEOLOGY 4. M20.

1 *New York Review of Books* From Augustine to John Donne theologians have worried about the logistics of the Second Coming. LIBERATION ***theologian***. ***natural theologian***: see NATURAL *adjective*. ***theologian of hope*** a proponent of the theology of hope (see THEOLOGY).

theologic /θɪəˈlɒdʒɪk/ *adjective.* LME.
[Old & mod. French *théologique* from ecclesiastical (medieval) Latin use of late Latin *theologicus*: see next, -IC.]
Theological.

theological /θɪəˈlɒdʒɪk(ə)l/ *adjective & noun.* LME.
[medieval Latin *theologicalis*, from late Latin *theologicus* (of non-Christian systems) from Greek *theologikos*, from *theologia* THEOLOGY: see -ICAL.]
▸**A** *adjective.* **1** Of or pertaining to the word of God or the Bible; scriptural. LME.
2 Of, pertaining to, or of the nature of theology; dealing with or treating of theology. L16.
3 *transf.* Pertaining to or characterized by dogma or theoretical principles. *derog.* M20.

1 theological virtue each of the three virtues of faith, hope, and charity (see 1 *Corinthians* 13:13), as distinct from the earlier cardinal four moral virtues. **2** H. MARTINEAU Frederick was a theological student in the university at Wilna. *Methodist Recorder* Theological explanations can help us to understand the experience of God.

▸**B** *noun.* †**1** In *pl.* Theological matters or principles. E17–L18.
2 A person trained at a theological college. *rare.* M19.

theologically /θɪəˈlɒdʒɪk(ə)li/ *adverb.* L16.
[from THEOLOGIC, THEOLOGICAL: see -ICALLY.]
In a theological manner; from a theological point of view; as regards or according to the principles of theology.

theologician /θɪələˈdʒɪʃ(ə)n/ *noun.* Now *rare.* M16.
[from Latin *theologicus* + -IAN: see -ICIAN.]
= THEOLOGIAN.

theologico- /θɪəˈlɒdʒɪkəʊ/ *combining form.* M17.
[Repr. Greek *theologikos* theological: see -O-.]
Forming words with the sense 'theologically-, theological and —', as ***theologico-metaphysical***, ***theologico-political***.

theologise *verb* var. of THEOLOGIZE.

theologism /θɪˈɒlədʒɪz(ə)m/ *noun.* Usu. *derog.* M19.
[from next or THEOLOGIZE: see -ISM.]
The action or product of theologizing; theological speculation.

theologist /θɪˈɒlədʒɪst/ *noun.* M17.
[medieval Latin *theologista*, from Latin *theologus*: see THEOLOGER, -IST.]
1 An expert in or student of a polytheistic religion; = THEOLOGER 2. Now *rare.* M17.
2 An expert in or student of a monotheistic religion. M17.

theologium /θɪələˈdʒʌɪəm/ *noun.* L19.
[mod. Latin from Greek *theologeion*, formed as THEO- + *logeion* speaking-place.]
GREEK ANTIQUITIES. A small balcony above the stage of a theatre, from which those impersonating the gods spoke.

theologize /θɪˈɒlədʒʌɪz/ *verb.* Also **-ise**. M17.
[In sense 1 from medieval Latin *theologizare*, from *theologia* THEOLOGY; in sense 2 perh. directly from THEOLOGY: see -IZE.]
1 *verb intrans.* Act the theologian; reason theologically; speculate in theology. M17.
2 *verb trans.* Conform to theology; treat theologically. M17.

1 EDWARD WHITE They do theologize . . on the question whether the . . human race owes its being to law or to grace. **2** A. FARRER It would . . be possible to suppose that the Galatian passage theologizes the story of Bethlehem.

■ **theologizer** *noun* L17.

theologoumenon /θɪələˈɡaʊmmən, -ˈɡuːm-/ *noun.* Pl. **-mena** /-mɪnə/. L19.
[Greek, use as noun of neut. of pres. pple pass. of *theologein* theologize, from *theologos*: see THEOLOGY.]
A theological statement or utterance reflecting personal opinion as opposed to defined dogma.

theologue /ˈθɪəlɒɡ/ *noun.* Also *-**log**. LME.
[Latin *theologus* from Greek *theologos*, formed as THEO- + *legein* to discourse: see -LOGUE.]
1 A theologian. Now *rare.* LME.
2 A theological student. *US colloq.* M17.

theology /θɪˈɒlədʒi/ *noun.* LME.
[Old & mod. French *théologie* from Latin *theologia* from Greek, from *theologos* a person who treats of the gods, a theologian, formed as THEO-: see -LOGY.]
1 The branch of knowledge that deals with Christian theistic religion; the organized body of knowledge dealing with the nature, attributes, and governance of God; divinity. LME.
2 The branch of knowledge that deals with non-Christian (esp. theistic) religions. M17.
3 A particular system or theory of esp. Christian religion. Also, the rational analysis of a religious faith. M17.
4 A system of theoretical principles; an esp. impractical or rigid ideology. *derog.* M20.

1 W. SHEED A doctorate in sacred theology from Rome itself. **2** J. L. ESPOSITO Muhammad ibn Abd al-Wahhab . . was trained in law, theology, and Sufism. **3** H. HALLAM The scholastic theology . . was . . an alliance between faith and reason.

Phrases: **biblical theology** (*a*) (now *rare*) theology as a non-dogmatic description of the religious doctrines contained in the Bible; (*b*) the exposition of biblical texts on the basis of a common biblical way of thinking. **dogmatic theology** Christian theology as authoritatively held and taught by the Church; the scientific statement of Christian dogma. ***EXEGETICAL theology***. LIBERATION ***theology***. ***natural theology***: see NATURAL *adjective*. ***pastoral theology***: see PASTORAL *adjective*. ***systematic theology***: see SYSTEMATIC *adjective*. **theology of hope** a theory, popularized by German theologians in the 1960s, which regards Christian hope as the basis for human action and eschatological salvation.

theomachy /θɪˈɒməki/ *noun.* L16.
[Greek *theomakhia*, formed as THEO-, -MACHY.]
†**1** A striving or warring against God; opposition to the will of God. L16–L17.
2 A battle among the gods (esp. with ref. to that narrated in Homer's *Iliad*). *rare.* E17.
■ **theomachist** *noun* (*rare*) a person who fights against God L18.

theomancy /ˈθɪəmansi/ *noun.* M17.
[Greek *theomanteia* spirit of prophecy, formed as THEO- + *manteia*: see -MANCY.]
A kind of divination based on the prophecies of oracles or oracular beings.

theomorphic /θɪəˈmɔːfɪk/ *adjective.* L19.
[from Greek *theomorphos*, formed as THEO-, -MORPH: see -IC.]
Having the form or likeness of God; of or pertaining to theomorphism.
■ **theomorphism** *noun* the doctrine that humankind has the form or likeness of God E19.

Theopaschite /θɪəˈpaskʌɪt/ *noun.* L16.
[ecclesiastical Latin *theopaschita* from ecclesiastical Greek *theopaskhitēs*, formed as THEO- + *paskhein* suffer: see -ITE¹.]
ECCLESIASTICAL HISTORY. A member of any of various 5th and 6th cent. sects who held that the divine nature of Christ suffered on the Cross.

theopathy /θɪˈɒpəθi/ *noun.* M18.
[ecclesiastical Greek *theopatheia* suffering of God: see THEO-, -PATHY.]
Sympathetic passive feeling excited by the contemplation of God; sensitiveness or responsiveness to divine influence; susceptibility to such feeling.
■ **theopaˈthetic** *adjective* of, pertaining to, or characterized by theopathy M18. **theoˈpathic** *adjective* = THEOPATHETIC M19.

theophany /θɪˈɒf(ə)ni/ *noun.* OE.
[ecclesiastical Latin *theophania* from Greek *theophaneia*, neut. pl. *theophania*, formed as THEO- + *phainein* to show: see -Y³.]
The visible manifestation of God or a god to humankind; an instance of this; *rare* a festival celebrating this, *spec.* Epiphany.

G. W. H. LAMPE He appears in heaven, or from heaven, in special visions and theophanies.

■ **theoˈphanic** *adjective* of or pertaining to theophany L19. **theophanism** *noun* theophany; belief in theophanies: M19.

theophilanthropist /ˌθɪəfɪˈlanθrəpɪst/ *noun.* L18.
[from THEO- + PHILANTHROPIST, after French *théophilanthrope*, irreg. formation meaning 'loving God and man'.]
ECCLESIASTICAL HISTORY. A member of a deistic sect founded in France in 1796.
■ **theoˈphilanthrope** *noun* = THEOPHILANTHROPIST E19. **theophilanˈthropic** *adjective* of or pertaining to theophilanthropy or theophilanthropists L18. **theophilanthropism** *noun* = THEOPHILANTHROPY E19. **theophilanthropy** *noun* the doctrine of the theophilanthropists L18.

Theophrastian /θɪəˈfrastɪən/ *adjective.* Also **-phrastan** /-ˈfrast(ə)n/. E20.
[from Latin *Theophrastus* from Greek *Theophrastos* (see below): see -AN, -IAN.]
Of, pertaining to, or characteristic of the Greek philosopher Theophrastus (fl. 4th cent. BC), or his writings, esp. his *Characters*, a set of thirty sketches on disagreeable aspects of human behaviour.
■ Also †**Theophrastical** *adjective*: only in M17.

theophylline /θɪəˈfɪliːn/ *noun.* L19.
[from mod. Latin *Thea* (see THEINE) + PHYLLO- + -INE⁵.]
CHEMISTRY. A bitter crystalline alkaloid, $C_7H_8N_4O_2$, isomeric with theobromine, which is found in small quantities in tea leaves.

theopneust /ˈθɪəpnjuːst/ *adjective.* M17.
[Greek *theopneustos*, formed as THEO- + *-pneustos* inspired, from *pneu-* stem of *pnein* breathe, blow.]
Divinely inspired.
■ Also **theopˈneustic** *adjective* (*rare*) E19.

theor /ˈθɪɔː/ *noun.* M19.
[Greek *theōros* spectator, envoy: see THEORY *noun*¹.]
GREEK HISTORY. An ambassador sent on behalf of a State, esp. to consult an oracle or perform a religious rite.

theorbo /θɪˈɔːbəʊ/ *noun.* Pl. **-os**, **-oes**. E17.
[Italian TIORBA, with alt. of ending as in some words in -ADO.]
A kind of large lute with a double neck and two sets of tuning-pegs, the lower holding the melody strings and the upper the bass strings, fashionable in the 17th cent. Also called ***archlute***.
■ **theorboed** *adjective* converted into a theorbo L19. **theorbist** *noun* a player on the theorbo E17.

theorem /ˈθɪərəm/ *noun & verb.* **M16.**
[French *théorème* or Latin *theorema* = Greek *theōrēma*, *-mat-* speculation, theory, proposition to be proved, from *theōrein* be a spectator, look at, from *theōros* THEOR.]
▶ **A** *noun.* **1** A general proposition or statement, not self-evident but demonstrable by argument or a chain of reasoning on the basis of given assumptions; *esp.* one in mathematics etc. expressed by symbols or formulae; GEOMETRY something to be proved. **M16.**
2 A stencil; *transf.* a design made with a stencil. *obsolete* exc. *Hist.* **E19.**
1 ***binomial theorem***, ***Jordan curve theorem***, ***Leibniz theorem***, ***Poynting's theorem***, ***Pythagoras's theorem***, etc.
▶ **B** *verb trans.* Express in or by means of a theorem. *rare.* **M19.**

theorematic /θɪərɪˈmatɪk/ *adjective.* **M17.**
[Greek *theōrēmatikos*, from *theōrēmat-*: see THEOREM, -IC.]
Pertaining to, by means of, or of the nature of a theorem.
■ **theorematically** *adverb* (*rare*) **M17.**

theoretic /θɪəˈrɛtɪk/ *adjective & noun.* **E17.**
[Late Latin *theoreticus* from Greek *theōrētikos*, from *theōrētos* that may be seen, from *theōrein*: see THEOREM, -IC.]
▶ **A** *adjective.* †**1** Speculative, conjectural. **E17–E18.**
2 = THEORETICAL 2. **M17.**
3 = THEORETICAL 3. **E18.**
3 GEO. ELIOT Her mind was theoretic, and yearned . . after some lofty conception of the world.
▶ **B** *noun sing.* & in *pl.* The theoretical side of a subject; theory as opposed to practice. **M17.**
English Review The British workman will never take up the theoretics of orthodox Marxianism.

theoretical /θɪəˈrɛtɪk(ə)l/ *adjective.* **E17.**
[formed as prec. + -AL[1].]
†**1** Contemplative. Only in **E17.**
2 a Of or pertaining to theory; of the nature of or consisting in theory as opposed to practice. **M17.** ▸**b** That is such according to theory; existing only in theory, ideal, hypothetical. **E19.**
3 a Of the mind or mental faculties: capable of forming theories; speculative. **M17.** ▸**b** Of a person: concerned with or specializing in theory; (given to) constructing or dealing with theories. **M19.**
2a J. W. KRUTCH No ready solution is available—not even a . . theoretical formulation which disregards all practical difficulties. M. KLINE The Greek genius for theoretical and abstract mathematics. **3b** J. J. C. SMART Theoretical physicists have far outstripped philosophers in their imaginativeness.
■ **theoretically** *adverb* (*a*) by means of or in relation to theory; (*b*) in theory, ideally, hypothetically: **E18.**

theoretician /θɪərɪˈtɪʃ(ə)n/ *noun.* **L19.**
[from THEORETIC + -IAN: see -ICIAN.]
A person who studies or is concerned with the theoretical side of a subject; a theorist.

theoreticism /θɪəˈrɛtɪsɪz(ə)m/ *noun.* **L20.**
[from THEORETIC + -ISM.]
PHILOSOPHY. A form of speculative idealism.
■ **theoreticist** *adjective* of or relating to theoreticism **L20.**

theoretico- /θɪəˈrɛtɪkəʊ/ *combining form.*
[Greek *theōrētikos* THEORETIC: see -O-.]
Forming words with the sense 'theoretical and —'.
■ **theoretico-hisˈtorical** *adjective* pertaining to both the theoretical and the historical sides of a subject **E20.** **theoretico-ˈpractical** *adjective* (*rare*) pertaining to or skilled in both the theory and the practice of a subject **M19.**

theoric /ˈθɪərɪk/ *noun & adjective*[1]. Now *arch. rare.* **LME.**
[Old & mod. French *théorique*, from medieval Latin *theorica* speculation, theory, use as noun of fem. of late and medieval Latin *theoricus* contemplative: cf. Patristic Greek *theōrikos* learned in spiritual matters: see -IC.]
▶ **A** *noun.* **1** = THEORY *noun*[1] 3, 4. **LME.** ▸†**b** In *pl.* Theoretical statements or notions. **M16–M17.**
†**2** A mechanical device theoretically representing or explaining a natural phenomenon. **L16–M17.**
†**3** A person devoted to contemplation; a member of a contemplative sect. **E17–L18.**
▶†**B** *adjective.* **1** = THEORETICAL 2. **M16–E19.**
2 = THEORETICAL 1, 3. **L16–M17.**
■ †**theorical** *adjective* = THEORIC *adjective*[1] **L16–M18.**

theoric /θɪˈɒrɪk/ *adjective*[2]. **E18.**
[Greek *theōrikos* pertaining to spectacles or display, from *theōria* viewing: see -IC.]
GREEK HISTORY. Pertaining to or provided for public spectacles or religious functions.

theorician /θɪəˈrɪʃ(ə)n/ *noun.* **M19.**
[from THEORIC *noun* + -IAN, after French *théoricien*.]
A holder of a theory; a theorist.

theoricon /θɪˈɔːrɪk(ə)n/ *noun.* **E19.**
[Greek *theōrikon* neut. of *theōrikos* THEORIC *adjective*[2].]
GREEK HISTORY. A fund in ancient Athens for theoric occasions.

theorise *verb* var. of THEORIZE.

theorism /ˈθɪərɪz(ə)m/ *noun. rare.* **E19.**
[formed as next + -ISM.]
Theorizing, speculation.

theorist /ˈθɪərɪst/ *noun.* **L16.**
[from THEORY *noun*[1] + -IST.]
1 An expert in the theory (as opposed to the practice) of a subject. **L16.**
2 A person who theorizes; a holder or propounder of a theory or theories. **M17.**
2 V. CRONIN Political theorists stressed the power of good laws to change society.

theorize /ˈθɪərʌɪz/ *verb.* Also **-ise.** **M17.**
[from next + -IZE.]
†**1** *verb trans.* Contemplate, survey. *rare.* Only in **M17.**
2 *verb intrans.* Form or construct theories; indulge in theories. **M17.**
3 *verb trans.* **a** Bring *into* or *out of* a condition by means of theory. **E19.** ▸**b** Construct a theory about; suppose by way of theory. **M19.**
2 R. JEBB He did not theorize without regard to facts and experience. *Marketing* It is always easier to theorise about these things than actually to go out and do them. **3a** J. R. LOWELL One thing that cannot be theorized out of existence . . is a lost campaign. **b** *Times Lit. Suppl.* Ethnic, national and religious conflict have not been successfully theorized by anyone.
■ **theoriˈzation** *noun* the action of theorizing, the construction of a theory or theories **E19.** **theorizer** *noun* **E19.**

theory /ˈθɪəri/ *noun*[1]. **L16.**
[Late Latin *theoria* from Greek *theōria* contemplation, speculation, sight, from *theōros* spectator (cf. THEOR), from base of *theasthai* look on, contemplate: see -Y[3].]
1 A mental scheme of something to be done, or of a way of doing something; a systematic statement of rules or principles to be followed. **L16.**
†**2** Mental view, contemplation. **E17–E18.**
3 a The knowledge or exposition of the general principles or methods of an art or science, esp. as distinguished from the practice of it; MATH. a set of theorems forming a connected system. **E17.** ▸**b** A system of ideas or statements explaining something, *esp.* one based on general principles independent of the things to be explained; a hypothesis that has been confirmed or established by observation or experiment and is accepted as accounting for known facts. **M17.**
4 (The formulation of) abstract knowledge or speculative thought; systematic conception of something. Freq. opposed to ***practice***. **E17.**
5 *loosely.* An unsubstantiated hypothesis; a speculative (esp. fanciful) view. **L18.**
1 DAY LEWIS My aunts and uncle had . . no theories about child upbringing. **3a** R. WARNER We studied the whole theory of flight. **b** A. KOESTLER Contradictory theories about the forces which make planets revolve. P. DAVIES The testing ground for Einstein's theory of curved space and time. ***atomic theory***, ***gauge theory***, ***theory of evolution***, ***theory of numbers***, ***theory of relativity***, etc. **4** A. DILLARD A terrifically abstract book of literary and aesthetic theory. **in theory** according to theory, theoretically. **5** E. M. FORSTER He had a theory that musicians are incredibly complex.
Comb.: **theory-laden** *adjective* designating a term, statement, etc., the use of which implies acceptance of some theory.

theory /θɪˈɔːri/ *noun*[2]. **M19.**
[Greek *theōria*: see prec., -Y[3].]
GREEK HISTORY. A group of theors sent by a State to perform a religious rite or duty.

theosis /θɪˈəʊsɪs/ *noun.* **L19.**
[medieval Latin from Greek *theōsis*.]
THEOLOGY. Deification.

theosoph /ˈθɪəsɒf/ *noun.* **E19.**
[French *théosophe* from medieval Latin *theosophus* from late Greek *theosophos* wise concerning God, formed as THEO- + *sophos* wise.]
A follower of theosophy.

theosophic /θɪəˈsɒfɪk/ *adjective.* **M17.**
[from THEOSOPHY + -IC.]
Pertaining to, of the nature of, or versed in theosophy.
■ **theosophical** *adjective* = THEOSOPHIC **M17.** **theosophically** *adverb* by means of or in accordance with theosophy **L17.**

theosophize /θɪˈɒsəfʌɪz/ *verb intrans.* Also **-ise.** **M19.**
[from next + -IZE.]
Practise or pretend to knowledge of theosophy; reason or discourse theosophically.

theosophy /θɪˈɒsəfi/ *noun.* **M17.**
[medieval Latin *theosophia* from late Greek = wisdom concerning God or things divine, from *theosophos*: see THEOSOPH, -Y[3].]
Any of various systems of belief which maintain that a knowledge of God may be achieved by spiritual ecstasy, direct intuition, or special individual revelations; *spec.* (*a*) such a system proposed by Jacob Boehme (1575–1624); (*b*) a modern system following some Hindu and Buddhist teachings, seeking universal brotherhood, and denying a personal god.
H. HALLAM His own models were the . . reveries of the Cabbala, and the theosophy of the mystics.
■ **theosopher** *noun* = THEOSOPHIST **M17.** **theosophism** *noun* the theory and practice of theosophy **L18.** **theosophist** *noun* a follower of theosophy **M17.** **theosoˈphistic** *adjective* of or pertaining to theosophy or theosophists **M19.** **theosoˈphistical** *adjective* theosophistic **E19.**

theotokion /θɪəˈtɒkɪɒn/ *noun.* Pl. ***-kia*** /-kɪə/. **M19.**
[ecclesiastical Greek, from *theotokos*: see next.]
ORTHODOX CHURCH. A short hymn or stanza addressed or referring to the Mother of God, usu. the last stanza in a series.

Theotokos /θɪˈɒtəkɒs/ *noun.* **L19.**
[ecclesiastical Greek (orig. adjective), formed as THEO- + *-tokos* bearing, bringing forth, from *tek-*, *tok-*, base of *tiktein* bear.]
CHRISTIAN CHURCH. Mother of God (as a title of the Virgin Mary).

theow /θuː/ *noun.* Long *obsolete* exc. *Hist.* Also **thew.**
[Old English *þīow*, *þēow*, *þēo* = Old High German *deo*, *dio*, Old Norse *þȳ*, Gothic *þius*, from Germanic.]
1 A slave, a bondman, a thrall. **OE.**
†**2** A female slave, a bondwoman. **OE–LME.**
■ **theowdom** *noun* the condition of a theow or slave; slavery, bondage: **OE.**

therapeusis /θɛrəˈpjuːsɪs/ *noun.* Now *rare.* **M19.**
[Back-form. from THERAPEUTIC after Greek nouns in *-sis* with adjectives in *-tikos*.]
MEDICINE. Therapy; treatment.

Therapeutae /θɛrəˈpjuːtiː/ *noun pl.* **L17.**
[ecclesiastical Latin from Greek *therapeutai* servants, attendants, (spiritual) healers, ult. from *therapeuein*: see next.]
Members of a Jewish mystical and ascetic sect, close to the Essenes, living in Egypt in the 1st cent. AD.

therapeutic /θɛrəˈpjuːtɪk/ *noun & adjective.* **M16.**
[French *thérapeutique* or late Latin *therapeutica* (pl.) from Greek *therapeutika* use as noun of neut. pl. of *therapeutikos*, from *therapeutēs* minister, from *therapeuein* minister to, treat medically: see -IC, -ICS.]
▶ **A** *noun.* **1** In *pl.* & †*sing.* The branch of medicine that deals with the treatment and cure of disease and ill health; the art of healing. **M16.**
2 A curative agent; a healing influence. **M19.**
▶ **B** *adjective.* **1** Of or pertaining to the healing of disease. Also *loosely*, health-giving, relaxing, stress-reducing. **M17.**
2 *Hist.* Of or pertaining to the Therapeutae. **L17.**
1 JANET MORGAN Hard physical work was in some respects therapeutic.
■ **therapeutical** *adjective* = THERAPEUTIC *adjective* 1 **E17.** **therapeutically** *adverb* in a therapeutic manner; in relation to therapeutics: **L19.** **therapeutist** *noun* a person who is skilled in therapeutics, a physician **E19.**

theraphosid /θɛrəˈfəʊsɪd/ *noun.* **L19.**
[from mod. Latin *Theraphosidae* (see below), from earlier *Theraphosae*, irreg. from Greek *thēraphion* small animal, insect, from *thēr* animal: see -ID[3].]
ZOOLOGY. A member of the family Theraphosidae of large hairy tropical mygalomorph spiders. Cf. TARANTULA 1b.

therapist /ˈθɛrəpɪst/ *noun.* **L19.**
[from THERAPY + -IST.]
A person who practises or administers therapy. Now *esp.*, a psychotherapist.
occupational therapist.

therapsid /θɛˈrapsɪd/ *noun & adjective.* **E20.**
[from mod. Latin *Therapsida* (see below), from Greek *thēr* animal + (*h*)*apsid-*, (*h*)*apsis* arch: see -ID[3].]
▶ **A** *noun.* A fossil synapsid reptile of the order Therapsida. **E20.**
▶ **B** *adjective.* Of, pertaining to, or designating this order. **E20.**

therapy /ˈθɛrəpi/ *noun.* **M19.**
[mod. Latin *therapia* from Greek *therapeia* healing.]
The medical treatment of (physical or mental) illness; (the application of) a system of treatments, activities, etc., intended for the alleviation and cure of a condition of ill health.
group therapy, ***ray therapy***, etc. ***chemotherapy***, ***hydrotherapy***, ***physiotherapy***, ***psychotherapy***, ***radiotherapy***, etc. ***deep therapy***: see DEEP *adjective*. ***occupational therapy***. ***physical therapy***: see PHYSICAL *adjective*. ***primal therapy***: see PRIMAL *adjective*.

Theravada /tɛrəˈvɑːdə/ *noun.* **L19.**
[Pali *theravāda* lit. 'doctrine of the elders'.]
A conservative form of Buddhism, practised in Myanmar (Burma), Thailand, and elsewhere in southern Asia. Also ***Theravada Buddhism***. Cf. HINAYANA, MAHAYANA.

therblig /ˈθəːblɪg/ *noun.* **E20.**
[Anagram of F. B. *Gilbreth*, Amer. engineer (1868–1924), who invented it.]
In time-and-motion study, a unit of work or absence of work into which an industrial operation may be divided; a symbol representing this.

For other words beginning with *theo-* see the entry for **theo-**

there /ðɛː, *unstressed* ðə/ *adverb, conjunction, pronoun, & noun.* Also (now *dial. & joc.*) **thar** /ðɑː/.
[Old English *þær, þēr* = Old Frisian *thēr*, Old Saxon *þar* (Dutch *daar*), Old High German *dar* (German *da*), cogn. with Old Norse, Gothic *þar*, from Germanic base also of THAT, THE.]
► **A** *adverb.* **I** *demonstr.* **1 a** In or at that place or position. OE. ▸**b** Indicating the fact, existence, or occurrence of something, *spec.* as being pointed out as present to the sight or perception. Freq. in unemphatic use, as (*a*) preceding *is, was,* etc.; (*b*) introducing a clause or sentence in which the verb precedes the subject; (*c*) (now *arch. & poet.*) following an aux. verb or occurring after the verb and before the subject in an interrog. clause or sentence; (*d*) (now *arch. & colloq.*) preceding a rel. clause with omission of the rel. pronoun; (*e*) *arch.* constituting an antecedent with omission of the following pronoun OE. ▸**c** Imparting emphasis in addressing a person; *esp.* (*a*) (following pers. pronoun, name, rank, etc.) attracting the attention of or summoning the person specified; (*b*) (following *hello, hi,* etc.) greeting a person. *colloq.* L16. ▸**d** Imparting emphasis preceding a noun qualified by *that, those*. *dial. & colloq.* M18.
2 To that place or position. OE.
3 †**a** In that case; then. OE–LME. ▸**b** In that matter or business; in that fact or circumstance; in that respect. OE. ▸**c** Referring to something said or done: in those words, in that act. L16.
4 At that point or stage in an argument, proceeding, situation, etc.; at that juncture. ME.

1a R. LEHMANN He won't move . . he just lies there. G. GREENE Looked up at the . . impassive eyes as if he might read there some hint. T. S. ELIOT In the mountains, there you feel free. V. SCANNELL Nottingham: We lived there for three years or so. **b** BYRON Lurk there no hearts that throb with . . pain. TENNYSON I will know if there be any faith in man. V. WOOLF There was Rebecca at the window. D. EDEN So there he was confined to the nursery. **c** OED Pass along there, please! J. BRAINE 'Hello there,' I said, 'What's new?' **d** SIR W. SCOTT That trunk is mine, and that there band-box. **2** J. H. NEWMAN When St. Hubert was brought there. OED Going to the meeting?—I am on my way there. J. B. PRIESTLEY Miss Trant shot a glance there too. **3b** J. P. DONLEAVY I'd agree with him there. A. TYLER For a while there I imagined I might outdistance him. **c** *Blackwood's Magazine* There you have hit the nail on the head. OED You have me there! I cannot tell you. **4** SHAKES. *Haml.* And there put on him What forgeries you please. G. FARQUHAR Brother! hold there, friend; I am no kindred to you.

►†**II** *rel.* **5** = WHERE *adverb* 4. OE–E16.
► **III** As *interjection*.
6 Expr. annoyance, confirmation, triumph, dismay, satisfaction, encouragement, etc. Also (esp. redupl.) used to soothe a child etc. M16.

6 J. S. WINTER But there, what's the good of talking about it. B. PYM There, let it go. B. NEIL This lady has fainted . . . There, there, my dear.

►†**B** *conjunction.* **1** = WHERE *conjunction* 1. OE–L16.
2 = WHEREAS *conjunction* 3. Only in LME.
► **C** *pronoun & noun.* That place or position; a place or position there. LME.

E. H. SEARS [Motion] requires a here and a there. V. NABOKOV The scene shifts . . to Old Russia, from there to England.

Phrases: ***all there***: see ALL *adverb* 1. ***all there is to it***: see TO *preposition*. ***and there's an end***: see END *noun*. **been there, done that, (bought the T-shirt)** *colloq.* expr. boredom, impatience, or total lack of interest due to overfamiliarity with something. **have been there before** *colloq.* have had previous experience of or be fully conversant with that matter or proceeding. ***here and there***: see HERE *adverb* etc. ***here, there, and everywhere***: see HERE *adverb* etc. **in there** *US slang* (*a*) (esp. of jazz music) excellent, superlative; (*b*) well-informed, conversant. ***neither here nor there***: see HERE *adverb* etc. ***out there***: see OUT *adverb*. **so there!** *colloq.*: expr. defiance or defiant triumph. **that there** *joc. colloq.* that matter, that behaviour. ***then and there***, ***there and then***: see THEN *adverb* etc. ***there is no saying***: see SAYING 1. ***there is nothing in it***: see NOTHING *pronoun & noun*. **there it is** that is the situation; nothing can be done about it. **there or thereabouts** in or very near that place or position; *fig.* something like that, approximately. **there's** (*a*) you are *a dear, a good girl*, etc., by virtue of present or future obedience or cooperation; (*b*) ***there's — for you***: expr. approval or disapproval of something; *Welsh dial.* how — someone or something is. ***there's a thing***: see THING *noun*[1]. **there you are** *colloq.* (*a*) = ***there you go*** below; (*b*) that process or action is or will be straightforward; the thing is done. **there you go** *colloq.* (*a*) this is what you wanted etc.; (*b*) expr. confirmation, triumph, resignation, etc. ***up there***: see UP *adverb*[2] & *adjective*[2].
Comb.: **thereabout**, **thereabouts** *adverbs* †(*a*) about or concerning or near that thing etc.; (*b*) about or near that place, in the neighbourhood, *fig.* approximately, (freq. in ***there or thereabouts*** above); **thereabove** *adverb* (*rare*) †(*a*) above or on top of that; more than that; (*b*) in that place above; in heaven; **thereafter** *adverb* (*a*) (now chiefly *formal*) after that (esp. in a book or document); (*b*) *arch.* accordingly; **thereagainst** *adverb* (*arch.*) against that; **thereamong** *adverb* (long *arch. rare*) among that, those, or them; **thereanent** *adverb* (*Scot. & north.*) about that matter; relating thereto; **thereat** *adverb* (*arch.*) (*a*) at that place; there; (*b*) on account of that, after that; **thereaway**, **thereaways** *adverbs* (chiefly *Scot. & north.*) †(*a*) to that place; (*b*) thereabouts; **therebeside** *adverb* (now *arch. & poet.*) by the side of that; next to that; nearby; **therefrom** *adverb* (*arch.*) from that; from that place; away from there; **therehence** *adverb* (*obsolete* exc. *dial.*) (*a*) from or out of that place; from there; †(*b*) from that source or origin; from that fact or circumstance; **thereinto** *adverb* (*arch.*) into that place; **thereon** *adverb* (*arch.*) (*a*) on that or it; †(*b*) in that, therein; (*c*) = ***thereupon*** below; **thereout** *adverb* (*a*) (long *rare* or *obsolete*) outside that place etc.; without; (*b*) (*arch.*) from or out of that, from that source; (*c*) (now *Scot.*) out of doors; in the open; abroad; in existence; (*d*) (now *Scot.*) out from that place etc.; **thereover** *adverb* (*arch.*) (*a*) over or above that; (*b*) *fig.* in reference to that, concerning that; **thereright** *adverb* (*obsolete* exc. *dial.*) straightaway, forthwith; **therethrough** *adverb* (*arch.*) (*a*) through that or it; (*b*) by means of that, by reason of that; thereby; **thereto** *adverb* (now chiefly *formal*) (*a*) to that or it; to that place etc.; (*b*) to that matter or subject; with regard to that point; (*c*) in addition to that; besides, moreover; **theretofore** *adverb* (long *formal*) before that time; previously to that; **theretoward** *adverb* (*rare*) toward that; **thereunder** *adverb* (*formal*) under that or it; (esp. in a book or document) under that title, heading, etc.; according to that; **thereunto** *adverb* (*arch.*) to that or it; **therewith** *adverb* (*arch.*) (*a*) with that (esp. of an addition to a document); in addition to that; besides; (*b*) on that being done or said; (directly) after that; thereupon; (*c*) (long *rare*) by means of that, thereby; (*d*) on account of that; in consequence of that; **therewithal** *adverb* (*arch.*) = ***therewith*** (a), (b) above; **therewithin** *adverb* (*arch.*) within or into that place; within there.
■ **thereness** *noun* the fact or condition of being there L17.

thereby /ðɛːˈbʌɪ/ *adverb.* Orig. two words. OE.
[from THERE + BY *preposition*.]
1 By that means, as a result of that; through that. OE.
2 Beside, adjacent to, or near that. Now *arch. & dial.* ME.
3 Thereabouts, approximately. *Scot.* M16.

1 *New York Times* Two great families would come together and thereby found a new line.

therefore /ˈðɛːfɔː/ *adverb & noun.* OE.
[from THERE + FORE *adverb & preposition*.]
► **A** *adverb.* Also (now the only form in sense 1, rare in sense 2) **therefor** /ðɛːˈfɔː/.
1 For that; for it; now *esp.*, for that object or purpose. Now chiefly *formal*. OE.
2 For that reason, on account of that; accordingly; consequently. ME.

1 W. MORRIS The love I had therefor. *Trade Marks Journal* Machines for resurfacing ice rinks and parts and fittings therefor. **2** M. ROBERTS Felix has failed, and is therefore destined for the . . secondary modern. G. PRIESTLAND Sometimes I think I only exist on paper—that I write, therefore I am.

► **B** *noun.* The word 'therefore' as marking a conclusion; an expressed conclusion or inference. M17.

therein /ðɛːrˈɪn/ *adverb.* Now chiefly *formal.* LOE.
[from THERE + IN *preposition*.]
► **I** *demonstr.* **1** In that place; *esp.* in that book or document; into that place. LOE.
2 In that matter, case, etc.; in that particular. ME.
3 Inside, indoors. *Scot.* E19.
►†**II** *rel.* **4** In which; wherein. LOE–LME.
Comb.: **thereinafter** in a later part of that document etc.; **thereinbefore** in an earlier part of that document etc.

theremin /ˈθɛrəmɪn/ *noun.* E20.
[Léon *Thérémin* (1896–1993), Russian engineer, its inventor.]
An electronic musical instrument in which the tone is generated by two high-frequency oscillators and the pitch controlled by the movement of the performer's hand towards and away from the circuit.

thereof /ðɛːrˈɒv/ *adverb.* Now chiefly *formal.* OE.
[from THERE *adverb* + OF *preposition*.]
1 Of that, concerning that. OE.
2 From that, from there. Now *rare*. ME.

1 D. MELTZER Dreams and analyses thereof to fill out his book. **2** MILTON Much more good thereof shall spring.

Theresian *noun & adjective* var. of TERESIAN.

thereupon /ðɛːrəˈpɒn/ *adverb.* Orig. two words. ME.
[from THERE + UPON *preposition*.]
1 Upon that or it. *arch.* ME.
2 On that being done or said; (directly) after that. LME.
3 In consequence of that; on that subject or matter; with reference to that. LME.

2 J. CONRAD I gave him the tip . . . Thereupon he lost all interest in me.

theri- *combining form* see THERIO-.

theriac /ˈθɪərɪak/ *noun & adjective. arch.* LME.
[Latin *theriaca*: see TREACLE *noun*.]
► **A** *noun.* An antidote to poison, esp. to the bite of a poisonous snake. Cf. TREACLE *noun* 1. LME.
►†**B** *adjective.* = THERIACAL. *rare.* Only in LME.

theriacal /θɪˈrʌɪək(ə)l/ *adjective.* Now *rare* or *obsolete.* E17.
[from prec. + -AL[1].]
Pertaining to or of the nature of a theriac; antidotal.

therian /ˈθɪərɪən/ *adjective & noun.* M20.
[from mod. Latin *Theria* (see below), from Greek *thēria* pl. of *thērion* wild animal: see -AN.]
ZOOLOGY. ► **A** *adjective.* Of or pertaining to the subclass Theria which includes all living mammals except monotremes (prototherians). M20.
► **B** *noun.* A mammal of this subclass. L20.

therio- /ˈθɪərɪəʊ/ *combining form.* Before a vowel **theri-**.
[Greek, from *thērion* wild animal: see -O-.]
Of, pertaining to, or resembling an animal, esp. (in ZOOLOGY) a mammal. Cf. THERO-.
■ **therian'thropic** *adjective* of or pertaining to a god represented as combining animal and human forms L19. **therioge'nology** *noun* the branch of veterinary science which deals with the reproductive systems of animals L20. **theri'olatry** *noun* the worship of animals or of theriomorphic gods L19. †**theriologic** *adjective* (*rare*) of or pertaining to the systematic study of animals; zoological: only in M17.

theriomorph /ˈθɪərɪə(ʊ)mɔːf/ *noun & adjective.* E20.
[from prec. + -MORPH.]
► **A** *noun.* **1** A representation of an animal form in art. E20.
2 = THEROMORPH. *rare.* E20.
► **B** *adjective.* Having the form or characteristics of an animal. M20.

theriomorphic /θɪərɪə(ʊ)ˈmɔːfɪk/ *adjective.* L19.
[formed as prec. + -IC.]
Esp. of a god: having the form of an animal.
■ **theriomorphism** *noun* representation of a person or god in the form of an animal; ascription of animal characteristics to a person: E20.

therm /θəːm/ *noun*[1]. Pl. **thermae** /ˈθəːmiː/, (*arch.*) **therms**. M16.
[Old French *thermes* (pl.) from Latin *thermae* from Greek *thermai* hot baths, from *thermē* heat.]
Chiefly CLASSICAL ANTIQUITIES. A public bath. Also (*rare*), a hot spring. Usu. in *pl.*

therm /θəːm/ *noun*[2]. L19.
[from Greek *thermos* hot, *thermē* heat.]
PHYSICS. †**1** = CALORIE (b). Only in L19.
2 A quantity of heat equal to 100,000 British thermal units or 1.055×10^8 joules, esp. as (formerly) used in the UK as the statutory unit of gas supplied. E20.

therm /θəːm/ *noun*[3] *& verb.* E18.
[Alt. of TERM *noun*.]
► **A** *noun.* **1** A pedestal for a bust or statue, esp. of a god. E18.
2 A rectangular tapering leg or foot of a chair, table, etc., fashionable in the 18th cent. L18.
► **B** *verb trans.* Make (a leg or foot of a chair, table, etc.) in a rectangular tapering form. L18.

therm /θəːm/ *noun*[4]. *colloq.* Now *rare* or *obsolete.* L18.
[Abbreviation.]
= THERMOMETER.

therm- *combining form* see THERMO-.

thermae *noun pl.* see THERM *noun*[1].

thermal /ˈθəːm(ə)l/ *adjective & noun.* M18.
[French, from Greek *thermē* heat + -AL[1]; in sense 1 partly formed as THERM *noun*[1].]
► **A** *adjective.* **1** Of, pertaining to, or of the nature of hot springs; (of a spring etc.) naturally hot or warm; having hot springs. M18.
2 *gen.* Of or pertaining to heat; determined, measured, caused, or operated by heat. M19. ▸**b** Of underwear etc.: promoting the retention of heat. L20.
Special collocations: **thermal agitation** = ***thermal motion*** below. **thermal analysis** CHEMISTRY analysis of a substance by examination of the way its temperature falls on cooling or rises on heating. **thermal barrier** AERONAUTICS = ***heat barrier*** s.v. HEAT *noun*. **thermal bremsstrahlung** electromagnetic radiation produced by the thermal motion of charged particles in a plasma. **thermal capacity** the capacity of a body to store heat, measured by the quantity of heat required to raise its temperature one degree. **thermal conductivity** the rate at which heat passes through a substance, expressed as the amount of heat that flows per unit time through unit area with a temperature gradient of one degree per unit distance. **thermal cycle** a cycle in which the temperature of a substance rises or falls and then returns to its initial value. **thermal death point** the lowest temperature at which a micro-organism can be killed by heat exposure under specified conditions. **thermal diffusion** diffusion occurring as a result of the thermal motion of atoms or molecules, esp. as a technique for separating gaseous compounds of different isotopes of an element (which diffuse at different rates in a temperature gradient). **thermal diffusivity** the thermal conductivity of a substance divided by the product of its density and its specific heat capacity. **thermal efficiency** the efficiency of an engine measured by the ratio of the work done by it to the heat supplied to it. **thermal equilibrium** a state in which no net gain, loss, or transfer of heat occurs. **thermal imaging** the technique of using the heat given off by objects or substances to produce an image of them or to locate them. **thermal inertia** resistance to change of temperature. **thermal lance** = ***thermic lance***. **thermal motion** motion of atoms or other particles due to their thermal energy. **thermal neutron** a neutron which is in thermal equilibrium with its environment (in contrast to a slow neutron). **thermal noise** ELECTRONICS electrical fluctuations arising from the random thermal motion of electrons. **thermal paper** heat-sensitive paper used in thermal printers. **thermal pollution** the production of heat, or the discharge of warm water, esp. into a river or lake, on a scale that is potentially harmful ecologically. **thermal printer** a printer having a matrix of fine pins as the printhead, which are selectively heated to form a character on heat-sensitive paper. **thermal radiation**:

emitted (esp. as infrared radiation) from the surface of a body and dependent on its temperature. **thermal reactor** a nuclear reactor in which the fission process relies upon thermal neutrons. **thermal resistance** resistance to the leakage of heat energy, esp. from an electrical conductor. **thermal runaway** *ELECTRONICS* a dramatic or destructive rise in the temperature of a transistor as a result of an increase in its temperature causing an increase in the current through it, and vice versa. **thermal shock** a sudden large application of heat energy. **thermal speed** the speed characteristic of a thermal neutron. **thermal storage** a system of storing water at high pressure and temperature in vessels above the boilers during off-peak hours in electricity generating stations; also used *attrib.* to designate appliances which store heat in other ways. **thermal unit** a unit of heat; ***British thermal unit***: see BRITISH *adjective*. **thermal velocity** = ***thermal speed*** above.

► **B** *noun*. **1** A rising current of relatively warm air, used by gliders and birds to gain height. **M20.**

2 In *pl.* Thermal underwear. **L20.**

■ **thermalling, -aling** *noun* soaring in thermals or warm rising air currents; the production of thermals: **M20. thermally** *adverb* in a thermal manner; by means of heat; as regards heat: **L19.**

thermalize /ˈθəːm(ə)lʌɪz/ *verb*. Also **-ise**. **M20.**

[from THERMAL *adjective* + -IZE.]

PHYSICS. **1** *verb trans.* Bring into thermal equilibrium with the environment. **M20.**

2 *verb intrans.* Attain thermal equilibrium with the environment. **M20.**

■ **thermaliˈzation** *noun* the process of thermalizing **M20.**

thermanaesthesia /ˌθəːmanɪsˈθiːzjə/ *noun*. Also ***-anes-**. **L19.**

[from THERM(O- + ANAESTHESIA.]

MEDICINE. Absence or loss of heat-perception; insensitivity to heat and cold.

thermantidote /θəːˈmantɪdəʊt/ *noun*. **M19.**

[from Greek *thermē* heat + ANTIDOTE *noun*.]

A thing which counteracts the effects of heat; *spec.* (***a***) in the Indian subcontinent, a rotating fan fixed in a window-opening within a dampened matting of cuscus roots; (***b***) (*rare*) a cooling medicine.

thermic /ˈθəːmɪk/ *adjective*. **M19.**

[from Greek *thermē* heat + -IC.]

Of or pertaining to heat; of the nature of heat; = THERMAL *adjective* 2.

thermic lance a steel pipe packed with steel wool through which a jet of suitable gas may be passed in order to burn away metal, concrete, etc., using heat generated by the burning of the pipe.

■ **thermical** *adjective* (*rare*) = THERMIC **M19. thermically** *adverb* (*rare*) thermally **L19. thermics** *noun* (*rare*) the branch of science that deals with heat, thermotics **M19.**

Thermidor /θəːmɪˈdɔː, *foreign* tɛrmidɔːr/ *noun*. **E19.**

[French, from Greek *thermē* heat + *dōron* gift.]

1 *Hist.* The eleventh month of the French Republican calendar (introduced 1793), extending from 19 July to 17 August. **E19.**

2 A moderate reaction following a revolution. **M20.**

Phrases: ***lobster Thermidor***: see LOBSTER *noun*[1].

¶ Thermidor was the month in 1794 in which Robespierre fell and the period of extreme repression and bloodshed ended.

Thermidorian /θəːmɪˈdɔːrɪən/ *noun & adjective*. **E19.**

[French *thermidorien*, from prec. + *-ien* -IAN.]

► **A** *noun*. **1** *FRENCH HISTORY.* A person taking part in the overthrow of Robespierre on the 9th Thermidor (27 July) 1794. **E19.**

2 A moderate opponent of a revolutionary movement; a counter-revolutionary. **L20.**

► **B** *adjective*. **1** Of, pertaining to, or characteristic of the month of Thermidor. **L19.**

2 *FRENCH HISTORY.* Of or pertaining to the Thermidorians (sense A.1 above). **L19.**

3 Of, pertaining to, or designating a moderate reaction following a revolution; counter-revolutionary. **M20.**

thermion /ˈθəːmɪɒn/ *noun*. **E20.**

[from THERM(O- + ION.]

PHYSICS. An electron or ion emitted from a surface at high temperature.

thermionic /θəːmɪˈɒnɪk/ *adjective*. **E20.**

[from prec. + -IC.]

PHYSICS. Of, pertaining to, or employing electrons emitted from a hot, esp. an incandescent, surface.

thermionic emission: of electrons from a heated surface. **thermionic valve** an electronic device consisting of an evacuated envelope containing two or more electrodes, such that a current can flow only in one direction as a result of thermionic emission from one electrode.

■ **thermionically** *adverb* **E20. thermionics** *noun* the branch of science that deals with thermionic emission **E20.**

thermistor /θəːˈmɪstə/ *noun*. **M20.**

[Contr. of *therm(al res)istor*.]

A small piece of semiconducting material the resistance of which falls with increasing temperature, enabling it to be used for sensitive temperature measurement and control.

thermite /ˈθəːmʌɪt/ *noun*. **E20.**

[from THERM(O- + -ITE[1].]

A mixture of finely divided aluminium with a metal oxide, esp. an iron oxide, which produces a very high temperature (*c* 3000°C) when ignited.

Comb.: **thermite process** (***a***) the reduction of finely divided oxides of iron or other metals by an exothermic reaction with finely divided aluminium; (***b***) thermite welding; **thermite welding** fusion welding in which the heat and the weld metal are produced by the thermite process.

thermo- /ˈθəːməʊ/ *combining form*. Before a vowel also **therm-**.

[Greek, from *thermos* hot, *thermē* heat: see -O-.]

Of, pertaining to, or connected with heat or temperature.

■ **thermoaˈcidophile** *noun* (*BIOLOGY*) an archaebacterium capable of surviving in conditions of high temperature and high acidity **L20. thermoˈchromic** *adjective* of, pertaining to, or displaying thermochromism **E20. thermoˈchromism** *noun* the phenomenon whereby certain substances undergo a reversible change of colour or shade when heated or cooled **E20. thermochromy** *noun* = THERMOCHROMISM **E20. thermocline** *noun* a temperature gradient; *esp.* an abrupt temperature gradient occurring in a body of water; a layer of water marked by such a gradient, the water above and below being at different temperatures: **L19. thermocoaguˈlation** *noun* (*MEDICINE*) the coagulation of tissue, esp. in the brain, by means of heat, as a form of treatment **M20. thermocomˈpression** *noun* the simultaneous application of heat and pressure, esp. in the making of solid-state devices **M20. thermoˈduric** *adjective* (*BIOLOGY*) (of bacteria etc.) capable of surviving high temperatures, esp. those of pasteurization **E20. thermo-eˈlastic** *adjective* of or pertaining to elasticity in connection with heat **E20. thermoforming** *noun* the process of heating a thermoplastic material and shaping it in a mould **M20. thermogalvaˈnometer** *noun* a thermoelectric instrument for measuring small electric currents **M19. thermoˈgenesis** *noun* the generation or production of heat, esp. in an animal body **L19. thermogeˈnetic, thermoˈgenic** *adjectives* of or pertaining to thermogenesis; produced by or producing heat: **L19. thermograviˈmetric** *adjective* of or pertaining to thermogravimetry **M20. thermograˈvimetry** *noun* (*PHYSICAL CHEMISTRY*) the chemical analysis of substances by measuring changes in weight as a function of increasing temperature **M20. thermoˈhaline** *adjective* [Greek *halinos* of salt] *OCEANOGRAPHY* of or pertaining to the temperature and salinity of seawater **M20. thermo-ˈhalocline** *noun* (*OCEANOGRAPHY*) a narrow layer of water separating layers of differing temperature and salinity **M20. thermo-ˈhardening** *adjective* thermosetting **M20. thermo-junction** *noun* the junction of two metals in a thermocouple **L19. thermokarst** *noun* (*PHYSICAL GEOGRAPHY*) topography in which the eventual melting of permafrost has produced hollows, hummocks, etc., reminiscent of karst **M20. thermoˈlabile** *adjective* liable to be destroyed or denatured when heated (opp. ***thermostable***) **E20. thermolaˈbility** *noun* thermolabile quality **E20. thermolumiˈnescence** *noun* luminescence resulting from the release at elevated temperatures of energy accumulated in a solid over time (by slow irradiation etc.), esp. as a method of dating ancient ceramic and other materials **L19. thermolumiˈnescent** *adjective* characterized by or pertaining to thermoluminescence **L19. thermoˈlysin** *noun* (*BIOCHEMISTRY*) a heat-stable proteolytic enzyme found in some thermophilic bacteria **M20. thermomagˈnetic** *adjective* pertaining to or involving thermomagnetism **E19. thermoˈmagnetism** *noun* magnetism caused or modified by the action of heat **E19. thermomeˈchanical** *adjective* both thermal and mechanical, involving both thermal and mechanical effects or (esp.) treatment of metals; *spec.* in *PHYSICS*, designating or pertaining to an effect observed in superfluid liquid helium (helium II) in which the liquid tends to flow from a region of lower to one of higher temperature: **M20. thermo-ˈmultiplier** *noun* (now *rare* or *obsolete*) a thermopile **M19. thermoˈnastic** *adjective* (*BOTANY*) of, pertaining to, or exhibiting thermonasty **M20. thermonasty** *noun* (*BOTANY*) (a) nastic movement, esp. the opening or closing of a flower, caused by a change in temperature **M20. thermoˈneutral** *adjective* (***a***) *BIOLOGY* (of an environment or its temperature) such that an organism is in thermal equilibrium without thermoregulation; (***b***) *CHEMISTRY* (of a reaction) accompanied by neither the absorption nor the emission of heat: **M20. thermoneuˈtrality** *noun* the condition of being thermoneutral **L19. thermophone** *noun* a device in which a sound pressure wave is generated by the heating effect of an electric current, used to calibrate microphones **L19. thermoˈphysical** *adjective* of or pertaining to thermophysics **M20. thermophysics** *noun* the branch of physics that deals with the physical properties of substances as they relate to (esp. high) temperature **M20. thermopile** *noun* a series of thermocouples closely packed together to combine their effect, esp. arranged for measuring small quantities of radiant heat **M19. thermopower** *noun* (*ELECTRICITY*) the thermoelectric electromotive force developed by a substance per degree difference in temperature **M20. thermoreceptor** *noun* (*PHYSIOLOGY*) a nerve ending that is sensitive to heat and cold **M20. thermoˈremanence** *noun* thermoremanent magnetism **M20. thermoˈremanent** *adjective* pertaining to or designating magnetism acquired, esp. by rock, as a result of cooling or solidifying in a magnetic field **M20. thermoscope** *noun* †(***a***) a thermometer; (***b***) any of various devices for indicating (esp. small) differences of temperature: **M17. thermoˈscopic** *adjective* of, pertaining to, or acting as a thermoscope **M18. thermoˈsensitive** *adjective* pertaining to or possessing sensitivity to heat **E20. thermosensiˈtivity** *noun* sensitivity to heat **E20. thermo-siphon** *noun* a siphon attachment by which the circulation in a system of hot-water pipes is increased or induced **M19. thermostaˈbility** *noun* the quality of being thermostable **E20. thermoˈstabilized** *adjective* (of food, esp. packaged food) heat-treated to delay any deterioration in quality **M20. thermoˈstable** *adjective* retaining its character or active quality at moderately high temperatures (opp. ***thermolabile***) **E20.** **thermo-therapy** *noun* a method of (esp. medical) treatment involving the application of heat **L19. thermoˈtolerant** *adjective* (of an organism) tolerant of but not requiring high temperature for growth **M20.**

thermochemistry /θəːməʊˈkɛmɪstri/ *noun*. **M19.**

[from THERMO- + CHEMISTRY.]

The branch of chemistry that deals with the relation of heat to chemical substances, esp. with the quantities of heat evolved or absorbed during chemical reactions.

■ **thermoˈchemical** *adjective* **L19. thermoˈchemically** *adverb* by means of or with reference to thermochemistry **E20. thermochemist** *noun* **L19.**

thermocouple /ˈθəːməʊkʌp(ə)l/ *noun*. **L19.**

[from THERMO- + COUPLE *noun*.]

A thermoelectric device for measuring temperature, consisting of two different metals joined at two points so that one junction develops a voltage dependent on the amount by which its temperature differs from that of the other end of each metal.

thermode /ˈθəːməʊd/ *noun*. **M20.**

[from THERMO- + -ODE[2].]

Chiefly *PHYSIOLOGY.* An object that is introduced into a medium, esp. living tissue, as a means by which heat may enter or leave it.

thermodynamic /ˌθəːmə(ʊ)dʌɪˈnamɪk/ *adjective*. **M19.**

[from THERMO- + DYNAMIC *adjective*.]

Of or pertaining to thermodynamics; involving the interconversion of heat and another form of energy, esp. mechanical energy.

■ **thermodynamical** *adjective* (*rare*) = THERMODYNAMIC **M19. thermodynamically** *adverb* as regards thermodynamics **L19. thermodynamicist** *noun* an expert in or student of thermodynamics **L19.**

thermodynamics /ˌθəːmə(ʊ)dʌɪˈnamɪks/ *noun*. **M19.**

[from THERMO- + DYNAMICS: see -ICS.]

The branch of physical science that deals with the relations between heat and other forms of energy (mechanical, electrical, chemical, etc.).

first law of thermodynamics the physical law to the effect that in a closed system the sum of all forms of energy remains constant (conserved), and that in an open system the increase of internal energy is equal to the sum of the work done on the system and the heat added to it. **second law of thermodynamics** the physical law stating that heat may not of itself pass from a cooler to a hotter body, entropy always being increased during an irreversible process. **third law of thermodynamics** Nernst's heat theorem (see NERNST *noun* 3).

thermoelectric /ˌθəːməʊɪˈlɛktrɪk/ *adjective & noun*. **E19.**

[from THERMO- + ELECTRIC *adjective*.]

► **A** *adjective*. **1** Of or pertaining to thermoelectricity; characterized by an electric current or potential produced by difference of temperature; operated by a current so produced. **E19.**

2 Of or involving both heat and electricity. **L19.**

► †**B** *noun*. A substance exhibiting thermoelectric effects. Only in **19.**

■ **thermoelectrical** *adjective* = THERMOELECTRIC **M19. thermoelectrically** *adverb* **L19.**

thermoelectricity /ˌθəːməʊɪlɛkˈtrɪsɪti/ *noun*. **E19.**

[from THERMO- + ELECTRICITY.]

Electricity generated in a body by difference of temperature in its parts; *esp.* an electric current produced in a closed circuit composed of two dissimilar metals when one of the points of union is kept at a temperature different from that of the rest of the circuit.

Thermogene /ˈθəːmədʒiːn/ *noun*. Also **t-**. **E20.**

[French *thermogène* THERMOGENIC *adjective*.]

(Proprietary name for) medicated cotton wool.

thermogram /ˈθəːməgram/ *noun*. **L19.**

[from THERMO- + -GRAM.]

1 A diagram recording variations in temperature; the trace produced by a recording thermometer. **L19.**

2 A photograph or image produced by the action of natural infrared radiation emanating from the subject. **M20.**

thermograph /ˈθəːməgrɑːf/ *noun*. **M19.**

[from THERMO- + -GRAPH.]

1 An image or tracing produced by the action of heat, esp. infrared radiation, on a prepared surface; now usu. *spec.*, = THERMOGRAM 2. Also, an apparatus for producing such images. **M19.**

2 = THERMOGRAM 1. **M19.**

3 A recording thermometer. **L19.**

thermographic /θəːmə(ʊ)ˈgrafɪk/ *adjective*. **M19.**

[from THERMO- + -GRAPHIC.]

Of, pertaining to, or obtained by a thermograph or thermography.

■ **thermoˈgraphically** *adverb* **M19.**

thermography /θəːˈmɒgrəfi/ *noun*. **M19.**

[formed as prec. + -GRAPHY.]

1 A process of writing, drawing, printing, photocopying, etc., in which the image is formed or developed by the influence of heat; *spec.* such a process which imitates embossing by creating a raised image. **M19.**

For other words beginning with *thermo-* see the main alphabetic sequence of entries

2 The taking or use of infrared thermograms, esp. to detect tumours. M20.

Thermolactyl /θəːmə(ʊ)ˈlaktɪl, -tʌɪl/ *noun*. Also **t-**. M20.
[French, from *thermo-* THERMO- + *lactyl* LACTYL.]
(Proprietary name for) a man-made fibre and fabric used for light thermal underwear.

thermology /θəːˈmɒlədʒi/ *noun*. Now *rare*. M19.
[from THERMO- + -LOGY.]
The branch of physics that deals with heat.
▪ **thermoˈlogical** *adjective* M19.

thermolysis /θəˈmɒlɪsɪs/ *noun*. L19.
[from THERMO- + -LYSIS.]
1 CHEMISTRY. The decomposition or dissociation of a compound by the action of heat. L19.
2 PHYSIOLOGY. The dissipation or dispersion of heat from the body. Now *rare*. L19.
▪ **thermoˈlytic** *adjective & noun* (**a**) *adjective* pertaining to or producing thermolysis; (**b**) *noun* (PHYSIOLOGY, *rare*) a thermolytic agent or substance: L19.

thermometer /θəˈmɒmɪtə/ *noun*. M17.
[French *thermomètre* or mod. Latin *thermometrum*, formed as THERMO-, -METER.]
1 An instrument for measuring temperature, esp. by means of a substance whose expansion and contraction under different degrees of heat and cold are capable of accurate measurement; *esp.* a narrow sealed glass tube marked with graduations, and having a bulb at one end filled with mercury or alcohol which expands along the tube on heating. M17.
2 *fig.* An indicator, a gauge. E19.

> 📖 **2** *Belfast Telegraph* A good thermometer of public opinion.

Phrases: **clinical thermometer** a glass mercury thermometer designed for measuring the temperature of the body, calibrated in degrees between 35° and 43.5°C (95° and 110°F), and usu. placed in the mouth or the rectum. *MAXIMUM* ***thermometer***. ***minimum thermometer***: see MINIMUM *noun*. *RESISTANCE* ***thermometer***. *REVERSING* ***thermometer***.
▪ **thermoˈmetric** *adjective* of or pertaining to the thermometer or its use; *rare* that acts as a thermometer: L18. **thermoˈmetrical** *adjective* = THERMOMETRIC M17. **thermoˈmetrically** *adverb* according to or by a thermometer; as regards thermometry: E19. **thermometry** *noun* the construction and use of thermometers; the scientific measurement of temperature: M17.

thermonuclear /θəːməʊˈnjuːklɪə/ *adjective*. M20.
[from THERMO- + NUCLEAR *adjective*.]
1 Designating, pertaining to, or involving a nuclear reaction that occurs only at very high temperatures (such as those inside stars), as fusion of hydrogen or other light nuclei. M20.
2 Pertaining to, characterized by, or possessing weapons that utilize thermonuclear reactions. M20.

thermophile /ˈθəːmə(ʊ)fʌɪl/ *adjective & noun*. Also **-phil** /-fɪl/. L19.
[from THERMO- + -PHILE.]
▶ **A** *adjective*. = THERMOPHILIC. L19.
▶ **B** *noun*. An organism, esp. a bacterium, growing optimally at high temperatures; a thermophilic organism. E20.

thermophilic /θəːmə(ʊ)ˈfɪlɪk/ *adjective*. L19.
[from THERMO- + -PHILIC.]
BIOLOGY. Requiring a high temperature (often above 50°C) for development, as certain bacteria. Also more widely, thriving at relatively high temperatures, preferring a warm environment.
▪ Also **thermophilous** /-ˈmɒfɪləs/ *adjective* L19.

thermoplastic /θəːməʊˈplastɪk/ *adjective & noun*. L19.
[from THERMO- + PLASTIC *adjective & noun*[3].]
▶ **A** *adjective*. Becoming soft and plastic when heated and hard and rigid when allowed to cool, esp. by a process which is reversible and indefinitely repeatable; made of such a substance. L19.
▶ **B** *noun*. A thermoplastic substance. E20.
▪ **thermoplaˈsticity** *noun* the quality of being thermoplastic M20.

Thermopylae /θəːˈmɒpɪliː/ *noun*. E20.
[A narrow pass on the north-east coast of Greece between Thessaly and Locris, scene of a battle in 480 BC in which a small Greek force temporarily withstood a Persian invasion.]
Heroic resistance against strong opposition; an instance of this.

thermoregulation /ˌθəːməʊrɛɡjʊˈleɪʃ(ə)n/ *noun*. E20.
[from THERMO- + REGULATION.]
Regulation of temperature, esp. of body temperature.
▪ **thermoˈregulate** *verb intrans*. regulate temperature, esp. body temperature E20. **thermoˈregulator** *noun* (**a**) an apparatus for regulating temperature, a thermostat; (**b**) an organism which thermoregulates: L19. **thermoregulatory** *adjective* of, pertaining to, or effecting thermoregulation M20.

Thermos /ˈθəːmɒs/ *noun*. Also **t-**. E20.
[Greek *thermos* warm, hot.]
(Proprietary name for) a vacuum flask. Also ***Thermos flask***.

thermoset /ˈθəːmə(ʊ)sɛt/ *adjective & noun*. M20.
[from THERMO- + SET *adjective*.]
▶ **A** *adjective*. Unable to be softened or melted by heat like a thermoplastic. Also = next. M20.
▶ **B** *noun*. A thermoset substance. M20.

thermosetting /ˈθəːməʊsɛtɪŋ/ *adjective*. M20.
[formed as prec. + SETTING *adjective*.]
Of a plastic: solidifying and becoming thermoset when heated.

thermosphere /ˈθəːməsfɪə/ *noun*. E20.
[from THERMO- + -SPHERE.]
1 †**a** The part of the atmosphere below about 8 km in which air density is largely dependent on temperature. *rare*. Only in E20. ▸**b** The part of the atmosphere between the mesopause and the height at which it ceases to have the properties of a continuous medium, characterized by an increase of temperature with height. M20.
2 The warmer upper part of the ocean. M20.
▪ **thermoˈspheric** *adjective* L20.

thermostat /ˈθəːməstat/ *noun & verb*. M19.
[from THERMO- + -STAT.]
▶ **A** *noun*. **1** An automatic apparatus for regulating temperature, esp. for keeping something at a constant temperature or for activating a device when the temperature reaches a certain point. M19.
2 A device which indicates undue increase of temperature; an automatic fire-alarm. Now *rare*. L19.
▶ **B** *verb trans*. Infl. **-tt-**. Provide with a thermostat; regulate the temperature of by means of a thermostat. M20.
▪ **thermoˈstatic** *adjective* of, pertaining to, or acting as a thermostat M19. **thermoˈstatically** *adverb* by means of a thermostat L19. **thermoˈstatics** *noun* equilibrium thermodynamics L19.

thermotaxis /θəːmə(ʊ)ˈtaksɪs/ *noun*. L19.
[from THERMO- + -TAXIS.]
†**1** PHYSIOLOGY. Thermoregulation. Only in L19.
2 BIOLOGY. Orientation or motion stimulated by external temperature. E20.
▪ **thermotactic** *adjective* of or pertaining to thermotaxis L19. **thermotaxic** *adjective* (*rare*) = THERMOTACTIC L19.

thermotic /θəːˈmɒtɪk/ *adjective*. Now *rare* or *obsolete*. M19.
[from Greek *thermōtikos* warming, calorific: see THERMO-, -OTIC.]
Of or pertaining to heat; *esp.* pertaining to thermotics.
▪ **thermotical** *adjective* (*rare*) = THERMOTIC M19. **thermotics** *noun* thermology M19.

thermotropic /θəːməˈtrəʊpɪk, -ˈtrɒpɪk/ *adjective*. L19.
[from THERMO- + -TROPIC.]
1 BIOLOGY. Of, pertaining to, or exhibiting thermotropism. *rare*. L19.
2 CHEMISTRY. Brought about by a change in temperature; *spec.* pertaining to or designating a mesophase which has its phase transitions effected by a change in temperature. E20.
▪ **thermoˈtropism** *noun* (BIOLOGY) the property of turning or bending in a given direction in response to heat L19.

thero- /ˈθɪərəʊ/ *combining form*.
[Greek *thēro-* combining form of *thēr* wild animal: see -O-.]
Of, pertaining to, or resembling an animal, esp. (in ZOOLOGY) a mammal. Cf. THERIO-.
▪ **therocephalian** /-sɪˈfeɪlɪən/ *adjective & noun* (**a**) *adjective* of or pertaining to an extinct group (Therocephalia) of carnivorous therapsids; (**b**) *noun* an animal of this group: E20. **theˈrology** *noun* (*rare*) = MAMMALOGY L19. **theromorph** *noun* (PALAEONTOLOGY, now *rare*) a synapsid, *esp.* a pelycosaur L19.

theroid /ˈθɪərɔɪd/ *adjective*. M19.
[from THERO- + -OID.]
Like or having the form of an animal; of animal nature or character.

therophyte /ˈθɪərəfʌɪt/ *noun*. E20.
[from Greek *theros* summer + -PHYTE.]
BOTANY. A plant which spends the winter or other period of unfavourable conditions during the life cycle as a seed.

theropod /ˈθɪərəpɒd/ *noun & adjective*. E20.
[from THERO- + -POD.]
PALAEONTOLOGY. ▶**A** *noun*. Any saurischian dinosaur of the group Theropoda, comprising mainly bipedal carnivores, including megalosaurs, tyrannosaurs, and the possible ancestors of present-day birds. E20.
▶ **B** *adjective*. Of or pertaining to the Theropoda; characteristic of a theropod. L20.
▪ **theˈropodous** *adjective* L19.

Thersitical /θəːˈsɪtɪk(ə)l/ *adjective*. *rare*. M17.
[from Greek *Thersitēs* Thersites (lit. 'the Audacious'), ugly and abusive member of the Greek force in the Trojan War, killed by Achilles + -ICAL.]
Resembling Thersites in language or behaviour; abusive, scurrilous.

thesauri *noun pl.* see THESAURUS.

thesaurosis /θɪsɔːˈrəʊsɪs/ *noun*. Now *rare*. Pl. **-roses** /-ˈrəʊsiːz/. M20.
[from Greek *thēsauros* store + -OSIS.]
MEDICINE. Any of various diseases caused by accumulation of foreign or abnormal substances in the tissues, esp. the lungs.

thesaurus /θɪˈsɔːrəs/ *noun*. Pl. **-ri** /-rʌɪ/, **-ruses**. L16.
[Latin from Greek *thēsauros* store, treasure, storehouse.]
1 A dictionary; an encyclopedia. L16. ▸**b** A collection of words arranged in lists or groups according to sense. Also (chiefly *N. Amer.*), a dictionary of synonyms (and occas. of antonyms). M19. ▸**c** A classified list of terms, esp. keywords, in a particular field, for use in indexing and information retrieval. M20.
2 A treasury, esp. of a temple. E19.

these /ðiːz/ *pronoun & adjective* (in mod. usage also classed as a *determiner*).
[Old English *þǣs* pl. of THIS: cf. THOSE. Extended forms with final *-e* appear in Middle English.]
▶ **A** *demonstr. pronoun pl.* Pl. of THIS; the things or people present, close at hand, indicated, already mentioned or understood; (in opposition to ***those***) the first of two or more sets of things, *esp.* the nearer or more immediate or obvious, the ones actually at hand. OE.

> 📖 SHAKES. *Temp.* These are devils. O, defend me! POPE Those call it Pleasure, and Contentment these. E. BOWEN I think these are your gloves. M. AMIS I've suffered some long moments . . but none longer . . than these.

▶ **B** *demonstr. adjective*. **1** Designating the things or people present, close at hand, indicated, already or about to be mentioned, or understood; the current; the well-known, the familiar; *colloq.* designating persons or things introduced into a narrative etc.; (in opposition to ***those***) designating the first of two or more sets of things, esp. the nearer or more immediate or obvious, etc. Cf. THIS *adjective*. OE.
2 With a (definite or indefinite) numeral in expressions of time referring to a period immediately past or immediately future. LME.

> 📖 **1** OED Do you think these scissors sharper than those you had yesterday? J. RHYS I thought all people were cruel but these three were kind. C. P. SNOW One can't rush these things. Q They thought we were these hip dance producers. ***not in these*** *TROUSERS*. ***one of these days***: see DAY *noun*. ***these days***: see DAY *noun*. **these her** —, **these my** —, etc., *arch.* these — of hers, mine, etc. **these kind of** —, **these sort of** — (with pl.): — of this kind (or sort). **2** H. JAMES She has been dead these twenty years.

Thesean /θiːˈsiːən/ *adjective*. E19.
[from *Theseus* (see below): see -AN, -EAN.]
Of, pertaining to, or characteristic of Theseus, a legendary hero-king of Athens whose exploits included killing the Minotaur and participating in the quest for the Golden Fleece.

thesis /ˈθiːsɪs; *in branch I also* ˈθɛsɪs/ *noun*. Pl. **theses** /ˈθiːsiːz/. LME.
[Late Latin from Greek = putting, placing; a proposition, an affirmation, from *the-* base of *tithenai* put, place.]
▶ **I 1** The syllable or part of a metrical foot that is unstressed (orig., CLASSICAL PROSODY, by lowered pitch or volume); the stressed beat in barred music. Opp. ARSIS. LME.
▶ **II 2** A proposition laid down or stated, *esp.* one maintained or put forward as a premiss in an argument, or to be proved; in Hegelian philosophy, a proposition forming the first stage in the process of dialectical reasoning (cf. ANTITHESIS, SYNTHESIS 2c); a statement, an assertion, a tenet. Formerly also, a general proposition of which a hypothesis forms a subordinate part (see HYPOTHESIS 2). L16. ▸**b** A theme for a school exercise, composition, etc. *rare*. L18.
3 A dissertation to maintain and prove a thesis or proposition; *esp.* one written or submitted by a candidate as the sole or principal requirement for a University degree. L16.

> 📖 **2** COLERIDGE A sort of metre, the law of which is a balance of thesis and antithesis. H. KUSHNER The thesis of this book is that there is a . . nourishment our souls crave. **3** A. GHOSH A PhD thesis on the textile trade . . in the nineteenth century.

Comb.: **thesis-novel** = *roman à thèse* s.v. ROMAN *noun*[3]; **thesis-play** a play which intentionally posits a particular proposition or thesis, esp. a social or political one; = PIÈCE À THÈSE.

Thesmophoric /θɛsmə(ʊ)ˈfɒrɪk/ *adjective*. *rare*. L19.
[Greek, from *thesmophoria*, neut. pl. from *thesmophoros*, from *thesmos* law + *-phoros* -bearing (an epithet of Demeter) + -IC.]
GREEK HISTORY. Of or pertaining to the Thesmophoria, an ancient Greek fertility festival held by women in honour of the goddess Demeter.

thesmothete /ˈθɛsməθiːt, -θɛt/ *noun*. E17.
[Greek *thesmothetēs*, pl. *-thetai*, from *thesmos* law + *thetēs* a person who establishes or lays down (the law).]
GREEK HISTORY. Each of the six inferior archons in ancient Athens, who were judges and lawgivers; *transf.* a person who lays down the law.

thesp /θɛsp/ *noun. colloq.* M20.
[Abbreviation.]
A Thespian.

Thespian /ˈθɛspɪən/ *adjective & noun.* L17.
[from Greek *Thespis* (see below) + -AN.]
▶ **A** *adjective.* Of or pertaining to Thespis, a Greek poet of the 6th cent. BC and the traditional founder of Greek tragedy; of or pertaining to tragedy or drama; tragic, dramatic. L17.
▶ **B** *noun.* A tragedian; an actor, an actress. E19.
▪ **Thespianism** *noun* the art or profession of acting E20.

Thess. *abbreviation.*
Thessalonians (New Testament).

Thessalian /θɪˈseɪlɪən/ *noun & adjective.* M16.
[from Latin *Thessalius*, *Thessalus* (Greek *Thessaleios*, *Thessalos*) adjectives, from Latin or Greek *Thessalia* Thessaly: see -AN, -IAN.]
GREEK HISTORY. ▶**A** *noun.* A native or inhabitant of Thessaly (now Thessalia), a region in northern Greece; the dialect of Greek spoken there. M16.
▶ **B** *adjective.* Of or pertaining to Thessaly or its people or dialect. L16.

Thessalonian /θɛsəˈləʊnɪən/ *noun & adjective.* E16.
[Irreg. from Latin *Thessalonica*, Greek *Thessalonikē* (see below) + -AN.]
▶ **A** *noun.* A native or inhabitant of ancient Thessalonica (now Salonica), a port in NE Greece. In *pl.* (treated as *sing.*), either of St Paul's two Epistles to the Thessalonians, books of the New Testament. E16.
▶ **B** *adjective.* Of or pertaining to ancient Thessalonica or its inhabitants. L19.

thet *pronoun, noun, conjunction, adjective, & adverb* see THAT.

theta /ˈθiːtə/ *noun.* LME.
[Greek *thēta*.]
1 The eighth letter (Θ, θ) of the Greek alphabet, also used in transliterating other languages; *transf.* a sign of doom, a death sentence (in allus. to the custom of using θ as standing for *thanatos* 'death' on the ballots used in voting on a sentence of life or death in ancient Greece). Also, the phonetic symbol θ, used *spec.* in the International Phonetic Alphabet to represent a voiceless dental fricative. LME.
2 CHEMISTRY. Used *attrib.* to designate the temperature of a polymer solution at which it behaves ideally as regards its osmotic pressure (also θ ***temperature***, Θ ***temperature***), and the conditions, solvent, etc., associated with such behaviour. M20.
3 PARTICLE PHYSICS. A meson that decays into two pions, now identified as a kaon. Also ***theta meson***, ***θ-meson***. M20.
Comb.: **theta activity**, **theta rhythm**, **theta waves** electrical activity observed in the brain under certain conditions, consisting of oscillations having a frequency of 4 to 7 hertz; **theta-function** MATH. (*a*) the sum of a series from $n = -\infty$ to $n = +\infty$ of terms denoted by $\exp(n^2a + 2na)$; a similar function of several variables; (*b*) a function occurring in probabilities, expressed by the integral $\int \exp(-t^2)\,dt$; ***theta meson***: see sense 3 above; **theta-phi diagram** a temperature-entropy diagram, which represents the heat-units converted into work per pound of working fluid (θ = absolute temperature; ϕ = entropy); **theta pinch** PHYSICS a toroidal pinch (PINCH *noun* 1d) in which the magnetic field follows the axis of the plasma and the current-carrying coils encircle it; ***theta rhythm***, ***theta waves***: see ***theta activity*** above.

thetatron /ˈθiːtətrɒn/ *noun.* M20.
[from prec. + -TRON.]
NUCLEAR PHYSICS. A fusion reactor employing a theta pinch in which the plasma is compressed axially by a sudden increase in the current in the coils, and so in the axial magnetic field.

thete /θiːt/ *noun.* M17.
[Greek *thēt-*, *thēs* villein, slave, thete.]
GREEK HISTORY. In ancient Athens, a freeman of the lowest class according to the constitution of Solon.

Thetford /ˈθɛtfəd/ *noun.* M20.
[A town in Norfolk, England.]
In full ***Thetford ware***. A type of Saxo-Norman pottery made in Thetford and in other parts of East Anglia.

thetic /ˈθɛtɪk/ *adjective.* L17.
[Greek *thetikos* such as is (fit to be) placed, positive, affirmative, from *thetos* placed, from *the-*: see THESIS, -IC.]
1 Involving direct or positive statement; (of a proposition, thesis, etc.) that has been laid down or stated; positive; dogmatic; arbitrary. L17.
2 CLASSICAL PROSODY. Of, bearing, or pertaining to the thesis. E19.
▪ **thetical** *adjective* = THETIC *adjective* 1 M17. **thetically** *adverb* M17.

Thetis /ˈθɛtɪs/ *noun.* LME.
[Greek.]
CLASSICAL MYTHOLOGY. One of the Nereids or sea-nymphs, the mother of Achilles; *poet.* the sea.

theurgic /θiːˈəːdʒɪk/ *adjective.* E17.
[Latin *theurgicus*, Greek *theourgikos* magical, formed as THEURGY: see -IC.]
Of or pertaining to theurgy.

> 🕮 F. O'BRIEN The animal . . was accorded the gift of speech by a secret theurgic process.

▪ **theurgical** *adjective* = THEURGIC M16. **theurgically** *adverb* M19.

theurgy /ˈθiːəːdʒi/ *noun.* M16.
[Late Latin *theurgia*, from Greek *theourgia* sorcery, from *theos* god + *-ergos* working: see -Y³.]
1 A system of white magic, originally practised by the Egyptian Neoplatonists, performed by the invocation and employment of beneficent spirits. Cf. GOETY. M16.
2 The operation or intervention of a divine or supernatural agency in human affairs; the results of such action in the phenomenal world. M19.
▪ **theurgist** *noun* a practitioner of or believer in theurgy; a magician: M17.

Thevenin's theorem /ˈtɛvənɛ̃z ˌθɪərəm/ *noun phr.* Also **Thé-**. L19.
[from M. L. *Thévenin*, 19th-cent. French engineer.]
ELECTRICITY. A theorem which states that a linear network with two terminals can be regarded for analytical purposes as a combination in series of an ideal voltage source and an impedance.

thew /θjuː/ *noun*¹. Now *literary.*
[Old English *þēaw* usage, conduct = Old Frisian *thaw*, Old Saxon *þau*, Old High German *thau*, *dau* discipline: ult. origin unkn.]
†**1** A custom, a usage, a general practice, *esp.* one observed by a group of people, a community, etc. OE–ME. ▸**b** In *pl.* Customs ordained; ordinances. LME–E17.
†**2** A habit; a person's manner of behaving or acting; a personal quality or characteristic; an attribute, a trait. Usu. in *pl.* OE–E19. ▸**b** A good quality or habit; a virtue. ME–L16.
3 *sing.* & (usu.) in *pl.* Attractive physical attributes or features; *esp.* good bodily proportions, parts, etc., as indicating physical strength; muscles, muscular development; might, vigour; *fig.* mental or moral vigour. ME.

> 🕮 **2** SOUTHEY In martial thewes . . To train the sons of Owen. **3** SHAKES. *Jul. Caes.* Romans now Have thews and limbs like to their ancestors. M. E. BRADDON Nature has been kinder to your brother in . . thew and sinew.

▪ **thewness** *noun* (*rare*) †(*a*) virtue; (*b*) vigour, robustness: ME. **thewy** *adjective* (*rare*) muscular, brawny: M19.

thew *noun*² var. of THEOW.

†**thew** *verb trans.* ME–E17.
[App. from THEW *noun*¹.]
Instruct in morals or manners; train; discipline, chastise.

thewed /θjuːd/ *adjective.* Now *literary.* ME.
[Orig. from THEW *verb* + -ED¹; later treated as from THEW *noun*¹ + -ED².]
†**1** Trained, instructed in morals or manners; having qualities or manners of a specified kind. ME–M17.
2 Having thews or muscles, esp. of a specified kind. M19.

> 🕮 **1** ***ill-thewed***, ***well-thewed***, etc. **2** R. GRAVES Clear-eyed and supple-thewed.

thewless /ˈθjuːlɪs/ *adjective. obsolete* exc. *Scot.* ME.
[from THEW *noun*¹ + -LESS. Cf. THIEVELESS, THOWLESS.]
†**1** Lacking morals or virtue; dissolute, profligate, immoral. ME–E16.
2 Lacking vigour or energy; inactive, spiritless, listless. E19.

they /ðeɪ/ *pers. pronoun, 3 pl. subjective (nom.), adjective, & adverb.* ME.
[Old Norse *þeir* (= Old English *þā* THO *pronoun*) nom. pl. masc. of *sá*, *sú*, *þat* THE, THAT; superseded Old English *hī*, *hīe*, pl. of *hē*, *hēo*, *hit*. Cf. THEIR, THEM.]
▶ **A** *pronoun.* **1 a** Subjective (the pl. of *he*, *she*, or *it*): the people, animals, or things previously mentioned or implied or easily identified. ME. ▸**b** Objective: them. Now *dial.* & *non-standard.* L17. ▸**c** As subj. of BE *verb* with pl. noun followed by a rel. clause as predicate: it. Now *rare.* E18.
2 a People in general; any persons, not including the speaker. ME. ▸**b** People in authority collectively, regarded as impersonal or oppressive. *colloq.* M19.
3 Demonstrative: those (chiefly as antecedent). *arch.* ME.
4 In relation to a singular noun or pronoun of undetermined gender: he or she. (Considered *erron.* by some.) LME.
5 Possessive: their, of them. *US dial.* E20.

> 🕮 **1a** V. WOOLF Eyes protruding as if they saw something to gobble in the gutter. I. MURDOCH She liked Paul's friends though they alarmed her. *Health Now* Once they have grown to a reasonable size cut the plants at ground level. ***they're off***: see OFF *adverb.* **b** A. GISSING I don't understand anything about they. **c** A. LANG They are small-minded . . people who are most shocked by . . 'vanity' in the great. **2a** *Country Living* In Morocco they use . . green China tea. *Fast Forward* A . . cop who doesn't exactly 'play it by the book' as they say in the US. **b** *Leicester Chronicle* 'They' are always doing you down. **3** TENNYSON They that know such things . . would call them masterpieces. **4** SCOTT FITZGERALD Ask anybody for Gordon Skerrett and they'll point him out to you. **5** J. C. OATES Coloreds crybabyin' about they skin.

▶ **B** *adjective.* Those; (now *rare*) the (qualifying pl. noun). Now *Scot. dial.* LME.

> 🕮 S. HOOD They Boers, they could shoot you . . at a couple of hundred yards.

▶ **C** *adverb.* There. *US dial.* L19.

> 🕮 H. HORNSBY They's more ways than one to skin a cat.

THI *abbreviation.*
Temperature–humidity index.

thi- *combining form* see THIO-.

thiabendazole /θʌɪəˈbɛndəzəʊl/ *noun.* M20.
[from THIA(ZOLE + BEN(ZENE + IMI)DAZOLE.]
MEDICINE & VETERINARY MEDICINE. An anthelmintic used esp. against intestinal nematodes.

thiamine /ˈθʌɪəmiːn/ *noun.* Also **-in** /-ɪn/. M20.
[from THIO- + AMINE.]
BIOCHEMISTRY. A water-soluble thermolabile sulphur-containing organic compound whose molecule contains a thiazole and a pyrimidine ring, present in many foods (esp. whole cereal grains, pork, and liver) and necessary for carbohydrate metabolism, and a deficiency of which causes beriberi. Also called ***vitamin*** B_1, ***aneurin***.
Comb.: **thiamine pyrophosphate** the active form of thiamine in which it acts as a co-enzyme.
▪ **thiaminase** *noun* an enzyme which catalyses the joining and splitting of the rings in thiamine molecules M20.

Thibet *noun*, **Thibetan** *noun & adjective* see TIBET etc.

thible *noun* var. of THIVEL.

thick /θɪk/ *adjective & noun.*
[Old English *þicce* = Old Frisian *thikke*, Old Saxon *þikki*, Old High German *dicki*, *dichi* (Dutch *dik*, German *dick*), Old Norse *þykkr*, from Germanic, of unkn. origin.]
▶ **A** *adjective.* **I 1** Of relatively great or specified extent or depth between opposite surfaces or sides; of large diameter; *spec.* (*a*) (of a line) broad, not fine; (of script or type etc.) consisting of such lines; (*b*) (of a garment) made of thick material. OE. ▸†**b** Esp. of water: deep. *rare.* OE–L17. ▸**c** Of a person or animal: thickset, stout. *obsolete* exc. *Scot.* & *dial.* ME.
2 *fig.* Excessive in some disagreeable quality; too much to tolerate. Formerly *esp.*, too gross or indelicate. Now chiefly in ***a bit thick*** below. *colloq.* L19.

> 🕮 **1** G. GREENE The man's . . fingers . . were short, blunt and thick. J. STEINBECK Eyes made huge by thick glasses. *New York Times* A template cut from quarter-inch-thick maple. *Sunday Times* My kilt . . is very thick; it can keep out snowdrifts. *Interview* I . . put on a thick layer of shaving cream.

▶ **II 3** Densely filled or covered, having a high density of constituent parts, (foll. by *with*); (of hair) bushy, luxuriant. OE.
4 Dense; arranged closely, crowded together, packed tightly; numerous, abundant. Usu. *pred.* Freq. in ***thick on the ground*** below. OE. ▸†**b** Of an action: occurring repeatedly in quick succession; frequent. LME–M17.
5 Of a liquid, semi-liquid, etc.: viscous; containing much solid matter; firm or stiff in consistency. OE. ▸**b** Of air, atmosphere, etc.: suffused with fumes or scent; full of moisture; stuffy. E17.
6 (Of mist, fog, smoke, etc.) dense; presenting a hindrance to vision; (of the weather etc.) characterized by mist or haze, cloudy, foggy, misty. Also, (of darkness) impenetrable by sight. OE.

> 🕮 **3** DRYDEN Thick as the galaxy with stars is sown. ADDISON A thick Forest . . of Bushes and . . Thorns. A. PATON The road was still thick with . . people going home. *Hair Styling* Your hair will become stronger, thicker. **4** BROWNING Lay me . . within some narrow grave . . But where such graves are thickest. T. KENEALLY The flies about it as thick almost as at high summer. **b** SHAKES. *Cymb.* He furnaces The thick sighs from him. **5** T. H. HUXLEY Not . . a clear bright spring but . . a thick stream laden with detritus. *Country Living* Simmer gently, . . until the mixture is thick and jammy. **b** J. CAREW The atmosphere was thick with smoke. *fig.*: V. BRITTAIN The air was thicker than ever with . . rumours. **6** SHAKES. *Macb.* Come thick Night, And pall thee in the dunnest smoke of hell. B. EMECHETA You could hardly see beyond a few feet in front of you, so thick was the fog. *Sea Classic International* If . . the weather suddenly turned thick, it might cost the chance of meeting the enemy.

▶ **III 7** Of the voice: hoarse; husky; indistinct; throaty. Also, (of an accent) marked; exaggerated. LME.

8 a Of the sight or hearing: lacking acuity or sensitivity. Now *dial.* E16. **▸b** Of a person (formerly also, of a person's wits or actions): slow; characterized by slowness of understanding; stupid, obtuse. Now *colloq.* L16.

9 Close in association; intimate, very friendly. Freq. in ***thick as thieves, thick as two thieves***. *colloq.* M18.

> 📖 **7** J. HARVEY He shouted in a thick clogged voice. *L.A. Style* Gomez . . donned a thick Spanish accent. **8b** SHAKES. *2 Hen. IV* His wit's as thick as Tewksbury mustard. J. HAYWARD Your thicke error in putting no difference betweene a magistrate and a king. B. MOORE You don't know what bourgeois means. You're too thick. **9** J. DOS PASSOS She and Mr. Spotman got to be quite thick, but he never tried to make love to her. *New Yorker* Some of the dealers are very thick with the burglars!

Phrases: **a bit thick** *colloq.* too much to tolerate; unreasonable; unfair. ***have a thick skin***: see SKIN *noun*. **thick as two planks**, **thick as two short planks** *colloq.* very stupid. **thick end of the stick** = ***dirty end of the stick*** s.v. DIRTY *adjective*. ***thick enough to trot a mouse on***: see TROT *verb*. **thick on the ground** *colloq.* numerous, abundant.

Special collocations & comb.: **thickback (sole)** a brown edible flatfish, *Microchirus variegatus*, of European offshore waters. **thick ear** *noun & adjective* (*slang*) (*a*) *noun* the external ear swollen by a sharp blow (freq. in ***give a person a thick ear***); (*b*) *adjective* designating literature etc. characterized by rough violence or knockabout humour. **thick end** *colloq. & dial.* the greater part *of* something. †**thick-eyed** *adjective* lacking acuity of vision, dim-sighted. **thick-film** *adjective* (of a process or device) using or involving a relatively thick solid or liquid film; *spec.* (ELECTRONICS) designating a miniature circuit etc. based on a metal film. **thick-knee** = ***stone curlew*** s.v. STONE *noun*. **thick-knit** *noun & adjective* (designating) a garment knitted from wool of greater thickness than double knitting. **thick-leaved** *adjective* (*a*) having or covered with dense foliage; (*b*) having thick fleshy leaves. **thick-lipped** *adjective* having thick or full lips. **thick register** the lowest register of the voice. **thick sandwich (course)** a sandwich course with an extended period of formal college instruction between two shorter periods of practical experience in industry etc. **thick-sighted** *adjective* not seeing clearly (*lit. & fig.*); having poor vision. **thickskin** (now *rare*) a thick-skinned person; **thick-skinned** *adjective* (*a*) (esp. of a plant or fruit) having a thick skin or outer layer; (*b*) *fig.* dull of sensation or feeling; obtuse; now *esp.*, oblivious, unresponsive, or insensitive to reproach or criticism. **thick-skull** a thick-skulled person. **thick-skulled** *adjective* (*a*) having a thick skull; (*b*) *fig.* dull, stupid; slow to learn. **thick space** TYPOGRAPHY a third of an em space used in separating words etc. in handsetting (cf. ***thin space*** s.v. THIN *adjective*). **thick-tongued** *adjective* speaking thickly. **thick 'un** *arch. slang* a gold sovereign; a crown or five-shilling piece; *rare* a pound sterling. **thick-witted** *adjective* dull, stupid; slow to learn. **thick woods** *Canad.* = ***strong wood(s)*** s.v. STRONG *adjective*.

▸ B *noun*. **I 1** A thicket. OE.

2 A stupid person. *colloq.* (orig. *School slang*). M19.

3 A thick fog. *Military slang*. M20.

> 📖 **1** *Horse & Hound* They had a good find in the thick at the bottom end. **2** S. O'CASEY The thick made out the Will wrong. M. BINCHY These awful country thicks wanted to take your stool.

▸ II *absol.* **4** The most densely occupied or crowded part *of* something. ME.

5 †a The more turbid or viscous part of a liquid, usu. that at the bottom. *rare*. LME–E18. **▸b** A drink of thick or dense consistency. *slang*. L19.

6 The thick part of a limb or of the body. Now *rare*. LME.

> 📖 **4** C. ACHEBE I . . got to a point in the thick of the crowd.

Phrases etc.: **in the thick of** at the most intense or busiest part of (an activity); heavily involved in or occupied with. **thick and thin** all conditions or circumstances; chiefly in ***through thick and thin***, in spite of all difficulties; under any circumstances. **thick-and-thin** *adjective* (*arch. slang*) constant, unwavering, steadfast, esp. in adherence to a political party or principles.

■ **thickish** *adjective* somewhat thick LME. **thickly** *adverb* in a thick manner; densely; closely; abundantly; indistinctly: ME. **thicky** *adjective* (*obsolete* exc. *poet.*) thick, dense, impenetrable ME.

thick /θɪk/ *verb*. Now *arch. & dial.*

[Old English *þiccian* (cogn. with Old High German *dicchen*, Middle High German *dicken*) from *þicce* THICK *adjective & noun*. Cf. THICKEN.]

1 *verb trans.* Make thick in consistency. OE.

2 *verb intrans.* Become thick, thicken. OE.

†**3** *verb intrans.* Move in crowds; flock, crowd. *rare*. OE–E16.

†**4** *verb trans.* Make (cloth etc.) close in texture by fulling. L15–M18.

> 📖 **2** W. DE LA MARE When dark hath thicked to night.

thick /θɪk/ *adverb*.

[Old English *þicce* = Old Saxon *þikko*, Old High German *diccho*, from Germanic base of THICK *adjective & noun*.]

1 So as to be thick; to a great depth. OE.

2 In a crowded state; closely, densely; in crowds; numerously, abundantly. OE.

3 In quick succession; frequently; quickly; fast. OE.

4 With indistinct articulation; with a husky or hoarse voice. Now *rare*. M16.

5 With a thick consistency. *rare* or *obsolete*. E18.

> 📖 **1** L. CARROLL The butter's spread too thick. **2** W. PETTY When England shall be thicker peopled. **3** W. LAW It will perhaps be thought . . that these hours of prayer come too thick.

Phrases & comb.: ***lay it on thick***, ***lay on thick***: see LAY *verb*[1]. **put it on thick**, **spread it on thick** do something to excess. **thick and fast**, (now *arch. & dial.*) **thick and threefold** in large numbers, and rapidly or in quick succession. **thick-cut** *adjective* cut in thick slices; containing such slices. **thick-sown** *adjective* sown or planted thickly; crowded, numerous, abundant.

thicken /ˈθɪk(ə)n/ *verb*. LME.

[from THICK *adjective* + -EN[5]. Cf. THICK *verb*.]

1 *verb trans. & intrans.* Make or become thick or thicker in consistency; (cause to) increase in density or concentration. LME.

†**2** *verb trans.* Make close or dense in arrangement of parts or constituents; fill up the spaces of. LME–E19.

3 *verb intrans.* Become dark or opaque; (of the weather) become cloudy or misty. E17.

4 a *verb trans. & intrans.* Make or become thicker in measurement; (cause to) increase in girth or bulk. E17. **▸b** *verb trans. fig.* Make more substantial; strengthen. E17.

5 *verb intrans. fig.* (Esp. of the plot in a book etc.) become more complex or intricate; increase in intensity. L17.

6 *verb intrans.* Become crowded, numerous, or frequent; gather thickly. E18.

> 📖 **1** J. E. T. ROGERS Oatmeal was used . . for thickening soup. A. LAMBERT The rain is thickening into sleet. **3** T. HARDY The dusk had thickened into darkness. D. NABOKOV The murk gradually thickened outside the window. **4a** G. GLENNY Earth in the alleys . . thrown up to thicken the soil above. M. WESLEY She had thickened, but her figure was still excellent. **5** C. RAYNER The silence they left behind thickened. **6** A. PRICE Home-going traffic from the coast was thickening.

■ **thickener** *noun* (*a*) a substance added to another to thicken it; (*b*) a machine or apparatus for the sedimentation of solids from suspension in a liquid: L16.

thickening /ˈθɪk(ə)nɪŋ/ *noun*. LME.

[from prec. + -ING[1].]

1 The action of THICKEN *verb*; an instance of this; the result of this action or process; a thickened substance or part. LME.

2 A substance used to thicken something; a thickener. M19.

> 📖 **1** P. HOLLAND Clouds are . . thickenings of . . vapourous aire. *Brain* External appearances of the brains were . . normal apart from the leptomeningeal thickening.

thicket /ˈθɪkɪt/ *noun*.

[Old English *þiccet*, from *þicce* THICK *adjective & noun* + -ET[2].]

A dense growth of shrubs, brushwood, and small trees; a place where trees or shrubs grow thickly tangled together.

> 📖 D. ATHILL A gloomy thicket of yew trees. *fig.*: E. HUXLEY The legal thickets of our housing, rent and mortgage laws. A. GHOSH I thrust . . through the thicket of trousered legs.

■ **thickety** *adjective* having many thickets; characterized by thickets: M17.

thickhead /ˈθɪkhɛd/ *noun*. E19.

[from THICK *adjective* + HEAD *noun*.]

1 A stupid or slow-witted person. *colloq.* E19.

2 Any of various Asian and Australasian perching birds of the family Pachycephalidae, which have large heads and robust bills; *esp.* (more fully ***buff-throated thickhead***) *Hylocitrea bonensis* of Sulawesi. M19.

■ **thickheaded** *adjective* (*a*) (esp. in names of animals and birds) having a short broad head; (*b*) *colloq.* stupid, slow-witted: E18. **thickheadedness** *noun* L19.

thickie /ˈθɪki/ *noun*. *colloq.* M20.

[from THICK *adjective & noun* + -IE.]

A stupid person.

thickness /ˈθɪknɪs/ *noun & verb*. OE.

[from THICK *adjective* + -NESS.]

▸ A *noun*. **1** The state or quality of being thick. OE.

2 The extent or distance between opposite surfaces of an object; the third dimension of a body or figure, distinct from length and breadth. OE.

3 The thick part of something; the part that lies between opposite surfaces. OE.

4 A layer of material of a certain thickness. E19.

> 📖 **1** J. WESLEY Mix juice of Celandine with Honey to the Thickness of Cream. *Which?* Spyros is conscious of the thickness of his lenses, and wanted frames to conceal this. *Hair* Jaw length bob, cut . . to give maximum thickness and volume. **2** *Mining Magazine* Reef thicknesses vary from . . 200mm to . . 3m. **3** A. LOVELL Steps made in the thickness of the Walls. R. BAGOT There was only the thickness of a floor between them. **4** N. GORDIMER Two huge wet pullovers . . were shaped to dry on thicknesses of newspaper.

▸ B *verb trans.* Reduce (wood, board, etc.) to a given thickness. Usu. in *pass.* L19.

> 📖 *Practical Woodworking* Every piece of wood . . had to be . . thicknessed by hand.

■ **thicknesser** *noun* a machine for thicknessing wood etc. E20.

thicko /ˈθɪkəʊ/ *noun*. *colloq.* Pl. **-os**. L20.

[from THICK *adjective & noun* + -O.]

A stupid person.

thickset /θɪkˈsɛt, *attrib.* ˈθɪksɛt/ *adjective & noun*. LME.

[from THICK *adverb* + *set* pa. pple of SET *verb*[1].]

▸ A *adjective*. **1** Densely planted or studded (*with*); set or growing close together. LME.

2 Of solid or heavy build; stocky. E18.

3 (Of a garment) made of thickset; (of fabric) having a short thick pile. Now *rare*. E18.

> 📖 **1** T. BUCKLEY They made a great fence around, with thick-set stakes. L. M. MONTGOMERY A huge cherry-tree . . so thick-set with blossoms that hardly a leaf was . . seen. **2** C. MUNGOSHI He was short, thickset, with a bullneck.

▸ B *noun*. **1** A strong corduroy fabric with a short thick pile. Also, a garment made of this material. Now *rare*. E18.

2 A thicket; a thickset plantation. M18.

thief /θiːf/ *noun*. Pl. **thieves** /θiːvz/.

[Old English *þiof*, *þēof* = Old Frisian *thiāf*, Old Saxon *þiof* (Dutch *dief*), Old High German *diob* (German *Dieb*), Old Norse *þjófr*, Gothic *þiufs*, from Germanic. Cf. THEFT.]

1 A person who steals or appropriates portable property etc. from another or others. Now chiefly, a person who does this by stealth and without using force or violence; a person who commits larceny. OE.

2 A rogue, a villain, a scoundrel. Now *Scot. & dial.* ME.

3 A protuberance in the snuff of a candle which causes the candle to gutter and waste. E17.

> 📖 **1** C. STOLL Now that securities are . . in a computer's memory, thieves go after the passwords. *Which?* A thief could enter the VW in five seconds. *fig.*: V. NABOKOV The moon is a thief: he steals his . . light from the sun.

Comb. & phrases: **auld thief**, **ill thief** *Scot. dial.* the Devil; ***stop thief!***: see STOP *verb*; **thief ant** a small ant belonging to the genus *Solenopsis* or a related genus which raids the nests of other species of ant or termite to steal food; **thief-catcher** (*a*) = ***thief-taker*** below; (*b*) a device formerly used to apprehend thieves; **thief-taker** a person who detects and captures a thief; *spec.* a member of an organized body of people formerly undertaking the detection and arrest of thieves; **thieves' hole** *Hist.* a dungeon reserved for thieves; ***thieves' kitchen***: see KITCHEN *noun*; ***thieves' Latin***: see LATIN *noun*; **thieves' market** a street market or bazaar at which cheap or stolen goods are sold; **thieves' vinegar** *Hist.* an infusion of rosemary tops, sage leaves, etc., in vinegar, valued as an antidote against the plague.

■ **thiefdom**, **thievedom** *noun* (*a*) *rare* theft, thieving, robbery; (*b*) the world or domain of thieves: M16. **thieflike** *adverb & adjective* (*a*) *adverb* in the manner of a thief; (*b*) *adjective* resembling (that of) a thief: E17.

Thiersch /tiːəʃ/ *noun*. L19.

[Karl *Thiersch* (1822–95), German surgeon.]

MEDICINE. Used *attrib.* and in *possess.* to designate a split-skin graft including only superficial layers, so that regeneration of the donor area can occur.

Thiersch graft, ***Thiersch's graft***, ***Thiersch's method***, ***Thiersch split-skin graft***, ***Thiersch's split-skin graft***, etc.

Thiessen /ˈθiːs(ə)n/ *noun*. E20.

[Alfred Henry *Thiessen* (1872–1956), US meteorologist.]

GEOGRAPHY & MATH. Used *attrib.* to designate Thiessen's method of analysing spatial distributions and concepts relating to this.

Thiessen polygon each of the polygons constructed around a set of points by drawing the perpendicular bisectors of the lines joining each point to its neighbours, so that every location in the polygon around a particular point is nearer to it than to any other such point.

thieve /θiːv/ *verb*.

[Old English *þēofian*, from THIEF.]

1 *verb intrans.* Act as a thief, commit theft. OE.

2 *verb trans.* Steal (something). L17.

■ **thieving** *noun* (*a*) the action of the verb; (*b*) *rare* an item of stolen property: M16.

thieveless /ˈθiːvlɪs/ *adjective*. *Scot.* M17.

[Perh. rel. to THEWLESS, THOWLESS.]

Lacking energy; ineffectual; spiritless; not serious; cold in manner.

thievery /ˈθiːv(ə)ri/ *noun*. M16.

[from *thieves* pl. of THIEF, or from THIEVE *verb*: see -ERY.]

1 The action or practice of stealing; an instance of this; (a) theft. M16.

2 The result or product of stealing; stolen property. *rare*. L16.

> 📖 **1** DEFOE Picking pockets, and other petty thieveries. **2** SHAKES. *Tr. & Cr.* Now with a robber's haste Crams his rich thievery up.

thieves *noun* pl. of THIEF.

thievish /ˈθiːvɪʃ/ *adjective*. LME.

[from *thieves* pl. of THIEF + -ISH[1].]

1 Of, pertaining to, or characteristic of a thief or thieves; furtive, stealthy. LME.

†**2** Esp. of a place: inhabited or frequented by thieves. LME–M17.

3 Given to thieving; dishonest. M16.

■ **thievishly** *adverb* LME. **thievishness** *noun* LME.

thig /θɪɡ/ *verb*. Long *obsolete* exc. *Scot.* Infl. **-gg-**.
[Old English *þicġ(e)an*, *þæġon*, *þeġen* repl. in Middle English by forms from Old Norse *þiggja*, *þǫgum*, *þágum*, *þegen* receive (Swedish *tigga*, Dutch *tigge* beg), from Germanic, from Indo-European.]
1 *verb trans.* Orig., take (esp. food), consume by eating or drinking. Later, take or appropriate for one's own use; borrow (with or without permission); plagiarize. **OE.**
2 *verb trans.* Orig., beg (alms, food, etc.). Now, solicit (gifts) from friends, esp. when setting up house etc. **ME.** ▸**b** *verb intrans.* Beg. **ME.**
†**3** *verb trans.* Crave or request (a boon, a favour, leave); invoke or call down (a curse). **LME–E18.**
■ **thigger** *noun*.

thigh /θʌɪ/ *noun & verb*.
[Old English *þēh*, *þēoh*, *þīoh* = Old Frisian *thiāch*, ODu. *thio* (Dutch *dij*), Old High German *dioh*, Old Norse *þjó*, from Germanic.]
▶ **A** *noun*. **1** The upper part of the human leg, from the hip to the knee. **OE.**
2 The part of an animal's hind leg anatomically equivalent to the human thigh; *loosely* the part corresponding to it in position or shape, as the tarsus of a bird. **ME.**
3 The part of a garment which covers the thigh. *rare.* **M16.**

📖 **1** ***hip and thigh, smite hip and thigh***: see **HIP** *noun*[1] 1. **2** ***second thigh***: see **SECOND** *adjective*. **3** B. MOORE The thigh of his worn jeans.

Comb.: **thigh-bone** the bone of the thigh, the femur; **thigh-boot** a boot with uppers reaching to the thigh; **thigh-high** *adjective & noun* (*a*) *adjective* thigh-length; (*b*) *noun* an item of clothing, esp. a garterless stocking, that reaches to a person's thigh; **thigh-length** *adjective* (of a garment, boot, etc.) extending down or up to the thigh; **thigh roll** a roll of padding on a horse's saddle, designed to prevent the girths from slipping backwards and to support the rider's legs in jumping and dressage; **thigh-slapper** *colloq.* an exceptionally funny joke, description, etc.
▶†**B** *verb trans.* Carve (a small game-bird) in preparation for eating. **LME–E19.**
■ **thighed** *adjective* having thighs (of a specified kind) **L15.**

thight /θʌɪt/ *adjective*. Now *dial.*
[Old English *þīht* corresp. to Old Norse *þéttr* watertight, of close texture, Middle Low German, Middle Dutch (whence German) *dicht* dense, close. In Middle English from Old Norse. Cf. **TIGHT** *adjective, adverb, & noun*.]
†**1** Tight, firm, solid. Only in **OE.**
2 (Of crops etc.) planted or growing closely together; (of rain) heavy. **OE.**
3 Of such close texture or construction as to be impervious to water; *spec.* (of a ship or boat) well-caulked, not leaky, watertight. Cf. **TIGHT** *adjective* 4. **E16.**
†**4** Close or dense in texture or structure. **M16–L17.**
■ †**thightness** *noun* **E17–L18.**

thigmokinesis /ˌθɪɡməʊkɪˈniːsɪs, -kʌɪ-/ *noun*. **M20.**
[from Greek *thigma* touch + -O- + **KINESIS**.]
ZOOLOGY. Movement of an organism in response to the absence of touch or body contact.

thigmotaxis /θɪɡməˈtaksɪs/ *noun*. **E20.**
[formed as prec. + **-TAXIS**.]
BIOLOGY. The way in which an organism moves or positions itself in response to a touch stimulus.
■ **thigmotactic** *adjective* of, pertaining to, or exhibiting thigmotaxis **E20.** **thigmotactically** *adverb* **L19.**

thigmotropism /θɪɡməˈtrəʊpɪz(ə)m/ *noun*. **E20.**
[formed as prec. + **-TROPISM**.]
BIOLOGY. The movement of (a part of) an organism in response to a touch stimulus; the habit of turning towards or away from an object on physical contact.
■ **thigmotropic** /-ˈtrəʊpɪk, -ˈtrɒpɪk/ *adjective* **E20.**

thikadar /teɪkəˈdɑː/ *noun*. Also ***theke-***. **E20.**
[Hindi.]
In the Indian subcontinent, a contractor, a middleman.

thilk /ðɪlk/ *adjective & pronoun*. Now *dial.* **ME.**
[App. from **THE** + **ILK** *adjective*[1] & *pronoun*[1].]
▶ **A** *demonstr. adjective*. **1** That; this. **ME.**
†**2** With pl. noun: these; those. **ME–L15.**
▶ **B** *pronoun*. That (or this) person or thing. **ME.**

thill /θɪl/ *noun*[1]. Also (*obsolete* exc. *dial.*) **fill** /fɪl/; (*dial.*) **sill** /sɪl/, **thrill** /θrɪl/, **trill** /trɪl/. **ME.**
[Origin unkn.]
The pole or shaft of a wagon, cart, etc., *esp.* either of a pair of shafts; *sing.* (now *US*) & in *pl.*, a pair of such shafts, the space between them.
Comb.: **thill-horse** a shaft-horse, a wheel-horse.
■ **thiller** *noun* a thill-horse **M16.**

thill /θɪl/ *noun*[2]. *local.* **ME.**
[Origin unkn. Cf. **SILL** *noun*[1] 4, **TILL** *noun*[3].]
(The thin stratum of clay etc. underlying) the floor or bottom of a seam of coal.

thimble /ˈθɪmb(ə)l/ *noun & verb*.
[Old English *þȳmel*, from **THUMB** *noun* + **-LE**[1].]
▶ **A** *noun*. †**1** A protective sheath for the finger; a finger-stall. Only in **OE.**
2 A cap of metal or plastic (formerly of leather), usu. with a closed end and a pitted surface, worn on the end of the finger to protect it and push the needle in sewing. Also, a similarly shaped cap of rubber used to facilitate counting money, turning pages, etc. **LME.** ▸**b** A thimble or similar article as used in the game of thimblerig. **E18.**
3 A ring or socket in the heel of a gate which turns on a hook or pin in the gatepost. *local.* **M16.**
4 *NAUTICAL.* A circular or heart-shaped metal ring, concave on the outside and fitting in a loop of spliced rope to lead a rope or to take a hook etc. **E18.**
5 *techn.* **a** *MECHANICS.* A short metal tube, sleeve, or ferrule. **L18.** ▸**b** *CERAMICS.* A rest on which to place the ware during glost-firing. **E20.** ▸**c** A printing unit used in electric typewriters and computer printers in which the characters are arranged on the outside of a cuplike shape. **L20.**
6 A watch. *Criminals' slang.* **E19.**
7 A thimbleful. **M19.**
8 *sing.* & in *pl.* The foxglove, *Digitalis purpurea*. Also more fully ***fairy thimble(s)***, ***witches' thimble(s)***. *dial.* **M19.**

📖 **2** ***hunt the thimble***: see **HUNT** *verb*. **7** *People* He is washing down sushi with a thimble of saké.

Comb.: **thimbleberry** any of several N. American blackberries and raspberries with thimble-shaped fruit, esp. *Rubus occidentalis* and *R. odoratus*; **thimble-eye** *NAUTICAL* an aperture in an iron plate with a rounded or built-up edge, so that a rope can be rove through it instead of through a sheave; **thimble-glass** a small thimble-shaped glass or tumbler; **thimble printer**: in which the printing unit is a thimble (see sense 5c above).
▶ **B** *verb intrans.* **1** Practise thimblerigging. **M17.**
2 Use a thimble in sewing. **L18.**
■ **thimbled** *adjective* (*a*) having or wearing a thimble; (*b*) *Criminals' slang* wearing a watch: **E19.** **thimbleful** *noun* as much as a thimble will hold; a small quantity (esp. of alcoholic drink): **E17.** **thimble-like** *adjective* resembling (that of) a thimble **M18.**

thimblerig /ˈθɪmb(ə)lrɪɡ/ *noun & verb*. **E19.**
[from **THIMBLE** *noun* + **RIG** *noun*[4].]
▶ **A** *noun*. A sleight-of-hand game or trick usually played with three inverted thimbles and a pea, the thimbles being moved about and bystanders encouraged to place bets or to guess as to which thimble the pea is under. Cf. ***shell-game*** s.v. **SHELL** *noun & adjective*. **E19.**
▶ **B** *verb*. Infl. **-gg-**.
1 *verb intrans.* Play the game or trick of thimblerig. Also *fig.*, cheat; behave in an adroit or underhand manner. **M19.**
2 *verb trans.* Manipulate or manage in an adroit or underhand manner. **M19.**

📖 **1** THACKERAY Juggling and thimblerigging with virtue and vice. **2** *Daily News* Lebret passes . . over the legal aspect of the case—thimblerigs it so to speak.

■ **thimblerigger** *noun* (*a*) a professional swindler who cheats by thimblerigging; (*b*) *fig.* an adroit manipulator: **M19.**

thin /θɪn/ *adjective, adverb, & noun*.
[Old English *þynne* = Old Frisian *thenne*, Old Saxon *þunni* (Dutch *dun*), Old High German *dunni* (German *dünn*), Old Norse *þunnr*, from Germanic from Indo-European base repr. also by Latin *tenuis*.]
▶ **A** *adjective*. Compar. & superl. **-nn-**.
1 Having the opposite surfaces relatively close together; of little thickness, depth, or diameter; *spec.* (*a*) lean, not plump; (*b*) (of a line) narrow, fine; (of script or type etc.) consisting of such lines; (*c*) (of a garment etc.) made of fine material. **OE.**
2 a Consisting of or characterized by sparsely placed individual constituents or parts; not dense; (of hair) not bushy or luxuriant. **OE.** ▸†**b** (Of the members of a group etc.) not numerous, few, scanty; (of a place) sparsely occupied or stocked, having only a small number *of*. **E16–M19.** ▸**c** (Of a gathering) poorly attended; (of a body of people) scant in number. **M17.**
3 a (Of a liquid or paste) containing little solid matter, having little density or consistency, watery; (of air or vapour) having low density, rare, tenuous. **OE.** ▸**b** *fig.* Insubstantial, intangible. **E17.** ▸**c** (Of a colour, (*arch.*) light, etc.): lacking depth or intensity; faint, weak; (of a sound) high-pitched and feeble. **M17.**
4 *fig.* Deficient in substance, quality, or vigour; scanty, meagre, insufficient. **ME.** ▸**b** *spec.* Of liquor: lacking body; having little flavour; low in alcohol, weak. (Cf. sense 3a above.) **LME.**
5 Penetrable by light or vision; *fig.* (of an excuse, argument, etc.) transparent, flimsy. **E17.**
6 *MOUNTAINEERING.* Of a rock face or a climb: having few good climbing holds. **M20.**
7 *ECONOMICS.* Of stocks or a stock market: in which trading is light. **M20.**

📖 **1** A. N. WILSON He ran his thin bony fingers through her hair. L. ELLMANN A bright thin crescent moon. R. RAYNER The tablecloth was thin and frayed. J. C. OATES Some are thin as pencil points. **2a** CONAN DOYLE A thin rain began to fall. M. DRABBLE The front stalls were a bit thin. **c** S. PEPYS There I found but a thin congregation. **3a** P. MATTHIESSEN I pant so in the thin air that I feel sick. **b** R. WELTON All the thin and airy delights of the world. **c** DAY LEWIS We hardly noticed the tired, thin quality of the voice. G. GORDON The blue is very thin, only just apparent. **4** S. BELLOW Family feeling is pretty thin by the time you get to the collateral relatives. *Video Today* Lumet fills out the thin storyline. **b** P. V. PRICE Wine diluted with water is thin. **5** J. TYNDALL Over the glacier hung a thin veil of fog. T. DREISER Clyde was lying. His story was too thin.

Phrases: **a thin time** *colloq.* a wretched or uncomfortable time or spell. ***have a thin skin***: see **SKIN** *noun*. ***on thin ice***: see **ICE** *noun*. ***the thin end of the wedge***: see **WEDGE** *noun* 3. **thin blue line** a line of policemen, *esp.* one which holds back a surging crowd; *transf.* the defensive barrier of the law. **thin-layer chromatography** *CHEMISTRY* chromatography in which compounds are separated on a thin layer of adsorbent material, now freq. a coating of silica gel on a glass plate or plastic sheet. **thin on the ground** *colloq.* not numerous. **thin on top** balding. ***thin red line***: see **RED** *adjective*. ***wear thin***: see **WEAR** *verb*[1].
▶ **B** *adverb*. Compar. & superl. **-nn-**. Thinly. **ME.**
Special collocations & comb. (of adjective & adverb): **thin air** a state of invisibility or non-existence; ***vanish into thin air***, disappear completely from sight or existence. **thin-cut** *adjective* cut in thin slices; containing such slices. **thin-film** *adjective* (of a process or device) using or involving a very thin solid or liquid film. **thin seam** *MINING* a narrow seam of coal. **thin section** a thin flat piece of rock or tissue prepared with a thickness of about 0.03 mm for examination with an optical microscope; a piece of tissue of the order of 30 nm thick prepared for electron microscopy. **thin-section** *verb trans.* make a thin section of (chiefly as ***thin-sectioning*** *verbal noun*). **thin-skinned** *adjective* (*a*) having a thin skin or rind; (*b*) *fig.* sensitive to reproach or criticism, easily upset. **thin-skinnedness** the condition or quality of being thin-skinned. **thin-sown** *adjective* sown or planted thinly; *fig.* widely-scattered, scarce. **thin space** *TYPOGRAPHY* a fifth of an em space used in separating words etc. in handsetting (cf. ***thick space*** s.v. **THICK** *adjective*). **thin-spun** *adjective* spun thinly; drawn out in spinning to a slender thread. **thin-worn** *adjective* made thin by wear.
▶ **C** *absol.* as *noun*. The thin part of something. *rare.* **ME.**
thick and thin: see **THICK** *noun*.
■ **thinly** *adverb* **ME.** **thinness** /-n-n-/ *noun* **OE.** **thinnish** *adjective* somewhat thin, tending to thinness **LME.**

thin /θɪn/ *verb*. Infl. **-nn-**.
[Old English *þynnian*, from **THIN** *adjective*.]
1 a *verb trans.* Reduce in thickness, depth, or diameter; spread *out* in a thin layer; gradually draw *off* or *down* to vanishing point. **OE.** ▸**b** *verb intrans.* Become thin or thinner; decrease in thickness, depth, or diameter. Also foll. by *out*, *off*, *away*. **E19.**
2 a *verb trans.* Make less dense or viscid; dilute. Also foll. by *down*. **OE.** ▸**b** *verb intrans.* Become less dense or viscid; grow tenuous or rare. **M19.**
3 a *verb trans.* Make less crowded or close by removing individual constituents or parts; make more sparse or sparsely occupied; reduce in number; *spec.* remove some of a crop of (seedlings, saplings, fruit, etc.) to improve the growth of the rest. Also foll. by *out*. **LME.** ▸**b** *verb intrans.* (Of a place) become less full or crowded; (of a crowd or anything consisting of many parts) become less dense or numerous. Also foll. by *off*, *out*. **L18.**

📖 **1a** HUGH WALPOLE A woman thinned and raddled by incessant jealousy. **b** T. HARDY Men thin away to insignificance and oblivion. **2a** L. BLUE I use curd cheese . . thinned down . . with yoghourt. **b** K. MANSFIELD The mist thinned, sped away, dissolved. **3a** J. C. OATES A thick pine and spruce forest he would not allow to be thinned. **b** E. MITTELHOLZER The rain . . began to thin off to a fine, steady drizzle. J. TROLLOPE Influenza arrived . . . The classrooms thinned out dramatically. A. MACRAE Now his hair was thinning.

■ **thinner** *noun* a person who or thing which thins; *spec.* (*a*) a machine for thinning a crop; (*b*) (in *pl.* & *sing.*) volatile liquid used to dilute paint, printing-ink, etc.: **M19.** **thinning** *noun* (*a*) the action of the verb; (*b*) that which is removed in the process of thinning (usu. in *pl.*): **OE.**

thine /ðʌɪn/ *possess. adjective* (in mod. usage also classed as a *determiner*) & *pronoun, 2 sing.* Now *arch.* & *dial.*
[Old English *þīn* used as genit. case of *þu* **THOU** *pers. pronoun & noun*[2] and as possess. adjective = Old Frisian *thīn*, Old Saxon *þīn* (Dutch *dijn*), Old High German *dīn* (German *dein*), Old Norse *þinn*, Gothic *þeins*, from Germanic from Indo-European base also of **THOU** *pers. pronoun & noun*[2]. Cf. **THY** *adjective*.]
▶ **A** *adjective*. = **THY** *adjective*. Used *attrib.* before a vowel or *h* or as the first of two or more possess. adjectives qualifying the same following noun. Also (*arch.*) used with emphatic force following any noun. Cf. **MINE** *adjective*. **OE.**
▶ **B** *pronoun*. [absol. use of the adjective.]
1 Your one(s), that or those belonging or pertaining to you; *spec.* your property. **OE.**
2 ***of thine***, belonging or pertaining to you. **LME.**
¶ See note s.v. **THOU** *pers. pronoun & noun*[2].

thing /θɪŋ/ *noun*[1].
[Old English *þing* = Old Frisian *thing*, Old Saxon *þing*, Old High German *ding* assembly for deliberation and/or business (German *Ding* affair, matter, thing), Old Norse *þing*, from Germanic.]
▶ **I** †**1** A meeting, an assembly; a court, a council. Only in **OE.**
2 a A matter brought before a court; a charge, a suit. *obsolete* exc. as passing into sense 3a. **OE.** ▸†**b** Cause, reason; sake. **OE–L16.**
3 a A matter with which one is concerned; an affair, a concern. Usu. in *pl.*, affairs in general; circumstances,

conditions. OE. ▸**b** With possess. adjective: one's particular interest or concern. M19. ▸**c** A preoccupation, an obsession; *spec.* a love affair, a romance. *colloq.* M20.

4 That which is done or to be done; a deed, an event, a happening, an experience. OE.

5 a That which is said; a saying, an utterance, an expression. OE. ▸**b** That which is thought; an opinion, an idea. M18.

†**6** Something; anything. ME–L17.

📖 **3a** J. RHYS Things are bad for a lot of people now. *Face* I'm definitely going to expand the publishing thing. P. FITZGERALD Frank was struck by her way of looking at things. **b** M. MARRIN It didn't sound like my kind of thing. **c** M. PIERCY I'm having an intense thing with a young man. G. SWIFT An independent girl with a thing about older . . men. **4** B. JOWETT Theft is a mean, and robbery a shameless thing. *New Scientist* Americans have been doing this sort of thing for years. *Atlantic* His recordings . . are treasurable souvenirs, but the great thing is to hear him live. **5a** *Village Voice* Saying the wrong thing at the wrong time. **b** A. DICKSON We may infer the same thing of the earth.

▸ **II** An entity of any kind.

7 *gen.* That which exists individually; that which is or may be an immaterial or abstract object of perception, knowledge, or thought; a being, an impersonal entity of any kind; a specimen or type of something. Also, an attribute or property of a being or entity. OE.

8 An inanimate material object, *esp.* (**a**) an unspecified object, one that it is difficult to denominate more exactly; (**b**) an inanimate object as distinct from an animate one; (usu. with specifying word) an animate entity, a living being; (freq. with cap. initial) a supernatural being, a monster. OE. ▸**b** A material substance (usu. of a specified kind); stuff, material. Now *esp.*, a foodstuff, a drink, a medicine. OE. ▸**c** Chiefly as a term of endearment, pity, or contempt: a person, *esp.* a woman, a child. ME. ▸**d** *euphem.* The genitals; *spec.* the penis. LME. ▸**e** An individual work of literature or art, a composition; a piece of writing or music etc. LME.

9 †**a** That which one possesses; property, wealth. OE–E16. ▸**b** A piece of property, an individual possession. Usu. in *pl.*, possessions, personal belongings or clothing; *esp.* (*colloq.*) those which one takes or puts on when going out, travelling, etc. ME. ▸**c** In *pl.* Equipment for some special use; utensils. L17.

10 *spec.* An actual being or entity as distinguished from a word, symbol, or idea by which it is symbolized or represented. LME.

📖 **7** F. A. KEMBLE Ignorance is an odious thing. J. S. MILL What is an action? Not one thing but a series of two things. O. HENRY The latest thing in suitings. L. PURVES There are a few things . . that I wish I had known earlier. **8** DICKENS Consideration of persons, things, times and places. TENNYSON Callest thou that thing a leg? J. CONRAD The hair of my head stirred . . I could see It—that Thing! A. DILLARD You enter its room . . holding a chair at the thing and shouting 'Simba!' *Today* Some of the things at the back don't seem to have been watered for days. *Buying Cameras* Spacious pockets . . secured to stop things popping out. **b** *Sunday Times* I lay in things I can shove in the oven. **c** A. BRONTË She's a nice, amusing little thing. D. CUSACK Poor thing . . She leads such a lonely life. **9b** V. WOOLF The maid had already unpacked her things. A. RANSOME Off with your things. Undies too. **c** J. HIGGINS The tray . . with the tea things on it. R. CARVER She's packed most of her kitchen things.

Phrases: **and things** *colloq.* and the like, et cetera. **any old thing** *colloq.* any thing whatever. ***a thing of nought***: see NOUGHT *pronoun & noun* 1. **be up to a thing or two** be knowing or shrewd. **do one's thing**, **do one's own thing** *colloq.* do what one wants, follow one's own interest or inclination. **do things to** *colloq.* affect remarkably. ***first things first***: see FIRST. **for one thing**, **for another thing** as one or an additional point to be noted. ***four last things***: see LAST *adjective*. **good thing** a fortunate occurrence or event. **have a thing about**, **have a thing for** *colloq.* be obsessed by; have a prejudice or fear about. ***know a thing or two***: see KNOW *verb*. ***if it's the last thing I do***: see LAST *adjective*. ***last thing (at night)***: see LAST *adjective*. ***last things***: see LAST *adjective*. **make a good thing of** turn to profit, make gain out of. **make a thing about**, **make a thing of** preoccupy oneself greatly with; make an issue of or a fuss about; regard as essential. ***material thing***: see MATERIAL *adjective*. ***near thing***: see NEAR *adjective*. ***new thing***: see NEW *adjective*. **no great things** *arch. colloq.* nothing great, of ordinary quality or character (cf. ***no great shakes*** s.v. SHAKE *noun*). ***no such thing***: see SUCH *adjective & pronoun*. ***not a thing***: see NOT *adverb*. **of all things** of all conceivable possibilities (often implying surprise). ***old thing***: see OLD *adjective*. ***one of those things***: see ONE *adjective, noun, & pronoun*. **OUTDOOR *things***. ***push things***: see PUSH *verb*. ***shape of things to come***: see SHAPE *noun*[1]. **show a person a thing or two**, **teach a person a thing or two**, **tell a person a thing or two**, etc., impart knowledge, experience, shrewdness, etc., to someone. ***sure thing***: see SURE *adjective*. ***take things as they come***: see TAKE *verb*. ***teach a person a thing or two***, ***tell a person a thing or two***: see ***show a person a thing or two*** above. ***the real thing***: see REAL *adjective*[2]. **there's a thing** *colloq.*: expr. astonishment at some object, event, etc. ***the sum of things***: see SUM *noun*. **the thing** (**a**) *pred.* what is proper, befitting, or fashionable; (of a person) on good form, up to the mark; (**b**) the special or important point; what is to be considered (esp. in ***the thing is***). ***the very thing***: see VERY *adjective*[1] *& adverb*. **thing in itself** PHILOSOPHY a thing as it is independently from human modes of perception and thought; a noumenon. **things of the mind** intellectual or cerebral matters. **things personal**, **things real** LAW personal or real property. ***too much of a good thing***: see TOO *adverb*.

Comb.: **thing-word** LINGUISTICS a noun referring to a material object; *spec.* a count noun.

■ **thinghood** *noun* the state or character of being a thing; existence as a thing; substantiality: M19. **thingifiˈcation** *noun* = REIFICATION M20. **thingify** *verb trans.* = REIFY E19. **thingliness** *noun* (*rare*) the quality of being thingly; existence as a thing: M17. **thingly** *adjective* of the nature of a thing M19. **thingness** *noun* the fact or character of being a thing, the essence of a thing L19.

Thing /θɪŋ/ *noun*[2]. M18.

[Old Norse *þing* (Danish, Norwegian, Swedish *ting*): see prec.]

Hist. In Scandinavian countries or settlements: a public meeting or assembly; *esp.* a legislative council, a parliament, a court of law. Cf. ALTHING.

Comb.: **Thingman** [Old Norse *þingmaðr*] a member of a Thing; *spec.* a housecarl.

thingamy *noun* var. of THINGUMMY.

thingum /ˈθɪŋəm/ *noun. colloq.* L17.

[from THING *noun*[1] + meaningless suffix *-um*.]

= THINGUMMY.

thingumabob /ˈθɪŋəməbɒb/ *noun. colloq.* Also **thingumbob** /ˈθɪŋəmbɒb/, **thingumebob**, & other vars. M18.

[Arbitrary extension of prec.]

= THINGUMMY.

thingumajig /ˈθɪŋəmədʒɪg/ *noun.* E19.

[formed as prec.]

= THINGUMMY.

thingumbob, **thingumebob** *nouns* vars. of THINGUMABOB.

thingummy /ˈθɪŋəmi/ *noun. colloq.* Also **thingamy** & other vars. L18.

[from THINGUM + -Y[6].]

A thing or person the name of which one cannot recall, does not know, or does not wish to specify.

thingy /ˈθɪŋi/ *noun.* L19.

[from THING *noun*[1] + -Y[6].]

1 A little thing. *Scot.* L19.

2 = THING *noun*[1]. Also = THINGUMMY. *colloq.* M20.

📖 **2** *Funny Fortnightly* What's that horrible black thingy doing in the washing machine?

thingy /ˈθɪŋi/ *adjective. colloq.* L19.

[from THING *noun*[1] + -Y[1].]

Resembling a thing; real, substantial. Also, concerned with actual things, practical.

■ **thinginess** *noun* L19.

think /θɪŋk/ *noun. colloq.* Also (*joc.*) **thunk** /θʌŋk/. M19.

[from THINK *verb*[2].]

An act of (continued) thinking. Also, what one thinks about something, an opinion.

📖 N. BALCHIN Have a think about it and let me know how you feel. **have another think coming** be greatly mistaken.

think /θɪŋk/ *verb*[1] *intrans. obsolete* exc. in METHINKS. Pa. t. & pple †**thought**.

[Old English *þyncan*, pa. t. *þūhte*, pa. pple *ġeþūht* = Old Saxon *þunkian* (Dutch *dunken*), Old High German *dunchen* (German *dünken*), Old Norse *þykkja*, Gothic *þugkjan*, from weak grade of Germanic verb, base also of next. In Middle English the forms of this and next became indistinguishable.]

Seem, appear.

think /θɪŋk/ *verb*[2]. Pa. t. & pple **thought** /θɔːt/, (*dial. & joc.*) **thunk** /θʌŋk/.

[Old English *þenċan*, pa. t. *þōhte*, pa. pple *ġeþōht* = Old Frisian *thenka*, *thinka*, Old Saxon *þenkian*, Old & mod. High German *denken*, Old Norse *þekkja*, Gothic *þagkjan*, factitive formation on strong grade of Germanic verb from Indo-European. Cf. prec., THANK *noun*, THOUGHT *noun*[1].]

▸ **I** Conceive in or exercise the mind.

1 *verb trans.* Form or have in the mind (a thought, notion, idea, etc., *that*); conceive of mentally. OE. ▸**b** Feel or experience (an emotion). Now *arch. & dial.* ME.

2 *verb trans.* **a** Meditate on, turn over in the mind, ponder. Foll. by *that* or (formerly) simple obj. OE. ▸**b** Have in mind, have one's thoughts full of, have as one's general perception, think in terms of. Freq. with adjective used absol. or adverb as obj. E19.

3 *verb intrans.* Exercise the mind, esp. the understanding, in a positive, active way; form connected ideas; meditate, cogitate; have the capacity to do this; (foll. by *about*, *of*, *over*, (*up*)*on*) have the mind occupied with, apply the mind to. OE.

4 a *verb trans.* Form or have an idea of in one's mind; imagine; conceive of mentally. ME. ▸**b** *verb intrans.* Foll. by *of*, (arch.) *on*: form or have an idea of something or someone in one's mind. Also, choose mentally. ME. ▸**c** *verb trans.* Form a clear mental impression of (something real); picture in the mind. M19.

5 *verb trans.* Bring into or out of a specified condition by thinking. Foll. by *away*, *down*, *into*, etc. L16.

📖 **1** S. SMILES They think great thoughts. **2a** A. TROLLOPE Mrs. Whortle began to think whether the visitor could have known of her intended absence. OED I am thinking what to do next. **b** A. LURIE I had begun to Think Small. **3** J. RHYS Will you tell him I think of him a lot. C. RAYNER Matters upon which he had thought many times. A. BROOKNER She forced herself to think ahead to the white bed that awaited her. D. W. WINNICOTT I . . have made mistakes that I hate to think about. *Sunday Times* I read and thought mostly in Latin. **4a** F. BURNEY You can't think how I'm encumbered with these ruffles! **b** J. FOWLES It was difficult not to think of it as meaningful. M. FORSTER I told her to think of herself as voluptuous, not fat. **5** R. INGALLS I'm too used to thinking myself into a part.

▸ **II** Call to mind, consider.

6 a *verb trans.* Call (someone or something) to mind; reflect (*that*); recollect, remember, (*that*, *to do*); *rare* bethink (oneself). OE. ▸**b** *verb intrans.* Consider the matter, reflect; (foll. by *of*, (arch.) (*up*)*on*) call someone or something to mind, remember, recollect. OE.

7 a *verb trans.* Contemplate, intend; now *esp.*, intend vaguely or half-heartedly. Foll. by *that*, *to do* or (arch.) simple obj. OE. ▸**b** *verb intrans.* Foll. by *of*, (arch.) (*up*)*on*: contemplate or intend doing something; now *esp.*, have a vague or half-hearted intention of doing something. L17. ▸**c** *verb intrans. spec.* Foll. by *of*: consider (a person) for a vacancy or as a prospective marriage partner. L17.

8 a *verb trans.* Devise, hit upon by mental effort; plan, plot. *arch.* ME. ▸**b** *verb intrans.* Foll. by *of*, (arch.) (*up*)*on*: devise a plan etc., plan, plot, or contrive something. L16.

9 *verb intrans.* Foll. by *of*, (arch.) (*up*)*on*: consider, have regard to something. ME.

📖 **6a** H. BELLOC To think that you can get to a place like that for less than a pound! M. LASKI What a fool I am, I never thought to look. **b** D. HALLIDAY Remember how Comer came bursting in one evening? It makes you think, doesn't it? D. H. LAWRENCE He thought of his boyhood in Teversham. **7a** TENNYSON You thought to break a country heart For pastime. T. HARDY He . . thought he would send for his mother. **b** A. BROOKNER I am thinking of joining the Open University. **c** C. PATMORE You, with your looks and catching air, To think of Vaughan! **8b** M. MOFFATT I could think of no other honest way of presenting such sensitive material. **9** T. F. POWYS He had his own character to think of—his own honour.

▸ **III** Be of opinion, deem, judge.

10 a *verb trans.* Hold the opinion, believe, judge; consider, suppose, often without any great assurance. OE. ▸**b** *verb intrans.* Hold a certain opinion. ME. ▸**c** *verb intrans.* Have a particular opinion of a person or thing. Foll. by *of* or (dial.) *to* and adverb or adverbial phrase. LME.

11 *verb trans.* Believe possible or likely; suspect; expect, anticipate. LME. ▸**b** *verb intrans.* Foll. by *of* or (now *rare*) *for* after *as* or *than*: expect, hope for, suppose. Now *rare*. L15.

12 *verb trans.* Judge or consider to exist; believe in the existence of. *rare.* M16.

📖 **10a** HOBBES Some, that have the ambition to be thought eloquent. W. CATHER I thought running water never froze. C. P. SNOW She thought I was both spoilt and neglected. B. KOPS No one thinks . . that you're going to die. M. AMIS I was at their mercy, or thought I was. G. GREENE Once I saw smoke coming out of a trench and I thought it was the dragon. **10b** A. B. GIAMATTI I am hardly the first to think so. **c** H. JAMES I like to be well thought of. **11** DEFOE He, thinking no harm, agreed. OED I little thought to find you here!

Phrases: ***be unable to hear oneself think***: see HEAR *verb*. ***come to think of it***: see COME *verb*. **I don't think** *slang* (after an ironical statement) I mean the opposite. **that's what you think**: expr. emphatic, sometimes scornful, disagreement. **think again** revise one's plans or opinions. **think the better of**, **think all the better of** form a higher opinion of. **think aloud** utter one's thoughts as soon as they occur. **think better of** change one's mind about (an intention) after reconsideration. ***think big***: see BIG *adverb*. ***think fit***: see FIT *adjective* 3. **think for oneself** form independent opinions, have an independent mind or attitude. **think highly of** = ***think much of*** below. ***think in terms of***: see TERM *noun*. ***think it much***. ***think it scorn***: see SCORN *noun*. **think little of** regard as insignificant or unremarkable. **think long** (*obsolete* exc. *dial.*) grow weary with waiting; long, yearn. ***think much***. **think much of** have a good opinion of. ***think nothing of***, ***think nothing of it***: see NOTHING *pronoun & noun*. **think on one's feet** react to events etc. quickly and effectively. ***think scorn***, ***think scorn of***: see SCORN *noun*. ***think shame***: see SHAME *noun*. ***think straight***: see STRAIGHT *adverb*[1]. ***think the world of***: see WORLD *noun*. **think twice (about)** hesitate, consider carefully, avoid acting hastily. **think with** agree with. **what do you think?**, **who do you think?** *colloq.*: introducing a surprising or exciting piece of information.

With adverbs in specialized senses: **think back** recall, reflect on; look back (*on* or *to*). **think out** find out or devise by thinking; produce or resolve by thinking; consider carefully. **think over** give careful and continued thought to in order to reach a decision. **think through** consider carefully and thoroughly. **think up** *colloq.* devise, produce by thought.

Comb.: **think-aloud** *adjective* (PSYCHOLOGY) designating or pertaining to data collected by asking a subject to express his or her thoughts out loud while performing a specific task; **think balloon** in a comic-strip cartoon, a circle floating above a character's head containing the character's thought in direct speech; **think box** *joc. & colloq.* the brain; **think bubble** = ***think balloon*** above. **think-in** a meeting, conference, etc., for thoughtful discussion; **think-piece** (chiefly JOURNALISM) an article containing discussion, analysis, opinion, etc., rather than facts or news; **think-tank** (*a*) *US colloq.* the brain; (*b*) a body of experts, as a research orginization, providing advice and ideas on specific national or commercial problems; (*c*) a meeting of experts; **think-tanker** *colloq.* a member of a think-tank.

thinkable /ˈθɪŋkəb(ə)l/ *adjective.* E19.
[from THINK *verb*² + -ABLE.]
1 Able to be deemed real or actual; imaginable as an existing fact. E19.
2 Able to be thought of; such as one can form an idea of; cogitable. M19.
¶ Earlier (LME) in UNTHINKABLE.
■ **thinkableness** *noun* (*rare*) L19. **thinkably** *adverb* in thought; conceivably; (earlier in UNTHINKABLY): M20.

thinker /ˈθɪŋkə/ *noun.* LME.
[from THINK *verb*² + -ER¹.]
1 A person who thinks, esp. in a specified way. Also, a person who has highly developed powers of thought. LME.
2 A thing which thinks; the mind, the brain. *rare.* M19.

📖 **1** G. CHALMERS Lloyd . . was an original thinker rather than the collector of the opinions of others. EDWARD WHITE Not one of them makes the slightest pretension to be a scholar or a thinker. ***freethinker***: see FREE *adjective, noun, & adverb.* ***wishful thinker***: see WISHFUL 2a.

thinking /ˈθɪŋkɪŋ/ *noun.* ME.
[from THINK *verb*² + -ING¹.]
1 a The action of THINK *verb*². ME. ▸**b** In *pl.* Thoughts; courses of thought. LME.
2 Opinion, judgement, belief. LME.

📖 **1a** *Time* Microcomputers have a central processing unit to do the thinking. R. D. LAING How does this type of psychiatric thinking affect clinical practice? ***freethinking***, ***lateral thinking***, ***positive thinking***, ***right-thinking***, etc. **good thinking**: expr. approval of a clever or well-thought-out plan, observation, etc. **high thinking** intellectual and idealistic opinions or attitudes; ***plain living and high thinking***: see LIVING *noun*¹. **put on one's thinking cap** *colloq.* meditate on a problem. ***vertical thinking***: see VERTICAL *adjective.* ***way of thinking***: see WAY *noun.* ***wishful thinking***: see WISHFUL 2a.

Comb.: **thinking-aloud** *adjective* (PSYCHOLOGY) = ***think-aloud*** s.v. THINK *verb*². **thinking-box** *colloq.* (*a*) = ***think box*** s.v. THINK *verb*²; (*b*) a room in which to think, a study; **Thinking Day** 22 February, the joint birthday of the first Chief Scout and Chief Guide, on which members of the Guides Association think of Guides all over the world; **thinking distance** the distance travelled by a motor vehicle from the time when the driver decides to stop until the time when he or she applies the brakes; **thinking part** *Theatrical slang* a theatrical role with no lines, a silent part.

thinking /ˈθɪŋkɪŋ/ *ppl adjective.* M17.
[formed as prec. + -ING².]
1 That thinks; having or using thought; cogitative. M17.
2 Given to thinking; thoughtful, reflective, intellectual. M17.
1 ***thinking subject***: see SUBJECT *noun* 5c.
■ **thinkingly** *adverb* in a thinking manner; with thought, deliberately; (earlier in UNTHINKINGLY): M19. **thinkingness** *noun* thinking quality or ability; thoughtfulness, intellectuality: L17.

thio- /ˈθʌɪəʊ/ *combining form.* Before a vowel also **thi-**, **thion-**. Also as attrib. adjective **thio**.
[from Greek *theion* sulphur: see -O-.]
Of, pertaining to, or containing sulphur; *spec.* in CHEMISTRY, forming names of compounds containing sulphur, esp. in place of oxygen in a molecular structure.
■ **thiaˈcetazone** *noun* [ACET(YL, SEMICARB)AZONE] PHARMACOLOGY a semicarbazone used as a bacteriostatic drug to treat tuberculosis and leprosy M20. **thiazide** *noun* [AZ(INE, OX)IDE] PHARMACOLOGY any of a class of sulphur-containing drugs that increase the excretion of sodium and chloride and are used as diuretics and auxiliary hypotensive agents M20. **thiazine** *noun* [AZINE] any of a class of dyes (e.g. thionine and methylene blue) whose molecules contain a ring of one nitrogen, one sulphur, and four carbon atoms L19. **thiazole** *noun* [AZO-, -OL] CHEMISTRY a foul-smelling liquid whose molecule is a ring of one nitrogen, one sulphur, and three carbon atoms L19. **thiaˈzolidine** *noun* [-IDINE] CHEMISTRY a liquid, C_3H_7NS, whose molecular structure is that of thiazole with an additional hydrogen atom attached to the nitrogen and each carbon atom; any compound containing this ring structure in its molecule: E20. **thio-acid** *noun* (CHEMISTRY) an acid, esp. an organic acid, in which one or more oxygen atoms in the molecule are replaced by divalent sulphur L19. **thio-ˈalcohol** *noun* (CHEMISTRY) a thiol having an ·SH group attached to an alkyl or cycloalkyl residue (cf. *thiophenol*) E20. **thiobacˈterium** *noun* = ***sulphur bacterium*** s.v. SULPHUR *noun* E20. **thioˈcarbamate** *noun* (CHEMISTRY) a salt of the ion NH_2CSO^- or a substituted derivative of this ion L19. **thioˈcarbamide** *noun* (CHEMISTRY) = THIOUREA L19. **thiochrome** *noun* (BIOCHEMISTRY) a yellow basic solid, $C_{12}H_{14}N_4OS$, formed by oxidation of thiamine and having a strong blue fluorescence in solution M20. **thiˈoctic** *adjective* [OCT(ANO)IC]: ***thioctic acid*** (CHEMISTRY), any of a series of isomeric fatty acids whose molecules contain eight carbon atoms and a ring formed by a disulphide group; *esp.* = ***LIPOIC acid***: M20. **thioˈcyanate** *noun* (CHEMISTRY) a salt or ester of thiocyanic acid L19. **thiocyˈanic** *adjective*: ***thiocyanic acid*** (CHEMISTRY), an unstable liquid, N·CSH, with a penetrating odour, the parent acid of thiocyanates L19. **thiodiˈglycol** *noun* (CHEMISTRY) a dihydric alcohol, $(CH_2CH_2OH)_2S$, used as a solvent and in chemical syntheses, including that of mustard gas L19. **thioˈester** *noun* (CHEMISTRY) the thio analogue of an ester, containing the group ·CO·S· M20. **thio-ˈether** *noun* (CHEMISTRY) a compound in which an atom of sulphur is bonded to two organic radicals. L19. **thioˈguanine** *noun* (BIOCHEMISTRY) a cytotoxic mercapto derivative of guanine, used to treat leukaemia (also more fully ***6-thioguanine***) M20. **thioˈketone** *noun* (CHEMISTRY) a thio analogue of a ketone, having the general formula RR′C=S (where R and R′ are alkyl groups) L19. **Thiokol** *noun* (proprietary name for) any of various polysulphide rubbers and liquids M20. **thioˈmersal** *noun* [MER(CURY, SAL(ICYLATE)] a bacteriostatic and fungistatic organomercury compound, $C_9H_9O_2SHgNa$, used as a medical disinfectant and as a preservative for biological products M20. **thionazin** /-ˈneɪzɪn/ *noun* [(PYR)AZINE] an organophosphorus compound, $C_8H_{13}N_2O_3PS$, used as an agricultural insecticide and nematocide M20. **thionine** *noun* a brownish-black dye, $C_{12}H_9N_3S$, used esp. as a stain in microscopy L19. **thionyl** *noun* (CHEMISTRY) the divalent group or radical :SO M19. **thiophanate** /θʌɪˈɒfəneɪt/ *noun* [formed as ALLOPHANE + -ATE¹] a colourless crystalline compound, $C_6H_4(NH{\cdot}CS{\cdot}NH{\cdot}COOC_2H_5)_2$, used chiefly as a veterinary anthelmintic; ***thiophanate-methyl***, an analogue of thiophanate containing methyl in place of the ethyl groups, used as a systemic fungicide, esp. in agriculture: L20. **thiophene** *noun* [after BENZENE] CHEMISTRY a colourless flammable liquid, C_4H_4S, whose molecule is a five-membered ring and which occurs in coal tar and petroleum L19. **thioˈphenol** *noun* (CHEMISTRY) a thiol having an ·SH group attached directly to a benzene ring (cf. ***thio-alcohol***); *spec.* the simplest of these, C_6H_5SH, a colourless liquid smelling of garlic: L19. **thioreˈdoxin** *noun* [REDOX] BIOCHEMISTRY any of several globular proteins which participate in intracellular electron-transfer by means of the sulphydryl groups of cysteine residues M20. **thioridazine** /-ˈdɛzɪːn/ *noun* [(PIPE)RID(INE, AZINE] PHARMACOLOGY a phenothiazine derivative, $C_{21}H_{26}N_2S_2$, used as a tranquillizer, esp. in the treatment of mental illness M20. **thiosemiˈcarbazide** *noun* (CHEMISTRY) the thio analogue, $NH_2{\cdot}CS{\cdot}NH{\cdot}NH_2$, of semicarbazide, used esp. as a rodenticide and as a stabilizer in organic liquids L19. **thiosemiˈcarbazone** *noun* (CHEMISTRY) a thio analogue of a semicarbazone, the oxygen of the latter being replaced by sulphur E20. **thioˈsulphate** *noun* (CHEMISTRY) any of the salts or esters of thiosulphuric acid, several of which are used in bleaching and photography (formerly called ***hyposulphite***) L19. **thiosulˈphuric** *adjective*: ***thiosulphuric acid*** (CHEMISTRY), an unstable acid, $H_2S_2O_3$, which is known only in solution and is the parent acid of thiosulphates L19. **thioˈtepa** *noun* (PHARMACOLOGY) the thio analogue of tepa, used to treat cancer M20. **thioˈuracil** *noun* (CHEMISTRY & PHARMACOLOGY) a mercapto derivative of uracil, sometimes used to inhibit thyroid secretion E20.

thioglycollic /ˌθʌɪə(ʊ)glʌɪˈkɒlɪk/ *adjective.* Also **-colic.** L19.
[from THIO- + GLYCOLLIC.]
CHEMISTRY. ***thioglycollic acid***, a colourless toxic liquid with a strong odour, $HSCH_2COOH$, which is a reducing agent used esp. in the pharmaceutical industry, in hair treatment products, and in analytical tests for ferric iron; mercaptoethanoic acid.
■ **thioˈglycollate** *noun* a salt or ester of thioglycollic acid L19.

thioindigo /θʌɪəʊˈɪndɪgəʊ/ *noun.* Pl. **-os.** E20.
[from THIO- + INDIGO.]
A red vat dye in which the two imino groups of indigotin are replaced by sulphur atoms. Also, = THIOINDIGOID *noun*.
■ **thioindigoid** *noun & adjective* (*a*) *noun* any of a class of mainly orange, red, and violet vat dyes that are substituted derivatives of thioindigo, used esp. in textile printing; (*b*) *adjective* of the nature of a thioindigoid: M20.

thiol /ˈθʌɪɒl/ *noun.* L19.
[from THIO- + -OL.]
CHEMISTRY. **1** The group ·SH, which is the sulphur analogue of the functional group of alcohols. Also called ***sulphydryl***. Usu. in *comb.* L19.
2 A compound containing an ·SH group; a mercaptan. E20.

thion- *combining form* see THIO-.

thionic /θʌɪˈɒnɪk/ *adjective.* L19.
[formed as THIO- + -IC (with -*n*- inserted or retained from Greek *theion*).]
CHEMISTRY. ***thionic acid***, any of a series of acids including dithionic acid and related acids represented by the formula $HSO_3(S)_nHSO_3$. Freq. with prefix indicating total number of sulphur atoms, as ***trithionic***, ***tetrathionic***, etc.
■ **thionate** *noun* (CHEMISTRY) a salt or ester of a thionic acid L19.

thiopental /θʌɪə(ʊ)ˈpɛnt(ə)l, -tal/ *noun.* Chiefly *US.* M20.
[from next: see -AL².]
PHARMACOLOGY. = next. Also ***thiopental sodium***.

thiopentone /θʌɪəˈpɛntəʊn/ *noun.* M20.
[from THIO- + PENT(OBARBIT)ONE.]
PHARMACOLOGY. A sulphur analogue of pentobarbitone; (more fully ***thiopentone sodium***) the sodium salt of this, used as a rapid-acting general anaesthetic and hypnotic.
¶ A proprietary name for this drug is PENTOTHAL.

thiourea /ˌθʌɪəʊjʊˈriːə/ *noun.* L19.
[from THIO- + UREA.]
CHEMISTRY. A crystalline compound, $SC(NH_2)_2$, used esp. in chemical synthesis, in photographic processes, and as a mould inhibitor. Also called ***thiocarbamide***.

thir /ðəː/ *pronoun & adjective. Scot. & north.* ME.
[Perh. from Old Norse *þeir* those.]
= THESE *pronoun & adjective.*

thiram /ˈθʌɪram/ *noun.* M20.
[Abbreviation of the systematic name: see THIURAM.]
CHEMISTRY. A sulphur-containing compound used as a fungicide and seed protectant; tetramethylthiuram disulphide, $(CH_3)_2N{\cdot}CS{\cdot}S_2{\cdot}SC{\cdot}N(CH_3)_2$.

third /θəːd/ *adjective, noun, & adverb (ordinal numeral).*
[Old English (late Northumbrian) *þird(d)a*, *-e*, *þridda* = Old Frisian *thredda*, Old Saxon *þriddio*, Old High German *dritto* (Dutch *derde*, German *dritte*), Old Norse *þriði*, Gothic *þridja*, from Germanic from Indo-European: cf. Latin *tertius*, Greek *tritos*.]
▶ **A** *adjective.* Next in order after the second, that is number three in a series, (represented by 3rd). OE.

📖 S. BELLOW I had been turned down twice and did not want it to happen a third time. *Blackwood's Magazine* We found our way into the city, the third largest in that country. *Gay Times*: *Gay Tattoo & Piercing Club.* Regular meetings, 3rd Fri each month, 9pm. ***third conjugation***, ***third declension***, etc. ***play third fiddle***: see FIDDLE *noun.* ***third law of thermodynamics***: see THERMODYNAMICS.

▶ **B** *noun.* **1** The third person or thing of a category, series, etc., identified contextually, as day of the month, (following a proper name) person, esp. monarch or pope, of the specified name, base in baseball, etc. OE. ▸**b** (A person having) a place in the third class in an examination list. E20. ▸**c** = ***third gear*** below. E20.
2 Each of three equal parts into which something is or may be divided; a fraction which when multiplied by three gives one, (= ***third part*** below). LME.
3 MUSIC. An interval embracing three consecutive notes in the diatonic scale; a note a third above another given note; a chord of two notes a third apart. LME.
4 A subdivision of a measure or dimension which has itself already been subdivided twice in the same ratio; the subdivision next below second (cf. SECOND *noun*² 6). *obsolete* exc. *Hist.* M16.
5 In *pl.* Goods of the third degree of quality. M18.
6 A third-class compartment, carriage, or section, on a train etc. M19.

📖 **1** *Sunday Correspondent* The general fired two warning shots . . and then a third. T. TRYON Junior rounded third and sprinted for home. ***law of excluded third***, ***principle of excluded third***: see EXCLUDE 5. **b** J. E. FLECKER I have got a third in Mods! **2** *Daily Telegraph* One third of the recruits were schizophrenic. B. CHATWIN Able to knock a third off the price. **on thirds** *Austral. & NZ* operating a system in farming, esp. sheep-farming, whereby a tenant farmer or employee does the work in return for one third of the profits. **third-and-fourth**, **thirds-and-fourths** *US* a system in cotton and corn farming, whereby the tenant partly pays for materials and the landowner receives a proportion of the crops.

Special collocations & comb.: (As ordinal.) Forming compound numerals with multiples of ten, as ***forty-third*** (43rd), ***five-thousand-and-third*** (5003rd), etc. (As adjective.) **third age** [French *troisième âge*] the period in life of active retirement; old age. **third-best** *adjective & noun* (a thing) of inferior or third-class quality. **third country** a Third-World country. ***third cousin***: see COUSIN *noun.* **third degree** *spec.* (*a*) the most serious category of burn; (*b*) *US* LAW the least serious category of crime; (*c*) a long and severe interrogation, esp. by the police, in order to bring about a confession or obtain information. **third-degree** *adjective & verb* (*a*) *adjective* (of a burn) of the most severe kind, affecting all layers of skin; *US* LAW (of a crime, as assault) next in culpability after second-degree; (*b*) *verb trans.* subject to a long and severe interrogation. **third ear** (esp. in PSYCHOANALYSIS) the ability to perceive intuitively what lies behind the words actually heard. ***Third Estate***: see ESTATE *noun.* **third eye** HINDUISM & BUDDHISM the eye of insight or destruction in the middle of the forehead of an image of a god, esp. Siva; *transf.* the power of intuitive insight. **third eyelid** the nictitating membrane of many animals. **third finger** the finger third from the thumb. **third floor** the floor of a building separated by two others or (*N. Amer.*) one other from the ground floor. **third flute** MUSIC a flute pitched a minor third above the ordinary flute. **third force** a political party or parties standing between two extreme or opposing parties; *gen.* any neutral power or third body or group. **third gear** the third in a sequence of forward gears in a motor vehicle, bicycle, etc. **third-generation** *adjective* (of a computer) distinguished by the introduction of integrated circuits and operating systems and belonging essentially to the period 1960–70. **third house** *US slang* the lobby in the American Congress. ***Third International***: see INTERNATIONAL *noun* 3. ***third last***: see LAST *adverb, adjective, & noun*⁵. **third man** (*a*) CRICKET (the position occupied by) a fielder placed near the boundary behind the slips; (*b*) LACROSSE (the position occupied by) a defence player placed behind the centre; (*c*) PHILOSOPHY [Greek *tritos anthrōpos*] an Aristotelian term for the first member of an infinite set of further forms said to be logically required by the Platonic theory that e.g. the form of man is itself a separate (archetypal) man (esp. in ***third man argument***); (*d*) *Boxing slang* the referee; (*e*) an unidentified third participant in a crime. **third market** *US* trade in stock undertaken outside the stock exchange. **third order** a religious order of lay members in a religious fraternity, not subject to the strict rules of the regulars. **third part** (now *rare*) = sense B.2 above. **third party** (*a*) a party or person besides the two primarily concerned; (*b*) a bystander. **third-party** *adjective* (of insurance) covering damage or injury suffered by a person other than the insured. ***third person***: see PERSON *noun.* **third position** BALLET the disposition of the body in which the feet are parallel and one behind the other, so that the heel of the front foot fits into the hollow of the instep of the back foot. ***third power***: see POWER *noun* 12. **Third Programme** *Hist.* one of the three national radio networks of the BBC from 1946 until

1967, when it was replaced by Radio 3. **third rail** in some electric railways, an extra rail which conveys the current (cf. CONDUCTOR-*rail*); also, an extra rail for trains with a wider gauge. **third-rail** *adjective* (*US slang*) designating highly intoxicating alcoholic liquor. **third reading** a third presentation of a bill to a legislature, in the UK to debate committee reports and in the US to consider it for the last time. ***Third Reich***: see REICH. ***third root***: see ROOT *noun*[1]. ***Third Secretary***: see SECRETARY *noun*. ***third sex***: see SEX *noun*. ***third slip***: see SLIP *noun*[3] 11. **thirdsman** a third person or party, *esp.* one called in as an intermediary or arbiter. **third stream** a style of music which combines elements of jazz and classical music. **third ventricle** the part of the central cavity of the brain that lies between the thalami and hypothalami of the two hemispheres. ***third water***: see WATER *noun* 10. **third way** a way of proceeding which is an alternative to two established or extreme approaches, esp. a political agenda which is centrist and consensus-based rather than left- or right-wing. THIRD WORLD. ***Third World War***: see WORLD *noun*.

▶ **C** *adverb*. Thirdly. **L19.**

> *Atlantic*: Third, the questions . . must be treated with seriousness.

■ **thirdly** *adverb* in the third place **E16**. **thirdness** *noun* **L19**.

third /θəːd/ *verb trans.* **LME.**
[from prec.]
1 Divide into three equal or corresponding parts; reduce to one third of the number or bulk. **LME.**
2 Support (a motion, proposition, etc.) as a third speaker; support a seconder. **M17.**

thirdborough /ˈθəːdbʌrə/ *noun*. Also †**thridborrow** & other vars. **L15.**
[Prob. corrupt. of *frithborh* s.v. FRITH *noun*[1].]
Hist. Orig., the chief of a frank-pledge. Later, the conservator of peace in a tithing, a petty constable. Cf. BORSHOLDER.

third class /θəːd ˈklɑːs; *as adjective also* ˈθəːdklɑːs/ *noun phr., adjective, & adverb*. As adjective & adverb also **third-class**. **M19.**
[from THIRD *adjective* + CLASS *noun*.]
▶ **A** *noun phr.* The third of a ranked series of classes into which people or things are grouped; the third-best accommodation in a train, boat, etc.; (a person with) a place in the third-highest division of an examination list. **M19.**
▶ **B** *adjective*. Belonging to, achieving, travelling by, etc., the class next below the second; of the third-best quality. **M19.**

> *Holiday Which?* The third class decks are crammed with backpackers.

▶ **C** *adverb*. By third-class accommodation in a train, boat, etc. **M19.**

> C. M. YONGE I will go third class, and walk from the station.

third hand /θəːd ˈhand; *as adjective also* ˈθəːdhand/ *noun phr. & adjective*. As adjective also **third-hand**. **M16.**
[from THIRD *adjective* + HAND *noun*.]
▶ **A** *noun phr.* ***at third hand***, †***at the third hand***, from a second intermediary; at the second remove from the original source. **M16.**
▶ **B** *adjective*. Obtained or drawn from a second-hand source; further from the original, and so less good, authoritative, etc., than something second-hand. **L16.**

> *Times* Early years of struggle: the rented flats, . . the third-hand bangers, the terrifying overdraft.

third-rate /θəːdˈreɪt; *as adjective also* ˈθəːdreɪt/ *adjective & noun*. Also (the usual form in sense A.1) **third rate**. **M17.**
[from THIRD *adjective* + RATE *noun*[1].]
▶ **A** *noun*. **1** *Hist.* The third of the rates or classes by which warships were distinguished according to the number of guns they carried; a warship of this rate or class. **M17.**
2 A person or thing of third-rate or inferior class. *rare*. **E19.**
▶ **B** *adjective*. **1** *Hist.* Of a warship: of the third rate. **M17.**
2 Of the third class in terms of quality or excellence; below second-rate; of very low or inferior quality. **E19.**

> **2** *Atlantic* An underpaid hack in a windowless annex of a third-rate institution.

■ **third-rater** *noun* a third-rate person or thing **E19**.

Third World /θəːd ˈwəːld/ *noun & adjectival phr.* Also **third world**. **M20.**
[from THIRD *adjective* + WORLD *noun*.]
▶ **A** *noun*. Those countries which are aligned with neither the (former) Communist nor the non-Communist bloc; *esp.* the developing countries of the world, usu. those of Africa, Asia, and Latin America. **M20.**
▶ **B** *attrib.* or as *adjective*. Of, pertaining to, or designating a country or countries forming part of the Third World. **M20.**

■ **Third Worlder** *noun* an inhabitant of the Third World **L20**. **Third Worldism** *noun* an ideology or policy of support for the Third World **L20**.

thirl /θəːl/ *noun*[1]. Long *obsolete* exc. *dial.*
[Old English *þȳrel*, from THROUGH *preposition & adverb* + -EL[1].]
1 A hole, a perforation; an aperture, an opening. **OE.**
2 *spec.* Either of the two holes or orifices of the nose, a nostril. **ME.**
1 ***nose-thirl***: see NOSTRIL *noun*.

thirl /θəːl/ *noun*[2]. *Scot.* **M16.**
[from THIRL *verb*[2]. Cf. THRILL *noun*[1].]
Astriction of lands and tenants to a particular mill (cf. THIRLAGE 2); the lands so astricted (cf. SUCKEN *noun* 2).

thirl /θəːl/ *verb*[1]. *obsolete* exc. *Scot. & dial.*
[Old English *þyrlian* (cf. Middle High German *dürkeln*), from THIRL *noun*[1]. Cf. THRILL *verb*[1].]
1 *verb trans.* Pierce (a body) with or as with a sharp-pointed instrument; bore a hole in; perforate. **OE.**
†**2** *verb trans. & intrans.* Pass through or *through*; penetrate (*into*). **ME–M16.**
3 *verb trans.* MINING. Cut through (a wall of coal etc.). **L17.**
4 *verb trans. & intrans.* Affect or pass *around* or *through* with a thrill of emotion etc. **E18.**

thirl /θəːl/ *verb*[2] *trans.* Chiefly *Scot.* **M16.**
[Metath. alt. of THRILL *verb*[2].]
†**1** Reduce to or hold in bondage or servitude; enslave. Only in **M16.**
2 SCOTS LAW. Bind or astrict (land or a tenant) to a servitude, esp. *to* a particular mill. Cf. THIRLAGE 2. **L16.**
3 Bind or oblige (a person) to work for or serve one particular party; *fig.* oblige or restrict in service to. Foll. by *to*. **E19.**

> **3** *Economist* He was in debt, and thirled to the production of two novels a year.

thirlage /ˈθəːlɪdʒ/ *noun*. *Scot.* **E16.**
[Metath. alt. of THRILLAGE.]
†**1** Bondage, servitude. **E16–E17.**
2 LAW. A servitude imposed on the tenants of certain lands, restricting their custom to a particular mill, forge, etc.; *spec.* the obligation of tenants to grind their corn at a particular mill and to pay the recognized dues or multure. **L17.** ▸**b** The multure exacted under this system. **L18.**

thirst /θəːst/ *noun*.
[Old English *þurst* = Old Saxon *þurst* (Dutch *dorst*), Old & mod. High German *durst*, from West Germanic (cf. Old Norse *þorsti*, Gothic *þaurstei*) from Indo-European base repr. also by Latin *torrere* dry, parch.]
1 The physical need to drink liquid; the uncomfortable or painful sensation caused by or the physical condition resulting from this. **OE.**
2 *fig.* A vehement desire *for*, *after*, *to do* something. **ME.**

> **1** A. CARTER My lips were already cracking with thirst. *Westminster Gazette* Orange wine is most refreshing and thirst-quenching. **2** C. V. WEDGWOOD The popular thirst for news stimulated by the Civil War.

Comb.: **thirst-country**, **thirst-land** a waterless tract of land, esp. in South Africa.

■ **thirstful** *adjective* (*rare*) thirsty **M19**. **thirstless** *adjective* having no thirst, not thirsty **L16**.

thirst /θəːst/ *verb*.
[Old English *þyrstan* = Old Saxon *þurstian* (Dutch *dorsten*), Old High German *dursten* (German *dürsten*), Old Norse *þyrsta*.]
†**1** *verb intrans. impers.* in **me thirsts**, **me thirsteth**, etc., I am thirsty. **OE–LME.**
2 *verb intrans.* Feel thirst, be thirsty; *transf.* (of ground or a plant) need moisture, be dry. **OE.**
3 *fig.* **a** *verb intrans.* Have a craving or strong desire *for*, *after*, *to do*. **OE.** ▸†**b** *verb trans.* Crave, long for. **OE–E18.**

> **3a** G. MACDONALD I entered, thirsting for the shade it promised.

■ **thirster** *noun* a person who thirsts *for* or *after* something **LME**.

thirsty /ˈθəːsti/ *adjective*.
[Old English *þurstig*, *þyrstig* = Old Saxon *þurstig*, Old High German *durstag* (German *durstig*): see THIRST *noun*, -Y[1].]
1 a Feeling thirst; having a need to drink liquid. **OE.** ▸**b** *transf.* Of ground or a plant: needing moisture, dry. **LME.**
2 *fig.* Having or characterized by a strong desire or craving. **OE.** ▸**b** Of a motor vehicle, engine, etc.: that has a high fuel-consumption rate. **L20.**
3 Causing thirst. Now *colloq.* **LME.**

■ **thirstily** *adverb* **M16**. **thirstiness** *noun* **L15**.

thirteen /θəːˈtiːn, ˈθəːtiːn/ *adjective & noun* (*cardinal numeral*).
[Old English *þrēotīene* = Old Saxon *thriutein* (Dutch *dertien*), Old High German *drīzehan* (German *dreizehn*), Old Norse *þrettán*: see THREE, -TEEN.]
▶ **A** *adjective*. **1** One more than twelve (a cardinal numeral represented by 13 in arabic numerals, xiii, XIII in roman). **OE.**
†**2** = THIRTEENTH *adjective*. **OE–E19.**
▶ **B** *noun*. **1** Thirteen persons or things identified contextually, as years of age, chances (in giving odds), minutes, shillings (now *Hist.*), pence, etc. **OE.**
2 One more than twelve as an abstract number; the symbols or figures representing this (13 in arabic numerals, xiii, XIII in roman). **LME.**
3 The thirteenth of a set or series with numbered members, the one designated thirteen, (usu. ***number thirteen***, or with specification, as ***book thirteen***, ***chapter thirteen***, etc.); a size etc. denoted by thirteen, a garment etc. of such a size (also ***size thirteen***). **E16.**
4 A set of thirteen; a thing having a set of thirteen as an essential or distinguishing feature. Formerly also *spec.* (*Anglo-Irish*), a silver shilling, from its being worth thirteen pence of Irish copper currency. **E18.**

> **1** S. GRAY At thirteen I was embarrassed to wear a swimming costume. ***old Thirteen***: see OLD *adjective*.
> **2** J. WOODFORDE The unlucky Number of thirteen sat down to dinner.

Comb.: Forming compound numerals with multiples of a hundred, as *513* (read ***five hundred and thirteen***, US also ***five hundred thirteen***) etc. In dates used for one thousand three hundred, as *1340* (read ***thirteen forty***), ***thirteen-eighties***, etc. With nouns + -ER[1] forming nouns with the sense 'something (identified contextually) being of or having thirteen —s', as ***thirteen-tonner*** etc. Special combs., as **thirteen-year cicada**, **thirteen-year locust** a periodical cicada of the race in the southern US whose nymphs emerge in a 13-year cycle (cf. SEVENTEEN-*year cicada*).

¶ That the number thirteen is unlucky is a widespread superstition.

■ **thirteener** *noun* (**a**) *Anglo-Irish* (now *rare*) a silver shilling (see THIRTEEN *noun* 4); (**b**) (BRIDGE etc.) the last unplayed card in a suit, after the other twelve have been played in tricks: **M18**.

thirteenth /θəːˈtiːnθ, ˈθəːtiːnθ/ *adjective & noun* (*ordinal numeral*).
[Old English *þrēotēoþa*, *prie-* repl. in northern Middle English by (metathesized and non-metathesized) forms of Old Norse *þrettánde* from which, in 16, the mod. form developed, as if from THIRTEEN + -TH[2].]
▶ **A** *adjective*. Next in order after the twelfth, that is number thirteen in a series, (represented by 13th). **OE.**

> W. STUBBS The thirteenth century is the golden age of English churchmanship. **thirteenth part** *arch.* = sense B.3 below.

▶ **B** *noun*. **1** The thirteenth person or thing of a category, series, etc., identified contextually, as day of the month, (following a proper name) person, esp. monarch or pope, of the specified name, etc. **OE.**
2 MUSIC. An interval embracing thirteen consecutive notes in the diatonic scale; a note a thirteenth above or below another given note; a chord of two notes a thirteenth apart, or based around the thirteenth of a note. **LME.**
3 Each of thirteen equal parts into which something is or may be divided, a fraction which when multiplied by thirteen gives one (= ***thirteenth part*** above); *spec.* (*Hist.*) a tax equal to one such part formerly imposed on personal property. **E17.**

> **1** A. DAY Tuesday being the thirteenth of this instant.

Comb.: Forming compound numerals with multiples of a hundred, as ***five-hundred-and-thirteenth*** (*513th*) etc.

■ **thirteenthly** *adverb* in the thirteenth place **E17**.

thirtieth /ˈθəːtɪɪθ/ *adjective & noun* (*ordinal numeral*).
[Old English *þrītigoþa*, *þritteogoþa*, repl. in Middle English by forms from THIRTY + -TH[2]. Cf. Old Norse *þrítugande*, *þrítugti*.]
▶ **A** *adjective*. Next in order after the twenty-ninth, that is number thirty in a series, (represented by 30th). **OE.**
thirtieth part *arch.* = sense B.2 below.
▶ **B** *noun*. **1** The thirtieth person or thing of a category, series, etc., identified contextually. **OE.**
2 Each of thirty equal parts into which something is or may be divided, a fraction which when multiplied by thirty gives one, (= ***thirtieth part*** above). **E19.**

Comb.: Forming compound numerals with multiples of a hundred, as ***two-hundred-and-thirtieth*** (*230th*) etc. and (*arch.*) with numerals below ten, as ***five-and-thirtieth*** etc.

thirty /ˈθəːti/ *adjective & noun* (*cardinal numeral*).
[Old English *þrītig* = Old Saxon *thrītig* (Dutch *dertig*), Old High German *drīzzug* (German *dreissig*), Old Norse *þrírtegr*, Gothic (accus.) *þrins tiguns*: see THREE, -TY[2].]
▶ **A** *adjective*. Three times ten (a cardinal numeral represented by 30 in arabic numerals, xxx, XXX in roman). **OE.**

> *Folk Roots* A . . festival . . with over thirty events. **the Thirty Years War**, **the Thirty Years' War** the religious wars of 1618–48 fought chiefly on German soil. **like thirty cents** *US slang* cheap, worthless.

▶ **B** *noun*. **1** Thirty persons or things identified contextually, as years of age, points, runs, etc., in a game, chances (in giving odds), minutes, etc. **OE.**
2 Three times ten as an abstract number; the symbols or figures representing this (30 in arabic numerals, xxx, XXX in roman). **OE.**
3 A set of thirty; a thing having a set of thirty as an essential or distinguishing feature. **LME.**
4 The thirtieth of a set or series with numbered members; the one designated thirty, (usu. ***number***

thirty, or with specification, as ***chapter thirty***, ***verse thirty***, etc.); a size etc. denoted by thirty, a garment etc. of such a size, (also ***size thirty***). **E16.**

5 In *pl.* The numbers from 30 to 39 inclusive, esp. denoting years of a century or units of a scale of temperature; *one's* years of life between the ages of 30 and 39. **L19.**

6 The end; *spec.* (JOURNALISM) 30 written at the bottom of an article etc. to indicate that it is finished. Chiefly *US slang.* **L19.**

> 📖 **5** B. W. ALDISS A delicate little woman in her early thirties. *attrib.*: J. MUNRO As English as a Thirties farce.

Comb.: Forming compound numerals (cardinal or ordinal) with numerals below ten, as ***thirty-nine*** (39), ***thirty-first*** (31st), etc., and (cardinals) with multiples of a hundred, as **430** (read ***four hundred and thirty***, US also ***four hundred thirty***), etc. With nouns + -ER¹ forming nouns with the sense 'something (identified contextually) being of or having thirty —s' as ***thirty seater***, ***thirty-tonner***, etc. Special combs., as ***the Thirty-nine Articles***: see ARTICLE *noun* 1; **thirty-one** a card-game resembling pontoon; **thirty-eight** a revolver of .38 calibre; ammunition for such a revolver; **thirty-pounder** a gun throwing a shot that weighs thirty pounds; **thirty-second note** MUSIC (chiefly *N. Amer.*) a demisemiquaver; ***thirty-SOMETHING***; **thirty-three (and a third)** (a microgroove gramophone record to be played at) 33(⅓) revolutions per minute; **thirty-two** (*a*) a plant-pot of which 32 are formed from one cast of clay; (*b*) a revolver of .32 calibre; (*c*) ***thirty-two-mo***, a size of book or paper in which each leaf is one-thirty-second of a standard printing-sheet; a book or leaf of this size.

■ **thirtyfold** *adjective & adverb* (*a*) *adjective* thirty times as great or as numerous; having thirty parts, divisions, elements, or units; (*b*) *adverb* to thirty times the number or quantity: **OE. thirtyish** *adjective* (*colloq.*) (*a*) about thirty (in age, measurements, etc.); (*b*) of, pertaining to, or characteristic of the 1930s; resembling or recalling the fashions etc. of the 1930s: **E20.**

this /ðɪs/ *pronoun, noun, adjective* (in mod. usage also classed as a *determiner*), *& adverb.*

[Old English *þis* neut., *þes* masc., *þēos* fem. (for masc. forms cf. Old Frisian *this*, Old High German *dese(r)*, Old Norse *þessi*), from West Germanic from bases of THAT, THE.]

▶**A** *pronoun & noun.* **I** *demonstr. pronoun & noun.* Pl. THESE, (formerly) THOSE.

1 The thing or person present, close at hand, indicated, already mentioned, or understood. With ref. to a person now denoting one actually present, or one speaking or (interrog.) being spoken to on a telephone etc., and always as subj. of *be*. **OE.**

2 The fact, action, circumstance, opinion, etc., implied or contained in the previous or immediately following statement. **OE.** ▸**b** The time of speaking or writing, now; the time or date (marked by an event or action) just mentioned. **OE.** ▸**c** The place where the speaker or writer is, here. Now *colloq.* **LME.**

3 In opposition to ***that***: the first of two or more things, esp. the nearer or more immediate or obvious, the thing actually at hand. Cf. sense B.2 below. **OE.** ▸**b** [A Latinism.] The latter. Cf. THAT *pronoun* 4b. Now *rare* or *obsolete.* **ME.**

> 📖 **1** CARLYLE No country for the Rich, this. TENNYSON This is my house and this my little wife. T. HARDY She kept a diary, and in this . . she sketched the changes of the land. J. STEINBECK This is the way to live. I. MURDOCH This is Marcus Fisher speaking. **2** SHAKES. *Haml.* This above all—to thine own self be true. M. ARNOLD This I say: A private loss here founds a nation's peace. E. WAUGH I can get court-martialled for this. **b** DEFOE Some time after this . . they fired three muskets. M. ROBERTS Helen does not remember what happened after this. **c** LYTTON The finest player . . between this and the Pyramids. **3** DRYDEN This is not fair; nor profitable that. W. MORRIS They sat . . and spoke of this or that.

▶**II** *noun.* Pl. **-es.**

4 A thing (rarely, a person) referred to as 'this'. **M17.**

▶**B** *demonstr. adjective.* Cf. THESE.

1 Designating the person or thing present, close at hand, indicated, already or about to be mentioned, or understood. **OE.** ▸**b** The presently existing, the current; of today; the well-known, the talked-about; the recently introduced, the topical. **OE.** ▸**c** Chiefly & now only LAW. Used before the current date, as ***this 20th April***. **L16.** ▸**d** (In narrative) designating a person or thing not previously mentioned or implied, a certain. *colloq.* **E20.**

2 In opposition to ***that*** and/or ***the other*** or ***the next***: designating the first of two or more things, esp. the nearer or more immediate or obvious, the thing actually at hand. **LME.**

> 📖 **1** J. C. POWYS This part of Wessex. W. BOYD At this stage the flow of traffic was considerable. **b** SHAKES. *Temp.* Where should they Find this grand liquor? BOSWELL We were told this Mr Waller was a plain country gentleman. OED This railway strike is a serious business. O. MANNING Sir Stafford Cripps who has done this thing. B. W. ALDISS There were six of us arriving at 2 a.m. this morning. **d** K. TENNANT They dug this great big trench. *Drive* I saw this car with the keys in the ignition. **2** GOLDSMITH He laughs this minute with one, and cries the next with another. E. A. FREEMAN The temporary . . superiority of this or that Bretwalda. T. HARDY I'll stand on this side of the wire-netting, and you keep on the other.

Phrases (of pronoun & adjective): **all this** all this sort of thing, this and everything of the kind. **like this** of this kind or nature; in this manner, thus. ***on this side (of)***: see SIDE *noun.* ***this AFTERNOON***. **this and that** = ***this or that*** below. ***this EVENING***. **this her** —, **this my** —, etc. *arch.* this — of hers, mine, etc. **this here** *slang* this particular —. ***this is it***: see IT *pronoun.* ***this lot***, ***this little lot***: see LOT *noun.* ***this MORNING***. **this much** as much as this; the amount or extent about to be stated. **this once** on this one occasion (only). **this or that**, **this, that, and the other**, **this, that, or the other** various things (of the kind specified or implied), every sort (of).

▶**C** *adverb.* †**1** In this way or manner; like this; thus. **LME–L16.**

2 To this extent or degree; as much as this; thus. **LME.**

> 📖 **2** J. P. NORRIS None of the portraits . . are dated this early. *Woman's Day (US)* I haven't felt this well in years. F. FORSYTH By being this shrewd . . Calthrop had managed to stay off every police file.

■ **thisness** *noun* (PHILOSOPHY) = HAECCEITY **M17.**

thisaway /ˈðɪsəweɪ/ *adverb. dial. & colloq.* **M19.**

[from THIS *adjective* + WAY *noun* with intrusive *a*.]

1 In this manner or respect. **M19.**

2 In this direction. **E20.**

thistle /ˈθɪs(ə)l/ *noun & verb.*

[Old English *þistel* = Old Saxon *þistil*, Old High German *distil(a)* (Low German *diestel*, *distel*, Dutch *distel*, German *Distel*), Old Norse *þistill*, from Germanic, of unkn. origin.]

▶**A** *noun.* **1** Any of numerous prickly-leaved and freq. also prickly-stemmed plants of the genera *Carduus*, *Cirsium*, and related genera of the composite family, which have tubular, chiefly purple flowers in globular heads; *spec.* any of those occurring as weeds. Also (usu. with specifying word), any of several prickly plants of other families. **OE.**

2 An image or figure of (the head of) a thistle, esp. as the national emblem of Scotland. **L15.** ▸**b** ***the Thistle***, the badge of a Scottish order of knighthood instituted by James II & VII in 1687 and revived by Queen Anne in 1703; (membership of) this order. **L17.**

3 A thing resembling a thistle in form or appearance; *fig.* a prickly and troublesome thing. **M17.**

1 ***blessed thistle***, ***Canada thistle***, ***carline thistle***, ***cotton-thistle***, ***globe thistle***, ***Mexican thistle***, ***plume thistle***, ***Russian thistle***, ***Scotch thistle***, ***spear thistle***, ***star-thistle***, etc.

Comb.: **thistle-bird** *dial.* a bird that feeds on thistle seeds; *esp.* the American goldfinch, *Carduelis tristis*; **thistle crown** *Hist.* an English gold coin of James I, bearing the figure of a thistle on the reverse, and worth about 4 shillings; **thistle-crown** the flower-head of a thistle; **thistle cup** a silver cup with an outward-turning rim (of a type formerly manufactured in Scotland); **thistle dollar** *Hist.* a Scottish silver coin of James VI, bearing the figure of a thistle on the reverse, and worth two marks (MARK *noun*² 2); **thistledown** (*a*) the light feathery down or pappus of a thistle seed; thistle seeds collectively, esp. as carried along by the wind; (*b*) *fig.* a very light and insubstantial thing; **thistle-finch** *dial.* a finch which feeds on thistle seeds; *esp.* the goldfinch, *Carduelis carduelis*; **thistle funnel** CHEMISTRY a kind of funnel with a large bulb between the conical flared part and the tube, suggesting the form of a thistle-head on its stalk; **thistle glass** a drinking-glass with a round bowl and an outward-turning rim; **thistle-head** the flower-head of a thistle.

▶**B** *verb trans.* Clear of thistles, weed out the thistles from. *rare.* **M18.**

■ **thistled** *adjective* covered or overgrown with thistles; decorated with figures of thistles: **M18. thistle-like** *adjective* resembling (the flower of) a thistle **M19. thistly** *adjective* of the nature of or resembling a thistle; spiny, prickly; consisting of thistles; overgrown with thistles: **L16.**

thiswise /ˈðɪswʌɪz/ *adverb.* Now *arch. rare.* **ME.**

[from THIS *adjective* + -WISE.]

In this manner, thus.

this world /ðɪs ˈwəːld/ *noun phr.* **OE.**

[from THIS *adjective* + WORLD *noun.*]

The present world; the present state or stage of existence as opposed to an imaginary or future existence; *esp.* mortal life as opposed to life after death.

■ **this-worldliness** *noun* the quality of being this-worldly **L19. this-worldly** *adjective* of or pertaining to this world; concerned with the things of this world or the present state of existence (opp. OTHERWORLDLY): **L19.**

thither /ˈðɪðə/ *adverb & adjective.* Now *arch. & literary.*

[Old English *þider* alt. (by assim. to HITHER) of *þæder*, corresp. to Old Norse *þaðra*, from Germanic base of THE, THAT + suffix meaning 'towards'. Cf. WHITHER *adverb.*]

▶**A** *adverb.* **1** To or towards that place; there. **OE.**

†**2** Up to that point (of time, a discourse, etc.); until then. **ME–E17.**

†**3** To that end or result. **ME–E17.**

> 📖 **1** H. I. JENKINSON The road thither leaves the main road at right angles. CLIVE JAMES He had obtained permission to visit a training camp . . and thither we went. ***hither and thither***: see HITHER *adverb* 1.

▶**B** *adjective.* Situated on that side; the further (of two). *rare.* **M19.**

thitherto /ðɪðəˈtuː/ *adverb.* Now *rare. arch. & literary.* **LME.**

[from prec. + TO *preposition* after HITHERTO.]

Up to that time; until then.

thitherward /ˈðɪðəwəd/ *adverb. arch.* **OE.**

[from THITHER + -WARD.]

1 Towards that place; in that direction; thither. **OE.**

†**2** On the way there; going there. **OE–M17.**

■ Also **thitherwards** *adverb* **OE.**

thitsi /ˈθɪtsiː/ *noun.* Also **theetsee.** **M19.**

[Burmese, from *thit* tree, wood + *asi* gum.]

A tree of tropical Asia, *Gluta usitata* (family Anacardiaceae); the varnish obtained from this tree, used in lacquer-work in Myanmar (Burma).

thiuram /ˈθʌɪjʊram/ *noun.* **M20.**

[from THIO- + UR(EA + AM(IDE.]

CHEMISTRY. The radical ·CSNR_2. Chiefly in ***thiuram disulphide***, any of a class of compounds of the formula $R_2N{\cdot}CS{\cdot}SS{\cdot}CS{\cdot}NR_2$ (where R is an alkyl group), used esp. to initiate polymerization reactions and accelerate vulcanization.

thivel /ˈθɪv(ə)l, ˈθʌɪv(ə)l/ *noun. Scot. & north.* Also **thible** /ˈθɪb(ə)l, ˈθʌɪb(ə)l/. **L15.**

[Origin unkn.]

A stick for stirring porridge or anything cooked in a pot.

thivish /ˈθʌɪvɪʃ/ *noun.* Also **tevish** /ˈtiːvɪʃ/. **M19.**

[Irish *taibhse* from Old Irish *taidbse* phantasm. Cf. TAISCH.]

A ghost, a spectre.

¶ Chiefly in the writings of W. B. Yeats.

thixotropy /θɪkˈsɒtrəpi/ *noun.* **E20.**

[from Greek *thixis* touching + -O- + Greek *tropē* turning + -Y³.]

CHEMISTRY. The property displayed by certain gels of becoming fluid when shaken, stirred, etc., and of reverting back to a gel when left to stand; reduction of viscosity in the presence of an applied stress.

■ **thixotropic** /-ˈtrəʊpɪk, -ˈtrɒpɪk/ *adjective* exhibiting or pertaining to thixotropy **E20. thixotropically** /-ˈtrəʊp-, -ˈtrɒp-/ *adverb* **M20.**

†**tho** *pronoun & adjective.*

[Old English *þā* nom. & accus. pl. of *se*, *sēo*, *þæt* THAT, THE. Cf. THOSE.]

▶**A** *pronoun.* **1** *demonstr. pronoun.* Those. **OE–L16.**

2 *rel. pronoun.* With pl. antecedent: that. **OE–LME.**

▶**B** *demonstr. adjective.* **1** Those. **OE–L16.**

2 With pl. noun: the. **OE–ME.**

tho /ðəʊ/ *adverb & conjunction.* Long *obsolete* exc. *dial.*

[Old English *þā* = Old Norse *þá*; orig. a case-form of the demonstr. stem *þa-* of THE, THAT, meaning 'that time' with ellipsis of noun.]

▶**A** *adverb.* Then, at that time. Formerly also, after that, thereupon. **OE.**

▶†**B** *conjunction.* When, at the time that. **OE–LME.**

tho' *adverb & conjunction* see THOUGH.

thoft /θɒft/ *noun.* Long *north.* Also **thaft** /θaft/.

[Old English *þofte* = Old Norse *þopta* (Norwegian, Danish *tofte*), Old High German *dofte*, Middle & mod. Low German *ducht* (German *Ducht*), Middle Dutch *dofte*, *dochte* (Dutch *doft*), from Germanic from Indo-European base meaning 'squat, sit low'. Cf. THOUGHT *noun*².]

A rower's bench, a thwart.

thole /θəʊl/ *noun.*

[Old English *þol(l)* = Old Frisian *tholl*, Middle Low German, Middle Dutch *dolle* (Dutch *dol*), Old Norse *þollr* fir tree, tree, peg.]

1 A vertical pin or peg in the side of a boat which serves as the fulcrum for an oar; *esp.* either of a pair forming a rowlock. Also ***thole-pin***. **OE.**

2 *gen.* A pin, a peg, *esp.* one by means of which the shafts are fastened to the carriage or axle of a cart etc. Also ***thole-pin***. **LME.**

thole /θəʊl/ *verb.*

[Old English *þolian* = Old Frisian *tholia*, Old Saxon *þolon*, *þolian*, Old High German *dolōn*, *dolēn*, Old Norse *þola*, Gothic *þulan*, from Germanic from Indo-European base meaning 'raise, remove'.]

1 *verb trans.* Be subjected or exposed to (something evil); be afflicted with; suffer, undergo. *arch.* **OE.**

2 *verb trans.* Endure passively, submit patiently to; put up with, tolerate. Now *Scot. & north.* **OE.** ▸**b** Admit of, bear; be capable of. *Scot. & north.* **L18.**

†**3** *verb trans.* Allow, permit. **OE–E18.**

4 *verb intrans.* Have patience, wait patiently. *dial.* **ME.**

5 *verb trans.* Bear to give; grant willingly. *dial.* **E18.**

2b thole amends admit of improvement.

tholeiite /ˈθəʊlɪʌɪt/ *noun.* **M19.**

[from *Tholei* (now *-ey*), a village in the Saar, Germany + -ITE¹.]

GEOLOGY. Orig., an olivine-poor basaltic rock containing plagioclase feldspar, pyroxene, and glass. Now, a basaltic rock containing augite and a calcium-poor pyroxene (pigeonite or hypersthene), and with a higher silica and lower alkali content than an alkali basalt.

■ **tholeiitic** /θəʊlɪˈɪtɪk/ *adjective* **E20.**

tholi, **tholoi** *nouns pl.* see THOLOS.

tholoid /ˈθəʊlɔɪd/ *noun*. Also (now *rare* or *obsolete*) **-oide**. E20.
[German *Tholoide*, from Greek *tholos*: see next, -OID.]
GEOLOGY. A dome-shaped steep-sided extrusion of hardened lava plugging the vent of a volcano.

tholos /ˈθɒlɒs/ *noun*. Pl. **-loi** /-lɔɪ/. Also (esp. in sense 1) **tholus** /ˈθəʊləs/, pl. **-li** /-lʌɪ/. M17.
[Latin *tholus*, Greek *tholos*.]
1 *ARCHITECTURE*. A circular domed building or structure; a dome, a cupola. M17.
2 *GREEK ANTIQUITIES*. A dome-shaped tomb, esp. of the Mycenaean period. Also ***tholos tomb***. L19.

Thomas /ˈtɒməs/ *noun*¹. E17.
[Male forename from late Latin *Thomas*, ecclesiastical Greek *Thōmas*, name of one of Christ's apostles.]
1 [cf. *John* 20:24–9.] A person who refuses to believe something without incontrovertible proof; a sceptic. Chiefly in ***doubting Thomas***. E17.
2 (A name for) a footman or a waiter. *colloq.* Now *rare* or *obsolete*. M19.
3 In full ***Thomas Atkins*** /ˈatkɪnz/. = TOMMY *noun*¹ 4. *colloq.* Now *rare* or *obsolete*. L19.

Thomas /ˈtɒməs/ *noun*². L19.
[H. O. *Thomas* (1834–91), English surgeon.]
MEDICINE. Used ***attrib.*** and in ***possess.*** to designate kinds of splint invented by Thomas; *spec.* one consisting of a soft ring encircling the thigh from which two rigid rods extend on each side of the leg and meet beyond the foot, allowing traction to be applied to the leg or the knee to be immobilized.

Thomism /ˈtəʊmɪz(ə)m/ *noun*. E18.
[from *Thomas* Aquinas (see next) + -ISM.]
THEOLOGY. The doctrines of Thomas Aquinas or of the Thomists.

Thomist /ˈtəʊmɪst/ *noun & adjective*. M16.
[medieval Latin *Thomista*, from *Thomas* Aquinas (see below): see -IST.]
THEOLOGY. ▶**A** *noun*. A follower or adherent of the Italian scholastic philosopher and theologian St Thomas Aquinas (1225–74), or of his system of philosophy and theology. M16.
▶**B** *adjective*. Of or pertaining to Thomism or Thomists. M19.
■ **Thoˈmistic** *adjective* = THOMIST *adjective* M19. **Thoˈmistical** *adjective* = THOMIST *adjective* M16.

Thompson /ˈtɒm(p)s(ə)n/ *noun*. E20.
[John T. *Thompson* (1860–1940), US general.]
In full ***Thompson sub-machine-gun***. (Proprietary name for) a sub-machine-gun of a type introduced by Thompson's company. Cf. TOMMY-GUN.

thomsenolite /ˈtɒms(ə)nəlʌɪt/ *noun*. M19.
[from Julius *Thomsen* (1826–1909), Danish chemist + -O- + -LITE.]
MINERALOGY. A monoclinic hydrated fluoride of aluminium, calcium, and sodium, usu. occurring as colourless crystals.

Thomsen's disease /ˈtɒms(ə)nz dɪˌziːz/ *noun phr.* L19.
[A. J. T. *Thomsen* (1815–96), Danish physician, who described the disease (by which he was himself affected).]
MEDICINE. = MYOTONIA ***congenita***.

Thomson /ˈtɒms(ə)n/ *noun*. L19.
[See below.]
1 *PHYSICS*. [William *Thomson*, Lord Kelvin: see KELVIN.] ***Thomson effect***, the phenomenon whereby the existence of a temperature gradient along an electrical conductor causes a potential gradient in the same or the contrary direction. L19.
2 [Joseph *Thomson* (1858–94), Scot. explorer.] ***Thomson's gazelle***, a small E. African gazelle, *Gazella thomsonii*, with a broad black lateral stripe. Cf. TOMMY *noun*¹ 5. L19.
3 *PHYSICS*. [J. J. *Thomson* (1856–1940), Brit. physicist.] ***Thomson scattering***, scattering of light by free electrons or other charged particles, in accordance with classical mechanics. M20.

Thomsonian /tɒmˈsəʊnɪən/ *adjective*. L19.
[from *Thomson* (see below) + -IAN.]
Of or pertaining to the Scottish poet James Thomson (1700–48); characteristic of Thomson or his style.

thomsonite /ˈtɒms(ə)nʌɪt/ *noun*. E19.
[from Thomas *Thomson* (1773–1852), Scot. chemist + -ITE¹.]
MINERALOGY. An orthorhombic mineral of the zeolite group, which is a hydrated silicate of aluminium, calcium, and sodium, and usu. occurs as white to reddish-brown fibrous radiated masses.

thon /ðɒn/ *pronoun & adjective*. *dial.* E19.
[App. alt. of YON with assimilation to *this*, *that*.]
= YON.

-thon *suffix* see -ATHON.

thong /θɒŋ/ *noun & verb*.
[Old English *þwang*, *þwong* = Old Frisian *thwang*, Middle Low German *dwank* constraint, Old High German *dwang* rein (German *Zwang* compulsion), from Germanic. See also WHANG *noun*¹, *verb*¹.]
▶**A** *noun*. **1** A narrow strip of hide or leather, for use esp. as a lace, cord, strap, or rein, or as the lash of a whip; *spec.* a whiplash of plaited hide. OE. ▶**b** A similar strip of another material, *esp.* one made from a plant stem or root. M17.
2 ***sea-thong***, any of several brown seaweeds with straplike fronds, esp. *Himanthalia elongata*. M17.
3 A sandal having a flat sole with straps, a flip-flop. Usu. in *pl.* *N. Amer.*, *Austral.*, & *NZ*. M20.
4 A skimpy bathing garment resembling a G-string. L20.

📖 **1** J. O'HARA The stick . . had a leather thong which he wrapped round his wrist. J. A. MICHENER Sandals with golden thongs clasping his ankles.

Comb.: **thong-weed** = sense 2 above.
▶**B** *verb trans.* **1** Provide with a thong or thongs; fasten or bind with a thong or thongs. Freq. as ***thonged*** *ppl adjective*. ME.
2 Flog or lash with a thong. M18.

thorac- *combining form* see THORACO-.

thoracal /ˈθɔːrək(ə)l/ *adjective*. M20.
[from THORACO- + -AL¹.]
= THORACIC.

thoraces *noun pl.* see THORAX.

thoracic /θɔːˈrasɪk, θə-/ *adjective*. M17.
[medieval Latin *thoracicus* from Greek *thōrakikos*, from *thōrak-* THORAX: see -IC.]
1 Of, pertaining to, or contained in the thorax; concerned with disease of the region or organs of the thorax. M17.
2 *ZOOLOGY*. (Of a fish) having the ventral fins situated directly beneath the pectoral; (of a ventral fin) so situated. M18.
3 Pertaining to, attached to, or forming part of the thorax of an arthropod. E19.
4 *ZOOLOGY*. Of a cirripede: belonging to the suborder Thoracica, in members of which the body consists of six thoracic segments, with a rudimentary abdomen. L19.
Special collocations: **thoracic cage** the skeleton of the thorax with its ligaments. **thoracic cavity** the space enclosed by the ribs, spine, and diaphragm, containing the heart, lungs, etc. **thoracic duct** the main trunk of the lymphatic system, passing upwards in front of the spine and draining into the left innominate vein near the base of the neck. **thoracic vertebra** each of the twelve vertebrae which articulate with a rib.
■ †**thoracical** *adjective* = THORACIC M17–M19. **thoracically** *adverb* in the thorax E20.

thoracico- /θəˈrasɪkəʊ/ *combining form* of THORACIC: see -O-.
■ **thoracicoˈlumbar** *adjective* (*ANATOMY* & *MEDICINE*) = THORACOLUMBAR L19.

thoraco- /ˈθɔːrəkəʊ/ *combining form* of Greek *thōrak-*, THORAX: see -O-. Before a vowel also **thorac-**.
■ **thoracentesis**, **thoracocentesis** /-sɛnˈtiːsɪs/ *nouns*, pl. **-teses** /-ˈtiːsiːz/. [Greek *kentēsis* pricking, from *kentein* prick] *MEDICINE* (an instance of) the insertion of a hollow needle into the pleural cavity in order to draw off fluid, pus, air, etc. M19. **thoracoˈlumbar** *adjective* (*ANATOMY* & *MEDICINE*) pertaining to the thoracic and lumbar regions, esp. of the spine; *spec.* designating the sympathetic nervous system: E20. **thoracoplasty** *noun* (*MEDICINE*) (an instance of) surgical repair of a diseased or damaged thorax L19. **thoracoscopy** /θɔːrəˈkɒskəpi/ *noun* (*MEDICINE*) examination of the pleural cavity using an endoscope L19. **thoracostomy** /θɔːrəˈkɒstəmi/ *noun* (*MEDICINE*) (an instance of) the surgical creation of an opening in the chest wall, esp. for the purpose of allowing drainage of fluid E20. **thoracotomy** /θɔːrəˈkɒtəmi/ *noun* (*MEDICINE*) (an instance of) surgical incision into the thorax L19.

thorax /ˈθɔːraks/ *noun*. Pl. **thoraces** /ˈθɔːrəsiːz/, **thoraxes**. LME.
[Latin from Greek *thōrax*, *-ak-*.]
1 *ANATOMY* & *ZOOLOGY*. The part of the body of a mammal between the neck and the abdomen, including the cavity enclosed by the ribs, breastbone, and dorsal vertebrae, and containing the chief organs of circulation and respiration; the chest. Also, the corresponding part of a bird, reptile, amphibian, or fish. LME.
2 *ZOOLOGY*. The middle section of the body of an arthropod, between the head and the abdomen. M18.
3 *GREEK ANTIQUITIES*. A breastplate, a cuirass. M19.

Thorazine /ˈθɔːrəziːn/ *noun*. M20.
[from TH(IO- + CHL)OR(O-² + AZINE.]
PHARMACOLOGY. (Proprietary name for) the drug chlorpromazine.

thoreaulite /ˈθɒrəʊlʌɪt/ *noun*. M20.
[from J. *Thoreau*, 20th-cent. Belgian geologist + -LITE.]
MINERALOGY. A monoclinic oxide of tin and tantalum usu. occurring as brown prismatic crystals.

Thoreauvian /θəˈrəʊvɪən/ *noun & adjective*. E20.
[from *Thoreauvius* Latinized form of *Thoreau* (see below) + -AN.]
▶**A** *noun*. An admirer or follower of the US naturalist and writer Henry David Thoreau (1817–62), or his work. E20.
▶**B** *adjective*. Resembling or characteristic of Thoreau or his work and beliefs. M20.

thoria /ˈθɔːrɪə/ *noun*. M19.
[from THORIUM after *alumina*, *magnesia*, etc.]
Thorium dioxide, ThO_2, an insoluble refractory white solid, used esp. in the manufacture of materials for high-temperature applications.

thorian /ˈθɔːrɪən/ *adjective*. M20.
[formed as prec. + -IAN.]
MINERALOGY. Having a constituent element partly replaced by thorium.

thorianite /ˈθɔːrɪənʌɪt/ *noun*. E20.
[from THORIA + *-n-* + -ITE¹.]
MINERALOGY. An impure form of thorium dioxide crystallizing in the cubic system and usu. occurring as dark grey to brownish-black crystals with a resinous lustre.

thoriated /ˈθɔːrɪeɪtɪd/ *adjective*. E20.
[from THORIUM + -ATE³ + -ED¹.]
Esp. of a tungsten valve filament: containing a proportion of thorium.

thorite /ˈθɔːrʌɪt/ *noun*. M19.
[from *Thor* Norse god of thunder + -ITE¹.]
MINERALOGY. A tetragonal silicate of thorium which forms orange-yellow, brown, or black crystals, usu. as a minor component of some intrusive igneous rocks.

thorium /ˈθɔːrɪəm/ *noun*. M19.
[formed as prec. + -IUM.]
A radioactive metallic chemical element, atomic no. 90, which is a member of the actinide series and occurs in monazite, thorite, and some other minerals. (Symbol Th.)
Comb.: **thorium-lead** designating a method of isotopic dating, and results obtained with it, based on the measurement of the proportions in rock of thorium-232 and its ultimate decay product, lead-208; **thorium series** the radioactive series of isotopes resulting from the decay of thorium-232 (the commonest natural isotope of thorium).

thorn /θɔːn/ *noun*.
[Old English *þorn* = Old Saxon *þorn* (Dutch *doorn*), Old & mod. High German *dorn*, Old Norse *þorn*, Gothic *þaurnus*, from Germanic from Indo-European.]
1 A stiff, sharp-pointed, straight or curved woody projection on the stem or other part of a plant; *spec.* (*BOTANY*) one that represents a modified branch (cf. PRICKLE *noun*¹ 3, SPINE 1). OE. ▶**b** *fig.* A cause of pain, grief, or trouble. ME.
2 A thorny bush, shrub, or tree; *spec.* a hawthorn, *Crataegus monogyna* (or allied species); a thorn tree, a thorn-bush. OE. ▶**b** Thorn-bushes or thorny branches collectively. Also, the wood of a thorn tree. ME. ▶**c** *fig.* (with allus. to *Matthew* 13:7). Something obstructing a course or way or choking growth. ME.
3 The letter Þ, þ, used in Old and Middle English, Gothic, and Old Saxon to represent the voiced and voiceless dental fricatives /ð/ and /θ/, later becoming similar and occas. identical in form to Y, resulting in *ye*, *yis*, etc., as variants of *the*, *this*, etc., and finally being superseded by the digraph *th* with the advent of printing; the letter Þ, þ, used in Old Norse and Icelandic to represent the voiceless dental fricative /θ/. Also, the phonetic symbol þ, used to represent this voiceless dental fricative, now usu. represented by the International Phonetic Alphabet symbol /θ/ (theta). Cf. ETH. OE.
4 A spine or spiny projection on an animal. ME.
5 With specifying word: any of certain geometrid moths, esp. of the genera *Ennomos* and *Selenia* (whose larvae feed on hawthorn or related plants). Also ***thorn moth***. M19.

📖 **1** *Proverb*: There is no rose without a thorn. ***crown of thorns (starfish)***: see CROWN *noun*. **b** I. MURDOCH All men . . carry within their minds some sharp thorn. **a thorn in one's flesh, a thorn in one's side, a thorn in the flesh, a thorn in the side** a constant annoyance or problem, a source of continual trouble or annoyance. **on thorns** in a painful state of anxiety or suspense, esp. in fear of being detected. **2** ***blackthorn***, ***box-thorn***, ***camel's thorn***, ***Christ's thorn***, ***Glastonbury thorn***, ***hawthorn***, ***Jerusalem thorn***, ***orange thorn***, etc. **c** W. IRVING The thorns which beset an author in the path of theatrical literature.

Comb.: **thorn-apple** a plant of the nightshade family, *Datura stramonium*, native to N. America, bearing large funnel-shaped white or mauve flowers; the fruit of this plant, a capsule covered with long spines and containing poisonous seeds; also called ***jimson-weed***, ***stink-weed***; **thornbill** (***a***) any of various S. American hummingbirds esp. of the genera *Chalcostigma* and *Rhamphomicron*, with relatively short bills; (***b***) any of several small Australian warblers of the genus *Acanthiza*; **thorn-bush** = ***thorn tree*** below; **thorn-hedge** a hedge of thorny shrubs; *spec.* a hedge of hawthorn sets; ***thorn moth***: see sense 5 above; **thorn-proof** *adjective* resistant to tearing or puncturing by thorns; **thorntail** any of various bright green S. American hummingbirds of the genus *Popelairia*, with projecting outer tail feathers; **thorn tree** a thorny tree, *esp.* a hawthorn or (in Africa) an acacia; **thornveld** *S. Afr.* veld in which acacias predominate; **thornwood** woodland composed of thorn trees, esp. (in Africa) acacias.
■ **thornless** *adjective* L18. **thornlike** *adjective* resembling (that of) a thorn; *esp.* shaped like a thorn: L19.

thorn /'θɔːn/ *verb trans.* LME.
[from the noun.]
1 Prick, pierce; make thorny, provide with thorns; *spec.* (now *rare*) protect (a hedge) with dead thorn-bushes. Freq. as ***thorned*** *ppl adjective.* LME.
2 Prick as with a thorn; vex. Now *rare.* L16.

thornback /'θɔːnbak/ *noun.* ME.
[from THORN *noun* + BACK *noun*[1].]
1 A ray, *Raja clavata*, of European waters, which has several rows of spines along its back and tail, and is caught for eating as skate; also ***thornback ray***. Also called ***roker***. ME. ▸**b** Any of certain similar fishes; *US* a Pacific guitar-fish, *Platyrhinoidis triseriata*; *Austral.* a ray, *Raja lemprieri* (also ***thornback skate***). M18.
2 An old maid. *slang.* Long *rare* or *obsolete.* L17.

thornen /'θɔːnən/ *adjective.* Long *obsolete* exc. *dial.*
[Old English *þyrnen*, from THORN *noun* + -EN[4].]
Of thorns or thorn; thorny.

thorny /'θɔːni/ *adjective.*
[Old English *þornig*, from THORN *noun* + -Y[1].]
1 Having many thorns; covered with thorns; prickly. OE.
2 Having many thorn-bearing or prickly plants; overgrown with thorns. Freq. *fig.* with allus. to *Matthew* 13:7. OE.
3 *fig.* Painful or distressing to the mind; vexatious, irritating. Now usu., having many points of difficulty; hard to handle; delicate. ME.

> 📖 **1** *fig.*: A. S. BYATT I have a sharp tongue and a thorny exterior. **thorny devil** *Austral.* = MOLOCH 2. **thorny oyster** = SPONDYLUS. ***thorny woodcock***: see WOODCOCK 3c. **2** L. NKOSI Pride and ambition led me into thorny paths. **3** D. CARNEGIE It was House's thorny task to break the unwelcome news. H. J. EYSENCK Using tricks in order to obtain a confession . . raises many thorny legal problems.

▪ **thornily** *adverb* L19. **thorniness** *noun* L17.

thoro- /'θɔːrəʊ/ *combining form* of THORIUM: see -O-.
▪ **thoro'gummite** *noun* [GUMMITE] *MINERALOGY* a tetragonal basic silicate of thorium, usu. also containing uranium, and occurring as microcrystalline aggregates, usu. yellowish-brown or greenish-grey L19. **Thorotrast** *noun* [CON)TRAST *noun*] *MEDICINE* (US proprietary name for) a colloidal solution of thorium dioxide used (esp. formerly) as a contrast medium in radiography M20.

thoron /'θɔːrɒn/ *noun.* E20.
[from THOR(IUM after *radon* etc.]
CHEMISTRY & PHYSICS. An isotope of radon, atomic weight 220, formed in the radioactive decay series of thorium.

thorough /'θʌrə/ *adjective & noun.* L15.
[Attrib. use of the adverb.]
▸**A** *adjective.* **1** That passes or extends through something. *obsolete* exc. in comb. (cf. THOROUGH-). Cf. THROUGH *adjective* 1a. L15.
2 Carried out through the whole of something; applied to or affecting every part or detail; not superficial; done with great care and completeness; (of a person) taking pains to do something carefully and completely. L15.
3 That is fully what is expressed by the noun; complete and unqualified; utter, absolute. M17.

> 📖 **2** GOLDSMITH A thorough knowledge of the world. A. C. BOULT His education had ceased at sixteen, and he wanted mine to be more thorough. E. O'BRIEN He was good at diagnosing, and very thorough. M. HOCKING The doctor . . had given Janet a thorough examination. **3** LYTTON The finest and most thorough gentleman I ever saw.

▸**B** *noun.* †**1** A man-made channel; a drainage ditch. Cf. THROUGH *noun*[2] 1. M–L16.
2 *Hist.* Thoroughgoing action or policy; *spec.* (**T-**) that of Strafford and Laud in England in the reign of Charles I. M17.
3 A furrow. *obsolete* exc. *dial.* M18.
▪ **thoroughly** *adverb* †(*a*) *rare* in a way that penetrates or goes right through; (*b*) in a thorough manner or degree; in every part or detail; in all respects; fully, completely, wholly, entirely, perfectly: ME. **thoroughness** *noun* M19.

thorough /'θʌrə/ *preposition & adverb.*
[Old English *þuruh*, disyllabic alt. of *þurh* THROUGH *preposition & adverb*, paralleled in *borough*, *furrow*, *marrow*, *sorrow*.]
▸†**A** *preposition.* = THROUGH *preposition.* OE–L19.
▸**B** *adverb.* = THROUGH *adverb.* Now only (*obsolete* exc. *dial.*), thoroughly (cf. THROUGH *adverb* 3). OE.

thorough- /'θʌrə/ *combining form.*
[Repr. THOROUGH *adverb*, *adjective.* Cf. THROUGH-.]
Forming combs. with verbs, adjectives, and nouns with the senses 'from one side to the other', 'throughout', 'through', 'thoroughly'.
▪ **thorough-bind** *verb trans.* bind (a wall etc.) with a stone or metal piece passing through from side to side L19. †**thorough-bore** *verb trans.* bore through, perforate OE–E18. **thorough-brace** *noun* (*US*) (*a*) either of a pair of strong straps connecting the front and back springs and supporting the body of a coach etc.; (*b*) a vehicle whose body is supported on such straps: M19. **thorough-drain** *verb trans.* drain (a field etc.) by means of trenches M19. **thorough-draught** *noun* (now *rare*) = THROUGH-DRAUGHT E19. †**thorough-go-nimble** *noun* (*slang*) diarrhoea M17–E19. **thorough-lights** *noun pl.* windows situated on opposite sides of a room so that light passes right through E17. **thorough-paced** *adjective* (*a*) *lit.* (of a horse) thoroughly trained, able to perform well at any pace; (*b*) *fig.* thoroughly trained or accomplished (in something); thoroughgoing, complete, thorough: M17. **thorough-pin** *noun* (*VETERINARY MEDICINE*) an inflamed swelling in the sheath of a tendon in a horse's hock, appearing on both sides so as to suggest a pin passing through L18. **thorough-sped** *adjective* (now *rare* or *obsolete*) thoroughly developed; complete: M18. **thorough-stitch** *adverb & adjective* (*obsolete* exc. *dial.*) (*a*) *adverb* through to the end; thoroughly, completely; (*b*) *adjective* thoroughgoing, out-and-out: L16.

thorough bass /'θʌrə beɪs/ *noun phr.* Also **thorough-bass**. M17.
[from THOROUGH *adjective* + BASS *noun*[2].]
MUSIC. **1** A bass part for a keyboard instrument extending through a piece of (esp. baroque) music, and notated with figures to indicate the harmony; *loosely* an accompaniment. Also, the method of indicating harmonies in this way. Also called ***figured bass***, ***continuo***, ***basso continuo***. M17.
†**2** [By confusion.] A loud or deep bass. M18–M19.

thoroughbred /'θʌrəbrɛd/ *adjective & noun.* In senses A.2a, B.1a also **T-**. E18.
[from THOROUGH *adverb* + BRED *adjective.*]
▸**A** *adjective.* **1** Thoroughly educated or accomplished; complete, thorough, out-and-out. Now chiefly as passing into sense A.3 below. E18.
2 a Of a horse: that is a thoroughbred (see sense B.1a below). L18. ▸**b** *gen.* Of an animal: of pure breed or stock. M19.
3 Resembling or suggestive of a thoroughbred horse; pure-bred; well-bred; distinguished; remarkable of its type; first-class. E19.

> 📖 **1** BURKE Nothing can be conceived more hard than the heart of a thoroughbred metaphysician. M. E. BRADDON He never handled a gun like a thoroughbred sportsman. **3** C. CLARKE In character he is a . . mongrel between the thoroughbred jester-clown and the cur errand-boy. *Times: Thoroughbred and Classic Cars* was the first of a series of magazines . . devoted to fostering the collectors' interest.

▸**B** *noun.* **1 a** A breed of horse originating from English mares and Arab stallions, whose ancestry for several generations is fully documented; a horse, esp. a racehorse, of this breed. M19. ▸**b** *gen.* A pure-bred animal. M19.
2 A person or thing regarded as resembling a thoroughbred horse; a well-bred, distinguished, or supremely talented person; a first-rate thing, esp. a vehicle. L19.

> 📖 **2** *Landscape* Veteran cars, and new post-vintage thoroughbreds and 'classic' models. *Q* A real thoroughbred of a record.

thoroughfare /'θʌrəfɛː/ *noun & adjective.* Also †**through-**. LME.
[from THOROUGH *adjective* + FARE *noun*[1].]
▸**A** *noun.* **1** *gen.* A passage, a way through. LME. ▸†**b** A place through which traffic passes; a town on a highway or route. LME–E19.
2 *spec.* A road, path, etc., forming a route between two places, a public way unobstructed and open at both ends; *esp.* a main road, a highway. M16. ▸**b** A navigable waterway, a channel for shipping. Chiefly *US.* L17.
†**3** The action of passing through something; the condition of being passed through; passage. M17–M19.

> 📖 **1** R. W. EMERSON They have made the island a thoroughfare; and London a shop. ***no thoroughfare***: see NO *adjective.* **2** H. READ Avoiding the main thoroughfare . . I took a . . less frequented street. INA TAYLOR The London street was a . . noisy thoroughfare.

▸**B** *attrib.* or as *adjective.* That is (on) a thoroughfare. Now *rare.* M16.

thoroughfare /'θʌrəfɛː/ *verb trans.* *rare.* Also (earlier) †**through-**. OE.
[from THROUGH *adverb* + FARE *verb.* In later use from the noun.]
Pass or travel through; form a thoroughfare in or across.

thoroughgoing /θʌrə'gəʊɪŋ/ *adjective.* E19.
[from THOROUGH *adverb* + *going* pres. pple of GO *verb.*]
Acting thoroughly or with completeness; thorough, uncompromising, out-and-out, absolute, complete.

> 📖 I. WATSON No one could be such a thoroughgoing liar. *Atlantic* The New Grove, in twenty volumes, was . . a thoroughgoing revision.

▪ **thoroughgoingly** *adverb* L19. **thoroughgoingness** *noun* M19.

thorough-stone *noun* var. of THROUGH-STONE *noun*[2].

thorough-wax *noun* var. of THOROW-WAX.

thoroughwort /'θʌrəwəːt/ *noun.* L16.
[from THOROUGH- + WORT *noun*[1], after THOROW-WAX.]
†**1** = THOROW-WAX. *rare.* Only in L16.
2 A N. American plant of the composite family, *Eupatorium perfoliatum*, having opposite leaves united at the base so that the stem appears to grow through them and corymbs of white flowers, which is valued for its tonic properties (also called ***boneset***). Also (with specifying word), any of various other N. American plants of this genus. E19.

thorow-wax /'θʌrəwaks/ *noun.* Also **thorough-**. M16.
[from THOROUGH- + WAX *verb*[1], from the stem appearing to grow through the leaves.]
An umbelliferous plant, *Bupleurum rotundifolium*, having perfoliate leaves and greenish-yellow flowers, formerly widespread as a cornfield weed.
false thorow-wax a southern European plant, *Bupleurum subovatum*, resembling thorow-wax and occasionally found in Britain.

thorp /θɔːp/ *noun.* Now *arch.* & *Hist.* Also **thorpe**.
[Old English *þrop*, (after Old Norse) *þorp* = Old Frisian *thorp*, Old Saxon *þorp* (Dutch *dorp*), Old & mod. High German *dorf*, Old Norse *þorp*, Gothic *þaurp* field, from Germanic.]
A hamlet, a small village.
¶ A common elem. in English place-names.

thortveitite /'θɔːtvʌɪtʌɪt, -veɪtʌɪt/ *noun.* E20.
[from O. *Thortveit*, 20th-cent. Norwegian mineralogist + -ITE[1].]
MINERALOGY. A rare monoclinic silicate of scandium and yttrium, usu. occurring as colourless or greyish crystals.

Thos. *abbreviation.*
Thomas.

those /ðəʊz/ *pronoun & adjective* (in mod. usage also classed as a *determiner*).
[Old English *þās* (southern Middle English *þōs*) pl. of THIS (cf. THESE); later (orig. in northern English) used as pl. of THAT, replacing THO *pronoun & adjective.*]
▸**A** *demonstr. pronoun pl.* †**1** Pl. of THIS; these. OE–ME.
2 Pl. of THAT; the things or persons indicated, mentioned, or understood; (in opposition to ***these***) the others of two sets of things, esp. the further or less immediate or obvious etc. ME.
3 As antecedent to a relative pronoun or adverb, or with following defining phr.: the things described or specified in some way, the ones, the persons. ME.

> 📖 **2** DRYDEN Lord of few Acres, and those barren too. J. CONRAD Gales . . and rain—those are the enemies of good Landfalls. **3** T. HARDY The sounds were chiefly those of pick-axes. S. T. WARNER He had . . sighed, as those do who must soon awaken. M. AMIS Money means as much to those who have it as to those who don't.

▸**B** *demonstr. adjective.* †**1** These. OE–ME.
2 Designating the persons or things indicated, named, mentioned, or understood; *emphatic* that are known or believed to be such as is stated; (in opposition to ***these***) designating the other of two sets of things, esp. the further or less immediate or obvious etc. Cf. THAT *adjective.* ME.
3 In concord with a pl. noun which is the antecedent to a relative (expressed or understood), which usu. specifies or completes the description. ME.
4 Such. Foll. by *that* (conjunction), †*as. arch.* E17.

> 📖 **2** GLADSTONE Some of those clergy who are called Broadchurchmen. T. HARDY In those days . . the country was densely wooded. C. TOMLINSON You see those three men working. *Daily Telegraph* Insurance to help pay those legal costs. *Plays International* I cannot compare those players with these at the Lyttleton. **those her** —, **those my** —, etc., *arch.* those — of hers, mine, etc. **those kind of** —, **those sort of** — (with pl. noun): — of that kind (or sort). **3** G. GORDON I am not one of those people who rise to a challenge. **4** N. LUTTRELL The town . . was reduced to those straights, that if not releived it must have surrendred.

thou /θaʊ/ *noun*[1]. *colloq.* Also **thou.** (point). Pl. same, **-s**. M19.
[Abbreviation.]
1 A thousand. M19.
2 A thousandth of an inch. E20.

thou /ðaʊ/, *unstressed* ðə/ *pers. pronoun, 2 sing. subjective (nom.), & noun*[2]. Now *arch.* & *dial.* Also †**ta**, (*dial.*) **tha** /ðaː/, *unstressed*, ðə/
[Old English *þu* = Old Frisian *thu*, Old Saxon *þu* (Low German *du*), Old & mod. High German *du*, Old Norse *þú*, Gothic *þu*, from Germanic from Indo-European base repr. also by Latin, Old Irish, Avestan *tū*, Greek (Doric) *tu*, (Attic) *su*, etc. Cf. THEE *pronoun & noun*, THINE.]
▸**A** *pronoun.* **1** Used by the speaker or writer to refer to the person he or she is addressing, as the subject of predication or in attributive or predicative agreement with that subject: you. Also with verb in 3rd person sing. OE.
2 As *interjection* in apposition to and preceding a noun: expr. esp. reproach or contempt. OE.

> 📖 **1** AV *Isa.* 14:12 How art thou fallen from heaven, O Lucifer. TENNYSON Thou—Lancelot!—thine the hand That threw me? T. HARDY O Lord, be thou my helper! **2** SHAKES. *Temp.* Thou liest, thou jesting monkey.

▸**B** *noun.* **1** The pronoun 'thou' as a word. Freq. in ***thees and thous***. LME.

2 A self; a person identical with the person addressed by the speaker or writer. **L17.**

> 📖 **1** S. WOODS She now used the familiar 'thou' only when it suited her.

¶ From Middle English *thee* and *thou* came to be regarded as familiar or (esp. in liturgical use) formal modes of address, being gradually supplanted in general use by *ye* and (now the current usage) *you*; *thy, thyself,* and *thine* were similarly supplanted by *your, yourself,* and *your(s)*.

thou /ðaʊ/ *verb trans. & intrans.* Pa. t. & pple **thou'd**. **LME.**
[from the pronoun.]
Use the pronoun 'thou' (to); address (a person) as 'thou'. Freq. in ***thee and thou***.

> 📖 N. MARSH Torrid blank verse and a good deal of theeing and thouing.

though /ðəʊ/ *adverb & conjunction.* Also (*informal*) **tho'**.
[Old English *þēah* superseded in Middle English by forms from Old Norse *þó* (*þau*), corresp. to Old Frisian *thach*, Old Saxon *þoh* (Dutch *doch*), Old High German *doh* (German *doch*), Gothic *þauh* or, yet, from Germanic formation on Indo-European base of **THE**, **THAT** + particle (Gothic *-uh*) repr. by Latin *-que*, Greek *te*, Sanskrit *ca*, Avestan *ča* and.]
▸ **A** *adverb.* **1** For all that; in spite of that; nevertheless, however, yet. Now *colloq.* **OE.**
2 Used as an intensive after a question or emphatic statement: indeed, truly. *colloq.* **E20.**

> 📖 **1** M. LAVIN As she had begun it, though, she had to end it. E. WAUGH One of the great characters of the Corps. He hadn't much use for me though. **2** G. VIDAL 'What a sad story!' said Maria. 'Isn't it, though?'

▸ **B** *conjunction.* **1** Introducing a subord. clause expressing a fact: notwithstanding that; in spite of the fact that, although. (Formerly with subjunct., now with indic.) Also foll. by †*that*. **OE.** ▸**b** Introducing a parenthetic subord. clause with ellipsis: in spite of being. **LME.**
2 Introducing a subord. clause expressing a supposition or possibility: even if; even supposing that; granting that. Also foll. by †*that*. **OE.**
3 Introducing a restricting or modifying subord. clause: and yet, but still, nevertheless, however. **ME.**
4 Introducing a subord. clause in which the fulfilment or non-fulfilment of a condition is left open: if. Long *obsolete* exc. in ***as though*** s.v. **AS** *adverb* etc. **ME.**

> 📖 **1** SHAKES. *Lear* Though that the Queen on special cause is here, Her army is mov'd on. DEFOE They are no kings, though they possess the crown. V. WOOLF She seems rather . . defenceless, though she is Gilbert Murray's daughter. **b** RUTHVEN TODD A neat though shabby home. B. PYM Some good furniture (though in need of polishing). **2** SHAKES. *John* Though that my death were adjunct to my act . . I would do it. ADDISON He would not accept of one [witness], tho' it were Cato himself. *ellipt.*: N. ROWE No Place, tho' e'er so holy, shou'd protect him. **3** BUNYAN Glad shall I be . . though I fear we are not got beyond all danger. V. S. PRITCHETT He did not take that as a joke, though he humored her with a small laugh. **4** G. GILLESPIE He cares not though the Church sinke.

thought /θɔːt/ *noun*[1].
[Old English *þōht*, *geþōht* = Old Saxon *giþāht* (Dutch *gedachte*), Old High German *gidāht*, from Germanic base of **THINK** *verb*[2]. Cf. synon. Old Norse *þótti*, *þóttr*, Gothic *þūhtus*.]
1 The action or process of thinking; mental activity; formation and arrangement of ideas in the mind. Also, the capacity for this. **OE.** ▸**b** The product of mental action or effort; what is in one's mind. **ME.** ▸**c** The intellectual activity or mode of thinking characteristic of or associated with a particular group, period, place, etc. Freq. with specifying word. **M19.**
2 An act or product of thinking; something that one thinks or has thought; an idea, a notion; *spec.* one suggested or recalled to the mind, a reflection, a consideration. **ME.**
3 a Consideration, attention, care, regard. Freq. in ***take thought*** below. **ME.** ▸**b** Meditation, mental contemplation. Freq. in ***lost in thought*** below. **ME.** ▸**c** Imagination, fancy. Chiefly *poet.* **ME.** ▸**d** The consideration of a project; the idea or notion of doing something; (an) intention, (a) purpose; *esp.* a partly-formed intention or hope (freq. with neg. expressed or implied). **ME.** ▸**e** Remembrance, memory. Long *obsolete* exc. as passing into sense 1. **ME.** ▸**f** Mental anticipation, expectation. (Now chiefly with neg. expressed or implied.) **ME.** ▸**g** An opinion, a judgement; a belief, a supposition; what one thinks of or about a thing or person. **LME.**
4 Anxiety, distress; grief, trouble, care, vexation. Also, a cause of distress or anxiety. *obsolete* exc. *Scot. & dial.* **ME.**
5 a A very small amount, a very little, a trifle. Chiefly & now only in adverbial relation to adjectives. **L16.** ▸**b** A very short length of time, a moment. Chiefly in adverbial phrs. *US.* **E20.**

> 📖 **1** J. NORRIS Whether Brutes are capable of thought? B. JOWETT Psychology . . analyses the transition from sense to thought. R. S. THOMAS Stripped of love And thought and grace. **b** ADDISON One . . may often find as much thought on the reverse of a Medal as in a Canto of Spenser. **c** L. C. KNIGHTS It has no significant relation with the best thought of the time. **2** L. M. HAWKINS I will collect my scattered thoughts. A. CLARE In some psychiatric disorders thoughts follow each other rapidly. DAY LEWIS The thought of eternal life can fill me with horror. **3a** T. HOOD Evil is wrought by want of Thought. **b** TENNYSON From deep thought himself he rouses. **c** MILTON O change beyond report, thought, or belief! **d** SHAKES. *Temp.* I do begin to have bloody thoughts. LD MACAULAY All thought of returning to the policy of the Triple Alliance was abandoned. **e** SHAKES. *Cymb.* Yourself So out of thought . . Cannot be question'd. **f** AV *Ps.* 49:11 Their inward thought is, that their houses shall continue for euer. OED I had no thought of meeting him there. **g** BROWNING My first thought was, he lied in every word. M. HASTINGS Quite a thought. It hadn't occurred to me, but it's a logical explanation. **5a** *Guardian* Mr Stewart looked a thought harassed.

Phrases: **give thought to** consider, think about. ***great thought***: see **GREAT** *adjective*. **lost in thought** absorbed in reverie or contemplation, abstracted. ***maiden thought***: see **MAIDEN** *noun & adjective*. ***New Thought***: see **NEW** *adjective*. **not give another thought to** not think any more about (someone or something), dismiss from one's mind. **not give a thought to** not think at all about (someone or something), dismiss from one's mind. ***penny for your thoughts***: see **PENNY** *noun*. ***second thoughts***: see **SECOND** *adjective*. ***stream of thought***: see **STREAM** *noun*. **take thought** consider matters, think things over.

Comb.: **thought control** the control of a person's thoughts; *esp.* the attempt to restrict ideas and impose opinions through censorship and the control of curricula; **thoughtcrime** [orig. in George Orwell's novel *Nineteen Eighty-Four*] unorthodox thinking considered as a criminal offence; **thought-executing** *adjective* †(*a*) acting with the rapidity of thought; (*b*) executing the thought or intention of a person; **thought-experiment** an experiment carried out only in the imagination; a mental assessment of the implications of a hypothesis; **thought-forms** (chiefly *THEOLOGY*) the combination of presuppositions, imagery, vocabulary, etc., current at a particular time or place and in terms of which thinking on a subject takes place; **thought model** a system of related ideas or images; **thought pattern** a set of assumptions and concepts underlying thought; a habitual way of thinking; in *pl.*, thought-forms; **thought police** in a totalitarian State, a police force established to suppress freedom of thought; **thought-provoking** *adjective* prompting serious thought; **thought-read** *verb* (*a*) *verb intrans.* practise thought-reading; (*b*) *verb trans.* subject to thought-reading; perceive by thought-reading; **thought-reader** a person supposedly able to perceive another's thoughts; **thought-reading** the supposed direct perception by one person of another person's thoughts; **thought reform** the systematic alteration of a person's mode of thinking; *spec.* in Communist China, a process of individual political indoctrination; **thought-saver** a trite expression used to save one the trouble of thinking of a more appropriate word, phrase, etc., a cliché; †**thought-sick** *adjective* sick with thinking or anxiety; **thought-stream** the continuous succession of a person's thoughts (cf. ***stream of consciousness***, ***stream of thought*** s.v. **STREAM** *noun*); **thought transference** supposed transference or communication of thought from one mind to another apart from the ordinary channels of sense; telepathy; **thought-wave** an undulation of the supposed medium of thought transference; **thoughtway** a customary way of thinking; an unconscious assumption or idea (usu. in *pl.*); **thought-world** the amalgam of mental attitudes, beliefs, presuppositions, and concepts about the world characteristic of a particular people, time, place, etc.

■ **thoughter** *noun* a person who has thoughts, esp. of a specified kind (orig. & chiefly in ***New Thoughter*** s.v. **NEW** *adjective*) **E20.** **thoughty** *adjective* (*obsolete* exc. *Scot. & US*) given to thought, thoughtful **LME.**

thought /θɔːt/ *noun*[2]. Now *dial.* Also **thaught**. **E17.**
[Alt. of **THOFT**. See also **THWART** *noun*[2].]
= **THWART** *noun*[2].

thought *verb*[1], *verb*[2] *pa. t. & pple*: see **THINK** *verb*[1], *verb*[2].

thoughted /ˈθɔːtɪd/ *adjective.* **L16.**
[from **THOUGHT** *noun*[1] + **-ED**[2].]
1 As 2nd elem. of comb.: having thoughts of a specified kind. Now chiefly *arch.* **L16.**
2 Affected with grief or anxiety; anxious, concerned. *Scot.* **M19.**
1 ***high-thoughted***, ***muddle-thoughted***, ***quick-thoughted***, etc.

†**thoughten** *adjective. rare* (Shakes.). Only in **E17.**
[Irreg. from *thought* pa. pple of **THINK** *verb*[2]: see **-EN**[6]. Cf. **BOUGHTEN** *adjective*.]
Having a thought or belief, thinking, *that*.

thoughtful /ˈθɔːtfʊl, -f(ə)l/ *adjective.* **ME.**
[from **THOUGHT** *noun*[1] + **-FUL**.]
1 Given to or engaged in thinking; absorbed in thought; pensive; preoccupied in mind; meditative. **ME.** ▸**b** Disposed to think about or consider matters; prudent; reflective. **ME.** ▸**c** Careful *to do*; mindful *of*. Now *rare* or *obsolete*. **L16.**
†**2** Anxious, distressed; sorrowful, melancholy, moody. **ME–M18.**
3 Showing thought or consideration for others; considerate, kindly. (Foll. by *of*.) **LME.**
†**4** Capable of thought; conscious, intelligent. *rare.* Only in **L17.**

> 📖 **1** W. BLACK Her calm and thoughtful look. G. M. FRASER Richey was watching me in silence, very thoughtful. **b** J. BUTLER Objections, which may appear very material to thoughtful men. F. TEMPLE Not beyond the reach of thoughtful enquiry. **c** SHAKES. *2 Hen. IV* They have been thoughtful to invest Their sons with arts. *Examiner* Thoughtful of enjoyments for ever left behind. **3** E. GASKELL His thoughtful wish of escorting them through the . . rough, riotous town. OED She is very unselfish and thoughtful of others.

■ **thoughtfully** *adverb* **E17.** **thoughtfulness** *noun* **L16.**

thoughtless /ˈθɔːtlɪs/ *adjective.* **L16.**
[formed as prec. + **-LESS**.]
1 Acting without thought or reflection; imprudent. **L16.** ▸**b** Unmindful, forgetful; heedless. Usu. foll. by *of*. Now *rare*. **E17.**
2 Deficient in or lacking thought; not given to thinking; stupid. Now *rare*. **L17.**
†**3** Free from care or anxiety. **M–L18.**
4 Lacking in consideration for others; inconsiderate. **L18.**

> 📖 **1** J. BUTLER Youth may be an excuse for rashness and folly . . as being naturally thoughtless. **b** DRYDEN A Snake . . Leaving his Nest . . thoughtless of his Eggs. **2** POPE A blockhead rubs his thoughtless skull. **3** GOLDSMITH So blest a life these thoughtless realms display. **4** OED It was very thoughtless of you to disturb her. W. HARRIS They're as thoughtless and irresponsible as hell.

■ **thoughtlessly** *adverb* **E18.** **thoughtlessness** *noun* **E18.**

thoughtness /ˈθɔːtnɪs/ *noun. rare.* **M19.**
[from *thought* pa. pple of **THINK** *verb*[2] + **-NESS**.]
The fact or quality of being thought or mentally discerned.

thoughtography /θɔːˈtɒɡrəfi/ *noun. rare.* **M20.**
[from **THOUGHT** *noun*[1] + **-OGRAPHY** after *photography*.]
The supposed production of a visible, usu. photographic, image by purely mental means.

thought-out /θɔːtˈaʊt/ *adjective.* **L19.**
[from *thought* pa. pple of **THINK** *verb*[2] + **OUT** *adverb*.]
Constructed or reached by thinking or mental effort; thoroughly considered. Usu. with qualifying adverb.
ill-thought-out, ***well-thought-out***, etc.

thousand /ˈθaʊz(ə)nd/ *noun & adjective* (in mod. usage also classed as a *determiner*), (*cardinal numeral*).
[Old English *þūsend* = Old Frisian *thūsend*, Old Saxon *þūsundig* (Dutch *duizend*), Old High German *thūsunt*, *dūsunt* (German *Tausend*), Old Norse *þúsund*, Gothic *þūsundi*, from Germanic, with cognates in Balto-Slavonic.]
▸ **A** *noun.* In senses 1 and 2 pl. now always same after numeral and often after quantifier, otherwise **-s**; as *sing.* usu. preceded by *a*, in emphatic use *one*.
1 Ten times one hundred units *of* a specified category or group (now almost always definite as ***a thousand of the***, ***a thousand of those***, etc., ***one thousand of her***, ***one thousand of his mother's***, etc.; orig. *genit. pl.*); ten times one hundred persons or things identified contextually, as pounds or dollars, years in dates, points in a game, chances (in giving odds), etc.; *pl.* after a quantifier, multiples of ten times one hundred such persons or things. Usu. treated as *pl.* **OE.** ▸**b** In *pl.* without specifying word: several thousand; *hyperbol.* large numbers. (Foll. by *of*.) **OE.**
2 Ten times one hundred as an abstract number, the symbol(s) or figure(s) representing this (1,000 in arabic numerals, m, M, in roman); *pl.* after a numeral, that number of multiples of ten times one hundred as an abstract number, the symbol(s) or figure(s) representing any such number (as 5,000). **LME.** ▸**b** In *pl.* The digits denoting the number of thousands. **LME.**

> 📖 **1** T. GAINSFORD A hundred well trained . . souldiers will beat a thousand of them. OED Bricks are sold by the thousand. J. K. JEROME An income of two thousand a year. ***upper ten thousand***: see **UPPER** *adjective*. **b** M. FORSTER Decisions involving thousands of pounds. *Japan Times* Thousands jostle each other in scores of dark water-tanks. ***hundreds and thousands***: see **HUNDRED** *noun* 1b.

▸ **B** *adjective.* After an article, possessive, etc.: ten times one hundred (a cardinal numeral represented by 1000 in arabic numerals, m, M, in roman); *hyperbol.* a great many. After a numeral or quantifier: multiples of ten times one hundred. **OE.**

> 📖 A. M. CLERKE A helium-envelope surrounds the sun to a depth of five thousand miles. *Nineteenth Century* The games . . which bring . . a thousand vexing cares. P. G. WODEHOUSE I was not going . . to cough up several thousand quid. *Discovery* The Babel of a thousand languages. H. FAST I raised a hundred and sixty thousand dollars.

Comb.: Forming compound numerals (cardinal or ordinal) with numerals below a thousand, as **1020** (read ***a thousand and twenty*** or ***one thousand and twenty***, (*N. Amer.*) also ***a thousand twenty*** or ***one thousand twenty***), **1020th** (read ***thousand and twentieth***, ***one thousand and twentieth***). Special combs., as **thousand-head kale**, **thousand-headed kale** a branching variety of kale, *Brassica oleracea* var. *fruticosa*, cultivated as fodder; **thousand island** [*Thousand Islands*, a large group of islands in the St Lawrence River, N. America] a mayonnaise salad-dressing made with ketchup; **thousand-jacket** *NZ* = **HOUHERE**; **thousand-legs** a millipede; **thousand-miler** *slang* a dark shirt that does not show the dirt; **thousand-year-old egg**, **thousand-year egg** a Chinese delicacy consisting of a pickled egg that has been kept in earth, lime, and chopped straw for some weeks; **Thousand-Year Reich** [German *tausendjähriges Reich*] the German Third

Reich (1933–45), as a regime envisaged by the Nazis as established for an indefinite period.

thousandfold /ˈθaʊz(ə)n(d)fəʊld/ *adjective & noun*. OE.
[from prec. + -FOLD.]
▶**A** *adjective*. A thousand times the amount or number. Now *rare*. OE.
▶**B** *noun*. A thousand times the amount or number. Freq. used adverbially. ME.

thousandth /ˈθaʊz(ə)nθ/ *adjective & noun*. M16.
[formed as prec. + -TH².]
▶**A** *adjective*. Next in order after the nine-hundred-and-ninety-ninth; that is number one thousand in a series, (represented by 1000th). M16.
> R. KIPLING The Thousandth Man will stand by your side To the gallows-foot—and after! **thousandth part** *arch*. = sense B. below.

▶**B** *noun*. Each of a thousand parts into which something is or may be divided, a fraction which when multiplied by one thousand gives one, (= ***thousandth part*** above). L18.
> *Scientific American* Reduced to less than a thousandth of its design specification.

†**thousandweight** *noun*. M16–M18.
[from THOUSAND + WEIGHT *noun*.]
A weight equal to 1000 pounds.

'thout /ðaʊt/ *adverb*. *colloq*. L19.
[Aphet.]
= WITHOUT.

thow *noun, verb* see THAW *noun, verb*.

thowless /ˈθaʊlɪs, ˈθuːlɪs/ *adjective*. *Scot*. LME.
[App. var. of THEWLESS.]
†**1** Lacking morals or virtue; dissolute, profligate, immoral. Also, thoughtless. LME–L15.
2 Lacking vigour or energy; inactive; spiritless, listless. E18.
■ **thowlessness** *noun* LME.

thowthistle /ˈθaʊθɪs(ə)l/ *noun*. Long *dial*.
[Old English *þūþistel* = Old High German *dūdistel*, formed as THISTLE, with unkn. 1st elem.]
A sowthistle or similar weed.

thra *adjective & adverb* var. of THRO.

Thracian /ˈθreɪʃ(ə)n/ *noun & adjective*. M16.
[from Latin *Thracius*, *Thracus* from Greek *Thraikios*, *Thraikē* Thrace (see below): see -AN, -IAN.]
▶**A** *noun*. **1** A native or inhabitant of Thrace, an ancient country lying west of Istanbul and the Black Sea and north of the Aegean, now part of modern Turkey, Greece, and Bulgaria. M16.
2 The Indo-European language of the ancient Thracians. L19.
▶**B** *adjective*. Of or pertaining to the Thracians or their language. L16.

thrack /θrak/ *verb trans*. Long *dial*. M17.
[Origin unkn.]
Pack full, cram; load.

Thraco- /ˈθreɪkəʊ/ *combining form*. E20.
[from (the same root as) THRACIAN: see -O-.]
Forming adjectives and nouns with the sense 'Thracian and —', as ***Thraco-Illyrian***, ***Thraco-Phrygian***.

thraldom /ˈθrɔːldəm/ *noun*. Now *literary & Hist*. Also **thrall-**. ME.
[from next + -DOM.]
The state or condition of being a thrall; servitude; captivity.
> *fig*.: *Nature* They have exchanged one kind of thraldom (to local authorities) for another.

thrall /θrɔːl/ *noun, adjective, & verb*. Now *literary & Hist*.
[Old English (late Northumbrian) *þræl* from Old Norse *þræll*, perh. from Germanic base meaning 'run' (cf. Gothic *þragjan* run, Old High German *dregil*, *drigil* servant, runner). Cf. THRILL *noun*¹.]
▶**A** *noun*. **1** A person in bondage to a lord or master; a villein, a serf, a slave; *loosely* a servant, a subject; *transf*. a person whose liberty is forfeit, a captive, a prisoner. OE.
2 The condition of being a thrall; thraldom, bondage, servitude; captivity. Freq. in ***in thrall*** (chiefly *fig*.). LME.
†**3** Oppression, trouble, misery, distress. M16–E19.
> **1** K. CROSSLEY-HOLLAND Nine thralls were working in a sloping field. *fig*.: C. LAMB The veriest thrall to sympathies, apathies, antipathies. **2** E. MUIR The marble cherubs . . Stand up more still, as if they kept all there . . in thrall.

▶**B** *adjective*. **1** That is a thrall; subject, captive, enslaved. ME.
†**2** Pertaining to or characteristic of thraldom; slavish, servile. LME–M16.
> **1** S. BARING-GOULD Male or female—free or thrall.

▶**C** *verb trans*. Make (a person) a thrall; subject to or hold in thrall. Now *rare*. ME.
■ **thralled** *adjective* (*a*) made a thrall, in thraldom; (*b*) resembling a thrall, servile: E16.

thralldom *noun* var. of THRALDOM.

thraneen *noun* var. of TRANEEN.

thranite /ˈθreɪnʌɪt/ *noun*. M19.
[Greek *thranitēs*, from *thranos* bench: see -ITE¹.]
GREEK HISTORY. A rower in one of the tiers of a trireme, generally believed to be the uppermost tier. Cf. THALAMITE, ZYGITE.

thrapple *noun, verb* vars. of THROPPLE *noun, verb*.

thrash /θraʃ/ *noun*. Also (now *rare*) **thresh** /θrɛʃ/. M17.
[from the verb.]
†**1** A threshing implement, a flail. Only in M17.
2 The action or an act of thrashing; a blow, a stroke; a beating. M19.
3 A party, *esp*. a lavish one. *slang*. M20.
4 a A short energetic usu. uncomplicated piece or passage of (jazz or rock) music, *esp*. one that is very fast and loud. *colloq*. M20. ▸**b** A style of fast loud harsh-sounding rock music, combining elements of punk and heavy metal. Also ***thrash metal***. *colloq*. L20.
5 A motor race, *esp*. one that is particularly fast and exciting. *colloq*. L20.
> **3** K. AMIS No quiet family party . . but a twenty-cover thrash.

thrash /θraʃ/ *verb*. Also (now *rare* exc. in senses 5, 7) **thresh** /θrɛʃ/. OE.
[Var. of THRESH *verb*.]
▶**I 1** See THRESH *verb*. OE.
▶**II 2** *verb trans*. Strike, knock. Long *obsolete* exc. as passing into sense 3 below. OE.
3 a *verb trans*. Beat or strike repeatedly as with a flail; *esp*. beat severely by way of punishment, esp. with a stick or whip. OE. ▸**b** *verb intrans*. Deliver or inflict blows as with a flail; strike or beat *on* or *at*. E19.
4 *verb trans*. Defeat thoroughly in a battle or contest. LME.
5 *verb intrans. & trans*. *NAUTICAL*. Sail to windward, make way against the wind or tide. M19.
6 *verb intrans*. Make wild movements like those of a flail or a whip; (foll. by *about*, *around*) move or fling the body, limbs, etc., about violently or in panic. M19.
7 *verb trans*. Foll. by *out*: discuss exhaustively; get at the truth of by discussion or argument. L19.
> **3a** *Manchester Examiner* The deacon . . thrashes him for wasting his time. F. FRANCIS The angler goes on threshing the water. **b** FILSON YOUNG Threshing at the nettles with his stick. **4** *Westminster Gazette* Hurrah, Wellington has thrashed Boney! *Pot Black* Griffiths was back in action . . thrashing Joe Johnson 5–0. **5** C. KINGSLEY The ship thrashed close-hauled through the rolling seas. **6** Z. TOMIN The vast wooden tub alive with fat carp thrashing about in agony. *fig*.: A. N. WILSON He thrashed about for ideas, wildly veering from one extreme to another.

¶ The form *thrash* was rare before E17.

thrasher /ˈθraʃə/ *noun*¹. Also (now *rare*) **thresher** /ˈθrɛʃə/. ME.
[Var. of THRESHER *noun*¹.]
▶**I 1** See THRESHER *noun*¹. ME.
▶**II 2** A person who thrashes or beats someone. E20.

thrasher /ˈθraʃə/ *noun*². Also **thresher** /ˈθrɛʃə/. E19.
[Prob. a survival of an English dial. name of the song thrush.]
Any of several N. American birds of the family Mimidae, with greyish or brownish plumage and a slightly down-curved bill; *esp*. (more fully ***brown thrasher***) *Toxostoma rufum*, which has a red-brown back and pale speckled underside.

thrashing /ˈθraʃɪŋ/ *noun*. Also **threshing** /ˈθrɛʃɪŋ/. LME.
[Var. of THRESHING.]
▶**I 1** See THRESHING. LME.
▶**II 2** The action of THRASH *verb* II; an instance of this; *spec*. (*a*) a thorough defeat in a battle or contest; (*b*) (a) severe beating by way of punishment, esp. with a stick or whip. E19.

Thraso /ˈθreɪsəʊ/ *noun*. Long *rare* or *obsolete*. Pl. **-o(e)s**. L16.
[See next.]
A braggart, a boaster.

thrasonical /θrəˈsɒnɪk(ə)l/ *adjective*. M16.
[from Latin *Thraso(n-)* from Greek *Thrasōn*, a boastful soldier in Terence's *Eunuchus*, from *thrasus* bold, spirited: see -ICAL.]
Resembling Thraso or his behaviour; bragging, boastful, vainglorious.
■ **thrasonic** *adjective* = THRASONICAL M17. **thrasonically** *adverb* L16.

thratch *verb & noun* var. of FRATCH.

thrave /θreɪv/ *noun*. Chiefly *Scot*. & *north*. Also **threave** /θriːv/. OE.
[Of Scandinavian origin: cf. Old Norse *þrefi*, Middle Swedish *þrave*, Swedish *trave*, Danish *trave*.]
1 Two shocks or stooks of corn etc., usu. containing twelve sheaves each, used as a measure of straw, fodder, etc. OE.
2 A large number; a company; a multitude, a lot. LME.
†**3** A bundle or handful tied up like a small sheaf. E–M17.
■ **thraver** *noun* a reaper paid according to the number of thraves cut LME. **thraving** *noun* the practice of paying reapers by the thrave E19.

thraw *noun, verb* see THROW *noun*², *verb*.

thraward /ˈθrɔːwəd/ *adjective*. *Scot*. L15.
[App. alt. of FROWARD.]
1 Disposed to turn aside from the proper way; refractory, perverse. *arch*. L15.
2 Twisted, crooked. *dial*. E19.

thrawing *verbal noun* see THROWING.

thrawn /θrɔːn/ *adjective*. Orig. & chiefly *Scot*. LME.
[from next.]
1 Perverse, contrary; cross-grained, ill-tempered. LME.
2 Twisted, crooked; misshapen, distorted. E16. ▸**b** Of the mouth or face: distorted by anger, ill temper, etc.; frowning. E16.
> **1** *Listener* They're a thrawn, bruised lot, these Le Carré heroes. **2** TOLKIEN A wide ravine, with . . rocky sides to which clung . . a few thrawn trees.

■ **thrawnly** *adverb* E16. **thrawnness** /-n-n-/ *noun* E19.

thrawn *verb pa. pple*: see THROW *verb*.

thread /θrɛd/ *noun*.
[Old English *þrǣd* = Old Saxon *thrād* (Dutch *draad*), Old High German *drāt* (German *Draht*), Old Norse *þráðr*, from Germanic base also of THROW *verb*.]
▶**I 1** A fine strand made by drawing out and twisting the fibres of flax, cotton, wool, silk, etc.; *spec*. a thin cord composed of two or more such strands twisted together. Also, a thin strand made by drawing out glass, metal, plastic, etc. OE. ▸**b** A sacred cord with which brahmins and Parsees are invested at initiation. L16.
2 Each of the threads forming the warp and weft of a woven fabric, esp. considered as an ultimate constituent of such a fabric; the least part of one's clothing. ME. ▸**b** A lineal measure of yarn: the length of a coil of the reel, varying according to material and locality. M17. ▸**c** *fig*. A single element interwoven with others. M19. ▸**d** In *pl*. Clothes. *slang* (orig. & chiefly *N. Amer*.). E20.
3 Material for weaving, sewing, knitting, etc., consisting of a wound thread or threads (freq. with specifying word). Also, a particular kind of such thread (usu. in *pl*.). ME. ▸†**b** *fig*. The material of which something is composed; quality, nature. M17–M18.
4 A very fine elongated piece of animal or plant tissue, as a fine ligament, a hair, a filament of a cobweb or of the byssus of a mollusc. LME. ▸**b** Anything resembling a thread in fineness and length, weakness, etc., as a thin continuous stream of liquid, a faint or weak continuity of sound, a feeble pulse; *spec*. a thin seam or vein of ore. L16. ▸**c** A degree of stickiness reached in boiling clarified syrup for confectionery. M19.
5 The spiral ridge of a screw; each complete turn of this; a similar ridge round the inside of a cylindrical hole, as in a nut or a screwhole. L17.
> **1** R. WELTON From these little Threads . . such strong Cables are form'd. G. R. PORTER Glass may be spun into very long . . threads. **2** R. WARNER I began to pull at the loose threads on the patchwork quilt. E. WILSON The fine threads part easily as the large needle passes through them. **c** ANNE STEVENSON Praise at home and prizes at school were threads she was already adeptly weaving into a 'web of happiness'. **d** *Just Seventeen* Coltrane . . togs up in his natty threads. **3** B. MALAMUD A darning needle and some thread to sew them with. ***cotton thread***, ***gold thread***, ***silk thread***, etc. **b** S. OCKLEY The language must be all of the same thread. **4** GOLDSMITH Threads, which are usually called the beard of the muscle. **b** *Westminster Gazette* Using her pleasant thread of voice agreeably. *Outlook* A little thread of unfrozen water . . tinkles feebly over the rocks. E. DAVID The cheese has softened and melted and is forming threads.

▶**II 6** †**a** A fine dividing line, a boundary line. LME–L17. ▸**b** The central line of the current of a stream, esp. as constituting a boundary line. L17.
7 The continued course of life, represented in classical mythology as a thread which is spun and cut off by the Fates. LME.
8 A thing which traces a path through a problem or intricate investigation, considered as fulfilling the function of the thread or clew in the Greek myth of Theseus in the labyrinth. L16.
9 A thing connecting successive points in a narrative, train of thought, etc.; the sequence of events or ideas continuing through the whole course of something. M17.
10 A continuous or persistent feature of something, *esp*. one combining with other features to form a pattern or texture. L17.
11 A means of connecting or holding together disparate elements. E19.
12 *COMPUTING*. A programming structure or process formed by linking a number of separate elements or subroutines; *esp*. each of the tasks executed concurrently in multi-threading. L20.

📖 **7** SWIFT Her Son . . to whom the Fates had assign'd a very short Thred. J. RATHBONE Strands in the thread of my life other than the bloody one of War. **8** W. KING Having . . that thread of knowledge, which might extricate me thence. A. TATE An Ariadne's thread that the poet will not permit us to lose. **9** R. G. COLLINGWOOD Interruptions, breaking the thread of the performance. P. GOODMAN Let us return to the thread of our argument. **10** B. JOWETT The continuous thread which appears and reappears throughout his rhetoric. **11** J. WESTON A thread uniting all the different parts of our legend. P. BOWLES The last possible suburb had been strung on the street's thread.

Phrases: ***hang by a thread***: see HANG *verb*. ***metallic thread***: see METALLIC *adjective*. ***square thread***: see SQUARE *adjective*. ***V-thread***: see V, V 2.

Comb.: **thread bag** *Jamaican* a small cloth bag, tied or drawn closed with a thread or string; **thread belay** MOUNTAINEERING a belay in which the rope or sling is passed through a hole in the rock before being secured again to the climber; **thread-board** SPINNING a board placed over the spindles of a ring-frame to hold the thread-guides; **thread-cell** a stinging cell in a coelenterate; a nematocyst; **thread-cutter** (*a*) a small blade attached to a sewing-machine etc. for severing a sewing-thread; (*b*) a tool or machine for cutting screw-threads; **thread-drawing** the process of ornamenting a textile fabric by drawing out some of the threads so as to form a pattern (cf. DRAWN-*threadwork*); **threadfin** any of various fishes having long narrow fins, *esp.* (*a*) a fish of the tropical family Polynemidae, characterized by narrow extensions of the pectoral fins; (*b*) a fish of the genus *Alectis*, as the African pompano; **thread-guide** a device in a sewing- or spinning-machine for directing the thread; **thread-lace** lace made of linen or cotton as opposed to silk thread; **thread mark** a distinguishing mark consisting of a thin line formed of highly coloured silk fibres, incorporated in banknote paper to prevent photographic counterfeiting; **thread-mill** *arch.* a factory manufacturing thread; **thread-paper** (*a*) (a strip of) thin soft paper folded to form separate divisions for different skeins of thread; (*b*) *arch.* a slender or thin person; **thread-wire** a wire thread-guide in a spinning-machine; **threadwork** ornamental work formed of threads, lacework; DRAWN-*threadwork*.

■ **threaden** *adjective* (now *arch. & dial.*) composed or made of (*spec.* linen) thread LME. **threadless** *adjective* E19. **threadlet** *noun* (*rare*) a little thread M19. **threadlike** *adjective* (*a*) resembling (that of) a thread; (*b*) *spec.* (of a pulse) thready: L18.

thread /θrɛd/ *verb*. Also (now *arch. & dial.*) **thrid** /θrɪd/, infl. **-dd-**. LME.
[from the noun.]

1 *verb trans.* Provide (a needle) with a sewing-thread by passing one end of the thread through the eye. Also, pass one end of a reel of thread through the thread-guides of (a sewing-machine). LME. ▸**b** Of a man: have sexual intercourse with (esp. a woman). *coarse slang*. M20.

2 a *verb trans.* Make one's way through (a narrow or obstructed passage, a crowd, etc.). L16. ▸**b** *verb trans. & intrans.* Make (one's way) through a narrow or obstructed passage, a crowd, etc. Freq. foll. by *through*. M17.

3 *verb trans.* Put (a bead etc.) on a thread by passing the thread through a central hole; connect (a number of things) by passing a thread through each; string *together*, or *on* a thread. L16. ▸**b** *verb trans. fig.* Run continuously through the whole length or course of; pervade. M19.

4 *verb intrans.* Flow in a thin stream; creep, twine, wind. *rare*. E17.

5 *verb trans.* Interweave or intersperse with or as with threads; *esp.* mark (hair) with streaks of a lighter or brighter shade. Usu. in *pass.* M19.

6 *verb trans.* Form a screw-thread on; provide with a screw-thread. M19.

7 *verb trans.* Stretch or fasten threads across, over, or round, esp. for protection. L19.

8 *verb trans.* Pass (film or tape) between the guides and other parts of a projector, tape-recorder, etc., so that it runs from one spool to another; = LACE *verb* 4e. Freq. foll. by *up*. L19.

📖 **1** M. FORSTER She . . began threading a needle. *transf.*: H. E. BATES She . . threaded the cowslip into my buttonhole. **2a** P. SCUPHAM Lizards thread the sunken maze. **b** D. H. LAWRENCE The scarlet men . . were threading among the men of the congregation. T. SHARPE He threaded his way through the shoppers. **3** F. FRANCIS Threading the bait upon the hook. OED The girl was threading beads on a string. **b** J. EARLE One spirit and purpose threads the whole. **5** D. H. LAWRENCE Her dark hair was threaded with grey.

Comb.: **thread-needle**, **thread-the-needle** a children's game in which the participants join hands in a line, and the player at one end of the line passes between the last two at the other end, the rest following.

■ **threader** *noun* a person who or thing which threads something; *esp.* (*a*) a person who threads a needle; (*b*) a device for threading a needle: LME. **threading** *verbal noun* (*a*) the action of the verb; an instance of this; (*b*) COMPUTING a programming technique in which processes are executed as a series of routines indicated by a sequence of instructions or words; *esp.* = MULTI-THREADING: L16.

threadbare /ˈθrɛdbɛː/ *adjective*. LME.
[from THREAD *noun* + BARE *adjective*.]

1 (Of cloth) so worn that the nap is lost and the threads of the warp and weft are visible; (of a garment etc.) made from threadbare cloth, worn-out, shabby. LME. ▸**b** Of a person: wearing threadbare clothes; shabby, seedy; impecunious. Now *rare* or *obsolete*. L16.

2 *fig.* Having lost effect, freshness, or force through overuse; trite from constant repetition; commonplace, hackneyed. L16.

📖 **1** E. WAUGH A . . shabby saloon car, upholstered in threadbare plush. I. MURDOCH The fine but . . threadbare Shiraz rug. **2** CHESTERFIELD The trite, threadbare jokes of those who set up for wit without having any. SIR W. SCOTT This quotation is rather threadbare.

■ **threadbareness** *noun* M16.

threaded /ˈθrɛdɪd/ *adjective*. ME.
[from THREAD *noun*, *verb*: see -ED[2], -ED[1].]

1 Provided with a thread or threads, esp. of a specified kind; that has been threaded. ME.

2 COMPUTING. **a** Of a list or tree: containing extra linkages as well as a pointer from each item to the following node. M20. ▸**b** Of a program etc.: formed from or involving a set of separate units, sections, modules, etc., which may be linked into a continuous sequence. Also *spec.* = MULTI-THREADED. L20.

threadle /ˈθrɛd(ə)l/ *verb trans. & intrans.* Long *dial.* M18.
[from THREAD *verb* + -LE[3].]
= THREAD *verb*.

Threadneedle Street /ˈθrɛdniːd(ə)l striːt, -ˈniːd-/ *noun phr.* E20.
[A street in the City of London where the Bank of England is located.]
The Bank of England or its directors. Cf. ***the Old Lady in Threadneedle Street*** s.v. OLD *adjective*.

threadworm /ˈθrɛdwəːm/ *noun*. E19.
[from THREAD *noun* + WORM *noun*.]
A worm with a very slender threadlike form; infection with such a worm; *spec.* = ***pinworm*** (a) s.v. PIN *noun*[1].

thready /ˈθrɛdi/ *adjective*. L16.
[from THREAD *noun* + -Y[1].]

1 Of, pertaining to, or of the nature of thread or threads; consisting or made of thread or threads; threadlike. L16.

†**2** Of a spindle or shuttle: full of thread. L16–M18.

3 Feeble, faint; *spec.* (*a*) (of the pulse) scarcely perceptible; (*b*) (of a sound, esp. the voice) lacking fullness, scarcely audible, faint. M18.

📖 **1** G. E. DAY The mucus will become very tough, and almost thready. G. MACDONALD Her black hair . . revealed a thready glitter of grey. **3** H. MCLEAVE [The doctor] placed his . . finger on the pulse. 'Thready and weak . .' he commented. *New Yorker* The thready whine of taped country music.

■ **threadiness** *noun* (*rare*) LME.

threap /θriːp/ *verb & noun*. Now *Scot. & north*. Also **threep**.
[Old English *þrēapian*, of unkn. origin.]

▶ **A** *verb*. **1** *verb trans.* Rebuke, reprove, scold, blame. OE.

2 *verb intrans.* Inveigh *against*; argue (*with*); quarrel, bicker; wrangle. ME.

3 *verb trans.* Persist in asserting, maintain, (something, *that*). LME. ▸**b** Insist on or persist in doing something. Foll. by *to do*. *rare*. E19.

4 †**a** *verb trans.* Impose (a belief etc.) *on* a person, esp. by persistent assertion. LME–E17. ▸†**b** *verb trans.* Impute, attribute, or ascribe (a specified quality) to a person. Foll. by *on*, *of*. M16–M18. ▸**c** *verb trans.* Thrust or press (something) *on* a person. L16. ▸**d** *verb intrans.* Urge some action of (a person); nag. Usu. foll. by *at*, *on*. E19.

▶ **B** *noun*. The action or an act of threaping. ME.

Comb.: **threap-ground**, **threap-land(s)** land of disputed ownership; *spec.* (*Hist.*) the tract between the Rivers Esk and Sark on the border between England and Scotland.

■ **threaper** *noun* L19.

threat /θrɛt/ *noun*.
[Old English *þrēat* (masc.) cogn. with Old Norse *þraut* (fem.) struggle, labour, from Germanic base of next.]

▶ **I** †**1** A throng or crowd of people; a troop, a band. OE–ME.

▶ **II** †**2** Oppression, compulsion; torment; distress, misery; danger. OE–LME.

3 A declaration of an intention to take some hostile action; *esp.* a declaration of an intention to inflict pain, injury, damage, or other punishment in retribution for something done or not done; CHESS a move that creates (esp. intentionally) the possibility of a capture or other advantageous move. Also, an indication of the approach of something unwelcome or undesirable; a person or thing regarded as a likely cause of harm etc. ME.

4 ZOOLOGY. Animal behaviour that keeps other animals at a distance or strengthens social dominance without physical conflict. M20.

📖 **3** SHAKES. *Jul. Caes.* There is no terror, Cassius, in your threats. E. WHARTON A threat of rain darkened the sky. R. SCRUTON The movement to reform the House of Lords has arisen in the face of a threat to abolish it. *New York Times* Coal mining in those areas was a threat to public safety. **under threat** at risk; exposed to the possibility *of* some specified adverse action or circumstance. ***4 threat display***, ***threat signal***, etc.

threat /θrɛt/ *verb*. Now *arch., Scot., & dial.*
[Old English *þrēatian* threaten, *þrēotan* trouble, Dutch *verdrieten* weary, Old High German *irdriozan* vex (German *verdriessen* annoy), Gothic *usþriutan* trouble, from Germanic, prob. cogn. with Latin *trudere* thrust.]

†**1** *verb trans.* Press, urge, try to force or induce, esp. by means of threats. Foll. by *that*, *to do*. OE–M17.

†**2** *verb trans.* Rebuke, reprove. OE–ME.

3 *verb trans.* = THREATEN 2. OE.

4 *verb trans.* = THREATEN 3, 5. ME.

5 *verb intrans.* = THREATEN 4. ME.

¶ Largely superseded by THREATEN.

threaten /ˈθrɛt(ə)n/ *verb*.
[Old English *þrēatnian*, from THREAT *noun* + -EN[5].]

†**1** *verb trans.* = THREAT *verb* 1. Only in OE.

2 *verb trans.* Make a threat or threats against (a person). Freq. foll. by *with* a specified action. ME. ▸†**b** Command sternly or strictly, esp. with threats of punishment or displeasure. (Chiefly in biblical translations.) LME–L16. ▸**c** Constitute a threat to; be likely to injure; be a source of harm or danger to. M17.

3 *verb trans.* Make a threat or threats *to do*; declare one's intention of inflicting (punishment, injury, etc.) in retribution for something done or not done. ME. ▸**b** In weakened sense: express an intention or promise *to do*. Freq. *joc.* E20.

4 *verb intrans.* Make or utter a threat or threats; declare one's intention of inflicting punishment, injury, etc. ME.

5 *verb trans.* Be a sign or indication of the approach of (something unwelcome or undesirable); presage, portend; appear likely *to do* something unwelcome or undesirable. M16.

📖 **2** HOBBES Threatning them with Punishment. DEFOE I won't be threatened neither. G. S. HAIGHT Mr. Jones was threatened with mob action. **c** R. L. FOX Hordes of Gauls pour into Greece . . and threaten her civilisation. **3** H. H. WILSON Reluctant to inflict the penalty that had been threatened. J. BERGER Your husband . . has just threatened to shoot me if I speak to you again. *Yorkshire Post* Head teachers threatened industrial action. N. HERMAN Mary threatened to leave home unless given her own room. **b** *New Yorker* His father didn't speak French but was always threatening to learn. **4** SHAKES. *Haml.* An eye like Mars, to threaten and command. G. NAYLOR Snow was threatening. **5** T. DREISER It even threatened snow at times. G. GREENE The conversation threatened to turn ugly.

¶ Largely superseding THREAT *verb*.

■ **threatener** *noun* LME. **threatening** *verbal noun* the action of the verb; an instance of this, a threat: ME. **threatening** *ppl adjective* that threatens; menacing: M16. **threateningly** *adverb* E17. **threateningness** *noun* (*rare*) L19.

threatened /ˈθrɛt(ə)nd/ *adjective*. M16.
[from prec. + -ED[1].]
That is or has been threatened; *spec.* (of a plant or animal) in danger of becoming rare or extinct.

📖 *Birds Magazine* The world's rare, endangered and threatened birds. N. BAWDEN I had always felt threatened when people . . did not agree with me.

threatful /ˈθrɛtfʊl, -f(ə)l/ *adjective*. *literary*. M16.
[from THREAT *noun* + -FUL.]
Full of threats; threatening.

■ **threatfully** *adverb* (*rare*) M16.

threave *noun* var. of THRAVE.

three /θriː/ *adjective & noun (cardinal numeral)*.
[Old English *þrī*, *þrie* masc., *þrīo*, *þrēo* fem., neut. = Old Frisian *thrē*, *thriā*, *thriū*, Old Saxon *þria*, *þrea*, *þriu* (Dutch *drie*), Old High German *drī*, *drīo*, *driu* (German *drei*), Old Norse *þrír*, *þriár*, *þriú*, Gothic *þrija*, from Germanic from Indo-European, whence also Latin *tres*, *tria*, Greek *treis*, *tria*, Sanskrit *trayah*, *trī*, Avestan *θrāyō*, *θri*.]

▶ **A** *adjective*. One more than two (a cardinal numeral represented by 3 in arabic numerals, iii, III in roman). OE.

📖 J. CONRAD Almayer . . had been three days in Macassar. D. HOGAN Camels . . greeted sandstorms with the same indifference as they had three thousand years before. *Woman* Three stylish colours, classic cream, elegant grey or chic black. *Japan Times* The maximum temperature in . . Tokyo is three degrees higher than in outlying areas. ***clogs to clogs in three generations***: see CLOG *noun*. ***drink the three outs***: see OUT *noun* 2. ***the three Estates of the Realm***: see ESTATE *noun*; ***the three Magi***: see MAGUS 2. ***the three R's***: see R, R 1. ***the three sisters***: see SISTER *noun*. **three ages** ARCHAEOLOGY the Stone, Bronze, and Iron Ages as basic divisions of the prehistoric period. ***three balls***: see BALL *noun*[1]. ***three cheers***: see CHEER *noun*[1] 7. **three faces under a hood**, **three faces in a hood** *dial.* the wild pansy, *Viola tricolor*. ***three figures***: see FIGURE *noun*. **three fourths** *arch.* (*a*) three-quarters; (*b*) the greater part, most of. **Three Hours (Service)** a devotional service lasting from 12 to 3 p.m. on Good Friday, intended to represent the hours of the Crucifixion; ***three monkeys***: see MONKEY *noun*. ***three musketeers***: see MUSKETEER. **three parts** three out of four equal parts, three-quarters. ***three sheets to the wind***: see SHEET *noun*[2]. **three wise men** (*a*) = *the Magi* s.v. MAGUS 2; (*b*) three advisers or arbitrators. ***three wise monkeys***: see MONKEY *noun*. ***two or three***: see TWO *adjective* 1.

▶ **B** *noun.* **1** Three persons or things identified contextually, as parts or divisions, years of age, points, runs, etc., in a game, chances (in giving odds), minutes, inches, shillings (now *Hist.*), pence, etc. **OE.**

2 One more than two as an abstract number; the symbol(s) or figure(s) representing this (3 in arabic numerals, iii, III in roman); a figure shaped like three, esp. in ice-skating. **OE.**

3 The time of day three hours after midnight or midday (on a clock, watch, etc., indicated by the numeral three displayed or pointed to). Also ***three o'clock***. **LME.**

4 A set of three; a thing having a set of three as an essential or distinguishing feature; *spec.* (*a*) a playing-card, domino, or side of a die marked with three pips or spots; (*b*) CRICKET a hit for which three runs are scored; (*c*) a unit of three soldiers in military drill, formed when executing a wheeling movement. **L15.**

5 The third of a set or series with numbered members, the one designated three (usu. ***number three***, or with specification, as ***book three***, ***chapter three***, etc.); a size etc. denoted by three, a shoe, glove, garment, etc., of such a size, (also ***size three***). **E16.**

6 Each of a set of three; *spec.* a large plant-pot of which three are formed from one cast of clay. **E19.**

▯ **1** DAY LEWIS I never revisited the place, which we left before I was three. *Which?* Not much legroom or headroom; just about width for three. ***rule of three***: see RULE *noun*. **Three in One** the Holy Trinity. **3** K. A. PORTER A storm came up at three in the morning. **4** *Field* The poachers' normal practice is to operate in twos and threes. **5** ***Radio Three***: see RADIO *noun* 3.

Comb.: Forming compound cardinal numerals with multiples of ten from twenty to ninety, as ***thirty-three***, (*arch.*) ***three-and-thirty***, etc., and (*arch.*) their corresponding ordinals, as ***three-and-thirtieth*** etc., and with multiples of a hundred, as *203* (read ***two hundred and three***, *US* also ***two hundred three***), etc. With nouns + -ER[1] forming nouns with the sense 'something (identified contextually) being of or having three —s', as ***three-seater***, ***three-wheeler***, etc. Special combs., as **three-address** *adjective* (COMPUTING) (employing instructions) having three addresses, two that specify the location of the two operands and one that specifies where the result is to be stored; **three-axis** *adjective* having or involving an ability to be rotated about each of three mutually perpendicular axes; **three-ball** *adjective & noun* (GOLF) (*a*) *adjective* (of a match) involving three players, each using a separate ball; (*b*) *noun* a three-ball golf match; **three-banded** *adjective* having or marked with three bands; ***three-banded armadillo***, an armadillo of the genus *Tolypeutes*, having three narrow ridged bands across the centre of the shell; **three-bar** *adjective* (*a*) GEOMETRY (of a curve) generated (as) by the motion of three bars pivoted together; (*b*) (of an electric fire) having three heating elements; **three-birds(-flying)** an ornamental toadflax, *Linaria triornithophora*, whose flowers suggest three birds perched on the spur; **three-body** *adjective* (MATH. & PHYSICS) involving or pertaining to three objects or particles; esp. in ***three-body problem***, the problem of determining the motion of three bodies mutually attracted by gravity; **three-card** *adjective* pertaining to or played with three cards; *spec.* (*a*) ***three-card monte***: see MONTE *noun* 1; (*b*) ***three-card trick***, in which a queen and two other cards are spread out face downwards, and bystanders invited to bet which is the queen (also called ***find the lady***); **three-colour** *adjective* (*a*) using or involving three distinct colours or wavelengths of light; esp. in ***three-colour process***, a means of reproducing a full range of colour by a combination of three primary colours in appropriate proportions; (*b*) designating *san ts'ai* ware; **three-corner** *adjective* three-cornered; **three-cornered** *adjective* (*a*) having three corners; triangular; (*b*) (of a contest etc.) between three individuals; (*c*) *fig.* (of a person) awkward, peevish; (*d*) ***three-cornered jack*** (*Austral.*), the fruit of the weed *Emex australis*, which bears three rigid spines; **three-cushion** *adjective* designating a type of billiards in which the cushion must be struck at least three times by a ball at each play in any one of four ways; **three-day** *adjective* consisting of or extending over three days; ***three-day event***, an equestrian competition, usu. consisting of three different events (dressage, cross-country, and show-jumping) taking place over three days; ***three-day eventer***, a horse participating in a three-day event; ***three-day week***, a reduced working week of only three days; **three-day fever**, **three-days fever** = DENGUE; **three-deck**, **three-decked** *adjectives* (esp. of a ship) having three decks; **three-decker** *noun & adjective* (designating) something with three decks, layers, or divisions; *spec.* (*a*) (designating) a warship with three gun-decks; (*b*) (designating) a three-volume novel; (*c*) (designating) a sandwich made with three slices of bread; **three-dimensional** *adjective* (*a*) having or appearing to have length, breadth, and depth; (*b*) *fig.* realistic, lifelike; believable; **three-dimensionality** three-dimensional quality; **three-dimensionally** *adverb* in a three-dimensional manner, in terms of three dimensions; **three-double** *adjective* (now *rare*) folded in three; consisting of three layers or thicknesses; **three-eight** *adjective & noun* (designating) time or rhythm with three quavers in a bar; **three-field** *adjective* designating a method of agriculture in which three fields are worked on a three-course system of two crops and a fallow; **three-foot** *adjective* †(*a*) three-footed; (*b*) measuring three feet in length, breadth, etc.; **three-footed** *adjective* having three feet; (esp. of a stool) having three supports; **three-four** *adjective & noun* (designating) time or rhythm with three crotchets in a bar; **three-gaited** *adjective* (of a horse) trained to walk, trot, and canter; **three-halfpence** *Hist.* a penny and a halfpenny, esp. of the old British currency before decimalization; **three-halfpenny** *adjective* (now *arch.* & *Hist.*) worth or costing three-halfpence; *fig.* paltry, contemptible; **three-halves power** the square root of the cube of a number; ELECTRONICS used *attrib.* to designate a law that the anode current of a valve is proportional to the three-halves power of the anode voltage; **three-in-hand** a carriage, coach, etc., drawn by three horses, a unicorn; **three-legged** *adjective* having three legs; ***three-legged mare***: see MARE *noun*[1]; ***three-legged race***, a race run between pairs, the right leg of one person being tied to the left leg of the other; **three-letter man** (*a*) *US* a person awarded a mark of distinction in three different sports; (*b*) *colloq.* an obnoxious person; **three-line**, **three-lined** *adjectives* having, consisting of, or marked with three lines; *spec.* (*a*) PRINTING (of a large capital letter) extending to the depth of three lines of text; (*b*) ***three-line whip***, a written notice, underlined three times to indicate great urgency, requesting the members of Parliament of a particular party to attend a parliamentary vote; the discipline of such a notice; **three-martini lunch** *N. Amer.* a lavish lunch, *esp.* one charged to a business expense account; **three-mast**, **three-masted** *adjectives* having three masts; **three-master** a three-masted ship; **three-one** *adjective & noun* (*arch.*) (*a*) *adjective* triune; (*b*) *noun* the Holy Trinity; **three-part** *adjective* (MUSIC) composed for three parts or voices; **three-piece** *adjective & noun* (*a*) *adjective* consisting of three matching items, as a suite of furniture or a suit of clothes; (of a band) comprising three instruments or players; (*b*) *noun* a three-piece suit; a three-piece suite; **three-piecer** (chiefly *N. Amer.*) a three-piece suit; **three-pile** *adjective & noun* (*a*) *adjective* (of velvet) having a pile made of three-ply yarn; (*b*) *noun* three-pile velvet; **three-piled** *adjective* (*a*) three-pile; thick; (*b*) *fig.* of the highest quality, refined; excessive, extreme, intense; **three-point** *adjective* (*a*) marked or graded with three points; (BASKETBALL) designating a goal shot from beyond a specified distance; (*b*) with contact at three points; ***three-point landing***, the landing of an aircraft on the two main wheels and the tail wheel or skid simultaneously; (*c*) involving the measurement of three known points to determine one's position in surveying, navigation, etc.; (*d*) ***three-point turn***, a method of turning a vehicle round in a narrow space, by moving in three arcs, forwards, backwards, then forwards again; **three-pointer** (*a*) a three-point landing; (*b*) a three-point turn; (*c*) BASKETBALL a three-point goal; **three-pounder** a gun throwing a shot that weighs three pounds; **three-pronged** *adjective* having three prongs or projecting points (***three-pronged bristletail***: see ***bristletail*** s.v. BRISTLE *noun*); **three-quarter** *noun & adjective* (*a*) *noun* (RUGBY FOOTBALL) (the position of) each of three or four players playing between the half-backs and the full-backs (also more fully ***three-quarter back***); (*b*) *adjective* consisting of three-quarters of something; measuring three-quarters of something identified contextually; (of a coat etc.) being three-quarters of the normal length (also more fully ***three-quarter length***); (of a portrait etc.) three-fourths of the area of a Kit-cat; showing the figure as far as the hips; ***three-quarter-face*** (esp. in PHOTOGRAPHY), the aspect between full face and profile; **three-quarters** *noun & adverb* (*a*) *noun* three of the four equal parts into which something is or may be divided; the greater part of something; (*b*) *adverb* to the extent of three quarters; almost, very nearly; **three-ring circus** (*a*) a circus having three rings for simultaneous performances; (*b*) *transf.* a showy or extravagant display; a scene of confusion or disorder; **threescore** *arch.* sixty; **three-sixty** (in various sports, aerobatics, etc.) a turn through 360 degrees; **three-space** three-dimensional space; ***three-spined*** STICKLEBACK; **three-spot** *US* a three-pipped playing-card; **three-square** (now *dial.* & *techn.*), †**three-squared** *adjectives* having three equal sides; (esp. of a file) equilaterally triangular in cross-section; **three-star** *adjective & noun* (*a*) *adjective* given three stars in a grading in which this denotes a high quality, usu. one grade below four-star; having or designating a military rank distinguished by three stars on the shoulder-piece of the uniform; (*b*) *noun* a thing given a three-star grading; **three strikes (and you're out)** [with ref. to baseball] (orig. in the US) denoting or relating to legislation providing that an offender's third felony is punishable by life imprisonment or other severe sentence; ***three-striper***: see STRIPER 1; **three-toed** *adjective* having three toes; ***three-toed sloth***, a sloth of the genus *Bradypus*, having three claws on each foot; ***three-toed woodpecker***, any of various woodpeckers having only three toes on each foot, esp. *Picoides tridactylus* of the northern hemisphere; **three-tongued** *adjective* (now *rare* or *obsolete*) (*a*) having three tongues; (*b*) trilingual; **three-two** *adjective & noun* (designating) time or rhythm with three minims in a bar; **three-valued** *adjective* having three values; *spec.* in PHILOSOPHY, designating a logical system or technique which incorporates a third value such as indeterminacy, uncertainty, half-truth, etc., in addition to the values of truth and falsehood customary in two-valued systems; **three-way** *adjective* (*a*) having or connecting with three ways, roads, etc.; situated where three ways meet; ***three-way cock***, ***three-way valve***: with an inlet and two alternative outlets; (*b*) involving three participants; (*c*) (of a loudspeaker) having three separate drive units for different frequency ranges.

■ **threefold** *adjective & adverb* (*a*) *adjective* three times as great or as numerous; having three parts, divisions, elements, or units; triple; (*b*) *adverb* to three times the number or quantity; triply; ***thick and threefold***: see THICK *adverb* 2: **OE.** **threefoldly** *adverb* in a threefold manner **OE.** **threeness** *noun* the fact, quality, or condition of being three in number or threefold; *esp.* the triune quality of the Holy Trinity: **E19.** **threesome** *noun & adjective* (*a*) *noun* a set of three persons or things; a group of three; a game for three; *esp.* in GOLF, a match in which one person plays against two opponents; (*b*) *adjective* consisting of three; for three; *esp.* (of a dance) performed by three people together: **LME.**

threep *verb & noun* var. of THREAP.

three-peat /ˈθriːpiːt/ *verb & noun. N. Amer.* **L20.**
[from THREE + RE)PEAT *verb*.]
▶ **A** *verb intrans.* Win a particular championship etc. three times, esp. consecutively. **L20.**
▶ **B** *noun.* A set of three such victories. **L20.**

threepence /ˈθrɛp(ə)ns, ˈθrʊ-, ˈθrʌ-/ *noun.* **L16.**
[from THREE *adjective* + PENCE. Cf. THRUPPENCE.]
Three pence, esp. of the old British currency before decimalization; *Hist.* a threepenny bit.

threepenny /ˈθrʌp(ə)ni, ˈθrʊ-/ *adjective & noun.* **LME.**
[from THREE + PENNY. Cf. THRUPPENNY.]
▶ **A** *adjective.* **1** Worth or costing threepence or three (new) pence. **LME.**
2 *fig.* Trifling, paltry, cheap. *arch.* **E17.**
1 threepenny bit *Hist.* a coin worth three old pence, orig. silver, later nickel brass and dodecagonal. **threepenny nail** [orig. costing threepence per hundred] a small nail.
▶ **B** *noun.* A coin worth threepence; a threepenny bit. **E18.**

threitol /ˈθriːɪtɒl/ *noun.* **M20.**
[from THREOSE + -ITOL.]
CHEMISTRY. A polyhydric alcohol, $HOCH_2(CHOH)_2CH_2OH$, formed by the reduction of threose.

threne /θriːn/ *noun.* Now chiefly *poet.* Also in Greek form **threnos** /ˈθriːnɒs/, pl. **-noi** /-nɔɪ/. **LME.**
[Greek *thrēnos* funeral lament.]
A song of lamentation; a dirge, a threnody. Formerly *spec.* (in *pl.*) = ***Lamentations (of Jeremiah)*** s.v. LAMENTATION 2.
■ **threˈnetic** *adjective* of, pertaining to, or of the nature of a threne; mournful: **M17.**

threnode /ˈθrɛnəʊd/ *noun. rare.* **M19.**
[Alt., after ODE.]
= next.

threnody /ˈθrɛnədi/ *noun.* **M17.**
[Greek *thrēnōidia*, from *thrēnos* THRENE + *ōidē* song, ODE: see -Y[3].]
A song of lamentation, esp. for the dead; a dirge.

▯ H. JACOBSON The low moaning threnody of fourteen million souls in exile.

■ **threnodial** /-ˈnəʊdɪəl/ *adjective* **E19.** **threnodic** /-ˈnɒdɪk/ *adjective* **L19.** **threnodist** *noun* a composer or performer of threnodies **E19.**

threnoi, **threnos** *nouns* see THRENE.

threonine /ˈθriːəniːn/ *noun.* **M20.**
[from next + -N- + -INE[5] (so named as having a similar molecular configuration to threose).]
BIOCHEMISTRY. A hydrophilic amino acid, $CH_3CH(OH)CH(NH_2)COOH$, widely present in proteins and essential in the human diet; 2-amino-3-hydroxybutanoic acid.

threose /ˈθriːəʊz, -s/ *noun.* **E20.**
[from ERYTHROSE by arbitrary rearrangement: see -OSE[2].]
CHEMISTRY. A hygroscopic solid tetrose sugar, $CHO{\cdot}(CHOH)_2{\cdot}CH_2OH$, existing as two optical isomers and differing from erythrose in having the hydroxyl groups on the second and third carbon atoms on opposite sides of the carbon chain.

thresh *noun* see THRASH *noun*.

thresh /θrɛʃ/ *verb.* Also **thrash** /θraʃ/. See also THRASH *verb*.
[Old English *þerscan* (late Old English with metathesis *þrescan*, *þryscan*) = Middle Low German, Middle Dutch *derschen* (Low German, Dutch *dorschen*), Old High German *dreskan* (German *dreschen*), Old Norse *þreskja*, Gothic *þriskan*, from Germanic, from Indo-European base repr. in Balto-Slavonic by words meaning 'crackle', 'crash', 'rattle'.]
▶ **I 1** *verb trans. & intrans.* Shake, beat, or mechanically treat (corn etc.) to separate the grain from the husk and straw, esp. with a flail or by the action of a revolving mechanism. **OE.**

▯ **1** P. KAVANAGH He should have his corn threshed by machine rather than . . flail. **thresh over** analyse (a problem etc.) in search of a solution.

▶ **II 2** See THRASH *verb*.

threshel /ˈθrɛʃ(ə)l/ *noun.* Now *dial.*
[Old English *perscel* cogn. with Old High German *driscil* (German *Drischel*): see prec., -EL[1].]
A flail.

thresher /ˈθrɛʃə/ *noun*[1]. Also **thrasher** /ˈθraʃə/. See also THRASHER *noun*[1]. **ME.**
[from prec. + -ER[1].]
▶ **I 1** A person who or thing which threshes corn etc. **ME.**
2 A shark, *Alopias vulpinus*, with a very long upper lobe to its tail with which it can lash the water to direct its prey. Also ***thresher shark***. **E17.**
▶ **II** See THRASHER *noun*[1].

Thresher /ˈθrɛʃə/ *noun*[2]. **E19.**
[See below.]
Hist. A member of an Irish political organization established in 1806, which issued manifestos signed 'Captain Thresher'.

thresher *noun*[3] var. of THRASHER *noun*[2].

threshing /ˈθrɛʃɪŋ/ *noun.* Also **thrashing** /ˈθraʃɪŋ/. See also THRASHING. **LME.**
[from THRESH *verb* + -ING[1].]
▶ **I 1** The action of THRESH *verb* I. Also (*rare*), grain obtained by threshing. **LME.**
▶ **II 2** See THRASHING.
Comb.: **threshing-floor** a prepared hard level surface on which corn etc. is threshed, esp. with a flail; **threshing-machine** a

power-driven machine for threshing corn etc.; **threshing-mill** a mill, worked by wind- or water-power, for threshing corn etc.

threshold /ˈθrɛʃəʊld, ˈθrɛʃhəʊld/ *noun.*
[Old English *þerscold*, *þrescold*, etc. = Old Norse *þreskǫldr*, *-kjǫldr*, Old High German *driscūfli* (German dial. *Drischaufel*): 1st elem. rel. to THRESH *verb*, 2nd elem. of unkn. origin.]
1 A sill of timber or stone forming the bottom of a doorway and crossed in entering a house or room; the entrance to a house, building, or room. OE.
2 The border or limit of a region; the point or line crossed on entry; *spec.* the beginning of the landing area on an airfield runway. OE. ▸**b** *fig.* A point of beginning or entry, the starting-point of an experience or undertaking. L16. ▸†**c** An obstacle, a stumbling-block. E17–E18.
3 A lintel. *rare.* E19.
4 A lower limit of some state, condition, or effect; the limit below which a stimulus is not perceptible or does not evoke a response; the magnitude or intensity that must be exceeded for a certain reaction, phenomenon, result, or condition to occur or be manifested. L19.
5 A step in a scale of wages or taxation, at which increases become due or obligatory, usu. operative under specific conditions, as rises in the cost of living etc. Freq. *attrib.* L19.

📖 **1** JOAN SMITH She went back to the door . . and paused on the threshold. **2** *Westminster Gazette* On what is known as 'the threshold of England', the Sussex coast. **b** M. SCAMMELL He seemed on the threshold of a brilliant career. *New Yorker* The Cold War was . . ending, and a threshold to something new was materialising. ***stumble at the threshold, stumble on the threshold***: see STUMBLE *verb* 1. **4** *Abingdon Herald* The 'vote threshold', below which candidates lose their deposit, should be reduced. A. STEVENS Many of our perceptions . . occur beneath the threshold of consciousness.

threshold /ˈθrɛʃəʊld, ˈθrɛʃhəʊld/ *verb trans.* M20.
[from the noun.]
In image processing, alter (an image) by reproducing it in two tones only, each part being dark or light according as the original is darker or lighter than some chosen threshold shade.

threst /θrɛst/ *verb. obsolete* exc. *Scot.*
[Old English *þræstan*, with no known cognates.]
†**1** *verb intrans.* Writhe, twist. Only in OE.
†**2** *verb trans.* Torture, torment; afflict; constrain. Only in OE.
3 *verb intrans.* Press; push; push one's way, jostle. Freq. foll. by *in*, *out*, etc. ME.
†**4** *verb trans.* Pierce, stab. ME–M16.
†**5** *verb trans.* Push forcibly or violently; thrust. ME–M16.

threw *verb pa. t.*: see THROW *verb.*

thribble /ˈθrɪb(ə)l/ *adjective & adverb, verb, & noun.* Also **thrible**. E19.
[Var. of TREBLE *adjective & adverb, verb, & noun.*]
▶ **A** *adjective & adverb.* Three times as much or as many; treble. *dial.* E19.
▶ **B** *verb intrans.* Become three times as much or as many as before; treble. *dial.* L19.
▶ **C** *noun.* In oil drilling, a 90-foot section of pipe consisting of three 30-foot lengths. Chiefly *US.* M20.

thrice /θrʌɪs/ *adverb & adjective.* Now chiefly *arch.* or *literary.*
[Old English *þriga*, *þrīwa* = Old Frisian *thria*, Old Saxon *þriwo*, *þrio*: see THREE, -S³. Cf. ONCE, TWICE. The spelling *-ce* is phonetic to retain the unvoiced sound denoted in the earlier spelling by *-s*.]
▶ **A** *adverb.* **1** Three times; on three successive occasions; to three times as much as the number or quantity; many times as much. OE.
2 Very, greatly, highly, extremely. L16.

📖 **1** TENNYSON With some surprise and thrice as much disdain. *Daily Herald* Barbara Hutton, the thrice-married Woolworth millionairess. A. T. ELLIS She took a long white scarf . . wound it thrice about her neck and went out. **2** TENNYSON Thrice blest whose lives are faithful prayers.

▶ **B** *adjective.* Performed or occurring three times; threefold, triple. Formerly also, very great. *rare.* LME.

📖 J. M. NEALE Till the thrice Confession Blot the thrice Denial out.

thrid *verb* see THREAD *verb.*

†**thridborrow** *noun* var. of THIRDBOROUGH.

thrift /θrɪft/ *noun*¹ & *verb.* ME.
[Old Norse *þrift*, formed as THRIVE *verb*: see -T³.]
▶ **A** *noun.* **1 a** The state or condition of thriving or being prosperous; prosperity, success. Also, fortune; luck. *obsolete* exc. *Scot.* ME. ▸**b** Vigorous growth. *rare.* ME. ▸**c** Means of thriving or prospering; industry; profitable occupation. Now *Scot. & dial.* L16. ▸**d** Growing-pains. *dial.* L18.
2 Savings, earnings; profit; acquired wealth. *arch.* ME.
3 Economical management; sparing use or careful expenditure of means; frugality. M16. ▸**b** A savings and loan association. *US.* L20.
4 A European plant of coasts and heaths, *Armeria maritima* (family Plumbaginaceae), having dense heads of small pink flowers, leafless stems, and dense rosettes of linear leaves (also called ***sea pink***). Also (with specifying word), any of several other plants of this genus or formerly included in it. L16.

📖 **1c** ALLAN RAMSAY Poor Vulcan hard at thrift. **2** C. ROSSETTI If much were mine, then manifold Would be the offering of my thrift. **3** J. A. MICHENER The earth uses its materials with uncanny thrift; it wastes nothing. P. P. READ The triumph of his generosity over his instinctive thrift.

Comb.: **thrift industry** *US* savings and loan associations regarded collectively; **thrift institution** *US* a savings and loan association; **thrift shop**, **thrift store** a shop selling second-hand goods (esp. clothes), usu. in aid of charity.

▶ **B** *verb trans.* Save thriftily, economize. *rare.* M19.

thrift /θrɪft/ *noun*². L19.
[Origin unkn.]
The (usu. wooden) handle of a mill-bill.

thriftless /ˈθrɪftlɪs/ *adjective.* LME.
[from THRIFT *noun*¹ + -LESS.]
†**1** Not thriving or prosperous; unsuccessful; unfortunate. Formerly also (*rare*), not flourishing in growth. LME–L17.
2 Unprofitable, worthless, useless. Now chiefly *Scot.* M16.
3 Wasteful, improvident, spendthrift. L16.

📖 **2** SHAKES. *Twel. N.* What thriftless sighs shall poor Olivia breathe! **3** C. S. PARKER He strove . . to wean his tenantry from thriftless habits.

■ **thriftlessly** *adverb* M19. **thriftlessness** *noun* M19.

thrifty /ˈθrɪfti/ *adjective.* LME.
[from THRIFT *noun*¹ + -Y¹.]
1 Characterized by success or prosperity; thriving, prosperous, successful; fortunate. LME.
†**2** (Of a person) worthy, estimable, respectable; (of an action or thing) decent, becoming, proper, seemly. LME–M17.
3 Thriving physically; growing healthily or vigorously; flourishing. LME.
4 Characterized by thrift or frugality; economical, careful of expenditure, sparing. E16. ▸†**b** Well-husbanded. *rare* (Shakes.). Only in E17.

📖 **1** E. BURRITT This is a thrifty, modern-looking town. **2** CHAUCER I sitte at hoom, I haue no thrifty clooth. **3** J. COX When choosing tomato seedlings . . pick those that are young, thrifty. **4** J. DOS PASSOS Concha was very thrifty and made Mac's pay go much further than he could. *Mining Magazine* A thrifty 6-cylinder Cummins diesel.

■ **thriftily** *adverb* LME. **thriftiness** *noun* E16.

†**thrill** *noun*¹. *Scot.* LME–L15.
[Alt. of THRALL *noun.* Cf. THIRL *noun*².]
A person who is bound in servitude, a thrall.

thrill /θrɪl/ *noun*² & *adjective.* L17.
[from THRILL *verb*¹.]
▶ **A** *noun.* **1** A sudden sensation of emotion or excitement producing a slight shudder or tingling feeling. L17. ▸**b** Thrilling property in a play, novel, speech, etc.; sensational quality. *rare.* L19. ▸**c** A thrilling or exciting experience or incident. M20.
2 The vibrating or quivering of something tangible or visible; a vibration, a pulsation, a throb. E19. ▸**b** *spec.* (MEDICINE) A vibratory movement felt when the hand is placed on the surface of the body. E19.

📖 **1** E. J. HOWARD A thrill of uncertainty and fear shot through her. B. VINE A small tic fluttered inside him. He was aware of an anticipatory thrill. **c** *House & Garden* A thrills and spills package involving a high-speed . . jetboat ride.

▶ **B** *attrib.* or as *adjective.* Of a crime: committed solely for the sake of the excitement experienced in carrying it out. *colloq.* E20.

📖 R. C. DENNIS The police think it was a thrill murder.

■ **thrilly** *adjective* (*a*) affected with a thrill; (*b*) having a thrilling or exciting quality: L19.

thrill *noun*³ see THILL *noun*¹.

thrill /θrɪl/ *verb*¹. ME.
[Metath. alt. of THIRL *verb*¹.]
▶ **I** Of material objects.
†**1** *verb trans. & intrans.* (with *through*). Pierce, bore, penetrate; break through (an enemy's line). ME–E18.
†**2** *verb trans.* Hurl (a pointed weapon). E–M17.

📖 **1** J. SYLVESTER Through . . Shirts of Mail His shaft shall thrill the Foes that him assail. **2** J. HEYWOOD Our . . Nymphs . . thrild their arrowie Iavelins after him.

▶ **II** Of immaterial forces.
†**3** *verb trans. & intrans.* (with *through*). Of a sound, an emotion, etc.: pierce, penetrate. ME–E18.
4 a *verb intrans.* Of an emotion, an event, etc.: produce a thrill; pass with a thrill *through.* L16. ▸**b** *verb intrans.* Feel or become affected by a thrill of emotion or excitement. Freq. foll. by *at*, *to.* L16. ▸**c** *verb trans.* Affect or move with a sudden sensation of emotion or excitement; *colloq.* (in *pass.*) be extremely pleased or delighted. E17.
5 a *verb trans.* Send out or utter thrillingly or tremulously. *rare.* M17. ▸**b** *verb intrans. & trans.* (Cause to) move tremulously or with vibration; (cause to) quiver or vibrate (as) with emotion. L18.

📖 **3** SPENSER With percing point Of pitty deare his hart was thrilled sore. **4a** S. LEACOCK A savage joy thrilled through me at the thought. **b** E. JOHNSON At fair time . . he had thrilled to the glorious smell of sawdust and orange peel. D. DAVIE The Anschluss, Guernica—all the names At which the poets thrilled or were afraid. **c** D. LEAVITT The magic . . of that meeting thrilled him still. *Architects' Journal* Many office workers are far from thrilled by the buildings they work in. **5b** T. HARDY The great valley of purple heath thrilling silently in the sun. P. KAVANAGH The song of the blackbird thrilled the evening.

■ **thrilling** *verbal noun* the action of the verb; an instance of this: E16. **thrilling** *adjective* that thrills; causing quivering, tingling, or shuddering; exciting: L16. **thrillingly** *adverb* E19. **thrillingness** *noun* M19.

†**thrill** *verb*² *trans. Scot.* LME–M16.
[from THRILL *noun*¹.]
Make a thrall of, enslave.
¶ Earlier form of THIRL *verb*².

†**thrillage** *noun. Scot.* LME–L15.
[from THRILL *noun*¹ + -AGE. Cf. THIRLAGE.]
Bondage, servitude.

†**thrillant** *adjective. rare* (Spenser). Only in L16.
[Irreg. from THRILL *verb*¹ + -ANT¹.]
Penetrating, piercing.

thriller /ˈθrɪlə/ *noun.* L19.
[from THRILL *verb*¹ + -ER¹.]
A person who or thing which thrills; *esp.* an exciting or sensational play, film, or novel, often involving crime or espionage.

📖 A. TYLER Those TV thrillers where spies rendezvoused in modern wastelands.

thrimble *verb* var. of THRUMBLE.

thrimsa /ˈθrɪmsə/ *noun.* Also **thrymsa**.
[Old English *þrimsa*, *þrymsa*, alt. of *trim(e)sa*, *trymesa* genit. pl. of *trimes*, *trymes* from late Latin *tremis* third part of an aureus, from *tres* three, after *semis* half (an as).]
Hist. An Anglo-Saxon gold or silver coin and money of account of uncertain value, representing the Roman tremissis. Also, a unit of weight equal to a drachm.

thrin /θrɪn/ *adjective & noun.* Also **thrinne**.
[Late Old English *þrinna* from early Old Norse *þrinnr* (later *þrennr*) triple, threefold, three, prob. from Germanic, cogn. with Sanskrit *trih*, Greek *tris* thrice. As noun, perh. a new formation after *twins*.]
▶†**A** *adjective.* Threefold, triple; three kinds of, three. LOE–ME.
▶ **B** *noun.* In *pl.* Triplets; three children or offspring at a birth. Chiefly *dial.* M19.

thring /θrɪŋ/ *noun*¹. *obsolete* exc. *dial.* Also **dring** /drɪŋ/.
[Old English *(ge)þring*, from THRING *verb.* Cf. DRONG, THRONG *noun.*]
A crowd, a press; a throng of people.

†**thring** *noun*². *rare.* ME–M19.
[App. alt.]
= DRENG.

thring /θrɪŋ/ *verb. obsolete* exc. *dial.* Also **dring** /drɪŋ/.
[Old English *þringan*, *þrungen* = Old Saxon *þringan* (Middle Low German, Dutch *dringen*), Old High German *dringan* (German *dringen*), Old Norse *þryngva*, *-gja*, from Germanic. Cf. DRONG, THRONG *verb.*]
†**1** *verb intrans.* Press, crowd, throng; move in a crowd; assemble. OE–E16. ▸†**b** *verb trans.* Crowd, gather or press closely around (a person). OE–E16.
2 *verb intrans.* Push forward, as against or through a crowd; force one's way hastily or eagerly; hasten, push on. OE.
3 *verb trans.* & †*intrans.* Press hard; use oppression (on); cause distress (to). ME.
4 *verb trans.* Thrust or drive violently; hurl; dash, knock. Usu. with adverb (phr.). ME. ▸**b** Foll. by *down*: throw down by force, knock down, overthrow (*lit. & fig.*); bring to ruin. LME.

thrinne *adjective & noun* var. of THRIN.

thrinter /ˈθrɪntə/ *adjective & noun.* Now *Scot. & north.* LME.
[Blend of THREE *adjective* and WINTER *noun.* Cf. TWINTER.]
▶ **A** *adjective.* Of a cow or sheep: of three winters; three years old. LME.
▶ **B** *noun.* A three-year-old sheep or (formerly) cow. LME.

thrip /θrɪp/ *noun*¹. *arch. slang.* L17.
[Abbreviation.]
Threepence; a threepenny bit.

thrip *noun*² var. of THRIPS.

thripple /ˈθrɪp(ə)l/ *noun.* Now *local.*
[Old English (Anglian) *þrēpel*, (West Saxon) *þrȳpel*, from unkn. 1st elem. + -LE¹.]
†**1** An execution cross; a framework. Only in OE.
2 A movable framework fitted on to a cart so as to increase its carrying capacity. LME.

thrips /θrɪps/ *noun.* Pl. same. Also **thrip**. L18.
[Latin (also used as mod. Latin genus name) from Greek *thrips*, pl. *thripes*, woodworm.]
Orig., any of various insect pests of plants. Now *spec.* a member of the order Thysanoptera of minute dark-coloured insects, typically having slender bodies and four fringed wings, many of which are pests of various plants. Also called ***thunderbug***, ***thunderfly***.

thrive /θrʌɪv/ *noun.* Long *obsolete* exc. *Scot.* & *dial.* L16.
[from the verb.]
Prosperity, thriving state; means of prospering, profitable occupation. Cf. THRIFT *noun*[1] 1a, c.

thrive /θrʌɪv/ *verb intrans.* Pa. t. **throve** /θrəʊv/, **thrived**; pa. pple **thriven** /ˈθrɪv(ə)n/, **thrived**. ME.
[Old Norse *þrífask* refl. of *þrífa* grasp, lay hold of suddenly.]
1 Orig., grow, increase. Later, grow or develop well and vigorously; *fig.* progress well, flourish, prosper. Freq. foll. by *on*. ME.
2 Increase in material wealth; be successful or fortunate; grow rich; (of a thing) be profitable or successful, turn out well. Freq. foll. by *on*. ME.

> **1** C. McCullough The baby thrived better than Meggie did, recovered faster from the birth ordeal. G. Tindall Daird had been born gregarious, . . had . . thrived on having people round him. P. Fussell Victorian . . chivalry throve . . on the mystique of monarchy. **2** *Harper's Magazine* Make your lives dependent upon your . . neighborhood, and household—which thrive by care and generosity. M. Robinson British industry had thriven . . on the labour of hungry and exhausted people.

■ **thriver** *noun* (*obsolete* exc. *dial.*) L16. **thrivingly** *adverb* in a thriving manner; prosperously, successfully, flourishingly: ME. **thrivingness** *noun* (*rare*) thriving condition, prosperity E19.

thriveless /ˈθrʌɪvlɪs/ *adjective. poet.* E16.
[from THRIVE *verb, noun*: see -LESS.]
Not thriving; lacking prosperity; unsuccessful, profitless.

thriven *verb pa. pple*: see THRIVE *verb*.

thro /θrəʊ/ *adjective & adverb. obsolete* exc. *Scot. dial.* Also **thra** /θrɑː/. ME.
[Old Norse *þrár*.]
▶ **A** *adjective.* **1** Stubborn, obstinate, persistent. ME.
†**2** Angry, furious, violent; keen, eager, earnest. ME–L15.
▶ **B** *adverb.* Obstinately; vigorously; boldly. LME.

thro' *preposition & adverb* var. of THROUGH *preposition & adverb*.

throat /θrəʊt/ *noun.*
[Old English *þrote*, *þrotu* = Old High German *drozza* (German *Drossel*: see THROTTLE *noun*), from Germanic, repr. also by Old Norse *þroti* swelling, Old English *þrūtian*, Old Norse *þrutna* to swell.]
▶ **I 1** The front of the neck beneath the chin and above the collar-bones, containing the upper parts of the gullet and windpipe, and blood-vessels serving the head. Also, the corresponding part in other vertebrates; occas., an analogous part in invertebrates. OE.
2 The passage which leads from the back of the mouth and nose to the gullet and windpipe in the front part of the neck; the pharynx and fauces. Also, the gullet, the windpipe. OE. ▸**b** A painful inflammation or infection of the throat. *colloq.* L19.
3 *fig.* The gullet, windpipe, or other passages, regarded as (***a***) the entrance to the stomach; (***b***) the voice or the source of the voice or speech; (***c***) the most vulnerable point of attack. Chiefly in phrs. below. ME.
†**4** *fig.* The devouring capacity of any destructive agency, as death, war, etc. L16–M18.

> **1** M. Keane Her hands were deeply sunburned and so was her throat. **2** Wilbur Smith Get me a beer, can't talk with a dry throat. A. Taylor His voice had almost gone from cancer of the throat. A. S. Byatt I have a sore throat. **4** Shakes. *Rich. III* He fights, Seeking for Richmond in the throat of death.

▶ **II** *transf.* **5** A narrow passage, esp. in or near the entrance of something; a narrow part in a passage. ME. ▸**b** SPORT. The part of a racket, bat, paddle, etc., which connects the head or blade to the shaft. E20. ▸**c** In a pistol, revolver, etc., the front section of the cylinder where it tapers towards the bore. M20.
6 ARCHITECTURE. **a** A groove or channel on the underside of a moulding, esp. to stop water reaching the wall; a moulding with such a channel. M17. ▸**b** The part in a chimney, furnace, etc., immediately above the fireplace, which narrows down to the neck. E19.
7 FORTIFICATION. = GORGE *noun*[1] 5. E18.
8 NAUTICAL. **a** The inward curve of a knee-timber. E18. ▸**b** The outside curve of the jaws of a gaff (now *rare*). Also, the forward upper corner of a fore-and-aft sail. L18.
9 BOTANY. The opening of a gamopetalous corolla, where the tube expands into the limb. M19.

> **5** N. Calder Plugs tend to form in the throat of the volcano. A. Brookner Decanters with silver throats and labels.

Phrases: ***a spark in one's throat***: see SPARK *noun*[1]. **be at each other's throats** quarrel violently. ***bur in the throat***: see BUR *noun*[1] 1. ***clergyman's sore throat***, ***clergyman's throat***: see CLERGY. **cut each other's throats** quarrel violently; engage in cutthroat or mutually destructive competition in trade etc. **cut one's own throat** bring about one's own downfall. **cut the throat of** kill (a person or animal) by severing essential veins or arteries in the neck; destroy, put an end to, (something). ***frog in the throat***: see FROG *noun*[1] 3. **have by the throat** *fig.* have a decisive grip on; ***have it by the throat***, ***have the game by the throat*** (*Austral. slang*), have the situation under control. ***jump down a person's throat***: see JUMP *verb*. **lie in one's throat** lie barefacedly or infamously. **pour down one's throat**, **pour down the throat** squander (property or money) in eating and drinking. **ram down a person's throat**, **thrust down a person's throat** force (an opinion, a thing, etc.) on a person's attention. ***stick in one's throat***: see STICK *verb*[1]. ***thrust down a person's throat***: see ***ram down a person's throat*** above.

Comb.: **throat-band** (***a***) = ***throat-lash*** below; (***b***) a band worn round the neck; a part of a garment encircling the neck; †**throat-bowl** the Adam's apple, the larynx; **throat-cutting** *noun & adjective* (***a***) *noun* the cutting of the throat; *fig.* mutually destructive competition in trade etc.; (***b***) *adjective* that cuts the throat; **throat-full** *adjective* (*rare*) full to the throat, stuffed, crammed; **throat halyard** NAUTICAL (in *pl.*) the ropes used to hoist or lower a gaff; **throat-lash**, **throat-latch** SADDLERY a strap passing under the horse's throat to help keep the bridle in position; **throat-mane** a growth of hair on the front of an animal's neck; **throat microphone**, (*colloq.*) **throat mike** a microphone attached to a speaker's throat and actuated by his or her larynx; **throat-pipe** (***a***) the windpipe; (***b***) the steam supply pipe in a steam engine; **throat-pouch** a gular sac in certain birds and animals; **throat-strap** = ***throat-lash*** above; **throat-wash** *rare* a medicinal gargle; **throatwort** any of several bellflowers reputed to cure sore throats, esp. *Campanula trachelium* and (more fully ***giant throatwort***) *C. latifolia*.

■ **throatal** *adjective* of, pertaining to, or produced in the throat E20. **throatful** *noun* as much as the throat can hold at once M19. **throatless** *adjective* without a throat, having no throat L19. **throatlet** *noun* an ornament or ornamental covering for the throat; a necklet, a small boa: M19.

throat /θrəʊt/ *verb trans.* LME.
[from prec.]
1 Cut the throat of (esp. a fish); slaughter, kill. *rare* exc. *techn.* LME.
2 Utter or articulate in or from the throat; express throatily. Also foll. by *out*. E17.
3 BUILDING. Provide with a throat or channel. Usu. in *pass.* E19.

> **2** R. Clay I was . . listening to . . cuckoos throating echoes from one side of the village to the other.

■ **throating** *noun* (***a***) the action of the verb; (***b***) *spec.* (BUILDING etc.) the cutting of a throat or channel, esp. on the underside of a moulding; the channel so cut: M18.

throated /ˈθrəʊtɪd/ *adjective.* M16.
[from THROAT *noun* or *verb* + -ED[2], -ED[1].]
Having or provided with a throat, esp. of a specified kind.
black-throated, ***deep-throated***, ***dry-throated***, etc.

throaty /ˈθrəʊti/ *adjective.* M17.
[from THROAT *noun* + -Y[1].]
1 Of a voice, vocal sound, etc.: produced or modified in the throat; guttural; hoarsely resonant, deep, husky. M17.
2 Of an animal: having loose pendulous skin about the throat; having a prominent or capacious throat. L18.

> **1** B. Emecheta The women were singing throaty gospel songs. G. Lees The big throaty baritone saxophone.

■ **throatily** *adverb* L19. **throatiness** *noun* L19.

throb /θrɒb/ *verb & noun.* LME.
[Prob. imit.]
▶ **A** *verb.* Infl. **-bb-**.
▶ **I** *verb intrans.* **1** Of the heart, pulse, etc.: beat, pulsate, esp. with more than the usual force or rapidity. LME. ▸**b** *transf.* Of an emotion etc.: pulsate strongly like or by means of the heart. Of a person, a body of people, etc.: feel or exhibit deep emotion; quiver. L18.
2 *gen.* Be moved or move rhythmically; pulsate or vibrate, esp. with a deep audible rhythm. M19.

> **1** H. Roth His heart throbbed in his ears. A. Burgess The noise made her head throb. *New Yorker* His arms throbbed from wrestling with the jack-hammer. **2** B. Mason The singing goes on, solid waves of sound, pulsing, throbbing.

▶ **II** *verb trans.* **3** Cause to throb or beat strongly. Formerly also, (of an emotion) pulsate strongly in reaction to (a misfortune etc.). *rare.* L16.
▶ **B** *noun.* **1** An act of throbbing; a usu. violent beat or pulsation of the heart etc. L16.
2 *transf.* & *fig.* A pulsating emotion; a (freq. audible) rhythmic beat or vibration. E17.

> **2** W. Irving He . . felt a throb of his old pioneer spirit. P. H. Gibbs The throb of the machines deep down in the basement. A. Hollinghurst The thump and throb of pop music could be heard.

■ **throbber** *noun* (*rare*) L19. **throbbingly** *adverb* in a throbbing manner; with pulsating heart or feeling: L17. **throbless** *adjective* (*rare*) without a throb or throbs; without feeling or emotion: M18.

throe /θrəʊ/ *noun & verb.* Also (earlier) †**throw(e)**. ME.
[Perh. rel. to Old English *þrēa*, *þrawu* threat, calamity, infl. by *þrōwian* suffer.]
▶ **A** *noun* (now usu. in *pl.*).
1 A violent physical spasm or pang, esp. in the pain and struggle of childbirth or death. Also, a spasm of feeling; mental agony; anguish. ME.
2 *transf.* & *fig.* An intense or violent struggle, esp. preceding or accompanying the production or creation of something. L17.

> **1** Sir W. Scott The throes of a mortal and painful disorder. C. Sangster Tumultuous throes Of some vast grief. **2** J. P. Stern Winter's last throes before spring sets in.

Phrases: **in the throes of** struggling with the task of, in the painful and violent process of.
▶ **B** *verb.* †**1** *verb trans.* Cause to suffer throes, agonize. *rare.* Only in 17.
2 *verb intrans.* Suffer throes, struggle painfully. E17.

Throgmorton Street /θrɒgˈmɔːt(ə)n striːt/ *noun phr.* E20.
[The street in the City of London where the Stock Exchange is located.]
The London Stock Exchange or its members.

thromb- *combining form* see THROMBO-.

thrombi *noun* pl. of THROMBUS.

thrombin /ˈθrɒmbɪn/ *noun.* L19.
[from Greek *thrombos* THROMBUS + -IN[1].]
BIOCHEMISTRY & PHYSIOLOGY. A plasma protein (normally present as inactive prothrombin) which acts as an enzyme to convert fibrinogen to fibrin and so cause the clotting of blood.

thrombo- /ˈθrɒmbəʊ/ *combining form.* Before a vowel also **thromb-**.
[from Greek *thrombos* THROMBUS: see -O-.]
Chiefly MEDICINE. Of, pertaining to, or involving the clotting of blood.

■ **thrombasˈthenia** *noun* a hereditary condition in which the number of platelets in the blood is normal but their clotting power is defective M20. **thromˈbectomy** *noun* (an instance of) surgical removal of a thrombus from a blood-vessel E20. **thrombocyte** *noun* a cell or particle which circulates in the blood of vertebrates and is responsible for its clotting; *spec.* a blood platelet: L19. **thrombocythaemia** /-sʌɪtˈhiːmɪə/ *noun* thrombocytosis, esp. due to proliferation of platelet-producing cells (megakaryocytes) M20. **thrombocytoˈpenia** *noun* reduction of the number of platelets in the blood E20. **thrombocytoˈpenic** *adjective* of or characterized by thrombocytopenia E20. **thrombocyˈtosis** *noun* a significant increase in the number of platelets in the blood M20. **thromboemˈbolic** *adjective* of, characterized by, or caused by thromboembolism M20. **thromboˈembolism** *noun* embolism of a blood-vessel caused by a thrombus dislodged from another site E20. **thromboˈgenic** *adjective* producing coagulation; *esp.* predisposing to thrombosis: L19. **thromboˈkinase** *noun* = THROMBOPLASTIN E20. **thromboˈpenia** *noun* = THROMBOCYTOPENIA E20. **thromboˈpenic** *adjective* = THROMBOCYTOPENIC M20. **thrombophleˈbitis** *noun* phlebitis involving secondary thrombosis in the affected vein L19. **thromboˈplastic** *adjective* causing or promoting the clotting of blood E20. **thromboˈplastin** *noun* a natural thromboplastic substance; now *spec.* an enzyme released from damaged cells, esp. platelets, which converts prothrombin to thrombin during the early stages of blood coagulation E20. **thrombosˈthenin** *noun* a contractile protein or mixture of proteins found in blood platelets M20. **thromˈboxane** *noun* any of several compounds formed from prostaglandin endoperoxides which, when released from blood platelets, induce platelet aggregation and arterial constriction L20.

thrombolite /ˈθrɒmbəlʌɪt/ *noun.* M19.
[from THROMBO- + -LITE.]
†**1** MINERALOGY. = ***pseudomalachite*** s.v. PSEUDO-. Only in M19.
2 GEOLOGY. A formation similar to a stromatolite but having a lumpy rather than a laminar structure. M20.

thrombolysis /θrɒmˈbɒlɪsɪs/ *noun.* M20.
[from THROMBO- + -LYSIS.]
MEDICINE. The dissolution or breaking down of a thrombus.

■ **thromboˈlytic** *adjective & noun* (***a***) *adjective* pertaining to or causing thrombolysis; (***b***) *noun* a thrombolytic agent: M20.

thrombose /θrɒmˈbəʊz, -s/ *verb.* L19.
[Back-form. from next.]
MEDICINE. **1** *verb trans.* Cause thrombosis in (a blood-vessel); affect with thrombosis. Chiefly as ***thrombosed*** *ppl adjective.* L19.
2 *verb intrans.* Of a blood-vessel: become occupied by a thrombus. M20.

thrombosis /θrɒmˈbəʊsɪs/ *noun.* Pl. **-boses** /-ˈbəʊsiːz/. E18.
[mod. Latin from Greek *thrombōsis* curdling, from *thrombousthai*, from *thrombos* THROMBUS: see -OSIS.]
Orig. (*rare*), a coagulation, a curdling. Now *spec.* (MEDICINE), (a) local coagulation or clotting of the blood in a part of the circulatory system; the formation of a thrombus. Also (*fig.*), traffic congestion.

■ **thrombotic** /θrɒmˈbɒtɪk/ *adjective* of, pertaining to, of the nature of, or caused by thrombosis M19.

thrombus /ˈθrɒmbəs/ *noun*. Pl. **-bi** /-bʌɪ/. L17.
[mod. Latin from Greek *thrombos* lump, piece, clot of blood, curd of milk.]
MEDICINE. †**1** *gen*. A small swelling caused by the coagulation of a body fluid, esp. blood. L17–E18.
2 *spec*. A clot which forms on the wall of a blood-vessel or a chamber of the heart, esp. so as to impede or obstruct the flow of blood. M19.

throne /θrəʊn/ *noun & verb*. Also (earlier) †**trone**. ME.
[Old French *trone* (mod. *trône*) from Latin *thronus* from Greek *thronos* elevated seat. Early in Middle English assim. to Latin form.]
▶ **A** *noun*. **1 a** A chair of State for a potentate or dignitary; *esp*. an ornate, elaborate, and usu. raised chair occupied by a sovereign on State occasions. ME. ▸**b** A chair for a deity, esp. God or Christ. ME. ▸**c** A ceremonial chair for a pope or bishop. LME. ▸**d** A chair provided by portrait-painters for their sitters. M19. ▸**e** A lavatory seat and bowl. *colloq*. (freq. *joc*.). E20.
2 *transf. & fig*. **a** The position, office, or dignity of a sovereign; sovereign power or authority. ME. ▸**b** A position of dominion or supremacy. M16. ▸**c** The occupant of a throne; the sovereign. M18.
3 In Christian theology, a member of the third order of the ninefold celestial hierarchy, ranking directly below the cherubim and above the dominations (usu. in *pl*.). ME.

> 🕮 **1a** D. JACOBSON The king's throne, an elaborate ivory-sheathed affair. **2a** B. BETTELHEIM The Archduke . . became heir to the throne. **b** *Ring* Thai junior flyweight champ . . barely kept his throne via a split decision. P. BAILEY That chair was her throne, from which she ruled over her brood.

Phrases: ***ascend the throne***: see ASCEND 7. ***power behind the throne***: see POWER *noun*. ***sit on the throne***: see *sit on* (e) s.v. SIT *verb*. **the Great White Throne** the throne of God (with allus. to *Revelation* 20:11). **throne and altar** the established civil and ecclesiastical systems in a State. **Throne of Grace** the place where God is conceived as sitting to answer prayer.
Comb.: **throne room** a room containing a throne; **Throne Speech** *Canad*. = ***the King's speech, the Queen's speech*** s.v. SPEECH *noun*.
▶ **B** *verb*. **1** *verb trans*. Place on or as on a throne; enthrone. LME.
2 *verb intrans*. Be enthroned; sit on or as on a throne. E17.

> 🕮 **1** POPE Th' eternal thunderer sat thron'd in gold. J. CONINGTON To throne him in the seat of power.

■ **thronedom** *noun* (*rare*) the dominion or authority of a throne E19. **throneless** *adjective* without a throne; deposed from a throne: E19.

throng /θrɒŋ/ *noun*.
[Old English *geþrang* throng, crowd, tumult, from ablaut stem *þring-*, *þrang-*, *þrung-*, shortened in Middle English: cf. Old Norse *þrǫng* throng, crowd. Cf. also THRING *noun*[1].]
1 A crowded mass of people, a crowd. OE. ▸**b** A great number of things crowded together; a multitude. M16.
2 Crowding of people; an act of thronging or crowding; crowded condition. ME.
3 Oppression; distress, woe; danger. Now *dial. rare*. ME.
4 Pressure, or a pressing amount, *of* work or business. Now *Scot. & dial*. M17.

> 🕮 **1** R. TRAVERS A vast throng of spectators crowded the high walls of the gaol. A. BRINK The summer throngs . . had overrun the place during the July festival.

throng /θrɒŋ/ *adjective & adverb*. Now *Scot. & north*. LME.
[from prec. Cf. Old Norse *þrongr* narrow, close, crowded.]
▶ **A** *adjective*. **1** Pressed closely together as a crowd; crowded, thronged. Formerly also, dense, thick. LME. ▸**b** Crowded with people etc.; thronged. M17.
2 Of a time, season, place, etc.: into which much is crowded; full, busy. M16.
3 Of a person: fully occupied in work or business; pressed, busy. E17.
4 Closely involved together; intimately associated. M18.

> 🕮 **2** J. GALT The street was as throng as on a market day.

▶ **B** *adverb*. Earnestly; busily; in large numbers. LME.

throng /θrɒŋ/ *verb*. ME.
[Perh. from Old English or from THRONG *noun*. Rel. to THRING *verb*.]
†**1** *verb trans*. Press violently; squeeze, crush. ME–E19.
†**2** *verb intrans*. Force one's way, press. ME–E17.
3 *verb intrans*. Assemble or move in a crowd or in large numbers. (Foll. by *round, through, towards*, etc.) E16.
4 *verb trans*. Crowd round and press against; jostle. M16.
5 *verb trans*. Bring or drive into a crowd, or into one place; collect closely, crowd. Chiefly as ***thronged*** *ppl adjective*. L16.
6 *verb trans*. Fill or occupy *with* many things or people or a large quantity of something; crowd, cram, stuff. Also, (of a multitude of people or things) fill completely, crowd. Freq. in *pass*. L16.

> 🕮 **3** W. S. MAUGHAM They lost one another in the crowd that thronged towards the exits. **6** J. BUCHAN A tiny lochan, thronged with wildfowl. R. C. HUTCHINSON People were thronging the pavements and spreading out into the road. SCOTT FITZGERALD The Dakota wheat thronged the valley. A. T. ELLIS All the chapels . . were thronged and full of singing.

■ **thronger** *noun* (*rare*) a person who throngs M17.

thropple /ˈθrɒp(ə)l/ *noun*. *Scot. & north*. Also **thrapple** /ˈθrap(ə)l/. LME.
[Origin unkn.]
The throat; *esp*. the windpipe or gullet, freq. of a horse or other animal.
■ **throppled** *adjective* (esp. of a horse) having a thropple, usu. of a specified kind; ***cock-throppled***: see COCK *noun*[1]: E17.

thropple /ˈθrɒp(ə)l/ *verb trans*. *Scot. & north*. Also **thrapple** /ˈθrap(ə)l/. L16.
[from prec.]
Throttle, strangle.

throstle /ˈθrɒs(ə)l/ *noun*.
[Old English *þrostle* = Old Saxon *þrosla*, Old High German *drōscala* (German *Drossel*), from Germanic from Indo-European base repr. also by Latin *turdus* thrush: cf. THRUSH *noun*[1].]
1 A thrush; *esp*. the song thrush, or formerly occas. the blackbird. Now *dial. & literary*. OE.
2 *Hist*. A kind of spinning-machine with a continuous action for drawing, twisting, and winding yarn (app. named from the humming sound it made). E19.
Comb.: **throstle-cock** the male throstle or song thrush; *dial*. the male mistle thrush.

throttle /ˈθrɒt(ə)l/ *noun*. M16.
[Perh. dim. of early form of THROAT *noun*. Cf. German *Drossel* dim. of Middle High German *drozze*, Old High German *drozza*.]
1 a The throat. Now chiefly *dial*. M16. ▸**b** The larynx. Now *rare*. E17.
2 a A valve controlling the flow of fuel, steam, etc., in an engine. Also more fully ***throttle-valve***. E19. ▸**b** A lever, pedal, or other control, esp. with its related apparatus, for opening or closing a throttle-valve. Also more fully ***throttle control, throttle-lever***. M19.

> 🕮 **1a** P. EGAN Floored by a heavy blow on the throttle. **2a** *Pilot* At the required altitude open the throttle to cruising power. **b** A. C. CLARKE Franklin pressed down the throttle and felt the surge of power.

Phrases: **at full throttle** at maximum power, at full speed. **full throttle** (at) maximum power, (at) full speed.

throttle /ˈθrɒt(ə)l/ *verb*. LME.
[Perh. from THROAT *noun* + -LE[3].]
1 *verb trans*. Stop the breath of by compressing the throat, strangle; *loosely* choke, suffocate. LME. ▸**b** *transf*. Tie something tightly round the neck of, so as to compress or restrict. M19.
2 *verb intrans*. Undergo suffocation; choke. M16.
3 *verb trans*. **a** Deliver or break off (an utterance) in a choking manner. L16. ▸**b** Stop forcibly utterance etc. of or by. M17.
4 a *verb trans*. Check or stop the flow of (a fluid in a tube etc.), esp. by means of a valve or by compression; control the flow of steam or gas to (an engine) in this way. Also foll. by *down*. L19. ▸**b** *verb intrans*. Foll. by *back, down*: close the throttle in order to slow down or stop. M20.

> 🕮 **1** M. WESLEY Hubert felt he could throttle her for cheating him. **2** *Westminster Gazette* The child throttled and died in my arms. **3b** E. M. FORSTER Margaret nearly spoke . . but something throttled her. **4a** C. A. LINDBERGH He throttled his motor and made a quick bank . . to the right. **b** K. M. PEYTON He throttled down sharply for the turning.

■ **throttleable** *adjective* (of an engine) that can be controlled by means of a throttle M20. **throttler** *noun* M19.

through /θrʌf, θrʊf, θrʌx/ *noun*[1]. *obsolete* exc. *Scot. & north*.
[Old English *þrūh* = Old Norse *þró* hollowed out receptacle, tube, chest, trough. Cf. Old High German *drūha*, *truhā*, Middle High German *trūhe* (German *Truhe*).]
†**1** A trough, pipe, or channel for water. Only in OE.
†**2** A hollow receptacle for a dead body; a coffin, a grave, a sepulchre. OE–L15.
3 A large slab of stone etc. laid on a tomb; a flat gravestone, *spec*. one resting on feet. ME.

through /θruː/ *noun*[2]. L18.
[from THROUGH *adverb* or *adjective*.]
1 An artificially constructed channel, trench, or passage. Cf. THOROUGH *noun* 1. *Scot. & dial*. L18.
2 = THROUGH-STONE *noun*[2]. E19.

through /θruː/ *attrib. adjective*. E16.
[Attrib. use of THROUGH *adverb*.]
1 a That passes or extends fully through something without obstruction. Cf. THOROUGH *adjective* 1. E16. ▸**b** That travels or covers the whole of a long distance or journey without interruption or change. E16.
2 = THOROUGH *adjective* 2, 3. *obsolete* exc. *Scot*. M16.

> 🕮 **1a** E. HALL A small front room . . and a through room from the passage to the scullery. ***no through road***: see NO *adjective*. **b** J. DAVIS The construction of this . . line would give us a through line from North to South. ***through passenger, through train***, etc. **through traffic** (*a*) rail traffic going on to a further destination; (*b*) road traffic which passes through a place without stopping.

through /θruː/ *verb*. *rare*. LME.
[from next, orig. with ellipsis of *go, get, pass*, etc.]
1 *verb intrans*. Get through; succeed. *Scot*. LME.
2 *verb trans*. Go through, pass through; traverse, penetrate. M16.
3 *verb trans*. Carry through, put through, effect. M17.

through /θruː/ *preposition & adverb*. Also **thro'**, (*non-standard*) **thru**.
[Old English *þurh* = Old Frisian *thruch*, Old Saxon *þurh*, *þuru*, Middle & mod. Dutch *door*, Old High German *duruh*, *-ih*, *dur* (German *durch*, *dial*. *dur*) from West Germanic. The metath. forms appear *c* 1300 and are standard from 15. Cf. THOROUGH *preposition & adverb*.]
▶ **A** *preposition*. **1** From one end, side, or surface of (a body or space) to the other, by passing within it; into one end, side, or surface of and out at the other. OE.
2 Between, among; along within. OE.
3 Over or about the whole extent of, all over; throughout; everywhere in. Cf. THROUGHOUT *preposition* 2a. OE.
4 a From beginning to end of; in or along the whole length or course of; *spec*. during the whole temporal extent of. Cf. THROUGHOUT *preposition* 2b. OE. ▸**b** To the end of. E17.
5 By means of, via; by the agency or (*arch*.) the action of. Also (*spec*.), as a usu. intermediate stage or member of (a list, sequence, etc.). OE.
6 By reason of, on account of, owing to. OE.
7 At a certain position or point reached with respect to, *esp*. at the end of; *spec*. (*a*) *lit*. at a point beyond, at the far end of; (*b*) *fig*. having finished or completed, done with. L18.
8 Up to and including, until. *N. Amer*. L18.
9 Above the sound of. E19.

> 🕮 **1** E. BOWEN She peered through gaps in the shrubbery. M. KEANE She climbed in through the window. D. ABSE Drawing air through their nostrils. A. CARTER The damp seeped through her thin shoes. M. ROBERTS The sun pours in through the big bay window. **2** KEATS The hare limp'd trembling through the frozen grass. T. HARDY He ploughed his way through beds of spear-grass. G. GREENE I would go for a walk through the rain. I. MCEWAN She swept her fingers through her hair. **3** M. SINCLAIR A bell clamoured suddenly through the quiet house. **4a** D. H. LAWRENCE Angry and stiff, she went through her last term. H. READ The mill . . was working through the night. L. BRUCE I would sit all alone through endless hours and days. B. GUEST The group . . arrived in Rome, where they stayed through Christmas. **b** G. BERKELEY Seven children . . came all very well through the small-pox. **5** G. GREENE We could find the address for you through the organisers. E. FIGES Hydrangea shading from pink through mauve to sky blue. *Truck* It drives through a Mack five-speed gearbox. **6** J. ROSENBERG Rembrandt enjoyed a rapid rise in his social position through his marriage. **7** V. WOOLF Halfway through dinner he made himself look across at Clarissa. S. TROTT When Maud's through work, she's coming over to see you. **8** L. DEIGHTON Deliveries . . only accepted between eight and eleven Monday through Friday.

▶ **B** *adverb*. **1 a** From end to end, side to side, or surface to surface of a body or space, by passing or extending within it. OE. ▸**b** All the way; to the end of a journey; to a destination. E17.
2 From beginning to end; to the end or conclusion. ME.
3 Through the whole extent, substance, or thickness; entirely, thoroughly. Used after (formerly before) adjectives or pa. pples. Cf. THOROUGH *adverb*. ME.
4 At or having reached a certain position or condition; *spec*. (*a*) *lit*. having penetrated or crossed a body or space; (*b*) *fig*. finished, at an end, having completed or accomplished something, *esp*. having passed an examination. L15.
5 So as to be connected by telephone. E20.

> 🕮 **1a** SCOTT FITZGERALD Rosemary waited on the outskirts while Dick fought his way through. **b** OED The train goes through to Edinburgh. **2** *Law Times* Having heard the case through and seen the witnesses. **3** M. LAVIN Charlotte was shot through with bitter regret. **4** SCOTT FITZGERALD With the new plan he could be through by spring. M. MARRIN That's it . . . I'm through I've had enough of this crew.

Phrases (of preposition & adverb): (of the many phrs. in which *through* forms an elem. in a phrasal verb or governs a noun, few are listed here: see the verbs and nouns) **be through**, **get through** have achieved, achieve, a pass mark in (an examination etc.). **be through with** have finished or completed; have done with; be tired of, have had enough of. ***get through***: see *be through* above. **go through one's hands**, **go through a machine**, etc., undergo some process or treatment, esp. as a stage of a larger process, be dealt with. ***go through the roof***: see ROOF *noun*. **pass through one's hands**, **pass through a machine**, etc. = ***go through one's hands, go through a machine*** above. ***shoot a person through***: see SHOOT *verb*. ***strike through***:

see STRIKE *verb*. ***talk through***: see TALK *verb*. **through and through** (*a*) [from THROUGH *preposition*] repeatedly through; right through, fully through; (*b*) [from THROUGH *adverb*] in all points or respects, thoroughly, entirely; repeatedly through the whole substance or entirety, through again and again. **through-the-lens** *adjective* (of light measurement) in which the light which is measured is that passing through the lens of the camera. ***wet through***: see WET *adjective*. ***worry through***: see WORRY *verb* 7.

through- /θruː/ *combining form*.

[Repr. THROUGH *preposition & adverb*. Cf. THOROUGH-.]

Forming combs. with verbs, adjectives, and (now usu.) nouns with the senses 'completely', 'thoroughly', 'from one end, side, etc., to the other'.

■ **through-ball** *noun* (FOOTBALL etc.) a forward pass which goes through the other team's defence M20. **through-band** *noun* a stone or other object extending through the breadth of a wall, dyke, etc., to bind the sides together E19. **through-bolt** *noun* a bolt passing fully through the pieces fastened by it, and secured at each end M19. **through-com'posed** *adjective* = DURCHKOMPONIERT L19. **through-deck** *noun* (*a*) a flight deck which runs the full length of a ship; (*b*) ***through-deck cruiser***, (a name for) a type of lightly armed aircraft carrier: M20. **through-draught** *noun* a draught or current of air passing through a room etc. E20. **throughfall** *noun* (FORESTRY) precipitation reaching the ground direct from the forest canopy (cf. ***stemflow*** s.v. STEM *noun*[1]) M20. **throughflow** *noun* the flowing of liquid, air, etc., through something M20. **through-gang** *verb & noun* (*obsolete exc. Scot.*) †(*a*) *verb trans.* go through, traverse; (*b*) *noun* a way or road through; a passage: LOE. **through-ganging** *adjective* (*Scot.*) that goes through a lot of work, active, energetic E19. **throughgoing** *noun & adjective* (*Scot.*) (*a*) *noun* passing through, a going through, a taking to task; (*b*) *adjective* that goes or passes through; *spec.* that goes through a lot of work, active, energetic: E19. **through-lounge** *noun* a lounge that extends from the front to the back of a house M20. **through-other** *adverb & adjective* (chiefly *Scot.*) (*a*) *adverb* (mingled) through one another; indiscriminately; in disorder; (*b*) *adjective* mixed up, confused, in disorder; (of a person etc.) wild, reckless, disordered: E16. **through-pass** *noun* = THROUGH-BALL M20. **through-passage** *noun* a passage through; a thoroughfare: M16. †**through-pierce** *verb trans.* pierce through, transfix L16–E17. **through-toll** *noun* (*Hist.*) a toll or duty levied on people etc. passing esp. through a town or territory; a toll which passes one through two or more turnpike gates: ME. **through-valley** *noun* (GEOLOGY) a flat depression consisting of two or more adjacent valleys whose separating features have been eroded E20.

througher /ˈθruːə/ *noun*. E18.

[from THROUGH *preposition* or *adverb* + -ER[1].]

MINING. A narrow passage cut in a coalmine.

†**throughfare** *noun & adjective*, *verb* see THOROUGHFARE *noun & adjective*, *verb*.

throughly /ˈθruːli/ *adverb*. *arch.* LME.

[from THROUGH *adverb* or *adjective* + -LY[2].]

1 Fully, completely, perfectly; thoroughly. LME.

2 Through the whole thickness, substance, or extent; throughout, all through. *arch. & poet.* M16.

throughout /θruːˈaʊt/ *preposition & adverb*. Also (*informal*) **thruout**, **thru-out**. LOE.

[Orig. two words, from THROUGH *preposition & adverb* + OUT *adverb*.]

▶**A** *preposition*. †**1** Through and out at the other side; right through. Also = THROUGH *preposition* 1, 2. LOE–E17.

2 a Through the whole of; in or to every part of; everywhere in. Cf. THROUGH *preposition* 3. ME. ▸**b** Through or during the whole time, extent, etc., of; from beginning to end of. Cf. THROUGH *preposition* 4a. ME.

> 🕮 **2a** R. G. MYERS Research seems to have become fashionable throughout the Third World. **b** *Japan Times* Throughout his trial, Otelo denied the charges.

▶**B** *adverb*. †**1 a** Right through, so as to penetrate completely. LOE–M16. ▸**b** Right through from beginning to end. LME–M17.

2 a Through the whole extent, substance, etc.; in every respect; in or to every part, everywhere. ME. ▸**b** Through the whole time or course; at every moment; all through. M18.

> 🕮 **2a** H. JAMES He was tall and lean, and dressed throughout in black.

throughput /ˈθruːpʊt/ *noun*. E19.

[from THROUGH- + PUT *noun*[1]. Cf. INPUT *noun*, OUTPUT *noun*.]

1 Energy, activity, capacity for work. *Scot.* E19.

2 The amount of material put through a process, esp. in manufacturing or computing. Also, processing or handling capacity. E20.

through-stone /ˈθrʌxstəʊn, ˈθrʌf-, ˈθrʊf-/ *noun*[1]. Now only *Scot. & north.* ME.

[from THROUGH *noun*[1] + STONE *noun*.]

= THROUGH *noun*[1] 3.

through-stone /ˈθruːstəʊn/ *noun*[2]. Also **thorough-** /ˈθʌrə-/. E19.

[from THROUGH- + STONE *noun*.]

BUILDING. A stone placed so as to extend through the thickness of a wall; a bondstone.

throughway /ˈθruːweɪ/ *noun*. Also ***thruway**. M20.

[from THROUGH- + WAY *noun*.]

A way through; *spec.* (*N. Amer.*) a motorway, an expressway.

throve *verb pa. t.*: see THRIVE *verb*.

†**throw** *noun*[1].

[Old English *þrāg*, *þrāh*: not repr. in any cogn. languages.]

1 The time at which anything happens; an occasion. OE–E16.

2 A space of time; a while. Later, a brief while, an instant, a moment. OE–L16.

> 🕮 **2** SPENSER Downe himselfe he layd Upon the grassy ground to sleepe a throw.

throw /θrəʊ/ *noun*[2]. Also (*Scot.*, the usual form in sense 7) **thraw** /θrɔː/. ME.

[from THROW *verb*.]

▶**I 1** The distance to which anything is or may be thrown. Freq. with specifying word, as ***stone's throw***. ME.

2 An act of throwing a missile etc.; a forcible propulsion or delivery from or as from the hand or arm. M16.

3 *spec.* **a** An act of throwing a net, fishing-line, etc. M16. ▸**b** An act of throwing a die or dice; the number thrown. M16. ▸**c** WRESTLING. The felling or throwing down of an opponent. E19. ▸**d** CRICKET. An illegitimate delivery considered to have been thrown rather than properly bowled. M19. ▸**e** A felling of timber; the direction in which a tree is caused to fall. L19.

4 GEOLOGY & MINING. A dislocation in a vein or stratum in which the part on one side of the fracture is displaced up or down; a fault. Also, the amount of such vertical displacement. L18.

5 A light rug or piece of decorative fabric used as a casual covering for furniture. Also, a shawl, a stole. Chiefly *N. Amer.* L19.

6 An item, or a turn or attempt at something, for which a fee is usu. charged. *colloq.* L19.

> 🕮 **1** R. FRAME There they were, a stone's throw away from her. **2** E. ALLEN A bouncing ball is difficult to handle . . , so it is best to let the throw continue. **5** B. T. BRADFORD Chairs . . had their arms draped with fluffy mohair throws from Scotland. **6** C. HOPE Knocking back pretty cocktails at a couple of quid a throw.

▶**II 7** An act of twisting or turning; the fact or condition of being twisted; a turn, a twist; a wrench. *Scot.* E16. ▸**b** *fig.* A perverse twist of temper or ill humour. *Scot.* L18.

8 A machine or device by or on which an object is turned while being shaped. M17.

9 MECHANICS. The action or motion of a slide-valve, or of a crank, eccentric wheel, or cam; the extent of this motion measured on a straight line passing through the centre of motion; the extent through which a switch or lever may be moved. Also, a crank-arm, a crank. E19. ▸**b** ELECTRICITY. The sudden deflection of the needle in an instrument, esp. a galvanometer. L19.

throw /θrəʊ/ *verb*. Pa. t. **threw** /θruː/, (*dial. & non-standard*) **throwed** /θrəʊd/; pa. pple **thrown** /θrəʊn/, (*dial. & non-standard*) **throwed**. Also (*Scot.*, the usual form in senses 1, 3, 4) **thraw** /θrɔː/, pa. pple **thrawn** /θrɔːn/.

[Old English *þrāwan* = Old Saxon *thrāian* (Dutch *draaien*), Old High German *drāen* (German *drehen*), from West Germanic from Indo-European base repr. also by Latin *terere* rub, Greek *teirein* wear out, *trēma* hole. Cf. THREAD *noun*.]

▶**I** Twist, turn, & derived senses.

1 a *verb trans.* Twist, wring; turn, esp. to one side; twist about, twine, wreathe. Now *Scot. & north.* OE. ▸**b** *verb intrans.* Turn, twist, twine, writhe. Chiefly *Scot.* OE.

2 *verb trans.* Fashion by means of a rotary or twisting motion; *spec.* (*a*) turn (wood etc.) in a lathe; (*b*) shape (round pottery) on a potter's wheel; (*c*) twist (silk fibres) into raw silk; prepare and twist the fibres of (raw silk etc.) into thread. LME.

3 *verb trans.* *fig.* Twist or pervert the meaning or intention of; distort the pronunciation of. *Scot.* M16.

4 a *verb intrans.* Act in opposition; be awkward or contrary; quarrel or contend *with*. *Scot.* L16. ▸**b** *verb trans.* Thwart, frustrate. Chiefly *Scot.* L18.

> 🕮 **1b** D. G. ROSSETTI The empty boat thrawed i' the wind. **2** *Crafts* The jugs . . like the bowls, are thrown on the wheel.

▶**II** Project or propel through the air, cast, drive, shoot (away), & related senses.

5 a *verb trans.* Project (something) through the air or space with usu. sudden force, from the hand or arm; cast, hurl, fling. ME. ▸**b** *verb intrans.* Hurl or fling something, as a missile, a weapon, etc. ME. ▸**c** *verb trans. & intrans.* CRICKET. Deliver (a ball) illegitimately, now esp. with a sudden straightening of the elbow. E19.

6 *verb refl.* & (now *rare*) *intrans.* Cast or precipitate oneself; fling oneself impetuously; spring, start, rush. ME.

7 *verb trans.* **a** Cause forcibly to fall; bring or break down (a thing); knock down or lay low (a person); *spec.* (WRESTLING), bring (an opponent) to the ground. ME. ▸**b** *fig.* Defeat in a contest; be the cause of defeat to. M19. ▸**c** Lose (a contest, race, etc.) deliberately. *colloq.* M19.

8 *verb trans.* Of the sea or wind: cast or drive violently (*on* or *on to*), cast away, wreck. ME.

9 a *verb intrans.* Play at dice. *rare.* ME. ▸**b** *verb trans.* Cause (a die or dice) to fall on to a surface, esp. by releasing or propelling from the hand; obtain (a specified number) by throwing a die or dice; (with cognate obj.) make (a throw) at dice. E17.

10 *verb trans. & intrans.* Of a gun etc.: hurl, project, shoot, (a missile or projectile). LME.

11 *verb trans.* & (*rare*) *intrans.* Give, deliver, aim, (blows). LME.

12 *verb trans.* Of a fountain, pump, etc.: eject or project (water). LME.

13 *verb trans.* Of a horse etc.: unseat, shake off, (a rider). Also in *pass.*, (of a rider) be unseated. M16.

14 *verb trans.* Project (a ray, beam, light) *on*, *over*, etc.; emit (light); cast (a shadow). L16.

15 *verb trans.* Direct (words, an utterance) *at*, *to*, *towards*, etc., esp. in hostility or contempt; cause (sound, a gesture) to pass or travel; blow (a kiss). Also, project (the voice), *spec.* as a ventriloquist. Cf. ***throw out*** (b) below. L16.

16 *verb trans.* Of a snake etc.: cast (its skin). Of a bird: moult (feathers). Of a horse: lose (a shoe). L16.

17 *verb trans.* **a** Play (a card) from one's hand; *esp.* discard (a card). M18. ▸**b** Make or cast (a vote) in an election etc. M18.

18 *verb trans. & intrans.* Foll. by *up*: vomit. *colloq.* Also (*Scot. & dial.*) without *up*. M18.

19 *verb trans. & intrans.* Put forth into water with a throwing action (a fishing net, line, or bait); cast. L18.

20 *verb trans.* **a** Perform or execute with force or suddenness (a somersault, leap, etc.). E19. ▸**b** Give or hold (a party), esp. spontaneously or informally. E20.

21 *verb trans.* Of a horse: lift (the feet) well in moving, esp. over rough ground. *US.* E19.

22 *verb trans.* Of an animal: produce as offspring, give birth to, drop. M19.

> 🕮 **5a** L. STEFFENS Ashbridge threw the letter into the street unread. P. FITZGERALD Throw some money out of the window to the organ-man. **6** D. HOGAN I'd . . gone to a window, tried to throw myself out. **7a** *British Medical Journal* [He] was thrown at football and hurt his knee. **c** *First Base* The Chicago White Sox . . threw the World Series against Cincinnati. **8** D. PELL They are thrown . . upon Rocks and Sands. **9b** S. FOOTE To throw six and four . . you must . . whirl the dice to the end of the table. **10** W. C. RUSSELL That gun'll throw about three quarters of a mile. **11** B. BOVA The youth on his left threw the first blow. **12** O. G. GREGORY A machine by which water is thrown upon fires. **13** G. ANSON One of their horses fell down and threw his rider. **14** J. STEINBECK A small electric globe threw a meagre yellow light. J. GARDNER The fuzzy shadows thrown by the nightlamp. **15** *Field* The hideous yells that were thrown at him. *Daily Graphic (Accra)* They threw several searching questions to me. *Listener* I can throw my voice. I could make a fortune as a medium. **17a** *Harper's Magazine* He can . . safely throw his queen on the ace. **20b** P. BAILEY He threw a farewell party, on the spur of the moment.

▶**III** *transf.* & *fig.* **23** *verb trans.* **a** Cause to pass, go, or come by a sudden or violent action; put or place with haste, suddenness, or force; *spec.* put *on* or take *off* (clothes etc.) hastily. ME. ▸**b** Foll. by *into*: add, include. L17. ▸**c** Construct (a bridge or arch) *over* a river, space, etc. M18. ▸**d** Lay or emit as a sediment or deposit. Usu. foll. by *down*. E19. ▸**e** Engage (the clutch or gears) of a motor vehicle (foll. by *in*, *into*); put (a vehicle) *into* gear. E20.

24 *verb trans.* **a** Cause to fall, pass, or come, usu. suddenly or forcefully, into or out of a certain state, condition, or relation; force, drive, thrust. Usu. foll. by *into*, *out of*. LME. ▸**b** Put deftly into a particular form or shape; express in a specified spoken or written form; change or translate *into*. E18. ▸**c** Break or make unusable (something mechanical). *colloq.* Chiefly *US.* M20.

25 Disconcert, confuse. *colloq.* M19.

> 🕮 **23a** ADDISON He threw off his Clothes. W. LONGMAN Philip threw every obstacle in the way of reconciliation. S. R. GARDINER Richard was carried to London and thrown into the Tower. E. SEGAL She threw her arms around him and they hugged. **e** N. SLATER He threw the cruising Alfa into third gear. **24a** B. HEAD He was so exciting . . that he threw her whole life into turmoil. **b** *Examiner* Two dress boxes . . were thrown into one. H. D. TRAILL Cædmon . . throws Scripture into metrical paraphrase. **25** C. HARKNESS She had such a shock . . that nothing could throw her again to that extent.

Phrases: ***not trust X as far as one can throw him or her***: see TRUST *verb*. **throw a fit** *slang* (*a*) have a fit; (*b*) *fig.* lose one's temper, overreact. **throw a glance**, **throw a look** turn or direct one's gaze, esp. briefly or hastily. **throw a punch** deliver a blow with a clenched fist. ***throw a slur on***: see SLUR *noun*[3] 1. ***throw a stone (at)***: see STONE *noun*. ***throw a veil over***: see VEIL *noun* 5. ***throw a wobbly***: see WOBBLY *noun*[2]. ***throw cold water on***: see COLD *adjective*. ***throw dust in a person's eyes***: see DUST *noun*. **throw good money after bad** incur further loss in trying to make good a loss already sustained. ***throw in a person's dish***: see DISH *noun* 1. ***throw in a person's lap***, ***throw into a person's lap***: see LAP *noun*[1]. ***throw into the scale***: see SCALE *noun*[1]. ***throw light on***: see LIGHT *noun* 5b. ***throw money at***: see MONEY *noun*. ***throw mud***: see MUD *noun*[1]. ***throw off one's stride***: see STRIDE *noun* 3b. ***throw off the scent***: see SCENT *noun*. **throw oneself at** seek blatantly as a spouse or sexual partner. **throw oneself into** (*a*) engage enthusiastically in; (*b*) ***throw oneself into the arms of***, blatantly start a sexual affair with. **throw oneself on**, **throw oneself upon** (*a*) rely completely on for help or protection; turn to unreservedly; (*b*) attack. **throw one's eye** = *throw a glance* above. ***throw one's hat into the ring***: see HAT *noun*. ***throw one's weight about***, ***throw one's weight around***, ***throw one's weight behind***: see WEIGHT *noun*. ***throw out of one's stride***: see STRIDE *noun* 3b. ***throw* OVERBOARD**. ***throw stones (at)***: see STONE *noun*. ***throw the book at***: see BOOK *noun*. ***throw the hatchet***: see HATCHET *noun* 1. **throw the switch** start or stop a process by operating a switch or lever. ***throw to the (four) winds***: see WIND *noun*[1]. ***throw to the wolves***: see WOLF *noun*.

With adverbs in specialized senses: **throw about**, **throw around** (*a*) throw in various directions; (*b*) spend (money) ostentatiously; (*c*) NAUTICAL (of a ship) turn about so as to face the other direction. **throw aside** cast aside as useless; discard, cease to use. **throw away** (*a*) discard as useless or unwanted; ***throw away the scabbard***: see SCABBARD *noun*[1] 1; (*b*) spend or use without adequate return; waste; fail to make use of; foolishly dispose of; (*c*) (of an actor or actress) deliver (lines) in a casual manner or with deliberate underemphasis. **throw back** (*a*) put back in time or condition; delay, make late; retard, check; (*b*) revert to an ancestral type or character; show atavism; (*c*) date back (*to*); (*d*) ***throw back on***, ***throw back upon***, compel to fall back on or resort to. **throw by** put aside decisively, reject. **throw down** (*a*) cause to fall, overthrow, demolish; (*b*) *fig.* (now *rare*) put down with force; humiliate; deject; (*c*) CRICKET knock down (a wicket) from a throw-in, with the intention of dismissing the batsman; ***throw down the gauntlet***: see GAUNTLET *noun*[1]; ***throw down the glove***: see GLOVE *noun*; (see also sense 23d above). **throw in** (*a*) put in as an addition, esp. at no extra cost; (*b*) insert or interject in the process of something; interpose (a remark); (*c*) WRESTLING give out or accept a challenge; (*d*) FOOTBALL throw (the ball) on to the pitch from the place where it has gone out of play; (*e*) CRICKET return (the ball) from the outfield; (*f*) CARDS give (a player) the lead, and so impose a disadvantage; (*g*) ***throw in one's hand***, retire from a card-game, *fig.* give up a contest or struggle; ***throw in one's lot with***: see LOT *noun*; ***throw in the sponge***: see SPONGE *noun*[1] 1; ***throw in the towel***: see TOWEL *noun*; (see also sense 23e above). **throw off** (*a*) rid or free oneself from by force or effort; shake off; cast off; discard; (*b*) HUNTING release (hounds, a hawk, etc.) for the chase; (of a hunter or hound) begin hunting; *fig.* make a start, begin; (*c*) eject, emit, esp. from the body or system; *rare* vomit; (*d*) produce and send forth (offspring, branches, etc.); (*e*) produce quickly and effortlessly (a literary or artistic work); utter in an offhand manner; (*f*) deduct from the total; knock off; (see also sense 23a above). **throw on** put on quickly or carelessly; (see also sense 23a above). **throw open** (*a*) make publicly accessible or available; (*b*) ***throw open one's doors***, become accessible, be hospitable or welcoming. **throw out** (*a*) put out forcibly or suddenly; eject, expel, turn out; (*b*) put forth vigorously from within; emit or radiate (heat or light); be the source of; send out (buds, shoots, etc.); project (the voice), esp. in singing; (*c*) cause to project or extend; build (something prominent or projecting, as a wing of a house, pier, etc.); (*d*) MILITARY send out (skirmishers etc.) a distance from the main body; (*e*) give expression to; *esp.* put forward tentatively; suggest; (*f*) put forth visibly, display, exhibit; (*g*) dismiss, reject, discard; *spec.* (of a legislative assembly etc.) reject (a bill or proposal); (*h*) put out of place or order by outrunning; (*i*) disturb (a person) from his or her train of thought, normal state of mind or ordinary course of action, etc.; put out; (*j*) CRICKET & BASEBALL put out (an opponent) by throwing the ball to the wicket or base; (*k*) move outwards from a centre; strike out; push out. **throw over** desert, abandon, reject. **throw to** close (a door etc.) with force. **throw together** (*a*) assemble hastily or roughly; (*b*) bring into casual contact or association. **throw up** (*a*) raise (the hands, eyes, etc.) quickly or suddenly; ***throw up your hands!***, surrender!; (*b*) erect or construct hastily; (*c*) bring to notice; make prominent or distinct; (*d*) give up, abandon, quit; (*e*) ***throw up against***, ***throw up at***, ***throw up to*** (colloq.), bring (something) up as an object of reproach or shame to (a person); (*f*) (of hounds) lift the head from the ground, having lost the scent; (*g*) *colloq.* produce, provide; (*h*) lift and open (a sash-window) quickly; (see also sense 18 above).

■ **throwable** *adjective* able to be thrown L19. **throwster** *noun* a person who or company which twists silk or manufactured filament yarn LME.

throw- /θrəʊ/ *combining form*.
[from THROW *noun*[2] or *verb*.]
Forming combs. with nouns or adverbs.
■ **throw-back** *noun* (*a*) a backward movement; (*b*) an arrest or reverse in a course or progress, a setback; (*c*) reversion to an earlier ancestral type or to the methods etc. of an earlier period; an instance of this: M19. **throw cushion** *noun* (*N. Amer.*) = ***scatter cushion*** s.v. SCATTER *verb* L20. **throw-down** *noun* (*a*) *slang* a fall, as in wrestling; *fig.* a comedown, a defeat; (*b*) *Austral.* & *NZ* a type of small firework, a squib: L19. **throw-forward** *noun* RUGBY FOOTBALL an illegal forward pass, a knock-on L19. **throw-in** *noun* (*a*) FOOTBALL an act of throwing the ball on to the pitch from the place where it has gone out of play; (*b*) CRICKET & BASEBALL an act of throwing in the ball from the outfield; (*c*) BRIDGE an end play in which the declarer throws the lead to an opponent who has to play into a tenace combination: M19. **throw-line**, **throw-net** *nouns* a fishing-line or net cast out by hand E20. **throw-off** *noun* (*a*) HUNTING the throwing-off or releasing of the hounds on a hunt, the start of a hunt; *gen.* the start of a race etc.; (*b*) an act of shaking off or getting free from; (*c*) a thing which is thrown off, an offshoot: M19. **throw-out** *noun* (*a*) an act of throwing out; *spec.* in CRICKET, the act of throwing out an opponent; (*b*) a thing thrown out; something discarded, a reject; (*c*) a page or bound insert in a book etc. which folds out beyond the normal page size, used esp. for maps and illustrations: L19. **throw-over** *noun* (*a*) an act or the result of throwing over something or someone; ***throw-over switch***, a switch by which each of two or more electric circuits may be brought into operation alternatively; (*b*) a wrap to throw over the shoulders, a loose outer garment: E19. **throw-stick** *noun* (*a*) a heavy usu. curved piece of wood used as a missile; (*b*) = ***throwing-stick*** (a) s.v. THROWING: M19. **throw weight** *noun* (MILITARY) the weight of warheads which a missile can carry to a target M20.

throw-away /ˈθrəʊəweɪ/ *noun* & *adjective*. Also **throwaway**. E20.
[from *throw away* s.v. THROW *verb*.]
▶ **A** *noun*. **1** An act of throwing something away. E20.
2 A thing which is thrown away; *spec.* one intended to be disposed of after use; a thing of brief lifespan. E20.

> 🕮 **2** *Daily Chronicle* This present rag of a throwaway that you can get for a halfpenny.

▶ **B** *adjective*. **1** Of a price: very low. E20.
2 Designating or pertaining to something designed to be thrown away after use, or of brief lifespan. E20.
3 Deliberately casual or understated. M20.

> 🕮 **2** J. HANSEN Two plastic-handled throwaway razors. *Smash Hits* 'Consistently great', they dribble, 'not like your modern throw-away pop star'. **3** *Fremdsprachen* The author . . simply mentions it in a throwaway remark.

†**throwe** *noun* & *verb* see THROE.

throwed *verb pa. t.* & *pple*: see THROW *verb*.

thrower /ˈθrəʊə/ *noun*. LME.
[from THROW *verb* + -ER[1].]
1 A person who fashions something by means of a rotary motion; *spec.* a person who shapes pottery on a potter's wheel. Cf. THROW *verb* 2. LME.
2 A person who or thing which casts, hurls, or throws something. LME.
2 *flame-thrower*, *knife-thrower*, *mud-thrower* etc.

throwing /ˈθrəʊɪŋ/ *verbal noun*. Also (*Scot.*) **thrawing** /ˈθrɔːɪŋ/. ME.
[formed as prec. + -ING[1].]
The action of THROW *verb*.
Comb.: **throwing-knife** a knife used as a missile, esp. among certain African peoples; **throwing-mill** a building in which silk is thrown; a machine for throwing silk; **throwing power** (*a*) the ability of a device etc. to propel something through the air; (*b*) the ability of an electrodepositing solution to produce an even coating on an irregularly shaped object; **throwing-stick** (*a*) a short wooden implement by which a dart or spear is thrown, in order to increase its speed; (*b*) a short club used as a missile; **throwing-table**, **throwing-wheel** a potter's wheel.

thrown *verb pa. pple*: see THROW *verb*.

thru *preposition* & *adverb* see THROUGH *preposition* & *adverb*.

†**thrum** *noun*[1].
[Old English *þrym*, cogn. with Middle Dutch *drom* pressure, squeezing, *drommel* a crush, a crowd. Cf. THRUM *verb*[1], THRUMBLE.]
1 A company or body of people; a host, a band, a troop; a crowd, a multitude. OE–LME.
2 Strength, might; magnificence, splendour, glory. OE–ME.

thrum /θrʌm/ *noun*[2].
[Old English *þrum* (only in (*under*)*tunge þrum*) = Middle Dutch *drom*, *drum* (mod. Dutch *dreum* thrum), Old High German *drum* end-piece, remnant (German *Trumm* end-piece, *Trümmer* remnants, ruins), from Germanic, from Indo-European base repr. also by Latin *terminus*, *termo*, Greek *terma* end, term.]
†**1** A ligament. Only in ***tongue thrum***, ***undertongue thrum***, ligament of the tongue. Only in OE.
2 A short piece of waste thread or yarn including the unwoven ends of the warp (see sense 3 below); *sing.* & in *pl.*, odds and ends of thread. Also, a short or loose end of thread projecting from the surface of a woven fabric; a tuft, tassel, or fringe of threads at the edge of a piece of cloth etc. ME. ▸**b** NAUTICAL. *sing.* & in *pl.* Short pieces of coarse woollen or hempen yarn, used for mops, mats, etc. LME. ▸**c** *fig.* A scrap, a shred; in *pl.* odds and ends. LME.
3 WEAVING. Any of the ends of the warp-threads left unwoven and remaining attached to the loom when the finished web is cut off; *sing.* & (usu.) in *pl.*, a row or fringe of such threads. LME.
4 a The central petals or florets of a composite or double flower; the stamens collectively. Also in *pl.* *obsolete* exc. in ***thrum-eyed*** below. L16. ▸†**b** A tuft or fringe of any threadlike structures, as hairs on a leaf, fibres of a root, etc. L16–L17. ▸**c** *ellipt.* A thrum-eyed plant. M20.
†**5** A ragged or poorly dressed person. *joc.* or *derog.* E17–E18.
Comb.: **thrum cap** (*a*) a cap made of thrums; (*b*) *Canad.* (*obsolete* exc. in place-names) a small island with a conical shape suggestive of a thrum cap; **thrum-eyed** *adjective* (of a heterostylous plant, esp. a primula, or its flowers) having the stamens inserted at the mouth of the corolla-tube and the style shorter than the tube (opp. ***pin-eyed***); **thrumwort** the star fruit, *Damasonium alisma*.
■ **thrummy** *adjective* (now *rare*) consisting of, characterized by, or covered with thrums; shaggy, downy, velvety: L16.

thrum /θrʌm/ *noun*[3]. L18.
[Imit. Cf. THRUM *verb*[3].]
A sound (as) of a guitar or similar instrument being strummed or thrummed. Also (*dial.*), the purring of a cat.

> 🕮 B. MASON Invisible hands crossed a lyre to make an unearthly, plangent thrum.

†**thrum** *verb*[1] *trans. rare.* Infl. **-mm-**. ME.
[App. rel. to THRUM *noun*[1], Flemish *drommen*, *dringhen* press together, compress. Cf. THRUMBLE.]
1 Compress, condense. Only in ME.
2 Crowd in, cram. Only in E16.

thrum /θrʌm/ *verb*[2]. Infl. **-mm-**. E16.
[from THRUM *noun*[2].]
1 *verb trans.* Provide or decorate with thrums or ends of thread; cover with thrums or small tufts, raise a nap on (cloth); fringe. E16.
†**2** *verb trans.* & *intrans.* Twist or curl (hair). *rare.* L16–M17.
3 *verb trans.* NAUTICAL. Sew or fasten bunches of hempen yarn over (a mat or sail) so as to produce a shaggy surface, suitable to prevent chafing or stop a leak. E18.

> 🕮 **1** SOUTHEY The . . sash of royalty . . is made of net work, and thrummed with red and yellow feathers.

thrum /θrʌm/ *verb*[3]. Infl. **-mm-**. L16.
[Imit. Cf. THRUM *noun*[3].]
1 a *verb intrans.* Play a stringed instrument idly, monotonously, or unskilfully; strum rhythmically without playing a tune. L16. ▸**b** *verb trans.* Play (a stringed instrument) idly, monotonously, or unskilfully; strum rhythmically on; produce (notes, a tune, etc.) by such playing. Also, pluck or twang (a string). E17.
2 *verb trans.* **a** Beat (a person). *slang*. Now *rare* or *obsolete*. E17. ▸†**b** Copulate with (a woman). *slang*. E17–M18.
3 a *verb trans.* Recite monotonously; say repeatedly. Also, hum through (a melody). E18. ▸**b** *verb intrans.* Speak or read monotonously, maunder on, mumble. L18.
4 *verb intrans.* Make a thrumming or humming sound, esp. continuously or monotonously. M18. ▸**b** Of a cat: purr. *dial.* E19.
5 a *verb trans.* Strike (something) with the fingers as if playing a stringed instrument; drum on (a table etc.). *rare*. M18. ▸**b** *verb intrans.* Drum idly. Freq. foll. by *on*. E19.

> 🕮 **1b** OUIDA The violin . . thrummed a gay melody. **3b** SIR W. SCOTT Boswell . . has thrummed upon this topic till it is threadbare. **4** *Westminster Gazette* Spinning-wheels are thrumming. *fig.*: M. GORDON The house in the morning thrummed with expectation.

■ **thrummer** *noun* E18. **thrumming** *verbal noun* the action of the verb; an instance of this: E17.

thrumble /ˈθrʌmb(ə)l/ *verb*. Chiefly & now only *Scot.* & *north*. Also **thrimble** /ˈθrɪmb(ə)l/. LME.
[Frequentative of THRUM *verb*[1].]
1 a *verb intrans.* Make one's way by pushing or jostling; push, jostle. LME. ▸**b** *verb trans.* Press, compress, squeeze; crowd or pile together. L15.
2 *verb trans.* Press or rub between the finger and thumb; handle. M17.

thrummed /θrʌmd/ *adjective*. M16.
[from THRUM *noun*[2], *verb*[2]: see -ED[2], -ED[1].]
1 Covered or decorated with thrums; having a nap or shaggy surface; fringed. *obsolete* exc. *dial.* M16.
2 NAUTICAL. Of a mat or sail: having pieces of hempen yarn sewn on or fastened through it so as to produce a dense shaggy surface. E18.

thrump /θrʌmp/ *noun*. L19.
[Imit.]
A heavy dull sound, a thump.

thrums /θrʌms/ *noun*. *slang*. Now *rare*. L17.
[Repr. colloq. or dial. pronunc. of THRUPPENCE.]
Threepence.

thruout, **thru-out** *preposition* & *adverb* see THROUGHOUT.

thruppence /ˈθrʌp(ə)ns, ˈθrʊ-/ *noun*. *colloq.* Now chiefly *Hist.* Also **thrupence**. L19.
[Repr. a pronunc.]
Threepence; a threepenny bit.

thruppenny /ˈθrʌp(ə)ni, ˈθrʊ-/ *adjective*. *colloq.* Now chiefly *Hist.* Also **thrupenny**. E20.
[Repr. a pronunc.]
Threepenny.

thrush /θrʌʃ/ *noun*[1].
[Old English *þryśce* rel. to synon. *þrǣśce*, Old High German *drōsca*; cf. THROSTLE.]
1 A songbird common in much of Europe, *Turdus philomelos*, which has a buff spotted breast and a loud repetitive song (also more fully ***song thrush***). Also = ***mistle thrush*** s.v. MISTLE 2. OE. ▸**b** Any of various other birds of the genus *Turdus* or related genera; *gen.* any bird of the family Turdidae. Freq. with specifying word. E18. ▸**c** Any of various birds which resemble the true thrushes, esp. of the families Timaliidae, Pachycephalidae, and Parulidae. Usu. with specifying word. M18.
2 *fig.* A female singer. *US colloq.* M20.
1b ***ground thrush***, ***hermit thrush***, ***olive thrush***, ***rock thrush***, ***Swainson's thrush***, ***whistling thrush***, ***wood thrush***, etc. **c** ***laughing-thrush***, ***New Zealand thrush***, ***quail-thrush***, ***shrike-thrush***, ***water-thrush***, etc.
Comb.: **thrush babbler** any of various babblers (birds) of equatorial Africa; **thrush nightingale** a songbird, *Luscinia luscinia*

(family Turdidae), which greatly resembles the nightingale and replaces it in NE Europe and central Asia; also called ***sprosser***.
■ **thrushlike** *adjective* resembling (that of) a thrush L19.

thrush /θrʌʃ/ *noun*[2]. M17.
[Origin unkn.: cf. in sense 1 Swedish *torsk*, Old Danish *tørsk*, Danish *troske*, in sense 2 FRUSH *noun*[2].]
1 MEDICINE. Candidiasis, esp. in infants, characterized by white patches on the inside of the mouth and on the tongue etc. (also called ***aphtha***, ***parasitic stomatitis***). Also, candidiasis affecting any other part, esp. the vagina. M17.
2 VETERINARY MEDICINE. An inflammation of the frog of a horse's hoof, causing it to soften and produce a fetid discharge. Cf. FRUSH *noun*[2]. M18.
Comb.: **thrush-fungus** the parasitic yeastlike fungus *Candida albicans*, which causes thrush (sense 1).

thrust /θrʌst/ *noun*. E16.
[from the verb.]
► **I 1** An act of pressing or pressure; *fig.* stress, difficulty, hardship; *Scot.* a squeeze, a hug, a bite, a chew. *obsolete* exc. *Scot.* E16.
†**2** Pressure or pushing of a crowd, jostling, crowding; a crowd, a throng. M16–E17.
3 A continuous pushing force; *spec.* (*a*) the lateral pressure exerted by an arch or other structure against an abutment or support; (*b*) MINING the crushing of pillars etc. due to the slow descent of the roof; (*c*) GEOLOGY a compressive strain in the earth's crust. E18. ▸**b** *fig.* Energy, vitality, drive. L20.
4 The propulsive force exerted by the propeller of a ship or aircraft, or developed by a jet or rocket engine. M19.

> 📖 **3b** *Opera Now* Mariana Nicolesco's intense . . sound combines power and thrust with plummy dark-hued richness.
> ***4 reverse thrust***: see REVERSE *adjective*. ***vectored thrust***: see VECTOR *verb*.

► **II 5 a** An attack, lunge, or stab with a pointed weapon. L16. ▸†**b** A contest or encounter with swords. E17–E19. ▸**c** *transf.* & *fig.* A thing having a piercing or attacking effect; *esp.* (*a*) a pointed or witty remark, a verbal sally; (*b*) a strong attempt to penetrate an enemy's line or territory, a concerted attack or effort. M17. ▸**d** The principal theme or gist *of* remarks, an argument, etc.; an aim, a purpose. Orig. *US*. M20.
6 A sudden or forcible push; an act of forcefully extending or projecting something. E19.
7 GEOLOGY. = ***thrust fault*** below. L19.

> 📖 **5a** R. L. Fox A dagger-wound . . which court gossip attributed to a thrust from King Darius. ***cut and thrust***: see CUT *noun*[2] 8. ***home thrust***: see HOME *adjective*. ***stop-thrust***: see STOP *noun*[2]. **thrust and parry** (*lit.* & *fig.*) attack and countermove. **c** J. Morley Those shrewd thrusts . . with which Voltaire pushed on his work of 'crushing the Infamous'. *Marketing Week* Our client . . wishes to introduce a bold marketing thrust to . . widen advertising appeal. **d** *Times* A main thrust of my address was the need to be sensitive to developing public attitudes. **6** N. Bawden She delivered this home truth with a proud thrust of her powerful jaw. M. Leitch With a single thrust of his leg, he kicked in the lock. PELVIC ***thrust***.

Comb.: **thrust augmentation** AERONAUTICS the action or process of increasing the thrust of a jet engine; **thrust augmentor** AERONAUTICS a procedure or modification used with a jet engine to increase its thrust; **thrust-bearing** ENGINEERING a bearing designed to take a load in the direction of the axis of a shaft; *spec.* the bearing in which revolves the foremost length of a propeller shaft in a ship and which transmits the thrust of the shaft to the hull; **thrust-block** a block or frame supporting a thrust-bearing; **thrust chamber** a chamber in a rocket engine in which the propellants are injected and burnt; **thrust fault** GEOLOGY a reverse fault, now *spec.* one of low angle in which the hanging wall overhangs the footwall; **thrust-plane** GEOLOGY the plane of dislocation in a thrust fault; **thrust reverser** AERONAUTICS a device for reversing the flow of gas from a jet engine so as to produce a retarding backward thrust; **thrust-shaft** a propeller-shaft; **thrust spoiler** AERONAUTICS a device for deflecting the flow of gas from a jet engine so as to reduce the thrust quickly without reducing the engine power; **thrust stage** THEATRICAL an open stage that projects into the auditorium giving audience seating around three sides; **thrust vector** a vector representing the direction (and magnitude) of the thrust produced by a jet engine, propeller, etc.; **thrust washer** a washer against which a thrust-bearing rests.
■ **thrustful** *adjective* energetic, ambitious, pushful E20. **thrustfulness** *noun* E20.

thrust /θrʌst/ *verb*. Pa. t. & pple **thrust**. ME.
[Old Norse *þrýsta*, which has been referred to Indo-European, whence Latin *trudere* thrust.]
► **I 1 a** *verb trans.* Exert physical force on or against (a body) so as to move it aside or away; shove, drive. Freq. with adverb or adverbial phr. ME. ▸**b** *verb trans. transf.* & *fig.* Compel (a person etc.) to confront something, give way, move aside, etc.; (foll. by *out*) expel, eject. Freq. with adverbs & prepositions. ME. ▸**c** *verb intrans.* Push against something; make a thrust. (*lit.* & *fig.*). ME.
†**2** *verb intrans.* Come *together* with force of impact; collide. *rare*. ME–E16.
3 a *verb intrans.* Make one's way forcibly or advance as through a crowd or against obstacles; crowd *in*; press onwards. LME. ▸†**b** *verb trans.* Press closely about; jostle. LME–M17. ▸†**c** *verb trans.* Pack (objects) into a confined space; fill (a space) tightly; cram. *rare*. LME–E17.
4 *verb trans.* Compress, squeeze; (*obsolete* exc. *Scot.*). Now *esp.* press (cheese). Cf. THRUTCH *verb* 1. LME.

> 📖 **1a** C. Odets The door . . is suddenly violently thrust open. **b** H. Guntrip We have been thrust up against . . fundamental problems. **3a** Sir W. Scott She thrust in between them. J. M. Coetzee Our soldiers have thrust deep into the enemy's territory.

► **II 5** *verb trans.* **a** Push with a sudden impulse or with force; cause to pierce or penetrate; place (something) forcibly or suddenly into a person's hand etc. ME. ▸**b** Extend or push (part of the body etc.) into somewhere or something; extend forward or throw out (a root, branch, spur of land, etc.) so as to project. LME.
6 †**a** *verb trans.* Strike with a pushing action; stab or pierce (a person etc.) *with* a pointed weapon or instrument. LME–L18. ▸**b** *verb intrans.* Pierce, stab; make a thrust or sudden lunge with a pointed weapon. L16.

> 📖 **5a** W. S. Maugham The knife had been thrust into his back. R. Park Carrie thrust a stack of plates into her daughter's hands. **b** A. Cross She had stood with her hands thrust into her coat pockets. *Scuba Times* Diamond Rock thrusts its . . summit sixty feet out of the water. **6b** W. S. Churchill The troopers turned upon him thrusting with their lances.

► **III 7** *verb trans. fig.* Force (a person) *into* some condition or course of action; *refl.* plunge oneself rashly *into* a situation. Also (*rare*), place (something) inappropriately or irregularly *into* some position; (foll. by *in*) introduce irrelevantly. LME.
8 *verb trans.* **a** Impose (a person, oneself) on others; enforce acceptance of (a person, oneself) in an office, position, or condition, or under certain circumstances. Freq. foll. by *on, into, upon*. M16. ▸**b** Press, enforce, or impose the acceptance of (something) *on* or *upon* a person. L16.

> 📖 **8a** W. K. Kelly A candidate . . would be thrust upon them by the Centre. W. Golding The man surely will not have the impertinence to thrust himself on me. **b** A. N. Wilson Hilaire and Marie were upset by . . another new way of life having been thrust upon them. ***thrust down a person's throat***: see THROAT *noun*.

■ **thrusting** *noun* (*a*) the action of the verb; (*b*) in *pl.*, white whey, thrutchings: LME.

thruster /ˈθrʌstə/ *noun*. L16.
[from prec. + -ER[1].]
1 A person who or thing which thrusts. L16.
2 a A person who thrusts himself or herself forward in the field, or rides too close to the hounds. *Hunting slang*. L19. ▸**b** A person who pushes himself or herself forward or imposes himself or herself on others; an aggressive or fiercely ambitious person. E20.
3 a ASTRONAUTICS. A small rocket engine on a spacecraft, used to make alterations in its flight path or altitude. M20. ▸**b** OIL INDUSTRY. Any of several jets or propellers on a drill ship or offshore rig, used for accurate manoeuvring and maintenance of position. L20.
4 A kind of surfboard or sailboard having one or more additional fins and a more streamlined shape than a standard model, and therefore capable of greater speed and manoeuvrability. Also (more fully ***thruster fin***), an additional fin on such a surfboard etc. L20.

> 📖 **2b** *Sport* Bustling Harry Stannard was a perpetual thruster at centre-forward.

thrutch /θrʌtʃ/ *noun*. Now *dial.* LME.
[from next. Cf. TRUDGE *noun* 1.]
An act of thrutching; a thrust, a push, a press, a squeeze. Also (*local*), a narrow gorge or ravine.

thrutch /θrʌtʃ/ *verb*. Now chiefly *dial.*
[Old English *þryććan* = Old High German *druchen* press, from West Germanic.]
1 *verb trans.* Press, squeeze, crush; crowd, throng; *fig.* oppress. Also *spec.*, press (cheese). OE.
2 *verb trans.* Thrust, push. ME.
3 *verb intrans.* Push, press, or squeeze into a place; jostle. M19.

> 📖 **3** C. Bonington I thrutched up the final crack to a small pinnacle . . of the High Rock.

■ **thrutching** *noun* (*a*) the action of the verb; (*b*) in *pl.*, white whey, thrustings: LME.

thruway *noun* see THROUGHWAY.

thrymsa *noun* var. of THRIMSA.

thuck /θʌk/ *noun*. M20.
[Imit.]
The sound of a missile, as an arrow, bullet, etc., hitting an object.

Thucydidean /ˌθjuːsɪdɪˈdiːən/ *adjective*. M18.
[from *Thucydides* (see below) + -EAN.]
Of, pertaining to, or characteristic of the Greek historian Thucydides (*c* 460–*c* 395 BC) or his work.

thud /θʌd/ *noun*. Orig. *Scot.* LME.
[from next.]
1 A blast of wind; a gust; a sudden squall. *Scot.* LME.
2 Orig., a loud sound, esp. as of a thunderclap. Now, a dull heavy sound, as of a blow on, or a solid object striking, a non-resonant surface. Also as *interjection*. M16.
3 A heavy blow; a thump with the fist. Also (*fig.*), a severe setback or affliction. *Scot.* & *north.* E18.

> 📖 **2** L. Spalding He dropped the bag . . with a soft thud on the new mats.

thud /θʌd/ *verb* & *adverb*. Orig. *Scot.* E16.
[Prob. identical with Old English *þyddan* thrust, push; rel. to Old English *þoddettan* push, beat, *þoden* violent wind.]
► **A** *verb*. Infl. **-dd-**.
1 *verb intrans.* Come with (the sound of) a blast or gust, as the wind or a sudden squall. *Scot.* E16.
2 *verb intrans.* Produce a thud or dull heavy sound; fall with a thud. L18. ▸**b** *verb trans.* Strike (a thing) so as to produce a thud. *rare*. L19.

> 📖 **2** I. Wallace His heart thudded inside his chest cavity. R. Frame Occasionally an apple thudded into the long grass. **b** W. Sansom A knock thudded the door.

► **B** *adverb*. With a thud. L19.

> 📖 R. Jefferies We heard an apple fall . . thud on the sward.

■ **thudding** *ppl adjective* (*a*) that thuds or produces a dull heavy sound; (*b*) *fig.* clumsy, heavy; emphatic: L18. **thuddingly** *adverb* E20.

thug /θʌg/ *noun* & *verb*. E19.
[Hindi *thag* cheat, swindler.]
► **A** *noun*. **1** *Hist.* (**T-**.) A member of a religious organization of professional robbers and assassins in India, who strangled their victims. E19.
2 A brutal or vicious ruffian. M19.

> 📖 **2** F. Forsyth A tattoo? Worn by young hooligans, punks, football thugs.

► **B** *verb*. Infl. **-gg-**.
1 *verb trans. Hist.* Assassinate by thuggee. M19.
2 *verb intrans.* Be a thug or ruffian. *US*. M20.

> 📖 **2** *Sun (Baltimore)* When I was thugging . . Middleton was the chief of the gang.

■ **thuggish** *adjective* characteristic of or resembling a thug M20. **thuggishly** *adverb* L20. **thuggishness** *noun* L20. **Thuggism** *noun* (*Hist.*) = THUGGEE M19.

thuggee /θʌˈgiː/ *noun*. Also **T-**. M19.
[Hindi *ṭhagī*, formed as prec.]
Hist. The system of robbery and assassination practised by the Thugs.

thuggery /ˈθʌg(ə)ri/ *noun*. M19.
[from THUG + -ERY.]
Being or acting as a thug; an instance of this.

> 📖 *Times Lit. Suppl.* Vishnevskaya writes . . about . . moral corruption and official thuggery.

thugyi /θəˈdʒiː/ *noun*. M19.
[Burmese.]
In Myanmar (Burma), the headman of a village.

thuja /ˈθjuːjə/ *noun*. M18.
[mod. Latin (see below): cf. THUYA.]
Any of various N. American and Far Eastern coniferous trees of the genus *Thuja*, allied to the cypresses (also called ***arbor vitae***). Also, the wood of any of these trees. Cf. THUYA.
oil of thuja a pale yellow essential oil obtained from thuja, having an odour like menthol and containing thujone; also called ***oil of arbor vitae***.
■ **thujaplicin** /-ˈplʌɪsɪn/ *noun* [from mod. Latin *Thuja plicata* (see below)] CHEMISTRY each of three isomers of isopropyltropolone, $C_3H_7 \cdot C_7H_5O_2$, which have fungicidal properties and occur in the giant arbor vitae, *Thuja plicata* M20. **thujone** *noun* (CHEMISTRY) a toxic liquid terpene, $C_{10}H_{16}O$, which is present in the oils of thuja, wormwood, etc., and is used as a solvent M19.

thula /ˈθuːlə/ *noun*. M20.
[Old Norse *þula*.]
A metrical list of names or poetic synonyms assembled in categories (orig. for oral recitation) to preserve traditional knowledge, esp. as in Old Norse.

Thule /ˈθjuːli, *in sense 2* θuːl, θjuːl/ *noun*. OE.
[Latin *Thule*, *Thyle* from Greek *Thoulē*, *Thulē*, of unkn. origin. In sense 2, from *Thule* (now Dundas), a settlement in NW Greenland.]
1 a ANTIQUITIES. A land (variously conjectured to be the Shetland Islands, Iceland, or part of Denmark or Norway) to the north of Britain, believed by ancient Greek and Roman geographers to be the most northerly region in the world. OE. ▸**b** *transf.* In full ***ultima Thule*** [Latin = farthest Thule]. The type of the extreme limit of travel and discovery; *fig.* the highest or uttermost point or degree attained or attainable, the (lowest) limit, the nadir. L18.
2 ARCHAEOLOGY. A prehistoric Eskimo culture widely distributed from Alaska to Greenland *c* AD 500–1400. Freq. *attrib.* E20.

📖 **1b** M. LOWRY You write off that behaviour as being the ultima Thule of ingratitude.

Thulean /ˈθ(j)uːlɪən/ *adjective.* **E20.**
[from prec. + **-AN**.]
GEOLOGY. Of, pertaining to, or designating a region of Tertiary volcanic activity which includes Iceland and much of Britain and Greenland.

thulia /ˈθ(j)uːlɪə/ *noun.* **L19.**
[from **THULIUM** + *-ia*, after **THORIA**, **YTTRIA**, etc.]
CHEMISTRY. The sesquioxide of thulium, Tm_2O_3, a dense white powder from which thulium is obtained.

thulite /ˈθ(j)uːlʌɪt/ *noun.* **E19.**
[from **THULE** + **-ITE**[1].]
MINERALOGY. A pink manganese-bearing variety of zoisite, which is sometimes fluorescent and was originally found in Norway.

thulium /ˈθ(j)uːlɪəm/ *noun.* **L19.**
[from **THULE** + **-IUM**.]
A rare metallic chemical element of the lanthanide series, atomic no. 69. (Symbol Tm.)

thumb /θʌm/ *noun.*
[Old English *þūma* = Old Frisian *thūma*, Old Saxon *þūma*, Middle Low German, Middle Dutch *dūme* (Dutch *duim*), Old High German *dūmo* (German *Daumen*), from West Germanic, repr. Indo-European base also of Latin *tumere* swell.]
1 a The short thick first digit of the human hand, opposable to the fingers, and distinguished from them by having only two phalanges; the first digit of the hand or foot of primates etc., esp. when it is opposable to or set apart from the other digits. **OE.** ▸**†b** The big toe. **LME–M17.** ▸**c** The inner digit of the forefoot in tetrapod animals; the first digit of the wing in birds, bearing the bastard wing. **E17.**
2 The breadth of the thumb as a measure, an inch. Also *thumb's breadth*. *obsolete* exc. *Scot. arch.* **LME.**
3 A thing analogous to or resembling a thumb, e.g. a projecting spur or stump of a woody plant, a diminutive animal or object, etc. **M18.**
4 A part of a glove etc. which is made to receive the thumb. **L19.**
Phrases: ***all fingers and thumbs***: see **FINGER** *noun*. **†bite the thumb at** insult (a person) by making the gesture of biting the thumb. ***DEAD MAN'S thumb***. ***green thumb***: see **GREEN** *adjective*. ***hop-o'-my-thumb***: see **HOP** *verb*[1]. ***miller's thumb***: see **MILLER** *noun*[1]. ***pricking of one's thumbs***, ***pricking in one's thumbs***: see **PRICKING** 1. ***rule of thumb***: see **RULE** *noun*. ***stand out like a sore thumb***, ***stick out like a sore thumb***: see **SORE** *adjective*[1]. ***tear-thumb***: see **TEAR** *verb*[1]. **thumbs down** (*a*) *ROMAN HISTORY* an indication of mercy or approval given by spectators during combats in the amphitheatre; (*b*) an indication of rejection, negation, or failure. **thumbs up** (*a*) *ROMAN HISTORY* an indication to show no mercy given by spectators in the amphitheatre; (*b*) an indication of acceptance, approval, or success. ***twiddle one's thumbs***: see **TWIDDLE** *verb*[1] 2. **under a person's thumb**, **under the thumb** entirely under a person's control, completely dominated by a person.
Comb.: **thumb-band** = *thumb-rope* below; **thumb-bottle** a small flask, a phial; **thumb-cleat** *NAUTICAL* a small cleat resembling a thumb in shape; **thumb-finger** (now *rare*) the thumb; **thumb-fingered** *adjective* clumsy, not dexterous; **thumb-flint** *ARCHAEOLOGY* = *thumbnail scraper* s.v. **THUMBNAIL** *noun*; **thumb index** a set of lettered or marked grooves cut or tabs fixed in the front edges of a book's leaves, so as to facilitate easy reference to any section by placing the thumb or finger on the appropriate letter etc.; **thumb-indexed** *adjective* (of a book) having a thumb index; **thumb-lancet**: having a broad two-edged blade; **thumb-lock** (*a*) a kind of lock which is opened by pressing with the thumb; (*b*) in *pl.*, thumbscrews; **thumb-mark** *noun & verb* (*a*) *noun* a mark made by a (dirty) thumb, esp. on the page of a book; a thumbprint; (*b*) *verb trans.* make a thumb-mark on, mark with the thumb; **thumb-nut** a nut shaped for turning with the thumb and forefinger; **thumb-pad** *ZOOLOGY* = ***NUPTIAL pad***; **thumb paper** *US* a small sheet of paper or card inserted in a book at the bottom of a page to protect it from thumb-marks; **thumb piano** *MUSIC* = **MBIRA**; **thumb pick** *MUSIC* a kind of plectrum worn on the thumb; **thumb-pin** = ***thumbtack*** below; ***thumb-piston***: see **PISTON** *noun* 2b; **thumb-pot** (*a*) a flowerpot of the smallest size; (*b*) *ARCHAEOLOGY* a Roman pot bearing the imprint of the potter's thumb; **thumb-ring** (*a*) a ring worn on the thumb; (*b*) a ring for the thumb on the guard of a dagger or sword; (*c*) *ARCHERY* a ring for the thumb to aid the drawing of a bow; **thumb-rope** (now *dial.*) a rope made by twisting hay or straw on the thumb; **thumb-stall** (*a*) a shoemaker's or sailmaker's thimble; (*b*) a sheath worn to protect an injured thumb; (*c*) *ECCLESIASTICAL HISTORY* a thimble of precious metal worn by a bishop after being dipped in consecrated oil, used for anointing in the rite of confirmation; **thumb-stick** a tall walking-stick with a forked thumb-rest at the top; **thumb-sucker** (*a*) a child who habitually sucks his or her thumb; (*b*) *journalists' slang* a serious article; a columnist; **thumbtack** *noun & verb* (*a*) *noun* a tack with a broad head; *N. Amer.* a drawing-pin; (*b*) *verb trans.* pin up with a thumbtack or thumbtacks.
▪ **thumbful** *noun* as much as a thumb can hold **M20.**

thumb /θʌm/ *verb.* **L16.**
[from prec.]
1 *verb trans.* Play (a wind instrument, a tune) (as) with the thumbs; perform ineptly. Now *rare*. **L16.**
2 *verb trans.* Feel (as) with the thumb; handle. **E17.**
3 a *verb trans.* Soil or wear (esp. a book) by repeated handling with the thumbs; read much or often. **M17.** ▸**b** *verb trans. & intrans.* Turn (pages) over (as) with the thumb in glancing through a book etc. Freq. foll. by *through*. **M20.**
4 *verb trans.* Press, move, touch, or spread with the thumb. **M18.**
5 *verb trans.* Request or obtain (a lift in a passing vehicle) by signalling with an outstretched thumb; signal to (a passing driver or vehicle) with the thumb; make (one's way) by thumbing lifts. Orig. *US*. **M20.**
6 *verb intrans.* Gesture with the thumb; *esp.* signal with the thumb in the hope of obtaining a lift in a passing vehicle. **M20.**

📖 **2** H. JAMES The brasses that Louis Quinze might have thumbed. **3a** LD MACAULAY Within a week . . it had been thumbed by twenty families. **b** J. HERBERT Ash thumbed through the local directory. **4** W. VAN T. CLARK 'I'm acting sheriff,' he said, thumbing out the badge on his vest. N. FARAH He . . massaged, thumbed and squeezed the hard joints. ***thumb one's nose at***: see **NOSE** *noun*. **5** Z. TOMIN The first three cars I thumbed didn't stop. **6** R. PRICE He turned to Yancey . . thumbing to the house—'Is that all . . old Rooster can afford?'

▪ **thumber** *noun* (*N. Amer. colloq.*) a person who thumbs a lift, a hitchhiker **M20.**

thumbed /θʌmd/ *adjective.* **E16.**
[from **THUMB** *noun*, *verb*: see **-ED**[2], **-ED**[1].]
1 Having thumbs (esp. of a specified kind). **E16.**
2 Of a book etc.: having the pages soiled or worn by the thumbs of readers; showing signs of much use. Freq. with adverb. **L18.**

📖 **2** *Sunday Times* One of the most thumbed through books in any stable.

thumbikins /ˈθʌmɪkɪnz/ *noun pl. Scot.* Also **thumbkins** /ˈθʌmkɪnz/. **L17.**
[from **THUMB** *noun* + **-KINS**.]
Hist. Thumbscrews.

thumbless /ˈθʌmlɪs/ *adjective.* **M17.**
[from **THUMB** *noun* + **-LESS**.]
1 Clumsy; incompetent. Cf. **HANDLESS** 2. Now *rare* or *obsolete*. **M17.**
2 Without a thumb or thumbs; *spec.* designating primates in which the thumb is rudimentary or functionless. **E18.**

thumbling /ˈθʌmlɪŋ/ *noun.* **M19.**
[from **THUMB** *noun* + **-LING**[1].]
A diminutive being; a dwarf, a pigmy; a Tom Thumb.

thumbnail /ˈθʌmneɪl/ *noun & verb.* **E17.**
[from **THUMB** *noun* + **NAIL** *noun*.]
▶ **A** *noun.* **1** The nail of a thumb. **E17.**
2 In full ***thumbnail sketch***. A drawing or sketch of the size of a thumbnail; *fig.* a concise or brief descriptive account. **M19.**

📖 **1** *Sounds* You could put the sum of my knowledge of CSN . . on your thumbnail. **2** L. CODY He answers quite neatly to your thumbnail of Leonard Margolin.

Comb.: **thumbnail scraper** *ARCHAEOLOGY* a kind of microlith made for scraping; ***thumbnail sketch***: see sense A.2 above.
▶ **B** *verb trans.* & (*rare*) *intrans.* Describe (a person) concisely by means of a thumbnail sketch. **M20.**

📖 *Times* Miss Ride—or 115 lb, blue-eyed, brunette . . Sally, as the papers thumbnail her.

thumbpiece /ˈθʌmpiːs/ *noun.* **M18.**
[from **THUMB** *noun* + **PIECE** *noun*.]
1 The part of a handle etc. intended to receive the thumb; a part of a mechanism operated by pressure of the thumb. **M18.**
2 A piece of bread, with cheese or meat, held between the thumb and finger. *Austral. & dial.* **M19.**
3 A protective covering for the thumb; the thumb of a glove etc. *rare*. **L19.**

thumbprint /ˈθʌmprɪnt/ *noun & verb.* **E20.**
[from **THUMB** *noun* + **PRINT** *noun*.]
▶ **A** *noun.* **1** An impression of the inner surface of the top joint of the thumb, made on a receptive surface and used esp. for identification. **E20.**
2 An identifying trait, a distinctive characteristic. **M20.**

📖 **2** M. MEYER The most difficult thing, if the translator is a creative writer . . is to . . resist leaving his thumbprint.

▶ **B** *verb.* **1** *verb trans.* Record the thumbprint or thumbprints of (a person). **L20.**
2 *verb intrans.* Make a thumbprint. **L20.**

thumbscrew /ˈθʌmskruː/ *noun & verb.* **L18.**
[from **THUMB** *noun* + **SCREW** *noun*[1].]
▶ **A** *noun.* **1** A screw with a flattened or winged head, for turning with the thumb and fingers; a small clamp adjusted by such a screw. **L18.**
2 An instrument of torture for crushing the thumbs. Usu. in *pl.* **E19.**

📖 **2** *fig.*: *Marketing* The thumbscrews are on for us to find . . alternatives to CFCs.

▶ **B** *verb trans.* Torture (as) with thumbscrews. **L18.**

thumby /ˈθʌmi/ *noun. colloq. & Scot.* **E19.**
[from **THUMB** *noun* + **-Y**[6].]
A little thumb; (a pet name for) a thumb.

thumby /ˈθʌmi/ *adjective. colloq.* **E20.**
[from **THUMB** *noun* + **-Y**[1].]
1 Soiled by thumb-marks. *rare.* **E20.**
2 Clumsy. **E20.**

†thummart *noun. Scot.* **L17–M19.**
[Alt. of **FOUMART**.]
A polecat.

Thummim /ˈθʌmɪm/ *noun.* **M16.**
[Hebrew *tummīm* pl. of *tōm* completeness.]
One of the two objects of a now unknown nature worn on the breastplate of a Jewish high priest (*Exodus* 28:30). Chiefly in ***Urim and Thummim***. Cf. **URIM**.

thump /θʌmp/ *noun.* **M16.**
[Imit.: see next.]
1 A heavy dull blow, esp. (as) with the fist or a blunt instrument; a deadened knock; the sound of such a blow or knock; *spec.* a knocking of machinery arising from slackness at a joint where there is reciprocal motion. **M16.** ▸**b** *spec.* In *pl.* A beating in the chest of a horse due to spasmodic contractions of the diaphragm, analogous to the hiccup in man. **E20.**
2 *euphem.* Hell. In exclamatory or imprecatory phrs. expr. strong disagreement, outrage, etc., or merely emphatic. Also as *interjection*. *dial.* (chiefly *north.*). **M20.**

📖 **1** G. SWIFT His lame leg . . knocked against the panelling . . with an oddly solid thump. R. PILCHER Roddy delivered an affectionate thump on Danus' shoulder. **2** *Melody Maker* What the thump have you done to your *hair*?

thump /θʌmp/ *verb & adverb.* **M16.**
[Imit. Cf. **JUMP** *verb*, **TUMP** *verb*[3].]
▶ **A** *verb.* **1** *verb trans.* **a** Strike or beat heavily, (as) with the fist or a blunt instrument; hammer, knock; (of a body, the feet) fall on or strike with a thump; put *down* with a thump. **M16.** ▸**b** Drive or force (a person or thing) *down*, *forward*, *off*, etc., or *into* some position or condition by thumping. Also, play (a tune etc.) with a heavy touch (usu. foll. by *out*). **L16.** ▸**c** Express by thumps or thumping. **E20.**
2 *verb intrans.* **a** Produce a thump or heavy deadened sound; fall or hit with a thump; deliver blows, esp. to attract attention (usu. foll. by *on*, *at*). **M16.** ▸**b** Tread heavily or noisily; (of a thing) move with thumps, bump along. **E17.** ▸**c** Esp. of the heart: pulsate violently or audibly; throb strongly. **L18.**
3 *verb trans.* Beat soundly in a fight; achieve a resounding victory over. *colloq.* **L16.**

📖 **1a** J. GATHORNE-HARDY She thumped the dishes down. *Times Lit. Suppl.* Chapple was moved to thump him on the jaw. **thump a cushion**, **thump the pulpit**, etc. (of a preacher) use violent gestures (cf. ***cushion-thumper*** s.v. **CUSHION** *noun*). **b** G. CHAPMAN Thrice th' Ajaces thumped him off. C. RYAN The bass drummer . . thumped out a . . beat in Morse code. **2a** R. BANKS I could . . hear the jukebox thumping . . in the background. A. DILLARD What monster of a . . June bug could . . thump so insistently at my window. **b** N. BAWDEN Marigold, thumping up the stairs. **c** A. GRAY My heart was thumping like a drum. **3** *Pot Black* Taylor ran off five straight victories to thump Thorburn.

Comb.: **thump-up** *slang* a punch-up.
▶ **B** *adverb.* With a thump. **E18.**
▪ **thumpety** *adverb* with a thump (usu. redupl. as ***thumpety-thump***) **M20.**

thumper /ˈθʌmpə/ *noun.* **M16.**
[from **THUMP** *verb* + **-ER**[1].]
1 a A person who or thing which thumps something. **M16.** ▸**b** *GEOLOGY.* A device for creating artificial seismic waves in the earth. **M20.**
2 A strikingly big thing of its kind, *esp.* a blatant or gross lie. *colloq.* **M17.**
3 A thumping or heavy blow. Long *rare* or *obsolete*. **L17.**
4 A motorcycle or trail bike designed to travel over rough terrain, *esp.* one with a single-cylinder, four-stroke engine which produces a characteristic 'thump' on the fourth power-stroke of the piston. *colloq.* **L20.**

📖 **1a** *Ambit* Behind the arrogant chest-thumper there was a humble and kindly man. **2** J. COLLINS They gives me a Thumper of a Christmas Box.

thumping /ˈθʌmpɪŋ/ *verbal noun.* **L16.**
[from **THUMP** *verb* + **-ING**[1].]
The action of **THUMP** *verb*; an instance of this.

thumping /ˈθʌmpɪŋ/ *adjective.* **L16.**
[from **THUMP** *verb* + **-ING**[2].]
1 That thumps; beating; pounding; throbbing. **L16.**
2 Of striking size, extent, or amount; exceptionally large or heavy; huge, prominent. Cf. **THWACKING** *adjective*, **WALLOPING** *adjective* 2, **WHACKING** *adjective*. *colloq.* **L16.**

1 *Which?* A thumping headache, a queasy tummy . . classic symptoms of a hangover. *Sky Magazine* Its thumping hip-house beat and psychedelic guitar riffs. **2** M. FOOT Brown, with a thumping majority at his back . . , could be a boorish bully. *Q* The director is making it up . . there is nothing else to explain its thumping non-sequiturs.

■ **thumpingly** *adverb* L17.

thumri /ˈθʊmri/ *noun*. M19.
[Hindi *ṭhumrī*.]
A light classical form of northern Indian vocal or instrumental music; a piece in this form.

thunbergia /θʌnˈbəːdʒə, -ˈbəːɡɪə/ *noun*. L18.
[mod. Latin (see below), from C. P. *Thunberg* (1743–1822), Swedish botanist + -IA[1].]
Any of various tropical chiefly climbing plants of the genus *Thunbergia*, of the acanthus family, which includes many species cultivated in greenhouses for their showy flowers.

thunder /ˈθʌndə/ *noun*.
[Old English *þunor* = Old Frisian *thuner*, Old Saxon *þunar* (Dutch *donder*), Old High German *donar* (German *Donner*), Old Norse *þórr*, from Germanic base repr. Indo-European base also of Latin *tonare* to thunder.]
1 a The loud crash or prolonged rumbling accompanying a flash of lightning, caused by the sudden heating and expansion of gases along the channel of the discharge, and heard a short interval after the lightning except at close quarters. Also, the meteorological conditions which give rise to thunderstorms. OE. ▸**b** Such a phenomenon regarded as a destructive force like lightning capable of striking objects etc.; a thunderbolt. Now *poet. & rhet.* OE. ▸**c** A peal of thunder, a thunderclap. Now *poet.* or *rhet.* OE. ▸**d** A thunderstorm. *obsolete* exc. *dial.* ME.
2 *fig.* **a** Threatening, terrifying, or forcible utterance; strong denunciation, censure, or invective; vehement or powerful eloquence; an instance of this. LME. ▸**b** Great force or energy (chiefly with allus. to *Job* 39:19). M16.
3 *transf.* Any loud deep rumbling or resounding noise. L16.
4 Used in phrs. expr. annoyance, anger, incredulity, etc. *colloq.* E18.

1b SHAKES. *Rich. II* Let thy blows . . Fall like amazing thunder on the casque Of thy . . pernicious enemy. **c** TENNYSON Low thunders bring the mellow rain. **2a** GIBBON He directed the thunders of the church against heresy. **b** T. GRAY With necks in thunder cloath'd. **3** J. WYNDHAM A thunder of trampling boots on the floor above. S. RUSHDIE The thunder of applause. **4** *Dandy* What in thunder are you idle scallywags doing?

Phrases: ***like a duck in thunder***: see DUCK *noun*[1]. **steal a person's thunder** appropriate another's idea, policy, etc., and spoil the effect the originator hoped to achieve by expressing it or acting upon it first. **thunder and lightning** (*a*) denunciation, invective; (*b*) *Hist.* a type of cloth, app. of garish colours, worn esp. in the 18th cent.; (*c*) *dial.* bread spread with clotted cream and golden syrup; (*d*) ANGLING a variety of artificial fly. **thunder-and-lightning** *adjective* (*a*) *Hist.* made of thunder and lightning cloth; (of clothes) flashy, garish, combining clashing colours; (*b*) melodramatic, startling, violent.

Comb.: **thunder-axe** *dial.* = CELT *noun*[2] (cf. THUNDERBOLT *noun* 3); **thunder-ball** (*a*) ball lightning; (*b*) *poet.* a thunderbolt; **thunder-bearer** (chiefly *poet.*) the bearer of thunder or thunderbolts, the god Jupiter; **thunder-bearing** *adjective* that brings or carries thunder; **thunder-bird** (*a*) *Austral.* either of two thickheads, *Pachycephala pectoralis* (the golden whistler) and *P. rufiventris* (the rufous whistler), which become noisy during thunderstorms; (*b*) a mythical bird thought by some N. American Indian peoples to cause thunder; **thunder-blast** (chiefly *poet.*) a peal or clap of thunder; a thunderbolt; **thunder-blasted** *adjective* blasted (as) with a thunderbolt, struck by lightning; **thunderboat** *US* an unlimited hydroplane; **thunder-box** *colloq.* a portable commode; a lavatory; **thunderbug** = THRIPS; **thunder-crack** *arch. & dial.* a thunderclap (*lit. & fig.*); †**thunder-dart** *rare* (Spenser) a thunderbolt; **thunder-dint** *arch.* a thunderbolt; **thunder-drop** any of the large scattered drops of rain which fall at the beginning of a thunder-shower; **thunder-drum** (*a*) a drum used in a theatre to imitate thunder; (*b*) *fig.* an imaginary drum represented as the source of thunder; **thunder egg** *N. Amer. & Austral.* a geode, esp. of chalcedony; **thunder-flash** *transf.* a harmless, very noisy, form of explosive used esp. in military exercises; a firework imitating such an explosive; **thunderfly** = THRIPS; **thunder-god** a god identified or specially associated with thunder; a god supposed to rule or control the thunder, as Jupiter in the Roman, or Thor in the Norse mythology; **thunder-gust** (chiefly *US*) a strong gust of wind accompanying a thunderstorm; **thunderhead** a rounded mass of cumulonimbus cloud projecting above the general body of cloud, and portending a thunderstorm; an anvil cloud; **thunder-mug** *slang* a chamber-pot (cf. *thunder-box* above); **thunder-plant** the houseleek, *Sempervivum tectorum*, believed to avert lightning from the roofs on which it was planted; **thunder-plump** [PLUMP *noun*[2]] (chiefly *Scot.*) a heavy and sudden shower accompanied by thunder and lightning; **thunder-pump**, **thunder-pumper** *N. Amer.* the American bittern, *Botaurus lentiginosus*, which has a distinctive booming call; †**thunder-rod** a lightning-conductor; **thunder run** THEATRICAL HISTORY a ramp fitted with two wooden troughs down which iron balls were rolled to imitate thunder; **thunder-sheet** THEATRICAL a piece of sheet metal shaken to imitate thunder; **thunder-shower** (now chiefly *N. Amer.*) a shower of rain accompanied by thunder and lightning; **thunder-snake** *US* the eastern king-snake, *Lampropeltis getulus*; **thunder stick** (a name supposedly given by peoples unfamiliar with firearms to) a rifle or cannon; **thunder-stone** (*a*) *arch.* a thunderbolt or supposed destructive bolt or shaft resulting from a lightning flash; (*b*) = THUNDERBOLT *noun* 3.

■ **thunderful** *adjective* (*rare*) thundery, full of thunder; sounding like thunder: M19. **thunderless** *adjective* M19.

thunder /ˈθʌndə/ *verb*.
[Old English *þunrian*, from prec.]
1 *verb intrans.* **a** *impers.* in ***it thunders***, ***it is thundering***, etc., thunder sounds, there is thunder. OE. ▸**b** Of a god, heaven, the sky, etc.: cause or emit thunder; sound with thunder. Now *poet. & literary.* OE.
2 *fig.* **a** *verb intrans.* Make vehement threats; utter censure or denunciation; inveigh powerfully *against*. Also, speak forcibly or with powerful eloquence; speak loudly, vociferate. ME. ▸**b** *verb trans.* Utter or communicate (threats, denunciation, approval, etc.) loudly or forcibly; shout out, roar. LME. ▸**c** *verb trans.* Make vehement threats against; denounce violently; put *down* by denunciation. Now *rare* or *obsolete.* L17.
3 *transf.* **a** *verb intrans.* Make or proceed with a loud resounding noise like thunder; rumble; roar by or along. LME. ▸**b** *verb trans.* Inflict (blows) noisily or forcibly; give out (a sound) powerfully; attack or overwhelm (a person, a place, etc.) with an overpowering noise or with action like a thunderbolt. M16.

1a CONAN DOYLE One day it thundered . . out of a cloudless sky. **b** SOUTHEY Earth shook, Heaven thunder'd. **2a** S. CHITTY A loud and leathery Lesbian . . who thundered continuously against the . . male. *EuroBusiness* The Kremlin . . stopped thundering about the . . Community being a thinly-veiled arm of the US military. **b** V. GLENDINNING Leo . . thundered, 'It's all in chapter four.' **3a** E. BOWEN The river . . thundered towards the mill-race. E. WAUGH Two lorries thundered past him. **b** W. WILKIE Learn to dread My vengeance thund'red on your wretched head.

thunderation /θʌndəˈreɪʃ(ə)n/ *noun & interjection. colloq.* (chiefly *US*). M19.
[from THUNDER *noun* + -ATION.]
Used (freq. in phrs.) to expr. irritation, anger, displeasure, etc.: damnation. Cf. THUNDER *noun* 4.

J. A. MICHENER: 'Thunderation!' Smith exploded . . . 'If only I could find seventeen men unafraid of mosquitoes.'

thunderbolt /ˈθʌndəbəʊlt/ *noun & verb*. LME.
[from THUNDER *noun* + BOLT *noun*[1].]
▶ **A** *noun*. **1 a** A flash of lightning, esp. when close enough for a simultaneous clap of thunder to be heard; a supposed bolt or shaft believed to be the destructive agent in a lightning-flash, esp. as an attribute of Jupiter, Thor, etc. Cf. BOLT *noun*[1] 2. LME. ▸**b** An imaginary or conventional representation of a thunderbolt as an emblem of a god, a heraldic bearing, etc. E18.
2 *fig.* Orig., a terrifying or awesome denunciation, censure, or threat proceeding from a high authority. Now *esp.* a sudden or unexpected and startling event or piece of news. Cf. THUNDERCLAP 3. M16. ▸**b** A person noted for violent or destructive action; a dynamic or furiously energetic person. L16. ▸**c** SPORT. A fast hard-struck shot or stroke. M20.
3 Any of various stones, fossils, or mineral concretions, formerly or popularly believed to be thunderbolts; *spec.* (*a*) a belemnite; (*b*) a flint celt or similar prehistoric implement; (*c*) a nodule of iron pyrites; (*d*) a meteorite. Chiefly *Scot. & dial.* E17.
4 Any of several plants believed to induce thunder if they were picked; *esp.* the corn poppy, *Papaver rhoeas*. *dial.* M19.

1a P. DALLY One might imagine the house, with its metal spires and crescents, to be a natural target for thunderbolts. **2** SPENSER To dart abroad the thunder bolts of warre. *Courier-Mail (Brisbane)* This news. It's a thunderbolt out of the blue. **b** R. W. EMERSON A thunderbolt in the attack, he was . . invulnerable in his entrenchments. **c** *Times* Heighway . . lashed a thunderbolt past Latchford from the edge of the box.

Comb.: **thunderbolt attack**, **thunderbolt raid** *colloq.* (now chiefly *Hist.*) a short but heavy air raid.

▶ **B** *verb trans.* Strike (as) with a thunderbolt; astonish, amaze; terrify. *rare.* L16.

thunderclap /ˈθʌndəklap/ *noun*. LME.
[from THUNDER *noun* + CLAP *noun*[1].]
1 A clap or loud crash of thunder. Formerly also, the impact of a lightning-flash, a thunderstroke. LME.
2 *transf.* A very loud sudden noise. E17.
3 *fig.* Something startling, unexpected, or terrifying. Cf. THUNDERBOLT *noun* 2. E17.

3 A. COOKE The family reacted to this thunderclap of tastelessness by getting rid of me.

thundercloud /ˈθʌndəklaʊd/ *noun*. L17.
[from THUNDER *noun* + CLOUD *noun*.]
1 A cumulonimbus cloud with a towering or spreading top, which is charged with electricity and produces thunder and lightning. L17.
2 *fig.* Something threatening or dreadful represented as or compared to a thundercloud. L18.

thundered /ˈθʌndəd/ *adjective*. E17.
[from THUNDER *noun*, *verb*: see -ED[2], -ED[1].]
†**1** Struck by a supposed thunderbolt or by lightning. *rare.* Only in E17.
2 Dealt or inflicted as by thunder; sounded with a noise like thunder. E19.
3 Affected by thunder; (of milk) turned sour by thundery weather. Chiefly *Scot.* L19.

thunderer /ˈθʌnd(ə)rə/ *noun*. LME.
[from THUNDER *verb* + -ER[1].]
1 a A god who rules or is believed to cause the thunder; *spec.* (***the Thunderer***) Jupiter. LME. ▸**b** THEATRICAL. A person employed to provide a mechanical imitation of thunder. Now *rare* or *obsolete.* E18.
2 *fig.* A mighty warrior; a powerful orator, an utterer of violent denunciation, invective, or censure; *spec.* (***the Thunderer***), the London newspaper *The Times*. L16.
3 A thing that makes a noise like thunder; *spec.* a bullroarer. M19.

thundering /ˈθʌnd(ə)rɪŋ/ *noun*. OE.
[from THUNDER *verb* + -ING[1].]
1 The action of THUNDER *verb*; *arch.* an instance of this, a clap of thunder. OE.
2 (An utterance or instance of) vehement threatening, invective, or censure. M16.

thundering /ˈθʌnd(ə)rɪŋ/ *adjective & adverb*. M16.
[from THUNDER *verb* + -ING[2].]
▶ **A** *adjective*. **1** That thunders (*lit. & fig.*); (of sound) as loud as thunder. M16.
2 Very energetic or forcible, violent. Now *esp.* very great or big, excessive, immense. *colloq.* E17.

1 W. SHEED Belloc's thundering affirmations gave . . Ward something to march to. **2** *Handgunner* Once again, it was a thundering success.

▶ **B** *adverb*. Excessively, immensely, exceedingly. *colloq.* E19.

Independent [Sowerbutts] was, as Geoffrey Smith puts it, 'a thundering good gardener'.

■ **thunderingly** *adverb* L17.

thunderlight /ˈθʌndəlʌɪt/ *noun*. Long *arch.* ME.
[from THUNDER *noun* + Old English *leyt*, *lait*, *lēget* lightning or LIGHT *noun*.]
Lightning.

thunderous /ˈθʌnd(ə)rəs/ *adjective*. E16.
[from THUNDER *noun* + -OUS.]
1 Of a sound: very loud, rumbling or resounding like thunder. E16.
2 Full of or charged with thunder; thundery. E16.
3 *fig.* Of threatening aspect; violent, powerful, or terrifying like thunder; charged with latent energy, like a thundercloud. M19.

1 *Sport* Jeers and catcalls had changed to thunderous applause. **2** A. SILLITOE The end of May had seen thunderous weather. **3** *Business* A thunderous speed boat race. A. S. BYATT He looked most horrid . . with veins standing on his brow and a most thunderous expression.

■ **thunderously** *adverb* M19. **thunderousness** *noun* E20.

thunderstorm /ˈθʌndəstɔːm/ *noun*. M17.
[from THUNDER *noun* + STORM *noun*.]
A storm with thunder and lightning, produced by electrically charged cumulonimbus clouds and usu. accompanied by heavy rain or hail.
like a duck in a thunderstorm, ***like a dying duck in a thunderstorm***: see DUCK *noun*[1].
■ **thunderstormy** *adjective* M20.

thunderstricken /ˈθʌndəstrɪk(ə)n/ *adjective*. L16.
[from THUNDER *noun* + STRICKEN *adjective*.]
1 = THUNDERSTRUCK *adjective* 1. L16.
2 = THUNDERSTRUCK *adjective* 2. M17.

thunderstrike /ˈθʌndəstrʌɪk/ *verb trans.* Pa. t. & pple **thunderstruck** /ˈθʌndəstrʌk/. E17.
[Back-form. from prec., that being taken as a pa. pple.]
1 Strike with lightning or a supposed thunderbolt. Long *rare* exc. *poet.* E17.
2 *fig.* Strike as with a thunderbolt; amaze, astonish greatly. *rare* exc. as in THUNDERSTRICKEN, THUNDERSTRUCK *adjectives*. E17. ▸**b** Inflict terrible vengeance, censure, etc., on. Also (*rare*), inflict damage on, batter severely. Long *rare* exc. *poet.* M17.

2 SOUTHEY The news . . thunderstruck all present.

thunderstroke /ˈθʌndəstrəʊk/ *noun. arch. & poet.* L16.
[from THUNDER *noun* + STROKE *noun*[1].]
1 A discharge or stroke of thunder; the impact of a lightning-flash. L16.
2 *transf. & fig.* Something resembling a thunderstroke in sound or effect; something startling, sudden, very loud, etc. L16.

📖 **2** G. O. TREVELYAN The thunder-stroke of such a confession . . could not be parried.

thunderstruck /ˈθʌndəstrʌk/ *adjective*. E17.
[A later equivalent of THUNDERSTRICKEN.]
1 Struck with sudden amazement, terror, etc.; extremely startled, astonished, or terrified. E17.
2 Struck by lightning or a supposed thunderbolt. Long *rare* or *obsolete*. M17.

📖 **1** I. WALLACE He sat thunderstruck, speechless and uncomprehending.

thunderstruck *verb pa. t. & pple of* THUNDERSTRIKE.

thundery /ˈθʌnd(ə)ri/ *adjective*. L16.
[from THUNDER *noun* + -Y[1].]
1 Of or pertaining to thunder; (of the weather, clouds, etc.) characterized by or presaging thunder. L16.
2 *fig.* Threatening a sudden outburst of anger, passion, or disturbance; gloomy, frowning. E19.

📖 **1** *Times* Brighter later with showers which may be thundery. **2** S. WILBERFORCE A thundery state of the political and social atmosphere.

thunk /θʌŋk/ *noun*[1], *verb*[1] *& adverb*. M20.
[Imit.]
► **A** *noun*. A sound of a dull blow or impact, as of solid bodies colliding. Also as *interjection*. M20.
► **B** *verb intrans*. Make a thunk; fall or land with a thunk. M20.
► **C** *adverb*. With a thunk. L20.

thunk *noun*[2] see THINK *noun*.

thunk *verb*[2] *pa. t. & pple*: see THINK *verb*[2].

Thur. *abbreviation*. Also **Thurs.**
Thursday.

†**thural** *adjective*. *rare*. E17–E18.
[from Latin *turalis*, from *t(h)us*, *t(h)ur-* incense: see THUS *noun*, -AL[1].]
Of, pertaining to, or of the nature of incense.

Thurberesque /θəːbəˈrɛsk/ *adjective*. M20.
[from *Thurber* (see below) + -ESQUE.]
Of or pertaining to the American cartoonist and writer James Thurber (1894–1961), the characters in his work, or his style of writing or drawing.

thurible /ˈθjʊərɪb(ə)l/ *noun*. LME.
[Old & mod. French, or Latin *t(h)uribulum*, from *t(h)us*, *t(h)ur-* incense: see THUS *noun*.]
A censer.

thuribuler /θjʊˈrɪbjʊlə/ *noun*. *rare*. E16.
[medieval Latin *thuribularius*, from Latin *thuribulum* THURIBLE + *-arius* -ER[2].]
= next.

thurifer /ˈθjʊərɪfə/ *noun*. M19.
[Late Latin from Latin *t(h)us*, *t(h)ur-*: see THUS *noun*, -FER.]
A person who carries a censer of burning incense in religious ceremonies. Cf. prec.

thuriferous /θjʊˈrɪf(ə)rəs/ *adjective*. *rare*. M17.
[formed as prec. + -OUS: see -FEROUS.]
That produces frankincense.

thurification /ˌθjʊərɪfɪˈkeɪʃ(ə)n/ *noun*. L15.
[Late Latin *thurificatio(n-)*, from *thurificare* THURIFY: see -ATION.]
The action or an act of thurifying a place, god, etc.; the burning or offering of, or perfuming with, incense.

thurify /ˈθjʊərɪfʌɪ/ *verb*. LME.
[French †*thurifier* or late Latin *thurificare*, from *t(h)us*, *t(h)ur-*: see THUS *noun*, -FY.]
†**1** *verb intrans*. = CENSE *verb*[1] 2. *rare*. Only in LME.
2 *verb trans*. = CENSE *verb*[1] 1. LME.

thuringer /ˈθjʊərɪŋə/ *noun*. Chiefly *US*. M20.
[German *Thüringer Wurst* Thuringian sausage (see next).]
A mildly seasoned summer sausage.

Thuringian /θjʊˈrɪndʒɪən/ *adjective & noun*. E17.
[from *Thuringia* (see below) + -AN.]
► **A** *adjective*. Of or pertaining to Thuringia, a region of central Germany (formerly a principality, and later a state under the Weimar Republic), its natives or inhabitants, or their Franconian dialect. E17.
► **B** *noun*. A native or inhabitant of Thuringia; the Franconian dialect of German spoken there. E17.

thurrock /ˈθʌrək/ *noun*. *obsolete* exc. *dial.*
[Old English *þurruc* bottom of a ship, bilge, corresp. to Dutch *durk*, of unkn. origin. In senses 2 and 3 perh. a different word.]
1 The bilge of a ship. OE.
2 A heap, *esp.* one of muck or dirt. *dial.* E18.
3 A covered drain. *dial.* M19.

Thursday /ˈθəːzdeɪ, -di/ *noun, adverb, & adjective*.
[Old English *þur(e)sdæg* for *þunresdæg* day of thunder from genit. of *þunor* THUNDER *noun*, partly assoc. with Old Norse *þórsdagr*, corresp. to Middle & mod. Dutch *donderdag*, Old High German *donarestac* (German *Donnerstag*), translating late Latin *Jovi dies* Jupiter's day.]
► **A** *noun*. The fifth day of the week, following Wednesday. OE.
Holy Thursday: see HOLY *adjective*. ***Maundy Thursday***. ***Sheer Thursday***. ***Skire Thursday***: see SKIRE *adjective*.
► **B** *adverb*. On Thursday. *colloq.* L18.
► **C** *attrib*. or as *adjective*. Of Thursday; characteristic of Thursday; taking place on Thursday(s). L18.
■ **Thursdays** *adverb* (*colloq.*) on Thursdays, each Thursday L20.

thurse /θəːs/ *noun*. Now *arch. & dial.*
[Old English *þyrs* = Old High German *duris*, *turs* (Middle High German *dürse*, *türse*, *turse*), Old Saxon *þuris* the rune þ, Old Norse *þurs*, from Germanic. Cf. HOBTHRUSH.]
Orig., a giant; the Devil, a demon. Later, a goblin, a hobgoblin.

Thurstone /ˈθəːstən/ *noun*. M20.
[Louis Leon *Thurstone* (1887–1955), US psychologist.]
PSYCHOLOGY. Used *attrib*. to denote tests or methods devised by Thurstone, esp. for the measurement of mental abilities and attitudes, for factor analysis, and the study of personality.

thus /θʌs, θuːs/ *noun*. LME.
[Latin *thus*, *thur-* var. of *tus*, *tur-* from Greek *thuos* sacrifice, incense.]
Frankincense, olibanum; a similar oleoresin from any of various coniferous trees. Also ***gum thus***.

thus /ðʌs/ *adverb*. Now chiefly *literary* or *formal*.
[Old English *þus* = Old Saxon *þus*, Middle & mod. Dutch *dus*, of unkn. origin.]
1 a In this way; as indicated; in the manner now being indicated or exemplified; as follows. OE. ▸**b** With ellipsis: thus says, thus said. *arch. & poet.* M16.
2 To this extent, number, or degree; so. OE.
3 Accordingly; consequently; therefore. OE.

📖 **1a** J. G. LOCKHART On the 13th he wrote thus to Captain Ferguson. C. BRONTË When I have . . kissed her, as thus. V. WOOLF If they eat thus in their exile, how must they eat at home? J. CONRAD Having been thus distinguished I could do no less than follow her with my eyes. N. MARSH Thus it was that Hal Cartell was thrown in the widow's path. **b** MILTON To whom thus Michael: Justly thou abhorr'st. **2** E. A. FREEMAN The legend . . has thus much of foundation. S. KAUFFMANN The little that the social scientists knew thus far. **3** F. SWINNERTON She thus heard at once of Anna's exploit. *New Internationalist* Tests can . . diagnose disorders in fetuses thus enabling early treatment.

Phrases: **thus and so** *dial. & US* (**a**) = SO-AND-SO *adjective* 1; (**b**) = SO-AND-SO *adverb* 1. **thus and thus** exactly in this way, just so.
■ **thusly** *adverb* (*colloq.*) thus M19. **thusness** *noun* (*joc. & colloq.*) the state of being thus M19. **thuswise** *adverb* in this way, thus ME.

thus-gate /ˈðʌsgeɪt/ *adverb*. *obsolete* exc. *Scot. arch.* ME.
[from prec. + GATE *noun*[2].]
In this way; thus.

thutter /ˈθʌtə/ *verb intrans*. *rare*. L19.
[Imit.]
Make a sputtering or rasping sound.

thuya /ˈθuːjə/ *noun*. E18.
[Irreg. repr. of Greek *thu(i)a*. Cf. THUJA, THYINE.]
The fragrant wood of a N. African tree allied to the cypresses, *Tetraclinis articulata* (formerly *Thuja*), which yields gum sandarac (cf. THYINE). Also = THUJA.

thwack /θwak/ *verb & noun*. LME.
[Imit.: cf. THACK *verb*[2], WHACK *verb*, *interjection*, *& adverb*.]
► **A** *verb trans*. **1** Beat or strike vigorously (as) with a stick, whack; thrash (*lit. & fig.*). LME.
2 Drive or force (as) by heavy blows. M16.
3 Pack, crowd, or cram (*together*). Formerly also (usu. foll. by *with*), pack, cram, (a place). M16.

📖 **2** SHAKES. *Wint. T.* We'll thwack him hence with distaffs.

► **B** *noun*. (The sound of) a heavy blow with a stick or the like. L16.
■ **thwacker** *noun* †(**a**) *rare* a huge lie; (**b**) a person who or thing which makes or delivers a thwack; *spec.* an implement for beating half-dried pantiles into shape on a thwacking-frame: L17.

thwacking /ˈθwakɪŋ/ *verbal noun*. M18.
[from prec. + -ING[1].]
The action of THWACK *verb*; an instance of this.
Comb.: **thwacking-frame** a stand on which pantiles are beaten into shape.

thwacking /ˈθwakɪŋ/ *adjective*. M16.
[formed as prec. + -ING[2].]
That thwacks; *colloq.* exceptionally large or formidable, big, strong. Cf. THUMPING *adjective* 2, WALLOPING *adjective* 2, WHACKING *adjective*.

thwaite /θweɪt/ *noun*. *dial.* Now *rare* exc. in place-names. ME.
[Old Norse *þveit(i)* piece of land, paddock (lit. 'cutting, cut-piece'), rel. to Old English *þwītan* to cut (off). Cf. THWITE.]
A piece of ground; *esp.* a piece of wild ground cleared from forest or reclaimed for arable.

thwart /θwɔːt/ *noun*[1]. Now *rare*. E17.
[from the verb.]
An act or instance of thwarting someone or something; a hindrance, an obstruction, a frustration.

thwart /θwɔːt/ *noun*[2]. M18.
[Var. of THOUGHT *noun*[2], infl. by THWART *verb*.]
A bench or seat (usu. a structural member) across a boat, on which a rower sits.

thwart /θwɔːt/ *adjective, adverb, & preposition*. ME.
[Old Norse *þvert* orig. neut. of *þverr* transverse, cross = Old English *þwe(o)rh* crooked, cross, perverse, Old High German *dwerh*, *twerh* (German *zwerch* in *Zwerchfell* diaphragm), Gothic *þwairhs* cross, angry, from Germanic from Indo-European base also of Latin *torquere* twist.]
► **A** *adjective*. **1 a** Of a person, attribute, etc.: disposed to offer resistance; cross-grained; perverse; obstinate, stubborn. ME. ▸**b** Of a thing: adverse, unfavourable, untoward, unpropitious; *spec.* (of a wind or current) cross. E17.
2 Lying or extending across something, transverse. LME.

📖 **1a** BACON Ignorance makes them churlish, thwart, and mutinous. R. L. STEVENSON The crass public or the thwart reviewer. **2** W. IRVING Thwart pieces from side to side about three inches thick. R. A. PROCTOR The actual rate of any star's thwart motion.

► **B** *adverb*. **1** = ATHWART *adverb* 2. Long *arch.* ME.
2 From one side to the other. Cf. ATHWART *adverb* 3. *arch.* E16.
†**3 a** NAUTICAL. To seaward *of*. M16–L17. ▸**b** Across the direction *of*. Only in M17.
► **C** *preposition*. **1** = ATHWART *preposition* 1. Now *arch. & poet.* LME.
2 Chiefly NAUTICAL. Across the course or direction of. Cf. ATHWART *preposition* 2. L15.

📖 **1** T. BUSBY When shines the God of Day, And thwart the darkened chamber darts his ray. W. MORRIS A pink-tinged cloud spread thwart the shore.

Comb.: **thwart-saw** (*obsolete* exc. *dial.*) a cross-cut saw; **thwartship** *adjective & adverb* (NAUTICAL) (placed, fixed, or facing) across the length of a ship; **thwart-ships** *adverb* (NAUTICAL) across a ship from side to side.
■ **thwartly** *adverb* (now *rare*) in a thwart manner, transversely, across LME. **thwartness** *noun* (long *rare*) the condition or quality of being thwart; *esp.* contrariness, perversity: M16. **thwartways** *adverb* (*rare*) thwartwise M17. **thwartwise** *adverb & adjective* cross(wise), transverse(ly) L16.

thwart /θwɔːt/ *verb*. ME.
[from (the same root as) prec.]
► **I 1 a** *verb trans*. Run counter to, go against; oppose, hinder. Now *rare* or *obsolete*. ME. ▸**b** *verb intrans*. Speak or act in contradiction or opposition; be at variance, conflict. Foll. by *with*. Now *rare* or *obsolete*. L15.
2 *verb trans*. Oppose (a person or purpose) successfully; prevent the accomplishment of (a purpose); foil, frustrate. L16.

📖 **1a** S. PARKER To what purpose does he . . taunt me for thwarting my own Principles. **b** F. HALL Those books do not thwart with the Veda. **2** V. NABOKOV The hangers were ingeniously fixed to their bars by coils of wire so as to thwart theft. *Atlantic* Holmes thwarts Roylott's attempt to kill the other stepdaughter by attacking the snake. A. T. ELLIS He hated to be thwarted and went white with rage when his car wouldn't start.

► **II 3 a** *verb trans*. Pass or extend across; traverse, cross; run at an angle to. Long *arch.* LME. ▸**b** *verb intrans*. Pass across, cross. Long *arch.* M16. ▸†**c** *verb trans*. Come across, meet. E17–E19.
†**4** *verb trans*. Lay (a thing) athwart or across; place crosswise; put (things) across each other. E16–M17.
5 *verb trans*. **a** In *pass*. Be crossed with a line, streak, band, etc. Long *arch.* E17. ▸**b** Cross-plough. M19.
6 *verb trans*. Place an obstacle across, block, (a road, course, etc.). *obsolete* exc. *fig.* (as passing into sense 2). E17.

📖 **6** E. K. KANE If no misadventure thwarted his progress.

■ **thwarter** *noun* a person who or thing which thwarts another, *esp.* a person who foils or frustrates another M17. **thwarting** *verbal noun* the action of the verb; *spec.* (**a**) the action of foiling someone or something, frustration, opposition; (**b**) cross-ploughing: LME. **thwarting** *ppl adjective* that thwarts; *spec.* (**a**) (long *arch.*) lying or passing crosswise, crossing, transverse; (**b**) conflicting, opposing, adverse; frustrating: LME. **thwartingly** *adverb* L16.

thwartle /ˈθwɔːt(ə)l/ *verb intrans*. Long *obsolete* exc. *dial.* M17.
[Dim. or frequentative of THWART *verb*: see -LE[3].]
Speak or act contradictorily.

thwart-over /ˈθwɔːtəʊvə/ *adjective*. *obsolete* exc. *dial.* ME.
[from THWART *adverb* + OVER *adjective* or *adverb*.]
That thwarts or obstructs someone or something; obstructive; perverse, self-willed. Formerly also, crossing, lying athwart.

†**thwick-thwack** *noun*. L16–L18.
[Redupl. of THWACK *noun*.]
The repetition or exchange of thwacks.

thwite /θwʌɪt/ *verb*. Long *obsolete* exc. *dial.*
[Old English *þwītan* cut (off), rel. to Old Norse *þveita* small axe, *þveit(i)* cut-off piece, parcel of land: cf. next, THWAITE.]
1 *verb trans.* Cut down, whittle, pare; cut away. OE.
2 *verb intrans.* Whittle away. Usu. foll. by *at*. L15.

thwittle /ˈθwɪt(ə)l/ *noun*. Long *obsolete* exc. *dial.* ME.
[from prec.: see -LE¹. Cf. next, prec., WHITTLE *noun*².]
A knife; *spec.* = WHITTLE *noun*².

thwittle /ˈθwɪt(ə)l/ *verb trans. & intrans.* Long *obsolete* exc. *dial.* L16.
[Frequentative or dim. of THWITE: see -LE³. Cf. prec.]
= THWITE.

thy /ðʌɪ/ *possess. adjective (in mod. usage also classed as a determiner), 2 sing.* Now *arch. & dial.* ME.
[Reduced form of THINE *adjective* (orig. before consonants except h).]
Of you; of yourself; which belongs or pertains to you. Cf. THINE *adjective*.

AV *Ruth* 1:16 Thy people shall be my people, and thy God my God. D. H. LAWRENCE Thou art my eldest son, and I am thy father. DAY LEWIS Thy songs were made for the pure and free.

¶ See note s.v. THOU *pers. pronoun & noun*².

Thyad /ˈθʌɪad/ *noun*. Pl. **-des** /-diːz/. E17.
[Greek *thuiad-*, *thuias* frenzied woman.]
GREEK ANTIQUITIES. A Bacchante.

Thyestean /θʌɪˈɛstɪən/ *adjective*. M17.
[Latin *Thyesteus* from Greek *Thuesteios*, from *Thuestēs* Thyestes, who in ancient Greek legend was tricked by his brother Atreus into eating the flesh of his own sons at a banquet: see -EAN.]
Cannibalistic; *spec.* involving the killing and eating of children.

thyine /ˈθʌɪɪn/ *adjective*. Long *rare*. LME.
[Latin *thyinus* from Greek *thuinos* of the tree *thu(i)a*: see THUYA, -INE¹.]
In biblical translations and allusions: of, pertaining to, or designating (the wood of) the thuya.

thylacine /ˈθʌɪləsiːn, -sʌɪn, -sɪn/ *noun*. M19.
[mod. Latin *Thylacinus* (see below), from Greek *thulakos* pouch: see -INE¹.]
A large doglike carnivorous marsupial, *Thylacinus cynocephalus*, of Tasmania, grey-brown with dark stripes over the rump (now very scarce or extinct). Also called ***Tasmanian tiger***, ***Tasmanian wolf***, ***zebra-wolf***.

thylakoid /ˈθʌɪləkɔɪd/ *noun & adjective*. M20.
[German *Thylakoid* from Greek *thulakoidēs* pouchlike, from *thulakos* pouch: see -OID.]
BOTANY. (Designating) any of the flattened sacs inside a chloroplast, bounded by pigmented membranes on which the light reactions of photosynthesis take place.

thymallus /θʌɪˈmaləs/ *noun*. L18.
[mod. Latin genus name, from Greek *thumallos*, name of a fish (said to be named from resemblance of its odour to thyme).]
= GRAYLING 1. Now chiefly as mod. Latin genus name.

thyme /tʌɪm/ *noun*. ME.
[Old & mod. French *thym* from Latin *thymum* from Greek *thumon*, *-mos*, from *thuein* burn, sacrifice.]
Any of various pungently aromatic dwarf labiate shrubs of the genus *Thymus*; esp. *T. vulgaris* (more fully ***garden thyme***), a low erect Mediterranean plant cultivated as a pot-herb, and *T. praecox* (more fully ***wild thyme***), a mat-forming plant of heaths, hill grassland, etc.; *collect.* the leaves of garden thyme, used as a flavouring. Also (with specifying word), any of several related or similar plants.
basil thyme: see BASIL *noun*¹. ***lemon thyme***: see LEMON *noun*¹. **oil of thyme** a fragrant volatile oil obtained from garden thyme, used as an antiseptic. ***water thyme***: see WATER *noun*.
Comb.: **thyme-leaved** *adjective* having small leaves like those of wild thyme; **thyme-oil** = *oil of thyme* above.

thymectomy /θʌɪˈmɛktəmi/ *noun*. E20.
[from THYMUS + -ECTOMY.]
Surgical removal of the thymus gland; an instance of this.
■ **thymectomize** *verb trans.* perform thymectomy on E20.

thymele /ˈθɪmɪli/ *noun*. M18.
[Greek *thumelē* altar, from *thuein* to sacrifice.]
The altar of Dionysus in the centre of the orchestra in an ancient Greek theatre.

thymi *noun pl.* see THYMUS.

thymiaterion /ˌθʌɪmɪəˈtɪərɪɒn/ *noun*. *rare*. Pl. **-ia** /-ɪə/. M19.
[Greek *thumiatērion*, from *thumian* burn incense.]
A kind of censer used by the ancient Greeks, and in the Greek Church.

thymic /ˈθʌɪmɪk/ *adjective*¹. M17.
[from THYMUS + -IC.]
ANATOMY & MEDICINE. Of, pertaining to, or connected with the thymus gland.

thymic /ˈθʌɪmɪk/ *adjective*². *rare*. M19.
[from THYME + -IC.]
CHEMISTRY. Of, pertaining to, or derived from thyme.
thymic acid = THYMOL.

thymidine /ˈθʌɪmɪdiːn/ *noun*. E20.
[from THYMINE + -IDINE.]
BIOCHEMISTRY. A nucleoside consisting of thymine linked to deoxyribose.

thymidylic /θʌɪmɪˈdɪlɪk/ *adjective*. M20.
[formed as prec. + -YL + -IC.]
BIOCHEMISTRY. ***thymidylic acid***, a nucleotide composed of a phosphoric acid ester of thymidine, present in most DNA.

thymine /ˈθʌɪmɪn/ *noun*. L19.
[from THYMIC *adjective*¹ + -INE⁵.]
BIOCHEMISTRY. A derivative of pyrimidine which is one of the bases of nucleic acids, paired with adenine in double-stranded DNA (and replaced by uracil in RNA); 5-methyluracil, $C_5H_6N_2O_2$.

thymitis /θʌɪˈmʌɪtɪs/ *noun*. M19.
[from THYMUS + -ITIS.]
MEDICINE. Inflammation of the thymus gland.

thymo- /ˈθʌɪməʊ/ *combining form*.
[from THYMUS: see -O-.]
Of or pertaining to the thymus gland.
■ **thymocyte** *noun* (PHYSIOLOGY) a lymphocyte found in the thymus gland E20. **thyˈmoma** *noun*, pl. **-mas**, **-mata** /-mətə/, MEDICINE a rare, usually benign tumour arising from thymus tissue and often associated with myasthenia gravis E20. **thymopoietin** /-pɔɪˈɛtɪn/ *noun* (BIOCHEMISTRY) a polypeptide hormone secreted by the thymus which stimulates the development of thymocytes L20. **thymosin** /ˈθʌɪməsɪn/ *noun* (PHYSIOLOGY) a mixture of polypeptides derived from the thymus gland which regulates development of T-lymphocytes M20.

thymol /ˈθʌɪmɒl/ *noun*. M19.
[from Greek *thumon* THYME + -OL.]
CHEMISTRY. A white crystalline compound present in oil of thyme and other volatile oils, used as a flavouring, preservative, etc., and in the synthesis of menthol; 2-isopropyl-5-methylphenol, $C_{10}H_{13}OH$.

thymoleptic /θʌɪməˈlɛptɪk/ *adjective & noun*. M20.
[from Greek *thumos* soul, spirit + *lēpsis* seizing: see -IC.]
PHARMACOLOGY. (Of or pertaining to) any of a group of antidepressant drugs or psychic energizers typically having a tricyclic molecule.

thymus /ˈθʌɪməs/ *noun*. Pl. **-muses**, **-mi** /-mʌɪ/. L16.
[Greek *thumos* warty excrescence like a thyme bud; the thymus gland.]
†**1** MEDICINE. A growth or tumour resembling a bud. *rare*. L16–L17.
2 ANATOMY & BIOLOGY. More fully ***thymus gland***. A glandular organ near the base of the neck which controls the early development of lymphoid tissue and is the site of maturation of T-lymphocytes, regressing during adulthood. E17.

thymy /ˈtʌɪmi/ *adjective*. E18.
[from THYME + -Y¹.]
1 Having much or overgrown with thyme. E18.
2 Pertaining to or of the nature of thyme; *esp.* having the scent of thyme. M18.

thyratron /ˈθʌɪrətrɒn/ *noun*. E20.
[from Greek *thura* door + -TRON.]
ELECTRONICS. A thermionic valve which uses an arc discharge in mercury vapour or low-pressure gas, and has a heated cathode and at least one grid.

thyreo- *combining form* see THYRO-.

thyristor /θʌɪˈrɪstə/ *noun*. M20.
[Blend of THYRATRON and TRANSISTOR.]
ELECTRONICS. A three-terminal semiconductor rectifier made up of four layers, *p-n-p-n*, so that when the fourth is positive with respect to the first a voltage pulse applied to the third layer initiates a flow of current through the device.

thyro- /ˈθʌɪrəʊ/ *combining form*. Also (now *rare* or *obsolete*) **thyreo-** /ˈθʌɪrɪəʊ/. M19.
[from THYROID: see -O-.]
ANATOMY & MEDICINE. Of, pertaining to, or connected with (*a*) the thyroid gland; (*b*) the thyroid cartilage.
■ **thyro-aryˈtenoid** *adjective* pertaining to or connecting the thyroid and arytenoid cartilages of the larynx; ***thyro-arytenoid folds***, ***thyro-arytenoid ligaments***, the vocal cords; ***thyro-arytenoid muscles***, a pair of muscles which relax the vocal cords: M19. **thyrocalciˈtonin** *noun* = CALCITONIN M20. **thyrocele** *noun* swelling of the thyroid gland L19. **thyroˈglobulin** *noun* a globular protein from which thyroid hormones are synthesized E20. **thyroˈhyoid** *adjective* pertaining to or connecting the thyroid cartilage and the hyoid bone; *esp.* designating ligaments forming part of the larynx, and a muscle that raises it: M19. **thyˈrotomy** *noun* (*a*) (an instance of) incision of the thyroid cartilage; (*b*) (an instance of) incision of the thyroid gland: L19. **thyroˈtoxic** *adjective* pertaining to or affected by (severe) thyrotoxicosis E20. **thyrotoxiˈcosis** *noun* a disorder involving overactivity of the thyroid gland E20.

thyroid /ˈθʌɪrɔɪd/ *adjective & noun*. E18.
[French †*thyroide* (now *thyréoïde*) or mod. Latin *thyroides*, irreg. from Greek (*khondros*) *thureoeidēs* shield-shaped (cartilage), from *thureos* oblong shield: see -OID.]
▶**A** *adjective*. **1** ANATOMY. Designating or pertaining to the thyroid (see sense B. below). E18.
2 *gen.* Having the form of a shield, shield-shaped; having a shield-shaped marking. L19.
1 thyroid gland, †**thyroid body** = sense B.2 below. **thyroid hormone** either or both of the two chief secretions of the thyroid gland, thyroxine and triiodothyronine.
▶**B** *noun*. **1** The largest of the cartilages of the larynx, consisting of two broad four-sided plates joined in front at an angle, enclosing the vocal cords and (in men) forming the Adam's apple. M19.
2 A large bilobed endocrine gland in the neck of vertebrates which secretes hormones regulating growth and development through control of the rate of metabolism. M19. ▸**b** MEDICINE. An extract prepared from animal thyroid glands and used to treat hypothyroid conditions (as goitre, cretinism, etc.). L19.
Comb.: **thyroid-stimulating** *adjective*: ***thyroid-stimulating hormone*** = THYROTROPIN.
■ **thyˈroidal** *adjective* of or pertaining to the thyroid cartilage or gland M19. **thyˈroideal** *adjective* = THYROIDAL E19. **thyroiˈdectomize** *verb trans.* perform thyroidectomy on M20. **thyroiˈdectomy** *noun* (an instance of) surgical excision of the thyroid gland L19. **thyˈroidic** *adjective & noun* (designating) a person with a disordered thyroid gland E20. **thyroiˈditis** *noun* inflammation of the thyroid gland L19.

thyronine /ˈθʌɪrəniːn/ *noun*. E20.
[from THYRO- + -n- + -INE⁵.]
CHEMISTRY. An amino acid, $C_{15}H_{15}NO_4$, of which the thyroid hormones can be regarded as derivatives.

thyrotropin /θʌɪrəˈtrəʊpɪn/ *noun*. Also **-trophin** /-ˈtrəʊfɪn/. M20.
[from THYRO- + -TROPIC, -TROPHIC + -IN¹.]
PHYSIOLOGY. A hormone secreted by the pituitary gland which regulates the production of thyroid hormones. Also called ***thyroid-stimulating hormone***.
Comb.: **thyrotropin-releasing factor**, **thyrotropin-releasing hormone** a tripeptide hormone secreted by the hypothalamus which stimulates release of thyrotropin; abbreviation *TRF*, *TRH*.
■ **thyrotrophic** /-ˈtrəʊfɪk, -ˈtrɒfɪk/ *adjective* regulating thryoid activity M20.

thyroxine /θʌɪˈrɒksiːn/ *noun*. Also (now *rare*) **-in** /-ɪn/. E20.
[from THYRO- + OXY- + INDOLE (from a misunderstanding of its chemical structure), alt. after -INE⁵.]
BIOCHEMISTRY. The chief hormone secreted by the thyroid gland, which increases the metabolic rate and regulates growth and development in animals; tetraiodothyronine, $C_{15}H_{11}NO_4I_4$.

thyrse /θəːs/ *noun*. E17.
[French from Latin THYRSUS.]
1 CLASSICAL ANTIQUITIES. = THYRSUS 1. E17.
2 BOTANY. = THYRSUS 2. Formerly also, a stem or shoot of a plant. M17.

thyrsi *noun* pl. of THYRSUS.

thyrsoid /ˈθəːsɔɪd/ *adjective*. M19.
[from THYRSUS + -OID.]
BOTANY. Of the form of or resembling a thyrsus.

thyrsus /ˈθəːsəs/ *noun*. Pl. **thyrsi** /ˈθəːsʌɪ, ˈθəːsiː/. L16.
[Latin from Greek *thursos* stalk of a plant, Bacchic staff.]
1 CLASSICAL ANTIQUITIES. A staff or spear tipped with an ornament like a pine cone, carried by Bacchus and his followers. L16.
2 BOTANY. Any of several forms of inflorescence; *spec.* †(*a*) a lax spike, as in some orchids; (*b*) a contracted kind of panicle, *esp.* one in which the individual branches form dichasia or monochasia, as in lilac and horse chestnut. E18.

thysanopteran /θʌɪsəˈnɒpt(ə)r(ə)n/ *adjective & noun*. L19.
[mod. Latin *Thysanoptera* (see below), from Greek *thusanos* tassel, fringe + *pteron* wing.]
ENTOMOLOGY. Of or pertaining to, an insect of, the order Thysanoptera, comprising the thrips or thunderflies.
■ **thysanopterous** *adjective* = THYSANOPTERAN *adjective* L19.

thysanuran /θʌɪsəˈn(j)ʊərən/ *adjective & noun*. M19.
[mod. Latin *Thysanura* (see below), from Greek *thusanos* tassel, fringe + *oura* tail: see -AN.]
ENTOMOLOGY. ▶**A** *adjective*. Of or pertaining to the order Thysanura of wingless (apterygote) insects including the silverfish and firebrat. M19.
▶**B** *noun*. An insect of this order. Also called ***three-pronged bristletail***. M19.
■ **thysanurous** *adjective* = THYSANURAN *adjective* M19.

thyself /ðʌɪˈsɛlf/ *pronoun*. Now *arch. & dial.* OE.
[from THEE *pers. pronoun* + SELF *adjective* (but long interpreted as THY + SELF *noun*).]
▶**I** Orig. *emphatic*.
1 In apposition to the subjective pronoun *thou* (or after a verb in the imper.): yourself. OE.
2 (Not appositional.) ▸**a** Subjective: you yourself (in emphatic use now *poet.*). Later also (pred., after *be* and after *than*, *as*), you (sing.). ME. ▸**b** Objective: you (sing.), yourself. LME.

📖 **1** SHAKES. *2 Hen. IV* Then get thee gone, and dig my grave thyself. W. COWPER Thou art of all thy gifts thyself the crown. **2a** AV *2 Chron.* 21:13 Thou . . hast slaine thy brethren . . which were better then thy selfe. G. MACDONALD It is thyself, and neither this nor that . . told, taught, or dreamed of thee. **b** J. HOWE My Soul take . . pleasure in such exertions of God, as thou dost now experience in thyself. G. B. BUBIER My God, I love Thee for Thyself.

▶**II** *refl.* **3** Refl. (direct, indirect, & after prepositions) corresp. to the subjective pronoun *thou*: (to, for, etc.) yourself. OE.

📖 **3** COVERDALE *Isa.* 53:14 To make thy self a glorious name. S. RICHARDSON Well, Child . . how dost find thyself? SHELLEY Be faithful to thyself. E. W. LANE Thou assertest thyself to be the son of the King.

¶ See note s.v. THOU *pers. pronoun.*

Ti *abbreviation.*
BIOLOGY. Tumour-inducing.

Ti *symbol.*
CHEMISTRY. Titanium.

ti /tiː/ *noun*[1]. *NZ.* M19.
[Polynesian: cf. KI.]
Any of various palmlike trees and shrubs of the genus *Cordyline*, of the agave family; *esp.* the cabbage tree, *C. australis* (also called ***ti-tree***).

Ti /tiː/ *noun*[2]. E20.
[Chinese *di* (Wade–Giles *ti*), lit. 'lord'.]
In early Chinese philosophy, (an honorific title given to) the supreme being, God. Also (*Hist.*), (an honorific title given to) an early Chinese ruler.

ti *noun*[3] var. of TE *noun*[1].

TIA *abbreviation.*
MEDICINE. Transient ischaemic attack.

Tiahuanaco /ˌtiːəwəˈnɑːkəʊ/ *adjective.* L19.
[A ruined city south of Lake Titicaca in Bolivia.]
ARCHAEOLOGY. Of or designating a pre-Incan culture, notable for its stonemasonry and distinctive pottery, which flourished in S. America in the first millennium AD.

tial /ˈtʌɪəl/ *noun. obsolete* exc. *Scot. & north.*
[Old English *tīgel* = Old High German *zugil* (German *Zügel*), Dutch *teugel*, Old Norse *tygell* (Danish *tøjle*), from Germanic, later infl. by TIE *verb*[1].]
1 A rope, rein, etc., used to pull or tow something. Long *rare.* OE.
2 A rope, cord, etc., used for tying something (up). M16.

Tia Maria /tiːə məˈriːə/ *noun.* M20.
[Spanish *Tía María* lit. 'Aunt Mary'.]
(Proprietary name for) a coffee-flavoured liqueur based on rum, made orig. in the W. Indies.

tian /tjɑ̃/ *noun.* Pl. pronounced same. M20.
[Provençal, ult. from Greek *tēganon* frying-pan, saucepan.]
A large oval earthenware cooking-pot traditionally used in Provence; a dish of finely chopped vegetables cooked in olive oil and then baked *au gratin.*

tiang /tiːˈaŋ/ *noun.* L19.
[Dinka.]
A topi (antelope) of a subspecies found in Sudan and adjacent parts of Ethiopia.

tiao /ˈtjɑːəʊ, tjaʊ/ *noun.* Pl. same. L19.
[Chinese *diào* (Wade–Giles *tiao*).]
Hist. A string of Chinese cash or copper coins, nominally equivalent to 1000 cash, but varying locally.

tiar /ˈtʌɪə/ *noun.* Chiefly *poet.* Now *rare.* E16.
[Prob. from French *tiare* tiara; later Anglicized from next.]
1 = TIARA 1. E16.
2 = TIARA 2. E17.
3 = TIARA 3. M17.

tiara /tɪˈɑːrə/ *noun.* M16.
[Latin from Greek, partly through Italian.]
1 *Hist.* Any of various head-dresses formerly worn in (the region of) Persia, *esp.* a kind of turban worn by kings in ancient Persia. M16.
2 A richly ornamental three-crowned diadem formerly worn by popes; *fig.* the office of pope, the papacy. Also more fully ***triple tiara.*** M17. ▶**b** HERALDRY. A charge in the form of a triple crown, representing the papal tiara. L18.
3 A woman's (usu. jewelled) ornamental coronet or headband worn on the front of the hair. E18.
4 The head-dress of the Jewish high priest. M19.

📖 **3** RIDER HAGGARD On her head was set a tiara of perfect pearls.

■ **tiaraed, -a'd** /-əd/ *adjective* wearing or adorned with a tiara E19.

tiare /tiːˈɑːreɪ/ *noun.* Pl. same. L19.
[Use of French *tiare* tiara.]
In Tahiti, any of several kinds of gardenia bearing fragrant white flowers.

tiarella /tɪəˈrɛlə/ *noun.* M18.
[mod. Latin (see below), from Latin TIARA + -ELLA.]
Any of various small chiefly N. American plants of the genus *Tiarella*, of the saxifrage family; *esp.* the foam flower, *T. cordifolia.*

Tib /tɪb/ *noun.* Now *rare.* M16.
[Perh. from pet-form of female forename *Isabel.*]
†**1** (A name for) a working-class woman. Also, a girlfriend, a sweetheart; *derog.* a promiscuous young woman, a prostitute. M16–L17.
2 *Hist.* In the game of gleek, the ace of trumps. M17.
Phrases: †**on St Tib's Eve**, †**on Tib's Eve** *dial.* never.

tibbin /ˈtɪbɪn/ *noun.* L19.
[Repr. a pronunc. of Arab. *tibn* straw.]
Hay, chopped straw.

Tiberian /tʌɪˈbɪərɪən/ *adjective.* E17.
[Latin *Tiberianus*, from *Tiberius* (see below) + *-anus* -AN.]
Hist. Of or pertaining to Tiberius (Roman emperor AD 14–37) or the town of Tiberias in Galilee (named after him).

Tibert /ˈtɪbət, ˈtʌɪbət/ *noun. arch.* L15.
[Old French, or from Flemish & Dutch *Tybert, Tibeert.*]
Orig., (the name of) the cat in the fable of Reynard the Fox. Later, any cat.

Tibet /tɪˈbɛt/ *noun.* Also (earlier, now *rare*) **Th-.** E19.
[A country in central Asia, now an autonomous region of China.]
Used *attrib.* to designate things found in, obtained from, or associated with Tibet, esp. (a garment made from) Tibetan cloth made from goat's hair, or later from wool.

Tibetan /tɪˈbɛt(ə)n/ *noun & adjective.* Also (earlier, now *rare*) **Th-.** E19.
[from prec. + -AN.]
▶**A** *noun.* A native or inhabitant of Tibet; the language of Tibet, a member of the Tibeto-Burman subfamily of Sino-Tibetan. E19.
▶**B** *adjective.* Of or pertaining to Tibet, its inhabitants, or their language. E19.
Tibetan antelope = CHIRU. **Tibetan cherry** a white-flowered cherry tree, *Prunus serrula*, native to western China. **Tibetan mastiff** (an animal of) a breed of large black-and-tan dog with a thick coat and drop ears. **Tibetan spaniel** (an animal of) a breed of small white, brown, or black dog with a silky coat of medium length. **Tibetan terrier** (an animal of) a breed of grey, black, cream, or particoloured terrier with a thick shaggy coat.
■ Also **Tibetian** /-ɛtɪən, -iːʃ(ə)n/ *noun & adjective* (now *rare*) M18.

Tibeto- /tɪˈbɛtəʊ/ *combining form.*
[from TIBET, TIBET(AN: see -O-.]
Forming adjectives and noun combs. with the meaning 'Tibetan (and)'.
■ **Tibeto-Burmese** *noun & adjective* = TIBETO-BURMAN M20. **Tibeto-Chinese** *adjective & noun* = SINO-TIBETAN E20. **Tibeto-Himalayan** *adjective & noun* (**a**) *adjective* of or pertaining to Tibet and the Himalayas; (**b**) *noun* a division of the Tibeto-Burman group of languages: L19.

Tibeto-Burman /ˌtɪbɛtəʊˈbəːmən/ *adjective & noun.* M19.
[from prec. + BURMAN.]
▶**A** *adjective.* Pertaining to Tibet and Burma (Myanmar); *spec.* designating or pertaining to a group of Sino-Tibetan languages spoken in Asia or the peoples speaking any of these languages. M19.
▶**B** *noun.* The Tibeto-Burman group of languages. M20.

Tibetology /tɪbɛˈtɒlədʒi/ *noun.* M20.
[from TIBET + -OLOGY.]
The branch of knowledge that deals with Tibetan culture.
■ **Tibetologist** *noun* M20.

tibia /ˈtɪbɪə/ *noun.* Pl. **-iae** /-ɪiː/. LME.
[Latin = shank, pipe, shin-bone.]
1 CLASSICAL ANTIQUITIES. A reed-pipe. LME.
2 ANATOMY. The inner and larger of the two bones of the lower leg, between the knee and the ankle, articulating at its upper end with the fibula; the shin-bone; the part of the leg including this; ZOOLOGY the corresponding part in other tetrapod animals; *esp.* the tibiotarsus of a bird. LME. ▶**b** ENTOMOLOGY. The section of an insect's leg between the femur and the tarsus. E19.

tibial /ˈtɪbɪəl/ *adjective & noun.* L16.
[from prec. + -AL[1].]
ANATOMY & ZOOLOGY. ▶**A** *adjective.* Of, pertaining to, or associated with the tibia. L16.
tibial tuberosity a rounded protuberance on the tibia just below the knee-joint.
▶**B** *noun. ellipt.* A tibial artery, muscle, etc. L19.
■ **tibialis** /-ˈeɪlɪs/ *noun* (ANATOMY) any of several muscles and tendons in the lower leg, involved in movement of the foot L19.

tibio- /ˈtɪbɪəʊ/ *combining form.*
[from TIBIA: see -O-.]
Chiefly ANATOMY. Of or pertaining to the tibia and (some other part), as ***tibio-fibular***, ***tibio-metatarsal***, etc.
■ **tibio'tarsal** *adjective* of or pertaining to the tibia and the tarsus; pertaining to the tibiotarsus: M19. **tibio'tarsus** *noun*, pl. **-tarsi**, ORNITHOLOGY the tibia of a bird's leg with the condyles formed by its fusion with the proximal bones of the tarsus L19.

tiburon /tɪbjʊˈrəʊn/ *noun. obsolete* exc. *Hist.* M16.
[French, Spanish, app. from an Amer. Indian lang. Cf. Portuguese *tubarão.*]
Any of various large sharks, esp. the bonnethead, *Sphyrna tiburo.*

Tiburtine /ˈtʌɪbəːtʌɪn/ *adjective.* LME.
[Latin *Tibertinus*, from *Tiburt-*, *Tiburs* Tibur (see below). Cf. TRAVERTINE.]
Of or pertaining to the region or district of Tibur (now Tivoli) in ancient Latium, Italy.
Tiburtine stone travertine.

tic /tɪk/ *noun.* E19.
[French from Italian *ticchio*: cf. TICK *noun*[5].]
1 (A disorder characterized by) a repeated habitual spasmodic twitching of one or more muscles, esp. of the face, largely involuntary and accentuated under stress. E19.
2 ***tic douloureux*** /duːləˈruː, -ˈrəː/ [French = painful], trigeminal neuralgia, in which spasms of pain are freq. accompanied by twitching of the facial muscles. E19.
3 A whim, a spontaneous reaction, an idiosyncrasy. Cf. TICK *noun*[5]. L19.

📖 **3** *Twentieth Century* An irritating tic of the British Left, this substitution of moral gestures for practical policies. C. P. SNOW The tic, common to many writers, of insisting that the table be kept . . tidy.

tical /tɪˈkɑːl, ˈtɪk(ə)l/ *noun.* M17.
[Portuguese, prob. from Marathi *takā* or Bengali *tākā* a coin (of varying value): cf. TAKA, TANGA *noun*[1].]
Hist. A silver coin used in Siam (Thailand) and (later also) Burma (Myanmar), roughly equivalent in value to the Indian rupee; the weight of this coin.

ticca *adjective* var. of TIKKA *adjective.*

tice /tʌɪs/ *verb & noun.* ME.
[Aphet. from Old French *atisier*: cf. ENTICE.]
▶**A** *verb trans.* Entice; induce by offering pleasure or advantage. *obsolete* exc. *Scot. & north.* ME.
▶**B** *noun.* An act of enticing a person, an enticement; *spec.* (**a**) CRICKET a yorker (now *rare*); (**b**) CROQUET a stroke tempting an opponent to aim at one's ball. M19.
■ **ticer** *noun* (*rare*) an enticer LME.

tich *noun* var. of TITCH.

Ticinese /tɪtʃɪˈniːz/ *adjective & noun.* M20.
[Italian, from *Ticino* (see below) + -ESE.]
▶**A** *adjective.* Of or pertaining to Ticino, an Italian-speaking canton in southern Switzerland, or its inhabitants. M20.
▶**B** *noun.* Pl. same. A native or inhabitant of Ticino. M20.

tick /tɪk/ *noun*[1].
[Old English *ticia.*]
1 Any of various bloodsucking acarids of the families Argasidae and Ixodidae, which attach themselves to the skin of dogs, cattle, and other mammals, and may transmit disease to humans. Also *loosely*, any of various parasitic flies (dipterans) of the families Hippoboscidae (infesting birds, sheep, etc.) and Nycteribiidae (infesting bats); a ked. OE. ▶**b** An unpleasant or despicable person. Freq. in ***little tick.*** *colloq.* M17.
2 In full ***tick-bean.*** A small-seeded variety of the horse-bean, *Vicia faba*, so called from the resemblance of the seed to a dog-tick. M18.
Phrases: **full as a tick**, **tight as a tick** *slang* full to repletion, *esp.* extremely drunk. ***hard tick***: see HARD *adjective.* ***new tick***: see NEW *adjective.* ***Rocky Mountain spotted fever tick***, ***Rocky Mountain spotted tick***, ***Rocky Mountain wood tick***: see ROCKY MOUNTAIN. ***soft tick***: see SOFT *adjective.*
Comb.: **tick-bean**: see sense 2 above; **tick-bird** a bird which feeds on ticks infesting large mammals, esp. (in Africa) an ox-pecker (genus *Buphagus*) or (in the W. Indies) the keel-bill, *Crotophaga ani*; **tick-borne** *adjective* transmitted by ticks; ***tick-borne fever***, a mild transient rickettsial fever of sheep, cattle, and goats; **tick fever** a fever (in humans or cattle) caused by the bites of ticks; **tick-fly** a parasitic fly (see sense 1); **tick paralysis**: caused by neurotoxin in the saliva of certain biting ticks; **tick pyaemia** a type of blood-poisoning in sheep, esp. lambs, caused by *Staphylococcus aureus* and leading to lameness or death; **tick-seed** any of various plants having seeds resembling ticks; *spec.* (*N. Amer.*) a coreopsis, esp. *Coreopsis lanceolata*; **tick-trefoil** any of various leguminous plants of the genus *Desmodium*, the pods of which break up into one-seeded joints which adhere to clothing, animals' fur, etc.; **tick typhus** = ROCKY MOUNTAIN (*spotted*) *fever.*
■ **tickicide** *noun* = ACARICIDE L20.

tick /tɪk/ *noun*[2]. LME.
[Prob. from Middle Low German, Middle Dutch *tēke*, and Middle Dutch *tīke* (Dutch *tijk*) rel. to Old High German *ziahha*, *ziehha* (German *Zieche* bedtick, pillowcase) from West Germanic from Latin *theca* from Greek *thēkē* case.]
A case or cover containing feathers etc., forming a mattress or pillow. Later also = TICKING 1.

tick /tɪk/ *noun*[3]. LME.
[Perh. rel. to Low German *tikk* touch, moment, instant, Dutch *tik* pat, touch, Middle High German *zic* slight touch from Germanic base. Cf. TIG *noun*[1].]

1 a A light but distinct touch; a light quick stroke or touch; a pat, a tap. *obsolete* exc. *dial.* LME. ▸**b** = TAG *noun*[2] 1. E17.
2 A distinct quick light dry sound, as of the collision of two small metal bodies; *esp.* the regular slight click made by a watch or clock. L17. ▸**b** A beat of the heart or pulse. *rare.* E19.
3 A small dash or other mark (now usu. '✓') made with a pen or pencil to draw attention to something, to check off an item in a list, to indicate the correctness of a written answer or remark, etc. M19. ▸**b** A small spot or speck of colour on the skin or coat of an animal. *Scot. rare.* L19. ▸**c** A ticked item on a list, esp. of birds to be observed. L20.
4 The time between two ticks of a clock; a moment, an instant. *colloq.* L19.
5 *STOCK EXCHANGE.* The smallest recognized amount by which a price (of a commodity, stock, etc.) may fluctuate. L20.

> 🕮 **3** G. GORER Questions . . that . . could be answered either with a simple tick or by writing. **c** *Bird Watching* Brian . . recorded his first Willow Warbler, while two Oxfordshire regulars both claimed new ticks. **4** E. W. HORNUNG I should have been spotted in a tick by a spy. E. REVELEY Just wait a tick while I tell George where we'll be. **in two ticks** in a very short time. **on the tick, to the tick** punctually, promptly.

tick /tɪk/ *noun*[4]. *colloq.* M17.
[App. abbreviation of TICKET *noun* in *on the ticket*.]
1 Credit; trust; reputation for solvency and honesty. Esp. in ***on tick***. M17.
2 A debit account; a bill, a reckoning. L17.

> 🕮 **1** THACKERAY When he had no funds he went on tick. R. D. BLACKMORE Giving tick unlimited, or even remission of all charges. **go on tick, run on tick** buy goods on credit, run into debt. **2** THACKERAY Some of my college ticks ain't paid now . . . Tailors' ticks.

tick /tɪk/ *noun*[5]. *rare.* E18.
[formed as TIC.]
1 *The* habit of crib-biting. E18.
2 A whim, a fancy; a peculiar notion. Cf. TIC 3. E20.

tick /tɪk/ *verb*[1]. ME.
[Prob. rel. to Dutch *tikken* pat, tick, Old High German *zekōn* pluck, Middle High German *zicken* push: cf. TICK *noun*[3], TICKLE *verb*, TIG *verb*.]
1 a *verb intrans.* Touch or tap a thing or person lightly; *spec.* pat a person affectionately or amorously. *obsolete* exc. *dial.* ME. ▸**b** *verb trans.* = TAG *verb*[2] 1. E20.
2 *verb intrans.* **a** Of a clock, watch, etc.: operate with or make a tick. E18. ▸**b** *spec.* Of a taximeter or taxi-cab: make a ticking sound while registering the fare. Usu. foll. by *away, up*. E20. ▸**c** Foll. by *over*: (of an internal-combustion engine) run or work with the propeller or gears disengaged, or at a low rate of revolutions; idle; *fig.* continue to function, work, etc., esp. at a low capacity or level. E20. ▸**d** Work, function, operate. Esp. in ***what makes a person tick***, what motivates a person. *colloq.* M20.
3 a *verb trans.* Bring to an end, pass, or consume (a period of time) (as) by the ticking of a clock etc. Freq. foll. by *away*. M19. ▸**b** *verb intrans.* Of time, events, etc.: pass, come to an end. Foll. by *by, away*. M20.
4 *verb trans.* **a** Mark (an answer, an item in a list, etc.) with a tick as noted, passed, checked, etc.; *colloq.* identify. Freq. foll. by *off*. M19. ▸**b** Foll. by *off*: reprimand, scold. *colloq.* (orig. *Military slang*). E20. ▸**c** Foll. by *off*: annoy; depress, dispirit. *N. Amer. slang.* M20.
5 *verb intrans.* Grumble, complain. *slang* (orig. *Military*). E20.

> 🕮 **1a** BUNYAN His sons . . ticking and toying with the daughters of their lord. **2a** G. GREENE A clock ticked with a cheap tinny sound. **ticking bomb** a time bomb. **b** B. PYM Do hurry, the taxi's ticking away. **c** *Times* Content to let the war tick over but . . refused to bring it to an end. *Airgun World* Guns ticking over at three-quarters of their full power will handle better. **d** *Independent* Dealing with her mail . . and generally keeping 113 Zia Road ticking along. **3a** R. BROUGHTON The clocks tick it [life] monotonously away. **b** G. BOYCOTT Each hour ticked away without any news. **4a** P. HOBSBAUM They're ticked, gone over, somehow rejected. I. MCEWAN He ticked off the . . days until the Christmas holidays. **b** B. BAINBRIDGE She . . ticked him off for digging his elbow into her shoulder. **c** E. SEGAL The coach is pretty ticked off that I'm cutting practice to work with this kid.

Comb.: **tick-off** *slang* a fortune-teller; **tick-over** the speed or state of an internal-combustion engine which is ticking over.

tick /tɪk/ *verb*[2]. *colloq.* M17.
[from TICK *noun*[4].]
1 a *verb intrans.* Buy goods on credit; run into debt, leave a debt unpaid. Now *rare.* M17. ▸**b** *verb trans.* Buy (goods) on credit; run up (a bill or debt). Also foll. by *up*. L17.
2 *verb intrans.* Give credit; supply goods or services on credit. E18.

†**tick** *verb*[3] *intrans. rare.* Only in 18.
[from TICK *noun*[5].]
Of a horse: have the habit of crib-biting.

tickameg *noun* var. of TITTYMEG.

tick-a-tick /ˈtɪkətɪk/ *noun.* E19.
[formed as TICK *noun*[3] with redupl.]
The sound of a clock or watch.

ticked /tɪkt/ *adjective.* L17.
[from TICK *noun*[1] + -ED[2].]
Of an animal, esp. a dog: having small markings or spots as if bitten by ticks.

†**tickel** *noun. rare.* L16–M18.
[from TICK *noun*[1] + -EL[1].]
= TICK *noun*[1] 1.

ticken *noun* see TICKING.

ticker /ˈtɪkə/ *noun. colloq.* E19.
[from TICK *verb* + -ER[1].]
1 A thing that ticks; *spec.* (*a*) (the pendulum of) a clock; (*b*) a watch; (*c*) (now *N. Amer.*) a tape machine, *esp.* one that prints news or stock prices. E19.
2 The heart; *US & Austral. slang* courage, guts. M20.
3 A person who ticks off items in a list etc.; *spec.* (*derog.*) a birdwatcher, a twitcher. L20.

> 🕮 **1** *New Yorker* The tickers . . are clattering as they print wire-service copy on continuous rolls. **2** *Sunday Sun (Brisbane)* The lady has ticker . . She didn't opt for the soft life. L. LOCHHEAD Nowt up with the ticker, any trouble with the waterworks?

Comb.: **ticker tape** (*a*) a paper strip on which messages are recorded in a tape machine; (*b*) (freq. *attrib.*) this or similar material thrown from windows to welcome a celebrity in a motorcade.

ticket /ˈtɪkɪt/ *noun & verb.* E16.
[Aphet. from French †*étiquet* from Old French *estiquet(te*, from *estiquier, estichier, estechier* fix, stick from Middle Dutch *steken*: see -ET[1]. Cf. ETIQUETTE.]
▸ **A** *noun.* **1** A short written document; a memorandum, a note. *obsolete* in *gen.* sense. E16. ▸**b** *spec.* A smelter's written tender for ore. *local.* L18. ▸**c** *STOCK EXCHANGE.* A document listing investors who have bought stocks or shares in the period up to the last account day. L19. ▸**d** An official documentary notification of an offence against traffic regulations; *spec.* a parking ticket. Orig. *US.* M20.
2 A certificate; a warrant, a licence, a permit. Now *rare* in *gen.* sense. E16. ▸**b** *spec.* A pay-warrant; a certificate of discharge from service, prison, the army, etc., *esp.* one certifying an amount of pay due. L16. ▸**c** *Hist.* = TICKET OF LEAVE. E19. ▸**d** *spec.* A certificate of qualification as a pilot, ship's master, etc. L19.
3 Orig., a notice posted in a public place. Now, a label attached to an object and giving its name, price, or other details. M16.
4 †**a** An acknowledgement of indebtedness; a promise to pay, *esp.* a promissory note; a note of money or goods received on credit; a debit account, a bill. L16–L18. ▸**b** *ellipt.* A pawn-ticket. M19.
5 A written or printed piece of paper, card, etc., making the holder entitled to enter a place, watch or take part in an event, travel to a destination (esp. by public transport), use a public amenity, eat a meal, etc., or eligible for a prize in a lottery etc. M17. ▸**b** A (counterfeit) pass or passport. *slang.* M20.
6 A visiting-card. Also ***visiting ticket***. *obsolete* exc. *dial.* L17.
7 *POLITICS.* A list of candidates for election put forward by a party, faction, etc. Also, the policies and principles of a party, an election platform. Orig. & chiefly *US.* E18.
8 *The* thing that is correct, needed, wanted, expected, etc.; *the* plan of action. *colloq.* M19.

> 🕮 **1d** S. BELLOW 'I'll park here . . . ,' said Emil. 'They can give me a ticket if they like.' C. DEXTER The penalty fixed for the traffic offence detailed on the ticket. **2d** R. HUNTFORD He had his Master's ticket; but he was still the frustrated naval officer. **3** THACKERAY The ticket in the window . . announced 'Apartments to Let.' J. FOWLES On each article stood the white ticket that announced its price. **5** P. P. READ He went into the station . . and bought a . . ticket. A. BROOKNER He . . presented his reader's ticket, and sat down at one of the desks. ***air ticket, bus ticket, lottery ticket, luncheon ticket, railway ticket, theatre-ticket.*** *attrib.*: ***ticket-agent, ticket booth, ticket-clerk, ticket-holder, ticket inspector, ticket money, ticket-pocket, ticket stub***, etc. *fig.*: *Modern Maturity* For many children in poor neighborhoods, drugs are seen as the only ticket out of poverty. **7** *Sunday Times* The two landslide victories he won on tickets of national pride and individual self-help. *Raritan* His abortive presidential campaign on the Progressive Party ticket. **8** F. MARRYAT 'What's the ticket, youngster—are you to go abroad with me?' D. LODGE No intention of dying yet . . . Living for ever is more the ticket.

Phrases etc.: ***big-ticket***: see BIG *adjective*. **clean ticket** *US* (the complete list of) all the official candidates of a political party. **have tickets on oneself** *Austral. colloq.* be vain or conceited. ***like a PAKAPOO ticket***. †**on ticket**, †**on the ticket** on credit, on trust (cf. TICK *noun*[4]). ***return ticket***: see RETURN *noun* 1b. ***round-trip ticket***: see ROUND *adjective*. ***split the ticket***: see SPLIT *verb*. ***straight ticket***: see STRAIGHT *adjective*[1]. TICKET OF LEAVE. ***visiting ticket***: see sense 6 above. **work one's ticket** contrive to obtain one's discharge from prison, the army, etc. **write one's own ticket** *colloq.* dictate one's own terms.

Comb.: **ticket barrier** the point at a railway station, sports stadium, etc., beyond which one cannot proceed without a ticket; **ticket benefit** an entertainment for which special tickets are sold, the proceeds going to a particular person, cause, etc.; **ticket chopper** *US* (a person in charge of) a machine which mutilates used tickets; **ticket-collector** an official who collects the tickets of passengers, spectators, etc., as or after they are used; **ticket-day** *STOCK EXCHANGE* the day before settling day, when a list of recent purchasers is given to stockbrokers (see sense 1c above); **ticket fine**: imposed on a motorist by the issuing of a ticket rather than by prosecution in court (see sense 1d above); **ticket office** an office or kiosk where tickets for transport, entertainment, etc., are sold; **ticket-porter** *Hist.* a member of a body of licensed street-porters in the City of London (opp. ***TACKLE-HOUSE porter***); **ticket-scalper** *US slang* = SCALPER *noun*[2] 2a, b; **ticket-splitter** *US* a person who votes for candidates of more than one party in an election; **ticket-splitting** *US* the practice of voting for candidates of more than one party in an election; ***ticket tout***: see TOUT *noun*[1] 3b.

▸ **B** *verb.* **I** *verb trans.* **1 a** Attach a ticket to; mark with a ticket, label. E16. ▸**b** *fig.* Describe or designate as by a ticket; characterize or categorize (*as*). M17. ▸**c** Attach a parking ticket to (a vehicle); serve (a person) with a ticket for a traffic or other offence. Orig. *US.* M20.
2 Issue (a person) with a ticket for travel. *N. Amer.* M19.

> 🕮 **1b** *Burlington Magazine* Having ticketed his style, they had no interest in its movements. E. HEMINGWAY I suppose . . I am ticketed as a Red . . and will be on the general blacklist. **c** R. BALLANTINE Cyclists have been ticketed for causing an obstruction.

▸ **II** *verb intrans.* **3** Make a written tender *for* tin or copper ore. Cf. sense A.1b above. *local.* L18.
■ **ticketed** *ppl adjective* marked with or bearing a ticket or tickets E17. **ticketer** *noun* (*rare*) a person who has a ticket L18. **ticketless** *adjective* M19.

ticket of leave /ˌtɪkɪt əv ˈliːv/ *noun phr.* M18.
[from TICKET *noun* + OF *preposition* + LEAVE *noun*[1].]
Hist. A ticket or document giving leave or permission; *spec.* (esp. in Australia) a conditional licence for a convict to be at large after the expiry of part of the sentence.
Comb.: **ticket-of-leave man** a prisoner or convict who had served part of his sentence and was granted certain concessions, esp. leave.
■ **ticket-of-leaver** *noun* a ticket-of-leave man M19.

tickety-boo /ˌtɪkɪtɪˈbuː/ *adjective. colloq.* M20.
[Origin uncertain; perh. from Hindi *ṭhīk hai* all right.]
In order, correct, fine.

> 🕮 A. BROOKNER His slang dated from before the war. 'Everything tickety-boo?' Yes, she would nod.

tickey /ˈtɪki/ *noun. S. Afr. colloq.* (now *Hist.*). Also **-cky**. L19.
[Origin unkn.]
A threepenny piece.

ticking /ˈtɪkɪŋ/ *noun.* Also (now *rare* or *obsolete*) **ticken** /ˈtɪk(ə)n/. M17.
[from TICK *noun*[2] + -ING[1].]
1 Fabric used for making a bedtick or for covering pillows, *esp.* a strong durable usu. striped linen or cotton. M17.
2 A bedtick. *rare.* L17.

tickle /ˈtɪk(ə)l/ *noun*[1]. *Canad. dial.* L18.
[Perh. from TICKLE *adjective* or *verb*.]
Around the coasts of Newfoundland and Labrador, a narrow difficult strait or channel.

tickle /ˈtɪk(ə)l/ *noun*[2]. E19.
[from the verb.]
1 An act of tickling a person or thing; a touch that tickles; a tickling sensation, a tickled or pleasantly excited feeling. E19.
2 A successful deal or crime. Cf. TICKLE *verb* 7d. *Criminals' slang.* M20.

> 🕮 **1** R. D. BLACKMORE I gave her a little tickle; and . . she began to laugh. J. C. OATES A curl of something in the pit of her belly, a tickle of sexual desire. ***slap and tickle***: see SLAP *noun*[2] 1.

tickle /ˈtɪk(ə)l/ *adjective & adverb.* Now *rare* exc. *dial.* ME.
[Prob. from the verb: cf. KITTLE *adjective*, *verb*[1].]
▸ **A** *adjective.* †**1** Pleasantly stirred or excited. Cf. TICKLE *verb* 1. Only in ME.
2 Unreliable; uncertain; changeable, capricious, fickle. *obsolete* exc. *dial.* ME.
3 Of a place, condition, etc.: insecure; precarious, slippery; dangerous. *arch.* LME. ▸**b** Of a thing: unsteady, unstable; easily overturned or set in motion; finely poised or balanced; delicate. Now *dial.* E16.
†**4** Easily moved or swayed, impressionable; easily tickled or tingled. Also, sexually promiscuous. LME–E17.
5 a Having delicate feelings or senses; fastidious, dainty, squeamish; touchy. Now *dial.* LME. ▸**b** = TICKLISH *adjective* 3. Now *dial.* M16. ▸**c** Of an animal: easily scared; shy, wild. *dial.* L19.

> 🕮 **2** C. COTTON His sons . . were best acquainted with his tickle & impatient humour. C. M. DOUGHTY Who can foresee the years to come, this world is so tickle.

▸ **B** *adverb.* Unsteadily, unstably; precariously. Long *rare* or *obsolete.* E17.

tickle /ˈtɪk(ə)l/ *verb.* ME.
[Origin uncertain: perh. frequentative of TICK *verb*[1] or a metath. alt. of KITTLE *verb*[1]. Cf. TITTLE *verb*[2].]
▶ **I** *verb intrans.* †**1** Be pleasantly stirred, excited, or thrilled. ME–M17.
2 Give a sensation as of being tickled, tingle, itch; *fig.* have a restless or urgent desire (*to do* something). LME.

📖 **1** HENRY MORE This pretty sport doth make my heart to tickle With laughter. **2** OED My foot tickles.

▶ **II** *verb trans.* **3** Excite agreeably, gratify, delight, (a person, sense of humour, appetite, etc.); amuse, divert. LME.
4 Lightly touch or stroke (a person or part of the body) so as to excite the nerves and (usually) cause laughter, spasmodic movement, irritation, or annoyance. LME. ▶**b** Catch (a trout or other fish) by light rubbing which causes the fish to move backwards into the hand. E17.
†**5 a** Arouse (as) by tickling; incite, provoke, prompt, (*to do* something). M–L16. ▶**b** Excite, affect; vex. M16–L17.
6 a Foll. by *up*: stir up, arouse by tickling, excite to action. M16. ▶**b** Get or move (a thing) *into* or *out of* some place, state, etc., as by tickling. L17.
7 Touch or play (an instrument's strings, keys, etc.), esp. with light touches. *colloq.* L16. ▶**b** Beat, punish. *colloq.* L16. ▶**c** Foll. by *up*: improve or decorate with light touches. M19. ▶**d** Rob, burgle. Esp. in ***tickle the peter***, rob the till or cash box. Cf. TICKLE *noun*[2] 2. *Criminals' slang* (chiefly *Austral.* & *NZ*). M20. ▶**e** CRICKET. Of a batsman: glance (a ball or bowler). Cf. GLANCE *verb* 8b. M20.
8 Puzzle, perplex. *Scot.* M19.
9 Improve the action of (a carburettor, esp. in a motorcycle) by depressing the float lightly to allow some petrol to pass in, esp. to allow a cold start. E20.

📖 **3** N. HAWTHORNE Something .. that thrilled and tickled my heart with a feeling partly sensuous and partly spiritual. H. BELLOC We are tickled by his irreverence .. we laugh. J. FANE Quaint old names tickled our fancy. **4** SHAKES. *Mids. N. D.* If my hair do but tickle me I must scratch. A. S. NEILL Tickling the ribs will often start a bout of happy laughter. *fig.*: M. FRAYN The cold air tickled her smoke-raw throat, and she suffered a .. fit of coughing. **7b** C. K. SHARPE These little rogues .. should be well tickled with the birch. **e** *Sunday Times* Brearley tickled Doshi away behind the wicket for three.

Phrases: **tickle in the palm** *colloq.* bribe. **tickle pink** *colloq.* amuse greatly, delight. ***tickle the ivories***: see IVORY *noun*. ***tickle the midriff***: see MIDRIFF 1. ***tickle the peter***: see sense 7d above.
Comb.: †**tickle-brain** (a supplier of) strong drink; **tickle-grass** any of several N. American grasses, *esp.* the rough bent, *Agrostis scabra*.

Ticklenburgs /ˈtɪklənbəːgz/ *noun.* Pl. same. L17.
[Alt. of *Tecklenburg* (see below).]
A kind of coarse linen, or linen and cotton, cloth from Tecklenburg, a town in Westphalia, Germany.

tickler /ˈtɪklə/ *noun.* E17.
[from TICKLE *verb* + -ER[1].]
1 A person who tickles something or someone; *spec.* (*colloq.*) a pianist. E17.
2 A thing which tickles or is used for tickling (*lit.* & *fig.*), as (*a*) a feather brush; (*b*) a birch, rod, etc., used to beat a person; (*c*) a device by which a small quantity of petrol is let into the carburettor to aid the starting of an engine; (*d*) a memorandum; (*e*) (more fully ***tickler coil***) an inductance coil in the anode circuit of a valve, giving positive feedback through another coil in the grid circuit. L17.
Comb.: **tickler coil** = sense 2(e) above.

ticklesome /ˈtɪk(ə)ls(ə)m/ *adjective.* Now *dial.* L16.
[from TICKLE *verb* + -SOME[1].]
That tends to tickle; delicate, precarious; ticklish.

tickle-tail /ˈtɪk(ə)lteɪl/ *noun. obsolete* exc. *dial.* LME.
[from TICKLE *adjective* or *verb* + TAIL *noun*[1].]
1 A promiscuous woman. LME.
2 A schoolteacher who beats a child across the buttocks; a birch rod used for this. L17.

tickling /ˈtɪklɪŋ/ *verbal noun.* ME.
[from TICKLE *verb* + -ING[1].]
1 The action of TICKLE *verb*; the state of being tickled (*lit.* & *fig.*); (a sensation of) irritation in the throat, a sensitive part of the skin, etc. ME.
2 *fig.* An itch to do something; a craving. M16.
Comb.: **tickling stick** *joc.* a feather duster or the like, used as a comedian's prop.

tickling /ˈtɪklɪŋ/ *ppl adjective.* M16.
[formed as prec. + -ING[2].]
That tickles (*lit.* & *fig.*); delicate, ticklish.

ticklish /ˈtɪklɪʃ/ *adjective* & *adverb.* L16.
[from TICKLE *adjective* or *verb* + -ISH[1].]
▶ **A** *adjective.* **1** Sensitive to tickling. L16.
2 Of a person: easily offended, irritated, or upset; touchy. Of a thing: unsteady, unstable; easily unbalanced or overturned. L16.
3 Needing very careful treatment, requiring cautious handling or action, tricky; delicate, precarious, hazardous. L16.

📖 **1** *Independent* I began to massage her feet .. She kept withdrawing them—she's very ticklish. **3** J. UPDIKE The ticklish relationship between publisher and writer. *City Limits* The case raises ticklish questions about the enforcement of drinking-up time.

▶ **B** *adverb.* Ticklishly. Long *rare.* M17.
■ **ticklishly** *adverb* in a ticklish manner, state, or position M17. **ticklishness** *noun* L16.

tickly /ˈtɪkli/ *adjective.* L15.
[from TICKLE *adjective* + -Y[1].]
Ticklish.

†**Tickney** *adjective.* L17–L19.
[from *Ticknal* (see below).]
Designating coarse earthenware of a kind formerly made at Ticknal near Derby in England.

tick-tack /ˈtɪktak/ *noun* & *verb.* Also (exc. in senses A.2, B.2) **tic-tac**. M16.
[Imit.]
▶ **A** *noun.* **1** A repeated ticking sound, *esp.* one made by a clock; the sound of the firing of small artillery. Also (earlier) as *interjection.* M16.
2 Any of various contrivances for making a clattering sound against a window or door as a practical joke, esp. at Hallowe'en. Chiefly *N. Amer.* L19.
3 A kind of manual semaphore signalling used by racecourse bookmakers to exchange information. Freq. *attrib.* L19.
Comb.: **tick-tack-toe** (*a*) *rare* a game in which each player, with eyes shut, brings a pencil down on a slate with numbers on it, scoring points equal to the number hit; (*b*) *N. Amer.* (a grid for playing) noughts and crosses.
▶ **B** *verb.* **1** *verb intrans.* = TICK-TOCK *verb*. M19.
2 *verb intrans.* & *trans.* Make a tick-tack clatter against (a window etc.). Cf. sense A.2 above. Chiefly *N. Amer.* E20.
3 *verb trans.* & *intrans.* RACING. Signal (information) by means of tick-tack semaphore. E20.
■ **tick-tacker** *noun* (RACING) a practitioner of tick-tack semaphore E20.

tick-tick /ˈtɪktɪk/ *verb* & *noun.* M18.
[Imit.: cf. next.]
▶ **A** *verb intrans.* Make a ticking sound. M18.
▶ **B** *noun.* A ticking sound, *esp.* of a clock or watch; (*colloq.*, esp. *nursery*) a clock or watch. L18.

tick-tock /ˈtɪktɒk/ *noun* & *verb.* M19.
[Imit.: cf. prec., TICK *verb*[1], TOCK.]
▶ **A** *noun.* The ticking of a clock, esp. a large one. Now also (*colloq.*, esp. *nursery*) a clock or watch. M19.
▶ **B** *verb intrans.* Of a clock etc.: make a rhythmic alternating ticking sound. E20.

ticky *noun* var. of TICKEY.

ticky /ˈtɪki/ *adjective.* M19.
[from TICK *noun*[1] + -Y[1].]
Full of or infested with ticks.

ticky-tacky /ˈtɪkɪˌtaki/ *noun* & *adjective.* Orig. *US.* M20.
[Prob. redupl. of TACKY *noun*, *adjective*[1].]
▶ **A** *noun.* Inferior or cheap material, esp. used in suburban building. M20.
▶ **B** *adjective.* Made of ticky-tacky; cheap, in poor taste. M20.

Tico /ˈtiːkəʊ/ *noun* & *adjective. slang* (chiefly *US*). E20.
[Amer. Spanish, from (esp. Costa Rican) Spanish *-tico* dim. suffix.]
▶ **A** *noun.* Pl. **-os**. = COSTA RICAN *noun*. E20.
▶ **B** *adjective.* = COSTA RICAN *adjective*. M20.

tic-polonga /tɪkpəˈlɒŋgə/ *noun.* E19.
[App. from Sinhalese *tit-polan̆gā*, from *tita* speckle, spot + *polan̆gā* viper.]
In Sri Lanka, Russell's viper.

tic-tac *noun* & *verb* see TICK-TACK.

Ticuna /tɪˈkuːnə/ *noun* & *adjective.* E19.
[Ticuna.]
▶ **A** *noun.* Pl. same, **-s**.
1 A member of a S. American Indian people inhabiting parts of the NW Amazon basin, mainly in Brazil and Colombia. E19. ▶**b** The language of this people. L19.
▶ **B** *adjective.* Of or pertaining to the Ticuna or their language. M19.

tid /tɪd/ *adjective. obsolete* exc. *dial.* E18.
[Origin uncertain: perh. from *tidbit* var. of TITBIT. Cf. TIDDLE *verb*[1], TIDLING.]
Tender, delicate, soft. Also, fond or careful *of*.

t.i.d. *abbreviation.*
MEDICINE. Latin *Ter in die* three times a day.

tidal /ˈtʌɪd(ə)l/ *adjective* & *noun.* E19.
[from TIDE *noun* + -AL[1].]
▶ **A** *adjective.* **1** Of, pertaining to, or affected by tides; ebbing and flowing periodically. E19.
2 Dependent on or regulated by the state of the tide or time of high water. M19.
3 *transf.* & *fig.* Periodic, intermittent; alternating, varying. L19.
Special collocations: **tidal air** PHYSIOLOGY the air which passes in and out of the lungs with each ordinary breath. **tidal basin**: accessible or navigable only at high tide. **tidal boat**: the sailings of which depend on the time of the tide. ***tidal bore***: see BORE *noun*[2] 2. **tidal flow** the regulated movement of esp. rush hour traffic in opposite directions on the same road lane, depending on the time of day and conditions. **tidal friction** frictional resistance to the motion of the tides, tending to retard the earth's rotation. ***tidal harbour***: see ***tidal basin*** above. **tidal river**: affected by the tide for some distance from its mouth. **tidal train**: running so as to connect with a tidal boat. **tidal wave** (*a*) = ***tidewave*** s.v. TIDE *noun*; (*b*) an exceptionally large ocean wave, *esp.* one caused by an underwater earthquake or volcanic eruption, or a hurricane (cf. TSUNAMI); (*c*) *fig.* a widespread or intense experience or manifestation of a feeling, opinion, etc.
▶ **B** *ellipt.* as *noun.* A tidal boat or train. M19.
■ **tidally** *adverb* in a tidal manner, in respect of the tides L19.

tidbit *noun* see TITBIT.

tiddle /ˈtɪd(ə)l/ *verb*[1]. *obsolete* exc. *dial.* or *slang.* M16.
[Origin uncertain: see -LE[3]. Cf. TID, TIDLING.]
1 *verb trans.* Indulge to excess, pet, pamper; tend carefully, nurse, cherish. M16.
2 *verb intrans.* Move or act aimlessly; fiddle *about*, fuss; potter. M18.

tiddle /ˈtɪd(ə)l/ *verb*[2] *intrans. colloq.* M19.
[Alt. of PIDDLE *verb*. Cf. TINKLE *verb*, WIDDLE *verb*[2].]
Urinate.

tiddledy-wink *noun* & *verb* var. of TIDDLYWINK.

tiddler /ˈtɪdlə/ *noun*[1]. *colloq.* L19.
[Prob. rel. to TITTLEBAT, TIDDLY *adjective*[2]: see -ER[1].]
A small fish, *esp.* a stickleback or minnow. Also, a child; any small person or thing.

📖 *Daily News* Boys .. fishing for tiddlers with .. bent pins. *Independent* British lotteries are confined to tiddlers run by local authorities, charities and clubs.

tiddler /ˈtɪdlə/ *noun*[2]. *slang.* E20.
[from *tiddle* var. of TITTLE *verb*[2] + -ER[1].]
A feather or feather brush for tickling someone, a tickler.

tiddler /ˈtɪdlə/ *noun*[3]. *US colloq.* M20.
[from TIDDL(YWINK + -ER[1].]
A tiddlywinks player.

tiddley *noun* & *adjective*[1], *adjective*[2], *adjective*[3] vars. of TIDDLY *noun* & *adjective*[1], *adjective*[2], *adjective*[3].

tiddley-om-pom-pom *interjection, adverb,* & *adjective* var. of TIDDLY-OM-POM-POM.

tiddly /ˈtɪdli/ *noun* & *adjective*[1]. *colloq.* Also **-ey**. M19.
[Origin uncertain: cf. TIDDLYWINK 1.]
▶ **A** *noun.* (An) alcoholic drink, *esp.* (a drink of) spirits. M19.
▶ **B** *adjective.* Slightly drunk, tipsy. E20.

📖 B. NICHOLS No more wine ... I shall be quite tiddly.

tiddly /ˈtɪdli/ *adjective*[2]. *colloq.* Also **-ey**. M19.
[Var. of TIDDY *adjective*.]
Very small, tiny.

tiddly /ˈtɪdli/ *adjective*[3]. *slang* (chiefly NAUTICAL). Also **-ey**. E20.
[Perh. from TIDY *adjective*.]
Smart, spruce.
tiddly suit one's best suit of clothes.

tiddly-om-pom-pom /tɪdlɪˈɒmpɒmpɒm/ *interjection, adverb,* & *adjective.* Also **tiddly-pom** /ˈtɪdlɪpɒm/, **tiddley-**. E20.
[Imit.: cf. POM-POM.]
▶ **A** *interjection* & *adverb.* Repr. the sound or regular beat of brass-band or similar music; with such a sound or beat. E20.
▶ **B** *adjective.* (**tiddly-pom**.) With a simple beat or tune, trite. M20.

tiddlypush /ˈtɪdlɪpʊʃ, tɪdlɪˈpʊʃ/ *noun. colloq.* E20.
[Origin unkn.]
A person or thing whose name is unknown or is unnecessary or indelicate to mention. Cf. THINGUMMY.

tiddlywink /ˈtɪdlɪwɪŋk/ *noun* & *verb.* Also ***tiddledy-** /ˈtɪd(ə)ldɪ-/. M19.
[Origin uncertain: perh. rel. to TIDDLY *noun* & *adjective*[1].]
▶ **A** *noun.* **1 a** An unlicensed public-house or pawnshop. *slang.* Now *rare.* M19. ▶**b** A drink (of alcohol). *rhyming slang.* L19.
2 a A game played with dominoes. M19. ▶**b** In *pl.*, a game in which small counters are flicked into a cup or similar receptacle by being pressed on the edge with a larger counter (freq. as a type of a useless or frivolous activity). In *sing.*, a counter (as) used in this game. L19.
▶ **B** *verb intrans.* Flip like a counter in tiddlywinks. Also, play tiddlywinks. M20.
■ **tiddlywinker** *noun* (*a*) *colloq.* a cheat; a trifler; (*b*) a tiddlywinks player: L19. **tiddlywinking** *adjective* & *noun* (*a*) *adjective colloq.* trifling, insignificant; (*b*) *noun* the activity of playing tiddlywinks; *colloq.* trifling or cheating behaviour: M19. **tiddlywinky** *adjective* (*dial.*) tiny, insignificant L19.

tiddy /ˈtɪdi/ *noun.* M17.
[Origin unkn.]
Hist. In the game of gleek, the four of trumps.

tiddy /ˈtɪdi/ *adjective. colloq.* or *nursery.* L18.
[Origin unkn.]
= TIDDLY *adjective*[2].

tiddy oggy /ˈtɪdɪ ɒgi/ *noun phr. dial. & NAUTICAL.* M20.
[Origin uncertain: perh. from TIDDLY *adjective*[2], TIDDY *adjective*.]
A Cornish pasty, *esp.* one containing a high proportion of potatoes to meat.

tide /tʌɪd/ *noun.*
[Old English *tīd* = Old Saxon *tīd* (Dutch *tijd*), Old High German *zīt* (German *Zeit*), Old Norse *tíð*, from Germanic word rel. to TIME *noun*. Branch II prob. after Middle Low German *(ge)tīde, tie*, Middle Dutch *ghetide* (Dutch *(ge)tij*) development of sense 'fixed time'.]
▶**I** Time.
1 = TIME *noun* 1, 2. *obsolete* exc. *Scot. & dial.* OE.
2 *spec.* = HOUR 1. Long *obsolete* exc. *Hist.* OE.
3 a = TIME *noun* 11, 12. *arch.* or *poet.* OE. ▶**b** = TIME *noun* 14. *arch.* OE.
4 A definite point, time, or season in a day, year, life, etc. Formerly also *spec.* = HOUR 3. *arch.* or *poet.* exc. in comb. OE.
†**5** *ECCLESIASTICAL.* = HOUR 5. OE–M16.
6 An anniversary or festival of the Church. Usu. in *comb.* OE. ▶**b** A village fair (taking place on the festival of the parish's patron saint). *dial.* E19.

📖 **3a** WORDSWORTH We will see it—joyful tide! Some day . . The mountain will we cross. **4** ***eventide, noontide, summer-tide***, etc. **6** ***Eastertide, Michaelmas tide, Whitsuntide***, etc.

▶**II** Tide of the sea.
7 The alternate rising and falling of the sea, usu. twice in each lunar day at each place, due to the attraction of the moon and sun; the alternate inflow and outflow produced by this on a coast, the flood and ebb; the seawater as affected by this. LME. ▶**b** *transf. & fig.* A (recurrent) flow, a rise and fall; something ebbing, or flowing, or turning, *esp.* a marked trend of opinion, fortune, or events. LME. ▶**c** *spec.* = ***flood-tide*** s.v. FLOOD *noun* 1. L16.
8 The time between two successive points of high water or between low water and high water; the part of this time during which the height of the water allows work etc. to be done. LME.
9 A body of flowing water etc.; a stream, a current, (*lit. & fig.*). Chiefly *literary*. L16.
10 The water of the sea. *poet. & dial.* L18.

📖 **7** J. MAIDMENT Waste lands bordering on the sea shore . . covered with water when the tide comes in. E. ARDIZZONE He noticed a little boat just afloat on the incoming tide. *Proverb*: Time and tide wait for no man. **b** SHAKES. *Jul. Caes.* There is a tide in the affairs of men Which, taken at the flood, leads on to fortune. D. FRASER In the autumn of 1918 the tide finally turned. **c** P. HOLLAND The River at every tide riseth to a great heigth. **9** O. HENRY The rush-hour tide of humanity.

Phrases: **acid tide** a temporary increase of acidity of the urine while fasting. **alkaline tide** a temporary decrease of acidity of the urine after eating, due to secretion of digestive juices. **cross tide** a tide running across the direction of another. ***double tides***: see DOUBLE *adjective & adverb*. ***ebb-tide***: see EBB *noun*. ***go with the tide***: see GO *verb*. ***high tide***: see HIGH *adjective*. ***holytide***: see HOLY *adjective*. ***lag of the tide***: see LAG *noun*[2] 4b. ***low tide***: see LOW *adjective*. ***priming of the tides***: see PRIMING *noun*[2]. ***rip tide***: see RIP *noun*[5]. ***save the tide***: see SAVE *verb*. ***stop the tide***: see STOP *verb*. ***swim against the tide***: see SWIM *verb*. ***turn the tide***: see TURN *verb*.
Comb.: **tide-boat** sailing with or by means of the tide; **tideland(s)** *N. Amer.* land(s) submerged at high tide; ***tideland spruce*** = *SITKA spruce*; **tidemark** (*a*) the mark left or reached by the tide at high or (occas.) low water; (*b*) a post etc. set up to mark the rise and fall of or the point reached by the tide; (*c*) a mark left on a surface, esp. a bath, at the limit reached by water; a line of dirt marking the extent to which a person's body has been washed; **tide-mill** a mill driven by the action of the tide on a water-wheel; **tide-rip** [RIP *noun*[5]] (a patch of) rough water, esp. as caused by opposing tides, or by a rapid rise of the tide, esp. over an uneven bottom; **tidesman** *Hist.* = ***tidewaiter*** below; **tide-surveyor** *Hist.* a customs official who supervised the tidewaiters; **tidetable** a table showing the times of high and low water at a particular place or places during a period; **tidewaiter** *Hist.* a customs officer who boarded ships on arrival (formerly with the tide) to enforce the customs regulations; **tidewater** *noun & adjective* (*a*) *noun* water brought by or affected by the tide, tidal water; *US* a region situated on tidewater; (*b*) *adjective* (*US*) designating a region, esp. eastern Virginia, situated on tidewater; **tidewave** the undulation of the surface of the sea which passes around the earth and causes high tide as its highest point reaches each successive place; **tideway** a channel in which a tide runs, *esp.* the tidal part of a river; the ebb and flow in such a channel.
■ **tideless** *adjective* L18. **tidelessness** *noun* E20.

tide /tʌɪd/ *verb*[1] *intrans.* & †*trans.* (with dative obj.). *arch.*
[Old English *(ge)tīdan* happen, come about, formed as prec.]
= BETIDE *verb* 1.

tide /tʌɪd/ *verb*[2]. L16.
[from TIDE *noun*.]
1 *verb intrans.* Flow or surge like the tide, flow to and fro, (*lit. & fig.*). L16.
2 *verb trans.* Carry like the tide. Usu. foll. by adverb. E17.
3 a *verb intrans. & trans.* (with *it*). Float or drift (as) on the tide; *spec.* (*NAUTICAL*), sail by taking advantage of favouring tides and anchoring when the tide turns. Usu. foll. by adverb. E17. ▶**b** *verb trans.* Make (one's way) by using the tides thus. M19.
4 *verb trans.* Foll. by *over*: get over, survive, ride out, (a difficult period, awkward situation, etc.); enable or help (a person etc.) to deal with a difficult period by giving temporary assistance. E19.
5 *verb trans.* Cause to flow like a tide or stream. *rare*. M19.

📖 **2** R. HAYMAN The feeling . . that other people were tiding him along . . in the right direction. **4** M. FORSTER They had some money saved and with judicious handling it would tide them over this crisis.

tided /ˈtʌɪdɪd/ *adjective. rare.* E19.
[from TIDE *noun* + -ED[2].]
Having tides, tidal; *dial.* done at a specified time, timed.

tideful /ˈtʌɪdfʊl, -f(ə)l/ *adjective.* Long *rare*. ME.
[from TIDE *noun* + -FUL.]
†**1** Of time: seasonable, opportune, right. Only in ME.
2 Having a full tide; filled with the tide. E17.

tidge /tɪdʒ/ *noun. colloq.* M20.
[Origin uncertain: cf. SMIDGE, TAD.]
A small amount or portion, a bit.

tiding /ˈtʌɪdɪŋ/ *noun.* Now chiefly *literary*.
[Late Old English *tīdung*, as if from Old English *tīdan* TIDE *verb*[1] + -ING[1], but prob. from Old Norse *tíðendi, -indi* (news of) events or occurrences, from *tíðr* occurring.]
1 The announcement of an event etc., a piece of news, (*arch.*). Now usu. in *pl.* (treated as *pl.* or (*arch.*) *sing.*), news, reports, information. LOE.
2 A thing that happens; an event, an incident, an occurrence. Now *rare*. ME. ▶†**b** An indication, a sign. *rare*. Only in ME.

📖 **1** J. GALT The glad tidings of salvation were first heard there. SAKI Messengers bearing tidings of misfortune and defeat.

¶ Sense 2 prob. the original.
■ **tidingless** *adjective* (*rare*) without tidings E19.

†**tidivate** *verb* see TITIVATE.

tidling /ˈtɪdlɪŋ/ *noun. obsolete* exc. *dial.* E16.
[Perh. from TIDDLE *verb*[1]: see -LING[1].]
A young or delicate child or animal; a pampered or spoilt child; a darling, a pet.

tidy /ˈtʌɪdi/ *adjective, noun, & adverb.* ME.
[from TIDE *noun* + -Y[1].]
▶**A** *adjective.* †**1** Timely, seasonable, opportune; in season. ME–E18.
2 Attractive in appearance; in good condition; fat, plump, healthy. Now *dial.* ME.
3 †**a** Good, excellent; worthy, able, skilful. ME–E17. ▶**b** Fairly satisfactory, reasonably good; agreeable, pleasing. *colloq.* M19. ▶**c** Considerable in amount or degree. *colloq.* M19.
4 a Of a person etc.: orderly in habits, methodically inclined, disposed to keep things or one's appearance neat. E18. ▶**b** Methodically or neatly arranged, with nothing in disorder or out of place. E19.

📖 **3c** G. SANTAYANA He had a tidy sum in the bank. **4a** R. RENDELL House-proud, passionately neat and tidy. JANET MORGAN Agatha had a tidy mind and was . . quick at sums. **b** L. MCINTOSH Incongruous in his neat suit and tidy hair among the tousled undergraduates. J. MOYNAHAN The work of major novelists rarely follows a tidy chronological pattern of development.

▶**B** *noun.* **1** Any of various things used to keep a thing or person tidy or neat; *spec.* (*a*) *dial.* a pinafore, an overall; (*b*) a receptacle for holding scraps, small objects, etc., esp. in a kitchen sink or on a desk; (*c*) (chiefly *US*) an ornamental loose covering for the back of a chair etc., an antimacassar. E19.
2 An act or spell of tidying something. Also ***tidy-up***. E20.

📖 **2** C. WHITMAN I bustled around . . giving my flat a rough tidy-up.

▶**C** *adverb.* Tidily. *dial. & colloq.* E19.
■ **tidily** *adverb* ME. **tidiness** *noun* M16.

tidy /ˈtʌɪdi/ *verb.* E19.
[from the adjective.]
1 *verb trans. & intrans.* Make (a room, oneself, etc.) tidy, put in good order, arrange neatly. Freq. foll. by *up*. E19.
2 *verb trans.* Put *away* or clear *up* for the sake of tidiness. M19.

📖 **1** W. PLOMER I . . hurriedly tidied my hair in the looking-glass. B. HEAD She busied herself tidying up and completing . . household chores. **2** A. LAMBERT In his orderly fashion he tidies away the remains of our meal.

■ **tidier** *noun* E20. **tidying** *verbal noun* the action of the verb; an instance of this: M19.

tie /tʌɪ/ *noun*[1]. Also (*obsolete* exc. in sense 2) **tye**.
[Old English *tēah* (*tēag-*), *tēg* = Old Norse *taug* rope from Germanic. Cf. TOW *noun*[2].]
1 A cord, rope, chain, etc., used for fastening or tying something; a knot, a bow, a ligature; *gen.* something joining two or more things together. OE. ▶**b** *ARCHITECTURE.* A beam or rod used to tie or bind together two parts of a building or other structure. LME. ▶**c** A transverse railway sleeper. *N. Amer.* M19.
2 *NAUTICAL.* **a** A rope or chain by which a yard is suspended. LME. ▶**b** A mooring rope. M19.
3 *fig.* Something uniting or restricting people or things; a restraint, a constraint; an obligation, a bond; a link, a connection. M16. ▶**b** *spec.* A binding contract obliging the licensee of a public house etc. to supply only the products of one particular brewery. Cf. TIED *adjective*[1] 2a. E20. ▶**c** *LOGIC.* Something uniting the elements of a linguistic construct, e.g. the verb 'to be'. E20.
4 *MUSIC.* A curved line placed above or below two notes of the same pitch to indicate that they are to be played for the combined duration of their time values. M17.
5 a Equality of score or position between competitors in a contest; a draw, a dead heat. L17. ▶**b** A match or fixture between competing players or teams, esp. in a knockout competition (freq. as ***cup-tie***). Also, a deciding match played after a draw. M19.
6 A knot of hair; a pigtail. Also = ***tie-wig*** s.v. TIE-. Now *rare* or *obsolete*. E18.
7 The action, fact, or method of tying something; the condition of being tied; an instance of this. E18. ▶**b** The linking or locking together of dog and bitch during copulation. M20.
8 Any of various strips of material, ribbons, scarves, etc., worn tied around the neck as decoration; a necktie; *spec.* a strip of material worn around the collar and folded or knotted at the front with the ends hanging down or tied in a bow. M18.
9 A kind of low shoe fastened with a tie or lace. Now *US*. E19.

📖 **1** DICKENS Great formal wigs, with a tie behind. *Garden* Secure the tree to the support with two . . ties. **3** J. R. GREEN The ties of a common blood, and a common speech. R. COLLIER We'd love to do an evening show . . but the children are *such* a tie. *Times* China intends to continue trade and economic ties with the United States. A. B. GIAMATTI A city is a place where ties of proximity . . assume the role of family ties. V. GLENDINNING Anthony has no ties and can be available when Leo wants. **5a** M. BRADBURY That would give us a tie, at ten ten. **8** *Lifestyle* Politicians, whose suits, ties and pot bellies typified the Establishment. ***bow-tie, kipper-tie***, etc. ***black tie***: see BLACK *adjective*. ***made-up tie***: see MADE *ppl adjective*. OLD SCHOOL ***tie***. ***white tie***: see WHITE *adjective*.

■ **tieless** *adjective* without a tie; *spec.* wearing no tie: E20.

tie *noun*[2] var. of TYE *noun*[1].

tie /tʌɪ/ *verb*[1]. Pa. t. & pple **tied** /tʌɪd/; pres. pple **tying** /ˈtʌɪɪŋ/, ***tieing**. Also †**tye**.
[Old English *tīgan* late form of West Saxon *tīegan*, Anglian *tēgan*, from Germanic.]
1 a *verb trans.* Attach or fasten (*to* another person or thing, *together*) by passing around a cord, rope, etc., and knotting it; confine or fasten (*back, up*, etc.) in this way. OE. ▶**b** *verb trans.* Draw together the parts of (a thing) with a knotted cord etc.; fasten (a garment etc.) in this way, esp. with strings already attached. Also, make or form (a cord, ribbon, shoelace, etc.) into a knot or bow, esp. to fasten something. LME. ▶**c** *verb trans.* Bind so as to imprison; prevent, check, or hinder the free movement or working of. LME. ▶**d** *verb trans. SURGERY.* Bind and constrict (an artery or vein) with a ligature to stop the flow of blood through it. L16. ▶**e** *verb trans.* Make or form (a knot, bow, etc.) by tying. M17. ▶**f** *verb intrans.* Admit of being tied or fastened. M19.
2 a *verb trans.* Join or connect (*to*) with material or immaterial links; *spec.* (*a*) *ARCHITECTURE* hold (rafters etc.) together with a crosspiece or tie; (*b*) (now *dial.*) unite in marriage; (*c*) *N. Amer.* brace (a railway track) with sleepers. OE. ▶**b** *verb trans. MUSIC.* Connect (written notes) by a tie or ligature. Also, perform (two notes) as one unbroken note. L16. ▶**c** *verb intrans.* (Of a dog and bitch) remain linked or locked together for a period during copulation; (of a dog) be linked with a bitch in this way. E20. ▶**d** *verb trans. PHILATELY.* Associate (a stamp) with an envelope or cover by overprinting the cancellation on both. M20.
3 *verb trans.* Restrain or constrain *to* or *from* an action etc.; limit or restrict as to behaviour, location, conditions, etc. ME. ▶†**b** Enslave (*lit. & fig.*). LME–E17. ▶**c** Bind or oblige (*to* a person for a service, *to do* something). Usu. in *pass.* Now *arch. & dial.* L16. ▶**d** Restrict (a business, dealer, etc.) to a particular source for articles sold. Chiefly as TIED *adjective*[1]. E19. ▶**e** Impose conditions on (foreign aid), esp. by restricting use *to* purchases from the source country. Freq. as TIED *adjective*[1]. M20.
4 *verb trans.* Make sure, confirm, ratify. Long *rare* or *obsolete*. E17.

5 a *verb intrans.* Finish a contest etc. equal in score or place (*with* a competitor). L17. **▸b** *verb trans.* Match or equal (a competitor, an existing record or score) in a contest etc. Chiefly *N. Amer.* M18.
6 *verb intrans.* HUNTING. Of a hound: linger on the scent instead of following it swiftly; loiter, lag. L18.

📖 **1a** *Western Folklore* One end of the rope may be tied to a tree. I. McEWAN They tied my hands together behind my back. R. J. CONLEY Foster . . had . . tied his horse to the hitching rail. D. LEVY Her hair is silver and she ties it back with a green ribbon. **b** V. WOOLF They tied their shoes . . and drew the bows . . tight. BEVERLEY CLEARY Her mother . . tied her sash in a nice fat bow. **e** E. DARWIN We tie a knot on our handkerchiefs to bring something into our minds. **f** A. D. SEDGWICK Straightly falling dress . . tying . . at the waist with a loosely knotted sash. **2a** W. LITHGOW Peloponnesus . . is tied to the continent by an Istmus. S. O'CASEY It's a terrible thing to be tied to a woman that's always grousin'. W. MARCH Her life was forever tied to his. **3** R. HOLME The White Friers . . were tyed to Fasting, Silence, and Canonical hours. **5a** P. LARKIN Cream Cracker and another competitor had tied for third place. **b** *New York Times* Real Madrid tied Internazionale of Milan, 1–1.

Phrases: **can you tie that?** *US slang* = **can you beat it?** s.v. BEAT *verb*[1] 5. ***fit to be tied***: see FIT *adjective*. ***have one's hands tied***: see HAND *noun*. ***ride and tie***: see RIDE *verb*. **tie a can on**, **tie a can to** *slang* reject or dismiss (a person), stop (an activity). ***tie hand and foot***: see HAND *noun*. ***tie in knots***: see KNOT *noun*[1]. **tie one on** *slang* (chiefly *N. Amer.*) get drunk. **tie the hands of** deprive of freedom of action. **tie the knot** *colloq.* get married; perform the marriage ceremony. ***tie the rap on***: see RAP *noun*[1]. ***tied to the apron-strings of***: see APRON-STRING.
With adverbs & prepositions in specialized senses: **tie down** (*a*) fasten down or confine by tying; (*b*) *fig.* limit or restrict (*to*), esp. by responsibilities etc.; commit (*to*). **tie in** (*a*) join *to* an existing structure or network; associate or be associated (*with*); (*b*) be in accordance or agreement (*with*). **tie into** *US colloq.* get to work vigorously on; consume (food or drink) enthusiastically. **tie off** (*a*) close (a tubular vessel) by tying something around it; (*b*) secure or make fast (a rope or line). **tie to** *US colloq.* rely on, trust in, attach oneself to. **tie up** (*a*) bind or fasten securely with a cord or band; (*b*) confine or secure (a person or animal) by tying or binding (*to* a fixed object etc.); (*c*) obstruct, prevent from acting freely; engage in unavoidable business etc., hold up, (usu. in *pass.*); (*d*) moor (a ship or boat); (*e*) invest or reserve (capital) so as to prevent immediate use; (*f*) associate or unite *with* or *to*; (*g*) bring (an undertaking etc.) to a satisfactory conclusion; (*h*) be in accordance or connected *with*.

tie *verb*[2] var. of TYE *verb*[1].

tie- /tʌɪ/ *combining form.* E16.
[from TIE *noun*[1] or *verb*[1].]
In combs. in various relations and with various senses, as 'that ties', 'functioning as or pertaining to a tie'.
tie and dye = *tie-dye* (a) below. **tie-back** a cord or strip for tying back a dress or holding a drawn curtain back from a window. **tie-bar** a bar acting as a tie or connection. **tie-beam** a horizontal beam acting as a tie in a building etc. **tie belt** a belt fastened by tying. **tie-bolt** *noun & verb* (*a*) *noun* a bolt which ties together the component parts of a structure; (*b*) *verb trans.* fasten with tie-bolts. **tie-break**, **tie-breaker** a means of deciding a winner out of contestants involved in a tie or draw. **tie-breaking** *adjective* functioning as a tie-break. **tie clasp**, **tie clip**, **tie-pin** a small ornamental clasp or pin for holding a tie in place against a shirt. **tie down** the state of being tied or fixed down on the ground; a device used to tie something down. **tie-dye** *noun & verb* (*a*) *noun* a method of producing a variegated dyed pattern by tying string etc. to protect parts of the fabric from the dye; a garment etc. dyed in this way; (*b*) *verb trans.* dye by this process. **tie game**, **tie match** a game or match resulting in a tie or played to decide a tie. **tie-in** (chiefly *N. Amer.*) (*a*) a connection or association (*with*), a link-up; (*b*) a sale made conditional on the purchase of an additional item or items from the same supplier; (*c*) a joint promotion of related items; an advertisement appearing in two different media; a book, film, or promotional item produced to take advantage of the appearance of a related work in another medium; (*d*) (the making of) a connection between two pipelines or sections of pipeline. **tie-line** (*a*) a line measured on the ground to check the accuracy of the principal lines of a triangulated survey; (*b*) a telephone line connecting two private branch exchanges; (*c*) a pipeline or transmission line connecting two distribution systems or two parts of a single system. ***tie match***: see *tie game* above. **tie-off** (*a*) SHOWJUMPING = ***jump-off*** (c) s.v. JUMP *verb*; (*b*) MOUNTAINEERING a method of reducing the leverage on a piton or other equipment placed in a rock by tying a short loop of rope or tape to it. **tie-on** *adjective* that is fastened on by tying. ***tie-pin***: see ***tie clasp*** above. **tie rod** (*a*) a rod acting as a tie in a building etc.; (*b*) a rod in the steering gear of a motor vehicle. **tie-up** (*a*) a ribbon, tape, etc., used for tying something up, a tie, a garter; (*b*) (chiefly *US*) a building or stall in which cattle are tied up for the night; (*c*) the action or an act of tying something up; the condition of being tied up, an entanglement; *spec.* (chiefly *US*) a stoppage of work or business, esp. on account of a lockout or strike; a traffic hold-up; (*d*) a connection, an association; *spec.* (*US*) a telecommunication link or network. **tie-wig** (chiefly *Hist.*) a wig having the hair gathered together behind and tied with a knot of ribbon.

tied /tʌɪd/ *adjective*[1]. L16.
[from TIE *verb*[1] + -ED[1].]
1 That has been tied, bound, or joined. L16. **▸b** MUSIC. Of notes: marked with a tie or ligature. E18.
2 *spec.* **a** Of a public house etc.: bound to supply the products of one particular brewery only (opp. ***free***). Of a house, esp. a cottage: occupied subject to the tenant working for the owner, as on a farm. L19. **▸b** Of an international loan etc.: given subject to conditions, esp. that it should be used for purchases from the source country. M20.

tied /tʌɪd/ *adjective*[2]. E20.
[from TIE *noun*[1] + -ED[2].]
Wearing a necktie (of a specified kind).

tied *verb pa. t. & pple* of TIE *verb*[1].

tief /tiːf/ *verb & noun. W. Indies.* L18.
[Repr. a pronunc. of THIEF, THIEVE.]
▸A *verb trans. & intrans.* Steal. L18.
▸B *noun.* A thief. L19.

tieing *verb pres. pple*: see TIE *verb*[1].

t'ien /tɪˈɛn, tjɛn/ *noun.* E17.
[Chinese *tiān* (Wade–Giles *t'ien*).]
In Chinese thought: heaven; God.

tienda /tɪˈɛndə/ *noun. US.* M19.
[Spanish = tent, awning, shop.]
In the south-western US: a shop, a stall, *esp.* a general store.

tiens /tjɛ̃/ *interjection.* M20.
[French, imper. sing. of *tenir* hold.]
Expr. surprise.

tienta /ˈtjenta/ *noun.* E20.
[Spanish, lit. 'probe'.]
In Spain, an occasion at which young bulls are tested for qualities suitable for stud and fighting bulls.

tiento /ˈtjento/ *noun.* Pl. **-os** /-ɒs/. E20.
[Spanish, lit. 'touch, feel'.]
MUSIC. In sixteenth- and seventeenth-cent. Spanish music: a contrapuntal piece resembling a ricercar, orig. for strings and later for organ.

Tientsin /tjɛnˈ(t)sɪn, tɪnˈ(t)sɪn/ *noun & adjective.* E20.
[A city and port in NE China.]
(Designating) a carpet made in or shipped from Tientsin.

Tiepolesque /tɪˌɛpə(ʊ)ˈlɛsk/ *adjective.* L19.
[from *Tiepolo* (see below) + -ESQUE.]
Characteristic of or resembling the work of Giovanni Battista Tiepolo (1696–1770) or his son Domenico (1727–1804), Italian painters famous esp. for frescos.

tier /tɪə/ *noun*[1] *& verb.* L15.
[Old & mod. French *tire* sequence, rank, order, from *tirer* draw (out) from Proto-Romance.]
▸A *noun.* **1** A row, rank, or course, usu. each of a series of rows placed one above another in a structure, as in theatre seating; *spec.* (*a*) *Hist.* a row of guns or a bank of oars in a warship; (*b*) *US* a line *of* contiguous plots, counties, states, etc.; (*c*) a rank of organ-pipes controlled by one stop; (*d*) *Austral.* in Tasmania, a mountainous scarp; a mountain; †(*e*) a decorative row of precious stones or fur on a garment; (*f*) each of a number of successively overlapping ruffles or flounces on a garment. L15. **▸b** *transf.* & *fig.* A rank, a grade; a stratum. L16.
2 NAUTICAL. **a** A row of ships moored or anchored at a particular place; an anchorage or mooring for such a row. M18. **▸b** A circle of coiled cable; a place for stowing this. L18.

📖 **1** D. LESSING The amphitheatres . . empty spaces, surrounded by tiers of circular stone seating. **b** *attrib.*: *Times* A two-tier system providing a first class letter service.

▸B *verb trans.* Arrange or place in tiers. L19.
■ **tiered** *adjective* arranged in or having tiers (freq. as 2nd elem. of comb., of a specified kind or number) E19. **tierer** *noun* (*rare*) E19. **tiering** *adjective* (*rare*) rising in or forming tiers L19. **tiering** *noun* arrangement in, or a system of, tiers; the formation of tiers: M20.

tier /ˈtʌɪə/ *noun*[2]. Also **tyer**. ME.
[from TIE *verb*[1] + -ER[1].]
1 A cord etc. used for tying something, a tie. ME.
2 A person who ties something. M17.
3 A competitor who ties with another in a contest. E19.
4 A pinafore or apron covering the whole front of a dress. See also TIRE *noun*[1] 3. *US.* M19.

tierce /tɪəs, *in sense 6c foreign* tjɛrs/ *noun*[1]. Also **terce** /təːs/. See also TERCE. LME.
[Var. of TERCE.]
▸I †**1 a** = THIRD *noun* 3. *rare.* Only in LME. **▸b** = THIRD *noun* 2. L15–M17.
2 *Hist.* A unit of capacity equal to one-third of a pipe, usu. equivalent to 35 gallons (approx. 159 litres); a cask or vessel of this capacity; a cask containing a certain quantity (varying with the goods) of provisions. L15.
†**3** A band or company of soldiers. Cf. TERCIO 1. L16–M17.
4 CARDS. Esp. in piquet, a sequence of three cards of the same suit. Cf. QUINT *noun*[2]. M17.
5 FENCING. The third of eight recognized parrying positions, defending the upper sword-arm portion of the body, with the sword-hand in pronation; a parry in this position. L17.
6 MUSIC. **a** = THIRD *noun* 4. Now *rare* or *obsolete*. L17. **▸b** The note two octaves and a major third above a fundamental note; an organ-stop giving tones at this interval above the normal pitch. L17. **▸c** ***tierce de Picardie*** /*foreign* də pikardi/ [French = of Picardy], a major third used instead of a minor in the final chord of a piece in a minor key. E19.
7 HERALDRY. A charge composed of three triangles, usu. of different tinctures and arranged in fesse. E19.
4 tierce major the highest three cards of a suit. **tierce minor** the lowest three cards of a suit. **5** ***quart and tierce***: see QUART *noun*[2] 1.
▸II See TERCE.

tierce *noun*[2] var. of TIERCÉ *noun*.

tiercé /ˈtɪəːseɪ, *foreign* tjɛrse/ *noun.* Also **tierce** /tɪəs/. M20.
[formed as next.]
Esp. in France, a method of betting requiring the first three horses in a race to be named in the correct order; a horse-race at which this method prevails.

tiercé /tjɛrse/ *adjective.* E18.
[French, pa. pple of Old & mod. French *tiercer* divide into three parts.]
HERALDRY. Of a field: divided into three equal parts of different tinctures.
■ Also **tierced** /tɪəst/ *adjective* M19.

tiercel /ˈtɪəs(ə)l/ *noun.* Also **tercel** /ˈtəːs(ə)l/. ME.
[Old French *tercel*, *terçuel* (mod. *tiercel*) from Proto-Romance dim. of Latin *tertius* THIRD *adjective* etc.; perh. so named from the belief that the third egg of a clutch produced a male, or from the male being a third smaller than the female. Spelling and pronunc. infl. by mod. French or TIERCE *noun*[1].]
FALCONRY. The male of any kind of falcon; *esp.* that of the peregrine falcon (in full ***tiercel-gentle***) or of the goshawk.
■ Also **tiercelet** /-lɪt/ *noun* LME.

tierceron /ˈtɪəsərɒn/ *noun.* M19.
[French, from *tiers* third + *-er-* connective + *-on* -OON.]
ARCHITECTURE. A subordinate rib springing from the point of intersection of two main ribs of a vault.

tiers état /tjɛrz eta/ *noun phr.* L18.
[French.]
Chiefly *Hist.* The French Third Estate (see ***Third Estate*** s.v. ESTATE *noun*).

tiers monde /tjɛr mɔ̃d/ *noun phr.* M20.
[French.]
= THIRD WORLD.

Tietze /ˈtiːtsə/ *noun.* M20.
[A. Tietze (1864–1927), Polish surgeon.]
MEDICINE. ***Tietze's disease***, ***Tietze's syndrome***, a condition involving painful swelling of one or more costal cartilages without evident cause.

TIFF /tɪf/ *abbreviation.*
COMPUTING. Tagged image file format, an image format widely used in desktop publishing.

tiff /tɪf/ *noun*[1]. *colloq. & dial.* Now *rare.* M17.
[Origin unkn.]
1 Liquor, *esp.* poor, weak, or diluted liquor. M17.
2 A sip or little drink of punch, beer, or diluted liquor. E18.

†**tiff** *noun*[2]. *rare.* Only in E18.
[from TIFF *verb*[1].]
The manner of dressing or arranging one's hair, wig, etc.

tiff /tɪf/ *noun*[3]. *colloq.* E18.
[Prob. orig. dial. Cf. TIFT *noun*[1].]
1 A slight outburst or fit of temper or peevishness. Now *rare.* E18.
2 A slight or petty quarrel, a temporary ill-humoured disagreement. M18.

📖 **2** L. M. ALCOTT More friendly than ever after their small tiff. ***lovers' tiff***, ***lover's tiff***: see LOVER.

†**tiff** *verb*[1]. ME.
[Old French *tif(f)er* (mod. *attifer*) adorn. Cf. TIFT *verb*[1].]
1 *verb trans.* Adorn, dress, deck *out*, (one's person, hair, etc.). ME–M18.
2 *verb intrans.* Adorn or dress oneself. E18–E19.
¶ Not recorded between LME and M17.

tiff /tɪf/ *verb*[2] *intrans. colloq.* See also TIFT *verb*[3]. E18.
[from TIFF *noun*[3].]
Be in a tiff or bad temper (now *rare*); have a tiff or petty quarrel.

tiff /tɪf/ *verb*[3] *trans. colloq. & dial.* Now *rare.* M18. See also TIFT *verb*[2].
[Origin unkn.]
Drink (usu. liquor), esp. slowly; sip.

tiff /tɪf/ *verb*[4] *intrans. Anglo-Indian.* E19.
[App. back-form. or abbreviation.]
= TIFFIN *verb* 2.

tiffany /ˈtɪf(ə)ni/ *noun*[1] & *adjective.* E17.
[Old French *tifanie* from ecclesiastical Latin *theophania* from Greek *theophaneia*: see THEOPHANY.]
▶ **A** *noun.* **1** Orig., a kind of thin transparent silk. Now usu., a transparent or translucent gauze muslin. E17.
2 An article or garment made of tiffany. E17.
3 *fig.* Something insubstantial or trivial. *arch.* E17.
▶ **B** *attrib.* or as *adjective.* Made of or resembling tiffany; *fig.* (*arch.*) insubstantial, trivial, flimsy. E17.

Tiffany /ˈtɪf(ə)ni/ *noun*[2]. L19.
[See below.]
Used *attrib.* and in *possess.* to designate articles made by or associated with: (*a*) Charles L. Tiffany (1812–1902), goldsmith and founder of the fashionable New York jewellers Tiffany & Co.; (*b*) his son Louis C. Tiffany (1848–1933), art nouveau decorator noted for his iridescent glassware.

tiffin /ˈtɪfɪn/ *noun & verb. Anglo-Indian.* E19.
[App. from *tiffing* verbal noun of TIFF *verb*[3] in specialized use.]
▶ **A** *noun.* A light meal, esp. at midday; lunch. E19.
▶ **B** *verb.* **1** *verb trans.* Provide with tiffin or lunch. M19.
2 *verb intrans.* Take tiffin, have lunch. L19.

tiffle /ˈtɪf(ə)l/ *verb*[1]. *obsolete* exc. *dial.* LME.
[Dim. or frequentative of TIFF *verb*[1]: see -LE[3].]
†**1** *verb trans.* Deck out, dress, or adorn in a trifling or time-wasting way. LME–E16.
2 *verb intrans.* Busy oneself aimlessly, fiddle, potter about. LME.
■ **tiffler** *noun* LME.

tiffle /ˈtɪf(ə)l/ *verb*[2] *trans.* Chiefly *dial.* Also **tifle**. M17.
[App. imit.]
Disorder, disarrange, entangle; (foll. by *out*) unravel.

tiffy /ˈtɪfi/ *noun. Nautical slang.* L19.
[Contr. of ARTIFICER.]
An engine-room artificer.

tiffy /ˈtɪfi/ *adjective. colloq.* Now *rare.* E19.
[from TIFF *noun*[3] + -Y[1].]
Peevish, moody, bad-tempered.

tifle /ˈtʌɪf(ə)l/ *verb*[1] *intrans.* Chiefly *dial.* E18.
[Origin unkn.]
Of a horse: get a strain in the back. Chiefly as ***tifled*** *ppl adjective*, suffering from such a strain.

tifle *verb*[2] var. of TIFFLE *verb*[2].

tift /tɪft/ *noun*[1]. *Scot. & dial.* L17.
[App. var.]
1 = TIFF *noun*[3]. L17.
2 A puff or breath of wind etc. M18.

tift /tɪft/ *noun*[2]. *Scot. & north.* E18.
[Origin uncertain: perh. rel. to TIFT *verb*[1].]
Condition, order; mood, humour. Freq. in ***in tift***, in good condition or humour.

tift /tɪft/ *verb*[1] *trans. obsolete* exc. *dial.* LME.
[Origin uncertain: perh. var. of TIFF *verb*[1]. Cf. TIFT *noun*[2].]
Prepare, make ready, put in order; dress.

tift /tɪft/ *verb*[2] *trans. Scot. & dial.* E18.
[Var.]
= TIFF *verb*[3].

tift /tɪft/ *verb*[3] *intrans. obsolete* exc. *dial.* L18.
[Var.]
= TIFF *verb*[2].

TIG *abbreviation.*
ENGINEERING. Tungsten inert gas (with ref. to welding with a tungsten electrode in an inert gas atmosphere).

tig /tɪg/ *noun*[1]. E18.
[from next: cf. TICK *noun*[3], TAG *noun*[2] & *adjective.*]
1 A light or playful touch, a tap, a pat. *Scot. & north.* E18.
2 A fit of bad temper. *colloq.* (orig. *Scot.*). L18.
3 = TAG *noun*[2] 1. E19.

tig *noun*[2] var. of TYG.

tig /tɪg/ *verb.* Infl. **-gg-**. LME.
[Var. of TICK *verb*[1].]
1 *verb intrans.* Give light or playful touches; *fig.* trifle or toy *with*, interfere or meddle *with*. *Scot. & north.* LME.
2 *verb trans. & intrans.* Touch in the game of tig or tag; *fig.* (chiefly *dial.*) annoy or tease by light touches or petty provocations. E18.
3 *verb intrans.* Run from place to place as if chased. *dial.* M19.
Phrases: ***tar and tig***, ***tig and tar***: see TAR *verb*[1] 2.
■ **tigger** *noun* (*rare*) L19.

tige /tiːʒ/ *noun.* M17.
[French = stalk, from Latin TIBIA.]
A stem, a stalk; ARCHITECTURE the shaft of a column.

tiger /ˈtʌɪgə/ *noun.* Also (*arch.*) **tyger**. ME.
[Old & mod. French *tigre* from Latin *tigris* from Greek.]
1 A large powerful carnivorous feline, *Panthera tigris*, tawny yellow in colour with blackish transverse stripes and a white belly, found in several races (some now extinct) in parts of Asia. ME.
2 Any of various other wild animals of the cat family as the jaguar, the puma, the leopard. Also, any of several other unrelated carnivores resembling tigers in size, build, or markings. Usu. with qualifying word. LME.
3 An image or representation of a tiger; this used as a badge or crest; an organization, society, team, etc., having this badge; a member of such a society. LME.
4 a A savage or bloodthirsty person; a person of great energy, strength, or courage; *spec.* (*colloq.*) (in full ***fen tiger***) a native of the Fens. Also, a fierce or rapacious animal. LME. ▸**b** Tigerish spirit or character. E19. ▸**c** A person with an insatiable appetite *for* something, as work or alcohol. *colloq.* (chiefly *Austral. & NZ*). L19. ▸**d** Alcoholic drink. *dial. & Austral. slang.* E20. ▸**e** An outstanding sportsman or sportswoman; *esp.* a climber of great skill and confidence. *slang.* E20. ▸**f** Any of the more successful small economies of eastern Asia, *esp.* those of Hong Kong, Singapore, Taiwan, and South Korea. *slang.* L20.
†**5** An overdressed person. Also, a hanger-on, a parasite. *slang.* M18–M19.
6 *ellipt.* = ***tiger moth***, ***tiger-shark***, ***tiger-snake***, etc.: see below. L18.
7 a A usu. liveried boy acting as a groom, footman, or other servant. *slang.* Now *rare* or *obsolete.* E19. ▸**b** A person engaged in menial employment; *spec.* a sheep-shearer. *Austral. slang.* M19. ▸**c** A captain's personal steward. *Nautical slang.* E20.
8 A shriek or howl, freq. of the word 'tiger', terminating a prolonged and enthusiastic cheer. *US slang.* M19.
9 CARDS. **a** Faro. *US slang.* M19. ▸**b** The lowest possible hand at poker. L19.
10 Any of various implements. M19.

> 🕮 **1** W. BLAKE Tyger! Tyger! burning bright In the forests of the night. *Honey* He fought like a tiger for the part . . in the film. **3** *Daily Mail* The Tigers . . expect a bigger attendance . . even though the game is on the last Saturday before Christmas. **4a** T. K. WOLFE Young tigers, all . . desperate to become astronauts. **b** T. HOOK The . . nonsense which the . . fools talked, had nearly roused the tiger.

Phrases: **a tiger in one's tank** [from a petrol advertising campaign] energy, spirit, animation. BENGAL ***tiger***. ***blind tiger***: see BLIND *adjective.* **buck the tiger**, **fight the tiger** *US slang* at faro or roulette, play against the bank; gamble, play cards. **have a tiger by the tail** have entered into an undertaking etc. which proves unexpectedly difficult but cannot easily or safely be abandoned. **heraldic tyger** HERALDRY a creature represented as having the body and tail of a lion, the neck of a horse, and a head like that of a wolf with the upper jaw bearing a small tusk. MANCHURIAN ***tiger***. ***paper tiger***: see PAPER *noun & adjective.* **ride a tiger** take on a responsibility or embark on a course of action which subsequently cannot easily or safely be abandoned. ***royal*** BENGAL ***tiger***. ***sabretooth tiger***, ***sabre-toothed tiger***: see SABRE *noun*[1]. SCARLET ***tiger (moth)***. SIBERIAN ***tiger***. ***Tasmanian tiger***: see TASMANIAN *adjective.*

Comb.: **Tiger balm** (proprietary name for) a mentholated ointment widely used in Eastern medicine for a variety of conditions; **tiger barb** any of several freshwater fishes of the genus *Barbus* of an orange colour with dark stripes; **tiger beetle** a member of the family Cicindelidae of active predatory beetles having elongated legs and freq. striped wing-cases; **tiger bittern** any of several bitterns having striped (esp. orange and black) plumage, as *Tigriornis leucolophus* of W. Africa, *Gorsachius melanolophus* of southern Asia, and members of the genus *Tigrisoma* of S. America; **tiger-cat** (*a*) any of several medium-sized members of the cat family, as the serval, the margay; *esp.* the dark-striped *Felis tigrina* of Central and S. America; (*b*) = DASYURE; (*c*) a tabby cat, *esp.* one having vertical stripes; **tiger-eye** = ***tiger's-eye*** below; **tiger-finch** the red avadavat, *Amandava amandava*; **tigerfish** any of several predatory marine and freshwater fishes, typically noted for aggressiveness or for striped markings; *esp.*: (*a*) a very large characin of the African genus *Hydrocynus*, esp. *H. vittatus*, a silvery game-fish; (*b*) the S. American *Hoplias malabaricus*; (*c*) the Indo-Pacific *Therapon jarbua*, a food fish in Japan; (*d*) an Indo-Pacific scorpion fish, *Pterois radiata*; **tiger-flower** = TIGRIDIA; **tiger heron** = ***tiger bittern*** above; **tiger-hunter** a person who hunts tigers; *US slang* a gambler; **tiger-iris** = ***tiger-flower*** above; **tiger lily** a Far Eastern lily, *Lilium tigrinum*, grown for its orange-red flowers marked with purple-black spots; **tiger maple** *N. Amer.* a kind of maplewood with strongly contrasting light and dark lines in the grain; **tiger moth** any of several boldly patterned moths of the family Arctiidae, esp. *Arctia caja*, a large scarlet and brown moth spotted and streaked with white; **tiger-nut** the tuber of the plant *Cyperus esculentus*, of the sedge family, used locally as food; also called ***rush-nut***; **tiger prawn** *Austral.* a large prawn marked with dark bands, of the genus *Penaeus*; **tiger salamander** a large N. American salamander, *Ambystoma tigrinum*, which is blackish with yellow patches or stripes; **tiger's-eye** (*a*) a yellowish-brown semiprecious variety of quartz with a silky or chatoyant lustre, formed by replacement of crocidolite; (*b*) *US* a crystalline pottery glaze with gold-coloured reflections; **tiger-shark** any of several voracious sharks marked with stripes or spots, as *Galeocerdo cuvieri* of warm seas and *Stegostoma tigrinum* of the Indian Ocean; **tiger-snake** (*a*) a venomous Australian elapid snake of the genus *Notechis*, esp. the brown and yellow *N. scutatus*; (*b*) a slightly venomous striped southern African colubrid snake of the genus *Telescopus*, esp. *T. semiannulatus*; **tiger-stripe** a striped pattern resembling that of a tiger's coat; a thing, *esp.* a domestic cat, having such a stripe; **tiger-striped** *adjective* marked with a tiger-stripe; **tiger-ware** stoneware with a mottled brown glaze, orig. from Germany; **tiger-wolf** the spotted hyena; **tiger-wood** any of several streaked woods used for cabinet-making; *esp.* (*US*) that of the African walnut, *Lovoa trichilioides*.

■ **tigerhood** *noun* the state or condition of being a tiger M19. **tigerine** *adjective* (*rare*) = TIGRINE E19. **tigerism** *noun* (*slang*, now *rare*) the qualities or attributes of a tiger or overdressed person; vulgar ostentation or affectation: M19. **tiger-like** *adjective & adverb* (*a*) *adjective* resembling (that of) a tiger, tigerish; (*b*) *adverb* in a tigerish manner: M16. **tigerly** *adjective* (*rare*) tiger-like, tigerish M17. **tigery** *adjective* (*rare*) tigerish, tiger-like M19.

tiger /ˈtʌɪgə/ *verb.* L19.
[from the noun.]
1 *verb intrans.* Act or behave like a tiger; prowl. *rare.* L19.
2 *verb trans.* Mark like a tiger with lines or streaks of contrasting colour, stripe. M20.
■ **tigering** *noun* a striated condition or appearance M20.

tigerish /ˈtʌɪg(ə)rɪʃ/ *adjective.* L16.
[from TIGER *noun* + -ISH[1].]
1 Resembling or of the nature of the tiger; cruel, fierce; relentless, determined. L16. ▸**b** Loud, ostentatious. *slang.* Now *rare.* M19.
2 Inhabited by or infested with tigers. E19.
■ **tigerishly** *adverb* L19. **tigerishness** *noun* M19.

tiggy /ˈtɪgi/ *noun.* Chiefly *Scot. & dial.* M19.
[from TIG *noun*[1] + -Y[6].]
= TAG *noun*[2] 1. Also ***tiggy touchwood***.

tight /tʌɪt/ *adjective, adverb, & noun.* ME.
[Prob. alt. of THIGHT.]
▶ **A** *adjective.* **1 a** Of a person: orig. (*rare*), physically fit, healthy; later, vigorous, capable, admirable. *obsolete* exc. *Scot. & dial.* ME. ▸**b** Neatly arranged or dressed; trim, smart; of a neat compact build, shapely. *arch. & dial.* L17.
†**2** = THIGHT 1. *rare.* Only in LME.
†**3** = THIGHT 4. *rare.* LME–L18.
4 Of such close texture or construction as to be impervious to a (specified) fluid etc., impermeable. Freq. as 2nd elem. of comb. LME. ▸**b** *spec.* Of a ship: well caulked, not leaky, watertight. M16. ▸**c** *transf. & fig.* Uncommunicative; secret; *spec.* in the OIL INDUSTRY, (of a well) about which little information is released. M17. ▸**d** Of a building: well-insulated or sealed against heat loss etc.; poorly ventilated. L20.
5 Firmly fixed or fastened in place; securely put together; not easily moved; *fig.* faithful, steadfast, constant. E16. ▸**b** On terms of close friendship, intimate. *US slang.* M20.
6 Of a rope, surface, etc.: drawn or stretched so as to be tense, not loose or slack, taut. L16. ▸**b** *fig.* Strict, stringent; severe. L19. ▸**c** Of an organization, (esp. popular music) group or member, etc.: strict, disciplined, well coordinated. M20.
7 Produced by or requiring great exertion or pressure; difficult to deal with or manage (esp. in ***tight corner***, ***tight spot***, ***tight squeeze***, etc., a position of difficulty). M18.
8 Of a garment etc.: fitting closely, tight-fitting. Also, fitting too closely. L18. ▸**b** Of a person: tough, hard; aggressive. *US dial. & slang.* E20. ▸**c** Of ground etc.: allowing little room for manoeuvre, lacking space. Of a turn, curve, etc.: having a short radius. M20.
9 a Of a contest: close. Of a bargain: with little margin of profit. E19. ▸**b** Of a person: mean, stingy. *colloq.* E19. ▸**c** Of money, materials, etc.: not easily obtainable, scarce. Of a money market etc.: in which money is scarce. Of a person: poor, hard up, (*dial. & slang*). E19.
10 Drunk, tipsy. *colloq.* M19.
11 a Closely packed; close together. Also (SPORT), keeping the opposition contained and allowing them little chance to score. M19. ▸**b** Of language, art, etc.: terse, concise, condensed; well-structured; cramped, inhibited. L19. ▸**c** Of a schedule etc.: packed with engagements; demanding. Of time, space, etc.: limited, restricted. M20.

> 🕮 **4** G. BERKELEY A tight house . . and wholesome food. ***air-tight***, ***gas-tight***, ***watertight***, etc. **5** *Automobile Engineer* Seam welding . . can be adopted . . when a tight joint is required. **6** S. WYNTER Hair scraped back into a tight bun. *Practical Health* A tourniquet (tight band round the limb). **b** *Daily Telegraph* Tight Whitehall control over life in Britain. B. MOORE Security was tight for the hotel had been bombed last year. **7** A. HOPKINS Wondering how the hero is going to get out of a tight situation. **8** P. HAINES A pencil skirt so tight she could barely walk. **9a** *Greyhound Star* The final . . saw the tightest of finishes. **c** S. ELDRED-GRIGG The Stevensons laid the old man off and money was tight for a while. C. PHILLIPS Long-haired, haversacked . . and clinging to a tight budget. **11a** *Royal Air Force Journal* They lived in dread of our fighters, and . . kept a tight formation. **b** *Scientific American* This small book of tight argument. **c** T. PARKS I have an awfully tight deadline on this rubbish I'm writing.

Phrases: ***tight as a tick***: see TICK *noun*[1]. **ton tight**, **tun tight** the space occupied by a tun cask of wine, used as a measure of a ship's capacity or tonnage.
▶ **B** *adverb.* **1** Tightly, in a tight manner. L17.
2 ***as tight as*** —, as quickly or rapidly as —. Cf. TITE *adverb. US dial.* M19.
3 Close *up to*, *after*, or *on*. *dial. & colloq.* L19.

📖 **1** T. L. CUYLER The tighter I clung the safer I felt. **sit tight** remain in one's seat; maintain one's position or point of view firmly. ***sleep tight***: see SLEEP *verb*.

Special collocations & comb. (of adjective & adverb): **tight-ass** *slang* (chiefly *N. Amer.*) an inhibited, strait-laced, or (occas.) stingy person. **tight-assed** *adjective* (*slang*, chiefly *N. Amer.*) inhibited, strait-laced, excessively conventional; occas., stingy, mean. **tight back** BOOKBINDING a book with a cover stuck directly to its spine. **tight barrel**, **tight cask** a barrel for liquids. **tight building syndrome** = ***sick building syndrome*** s.v. SICK *adjective*. ***tight cask***: see ***tight barrel*** above. ***tight corner***: see sense A.7 above. **tight end** AMER. FOOTBALL (the position of) an offensive end who lines up close to the tackle. **tight-fisted** *adjective* mean, parsimonious, stingy. **tight-fitting** *adjective* (of a garment etc.) fitting (too) close to the body. **tight head** RUGBY FOOTBALL (the position of) the prop forward supporting the hooker on the opposite side of the scrum from the loose head. **tight junction** CYTOLOGY a specialized connection of two adjacent animal cell membranes such that the space usually lying between them is absent. **tight-laced** *adjective* (*a*) that is laced tightly; *Hist.* (constricted by) wearing tightly laced stays; (*b*) *fig.* excessively strict concerning morality or propriety, strait-laced. **tight-lacing** the action or process of lacing tightly; *spec.* (*Hist.*) the practice of wearing tightly laced stays to reduce or preserve the form of the waist. **tight-lipped** *adjective* having the lips firmly closed, esp. to restrain emotion or speech; determinedly reticent or uncommunicative, severe. ***tight ship***: see SHIP *noun* 1. ***tight spot***, ***tight squeeze***: see sense A.7 above. **tightwad** *slang* (chiefly *N. Amer.*) a mean or miserly person.

▶ **C** *noun*. **1** In *pl.* ▸**a** Tight-fitting breeches worn by men in the 18th and 19th cents. and still forming part of ceremonial court dress. **E19.** ▸**b** A woman's or girl's one-piece close-fitting stretchable undergarment of wool, nylon, etc., covering the legs and lower torso and worn in place of stockings. Also, a similar garment worn by dancers, acrobats, etc. **M19.**

2 a *ellipt.* An awkward situation, a tight spot. Chiefly in ***in a tight***. *US dial. & colloq.* **L19.** ▸**b** RUGBY FOOTBALL. = SCRUM *noun* 1. Chiefly in ***in the tight***. **E20.**

■ **tightish** *adjective & adverb* somewhat tight(ly) **M18.**

tight /tʌɪt/ *verb trans.* Now *dial.* **M16.**
[from TIGHT *adjective*.]
†**1** Make (a vessel etc.) watertight. Also, tighten, draw tight, compress. **M16–M17.**
2 Put in order, make tidy or neat. **L18.**

tighten /ˈtʌɪt(ə)n/ *verb*. **E18.**
[from TIGHT *adjective* + -EN[5].]
1 *verb trans.* Make tight or tighter; pull taut, fix tightly, secure; press closely together, compress; make more stringent or severe. Freq. foll. by *up*. **E18.**
2 *verb intrans.* Become tight or tense; be stretched tight or drawn close. Freq. foll. by *up*. **M19.**

📖 **1** S. MATEER The strings are tightened . . to produce a musical note when struck. C. EASTON The illness tightened its grip. ***tighten one's belt***: see BELT *noun*. ***tighten the purse-strings***: see PURSE-STRING. **2** W. CATHER Mrs Forrester's hand tightened on his arm.

■ **tightener** *noun* **E19.**

tightly /ˈtʌɪtli/ *adverb*. **LME.**
[from TIGHT *adjective* + -LY[2].]
In a tight manner; with constriction, tension, or compression; closely, tensely; firmly, securely; (now *dial.*) soundly, properly, well.

tightness /ˈtʌɪtnɪs/ *noun*. **E18.**
[formed as prec. + -NESS.]
The quality or condition of being tight; *spec.* constriction felt in breathing.

tightrope /ˈtʌɪtrəʊp/ *noun & verb*. **E19.**
[from TIGHT *adjective* + ROPE *noun*[1].]
▶ **A** *noun*. A rope or wire stretched tightly high above the ground, on which acrobats perform. Opp. ***slack-rope*** s.v. SLACK *adjective*. **E19.**

📖 *fig.*: *Jazz FM* To walk the tightrope between careful preparation and uninhibited abandonment.

▶ **B** *verb intrans. & trans.* Perform on a tightrope; walk along or traverse as if on a tightrope. **M19.**

tiglic /ˈtɪglɪk/ *adjective*. **L19.**
[from mod. Latin specific epithet of the tree *Croton tiglium*, whose seeds yield croton oil, from medieval Latin *tiglium*: see TILLY *noun*[1], -IC.]
CHEMISTRY. ***tiglic acid***, an unsaturated acid isomeric with angelic acid, obtained from croton oil and an intermediate in the breakdown of isoleucine; 2-methyl-*trans*-but-2-enoic acid, $C_5H_8O_2$.

tiglon *noun* var. of TIGON.

tignon /ˈtiːjɒn/ *noun*. **L19.**
[Louisiana French, from French *tigne* dial. var. of *teigne* moth.]
A handkerchief worn as a turban head-dress esp. in Louisiana by Creole women.

tigon /ˈtʌɪg(ə)n/ *noun*. Also **tiglon** /ˈtʌɪgl(ə)n/, **tigron** /ˈtʌɪgr(ə)n/. **E20.**
[Blend of TIGER *noun* and LION *noun*.]
An animal born of a mating between a tiger and a lioness. Cf. LIGER.

Tigray /ˈtɪgreɪ/ *noun & adjective*. **M19.**
[from base of TIGRINYA.]
= TIGRINYA.

Tigre /ˈtɪgreɪ/ *noun & adjective*. Also **Tigré**. **L19.**
[Tigre.]
▶ **A** *noun*. A Semitic language spoken in northern Ethiopia and adjoining parts of Sudan (distinguished from Tigrinya, spoken in Tigre itself). **L19.**
▶ **B** *adjective*. Of or pertaining to the province of Tigre in northern Ethiopia, or the language Tigre. **L20.**
■ **Tigrean** *noun & adjective* (*a*) *noun* a native or inhabitant of Tigre; (*b*) *adjective* of or pertaining to Tigre or its people: **M19.**

tigress /ˈtʌɪgrɪs/ *noun*. **L16.**
[from TIGER *noun* + -ESS[1], after French *tigresse*.]
1 A female tiger. **L16.**
2 *fig.* A fierce, cruel, or intensely passionate woman. **E18.**

tigridia /tʌɪˈgrɪdɪə/ *noun*. **M19.**
[mod. Latin (see below), from Latin or Greek *tigrid-* var. stem of *tigris* TIGER *noun* + -IA[1].]
Any of various bulbous chiefly Central American plants of the genus *Tigridia*, of the iris family, which are characterized by flamboyant, usu. red or orange flowers with a spotted base (also called ***tiger-flower***); *esp.* a plant of this genus grown for ornament, spec. *T. pavonia* (the peacock tiger-flower).

tigrine /ˈtʌɪgrʌɪn/ *adjective*. **M17.**
[Latin *tigrinus*, from *tigris* TIGER *noun* + -INE[1].]
Of, pertaining to, or resembling a tiger, esp. in marking or colouring, or (chiefly *fig.*) in powerful ferocity.

Tigrinya /tɪˈgriːnjə/ *noun & adjective*. **L19.**
[Tigrinya.]
(Of) a Semitic language spoken in the province of Tigre in northern Ethiopia. Also called ***Tigray***. Cf. TIGRE.

tigroid /ˈtʌɪgrɔɪd/ *adjective*. **L19.**
[Greek *tigroeidēs* like a tiger: see -OID.]
Resembling a tiger or tiger's skin; marked or striped like a tiger.
tigroid body ANATOMY (now *rare* or *obsolete*) = ***Nissl body***.
■ **tiˈgrolysis** *noun* = ***Nissl degeneration*** **E20.**

tigron *noun* var. of TIGON.

Tigua *noun & adjective* var. of TIWA.

Tigurine /ˈtɪgjʊrʌɪn/ *adjective & noun*. **M16.**
[Latin *Tigurinus* in *Tigurinus pagus* a district of ancient Helvetia.]
▶ **A** *adjective*. Of or pertaining to Zurich in Switzerland. Also = ZWINGLIAN *adjective*. **M16.**
▶ **B** *noun*. = ZWINGLIAN *noun*. *rare*. **L17.**

tika /ˈtiːkɑː, ˈtɪkɑː/ *noun*. Also **tikka**. **L19.**
[Hindi *ṭīkā*, Panjabi *ṭikkā*.]
Among Hindus, a mark on the forehead (esp. of a woman) indicating caste, status, or worn by both sexes as an ornament. Also ***tika dot***, ***tika mark***. Cf. TILAK.

tike *noun* var. of TYKE.

tiki /ˈtɪki/ *noun*. **L18.**
[Maori = image: cf. HEI-TIKI.]
A large wooden or small ornamental greenstone image of an ancestor or any human figure.
Comb.: **tiki bar** (orig. & chiefly *US*) a tropical-style bar as on islands of the South Pacific; **tiki torch** (orig. & chiefly *US*) an outdoor lamp burning solid fuel and consisting of a bowl on top of a pole inserted in the ground.

tikinagun /tɪkəˈnag(ə)n/ *noun*. *Canad.* **M19.**
[Cree *tikina:kan*.]
= ***cradle-board*** s.v. CRADLE *noun*.

tikka /ˈtɪkə, ˈtiːkə/ *noun*[1]. **M20.**
[Panjabi *ṭikkā*.]
INDIAN COOKERY. (A dish of) small pieces of meat or vegetable marinaded in spices and cooked on a skewer. Freq. with qualifying word, as ***chicken tikka***, ***lamb tikka***.

tikka *noun*[2] var. of TIKA.

tikka /ˈtiːkɑː, ˈtɪkə/ *adjective*. Also **ticca**. **E19.**
[Hindi *ṭhīkā* contract work, hire, fare.]
In the Indian subcontinent: engaged on contract, hired. Esp. in ***tikka gharry***, a hired carriage.

Tikopian /tɪˈkəʊpɪən/ *noun & adjective*. **M19.**
[from *Tikopia* (see below) + -AN.]
▶ **A** *noun*. A native or inhabitant of Tikopia, one of the Solomon Islands. **M19.**
▶ **B** *adjective*. Of or pertaining to Tikopia. **M19.**

til /tɪl/ *noun*. **M19.**
[Sanskrit *tila*.]
In the Indian subcontinent, the sesame plant, *Sesamum indicum*. Chiefly in ***til oil***, ***til seed***.
black til the ramtil, *Guizotia abyssinica*, which yields a similar oil-seed.

'til /tɪl/ *preposition & conjunction*. **M20.**
[Contr.]
= UNTIL *preposition & conjunction*.

tilak /ˈtɪlək/ *noun*. **L19.**
[Sanskrit *tilaka*.]
Among Hindus, a mark or large symbol on the forehead indicating caste, status, etc., or worn as an ornament. Cf. TIKA.

tilapia /tɪˈleɪpɪə/ *noun*. Pl. same, **-s**. **M19.**
[mod. Latin (see below), of unkn. origin.]
A freshwater cichlid fish belonging to the genus *Tilapia* or a related genus (esp. *Sarotherodon*), native to Africa but introduced elsewhere as a food fish or an aquarium species.

tilbury /ˈtɪlb(ə)ri/ *noun*. **L18.**
[In sense 1 from *Tilbury*, a town in Essex on the River Thames; in sense 2 from *Tilbury* inventor of the carriage.]
†**1** A sixpenny piece; sixpence. *slang*. **L18–E19.**
2 *Hist.* A light open two-wheeled carriage, fashionable in the first half of the 19th cent. **E19.**

tilde /ˈtɪldə/ *noun*. **M19.**
[Spanish from (with metathesis) Latin *titulus* TITLE *noun*.]
1 a The diacritic mark ˜ placed in Spanish above *n* to indicate the palatalized sound /ɲ/, as in *señor*; a similar mark in Portuguese above *a* and *o* and in some phonetic transcriptions to indicate nasality. **M19.** ▸**b** The diacritic mark ˜ placed above a letter to indicate contraction of a following *n* or *m*. **M20.**
2 This mark used as a symbol in mathematics and logic, chiefly to indicate negation. **M20.**

tile /tʌɪl/ *noun*.
[Old English *tiġele* (*tiġule*) corresp. to Old Saxon *tiegla* (Dutch *tegel*), Old High German *ziagal*, *-ala* (German *Ziegel*), Old Norse *tigl* from Latin *tegula* from Indo-European base meaning 'cover'.]
1 A thin slab of baked clay usu. of a regular shape and used in a series for covering a roof, paving a floor, lining a wall or fireplace, etc. Now also, similar covering made of other material such as concrete, glazed pottery, marble, cork, linoleum, etc. **OE.** ▸**b** METALLURGY. A small flat piece of earthenware used to cover a vessel in which metals are fused. **M18.** ▸**c** A hollow cylindrical or semi-cylindrical section made of clay, concrete, etc., used for draining land, roads, buildings, etc. **M19.**
2 The material of which tiles or bricks consist, baked clay; tiles collectively. Now *rare*. **ME.**
3 A hat. *slang*. **E19.**
4 A thin flat piece used in a game, esp. in mah-jong or Scrabble; a domino. **M19.**
5 MATH. A plane shape used in tiling. **L20.**

📖 **1** V. SACKVILLE-WEST The damaged tiles were . . half-stripped from the roof. E. WELTY The . . floral tiles that paved the front gallery. ***bathroom tile***, ***carpet tile***, ***cork tile***, etc. **2** DICKENS Well-paved roads, and foot-ways of bright tile.

Phrases: ***Dutch tile***: see DUTCH *adjective*. **have a tile loose** *slang* be slightly crazy. ***hip-tile***: see HIP *noun*[1]. **on the tiles** [after the nocturnal activities of cats] *slang* having a spree, on a debauch. ***Penrose tile***.
Comb.: **tile-drain** *noun & verb* (*a*) *noun* a drain constructed of tiles; (*b*) *verb trans.* drain (a field etc.) by means of tiles; **tile-drainage**: constructed of tiles; **tilefish** any of various fishes of the family Malacanthidae (or Branchiostegidae), having elongated or compressed bodies, esp. the brightly coloured *Lopholatilus chamaeleonticeps*, caught for food off the US Atlantic coast; **tile game**: played with flat pieces; **tile-hanging** tiling fixed vertically to an outside wall; **tile-kiln**: in which tiles are baked; **tile-maker** a person whose trade is the making of tiles; **tile-ore** cuprite; **tile-sherd** (*obsolete* exc. *dial.*) a broken piece or fragment of tile; **tile-work** (*a*) work consisting of tiles; (*b*) in *pl.* (treated as *sing.*), a factory making tiles; **tile-yard** a place where tiles are made.
■ **tilery** *noun* a place where tiles are made **M19.**

tile /tʌɪl/ *verb trans.* In sense 2 usu. **tyle**. **LME.**
[from the noun; in sense 2, back-form. from TILER.]
1 Cover with or as with tiles; overlay, overlap. Also foll. by *over*, *up*. **LME.**
2 FREEMASONRY. Protect (a lodge or meeting) from interruption and intrusion, so as to keep its proceedings secret, by placing a tiler or doorkeeper at the door. Also (*transf.*), bind (a person) to secrecy; keep (a meeting) strictly secret. Chiefly as **tyled** 2. **E18.**

tiled /tʌɪld/ *ppl adjective*. **LME.**
[from prec. + -ED[1].]
1 Covered, roofed, lined, or laid with tiles. **LME.** ▸**b** BOTANY & ZOOLOGY. Covered with or made of overlapping leaves, scales, etc.; imbricated. Now *rare* or *obsolete*. **M18.**
2 FREEMASONRY. Protected from interruption; kept secret. See TILE *verb* 2. **M18.**
3 Designating a fish dried and cured in the sun. *Scot.* **L18.**
4 COMPUTING. Pertaining to or involving the use of tiling to display windows (cf. TILING 4). **L20.**

📖 **1** D. BOGARDE The tiled floor was cool to her bare feet. **3** SIR W. SCOTT Dined . . on tiled haddocks very sumptuously.

tiler /ˈtʌɪlə/ *noun.* In sense 2 usu. **tyler**. ME.
[from TILE *noun, verb* + -ER[1].]
1 A person who makes or lays tiles. ME.
2 FREEMASONRY. A doorkeeper who keeps the uninitiated from intruding on the secrecy of a lodge or meeting. M18.

tilestone /ˈtʌɪlstəʊn/ *noun.*
[Late Old English *tigelstān*, from *tigele* TILE *noun* + *stān* STONE *noun*.]
†**1** (A tile or brick of) baked clay. LOE–L17.
2 GEOLOGY. A laminated flagstone which splits into layers thicker than slate, suitable for roofing-tiles; a tile made of this. M17.

tiling /ˈtʌɪlɪŋ/ *noun.* LME.
[from TILE *noun, verb* + -ING[1].]
1 The action of TILE *verb*; the covering of a roof etc. with tiles. LME.
2 Work consisting of tiles; *collect.* the tiles forming the covering of a roof, floor, etc. E16. ▸**b** MATH. A way of arranging identical plane shapes so that they completely cover an area without overlapping. L20.
3 The process of tile-draining land. M20.
4 COMPUTING. A technique for displaying several non-overlapping windows on a screen. L20.
2b PENROSE *tiling*.

till /tɪl/ *noun*[1]. LME.
[Origin unkn.]
1 A small box or compartment forming part of a larger box, chest, or cabinet, and used for keeping valuables, documents, etc.; a drawer. Now *rare*. LME. ▸**b** *spec.* A drawer or similar receptacle for money in a shop or bank, in which cash for daily transactions is temporarily kept; *esp.* a cash register. (The usual sense.) L17.
2 PRINTING. = SHELF *noun*[1] 3a. E19.
1b *have one's hand in the till*: see HAND *noun*.
Comb.: **till-alarm** a device on a cash till by which a bell is automatically rung when the till is opened; **till-roll** a roll of paper recording an account of the transactions made at the till to which it is attached; **till-tapper** *rare* a person who steals money from a till.

till /tɪl/ *noun*[2]. E17.
[Origin unkn.]
PRINTING. In early wooden hand printing-presses, a shelf, divided in two, that clasps the hose and causes it to descend perpendicularly, without any play.

till /tɪl/ *noun*[3]. Orig. & chiefly *Scot.* L17.
[Origin unkn. Cf. THILL *noun*[2].]
1 Shale. *rare.* L17.
2 A stiff clay, more or less impervious to water, esp. as forming a subsoil difficult to work. M18. ▸**b** GEOLOGY. = ***boulder-clay*** s.v. BOULDER *noun*. M19.

till /tɪl/ *verb*[1].
[Old English *tilian* = Old Frisian *tilia* get, cultivate, Old Saxon *tilian*, *tilon* obtain (Dutch *telen* produce, cultivate), Old High German *zilōn*, *zilēn* (German *zielen* aim, strive), Gothic *gatilon* from Germanic base also of TILL *preposition & conjunction*.]
▶ **I** Labour, cultivate.
†**1** *verb intrans.* Strive, exert oneself, work. OE–ME.
†**2** *verb trans.* Labour or seek after, provide; obtain by effort. Later also, get, obtain. OE–LME.
†**3** *verb trans.* Attend to medically; treat (a patient or disease), take care of. Only in OE.
4 *verb trans.* & (*rare*) *intrans.* Do work such as ploughing, manuring, etc., on (land) in preparation for growing crops; cultivate (soil, a field, etc.). ME. ▸**b** *verb trans. spec.* Plough (land). LME.
†**5** *verb trans.* Produce or raise (a crop); tend and cultivate (a plant) to promote growth. ME–L15.
6 *verb trans.* Improve and develop (a person's mind, a field of knowledge, a virtue, etc.). ME.
▶ **II** Prepare.
7 *verb trans.* Spread (a net), set (a trap). Also, set in any position. Now *dial.* ME.
†**8** *verb trans.* Pitch (a tent); set (a sail). LME–E17.
■ **tillable** *adjective* able to be tilled or cultivated; *esp.* able to be ploughed: L16.

till /tɪl/ *verb*[2] *trans. rare.* M19.
[from TILL *noun*[1].]
Put (money) into a till.

till /tɪl/ *preposition & conjunction.*
[Old English (Northumbrian) *til* preposition with dat. = Old Frisian *til* (with dat.), Old Norse *til* (with genit.); prob. from adverbial use of Germanic noun meaning 'aim, goal' (cf. TILL *verb*[1]) repr. by Old English *till* fixed point. Cf. UNTIL, UNTO.]
▶ **A** *preposition.* **1** To (expressing position, direction, relationship, etc.); as far as. Now only *Scot. & north.* OE.
2 a Onward to (a specified time); up to the time of (an event); during the time before. Freq. with adverb or adverbial phr. of time. ME. ▸**b** Used in stating the time of day: to. *US.* M20.
3 Introducing an inf.: to. Now only *Scot.* ME.
4 After a neg.: before (a specified time). Cf. UNTIL *preposition* 5. L16.

📖 **1** T. FULLER He was . . restored till his liberty and archbishoprick. **2a** C. KINGSLEY A plant till then unknown to me. J. BUCHAN I had not . . heard his name till that afternoon. **b** H. KURATH In . . the Midland . . *quarter till eleven* is current. **3** SIR W. SCOTT An ye had wussed till hae been present. **4** DEFOE [He] begged of me not to go on shore till day.

▶ **B** *conjunction.* **1** To the time that; up to the point when. Formerly also foll. by *that*. ME.
2 = UNTIL *conjunction* 2. ME.
†**3** During the time that; so long as; while. ME–E17.
4 After a neg.: before the time that; before; when. Cf. UNTIL *conjunction* 3. Now *dial. & US.* LME.
5 In order that (one) may, so that. *Scot. & Anglo-Irish.* L19.

📖 **1** SPENSER They traveiled . . Till that at last they to a Castle came. V. WOOLF We talked till I left at 8. **2** MRS H. WARD Bessie ran till she was out of breath. **4** W. LITHGOW Scarcely were wee well advanced in our way, till wee were beset with . . three hundred Arabs. **5** A. J. CRONIN Come till I give ye a grand, big hug.

Phrases: **till and frae** (long *obsolete* exc. *Scot.*) to and fro. ***up till***: see UP *adverb*[1].

tillage /ˈtɪlɪdʒ/ *noun.* L15.
[from TILL *verb*[1] + -AGE.]
1 a The state or condition of being tilled or cultivated. L15. ▸**b** The operation or art of tilling land to prepare it for raising crops; cultivation, agriculture, husbandry. M16.
2 Tilled or ploughed land; land under crops as opp. to pasturage; crops growing on tilled land. M16.
3 The improvement and development of the mind or spirit. M16.
4 Sexual intercourse with a woman. *poet. rare.* L16.

📖 **4** SHAKES. *Sonn.* Where is she so fair whose unear'd womb Disdains the tillage of thy husbandry?

Tillamook /ˈtɪləmuːk/ *noun & adjective.* Also (earlier) **Killa-** /ˈkɪlə-/. E19.
[Chinook *t'ílilmuks* people of Nehalem; the final *-s* was taken in English as the pl. ending (Chinook pl. *-uks*). In sense 3 directly from *Tillamook* County, NW Oregon.]
▶ **A** *noun.* Pl. **-s**, same.
1 A member of a Salish people formerly inhabiting coastal areas of north-west Oregon. E19.
2 The Salish language of this people. E20.
3 In full ***Tillamook cheese***. (Proprietary name for) a crumbly, sharp-tasting variety of Cheddar cheese made in Tillamook. Chiefly *N. Amer.* E20.
▶ **B** *adjective.* Of or pertaining to the Tillamooks or their language. M19.

tillandsia /tɪˈlandzɪə/ *noun.* M18.
[mod. Latin (see below), from Elias *Tillands* (1640–93), Swedish botanist + -IA[1].]
Any of various bromeliads of the genus *Tillandsia* of tropical and subtropical America, which includes epiphytes such as Spanish moss, *Tillandsia usneoides*.

tiller /ˈtɪlə/ *noun*[1].
[Old English *tilia*, from *tilian* TILL *verb*[1]; later from TILL *verb*[1] + -ER[1].]
1 A person who tills soil or cultivates a crop or plant; a farmer, a farm labourer. Now *arch.* or *literary.* OE.
2 An implement or machine for breaking up soil; a mechanical cultivator. M20.

tiller /ˈtɪlə/ *noun*[2]. LME.
[Anglo-Norman *telier* weaver's beam from medieval Latin *telarium* from Latin *tela* web: see -ER[2].]
1 ARCHERY. In a wooden crossbow: a beam grooved to hold the arrow or drilled for the bolt; the stock. In a longbow: the place on the limb which is the actual point of balance of forces of the bow. LME. ▸**b** A device made of a straight piece of wood with a notch at one end and notches on the upper side in which a bow is placed and drawn so as to bend the bow and balance it. Cf. TILLERING. M16. ▸†**c** A stock or shaft fixed to a longbow to enable it to be used as a crossbow and to provide greater convenience or precision of aim. Also, a bow fitted with such a tiller. L16–L17.
2 NAUTICAL. A horizontal bar attached to the head of a vessel's rudder, acting as a lever by which the rudder is moved for steering. LME.
Comb.: **tiller-chain** NAUTICAL: serving the same purpose as a tiller-rope; **tiller-head** NAUTICAL the extremity of the tiller to which are secured the two ends of the tiller-rope or tiller-chain; **tiller-lines** NAUTICAL two lines or ropes fastened each to one arm of the tiller in a vessel; **tillerman** *US* a fire-fighter who controls the rear portion of a long ladder-truck; **tiller-rope** NAUTICAL (*a*) a rope connecting the tiller-head with the drum or barrel of a vessel's steering-gear; (*b*) a rope leading from the tiller-head to each side of the deck, to assist in steering in rough weather; (*c*) in *pl.*, = ***tiller-lines*** above; **tiller soup** *Nautical slang* the wielding of a tiller as a threat by the coxswain to encourage a crew.
■ **tillering** *noun* (ARCHERY) the putting of a bow on a tiller to stretch or bend, and thus balance, the bow M16. **tillerless** *adjective* (*rare*) L19.

tiller /ˈtɪlə/ *noun*[3] & *verb.* Also (*dial.*) **teller** /ˈtɛlə/, **tellow** /ˈtɛləʊ/. M17.
[App. repr. Old English *telgor*, *tealgor*, *telgra* extended from *telga* branch, bough, twig.]
▶ **A** *noun.* †**1** A young tree, a sapling; *esp.* one arising from the stool of a felled tree. Now chiefly *dial.* M17.
2 A lateral shoot from the base of the stem, esp. of a cereal grass. Also ***tiller shoot***. M18.
▶ **B** *verb intrans.* Esp. of a cereal grass: send out tillers or lateral shoots. Also foll. by *out*. L17.
■ **tillered** *adjective* having lateral shoots, *esp.* several from one root M18.

tillet /ˈtɪlɪt/ *noun.* Also **tillot** /ˈtɪlət/. LME.
[App. from Old French *tellette* var. of *teilete*, *toilete* a wrapper of cloth: cf. TOILET *noun*.]
A coarse linen fabric formerly used for linings, wrapping up textile fabrics, and making awnings.

tilleul /tiˈjəːl/ *noun & adjective.* M16.
[French, from Latin dim. form from *tilia* linden.]
▶ **A** *noun.* **1** A lime or linden tree. M16.
2 A pale yellowish-green colour. Also ***tilleul green***. L19.
▶ **B** *adjective.* Of a pale yellowish-green colour. L19.

Tilley lamp /ˈtɪlɪ lamp/ *noun phr.* M20.
[Name of the manufacturers.]
(Proprietary name for) a portable oil or paraffin lamp in which air pressure is used to supply the burner with fuel.

tillicum /ˈtɪlɪkəm/ *noun.* *N. Amer.* (chiefly *dial.*). M19.
[Chinook Jargon *tilikum* people from Chinook *tilxam*, from *t-* pl. prefix + *ilxam* village.]
1 A member of one's own tribe or people; in *pl.*, the people, ordinary people. M19.
2 A friend. M19.

tillite /ˈtɪlʌɪt/ *noun.* E20.
[from TILL *noun*[3] + -ITE[1].]
GEOLOGY. A sedimentary rock composed of glacial till compacted into hard rock.
■ **tilloid** *noun* (GEOLOGY) a sedimentary rock resembling a tillite but not known to be of glacial origin M20.

tillot *noun* var. of TILLET.

tilly /ˈtɪli/ *noun*[1]. Now *rare.* E18.
[French *tilli* from medieval Latin *tiglium* (Italian *tiglia*). Cf. TIGLIC.]
More fully ***tilly-seed***. The seed of the tree *Croton tiglium*, which yields croton oil.

tilly /ˈtɪli/ *noun*[2]. E20.
[Irish *tuilleadh* additional quantity, supplement.]
In Ireland and places of Irish settlement, an additional article or amount unpaid for by the purchaser as a gift from the vendor.

tilly /ˈtɪli/ *adjective.* L18.
[from TILL *noun*[3] + -Y[1].]
Composed of, or of the nature of, till or stiff clay.

tilly-vally /ˈtɪlɪvali/ *interjection. arch.* E16.
[Origin unkn.]
Nonsense! Fiddlesticks!

tilma /ˈtɪlmə/ *noun.* M19.
[Mexican Spanish, from Nahuatl *tilmatli*.]
A simple cloak or blanket secured with a knot, worn by Mexican Indians.

Tilsit /ˈtɪlsɪt/ *noun.* M20.
[Former name of Sovetsk, near the Baltic coast.]
More fully ***Tilsit cheese***. A semi-hard cheese orig. made at Tilsit.
■ Also **Tilsiter** /ˈtɪlsɪtə/ *noun* M20.

tilt /tɪlt/ *noun*[1]. Orig. †**teld**.
[Old English *teld* = Old High German *zelt* (German *Zelt*) tent, perh. infl. by TENT *noun*[1].]
1 A covering of coarse cloth, orig. of hair-cloth; an awning; a tent, a tabernacle. OE. ▸**b** *spec.* An awning or cover for a boat, cart, or motor vehicle, usu. of canvas or tarpaulin. ME.
2 In Labrador and Newfoundland: a fisherman's or woodcutter's hut; a lean-to shelter. E17.

tilt /tɪlt/ *noun*[2]. E16.
[from next.]
▶ **I 1 a** *Hist.* A combat for exercise or sport between two knights or armed men on horseback with lances, the aim of each being to throw his opponent from the saddle; a joust. Also, the exercise of riding with a lance at a mark, as the quintain. E16. ▸**b** *transf.* A combat, a contest, a duel; a debate, a public dispute or discussion. M16. ▸**c** A thrust of a weapon, as at a tilt; now *esp.* (*fig.*) a forceful effort, a verbal attack. E18.
2 *Hist.* A place for holding tilts or jousts; a tilting ground or yard; a barrier in such a place. E16.

📖 **1b** *Irish Press* Mayo could lose . . in tomorrow's championship tilt with Roscommon. **c** E. PAUL After a lively tilt in the newspapers . . the plan was . . abandoned.

▶ **II 3** The action of tilting or condition of being tilted; a sudden divergence from the normal vertical or horizontal position; inclination upward or downward. Earliest in ***on the tilt, upon the tilt***, in a tilted position, raised on one side. M16. ▸**b** *spec.* in GEOLOGY. An abrupt upheaval of strata to a considerable angle from the horizontal. M19.

4 a A slope of the surface of the ground. M19. ▸**b** *fig.* An inclination; a bias. L20.

5 = TILT-HAMMER. M19.

6 A device used in N. America in fishing through a hole in the ice, in which a stick or crosspiece is tilted up when the fish takes the hook. Also called ***tip-up***. L19.

7 On a pinball machine, a device that stops the game if the machine is jarred or lifted. Also ***tilt mechanism***. M20.

8 CINEMATOGRAPHY & TELEVISION. The upward or downward pivoting movement of a camera across the screen. M20.

> 🕮 **3** C. SAGAN The . . changing direction between the tilt of the Earth's rotational axis and its orbit. *Raritan* Her head angled coyly to one side in a suggestive tilt. **4b** R. H. TAWNEY The enormous tilt of economic power from south and east to north and west.

▸**III 9** The American black-necked stilt, *Himantopus mexicanus* (from its jerking motion). Cf. ***tilt-up*** (a) s.v. TILT *verb*^{1}. *US. rare.* E19.

Phrases: **at full tilt**, **full tilt** at full speed and with direct thrust; with full force or impetus. **light up and say 'tilt'** *colloq.* register by one's look or reaction that something is wrong. ***on the tilt***: see sense 3 above. **run at tilt**, **run at the tilt**, **run tilt** ride in a tilt or joust. **say 'tilt'** = ***light up and say 'tilt'*** above. ***upon the tilt***: see sense 3 above.

Comb.: **tilt cab** a cab of a lorry etc., which can tilt forwards; **tilt guard** = ***Tilt Yard guard*** below; **tiltmeter** GEOLOGY an instrument for measuring oblique shifts in the position of a mass of rock, etc; **tilt rotor** AERONAUTICS a tilting rotor (see TILT *verb*^{1}); an aircraft fitted with these (freq. *attrib.*); **tilt-top** *adjective* having a top that tilts; **tilt-wheel** *US* a steering wheel that tilts; **tilt-wing** *adjective & noun* (designating) an aircraft with wings that tilt; **tilt-yard** *Hist.* a yard or enclosed space for tilts and tournaments; **Tilt Yard guard** the guard mounted on the site of the tilt-yard of the old Royal Palace of Whitehall in London.

tilt /tɪlt/ *verb*^{1}. LME.
[Perh. repr. Old English form rel. to *tealt* unsteady (whence *tealtian* totter), or of Scandinavian origin (cf. Norwegian *tylten* unsteady, Swedish *tulta* totter). Branch III is from TILT *noun*^{2}, branch IV from TILT-HAMMER.]

▸**I** †**1** *verb trans.* Cause to fall; push over, throw down; overthrow, overturn. LME–L16.

†**2** *verb intrans.* Fall over, tumble; be overthrown. Only in LME.

3 *verb intrans.* Move unsteadily up and down; *esp.* (of waves or a ship at sea) pitch. L16.

▸**II 4 a** *verb trans. & intrans.* (Cause to) lean from the vertical or incline from the horizontal; move into a slanted position, slope; tip *up*. Also (*fig.*), incline towards a particular opinion. L16. ▸**b** *verb trans.* Pour or empty *out* (the contents of a container); cause (contents) to flow to one side by tipping the container. E17.

5 *verb trans.* CINEMATOGRAPHY & TELEVISION. Move (a camera) in a vertical plane. E20.

> 🕮 **4a** ALDOUS HUXLEY Leaning backwards, his chair tilted on its hind legs. I. ASIMOV The desk top tilted to an angle of forty-five degrees. F. KING She tilted her head back to gaze up at the . . sky. *New Yorker* He is . . tilting towards a new economic course. **b** A. HOLLINGHURST I tilted out the rest of the champagne.

▸**III 6** *verb intrans.* **a** *Hist.* Engage in a tilt or joust. L16. ▸**b** Engage in a contest, combat, or dispute (*with*); strike *at* with a weapon; argue *against*. L16. ▸**c** Charge into a place or at a person; run *against*, rush or burst *in*, *through*, etc. M19.

7 *verb trans.* **a** Drive or thrust with violence; rush at, charge. L16. ▸**b** Poise (a lance) for a thrust. E18.

> 🕮 **6b** *New Yorker* She was . . tilting against . . what the Eurocrats . . were proposing. ***tilt at windmills***: see WINDMILL *noun* 1.

▸**IV 8** *verb trans.* Forge or work with a tilt-hammer. E19.

Phrases: **tilting fillet** a wedge-shaped slip of wood placed under the front edge of the first or lowest course of slates in a roof, to give that course the same inclination as in the courses above. **tilting furnace** a furnace with a tilting mechanism for pouring. **tilting rotor** AERONAUTICS a rotor which may be tilted to function as a propeller during cruising flight.

Comb.: **tilt-up** *noun & adjective* (*a*) *noun* (*US*) = PEETWEET; (*b*) *adjective* that tilts up; tip-up.

■ **tiltable** *adjective* M20.

tilt /tɪlt/ *verb*^{2} *trans.* L15.
[from TILT *noun*^{1}.]
Cover with a tilt or awning.

tilt-boat /ˈtɪltbəʊt/ *noun.* LME.
[from TILT *noun*^{1} (or short for *tilted*) + BOAT *noun*.]
A large rowing boat having a tilt or awning, formerly used on the River Thames, esp. as a passenger boat between London and Gravesend.

tilter /ˈtɪltə/ *noun.* L16.
[from TILT *verb*^{1} + -ER^1.]

1 A person who tilts or jousts; a combatant, a contestant; a participant in a dispute or critical attack. L16. ▸†**b** A rapier; a sword. *slang.* L17–E18.

2 A person who or thing which inclines or slopes (something) up or down; *spec.* (*a*) an apparatus for tilting a cask to empty it without stirring up the dregs; (*b*) a worker who empties out coal into trucks at a pit's mouth. M17.

3 A person who works with a tilt-hammer. E19.

tilter /ˈtɪltə/ *verb intrans. Scot. & dial.* M19.
[App. frequentative of TILT *verb*^{1}: cf. Old English *tealtrian* be unsteady, shake, totter, extended form of *tealtian*. See -ER^5.]
Sway up and down.

tilth /tɪlθ/ *noun & verb.*
[Old English *tilþ*, *tilþe*, from *tilian* TILL *verb*^{1} + -TH^1.]

▸**A** *noun.* **1** Labour or work in the cultivation of the soil; tillage, agricultural work, husbandry. OE. ▸**b** The condition of being under cultivation or tillage; *transf.* the condition of land under tillage. L15. ▸**c** An act of tilling; a ploughing or other agricultural operation. M16.

†**2** The result or produce of tillage; crops, harvest. OE–L18.

3 *fig.* The cultivation of knowledge, morality, the mind, etc. ME.

4 Land under cultivation, arable land; a piece of tilled land, a ploughed field. ME. ▸**b** The prepared surface soil; the depth of soil dug or cultivated. M18.

▸**B** *verb trans.* Till, cultivate. Now *rare* or *obsolete*. LME.

tilt-hammer /ˈtɪlthamə/ *noun.* M18.
[from TILT *noun*^{2} or *verb*^{1} + HAMMER *noun*.]
A heavy pivoted hammer used in forging, raised by mechanical means and allowed to drop on the metal being worked.

TIM /tɪm/ *noun*^{1}. M20.
[First three letters from TIME *noun*.]
Hist. The dialling code formerly used to obtain the telephone service giving the correct time in words; this telephone service itself.

Tim /tɪm/ *noun*^{2}. *Scot. colloq.* Freq. *derog.* M20.
[Abbreviation of male forename *Timothy*.]
(A nickname for) a Roman Catholic; *spec.* a supporter of Glasgow Celtic football club.

Tim. *abbreviation.*
Timothy (New Testament).

timar /tɪˈmɑː/ *noun.* L16.
[Turkish, from Persian *tīmār* attendance, custody.]
Hist. **1** = TIMARIOT. L16.
2 In the Turkish feudal system, a fief held by military service. E17.

timarchy /ˈtʌɪmɑːki/ *noun. rare.* M17.
[Greek *timarkhia*, from *timē* honour, value + *arkhia* government.]
= TIMOCRACY.

timariot /tɪˈmɑːrɪət/ *noun.* E17.
[French, from Italian *timariotto* from Persian *tīmār*: see TIMAR, -OT^2.]
Hist. The holder of a timar.

timbal /ˈtɪmb(ə)l/ *noun.* Also **tym-**. L17.
[French *timbale* alt. after *cymbale* cymbal of †*tamballe* from Spanish *atabal* (with assim. to *tambour* drum): see ATABAL.]
1 A kettledrum. *arch.* L17.
2 = TIMBALE 2. E20.

timbale /tamˈbɑːl, tɛ̃bal (*pl. same*); *in sense 3* tɪmˈbɑːli/ *noun.* E19.
[French: see prec. In sense 3, perh. from Spanish *timbal*, pl. *timbales* of same origin.]

1 A drum-shaped dish made of finely minced meat, fish, etc., cooked in a pastry crust or a mould. Also (in full ***timbale mould***), the mould or crust in which this dish is served. E19.

2 ENTOMOLOGY. A membrane which forms part of the sound-producing organ in various insects, as the cicada. M19.

3 In *pl.* Two single-headed drums played as a pair with drumsticks. E20.

timber /ˈtɪmbə/ *noun*^{1} *& adjective.*
[Old English *timber* = Old Frisian *timber*, Old Saxon *timbar*, Old High German *zimbar* (German *Zimmer* room), Old Norse *timbr*, from Germanic (cf. Gothic *timrjan* build, *timrja* builder), from Indo-European base meaning 'build'.]

▸**A** *noun.* †**1** A building, a structure, a house. OE–ME.

2 Building material; the matter of which anything is built or composed; material, stuff. Now only *spec.*, wood as a building material. OE. ▸**b** Wood as a substance, or as the material of small articles. Now *Scot. & dial.* M16.

3 *sing. & (rare) in pl.* The wood of large growing trees able to be used for structural purposes; the trees themselves. OE. ▸**b** LAW. Trees growing on land and forming part of a freehold inheritance, *esp.* oak, ash, or elm trees of the age of twenty years or more. M18. ▸**c** *collect.* Trees in their natural state not considered as building material; an area of woodland or forest. L18.

4 A beam or piece of wood forming or capable of forming part of any structure. ME. ▸**b** NAUTICAL. In *pl.* The pieces of wood composing the ribs, bends, or frames of a ship's hull. M18.

5 Any object made wholly or chiefly of wood, as a ship, a gate or fence jumped in hunting, a cricket wicket, etc. Freq. *colloq.* LME. ▸**b** *spec.* A wooden leg; *transf.* a leg. *slang.* E19.

6 Orig., bodily structure, frame, build. Later, personal quality or character; suitable quality or character for a specified office etc. Chiefly *US.* E17.

7 As *interjection.* A warning call that a tree is about to fall. E20.

> 🕮 **2** M. EDWARDES Buy the timber, saw it into logs, and sell it. ***rift timber***: see RIFT *noun*^{1} 3. ***rough timber***: see ROUGH *adjective*. ***round timber***: see ROUND *adjective*. **3** *Forestry* Epicormic shoots which adversely affect the quality . . of the timber. **c** *Times* The timber attenuates into a sub-Arctic forest. ***TALL timber***. **4** J. FRAME The timbers of the house . . had 'settled' and shrunk. **b** M. HOCKING Groaned like the straining of a ship's timbers in a gale. ***shiver my timbers***: see SHIVER *verb*^{1} 1. **5** *Sunday Times* Ability to hit timber . . earns Indian spinners respect wherever cricket is played. *Irish Times* The . . horse has experience over timber. **6** R. S. CHURCHILL His parliamentary stature . . proved that he was of Cabinet timber.

▸**B** *adjective.* **1** Made or consisting of wood; wooden. E16.

2 Unmusical; dull, wooden; unimpressionable. *Scot.* E19.

Comb.: **timber beast** *N. Amer.* a logger; **timber-beetle** any beetle which, as a larva or adult, is destructive to timber; **timber berth** *Canad.* a tract of forested land with bounds established by the government which leases or sells the rights to fell and remove timber; **timber carriage**, **timber cart** a high-wheeled cart for carrying heavy timber, which is slung under the axles; **timber cruise** *N. Amer.* = CRUISE *noun* 3; **timber-cruiser** *N. Amer.* a timber prospector; **timber-dog** a short iron rod with both ends turned down and sharpened, used for holding together timbers in tunnelling or the timbering of trenches; **timber-doodle** (*a*) *N. Amer. dial.* the American woodcock, *Scolopax minor*; (*b*) *slang* alcoholic spirit; **timber drive** *N. Amer.* an organized floating of loose timber down a waterway; **timber due** *Canad.* a tax paid to the government on each tree taken out of a timber berth; **timber-framed** *adjective* having a frame of timber, framed in wood; **timber-grouse** *US* any kind of grouse which frequents woodlands; **timber-head** (*a*) NAUTICAL the head or end of any timber; *spec.* such an end rising above the deck and serving as a bollard; (*b*) *slang* a stupid person, a blockhead; **timber hitch** a knot used in attaching a rope to a log or spar for hoisting or towing it; **timberjack** *N. Amer.* a lumberjack or logger; **timber jam** = LOG-JAM 1; **timber-jumper** *Hunting slang* a horse good at jumping over gates and fences; **timberland** *US* land covered with forest yielding timber; **timber licence** *Canad.* a licence to cut timber on a timber berth on payment of dues to the government; **timber-limit**: (*a*) *Canad.* = ***timber berth*** above; (*b*) any tract of forested land suitable for lumbering; (*c*) = ***timberline*** below; **timberline** (chiefly *N. Amer.*) (*a*) the line or level on a mountain above which no trees grow; (*b*) in the northern hemisphere, the line north of which no trees grow; **timber rattler**, **timber rattlesnake** a venomous snake, *Crotalus horridus*, of the north-eastern US, marked with dark bands or blotches; **timber-toe** *slang* a wooden leg; **timber-topper** = ***timber-jumper*** above; **timber tree**: yielding wood fit for building or construction; ***timber wolf***: see WOLF *noun* 1; **timber-work** work in timber; the wooden part of any structure; **timber-yard** an open yard or place where timber is stacked or stored.

■ **timberless** *adjective* (*rare*) without timber; devoid of forest trees: M19.

timber /ˈtɪmbə/ *noun*^{2}. ME.
[Old French *timbre*, medieval Latin *timber*, *timbra*, *-ia*, *-ium*, Middle Low German *timber*, supposed to be ult. a special use of prec.]
A definite quantity of furs; a package containing 40 skins of ermine, sable, marten, etc.

timber /ˈtɪmbə/ *verb.*
[Old English *timbran*, *timbrian*: cf. TIMBER *noun*^{1}.]

1 a *verb trans.* Build or construct (a house, ship, etc.), later *spec.* of wood. Long *arch.* OE. ▸**b** *verb intrans.* Of a bird: build a nest. Long *rare* or *obsolete*. OE.

†**2** *verb trans.* Bring about, bring into operation (an action, condition, etc.); form, cause, do. OE–M17.

†**3** *verb trans.* Make up or add fuel to (a fire). L15–L17.

4 *verb trans.* **a** Put in or apply timber to support (a roof, shaft, trench, etc.). E18. ▸**b** Cover or frame with timber. M19.

■ **timbering** *noun* (*a*) the action of the verb; (*b*) building material, esp. of wood; timber-work: ME.

timbered /ˈtɪmbəd/ *adjective.* LME.
[from TIMBER *noun*^{1}, *verb*: see -ED^2, -ED^1.]

1 Constructed of timber; built or made of wood, wooden. LME.

2 (Of a thing) having a structure of a specified kind, constructed, made; (of a person or animal) having a particular bodily structure or constitution, framed, built. L16.

3 Stocked with growing trees; wooded. E18.

timberman /ˈtɪmbəman, -mən/ *noun.* Pl. **-men**. LME.
[from TIMBER *noun*^{1} + MAN *noun*.]

1 Orig., a man supplying or dealing in timber. Later, a man employed in handling timber. LME. ▸**b** An owner or manager of a company engaged in lumbering. *Canad.* L19.

†**2** A person who makes things from timber; a carpenter. *Scot.* LME–M17.

3 A man employed in timbering the shafts or roofs of a mine, the sides of a trench, etc. **M19.**

4 A longhorn beetle with wood-boring larvae; *spec.* *Acanthocinus aedilis*, which has extremely long antennae and lives in the trunks of conifers. **L19.**

timbo /tiːmˈbəʊ/ *noun*. **E17.**

[Spanish & Portuguese *timbó* from Tupi-Guarani.]

1 Any of several Amazonian woody vines which yield fish poisons, esp. *Paullinia pinnata* (family Sapindaceae) and the cube (genus *Lonchocarpus*). **E17.**

2 A leguminous timber tree of Argentina and neighbouring regions, *Enterolobium contortisiliquum*; the soft red wood of this tree, used for making furniture. **E20.**

†timbre *noun*¹. **ME–L16.**

[Old French, from Proto-Romance from medieval Greek *timbanon* timbrel, kettledrum = Greek *tumpanon* TYMPANUM.]

= TIMBREL *noun*.

timbre /ˈtɪmbə/ *noun*² & *verb*. *obsolete* exc. *Hist.* Also **tymber**. **LME.**

[Old & mod. French, same word as prec.]

▶ **A** *noun*. The crest of a helmet; the helmet, crest, and other exterior ornaments placed around the shield in heraldic arms. **LME.**

▶ **B** *verb trans.* Decorate with a crest; surmount as a crest. **E16.**

■ **timbred** *adjective* having a timbre of a specified kind **M20.**

timbre /ˈtambə, *foreign* tɛ̃br/ *noun*³. See also TAMBER. **M19.**

[French, same word as TIMBRE *noun*¹.]

The distinctive character or quality of a musical or vocal sound apart from its pitch and intensity, due mainly to the extent to which harmonics are present.

🕮 *Making Music* A great keyboard, with . . good, clear, precise timbres. H. NORMAN Charlotte's voice was of a fragile, hesitant timbre.

■ **timbreless** *adjective* (of the voice) lacking timbre, having no distinctive quality; without depth or variation, monotonic: **E20.** **timbrous** *adjective* sonorous, resonant **E20.**

timbrel /ˈtɪmbr(ə)l/ *noun* & *verb*. *arch.* **E16.**

[Perh. dim. of TIMBRE *noun*¹: see -EL².]

▶**A** *noun*. A musical percussion instrument, *esp.* one able to be held up in the hand, as a tambourine. **E16.**

▶ **B** *verb trans.* & *intrans.* Infl. **-ll-**, *-**l**-. Play or accompany on a timbrel. **E17.**

Timbuctoo /tɪmbʌkˈtuː/ *noun*. Also **Timbuktu**. **M19.**

[*Timbuktu*, a town on the edge of the Sahara in Mali, W. Africa.]

Any extremely distant or remote place.

time /tʌɪm/ *noun*.

[Old English *tīma* = Old Norse *tími* time, good time, prosperity, from Germanic, from base of TIDE *noun*, which was superseded by *time* in the strictly temporal senses.]

▶ **I 1** A finite extent of continued existence; e.g. the interval between two events, or the period during which an action or state continues; a period referred to in some way. **OE.** ▶**b** In biblical translations: a space of time, usu. taken to be a year. **LME.** ▶**c** *ellipt.* A long time. **M19.**

2 *sing.* & (now usu.) in *pl.* A period in history, a period in the existence of the world; an age, an era; ***the time(s)***, the present age, the age being considered. **OE.**

3 With possess. or *of*: the period contemporary with the person specified. **OE.**

4 A period of existence or action; *spec.* a person's lifetime. **OE.** ▶**b** The period of a woman's pregnancy or an animal's gestation. Cf. sense 13 below. **OE.** ▶**c** *sing.* & (usu.) in *pl.* A woman's periods; menstruation. **M16.** ▶**d** A person's term of apprenticeship. **M17.** ▶**e** FENCING. The period of initiation and performance of an action, e.g. an opportunity to attack given by an opponent's making of a movement. **E18.** ▶**f** A period of imprisonment. Chiefly in ***do time***. *slang*. **L18.**

5 Length of time sufficient, necessary, or desired; available time, time at one's disposal; BROADCASTING time in a transmission that can be bought, e.g. for advertising. **ME.** ▶**b** Length of time taken to run a race or complete an event; progress in a race or journey. **M19.**

6 *sing.* & (usu.) in *pl.* The prevailing conditions of a period or a person's life. Freq. in phrs. & (in *pl.*) in titles of newspapers. **L15.**

7 An experience of a specified (good, bad, etc.) nature; (without specification) a good or bad experience of some duration; *N. Amer.* a party, a wildly enjoyable time; *US colloq.* a fuss (only in ***make a time***). **E16.**

8 a MUSIC. Orig., the duration of a breve relative to that of a semibreve. Later, the duration of a note; the rhythm of a piece of music, as shown by division into bars and expressed by a time signature; the rate at which a piece is performed, the tempo; the characteristic rhythm and tempo of a particular kind of composition. **M16.** ▶**b** MILITARY. The rate of marching, expressed as so many paces per minute. **E19.**

9 CLASSICAL PROSODY. A unit of time measurement. **L16.**

10 Pay for a period of time spent working. **L18.**

🕮 **1** A. RADCLIFFE Annette . . was absent a considerable time. G. BORROW I will lead you to Finisterre in no time. B. JOWETT All times of mental progress are times of confusion. I. MURDOCH For some time I stood as one enchanted in the middle of the room. W. TREVOR The time taken had been half a minute. **c** J. LE CARRÉ My God, you've been a time! **2** E. A. FREEMAN An act which ran counter to the religious feelings of the time. W. C. SMITH A folly, . . A superstition of these modern times. *New Scientist* Leaves . . which Egyptians have used to treat . . diseases since ancient times. **3** WORDSWORTH In great Eliza's golden time. **4** SHAKES. *A.Y.L.* One man in his time plays many parts. A. THIRKELL I've seen some rum places in my time. **5** P. INCHBALD After work tonight? I can't keep doing this in the firm's time. P. MARSHALL She needed some time to herself. G. TINDALL *Not* that I would have had time to read them. **b** O. S. NOCK A continuation . . of longer locomotive workings, shorter turn-round times at running sheds. **6** J. H. NEWMAN When times grew cold and unbelieving. B. DYLAN The times they are a-changin'. **7** E. WAUGH Imagine what a time we've had with reporters and people. R. MACAULAY Maurice and she had had good times together. **8a** *Listener* The first theme of the . . opening movement, expounded in three-four time. W. GOLDING Musicians began to play, catching the time from the dancers. **10** *Daily Telegraph* They want holiday pay, at . . single time, increased to time and a third.

▶ **II** Time when: a point in time; a space of time treated without ref. to duration.

11 a A recognizable part of the year, the cycle of seasons, or the day; a point in the moon's age. **OE.** ▶**b** A point in the course of a period, esp. a day (expressed by hours and minutes past midnight or noon). **ME.** ▶†**c** A season considered with reference to the weather experienced; weather. *rare*. **LME–E16.**

12 A point in time marking or marked by some event or condition; a point when something happens, an occasion. **OE.**

13 A moment or (short) period appointed for a particular purpose or event; the due or proper time; *ellipt.* the date or time at which a woman gives birth (cf. sense 4b above); the date or time of a person's death. **OE.** ▶**b** The moment when a boxing bout is due to begin or end. **E19.** ▶**c** The moment when a public house is legally obliged to stop selling drink. **E20.**

14 A favourable, convenient, or appropriate time for doing something; the right moment or occasion; an opportunity. **OE.**

15 Each occasion of a recurring action. **ME.**

16 In *pl.* preceded by a cardinal numeral. ▶**a** Followed by a number or an expression of quantity: expr. the multiplication of the latter by the former. **LME.** ▶**b** Followed by an adjective or adverb in the compar. degree, or in the positive by *as* (formerly †*so*) with an adjective or adverb: expr. comparison. **M16.**

†**17** GRAMMAR. The tense of a verb. **LME–E17.**

18 HORSEMANSHIP. A single completed motion or action of a horse's movement. **M18.**

🕮 **11a** T. HOOK Showers of rain, unseasonable at the time of year. ***daytime***, ***holiday time***, ***night-time***, ***springtime***, ***summertime***, etc. **b** V. WOOLF He took out his . . watch and told her the time. J. BRAINE 'Good evening,' she said. 'Have you the time please?' **12** J. CONRAD I interrupted again and this time bitterly. I. MURDOCH By the time we got back . . it was nearly dark. G. GREENE There are times . . when Shakespeare is a little dull. N. MOSLEY Christian attitudes at the time of the Crusades. **13** J. L. WATEN Sunday afternoon was our time for entertaining. DYLAN THOMAS Half past eleven is opening time. J. WAIN The time had come for him to take control. **c** T. S. ELIOT Hurry up please its time. **14** *Practical Gardening* This . . was the time to . . plant a chamomile path. **15** D. HAMMETT Twice Mimi started to say something, but each time broke off to listen. G. BOYCOTT I lost count of how many times I changed batting gloves. G. M. FRASER I went up the steps . . four at a time. **16a** M. E. G. DUFF Territories . . more than twenty-one times the size of Scotland. **b** *Engineer* Rear tyres can last between two and four times as long.

▶ **III** In generalized sense.

19 Duration conceived as having a beginning and an end; finite duration as distinct from eternity. **ME.**

20 Indefinite continuous duration regarded as that in which the sequence of events takes place. **LME.**

21 A basis of reckoning time based on the occurrence of noon at a particular place or meridian. Freq. with preceding place-name. **E18.**

🕮 **19** *Sporting Magazine* That famous horse . . whose excellence . . will be, perhaps, transmitted to the end of time. **20** E. H. PORTER The doctor . . said that time alone could tell. X. FIELDING An outlaw whom the passage of time had glamourized. L. PAYNE I worked swiftly. Time was not on my side. **21** ***Atlantic Time***, ***Central Time***, ***Greenwich Mean Time***, ***local time***, etc.

Phrases etc.: **about time** approximately the appropriate or expected time; *iron.* long past such a time; freq. with ellipsis of *be*, this is long overdue (also ***about time too***). ***against time***: see AGAINST *preposition*. **ahead of one's time** having ideas too enlightened or too advanced to be accepted by one's contemporaries. **ahead of time** sooner than expected or due. ***all in good time***: see GOOD *adjective*. **all the time** (*a*) constantly, continually; at all times; (*b*) during the whole of the period referred to (freq. implying a contrary expectation). **all the time in the world** plenty of time, more time than is needed. ***apparent solar time***, ***apparent time***: see APPARENT *adjective* 4. ***arrow of time***: see ARROW *noun* 1. **at a time** (*a*) at the same time, simultaneously; at one time; *esp.* in successive groups of a specified number each (***one at a time***, singly, one by one); †(*b*) *rare* (Shakes.), at times, occasionally. — **a time** (a specified price) on each occasion or for each item. **at one time** (*a*) in or during an unspecified period; once, formerly; ***at one time and another***, ***at one time with another***, on various occasions; (*b*) at a time, simultaneously. **at that point in time** at that particular moment, then. ***at the best of times***: see BEST *adjective* etc. **at the same time** (*a*) during the same period, at the same moment; simultaneously; (*b*) nevertheless, however. **at this moment in time**, **at this point in time** at this particular moment, now. **at times** occasionally, intermittently. **at what time**, **what time** when (now only (exc. *poet.*) *interrog.*), esp. as specified in hours and minutes (time of the clock). ***beat time***: see BEAT *verb*¹ 17. **before one's time** prematurely. **behind the times** old-fashioned, out of date. ***behind time***: see BEHIND *preposition* 5. BETWEEN ***times***. ***big time***: see BIG *adjective*. ***borrowed time***: see BORROW *verb*¹. ***by process of time***: see PROCESS *noun*. †**by times** (*a*) in good time, early; = BETIMES; (*b*) at various times; now and then. ***common time***: see COMMON *adjective*. ***compound time***: see COMPOUND *adjective*. ***dead time***: see DEAD *adjective* etc. ***do time***: see sense 4f above. ***double time***: see DOUBLE *adjective* & *adverb*. ***equation of time***: see EQUATION 4. ***every time***: see EVERY *adjective* 1. ***extra time***: see EXTRA *adjective*. **Father Time** time personified as an old man carrying a scythe and an hourglass, and bald except for a forelock. **for all time** for ever. ***for old times' sake***: see SAKE *noun*¹. ***for the first time***, ***for the second time***: see FOR *preposition*. ***for the time being***: see BE. ***from time to time***: see FROM *preposition*. ***full time***: see FULL *adjective*. **give a person the time of day** *colloq.* exchange a greeting or casual remarks with a person. **give a person time** be patient with a person, esp. in expectation of a change or achievement; usu. in *imper.* ***go with the times***: see GO *verb*. **half the time** *colloq.* as often as not. ***have a good time***: see GOOD *adjective*. **have a lot of time for**, **have no time for** *colloq.* have much (or no) respect, admiration, or liking for (a person). **have a time of it** undergo trouble or difficulty. **have the time** (*a*) be able to spend the time needed (*to do*, *for*); (*b*) know from a watch etc. what time it is; (*c*) ***have the time of one's life***: see LIFE *noun*. ***high old time***: see ***a high old time*** s.v. HIGH *adjective*, *adverb*, & *noun*. ***in good time***: see GOOD *adjective*. ***in jig time***: see JIG *noun*¹. ***in less than no time***: see LESS *adjective* etc. **in no time** = ***in less than no time*** above. **in one's own good time** at a time and rate of one's own choosing. **in one's own time** outside working hours. ***in process of time***: see PROCESS *noun*. ***in the nick of time***, ***in the very nick of time***: see NICK *noun*¹. **in time** (*a*) sooner or later, eventually; (*b*) soon or early enough, not too late; (*c*) MUSIC in the correct rhythm and tempo; (*d*) *US colloq.* = ***on earth*** s.v. EARTH *noun*¹. **it takes a person all his or her time** *colloq.* it presents a person with great difficulties, it requires great effort from a person (*to do*). ***just in time***: see JUST *adverb*. **keep good time**, **keep bad time**, etc., (of a timepiece) show (or not show) the passage of time accurately, neither gaining nor losing; (of a person) be (or not be) habitually punctual. **keep time** (*a*) MUSIC mark rhythm by one's movements; (of a performer) adhere to the correct rhythm and tempo of the music; keep pace *with* a measure or another performer; (*b*) = ***keep good time*** above. **know the time of day** *colloq.* be well informed. ***long time (no see)***: see LONG *adjective*¹. **lose no time** act promptly (*in doing*). ***make a time***: see sense 7 above. ***make good time***: see MAKE *verb*. ***make time***: see MAKE *verb*. **many a time** on many occasions, in many instances; often. **many a time and oft**, **many a time and often** *arch.* = ***many a time*** above. **many's the time** (with following clause) = ***many a time*** above. ***mark time***: see MARK *verb*. ***mean solar time***, ***mean time***: see MEAN *adjective*². ***move with the times***: see MOVE *verb*. ***nick of time***: see NICK *noun*¹. ***nine times out of ten***: see NINE *adjective*. **not before time** not soon enough, long overdue. **not give a person the time of day** *colloq.* not help or cooperate with a person, be offhand with a person. **no time** *colloq.* a very short interval (see also ***in less than no time*** s.v. LESS *adjective*). **on time** (*a*) punctually; (*b*) *N. Amer.* on credit. ***once upon a time***: see ONCE *adverb* etc. ***one at a time***: see ***at a time*** (a) above. **out of one's time** in an era unsympathetic to one's attitudes, aspirations, etc. **out of time** (*a*) at an inappropriate time; (*b*) after the prescribed period has elapsed, too late; ***knock out of time*** in boxing, disable (an opponent) so that he cannot resume fighting before the end of the count or the round; *gen.* thoroughly overcome; (*c*) MUSIC not in time. **out-of-time** *adjective* unseasonable. **over time** during a period of time, gradually. ***pass the time of day***: see PASS *verb*. ***play for time***: see PLAY *verb*. **pressed for time** short of time, in a hurry. ***quadruple time***: see QUADRUPLE *adjective*. ***quick time***: see QUICK *adjective* & *adverb*. ***real time***: see REAL *adjective*². ***serve one's time***, ***serve the time***, ***serve time***: see SERVE *verb*¹. ***sign of the times***: see SIGN *noun*. ***simple time***: see SIMPLE *adjective*. ***slow time***: see SLOW *adjective* & *adverb*. ***snatch one's time***: see SNATCH *verb* 2. ***solar time***: see SOLAR *adjective*¹. ***standard time***: see STANDARD *noun* & *adjective*. ***stand the test of time***: see TEST *noun*¹. **take one's time** allow oneself enough time, proceed without hurry; be too long in doing something. ***take time by the forelock***: see FORELOCK *noun*¹. ***the nick of time***, ***the very nick of time***: see NICK *noun*¹. ***this long time***: see LONG *adjective*¹. **time about** (chiefly *Scot.* & *north.*) alternately, in turns. **time after time** on many occasions, repeatedly. ***time and again***: see AGAIN *adverb* 4. **time and a half** a rate of pay at one and a half times the normal rate. **time and tide** [alliterative redupl.] time; now *rare* exc. in proverbial phrs. ***time and time again***: see AGAIN *adverb* 4. **time enough** soon enough, sufficiently early. **time immemorial** LAW (since) a time up to the beginning of the reign of Richard I in 1189; *gen.* = ***time out of mind*** (a) below. **time of day** (*a*) the time (in hours and minutes) as shown by clocks and watches; *colloq.* a point or stage in a period or course of events; (*b*) *slang* the prevailing aspect of affairs; the right way of doing something. **time off** time away from one's work, school, etc., when one can rest or take recreation; time taken off the length of a prison sentence. ***time of ignorance***: see IGNORANCE 1b. **time of life** a person's age; *spec.* the age when a woman's menopause is likely; middle age. **time of one's life** a period or occasion of exceptional enjoyment. **time on one's hands** time in which a person has nothing to do. **time out** (chiefly *N. Amer.*) (*a*) time that is not counted towards the duration of a game; (*b*) time off from an occupation, activity, etc.; (see also *time-out* below). **time out of mind** (*a*) (since or for) a longer time than anyone can remember or trace, (for) a very long (past) time (cf. *time immemorial* above); (*b*) on many occasions, many times. *time's arrow*: see ARROW *noun* 1. **times without number** = *many a time* above. **time was** there was a time (*when*). **to time** †(*a*) for ever; (*b*) within prescribed time-limits. *triple time*: see TRIPLE *adjective & adverb*. **two times (table)**, **three times (table)**, etc., the multiplication table of the number specified. *unity of time*: see UNITY *noun*[1] 8. *what time*: see *at what time* above. *withstand the test of time*: see TEST *noun*[1].

Comb.: **time adverbial** LINGUISTICS: expressing time; **time-and-motion** *adjective* designating, of, or pertaining to a study concerned with measuring the efficiency of industrial and other operations; **time average** PHYSICS & MATH.: evaluated over a period of time; **time-ball** a sphere which at a certain moment each day is allowed to fall down a vertical rod placed in a prominent position, so as to give an accurate indication of time; **time-bargain** a contract for the sale or purchase of goods or stock at an agreed price at a certain future date; **time-barred** *adjective* disqualified or invalid by reason of arriving or being presented after the expiry of a time-limit; **time base** ELECTRONICS a signal for uniformly and repeatedly deflecting the electron beam of a cathode-ray tube; a line on the display produced in this way and serving as a time axis; (also *time-base generator*) a circuit for generating such a signal; **time-bill** a timetable of trains, buses, etc.; **time bomb** (*a*) a bomb timed to explode at a pre-set time; (*b*) COMPUTING a series of instructions hidden in a program so as to be executed at a particular time, usually with deleterious results; **time capsule** a box etc. containing a selection of objects chosen as representative of life at a particular time, and buried for discovery in the future; **time charter** an agreement to charter a ship for a certain period of time, the charterer being responsible for its loading and unloading; **time check** an act of stating or ascertaining the exact time, esp. over the air; **time clock** (*a*) a clock with a mechanism for recording employees' times of arrival and departure; (*b*) a clock which can be set to switch an appliance on or off at pre-set times; **time code** a coded signal on videotape or film giving information about frame number, time of recording or exposure, scene, camera, etc.; **time constant** PHYSICS & ENGINEERING the time taken by an exponentially varying quantity to change by a factor $1-1/e$ (approx. 0.6321), regarded as a parameter of the system in which the variation occurs; a time taken as representative of the speed of response of a system; **time-consuming** *adjective* taking up a lot of time; **time-course** the period of time in which something happens or over which something is monitored; **time-delay** a time-lag, *esp.* one that has been deliberately introduced; **time deposit** (a deposit in) a bank account from which money cannot be drawn before a set date or for which notice of withdrawal is required; **time depth** LINGUISTICS the length of time that something has existed or since which it first arose; **time dilatation** SCIENCE the relativistic slowing down of the passage of time in a frame of reference moving relative to the observer; **time-division** *adjective* (TELECOMMUNICATIONS) designating a technique in which a number of signals are transmitted successively in rapid rotation over the same channel; **time domain** time considered as an independent variable in the analysis or measurement of time-dependent phenomena (freq. *attrib.*); *time domain* REFLECTOMETER; **time-expired** *adjective* whose term of engagement has expired; (of a convict) whose term of sentence has expired; (of perishable goods) of which the term of safe storage has expired; **time exposure** PHOTOGRAPHY exposure for a relatively long time, *esp.* one in which the shutter is closed by a separate operation after it is opened; **time factor** the passage of time as setting a limit on what can be achieved; **time-fellow** *arch.* a contemporary; **Timeform** RACING (proprietary name for) a numerical rating based on past performance given to racehorses by the periodical *Timeform*; **time-frame** a limited and established period of time during which an event etc. took place or is planned to take place; **time-fuse**: set to burn out after a predetermined length of time; **time hit** FENCING a hit made on a time thrust; **time-honoured** *adjective* revered or respected on account of long existence; **time-killer** a person who or thing which kills time; an amusement, a diversion; *time-lag*: see LAG *noun*[2] 4b; **time-lapse** *adjective & noun* (designating or pertaining to) a technique of taking a sequence of photographs at set intervals to record changes that take place slowly; **time-limit** the limit of time within which a task must be done or an event happen; **time lock** a lock with a timer which prevents its being unlocked until a set time; **time machine** an imaginary machine capable of transporting a person backwards or forwards in time; **time-notice** a notice given a definite time beforehand; **time-of-flight** *adjective* (PHYSICS) designating techniques and apparatus that depend on the time taken by subatomic particles to traverse a set distance; **time-out** (*a*) (chiefly *US*) a usually brief break in play in a game; (*b*) COMPUTING a cancellation or cessation that automatically occurs when a predefined interval of time has passed without a certain event occurring; (see also *time out* in Phrases above); **time ownership** = TIME-SHARING 2; **time-payment** (*a*) payment by instalments; (*b*) payment on the basis of time worked; **time pencil** a type of delayed-action firing-switch or detonator for setting off explosive devices; **time policy** an insurance policy providing cover for a specified period of time only; **time-rate** (*a*) rate in time; (*b*) rate of payment on the basis of time worked; **time-release** *adjective* denoting something, esp. a drug preparation, that releases an active substance gradually; **time-resolved** *adjective* (CHEMISTRY & PHYSICS) produced by or pertaining to a spectroscopic technique in which a spectrum is obtained at a series of time intervals after excitation of the sample; **time reversal** PHYSICS a transformation in which the passage of time, and so all velocities, are represented as reversed (*time reversal invariance*, invariance of laws of nature under this transformation); **time-saver** a thing that saves a lot of time; **time-scale** the time allowed for or taken by a sequence of events; **time-series** a series of values of a quantity obtained at successive times (often with equal intervals between them); *time-series analysis*, the statistical analysis of such series; **time-served** *adjective* having completed a period of apprenticeship or training; **time-server** a person who adapts his or her conduct or views to suit prevailing circumstances, fashion, etc.; **time-serving** *noun & adjective* (*a*) *noun* the action or conduct of a time-server; (*b*) *adjective* behaving like a time-server, temporizing; **time-servingness** the character of being a time-server; **time sheet** a paper for recording the names of workers and the hours they work; **time-shift** *noun & verb* (*a*) *noun* a shift in time; (*b*) *verb trans.* make a video recording of (a television programme) in order to watch it at a more convenient time; **time signal** an audible or visible signal to indicate the exact time of day; *esp.* that broadcast by the BBC at certain times; **time signature** MUSIC a sign placed at the beginning of a piece of music or where the time changes to show the rhythm, consisting of a fraction whose denominator defines a note (in terms of the number in a semibreve) and whose numerator gives the number of such notes in a bar; **time slice** COMPUTING each of the short intervals of time during which a computer or its central processor deals uninterruptedly with one user or program, before switching to another; **time-slicing** the division of processor running time into a succession of short intervals that are allocated in turn to different users or programs; **time slot** a portion of time allocated to a purpose or person, esp. to an individual broadcast programme; **time-span** the full extent of a thing in time; **time-spirit** = ZEITGEIST; **times table** a multiplication table (cf. sense 16a above); **time-stamp** *noun & verb* (*a*) *noun* (the impression made by) a device for stamping documents with the date and time of receipt; (*b*) *verb trans.* mark with a time-stamp; **time-stratigraphic** *adjective* (GEOLOGY) = CHRONOSTRATIGRAPHIC; **time study** a time-and-motion study; the close observation of industrial or other processes with a view to introducing more efficient procedures; **time switch** a switch that acts automatically at a pre-set time; **time-taking** *adjective* that takes time; leisurely, slow; **time thrust** FENCING a counter-stroke made during an opponent's attack, preventing the opponent from scoring from it; **time train** the set of wheels that turn the hands of a clock or watch; **time-traveller** a person who travels into the past or the future; **time-travelling** the (imagined) activity of travelling into the past or future; **time trial** a test of individual speed over a set distance; a race in which competitors are separately timed; **time warp** an imaginary or hypothetical distortion of space–time that causes or enables a person to remain stationary in time or to travel backwards or forwards in time; **time-work** work which is paid for by the time it takes; **time-worn** *adjective* impaired by age; **time zone** a range of longitudes throughout which the same standard time is adopted, differing from GMT by a whole number of hours.

■ **timelike** *adjective* (PHYSICS) designating or relating to an interval between two points in space–time that lie inside one another's light cones (so that a signal or observer can pass from one to another) E20.

time /tʌɪm/ *verb*. ME.
[from the noun.]

▶†**I 1** *verb intrans.* **a** Happen, occur. Usu. *impers.* in *it times* etc. Only in ME. ▸**b** Fare (*well* or *ill*); *spec.* fare well, prosper. Only in ME.

▶**II 2** *verb trans.* Arrange the time of (an action or event); choose the occasion for; *esp.* do (a thing) at the right time. LME.

3 *verb trans.* Mark the rhythm or measure of, as in music; sing or play in (good or bad) time. L15. ▸**b** *verb trans.* Set the time of; regulate the rate or rhythm of; arrange the time of arrival of (a train etc.); cause to coincide in time with something (foll. by *to*). M17. ▸**c** *verb intrans.* Keep time *to*; sound or move in unison or harmony *with*. *poet.* M19.

4 *verb trans.* Fix the duration of; regulate the operation of (a mechanism etc.) as to duration or time of operation; adjust (a clock etc.) to keep accurate time. L16.

5 *verb trans.* Ascertain the time at which (something) is done or happens; ascertain the time taken by (an action or the person doing it). L17.

6 *verb trans. & intrans.* FENCING. Attack (an opponent) in time (TIME *noun* 4e). E19.

> 📖 **2** C. CHAPLIN I would time the moment that she left . . so as to meet her. **3** R. P. GRAVES Life was dominated and timed by the . . church bells. **b** J. TYNDALL Timing the pull to the lurching of the ship. *Punch* Special trains, timed to take . . half-an-hour longer. **4** C. STOLL A . . bomb . . timed to blow up sometime in the future. **5** R. K. NARAYAN He held a watch . . and timed my run.

time /tʌɪm/ *conjunction*. *US colloq.* E20.
[Ellipt.]
At or by the time that; as soon as; when.

timeful /ˈtʌɪmfʊl, -f(ə)l/ *adjective*. Now *rare*. ME.
[from TIME *noun* + -FUL.]
1 Seasonable, timely. ME.
†**2** Early in season. Only in LME.
3 Occurring in or consisting of time; temporal. LME.
■ **timefully** *adverb* with timely action M19. **timefulness** *noun* M20.

timekeeper /ˈtʌɪmkiːpə/ *noun*. L17.
[from TIME *noun* + KEEPER *noun*.]
1 An instrument for measuring the passage of time, a timepiece. Formerly *spec.* a chronometer. L17.
2 A person who measures or records time or time taken, e.g. in a sporting contest. L18.
3 With specifying word: a person who or thing which keeps (good or bad) time. E19.
■ **timekeeping** *noun* the keeping of time; punctuality: E19.

timeless /ˈtʌɪmlɪs/ *adjective, adverb, & noun*. M16.
[from TIME *noun* + -LESS.]
▶**A** *adjective*. **1** Unseasonable, ill-timed; *esp.* occurring or done prematurely. Now *rare* or *obsolete*. M16.
2 Not subject to time; not affected by the passage of time; eternal. E17.

> 📖 **2** R. CHURCH The calm and timeless atmosphere of the old village.

▶**B** *adverb*. Timelessly. *poet.* L16.
▶**C** *absol.* as *noun*. An eternal thing; ***the Timeless***, God. E19.
■ **timelessly** *adverb* (*a*) (now *rare* or *obsolete*) unseasonably, out of due time; (*b*) without reference to time, independently of the passage of time: E17. **timelessness** *noun* L19.

timely /ˈtʌɪmli/ *adjective*. ME.
[from TIME *noun* + -LY[1].]
1 a Occurring, done, or made at an appropriate or suitable time; opportune. ME. ▸**b** Occurring or appearing in good time; early. Now *rare* or *obsolete* exc. as passing into sense 1a. LME.
†**2** Of or in time, as opp. to eternity; temporal, earthly. *rare*. ME–E17.
†**3 a** Pertaining to the time of day. *rare* (Spenser). Only in L16. ▸**b** Keeping time or measure. *rare* (Spenser). Only in L16.

> 📖 **1a** S. NAIPAUL The mutineers were stopped by the timely intervention of one coast-guard vessel.

■ **timeliness** *noun* L16.

timely /ˈtʌɪmli/ *adverb*. LOE.
[from TIME *noun* + -LY[2].]
1 Early, in good time; soon, quickly. *arch.* LOE.
2 Formerly, soon enough, in time. Now, at the right time. ME.

> 📖 **2** *European Sociological Review* They seemed . . to move the Socialists slightly, but timely, to the Right.

timenoguy /ˈtɪmɪnɒgi/ *noun*. L18.
[Prob. ult. based on Old & mod. French *timon* wagon-pole, tiller and GUY *noun*[1].]
NAUTICAL. A taut rope running between different parts of a ship to prevent tangling or fouling, as to deflect rigging from anchors, windlasses, etc. Also, a gadget, a thingummy.

timeous /ˈtʌɪməs/ *adjective & adverb*. Chiefly *Scot.* Also **timous**. LME.
[from TIME *noun* + -OUS.]
▶**A** *adjective*. **1** Done, occurring, or appearing early, or sufficiently early. LME.
2 Timely, opportune. E17.
▶**B** *adverb*. Early. Now *dial.* L16.
■ **timeously** *adverb* †(*a*) early, in good time; (*b*) soon enough, in time; at the right time: LME.

timepiece /ˈtʌɪmpiːs/ *noun*. M18.
[from TIME *noun* + PIECE *noun*.]
An instrument (as a clock or watch) for measuring the passage of time.

timer /ˈtʌɪmə/ *noun*. L15.
[from TIME *noun*, *verb* + -ER[1].]
▶**I** †**1** A person skilled in musical time, a musician. *rare*. L15.
2 a A watch or clock that is a (good or bad) timekeeper. L19. ▸**b** A person who acts as timekeeper in a sporting event. L19.
3 An instrument for automatically timing a process or activating a device at a pre-set time. E20.
▶**II 4** As 2nd elem. of comb.: a person who or thing which does something in or for a specified time. L19.

> 📖 **4** *Essentials* The over-30 first-timers ran a greater risk of needing a Caesarian. ***full-timer***, ***old-timer***, ***part-timer***, etc.

times /tʌɪmz/ *adverb*. L19.
[Ellipt.]
At times; sometimes; many times.

time-sharing /ˈtʌɪmʃɛːrɪŋ/ *verbal noun*. M20.
[from TIME *noun* + *sharing* verbal noun of SHARE *verb*[2].]
1 COMPUTING. The automatic sharing of processor time so that a computer can serve several users or devices concurrently, rapidly switching between them so that each user has the impression of continuous exclusive use. M20.
2 The right to use a property (esp. as a holiday home) for a fixed limited time each year. L20.
■ **time-share** *noun & verb* (*a*) *noun* = TIME-SHARING 2; a share in a property under a time-sharing scheme; (*b*) *verb trans.* use concurrently with others on a time-sharing basis: M20.

time–space /tʌɪmˈspeɪs/ *noun & adjective*. E20.
[from TIME *noun* + SPACE *noun*.]
= SPACE–TIME.

timetable /ˈtʌɪmteɪb(ə)l/ *noun & verb*. E19.
[from TIME *noun* + TABLE *noun*.]
▶**A** *noun*. A list of the times at which successive things are to be done or to happen, or of the times occupied by a

process; *spec.* (**a**) a printed table or book of tables showing the departure and arrival times of trains, buses, etc.; (**b**) a table showing how the time of a school or college is allotted to the various subjects, classes, or lectures. E19.

Sun (Baltimore) Both houses should figure out a timetable for action.

▶ **B** *verb trans.* Plan or arrange according to a timetable; include in a timetable. E20.

timewise /ˈtʌɪmwʌɪz/ *adverb.* M20.
[from TIME *noun* + -WISE.]
With regard to time.

timid /ˈtɪmɪd/ *adjective.* M16.
[French *timide* or Latin *timidus*, from *timere* to fear: see -ID¹.]
1 Easily frightened; lacking boldness or courage; fearful, timorous. M16.
2 Characterized by or indicating fear. M18.

2 W. BLACK She has given him some timid encouragement.

■ **tiˈmidity** *noun* the quality of being timid L16. **timidly** *adverb* M18. **timidness** *noun* (*rare*) E19.

timing /ˈtʌɪmɪŋ/ *noun.* ME.
[from TIME *verb* + -ING¹.]
†**1** Happening, occurrence; (good or ill) fortune; an event, an occurrence. Only in ME.
2 The fixing, ascertaining, noting, or recording of time or times; the way something is timed, esp. when considered in relation to others. L16.
3 In an internal-combustion engine, the times when the valves open and close, and the time of the ignition spark, in relation to the movement of the piston in the cylinder. L19.

2 S. RADLEY He had . . wanted her to establish the timing of Alison's movements. V. S. PRITCHETT She has a wonderful sense of timing—when to be in the spotlight.

timist /ˈtʌɪmɪst/ *noun.* E17.
[from TIME *noun* + -IST.]
†**1** A time-server. E–M17.
2 A person who keeps correct time in music. M18.

timocracy /tɪˈmɒkrəsi/ *noun.* L15.
[Old & mod. French *timocratie* from medieval Latin *timocratia* from Greek, from *timē* honour, value: see -CRACY.]
1 Government with a property qualification for the ruling class; a society governed by such people. L15.
2 Government in which love of honour is the dominant motive of the ruling class; a society governed by such people. M17.
■ **timoˈcratic** *adjective* M19. **timoˈcratical** *adjective* M17.

timolol /ˈtɪməlɒl/ *noun.* L20.
[from *tim*-, of unkn. origin + PROPRAN)OLOL.]
PHARMACOLOGY. A beta blocker used to treat hypertension, migraine, and some eye conditions.

Timon /ˈtʌɪmən/ *noun.* E18.
[Main character in Shakespeare's *Timon of Athens*.]
A misanthrope.

timoneer /tʌɪməˈnɪə/ *noun. rare.* M18.
[Old & mod. French *timonier*, from *timon* helm from Latin *temon-*, *temo*: see -EER.]
A helmsman.

timor /ˈtɪmə/ *noun*¹. *rare.* L16.
[Latin.]
Fear.

Timor /ˈtiːmɔː/ *noun*². E19.
[See below.]
Used *attrib.* to designate animals native to Timor, an Indonesian island off the north-west coast of Australia.
Timor deer = RUSA *noun*¹. **Timor pony** a small stocky horse of a breed from Timor.

Timorese /tiːmɔːˈriːz/ *noun & adjective.* M19.
[from prec. + -ESE.]
▶ **A** *noun.* Pl. same. A member of the indigenous people of Timor (see prec.). M19.
▶ **B** *adjective.* Of, pertaining to, or characteristic of Timor or its inhabitants. L19.

timorous /ˈtɪm(ə)rəs/ *adjective.* LME.
[Old French *temoros*, *-reus* from medieval Latin *timorosus*, from Latin *timor* fear, from *timere*: see TIMID, -OUS.]
1 a Feeling fear; frightened, apprehensive, afraid. (Foll. by *of*, *to do*, *lest*.) Now *rare.* LME. ▸**b** Subject to fear; easily frightened, timid. Formerly also, modest, reverential. L15. ▸**c** Proceeding from or indicating fear; characterized by timidity. L16.
†**2** Causing fear or dread. LME–M17.

1a DICKENS He . . was rather timorous of venturing. **b** ARNOLD BENNETT She was . . a timorous young thing, defenceless and trembling.

■ **timorously** *adverb* LME. **timorousness** *noun* L15.

timorsome /ˈtɪməs(ə)m/ *adjective.* Now *dial.* L16.
[from prec., by substitution of -SOME¹ for *-ous*.]
Subject to or characterized by fear; timorous, timid.

timothy /ˈtɪməθi/ *noun.* M18.
[*Timothy* Hanson, who introduced the grass from New York to Carolina *c* 1720.]
More fully ***timothy grass***. A meadow grass, *Phleum pratense*, widely grown for fodder. Also called ***meadow cat's-tail***.

timous *adjective & adverb* var. of TIMEOUS.

timpani /ˈtɪmpəni/ *noun pl.* Also **tym-**. L19.
[Italian, pl. of *timpano* kettledrum, from Latin *tympanum* drum.]
Kettledrums.

timpanist /ˈtɪmpənɪst/ *noun.* Also **tym-**. M20.
[from prec. + -IST.]
A person who plays the kettledrums.

timps /tɪm(p)s/ *noun pl. colloq.* M20.
[Abbreviation.]
= TIMPANI.

Timucua /tɪməˈkuːə/ *noun & adjective.* M19.
[The name of the people as recorded by Spanish chronicles.]
▶ **A** *noun.* Pl. **-s**, same.
1 A N. American Indian language once spoken in Florida, extinct from the 18th cent. M19.
2 A member of the people that spoke this language. L19.
▶ **B** *attrib.* or as *adjective.* Of or pertaining to the Timucuas or their language. L19.
■ **Timucuan** *adjective* = TIMUCUA *adjective* M20.

Timurid /ˈtɪmjʊrɪd/ *adjective & noun.* L19.
[from *Timur* (see below) + -ID³.]
Hist. ▶**A** *adjective.* Descended from Timur or Tamerlane (1336–1405), the Mongol conqueror of much of Asia; of or pertaining to the Turkic dynasty founded by him, which ruled in central Asia until the 16th cent. L19.
▶ **B** *noun.* A descendant of Timur; a member of the Timurid dynasty. E20.

†**timwhisky** *noun.* M18–M19.
[from unkn. 1st elem. + WHISKY *noun*².]
= WHISKY *noun*².

tin /tɪn/ *noun & adjective.*
[Old English *tin* = Old Frisian, Middle & mod. Low German, Middle & mod. Dutch *tin*, Old High German *zin* (German *Zinn*), Old Norse *tin*, from Germanic.]
▶ **A** *noun.* **1** A silvery lustrous malleable metal which is a chemical element, atomic no. 50, occurs chiefly in the mineral cassiterite, resists atmospheric corrosion, and is used in making alloys (e.g. bronze, pewter) and tin plate. (Symbol Sn.) OE.
2 A container made of tin or (more usually) tin plate or aluminium; *spec.* one in which food (or drink) is hermetically sealed for preservation, a can; the contents of this. Also (*Scot.*), a mug. L18. ▸**b** Tin plate as the material of such containers. L19. ▸**c** *colloq.* A metal rectangle with a number painted on it which is set on the scoreboard to show the score etc. during a cricket match. Usu. in *pl.* E20. ▸**d** ***the tin***, a strip fitted along the bottom of the front wall of a squash court which resounds when struck by the ball, showing it to have dropped out of play. M20.
3 Money, cash. *slang.* M19.
4 The badge or shield of a policeman. *US slang.* M20.
5 *ellipt.* = ***tin-loaf*** below. M20.

1 black tin tin ore prepared for smelting. ***block tin***: see BLOCK *noun*. ***grey tin***: see GREY *adjective*. ***white tin***: see WHITE *adjective*. **2 *baking tin*, *biscuit tin*, *loaf tin*, *sardine tin*, *etc.*.** H. C. RAE She cooked up a tin of Ravioli.

▶ **B** *attrib.* or as *adjective.* **1** Made or consisting of tin; pertaining to tin or its production. L15.
2 Shoddy, mean, petty. L19.
3 Designating buildings with a roof of corrugated iron, esp. Nonconformist chapels. L19.
Comb., special collocations, & phrases: **little tin god**, **tin god** (**a**) an object of unjustified veneration; (**b**) a self-important person; ***put the tin lid on***: see LID *noun*; **tin-arsed** *adjective* (*Austral. & NZ slang*) very lucky; **tin-bounding** the marking out of the boundaries of a piece of ground for tin-mining; **tin can** (**a**) a can, esp. an empty one; (**b**) *slang* (chiefly *US*), a warship, esp. a destroyer; a submarine; **tin-canning** *NZ* a greeting or serenading on a special occasion by the beating of tin cans; **tin disease** = ***tin pest*** below; **tin ear** (**a**) *slang* = ***cauliflower ear*** s.v. CAULIFLOWER *noun*; (**b**) ***have a tin ear*** (colloq.), be tone-deaf; **tin-enamel** white tin-glaze decorated in enamel colours; ***tin fish***: see FISH *noun*¹ 1b; **tin-glass** (now *rare* or *obsolete*) bismuth; **tin-glaze** a glaze made white and opaque by the addition of tin oxide; ***tin god***: see ***little tin god*** above; TIN HAT; **tin helmet** = TIN HAT *noun phr.*; **tin-kettle** *noun & verb* (**a**) *noun* a kettle of tinned iron; (**b**) *verb trans.* serenade roughly by beating a tin-kettle etc.; ***tin Lizzie***: see LIZZIE 2; **tin-loaf** a (freq. rectangular) loaf baked in a tin; **tin-mouth** = CRAPPIE; **tin-opener** an instrument for opening tins; **tin-pan alley** *colloq.* (**a**) the world of composers and publishers of popular music; (**b**) (**T- P- A-**) a district containing many song publishing houses; **tin-panny** *adjective* (*US*) producing a tinny sound; **tin pest** the crumbling of pure tin that occurs at low temperatures as the ordinary white allotrope changes to grey tin; **tin plate** (a plate of) sheet iron or sheet steel coated with tin; **tin-plate** *verb trans.* coat with tin; **tinsmith** a worker in tin, a maker of tin utensils; **tinsmithing** the work of a tinsmith; **tinsnips** hand-held clippers used for cutting metal; **tin soldier** a toy soldier made of metal; **tin-stone** cassiterite; formerly, a rock made of this, a lump of tin ore; **tin-stream** *noun & verb intrans.* (a flow of water used to) wash tin from a sand or gravel deposit; **tin-tack** a tack or short nail coated with tin; **tinware** articles made of tin or tin plate; **tin wedding** (orig. *US*) the tenth anniversary of a wedding; **tin whistle** = ***PENNY whistle***.
■ **tinful** *noun* as much as a tin will hold L19. **tinning** *noun* (**a**) the action of the verb; (**b**) a tin coating or lining; (**c**) tin-mining: LME.

tin /tɪn/ *verb*¹ *trans.* Infl. **-nn-**. LME.
[from the noun.]
1 Cover with a thin layer of tin; coat or plate with tin. LME. ▸**b** Melt a thin layer of solder on to (an object) prior to soldering it to something else or using it for soldering. L19.
2 Seal in an airtight tin for preservation; = CAN *verb*² 1. L19.

1b *Practical Wireless* Never start soldering unless the iron is well tinned.

tin *verb*² var. of TIND.

TINA /ˈtiːnə/ *abbreviation.*
There is no alternative (orig. with ref. to the policies of Margaret Thatcher, British Prime Minister 1979–90).

tinaja /tɪˈnɑːhə, *foreign* tiˈnaxa/ *noun.* Pl. **-as** /-əz, *foreign* -as/. L16.
[Spanish, augm. of *tina*, *tino* vat from Latin *tina*.]
1 In Spain: a large earthenware jar for holding wine, oil, olives, or salted fish or meat. In parts of Latin America: such a jar used for storing water. L16.
2 In the south-western US: a rock hollow where water is retained; any temporary or intermittent pool. M19.

tinamou /ˈtɪnəmuː/ *noun.* L18.
[French from Carib *tinamu*.]
A bird of the S. American family Tinamidae (order Tinamiformes), comprising plump ground-dwelling birds resembling grouse but related to the rheas.

tincal /ˈtɪŋk(ə)l/ *noun.* Also †**tincar**. M17.
[Prob. from Portuguese *tincal*, *tincar* from Persian & Urdu *tinkār*, *tankār* ult. from Sanskrit *ṭaṅkaṇa*.]
Crude borax, found in lake-deposits in some Asian countries.

tinchel /ˈtɪŋk(ə)l/ *noun. Scot.* Also **tainchel(l)**. M16.
[Gaelic *timchioll*.]
In Scotland, a wide circle of hunters driving together a number of deer by gradually closing in on them.

tinct /tɪŋkt/ *noun.* Now only *poet.* LME.
[Latin *tinctus* a dyeing, from *tingere*: see TINGE *verb*.]
1 Colour; a colouring matter; = TINCTURE *noun* 1, 2a. LME.
†**2** ALCHEMY. A transmuting elixir; = TINCTURE *noun* 3a. L15–E17.
†**3** *fig.* A touch or tinge *of* something; = TINCTURE *noun* 4c. M–L18.

tinct /tɪŋkt/ *verb trans.* Pa. t. & pple **tinct** (*poet.*), **tincted**. LME.
[Latin *tinct-* pa. ppl stem of *tingere*: see TINGE *verb*.]
1 Colour; dye; tinge, tint. Long only as pa. t. & pple. LME.
2 *transf.* & *fig.* Imbue or impregnate *with* a substance or quality, esp. in a slight degree. Long only as pa. t. & pple. LME.
†**3** ALCHEMY. Subject to a transmuting elixir. LME–M17.

tinctorial /tɪŋ(k)ˈtɔːrɪəl/ *adjective.* M17.
[from Latin *tinctorius*, from *tinctor* dyer, formed as prec.: see -AL¹.]
Of, pertaining to, or used in dyeing; yielding or using dye or colouring matter.
■ **tinctorially** *adverb* L19.

tincture /ˈtɪŋ(k)tʃə/ *noun.* LME.
[Latin *tinctura* dyeing, formed as TINCT *verb*: see -URE.]
†**1** A colouring matter, a dye, a pigment; *spec.* one used as a cosmetic. LME–E19.
2 a Hue, colour, esp. as imparted by something that stains; a tinge, a tint. Now *rare.* L15. ▸†**b** The action of dyeing, staining, or colouring something; *fig.* a stain, a blemish. L15–L17. ▸**c** HERALDRY. A colour, metal, or fur used in coats of arms and in blazons. E17.
3 †**a** ALCHEMY. A supposed spiritual principle or immaterial substance whose character may be infused into material things; the quintessence, spirit, or soul of a thing. L15–L17. ▸**b** CHEMISTRY. The active principle of a substance; a solution of this, an essence. Now only (PHARMACOLOGY), a medicinal solution, usually in alcohol, of the active constituents of a naturally occurring substance, esp. one of plant origin. L17.
4 †**a** An imparted quality likened to a colour or dye; a quality or character with which something is imbued, esp. a derived quality. L16–E19. ▸†**b** A physical quality other than colour communicated to something. E17–E18. ▸**c** A slight infusion *of* an element or quality; a tinge, a trace; a smattering *of* knowledge etc. E17.
5 An alcoholic drink, a snifter. *colloq.* E20.

📖 **3a universal tincture** = ELIXIR 2. **4a** STEELE Goodness mixed with Fear, gives a Tincture to all her Behaviour. **c** H. A. L. FISHER The peoples of Russia . . had received but a faint initial tincture of Christianity. C. P. SNOW Henry always had a tincture of detached radicalism.

tincture /ˈtɪŋ(k)tʃə/ *verb trans.* E17.
[from the noun.]
1 Colour, tinge; add a small amount of (a substance) to. (Foll. by *with*.) Usu. in *pass.* E17.
2 Imbue with a mental, moral, or (formerly) physical quality; affect slightly, tinge, taint. (Foll. by *with*.) Usu. in *pass.* M17.

📖 **1** WORDSWORTH Homespun wool But tinctured daintily with florid hues. W. CATHER Drinking raw alcohol, tinctured with oil of cinnamon. **2** *Times Lit. Suppl.* The boldness was tinctured with uncertainty.

tind /tɪnd/ *verb. obsolete* exc. *dial.* Also **teen(d)** /tiːn(d)/, **tin** /tɪn/.
[Old English *tendan*, in compounds (*ontendan*, *fortendan*, etc.) and in *tending* verbal noun, from Germanic (whence Gothic *tandjan* kindle), from base also of TINDER.]
1 *verb trans.* = KINDLE *verb*¹ 1, 3. OE.
2 *verb intrans.* = KINDLE *verb*¹ 5. OE.

tindal /ˈtɪnd(ə)l/ *noun.* L17.
[Malayalam *taṇḍal*, Telugu *taṇḍelu*.]
In the Indian subcontinent and the Malay archipelago: a petty officer of a crew of lascars; a foreman.

tinder /ˈtɪndə/ *noun.*
[Old English *tynder*, *tyndre*, corresp. (with variation in suffix and gender) to Middle & mod. Low German *tunder* (Dutch *tonder*), Old High German *zuntara* (German *Zunder*), Old Norse *tundr*, from Germanic base also of TIND.]
1 A dry flammable substance that readily ignites from a spark; *esp.* that made from partially charred linen and from the hyphae of certain fungi, formerly used to catch the spark struck from a flint with a steel. OE.
†**2** *transf.* Fire; a spark; a tinder-box. L16–E17.
Comb.: **tinder-box** a box in which was kept tinder and usu. also a flint and steel; *fig.* a thing that is readily ignited; a person who is readily aroused, esp. to anger; **tinder-dry** *adjective* extremely dry (and flammable).
▪ **tinder-like** *adjective* readily ignited or (*fig.*) aroused E17. **tindery** *adjective* of the nature of or resembling tinder, tinder-like M18.

tine /tʌɪn/ *noun*¹.
[Old English *tind* = Middle Low German *tind*, Old High German *zint*, Old Norse *tindr*, rel. to synon. Middle Low German *tinne*, Old High German *zinna* (German *Zinne* pinnacle). In sense 3 from the verb.]
1 Any of a series of projecting points on a weapon or implement; *esp.* (*a*) any of the prongs of a fork; (*b*) any of the teeth of a comb. OE.
2 Orig., a small branch, a twig. Later, any of the branches of a deer's horn. ME.
3 The action or an act of tining or harrowing ground. L18.
▪ **tined** *adjective* having tines, freq. of a specified number or kind LME.

tine /tʌɪn/ *noun*². Long *obsolete* exc. *Scot.* ME.
[from TINE *verb*².]
Loss. Now only in ***till tyne***, in vain.

tine /tʌɪn/ *noun*³. *obsolete* exc. *dial.* LME.
[Origin unkn.]
Any of several vetches which twine around corn; *esp.* the hairy tare, *Vicia hirsuta*. Also more fully ***tine-tare***.

†**tine** *noun*⁴. *rare* (after Spenser). L16–E17.
[By-form of TEEN *noun*¹; perh. from Norse (cf. Norwegian dial. *tyne* injury).]
Affliction, trouble, sorrow.

†**tine** *adjective* & *noun*⁵. LME.
[Origin unkn.]
▶ **A** *adjective.* Very small, diminutive, tiny. Only in ***little tine***. LME–E17.
▶ **B** *noun.* A very little space, time, or amount. Only in ***a little tine***. LME–M16.

tine /tʌɪn/ *verb*¹ *trans.* Long *obsolete* exc. *dial.* Also **tyne**.
[Old English *tȳnan* = Old Frisian *tēna*, Middle Dutch *tūnen* (Dutch *tuinen*), Old High German *zūnen* (German *zäunen*), from West Germanic verb, from *tūn-* enclosure: see TOWN *verb*.]
1 Close, shut. Also foll. by *to*. OE.
2 Enclose; hedge or fence in. OE. ▸**b** Make or repair (a hedge etc.). E16.

📖 **1** T. HARDY Cainy and I haven't tined our eyes to-night.

tine /tʌɪn/ *verb*². Chiefly & now only *Scot.* & *north.* Also **tyne**. Pa. t. & pple **tint**, **tynt** /tɪnt/. ME.
[Old Norse *týna*, from *tjón* loss, damage, cogn. with Old English *tēon*: see TEEN *noun*¹, *verb*¹.]
1 *verb intrans.* = LOSE *verb* 1. ME.
†**2** *verb trans.* = LOSE *verb* 2a. ME–L16.
3 *verb trans.* Lose; suffer deprivation of. ME. ▸**b** Fail to obtain or win; miss. ME. ▸**c** = LOSE *verb* 6. ME. ▸†**d** = LOSE *verb* 8a. LME–L16. ▸**e** = LOSE *verb* 3b. E16.
4 *verb intrans.* = LOSE *verb* 5. ME.

📖 **3** R. BURNS Tam tint his reason a'thegither.

tine /tʌɪn/ *verb*³ *trans.* E16.
[from TINE *noun*¹.]
1 Provide with tines or prongs. E16.
2 Rake over or harrow (ground). M18.

tinea /ˈtɪnɪə/ *noun.* LME.
[Latin = gnawing worm or grub, moth, bookworm.]
1 MEDICINE. = RINGWORM. Freq. with mod. Latin specifying word, as ***tinea capitis*** /ˈkapɪtɪs/ [Latin = of the head], ***tinea pedis*** /ˈpɛdɪs/ [Latin = of the foot], etc. LME.
2 (T-.) ENTOMOLOGY. Orig., any of various destructive insects and other small creatures. Later *spec.* a moth of the genus *Tinea*, the larvae of which are very destructive to cloth, feathers, soft paper, decaying wood, museum specimens, etc., including some common clothes-moths. Now only as mod. Latin genus name. LME.
▪ **tineid** *adjective* & *noun* (*a*) *adjective* of or pertaining to the family Tineidae of small moths, including clothes-moths; (*b*) *noun* a member of this family: M19.

tin foil /ˈtɪnfɔɪl/ *noun* & *verb.* Also **tin-foil**, **tinfoil**. LME.
[from TIN *noun* + FOIL *noun*¹.]
▶ **A** *noun.* Tin hammered or rolled into a thin sheet. Now also, foil made of tin alloy or aluminium, used esp. for wrapping food to be cooked or stored. LME.

📖 D. MADDEN A chocolate egg wrapped in brightly coloured tin foil. *attrib.*: D. LEAVITT Walter spooned reheated gourmet frozen dinners from tin foil containers.

▶ **B** *verb trans.* Cover or coat with tin foil. Chiefly as ***tin-foiled*** *ppl adjective.* L16.

ting /tɪŋ/ *noun*¹ & *interjection.* Also redupl. **ting-ting**. E17.
[from the verb.]
(Repr.) the thin high-pitched sound made by a small bell, glass, etc., when struck.
ting-a-ling(-ling) *noun* & *interjection* (repr.) the sound of the repeated ringing of a small bell etc.

Ting /tɪŋ/ *noun*² & *adjective.* E20.
[County of origin in Hebei province, China.]
In full ***Ting yao*** /jaʊ/ [*yáo* pottery]. (Designating) a type of white Chinese protoporcelain, freq. with carved decoration, produced during the Tang and Song dynasties.

ting /tɪŋ/ *noun*³. E20.
[Chinese *dǐng* (Wade–Giles *ting*).]
A Chinese Bronze Age vessel, usu. with two looped handles and three or four feet.

ting /tɪŋ/ *verb.* LME.
[Imit.]
1 *verb intrans.* (Of a bell, glass, etc.) emit a thin high-pitched ringing sound when struck; (of a person) make this sound *with* a bell etc. LME.
2 *verb trans.* Cause (a bell, glass, etc.) to emit a thin high-pitched ringing sound, esp. by striking the surface. Also *spec.* (*dial.*), make this sound at (a bee swarm) to induce it to settle. L15.

📖 **1** J. SCOTT Machines that ping and ting . . as the little ball goes round.

t'ing /tɪŋ/ *noun.* M19.
[Chinese *tíng* (Wade–Giles *t'ing*).]
In China, a small open pavilion used as a place to rest or view the landscape.

tinge /tɪn(d)ʒ/ *verb* & *noun.* L15.
[Latin *tingere* dye, colour.]
▶ **A** *verb.* Pres. pple **tinging**, **tingeing**.
1 *verb trans.* Give a slight shade of some (specified) colour to; tint or modify the colour of. Freq. foll. by *with*. L15. ▸**b** *transf.* Give a slight taste or smell to. Usu. foll. by *with*. L17.
2 *verb intrans.* Become modified in colour; take a (usu. specified) shade. M17.
3 *verb trans. fig.* Qualify or modify by the admixture of some slight characteristic or quality. Usu. foll. by *with*. Freq. as ***tinged*** *ppl adjective.* L17.

📖 **1** J. L. WATEN Black hair, tinged with grey. A. CARTER His blood tinged the water pink. **3** R. P. GRAVES An unhappy . . love-affair . . had tinged his work with romantic melancholy. J. WAINWRIGHT It was an envy tinged with admiration.

▶ **B** *noun.* **1** A slight shade of colouring, *esp.* one modifying a tint or colour. Usu. with specifying word. M18. ▸**b** *transf.* A small amount of colouring or dye. L18.
2 *fig.* A slight admixture of some qualifying property or characteristic; a touch or trace *of* some quality. L18.

📖 **1** C. THUBRON His face has acquired an unhealthy lemon tinge. **2** C. P. SNOW In his last years there was a dark tinge of disappointment.

▪ **tingent** *adjective* (now *rare* or *obsolete*) that tinges, colouring M17. **tinger** *noun* E19. **tingible** *adjective* (*rare*) M17.

tingle /ˈtɪŋg(ə)l/ *noun*¹. ME.
[App. from stem of unrecorded Old English verb = Old Norse *tengja* fasten, tie + -LE¹; = Middle High German *zingel* small tack or hook, Low German *tingel*.]
techn. **1** More fully ***tingle nail***. A very small nail; the smallest size of tack. ME.
2 a An S-shaped metal clip used to support heavy panes of glass on a roof. L19. ▸**b** A metal, usu. copper, sheet used for temporary boat repairs. E20.
3 Any of a series of small loops on a bricklayer's line which are wedged between layers of bricks to keep it horizontal. L19.

tingle /ˈtɪŋg(ə)l/ *noun*². L19.
[Origin unkn.: earliest in *whelk-tingle*.]
Any of several marine molluscs which bore holes in the shells of oysters and other molluscs, as (in full ***smooth tingle***) the dog-whelk *Nucella lapillus*, and (in full ***American tingle***) the oyster drill *Urosalpinx cinerea*.

tingle /ˈtɪŋg(ə)l/ *verb* & *noun*³. LME.
[Perh. var. of TINKLE *verb*, by assoc. with RING *verb*¹. Cf. DINDLE, DINGLE *verb*, PRINGLE.]
▶ **A** *verb.* **I 1** *verb intrans.* (Of a part of the body) be affected with a slight prickling or stinging sensation; smart, thrill; (of the ears) be (as) so affected on hearing something especially pleasant or unpleasant. LME. ▸**b** Of the cheeks: smart or redden with shame, indignation, etc. M16.
2 *verb trans.* Cause to tingle; sting, excite, stimulate. L16.
3 *verb intrans.* Cause a slight prickling or stinging sensation *in* a part of the body; pass *through* with a tingling or thrilling sensation. E19.

📖 **1** *American Accent* The Colonel banged down the receiver so hard his hand tingled. C. BUCKLEY Charley's nostrils tingled from the vapors. **2** M. O. W. OLIPHANT It tingled her to her very fingers' ends. **3** A. MAUPIN Feeling the blood tingle in her limbs.

▶ **II** Now *rare* exc. *Scot.*
4 *verb intrans.* Make a continued light ringing sound. LME.
5 *verb trans.* Ring (a bell etc.) lightly. M17.
▶ **B** *noun.* The action or condition of tingling; an instance of this, a tingling sensation in part of the body. L17.

📖 V. NABOKOV The tingle and tang of reality.

▪ **tingler** *noun* a thing which causes tingling, *esp.* a smarting blow E19. **tinglish** *adjective* (*rare*) = TINGLY M19. **tingly** *adjective* characterized by tingling L19.

tingle-tangle /ˈtɪŋg(ə)ltaŋg(ə)l/ *noun*¹. M17.
[Redupl. of TINGLE *noun*³.]
A confused tinkling or ringing, as of several bells.

tingle-tangle /ˈtɪŋg(ə)ltaŋg(ə)l/ *noun*². E20.
[German *Tingeltangel*.]
Esp. in Germany, a cheap or disreputable nightclub etc.; a cabaret.

ting-tang /ˈtɪŋtaŋ/ *noun.* L17.
[Imit.]
A succession of two different ringing sounds, as that made by the ringing of a small bell; *transf.* a small bell.
Comb.: **ting-tang clock**: striking the quarter or half hours with only two bells.

ting-ting *noun* & *interjection* see TING *noun*¹ & *interjection*.

tin hat /tɪn ˈhat/ *noun* & *adjectival phr. slang.* E20.
[from TIN *adjective* + HAT *noun*.]
▶ **A** *noun phr.* A metal hat; *esp.* (MILITARY) a protective steel helmet. E20.
put the tin hat on = *put the lid on*, *put the tin lid on* s.v. LID *noun*.
▶ **B** *adjectival phr.* In *pl.* Drunk. Chiefly MILITARY. E20.
▪ **tin-hatted** *adjective* wearing a metal helmet or helmets E20.

tinhorn /ˈtɪnhɔːn/ *adjective* & *noun. slang* (chiefly *US*). L19.
[from TIN *noun* + HORN *noun*.]
▶ **A** *adjective.* Inferior, contemptible; pretentious, flashy. L19.

📖 R. STOUT You tin-horn Casanova. **tinhorn gambler** a cheap gambler; a person who gambles for low stakes. **tinhorn sport** a contemptible person.

▶ **B** *noun.* A contemptible person, *esp.* one who is pretentious or flashy. Also *ellipt.*, = ***tinhorn gambler*** above. L19.

📖 S. LEWIS Those tin-horns that spend all they got on dress-suits.

Tinikling /tɪnɪˈklɪŋ/ *noun.* M20.
[Tagalog, from *tikling* the Philippine rail (bird) + infix *-in-* done in the manner of.]
A Philippine folk-dance in which the dancer steps between two wooden poles moved alternately together and apart.

tining /ˈtʌɪnɪŋ/ *noun*¹. Now only *Scot.* & *north.* Also **tyn-**. ME.
[from TINE *verb*² + -ING¹.]
The action or an act of losing, (a) loss.

tining /ˈtʌɪnɪŋ/ *noun*². Long *obsolete* exc. *dial.* LME.
[from TINE *verb*¹ + -ING¹.]
1 A hedge, a fence, *esp.* one made of dead thorns. LME.
2 Fencing, hedging; the making or repairing of a hedge. E16.

tining /ˈtʌɪnɪŋ/ *noun*³. E18.
[from TINE *noun*¹, *verb*³ + -ING¹.]
1 In *pl.* The tines or teeth of a harrow. E18.
2 The action or an act of harrowing. M18.

tink /tɪŋk/ *noun*¹ & *interjection.* Also redupl. **tink-tink**. E17.
[Imit.]
(Repr.) an abrupt ringing sound as of metal being struck with a hard light object.

tink /tɪŋk/ *noun*². *colloq.* (chiefly *Scot.*), *derog.* M19.
[Abbreviation.]
= TINKER *noun* 1b.

tink /tɪŋk/ *verb*¹. LME.
[Imit. Cf. TINK *noun*¹ & *interjection*, TINKLE *verb*.]
1 *verb intrans.* Esp. of metal: emit an abrupt ringing sound when struck; tinkle. Also, chink, clink. Long *rare* or *obsolete*. LME. ▸**b** *verb intrans.* Of a person: make such a sound by striking upon resonant metal etc. Long *rare* or *obsolete*. LME.
2 *verb trans.* Cause to emit an abrupt ringing sound. Also, tinkle (a bell etc.). Long *rare*. L15.

tink /tɪŋk/ *verb*². *non-standard.* Pa. t. & pple **tought** /tɔːt/. M18.
[Repr. dial. or foreign pronunc.]
= THINK *verb*².

tinker /ˈtɪŋkə/ *noun.* ME.
[Origin unkn.: earliest in Anglo-Latin surname. Cf. TINKLER *noun*¹.]
1 A (usu. itinerant) pedlar or repairer of pots, kettles, etc. ME. ▸**b** In Scotland and Ireland, a member of a travelling people, a gipsy; *transf.* (*derog.*) a disreputable or abusive person. M16. ▸**c** A clumsy or unskilful worker; a botcher. M17. ▸**d** A mischievous person or animal, esp. a child; a rascal. Freq. *joc.* E20.
2 Any of various fishes, birds, etc., as a skate, a stickleback, a mackerel, a guillemot, *Canad.* a razor-billed auk. *dial.* L18.
3 [from the verb.] An act of tinkering; an (esp. unskilful) attempt at repairing something. M19.
1 not care a tinker's curse, **not care a tinker's damn**, **not care a tinker's** care little or not at all. **not worth a tinker's curse**, **not worth a tinker's damn**, **not worth a tinker's** worthless, of little significance.
Comb.: **tinker-bird** any of several African birds having a call like repetitive hammering, *esp.* a barbet of the genus *Pogoniulus*.
■ **tinkerdom** *noun* the domain of tinkers; the condition or practice of a tinker: M19.

tinker /ˈtɪŋkə/ *verb.* L16.
[from prec.]
1 *verb intrans.* Work as a tinker; repair metal utensils etc. Chiefly as ***tinkering*** *verbal noun* & *ppl adjective*. L16.
2 *verb intrans. transf.* Work on anything clumsily or imperfectly, esp. in an attempt at improvement. Also, occupy oneself aimlessly; trifle, potter. Usu. foll. by *at*, *with*. M17.
3 *verb trans.* Repair as a tinker; repair or attempt to improve clumsily or imperfectly; patch *up*. M18.

> 🕮 **2** G. SWIFT Does he loiter . . with his motor-bike . . tinker with it? ANNE STEVENSON Discarding weak poems, tinkering with the title.

■ **tinkerer** *noun* L19.

tinkle /ˈtɪŋk(ə)l/ *verb, noun, & interjection.* LME.
[Frequentative of TINK *verb*¹: see -LE³.]
▸ **A** *verb.* **I 1** *verb intrans.* Tingle; (of the ears) ring. Now *rare*. LME.
▸ **II 2** *verb intrans.* Emit a succession of short light ringing sounds; (of a person) produce this sound on a bell, musical instrument, etc. LME. ▸**b** *transf.* Of writing: jingle. E17. ▸**c** *fig.* Talk without substance or sense; prate. M17. ▸**d** Move or proceed making this sound. E19.
3 *verb trans.* **a** Call attention to or express by tinkling. M16. ▸**b** Attract or summon by tinkling. L16.
4 *verb trans.* Cause to tinkle or emit short light ringing sounds. E17.
5 *verb intrans.* Urinate. *colloq.* M20.

> 🕮 **2** C. BROWN There was a piano in the auditorium . . sometimes . . I'd just tinkle on it softly. W. GOLDING She dropped her arms and the bracelets tinkled as they fell to her wrists. **c** K. MANSFIELD As to Proust with his Morceaux de Salon . . let him tinkle away. **d** ALDOUS HUXLEY Let her merely tinkle about among the coffee cups. **3** B. BAIN The piano tinkles out its tinkle / reminders of their night / of dreams. **4** C. MCCULLERS A breeze tinkled the glass pendants of the little Japanese pagoda on the table.

▸ **B** *noun & interjection.* **I** *noun & interjection.* Also redupl. **tinkle-tinkle**.
1 (Repr.) a tinkling sound. L17.
▸ **II** *noun.* **2** *gen.* The action or an act of tinkling. E19. ▸**b** An act of urinating. *colloq.* M20.
3 A telephone call. Chiefly in ***give a person a tinkle***. *colloq.* M20.

> 🕮 **2** R. BRADBURY The tinkle of ice in a lemonade pitcher. A. HIGGINS The priest genuflected . . and the bell rang again, a single tinkle. **3** B. BAINBRIDGE Next time you're in London . . give me a tinkle.

Phrases: **tinkling grackle** *Jamaican* a grackle, *Quiscalus niger*, so called from its call.
■ **tinkling** *noun* (*a*) the action of the verb; an instance of this, a tinkling sound; (*b*) = ***tinkling grackle*** above: L15. **tinkly** *adjective* characterized by tinkling L19.

tinkler /ˈtɪŋklə/ *noun*¹. *Scot. & north.* ME.
[Origin unkn.: earliest in Anglo-Latin surname; relation to TINKER *noun* obscure.]
= TINKER *noun* 1.

tinkler /ˈtɪŋklə/ *noun*². E17.
[from TINKLE *verb* + -ER¹.]
A person who or thing which tinkles; *esp.* a small bell.

tinkle-tankle /ˈtɪŋk(ə)ltaŋk(ə)l/ *noun & verb.* E17.
[Redupl. of TINKLE *noun*.]
(Emit) a tinkling with alternation of sound.

tinktinkie /tɪŋkˈtɪŋki/ *noun. S. Afr.* L19.
[Afrikaans: imit., with *-ie* dim. suffix.]
A small bird whose call is a single repetitive note, *esp.* any of several common warblers.

tinman /ˈtɪnmən/ *noun.* Pl. **-men**. E17.
[from TIN *noun* + MAN *noun*.]
A tinsmith; a dealer in tinware.
Comb.: **tinman's solder**: composed of equal proportions of tin and lead; **tinmen's snips** = *tinsnips* s.v. TIN *noun* & *adjective*.

tinned /tɪnd/ *adjective.* LME.
[from TIN *noun*, *verb*¹: see -ED², -ED¹.]
1 Coated or plated with tin. LME.
2 Preserved or contained in an airtight tin; canned. M19. ▸**b** *fig.* = CANNED *adjective* 2. E20.
3 Baked in a tin. *rare*. L19.
2 tinned air *Nautical slang* air supplied by an artificial ventilation system. **tinned dog** *Austral. slang* canned meat.

tinner /ˈtɪnə/ *noun.* ME.
[from TIN *noun* or *verb*¹ + -ER¹.]
1 A tinsmith. ME.
2 A tin-miner. E16.
3 A person who tins foodstuffs; a canner. E20.

tinnery /ˈtɪn(ə)ri/ *noun.* M18.
[from prec. + -Y³, or from TIN *noun* + -ERY.]
Tin-mining; a tin-mine. Now also, a cannery.

tinnet /ˈtɪnɪt/ *noun. obsolete* exc. *dial.* M17.
[Repr. unrecorded Old English form, formed as TINE *verb*¹ + -ET².]
Brushwood for making or repairing a hedge etc.

tinnie *noun* var. of TINNY *noun*.

†tinnient *adjective.* M17–M18.
[Latin *tinnient-* pres. ppl stem of *tinnire* ring, tinkle: see -ENT.]
Ringing, resonant.

tinnitus /tɪˈnʌɪtəs, ˈtɪnɪtəs/ *noun.* M19.
[Latin, from *tinnire* ring, tinkle, of imit. origin.]
MEDICINE. A sensation of ringing or buzzing in the ears.

tinny /ˈtɪni/ *noun.* Also **tinnie**. E19.
[from TIN *noun* + -Y⁶.]
1 A small tin mug, *esp.* one for a child. Chiefly *Scot.* E19.
2 A can of beer. *Austral. colloq.* M20.
3 A usu. small boat with an aluminium hull. *Austral.* L20.

tinny /ˈtɪni/ *adjective.* M16.
[from TIN *noun* + -Y¹.]
1 Orig., made of tin. Now (of ore etc.) consisting of or yielding tin. M16.
2 Characteristic of or resembling (that of) tin; hard, crude, metallic; *esp.* (of sound) of poor quality, missing the lower frequencies; (of a device) producing sound of this quality. L19. ▸**b** Tasting or smelling of tin. L19.
3 Rich, wealthy. *slang*. L19.
4 Lucky. *Austral. & NZ slang*. E20.

> 🕮 **2** P. ACKROYD The tinny sounds of a small orchestra. A. DILLARD The looping plane had sounded tinny, like a kazoo.

■ **tinnily** *adverb* with a tinny sound E20. **tinniness** *noun* L19.

tinpot /ˈtɪnpɒt/ *noun & adjective.* L18.
[from TIN *noun* + POT *noun*¹.]
▸ **A** *noun.* **1** (As two words.) A pot made of tin or tin plate. L18.
2 The pot of molten tin into which a sheet of iron is dipped in the manufacture of tin plate. M19.
▸ **B** *adjective.* Of inferior quality, importance, etc.; cheap, shoddy. M19.

> 🕮 *Times* 'Bourgeois Latvia' was . . advanced, and far from being a tinpot European state.

tinsel /ˈtɪns(ə)l/ *noun*¹. Now *Scot.* ME.
[Prob. formed as TINE *verb*² + Old Norse suffix *-sla*; cf. Norwegian *tynsla* destruction, damage.]
1 The sustaining of damage or detriment; loss. Now *rare* or *obsolete*. ME.
†**2** Perdition, damnation. Only in ME.
3 SCOTS LAW. Forfeiture or deprivation of a right etc. Now only in phrs. *arch.* LME.

†tinsel *noun*². LME–L19.
[formed as TINE *verb*¹ + Old Norse suffix *-sl*.]
= TINNET.

tinsel /ˈtɪns(ə)l/ *noun*³, *adjective, & verb.* LME.
[Old French (or *estincelé* ppl adjective, from *estinceler* sparkle, from) *estincele* (mod. *étincelle*) spark, repr. popular Latin form of Latin SCINTILLA.]
▸ **A** *noun.* †**1** Fabric interwoven with metallic thread or decorated with spangles etc. LME–M18.
2 Spangles, metallic threads, etc., used for decoration to give a sparkling effect; *esp.* glittering metallic strips woven into strands for decorating a Christmas tree etc. L16.
3 *fig.* Superficial brilliance or splendour; showiness, glitter. M17.

> 🕮 **2** *New Yorker* A cheerful shopwindow still hung with Christmas tinsel. **3** C. THUBRON You're besotted by her glamour. I can't believe it. It's just tinsel.

▸ **B** *adjective* (passing into *attrib.* use of the *noun*). Decorated with tinsel; sparkling, glittering; *fig.* showy, flashy. L15.

> 🕮 *Times* The tinsel world of Hollywood. L. ERDRICH Tinsel garlands left over from Christmas.

Comb.: **Tinseltown** *noun & adjective* (*colloq.*) (*a*) *noun* Hollywood; *transf.* a superficially glamorous town; (*b*) *adjective* (chiefly *derog.*) superficially brilliant or glamorous, showy, flashy.
▸ **C** *verb trans.* Infl. **-ll-**, *-**l**-.
1 Apply tinsel to; make glittering or sparkling. L16.
2 Give a speciously attractive or showy appearance to. M18.
■ **tinselled** *adjective* (*a*) decorated with tinsel, glittering, sparkling; (*b*) *fig.* superficially brilliant or splendid, showy, flashy: M16. **tinselly** *adjective* characterized by or heavily decorated with tinsel; gaudy: E19. **tinselry** *noun* showy or gaudy decoration etc. M19.

tinsey /ˈtɪnsi/ *noun & adjective. colloq.* L17.
[Alt.]
= TINSEL *noun*³ & *adjective*.

tint /tɪnt/ *noun & verb*¹. E18.
[Alt. (perh. by assim. to Italian *tinta*) of TINCT *noun*.]
▸ **A** *noun.* **1** A (usu. slight or delicate) colour; a hue, a tinge; *esp.* a faint colour spread over a surface or added to give a specified tinge to a different colour. E18. ▸**b** *fig.* Quality, character; a hint or tinge *of* something. M18. ▸**c** (An application of) a semi-permanent artificial colouring for the hair. E20.
2 *spec.* **a** In painting, a variety of a colour formed by adding white to a base colour. M18. ▸**b** In print-making, a uniform halftone effect produced by a series of lines or dots. E19.

> 🕮 **1** T. THOMSON It is nearly colourless, having only a slight tint of yellow. E. H. GOMBRICH We . . see . . a bright medley of tints which blend in our eye. **b** BYRON Our inborn spirits have a tint of thee.

Comb.: **tint-block** a wooden or metal block engraved with fine parallel lines for printing tints; **tint-tool** an implement for engraving a tint-block.
▸ **B** *verb.* **1** *verb trans.* Apply or give a tint to; tinge. L18. ▸**b** *verb trans.* Colour (the hair) with a tint. E20.
2 In painting, add white to (a base colour). M19.
3 *verb intrans.* Become tinted or coloured. L19.

> 🕮 **1** J. TYNDALL The sun . . tinted the clouds with red and purple. **b** N. FARAH Nails neatly varnished, hair tinted.

■ **tintable** *adjective* L20. **tinted** *ppl adjective* coloured, tinged, (freq. with defining word); *spec.* (of gloss) coloured to reduce the strength of light passing through: M18. **tinter** *noun* a person who or thing which tints; *esp.* an artist skilful in the use of tints: E19. **tinting** *noun* (*a*) the action of the verb; (*b*) tint or tints; colouring: M19. **tintless** *adjective* L18. **tinty** *adjective* having too prominent or clashing tints L19.

tint *verb*² *pa. t. & pple* of TINE *verb*².

tintamarre /tɪntəˈmɑː/ *noun.* M16.
[French, of unkn. origin.]
A confused and noisy uproar; clamour, racket.

> 🕮 C. MACKENZIE The tintamarre of plates, knives, and forks.

†tint for tant *noun phr.* E17–E19.
[Alt. of †*taunt for taunt*, perh. after earlier *tit for tat*.]
= ***tit for tat*** s.v. TIT *noun*³ 1.

tintinnabula *noun* pl. of TINTINNABULUM.

tintinnabulate /*as adjective* tɪntɪˈnabjʊlət, *as verb* tɪntɪˈnabjʊleɪt/ *adjective & verb.* L19.
[Latin *tintinnabulatus* having a bell or bells, formed as next: see -ATE².]
▸ **A** *adjective.* Bell-shaped. *rare*. L19.
▸ **B** *verb intrans.* Ring, tinkle. E20.

> 🕮 J. UPDIKE Her ankle-rings of bronze and silver tintinnabulated.

tintinnabulation /ˌtɪntɪnabjʊˈleɪʃ(ə)n/ *noun.* M19.
[formed as next + -ATION.]
(The sound of) a ringing or tinkling (as) of bells.

> 🕮 A. CARTER Accompanied by a faint tintinnabulation of jewellery, he approached.

tintinnabulum /tɪntɪˈnabjʊləm/ *noun*. Pl. **-la** /-lə/. L16.
[Latin = bell, from *tintinnare* ring + *-bulum* suffix of instrument.]
A small (esp. tinkling) bell.
■ **tintinnabulant** *adjective* (*rare*) ringing, tinkling E19. **tintinnabular** *adjective* = TINTINNABULARY M18. **tintinnabulary** *adjective* of, pertaining to, or characterized by bells or bell-ringing L18. **tintinnabulatory** *adjective* (*rare*) = TINTINNABULARY E19. **tintinnabulous** *adjective* = TINTINNABULARY L18.

tintinnid /tɪnˈtɪnɪd/ *noun*. M20.
[Latin *Tintinnidae* (see below), formed as prec.: see -ID[3].]
ZOOLOGY. A ciliate protozoan of the family Tintinnidae or the suborder Tintinnina, often distinguished by a bell-shaped chitinous test.

†**tintirinties** *noun* see CHINCHERINCHEE.

tinto /ˈtɪntəʊ/ *noun*. Pl. **-os**. L16.
[Spanish = tinted, dark-coloured.]
= TENT *noun*[4]. Now also *gen.*, (a drink of) any red wine.

Tintometer /tɪnˈtɒmɪtə/ *noun*. L19.
[from TINT *noun* + -OMETER.]
(Proprietary name for) a form of colorimeter for the exact determination of colour.

tin-type /ˈtɪntʌɪp/ *noun*. M19.
[from TIN *noun* + TYPE *noun*.]
PHOTOGRAPHY (now *Hist.*). A photograph taken as a positive on a thin tin plate.
not on your tin-type *colloq.* certainly not.

tiny /ˈtʌɪni/ *adjective* & *noun*. L16.
[Extension with -Y[1] of synon. TINE *adjective* & *noun*[5].]
▶ **A** *adjective*. Very small or slight; minute. L16.

K. VONNEGUT We were a very tiny family. *Social History of Medicine* These figures represented only a tiny fraction of those . . with the disease.

Special collocations & phrases: **tiny garment**: made for an expected baby. **tiny mind** (chiefly *derog.*) a feeble or inferior mind, esp. one lacking common sense. ***the patter of tiny feet***: see PATTER *noun*[2].
▶ **B** *noun*. †**1** A very small amount. *rare*. Only in M17.
2 a A very small child, an infant. Usu. in *pl.* L18. ▸**b** (A nickname for) a very large or tall person. *joc.* M20.

2a *Mother* Real tinies can fish . . out of a bowl.

■ **tinily** *adverb* in a tiny degree; minutely, diminutively: M19. **tininess** *noun* L17.

-tion /ʃ(ə)n/ *suffix*.
[Repr. (French *-tion* from) Old French *-cion* from Latin *-tio(n-)*, combining with verb stems in *-t*: see -ATION, -ION.]
Forming nouns denoting (an instance of) action, or a resulting state or condition, as ***completion***, ***protection***, ***relation***, etc.

tiorba /ˈtjɔrba/ *noun*. Pl. **-be** /-be/. M20.
[Italian.]
= THEORBO.

-tious /ʃəs/ *suffix*.
[Repr. Latin *-tiosus*, combining *-iosus* -IOUS with verb stems in *-t*.]
Forming adjectives with the sense 'full of, characterized by', corresponding to nouns in *-tion*, as ***ambitious***, ***nutritious***, ***superstitious***, etc. See -IOUS, -OUS.

tip /tɪp/ *noun*[1]. LME.
[Old Norse *typpi* noun (*typpa* verb, *typptr* tipped, topped, *typpingr* edging), from Germanic base also of TOP *noun*[1].]
1 a The extremity or end of a thing; *esp.* the pointed or rounded end of a slender or tapering thing. LME. ▸†**b** The highest point or level *of* something; the apex. M16–E17.
2 *gen.* A small piece or part attached to or forming the end of a thing. LME. ▸**b** *ANGLING*. The topmost joint of a fishing-rod. L19. ▸**c** A leaf-bud of tea. Usu. in *pl.* L19. ▸**d** Orig., a paper band round the mouth end of a cigarette. Now, = FILTER *noun* 4(c). L19.
3 A thin flat brush (orig. made from the tip of a squirrel's tail) used to lay gold leaf. E19.
4 A light horseshoe covering only the front half of the hoof. M19.

1a B. BREYTENBACH The cigar tip glowed. J. C. OATES The tips of her fingers had gone icy.

Phrases: ***arse over tip***: see ARSE *noun* 1. ***felt tip***: see FELT *adjective*[1]. **from tip to toe** from top to bottom. **on the tip of one's tongue** on the point of being spoken, esp. after difficulty in remembering. ***tip of the iceberg***: see ICEBERG 4.
Comb.: **tip loss** loss of aerodynamic lift at the tip of an aerofoil, due to vortex formation; **tip speed** *AERONAUTICS* (*a*) the velocity of vertical oscillation of a wing-tip; (*b*) the angular velocity of a rotor multiplied by its radius; **tip-tilted** *adjective* turned up at the tip; **tip-touch** *verb trans.* touch with one's fingertips.
■ **tipless** *adjective*[1] E20. **tiplet** *noun* a small tip or point L19.

tip /tɪp/ *noun*[2]. LME.
[App. from TIP *verb*[1].]
An act of tipping; (esp. *BASEBALL*) a light stroke or tap .
foul tip *BASEBALL* a foul hit in which the ball is only grazed. †**tip for tap** = ***tit for tat*** s.v. TIT *noun*[3] 1.

†**tip** *noun*[3]. *slang*. E17–M18.
[from TIP *verb*[2].]
(A drink of) alcoholic liquor.

tip /tɪp/ *noun*[4]. L17.
[from TIP *verb*[2].]
†**1** In skittles, the knocking over of a pin by another which falls or rolls against it. L17–E19.
2 *gen.* An act of tipping or tilting, the fact of being tipped; a slight push or tilt. M19.
3 A place where the contents of a truck etc. are tipped and discharged; *esp.* a place where refuse is tipped, a dumping-ground; *fig.* an extremely untidy place. M19. ▸**b** A truck etc. whose contents are discharged by tipping. M19.

2 tip of the hat *N. Amer.* an acknowledgement of achievement; an expression of thanks etc.
3 V. GLENDINNING She lives in an absolute tip of a flat. *Earth Matters* The report . . surveyed a 100 . . waste tips.

tip /tɪp/ *noun*[5]. M18.
[from TIP *verb*[4]. Cf. next.]
A small present of money given esp. for a service rendered or expected; a gratuity.

J. TROLLOPE They give me vast tips, especially the Yanks.

■ **tipless** *adjective*[2] E20.

tip /tɪp/ *noun*[6]. *colloq.* M19.
[from TIP *verb*[5].]
1 A piece of useful private or special information, *esp.* a forecast upon which to base betting or stock investment etc.; *gen.* a casual piece of advice, a hint. M19.
2 The object of such a piece of information; *esp.* the predicted winner in a horse race. L19.

1 *New York Times* A new collection of managerial tips, with chapters on selling, negotiating, managing. *Decanter* My tip is, 'Buy 1985s'.

Phrases: **miss one's tip** miss one's cue; *fig.* fail in one's object. **straight tip** a direct or honest piece of advice, a strong hint, (freq. in ***the straight tip***).

tip /tɪp/ *verb*[1]. Infl. **-pp-**; pa. t. & pple **tipped**, (*arch.*) **tipt**. ME.
[Perh. from TIP *noun*[1] in sense 'touch (as with) a point'; cf. Low German, Dutch *tippen*. Cf. TIP *verb*[4], *verb*[5], TIP *noun*[2].]
1 *verb trans.* Strike or touch lightly; tap noiselessly. ME. ▸**b** *CRICKET*. Hit (a ball) lightly, esp. with the edge of the bat. E19. ▸**c** *BASKETBALL* & *ICE HOCKEY*. Net (the ball or puck) with a light touch or push. Freq. foll. by *in*, *into*. M20.
2 *verb intrans.* Step or dance lightly; walk on tiptoe; trip. Now *Scot.*, *dial.*, & *US*. E19.
3 *verb intrans.* *MUSIC*. = TONGUE *verb* 9b. Chiefly as ***tipping verbal noun***. L19.

1 G. GREENE He tipped off a satisfactory length of ash. **tip-and-run** a form of cricket in which the batsman must run for every hit.

tip /tɪp/ *verb*[2]. Infl. **-pp-**; pa. t. & pple **tipped**, (*arch.*) **tipt**. Orig. †**type**. LME.
[Prob. of Scandinavian origin, perh. with inf. later infl. by pa. pple *tipt* or TIP *verb*[1]. Cf. TIP *noun*[4], *noun*[3].]
▶ **I** *verb intrans.* **1** Orig., be overthrown, fall. Later, fall by overbalancing, be overturned or upset (also foll. by *over*). LME.
2 Assume a slanting or sloping position; incline, tilt; tilt up at one end and down at the other (usu. foll. by *up*). M17.

1 L. ERDRICH Two men saw the boat tip. **2** JAYNE PHILLIPS The seat tipped at an odd angle.

▶ **II** *verb trans.* **3** Cause to overbalance or fall over; overturn, upset. LME. ▸†**b** Of a skittle pin: knock down another pin by falling or rolling against it. L17–L19.
4 Cause to incline or tilt; raise or push into a slanting position. Also foll. by *up*. E17. ▸†**b** *fig.* Make unsteady; intoxicate. *slang*. E17–E18. ▸**c** *BOOKBINDING*. Foll. by *in*: paste (a single leaf) to a leaf that is part of a section of a book at the inside edge. E20.
5 Drink; drink up (foll. by *off*). *slang* & *dial.* L17.
6 Empty out (a container or its contents) by tilting up or overturning. Also foll. by *out*. M19.
7 Foll. by *off*: dispose of; kill. *slang*. E20.

3 *Which?* A child tipping a pan over. **4** E. DAVID Tip the pan towards you. A. TYLER She . . tipped her head back for a long . . swig. **6** P. FARMER I'd have tipped that bowl and all its contents over Becky. V. GLENDINNING Bags of rubble were being tipped into the skip.

Phrases & comb.: **tipcat** (*a*) a game in which a player strikes a tapered piece of wood at one end, causing it to spring up, before hitting it away; (*b*) the piece of wood used in this game. **tip off** *slang* & *dial.* die. **tip one's hand(s)**, **tip one's mitt** (*slang*, chiefly *US*) reveal one's intentions inadvertently. **tip one's hat**, **tip one's cap** *N. Amer.* raise or touch one's hat or cap in greeting or acknowledgement. ***tip the balance***: see BALANCE *noun*. ***tip over the perch***, ***tip the perch***: see PERCH *noun*[2]. ***tip the scale(s)***: see SCALE *noun*[1].
■ **tippable** *adjective*[1] (of a seat etc.) able to be tilted or tipped up M20. **tipper** *noun*[1] (*a*) a worker employed in tipping or emptying out trucks etc.; (*b*) a device for tipping or tilting, *esp.* one for tipping and emptying a truck etc.; (*c*) a truck etc. designed to tip to unload its contents: M19. **tipping** *noun*[1] (*a*) the action of the verb; (*b*) (in *pl.*) material tipped or emptied out from a quarry etc.; (*c*) ***tipping point***, the point at which the build-up of minor incidents reaches an unbearable level, causing someone to act in a way that they had formerly resisted: E19.

tip /tɪp/ *verb*[3] *trans.* Infl. **-pp-**; pa. t. & pple **tipped**, (*arch.*) **tipt**. LME.
[from TIP *noun*[1], partly repr. Old Norse *typpa* (see TIP *noun*[1]).]
Provide with a tip; attach something to the tip or end of. Also, colour at the tip or edge. Freq. foll. by *with*. Chiefly as ***tipped ppl adjective***.

A. PATON The sun tips with light the mountains of Ingeli. *Hippocrates* Wooden gouges tipped with stainless steel needles.

■ **tipping** *noun*[2] (*a*) an additional usu. contrasting piece forming a tip to something; (*b*) *Scot.* = TIPPET *noun* 2c; (*c*) the action of the verb: ME. **tipping** *adjective* (*dial.* & *arch. slang*) excellent L19.

tip /tɪp/ *verb*[4]. Infl. **-pp-**; pa. t. & pple **tipped**, (*arch.*) **tipt**. E17.
[Prob. from TIP *verb*[1].]
1 *verb trans.* Give, let have; hand, pass. Also foll. by *up*. *slang*. E17. ▸**b** *verb intrans.* Foll. by *up*: hand over money, pay up. *slang*. M19.
2 *verb trans.* Give a tip or gratuity to, esp. in return for a service. E18. ▸**b** *verb intrans.* Give a gratuity or gratuities. E18.

1 tip the wink to give private information or warning to (as) by a wink. **2** D. SHIELDS I tipped the cabby. **b** C. M. WESTMACOTT He used to tip pretty freely.

Comb.: **tip-it** a game in which an object hidden in a player's hand has to be detected by a player on the opposite side.
■ **tippable** *adjective*[2] able to receive a gratuity E20. **ti'ppee** *noun*[1] the receiver of a gratuity L19. **tipper** *noun*[2] a person who gives tips or gratuities, esp. systematically L19.

tip /tɪp/ *verb*[5]. Infl. **-pp-**. L19.
[Prob. from TIP *verb*[1].]
1 *verb trans.* Give a piece of private information or advice about; *esp.* name as a likely winner, a profitable speculation, etc. *colloq.* L19.
2 *verb trans.* Provide with private information or advice; warn, alert, inform. Freq. foll. by *off*. *slang*. L19.
3 *verb intrans.* Give out tips or private information; be a tipster. *colloq.* E20.

1 *Stage* Phillips is tipped as a hot favourite to get an Oscar Award. **2** J. CAREW They suspected that she had tipped off the police.

■ **ti'ppee** *noun*[2] (chiefly *US*) a person who uses inside information about a company or business enterprise to trade profitably M20. **tipper** *noun*[3] = TIPSTER 1 L19.

†**tipe** *noun*. M16.
[Origin uncertain; sense 2 app. synon. with TIP *noun*[1] 1a.]
1 A small cupola or dome. M16–E18.
2 *fig.* The highest point *of* something; the acme. M16–E17.

†**tiphe** *noun*. L16–L18.
[Greek *tiphē*.]
Einkorn wheat, *Triticum monococcum*.

tipi *noun* var. of TEPEE.

tip-in /ˈtɪpɪn/ *noun*. M20.
[from *tip in*: see TIP *verb*[1], *verb*[2].]
1 = ***paste-in*** s.v. PASTE *verb*. M20.
2 *BASKETBALL*. A score made by tipping a rebound into the basket. *US*. M20.

tipiti /tɪpɪˈtiː/ *noun*. M19.
[Portuguese from Tupi *typyty*.]
A strainer used by S. American Indians to express cassava juice.

tipitiwitchet /ˌtɪpɪtɪˈwɪtʃɪt/ *noun*. *US*. M18.
[Origin unkn.]
= ***Venus fly-trap*** s.v. FLY-TRAP 1.

tiple /ˈtiːpleɪ, *foreign* ˈtiple/ *noun*. M20.
[Spanish = treble.]
1 In Spain and Spanish America, a high-pitched stringed instrument resembling a small guitar. M20.
2 A Catalan wind instrument derived from the shawm. M20.

tip-off /ˈtɪpɒf/ *noun*. E20.
[from *tip off*: see TIP *verb*[5].]
1 *slang*. **a** A piece of information, *esp.* one given to the police about criminal activity. E20. ▸**b** A person supplying such information. *slang*. M20.
2 *BASKETBALL*. A method of (re)starting play, in which two opposing players contest a jump-ball; an instance of this. E20.

tippet /ˈtɪpɪt/ *noun*. ME.
[Prob. from Anglo-Norman deriv. of TIP *noun*[1]: see -ET[1].]
1 *Hist.* **a** A long narrow piece of cloth formerly attached to a hood or sleeve, or worn loose around the neck. ME. ▸**b** = CAMAIL 2. *rare*. LME. ▸**c** A short cape or stole worn around the (neck and) shoulders. L15. ▸**d** *ECCLESIASTICAL*. = SCARF *noun*[2] 1b. M16.
2 *transf.* †**a** A hangman's rope. *joc.* LME–E19. ▸**b** A structure in an animal or bird resembling or suggesting a

tippet; *esp.* = RUFF *noun*[1] 3. E19. ▸**c** A length of twisted hair or gut to which a fishing-hook is attached. *Scot.* E19.

■ **tippeter** *noun* (*Hist.*) a member of New College, Oxford, who wore a tippet L17.

tippet /ˈtɪpɪt/ *verb intrans.* E20.
[Perh. alt. of TIPTOE *verb*.]
= TIPTOE *verb* 2.

tipple /ˈtɪp(ə)l/ *verb*[1] & *noun*. L15.
[Back-form. from TIPPLER *noun*[1].]
▸ **A** *verb*. †**1** *verb trans. & intrans.* Sell (alcoholic drink) by retail. L15–M17.
†**2** *verb trans.* Intoxicate. M16–M17.
3 *verb intrans.* Drink alcoholic liquor, esp. habitually. M16. ▸**b** *transf.* Drink, sip. *rare. poet.* M17.
4 *verb trans.* Drink (alcohol), esp. repeatedly in small quantities. L16. ▸**b** Foll. by *away*. Spend or squander by tippling. E17.
5 *verb intrans.* Rain heavily; pour. Usu. foll. by *down*. E20.

> 🕮 **3** R. DAVIES There was plenty of brandy, for . . Lind loved to tipple. D. LESSING The glass stained sour with his father's tippling. **4** A. H. CLOUGH We sit . . and tipple champagne. **5** J. PORTER It was tippling down . . absolutely tippling.

Comb.: **tippling-house** (*obsolete* exc. *Hist.*) an ale-house, a tavern.
▸ **B** *noun*. Drink, *esp.* alcoholic liquor; an alcoholic drink. *colloq.* L16.

> 🕮 S. HOOD It's a single malt . . but it's my favourite tipple. B. W. ALDISS We'll have a bit of a tipple.

tipple /ˈtɪp(ə)l/ *verb*[2]. Orig. & chiefly *dial.* M19.
[Frequentative of TIP *verb*[2]: see -LE[3].]
1 *verb intrans.* Tumble; topple *over*. M19.
2 *verb trans.* Throw; tip up or over. L19.

tippler /ˈtɪplə/ *noun*[1]. LME.
[Origin unkn. Cf. Norwegian dial. *tipla* drip slowly, *tippa* drink in small quantities.]
†**1** A retailer of alcoholic liquor, esp. ale; a tapster. LME–M17.
2 A person who tipples; a habitual drinker of alcohol, esp. in small quantities. L16.

tippler /ˈtɪplə/ *noun*[2]. M19.
[from TIPPLE *verb*[2] + -ER[1].]
1 A revolving frame or cage in which a truck etc. is inverted to discharge its load. M19.
2 A tumbler pigeon. M19.

tippy /ˈtɪpi/ *noun* & *adjective*[1]. *colloq.* L18.
[from TIP *noun*[1] + -Y[1].]
▸ **A** *noun. obsolete* exc. *Scot.*
1 *The* height of fashion; *the* fashionable thing. L18.
2 A dandy. L18.
▸ **B** *adjective*. **1** Very fashionable; stylish, smart. Now *rare* exc. *Scot.* E19.
2 Highly ingenious or clever. Now *rare*. M19.
3 Of tea: containing a large proportion of leaf-buds. L19.

tippy /ˈtɪpi/ *adjective*[2]. *US colloq.* L19.
[from TIP *verb*[2] + -Y[1].]
Inclined to tip or tilt; unsteady.

tippy-toe /ˈtɪpɪtəʊ/ *noun, verb, adverb, & adjective. colloq.* L19.
[Alt. of TIPTOE.]
▸ **A** *noun*. In *pl.* & (occas.) *sing.* = TIPTOE *noun*. L19.
▸ **B** *verb intrans.* Pres. pple & verbal noun **-toeing**. = TIPTOE *verb* 2. E20.
▸ **C** *adverb*. On tiptoe. E20.
▸ **D** *adjective*. = TIPTOE *adjective*. M20.

tipstaff /ˈtɪpstɑːf/ *noun*. Pl. **-staffs**, **-staves** /-steɪvz/. M16.
[Contr. of *tipped staff*.]
1 A metal-tipped staff carried as a symbol of office. M16.
2 *transf.* An official carrying a tipped staff; *esp.* a sheriff's officer, a bailiff. L16.

tipster /ˈtɪpstə/ *noun*. M19.
[In sense 1 from TIP *noun*[6] + -STER; in sense 2 from TIP *noun*[5] + -STER.]
1 A person who provides tips or confidential information, esp. about betting in horse-racing etc. M19.
2 = TIPPER *noun*[2]. L19.

tipsy /ˈtɪpsi/ *adjective* & *verb*. L16.
[from TIP *verb*[2] + -SY.]
▸ **A** *adjective*. **1** Partly intoxicated, so as to be unsteady on one's feet; *euphem.* intoxicated, drunk. L16.
2 *transf.* Characterized by intoxication; causing or caused by intoxication. M17.
3 *fig.* Inclined to tip or tilt; unsteady. M18.

> 🕮 **1** C. HARKNESS Euphorically tipsy on ale, the vicar mistook his way to the . . lavatories. **2** W. SHEED City strays would . . hurl tipsy taunts at my parents. *San Francisco Focus* I . . make a tipsy beeline for the . . counter.

Comb.: **tipsy-cake** a cake soaked in alcohol, freq. served with custard.
▸ **B** *verb trans.* Make tipsy. Long *rare*. L17.

■ **tipsify** *verb trans.* make tipsy, intoxicate E17. **tipsily** *adverb* in a tipsy or intoxicated manner, unsteadily E19. **tipsiness** *noun* L16.

tipt *verbs pa. t. & pple*: see TIP *verb*[1], *verb*[2], *verb*[3], *verb*[4].

tip-tap /ˈtɪptap/ *adjective, verb, & noun*. E17.
[Redupl. of TAP *noun*[2] or *verb*[2].]
▸ **A** *adjective*. That taps repeatedly. *rare*. E17.
▸ **B** *verb intrans.* Infl. **-pp-**. Tap repeatedly or in alternation. M19.

> 🕮 E. BIRNEY The chess-carver tiptapping / in his brick cave.

Comb.: **tip-tap-toe** *dial.* tick-tack-toe, noughts and crosses.
▸ **C** *noun*. (The sound of) a repeated tapping of alternating character. L19.

tiptoe /ˈtɪptəʊ/ *noun, adverb, adjective, & verb*. Also **tip-toe**. LME.
[from TIP *noun*[1] + TOE *noun*.]
▸ **A** *noun sing.* & in *pl.* The tips of the toes. Chiefly in ***on tiptoe(s)***, ***upon tiptoe(s)***, ***on one's tiptoe(s)***, ***upon one's tiptoe(s)***, with the heels raised so that the weight of the body is on the balls of the feet; *fig.* with eager expectation. LME.

> 🕮 ALDOUS HUXLEY Standing on tiptoe he could just reach the wooden latch. J. CASEY She . . began to dance slowly . . up on her tiptoes.

▸ **B** *adverb*. On tiptoe. Now *rare*. L16.
▸ **C** *adjective*. (Characterized by) standing or walking on tiptoe; *fig.* eagerly expectant; extremely cautious or careful. L16.

> 🕮 M. EDGEWORTH Grace . . made her tiptoe approaches. A. MORICE We were being very tiptoe and courteous to each other.

▸ **D** *verb*. Pres. pple & verbal noun **-toeing**.
1 *verb intrans.* Raise oneself or stand on tiptoe. Now *rare*. M17.
2 *verb intrans.* & †*trans.* (with *it*). Go or walk on tiptoe; step lightly or stealthily. M18.

> 🕮 **2** B. A. MASON I used to hear her tiptoeing in late at night. **tiptoe around** cautiously avoid mention or consideration of.

■ **tiptoed** *adjective* (*literary*) raised on tiptoe M17.

tiptop /tɪpˈtɒp/ *noun, adjective, & adverb. colloq.* Also **tip-top**. E18.
[Redupl. of TOP *noun*[1], prob. with assoc. of TIP *noun*[1].]
▸ **A** *noun*. **1** The very top; the highest point or part; the height or acme *of* something. E18.
2 *sing.* & in *pl.* People of the highest quality or rank. Now *rare* or *obsolete*. M18.
3 A line guide on a fishing-rod. *N. Amer.* M20.

> 🕮 **1** S. O'FAOLÁIN Beeches with the rooks' nests in their tiptops.

▸ **B** *adjective*. At the very top; *fig.* of the highest rank or quality; first-rate. E18.

> 🕮 B. CHATWIN The members treated themselves to a tip-top luncheon. M. AMIS I leapt out of bed feeling . . really tiptop.

▸ **C** *adverb*. In the highest degree; superlatively. L19.
■ **tip-topmost** *adjective* highest; best: M20. **tip-topper** *noun* a high-ranking or excellent person or thing E19.

tipula /ˈtɪpjʊlə/ *noun*. Pl. †**-lae**. M18.
[Latin *tippula* water spider, water bug, adopted by Linnaeus as genus name (see below).]
ENTOMOLOGY. A crane-fly. Now only as mod. Latin genus name.
■ **tipulid** *adjective* & *noun* (**a**) *adjective* of or pertaining to the dipteran family Tipulidae, which comprises the crane-flies; (**b**) *noun* a tipulid fly, a crane-fly: L19.

tip-up /ˈtɪpʌp/ *noun* & *adjective*. M19.
[from TIP *verb*[2] + UP *adverb*[1].]
▸ **A** *noun*. A thing which tips or tilts up; *spec.* (**a**) *N. Amer.* any of various sandpipers; (**b**) *N. Amer.* = TILT *noun*[2] 6; (**c**) *ellipt.* a tip-up seat. M19.
▸ **B** *adjective*. Designed to tip or tilt up; *esp.* (**a**) (of a container) designed to discharge its contents by tipping; (**b**) (of a seat in a theatre etc.) designed to tilt up when not occupied to give room for passing. L19.

TIR *abbreviation*.
French *Transport international routier* international road transport (esp. with ref. to EU regulations).

tirade /tʌɪˈreɪd, tɪ-/ *noun* & *verb*. E19.
[French from Italian *tirata* volley, from *tirare* from Proto-Romance verb meaning 'draw': cf. TIRE *verb*[2].]
▸ **A** *noun*. **1** A long vehement speech on some subject; a declamation, a denunciation. E19.
2 A passage of a poem dealing with a single theme or idea. E19.
3 MUSIC. An ornamental run or flourish filling an interval between two notes. L19.

> 🕮 **1** P. CAREY Her mother delivered a long tirade against Irishmen.

▸ **B** *verb intrans.* Utter or write a tirade; declaim vehemently. L19.

tirage /tɪˈrɑːʒ, *foreign* tiraːʒ/ *noun*. Pl. pronounced same. L19.
[French = drawing, bringing out, printing, from *tirer* draw etc.: see TIRE *verb*[2], -AGE.]
A reprint of a book from the same type; = IMPRESSION 5d.

tirailleur /tɪrʌɪˈəː/ *noun*. L18.
[French, from *tirailler* fire in skirmishing order, from *tirer* draw, shoot (see TIRE *verb*[2]) + *-eur* -OR.]
FRENCH HISTORY. Any of a body of skirmishers employed in the French Revolutionary War in 1792; a skirmisher, a sharpshooter; a soldier trained for independent action.

tiramisu /tiːrəmɪˈsuː/ *noun*. L20.
[Italian, from phr. *tira mi sù* pick me up.]
An Italian dessert consisting of layers of sponge cake soaked in coffee and brandy or liqueur with powdered chocolate and mascarpone cheese.

tire /tʌɪə/ *noun*[1]. ME.
[Aphet. from ATTIRE *noun*.]
1 Dress, apparel, attire. Formerly also, apparatus, equipment. *arch.* ME–E18.
2 A covering or ornament for a woman's head; a head-dress. *arch.* LME.
3 A pinafore or apron worn to protect a dress; = TIER *noun*[2] 4. *US.* M19.

tire /tʌɪə/ *noun*[2]. See also TYRE *noun*. L15.
[Perh. a use of prec.]
†**1** *collect.* The curved pieces of iron plate (see STRAKE *noun* 1) with which cart and carriage wheels were formerly shod. L15–E19.
2 A continuous circular band of iron or steel placed round the wheel of a vehicle to strengthen it. L18.

†**tire** *noun*[3]. L16–L17.
[French *tir* shot, volley, from *tirer*: see TIRE *verb*[2].]
The simultaneous discharge of a battery of artillery; a volley, a broadside; *transf.* a rumble of thunder.

> 🕮 MILTON To displode their second tire Of Thunder.

tire /tʌɪə/ *noun*[4]. Also **tyer**. E17.
[Tamil *tayir*.]
In S. India, curdled milk or cream beginning to sour.

tire /tʌɪə/ *noun*[5]. E19.
[from TIRE *verb*[1].]
1 Tiredness, fatigue. *Scot., dial., & colloq.* E19.
2 In *pl.* = ***milk-sickness*** s.v. MILK *noun* & *adjective*. E19.

tire /tʌɪə/ *verb*[1].
[Old English *tēorian*, freq. in compounds *ātēorian*, *ġetēorian*, of unkn. origin.]
▸ **I** *verb intrans.* †**1** Fail, cease supply; diminish, give out, come to an end. OE–E17.
2 Become weak or exhausted from exertion; be worn out. OE.
3 Have one's interest or patience exhausted by excess or monotony; be weary or sick *of* a person or thing. E16.
4 Become weary with waiting *for* something; long *after*, *for*, *to do* something. Orig. & chiefly *Scot.* L18.

> 🕮 **2** G. GREENE I lay down . . —I still tired easily—and fell asleep. **3** S. CHITTY She was now tiring of her and dreamed of more stimulating company. L. KENNEDY I was also, as my mother never tired of telling me, inclined to fecklessness.

▸ **II** *verb trans.* **5** Wear down by exertion; fatigue, exhaust. Also foll. by *out*. OE.
6 Exhaust the interest or patience of (a person) by excess or monotony; satiate, bore. E16. ▸**b** Exhaust, wear out (an object, a person's patience, time, etc.). *arch.* or *poet.* L16.

> 🕮 **5** F. O'CONNOR He wore his mother's glasses. They tired his eyes. M. SARTON Don't you tire yourself out with talking. T. MCGUANE The sun had tired James, and he slept. **6** SHAKES. *Much Ado* Thou wilt . . tire the hearer with a book of words.

■ **tiring** *adjective* wearying, fatiguing L16. **tiringly** *adverb* in a tiring manner, to a wearisome degree L19.

tire /tʌɪə/ *verb*[2]. Long *arch.* ME.
[French *tirer* draw from Proto-Romance, of unkn. origin.]
†**1** *verb intrans. & trans.* Draw, pull, tug. ME–L16.
2 *verb intrans.* Of a hawk: pull or tear with the beak at a tough morsel given to it; tear flesh in feeding. Foll. by *on*, *upon*. ME.
†**3** *verb intrans.* **a** Prey *upon* a person's mind, heart, etc. L16–E17. ▸**b** Exercise oneself *upon* (in thought or action). *rare* (Shakes.). Only in E17.

tire /tʌɪə/ *verb*[3]. ME.
[Aphet. from ATTIRE *verb*.]
†**1** *verb refl.* Get oneself ready *to do* something; prepare to go somewhere; go. Only in ME.
2 *verb trans.* †**a** Equip, fit out; arm. Only in ME. ▸†**b** Clothe, dress, adorn. ME–E18. ▸**c** Dress (the hair or head), esp. with a tire or head-dress. *arch.* LME.
3 *verb trans.* Plaster or decorate (a building). Now *dial.* LME.

†**4** *verb trans.* Prepare, cut, or dress (an egg) as food. LME–M18.

■ **tiring** *noun* (*arch.*) (*a*) the action of the verb (*tiring-house, tiring-room*, a dressing-room, esp. in a theatre); (*b*) attire, apparel: M16.

tire /tʌɪə/ *verb*[4] *trans.* See also TYRE *verb*. L18.
[from TIRE *noun*[2].]
Put a tire or tires on (a wheel or cart).

tired /ˈtʌɪəd/ *adjective*. LME.
[from TIRE *verb*[1] + -ED[1].]
1 Weakened by exertion etc.; exhausted, fatigued (also *tired out*). Also, sick or weary *of*, impatient *with*; *slang* habitually or incorrigibly lazy. LME.
2 Overused, exhausted; (of language) hackneyed, trite. M18. ▸**b** (Of food, flowers, etc.) limp, no longer fresh; (of clothes) crumpled, shapeless, baggy through long wear. L19.

> **1** J. BUCHAN In about a week I was tired of seeing sights. J. STEINBECK He . . massaged the tired muscles. *Lebende Sprachen* I am tired enough to drop. **2** V. S. REID When one whole family must live off a little acre, soon the acre will be tired. *Hair* A good brush through . . brings back . . life to a tired style. *She* It's a tired old joke that women become like their mothers.

Phrases & special collocations: **make tired** *slang* (orig. *US*) get on the nerves of, irritate. ***sick and tired of***: see SICK *adjective*. **the tired businessman** *iron.* a businessman with short working hours and pleasure-loving habits. **tired and emotional** *joc. euphem.* drunk. **tired Tim** [with allus. to two tramps (the other *weary Willie*), characters in the comic magazine *Illustrated Chips*] a tramp, a work-shy person.

■ **tiredly** *adverb* M17. **tiredness** *noun* M16.

tireless /ˈtʌɪəlɪs/ *adjective*. L16.
[from TIRE *verb*[1] + -LESS.]
Having inexhaustible energy; untiring, indefatigable.

■ **tirelessly** *adverb* M19. **tirelessness** *noun* L19.

†**tireling** *noun & adjective*. L16–E17.
[formed as prec. + -LING[1]: cf. *hireling, shaveling*.]
(Designating) a tired person or animal.

> SPENSER His tyreling iade he fiercely forth did push.

tiresome /ˈtʌɪəs(ə)m/ *adjective*. E16.
[formed as prec. + -SOME[1].]
1 Wearisome, tedious, boring. Formerly also, physically tiring. E16.
2 Troublesome, unpleasant; irksome, annoying. *colloq.* L18.

> **1** BEVERLEY CLEARY Standing still doing nothing was tiresome. **2** J. TROLLOPE How tiresome virtue is . . blocking every path to pleasure.

■ **tiresomely** *adverb* L18. **tiresomeness** *noun* M17.

tiretaine /ˈtɪətɛn/ *noun*. ME.
[Old & mod. French, perh. from Old French *tiret, tire* silk stuff from Latin *tyrius* from place-name *Tyre*: cf. TARTAN *noun*[1].]
A strong heavyweight cloth woven of wool mixed with linen or cotton; linsey-woolsey.

¶ Not recorded between ME and M19.

tire-woman /ˈtʌɪəwʊmən/ *noun*. *arch.* Pl. **-women** /-wɪmɪn/. E17.
[from TIRE *noun*[1] + WOMAN *noun*.]
A lady's maid. Formerly also, a dressmaker, a costumier.

tiring-iron /ˈtʌɪrɪŋˌʌɪən/ *noun*. Also †**tarrying-**. E17.
[from TIRE *verb*[1] + -ING[2] + IRON *noun*.]
A puzzle consisting of a number of attached rings on a closed wire loop, the object of the puzzle being to remove the rings from the loop. Usu. in *pl.*

tirl /təːl/ *noun*[1]. Chiefly *Scot.* L15.
[App. rel. to TIRL *verb*[3].]
†**1** ***tirl-bed***, a trundle- or truckle-bed on low wheels or castors. *rare*. Only in L15.
2 An experience or turn at doing something; a trial, a taste. M17.
3 A revolving mechanism like a turnstile; a wheel. L17.
4 An act of rotating; a twirl, a whirl. L18.

tirl /təːl/ *noun*[2]. *Scot.* E19.
[from TIRL *verb*[3].]
An act of rattling, knocking, or tapping.

tirl /təːl/ *verb*[1]. *Scot.* LME.
[Origin unkn.]
†**1** *verb intrans.* Pluck *at*; *esp.* pluck the strings of a harp etc. LME–M16.
2 *verb trans.* Pluck (a string etc.) so as to cause vibration; sound (a stringed instrument). L19.

tirl /təːl/ *verb*[2] *trans.* *Scot. & north.* L15.
[App. rel. to TIRR.]
1 Roll or turn back (bedclothes etc.), pull or strip off (a garment, roof, etc.). L15.
2 Roll back the covering of; strip (a person) naked; unroof (a building); uncover. E18. ▸**b** Uncover (peat, stone, etc.) by removing surface soil, overlying earth, etc.; lay bare. E19.

tirl /təːl/ *verb*[3]. Now chiefly *Scot. & north.* E16.
[Metathetic var. of TRILL *verb*[2].]
▸**I 1** *verb trans.* Cause to move round or rotate; twirl, spin, turn; turn over, move by rolling. E16.
2 *verb intrans.* Turn over, rotate; roll, whirl, spin. M18.
▸**II 3** *verb intrans.* Make a rattling noise by turning or moving something rapidly to and fro or up and down. E16.
4 *verb trans.* Rattle or knock on (a door etc.). *Scot. rare.* L18.

3 tirl at the pin make a rattling noise on a gate or door in order to gain admittance.

tirlie /ˈtəːli/ *noun & adjective*. *Scot.* Also **tirly**. E19.
[from TIRL *noun*[1], *verb*[3]: see -IE.]
▸**A** *noun*. Anything that turns, curls, or spins. E19.
▸**B** *adjective*. Full of twirls or whirls. E19.

Comb.: **tirlie-whirlie** a whirled figure, ornament, or pattern; a whirligig; a musical twirl.

Tir-na-nog /ˈtɪənanəʊg/ *noun*. L19.
[Irish *Tír na nÓg* land of the young.]
IRISH MYTHOLOGY. A fabled land of perpetual youth; an Irish version of Elysium.

tiro /ˈtʌɪrəʊ/ *noun*. Also **tyro**. Pl. **-o(e)s**. LME.
[Latin *tiro(n-)* (in medieval Latin often spelt *tyro*) young soldier, recruit, beginner.]
A beginner, a learner, a novice.

tirocinium /tʌɪrəʊˈsɪnɪəm/ *noun*. Also **tyro-**. Pl. **-nia** /-nɪə/. E17.
[Latin, first military service on campaign, young troops, from prec.]
1 First experience of anything; training, apprenticeship; *transf.* inexperience, rawness. E17.
2 A band of novices or recruits. M17.

Tironensian /tɪrəˈnɛnsɪən/ *adjective & noun*. Also **Ty-**. L18.
[medieval Latin *tironensis* of Tiron, a village in France (see below): see -IAN.]
▸**A** *adjective*. Of or pertaining to a Benedictine congregation founded by St Bernard of Tiron (*c* 1046–1117). L18.
▸**B** *noun*. A member of the Tironensian congregation. L18.

Tironian /tʌɪˈrəʊnɪən/ *adjective*. E19.
[Latin *Tironianus* in *notae Tironianae* Tironian notes: see -IAN.]
Of or pertaining to Tiro, the freedman of Cicero. Orig. & chiefly in ***Tironian notes***, a system of shorthand in use in ancient Rome, said to have been invented or introduced by Tiro.

tirr /təː/ *verb*. *Scot. & north.* M16.
[App. reduced form of TIRVE. Cf. TIRL *verb*[2].]
1 a *verb trans.* Strip (a person) naked, undress; uncover, unroof (a house etc.). M16. ▸**b** *verb intrans.* Take off one's clothes; strip, undress. L18.
2 *verb trans.* Bare (land) of its surface covering; remove (turf or surface soil) from land; lay bare. M16.
3 *verb trans.* Strip or tear off (a covering, esp. roofing). L16.

tirra-lirra /tɪrəˈlɪrə/ *verb & noun*. L16.
[Imit.]
▸**A** *verb intrans.* Of a skylark etc.: sing tirra-lirra (see below). L16.
▸**B** *noun*. A representation of the note of the skylark, or of a similar sound uttered as an exclamation of delight. E17.

tirrit /ˈtɪrɪt/ *noun*. *rare.* L16.
[Origin uncertain: perh. alt. of *terror*.]
A fit of fear or temper; an upset, a disturbance.

> SHAKES. *2 Hen. IV* Here's a goodly tumult! I'll forswear keeping house afore I'll be in these tirrits and frights.

tirrivee /tɪrɪˈviː/ *noun*. *Scot.* E19.
[Origin unkn.]
A fit of rage, a display of bad temper; an unchecked outburst, a tantrum.

tirshatha /təːˈʃɑːθə/ *noun*. Also **T-**. LME.
[Hebrew *tiršāṯā* from Old Persian: cf. Avestan *taršta* his reverence.]
(The title of) a viceroy or prefect of ancient Persia; in the Old Testament and Hebrew Scriptures, Nehemiah.

Tirthankara /tɪəˈtaŋkərə/ *noun*. M19.
[Sanskrit, lit. 'maker of a ford', from *tīrtha* ford, passage + *kara* maker.]
JAINISM. Any of twenty-four Jinas venerated as having by their teaching made a path for others to follow.

tirve /təːv/ *verb trans.* Long *obsolete* exc. *Scot.* ME.
[Origin unkn.]
= TIRR *verb* 1a, 3.

'tis *verb* see IT *pronoun*.

tisane /tɪˈzan/ *noun*. Also (now *rare* or *obsolete*) **ptisan(e)**. LME.
[Old & mod. French *tisane*, †*ptisane*, from Latin (*p*)*tisana* from Greek *ptisanē* peeled barley, barley-water, rel. to *ptissein* peel.]
A wholesome or medicinal drink or infusion, orig. *spec.* made with barley; now (*esp.*), a herbal tea.

¶ The spelling *pt-* arose in E16 and was common in 17. The word became rare until reintroduced from French.

Tisha b'Av /tɪʃə ˈbav/ *noun phr.* Also **Tisha b'Ab**, **Tisha Bov** /ˈbɒv/. M20.
[Hebrew *tišʿāh bĕʾāḇ*.]
The ninth day of the month Ab, on which both the First and the Second Temples are said to have been destroyed, observed by Jews as a day of mourning.

Tishri /ˈtɪʃriː/ *noun*. Also **Tisri** /ˈtɪzriː/. M17.
[Late Hebrew *tišrī*, from Aramaic *šĕrā* begin.]
In the Jewish calendar, the first month of the civil and seventh of the religious year, usu. coinciding with parts of September and October. Formerly called ***Ethanim***.

tisicky /ˈtɪzɪki/ *adjective*. E19.
[Alt. of PHTHISICKY.]
Wheezy, asthmatic. Also, delicate, squeamish.

Tisri *noun* var. of TISHRI.

tisso *noun* var. of TEESOO.

tissual /ˈtɪʃʊəl, ˈtɪsjʊəl/ *adjective*. *rare.* M19.
[from next + -AL[1].]
Of or pertaining to (living) tissue; tissular.

tissue /ˈtɪʃuː, ˈtɪsjuː/ *noun*. LME.
[Old French *tissu* use as noun of pa. pple of *tistre* from Latin *texere* weave.]
1 a A rich cloth, often interwoven with gold or silver. *obsolete* exc. *Hist.* LME. ▸**b** Any of various rich or fine materials of a delicate or gauzy texture. M18.
†**2** A band or girdle of rich material. LME–E17.
3 A woven fabric. M16.
4 A thing that conveys the impression of being woven as if produced by the intertwining of separate elements; an intricate mass, structure, or network *of* things; *spec.* a connected series *of* errors, lies, etc. E18.
5 BIOLOGY. The material of which an animal or plant body, or any of its parts or organs, is composed, consisting of an aggregation of cells, or of modifications or products of cells; (usu. with qualifying word) a particular type or form of this. L18.
6 a = *tissue-paper* below. L18. ▸**b** RACING. A sheet of paper showing the form of the horses competing in a race. M19.
7 PHOTOGRAPHY. Paper made in strips coated with a film of gelatin containing a pigment, used in carbon printing. Now *rare* or *obsolete*. L19.
8 a A disposable piece of soft absorbent paper used as a handkerchief, for drying or cleaning the skin, etc. E20. ▸**b** A cigarette paper. *Austral. & NZ slang.* M20.

> **4** K. AMIS The sun shone through a tissue of cloud. *Irish Press* Sheridan's evidence was a tissue of lies. **5 *areolar tissue, connective tissue, granulation tissue, palisade tissue, reticular tissue***, etc. **8a** P. USTINOV 'Funny? Listen, it's hysterical,' said the President, drying his eyes on a tissue.

Comb.: **tissue-bank** a place where a supply of human or animal tissue for grafting is stored; **tissue culture** a culture of cells derived from tissue; the practice of culturing such cells; **tissue fluid** extracellular fluid which bathes the cells of most tissues, arriving via blood capillaries and being removed via the lymphatic vessels; **tissue-lymph**: derived from the tissues (not directly from the blood); **tissue-matching** = *tissue-typing* below; **tissue-paper** thin soft gauzelike unsized paper, used esp. for wrapping or protecting fragile or delicate articles; **tissue type** MEDICINE a class of tissues which are immunologically compatible with each other; **tissue-type** *verb trans.* determine the tissue type of; **tissue typing** MEDICINE the assessment of the immunological compatibility of tissue from separate sources, esp. prior to transplantation.

■ **tissuey** *adjective* having the quality or texture of tissue M19.

tissue /ˈtɪʃuː, ˈtɪsjuː/ *verb trans.* L15.
[from the noun.]
1 Make into a tissue, weave; *spec.* weave with gold or silver threads. Also, adorn or cover with tissue. Now *rare*. L15.
2 Wipe (*off*) with a tissue. M20.

tissular /ˈtɪsjʊlə/ *adjective*. M20.
[Irreg. from TISSUE *noun* + *-ular* after *muscular, nodular*, etc.]
MEDICINE & PHYSIOLOGY. Of or pertaining to (living) tissue; tissual.

tiswas /ˈtɪzwɒz/ *noun*. *slang.* M20.
[Perh. fanciful enlargement of TIZZ.]
A state of nervous agitation or confusion.

tiswin /tɪzˈwiːn, tɪs-/ *noun*. *US.* L19.
[Amer. Spanish *texguino*.]
An alcoholic drink made by American Indians from maize, wheat, or mesquite beans.

tit /tɪt/ *noun*[1].
[Old English *tit*, corresp. to Middle & mod. Low German *titte*, Dutch *tit*, Middle & mod. High German *zitze*.]
1 = TEAT 1. Now *obsolete* exc. *dial.* OE.
2 A woman's breast. Usu. in *pl. slang* (orig. *US*). E20.
3 A nipple; *spec.* (orig. *Military slang*) a push-button, esp. one used to fire a gun or release a bomb. *colloq.* M20.

📖 **2** T. PARKS She had the best small pointed tits in the whole world.

Phrases & comb.: ***arse over tit***: see ARSE *noun* 1. ***dummy tit***: see DUMMY *noun & adjective*. **get on a person's tit(s)** *slang* cause intense irritation, get on a person's nerves. ***suck the hind tit***: see SUCK *verb*. **tit and ass, tit and arse** *slang* (designating) crude sexuality; ***tit and ass magazine*** = ***tit magazine*** below. **tit magazine** *slang* a magazine containing photographs of nude women. **tits and ass, tits and arse, tits and bums** *slang* = ***tit and ass*** above.

tit /tɪt/ *noun*[2]. *dial.* (chiefly *Scot.*). ME.
[Rel. to TIT *verb*[1], of unkn. origin.]
A short sharp pull; a tug, a jerk, a twitch.

tit /tɪt/ *noun*[3]. M16.
[Rel. to TIT *verb*[2]. In sense 1 var. of earlier †*tip for tap*: see TIP *noun*[2].]
1 ***tit for tat***, one blow or stroke in return for another; an equivalent given in return; retaliation. Also (*rhyming slang*), a hat (cf. TITFER). M16.
2 A light stroke or tap; a slap. E19.

📖 **1** *attrib.*: R. OWEN Anglo-Soviet relations plummeted . . after a series of tit for tat expulsions.

Comb.: **tit-tat-toe** a children's game; *esp.* (chiefly *US*) noughts and crosses.

tit /tɪt/ *noun*[4]. M16.
[Prob. of Scandinavian origin, earliest in TITLING *noun*[1], TITMOUSE: cf. Old Norse *titlingr*, Icelandic *titlingur* sparrow, Norwegian dial. *titling* small size of stockfish.]
1 A small horse, a horse that is not fully grown; later *gen.* (*derog.*), any horse; a nag. Now *rare*. M16.
2 A girl, a young woman; *loosely* a woman of any age. Now (*esp.*), a woman of loose character, a hussy, a minx. L16.
3 A small active passerine bird of the genus *Parus* or the family Paridae, mainly of the northern hemisphere. Also (in comb. or with qualifying word), any of various similar small birds of other families. E18.
bearded tit, blue tit, bush-tit, coal-tit, long-tailed tit, marsh tit, penduline tit, scrub-tit, shrike-tit, Siberian tit, willow tit, etc. **great tit** a common tit, *Parus major*, of Eurasia and N. Africa, with a black and white head, greyish wings, and yellow underparts.
Comb.: **tit-babbler** any of several small Asian babblers chiefly of the genus *Macronous*; **tit-bell** a bell-shaped container filled with seeds, fat, etc., hung out of doors to supply food to tits and other small birds; **tit-pipit** the meadow pipit, *Anthus pratensis*; **tit warbler** (*a*) an Old World warbler of the African genus *Parisoma* or the Asian genus *Leptopoecile*; (*b*) (more fully ***fire-capped tit warbler***), a penduline tit of central Asia, *Cephalopyrus flammiceps*.

tit /tɪt/ *noun*[5]. *slang*. M20.
[Origin uncertain: perh. from TIT *noun*[1]: cf. TIT *noun*[4], TWIT *noun*[1].]
A foolish or ineffectual person, a nincompoop.

📖 R. H. MORRIESON We'll go an' see the silly old tit.

tit /tɪt/ *verb*[1]. *dial.* (chiefly *Scot.*). Infl. **-tt-**. ME.
[Rel. to TIT *noun*[2], of unkn. origin.]
1 *verb trans. & intrans.* Pull or tug (*at*) forcibly; snatch (*at*). ME.
†**2** *verb trans.* Pull *up*, esp. in a halter; hang (*up*). LME–M17.

tit /tɪt/ *verb*[2]. Now *dial.* Infl. **-tt-**. L16.
[Rel. to TIT *noun*[3]: app. an onomatopoeic match to *tat*.]
1 *verb trans. & intrans.* Tap lightly, pat. L16.
2 *verb trans.* Upbraid, scold. Orig. & chiefly in ***tit in the teeth***. L16.

Tit. *abbreviation*.
Titus (New Testament).

Titan /ˈtʌɪt(ə)n/ *noun & adjective*. LME.
[Latin from Greek, name of the elder brother of Kronos.]
▶ **A** *noun*. **1** The sun-god; the sun personified. Chiefly *poet.* LME.
2 GREEK MYTHOLOGY. A member of a family of giants, the offspring of Uranus (Heaven) and Gaia (Earth), who contended for the sovereignty of heaven and were overthrown by Zeus. Usu. in *pl.* L15.
3 *transf.* (Usu. **t-**.) ▸**a** A person resembling a Titan in great stature, physical strength, intellectual power, etc.; a giant. Cf. OLYMPIAN *noun* 3. E19. ▸**b** A machine of great size and power, as a dredger or crane. L19.

📖 **3a** *Time* A Titan of music was gone, an era ended. *Yorkshire Post* This battle of the High Street titans is about . . the need to shift market targets.

▶ **B** *adjective*. (Usu. **t-**.) Titanic, gigantic. M17.
■ **Titaˈnesque** *adjective* resembling or having characteristics of the Titans; colossal, gigantic: L19. **Titaness** *noun* a female Titan; a giantess: L16.

titan- *combining form* see TITANO-[2].

titanate /ˈtʌɪtəneɪt/ *noun*. M19.
[from TITANIUM + -ATE[1].]
CHEMISTRY. A salt containing oxyanions of titanium.

titania /tʌɪˈteɪnɪə, tɪ-/ *noun*. E20.
[from TITANIUM, after *magnesia*, *zirconia*, etc.]
CHEMISTRY. = TITANIUM ***dioxide***.

Titanian /tʌɪˈteɪnɪən/ *adjective*[1]. E17.
[from Latin *Titanius* of or belonging to the Titans: see TITAN, -IAN.]
Of, pertaining to, or like the Titans; Titanic. Formerly also, of the sun-god; solar, sunlike.

titanian /tʌɪˈteɪnɪən, tɪ-/ *adjective*[2]. E19.
[from TITANIUM + -IAN.]
CHEMISTRY. †**1** Of or pertaining to titanium; = TITANIC *adjective*[2]. E–M19.
2 MINERALOGY. Having a constituent element partly replaced by titanium. M20.

Titanic /tʌɪˈtanɪk/ *adjective*[1]. Also **t-**. M17.
[Greek *titanikos*, from *Titanes* pl. of *Titan*: see TITAN *noun & adjective*, -IC.]
†**1** Of or pertaining to the sun. *rare*. Only in M17.
2 Pertaining to, resembling, or characteristic of the Titans of mythology; gigantic, colossal. E18.

📖 **2** ISAIAH BERLIN Great men, Titanic figures, who . . achieve superhuman results—Napoleon, Bismarck. E. SEGAL Barney made a Titanic effort to appear calm.

■ †**Titanical** *adjective* (*rare*) = TITANIC *adjective*[1] 2 M17–L17. **Titanically** *adverb* E19.

titanic /tʌɪˈtanɪk, tɪ-/ *adjective*[2]. E19.
[from TITANIUM + -IC.]
Of, pertaining to, or derived from titanium; containing titanium, esp. in the tetravalent state.

Titanic /tʌɪˈtanɪk/ *adjective*[3] *& noun*. E20.
[A giant Brit. liner which sank on its maiden voyage in 1912 after collision with an iceberg.]
(Designating or pertaining to) a vast and supposedly indestructible organization fated to disaster.

titaniferous /tʌɪtəˈnɪf(ə)rəs/ *adjective*. E19.
[from TITANIUM: see -FEROUS.]
MINERALOGY. Containing or yielding titanium.

Titanism /ˈtʌɪtənɪz(ə)m/ *noun*. M19.
[French *titanisme* formed as TITAN + -ISM.]
The character of a Titan; *spec.* (*a*) revolt against the order of the universe; (*b*) titanic force or power.

titanite /ˈtʌɪtənʌɪt/ *noun*. L18.
[from next + -ITE[1].]
MINERALOGY. †**1** = RUTILE. L18–E19.
2 = SPHENE. M19.

titanium /tʌɪˈteɪnɪəm, tɪ-/ *noun*. L18.
[from TITAN + -IUM, after *uranium*.]
A chemical element, atomic no. 22, which is one of the transition metals, occurring naturally in various clays and other minerals and used to make strong, light, corrosion-resistant alloys. (Symbol Ti.)
Comb.: **titanium dioxide** the oxide TiO_2, an inert compound occurring naturally as the minerals rutile, anatase, and brookite, and used esp. as a white pigment and opacifier; **titanium white** a white pigment consisting chiefly or wholly of titanium dioxide.

titano- /tʌɪˈtanəʊ, ˈtʌɪtənəʊ/ *combining form*[1].
[from (the same root as) TITANIC *adjective*[1]: see -O-.]
Gigantic, huge.
■ **titanosaur** *noun* PALAEONTOLOGY any of various gigantic sauropod dinosaurs, mainly of the Cretaceous period, including *Titanosaurus* L19. **titanothere** *noun* [Greek *thērion* wild animal] PALAEONTOLOGY any of a group of extinct ungulate mammals like rhinoceros, of the Tertiary period M20.

titano- /ˈtʌɪtənəʊ/ *combining form*[2]. Before a vowel or *h* also **titan-**.
[from TITANIUM: see -O-.]
CHEMISTRY & MINERALOGY. Containing titanium.
■ **titaˈnaugite** *noun* (MINERALOGY) a variety of augite containing titanium M20. **titanoˈhaematite**, **titanhaem-** *noun* (MINERALOGY) a variety of haematite containing titanium dioxide in solid solution M20.

titanous /ˈtʌɪtənəs/ *adjective*. M19.
[from TITANIUM after *ferrous* etc.]
CHEMISTRY. Containing titanium, esp. in the trivalent state. Cf. TITANIC *adjective*[2].

titar /ˈtiːtɑː/ *noun*. Also **tetur**, **teetar**. L19.
[Hindi *tītar*, from Sanskrit *tittira* partridge, rel. to Greek *tetraōn*, Latin *tetrao* guinea-fowl, grouse.]
In the Indian subcontinent: the grey francolin of southern Asia, *Francolinus pondicerianus*.

titbit /ˈtɪtbɪt/ *noun*. Also (now chiefly *N. Amer.*) **tidbit** /ˈtɪdbɪt/. M17.
[In 16 *tyd bit*, perh. from dial. *tid* tender, soft + BIT *noun*[2].]
1 A small piece of food; a dainty morsel, a delicacy. M17.
2 An interesting or piquant item of news or information. E18.

📖 **1** *Mother & Baby* Don't let your child feed your dog . . with titbits from his plate. **2** M. FORSTER Haydon told her many indiscreet tit-bits about Mrs Norton.

■ **titˈbitical**, **titbitty** *adjectives* of the nature of or full of titbits L19.

titch /tɪtʃ/ *noun*. *colloq.* Also **tich**. M20.
[from Little *Tich*, stage name of the tiny music hall comedian Harry Relph (1868–1928).]
(A name for) a small person.

titchy /ˈtɪtʃi/ *adjective*. *colloq.* M20.
[from prec. + -Y[1].]
Very small, minute, tiny.

tite /tʌɪt/ *adverb*. *obsolete* exc. *Scot. & dial.* ME.
[Of Scandinavian origin: cf. Old Norse *títt* frequently, Old Swedish *tid* repeatedly, quickly, Norwegian and Swedish dial. *tidt* quickly.]
Quickly, directly, soon. *obsolete* exc. in ***as tite as***, as soon or as willingly as.
■ Also **titely** *adverb* (*obsolete* exc. *dial.*) ME.

titer *noun* see TITRE.

titfer /ˈtɪtfə/ *noun*. *slang*. E20.
[Shortened from *tit for tat* used as rhyming slang: see TIT *noun*[3] 1.]
A hat.

tithe /tʌɪð/ *adjective & noun*.
[Old English *tēoþa* contr. of *teogoþa*: see TENTH *adjective & noun*.]
▶ **A** *adjective*. Designating a division or part which constitutes one tenth of the whole. Formerly also, tenth in a series. OE.

📖 SHAKES. *All's Well* One good woman in ten . . . We'd find no fault with the tithe-woman. *Westminster Review* We have not space to follow Dr. Newman through a tithe part of his illustrations.

▶ **B** *noun*. **1** One tenth of the annual produce of agriculture etc., formerly taken as a tax (orig. in kind) for the support of the church and clergy. Later also, in certain religious denominations: a tenth of an individual's income, pledged to the church. OE. ▸**b** *gen.* Any levy, tax, or tribute of one tenth. E17.
2 A tenth of anything; *loosely* a very small part. L15.

📖 **2** W. BLACK I cannot tell you a tithe of what he said.

Comb.: **tithe-barn**: built to hold a parson's corn or other tithes paid in kind; **titheman** *Hist.* a collector of tithes; **tithe-pig**: due or taken as tithe; ***tithe-proctor***: see PROCTOR *noun* 1.
■ **titheless** *adjective* E17.

tithe /tʌɪð/ *verb*.
[Old English *tēoþian*, *teogoþian*, from prec.]
1 *verb trans.* **a** Grant or pay one tenth of (one's produce, earnings, etc.), esp. towards the support of the church and clergy; pay tithes on (one's produce, land, etc.). OE. ▸**b** Pay or give (a tenth of one's produce, earnings, etc.) as tithe; *gen.* pledge or contribute as a levy. OE.
†**2** *verb trans.* **a** Take every tenth thing or person from (the whole number); take one tenth of (the whole); divide into tenths. OE–M17. ▸**b** *spec.* Reduce (a community or group of people) to one tenth of its number by keeping only every tenth person alive. Later also, reduce the number of (a body of people) by putting to death one in every ten; *rhet.* destroy a large proportion of. LME–L17.
3 *verb intrans.* Pay tithe, esp. to the church. ME.
4 *verb trans.* **a** Impose the payment of tithe on (a person); exact tithe from. LME. ▸**b** Collect one tenth from (goods or produce) by way of tithe. L16.
■ **tithable** *adjective & noun* (a person or thing) subject to the payment of tithes LME.

tither /ˈtʌɪðə/ *noun*[1]. LME.
[from prec. + -ER[1].]
1 A person who pays tithes. Now *rare*. LME.
2 A collector of tithes. Also, a supporter of the system of ecclesiastical tithes. L16.

tither /ˈtɪðə/ *noun*[2]. M20.
[Origin unkn.: cf. DITHER *noun*.]
A state of feverish excitement.

tithing /ˈtʌɪðɪŋ/ *noun*.
[Old English *tēoþung*, from *tēoþa* TITHE *noun* or *tēoþian* TITHE *verb*: see -ING[1], -ING[3].]
1 = TITHE *noun* 1. OE.
2 *Hist.* Orig., a company of ten householders in the system of frank-pledge; later, a rural division originally regarded as one tenth of a hundred. OE.
†**3** A tenth part of anything. ME–E17.
Comb.: **tithingman** *Hist.* (*a*) orig., the chief man of a tithing (see sense 2 above); later, a parish peace-officer or petty constable; (*b*) in Maryland and New England: an elective officer of a township, whose functions included the prevention of disorderly conduct or enforcement of order during religious services.

†**tithymal** *noun*. LME–E18.
[Latin *tithymal(l)us* spurge, *tithymalis* sea spurge, from Greek *tithumalos*, *-malis*. Cf. Old French *tintinmalle* (mod. *tithymale*) cypress spurge.]
Any plant of the genus *Euphorbia*; a spurge.

titi /ˈtiːtiː/ *noun*[1]. M18.
[Aymara.]
Any of several small long-coated monkeys of the genus *Callicebus*, native to the tropical forests of S. America.

titi /ˈtʌɪtʌɪ, ˈtiːtiː/ *noun*[2]. E19.
[Perh. of Amer. Indian origin.]
Any of several evergreen trees and shrubs of the family Cyrillaceae, native to the south-east US; esp. (more fully

black titi) *Cliftonia monophylla* and (more fully ***red titi***, ***white titi***) *Cyrilla racemiflora*.

titi /ˈtiːtiː/ *noun*³. *NZ*. Also **teetee**. L19.
[Maori.]
The sooty shearwater, *Puffinus griseus*. Also, any of several other New Zealand petrels.

Titian /ˈtɪʃ(ə)n/ *noun & adjective*. E19.
[Anglicized from *Tiziano* Vecelli (d. 1576), Venetian painter.]
▸ **A** *noun*. **1** A picture by Titian. E19.
2 A person, esp. a woman, with Titian hair (see below). E20.
▸ **B** *attrib.* or as *adjective*. **1** Painted by or characteristic of the style of Titian. M19.
2 Of hair: of a bright golden auburn colour favoured by Titian in his pictures. L19.
Comb.: **Titian-haired** *adjective* having bright golden auburn hair.
■ **Titiaˈnesque** *adjective* in the style of Titian E19.

titihoya /tɪtɪˈhɒjə/ *noun*. *S. Afr.* M20.
[Zulu *ititihoye*, of imit. origin.]
Any of various plovers having a distinctive cry.

titillate /ˈtɪtɪleɪt/ *verb trans.* E17.
[Latin *titillat-* pa. ppl stem of *titillare* tickle: see -ATE³.]
1 Excite or stimulate as by tickling; *esp.* excite pleasantly, gratify (a sense, the imagination, etc.); exhilarate. E17.
2 Touch lightly; irritate slightly; tickle. M19.

> 🕮 **1** E. SEGAL A . . hysteric, who gets frightened when she titillates a man. N. ANNAN American style began to titillate Europe.

■ **titillatingly** *adverb* in a titillating manner L19. **titillator** *noun* E19. **titillatory** *adjective* pertaining to or characterized by titillation M18.

titillation /tɪtɪˈleɪʃ(ə)n/ *noun*. LME.
[Old & mod. French, or Latin *titillatio(n-)*, formed as prec.: see -ATION.]
1 Excitation or stimulation of the mind or senses; *esp.* pleasing excitement, gratification. LME.
2 A sensation of being tickled; a tingling, an itching. E17.
3 The action of touching lightly or tickling. E17.

Titius–Bode law /tɪʃəsˈbəʊd lɔː, -ˈbəʊdə-/ *noun phr.* M20.
[Johann D. *Titius* (1729–96), its discoverer + J. E. *Bode*: see BODE'S LAW.]
ASTRONOMY. = BODE'S LAW.

titivate /ˈtɪtɪveɪt/ *verb*. *colloq.* Also **titt-**, (earlier) †**tid-**. E19.
[Perh. from TIDY *adjective* after *cultivate*.]
1 a *verb trans.* Make small enhancing alterations or attractive additions to; smarten, adorn; put the finishing touches to. Also foll. by *off*, *up*. E19. ▸**b** *verb intrans.* Make oneself smart; smarten up. M19.
2 *verb trans.* = TITILLATE *verb* 1. (Freq. considered *erron.*) E20.

> 🕮 **1a** R. FRAME She slapped on her warpaint and titivated her hair.

■ **titiˈvation** *noun* E19. **titivator** *noun* a person who titivates E20.

titivil /ˈtɪtɪvɪl/ *noun*. *obsolete* exc. *Hist.* LME.
[medieval Latin *Titivillus*, *Tutivillus*, of unkn. origin.]
A devil in mystery plays who collected words dropped by priests in careless recitation of the church service and carried them to hell; *transf.* a scoundrel, a gossip-monger.

titlark /ˈtɪtlɑːk/ *noun*. M17.
[from TIT *noun*⁴ + LARK *noun*¹.]
A pipit; *esp.* the meadow pipit, *Anthus pratensis*.

title /ˈtʌɪt(ə)l/ *noun*. OE.
[Old French (mod. *titre*), from Latin *titulus* placard, inscription, title.]
†**1** An inscription placed on or over an object, giving its name or describing it; a placard giving written information. OE–M17.
2 The descriptive heading of each section or subdivision of a book (now only in law-books); the formal heading of a legal document; *transf.* a division of a book, statute, etc. ME.
3 a The name of a book, poem, or other composition; an inscription at the beginning of a book indicating its subject or contents and usu. the name of the author, publisher, and place and date of publication. Also = ***title-page*** below. ME. ▸**b** The label or panel on the back or spine of a book giving its title. L19. ▸**c** Chiefly *PUBLISHING*. A book, a magazine, a newspaper; a recording. L19.
4 That which justifies or substantiates a claim; grounds for a claim; an alleged or recognized right, an entitlement. ME. ▸**b** *spec.* in *LAW*. Legal right to the possession of land or property; the evidence of such right; title-deeds. LME. ▸†**c** An assertion of right; a claim. LME–E18.
5 a A descriptive or distinctive appellation; a name, a denomination, a style. LME. ▸**b** An appellation attached to an individual or family in virtue of rank, office, attainment, etc.; *esp.* an appellation of honour pertaining to a person of high rank. Also (*colloq.*), a person with a title. LME.
6 *ECCLESIASTICAL*. A certificate of presentment to a benefice; a guarantee of support usu. required by a bishop from a candidate for ordination. LME.
7 *ECCLESIASTICAL*. Each of the principal or parish churches in Rome, the incumbents of which are cardinal priests. LME.
8 In assaying, the expression in carats of the degree of purity of gold. L19.
9 A piece of written material in a film or television programme explaining action or representing dialogue; a caption; *spec.* a subtitle. Also = ***credit title*** s.v. CREDIT *noun*. E20.
10 *SPORT*. The championship in a contest or competition; the game or contest in which this is decided. E20.

> 🕮 **3a** M. ESSLIN *L'Aveu* . . published in English, under the title 'the endless humiliation'. ***running title***: see RUNNING *adjective*. **c** *Campaign* A new monthly title . . will hit the newsstands at the end of July. **4** JOHN BROOKE No king has ever had a better title to his crown than King George I. A. S. BYATT You should be able to prove your title to the whole collection. **b** ***progress of titles***: see PROGRESS *noun* 3. **5a** O. HENRY His personality secured him the title of 'Black Eagle'. **b** F. FORSYTH He knew Sir Harry . . well enough to drop titles in private. H. CARPENTER He was attracted by good looks and titles. **10** *Swimming Times* Martin Mansell . . took 5 titles, two of which were world bests.

Comb.: **title catalogue** a library catalogue in which entries are arranged alphabetically according to the chief word of the title; **title-deed** a deed or document containing or constituting evidence of ownership (usu. in *pl.*); **title entry**: made for a book in a library catalogue under the title (as opp. to under the author's name); **title fight** *BOXING* a match held to decide a championship; **title-holder** (*a*) a person who holds title-deeds; (*b*) the reigning champion in a particular field of sport; **title insurance** *US*: protecting the owner or mortgagee of land or property against lawsuits arising from defective title; **title-music**: played during the credits at the beginning of a film or television programme; **title-page** the page at or near the beginning of a book which bears the title; **title-part**, **title-role** the part in a play etc. from which the title of the piece is taken; **title-piece** an essay, piece of music, etc., giving its name to the collection of which it forms part; ***title-role***: see ***title-part*** above. **title song**, **title track** the song or track giving its name to a long-playing record or CD.
■ **titleless** /-l-l-/ *adjective* LME. **titleship** *noun* (*rare*) possession of a title; right of ownership: L18. **titlist** *noun* (chiefly *US*) a title-holder, a champion in some sport E20.

title /ˈtʌɪt(ə)l/ *verb trans.* ME.
[from the noun.]
†**1** Write or arrange under titles or headings; make a list of; set down in writing, inscribe, record. ME–M16.
†**2** = ENTITLE *verb* 4. *rare*. ME–M17.
†**3** Dedicate (by name); assign, ascribe. ME–L16.
4 Give a title to (a book or other composition); inscribe the title on, write the heading or headings to. LME.
5 Designate by a certain name indicative of relationship, character, office, etc.; speak of or describe as, style, call. L16. ▸**b** Endow or dignify with a title of rank; speak of by an honorific title. Chiefly as ***titled*** *ppl adjective*. M18.

titler /ˈtʌɪtlə/ *noun*. L16.
[App. from TITLE *noun* + -ER¹.]
†**1** A person who claims or asserts a legal title. L16–M17.
2 *COMMERCE*. A truncated cone of refined sugar. Usu. in *pl.* M19.
3 a A person who writes titles, esp. on film or slides. Now *rare*. E20. ▸**b** A device for providing a film, video recording, etc., with captions or titles. M20.

titling /ˈtɪtlɪŋ/ *noun*¹. LME.
[from TIT *noun*⁴ + -LING¹.]
†**1** A small stockfish. LME–M19.
2 Any of various tits, pipits, and similar small birds, *esp.* a dunnock. Now only *Scot. & north*. M16.

titling /ˈtʌɪtlɪŋ/ *noun*². LME.
[from TITLE *verb* + -ING¹.]
1 The action of TITLE *verb*. LME.
2 *PRINTING*. A type font comprising only capitals and numerals occupying the whole body, used esp. for titles and headings. L19.

titman /ˈtɪtmən/ *noun*. *US dial.* Pl. **-men**. E19.
[from TIT *noun*⁴ + MAN *noun*.]
The smallest pig etc. of a litter; *transf.* a man who is physically or mentally stunted.

titmouse /ˈtɪtmaʊs/ *noun*. Pl. **-mice** /-mʌɪs/. ME.
[from TIT *noun*⁴ + Old English *māse* = Middle Low German, Middle Dutch *mēse* (Dutch *mees*), Old High German *meisa* (German *Meise*), from West Germanic; assim. to MOUSE *noun* in 16.]
1 A bird of the genus *Parus* or the family Paridae; = TIT *noun*⁴ 3. Freq. with specifying word. ME.
2 A small, petty, or insignificant person or thing. Long *rare*. L16.

1 ***blue titmouse***, ***coal titmouse***, ***great titmouse***, ***long-tailed titmouse***, etc.

Titoism /ˈtiːtəʊɪz(ə)m/ *noun*. M20.
[from *Tito*, name adopted by Josip Broz (1892–1980) + -ISM.]
Hist. The ideas or policies associated with Marshal Tito, premier of Yugoslavia 1945–80; *spec.* a form of Communism which concentrated on the national interest without reference to the Soviet Union.

Titoist /ˈtiːtəʊɪst/ *noun & adjective*. M20.
[formed as prec. + -IST.]
Hist. ▸**A** *noun*. A follower or adherent of Titoism. M20.
▸ **B** *adjective*. Of, pertaining to, or resembling Titoism. M20.
■ **Titoite** *noun & adjective* (usu. *derog.*) = TITOIST M20.

titoki /ˈtiːtəʊki/ *noun*. M19.
[Maori.]
A New Zealand tree, *Alectryon excelsum* (family Sapindaceae), with tough timber, reddish flowers, and leaves like those of the ash. Also called ***New Zealand ash***.

titrant /ˈtʌɪtr(ə)nt/ *noun*. M20.
[from next + -ANT¹.]
CHEMISTRY. A reagent added in titration.

titrate /tʌɪˈtreɪt, tɪ-/ *verb trans.* L19.
[French *titrer*, from *titre* title, qualification, fineness of alloyed gold or silver, etc.: see TITLE *noun*, -ATE³.]
CHEMISTRY. Measure the amount of a constituent in (a solution) by slowly adding measured volumes of a suitable specific reagent of known concentration, until the point is reached at which a reaction just begins or ceases to occur (often marked by a change in colour of a reagent or of an added indicator). Also (*MEDICINE*), continuously measure and adjust the balance of (physiological functions or drug dosages).
■ **titratable** *adjective* able to be measured by titration E20. **titrator** *noun* an apparatus for performing titration automatically M20.

titration /tʌɪˈtreɪʃ(ə)n, tɪ-/ *noun*. M19.
[formed as prec.: see -ATION.]
The action or process of titrating something; (an instance of) volumetric analysis.

titre /ˈtʌɪtə, ˈtiːtə/ *noun*. Also ***titer**. M19.
[French: see TITRATE.]
1 Orig., the fineness of gold or silver. Now (*CHEMISTRY*), the concentration of a solution as determined by titration; the minimum volume of a solution needed to reach the end-point in a titration; *MEDICINE* the concentration of an antibody, as measured by the extent to which it can be diluted before ceasing to give a positive reaction with antigen. M19.
2 *CHEMISTRY*. The highest temperature reached during controlled crystallization of free insoluble fatty acids in an oil. L19.

ti-tree /ˈtiːtriː/ *noun*. *NZ*. M19.
[from TI *noun*¹ + TREE *noun*.]
The cabbage tree, *Cordyline australis*: = TI *noun*¹. Also, by confusion, = TEA-TREE 2b.

titrimetry /tʌɪˈtrɪmɪtri, tɪ-/ *noun*. L19.
[from TITRE + -I- + -METRY.]
CHEMISTRY. Titration.
■ **titriˈmetric** *adjective* of or pertaining to titrimetry L19. **titriˈmetrically** *adverb* by means of titrimetry M20.

titter /ˈtɪtə/ *noun*¹. E18.
[from TITTER *verb*¹.]
An act of tittering; a stifled laugh, a giggle.

titter /ˈtɪtə/ *noun*². *slang*. E19.
[Origin uncertain: cf. TIT *noun*¹, TIT *noun*⁴.]
A young woman, a girl.

titter /ˈtɪtə/ *verb*¹. E17.
[Imit.]
1 *verb intrans.* Laugh in a suppressed, nervous, or secretive manner; giggle. E17.
2 *verb trans.* Utter with suppressed laughter. L18.

> 🕮 **1** B. BEHAN The prisoners tittered and had to laugh aloud sometimes at his jokes.

■ **titterer** *noun* E19. **titteringly** *adverb* in a tittering manner M19.

titter /ˈtɪtə/ *verb*² *intrans.* Now *dial.* See also TEETER *verb*. LME.
[= Old Norse *titra* shake, shiver, cogn. with Old High German *zittarōn* (German *zittern* tremble).]
1 Move unsteadily; totter, reel; sway to and fro. LME.
2 See-saw, swing up and down. E19.

titter /ˈtɪtə/ *adverb*. Now only *north*. ME.
[Compar. of TITE with shortened vowel: cf. *elder*, *latter*, *utter*.]
1 More quickly; sooner, earlier. ME.
2 More readily, more willingly, rather. ME.

titter-totter /ˈtɪtətɒtə/ *noun, adverb, & verb*. Now *dial.* M16.
[Redupl. of TITTER *verb*² or TOTTER *verb*.]
▸ **A** *noun*. The pastime of playing see-saw. Also, a see-saw. M16.
▸ **B** *adverb*. In a tottering manner; unsteadily; *fig.* hesitatingly, waveringly. E18.
▸ **C** *verb intrans.* See-saw. E19.

tittery /ˈtɪt(ə)ri/ *noun. slang.* Now *rare.* E18.
[App. from TITTER *verb*^{2}.]
Gin.

tittery /ˈtɪt(ə)ri/ *adjective.* M20.
[from TITTER *noun*^{1} or *verb*^{1} + -Y^{1}.]
Of laughter, a remark, etc.: having a nervous, tittering quality.

tittivate *verb* var. of TITIVATE.

tittle /ˈtɪt(ə)l/ *noun.* LME.
[Latin *titulus* TITLE *noun*, in medieval sense of 'little stroke', 'accent'.]
1 A small stroke or point in writing or printing, as a tilde, a cedilla, a punctuation or diacritic mark, the dot over the letter i, etc.; *gen.* any stroke or tick with a pen. LME. ▸†**b** The three dots (...) following the letters and contractions in the alphabet on hornbooks, usu. followed by *Est Amen.* M16–M17.
2 The smallest or a very small part of something; a minute amount, a whit. Freq. in ***not one jot or tittle*** [after *Matthew* 5:18]. LME.
Phrases: **to a tittle** with minute exactness, to the smallest particular, to a T.

tittle /ˈtɪt(ə)l/ *verb*^{1} *intrans. & trans.* Now *Scot., dial., & colloq.* LME.
[Imit.: app. parallel to TATTLE *verb*, expr. a lighter sound (cf. TITTLE-TATTLE).]
Speak in a low voice, whisper. Also, tell (news) by way of tattle or gossip.

tittle /ˈtɪt(ə)l/ *verb*^{2} *trans. & intrans. dial.* Also **tiddle** /ˈtɪd(ə)l/. LME.
[Alt. of TICKLE *verb*. Cf. TIDDLER *noun*^{2}.]
Tickle.

tittlebat /ˈtɪt(ə)lbat/ *noun. nursery & colloq.* E19.
[Child's var. of STICKLEBACK.]
A stickleback.

tittle-tattle /ˈtɪt(ə)ltat(ə)l/ *noun, verb, & adjective.* E16.
[Redupl. of TATTLE: cf. Low German *titel-tateln* verb, PRITTLE-PRATTLE *noun & verb*.]
▸ **A** *noun.* **1** Talk, chatter, prattle; *esp.* idle talk, petty gossip. E16. ▸**b** A period of idle talk; an item of gossip. L16.
†**2** A habitual tattler, a gossip. L16–E18.
▸ **B** *verb intrans.* Chatter, prate, talk idly; gossip. M16.
▸ **C** *adjective.* Characterized by or addicted to tattling; gossiping. L16.
■ **tittle-tattler** *noun* E17.

tittup /ˈtɪtəp/ *noun.* Chiefly *dial.* L17.
[App. imit., from the sound of the horse's feet.]
A canter, a hand-gallop. Also, a curvet.

tittup /ˈtɪtəp/ *verb intrans.* Infl. **-p(p)-**. L18.
[Rel. to the noun.]
Progress with an up-and-down or jerky movement; walk in an affected manner, mince, prance. Also (of a horse etc.), canter, gallop easily.

📖 P. LAURIE Police horses tittup round .. the Embassy. *Observer* A slim .. figure tittupping around the flat on stiletto heels.

tittupy /ˈtɪtəpi/ *adjective. colloq.* L18.
[from TITTUP *noun* or *verb* + -Y^{1}.]
Apt to tip up; unsteady, shaky.

titty /ˈtɪti/ *noun*^{1}. Chiefly *Scot. colloq.* E18.
[Origin uncertain: perh. repr. a childish pronunc., perh. rel. to TIT *noun*^{4}.]
A sister; a young woman or girl.

titty /ˈtɪti/ *noun*^{2}. Now *colloq.* M18.
[Dial. & nursery dim. of TEAT or TIT *noun*^{3}: see -Y^{6}.]
A woman's breast; a nipple.

📖 G. PALEY Every wild boy on the block has been leaning his thumbs on her titties. ***tough titty***: see TOUGH *adjective*.

Comb.: **titty-bag** a sweetened object given to a baby to suck; **titty-bottle** a baby's feeding bottle with a teat.

titty /ˈtɪti/ *adjective. dial. & colloq.* L19.
[from TIT *noun*^{4} + -Y^{1}.]
Diminutive, insignificant.
Comb.: **titty-totty** *adjective* (*dial.*) = TITTY *adjective*.

tittymeg /ˈtɪtɪmɛg/ *noun. N. Amer.* Also **tickameg** /ˈtɪkəmɛg/. M18.
[from Ojibwa *adikameg*.]
A whitefish of N. American lakes, esp. *Coregonus clupeaformis*.

titubancy /ˈtɪtjʊb(ə)nsi/ *noun. rare.* E19.
[Latin *titubantia*, formed as next: see -ANCY.]
The condition of being titubant; unsteadiness, tipsiness.

titubant /ˈtɪtjʊb(ə)nt/ *adjective. rare.* E19.
[Latin *titubant-* pres. ppl stem of *titubare*: see next, -ANT^{1}.]
Staggering, reeling, unsteady; stammering; tipsy; hesitating, faltering.

titubate /ˈtɪtjʊbeɪt/ *verb intrans. rare.* L16.
[Latin *titubat-* pa. ppl stem of *titubare* stagger: see -ATE^{3}.]
1 Stagger, reel, totter, stumble; rock, roll. L16.
2 Stammer; falter in speaking. E17.

titubation /tɪtjʊˈbeɪʃ(ə)n/ *noun. rare.* M17.
[Latin *titubatio(n-)*, formed as prec.: see -ATION.]
The action or an act of staggering or reeling; MEDICINE rhythmic nodding of the head and trunk, often with a stumbling gait, due to cerebellar disease; *fig.* hesitancy, perplexity, embarrassment. Formerly also, stammering.

titular /ˈtɪtjʊlə/ *adjective & noun.* L16.
[French *titulaire* or mod. Latin *titularis*, from *titulus* TITLE *noun*: see -ULAR.]
▸ **A** *adjective.* **1** That exists or is such only in title or name; holding or bearing a title without exercising the functions implied by it; nominal. L16.
2 Pertaining to, consisting of, or denoted by a title of dignity; (of a person) having a title of rank, titled; bearing or conferring the appropriate title. E17.
3 Of or pertaining to a title or name; of the nature of or constituting a title. M17.
4 From whom or which a title or name is taken; *spec.* designating or pertaining to any of the principal or parish churches of Rome from which the titles of the cardinals are derived. M17.

📖 **1** C. MCCULLOUGH She dismissed the titular head of her department as an incubus around the Departmental neck. **titular abbot** a person holding the title of abbot from a monastery that no longer exists as a religious community. **titular bishop** (*a*) a bishop deriving his title from a Christian see no longer in existence; (*b*) a suffragan bishop. **3 titular character** the title role.

▸ **B** *noun.* **1** SCOTS LAW. A layman who became possessor of the title to the tithes of an ecclesiastical benefice after the Reformation. Also ***titular of the teinds***, ***titular of the tithes***. E17.
2 A person holding a title to an office, benefice, or possession, irrespective of the functions, duties, or rights attaching to it. Also = ***titular bishop*** above. E17.
3 a A person who bears a title of rank; a titled person. M18. ▸**b** A person bearing a particular title or name. E19.
■ **tituˈlarity** *noun* (*rare*) the quality or state of being titular M17. **titularly** *adverb* in respect of title, name, or style; *esp.* in name only, nominally: E17.

titulary /ˈtɪtjʊləri/ *adjective & noun.* Now *rare.* E17.
[Var. of prec. by substitution of -ARY^{2} or -ARY^{1}.]
▸ **A** *adjective.* = TITULAR *adjective.* E17.
▸ **B** *noun.* = TITULAR *noun* 2, 3. E18.

titulature /ˈtɪtjʊlətjʊə/ *noun.* L19.
[from late Latin *titulatum* pa. pple of *titulare* give a title to, from *titulus* TITLE *noun*, + -URE.]
Hist. The set of titles borne by an official; the title by which an official is known.

titule /ˈtɪtjuːl/ *verb trans.* M16.
[Late Latin *titulare*: see prec.]
= TITLE *verb*.

titulus /ˈtɪtjʊləs/ *noun.* Pl. ***-li*** /-lʌɪ, -liː/. E20.
[Latin: see TITLE *noun*.]
An inscription on or over something; *esp.* the inscription on the Cross.

tityra /ˈtɪtɪrə/ *noun.* E20.
[mod. Latin (see below) from Greek *tituras* a kind of bird.]
A tropical American tyrant-flycatcher of the genus *Tityra*, with mainly black and white plumage and a croaking or grunting call.

†**tityre-tu** *noun.* E17–M19.
[Latin *Tityre tu* you Tityrus, the first two words of Virgil's first eclogue, addressed to a man lying at ease beneath a tree.]
Any of a group of well-to-do ruffians on the streets of London in the 17th cent.

Tityrus /ˈtɪtɪrəs/ *noun.* Pl. **-ri** /-rʌɪ, -riː/. E17.
[Latin, name of a shepherd, from Greek *Tituros* said to be Doric for *saturos* satyr.]
MYTHOLOGY. A fictitious monster supposed to be bred from a sheep and a goat.

ti-tzu /ˈtiːtsuː/ *noun.* L19.
[Chinese *dízi* (Wade–Giles *ti-tzu*).]
MUSIC. A Chinese bamboo transverse flute.

Tiv /tɪv/ *noun & adjective.* M20.
[Bantu.]
▸ **A** *noun.* Pl. **-s**, same.
1 A member of a people of central Nigeria living on either side of the Benue river. M20.
2 The Niger-Congo language of this people. L20.
▸ **B** *adjective.* Of or pertaining to this people or their language. M20.

tivy /ˈtɪvi/ *interjection & verb. rare.* M17.
[Prob. imit. Cf. TANTIVY.]
▸ **A** *interjection.* = TANTIVY *interjection.* M17.
▸†**B** *verb.* = TANTIVY *verb.* Only in M19.

Tiwa /ˈtiːwə/ *noun & adjective.* Also **Tigua**. E18.
[Tiwa.]
▸ **A** *noun.* Pl. same, **-s**.
1 A member of a Pueblo Indian people living in the region of Taos, New Mexico. E18.
2 The Tanoan language of this people. M20.
▸ **B** *adjective.* Of or pertaining to this people or their language. E20.

Tiwi /ˈtiːwi/ *noun & adjective.* M20.
[Tiwi, pl. of *tina* man, *tiŋa* woman.]
▸ **A** *noun.* Pl. same.
1 A member of an Aboriginal people inhabiting the Melville and Bathurst Islands in northern Australia. M20.
2 The language of this people. M20.
▸ **B** *adjective.* Of or pertaining to this people or their language. M20.

tiyin /tiːˈjɪn/ *noun.* Pl. same, **-s**. L20.
[Kirghiz.]
A monetary unit of Kyrgyzstan, equal to one-hundredth of a som.

tizz /tɪz/ *noun. colloq.* Also **tiz**. M20.
[Abbreviation.]
= TIZZY *noun*^{2}.

tizzy /ˈtɪzi/ *noun*^{1}. *slang* (now *Hist.*). E19.
[Origin unkn.]
A sixpence.

tizzy /ˈtɪzi/ *noun*^{2}. *colloq.* (orig. *US*). M20.
[Origin unkn.]
A state of nervous agitation. Freq. in ***in a tizzy***.

tizzy /ˈtɪzi/ *adjective. colloq.* L20.
[Prob. ult. imit.]
Of a sound: high-pitched and buzzing or distorted.
■ **tizziness** *noun* L20.

tjaele /ˈtʃeɪlə, ˈʃeɪ-/ *noun.* Also **tae-** /ˈteɪ-/. E20.
[Swedish *tjäle* ice in frozen ground.]
A frozen surface at the base of the active layer in a periglacial environment, which moves downwards as thaw occurs. Freq. *attrib.*

tjalk /tjɑːlk/ *noun.* M19.
[Dutch & Low German from West Frisian *tsjalk*, perh. dim. of *kjal* KEEL *noun*^{2}.]
A flat-bottomed Dutch sailing boat for use in shallow water.

tjanting /ˈtʃantɪŋ/ *noun.* E19.
[Javanese.]
A small hand-held metal instrument for the application of melted wax in batik work.

tjurunga /tʃəˈrʊŋgə/ *noun.* Also **churinga** /tʃəˈrɪŋgə/. Pl. **-s**, same. L19.
[Aranda *tywerrenge*.]
Among Australian Aborigines, a sacred object, *spec.* an amulet.

TKO *abbreviation.*
BOXING. Technical knockout.

TL *abbreviation.*
Thermoluminescence; thermoluminescent (dating technique).

Tl *symbol.*
CHEMISTRY. Thallium.

tlachtli /ˈtlatʃtliː/ *noun.* L19.
[Nahuatl.]
Chiefly *Hist.* Among the Aztecs, Mayas, and other Central American Indian peoples: a ball game, played on an I-shaped court, in which players use knees, hips, and elbows to direct a solid rubber ball into the opponent's end of the court or through either of two vertically-placed rings. Also called ***pok-ta-pok***.

Tlapanec /ˈtlapənɛk/ *noun & adjective.* L19.
[Spanish *tlapaneca*, *-neco* from Nahuatl *tlapanecatl*.]
▸ **A** *noun.* Pl. **-s**, same.
1 A member of an American Indian people of SW Guerrero, Mexico. L19.
2 The language of this people. L19.
▸ **B** *attrib.* or as *adjective.* Of or pertaining to the Tlapanecs or their language. E20.

Tlaxcalan /tlɑːsˈkɑːlən/ *noun & adjective.* Also **Tlascalan**, **Tlaxcaltec** /-ˈkɑːltɛk/. L18.
[from *Tlaxcala* a city and State in Mexico + -AN; *-tec* from Spanish *tlaxcalteca* from Nahuatl.]
(Of or pertaining to) a member of a Nahuatl-speaking people in central Mexico.

TLC *abbreviation.*
1 Tender loving care. *colloq.*
2 CHEMISTRY. Thin-layer chromatography.

Tlingit /ˈklɪŋkɪt, ˈklɪŋgɪt, tl-/ *noun & adjective.* M19.
[Tlingit *łi:ngít* person, Tlingit.]
▸ **A** *noun.* Pl. same, **-s**.
1 A member of a N. American Indian people of the coasts and islands of SE Alaska. M19.

2 The Na-Dene language of this people. E20.
▸ **B** *adjective.* Of or pertaining to the Tlingit or their language. L19.

TLR *abbreviation.*
Twin-lens reflex (camera).

TM *abbreviation.*
1 Trade mark.
2 Transcendental meditation.
3 Trench mortar.

Tm *symbol.*
CHEMISTRY. Thulium.

tmesis /ˈtmiːsɪs/ *noun.* Pl. **tmeses** /ˈtmiːsiːz/. M16.
[Greek *tmēsis* cutting, from *temnein* cut.]
GRAMMAR & RHETORIC. The separation of the elements of a word, esp. a compound word, by the interposition of another word or words.

TMO *abbreviation.*
Telegraph money order.

TMV *abbreviation.*
Tobacco mosaic virus.

TN *abbreviation*[1].
Tennessee.

tn *abbreviation*[2].
1 Ton(s). *US.*
2 Town.

TNT *abbreviation.*
Trinitrotoluene.

TO *abbreviation.*
Turn over (cf. PTO).

to /tɔː/ *noun.* Now *rare.* Pl. same. L19.
[Japanese.]
A Japanese unit of capacity equal to ten sho, equivalent to approx. 18.0 litres or 3.97 gallons.

to /tuː/ *adjective.* Long *obsolete* exc. *dial.* ME.
[Shortening of TONE *adjective.*]
One, esp. *the* one as opp. to *the* other.

to /tʊ, tuː, *unstressed* tə/ *preposition, adverb, & conjunction.* Also before a vowel (*arch.*) **t'** /t(ə)/.
[Old English *tō* adverb & preposition (mainly with dat.) = Old Frisian, Old Saxon *to* (Dutch *toe* adverb), Old High German *zō*, *zuo* (German *zu*), from West Germanic (essentially adverbial). Partly also repr. Old English *te* = Old Frisian, Old Saxon *te*, *ti* (Dutch *te*), Old High German *ze*, *zi*, *za*, from West Germanic (preposition).]
▸ **A** *preposition.* **I** Introducing a noun or pronoun.
1 Expr. a spatial or local relation. ▸**a** Indicating the place, thing, person, condition, etc., approached and reached (also with adverb prefixed, or with another preposition following); *ellipt.* (*a*) (chiefly *arch.*) with ellipsis of *go, come,* etc., esp. in *imper.* or after an aux. verb; (*b*) (chiefly *dial.*) gone to; on the way to; (*c*) after a noun implying or suggesting motion: that goes to, that takes one to. OE. ▸**b** Expr. direction (*lit. & fig.*): in the direction of, towards (*arch.*, introducing a noun suffixed by *-ward* or *-wards*). Also (*obsolete* exc. *dial.* following *look, smell,* etc.), at. OE. ▸**c** Indicating the limit of a movement or extension in space: as far as. Also, indicating the remote limit after an expression of distance. OE. ▸**d** Expr. local and spatial position: at, in. Now *dial. & US colloq.* OE. ▸**e** Expr. the relation of contact etc.; *spec.* (*a*) into or in contact with; on, against; (*b*) expr. contiguity or close proximity: by, beside. OE.
2 Expr. a relation in time. ▸**a** (Indicating a final limit in time, or the end of a period) till, until; so long before a definite future time, *esp.* (in stating the time of day) so many minutes, or a quarter or half of an hour, before a particular hour (specified or *ellipt.* understood). See also FROM 3. OE. ▸**b** At a particular time (now *dial.* exc. in ***today, tomorrow, tonight***); *arch.* (indicating the precise time for an event or action) precisely or punctually at or on. Formerly also, during. OE.
3 Expr. the relation of purpose, destination, result, effect, resulting condition or status. ▸**a** (Indicating aim, purpose, intention, or design) for; for the purpose of; with the view or end of; in order to; towards or for the making of; as a contributory element or constituent of. Also, indicating the crop with which ground is planted. OE. ▸**b** Indicating result, effect, or consequence: so as to produce, cause, or result in. OE. ▸**c** (Indicating a state or condition resulting from some process) so as to become; *colloq.* reduced to the condition of, having become. Also (now *arch. & formal*), (indicating resulting position, status, or capacity) for, as, by way of, in the capacity of. OE. ▸**d** Indicating destination, or an appointed or expected end or event. ME. ▸**e** Indicating that to which something tends or points; *spec.* (*a*) indicating the object of inclination, desire, need, etc.; (*b*) indicating the object of a right or claim. ME.
4 Expr. a limit in extent, amount, or degree. ▸**a** Indicating a limit or point attained in degree or amount: as far as; to the point of; down to. Also, indicating the final point or second limit of a series, or of the extent of a variable quantity or quality. OE. ▸**b** (Indicating the full extent, degree, or amount) so as to reach, complete, or constitute; so far or so much as to cause. Also, expr. the amount, extent, space, etc. *to* which something is limited or restricted. OE.
5 Indicating addition, attachment, accompaniment, or possession. ▸**a** In addition to, besides, with (now esp. (chiefly *dial.*) indicating food taken as an addition to a specified dish or meal). Also, to the accompaniment of; as an accompaniment to (esp. indicating a tune to which words are set). OE. ▸**b** Indicating attachment or adherence (*lit. & fig.*). OE. ▸**c** Indicating the relation of belonging to or being possessed by. OE.
6 Expr. relation to a standard or to a stated term or point. ▸**a** Expr. comparison: in comparison with, as compared with. OE. ▸**b** (Connecting two expressions of number or quantity which correspond to each other, or of which one constitutes the amount or value of the other) in, making up; (now *rare* or *obsolete*) introducing an expression denoting price or cost) for, at. Also, (connecting the names of two numbers, quantities, etc., compared or opposed to each other in respect of amount or value) (as) against. OE. ▸**c** Expr. agreement or adaptation: in accordance with, according to, after, by. OE. ▸**d** Expr. the relation of comparison, proportion, correspondence, agreement, disagreement, etc. Also (now *rare* or *obsolete*), than. ME. ▸**e** Expr. a gen. relation: in respect of, concerning, about, of, as to. Now *rare.* ME. ▸**f** Esp. in GEOMETRY: expr. relative position. L16.
7 Expr. the relation to a specified object of speech, action, etc. ▸**a** Indicating the object of speech, address, etc.; in honour of; for the worship of. OE. ▸**b** Indicating the object of application, attention, etc. Also (*arch. & rhet.*), with ellipsis of *go, betake oneself,* etc. (in imper., or following an aux. verb). ME. ▸**c** (Expr. impact or attack) at, against, upon. Also (*arch.*), (indicating opposition, hostility, etc.) against, towards. ME. ▸**d** Expr. response to a statement, question, command, etc. Also (chiefly *poet.*), indicating the causative agent of an involuntary reaction or responsive action. ME. ▸**e** Expr. exposure of something to a physical agent. LME.
8 Repr. an original dative. ▸**a** Used in the syntactical construction of intrans. verbs; (after *testify, witness, swear, confess,* etc.) in support of; in assertion or acknowledgement of. (See also preceding senses, and the verbs themselves.) OE. ▸**b** Used in the syntactical construction of many translating verbs, introducing the indirect or dative object. (See also preceding senses, and the verbs themselves.) OE. ▸**c** Used after *be, become, seem, appear, mean,* etc., to indicate the recipient of an impression or the holder of a view or opinion; ***be something to***, be something in the view or opinion of; be of importance or concern to (freq. in ***what is that to you?***). Also, introducing the recipient of something given, or the person or thing on whom or which an event acts or operates. OE. ▸**d** Indicating the person or thing towards which an action, feeling, etc., is directed, or for whose benefit, use, disposal, etc., something is done or exists. OE. ▸**e** Expr. the relation of an adjective (or derived adverb or noun) to a noun denoting a person or thing to which its application is directed or limited. Also, introducing the agent-noun. after a passive verb (chiefly after pa. pple expr. a continuing action, esp. with *known, unknown*). OE. ▸**f** Prefixed to a debit entry in accounting. L18. ▸**g** Indicating a person etc. using a specified name or expression: in the language or usage of. E20.

📖 **1a** GOLDSMITH To reclaim a lost child to virtue. A. URE Ridges from the top to near the bottom. LD MACAULAY If he asked his way to St. James's. BROWNING To Ispahan forth-with! OED Come here to me. *Chambers's Journal* Beyond the harbour, away to the east. A. WHITE They are not sending me to Liverpool after all. **b** M. EDGEWORTH Standing with his back to me. *Blackwood's Magazine* He pointed to a clump of trees. R. CONQUEST Miles away to the west. G. HOUSEHOLD The wind . . had gone round to the north. **c** SHAKES. *Macb.* How far is't call'd to Forres? *Fraser's Magazine* Protestant to the backbone. H. B. TRISTRAM Wet to the skin. OED Eleven miles . . to Witney. **d** *Harper's Magazine* You can get real handsome cups and saucers to Crosby. **e** DICKENS Applying plenty of yellow soap to the towel. LD MACAULAY I sit down to table. **2a** WORDSWORTH Some maintain . . to this day. E. BOWEN Mrs. Heccomb always shopped from ten-thirty to midday. A. CARTER The . . clock . . had stopped at five minutes to three. R. PETRIE It's twelve minutes to. **b** J. HOOPER In no parish . . shall the bells be rung to noon upon the Saturdays. *Chambers's Journal* Ainsworth came to his time. **3a** A. HUNTER You sit down to writing at your bureau. *Harper's Magazine* Whole gardens of roses go to one drop of the attar. J. GALSWORTHY He went out to dinner. L. KANNER A means to an end. *Daily Telegraph* The area sown to winter barley was . . increased. **b** W. GOUGE Fire brake out to the destruction of many. R. BAGOT Now, to his despair, he felt . . his patient . . fighting against his skill. **c** CAPT. J. SMITH Tops of Deeres hornes boyled to a jelly. A. C. SWINBURNE I take to witness four . . poems. G. GREENE The half where the hotels used to stand had been blasted to bits. I. MURDOCH The sky had dulled to a . . dark lightless white netted over with grey. **d** DRYDEN Born to bitter Fate. **e** SIR W. SCOTT 'To your health, mother!' said Hamish. *Pall Mall Gazette* The claimant to the Imamship of Sanaa. **4a** GOLDSMITH Sir Tomkin . . swore he was hers to the last drop of his blood. J. LEYLAND Every style from early Norman to late perpendicular. B. MONTGOMERY Three months to a day since the beginning of the Alamein battle. *Times* Thorn EMI, the electronics to showbusiness group. **b** HENRY FIELDING She was in love with him to distraction. *Law Times* The widow's absolute interest to a life estate. *Daily Chronicle* Generous . . to a fault. E. SYKES Notes to the value of 550,000,000 marks. E. S. DUCKETT A man . . thin to emaciation. I. MURDOCH The boy . . resembled him to a singular degree. **5a** I. WALTON Mix these together, and put to them either Sugar, or Honey. C. WATERTON An old song, to the tune of La Belle Catharine. J. RUSKIN He can't have cream to his tea. **b** W. COWPER As creeping ivy clings to wood or stone. B. JOWETT To that opinion I shall always adhere. I. MURDOCH If I could find anything to tie it to. **c** W. CAMDEN Katherine, wife to Charles Brandon, Duke of Suffolke. R. H. DANA Without clothing to his back, or shoes to his feet. ARNOLD BENNETT She belonged to the middle class. L. C. DOUGLAS There is a lot to him that doesn't show up on the surface. R. MACNEIL He served as secretary to the prolocutor. **6a** SHAKES. *Haml.* So excellent a king, that was to this Hyperion to a satyr. **b** JER. TAYLOR Three weeks of five days to the week. W. HUNTINGTON Thirteen to the dozen. THACKERAY Delicious little Havannahs, ten to the shilling. *Daily Express* Odds of nine to two. *National Observer (US)* 297 electoral votes to 241. C. THUBRON Crammed together, sometimes two or three families to a room. **c** LD MACAULAY Temple is not a man to our taste. E. WAUGH To my certain knowledge she's driven three men into the bin. I. MURDOCH Hugh mended his pace to hers. A. CARTER Prone upon her mattress dallying, to all appearances, with her inamorato. **d** J. F. COOPER Strangely contrasted to the chill aspect of the lake. LD MACAULAY Lewis was not inferior to James in generosity and . . far superior to James in . . abilities. PERCY WHITE A . . repast, fashioned on a smaller scale to that provided at Langdale. A. CARTER The next day was Christmas Eve but it was no different to any other day. **e** J. EDWARDS Being conscious to my own inabilities. J. BUCHAN He is a horse-thief to trade. **f** R. HAKLUYT Parallel to the equinoctiall. R. HARDY They formed an angle to the bivouac. **7a** SHELLEY Hail to thee, blithe Spirit! STEELE With continual toasting Healths to the Royal Family. T. HARDY I don't see any monument . . to the late Mr. Bellston. **b** DEFOE We fell to digging. *Blackwood's Magazine* Come, lads, all hands to work! **c** TINDALE *Col.* 3:13 If eny man have a quarrel to a nother. L. CARROLL 'Take a stick to him!' shouted the Vice-Warden. G. DOUGLAS He had a triple wrath to his son. **d** SIR W. SCOTT Little waves . . sparkling to the moonbeams. TENNYSON The dead leaf trembles to the bell. **e** R. HARDY Abandoning . . fertile land to the needs of wild animals. **8a** GOLDSMITH Homage to which they had aspired. R. BAGOT You could swear to its authenticity? M. BANTON He . . can attend to less pressing matters. **b** LD MACAULAY Admit Roman Catholics to municipal advantages. G. HEYER Devoted . . the afternoon to the composition of a formal invitation. **c** W. PAINTER Great dishonour would redound to us. WORDSWORTH A primrose by a river's brim A yellow primrose was to him, And it was nothing more. J. H. NEWMAN Faith has one meaning to a Catholic. A. BIRRELL Lost his heart to Peg Woffington. **d** R. A. KNOX A carriage all to himself. W. MCILVANNEY A woman cleans to this fella's wife. **e** SHAKES. *Merry W.* A man long known to me. MILTON Grateful to Heaven. J. DUNCAN Pervious to air and moisture. LD MACAULAY Under no authority known to the law. **g** *Outlook* Owen Glyn Dwr—Glendower to the Anglo-Saxon. *Transatlantic Review* Lindy (Miss Hoffmann to the kids) had to glide it back down to them.

▸ **II** Introducing an infinitive.
9 With inf. in adverbial relation. ▸**a** Indicating a specified purpose, use, function, or intention. OE. ▸**b** Indicating a specified object or application. OE. ▸**c** Indicating occasion or condition: expr. a fact, supposition, or cause. OE. ▸**d** Indicating potential or actual result or consequence. OE. ▸**e** Indicating a settled, expected, or actual event or outcome. LME.
10 With inf. in adjectival relation. ▸**a** Expr. an intended or future action or state. OE. ▸**b** Expr. possibility or potential action. ME. ▸**c** Expr. duty, obligation, or necessity. LME. ▸**d** Expr. quality or character. LME. ▸**e** With inf. equiv. to a rel. clause with indic.; chiefly after *first, last,* etc., as ***the first to come, the last to speak.*** M16.
11 With inf. in use as noun. OE.
12 With inf. equiv. to a finite verb or clause OE.
13 Other constructions. ▸†**a** Introducing an inf. in a dependent clause when the inf. in the main clause was not so introduced. ME–E17. ▸**b** Introducing an inf. immediately preceded by an adverb or adverbial phr., esp. for emphasis (sometimes considered *erron.*). ME. ▸**c** Used *absol.* at the end of a clause, with ellipsis of the inf. (to be supplied from the prec. clause). Now *colloq.* ME. ▸†**d** Introducing a verbal noun in place of dative inf. (perh. with the idea of a future action). LME–L15.

📖 **9a** DEFOE I gave a soldier five dollars to carry them news. ADDISON But to return to our Subject. OED Are they quite good to eat? *Listener* Now is the time to sow schizanthus. U. CURTISS Sarah went to meet her at . . a saunter. **b** EVELYN The fittest to be chosen. GEO. ELIOT Increased disinclination to tell his story. L. KUPER I try to do my vacuuming quickly. K. WEATHERLY When he was ready to go. **c** SHAKES. *Temp.* I have broke your hest to say so! GOLDSMITH I could not but smile to hear her talk. SIR W. SCOTT Deadly to hear, and deadly to tell. **d** J. RUSKIN He has only to speak a sentence . . to be known for an illiterate. A. LA BERN Ashtrays too heavy to steal. **e** T. GRAY Many a flower is born to blush unseen. BYRON When we two parted . . To sever for years. **10a** SMOLLETT He has a son to educate. *Fraser's Magazine* Leopold was to be appointed Viceroy. BROWNING The best is yet to be. **b** SHAKES. *3 Hen. VI* Sweet Duke of York, our prop to lean upon. WORDSWORTH A maid whom there was none to praise. R. KIPLING The gates are mine to open. E. WALLACE One never-to-be-forgotten occasion. **c** A. RADCLIFFE They had no time to lose. GEO. ELIOT Not . . a thing to make a fuss about. **d** SIR W. SCOTT Crackenthorp was not a man to be brow-beaten. GEO. ELIOT Not the woman to misbehave towards her betters. **e** MILTON He came, and with him Eve, more loth, though first To offend. J. F. COOPER Harper was the last to appear. **11** MILTON God hath pronounc't it death to taste that Tree. POPE Talking is not always to converse. G. CRABBE He fear'd to die. W. H. MALLOCK Not to affirm is a very different thing from to deny. **12** SHAKES. *Haml.* To be, or not to be—that is the question. SWIFT I desire the Reader to attend. SIR W. SCOTT O'er Roslin . . A wondrous blaze was seen to gleam. BROWNING Oh, to be in England! W. MORRIS Ah, what to do? **13a** LD BERNERS A . . prince that wil . . governe wel, and not to be a tyraunt. **b** E. CLARK This answer seemed to seriously offend him. **c** W. D. HOWELLS I kept on . . I had to. F. M. CRAWFORD I wanted to turn round . . It was an effort not to.

Phrases: ***as to***: see AS *adverb* etc. ***nothing to it***: see NOTHING *pronoun & noun*. **that is all there is to it** it is that and nothing more. ***there is nothing to it***: see NOTHING *pronoun & noun*. **to work** *US colloq.* at work, working. ***up to***: see UP *adverb*[1].

▸ **B** *adverb*. †**1** Expr. motion resulting in arrival: to a place etc. implied or indicated by the context. OE–LME.

2 Expr. contact: so as to come close against something. Now *arch. & colloq.* ME.

3 Expr. attention or application. ME.

4 a In conjunction with other adverbs of direction: in one direction as opp. to the other. Long only in TO AND FRO. ME. ▸**b** Expr. direction: towards a thing or person implied. L19.

†**5** Up to a time indicated by the context; till then. ME–M16.

6 Expr. attachment, application, or addition. Now *dial. & colloq.* LME.

†**7** Expr. assent or adhesion: in assent to or favour of something implied. Only in LME.

📖 **2** G. B. SHAW She . . pulls the outside shutters to. **4a** SHAKES. *Ant. & Cl.* This common body, Like to a vagabond flag upon the stream, Goes to and back. **b** *American Naturalist* Owls with their feathers turned wrong end to.

Phrases: ***to and again***: see AGAIN *adverb*.

▸†**C** *conjunction*. **1** To the time that or *that*; till, until, (*that*). ME–E17.

2 During the time that; while; till. (Also foll. by *that*.) *rare*. Only in LME.

to- /tuː, *unstressed* tə/ *prefix*[1] (not productive).

[Old English *to-* = Old Frisian *ti-*, *te-*, Old Saxon *ti-* (*te-*), Old High German *zi-*, *za-*, *ze-* and *zir-*, *zar-* (German *zer-*), from West Germanic from Germanic = Latin *dis-*: see DIS-.]

Forming chiefly verbs with the senses 'asunder, apart, to or in pieces', and 'away, about, abroad, here and there'. Also with intensive force, 'completely, entirely, thoroughly, greatly, severely'.

to- /tuː, *unstressed* tə/ *prefix*[2] (not productive). ME.

[from TO *preposition & adverb*.]

Used in verbs, nouns, adjectives, and adverbs, in the sense of 'motion, direction, or addition to', or as the mark of the infinitive.

toa /ˈtəʊə/ *noun*[1]. Also **tooa** /ˈtuːə/. L18.

[Polynesian.]

A casuarina of the South Sea islands, *Casuarina equisetifolia*, with a hard wood used to make clubs.

toa /ˈtəʊə, *foreign* ˈtɔːa/ *noun*[2]. *NZ*. Pl. same, **-s**. M19.

[Maori.]

Chiefly *Hist.* A brave warrior.

toad /təʊd/ *noun*.

[Old English *tāda*, *tādde*, shortening of *tādige*, *tādie*; of unkn. origin.]

1 Any of numerous amphibians of the order Anura (formerly Salientia), which develop from tadpoles and are tailless as adults; *esp.* (as distinct from *frog*) any of those that have a dry warty skin, walk rather than leap, and were formerly reputed to have poisonous attributes. Freq. *spec.* the European common toad, *Bufo bufo*. OE. ▸**b** With specifying word: any of various animals held to resemble the toad in appearance or habits. L19.

2 A repulsive or detestable person. Freq. *joc.* ME.

3 = TOADY *noun* 2. M19.

1 ***clawed toad***, ***giant toad***, ***midwife toad***, ***natterjack toad***, ***Suriname toad***, etc. **running toad** = NATTERJACK. **toad in the hole** (*a*) sausages or other meat baked in batter; (*b*) any of various children's games, *esp.* a form of hide-and-seek and a game in which lead discs are thrown at holes in a wooden structure. ***b horned toad***.

Comb.: **toad bug** *N. Amer.* any small predacious water bug of the genus *Gelastocoris*; **toad-frog** (*a*) any anuran of the family Pelobatidae, intermediate between toads and frogs; (*b*) *US dial.* = sense 1 above; **toad-headed** *adjective* having a head like a toad; ***toad-headed lizard***, any of several viviparous agamid lizards of the genus *Phrynocephalus*, of the Near East; **toad-lily** any of various Far Eastern lilies constituting the genus *Tricyrtis*, with purple-spotted flowers, several of which are grown for ornament; **toad-rush** a small annual rush, *Juncus bufonius*, of bare muddy places; **toad's cap** *dial.* a toadstool; **toad's cheese** *dial.* any poisonous fungus; **toad's eye tin** a variety of cassiterite resembling wood-tin; †**toadskin** *N. Amer. slang* (*a*) a five-cent stamp; (*b*) a banknote; **toad-snatcher** *dial.* the reed bunting; **toad-spit**, **toad-spittle** = *cuckoo-spit* s.v. CUCKOO *noun*; **toad-stabber**, **toad-sticker** *US slang* a large knife; **toad-strangler** *US dial.* a heavy downpour of rain.

■ **toadery** *noun* (*rare*) a place where toads live or are reared M18. **toadish** *adjective* (*rare*) †(*a*) venomous; (*b*) of the nature of or resembling a toad: E17. **toadless** *adjective* (*rare*) E20. **toadlet** *noun* a small or young toad E19. **toadlike** *adjective* resembling (that of) a toad L16. **toadling** *noun* = TOADLET LME. **toadship** *noun* (with possess. adjective, as ***his toadship*** etc.) a mock title of respect given to a toad L18.

toad-eat /ˈtəʊdiːt/ *verb trans. & intrans. rare*. Infl. as EAT *verb*; pa. t. usu. **-ate** /-eɪt, -ɛt/, pa. pple usu. **-eaten** /-iːt(ə)n/. M18.

[Back-form. from next.]

Behave servilely to (a person), fawn on (a person). Chiefly as ***toad-eating*** *verbal noun & ppl adjective*.

toad-eater /ˈtəʊdiːtə/ *noun*. E17.

[from TOAD + EATER.]

1 A person who eats toads; orig. *spec.* a charlatan's attendant who ate or pretended to eat toads (regarded as poisonous) to demonstrate the charlatan's skill in expelling poison. E17.

2 A fawning flatterer, a sycophant; = TOADY *noun* 2. Also (*derog.*, now *rare*), a humble friend or dependant. M18.

toadfish /ˈtəʊdfɪʃ/ *noun*. Pl. **-es** /-ɪz/, (usu.) same. E17.

[from TOAD + FISH *noun*[1].]

1 A puffer fish; *esp.* the poisonous *Sphoeroides hamiltoni* (more fully ***common toadfish***) of Australasian waters; a porcupine fish. E17.

2 A frog-fish; *esp.* (chiefly *S. Afr.*) one of the family Antennariidae. M17.

3 Any of various bottom-dwelling fishes of the family Batrachoididae, which have a wide flattened head and large mouth, and are found in warm shallow seas; *esp.* (more fully ***oyster toadfish***) *Opsanus tau* of the US Atlantic coast (also called ***oyster-fish***). E18.

toadflax /ˈtəʊdflaks/ *noun*. L16.

[from TOAD + FLAX *noun*.]

1 (More fully ***yellow toadflax***) a plant of the figwort family, *Linaria vulgaris*, resembling a snapdragon but with spurred yellow flowers and leaves like those of flax. Also, usu. with specifying word, any of various other plants, sometimes with leaves of a different shape, belonging to this genus or formerly included in it. L16.

2 ***bastard toadflax***, a small semiparasitic plant of chalk or limestone grassland, *Thesium humifusum*, of the sandalwood family, with linear leaves and small yellowish flowers. L16.

1 ***ivy-leaved toadflax***: see ***ivy-leaved*** s.v. IVY *noun*.

toado /ˈtəʊdəʊ/ *noun*. *Austral.* Pl. **-oes**. E20.

[from TOAD(FISH + -O.]

= TOADFISH 1.

toadstone /ˈtəʊdstəʊn/ *noun*[1]. M16.

[from TOAD + STONE *noun*, translating Latin *batrachites*, Greek *batrakhitēs* or medieval Latin *bufonitis*, *crapaudinus*, French *crapaudine*. Cf. BUFONITE, CRAPAUDINE.]

A stone or stonelike object, esp. a fossil fish tooth, supposed to have been formed in the head or body of a toad, formerly used as an amulet etc. and credited with therapeutic or protective properties.

toadstone /ˈtəʊdstəʊn/ *noun*[2]. *local*. L18.

[Perh. repr. German *to(d)tes Gestein* dead rock.]

A dark brownish-grey vesicular basalt, occurring in the metalliferous limestone area of Derbyshire, England.

toadstool /ˈtəʊdstuːl/ *noun & verb*. LME.

[from TOAD + STOOL *noun*, a fanciful name: cf. ***paddock-stool*** s.v. PADDOCK *noun*[1].]

▸ **A** *noun*. **1** Any of various basidiomycetous fungi in which the fruiting body consists of a round flat cap and a slender stalk; *esp.* one that is poisonous or inedible (cf. MUSHROOM *noun* 1). *colloq.* LME.

2 *fig.* Something of rapid growth and short duration. E19.

📖 **1** K. MANSFIELD If only one could tell true love from false as one can tell mushrooms from toadstools.

▸ **B** *verb intrans*. Grow up like a toadstool; expand or increase rapidly. Cf. MUSHROOM *verb* 3. *rare*. M20.

toady /ˈtəʊdi/ *noun & verb*. L17.

[from TOAD + -Y[6]. In sense 2 perh. back-form. from TOAD-EATER.]

▸ **A** *noun*. **1** A toad, formerly *spec.* a small or young toad. Long *rare* or *obsolete*. L17.

2 A person who behaves servilely to or fawns on another; a sycophant, an obsequious hanger-on. Also (*derog.*, *rare*), a humble friend or dependant. E19.

▸ **B** *verb trans. & intrans.* Be a toady (to); behave servilely to or fawn on (a person). E19.

■ **toadyish** *adjective* E20. **toadyism** *noun* behaviour characteristic of a toady M19.

toady /ˈtəʊdi/ *adjective*. *rare*. E17.

[from TOAD + -Y[1].]

†**1** Resembling a toad. E17–E18.

2 Having many toads. L19.

to and fro /tuː ənd ˈfrəʊ/ *adverbial, noun, prepositional phr.* ME.

[from TO *adverb* + AND *conjunction*[1] + FRO *adverb*.]

▸ **A** *adverbial phr.* **1** Successively to and from a place etc.; with alternating movement; backwards and forwards. ME.

†**2** In places lying in opposite or different directions; here and there. LME–L17.

†**3** For and against a question etc.; pro and con. M16–L17.

▸ **B** *noun phr.* Pl. **tos and fros**.

1 Orig., discussion for and against a question. Later, indecision, vacillation. M16.

2 Movement to and fro; an instance of this. M19.

▸ **C** *prepositional phr.* To and from. Now *rare*. L16.

▸ **D** *adjectival phr.* (Usu. with hyphens.) That moves to and fro; characterized by movement to and fro. M18.

¶ See also TOING AND FROING.

toast /təʊst/ *noun*[1]. LME.

[from TOAST *verb*[1]. Branch II derives from the idea that a woman's name flavours the drink as spiced toast would.]

▸**I 1 a** A slice or piece of bread browned on both sides by exposure to an open fire, a grill, or other source of radiant heat. Now *rare* or *obsolete*. LME. ▸**b** Bread in slices dried and browned by exposure to an open fire, a grill, or other source of radiant heat. M18.

2 This as the type of what is hot and dry. M16.

†**3** In full ***old toast***. A person who drinks to excess; a fellow drinker, a boon companion. *slang*. M17–E18.

4 A light brown, *esp.* the golden-brown colour of toasted bread. E20.

1b be toast *slang* be or be likely to become finished, defunct, or dead. ***French toast***: see FRENCH *adjective*. ***Melba toast***: see MELBA 3. **on toast** served up on a slice of toast; ***have a person on toast*** (*colloq.*), be able to deal with a person as one wishes.

▸**II 5** A person (orig. esp. a woman), institution, etc., in whose honour a company is requested to drink; (*arch.*) *the* reigning beauty of a place etc. E18.

6 A call to a company to drink or an instance of drinking in honour of a person (orig. esp. a woman), institution, etc. M18.

📖 **5** F. BURNEY The present beauty . . a Mrs. Musters . . the reigning toast of the season. **6** G. DALY A round of toasts followed the cutting of the cake. ***loyal toast***: see LOYAL *adjective* 2.

Comb.: **toast-and-water** toast steeped in water, formerly used as a food for invalids; **toast-colour** = sense 4 above; **toastmaster** an official responsible for proposing or announcing toasts at a public occasion; ***toastmaster glass***, ***toastmaster's glass***, a drinking-glass of apparently large capacity with a thick bowl on a tall stem; ***toast Melba***: see MELBA 3; **toastmistress** a female toastmaster; **toast rack** (*a*) a rack for holding slices of toast at table; (*b*) *colloq.* a vehicle, esp. a tram, with full-width seats and (usu.) open sides.

■ **toastie** *noun* (*colloq.*) a toasted snack or sandwich L20. **toasty** *adjective* (chiefly *colloq.*) resembling toast, *esp.* warm and comfortable L19.

toast /təʊst/ *noun*[2]. Chiefly *US & W. Indies*. M20.

[Perh. the same word as prec.]

1 A type of long narrative poem recited extempore. M20.

2 In reggae music, a performance by a disc jockey who speaks or shouts while playing a record. L20.

toast /təʊst/ *verb*[1]. LME.

[Old French *toster* roast, grill from Proto-Romance from Latin *tost-* pa. ppl stem of *torrere* parch. In branch II directly from TOAST *noun*[1].]

▸**I 1** *verb trans.* Burn as the sun does, parch; heat thoroughly. *obsolete* exc. as passing into sense 2. LME.

2 *verb trans.* Brown (bread, cheese, etc.) by exposure to an open fire, a grill, or other source of radiant heat. LME. ▸**b** Warm (one's feet, oneself, etc.) at a fire. M19.

3 *verb intrans.* **a** Warm oneself thoroughly. E17. ▸**b** Of bread, cheese, etc.: become brown by being toasted; admit of being toasted. Cf. earlier TOASTER *noun*[1] 3. E20.

📖 **1** BACON The grass is soon parched with the Sun and toasted. **2** W. MCILVANNEY She toasted one slice of bread. **toasting-fork** a long-handled fork for toasting bread etc. over a fire. **b** W. TREVOR Pulvertaft stood toasting his back at the fire. **3** OED This cheese toasts well.

▸**II 4** *verb intrans.* Propose or drink a toast (*to*). Now *rare* or *obsolete*. L17.

5 *verb trans.* Propose or drink a toast to (a person, orig. esp. a woman, institution, etc.). E18.

📖 **4** F. MANNING When ere I Toast . . I'll begin No Giant's Health. **5** L. MACNEICE People . . toasting the King, Red lozenges of light as each one lifts his glass. C. SIMMONS I . . held up my glass to toast the proposal. **toasting glass** a glass used for drinking toasts.

toast /təʊst/ *verb*[2] *trans. & intrans.* L20.
[from TOAST *noun*[2].]
Accompany (reggae music) by speaking or shouting. Freq. as ***toasting*** *verbal noun.*

toaster /ˈtəʊstə/ *noun*[1]. L16.
[from TOAST *verb*[1] + -ER[1].]
▶ **I 1** A person who toasts bread etc. L16.
2 A thing which toasts bread etc.; *spec.* (*a*) a toasting-fork; (*b*) an electric appliance for making toast. L17.
3 Bread, cheese, etc., that admits of being toasted. Freq. with specifying word. L17.
▶ **II 4** A person who proposes or joins in a toast; *spec.* a toastmaster. E18.
Comb.: **toaster-oven** a small oven suitable for toasting, broiling, and baking.

toaster /ˈtəʊstə/ *noun*[2]. L20.
[from TOAST *verb*[2] + -ER[1].]
A person who accompanies reggae music by speaking or shouting.

toa-toa /ˈtəʊətəʊə/ *noun.* M19.
[Maori.]
A small New Zealand coniferous tree, *Phyllocladus glaucus*, a kind of celery-top pine.

Toba /ˈtəʊbə/ *noun & adjective.* E19.
[Origin unkn.]
▶ **A** *noun.* **1** A member of a S. American Indian people inhabiting areas of the Gran Chaco in Argentina and Bolivia. E19.
2 The Guaycuruan language of this people. L19.
▶ **B** *adjective.* Of or pertaining to this people or their language. M20.

tobacco /təˈbakəʊ/ *noun.* Pl. **-o(e)s**. M16.
[Spanish *tabaco*, reputedly from a Carib word meaning a pipe through which the smoke was inhaled or from a Taino word for a primitive cigar, but perh. from Arab.]
1 A preparation of the dried leaves of the plants *Nicotiana tabacum* or *N. rustica* (see sense 2), which is smoked in pipes, cigarettes, cigars, etc., for its pleasantly relaxing effects, taken as snuff, or chewed; a particular form of this. M16. ▶**b** A similar preparation of the dried leaves of other plants. L19. ▶**c** A deep shade of brown; = TABAC *noun*[1]. E20.
2 Either of the plants (of tropical American origin) which furnish the leaves for this preparation: *Nicotiana tabacum*, of the nightshade family, the kind now most commonly cultivated, and the allied *N. rustica* (more fully ***green tobacco***, ***wild tobacco***). Also (with specifying word), any of various plants whose dried leaves are smoked in a similar way. L16.

> 📖 **1** BYRON Sublime Tobacco! Which from east to west Cheers the tar's labour or the Turkman's rest. ***Latakia tobacco***, ***negro-head tobacco***, ***plug tobacco***, ***Turkish tobacco***, ***Virginia tobacco***, etc. **2** ***Indian tobacco***: see INDIAN *adjective.* ***rabbit tobacco***: see RABBIT *noun.*

Comb.: **tobacco beetle** a small beetle, *Lasioderma serricorne* (family Anobiidae), which infests stored tobacco and other dried products; **tobacco-box** (*a*) a box for holding tobacco, *esp.* a small flat box to be carried in the pocket; (*b*) either of two flattened N. American fishes, the little skate, *Raja erinacea*, and the pumpkinseed, *Lepomis gibbosus*; **tobacco-cutter** †(*a*) a person employed in cutting tobacco; (*b*) a machine or knife for cutting tobacco; **tobacco dove** a small light brown dove, *Columbina passerina*, found from south-eastern US to northern S. America; also called ***common ground dove***; **tobacco-fish** a sea bass, *Serranus tabacarius*, found off the Atlantic coasts of America; **tobacco flea-beetle** a small American leaf-beetle, *Epitrix hirtipennis*, the adults of which feed on tobacco leaves and are a serious pest; **tobacco fly** *US* (the adult of) either the tobacco hornworm or the tomato hornworm; **tobacco heart** MEDICINE a condition caused by the excessive use of tobacco, characterized by a rapid and irregular pulse, pain in the chest, breathlessness, etc.; **tobacco hornworm** a large American hawkmoth, *Manduca sexta*, the larvae of which feed on the leaves of tobacco and related plants; also called ***southern hornworm***; **tobacco house** †(*a*) a place of public resort for the sale and smoking of tobacco; (*b*) a building for the storage of tobacco; **tobacco-leaf** (*a*) a leaf of the tobacco plant; (*b*) a form of 18th-cent. Chinese porcelain decorated with a floral pattern including tobacco-leaves (freq. *attrib.*); **tobacco lord** SCOTTISH HISTORY a wealthy tobacco merchant of Glasgow; **tobacco-man** (long *rare* or *obsolete*) a seller of tobacco, a tobacconist; **tobacco mosaic virus** an RNA virus that causes mosaic disease in tobacco and similar effects in other plants, much used as an experimental subject; abbreviation ***TMV***. **tobacco moth** a pyralid moth, *Ephestia elutella*, the larvae of which feed on stored products including tobacco, cocoa, nuts, etc.; also called ***cocoa moth***; **tobacco-pipe** (*a*) a pipe for smoking tobacco; (*b*) *US local* = ***Indian pipe*** s.v. INDIAN *adjective*; (*c*) ***tobacco-pipe fish***, a pipefish, *Fistularia tabacaria* (family Fistulariidae), occurring in the tropical W. Atlantic; **tobacco plant** either of the plants which yield tobacco; also, any of various plants of the genus *Nicotiana* grown for their night-scented flowers; **tobacco-pouch** a pouch for carrying tobacco for smoking or chewing; **tobacco-root** the root of either of two N. American plants: the bitter-root *Lewisia rediviva*, and a valerian, *Valeriana edulis*, which has a tobacco-like smell when cooked; **tobacco-shop** (*a*) a shop for the sale of tobacco; †(*b*) a place of public resort for smoking tobacco; **tobacco-stopper** an instrument for pressing down the tobacco in the bowl of a pipe for smoking; **tobacco streak** a streak disease of tobacco and many other plants, caused by an RNA virus; **tobacco-water** an infusion of tobacco in water, used esp. for sprinkling on plants to rid them of insect pests; **tobacco whitefly** a whitefly, *Bemisia tabaci*, which infests tobacco leaves; **tobacco worm** *US* (the larva of) either the tobacco hornworm or the tomato hornworm.

■ **tobaccoless** *adjective* (*rare*) M19. **tobaccoˈnalian** *adjective & noun* (*rare*) [app. after *bacchanalian*] (*a*) *adjective* of or pertaining to tobacco-smoking; (*b*) a person addicted to tobacco-smoking: M19.

tobacconist /təˈbak(ə)nɪst/ *noun.* L16.
[from prec. + euphonic *-n-* + -IST.]
†**1** A person addicted to the use of tobacco; *esp.* a habitual tobacco-smoker. L16–M18.
2 A retail dealer in tobacco, cigarettes, etc. M17.

Tobagonian /təbeɪˈgəʊnɪən/ *noun & adjective.* M20.
[from *Tobago* (see below) + euphonic *-n-* + -IAN.]
▶ **A** *noun.* A native or inhabitant of Tobago, an island in the W. Indies, part of the State of Trinidad and Tobago. M20.
▶ **B** *adjective.* Of or pertaining to Tobago or its inhabitants. M20.

tobe /təʊb/ *noun.* M19.
[Arab. *tawb* garment, cloth.]
In northern and central Africa: a length of cotton cloth worn as an outer garment.

to-be /təˈbiː/ *adjective & noun.* L16.
[from TO *preposition* + BE.]
▶ **A** *adjective.* That is yet to be or to come; future (freq. as 2nd elem. of comb. expr. family relationship). L16.
bride-to-be, ***husband-to-be***, ***mother-to-be***, etc.
▶ **B** *noun.* That which is to be; the future. E19.

tober /ˈtəʊbə/ *noun. slang.* L19.
[Shelta *tobar* road. Cf. TOBY *noun*[2].]
The site occupied by a circus, fair, or market.

Tobias night /təʊˈbʌɪəs nʌɪt/ *noun phr. rare.* M20.
[translating German *Tobiasnacht*, with allus. to *Tobit* 8:1–3.]
Chiefly *Hist.* A night during which the consummation of a marriage is postponed. Usu. in *pl.*

Tobin bronze /ˈtəʊbɪn brɒnz/ *noun phr.* L19.
[from John A. *Tobin* (fl. 1882), US inventor and naval officer + BRONZE *noun.*]
METALLURGY. = ***NAVAL brass***.

Tobin's tube /ˈtəʊbɪnz tjuːb/ *noun phr.* L19.
[from Martin *Tobin* of Leeds, the inventor, + -'S[1] + TUBE *noun.*]
A device for admitting fresh air in an upward direction into a room.

toboggan /təˈbɒg(ə)n/ *noun & verb.* E19.
[Canad. French *tabaganne* from Micmac *topağan* sled. Cf. PUNG *noun*[1], TOM PUNG. In sense A.2 directly from the verb.]
▶ **A** *noun.* **1** A long light narrow sledge, orig. made of a thin strip of wood upcurved in front and used for transport over snow, now usu. consisting of a frame with low runners and used for sliding downhill esp. over compacted snow or ice. E19.
2 The practice or sport of tobogganing. L19.
3 *fig.* A rapid decline, a progression towards disaster. Freq. in ***on the toboggan***. *US slang.* E20.
4 A long woollen cap, as worn when tobogganing. Also ***toboggan-cap***. *US.* E20.
Comb.: ***toboggan-cap***: see sense 4 above; **toboggan-chute**, **toboggan-slide** a steep incline for tobogganing.
▶ **B** *verb intrans.* **1** Ride on a toboggan, esp. downhill over compacted snow or ice. M19.
2 *fig.* Slide swiftly and uncontrollably; progress towards disaster; (of prices) fall steeply. L19.
■ **tobogganer** *noun* a person who toboggans L19. **tobogganist** *noun* a tobogganer L19.

†**to-brake** *verb* see TO-BREAK.

Tobralco /təˈbralkəʊ/ *noun.* E20.
[from Tootal Broadhurst Lee Company Ltd, the manufacturers.]
(Proprietary name for) a type of cotton fabric.

tobramycin /tɒbrəˈmʌɪsɪn/ *noun.* L20.
[from *to-* of unkn. origin + Latin *tene)bra(rius* belonging to darkness (see below), from *tenebrae* darkness: see -MYCIN.]
PHARMACOLOGY. An antibiotic produced by the bacterium *Streptomyces tenebrarius* which is active mainly against Gram-negative bacteria and is used esp. to treat pseudomonas infections.

†**to-break** *verb.* Pa. t. **-brake**, **-broke**, pa. pple **-broke(n)**. OE.
[from TO-[1] + BREAK *verb.*]
1 *verb trans.* Break to pieces; shatter, rupture; destroy, demolish. OE–L17. ▶**b** Break (a commandment, promise, etc.). OE–LME. ▶**c** Rend, tear (clothes or the like). Only in ME.
2 *verb intrans.* Break apart or into pieces; be ruptured, shattered, or fractured. ME–E16.

to-burst /tʊˈbəːst/ *verb.* Long *obsolete* exc. *dial.* Infl. as BURST *verb*; pa. t. & pple usu. **-burst**. OE.
[from TO-[1] + BURST *verb.*]
1 *verb intrans.* Burst apart or into pieces, be shattered. OE.
†**2** *verb trans.* Cause to burst apart or into pieces, shatter. OE–M16.

toby /ˈtəʊbi/ *noun*[1]. L17.
[Pet-form of male forename *Tobias.*]
1 The buttocks. Freq. in ***tickle a person's toby***. *slang.* Now *rare* or *obsolete.* L17.
2 More fully ***toby jug***. A jug or mug in the form of a stout old man wearing a long and full-skirted coat and a three-cornered hat. M19.
3 a More fully ***toby dog***. The trained dog in the Punch-and-Judy show, which wears a frill round its neck. M19. ▶**b** ***toby collar***, ***toby frill***, a broad turned-down pleated or goffered collar like the frill worn by Punch's dog. L19.
4 In full ***toby tub***. A colour-printing machine for textiles. M19.
5 An inferior kind of cigar. *US slang.* L19.
6 A stick of ochre used for marking sheep which have not been shorn to the owner's satisfaction. *Austral. slang.* E20.
7 THEATRICAL. (**T-**.) A blundering yokel as a stock character of American comedy. M20.
8 ANGLING. (**T-**.) A type of lure used in spinning. M20.

toby /ˈtəʊbi/ *noun*[2] *& verb. arch. slang.* E19.
[App. alt. of Shelta *tobar*: see TOBER.]
▶ **A** *noun.* The public highway, esp. as frequented by robbers. E19.
the high toby (*a*) highway robbery by a mounted thief; (*b*) the public highway. **the low toby** robbery by a footpad.
▶ **B** *verb trans.* Rob (a person) on the public highway. E19.
Comb.: **tobyman** a highwayman.

toc /tɒk/. L19.
Arbitrary syllable used for the letter *t* in spoken telecommunication messages and in the oral spelling of code messages.
toc emma *Military slang* a trench mortar. **Toc H** [from Talbot House, a military rest-house and club for soldiers] an association, orig. of ex-servicemen, founded after the war of 1914–18 to embody Christian fellowship and service.

toccata /təˈkɑːtə/ *noun.* E18.
[Italian, use as noun of fem. pa. pple of *toccare* touch.]
MUSIC. A composition for a keyboard instrument, intended to exhibit the performer's touch and technique and having the air of an improvisation. Also, a fanfare for brass instruments.

toccatina /tɒkəˈtiːnə/ *noun.* M18.
[Italian, dim. of TOCCATA.]
MUSIC. A short toccata.

Tocharian /təˈkɛːrɪən, -ˈkɑːrɪən/ *adjective & noun.* Also **Tokh-**. E20.
[French *tocharien* from Latin *Tochari* from Greek *Tokharoi* a Scythian tribe in central Asia.]
▶ **A** *adjective.* Of, pertaining to, or designating an extinct Indo-European language of a central Asian people in the first millennium AD, of which remains have been discovered in Chinese Turkestan. E20.
▶ **B** *noun.* **1** The Tocharian language. M20.
2 A member of the central Asian people or peoples speaking this language. M20.
1 Tocharian A the western dialect of this language, = TURFANIAN. **Tocharian B** the eastern dialect of this language, = KUCHAEAN.
■ **Tocharish** /təˈkɑːrɪʃ, -ˈkɛːrɪʃ/ *noun* [German *Tocharisch*] the Tocharian language E20.

tocher /ˈtɒxə/ *noun & verb. Scot. & north.* L15.
[Irish *tochra*, Gaelic *tochradh*.]
Chiefly *Hist.* ▶**A** *noun.* A woman's marriage portion; a dowry. L15.
Comb.: **tocher-band** a marriage settlement; **tocher-good** property given as tocher or dower.
▶ **B** *verb trans.* Provide with a tocher; dower. L16.
■ **tochered** *adjective* provided with a tocher, dowered (freq. with specifying word) E18. **tocherless** *adjective* L18.

tochis *noun* var. of TOKUS.

tock /tɒk/ *noun & verb.* Also redupl. **tock-tock**. M19.
[Imit. Cf. TICK-TOCK.]
▶ **A** *noun.* A short hollow sound, deeper and more resonant than a tick. (Earliest in TICK-TOCK.) M19.
▶ **B** *verb intrans.* Make such a sound. E20.

toco /ˈtəʊkə/ *noun*[1]. Pl. **-os**. L18.
[Portuguese from Tupi; cf. TOUCAN.]
ORNITHOLOGY. In full ***toco toucan***. A large toucan, *Ramphastos toco*, which has mainly black and white plumage and a massive orange black-tipped bill, and is found in the lowland forests of S. America.

toco /ˈtəʊkəʊ/ *noun*[2]. *arch. slang.* Also **toko**. E19.
[Hindi *ṭhōkō* imper. of *ṭhoknā* thrash, hit.]
Chastisement, corporal punishment.

toco- /ˈtɒkəʊ/ *combining form.* Also **toko-**.
[from Greek *tokos* offspring: see -O-.]
Chiefly MEDICINE. Of or pertaining to parturition or obstetrics.

■ **tocodyna'mometer** *noun* an instrument for measuring uterine contractions during childbirth **E20. toco'logical** *adjective* (now *rare*) = OBSTETRIC **E20. to'cologist** *noun* (now *rare*) = OBSTETRICIAN **E20. to'cology** *noun* (now *rare*) = OBSTETRICS **E19.**

tocopherol /tɒˈkɒfərɒl/ *noun.* **M20.**
[from prec. + Greek *pher(ein* to bear + -OL.]
BIOCHEMISTRY. Any of a group of related fat-soluble alcohols that occur in plant oils, wheat germ, egg-yolk, etc., and are antioxidants essential in the diets of many animals and probably of humans. Also called ***vitamin E.***

tocsin /ˈtɒksɪn/ *noun.* **L16.**
[Old French *touquesain, toquassen* (mod. *tocsin*) from Provençal *tocasenh*, from *tocar* strike, TOUCH *verb* + *senh* bell.]
1 A signal, esp. an alarm-signal, sounded by ringing a bell or bells. **L16.**
2 A bell used to sound an alarm. **M19.**

tocusso /tɒˈkʊsəʊ/ *noun.* **L18.**
[Amharic *tokusso.*]
In Ethiopia: the finger millet, *Eleusine coracana.*

tod /tɒd/ *noun*[1]. *Scot. & north.* **ME.**
[Origin unkn.]
1 A fox. **ME.**
2 *fig.* A sly or crafty person. **E16.**
Comb.: **tod-hole** a fox's earth; *fig.* a secret hiding place; **tod-tails, tods'-tails** stag-horn moss, *Lycopodium clavatum.*

tod /tɒd/ *noun*[2]. *arch.* **LME.**
[Prob. of Low Dutch origin (cf. Low German *todde* bundle, pack); cf. Old Norse *toddi* bit, piece, Old High German *zot(t)a, zata,* Middle High German *zotte* tuft of wool.]
1 A unit of weight of wool, usu. equal to 28 pounds (approx 12.7 kg). **LME.** ▸**b** A load. **M16.**
2 A bush, esp. of ivy; a mass of foliage. **M16.**

tod /tɒd/ *noun*[3]. *US colloq.* **L18.**
[Abbreviation.]
= TODDY 2.

tod /tɒd/ *noun*[4]. *slang.* **M20.**
[Short for *Tod Sloan* (a US jockey, 1874–1933), rhyming slang.]
on one's tod, alone, on one's own. Cf. PAT MALONE.

tod /tɒd/ *verb intrans. dial.* Infl. **-dd-. E17.**
[from TOD *noun*[2].]
Of (a specified number of) sheep or fleeces: produce a tod of wool. Freq. in ***tod threes*** (etc.), produce a tod from every three (etc.) sheep.

Toda /ˈtəʊdə/ *noun & adjective.* **M19.**
[Toda.]
▸**A** *noun.* Pl. **-s**, same.
1 A member of a people of southern India. **M19.**
2 The language of this people, a Dravidian language closely related to Tamil. **M20.**
▸**B** *adjective.* Of or pertaining to this people or their language. **M19.**

today /təˈdeɪ/ *adverb, noun, & adjective.* **OE.**
[from TO *preposition* + DAY *noun.* Cf. TONIGHT.]
▸**A** *adverb.* **1** On or in the course of this present day. **OE.**
2 In the present age; in modern times; nowadays. **ME.**

> **1** E. WAUGH You won't get in today Come back tomorrow morning. J. KOSINSKI Mr. Rand is ill and must forgo the pleasure of your company . . today. **today . . . tomorrow** on one day . . . on the next day. **today week, today fortnight** a week, fortnight, from today. ***here today, gone tomorrow***: see HERE *adverb.* **2** *Which?* The vast majority of new family cars sold today are front-wheel drive.

▸**B** *noun.* **1** This present day. **ME.**
2 This present age; modern times. **M19.**

> **1** *Sun* If you have all today's numbers call our hotline. **2** *Plays International* John Godber's play about today's teaching profession. *Midwest Living* Combines the charm of yesteryear with the comforts of today.

▸**C** *adjective.* Modern; characteristic of or suitable for the present day. *colloq.* **M20.**

> J. WAINWRIGHT The today song-smiths . . wrote boy-girl-and-bed words.

■ **todayish** *adjective* (*rare*) of or pertaining to the present time; characteristically modern: **M19.**

Todd-AO /tɒdeɪˈəʊ/ *noun.* **M20.**
[from Mike *Todd* (1907–58), US stage and film producer + the initials of American Optical Co.]
CINEMATOGRAPHY. (US proprietary name for) a cinematic process producing a wide-screen image.

todder /ˈtɒdə/ *noun. obsolete* exc. *dial.* **E17.**
[Origin unkn.]
Spawn of a frog or toad; slimy gelatinous matter.

toddle /ˈtɒd(ə)l/ *noun.* **E19.**
[from next.]
1 The action or an act of toddling; *transf.* a leisurely walk, a stroll. **E19.**
2 A toddler. Now *rare.* **E19.**

> **1** J. I. M. STEWART Lempriere had . . quickened his toddle—with his walking-stick pointing . . ahead.

■ **toddlekins** *noun* a toddler **M19.**

toddle /ˈtɒd(ə)l/ *verb.* **E16.**
[Origin unkn.: sense 1 may be a different word.]
†**1** *verb intrans.* Play or toy *with. rare.* Only in **E16.**
2 *verb intrans.* Esp. of a small child: walk or run with short unsteady steps. **L16.**
3 *verb intrans.* Take a casual or leisurely walk; stroll; depart, go (usu. foll. by *off*). **E18.** ▸**b** *verb trans.* Cause to toddle. *rare.* **L18.**

> **2** P. MARSHALL Marion was weaned and could toddle around. **3** I. MURDOCH I wondered if you and your wife would . . toddle over . . and have a drink.

toddler /ˈtɒdlə/ *noun.* **L18.**
[from TODDLE *verb* + -ER[1].]
A person who toddles; *esp.* a child who is just beginning to walk.
■ **toddlerhood** *noun* the condition of being a toddler **M20.**

toddy /ˈtɒdi/ *noun.* **E17.**
[Marathi *tāḍī*, Hindi *tāṛī* from Sanskrit *tāḍī* palmyra.]
1 The sugary sap from any of certain palm trees, *esp.* the jaggery palm *Caryota urens*, the palmyra *Borassus flabellifer*, and the coconut palm *Cocos nucerifa*, which is used as a drink in tropical countries; *esp.* the sap of such a palm fermented to produce an arrack. **E17.**
2 a A drink consisting of whisky or other spirits with hot water and sugar or spices. **L18.** ▸**b** A drink or glass of toddy. **M19.**
2a ***brandy-toddy, rum-toddy, whisky-toddy***, etc.
Comb.: **toddy-bird** a weaver, *Ploceus philippinus*, which is found in southern Asia and feeds on the sap of palms; **toddy cat** the common palm civet, *Paradoxurus hermaphroditus*, of southern Asia and Indonesia; **toddy-ladle** a small ladle used to transfer hot toddy from a bowl to a glass; **toddy-lifter** a device used in the manner of a pipette to transfer hot toddy from a bowl to a glass; **toddy palm** any palm that yields toddy, spec. *Caryota urens*; **toddy-stick** a spatula, usu. of glass or metal, for stirring hot toddy; **toddy-tapper** a person who collects or prepares toddy from palms; **toddy-tapping** the collection of toddy from palms; **toddy-tree** = *toddy-palm* above.

todea /ˈtəʊdiːə/ *noun.* **L19.**
[mod. Latin (see below), from H. J. *Tode* (1733–97), German botanist.]
Any of several Australasian ferns belonging to the genus *Todea*, allied to the royal fern, or (as the crape-fern, *Leptopteris superba*) formerly included in it.

todger /ˈtɒdʒə/ *noun. slang.* Also **tadger** /ˈtadʒə/. **M20.**
[Origin unkn.]
The penis.

to-do /təˈduː/ *noun.* **L16.**
[from *to do* s.v. DO *verb* 33.]
(A) commotion, (a) fuss; bustle.

> J. BRAINE You make a great to-do about your humble beginnings.

tody /ˈtəʊdi/ *noun.* **L18.**
[F. *todier*, from Latin *todus* a small bird.]
Any of several small insectivorous Caribbean birds constituting the genus *Todus* and family Todidae, which have green backs and red throats and are allied to the kingfishers.

toe /təʊ/ *noun.*
[Old English *tā* = Middle Low German *tē*, Middle & mod. Dutch *tee*, Old High German *zēha* (German *Zeh, Zehe*), Old Norse *tá*, from Germanic.]
1 a Each of the five terminal members of the human foot. **OE.** ▸**b** Speed, energy. *Austral. & NZ slang.* **L19.**
2 a Each of the digits of the foot of a quadruped or bird. **LME.** ▸**b** The front part of the hoof (or shoe) of a horse. **M16.**
3 A part resembling a toe or the toes, in shape or position; *esp.* the lower extremity, end, tip, or point of something. **LME.** ▸**b** The lower extremity of a spindle or screw, as in a press; a projection on the bolt of a lock etc., against which the key or a cam presses. **L17.** ▸**c** A projection at the base of a wall; the foot or base of a cliff or embankment; *ARCHITECTURE* a projection from the foot of a buttress etc. to give stability. **M19.** ▸**d** The peen of a hammer head; the tip of the head of a golf club or hockey-stick. **L19.** ▸**e** A flattish portion at the foot of an otherwise steep curve on a graph. **M20.** ▸**f** *HORTICULTURE.* A section of a fleshy root. **M20.**
4 The part of a shoe, sock, etc., which covers the toes; a cap for the toe on a stirrup. **LME.**
Phrases: ***big toe***: see BIG *adjective.* ***dig in one's toes***: see ***dig in*** s.v. DIG *verb.* **dip one's toe in (the water), dip one's toes in (the water)** test (a new or unfamiliar situation) before ultimate commitment to a course of action; make a tentative preliminary move. ***from head to toe***: see HEAD *noun.* ***from tip to toe***: see TIP *noun*[1]. ***from top to toe***: see TOP *noun*[1]. ***great toe***: see GREAT *adjective.* **have it on one's toes** *slang* run away. **kiss the Pope's toe** *Hist.* kiss the golden cross of the sandal on the Pope's right foot, as a mark of respect (the customary salutation of non-royal people granted an audience). ***little toe***: see LITTLE *adjective.* ***nigger toe***: see NIGGER *adjective & noun.* **on one's toes** alert, eager. ***seedy toe***: see SEEDY *adjective.* †**stand upon one's toes** stand on tiptoe. **step on a person's toes** = ***tread on a person's toes*** s.v. TREAD *verb.* ***the light fantastic toe***: see FANTASTIC *adjective* 5b. **toe and heel** (*a*) a style of dancing in which the toe and heel tap rhythmically on the ground; (*b*) = *heel-and-toe* s.v. HEEL *noun*[1]. **toe in the door** a (first) chance of ultimate success, an opportunity to progress, esp. in ***have a toe in the door, have one's toe in the door***; cf. ***foot in the door*** s.v. FOOT *noun.* **toe of Italy** the SW extremity of Italy (which country resembles a leg and foot in shape). **toe to toe** (*a*) (carried on) in close combat, at close quarters; (*b*) neck and neck. ***tread on a person's toes***: see TREAD *verb.* **turn up one's toes** *colloq.* die.
Comb.: **toe-board** a board for the feet to rest on; a board marking the limit of the thrower's run in putting the shot etc.; **toe-boot** a boot to protect the forefeet of a trotting horse from injury by the hind feet; **toe box** a piece of stiffened material between the lining and the toecap of a shoe; **toe brake** *AERONAUTICS* in an aircraft, a brake that is operated with the foot; **toecap** the (usu. reinforced) outer covering of the toe of a boot or shoe; **toe-clip** a clip on a bicycle pedal to receive the toe of the shoe so as to prevent the foot from slipping; **toe-cover** *slang* a useless or worthless present; **toe-crack** a fissure in the front of a horse's hoof; **toe-curling** *adjective* excessively sentimental; nauseating; **toe-dancer** a (ballet) dancer who dances on points; **toe-dancing** dancing on points; **toe-end** *verb trans.* kick with the point of one's foot; **toe-hold** (*a*) *WRESTLING* a hold in which the opponent's toe is seized and the leg forced backwards; (*b*) a small foothold, esp. to facilitate climbing; *fig.* a (relatively insignificant) basis from which advantage may be gained or influence or support increased; cf. ***foothold*** s.v. FOOT *noun*; **toe-in-the-water** *adjective* tentative; experimental; **toe jump** *SKATING* a jump initiated with the help of the toe of the non-skating foot; **toe loop** (*a*) *SKATING* a loop jump that is also a toe jump (also more fully ***toe loop jump***); (*b*) a loop on a sandal through which a toe is placed; **toenail** *noun & verb* (*a*) *noun* each of the nails of the toes; a nail driven obliquely through the end of a beam etc.; (*b*) *verb trans.* fasten (beams) with toed nails (see TOED 2); **toe-piece** a toecap; a toe-plate; the (lengthened tip of the) toe of a solleret; **toe-plate** (*a*) an iron plate on the sole of the toe of a boot or shoe; (*b*) a metal plate worn as a remedy for a hammer-toe; **toe-puff** a stiffener for the toe of the upper of a shoe; **toe rake** *SKATING* a set of teeth at the front of the blade of a skate; **toe-ring** (*a*) a ring worn on the toe; (*b*) *US* a stout ferrule on the end of a cant-hook; **toe-rubber** *N. Amer.* a rubber overshoe that covers only the front part of a shoe; **toe shoe** *N. Amer.* a ballet shoe with a reinforced toe; a point shoe; **toe-spin** *SKATING* a spin performed on the toe; **toe-strap** (*a*) a strap or thong securing the toe of an item of footwear; (*b*) a strap on a bicycle pedal to prevent the foot from slipping; (*c*) a band fixed to a sailing boat or a surfboard and serving to hold the foot of someone leaning out; **toe-tapping** *verbal noun & adjective* (*a*) *verbal noun* the tapping of feet in time to music; (*b*) *adjective* (of music) lively; that makes one want to tap one's feet; **toe-tip** the tip of a toe; **toe wall** a low retaining wall built at the foot of an embankment; **toe-weight** a small knob of metal attached to the hoof or shoe of a horse to modify the gait in trotting.
■ **toeless** *adjective* (esp. of footwear) without toes **L19.**

toe /təʊ/ *verb.* Pres. pple & verbal noun **toeing. E17.**
[from the noun.]
1 *verb trans.* Provide with a toe or toes; mend the toe of (a sock etc.). **E17.**
2 *verb trans.* Touch (esp. a starting-line before a race) with the toes. Chiefly in ***toe the line*** below. **E19.** ▸**b** Kick with the toe. **M19.** ▸**c** *GOLF.* Strike (the ball) with the toe or tip of the club. **M19.**
3 *verb intrans. & trans.* (with *it*). Move the toe, tap rhythmically with the toe in dancing. Chiefly in ***toe and heel (it)***, dance. **E19.**
4 a *verb intrans.* Turn the toes *in* or *out* when walking. **L19.** ▸**b** *verb intrans. & trans.* Of a pair of wheels: have a slight forward convergence (***toe in***) or divergence (***toe out***). Also, cause (a pair of wheels) to behave thus. **E20.**
5 *verb trans. CARPENTRY.* Secure or join (a brace etc.) to a beam by nails driven obliquely; drive (a nail) obliquely. **L19.**

> **1** *fig.*: G. M. HOPKINS A heavy fall of snow. It tufted and toed the firs and yews. **2** A. BEATTIE Mary sat on the bench and toed the dust like a sad horse. **toe the line** (*a*) line up before a race with the toes touching the starting-line; (*b*) *fig.* conform to a political party's policy or to generally accepted standards or principles, esp. under pressure.
> **4a** B. MACDONALD She toed out and had trouble with her arches.

toea /ˈtəʊeɪə/ *noun.* Pl. same. **L20.**
[Motu, lit. 'cone-shaped shell, shell armlet' (formerly used as currency).]
A monetary unit of Papua New Guinea, equal to one-hundredth of a kina.

toed /təʊd/ *adjective.* **E17.**
[from TOE *noun, verb*: see -ED[2], -ED[1].]
1 Having a toe or toes; (as 2nd elem. of comb.) having toes of a specified number or kind; having a part resembling a toe; (of a stocking) having separate divisions for the toes. **E17.**
2 *CARPENTRY.* (Of a brace etc.) secured or joined to a beam by nails driven obliquely; (of a nail) driven obliquely. **L19.**
1 ***even-toed, odd-toed, pigeon-toed, web-toed***, etc.

toe-in /ˈtəʊɪn/ *noun.* **E20.**
[from *toe in*: see TOE *verb* 4b.]
A slight forward convergence of a pair of wheels so that they are closer together in front than behind.

toenadering /ˈtunɑːdərɪŋ/ *noun. S. Afr.* E20.
[Dutch, from *toe* TO *adverb* + *nadering* approach (from *na* NEAR *adverb*[2]).]
Rapprochement, esp. between political parties or factions.

toe-out /ˈtəʊaʊt/ *noun.* M20.
[from *toe out*: see TOE *verb* 4b.]
A slight forward divergence of a pair of wheels so that they are closer together behind than in front.

Toepler pump *noun phr.* var. of TÖPLER PUMP.

toerag /ˈtəʊrag/ *noun. slang.* M19.
[from TOE *noun* + RAG *noun*[1].]
1 A rag wrapped round the foot and worn by tramps in place of a sock. M19.
2 Orig., a tramp or vagrant. Now (*derog.*), a despicable or worthless person. L19.
■ **toe-ragger** *noun* (*Austral. slang*) a tramp, a vagrant L19.

toering /ˈtuːrɪŋ/ *noun. S. Afr.* M19.
[Afrikaans from Malay *tudong* (now *tudung*) cover, lid, sun-hat.]
A wide-brimmed conical hat of straw, formerly worn by Cape Malays.

toey /ˈtəʊi/ *adjective. slang* (chiefly *Austral.*). M20.
[from TOE *noun* + -Y[1].]
(Of a horse, a runner) speedy; (of a horse) eager to race; (of a person) nervously impatient, anxious, touchy.

to-fall /ˈtuːfɔːl/ *noun.* LME.
[from TO *preposition* + FALL *noun*[2] or *verb*.]
1 A supplementary structure with a sloping roof attached to the wall of a main building; a lean-to; a shed. *Scot. & north.* LME. ▸**b** *fig.* A dependent thing or person; a shelter. LME.
2 The act of coming to a close. Only in ***to-fall of the day***, ***to-fall of the night***, the close of day, evening, nightfall. *Scot. & poet.* E18.

toff /tɒf/ *noun & verb. slang.* M19.
[Perh. alt. of TUFT *noun*.]
▸**A** *noun.* **1** A well-dressed or smart person; a person of some wealth or social standing. M19.
2 A person who behaves generously; a loyal or stalwart person. *rare.* L19.
▸**B** *verb trans. & refl.* Dress (oneself) *up* like a toff; dress smartly or expensively. E20.
■ **toffish**, **toffy** *adjectives* resembling or characteristic of a toff, stylish, well-to-do L19.

toffee /ˈtɒfi/ *noun & adjective.* Also **toffy**. E19.
[Alt. of TAFFY *noun*[2], of unkn. origin.]
▸**A** *noun.* **1 a** A firm or hard sweet softening when chewed or sucked, made by boiling together sugar or treacle with butter, often with other ingredients or flavourings added, such as nuts etc. E19. ▸**b** A small, shaped piece of toffee, usu. sold wrapped. M20.
2 Nonsense, rubbish. E20.
3 A medium shade of brown. Also **toffee-brown**. M20.
Phrases: EVERTON TOFFEE. **for toffee** *colloq.* at all; even tolerably well; (only in neg. contexts). ***Harrogate toffee***: see HARROGATE 2.
Comb.: **toffee-apple** (*a*) an apple thinly coated with toffee and mounted on a stick; (*b*) *arch. slang* a bomb similar in shape to a toffee-apple fired from a trench mortar; **toffee-brown** = sense 3 above; **toffee hammer** a miniature hammer used esp. to break pieces of toffee; **toffee-nose** *slang* a snob; a pretentiously superior person; **toffee-nosed** *adjective* (*slang*) snobbish; pretentiously superior.
▸**B** *adjective.* Toffee-coloured; medium brown. M20.
■ **toffee-like** *adjective* resembling (that of) toffee E20.

to-flight /ˈtuːflʌɪt/ *noun.* Long *obsolete* exc. *Scot.* ME.
[from TO-[2] + FLIGHT *noun*[2], corresp. to Old High German, Middle High German *zuofluht* (German *Zuflucht*, Dutch *toevlucht*) refuge, shelter, resource.]
A shelter, a refuge.

†**tofore** *preposition, adverb, & conjunction.* OE–M17.
[Old English *tōforan* = Old Frisian *tofora*, Old Saxon *teforan*, Middle High German *zevor*, *zuovor(n)* (German *zuvor*), from Germanic: see TO *preposition, conjunction, & adverb*, FORE *adverb & preposition*.]
= BEFORE.
¶ 2nd elem. of *heretofore*, *theretofore*.

Tofranil /ˈtɒfrənɪl/ *noun.* M20.
[Origin unkn.]
PHARMACOLOGY. (Proprietary name for) the drug imipramine.

to-fro /ˈtuːfrəʊ/ *adjective & noun. poet.* L19.
[from TO AND FRO.]
▸**A** *adjective.* Moving alternately in opposite directions; passing to and fro. L19.
▸**B** *noun.* Alternating movement; the action or an act of passing to and fro. *rare.* M20.

toft /tɒft/ *noun*[1]. OE.
[from Old Norse *topt*.]
1 A homestead, the site of a house and its outbuildings. Freq. in ***toft and croft***, an entire holding, consisting of the homestead and attached plot of arable land. OE.
2 An entire homestead and croft; a field or piece of land larger than the site of a house. LME.
3 A knoll or hillock in a flat region, *esp.* one suitable for the site of a house or tower. Now *local.* LME.
Comb.: **toftman** the owner or occupier of a toft; **toftstead** = sense 1 above.

Toft /tɒft/ *noun*[2]. L19.
[Staffordshire family name.]
In full ***Toft ware*** etc. (A style of) lead-glazed slip-ware made in Staffordshire in the late 17th cent. by the Toft family, esp. Thomas Toft (d. 1689).

tofu /ˈtəʊfuː/ *noun.* L18.
[Japanese *tōfu* from Chinese *dòufu*, from *dòu* beans + *fǔ* rot, turn sour.]
A curd made from mashed soya beans; bean curd.

tog /tɒg/ *noun.* E18.
[App. abbreviation of TOGEMANS. In sense 3, modelled on CLO.]
1 A coat; any outer garment. *slang* (chiefly *Criminals'*). E18.
2 *sing.* & (usu.) in *pl.* An item of clothing (*colloq.*); *Austral. & NZ colloq.* a swimming costume. L18.
3 A unit of thermal resistance used to express the insulating properties of clothes and quilts. M20.

> 🕮 **1** *Sporting Magazine* Curtis, in a new white upper tog. **2** D. HOGAN Black oversize togs which garbed . . my body. ***long togs***: see LONG *adjective*[1]. **3** *Home & Freezer Digest* A light, quilted bedspread, tog rating six.

■ **togless** *adjective* (*rare*) without togs or clothes; naked: M19.

tog /tɒg/ *verb.* Infl. **-gg-**. L18.
[Prob. from prec.: earliest as *togged* ppl adjective.]
1 *verb trans.* Clothe; dress, esp. elaborately or stylishly. Usu. foll. by *out*, *up*. L18.
2 *verb intrans.* Put on one's clothes; dress, esp. elaborately or stylishly. Usu. foll. by *out*, *up*. E19.

> 🕮 **1** *Listener* They were togged out as officers.

toga /ˈtəʊgə/ *noun.* E17.
[Latin, rel. to *tegere* cover.]
1 ROMAN HISTORY. A loose flowing outer garment worn by a Roman citizen, made of a single piece of cloth and covering the whole body apart from the right arm. E17.
2 *transf. & fig.* A robe of office; a professional gown; a mantle of responsibility etc. M18.

> 🕮 **1** ***toga praetexta***: see PRAETEXTA *adjective*. **toga virilis** /vɪˈrʌɪlɪs/ [lit. 'of a man, virile'] a white toga donned as a sign of manhood at the age of 14. **2** J. MACFARLANE Can they be expected to don the togas of the geologist, . . the chemist, the linguist? *Time* Swaziland's Prime Minister . . wore a red printed toga.

■ **togaed** *adjective* wearing a toga M19.

togate /ˈtəʊgeɪt/ *adjective.* M19.
[Latin *togatus*, formed as prec.: see -ATE[2].]
Togaed; belonging or relating to ancient Rome.

togated /ˈtəʊgeɪtɪd/ *adjective.* M17.
[formed as prec. + -ED[1].]
Togaed; wearing a toga as opp. to being dressed for war; peaceful.

togavirus /ˈtəʊgəvʌɪrəs/ *noun.* L20.
[from TOGA + VIRUS.]
MEDICINE. Any of various RNA viruses of the family Togaviridae, which have enveloped icosahedral capsids, are mostly arthropod-borne, and include the viruses of rubella, swine fever, yellow fever, equine encephalitis, etc.

†**toge** *noun.* LME–L17.
[French (also †*togue*) from Latin TOGA.]
A Roman toga; a cloak, a loose coat.

toged /ˈtəʊgd/ *adjective. arch. rare.* E17.
[from prec. + -ED[2].]
Togaed; robed.

†**togemans** *noun. Criminals' slang. rare.* Also **tog(e)man**. M16–L18.
[from TOGE or Latin TOGA + *-mans*, as in DARKMANS, LIGHTMANS.]
A cloak, a loose coat.

together /təˈgɛðə/ *adverb, preposition, & adjective.*
[Old English *tōgædere* = Old Frisian *togadera*, *-ere*, Middle Dutch *tegadere* (Dutch *-er*), ult. from TO *preposition* + West Germanic base also of Old English *gæd* fellowship, *ġegada* companion, cogn. with Middle Dutch *ghegade* (Dutch *gade*) comrade. Cf. GADLING *noun*[1], GATHER *verb*.]
▸**A** *adverb.* **1** Into one gathering, company, or body; (of two persons, things, separate parts, etc.) into association, proximity, contact, or union. OE.
2 In company, as a body; (of two persons, things, separate parts, etc.) in union, conjunction, association, or contact. OE. ▸**b** In notional combination; collectively. L18.
3 With coherence or combination of parts or elements belonging to a single body or thing; so as to form a connected, united, or coherent whole. ME.
4 At the same time, simultaneously. ME.
5 Without interruption, continuously, consecutively. ME.
6 In concert; with unity of action; unitedly. ME.
7 One with another; mutually, reciprocally; to one another (freq. in ***belong together***). ME.

> 🕮 **1** SCOTT FITZGERALD They both . . arrived . . as though a series of pure accidents had driven them together. I. MURDOCH He put his hands together in an attitude of prayer. T. TRYON This ragtag-and-bobtail lot was no brotherhood . . come together in a ceremony of . . friendship. **2** M. DE LA ROCHE They wished always to be together, but, as Finch was still at school, . . this was impossible. E. BOWEN The two old friends entered the house together. **b** *Highlife* More geysers . . than the rest of the globe put together. **3** B. FUSSELL Sometimes the cheese just doesn't hold together. *Daily Star* Ready to fight to keep his crumbling empire together. **4** LD MACAULAY The two things he most desired could not be possessed together. BEVERLEY CLEARY 'Boi-i-ing!' shouted the two boys together. **5** W. GRESLEY He . . never slept twice together in the same apartment. C. P. SNOW For minutes together, Luke gave orders for a new start. **6** WORDSWORTH Together we released the Cloak. **7** T. T. LYNCH Yet sometimes . . My work and I have fallen out together.

Phrases: (A selection of cross-refs. only is included.) ***get one's act together***: see ***get together*** s.v. GET *verb*. ***grow together***: see GROW *verb*. ***hang together***: see HANG *verb*. ***hold together***: see HOLD *verb*. ***lay their heads together***: see HEAD *noun*. ***live together***: see LIVE *verb*. ***not have two pennies to rub together***: see RUB *verb*. ***put two and two together***: see TWO *noun* 2. ***speak together***: see SPEAK *verb*. ***stick together***: see STICK *verb*[1]. **together with** along with; in combination with; as well as; at the same time as.
▸†**B** *preposition.* Along with, with the addition of, with. *rare.* M16–M17.
▸**C** *adjective.* Composed, well-organized, self-assured; free of emotional difficulties or inhibitions. *colloq.* M20.

> 🕮 *New Yorker* A young lady . . has got to be a very together person to survive. *Blitz* Lively, together . . people only need apply.

■ **togetherness** *noun* (*a*) the state or condition of being together or being united; (*b*) the fact of getting on well together; a feeling of well-being or comfort from being together or in association, fellowship: M17.

Toggenburg /ˈtɒgənbəːg/ *adjective & noun.* L19.
[A valley in the canton of St Gallen, Switzerland.]
(Designating) (an animal of) a hornless light brown breed of goat developed in the region of Toggenburg.

toggery /ˈtɒg(ə)ri/ *noun. colloq.* E19.
[from TOG *noun* + -ERY.]
1 Garments; clothes collectively; *esp.* (with specifying word.) professional or official dress. E19.
2 The trappings of a horse; harness. *rare.* L19.

> 🕮 **1** H. JAMES Dressed as a workman in his Sunday toggery.

toggle /ˈtɒg(ə)l/ *noun & verb.* M18.
[Origin unkn.]
▸**A** *noun.* **1** NAUTICAL. A short pin passed through a loop or the eye of a rope, a link of a chain, etc., to keep it in place, or for the attachment of a line. M18.
2 A crosspiece on the end of a line or chain, or fixed in a belt or strap for attaching a weapon etc. by a loop or ring. Now *esp.*, a short rod-shaped piece secured to cloth and pushed through a loop and twisted so as to act as a fastener on a garment. L19. ▸**b** A movable pivoted crosspiece serving as a barb in a harpoon. L19. ▸**c** A toggle joint. E20. ▸**d** A kind of wall fastener for use on open-backed plasterboarding etc., having a part that springs open or turns through 90 degrees after it is inserted, so as to prevent withdrawal. Also ***toggle-bolt***. M20. ▸**e** ELECTRONICS. = LATCH *noun*[1] 2b. Also ***toggle circuit***. M20. ▸**f** COMPUTING. A key or command that is always operated in the same way but has opposite effects on successive occasions. Also ***toggle switch***. L20.
Comb.: **toggle-bolt** (*a*) a bolt having a hole through the head to receive a toggle; (*b*) = sense 2d above; ***toggle circuit***: see sense 2e above; **toggle-harpoon**, **toggle-iron** a harpoon with a pivoted toggle instead of barbs; **toggle joint** a joint consisting of two pieces hinged endwise, operated by applying pressure at the elbow; **toggle switch** (*a*) an electric switch operated by means of a projecting lever that is moved with a snap action, usu. up and down; (*b*) see sense 2f above.
▸**B** *verb.* **1** *verb trans.* Secure or fasten by means of a toggle or toggles. M19.
2 *verb trans.* Provide with a toggle or toggles. L19.
3 ELECTRONICS. **a** *verb intrans.* Of a bistable circuit: change from one stable state to the other. M20. ▸**b** *verb trans.* Cause (a circuit, a bit) to change state. L20.
4 **a** *verb trans.* Operate (a toggle switch). L20. ▸**b** *verb trans. & intrans.* Switch *on*, *off*, or into one of (usu. two) distinct states by means of a toggle switch. L20.

toggy /ˈtɒgi/ *noun.* Long *rare* (chiefly *N. Amer.*). Also **tuggy**. M18.
[Origin uncertain: perh. rel. to TOG *noun* or TOGA.]
A kind of overcoat, usu. made of skins or leather, worn in regions of extreme cold.

toghe /təʊ/ *noun. obsolete* exc. *Hist.* Also **toughe**. L16.
[Irish TUATH.]
In Ireland: a territory, a district.

togidashi /tɒgɪˈdaʃi/ *noun & adjective.* **L19.**
[Japanese, from *togu* whet, grind + *dasu* produce, let appear.]
(Made of) a kind of Japanese lacquer in which gold or silver designs are overlaid with several coats of lacquer which are then rubbed and ground down, revealing the underlying design as if floating below the lacquer surface.

†togman *noun* var. of TOGEMANS.

Togolese /təʊgəʊˈliːz/ *adjective & noun.* **M20.**
[from *Togo* (see below) + -ESE, after French *togolais.*]
▶ **A** *adjective.* Of or pertaining to the State of Togo (formerly Togoland) in W. Africa. **M20.**
▶ **B** *noun.* Pl. same. A native or inhabitant of Togo. **M20.**

togt /tɒxt/ *noun. S. Afr.* **M19.**
[Afrikaans from Dutch *tocht* expedition, journey.]
†**1** A trading expedition or venture. Only in **M19.**
2 Casual labour, hired for a specific job. **E20.**
Comb.: **togt boy** a casual labourer; **togt-ganger** a travelling trader; **togt licence** a licence authorizing the holder to undertake casual labour.

togue /təʊg/ *noun.* **L19.**
[Canad. French, perh. from Micmac *atoğwa:su.*]
The American lake trout, *Salvelinus namaycush.*

toheroa /ˈtəʊərəʊə/ *noun.* **L19.**
[Maori.]
A large edible bivalve mollusc, *Mesodesma ventricosum*, common on some coasts of New Zealand.

to-ho /təʊˈhəʊ/ *interjection.* **E19.**
[from HO *interjection*[2].]
SPORT. Ordering a pointer or setter to stop.

tohu-bohu /təʊhuːˈbəʊhuː/ *noun.* **E17.**
[from Hebrew *thōhū wa-bhōhū* emptiness and desolation (*Genesis* 1:2).]
That which is empty and formless; chaos; utter confusion.

tohunga /ˈtɔhʊŋə, ˈtəʊhʊŋə/ *noun.* **M19.**
[Maori.]
A Maori priest or doctor.

toich /tɔɪk, -x/ *noun.* **M20.**
[Dinka *toc* swamp.]
GEOGRAPHY. In southern Sudan, a stretch of flat land near a river that is subject to annual flooding.

Toidey /ˈtɔɪdi/ *noun.* Also **t-**. **E20.**
[Origin unkn.]
(US proprietary name for) a toilet-training device that can be clipped or strapped on to an ordinary lavatory seat.

toil /tɔɪl/ *noun*[1]. **ME.**
[Anglo-Norman = Old French *tooil, touil, tueil* bloody mêlée, trouble, confusion, from *tooillier* TOIL *verb*[1].]
1 In *pl.* & †*sing.* Battle, strife, mêlée, turmoil. Formerly also, verbal contention, dispute, controversy. *arch.* **ME.**
2 a Intensive labour; hard or prolonged exertion which is physically or mentally taxing. **M16.** ▸**b** The result of toil; something produced or accomplished by hard or prolonged exertion. *rare.* **E18.**
3 A struggle; a spell of intensive physical or mental labour; a laborious task or operation. *arch.* **L16.**

> **1** LONGFELLOW Weapons, made For the hard toils of war. **2a** J. HERBERT His body flagged with the very toil of breathing. **3** C. KINGSLEY Many a toil must we bear ere we find it.

Comb.: **toil-worn** *adjective* worn or worn out by toil.
■ **toilful** *adjective* (*arch.*) (*a*) labouring; hard-working; (*b*) involving toil or hard work, toilsome: **L16.** **toilfully** *adverb* **M19.** **toilless** /-l-l-/ *adjective* (*rare*) †(*a*) not entailing toil; (*b*) free from toil; that acts without exertion: **E17.**

toil /tɔɪl/ *noun*[2]. **E16.**
[Old French *toile, teile* (mod. *toile*) cloth, linen, web from Latin *tela*, from base also of *texere* weave.]
1 *sing.* & (now usu.) in *pl.* A net or nets forming an enclosed area into which a hunted quarry is driven, or within which game is known to be. Now chiefly *fig.* **E16.**
†**2** A trap, a snare. *rare.* **E17–E18.**

> **1** SHAKES. *Ant. & Cl.* As she would catch another Antony In her strong toil of grace. E. BIRNEY Soldiers in the toils of civilian law for thefts.

toil /tɔɪl/ *verb*[1]. **ME.**
[Anglo-Norman *toiler* dispute, wrangle = Old French *tooillier* (mod. *touiller* mix, stir up) from Latin *tudiculare* stir about, from *tudicula* machine for crushing olives, from base of *tundere* beat, crush.]
▶†**I 1** *verb intrans.* Contend verbally, dispute, argue. Also, contend in battle; fight, struggle. Only in **ME.**
2 *verb trans.* Pull, drag, tug about. Only in **ME.**
▶**II 3** *verb intrans.* Struggle towards an aim or for a living; engage intensively in hard or prolonged labour or exertion; *fig.* struggle mentally. **LME.** ▸**b** Make slow, laborious, or painful progress. Foll. by *along, through, up*, etc. **L18.**
4 *verb trans.* & (now *Scot.*) *refl.* Cause to work hard; tire (a person, oneself, etc.), esp. with work; (foll. by *out*) exhaust with toil. *arch. & dial.* **M16.**
†**5** *verb trans.* Labour upon; *esp.* till (the earth, the soil). *rare.* **M16–E17.**
6 *verb trans.* Bring into some condition or position, or obtain, by toil; (foll. by *out*) accomplish by toil. *rare.* **M17.**

> **3** SCOTT FITZGERALD Servants . . toiled all day with mops and scrubbing-brushes. A. N. WILSON He toiled at his treatise on volcanoes. **b** R. P. JHABVALA We . . toiled up the rocky, . . barren and exposed path. **4** SIR W. SCOTT Physicians had to toil their wits to invent names for imaginary maladies. **6** COLERIDGE When, at last, the thing is toiled and hammered into fit shape.

▶†**III 7** *verb trans.* Stir (food), mix (ingredients etc.) by stirring. **LME–M16.**
■ **toiler** *noun* a person who toils, a hard worker **M16.** **toiling** *verbal noun* the action of the verb; an instance of this: **ME.** **toilingly** *adverb* in a toiling manner **E19.**

toil /tɔɪl/ *verb*[2] *trans. arch. & dial.* **L16.**
[from TOIL *noun*[2].]
Trap or enclose in toils; drive (game) into toils; *fig.* entrap; *dial.* set (a trap).

toile /twaːl/ *noun.* **LME.**
[French: see TOIL *noun*[2].]
1 †**a** Cloth; cloth or canvas used for painting on. *rare.* **LME–L16.** ▸**b** A painting on canvas. **E20.**
2 Any of various linen or cotton fabrics. Freq. with French specifying word. **L18.**
3 A reproduction of a fashion garment made up in muslin or other cheap material so that fitting alterations or copies can be made. **M20.**
2 toile de Jouy /də ʒwiː/ a type of printed calico usu. with a characteristic floral, figure, or landscape design on a light background, made from the mid 18th cent. at Jouy-en-Josas near Paris.

toilé /twale/ *noun.* **M19.**
[French, from prec.]
In lace-making, an area with a closely-worked inwrought pattern.

toilenette *noun* var. of TOILINET.

toilet /ˈtɔɪlɪt/ *noun.* In senses 5, 6 also **toilette** /twaːˈlɛt/. **M16.**
[French *toilette* cloth, wrapper, dim. of TOILE *noun*: see -ET[1], -ETTE.]
†**1** A piece of fabric used as a wrapper for clothes; (*rare*) a cloth used to cover the shoulders during hairdressing. Also (only in Dicts.), a bag or case for nightclothes. **M16–M19.**
2 The articles required or used in applying make-up, arranging the hair, dressing, etc.; a toilet set. Formerly also, a case containing these. **M17.**
3 A cloth cover for a dressing-table. Also ***toilet-cover***. **L17.**
4 More fully ***toilet table***. A dressing-table. **L17.**
5 The action or process of washing, dressing, arranging the hair, etc. **L17.** ▸**b** *Hist.* In the 18th cent., the reception of visitors by a lady during the concluding stages of her toilet. **E18.**
6 Manner or style of dressing; costume; a dress or costume. Now *rare.* **M18.**
7 A dressing-room; *esp.* (*US*) a dressing-room furnished with washing facilities. Also ***toilet-room***. **E19.**
8 (A room or cubicle containing) a lavatory. **E20.**

> **2** E. K. KANE My entire toilet, a tooth-brush, a comb, and a hair-brush. **4** SIR W. SCOTT On the toilette beside, stood an old-fashioned mirror. **5** M. FORSTER Only by sticking . . to the set routines of her mistress's toilet . . could she steady herself. **6** *Truth* Lady Dudley's black toilette was much admired. DEMI-TOILETTE. **8** *Today* The little girl had wanted to go to the toilet. J. UPDIKE Mailing letters, flushing a toilet . . all have this sweetness of riddance. *fig.*: K. VONNEGUT That document was all I needed to . . understand that my tenure was down the toilet.

Comb.: **toilet box** a box containing toilet articles; **toilet brush** (*a*) a nail-brush; (*b*) a lavatory brush; **toilet-case** a toilet box; **toilet-cover** = sense 3 above; **toilet-glass** a dressing-table mirror; **toilet humour** = *lavatory humour* s.v. LAVATORY noun; **toilet paper** †(*a*) paper used for shaving, hair-curling, etc.; (*b*) paper (in sheets or on a roll) for cleaning oneself after urination or defecation; **toilet roll** a roll of toilet paper; ***toilet-room***: see sense 7 above; **toilet set** a set of hairbrushes, combs, etc., used in arranging the hair; **toilet soap**: for washing oneself; ***toilet table***: see sense 4 above; **toilet tent** a temporary lavatory at a fête etc. consisting of a tent and one or more chemical lavatories; **toilet tissue** = ***toilet paper*** (b) above; **toilet-train** *verb trans.* cause (a child) to adopt acceptable habits of urination and defecation; train (a child) to use a lavatory; **toilet-training** the training of a child to control his or her urination and defecation and to use a lavatory; **toilet water** a dilute and refreshing form of perfume; eau-de-Cologne.

toilet /ˈtɔɪlɪt/ *verb.* **M19.**
[from prec.]
1 *verb intrans.* Carry out one's toilet, wash and dress oneself. **M19.**
2 *verb trans.* Assist or supervise (a child, an invalid, etc.) in using a lavatory; *refl.* use a lavatory unaided. **M20.**
■ **toileting** *verbal noun* the action of the verb; an instance of this: **M20.**

toiletry /ˈtɔɪlɪtri/ *noun.* **M19.**
[from TOILET noun + -RY.]
1 The carrying out of one's toilet. *rare.* **M19.**
2 = TOILET *noun* 2. *rare.* **L19.**
3 Any of various articles, cosmetics, or products used in washing, dressing, etc. Usu. in *pl.* **E20.**

toilette *noun* see TOILET *noun.*

toilinet /ˈtwaːlɪnɛt/ *noun & adjective.* Also **-ette**, **toilenette**. **L18.**
[App. from TOILE *noun* after SATINETTE.]
(Made of) a kind of fine cloth with a silk or cotton warp and a woollen weft used esp. for fancy waistcoats and dresses in the 18th and 19th cents.

toilsome /ˈtɔɪls(ə)m/ *adjective.* **L16.**
[from TOIL *noun*[1] + -SOME[1].]
1 Characterized by or involving toil; laborious, tiring. **L16.**
†**2** Caused by toil. *rare* (Spenser). Only in **L16.**
3 Hard-working; labouring. *arch.* **E17.**

> **1** R. L. STEVENSON Even for a man unburthened, the ascent was toilsome and precarious. P. G. WODEHOUSE Cooley . . by means of a toilsome youth . . had amassed a large amount of money.

■ **toilsomely** *adverb* **E17.** **toilsomeness** *noun* **L16.**

to-infinitive /ˈtuːɪn,fɪnɪtɪv/ *noun.* **M20.**
[from TO *preposition* + INFINITIVE *noun.*]
LINGUISTICS. The infinitive form of the verb immediately preceded by *to.*

toing and froing /tuːɪŋ (ə)nd ˈfrəʊɪŋ/ *noun phr.* Pl. **toings and froings**. **M19.**
[from TO AND FRO + -ING[1].]
Constant movement to and fro; bustle, dispersed activity; an instance of this.

toise /tɔɪz/ *noun.* **L16.**
[French from Old French *teise* = Italian *tesa* from late Latin *tesa, tensa* (sc. *brachia*) lit. 'the outstretched arms', use as noun of neut. pl. pa. pple (taken as fem. sing.) of Latin *tendere* stretch.]
Chiefly MILITARY. A former French unit of length equal to about 1.949 metres.

toisech /ˈtɒʃək, -x/ *noun.* **M18.**
[Gaelic *tóisech* lord, chief = Welsh *tywysog* leader, prince. Cf. TAOISEACH.]
SCOTTISH HISTORY. In Celtic Scotland: a dignitary or official ranking below a mormaor: corresponding to the later chief of a clan or thane.

toison d'or /twazɔ̃ dɔr/ *noun phr.* **E17.**
[French = fleece of gold.]
HERALDRY & GREEK MYTHOLOGY. The Golden Fleece.

toit *verb* var. of TOYTE.

toi-toi /ˈtɔɪtɔɪ/ *noun.* **M19.**
[Maori.]
Any of various tall reedlike grasses and sedges occurring in New Zealand; *esp.* the grass *Arundo conspicua.*

Tojo /ˈtəʊdʒəʊ/ *noun. Military slang* (chiefly *US & Austral.*). Pl. **-os**. **M20.**
[Hideki *Tōjō* (1884–1948), Japanese minister of war and prime minister during the war of 1939–45.]
A Japanese serviceman; Japanese forces collectively.

tokamak /ˈtəʊkəmak/ *noun.* **M20.**
[Russian, from *toroidal'naya kamera s magnitnym polem*, toroidal chamber with magnetic field.]
PHYSICS. A toroidal apparatus for producing controlled fusion reactions in a hot plasma, in which the controlling magnetic field is the sum of a toroidal field and a poloidal field.

Tokarev /ˈtɔːkərjɛf/ *noun & adjective.* **M20.**
[F. V. *Tokarev* (1871–1968), Russian designer of firearms.]
(Designating) any of a range of automatic and semi-automatic firearms designed or developed by Tokarev.

Tokay /təʊˈkeɪ/ *noun*[1]. **E18.**
[*Tokaj* in Hungary (see below).]
A rich sweet aromatic wine made near Tokaj (also ***Tokay wine***); a similar wine made elsewhere, esp. in California and Australia. Also, in Alsace, the Pinot Gris vine or grape (more fully ***Tokay d'Alsace*** /dalˈsas/); a light white wine made from these grapes.

tokay /ˈtəʊkeɪ/ *noun*[2]. **M18.**
[Malay dial. *toke'* from Javanese *tekèk* of imit. origin. Cf. GECKO.]
More fully ***tokay gecko***. The largest of the geckos, *Gekko gecko*, which has a grey body with blue and orange spots, has a loud call resembling the name, and is found in southern Asia and Indonesia.

toke /təʊk/ *noun*[1]. *slang.* **M19.**
[Origin unkn.]
(A piece of) bread.

toke /təʊk/ *noun*[2] *& verb. N. Amer. slang.* **M20.**
[Origin unkn.]
▶ **A** *noun.* A pull on a cigarette or pipe, esp. one containing marijuana or other narcotic substance. **M20.**
▶ **B** *verb intrans. & trans.* Take a pull on (a cigarette or pipe, esp. one containing marijuana). **M20.**

toke /təʊk/ *noun*³. *N. Amer. slang.* L20.
[Origin uncertain: perh. abbreviation of TOKEN *noun*.]
A gratuity, a tip.

token /ˈtəʊk(ə)n/ *noun & adjective.*
[Old English *tāc(e)n* = Old Frisian *tēk(e)n*, Old Saxon *tēcan* (Dutch *teeken*), Old High German *zeihhan* (German *Zeichen*) Old Norse *teikn*, Gothic *taikns*, from Germanic base rel. to TEACH *verb*.]
▶ **A** *noun.* **1** A thing serving as a sign or symbol; a visible or tangible representation of something abstract or immaterial. OE. ▸†**b** Any of the twelve signs of the zodiac. *rare.* OE–M16. ▸**c** A thing given as an expression of affection, or to be kept as a memento, *esp.* a keepsake given at parting. LME. ▸**d** LINGUISTICS. A particular example of a linguistic unit, as an individual occurrence in speech or writing, as opp. to the type or class of linguistic unit of which it is an instance. Cf. TYPE *noun* 10. E20. ▸**e** COMPUTING. The smallest meaningful unit of information in a sequence of data. M20. ▸**f** COMPUTING. A marker whose presence or absence at a point in a system indicates the status of that point. L20.
2 a A mark or indication serving to distinguish an object from others; a characteristic or distinctive mark. *arch.* OE. ▸**b** A spot on the body indicating disease, esp. the plague. *obsolete* exc. *Hist.* ME.
3 a A thing serving as proof of a fact or statement; a piece of evidence. *arch.* OE. ▸†**b** A vestige or trace bearing evidence as to something which formerly existed. ME–E17.
4 a = SIGN *noun* 7b. OE. ▸**b** = SIGN *noun* 7a. OE.
5 A signal; a sign or gesture to attract attention or give an order. Now *rare* or *obsolete.* OE.
6 A mark, word, or object conferring authority on or serving to authenticate the holder or speaker; a password. ME.
7 A badge or favour worn to indicate service or allegiance to a person or party. L15.
8 An object representing evidence of entitlement to a right or privilege, which when presented enables the right or privilege to be exercised (long *rare* or *obsolete*); *spec.* (now chiefly *Hist.*) a stamped piece of lead etc. given as a voucher of fitness to receive Holy Communion. M16.
9 a Chiefly *Hist.* A stamped piece of metal, often similar in appearance to a coin, issued as a medium of exchange by an employer, trader, or company, on the undertaking to take it back at its nominal value, giving goods or legal currency for it. L16. ▸**b** A voucher exchangeable for goods, usu. given as a gift. Freq. with specifying word. E20. ▸**c** A small metal or plastic disc to be used in operating a machine or in exchange for services. Freq. with specifying word. M20.
10 PRINTING (now *Hist.*). A measure of presswork completed; a certain number of sheets of paper (usu. 250) passed through the press. L17.
11 A person chosen as a nominal representative of a minority or under-represented group. *US.* M20.

> 📖 **1** F. BURNEY A cordial slap on the back, and some other equally gentle tokens of satisfaction. E. H. GOMBRICH The power of art to rouse the passions is . . a token of its magic. **c** J. AIKEN Notes and tokens are fine, but it is your dear presence that I . . need. **2a** SIR W. SCOTT The tokens on his helmet tell The Bruce, my Liege. **3a** J. BARNES What the expedition should take as tokens of goodwill . . to the peasants. **5** SWIFT Tokens to let them know, that they might do with me what they pleased. **6** F. HERBERT I give you the . . ducal signet as token that I write truly. **9b** *book token, gift-token, record token*, etc. **c** *Washington Post* 10-cent student bus tokens.

▶ **B** *adjective.* Serving to acknowledge a principle only; done as a matter of form; constituting a symbolic or tokenist gesture; nominal, perfunctory. OE.

> 📖 S. WYNTER His resistance was only a token gesture before surrender. *City Limits* The token black on a Madison Avenue team . . becomes chairman. J. TROLLOPE Nelson stirred in his basket out of token politeness. *Sanity* To have moved token American forces into Saudi Arabia to reinforce the warning . . to Iraq.

Phrases: **by the same token**, (*arch.*) **by this token**, **by that token** (*a*) for the same reason; in the same way; similarly; (*b*) (now *arch. & dial.*) the proof of this being that. **in token of** as a sign, symbol, or evidence of. **more by token** *arch.* still more, the more so.
Comb. & special collocations: **token booth** *US* a booth from which tokens are sold, esp. those for obtaining subway tickets; **token economy** PSYCHIATRY the principle or practice of rewarding desirable behaviour with tokens which can be exchanged for goods or privileges, and sometimes punishing undesirable behaviour by withholding or withdrawing such tokens; **token estimate** a provisional statement of a sum of money, placed before Parliament to allow discussion to proceed; **token payment** (*a*) the payment of a small proportion of a sum due, to acknowledge that the debt has not been repudiated; (*b*) a nominal payment; **token-reflexive** *noun & adjective* (LOGIC) (denoting) a word the referent or temporal or spatial orientation of which is contextually determined, as *I, now, today*; **token ring** (*a*) a ring worn as a token of an engagement or pledge; (*b*) COMPUTING an arrangement with a circulating sequence of bits acting as a token for the ability of a point to transmit information; **token stoppage**, **token strike** a brief strike to demonstrate strength of feeling only; **token vote** a parliamentary vote of money on the basis of a token estimate.
■ **tokenize** *verb trans.* (COMPUTING) divide (a sequence of data) into separate tokens L20. **tokenless** *adjective* (*rare*) M18.

token /ˈtəʊk(ə)n/ *verb trans.*
[Old English *tācnian* = Middle Low German *tēkenen*, Old High German *zeihhanen*, *-ōn* (German *zeichnen*), Gothic *taiknjan*, from Germanic base of prec.]
1 Be a token or sign of; represent, betoken. OE.
2 Be a type or symbol of; typify, symbolize. OE.
†**3** Mark with a sign or distinctive mark. ME–E17.
4 Betroth, promise in marriage. *arch. & dial.* L19.

> 📖 **1** D. AVERY These reforms . . tokened a new determination to solve some of the . . problems. **2** *Mind* The content of the belief is tokened in a language of thought. **4** N. MARSH She's going to be tokened to . . Andersen.

tokening /ˈtəʊk(ə)nɪŋ/ *noun.* Now *rare.* OE.
[from TOKEN *verb* + -ING¹.]
1 The action of TOKEN *verb*; representation, signification, symbolization, presaging; an instance of this. OE.
2 A token, a sign, a mark; a portent; a signal. Formerly also, a zodiacal sign. OE.

tokenism /ˈtəʊk(ə)nɪz(ə)m/ *noun.* Orig. *US.* M20.
[from TOKEN *noun* + -ISM.]
The principle or practice of granting minimal concessions, esp. to minority or under-represented groups as a token gesture to appease radical demands, comply with legal requirements, etc.

> 📖 *Isis* The . . donation . . to Ethiopia proved controversial. It was denounced as mere tokenism. *Art* Are we . . happier with the tokenism of four per cent for ethnic art?

■ **tokenist**, **tokenistic** *adjectives* of the nature of tokenism L20.

token-money /ˈtəʊk(ə)nmʌni/ *noun.* M16.
[from TOKEN *noun* + MONEY *noun*.]
1 ECCLESIASTICAL HISTORY. The payment made for a token or voucher of fitness to receive Easter Holy Communion. M16.
2 Private tokens issued by a trader or company to serve as a fractional currency and temporary medium of exchange between trader and customer. L19.
3 State-issued coins having a higher face value than their worth as metal. L19.

Tokharian *adjective & noun* var. of TOCHARIAN.

toki /ˈtɒki/ *noun. NZ.* M19.
[Maori.]
A Maori war adze or axe, usu. of stone.

tokkin /tɒˈkɪn/ *noun.* Pl. same, **-s.** L20.
[Japanese acronym.]
In Japan: a type of short-term corporate investment fund managed by a trust bank, providing a reduction of tax liability and other financial advantages. Also ***tokkin fund***.

toko *noun* var. of TOCO *noun*².

toko- *combining form* var. of TOCO-.

tokoloshe /tɒkəˈlɒʃi/ *noun.* M19.
[Sesotho *thokolosi*, *t(h)ikoloshi*, Xhosa *uThikoloshe*, Zulu *utokoloshe*.]
In southern African folklore, a mischievous and lascivious hairy manlike creature of short stature.

tokonoma /tɒkəʊˈnəʊmə/ *noun.* E18.
[Japanese.]
In a Japanese house, a recess or alcove, usu. a few inches above floor-level, for displaying flowers, pictures, ornaments, etc.

Tok Pisin /tɒk ˈpɪsɪn/ *noun.* M20.
[Pidgin English = talk pidgin.]
A Melanesian English-based pidgin spoken in Papua New Guinea.

Tokugawa /tɒkuːˈɡɑːwɑː/ *adjective & noun.* L19.
[from Ieyasu *Tokugawa* (1543–1616), Japanese military ruler and founder of a shogunate.]
▶ **A** *adjective.* Of or pertaining to the Japanese ruling dynasty (1603–1867) founded by Tokugawa, characterized by internal political and economic stability, a rigid feudal social order, and international isolation. L19.
▶ **B** *noun.* The Tokugawa dynasty of rulers collectively; their period of rule. M20.

tokus /ˈtəʊkəs/ *noun. N. Amer. slang.* Also **tochis** /ˈtəʊkɪs, ˈtɒk-/, **tuchis** /ˈtuːkɪs/. E20.
[Yiddish *tokhes* from Hebrew *tahat* beneath.]
The buttocks; the anus.

Tokyoite /ˈtəʊkjəʊʌɪt, -kɪəʊ-/ *noun.* L20.
[from *Tokyo*, the capital of Japan + -ITE¹.]
A native or inhabitant of Tokyo.

tola /ˈtəʊlə/ *noun.* E17.
[Hindi *tolā* from Sanskrit *tolaka*.]
In the Indian subcontinent: a unit of weight chiefly used for precious metals, formerly varying and now equal to 180 grains (about 11.7 grams). Also, a coin of this weight.

Tolai /ˈtəʊlʌɪ/ *adjective & noun.* M20.
[Tolai *to lai* interjection and greeting, lit. 'O friend!']
▶ **A** *adjective.* **1** Designating or pertaining to a people or group of peoples inhabiting the Gazelle peninsula in north-east New Britain, Bismarck archipelago (SW Pacific). M20.
2 Of or pertaining to the Austronesian language of this people, adopted widely by missions throughout New Britain and New Ireland. M20.
▶ **B** *noun.* Pl. same. The Tolai people; the Austronesian language of the Tolai. M20.

tolar /ˈtɒlɑː/ *noun.* L20.
[Slovene, from German *Taler* DOLLAR.]
The basic monetary unit of Slovenia, equal to 100 stotins.

tolazamide /təˈleɪzəmʌɪd/ *noun.* M20.
[from TOL(UENE + AZ(O- + AMIDE.]
PHARMACOLOGY. A sulphonylurea, $C_{14}H_{21}N_3O_3S$, used as a hypoglycaemic drug to treat diabetes.

tolazoline /təˈleɪzəliːn/ *noun.* M20.
[from TOL(YL + *imid*)*azoline*, from IMIDAZOLE + -INE⁵.]
PHARMACOLOGY. An imidazole derivative, $C_3H_5N_2{\cdot}CH_2C_6H_5$, used as an adrenergic blocking agent and vasodilator, esp. to treat spasm of the peripheral arteries.
¶ Proprietary names for this drug include PRISCOL, (*US*) PRISCOLINE.

tolbooth *noun* var. of TOLLBOOTH.

tolbutamide /tɒlˈbjuːtəmʌɪd/ *noun.* M20.
[from TOL(UENE + BUT(YL + AMIDE.]
PHARMACOLOGY. A sulphonylurea used as a hypoglycaemic drug to treat diabetes; 1-butyl-3-tosylurea, $C_{12}H_{18}N_2O_3S$.

told /təʊld/ *ppl adjective.* ME.
[pa. pple of TELL *verb*.]
Related, narrated, recounted; counted, reckoned. Chiefly as 2nd elem. of comb., as ***oft-told***, ***twice-told***, etc.
told out *colloq.* counted out; played out, exhausted.
¶ Earlier in UNTOLD.

told *verb pa. t. & pple* of TELL *verb*.

tol-de-rol /ˈtɒldɪrɒl/ *noun & interjection.* M18.
[Origin unkn.]
Used as a meaningless refrain in songs. Also, expr. jollity etc.

toldo /ˈtoldo/ *noun.* Pl. **-os** /-ɔs/. M19.
[Spanish = awning, canopy, penthouse.]
1 In Spanish-speaking countries, a canopy. M19.
2 A S. American Indian tent, hut, or other simple dwelling. M19.

tole /təʊl/ *noun & adjective.* Also **tôle** /toːl/. M20.
[French *tôle* sheet iron from dial. *taule* table from Latin *tabula* a flat board.]
▶ **A** *noun.* Enamelled or lacquered tin-plated sheet iron used for making decorative metalwork. Also ***tôle peinte*** /pɛ̃ːt/. M20.
▶ **B** *attrib.* or as *adjective.* Made of tole. M20.

tole *verb*¹ var. of TOLL *verb*¹.

tole *verb*² *pa. t. & pple*: see TELL *verb*.

Toledan /tɒˈleɪd(ə)n, təˈliːd(ə)n/ *noun & adjective.* M19.
[formed as next + -AN. Cf. earlier TOLETAN.]
▶ **A** *noun.* A native or inhabitant of Toledo in Spain. M19.
▶ **B** *adjective.* Of or pertaining to Toledo. M19.

Toledo /tɒˈleɪdəʊ, təˈliːdəʊ/ *noun.* Pl. **-os.** L16.
[A city in Spain, long famous for the manufacture of finely tempered sword-blades.]
A sword with a finely tempered blade, *esp.* one made at Toledo. Also ***Toledo sword***.

tolerable /ˈtɒl(ə)rəb(ə)l/ *adjective & adverb.* LME.
[Old & mod. French *tolérable* from Latin *tolerabilis*, from *tolerare* TOLERATE: see -ABLE.]
▶ **A** *adjective.* **1** Able to be tolerated or endured; supportable; bearable, endurable. LME.
2 Moderate in degree, quality, or character; mediocre, passable; now *esp.*, fairly good or agreeable. L15.
3 Such as to be tolerated or countenanced; permissible, allowable. Long *rare* or *obsolete.* M16.
4 *pred.* In fair health; passably well. *colloq.* E19.

> 📖 **1** T. HARDY Winter in a solitary house in the country, without society, is tolerable . . given certain conditions. *Which?* The World Health Organization . . has drawn up a tolerable weekly intake for aluminium. **2** E. GASKELL He had eaten a very tolerable lunch. H. J. LASKI There was already a tolerable certainty of his success. **3** BACON The most Tolerable . . Reuenge is for those wrongs which there is no Law to remedy. **4** C. BRONTË We're tolerable, sir, I thank you.

▶ **B** *adverb.* Tolerably, passably, moderately. Now chiefly *colloq. & dial.* E17.

> M. TWAIN Her sister, Miss Watson, a tolerable slim old maid.

■ **tolera'bility** *noun* the quality or state of being tolerable; tolerableness: M17. **tolerableness** *noun* E17. **tolerablish** *adjective* (*colloq. rare*) somewhat tolerable, just passable L18. **tolerably** *adverb* in a tolerable manner or way; passably, moderately, fairly well: LME.

tolerance /'tɒl(ə)r(ə)ns/ *noun*. LME.
[Old & mod. French *tolérance* from Latin *tolerantia*, from *tolerant-* pres. ppl stem of *tolerare* TOLERATE: see -ANCE.]
1 The action or practice of bearing pain or hardship; the power or ability to endure something. Now *rare* exc. as passing into other senses. LME. ▸**b** *PHYSIOLOGY.* The power (constitutional or acquired) of enduring large doses of active drugs, or of resisting the action of a toxin etc.; diminution in the response to a drug after continued use. Also foll. by *to*. L19. ▸**c** *BIOLOGY.* The ability of an organism to withstand some particular environmental condition; *spec.* in *FORESTRY*, the capacity of a tree to endure shade. Foll. by *to*. L19. ▸**d** *BIOLOGY.* The ability of an organism to survive or flourish despite infection or infestation. E20. ▸**e** *IMMUNOLOGY.* The ability to accept a graft, transplant, antigen, etc., without an immunological reaction. M20.
2 The action of allowing something or granting permission. *obsolete* exc. *Scot.* LME.
3 The disposition or ability to accept without protest or adopt a liberal attitude towards the opinions or acts of others; toleration; forbearance. Cf. earlier TOLERANCY. M18.
4 a = REMEDY *noun* 3. M19. ▸**b** *ENGINEERING* etc. An allowable amount of variation in the dimensions of a machine or part. More widely, the allowable amount of variation in any specified quantity. E20.

> **1** BACON Diogenes, one terrible frosty Morning, . . stood Naked shaking to shew his Tolerance. **3** Y. MENUHIN To meet a tolerance that accepted the odd man out . . was a heartwarming experience. P. BAILEY My grandmother had no tolerance of illness; regarded it, indeed, as a vice, an indulgence.

Comb.: **tolerance dose** *MEDICINE* a dose, esp. of radiation, believed to be received or taken without harm; **tolerance level** the level (of noise etc.) that can be tolerated or is acceptable; *spec.* in *MEDICINE* = ***tolerance dose*** above; **tolerance limit** a limit laid down for the permitted variation of a parameter of a product.

tolerance /'tɒl(ə)r(ə)ns/ *verb trans.* M20.
[from the noun.]
ENGINEERING etc. Specify a tolerance for (a machine part etc.). Chiefly as ***toleranced*** *ppl adjective*, ***tolerancing*** *verbal noun*.

tolerancy /'tɒl(ə)r(ə)nsi/ *noun*. *rare*. M16.
[from Latin *tolerantia*: see TOLERANCE *noun*, -ANCY.]
The quality or disposition of being tolerant to the opinions or practices of others. Cf. TOLERANCE *noun* 3.

tolerant /'tɒl(ə)r(ə)nt/ *adjective & noun*. L18.
[French *tolérant* pres. pple of *tolérer* from Latin *tolerare* TOLERATE: see -ANT¹. Cf. earlier INTOLERANT.]
▸**A** *adjective*. **1** Disposed to accept without protest the opinions or acts of others; (foll. by *of*) patient; showing forbearance or adopting a liberal attitude towards. L18.
2 Of a thing: capable of bearing or sustaining something. Foll. by *of*. *rare* exc. as passing into senses below. M19.
3 *PHYSIOLOGY.* Able to endure the action of a drug, toxin, etc., without being affected. L19.
4 *BIOLOGY.* Capable of withstanding a particular environmental condition; *spec.* in *FORESTRY*, capable of enduring shade. L19.
5 *BIOLOGY.* Of an organism: exhibiting tolerance to infection or infestation. E20.
6 *IMMUNOLOGY.* Exhibiting immunological tolerance to grafts, transplants, antigens, etc. Foll. by *of*, *to*. M20.

> **1** E. M. FORSTER He was infinitely tolerant of the young, and had no desire to snub George. A. STORR It was his own experience of feeling ill at ease which made Snow so tolerant.

▸**B** *noun*. A person who tolerates opinions or practices different from his or her own; a person free from bigotry. *rare*. L18.
■ †**tolerantism** *noun* (*rare*) the principles or practice of a tolerant: only in E19. **tolerantly** *adverb* in a tolerant manner; forbearingly: E19.

tolerate /'tɒləreɪt/ *verb trans.* E16.
[Latin *tolerat-* pa. ppl stem of *tolerare* bear, endure: see -ATE³.]
1 Endure or bear (pain or hardship). E16. ▸**b** *PHYSIOLOGY.* Endure without ill effects the action of (a toxin or strong drug). L19.
2 Allow the existence, occurrence, or practice of (esp. a particular religion) without authoritative interference; *gen.* allow, permit. M16. ▸†**b** Allow or permit (a person) *to do* something. L16–E19.
3 Treat with forbearance; find endurable, adopt a liberal attitude towards; accept without protest. L16.

> **1** L. DEIGHTON It was incredible that they could tolerate the intense heat. **2** C. HILL Baptists were suggesting the possibility of tolerating more than one brand of religious worship. *Pen International* No controversial subject is tolerated and the approval of the authorities is required for every new . . production. **b** R. COKE Berta . . wife of Ethelbert . . was tolerated to observe the rites of Christian religion. **3** D. MURPHY They were very happy together, each amiably tolerating the other's foibles.

■ **toleratingly** *adverb* in a tolerating manner L19. **tolerator** *noun* a person who tolerates something M17.

toleration /tɒlə'reɪʃ(ə)n/ *noun*. L15.
[French *tolération* from Latin *toleratio(n-)*, formed as prec.: see -ATION.]
1 †**a** The action of allowing something or granting permission by authority; licence. L15–E18. ▸**b** *spec.* Licence to gather oysters or maintain oyster-beds. *US local*. L18.
2 †**a** The action of enduring or bearing pain, hardship, etc. M16–E17. ▸**b** *PHYSIOLOGY.* = TOLERANCE *noun* 1b. Now *rare* or *obsolete*. L19.
3 The action or practice of finding something endurable or accepting something without protest; adoption of a liberal attitude; forbearance, tolerance. L16.
4 *spec.* State sanction for the expression of religious opinion or freedom to practise forms of religion at variance from those officially established or recognized. E17.
5 = TOLERANCE *noun* 4a. L19.
4 Act of Toleration an act or statute granting religious toleration; *spec.* (*ENGLISH HISTORY*) a bill of 1689 by which freedom of religious worship was granted, on certain prescribed conditions, to Dissenting Protestants.
Comb.: **Toleration Act** = ***Act of Toleration*** (see sense 4 above).
■ **tolerationism** *noun* (*rare*) the principles or practice of religious toleration L19. **tolerationist** *noun* an advocate or supporter of religious toleration M19.

tolerize /'tɒlərʌɪz/ *verb trans.* Also **-ise**. M20.
[from TOLER(ANT + -IZE.]
IMMUNOLOGY. Render immunologically tolerant to grafts, transplants, antigens, etc.
■ **toleri'zation** *noun* L20.

tolerogen /'tɒl(ə)rədʒ(ə)n/ *noun*. M20.
[from TOLER(ANCE *noun* + -OGEN.]
IMMUNOLOGY. A substance inducing immunological tolerance.
■ **tolero'genic** *adjective* that induces immunological toleration M20. **toleroge'nicity** *noun* the quality or capacity of inducing immunological toleration L20.

Toletan /'tɒlɪt(ə)n/ *adjective*. *rare*. LME.
[Latin *Toletanus*, from *Toletum* Toledo: see -AN. Cf. TOLEDAN.]
Of or pertaining to Toledo in Spain. Chiefly *Hist.* in ***Toletan tables***, Alphonsine tables (see ALPHONSINE).

tolfraedic /tɒʊl'friːdɪk/ *adjective*. E19.
[from Old Norse *tólf-rœðr* (only in *tólfrætt hundrað* a hundred of twelve tens), from *tólf* twelve + *ræða* speak: see -IC.]
Hist. Duodecimal: designating the ancient Scandinavian system of reckoning, in which twelve tens were counted as a hundred.

tolguacha *noun* var. of TOLOACHE.

tolidine /'tɒlɪdiːn/ *noun*. L19.
[from TOL(YL + BENZ)IDINE.]
CHEMISTRY. A benzidine derivative, $(NH_2(CH_3)C_6H_3)_2$, which is the parent compound of a group of azo dyes and is used as a reagent in chemical analysis.

tolite /'tɒlʌɪt/ *noun*. E20.
[from TOL(UENE + -ITE¹.]
= TRINITROTOLUENE.

tolkach /'tolkatʃ/ *noun*. Pl. **-i** /-i/. M20.
[Russian, from *tolkat'* push, jostle.]
In countries of the former USSR, a person who negotiates difficulties or arranges things, a fixer.

Tolkienian /tɒl'kiːnɪən/ *adjective*. M20.
[from *Tolkien* (see below) + -IAN.]
Of or pertaining to the philologist and author of fantasy literature John Ronald Reuel Tolkien (1892–1973); characteristic of Tolkien or his writings.
■ **Tolkie'nesque** *adjective* characteristic of Tolkien or his writings L20.

toll /təʊl/ *noun*¹.
[Old English *toll* = Old High German *zol* (German *Zoll*), Old Norse *tollr* (masc.), with by-forms Old English *toln*, Old Frisian *tol(e)ne*, Old Saxon *tolna* (fem.), from medieval Latin *toloneum* alt. of late Latin *teloneum* from Greek *telōnion* toll-house, from *telōnēs* tax-collector, from *telos* tax.]
1 A charge, a payment, a tax, a duty; *spec.* (**a**) (*obsolete* exc. *Hist.*) a payment exacted by a feudal superior or other authority as a tribute or in return for protection; (**b**) a fee, percentage, etc., taken by an agent effecting some transaction (as the collection of a tax or duty). Now chiefly as in sense 2 below. OE.
2 A charge for permission to pass a barrier or to proceed along a road, over a bridge, etc. OE. ▸**b** A charge or payment for provision of a service, as (**a**) (long *obsolete* exc. *dial.*) a proportion of the grain or flour ground by a miller, taken as payment for grinding; (**b**) a charge for the right to bring goods to or sell goods in a place, esp. a market. OE. ▸**c** A charge for a telephone call, esp. a long-distance call. Chiefly *N. Amer.* L19.
3 *fig.* A cost; a loss; damage; *esp.* (the number or a list of) deaths or casualties resulting from a battle, natural disaster, etc. (*rare* before L19.) LME.

> **1** TENNYSON Tax and toll, From many an inland town and haven large. LD MACAULAY Forfeitures went to Sunderland. On every grant toll was paid to him. **toll and team** (*LAW*, now *Hist.*) in Anglo-Saxon England, the right to charge toll together with the right of jurisdiction granted in a suit of team (see TEAM *noun* 7b). **3** *Listener* A . . programme aimed at reducing the toll on the roads. *Times* The death toll in the train disaster . . could be more than 1,000. **take a toll**, **take its toll** cause or be accompanied by loss, damage, injury, etc., (foll. by *of*, *on* a person).

Comb.: **toll-bar** a barrier across a road or bridge, where a toll is collected; †**toll-book**: containing a register of animals or goods for sale at a market or fair and the tolls payable for them; **toll-bridge**: at which a toll is charged for the right to cross; **toll call** †(**a**) a telephone call for which an individual charge was made; (**b**) *N. Amer.* a long-distance telephone call, a call between different telephone areas; **toll-dish** a dish or bowl for measuring the toll of grain at a mill; **toll-farmer**: of the tolls at a certain place (cf. FARMER *noun* 1); **toll-free** *adjective & adverb* (**a**) *adjective* exempt from payment of a charge or toll; (**b**) *adverb* without having to pay a charge; **toll-gate**: across a road preventing passage until a toll is paid; †**toll-gatherer** a person who collects tolls, *esp.* = PUBLICAN *noun*¹ 1; **toll-house** a house, booth, etc., where tolls are collected, *esp.* a house by a toll-gate or toll-bridge; **toll-keeper** the keeper of a toll-gate or toll-house; **tollman** a man who collects tolls, the keeper of a toll-gate; **toll plaza** *US* a row of toll-booths on a toll-road; **toll-road** a road maintained by the tolls collected on it; **toll TV** = ***pay-television*** s.v. PAY-; **tollway** *US* a highway for the use of which a charge is made; **toll-taker** a toll-collector.
■ **toller** *noun*¹ (now *rare*) a toll-collector OE.

toll /təʊl/ *noun*². LME.
[from TOLL *verb*³.]
The action of tolling a bell; the sound made by this. Also, (the sound of) a single stroke of a bell.

†**toll** *noun*³. *rare*. L15–E19.
[from TOLL *verb*¹.]
A lure.

toll /təʊl/ *noun*⁴. *rare*. *obsolete* exc. *dial.* M17.
[Origin unkn.]
A clump of trees.

toll /təʊl/ *verb*¹. Now *dial.* & *US*. Also **tole**. ME.
[Rel. to Old English *for*|*tyllan* seduce.]
1 *verb trans.* Attract, entice, allure. Formerly also, incite. ME. ▸**b** *verb trans.* *spec.* Lure or decoy (a duck, fish, etc.) for the purpose of capture. *N. Amer.* M19. ▸**c** *verb intrans.* Of an animal: admit of being lured. *N. Amer.* M19.
2 *verb trans.* Pull, drag, draw. Long *rare* or *obsolete*. LME.
Comb.: **toll-bait** *US* chopped bait thrown into the water to attract fish.
■ **toller** *noun*² †(**a**) *rare* a person who entices another; (**b**) *US* a decoy, *esp.* a dog of a small breed used in decoying ducks: LME.

toll /təʊl/ *verb*². Now *rare*. ME.
[from TOLL *noun*¹.]
▸**I** *verb intrans.* **1** Take, collect, or exact a toll. ME.
†**2** Pay a toll. Freq. in ***toll for***, enter (a horse etc.) for sale in the toll-book of a market. LME–M17.
▸**II** *verb trans.* **3 a** Exact a portion of (produce, a crop, etc.). LME. ▸**b** Impose a toll on, exact a toll from, (a person etc.). L16. ▸**c** Charge a toll for the use of (a bridge, crossing, etc.). Chiefly as ***tolled*** *ppl adjective*. L20.

> **3a** *fig.*: SHAKES. *2 Hen. IV* The bee, tolling from every flower The virtuous sweets.

■ **tollable** *adjective* (*rare*) requiring payment of a toll E17.

toll /təʊl/ *verb*³. LME.
[Prob. orig. a particular use of TOLL *verb*¹ 2.]
1 *verb trans.* (Of a bell or bell-ringer) sound (a solemn tone, esp. a knell); (of a clock) strike (the hour) with a slow uniform succession of strokes. LME.
2 *verb trans. & intrans.* Cause (a large or deep-toned bell) to toll, now esp. on the occasion of a death or funeral. (Foll. by *for*.) L15. ▸**b** *verb trans.* Announce (a death etc.) by tolling; toll for (a dying or dead person). L16.
3 *verb intrans.* (Of a bell) sound with a slow uniform succession of strokes (*for* a purpose); (of a clock) strike the hour on a deep-toned bell. M16. ▸**b** Make a deep-toned or monotonously repeated sound like the tolling of a bell. M18.
4 *verb trans.* Summon or dismiss by tolling. E17.

> **1** J. BEATTIE Slow tolls the village-clock the drowsy hour. SIR W. SCOTT And bells toll'd out their mighty peal. **2** W. COWPER Toll for the brave! The brave that are no more! TENNYSON Toll ye the church-bell sad and slow. **3** C. HARMAN The bell of Harrow School Chapel was tolling for . . Professor Tindall, who had died. H. L. KLAWANS A bell from a nearby church began to toll for midnight mass. **4** THACKERAY The bells were . . tolling the people out of church.

Phrases: **toll in** summon a congregation by tolling, esp. shortly before the start of a service.

■ **tolling** *noun* (*a*) the action of the verb; (*b*) the sound made by this: L15.

toll /təʊl/ *verb*[4] *trans.* Now *rare* or *obsolete.* LME.
[Anglo-Norman *toller, toler, touller* from Latin *tollere* take away.]
LAW. Take away, annul.
toll an entry take away the right of entry.

tollage /ˈtəʊlɪdʒ/ *noun.* L15.
[Perh. from TOLL *verb*[2] + -AGE.]
1 A fee, a toll; exaction or payment of (a) toll. L15.
†**2** = TALLAGE *noun.* M16–M17.

tollbooth /ˈtəʊlbuːð, -buːθ/ *noun.* Also **tolbooth**. ME.
[from TOLL *noun*[1] + BOOTH.]
1 A booth, stall, or office at which tolls or customs are collected; *spec.* a roadside booth at which a toll for right of passage is collected. ME.
2 Chiefly *Scot. arch.* ▸**a** A town hall, a guildhall. LME. ▸**b** A town jail. LME.

Tollens /ˈtɒlənz/ *noun.* E20.
[Bernhard Christian Gottfried *Tollens* (1841–1918), German chemist.]
CHEMISTRY. ***Tollens' reagent***, ***Tollens's reagent***, a solution of ammoniacal silver nitrate and sodium hydroxide; ***Tollens' test***, a test for aldehydes, which give a silver precipitate when heated with Tollens' reagent.

tollent /ˈtɒl(ə)nt/ *adjective. rare.* L18.
[Latin *tollent-* pres. ppl stem of *tollere* lift, take away: see -ENT.]
LOGIC. That denies or negates. Opp. PONENT *adjective* 2.

tolley /ˈtɒli/ *noun.* L20.
[Blend of TAW *noun*[4] and ALLY *noun*[2].]
= TAW *noun*[4] 1.

tol-lol /tɒlˈlɒl/ *adjective. slang.* Also **toll-**, **-loll**. L18.
[from TOL(ERABLE with rhyming extension.]
Tolerable, fairly good, passable, (esp. with ref. to health).
■ **tol-lol-ish** *adjective* M19.

tollon *noun* var. of TOYON.

Tolman /ˈtɒlmən/ *noun.* E19.
[Surname of a US fruit-grower.]
In full ***Tolman sweet***, ***Tolman sweeting***, ***Tolman's sweet***, ***Tolman's sweeting***. A yellow-skinned variety of apple originally developed in Rhode Island; a tree bearing this apple.

toloache /tɒlˈwatʃi/ *noun.* Also **tolguacha** /tɒlˈgwatʃə/. L19.
[Mexican Spanish from Nahuatl *toloatzin*, from *toloa* bow the head + honorific particle *-tzin*, the plant being revered by the Indians.]
A large-flowered datura, *Datura inoxia*, of south-western N. America; a hallucinogenic preparation of this plant, used in initiation ceremonies.

tolsel /ˈtəʊls(ə)l/ *noun. local.* Also **tolzey** /ˈtəʊlzi/. LME.
[from TOLL *noun*[1]: cf. Old English *seld* seat, *sele* hall, *tollsetl* toll-booth, custom-house.]
A guildhall; (a court held in) a borough court-house.

Tolstoyan /ˈtɒlstɔɪən, -ˈstɔɪən/ *adjective & noun.* Also **-oian**. L19.
[from *Tolstoy* (see below) + -AN.]
▶ **A** *adjective.* Of, pertaining to, or characteristic of Count Leo N. Tolstoy (1828–1910), Russian writer and social reformer. L19.
▶ **B** *noun.* A follower of Tolstoy or his teachings. E20.
■ **Tolstoyanism** *noun* (adherence to) the principles of social and moral reform proposed by or associated with Tolstoy E20.

tolt /təʊlt/ *noun.* E17.
[Anglo-Norman *to(u)lte* = Anglo-Latin *tolta*, from Latin *tollere* take away.]
LAW (now *Hist.*). A writ by which a case was removed from a court-baron to the county court.

Toltec /ˈtɒltɛk/ *noun & adjective.* L18.
[Spanish *tolteca* from Nahuatl *toltecatl* lit. 'person from Tula' (ancient Toltec city).]
Hist. ▶**A** *noun.* A member of a Nahuatl people dominant in Mexico before the arrival of the Aztecs. L18.
▶ **B** *adjective.* Of or pertaining to this people. L19.
■ **Toltecan** *adjective* M19.

tolu /təˈluː, ˈtəʊluː/ *noun.* Also (in *balsam of tolu* usu.) **T-**. L17.
[Santiago de *Tolú*, Colombia.]
In full ***tolu balsam***, ***balsam of tolu***. A balsam from the bark of *Myroxylon balsamum*, a leguminous tree of Central and S. America, used in perfumery, as a flavouring in cough mixtures, etc.

toluene /ˈtɒljuiːn/ *noun.* L19.
[from prec. + -ENE.]
CHEMISTRY. A colourless liquid cyclic hydrocarbon, $C_6H_5CH_3$, which is obtained from coal tar and petroleum and is used as a solvent and in the manufacture of many organic compounds. Also called ***methylbenzene***, ***toluol***.
■ **toluic** /təˈl(j)uːɪk, ˈtɒl-/ *adjective*: ***toluic acid***, each of three crystalline isomeric cyclic acids, $CH_3C_6H_4COOH$, which are produced from toluene, cymene, or xylene; methylbenzoic acid: M19. **toluol** *noun* = TOLUENE M19. **toluyl** /ˈtɒl(j)ʊʌɪl, -uːɪl/ *noun* each of three isomeric cyclic radicals, $CH_3C_6H_4CO\cdot$, derived from a toluic acid M19. **toluylic** *adjective*: ***toluylic acid*** = ***toluic acid*** M19.

toluidine /ˈtɒljʊɪdiːn, tɒˈljuː-/ *noun.* M19.
[from TOLU(ENE + -IDINE.]
CHEMISTRY. Each of three isomeric bases of formula $CH_3C_6H_4NH_2$, which occur as toxic flammable liquids or solid flakes and are used in making diazo dyes and organic chemicals.
Comb.: **toluidine blue** a thiazine dye, $C_{15}H_{16}ClN_3S$, now used chiefly as a biological stain.

†**tolutation** *noun. rare.* M17–L18.
[from Latin *tolut-* stem of *tolutim* at a trot + -ATION.]
The action of ambling or trotting (*lit.* & *fig.*).

tolyl /ˈtɒlʌɪl, -lɪl/ *noun.* M19.
[from TOL(UENE + -YL.]
CHEMISTRY. Each of three isomeric cyclic radicals, $CH_3C_6H_4\cdot$, derived from toluene. Formerly also = BENZYL.

tolzey *noun* var. of TOLSEL.

Tom /tɒm/ *noun*[1] & *verb.* LME.
[Abbreviation of male forename *Thomas*.]
▶ **A** *noun.* **1** (A name for) a male representative of the common people; (a name for) an ordinary man. LME. ▸†**b** = ***Tom o' Bedlam*** s.v. BEDLAM *noun* 2. M16–L17. ▸**c** (**t-**.) A girl, a woman. *Austral. slang.* E20. ▸**d** (Freq. **t-**.) A prostitute. *slang.* M20. ▸**e** = UNCLE TOM *noun. US slang.* M20.
2 (Used in the name of) any of various exceptionally large bells. E17.
3 (Usu. **t-**.) The male of various animals; *esp.* a male cat. M18.
Phrases: ***Long Tom***: see LONG *adjective*[1]. ***Old Tom***: see OLD *adjective*. **Tom, Dick, and Harry** (freq. *derog.*) ordinary people taken at random. ***Tom o'Bedlam***: see BEDLAM *noun* 2.
Comb.: **tomcod** (chiefly *N. Amer.*) any of various small marine fishes; now *esp.* either of two gadid fishes of the genus *Microgadus*, *M. tomcod* of the W. Atlantic and *M. proximus* of the E. Pacific, and the related *Urophycis floridana* (also called ***southern hake***); ***Tom Collins***: see COLLINS *noun*[1]; **Tom Jones** *adjective* designating a garment, hairstyle, etc., considered suggestive of 18th-cent. fashions, esp. as represented in the 1963 film version of Fielding's novel *History of Tom Jones* (1749); **Tom-noddy** (*a*) *Scot.* & *north.* the puffin; (*b*) a foolish or stupid person; **tompot (blenny)** a blenny, *Blennius gattorugine*, found among kelp off rocky coasts of the E. Atlantic and Mediterranean; **Tom Pudding** *slang* any of several boxlike iron boats coupled together and towed by a tug to carry coal on canals; **Tom Thumb** (*a*) a very short male person; (*b*) *derog.* an insignificant person; (*c*) a dwarf variety of certain flowering plants (esp. nasturtium or snapdragon) and vegetables; **Tom Tiddler's ground** (*a*) a children's game in which one player tries to catch the others who run on to his or her territory crying 'We're on Tom Tiddler's ground, picking up gold and silver'; (*b*) a place where money or profit is readily made.
▶ **B** *verb.* Infl. **-mm-**.
1 *verb trans.* Address familiarly as 'Tom'. *colloq.* (*rare*). E20.
2 *verb intrans.* (with *it*). = UNCLE TOM *verb. US slang.* M20.
3 *verb intrans.* (**t-**.) Practise prostitution, behave promiscuously; copulate. *slang.* M20.

tom /tɒm/ *noun*[2]. *colloq.* E20.
[Abbreviation.]
= TOMATO 1.

tom /tɒm/ *noun*[3]. *slang.* M20.
[Abbreviation.]
= TOMFOOLERY (b).

tom /tɒm/ *noun*[4]. *slang.* L20.
[Abbreviation.]
= TOM-TOM *noun* 1b.

tomahawk /ˈtɒməhɔːk/ *noun.* Also **tommyhawk** /ˈtɒmɪhɔːk/. E17.
[Virginia Algonquian.]
1 A N. American Indian axe with a stone or (later) iron head, *esp.* one used as a weapon. E17.
2 *transf.* Any similar weapon or tool used elsewhere; *spec.* (*a*) (chiefly *Hist.*) a sailor's poleaxe; (*b*) *Austral.* & *NZ* a hatchet. L17.
3 *fig.* An (imaginary) instrument of a savage or vindictive attack. E19.

> 📖 **2** K. MANSFIELD Down came the little tomahawk and the duck's head flew off. **3** H. ROGERS That age of . . savage controversy, of the tomahawk and scalping-knife.

Phrases: **bury the tomahawk** lay down one's arms, cease hostilities. **dig up the tomahawk** take up arms, commence hostilities. **lay aside the tomahawk** = ***bury the tomahawk*** above. **take up the tomahawk** = ***dig up the tomahawk*** above.

tomahawk /ˈtɒməhɔːk/ *verb trans.* E18.
[from the noun.]
1 Strike, cut, or kill with a tomahawk. E18. ▸**b** *fig.* Make a savage or vindictive verbal attack on (a person, book, etc.). E19.
2 Cut (a sheep) while shearing. *Austral.* & *NZ.* M19.
■ **tomahawker** *noun* E19.

tomalley /ˈtɒmali/ *noun.* Chiefly *N. Amer.* Also †**taumaly**. M17.
[French *taumalin* from Carib *taumali*.]
The liver (hepatopancreas) of the lobster, which makes a green sauce when cooked.

toman /təˈmɑːn/ *noun*[1]. M16.
[Persian *tūmān* from Old Turkish *tümen* from Tocharian A *tmān*, prob. ult. from base of Chinese *wàn* 10,000.]
1 a A former Persian gold coin and money of account, nominally worth 10,000 dinars. M16. ▸**b** In Iran, a coin and unofficial monetary unit equal to ten rials. M20.
2 *Hist.* In Persia, Turkey, etc.: a military division of 10,000 men. Now *rare* or *obsolete.* L17.

toman /ˈtəʊmən/ *noun*[2]. E19.
[Gaelic, dim. of *tom* hill.]
A hillock; a mound, *esp.* one formed of glacial moraine.

Tom-and-Jerry /tɒm(ə)n(d)ˈdʒɛri/ *verb & noun. colloq.* As noun also **Tom and Jerry**. E19.
[With allus. to the chief characters in Pierce Egan's *Life in London* (1821).]
▶ **A** *verb intrans.* Drink and behave riotously. Now *rare.* E19.
▶ **B** *noun.* **1** A kind of hot rum cocktail or highly spiced punch. Orig. *US.* E19.
2 More fully ***Tom and Jerry shop***. A rough public house or tavern. Now *rare.* M19.
■ **Tom-and-Jerryism** *noun* drunken revelling M19.

†**tomasha** *noun* var. of TAMASHA.

tomata, †**tomate** *nouns* see TOMATO *noun.*

tomatillo /tɒməˈtɪl(j)əʊ, *foreign* tomaˈtiʎo/ *noun.* Orig. & chiefly *US.* Pl. **-os** /-əʊz, *foreign* -ɒs/. E20.
[Spanish, dim. of *tomate* TOMATO *noun.*]
The edible purplish fruit of a kind of ground cherry, *Physalis philadelphica*; the plant bearing this fruit, a native of Mexico.

tomatine /ˈtɒmətiːn/ *noun.* Also **-in** /-ɪn/. M20.
[from TOMAT(O + -INE[5].]
BIOCHEMISTRY. An alkaloid which is a steroidal glycoside present in the stems and leaves of the tomato and related plants.

tomato /təˈmɑːtəʊ/ *noun & adjective.* E17.
[French, Spanish, or Portuguese *tomate* from Nahuatl *tomatl*.]
▶ **A** *noun.* Pl. **-oes**. Orig. †**tomate**; also (*arch.*) **tomata** /təˈmɑːtə/.
1 The glossy, usu. bright red and spherical, pulpy fruit of a plant of the nightshade family, *Lycopersicon esculentum*, eaten in salads, as a cooked vegetable, etc.; the plant bearing this fruit, a native of the Andes. E17. ▸**b** The bright red colour of a ripe tomato. E20. ▸**c** An attractive girl. *slang* (orig. *US*). E20.
2 With specifying word: (the plant bearing) any of several special varieties of this fruit; (the plant bearing) any of certain related fruits. M19.
2 ***beef tomato***, ***cherry tomato***, ***currant tomato***, ***plum tomato***, ***strawberry tomato***, ***tree tomato***, etc.
Comb.: **tomato hornworm** a large N. American hawkmoth, *Manduca quinquemaculata*, the larvae of which feed on the leaves of tomato, tobacco, etc.; also called ***northern hornworm***; **tomato juice** the juice from tomatoes, a drink of this; **tomato moth** a European noctuid moth, *Lacanobia oleracea*, the larvae of which sometimes feed on tomato leaves; also called ***bright-line brown-eye***; ***tomato pinworm***: see PINWORM (b) s.v. PIN *noun*[1]; **tomato vine** *US* a tomato plant; **tomato worm** (*a*) (the larva of) the noctuid moth *Helicoverpa armigera*, which sometimes bores into tomato fruits (also called ***scarce bordered straw***, ***Old World bollworm***); (*b*) *N. Amer.* (the larva of) the tomato hornworm.
▶ **B** *adjective.* Of a bright red colour. Cf. sense A.1b above. L20.

> 📖 M. KENYON Her rosy cheeks turned tomato with indignation.

■ **tomatoey** *adjective* having the taste or flavour of tomatoes L20.

tomb /tuːm/ *noun & verb.* ME.
[Anglo-Norman *tumbe* or Old & mod. French *tombe*, from late Latin *tumba* from Greek *tumbos* mound, tomb.]
▶ **A** *noun.* **1** A burial place; *spec.* (*a*) an enclosure cut in the earth or in rock to receive a dead body; (*b*) a (partly or wholly underground) vault for burying the dead; (*c*) *ANTIQUITIES* a tumulus or mound raised over a corpse. ME.
2 A monument to the memory of a dead person, usu. erected over his or her burial place. Also *occas.*, a cenotaph. ME.
3 The final resting-place of a person; ***the tomb*** (*poet.*), death. M16.

> 📖 **1** R. L. FOX They were buried in vaulted underground tombs. *fig.*: W. H. AUDEN The muttering tomb / of a museum reading-room. **2** *Guardian* A wreath on the tomb of the unknown soldier. **3** J. LOCKE Our Minds represent to us those Tombs, to which we are approaching. T. GRAY *Charity*, that glows beyond the tomb.

Phrases: ***mastaba tomb***: see MASTABA 2. ***the tomb***: see sense 3 above. **the Tombs** *US slang* New York City prison. ***tholos tomb***: see THOLOS 2. ***watery tomb***: see WATERY 7.
Comb.: **tomb bat** any of several bats of the genus *Taphozous* (family Emballonuridae), which are related to the sac-winged bats and frequent tombs in Africa and Asia.
▶ **B** *verb trans.* Deposit (a body) in a tomb; bury (*lit.* & *fig.*). Now *rare.* ME.
■ **tombic** /ˈtuːmbɪk, ˈtɒm-/ *adjective* (*rare*) of, pertaining to, or connected with a tomb or tombs L19. **tombless** *adjective* L16.

tombac /ˈtɒmbak/ *noun*. **E17**.
[French from Portuguese *tambaca* from Malay *tembaga* copper, brass, perh. from Sanskrit *tāmraka* copper. Cf. TUMBAGA.]
METALLURGY. A brittle brass alloy originally produced in Indo-China, containing from 72 to 99 per cent of copper and from 1 to 28 per cent of zinc, used in the east for gongs and bells, and in the west for cheap jewellery etc. Also called ***red brass***.
red tombac: containing 97.5 per cent of copper. **white tombac**: containing arsenic.

†tombaga *noun* var. of TUMBAGA.

tombarolo /tombaˈroːlo/ *noun*. Pl. ***-li*** /-li/. **L20**.
[Italian, from *tomba* tomb, grave.]
A grave-robber.

tombo /ˈtɒmbəʊ/ *noun*. **E18**.
[W. African name.]
In W. Africa, the fruit of the wine palm, *Raphia hookeri*; the wine obtained from this palm.

tombola /tɒmˈbəʊlə/ *noun*. **L19**.
[French or Italian, from Italian *tombolare* turn a somersault, tumble.]
A kind of lottery with tickets usually drawn from a turning drum-shaped container, esp. at a fête or fair.

tombolo /ˈtɒmbələʊ/ *noun*. Pl. **-os**. **L19**.
[Italian = sand-dune.]
PHYSICAL GEOGRAPHY. A bar of shingle, sand, etc., joining an island to the mainland.

tombotie *noun* var. of TAMBOTI.

tomboy /ˈtɒmbɔɪ/ *noun*. **M16**.
[from TOM *noun*[1] + BOY *noun*.]
†**1** An uncouth or boisterous boy. **M–L16**.
†**2** A forward or immodest woman. **L16–L18**.
3 A girl who behaves in a (usu. rough or boisterous) boyish way. **L16**.
▪ **tomboyish** *adjective* **M19**. **tomboyishly** *adverb* **M20**. **tomboyishness** *noun* **L19**. **tomboyism** *noun* tomboyish conduct **L19**.

tombstone /ˈtuːmstəʊn/ *noun*. **M16**.
[from TOMB *noun* + STONE *noun*.]
1 Orig., (the cover of) a stone coffin. Later, a horizontal stone covering a grave. Now, any monument placed as a memorial over a person's grave; *esp*. a gravestone. **M16**.
2 *slang*. **a** A pawn-ticket. **L19**. ▸**b** A projecting tooth, *esp*. a discoloured one. **E20**.
3 COMMERCE. An advertisement listing the underwriters or firms associated with a new share issue etc. Freq. *attrib*. **M20**.

tom-cat /ˈtɒmkat/ *noun & verb*. Also (the usual form in sense A.2) **tomcat**. **E19**.
[from TOM *noun*[1] + CAT *noun*[1].]
▶**A** *noun*. Orig. two words.
1 A male cat. **E19**.
2 A lecherous or sexually aggressive man, a womanizer. *colloq*. (orig. *US*). **M20**.
▶**B** *verb intrans*. Infl. **-tt-**. Pursue women promiscuously for sexual gratification. Freq. foll. by *around*. *N. Amer. slang*. **E20**.

> W. P. McGIVERN A guy tom-catting around while his wife's away.

tome /təʊm/ *noun*. **E16**.
[French from Latin *tomus* from Greek *tomos* slice, piece, roll of papyrus, volume, rel. to *temnein* to cut.]
†**1** Each of the separate volumes of a literary work; *rare* each of the largest parts or sections of a single volume. **E16–M18**.
2 A book, a volume; *esp*. a large, heavy, or learned one. **L16**.
3 ECCLESIASTICAL HISTORY. [translating Latin *tomus*.] A papal letter. **L18**.

> **1** N. UDALL The second tome or volume of the Paraphrase of Erasmus. **2** C. HARKNESS He writes endless tomes in Latin. **3** GIBBON The tome of Leo was subscribed by the Oriental bishops.

▪ **tomelet** *noun* a small volume **M19**.

-tome /təʊm/ *suffix*.
[In sense 1 from Greek *-tomon* neut. of *-tomos* that cuts: see -TOMY. In sense 2 from Greek *tomē* a cutting.]
1 Chiefly MEDICINE. Forming the names of instruments used for cutting, esp. ones used in surgical operations denoted by the corresponding word in *-tomy*, as ***craniotome***, ***microtome***, ***osteotome***, etc.
2 ANATOMY & ZOOLOGY. Forming nouns denoting a distinct section or segment of a body or part, as ***harmotome***, ***myotome***, ***nephrotome***, etc.

tomentose /təˈmɛntəʊs, ˈtəʊməntəʊs/ *adjective*. **L17**.
[from next + -OSE[1].]
1 BOTANY & ZOOLOGY. Closely covered with short matted hairs. **L17**.
2 ANATOMY. Flocculent in appearance esp. due to the presence of fine capillaries. **M19**.
▪ Also **toˈmentous** *adjective* (now *rare*) **E19**.

tomentum /təˈmɛntəm/ *noun*. **L17**.
[Latin = stuffing for cushions.]
1 BOTANY. Dense short matted pubescence on the stem, leaves, etc. **L17**.
2 ANATOMY. A downy covering; *spec*. (more fully ***tomentum cerebri*** /ˈsɛrɪbrʌɪ, -briː/ [= of the brain]) the flocculent inner surface of the pia mater, consisting of numerous minute capillaries. Now *rare*. **E19**.
▪ **tomentulose** *adjective* (BOTANY) minutely tomentose **L19**.

tomfool /tɒmˈfuːl, *as adjective usu*. ˈtɒmfuːl/ *noun, adjective, & verb*. **LME**.
[from TOM *noun*[1] + FOOL *noun*[1].]
▶**A** *noun*. **1** (A name for) a person with a mental handicap. Long *rare*. **LME**.
2 A person who plays the part of a fool, a buffoon; *spec*. a buffoon who accompanies morris dancers. **M17**.
3 A (very) foolish or silly person. **E18**.
▶**B** *attrib*. or as *adjective*. Foolish, silly, stupid, daft. **M18**.
▶**C** *verb intrans*. Play the fool. **E19**.
▪ **tomˈfoolery** *noun* (*a*) (an instance of) foolish, silly, or daft behaviour; (*b*) *rhyming slang* jewellery: **E19**. **tomˈfoolish** *adjective* of, pertaining to, or of the nature of a tomfool **L18**. **tomˈfoolishness** *noun* **L19**.

tomium /ˈtəʊmɪəm/ *noun*. Pl. **tomia** /ˈtəʊmɪə/. **M19**.
[from Greek *tomos* cutting, sharp + -IUM. Cf. Greek *tomion* a sacrifice cut up.]
ORNITHOLOGY. Each of the cutting edges of a bird's bill.
▪ **tomial** *adjective* **L19**.

tomme /tɔm/ *noun*. Pl. pronounced same. **M20**.
[French.]
Any of various cheeses made in Savoy, a region of SE France.

Tommy /ˈtɒmi/ *noun*[1]. Also (the usual form in senses 1, 3) **t-**. **L18**.
[Dim. or pet-form of TOM *noun*[1] (and THOMSON): see -Y[6].]
1 Brown bread formerly supplied to soldiers as rations; *dial*. a loaf of bread. Also more widely, provisions; *spec*. (*a*) food taken to work or school each day for lunch etc.; (*b*) goods supplied to employees under the truck system. **L18**.
2 A simpleton. *dial*. **E19**.
3 A thing that is small of its kind; *spec*. = ***tommy-bar*** below. **E19**.
4 [*Thomas Atkins*, used in specimens of completed official forms.] (A name for) the typical private soldier in the British army. Also more fully ***Tommy Atkins***. Cf. THOMAS *noun*[1] 3. *colloq*. **L19**.
5 = ***Thomson's gazelle*** s.v. THOMSON 2. *colloq*. **E20**.

> **4** *Sun (Baltimore)* The British Tommy's traditional stubbornness—born of centuries of defensive fighting.

Phrases: ***hell and Tommy***: see HELL *noun*. **soft Tommy** (*a*) *arch. slang* rations of bread as opp. to biscuits; (*b*) soft solder used by jewellers.
Comb.: **Tommy-bag**: in which a schoolchild or worker carries his or her lunch etc.; **Tommy-bar** a short bar which is inserted into a hole in a box spanner or screw to help turn it; **Tommy-cooker** *Military slang* a small portable spirit stove; **Tommy-rot** nonsense, rubbish; **Tommy-shop** *Hist*. = ***truck-shop*** s.v. TRUCK *noun*[2]; **Tommy system** = ***truck system*** s.v. TRUCK *noun*[2] 4; **Tommy talker** *colloq*. = KAZOO.

tommy /ˈtɒmi/ *noun*[2]. *Austral. & NZ colloq*. **L19**.
[Abbreviation of TOMAHAWK *noun*.]
More fully ***tommy-axe***. A hatchet.

tommy-gun /ˈtɒmɪɡʌn/ *noun & verb*. *colloq*. **E20**.
[Familiar abbreviation of THOMPSON + GUN *noun*.]
▶**A** *noun*. A Thompson or other sub-machine-gun. **E20**.
▶**B** *verb trans*. Infl. **-nn-**. Fire on or kill with a tommy-gun. **M20**.
▪ **tommy-gunner** *noun* **M20**.

tommyhawk *noun* var. of TOMAHAWK *noun*.

tomo /ˈtəʊməʊ/ *noun*. *NZ*. Pl. **-os**. **M20**.
[Maori.]
A depression or hole in limestone terrain.

tomography /təˈmɒɡrəfi/ *noun*. **M20**.
[from Greek *tomos* slice, section + -GRAPHY.]
Chiefly MEDICINE. Any of various techniques which provide images of successive plane sections of the human body or other solid objects using X-rays or ultrasound, now freq. processed by computer to give a three-dimensional image.
▪ **ˈtomogram** *noun* a visual record taken by tomography **M20**. **ˈtomograph** *noun* (*a*) a tomogram; (*b*) an apparatus for carrying out tomography: **M20**. **tomographer** *noun* a practitioner of tomography **L20**. **tomoˈgraphic** *adjective* **M20**. **tomoˈgraphically** *adverb* by means of tomography **M20**.

to-morn /təˈmɔːn/ *adverb & noun*. Now *arch. & dial*. Orig. two words. **OE**.
[from TO *preposition* + MORN.]
= TOMORROW.

tomorrer /təˈmɒrə/ *adverb*. *colloq. & dial*. **E20**.
[Repr. a pronunc.]
= TOMORROW *adverb*.

tomorrow /təˈmɒrəʊ/ *adverb & noun*. Orig. two words. **ME**.
[from TO *preposition* + MORROW.]
▶**A** *adverb*. On the day after today; on the morrow. Also *fig*., in the (near) future. **ME**.

> *Listener* An accelerated movement towards independence: Ghana yesterday; Nigeria . . tomorrow. ***here today, gone tomorrow***: see HERE *adverb*. ***jam tomorrow***: see JAM *noun*[2]. ***today . . . tomorrow***: see TODAY *adverb* 1.

▶**B** *noun*. The day after today; the next day; the morrow. Now also *fig*., the future, (in *pl*.) future days. **ME**.

> B. FRANKLIN One to-day is worth two to-morrows. S. BRIGGS A highly successful retailer who believed . . today's luxuries should become tomorrow's necessities. *Telegraph (Brisbane)* Tomorrow's international formula one race. B. PYM He . . missed his opportunity. Still, tomorrow was another day. **as if there was no tomorrow**, **as though there were no tomorrow**, etc., with no regard for the future, recklessly.

Comb.: **tomorrow afternoon**, **tomorrow evening**, **tomorrow morning**, **tomorrow night**, etc., (during) the afternoon, evening, morning, night, etc., of tomorrow.
▪ **tomorrower** *noun* a procrastinator **E19**.

Tompion /ˈtɒmpɪən/ *noun*[1]. **E18**.
[from *Tompion* (see below).]
A clock or watch (of a kind) made by the English clockmaker Thomas Tompion (1639–1713).

tompion *noun*[2] var. of TAMPION.

tom pung /tɒm ˈpʌŋ/ *noun phr*. *N. Amer*. Now *rare* or *obsolete*. **E19**.
[from (Algonquian base of) TOBOGGAN *noun*. Cf. PUNG *noun*[1].]
= PUNG *noun*[1].

tomtit /ˈtɒmtɪt/ *noun*. **E18**.
[from TOM *noun*[1] + TIT *noun*[4].]
1 Any of several small British birds, esp. tits; *spec*. the blue tit, *Parus caeruleus*. Also, any of various similar birds elsewhere; *esp*. (*a*) *N. Amer*. a chickadee, *P. atricapillus*; (*b*) *Austral*. a thornbill, *Acanthiza chrysorrhoa* (family Acanthizidae); (*c*) *NZ* a small black and white flycatcher, *Petroica macrocephala* (family Eopsaltridae). **E18**. ▸**b** *transf*. A little man or boy. *rare*. **M18**.
2 A small sailing boat. **M19**.
3 = SHIT *noun*. *rhyming slang*. **M20**.

tom-tom /ˈtɒmtɒm/ *noun*. **L17**.
[Telugu *ṭamaṭama*, Hindi *ṭam ṭam* (imit.).]
1 A simple hand-beaten drum associated with American Indian, African, or Eastern cultures. **L17**. ▸**b** A tall low-toned hand-beaten drum used esp. by pop, rock, and jazz groups. **M20**.
2 (The sound of) the beating of a drum. **L19**.

tom-tom /ˈtɒmtɒm/ *verb intrans. & trans*. Infl. **-mm-**. **M19**.
[Partly from the noun, partly imit.]
Play or perform on a tom-tom or tom-toms; drum.

-tomy /təmi/ *suffix*.
[from Greek *-tomia*, from *-tomos* cutting, from *temnein* to cut: cf. -ECTOMY, -STOMY.]
1 MEDICINE. Forming nouns denoting surgical operations in which an incision is made into an organ or part, as ***cystotomy***, ***laparotomy***, ***tracheotomy***, etc.
2 Forming nouns with the sense 'cutting up', as ***anatomy***, ***zootomy***.
3 Forming nouns with the sense 'division into parts', as ***dichotomy***, etc.

ton /tʌn/ *noun*[1]. Also †**tun**. See also TUN *noun*[1]. **ME**.
[Var. of TUN *noun*[1].]
▶**I 1** See TUN *noun*[1]. **ME**.
▶**II 2** A unit of measurement of the carrying capacity, cargo, or weight of a ship. Orig., the space occupied by a tun cask of wine. Now, (*a*) (in full ***displacement ton***) a unit of measurement of a ship's weight or volume in terms of its displacement of water with the loadline just immersed, equal to 2240 pounds (approx. 1016 kg) or to 35 cubic feet (approx. 0.99 cubic metre); (*b*) (in full ***freight ton***) a unit of weight or volume of cargo, equal to a metric ton (1000 kg, approx. 2205 lb) or to 40 cubic feet (approx. 1.13 cubic metre); (*c*) (in full ***gross ton***) a unit of gross internal capacity, equal to 100 cubic feet (approx. 2.83 cubic metre); (*d*) (in full ***net ton***, ***register ton***) an equivalent unit of net internal capacity. Cf. TONNAGE *noun*. **LME**.
3 Any of several units of measurement of capacity for various solid materials or commodities; *esp*. 40 cubic feet of timber. Now *rare* or *obsolete*. **LME**.
4 A unit of measurement of weight, varying according to period, locality, and commodity, but now generally 20 hundredweight; *esp*. (*a*) (in full ***long ton***) a unit equal to 2240 pounds (approx. 1016 kg); (*b*) chiefly *N. Amer*. (in full ***short ton***) a unit equal to 2000 pounds (approx. 907 kg); also, a tonne; (*c*) (in full ***metric ton***) a tonne (1000 kg). **LME**. ▸**b** A unit of refrigerating power equal to that needed to freeze one (short) ton of water at 0°C in 24 hours. **M20**.
5 a A very large amount or number *of*; (also *adverbial*) a great deal, a lot. Usu. in *pl*. *colloq*. **L18**. ▸**b** One hundred; *spec*. (*slang*) (*a*) CRICKET a century; (*b*) a sum of a hundred

pounds; (*c*) a speed of 100 m.p.h. (esp. with ref. to a motorcycle). **M20.**

> 🕮 **5a** J. M. BARRIE 'Do you kill many [pirates]?' 'Tons.'

Phrases: **do a ton**, **do the ton** *slang* travel at a speed of 100 m.p.h. ***like a ton of bricks***: see BRICK *noun*. **weigh a ton** *colloq.* be very heavy.

Comb.: **ton-force**, pl. **tons-force**, a unit of force equal to the weight of a mass of one ton, esp. under standard gravity; **ton-mile** the equivalent of the work done by a vehicle etc. in carrying a ton the distance of a mile; **ton-mileage** amount of or reckoning in ton-miles; charge per ton-mile; ***ton tight***: see TIGHT *adjective*; **ton weight** (*a*) the weight of one ton; (*b*) *colloq.* a very heavy object or burden (*lit. & fig.*).

ton /tɔ̃/ *noun*[2]. **M18.**
[French from Latin *tonus* TONE *noun*.]
1 *The* fashion, *the* vogue; fashionableness, style. **M18.** **2** Fashionable people collectively; the fashionable world. Treated as *sing.* or *pl.* **M18.**

> 🕮 **2** J. AIKEN It is the most elegant establishment . . , and half the ton was there.

-ton /t(ə)n/ *suffix.*
[After place-names and surnames in *-ton* unstressed devel. of TOWN *noun*.]
Forming descriptive nouns, as ***simpleton***, ***singleton***.

tonadilla /tonaˈdiʎa, tɒnəˈdiːljə/ *noun.* Pl. **-as** /-as, -əz/. **M19.**
[Spanish, dim. of *tonada* tune, song.]
A light operatic interlude of the mid 18th to early 19th cents., performed orig. as an intermezzo but later independently.

tonal /ˈtəʊn(ə)l/ *adjective.* **L18.**
[medieval Latin *tonalis*, from Latin *tonus* TONE *noun*: see -AL[1].]
1 *MUSIC.* †**a** Designating church music in any of the plainsong modes. *rare.* Only in **L18.** ▸**b** Of a sequence or a fugal answer: varying the intervals so as to preserve the key of the original melody or subject. Cf. REAL *adjective*[2] 4c. **M19.** ▸**c** Designating or pertaining to music written in a key or keys. **L19.** **2** Of or pertaining to tone, characterized by tonality; *spec.* (of speech or a language) expressing semantic differences by variation of tone. **M19.**

> 🕮 **2** E. A. NIDA In Ngbandi . . tense distinctions are generally indicated by tonal differences. F. SPALDING His fluent handling of paint, his control of tonal values. *Rhythm* The tonal characteristics you . . expect from a brass shelled drum.

■ **tonally** *adverb* in respect of tone **L19.**

tonalism /ˈtəʊn(ə)lɪz(ə)m/ *noun.* **L19.**
[from prec. + -ISM.]
ART & MUSIC. A style or technique of composition characterized by a concern for tone or tonality.

tonalist /ˈtəʊn(ə)lɪst/ *noun & adjective.* **E20.**
[formed as prec. + -IST.]
▸ **A** *noun.* **1** *ART.* A painter who concentrates on achieving a harmonious arrangement of colour, light, and tone; *spec.* one belonging to a group of American landscape painters of the late 19th and early 20th cents. **E20.** **2** *MUSIC.* A composer whose work is consciously based on tonality and (traditional) harmonies. **L20.**
▸ **B** *attrib.* or as *adjective.* Designating or pertaining to (the work or style of) a tonalist. **L20.**

tonalite /ˈtəʊn(ə)lʌɪt/ *noun.* **L19.**
[from *Tonal(e Pass*, northern Italy + -ITE[1].]
GEOLOGY. Orig., (a variety of) quartz-diorite. Now *spec.* a coarse-grained plutonic rock consisting essentially of sodic plagioclase, quartz, and hornblende or other mafic minerals.
■ **tonaˈlitic** *adjective* **M20.**

tonality /tə(ʊ)ˈnalɪti/ *noun.* **M19.**
[from TONAL + -ITY.]
1 *MUSIC.* **a** The sum of relations between the tones or notes of a scale or key; a particular scale or key. **M19.** ▸**b** The principle or practice of organizing musical composition around a keynote or tonic. **M20.** **2** The tonal quality or colour scheme of a picture. **M19.** **3** *PHONETICS.* The differentiation of words, syllables, etc., by a change of vocal pitch; the property of being a tone language. **M20.**
■ **tonalitive** *adjective* (*MUSIC*, now *rare* or *obsolete*) of or pertaining to tonality **E20.**

to-name /ˈtuːneɪm/ *noun. obsolete* exc. *dial.* **OE.**
[from TO-[2] + NAME *noun*.]
A name or epithet added to an original name, esp. (*Scot.*) to distinguish individuals having the same forename and surname; a cognomen, a nickname.

tonant /ˈtəʊnənt/ *adjective. rare.* **L19.**
[Latin *tonant-* pres. ppl stem of *tonare* make a loud noise, thunder: see -ANT[1].]
Thundering, loud.

tonari gumi /təʊˈnɑːrɪ ˈguːmi/ *noun phr.* Pl. same. **M20.**
[Japanese, from *tonari* next door + *kumi* group.]
In Japan, a small association of neighbouring households, taking responsibility for various common concerns.

Tonbridge *adjective* see TUNBRIDGE.

tondi *noun pl.* see TONDO.

tondino /tonˈdiːno/ *noun.* Pl. **-ni** /-ni/. **E18.**
[Italian, dim. of TONDO.]
1 *ARCHITECTURE.* A round moulding resembling a ring. **E18.** **2** *CERAMICS.* A majolica plate with a wide flat rim and deep centre. **L19.**

tondo /ˈtɒndəʊ/ *noun.* Pl. **-di** /-di/, **-dos.** **L19.**
[Italian = a round, a circle, a compass, shortened from *rotondo* round.]
An easel painting of circular form; a carving in relief within a circular space.

tone /təʊn/ *noun & verb.* **ME.**
[(Old & mod. French *ton* from) Latin *tonus* from Greek *tonos* tension, tone, from *teinein* stretch.]
▸ **A** *noun.* **1** A characteristic sound made by a voice, instrument, etc. (with ref. to its aurally perceived qualities). **ME.** **2** †**a** *MUSIC.* (Correct) pitch. **ME–E18.** ▸**b** A sound having a definite pitch and character; *spec.* (*a*) a musical note; (*b*) *PHYSICS* a sound produced by a regular vibration, esp. (more fully ***pure tone***) a simple sinusoidal waveform of specific frequency; (*c*) *TELEPHONY* an automatically generated sound conveying information to a caller about a required line, number, etc. **LME.** **3** **a** The quality or luminosity of a colour; a tint, a shade. **L15.** ▸**b** The general effect of the combination of light and shade or of colour in a painting etc. **E19.** **4** *MUSIC.* Any of the larger intervals between successive notes of a diatonic scale, a major second. **E17.** ▸†**b** *transf.* In Pythagorean thought, the distance between the earth and the moon. *rare.* **E–M17.** **5** **a** A distinctive vocal quality, modulation, or intonation expressing or indicating an attitude, emotion, etc. **E17.** ▸**b** A distinctive way of pronouncing words, an accent. *arch.* **L17.** ▸**c** A style of speech or writing regarded as reflecting a person's mood, attitude, or personality; a mood or attitude conveyed by an author's style. **M18.** **6** *PHYSIOLOGY.* The normal firmness or functioning of healthy organs and tissues; *spec.* the normal tension and resistance to passive stretching of resting muscle. **M17.** **7** A particular style or spirit of thought, behaviour, etc., *esp.* the prevailing mores of a society or community; a mood, a disposition. Now also (*colloq.*), distinction, class. **M17.** **8** **a** *LINGUISTICS.* A unit of sound in many languages which distinguishes words by the different pitches of successive syllables. **L17.** ▸**b** *PHONETICS.* (An accent on) a stressed syllable of a word. **L19.** **9** *MUSIC.* Each of nine psalm-tunes traditionally used in plainsong. **L18.**

> 🕮 **1** A. BAIN Instruments and voices are distinguished by . . their individual tones. **2b** R. CRASHAW She Carves out her dainty voice . . Into a thousand sweet distinguish'd tones. ***dialling tone***, ***ringing tone***, etc. *COMBINATION* ***tone***. ***fundamental tone***: see FUNDAMENTAL *adjective*. ***leading tone***: see LEADING *adjective*. ***partial tone***: see PARTIAL *adjective & noun*. ***prime tone***: see PRIME *adjective*. ***resultant tone***: see RESULTANT *adjective*. ***side tone***: see SIDE *noun*. ***Touch Tone***: see TOUCH *noun*. **3a** H. E. BATES A . . redness in the soil, the strata of ore emerging in warm brown tones. *attrib.*: K. AMIS A boy with a two-tone sweater. **b** R. FRASER The prevailing tones in this landscape are dark and wintry. **5a** T. LEDIARD The tone of your voice has become more masculine. E. BLISHEN Anger . . gave an odd tone to his voice. R. RENDELL He heard her voice . . and the tone seemed . . soft and yearning. **c** H. WILSON He determined . . to adopt a tone of conciliation. J. MARTINEAU His book . . is bright and joyous in tone. A. LAMBERT Should I believe the cold tone of this letter? **7** *Times* The tone of the market is . . dull. R. LOWELL The school's tone . . was a blend of the feminine and the military. *Economist* To set the tone for the week with a short keynote speech. S. TROTT He couldn't . . fire her because she added such tone to the place. **8a** *Scientific American* Standard Chinese has . . four tones: rising, falling, level and dipping. **9** ***Gregorian tones***: see GREGORIAN *adjective* 2. ***peregrine tone***: see PEREGRINE *adjective*.

Comb.: **tonearm** orig., the tubular arm connecting the soundbox of a gramophone to the horn; now, a pick-up arm; **toneburst** an audio signal used in testing the transient response of audio components; **tone cluster** *MUSIC* a group of adjacent notes on a piano played simultaneously; **tone-colour** *MUSIC* timbre; **tone control** the adjustment of the proportion of high and low frequencies in reproduced sound; a device or manual control for achieving this; **tone-deaf** *adjective* (*a*) unable to perceive differences of musical pitch accurately; (*b*) *fig.* insensitive; **tone-deafness** the condition of being tone-deaf; **tone dialling** *TELEPHONY*: in which each digit is transmitted as a particular combination of tones (opp. ***pulse dialling***); **tone generator** an apparatus for electronically producing tones of a desired frequency; **tone-group** *LINGUISTICS* a distinctive sequence of pitches or tones in an utterance; **tone language** *LINGUISTICS*: in which variations in pitch distinguish different words; **tone-on-tone** *adjective* (designating a fabric, design, etc.) composed of harmonizing rather than contrasting hues of colour; **tone-painting** the art of composing descriptive music; **tone poem** *MUSIC* = *symphonic poem* s.v. SYMPHONIC 3; **tone poet** *MUSIC* a composer, esp. of tone poems; **tone-row** *MUSIC* an arrangement of notes of the chromatic scale (usu. all twelve) in a fixed order used to form the basis of a composition (cf. SERIES *noun* 18); **tone sandhi** *LINGUISTICS* in a tone language, modification of tone caused by the influence of contiguous tonal patterns; **tone separation** *PHOTOGRAPHY* a method of increasing the contrast of a print by using a limited range of tones; posterization; **tone-syllable** the accented syllable of a word.

▸ **B** *verb.* †**1** *verb trans. MUSIC.* Sound with the proper tone; intone. **ME–L16.** **2** *verb intrans.* Of words etc.: come out in musical tones. *rare.* **LME.** **3** *verb trans.* Utter with a particular (esp. musical) tone. **M17.** **4** **a** *verb trans.* Modify or adjust the tone of, give a desired tone to; *spec.* alter the tone or tint of (a monochrome photograph) by means of a chemical solution. Also, give (improved) tone to, strengthen, improve. **E19.** ▸**b** *verb intrans.* Esp. of a photograph: undergo a change of tone or colour. **M19.** **5** *verb intrans.* Harmonize *with* in colouring. Also foll. by *in.* **L19.**

> 🕮 **3** T. D'URFEY With pleasing Twang he tones his Prose. **4a** SHELLEY A degree of solemnity . . toned his voice as he spoke. *Hair Flair* The hair was toned using beige shades. **5** M. FORSTER A . . greyish colour that toned in well with the yellow sandstone. *Practical Householder* Colours for . . woodwork that . . gently tone with the colour of walls.

Phrases & comb.: **tone down** (*a*) lower or soften the tone of, make less emphatic; (*b*) become lower, weaker, or softer in tone. **tone up** (*a*) *verb phr. trans. & intrans.* make or become stronger in tone of sound or colour, strengthen, improve; (*b*) *verb phr. trans.* make (a statement etc.) more emphatic. **tone-up** a strengthening, an improvement.

■ **toneful** *adjective* full of musical sound, tuneful **M19.** **toneless** *adjective* (*a*) soundless, mute; (*b*) having no distinctive tone, expressionless; (*c*) lacking energy, listless, dull: **L18.** **tonelessly** *adverb* **L19.** **tonelessness** *noun* **L19.** **toner** *noun* a person who or thing which tones something; *spec.* (*a*) *PHOTOGRAPHY* a chemical bath for changing the tone or colour of a print; (*b*) particles of pigment used in xerographic processes to render an electrostatic image visible; (*c*) any of various cosmetic preparations used for modifying hair colour or conditioning the skin: **L19.**

tone /təʊn/ *pronoun & attrib. adjective.* Long *obsolete* exc. *dial.* **ME.**
[from misdivision of neut. of THE (Old English *þæt*) + ONE *adjective, noun, & pronoun*. See also TO *adjective*.]
(*The*) one — of two. Usu. opp. ***tother***.

toned /təʊnd/ *adjective.* **LME.**
[from TONE *noun & verb*: see -ED[1], -ED[2].]
1 That has been toned; *spec.* (*a*) (of body or mind) brought into tone; (*b*) slightly coloured, tinted. **LME.** **2** As 2nd elem. of comb.: having a tone of a specified kind or quality. **L18.**

> 🕮 **1** LD MACAULAY A . . being whose mind was . . as firmly toned at eighty as at forty. C. POTOK A huge canvas toned in a wash of burnt sienna. **toned paper** off-white paper. **2** ***deep-toned***, ***fine-toned***, etc.

Comb.: **toned-down** *adjective* reduced in intensity or harshness.

tonel /ˈtʌn(ə)l/ *noun.* Also **-ell**, **tonn-**. **ME.**
[Earlier form of TUNNEL *noun*; in spec. sense repr. Portuguese *tonel*.]
A cask, a barrel, esp. of wine (now *Hist.*); *spec.* (**tonel**) a large cask used during the production of port wine.

toneme /ˈtəʊniːm/ *noun.* **E20.**
[from TONE *noun*: see -EME.]
LINGUISTICS. A tone or set of tones functioning as a distinctive phoneme in a language.
■ **toˈnemic** *adjective* of or pertaining to a toneme or tonemes **E20.** **toˈnemically** *adverb* with regard to or in terms of tonemes **E20.**

tonetic /tə(ʊ)ˈnɛtɪk/ *adjective & noun.* **E20.**
[from TONE *noun*, after *phonetic*: see -ETIC.]
LINGUISTICS. ▸**A** *adjective.* Of or pertaining to the use of tones; of or relating to intonation. **E20.**
▸ **B** *noun.* In *pl.* (treated as *pl.* or, now usu., *sing.*). The branch of linguistics that deals with the phonetics of tones. **E20.**
■ **tonetically** *adverb* **M20.**

tonette /təʊˈnɛt/ *noun.* **M20.**
[from TONE *noun* + -ETTE.]
A simple end-blown wind instrument resembling a small flute.

toney *adjective* var. of TONY *adjective*.

tong /tɒŋ/ *noun*[1]. **L19.**
[Imit. Cf. TONG *verb*[1].]
A resonant sound (as) of a large bell; a stroke producing this.
¶ Usu. repr. a sound deeper than *tang* but sharper than *dong*.

tong /tɒŋ/ *noun*². L19.
[Chinese (Cantonese) *t'ŏng*, (Mandarin) *táng*) hall, meeting place.]
An association or secret society of Chinese in the US, orig. formed as a benevolent or protective society but freq. associated with underworld criminal activity.

tong *noun*³ see TONGS.

tong /tɒŋ/ *verb*¹ *intrans. & trans.* L16.
[Imit. Cf. TONG *noun*¹.]
Emit or cause (a bell etc.) to emit a deep ringing sound.
¶ See note s.v. TONG *noun*¹.

tong /tɒŋ/ *verb*² *trans. & intrans. US.* M19.
[from TONGS.]
Grasp, gather, or handle (something) with tongs; *spec.* style (hair etc.) with curling tongs.
■ **tonger** *noun* a person who gathers oysters with oyster-tongs L19. **tonging** *verbal noun* the use of tongs; *spec.* the gathering of oysters with oyster-tongs: M19.

Tonga /ˈtɒŋə, ˈtɒŋgə/ *noun*¹ *& adjective.* M19.
[Tonga.]
▶ **A** *noun.* Pl. same, **-s**. A member of any of several African peoples living chiefly in southern Mozambique, Malawi, and Zambia; the Bantu language spoken by these peoples. Cf. TSONGA. M19.
▶ **B** *adjective.* Of or pertaining to these peoples or their language. M19.

tonga /ˈtɒŋgə/ *noun*². L19.
[Hindi *tãgā*.]
A small light two-wheeled horse- or pony-drawn carriage or cart originating in India.

Tongan /ˈtɒŋən/ *noun & adjective.* M19.
[from *Tonga* (see below) + -AN.]
▶ **A** *noun.* A native or inhabitant of the island kingdom of Tonga in the SW Pacific Ocean. Also, the Polynesian language spoken in Tonga. M19.
▶ **B** *adjective.* Of or pertaining to Tonga or the language spoken there. M19.

tongkang /tɒŋˈkaŋ/ *noun.* M19.
[Malay.]
A seagoing barge used as a cargo boat in the Malay archipelago.

tongs /tɒŋz/ *noun pl.* Also (long *obsolete* exc. in sense 1b) in sing. **tong**.
[Old English *tang(e)* corresp. to Old Frisian *tange*, Old Saxon *tanga*, Old High German *zanga* (Dutch *tang*, German *Zange*), Old Norse *tǫng*, from Germanic from Indo-European base repr. also by Greek *daknein* bite, Sanskrit *daṃś-*.]
1 Treated as *pl.* or (*rare*, chiefly *Scot.*) *sing.* An implement consisting of two long limbs or legs, often with flattened or shaped ends, connected by a hinge, pivot, or spring by which their lower ends can be brought together to grasp or take up objects which it is impossible or inconvenient to lift with the hand. Also ***pair of tongs***. OE. ▸**b** *sing.* **tong**. One half of a pair of tongs. *joc.* M19.
2 Anything, esp. a gripping device, having two long limbs hinged at one end. LME. ▸**b** A pair of hand-shears. *Austral. & NZ slang.* L19. ▸**c** OIL INDUSTRY. A large pipe wrench used for making up or breaking out lengths of pipe or casing. E20.

> 📖 **1** R. P. JHABVALA She dropped several lumps of sugar into her tea with a pair of silver tongs. K. AMIS Jacob put the log back with a pair of tongs.

Phrases & comb.: CURLING-*tongs*. *fire-tongs*: see FIRE *noun*. ***hammer and tongs***: see HAMMER *noun*. ***lazy-tongs***: see LAZY *adjective*. ***oyster-tongs***: see OYSTER *noun*. SPAGHETTI ***tongs***. ***sugar-tongs***: see SUGAR *noun*. **tongman** *US* a person who gathers oysters with tongs. **tongsman** (*a*) = *tongman* above; (*b*) OIL INDUSTRY a person who handles the tongs (sense 2c above). **would not touch with a pair of tongs** would not have anything to do with (expr. repugnance).

tongue /tʌŋ/ *noun.*
[Old English *tunge* = Old Frisian *tunge*, Old Saxon *tunga*, Old High German *zunga* (Dutch *tong*, German *Zunge*), Old Norse *tunga*, Gothic *tuggō*, from Germanic, rel. to Latin *lingua*.]
▶ **I** A part of the body.
1 A blunt, tapering, muscular, soft, fleshy organ situated on the floor of the mouth, bearing taste buds and important in taking in and swallowing food and in articulating speech; the corresponding organ of most vertebrate animals, freq. protrusible and freely mobile and aiding in the sensing and manipulation of food; any analogous organ in the mouth of an invertebrate. OE.
2 The tongue of an animal as an article of food; *esp.* an oxtongue. LME.
3 A figure or representation of this organ. L15.

> 📖 **1** C. BUTLER The Nectar . . the Bees gather with their tongues. W. MOTLEY Ang thumbed her nose at him and stuck out her tongue. **2** E. M. FORSTER Followed by the tongue—a freckled cylinder of meat, with . . jelly at the top.

▶ **II** With ref. to speech.
4 The tongue as the principal organ of speech; the faculty of speech; the power of articulation or vocal expression or description. OE.
5 The action of speaking; speech, talking, voice. Also, what is spoken or uttered; words, talk. OE. ▸**b** Speech as contrasted with thought, action, or fact; mere words. LME. ▸†**c** An opportunity to speak, a voice, a vote. *rare* (Shakes.). Only in E17.
6 A language; the speech or language of a people or race, or of a particular class or locality; ***the tongues*** (*arch.*), foreign languages, *spec.* classical Latin, Greek, and Hebrew. OE. ▸**b** In biblical use, a people or nation having a language of their own. Usu. in *pl.* LME. ▸**c** The knowledge or use of a language. Also, a language or form of vocalization characteristic of glossolalia (freq. *collect. pl.*, treated as *sing.* or *pl.*), esp. in ***in tongues***. Cf. ***the gift of tongues*** below. LME.
7 Manner of speaking; mode of expression; (now *rare*) the sound of the voice. LME.
8 The bark or howl of a dog; *spec.* the hunting-cry of a hound in pursuit of game. Chiefly in ***give tongue*** below. L18.

> 📖 **4** TENNYSON I would that my tongue could utter the thoughts that arise in me. **5** A. C. AMOR Gabriel with his indiscreet tongue had betrayed them all again. **6** ADDISON Celebrated Books, either in the learned or the modern Tongues. *New Scientist* Nostratic, an ancient tongue that gave rise to several major language families. **c** *Redemption* Frank didn't ask what was wrong. He simply prayed in tongues. **7** *Punch* She is famed principally for the acidity of her tongue.

▶ **III** A thing resembling a tongue.
9 A tapering or flickering jet of flame (earliest with ref. to the miraculous tongues of fire at Pentecost: *Acts* 2:3). OE.
10 An elongated, often flattened projecting object or part of a thing, esp. when mobile, or attached at one end or side. ME.
11 The pin of a buckle or brooch. ME.
12 A projecting piece forming a tab or flap, or a means of fastening; *spec.* a broad flat strip of leather etc. covering the opening in the front of a boot or shoe, across which the laces, buttons, etc., may be fastened. ME.
13 The clapper of a bell. LME.
14 A thin flexible strip of metal covering the aperture of a reed in an organ-pipe. Also, a reed in an oboe or bassoon; a plectrum or jack in a harpsichord. M16.
15 The pole by which a wagon or other vehicle may be drawn along. L16.
16 A young or small sole (fish). Cf. ***tongue-fish***, ***tongue-sole*** below. E19.
17 The movable tapered piece of rail in a railway switch. M19.
18 A projecting flange, rib, or strip; *esp.* a projecting tenon along the edge of a board, to be inserted into a groove or mortise in the edge of another board; a connecting slip joining two grooved boards. M19.
19 = TANG *noun*¹ 2. *rare.* M19.
20 MUSIC. = PLAQUE 6. M20.

> 📖 **9** J. C. POWYS A solitary tongue of orange-coloured flame dancing . . on the top of the black coals. **12** S. PLATH Flat brown leather shoes with fringed tongues lapping down over the front. **15** T. PYNCHON Market wagons stand unhitched with tongues tilted to the ground.

▶ **IV 21** A narrow strip of land running into the sea or a lake, or enclosed by two branches of a river, or projecting from one area into another (distinguished by topography, vegetation, land use, etc.). Also, a narrow inlet of the sea or other body of water; a long extension from the lower part of a glacier or iceberg. LME. ▸**b** A deep narrow part of the current of a river, running smoothly and rapidly between rocks. L19. ▸**c** GEOLOGY. A part of a formation that projects laterally into an adjacent formation, becoming thinner in the direction of its length. E20.

> 📖 **21** *Climber* Blaven . . stands aloof and majestic on the tongue of land separating Lochs Scavaig and Slappin.

Phrases etc.: ***dead-tongue***: see DEAD *adjective*. **find one's tongue** be able to express oneself after a shock etc. **get one's tongue around**, **get one's tongue round** pronounce, articulate. **give tongue** speak out, esp. loudly; (of a dog) bark; *spec.* (of a hound) give a loud cry when on the scent or in sight of the quarry. HART'S TONGUE. **hold one's tongue** (now. usu. *colloq.*) be silent. ***hound's-tongue***: see HOUND *noun*¹. **keep a civil tongue in one's head** avoid rudeness. ***keep a still tongue in one's head***: see STILL *adjective*. ***long tongue***: see LONG *adjective*¹. **lose one's tongue** be unable to express oneself after a shock etc. ***mother tongue***: see MOTHER *noun*¹ *& adjective*. ***oil one's tongue***: see OIL *verb* 2. ***on the tip of one's tongue***: see TIP *noun*¹. ***silver tongue***: see SILVER *noun & adjective*. ***slip of the tongue***: see SLIP *noun*³ 8. **speak in tongues**, **speak with tongues** CHRISTIAN CHURCH practise glossolalia (see ***the gift of tongues*** below). ***string of the tongue***: see STRING *noun*. **the gift of tongues** CHRISTIAN CHURCH the ability to speak in a language unknown to the speaker, or to vocalize freely, usu. in the context of religious (esp. pentecostal or charismatic) worship, identified as a gift of the Holy Spirit (cf. *Acts* 10:46, 19:6, 1 *Corinthians* 14:6, 23); glossolalia. ***the rough edge of one's tongue***, ***the sharp edge of one's tongue***: see EDGE *noun*. ***the rough side of one's tongue***: see ROUGH *adjective*. **throw one's tongue** = ***give tongue*** above. ***tongues wag***: see WAG *verb*. ***whip and tongue grafting***: see WHIP *noun*. **with one's tongue hanging out**, **with tongue hanging out** *colloq.* with great thirst or (*fig.*) eager expectation. **with one's tongue in one's cheek**, **with tongue in cheek** with sly irony or humorous insincerity (cf. ***tongue-in-cheek*** below). ***wooden tongue***: see WOODEN *adjective*. ***woody tongue***: see WOODY *adjective*.
Comb.: **tongue-and-groove** *adjective* designating or pertaining to (a joint between) boards in which a tongue along one edge fits into a groove along the edge of its neighbour; **tongue-bang** *verb trans.* scold (chiefly as ***tongue-banging*** *verbal noun*); **tongue-bit** a bridle bit having a plate attached to stop the horse putting its tongue over the mouthpiece; **tongue-depressor** MEDICINE an instrument for pressing down the tongue, esp. to allow inspection of the mouth or throat; **tongue-fish** a sole; *esp.* a tongue-sole of the genus *Symphurus*, of the W. Atlantic and Caribbean; **tongue-in-cheek** *adjective & adverb* (*a*) *adjective* ironic, slyly humorous; (*b*) *adverb* = ***with one's tongue in one's cheek*** above; **tongue-lash** *verb trans.* scold or abuse verbally, esp. loudly or at length (freq. as ***tongue-lashing*** *verbal noun*); **tongue-pad** *noun & verb* (now *arch. & dial.*) (*a*) *noun* a talkative person; (*b*) *verb intrans. & trans.* scold; **tongue-shot** speaking distance, voice-range; **tongue-slip** a slip of the tongue; **tongue-sole** any small tropical flatfish of the family Cynoglossidae; **tongue-tacked** *adjective* (*Scot.*) = ***tongue-tied*** below; ***tongue thrum***: see THRUM *noun*² 1; **tongue-tie** *noun & verb* (*a*) *noun* a thing which restrains the tongue; *spec.* congenital shortness of the frenulum of the tongue, once incorrectly supposed to be the cause of feeding or breathing difficulty in infants; (*b*) *verb trans.* make inarticulate, render speechless, restrain from speaking; **tongue-tied** *adjective* speechless, esp. from shyness or other emotion; restrained from free speech; (now *rare*) inarticulate due to shortness of the frenulum of the tongue; **tongue-tiedness** a state of being tongue-tied; **tongue-twister** a sequence of words, often alliterative, which is difficult to articulate quickly; **tongue-twisting** *adjective* difficult to articulate; **tongue-work** (*a*) *rare* work on languages, philological study; (*b*) debate, dispute; (*c*) chatter, gossip; **tongue-worm** (*a*) = PENTASTOMID *noun*; (*b*) = LYTTA.
¶ The mod. spelling arose from 15th-cent. var.
■ **tongueless** *adjective* without a tongue; dumb: LME. **tonguelet** *noun* a little tongue or tonguelike object M19. **tonguelike** *adjective* resembling (that of) a tongue M19. **tonguer** *noun* (*a*) *rare* a speaker; (*b*) *NZ slang* (*obsolete* exc. *Hist.*) a person who assisted in cutting up a whale carcass and was entitled to the tongue as payment: E19. **tonguester** *noun* a great talker, a gossip L19.

tongue /tʌŋ/ *verb.* LME.
[from the noun.]
1 *verb trans.* Assail with words; reproach, scold; gossip about (a person), slander. Now chiefly *dial.* LME.
2 *verb intrans. & trans.* (with *it*). Use the tongue, speak, talk, esp. volubly; (of a hound) give tongue. E17.
3 *verb trans.* Utter, say; pronounce, articulate with the tongue. E17.
4 *verb trans.* Provide with the power of speech; give utterance to. *poet.* E17.
5 *verb trans.* Touch or move with the tongue; lick (*up*). L17. ▸**b** *verb trans. & intrans.* Kiss with the tongue; give a French kiss. Also = FRENCH *verb* 5. *slang.* E20.
6 *verb trans.* Cut a tongue into (a piece of wood etc.); provide with a tongue-like projection. M18.
7 *verb trans.* Join or fit together by means of a tongue and groove or tongue and socket. E19.
8 *verb intrans.* Project as a protruding tongue; throw out tongues (of flame). E19.
9 MUSIC. **a** *verb trans.* Articulate or rapidly repeat (a note on a wind instrument) by interrupting the airflow briefly with the tongue. M20. ▸**b** *verb intrans.* Articulate notes on a wind instrument with the tongue. L20.

> 📖 **3** SHAKES. *Cymb.* 'Tis still a dream, or else such stuff as madmen Tongue. O. W. HOLMES The Colonel raged . . and tongued a few anathemas. **5** R. COOVER She tongued a wad of sweet roll out of one of the gaps in her teeth. **9a** ***double tonguing***: see DOUBLE *adjective & adverb*. ***flutter-tongue***: see FLUTTER *noun*. ***slap-tongue***: see SLAP *verb*¹. ***triple tonguing***: see TRIPLE *adjective & adverb*. **b** *Early Music* Instead of tonguing, articulate the music by playing bagpipe-type grace notes.

tongued /tʌŋd/ *adjective.* LME.
[from TONGUE *noun* or *verb*: see -ED¹, -ED².]
Having a tongue or tongues (in various senses). ***double-tongued***, ***honey-tongued***, ***long-tongued***, ***sharp-tongued***, etc. **tongued and grooved** fitted with a tongue-and-groove joint.

tonguey /ˈtʌŋi/ *adjective.* LME.
[from TONGUE *noun* + -Y¹.]
1 Talkative. Now *US & dial.* LME.
2 Characterized by or pertaining to the tongue; (of voice quality) modified by the tongue. M19.

> 📖 **1** J. LOMAX Kind of cute and smart and tonguey. Guess he was a graduate.

■ **tonguiness** *noun* E17.

toni /ˈtəʊni/ *noun.* Also **tony**. L16.
[Tamil, Malayalam *tōṇi* rel. to DHONEY.]
A small or medium-sized seagoing boat used on the coast of southern India; now *esp.* a ferry-boat.

tonic /ˈtɒnɪk/ *adjective, noun, & verb.* M17.
[French *tonique* from Greek *tonikos* of or for stretching, from *tonos* TONE *noun*: see -IC.]
▶ **A** *adjective.* **1** MEDICINE & PHYSIOLOGY. Of, pertaining to, or producing physical tension, esp. muscle contraction; *spec.*

designating or involving continuous muscular contraction without relaxation (opp. ***clonic***). **M17.**
2 Of or pertaining to the normal tone or healthy condition of the tissues or organs, esp. the muscles. **L17.**
3 Having the property of increasing or restoring the tone or healthy condition and activity of the organs or the body as a whole; strengthening, invigorating, bracing. **M18.**
4 *MUSIC.* Designating, pertaining to, or based on the tonic or keynote of a composition; (of a chord) having the tonic for its root. **M18.**
5 a Pertaining to musical tone or quality. *rare.* **L18.** ▸**b** Pertaining to tone or pitch of the voice in speech; characterized by distinctions of tone or accent; tonal. Also (*PHONETICS*) (of a syllable) carrying the primary stress or accent in its tone-group. **M19.**

> 🕮 **1** ***tonic contraction, tonic convulsion, tonic spasm***, etc. **3** S. T. WARNER While it lasted . . it was tonic. But now everyone is dead tired. J. FANE Their company . . always . . had a tonic effect.

▸ **B** *noun.* **1** *MEDICINE.* A medicine or medicinal agent intended to have a general tonic or invigorating effect. **L18.** ▸**b** An invigorating or bracing influence. **M19.** ▸**c** *ellipt.* = ***tonic water*** below. **M20.**
2 *MUSIC.* **a** The note on which a key or scale is based; = **KEYNOTE** *noun* 1. **E19.** ▸**b** The principal key of a musical composition or passage; the home key. **L19.**
3 *PHONETICS.* The syllable of a tone-group which carries the primary stress or accent; = **NUCLEUS** *noun* 10a. **M20.**

> 🕮 **1** F. PERRY The plants contain a bitter principle and when dried are used as a tonic. **b** E. ROOSEVELT His speeches were a tonic to us. ***c gin and tonic, vodka and tonic***, etc. **2a** E. PROUT The seventh note of the scale . . has a very strong tendency to lead up . . to the tonic.

Comb. & special collocations: **tonic-clonic** *adjective* (*MEDICINE*) of or characterized by successive phases of tonic and clonic spasm (as in *grand mal* epilepsy); **tonic major**, **tonic minor** the major, minor key having a given note, esp. the tonic note of a composition, as tonic; **tonic sol-fa** a system of teaching music, esp. vocal music, in which the seven notes of the major scale in any key are denoted (in ascending order) by sung syllables variously written *doh, ray, me, fah, soh, lah, te* and noted by the initials *d, r, m*, etc., *doh* always denoting the tonic or keynote; **tonic water** a non-alcoholic carbonated drink containing quinine or another bitter flavouring, orig. intended as a stimulant of appetite and digestion; a drink or glass of this; **tonic wine** weak flavoured wine sold as a medicinal tonic.
▸ **C** *verb trans.* Infl. **-ck-**. Act as a tonic on, invigorate. Also, administer a tonic to. **E19.**

tonical /ˈtɒnɪk(ə)l/ *adjective.* **L16.**
[formed as **TONIC** *adjective* + **-ICAL**.]
†**1** = **TONIC** *adjective* 1. **L16–M18.**
2 = **TONIC** *adjective* 3, 4. Long *rare.* **M17.**

tonically /ˈtɒnɪk(ə)li/ *adverb.* **L19.**
[from **TONIC** *adjective* or prec.: see **-ICALLY**.]
1 *MEDICINE & PHYSIOLOGY.* By or in relation to tension; by tonic contraction. **L19.**
2 As a tonic; for invigoration. **L19.**

tonicity /tə(ʊ)ˈnɪsɪti/ *noun.* **E19.**
[from **TONIC** *adjective* + **-ITY**.]
1 *MEDICINE & PHYSIOLOGY.* Muscle tone; tone or condition of any tissue or organ. Also, state or quality as regards osmotic pressure. **E19.** ▸**b** Tonic quality (of contraction). **L19.**
2 *PHONETICS.* The fact or property of having a phonetic emphasis at a certain place in an intonation pattern. **M20.**

tonify /ˈtəʊnɪfʌɪ/ *verb trans.* **L18.**
[from **TONE** *noun* or French *ton*: see **-FY**. Cf. **TONISH**, **TONY** *adjective*.]
1 Make fashionable or stylish. *rare.* **L18.**
2 Impart tone to (a part of the body). **M19.** ▸**b** *ACUPUNCTURE.* Stimulate (a point or meridian) to produce an increase of energy; increase the energy of (a part of the body) in this way. Opp. **SEDATE** *verb* 2b. **M20.**
■ **tonifiˈcation** *noun* **M20.**

tonight /təˈnʌɪt/ *adverb & noun.* Also **to-night**, (now *rare* or *obsolete*) **to night**. See also **TONITE** *adverb.* **OE.**
[from **TO** *preposition* + **NIGHT** *noun.* Cf. **TODAY**.]
▸ **A** *adverb.* **1** On the night following this day; *colloq.* on the evening of today, this evening (i.e. later). **OE.**
2 On this very night (i.e. now, at night); *colloq.* on this very evening. **ME.**
3 On the night just past, last night. Long *obsolete* exc. *dial.* **ME.**

> 🕮 **1** G. GREENE Will you have dinner with me to-night? **2** M. ARNOLD Lovely all times she lies, lovely tonight. G. VIDAL But tonight Philip was not . . interested in finding a companion. M. GILBERT He was in the pub tonight. **3** SHAKES. *Rom. & Jul.* I dreamt a dream tonight.

▸ **B** *noun.* This night; the night after this day. Also, this evening. **ME.**

> 🕮 WORDSWORTH To-night will be a stormy night. *Guardian* Tonight's papers are full of . . interviews with the . . survivors.

†**Tonika** *noun* var. of **TUNICA** *noun*^{2}.

tonish /ˈtɒnɪʃ/ *adjective.* Now *rare* or *obsolete.* Also **tonnish**. **L18.**
[from **TON** *noun*^{2} + **-ISH**^{1}.]
Fashionable, stylish.

tonist /ˈtəʊnɪst/ *noun. rare.* **L19.**
[from **TONE** *noun*, after *colourist*.]
An artist skilled in the use of tone.

tonite /ˈtəʊnʌɪt/ *noun.* **L19.**
[from Latin *tonare* to thunder + **-ITE**^{1}.]
A high explosive made of pulverized gun-cotton impregnated with barium nitrate.

tonite /təˈnʌɪt/ *adverb. colloq.* (chiefly *commercial*). **M20.**
[Phonetic spelling, after *nite*.]
= **TONIGHT** *adverb.*

tonitruant /təˈnɪtrʊənt/ *adjective. rare.* Also **-trant** /-tr(ə)nt/. **L16.**
[Late Latin *tonitruant-* pres. ppl stem of *tonitruare* to thunder, from *tonitrus* thunder: see **-ANT**^{1}.]
Of or like thunder, thundering (chiefly *fig.*).
■ Also **tonitruous** *adjective* **E17.**

tonjon /ˈtɒndʒɒn/ *noun. Anglo-Indian.* **E19.**
[Origin unkn.]
An open sedan chair slung on a single pole and carried by four bearers.

tonk /tɒŋk/ *noun*^{1} *& verb. slang* (chiefly *SPORT*). **E20.**
[Imit.]
▸ **A** *noun.* A powerful stroke or hit, esp. with a bat (or racket). **E20.**
▸ **B** *verb trans.* Strike, esp. vigorously. Also (in *pass.*), be beaten or defeated. **E20.**
■ **tonker** *noun* (*Cricket slang*) a person who strikes the ball hard, a batsman who has a hard-hitting cavalier style **L20.**

tonk /tɒŋk/ *noun*^{2}. *slang.* **M20.**
[Origin unkn.]
1 As a term of abuse: a fool, an idiot. Also (*arch.*), a homosexual man. Chiefly *Austral.* **M20.**
2 The penis. **L20.**

tonk /tɒŋk/ *noun*^{3}. *colloq.* **M20.**
[Abbreviation.]
= **HONKY-TONK** *noun* 1.

tonka bean /ˈtɒŋkə biːn/ *noun phr.* Also **tonquin bean** /ˈtɒŋkɪn/. **L18.**
[from *tonka* Guyanese name + **BEAN** *noun*.]
Any of the black fragrant seeds of a large S. American leguminous tree, *Dipteryx odorata*, which are used for scenting tobacco and snuff and as an ingredient in perfumes. Also, the tree from which these seeds are obtained.

Tonkawa /ˈtɒŋkəwə/ *noun & adjective.* Also †**-way**. **E19.**
[Amer. Spanish *tancahues, tancagueis*, prob. from Wichita.]
▸ **A** *noun.* Pl. same, **-s**. A member of a N. American Indian people of central Texas. Also, the language formerly spoken by this people. **E19.**
▸ **B** *attrib.* or as *adjective.* Of or pertaining to this people or their language. **L19.**

Tonkinese /tɒŋkɪˈniːz/ *noun & adjective.* **L17.**
[from *Tonkin* var. of *Tongking* (see below) + **-ESE**.]
▸ **A** *noun.* Pl. same.
1 A native or inhabitant of Tongking, a region and former French protectorate of northern Vietnam bordering China. **L17.**
2 The chief northern dialect of Vietnamese. **M20.**
▸ **B** *adjective.* Of or pertaining to the Tonkinese or their language. **L19.**

tonlet /ˈtʌnlɪt/ *noun.* **L15.**
[Old French *tonnel(l)et, tonlet* dim. of *tonneau* cask.]
Hist. A short skirt of armour; each of the overlapping horizontal bands of which this was sometimes made.

tonnage /ˈtʌnɪdʒ/ *noun.* In sense 1 also **tunn-**. **LME.**
[In sense 1 from Old French *tonnage* (Anglo-Latin *tonnagium*), from *tonne* **TUN** *noun*^{1}; in other senses from **TON** *noun*^{1} + **-AGE**.]
1 *Hist.* A duty or tax of so much per tun levied on wine imported to England in tuns or casks between the 14th and 18th cents. **LME.**
†**2** A charge for the hire of a ship of so much per ton of capacity per week or month. Only in **16.**
3 A charge or duty payable at so much per ton on cargo or freight. **E17.**
4 Ships collectively, shipping (considered in respect of carrying capacity, or of weight of cargo carried). **E17.**
5 The internal capacity of a ship expressed in tons of 100 cubic feet or 2.83 cubic metres (orig., the number of tun casks of wine which a merchant ship could carry); the size, weight, or capacity of a ship, variously calculated in terms of cubic capacity or weight of water displaced when afloat. Cf. **TON** *noun*^{1} 2. **E18.**
6 Weight in tons; *loosely* (great) weight. **L18.**

> 🕮 **4** *Ships Monthly* Recently, cruise operators have been flooding shipyards with orders for new tonnage. **5** R. L. STEVENSON A steamship of considerable tonnage. **deadweight tonnage** the weight of cargo carried by a ship when submerged to a given Plimsoll mark. **displacement tonnage** the weight of a ship, calculated by the volume of water displaced when afloat. **gross tonnage** the tonnage of a ship calculated as one-hundredth of its cubic capacity in cubic feet below the upper deck. **net tonnage** the tonnage of a ship adjusted to allow for space not used for cargo. **register tonnage** the tonnage of a ship (gross or net) entered on a registration certificate. **6** J. HARVEY A sunlit tower block, all its iron and concrete tonnage turned to lightness.

tonnage /ˈtʌnɪdʒ/ *verb trans.* **M17.**
[from the noun.]
1 Impose tonnage (duty) on. *rare* (now *Hist.*). **M17.**
2 Have a tonnage (capacity) of (so much); provide with shipping capacity. **M19.**

tonne /tʌn/ *noun*^{1}. **L19.**
[French. Cf. **TON** *noun*^{1}.]
A metric unit of measurement of weight, equal to 1000 kilograms (approx. 2205 pounds); a metric ton.

†**tonne** *noun*^{2}, *verb* vars. of **TUN** *noun*^{1}, *verb.*

tonneau /ˈtɒnəʊ/ *noun.* Pl. **-s**, in sense 1 also †**-x**. **L18.**
[French = barrel, cask.]
1 A unit of capacity for French (esp. Bordeaux) wine, usu. equal to 900 litres (198 gallons). **L18.**
2 The rounded rear body of some vintage motor-cars (orig. with the door at the back); the rear part of a car with front and rear compartments, or of an open car or carriage. Also, a car having a tonneau. **E20**
Comb.: **tonneau cover** a removable flexible cover for protecting the rear or passenger seats in an open car when not in use; a similar cover for the cockpit of a small aeroplane, a cabin cruiser, etc.

tonnel *noun* var. of **TONEL**.

tonnelle /tɒnɛl/ *noun.* Pl. pronounced same. **M19.**
[French = **TUNNEL** *noun*.]
An arbour.

tonner /ˈtʌnə/ *noun.* **M19.**
[from **TON** *noun*^{1} + **-ER**^{1}.]
A vessel having a burden or capacity of a specified number of tons; a lorry having a weight of a specified number of tons.

tonnish *adjective* var. of **TONISH**.

tono- /ˈtəʊnəʊ/ *combining form.*
[Greek *tono-* combining form of *tonos* **TONE** *noun*: see **-O-**.]
Stretching, tension, tone.
■ **tonofibril** *noun* (*CYTOLOGY*) a bundle of tonofilaments **E20.** **tonofiˈbrilla** *noun*, pl. **-llae** /-liː/, (*a*) *CYTOLOGY* = **TONOFIBRIL**; (*b*) *ZOOLOGY* a non-contractile fibril in an insect that passes from a myofibril through the epidermis into the cuticle: **E20.** **tonoˈfilament** *noun* (*CYTOLOGY*) each of the minute supportive or non-contractile filaments that occur in aggregated networks in the cytoplasm of many epithelial cells, esp. in the epidermis **M20.** **tonograph** *noun* (*MEDICINE*) a recording tonometer **L19.** **tonoˈlogical** *adjective* of or pertaining to tonology **M20.** **toˈnology** *noun* the branch of linguistics that deals with tones and intonation in speech **L19.** **tonoplast** *noun* (*BOTANY*) the membrane which bounds the chief vacuole of a plant cell **L19.** **tonoˈtactic** *adjective* of or pertaining to tonotaxis **E20.** **tonoˈtaxis** *noun* (*BIOLOGY*) a taxic response to the osmotic condition of the surroundings **L19.** **tonoˈtopic**, **tonoˈtopical** *adjectives* (*ANATOMY*) (of features of the auditory system) exhibiting a spatial correspondence with the frequency of heard sound **M20.** **tonoˈtopically** *adverb* in a tonotopic manner **L20.**

tonometer /təʊˈnɒmɪtə/ *noun.* **E18.**
[from **TONO-** + **-METER**.]
1 *MUSIC.* An instrument for determining the pitch of tones; *spec.* a tuning-fork, or a graduated set of tuning-forks, for determining the exact frequency of vibration which produces a given tone. **E18.**
2 *PHYSIOLOGY & MEDICINE.* An instrument for measuring the pressure in the eyeball (to test for glaucoma), or that in a blood-vessel etc. **L19.**
■ **tonoˈmetric** *adjective* of or pertaining to tonometry **E20.** **tonometry** *noun* the use of a tonometer **L19.**

tonquin bean *noun phr.* var. of **TONKA BEAN**.

tonsil /ˈtɒns(ə)l, ˈtɒnsɪl/ *noun.* **L16.**
[French *tonsilles* (pl.) or Latin *tonsillae* (pl.).]
ANATOMY. **1** Either of two oval masses of lymphoid tissue situated on either side of the fauces of the throat. Also, each of four other paired lymphoid structures around the pharynx, esp. the adenoids. Freq. in *pl.* **L16.**
2 Any of various other small rounded masses of esp. lymphoid tissue; *spec.* (in full ***tonsil of the cerebellum***) a lobe on the underside of each hemisphere of the cerebellum. **L19.**
■ **tonsillar** /ˈtɒnsɪlə/ *adjective* of or pertaining to the tonsils **M19.** **tonsiˈllectomy** *noun* (an instance of) surgical removal of the tonsils **L19.** **tonsiˈllotomy** *noun* (an instance of) surgical removal of the tonsils or (now *spec.*) part of a tonsil **L19.**

†tonsile *adjective.* M17–M19.
[from Latin *tonsilis*, from *tons-*: see TONSURE, -ILE.]
Of a shrub, tree, etc.: that may be clipped to shape.

tonsillitis /tɒnsɪˈlʌɪtɪs/ *noun.* E19.
[from TONSIL + -ITIS.]
MEDICINE. Inflammation of the tonsils, caused by bacterial or viral infection.
■ **tonsiˈllitic** *adjective* (*a*) *rare* = TONSILLAR; (*b*) affected with tonsillitis: M19.

tonsor /ˈtɒnsə/ *noun. joc.* M17.
[Latin: see next.]
A barber.

tonsorial /tɒnˈsɔːrɪəl/ *adjective.* Chiefly *joc.* E19.
[from Latin *tonsorius*, from *tonsor* barber, from *tons-*: see TONSURE, -IAL.]
Of or pertaining to a barber or hairdressing.
📖 THACKERAY A tonsorial practitioner in the Waterloo Road.
■ **tonsorialist** *noun* (*joc.*) a barber M19.

tonstein /ˈtɒnstʌɪn/ *noun.* M20.
[German, lit. 'clay stone'.]
GEOLOGY. A rock composed mainly of kaolinite, commonly associated with certain coal seams; a thin band of this.

tonsure /ˈtɒnsjə, ˈtɒnʃə/ *noun & verb.* LME.
[Old & mod. French, or Latin *tonsura*, from *tons-* pa. ppl stem of *tondere* shear, clip: see -URE.]
▶ **A** *noun.* **1** The action or process of clipping the hair or shaving the head; the state of being shorn. LME.
2 *spec.* The shaving of the head or part of it as a religious practice or rite, esp. as a preparation to entering the clergy or a religious order. LME. ▸**b** The part of a priest's or monk's head left bare by shaving the hair, in the Western Christian church typically a round patch on the crown. LME.
†**3** The clipping of coins, or of shrubs or hedges; the state of being clipped. *rare.* L15–L17.
▶ **B** *verb trans.* Clip or shave the hair of; usu. *spec.* give a tonsure to; *fig.* make bald-headed. L18.
■ **tonsurate** *noun* (*ECCLESIASTICAL HISTORY*) the state or quality of being tonsured, esp. in preparation for orders L19. **tonsured** *adjective* that has received the (ecclesiastical) tonsure; *fig.* partly bald; (of a shrub) clipped: E18.

tontine /tɒnˈtiːn/ *noun & adjective.* M18.
[French, from Lorenzo *Tonti* (1630–95), Neapolitan banker, who started such a scheme to raise government loans in France around 1653.]
▶ **A** *noun.* **1** A financial scheme by which subscribers to a loan or common fund each receive an annuity for life, the amount increasing as each dies, till the last survivor enjoys the whole income. Also, the share or right of each subscriber in such a scheme; the subscribers collectively; the fund so established. M18.
2 A scheme for life assurance in which the beneficiaries are those who survive and maintain a policy to the end of a given period. L19.
▶ **B** *attrib.* or as *adjective.* Of, pertaining to, or of the nature of a tontine. L18.

tonto /ˈtɒntəʊ/ *noun & adjective. colloq.* (orig. *US*). L20.
[Spanish.]
▶ **A** *noun.* Pl. **-os**. A foolish or stupid person. L20.
▶ **B** *adjective.* Foolish, crazy; mad. L20.

Tonton /tɔ̃tɔ̃, ˈtɔ̃tɔ̃/ *noun.* Pl. pronounced same. M20.
[Shortened from next.]
= next.

Tonton Macoute /tɔ̃tɔ̃ makut, ˌtɔ̃tɔ̃ məˈkuːt/ *noun.* Pl. ***-s -s*** (pronounced same). M20.
[Haitian French, said to allude to an ogre of folk-tales.]
A member of a militia formed in 1961 by President F. Duvalier of Haiti, notorious for its brutal and arbitrary behaviour and disbanded in 1986.

ton-up /ˈtʌnʌp/ *noun & adjective. slang.* M20.
[from TON *noun*[1] + UP *adverb*[2].]
▶ **A** *noun.* A speed of 100 m.p.h.; a motorcyclist who achieves this. Also, a score of 100 in a game. M20.
▶ **B** *attrib.* or as *adjective.* **1** Designating a young motorcyclist who enjoys travelling at high speed. M20.
2 Achieving a speed or score of 100 in other contexts. M20.

tonus /ˈtəʊnəs/ *noun.* L19.
[Latin from Greek *tonos* TONE *noun.*]
PHYSIOLOGY & MEDICINE. **1** The normal condition of constant low-level activity of a tissue; *spec.* muscular tone. L19.
2 A tonic spasm. *rare.* L19.

Tony /ˈtəʊni/ *noun*[1]. Pl. in sense 1 **Tonies**, in sense 2 **Tonys**. M17.
[In sense 1, a particular application of a familiar abbreviation of male forename *Ant(h)ony*; in sense 2 from the nickname of Antoinette Perry (1886–1946), US actress and producer.]
†**1** A fool; a simpleton. *slang.* M17–E19.
2 Any of the medallions awarded annually by the American Theatre Wing (New York) for excellence in some aspect of the theatre. Also ***Tony award***. M20.

tony *noun*[2] var. of TONI.

tony /ˈtəʊni/ *adjective. colloq.* (orig. *US*). Also **toney**. L19.
[from TONE *noun* + -Y[1].]
Having a high or fashionable tone; high-toned, stylish.
📖 *Forbes* From plebeian coach class to the tonier and more sophisticated business and first classes.

Tony Curtis /təʊnɪ ˈkəːtɪs/ *noun.* M20.
[The film-name of Bernard Schwarz (b. 1925), US actor.]
A style of man's haircut popular in the 1950s, the hair at the sides of the head being combed back and that at the front curled forward on the forehead.

too /tuː/ *adverb.* OE.
[Stressed form of TO *preposition*, spelt *too* from 16th cent.]
▶ **I 1** In addition; furthermore, besides, also. OE. ▸**b** At the beginning of a clause: moreover. (*rare* or *obsolete*. 17–E20.) Now chiefly *N. Amer.* ME. ▸**c** Certainly, indeed (used emphatically to reassert a command or counter a negative). *colloq.* (orig. & chiefly *N. Amer.*). E20.
📖 **1** J. BETJEMAN You'd hate it too if you were me. M. AMIS I too saw what he saw. **b** R. LUDLUM Too, the windows were not that close to one another. **c** A. MALING 'You can't really believe in both,' she said. 'You can too!' Frances said hotly.
▶ **II 2** Qualifying a following adjective or adverb: in excess; to a greater degree than is right, desirable, permissible, or necessary. Freq. foll. by *to do, for*. Cf. ***too much*** below. OE. ▸**b** Qualifying a verb: too much, to excess. *literary. rare.* E16.
3 Modifying an adjective: to a lamentable or reprehensible extent; regrettably, painfully. Esp. in ***too true, all too, but too, only too***, or redupl., with intensive force. ME. ▸**b** As a mere intensive: extremely, exceedingly, very. Also ***only too, but too***, or (now freq. *affected*) redupl. ME.
📖 **2** M. SINCLAIR She was too tired to listen. J. STEINBECK The coat was too big, the trousers too short, for he was a tall man. H. SECOMBE Perhaps I'm pushing things a bit too far. **b** BROWNING I have too trusted my own lawless wants, Too trusted my vain self. **3** LD MACAULAY At best a blunderer, and too probably a traitor. S. DOUGLAS Tracers . . indicating all too clearly that the enemy . . was on the attack. N. FREELING 'Rare, that sort of saint.' 'Too true.' **b** M. LASKI We shall be happy, only too happy to open an account for Madame. D. CUSACK I think male animals are simply too disgusting.
Phrases & comb.: Prefixed to adjectives and adverbs to form adjectival phrs. and adverbial phrs., freq. with other qualifiers, as ***all-too-familiar, not-too-bright, too-hastily***, etc. ***just too bad***: see JUST *adverb.* ***none too***: see NONE *adverb* 2. ***too bad***: see BAD *adjective.* ***too big for one's boots, too big for one's breeches***: see BIG *adjective.* ***too clever by half***: see HALF *noun.* ***too — for words***: see WORD *noun.* ***too good to be true***: see GOOD *adjective.* ***too hot to hold one***: see HOT *adjective.* ***too*** MANY ***for***. **too much** (*a*) = sense 2 above (now only qualifying verbs, verbal phrs., or ppl adjectives); (*b*) *pred.* more than necessary or desirable, excessive; ***too much of a good thing***, an excess of something otherwise desirable; (*c*) as *interjection* (orig. *US*), excellent! **too much for** more than a match for, such as to overwhelm or subdue. ***too right***: see RIGHT *adjective.*

tooa *noun* var. of TOA *noun*[1].

†tooart *noun* var. of TUART.

toodle-oo /tuːd(ə)lˈuː/ *interjection. colloq.* E20.
[Origin uncertain: perh. alt. of French *à tout à l'heure* see you soon!]
Goodbye. Cf. TOORALOO.
■ Also **toodle-pip** *interjection* [cf. PIP-PIP] L20.

took *verb pa. t.* of TAKE *verb.*

tool /tuːl/ *noun.*
[Old English *tōl* = Old Norse *tól* pl., from Germanic base meaning 'prepare': cf. TAW *verb.*]
1 A thing used to apply manual force to an object or material, esp. a device designed for some particular mechanical function in a manual activity, as a hammer, a saw, a fork; an implement. Now also, a powered machine used for a similar purpose. OE. ▸**b** A weapon; formerly *esp.* (now *arch.*) a sword; now *esp.* (*slang*) a gun. LME. ▸**c** Orig. (*rare*), the blade of a knife. Now, the cutting or shaping part of a machine tool. M17. ▸**d** A small stamp or roller used for impressing an ornamental design on leather, esp. in bookbinding. Also, a design so made. M18. ▸**e** *spec.* A large kind of chisel. Also, a large paintbrush, as used in house-painting. E19. ▸**f** In *pl.* Eating utensils. *slang.* E20.
2 *transf. & fig.* A thing (concrete or abstract) used in the carrying out of some occupation or pursuit; a means of effecting a purpose or facilitating an activity. OE. ▸**b** The penis. Now *slang.* LME. ▸**c** *COMPUTING.* A utility program employed in the development and maintenance of software and (less frequently) hardware; an item of software for interactive applications. L20.
3 *fig.* **a** A person used by another as a mere instrument for some purpose. M17. ▸**b** An unskilful worker; a shiftless person. Freq. in ***poor tool***. *slang* or *dial.* L17. ▸**c** A pickpocket; the member of a pair or team of pickpockets who actually picks pockets. M19.
📖 **1** *Scientific American* He has found two teeth . . in a deposit together with crudely chipped stone tools. *Garden Answers* The garden rake is a tool that is in demand all year round. **c** *Which?* Steel sheet . . is squeezed between shaped blocks known as tools. **2** HOBBES They . . make use of Similitudes . . and other tooles of Oratory. R. NIEBUHR Education is . . both a tool of propaganda . . and a means of emancipation. D. R. COX One of the main mathematical tools . . is the Laplace transform. J. D. WATSON Used X-ray diffraction as his principal tool of research. **b** J. SEABROOK He was always waving his tool about in front of me. **3** CONAN DOYLE The fellow . . sends his tools to keep watch upon me.
Phrases: ***edge-tool***: see EDGE *noun.* **hand tool** a hand-held tool as distinct from a machine tool. ***machine tool***: see MACHINE *noun.* ***power tool***: see POWER *noun.* ***string of tools***: see STRING *noun* 22b. **the tools of the trade** the basic equipment required for a particular occupation.
Comb.: **tool-bar** (*a*) a frame fitted to a tractor on which interchangeable implements may be mounted; (*b*) *COMPUTING* a strip of icons, usu. along the top of a window, which represent the tools available within the program being used; **tool-box** (*a*) a box or other container for keeping tools in; (*b*) the steel box in which the cutting tool of a planing or other machine is clamped; (*c*) *COMPUTING* a set of software tools; the set of programs or functions accessible from a single menu; **tool-crib** a place from which tools or other stores are issued to workers; **tool-dresser** *OIL INDUSTRY* = ROUSTABOUT *noun* 3; **tool head** a part of a machine that carries a tool or tool-holder and can be moved to bring the tool to bear on the work; **tool-holder** (*a*) a handle by which a tool is held in the hand, *esp.* a detachable handle for various tools; (*b*) a tray with a rack for holding a set of tools; (*c*) a device for holding a tool firmly in place, as in a lathe, or when being ground on a grindstone; **tool-house** a tool-shed; **toolkit** (*a*) a set of tools; (*b*) *COMPUTING* a set of software tools, esp. designed for a specific application; **tool-maker** a maker of tools; a person who makes and maintains industrial tools; **tool-man** (*a*) a worker with tools; a toolroom worker; (*b*) *slang* a lock-picker, a safe-breaker; **tool-mark** the mark of a tool on any object that has been shaped or worked by it; **tool-post** the post of a machine tool which holds a cutting tool steady; **tool-pusher** a person who directs the drilling on an oil rig; **toolroom** a room in which tools are made or kept; **tool-shed**: for keeping tools in (esp. gardening and household implements); **tool steel** hard steel of a quality used for making cutting tools.
■ **toolless** /-l-l-/ *adjective* M19.

tool /tuːl/ *verb.* E19.
[from the noun.]
▶ **I 1** *verb trans.* Work or shape with a tool; *spec.* (*a*) smooth the surface of (a building stone) with a large chisel; (*b*) impress an ornamental design on (leather) with a special tool. Freq. as ***tooled*** *ppl adjective.* M19.
2 *verb intrans.* Work with a tool or tools (esp. in bookbinding). L19.
3 *verb trans. & intrans.* Equip (a factory) with the machine tools needed for a particular product; provide the tools needed for (a new product). Usu. foll. by *up*. E20. ▸**b** *verb intrans.* Foll. by *up*: arm oneself. Freq. as ***tooled-up*** *ppl adjective. slang.* M20.
📖 **3b** *Loaded* He . . gets his leg ground to bits by tooled up cocaine smugglers.
▶ **II 4 a** *verb trans.* Drive (a team of horses, a vehicle, a person in a vehicle). Also, (of a horse) draw (a person) in a vehicle. E19. ▸**b** *verb intrans.* Travel in a vehicle (orig. *spec.* in a horse-drawn vehicle); drive; (of a vehicle) travel, go *along*. M19.
5 *verb intrans.* Of a person: go (or come) in an easy manner; go *off* quickly. *slang.* M19.
6 *verb intrans.* Play *around*; behave in an aimless or irresponsible manner. *slang.* M20.
📖 **4b** A. MACRAE Tooling around town it did maybe eight miles to the gallon.
■ **tooler** *noun* (*a*) *rare* a broad chisel used by stonemasons for random tooling; (*b*) a person who tools the covers of books: E19.

toolache /ˈtuːlatʃ, tuːˈleɪtʃi/ *noun. Austral.* Also **toolach** /ˈtuːlatʃ/. L19.
[Aboriginal.]
A grey wallaby, *Macropus greyi*, of southern Australia, now extinct. Also ***toolache wallaby***.

toolie /ˈtuːli/ *noun. slang.* M20.
[from TOOL *noun* + -IE.]
OIL INDUSTRY. = ***tool-dresser*** s.v. TOOL *noun.*

toolies /ˈtuːlɪz/ *noun pl. Canad.* M20.
[Alt. of *tules* pl. of TULE.]
The backwoods; remote or thinly populated regions.

tooling /ˈtuːlɪŋ/ *verbal noun.* L17.
[from TOOL *verb* + -ING[1].]
†**1** Provision of tools; tools collectively. Only in L17.
2 The action of TOOL *verb*; workmanship performed with some special tool; *spec.* (*a*) the dressing of stone with a broad chisel; elaborate ornamental carving in stone or wood; (*b*) the impressing of ornamental designs on leather (esp. on the covers of books) with heated tools or

stamps; the designs so formed. L17. ▸**b** The process of designing and supplying the machine tools needed for a product or model; these tools collectively. M20.
2 *blind tooling*: see BLIND *adjective*.

toom /tu:m/ *adjective*. Now only *Scot. & north.*
[Old English *tōm* = Old Norse *tómr*, Old Saxon *tōm(i*, Old High German *zuomig*, from Germanic base also of TEEM *verb*[2].]
Empty (*lit. & fig.*).

toom /tu:m/ *verb trans. Scot. & north.* E16.
[from the adjective, repl. earlier TEEM *verb*[2].]
1 Empty (a vessel, receptacle, etc.). E16.
2 Empty out (the contents of a vessel etc.). M16.

toon /tu:n/ *noun*[1]. Also **tun**. E19.
[Hindi *tun*, *tūn* from Sanskrit *tunna*.]
An Indo-Malayan and Australian tree, *Toona ciliata* (family Meliaceae), which yields a timber resembling mahogany; the wood of this tree. Also called ***red cedar***.

toon /tu:n/ *noun*[2]. *dial. & colloq.* E20.
[Repr. a pronunc.]
= TUNE *noun*.

toon /tu:n/ *noun*[3]. *colloq.* M20.
[Abbreviation.]
= CARTOON *noun* 2, 2b. Also, a cartoon character.
¶ Earliest in comb. *Terry-Toon*, name given to the cartoons produced by Paul Terry and his company in the US.

toonie /'tu:ni/ *noun*. E20.
[from *toon* repr. Scot. pronunc. of TOWN *noun* in local (Shetland) sense of 'arable land on a croft': see -IE.]
In full ***toonie dog***. = ***Shetland sheepdog*** s.v. SHETLAND *adjective* 1.

tooraloo /tu:rə'lu:/ *interjection. colloq.* E20.
[Var. of TOODLE-OO.]
Goodbye.

toot /tu:t/ *noun*[1]. Now chiefly *dial.* Also **tote**, **tout**. LME.
[from TOOT *verb*[1].]
An isolated hill or man-made mound suitable as a place of observation; a lookout. Also ***toot-hill*** (*arch.* exc. in place-names).

toot /tu:t/ *noun*[2]. M17.
[from TOOT *verb*[2].]
An act of tooting; a note or short blast on a horn (now esp. that of a vehicle), or a wind instrument.

> 🕮 S. T. HAYMON The Post Office van . . whizzed past with a cheery toot.

toot /tu:t/ *noun*[3]. Also **tout**. L18.
[from TOOT *verb*[3].]
1 A copious draught; a swig, a tipple. *Scot. colloq.* L18.
2 A drinking session; a binge, a spree; a convivial occasion. *slang* (orig. *Scot.*). L18.
3 Cocaine; a 'snort' of cocaine. *US slang.* L20.

> 🕮 **2** P. G. WODEHOUSE He's away on a toot somewhere, and won't be back for days.

toot /tu:t/ *noun*[4]. *NZ.* M19.
[Alt. of Maori TUTU *noun*[1].]
The tutu, *Coriaria arborea*.

toot /tu:t/ *noun*[5]. *dial. & US.* L19.
[Origin unkn.]
An idle or worthless person; a fool.

toot /tu:t/ *verb*[1] *intrans.* Long *obsolete* exc. *dial.* (now *rare*).
[Old English *tōtian* from Germanic base also of TOUT *verb*[1].]
1 Protrude, stick *out* so as to be seen, peep *out*. OE.
2 Peer, look out; gaze; look inquisitively, pry. ME.

toot /tu:t/ *verb*[2]. E16.
[Prob. from Middle Low German *tūten*, unless a parallel imit. formation.]
▸**I** *verb intrans.* **1** Of a wind instrument: make its characteristic sound; *esp.* give out one or more short notes or blasts. E16.
2 Of a person: sound or blow a horn or similar wind instrument; now *esp.*, sound the horn or whistle of a motor car, train, etc. M16.
3 Of an animal: make a sound like that of a horn etc.; trumpet as an elephant, bray as an ass. Of a male grouse: give its characteristic mating call. E19.

> 🕮 **2** J. FRYER Tooting with their trumpets. J. MANN Tamara tooted on her horn, and turned towards the . . village.

▸**II** *verb trans.* **4** Call out aloud, shout (something); proclaim loudly, trumpet abroad. Chiefly *Scot.* L16.
5 Sound (notes, a tune, etc.) on a horn, pipe, etc. E17.
6 Sound (a horn, whistle, etc.). L17.

> 🕮 **4** R. TANNAHILL Ilk rising generation toots his fame. **5** M. MACHLIN The tugs . . tooted their farewell. **6** *Daily Graphic* The Monmouth's whistle was tooted vigorously.

toot /tu:t/ *verb*[3]. *colloq.* Also **tout**. L17.
[Origin unkn.]
1 *verb intrans.* Drink copiously; quaff; tipple. *Scot.* L17.
2 *verb trans.* Empty (a vessel) by drinking its contents; drink up (liquor). Foll. by *off*, *out*, *up*. *Scot.* Now *rare* or *obsolete*. L18.
3 *verb intrans.* Go on a spree. Chiefly *US*. L19.
4 *verb trans. & intrans.* Inhale (cocaine). *US slang.* L20.

tooter /'tu:tə/ *noun*. E17.
[from TOOT *verb*[2] + -ER[1].]
1 A person who toots, or plays on a wind instrument; a trumpeter, a piper. E17.
2 A horn, a wind instrument. M19.
3 A person who proclaims something loudly; *spec.* = TOUT *noun*[1] 3a. *US.* M19.

tooth /tu:θ/ *noun*. Pl. **teeth** /ti:θ/.
[Old English *tōþ*, pl. *tēþ* = Old Frisian *tōth*, Old Saxon (Dutch) *tand*, Old High German *zan(d)* (German *Zahn*), Old Norse *tọnn*, from Germanic (cf. Gothic *tunþus*), from Indo-European base repr. also by Latin *dent-*, Greek *odont-*, Sanskrit *dant-*.]
▸**I 1** Each of the hard dense projections in the mouth of most vertebrates except birds, typically attached to each jaw in one or more rows, having points, edges, or grinding surfaces, often coated with enamel, and serving primarily for biting, tearing, or crushing solid food, and secondarily as weapons etc. Also, a similar biting, grinding, or scraping projection attached within the mouth or throat in various animals. OE. ▸**b** *spec.* An elephant's tusk (projecting upper incisor tooth), as a source of ivory. OE.
2 Appetite, the action of eating; *esp.* one's taste (*lit. & fig.*), liking, palate. Now chiefly in ***sweet tooth*** s.v. SWEET *adjective & adverb*. LME.
3 *fig.* A thing which bites or gnaws; a hostile, destructive, or devouring agency or quality; *esp.* the full force of a strong wind. M16. ▸**b** In *pl.* The effectiveness of a law, treaty, institution, etc. in enforcing its provisions, esp. by the exaction of penalties etc. E20. ▸**c** In *pl.* The combatant personnel of an armed force. Cf. TAIL *noun*[1] 6(a). M20.

> 🕮 **1** A. N. WILSON She smiled . . , showing a mouthful of magnificent pearly teeth. ***buck-tooth***, ***deciduous tooth***, ***eye-tooth***, ***foal-tooth***, ***incisor tooth***, ***jaw-tooth***, ***milk tooth***, ***pavement-tooth***, ***permanent tooth***, ***scissor-tooth***, ***second tooth***, ***temporary tooth***, ***wisdom tooth***, etc. **2** C. COTTON Keep the best o' th' meat . . For your Worships dainty tooth. **3** J. BARTH Launching a new rowboat into the teeth of a nor'easter. **b** *New Scientist* The copyrighting of microcode really doesn't seem to have a lot of teeth.

▸**II 4** A projecting part, esp. one of a row, in an artificial structure, as an implement, a machine, etc.; *esp.* (***a***) each of the pointed projections of a comb, saw, or file; a prong, a tine; (***b***) each of the series of projections on the edge of a cog-wheel, pinion, etc., which engage with corresponding ones on another. LME. ▸**b** In *pl.* A ship's guns. *Nautical slang.* E19. ▸**c** In *pl.* The lower zone of facets in a rose-cut diamond. L19.
5 A projecting part in a natural structure; a sharp prominence; *spec.* (***a***) a projecting point on the upper part of the bill in some birds; (***b***) each of a row of small projections on the edge of one valve of a bivalve's shell; (***c***) each of the pointed processes on the margin of leaves or other parts in many plants. LME.
6 (Without *pl.*) A rough quality of the surface of paper, canvas, wood, etc., which enables pencil-marks, paints, glue, etc. to adhere. E19.

> 🕮 **4** B. MALAMUD He combed his hair and beard until the teeth of the comb fell out. *Which?* The teeth of the blade are bent alternately from side to side. **5** GLYN EVANS Dung beetles have well-developed teeth on the fore legs to assist them in digging.

Phrases: ***a kick in the teeth***: see KICK *noun*[1] 2. ***armed to the teeth***: see ***to the teeth*** below. ***as scarce as hen's teeth***: see HEN *noun*. ***by the skin of one's teeth***: see SKIN *noun*. **cast in a person's teeth**, **fling in a person's teeth**, etc., reject defiantly or refer reproachfully to (a previous action, statement, etc., of that person). ***cut one's eye-teeth***: see CUT *verb*. ***dog's tooth***. ***dragon's teeth***. ***false teeth***: see FALSE *adjective*. ***fed to the teeth***, ***fed to the back teeth***: see FED *ppl adjective*. ***fight tooth and nail***: see ***tooth and nail*** below. ***fine-tooth comb***: see FINE *adjective & adverb*. **get one's teeth into** become engrossed in, come to grips with, begin serious work on. **in spite of one's teeth** (now chiefly *dial.*) in spite of one's opposition. **in the teeth of** in direct opposition to, so as to face or confront, straight against; in defiance of, in spite of; in the face of (usu. implying hostility or danger). ***long in the tooth***: see LONG *adjective*[1]. ***make a person's teeth water***: see WATER *verb*. ***old woman's tooth***. ***one's teeth water***: see WATER *verb*. **say between one's teeth** say while (half-)clenching one's teeth with anger, effort, etc. ***set a person's teeth on edge***: see EDGE *noun*. **set one's teeth** clench one's teeth firmly together from indignation, or in determination as in facing danger, opposition, or difficulty. **show one's teeth** *lit.* uncover one's teeth by drawing back the lips, esp. as an animal in readiness for attack; *fig.* show hostility or malice, behave threateningly; reveal one's aggressive power. ***sweet tooth***: see SWEET *adjective & adverb*. ***take the bit between one's teeth***: see BIT *noun*[1] 6. ***the run of one's teeth***: see RUN *noun*. **to a person's teeth** to a person's face, directly, openly, defiantly. **tooth and nail**, †**with tooth and nail** occas., with one's teeth and nails as weapons; by biting and scratching; chiefly (*fig.*), vigorously, fiercely, with utmost effort, with all one's might (chiefly in ***fight tooth and nail***). **to the teeth** very fully or completely; esp. in ***armed to the teeth***. **up to the teeth** = ***to the teeth*** above. ***with the skin of one's teeth***: see SKIN *noun*.
Comb.: **teeth ridge** the ridge of the upper gums behind the front teeth, the alveolar ridge; **tooth-billed** *adjective* (ORNITHOLOGY) (of a bird) having one or more toothlike projections on the edge of the bill; **toothcarp** any of numerous small, mainly freshwater fishes resembling carp but possessing small teeth, esp. of the families Cyprinodontidae and Poeciliidae; **tooth-comb** *noun & verb* (***a***) *noun* = ***fine-tooth comb*** s.v. FINE *adjective & adverb*; (***b***) *verb trans.* investigate minutely; **tooth fairy** in nursery-tales, a fairy said to take away children's milk teeth and leave a small sum of money; **tooth-glass** (***a***) a glass used to hold false teeth; (***b***) a small glass used to wash out the mouth, hold toothbrushes, etc.; **tooth-mark**, pl. **tooth-marks**, **teeth-marks**, a mark made by a tooth in biting, or by an edged tool; **tooth-marked** *adjective* bearing tooth-marks; **tooth-mug** a mug used like a tooth-glass; **toothpaste** a paste used for cleaning the teeth; **tooth-plate** DENTISTRY = PLATE *noun* 12; **tooth powder** a powder used for cleaning the teeth, a dentifrice; **tooth-pulp**: in the cavity at the centre of a tooth; **tooth shell** = ***tusk shell*** s.v. TUSK *noun*[1]; **toothwort** either of two plants having rhizomes with toothlike scales, *Lathraea squamaria*, a leafless fleshy plant of the broomrape family parasitic on the roots of trees, and coral-root, *Cardamine bulbifera*.
■ **toothful** *noun* a small mouthful, esp. of liquor L18. **toothlet** *noun* (BOTANY & ZOOLOGY, *rare*) a small tooth or toothlike projection, a denticulation L18. **toothlike** *adjective* resembling (that of) a tooth M19.

tooth /tu:θ/ *verb*. LME.
[from the noun.]
1 *verb intrans.* Grow or cut teeth; teethe. Chiefly as ***toothing*** *verbal noun*. Now *rare* or *obsolete*. LME.
2 *verb trans.* Supply with teeth; fit or fix teeth into; cut teeth in or on. L15.
3 *verb trans.* Bite, gnaw, chew. L16.
4 *verb trans. & intrans.* Fit or fix into something using projections like teeth, or in the manner of teeth; interlock. E18.

toothache /'tu:θeɪk/ *noun*. LME.
[from TOOTH *noun* + ACHE *noun*[1].]
An ache or prolonged pain in a tooth or the teeth.
Comb.: **toothache tree** either of two N. American kinds of prickly ash, *Zanthoxylum americanum* and *Z. clava-Herculis*, the pungent bark and fruits of which were formerly chewed to relieve toothache.
■ **toothachy** *adjective* (*colloq.*) affected with toothache M19.

toothbrush /'tu:θbrʌʃ/ *noun*. L17.
[from TOOTH *noun* + BRUSH *noun*[2].]
A small brush with a long handle, usu. having stiff bristles sticking out at right angles from the end, used for cleaning the teeth.
Comb.: **toothbrush moustache** a short bristly moustache trimmed to a rectangular shape; **toothbrush tree** a small tree, *Salvadora persica* (family Salvadoraceae), of tropical Asia and Africa, the twigs of which are used as a chew-stick.

toothed /tu:θt/ *adjective*. ME.
[from TOOTH *noun* or *verb*: see -ED[2], -ED[1].]
1 Of a person, an animal, etc.: having teeth (freq. of a specified kind). ME.
2 Having natural projections or processes like teeth; dentate; indented; jagged. LME.
3 Made or fitted artificially with teeth or toothlike projections; *spec.* (of a wheel) having cogs. LME.
1 **toothed whale** a whale of the suborder Odontoceti, characterized by having teeth rather than baleen plates, and including sperm whales, killer whales, and dolphins and porpoises.

toothily /'tu:θɪli/ *adverb*. M20.
[from TOOTHY + -LY[2].]
In a toothy manner; so as to display the teeth.

toothing /'tu:θɪŋ/ *noun*. LME.
[from TOOTH *noun* or *verb* + -ING[1].]
1 Cutting of the teeth, teething. Now *rare* or *obsolete*. LME.
2 A structure or formation (natural or artificial) consisting of teeth or toothlike projections; such teeth collectively; dentation, serration. E17. ▸**b** *spec.* Bricks or stones left projecting from a wall to form a bond for additional work to be built on; (the construction of) a join so made. L17.
3 The process of forming teeth or serrations (as on a saw etc.). M19.
Comb.: **toothing-plane** a plane having a blade with a serrated edge, used to score and roughen a surface.

toothless /'tu:θlɪs/ *adjective*. LME.
[from TOOTH *noun* + -LESS.]
1 a Having the teeth still undeveloped; that has not yet cut its teeth. LME. ▸**b** Having lost the teeth, as from age. LME. ▸**c** That is naturally without teeth; not developing teeth. L19.
2 *fig.* **a** Destitute of keenness or edge; not biting. L16. ▸**b** Lacking the means of compulsion or enforcement; ineffectual. M20.
3 Not jagged, serrated, or dentate. E19.
■ **toothlessly** *adverb* L19. **toothlessness** *noun* M17.

toothpick /'tu:θpɪk/ *noun & adjective*. L15.
[from TOOTH *noun* + PICK *noun*[1].]
▸**A** *noun*. **1** An instrument for picking the teeth, usually a pointed quill or small sliver of wood, sometimes of metal or other material. L15.
2 A Mediterranean umbelliferous plant, *Ammi visnaga*, the hardened rays of the umbel of which are or have

been used as toothpicks. Also more fully ***Spanish toothpick***. *rare* (only in Dicts.). **L16.**

3 In *pl.* Splinters, matchwood. Only in *hyperbol.* phrs., as ***smashed into toothpicks***. **M19.**

4 A bowie-knife. Also ***Arkansas toothpick***. *US slang.* **M19.**

5 A very narrow pointed boat. *slang.* **L19.**

▶ **B** *attrib.* or as *adjective.* †**1** Affording sufficient leisure to allow the use of a toothpick, idle, casual. Only in **M18.**

2 Of very narrow pointed shape. **L19.**

toothsome /ˈtuːθs(ə)m/ *adjective.* **M16.**
[from TOOTH *noun* + -SOME[1].]

1 Pleasant to the taste, appetizing, palatable. **M16.** ▸**b** *fig.* Pleasant, attractive. **M16.**

2 Dainty in appetite. *rare.* **M19.**

■ **toothsomely** *adverb* **L19.** **toothsomeness** *noun* **E17.**

toothy /ˈtuːθi/ *adjective.* **M16.**
[from TOOTH *noun* + -Y[1].]

1 Having numerous, large, or prominent teeth; displaying the teeth. **M16.**

2 Having many teeth or toothlike projections; toothed. **E17.**

3 *fig.* Biting, ill-natured, peevish. *Scot. & north.* **L17.**

4 = TOOTHSOME 1. *rare.* **M19.**

📖 **1** *Today* A little girl with a big toothy grin.

toothy-peg /ˈtuːθɪpɛɡ/ *noun. nursery & joc.* **E19.**
[from TOOTH *noun* + -Y[6] + PEG *noun*[1].]

A tooth, *esp.* one just appearing through the gum.

tooting /ˈtuːtɪŋ/ *ppl adjective.* **M17.**
[from TOOT *verb*[2] + -ING[2].]

1 That toots, as a horn, siren, etc. **M17.**

2 Used as an emphatic affirmative or intensive. Usu. with preceding adverb or adjective, as ***darn tooting***, ***plumb tooting***, etc. *N. Amer. slang.* **M20.**

📖 **1** ***rootin' tootin'***: see ROOT *verb*[2]. **2** B. MALAMUD You're plumb tootin' crazy.

tootle /ˈtuːt(ə)l/ *verb & noun.* **E19.**
[from TOOT *verb*[2] + -LE[3].]

▶ **A** *verb.* **1** *verb intrans.* Toot continuously; produce a succession of notes (as) on a wind instrument. Freq. *joc.* **E19.**

2 *verb trans.* Play (a wind instrument); play (music) on a wind instrument. *joc. & colloq.* **L19.**

3 *verb intrans.* Write trivial or inconsequential matter; talk twaddle. **L19.**

4 *verb intrans.* Walk, ride, etc., casually or aimlessly; drive, esp. in a small or slow car. (Foll. by *along*, *around*, *off*, etc.) *colloq.* **E20.**

📖 **1** O. SEAMAN The lark is tootling in the sky. **2** J. GALWAY I had tootled my flute to some purpose. **4** *Listener* Veteran cars tootle down country lanes.

▶ **B** *noun.* **1** An act or the action of tootling; a succession of little musical notes. Freq. *joc.* **M19.**

2 Trivial or inconsequential speech or writing; verbiage, twaddle. **L19.**

📖 **1** *New Yorker* I could hear a saxophone's preparatory tootles down the hall. **2** M. MITCHELL Will was talking common sense instead of a lot of tootle.

too-too /ˈtuːtuː, tuːˈtuː/ *adjective. affected.* Also **too too**. **L19.**
[Redupl. of TOO.]

Extreme, very good, exquisite. Also, affected, pretentiously artificial.

too-too /tuːˈtuː/ *verb intrans.* Chiefly *depreciative.* **E19.**
[Imit.]

Make a tooting or hollow sound with the voice, a musical instrument, etc.

📖 THACKERAY An unequal and disagreeable tootooing on a horn.

toots /tʊts/ *noun. slang* (orig. & chiefly *N. Amer.*). **M20.**
[Prob. abbreviation of TOOTSY.]

Used as a familiar form of address, esp. to a woman or girl.

tootsey, **tootsie** *nouns* vars. of TOOTSY.

toot sweet /tuːt ˈswiːt/ *adverb. colloq.* **E20.**
[Anglicized from French *tout de suite*.]

Straightaway, immediately; promptly, quickly.

tootsy /ˈtʊtsi/ *noun.* Also **-sie**, **-sey**; redupl. **tootsy-wootsy** /tʊtsɪˈwʊtsi/. **M19.**
[from alt. of FOOT *noun* + -Y[6].]

1 A foot, a toe. Usu. in *pl. nursery & joc.* **M19.**

2 A woman, a girl; a sweetheart, a lover. Freq. as a familiar form of address. *slang* (chiefly *US*). **L19.**

📖 **1** M. WESLEY You can rest your tootsies while I listen to music.

top /tɒp/ *noun*[1] *& adjective.*
[Late Old English *topp* = Old Frisian *topp* tuft, Middle & mod. Dutch *top* crest, summit, tip, Old & mod. High German *zopf* plait, tress, Old Norse *toppr* top, tuft, from Germanic: cf. TIP *noun*[1], TOUPEE.]

▶ **A** *noun.* **I** The highest or uppermost part.

1 a The highest or uppermost point or part of a material thing; the upper surface of a thing, esp. a table; in *pl.*, the highest part of a moor, the peaks of a mountain range. **LOE.** ▸**b** The highest part of anything, considered as a position in space; the end of something (conventionally) perceived as higher. **ME.**

2 The uppermost part of the body; the head, *esp.* the crown (now only in phrs. below). **ME.** ▸**b** The uppermost branch of a deer's horn. Chiefly in ***on top***. *rare.* **LME.**

3 a The hair on (the crown of) the head; a bird's crest; an animal's forelock. *obsolete* exc. *Scot. & north.* **ME.** ▸**b** A tuft of hair, wool, fibre, etc.; *esp.* the portion of flax or tow put on the distaff. *obsolete* exc. *Scot. & north.* **ME.** ▸**c** A bundle of combed wool prepared for spinning. Usu. in *pl.* **M17.**

4 *sing.* & in *pl.* The smaller branches and twigs of a tree as distinct from the timber. **LME.**

5 The (slender) end of a growing part; *transf.* the narrower end of anything tapering, the tip. **L15.**

6 *sing.* & (usu.) in *pl.* The leaves, stems, and shoots of a plant; *esp.* those of a vegetable grown for its root. Cf. ***turnip-tops*** s.v. TURNIP. **E16.**

7 The inside of a roof; a ceiling. Now *dial.* **E18.**

8 *techn.* **a** The part of a cut gem above the girdle. **E18.** ▸**b** BOOKBINDING. The upper edge or edges of a page or pages in a book. **M19.**

9 A circus tent. Chiefly in ***big top*** s.v. BIG *adjective.* **M20.**

📖 **1** E. HEMINGWAY The wind blew in the tops of the pine trees. J. KOSINSKI I climbed to an upper terrace . . and then to the very top. R. PILCHER He glanced up . . over the top of his spectacles. **b** DAY LEWIS Standing at the top of the garden. A. CHRISTIE They had come almost to the top of the path. **2** B. EMECHETA The gravediggers stood . . their tops bared.

▶ **II** A part placed on or fitted to something, and forming the upper part or covering.

10 NAUTICAL. A platform round the head of each of the lower masts of a ship, serving to extend the upper rigging or carry guns etc. Also (now *rare* exc. *attrib.*), a topsail; a topmast. **LME.**

11 Orig., the upper part of the leg of a high boot, esp. when widened out or turned over. Now, (esp. on hunting-boots) a broad band of a different colour or material simulating this; in *pl.*, top-boots. Also, the upper part of a shoe. **E17.**

12 The roof, esp. a folding one, of a carriage, pram, or car. **E17.**

13 An ear-stud, *esp.* one also having a drop. Now *rare.* **E18.**

14 A metal button with a gilt or silvered face. Now *rare.* **M19.**

15 The stopper of a bottle; the lid or cover of a jar, tin, etc., *esp.* the foil cover of a milk bottle. **M19.**

16 A (woman's) garment for the upper body (as a blouse, jumper, etc.), to be worn with a separate garment for the lower body. **E20.**

📖 **15** A. SILLITOE Screwing the top back on the flask. *Daily Mirror* The retail price of . . silver top milk goes up. **16** *Jackie* That top . . would go perfectly with my new skirt.

▶ **III** The first in time, order, or precedence.

17 The earliest part of a period of time; the beginning. Now *rare.* **LME.**

18 The highest pitch or degree; the height. **M16.** ▸**b** A thing which is the highest example *of* a class of things. **L16.** ▸**c** AUDIO. High-frequency sound, esp. as regards its characteristics in sound reproduction. **M20.**

19 The highest place or rank; a person or thing occupying this. **E17.** ▸**b** The highest gear in a vehicle. **E20.** ▸**c** BRIDGE. A high card; the highest card in a suit in a player's hand. **E20.**

20 The highest point in a progression; the peak. Now *arch. & dial.* **M17.**

21 a The best or choicest part. Now chiefly in ***the top of the morning*** (*Anglo-Irish*): a morning greeting. **M17.** ▸**b** In *pl.* The best sheep or lambs in a flock (now *dial.*); *colloq.* (*pred.*) the best person or thing. **M19.**

22 PARTICLE PHYSICS. (A quark carrying) a possible sixth quark flavour, associated with a charge of + ⅔. Also called ***truth***. (Symbol *t*.) **L20.**

📖 **18** A. POWELL He was not feeling at the top of his form. **b** G. HICKES The episcopate is the top of all the honours among men. **19** E. ROOSEVELT Often businessmen go into government with the idea that they will be men at the top. J. F. HENDRY He was top of his class. Z. TOMIN Whatever is happening at the top, it is the citizens who are the . . creators of . . society. **21b** *Lydney (Glos.) Observer* Pubs were . . voted tops for . . service and friendly atmosphere. U. HOLDEN You're wonderful, you're the tops.

▶ **IV** [from TOP *verb*[1].]

23 a ***top-up***, an addition, something serving to top up something (esp. a partly full glass). **L19.** ▸**b** GOLF. A stroke in which the ball is (usu. inadvertently) struck above the centre. **L19.** ▸**c** ***top-off***, an informer. *Austral. slang.* **M20.**

24 Topspin. **E20.**

Phrases: **at the top** in a position of power or authority; in the highest rank of a profession etc. (cf. ***at the top of the tree*** s.v. TREE *noun*). ***at the top of one's voice***: see VOICE *noun.* **at tops** = TOPS *adverb.* ***big top***: see BIG *adjective.* ***blow one's top***: see BLOW *verb*[1]. ***brown top***: see BROWN *adjective.* ***bunchy top***: see BUNCHY 2. ***double top***: see DOUBLE *adjective & adverb.* **from top to bottom**, **from top to toe** from head to foot; in every part; completely, throughout. ***lop and top***: see LOP *noun*[2] 1. ***off the top of one's head***: see HEAD *noun.* **on a person's top** (now *Scot.*) attacking a person (physically or verbally). **on top** (*a*) on or in the top of something; (*b*) in a superior position; supreme, dominant; (*c*) on the upper part of the head. **on top of** (*a*) in addition to; (*b*) in very close proximity to; (*c*) in control of; (*d*) ***get on top of***, overwhelm, depress; ***on top of the world*** (*colloq.*), exuberant, elated. **over the top** (*a*) (chiefly *Hist.*) over the parapet of a trench (and into battle); (*b*) into a final or decisive state; (*c*) beyond reasonable limits, too far. ***thin on top***: see THIN *adjective.* **top of the milk** the cream that rises to the top of milk when left undisturbed. ***top of the pops***: see POP *noun*[6] 1. ***up top***: see UP *adverb*[2] *& adjective*[2].

▶ **B** *adjective.* **1** At, on, or forming the top; highest in position, degree, or importance. Earlier in TOPSAIL. **L15.**

2 Having or fitted with a top. **M19.**

📖 **1** A. LEE I arranged myself on my lumpy top bunk. *She* Top prize for ingenuity must go to the French. *Sun* Pianos are big business. The repair bill for a top make can be £7,000. **2** W. WHITMAN Queer old one-horse top-wagons.

Special collocations & comb.: ***top banana***: see BANANA 3. **top board** CHESS the principal player of a team in a match or tournament. **top-boot** (chiefly *Hist.*) a long boot, *esp.* one with a top of a different material or colour. ***top brass***: see BRASS *noun* 4. **topcoat** (*a*) an overcoat, a greatcoat, an outer coat; (*b*) a layer of paint etc. applied after the undercoat. **top copy** the original typescript of a document, of which the undersheets are carbon copies. **top-cut** reduction in the strength of the higher-frequency components of an audio signal. **top cutter** *US Military slang* = ***top sergeant*** below. **top cymbal** MUSIC a ride cymbal. **top dead centre** MECHANICS the point at which a piston is about to change from an upward to a downward stroke. **top deck** the upper deck of a ship. **top dog** *colloq.* a victor, a master. **top dollar** *N. Amer. colloq.* a high or the highest price. **top-down** *adjective* (*a*) COMPUTING working from the top or root of a tree towards the branches (with or without backtracking); (*b*) proceeding from the top downwards; hierarchical. **top-drawer** (*a*) *colloq.* upper-class; of high social standing; (*b*) of the highest level. **top-dress** *verb trans.* apply manure or fertilizer on the top of (land or a crop) instead of ploughing it in. **top-dressing** (*a*) the application of manure or fertilizer on the top of land or a crop (***aerial top-dressing***: see AERIAL *adjective* 4c); (*b*) the manure or fertilizer so applied; (*c*) *fig.* a superficial show. **top edge** (*a*) BOOKBINDING = sense A.8b above; (*b*) CRICKET the upper edge of a bat as held by the batsman; a shot hit off this edge. **top-edge** *verb trans. & intrans.* (CRICKET) unintentionally hit (the ball) with the top edge. **Top End** *Austral. colloq.* (the northern part of) the Northern Territory. **top fermentation** BREWING a process in which the yeast rises to the surface during fermentation, characteristic of British-type beers. **top-fermented** *adjective* (BREWING) designating a beer brewed by top fermentation. **top-flight** *adjective* in the highest rank of achievement (cf. ***in the top flight*** s.v. FLIGHT *noun*[1]). **top fruit** fruit growing on trees as distinct from on bushes or the ground. **top-full** *adjective* (now *rare*) full to the top; brim-full. **top gear** the highest gear in a motor vehicle or bicycle. **top-graft** *verb trans.* = ***top-work*** below. **top-hamper** an encumbrance on top, *esp.* (NAUTICAL) the upper sails and rigging of a ship. **top hand** *N. Amer. colloq.* an experienced or proficient ranch-worker. **top hat** a man's silk hat with a high cylindrical crown, worn esp. on formal occasions; *transf.* an important person. **top-hat** *adjective* shaped like a top hat. **top-hatted** *adjective* wearing a top-hat. **top-hole** *adjective* (*colloq.*) first-rate, excellent. **top kick** *US Military slang* = ***top sergeant*** below. **top-land** high or elevated land. **top-level** *adjective* of the highest level of importance, prestige, etc. **top light** a skylight. **top-lighted**, **top-lit** *adjectives* lit by a skylight. **top line** (*a*) in cattle, the profile line of an animal's back from the centre of the shoulders to the end of the hip-bones; (*b*) (freq. *attrib.*) the head item on a bill of entertainment; the headline of a newspaper; ***on the top line*** (*slang*), at the peak of readiness, alertness, perfection, etc. **top-liner** an important or famous person or thing, a star. ***top-lit***: see ***top-lighted*** above. **top-loader** (*a*) *N. Amer.* a lumberjack who works at the top of a load of logs; (*b*) a machine, esp. a washing machine, which is loaded from the top (instead of from the front). **topman** (*a*) = ***top-sawyer*** below; (*b*) NAUTICAL a sailor on duty in a top, attending to the upper sails or acting as a marksman; (*c*) a miner working at the top of a shaft; (*d*) *slang* a demolition worker who demolishes walls etc. from the top. **topminnow** = KILLIFISH. **top notch** *adjective* (*colloq.*) first-rate, excellent. **top-notcher** *colloq.* a first-rate person or thing. **top note** (*a*) the highest note in a singer's range; (*b*) in a perfume, those scents which are most dominant, or which are the first to be smelt. **top onion** a form of tree onion, bearing small bulbs as well as flowers in the inflorescence. **top people** high-ranking or influential people. **top-sawyer** (*a*) a sawyer who works the upper handle of a pit-saw; (*b*) *fig.* a person who holds a superior position; a distinguished person. **top-score** *verb intrans.* (CRICKET) make the greatest number of runs of an innings. **top scorer** (esp. SPORT) a person who achieves the greatest score. **top secret** *adjectival phr.* of the highest secrecy. **top sergeant** *US Military slang* first sergeant. **topset** *adjective* (GEOLOGY) designating a near-horizontal bed or stratum deposited on top of other beds in a delta. **top-slicing** (*a*) MINING a method of working in which successive slices are mined from the top of an ore body downwards, the material overlying each slice being made to cave in after its completion; (*b*) a method of assessing tax chargeable on a lump sum by averaging it out over the years for which it has accrued and charging tax accordingly. **topsman** (*a*) *Scot. & north.* a head man; *esp.* the chief drover in charge of a herd of cattle on the road; (*b*) *arch. slang* a hangman. **topsoil** *noun & verb* (*a*) *noun* the surface layer of soil (opp. SUBSOIL); (*b*) *verb trans.* remove the topsoil from; dress with topsoil. **topspin** a fast forward spinning motion imparted to a ball when throwing or hitting it. **top-spinner** CRICKET a ball delivered with topspin. **top-stitch** *verb trans.* make a row of stitches on (the right side of) a garment etc., esp. for decoration. **top-stitching** stitching (esp. for decoration) on the right side of a garment etc. **top-stone** a stone placed on or forming the top of something; a capstone. **top table** at a formal dinner, the table at which the chief guests are placed. **top ten**, **top twenty**, etc., the first ten, twenty, etc., recordings in the popular music charts. **top-timber** any of the uppermost timbers in the side of a ship. **top view** = *plan view* s.v. PLAN *noun*. **top-water** *noun & adjective* (*a*) *noun* water percolating through the roof of a mine; (*b*) *adjective* (of a bait) that floats on top of the water. **top-weight** the heaviest weight carried by a horse in a race; a horse carrying this weight. **top-work** *verb trans.* replace part or all of the top of (a fruit tree) by grafts of another variety. **top yeast** a yeast that rises to the surface during fermentation.

■ **topness** *noun* (*a*) *rare* the state of being (at the) top; pre-eminence; (*b*) PARTICLE PHYSICS the property attributed to the top quark (see TOP *noun*[1] 22): M20.

top /tɒp/ *noun*[2].
[Late Old English *top*, of unkn. origin.]
1 A wooden, metal, or plastic toy, usu. conical, spherical, or pear-shaped, with a point on which it spins when set in motion by a string, a spring, the hand, etc. LOE.
2 More fully ***top-shell***. (The shell of) a gastropod of the family Trochidae, which comprises marine forms with a short conical shell. L17.
3 A conical piece of wood with lengthwise grooves in which the strands of a rope run when being twisted. L18.
1 ***sleep like a top***: see SLEEP *verb*.
¶ Rare before LME.
■ **topwise** *adverb* in the manner of a top LME.

top /tɒp/ *verb*[1]. Infl. **-pp-**. ME.
[from TOP *noun*[1].]
▶†**I 1** *verb intrans.* Fight, struggle. Only in ME.
▶**II** †**2** *verb trans.* Cut *off* (the hair of the head); crop (a person). ME–M17.
3 *verb trans.* Remove the top from (a growing plant), prune (a branch), esp. to improve growth; remove the withered calyx from (a fruit or vegetable) in preparation for cooking (chiefly in ***top and tail*** below). E16.
†**4** *verb trans.* Snuff (a candle). M16–M19.
5 *verb trans.* Execute by hanging; *gen.* kill; *refl.* commit suicide. *slang.* E18.
6 *verb trans.* Shorten the teeth of (a toothed wheel). L19.

> 🕮 **5** *Daily Telegraph* I'd rather be topped than do 20 years behind bars. *Sun* I have been desperately unhappy . . but I have never given a thought to topping myself.

▶**III 7** *verb trans.* Provide with a top; cover, surmount or crown (*with*). Usu. in *pass.* (Not always distinguishable from sense 13 below.) LME.
8 a *verb trans.* Complete by putting the top on or forming the top of; *esp.* put the finishing touch to, finish off. Usu. foll. by *off*, *up*. E16. ▶**b** *verb intrans.* Foll. by *off*, *up*: finish *up* or *off with*. *colloq.* M19.
9 *verb trans.* Of a male animal: copulate with. Cf. TUP *verb*. *obsolete* exc. *US*. E17.
†**10 a** *verb intrans.* Cheat at dice by palming the die; *gen.* cheat, trick, impose *upon*. *slang.* M17–E18. ▶**b** *verb trans.* Impose (a thing) *upon* a person. *slang.* L17–M18. ▶**c** *verb trans.* Insult. *slang.* L17–L18.

> 🕮 **7** A. CARTER A stout wall topped with barbed wire. JILLY COOPER The wedding cake is topped by a . . replica of the bride and groom. **8a** A. WEST Festivities, topped off by a big dinner. G. PRIESTLAND A hearty meal . . topped off with a . . knickerbocker glory. **b** RIDER HAGGARD Everything went wrong . . and to top up with I got . . fever.

▶**IV 11** *verb trans.* **a** Exceed in height, weight, amount, etc. L16. ▶**b** Surpass, better. L16.
12 *verb trans.* Reach the top of (a hill etc.). E17.
13 *verb trans.* Be at the top of; *fig.* be the best of; *transf.* appear as the chief performer at. (Not always distinguishable from sense 7 above.) E17. ▶**b** Now chiefly *US* SPORT. Get the better of. M17.
14 *verb trans.* Get over the top of; rise above. M18.
15 *verb trans. & intrans.* Chiefly GOLF. Hit (a ball) above the centre; play (a stroke) in this way. L19.

> 🕮 **11** T. C. WOLFE He already topped his mother by an inch or two. *Japan Times* Petroleum imports . . topped 8 million barrels a day. **b** R. DAVIES The Ace of Spades; there was no card to top it. *Sunday Times* Every offer . . was . . topped by an undisclosed bidder. **12** J. S. CORBETT They topped the crags that overhung the tarn. **13** W. H. DIXON In character as in intellect Bacon tops the list. *Sounds* Led Zeppelin remain favourites to top a . . festival at Wrotham Park. **14** R. D. BLACKMORE My head topped the platform of rock.

With adverbs in specialized senses, & phrases: **top and tail** (*a*) remove the stalk and withered calyx from (a fruit or vegetable) in preparation for cooking; (*b*) *colloq.* wash the face and bottom of (a baby or small child). **top off** (*a*) *colloq.* (chiefly *US*) (of a ship, aircraft, etc.) fill up or complete a cargo; (*b*) *US colloq.* fill up (a partly full tank) with fuel; (*c*) = ***top out*** (b) below; (*d*) *Austral. slang* inform on; (see also sense 8 above). **top one's part** (chiefly THEATRICAL) play one's part to perfection. **top out** (*a*) put the highest structural feature on (a building), esp. ceremonially; (*b*) reach a peak, cease rising. **top up** (*a*) fill to the top (a partly full glass or other container); fill up a partly full glass for (a person); (*b*) add to, bring (a number or amount) up to a certain level; (see also sense 8 above).

top /tɒp/ *verb*[2]. Infl. **-pp-**. M16.
[Dutch *toppen* top or peak (a yard), of unkn. origin. Branch II prob. a different word.]
▶**I** NAUTICAL. **1** *verb trans.* Slant (a yard) by tilting up one arm and depressing the other; tilt up (a yard) vertically; *gen.* alter the position of (a yard) in any way. M16.
2 *verb intrans.* Foll. by *up*: assume a slanting position. M19.
1 topping-lift either of a pair of lifts by which a yard may be topped.
▶**II 3** *verb intrans.* Topple over, overbalance. Cf. TOPE *verb*[1] 3. Long *rare* or *obsolete*. M16.
4 *verb trans.* Tip over, overturn. Cf. TOPE *verb*[1] 2. *obsolete* exc. *dial.* M17.

toparch /ˈtɒpɑːk/ *noun*. M17.
[Greek *toparkhēs*, from *topos* place + *-arkhēs* -ARCH.]
The ruler of a small district, city, or state.
■ **toparchy** *noun* [Latin *toparchia*, Greek *toparkhia*] the territory ruled by a toparch E17.

topass /ˈtəʊpəs/ *noun*. L17.
[Portuguese *topaz* app. from Tamil *tupās*, *tupāci* from Hindi *duhbhāṣī* man of two languages, interpreter (cf. DUBASH).]
Hist. In the Indian subcontinent: a person of mixed Indian and Portuguese descent.

topaz /ˈtəʊpaz/ *noun & adjective*. ME.
[Old French *topace*, (also mod.) *topaze* from Latin *topazus*, *-azius*, *-azion* from Greek *topazos*, *-azion*.]
▶**A** *noun*. **1** Orig. (esp. with ref. to classical authors), a yellow sapphire (also ***yellow topaz***, ***oriental topaz***); also, a green chrysolite. Now, an orthorhombic fluosilicate of aluminium that usu. occurs as transparent and lustrous yellow, colourless, or pale blue prismatic crystals, and is valued as a precious stone (also ***true topaz***, ***occidental topaz***). ME. ▶**b** With specifying word: any of several varieties of quartz turned yellow, red, or brown, esp. by heating. L18.
2 The dark yellow colour of a topaz; HERALDRY (now *Hist.*) the tincture topaz in the fanciful blazon of arms of peers. L16.
3 Either of two S. American hummingbirds of the genus *Topaza*, which have black heads, metallic yellow or green throats, and crimson or orange-red underparts. Also ***topaz hummingbird***. L18.
1b ***false topaz***, ***Scotch topaz***, ***smoky topaz***, ***Spanish topaz***.
▶**B** *attrib.* or as *adjective*. Resembling a topaz in colour, dark yellow; made or consisting of topaz; set or provided with a topaz or topazes. E19.
■ **topazine** /-ɪn, -ʌɪn/ *adjective* resembling or of the colour of topaz E19. **topazy** *adjective* (*rare*) of the colour of topaz L19.

topazolite /təʊˈpazəlʌɪt/ *noun*. E19.
[from TOPAZ + -O- + -LITE.]
MINERALOGY. A yellowish-green variety of andradite garnet.

topchee /ˈtəʊptʃiː/ *noun*. Also **topgi** /ˈtəʊpdʒiː/. E17.
[Persian, Urdu *topchī*, Turkish *topçu*, from Turkish *top* gun, cannon.]
Hist. In the Ottoman Empire: a gunner, an artillery soldier.

tope /təʊp/ *noun*[1]. L17.
[Origin uncertain: perh. from Cornish.]
Either of two small sharks of the genus *Galeorhinus*, *G. galeus* (also called **soupfin**) and the school shark, *G. australis*.

tope /təʊp/ *noun*[2]. L17.
[Telugu *tōpu*, Tamil *tōppu*.]
In the Indian subcontinent: a grove or plantation of trees, esp. mango trees.

tope /təʊp/ *noun*[3]. E19.
[Panjabi *thūp*, *thop* barrow, mound, app. rel. to Sanskrit *stūpa* STUPA.]
In the Indian subcontinent: a mound or barrow, *esp.* the ruins of an ancient stupa.

tope /təʊp/ *verb*[1]. M17.
[Origin uncertain: cf. TOP *verb*[2].]
†**1** *verb trans.* = TOP *verb*[2] 1. Only in M17.
2 *verb trans.* = TOP *verb*[2] 4. *obsolete* exc. *dial.* L17.
3 *verb intrans.* Incline or fall to one side; topple over; fall asleep; die. Cf. TOP *verb*[2] 3. *dial.* L18.

tope /təʊp/ *verb*[2] *trans. & intrans.* Now *arch. & literary.* M17.
[Perh. alt. of TOP *verb*[2].]
Drink (alcohol) in large quantities, esp. habitually.
■ **toper** *noun* L17.

topectomy /təˈpɛktəmi/ *noun*. Now *rare*. M20.
[from TOP(O- + -ECTOMY.]
MEDICINE. (An instance of) a surgical operation in which selected areas are removed from the cerebral cortex as a treatment for mental illness.

topee *noun* var. of TOPI *noun*[1].

topgallant /tɒpˈgal(ə)nt, təˈgal-/ *adjective & noun*. E16.
[from TOP *noun*[1] + GALLANT *adjective*, as making a gallant show in comparison with the lower tops.]
▶**A** *adjective*. **1** NAUTICAL. Designating or pertaining to a part of the mast next above the topmast. E16. ▶**b** Of a wind or the weather: allowing topgallant sails to be used. L17. ▶**c** Of a rail, deck, etc.: extending above the adjoining parts. M19.
2 *fig.* Grand, fine, excellent. *arch.* E17.
1 ***topgallant mast***, ***topgallant sail***, ***topgallant yard***, etc.
▶**B** *noun*. †**1** NAUTICAL. A top or platform at the head of a topmast (see TOP *noun*[1] 10). Only in 16.
2 NAUTICAL. A topgallant mast; a topgallant sail. L16.
3 *transf. & fig.* The most elevated part *of* anything; the highest point or pitch. *arch.* L16.

topgi *noun* var. of TOPCHEE.

toph /təʊf/ *noun*. Now *rare*. Also **tophe**. M16.
[from TOPHUS.]
†**1** In full ***toph stone***. = TOPHUS 1. M16–E19.
2 MEDICINE. = TOPHUS 2. L16.
■ **toˈphaceous** *adjective* †(*a*) sandy, gritty; rough, stony; (*b*) MEDICINE gritty or calcareous, as the matter deposited in gout: L17.

tophaike /təʊˈfeɪk/ *noun*. E19.
[Colloq. Turkish *tüfek* (literary Turkish *tüfenk* from Persian *tufang*), perh. from Persian *tufak* from Old Turkish *tüvek* blowpipe.]
Hist. A Turkish musket.

tophe *noun* var. of TOPH.

top-heavy /tɒpˈhɛvi/ *adjective*. M16.
[from TOP *noun*[1] + HEAVY *adjective*.]
1 Disproportionately heavy at the top, esp. so as to be in danger of overbalancing. M16.
2 Of a person: drunk. *arch. slang.* L17.
3 *transf.* **a** Of a business, organization, etc.: having a disproportionately large number of people in senior administrative positions; overcapitalized. M20. ▶**b** Of a woman: having a disproportionately large bust. *colloq.* L20.

> 🕮 **1** *Which?* The Moulinex was . . top heavy and could easily fall over if knocked. *fig.*: S. NAIPAUL That lengthy charter so top-heavy with ringing preambles.

■ **top-heavily** *adverb* E20. **top-heaviness** *noun* M19.

Tophet /ˈtəʊfɪt/ *noun*. LME.
[Hebrew *Tōpet*, a place in the Valley of Hinnom near Jerusalem, used for idolatrous worship and later for burning refuse.]
1 Hell. LME.
2 *fig.* A place or state of misery or turmoil. E17.
■ **To'phetic** *adjective* (*rare*) = TOPHETICAL E20. **To'phetical** *adjective* of, pertaining to, or of the nature of Tophet L17.

tophus /ˈtəʊfəs/ *noun*. Pl. **tophi** /ˈtəʊfʌɪ/. M16.
[Latin *tophus*, *tofus* loose porous stones of various kinds, whence Italian *tufo*, French *tuf*: see also TUFA, TUFF *noun*.]
1 A porous stone deposit; tufa, travertine. M16.
2 MEDICINE. A deposit of sodium urate which forms around a joint, in the pinna of the ear, etc., in cases of gout. Also, gravel, or a stone or calculus, formed within the body. E17.
■ †**tophous** *adjective* of the nature of a stony or calcareous concretion M17–M18.

topi /ˈtəʊpi/ *noun*[1]. *Anglo-Indian.* Also **topee**. M19.
[Hindi *topī* hat.]
A hat; *spec.* a pith helmet, a sola topi.

topi /ˈtəʊpi/ *noun*[2]. L19.
[Mende.]
A large African antelope, *Damaliscus lunatus*, which is usu. reddish-brown with black patches, has a sloping back, and is found widely on grassland and savannah; *spec.* the race of this occurring in the coastal region of E. Africa. Cf. KORRIGUM, TIANG, TSESSEBI.

topiaria /təʊpɪˈɛːrɪə/ *noun*. *rare*. L16.
[Latin, fem. of *topiarius*: see TOPIARY.]
The art of topiary.

topiarius /təʊpɪˈɛːrɪəs/ *noun*. *rare*. Pl. ***-rii*** /-rɪʌɪ, -rɪiː/. E18.
[Latin: see next.]
An ornamental gardener; a topiarist.

topiary /ˈtəʊpɪəri/ *adjective & noun*. L16.
[French *topiaire* from Latin *topiarius* (adjective) of or pertaining to ornamental gardening, (noun) ornamental gardener, from *topia* (sc. *opera*) ornamental gardening from Greek *topia* pl. of *topion* dim. of *topos* place: see -ARY[1].]
▶**A** *adjective*. Concerned with, involving, or formed by the clipping of shrubs, trees, etc., into ornamental geometric, animal, or other shapes. L16.
▶**B** *noun*. The art of clipping shrubs etc. into ornamental shapes; an example of this, a piece of topiary work. E20.
■ **topiarian** /-pɪˈɛːrɪən/ *adjective & noun* (*a*) *adjective* = TOPIARY *adjective*; (*b*) *noun* = TOPIARIST: L17. **topiarist** *noun* a practitioner of the art of topiary E20.

topic /ˈtɒpɪk/ *noun & adjective*. L15.
[As noun from Latin *topica*, from Greek *topika* (adjective) in *ta topika* lit. 'matters concerning commonplaces' (title of a treatise by Aristotle), from *topos* place, commonplace; as adjective from Greek *topikos*, from *topos*.]
▶**A** *noun*. **I 1** RHETORIC. In *pl.* A set of general rules, maxims, or ideas on various subjects; a work containing these, *spec.* that by Aristotle. Now *rare*. L15.

2 †**a** An argument, *esp.* a stock argument. M17–M19. ▸**b** A category under which arguments or subjects may be arranged. *obsolete* exc. as in sense 3. M17.

3 A theme or subject for a book, essay, sermon, lecture, conversation, etc. E18. ▸**b** *LINGUISTICS.* A part of a sentence which indicates what is being talked about and about which the rest of the sentence makes a statement, asks a question, etc. Opp. COMMENT *noun* 5. Cf. THEME *noun* 1c. M20.

> **2a** SIR W. SCOTT Interrupting those tears to suggest topics of hope and comfort. **3** A. J. CRONIN Giving Miss Page matter for serious reflection and another topic to discuss. J. BERGER The scandal . . was still a topic of conversation. A. KENNY He had decided and outspoken views on a variety of topics.

▸†**II 4** *MEDICINE.* A remedy applied externally to a particular part of the body. L16–M18.

▸†**B** *adjective.* **I 1** Of a rule or argument: applicable in most but not all cases; not demonstrative, but merely probable. L16–M17.

▸**II 2** = TOPICAL *adjective* 1. E17–L18.

3 *MEDICINE.* = TOPICAL *adjective* 2. Only in 17.

topical /ˈtɒpɪk(ə)l/ *adjective & noun.* L16.
[from Greek *topikos* + -AL[1]: see prec.]
▸**A** *adjective.* **I 1** Of or pertaining to a place; local. L16.

2 *MEDICINE.* Affecting or applied externally to a particular part of the body. E17.

> **2** *Chicago Sun-Times* Topical anesthetics containing benzocaine . . take the sting out of sunburns.

▸**II** †**3** = TOPIC *adjective* 1. L16–E18.

4 Of or pertaining to a topic or subject of an essay, conversation, etc. M19.

5 Of or pertaining to current affairs or a subject in the news etc. L19.

> **5** M. MOORCOCK Topical songs about our defeats and victories in the War. I. MURDOCH Nor was he interested in politics, or topical matters generally.

▸**B** *noun.* †**1** *MEDICINE.* = TOPIC *noun* 4. *rare.* Only in M17.

2 *Hist.* A film dealing with topical events. E20.

■ **topiˈcality** *noun* the quality of being topical or current E20. **topicaliˈzation** *noun* (*LINGUISTICS*) the action of topicalizing a part of a sentence M20. **topicalize** *verb trans.* (*LINGUISTICS*) make (a part of a sentence) into a topic L20. **topically** *adverb* M17.

topinambour /tɒpɪˈnambʊə/ *noun.* Also (earlier) †**-bou**. M17.
[French †*topinambou*, now *-bour*, from Portuguese *tupinambo(r)* alt. of *tupinamba* TUPINAMBA *adjective* (sc. *batata* potato).]
The Jerusalem artichoke, *Helianthus tuberosus*.

topknot /ˈtɒpnɒt/ *noun.* L17.
[from TOP *noun*[1] + KNOT *noun*[1].]
1 a Chiefly *Hist.* A decorative knot or bow of ribbon worn on the top of the head esp. in the 18th cent. L17. ▸**b** A tuft or crest of hair growing on the top of the head; a bun or short pony-tail worn on the crown of the head; a crest on the head of a bird; *Austral. & NZ* wool shorn from the top of a sheep's head. E18. ▸**c** The head. *slang.* M19.

2 *transf.* **a** A person who wears a topknot. *rare.* L17. ▸**b** Any of several small flatfishes of the genera *Zeugopterus* and *Phrynorhombus* (family Scopthalmidae), which have the dorsal and anal fins continuing as lobes under the tail, and occur locally off NE Atlantic coasts; esp. *Z. punctatus*, of British and French waters. M19.

Comb.: **topknot pigeon** either of two Australian crested pigeons, *Ocyphaps lophotes*, which has a slender crest, and (*spec.*) *Lopholaimus antarcticus*, which has a flattened crest and typically occurs in flocks in eastern Australian forests.

■ **topknotted** *adjective* (of a bird) having a topknot M19.

Töpler pump /ˈtəːplə pʌmp/ *noun phr.* Also **Toepler pump**. L19.
[from August Joseph Ignaz *Töpler* (1836–1912), German physicist + PUMP *noun*[1].]
PHYSICS. A pump in which the vessel to be evacuated is connected via a valve to a reservoir, which is connected to a reservoir of mercury, so that lowering the last draws gas out of the vessel into the reservoir and raising it expels the gas.

topless /ˈtɒplɪs/ *adjective.* L16.
[from TOP *noun*[1] + -LESS.]
1 Having no top. L16.

2 *fig.* Seeming to have no top; immensely or immeasurably high. L16. ▸†**b** Supreme, paramount. *rare* (Shakes.). Only in E17.

3 a Designating or pertaining to a (woman's) garment that does not cover the breasts and upper body. M20. ▸**b** Esp. of a woman: naked or almost naked above the waist; bare-breasted. M20. ▸**c** Involving or portraying a topless woman or topless women; performed topless; (of a place, esp. a beach) at which women go topless; (of a bar) employing topless waitresses. M20.

> **3c** *Times* Topless sunbathing is . . well-established . . on a great many British beaches. *Daily Mirror* Releasing a topless photograph of her to newspapers. *New Scientist* Testifying in court on behalf of a topless restaurant.

■ **toplessness** *noun* M20.

toploftical /ˌtɒpˈlɒftɪk(ə)l/ *adjective. arch. joc.* E19.
[App. from TOP *adjective* + LOFT *noun* (in sense gallery or (upper) storey) + -ICAL, after *tyrannical* etc.]
Haughty.

toplofty /tɒpˈlɒfti/ *adjective. colloq.* (chiefly *US*). M19.
[App. from TOP *noun*[1] + LOFTY *adjective*, or formed as prec.]
Haughty.
■ **toploftiness** *noun* L19.

topmast /ˈtɒpmɑːst, -məst/ *noun.* L15.
[from TOP *adjective* + MAST *noun*[1].]
NAUTICAL. A mast attached to the top of a lower mast; *spec.* the second section of a mast above the deck, formerly the uppermost mast, later surmounted by the topgallant mast.

topmost /ˈtɒpməʊst/ *adjective.* L17.
[from TOP *adjective* + -MOST.]
Uppermost, highest.

topo /ˈtɒpəʊ/ *adjective & noun. US colloq.* L20.
[Abbreviation.]
▸**A** *adjective.* Topographic. L20.
▸**B** *noun.* Pl. **-os**. A topographic map. L20.

topo- /ˈtɒpəʊ/ *combining form* of Greek *topos* place: see -O-. Before a vowel also **top-**.
■ **topoˈcentric** *adjective* (*ASTRONAUTICS*) (of a parameter of a spacecraft or an orbit) measured relative to a point on the earth's surface; cf. GEOCENTRIC: M20. **topocline** *noun* (*BIOLOGY*) a cline associated with variations in a taxon through its geographical range M20. **toˈpogenous** *adjective* (*ECOLOGY*) (of a bog, peat, etc.) formed as the result of geographical features (cf. OMBROGENOUS, SOLIGENOUS): M20. **topoinhiˈbition** *noun* (*BIOLOGY*) the inhibition of cell multiplication by contact with other cells L20. **topoˈisomer** *noun* (chiefly *BIOCHEMISTRY*) a topologically distinct isomer L20. **topoiˈsomerase** *noun* (*BIOCHEMISTRY*) an enzyme which alters the supercoiled form of a DNA molecule L20. **topotype** *noun* (*TAXONOMY*) a specimen from the locality where the original type specimen was obtained L19.

topochemical /tɒpəʊˈkɛmɪk(ə)l/ *adjective.* E20.
[from prec. + CHEMICAL *adjective*.]
1 *ENTOMOLOGY.* Pertaining to or designating an insect's capacity to perceive spatial relationships through the sense of smell. E20.

2 *CHEMISTRY.* Of or pertaining to topochemistry. E20.
■ **topochemically** *adverb* M20.

topochemistry /tɒpəʊˈkɛmɪstri/ *noun.* M20.
[from TOPO- + CHEMISTRY.]
The chemistry of reactions as affected by local variations in the structure of the medium on or in which they occur.

topograph /ˈtɒpəgrɑːf/ *noun.* M19.
[from TOPO- + -GRAPH.]
1 A representation or description of the places in a particular area. *rare.* M19.

2 *CRYSTALLOGRAPHY.* A photograph taken, usu. with X-rays, to exhibit the variation over the surface of a crystal of some physical or structural characteristic. M20.

topography /təˈpɒgrəfi/ *noun.* LME.
[Late Latin *topographia* from Greek, formed as TOPO-: see -GRAPHY.]
1 A detailed description, delineation, or representation on a map of the features of a place. LME.

2 The detailed description or mapping of the natural and artificial features of a town, district, etc. LME. ▸**b** *transf.* The identification of the locality or local distribution of a thing. *rare.* M17.

3 The surface features of a place or region collectively. M17.

4 *ANATOMY & ZOOLOGY.* The determination and description of the arrangement of parts in a region of the body, or of the external anatomy of an animal. M19.

> **2** R. G. COLLINGWOOD Literature . . devoted to sentimental topography: books about the charm of Sussex, the magic of Oxford. *Modern Painters* Landscape was . . more than a matter of topography. **3** O. HENRY As straight as the topography of West Texas permitted. *fig.*: T. REID I am not so well acquainted with the topography of the mind.

■ **topographer** *noun* E17. **topoˈgraphic** *adjective* M17. **topoˈgraphical** *adjective* L16. **topoˈgraphically** *adverb* in a topological manner, with respect to topography E17. **topographist** *noun* (*rare*) L18. **topographize** *verb* (*rare*) (**a**) *verb trans.* describe topographically; (**b**) *verb intrans.* undertake topographical research: L18.

topoi *noun* pl. of TOPOS.

topological /tɒpəˈlɒdʒɪk(ə)l/ *adjective.* E18.
[from next + -ICAL.]
Of or pertaining to topology.
topological invariant, **topological property** *MATH.* a thing which is invariant under a topological transformation. **topological space** *MATH.* an abstract space together with a topology (sense 3b) on it. **topological transformation** *MATH.* = HOMOEOMORPHISM 2.
■ **topologic** *adjective* = TOPOLOGICAL L19. **topologically** *adverb* E18. **topologiˈzation** *noun* (*MATH.*) the process of topologizing something M20. **toˈpologize** *verb trans.* (*MATH.*) make into a topological space; chiefly as **topologized** *ppl adjective*: M20.

topology /təˈpɒlədʒi/ *noun.* M17.
[from TOPO- + -LOGY.]
†**1** The branch of botany that deals with the habitats of plants. Only in M17.

2 The branch of knowledge that deals with the topography of a particular region and esp. how this reflects its history. M19.

3 *MATH.* **a** The branch of mathematics that deals with those properties of figures and surfaces which are independent of size and shape and are unchanged by any deformation that is continuous, and with those of abstract spaces that are invariant under homoeomorphic transformations. L19. ▸**b** A family of open subsets of an abstract space such that the union of any of the subsets and the intersection of any two of them are members of the family, together with the space itself and the null set. M20.

4 a (The branch of mathematics that deals with) the topological properties *of* something. E20. ▸**b** The way in which constituent parts are interrelated or arranged. M20.
■ **topologist** *noun* E20.

toponium /tɒˈpəʊnɪəm/ *noun.* L20.
[from TOP *noun*[1] + -ONIUM, after *positronium*.]
PARTICLE PHYSICS. A bound state of a top quark and a top antiquark.

toponomastic /ˌtɒpɒnəˈmastɪk/ *noun & adjective.* E20.
[from TOPO- + ONOMASTIC.]
▸**A** *noun sing.* & (*rare*) in *pl.* = TOPONYMY. E20.
▸**B** *adjective.* Of or pertaining to place-names. E20.

toponym /ˈtɒpənɪm/ *noun.* L19.
[from TOPO- + -NYM.]
1 *ZOOLOGY & ANATOMY.* A name for a region of the body. Now *rare.* L19.

2 A place-name, esp. a descriptive one, usu. derived from a topographical feature of the place. Also, any name, as a personal name etc., derived from a place-name. M20.
■ **topoˈnymic** *adjective & noun* (**a**) *adjective* of or pertaining to toponymy; (**b**) *noun* = TOPONYM 2: L19.

toponymy /tɒˈpɒnɪmi/ *noun.* L19.
[formed as prec. + -Y[3].]
The branch of knowledge that deals with place-names.
■ **toponymist** *noun* M19.

topos /ˈtɒpɒs/ *noun.* Pl. **-poi** /-pɔɪ/. M20.
[Greek: see TOPIC.]
A traditional theme in a literary composition; a rhetorical or literary formula.

toposcope /ˈtɒpəskəʊp/ *noun.* E20.
[from TOPO- + -SCOPE.]
1 A board, dial, etc., erected at a viewpoint to show the direction of designated features of the landscape. E20.

2 *MEDICINE.* An instrument used for toposcopy. M20.
■ **topoˈscopic** *adjective* (*MEDICINE*) of or pertaining to toposcopy M20. **toposcopy** /tɒˈpɒskəpi/ *noun* (*MEDICINE*) simultaneous observation of the electrical activity in different areas of the brain by means of electrodes connected to separate oscilloscopes etc. M20.

topotaxy /ˈtɒpəʊtaksi/ *noun.* M20.
[from TOPO- + -TAXY, after *epitaxy*.]
CRYSTALLOGRAPHY. A solid state reaction or process whereby crystals are produced having the same orientation as those in the original substance.
■ **topoˈtactic** *adjective* of or pertaining to topotaxy L20. **topoˈtactical** *adjective* = TOPOTACTIC M20. **topoˈtactically** *adverb* by means of topotaxy M20.

topped /tɒpt/ *adjective.* LME.
[from TOP *noun*[1], *verb*[1]: see -ED[2], -ED[1].]
1 Having a top or tops, esp. of a specified kind. LME.

2 That has been topped; having the top removed. E18.

> **1** *Horse & Rider* Scarlet jacket with topped boots and cap. ARTHUR LYONS A glass-topped drawerless desk.

topper /ˈtɒpə/ *noun & verb.* L17.
[from TOP *noun*[1], *verb*[1] + -ER[1].]
▸**A** *noun.* **I 1** A person who or thing which tops something; *esp.* a machine which removes the tops from growing crops. L17. ▸**b** A person who makes or adds the top to something. L19.

2 A culminating action or remark; *esp.* an outrageous one, or one that cannot be capped. M20.

3 A hard protective lightweight cover or shell mounted on the back or bed of a pick-up truck. Also, a type of camper mounted on a truck bed. *US.* M20.

▸**II 4** An exceptionally good person or thing; the best or one of the best of the kind. *colloq.* E19.

5 A blow on the head. *arch. slang.* L18.

6 A top hat. *colloq.* E19. ▸**b** A woman's short loose jacket or coat. Chiefly *N. Amer.* M20.

7 A cigar- or cigarette-end. *slang.* L19.

For other words beginning with *topo-* see the main alphabetic sequence of entries

▶ **B** *verb trans.* Knock on the head; kill by a blow on the head. *arch. slang.* **E19.**

toppie /ˈtɒpi/ *noun. S. Afr.* **L19.**
[Perh. from **TOPKNOT.**]
Any small dark-headed bulbul of the genus *Pycnonotus*, found in southern Africa, esp. the Cape bulbul, *P. capensis*.

topping /ˈtɒpɪŋ/ *noun.* **ME.**
[from **TOP** *verb*¹ + **-ING**¹.]
▶ **I 1 a** A thing forming a top to something else. **ME.** ▶**b** *spec.* A top layer or garnish put on food. **E20.**
2 In *pl.* The branches, shoots, etc., cut off from the tops of trees or plants. **M17.**
3 ANGLING. A feather from the crest of a golden pheasant used in some fishing-flies. **M19.**
4 A hill. Chiefly in place-names. *north.* **L19.**

📖 **1b** J. HELLER He ordered cheesecake with strawberry topping. *Which?* Pizza bases with .. cheese and tomato toppings.

▶ **II 5** The action of **TOP** *verb*¹. **E16.**

topping /ˈtɒpɪŋ/ *adjective.* **L17.**
[from **TOP** *verb*¹ + **-ING**².]
†**1** Very high. **L17–E18.**
2 *fig.* Very high in position, rank, estimation, etc.; pre-eminent, distinguished. **L17.**
3 Of high quality; excellent. *arch. slang.* **E18.**
4 Domineering; boastful. *US colloq.* **E19.**
■ **toppingly** *adverb* (*arch. slang*) **M18.** **toppingness** *noun* (*US colloq., rare*) **L19.**

toppish /ˈtɒpɪʃ/ *adjective. Stock Exchange slang.* **L20.**
[from **TOP** *noun*¹ + **-ISH**¹.]
= **TOPPY** 4.

topple /ˈtɒp(ə)l/ *noun*¹. Long *dial. rare.* **LME.**
[from **TOP** *noun*¹ + **-LE**¹.]
A crest, a tuft.

topple /ˈtɒp(ə)l/ *noun*². *rare.* **E20.**
[from the verb.]
An act of toppling.

topple /ˈtɒp(ə)l/ *verb.* **M16.**
[from **TOP** *verb*¹ + **-LE**³.]
†**1** *verb intrans.* Roll or tumble about. Only in **M16.**
2 *verb intrans.* Fall over from a great height or as if top-heavy; fall headlong. Usu. foll. by adverbs & prepositions. **L16.** ▶**b** Turn somersaults. *dial.* **E19.**
3 *verb trans.* Cause to fall over; *esp.* (*fig.*) overthrow (a government etc.). **L16.**
4 *verb trans.* Cause to lean unsteadily. *rare.* **M17.**
5 *verb intrans.* Lean over unsteadily; totter as if on the point of falling. **E19.**

📖 **2** E. BLUNDEN A church steeple in flames, finally toppling to earth. A. CARTER I lost balance and toppled forward into a .. shallow pool. *New Musical Express* The .. bus caught fire after toppling down an embankment. **3** N. FARAH I'll be in this country .. until this dictatorship is toppled by another. D. LEAVITT A pyramid of toilet paper that she had accidentally toppled. F. FORSYTH If someone toppled King Fahd .. who would it likely be? **5** K. CROSSLEY-HOLLAND Cauldrons toppled and fell from the shelf.

■ **topply** *adjective* liable to topple over **E20.**

toppy /ˈtɒpi/ *adjective. colloq. & slang.* **M16.**
[from **TOP** *noun*¹ + **-Y**¹.]
†**1** Having a top or tops. *rare.* Only in **M16.**
2 Of an animal: of superior quality. *US.* **L19.**
3 MUSIC. Containing too much treble. **M20.**
4 Of a market, currency, etc.: high and unstable. *Stock Exchange slang.* **M20.**

TOPS /tɒps/ *abbreviation.*
Hist. Training opportunities scheme (a system of government-funded vocational training programmes).

tops /tɒps/ *adverb. colloq.* **M20.**
[Pl. of **TOP** *noun*¹.]
At the most; at the latest.

📖 *New Yorker* You'll be back .. by four, tops. Q The crowd stiffens. Bob Dylan is five feet, tops.

topsail /ˈtɒpseɪl, ˈtɒps(ə)l/ *noun.* **LME.**
[from **TOP** *adjective* + **SAIL** *noun*¹.]
NAUTICAL. In a square-rigged vessel, the sail, or (in larger ships) either of two sails, next above the lower sail. In a fore-and-aft rigged vessel, a square or triangular sail set above the gaff.

topside /ˈtɒpsʌɪd/ *noun & adverb.* **L16.**
[from **TOP** *adjective* + **SIDE** *noun.*]
▶ **A** *noun.* **1** The upper side of something; *esp.* the upper part of a ship's side. **L16.**
2 The outer side of a round of beef, cut from between the leg and the aitchbone. **L19.**
3 (**T-**.) *The* upper or ruling class, the Establishment. *rare.* **M20.**
4 METEOROLOGY. The part of the ionosphere above the height at which the concentration of free electrons is greatest, i.e. above about 300 km (200 miles). Freq. *attrib.* **M20.**
5 In offshore drilling, an installation or piece of equipment above water. Freq. *attrib.* **L20.**
▶ **B** *adverb.* Also **-sides.** On or to the top; *esp.* on or to the upper deck of a ship. *colloq.* **L19.**

Topsider /ˈtɒpsʌɪdə/ *noun.* Also **t-.** **M20.**
[from prec. + **-ER**¹.]
A casual shoe, usu. made of canvas with a rubber sole. Usu. in *pl.*
¶ Proprietary name in the US.

topsy *noun* var. of **TUPSEE.**

topsy-turn /ˈtɒpsɪtəːn/ *verb trans.* Now *rare.* **L16.**
[from next: see **TURN** *verb.*]
Turn upside down; *fig.* throw into confusion.

topsy-turvy /tɒpsɪˈtəːvi/ *adverb, noun, adjective, & verb.* **E16.**
[1st elem. prob. from **TOP** *noun*¹, 2nd elem. prob. from **TERVE**, with **-Y**¹ added to both elems. to make a jingle: cf. **ARSY-VERSY.**]
▶ **A** *adverb.* Also (*Scot.*) **tapsalteerie** /taps(ə)lˈtiːri/. Upside down; with inversion of the natural or proper order, in or into utter confusion. **E16.**

📖 DICKENS A chaos of carts .. lay topsy-turvy at the bottom of a .. hill. P. H. JOHNSON It's rather topsy-turvy, though—Sausage rolls after jam tarts.

▶ **B** *noun.* An act of turning upside down; *fig.* inversion of the proper order, a state of utter confusion. **L16.**

📖 E. O'NEILL It's a shame .. to .. have to start in with things in such a topsy-turvy.

▶ **C** *adjective.* Turned upside down; *fig.* utterly confused. **E17.**

📖 BEVERLEY CLEARY Full of .. questions .. to ask about this topsy-turvy household.

▶ **D** *verb trans.* Turn upside down; *fig.* throw into utter confusion. **E17.**

📖 *Guardian* Some addict has topsy turvied a litter-bin.

■ **topsy-turvily** *adverb* in a topsy-turvy manner **L19.** **topsy-turviness** *noun* topsy-turvy quality or condition **M19.** **topsy-turvydom** *noun* utter confusion **L19.** **topsy-turvyhood** *noun* (*rare*) = **TOPSY-TURVINESS** **L18.**

topsy-versy /tɒpsɪˈvəːsi/ *adverb. colloq. rare.* **M18.**
[Blend of **TOPSY-TURVY** and **ARSY-VERSY.**]
Upside down.

toque /təʊk/ *noun.* **E16.**
[French, corresp. obscurely to Italian *tocca, tocco*, Spanish *toca*, Portuguese *touca* cap, woman's head-dress, of unkn. origin.]
1 Orig. (*Hist.*), a type of hat with a full pouched crown and a narrow closely turned-up brim, fashionable amongst both sexes in the 16th cent. Now, a small hat without a projecting brim, or with a very small or closely turned-up brim. **E16.** ▶**b** *Hist.* A pad used in hairdressing to give additional height. *rare.* **E19.**
2 = **TUQUE.** *Canad.* **L19.**
3 A tall white hat with a full pouched crown, worn by chefs. **M20.**
Comb.: **toque macaque**, **toque monkey** a Sri Lankan macaque, *Macaca sinica*, which resembles the bonnet macaque of southern India.

toquilla /təˈkiːjə/ *noun.* **L19.**
[Amer. Spanish use of Spanish = small gauze head-dress, dim. of *toca* **TOQUE.**]
The jipijapa plant, *Carludovica palmata*; the fibre obtained from this plant.

tor /tɔː/ *noun.*
[Old English *torr*, perh. of British origin (cf. Old Welsh *torr* bulge, belly, Gaelic *tòrr* bulging hill).]
A rocky peak or hill, esp. in Cornwall or Devon (freq. in place-names). Formerly also, a (pile of) rocks on the top of a hill.
Comb.: **tor ouzel** the ring ouzel.

tora /ˈtɔːrə/ *noun.* **L19.**
[Amharic.]
A hartebeest, *Alcelaphus buselaphus*, of a rare subspecies found in NE Africa. Also ***tora hartebeest***.

Toradja /tɒˈrɑːdʒə/ *noun & adjective.* **E20.**
[Toradja.]
▶ **A** Pl. same, **-s.**
1 A member of an Austronesian people of central Sulawesi, Indonesia. **E20.**
2 The language of this people. **M20.**
▶ **B** *attrib.* or as *adjective.* Of or pertaining to the Toradja or their language. **M20.**

Torah /ˈtɔːrə, ˈtəʊ-/ *noun & adjective.* **L16.**
[Hebrew *tōrāh* direction, instruction, doctrine, law, from *yārāh* throw, show, direct, instruct.]
▶ **A** *noun.* (The teaching of) the will of God as revealed in Mosaic law; (a scroll containing) the Pentateuch. **L16.**
▶ **B** *adjective.* Of or pertaining to the Torah; *esp.* enclosing or decorating the scroll of the Torah. **E20.**

torana /ˈtɔːrana/ *noun.* **L19.**
[Sanskrit *toraṇa* gate, arched portal.]
In the Indian subcontinent, a sacred Buddhist gateway, consisting of a pair of uprights with one or more (usu. three) crosspieces and elaborate carving.

torba /ˈtɔːbə/ *noun.* **E20.**
[Arab. *turba* dust, soil.]
A cement made from crushed limestone used as a traditional flooring in Malta.

torbanite /ˈtɔːbənʌɪt/ *noun.* **M19.**
[from *Torbane* Hill, West Lothian, Scotland: see **-ITE**¹.]
GEOLOGY. A deep brown shale containing the remains of microscopic algae and yielding straight-chain hydrocarbons and gas.

torbernite /ˈtɔːbənʌɪt/ *noun.* **M19.**
[from *Torbernus* Latinized form of *Torbern* O. Bergman (d. 1784), Swedish chemist + **-ITE**¹.]
MINERALOGY. A hydrated copper uranium phosphate occurring as bright green tabular crystals of the tetragonal system.

torc *noun* var. of **TORQUE** *noun*¹.

torch /tɔːtʃ/ *noun & verb.* **ME.**
[Old & mod. French *torche* from Proto-Romance, from Latin *torqua* var. of *torques* necklace, wreath, from *torquere* twist.]
▶ **A** *noun.* **1** A portable hand-held light or lamp; *spec.* (***a***) a piece of wood, cloth, etc., soaked in tallow or other flammable substance and lit for illumination; (***b***) a small battery-powered electric lamp (also ***electric torch***). **ME.** ▶**b** Any portable appliance which burns with a concentrated intense flame used for welding, stripping paint, etc.; *spec.* (chiefly *N. Amer.*) a blowlamp. **E20.** ▶**c** An arsonist. *US slang.* **M20.**
2 The great mullein, *Verbascum thapsus*, so called from its tall spike of yellow flowers. Usu. in *pl.* **M16.**
3 *fig.* A source of heat, illumination, enlightenment, etc. **M17.**

📖 **1** W. STYRON Torches made of .. stakes and rags soaked in .. turpentine. P. D. JAMES Follow the jerking moon of her torch's beam. **3** BOSW. SMITH The torch of Greek learning and civilization was to be extinguished.

Phrases: **carry a torch for**, **hold a torch for** feel (esp. unrequited) love for. **hand on the torch**, **pass on the torch** pass on a tradition, learning, etc. **put to the torch** destroy by burning. **take up the torch** continue a tradition, take up a worthy cause.
Comb.: **torch-bearer** a person carrying a torch in a ceremony, demonstration, etc.; *fig.* a person giving guidance or enlightenment; **torch-carrying** the harbouring of (esp. unrequited) love; **torch-fish** a deep-sea angler-fish of the family Linophrynidae, having a luminous bulb on the first dorsal spine, above the eye; **torch-fishing** fishing by torchlight at night; **torch-flower** any of several plants bearing bright red or yellow flowers on a tall stem, suggesting a torch; *esp.* = ***torch-lily*** below; **torch-holder** (***a***) a torch-bearer; (***b***) a bracket or other device for supporting a torch; **torch lily** the red-hot poker (plants of the genus *Kniphofia*); **torch-man** (***a***) a torch-bearer; (***b***) *slang* an arsonist; **torch-race** GREEK HISTORY a race held at certain festivals, in which the runners carried lighted torches; **torch singer** a singer of torch songs; **torch singing** the singing of torch songs; **torch song** a popular song of unrequited love; **torch-thistle** any of several treelike cacti of the genus *Cereus* (or formerly included in it), used by American Indians as torches; **torchwood** (***a***) resinous wood suitable for making torches; (***b***) any of several trees of the genus *Amyris* of the rue family, having resinous wood, esp. *A. balsamifera*, of the W. Indies and Florida.

▶ **B** *verb.* **1** *verb intrans.* Flare like a torch; catch fire. *dial.* **M19.**
2 *verb intrans.* Catch fish etc. by torchlight. *N. Amer.* **L19.**
3 *verb trans.* Set alight, set fire to; destroy by fire. *slang.* **M20.**

📖 **3** M. AMIS Half way through the .. coffee I torched a cigarette. *New Yorker* He had torched his office to collect on the insurance.

■ **torched** *adjective* provided with or illuminated by a torch or torches **E19.** **torcher** *noun* (***a***) *rare* a torch-bearer; (***b***) *US slang* a torch singer: **E17.** **torchless** *adjective* **E19.** **torchy** *adjective* (***a***) *rare* full of torches; (***b***) *colloq.* (chiefly *N. Amer.*) of, pertaining to, or characteristic of a torch song or torch singer: **E17.**

torchère /tɔːˈʃɛː, *foreign* tɔrʃɛːr/ *noun.* Pl. pronounced same. **E20.**
[French, formed as **TORCH** *noun.*]
A tall ornamental flat-topped stand for a candlestick.

torchlight /ˈtɔːtʃlʌɪt/ *noun & adjective.* **ME.**
[from **TORCH** *noun* + **LIGHT** *noun.*]
▶ **A** *noun.* **1** The light of a torch; illumination by a torch or torches. Formerly also (*rare*), a torch. **ME.**
2 Dusk. Long *rare* or *obsolete.* **M17.**
▶ **B** *adjective.* Performed or taking place by torchlight. **M19.**

📖 *New York Review of Books* He .. marched in a torchlight parade.

torchon /ˈtɔːʃ(ə)n, *foreign* tɔrʃɔ̃/ *noun.* **M19.**
[French = duster, dish-cloth, from *torcher* wipe.]
In full ***torchon lace***. A coarse loose-textured kind of bobbin lace with geometrical designs.

torcular /ˈtɔːkjʊlə/ *noun & adjective.* Now *rare* or *obsolete.* M17.
[Latin = press for wine or oil.]
ANATOMY. ▶**A** *noun.* In full ***torcular Herophili*** /hɛˈrɒfɪlʌɪ/ [of Herophilus]. The depression in the occipital region at which the sinuses of the dura mater meet. M17.
▶**B** *adjective.* Of or pertaining to this depression. M17.

tordion /ˈtɔːdɪən/ *noun.* Now *Hist.* Also **tour-**. M16.
[French from Old French *tourdion*, *-eon*, from *tordre* twist.]
MUSIC. A dance similar to a 16th-cent. galliard but less vigorous.

tore /tɔː/ *noun*[1]. M17.
[French formed as TORUS.]
1 ARCHITECTURE. = TORUS 1. M17.
2 GEOMETRY. = TORUS 4. *rare.* M19.

tore /tɔː/ *noun*[2]. Chiefly *dial.* E18.
[Origin unkn.: cf. TOR-GRASS.]
Long coarse grass remaining in the field in winter or spring. Also ***tore grass***.

tore *verb pa. t. & pple*: see TEAR *verb*[1].

toreador /ˈtɒrɪədɔː, ˌtɒrɪəˈdɔː/ *noun.* Pl. **-s**, **-es** /-ɪz/. E17.
[Spanish, from *torear* fight bulls, from TORO.]
A bullfighter, *esp.* one on horseback. Cf. TORERO.
Comb.: **toreador pants** (chiefly *US*) tight-fitting calf-length women's trousers.

torenia /tɒˈriːnɪə/ *noun.* M19.
[mod. Latin (see below), from Olaf *Torén* (1718–53), chaplain to the Swedish East India Company + -IA[1].]
Any of various plants of the genus *Torenia*, of the figwort family native to subtropical and tropical Africa with tubular two-lipped blue, purple, etc., flowers; *esp.* one grown for ornament.

tore-out /ˈtɔːraʊt/ *noun.* E20.
[from *tore* dial. pa. pple of TEAR *verb*[1] + OUT *adverb*.]
A small sailing boat.

torero /tɒˈrɛːrəʊ, *foreign* toˈrero/ *noun.* Pl. **-os** /-əʊz, *foreign* -ɔs/. E18.
[Spanish, from TORO.]
A bullfighter, *esp.* one on foot. Cf. TOREADOR.

toreutic /təˈruːtɪk/ *adjective.* M19.
[Greek *toreutikos*, from *toreuein* work in relief etc.: see -IC.]
Of or pertaining to toreutics.

toreutics /təˈruːtɪks/ *noun.* M19.
[from prec.: see -ICS.]
The art of working in metal or ivory, *esp.* the art of chasing, carving, and embossing metal as practised in ancient cultures.

torfle /ˈtɔːf(ə)l/ *verb intrans.* Long *rare* or *obsolete* exc. *Scot.* L16.
[Origin unkn.]
1 Decline in health, pine away. L16.
2 Tumble, toss about. E19.

torgant /ˈtɔːg(ə)nt/ *adjective. rare.* E19.
[App. from Latin *torquent-* pa. ppl stem of *torquere*: see TORQUED, -ENT.]
HERALDRY. S-shaped. Cf. TORQUED 1.

torgoch /ˈtɔːgɒk, -x/ *noun.* E17.
[Welsh = red-belly.]
A red-bellied form of the char, *Salvelinus alpinus*, found in certain Welsh lakes.

tor-grass /ˈtɔːgrɑːs/ *noun.* M20.
[Prob. specific use of *tore grass* (see TORE *noun*[2]), erron. assoc. with TOR.]
A tall tussock-forming grass of chalk and limestone pasture, *Brachypodium pinnatum*.

torgsin /ˈtɔːgsɪn/ *noun & adjective.* M20.
[Russian, contr. of *vsesoyuznoe ob"edinenie po torgovlya s inostrantsami* the All-Union Association for Trade with Foreigners.]
Hist. (Of, pertaining to, or designating) a Soviet trading organization in the 1930s which sold goods for foreign currency.

Torgut /ˈtɔːgʊt/ *noun & adjective.* L19.
[Prob. from Mongolian.]
Hist. ▶**A** *noun.* Pl. **-s**, same. A member of a migratory Mongol people whose descendants settled in China. L19.
▶**B** *attrib.* or as *adjective.* Of or pertaining to this people. L19.

tori /ˈtɔːri/ *noun*[1]. M20.
[Japanese, lit. 'taking'.]
JUDO. The active partner in the performance of a hold, throw, etc.
¶ Cf. SUMOTORI.

tori *noun*[2] *pl.* see TORUS.

toric /ˈtɒrɪk, ˈtɔːrɪk/ *adjective & noun.* L19.
[from TORUS + -IC.]
▶**A** *adjective.* Pertaining to or having the form of (part of) a torus; *spec.* (esp. of a lens) having a surface curved like part of a torus, the radius of curvature having a minimum value in one direction and a maximum value in the direction at right angles to this. L19.
▶**B** *noun.* A lens with a toric curvature. M20.

torii /ˈtɔːriː/ *noun.* Pl. same. E18.
[Japanese, from *tori* bird + *i* sit, perch.]
A ceremonial gateway of a Japanese Shinto shrine, with two uprights and two crosspieces.

toril /toˈril/ *noun.* Pl. **-es** /-ɛs/. L19.
[Spanish.]
Any of a series of pens confining the bull before a bull-fight, *esp.* the last pen leading to the ring.

Torinese /tɒrɪˈniːz/ *adjective & noun.* Also **Tur-** /t(j)ʊr-/. L19.
[Italian, from *Torino* Turin (see below): see -ESE.]
▶**A** *noun.* Pl. same.
1 A native or inhabitant of the city of Turin, NW Italy. L19.
2 The dialect of Italian spoken in Turin. M20.
▶**B** *adjective.* Of, pertaining to, or characteristic of Turin, its inhabitants, or dialect. L19.

torma /ˈtɔːmə/ *noun.* Pl. same, **-s**. L19.
[Tibetan.]
A sacrificial offering burned in a Tibetan Buddhist ceremony.

torment /ˈtɔːmɛnt/ *noun.* ME.
[Old French *torment*, (mod. also) *tourment*, from Latin *tormentum* engine for throwing missiles etc., instrument of torture, from *torquere* twist. Cf. TOURMENTE.]
▶**I 1** Orig., the infliction or suffering of torture. Later, (the condition of enduring) extreme pain or suffering; physical or mental agony. ME. ▶†**b** *spec.* Colic; = TORMINA. LME–L17.

📖 **1** G. STEIN Jeff . . always had this torment going on inside him. M. DAS I deserve all the torments hell can inflict.

▶**II 2** A cause of extreme pain, suffering, or anguish. Also, a source of worry or annoyance; a troublesome person. ME.
†**3** A violent storm; a tempest. Cf. TOURMENTE. ME–E17.
†**4** A missile-throwing device worked by torsion. LME–M16.

torment /tɔːˈmɛnt/ *verb trans.* ME.
[Old French *tormenter*, (mod. also) *tourmenter*, formed as prec. Cf. late Latin *tormentare*.]
1 Inflict torment on; afflict with extreme pain, suffering, or anguish. Now also, worry excessively, trouble, annoy. ME.
2 Agitate, disturb; shake or stir up (*lit. & fig.*). Now *rare* or *obsolete.* LME. ▶**b** *fig.* Twist, distort. *rare.* M17.

📖 **1** D. L. SAYERS Those nightmare doubts that . . torment us. O. MANNING Nothing could repel the tormenting flies that . . hit one's face. ISAIAH BERLIN History will not . . solve the great questions which have tormented . . every generation.

■ **tormented** *adjective* (*a*) tortured, pained, vexed; (*b*) *US slang* = DAMNED *adjective* 4: M16. **tormentedly** *adverb* L19. **tormentingly** *adverb* in a tormenting manner L16. †**tormentous** *adjective* (*rare*) = TORMENTUOUS L16–M17. **tormentress** *noun* a female tormentor LME. **tormentuous** *adjective* (*rare*) tormenting, torturing L16.

tormentil /ˈtɔːm(ə)ntɪl/ *noun.* LME.
[Old & mod. French *tormentille* from medieval Latin *tormentilla*, of uncertain origin.]
A small potentilla of heaths and moors, *Potentilla erecta*, having four-petalled yellow flowers and strongly astringent roots.

tormentor /tɔːˈmɛntə/ *noun.* ME.
[(Anglo-Norman *tormentour* from) Old French *tormenteor*, formed as TORMENT *verb*: see -OR.]
1 A person who or thing which causes torment; a source of extreme pain, suffering, or annoyance. ME.
2 *transf.* **a** A sharp or long-handled implement, as a long-handled fork etc.; in *pl.* (treated as *sing.*), a pair of cook's tongs. Now *rare* or *obsolete.* E17. ▶**b** THEATRICAL. Either of two vertical borders inside the proscenium arch which mask the wings from the audience. Cf. TEASER 3e. Chiefly *US.* L19.

tormentry /ˈtɔːm(ə)ntri/ *noun.* Now *rare* or *obsolete.* ME.
[Old French *tormenterie*, from *tormenteor* TORMENTOR: see -RY.]
†**1** A body of tormentors or executioners. *rare.* Only in ME.
2 Extreme pain or suffering; torment. Formerly also, the infliction of this. LME.

tormina /ˈtɔːmɪnə/ *noun pl.* Now *rare.* M17.
[Latin, ult. from *torquere* twist.]
MEDICINE. Acute wringing pains in the abdomen; colic, gripes.

torn /tɔːn/ *adjective.* LME.
[pa. pple of TEAR *verb*[1].]
1 That has been torn or pulled violently apart; rent, riven. LME.
2 BOTANY. Deeply and irregularly divided. L19.
Comb.: **torn-down** *adjective* (*a*) torn or pulled down; (*b*) *dial. & US* rough, riotous, boisterous.

torn *verb* pa. pple of TEAR *verb*[1].

tornada /tɔːˈnɑːdə, *foreign* torˈnada/ *noun.* E19.
[Provençal, from *tornar* turn.]
A three-line envoi incorporating all the verse-endings of the preceding stanzas.

tornado /tɔːˈneɪdəʊ/ *noun.* Pl. **-oes**. M16.
[Perh. alt. of Spanish *tronada* thunderstorm, from *tronar* thunder, later assim. to *tornar* turn: see -ADO.]
1 A violent thunderstorm of the tropical Atlantic. Now *rare* exc. as passing into sense 2. M16.
2 A violent storm over a limited area, with whirling winds, a cyclone; in W. Africa, a thundery squall at the beginning or end of the rainy season. Now usu. *spec.*, a destructive vortex of rotating winds of up to 300 miles per hour, forming a funnel-shaped cloud like a water-spout, which advances overland in a narrow path below a large thunderstorm, esp. in the southern plains of the US. E17.
3 *fig.* A violent or devastating person or thing; a sudden outburst, a volley. E19.
Comb.: **tornado-cellar** an underground shelter from tornadoes; **tornado-lamp**, **tornado-lantern** a hurricane-lamp; **tornado-pit** = *tornado-cellar* above.
■ †**tornade** *noun* (*rare*) = TORNADO M17–E19. **tornadic** /-ˈnadɪk/ *adjective* of, pertaining to, or resembling (that of) a tornado; violent, devastating: L19.

tornaria /tɔːˈnɛːrɪə/ *noun.* L19.
[mod. Latin, from Greek *tornos* or Latin *tornus* (from the shape): see TORNUS.]
ZOOLOGY. The free-swimming ciliated larva of an acorn-worm or enteropneust (hemichordate).

torni *noun* pl. of TORNUS.

tornillo /tɔːˈnɪl(j)əʊ/ *noun. US.* Pl. **-os**. Also **-lla** /-l(j)ə/. M19.
[Spanish, lit. 'screw', dim. of *torno* a turn.]
The screw-bean, *Prosopis pubescens*.

tornus /ˈtɔːnəs/ *noun.* Pl. **-ni** /-nʌɪ/. L19.
[Latin = potter's wheel, lathe, from Greek *tornos*.]
ENTOMOLOGY. The angle at the outer back corner of the wing of an insect, esp. of the hindwing of a moth.
■ **tornal** *adjective* L19.

toro /ˈtɔːrəʊ, *foreign* ˈtoro/ *noun.* Pl. **-os** /-əʊz, *foreign* -ɔs/. M17.
[Spanish from Latin *taurus* bull.]
A bull used in bullfighting.

toroid /ˈtɒrɔɪd, ˈtɔː-/ *noun.* L19.
[from TORUS + -OID.]
GEOMETRY. An object having the shape of a torus (TORUS 4); a toroidal object.

toroidal /tɒˈrɔɪd(ə)l, tɔː-/ *adjective.* L19.
[formed as prec. + -AL[1].]
GEOMETRY. Pertaining to or of the shape of a torus (TORUS 4); ring-shaped with a circular cross-section. Also = TORIC *adjective*.
■ **toroidally** *adverb* M20.

Toronto blessing /təˈrɒntəʊ ˌblɛsɪŋ/ *noun phr.* L20.
[from *Toronto*, city in Canada, site of a church where the phenomenon was observed in 1994 + BLESSING.]
A euphoric manifestation of mass hysteria associated with a charismatic revival among evangelical Christians.

Torontonian /tɒrɒnˈtəʊnɪən/ *noun.* L19.
[from *Toronto* (see below) + -IAN.]
A native or inhabitant of Toronto, the capital of Ontario, Canada.

torori /ˈtɔːrɒri/ *noun. NZ.* E20.
[Maori *tōrori*.]
Native-grown Maori tobacco.

torose /tɒˈrəʊs, tɔː-/ *adjective.* M18.
[Latin *torosus* from *torus* bulge, brawn: see -OSE[1]. Cf. TORULOSE.]
Chiefly BOTANY. Bulging, protuberant; roughly cylindrical with a series of bulges and constrictions; knobby.

torous /ˈtɔːrəs/ *adjective.* Long *rare* or *obsolete.* M17.
[from Latin *torosus* fleshy, brawny: see prec., -OUS.]
Bulging, swollen, knobby; torose.

torp /tɔːp/ *noun. slang.* E20.
[Abbreviation.]
= TORPEDO *noun* 2.

torpedo /tɔːˈpiːdəʊ/ *noun & verb.* E16.
[Latin = stiffness, numbness; also, the electric ray, from *torpere*: see TORPID.]
▶**A** *noun.* Pl. **-oes**.
1 An electric ray (fish), *esp.* one of the genus *Torpedo*. Also ***torpedo ray***. E16. ▶**b** *fig.* A person who or thing which has a numbing effect. L16.
2 Orig., a timed explosive device designed to detonate under water. Now, a self-propelled submarine missile, usu. cigar-shaped, designed to explode on impact with a target. L18. ▶**b** In full ***aerial torpedo***. A shell designed to be dropped from an aircraft and explode on impact. L19.

3 Any of various explosive devices; *spec.* (*a*) an explosive shell buried underground, detonated by pressure from above; (*b*) a firework exploding on impact with a hard surface; (*c*) a cartridge exploded in an oil-well to renew or increase the flow; (*d*) a device on a railway line detonated by pressure to give a danger signal. *US*. L18. ▸**b** *transf.* A gangster, a gunman. *US colloq.* E20.

4 a (A vehicle with) a motorcar body tapered at both ends. Also ***torpedo-body***. E20. ▸**b** A tablet or capsule of a narcotic drug. *slang*. E20.

Comb.: **torpedo beard** a pointed beard; **torpedo boat** a small fast lightly armed warship for carrying and discharging a torpedo or torpedoes; ***torpedo-boat catcher***, ***torpedo-boat destroyer*** a small fast warship designed to defend a fleet against torpedo boats; ***torpedo-body***: see sense 4a above; **torpedo-bomber** an aircraft carrying aerial torpedoes; **torpedo-catcher** (*a*) a defensive device to deflect or detonate a torpedo; (*b*) a torpedo-boat catcher; **torpedo destroyer** a torpedo-boat destroyer; **torpedo juice** *slang* (*a*) alcohol extracted from torpedo fuel; (*b*) any strong home-made alcohol; **torpedoman** (*a*) a naval rating with a non-substantive qualification trained in the maintenance and use of torpedoes; (*b*) *US* a person employed to clear an oil-well with torpedoes; **torpedo-net** a steel-wire net suspended round a ship to protect against torpedoes; **torpedo-tube** a tube from which a torpedo is fired by using compressed air or an explosive charge.

▸ **B** *verb trans.* †**1** Benumb, deaden. *rare*. Only in L18.

2 Attack with a torpedo; destroy or damage by this means. Freq. in *pass.* L19. ▸**b** *fig.* Cause to stop or fail suddenly; make inoperative or ineffective; destroy. L19. ▸**c** Lay (a channel etc.) with torpedoes or submarine mines. L19.

3 Explode a torpedo at the bottom of (an oil-well) to renew or increase the flow. *US*. L19.

> 📖 **2** H. CARPENTER The ship on which he was travelling was torpedoed. **b** *Times* The project was torpedoed by the Reagan-Gorbachov summit. *Natural History* How long before another oil shock torpedoes our economy?

■ **torpedoist** *noun* (*rare*) an expert in or advocate of the use of torpedoes L19. **torpedo-like** *adverb & adjective* (*a*) *adverb* in the manner of a torpedo; (*b*) *adjective* resembling a torpedo, like (that of) a torpedo: E18.

torpefy /ˈtɔːpɪfʌɪ/ *verb trans.* E19.
[Latin *torpefacere*, from *torpere* (see TORPID) + *facere* make.]
Make torpid; benumb, deaden.

torpent /ˈtɔːp(ə)nt/ *adjective & noun.* Now *rare* or *obsolete*. M17.
[Latin *torpent-* pres. ppl stem of *torpere*: see TORPID, -ENT.]
▸ **A** *adjective.* = TORPID *adjective.* Long *rare*. M17.
▸ **B** *noun.* MEDICINE. A medicine which soothes an irritation or subdues a reaction. Only in Dicts. L19.

torpex /ˈtɔːpɛks/ *noun.* M20.
[from TORP(EDO *noun* + EX(PLOSIVE *noun*.]
An explosive consisting largely of TNT, cyclonite, and aluminium, used for depth charges.

torpid /ˈtɔːpɪd/ *adjective & noun.* LME.
[Latin *torpidus*, from *torpere* be sluggish: see -ID[1].]
▸ **A** *adjective.* **1** Inactive, apathetic; slow, sluggish; dull. LME.
2 (Of a part of the body etc.) numb; (of an animal) dormant, esp. in hibernation etc. E17.

> 📖 **1** V. WOOLF My powers flag; I become torpid. P. MARSHALL There was a torpid sun outside.

▸ **B** *noun.* In *pl.* Annual boat races between Oxford college eights, now held in the spring term. Also (*sing.*), a crew or boat taking part in such a race. E20.

■ **tor'pidity** *noun* the condition or quality of being torpid; torpor: E17. **torpidly** *adverb* E19. **torpidness** *noun* L17.

torpitude /ˈtɔːpɪtjuːd/ *noun.* E18.
[Irreg. from Latin *torpere* (see TORPID) + -TUDE.]
= TORPIDITY.

torpor /ˈtɔːpə/ *noun.* LME.
[Latin, from *torpere* be sluggish: see -OR.]
Torpid condition or quality; apathy, listlessness, dullness; indifference; *spec.* (MEDICINE) a state of sluggishness and low responsiveness (less marked than stupor); BIOLOGY a state of physical and physiological inactivity, esp. in conditions of excessive heat or cold. Also, an instance of this.

> 📖 A. BURGESS Torpor has kept me in bed until noon. B. CHATWIN There was an oriental torpor in her movements.

■ **torpo'rific** *adjective* causing torpor; stupefying, deadening: M18.

torquate /ˈtɔːkweɪt/ *adjective. rare.* M17.
[Latin *torquatus* wearing a torque, formed as TORQUES: see -ATE[2].]
Of an animal or bird: having a ring of distinctive colour or texture of hair or plumage around (part of) the neck; collared.

torquated /tɔːˈkweɪtɪd/ *adjective. rare.* E17.
[formed as prec. + -ED[1].]
1 Wearing a torque. E17.
2 Formed like a torque; twisted. M19.

torque /tɔːk/ *noun*[1]. Also **torc**. M19.
[French, formed as TORQUES.]
Hist. A neck ornament formed from a twisted band of (usu. precious) metal, worn esp. by the ancient Celts.

torque /tɔːk/ *noun*[2]. L19.
[from Latin *torquere* twist.]
PHYSICS & MECHANICS. A twisting or rotating force, esp. in a mechanism; the moment of a system of forces producing rotation.

Comb.: **torque converter** a device that varies or multiplies torque, esp. as part of an automatic transmission system in a motor vehicle; **torque motor** ELECTRICAL ENGINEERING an electric motor designed to exert a torque without continuous rotation; **torque wrench** a tool for setting and adjusting the tension of nuts and bolts.

■ **torquey** *adjective* (of an engine) producing plenty of torque, able to pull well L20.

torque /tɔːk/ *verb trans.* M20.
[from TORQUE *noun*[2].]
Apply torque or twisting force to.

torqued /tɔːkt/ *adjective.* L16.
[After French †*torqué* pa. pple of †*torquer* from Latin *torquere* twist.]
1 = TORQUATED 2; *spec.* (HERALDRY) S-shaped; wreathed. L16.
2 *fig.* Upset, angry; overexcited. Also ***torqued up***. *US slang*. M20.

> 📖 **2** M. MILLAR Can't I even ask a question without you getting torqued up.

torques /ˈtɔːkwiːz/ *adjective & noun.* M16.
[Latin, from *torquere* twist.]
▸†**A** *adjective.* Twisted, bent. *rare*. Only in M16.
▸ **B** *noun.* = TORQUE *noun*[1]. L17.

torr /tɔː/ *noun.* Pl. same. M20.
[from *Torr(icelli*: see TORRICELLIAN.]
PHYSICS. A unit of pressure used chiefly in measuring partial vacuums, equal to 133.32 newtons per square metre.

torrefy /ˈtɒrɪfʌɪ/ *verb trans.* E17.
[French *torréfier* from Latin *torrefacere* dry by heat, from *torrere* scorch: see -FY.]
Roast, scorch; heat (a substance, esp. an ore or a drug) to drive off all moisture or volatile impurities.

■ **torre'faction** *noun* the action or process of drying or roasting something by heat; the fact or condition of being dried or roasted: E17.

Torrens system /ˈtɒr(ə)nz sɪstəm/ *noun phr.* M19.
[Sir Robert *Torrens* (1814–84), first Premier of South Australia.]
A system of land title registration adopted orig. in Australia.

torrent /ˈtɒr(ə)nt/ *noun & adjective.* L16.
[French from Italian *torrente* from Latin *torrent-*, use as noun of pres. ppl stem of *torrere* scorch: see -ENT.]
▸ **A** *noun.* **1** A fast-flowing stream of water; *esp.* an intermittently high and fast-flowing mountain stream. L16. ▸**b** *transf.* A forcible or fast-moving body of lava, stones, etc.; a violent downpour of rain. L18.
2 *fig.* A violent rush or outpouring of words etc. M17. ▸**b** A hanging mass of foliage, drapery, etc. M19.

> 📖 **1b** C. HARKNESS It poured with rain—it . . came down in torrents all day. **2** C. HARMAN Nora poured out a torrent of reproaches, regrets, woes.

Comb.: **torrent-duck** a duck, *Merganetta armata*, of fast-flowing rivers in the Andes.

▸ **B** *adjective.* Rushing; forceful. *poet.* M17.

torrential /təˈrɛnʃ(ə)l/ *adjective.* M19.
[from prec. + -IAL.]
1 Of, pertaining to, or produced by a torrent. M19.
2 Resembling or characteristic of a torrent; rushing; fast-moving; violent, copious. L19.

> 📖 **2** F. FORSYTH It had rained the previous night, a torrential downpour.

■ **torrentially** *adverb* L19.

torrentuous /təˈrɛntjʊəs/ *adjective.* M19.
[French *torrentueux*, formed as TORRENT: see -UOUS.]
Rushing, torrential; impetuous.

torret /ˈtɒrɪt/ *noun. obsolete* exc. *dial.* LME.
[Var. of TERRET.]
†**1** = TERRET 1. Only in LME.
†**2** = TERRET 3. LME–M16.
3 A ring etc. by which an object can be attached to a chain. LME.
4 = TERRET 4. LME.

Torricellian /tɒrɪˈtʃɛlɪən, -sɛl-/ *adjective.* M17.
[from *Torricelli* (see below) + -IAN.]
Of or pertaining to (the work of) Evangelista Torricelli (1608–1647), Italian scientist.

Torricellian experiment: by which Torricelli demonstrated that a column of mercury in an inverted closed tube is supported by the pressure of the atmosphere on the mercury in the vessel at the bottom, the height of the column corresponding to the atmospheric pressure (about 76 cm, 30 inches, under standard conditions). **Torricellian vacuum**: formed above a column of mercury in a barometer etc., as when the tube is longer than the height of mercury supportable by the ambient pressure.

torrid /ˈtɒrɪd/ *adjective.* L16.
[French *torride* or Latin *torridus*, from *torrere* scorch: see -ID[1].]
1 Scorched, burned; intensely hot, scorching. L16.
2 *fig.* Ardent, zealous; fiercely passionate. M17.

> 📖 **1** C. MCCULLERS The nights were torrid as in midsummer. **torrid zone** the region of the earth between the tropics of Cancer and Capricorn. **2** ANNE STEVENSON She was . . carrying on a torrid affair with Richard.

■ **to'rridity** *noun* the state, condition, or quality of being torrid; intense heat or passion: M19.

Torridonian /tɒrɪˈdəʊnɪən/ *adjective & noun.* L19.
[from Loch *Torridon* in NW Scotland + -IAN.]
GEOLOGY. ▸**A** *adjective.* Of, pertaining to, or designating (the period of deposition of) the later of the two main series of Precambrian rocks in NW Scotland, running in a narrow belt from Cape Wrath to Skye and consisting chiefly of sandstones, grits, and shales. L19.
▸ **B** *noun.* The Torridonian series. M20.

torry /ˈtɒri/ *verb trans. rare.* M20.
[Spanish *torear*.]
Provoke and fight (a bull).

torsade /tɔːˈseɪd/ *noun.* L19.
[French, from Latin *tors-* pa. ppl stem of *torquere* twist: see -ADE.]
A decorative twisted braid, ribbon, etc., used as trimming; an artificial plait of hair.

torsade de pointes /torsad də pwɛ̃t, tɔːˌsɑːd də ˈpwant/ *noun phr.* M20.
[French, lit. 'torsade of spikes': see prec.]
MEDICINE. A form of tachycardia characterized by a cyclical variation in the strength of the electric pulse arising in the ventricles of the heart, giving a characteristic electrocardiogram resembling a twisted fringe of spikes.

Torschlusspanik /ˈtoːrʃlʊsˌpaːnɪk/ *noun.* M20.
[German = last-minute panic (lit. 'shut door (or gate) panic').]
A sense of alarm or anxiety at the passing of life's opportunities, said to be experienced in middle age.

torse /tɔːs/ *noun*[1]. L16.
[French †*torse*, †*torce*, from Proto-Romance, from Latin *torta* fem. pa. pple of *torquere* twist.]
HERALDRY. A twisted band or wreath around the join of a crest to a helmet, often depicted under a crest without a helmet.

torse /tɔːs/ *noun*[2]. Now *rare*. E17.
[French from Italian *torso* TORSO.]
= TORSO.

torsel *noun* var. of TASSEL *noun*[2].

torsibility /tɔːsɪˈbɪlɪti/ *noun.* M19.
[from TORSION + -IBILITY.]
The degree to which an object, esp. a rope, can be twisted.

torsion /ˈtɔːʃ(ə)n/ *noun.* LME.
[Old & mod. French from late Latin *torsio(n-)* by-form of *tortio(n-)* from *tort-* pa. ppl stem of *torquere* twist: see -ION.]
†**1** MEDICINE. Pain in the abdomen, colic. LME–L17.
2 MEDICINE. A twisting of the body or a part of it, esp. of a loop of intestine, or of a testis in the scrotum. LME.
3 *gen.* The action of twisting an object by the operation of two opposing turning forces acting at right angles to its axis; a twisted condition (as) produced by this action. M16. ▸**b** SURGERY. The twisting of the cut end of an artery to stop bleeding. M19. ▸**c** MATH. The degree to which a curve departs from being planar at any given point, measured by the rate of change of the angle of the osculating plane with respect to distance along the curve. M19. ▸**d** ZOOLOGY. The spontaneous twisting of the visceral hump of a gastropod mollusc through 180 degrees at a certain stage of larval development. L19.

Comb.: **torsion-balance** an instrument for measuring minute horizontal forces by means of the angle through which they twist a thin wire or filament; **torsion bar** a bar that is subject to torque; *spec.* one in the suspension of some motor vehicles, fixed so that vertical motion of the wheel assembly tends to twist the bar and is thereby absorbed; **torsionmeter** an instrument which measures the torsion in a rotating shaft, thus providing information about the power output of the engine driving it; **torsion pendulum**: working by rotating back and forth, not swinging; **torsion test** ENGINEERING a test in which a material is subjected to torsion.

■ **torsiograph** *noun* (MECHANICS) an instrument for measuring torsional oscillations of the crankshaft of an engine M20. **torsional** *adjective* of or pertaining to torsion; caused by or resulting from torsion: M19. **torsionally** *adverb* in respect of torsion L19.

torsk /tɔːsk/ *noun.* Also (earlier) **tusk** /tʌsk/. E18.
[Norwegian *torsk*, *tosk*, from Old Norse *þorskr*, *þoskr*, prob. from base of *þurr* dry.]
A gadid fish, *Brosme brosme*, with a single dorsal fin, which is found in the N. Atlantic and is fished commercially. Also called ***cusk***.

torso /ˈtɔːsəʊ/ *noun*. Pl. **-os**. L18.
[Italian = stalk, stump, trunk of a statue, formed as THYRSUS.]
1 The trunk of a statue, without or considered independently of head and limbs. Also, the trunk of the human body. L18.
2 *fig.* An incomplete or mutilated thing. E19.

📖 **1** R. RAYNER He . . stripped off his shirt to reveal bronzed torso and . . gold chains. **2** *Gramophone* The . . first movement torso of a projected Symphony.

Comb.: **torso-tosser** *slang* a lively esp. erotic dancer.

tort /tɔːt/ *noun*. ME.
[Old French from medieval Latin *tortum* use as noun of neut. of Latin *tortus*: see next.]
†**1** Injury, wrong. ME–M18.
2 LAW. A breach of a duty imposed by law (rather than by contract) which gives a right of action for damages. L16.

†**tort** *ppl adjective*. LME–M18.
[Latin *tortus* pa. pple of *torquere* twist.]
Twisted.

torte /tɔːt/ *noun*. Pl. **tortes**, **torten** /ˈtɔːt(ə)n/. ME.
[In sense 1 prob. from late Latin *torta* round loaf, cake. In sense 2 from German *Torte* tart, pastry, cake from Italian *torta* from late Latin: cf. TOURTE.]
†**1** A round cake of bread. *rare*. ME–M16.
2 An elaborate sweet cake or tart. M18.
2 *Linzertorte*, *Sachertorte*, etc.

torteau /ˈtɔːtəʊ/ *noun*. Also (earlier) †**tortel**. Pl. **-eaux** /-əʊ(z)/. L15.
[Old French *tortel*, mod. French *torteau* large cake, from *tourte* from late Latin *torta*: see prec.]
HERALDRY. A roundel gules representing a round loaf of bread.

tortellini /tɔːtɪˈliːni/ *noun pl.* M20.
[Italian, pl. of *tortellino* dim. of *tortello* small cake, fritter.]
Small squares of pasta stuffed with meat, cheese, etc., rolled and shaped into rings; an Italian dish consisting largely of this and usu. a sauce.

torten *noun pl.* see TORTE.

tortfeasor /ˈtɔːtfiːzə/ *noun*. M17.
[Old French *tort-fesor*, *-faiseur*, etc., from *tort* wrong, evil (see TORT *noun*) + *fesor*, *faiseur* doer.]
LAW. A person guilty of a tort; a wrongdoer.

torticollis /tɔːtɪˈkɒlɪs/ *noun*. E19.
[mod. Latin from Latin *tortus* crooked, twisted + *collum* neck.]
MEDICINE. A condition in which the head is persistently or intermittently turned or twisted to one side; wryneck.

tortie /ˈtɔːti/ *noun*. *colloq.* M20.
[Dim. of TORTOISESHELL: see -IE.]
= TORTOISESHELL *cat*.

tortile /ˈtɔːtɪl, -ʌɪl/ *adjective*. Chiefly *poet.* M17.
[Latin *tortilis*, from *tort-* pa. ppl stem of *torquere* twist: see -ILE.]
Twisted, coiled; winding.

tortilla /tɔːˈtiːjə/ *noun*. L17.
[Spanish, dim. of *torta* cake from late Latin: see TORTE.]
Esp. in Mexican cookery, a thin round cake made with either cornmeal or wheat flour and freq. filled with meat, cheese, beans, etc. Also, in Spanish cookery, a thick flat omelette freq. eaten cold in wedges.
Comb.: **tortilla chip** a fried segment of corn tortilla, eaten cold, or sprinkled with cheese etc. and heated (usu. in *pl.*).

tortillon /tɔːˈtɪljən/ *noun*. L19.
[French, from *tortiller* twist, twirl.]
= STUMP *noun*².

tortilly /tɔːˈtɪli/ *adjective*. Orig. †**tortillé**. E19.
[French *tortillé* pa. pple of *tortiller*: see prec.]
HERALDRY. Of an ordinary: wreathed.

tortious /ˈtɔːʃəs/ *adjective*. LME.
[Anglo-Norman *torcious*, from stem of *torcion*, *tortion* extortion, violence, from late Latin *tortio(n-)* torture: see -OUS.]
†**1** Wrongful, injurious; illegal. LME–M18.
2 LAW. Of or pertaining to a tort; constituting a tort. M16.
■ **tortiously** *adverb* L18.

tortive /ˈtɔːtɪv/ *adjective*. *rare*. E17.
[French †*tortif* or Latin *tortivus* pressed, squeezed out.]
Tortuous.

tortoise /ˈtɔːtəs, -tɔɪz/ *noun & adjective*. LME.
[Old & mod. French *tortue*, Spanish *tortuga*, from medieval Latin *tortuca* of uncertain origin.]
▶ **A** *noun*. **1** A slow-moving four-limbed reptile of the family Testudinidae (order Chelonia), in which the main part of the body is enclosed in a shell consisting of a domed carapace and a flat plastron formed by the dorsal vertebrae, ribs, and sternum, into which the head and feet may be withdrawn for protection, the skin being covered with large leathery or horny plates (also *land tortoise*). Also more widely, any chelonian; a turtle, a terrapin. LME.
2 *Hist.* = TESTUDO 3. LME. ▸**b** A representation of a tortoise. M17. ▸**c** *fig.* A slow-moving person or thing. E19.
3 Tortoiseshell; tortoiseshell colour. E18.

📖 **1** G. STIMPSON Unquestionable proof that . . Galapagos tortoises have lived 150 years. **2c** A. THEROUX The tortoise of the hour hand, the hare of the minute hand. **3** J. KRANTZ Her smokey eyes . . striped with faint horizontal lines of tortoise and dark brown.

Comb.: **tortoise-beetle** a leaf-beetle belonging to the genus *Cassida* or a related genus, whose enclosing carapace resembles that of a tortoise; **tortoise core** *Archaeol.*: resembling a tortoise in shape; **tortoise-pace** a very slow or sluggish pace; **tortoise race**: in which the last person home wins.
▶ **B** *adjective*. Made of or of the colour of tortoiseshell. M17.
■ **tortoise-like** *adjective & adverb* (*a*) *adjective* resembling a tortoise, like (that of) a tortoise; (*b*) *adverb* in the manner of a tortoise: E17.

tortoiseshell /ˈtɔːtəʃɛl/ *noun & adjective*. E17.
[from prec. + SHELL *noun*.]
▶ **A** *noun*. **1** The shell, esp. the plates of the upper shell or carapace, of a tortoise. E17. ▸**b** The material of the shell of certain (mainly marine) tortoises, esp. of the hawksbill turtle, *Eretmochelys imbricata*, which is semi-transparent, with a mottled or clouded yellow-brown coloration, and was formerly used extensively in ornamental work. Also, the colour of this; a substance made in imitation of this. M17.
†**2** = TORTOISE *noun* 2. M17–E18.
3 **a** = *tortoiseshell cat* below. M19. ▸**b** Any of several nymphalid butterflies with brownish mottled wings, esp. of the genera *Nymphalis* and *Aglais*. Also more fully *tortoiseshell butterfly*. L19.
3b *large tortoiseshell* the Eurasian butterfly *Nymphalis polychloros*, now rare in Britain. *small tortoiseshell* the small Eurasian butterfly *Aglais urticae*.
▶ **B** *attrib.* or as *adjective*. Made of tortoiseshell; resembling tortoiseshell in colour or appearance; mottled or variegated with black or brown, yellow, red, etc. M17.
Special collocations: **tortoiseshell butterfly**: see sense A.3b above. **tortoiseshell cat** a domestic cat with a mottled black and brownish-yellow coat (often with white or cream). **tortoiseshell turtle** a turtle, esp. the hawksbill turtle from which tortoiseshell is obtained. **tortoiseshell ware** a fine kind of pottery coloured with copper and manganese oxides.

Tortolan /tɔːˈtəʊlən/ *adjective & noun*. E20.
[from *Tortola* (see below) + -AN.]
▶ **A** *adjective*. Of or pertaining to Tortola, the largest of the British Virgin Islands. E20.
▶ **B** *noun*. A native or inhabitant of Tortola. M20.

Tortoni /tɔːˈtəʊni/ *noun & adjective*. E20.
[Surname of an Italian café-owner in Paris in the 18th cent.]
(Designating) a kind of ice-cream flavoured with macaroons etc.

tortrices *noun* pl. of TORTRIX.

tortricid /tɔːˈtrɪsɪd, ˈtɔːtrɪsɪd/ *adjective & noun*. L19.
[from next: see -ID³.]
ENTOMOLOGY. ▶**A** *adjective*. Of, pertaining to, or designating the large family Tortricidae of small, mainly nocturnal greyish or brownish moths with fringed wings held over the body when at rest, the larvae often living as leaf-rollers or leaf-miners. L19.
▶ **B** *noun*. A moth of this family. E20.

tortrix /ˈtɔːtrɪks/ *noun*. Pl. **-trices** /-trɪsiːz/. L18.
[mod. Latin (see below), fem. of *tortor* in sense 'twister' (with ref. to the leaf-rolling habits of the larvae): see -TRIX.]
A tortricid moth, esp. of the genus *Tortrix*; a leaf-roller moth. Chiefly as mod. Latin genus name.

tortuose /ˈtɔːtjʊəʊs/ *adjective*. *rare*. E19.
[Latin *tortuosus*: see TORTUOUS, -OSE¹.]
Tortuous, twisted.

tortuosity /tɔːtʃʊˈɒsɪti, ˈtɔːtjʊ-/ *noun*. LME.
[Late Latin *tortuositas*, from Latin *tortuosus*: see next, -ITY.]
1 The quality or condition of being tortuous; twistedness, sinuosity; an instance of this. LME.
2 A twisted or sinuous thing; a twist, a turn (*lit. & fig.*). M17.
3 A measure of the degree to which a pathway, esp. a pore in a material, is convoluted, calculated as the ratio of its actual length to the straight-line distance between its ends. M20.

tortuous /ˈtɔːtʃʊəs, -jʊəs/ *adjective*. LME.
[Old French (mod. *tortueux*) from Latin *tortuosus*, from *tortus* twisting, from *tort-* pa. ppl stem of *torquere* twist: see -UOUS.]
1 Full of twists or turns; twisted, winding, sinuous. LME. ▸**b** Not direct or straightforward; devious, circuitous. E19.
2 [By confusion.] ▸**a** = TORTIOUS 1. Now *rare* or *obsolete*. L16. ▸**b** = TORTUROUS. E20.

📖 **1** W. HORWOOD The route from Avebury is slow and tortuous. **b** *Economist* The next step in this tortuous process is to be a series of bilateral meetings.

■ **tortuously** *adverb* M19. **tortuousness** *noun* E19.

torture /ˈtɔːtʃə/ *noun & verb*. LME.
[Old & mod. French, or late Latin *tortura* twisting, writhing, torment, from *tort-*: see TORTUOUS, -URE.]
▶ **A** *noun*. **1** Orig., (a disorder characterized by) contortion, distortion, or twisting. Later, (the infliction of) severe physical or mental suffering; anguish, agony, torment. LME. ▸**b** *transf.* A cause of severe pain or anguish. E17.
2 The infliction of severe bodily pain as a punishment or as a means of interrogation or persuasion; a form or instance of this. M16. ▸†**b** *transf.* An instrument or means of torture. E17–E18.

📖 **1** J. MOYNAHAN His tension mounts, and the last quarter hour before they meet is sheer torture. **b** *Business Traveller* If you're tall you'll find the tiny . . beds . . torture. **2** *Holiday Which?* Its gruesome collection of instruments of torture. *European* The torture of the *falanga*, or beating on the soles.

Phrases: **judicial torture** torture inflicted by a judicial authority in order to force a confession or extract information. ***physical torture***: see PHYSICAL *adjective*. **put to the torture**, **put to torture** *arch.* subject to torture.
Comb.: **torture chamber** a room set aside for the infliction of torture.
▶ **B** *verb trans.* **1** Subject to torture as a punishment or as a means of interrogation or persuasion. L16.
2 Inflict severe mental or physical suffering on; cause anguish in; torment. Also, puzzle or perplex greatly. L16.
3 *fig.* Force violently out of the original state or form; twist, distort; pervert. Also foll. by *into*. E17.
4 Extract by torture. L17.

📖 **1** R. RENDELL He's being put through a fairly heavy interrogation, but not tortured. **2** P. H. GIBBS Those absurd dreams which had tortured his brain. **3** J. GROSS To torture the facts . . to make them fit his pre-ordained theories.

■ **torturable** *adjective* (*rare*) M17. **tortured** *adjective* that has been subjected to torture; twisted, distorted, perverted: E17. **torturer** *noun* a person who or thing which inflicts or causes torture, esp. a person who inflicts judicial torture L16. **torturesome** *adjective* (*rare*) = TORTUROUS 1 L19.

torturous /ˈtɔːtʃ(ə)rəs/ *adjective*. L15.
[Anglo-Norman = Old & mod. French *tortureux*, from *torture* TORTURE *noun*: see -OUS. In mod. use from TORTURE *noun* + -OUS.]
1 Characterized by, involving, or causing torture; tormenting, excruciating. L15.
2 *fig.* Violently twisted or distorted; perverted. Also (by confusion) = TORTUOUS 1. M19.

📖 **1** R. MISTRY Another torturous night of mosquitoes. **2** J. RABAN However torturous your route, you will eventually find your way out.

■ **torturously** *adverb* M19.

torula /ˈtɔruːlə, -(j)ʊlə/ *noun*. Pl. **-lae** /-liː/. M19.
[mod. Latin, dim. (with change of gender) of TORUS: see -ULE.]
BIOLOGY. Any of various yeastlike fungi now or formerly included in the genus *Torula*, several of which grow on dead vegetation and may cause infections; each of the rounded cells of these organisms, often arranged in chains. Also (in full ***torula yeast***), a yeast, *Candida utilis*, cultured for use in medicine and as a food additive, esp. as a source of vitamins and protein.
■ **toruˈlosis** *noun* (MEDICINE) infection with the fungus *Torula histolytica* (= *Cryptococcus neoformans*); = CRYPTOCOCCOSIS: E20.

torulose /ˈtɔːjʊləʊs, ˈtɒr(j)ʊləʊs/ *adjective*. E19.
[formed as TORULA + -OSE¹. Cf. TOROSE.]
BOTANY & ZOOLOGY. Cylindrical with small rounded swellings at intervals.
■ Also **torulous** *adjective* (*rare*) M18.

torus /ˈtɔːrəs/ *noun*. Pl. **-ri** /-rʌɪ/, **-ruses**. M16.
[Latin = swelling, bolster, round moulding.]
1 ARCHITECTURE. A large convex moulding, usu. semicircular in cross-section, esp. at the base of a column. M16.
2 BOTANY. **a** The receptacle of a flower. E19. ▸**b** A central thickened area of the pit membrane in a bordered pit of a gymnosperm. L19.
3 ZOOLOGY. A protuberant part or organ, as the ventral parapodia in some annelids; ANATOMY a smooth rounded ridge. L19.
4 GEOMETRY. Orig., a surface or solid generated by the revolution of a circle or other conic about any axis. Now *spec.* a surface or solid generated by the circular motion of a circle about an axis outside itself but lying in its plane; a solid ring of circular cross-section; a body topologically equivalent to this, having one hole in it but not necessarily circular in form or cross-section. L19.

torve /tɔːv/ *adjective*. *literary*. M17.
[Latin *torvus*.]
Stern or grim in appearance.
■ **torvid** *adjective* = TORVE M17. **torvity** *noun* grimness or sternness of appearance E17. **torvous** *adjective* = TORVE L17.

Tory /ˈtɔːri/ *noun & adjective*. M17.
[Prob. from Irish *toraidhe* a pursued person, a highwayman, from *tóir* pursue (cf. *tóraigheacht* act of pursuing, pursuit).]
▶ **A** *noun*. **1** *Hist.* Any of the Irish people dispossessed by English settlers who became outlaws in 17th-cent.

Ireland. Later also (*derog.*), an Irish Catholic or Royalist. M17.

2 *Hist.* (A nickname for) a person opposing the exclusion of James II from the succession. Opp. WHIG *noun*² 2. L17.

3 Orig. (now *Hist.*), a member of the English, later British parliamentary party supporting the established religious and political order, that gave rise to the Conservative Party in the 1830s (opp. WHIG *noun*² 3). Now, a member or supporter of the British Conservative Party. E18.

4 *US HISTORY.* **a** An American colonist loyal to Britain during the American Revolution. L18. ▸**b** A Union sympathizer in the Confederate States during the American Civil War. M19.

5 *transf.* A member or supporter of a political party analogous to the British Conservative Party; a person of conservative views or temperament. L18.

▸ **B** *adjective.* That is a Tory; of, pertaining to, or characteristic of a Tory or Tories; Conservative. L17.

E. PAUL The Tory *Petit Journal* came out as a handbill. M. B. BROWN The evolution of a working class, Tory voter in Britain.

Special collocations: **Tory democracy** (chiefly *Hist.*) democracy under Tory leadership; reforming or progressive Conservatism. **Tory democrat** (chiefly *Hist.*) an advocate or supporter of Tory democracy.

■ **Torydom** *noun* the realm or rule of Tories M19. **Toryfy** *verb trans.* (freq. *joc.*) make Tory, convert to Toryism M18. **Toryish** *adjective* somewhat Tory; inclined to Toryism: L17. **Toryishly** *adverb* L17. **Toryism** *noun* the principles or practices of Tories; an instance of this: L17. **Toryize** *verb trans.* = TORYFY L19.

†tory-rory *adverb & adjective.* M17.
[Origin unkn.]
▸ **A** *adverb.* Uproariously, boisterously. M–L17.
▸ **B** *adjective.* **1** Roaring, uproarious, roistering, boisterous. L17–E18.
2 Ruffianly. L17–E19.

Tosa /ˈtəʊsə/ *noun*¹. L19.
[An aristocratic Japanese family of court painters.]
Used *attrib.* to designate a school of Japanese painting characterized by traditional themes and techniques, which flourished from the mid 15th to the late 19th cents.

Tosa /ˈtəʊsə/ *noun*². M20.
[Former province on the island of Shikoku, Japan.]
(An animal of) a black, tan, or brindled breed of mastiff orig. bred as a fighting dog in Japan.

tosafist /ˈtəʊsəfɪst/ *noun.* L19.
[from Hebrew *tōsāphōth* pl. of *tōsāphāh* addition, from *yāsaph* add: see -IST.]
A medieval writer of critical and explanatory notes on the Talmud.

tos and fros *noun phr.* pl. of TO AND FRO *noun phr.*

tosh /tɒʃ/ *noun*¹. *Criminals' slang.* M19.
[Origin unkn. Cf. TOSHER¹.]
Valuables retrieved from drains and sewers.

tosh /tɒʃ/ *noun*² *& verb. School slang.* L19.
[Origin unkn.]
▸ **A** *noun.* A bath; a bath-tub. L19.
▸ **B** *verb.* **1** *verb trans.* Splash, souse. L19.
2 *verb intrans.* Bathe. E20.

tosh /tɒʃ/ *noun*³. *colloq.* L19.
[Origin unkn.]
Nonsense, rubbish. Also as *interjection.*
■ **toshy** *adjective* worthless, rubbishy E20.

tosh /tɒʃ/ *noun*⁴. *slang.* E20.
[Abbreviation.]
= TOSHEROON. Also *gen.*, money.

tosh /tɒʃ/ *noun*⁵. *slang.* M20.
[Origin unkn.]
Used as a form of address, usu. to an unknown person.

tosher /ˈtɒʃə/ *noun*¹. *Criminals' slang.* M19.
[Origin unkn. Cf. TOSH *noun*¹.]
1 A person who searches for valuables in drains and sewers. M19.
2 A thief stealing copper from the bottoms of ships. Now *rare* or *obsolete.* M19.

tosher /ˈtɒʃə/ *noun*². L19.
[Perh. rel. to TOSH *verb.*]
A small fishing smack.

tosher /ˈtɒʃə/ *noun*³. *slang.* Now *rare* or *obsolete.* L19.
[Joc. alt. of *unattached* + -ER⁶.]
A student not attached to a college at a collegiate university.

tosheroon /tɒʃəˈruːn/ *noun. slang* (*obsolete* exc. *Hist.*). M19.
[Origin unkn.]
A half-crown.

Tosk /tɒsk/ *noun & adjective.* M19.
[Albanian *Toskë.*]
▸ **A** *noun.* Pl. same, **-s**. A member of a people of southern Albania; the language spoken by this people. M19.
▸ **B** *adjective.* Of or pertaining to this people or their language. E20.

toss /tɒs/ *noun.* M17.
[from the verb.]
1 The action or an act of tossing; a throw; a fall from a horse. M17.
†2 A state of agitation or commotion. M17–M19.
3 A sudden jerk, esp. of the head; an act of tossing the hair; a mass of hair. L17.
4 In neg. contexts: a jot, a very small amount. Chiefly in ***not care a toss, not give a toss***. Cf. TOSSER *noun* 3. *colloq.* L19.

1 G. BOYCOTT Botham won the toss and put West Indies in to bat. *Tennis* I recommend a toss that reaches its apex just before your racquet meets the ball. 4 J. BARNES What makes you think I give a toss about the effing phone bill?

Phrases: **argue the toss** dispute a decision or opinion. **take a toss** suffer a fall from a horse.

Comb.: **toss pillow** *US* a scatter cushion; **toss-up** (*a*) the tossing of a coin; (*b*) *colloq.* an even chance; a close thing; a doubtful matter.

toss /tɒs/ *verb.* Pa. t. & pple **tossed**, (*arch. & poet.*) **tost**. E16.
[Origin unkn.]
▸ **I** *verb trans.* **1** Throw at random or here and there; fling about from side to side; buffet. E16. ▸**†b** Turn over and over; leaf through (a book). M16–M18.
2 Shake, shake up, stir up; set in commotion; disturb, agitate; disquiet in mind. E16. ▸**b** *COOKERY.* Stir or turn (food) over, esp. to provide a coating of butter, oil, etc. E18.
3 Throw or hit (a ball etc.) back and forth between two or more persons; throw or hit (a ball etc.) to another. E16. ▸**b** Bandy (a subject or question) about in debate; discuss; make the subject of talk. M16.
4 Throw up, throw into the air; *esp.* throw (a coin etc.) up to decide a choice by the side which is uppermost on landing; (of a bull etc.) catch with a horn and throw into the air; (of a horse) throw or fling off (its rider); turn (a pancake) by throwing into the air so as to land in the pan with the other side up. E16. ▸**b** Wager with (a person) on the toss of a coin. Usu. foll. by *for* something. M19. ▸**c** Release (a homing pigeon) in a race or trial flight. L19.
5 *gen.* Throw, fling, or hurl; throw carelessly. Freq. foll. by adverbs. L16. ▸**b** Throw away, discard. *colloq.* L20.
6 Lift or jerk up suddenly without letting go; *spec.* (*a*) brandish (a weapon); (*b*) raise (a cup etc.) to the lips in order to drink. Now *rare.* L16.
7 Raise or jerk (the head etc.) with an impatient or spirited movement. L16.
8 Search in the course of a police investigation. *US slang.* M20.

1 AV *Eph.* 4:14 Be no more children, tossed to and fro, and caried about with euery winde of doctrine. B. VINE When reproved, she . . whined, tossing herself this way and that. **2b** H. C. RAE Tossed green salad and cold lake trout. **3** *Globe & Mail (Toronto)* Quarterback . . Chudziak tossed a 38-yard pass to . . Lytwynec. *fig.*: *Classic CD* The Scherzo is quintessentially Mendelssohn, . . the short motif being tossed to and fro among the players. **4** J. BUCHAN I tossed a coin—heads right, tails left—and it fell heads. ***tossing the caber.*** **5** S. TROTT He'd picked up . . pebbles and was tossing them into the . . water. **6** ***toss oar(s), toss one's oar(s)*** raise one's oar(s) to an upright position in salute. **7** R. L. STEVENSON He would . . toss back his shock of hair.

▸ **II** *verb intrans.* **†9** Be in mental agitation; be disquieted. Only in 16.
10 a Move about restlessly. Now freq. in ***toss and turn.*** M16. ▸**b** Be flung about; be kept in motion. L16.
11 Fling oneself *into* or *out of* a place etc. E18.
12 Toss a coin, toss up. M19.

10a E. LANGLEY Excited by the events . . , I tossed beside him and could not sleep. **b** LD MACAULAY A fleet of merchantmen tossing on the waves.

With adverbs in specialized senses: **toss in** *NZ slang* = ***chuck in*** s.v. CHUCK *verb*². **toss off** (*a*) *verb phr. trans.* drink off with gusto; (*b*) *verb phr. trans.* do or make rapidly or without effort; (*c*) *verb phr. trans. & intrans.* (*coarse slang*) masturbate. **toss up** †(*a*) prepare hastily; (*b*) = sense 12 above.

tosser /ˈtɒsə/ *noun.* E17.
[from prec. + -ER¹.]
1 A person who or thing which tosses something. E17.
2 A contemptible person. *coarse slang.* M20.
3 A coin of small value. Also, a jot. Cf. TOSS *noun* 4. Usu. in neg. contexts. *colloq.* M20.

tosspot /ˈtɒspɒt/ *noun.* M16.
[from TOSS *verb* + POT *noun*¹.]
A heavy drinker; a drunkard.

tost *verb pa. t. & pple:* see TOSS *verb.*

tostada /tɒˈstɑːdə/ *noun.* Also **-do** /-dəʊ/, pl. **-os**. M20.
[Spanish, pa. pple of *tostar* to toast.]
A deep-fried cornmeal pancake topped with a seasoned mixture of beans, mincemeat, and vegetables.

tosticate /ˈtɒstɪkeɪt/ *verb trans.* Chiefly *dial.* M17.
[Alt. of INTOXICATE *verb.*]
1 Intoxicate. Chiefly as ***tosticated*** *ppl adjective.* M17.
2 Distract, perplex. Chiefly as ***tosticated*** *ppl adjective.* E18.

toston /tɒsˈtɒn/ *noun.* L19.
[Amer. Spanish from Latin *testa*: see TESTON.]
A silver coin formerly in use in some Latin American countries.

tosyl /ˈtəʊsʌɪl, -sɪl/ *noun.* M20.
[German, from toluol TOLUOL + sulfonyl SULPHONYL.]
CHEMISTRY. The *para* isomer of the monovalent radical toluene-4-sulphonyl, $CH_3C_6H_4SO_2\cdot$. Usu. in *comb.*
■ **tosylate** *noun & verb* (*a*) *noun* an ester of the tosyl group; (*b*) *verb trans.* introduce a tosyl group into (a compound or group): M20. **tosyˈlation** *noun* the process of tosylating something M20.

†tot *noun*¹. LME–L18.
[from (the same root as) TOT *verb*¹.]
The word *tot* or letter T written against an item in an account to indicate receipt of the amount specified; an item in an account; a note, a jotting.

tot /tɒt/ *noun*². *colloq.* (orig. *dial.*). E18.
[Perh. from TOTTER *verb* or abbreviation of TOTTERER.]
1 A very small child. E18.
2 A very small drinking-vessel; a child's mug. Chiefly *dial.* E19.
3 A minute quantity of something, *esp.* a dram of liquor; a very small object. E19.

1 K. AMIS We were eleven at table, including the two tots. **3** A. CARTER She decided to give up rum, except for a single tot . . at night.

Comb.: **tot lot** *N. Amer.* a playground for small children.

tot /tɒt/ *noun*³. *arch.* M18.
[Abbreviation of TOTAL *noun* or Latin *totum.*]
A total; a set of figures to be added up.

tot /tɒt/ *noun*⁴. *slang.* L19.
[Origin unkn.]
Orig., a bone. Later, any article worth salvaging from a dustbin, refuse heap, etc.; such articles collectively.

†tot *verb*¹ *trans.* Infl. **-tt-**. LME–L18.
[from Latin *tot* so much. Cf. TOT *noun*¹.]
Put a mark by (an item in an account), orig. to indicate receipt of the amount specified; jot down in writing.

tot /tɒt/ *verb*² *trans. & intrans.* Infl. **-tt-**. M18.
[from TOT *noun*³.]
Add up. Usu. foll. by *up.*
totting up *spec.* the procedure under which past endorsements of a person's driving licence can contribute towards disqualification when a further motoring offence is committed.

tot /tɒt/ *verb*³ *intrans.* Infl. **-tt-**. L19.
[from TOT *noun*⁴.]
Orig., pick up bones. Later, salvage saleable items from dustbins, refuse heaps, etc. Chiefly as ***totting*** *pres. pple.*

tot *verb*⁴ var. of TOYTE.

total /ˈtəʊt(ə)l/ *adjective & noun.* LME.
[Old & mod. French from medieval Latin *totalis*, from *totum* the whole, use as noun of neut. of Latin *totus* entire, whole.]
▸ **A** *adjective.* **1** Of or pertaining to the whole of something. LME.
2 Constituting or comprising a whole; whole, entire. LME.
3 a Complete in extent or degree; absolute, utter. LME. ▸**b** Complete in nature; involving all resources or aspects; manifesting every characteristic or the whole nature of an activity, person, etc. M20.

1 *Practical Health* Offered hormone replacement therapy . . after a total hysterectomy. **2** *Which?* The total hire charge for one day . . varied from £13 . . to £35. **3a** J. C. OATES Of course I understand, I'm not a total fool. M. AMIS Kasimir and I sat . . in total silence for forty-five minutes. **b** J. D. MACDONALD How any platonic relationship between Mike and this total woman would be possible.

Special collocations: **total abstainer** a teetotaller. **total abstinence** complete abstinence from alcoholic drink. **total allergy syndrome** a condition involving a wide range of symptoms and thought to be caused by sensitivity to chemical substances encountered in the modern environment. **total eclipse**: in which the whole disc of a celestial object is obscured. **total harmonic distortion** the distortion produced by an amplifier etc., as measured in terms of the harmonics of the sinusoidal components of the signal that it introduces. **total heat** *PHYSICS* = ENTHALPY. **total internal reflection** *PHYSICS* reflection of all the light reaching an interface with a less dense medium when the angle of incidence exceeds the critical angle. **total quality management** a management system based on the principle that every member of staff must be committed to maintaining high standards of work in every aspect of a company's operations. **total recall** the ability to remember every detail of a past event, experience, etc. ***total sum***: see SUM *noun.* **total war** a war in which all available resources of weapons and personnel are employed; a war conducted without scruple or limitation.
▸ **B** *noun.* The aggregate, the whole sum or amount; a whole. LME.

Phrases: ***grand total***: see GRAND *adjective*¹. **in total** all together, entirely. SUM TOTAL.

■ **tota'listic** *adjective* total; all-embracing; *esp.* concerned with the whole social environment: M20. **totalness** *noun* (*rare*) totality E18. **totally** *adverb* (*a*) completely, entirely, altogether; (*b*) *colloq.* (as an intensive) utterly, really: E16.

total /ˈtəʊt(ə)l/ *verb*. Infl. **-ll-**, *-l-. L16.
[from prec.]
1 *verb trans.* Find the total of, add up. Also (*US*), work *out*. L16.
2 a *verb trans.* Amount in number to. M19. ▸**b** *verb intrans.* Amount to, mount *up to*. L19.
3 *verb trans.* Damage beyond repair; demolish, wreck; kill, injure severely. Chiefly *N. Amer. slang*. L19.

🕮 **1** G. BROWN I had to total up contributions to see how much each member was in arrears. **2a** E. PAWEL The city's population totaled 303,000. **b** M. PUZO The contents of the . . purse . . totaled up to over twenty thousand dollars. **3** A. T. ELLIS If you've totalled my bike you'll have to buy me another.

totalisator *noun*, **totalise** *verb* vars. of TOTALIZATOR, TOTALIZE.

totalitarian /ˌtəʊtalɪˈtɛːrɪən, təʊˌtalɪ-/ *adjective & noun*. E20.
[from TOTALITY + -ARIAN, after Italian *totalitario*.]
▶ **A** *adjective*. Of or pertaining to an authoritarian system of government which tolerates only one political party, to which all other institutions are subordinated, and which usu. demands the complete subservience of the individual to the State. E20.
▶ **B** *noun*. A leader or member of a totalitarian party; an adherent or advocate of totalitarianism. M20.
■ **totalitarianism** *noun* totalitarian theory and practice; the advocacy of totalitarian government; *transf.* authoritarianism; monolithic character: E20. **totalitariani'zation** *noun* the action or process of making something totalitarian; the fact of becoming totalitarian: M20.

totality /təʊˈtalɪti/ *noun*. L16.
[medieval Latin *totalitas*, from *totalis* TOTAL *adjective*: see -ITY.]
1 The total number or amount, the aggregate. L16.
2 The quality of being total; entirety. E17. ▸**b** ASTRONOMY. Total obscuration of a celestial object in an eclipse; the moment or duration of this. M19.

totalizator /ˈtəʊt(ə)lʌɪzeɪtə/ *noun*. Also **-isa-**. L19.
[from next + -ATOR, after French *totalisateur*.]
An apparatus showing the number and amount of bets placed on each participant in a race, to facilitate the division of the total among those backing the winner; a system of betting based on this. Also, any totalizer.

totalize /ˈtəʊt(ə)lʌɪz/ *verb trans*. Also **-ise**. E19.
[from TOTAL *adjective* + -IZE.]
Make total; combine into a total or aggregate. Also, find the total of.
■ **totali'zation** *noun* the action or process of totalizing something; the condition of being totalized: L19. **totalizer** *noun* an apparatus that registers totals; a totalizator: L19.

totara /ˈtəʊt(ə)rə/ *noun*. M19.
[Maori *tōtara*.]
A large New Zealand podocarpus, *Podocarpus totara*; the light, durable, dark red timber of this tree, valued for building, cabinet work, etc.

tote /təʊt/ *noun*¹. L17.
[Prob. from TOOT *verb*¹.]
The handle of a carpenter's plane.

tote /təʊt/ *noun*². L18.
[Abbreviation.]
1 A total. Usu. pleonastic in ***the whole tote***. Now *dial.* L18.
2 A total abstainer. *dial. & colloq.* M19.
3 A totalizator; *the* system of betting using this; *Austral. & NZ* a lottery. *colloq.* L19.

tote *noun*³ var. of TOOT *noun*¹.

tote /təʊt/ *verb & noun*⁴. *colloq.* (chiefly *N. Amer.*). L17.
[Prob. of dial. origin.]
▶ **A** *verb trans.* Carry; transport; wear or carry regularly as part of one's equipment. L17.
tote fair carry one's fair share; *fig.* act fairly or honestly.
▶ **B** *noun*. In full ***tote bag***. A large bag for shopping. E20.
Comb.: **tote bag**: see above; **tote box** a portable box for small items; **tote road** a rough temporary road.
■ **toter** *noun* (*a*) a carrier or wearer of something; a person whose role it is to carry or transport things; (*b*) *N. Amer.* a container, a tray: E19.

totem /ˈtəʊtəm/ *noun*. M18.
[Ojibwa *nindoodem* my totem.]
1 An animal or other natural object which a group of N. American Indians regards as specially associated with itself and from which it takes its name; a representation of this as an emblem or badge; a group of Indians within a nation sharing the same totem. M18. ▸**b** In full ***totem-pole***. A post on which totems are carved or hung. E20.
2 ANTHROPOLOGY. A people divided into groups named after animals; an animal that gives its name to such a group. L19.
3 An emblem, a badge; a symbol, a token. L19.

🕮 **3** M. GEE A fairy godmother scattering beads and feathers, . . small . . totems of love. *Rail Enthusiast* A . . lion and wheel totem was carried on the non-driving cab sides.

■ **to'temic** *adjective* of, pertaining to, or of the nature of a totem or totems; characterized by or having totems: M19. **to'temically** *adverb* in reference to totems or totemism; after the manner of a totem: E20. **totemism** *noun* the use of totems; belief in totems: L18. **totemist** *noun* (*a*) a person who belongs to a totem group or has a totem; (*b*) an expert in or student of totemism: L19. **tote'mistic** *adjective* of, pertaining to, or characterized by totemism L19. **totemite** *noun* = TOTEMIST (a) E20.

Totentanz /ˈtotəntants/ *noun*. Pl. ***-tänze*** /-tɛntsə/. L18.
[German, lit. 'death dance'.]
= ***Dance of Death*** s.v. DANCE *noun*.

tother /ˈtʌðə/ *pronoun & adjective*. Now chiefly *dial.* & *joc.* Also **t'other**. ME.
[from misdivision of neut. of THE (Old English *þæt*) + OTHER *adjective, pronoun, noun*. Cf. TONE *pronoun & adjective*.]
▶ **A** *pronoun*. **1** The other one. ME.
†**2** The second one (of two or more). Only in ME.
†**3** *sing.* & (*rare*) in *pl.* The others, the rest. ME–L17.
1 tell tother from which tell one from the other.
▶ **B** *attrib. adjective*. **1 a** The other. ME. ▸†**b** After a possess.: other. L15–E18.
2 †**a** The second (of two or more). Only in ME. ▸**b** Additional, another, one more. *obsolete* exc. *Scot.* E17.

🕮 **2b** I. WALTON Each man drink the tother cup and to bed.

1a tother day, the tother day, tother year, the tother year, etc. †(*a*) the following day, year, etc.; †(*b*) the preceding day, year, etc.; (*c*) the other day etc., a few days etc. ago. **tother school, tother 'un** *School slang* a preparatory school, a school one attended before public school.
Comb.: **tothersider** (chiefly *Austral.*) a person from the other side, esp. an eastern state.
¶ Esp. in Sc. & north. use also ***the tother***.

totidem verbis /ˌtɒtɪdɛm ˈvəːbiːs/ *adverbial phr.* M17.
[Latin.]
In so many words.

totient /ˈtəʊʃ(ə)nt/ *noun*. L19.
[from Latin *toties, totiens* as often, so often (from *tot* so many), after QUOTIENT.]
MATH. The number of positive integers less than and prime to a given number. Also called ***indicator***.
■ **totitive** /ˈtɒtɪtɪv/ *noun* any such integer in relation to the given number L19.

toties quoties /ˌtɒtɪeɪz ˈkwɒtɪeɪz, ˌtəʊʃiːz ˈkwəʊʃiːz/ *adverbial phr.* LME.
[Latin = so often as often.]
As often as something happens or occasion demands.

totipalmate /təʊtɪˈpalmeɪt/ *adjective*. L19.
[formed as next + PALMATE.]
ORNITHOLOGY. Having all the toes connected by a membrane reaching to the extremities.

totipotent /təʊˈtɪpət(ə)nt/ *adjective*. E20.
[from *toti-* combining form of Latin *totus* whole + POTENT *adjective*².]
BIOLOGY. Capable of differentiating into any other related kind of cell or (in some organisms) a complete individual.
■ **totipotence** *noun* totipotency E20. **totipotency** *noun* the property of being totipotent E20. **totipo'tential** *adjective* = TOTIPOTENT M20.

toto /ˈtəʊtəʊ/ *noun*¹. Pl. **-os**. E20.
[Kiswahili *mtoto* offspring, child.]
In E. Africa: a child; a baby; a young animal; a young servant.

toto /ˈtəʊtəʊ/ *noun*². *Military slang*. Pl. **-os**. E20.
[French.]
A louse.

toto caelo /təʊtəʊ ˈsiːləʊ, ˈkʌɪləʊ/ *adverbial phr.* L17.
[Latin, lit. 'by the whole heaven'.]
Entirely, utterly.

totok /ˈtɒtɒk/ *noun*. Pl. **-s**, same. M20.
[Malay, lit. 'genuine, pure-blooded'.]
A Chinese immigrant in Indonesia who retains a cultural affiliation with China.

Totonac /təʊtəˈnak/ *noun & adjective*. L18.
[Spanish *Totonaca* from Nahuatl *Totonacatl*, pl. *Totonaca*.]
▶ **A** *noun*. Pl. same, **-s**.
1 A member of an American Indian people of east central Mexico. L18.
2 The language of this people. E20.
▶ **B** *adjective*. Of or pertaining to the Totonac or their language. E20.
■ **Totonacan** *adjective & noun* (of or pertaining to) the language family of which Totonac is a member M20.

totora /təʊˈtɔːrə/ *noun*. E17.
[Quechua, Aymara *t'otóra*.]
A bulrush of alpine lakes in Peru and Bolivia, *Scirpus totora*, used to build boats, houses, etc.

¶ In isolated use before E20.

tot siens /tɒt ˈsins, tɒt ˈsiːns/ *interjection & noun*. *S. Afr.* M20.
[Afrikaans *tot (weer)siens* until we meet again, from Dutch *tot* until + *zien* see.]
(Goodbye) until we meet again; an utterance of this.

totsy /ˈtɒtsi/ *noun*. *slang*. M20.
[from TOT *noun*² + -SY.]
A sexually attractive or provocative woman.

Tottenham Pudding /tɒt(ə)nəm ˈpʊdɪŋ/ *noun phr.* M20.
[*Tottenham* in north London, where the feed was first produced.]
Feed for pigs or poultry consisting of sterilized kitchen waste.

Totten trust /tɒt(ə)n ˈtrʌst/ *noun phr. US*. M20.
[H. B. *Totten*, party to a court case in 1902 concerning an estate of which he was administrator.]
LAW. A tentative trust in the form of a savings account opened by one person acting as trustee for another, but revocable by the former at any time.

totter /ˈtɒtə/ *noun*¹. LME.
[from the verb.]
†**1** A swing. LME–M16.
2 The action or an act of tottering; an unsteady movement or gait. M18.
Comb.: **totter-grass** quaking-grass, *Briza media*.

totter /ˈtɒtə/ *noun*². L19.
[from TOT *verb*³ + -ER¹. Cf. TATTER *noun*³.]
A rag-and-bone collector; a person who goes totting.

totter /ˈtɒtə/ *verb*. ME.
[Middle Dutch *touteren* swing (so Dutch *touter* noun) from Old Saxon, corresp. to Old English *tealtrian* totter, stagger.]
†**1** *verb intrans.* Move or swing to and fro or up and down; *spec.* be hanged; *fig.* waver, vacillate. ME–M17.
2 *verb intrans.* Rock or shake as if about to overbalance or collapse; (of an institution, government, etc.) be insecure or about to collapse. Formerly also, tremble. LME.
3 *verb intrans.* Walk with unsteady steps or with difficulty; move or go shakily or feebly; reel, stagger. E17.
†**4** *verb trans.* Cause to shake to and fro, rock; make unstable. Cf. TOTTERED 2. Only in 17.

🕮 **2** U. SINCLAIR Whose delicatessen store was tottering on the brink of ruin. **3** W. BLACK A tottering white-headed old man. V. CRONIN He tottered back to bed and . . that afternoon he died.

■ **totterer** *noun* E18. **totteringly** *adverb* in a tottering manner M17. **tottery** *adjective* given to tottering; shaky, unsteady: M19.

†**tottered** *adjective*. L16.
[Orig. a var. of TATTERED. Later assoc. with TOTTER *verb*.]
1 = TATTERED 1, 4. L16–L17.
2 Of a building or ship: battered and shaken, in a tottering condition. Cf. TATTERED 5. E17–E19.

Tottie /ˈtɒti/ *noun*. *S. Afr. colloq.* (now considered *offensive*). M19.
[Abbreviation of HOTTENTOT *noun*: see -IE.]
A Nama.

totting /ˈtɒtɪŋ/ *noun*. L19.
[from TOT *verb*³ + -ING¹. Cf. TATTING *noun*².]
The action of TOT *verb*³; the salvaging of items from refuse etc. as a living.

tottle /ˈtɒt(ə)l/ *verb*. M18.
[In sense 1 app. imit. In senses 2, 3 by-form of *toddle, topple*, or *totter*.]
1 a *verb intrans.* Move and bubble like a boiling liquid or a brook; simmer. *Scot.* M18. ▸†**b** *verb trans.* Cause to simmer or boil. *Scot.* M–L18.
2 *verb intrans.* Move unsteadily with faltering steps. Chiefly *Scot.* E19.
3 *verb intrans.* = TOPPLE *verb* 2. *dial.* M19.
■ **tottling** *ppl adjective* that tottles; apt to topple over; shaky; *fig.* feeble-minded: M18. **tottlish** *adjective* unsteady, tottery M19.

totty /ˈtɒti/ *noun*. E19.
[from TOT *noun*² + -Y⁶.]
1 = TOT *noun*² 1. E19.
2 A girl or woman, esp. one regarded as sexually desirable; such girls or women collectively. *slang*. L19.

🕮 **2** M. SYAL If . . Martin could keep a high-maintenance totty like Tania happy, he must be doing something right. S. INGHAM Clever me, I've scored the most glorious bit of totty.

Comb.: **totty-pot** *slang* = POTTY *noun*.

totty /ˈtɒti/ *adjective*. Now *dial.* LME.
[App. from *tot-* as in TOTTER *verb* + -Y¹.]
Tottery; weak in the head; dizzy, dazed; tipsy.

totum /ˈtəʊtəm/ *noun*¹. Long *rare*. M17.
[Latin.]
A, or the, whole.

totum /ˈtəʊtəm/ *noun*². Now *dial.* E18.
[Latin: see TEETOTUM.]
(A game played with) a teetotum.

tou /tuː/ *noun*. L19.
[Chinese *dòu* (Wade-Giles *tou*).]
CHINESE ANTIQUITIES. A hemispherical pedestalled bowl with a lid of similar shape, used as a container for food, esp. during a sacrificial rite.

toubab /ˈtuːbɑːb/ *noun*. Freq. considered *derog*. Also **-bob** /-bɒb/. Pl. **-s**, same. L20.
[French *toubabe* from Wolof *tubaab* European.]
In central and west Africa: a white person, a western-ized person; a European.

toucan /ˈtuːk(ə)n/ *noun*. M16.
[French from Portuguese *tucano* from Tupi *tucan*, imit. of the bird's call.]
1 Any of various tropical American fruit-eating birds of the family Ramphastidae, distinguished by an enormous, usu. coloured, beak and brightly coloured plumage; *esp*. one of the genus *Ramphastos* or *Andigena*. M16.
2 (Usu. **T-**.) *The* constellation Tucana. M17.
1 toco toucan: see TOCO *noun*[1].
■ **toucanet** *noun* any of the smaller birds of the toucan family belonging to the genera *Aulacorhynchus*, *Selenidera*, and *Baillonius* E19.

Toucana *noun* see TUCANA.

touch /tʌtʃ/ *noun*. ME.
[Orig. from Old French *touche*, formed as TOUCH *verb*. In some later uses directly from TOUCH *verb*.]
▸ **I 1** The action or an act of touching, esp. with the hand or body; a very slight blow; RUGBY FOOTBALL (now *rare*) a touch-down; a hit, a knock (long *rare* or *obsolete*); *euphem*. (long *rare* or *obsolete*) sexual contact. ME. ▸**b** The fact or state of touching or being touched; contact. LME. ▸**c** *fig*. A stroke of wit, satire, etc. E16.
2 The faculty of perceiving by physical contact with part of the body. LME. ▸**b** The sensation produced by touching something; the quality of a thing as perceived by touching. LME.
3 The action or manner of playing a musical instrument, esp. a keyboard one; style of playing, esp. on a keyboard; *poet*. a note or snatch of music. LME. ▸†**b** A toccata. E17–L18. ▸**c** The manner in which a keyboard instrument responds to a player's touch. E19.
4 = TAG *noun*[2] 1. E19.

📖 **1** J. C. OATES Eddy . . feels a shy touch at his wrist. **b** W. COWPER The flax That falls asunder at the touch of fire. **2** J. MOYNAHAN For Lawrence touch is . . more powerful . . than sight. **3** P. V. WHITE To perform, with admirably light touch, . . the piano pieces of Mendelssohn.

▸ **II 5 a** The purity of gold or silver as tested with the touchstone and indicated by the official mark; *fig*. quality, kind, sort, 'stamp'. ME. ▸**b** An official mark on gold or silver indicating that it has been found to be of standard purity; a die, punch, or stamp for making this. Also, an official mark stamped on pewter. LME.
6 A mention, an allusion; a short statement. Now *rare* or *obsolete*. LME.
7 Orig. (*rare*), an iron rod used to ignite gunpowder. Later, something which ignites quickly, touchwood (*lit*. & *fig*.). LME.
8 A turn at something, a go. Formerly also, a mean or deceitful act. Now *rare*. L15.
9 = TOUCHSTONE 1; *esp*. black stone used in monuments. L15.
10 A distinguishing quality or characteristic. E16. ▸**b** A person's characteristic skill or aptitude in an activity, esp. a sport. E20.
†**11** (A) reproach; blame. M16–E17.
12 An affecting influence, *esp*. a slight one. L16. ▸**b** A sense, a feeling, (*of* an emotion etc.). L16.
13 An act of testing, a test; a criterion. Now *arch*. *rare* in ***put to the touch***. L16.
14 A very small quantity, a very slight amount; a dash, a trace; a slight attack *of* a condition affecting the body, a twinge. L16.
15 A light or quick stroke with a brush, pencil, chisel, etc.; a detail in a work of art; a slight effort in altering or improving a work. Usu. in *pl*. E17. ▸**b** A person's ability to use a brush, pencil, etc.; artistic skill; style or quality of artistic work. E19.
16 SHIPBUILDING. The angle at the broadest part of a plank that tapers towards both ends. E18.
17 a With preceding sum of money: a thing that costs or will sell for the sum specified. *slang*. E18. ▸**b** An act of theft; an act of asking for and getting money from a person. *slang*. M19.
18 The part of the pitch immediately beyond the touch-lines and goal-lines (in RUGBY & SOCCER, freq. in ***in touch***, ***into touch***, etc.) or formerly between the goal-lines and the end lines (in AMER. FOOTBALL). M19.
19 A close relationship of communication, agreement, or understanding. Only in ***in touch***, ***out of touch***, ***keep in touch***, ***lose touch*** below. L19.
20 CAMPANOLOGY. A series of changes less than a peal. L19.
21 STOCK EXCHANGE. The amount by which the lowest offer or selling price exceeds the highest bid or buying price. M20.

📖 **10** *Granta* It's little touches like that that'll show you the trained soldier. *Rolling Stone* Such classic pop touches as the glockenspiel . . flesh out the . . sound. **b** A. S. BYATT Alexander, reasonably good with boys, had less touch with adults. **11** H. JAMES Vineyards red with the touch of October. **13** G. GREENE A roast with a touch of garlic. S. J. PERELMAN Suffering from a touch of insomnia. F. WELDON Its sound was New Orleans Revival with a touch of folk. I. MURDOCH A little touch of brightness . . had been Patrick's red pyjamas. **14** H. JAMES He added a touch . . and then gave her his sketch. **b** ANNE STEVENSON Her touch, particularly in poetry, had been less sure. **16** JOYCE There was a dosshouse . . but it was only a tanner touch. **b** R. CHANDLER Make a quick touch on the Sternwoods for travel money. **17** B. BEAUMONT Woodward chased across . . to tap a rolling ball into touch.

Phrases: — **as touch** perfectly or absolutely — **at a touch** if touched even very lightly. **a touch** — = *a bit* — s.v. BIT *noun*[2]. **be in touch**, **be out of touch** show, or not show, one's customary skill; (see also ***in touch***, ***out of touch*** below). **easy touch** *slang* a person easily manipulated, *esp*. one easily induced to part with money; a task or opponent easily handled. ***finishing touch***: see FINISHING *ppl adjective*. **in touch** in communication or contact (*with*); in sympathy (*with*); ***in touch with***, aware of, informed about; chiefly in ***be in touch (with)***, ***get in touch (with)***, ***keep in touch (with)***; (see also **be in touch** above). †**keep touch** keep faith, keep one's promise. ***light touch***: see LIGHT *adjective*[1]. **lose one's touch** not show one's customary skill. **lose touch** cease to be in contact (*with* a person etc.); ***lose touch with***, cease to be informed about. ***Nelson touch***: see NELSON *noun*[1]. **out of touch** not in communication or contact; lacking in awareness or sympathy; not up to date or modern; (foll. by *with*). ***personal touch***: see PERSONAL *adjective*. **soft touch** *slang* = ***easy touch*** above. **to the touch** when touched. **touch of nature** (*a*) a natural trait; (*b*) *colloq*. [from a misinterpretation of Shakes. *Tr. & Cr.* III. iii. 175] a manifestation of human feeling with which others sympathize. **within touch** near enough to touch; within reach (*of*); accessible.

Comb. (partly from the verb): **touch box** (*obsolete* exc. *Hist*.) a box for priming powder, formerly forming part of a musketeer's equipment; **touch-dancing** dancing in which the partner is held close; **touch-finder** RUGBY FOOTBALL a person who or a kick which succeeds in driving the ball into touch; **touch football** a form of American football in which touching takes the place of tackling; **touch-hole** a small hole in the breech of a firearm through which the charge is ignited; **touch-in-goal** RUGBY FOOTBALL (*a*) (more fully ***touch-in-goal line***) either of the boundary lines of the in-goal area, extending from the goal-line to the dead ball line; (*b*) the part of the pitch immediately beyond the in-goal area; **touch judge** RUGBY FOOTBALL a person who performs duties equivalent to those of a linesman in other ball games; **touch-kick** RUGBY FOOTBALL: that sends the ball into touch; **touch-mark** an official stamp on pewterware, *esp*. one identifying the maker; **touch-needle** each of a set of slender bars of gold or silver alloy used as standards when testing other alloys on a touchstone; **touch-pad** a computer input device in the form of a small touch panel; **touch panel** a panel containing different areas that need only to be touched to operate an electrical device; **touch-paper** paper impregnated with saltpetre so as to burn slowly, used for igniting fireworks, gunpowder, etc.; **touch-piece** *Hist*. a coin or medal given by the sovereign to each person touched for scrofula ('king's evil'); †**touch-powder** fine gunpowder for priming a gun; **touch rugby** a form of rugby in which touching takes the place of tackling; **touch screen** COMPUTING a VDU screen that is also an input device operated by touching it; **touch shot** TENNIS a shot without any force; **touch tablet** COMPUTING a touch-pad which responds to the position of a finger etc. in contact with it in the same way as a conventional tablet does that of a mouse; **Touch-Tone** (proprietary name for) a telephone in which push-buttons take the place of a dial; **touch-type** *verb intrans*. type without looking at the keys.
■ **touchless** *adjective* (*a*) lacking a sense of touch; (*b*) intangible: E19.

touch /tʌtʃ/ *verb*. ME.
[Old French *tochier*, *tuchier* (mod. *toucher*), from Proto-Romance word of imit. origin.]
▸ **I** Senses in which physical contact is the dominant idea.
1 *verb trans*. Put the hand, finger, or other part of the body on (a thing); make physical contact with (a thing) *with* the hand, an instrument, etc.; bring (two things) into mutual contact. ME. ▸**b** Foll. by *to*: bring into physical contact with. ME.
2 *verb trans*. Come into, or be in, physical contact with, without voluntary action. ME. ▸**b** *verb trans*. GEOMETRY. Of a line: meet (another line or surface) at a point without intersecting it, even if produced; be tangent to. L16. ▸**c** *verb intrans*. Of two things: come into, or be in, physical contact with each other. E17.
3 *verb trans*. Strike lightly. ME.
4 a *verb trans*. Be immediately adjacent to; adjoin, border on. LME. ▸**b** *verb intrans*. Orig., be immediately adjacent. Now only *fig*., have mutual contact or common ground. LME.
5 *verb intrans*. Touch a thing. LME.
6 *verb trans*. Affect physically by contact in a way specified or implied by the context; cut; clean; decompose. LME.
7 *verb trans*. Bring *into* a specified condition by touching. Also foll. by *to*. E19.

📖 **1** A. DAVIES She touched my shoulder lightly. I. MURDOCH I touched the . . glass with my finger. **b** *Observer* He touches the wires to the terminals. **2** DAY LEWIS The . . skirt of her costume touches the ground. **c** N. FARAH They walked . . with their shoulders nearly touching. **4a** DICKENS Part of the road where it touched the river. **5** *New Yorker* After . . promising not to touch, I was allowed into the roped-off sanctum. **6** J. MOXON So hard that a File will not touch it.

▸ **II** Senses in which physical contact is present but not dominant.
8 *verb trans*. & †*intrans*. (with *with*, *at*). In neg. contexts: lay hands on so as to harm; harm or physically disturb in any way; meddle with. ME. ▸**b** *verb trans*. & †*intrans*. (with *with*, *at*). Have to do with in any way, have any dealings with. Usu. in neg. contexts. LME. ▸**c** *verb trans*. Consume; consume any of; make use of any of. Usu. in neg. contexts. LME.
9 a *verb intrans*. Of a ship, traveller, etc.: stop briefly at a place on the way. Usu. foll. by *at*. E16. ▸**b** *verb trans*. Visit in passing, call briefly at. L16.
10 *verb trans*. Affect deleteriously, esp. to a slight degree. Usu. in *pass*. L16.
11 *verb trans*. Slightly affect the colour or appearance of; slightly alter (a painting etc.). L16. ▸**b** Add (a detail) to a work of art, esp. a picture by lightly touching with the brush etc. L17.
12 *verb trans*. **a** Take, receive, obtain, (money); steal. Now *slang*. E17. ▸†**b** Bribe. M–L18. ▸**c** Ask for and get money from; obtain a loan or gift from. Usu. foll. by *for*. M18.
13 *verb intrans*. With compl. Feel to the touch. *rare*. L18.

📖 **8** SHAKES. *1 Hen. IV* The lion will not touch the true prince. R. SILVERBERG Anyone here touches you, you let me know, I'll make him sorry. **b** CONAN DOYLE 'It is only for the young lady's sake that I touch your case at all,' said Holmes. *Homes & Gardens* West has nine tricks in his hand without touching East's hearts. S. ELDRED-GRIGG Don't touch that . . . That's for your aunty Millie. **c** E. GLASGOW She hasn't touched a morsel all day. S. MILES The . . plate of liver and rice which I have not touched. **9a** R. HUNTFORD *Nimrod* touched first at Torquay. **b** A. MILLER I was . . on a freighter touching the Gulf ports. **10** C. BRONTË Two bottles of . . ale, and a double quart of Porter . . and I'm not a bit touched. **11** P. H. GIBBS Her rather full lips were touched with rouge. E. WELTY A flicker of amusement touched the young man's face. **12a** E. WALLACE He touched a purse from a stout old lady. **c** O. WELLES I . . touched him for the price of a first-class ticket to Monte Carlo.

▸ **III** Non-physical senses.
†**14** *verb trans*. Guess or state correctly; hit on. ME–L18.
15 *verb trans*. Produce tender or painful feelings in. (Foll. by *with*.) ME.
16 *verb trans*. & †*intrans*. (with *to*, *on*). Be the business of, be a concern of, (now *rare*); be of concern to, make a difference to, affect. ME.
17 *verb trans*. Imbue with a specified quality; affect mentally or morally. Usu. in *pass*., foll. by *with*. LME. ▸**b** Make slightly insane, slightly impair in intelligence. Usu. in *pass*. (cf. TOUCHED). E18.
†**18** *verb trans*. Affect (an organ of sense, a sense). LME–M17.
19 *verb trans*. = ***touch on*** below. Now *rare*. LME.
20 *verb trans*. Get as far or as high as, esp. briefly; reach. LME. ▸**b** Approach in excellence etc. Usu. in neg. contexts. M19.
21 *verb intrans*. Draw very near, verge. Usu. foll. by *on* (also *at*, *to*). LME. ▸**b** *verb trans*. NAUTICAL. Keep as close to (the wind) as possible. M16.
†**22** *verb trans*. Rebuke; criticize; say something telling about (a person). E16–M19.
23 *verb trans*. Formerly, grieve, upset. Now, annoy, nettle. M16.
24 *verb trans*. †**a** Influence (a person) in mind or will. L16–M17. ▸**b** Of feeling: affect (a person). M17.

📖 **15** L. BLUE I have always been touched by this Christian voice from the past. M. MARRIN I was touched at the kindness. **16** COVERDALE *Eccles*. 12:14 Feare God, and kepe his commaundements, for that toucheth all men. C. PEBODY Till . . a few years ago . . the Provincial Press was hardly touched. *Boston Globe* I never realized my drug addiction ever touched anyone else. **17** TENNYSON High nature amorous of the good, But touch'd with no ascetic gloom. **b** N. MARSH I thought he was a bit touched. **18** SHAKES. *Merch. V.* If . . any air of music touch their ears. **19** G. SARTON One point, however, that I would like to touch. **20** L. DEIGHTON The Mercedes touched seventy-five. **b** J. B. PRIESTLEY Never 'eard anybody to touch Tommy with a mouth-organ. **21** BURKE A political life just touching to its close. **23** J. ARCH It touched scores . . of labourers on the raw. **24b** SIR W. SCOTT Touched with pity and remorse, He sorrowed o'er the expiring horse.

▸ **IV** Contextual and technical uses.
25 a *verb trans*. & *intrans*. (with *to*). Have sexual contact with. Cf. ***touch up*** below. Long *rare* or *obsolete*. ME. ▸**b** *verb trans*. Finger so as to excite sexually; *refl*. masturbate. E20.
26 *verb trans*. Mark (metal) to show that it has officially been found to be of standard purity. LME. ▸**b** *verb trans*.

Test (gold or silver) for purity by rubbing it on a touchstone. M16. ▸†**c** *verb intrans.* Prove to be of standard purity when tested; *fig.* stand the test. E17–E18.

27 *verb trans.* Strike the keys or strings of (a musical instrument); strike (keys or strings); play on, cause to sound; produce (music) in this way. LME.

28 *verb trans. & intrans.* Lay one's hand on (a person) to cure scrofula. E17.

29 *verb trans.* Apply a substance lightly to (a part of the body) for medicinal purposes. E17.

†**30** *verb trans.* Magnetize by contact. E17–L18.

31 *verb trans. SCOTTISH HISTORY.* Give royal assent to (a bill) by touching it with the sceptre. L17.

32 *verb trans. RUGBY FOOTBALL.* = **touch down** (a) below. M19.

> 📖 **29** B. SPOCK The doctor may recommend touching it with an antiseptic powder.

Phrases: ***touch a nerve***: see NERVE *noun*. **touch base** *N. Amer.* make (personal) contact (*with*). ***touch bottom***: see BOTTOM *noun*. ***touch one's hat***: see HAT *noun*. ***touch on the raw***: see RAW *noun*. ***touch the ark***: see ARK 2. **touch the spot** *colloq.* find out or do exactly what was needed. **touch wood** touch something wooden with the hand to avert ill luck; freq. as an exclamation accompanying the action. ***would not touch with a bargepole***: see ***bargepole*** s.v. BARGE *noun*. ***would not touch with a pair of*** TONGS. ***would not touch with a ten-foot pole***, ***would not touch with a forty-foot pole***: see POLE *noun*[1] 1.

With adverbs in specialized senses: **touch down** (*a*) *verb phr. trans. & intrans.* (*RUGBY FOOTBALL*) bring (the ball) while held in the hands into contact with the ground behind the goal, usually that of the opposing side; (*b*) *verb phr. trans. & intrans.* (*AMER. FOOTBALL*) pass or carry (the ball) into the end zone of the opposing side. (*c*) *verb phr. intrans.* (*AERONAUTICS*) make contact with the ground in landing; land. **touch in** insert (a detail) in a painting etc. by touching with the pencil, brush, etc. **touch off** (*a*) represent exactly; (*b*) fire (a cannon etc.), orig. by putting a match to it; *fig.* provoke (a reaction), initiate suddenly. **touch on** mention lightly or in passing, allude to; formerly, speak or write of, relate; (see also sense 21 above). **touch up** (*a*) improve, finish, or modify by adding light strokes; put finishing touches to; (*b*) stimulate by striking lightly or sharply, esp. (a horse) with a whip or spur; *fig.* remind; jog (the memory); (*c*) *slang* finger or caress so as to excite sexually; sexually molest.

Comb.: **touch-back** in rugby football, an act of touching the ground with the ball on or behind the player's own goal-line after it has been driven there by the opposing side; a similar action in some other ball games; **touch-last** = TAG *noun*[2] 1; **touch-up** an act of touching something up; a stroke added by way of improvement or finish.

■ **toucha'bility** *noun* the quality of being touchable; suitability to be touched: M20. **touchable** *adjective* (*a*) affecting the sense of touch; tangible; (*b*) able to be affected in mind or feeling: LME. **touchableness** *noun* (long *rare*) = TOUCHABILITY E17.

touch and go /tʌtʃ (ə)nd ˈɡəʊ/ *noun & adjectival phr.* Also (esp. as attrib. adjective) **touch-and-go**. M17.

[from TOUCH *verb* + AND *conjunction*[1] + GO *verb*.]

▸ **A** *noun phr.* Pl. **touch and goes**.

1 a The action of touching something momentarily; a thing done quickly or instantaneously. *rare*. M17. ▸**b** *AERONAUTICS.* A manoeuvre in which an aircraft touches the ground as in landing and immediately takes off again. M20.

2 A precarious or delicate situation. M19.

▸ **B** *adjectival phr.* **1** Uncertain as to the outcome; precarious. M17.

2 Involving or characterized by rapid or superficial execution; sketchy; casual; expeditious. M19.

> 📖 **1** F. HOYLE It's going to be a touch and go business. *Sun* It was touch and go when Michael was born. **2** V. W. BROOKS In one of those *dégagé* touch and go sketches in which he . . sums up . . history.

touchdown /ˈtʌtʃdaʊn/ *noun*. M19.

[from ***touch down*** s.v. TOUCH *verb*.]

1 *RUGBY & AMER. FOOTBALL.* An act of touching the ground behind the opposing side's goal with the ball while it is held in the hands, to score points. Also (*AMER. FOOTBALL*), a score made by carrying or passing the ball into the end zone of the opposing side. M19.

2 *AERONAUTICS.* The action or an act of making contact with the ground during landing. M20.

touché /tuːˈʃeɪ/ *interjection*. E20.

[French, pa. pple of *toucher* to touch.]

1 *FENCING.* Acknowledging a hit by one's opponent. E20.

2 Expr. good-humoured acknowledgement of a valid point or justified accusation made by another person. E20.

> 📖 **2** A. S. BYATT 'You haven't contributed much.' . . 'How could I have?' 'Touché. I do go on.'

touched /tʌtʃt/ *ppl adjective*. LME.

[from TOUCH *verb* + -ED[1]. Cf. TETCHED.]

That has been touched; *spec.* (*a*) affected with tender or painful feelings; (*b*) slightly insane, slightly impaired in intelligence.

touched gold the touch-piece given by the monarch when he or she touched for scrofula, supposed to retain healing properties. **touched proof** a proof from an engraved or etched plate approaching completion, submitted to the artist of the original picture for approval or comment.

toucher /ˈtʌtʃə/ *noun*. LME.

[formed as prec. + -ER[1].]

1 A person who or thing which touches; *spec.* (*a*) *slang* a person who seeks to obtain loans of money or gifts; (*b*) a person who touches other people more than most. LME.

2 *BOWLS.* A bowl which touches the jack. E17.

3 A case of close contact, an exact fit; a very near approach, a near thing. *slang.* E19.

3 as near as a toucher very nearly, all but.

touching /ˈtʌtʃɪŋ/ *adjective*. E16.

[formed as prec. + -ING[2].]

That touches; *esp.* such as to excite tender feeling or sympathy; moving, pathetic.

> 📖 T. H. HUXLEY A touching faith in the efficacy of . . parliament. E. WAUGH The delight of these simple people . . is very touching.

■ **touchingly** *adverb* E18. **touchingness** *noun* M18.

touching /ˈtʌtʃɪŋ/ *preposition*. Now *literary*. LME.

[Old & mod. French *touchant* pres. pple of *toucher* to touch.]

In reference or relation to; respecting, regarding, concerning; (in concord with a preceding noun or pronoun, also) that refers or relates to. Also ***as touching***.

> 📖 STEELE A late Request . . touching the Care of a young Daughter. G. K. CHESTERTON Discoveries . . touching the neglected traditions of the London Boroughs.

touch-line /ˈtʌtʃlʌɪn/ *noun*. M16.

[from TOUCH *noun*, *verb* + LINE *noun*[2].]

†**1** *GEOMETRY.* A tangent. M16–L17.

2 In various sports, the boundary line on each side of the field of play, usu. extending from goal-line to goal-line. M19.

touch-me-not /ˈtʌtʃmɪnɒt/ *noun & adjective*. L16.

[from *touch me not*, translating Latin NOLI ME TANGERE.]

▸ **A** *noun*. †**1** The squirting cucumber, *Ecballium elaterium*. L16–M18.

2 A balsam or impatiens whose ripe capsules split open with a jerk on being touched; esp. *Impatiens noli-tangere*. M17.

▸ **B** *adjective*. Esp. of a person: that does not allow or invite touching. L16.

> 📖 J. SCOTT Who knows why a woman, hitherto touch-me-not, suddenly yields?

touchous /ˈtʌtʃəs/ *adjective*. *dial.* M19.

[formed as next + -OUS.]

Easily offended, touchy.

touchstone /ˈtʌtʃstəʊn/ *noun*. L15.

[formed as next + STONE *noun*, after Old French *touchepierre* (mod. *pierre de touche*).]

1 A smooth dark mineral, esp. a form of jasper, used for testing the quality of gold and silver alloys by rubbing it with the alloy and noting the colour of the mark made; a piece of such stone used for this purpose. Also, any smooth dark stone. L15.

2 *fig.* A thing which serves to test the genuineness or value of anything; a test, a criterion. M16.

> 📖 **2** G. BROWN The touchstone of political action is whether it is in line with their current dogma.

touchwood /ˈtʌtʃwʊd/ *noun*. L16.

[from TOUCH *noun*, *verb* + WOOD *noun*[1].]

1 The pale soft crumbly substance into which wood is converted by the action of certain fungi, esp. *Polyporus squamosus*, and which will burn for many hours when once ignited. L16.

2 Any of various bracket fungi, esp. *Fomes fomentarius* and *Phellinus igniarius*, used to make tinder; the tinder (amadou) made from such a fungus. L16.

3 A person who or thing which readily ignites (*lit.* & *fig.*); *esp.* an irascible or passionate person. Now *rare*. E17.

touchy /ˈtʌtʃi/ *adjective*. E17.

[formed as prec. + -Y[1]. In sense 1 perh. alt. of TETCHY.]

1 Easily moved to anger; apt to take offence on slight cause; irascible, irritable, tetchy. E17.

2 Sensitive to touch. E17. ▸**b** Easily ignited. M17.

3 Not to be touched without danger, requiring careful handling; ticklish, risky. E17.

4 Of a drawing etc.: characterized by or composed of distinct touches or light strokes. E19.

> 📖 **1** J. BARTH My landlord's right touchy about receiving calls for me. M. HOLROYD He was increasingly touchy about publicity. **3** J. BLUME This is a touchy subject, and I have to approach it carefully.

Comb.: **touchy-feely** *adjective* (*colloq.*) openly expressing affection or other emotions, esp. through physical contact; characteristic of or relating to such behaviour.

■ **touchily** *adverb* M17. **touchiness** *noun* M17.

tough /tʌf/ *adjective, adverb, noun, & verb*.

[Old English *tōh* = Old High German *zāh*, Middle Low German *tā*, from base also of Middle Low German *tei*, Dutch *taai*, Old High German *zāhi* (German *zäh*). Cf. TAUT *adjective*.]

▸ **A** *adjective*. **1** Of closely cohesive substance or texture, pliable or ductile rather than brittle; not easily broken or divided, strong, durable; (of food) difficult to chew. OE.

2 Viscous, sticky, glutinous. Now *rare*. OE.

3 Severe, rigorous; (of a contest etc.) strenuously and competitively maintained. ME.

4 Able to resist hardship, pain, fatigue, etc., having great physical and mental endurance, hardy. ME.

5 a Difficult to influence or affect; persistent, stubborn, uncompromising; hardened. ME. ▸**b** Uncompromising or severe towards opposition etc.; stern, strict, inflexible. (Foll. by *on*.) E20.

6 Difficult to accomplish or deal with; demanding, laborious, taxing; *colloq.* (of circumstances, luck, etc.) distressing, unfortunate, unjust (also as *interjection*, freq. *iron.*). (Foll. by *on*.) ME. ▸**b** Hard to believe or understand; taxing credulity or comprehension. Now *rare*. E19.

7 Violent, rough, or aggressive, esp. criminally so. L19.

8 Very good, excellent, fine. *US slang*. M20.

> 📖 **1** *Health Now* The dermis, the tough fibrous tissue of the skin. *Skin Diver* A tough impact-resistant thermoplastic housing. **3** *Times* Mrs. Marshall had a tough fight in her semi-final. **4** A. WILSON One of those frail-looking . . women who are in fact tough and wiry. **5a** B. HOLIDAY The first woman police judge, . . a tough hard-faced old dame. **b** *Crisis* Tough new measures to deal with this new wave of . . terrorism. **6** R. RAYNER To tell you how tough it is to break into screenwriting. N. SHERRY The trek to Zigita was short . . but extremely tough. I. BANKS That's all there is to it and if you don't like it, tough. **7** W. T. STEAD A district which was decidedly tough. I. MCEWAN They would all be tough gangsters . . hard men.

Phrases: **tough as old boots**, **tough as leather** *colloq.* very tough.

Special collocations & comb.: **tough guy** *colloq.* (*a*) a rough or violent person; (*b*) a hard or uncompromising person, a person not easily thwarted. **tough love** promotion of a person's welfare by enforcing certain constraints on them or requiring them to take responsibility for their actions; (*N. Amer.*) a political policy designed to encourage self-help by restricting state benefits. **tough luck** (*a*) bad luck, misfortune; (*b*) as *interjection* (freq. *iron.*), hard luck! too bad! **tough-minded** *adjective* realistic, sceptical, not sentimental or idealistic. **tough-mindedness** the quality of being tough-minded. ***tough nut***: see NUT *noun*. **tough pitch** commercially pure copper in which the amount of cuprous oxide is reduced by poling to minimize brittleness. **tough shit**, **tough stuff**, **tough titty** *slang* (chiefly *N. Amer.*) = ***tough luck*** (b) above.

▸ **B** *adverb*. †**1** Vigorously, stoutly; persistently. LME–E19.

2 In an uncompromising, aggressive, or unyielding manner. *colloq.* M20.

▸ **C** *noun*. A tough person, *esp.* a rough, violent, or criminal one; a thug, a ruffian. M19.

▸ **D** *verb trans.* Foll. by *out*: withstand or endure (difficult conditions etc.) to the end without flinching. Freq. with *it*. M19.

> 📖 *Observer* Fraser, it is assumed, will tough out this . . crisis. R. HARRIES Lewis, as it were, bit the bullet and toughed it out.

■ **toughish** *adjective* somewhat tough L18. **toughly** *adverb* LME. **toughness** *noun* LME.

toughe *noun* var. of TOGHE.

toughen /ˈtʌf(ə)n/ *verb*. L16.

[from TOUGH *adjective* + -EN[5].]

1 *verb trans.* Make tough. Freq. foll. by *up*. L16.

2 *verb intrans.* Become tough. Freq. foll. by *up*. E18.

> 📖 **1** C. HARKNESS I hate my school . . but Daddy was adamant. He said it would toughen me up. P. D. JAMES Old sandals, the leather stained and toughened by sea water. **2** C. LASSALLE You must toughen up, Laura. Or you'll go under.

■ **toughener** *noun* L19.

toughie /ˈtʌfi/ *noun*. *colloq.* Also **-ghy**. E20.

[formed as prec. + -IE.]

1 A tough person, *esp.* a rough, violent, or uncompromising one. E20.

2 A difficult problem, enterprise, etc. M20.

toughra *noun* var. of TUGHRA.

tought /tɔːt/ *noun*. Now *dial.* L17.

[Origin unkn.]

A length or section of an angler's hairline. Also, a piece of spun yarn.

tought *verb pa. t. & pple* of TINK *verb*[2].

toughy *noun* var. of TOUGHIE.

toujours /tuʒuːr/ *adverb*. E18.

[French.]

Always. Chiefly in phrs. below.

toujours gai /ɡe/, always cheerful, cheerful under all circumstances. ***toujours perdrix*** /pɛrdri/ [lit. 'always partridge']: implying that one can have too much of a good thing.

touladi /ˈtuːlədiː/ *noun*. Also (earlier) **tu-**. M19.

[Canad. French, perh. from Algonquian.]

The N. American lake trout, *Salvelinus namaycush*.

Toulousain /tʊ'lu:zeɪn; *foreign* tuluzɛ̃ (*pl. same*)/ *noun & adjective*. **L19.**
[from *Toulouse* (see below) + *-ain* **-AN.**]
▶ **A** *noun.* Also (fem.) **-aine** /-eɪn; *foreign* -ɛn (*pl. same*)/. A native or inhabitant of Toulouse, a city in SW France. **L19.**
▶ **B** *adjective.* Of, pertaining to, or characteristic of Toulouse. **L19.**

toup /tu:p/ *noun. slang.* **M20.**
[Abbreviation.]
= next.

toupee /'tu:peɪ/ *noun.* Also **-ée.** **E18.**
[Alt. of French *toupet* tuft of hair, from Old French *toup* tuft (from base also of **TOP** *noun*[1]): see **-ET**[1].]
Orig., a curl or artificial lock of hair worn on the top of the head, esp. as part of a wig; a wig with the front hair combed up over a pad into such a topknot; natural hair dressed in this way. Now usu., a patch of false hair or a small wig to cover a bald spot. Formerly also, a wearer of a toupee or topknot, a fashionable person.
■ **toupeed** *adjective* wearing a toupee **M19.**

toupet /'tu:peɪ, -pɪt, *foreign* tupɛ (*pl. same*)/ *noun.* **E18.**
[French: see prec.]
= prec.

tour /tʊə, *in sense 2b also foreign* tur (*pl. same*)/ *noun.* **ME.**
[Old & mod. French *tour*, earlier *tor*, *torn*: see **TURN** *noun.*]
1 One's turn to do something. Now usu. *spec.*, a spell of work or duty on military or diplomatic service, on an oil rig, etc.; the period of time to be spent at a particular post (also *tour of duty*). **ME.**
2 †**a** A circular movement, a revolution. *rare.* **ME–E18.** ▸**b** In a cotillion, a circular movement by the dancers. In *BALLET*, a turn by a solo dancer, usu. *en l'air.* **M19.**
†**3 a** A course to which one may turn, an expedient. **M16–L17.** ▸**b** A turn of phrase; a manner of expressing or presenting something; an aspect given to a matter. **L17–M18.**
4 A journey or period of travel from place to place, *esp.* a holiday comprising visits to a number of places on a route through an area. Also, a series of performances, matches, etc., at different places on a route. **M17.** ▸**b** A round, circuit, or survey *of*; an excursion, an outing, a ramble. **M17.** ▸**c** *MOTOR RACING* etc. A circuit of a racetrack, a lap. **M20.**
5 A crescent of false hair worn around the head. *obsolete* exc. *Hist.* **L17.**
6 A trill, variation, or change in the song of a trained canary. **E20.**

> 🕮 **1** *New Yorker* Schwarzkopf returned to Vietnam for a second tour. **4** *Spin* His solo tour, across four continents, will feature fifteen musicians. R. GITTINGS On a walking tour . . through the Lake District. ***conducted tour, grand tour, guided tour, package tour***, etc. ***on tour*** (esp. of a musical or dramatic group, sports team, etc.) touring. **b** R. RENDELL He . . made a careful tour of the house, checking . . everything.

Comb.: **tour operator** a travel agent specializing in package holidays.

tour /tʊə/ *verb.* **M18.**
[from the noun.]
1 *verb intrans.* Make a tour, esp. for a series of performances or matches or as a holiday. **M18.** ▸**b** *MOTOR RACING* etc. Of a car: travel very slowly. **E20.**
2 *verb trans.* Make a tour of (an area etc.). **L19.** ▸**b** Take (a play, entertainment, etc.) on tour; arrange for (a performer etc.) to tour. **L19.**

> 🕮 **1** H. WYNDHAM Godfrey . . has decided not to tour, . . so I shall ask Anthony. W. C. HANDY Playing for dances, touring on the road . . and giving concerts. **2** *Times Lit. Suppl.* We borrowed . . from municipal galleries and the exhibitions toured these. *Country Homes* The critically acclaimed production of *Showboat* . . is touring the country. **b** *Tucson Magazine* Performing groups will tour this production.

Comb.: **touring-car** a car with room for passengers and much luggage.

touraco *noun* var. of **TURACO.**

Tourangeau /turɑ̃ʒo/ *noun & adjective.* Pl. ***-eaux*** /-o/. **L19.**
[French, from *Touraine* (see below).]
(A native or inhabitant) of Touraine, a former province of France corresponding more or less to the modern department of Indre-et-Loire, or of its chief town Tours.
■ Also ***Tourangeois*** /turɑ̃ʒwa (*pl. same*)/ *adjective & noun* **M19.**

tourbillion /tʊə'bɪljən/ *noun.* Also (esp. in sense 3) **tourbillon** /tʊə'bɪlən, -'bɪjən; *foreign* turbijɔ̃ (*pl. same*)/. **L15.**
[French *tourbillon* from Old French *torbeillon*, from Latin *turbellae* bustle, stir, blended with *turbo* whirlwind.]
1 A whirlwind, a whirling storm. Now usu. *transf.* & *fig.*, a vortex, a whirl; an eddy, a whirlpool. **L15.**
2 A kind of firework which spins as it rises. **M18.**
3 *WATCHMAKING.* A revolving carriage in which the escapement is fitted to counteract position errors. **L19.**

tour de force /tʊə də 'fɔ:s, *foreign* turdəfɔrs/ *noun phr.* Pl. **tours de force** (pronounced same). **E19.**
[French.]
A feat of strength or skill; an impressive achievement or performance.

tour d'horizon /tur dɔrizɔ̃/ *noun phr.* Pl. ***tours d'horizon*** (pronounced same). **M20.**
[French, lit. 'tour of the horizon'.]
An extensive tour. Chiefly *fig.*, a broad general survey.

tourdion *noun* var. of **TORDION.**

tourelle /tʊ'rɛl/ *noun.* **ME.**
[French, dim. of *tour* **TOWER** *noun*[1]: see **-EL**[2].]
A turret.

tourer /'tʊərə/ *noun.* **E20.**
[from **TOUR** *verb* + **-ER**[1].]
1 A means of transport used (and specially designed) for touring, as a car, bicycle, caravan, etc. **E20.**
2 A person who tours or goes on tour. **M20.**

Tourette /tʊə'rɛt/ *noun.* **L19.**
[Gilles de la *Tourette* (1857–1904), French neurologist.]
MEDICINE. ***Tourette's syndrome, Tourette's disease, Tourette syndrome, Tourette disease***, a neurological disorder characterized by tics, involuntary vocalization, and often by the compulsive utterance of obscenities.
■ **Touretter** *noun* a person with Tourette's syndrome **L20.** **Tourettic** *adjective* pertaining to or characteristic of Tourette's syndrome **L20.** **Tourettism** *noun* Tourette's syndrome **L20.**

tourism /'tʊərɪz(ə)m/ *noun.* **E19.**
[from **TOUR** *noun* + **-ISM.**]
The theory and practice of touring; travelling for pleasure. Now *esp.*, the business of attracting tourists and providing accommodation and entertainment; the organization and operation of (foreign) holidays, esp. commercially.

> 🕮 J. CARTWRIGHT This is the age of tourism, not travel. *Holiday Which?* Soviet tourism is still geared to groups.

tourist /'tʊərɪst/ *noun & verb.* **L18.**
[formed as prec. + **-IST.**]
▶ **A** *noun.* **1** A person making a tour or visit as a holiday, often as part of a group; a person travelling for pleasure, esp. abroad. Also, a member of a touring sports team (usu. in *pl.*). **L18.**
2 *ellipt.* = ***tourist class*** below. **M20.**

> 🕮 **1** *Times* The . . Rugby Union tourists beat South West Africa . . in their match. P. THEROUX Guidebooks . . repeat falsifications . . for credulous tourists. B. VINE Conducting parties of tourists round Rome and Florence.

Comb.: **tourist class** the lowest class of passenger accommodation in a ship, aircraft, etc.; **tourist track** (*a*) a route from place to place frequented by tourists; (*b*) *NZ* a track through the bush for walkers; **tourist trap** *colloq.* (*a*) an object sold to tourists at an excessively high price; (*b*) somewhere regarded as a place where tourists are exploited.
▶ **B** *verb intrans.* Travel for pleasure, as a tourist. *rare.* **L19.**

touristic /tʊə'rɪstɪk/ *adjective.* **M19.**
[from prec. + **-IC.**]
Of, pertaining to, or of the nature of tourists or tourism, appealing to tourists.
■ **touristical** *adjective* = **TOURISTIC M19.** **touristically** *adverb* **E20.**

touristy /'tʊərɪsti/ *adjective. colloq.* (usu. *derog.*). **E20.**
[formed as prec. + **-Y**[1].]
Characteristic of, designed for, or appealing to tourists; consisting of or much visited by tourists.

tour jeté /tʊə ʒɛ'teɪ/ *noun phr.* **M20.**
[from French *tour* turn + *jeté* thrown: see **JETÉ.** Not found in French.]
BALLET. = ***JETÉ en tournant.***

tourmaline /'tʊəməlɪn, -i:n/ *noun & adjective.* **M18.**
[French *tourmaline*, German *Turmalin*, Dutch *toermalijn*, Spanish, Italian, *turmalina*, ult. from Sinhalese *tōramalli* cornelian.]
▶ **A** *noun.* **1** *MINERALOGY.* A brittle boron aluminosilicate mineral with a glassy lustre, occurring as prismatic crystals of the trigonal system, in compact or columnar masses, and in esp. granitic rocks, usually blackish and opaque (schorl), but also valued as a semi-precious stone in semi-transparent forms of various shades, and used (esp. for its pyroelectric and polarizing properties) in electrical and optical instruments. **M18.** ▸**b** A specimen or gem of this mineral. **E19.**
2 (Proprietary name for) a mink fur of a pale beige colour; the colour of this. **M20.**
▶ **B** *attrib.* or as *adjective.* Of the colour of tourmaline (sense A.2 above), pale beige. **M20.**
■ **tourmalinize** *verb trans.* (*GEOLOGY*) alter (granitic rock) into a form rich in tourmaline, esp. by hydrothermal veining (chiefly as ***tourmalinized*** *ppl adjective*, ***tourmalinizing*** *verbal noun*) **L19.** **tourmalini'zation** *noun* the process or state of being tourmalinized **L19.**

tourmente /turmɑ̃:t/ *noun.* Pl. pronounced same. **M19.**
[French: see **TORMENT** *noun.*]
A whirling storm or eddy of snow. Cf. **TORMENT** *noun* 3.

tourn /tʊən/ *noun.* **LME.**
[Anglo-Norman, from Old & mod. French *tourner* **TURN** *verb.*]
Hist. The twice-yearly tour or circuit made by the sheriff of a county, in which he presided at the court in each hundred; the court of record held on such an occasion. Cf. **TURN** *noun* 11b.

Tournai /'tʊəneɪ/ *noun.* Also **Tournay.** **M19.**
[See below. Cf. **DORNICK** *noun*[1].]
1 A kind of printed woven fabric produced in the Belgian town of Tournai and used for upholstery. **M19.**
2 More fully ***Tournai porcelain*** etc. A kind of porcelain manufactured in Tournai. **L19.**

tournament /'tʊənəm(ə)nt/ *noun.* **ME.**
[from Anglo-Norman vars. of Old French *torneiement*, *tur-*, from *torneier*: see **TOURNEY** *verb*, **-MENT.**]
1 *Hist.* A meeting or pageant at which mounted and armoured combatants jousted or fought with blunted weapons, originally in two groups but later in a series of single combats. **ME.** ▸**b** A display of military techniques, exercises, etc. **E18.**
2 *fig.* An encounter, a trial of strength. **M17.**
3 A contest in a game of skill between a number of competitors, *esp.* one played in heats. **M18.**
4 *MATH.* A set of points each of which is joined by a directed line to every other point, forming a digraph used esp. in modelling pairwise choices, contests, etc. Also ***tournament graph.*** **M20.**
3 ***chess tournament, tennis tournament***, etc.
■ **tournamental** *adjective* of or pertaining to a tournament **E19.**

tournasin /'tʊənəsɪn/ *noun.* **M19.**
[French *tournas(s)in*, from *tournas(s)er* turn pottery on a wheel from *tourner* **TURN** *verb.*]
A knife or spatula used to remove partially dried excess slip from decorated pottery.

Tournay *noun* var. of **TOURNAI.**

tournedos /'tʊənədəʊ, *foreign* turnədo/ *noun.* Pl. same /-dəʊz, *foreign* -do/. **L19.**
[French, from *tourner* to turn + *dos* back.]
A small round thick cut from a fillet of beef, with a surrounding strip of fat.
tournedos Rossini /rɒ'si:ni/ [see **ROSSINIAN**]: served with a croûton and pâté and a Madeira sauce.

tournee /'tʊəni/ *noun.* Also ***tournée*** /turne (*pl. same*)/. **L18.**
[French.]
A round, a circuit, a tour.

tournesol *noun* var. of **TURNSOLE.**

tournette /tʊə'nɛt/ *noun.* **E20.**
[French, from *tourner* to turn + *-ette* **-ETTE.**]
ARCHAEOLOGY. A rotating disc resembling a simple form of potter's wheel.

tourney /'tʊəni, 'tə:ni/ *noun.* **ME.**
[Old French *tornei* (mod. *tournoi*), from *torneier*: see next.]
1 = **TOURNAMENT** 1. **ME.**
2 = **TOURNAMENT** 3. **L19.**

tourney /'tʊəni, 'tə:ni/ *verb intrans.* **ME.**
[Old French *torneier*, ult. from Latin *tornus* **TURN** *noun.*]
Take part in a tourney or tournament.
■ **tourneyer** *noun* **ME.**

tourniquet /'tʊənɪkeɪ/ *noun.* **L17.**
[French, perh. alt. of Old French *tournicle* var. of *tounicle*, *tunicle* coat of mail, **TUNICLE**, by assoc. with *tourner* **TURN** *verb.*]
1 A device for stopping or slowing the flow of blood through an artery by compression, often with a bar twisted through a bandage, or a cord or rubber tube. **L17.**
2 A turnstile. *rare.* **E18.**

Tournois /'tʊənwɑ:, *foreign* turnwa/ *noun & adjective.* **LME.**
[French, from Latin *Turonensis* of Tours (see below). Cf. **TURNER** *noun*[2].]
Hist. ▶ **A** *noun.* Pl. same. Money or a coin struck at Tours (a city in France), one-fifth less in value than that coined at Paris. **LME.**
▶ **B** *postpositive adjective.* Coined at Tours. **L15.**

tournure /'tʊənjʊə, *foreign* turny:r (*pl. same*)/ *noun.* **M18.**
[French from Old French *torneure* from popular Latin *tornatura*, from Latin *tornare* **TURN** *verb*: see **-URE.**]
1 Graceful manner or bearing, deportment. **M18.**
2 The turning of a phrase, mode of expression. *rare.* **E19.**
3 The contour or shape of a limb etc. **E19.**
4 *Hist.* = **BUSTLE** *noun*[2]. Also, a kind of corset. **M19.**

> 🕮 **1** H. JAMES Drawing her muslin furbelows over the gravel . . she had the *tournure* of a princess.

tours de force *noun phr.* pl. of **TOUR DE FORCE.**

tours d'horizon *noun phr.* pl. of **TOUR D'HORIZON.**

tourte /tʊət, *foreign* turt (*pl. same*)/ *noun*[1]. **M17.**
[French from late Latin *torta* round loaf, cake. Cf. **TORTE.**]
A pie, a tart, a flan.

Tourte /tʊət, *foreign* turt (*pl.* same)/ *noun*[2]. L19.
[See below.]
A violin bow made by or to the design of François Tourte (1747–1835), perfecter of the modern bow. Also ***Tourte bow***.

tourtière /tʊətɪ'ɛː, *foreign* turtjɛːr (*pl.* same)/ *noun*. M20.
[French, formed as TOURTE *noun*[1].]
1 A kind of meat pie traditionally eaten at Christmas in Canada. M20.
2 A tin or round baking-sheet for tarts and pies. M20.

touse /taʊz/ *verb & noun*. Also **towse**, **-ze**. ME.
[Corresp. to Low German *tûsen* pull or shake about, Old High German *zirzuson*, *erzûsen* tear to pieces, German *zausen*: prob. already in Old English. In Middle English only with prefixes *be-*, *to-*. Cf. next.]
▶ **A** *verb*. **1** *verb trans.* Pull roughly about, handle roughly, = TOUSLE *verb* 1; (of a dog) tear at, worry. Now *Scot. & dial.* ME. ▸†**b** Pull out of joint, rack. *rare* (Shakes.). Only in E17.
†**2** *verb intrans.* Tussle; *fig.* rummage. M16–L17.
3 *verb trans.* Tease (wool). Long *obsolete* exc. *Scot.* L16.
▶ **B** *noun*. **1** Rough pulling about, horseplay; commotion, uproar, fuss. *dial.* L18.
2 = TOUSLE *noun* 2. *dial.* L19.
■ **tousing** *noun* (chiefly *dial.*) (**a**) the action of the verb; an instance of this; (**b**) a beating, a defeat: M16.

tousle /'taʊz(ə)l/ *verb & noun*. Also (now *rare*) **touzle**, **tow-**. LME.
[Frequentative of prec.: see -LE[3]. Cf. TUSSLE.]
▶ **A** *verb*. **1** *verb trans.* Pull about roughly, handle (esp. a woman) roughly or rudely; disorder or dishevel (esp. the hair); *fig.* abuse, maltreat. Also foll. by *about*, *out*, *up*. Freq. as ***tousled*** *ppl adjective*. LME.
2 *verb intrans.* Toss oneself about; *fig.* rummage. M19.

> **1** R. P. JHABVALA Undid her hair and tousled it with her fingers. J. AIKEN Two female figures with tousled hair.

▶ **B** *noun*. **1** A struggle, a tussle; a romp. *Scot.* M18.
2 A tousled mass or mop of hair etc. Freq. in ***tousle-haired***, ***tousle-headed*** *adjectives*. L19.
■ **tously** *adjective* characterized by being tousled or dishevelled; having tousled hair or clothes: M19.

tous-les-mois /tuːleɪ'mwa/ *noun*. *W. Indies*. M19.
[French = all the months, every month, but prob. alt. of *toloman* the name in the French Antilles.]
Any of several cannas with an edible starchy rhizome, esp. *Canna edulis*; the starch obtained from this rhizome.

Toussaint /'tuːsɛ̃/ *noun*. M20.
[French, from *tous* pl. of *tout* all + *saint* saint.]
Esp. in the W. Indies: *the* feast of All Saints (1 November).

tousy /'taʊzi/ *adjective*. Chiefly *Scot. & north*. Also **towsy**, **-zy**. L18.
[from TOUSE *verb* + -Y[1].]
1 Dishevelled, unkempt, tousled; shaggy, rough. L18.
2 Abundant, prolific. M19.

tout /taʊt/ *noun*[1]. E18.
[from TOUT *verb*[1].]
1 A thieves' scout or watchman. *slang*. Now *rare*. E18.
2 Watch. Only in ***keep tout***, ***keep the tout***. *slang*. Now *rare*. E19.
3 a A person who solicits custom. M19. ▸**b** In full ***ticket tout***. A person who buys up tickets for sporting, musical, etc., events in order to resell them at a profit. M20.
4 a A person who spies on the movements and condition of racehorses in training. Also ***racing tout***. M19. ▸**b** An informer; a spy. Chiefly *Scot. & N. Irish*. L19.

> **3a** R. CAMPBELL Pestered . . by . . those touts for houses of ill-fame. **b** *Scottish Rugby* Blame the ticket touts for ruining this . . for the . . fans.

tout /taʊt/ *noun*[2]. *Scot.* L18.
[Origin unkn. Cf. TOUT *verb*[2].]
1 A fit of ill humour, a sulk. L18.
2 A slight bout of illness. E19.

tout *noun*[3], *noun*[4] vars. of TOOT *noun*[1], *noun*[3].

tout /tu/ *adjective*, *noun*[5], *& adverb*. E18.
[French.]
All, everything; quite, entirely. Chiefly in phrs. below.
CAPABLE DE TOUT. DU TOUT. MALGRÉ ***tout***. ***tout au contraire*** /tut o kɔ̃trɛːr/ quite the contrary. ***tout compris*** /tu kɔ̃pri/ all included, inclusive. ***tout court*** /tu kuːr/ in short, simply, without qualification or addition. ***tout de suite*** /tu də sɥit/ at once, immediately, (cf. TOOT SWEET). ***tout le monde*** /tu lə mɔ̃d/ all the world, everyone. TOUT ENSEMBLE. TOUT PARIS. ***tout seul*** /tu sœl/ quite alone, on one's own. ***tout simple***, ***tout simplement*** /tu sɛ̃pl, sɛ̃pləmɑ̃/ quite simply, just that.

tout /taʊt/ *verb*[1].
[Old English *tȳtan* from Germanic base repr. also in Middle Low German *tûte* horn, funnel (Low German *tût(e)* spout), Middle Dutch *tûte* (Dutch *tuit* spout, nozzle), Old Norse *tûta* nipple, teat. Cf. TOOT *verb*[1].]
†**1** *verb intrans.* **a** Peep, peer, look out; gaze. OE–L17. ▸**b** Keep watch; be on the lookout. *slang*. L17–E18.
2 *verb trans.* **a** Watch, spy on. *slang*. L17. ▸**b** Spy on the movements and condition of (a racehorse in training) with a view to using the information for betting purposes. E19.
3 a *verb intrans.* Act as a tout or person soliciting custom; (foll. by *for*) solicit custom, employment, etc., pester customers; (chiefly *US & Austral.*) canvass *for* votes. M18. ▸**b** *verb trans.* Solicit the custom etc. of (a person); solicit custom for (a thing), try to sell; *gen.* recommend, advocate, extol. E20.

> **3a** R. MACAULAY A guide stood . . touting, calling out to . . people. W. GOLDING Trams which went up and down . . touting for custom. **b** A. TAN I was touted as the Great American Hope. *Japan Times* The . . researcher . . touted Retin-A as a wrinkle reducer.

tout /taʊt/ *verb*[2]. *Scot.* M16.
[Origin unkn. Cf. TOUT *noun*[2].]
1 *verb trans.* Toss or throw about in disorder; *fig.* canvass, discuss. M16.
2 a *verb trans.* Irritate, vex, tease. E18. ▸**b** *verb intrans.* Become irritated or unwell. E19.

tout ensemble /tut ɑ̃sɑ̃mbl/ *noun phr.* E18.
[French, from TOUT *adjective*, *noun*[5], & *adverb* + ENSEMBLE *noun*.]
= ENSEMBLE *noun* 1.

touter /'taʊtə/ *noun*. M18.
[from TOUT *verb*[1] + -ER[1].]
1 = TOUT *noun*[1] 3a. M18.
2 = TOUT *noun*[1] 4a. E19.
3 = TOUT *noun*[1] 1. *slang*. Now *rare*. M19.

tout Paris /tu pari/ *noun phr.* Also ***le tout Paris*** /lə/. L19.
[French, lit. 'all Paris, the whole of Paris'.]
Everyone of importance in Paris, Parisian high society; *transf.* everyone of importance in a specified place or community.

> *Times* The talk of le tout Paris in the French business world.

tou ts'ai /tuː 'tsʌɪ/ *noun & adjective*. M20.
[Chinese *dòucǎi* (Wade–Giles *tou ts'ai*) lit. 'contrasting colours'.]
CERAMICS. (Designating) a kind of Chinese porcelain delicately decorated with a blue underglaze overlaid with coloured enamels, developed in the reign of Ch'êng Hua (1465–87); (of or designating) this style of decoration.

touzle *verb & noun* see TOUSLE.

tovarish /tɒ'vaːrɪʃ/ *noun*. Also **-rich**. E20.
[Russian *tovarishch* from Turkic (perh. Tartar).]
In the former USSR, comrade. Freq. as a form of address.

TOW *abbreviation*.
MILITARY. Tube-launched, optically tracked, wire-guided (missile).

tow /təʊ/ *noun*[1].
[Old English *tow-* in *towcræft* spinning, *towhūs* spinning-house, rel. to Middle Low German *touw*, Old Saxon *tou*, Old Norse *tó* wool, tow, ult. from Germanic.]
1 The fibre of flax, hemp, or jute prepared for low-grade spinning. OE. ▸**b** *spec.* The short coarse fibres of flax or hemp, separated by the hackle from the finer part. Cf. LINE *noun*[1] 1, OAKUM. M16.
2 A bundle of untwisted natural or man-made fibres. M20.
1 have tow on one's distaff, **have tow on one's rock** *arch.* have business to attend to.
Comb.: **tow-coloured** *adjective* (of hair) very light in colour; **tow-head** (**a**) a person having) a light-coloured or unkempt head of hair; (**b**) *US* the hooded merganser, *Mergus cucullatus*, the male of which has a semicircular crest with a white patch; (**c**) *US* a sand bar or shoal causing ripples in a river or stream; **tow-headed** *adjective* having light-coloured or unkempt hair.
■ **towy** *adjective* like or of the nature of tow E17.

tow /təʊ/ *noun*[2]. Chiefly *Scot. & dial.* ME.
[Corresp. to Old Frisian *tow*, Middle Low German *touwe* (Dutch *touw*, German *Tau*), Old Norse *tog* (Norwegian *tog*, Swedish *tåg*, Danish *toug*, *tov*); rel. to TIE *noun*[1].]
1 A rope; a line, a chain, a cable. ME.
2 *spec.* A hangman's rope, a halter. L16.

tow /təʊ/ *verb*[1] & *noun*[3].
[Old English *togian* = Old Frisian *togia*, Middle Low German *togen*, Old High German *zogōn*, Old Norse *toga*, from Germanic. Perh. also partly from TOW *noun*[2]. Cf. TEW *verb*[2], TUG *verb*.]
▶ **A** *verb*. †**1** *verb trans.* Draw by force, drag; convey or carry (to a place). OE–L16. ▸**b** Draw *up* or let *down* with a rope. *Scot.* L16–M18.
2 *verb trans.* Of a vessel, vehicle, etc.: draw or pull (a vessel, vehicle, etc.) along on the water, ground, etc., by a rope, line, or bar. LME.
3 *verb intrans.* Advance or proceed by towing or being towed. E17.
4 *verb trans.* Drag (a person, animal, etc.) along behind one (as) by a line. Freq. *joc.* M17. ▸**b** ATHLETICS. Bring (other competitors) along rapidly by setting a fast pace. M20.

> **2** A. HARDY Tugs used to tow the smacks out of harbour. *Drive* It was the runner we towed away. The wreck was in the garage. *Earth Matters* An aeroplane towing a banner. **3** A. RANSOME The *Goblin*'s wake lengthened . . under *Wizard*, the sailing dinghy, towing astern. **4** BETTY SMITH Little girls towed baby brothers and sisters along.

▶ **B** *noun*. **1** A rope or line used for towing a vessel etc. E17.
2 The action of towing, the fact of being towed; an instance of this. Freq. in ***have in tow***, ***have on tow***, be towing (a thing or person); *fig.* have (a person etc.) in one's company, freq. as one's charge or responsibility. E17. ▸**b** = ***ski tow*** s.v. SKI *noun*. M20.
3 a A vessel etc. being towed; a string of boats, barges, etc., being towed. Also, a string of barges being pushed rather than pulled. E19. ▸**b** A vessel that tows something, a tug. L19.

> **2** DAY LEWIS Oh, he's got one of his Swedish blondes in tow. R. KIPLING Do you want a tow to Brixham? *Parents* The problems of shopping with a . . toddler in tow. *Ships Monthly* The intended tow of the trials/target ship . . to Rosyth . . did not take place.

Comb.: **towaway** *N. Amer.* the towing away of an illegally parked vehicle (***towaway zone***, an area from which such vehicles may be towed away); **tow-bar** a bar used in towing esp. a trailer or caravan; **tow-boat** a boat, *spec.* a tug, used for towing others; **tow-boating** *US* the piloting or operating of a tow-boat; **towfish** a housing for measuring or detecting instruments, designed to be towed underwater behind a ship; **tow-line** a line, rope, or cable used for towing anything; **tow-net** *noun & verb* (**a**) *noun* a drag-net or dredge used for the collection of natural specimens; (**b**) *verb trans. & intrans.* drag with a tow-net; **towpath** a path by the side of a canal or navigable river for use in towing; **tow-plane** an aircraft that tows gliders; **tow rope** a rope, hawser, cable, etc., used in towing; **tow-start** *verb trans.* tow (a vehicle) in order to start the engine.
■ **towability** *noun* M20. **towable** *adjective* able to be towed E20.

tow /təʊ/ *verb*[2] *trans.* Now *rare*. E17.
[from TOW *noun*[1].]
1 Comb or card (flax); bring to the state of tow or fibre. E17.
2 POTTERY. Smooth the surface of (earthenware or china) before firing, by rubbing with tow, sandpaper, or flannel. L19.

towage /'təʊɪdʒ/ *noun*. ME.
[Partly from Anglo-Norman *towage*, Anglo-Latin *towagium*; partly directly from TOW *verb*[1]: see -AGE.]
1 The action or process of towing or being towed. ME.
2 A charge or payment for towing a vessel. M16.

towai /'təʊwʌɪ/ *noun*. M19.
[Maori.]
A large New Zealand timber tree, *Weinmannia silvicola* (family Cunoniaceae), allied to the kamahi.

towan /'taʊən/ *noun*. E19.
[Cornish. Cf. Welsh *tywyn*, Breton *tevenn*.]
In Cornwall, a coastal sand-hill, a dune.

toward /*as adjective* 'təʊəd, *as adverb* tə'wɔːd, tɔːd/ *adjective & adverb*.
[Old English *tōweard* = Old Saxon *tōward*, Old High German *zuowart*, *-wert* directed forwards: see TO *preposition*, -WARD.]
▶ **A** *adjective*. †**1** That is to come, going to be; coming, future. OE–E17.
2 Approaching, imminent, impending. Usu. *pred.* Now *arch. & dial.* OE. ▸†**b** Forthcoming, ready at hand; in existence. LME–M16. ▸**c** In progress, going on; being done. *arch.* M19.
3 a Chiefly of a young person: disposed or willing to learn, promising. *arch.* ME. ▸**b** Compliant, obliging, docile. Now *arch. & dial.* ME. ▸**c** Of a thing: favourable, propitious. Opp. ***untoward***. *rare*. LME.
4 Left as opp. to right. *dial.* M19.

> **2** SHAKES. *A.Y.L.* There is, sure, another flood toward, and these couples are coming to the ark.

▶ **B** *adverb*. **1** In a direction towards oneself or something aimed at. Long *arch.* OE. ▸**b** To the left side or nearside of a horse etc. *dial.* E18.
2 Onward in a course, forward. Long *dial.* LME.
■ **towardness** *noun* (*arch.*) LME.

toward /tə'wɔːd, tɔːd/ *preposition*. OE.
[from TOWARD *adjective*.]
1 = TOWARDS *preposition* 1. OE. ▸†**b** = TOWARDS *preposition* 1b. LME–E17.
2 = TOWARDS *preposition* 2. OE. ▸†**b** = TOWARDS *preposition* 2b. LME–E17.
3 = TOWARDS *preposition* 3. OE. ▸**b** = TOWARDS *preposition* 3b. Now *dial.* E16.
4 = TOWARDS *preposition* 4. ME.
5 = TOWARDS *preposition* 7. LME.
6 a In preparation for; on the point of. Long *arch.* LME. ▸†**b** In store for, imminently threatening. LME–E17.
7 = TOWARDS *preposition* 5. LME.

towardly /ˈtəʊədli/ *adjective.* Now *arch. & dial.* LME.
[from TOWARD *adjective* + -LY[1].]
1 Favourably disposed, friendly, affable. LME.
2 Promising success, propitious; favourable, advantageous. E16.
3 = TOWARD *adjective* 3a, b. E16.
■ **towardliness** *noun* M16.

towardly /ˈtəʊədli/ *adverb.* Now *arch. & dial.* LME.
[formed as prec. + -LY[2].]
In a toward or towardly manner, obligingly.

towards /təˈwɔːdz, ˈtwɔːdz, ˈtɔːdz/ *preposition, adjective, & adverb.* OE.
[formed as TOWARD *adjective & adverb* + -S[3]: see -WARDS.]
▶ **A** *preposition.* **1** In the direction of, on the way to, so as to approach. OE. ▸†**b** To, so as to reach. LME–E17. ▸†**c** On the way to (a place). *rare* (Shakes.). Only in E17.
2 Directed to, facing, on the side next to. LME. ▸†**b** In attendance on, beside, with. LME–M17.
3 As regards, in relation to, in respect of. LME. ▸**b** Compared to, in comparison with. Now *dial.* M16. ▸**c** ***towards X, towards X's health***: used as a toast. Now *arch. & dial.* M18.
4 Nearly as late or as far on as, shortly before, near. LME.
5 As a contribution to; for making up or assisting a sum, total, etc. L15.
†**6 a** In prospect of or approaching an event, acquisition, etc. E16–L17. ▸**b** Coming up or in store for. M16–M18.
7 Verging on, nearly as much or as many as. L16.

> **1** D. ABSE My mother walked over towards me. E. BOWEN The Jaguar must have been nosing towards it for some time. J. HERBERT He lolled his head towards her. M. AMIS Joggers heading towards the park. *fig.*: *Times Educ. Suppl.* Ministers were not considering moving towards a baccalaureate. **2** A. HELPS A.. seat in a sheltered nook towards the south. E. WAUGH Mrs Stitch turned her face.. towards her visitor. **3** J. SIMMS I grew bitter towards my sister. *Lifestyle* Modern attitudes towards homosexuality are.. wrong. **4** V. S. PRITCHETT The sea-fog began to lift towards noon. *Linguist* Towards the end of the century, Romanticism made a come-back. **5** W. LAW She pays.. something yearly towards their clothing. I. COLEGATE To offer.. a small cheque towards the expenses. **7** J. H. NEWMAN When he is towards fifty, Mr. Wesley marries.

▶ **B** *pred. adjective.* = TOWARD *adjective* 2. LME–L18.
▶ **C** *adverb.* **1** = TOWARD *adverb* 2. *arch.* LME.
†**2** Towards an end or purpose, as a contribution towards something. Only in L15.

towel /ˈtaʊəl/ *noun & verb.* ME.
[Old French *toail(l)e* (mod. *touaille*), from Germanic base also of Old English *þwēan*, Old Saxon *þwahan*, Old High German *dwahan*, Old Norse *þvá* Gothic *þwahan* wash.]
▶ **A** *noun.* **1** A piece of rough-surfaced absorbent cloth used for drying a person or thing after washing or wetting. Also, a cloth or piece of absorbent paper used to dry plates, dishes, spillages, etc.; a tea towel. ME.
2 ECCLESIASTICAL. A cloth of linen, silk, etc., for use at communion or for covering the altar. Now *rare* or *obsolete.* ME. ▸†**b** A cloth used as a head-dress, girdle, etc. LME–M17.
3 In full ***oaken towel***. A stick, a cudgel. *slang.* M18.
4 = SANITARY ***towel***. L19.
1 ***bath towel***, ***hand-towel***, ***kitchen towel***, ***paper towel***, ***roller towel***, etc. **chuck in the towel**, **throw in the towel** *colloq.* (orig. BOXING) give up, admit defeat. ***Turkish towel***: see TURKISH *adjective.*
Comb.: **towel-gourd** the loofah or dishcloth gourd, *Luffa aegyptiaca*; **towelhead** *slang, offensive* a person who wears a head-cloth or turban; **towel-horse** a frame or stand on which to hang towels; **towel rail**, **towel ring**: on which to hang towels.
▶ **B** *verb.* Infl. **-ll-**, *__-l-__.
1 *verb trans.* Beat, cudgel, thrash. Also (*Austral.*) foll. by *up*. *slang.* E18.
2 *verb trans. & intrans.* Rub, wipe, or dry (esp. oneself) with a towel. Also foll. by *at*, *down*, *off*. M19.

> **2** M. CRICHTON The girls got out of the pool.. and began toweling off. *Times* Miller towelled himself.. as if he had just emerged from a shower.

■ **towelette** *noun* a small towel; *esp.* a small paper or cloth towel, pre-moistened and in a sealed package, used for cleansing: E20. **towelled** *adjective* wrapped in a towel E20.

towelling /ˈtaʊəlɪŋ/ *noun & adjective.* Also *__-eling__. L16.
[from prec. + -ING[1].]
▶ **A** *noun.* **1** Absorbent cloth, esp. cotton or linen with uncut loops, used as material for towels. L16.
2 The action or an act of towelling something; *spec.* (*a*) a rubbing or wiping with a towel; (*b*) *slang* a beating, a thrashing. M19.
1 ***terry towelling***: see TERRY *adjective.*
▶ **B** *attrib.* or as *adjective.* Made of towelling. M20.

tower /ˈtaʊə/ *noun*[1].
[Old English *torr*, reinforced in Middle English by Anglo-Norman, Old French *tur*, *tor*, (also mod.) *tour*, from Latin *turris* from Greek *turris*, *tursis*.]
1 A tall narrow building or structure, usu. of square, circular, or rectangular section, either standing alone or forming part of a castle, church, etc. (freq. with specifying word). OE.
2 A fortress or stronghold comprising or including such a tower. OE.
3 A structure resembling a tower; *spec.* (*a*) *Hist.* a tall movable structure used in storming a fortified place; a similar structure carried on the back of an elephant; †(*b*) CHESS = ROOK *noun*[2]; (*c*) *Hist.* a woman's very high head-dress built up in the form of a tower (cf. TOUR *noun* 5); (*d*) a tall structure used in an industrial process, for housing machinery, etc.; (*e*) *US* a railway signal-box; (*f*) (in full ***control tower***) a high building at an airport etc. from which air traffic is controlled by radio etc.; (*g*) = PYLON 4; (*h*) (in full ***tower block***) a tall modern building containing many flats or offices. ME.
4 *transf.* A lofty pile or mass. ME.
5 ASTROLOGY. = HOUSE *noun*[1] 9. *rare.* LME.
6 a Very high flight, soaring. Cf. TOWER *verb* 3. *arch.* LME. ▸**b** The vertical ascent of a wounded bird. L19.

> **1** M. ARNOLD And the eye travels down to Oxford's towers. W. PERRIAM The tower was Gothic, complete with pointed arches. ***bell tower***, ***church tower***, ***clock tower***, ***Martello tower***, ***round tower***, ***watch-tower***, etc. **4** L. BLUE Unsteady towers of reference books.

Phrases: IVORY ***tower***. **the Tower** the Tower of London; ***Lieutenant of the Tower***: see LIEUTENANT. **Tower of Babel** = BABEL 3. **tower of silence** a tall open-topped structure on which the dead are placed in accordance with Parsee tradition. **tower of strength** a person, institution, etc., giving strong and reliable support. **town and tower** *poet.* inhabited parts of a country or region.
Comb.: ***tower block***: see sense 3(f) above; **tower-cress** a cruciferous plant, *Arabis turrita*, similar to tower mustard; **tower karst** PHYSICAL GEOGRAPHY a type of karst characterized by isolated steep-sided hills; **tower mustard** (*a*) a narrowly erect cruciferous plant of sandy banks, *Arabis glabra*, with an inflorescence which elongates in fruit; (*b*) = ***tower-cress*** above; **Tower pound** [from the standard pound being kept in the Tower of London] *Hist.* a pound of 5400 grains (= 11¼ troy ounces), used as the legal unit of weight for precious metals etc. until the adoption of the troy pound in 1526; **Tower weight** *Hist.* weight expressed in terms of the Tower pound.
■ **towerless** *adjective* E19. **towerlike** *adjective* resembling (that of) a tower M16.

tower /ˈtəʊə/ *noun*[2]. E17.
[from TOW *verb*[1] + -ER[1].]
A person who tows or pulls something with a rope etc., esp. a boat on a river or canal.

tower /ˈtaʊə/ *verb.* LME.
[from TOWER *noun*[1].]
†**1** *verb trans.* Provide with a tower or towers. LME–M16.
2 *verb intrans.* Rise to or reach a great height, stand high; *fig.* be eminent or superior. Freq. foll. by *above*, *over*. L16.
3 *verb trans.* Raise or uplift to a height; *fig.* exalt. L16.
4 a *verb intrans.* Esp. of a bird: soar aloft; *spec.* in FALCONRY, (of a hawk) soar up and hover so as to be able to swoop down on the quarry. L16. ▸†**b** *verb trans.* Soar up in, rise up to. E–M17. ▸**c** *verb intrans.* Of a wounded bird: rise vertically. L18.

> **2** R. CHURCH Great elms towering up. G. DALY Turner, the aged.. recluse who towered over British painting. R. RENDELL On high heels.. she towered over Robin.

towered /ˈtaʊəd/ *adjective.* LME.
[from TOWER *noun*[1], *verb*: see -ED[2], -ED[1].]
1 Having a tower or towers; raised or rising like a tower. LME.
2 Of a wounded bird: that has risen vertically. E19.

> **1** TENNYSON The river winding clearly Down to tower'd Camelot.

towering /ˈtaʊərɪŋ/ *adjective.* L16.
[from TOWER *verb* + -ING[2].]
1 That towers or rises high; very high or tall, lofty. L16.
2 Rising to a high pitch of intensity, violent. E17.
3 *fig.* Extremely eminent, exalted; aiming high, ambitious. E17.

> **1** R. PILCHER That world of endless moors and towering hills. R. BANKS A towering grim man in overalls. **2** B. CHATWIN He flew into a towering rage. **3** C. THIRLWALL A man.. of towering ambition. A. STEVENS In contrast to the.. inadequate pastor, Freud was a towering figure.

■ **toweringly** *adverb* E19.

towery /ˈtaʊəri/ *adjective.* Chiefly *poet.* M16.
[from TOWER *noun*[1] + -Y[1].]
1 Characterized by, resembling, or having towers. M16.
2 Towering, lofty, exalted. M18.

towhee /ˈtəʊ(h)iː, ˈtaʊ-/ *noun. N. Amer.* M18.
[Imit. of the call of *Pipilo erythrophthalmus* (see below).]
Any of several buntings of the genus *Pipilo*, of brush and woodland in N. America, *esp.* (in full ***rufous-sided towhee***) the most widespread, the brightly coloured *P. erythrophthalmus* (also called ***chewink***, ***ground robin***, ***swamp robin***).

towing /ˈtəʊɪŋ/ *noun.* LME.
[from TOW *verb*[1] + -ING[1].]
The action or process of TOW *verb*[1]; *spec.* the drawing of a fine net behind a boat to capture marine zoological specimens; in *pl.*, the proceeds of this, the specimens captured.
Comb.: **towing hook**: to which a towline is fastened; **towing light**: to indicate that a vessel is towing or being towed; **towing line** = ***tow-line*** s.v. TOW *verb*[1] & *noun*[3]; **towing net** = ***tow-net*** s.v. TOW *verb*[1] & *noun*[3]; **towing path** = ***towpath*** s.v. TOW *verb*[1] & *noun*[3]; **towing rope** = ***tow rope*** s.v. TOW *verb*[1] & *noun*[3].

towkay /ˈtaʊkeɪ/ *noun.* M19.
[Malay *tauke* from Chinese dial. *thâu-ke*.]
A Chinese businessman or employer, esp. in Malaysia.

town /taʊn/ *noun.*
[Old English *tūn* = Old Frisian, Old Saxon *tūn*, Old High German *zūn* (Dutch *tuin* garden, German *Zaun*) fence, hedge, Old Norse *tún* from Germanic, rel. to Celtic, Old Irish *dún*, Welsh *din* (in place-names) fort, camp, castle, fortified place. Cf. TOONIE.]
1 †**a** An enclosed piece of ground, an enclosure; a field, a garden, a courtyard. OE–LME. ▸**b** *spec.* The enclosed land surrounding or belonging to a single dwelling; a farm with its farmhouse. Long *obsolete* exc. *Scot.* OE.
2 The house or group of houses or buildings on an area of enclosed land; a farmstead, a homestead. Now chiefly *Scot.* OE.
3 A cluster of houses or other buildings; a small village, a hamlet. Now *Scot., dial., & Austral.* OE.
4 An inhabited place larger and more regularly built and with more complete and independent local government than a village but not created a city. Also without article (and freq. preceded by a preposition): (the centre of) some village, town, or city understood or identified contextually; the chief town of a district or province, the capital, *spec.* London. OE. ▸**b** *The* areas in and around cities and conurbations, *the* part of a State in and near the capital, *spec.* as distinguished from the country. OE.
5 The people or entire community of a town, the townspeople; *arch.* the fashionable society of London or some other large city. ME. ▸**b** The civic community inhabiting a place as opp. to resident members of a university in the place (esp. Oxford or Cambridge). Chiefly in ***town and gown*** s.v. GOWN *noun* 1c. M17.
6 a A division of a county, which may contain one or more villages or towns; a township; the inhabitants of such a division. *N. Amer.* M17. ▸**b** A municipal corporation, having its own geographical boundaries. *US.* E19.
7 A concentration of burrows of prairie dogs. Cf. VILLAGE 3. E19.

> **4** J. S. WINTER In time to catch the next train up to Town. A. GORDON In the little town of Kail.. there were three.. markets. D. LESSING He had gone into town. DAY LEWIS Down the steep hill into the centre of town. ***country town***, ***garrison town***, ***market town***, ***mill town***, etc. **b** BURKE The quiet of the town is purchased by the ruin of the country. **5** LD MACAULAY His Absolom and Achitophel.. had amazed the town.

Phrases: ***corporate town***: see CORPORATE *adjective* 1. ***down town***: see DOWN *preposition*. ***girl about town***, ***girl of the town***: see GIRL *noun*. **go to town** *colloq.* do something energetically, enthusiastically, or extravagantly. **man about town**, **woman about town** a person who is constantly in the public eye or in the round of social functions, fashionable activities, etc. ***new town***: see NEW *adjective*. ***old town***: see OLD *adjective*. **on the town** (*a*) enjoying the entertainments, esp. the night life, of a town, celebrating; (*b*) getting a living by prostitution, thieving, etc. ***open town***: see OPEN *adjective*. **out of town** away from a town, outside a town (cf. OUT-OF-TOWN); ***ride out of town on a rail***, ***run out of town on a rail***: see RAIL *noun*[2]. ***paint the town red***: see PAINT *verb*. ***paper town***: see PAPER *noun & adjective*. ***satellite town***: see SATELLITE *noun* 3b. ***the talk of the town***: see TALK *noun*[1]. **town and country planning** the preparation of plans involving the development of towns and countryside (cf. ***town planning*** below). ***town and tower***: see TOWER *noun*[1]. ***twin town***: see TWIN *adjective & noun*. ***woman about town***: see ***man about town*** above. **woman of the town** *arch.* a prostitute.
Comb.: **town ball** *US* (now *rare* or *obsolete*) a game resembling baseball; **town-bull** *Hist.*: formerly kept in turn by the cow-keepers of a village; **town car** *US* a four-door car with a passenger compartment which is permanently enclosed and a driver's compartment which is not; **town clerk** (now *Hist.*) the secretary and legal adviser of a town corporation in charge of records, correspondence, municipal elections, etc. (in Britain until 1974); **town clown** *US slang* a policeman working in a village or small town; **town council** the elective governing and administrative body in a municipality; **town councillor** an elected member of a town council; ***town crier***: see CRIER 2a; **town-end** (now *Scot. & dial.*) the end of the main street of a town or village; **town gas**: manufactured and supplied for domestic or commercial use, based on coal gas; **town-guard** (*a*) SCOTTISH HISTORY the military guard of a town; (*b*) the guard policing a garrison town; **town hall** a large hall or building used for the administration of local government, the holding of court sessions, public meetings, entertainments, etc.; ***town-hall clock(s)***, the plant moschatel, *Adoxa moschatellina*, which has a head of four green flowers each facing in a different direction, with a fifth on top; **town home** *US* = ***town-house*** (c) below; **town house** (*a*) a town hall; (*b*) a residence in a town, esp. as opp. to one in the country; (*c*) a terrace house, esp. of a stylish modern type; **townland** esp. in Ireland, a division of land of varying extent; a territorial division, a township; **town-major** *Hist.* (*a*) the major of a town-guard; (*b*) the

chief executive officer in a garrison town or fortress; (*c*) the chief magistrate or administrative officer of a foreign town; (*d*) an officer responsible for liaison between troops stationed in a town and the townspeople; **townman** †(*a*) a villein; (*b*) a man living in a town, *esp.* one following town ways; **town marshal** *US* a sheriff; **town mayor** the chair of a town council; **town-meeting** a general assembly of the inhabitants of a town; *spec.* in *US*, a legal meeting of the qualified voters of a town for the administration of local government; ***town mouse***: see MOUSE *noun*; **town plan** a ground-plan showing the positions of the streets and buildings in the proposed development of a town; **town-plan** *verb trans. & intrans.* prepare a plan for the construction or development of (a building etc.) in a town; **town planner** a person whose occupation is town planning; **town planning** the preparation of plans involving the construction and growth of a town, taking into account conditions of housing and traffic, the convenient situation of public buildings, open spaces, etc.; **townscape** (*a*) a picture or view of a town; (*b*) the arrangement and overall appearance of the buildings and other features of a town; **townscaping** the planning of a townscape; **townsfolk** = *townspeople* below; **townsman** †(*a*) = *townman* (a) above; (*b*) a man living in a town or city, a citizen; (*c*) an ordinary citizen or resident of a university town as opp. to a gownsman or member of the university; (*d*) (usu. with *possess.*) a man of one's own town; (*e*) = *selectman* s.v. SELECT *adjective & noun*; **townspeople** (*a*) people who live in a town; (*b*) (usu. with *possess.*) people living in the same town; fellow-townsmen; **townsperson** a townsman, a townswoman; **townswoman** a woman inhabitant of a town; ***Townswomen's Guild***, an urban organization of women engaging in educational and social activities; **town-talk** the common talk or gossip of the people of a town; **town-traveller** a commercial traveller whose operations are confined to the town which is his or her employer's place of business; **town twinning** the establishment of regular contacts between two towns in different countries; **town-way** (*rare*, Shakes.) the way to the town.

■ **townful** *noun* as many as a town contains or will contain M19. **townhood** *noun* the condition or status of a town M19. **townify** *verb trans.* (*colloq.*) cause to resemble a town, give characteristics of a town to L18. **townish** *adjective* †(*a*) situated or existing in a town; urban; (*b*) characteristic of the town or town life, esp. as opp. to the country; having the manners or habits of town-dwellers: LME. **townishness** *noun* M19. **townless** *adjective* LME. **townlet** *noun* a very small town M16. **townly** *adjective* pertaining to or characteristic of a town; having the manners or habits of a town-dweller: M18. **townward** *adverb & adjective* (*a*) *adverb* [orig. *to the townward*] in the direction of a town; (*b*) *adjective* going or directed toward a town: LME. **townwards** *adverb* = TOWNWARD *adverb* L19.

town /taʊn/ *verb trans. rare.* L16.
[from the noun.]
1 Provide with a town or towns. L16.
2 Make (a community) into a town. L19.

townee /ˈtaʊni, taʊˈniː/ *noun & adjective.* Freq. *derog.* M19.
[from TOWN *noun* + -EE¹. Cf. TOWNY.]
▶ **A** *noun.* A person living in a town, esp. as opp. to a member of a university or a country-dweller. M19.
▶ **B** *adjective.* Of, pertaining to, or characteristic of a town-dweller or a town. M20.

townie *noun & adjective* var. of TOWNY.

Townsend /ˈtaʊnzɛnd/ *noun.* M20.
[Sir John *Townsend* (1868–1957), Irish physicist.]
PHYSICS. Used *attrib.* with ref. to phenomena and concepts related to Townsend's work on the conduction of electricity through gases.
Townsend avalanche: see AVALANCHE *noun* 2b. **Townsend current**, **Townsend discharge** a dark, low-current electric discharge in a gas that depends on an external source of ionization for its continuance.

township /ˈtaʊnʃɪp/ *noun.* OE.
[from TOWN *noun* + -SHIP.]
†**1** The inhabitants of a village collectively; the community occupying an enclosed piece of ground. OE–ME.
2 a The community inhabiting a particular manor or parish; such a manor or parish as a territorial division. Now chiefly *Hist.* LME. ▸**b** *spec.* Each of the local divisions or districts of a large parish, each containing a village or small town, usu. having its own church. M16.
3 An independent or self-governing town or village, orig. in ancient Greece or Italy, later in certain other countries in medieval or modern times. E17.
4 A division of a county (now usu. six miles square) having certain corporate powers of local administration; *gen.* = TOWN *noun* 6a. *N. Amer.* L17.
5 A site reserved for and laid out as a town (*Hist.*); a settlement at an early stage of development; a small town, a village, a hamlet. *Austral. & NZ.* L18.
6 A farm held in joint tenancy. *Scot.* E19.
7 *Hist.* A basic unit of local or social organization in the Anglo-Saxon period. M19.
8 In South Africa, an area set aside for non-white occupation. M20.

Townsville /ˈtaʊnzvɪl/ *noun.* M20.
[A town on the coast of Queensland, Australia.]
Townsville stylo [STYLO *noun*²], (now *rare*) ***Townsville lucerne***, a trifoliate leguminous plant, *Stylosanthes sundaica*, grown as a fodder plant in northern Australia and other tropical regions.

towny /ˈtaʊni/ *noun & adjective. colloq.* Also **townie**. E19.
[from TOWN *noun*: see -Y⁶, -Y¹. Cf. TOWNEE.]
▶ **A** *noun.* **1** A town-bred person; a person accustomed to town life. Freq. *derog.* E19.
2 A townsperson as opp. to a member of the university in a town. *US slang.* M19. ▸**b** A town-dweller as opp. to a person travelling with a circus or carnival. *N. Amer. slang.* M20.
3 A fellow-townsman or -townswoman. *slang.* M19.

📖 **1** *Satellite Times* Enough skyscrapers to keep even the most dedicated of townies happy.

▶ **B** *adjective.* Of, pertaining to, or characteristic of a town; townish. Freq. *derog.* M19.

📖 R. JAFFE He just hoped he didn't look like a townie thug.

■ **towniness** *noun* L19.

tow-row /taʊˈraʊ/ *adjective, verb, & noun.* Orig. *dial.* E18.
[Redupl. of ROW *noun*³.]
▶† **A** *adjective.* Intoxicated. *slang.* Only in E18.
▶ **B** *verb intrans.* Make a din. M19.
▶ **C** *noun.* An uproar, a hubbub, a din. L19.

towse *verb & noun* var. of TOUSE.

towser /ˈtaʊzə/ *noun. arch.* Also **T-**. L17.
[from *towse* var. of TOUSE + -ER¹.]
A large dog, esp. of the kind formerly used in bear- or bull-baiting; *transf.* a savage, violent person, a rough uncouth person.

towsy *adjective*, **towze** *verb & noun* vars. of TOUSY, TOUSE.

towzle *verb & noun* see TOUSLE.

towzy *adjective* var. of TOUSY.

tox- /tɒks/ *combining form* repr. TOXI- or TOXO-² before a vowel. Cf. TOXICO-.
■ **toˈxalbumin** *noun* any of various toxic albumins found in some fungi, animal venoms, and bacterial cultures, many of which are neurotoxins L19. **toxaphene** *noun* (CHEMISTRY) chlorinated camphene, a toxic amber waxy solid which has an odour of chlorine and camphor and is used chiefly as an insecticide M20.

toxaemia /tɒkˈsiːmɪə/ *noun.* Also ***toxemia**. M19.
[from prec. + Greek *haima* blood: see -IA¹.]
1 MEDICINE & VETERINARY MEDICINE. An illness or condition caused by the spread of bacterial or other toxins by the bloodstream. M19.
2 MEDICINE. In full ***toxaemia of pregnancy***. Any of various metabolic disorders occurring in pregnant women, resulting in pre-eclampsia or eclampsia. E20.

toxi- /tɒksi/ *combining form* of TOXIC or TOXIN: see -I-. Cf. TOX-, TOXICO-, TOXO-².
■ **toxiˈgenic** *adjective* producing a toxin or toxic effect; caused by a toxin: E20. **toxigeˈnicity** *noun* the state of being toxigenic; the degree to which something is toxigenic: E20. **toxiˈphobia** *noun* irrational fear of being poisoned L19.

toxic /ˈtɒksɪk/ *adjective & noun.* M17.
[medieval Latin *toxicus* poisoned, from classical Latin *toxicum* poison from Greek *toxikon pharmakon* poison for smearing arrows (*toxikos* orig. meaning 'of or pertaining to the bow', from *toxon* bow).]
▶ **A** *adjective.* **1** Of the nature of a poison; poisonous. M17.
2 Caused or produced by a poison; due to poisoning. L19.
2 **toxic shock syndrome** MEDICINE a state of acute shock in women due to septicaemia, freq. caused by bacterial infection resulting from a retained tampon, IUD, etc.
▶ **B** *noun.* = TOXIN. Now *rare.* L19.
■ **toxical** *adjective* (now *rare* or *obsolete*) of toxic nature or character E17.

toxic- *combining form* see TOXICO-.

toxicant /ˈtɒksɪk(ə)nt/ *adjective & noun.* L19.
[Var. of INTOXICANT with differentiation of meaning: see -ANT¹. Cf. next.]
▶ **A** *adjective.* Poisonous, toxic. *rare.* L19.
▶ **B** *noun.* A toxic substance, a poison; formerly *spec.*, a narcotic drug. L19.

toxication /tɒksɪˈkeɪʃ(ə)n/ *noun.* E19.
[Var. of INTOXICATION 1.]
Poisoning, esp. by the toxins of pathogenic micro-organisms.

toxicity /tɒkˈsɪsɪti/ *noun.* L19.
[from TOXIC + -ITY.]
Toxic or poisonous quality, esp. in relation to its degree or strength.

toxico- /ˈtɒksɪkəʊ/ *combining form.* Before a vowel also **toxic-**.
[from Greek *toxikon* poison (see TOXIC) or TOXIC: see -O-. Cf. TOX-, TOXI-, TOXO-².]
■ **toxicoˈgenic** *adjective* = TOXIGENIC L19. **toxiˈcosis** *noun*, pl. **-coses**, a disease or condition produced by the action of a toxin; poisoning: M19.

toxicodendron /ˌtɒksɪkəˈdɛndrɒn/ *noun.* E18.
[mod. Latin genus or species name (see below), formed as prec. + Greek *dendron* tree.]
Any of several N. American sumacs (genus *Rhus*), formerly (and still sometimes) regarded as forming a separate genus *Toxicodendron*; *spec.* the poison-oak, *Rhus toxicodendron* (formerly *Toxicodendron toxicaria*).

toxicology /tɒksɪˈkɒlədʒi/ *noun.* M19.
[from TOXICO- + -LOGY.]
The branch of science that deals with the nature, effects, and detection of poisons.
■ **ˌtoxicoˈlogical** *adjective* M19. **ˌtoxicoˈlogically** *adverb* L19. **toxicologist** *noun* M19.

toxin /ˈtɒksɪn/ *noun.* L19.
[from TOXIC: see -IN¹.]
Any poisonous antigenic substance produced by or derived from micro-organisms, which causes disease when present at low concentration in the body. Also more widely, any antigenic poison or venom of plant or animal origin.
Comb.: **toxin-antitoxin** a mixture of a toxin and an antitoxin which is sometimes used in immunization.

toxo- /tɒksəʊ/ *combining form*¹ of Greek *toxon* bow: see -O-.

toxo- /ˈtɒksəʊ/ *combining form*² of TOXIN, or instead of TOXICO-: see -O-. Cf. TOX-, TOXI-.
■ **toxophore** *noun & adjective* (*a*) *noun* a toxophoric group; (*b*) *adjective* = TOXOPHORIC: L19. **toxoˈphoric**, **toˈxophorous** *adjectives* poison-bearing; designating a particular group of atoms in the molecule of a toxin to which its toxic properties are due: E20.

toxocara /tɒksəˈkɑːrə/ *noun.* Also **T-**. M20.
[mod. Latin (see below), from TOXO-¹ + Greek *kara* head.]
Chiefly VETERINARY MEDICINE. Any of various parasitic nematode worms of the genus *Toxocara*, esp. *T. canis* and *T. cati*, which are the common roundworms of dogs and cats respectively and are transmissible to humans. Also, toxocariasis.
■ **toxocaral** *adjective* M20. **toxocariasis** /-kəˈrʌɪəsɪs/ *noun*, pl. **-ases**, infestation with any nematode worm of the genus *Toxocara*, the larvae of which can cause damage to various tissues and organs including the eye M20.

Toxodon /ˈtɒksədɒn/ *noun.* M19.
[mod. Latin (see below), from TOXO-¹ + -ODON.]
PALAEONTOLOGY. Any large notoungulate of the extinct genus *Toxodon*, which is characterized by strongly curved molar teeth and whose remains are found in Pliocene and Pleistocene deposits in S. America.
■ **toxodont** *adjective & noun* (*a*) *adjective* belonging to or having the characters of the genus *Toxodon* or the suborder Toxodontia; (*b*) *noun* a notoungulate of this suborder: L19.

toxoid /ˈtɒksɔɪd/ *noun.* E20.
[from TOX(IN + -OID.]
MEDICINE. A chemically modified toxin from a pathogenic micro-organism, which is no longer toxic but is still antigenic and can be used as a vaccine.

toxology /tɒkˈsɒlədʒi/ *noun.* M19.
[from TOXO-¹ + -LOGY.]
The branch of knowledge that deals with archery and the history of the bow.

toxophilite /tɒkˈsɒfɪlʌɪt/ *adjective & noun.* L18.
[from *Toxophilus* title of Ascham's book (1545) intended to mean 'lover of the bow' (from TOXO-¹ + Greek *philos*: see -PHIL): see -ITE¹.]
▶ **A** *adjective.* Of or pertaining to archers or archery. L18.
▶ **B** *noun.* A devotee of archery, an archer. E19.
■ **toxophiˈlitic** *adjective* pertaining or relating to archers or archery L18. **toxophily** *noun* the practice or love of archery L20.

toxoplasma /tɒksəˈplazmə/ *noun.* Pl. **-mas**, **-mata** /-mətə/. E20.
[mod. Latin (see below), formed as TOXO-² + PLASMA.]
BIOLOGY. Any of various protozoans of the genus *Toxoplasma*, which comprises crescentic uninucleate sporozoans that are internal parasites of vertebrates.
■ **toxoplasmic** *adjective* M20. **toxoplasmin** *noun* an antigenic preparation of toxoplasma used in skin testing M20. **toxoplasmosis** *noun*, pl. **-oses**, infection with, or a disease caused by, *Toxoplasma gondii*, which can lead to jaundice, brain lesions, etc., and can be fatal M20.

toy /tɔɪ/ *noun.* LME.
[Origin unkn.: Middle Dutch *toi* (Dutch *tooi*) attire, finery agrees in form but not sense.]
▶ **I** An action, a feeling.
1 a A frivolous speech or piece of writing; a foolish or idle tale; a funny remark, a jest, a joke. *arch.* LME. ▸**b** A light, frivolous, or lively tune. Long *rare.* L16.
†**2** A playful or frisky movement; a piece of amusement or entertainment; an antic, a trick. L15–L18.
†**3** A foolish or idle fancy; a whim, a caprice; *spec.* a foolish or unreasoning aversion. M16–L17.
†**4** Amorous play, dallying, toying; a light caress. M16–E18.
▶ **II** A thing, an object.
5 A thing of little or no importance, a trifle; a foolish affair, a piece of nonsense; (in *pl.*) trumpery, rubbish. M16.
6 An object to play with, often a model or miniature replica of something and esp. for a child; something intended for amusement rather than for practical use; a plaything. (Now the usual sense.) L16.

7 a A small article of little value but prized as an ornament or curiosity; a knick-knack, a trinket; anything small or inferior *of* its kind. L16. ▸**b** Any small steel article or tool, as a hammer, buckle, hook, nail, etc. L18. ▸**c** A watch. *Criminals' slang.* E19. ▸**d** A small tin or jar containing opium; the quantity of opium held in such a container. *US slang.* E20.

8 A person, esp. considered as a plaything. Freq. *derog.* L16.

9 A close-fitting women's cap or head-dress with flaps coming down to the shoulders. SCOTTISH HISTORY. E18.

10 In *pl.* At Winchester College, a bureau, a desk. Also more widely, a cubicle used as a study. E19.

11 (An animal of) a diminutive breed or variety, esp. of a dog or pigeon. M19.

📖 **5** SHAKES. *Macb.* There's nothing serious in mortality— All is but toys. **6** R. L. STEVENSON Lead soldiers, dolls, all toys . . are in the same category. R. GODDEN The end of our childhood; soon, even Rose would not want toys any more. ***soft toy***: see SOFT *adjective*. **7a** W. BLACK Perched on the . . hill was a conspicuous toy of a church. **8** A. HOLLINGHURST I saw him becoming . . my slave and my toy.

Attrib. & comb.: In the sense 'being a (usu. small) model for playing with', as ***toy car***, ***toy gun***, ***toy trumpet***, etc.; in the sense 'diminutive in size', as ***toy dog***, ***toy poodle***, ***toy village***, etc. Special combs., as **toy boy** *colloq.* a woman's much younger male lover; **toy library** a collection of toys which may be borrowed by or for children; **toyman** a man who sells toys or keeps a toy-shop; **toy-shop** a shop for selling toys; **toy soldier** (*a*) a small model of a soldier; (*b*) *colloq.* a soldier in a peacetime army; **toy theatre** a miniature theatre in which the characters are represented by printed pictures mounted on card or wood; **toytown** *noun & adjective* (*a*) *noun* a model of a town used as a plaything; *fig.* a small or insignificant town; (*b*) *adjective* resembling a model of a town; toylike; insignificant.

■ **toyful** *adjective* (now *rare* or *obsolete*) full of fun, playful; amusing: L19. **toyish** *adjective* (now *rare*) †(*a*) flirtatious; playful, frisky; (*b*) trivial, worthless; foolish, nonsensical; (*c*) of a humorous character; (*d*) toylike, diminutive: M16. **toyless** *adjective* L19. **toylike** *adjective* resembling (that of) a toy E19.

toy /tɔɪ/ *verb.* E16.

[from the noun.]

1 *verb intrans.* Deal lightly or frivolously *with*; trifle, amuse oneself (*with* a person, activity, etc.); play about. Also (foll. by *with*), consider superficially (an idea etc.). E16. ▸**b** Foll. by *with*: handle or finger idly. E19.

2 *verb intrans.* Behave in a superficially amorous manner (*with* a person); dally, flirt. M16.

3 *verb trans.* Foll. by *away*, *out*: spend or waste (time) in toying. *rare.* L16.

📖 **1** *Times* He had toyed with many crafts. A. S. BYATT Cropper toyed with the idea of writing an autobiography. **b** J. CONRAD Mill's hand was toying absently with an empty glass. L. URIS He toyed with the soup . . but . . had no appetite.

■ **toyer** *noun* a person who toys; a trifler: E18.

to-year /tə'jɪə/ *adverb.* Now *dial.* ME.

[from TO *preposition* + YEAR *noun*[1]: cf. *today*, *tonight*.]

This year.

Toynbeean /'tɔɪnbiːən/ *adjective.* M20.

[from *Toynbee* (see below) + -AN.]

Of or pertaining to the English historian Arnold Joseph Toynbee (1889–1975), his style, or his theories of the rise and decline of civilizations.

toyon /'tɔɪɒn/ *noun.* Also **tollon**. M19.

[Mexican Spanish *tollón*.]

A Californian evergreen shrub of the rose family, *Heteromeles arbutifolia*, the fruiting branches of which are used for Christmas decorations. Also called ***Californian holly***.

toyte /tɔɪt/ *verb intrans. Scot. & north.* Also **toit**, **tot** /tɒt/ (infl. **-tt-**). L18.

[Origin uncertain: perh. alt. of TOTTER *verb*.]

Totter, walk feebly or unsteadily.

toze /təʊz/ *verb*[1] *trans. obsolete* exc. *dial.* ME.

[from base of TEASE *verb*. Cf. next.]

1 Pull apart; separate or unravel the fibres of; comb, card (wool etc.); tease. ME.

†**2** *fig.* Search out; analyse; elicit, tease out. LME–M17.

toze /təʊz/ *verb*[2] *trans.* Now *rare.* M18.

[Perh. same word as prec.]

MINING. Separate (tin ore) from the gangue by stirring in water and allowing the heavier particles to settle.

†tozy *adjective & noun. rare.* E18–E19.

[App. from TOZE *verb*[1] + -Y[1].]

(Something) soft as teased wool.

TPR *abbreviation.*

MEDICINE. Temperature, pulse, and respiration.

Tpr. *abbreviation.*

Trooper.

TQM *abbreviation.*

Total quality management.

TR *abbreviation.*

ELECTRONICS. Transmit–receive.

trabaccolo /trə'bakələʊ/ *noun.* Pl. **-los**, **-li** /-liː/. E19.

[Italian from medieval Latin from Latin *trab-*, *trabs* beam, timber.]

An Italian ship (esp. of the Adriatic coast) of medium size; a small coasting vessel.

trabant /trə'bant/ *noun.* E17.

[German = lifeguard, armed attendant, of Turkish (orig. Persian) origin: see DRABANT.]

1 (Usu. **T-**.) In some European countries, a guard, an armed attendant, a member of an important person's staff or retinue. Now chiefly *Hist.* E17.

2 CYTOLOGY. = SATELLITE *noun* 6. E20.

trabea /'treɪbɪə/ *noun.* Pl. **-eae** /-ɪiː/. E17.

[Latin.]

ROMAN ANTIQUITIES. A toga ornamented with horizontal purple stripes, worn as a State robe by kings, consuls, and other men of rank in ancient Rome.

trabeate /'treɪbɪeɪt/ *adjective.* L19.

[Irreg. from Latin *trab-*, *trabs* beam, timber + -ATE[2], prob. confused with Latin *trabeatus* wearing a trabea.]

ARCHITECTURE. = next.

trabeated /'treɪbɪeɪtɪd/ *adjective.* M19.

[formed as prec. + -ED[1].]

ARCHITECTURE. Constructed with beams; having beams or long squared stones as lintels and entablatures; covered with a beam or entablature, as a doorway.

trabeation /treɪbɪ'eɪʃ(ə)n/ *noun.* M16.

[formed as TRABEATE: see -ATION.]

ARCHITECTURE. Orig., a horizontal beam; an entablature. Later, construction with horizontal beams etc. as opp. to arches or vaults.

trabecula /trə'bɛkjʊlə/ *noun.* Pl. **-lae** /-liː/. M19.

[Latin, dim. of *trab-*, *trabs* beam, timber: see -CULE.]

1 ANATOMY & ZOOLOGY. Each of a series or group of bands or columns of connective tissue; *esp.* (*a*) a plate of the calcareous tissue forming cancellous bone; (*b*) a ridge of muscular tissue on the inside of a ventricle of the heart; (*c*) a fibrous band forming part of the framework of soft organs; (*d*) a pillar of microscopic calcareous fibres which builds up the skeleton of a coral. Usu. in *pl.* M19.

2 BOTANY. Any of certain rodlike structures in plants; *esp.* (*a*) a rodlike part of a cell wall projecting radially across the lumen; (*b*) any of the strands of sterile tissue dividing the cavity in a sporangium of a quillwort. M19.

■ **trabecular** *adjective* pertaining to or of the nature of a trabecula; composed of or furnished with trabeculae: M19. **trabeculate** *adjective* = TRABECULATED M19. **trabeculated** *adjective* provided with or having trabeculae L19. **trabecu'lation** *noun* formation of trabeculae; a reticulated or barred condition, as of the muscle fibres in the wall of a hypertrophied urinary bladder: E20.

trabuch /trə'bʊk/ *noun. obsolete* exc. *Hist.* L15.

[Old French *trabuc*, from *tra-*, *tres-* (from Latin *trans* expr. displacement) + *buc* trunk (of the body), bulk, from Frankish *būk* belly.]

A medieval engine used in battle for throwing large stones against walls etc. Cf. TREBUCHET.

trac /trak/ *noun.* E20.

[Origin unkn.]

BASKET-MAKING. More fully ***trac border***. A basketwork border made by taking the remaining length of an upright and weaving it in and out of the following uprights before repeating the process with the next.

tracasserie /trə'kas(ə)ri/ *noun.* M17.

[French, from *tracasser* bustle, worry oneself: see -ERY.]

A state of disturbance or annoyance; a fuss; a petty quarrel. Usu. in *pl.*

trace /treɪs/ *noun*[1] *& adjective.* ME.

[Old & mod. French, formed as TRACE *verb*[1].]

▸ **A** *noun.* †**1** The way or path which a person, animal, or thing takes; a course, a road; *fig.* a course of action or conduct, a way of proceeding. ME–M18.

2 A footprint left by an animal, esp. a deer (usu. in *pl.*). Later *gen.*, the track made by the passage of any person or thing; *US* a beaten path, a trail. ME.

3 a A mark indicating the (usu. former) presence or action of something; a vestige, an impression. ME. ▸**b** PSYCHOLOGY. A change in the cells of the brain which is the physical manifestation of learning and memory. L17. ▸**c** The presence of a minute amount of some constituent in a substance; a quantity too small to measure; *gen.* a very small amount. E19. ▸**d** LINGUISTICS. A phonetically null element considered to have been left in the position from which an element has been moved. L20.

4 A non-material indication of the presence or existence of something, or of a former event or condition; an impression or hint of a quality etc.; a sign, a suggestion. LME.

†**5** A series of steps in dancing; a measure; a dance. LME–L16.

6 a A line or figure drawn, a sketch; the traced record of a self-recording instrument; FORTIFICATION the ground-plan of a work. M18. ▸**b** The luminous line or pattern on the screen of a cathode-ray tube, esp. an oscilloscope or a radarscope. M20.

7 GEOMETRY. The intersection of a surface, or of (the projection plane of) a line in space, with a coordinate plane; the projection of a curve on a given plane. M19.

8 MATH. The sum of the elements in the principal diagonal of a matrix; the sum of the conjugates of an algebraic number. M20.

9 COMPUTING. The detailed examination of the execution of a program in order to investigate a fault, using another program to cause individual instructions, operands, and results to be printed or displayed as they are reached by the first program; the analysis so obtained. Also, = ***trace program*** below. M20.

10 A request for information to be sought concerning a particular person or thing; an investigation which traces information (freq. to discover the source of a telephone call). L20.

📖 **2** CONAN DOYLE 'No footsteps, you say?' 'The ground was iron hard, sir. There were no traces.' M. MITCHELL I knew a wagon trace that winds off from the main Jonesboro road. **on a person's traces** in pursuit of a person. **3a** H. WOUK Traces of the war in these quiet hills were few. J. WINTERSON The ground still had traces of snow. **4** L. DEIGHTON He allowed a trace of his anger to show. A. DAVIS They had purged themselves of every trace of emotion. A. BROOKNER Owen had left no trace in my life. **10** *Daily Telegraph* An automatic trace on a complainant's line . . to log each call and the source.

▸ **B** *attrib.* or as *adjective.* Pertaining to a trace or traces; *esp.* present or required only in traces. M20.

trace element: that is present (esp. in the soil or in rocks), or is required by living organisms, only in minute amounts. **trace fossil** PALAEONTOLOGY a fossil of the track, trail, or burrow of an animal rather than of the animal itself. **trace program**, **trace routine** COMPUTING: by which a trace is carried out on another program (see sense A.9 above).

■ **traceless** *adjective* (*a*) leaving no trace or track; that cannot be traced; (*b*) MATH. (of a tensor etc.) having a trace equal to zero: M17. **tracelessly** *adverb* M19.

trace /treɪs/ *noun*[2]. ME.

[Old French *trais* pl. of *trait* draught, harness-strap, formed as TRACT *noun*[3].]

1 Orig., a pair of ropes, chains, or leather side-straps by which the collar of a horse or other draught animal is fastened to a crossbar or swingletree; now only, each of the individual ropes or straps so used (usu. in *pl.*). ME.

2 a ANGLING. A length of nylon monofilament or wire (previously gimp or gut) attached to the end of a reel line. M19. ▸**b** In an organ, a rod connecting the draw-stop rod with the trundle, or the trundle with the lever moving the slider. M19. ▸**c** BOTANY. = ***leaf-trace*** s.v. LEAF *noun*[1]. L19.

📖 **1** W. STYRON The four wagons . . were ready, waiting, the mules stamping . . in their traces. ***kick over the traces***: see KICK *verb*[1].

Comb.: **trace-chain**: forming a trace; **trace-horse** a horse put in traces to pull a vehicle (cf. ***shaft-horse*** s.v. SHAFT *noun*).

trace /treɪs/ *verb*[1]. LME.

[Old French *tracier* (mod. *tracer*) from Proto-Romance, from Latin *tractus*: see TRACT *noun*[3].]

▸ **I 1** *verb intrans.* Make one's way, proceed; walk, go; wander. *obsolete* exc. *dial.* LME.

†**2** *verb intrans.* Perform a step in dancing; tread a measure; dance. LME–E19.

†**3** *verb trans.* Travel or pass over; go around or through; tread, traverse. LME–E19.

▸ **II 4** *verb trans.* Follow the traces of, track; follow (footprints etc.). Also, pursue, shadow. LME.

5 *verb trans.* **a** Discover, find by investigation; ascertain, search out. LME. ▸**b** Discover evidence of the existence or occurrence of; find traces of. L17. ▸**c** COMPUTING. Subject (a program) to a trace (TRACE *noun*[1] 9). M20.

6 a *verb trans.* Follow the development or history of; follow (a course of development). (Foll. by *back*, *to*.) M17. ▸**b** *verb intrans.* Go back in time (*to*); date *back*. L19.

7 *verb trans.* **a** Make out or follow the course of (something) with one's eyes, finger, mind, etc.; ascertain (a course or line). E18. ▸**b** Discern, decipher (obscure writing). M18. ▸**c** Make a tracing of (a listed item); derive (a tracing) *from* an index or catalogue. E20.

📖 **4** A. MACLEAN The hounds traced him along the east side of the village. F. SMYTH The police . . traced bloodstained footsteps across the road. **5a** A. MACLEAN I think I've traced the source of the poison. *She* They helped me trace which hospital my mum was in. **6a** N. O. BROWN Psycho-analysts . . trace the origin of Swift's neurosis to his earliest childhood. F. WELDON He could trace his ancestry back to King David. G. TINDALL I cannot now trace the exact route by which Anna came into my life. **7a** R. P. WARREN His right forefinger traced each line as he read it. P. THEROUX I dug out my map and traced the railway line from Veracniz.

▸ **III 8** *verb trans.* Mark, make marks on; *esp.* ornament with lines, figures, or characters. LME.

9 *verb trans.* Make a plan, diagram, or chart of; mark out the course of (a road etc.). Also (*fig.*), devise (a plan of action), map out (a policy). LME. **10** *verb trans.* **a** Draw; draw an outline of; write. LME. ▸**b** Copy (a drawing, plan, etc.) by following the lines of the original drawing on a transparent sheet placed over it; make a tracing of. M18.

> **8** R. FIRBANK A cream . . sunshade traced at the borders with . . lines of blue. **9** *Atlantic* Above my father's head an electric monitor traced his heartbeat. **10a** A. CHRISTIE Henrietta . . traced a pattern with her toe. G. GREENE To trace with his pencil a path to the centre of the maze.

■ **traceable** *adjective* able to be traced (cf. earlier UNTRACEABLE) M18. **tracea'bility** *noun* the quality of being traceable L19. **traceably** *adverb* in a manner that can be traced M19.

trace /treɪs/ *verb*² *trans. obsolete* exc. *local.* LME.
[Perh. alt. of TRESS *verb.*]
Plait, interweave, braid. Also foll. by *up*.

tracer /'treɪsə/ *noun*¹. E16.
[from TRACE *verb*¹ + -ER¹.]
1 A person who investigates, searches out, or follows the track of something; *spec.* a person whose business is the tracing of missing persons, property, etc. E16.
2 A person who or thing which traces lines or makes tracings; *spec.* (*a*) a person whose work it is to trace copies of drawings or plans, or patterns for embroidery; (*b*) a tool for marking out or engraving designs. L18.
3 A thing used in investigating or following the track of something; *spec.* (*a*) ANATOMY (now *rare*) = SEEKER 2(a); (*b*) *N. Amer.* an inquiry form on which the successive movements of a missing car, parcel, etc., are recorded; (*c*) a substance (as a radioactive isotope or a dye) with distinctive properties that is introduced into a system so that its subsequent distribution may be readily followed; (*d*) a device which transmits a signal and can be traced when attached to a moving vehicle etc. L19.
4 A bullet or shell whose course is made visible by a trail (of smoke, flames, etc.) emitted during flight; such bullets or shells collectively. E20.

tracer /'treɪsə/ *noun*². M19.
[from TRACE *noun*² + -ER².]
A trace-horse.

tracery /'treɪs(ə)ri/ *noun.* LME.
[from TRACE *verb*¹ or TRACER *noun*¹: see -ERY.]
†**1** A place for tracing or drawing. *rare.* Only in LME.
2 ARCHITECTURE. Ornamentation in the upper part of a Gothic window, consisting of a perforated design or of an intersecting pattern formed by the elaboration of the mullions; the interlaced work of a vault, panel, etc. M17.
3 Any delicate interweaving of lines or threads; an interlacing of foliage etc.; openwork. E19.
2 bar tracery: in which the mullions are elaborated into simple intersecting bars. ***plate tracery***: see PLATE *noun.*
■ **traceried** *adjective* ornamented with or characterized by tracery M19.

trachea /trə'kiːə, 'treɪkɪə/ *noun.* Pl. **-eae** /-iːiː/. LME.
[medieval Latin from late Latin *trachia* from Greek *trakheia* (fem. of *trakhus* rough), short for *artēria trakheia* rough artery, (in medieval Latin *arteria trachea*).]
1 ANATOMY & ZOOLOGY. A large membranous tube extending from the larynx to the bronchi, which is strengthened by cartilaginous (or bony) rings and conveys air to and from the lungs; the windpipe. LME.
2 BOTANY. A tracheary element. Now *Hist.* M18.
3 ZOOLOGY. A fine chitinous tube leading from a spiracle (or gill) in an insect or other arthropod, which is freq. spirally ringed and conveys air direct to the tissues. Usu. in *pl.* E19.
■ **trachean** *adjective* †(*a*) = TRACHEAL; (*b*) (now *rare*) = TRACHEATE *adjective* 1, 2: E17.

tracheal /'treɪkɪəl, trə'kiːəl/ *adjective.* E18.
[from prec. + -AL¹.]
ANATOMY, ZOOLOGY, & BOTANY. Pertaining to or connected with the trachea; pertaining to, of the nature of, or composed of tracheae.

tracheary /'treɪkɪəri/ *noun & adjective.* M19.
[mod. Latin *trachearius*: cf. TRACHEA, -ARY².]
▸†**A** *noun.* = TRACHEATE *noun. rare.* Only in M19.
▸**B** *adjective.* **1** ZOOLOGY. = TRACHEATE *adjective* 1. *rare.* L19.
2 BOTANY. Of the nature of or pertaining to tracheae; tracheal. Chiefly in ***tracheary element*** below. L19.
2 tracheary element any of the water-conducting cells, whether tracheids or vessel elements, in the xylem of a vascular plant (formerly supposed to serve for the passage of air).

tracheate /'treɪkɪeɪt/ *adjective & noun.* L19.
[mod. Latin *Tracheata* (see below), from *tracheatus* having tracheae, from TRACHEA: see -ATE².]
ZOOLOGY. ▸**A** *adjective.* **1** Of an arthropod: having tracheae; *spec.* belonging to the former order Tracheata, comprising arachnids which breathe by tracheae alone. L19.
2 Of respiration: by means of tracheae. L19.
▸**B** *noun.* A tracheate arthropod. L19.
■ **tracheated** *adjective* (of an arthropod, its gill, etc.) provided with or having tracheae L19.

tracheid /'treɪkɪɪd/ *noun.* Also (now *rare*) **-cheide**. L19.
[German *Tracheide*, from TRACHEA + *-ide* -ID².]
BOTANY. A type of tracheary element (found esp. in gymnosperms and ferns) which lacks a perforation plate. Cf. VESSEL *noun*¹ 5b.
■ **tracheidal** /trə'kiːɪd(ə)l/ *adjective* L19.

tracheitis /treɪkɪ'ʌɪtɪs/ *noun.* M19.
[from TRACHEA + -ITIS.]
MEDICINE. Inflammation of the trachea, usu. secondary to a nose or throat infection.

trachelate /'trakɪleɪt/ *adjective.* E19.
[from Greek *trakhēlos* + -ATE².]
ENTOMOLOGY. Having a neck, or a constriction like a neck.

tracheo- /trə'kiːəʊ, 'trakɪəʊ, 'treɪkɪəʊ/ *combining form* of TRACHEA: see -O-.
■ **tracheobronchial** /-'brɒŋkɪəl/ *adjective* (ANATOMY & ZOOLOGY) pertaining to (the junction of) the trachea and the bronchi L19. **tracheobron'chitis** *noun* (MEDICINE) inflammation of the trachea and bronchi M19. **tracheophone** *noun & adjective* (ZOOLOGY) (a passerine bird) having the syrinx situated entirely or chiefly in the trachea L19. **trache'oscopy** *noun* (MEDICINE) inspection or examination of the trachea, as with a laryngoscope L19. **trache'ostomy** *noun* (MEDICINE) (an instance of) a surgical operation to make an opening in the trachea, esp. so that the patient can breathe through it via a curved tube; the opening so made: M20. **trache'otomy** *noun* (MEDICINE) = TRACHEOSTOMY E18.

tracheole /'treɪkɪəʊl/ *noun.* E20.
[from TRACHEA + -OLE¹.]
ENTOMOLOGY. A microscopic terminal branch of a trachea, adjacent to the cell of the tissue which it supplies.
■ **trache'olar** *adjective* pertaining to a tracheole; consisting of tracheoles: E20.

trachle /'trɑːx(ə)l/ *verb & noun. Scot.* Also **trauchle**. M16.
[Origin unkn.: cf. Western Flemish *tragelen, trakelen* walk with difficulty.]
▸**A** *verb.* **1** *verb trans.* Bedraggle, dishevel; damage by trampling etc. M16.
2 a *verb trans.* Tire out by long walking; exhaust by over-exertion; *fig.* distress. L16. ▸**b** *verb intrans.* Tire oneself out; drudge, toil. Also, walk slowly and wearily, trudge. E19.
▸**B** *noun.* **1** An exhausting journey or effort; bother, trouble. L17.
2 A careless or incompetent person. L19.

trachoma /trə'kəʊmə/ *noun.* L17.
[Greek *trakhōma* roughness, from *trakhus* rough: see -OMA.]
MEDICINE. A chronic contagious disease of the eye caused by the virus-like bacterium *Chlamydia trachomatis*, characterized by inflammation and granulation of the conjunctiva of the eyelids, common in tropical countries, and freq. leading to blindness.
■ **trachomatous** *adjective* pertaining to, of the nature of, or affected by trachoma L19.

trachy- /treɪki/ *combining form.*
[In sense 1 directly from Greek *trakhus* rough; in sense 2 from next.]
1 Chiefly BOTANY. Forming nouns and adjectives with the sense 'rough', as ***trachycarpous***, ***trachyspermous***.
2 GEOLOGY. Forming names of igneous rocks with the sense 'intermediate between trachyte and', as ***trachybasalt***, ***trachyrhyolite***.

trachyte /'treɪkʌɪt, 'trakʌɪt/ *noun.* E19.
[from Greek *trakhus* rough or *trakhutēs* roughness: cf. -ITE¹.]
GEOLOGY. Orig., any of a group of volcanic rocks having a characteristically rough or gritty surface. Now *spec.* any fine-grained volcanic rock of the alkaline series of intermediate rocks.
■ **trachytic** /trə'kɪtɪk/ *adjective* consisting of, of the nature of, or containing trachyte E19.

tracing /'treɪsɪŋ/ *noun.* LME.
[from TRACE *verb*¹ + -ING¹.]
1 a Drawing, delineation; the copying of a drawing etc. by means of a transparent sheet placed over it. LME. ▸**b** That which is produced by tracing or drawing; *spec.* a copy made by tracing; a recording from a self-registering instrument. LME. ▸**c** The marking out of a figure on the ice when skating; a pattern thus made. E20.
2 The following of traces, tracking. Formerly also (in *pl.*), traces, tracks. E16.
3 The procedure of making a list of all the headings under which a given item occurs in an index or catalogue; an entry in such a list. E20.
4 The following of the course of the groove on a gramophone record by a stylus. Freq. in ***tracing distortion*** below. M20.
5 COMPUTING. The process of performing a trace (TRACE *noun*¹ 9). M20.
Comb.: **tracing distortion**: occurring when a stylus does not describe exactly the same path as the groove on a gramophone record; **tracing-paper** translucent paper for copying drawings etc. by tracing; **tracing table**: having a translucent top illuminated from underneath; **tracing-wheel** a toothed wheel or roulette for marking out patterns.

track /trak/ *noun.* L15.
[Old & mod. French *trac* perh. from Low Dutch (Middle Dutch, Low German) *tre(c)k* drawing, draught, pull (cf. TREK *noun*).]
▸**I 1 a** The mark or marks left by a person, animal, or thing in passing; a trail, a wheel-rut, the wake of a ship, a series of footprints, etc. L15. ▸**b** PARTICLE PHYSICS. A line (in a cloud chamber, on a film, etc.) marking the path taken by an atomic or subatomic particle. E20. ▸**c** A line on the skin made by the repeated injection of an addictive drug. *slang.* Usu. in *pl.* M20.
2 a A line of travel, passage, or motion; the actual course or route followed by something. M16. ▸**b** AERONAUTICS. A projection on the earth's surface of the (intended) course of an aircraft; a representation of this on a chart. E20. ▸**c** AERONAUTICS. The plane in which the blades of a propeller are intended to rotate. E20. ▸**d** An assembly line; = LINE *noun*² 7c. M20. ▸**e** EDUCATION. = STREAM *noun* 5d. *US.* M20.
3 *fig.* **a** A course of action or conduct; a way of proceeding. M17. ▸**b** A train or sequence of events, thoughts, etc. L17.
†**4** *fig.* A trace, a sign, evidence of the existence of. M–L17.
5 A rough path, *esp.* one beaten by use. M17.
6 a *sing.* & in *pl.* A continuous pair of parallel rails and the space between them, on which railway vehicles travel, *spec.* as distinguished from one or more such pairs comprising a line covering a particular route. Also, a similar pair of rails on which anything moves. E19. ▸**b** The transverse distance between a vehicle's wheels. M19. ▸**c** A continuous articulated band passing round the wheels of a heavy vehicle, as a tank, and facilitating travel over rough or soft ground. Cf. CATERPILLAR 4. L19. ▸**d** A metal or plastic strip from which something, as a curtain or spotlight, may be hung or fitted. L20.
7 a A course prepared or laid out for runners; a racecourse for horses, dogs, etc. Also, any course or path laid out for a special purpose. Freq. with specifying word. M19. ▸**b** *collect.* Track events (in athletics). Orig. *US.* E20. ▸**c** A ballroom, a dancehall. *US slang.* M20. ▸**d** CRICKET. The ground between and around the wickets; the wicket. L20.
8 a A groove on a gramophone record (now *rare*); a single recorded item, esp. of popular music (on a gramophone record consisting of a band of grooves close together). E20. ▸**b** A lengthwise strip of magnetic tape containing a single sequence of signals; *esp.* = ***soundtrack*** *noun* s.v. SOUND *noun*². More widely, a linear path in an information storage device that accommodates one sequence of signals or corresponds to one head. M20.

> **1a** DICKENS The walls . . tapestried with the tracks of snails. R. SILVERBERG He was beginning to weep, and . . wet tracks gleamed on his face. **3a** G. A. BELLAMY You see me now entered into a new track of life. **5** R. MACAULAY Rough tracks climbed . . through the heather. C. MCCULLOUGH The Wahine road was a wheel-rutted earthen track. **6a** L. SPALDING My mother grew up . . near railroad tracks. P. THEROUX Somewhere down the line there was a break in the tracks. **c** *Surveyor* The . . mini-excavator . . is fitted with rubber tracks. **d** S. DELANEY On tracks under the awning . . butcher hooks swung. *Practical Householder* Both bi-fold and sliding doors require some form of track. **7a** R. DAHL At the other end of the track, beyond the winning-post. *Racing Monthly* Racecourses will be able to omit water jumps from their tracks. I. MURDOCH They reached the cycle track. **b** M. J. BRUCCOLI He left . . with medals for elocution and track. **8a** *Dirty Linen* The LP will have 12 tracks. **b** *ZX Computing Monthly* There are 18 sectors on each track. *Punch* The backing tracks . . are . . less full-bodied.

▸**II** Used by confusion for TRACT *noun*³.
9 A feature, a trait. Cf. TRACT *noun*³ 5. *Scot.* Long *rare.* E16.
10 A stretch of land; a period of time. Cf. TRACT *noun*³ 1a, 2a. L17.
Phrases: **across the tracks** in the socially inferior part of town. **cover a person's tracks**, **cover up a person's tracks** conceal or screen a person's movements etc. ***down the track***: see DOWN *preposition*. ***fly the track***: see FLY *verb*. **in one's tracks** where one is at that moment; there and then, instantly, immediately. ***inside track***. **keep track of** follow the course or development of; keep account of. **lose track** fail to follow the course or development (of). **make tracks** *colloq.* go or run away. **make tracks for** *colloq.* go in pursuit of, go towards. MULTI-TRACK. **off the track** derailed; *fig.* away from the subject. ***one-track***: see ONE *adjective, noun, & pronoun*. **on the right track** having the right idea; following the right line of enquiry. **on the track** *Austral.* on the move in search of work; ***on the wallaby track***: see WALLABY 1. **on the track (of)** in pursuit (of); having a clue (to). **on the wrong track** having the wrong idea; following the wrong line of enquiry. **on track** *N. Amer.* on course; achieving or doing what is required. ***outside track***: see OUTSIDE *adjective*. ***plumb a track***: see PLUMB *verb* 3. ***single track***: see SINGLE *adjective & adverb*. ***the beaten track***: see BEATEN *adjective* 3. **the wrong side of the tracks** *colloq.* the socially inferior part of town. **track and field** track events and field events (in athletics).
Comb.: **track athlete** an athlete specializing in track events; **track-bed** the layer of gravel, clay, etc., on which railway lines are laid; **track-brake** a railway brake which acts on or from the track, esp. by pressure from electromagnets; **track circuit** an electric circuit formed by the two rails of a railway line, so that the short-circuit produced by a train can control the signals;

track-circuit *verb trans.* provide with or make into a track circuit; **track-clearer** a blade or bar fixed to the front of a vehicle to push obstacles etc. aside and clear the way ahead; **track event** an athletic event taking place on a running track (cf. ***field event*** s.v. FIELD *noun*); **track-in** CINEMATOGRAPHY & TELEVISION the movement of a camera towards a subject; **tracklayer** (*a*) a person who lays or repairs railway track, a platelayer; a railway truck with machinery for laying rails; (*b*) a tractor or other vehicle which travels on continuous tracks; **track-laying** *noun & adjective* (*a*) *noun* the laying of railway track; CINEMATOGRAPHY the assembling of the soundtrack that is to accompany a picture; (*b*) *adjective* that lays railway track; (of a vehicle) having continuous tracks; **track lighting**: in which the lights are fitted on tracks, allowing variable positioning; **track-line** the line or route of a (former) track or path; **track-man** (*a*) a man who constructs or maintains railways; (*b*) a track athlete; **track record** (*a*) the best recorded performance in a particular athletics event at a particular track; (*b*) the performances achieved by a particular athlete in the past; *transf.* a person's past achievements or behaviour taken as a guide to future performance; **track rod** a rod that connects the two front wheels of a motor vehicle and transmits the steering action from the steering column to the wheels; **track-shoe** = ***running shoe*** s.v. RUNNING *noun*; **trackside** *noun & adjective* (located in) the area beside a railway line or running track; **track-suit** a loose warm two-piece suit worn for exercising or jogging or before and after athletic events; **track-suited** *adjective* wearing a track-suit; **track-walker** a person who regularly walks along and examines a certain length of railway track; **trackway** (*a*) a path beaten by use, a track; (*b*) an ancient British roadway, a ridgeway; **track-work** (*a*) the construction of a railway track or line; (*b*) action on an athletic or racing track.
■ **trackster** *noun* (*US*) a track athlete L20.

track /trak/ *verb*¹. E16.
[from prec. or from French *traquer*.]
▶†**I** Used by confusion for TRACT *verb*.
1 *verb trans.* Put off, delay. Cf. TRACT *verb* 2. Only in E16.
▶ **II 2 a** *verb trans.* Follow the track of; trace the course or movements of. Also, find and follow (a track, course, etc.). M16. ▸**b** *verb intrans.* Follow up a track or trail. E19. ▸**c** *verb intrans.* ELECTRONICS. Of a tunable circuit or component: vary in frequency in the same way as another circuit or component, so that the frequency difference between them remains constant. M20.
3 *verb trans.* **a** Mark out (a path or way), esp. by repeated use, mark with tracks, beat. Also, indicate the path or course of. L16. ▸**b** Make one's way through or across; traverse. L18.
4 a *verb intrans.* Follow a track or path; pass, go, travel. Now *US slang.* L16. ▸**b** *verb intrans. & trans.* Of a gramophone stylus: follow (the groove of a record or the sound produced by this). E20. ▸**c** *verb intrans.* Of a film or television camera, or its operator: move in relation to the subject being filmed. Freq. foll. by *back, in.* M20.
5 *verb intrans.* Of the wheels of a vehicle etc.: run so that the back ones are in the same track as the front ones; be in alignment (*with*). Of the feet: be placed in walking in the same straight line. E19.
6 *verb trans.* Leave a trail of footprints on (a floor); make a track with (dirt or snow) from the feet. *N. Amer.* M19.
7 *verb intrans.* **a** Keep company *with*, esp. as a companion or lover; consort *with*. *Austral.* E20. ▸**b** Be or feel emotionally involved (*with*), enjoy a rapport, relate. *US.* L20.

> 🕮 **2a** SIR W. SCOTT Misfortunes which track my footsteps like slot-hounds. *Daily Telegraph* Every . . aircraft flying over Europe can be tracked by radar. M. BRADBURY You track me, you spy on me. *Scientific American* During a head turn the eyes often track a single point. **track down** reach or capture by tracking; find, locate. **3a** *New Scientist* Dusty trails tracked by mammoth and horses. **4b** *Gramophone* This cartridge successfully tracks all types of records. **5** E. HOUGH His feet . . do not 'track', but cross each other weakly. *Dirt Bike* A firmer fork will help the bike track better. **6** J. REED The mud underfoot was deep . . tracked everywhere by heavy boots. **track in** bring in (dirt etc.) on the feet. **track up** mess up or dirty with the feet. **7b** *Newsweek* He tracks better with reporters than did his phlegmatic predecessor.

Comb.: **track-ball** COMPUTING a small ball that is rotated in a holder to move a cursor on a screen; a tracker ball.
■ **tracka'bility** *noun* the ability of a stylus or cartridge to track adequately L20.

track /trak/ *verb*². E18.
[App. from Dutch *trekken* draw, pull, etc. (see TREK *verb*), assim. in form to prec.]
1 *verb trans.* Tow (a boat, now usu. a canoe), esp. from a bank or towpath. Cf. TRACT *verb* 1. E18.
2 *verb intrans.* Proceed by being towed. M19.

> 🕮 **1** M. H. MASON Tracking . . the boat was impossible, for the banks were perpendicular mud.

Comb.: **track line**, **track rope**: used to tow a boat.
¶ Earlier in TRACK-BOAT.

trackage /'trakɪdʒ/ *noun*¹. E19.
[from TRACK *verb*² + -AGE.]
The action or process of tracking or towing, the fact of being tracked.

trackage /'trakɪdʒ/ *noun*². *US.* L19.
[from TRACK *noun* + -AGE.]
The tracks or lines of a railway system collectively.

track-boat /'trakbəʊt/ *noun.* M17.
[translating Dutch *trek-schuit*: cf. TRACK *verb*², BOAT *noun*.]
A boat which is tracked or towed; a tow-boat.

tracker /'trakə/ *noun*¹. E17.
[from TRACK *verb*¹ + -ER¹.]
A person who or thing which tracks; *spec.* (*a*) = ***black tracker*** s.v. BLACK *adjective*; (*b*) a tracker dog.
Comb.: **tracker ball** COMPUTING = ***track-ball*** s.v. TRACK *verb*¹; **tracker dog** a (police) dog trained to pick up and follow a scent.

tracker /'trakə/ *noun*². L18.
[from TRACK *verb*² + -ER¹.]
1 A person who tracks or tows a boat. Also, a boat which tows another, a tugboat. L18.
2 A wooden connecting-rod with a pulling action in the mechanism of an organ. M19.

tracking /'trakɪŋ/ *noun.* E16.
[from TRACK *verb*¹ + -ING¹.]
The action of TRACK *verb*¹; *spec.* (*a*) the formation or occurrence of electrically conducting paths over the surface of an insulating material; (*b*) ELECTRONICS the maintenance of a constant difference in frequency between two or more connected circuits or components; (*c*) EDUCATION (*US*) the streaming of school pupils; (*d*) the alignment of a vehicle's wheels.
parallel tracking: see PARALLEL *adjective*.
Comb.: **tracking error** the error that occurs in gramophone reproduction when the stylus is not fully in line with the groove; **tracking shot** CINEMATOGRAPHY & TELEVISION a shot during which the camera tracks; **tracking station** an establishment set up to track objects in the sky; **tracking weight** the weight with which a stylus rests on a gramophone record.

tracklement /'trak(ə)lm(ə)nt/ *noun.* M20.
[Origin unkn.]
An article of food, *spec.* a jelly, served with meat.

trackless /'traklɪs/ *adjective.* M17.
[from TRACK *noun* + -LESS.]
1 Without a track or path; not marked by a track; untrodden. M17.
2 Leaving no track or trace. L17.
3 Not running on a track or rails, but powered from overhead cables. E20.
3 trackless trolley *US* a trolley bus.
■ **tracklessly** *adverb* M19.

tract /trakt/ *noun*¹. OE.
[App. abbreviation of Latin *tractatus* TRACTATE.]
1 A book or written work treating of a particular topic; a treatise, a dissertation, a tractate. Formerly also, literary treatment or discussion. Now *rare*. OE.
2 A short pamphlet, esp. on a religious or political topic, suitable for distribution or propaganda. E19.

> 🕮 **2** G. M. TREVELYAN Tracts in favour of temperate drinking were . . circulated by religious bodies and anxious patriots. M. HOLROYD Each day . . continued with such improving tracts as *Jessica's First Prayer*. ***Oxford Tracts***: see OXFORD *adjective*.

■ **tractlet** *noun* a small tract L19.

tract /trakt/ *noun*². LME.
[from medieval Latin TRACTUS. Cf. next.]
ROMAN CATHOLIC CHURCH (now *Hist.*). An anthem of verses of Scripture formerly sung or recited instead of the alleluia in the Mass on certain penitential days and at requiems.

tract /trakt/ *noun*³. LME.
[Latin *tractus* drawing, draught, from *tract-* pa. ppl stem of *trahere* draw, drag. Cf. prec., TRACTUS.]
▶ **I 1 a** Duration, continuance, course, *of* some action or state, or (formerly) *of* time (now *rare* or *obsolete*). Also (*arch.*), a period of time. LME. ▸†**b** Protraction *of* time, delay. E16–E17.
2 a A (usu. large) stretch or expanse *of* land, territory, water, etc.; a region, a district. M16. ▸**b** A plot of land with definite boundaries, esp. one for development. Also, an estate. *US.* E20.
3 A region or area of some natural structure, as a mineral formation, or the body of an animal or plant, *esp.* one which extends longitudinally; *spec.* the whole extent of a continuous longitudinal anatomical structure, as the gut, a bundle of associated nerve fibres in the brain or spinal cord; ORNITHOLOGY a defined feathered area or pteryla on the skin of a bird. L17.

> 🕮 **1a** E. HALL This short tyme and small tract of my mortal life. N. BACON The seasons now in tract were of short continuance. **2** A. MOOREHEAD The tremendous unexplored tract, . . an area more than half the size of Europe. A. J. TOYNBEE Vast tracts of the Australian continent are barren. P. DALLY He owned large estates and tracts of land. **b** F. L. WRIGHT The plan . . for a housing project on a 100 acre tract. **3** ***digestive tract***, ***optic tract***, ***pyramidal tract***, ***respiratory tract***, ***urinary tract***, etc.

▶ **II** Drawing; a drawn thing.
†**4** HERALDRY. A tressure. LME–E17.
†**5** A lineament, a feature, a trait. E17–L18.
†**6** The action of drawing or pulling; *fig.* attraction. *rare.* Only in E17.
▶ **III** Senses related to TRACK *noun*, TRACE *noun*¹.
7 A course, path, or route, esp. as traversed or followed by something; = TRACK *noun* 2a. Now *rare* or *obsolete*. M16.
8 *fig.* A course of action etc.; a way of proceeding; = TRACK *noun* 3a. Now *rare* or *obsolete*. M16.
9 a A mark or impression indicating the course of a person, animal, or thing; a trace. Cf. TRACK *noun* 1a. Now *rare* or *obsolete*. M16. ▸†**b** A mark remaining where something has been; a trace, a vestige. L16–L17.
Comb.: **tract home**, **tract house** *US* a home or house built on a tract or estate.

†**tract** *verb.* E16.
[from Latin *tract-*: see prec.]
1 *verb trans.* Draw, pull along, haul, tow; = TRACK *verb*² 1. E16–M18.
2 *verb trans.* Lengthen out, prolong, protract (time); delay, put off. E16–M17.
3 Pursue or follow up by the track or traces left; track, trace. L16–M17.

tractable /'traktəb(ə)l/ *adjective.* LME.
[Latin *tractabilis*, from *tractare* handle etc., frequentative of *trahere* draw, drag: see -ABLE. Cf. TREAT *verb*.]
†**1** Capable of contracting, esp. in response to a stimulus. *rare.* Only in LME.
2 a Of a person, animal, etc.: easily managed; docile, compliant, controllable. E16. ▸**b** Easily led or persuaded *to* something. Long *rare* or *obsolete*. E16. ▸**c** Of a thing: easy to manage or deal with; *spec.* (of a material) pliant, malleable. M16.
†**3** That can be handled or felt. Only in 17.
†**4** That can be tolerated or endured. Only in 17.

> 🕮 **2a** G. ORWELL Bulls which had always been tractable suddenly turned savage. B. DUFFY Thoroughly tractable men trained from boyhood to endure hours of stupefying memorization. **c** T. S. ELIOT Made into something precise, tractable, under control.

■ **tracta'bility** *noun* the quality of being tractable; manageableness: L15. **tractableness** *noun* tractability M16. **tractably** *adverb* (*rare*) E17.

tractarian /trak'tɛːrɪən/ *noun & adjective.* E19.
[from TRACT *noun*¹ + -ARIAN.]
▶ **A** *noun.* **1** A writer, publisher, or distributor of tracts. *rare.* E19.
2 *Hist.* (Usu. **T-**.) A supporter of the High Church principles advocated in the Oxford Tracts; a member of the Oxford Movement. M19.
▶ **B** *adjective.* *Hist.* (Usu. **T-**.) Of or belonging to the Tractarians. M19.
■ **Tractarianism** *noun* the tenets or principles of the Tractarians; adherence to or support of these: M19.

tractate /'trakteɪt/ *noun.* L15.
[Latin *tractatus*, from *tractat-* pa. ppl stem of *tractare*: see TRACTABLE, -ATE¹.]
A book or literary work treating of a particular subject; a treatise.

tractator /'trakteɪtə/ *noun.* M17.
[Late Latin, from Latin *tractat-*: see prec., -OR.]
†**1** A person who treats of a subject; the writer of a tractate. M17–E18.
2 *Hist.* A writer of any of the Oxford Tracts. M19.

tractatule /'traktətjuːl/ *noun. rare.* L19.
[from TRACTATE or Latin *tractatus* + -ULE.]
A small tractate or treatise.

tractile /'traktɪl, -ʌɪl/ *adjective. rare.* E17.
[formed as TRACT *verb* + -ILE. Cf. DUCTILE.]
†**1** Able to be drawn out to a thread. Only in E17.
2 Capable of drawing or pulling. M19.
3 Able to be drawn, as money from a bank. L19.
■ **trac'tility** *noun* the quality of being tractile E18.

traction /'trakʃ(ə)n/ *noun.* LME.
[French, or medieval Latin *tractio(n-)*, formed as prec.: see -ION.]
1 a The action of drawing or pulling; orig. *spec.* (PHYSIOLOGY & MEDICINE) a pulling by contraction, as of a muscle. Also, a drawing or pulling movement used in massage. LME. ▸**b** *fig.* Drawing power, attraction. M17. ▸**c** MEDICINE. A sustained pull applied to a part of the body to maintain the positions of fractured bones, correct deformity, etc.; the state of being subjected to such a pull. Freq. in ***in traction***. L19.
2 The action of drawing a vehicle or load along a road or track, esp. with ref. to the means or power used. E19. ▸**b** Transportation by a public railway or tramway system. Chiefly in ***traction company***, ***traction system***. *US.* L19.
3 The force or amount of force required for traction; the grip of a tyre on a road, a wheel on a rail, etc. Also ***force of traction***. E19.
4 PHYSICAL GEOGRAPHY. The rolling and dragging of particles along the ground by a stream or the wind. E20.

> 🕮 **2** ***horse traction***, ***steam traction***, etc. **3** *Daily Telegraph* Each wheel receives the correct amount of power for maximum traction and roadholding.

Comb.: **traction-engine** a steam or diesel engine used to draw heavy loads on roads, in fields, etc.; **traction-load** the weight of

a locomotive engine or motor vehicle which presses the driving-wheels down on the rail or ground and produces the required friction to prevent the wheel from slipping; **traction motor** an electric motor designed to draw heavy loads; **traction splint** *MEDICINE* a splint with an attachment for pulling on a limb; **traction-wheel** the driving-wheel of a locomotive etc.
■ **tractional** *adjective* of or pertaining to traction **L19**.

tractive /ˈtraktɪv/ *adjective*. **E17**.
[formed as TRACT *verb* + -IVE.]
Having the property of drawing or pulling; used for traction.

📖 *Which?* They measured the test car's tractive power on packed snow.

tractless /ˈtraktlɪs/ *adjective*. *arch. rare*. **E17**.
[from TRACT *noun*[3] + -LESS.]
Without a tract or tracts; *spec.* = TRACKLESS.

tractor /ˈtraktə/ *noun*. **L18**.
[formed as TRACT *verb* + -OR.]
1 In *pl.* In full ***metallic tractors***. A pair of pointed rods of different metals, as brass and steel, believed to relieve rheumatic or other pain by being drawn over the skin. *obsolete* exc. *Hist.* **L18**.
2 a *gen.* A person who or thing which draws or pulls something. **L18**. ▸**b** A traction-engine. Now usu., a sturdy, powerful motor vehicle freq. with large rear wheels and an elevated driving seat, used esp. for hauling farm machinery. **E20**. ▸**c** *AERONAUTICS*. An airscrew mounted at the front of an aircraft so as to exert a pull; an aircraft having this. Usu. *attrib.* Cf. PUSHER 2c. **E20**. ▸**d** The driving section of an articulated lorry. **E20**. ▸**e** *COMPUTING*. A mechanism that draws the paper through a printer. Also ***tractor feed***. **L20**.

📖 **2b** *Detroit Free Press* Grounds maintenance tractor . . designed for big jobs where you need rugged, dependable power. **c** *Flying* If you increase power at high angles of attack, a tractor propellor tends to pull the nose upward.

Comb.: ***tractor feed***: see sense 2e above; **tractor-trailer** *N. Amer.* an articulated lorry.
■ **tractoˈration** *noun* (*obsolete* exc. *Hist.*) the use of metallic tractors **E19**. **tractorcade** *noun* a procession of tractors **L20**. **tractoring** *noun* ploughing or cultivating by means of a farm tractor **E19**.

†**tractory** *noun*. **E17–L19**.
[from Latin *tractorius* of or for drawing, formed as prec.: see -ORY[2].]
1 A part of a plough. *rare*. Only in **E17**.
2 *ECCLESIASTICAL HISTORY*. A letter from a synod or council of bishops. *rare*. Only in **E18**.
3 *GEOMETRY*. = TRACTRIX. Only in **19**.

tractotomy /trakˈtɒtəmi/ *noun*. **M20**.
[from TRACT *noun*[3] + -O- + -TOMY.]
MEDICINE. A surgical operation in which certain nerve tracts in the brain or spinal cord are severed or destroyed.

tractrix /ˈtraktrɪks/ *noun*. Pl. **-trices** /-trɪsiːz/. **E18**.
[mod. Latin, fem. of TRACTOR: see -TRIX. Cf. DIRECTRIX.]
GEOMETRY. A curve whose tangents all intercept the *x*-axis at the same distance from the point of contact, being the involute of a catenary. Also, each of a class of curves similarly traced by the end of a rigid rod moving along a fixed line or curve.

tractus /ˈtraktəs/ *noun*. **LME**.
[medieval Latin (sc. *cantus*) lit. 'drawn-out (song)', formed as TRACT *noun*[3].]
ROMAN CATHOLIC CHURCH (now *Hist.*). = TRACT *noun*[2].

trad /trad/ *noun* & *adjective*. *colloq.* **M20**.
[Abbreviation.]
▸ **A** *noun*. **1** Traditional jazz. **M20**.
2 = TRADITIONALIST. **M20**.
▸ **B** *adjective*. = TRADITIONAL *adjective*. **M20**.

📖 *Expression!* The restaurant has a deserved reputation for Very Trad British Fare.

tradable /ˈtreɪdəb(ə)l/ *adjective*. Also **tradeable**. **L16**.
[from TRADE *noun* or *verb* + -ABLE.]
That may be traded or used in trading; marketable.
■ **tradaˈbility** *noun* **L20**.

tradal /ˈtreɪd(ə)l/ *adjective*. **L19**.
[Irreg. from next + -AL[1].]
Of or pertaining to trade; commercial.

trade /treɪd/ *noun*. **LME**.
[Middle Low German = track, corresp. to Old Saxon *trada*, Old High German *trata* from West Germanic, whence also TREAD *verb*.]
▸ **I 1** Buying and selling or exchange of commodities for profit, *spec.* between nations; commerce, trading, orig. conducted by passage or travel between trading parties; an instance or example of this. **LME**.
2 a Passage to and fro; coming and going; *fig.* mutual communication, dealings. Cf. TREAD *noun* 7. *obsolete* exc. *dial.* **L16**. ▸**b** Fuss, commotion; trouble. Cf. TREAD *noun* 7. *dial.* **M19**.
3 Goods, materials, commodities. Now *dial.* & (usu.) *derog.*, rubbish, trash. **M17**.
†**4** A fleet of trading ships under convoy. **M18–E19**.
5 A trade wind. Usu. in *pl.* **L18**.
6 An act of trading, a transaction, a bargain; *spec.* a deal, a swap. Orig. *US*. **E19**.
7 Commodities for use in bartering with primitive peoples; native produce for barter. **M19**.
8 A prostitute used by a homosexual; a homosexual partner. Also, such people collectively. *slang*. **M20**.
9 Enemy aircraft, *esp.* those open to aerial combat or destruction. **M20**.

📖 **1** *Country Homes* A refreshment tent . . is doing a roaring trade in halves of scrumpy. J. MASSON There was no black market or street trade in any psychiatric drugs. *People* The British established a rich trade with Portugal for this . . wine. *Time* An illegal . . weapons trade is growing. **5** D. DIVINE The trade that had been blowing . . died off. **6** M. C. SMITH Arkady handed over the envelope . . the first trade was completed.

▸ **II** †**10** A course, a way, a path. Cf. TREAD *noun* 3. **LME–E17**. ▸**b** The track or trail of a person or animal. Cf. TREAD *noun* 2. **L15–L16**.
11 A way or manner of life; a course of action. Also, a habitual way of proceeding, a habit. Cf. TREAD *noun* 6. *obsolete* exc. *Scot.* & *dial.* **LME**.
12 a The habitual practice of an occupation, business, or profession, esp. as a means of livelihood or gain. Now usu., a mercantile occupation or skilled handicraft (*esp.* one requiring an apprenticeship), as distinct from a profession, or a skilled handicraft, as distinct from any other occupation. Cf. TREAD *noun* 8. **M16**. ▸**b** Anything practised for a livelihood; *spec.* (*slang*) prostitution. **M17**.
13 a *The* people engaged in a particular trade or business; *spec.* (*a*) publishers and booksellers; (*b*) licensers and victuallers. **L17**. ▸**b** Any of the usu. seven corporations of craftsmen in a Scottish burgh, each of which formerly elected one or more members of the town council. **L18**. ▸**c** *The* submarine service of the Royal Navy. *slang*. **E20**. ▸**d** *The* secret service. *slang*. **M20**.
14 In *pl.* The trade papers or magazines of the entertainment world. Orig. & chiefly *US*. **M20**.

📖 **12a** S. BUTLER Mr Pontifex was a carpenter by trade. J. R. ACKERLEY The girls took jobs as teachers, the boys were put to trades. P. ANGADI He had built up a considerable empire in the furniture trade. *Jazz FM* To ply the trade of professional jazz musician. **13a** C. E. PASCOE Some . . publishing houses . . are as ready to sell to the general public as to 'the trade'. **14** N. SEDAKA I bought the latest trades and began to circle the new records.

Phrases: **blow trade** (now *rare*) (of the wind) blow in a habitual course or constantly in the same direction. ***balance of trade***: see BALANCE *noun*. **domestic trade** trade or commerce occurring within a country. ***fair trade***: see FAIR *adjective*. **foreign trade** trade or commerce with other countries, international trade. ***free trade***: see FREE *adjective*. **in trade** (now usu. *derog.*) following a mercantile occupation, esp. that of a shopkeeper. ***Jack of all trades***: see JACK *noun*[1]. ***RESTRAINT of trade***. ***rough trade***: see ROUGH *adjective*. ***terms of trade***: see TERM *noun*. ***the tools of the trade***: see TOOL *noun*. ***triangular trade***: see TRIANGULAR *adjective* 4. ***wet trade***: see WET *adjective*.
Comb.: **trade allowance** discount allowed to dealers or retailers; **trade barrier** a policy or regulation that restricts international trade; **Trade Board** *Hist.* a statutory body for settling disputes etc. in certain industries; **trade book**: published by a commercial publisher and intended for general readership; **trade card** a tradesman's or -woman's card bearing his or her name, trade, and place of business; **tradecraft** (*a*) skill or art in connection with a trade or calling; *spec.* (*slang*) skill in espionage and intelligence work; (*b*) the craft or art of trading or dealing; **trade cycle** recurring periods of increased and decreased economic activity; **trade deficit** = ***trade gap*** below; **trade discount**: allowed or agreed between traders, usually in the same line of business, or to a retailer by a wholesaler etc.; **trade dispute** a dispute among workers or between employers and workers connected with conditions of employment, the employment of a particular individual, etc.; **trade-edition** (*a*) a book where copyright is jointly held by several parties; (*b*) an edition of a book intended for general sale rather than for book clubs or specialist suppliers; **trade effluent** effluent other than domestic sewage; *esp.* effluent produced by a trade or industry; **trade-English** a pidgin English used in Africa between English traders and Africans, and between Africans speaking different languages; †**trade-fallen** *adjective* fallen or broken in trade, bankrupt; **trade gap** the extent by which a country's imports exceed its exports; **trade journal**, **trade magazine**, **trade paper**: containing information relating to a particular trade; **trade-language** a language used between people normally speaking different languages; **trade-last** *US* a compliment offered in exchange for one paid to the speaker; *loosely* any compliment; ***trade magazine***: see ***trade journal*** above; **trade-master** a person who instructs a class in a trade or handicraft; **trade mission** a mission sent by one country to another to promote trade with it; **trade name** (*a*) a name given to a proprietary article; (*b*) the name by which an article or substance is known in a trade; (*c*) the name or style under which a business trades; ***trade paper***: see ***trade journal*** above; **trade plate** a temporary number-plate for an unlicensed vehicle (usu. in *pl.*); **trade price** the price at which a wholesale dealer sells to a retailer; **trade reduction** = ***trade discount*** above; **trade-room** a room, esp. on board ship, for the storage and exchange of trade goods; **trade-route** a route followed by traders or trading ships; **trade-sale** an auction held by and for a particular trade; **trade school** a school in which manual skills are taught; **trade secret** a secret device or technique used esp. in a particular trade; *loosely* (freq. *joc.*) any secret; **tradesfolk** people engaged in trade; tradespeople; *spec.* artisans, shopkeepers; **trade show** *CINEMATOGRAPHY* a private advance showing to the trade of a new film; **trade-show** *verb trans.* (*CINEMATOGRAPHY*) show (a film) to the trade before it goes on general release; **tradespeople** people engaged in trade; tradesmen or -women and their families; **tradesperson** a tradesman or tradeswoman; **trade surplus** the extent by which a country's exports exceed its imports; **trade term** an expression chiefly used within a particular trade; **trade-test** *verb trans.* & *intrans.* test the ability of (an individual) in a given trade; **trade war** a situation in which governments act aggressively in international markets to promote their own countries' trading interests; **trade waste** = ***trade effluent*** above; **trade-weighted** *adjective* (esp. of exchange rates) weighted according to the importance of the trade with the various countries involved. See also TRADE MARK, TRADESMAN, TRADESWOMAN, TRADE UNION, TRADE WIND.
■ **tradeful** *adjective* (*arch.*) full of trade; fully occupied or engaged in trading: **L16**. **tradeless** *adjective* (*a*) without a trade; unskilled in any trade; (*b*) without trade or commerce: **E18**.

trade /treɪd/ *verb*. **M16**.
[from prec.]
†**1 a** *verb trans.* Tread (a path); cross (the sea); *fig.* lead (one's life). **M16–M17**. ▸**b** *verb intrans.* Tread, walk, go. **L16–M17**.
†**2** *verb trans.* Follow (a course) habitually; use (something) regularly. **M16–M17**.
†**3** *verb trans.* Familiarize with something; accustom *to* or *to do*; train *in* or *with*. **M16–M17**.
†**4** *verb intrans.* **a** Have dealings; communicate, converse; negotiate. Freq. foll. by *with*. **M16–L17**. ▸**b** Foll. by *in*: occupy oneself with, be concerned with, have dealings in. **E17–E19**.
5 a *verb intrans.* & †*trans.* Go to or *to* a place for purposes of trade. **L16**. ▸**b** *verb intrans.* Engage in trade or commerce, pursue trade; *spec.* engage in illegal trade. (Foll. by *with* a person etc., *in* or *for* a commodity.) **L16**.
6 *verb trans.* Use as the object of trade; buy and sell, barter, exchange; *fig.* exchange (insults, blows, etc.). **E17**. ▸**b** *spec.* (*N. AMER. SPORT*). Exchange (a player) between clubs or teams, esp. *for* another. **L19**.
7 *verb intrans. COMMERCE*. Of a share or currency: be bought and sold (*at* a certain price etc.). **L20**.

📖 **5a** H. H. WILSON They traded with profit only to China. **b** CAPT. COOK Those who remained in the canoes traded with our people very fairly. SIR W. SCOTT I only trade now as wholesale dealer. *New Yorker* Garland generally trades for his dogs, but he occasionally pays cash. **6** J. MCPHEE They trade mud-shark livers for seal oil. *Arizona Daily Star* He traded his first horse at age 12. S. NAIPAUL Clara did not trade gossip with the neighbours. *Times* He and the Zulu chief were soon within an ace of trading punches across the table. **trade places** *N. Amer.* change places. **7** *Times* The dollar was trading back where it was in January.

With adverbs & prepositions in specialized senses: **trade down** buy or sell cheaper goods than before or than usual; sell something and buy a cheaper replacement. **trade in** exchange (a used car etc.) as payment or esp. part-payment *for* a new one. **trade off** dispose of by barter; *fig.* exchange for something else, esp. as a compromise. **trade on** make use of for one's own ends; profit by; take advantage of (a person's credulity, one's reputation, etc.). **trade up** buy or sell dearer goods than before or than usual; sell something and buy a dearer replacement.
Comb.: **trade-in** (*a*) a transaction in which something is traded in; a part-exchange; (*b*) an item traded in, *esp.* a used car; (*c*) a sum allowed in return for this; **trade-off** a balance achieved between two desirable but incompatible features; a bargain, a compromise.

tradeable *adjective* var. of TRADABLE.

traded /ˈtreɪdɪd/ *adjective*. **M16**.
[from TRADE *noun* or *verb* + -ED[1], -ED[2].]
That has been traded; having a (specified) trade; subject to trading. Formerly *spec.* (*a*) versed, skilled, experienced; conversant, familiar; (*b*) (of a road or way) much or habitually used; (*c*) (of a place) frequented for trading.
traded option *COMMERCE* an option on a stock exchange which can itself be bought and sold.

trade mark /ˈtreɪd mɑːk/ *noun* & *verb*. Also (esp. as verb) **trademark**. **M19**.
[from TRADE *noun* + MARK *noun*[1].]
▸ **A** *noun*. **1** A device, word, or combination of words, secured by legal registration or established by use, used to distinguish the goods of or to represent a particular manufacturer or trader. **M19**.
2 *transf.* A distinctive mark or characteristic. **M19**.

📖 **1** *Scientific American* Inadequate protection abroad of our patents, copyrights, trademarks, and trade secrets. **2** *Daily Telegraph* Judge James Pickles, whose outspoken views have become a trade mark.

▸ **B** *verb trans.* Affix a trade mark on, provide with a trade mark. Chiefly as ***trademarked*** *ppl adjective*. **E20**.

trader /ˈtreɪdə/ *noun*. **L16**.
[from TRADE *verb* + -ER[1].]
1 A person engaged in commerce or trading. **L16**. ▸**b** A prostitute. *slang* (now *rare*). **L17**. ▸**c** A ship engaged in trading; a merchant ship. **E18**.

†**2** A person who is occupied or concerned *in* something. M17–E19.

> 1 *Daily Nation (Nairobi)* He warned traders that it was an offence to operate a business without a licence. ***fair-trader, free-trader, slave-trader***, etc.

tradescantia /tradɪˈskantɪə/ *noun.* M18.
[mod. Latin (see below), from John *Tradescant* (the Elder, d. *c* 1637), English gardener, naturalist, and collector: see -IA[1].]
Any plant of the American genus *Tradescantia* (family Commelinaceae), characterized by triangular three-petalled purple, blue, pink, etc., flowers; *esp.* any of those grown for ornament, e.g. *T. virginiana* of the eastern US, and its hybrid derivative *T.* × *andersoniana*.

tradesman /ˈtreɪdzmən/ *noun.* Pl. **-men**. L16.
[from TRADE *noun* + -S[1] + MAN *noun*.]
1 A person who is skilled in and follows a trade or a skilled handicraft; an artisan, a craftsman. Now chiefly *Scot. & Austral.* L16.
2 A person who is engaged in trade or the sale of commodities; *esp.* a shopkeeper. E17.
Comb.: **tradesman's door, tradesman's entrance** a minor or side entrance to a property for use by tradesmen or workmen.
■ **tradesmanlike** *adjective* resembling or characteristic of a tradesman L18. **tradesmanship** *noun* the fact of being a tradesman; the character of a tradesman; tradesmen collectively: E19.

tradeswoman /ˈtreɪdzwʊmən/ *noun.* Pl. **-women** /-wɪmɪn/. E18.
[formed as prec. + WOMAN *noun*.]
A woman engaged in trade, or in a particular trade. Also (now *rare*), the wife of a tradesman.

trade union /treɪd ˈjuːnjən, -ɪən/ *noun phr.* Also **trades union** /treɪdz/. M19.
[from TRADE *noun* + UNION *noun*[2].]
An organized association of the workers in a trade, group of trades, or profession for the protection and furtherance of their interests, rights, and working conditions, and for the provision of financial assistance during strikes, sickness, unemployment, etc. Cf. UNION *noun*[2] 7b.
Comb.: **trade union congress** (*a*) a national delegate conference of British trade unions, held annually since 1868; (*b*) (with cap. initials) the national confederation of British trade unions, originally formed to organize the annual congress.
■ **trade-unionism** *noun* the system, principles, or practice of trade unions M19. **trade-unionist** *noun* a member of a trade union M19. **trade-unionized** *adjective* enrolled in a trade union; formed into or having a trade union: M20.

trade wind /ˈtreɪd wɪnd/ *noun phr.* M17.
[from TRADE *noun*[1] + WIND *noun*[1]. App. originating in phr. *blow trade*: see TRADE *noun*.]
Orig., a wind that blows steadily in the same direction. Now *spec.*, a wind blowing constantly towards the equator from the north-east or south-east. Formerly, a seasonal wind of the Indian Ocean, a monsoon. Cf. ANTITRADE *wind*.

trading /ˈtreɪdɪŋ/ *noun.* L16.
[from TRADE *verb* + -ING[1].]
The action of TRADE *verb*; *esp.* buying and selling; commerce, trade.
Comb.: **trading account** an account giving details of sales during a period, including the revenue gained, the cost, the stock held, and the overall profit or loss; **trading card** each of a set of picture cards, featuring e.g. popular cartoon characters, that are collected and traded, esp. by children; **trading estate** an area of land specially developed for commerce or light industry; **trading floor** the area in a stock exchange where dealing is done; **trading-house** *Hist.* a building where bartering with N. American Indians took place; **trading-place** a place visited, esp. for trade; **trading post** (*a*) see POST *noun*[4] 3c; (*b*) a post or position on a stock exchange floor where particular stocks are bought and sold; **trading profit** profit as shown in a trading account; **trading stamp** a stamp given to a customer in some stores which is exchangeable in large numbers for various articles (cf. STAMP *noun* 8b(c)).

tradition /trəˈdɪʃ(ə)n/ *noun.* LME.
[Old & mod. French *tradicion*, *-tion* or Latin *traditio(n-)*, from *tradere* hand over, deliver, formed as TRANS- + *dare* give: see -ITION.]
1 Delivery, esp. oral, of information or instruction. Formerly also, an orally delivered ordinance. Now *rare*. LME.
2 a A statement, belief, custom, etc., handed down by non-written (esp. oral) means from generation to generation; such beliefs etc. collectively. LME. ▸**b** The action of handing down something, from generation to generation; transmission of statements, beliefs, customs, etc., esp. by word of mouth or unwritten custom; the fact of being handed down thus. Freq. in ***by tradition***. L16. ▸**c** A long established and generally accepted practice or custom; immemorial usage. Also *spec.*, the principles held and generally followed by any branch of art or literature, acquired from and handed down by experience and practice. L16.
3 THEOLOGY. (A) doctrine usu. regarded as having divine authority without written evidence; *spec.* (*a*) any one or all of the laws held by the Pharisees to have been delivered by God to Moses, handed down orally from generation to generation and embodied in the Mishnah; (*b*) the oral teachings of Christ and the apostles, transmitted by word of mouth from generation to generation; (*c*) (usu. **T-**) the words and deeds of Muhammad not contained in the Koran but transmitted at first orally, and later recorded; *esp.* those accepted by the Sunnites but rejected by the Shiites, the Sunna. LME.
4 †**a** The giving up, surrender, or betrayal of something or someone. L15–M17. ▸**b** *spec.* (ECCLESIASTICAL HISTORY). Surrender of sacred books etc. in times of persecution. Cf. TRADITOR 2. M19.
5 The action of handing over something material to another; *spec.* (LAW) the formal delivery of property etc. M16.

> **2a** R. MACAULAY Wrapping their heads up is a religious tradition that goes very deep. J. CARTWRIGHT We use local skills and time-honoured traditions. **b** H. HALLAM The memory of Greece and Rome would have been . . preserved by tradition. F. HOYLE Unable to leave a written record, they . . had no recourse except to tradition. **c** *Ashmolean* The more avant-garde painters . . had broken with realist tradition. *Farmers Weekly* Jackarooing is one of the oldest . . traditions in Australian agriculture.

Comb.: **tradition-directed** *adjective* governed by social conventions.
■ **traditioned** *adjective* (*rare*) having traditions of a specified kind or degree M19. **traditioner** *noun* (*rare*) = TRADITIONIST M17. **traditionism** *noun* (*rare*) = TRADITIONALISM 1 M19. **traditionless** *adjective* having no traditions M19.

tradition /trəˈdɪʃ(ə)n/ *verb trans. rare.* M17.
[from prec.]
Transmit by tradition; relate as a tradition.

traditional /trəˈdɪʃ(ə)n(ə)l/ *adjective & noun.* L16.
[formed as prec. + -AL[1].]
▸ **A** *adjective.* **1 a** Belonging to or of the nature of tradition; handed down by or derived from tradition; *loosely* customary, conventional. L16. ▸**b** That is such according to tradition; asserted or related by tradition. M19. ▸**c** *spec.* Designating jazz of the earliest style, dating from the early 20th cent. Cf. TRAD *noun* 1. M20.
†**2** Observant of or bound by tradition. *rare.* L16–M17.

> **1a** J. STEINBECK The traditional dark cypresses wept around the edge of the cemetery. P. FITZGERALD I'm not familiar with traditional sayings. INA TAYLOR She preferred the traditional methods to any new-fangled ideas. *Which?* With a traditional . . bank account, there are three main types of charges.

▸ **B** *noun.* A traditional belief, practice, etc. *rare.* M17.

> *Time Out* Wanted urgently — six boys and girls as performers of folklore traditionals.

■ **traditioˈnality** *noun* traditional quality or character; a traditional belief or principle: M19. **traditionally** *adverb* M17.

traditionalise *verb* var. of TRADITIONALIZE.

traditionalism /trəˈdɪʃ(ə)n(ə)lɪz(ə)m/ *noun.* M19.
[French *traditionalisme* or from TRADITIONAL + -ISM.]
1 Adherence to traditional doctrine or theory; excessive respect for tradition, esp. in religious matters. M19.
2 A system of philosophy according to which all human or esp. religious knowledge is derived by traditional instruction from an original divine revelation. L19.

traditionalist /trəˈdɪʃ(ə)n(ə)lɪst/ *noun.* L19.
[from TRADITIONAL + -IST.]
1 An adherent of traditionalism; an upholder of the authority of tradition. L19.
2 A person who plays, appreciates, or supports traditional jazz. M20.

> **1** F. FITZGERALD A traditionalist who looked . . backwards into the old stream of Confucian civilization. *attrib.*: T. B. BOTTOMORE A traditionalist revival of ancient values and ways of life.

■ **traditionaˈlistic** *adjective* of or pertaining to traditionalists or traditionalism L19.

traditionalize /trəˈdɪʃ(ə)n(ə)lʌɪz/ *verb trans.* Also **-ise**. L19.
[from TRADITIONAL + -IZE.]
Make traditional; fill with or constrain by tradition.
■ **traditionaliˈzation** *noun* M20.

traditionary /trəˈdɪʃ(ə)n(ə)ri/ *noun & adjective.* L16.
[from TRADITION *noun* + -ARY[1].]
▸ **A** *noun.* A traditionalist, esp. in religious matters. *rare.* L16.
▸ **B** *adjective.* †**1** = TRADITIONAL *adjective* 2. E–M17.
2 = TRADITIONAL *adjective* 1, 1b. M17.

traditionist /trəˈdɪʃ(ə)nɪst/ *noun.* M17.
[from TRADITION *noun* + -IST.]
1 A person who adheres to or maintains the authority of tradition, *esp.* one who accepts the Muslim or Jewish doctrine of tradition (see TRADITION *noun* 3). M17.
2 A person who perpetuates or records a tradition; a relater of traditions. M18.

traditive /ˈtradɪtɪv/ *adjective.* Now *rare.* E17.
[French †*traditif* traditional, from late Latin *traditus* oral transmission: see -IVE.]
Characterized by, belonging to, or transmitted by tradition; traditional.

traditor /ˈtradɪtə/ *noun.* LME.
[Latin: see TRAITOR.]
1 A betrayer, a traitor. *obsolete* exc. in sense 2 below. LME.
2 ECCLESIASTICAL HISTORY. An early Christian who surrendered sacred books and vessels or betrayed fellow-Christians in times of persecution to save his or her own life. Cf. TRADITION *noun* 4b. L16.

traduce /trəˈdjuːs/ *verb trans.* M16.
[Latin *traducere*, formed as TRANS- + *ducere* to lead.]
†**1** Convey from one place to another; transport. M16–L17. ▸**b** Put into another form; translate into another language; alter, modify. M16–M19. ▸**c** Transfer. M16–M17.
†**2** Pass on to offspring, esp. by generation; transmit. M16–M18. ▸**b** *transf.* Generate, propagate, produce as offspring. L16–E18. ▸**c** Obtain *from* a source. E17–E18.
3 Speak ill of, malign, slander, misrepresent. Formerly also, state slanderously; blame *for*, accuse *of*. L16.

> **3** J. MCPHEE This deprecated, defamed, traduced, and disparaged metropolis.

■ **traducement** *noun* the action or an act of traducing a person or thing; defamation, slander: L16. **traducer** *noun* E17.

traducian /trəˈdjuːsɪən, -ʃ(ə)n/ *noun.* E18.
[ecclesiastical Latin *Traduciani* use as noun of pl. of *traducianus* transmitting, transmitter, deriv. of Latin *tradux* vine-shoot for propagation, also in transf. sense: see -IAN.]
A person who maintains that the soul of a child, like the body, is propagated by or inherited from the parents. Also (*rare*), a person who maintains that original sin is transmitted from parent to child.
■ **traducianism** *noun* (*a*) the doctrine of the transmission of the soul from parents to child; (*b*) *rare* the doctrine of the hereditary transmission of original sin: M19. **traducianist** *noun* a believer in traducianism M19.

†**traduct** *verb trans.* E–M17.
[Latin *traduct-* pa. ppl stem of *traducere* TRADUCE.]
Transmit, esp. by generation; propagate.

traduction /trəˈdʌkʃ(ə)n/ *noun.* E16.
[Old & mod. French, or Latin *traductio(n-)* leading across, transference, in Christian Latin also in sense 3, from *traduct-*: see prec., -ION.]
†**1** Conveyance from one place to another; transportation, transference. E16–L17.
†**2** Translation into another language; a translation. M16–E19.
3 Transmission, handing down; *spec.* transmission by generation to offspring or posterity. Now *rare* or *obsolete*. L16. ▸†**b** *transf.* Something transmitted. M17–L18.
4 The action of traducing or defaming a person or thing; slander, calumny. *rare.* M17.
5 LOGIC. Transference or transition from one order of reasoning to another. M19.

traductive /trəˈdʌktɪv/ *adjective.* M17.
[from TRADUCTION 3 + -IVE.]
1 Having the property of being traduced or transmitted; passing on to another. Now *rare* or *obsolete*. M17.
2 LOGIC. Involving traduction. *rare.* M19.

traductor /trəˈdʌktə/ *noun.* Also †**-er**. L17.
[from TRADUCT + -OR, -ER[1].]
†**1** A person who traducts something. Only in L17.
2 A device on the side of a railway carriage that picks up and deposits mailbags while the train is moving. M20.

Trafalgar /trəˈfalgə, traf(ə)lˈgɑː/ *noun.* E19.
[A cape on the south coast of Spain, famed for a British naval victory over the combined fleets of France and Spain in 1805.]
▸ **I 1** Used *attrib.* to designate things pertaining to or named after (the battle of) Trafalgar. E19.
1 Trafalgar chair a light graceful Regency chair often decorated with anchors or other nautical motifs. **Trafalgar Day** 21 October, the anniversary of the battle of Trafalgar. **Trafalgar Square** *verb phr. trans.* (*joc.*) harangue (from the practice of soap-box oratory in such places as Trafalgar Square in London).
▸ **II 2** A size of type one size larger than two-line double pica and one size smaller than canon. Now *Hist.* M19.

traffic /ˈtrafɪk/ *noun.* Also (*arch.*) **-ck**. E16.
[French †*traff(f)ique* (now *trafic*), Spanish *tráfico*, Italian *traffico*, of unkn. origin.]
1 The commercial transportation of merchandise or passengers by road, rail, sea, air, etc.; the people or goods so transported. Also, trade as an international or large-scale activity. E16.
2 The buying and selling or exchange of goods for profit; barter; commerce. Also (*rare*), an instance of this; a commercial transaction; a line of business or trade. M16.

▸**b** Dealing or trade of an illicit or disreputable nature. **M17.**

3 Social intercourse; interpersonal communication or dealings. **M16.**

4 †**a** Merchandise in which trade is done; saleable commodities. **M16–L18.** ▸†**b** A prostitute. *rare.* **L16–M17.** ▸**c** Worthless stuff, trash. Also, persons of the lowest class, rabble. *Scot. & dial.* **E19.**

5 a The passage to and fro of vehicles, people, ships, planes, etc.; the flow or movement of vehicles etc. along a route, as a road, sea-lane, etc.; such vehicles etc. collectively. **E19.** ▸**b** The amount of business done in terms of goods or number of passengers carried by a railway or other transport operation; a statement of revenue or volumes from such business. **M19.** ▸**c** The messages, signals, etc., transmitted through a communications system; the flow or volume of such business. **L19.** ▸**d** The division of an organization responsible for traffic management; a traffic department. Chiefly *US.* **L19.** ▸**e** *SPORT.* A crowding or bunching together of participants in a team game, race, etc. Orig. *US.* **L20.**

📖 **1** J. L. MOTLEY Cadiz . . where the ancient and modern systems of traffic were blending. **2** EVELYN Antient Moneys . . first used in Trafick. *fig.*: J. HILTON Serene friendships, a long and kindly traffic of the mind. **as much as the traffic will bear, as much as the traffic will stand** as much as the trade or market will tolerate, as much as is economically viable. **b** S. BRILL The murders had to do with drug traffic. **3** T. STAFFORD The President . . returned him no Answer . . . utterly refusing any further traffique with him. **5a** *Belle (Australia)* Replace the carpet on the . . stair . . if it takes a lot of traffic. A. GHOSH The traffic packed . . tight . . all the way to the Dhakuria overbridge. *attrib.*: *Daily Telegraph* There's stress enough in modern traffic conditions. ***through traffic***: see **THROUGH** *adjective* 1b. **b** *Holiday Which?* Air UK . . recorded a 39% growth in passenger traffic. ***MIXED-traffic***. **c** *Times Lit. Suppl.* British Intelligence could decipher German . . cipher traffic.

Comb.: **traffic analysis** *US* in cryptography, the obtaining of information through analysis of patterns of communication without the decipherment of individual messages; **traffic analyst** *US* a person engaged in traffic analysis; **traffic artery** (orig. *US*) a main or arterial road; **traffic calming** [German *Verkehrsberuhigung*] the deliberate slowing of road traffic, esp. through residential areas, as by narrowing or obstructing roads; **traffic circle** (chiefly *N. Amer.*) a traffic roundabout; **traffic cone** = **CONE** *noun* 11; **traffic control** the regulation of traffic movement through the use of signals or direct commands; a service with this responsibility (esp. in ***air traffic control***); **traffic controller** a person or automatic device for regulating traffic movement (esp. in ***air traffic controller***); **traffic cop** *slang* a member of the traffic police; **traffic court** (orig. *US*) a court of law with jurisdiction over motoring offences; **traffic engineer** a person engaged in the design and planning of roads and the control of traffic; **traffic engineering** the design and planning of roads and the control of traffic; ***traffic island***: see **ISLAND** *noun*[1] 2b; **traffic jam** a condition in which the flow of road traffic is obstructed and comes to a (virtual) standstill; a build-up of traffic caused by this; the vehicles caught in such a build-up; **traffic-jammed** *adjective* caught in a traffic jam; **traffic lane** a road carriageway for a single line of moving vehicles; an air or sea route designated as a set course for shipping or aircraft in order to avoid collisions; **traffic light** (*a*) *rare* a light used for the guidance of aircraft; (*b*) (each of) a set of automatic lights (usu. red, amber, and green) for controlling road traffic, esp. at junctions (freq. in *pl.*); **traffic offence** an infringement of the law by the driver of a motor vehicle; **traffic officer** = ***traffic policeman*** below; **traffic pattern** (*a*) a pattern in the air above an airport of permitted lanes for aircraft to follow after take-off or prior to landing; (*b*) the characteristic distribution of traffic on a route; **traffic police** the branch of a police force concerned with the enforcement of traffic regulations and road traffic control; **traffic policeman** a (male) member of the traffic police; **traffic-proof** *adjective* (of a horse or pony) trained so as to be ridden or driven safely in traffic; **traffic-proof** *verb trans.* train (a horse or pony) to be ridden or driven safely in traffic; **traffic sign** a roadside sign conveying information, a warning, etc., to drivers of motor vehicles; **traffic signal** = ***traffic light*** (b) above; **traffic snarl** *colloq.* a traffic jam; **traffic ticket** *US* an official notification of a traffic offence, issued by a traffic warden or the police; **traffic violation** *US* = ***traffic offence*** above; **traffic warden** a uniformed official employed to help control road traffic and to enforce regulations about the parking of motor vehicles.

■ **trafficless** *adjective* devoid of traffic **L19.**

traffic /ˈtrafɪk/ *verb.* Also (*arch.*) **-ck.** Infl. **-ck-. M16.**
[French *traf(f)iquer*, Spanish *traficar*, Italian *trafficare*; of unkn. origin.]

1 *verb intrans.* Carry on trade, buy and sell; have commercial dealings *with* a person etc. Also (now *rare* or *obsolete*), resort *to* a place for the purpose of trade. **M16.** ▸**b** Deal or trade *in* something of an illicit or disreputable nature. **M17.**

2 *verb intrans.* Conduct secret dealings; intrigue or conspire (*with* a person). Also, communicate or have social dealings (*with* a person), conduct negotiations; be concerned (*in* a matter). **M16.**

†**3** *verb trans.* Travel across or frequent for the purpose of trading; carry on trade in (a place). **M16–E17.** ▸**b** *verb trans. & intrans.* Pass to and fro (on), frequent (a road etc.). *dial. rare.* **E19.**

4 *verb trans.* Carry on a trade in; barter; deal in, *esp.* illicitly. **L16.**

📖 **1** CAPT. COOK They trafficked with us for cocoa-nuts. S. NAIPAUL The smaller ships . . trafficked among the islands. **b** *Times Lit. Suppl.* They traffick in white slaves. **2** G. VIDAL You can't be President and traffic with parlour pinks and socialists. **4** *Daily Telegraph* Diplomats have helped traffic gold into India where legal import is banned.

■ **trafficker** *noun* a person who trades or traffics, esp. in something of an illicit or disreputable nature **L16.**

trafficable /ˈtrafɪkəb(ə)l/ *adjective.* **E17.**
[from **TRAFFIC** *noun, verb* + **-ABLE.**]

†**1** Adapted or suitable for traffic or trading. *rare.* Only in **E17.**

2 Able to be bought or sold; marketable. **M17.**

3 Of a road: suitable for the passage of vehicular traffic. **L19.**

■ **traffica'bility** *noun* suitability for the passage of vehicular traffic **L19.**

trafficator /ˈtrafɪkeɪtə/ *noun.* **M20.**
[from **TRAFFIC** *noun* + **INDIC)ATOR.**]

A signal arm of a type formerly attached to each side of a motor vehicle, which could be raised and illuminated automatically to act as an indicator when the vehicle was about to change direction.

trafficked /ˈtrafɪkt/ *adjective.* **M16.**
[from **TRAFFIC** *noun, verb*: see **-ED**[2], **-ED**[1].]

†**1** That has trafficked or traded abroad; experienced in trading. *rare.* Only in **M16.**

†**2** Travelled over or explored for traffic or trade. *rare.* Only in **E17.**

3 Made the subject of traffic or trade; dealt in as merchandise. **L19.**

4 Of a road, route, transport service, etc.: used by vehicular or passenger traffic. Freq. with specifying word. **E20.**

📖 **4** *Times* British Rail wants to close it because it . . is duplicated by a . . more heavily trafficked line.

tragacanth /ˈtragəkanθ/ *noun.* **L16.**
[French *tragacante* from Latin *tragacantha* from Greek *tragakantha* goat's-thorn, from *tragos* male goat + *akantha* thorn.]

1 In full ***gum tragacanth***. A gum or mucilaginous mixture of polysaccharides obtained from several shrubs of the genus *Astragalus* (see sense 2 below) by natural exudation or incision, in the form of whitish strings or flakes partly soluble in water, and used as a vehicle for drugs, as a food additive, and in numerous industrial products. **L16.**

2 Any of several low spiny leguminous shrubs of the genus *Astragalus* found in western and central Asia, from which gum tragacanth is derived. *rare.* **E17.**

1 Indian tragacanth = ***KARAYA gum***.

tragal /ˈtreɪg(ə)l/ *adjective.* **L19.**
[from **TRAGUS** + **-AL**[1].]

ANATOMY. Of, pertaining to, or situated on the tragus.

tragedian /trəˈdʒiːdɪən/ *noun.* **LME.**
[Old French *tragediane*, French *tragédien* from Old & mod. French *tragédie* **TRAGEDY**: see **-IAN.**]

1 A writer of tragedy; a tragic poet or dramatist. **LME.**

2 A tragic actor. **L16.**

†**3** *fig.* A person involved in a tragic or dreadful calamity; the victim, or inflicter, of a tragic fate. **L16–M17.**

tragedical /trəˈdʒiːdɪk(ə)l/ *adjective. rare.* **M16.**
[from Greek *tragōidikos* befitting tragedy + **-AL**[1].]

Of a tragic character; tragic.

tragédie lyrique /traʒedi lirik/ *noun phr.* Pl. **-s -s** (pronounced same). **E20.**
[French, lit. 'lyric tragedy'.]

A type of serious French opera of the 17th and 18th cents. making use of tragic mythological or epic subjects; an example of this. Cf. **OPERA SERIA.**

tragédienne /trədʒiːdɪˈɛn/ *noun.* **M19.**
[French, fem. of *tragédien* **TRAGEDIAN.**]

A tragic actress.

tragédies lyriques *noun phr.* pl. of **TRAGÉDIE LYRIQUE.**

tragedietta /trədʒiːdɪˈɛtə/ *noun.* **L19.**
[Italian, from *tragedia* **TRAGEDY** + *-etta* **-ET**[1].]

A slight or short tragedy; a dramatic sketch of tragic character.

tragedious /trəˈdʒiːdɪəs/ *adjective.* Long *rare.* **L15.**
[from Latin *tragœdia* **TRAGEDY** + **-OUS.**]

Full of, or having the character of, tragedy; calamitous, tragic.

tragedize /ˈtradʒɪdʌɪz/ *verb.* Also **-ise. L16.**
[from next + **-IZE.**]

1 *verb trans.* Act or perform (a play etc.) as a tragedy; conduct tragically; treat tragically. **L16.**

2 *verb intrans.* Perform as a tragedian; act or speak in tragic style. **M18.**

3 *verb trans.* Convert into a tragedy; dramatize in tragic form. **M18.**

tragedy /ˈtradʒɪdi/ *noun.* **LME.**
[Old & mod. French *tragédie* from Latin *tragœdia* from Greek *tragōidia* app. from *tragos* goat + *ōidē* **ODE** song.]

1 †**a** A serious medieval narrative or narrative poem written in an elevated style and typically dealing with the downfall of an important or powerful person. **LME–L16.** ▸**b** In classical and Renaissance drama, a serious verse play (orig. a Greek lyric song), written in an elevated style, in which the protagonist (usu. a political leader or royal personage) is drawn to disaster or death by an error or fatal flaw. Later, a drama of a similarly serious nature and unhappy ending but typically dealing with an ordinary person or people; any literary composition with similar characteristics. **LME.**

2 A genre of drama etc. characterized by its depiction of characters involved in unhappy or disastrous events, and a serious or elevated style. **LME.**

3 An unhappy, terrible, or fatal event in life; a calamity, a disaster (freq. *hyperbol.*); such events collectively. **LME.** ▸†**b** Misery, misfortune; *esp.* sorrowful or violent end. Chiefly with possess. **LME–M18.** ▸†**c** A distressing or dreadful tale; a passionate lamentation. **M16–M17.**

📖 **1b** *Guardian* The . . horror of Webster's revenge tragedy is beautifully tempered by a touching realism in . . [this] production. **2** *Bulletin of Hispanic Studies* Types of serious drama—political tragedy, heroic drama, . . and the peasant play. **3** *Indian Bookworm's Journal* It is a tragedy that our best young men are not joining the Defence Services. **b** J. WESLEY See the Wicked's dismal Tragedy. **c** HENRY MORE Some would raise such Stirres and Tragedies about.

¶ Cf. **COMEDY.**

■ **tragedist** *noun* (*rare*) = **TRAGEDIAN** 1 **E19.**

tragelaph /ˈtragɪlaf/ *noun.* **LME.**
[Latin *tragelaphus* from Greek *tragelaphos*, from *tragos* goat + *elaphos* deer.]

1 a Any of various antelopes or other horned animals vaguely known to ancient writers. *obsolete* exc. *Hist.* **LME.** ▸**b** A mythical or fictitious composite animal represented as a combination of a goat and a stag. **M17.**

2 *ZOOLOGY.* An antelope of the modern genus *Tragelaphus*, as the bushbuck, the kudu, the eland, etc. **L19.**

■ **tragelaphine** /trəˈgɛləfʌɪn/ *adjective & noun* (*a*) *adjective* of or designating the subfamily Tragelaphinae of antelopes, typified by the genus *Tragelaphus*; (*b*) *noun* an antelope of this group: **L19.**

trageremics /treɪgəˈriːmɪks/ *noun.* **M20.**
[from *Trager* (see **TRAGER–SMITH**) after **PHONEMICS.**]

LINGUISTICS. (A mock-technical term for) the approach to phonemic analysis characteristic of the American linguist George L. Trager.

Tragerian /treɪˈgɪərɪən/ *adjective & noun.* **M20.**
[from *Trager* (see next) + **-IAN.**]

LINGUISTICS. ▸**A** *adjective.* Of, pertaining to, or characteristic of the approach to phonemic analysis of George L. Trager. **M20.**

▸**B** *noun.* An adherent or practitioner of Tragerian analysis. *rare.* **M20.**

Trager–Smith /treɪgəˈsmɪθ/ *noun.* Also **Smith–Trager** /smɪθˈtreɪgə/. **M20.**
[from George L. *Trager* (1906–94) + Henry L. *Smith* (1913–72), American linguists and co-authors of *An Outline of English Structure* (1951).]

LINGUISTICS. Used *attrib.* to designate the method of linguistic analysis and phonemic transcription exemplified in *An Outline of English Structure.*

traghetto /traˈgɛtəʊ/ *noun.* Pl. **-tti** /-ti/. **E17.**
[Italian.]

In Venice, a landing-place or jetty for gondolas. Now also, a gondola.

tragi *noun* pl. of **TRAGUS.**

tragi- /ˈtradʒi/ *combining form.*
[from **TRAGIC** after **TRAGICOMEDY**: see **-I-**. Cf. **TRAGICO-.**]

Forming nouns and adjectives with the sense 'tragic and'.

■ **tragi'comic** *adjective* having the character of a tragicomedy **L17.** **tragi'comical** *adjective* of a tragicomic nature **M16.** **tragi'comically** *adverb* in a tragicomic manner **M18.** **tragica'tastrophe** *noun* an event which is partly tragic and partly catastrophic **E19.** **tragi-farce** *noun* an event or literary work which is partly tragic and partly farcical **L19.**

tragic /ˈtradʒɪk/ *adjective & noun.* **M16.**
[French *tragique* from Latin *tragicus* from Greek *tragikos*, from *tragos* goat (but assoc. with *tragōidia* **TRAGEDY**): see **-IC.**]

▸**A** *adjective.* **1** Of, pertaining to, or in the style of tragedy; befitting tragedy. **M16.**

2 Resembling the ending of a tragedy; calamitous, disastrous, terrible, fatal, (freq. *hyperbol.*). **M16.**

3 Relating to or expressing fatal or sorrowful events; causing sorrow; extremely distressing; sad. **L16.**

📖 **1** JONSON Comic matter will not be exprest In tragic verse. J. G. LOCKHART Her . . tragic exclamation . . , 'You've brought me water, boy, I asked for beer'. **2** *Folk Roots* It would be tragic to ignore this . . singer / songwriter's debut. **3** L. H. TRIBE She has no alternative other than the tragic one of ending the fetus's life.

Special collocations: **tragic-comedy** (long *rare*) = TRAGICOMEDY. **tragic flaw** = HAMARTIA. **tragic irony** a device, orig. in Greek tragedy, by which the tragic or fatal significance of a character's words or actions is revealed to the audience but unknown to the character himself or herself.

▶ **B** *noun*. **1 a** = TRAGEDIAN 2. L16. ▸**b** = TRAGEDIAN 1. L16.

2 Orig., a tragic fate. Later, a tragic event, a disaster. *rare*. L17.

3 A tragic literary work, a tragedy. Long *rare* or *obsolete*. E18.

¶ Cf. COMIC.

tragical /ˈtradʒɪk(ə)l/ *adjective*. L15.
[formed as prec. + -AL¹.]

1 = TRAGIC *adjective* 3. Now *rare*. L15.

†**2** Of style, subject, etc.: elevated; serious. Also, grandiose; (of language) grandiloquent, rhetorical; (of aspect or manner) grave. M16–L17.

3 = TRAGIC *adjective* 2. M16.

†**4** = TRAGIC *adjective* 1. L16–E17.

▪ **tragiˈcality** *noun* (*rare*) = TRAGICALNESS M19. **tragicalness** *noun* tragic quality M17.

tragically /ˈtradʒɪk(ə)li/ *adverb*. L16.
[from TRAGICAL *adjective* or TRAGIC *adjective*: see -ICALLY.]
In a tragic manner, in a manner befitting tragedy.

tragico- /ˈtradʒɪkəʊ/ *combining form*.
[from Greek *tragikos* TRAGIC: see -O-. Cf. TRAGI-.]
Forming chiefly adjectives with the sense 'tragic and'.
▪ **tragico-ˈfarcical** *adjective* combining tragic and farcical elements E20. †**tragico-heroi-comic** *adjective* (*rare*) combining tragic, heroic, and comic elements M18. **tragico-hiˈstorical** *adjective* combining tragic and historical elements E20.

tragicomedy /tradʒɪˈkɒmɪdi/ *noun*. Also **tragi-comedy**. L16.
[French *tragicomédie* or Italian *tragicommedia* from late Latin *tragicomœdia*, for *tragicocomœdia*: see TRAGEDY, COMEDY.]

1 A literary work, usu. a play, combining the qualities of a tragedy and a comedy, or containing both tragic and comic elements. Also, a genre of drama etc. characterized by tragic and comic qualities or elements. L16.

2 An event or series of events of mixed tragic and comic character; a combination of sad and humorous elements in life. E17.

tragopan /ˈtragəpan/ *noun*. M19.
[mod. Latin (see below) from Greek name of a horned bird, from *tragos* goat + *Pan* the god Pan.]
Any of several partly arboreal pheasants of the genus *Tragopan* of southern and eastern Asia, the males of which have a pair of erectile fleshy horns on the head, used for display.

tragulid /ˈtragjʊlɪd/ *noun & adjective*. L19.
[mod. Latin *Tragulidae* (see below), from *Tragulus* genus name, dim. of Latin *tragus* from Greek *tragos* goat: see -ULE, -ID³.]
ZOOLOGY. ▶**A** *noun*. A ruminant mammal of the family Tragulidae, which includes modern chevrotains. L19.
▶ **B** *adjective*. Of, pertaining to, or designating this family. M20.

tragus /ˈtreɪgəs/ *noun*. Pl. **-gi** /-gʌɪ, -dʒʌɪ/. L17.
[Late Latin from Latin from Greek *tragos* goat (with ref. to a tuft of hair which the structure often bears, compared to a goat's beard).]
ANATOMY & ZOOLOGY. A prominence on the inner side of the external ear, in front of and partly closing the passage to the organs of hearing.

trahison /traizɔ̃/ *noun*. M19.
[French.]
Treason, treachery. Chiefly in ***trahison des clercs*** /de klɛːr/ [from *La trahison des clercs*, a work by Julien Benda (1927)], a compromise of intellectual integrity or betrayal of standards by writers, artists, and thinkers.

traik /trɛk/ *noun*. *Scot*. E16.
[Origin unkn.: sense 2 may be a different word. Cf. next.]

1 An illness, esp. of an epidemic nature; a plague; mischief, disaster. Also, an annoying person, a pest. E16.

2 Meat from sheep that died from disease or exhaustion. E19.

▪ **traiky** *adjective* weak, worn out, exhausted E19.

traik /trɛk/ *verb intrans*. *Scot*. E16.
[Origin uncertain: perh. rel. to Swedish *tråka* rub on, tug, drudge, Norwegian *traaka* struggle against, go slowly or with difficulty, *traakes* become tired or exhausted. Cf. prec.]

1 Decline in health; waste away; become worn out or exhausted; decay, collapse. E16.

2 Wander, stray, go astray; come *after*, follow. E19.

▪ **traiked** *ppl adjective* (*a*) wasted; worn out; (*b*) (of sheep or cattle) having died a natural death: E16.

trail /treɪl/ *noun*¹. ME.
[App. from TRAIL *verb*. In sense 10 = Latin *tragula*.]
▶**I 1** Orig., the train of a robe or other garment. Later, a trailing or hanging garment; a trailing or loosely hanging length of hair etc. ME. ▸**b** A woman who trails her dress along the ground; a slattern, a slut. *Scot*. E19.

2 a A carved, moulded, or embroidered ornament in the form of a trailing wreath or spray of foliage or tendrils. LME. ▸**b** A wreath or spray of leaves etc.; a trailing tendril or branch. L16.

> 🕮 **1** E. B. BROWNING Cheeks.. Which a trail of golden hair Keeps from fading. **2b** H. MARTINEAU They.. entangled their feet in trails of the blue convolvulus.

▶**II 3** A sledge. *obsolete* exc. *Scot. & dial*. LME.

4 A track or scent, esp. as followed in hunting, or in seeking a person or thing. Also (*rare*), a strong-smelling drag or lure drawn along the ground for hounds to follow. L16.

5 A thing drawn along behind as an appendage; a body or collection *of* things or people drawn along by or following in the wake of a person or thing, esp. in a lengthened formation. E17.

6 A mark, trace, or track, remaining on a surface etc. after a thing or person has passed by or along. E17. ▸**b** *spec*. The trace produced by the motion of the image of a star across a photographic film during long exposure. L19.

7 More fully ***trail-net***. A drag-net. E18.

8 The rear end of the stock of a gun-carriage, which rests or slides on the ground when the carriage is unlimbered. M18.

9 A beaten path or track, esp. in a wild or uninhabited region. Also, a marked route through countryside, around a town, etc., indicating points of interest or historical significance. E19.

10 *GEOLOGY*. An accumulation of eroded material, esp. deposited in a rough line by a moving glacier. M19.

11 The distance, measured fore and aft, between the centre of a steered wheel (on a car, bicycle, etc.) and the point of intersection of the steering axis with the ground. E20.

12 = TRAILER *noun* 7. L20.

> 🕮 **4** *Times* The hound.. took up the stale trail over some.. trying ground. B. CHATWIN There was a.. reporter on the trail of a Peruvian terrorist. **5** R. FISK A fast diesel pulling a trail of.. carriages. **6** S. O'FAOLÁIN A.. slug.. drew his silver trail inch by inch. *fig*.: A. TYLER She darted in and out.. leaving a trail of irresponsible remarks. ***vapour trail***: see VAPOUR *noun*. **9** ***blaze the trail***: see BLAZE *verb*³. ***hit the trail***: see HIT *verb*. ***nature trail***: see NATURE *noun*. **12** *Radio Times* A couple of 30-second trails asking viewers to write in with their case studies.

▶**III 13** The action of dragging oneself or something along, or of creeping or crawling. Also (*dial*.), a tiring walk. *rare*. M16.

14 The action of hunting game by trailing or tracking; chase by the track or scent. *rare*. M17.

15 *MILITARY*. The act of trailing a rifle etc., the position of the weapon when trailed (see TRAIL *verb* 5). M19.

15 at the trail *MILITARY* with a rifle etc. grasped in the trailed position.

Comb.: **trail bike** (orig. *US*) a light motorcycle for use on rough terrain; **trail-blazer** (*a*) a person who marks out a new track through wild or inhospitable country; (*b*) a pioneer, an innovator; **trail-blazing** *noun & adjective* (*a*) *noun* the act or process of blazing a trail; (*b*) *adjective* that blazes a trail; pioneering; **trail boss** *US* a foreman in charge of a cattle-drive; **trail head** *N. Amer*. (an organizational centre at) the beginning of a trail for walkers; **trail-hound** a small hound bred or kept for its ability to track hunted animals (freq. *fig*.); **trail mix** a mixture of dried fruit and nuts eaten as a snack food, esp. by walkers, campers, etc.; ***trail-net***: see sense 7 above; **trail-riding** motorcycling with a trail bike; **trail-rope** (*a*) *US* a long rope used for tethering animals loosely; (*b*) = PROLONGE; (*c*) a rope trailed on the ground to check the speed of a hot-air balloon; **trailside** *adjective & noun* (*a*) *adjective* situated beside a track or trail; (*b*) *noun* (*rare*) the side of a track or trail, the strip of land beside a track or trail; **trailway** *N. Amer*. a route through rough country cleared and maintained for recreational walking.

▪ **trailless** /-l-l-/ *adjective* (*rare*) trackless, pathless L19.

†**trail** *noun*². LME.
[Old & mod. French *treille* from Latin *trichila* bower, arbour.]

1 A latticed structure on which climbing plants may be trained; a trellis. LME–E18.

2 A lattice; a grating; a grill. L15–M16.

trail /treɪl/ *noun*³. M18.
[Aphet. from ENTRAIL *noun*¹.]
Entrails collectively; *esp*. those of certain game-birds, as woodcock and snipe, and fish, as red mullet, which are cooked and eaten with the rest of the flesh.

trail /treɪl/ *verb*. ME.
[from Old French *traillier* tow, or Middle Low German, Middle Flemish *treilen* haul (a boat), ult. from Latin *tragula* drag-net. Cf. DRAIL, TRAWL *verb*.]
▶**I 1** *verb intrans*. Hang down so as to drag along a surface, esp. the ground; be drawn or dragged along behind something in motion. ME.

2 *verb intrans*. **a** Walk slowly or wearily as if dragged along; follow along behind, esp. passively or in a lengthened formation; (*rare*) creep, crawl. Formerly also, walk with long trailing garments. ME. ▸**b** Orig., (of liquid) flow slowly. Later, (of a thing) move along slowly; drift; form a trail. L15. ▸**c** Extend in a straggling line. E17. ▸**d** *CARDS*. In cassino, play a card that is useless for gaining a point. E20.

3 *verb intrans*. (Of a garment, hair, etc.) hang down or fall loosely; (of a plant, branch, stem, etc.) grow decumbently to a considerable length so as to rest on the ground, hang over a wall, etc. LME.

4 a *verb trans*. Draw along behind; drag (a garment etc.) along, esp. over the ground. LME. ▸**b** *verb trans*. Of a vehicle: carry or convey by drawing or dragging. Now *esp*. tow (a trailer, a caravan, etc.); transport (a boat etc.) on a trailer behind a motor vehicle. LME. ▸**c** *verb trans*. Drag (the body or limbs) along wearily or with difficulty; *refl*. drag oneself along. M16. ▸**d** *verb intrans*. Fish by trailing or dragging a bait from a moving boat. M19. ▸**e** *verb trans*. *BOWLS*. Drive (the jack) further up the green by carrying it along with the force of the shot. E20.

5 *verb trans*. *MILITARY*. Orig., carry (a pike or similar weapon) in the right hand at an oblique angle with the butt nearly touching the ground; carry (a pike) reversed, with the pointed head dragging along the ground, as at a military funeral. Later, carry (a rifle etc.) in a horizontal position in the right hand with the arm fully extended downward, or (*US*) in an oblique position, grasping it just above the balance with the arm extended downward and slightly bent. M16.

6 *verb trans*. *fig*. Draw out, protract; drag forcibly *to* a course of action; cause (a person) to accompany or follow one, esp. reluctantly. E17. ▸**b** Lead on as by persuasion; *arch. colloq*. ridicule, make a fool of. E18.

7 *verb intrans*. Tail off indefinitely or inconclusively; peter out; gradually diminish. Usu. foll. by *off*, *away*. M19.

8 *verb trans*. Advertise or publicize (esp. a film, a radio or television programme) with a trailer or trailers. Cf. TRAILER *verb* 1. M20.

> 🕮 **1** P. NORMAN The curtain.. is.. so long that it trails on the ground. E. FIGES Leaning back in the.. boat with his hand trailing in the water. **2a** A. W. KINGLAKE The cavalcade which had trailed in his wake. J. TROLLOPE Henry.. was trailing dismally at the rear. **3** J. UGLOW The guelder roses trailing through the windows. **4a** DAY LEWIS Black engines with funnels.. trailing an ostrich feather of white smoke. R. DAHL The rest of us sat in the boat trailing our fingers in the clear water. **c** A. DAVIES She stood on our doorstep.. trailing her mangled leg. **6** D. RUTHERFORD Sally.. trailing a reluctant Josie, was heading for the exit. **7** W. GOLDING Mr Pedigree's voice trailed off. **8** *Media Week* Trailed beside relevant sports programmes.. the Sportsyear series will reach a wide.. audience.

▶**II 9** *verb trans*. Decorate or cover with a trailing pattern or ornament. Foll. by *with*. Now chiefly as ***trailed*** *ppl adjective*. LME. ▸**b** *CERAMICS*. Apply (slip) through a nozzle or spout to decorate pottery. M20.

10 a *verb intrans*. Follow the trail or track of hunted game. LME. ▸**b** *verb trans*. Follow the trail or track of, track; *gen*. follow. L16. ▸**c** *verb trans*. Lag behind (someone or something) in a contest, comparison, etc. M20. ▸**d** *verb intrans*. Be losing or lagging behind in a contest, comparison, etc. M20.

11 *verb trans*. Mark or beat out (a trail or track); make trails or tracks in; *US* tread down (grass) to make a path or track. L16. ▸**b** Drive or herd (livestock) along a trail. *US*. E20.

> 🕮 **10b** A. LURIE The dog that is trailing Vinnie.. is her familiar demon. **c** *Times* Another poll.. showed them trailing the Liberals.. by 54 per cent to 23 per cent. **d** *Times* Hansen's best work came after he had trailed for the first four rounds.

Phrases: **trail a pike** *arch*. serve as a soldier. ***trail one's coat(-tails)***: see COAT *noun*.

▪ **trailable** *adjective* (*US & Austral*.) (of a boat) that may be towed on a trailer behind a motor vehicle M20. **trailing** *noun* (*a*) the action of the verb; an instance of this; (*b*) a form of bowls in which the object is to trail or carry the jack into a semicircle drawn beyond two bowls placed three feet apart; (*c*) a trailing branch or shoot of a plant; a long trailing part or appendage: ME.

trailbaston /ˈtreɪlbast(ə)n/ *noun*. ME.
[Anglo-Norman *traille-baston*, from *traille* imper. of Old French *traillier* TRAIL *verb* + BASTON, lit. 'person who trails or carries a club or cudgel'.]
Hist. Any of a class of violent brigands or hired ruffians active in the reign of Edward I, during his absence or absorption in foreign wars. Also, the system of violence of these brigands; an ordinance issued against them; an inquisition, trial, court, or justice appointed for their suppression.

trailer /ˈtreɪlə/ *noun & verb*. L16.
[from TRAIL *verb* + -ER¹.]
▶**A** *noun*. †**1** A person who travels on foot; *esp*. (*slang*) a footpad. *rare*. L16–M17.

2 A hound or hunter that hunts by the trail; a person who follows a trail, a tracker. L16.

3 A thing that trails, drags along, or hangs loosely; *esp*. a trailing plant or branch. E17.

4 A person who trails or drags something. E18.

5 A rear wheel of a front-driven vehicle or locomotive, as opp. to the driving-wheel; a trailing wheel. L19.

6 Any of various vehicles designed to be drawn along or towed by another; *esp*. (*a*) a small unpowered vehicle or open cart towed behind a car or truck; (*b*) the rear section of an articulated lorry; (*c*) a usu. two-wheeled platform for transporting a boat etc.; (*d*) *N. Amer.* a caravan. L19.

7 A piece of advance publicity, freq. consisting of or including a brief excerpt, shown or broadcast to advertise a film, radio or television programme, etc. Cf. TRAIL *noun*¹ 12. E20.

📖 **3** *Which?* Hanging baskets . . planted with . . trailers to grow out through the mesh.

Comb.: **trailer camp**, **trailer court** *N. Amer.* a caravan site; **trailer home**, **trailer house** *N. Amer.* a mobile home; **trailer park** *N. Amer.* = *trailer camp* above; **trailer-sailer** *Austral. & NZ* a small sailing boat which can be transported on a trailer; **trailer tent** a tent which is attached to, transported, and erected on a trailer; **trailer trash** (*US, derog. & offensive*) a poor, lower-class white person, typified as living in a mobile home; such persons collectively; **trailer-truck** *US* an articulated lorry.

▶ **B** *verb.* **1** *verb trans. & (rare) intrans.* Advertise or publicize (esp. a film, radio or television programme) with a trailer or trailers. Cf. TRAIL *verb* 8. M20.

2 *verb intrans.* Travel or live in a caravan or trailer. Chiefly as ***trailering*** *verbal noun*. Chiefly *N. Amer.* M20.

3 *verb trans.* Transport on a trailer. Chiefly *N. Amer. & Austral.* L20.

📖 **1** *Times* The keynote speech . . had been much trailered.

■ **trailerable** *adjective* (chiefly *N. Amer. & Austral.*) (of a boat) that may be transported on a trailer attached to a motor vehicle L20. **trailerite** *noun* (*N. Amer.*) a person who lives in or travels by caravan M20.

trailing /ˈtreɪlɪŋ/ *ppl adjective.* ME.

[from TRAIL *verb* + -ING².]

That trails or drags; drifting along; hanging loosely; following passively; *spec.* (of a plant) having an elongated decumbent manner of growth.

trailing AZALEA. **trailing edge** (*a*) the rear edge of a moving body, esp. an aircraft wing or propeller blade; (*b*) ELECTRONICS the part of a pulse in which the amplitude diminishes. **trailing vortex**: formed behind the trailing edge of an object, esp. a wing, propeller, etc. **trailing wheel** a wheel to which motive force is not directly applied, esp. when behind the driving-wheel or -wheels.

■ **trailingly** *adverb* L16.

traily /ˈtreɪli/ *adjective. dial. & colloq.* M19.

[from TRAIL *noun*¹ + -Y¹.]

Characterized by trailing; slovenly, lazy; languid.

train /treɪn/ *noun*¹. ME.

[Old & mod. French *train* masc., *traine* fem. (mod. *traîne*), from Old French (orig.) *trahiner*, *trainer* (mod. *traîner*), from Proto-Romance from Latin *trahere* draw.]

▶†**I 1** Waiting, delay. Freq. in ***for a train***, for a while. ME–M16.

2 A horse's gait paced between an amble and a trot; a horse's course or manner of running; a period of riding. M16–L17.

▶ **II 3 a** A trailing section at the back of a ceremonial robe, an evening dress, etc., which is drawn along on the ground behind the wearer. LME. ▶**b** The tail or tail feathers of a bird, esp. the long trailing tail feathers of the peacock; in FALCONRY, the tail of a hawk. Formerly also, the tail of a quadruped. L16. ▶**c** The tail of a comet; a luminous trail, such as that following a meteor. E17.

†**4** A drag or strong-smelling lure for hounds; a trail of carrion for luring wolves, foxes, etc., into a trap. LME–E18.

5 Any of various material objects that are dragged; *spec.* †(*a*) a drag-net; (*b*) the trail of a gun-carriage; (*c*) a rough kind of sledge or sleigh used in Canada for transport. L16.

6 A thing resembling the train of a robe, as the winding course of a river, a snake's body, etc. *poet.* M17.

📖 **3a** BARONESS ORCZY The long train of her . . gown swept the dead leaves off the steps. **6** SIR W. SCOTT Like streamlet . . winding slow its silver train.

▶ **III 7 a** A body of attendants or followers; a retinue; a series of vehicles conveying a retinue. LME. ▶**b** MILITARY. Artillery, supplies, and other equipment for battle or siege, together with transport vehicles and men, travelling in support of an army. E16. ▶**c** *fig.* A set of attendant circumstances or conditions; a series of consequences. Freq. in ***in the train of*** below. L16.

8 A body of people, animals, vehicles, etc., travelling together in a long line or procession. L15.

9 a A course of action in relation to its manner or purpose; method of procedure; way of life; course or direction of an argument etc. *obsolete* exc. as passing into sense 9b. L15. ▶**b** A series, succession, or chain of actions, events, thoughts, or phenomena; a line of reasoning comprised of successive ideas. Freq. in ***train of thought***. M17.

10 A line of gunpowder etc. laid as a fuse to detonate a mine or charge. M16.

11 An extended series or row of material objects; *esp.* a series of things arranged in a definite order for a particular purpose. E17. ▶**b** OIL INDUSTRY. A set of interconnected units for carrying out a specific process, esp. the liquefaction of natural gas. M20.

12 A series of connected parts of machinery which actuate one another in succession; *esp.* the set of wheels and pinions in a clock or watch which turns the hands, or that which actuates the striking part. L18.

13 Orig. ***train of carriages***. A set or series of railway carriages, vans, or trucks coupled together and moved by a locomotive or powered carriage. Freq. with specifying word. E19. ▶**b** A line of coupled vehicles, barges, etc. L19.

📖 **7a** STEELE She has ever had a Train of Admirers. **8** J. GILMOUR Camels, trains of which . . may be seen making their way along the crowded streets. **9a** I. BARROW God . . by . . undiscernable trains, ordereth all events. **b** H. M. ROSENBERG The . . re-radiated wave trains from each of the three atoms. P. FUSSELL Through a whole train of oversights . . it took four days for awareness to sink in. S. HILL The boy had been vague, . . had lost his train of thought several times. **11** W. ABNEY A train of prisms . . set to the angle of minimum deviation. **12** ***going train***, ***striking train***, etc. **13** *Daily Telegraph* Trains were running up to 30 minutes late. J. FANE I used to take the train to Salisbury. ***express train***, ***fast train***, ***goods train***, ***local train***, ***passenger train***, ***slow train***, ***stopping train***, etc. *attrib.*: ***train crash***, ***train driver***, ***train fare***, ***train ride***, ***train robber***, etc.

Phrases: **in a person's train** following behind a person. **in the train of** as a sequel to or consequence of. **in train** properly directed or arranged; in proper order; on course. ***pull a train***: see PULL *verb*. ***train of carriages***: see sense 13 above.

Comb.: **train-bearer** an attendant who carries the train of a robe etc.; **train-ferry**: for conveying railway trains across water; **train-guard** (*a*) a train of attendants forming a guard; a body of soldiers guarding the train of an army; (*b*) the guard of a railway train; **train-jumper** (orig. *US*) a person who travels by train without paying the fare; **trainmaster** *US* a person in charge of a train or trains; *spec.* a railway official responsible for the movement of all trains over a certain stretch of line; **train-mile** one mile travelled by one train on a railway, as a unit in estimating amount of traffic, working expenses, etc.; **train set** (*a*) a set of trains, tracks, etc., making up a model railway; (*b*) a set of wagons or carriages, sometimes with a locomotive, coupled together; a train; **train-shed** *US* a roof supported by posts forming a shelter for one or more platforms at which trains stop; a roughly built or unenclosed railway station; **trainsick** *adjective* affected with trainsickness; **trainsickness** nausea caused by the motion of a train; **trainside** *adjective* (*US*) beside or near a train, taking place next to a train; **train-spot** *verb intrans.* pursue the hobby of train-spotting; **train-spotter** a person whose hobby is observing trains and recording locomotive numbers; **train-spotting** the hobby of observing trains and recording locomotive numbers; **train-stop** (*a*) an automatic device, operating in conjunction with a railway signal, for stopping a train; (*b*) the state of a train's being at a stop; a railway halt; **train ticket** (*a*) a ticket given to a train driver as authority to travel over a single-track section of railway (cf. STAFF *noun*¹ 10); (*b*) a ticket purchased to authorize a passenger to travel on a train.

■ **trainful** *noun* as much or as many as a railway train will hold M19. **trainless** *adjective* (*a*) (of a robe etc.) without a train; (*b*) devoid of railway trains; on which no trains are running: M19.

†**train** *noun*². ME.

[Old French *traine* guile, deceit, ruse, from *traïr* (mod. *trahir*) betray: see TRAY *verb*.]

1 a An act or scheme designed to deceive or entrap someone; a trick, a stratagem. ME–M18. ▶**b** Treachery, guile, deceit, trickery. LME–L16.

2 A trap, a snare, (*lit. & fig.*). Freq. in ***lay a train***, set a trap. LME–L17.

3 A thing intended to entice an animal into a trap or snare; a lure, a bait, a decoy. LME–E17.

4 A live bird attached to a line, or a lame and disabled bird, given as an enticement to a young hawk during its training. L15–E17.

📖 **1** SHAKES. *Macb.* Macbeth By many of these trains hath sought to win me Into his power.

†**train** *noun*³. LME–E19.

[Middle & mod. Low German *trān*, Middle Dutch *traen* (Dutch *traan*) = German *Tran* rel. to *träne* tear, drop.]

= TRAIN-OIL.

train /treɪn/ *verb*. LME.

[Old French *trahiner*, *trainer* (mod. *traîner*): see TRAIN *noun*¹.]

▶ **I 1 a** *verb trans.* Draw or pull along; drag, haul, trail. *arch.* LME. ▶**b** *verb intrans.* Of a garment etc.: hang down, esp. so as to trail on the ground. Now *rare*. L16.

2 *verb trans. fig.* ▶†**a** Drag out, protract, spin out; spend or pass (time, one's life) slowly or tediously. LME–M17. ▶†**b** Draw along *with*; involve as a consequence. L16–E17. ▶**c** Lengthen, drawl, utter slowly, (a word, phrase, etc.). Long *rare*. M17.

3 *verb trans. fig.* Induce by enticement, decoy; lead *on* or astray, deceive. *arch.* LME. ▶†**b** Induce by persuasion; persuade, convert. Freq. foll. by *to*. E16–E17.

†**4** *verb trans.* Lead, conduct, bring. M16–M19.

📖 **1a** SIR W. SCOTT To train me to prison under false pretexts. **b** N. HOOKE Ceres was represented . . with a long training robe. **3** J. TILLOTSON Being insensibly trained on from one degree of wickedness to another. **4** M. HERBERT His chosen troopes with triumph on he traines.

▶ **II 5** *verb trans.* Control or direct so as to bring to a required form; *spec.* cause (a plant or branch) to grow in a desired shape, manner, or direction, esp. against a wall or up a trellis. LME.

6 *verb trans.* **a** Provide (esp. a young person) with a moral and disciplined upbringing; educate, rear. Also foll. by *up*. M16. ▶**b** Orig. *spec.*, provide (soldiers) with military discipline; drill. Now, instruct in or for a particular skill, profession, occupation, etc., esp. by practice or practical experience; make proficient by such instruction and practice. Also, make (the mind, eye, etc.) sharp and discerning as a result of instruction, practice, etc. (chiefly as ***trained*** *ppl adjective*). (Foll. by *for*, *in*, *to*, *to do*.) M16. ▶**c** Discipline and teach (an animal) to obey orders or perform tricks; school and prepare (a horse, esp. a racehorse) for competition. Freq. foll. by *to do*. E17. ▶**d** Bring by a course of diet and exercise to a state of physical fitness and efficiency, esp. to participate in a sport or to compete in a sporting event. M19.

7 *verb intrans.* Orig. *spec.*, perform military drill. Now, undergo or follow a course of instruction, esp. by practice; undertake physical exercise; attain a certain physical condition or level of fitness through diet, exercise, etc. Also, practise the schooling and preparation of horses or racehorses as a profession. E17.

📖 **5** E. WILSON They have . . trained . . crimson ramblers over their houses. **6a** AV *Prov.* 22:6 Traine vp a childe in the way he should goe. R. ALTER She has been trained to be . . a beautiful flower in a social world actuated by . . money. **b** W. HARRIS His penetrating trained eye saw every rock. J. MCGAHERN They took two years to train us as teachers. J. L. ESPOSITO Muhammad . . was trained in law, theology, and Sufism at Mecca and Medina. J. LE CARRÉ I am . . a professional, trained to listen and remember. **c** *Reader's Digest* Pit bull terriers, trained to kill by a drug dealer. **d** J. H. BURN Those who train young men for athletic events. **7** S. TROTT I've decided to train for a marathon. D. ARKELL He was now a sergeant, training to be an officer.

▶ **III 8** *verb trans.* †**a** Hunt or pursue by following a trail; track. *rare*. Only in L16. ▶**b** MINING. Trace (a vein of ore etc.) to the source. E18.

9 *verb trans.* Point or aim (a gun, camera, etc.). Freq. foll. by *on*. M19.

10 a *verb intrans. & trans.* (with *it*). Go by train, travel by railway. *colloq.* M19. ▶**b** *verb trans.* Transport by rail. *rare*. L19.

11 *verb intrans.* Associate, ally, or cooperate *with*. *N. Amer. colloq.* L19.

📖 **9** J. REED The cruisers . . are anchored . . , their guns trained on the approaches to the city. *fig.*: A. BROOKNER Menfolk on whom they trained their batteries of silent accusation. **10a** J. WAINWRIGHT He was at King's Cross . . he'd just trained down from the North. I. BANKS We heard things were happening in Berlin so we hitched and trained it.

With adverbs in specialized senses: **train down** reduce one's weight by diet or exercise so as to get fit for a sporting event etc. †**train off** get out of condition, lose one's strength or skill, as by overtraining. **train on** improve in fitness or condition by training.

■ **trainage** *noun* (*rare*) the action of drawing or hauling something along; conveyance by train: E17.

trainable /ˈtreɪnəb(ə)l/ *adjective.* M16.

[from TRAIN *verb* + -ABLE.]

Able to be trained; amenable to discipline and instruction.

■ **trainability** /-ˈbɪlɪti/ *noun* M20.

trainante /trɛnɑ̃ːt/ *adjective.* Now *rare*. E19.

[French *traînante* fem. adjective from pres. pple of *traîner* drag: see TRAIN *verb*.]

Of a vocal or musical sound: drawn out, lengthened, drawling.

trainband /ˈtreɪnband/ *noun.* Also **train-band**. M17.

[Abbreviation of *trained band* from TRAINED *ppl adjective*² + BAND *noun*³.]

Hist. Any of several divisions of civilian militia organized in London and other areas from the 16th to the 18th cents. Also, any of various similar forces in other countries.

traineau /treɪˈnəʊ, *foreign* trɛno/ *noun.* Pl. **-eaux** (pronounced same). M17.

[French *traîneau*, from *traîner*: see TRAIN *verb*.]

A sledge, a sleigh, *esp.* one drawn by one or more horses or dogs over snow or ice.

trained /treɪnd/ *adjective*¹. L16.

[from TRAIN *noun*¹ + -ED².]

(Of a robe or formal dress) having a train or long trailing section; (of a meteor) having a luminous tail.

trained /treɪnd/ *ppl adjective*². L16.

[from TRAIN *verb* + -ED¹.]

†**1** Drawn or dragged along; *fig.* enticed. *rare* (Spenser). Only in L16.

2 Orig. *spec.*, subjected to military discipline, drilled. Now, instructed, educated; made proficient in a specific skill etc. by discipline and instruction. L16.

3 Of a plant: caused to grow in a required form or direction. M18.
2 trained band *Hist.* = TRAINBAND.
¶ Earlier in UNTRAINED.

trainee /treɪˈniː/ *noun.* M19.
[from TRAIN *verb* + -EE¹.]
A person (orig. an animal) undergoing training. Freq. *attrib.*
■ **traineeship** *noun* the position of a trainee, a post as a trainee M20.

†trainel *noun.* ME.
[Old French.]
1 Part of a horse's harness; a hobble, a trammel. Only in ME.
2 A drag-net. Also ***trainel-net***. L16–E18.

trainer /ˈtreɪnə/ *noun.* L16.
[from TRAIN *verb* + -ER¹.]
1 A person who trains or instructs a person or animal; an instructor; a person who trains athletes, footballers, racehorses, etc., as a profession. Also, a piece of equipment used for training; an exercise machine. L16. ▸**b** *spec.* An aircraft or simulator used to train pilots or other aircrew. M20.
2 *Hist.* A member of a trainband, esp. when assembled for training or drill; a militiaman. L16.
3 A soft running or sports shoe without spikes or studs and usu. made of leather or canvas, worn for training rather than the sport itself; a shoe of a similar or exaggerated style worn for leisure or as a fashion item; a training shoe. L20.

📖 **1** *Practical English Teaching* A freelance teacher trainer and materials writer. *Interview* What's the difference between a dog trainer and a dog psychiatrist? **3** *Listener* The Intourist taxi driver in his Western trainers.

training /ˈtreɪnɪŋ/ *noun.* LME.
[from TRAIN *verb* + -ING¹.]
1 The action of TRAIN *verb*; esp. (*a*) the act or process of providing or receiving instruction in or for a particular skill, profession, occupation, etc.; (*b*) the process of developing physical fitness and efficiency by diet and exercise. LME.
2 Military drill; *esp.* (*Hist.*) a public meeting or muster at a stated time for drill of militia and volunteer forces. L16.
Phrases: **go into training** begin physical training. **in training** undergoing physical training; physically fit as a result of such training. ***physical training***: see PHYSICAL *adjective*. ***Officers Training Corps***: see OFFICER *noun*. **out of training** no longer undergoing physical training; physically unfit. ***transfer of training***: see TRANSFER *noun* 2c.
Comb.: **training-college** a college for training prospective entrants to a particular profession; *spec.* a college for training teachers (cf. ***training-school*** below); **training-day** a day devoted to training; *spec.* (*Hist.*), a stated or legally appointed day for the drilling of militia and volunteer forces; **training-school** a school in which pupils are trained in a particular profession or occupation; *spec.* (*a*) a school for training teachers; (*b*) *N. Amer.* a vocational institution for juvenile delinquents; **training-ship**: on which young people are trained in seamanship; **training shoe** = TRAINER 3.

trainman /ˈtreɪnmən/ *noun.* Pl. **-men** /-mən/. Also **train man**. M17.
[from TRAIN *noun*¹ or *verb* + MAN *noun*.]
†1 A man belonging to a trainband. Only in M17.
2 A railway employee working on a train. Orig. *US.* L19.

train-oil /ˈtreɪnɔɪl/ *noun.* Also **train oil**. M16.
[from TRAIN *noun*³ + OIL *noun*.]
Oil obtained by boiling the blubber of whales, esp. of the right whale. Formerly also, oil obtained from the blubber of seals or from various fishes.

†train-scent *noun.* E17.
[from TRAIN *noun*¹ or *verb* + SCENT *noun*.]
A drag or train for hounds (TRAIN *noun*¹ 4); the sport of exercising hounds or horses by means of following such a drag.

traipse /treɪps/ *noun. colloq. & dial.* Also **trapes**. L17.
[Rel. to next.]
1 A slovenly woman or girl; a slattern. L17.
2 An act of traipsing; a tedious or wearying journey on foot. M19.

📖 **2** A. WILSON It means a traipse upstairs to the members' bar.

traipse /treɪps/ *verb. colloq.* Also **trapes**. L16.
[Origin unkn. Cf. TRAPE.]
1 *verb intrans.* Tramp or trudge wearily; walk about aimlessly or needlessly; go about; go on errands (freq. foll. by *about*). Also, (esp. of a woman or child) go about dressed in a slovenly way. L16. ▸**b** Trail along the ground; hang untidily. Chiefly *dial.* L18.
2 *verb trans.* **a** Walk or tramp over; tread or tramp (the fields, streets, etc.). Chiefly *dial.* M18. ▸**b** Carry or drag about in a wearying way. *rare.* E19.

📖 **1** D. LODGE I've had enough of traipsing round churches. *Woman* Marie Christine adores traipsing off to far-flung corners of the globe. **2a** H. CAINE It's bad weather to trapes the fells.

traist /treɪst/ *adjective.* Orig. *Scot. & north.* ME.
[App. from Old Norse *treystr* pa. pple of *treysta* make firm or strong, used in the sense of Old Norse *traustr* firm, strong, safe, secure, trusty.]
†1 Assured, sure, confident, full of trust. Also (*rare*), strong, safe. ME–L15.
2 Trusty, trustworthy; faithful, true. Long *obsolete* exc. *poet.* ME.
¶ Obsolete after E17; revived E20 by Ezra Pound.

trait /treɪ, treɪt/ *noun.* L15.
[French from Latin *tractus* drawing, draught: see TRACT *noun*³. Cf. TRET.]
†1 Arrows; missiles of any kind. *rare.* Only in L15.
†2 = TRACT *noun*³ 1b. *rare.* Only in M16.
3 A stroke of the pen or pencil; a short line; a touch in a picture. Also (*rare*), a stripe. M16. ▸**†b** A line, passage, or piece of writing. *rare.* L16–M18.
4 †a A stroke of skill or cunning. Chiefly in ***double trait***, a stroke of double dealing. Only in E17. ▸**b** An instance or expression of wit, sarcasm, etc. *arch.* E18.
5 A characteristic feature of mind or character; a distinguishing quality, esp. of a person, culture, or social group. Also, a distinctive feature characterizing a thing. M18. ▸**b** A touch or trace *of* a quality. Now *rare.* E19.
6 A distinctive facial configuration or feature. L18.

📖 **3** *fig.*: B. F. WESTCOTT The picture which he draws can be completed by traits taken from the other Evangelists. **4b** HOR. WALPOLE In Voltaire's letters are some bitter traits on the King of Prussia. **5** M. MEYER Several of these early traits—withdrawnness, social formality . . —he was to retain until his death. *Profession* There is no essential trait or quality . . that marks the 'literariness' of a text. **6** SHELLEY Her face is . . altered. The traits have become more delicate.

trait d'union /trɛ dynjɔ̃/ *noun phr.* Pl. ***traits d'union*** (pronounced same). E20.
[French, lit. 'hyphen'.]
A link or point of contact between or amongst otherwise unconnected characteristics or parties.

traiteur /trɛtœːr/ *noun.* Pl. pronounced same. M18.
[French, from *traiter* treat, supply with food for money + *-eur* -OR.]
Orig., (a person running) a restaurant in France, Italy, etc., supplying or sending out meals to order. Now, a caterer; (a person who runs) a delicatessen selling prepared meals.

traitor /ˈtreɪtə/ *noun & verb.* ME.
[Old French *traitour, -ur* from Latin *traditor* (whence Old French *traitre*, mod. *traître*), from *tradere* deliver, betray, formed as TRANS- + *dare* give: see -OR.]
▸ **A** *noun.* A person who betrays (the trust of) another, a cause, etc.; a disloyal or treacherous person; *spec.* a person who commits or is judged to be guilty of treason against his or her sovereign or country. Freq. foll. by *to.* ME.

📖 O. HENRY I'm no traitor to a man that's been my friend. D. H. LAWRENCE Tolstoi was a traitor To the Russia that needed him most.

▸ **B** *verb.* **1** *verb trans.* Make (a person) a traitor. Now also (*Black English*), betray. E17.
†2 *verb intrans.* Act as a traitor. *rare.* Only in M17.
■ **traitorhood** *noun* (*rare*) the state or condition of a traitor; treachery: LME. **traitorism** *noun* the practice or principles of a traitor L16. **traitorship** *noun* (*rare*) †(*a*) (with possess. adjective, as ***his traitorship*** etc.): a mock title of respect given to a traitor; (*b*) the state or condition of a traitor; treachery, treason: L16.

traitoress *noun* var. of TRAITRESS.

†traitorly *adjective.* E16–M17.
[from TRAITOR *noun* + -LY¹.]
= next.

traitorous /ˈtreɪt(ə)rəs/ *adjective.* ME.
[Old & mod. French *traîtreux*, from *traître* TRAITOR *noun*: see -OUS.]
Characteristic or having the character of a traitor; treacherous.

📖 R. OWEN The suppression of deviant views as traitorous and unpatriotic. *Vanity Fair* It would be traitorous of me to leave my upbringing behind.

■ **traitorously** *adverb* ME. **traitorousness** *noun* L16.

traitress /ˈtreɪtrɪs/ *noun.* Also **traitoress** /ˈtreɪt(ə)rɪs/. LME.
[Old & mod. French *traîtresse* fem. of *traître* TRAITOR *noun*: see -ESS¹. In form *traitoress* from TRAITOR *noun* + -ESS¹.]
A female traitor; a traitorous or treacherous woman.

📖 R. L. STEVENSON [Knox] solemnly proclaims all reigning women to be traitoresses and rebels against God.

traits d'union *noun phr.* pl. of TRAIT D'UNION.

Trajanic /treɪˈdʒanɪk/ *adjective.* E20.
[from Latin *Traianus* Trajan (see below) + -IC.]
Of or pertaining to the Roman emperor Marcus Ulpius Traianus (AD 53–117), esp. to the style of triumphal art associated with him.

traject /ˈtradʒɛkt/ *noun.* Now *rare.* M16.
[Latin *trajectus* passing over, place for crossing, from *traicere* throw across, formed as TRANS- + *jacere* throw. Cf. TRANECT.]
1 A way or place of crossing over; *esp.* a crossing-place of a river, strait, etc. M16.
2 The action or an act of crossing over a stretch of water or land; (a) passage. L18.

📖 **1** SIR W. SCOTT He would not . . put foot in a boat till he had discovered the shortest possible traject. **2** E. O'DONOVAN During the whole traject I met with no living things.

traject /trəˈdʒɛkt/ *verb. arch.* E17.
[Latin *traject-* pa. ppl stem of *traicere*: see prec.]
†1 *verb trans. & intrans.* Pass across, cross (a river, sea, etc.). E17–E18.
2 *verb trans.* **†a** Carry or convey across or over; transport (a material thing). M–L17. ▸**b** Transmit or project (light, colour, thought, words, etc.). M17.

📖 **2b** C. CLARKE The power of trajecting his soul into the body of any individual.

trajectile /trəˈdʒɛktʌɪl, -tɪl/ *adjective & noun. rare.* M19.
[Prob. from TRAJECTORY after *projectile*.]
▸ **A** *adjective.* Capable of throwing or impelling something across a distance. M19.
▸ **B** *noun.* An object so thrown, a projectile. M19.

trajection /trəˈdʒɛkʃ(ə)n/ *noun.* Now *rare.* L16.
[Latin *trajectio(n-)*, formed as TRAJECT *verb*: see -ION.]
†1 A perception conveyed to the mind; an impression, a mental image. *rare.* L16–M17.
2 Transposition; metathesis. E17.
3 The action or an act of passing across something or of being transmitted; transmission through a medium or through space; transmission of light, heat, etc. Formerly also, passage across a river etc. M17.

trajectitious /tradʒɛkˈtɪʃəs/ *adjective.* Long *rare.* M17.
[Late Latin *trajecticius* that is carried over (sea), from Latin *traject-*: see TRAJECT *verb*, -ITIOUS¹.]
Characterized by passage across the sea; foreign.

trajectory /trəˈdʒɛkt(ə)ri, ˈtradʒɪkt(ə)ri/ *adjective & noun.* M17.
[medieval Latin *trajectorius* pertaining to trajection, formed as TRAJECT *verb*: see -ORY².]
▸ **A** *adjective.* PHYSICS etc. Of or pertaining to anything which is thrown or hurled through the air or space. M17.
▸ **B** *noun.* **1** PHYSICS etc. The path of any body moving under the action of given forces, esp. one not known to be moving in a closed curve or orbit; *esp.* the curve described by a projectile in its flight through the air. L17.
2 GEOMETRY. A curve or surface passing through a given set of points, or intersecting each of a given series of curves or surfaces according to a given law (e.g. at a constant angle). L18.

trajet /ˈtradʒɪt, *foreign* traʒɛ (*pl. same*)/ *noun.* M18.
[French from Latin *trajectus* TRAJECT *noun*.]
1 A crossing, a passage. Cf. TRAJECT *noun* 2. M18.
2 The course of a nerve, blood-vessel, etc. *rare.* M19.

Trakehner /traˈkeɪnə/ *noun.* In sense 2 also **t-**, **trakener**. E20.
[German, from the *Trakehnen* stud (see below).]
1 (An animal of) a breed of saddle horse first developed at the Trakehnen stud near Kaliningrad in Russia. E20.
2 A type of fence, consisting of a ditch spanned by centre rails, in the cross-country section of an equestrian three-day event etc. M20.

tra-la-la /trɑːlɑːˈlɑː, trɑːlɑːˈlɑː/ *interjection & noun.* Also **tra-la** /ˈtrɑːlɑː/. E19.
[Imit. a refrain of a song or a fanfare.]
▸ **A** *interjection.* Expr. gaiety or joy. E19.
▸ **B** *noun.* **1** An utterance of 'tra-la-la'; a cadence or fanfare on a horn or similar instrument. L19.
2 A lively or showy celebration; a fuss, a commotion. *colloq.* M20.

tralatitious /traləˈtɪʃəs/ *adjective.* Now *rare.* M17.
[Latin *tralaticius*, *trans-*, from *translat-* pa. ppl stem of *transferre* TRANSFER *verb*: see -ITIOUS¹.]
1 Characterized by transference; *esp.* (of a word or phrase) metaphorical, figurative. M17.
2 Handed down from generation to generation; traditional. L18.

tralucent /trəˈluːs(ə)nt/ *adjective.* Long *rare.* L16.
[Latin *tralucent-* pres. ppl stem of *tralucere*, *trans-* shine across or through: see -ENT.]
Translucent.

tram /tram/ *noun*¹. LME.
[Old & mod. French *trame* woof, (fig.) contrivance from Latin *trama* woof.]
▶†**I 1** A cunning contrivance or device; a plot, a scheme. Chiefly *Scot. & north.* LME–M19.
2 A mechanical contrivance; a machine; a tool. Usu. in *pl.* Chiefly *Scot. & north.* Only in LME.
▶**II 3** Weft; *spec.* (more fully ***tram silk***) double silk thread used for the weft of some velvets and silks. L17.

tram /tram/ *noun*² *& verb*. E16.
[Middle Low German, Middle Dutch *trame* balk, beam: ult. origin unkn.]
▶**A** *noun*. **I 1** Either of the two shafts of a cart, wagon, wheelbarrow, etc. *Scot.* E16.
2 Either of the two upright posts of a gallows (usu. in *pl.*); *joc.* a person's leg. *Scot.* Now *rare*. M17.
▶**II 3** Orig., a frame, barrow, etc., for the transport of corves in a coalmine. Later, a four-wheeled vehicle used for this purpose. E16. ▸**b** A person in charge of a such tram; the work performed by such a person. M19.
4 A frame or bench on four legs or blocks, constituting a stand for casks, a workbench, etc. E19.
▶**III** †**5** A road, a highway. *rare*. Only in M16.
6 Each of a parallel line of wooden, stone, or metal wheel-tracks, in or from a coalmine. E19.
7 A road with wooden, stone, or metal wheel-tracks, orig. in or from a coalmine. Also ***tram-road***. M19.
▶**IV 8** An electrically powered passenger vehicle running on rails laid in a public road or street. Also ***tramcar***. L19.
Comb.: **tramcar**: see sense A.8 above; **tramline** (usu. in *pl.*) (*a*) a road or rail for a tram; (*b*) *colloq.* either of a pair of parallel lines, esp. at either side of a tennis-court (the inner of each pair marking the boundary of the court for singles and the outer for doubles); a similar line at the side or back of a badminton court; (*c*) an inflexible, predetermined, or restrictive course of action, principle, etc.; **tram-plate** a flat or flanged iron plate used in a tramway; **tram-rail** (*a*) a plate-rail; (*b*) each of the rails of a tramway; **tram-road** (chiefly *Hist.*) (*a*) a road with wooden, stone, or metal wheel-tracks; (*b*) a prepared track or narrow railroad for wagons etc., as distinguished from a tramway laid down on a road or street for tramcars; **tramway** (*a*) (chiefly *Hist.*) = ***tram-road*** (a) above; (*b*) a railway laid down on a public road or street for tramcars, as distinguished from a tram-road for wagons etc.; (*c*) a tramcar system.
▶**B** *verb*. Infl. **-mm-**.
1 *verb intrans. & trans.* (with *it*). Travel by tram. *rare*. E19.
2 *verb trans.* Convey coal, ore, etc. by tram (chiefly as ***tramming*** *verbal noun*); cause (a tram) to move. *rare*. L19.
■ **tramless** *adjective* M19. **trammer** *noun* a person or animal working on a tramway; *spec.* = PUTTER *noun*¹ 1b: M19. **trammie** *noun* (*colloq.*, chiefly *Austral. & NZ*) the conductor or driver of a tramcar E20.

trama /ˈtreɪmə, ˈtrɑːmə/ *noun*. Pl. **-mae** /-miː/. M19.
[Latin = warp threads of a loom, (in later use app.) weft.]
BOTANY. In a hymenomycetous fungus, the innermost tissue of a lamella, composed of elongated cells whose long axes are parallel to the hymenium.
■ **tramal** *adjective* L19.

†**tramble** *verb*. E17.
[Origin uncertain. Cf. Swedish dial. *tramla*, *trumla* fall.]
1 *verb intrans.* Tumble, fall headlong. *rare*. Only in E17.
2 *verb trans.* = BUDDLE *verb*. L17–E18.

Traminer /trəˈmiːnə/ *noun*. M19.
[German, from *Tramin* (Italian *Termeno*) a village in N. Italy.]
(Any of several vines bearing) a white grape used in wine-making esp. in Germany and Alsace; the white wine with perfumed bouquet made from this grape.

trammel /ˈtram(ə)l/ *noun & verb*. LME.
[In sense 1 Old & mod. French *tramail* (mod. *trémail*) from medieval Latin *tramaculum* var. of *tremaculum*, *trimaculum*, perh. formed as TRI- + *macula* spot, mesh. Later senses may represent different words.]
▶**A** *noun*. **I 1** A triple drag-net for fish, designed so that a fish entering through one of the large-meshed outer sections will push part of the fine-meshed central section through the large meshes on the further side, forming a pocket in which the fish is trapped. Also ***trammel-net***. LME. ▸**b** A net for catching wild birds. Also ***trammel-net***. M16.
▶**II** †**2** A hobble for a horse. M16–M18.
3 *transf. & fig.* An impediment to free action; a constraint, a hindrance. Usu. in *pl.* M17.
4 MECHANICS. An instrument for drawing ellipses etc. with a bar sliding in two upright grooves. Also, a beam-compass. E18.
📖 **3** R. FRY The freedom of art from all trammels and tyrannies.
▶**III 5** A chain, hook, or similar device suspended in a chimney for a kettle etc. Now *dial. & US*. M16.
†**6** A plait, braid, or tress of hair. Usu. in *pl.* L16–L17.
▶**B** *verb*. Infl. **-ll-**, *-l-.
†**1** *verb trans.* Bind up (a corpse). Only in M16.
2 *verb trans. & intrans.* Catch (fish or birds) with a trammel-net. Chiefly as ***trammelling*** *verbal noun*. L16.
▸**b** *verb trans. fig.* Entangle or fasten *up* as in a trammel-net. E17.
3 *verb trans.* Hobble (a horse, a horse's legs). Long *rare* or *obsolete*. E17.
4 *verb trans. fig.* Impede the free action of; hinder, constrain. E18.
📖 **2b** SHAKES. *Macb.* If th' assassination Could trammel up the consequence, and catch . . success. **4** G. S. HAIGHT Feelings could not be trammelled by legal bonds.
■ **trammelled** *adjective* confined, caught, or impeded (as) by trammels; that has been trammelled: E17. **trammeller** *noun* (*rare*) LME.

tramontane /trəˈmɒnteɪn/ *adjective & noun*. In sense A.3 now usu. **tramontana** /tramɒnˈtɑːnə/. ME.
[Italian *tramontana* north wind, polestar, *tramontani* dwellers beyond the mountains, from Latin *transmontanus*, formed as TRANS- + *mont-*, *mons* MOUNT *noun*¹: see -ANE.]
▶**A** *noun*. †**1** The polestar (orig. so called because visible beyond the Alps from Italy); *fig.* a guiding star. ME–M17.
2 A person living or originating from beyond the mountains, esp. the Alps as seen from Italy; (esp. from the Italian point of view) a stranger, a foreigner, a barbarian. L16.
3 In the Mediterranean and esp. in Italy, the north wind (as coming from beyond the Alps). More widely, a cold wind from across a mountain range. E17.
▶**B** *adjective*. **1** Living, situated, or originating from beyond the mountains, esp. the Alps as seen from Italy. Also (esp. from the Italian point of view), foreign; barbarous. L16.
2 Of wind: coming across or from beyond the mountains (esp. the Alps). E18.

tramp /tramp/ *noun*. M17.
[from the verb.]
1 A person who travels from place to place on foot, in search of employment or as a vagrant or beggar. M17. ▸**b** A promiscuous woman. *slang* (orig. *US*). E20.
2 A journey on foot, *esp.* a long, tiring, or protracted one; a trudge; *colloq.* a long walk in rough country for recreation. L18.
3 An act of tramping; a heavy or forcible tread, a stamp. E19. ▸**b** More fully ***axle tramp***. Alternate bouncing of wheels on the same axle. M20.
4 The sound of a heavy footfall, esp. of the measured and continuous tread of a body of people or animals. Also redupl. E19.
5 An iron plate worn to protect the sole of a boot in digging. Also, the part of a spade etc. pressed on by the foot in digging. E19.
6 a In full ***ocean tramp***, ***tramp steamer***. A cargo vessel, esp. a steamship, taking available cargoes for any port instead of trading regularly between fixed ports. L19. ▸**b** An aircraft plying commercially according to demand. E20.
📖 **1b** J. WELCOME You can usually tell . . the nice girls from the tramps. **2** G. STEIN Joyous, country tramps . . over rolling hills and cornfields. P. SCOTT Sensible shoes she had not worn since she . . last went for a tramp. **on the tramp**, **on tramp** on one's way from place to place on foot, esp. in search of employment or as a vagrant or beggar. **3** BROWNING The reed Is crushed beneath its tramp. **6a** W. S. MAUGHAM The skipper of a tramp from Shanghai.
■ **trampdom** *noun* the world of tramps; tramps collectively: L19. **tramphood** *noun* (*rare*) the state or condition of being a tramp M20. **trampish** *adjective* of the nature or character of a tramp M19.

tramp /tramp/ *verb*. LME.
[Prob. of Low Dutch origin from Germanic base: cf. Middle Low German *trampen*. See also TRAMPOOSE, TROMP.]
1 *verb intrans.* Tread or walk with a firm heavy resonant step. LME.
2 *verb trans.* Press or compress by treading; tread or trample on. Freq. foll. by *down*. LME. ▸**b** Tread (washing) in a tub of soapy water. *Scot.* L18.
3 *verb intrans.* Tread heavily or with force *on*; stamp (*on*). L16.
4 *verb intrans. & trans.* (with *it*). ▸**a** Walk steadily; trudge; travel on foot; *colloq.* walk long distances in rough country for recreation. M17. ▸**b** Live as a tramp. *colloq.* M19.
5 *verb trans.* **a** Walk through or over, esp. heavily or wearily; cover (a specified distance) in this way. L18. ▸**b** Bring into or out of a specified condition by walking vigorously or steadily. M19.
6 *verb intrans.* Make a voyage on a tramp steamer. *colloq.* L19. ▸**b** Transport goods by road to varying destinations as the load requires. M20.
7 *verb trans.* Dismiss (a person) from employment; sack. *Austral. slang*. M20.
📖 **1** M. GEE Endless heavy boots going tramping up the stairs. **2** LYTTON No horse tramps the seeds we have sown. **3** N. FLEMING Melanie . . tramped on the accelerator. **4** J. P. HENNESSY School, to and from which he would tramp in all weathers. A. MACRAE He had spent several days tramping and climbing at National Park. **5a** V. WOOLF They tramped miles along the roads. L. GORDON Eliot was tramping the pavements of Clerkenwell. **b** *Field* You will tramp your boots and feet into order.
■ **tramping** *verbal noun* the action of the verb; an instance of this: L18.

tramp /tramp/ *adverb*. Also redupl. **tramp-tramp**. L18.
[from TRAMP *verb*.]
With a firm heavy resonant tread.

tramper /ˈtrampə/ *noun*. E18.
[from TRAMP *verb* + -ER¹.]
1 A person who tramps; *spec.* (*a*) a person with a heavy resonant tread; (*b*) a person who travels on foot; a tramp; *colloq.* a person who walks long distances in rough country for recreation. E18.
2 A thing which tramps; *spec.* (in *pl.*) heavy boots for walking. *Scot.* E18.

trample /ˈtramp(ə)l/ *verb & noun*. LME.
[from TRAMP *verb* + -LE³. Cf. Middle & mod. High German, Low German *trampeln*.]
▶**A** *verb*. **1** *verb intrans.* Tread or walk heavily; tramp, stamp. LME. ▸†**b** *verb trans. & intrans.* Tread or walk on (a path etc.). *rare*. L16–L17.
2 *verb trans.* Tread heavily and esp. damagingly on; crush or break down by heavy treading. M16.
3 *verb intrans.* Foll. by *on*, *over*: tread on repeatedly with heavy or crushing steps; *fig.* treat with contempt; disregard the rights or feelings of. L16.
4 *verb trans.* Bring into or out of a specified condition by trampling; *esp.* put *out* (a fire) in this way. L16.
📖 **1** F. TUOHY Those appalling louts trampling around the house! **2** S. BELLOW The hijackers tore his clothes . . and trampled him. R. M. WILSON Bodies are trampled in the . . rush to escape that horror. *fig.*: J. MASEFIELD Men trample women's rights at will. **3** *New Yorker* People who trample on the rights of others. P. BAILEY They . . trampled on my satchel. **4** B. CHATWIN This trio . . trampled slush into the carpet.
▶**B** *noun*. The action or an act of trampling. E17.
📖 R. A. VAUGHAN The earth shakes with the trample of a myriad hoofs.
■ **trampled** *adjective* that has been trampled; crushed by trampling; *fig.* downtrodden, oppressed: LME. **trampler** *noun* L16. **trampling** *verbal noun* the action of the verb; an instance of this. LME.

trampoline /ˈtrampəliːn/ *noun & verb*. L18.
[Italian *trampolino*, from *trampoli* stilts.]
▶**A** *noun*. An apparatus consisting of a strong fabric sheet connected by springs to a horizontal frame, used by gymnasts etc. as a springboard and landing area in acrobatic exercises. L18.
▶**B** *verb intrans.* Perform on a trampoline, use a trampoline. M19.
■ **trampolinist** *noun* a performer on a trampoline M19.

trampoose /tramˈpuːz/ *verb intrans.* *US slang*. Now *rare* or *obsolete*. L17.
[App. alt. of TRAMP *verb*. Cf. VAMOOSE.]
Tramp, trudge.

tramp-tramp *adverb* see TRAMP *adverb*.

trance /trɑːns/ *noun*. LME.
[Old French *transe* (mod. *trance*), from *transir* depart, die, fall into a trance from Latin *transire*: see TRANSIENT.]
†**1** A state of extreme apprehension or dread; a state of doubt or suspense. LME–L16.
2 An unconscious or insensible condition; a faint; a half-conscious state characterized by a lack of response to stimuli; a cataleptic or hypnotic condition. Also (SPIRITUALISM), such a state as entered into by a medium. LME.
3 An intermediate state between sleeping and waking; half-awake condition; a stunned or dazed state. LME.
4 A state of mental abstraction from external things; absorption, exaltation, rapture, ecstasy. LME.
5 More fully ***trance music***. A type of electronic dance music characterized by hypnotic rhythms and sounds. L20.
📖 **1** CAXTON She was in a traunce what she shold saye to her. **2** H. A. L. FISHER He went into trances . . and visions appeared to him. O. SACKS Indications of catatonia or trance, impeding all movement and speech and thought. **3** T. GRAY Glo'ster stood aghast in speechless trance. **4** Y. MENUHIN I played . . automatically in a . . happy trance. G. DALY A religious trance that seems to border on sexual ecstasy. **5** *Big Issue* Block and Lisa Lashes . . pump those burned little brains with an ungodly diet of non-stop trance.
■ **tranceful** *adjective* (*rare*) full of trances; entrancing: L19. **trancelike** *adjective* resembling a trance; like that of a trance: E19.

trance /trɑːns/ *verb*¹. ME.
[In sense 1 from Old French *transir* depart, die; in sense 2 from prec.]
†**1** *verb intrans.* Be in a trance, fall into a trance. Also (*rare*), die. ME–M17.
2 *verb trans.* Put into a trance; entrance. Chiefly *poet.* L16.

■ **tranced** /trɑːnst, *poet.* ˈtrɑːnsɪd/ *adjective* (chiefly *poet.*) in a trance; entranced: E17. **trancedly** /ˈtrɑːnsɪdli/ *adverb* (chiefly *poet.*) M19. **trancing** *adjective* (chiefly *poet.*) that trances someone; *esp.* entrancing: E17.

trance /trɑːns/ *verb*² *intrans.* Long *obsolete* exc. *dial.* LME.
[Origin unkn. Cf. TROUNCE *verb*².]
Move about actively or briskly; prance, skip.

†**tranch** *verb trans.* E16–M19.
[French *trancher* to cut: see TRENCH *verb*.]
Carve (a fish, esp. a sturgeon).

tranchant /trɑ̃ʃɑ̃/ *adjective. literary.* E16.
[French: see TRENCHANT.]
Cutting (chiefly *fig.*); incisive. Also, (of a colour) glaring, crude.
¶ Formerly fully naturalized.

tranche /trɑːnʃ, trɑ̃ːʃ/ *noun.* Pl. pronounced same, /-ɪz/. L15.
[Old & mod. French, from *trancher*: see TRENCH *verb*.]
1 A cutting, a cut; a piece cut off, a slice. L15.
2 Chiefly ECONOMICS. A portion of something, esp. of income; an instalment of a loan; a block of shares or of government stock. M20.
Phrases: **tranche de vie** /də ˈviː/ [lit. 'slice of life'] a representation of daily life, esp. in literature or painting.

tranché /ˈtrɑːnʃi/ *adjective.* M17.
[French, pa. pple of *trancher*: see TRENCH *verb*.]
HERALDRY. Of a shield: divided into parts of different tinctures by the line of a bend. Usu. *postpositive*.

tranchet /ˈtrɑːnʃɪt, *foreign* trɑ̃ʃɛ (*pl. same*)/ *noun.* M19.
[French, from *trancher*: see TRENCH *verb*, -ET¹.]
†**1** A cobbler's knife. Only in M19.
2 ARCHAEOLOGY. A chisel-shaped flint implement of some mesolithic and neolithic cultures. L19.

tranchette /trɑːnˈʃɛt/ *noun.* L20.
[from TRANCHE *noun* + -ETTE.]
ECONOMICS. A small tranche; *esp.* a limited issue of government stocks. Cf. TAPLET.

†**tranect** *noun. rare* (Shakes.). Only in L16.
[Prob. var. of TRAJECT *noun*.]
A ferry.

traneen /trəˈniːn/ *noun. Anglo-Irish.* Also **thra-** /θrə-/. M19.
[Anglicized spelling of Irish *tráithnín* a little stalk of grass.]
The crested dog's-tail grass, *Cynosurus cristatus*. Freq. *fig.*, a thing of little or no value, a jot, an iota.
🕮 L. ROBINSON I don't care a thraneen about Doctor Johnson.

tranexamic /tranɛkˈsamɪk/ *adjective.* M20.
[from elements of the systematic name, *trans-4-aminomethylcyclohexanecarboxylic acid*.]
PHARMACOLOGY. ***tranexamic acid***, a white crystalline cyclohexane derivative, $NH_2CH_2C_6H_{10}COOH$, which inhibits fibrinolysis and is used to treat haemorrhage.

†**trangam** *noun.* Chiefly *derog.* M17–E19.
[Origin unkn.]
An odd or intricate contrivance of some kind; a knick-knack, a puzzle; a toy, a trinket.

trangle /ˈtraŋg(ə)l/ *noun.* E18.
[Obsolete French, var. of Old & mod. French *tringle*. Cf. TRINGLE.]
HERALDRY. A narrow fess; a bar, a barrulet.

trank /traŋk/ *noun*¹. M19.
[Perh. formed as TRANCHE.]
An oblong piece of kid etc. from which a glove is to be cut out; a glove-shape cut from this, before being sewn.

trank /traŋk/ *noun*². *slang.* M20.
[Abbreviation.]
= TRANQUILLIZER.
■ **tranked** *adjective* having taken or affected by a tranquillizer L20.

†**trankum** *noun. rare.* Only in E19.
[from TRINKUM-TRANKUM.]
A personal ornament; a trinket.

tranky /ˈtraŋki/ *noun.* E18.
[Origin unkn.]
An undecked boat used in pearl-fishing in the Persian Gulf.

trannie /ˈtrani/ *noun*¹. *slang.* L20.
[Abbreviation: see -IE.]
A transvestite.

trannie *noun*², *noun*³ see TRANNY *noun*¹, *noun*³.

tranny /ˈtrani/ *noun*¹. *colloq.* Also **trannie**. M20.
[Abbreviation: see -Y⁶, -IE.]
A transistor radio.

tranny /ˈtrani/ *noun*². *colloq.* (chiefly *US*). M20.
[Abbreviation: see -Y⁶.]
The transmission of a motor vehicle, esp. a truck or van.

tranny /ˈtrani/ *noun*³. *colloq.* Also (*rare*) **trannie**. L20.
[Abbreviation: see -Y⁶, -IE.]
A photographic transparency, a slide.

tranquil /ˈtraŋkwɪl/ *adjective.* LME.
[French *tranquille* or Latin *tranquillus*.]
Free from agitation or disturbance; calm, serene, peaceful.
🕮 H. A. L. FISHER They withdrew . . into the tranquil light of the Christian paradise. I. MURDOCH A tranquil orderly house in which he could work.
■ **tranquilly** *adverb* M18. **tranquilness** *noun* (*rare*) E19.

tranquility *noun* var. of TRANQUILLITY.

tranquilize *verb*, **tranquilizer** *noun* see TRANQUILLIZE, TRANQUILLIZER.

tranquilli *noun pl.* see TRANQUILLO.

tranquillise *verb*, **tranquilliser** *noun* vars. of TRANQUILLIZE, TRANQUILLIZER.

tranquillity /traŋˈkwɪlɪti/ *noun.* Also ***tranquility**. LME.
[Old & mod. French *tranquillité* from Latin *tranquillitas*, from *tranquillus* tranquil: see -ITY.]
The quality or state of being tranquil; calmness, serenity.

tranquillize /ˈtraŋkwɪlʌɪz/ *verb.* Also **-ise**, ***tranquilize**. E17.
[from TRANQUIL + -IZE.]
1 *verb trans.* Make tranquil, esp. by a drug. E17.
2 *verb intrans.* Become tranquil. *arch.* M18.
🕮 **1** K. AMIS Does he get . . therapy, or . . just go on being tranquillized?
■ **tranquilliˈzation** *noun* the action or an act of tranquillizing a person or thing L18.

tranquillizer /ˈtraŋkwɪlʌɪzə/ *noun.* Also **-iser**, ***tranquilizer**. E19.
[from prec. + -ER¹. Cf. TRANK *noun*².]
A person who or thing which tranquillizes someone or something; *spec.* a drug for the reduction of tension or anxiety.
🕮 I. ILLICH Dependence on prescribed tranquillizers has risen. **major tranquillizer** a tranquillizer of the kind used to treat psychotic states. **minor tranquillizer** a tranquillizer of the kind used to treat anxiety states; *esp.* a benzodiazepine.

tranquillo /tranˈkwɪləʊ/ *adverb, adjective, & noun.* M19.
[Italian from Latin *tranquillus*.]
MUSIC. ▶**A** *adverb & adjective.* A direction: in a tranquil style or tempo; tranquil(ly). M19.
▶ **B** *noun.* Pl. **-llos**, **-lli** /-li/. A movement or piece in a tranquil style or tempo. M19.

trans /trɑːnz/ *noun. colloq.* L19.
[Abbreviation.]
1 = TRANSLATION 2. *US.* L19.
2 = TRANSCONTINENTAL *noun. Austral.* M20.
3 = TRANSMISSION 3. M20.

trans- /trans, trɑːns, -nz; *see note below*/ *prefix.* In sense 2 also as attrib. adjective **trans**.
[Latin, from *trans* preposition 'across, over'.]
1 Used in words adopted from Latin and in English words modelled on these, and as a freely productive prefix, with the senses 'across, beyond', as ***transfer***, ***transmarine***, 'on or to the other side of' (opp. CIS-), as ***transalpine***, ***transatlantic***, ***Transkei***, 'into another state or form', as ***transform***, ***transcribe***, 'surpassing, transcending', as ***transfinite***.
2 CHEMISTRY. (Usu. italicized.) Designating compounds in which two atoms or groups are situated on opposite sides of a given plane in the molecule (opp. CIS-). Also in GENETICS, designating alleles at different loci, esp. on different chromosomes.
3 BIOLOGY & CHEMISTRY. Used in words with the sense 'of or pertaining to transfer', as ***transamination***, ***transgenic***.
4 PHYSICS & CHEMISTRY. Used in words with the sense 'lying beyond in the periodic table, having a higher number than', as ***transuranic***.
¶ With some exceptions, the pronunc. with /s/ is more usual that that with /z/ before /f/, /k/, /l/, /p/, /s/, /ʃ/, /t/, /θ/, and unstressed vowels.
■ **transacetylase** /-əˈsɛtɪleɪz/ *noun* (BIOCHEMISTRY) an enzyme which catalyses the transfer of an acetyl group from one molecule to another M20. **transˈannular** *adjective* (CHEMISTRY) situated or occurring between non-adjacent atoms in a ring E20. **trans-bay** *adjective* (*US*) that crosses a bay, *spec.* San Francisco Bay M20. **transboard** *verb trans.* (*rare*) transfer (people, goods, etc.) from one ship to another; tranship: E19. **trans-ˈborder** *adjective* of, pertaining to, or situated on the further side of a border; that crosses a border: L19. **transˈboundary** *adjective* that crosses a boundary or boundaries L20. **trans-ˈchannel** *adjective* that crosses a channel, esp. the English Channel L19. **transˈcode** *verb trans. & intrans.* convert from one form of coded representation or signalling to another M20. †**transcoloration** *noun* the action or process of changing the colour of something or of causing something to change colour; an instance of this: M17–E19. †**transcolour** *verb trans.* (*rare*) change the colour of; cause to change colour: M17–M19. **transconˈfessional** *adjective* extending across religious denominations; interdenominational: L20. **transconforˈmation** *noun* (BIOCHEMISTRY) change in the conformation of a protein molecule M20. **transˈconjugant** *noun* (BIOLOGY) a plasmid or a bacterial cell which has received genetic material by conjugation with another bacterium L20. **transˈcortical** *adjective* (ANATOMY & MEDICINE) transversing the cortex of the brain; pertaining to or designating nervous transmission, or lesion, involving (a cross-section of) the cerebral cortex: E20. **transcreˈate** *verb trans.* (*rare*) create by or in the manner of transmission M19. **tranˈscribble** *verb trans.* (*rare*) transcribe carelessly or hastily M18. **tranˈscribbler** *noun* a careless or hasty transcriber M18. **transˈcrystalline** *adjective* (of a fracture) passing through individual crystals of a metal rather than following grain boundaries E20. **transˈcultural** *adjective* pertaining to or involving more than one culture; cross-cultural; ***transcultural psychiatry***, the comparative study of mental illness in different cultures: M20. **transcultuˈration** *noun* the state of being transcultural; acculturation: M20. **transˈcurrence** *noun* †(*a*) *rare* a swift passage across, over, or through; (*b*) GEOLOGY the phenomenon of transcurrent faulting: M17. **transˈcurrent** *adjective* †(*a*) *rare* passing swiftly across, over, or through; (*b*) ENTOMOLOGY (*rare*) extending or running transversely; (*c*) GEOLOGY designating or pertaining to a fault primarily due to horizontal displacement; *esp.* one of large dimensions and with a nearly vertical inclination: E17. **transcuˈtaneous** *adjective* existing, applied, or measured across the depth of the skin M20. **transdenomiˈnational** *adjective* = TRANSCONFESSIONAL L20. **transderiˈvational** *adjective* (LINGUISTICS) relating to or involving more than one derivation L20. **transˈdermal** *adjective* (MEDICINE) occurring or applied through the skin; *esp.* (of a medicine) applied in an adhesive patch so as to be absorbed slowly into the body: L20. **transdetermiˈnation** *noun* (BIOLOGY) alteration of the development of an imaginal disc during culture of *Drosophila* tissue so that it gives rise to a structure normally developed from a different disc M20. **transˈdialect** *verb trans.* (*rare*) translate from one dialect into another L17. **transdisciplinarity** *noun* the condition of being transdisciplinary L20. **transdisciˈplinary** *adjective* of or pertaining to more than one discipline or branch of learning; interdisciplinary: L20. **transearth** *adjective* (ASTRONAUTICS) of or pertaining to space travel or a trajectory towards the earth from the moon or another planet M20. **transˈelement** *verb trans.* change or transmute the elements of (esp. the Eucharist) M16. **transˈelementate** *verb trans.* transelement L16. **transelemenˈtation** *noun* the action or process of transelementing something; an instance of this: M16. **transemˈpirical** *adjective* (*rare*) pertaining to things beyond the range of experiential knowledge; metempirical: E20. **transequaˈtorial** *adjective* that crosses the equator; situated on the further side of the equator: E20. **transeˈssentiate** *verb trans.* (*rare*) change (a thing) from one essence or being into another L17. **transˈfashion** *verb trans.* change the fashion of, transform E17. **trans-fat** *noun* (CHEMISTRY) = TRANS-FATTY ACID L20. **trans-fatty acid** *noun* (CHEMISTRY) any unsaturated fatty acid with a *trans* arrangement of atoms about its double bonds, such acids occurring in margarines and cooking oils as a side-effect of manufacturing and being thought to increase the risk of coronary heart disease M20. **transfeminate** /-ˈfɛmɪneɪt/ *verb trans.* (*rare*) change the sex of M17. **transˈfluvial** *adjective* situated or living across or beyond a river E19. **trans-ˈfrontier** *adjective* living, situated, or occurring beyond or across the frontiers of a country L19. **transˈglobal** *adjective* that travels across or round the world M20. **transhiˈstorical** *adjective* (having significance) that transcends the historical; universal, eternal: E20. **transhyˈdrogenase** *noun* (BIOCHEMISTRY) an enzyme which catalyses the transfer of hydrogen from one organic substrate to another M20. **transindiˈvidual** *adjective* not confined to any particular thing or person, more than individual M20. **transˈinsular** *adjective* (*a*) crossing or going across an island; (*b*) ANATOMY (of a fissure of the brain) that traverses the insula: L19. **trans-ˈisthmian** *adjective* crossing or extending across an isthmus, esp. the isthmus of Panama L19. **transketolase** /-ˈkiːtəleɪz/ *noun* (BIOCHEMISTRY) an enzyme which catalyses the transfer of a ketonic alcohol group, esp. that of the glycol aldehyde group during photosynthesis M20. **transˈlunar** *adjective* (*a*) = TRANSLUNARY; (*b*) ASTRONAUTICS of or pertaining to space travel or a trajectory (from the earth) towards the moon: E20. **transˈlunary** *adjective* lying or originating beyond the moon (opp. *sublunary*); *fig.* beyond the earthly, visionary: E17. **transˈmake** *verb trans.* [translating Greek *metapoiein*] (chiefly THEOLOGY) make into something different, refashion; transelement: M19. **transˈmarginal** *adjective* beyond the margin of normal consciousness, subliminal E20. **transmaˈterial** *adjective* (*rare*) beyond or transcending what is material E20. **transˈmembrane** *adjective* (BIOLOGY) existing or occurring across a cell membrane M20. **transmethyˈlation** *noun* (CHEMISTRY) the transfer of a methyl group from a molecule of one compound to one of another M20. **transˈmortal** *adjective* (chiefly *poet.*) beyond what is mortal, immortal M20. **transˈmundane** *adjective* that is or lies beyond the world L18. **transˈmural** *adjective* (*a*) situated beyond a wall or walls, esp. beyond (i.e. north of) a Roman boundary wall in northern Britain; (*b*) MEDICINE existing or occurring across the (entire) wall of an organ or blood-vessel: M19. **transˈnational** *adjective & noun* (*a*) *adjective* (having interests) extending beyond national bounds or frontiers; (*b*) *noun* a transnational company: E20. **transˈnationally** *adverb* in a transnational manner E20. **transˈnatural** *adjective* †(*a*) supernatural; (*b*) *rare* of transmuted nature: M16. **transˈnature** *verb trans.* (long *rare* or *obsolete*) change the nature of M16. **transˈnormal** *adjective* beyond or above what is normal M19. **transˈocean** *adjective* = TRANSOCEANIC 2 E20. **transˈocular** *adjective* across the eye L19. **transoid** *adjective* (CHEMISTRY) designating a compound, group, or structure in which two like atoms or groups lie on opposite sides of a single bond or line of bonds M20. **transˈorbital** *adjective* between the eye sockets M19. **trans-Paˈcific** *adjective* (*a*) across or crossing the Pacific Ocean; (*b*) on the other side of the Pacific Ocean: L19. **tranˈspeciate** *verb trans.* (now *rare*) change into (a different form or species); transform: M17. **transˈpeptidase** *noun* (BIOCHEMISTRY) an enzyme which catalyses transpeptidation M20. **transpeptidation** /-pɛptʌɪˈdeɪʃ(ə)n/ *noun* (BIOCHEMISTRY) a reaction in which a peptide bond is broken and a new one formed with another molecule M20. **transˈpersonal** *adjective* transcending the personal, transindividual; *spec.* designating a form of psychology or psychotherapy which seeks to explore transcendental experiences and states of consciousness that go beyond normal personal identity and desires: E20. **transpheˈnomenal** *adjective*

(PHILOSOPHY) transcending or beyond the phenomenal L19. **transphosphory'lation** *noun* (BIOCHEMISTRY) the transfer of a phosphate group from a molecule of one compound to one of another M20. **transplu'tonium** *adjective* (CHEMISTRY) (of an element) having a higher atomic number than plutonium (i.e. 95 or over) M20. **trans'polar** *adjective* crossing the pole or polar region M19. **transpo'litical** *adjective* transcending or crossing political boundaries L20. **trans'prose** *verb trans.* (chiefly *joc.*) translate or turn into prose L17. **transpro'vincial** *adjective* crossing a province E20. **trans'pulmonary** *adjective* acting or operated through the lungs; ***transpulmonary pressure***, the difference between the pressure in the lungs and that in the pleural cavity: E20. **transqualify** *verb trans.* (*rare*) change in quality M17. **trans'racial** *adjective* across or crossing racial boundaries L20. **trans'riverine** *adjective* situated across a river, transfluvial E20. **trans-'shape** *verb trans.* (*arch.*) alter the shape or form of L16. **trans-Si'berian** *adjective & noun* (*a*) *adjective* crossing Siberia; (*b*) *noun* the trans-Siberian railway or express: L19. **trans-'species** *adjective* (BIOLOGY) trans-specific L20. **trans-specific** *adjective* (BIOLOGY) (*a*) (of evolution) involving change from one species to another; (*b*) (of communication, fertilization, infection, etc.) passing or occurring between animals of different species: M20. **trans-'stellar** *adjective* existing or situated beyond the stars L19. **trans-sub'jective** *adjective* transcending or beyond subjective experience L19. **trans-sy'naptic** *adjective* (PHYSIOLOGY) involving transmission of a nerve impulse across a synapse M20. **transtage** *noun* (ASTRONAUTICS) a final stage of a multistage rocket that can be restarted in order to change the flight path or orbit M20. **transtho'racic** *adjective* (MEDICINE) occurring or performed through the wall of the thorax or across the thoracic cavity E20. **transu'rethral** *adjective* (MEDICINE) performed via the urethra M20. **transvalu'ation** *noun* (an) alteration of values, (a) revaluation L19. **trans'value** *verb trans.* alter the value of, re-value L19. **trans'venom** *verb trans.* (*rare*) transform *into* something poisonous M17. **transver'bation** *noun* (*rare*) verbal translation; translation word for word: L19. **trans-world** *adjective* (travelling etc.) across the world, worldwide M20.

transaccidentation /trans,aksɪdɛn'teɪʃ(ə)n, trɑːns-, -nz-/ *noun*. L16.
[medieval Latin *transaccidentatio(n-)*, after *transubstantiatio(n-)* TRANSUBSTANTIATION: see TRANS-, ACCIDENT, -ATION.]
THEOLOGY. The conversion into the body and blood of Christ of the accidents and not only the substance of the Eucharistic elements. Cf. TRANSUBSTANTIATION.

transact /tran'zakt, trɑːn-, -'sakt/ *verb & noun*. L16.
[Latin *transact-* pa. ppl stem of *transigere* drive through, accomplish, formed as TRANS- + *agere* drive, do.]
▶ **A** *verb*. **1** *verb intrans.* Carry through negotiations; have dealings or do business *with*. Now *rare*. L16.
†**2** *verb trans.* Carry, hand, or take over; transfer. E17–L19.
3 *verb trans.* Carry through, perform, or conduct (esp. business). M17. ▸†**b** *verb intrans.* Esp. of business: be carried through, performed, or conducted. M17–M18.
4 *verb trans.* Deal in or with; handle, treat; discuss. *arch.* M17.

📖 **1** T. LUPTON Departments or individuals, that transact with each sub-environment. **2** *Science* A paper . . from which the following passages are transacted. **3** R. L. STEVENSON The business was speedily transacted. D. JACOBSON Gathering . . around the king, while he transacts the business of the state. **b** O. CROMWELL Whilst these things have been thus transacting here. **4** THACKERAY While these delicacies were being transacted below.

▶ **B** *noun*. A transaction. Long *obsolete* exc. *Scot. & dial.* M17.
■ **transactor** *noun* (*a*) a person who transacts something; (*b*) a device for carrying out transactions; *spec.* in COMPUTING, (**T-**, US proprietary name for) a data input and display device: E17.

transaction /tran'zakʃ(ə)n, trɑːn-, -'sak-/ *noun*. LME.
[Late Latin *transactio(n-)*, formed as prec.: see -ION.]
1 ROMAN & CIVIL LAW (now *Hist.*). The adjustment of a dispute between parties by mutual concession; an agreement, a covenant. LME.
†**2** The action of passing or making over a thing from one person etc. to another; transference. Only in 17.
3 The action of transacting or fact of being transacted; the carrying on or completion of business etc. M17.
4 That which is or has been transacted, esp. a piece of business; a deal. M17. ▸†**b** A physical operation, action, or process. M17–L18.
5 In *pl.* Published reports of discussions, papers read, etc., at the meetings of a learned society. M17.

📖 **1** P. MASSINGER This transaction, Drawn in express and formal terms. **2** J. HOWELL The transaction of these Provinces which the King . . made as a dowry. **3** F. BURNEY After the transaction of this affair. **4** C. CHAPLIN The transaction was simple . . and the car was mine. *Which?* An up to date record of all your transactions. **5** A. B. EDWARDS Scientific journals and the transactions of learned societies.

transactional /tran'zakʃ(ə)n(ə)l, trɑːn-, -'sak-/ *adjective*. M19.
[from prec. + -AL[1].]
1 Of, pertaining to, of the nature of, or involving a transaction; taking place in fact or reality. M19.
2 PSYCHOLOGY. Of, pertaining to, or involving interpersonal communication viewed as transactions of attitude between the participants; *spec.* in ***transactional analysis***, psychotherapeutic analysis based on the role-playing revealed in such transactions (esp. in relation to the roles of parent, adult, and child). M20.
■ **transactionalist** *noun* an advocate of a theory of social transactions L20. **transactionally** *adverb* by means or by way of a transaction; practically: M19.

transactivation /,transaktɪ'veɪʃ(ə)n, ,trɑːns-, -nz-/ *noun*. M20.
[from TRANS- + ACTIVATION.]
Chiefly BIOCHEMISTRY. Activation of one entity by another which is *trans* to it; *spec.* activation of a gene at one locus by the presence of a particular gene at another locus, esp. following infection by a virus.

transalpine /tranz'alpʌɪn, trɑːnz-, -ns-/ *adjective*. L16.
[Latin *transalpinus*, formed as TRANS- + ALPINE *adjective & noun*[2]. Cf. CISALPINE.]
1 Of, pertaining to, or situated on the further (not the Roman) side of the Alps. L16. ▸**b** Beyond the Alps from the English point of view; Italian. *arch.* E17.
2 That crosses the Alps. *rare*. M17.

transaminase /tran'zamɪneɪz, trɑːn-, -'sa-/ *noun*. M20.
[from next + -ASE.]
BIOCHEMISTRY. An enzyme which catalyses transamination.

transamination /,transamɪ'neɪʃ(ə)n, ,trɑːns-, -nz-/ *noun*. M20.
[from TRANS- + AMINO- + -ATION.]
BIOCHEMISTRY. The transfer of an amino group from one molecule to another, esp. from an amino acid to a keto-acid.
■ **transaminate** *verb trans. & intrans.* subject to or undergo transamination M20.

transanimation /,transanɪ'meɪʃ(ə)n, ,trɑːns-, -nz-/ *noun*. Now *rare*. L16.
[ecclesiastical Latin *transanimatio(n-)*, from Latin TRANS- + *anima* soul: see -ATION.]
Metempsychosis.

transatlantic /tranzat'lantɪk, trɑːnz-, -ns-/ *adjective & noun*. L18.
[from TRANS- + ATLANTIC.]
▶ **A** *adjective*. **1** That crosses the Atlantic. L18.
2 Of, pertaining to, or situated on the further side of the Atlantic; (from a British or European point of view) American; (from an American point of view) British or European. L18.
▶ **B** *noun*. A transatlantic person or thing. E19.
■ **transatlantically** *adverb* in a transatlantic manner M19. **transatlantician** /-'tɪʃ(ə)n/ *noun* = TRANSATLANTIC *noun* M19. **transatlanticism** *noun* transatlantic character, nationality, or behaviour; a transatlantic idiom: M19.

transaxle /'tranzaks(ə)l, 'trɑːnz-, -ns-/ *noun*. Orig. *US*. M20.
[from TRANS(MISSION + AXLE.]
An integral driving axle and differential gear in a motor vehicle.

transcalent /'transkəl(ə)nt, tran'skeɪl(ə)nt, trɑː-, -nz-/ *adjective*. M19.
[from TRANS- + Latin *calent-* pres. ppl stem of *calere* be hot, glow: see -ENT.]
Freely conducting radiant heat; diathermanous.
■ **transcalency** *noun* the property of being transcalent, diathermcy M19.

Transcash /'tranzkaʃ, 'trɑːnz-, -ns-/ *noun*. Also **t-**. L20.
[from TRANS- or TRANS(FER *verb* + CASH *noun*[1].]
A National Girobank facility whereby bills may be paid at a post office to any firm, public service, etc., that has a Girobank account.

transceiver /tran'siːvə, trɑːn-/ *noun*. M20.
[from TRANS(MITTER + RE)CEIVER.]
A combined radio transmitter and receiver.

transcend /tran'sɛnd, trɑːn-/ *verb*. ME.
[Old French *transcendre* or Latin *trans(s)cendere* climb over, surmount, formed as TRANS- + *scandere* climb.]
1 *verb trans.* Go beyond or exceed the limits of (something immaterial); *esp.* be beyond the range or grasp of (human experience, reason, belief, etc.). ME. ▸**b** Be above and independent of; (esp. of God) exist apart from the limitations of (the material universe). L19.
2 *verb trans.* Surpass, excel, or exceed, esp. in a specified quality or attribute. LME.
†**3** *verb trans.* Cross or surmount (a physical obstacle or limit, as a river, mountain, etc.). LME–L17.
†**4** *verb intrans.* Ascend, go up, rise. LME–E17.
5 *verb intrans.* Be transcendent; excel. *arch.* E16.

📖 **1** H. READ The ultimate values of art transcend the individual and his time. *Times Lit. Suppl.* The heavenly perception . . transcends all present experiences. **3** G. SANDYS Mountaines not to be transcended without much difficulty. **5** J. SHEFFIELD Nor wherein Man so transcends, except in arrogance.

■ **transcendible** *adjective* (*rare*) able to be transcended L17. **transcendingly** *adverb* in a transcending manner, transcendently E16. **transcendingness** *noun* the state of being transcending, transcendence M18.

transcendence /tran'sɛnd(ə)ns, trɑːn-/ *noun*. E17.
[Late Latin *transcendentia*, from *transcendent-*: see next, -ENCE.]
1 The action or fact of transcending; the condition or quality of being transcendent; an instance of this. E17.
†**2** Exaggeration, hyperbole. *rare*. E–M17.
3 MATH. The fact of being transcendental (see TRANSCENDENTAL *adjective* 4). E20.
■ **transcendency** *noun* (a) transcendence E17.

transcendent /tran'sɛnd(ə)nt, trɑːn-/ *adjective & noun*. LME.
[Latin *transcendent-* pres. ppl stem of *transcendere* TRANSCEND: see -ENT.]
▶ **A** *adjective*. **1** That transcends; surpassing or excelling others of its kind, supreme; beyond the range or grasp of human experience, reason, belief, etc. Formerly also, greatly superior *to*. LME. ▸**b** Of God: existing apart from, and not subject to the limitations of, the material universe (cf. **immanent**). L19.
2 PHILOSOPHY. **a** In scholastic philosophy, higher than or not included in any of Aristotle's ten categories. L17. ▸**b** In Kantian philosophy, not realizable in human experience. E19.
3 MATH. = TRANSCENDENTAL *adjective* 4. E20.

📖 **1** MILTON That transcendent Apostle Saint Paul. POPE Nausicaa . . shone transcendent o'er the beateous train. S. RICHARDSON Such transcendent goodness of heart.

▶ **B** *noun*. **1** Chiefly PHILOSOPHY. A transcendent person or thing; *spec.* (*a*) (in scholastic philosophy) a transcendent predicate; (*b*) (in Kantian philosophy) something not realizable in experience. LME.
2 MATH. A transcendental expression or function; a non-algebraic function. E19.

📖 **1** A. MASON He had challenged the Transcendent for a sign.

■ **transcendently** *adverb* E17. **transcendentness** *noun* (*rare*) E17.

transcendental /transɛn'dɛnt(ə)l, trɑːn-/ *adjective & noun*. E17.
[medieval Latin *transcendentalis*, formed as prec.: see -AL[1].]
▶ **A** *adjective*. †**1** Of, pertaining to, or belonging to the divine as opp. to the natural or moral world. Only in E17.
2 PHILOSOPHY. **a** In scholastic philosophy, = TRANSCENDENT *adjective* 2a. M17. ▸**b** Chiefly in Kantian philosophy, presupposed in and necessary to experience; a priori. L18. ▸**c** In Schellingian philosophy, explaining matter and objective things as products of the subjective mind. E20.
3 = TRANSCENDENT *adjective* 1. E18. ▸**b** Superrational, superhuman, supernatural. E19. ▸**c** Abstract, metaphysical; vague, obscure. M19. ▸**d** Esp. in Emersonian thought: regarding the divine as the guiding principle in man. M19.
4 MATH. Not able to be produced by (a finite number of) the ordinary algebraical operations of addition, multiplication, involution, or their inverse operations; expressible, in terms of one variable, only in the form of an infinite series (as, for example, the logarithmic, sine, and exponential functions). E18.

📖 **3** *iron.*: BURKE These considerations . . were below the transcendental dignity of the Revolution Society. **b** A. GUINNESS I had witnessed something . . transcendental and very human. **c** B. JOWETT An unmeaning and transcendental conception.

Special collocations: **transcendental argument**: to prove the existence of something as a necessary presupposition. **Transcendental Meditation** a method of silent meditation and the repetition of a mantra, based on Eastern mysticism, used to promote relaxation and detachment. **Transcendental Meditator** a person who practises Transcendental Meditation. **transcendental object** a real (unknown and unknowable) object. **transcendental unity** unity brought about by cognition.
▶ **B** *noun*. A transcendental conception, term, or quantity. E17.
¶ *Transcendental Meditation* is a proprietary name in the US.
■ **transcenden'tality** *noun* (*rare*) transcendental quality M19. **transcendentali'zation** *noun* the action or an act of transcendentalizing; an instance of this: M20. **transcendentalize** *verb trans.* make transcendent or transcendental M19. **transcendentally** *adverb* E19.

transcendentalism /transɛn'dɛnt(ə)lɪz(ə)m, trɑːn-/ *noun*. E19.
[from prec. + -ISM.]
1 Transcendental philosophy or thought; a system of this. E19.
2 Exalted or visionary language; an instance of this. M19.
3 (A) transcendent quality or character; (a) transcendency. *rare*. M19.
■ **transcendentalist** *noun & adjective* (*a*) *noun* an adherent of transcendentalism; (*b*) *adjective* of or pertaining to transcendentalists or transcendentalism: E19. **transcendenta'listic** *adjective* transcendentalist L19.

transcension /tran'sɛnʃ(ə)n, trɑːn-/ *noun*. *rare*. E17.
[from TRANSCEND after *ascend*, *ascension*.]
The action or process of transcending; an instance of this; (a) transcendence.

†**transcolate** *verb trans. rare.* E17–E19.
[from TRANS- + PER)COLATE *verb*.]
= PERCOLATE *verb* 1.
■ †**transcolation** *noun* M17–E19.

transconductance /transkən'dʌkt(ə)ns, trɑːns-, -nz-/ *noun.* M20.
[from TRANS(FER *noun* + CONDUCTANCE.]
ELECTRONICS. The ratio of the (change in) current at one electrode or terminal of an active device, esp. the output, to the (change in) voltage at another, esp. the input; *spec.* = ***mutual conductance*** s.v. MUTUAL *adjective*.

transcontinental /ˌtranzkɒntɪ'nɛnt(ə)l, trɑːnz-, -ns-/ *adjective & noun.* M19.
[from TRANS- + CONTINENTAL.]
▶ **A** *adjective.* That crosses a continent; *esp.* (of a railway etc.) extending across a continent. Also, of or pertaining to the further side of a continent. M19.
▶ **B** *ellipt.* as *noun.* A transcontinental railway, a transcontinental train. Chiefly *Canad.* E20.
■ **transcontinentally** *adverb* M20.

transcribe /tran'skrʌɪb, trɑːn-/ *verb.* M16.
[Latin *transcribere*, formed as TRANS- + *scribere* write.]
1 *verb trans.* **a** Make a copy of in writing. M16. ▸**b** Quote or cite from a specified source. Now *rare.* M17. ▸**c** *BIOLOGY.* Synthesize (a nucleic acid, usu. RNA) using an existing nucleic acid (usu. DNA) as a template, so that the genetic information in the latter is copied. Foll. by *into* (the second molecule), *from*, *off* (the first molecule). M20.
†**2** *verb trans.* Attribute or ascribe *to* another. M16–M17.
3 *verb trans.* Transliterate; write out (shorthand, notes, etc.) in ordinary characters or continuous prose. Formerly also, translate. M17.
†**4** *verb trans. fig.* Copy or imitate (a person, quality, action, etc.); reproduce. M17–E18.
†**5** *verb trans. ROMAN LAW.* Transfer, assign, or make over *to* another. Only in L19.
6 *MUSIC.* **a** *verb trans.* Adapt (a composition) for a different voice or instrument. L19. ▸**b** *verb intrans.* Of a composition: admit of being transcribed. L19.
7 *verb trans.* Record for subsequent reproduction; broadcast in this form. Also (*rare*), record from a secondary source. M20.

> 🕮 **1a** B. TRAPIDO Carefully transcribing the rough draft of my essay. *absol.*: LD MACAULAY Tomorrow I shall begin to transcribe again and to polish. **b** J. WESLEY Plain, easy rules. Chiefly transcribed from Dr Cheyne. **2** R. ABBOT The Papists . . who haue transcribed the authority of Religion to mortall Men. **3** A. LURIE I have to transcribe two more interviews. *absol.*: C. STEAD Transcribing out of a notebook of beautiful . . shorthand. **4** I. WATTS Such love, and meekness . . , I would transcribe, and make them mine. **6a** R. CHURCH The concertos of Vivaldi, transcribed by Bach for the organ.

■ **transcribable** *adjective* able to be transcribed; (*spec.* in *BIOLOGY*) susceptible to transcription: M20. **transcriber** *noun* (*a*) a person who or thing which transcribes something; a copyist, a copier; (*b*) a machine that plays dictated matter for transcription: E17.

transcript /'transkrɪpt, 'trɑːn-/ *noun.* Also (earlier) †**transcrit**. ME.
[Old & mod. French *transcrit* assim. to Latin *transcriptum* use as noun of neut. pa. pple of *transcribere* TRANSCRIBE.]
1 A thing that has been transcribed; a written or printed copy. Also (*LAW*), a copy of a legal record, esp. court proceedings. ME.
2 *transf. & fig.* A copy, an imitation, a reproduction; a representation, an interpretation. E17.
3 *BIOLOGY.* A length of RNA or DNA which has been transcribed from a DNA or RNA template (respectively). M20.

> 🕮 **1** S. BRILL Subcommittee transcripts . . revealed that the two Fitzsimmons told different stories. L. KENNEDY A transcript of the Suez programme reached . . *The Times.* **2** K. CLARK Courbet painted some of the most literal transcripts of nature.

transcript /tran'skrɪpt, trɑːn-/ *verb trans.* Long *rare* or *obsolete.* L16.
[Latin *transcript-*: see TRANSCRIPTION.]
Transcribe.
■ **tran'scriptor** *noun* (*rare*) a transcriber E17.

transcriptase /tran'skrɪpteɪz, trɑːn-/ *noun.* M20.
[from TRANSCRIPT(ION + -ASE.]
BIOCHEMISTRY. A polymerase which catalyses the formation of RNA from a DNA template during transcription; ***reverse transcriptase***, a polymerase which catalyses the formation of DNA from an RNA template in reverse transcription.

transcription /tran'skrɪpʃ(ə)n, trɑːn-/ *noun.* L16.
[French, or late Latin *transcriptio(n-)*, from Latin *transcript-* pa. ppl stem of *transcribere* TRANSCRIBE: see -ION.]
1 The action or process of transcribing something; an instance of this. L16.
2 The result of transcribing something; a transcript; a copy. M17.
†**3** *ROMAN LAW.* A transfer or assignment of a debt or obligation. L17–L19.
4 *BIOLOGY.* The process by which genetic information, represented by the sequence of nucleotides of DNA, is copied into molecules of RNA which are synthesized, with the DNA serving as a template. M20.

> 🕮 **1** J. HEALEY The error was committed in the transcription of the copy from Ptolomies library. J. KENNEDY Evidence which no transcription can corrupt. **2** W. RUMSEY Most medicinal Books are . . transcriptions from former Writers. W. S. ALLEN Transcriptions into Prakrit (Middle Indian) on coins of the Greek kings of . . India. **4 reverse transcription**, the reverse process to ordinary transcription (occurring in some RNA viruses), by which DNA is synthesized from an RNA template.

■ **transcriptional** *adjective* of, pertaining to, or of the nature of transcription L19. **transcriptionally** *adverb* E20. **transcriptionist** *noun* a person who makes a transcription; *US* an audio typist: L20.

transcriptitious /transkrɪp'tɪʃəs, trɑːn-/ *adjective. rare.* M17.
[formed as TRANSCRIPT *verb* + -ITIOUS[1].]
Resulting from transcription; of the nature or character of a transcript.

transcriptive /tran'skrɪptɪv, trɑːn-/ *adjective.* M17.
[from TRANSCRIPTION after *description*, *descriptive*: see -IVE.]
1 Serving to transcribe; characterized by or tending to transcription. M17.
†**2** *ROMAN LAW.* Transferring a debt or obligation. *rare.* Only in L19.

†**transcrit** *noun* see TRANSCRIPT *noun*.

transduce /tranz'djuːs, trɑːnz-, -ns-/ *verb trans.* M20.
[Back-form. from next.]
1 Convert (energy, esp. in the form of a signal) into a different medium or form of energy. M20.
2 *MICROBIOLOGY.* Transfer (genetic material) from one cell to another with a virus or virus-like particle as the vector; subject (a cell) to such transfer. M20.

transducer /tranz'djuːsə, trɑːnz-, -ns-/ *noun.* E20.
[from Latin *transducere* lead across, transfer, formed as TRANS- + *ducere* lead: see -ER[1].]
A device for converting variations in one physical quantity, as pressure, brightness, etc., quantitatively into variations in another, as voltage, position, etc; *esp.* a device for converting a non-electrical to an electrical signal.

transduction /tranz'dʌkʃ(ə)n, trɑːnz-, -ns-/ *noun.* M17.
[Latin *transductio(n-)*, from *transduct-* pa. ppl stem of *transducere*: see prec., -ION.]
1 The action of leading or bringing across. *rare.* M17.
2 The action or process of transducing a signal. M20.
3 *MICROBIOLOGY.* The transfer of genetic material from one cell to another by a virus or virus-like particle. M20.
■ **transductant** /-'dʌkt(ə)nt/ *noun* (*MICROBIOLOGY*) a cell into which genetic material has been transduced M20. **transductional** *adjective* of or pertaining to (genetic) transduction M20.

transductor /tranz'dʌktə, trɑːnz-, -ns-/ *noun.* L19.
[Latin, from *transduct-*: see prec., -OR.]
†**1** *ANATOMY.* A muscle of the big toe. Only in L19.
2 *ELECTRICITY.* A type of reactor having a direct current winding which controls the magnetic flux saturation of a core and hence can produce large changes in an associated alternating current winding. M20.

transect /'transɛkt, 'trɑːn-/ *noun.* E20.
[from the verb.]
SCIENCE (orig. *ECOLOGY*). A line or strip across the earth's surface along which a survey is made; a linear survey. Also, a straight line or narrow section through any object, natural feature, etc., along which a series of observations or measurements is made.

transect /tran'sɛkt, trɑːn-/ *verb trans.* M17.
[from Latin TRANS- + *sect-* pa. ppl stem of *secare* cut.]
Cut across; divide by passing across; cut transversely.

> 🕮 *Nature* Gorge-like melt-water channels transecting the Mendip ridge.

■ **transection** *noun* the action of transecting; a transverse section: L19.

transept /'transɛpt, 'trɑːn-/ *noun.* Also in Latin form †**transeptum**. M16.
[mod. Latin (Anglo-Latin) *transeptum*, formed as TRANS- + SEPTUM.]
The transverse part of a cruciform church at right angles to the nave; either of the two arms of this (more fully ***north transept*** and ***south transept***).
■ **tran'septal** *adjective* of, pertaining to, or of the nature of a transept M19. **tran'septed** *adjective* (*ARCHAEOLOGY*) (*spec.* designating a type of gallery grave) having side chambers resembling transepts M20.

transeunce *noun*, **transeunt** *adjective* see TRANSIENCE, TRANSIENT.

transexual *adjective & noun* see TRANSSEXUAL.

transfection /trans'fɛkʃ(ə)n, trɑːns-, -nz-/ *noun.* M20.
[from TRANS- or TRANS(FER *noun* + IN)FECTION.]
MICROBIOLOGY. The introduction of free nucleic acid into a eukaryotic cell.
■ **transfect** *verb trans.* infect (a cell) with free nucleic acid; introduce (genetic material) by transfection: M20.

transfer /'transfəː, 'trɑːns-, -nz-/ *noun.* L17.
[from the verb.]
1 *LAW.* Conveyance of property, esp. of stocks or shares, from one person to another. L17.
2 *gen.* The action of transferring or fact of being transferred; conveyance or removal from one place, person, etc., to another. Also *spec.*, the removal of a worker, player, etc. from one location, sphere, club, etc., to another; a change of place of employment within an organization. L18. ▸**b** *NAUTICAL.* The distance moved at right angles to the direction of travel during tacking. L19. ▸**c** *PSYCHOLOGY.* The carrying over of the effects of training or practice from the learning of one function to help or hinder the learning of another. Also more fully ***transfer of practice***, ***transfer of training***. E20.
3 A person who or thing which is or has been transferred; *spec.* a design etc. conveyed or to be conveyed from one surface to another, esp. a small usu. coloured picture or design on paper or plastic film, which is transferable to another surface. M19.
4 A means or place of transfer; *spec.* a change between lines or routes on a transport service. Also, a ferry service; a ticket entitling a passenger to make such a change. Chiefly *N. Amer.* L19.

> 🕮 **1** INA TAYLOR Arranging the transfer of some of his business assets to his son. **2** *Atlantic* An automatic transfer from junior high to high school. JULIA HAMILTON I've applied for a transfer to go out as an interpreter. *Independent* Rangers will expect a fee for the transfer of their most accomplished striker. **3** *Which?* The . . transfer had to be stuck on with water. *Opera Now* CD transfers of recordings originally released in the 1970s.

Phrases: *CERTIFIED* ***transfer***. ***negative transfer***: see NEGATIVE *adjective*. ***positive transfer***: see POSITIVE *adjective*. ***transfer of practice***, ***transfer of training***: see sense 2c above.
Comb.: **transfer-book** a register of transfers of property, shares, etc.; **transfer case** (*a*) a case in(to) which materials are transferred; (*b*) *MECHANICS* (the housing of) a mechanism for dividing the power between two or more driving axles of a motor vehicle; **transfer company** *US* a company conveying passengers or luggage between stations; **transfer factor** *IMMUNOLOGY* a substance released by antigen-sensitized lymphocytes and capable of transferring the response of delayed hypersensitivity to a non-sensitized cell or individual into which it is introduced; **transfer fee** (*a*) that charged by a joint-stock company for registering a transfer; (*b*) (*SPORT*, esp. *FOOTBALL*) a sum of money paid by one club to another in exchange for the transfer of a professional player; **transfer function** (*a*) *MATH.* a mathematical function relating the output or response of something to the input or stimulus; (*b*) *ELECTRONICS* a ratio of two quantities measured simultaneously at two different points of a circuit or device; **transfer ink** ink used for writing or drawing on lithographic transfer paper or for taking prints for transferring to lithographic stone; **transfer line** *ENGINEERING* a line of workstations along which a part is automatically conveyed for a sequence of automatic machining operations; **transfer list** a list of footballers available for transfer; **transfer machine** *ENGINEERING* a composite machine that performs a series of operations without the intervention of the operator; **transfer mould** the mould cavity in transfer moulding; **transfer-mould** *verb trans.* make by transfer moulding; **transfer moulding** a moulding process used chiefly for thermosetting plastics in which the material is softened and then forced into a closed mould cavity where it sets; **transfer orbit** *ASTRONAUTICS* an orbit that touches two given orbits and so provides a trajectory by which a spacecraft can pass from one orbit to the other; **transfer-paper** specially coated paper used for lithographic writing or drawing, or for taking impressions to be transferred to lithographic stone; **transfer payment** *ECONOMICS* a payment made or income received in which no goods or services are being paid for, such as a benefit payment or subsidy; **transfer-printed** *adjective* (esp. of ceramics) having a ready-made design printed on as a transfer during manufacture; **transfer RNA** *BIOLOGY* RNA consisting of folded molecules which transport amino acids from the cytoplasm of a cell to a ribosome and bind to an mRNA strand, so ordering the assembly of a polypeptide or protein; abbreviation ***tRNA***.

transfer /trans'fəː, trɑːns-, -nz-/ *verb.* Infl. **-rr-**. LME.
[French *transférer* or Latin *transferre*, formed as TRANS- + *ferre* bear, carry.]
1 *verb trans.* Move, take, or convey from one place, person, situation, time of occurrence, etc., to another; transmit, transport; give or hand over from one to another. LME. ▸**b** *fig.* Use (a word) in a sense different from the original or literal sense, esp. in a different but comparable context; alter or extend (the sense of a word) in this way. Chiefly as ***transferred*** *ppl adjective*. LME.
2 *verb trans. LAW.* Convey or make over (title, right, or property) by deed or legal process. L16.
3 *verb intrans.* Make or undergo a transfer. M17.
4 *verb trans.* Convey or apply (a drawing or design) from one surface to another, esp. from a prepared sheet to stone, pottery, cloth, etc. M19.

1 E. FEINSTEIN Secretly transferring funds to a Swiss bank. *She* I was transferred to . . hospital. P. LOMAS Transferring on to me an image of her past. **b transferred epithet** a figure of speech in which a word or phrase is used to qualify a noun other than that to which it literally applies (as 'a sleepless night', 'his weary way', etc.); hypallage. **3** *New Yorker* Bouza was considering transferring out of the police force. S. BRETT Not impossible that the play should transfer to the West End.

transferable /trans'fəːrəb(ə)l, 'transf(ə)r-, trɑː-, -nz-/ *adjective*. Also **-rr-**. M17.
[from prec. + -ABLE.]
Able to be transferred; *esp.* (of a bill, ticket, cheque, etc.) able to be legally made over to another, assignable from one person to another; negotiable.
transferable vote a vote that may be transferred to a second or further competing candidate if the candidate of first choice is eliminated during a succession of counts or has more votes than are needed for election (freq. in ***single transferable vote***).
■ **transfera'bility** *noun* L18.

transferase /'transf(ə)reɪz, 'trɑːns-, -nz-/ *noun*. M20.
[from TRANSFER *verb* + -ASE.]
BIOCHEMISTRY. An enzyme which catalyses the transfer of a particular group from one molecule to another.

transferee /transfəː'riː, trɑːns-, -nz-/ *noun*. M18.
[from TRANSFER *verb* + -EE[1].]
1 Chiefly *LAW*. A person to whom a transfer is made. Correl. to ***transferor*** or ***transferrer***. M18.
2 A person who is transferred or removed (from one position or grade to another). L19.

transference /'transf(ə)r(ə)ns, 'trɑːns-, -nz-/ *noun*. L17.
[from TRANSFER *verb* + -ENCE.]
1 *SCOTS LAW*. The procedure by which a depending action is transferred from a deceased defender to his or her representative. L17.
2 The action or process of transferring; conveyance from one place, person, or thing to another; transfer. M18. ▸**b** *PSYCHOANALYSIS*. The transfer to an analyst from a patient of powerful emotions previously (in childhood) directed at some other person or thing and since repressed or forgotten; *loosely* the emotional aspect of a patient's relationship to an analyst. E20.
2b ***negative transference***: see NEGATIVE *adjective*. ***positive transference***: see POSITIVE *adjective*.
Comb.: **transference neurosis** *PSYCHOANALYSIS* a neurotic state induced by transference and considered beneficial to the therapy; **transference number** *PHYSICAL CHEMISTRY* (chiefly *US*) = ***transport number*** s.v. TRANSPORT *noun*.
■ **transfe'rential** *adjective* of or pertaining to transference L19.

transferer *noun* var. of TRANSFERRER.

transferor /trans'fəːrə, 'transf(ə)rə, trɑːns-, -nz-/ *noun*. L19.
[from TRANSFER *verb* + -OR.]
Chiefly *LAW*. A person who makes a transfer of property etc. Correl. to ***transferee***.

transferrable *adjective* var. of TRANSFERABLE.

transferral /trans'fəːr(ə)l, trɑːns-, -nz-/ *noun*. L18.
[from TRANSFER *verb* + -AL[1].]
The action or fact of transferring; transfer.

transferrer /trans'fəːrə, trɑːns-, -nz-/ *noun*. Also **-ferer**. M18.
[formed as prec. + -ER[1].]
A person who or thing which transfers something. Correl. to ***transferee***.

transferrin /trans'fɛrɪn, trɑːns-, -nz-/ *noun*. M20.
[from TRANS- or TRANSFER *verb* + FERRO- + -IN[1].]
BIOCHEMISTRY. A beta globulin which binds and transports iron in blood serum. Also called ***siderophilin***.

transfigurate /trans'fɪgjʊreɪt, trɑːns-, -nz-/ *verb trans*. Now *rare*. LME.
[Latin *transfigurat-* pa. ppl stem of *transfigurare* TRANSFIGURE: see -ATE[3].]
= TRANSFIGURE.

transfiguration /ˌtransfɪgə'reɪʃ(ə)n, ˌtrɑːns-, -gjʊr-, -nz-/ *noun*. LME.
[Old & mod. French, or Latin *transfiguratio(n-)*, formed as prec.: see -ATION.]
1 (Freq. **T-**.) The dazzling change in the appearance of Jesus when on a mountain with three of his disciples (*Matthew* 17:1–8; *Mark* 9:2–8; *Luke* 9:28–36); a picture or representation of this. Also, the church festival commemorating this event, observed on 6 August. LME.
2 *gen*. The action of transfiguring or state of being transfigured; metamorphosis. M16.

transfigure /trans'fɪgə, trɑːns-, -nz-/ *verb trans*. ME.
[Old & mod. French *transfigurer* or Latin *transfigurare*, formed as TRANS- + *figura* FIGURE *noun*.]
1 Alter or change the appearance of; transform. Freq. in *pass*. ME.
2 *fig*. Change into a more elevated, glorious, or spiritual form. LME.

1 D. CUSACK Her gentle face is transfigured.

■ **transfigurative** *adjective* (*rare*) having the quality of transfiguring L19. **transfigurement** *noun* (*rare*) = TRANSFIGURATION 2 M19.

transfinalization /trans,fʌɪn(ə)lʌɪ'zeɪʃ(ə)n, trɑːns-, -nz-/ *noun*. Also **-isation**. M20.
[from TRANS- + FINALIZATION.]
CHRISTIAN THEOLOGY. The change undergone by the bread and wine at the Eucharist understood or expressed teleologically in terms of changed purpose or function. Cf. TRANSIGNIFICATION.

transfinite /trans'fʌɪnʌɪt, trɑːns-, -nz-/ *adjective*. E20.
[from TRANS- + FINITE *adjective & noun*.]
MATH. Pertaining to or designating a number corresponding to an infinite set in the way that a natural number denotes or counts members of a finite set.

transfix /trans'fɪks, trɑːns-, -nz-/ *verb trans*. L16.
[Latin *transfix-* pa. ppl stem of *transfigere*, formed as TRANS- + *figere* fix, fasten.]
1 Pierce through with or impale on a sharp pointed object; fix or fasten by piercing. L16.
2 *fig*. Affect deeply esp. with pain, grief, or other emotion. Also, make motionless (with fascination, astonishment, fear, etc.). M17.

1 W. PALEY The butcher-bird transfixes its prey upon the spike of a thorn. **2** R. HOLMES I stared at these photographs for hours, transfixed.

■ **transfixedly** /-'fɪksɪdli/ *adverb* M19. **transfixture** *noun* (*rare*) the state or condition of being transfixed, esp. with emotion L19.

transfixion /trans'fɪkʃ(ə)n, trɑːns-, -nz-/ *noun*. E17.
[from prec.: see -ION.]
1 The action of transfixing, the state of being transfixed. E17.
2 *MEDICINE*. A method of amputation by piercing a limb transversely and cutting outward from within. Now *rare* or *obsolete*. L19.

transfluence /'transfluəns, 'trɑːns-, -nz-/ *noun*. M20.
[from next: see -ENCE.]
PHYSICAL GEOGRAPHY. The flow of glacial ice across a preglacial watershed, with consequent severe erosion.

transfluent /'transfluənt, 'trɑːns-, -nz-/ *adjective*. E19.
[Latin *transfluent-* pres. ppl stem of *transfluere*, formed as TRANS- + *fluere* flow: see -ENT.]
1 Flowing across or through; *spec*. in *HERALDRY*, (of a stream) flowing under a bridge. *rare*. E19.
2 *PHYSICAL GEOGRAPHY*. Of glacial ice: undergoing transfluence. M20.

transform /'transfɔːm, 'trɑːns-, -nz-/ *noun*. M19.
[from the verb.]
1 A thing derived from another by transformation; *esp*. (*MATH*.) an expression or (*LINGUISTICS*) a syntactic structure derived by the application of a transformation. M19.
2 *GEOLOGY*. In full ***transform fault***. A transcurrent fault terminating abruptly at both ends, *esp*. one that connects two segments of an oceanic ridge. Also, any transcurrent fault associated with two lithospheric plates sliding past one another. L20.
1 ***Fourier transform***. ***Laplace transform***.
Comb.: ***transform fault***: see sense 2 above; **transform faulting** the generation of transform faults.

transform /trans'fɔːm, trɑːns-, -nz-/ *verb*. ME.
[Old & mod. French *transformer* or Latin *transformare*, formed as TRANS- + FORM *verb*[1].]
1 *verb trans*. Change the form, shape, or appearance of; alter the character or nature of. ME.
2 *verb intrans*. Undergo a change of form or nature; change; *MATH*. undergo transformation. L16.
3 *verb trans*. & *intrans*. *MATH*. Alter (a figure, expression, etc.) to another differing in form, but equal in significance or value; subject to a transformation. M18.
4 *verb trans*. *ELECTRICITY*. Change a current in potential, as from high voltage to low voltage, or in type, as from alternating to direct current. L19.
5 *verb trans*. *BIOLOGY*. ▸**a** Change the genotype of (a cell, orig. a bacterium) by the permanent introduction of DNA from another source, esp. by means of a plasmid. E20. ▸**b** Cause (a cell) to undergo transformation into a cancer-like cell. M20.

1 D. CARNEGIE He repeatedly took some drab little creature . . and transformed her . . into a glamorous vision. ISAIAH BERLIN The energetic social legislation . . transformed the social order. R. P. JHABVALA The cross expression on her face was . . transformed to one of joy. J. HALPERIN The railway . . was beginning to transform both life and countryside in many parts of England. **2** P. W. ATKINS We can construct matrix representatives . . very simply because we know how the components transform. **4 transform down** lower the voltage (while increasing the current). **transform up** raise the voltage (while decreasing the current).

■ **transforma'bility** *noun* ability to be transformed E19. **transformable** *adjective* L17. **transformance** *noun* (*rare*) transformation E17. **transformant** *noun* (*BIOLOGY*) (an organism derived from) a transformed cell M20.

transformation /transfə'meɪʃ(ə)n, trɑːns-, -nz-/ *noun*. LME.
[Old & mod. French, or late Latin *transformatio(n-)*, from Latin *transformat-* pa. ppl stem of *transformare*: see prec., -ATION.]
▸**I 1** The action of changing in form, shape, or appearance; metamorphosis. LME.
2 A complete change in character, nature, etc. L16.
3 *THEATRICAL*. More fully ***transformation scene***. A scene in a pantomime in which (part of) the scenery is dramatically altered in the sight of the audience; *esp*. (now *Hist*.) one in which the principal performers became the players of an ensuing harlequinade. M19.
4 A woman's wig. Now *rare*. E20.

1 G. DALY The transformation of Galatea from statue to living being. **2** *Independent* The political transformation of Eastern Europe has . . already happened. The economic transformation . . has hardly begun.

▸**II** *techn*. **5** *MATH*. A change of any mathematical entity in accordance with some definite rule or set of rules; the rules themselves; *spec*. (***a***) change of form without alteration of significance or value; substitution of one geometrical figure for another of equal magnitude but different form, or of one algebraic expression or equation for another of the same value; (***b***) the introduction of a new set of coordinates; (***c***) = MAPPING 2. Formerly also, truncation of the vertices of a solid figure. L16.
6 Natural change of form in a living organism; = METAMORPHOSIS 3a. M17.
7 *CHEMISTRY*. Change of chemical structure, esp. by rearrangement of atoms in a molecule to form a compound of a different type; a reaction in which this occurs. M19.
8 *ELECTRICITY*. Change of a current into one of different potential, or different type, or both, as by a transformer. L19.
9 *PHYSICS*. Change of one element into another by nuclear bombardment or radioactive decay; transmutation. E20.
10 *BIOLOGY*. The genetic alteration of a cell (orig. a bacterium) by the introduction or absorption of extraneous DNA, esp. by means of a plasmid. E20.
11 *CYTOLOGY* & *MEDICINE*. The heritable alteration of a eukaryotic cell so that it comes to possess some or all of the characteristics of a cancer cell. M20.
12 *LINGUISTICS*. The conversion of one syntactic structure into another by the application of specific rules; a rule converting deep structure to surface structure. M20.

5 ***Laplace transformation***. ***Lorentz transformation***. **6** D. ATTENBOROUGH They grow by a series of moults but never . . undergo transformation.

Comb.: **transformation card** a playing-card on which the suit signs are incorporated into a decorative design or picture; ***transformation scene***: see sense 3 above.
■ **transformationist** *noun* (***a***) = TRANSFORMIST; (***b***) = TRANSFORMATIONALIST *noun*: L19.

transformational /transfə'meɪʃ(ə)n(ə)l, trɑːns-, -nz-/ *adjective*. L19.
[from prec. + -AL[1].]
Of or pertaining to transformation; *spec*. in *LINGUISTICS* (more fully ***transformational-generative***) designating or pertaining to a linguistic rule for converting structures, or a model or method of analysis based on the generation of one structure from another by transformations.
transformational cycle: see CYCLE *noun* 3c.
■ **transformationalism** *noun* transformational theory M20. **transformationalist** *noun & adjective* (***a***) *noun* an adherent of transformational theory; (***b***) *adjective* pertaining to or characteristic of transformationalists: M20. **transformationally** *adverb* by means of transformation(s), according to transformational rules M20.

transformative /trans'fɔːmətɪv, trɑːns-, -nz-/ *adjective*. L17.
[medieval Latin *transformativus*, from Latin *transformat-*: see TRANSFORMATION, -ATIVE.]
1 Capable of transforming something. L17.
2 *LINGUISTICS*. = TRANSFORMATIONAL *adjective*. Freq. in ***transformative-generative***. M20.

transformer /trans'fɔːmə, trɑːns-, -nz-/ *noun*. L16.
[from TRANSFORM *verb* + -ER[1]. In sense 2 orig. translating French *transformateur*.]
1 A person who or thing which transforms something. L16.
2 *spec*. in *ELECTRICITY*. An apparatus for changing the voltage of an alternating current or (formerly) a direct current. Formerly also, one for changing alternating into direct current or vice versa. L19.
3 (**T-**.) (Proprietary name for) a child's toy consisting of a model robot whose components can be rebuilt to form another toy (as a motor vehicle, a gun, etc.). Usu. in *pl*. L20.
Comb.: **transformer oil** a high-grade oil with a low sludge content used to cool and insulate transformers etc.
■ **transformerless** *adjective* M20.

transformism /trans'fɔːmɪz(ə)m, trɑːns-, -nz-/ *noun*. L19.
[French *transformisme*, from *transformer* TRANSFORM *verb*: see -ISM.]
1 *BIOLOGY*. The hypothesis that existing species are the product of the gradual transformation of other forms of living beings; *loosely* such transformation; the doctrine of evolution of species. Now chiefly *Hist*. L19.
2 The doctrine of gradual evolution of morals and social relations; *loosely* such evolution. L19.
▪ **transformist** *noun* an adherent or advocate of transformism L19.

transfretation /transfrɪ'teɪʃ(ə)n, trɑːns-, -nz-/ *noun*. Long *obsolete* exc. *Hist*. M16.
[Latin *transfretatio(n-)*, from *transfretat-* pa. ppl stem of *transfretare*, formed as TRANS- + *fretum* strait: see -ATION.]
The action of crossing a strait; *esp*. the crossing of the English Channel by a monarch.

transfuse /trans'fjuːz, trɑːns-, -nz-/ *verb trans*. LME.
[Latin *transfus-* pa. ppl stem of *transfundere*, formed as TRANS- + *fundere* pour.]
1 Cause to pass from one person or thing to another; cause to have gradual and complete influence; instil. LME.
2 *lit*. Pour (a liquid) from one vessel or receptacle into another. Now *rare*. E17.
3 Transfer (blood or a cell suspension) from one person or animal into another; inject (blood or other fluid) into the veins. M17. ▸**b** Treat (a person) with a transfusion of blood etc. L19.

📖 **1** A. B. EDWARDS The sun . . at its highest and the air transfused with light.

▪ **transfusible** *adjective* (*rare*) able to be transfused M17. **transfusive** /-'fjuːsɪv, -zɪv/ *adjective* (*rare*) that transfuses; capable of transfusing some influence etc.: L17.

transfusion /trans'fjuːʒ(ə)n, trɑːns-, -nz-/ *noun*. L16.
[Latin *transfusio(n-)*, formed as prec.: see -ION.]
1 The action of transfusing something or of being transfused; gradual transfer, permeation; transmission. L16.
2 *spec*. The process of transferring blood or a cell suspension from one person or animal into the veins of another (more fully ***blood transfusion***); the injection of blood or other fluid into the veins. Also, an instance of this. M17.
Comb.: **transfusion tissue** a tissue, composed of tracheids and parenchyma cells, which surrounds the vascular bundle in gymnosperm leaves and is believed to serve for the transport of nutriment between the vascular bundle and the mesophyll.
▪ **transfusional** *adjective* occurring as a result of or by means of transfusion M20. **transfusionist** *noun* a person who advocates or uses the process of transfusion of blood L19.

transgender /trans'dʒɛndə, 'trɑːns-/ *noun & adjective*. L20.
[from TRANS- + GENDER *noun*.]
▸**A** *noun*. A person whose identity does not conform to conventional notions of male or female gender, but combines or moves between these identities; a transvestite or transsexual. L20.
▸**B** *adjective*. Relating to or designating a transgender or transgenders; *spec*. undergoing or having undergone sex change procedures. L20.
▪ **trangendered** *adjective* = TRANSGENDER *adjective* L20. **transgenderist** *noun* = TRANSGENDER *noun* L20.

transgenic /tranz'dʒɛnɪk, trɑːnz-, -ns-/ *adjective & noun*. L20.
[from TRANS- + GENE + -IC.]
BIOLOGY. ▸**A** *adjective*. Of, pertaining to, or designating an organism containing genetic material into which DNA from an unrelated organism has been artificially introduced. L20.
▸**B** *noun*. **1** In *pl*. (usu. treated as *sing*.). The branch of biology concerned with transgenic organisms. L20.
2 A transgenic organ. L20.
▪ **'transgene** *noun* a gene which is or has been introduced into the genome of another organism L20. **transgenosis** /-dʒɪ'nəʊsɪs/ *noun*, pl. **-noses** /-'nəʊsiːz/, the transfer of genes from an organism to another unrelated one and their subsequent expression L20.

transgredient /tranz'griːdɪənt, trɑːnz-, -ns-/ *adjective*. *rare*. M19.
[Latin *transgredient-* pres. ppl stem of *transgredi*: see TRANSGRESS *verb*, -ENT.]
That transgresses.

†transgress *noun*. *rare*. LME–M19.
[Orig. from French †*transgrès*; later from the verb.]
(A) transgression, (a) trespass.

transgress /tranz'grɛs, trɑːnz-, -ns-/ *verb*. L15.
[Old & mod. French *transgresser* or Latin *transgress-* pa. ppl stem of *transgredi*, formed as TRANS- + *gradi* proceed, walk.]
1 a *verb intrans*. Break a law or command; trespass, offend. (Foll. by *against*.) L15. ▸**b** *verb trans*. Go beyond the bounds or limits prescribed by (a law, command, etc.); violate, contravene. E16.
2 a *verb trans*. Go or pass beyond (any limit or bounds), exceed; *GEOLOGY* (of the sea) spread over (the land). E17. ▸†**b** *verb intrans*. Trespass (*on*); wander, digress. M–L17.

▪ **transgressible** *adjective* (*rare*) able to be transgressed (earlier in INTRANSGRESSIBLE) M19. **transgressor** *noun* a person who transgresses, a lawbreaker, a sinner LME.

transgression /tranz'grɛʃ(ə)n, trɑːnz-, -ns-/ *noun*. LME.
[Old & mod. French from Latin *transgressio(n-)*, from *transgress-*: see prec., -ION.]
1 The action or an act of transgressing or passing beyond the bounds of legality or right; a violation of law, duty, or command; disobedience, trespass, sin. LME.
2 The action of overstepping a limit or boundary. *rare*. E17.
3 *GEOLOGY*. The spread of the sea or of marine sediment over the land. L19.

📖 **1** AV *Isa*. 53:5 He was wounded for our transgressions . . bruised for our iniquities. *Studies in English Literature* Sir Thomas . . commits glaring transgressions against his own moral principles. **2** *Scientific American* The stratification of sedimentary deposits suggested successive marine transgressions onto the continents.

transgressive /tranz'grɛsɪv, trɑːnz-, -ns-/ *adjective*. M17.
[from TRANSGRESS *verb* + -IVE.]
1 Involving or pertaining to transgression; in mod. use *spec*. denoting or relating to writing, cinema, or art in which orthodox cultural, moral, or artistic boundaries are challenged by the representation of unconventional behaviour and the use of experimental forms. M17.
2 *GEOLOGY*. Of a stratum: overlapping or overlapped by another stratum unconformably, esp. as a result of marine transgression. M19.

📖 **1** *Times Lit. Suppl*. The enormous transgressive force of the poem has been lost.

¶ In 19 only in *GEOLOGY* use.
▪ **transgressively** *adverb* M19.

tranship *verb* var. of TRANSSHIP.

transhuman /tranz'hjuːmən, trɑːnz-, -ns-/ *adjective*. E19.
[from TRANS- + HUMAN *adjective*, after Italian *trasumanar* (Dante).]
Beyond what is human; superhuman.
▪ **transhumanate** *verb trans*. = TRANSHUMANIZE M19. **transhuma'nation** *noun* a making or becoming transhuman M19. **transhumanize** *verb trans*. make transhuman L19.

transhumance /tranz'hjuːməns, trɑːnz-, -ns-/ *noun*. E20.
[French, from *transhumer* (ult. from Latin TRANS- + *humus* ground): see -ANCE.]
The seasonal transfer of grazing animals to different pastures, often over long distances.
▪ **transhumant** *adjective* migrating between regions with differing climates; *spec*. of or pertaining to transhumance: M20.

transience /'transɪəns, 'trɑːns-, -nz-/ *noun*. In sense 2 also **transeunce**. M18.
[formed as TRANSIENT: see -ENCE.]
1 The condition or state of being transient or short-lived; the fact of passing away soon or in a short time; transiency. M18.
2 *PHILOSOPHY*. The quality of being transient or transitive. Opp. ***immanence***. L19.

transiency /'transɪənsi, 'trɑːns-, -nz-/ *noun*. M17.
[formed as prec.: see -ENCY.]
1 The state or condition of being (a) transient; transience. M17.
2 A transient thing or being. *rare*. M19.

transient /'transɪənt, 'trɑːns-, -nz-/ *adjective & noun*. In sense A.2 also **transeunt**. L16.
[from Latin *transiens*, *transeunt-* pres. pple of *transire* go across, pass over, formed as TRANS- + *ire* go.]
▸**A** *adjective*. **1** Passing away with time, not durable or permanent; temporary, transitory; *esp*. passing away quickly or soon, brief, momentary. L16.
2 *PHILOSOPHY*. Operating beyond itself; having an external effect. Opp. ***immanent***. Cf. TRANSITIVE *adjective* 3. E17.
3 Passing through; passing from one thing or person to another. Now *rare*. E17.
4 Passing through a place without staying in it, or staying only for a short time; *spec*. (*US colloq*.) designating or pertaining to a short-stay guest at a hotel etc. L17.
5 *MUSIC*. Of a note, a chord, etc.: introduced in passing, not belonging to the harmony or key of the passage. E19.
6 Esp. of printed matter: occasional, isolated, one-off, individual. *US*. M19.

📖 **1** T. HARDY She was but a transient impression, half forgotten. **transient ischaemic attack** *MEDICINE* a brief episode of neurological dysfunction, involving weakness, numbness, speech or vision difficulties, etc., resulting from an interruption in the blood supply to the brain or eye.

▸**B** *noun*. **1** A transient thing or being; something passing or transitory, not permanent; *CHEMISTRY* a short-lived species, such as a free radical, an excited state, etc. M17.
2 A person who passes through a place, or stays in it for only a short time. Also, a traveller, a tramp, a migrant worker. *colloq*. (orig. *US*). L19.
3 *SCIENCE*. A transient variation in current or voltage, or in any waveform, esp. at the beginning of a signal; a momentary disturbance of a system; a very brief surge, esp. (in sound reproduction) of volume. E20.

📖 **2** P. D. JAMES The original tenants . . replaced by the transients of the city, the peripatetic young.

▪ **transiently** *adverb* M17. **transientness** *noun* M17.

transignification /ˌtransɪgnɪfɪ'keɪʃ(ə)n, ˌtrɑːn-, -ˌsɪg-/ *noun*. M20.
[from TRANS- + SIGNIFICATION.]
CHRISTIAN THEOLOGY. The change undergone by the bread and wine at the Eucharist understood or expressed in terms of their sacramental significance. Cf. TRANSFINALIZATION.

transilience /tran'sɪlɪəns, trɑːn-/ *noun*. *rare*. M17.
[formed as next: see -ENCE.]
A leaping from one thing to another; an abrupt transition.

transilient /tran'sɪlɪənt, trɑːn-/ *adjective*. E19.
[Latin *trans(s)ilient-* pres. ppl stem of *trans(s)ilire* leap across, formed as TRANS- + *salire* leap: see -ENT.]
Leaping or passing from one thing or condition to another; *esp*. (*MINERALOGY*) (of a rock or mineral) passing abruptly into another.

transilluminate /transɪ'luːmɪneɪt, trɑːns-, -'ljuː-, -nz-/ *verb*. E20.
[from TRANS- + ILLUMINATE *verb*.]
1 *verb trans*. Cause light to pass through; *MEDICINE* shine strong light or other radiation through (an organ or part) to detect disease or abnormality. E20.
2 *verb intrans*. Appear or show up during transillumination. *rare*. L20.
▪ **transillumi'nation** *noun* the action or process of transilluminating L19. **transilluminator** *noun* (*a*) an instrument for examining the conjunctiva and the sclerotic of the eyeball by shining light through them; (*b*) an instrument for making spots on chromatography plates and electrophoresis gels visible by shining ultraviolet light through them: E20.

transire /tran'zʌɪə, trɑː-, -s-, -ʌɪri/ *noun*. L16.
[Use as noun of Latin inf.: see TRANSIENT.]
LAW. A customs permit for the passage of goods.

transistor /tran'zɪstə, trɑːn-, -'sɪ-/ *noun*. M20.
[Blend of TRANSFER *verb* and RESISTOR.]
1 A semiconductor device, usu. having three terminals and two junctions, in which the load current can be made to be proportional to a small input current, and capable of amplification and rectification (functionally equivalent to a valve). M20.
2 In full ***transistor radio***. A small portable radio having transistors and other solid-state devices in place of valves. M20.

📖 **1** ***field-effect transistor***, ***junction transistor***, ***mesa transistor***, ***power transistor***, ***Schottky transistor***, etc.
2 S. BELLOW The Puerto Rican sweepers carried transistors playing Latin music.

Comb.: ***transistor radio***: see sense 2 above; **transistor set** a radio or television set having transistors instead of valves; **transistor–transistor logic** *ELECTRONICS* logic in which transistors take the place of many of the coupling resistors.
▪ **transistori'zation** *noun* the use of transistors in electronic apparatus M20. **transistorize** *verb trans*. design or make with transistors (rather than valves etc.) (chiefly as ***transistorized*** *ppl adjective*.) M20.

transit /'transɪt, 'trɑːns-, -nz-/ *noun*. LME.
[Latin *transitus*, formed as next.]
1 The action of passing across or through; passage or journey from one place or point to another. Freq. in ***in transit***. LME. ▸**b** A way for passing; a river crossing. *rare*. LME. ▸**c** The passage or carriage of people or goods from one place to another; *spec*. (chiefly *N. Amer*.) public passenger transport. E19.
2 *fig*. A passing across; a transition, a change; *esp*. the passage from this life to the next by death. M17.
3 *ASTRONOMY*. **a** The passage of an inferior planet (Mercury or Venus) across the sun's disc, or of a satellite or its shadow across the disc of a planet. Formerly also, an occultation of a star or planet by the moon, or of a star by a planet. M17. ▸**b** The passage of a celestial object across a meridian. E19.
4 *ASTROLOGY*. The passage of a planet across some special point or region of the zodiac. L17.
5 *ellipt*. A transit-instrument; a transit-theodolite. *colloq*. M19.
Comb.: **transit camp** a camp for the temporary accommodation of servicemen awaiting posting, refugees, prisoners-of-war, etc.; **transit-circle** = ***meridian circle*** *noun*[1] s.v. MERIDIAN *noun*; **transit-duty**: paid on goods passing through a country; **transit-instrument** an astronomical telescope mounted on a fixed east-and-west axis, by which the time of the passage of a celestial object across the meridian may be determined; **transit lounge** a waiting-room for transit passengers at an airport; **transit man** *N. Amer*. a surveyor who uses a transit-theodolite; **transit-pass** a warrant to pass through a country without payment of duty; **transit passenger**: making a brief stop at an airport in transit to another destination; **transit-theodolite** an instrument resembling a theodolite, used in surveying for the measurement

of horizontal angles; **transit-trade**: arising out of the passage of foreign goods through a country; **transit visa**: permitting the holder to pass through a country but not to stay there.

transit /ˈtransɪt, ˈtrɑːns-, -nz-/ *verb*. LME.
[Latin *transit-* pa. ppl stem of *transire*: see TRANSIENT.]
1 *verb intrans.* Pass through or over; pass away. LME.
2 *verb trans. & intrans.* ASTROLOGY. Pass across (a sign, house, or special point of the zodiac). M17.
3 *verb trans.* Pass across or through (something); traverse, cross. L17.
4 *verb trans. & intrans.* ASTRONOMY. Pass across (the disc of a celestial body, the meridian, the field of view of a telescope); make a transit (of). L17.

📖 **1** T. MORGAN Maugham was transiting through America on one of his journeys to Asia. **3** *Chicago Tribune* Transiting the Strait of Magellan takes . . 36 hours. **4** *Nature* In 1910 Halley's comet . . transited the Sun.

■ **transitable** *adjective* (*rare*) passable, crossable M19.

transitation /tranzɪˈteɪʃ(ə)n, trɑːnz-, -ns-/ *noun. rare.* E17.
[App. from TRANSIT *verb* + -ATION (orig. a humorous formation).]
The action of passing; passage.

transition /tranˈzɪʃ(ə)n, trɑːn-, -ˈsɪʃ-/ *noun.* M16.
[Old & mod. French, or directly from Latin *transitio(n-)*, formed as TRANSIT *verb*: see -ION.]
1 The action or process of passing or passage from one condition, action, or (occas.) place, to another; change; an instance of this. M16.
2 Passage in thought, speech, or writing from one subject to another; a figure or phrase used in this. M16.
3 MUSIC. †**a** Going from one chord to another by means of a passing note. Only in M17. ▸**b** (A) momentary modulation from one key to another. Also, modulation into a remote key. M18.
4 Passage from an earlier to a later stage of development or formation; *esp.* (*a*) ARCHITECTURE change from an earlier to a later style; a style having intermediate or mixed character; (*b*) PHILOLOGY the historical passage of a language from one well-defined stage to another (as from Old English to Middle English); the interval occupied by this; the intermediate form of the language during this interval. Formerly also (GEOLOGY), a series of early stratified rocks now classified as Silurian. Freq. *attrib.* E19.
5 PHYSICS. A change of an atomic nucleus or an orbital electron from one quantized state to another, with the emission or absorption of radiation of a characteristic wavelength. E20.
6 BIOLOGY. The occurrence in a nucleic acid of one purine in place of another, or of one pyrimidine in place of another. Cf. TRANSVERSION *noun*[1] 2. M20.

📖 **1** P. CAMPBELL He made the transition from politics to business. *Guardian* Transition to a market economy must be carried out in several . . stages. *attrib.*: *Nature* Binding sites . . bind selectively to the transition stage of the substrate. ***transition period, transition process, transition zone***, etc.

Comb.: **transition curve** (ENGINEERING etc.) a curve of constantly changing radius, used to connect a circular arc to a straight line or to an arc of different curvature; **transition element** CHEMISTRY †(*a*) = ***transitional element*** s.v. TRANSITIONAL *adjective*; (*b*) any of a large class of metallic elements occupying the central block of the periodic table, characterized by atoms or cations containing partly filled *d* or *f* orbitals and commonly exhibiting variable valency and forming coloured complexes; **transition fit** ENGINEERING a fit between two mating parts such that, within the specified tolerances, there may be either interference or clearance between them; **transition metal** CHEMISTRY = ***transition element*** (b) above; **transition probability** PHYSICS the probability of a transition between two given states of a system (esp. an atom); **transition series** CHEMISTRY the series of transition elements; **transition temperature** PHYSICS the temperature at which a substance acquires or loses some distinctive property, esp. superconductivity.

transition /tranˈzɪʃ(ə)n, trɑːn-, -ˈsɪʃ-/ *verb.* L20.
[from the noun.]
1 *verb intrans.* Make or undergo a transition (from one state, system, etc. *to* or *into* another); change over, switch. L20.
2 *verb trans.* Cause to undergo transition; bring from one state to another, convert. L20.

📖 **1** *Aviation Week* Transitioning to the advanced displays from the basic dial indicators . . sometimes causes minor confusion. **2** *Applied Linguistics* Bilingual programs . . that transition children into English as quickly as possible.

transitional /tranˈzɪʃ(ə)n(ə)l, trɑːn-, -ˈsɪʃ-/ *adjective & noun.* E19.
[from TRANSITION *noun* + -AL[1].]
▶ **A** *adjective.* Of or pertaining to transition; characterized by or involving transition; intermediate; *esp.* of, pertaining to, or designating an intermediate artistic style, as between (*a*) Norman (Romanesque) and Early English (Gothic) architecture (late 12th cent.); (*b*) Ming and Qing dynasty Chinese ceramics (mid 17th cent.). E19.

📖 H. MOORE We live in a transitional age, between one economic structure . . and another. **transitional case** GRAMMAR in some languages, a case expressing motion toward. **transitional element** CHEMISTRY (now *Hist.*) each of the nine metallic elements now classed in group VIII (or groups 8–10) of the periodic table.

▶ **B** *ellipt.* as *noun.* A transitional thing, period, etc. *rare.* E20.
■ **transitionally** *adverb* L19. **transitionalness** *noun* L19. **transitionary** *adjective* (*rare*) = TRANSITIONAL *adjective* L17.

transitival /transɪˈtʌɪv(ə)l, trɑːns-, -nz-/ *adjective. rare.* L19.
[from next + -AL[1].]
GRAMMAR. = TRANSITIVE *adjective* 2.

transitive /ˈtransɪtɪv, ˈtrɑːns-, -nz-/ *adjective & noun.* M16.
[Late Latin *transitivus*, formed as TRANSIT *verb*: see -IVE. In sense 1 app. from Old French *transitif* transient.]
▶ **A** *adjective.* †**1** Passing or liable to pass into another condition, changeable; transient, transitory. *rare.* M16–E20.
2 GRAMMAR. Of verbs and their construction: expressing an action which passes over to an object; taking a direct object to complete the sense. L16.
3 PHILOSOPHY. = TRANSIENT *adjective* 2. Opp. ***immanent***. E17.
4 Characterized by or involving transition; passing through stages; forming a transition between two stages, positions, or conditions; transitional, intermediate. Now *rare* or *obsolete.* M17.
†**5** Of the application of a word: transferred. *rare.* Only in E19.
6 MATH. & LOGIC. Of a relation: such that if it holds between every pair of successive members of a sequence, then it necessarily holds between any two members. Of a group: containing elements in transitive relation. M19.
▶ **B** *noun.* A transitive verb. E17.
■ **transitiveness** *noun* M19.

transitively /ˈtransɪtɪvli, ˈtrɑːns-, -nz-/ *adverb.* L16.
[from prec. + -LY[2].]
1 GRAMMAR. In a transitive sense or construction; with a direct object. L16.
2 In a manner involving (*a*) transition; (*b*) transitive action. M17.
3 MATH. & LOGIC. By or in a transitive relation. L19.

transitivise *verb* var. of TRANSITIVIZE.

transitivism /ˈtransɪtɪvɪz(ə)m, ˈtrɑːns-, -nz-/ *noun.* E20.
[from TRANSITIVE *adjective* + -ISM.]
PSYCHIATRY. A mental state or condition in which a patient attributes to others his or her own experiences and sensations.

transitivity /transɪˈtɪvɪti, trɑːns-, -nz-/ *noun.* L19.
[formed as prec. + -ITY.]
Chiefly GRAMMAR, MATH., & LOGIC. The state or condition of being transitive; transitive quality. Also, state or condition as regards being either transitive or intransitive.

transitivize /ˈtransɪtɪvʌɪz, ˈtrɑːns-, -nz-/ *verb trans.* Also **-ise**. M20.
[formed as prec. + -IZE.]
GRAMMAR. Make (a verb) transitive.
■ **transitivizer** *noun* an affix that makes a verb transitive L20.

transitory /ˈtransɪt(ə)ri, ˈtrɑːns-, -nz-/ *adjective & noun.* LME.
[Anglo-Norman *transitorie*, Old & mod. French *transitoire*, from Christian Latin *transitorius*, formed as TRANSIT *verb*: see -ORY[2].]
▶ **A** *adjective.* **1** Not permanent or lasting; fleeting, momentary, brief; transient. LME.
2 Of the nature of a passage or transition; transitional. *rare.* L16.
3 LAW. ***transitory action***, an action that may be brought in any country irrespective of where the transaction etc. originated. M17.
†**4** Trifling, of little moment. Only in L17.
▶† **B** *noun.* **1** A device for viewing an astronomical transit; orig., the transverse piece of a cross-staff. L16–M18.
2 A transitory or fleeting thing. Usu. in *pl.* Only in M17.
■ **transitorily** *adverb* E17. **transitoriness** *noun* L16.

transitron /ˈtransɪtrɒn, ˈtrɑːns-, -nz-/ *noun.* M20.
[from TRANS(CONDUCTANCE + -*i*- + -TRON.]
ELECTRONICS. A pentode in which the suppressor grid is used as the control grid so that the valve exhibits negative transconductance.

Transjordanian /ˌtranzdʒɔːˈdeɪmɪən, ˌtrɑːnz-, -ns-/ *noun & adjective.* E20.
[from TRANS- + *Jordan* (see below) + -IAN.]
▶ **A** *noun.* A person from beyond the River Jordan; *spec.* a native or inhabitant of Transjordan (Transjordania), a territory east of the River Jordan, now part of the kingdom of Jordan. Now *Hist.* E20.
▶ **B** *adjective.* Of or pertaining to the land beyond the Jordan; *spec.* (now *Hist.*) of or pertaining to Transjordan. E20.

Transkeian /transˈkʌɪən, trɑːns-, -nz-/ *adjective & noun.* L19.
[from *Transkei* (see below), from TRANS- + *Kei* a river in eastern South Africa + -AN.]
(A native or inhabitant) of the Transkei, a former black African homeland within the Republic of South Africa.

For other words beginning with *trans-* see the entry for **trans-**

†**translate** *noun.* L16–E19.
[from Latin *translatus* pa. pple: see next.]
A translation.

translate /transˈleɪt, trɑːns-, -nz-/ *verb.* ME.
[Orig. from Latin *translatus* pa. pple of *transferre* TRANSFER *verb*, perh. reinforced by Old French *translater*, medieval Latin *translatare*: see -ATE[3].]
1 *verb trans.* Bear, convey, or remove from one person, place, time, or condition to another; transfer, transport; *spec.* move (a bishop) from one see to another; *Scot.* move (a minister) from one pastoral charge to another. Also, move the remains of (a famous person, esp. a saint), from one place to another. ME. ▸**b** Carry or convey to heaven, orig. esp. without death. LME. ▸**c** MEDICINE. Move the seat of (a disease) from one person, or part of the body, to another. Now *rare* or *obsolete.* M18.
2 a *verb trans.* Turn from one language into another; express the sense of in another language. Also, express in other words, paraphrase. ME. ▸**b** *verb intrans.* Perform translation; change from one language or form of words into another. Also (of language, an author's work, etc.) admit of translation. LME. ▸**c** *verb trans.* Expound the significance of (something not expressed in words); interpret, explain. Also, express in terms of something else, or by a different medium or mode of expression. L16. ▸**d** *verb trans.* BIOLOGY. Convert (the sequence of nucleotides in messenger RNA) to the amino-acid sequence of a protein or polypeptide during synthesis. M20.
3 Change in form, appearance, or substance; transform, alter; renovate or reform (an old garment etc.). Now *rare.* LME.
4 Transport by strength of feeling; enrapture, entrance. *arch.* M17.
5 *verb intrans. & trans.* PHYSICS etc. (Cause to) undergo translational motion. M20.
6 *verb intrans.* Foll. by *into*: result in, be converted into, manifest itself as. L20.

📖 **1** G. BURNET First bishop of Worcester, and soon after . . translated to Winchester. **b** D. CECIL Her mother, now translated into a better world. **2a** T. GUNN He was translating books from French into English. **b** M. C. SMITH Almost no one in the West reads Mandelstam. He's too Russian. He doesn't translate. **c** G. GREENE Try to translate Dostoievsky's novels into film terms. **6** *Oxford Today* Academic research didn't readily translate into practical industrial use.

■ **translataˈbility** *noun* ability to be translated M19. **translatable** *adjective* (earlier in UNTRANSLATABLE) M18. **translaˈtese** *noun* = TRANSLATIONESE M20.

translation /transˈleɪʃ(ə)n, trɑːns-, -nz-/ *noun.* ME.
[Old & mod. French, or directly from Latin *translatio(n-)*, from *translat-* pa. ppl stem of *transferre* TRANSFER *verb*: see -ATION.]
1 Removal or conveyance from one person, place, time, or condition to another; transfer, transferral; *spec.* the removal of a bishop from one see to another; *Scot.* the removal of a minister from one pastoral charge to another. Also, the removal of the remains of a famous person, esp. a saint, to another place. ME. ▸**b** Removal from earth to heaven, orig. esp. without death. LME. ▸**c** MEDICINE. Transference of a disease from one person or part of the body to another. Now *rare* or *obsolete.* M17. ▸**d** PHYSICS etc. Movement of a body or form of energy from one point of space to another, esp. by direct linear motion without (or considered apart from) rotation. E18.
2 The action or process of expressing the sense of a word, passage, etc., in a different language. Also, the product of this; a version in a different language. ME. ▸**b** The expression or rendering of something in another medium, form, or mode of expression. Also, the result of this. L16. ▸**c** BIOLOGY. The process by which genetic information represented by the sequence of nucleotides in messenger RNA gives rise to a definite sequence of amino acids during the synthesis of a protein or polypeptide. M20.
3 Transformation, alteration, change; changing or adapting to another use; renovation. Now *rare.* LME.
4 LAW. A transfer of property; *spec.* alteration of a bequest by transferring the legacy to another person. LME.
†**5** RHETORIC. Transference of meaning; metaphor. M16–M17.
6 TELEGRAPHY. The automatic retransmission of a message by means of a relay. M19.

📖 **1d** *Nature* In a sea which covers tidal flats the tidal currents cause . . a periodical translation of water masses. **2** W. GOLDING Perfect translation from one language into another is impossible. **b** W. S. HATCHER Semantic notions . . rendered syntactically by means of *translations* from one theory into another.

Comb.: **translation loan**, **translation loanword** = ***loan-translation*** s.v. LOAN *noun*[1]; **translation table** COMPUTING a table of stored information used in translating one code into another; **translation wave** an ocean wave with a propelling or forward impulse.

translational /trans'leɪʃ(ə)n(ə)l, trɑːns-, -nz-/ *adjective.* E19.
[from prec. + -AL[1].]
1 Pertaining to or consisting in translation from one language into another. E19.
2 PHYSICS etc. Consisting in or pertaining to linear or onward motion, as distinct from rotation, vibration, oscillation, etc. M19.
▪ **translationally** *adverb* as regards or by means of translation E20.

translationese /trans,leɪʃə'niːz, trɑːns-, -nz-/ *noun.* M20.
[from TRANSLATION + -ESE.]
A style of language supposed to be characteristic of (esp. bad) translations; unidiomatic language in a translation.

translative /trans'leɪtɪv, 'translətɪv, trɑːns-, -nz-/ *adjective.* L16.
[medieval Latin *translativus* pertaining to transference of meaning, from Latin *translat-*: see TRANSLATION, -IVE.]
†**1** Involving transference of meaning; metaphorical. Only in L16.
2 Involving transference from one place to another; PHYSICS (of motion) translational. Now *rare.* L17.
3 Serving to translate; relating to translation, translational. M18.
4 LAW. Expressing or constituting a transfer of property. L19.
5 GRAMMAR. In some languages, of or designating a case expressing becoming or passing into a state. L19.

translator /trans'leɪtə, trɑːns-, -nz-/ *noun.* ME.
[In sense 1 orig. from Old French *translator, -our* (mod. *-eur*) or late Latin *translator*, from Latin *translat-*; later directly from TRANSLATE *verb*: see -OR.]
1 A person who translates from one language into another; the author of a translation. ME. ▸**b** A person who transfers something from one medium to another, as a painting by engraving, etc. M19. ▸**c** COMPUTING. A program that translates from one (esp. programming) language into another. M20.
†**2** A person who transfers or transports something. M16–M17.
3 A person who transforms, changes, or alters something; *spec.* a cobbler who renovates old shoes. Now *rare.* L16. ▸**b** A transducer. *rare.* L19.
4 a TELEGRAPHY. An automatic repeater. M19. ▸**b** A relay set or station which receives television signals and retransmits them without demodulating them. M20.
▪ **translatorese** *noun* = TRANSLATIONESE E20. **translatorship** *noun* the position or function of a translator L16. **translatress** *noun* a female translator M17. **translatrix** *noun* = TRANSLATRESS L19.

translatory /trans'leɪt(ə)ri, 'translət(ə)ri, trɑːns-, -nz-/ *adjective.* E18.
[from Latin *translat-* (see TRANSLATION) + -ORY[2].]
†**1** Characterized by transferring something from one person to another. *rare.* Only in E18.
2 = TRANSLATIONAL 2. M19.

transliterate /trans'lɪtəreɪt, trɑːns-, -nz-/ *verb trans.* M19.
[from TRANS- + Latin *litera* letter + -ATE[3].]
Replace (letters or characters of one language) by those of another used to represent the same sounds; write (a word etc.) in the closest corresponding characters of another alphabet or language.
▪ **transliteˈration** *noun* the action or process of transliterating; the rendering of the letters or characters of one alphabet in those of another; the result of this: M19. **transliterator** *noun* a person who transliterates something M19.

translocate /'transləʊkeɪt, trɑːns-, -nz-/ *verb.* E19.
[from TRANS- + LOCATE, prob. partly as back-form. from next.]
1 *verb trans.* Move from one place to another; relocate; rearrange; *esp.* transfer (wild animals) to another part of their (former) range. E19.
2 *verb trans.* PHYSIOLOGY & BIOCHEMISTRY. Subject (a substance) to translocation. Usu. in *pass.* E20.
3 *verb trans.* GENETICS. Move (a portion of a chromosome) *to* a new position on the same or a different chromosome. M20.
4 *verb intrans.* Move, change location. L20.
▪ **translocatable** *adjective* (GENETICS) able to be translocated L20.

translocation /translə'keɪʃ(ə)n, trɑːns-, -nz-/ *noun.* E17.
[from TRANS- + LOCATION, orig. perh. after *translation.*]
1 Removal from one place to another; displacement; *esp.* relocation of wild animal populations. E17.
2 PHYSIOLOGY & BIOCHEMISTRY. Transport of dissolved substances within an organism, esp. in the phloem of a plant. Also, diffusion of a substance across a cell membrane, assisted by a transport process. L19.
3 GENETICS. Removal of a section of a chromosome and its insertion into a new position on the same or a different chromosome; an instance of this; a portion of a chromosome that is so moved. E20.

📖 **1** *National Geographic* The translocation of three troops [of baboons] . . to . . sparsely inhabited country.

▪ **'translocase** *noun* [-ASE] BIOCHEMISTRY an enzyme which catalyses translocation of a substance across a membrane M20. **translocational** *adjective* M20.

translucence /trans'luːs(ə)ns, trɑːns-, -nz-/ *noun.* LME.
[from Latin *translucent-* pres. ppl stem of *translucere* shine through formed as TRANS- + *lucere* shine: see -ENCE.]
1 (Partial) transparency; translucent quality. LME.
2 The action of shining through something. E19.

translucency /trans'luːs(ə)nsi, trɑːns-, -nz-/ *noun.* L16.
[formed as prec.: see -ENCY.]
= TRANSLUCENCE 1.

translucent /trans'luːs(ə)nt, trɑːns-, -nz-/ *adjective.* L16.
[from (the same root as) TRANSLUCENCE: see -ENT.]
†**1** That shines through something; brightly shining. Also, brightly lit. L16–L18.
2 a Through which light passes; transparent. Now *rare* or *obsolete.* E17. ▸**b** Allowing light (or X-rays etc.) to pass through diffusely; semi-transparent. Also *loosely*, emitting or reflecting a diffuse light. L18.

📖 **2a** J. RABAN The water is . . as clear as a block of translucent quartz. I. MCEWAN The skin was so pale and fine it was almost translucent. **b** *Independent* Bathed in autumn beauty, with translucent green fields.

▪ **translucently** *adverb* M19.

translucid /trans'luːsɪd, trɑːns-, -nz-, -'ljuː-/ *adjective.* E17.
[Latin *translucidus*, formed as TRANS- + *lucidus* LUCID.]
= TRANSLUCENT 2.
▪ **transluˈcidity** *noun* translucent quality L17.

transmarine /tranzmə'riːn, trɑːnz-, -ns-/ *adjective & noun.* L16.
[Latin *transmarinus*, formed as TRANS- + *marinus*: see MARINE *adjective.*]
▸ **A** *adjective.* **1** That is beyond the sea; situated or originating on the other side of the sea. L16.
2 Crossing or extending across the sea. M19.
▸†**B** *noun.* A person born or living beyond the sea. L16–M17.

transmew /tranz'mjuː, trɑːnz-, -ns-/ *verb trans. & intrans.* Now *arch. & dial.* Also †**-mue**. LME.
[Old & mod. French *transmuer* from Latin *transmutare* TRANSMUTE.]
= TRANSMUTE 1, 2.

transmigrant /tranz'mʌɪgr(ə)nt, trɑːnz-, -ns-/ *noun & adjective.* E17.
[Latin *transmigrant-* pres. ppl stem of *transmigrare*: see next, -ANT[1].]
▸ **A** *noun.* †**1** = EMIGRANT. Only in E17.
2 Orig., a person passing through a country or place temporarily during the process of emigration from one country to another. Now also, a person who is subjected to resettlement in a different part of a country. L19.

📖 **2** *New Scientist* Indonesian transmigrants starving . . but too destitute to return to their original homelands.

▸ **B** *adjective.* That transmigrates. *rare.* M17.

transmigrate /tranzmʌɪ'greɪt, trɑːnz-, -ns-/ *verb.* LME.
[Latin *transmigrat-* pa. ppl stem of *transmigrare*, formed as TRANS- + *migrare* MIGRATE.]
1 *verb trans.* In *pass.* Be transferred, be transported. Now only as in sense 3. LME.
2 *verb intrans.* Move or pass from one place to another; *esp.* (of a person, a tribe, etc.) move from one place of abode to another, migrate; be subject to transmigration. E17.
3 *verb intrans. spec.* Of the soul: pass at or after death into another body (human or other). E17.
▪ **transmigrator** *noun* (*rare*) a person who or thing which transmigrates M18.

transmigration /tranzmʌɪ'greɪʃ(ə)n, trɑːnz-, -ns-/ *noun.* ME.
[Late Latin (Vulgate) *transmigratio(n-)*, formed as prec.: see -ATION.]
†**1** The captivity of the Jews in Babylon. Also, those who underwent it. ME–E17.
2 Passage or removal from one place to another, esp. from one country to another. Also, the action or practice of transmigrating or causing people to transmigrate to different parts of a country; resettlement. LME.
†**3** Transition from one state or condition to another; *esp.* passage from this life by death. Also *loosely*, transformation, transmutation. L16–L17.
4 *spec.* Passage of the soul at or after death into another body; metempsychosis. L16.
5 MEDICINE. = DIAPEDESIS. *rare.* L19.
▪ **transmigrationism** *noun* the theory or doctrine of transmigration of souls L19. **transmigrationist** *noun & adjective* (*a*) *noun* an exponent or adherent of transmigrationism; (*b*) *adjective* of or pertaining to transmigrationism or transmigrationists: L19. **transˈmigrative** *adjective* of, pertaining to, or characterized by transmigration E18. **transˈmigratively** *adverb* by way of transmigration (of the soul) E19. **transˈmigratory** *adjective* of or pertaining to transmigration E19.

transmiss /'tranzmɪs, 'trɑːnz-, -ns-, -'mɪs/ *noun. obsolete* exc. *Hist.* L17.
[from Latin *transmissus* pa. pple of *transmittere*: see TRANSMIT *verb.*]
A copy of an Irish Bill returned to the Irish parliament with the king's approval from the 16th to the 19th cent.

transmissibility /tranz,mɪsɪ'bɪlɪti, trɑːnz-, -ns-/ *noun.* E19.
[from next: see -BILITY.]
The quality or degree of being transmissible. Also occas., transmissivity.

transmissible /tranz'mɪsɪb(ə)l, trɑːnz-, -ns-/ *adjective.* M17.
[from TRANSMIT *verb* after *admit, admissible*, etc., perh. infl. by French *transmissible.*]
Able to be transmitted or transferred; *esp.* (of a gene, a trait, etc.) heritable, (of a disease) able to pass from one affected person to another, communicable, contagious.

transmission /tranz'mɪʃ(ə)n, trɑːnz-, -ns-/ *noun.* E17.
[Latin *transmissio(n-)* formed as TRANS- + *missio(n-)*: see MISSION *noun.*]
1 Conveyance or transfer from one person or place to another; the action or process of passing from one person, organism, generation, etc., to another, as by personal contact, stored information, genetic inheritance, etc. E17.
2 Conveyance or passage through a medium, as of light, heat, sound, etc. Also *spec.*, the sending out of electrical signals or electromagnetic waves; the broadcasting of radio or television programmes; an instance of this, a series of transmitted signals, a broadcast. E18.
3 MECHANICS. Transfer of motive force from one place to another; a device for effecting this; *spec.* (in full ***transmission-gear***) a mechanism for transmitting the power of an engine etc., esp. to the axle of a motor vehicle. E20.

📖 **1** DE QUINCEY One link in the transmission of the Homeric poems. *Independent* The most common mode of transmission was heterosexual intercourse. **2** C. G. BURGE The number of channels available for radio transmission is limited. *Financial Times* The poor quality of the connection makes most data transmission impossible.

Comb.: **transmission electron microscope** a form of electron microscope in which an image is derived from electrons which have passed through the specimen; *spec.* one in which the whole image is formed at once, not by scanning; ***transmission-gear***: see sense 3 above; **transmission line** a conductor or set of conductors designed to carry electricity (esp. on a large scale) or electromagnetic waves with minimum loss and distortion; **transmission loss** dissipation of electrical or acoustic power during its passage from one point to another.
▪ **transmissional** *adjective* M20.

transmissive /tranz'mɪsɪv, trɑːnz-, -ns-/ *adjective.* M17.
[from TRANSMIT *verb* after *permit, permissive*, etc.]
Of or pertaining to transmission; that transmits something. Also, that is or can be transmitted, transmissible.

transmissivity /tranzmɪ'sɪvɪti, trɑːnz-, -ns-/ *noun.* E20.
[from prec.: see -ITY.]
PHYSICS etc. The degree to which a medium allows something, esp. electromagnetic radiation, to pass through it.

transmissometer /tranzmɪ'sɒmɪtə, trɑːnz-, -ns-/ *noun.* M20.
[from TRANSMISS(ION + -OMETER.]
An instrument for measuring the degree to which light is transmitted through a medium without absorption.

transmit /'tranzmɪt, 'trɑːnz-, -ns-/ *noun.* L17.
[from the verb.]
1 An act of transmitting; an order of transmission. *rare.* L17.
2 A transmit button or switch. M20.

transmit /tranz'mɪt, trɑːnz-, -ns-/ *verb.* Infl. **-tt-**. LME.
[Latin *transmittere*, formed as TRANS- + *mittere* send.]
1 *verb trans.* Cause (a thing) to pass, go, or be conveyed to another person, place, or thing; send across an intervening space; convey, transfer. LME.
2 *verb trans.* Convey or communicate (usually something immaterial) *to* another or others; pass on, esp. by inheritance or heredity; hand down. E17.
3 a *verb trans.* SCIENCE. Cause (light, heat, sound, etc.) to pass through a medium; (of a medium) allow (light etc.) to pass through; conduct. Also, convey (force or movement) from one part of an object or mechanism to another. M17. ▸**b** *verb trans. & intrans.* Send out electric signals or electromagnetic waves corresponding to (an image, a programme, a message, etc.). L19.

📖 **1** C. R. MARKHAM They . . transmitted my letter to the Secretary of State. **2** H. READ Modern methods of transmitting information, especially the camera, television and the cinema. H. L. MENCKEN A criminal may not transmit his evil traits to offspring. *Japan Times* Leprosy . . is transmitted after prolonged and close physical contact. **3b** G. ORWELL The telescreen received and transmitted simultaneously.

Phrases & comb.: **on transmit** (of a radio transceiver) in the state of being able to transmit radio signals, with the transmitter switched on. **transmit button**, **transmit switch**: used to activate a radio transmitter.

transmittable /tranzˈmɪtəb(ə)l, trɑːnz-, -ns-/ *adjective. rare.* E17.
[from TRANSMIT *verb* + -ABLE.]
That may be transmitted; transmissible.

transmittal /tranzˈmɪt(ə)l, trɑːnz-, -ns-/ *noun.* E18.
[from TRANSMIT *verb* + -AL¹.]
The action of transmitting; transmission.
letter of transmittal *US* an official letter in which the recipient is informed that certain documents are transferred to his or her custody.

transmittance /tranzˈmɪt(ə)ns, trɑːnz-, -ns-/ *noun.* M19.
[formed as prec. + -ANCE.]
1 The action of transmitting; transmission. *rare* (only in Dicts.). M19.
2 PHYSICS. The ratio of the transmitted luminous flux to the incident luminous flux. E20.
■ **transmittancy** *noun* the ratio of the transmittance of a solution to that of a similar body of solvent E20.

transmitter /tranzˈmɪtə, trɑːnz-, -ns-/ *noun.* E18.
[from TRANSMIT *verb* + -ER¹.]
1 *gen.* A person who or thing which transmits something. E18.
2 *spec.* The part of a telegraphic or telephonic apparatus by means of which messages are transmitted; a transmitting instrument; *esp.* an apparatus for transmitting radio or television signals. M19.
3 PHYSIOLOGY. = NEUROTRANSMITTER. M20.
Comb.: **transmitter-receiver** = TRANSCEIVER.

transmogrify /tranzˈmɒɡrɪfʌɪ, trɑːnz-, -ns-/ *verb trans.* Chiefly *joc.* M17.
[Origin uncertain; perh. alt. of *transmigrate* after verbs in -FY.]
1 Alter or change (orig. *spec.* a person) in form or appearance; transform, esp. in a grotesque, strange, or surprising way. M17.
2 Astonish utterly, confound. *dial.* L19.
■ **transmogrifiˈcation** *noun* the action of transmogrifying someone or something, (a) transformation M17. **transmogrifier** *noun* L17.

transmontane /tranzˈmɒnteɪn, trɑːnz-, -mɒnˈteɪn, -ns-/ *adjective.* LME.
[Latin *transmontanus*: see TRAMONTANE.]
1 Living, originating, or situated beyond, or on the other side of, a range of mountains; tramontane. LME.
2 Across or over the mountains. L19.

†**transmove** *verb trans. rare* (Spenser). Only in L16.
[App. from TRANS- + MOVE *verb*, but used for *transmue*, TRANSMEW.]
Transmute.

†**transmue** *verb* var. of TRANSMEW.

transmutable /tranzˈmjuːtəb(ə)l, trɑːnz-, -ns-/ *adjective.* LME.
[medieval Latin *transmutabilis*, from Latin *transmutare* TRANSMUTE: see -ABLE.]
1 Able to be transmuted or changed into something else. LME.
†**2** Liable to change, changeable, mutable. LME–E16.
■ **transmutaˈbility** *noun* E17.

transmutation /tranzmjuːˈteɪʃ(ə)n, trɑːnz-, -ns-/ *noun.* LME.
[Old & mod. French, or directly from late Latin *transmutatio(n-)*, from Latin *transmutat-* pa. ppl stem of *transmutare* TRANSMUTE: see -ATION.]
1 Change of condition; alternation between conditions. Long *arch. rare.* LME.
2 Change of one thing into another; conversion into something different; alteration, transformation. Also, an instance of this. LME.
3 Orig. in ALCHEMY, the (supposed) conversion of one element or substance into another, esp. of a baser metal into gold or silver. Now also in PHYSICS, the (actual) change of one element or isotope into another, esp. by irradiation or bombardment (as opp. to spontaneous decay). LME.
4 LAW. Transfer, esp. of ownership. L15.
†**5 a** RHETORIC. Transferred use of a word; metonymy. *rare.* Only in M16. ▸**b** = TRANSMIGRATION 4. *rare.* Only in L16. ▸**c** HERALDRY. Counterchanging. *rare.* E17–E18.
6 BIOLOGY. Conversion or transformation of one species into another. (Now chiefly *Hist.*) E17.
7 MATH. Transformation. Formerly also, permutation. Now *rare* or *obsolete.* L17.
■ **transmutational** *adjective* of or pertaining to transmutation (esp. that of biological species) M19. **transmutationist** *noun* (now chiefly *Hist.*) an advocate or adherent of a theory of transmutation, esp. that of biological species M19.

transmutative /tranzˈmjuːtətɪv, trɑːnz-, -ns-/ *adjective.* E17.
[from medieval Latin *transmutativus*, from Latin *transmutat-*: see TRANSMUTATION, -IVE.]
Having the quality of transmuting; able to transmute (something else); characterized by transmutation.

transmute /tranzˈmjuːt, trɑːnz-, -ns-/ *verb.* LME.
[Latin *transmutare*, formed as TRANS- + *mutare* change.]
1 *verb trans.* Alter or change in nature, properties, appearance, or form; transform, convert, turn. Freq. with *fig.* allusion to sense 1b. LME. ▸**b** Orig. in ALCHEMY, change (a substance) into another substance, esp. a baser metal into gold or silver. Now also in PHYSICS, change (one element or isotope) *into* or *to* another, esp. by irradiation or bombardment; change (a subatomic particle) *into* another particle. E17.
2 *verb intrans.* Undergo transmutation; be transformed; change or turn *into* something else. L17.
†**3** *verb trans.* Remove from one place to another; transport. *rare.* L17–E19.

> 🕮 **1a** J. LONDON A great task to transmute feeling and sensation into speech. F. POHL The slim, smiling bride . . was now transmuted into a plump, faded woman. **b** E. J. KORMONDY Hydrogen is transmuted to helium with a . . release of considerable radiant energy. **2** *Nature* An up quark transmutes into a down.

■ **transmuted** *ppl adjective* (*a*) HERALDRY counterchanged; (*b*) changed in form or nature, altered, transformed: L15. **transmuter** *noun* E19.

†**transnomination** *noun.* M16–E18.
[Late Latin *transnominatio(n-)*, from Latin TRANS- + *nominatio(n-)* NOMINATION, translating Greek *metōnumia* METONYMY.]
= METONYMY.

transoceanic /ˌtransəʊʃɪˈanɪk, trɑː-, -ns-, -sɪ-/ *adjective.* E19.
[from TRANS- + OCEANIC.]
1 Existing or situated beyond the ocean. E19.
2 Crossing the ocean. M19.

transom /ˈtrans(ə)m/ *noun.* Also (earlier) †**traversayn.** LME.
[Old & mod. French *traversin*, formed as TRAVERSE *noun.*]
†**1** A type of bolster for a bed. LME–E16.
2 *gen.* A supporting or strengthening crossbar in any structure; a lintel. LME. ▸**b** A cross-beam in a ship's frame; *spec.* any of several transverse beams across the stern-post of a ship. LME. ▸†**c** The transverse bar in a cross. L16–M19. ▸**d** Any of the cross-timbers laid between railway sleepers. M19. ▸**e** A beam across a saw-pit to support a log. L19.
3 A horizontal bar of wood or stone across a mullioned window or between a door and fan-light. LME. ▸**b** = **transom window** below. *US.* M19.
4 The seat of a throne; a seat at the side of a ship's cabin or state-room. M19.
Comb.: **transom-knee** any of the timbers or irons attaching the transoms to the stern-timbers; **transom-stern** a ship's stern formed by or taking its shape from a transom; **transom-window** (*a*) a window divided by a transom; (*b*) a small window above a door lintel or above a larger window.
■ **transomed** *adjective* divided by or having a transom or transoms L16.

†**transon** *verb trans.* E16–E18.
[French †*transonner*, *tronçonner* var. of *tronçonner* cut up, carve, from *tronçon* TRUNCHEON *noun.*]
Carve (an eel).

transonic /tranˈsɒnɪk, trɑːn-/ *adjective.* M20.
[from TRANS- + SONIC, after *supersonic*, *ultrasonic*.]
Pertaining to, involving, or designating speeds close to that of sound; (of aircraft) able to fly at such speeds.

transpadane /ˈtranspədeɪn, ˈtrɑːns-, -nz-/ *adjective.* E17.
[Latin *transpadanus*, formed as TRANS- + *padanus* of the Po (*Padus*): see -ANE.]
Situated to the north of the River Po. Opp. CISPADANE.

transparence /transˈpar(ə)ns, trɑːns-, -nz-, -ˈpɛːr(ə)ns/ *noun.* L16.
[formed as next: see -ENCE.]
1 Transparency, translucence. L16.
†**2** *transf.* A transparent object. *rare.* M17–L18.

> 🕮 **1** J. UPDIKE A kind of altar of Plexiglas demonstrated with its transparence that no body existed beneath the head.

transparency /tranˈspar(ə)nsi, trɑː-, -ˈspɛː-/ *noun.* L16.
[medieval Latin *transparentia*, from *transparent-*: see next, -ENCY.]
1 A transparent object or medium. Now *rare* in *gen.* sense. L16. ▸**b** A picture, inscription, etc., on translucent material, made visible by light from behind. L18. ▸**c** A positive transparent image on glass, photographic film, etc., to be viewed using a light-transmitting projector. M19.
2 The quality or condition of being transparent; *spec.* (ECONOMICS) ease of assessment of information etc. L16. ▸**b** The state or quality of transmitting sound waves without distortion. L20.
†**3** HERALDRY. An outline figure of a charge of a darker shade than that of the field. E17–E18.
4 [translating German *Durchlaucht*.] A jocular honorific title or form of address. *rare.* M19.

> 🕮 **1b** *Islander (Victoria, BC)* The whole town . . a blaze of light, with a plenitude of transparencies. **c** *Bon Appetit* Hand-colored photo transparencies of 1930's bathing beauties. *attrib.*: *Practical Photography* ORWO is a high quality transparency film (for colour slides). **2** D. ADAMS The . . dome . . fades into transparency, revealing a dark and sullen sky. *Times* The Deutsche Aktienindex . . will be calculated every minute during the . . session, to increase market transparency.

transparent /tranˈspar(ə)nt, trɑː-, -ˈspɛː-/ *adjective.* LME.
[Old & mod. French from medieval Latin *transparent-* pres. ppl stem of *transparere* shine through, from Latin TRANS- + *parere* come into view: see -ENT.]
1 Having the property of transmitting light, so as to make objects lying beyond clearly visible; pellucid; diaphanous. Formerly also, visible through something. LME. ▸†**b** Of light: shining through; penetrating. *rare* (Shakes.). Only in L16. ▸**c** Allowing the passage of radiant heat or any other specified kind of radiation; allowing the passage of sound waves without distortion. L19. ▸**d** COMPUTING. Of a program or process: not revealing its presence to the general user. L20.
2 *fig.* Easily seen through or understood; easily discerned; evident, obvious; (of a person, statement, etc.) frank, open, ingenuous. L16. ▸**b** PHONOLOGY. Of a rule: that can be extrapolated from every occurrence of the phenomenon; to which there are no exceptions. Opp. OPAQUE *adjective* 3b. L20.
3 Of sound: clear, not blurred; without tonal distortion. M20.

> 🕮 **1** M. GEE A shocking pink transparent shorty nighty. L. SPALDING We can see their hearts beating through their thin, transparent skin. **b** SHAKES. *2 Hen. VI* Like to the glorious sun's transparent beams. **2** J. FRAME Someone spoke of a place . . with such transparent love. A. BROOKNER I was straightforward, transparent. **3** *Keyboard Player* You hear solid brass with transparent mid-range and treble.

■ **transparently** *adverb* E17. **transparentness** *noun* (*rare*) E18.

transphasor /transˈfeɪzə, trɑːns-, -nz-/ *noun.* L20.
[from TRANS(IST)OR with insertion of PHASE *noun.*]
ELECTRONICS. A semiconductor device in which one light beam can be modulated by another.

transpicuous /tranˈspɪkjʊəs, trɑːn-/ *adjective.* M17.
[mod. Latin *transpicuus*, from Latin *transpicere* look through, formed as TRANS- + *specere* look: see -OUS.]
1 That can be seen through; transparent. M17.
2 *fig.* Easily understood, lucid. L19.
■ **transpicuously** *adverb* M19.

transpierce /transˈpɪəs, trɑːns-, -nz-/ *verb trans.* L16.
[from TRANS- + PIERCE *verb*, after Old & mod. French *transpercer*.]
1 Pierce through from side to side. Chiefly *literary.* L16.
2 Pass or extend through; penetrate. *rare.* E17.

transpiration /transpəˈreɪʃ(ə)n, trɑːns-/ *noun.* LME.
[French, formed as TRANSPIRE: see -ATION.]
1 The action or process of transpiring through the skin or surface of the body; insensible perspiration. Also, the matter transpired. LME.
2 BOTANY. The loss of moisture by evaporation from the surface of a plant, esp. from the stomata of the leaves. M16.
3 The action or fact of becoming indirectly known. *rare.* E19.
4 PHYSICS. The passage of a gas or liquid through a capillary tube or porous substance. Now *rare.* M19.
Comb.: **transpiration stream** the flow of water through a plant, from the roots to the leaves, via the xylem vessels.

†**transpirative** *adjective. rare.* L16–M18.
[from medieval Latin *transpirat-* pa. ppl stem of *transpirare* TRANSPIRE + -IVE.]
Transpiring; tending to transpire.

transpire /tranˈspʌɪə, trɑːn-/ *verb.* LME.
[French *transpirer* or medieval Latin *transpirare*, from Latin TRANS- + *spirare* breathe.]
1 *verb trans.* **a** Emit or cause (a gas or liquid) to pass as vapour through the walls or surface of a body; *esp.* (of an animal) give off or discharge (waste matter etc.) through the skin; (of a plant) give off (watery vapour) through the leaf stomata etc. Also, exhale (an odour); breathe forth (vapour or fire). LME. ▸**b** PHYSICS. Cause (a gas or liquid) to pass through the pores or walls of a vessel. Now *rare.* M19.
2 *verb intrans.* **a** Of a body: emit vapour or perfume; give out an exhalation. Of an animal body: give off moisture through the skin; perspire. Now *rare* or *obsolete.* M17. ▸**b** Of a plant: give off watery vapour through the stomata of the leaves etc. L19.
3 *verb intrans.* Of a volatile substance, water, etc.: pass out as vapour through pores; evaporate. M17.

4 *verb intrans. fig.* Become known indirectly or unintentionally; leak out. Also, prove to be the case, turn out. **M18.** ▸**b** Occur, happen. **L18.**

> 📖 **4** N. FARAH It transpired . . that Soyaan had been to Beydan's. F. KING I wondered—unworthily, as it later transpired—if he would make a compensating adjustment to the bill. **b** S. TROTT I began to think . . about . . what had transpired between us.

▪ **transpirable** *adjective* **L16.**

transplace /trans'pleɪs, trɑːns-, -nz-/ *verb trans.* Now *rare.* **E17.**
[from TRANS- + PLACE *verb.*]
Transpose, interchange; displace.

transplant /*as verb* trans'plɑːnt, trɑːns-, -nz-; *as noun* 'tra-, 'trɑː-/ *verb & noun.* **LME.**
[Late Latin *transplantare*, formed as TRANS- + *plantare* PLANT *verb.*]
▶ **A** *verb.* **1** *verb trans.* Remove and reposition (a plant). **LME.**
2 *verb trans.* Convey or remove elsewhere; *esp.* transport to another country or place of residence. Freq. foll. by *into, to.* **M16.**
†**3** *verb intrans.* Settle in another place of residence; emigrate. **E–M17.**
4 *verb trans.* MEDICINE. Transfer (an organ or portion of tissue) from one part of the body, or from one person or animal, to another. **L18.**
5 *verb intrans.* Admit of being transplanted. **L18.**

> 📖 **1** *Practical Gardening* Sowing in a pot of seed compost . . and then transplanting the seedlings.

▶ **B** *noun.* **1** A transplanted person or thing; *spec.* (**a**) a seedling transplanted one or more times; (**b**) MEDICINE an organ, tissue, etc., which has been surgically transplanted. **M18.** ▸**b** A person not native to his or her place of permanent residence. *US.* **M20.**
2 MEDICINE. (An instance of) a surgical operation in which an organ, tissue, etc., is transplanted. **M20.**

> 📖 **1** *Tree News* The Forestry Commission confirmed that smaller transplants . . are easier to establish. F. PARRISH [His] hair was . . a wig, or at least a transplant. **b** *Los Angeles Times* One of the hottest places for trendy California transplants.

▪ **transplanta'bility** *noun* ability to be transplanted **E19.** **transplantable** *adjective* able to be transplanted **M17.** **transplanter** *noun* (**a**) a person who transplants plants; (**b**) a tool used for transplanting plants; (**c**) a surgeon carrying out transplant operations: **E17.**

transplantation /transplɑːn'teɪʃ(ə)n, trɑːns-, -plant-, -nz-/ *noun.* **E17.**
[from prec. + -ATION.]
1 *gen.* The action or an act of transplanting a person or thing. **E17.** ▸**b** = TRANSPLANT *noun* 2. **E19.**
2 The supposed curing of a disease by causing it to pass to another person etc. *obsolete exc. Hist.* **M17.**
3 A transplanted person or thing. **M17.**

transplendent /tran'splɛnd(ə)nt, trɑːn-/ *adjective. rare.* **M16.**
[from TRANS- + SPLENDENT. Cf. RESPLENDENT.]
Resplendent in the highest degree.
▪ **transplendency** *noun* (*rare*) **M17.**

transponder /tran'spɒndə, trɑːn-, -nz-/ *noun.* **M20.**
[from TRANS(MIT *verb* + RES)POND *verb* + -ER[1].]
1 RADIO & RADAR. A device which automatically transmits a pulse or signal on receiving one from an interrogator. **M20.**
2 TELECOMMUNICATIONS. A device on a satellite which receives communication or broadcast signals and transmits them back to earth; a device on an aircraft which receives a signal and responds by transmitting certain information. **M20.**

transpontine /trans'pɒntʌɪn, trɑːns-, -nz-/ *adjective.* **M19.**
[from TRANS- + (in sense 1) Latin *pont-*, *pons* bridge, (in sense 2) Latin *pontus* sea: see -INE[1].]
1 That is across or over a bridge or bridges; *spec.* in London, south of the River Thames (opp. *cispontine*). **M19.**
2 On or from the other side of the ocean; *spec.* North American. **L19.**

transport /'transpɔːt, 'trɑːns-/ *noun.* **LME.**
[from the verb, or from Old & mod. French (cf. medieval Latin *transportus* transfer).]
1 †**a** LAW. Transfer or conveyance of property. **LME–L17.** ▸**b** *gen.* The carrying or conveyance of a person or thing from one place to another. **E17.**
2 The state of being affected by strong (now esp. pleasurable) emotion; exaltation, rapture, ecstasy; *sing.* & in *pl.*, an instance of this. **M17.**
3 A system or means of transportation or conveyance of people, goods, etc.; *spec.* (MILITARY) a ship, aircraft, etc., used to carry soldiers or supplies (also *transport-ship, transport-plane*, etc.). **L17.**
4 A transported convict; a person under sentence of transportation. *obsolete exc. Hist.* **M18.**

> 📖 **1b** INA TAYLOR Canals dug . . to facilitate the transport of coal. *Psychology Today* Anxiety triggers the transport of fat out of storage and into the blood. **2** P. MATTHIESSEN That crazy joy, that transport. P. L. FERMOR I let in more hot water and wallowed in transports of luxury. **3** S. RADLEY I haven't any transport and it's all of seventeen miles. *National Trust Magazine* Mountain bikes have proved to be the latest . . method of 'green' transport. ***PUBLIC transport.***

Comb.: **transport café** a roadside café used esp. by lorry-drivers; **Transport House** [former headquarters of the Labour Party] the British Labour Party leadership; **transport number** PHYSICAL CHEMISTRY the proportion of a current flowing through a particular electrolytic solution which can be attributed to the movement of any given ion species; ***transport-plane***: see sense 3 above; **transport property** PHYSICS a property of a gas or liquid which determines its characteristics regarding the movement of matter and energy, as viscosity, thermal conductivity, and diffusion (usu. in *pl.*); ***transport-ship***: see sense 3 above.

transport /tran'spɔːt, trɑːn-/ *verb.* **LME.**
[Old & mod. French *transporter* or Latin *transportare*, formed as TRANS- + *portare* carry.]
1 *verb trans.* Move or carry from one place or person to another; convey across; *transf.* cause (a person) to imagine himself or herself in a different place or time. Formerly also *spec.* (LAW), transfer (property). **LME.** ▸†**b** *verb intrans.* Change one's place of residence; emigrate. **M16–L17.** ▸**c** *verb trans.* Convey (a convict) to a penal colony; convey into slavery in another country etc.; deport. **M17.**
2 *verb trans. fig.* Affect strongly with an emotion; cause exaltation or ecstasy in, enrapture. **E16.**
3 *verb trans. Scot.* ▸**a** Move (a minister) to another pastoral charge. **M17.** ▸**b** ECCLESIASTICAL LAW. Remove (a church) to another site within a parish. **E18.**

> 📖 **1** D. HOGAN She'd been transported there by a slow bus. **2** A. BEATTIE I was reluctant to let language transport me.

▪ †**transportage** *noun* transportation, conveyance **M16–M17.** **transportal** *noun* (*rare*) = TRANSPORTATION 1 **M19.** **transportance** *noun* (long *rare*) transportation, conveyance **E17.** **tran'sportative** *adjective* (*rare*) (**a**) transportable; (**b**) transporting: **M17.** **transpor'tee** *noun* (*obsolete* exc. *Hist.*) a transported convict **L19.** **transportive** *adjective* (*rare*) that transports, transporting **E17.**

transportable /tran'spɔːtəb(ə)l, trɑːn-/ *adjective & noun.* **L16.**
[from TRANSPORT *verb* + -ABLE.]
▶ **A** *adjective.* **1** Able to be transported; *spec.* (**a**) COMPUTING. = PORTABLE *adjective* 1e; (**b**) (of a television set, computer, etc.) heavier than a portable, movable but not by hand. **L16.**
2 Of an offence: punishable by transportation. *obsolete exc. Hist.* **M18.**
▶ **B** *noun.* A transportable television set, computer, etc. **M20.**
▪ **transporta'bility** *noun* **M17.** **transportableness** *noun* **E18.**

transportation /transpɔː'teɪʃ(ə)n, trɑːns-/ *noun.* **M16.**
[from TRANSPORT *verb* + -ATION.]
1 The action or process of transporting something; conveyance of people, goods, etc., from one place to another; *spec.* (*Hist.*) the action or system of transporting convicts to a penal colony. **M16.** ▸**b** GEOLOGY. The movement of particulate or dissolved material by water, ice, wind, etc. **M19.**
†**2** = TRANSPORT *noun* 2. Only in **17.**
3 = TRANSPORT *noun* 3. *N. Amer.* **M19.** ▸**b** A ticket or pass for travelling by public transport. *US.* **E20.**

> 📖 **1** L. STRACHEY This sentence . . was commuted for one of transportation for life. *Sun (Baltimore)* Roads will face competition from other modes of transportation. **3** S. BELLOW I hope you don't take public transportation to work.

▪ **transportational** *adjective* of or pertaining to transportation **L19.** **transportationist** *noun* (*Hist.*) an advocate of the transportation of convicts **M19.**

transporter /tran'spɔːtə, trɑːn-/ *noun.* **M16.**
[from TRANSPORT *verb* + -ER[1].]
A person or thing which transports people, goods, etc.; now *esp.* a vehicle used to transport other vehicles, large pieces of machinery, etc., by road.
Comb.: **transporter-bridge** a bridge carrying vehicles etc. across water on a moving platform or carriage suspended from supports.

transposable /trans'pəʊzəb(ə)l, trɑːns-, -nz-/ *adjective.* **M19.**
[from TRANSPOSE *verb* + -ABLE.]
Able to be transposed; interchangeable.
▪ **transposa'bility** *noun* **E20.**

transposase /'transpəzeɪz, trɑːns-, -nz-/ *noun.* **L20.**
[from TRANSPOS(ITION + -ASE.]
BIOCHEMISTRY & GENETICS. An enzyme which catalyses chromosomal transposition.

transpose /trans'pəʊz, trɑːns-, -nz-/ *verb & noun.* **LME.**
[Old & mod. French *transposer*, formed as TRANS- + POSE *verb*[1].]
▶ **A** *verb.* †**1** *verb trans.* Transform, transmute, convert. Freq. foll. by *to.* **LME–E17.**
†**2** *verb trans.* Change in style or expression; translate; adapt. Usu. foll. by *into.* **LME–M19.**
3 *verb trans.* Alter the order of (items) or the position of (a thing) in a series; cause (two or more things) to change places; *esp.* alter the order of letters in a word or of words in a sentence. **LME.** ▸**b** MATH. Transfer (a quantity) from one side of an equation to the other, with change of sign. **E19.**
†**4** *verb trans.* Change the application or use of. Also, pervert, misapply. **E16–M17.**
5 *verb trans.* Transfer to a different place or time. Usu. foll. by *into, to.* **E16.**
6 *verb trans. & intrans.* MUSIC. Write or perform (a piece of music) in a different key from the original. Also foll. by *down, up.* **E17.**

> 📖 **3** P. BROOK In many plays there are scenes . . that can easily be . . transposed. *Which Computer?* Commands can transpose rows and columns. **5** P. ZWEIG The nineteenth century transposed the religious quest for salvation into . . secular idioms. **6** *Early Music* Lutenists with G lutes will . . use this edition without making . . singers transpose. *Classic CD* Viola music is not just violin music transposed down a fifth. **transposing instrument** MUSIC (**a**) a piano etc. with a mechanical transposing device; (**b**) an instrument producing notes different in pitch from those written.

▶ **B** *noun.* †**1** Transposition. *rare.* **L16–E17.**
2 MATH. A matrix obtained from a given matrix by interchanging each row and the corresponding column. **M20.**
▪ **transposal** *noun* (*rare*) transposition **L17.** **transposer** *noun* **L19.**

transposition /transpə'zɪʃ(ə)n, trɑːns-, -nz-/ *noun.* **M16.**
[French, or late Latin *transpositio(n-)*, from Latin TRANS- + *positio(n-)* POSITION *noun.*]
1 *gen.* The action or an act of transposing; the condition of being transposed. **M16.**
2 Alteration of order or interchange of position (of letters or words) in a series; metathesis; the result of this, a transposed word or sentence. **L16.** ▸**b** MATH. The interchange of each row of a matrix with the corresponding column. **M19.**
3 MUSIC. The writing or performance of a piece in a different key from the original; a transposed piece. **E17.** ▸†**b** Inversion of parts in counterpoint. **E17–L19.**
4 MATH. Transfer of a quantity from one side of an equation to the other. **M17.**
5 ANATOMY. = HETEROTAXY 1. **M19.**
6 ELECTRICITY. An alteration of the relative positions of power lines or telephone lines at intervals along their length, in order to minimize effects of mutual inductance and capacitance. **E20.**
7 GENETICS. The transfer of a chromosomal segment to a new position on the same or another chromosome. **E20.**
Comb.: **transposition cipher**: in which the letters of the plain text are rearranged in a different sequence as an anagram.

transpositive /trans'pɒzɪtɪv, trɑːns-, -nz-/ *adjective.* **L18.**
[from TRANSPOSE *verb* after *positive* etc.]
Characterized by or given to transposition.
▪ **transpositively** *adverb* **M20.**

transposon /trans'pəʊzɒn, trɑːns-, -nz-/ *noun.* **L20.**
[from TRANSPOS(ITION + -ON.]
GENETICS. A chromosomal segment that can undergo transposition; *spec.* a segment of bacterial DNA that can be translocated *en bloc* between chromosomal, phage, and plasmid DNA in the absence of a complementary sequence in the host DNA.

transputer /trans'pjuːtə, trɑːns-, -nz-/ *noun.* **L20.**
[from TRANS(ISTOR + COM)PUTER.]
ELECTRONICS. A chip that incorporates all the functions of a microprocessor, including memory.

transreceiver /tranzrɪ'siːvə, trɑːnz-, -ns-/ *noun.* **M20.**
[from TRANS(MITTER + RECEIVER.]
= TRANSCEIVER.

transrhenane /tranz'riːneɪn, trɑːnz-, -ns-/ *adjective.* **E18.**
[Latin *transrhenanus*, formed as TRANS- + *Rhenanus* of the river Rhine: see -ANE.]
Situated on, or originating from, the far side of the river Rhine; *spec.* German (as opp. to Roman or French).

transsexual /trans'sɛksjʊəl, -trɑːns-, -nz-, -ʃʊəl/ *adjective & noun.* In senses A.1 and B. also **transexual.** **M20.**
[from TRANS- + SEXUAL.]
▶ **A** *adjective.* **1** Having the physical characteristics of one sex but a strong and persistent desire to belong to the other; of or pertaining to transsexualism. **M20.**
2 Of or pertaining to both sexes; intersexual. **L20.**
▶ **B** *noun.* A transsexual person; a person whose sex has been changed by surgery. **M20.**
▪ **transsexualism** *noun* the state or condition of being transsexual **M20.** **transsexualist** *noun & adjective* (**a**) *noun* = TRANSSEXUAL *noun*; (**b**) *adjective* = TRANSSEXUAL *adjective* 1: **M20.** **transsexu'ality** *noun* transsexualism; *loosely* bisexuality: **M20.**

transship /trans'ʃɪp, trɑːns-, -nz-/ *verb.* Also **tranship** /tran'ʃɪp, trɑːn-/. Infl. **-pp-.** **L18.**
[from TRANS- + SHIP *verb.*]
1 *verb trans. & intrans.* Transfer (cargo etc.) from one ship or form of transport to another. **L18.**

For other words beginning with *trans-* see the entry for **trans-**

2 *verb intrans.* Of a passenger: change from one ship or form of transport to another. L19.
▪ **transshipment** *noun* the action or process of transshipping L18.

transubstantial /transəbˈstanʃ(ə)l, trɑːn-/ *adjective.* M16.
[medieval Latin *transubstantialis*, formed as TRANS- + Christian Latin *substantialis* SUBSTANTIAL.]
1 Changing or changeable from one substance into another. M16.
2 Made of something beyond substance; non-material, incorporeal. M16.
▪ **transubstantialism** *noun* (THEOLOGY) the theory or doctrine of transubstantiation M19. **transubstantialist** *noun* (THEOLOGY) a believer in transubstantiation M19. **transubstantialize** *verb* †(*a*) *verb trans.* transubstantiate, transform; (*b*) *verb intrans.* (THEOLOGY) profess the doctrine of transubstantiation: M17. **transubstantially** *adverb* L16.

transubstantiate /transəbˈstanʃɪeɪt, trɑːn-/ *verb.* Pa. pple & ppl adjective **-iated**, (*arch.*) **-iate**. LME.
[medieval Latin *transubstantiat-* pa. ppl stem of *transubstantiare*, formed as TRANS- + Latin *substantia* SUBSTANCE.]
1 *verb trans.* Change the substance of; transform, transmute; *spec.* (THEOLOGY) convert (the Eucharistic elements) wholly into the blood and body of Christ (see TRANSUBSTANTIATION). Freq. foll. by *into*. LME.
2 *verb intrans.* Cause a thing to change in substance; effect transubstantiation. L16.
3 *verb intrans.* Become transubstantiated. *rare.* M19.
▪ **transubstantiative** *adjective* (*rare*) of or pertaining to transubstantiation E19. †**transubstantiator** *noun* = TRANSUBSTANTIALIST M16–L17.

transubstantiation /ˌtransəbstanʃɪˈeɪʃ(ə)n, ˌtrɑːn-, -sɪˈeɪʃ(ə)n/ *noun.* LME.
[medieval Latin *tran(s)substantiatio(n-)*, formed as prec.: see -ION.]
1 The changing of one substance into another. LME.
2 THEOLOGY. The conversion of the whole substance of the Eucharistic elements into the body and blood of Christ, only the appearance of bread and wine remaining. Cf. CONSUBSTANTIATION. M16.
▪ **transubstantiationist** *noun* (THEOLOGY) = TRANSUBSTANTIALIST M19.

transudation /transjuːˈdeɪʃ(ə)n, trɑːns-/ *noun.* E17.
[from French *transsudation*, from *transsuder*: see TRANSUDE, -ATION.]
1 The action or process of transuding; the passing off or oozing out of a liquid through the pores of a substance. E17.
2 = TRANSUDATE. M17.
▪ **ˈtransudate** *noun* a substance which is transuded; *spec.* (MEDICINE) watery fluid of non-inflammatory origin which has collected in a body cavity etc. (cf. EXUDATE *noun*): L19. **tranˈsudatory** *adjective* (*rare*) having the quality of transuding; characterized by transudation: M18.

transude /tranˈsjuːd, trɑːn-/ *verb.* M17.
[French *transsuder* refash. of Old French *tressuer*, from Proto-Gallo-Romance base from Latin TRANS- + *sudare* sweat.]
1 *verb intrans.* Ooze through or out like sweat; exude through pores (in the skin, blood-vessels, etc., or anything permeable). M17.
2 *verb trans.* †**a** Ooze through (something) like sweat. L18–E19. ▸**b** Cause (something) to ooze through. M19.

transume /tranˈsjuːm, trɑːn-/ *verb trans.* L15.
[Latin *tran(s)sumere* (in medieval Latin) transcribe, copy, formed as TRANS- + *sumere* take, seize.]
1 Make an official copy of (a legal document). *obsolete* exc. *Hist.* L15.
†**2** Transfer; convert, transmute. Freq. foll. by *into*. L15–M17.

transumpt /tranˈsʌm(p)t, trɑːn-/ *noun.* Chiefly *Scot. obsolete* exc. *Hist.* LME.
[medieval Latin *trans(s)sumptum* use as noun of pa. pple of *trans(s)umere*: see prec.]
A copy, a transcript; *esp.* one of a legal document.

transumption /tranˈsʌm(p)ʃ(ə)n, trɑːn-/ *noun.* Long *rare.* LME.
[Latin *transumptio(n-)* (in medieval Latin) copying, from *transumpt-* pa. ppl stem of *transumere*: see prec., -ION.]
†**1** (A) transcription, (a) copy; (a) quotation. LME–E18.
2 = METALEPSIS. LME.
†**3** Transference or translation to another place etc. Only in 17.

transumptive /tranˈsʌm(p)tɪv, trɑːn-/ *adjective.* Long *rare.* LME.
[Latin *transumptivus*, from *transumpt-*: see prec., -IVE.]
Of or pertaining to transumption; metaleptic.

transuranic /transjʊˈranɪk, trɑːns-, -nz-/ *adjective.* M20.
[from TRANS- + URAN(IUM + -IC.]
Of a chemical element: having a higher atomic number than uranium (i.e. 93 or over).
▪ **transuranian** (*rare*), **transuranium** *adjectives* (*a*) = TRANSURANIC; (*b*) of, pertaining to, or resembling transuranic elements: M20.

Transvaal daisy /tranzvɑːl ˈdeɪzi, trɑːnz-, -ns-/ *noun.* E20.
[from *Transvaal* (see next) + DAISY.]
A South African plant, *Gerbera jamesonii*, grown for ornament. Also called ***gerbera***.

Transvaaler /tranzˈvɑːlə, trɑːnz-, -ns-/ *noun.* L19.
[from *Transvaal* (see below), separated from the Orange Free State by the River Vaal, + -ER[1].]
A native or inhabitant of Transvaal, a north-eastern province of South Africa (formerly a Boer republic).

Transvaalian /tranzˈvɑːlɪən, trɑːnz-, -ns-/ *adjective.* L19.
[formed as prec. + -IAN.]
Of or pertaining to the Transvaal in South Africa.

transversal /tranzˈvəːs(ə)l, trɑːnz-, -ns-/ *adjective & noun.* LME.
[medieval Latin *transversalis*, from Latin *transversus*: see TRANSVERSE *adjective*, -AL[1].]
▸**A** *adjective.* = TRANSVERSE *adjective.* LME.
▸**B** *noun.* **1** = TRANSVERSE *noun* 2. LME.
2 MATH. A straight line intersecting two or more other straight lines. Also, a curve that satisfies a transversality condition. L19.
3 ROULETTE. A bet placed on three numbers forming a crosswise row. L19.
▪ **transverˈsality** *noun* the condition or state of being transversal; ***transversality condition*** (MATH.): that the shortest line segment joining a point to a curve must be orthogonal to the curve at the point where the segment meets it: M19. **transversally** *adverb* LME.

transversary /tranzˈvəːs(ə)ri, trɑːnz-, -ns-/ *adjective & noun. obsolete* exc. *Hist.* LME.
[Latin *transversarius*, formed as next: see -ARY[1].]
▸†**A** *adjective.* Transverse. *rare.* Only in LME.
▸**B** *noun.* A crosspiece on a cross-staff. L16.

transverse /ˈtranzvəːs, ˈtrɑːnz-, -ns-/ *adjective, noun, & adverb.* LME.
[Latin *transversus* pa. pple of *transvertere* TRANSVERT.]
▸**A** *adjective.* Extending or proceeding in a crosswise direction; lying or running across; (also foll. by *to*). having a breadth greater than the length or height; *spec.* in PHYSICS (of a vibration, wave, etc.) involving displacement at right angles to the direction of propagation. Opp. ***longitudinal***. LME.
Special collocations: **transverse alliteration** a type of alliteration using two interwoven patterns, found esp. in early Germanic verse. **transverse axis** (*a*) an axis transverse to the longitudinal axis; (*b*) MATH. = ***principal axis*** (a) s.v. PRINCIPAL *adjective.* **transverse colon** ANATOMY that part of the colon which crosses the front of the abdomen from right to left below the stomach. **transverse flute**: having the mouthpiece in the side near one end. **transverse Mercator** a map projection obtained like the Mercator but such that the central horizontal line is a pair of meridians rather than the equator. **transverse myelitis** MEDICINE myelitis which extends across a section of the spinal cord. **transverse process** ANATOMY a lateral process of a vertebra. **transverse suture** ANATOMY the suture between the frontal and facial bones.
▸**B** *noun.* †**1** Crosswise direction or position. *rare.* LME.
2 A thing lying or extending crosswise; a crosspiece. LME.
▸**C** *adverb.* In a transverse direction or position; across, crosswise. *rare* exc. *poet.* M17.
▪ **transversely** *adverb* M16. **transverseness** *noun* M19.

transverse /tranzˈvəːs, trɑːnz-, -ns-/ *verb*[1] *trans.* Now *rare* or *obsolete.* LME.
[Old French *transverser* (mod. *traverser*) from medieval Latin *transversare*, from Latin *transvers-* pa. ppl stem of *transvertere* TRANSVERT.]
1 Extend or proceed across; cross, traverse, intersect. Formerly also *fig.*, cross, thwart. LME.
2 Turn upside down or backwards; overturn. E16. ▸**b** Transform, transmute. L17.

transverse /tranzˈvəːs, trɑːnz-, -ns-/ *verb*[2] *trans.* L17.
[from TRANS- + VERSE *noun.*]
Translate or render in verse.

transversion /tranzˈvəːʃ(ə)n, trɑːnz-, -ns-/ *noun*[1]. M17.
[from TRANSVERT *verb* after *convert, conversion*, etc.]
1 (An) intersection. Also, (a) conversion, (a) transformation. *rare.* M17.
2 BIOLOGY. The occurrence in a nucleic acid of a purine in place of a pyrimidine or vice versa. Cf. TRANSITION *noun* 6. M20.

transversion /tranzˈvəːʃ(ə)n, trɑːnz-, -ns-/ *noun*[2]. L18.
[from TRANSVERSE *verb*[2] + -ION.]
(A) translation or rendition in verse.

transversive /tranzˈvəːsɪv, trɑːnz-, -ns-/ *adjective. rare.* M19.
[from Latin *transvers-* pa. ppl stem of *transvertere* TRANSVERT + -IVE.]
Crossing, thwarting.

†**transvert** *verb trans.* LME–M17.
[Latin *transvertere* turn across, formed as TRANS- + *vertere* turn.]
Traverse, intersect; transform, convert.

For other words beginning with *trans-* see the entry for **trans-**

Transverter /tranzˈvəːtə, trɑːnz-, -ns-/ *noun.* Also **t-**. E20.
[from TRANS(FORMER + CON)VERTER.]
ELECTRICAL ENGINEERING. An apparatus for converting alternating current into high-voltage direct current, and vice versa.
¶ Proprietary name in the US.

transvestic /tranzˈvɛstɪk, trɑːnz-, -ns-/ *adjective.* M20.
[from next or TRANSVESTITE: see -IC.]
= TRANSVESTITE *adjective.*
▪ **transvesticism** /-sɪz(ə)m/ *noun* (*rare*) = TRANSVESTISM M20.

transvestism /tranzˈvɛstɪz(ə)m, trɑːnz-, -ns-/ *noun.* E20.
[formed as next: see -ISM.]
The practice of wearing or desire to wear the clothes of the opposite sex, esp. as a sexual stimulus.
▪ **transvestist** *noun & adjective* = TRANSVESTITE *noun & adjective* M20.

transvestite /tranzˈvɛstʌɪt, trɑːnz-, -ns-/ *noun & adjective.* E20.
[from TRANS- + Latin *vestire* clothe + -ITE[1].]
▸**A** *noun.* A person given to transvestism. E20.
▸**B** *adjective.* Of or pertaining to transvestism or transvestites; (of a person) given to transvestism. E20.

transvestitism /tranzˈvɛstɪtɪz(ə)m, trɑːnz-, -ns-/ *noun.* M20.
[formed as prec.: see -ISM.]
= TRANSVESTISM.
▪ **transvestitic** *adjective* (*rare*) = TRANSVESTITE *adjective* L20.

Transylvanian /transɪlˈveɪnɪən, trɑːn-/ *noun & adjective.* M17.
[from *Transylvania* (see below) + -AN.]
▸**A** *noun.* A native or inhabitant of Transylvania, formerly part of Austria-Hungary, now in western Romania. M17.
▸**B** *adjective.* Of, pertaining to, or characteristic of Transylvania. M19.

tranter /ˈtrantə/ *noun. obsolete* exc. *dial.* Also (earlier) †**traventer**. LME.
[Anglo-Norman *traventer* = Anglo-Latin *trave(n)tarius*, of unkn. origin.]
A person who buys up goods to sell elsewhere; a pedlar, a hawker, formerly *esp.* one travelling by horse and cart. Orig. also, a retailer of ale.
▪ **trant** *verb intrans.* (*rare*) [back-form.] make one's living as a tranter LME. **trantery** *noun* the occupation of a tranter ME.

tranylcypromine /tranʌɪlˈsʌɪprəmiːn, -nɪl-/ *noun.* M20.
[from TRAN(S- + PHEN)YL + CY(CLO- + PRO(PYL + A)MINE, elems. of the systematic name.]
PHARMACOLOGY. A monoamine oxidase inhibitor, $C_9H_{11}N$, used to treat severe depression.
¶ A proprietary name for this drug is PARNATE.

trap /trap/ *noun*[1].
[Old English *træppe* (in *coltetræppe* Christ's thorn), *treppe*, corresp. to Middle Dutch *trappe*, Flemish *trape*, medieval Latin *trappa*, Old French *trape* (mod. *trappe*), Provençal, Portuguese *trapa*, Spanish *trampa*.]
1 A device or enclosure, often baited, designed to catch and retain or kill game or vermin, either by allowing entry but not exit, or by catching hold of the body; a gin, a snare. OE. ▸**b** *fig.* A trick betraying a person into an unintended action or speech. ME. ▸**c** *transf.* A person who catches offenders; a detective, a police officer. *slang* (now only *Austral.*). E18. ▸**d** A device allowing a pigeon to enter but not leave a loft. L19. ▸**e** An arrangement to catch an unsuspecting person; *esp.* a police device to detect a motorist exceeding the legal speed limit (also ***speed trap***). E20.
2 A covering over a pit or floor opening, designed to fall when stepped on; a trapdoor. ME. ▸**b** The mouth. Chiefly in ***keep one's trap shut, shut your trap!*** below. *slang.* L18. ▸**c** A concealed compartment; *spec.* a hiding place for stolen or illegal goods. *US slang.* M20.
3 a A shoe-shaped wooden device with a pivoted bar used in the game of trap-ball. Also = TRAP-BALL 1. L16. ▸**b** A device for suddenly releasing and hurling an object, esp. a clay pigeon, into the air to be shot at. E19. ▸**c** A compartment from which a greyhound is released at the start of a race. E20.
4 Deceit; trickery; fraud. *slang.* L17.
5 Chiefly *Hist.* A light usu. two-wheeled spring carriage. *colloq.* L18.
6 a A device in a waste pipe for preventing the upward escape of noxious gases etc., as a double curve or U-shaped section in which water stands. M19. ▸**b** Any of various devices for preventing the passage of steam, water, silt, etc. Also, a ventilation door in a mine. L19. ▸**c** GEOLOGY. An underground rock formation in which an accumulation of oil or gas is trapped. Also ***gas trap, oil trap***. E20. ▸**d** RADIO. A resonant circuit used as a rejector or acceptor circuit to block or divert signals of a specific frequency, esp. to reduce interference in a receiver tuned to a nearby frequency. Also ***wave trap***. E20.
7 a A recess for carrying accessories in the butt of a rifle etc. M19. ▸**b** = ***trap-net*** below. *US.* L19. ▸**c** GOLF. A bunker. Chiefly *N. Amer.* L19.

8 (A fault resulting from) a break in the warp threads of a piece of weaving. **L19.**
9 PHYSICS. A site in a crystal lattice which is capable of temporarily immobilizing a moving electron or hole. **M20.**
10 AMER. FOOTBALL. A tactic in which an attacking team allows a defending player to cross the line of scrimmage and blocks him from the side, enabling the player with the ball to go unopposed through the gap created. Also more fully ***trap-play***. **M20.**

🕮 **1** C. MUNGOSHI His grandfather setting the traps with the stone and two sticks. **b** M. L. KING I almost fell into the trap of accepting uncritically everything he wrote. **e** C. MACKENZIE Slow down a bit. There's a trap somewhere along here.

Phrases: **be up to trap** be knowing or cunning. DEATH-*trap*. **keep one's trap shut** *slang* remain silent. ***leg trap***: see LEG *noun*. RAT-TRAP. **shut your trap!** *slang* be quiet! ***speed trap***: see sense 1e above. ***tourist trap***: see TOURIST *noun*. **trap and ball** = TRAP-BALL 1. ***vampire trap***: see VAMPIRE *noun* 4.
Comb.: **trap-bat** (*a*) a bat used in trap-ball; (*b*) the game of trap-ball; **trap boat** *N. Amer.* a fishing boat using trap-nets; **trap cage**: fitted with a spring device to catch and retain a bird etc. inside; **trap-cellar** the space beneath the trapdoors in a theatre stage; **trap-crop** a crop planted to attract insect pests etc. from another crop, *esp.* one in which the pests fail to survive or reproduce; **trapfall** a trapdoor or covering over a pit etc. designed to give way beneath the feet; **trap-gun** (*a*) a gun set with an automatic trip device; (*b*) a gun used in trap-shooting; **trap-hatch**: covered with a trap or trapdoor; **trap-hook** a snap-hook; **trap-house** a shelter from which clay pigeons are released in trap-shooting; **trap-light**: fitted with a device for trapping moths etc.; **trap-line** (*a*) the ensnaring filament in a spider's web; (*b*) *N. Amer.* a series of game traps; **trap-match** a trap-shooting match; **trap-nest** *noun & verb* (*a*) *noun* a nesting-box allowing a hen to enter but not leave until released; (*b*) *verb trans.* enclose (a hen) in a trap-nest; **trap-net** a large fishing net with a funnel-shaped neck; ***trap-play***: see sense 10 above; **trap-point** a safety-point preventing unauthorized movement of a train etc. from a siding on to the main line; **trapshoot** *N. Amer.* a sporting contest or event involving shooting clay pigeons etc.; **trap-shooter** a person who shoots clay pigeons etc. as a sport; **trap-shooting** the sport of shooting clay pigeons etc. released from a spring trap; **trap-shot** = ***trap-shooter*** above; **trap-shy** *adjective* (of an animal) reluctant to approach a trap; **trap-siding**: intended to intercept and derail breakaway train carriages; **trapskiff** *N. Amer.*, *rare* = ***trap boat*** above; **trapstick** a stick used in trap-ball; **trap-tree** a tree deadened or felled in order to localize insect infestation; **trap-yard** an enclosure into which horses, sheep, etc., are driven and confined.
■ **trappy** *adjective* (*colloq.*) inclined to act as a trap or snare; containing a trap or traps: **L19.**

†trap *noun*². **ME–E18.**
[Alt. of Old & mod. French *drap*: see DRAPE *verb*.]
= TRAPPING 1. Usu. in *pl.*

trap /trap/ *noun*³. Long *obsolete* exc. *Hist.* **LME.**
[Old French *trappe*.]
A tin or dish for baking.

trap /trap/ *noun*⁴. Also **trapp**. **L18.**
[Swedish *trapp*, from *trappa* stair (with ref. to the appearance often presented by the rock). Cf. next.]
GEOLOGY. Orig., a dark-coloured igneous rock more or less columnar in structure. Now, any igneous rock which is neither granitic nor of recent volcanic formation. Also ***trap rock***.

trap /trap/ *noun*⁵. *Scot.* **E19.**
[App. from Dutch & Middle Flemish = flight of steps, stair. Cf. prec.]
A ladder leading to a loft etc. Also ***trap-ladder***.
Comb.: **trap-cut** *noun & adjective* = ***step-cut*** s.v. STEP *noun*¹.

trap /trap/ *noun*⁶. *colloq.* **E20.**
[Prob. from TRAP *noun*¹.]
sing. & (usu.) in *pl.* In a jazz or dance band, percussion instruments; these together with a standard drum-kit.
Comb.: **trap-drum(s)** a drum-kit used in a jazz or dance band; **trap-drummer** a musician who plays the trap-drums.

trap /trap/ *noun*⁷. *Body-builders' slang.* **M20.**
[Abbreviation.]
= TRAPEZIUS. Usu. in *pl.*

trap /trap/ *verb*¹ *trans. arch.* Infl. **-pp-**. **LME.**
[from TRAP *noun*².]
Put trappings on (a horse etc.); caparison. Chiefly as TRAPPED *ppl adjective*.

trap /trap/ *verb*². Infl. **-pp-**. **LME.**
[from TRAP *noun*¹. Cf. earlier BETRAP.]
▶ **I** *verb trans.* **1** Catch (as) in a trap; entrap, ensnare. Also (chiefly *techn.*), retain in or separate out with a trap. **LME.** ▸**b** *fig.* Catch out (a person), esp. by a deliberate trick or plan. **M17.**
2 Provide or set with a trap or traps. **M19.**
3 a BASEBALL & AMER. FOOTBALL. Catch (the ball) just after it has hit the ground. Also, hem (a runner) between two fielders. **L19.** ▸**b** CRICKET. Cause (a batsman) to be dismissed, freq. leg before wicket. **E20.** ▸**c** FOOTBALL. Receive and control (the ball). **M20.**

🕮 **1** D. MADDEN A bee had flown into the church, and was trapped at this window. G. DALY Her young friend was trapped in a loveless marriage. **b** G. GREENE I don't know who trapped you into it.

▶ **II** *verb intrans.* **4** Catch wild animals in traps for their furs; set traps for game. **E19.**
5 Use or work a trap or traps, esp. in trap-shooting. **M19.**
6 a Of a greyhound: leave the trap at the start of a race. **M20.** ▸**b** Of a pigeon: enter the trap of a loft. **L20.**

🕮 **4** D. WALLACE Tom Blake . . had trapped at the . . western end of Grand Lake.

†trapan *noun* see TREPAN *noun*².

†trapan *verb* var. of TREPAN *verb*².

trap-ball /ˈtrapbɔːl/ *noun*. **M17.**
[from TRAP *noun*¹ + BALL *noun*¹.]
1 A game in which a ball placed on one end of a trap (see TRAP *noun*¹ 3a) is thrown into the air by striking the other end with a bat, then hit away with the bat. **M17.**
2 A ball used in this game. *rare*. **E18.**

trapdoor /trapˈdɔː/ *noun*. **LME.**
[from TRAP *noun*¹ + DOOR.]
1 A door or hatch, usu. flush with the surface, in a floor, roof, ceiling, or theatre stage. **LME.** ▸**b** *spec.* A door directing the ventilating current in a mine. **M19.**
2 COMPUTING. A feature or defect of a computer system which allows surreptitious unauthorized access to data belonging to other users of a computer. **L20.**
3 CRYPTOGRAPHY. A piece of secret information that makes it easy to solve an otherwise very difficult code. Freq. *attrib.* **L20.**
Comb.: **trapdoor spider** any of various mygalomorph spiders of the family Ctenizidae, which live in burrows closed with a hinged lid and are found in most warm areas.

trape /treɪp/ *verb intrans.* Now *rare*. Long *obsolete* exc. *dial.* **E18.**
[Origin unkn. Cf. TRAIPSE *verb*.]
= TRAIPSE *verb* 1.

trapes *noun*, *verb* vars. of TRAIPSE *noun*, *verb*.

trapeze /trəˈpiːz/ *noun*. **M19.**
[French *trapèze* formed as TRAPEZIUM.]
1 An apparatus consisting of a crossbar or set of crossbars suspended by ropes, used as a swing to perform acrobatics. **M19.** ▸**b** *Sailing*. A sliding support used for outboard balancing on a yacht etc. **M20.**
2 A (style of) garment with a trapezium-shaped outline, popular in the 1960s. Also ***trapeze-line***. **M20.**
Comb.: **trapeze artist** = TRAPEZIST; **trapeze harness**: worn by a crew member balancing a yacht etc. with a trapeze; ***trapeze-line***: see sense 2 above.
■ **trapezing** *noun* the action of performing on or using a trapeze **L19.** **trapezist** *noun* a performer on the trapeze **L19.**

trapezii *noun* pl. of TRAPEZIUS.

trapezium /trəˈpiːzɪəm/ *noun*. Pl. **-zia** /-zɪə/, **-ziums**. **L16.**
[Late Latin from Greek *trapezion* from *trapeza* table.]
1 GEOMETRY. **a** Any quadrilateral that is not a parallelogram. Now *rare*. **L16.** ▸**b** A quadrilateral having one pair of opposite sides parallel. **L17.** ▸**c** = TRAPEZOID *noun* 1a. Now chiefly *N. Amer.* **L18.**
2 ANATOMY & ZOOLOGY. The first distal carpal bone of the wrist, articulating with the metacarpal bone of the thumb; the corresponding bone in other mammals. Also ***trapezium bone***. **M19.**
3 ASTRONOMY. An asterism in the form of a trapezium; *spec.* the multiple star θ Orionis in the Great Nebula of Orion. **M19.**
4 = TRAPEZE 1. *rare*. **M19.**
■ **trapezial** *adjective* (*a*) of or pertaining to a trapezium; having the form of a trapezium, trapeziform; (*b*) ANATOMY pertaining to the trapezium or the trapezius: **L17.** **trapeziform** *adjective* having the form of a trapezium; quadrilateral with only two sides parallel: **L18.**

trapezius /trəˈpiːzɪəs/ *noun*. Pl. **-zii** /-zɪʌɪ/. **E18.**
[mod. Latin formed as prec.]
ANATOMY. Either of a pair of large flat triangular muscles which together form the figure of a trapezium, extending over the back of the neck and adjacent parts. Also ***trapezius muscle***.

trapezohedron /ˌtrapɪzə(ʊ)ˈhiːdrən, -ˈhɛd-/ *noun*. Pl. **-dra** /-drə/, **-drons**. **E19.**
[from TRAPEZ(IUM + -O- + -HEDRON, after *tetrahedron* etc.]
GEOMETRY & CRYSTALLOGRAPHY. A solid figure whose faces are trapeziums or trapezoids.
■ **trapezohedral** *adjective* **M19.**

trapezoid /ˈtrapɪzɔɪd, trəˈpiːzɔɪd/ *noun & adjective*. **E18.**
[mod. Latin *trapezoides* from late Greek *trapezoeidēs* from *trapeza* table: see -OID.]
▶ **A** *noun*. **1** GEOMETRY. **a** An irregular quadrilateral having neither pair of opposite sides parallel. **E18.** ▸†**b** An irregularly quadrate solid with no pair of sides parallel. Only in **18.** ▸**c** = TRAPEZIUM 1b. Now chiefly *N. Amer.* **L18.**
2 ANATOMY. The second distal carpal bone of the wrist. **M19.**
▶ **B** *adjective*. = TRAPEZOIDAL. **E19.**

trapezoidal /trapɪˈzɔɪd(ə)l/ *adjective*. **L18.**
[from prec. + -AL¹.]
1 GEOMETRY. Of a plane figure: having the form of a trapezoid or (esp. *N. Amer.*) of a trapezium. **L18.**
2 Of a solid: having trapezoidal faces; trapezohedral. **L18.**
1 trapezoidal rule MATH. a method for the approximate numerical integration of the area under a curve, which is treated as a number of trapezia.

Trapezuntine /trapɪˈzʊntʌɪn/ *noun & adjective*. **E20.**
[from Latin *Trapezunt-*, *Trapezus* Trabzon (see below) + -INE¹.]
▶ **A** *noun*. A native or inhabitant of the city of Trabzon in north-eastern Turkey. **E20.**
▶ **B** *adjective*. Of or pertaining to Trabzon or its inhabitants. **E20.**

trapiche /trəˈpitʃe/ *noun*. **M17.**
[Amer. Spanish, from Latin *trapetum* oil-press.]
A sugar cane mill.

†trapish *adjective*. **E–M18.**
[from TRAIPSE *noun* + -ISH¹.]
Slovenly, slatternly.

trapp *noun* var. of TRAP *noun*⁴.

trappean /ˈtrapɪən/ *adjective*. **E19.**
[from TRAP *noun*⁴ + -EAN.]
GEOLOGY. Pertaining to, of the nature of, or consisting of trap rock.

trapped /trapt, *poet.* ˈtrapɪd/ *adjective*. **LME.**
[from TRAP *noun*², *verb*¹ + -ED², -ED¹.]
Esp. of a horse: provided or adorned with trappings.

trapper /ˈtrapə/ *noun*¹. *obsolete* exc. *Hist.* **ME.**
[Anglo-Norman var. of Old French *drapure*, from *drap*: see DRAPE *verb*.]
= TRAPPING 1.

trapper /ˈtrapə/ *noun*². **M18.**
[from TRAP *noun*¹, *verb*² + -ER¹.]
1 A person who sets traps or snares, esp. one who traps wild animals for their furs. **M18.**
2 A boy engaged to work a trapdoor to allow the passage of trams in a coalmine. *obsolete* exc. *Hist.* **E19.**
3 A person managing a trap in trap-shooting. **L19.**
4 A horse which draws a trap or gig. *colloq.* **L19.**

trapping /ˈtrapɪŋ/ *noun*. **LME.**
[from TRAP *noun*², *verb*¹ + -ING¹.]
1 (A covering spread over) the harness or saddle of a horse etc., *esp.* an ornamental one; a caparison. Now only in *pl.* **LME.**
2 *transf.* In *pl.* & †*sing.* External usu. decorative features, dress, etc., esp. as an indication of some status or position. **L16.**

🕮 **2** N. BARBER He loved the trappings of office. *Time* Eschewing the fancy trappings of power, 'Mr. Sam' drove an '88 Ford pickup truck. *Daily Telegraph* He did not aspire to such trappings as a 'set' in Albany.

Trappist /ˈtrapɪst/ *noun*¹ & *adjective*. **E19.**
[French *trappiste* from *La Trappe* (see below): see -IST.]
▶ **A** *noun*. A member of the branch of the Cistercian order of monks established in 1664 at La Trappe in Normandy, noted for an austere rule including a vow of silence. **E19.**
▶ **B** *adjective*. Of or pertaining to this monastic branch. **M19.**

trappist /ˈtrapɪst/ *noun*². **L19.**
[from TRAP *noun*¹, *verb*² + -IST.]
= TRAPPER *noun*² 1.

Trappistine /ˈtrapɪstɪn, -iːn/ *adjective & noun*. **M19.**
[from TRAPPIST *noun*¹ + -INE³.]
▶ **A** *adjective*. Of or pertaining to an order of nuns affiliated with the Trappists, founded in 1827. **M19.**
▶ **B** *noun*. **1** A member of the Trappistine order. **L19.**
2 A liqueur made by the Trappists. **L19.**

trappoid /ˈtrapɔɪd/ *adjective*. **M19.**
[from TRAP *noun*⁴ + -OID.]
GEOLOGY. Resembling or allied to trap rock.

traps /traps/ *noun pl. colloq.* **E19.**
[Origin uncertain; perh. contr. of *trappings*: see TRAPPING.]
Personal effects, belongings; baggage.

trapunto /trəˈpʊntəʊ, -ˈpʌntəʊ/ *noun*. **E20.**
[Italian, use as noun of pa. pple of *trapungere* embroider.]
A kind of quilting in which the design is padded by pulling or cutting the threads of the underlying fabric to insert stuffing.

tra-ra /ˈtrɑːrɑː, trɑːˈrɑː/ *interjection & noun*. **M19.**
[Imit.]
(Repr.) the sound of a horn, trumpet, etc. Cf. TRA-LA-LA.

trascinando /traʃɪˈnandəʊ/ *adverb & adjective*. **L19.**
[Italian, pres. pple of *trascinare* drag, pull.]
MUSIC. = RALLENTANDO *adverb & adjective*.

trasformismo /trasfor'mizmo/ *noun*. **E20**.
[Italian, from *trasformare* change, transform.]
In Italy, a system of shifting political alliances to form a stable administration or a workable policy.

trash /traʃ/ *noun*[1]. **LME**.
[Origin unkn.]
1 A thing of little or no value; worthless or poor quality stuff, esp. literature; rubbish. **LME**. ▸†**b** Money, cash. *slang*. **L16–E19**. ▸**c** In full ***trash rock***. Rock music with a raucous sound or of a throwaway nature. Chiefly *US*. **L20**.
†**2** More fully ***trash nail***. A small nail or tack, used esp. in fixing up staging or scenery. **L15–E17**.
3 a Material (as twigs, leaves, etc.) broken or lopped off and discarded in preparing something for use. **M16**. ▸**b** *spec*. The refuse of crushed sugar canes and the dried stripped leaves and tops of sugar canes, used as fuel. **E18**.
4 A worthless or disreputable person. Now *esp*., such people collectively. **E17**.
5 An old worn-out shoe. *dial*. **M18**.
6 Domestic refuse, garbage. Also, a receptacle for this, a dustbin. **E20**.

🕮 **1** THACKERAY New pictures, in the midst of a great quantity of trash. E. HARDWICK Out of the apartment went the . . trash of . . decades. H. CARPENTER Pious trash that the Sunday Schools handed out as 'reward books'. **4** K. GIBBONS Marry trash and see what comes of you. **white trash** *N. Amer.* (usu. *derog.*) the poor white population, esp. in the southern US. **6** U. SINCLAIR He was flung aside, like a bit of trash. *New Yorker* Truckloads of trash were taken to the prison dump. L. SPALDING I had not . . emptied the trash.

Comb.: **trash can** *N. Amer.* a dustbin. **trash fish** *US*: sold for animal feed etc. rather than human consumption. **trash-house** a building on a sugar-plantation for storing sugar cane trash; **trash-ice** (on a sea, lake, etc.) broken ice mixed with water; **trashman** *N. Amer.* a dustman; ***trash nail***: see sense 2 above; **trash-rack**: set in a stream to prevent the passage of floating debris; ***trash rock***: see sense 1c above; **trash talk** *US colloq.* insulting or boastful speech intended to demoralize, intimidate, or humiliate someone, esp. an opponent in a game; **trash-talk** *verb trans. & intrans.* (*US colloq.*) use trash talk towards (someone); **trash-talker** *US colloq.* a person who trash-talks, esp. in a particularly ostentatious or effective manner.

¶ Senses 2 and 4 now usu. regarded as *fig.* of sense 6.
■ **trashery** *noun* trash, rubbish, refuse **M16**. **trashtrie** *noun* (*Scot.*) = TRASHERY **L18**.

trash /traʃ/ *noun*[2]. Now *dial*. **E17**.
[Rel. to next.]
A leash used to check dogs in training them. Also ***trash-cord***.

trash /traʃ/ *verb*[1] *trans*. **E17**.
[Origin unkn. Cf. prec.]
†**1** Check (a dog) with a leash; *gen.* restrain, hinder. **E17–M19**.
2 Efface, obliterate. *US dial.* **M19**.

trash /traʃ/ *verb*[2]. *obsolete* exc. *dial*. **E17**.
[App. of Scandinavian origin: cf. Sw *traska*, Norwegian *traske*.]
1 *verb intrans*. Walk or run at an exhausting speed, esp. through mud. **E17**.
2 *verb trans*. Exhaust with walking, running, or exertion. **L17**.

trash /traʃ/ *verb*[3] *trans*. **M18**.
[from TRASH *noun*[1].]
1 Strip the outer leaves from (growing sugar canes) to speed up the ripening process. **M18**.
2 Throw away, discard. *colloq.* **E20**.
3 Damage, wreck, vandalize. Also foll. by adverbs. *colloq.* (chiefly *N. Amer.*). **L20**.
4 Injure seriously, destroy; kill. *US colloq.* **L20**.
5 Impair the quality of (a work of art); expose the worthless nature of; disparage. **L20**.

🕮 **2** J. SCOTT He junked the car, he trashed his clothes. **3** L. CODY He . . wanted to trash her place over by way of revenge. N. SEDAKA The toughs . . started trashing the auditorium. *Practical Computing* Turning off the power supply . . trashes all the data in chips. **4** W. P. MCGIVERN Jules Levy . . trashed the pusher who murdered your son. **5** V. GORNICK She is about to trash the book I gave her to read.

■ **trasher** *noun* (*a*) a person who trashes sugar cane; (*b*) *colloq.* a vandal, a wrecker: **E20**.

trashy /'traʃi/ *adjective*. **E17**.
[from TRASH *noun*[1] + -Y[1].]
1 Of poor quality; worthless; rubbishy. **E17**.
2 Of a person: worthless, disreputable. *colloq.* **M19**.

🕮 **1** S. TROTT Manufacturing trashy plastic furniture. E. JONG It was merely a trashy 'Hollywood novel'. **2** *Detroit Free Press* I . . couldn't believe such things happened except in low class trashy families.

■ **trashily** *adverb* **M19**. **trashiness** *noun* **M19**.

Traskite /'traskʌɪt/ *noun*. **E17**.
[from John *Trask* (fl. 1617), English religious leader: see -ITE[1].]
ECCLESIASTICAL HISTORY. A member of a Baptist sect observing Saturday as the Sabbath.

†**trason** *verb intrans*. **L15–M19**.
[Origin uncertain: 1st elem. prob. from Old French *tras-*, *tres-* (from Latin *trans* across), repr. in *trespass* etc.]
HUNTING. Of a roe: cross or double before the hounds.

trass /tras/ *noun*. **L18**.
[Dutch *tras*, German *Trass*.]
= TARRAS *noun*.

tratt /trat/ *noun*. *colloq.* Also **trat**. **M20**.
[Abbreviation.]
A trattoria.

trattles /'trat(ə)lz/ *noun pl*. *local*. Also **trott-** /'trɒt-/. **M16**.
[Prob. rel. to TREDDLE *noun*[1].]
The rounded droppings of sheep, rabbits, etc.

trattoria /tratə'riːə/ *noun*. **E19**.
[Italian.]
An Italian restaurant.

trauchle *verb & noun* var. of TRACHLE.

traulism /'trɔːlɪz(ə)m/ *noun*. *rare*. Also in Latin form **-ismus** /-ɪzməs/. **M17**.
[Greek *traulismos*, from *traulizein* to lisp.]
Stuttering; a stutter.

trauma /'trɔːmə, 'traʊmə/ *noun*. Pl. **-mas**, **-mata** /-mətə/. **L17**.
[Greek = wound.]
1 MEDICINE. Orig., a physical wound. Now, external or internal injury; a state or condition resulting from this, e.g. shock. **L17**.
2 PSYCHOANALYSIS. A psychic injury, *esp.* one caused by emotional shock the memory of which may be either repressed and unresolved, or disturbingly persistent; a state or condition resulting from this. **L19**.
3 *gen.* Distress; (a) disturbance. **L20**.

🕮 **2** *Daily Telegraph* A hand-written notice which said 'Traumas Treated'. **3** J. CAREY Finding the right desk on the first morning was the major trauma.

traumatic /trɔː'matɪk, traʊ-/ *adjective*. **M17**.
[Late Latin *traumaticus* from Greek *traumatikos*, formed as prec.: see -IC.]
1 †**a** Used for the healing of wounds; vulnerary. **M–L17**. ▸**b** MEDICINE. Of, pertaining to, causing, or resulting from a physical wound or external injury; pertaining to the treatment of wounds. **M19**.
2 PSYCHOANALYSIS. Of, pertaining to, or caused by a psychic wound or emotional shock, esp. leading to or causing behavioural disturbance. **L19**.
3 *gen.* Distressing, emotionally disturbing. **M20**.

🕮 **3** G. DALY Her nerves had never recovered from the traumatic experience of being married to him.

Special collocations: **traumatic acid** a wound hormone found in some plants, $HOOC(CH_2)_8CH{=}CHCOOH$.
■ **traumatically** *adverb* **M19**.

traumatism /'trɔːmətɪz(ə)m, 'traʊ-/ *noun*. **M19**.
[from Greek *traumat-*, *trauma* wound + -ISM.]
1 MEDICINE. The effects of a physical wound or external injury on the body or injured part; the condition resulting from this. Now *rare*. **M19**.
2 PSYCHOANALYSIS. A condition of the psyche resulting from repression to the unconscious mind of emotional wounds which are unacceptable to the conscious mind. **L19**.
■ **traumati'zation** *noun* the action of traumatizing someone or something; the state of being traumatized: **M20**. **traumatize** *verb trans.* inflict a (physical or emotional) wound on; wound; damage psychologically: **E20**.

traumatology /trɔːmə'tɒlədʒi, traʊ-/ *noun*. **L19**.
[formed as prec. + -OLOGY.]
MEDICINE. Orig., the scientific description of wounds. Now, the branch of medicine that deals with the treatment of wounds and serious injuries and with the disabilities they cause.
■ **traumatologist** *noun* **M20**.

traumatotropism /trɔːmətə'trəʊpɪz(ə)m/ *noun*. **M20**.
[formed as TRAUMATISM: see -O-, -TROPISM.]
BOTANY. Abnormal growth or curvature of a plant resulting from a wound.
■ **traumatotropic** /-'trəʊpɪk, -'trɒpɪk/ *adjective* of, pertaining to, or of the nature of traumatotropism **M20**. **traumatropic** /-'trəʊpɪk, -'trɒpɪk/ *adjective* = TRAUMATOTROPIC **L19**. **trauma'tropism** *noun* = TRAUMATOTROPISM **L19**.

trautonium /traʊ'təʊnɪəm/ *noun*. **M20**.
[from Friedrich *Trautwein* (1888–1956), German scientist and inventor, after *euphonium*.]
An electronic musical instrument capable of producing notes of any pitch.

travail /'traveɪl/ *noun*[1]. Now chiefly *literary*. Also †**travel**. See also TRAVEL *noun*. **ME**.
[Old & mod. French, formed as TRAVAIL *verb*.]
▸**I 1** Physical or mental work; *esp.* painful exertion; hardship; suffering; an instance of this. **ME**.
†**2** A painful or laborious task; in *pl.*, labours. **ME–E18**.
3 The pains of childbirth; labour. **ME**.
†**4** The product or result of toil or work; *esp.* a literary work. **LME–E17**.

🕮 **1** *Observer* Some . . took refuge from the travails of modern life. **3** C. MACKENZIE The shock brought on a premature travail, and she was delivered of a boy. *fig.*: A. C. CLARKE The entire ocean seemed to be in travail as the shock waves . . were reflected back and forth.

▸**II** See TRAVEL *noun*.

†**travail** *noun*[2]. **L16–L18**.
[French, perh. ult. from Latin *trabs*, *trabem* beam.]
= TRAVE 2, TRAVIS 1.

travail /trə'vʌɪ/ *noun*[3]. *N. Amer.* **E19**.
[French: perh. same word as prec. Cf. TRAVOIS.]
= TRAVOIS.

travail /'traveɪl/ *verb*. Also †**travel**. See also TRAVEL *verb*. **ME**.
[Old & mod. French *travailler* from Proto-Romance verb from medieval Latin *trepalium* instrument of torture, prob. from Latin *tres* three + *palus* stake.]
▸**I 1** *verb trans*. Torment, distress, afflict; weary, tire. Now *rare* or *obsolete*. **ME**.
2 *verb intrans.* & †*refl*. Exert or apply oneself, work hard, toil. (Foll. by *about*, *for*, *in*, *to do*.) *arch.* **ME**. ▸†**b** *verb trans*. Put to work; employ. **LME–M17**. ▸†**c** *verb intrans*. Gain knowledge *in* a subject through study. Chiefly as ***travailed*** *ppl adjective*. **M16–M18**.
3 *verb intrans*. Suffer the pains of childbirth; be in labour. **ME**.
▸**II** See TRAVEL *verb*.

travailer /'traveɪlə/ *noun*. Also †**traveller**. See also TRAVELLER. **LME**.
[from prec. + -ER[1].]
1 A person who travails or labours. Long *arch.* or *obsolete*. **LME**.
2 See TRAVELLER.

travailous /'traveɪləs/ *adjective*. *arch.* **ME**.
[Old French *travaillos*, *-eus*, formed as TRAVAIL *noun*[1]: see -OUS.]
Laborious; wearisome.

travaux préparatoires /travo preparatwaːr/ *noun phr. pl.* **M20**.
[French, lit. 'preparatory works'.]
LAW. Drafts, records of discussions, etc., relating to legislation or a treaty under consideration.

trave /treɪv/ *noun*. *obsolete* exc. *dial*. **LME**.
[In sense 1 from Old French *trave* beam; with sense 2 cf. French *entrave* clog, restraint, etc.]
1 A wooden beam. **LME**. ▸**b** Either of the shafts of a cart; the shafts collectively. *dial.* **E19**.
2 = TRAVIS 1. **LME**.

travel /'trav(ə)l/ *noun*. Also †**travail**. See also TRAVAIL *noun*[1]. **LME**.
[Var. of TRAVAIL *noun*[1].]
▸**I 1** See TRAVAIL *noun*[1]. **LME**.
▸**II 2** The action of travelling or journeying, esp. in foreign parts. **LME**.
3 A journey, a spell of travelling, esp. in foreign parts. Now only in *pl.*, exc. *dial.* **M16**. ▸**b** In *pl.* A written account of such journeys. *arch.* **E18**.
4 Movement in a course or over a distance; *esp.* the range, rate, or manner of movement of a part in machinery. **L16**. ▸**b** Traffic. *rare*. **L18**.

🕮 **2** H. ACTON Despite her . . aversion to modern travel Nancy continued on her round of . . visits. P. FITZGERALD To broaden his mind a bit, . . that was what travel was for. D. PROFUMO It had taken them two days of travel to reach the Lodge. **3** I. MURDOCH The two were full of their travels. P. ACKROYD The whole family . . began their Italian travels. **4** *Design Engineering* A lead screw having . . a total travel of 100mm. J. E. GORDON The gauge . . needle had gone right round its full travel. *Practical Woodworking* The table . . has travel in all three directions of 100mm.

Comb.: **travel agency** a firm which makes transport, accommodation, etc., arrangements for travellers, and which acts as an agent for tour operators; **travel agent** (*a*) a person who works for a travel agency; (*b*) a travel agency; **travel allowance** (*a*) an allowance to cover the expenses of a journey; (*b*) *Hist.* the maximum amount of money travellers were allowed to take out of the UK during the period 1946–80; **travel brochure**: advertising travel and describing the features and amenities of holiday resorts etc.; **travel bureau** = ***travel agency*** above; **travel card** a prepaid card allowing unlimited travel on buses or trains for a (specified) period of time; **travel folder** = ***travel brochure*** above; **travel-sick** *adjective* affected by travel-sickness; **travel-sickness** nausea caused by the motion of a vehicle; **travel trailer** *N. Amer.* a large well-equipped caravan.

travel /'trav(ə)l/ *verb*. Infl. **-ll-**, ***-l-**. Also †**travail**. See also TRAVAIL *verb*. **ME**.
[Var. of TRAVAIL *verb*.]
▸**I 1** See TRAVAIL *verb*. **ME**.
▸**II 2** *verb intrans*. Go from one place to another; make a journey, esp. of some length or abroad. **ME**. ▸**b** Of a Methodist preacher: go round a circuit. **L18**. ▸**c** Go from place to place as a sales representative, working *for* a particular firm or dealing *in* a specified commodity. **M19**.

▸**d** Of an animal, esp. a deer: move onwards in feeding. **L19.**

3 *verb trans.* Journey through (a country etc.); journey along or follow (a road or path). **ME.** ▸**b** Cover (a specified distance) in travelling. **LME.**

4 *verb intrans.* Move; proceed; pass, esp. deliberately or systematically from point to point; *SCIENCE* be transmitted. Usu. foll. by adverb or preposition. **ME.** ▸**b** Of a machine or mechanical part: move, or admit of being moved, along a fixed course. **E19.** ▸**c** Move quickly. *colloq.* **L19.** ▸**d** *BASKETBALL.* Make progress in any direction while carrying the ball, in violation of the rules. **M20.**

5 *verb trans.* Drive or transport (esp. livestock) from one place to another; convey. **LME.** ▸**b** *THEATRICAL.* Take (props etc.) with one from place to place. **M20.** ▸**c** *PUBLISHING.* Take (books) from place to place in order to promote and sell them. **M20.**

6 *verb intrans.* Esp. of a commodity: withstand a long journey. *colloq.* **M19.**

📖 **2** V. BRITTAIN We . . travelled together from Leicester to Oxford. R. C. HUTCHINSON Half the passengers . . were travelling fourth-class. A. GRAY I would like to travel . . , visit Paris, Vienna, Florence. A. TYLER They were travelling through farm country. **c** E. BOWEN An ex-officer travelling in vacuum cleaners. E. WELTY Bowman, who . . travelled for a shoe company through Mississippi. **3** N. SHUTE I had travelled the world. *Scientific American* The street is . . heavily traveled in the . . rush hours. **b** C. ISHERWOOD He could have travelled hundreds of miles across nowhere. **4** R. J. GRAVES Pains commencing in particular parts . . and travelling back towards the spine. T. HARDY From the . . library . . his gaze travelled on to the various spires, halls, gables. J. M. COETZEE My soapy hand travels between her thighs. *Guardian* Nearly one in five thought sound travelled faster than light. **5** *Daily Telegraph* 'Meat' ponies should be travelled no further than to the nearest slaughterhouse. **6** J. WELCOME A charming wine, . . though they tell me it doesn't travel. M. HEBDEN Like a delicate wine, Pel . . didn't travel well.

■ **travellable** *adjective* (of a road etc.) able to be travelled along **E17.** **travelled** *ppl adjective* (*a*) that has travelled; that has been travelled; (*b*) *GEOLOGY* (of blocks, boulders, etc.) transported to a distance from their original site, esp. by glacial action; erratic: **LME.**

travelator /ˈtravəleɪtə/ *noun.* Chiefly *US.* Also **travolator**, (proprietary) **Trav-o-lator**. **M20.**
[from prec. after ESCALATOR.]
A moving walkway for use esp. in airports.

traveling *verbal noun, ppl adjective* see TRAVELLING *verbal noun, ppl adjective.*

traveller /ˈtrav(ə)lə/ *noun.* Also †**travailer**, ***traveler**. See also TRAVAILER. **LME.**
[from TRAVEL *verb* + -ER¹.]
▸**I 1** See TRAVAILER. **LME.**
▸**II 2 a** A person who is travelling or on a journey; a person who travels or journeys, esp. abroad. **LME.** ▸**b** An itinerant beggar, a hawker, (now *dial.*); a Gypsy; *Austral.* an itinerant worker. **L16.** ▸**c** A representative of a company who visits shops etc. to show samples and gain orders. Also ***commercial traveller***. **L18.**

3 An animal that can go quickly or for long distances. **M17.**

4 A device or mechanism which moves or runs along a rope, groove, etc., or acts as a guide for something else to move or run along; *esp.* a travelling crane. Also *spec.* (*NAUTICAL*), an iron ring able to move freely along a mast, spar, or rope. **M18.** ▸**b** A tool for measuring the circumference esp. of a wheel. Now *dial.* **L19.**

5 A piece of luggage; a suitcase, a trunk, a bag. Chiefly *US.* **L19.**

Phrases: ***commercial traveller***: see sense 2c above. ***New Age traveller***. **traveller's cheque**, **travellers' cheque**, **travellers cheque** a cheque for a fixed amount of money which may be cashed or used in payment abroad, on the holder's signature. **traveller's joy** a woody climbing plant of the buttercup family, *Clematis vitalba*, of hedges on chalk and limestone, with greenish-white flowers and feathery fruiting styles; also called ***old man's beard***. **traveller's palm**, **traveller's tree** a palmlike tree, *Ravenala madagascariensis* (family Strelitziaceae), native to Madagascar and valued by travellers for the rainwater held in the bases of the leaf-stalks. **traveller's tale** an incredible and probably untrue story.

■ **travelleress** *noun* (*rare*) a female traveller **E19.**

travelling /ˈtrav(ə)lɪŋ/ *verbal noun.* Also ***traveling**. **LME.**
[from TRAVEL *verb* + -ING¹.]
The action of TRAVEL *verb.*

Attrib. & comb.: In the senses 'of travelling', '(adapted to be) used in travelling, taken with one when travelling', as ***travelling bag***, ***travelling companion***, ***travelling dress***, etc. Special combs., as **travelling fellowship**: given to enable the holder to travel for the purpose of study or research; **travelling rug**: used for warmth on a journey; **travelling scholarship**: given to enable the holder to travel for the purpose of study or research.

travelling /ˈtrav(ə)lɪŋ/ *ppl adjective.* Also ***traveling**. **ME.**
[from TRAVEL *verb* + -ING².]
That travels.

travelling crane a crane able to move on rails, esp. along an overhead support. **travelling library** a mobile library. **travelling salesman** = TRAVELLER 2c; ***travelling salesman problem*** (*MATH.*), the problem of determining the shortest route that passes through each of a set of given points once only and returns to the starting-point. **travelling stock** *Austral. & NZ* livestock which is driven from place to place (freq. *attrib.*). **travelling wave** *PHYSICS* a wave in which the positions of maximum and minimum amplitude travel; ***travelling-wave tube***, an electron tube in which a guided electromagnetic wave is amplified by interaction with a beam of electrons travelling at about the same velocity.

travelogue /ˈtravəlɒɡ/ *noun.* Also ***-log**. **E20.**
[from TRAVEL *noun* + -LOGUE.]
A film or illustrated lecture about places etc. encountered in the course of travel or travels.

†**traventer** *noun* see TRANTER.

travers /travɛːr, ˈtravəs/ *noun.* Pl. same. **L19.**
[French *pied de travers* foot askew, from *travers* breadth, irregularity, from *traverser* TRAVERSE *verb.*]
HORSEMANSHIP. A movement in which a horse walks parallel to a wall with its head and neck facing forward and its hindquarters curved out from the wall.

traversal /trəˈvəːs(ə)l, ˈtravəs(ə)l/ *noun.* **E20.**
[from TRAVERSE *verb* + -AL¹.]
= TRAVERSE *noun* 11.

†**traversayn** *noun* see TRANSOM.

traverse /ˈtravəs, trəˈvəːs/ *noun.* Also †**travis**. See also TRAVIS. **LME.**
[Old & mod. French *travers* (masc.), *traverse* (fem.), partly from *traverser* (see the verb), partly from medieval Latin *tra(ns)versum* use as noun of neut. pa. pple of *transversare* TRANSVERSE *verb*¹, partly repr. late Latin *traversa* use as noun of fem. pa. pple of Latin *transvertere* turn across.]
▸**I** An immaterial obstruction or obstacle; opposition.

1 An impediment, an obstacle, a difficulty; a mishap; an adversity. Now *rare.* **LME.**

2 *LAW.* A formal denial in pleading, esp. of an allegation made by the other side. **LME.**

†**3** (A) dispute. **LME–M17.**

†**4** = PASSAGE *noun* 15b. **L16–M17.**

📖 **1** W. PENN It is my lot to meet with traverses and disappointments.

▸**II** A structure placed or extending across something.

5 A curtain or screen partitioning a room, hall, or theatre. Now chiefly *Hist.* **LME.**

6 A small area shut off or enclosed by a curtain or screen in a church, house, etc. Now chiefly *spec.*, a gallery extending from side to side across a church or room. **L15.**

†**7** A bar, a barrier. **L16–M18.**

8 *FORTIFICATION.* A defensive barricade across an approach, line of fire, etc.; *spec.* a bank of earth on the terreplein of a rampart or the covered way of a fortress, or either of two right-angled bends in a trench, serving to protect against enfilade. **L16.**

9 Anything laid or fixed across something else, as a transom, a rung on a ladder, etc. **E18.**

▸**III** Movement across or through; a manner or means of doing this.

10 a (A) sideways movement. Now only *spec.* of a part in a machine, or as in senses 10b, c below. **M16.** ▸**b** The lateral movement of a gun etc. on a pivot or mount; the capacity for such movement. **L19.** ▸**c** *MOUNTAINEERING.* A sideways movement, or a series of such movements, across a rock-face or slope from one practicable line of ascent or descent to another; a place where this is necessary. **L19.**

11 The action or an act of crossing or passing through a region etc. **L16.** ▸**b** A toll paid on crossing the boundary of a town etc. *obsolete* exc. *Hist.* **L16.**

12 *NAUTICAL.* A zigzag line taken by a ship because of contrary winds or currents; each of the runs in tacking. **L16.** ▸**b** *SKIING.* A zigzag course followed in descending a slope; each of the diagonal runs made in this; a slope on which such runs are necessary. **E20.**

13 A way across or through; a pass, a crossing. **L17.**

14 *SURVEYING.* A line of survey plotted from compass bearings and measured distances between successive points; a tract of country surveyed in this way. **E19.**

📖 **10c** A. GILCHRIST A . . dangerous cliff face, followed by a traverse and then an upward climb. **11** *Country Walking* A traverse of the complete Snowdon horseshoe. **13** P. MATTHIESSEN We walk a long eastward traverse, then west again.

Comb.: **traverse-board** *NAUTICAL* (chiefly *Hist.*) a circular board marked with the compass points and used to indicate the course of a ship; **traverse-book** *NAUTICAL* a logbook; **traverse jury**: empanelled to adjudicate on an appeal from another jury; **traverse-map** a rough map with the main points determined by traversing; **traverse rod** *US* a curtain rail; **traverse-survey** *SURVEYING* = sense 14 above. **traverse-table** (*a*) *NAUTICAL* a table for calculating the difference of latitude and departure corresponding to a given course and distance; (*b*) = TRAVERSER (b).

traverse /ˈtravəs, trəˈvəːs/ *adjective. rare.* **LME.**
[Old French *travers* from medieval Latin *tra(ns)versus* formed as TRANSVERSE *adjective.*]
1 Lying, passing, or extending across; transverse. **LME.**
†**2** Slanting; oblique. **E–M17.**

■ **traversely** *adverb* **M16.**

traverse /ˈtravəs, trəˈvəːs/ *verb.* **ME.**
[Old & mod. French *traverser* from late Latin *tra(ns)versare*, formed as TRANSVERSE *noun, adjective, & adverb.*]
▸**I** Act or direct oneself against.

1 *verb trans. LAW.* Deny (an allegation) in pleading; deny the validity of. **ME.** ▸†**b** Affirm, by way of contradicting a charge or allegation. **L15–M17.**

2 *verb trans.* Act against; oppose, thwart, or frustrate (a plan etc.). **ME.**

†**3** *verb trans.* Dispute; discuss. **LME–L16.**

▸**II** Run across or through.

4 *verb trans.* **a** Of a sharp object or weapon: penetrate, pierce. Formerly also, (of a person) stab *with* a weapon. Now *rare.* **LME.** ▸**b** Cross with a line, stripe, barrier, etc. Now *rare.* **LME.**

5 *verb intrans.* Move across; cross; (of a ship) tack. **LME.**

6 *verb trans.* Cross (a mountain, river, etc.) in travelling; journey over, along, or through; cover (a distance) in journeying. **LME.**

7 *verb trans. fig.* Go through (life, time, the mind, etc.); *esp.* consider or discuss the whole extent of (a subject etc.). **L15.**

8 *verb trans.* Lie or extend across (something). **L15.**

9 *verb intrans.* Move from side to side; dodge. *arch.* **L15.**

10 a *verb intrans.* Of a horse: advance obliquely. **M16.** ▸**b** *verb trans. & intrans. SKIING.* Ski diagonally across (a slope). **E20.**

11 *verb trans.* Go to and fro over or along; cross and recross. **L16.** ▸**b** *verb intrans.* Advance in a zigzag line. *rare.* **L18.**

12 *verb trans.* Move or turn sideways; *esp.* turn (a gun) sideways to take aim. **E17.** ▸†**b** *verb trans. CARPENTRY.* Plane (wood) across the grain. **L17–E18.**

13 *verb intrans.* Run freely in a socket, ring, or groove; turn freely (as) on a pivot. **L18.**

14 *verb intrans. MOUNTAINEERING.* Cross a rock-face or slope by means of a series of sideways movements. **L19.**

15 *verb trans. SURVEYING.* Make a traverse of (a region); delimit (an area) by determining the position of boundary points in this way. **L19.**

📖 **5** E. BLOWER He traversed backwards and forwards from the window to the door. **6** R. FRY We traverse wide stretches of country. P. FITZGERALD The pedlars . . traversed every street. W. HORWOOD The ground rose . . and became hard to traverse. **7** SIR W. SCOTT Thoughts which hastily traversed the mind of young Durward. **8** D. ADAMS A moving catwalk that traversed a vast cavernous space. I. MURDOCH The sun today was . . occluded . . , traversed by a film of mist. **14** *High Magazine* They will be climbing . . to the SW summit and then hope to traverse to the NE summit.

■ **traversable** *adjective* †(*a*) *rare* moving to and fro, confused; (*b*) able to be traversed: **L15.** **traversed** *adjective* (*a*) that has been traversed; †(*b*) (of a horse) having two white feet on one side or one white foot diagonally opposite another white foot: **L16.** **traverser** *noun* (*a*) a person who or thing which traverses; (*b*) a sideways-moving platform for shifting a railway carriage or engine from one set of rails to another parallel set: **E17.**

†**traverse** *adverb.* **LME–E18.**
[from TRAVERSE *adjective.*]
Across; crosswise.

traverso /trəˈvəːsəʊ/ *noun.* Pl. **-os**. **E19.**
[Italian.]
MUSIC. A transverse flute.

travertine /ˈtravətɪn/ *noun.* Also **-in**. **L18.**
[Italian *travertino*, older *tivertino*, from Latin *tiburtinus* TIBURTINE.]
A white or light-coloured concretionary limestone, usually hard and semi-crystalline, precipitated in hot springs, caves, etc., from water holding calcium carbonate in solution, and sometimes used for building (also ***travertine stone***). Also, a porous, sponge-textured stone formed in the same way (also called ***calc-sinter***, ***tufa***).

†**travested** *adjective.* **M17–M18.**
[Prob. from Italian *travestito*, French *travesti* after *vested* etc. Cf. TRAVESTY *verb.*]
Disguised; ridiculed by parody or imitation.

travestiment /ˈtravɪstɪm(ə)nt/ *noun. rare.* **M19.**
[from TRAVESTY *verb* + -MENT.]
= next. Also, an instance of this.

travestissement /travɛstismɑ̃/ *noun. rare.* **M20.**
[French, lit. 'disguise, travesty'.]
The action of travestying a person or thing; the wearing of the dress of the opposite sex. Cf. prec.

travesty /ˈtravɪsti/ *adjective & noun.* **M17.**
[French *travesti* pa. pple of *travestir* from Italian *travestire*, from *tra-* TRANS- + *vestire* clothe.]
▸†**A** *adjective.* Dressed so as to be made ridiculous; burlesqued, parodied. **M17–L18.**
▸**B** *noun.* **1** (A) derisive or ludicrous imitation of a serious literary work. Now chiefly *transf.*, a grotesque misrepresentation or imitation (*of* a thing). **L17.**

2 Orig., an alteration of dress; a disguise. Now *spec.* (chiefly *THEATRICAL*), (dressing in) the clothes or style of clothing of members of the opposite sex (see also EN TRAVESTI). M18.

> 📖 **1** A. G. GARDINER A travesty of justice—a premium upon recklessness. I. ASIMOV His drooping eyelid dipped . . in a ghastly travesty of a wink.

Comb.: **travesty role** THEATRICAL: designed to be played by a performer of the sex opposite to that of the character represented.

travesty /ˈtravɪsti/ *verb trans.* L17.
[Orig. pa. pple, from French *travesti*: see prec.]
1 Alter in dress or appearance; disguise by such alteration. L17.
2 Make a travesty of; imitate or misrepresent ludicrously or grotesquely. L17.

> 📖 **2** J. MOYNAHAN 'None of That' travesties Mabel Dodge's lust for willed experience. E. DAVID Altering, travestying and degrading the dish itself.

▪ **travestier** *noun* L19.

travis /ˈtravɪs/ *noun*. Now *dial*. Also **trevis** /ˈtrɛvɪs/. LME.
[Var. of TRAVERSE *noun*.]
▶ **I 1** A railed enclosure into which restive horses are put to be shod. LME.
2 A wooden partition separating two stalls in a stable. E18.
3 A horse's stall in a stable. E18.
▶ **II** See TRAVERSE *noun*.

travisher /ˈtravɪʃə/ *noun*. E20.
[Perh. from dial. form of TRAVERSE *verb*.]
A carpenter's shave used for the final smoothing of chair seats.

travois /trəˈvɔɪ/ *noun*. *N. Amer.* Pl. same /-ˈvɔɪz/. M19.
[Alt. of TRAVAIL *noun*³. Cf. TRAVOY.]
A traditional N. American Indian vehicle consisting of two joined poles pulled by a horse etc.

travolator, **Trav-o-lator** *nouns* see TRAVELATOR.

travoy /trəˈvɔɪ/ *noun & verb*. *N. Amer.* L19.
[Repr. French Canad. pronunc. of French *travail*: see TRAVAIL *noun*³, TRAVOIS.]
▶ **A** *noun*. A small basic sledge used in dragging logs. L19.
▶ **B** *verb trans. & intrans.* Haul (a log or logs) by means of a travoy. L19.

trawl /trɔːl/ *noun*. M17.
[In branch I from TRAWL *verb*; in branch II perh. from TRAWL *verb* but cf. Middle Dutch *draghel* drag-net.]
▶ **I 1** An act of trawling for fish. *rare*. M17.
2 An exhaustive or extensive search. L20.

> 📖 **2** *Out of Town* A trawl through the display cases could reveal . . many . . items.

▶ **II 3** A large fishing net, *esp.* a conical one with a wide mouth, dragged along the bottom of the sea or a river by a boat. Also *trawl-net*. L17.
4 A long buoyed sea-fishing line having many short lines with baited hooks attached at intervals. Also ***trawl-line***. *US*. M19.

Comb.: **trawl-beam**: for holding open the mouth of a trawl; **trawl-buoy**: for buoying up a trawl; **trawl-head** either of two metal frames supporting the trawl-beam; ***trawl-line***: see sense 4 above; ***trawl-net***: see sense 3 above; **trawl-warp** a rope by which a trawl-net is dragged along.

trawl /trɔːl/ *verb*. M16.
[Prob. from Middle Dutch *traghelen* drag, rel. to *traghel* drag-net, perh. from Latin *tragula* drag-net, obscurely from *trahere* draw. Cf. prec., TRAIL *verb*.]
1 *verb intrans.* Fish (*for*) with a trawl. M16.
2 *verb intrans.* Fish by drawing bait along in the water; troll. E18.
3 *verb intrans.* Fish with a seine. M19.
4 *verb trans.* Catch with a trawl. M19.
5 *fig.* **a** *verb trans.* Search through or amongst exhaustively or extensively, esp. for a suitable candidate for a job etc. E20. ▸**b** *verb intrans.* Engage in an exhaustive or extensive search *for*; *esp.* search for a suitable candidate for a job etc. by sifting through a large number. L20.

> 📖 **5a** *Empire* Soderbergh . . trawls his psyche for material. *Management Today* Trawling the market to find out who does what particularly well. **b** *Guardian* UK Press Gazette . . is currently trawling for an editor.

trawler /ˈtrɔːlə/ *noun*. L16.
[from prec. + -ER¹.]
1 A person who fishes with a trawl. L16.
2 A boat used in fishing with a trawl. M19.

Traxcavator /ˈtrakskəveɪtə/ *noun*. M20.
[Blend of TRACK *noun* or TRACTOR and EXCAVATOR.]
(Proprietary name for) a type of mechanical excavator moving on endless steel bands or tracks.

tray /treɪ/ *noun*¹.
[Late Old English *trīg* = Old Swedish *trø* corn-measure, from Germanic base also of TREE *noun*.]
1 A utensil consisting of a thin flat piece of wood, metal, or plastic with a raised rim, used for carrying dishes, cups, glasses, etc.; a shallow flat receptacle, or lidless box, esp. for containing small articles, papers, etc.; *spec.* such a box forming a compartment in a trunk. LOE. ▸**b** *transf.* A light meal served on and eaten off a tray. E20. ▸**c** A drawer in which a body is stored within a refrigerated cabinet or chamber at a mortuary. *US*. M20.
†**2** A mason's hod for mortar. LOE–E17.
3 A hurdle. *dial*. E19.
4 The part of a truck on which goods are carried. *Austral.* M20.

> 📖 **1** B. BAINBRIDGE She regarded the trays of plastic brooches. N. FARAH The orderly . . walked in carrying a tray of drinks. P. FITZGERALD The . . clash of metal trays in the canteen. M. MARRIN I put . . unanswered mail into a full tray. ***in-tray***, ***out-tray***, ***safe tray***, ***tea-tray***, etc. **b** E. F. BENSON My maid would bring me a tray instead of dinner.

Comb.: **tray-buggy** *US* a buggy with a body shaped like a tray; **traymobile** *Austral. & NZ* a trolley, *esp.* a tea trolley; **tray stand** a small table on which to rest a tray; **tray table** a tray with legs which can be folded out, forming a stand or table; **tray top** (*a*) a rimmed tabletop which can be removed and used separately as a tray; (*b*) *Austral.* a truck with a pick-up body.
▪ **trayful** *noun* as much as a tray will hold M17.

tray /treɪ/ *noun*². E19.
[Var. of TREY after BAY *noun*⁸.]
The third branch of a stag's horn.

tray *noun*³ var. of TREY.

†**tray** *verb trans.* ME–M16.
[Old French *trair* (mod. *trahir*) from Proto-Romance alt. of Latin *tradere* deliver, formed as TRANS- + *dare* give.]
Betray.

treacher /ˈtrɛtʃə/ *noun*. Long *rare*. ME–M18.
[Old French *trecheor*, *trich-* (mod. *tricheur*), from *trechier*, (also mod.) *tricher* to cheat or trick: see TRICK *noun & adjective*, -ER², -OR.]
A deceiver, a cheat; a traitor.

†**treacherer** *noun*. L16–E17.
[App. from TREACHERY + -ER¹. Cf. TREACHETOUR.]
= prec.

treacherous /ˈtrɛtʃ(ə)rəs/ *adjective*. ME.
[Old French *trecherous*, *tricher-*, formed as TREACHER: see -OUS.]
1 Guilty of or involving treachery; disloyal, traitorous. ME.
2 *fig.* Deceptive, unreliable; *esp.* (of ground, ice, conditions, etc.) dangerous, hazardous. E17.

> 📖 **1** CONAN DOYLE A treacherous friend and a fickle wife. **2** R. K. NARAYAN He found the subject as treacherous as a bog at night. R. FRAME The road was treacherous after rains.

▪ **treacherously** *adverb* ME. **treacherousness** *noun* E17.

treachery /ˈtrɛtʃ(ə)ri/ *noun*. ME.
[Old French *trecherie*, (also mod.) *tricherie*, from *trechier*, *trichier*: see TRICK *noun & adjective*, -ERY.]
1 Violation of faith or betrayal of trust; perfidy; *spec.* treason. ME.
2 An instance of or an act involving this. ME.
3 *transf.* Ground that gives way under the feet. L19.

> 📖 **1** JULIA HAMILTON His tender concern made her . . aware of her own treachery. **2** N. MONSARRAT Guiscard stole . . , used any treachery, sealed and then betrayed any bargain. **3** G. ALLEN The . . belt [of mud] was one huge . . expanse of liquid treachery.

†**treachetour** *noun*. *rare* (Spenser). Only in L16.
[Alt. of TREACHERER.]
A deceiver; a traitor.

treacle /ˈtriːk(ə)l/ *noun & verb*. ME.
[Old French *triacle* (with parasitic *l*) from Latin *theriaca* from Greek *thēriakē* (sc. *antidotos* antidote) use as noun of fem. of adjective from *thērion* wild or venomous animal.]
▶ **A** *noun*. **I** Original sense.
†**1** PHARMACOLOGY. Any of various medicinal salves formerly used as antidotes to poisons, venomous bites, etc. Cf. THERIAC. ME–E19.
2 *fig. & gen.* A person or thing believed to have antidotal properties; an effective remedy. Long *arch.* or *obsolete*. ME.
3 With specifying word, any of several plants formerly credited with medicinal properties. Cf. ***treacle mustard*** below. *obsolete* exc. *dial.* LME.
1 *VENICE treacle*. **3** ***countryman's treacle***, ***English treacle***, ***poor man's treacle***, etc.
▶ **II** Current sense.
4 Uncrystallized syrup drained from partly refined sugar, golden syrup; uncrystallized syrup drained from raw sugar in refining, molasses (freq. distinguished as ***black treacle***). L17.
5 Any syrup obtained from various trees and plants. M18.
6 *fig.* Cloying sentimentality or flattery. L18.

> 📖 **6** V. NABOKOV A note in a blue-margined envelope, a nice mixture of poison and treacle. S. BRETT They flipped through the [cassette] tape . . , but the same unremitting treacle covered both sides.

Comb.: **treacle mustard** (*a*) any of various yellow-flowered cruciferous plants of the genus *Erysimum*, esp. the weed *E. cheiranthoides*; †(*b*) penny cress, *Thlaspi arvense*, so called on account of its supposed medicinal properties; **treacle sleep** *colloq.* a deep unbroken sleep.

▶ **B** *verb*. †**1** *verb trans.* Make into a salve or antidote. *rare*. Only in L15.
2 *verb trans.* Smear with treacle; *rare* dose with brimstone and treacle. M19. ▸**b** *verb trans. & intrans.* Smear (a tree) with treacle to catch moths. E20.
3 *verb intrans.* Flow like treacle. *joc.* L19.
▪ **treacly** *adjective* resembling treacle in quality or appearance; *fig.* cloyingly sweet or sentimental, honeyed: M18.

tread /trɛd/ *noun*. ME.
[from the verb.]
▶ **I 1** A footprint. *rare*. ME.
†**2** A line of footprints, a track, a trail. Cf. TRADE *noun* 10b. LME–E19.
3 A trodden way, a path. Chiefly *fig.* Cf. TRADE *noun* 10. LME.
4 The action or an act of treading or walking; the manner or sound of this; a step. LME. ▸**b** An act of treadling. *rare*. L17.
†**5** The action of a male bird in copulation. L17–M18.

> 📖 **4** J. LE CARRÉ The youthful springiness of his tread. JULIA HAMILTON She sat . . listening to Edmund's firm tread crossing the hall.

▶ **II 6** A course or manner of action, *esp.* a regular one; a habit, a custom. Cf. TRADE *noun* 11. Chiefly *Scot.* (now *dial.*). M16.
7 Coming and going; communication, dealings. Also, fuss, trouble. Cf. TRADE *noun* 2a, b. *Scot.* (now *dial.*). M16.
8 = TRADE *noun* 12a. *Scot.* L16.
▶ **III 9** The chalaza of an egg. Now *rare*. L16.
10 A bruise or wound of the coronet of a horse's foot, caused by setting one foot on another. M17.
11 The horizontal upper surface of a step or a stair; the width of this from front to back. Also ***tread board***. E18. ▸**b** FORTIFICATION. A terrace at the back of a parapet, from which to fire. M19. ▸**c** PHYSICAL GEOGRAPHY. The approximately horizontal part of each of a series of steplike landforms, as in a glacial stairway or river terrace. E20.
12 The part of the sole of the foot or of a shoe which comes in contact with the ground in walking. E18.
13 a A wheel track, a rut (*dial.*); the transverse distance between two wheels on a vehicle. Now *esp.*, the part of a wheel on a vehicle that touches the ground or a rail; the part of a rail that the wheels of a vehicle touch. M18. ▸**b** The thick moulded surface of a pneumatic tyre designed to grip the road. L19.

> 📖 **11** K. AMIS Mr Pastry's tennis-ball lying . . on the second tread from the top. **13b** *attrib.*: *Mountain Biker* The open tread pattern on this new Fisher tyre.

▪ **treaded** *adjective* (of a tyre) having a moulded tread E20. **treadless** *adjective* (esp. of a tyre) having no tread M20.

tread /trɛd/ *verb*. Pa. t. **trod** /trɒd/, (*rare*) **treaded**; pa. pple **trodden** /ˈtrɒd(ə)n/, **trod**.
[Old English *tredan* = Old Frisian *treda*, Old Saxon *tredan*, Old High German *tretan* (Dutch *treden*, German *treten*), from West Germanic. Cf. TRADE *noun*.]
1 *verb trans.* Walk on (the ground etc.); walk in or about (a place). OE.
2 *verb trans.* Walk along, follow, (a path or road). OE.
3 *verb intrans.* Walk; set down the feet in walking. Freq. foll. by adverbs. OE. ▸**b** Step *on*, put one's foot down *on* accidentally or intentionally. LME.
4 *verb trans.* **a** Step or walk with pressure on, esp. so as to crush or destroy; trample. Now only foll. by *down* or in phrs. and sense 4b below. OE. ▸**b** *spec.* Thresh (corn), press out the juice of (grapes), by trampling (also foll. by *out*); wash (clothes) by trampling. LME. ▸**c** *fig.* Oppress; treat harshly. Usu. foll. by *down*. Cf. DOWNTRODDEN. E16.
5 *verb intrans.* Foll. by *on*: trample on; *fig.* suppress, subdue mercilessly. OE.
6 a *verb trans.* Of a male bird: copulate with (a hen). ME. ▸**b** *verb intrans.* Of birds: copulate. L15.
7 *verb trans.* Press down and firm (soil) with the feet. LME. ▸**b** *verb intrans.* Of soil: yield or give under foot. *dial.* M19.
8 *verb trans.* Make or form (esp. a path) by the action of the feet in walking (usu. foll. by *out*); make a track with (dirt etc.) from the feet. LME.
9 *verb trans.* With adverbs: bring into a specified position or condition by treading. M16.
10 *verb trans.* Press on (a treadle). L17.

> 📖 **1** H. JAMES She trod the place like a reigning queen. J. CONRAD He trod the pavement heavily with his shiny boots. **2** N. FARAH A path trodden a million times. **3** R. BROOKE Around me the feet of thy watchers tread. R. PARK Ann came shyly after, treading too closely behind her mother. W. GOLDING Softly they . . trod, almost on tiptoe, down the garden path. *fig.*: G. GREENE They had to tread carefully for a lifetime, never speak without thinking twice. **b** SHAKES. *Meas. for M.* The poor beetle that we tread upon. V. WOOLF He . . trod on the lace of my petticoat. **9** JOYCE The heels of her . . boots were trodden down all to one side. M. FORSTER The carpet there. It's ruined . . . Susan's nephews have dropped . . gunge on it and it's all trodden in.

Phrases: **tread a measure**, **tread a dance** *arch.* perform a dance in a rhythmic or stately manner. ***tread on air***, ***tread as if on air***:

see AIR noun[1] 1. **tread on a person's toes**, **tread on a person's corns** offend or irritate a person, esp. by impinging on his or her area of responsibility. *tread on eggs*: see EGG noun. **tread the boards**, **tread the stage** be an actor or actress; appear on the stage. *tread under foot*: see FOOT noun. **tread water** maintain an upright position in water by moving the feet as if walking and the hands with a downward circular motion.

Comb.: **treadmill** (*a*) an apparatus for producing motion by the weight of a person or animal continuously stepping on steps arranged around the inner surface of a revolving upright wheel; (*b*) *fig.* a monotonous routine or round of work etc.; **treadmilling** (*a*) *rare* labouring on a treadmill; (*b*) BIOLOGY the continual transfer of tubulin subunits from one end of a microtubule to the other; **tread-softly** the spurge nettle, *Cnidoscolus stimulosus*. **treadwheel** = *treadmill* (a) above.

■ **treader** noun ME. **treading** noun (*a*) the action of the verb; an instance of this; (*b*) (long *rare* or *obsolete*) a thing made by treading: LME.

treadle /ˈtrɛd(ə)l/ *noun & verb*. Also **treddle**.
[Old English *tredel*, from *tredan*: see prec., -LE[1].]
▶ **A** *noun*. †**1** A step, a stair. *rare*. OE–M19.
2 A lever worked by the foot and imparting motion to a part of a machine. LME. ▸**b** A pedal, as on a bicycle etc. L19. ▸**c** Any device activating a mechanism (e.g. a traffic signal or exit door) when stepped on or otherwise depressed. E20.
†**3** = TREAD noun 9. M17–L18.

📖 **2** *attrib.*: D. MADDEN Her aunt's workroom, with its . . treadle sewing machine.

▶ **B** *verb intrans.* Work a treadle; *rare* move the feet as if doing this. L19.

†**treague** *noun*. L16–M17.
[medieval Latin *trege*, *treuge* = Old English *treowa*, Old Saxon *treuwa*, Gothic *triggwa*: see TRUCE noun.]
A truce.

treason /ˈtriːz(ə)n/ *noun & verb*. ME.
[Anglo-Norman *treisoun*, *tres(o)un*, Old French *traison* (mod. *trahison*) from Latin *traditio(n-)*: see TRADITION noun.]
▶ **A** *noun*. **1** The action of betraying a person etc., betrayal of trust, treachery. ME.
2 LAW. **a** Violation by a subject of allegiance to the sovereign or to the State, esp. by attempting or plotting to kill or overthrow the sovereign or overthrow the Government. Formerly also ***high treason***. ME. ▸**b** *Hist.* ***petit treason***, ***petty treason***, murder of a person, esp. a master or husband, thought to be owed allegiance. L15.
3 An act or kind of treason. Now *rare*. ME.

📖 **1** M. PUZO Always alert for treason, always believing that women would betray and desert him.

Phrases & comb.: ***high treason***: see sense 2a above. ***misprision of treason***: see MISPRISION noun[1] 2. ***petit treason***, ***petty treason***: see sense 2b above. **treason felon** LAW a person convicted of treason felony. **treason felony** LAW an offence orig. classed as treason but removed from this category by an act of 1848 and made a felony. **treason of the clerks** = *TRAHISON des clercs*.
▶ **B** *verb trans.* Act treasonably towards, betray. *rare*. ME.
¶ The offence of *petty treason* was abolished in 1828, *treason* taking on the meaning of *high treason*.

treasonable /ˈtriːz(ə)nəb(ə)l/ *adjective*. LME.
[from TREASON noun + -ABLE.]
Of the nature of treason, guilty of or involving treason, treacherous.

📖 S. RICHARDSON So, Pamela, we have seized . . your treasonable papers? H. HALLAM Their participation in a treasonable conspiracy being manifest.

■ **treasonableness** noun L17. **treasonably** adverb LME.

treasonous /ˈtriːz(ə)nəs/ *adjective*. LME.
[formed as prec. + -OUS.]
Treasonable.
■ **treasonously** adverb LME.

treasurable /ˈtrɛʒ(ə)rəb(ə)l/ *adjective*. E17.
[from TREASURE verb + -ABLE.]
Fit or worthy to be treasured; valuable, precious.
■ **treasurableness** noun (*rare*) L19.

treasure /ˈtrɛʒə/ *noun*. ME.
[Old & mod. French *trésor* from Proto-Romance from Latin THESAURUS.]
1 *sing.* & in *pl.* Wealth or riches stored or accumulated, esp. in the form of gems, precious metals, or gold or silver coin. Also (*sing.*), a hoard of such wealth. ME. ▸†**b** A store or stock *of* anything valuable. LME–E18.
2 A thing valued and kept for its rarity, workmanship, associations, etc.; *colloq.* a much loved or highly valued person. ME.
†**3** A treasury; a treasure-house, a treasure chest. *rare*. LME–L16.

📖 **1** BYRON Goods, and jewels, and all kinds of treasure. P. FLEMING A fruitless search . . for the buried treasure of the Kandyan Kings. **2** C. E. MATHEWS A treasure not only to Devonians, but to book lovers generally. *Security Gazette* Ireland's greatest art treasure, the 1,000 year old 'Book of Kells'. *New Yorker* The STACK-A-SHELF system is perfect for showcasing your personal treasures. J. FANE The Whitakers' daily lady . . is the proverbial treasure.

Comb.: **treasure chest** a chest for holding or storing treasure; **treasure-flower** a gazania, *Gazania rigens*, grown for ornament; **treasure-house** a building or room in which treasure is kept, a treasury; **treasure hunt** a hunt for treasure; a game in which hidden objects are searched for, often by following a trail of clues; **Treasure State** US the State of Montana; **treasure trove** [Anglo-Norman *tresor trové* treasure found] LAW treasure found hidden in the ground etc. but of unknown ownership, and so belonging to the Crown (though sometimes in part returned or recompensed); *gen.* a hidden store of valuables.
■ **treasureless** adjective L16.

treasure /ˈtrɛʒə/ *verb trans*. LME.
[from the noun.]
1 Lay aside or store (something valuable) for preservation or future use. Freq. foll. by *up*. LME.
†**2** Provide or endow with treasures; enrich. *rare*. L16–M17.
3 Keep as precious; value (esp. a long-kept possession etc.) highly; cherish, prize. E20.

📖 **1** *fig.*: I. WATTS To acquire and treasure up a large store of ideas. **3** LYNDON B. JOHNSON A silver desk set I will always treasure. S. DESHPANDE I'd always treasured my hours of solitude. J. FRAME Madge would soon be leaving her treasured home.

treasurer /ˈtrɛʒ(ə)rə/ *noun*. ME.
[Sense 1 from Anglo-Norman *tresorer*, Old & mod. French *trésorier*, from *trésor* TREASURE noun after late Latin *thesaurarius*: see -ER[2]. Sense 2 from TREASURE verb + -ER[1].]
1 A person appointed to administer the funds of a society, company, municipality, etc.; an officer having responsibility for paying and receiving public revenues; *spec.* (usu. **T-**) (*a*) *Hist.* (in full ***Lord High Treasurer***, ***Lord Treasurer***) the head of the exchequer; (*b*) *Austral.* the minister of finance. ME.
2 A person who treasures something, a hoarder or keeper *of* something precious. *rare*. L16.

📖 **1** *fig.*: SIR W. SCOTT The secrets of which thou seemest . . a too faithful treasurer.

■ **treasurership** noun the office of treasurer L15. **treasuress** noun (now *rare*) a female treasurer LME.

treasury /ˈtrɛʒ(ə)ri/ *noun*. ME.
[Old French *tresorie* (formed as TREASURE noun) after medieval Latin *thesaur(ar)ia*, *-ium*: see -Y[3].]
1 A room or building where treasure is stored, a place or receptacle for money or valuables. Also, the funds or revenue of a State, institution, society, etc. ME.
†**2** A treasure. ME–L17.
3 A repository or collection of valuable or pleasing things. LME.
4 (**T-**.) The department of State responsible for the collection, management, and expenditure of the public revenue of a country; the staff of this department; the building from which this department is run. LME.
5 In full ***treasury bill***. A bill of exchange issued by the Government to raise money for temporary needs. Usu. in *pl.* L18.
6 The weekly payment of a company of actors. *Theatrical slang*. L19.

📖 **3** W. SHEED The treasury of great songs written . . between the wars. **4 First Lord of the Treasury** in Britain, the Prime Minister. **Secretary of the Treasury** the head of the US Treasury Department.

Comb.: **Treasury bench** the front bench on the right hand of the Speaker in the House of Commons, occupied by the Prime Minister, the Chancellor of the Exchequer, and other members of the Government; *treasury bill*: see sense 5 above; **treasury-bond** a government bond issued by the Treasury; **Treasury Department** the US government finance department; **treasury note** (*Hist.* exc. *US*) a note issued by the Treasury for use as currency; **treasury tag** a small tag used to fasten papers together, consisting of a length of string with a metal bar at each end.
■ **treasuryship** noun = TREASURERSHIP E18.

treat /triːt/ *noun*[1]. *obsolete* exc. *dial.* & *Hist.* Also **treet**, **trete**. ME.
[Origin uncertain: perh. from French *trait* withdrawn, extracted.]
The second quality of bran removed by sieving from wheatmeal.
bread of trete the second lowest and cheapest quality of bread specified in the regulations of the 13th cent.

treat /triːt/ *noun*[2]. LME.
[from the verb.]
▶ **I** †**1** The action or an act of treating or discussing terms; (a) negotiation, (an) agreement. LME–L16.
†**2** An entreaty. E–M17.
3 a An entertainment, meal, outing, etc., provided by a person for the enjoyment of another or others. M17. ▸**b** The action or an act of treating or entertaining; (with *possess.*) one's turn to treat. L17. ▸**c** An event, circumstance, gift, etc., esp. when unexpected or unusual, that gives great pleasure. L18. ▸**d** ***a treat***, so as to gratify highly, extremely good or well. *colloq.* L19.
†**4** = TREATMENT 1. L17–E18.

📖 **3a** S. HOOD A Christmas treat for the village children in the village hall. ***Dutch treat***: see DUTCH adjective. **b** J. CROWNE The treat to-night is mine, and I invite all this good company. **stand treat** bear the expense of a treat. **c** W. G. GRACE It was a treat to watch him punish the bowling. N. FREELING Smoking a small Dutch cigar as a treat. J. COX Occasionally . . a worm. What a treat for the birds. ***a fair treat***: see FAIR adjective. **d** A. SILLITOE The sports ground looked a treat. *Guardian* He had a stroke . . but he's come on a treat.

▶ **II 5** A plaster or ointment spread on a cloth; a poultice. Long *obsolete* exc. *Scot. dial.* LME.
†**6** = TREATISE 1. LME–M16.

treat /triːt/ *verb*. ME.
[Anglo-Norman *treter*, Old French *tretier*, *traitier* (mod. *traiter*) from Latin *tractare* drag, manage, handle, from pa. ppl stem of *trahere* draw.]
1 a *verb intrans.* Discuss terms, carry on negotiations, (*with*); bargain, negotiate, (*for*); (with adverbial) bring into or out of a place etc. by negotiation. ME. ▸†**b** *verb trans.* Negotiate for or about, arrange, plan. LME–E18.
2 a *verb trans.* Deal with or represent (a subject) in literature, art, etc.; discuss or present in speech or writing. ME. ▸**b** *verb intrans.* Conduct discussion in speech or writing, discourse, (*of* or *on* a subject, *with* a person or subject). LME.
3 *verb trans.* & *intrans.* Entreat, beseech, request, (a person). Long *obsolete* exc. *Scot.* LME.
†**4** *verb trans.* Apply oneself to, work at, carry out; handle; manage, rule, lead, (a person). LME–E17.
5 a *verb trans.* Deal with or behave or act towards in a specified way; regard in a particular way and deal with accordingly (freq. foll. by *as*, *like*). LME. ▸†**b** *verb intrans.* Deal *with* in a specified way. LME–E18.
6 *verb trans.* **a** Apply medical care or attention to (a person, part of the body, or ailment). (Foll. by *with* a remedy, *for* a disease etc.) LME. ▸**b** Subject to chemical etc. action; act upon to obtain a particular result. (Foll. by *with*.) E19.
†**7** *verb trans.* Show kindness or respect to; indulge, favour; honour. LME–L16.
8 a *verb trans.* Provide with food, drink, entertainment, etc., esp. at one's own expense; show hospitality to, regale. (Foll. by *to* or *with* the thing provided.) E16. ▸**b** *verb intrans.* Provide food etc. as a treat. E18.

📖 **1a** T. ARNOLD They began to treat with Marcellus for the surrender of Syracuse. **2a** A. B. JAMESON The life of St Stephen . . has been treated in mural frescoes. R. G. COLLINGWOOD Books in which religion was treated from a psychological point of view. **b** U. ELLIS-FERMOR Those books which treat mainly . . with our particular theme. *Nature* He could usually treat with professionals on equal terms. **5a** R. KIPLING At least she did not treat me like a child. A. S. NEILL The villagers treated the affair . . as a huge joke. V. WOOLF Don't you think it . . cruel the way they treat dogs in this country? R. P. JHABVALA The Nawab treated him with . . exaggerated courtesy. *Daily Telegraph* Any information would be treated in the strictest confidence. ***treat like dirt***: see DIRT noun. ***treat like a lord***: see LORD noun. **6a** ANTHONY SMITH She was treated for the wound. R. GODDEN Unless treated quickly rabies is certain death. **b** J. R. MCCULLOCH Potato-starch when treated with sulphuric acid becomes sugar. A. CARTER It was made of papier mâché specially treated to withstand the weather. **8a** K. ISHIGURO I treated Ichiro to another ice-cream. M. WESLEY Blanco pointed at the . . cream cakes. 'My mother sent me some money. I'll treat you.' *iron.*: K. AMIS I've been treating young Charlie to a . . lecture on . . health. **b** A. LURIE When you're in work you treat. Everyone knows that.

■ **treatee** noun (*rare*) a person who is treated or entertained M19. **treater** noun LME.

treatable /ˈtriːtəb(ə)l/ *adjective*. ME.
[Old & mod. French *traitable* from Latin *tractabilis* TRACTABLE; in some senses from prec. + -ABLE.]
1 a Of a person etc.: easily dealt with; open to appeal or argument; reasonable, affable. *arch.* ME. ▸†**b** Of an action, utterance, etc.: moderate, deliberate; gentle; clear, distinct. LME–L17.
2 Able to be treated or dealt with. Freq. in MEDICINE, able to be treated with success, yielding to treatment. ME.
†**3** Able to be handled or touched, tangible; exposed to touch. *rare*. LME–M16.
■ **treataˈbility** noun M20. **treatableness** noun E16. **treatably** adverb LME.

treatise /ˈtriːtɪs, -ɪz/ *noun & verb*. LME.
[Anglo-Norman *tretis*, from Old French *traitier* TREAT verb: see -ISE[1].]
▶ **A** *noun*. **1** A written work dealing formally and methodically with a subject. Formerly also *gen.*, a literary work, a book. LME. ▸†**b** A spoken or written story or narrative. LME–E17. ▸†**c** A description or account (*of* something). L16–L17.
†**2 a** Negotiation, discussion or arrangement of terms. LME–M17. ▸**b** A treaty. LME–M16.

📖 **1** J. AIKEN To write a treatise on the structuralist elements in Heidegger.

▶†**B** *verb trans.* & *intrans.* Write a treatise (on). E16–E17.
■ †**treatiser** noun E–M17.

treatment /'triːtm(ə)nt/ *noun*. M16.
[from TREAT *verb* + -MENT.]
1 The process or manner of behaving towards or dealing with a person or thing. (Foll. by *of*.) M16.
2 = TREAT *noun*[2] 3a. *obsolete* exc. *dial*. M17.
3 a The application of medical care or attention to a patient, ailment, etc. (Foll. by *of*, *with*.) M18. ▸**b** Subjection to the action of a chemical, physical, or biological agent etc. (Foll. by *of*, *with*.) E19.
4 Discussion or arrangement of terms, negotiation. *rare*. E19.
5 A manner or instance of dealing with a subject or work in literature, art, etc.; literary or artistic handling, written or spoken discussion. M19. ▸**b** CINEMATOGRAPHY. A preparatory version of a screenplay, including descriptions of sets and of the camerawork required. E20.
6 In full ***the full treatment***. The most elaborate or extensive way of dealing with a subject, situation, person, etc. Freq. in ***get the full treatment***, ***give the full treatment***. *colloq*. M20.

> **1** ROBERT WATSON The troops, discontented with his treatment of them . . refused to obey. COLERIDGE Had Luther been . . a prince, he could not have desired better treatment. *New York Review of Books* Concern over the shabby treatment of Hong Kong. **3a** V. BRITTAIN The Devonshire Hospital . . for the treatment of rheumatic complaints. *Practical Health* Patients under treatment for leukaemia. **b** ***heat treatment***, ***insulin treatment***, ***primary treatment***, ***solution treatment***, etc. **5** W. Y. SELLAR His treatment of the subjects taken from the Greek mythology. **6** E. HEMINGWAY We'll give breakfast the full treatment.

treaty /'triːti/ *noun & verb*. LME.
[Anglo-Norman *treté*, Old & mod. French *traité* from Latin *tractatus* TRACTATE: see -Y[5].]
▶ **A** *noun*. †**1 a** Literary or artistic treatment, written or spoken discussion. LME–M17. ▸**b** = TREATISE *noun* 1. LME–E18.
2 Discussion of terms, negotiation. Now *rare* or *obsolete* exc. in ***in treaty***. LME.
3 a An agreement or contract between individuals or parties. *obsolete* exc. in ***private treaty*** s.v. PRIVATE *adjective*. LME. ▸**b** A formally concluded and ratified agreement or compact between two or more States, relating to peace, alliance, commerce, etc.; a (notional) document embodying such an agreement. LME.
†**4** Entreaty, persuasion, request. LME–M17.

> **3b** C. HILL The Treaties of Westphalia in 1648 had ended the German war. LYNDON B. JOHNSON The signing of a treaty to prohibit weapons . . in outer space. ***extradition treaty***, ***peace treaty***, etc.

Comb.: **treaty Indian** *N. Amer.* (now chiefly *Canad.*): whose people have signed a treaty with the government; **treaty port** *Hist.*: bound by treaty to be open to foreign trade.
▶ **B** *verb*. **1** *verb intrans*. Make a treaty. M19.
2 *verb trans*. Bind or affect by a treaty. L19.
■ **treatyless** *adjective* L19.

Trebbiano /trɛbɪ'ɑːnəʊ/ *noun*. L19.
[Italian, from the River *Trebbia* in northern central Italy.]
A variety of vine and grape widely cultivated in Italy and elsewhere; the dry aromatic white wine produced from this grape.

treble /'trɛb(ə)l/ *noun*. ME.
[Old French, use as noun of adjective: see next. Cf. TRIPLUM.]
▶ **I 1** The highest singing voice, esp. as possessed by a boy; a part written for or sung by such a voice; a person having a treble voice or singing a treble part; the highest part in musical composition. ME.
2 (A) high-pitched or shrill voice, sound, or note; the high-frequency component of recorded or transmitted sound. E16.
3 An instrument, string, bell, etc., of treble pitch. M16.

> **1** K. AMIS Boy trebles of thirteen or fourteen. **2** TENNYSON I chatter over stony ways, In little sharps and trebles. R. RENDELL Voices could be heard, the clamorous treble of children. *Empire* Adjusting the treble or bass can make a footstep heavier or lighter.

▶ **II 4** A threefold number, quantity, etc.; a thing consisting of three parts; a sum or quantity three times as great as another. LME. ▸**b** PAPER-MAKING. A frame on which hand-made paper is hung to dry. *obsolete* exc. *Hist*. M18. ▸**c** A method of crocheting in which three loops of thread are carried on the hook; a line or chain of crochet work done by this method. L19. ▸**d** = ***treble hook*** s.v. TREBLE *adjective*. L19. ▸**e** RACING. A bet on three races, in which the winnings and stake from the first race are transferred to the second and then (if successful) to the third. Also, a total of three races won by the same horse. E20. ▸**f** DARTS. (A throw into) the narrow space enclosed by the two middle circles of a dartboard, worth treble. M20. ▸**g** SPORT. A total of three victories, championships, etc., esp. by a football club during a season. M20. ▸**h** A drink of spirits of three times the standard measure. M20.

> **4g** *Listener* The treble of League, Cup, and European Cup seemed . . a possibility.

treble /'trɛb(ə)l/ *adjective & adverb*. ME.
[Old French from Latin *triplus* TRIPLE *adjective*.]
▶ **A** *adjective*. **1** Consisting of three members, things, sets, etc., threefold; existing or occurring three times or in three ways; of three kinds; triple. ME.
2 Three times as much or as many; of three times *the* number or amount. ME. ▸**b** *spec*. Of a drink of spirits: constituting three times the standard measure. M20.
3 Of, pertaining to, or designating the highest singing voice (esp. of a boy) or musical part or frequency of sound; designating a musical instrument, string, etc., of the highest pitch; soprano. LME. ▸**b** High-pitched, shrill. M16.

> **1** GIBBON A treble inclosure of brick walls. SIR W. SCOTT It was attended with a treble difficulty. F. HARRISON Every . . episode has its double and treble meaning. **2** T. JEFFERSON It sells . . for treble the price of common whale oil. A. URE The roller A, moving with a treble surface velocity. **b** L. DEIGHTON He . . ordered three treble brandies. **3** HARPER LEE The town fire siren wailed up the scale to a treble pitch. *Daily Telegraph* Twin . . loudspeaker enclosures, each containing 2 speakers (bass and treble).

Special collocations: **treble agent** a person ostensibly spying for three countries, although in fact loyal to only one. **treble bell** the smallest bell of a peal or set. **treble chance** a form of football pool in which different numbers of points are awarded for a draw, an away win, and a home win. **treble clef**: placing German above middle C on the second lowest line of the staff. **treble hook** a fish-hook with three points. **treble rhyme**: including three syllables.
▶ **B** *adverb*. **1** To three times the amount or extent; three times over; trebly. ME.
2 In a high-pitched tone, shrilly. L16.
■ **trebleness** *noun* (*rare*) (**a**) treble quality of sounds, high pitch; (**b**) the quality of being threefold: E17.

treble /'trɛb(ə)l/ *verb*. ME.
[from prec.]
1 *verb trans*. Make three times as much or as many; multiply by three. ME. ▸**b** Fold in three thicknesses; make in three layers. L16. ▸**c** Amount to three times as many or as much as. E17.
2 *verb intrans*. Emit a high-pitched or shrill sound. Also (foll. by *upon*), sing the treble part to the lower parts in a composition. *rare*. LME.
3 *verb intrans*. Become three times as much or as many. E17.

> **1** SHAKES. *Merch. V.* Double six thousand, and then treble that. *Listener* Pre-packaging . . trebles a shop assistant's throughput. **c** G. BORROW The Carlists . . whose numbers more than trebled his own. **3** C. PEBODY Mr Levy reduced the price of the paper . . . The circulation doubled, trebled, quadrupled.

trebly /'trɛbli/ *adjective*. L20.
[from TREBLE *noun* + -Y[1].]
Esp. of reproduced music: having too much treble; tinny.

trebly /'trɛbli/ *adverb*. L16.
[from TREBLE *adjective* + -LY[2].]
In a treble or threefold degree or manner, three times as much, triply.

> TENNYSON This hath made them trebly dear.

trebuchet /'trɛbjʊʃɛt, -bəʃɛt, *foreign* trebyʃɛ (*pl. same*)/ *noun*. Also **trebucket** /'triːbʌkɪt, 'trɛ-/. ME.
[Old & mod. French *trébuchet* (medieval Latin *trebuchetum*, *tra-*), from *trébucher* overturn, overthrow, stumble, fall, ult. formed as TRABUCH: see -ET[1].]
1 *Hist*. A medieval military machine used in siege warfare for hurling heavy stones and other missiles. ME.
2 A small delicately poised balance or pair of scales. M16.
3 *Hist*. = ***cucking-stool*** s.v. CUCK *verb*[1]. M17.

trecento /treɪ'tʃɛntəʊ/ *noun*. M19.
[Italian = three hundred.]
The fourteenth century as a period of Italian art, architecture, literature, etc.; the style of the art etc. of this period.
■ **trecentist** *noun*, pl. **-tisti** /-'tɪsti/, an Italian artist, author, etc., of the 14th cent. E19.

treckschuit *noun* var. of TREKSCHUIT.

tre corde /treɪ 'kɔːdeɪ/ *adverbial & adjectival phr*. M20.
[Italian = three strings.]
A direction in music for the piano: with release of the soft pedal; (to be) played with such release. Cf. UNA CORDA.

treddle /'trɛd(ə)l/ *noun*[1]. Now *dial*.
[Old English *tyrdel* dim. of *tord* TURD: see -LE[1].]
A pellet of sheep's or goat's dung. Usu. in *pl*.
■ Also **treddling** *noun* (*dial*.) (usu. in *pl*.) LME.

treddle *noun*[2] & *verb* var. of TREADLE.

†**tredecile** *adjective & noun*. M17–E19.
[mod. Latin *tredecilis*, from Latin *tres* three + *decem* ten: see -ILE.]
ASTROLOGY. (Designating) the aspect of two planets which are three-tenths of a circle (108°) apart in the sky. Cf. DECILE.

tredrille /trɛ'drɪl/ *noun*. Also **-dille** /-'dɪl/. M18.
[from QUADRILLE *noun*[1] with *tre-* three for *qua(d)-* four.]
An adaptation of the card-game quadrille for three players, usu. with thirty cards.

tree /triː/ *noun & adjective*.
[Old English *trēo(w)* = Old Frisian *trē*, Old Saxon *trio*, *treo*, Old Norse *tré*, Gothic *triu*, from Germanic var. of Indo-European base repr. by Sanskrit *dāru*, *dru-* tree, Greek *doru* wood, spear, *drus* tree, oak.]
▶ **A** *noun*. **1** A woody perennial plant, typically having a single stem or trunk growing to a considerable height and bearing lateral branches at some distance from the ground. Cf. SHRUB *noun*[1] 1. OE. ▸**b** More widely, any bush or shrub of erect growth with a single stem. Also, any of certain herbaceous plants, such as the banana, with a very tall but not woody stem. ME. ▸**c** = ***Christmas tree*** (a) s.v. CHRISTMAS *noun*. M19.
2 Wood, esp. as a material; timber. *arch*. OE.
3 A branch or trunk of a tree as shaped for some purpose; a wooden pole, stake, bar, etc., forming part of a structure. Usu. as 2nd elem. of comb., as ***axle-tree***, ***cross-tree***, ***roof-tree***, ***summer tree***, etc. OE. ▸**b** A stick used as a staff or club. *obsolete* exc. *Scot*. OE.
4 a The cross on which Jesus was crucified. *arch. & poet*. OE. ▸**b** A gallows. ME.
5 a A genealogical tree; *fig*. a family, a lineage, a stock. ME. ▸**b** MATH. & COMPUTING etc. A branching figure or graph in which processes, relationships, etc., are represented by points or nodes joined by lines (also ***tree diagram***); a process, analysis, etc., having this structure; a dendrogram. M19.
6 a The wooden shaft of a spear; the handle of an implement. Formerly also, a spear, a lance. Now *dial*. ME. ▸†**b** A wooden structure, *esp*. a ship. LME–L16. ▸**c** The framework of a saddle, a saddle-tree; a block for keeping a shoe in shape when not worn, a shoe- or boot-tree. L15. ▸**d** A wooden vessel; a barrel, a cask. *Scot*. E16.
7 Any natural or artificial structure of branched form; *spec*. (**a**) CHEMISTRY a treelike mass of crystals forming from a solution; a dendrite; (**b**) ANATOMY any branching system of vessels, nerves, etc., in the body; (**c**) ZOOLOGY (in full ***respiratory tree***) a branched respiratory organ in the body cavity of holothurians; (**d**) OIL INDUSTRY a valve manifold on the casing of an oil or gas well (= ***Christmas tree*** (c) s.v. CHRISTMAS *noun*). E18.

> **1** J. BUCHAN A biggish clump of trees—firs mostly, with a few ashes and beeches. ***apple tree***, ***fir-tree***, ***oak tree***, etc. **b** ***currant-tree***, ***rose tree***, etc.

Phrases: **at the top of the tree** in the highest rank of a profession etc. ***bark up the wrong tree***: see BARK *verb*[1]. ***Christmas tree***: see CHRISTMAS *noun*. ***FAMILY-tree***. ***GENEALOGICAL tree***. **grow on trees** be freely or easily obtainable (usu. with neg.). ***not see the wood for the trees***: see WOOD *noun*[1]. **out of one's tree** *slang* (chiefly *N. Amer.*) mad, crazy. ***respiratory tree***: see sense 7(c) above. ***see the wood for the trees***: see WOOD *noun*[1]. **tree of Diana** a treelike mass of crystals formed in a solution of silver salts etc. **tree of heaven** a Chinese ailanthus, *Ailanthus altissima*, grown as an ornamental tree. ***tree of Jesse***: see JESSE *noun*[1]. **tree of knowledge** (**a**) the tree in the Garden of Eden bearing the apple eaten by Eve (also ***tree of the knowledge of good and evil***); (**b**) knowledge in general, comprising all its branches. **tree of liberty** a tree planted in celebration of a revolution or victory securing liberty. **tree of life** (**a**) a tree symbolic of life or immortality, *esp*. that found in the Garden of Eden (*Genesis* 2:9); (**b**) ANATOMY = ARBOR VITAE 2; (**c**) a representation of a tree or shrub used as a motif, esp. in oriental art. ***triple tree***: see TRIPLE *adjective & adverb*. ***TYBURN tree***. **up a tree** *colloq*. (chiefly *N. Amer.*) unable to escape, in a predicament, in great difficulties (cf. ***up a gum tree*** s.v. GUM *noun*[2]). ***wolf tree***: see WOLF *noun* 9.
Comb.: **tree agate**: bearing treelike markings; **tree babbler** any of various SE Asian babblers of the genera *Stachyris* and *Malcopteron*, which inhabit the ground levels of mature forests; **tree-bear** *US dial*. the racoon; **tree boa** any of several American arboreal boas of the genus *Corallus*, which have prehensile tails; **tree-calf** BOOKBINDING a binding made of calf stained with a treelike design; **tree-cat** (**a**) any small arboreal cat; (**b**) a palm civet; (**c**) *N. Amer. dial*. = FISHER 2b; **tree civet** a palm civet, *esp*. the African *Nandinia binotata*; **tree-crab** the coconut crab; **tree cranberry** the bush cranberry, *Viburnum trilobum*; **treecreeper** (**a**) any of various small passerine birds of the genus *Certhia* (family Certhiidae), which have down-curved bills and creep on the trunks and branches of trees; *esp*. the common *C. familiaris* of Eurasia and *C. americana* of North and Central America; (**b**) any similar bird of the Australian family Climacteridae; (**c**) = ***woodcreeper*** s.v. WOOD *noun*[1] & *adjective*[1]; **tree cricket** any of numerous arboreal crickets constituting the subfamily Oecanthinae; **tree-crow** = ***tree pie*** below; **tree cult** = ***tree-worship*** below; **tree daisy** = ***daisy-bush*** s.v. DAISY *noun*; **tree deity** a tree god or goddess; ***tree diagram***: see sense 5b above; **tree doctor** = ***tree surgeon*** below; **tree duck** = ***whistling duck*** s.v. WHISTLING *ppl adjective*; **tree-feeder** an animal that feeds on the foliage of trees, or on the insects living on leaves or bark; **tree-fern** any of various tree-sized tropical or subtropical ferns, esp. of the family Cyatheaceae, bearing a crown of fronds at the top of a stem resembling a tree-trunk; **tree fox** (**a**) the grey fox; (**b**) *N. Amer. dial*. = FISHER 2b; **tree frog** an arboreal frog; *spec*. one of

the large family Hylidae, which comprises mainly small species with adhesive discs on the tips of the toes; **tree god**, **tree goddess** a god, goddess, supposed to inhabit a tree; a tree which is an object of worship; **tree-goose** (*obsolete* exc. *Hist.*) the barnacle goose; **tree heath** = BRIER *noun*² 1; **tree hoopoe** = ***wood hoopoe*** s.v. WOOD *noun*¹ & *adjective*¹; **tree hopper** any of various mainly tropical homopteran bugs of the family Membracidae, which live chiefly on trees; **tree house** (*a*) a house built in a tree for security against enemies; (*b*) a structure or hut built in a tree for children to play in; **tree-hugger** *colloq.* (*a*) a person who cares for trees or the environment generally; an environmentalist (usu. *derog.*); (*b*) a person who adopts a position embracing a tree to prevent it from being felled; **tree kangaroo** any of several arboreal wallabies constituting the genus *Dendrolagus*, which are found in New Guinea and tropical Queensland; **tree limit**, **tree line** (*a*) the line or level of altitude or latitude above which no trees grow (cf. ***snowline*** s.v. SNOW *noun*¹); (*b*) a row of trees, the edge of a wood; **tree-louse** an aphid; **tree lupin** a shrubby yellow-flowered Californian lupin, *Lupinus arboreus*, often planted to reclaim sandy land; **tree mallow** a tall woody-stemmed European mallow, *Lavatera arborea*, of cliffs and maritime rocks; **tree martin** an Australian swallow, *Hirundo nigricans*, which nests in trees; **tree medick** a shrubby medick, *Medicago arborea*, native to Greece and Turkey and grown for ornament; **tree-moss** (*a*) any of various lichens or mosses growing as epiphytes on trees; (*b*) any of several clubmosses resembling a miniature tree; *esp.* fir clubmoss, *Huperzia selago*; **tree mouse** any of various arboreal mice, esp. of the genera *Dendromus* (of Africa) and *Pogonomys* (of New Guinea); **tree network** (chiefly COMPUTING) a network having a tree structure; **tree onion** a variety of onion, *Allium cepa* var. *proliferum*, which bears small bulbs as well as flowers in the inflorescence; also called ***top onion***; **tree-oyster** an oyster found on the roots of mangroves; **tree partridge** any of various SE Asian partridges of the genera *Arborophila* and *Tropicoperdix*, which inhabit forests and scrub; **tree peony** any of several shrubby peonies, *esp.* the moutan, *Paeonia suffruticosa*; **tree pie** any of several Asian long-tailed arboreal crows of the genus *Dendrocitta* and related genera; **tree pipit** a common Old World pipit, *Anthus trivialis*, which inhabits open country with scattered trees; **tree porcupine** any of various arboreal porcupines of the genus *Coendou*, which are found in the forests of Central and S. America and have prehensile tails; **tree rat** (*a*) an arboreal rat; (*b*) *W. Indies* = HUTIA; (*c*) *colloq.* the grey squirrel; **tree ring** a ring in the cross-section of a tree-trunk, indicating a year's growth; **tree-rune** a rune of branched or treelike form; **treerunner** (*a*) any of several small Central and S. American birds of the genus *Margarornis* (ovenbird family); (*b*) *Austral.* the varied sitella, *Neositta chrysoptera*; **treescape** (a painting or drawing of) a landscape or scene consisting of or filled with trees; **tree search** COMPUTING a search in which a situation or entity is represented by a tree diagram, e.g. to facilitate efficient searching; **tree shrew** any of various small insectivorous arboreal mammals with pointed snouts and bushy tails, constituting the order Scandentia, which are found in the forests of SE Asia and are often regarded as close relatives of the primates; **tree snake** any of various slender non-venomous arboreal snakes of the subfamily Colubrinae, esp. of the genera *Dryophis* (of Asia), *Leptophis* (of S. America), and *Dendrelaphis* (of Australia); **tree sparrow** (*a*) a Eurasian sparrow, *Passer montanus*, which inhabits agricultural land and has a chestnut crown in both sexes; (*b*) a sparrow-like emberizid, *Spizella arborea*, which breeds on the edge of the tundra in N. America; **tree squirrel** an arboreal squirrel, *esp.* any of the genera *Sciurus* (of America and Eurasia), *Funisciurus* (of Africa), and *Callosciurus* (of SE Asia); **tree structure** (chiefly COMPUTING) a structure in which there are successive branchings or subdivisions (cf. ***tree diagram*** above); **tree surgeon** a practitioner of tree surgery; **tree surgery** the pruning and treatment of damaged or decayed trees in order to preserve them; **tree swallow** a N. American swallow, *Tachycineta bicolor*, which nests in trees etc.; **tree swift** each of three Asian crested swifts of the genus *Hemiprocne* and family Hemiprocnidae, which make a tiny nest of plant fragments and saliva attached to a tree branch; **tree toad** = ***tree frog*** above; **tree tomato** a Peruvian shrub of the nightshade family, *Cyphomandra crassicaulis*, grown in tropical and subtropical countries; the red or yellow egg-shaped fruit of this shrub; also called ***tamarillo***; **treetop** the top of a tree, the uppermost branches of a tree, (freq. in *pl.*); **tree trunk** the trunk of a tree; **tree warbler** any Old World warbler of the genus *Hippolais*, found in open country with scattered trees and scrub; **tree wasp** a European social wasp, *Dolichovespula sylvestris*, which makes a rounded nest suspended from a branch; **tree-worship** worship of trees or of the gods, spirits, etc., supposed to inhabit them.

▶**B** *attrib.* or as *adjective.* Made of wood, wooden. *obsolete* exc. *dial.* LME.

■ **treeful** *noun & adjective* (*rare*) (*a*) *noun* as much or as many as will fill or crowd a tree; (*b*) *adjective* full of or covered with trees: M19. **treeless** *adjective* destitute of trees, containing no trees L18. **treelessness** *noun* M19. **treelike** *adjective* resembling (that of) a tree M17. **treey** *adjective* (*rare*) covered or filled with trees, well wooded M19.

tree /triː/ *verb.* Pa. t. & pple **treed**. L16.
[from the noun.]
1 *verb trans.* Force (a hunted animal etc.) to take refuge in a tree, drive into or up a tree; *fig.* (chiefly *US*) put into a difficult or awkward situation. L16.
2 *verb intrans.* Climb up or perch in a tree, esp. to take refuge from a hunter etc. L17.
3 *verb trans.* Stretch or trim (a shoe or boot) on a shoe-tree; provide or fit with a wooden tree or shaft; support with timbers or beams. M18.
4 *verb trans.* Plant or cover with trees. Chiefly as ***treed*** *ppl adjective.* L19.
5 *verb intrans.* Take a treelike or branching form, as a deposit from a solution under the influence of an electric current. L19.

> 📖 **1** K. VONNEGUT His father . . was treed by a grizzly in Yellowstone Park.

treen /triːn, *as adjective also* 'triːən/ *adjective & noun.*
[Old English *trēowen*, formed as TREE *noun* + -EN⁴.]
▶**A** *adjective.* **1** Made of wood, wooden. *obsolete* exc. *dial.* OE.
†**2** Of or pertaining to a tree or trees. *rare.* LME–L17.
▶**B** *noun pl.* (*collect.*) Small domestic wooden objects, esp. when regarded as antiques. E20.

treenail /'triːneɪl/ *noun & verb.* Also **trenail** /'trɛn(ə)l/. ME.
[from TREE *noun* + NAIL *noun.*]
▶**A** *noun.* A cylindrical pin of hard wood used in fastening timbers together, esp. in shipbuilding. ME.
▶**B** *verb trans.* Fasten or secure with a treenail or treenails. E17.

treet *noun* var. of TREAT *noun*¹.

tref /trɛv/ *noun.* M19.
[Welsh.]
Hist. A Welsh social unit consisting of a hamlet or homestead.

trefa /'treɪfə/ *noun & adjective.* Also **trifa** /'trʌɪfə/, **tref** /treɪf/, & other vars. M19.
[Hebrew *ṭĕrēpāh* flesh of an animal torn or mauled, from *ṭārap* tear, rend.]
▶**A** *noun.* Meat forbidden to Jews because of coming from an animal not slaughtered according to Jewish law; *gen.* any food that is not kosher. M19.
▶**B** *attrib.* or as *adjective.* Of food: not prepared according to Jewish law, forbidden to Jews, not kosher. M19.

treff /trɛf/ *noun. slang.* M20.
[German *Treff* meeting(-place), *Treffpunkt* rendezvous, from *treffen* meet, strike.]
In espionage, a secret meeting or meeting-place, esp. for the transfer of goods or information.

treffend /'trɛfənt/ *adjective. rare.* M19.
[German.]
Apposite, fitting, pertinent.

trefid *adjective* see TRIFID.

trefle /'trɛf(ə)l/ *noun.* E16.
[Old & mod. French *trèfle* from Greek *triphullon*: see -LE². Cf. TREFOIL.]
†**1** = TREFOIL *noun* 1. Only in E16.
2 MILITARY HISTORY. A mine having three chambers. M18.
3 = TREFOIL *noun* 2. L19.

treflé /'trɛfleɪ/ *adjective.* Also **-fly** /-fli/. E18.
[French *tréflé.*]
HERALDRY. = BOTONY.

trefoil /'trɛfɔɪl, 'triːfɔɪl/ *noun & adjective.* ME.
[Anglo-Norman *trifoil* from Latin *trifolium* (whence Old French *trefeuil*), formed as TRI- + *folium* leaf, FOIL *noun*¹.]
▶**A** *noun.* **1** Any of various mainly leguminous plants, esp. clovers (genus *Trifolium*), having leaves composed of three leaflets; *esp.* any of several small yellow-flowered plants of this kind. ME.
2 An ornamental figure representing or resembling a trifoliate leaf, *spec.* (ARCHITECTURE) in a tracery window; *gen.* a thing arranged in or having three lobes, a set or group of three. ME. ▸**b** HERALDRY. A charge representing a clover-leaf with its stalk. M16.
1 ***bean trefoil***, ***bird's-foot trefoil***, ***hop trefoil***, ***tick-trefoil***, etc.
▶**B** *adjective.* Consisting of three leaflets or lobes, trifoliate; having the shape of a trefoil, decorated with a trefoil or trefoils. M18.
■ **trefoiled** *adjective* = TREFOIL *adjective* LME. **trefoliated** *adjective* = TRIFOLIATE M19.

tregetour /'trɛdʒətə/ *noun. arch.* ME.
[Old French *tre(s)geteo(u)r*, from *tre(s)geter* throw across or to and fro, ult. from Latin *trans* TRANS- + *jactare* throw.]
A conjuror, a juggler, a magician; a trickster, a deceiver.

trehala /trɪ'hɑːlə/ *noun.* M19.
[Turkish *tigale* from Persian *tigāl.*]
A sweet substance obtained from the cocoons of a Middle Eastern weevil, *Larinus maculatus*, and used as a sugar substitute. Also ***trehala manna***.

trehalose /'triːhələʊs, trɪ'hɑːləʊs, -əʊz/ *noun.* M19.
[from prec. + -OSE².]
CHEMISTRY. A disaccharide orig. obtained from trehala and found in fungi, yeasts, etc.
■ **trehalase** *noun* (BIOCHEMISTRY) an enzyme which catalyses the hydrolysis of trehalose to glucose L19.

treillage /'treɪlɪdʒ/ *noun.* L17.
[French, formed as TRAIL *noun*²: see -AGE.]
A trellis.
■ **treillaged** *adjective* (*rare*) trellised E19.

trek /trɛk/ *noun.* M19.
[Afrikaans, Dutch, formed as next.]
1 Travel by ox-wagon; a journey, esp. an organized migration or expedition, made in this way; a stage of such a journey. *S. Afr.* (chiefly *Hist.*). M19.
2 *gen.* A long and arduous journey or expedition, *esp.* one made on foot or by inconvenient means. L19.

> 📖 **2** S. ELDRED-GRIGG Every time we wanted water it was a trek.

Comb.: **trek Boer** *S. Afr.* HISTORY (*a*) a Boer who moved his family and grazing stock from place to place; a nomadic grazier; (*b*) = VOORTREKKER; **trekbok**, pl. **-bokke** /-kə/, **-bokken** /-kən/, *S. Afr.* an antelope, esp. a springbok, in a migrating herd; **trek-cart** a light cart used by boy scouts for transporting stores etc.; **trek chain** *S. Afr.* = TREK-TOW; **trek farmer** = ***trek Boer*** (a) above; **trek fever** *S. Afr.* wanderlust, an urge to be on the move; **trek net** *S. Afr.* = SEINE *noun*; **trek netter** *S. Afr.* a fisherman using a trek net; **trek ox** *S. Afr.* a draft ox; **trek wagon** *S. Afr.* a large covered wagon for long journeys.

trek /trɛk/ *verb.* Infl. **-kk-**. M19.
[Afrikaans, Middle & mod. Dutch *trekken* draw, pull, travel.]
1 *S. Afr.* **a** *verb intrans.* Migrate or journey by ox-wagon with one's belongings (chiefly *Hist.*); *slang* go away, depart. M19. ▸**b** *verb trans.* Cover (ground, a distance) by travelling thus. L19.
2 *verb trans.* Of an ox etc.: draw or pull (a vehicle or load). Also, drive (oxen etc.) to new pasture etc. *S. Afr.* M19.
3 *verb intrans.* Make a long and arduous journey or expedition, esp. on foot or by inconvenient means. E20.

> 📖 **3** C. MCCULLOUGH It would mean trekking down to the kitchen again.

■ **trekking** *verbal noun* the action of going on a trek or journey; *spec.* = ***pony-trekking*** s.v. PONY *noun*: M19.

trekker /'trɛkə/ *noun.* M19.
[from prec. + -ER¹.]
1 A person who treks (chiefly *S. Afr.*). Also (*slang*) = TREKKIE 2. M19.
2 A person travelling a long distance, esp. on foot; *spec.* a rambler, a hiker. M20.
2 ***pony-trekker***: see PONY *noun.*

trekkie /'trɛki/ *noun.* L19.
[Sense 1 from TREK *noun* + -IE. Sense 2 from *Star Trek* (see below) + -IE.]
1 A small group of trekkers. *S. Afr. rare.* L19.
2 (Also **T-**.) An admirer of the US science fiction television programme *Star Trek*; a person interested in space travel or science fiction. *slang.* L20.

trekschuit /'trɛkskʊɪt, *foreign* -sxœyt/ *noun.* Also **treck-** & other vars. L17.
[Dutch, formed as TREK *verb* + SCHUIT.]
A Dutch horse-drawn canal-boat or riverboat.

trek-tow /'trɛktəʊ/ *noun. S. Afr.* Also **-tou**. E19.
[Afrikaans, formed as TREK *noun* or *verb* + Dutch *touw* TOW *noun*².]
The central cable of twisted hide attached to the pole of an ox-wagon, to which the yokes of the oxen are fastened.

trellis /'trɛlɪs/ *noun & verb.* LME.
[Old French *trelis*, *-ice* from Proto-Romance from Latin *trilic-*, *trilix*, formed as TRI- + *licium* thread of a warp.]
▶**A** *noun.* **1** = LATTICE *noun* 1. Now *rare.* LME. ▸**b** HERALDRY. A charge representing a trellis. E19. ▸**c** = ***trellis stitch*** below. E20.
2 A lattice or framework of light wooden, metal, etc., bars used esp. as a support for fruit trees or creepers and freq. fastened against a wall. E16.
1b in trellis with the pieces of which the charge is composed crossing and nailed at the joints, not interlacing.
Comb.: **trellis drainage (pattern)** PHYSICAL GEOGRAPHY: that consists of roughly parallel streams joined at right angles by tributaries; **trellis stitch** in embroidery or knitting, an arrangement of stitches between parallel lines to give a lattice effect; **trellis window**: fitted with a trellis or grating; **trellis-work** light interlacing strips of wood, metal, etc., forming a trellis or lattice.
▶**B** *verb trans.* Infl. **-s-**, **-ss-**.
1 Provide with a trellis or lattice; enclose in a trellis or grating. LME.
2 Train (a plant) on a trellis, support (as) with a trellis. E19.
■ **trellising** *noun* (*a*) the action of the verb; (*b*) trellis-work, a trellis: L15.

trellised /'trɛlɪst/ *adjective.* Also **-ss-**. L15.
[from TRELLIS *noun*, *verb*: see -ED², -ED¹.]
1 Provided with a trellis or lattice; formed of trellis-work; trained upon a trellis. L15.
2 Shaped or arranged like a trellis; having a pattern or markings resembling a trellis. M17. ▸**b** HERALDRY. Barred vertically and horizontally to give a trellis or lattice, and sometimes with the bars nailed rather than interlaced at each intersection; portcullised. M19. ▸**c** PHYSICAL GEOGRAPHY. Of a drainage pattern: consisting of roughly parallel streams joined at right angles by tributaries. L19.

trem /trɛm/ *noun. slang.* M20.
[Abbreviation.]
A tremolo fitted to an electric guitar. Also ***trem arm***.

trematode /'trɛmətəʊd/ *noun & adjective.* M19.
[mod. Latin *Trematoda* (see below), from Greek *trēmatōdēs* perforated, from *trēma* hole, orifice (with ref. to the perforated skin of many flukes): see -ODE¹.]

ZOOLOGY. ▶**A** *noun.* Any parasitic flatworm of the class Trematoda, which orig. comprised all flukes but now only includes the endoparasitic species, most of which are digenean; a fluke. M19.
▶**B** *adjective.* Of, pertaining to, or designating (flukes of) the class Trematoda. M19.

tremblant /ˈtrɛmbl(ə)nt/ *adjective.* L20.
[from TREMBLE *verb* + -ANT[1].]
Of an ornament, jewel, etc.: incorporating springs or fine projecting wires which tremble or vibrate when affected by movement.

tremble /ˈtrɛmb(ə)l/ *verb & noun.* ME.
[Old & mod. French *trembler* from medieval Latin *tremulare* rel. to Latin *tremulus* TREMULOUS: see -LE[3].]
▶**A** *verb.* **1** *verb intrans.* Shake involuntarily with a slight rapid motion, as from fear, excitement, weakness, etc.; quake, quiver, shiver; (of the voice, light, etc.) be unsteady or tremulous. ME. ▸**b** Be in a state of extreme dread, apprehension, awe, etc.; shudder. (Foll. by *at, to do.*) LME.
†**2** *verb trans.* Regard with dread, apprehension, etc., tremble at. *rare.* LME–M16.
3 *verb trans.* Cause to tremble or shake. LME.
4 *verb intrans.* Move in a trembling or quivering manner. Chiefly *poet.* M18.

> 🕮 **1** B. POTTER Peter . . was out of breath and trembling with fright. J. C. OATES Iris's hand trembles but she concentrates on the task. **b** R. HAKLUYT Into what dangers . . they plunged themselves . . I tremble to recount. A. W. KINGLAKE Nations trembled at the coming of the Golden Horde. **3** E. B. BROWNING She trembles her fan. **4** TENNYSON A teardrop trembled from its source.

▶**B** *noun.* **1** The action of trembling; an act or instance of this, a tremor, a quiver; tremulousness or unsteadiness of the voice etc. E17.
2 ***the trembles***, any disease or condition characterized by involuntary trembling, as malaria, palsy (esp. in sheep), delirium tremens, etc. (cf. ***the shakes*** s.v. SHAKE *noun*); *US* milk-sickness. *colloq.* E19.

> 🕮 **1** DICKENS A terrible tremble crept over her whole frame. *Punch* I could sense a tremble of joy in children everywhere. **all in a tremble**, **all of a tremble**, **in a tremble**, **of a tremble** *colloq.* trembling all over; extremely agitated or excited.

■ **trembling** *verbal noun* (*a*) the action of the verb; an instance or act of this; (*b*) the trembles: ME. **trembling** *ppl adjective* that trembles; characterized or accompanied by trembling; ***trembling poplar***, either of two aspens, *Populus tremula* and the N. American *P. tremuloides*, noted for their tremulous leaves: LME. **tremblingly** *adverb* M16. **tremblingness** *noun* (*rare*) E18.

tremblement /ˈtrɛmb(ə)lm(ə)nt, *in sense 3 foreign* trɑ̃bləmɑ̃ (*pl. same*)/ *noun.* L17.
[French, formed as prec.: see -MENT.]
1 = TREMBLE *noun.* L17.
2 A cause of trembling; a terror. *rare.* L17.
3 MUSIC. A trill. L19.

trembler /ˈtrɛmblə/ *noun.* ME.
[from TREMBLE *verb* + -ER[1].]
1 A person who trembles, esp. with fear; a timorous or terrified person. ME.
2 A member of a religious sect having devotional exercises accompanied by trembling, quaking, or shaking; *spec.* a Quaker. *obsolete* exc. *Hist.* L17.
3 Any of several thrashers (birds) of the genera *Cinclocerthia* and *Ramphocinclus* which have the habit of violent shaking, found in the Lesser Antilles. M19.
4 ELECTRICITY. A vibrating spring blade which alternately makes and breaks the circuit in an induction coil; such a blade used as a security device sensitive to physical disturbance. L19.
Comb.: **trembler bell** an electric bell rung by a hammer attached to a trembler.

trembleuse /trɛmˈbləːz/ *noun.* M19.
[French, fem. of *trembleur* trembler.]
More fully ***trembleuse cup***. A cup having a saucer with a well into which it fits.

tremblor /ˈtrɛmblɔː/ *noun.* Chiefly *US.* E20.
[Alt. of Spanish *temblor* shudder, (in Amer. Spanish) earthquake, infl. by TREMBLER: see -OR.]
An earthquake, an earth tremor.

trembly /ˈtrɛmbli/ *adjective. colloq.* M19.
[from TREMBLE *verb* or *noun* + -Y[1].]
Full of trembling; tremulous, shaky, agitated.

> 🕮 DICKENS Trembly and shaky from head to foot. E. MITTELHOLZER His eyes . . flashed in such a way. It made you feel . . trembly inside.

Tremcard /ˈtrɛmkɑːd/ *noun.* L20.
[from TR(ANSPORT *noun* + EM(ERGENCY *noun* + CARD *noun*[2].]
A card carried in goods vehicles transporting hazardous loads, giving information on the nature of the load and on measures to be taken in an emergency.

tremella /trɪˈmɛlə/ *noun.* L18.
[mod. Latin (see below), dim. of Latin *tremulus* TREMULOUS.]
Any of various fungi of the genus *Tremella* (class Hymenomycetes) with gelatinous basidiocarps, which form jelly-like masses esp. on decayed wood.
■ **ˈtremelloid** *adjective* resembling *Tremella* in form or substance M19.

tremendous /trɪˈmɛndəs/ *adjective.* M17.
[from Latin *tremendus* gerundive of *tremere* tremble (at), rel. to TREMOR: see -OUS. Cf. *horrendous, stupendous.*]
1 Inspiring dread or awe; fearsome, terrible; majestically impressive. Now *literary.* M17.
2 Extremely large or good, very considerable or substantial, excellent; remarkable, extraordinary. *colloq.* E19.

> 🕮 **1** EVELYN Not blaspheming the tremendous name of God. J. PORTER The air . . was rendered livid and tremendous by long spires of fire. **2** J. COX A tremendous boom left an eerie silence in its wake. *Modern Maturity* Every major city . . is having tremendous problems. *Gardener* Old . . twigs make tremendous stakes and supports.

■ **tremendously** *adverb* awe-inspiringly, fearsomely; *colloq.* exceedingly, extremely, very greatly: L17. **tremendousness** *noun* E18.

tremendum /trɪˈmɛndəm/ *noun.* E20.
[Ellipt.]
= MYSTERIUM TREMENDUM.

tremie /ˈtrɛmi/ *noun.* E20.
[French *trémie* from Old French *tremuie* (mill-)hopper, from Latin *trimodia* a three-peck measure, from *tri-* three + *modius* peck.]
ENGINEERING. A movable metal tube, widening at its upper end into a large hopper, for depositing concrete under water.

tremissis /trɪˈmɪsɪs/ *noun.* Pl. **tremisses** /trɪˈmɪsiːz/. Also **tremis** /ˈtrɛmɪs/. LME.
[Late Latin, genit. sing. of *tremis*, from *tres* three, after *semis* half an as. Cf. SEMIS *noun*[1].]
ANTIQUITIES. A late Roman or early Byzantine gold coin, the third part of a solidus; a Merovingian or other imitation of this.

tremogram /ˈtrɛməgram/ *noun.* Now *rare.* L19.
[from Greek *tremein* tremble, quiver + -O- + -GRAM.]
1 A tracing made by means of a tremograph. L19.
2 An irregularity characterizing a person's handwriting. E20.
■ **tremograph** *noun* an instrument for recording involuntary muscular tremor L19.

tremolando /trɛməˈlandəʊ/ *noun, adverb, & adjective.* M19.
[Italian, pres. pple of *tremolare* tremble.]
MUSIC. ▶**A** *noun.* Pl. **-dos**, **-di** /-di/. = TREMOLO *noun* 1, 2a. M19.
▶**B** *adverb & adjective.* (A direction:) with tremolo. M19.

tremolant /ˈtrɛm(ə)l(ə)nt/ *noun.* M19.
[German, from Italian *tremolante* TREMULANT.]
= TREMOLO *noun* 2a.

tremolist /ˈtrɛm(ə)lɪst/ *noun.* E20.
[from TREMOLO + -IST.]
MUSIC. A user of tremolo.

tremolite /ˈtrɛm(ə)lʌɪt/ *noun.* L18.
[from *Tremola* Valley in Switzerland + -ITE[1].]
MINERALOGY. A white to grey amphibole mineral related to actinolite but containing no iron, which is widespread in igneous rocks and characteristic of metamorphosed dolomitic limestones.
■ **tremolitic** /-ˈlɪtɪk/ *adjective* L19.

tremolo /ˈtrɛm(ə)ləʊ/ *noun, adjective, adverb, & verb.* M18.
[Italian, formed as TREMULOUS.]
MUSIC. ▶**A** *noun.* Pl. **-os**.
1 A tremulous or vibrating effect produced on musical instruments or in singing by rapid reiteration of a single note (esp. on a stringed instrument) or rapid alternation between two notes. Cf. VIBRATO. M18.
2 a A mechanical device fitted in an organ to produce such an effect; a tremulant. Also ***tremolo stop***. M19. ▸**b** A device, esp. a lever, fitted to an electric guitar to produce a similar effect (also ***tremolo arm***); an electrical device of similar effect in an amplifier etc. M20.
▶**B** *adjective & adverb.* A musical direction: with tremolo. L19.
▶**C** *verb intrans.* Play or perform with a tremolo effect. *rare.* E20.

tremor /ˈtrɛmə/ *noun & verb.* LME.
[Old French *tremour*, Latin *tremor* rel. to *tremere*, Greek *tremein* tremble: see -OR.]
▶**A** *noun.* †**1** Terror. LME–L15.
2 Trembling or involuntary shaking of the body, limbs, etc.; unsteadiness, agitation; an instance of this, a quiver; a shiver or thrill of fear, excitement, etc. E17.
3 (A) vibration or shaking caused by an external impulse; *spec.* a slight earthquake (also ***earth tremor***). M17.

> 🕮 **1** *Times* The weakness and tremor of Parkinson's disease. R. RENDELL He felt a tremor of apprehension. **3** *Times* The tremor . . damaged many buildings in the old part of the city.

Comb.: **tremor disc** ASTRONOMY the telescopic or photographic image of a star as enlarged by atmospheric tremor.
▶**B** *verb intrans.* Be agitated by a tremor or tremors; shake, tremble. E20.
■ **tremorless** *adjective* M19. **tremorlessly** *adverb* L19.

tremorine /ˈtrɛməriːn/ *noun.* M20.
[from TREMOR *noun* + -INE[5].]
PHARMACOLOGY. A bicyclic compound, $(C_4H_8N{\cdot}CH_2{\cdot}C{\equiv})_2$, derived from pyrrolidine and used in research into Parkinsonism.

tremulant /ˈtrɛmjʊlənt/ *adjective & noun.* LME.
[As adjective var. of TREMULOUS with substitution of -ANT[1]; as noun from Italian *tremolante*.]
▶**A** *adjective.* Tremulous, trembling. LME.
▶**B** *noun.* MUSIC. = TREMOLO 1, 2a. M19.
¶ Not recorded between LME and M19.

tremulate /ˈtrɛmjʊleɪt/ *verb intrans. & trans.* M17.
[Late Latin *tremulat-* pa. ppl stem of *tremulare* tremble: see -ATE[3].]
(Cause to) tremble, vibrate, or quiver.
■ **tremuˈlation** *noun* the action or condition of trembling; an instance of this: M17.

tremulous /ˈtrɛmjʊləs/ *adjective.* E17.
[from Latin *tremulus*, from *tremere* tremble: see -ULOUS.]
1 Characterized or affected by trembling, shaking, or quivering; *transf.* fearful, timid, vacillating. E17.
2 Ready to vibrate in response *to* an influence; tremblingly sensitive or responsive *to*. L18.
3 Of writing, a line, etc.: produced by a tremulous hand; finely wavy. L19.

> 🕮 **1** SOUTHEY His barkings loud . . Amid their tremulous bleat. W. WATSON The tremulous hand of age. G. DALY A slim, tremulous young man who barely dares to touch his creation.

■ **tremulously** *adverb* M18. **tremulousness** *noun* E18.

trenail *noun & verb* var. of TREENAIL.

trenbolone /ˈtrɛnbələʊn/ *noun.* L20.
[from TR(I)ENE + ANA)BOL(IC + -ONE.]
PHARMACOLOGY & VETERINARY MEDICINE. A synthetic anabolic steroid which has been used as an animal growth hormone.

trench /trɛn(t)ʃ/ *noun.* LME.
[Old French *trenche* cutting, cut, ditch, slice, from *trenchier*: see next.]
†**1** A path or track cut through a wood or forest. LME–L16.
2 A long narrow (usu. deep) ditch or furrow cut out of the ground. L15.
3 MILITARY. **a** Orig., a deep narrow ditch dug by troops, the earth from which is thrown or banked up in front as a defensive parapet. Later also, such a ditch together with its defensive parapet. Now chiefly (in *pl.*), the connected series or system of such defences forming an army's line. L15. ▸†**b** The parapet or bank of earth in front of a trench. M16–E18. ▸**c** *fig.* A defensive position or barrier; in *pl.*, the front line. E17. ▸**d** In full ***trench coat***. Orig. (in the war of 1914–18), a soldier's long padded or lined waterproof overcoat. Now also, any long loose belted double-breasted raincoat. E20.
4 Anything resembling a trench; *spec.* (*a*) a cut, scar, or deep wrinkle in the face; (*b*) ANATOMY & ZOOLOGY (now *rare*) a cavity, pit, or fossa; (*c*) CARPENTRY a part of a joint in the form of a long narrow slot cut across the grain. L16.
†**5** A bridoon or snaffle used in conjunction with a curb-bit. Also more fully ***flying trench***. E17–E18.
6 An elongated natural channel in the seabed; *spec.* a very long one several kilometres deep, running parallel to the edge of a continent or an island arc and believed to mark a subduction zone. M20.

> 🕮 **2** *Green Cuisine* To plant potatoes . . lay them in trenches 6in . . deep. *Build It!* A professional groundworker digging the trenches and putting down the concrete. **3a** *Times* The German barrage fire on the trenches . . was of extreme severity. **c** *Rolling Stone* He has been in the trenches too long not to be a master at mixing sincerity with evasiveness. **d** *Vogue* Updated Trenches styled in luxury gaberdine. **4** SHAKES. *Tit. A.* Witness these trenches made by grief and care.

Comb.: **trench boot**: combined with leggings; ***trench coat***: see sense 3d above; **trench-coated** *adjective* wearing a trench coat; **trench feet** = ***trench foot*** below; **trench fever** an epidemic louse-borne rickettsial disease that was common among soldiers in the war of 1914–18, causing splenomegaly and recurrent fever; **trench foot** a painful condition of the feet caused by prolonged immersion in cold water or mud and marked by blackening and death of surface tissue; **trench-knife** (orig. MILITARY): having a double-edged blade; **trench mortar** MILITARY a small mortar for throwing bombs from a front trench into enemy trenches; **trench mouth** MEDICINE ulcerative gingivitis; **trench-rat** the brown or Norway rat, *Rattus norvegicus*; **trench warfare** (*a*) hostilities carried on from more or less permanent trenches; (*b*) *fig.* a protracted dispute in which the parties maintain entrenched positions while persistently attacking their opponents.
■ **trenchful** *noun* (chiefly MILITARY) as much or as many as a trench will hold E20. **trenchless** *adjective* (esp. of pipe-laying or draining machinery) that dispenses with the cutting of a trench M20.

trench /trɛn(t)ʃ/ *verb*. LME.
[In branch I from Old French *trenchier* (mod. *trancher*) cut, ult. from Latin *truncare*: see TRUNCATE *verb*. In branch II from or infl. by prec.]
► **I 1** *verb trans.* Cut (in pieces); divide or sever by cutting; make a cut in. LME. ▸**†b** Cut or carve *in* or *into* a material; make (a wound) *in*. *rare*. L16–E17.
2 *verb trans.* Cut (a channel) through a ridge or raised surface; cut through (a ridge etc.). E17.
> 📖 **1** POPE Trench the black earth a cubit long and wide. **b** SHAKES. *Ven. & Ad.* The wide wound that the boar had trench'd In his soft flank. **2** A. GEIKIE In the .. denudation of the country, deep valleys have been trenched through it. *fig.*: R. H. HORNE Oft have I marked a deep awe trench his face.

► **II 3 a** *verb trans.* Cut or dig a trench or trenches in (the ground); *spec.* (AGRICULTURE & HORTICULTURE) turn over the soil of (a field, garden, etc.) by digging a series of adjoining trenches. M16. ▸**b** *verb intrans.* Dig a trench or trenches. L18.
4 *verb trans.* MILITARY. Surround or fortify with a trench. Also foll. by *about*, *around*. Now *rare* or *obsolete*. M16. ▸**b** *fig.* = ENTRENCH 2. Chiefly as ***trenched ppl adjective***. E17.
5 *verb trans.* **†a** Divert (a river) by digging a trench. *rare* (Shakes.). Only in L16. ▸**b** Drain (land) by means of open trenches. E19.
6 *verb intrans.* Foll. by *on*, *upon*: encroach; border closely, verge; have a bearing. Cf. ENTRENCH 5. *arch.* E17.
†7 *verb intrans.* Of land: extend, stretch. *rare*. Only in 18.
> 📖 **6** JAS. ROBERTSON This scheme .. may seem to trench on the liberty of individuals. DISRAELI Some unlucky jest, trenching on treason. C. M. DAVIES The opinions of this school—where they trench most closely on orthodoxy.

trenchant /ˈtrɛn(t)ʃ(ə)nt/ *adjective*. ME.
[Old French (mod. *tranchant*), pres. pple of *trenchier*: see prec., -ANT[1].]
1 Cutting, adapted for cutting; having a sharp edge. *arch.* or *poet.* ME. ▸**b** ZOOLOGY. Of a tooth, beak, etc.: having a cutting edge, sectorial. *rare*. M19.
2 Of language, style, etc.: incisive; vigorous and clear; effective, energetic. ME.
3 Sharply defined, clear-cut. M19.
> 📖 **2** M. R. MITFORD Trenchant repartee, that cuts .. like a razor. S. J. OWEN For all these evils .. Wellesley devised prompt and trenchant remedies. **3** *Burlington Magazine* Pictures .. showing .. a less trenchant treatment of light and drapery.

■ **trenchancy** *noun* the quality of being trenchant in style or tone M19. **trenchantly** *adverb* ME.

trencher /ˈtrɛn(t)ʃə/ *noun*[1]. ME.
[Anglo-Norman *trenchour*, Old French *trencheoir*, from *trenchier*: see TRENCH *verb*, -ER[2].]
†1 A cutting instrument; a knife. ME–M16.
2 A flat piece of wood for cutting and serving meat (*obsolete* exc. *Hist.*); (*arch.* or *Hist.*) a plate, a platter. ME. ▸**†b** A slice of bread used as a plate or platter. LME–E16. ▸**c** A trencher with food on it; a supply of food. *arch.* L16.
3 *transf.* Any flat board. Now *rare* or *obsolete* exc. as in sense 3b. E16. ▸**b** *ellipt.* = ***trench cap*** (a) below. M19.
Phrases: **lick the trencher** toady, be a parasite.
Comb.: **trencher cap** (*a*) a stiff square academic hat, a mortar-board; **†**(*b*) a student who wears a trencher cap; **†trencher-friend** a parasite, a toady; **trencherwoman** a woman with a hearty appetite.
■ **trencherful** *noun* as much as a trencher will hold M17. **†trenchering** *noun* (*a*) (*rare*) eating, feasting; (*b*) (*rare*, Shakes.) trenchers collectively: L16–E17.

trencher /ˈtrɛn(t)ʃə/ *noun*[2]. E17.
[from TRENCH *verb* + -ER[1].]
†1 A person who carves meat etc. *rare*. Only in E17.
2 A person who cuts or digs trenches; a person who trenches ground. L19.
3 A machine or attachment used for digging trenches. M20.

trencherman /ˈtrɛn(t)ʃəmən/ *noun*. Pl. **-men**. L16.
[from TRENCHER *noun*[1] + MAN *noun*.]
1 A feeder, an eater, (of a specified kind). Esp. in ***good trencherman***, ***stout trencherman***, ***valiant trencherman***, a person with a hearty appetite. L16.
2 A person who cadges free meals, a parasite. Now *rare* or *obsolete*. L16.

trenchman /ˈtrɛn(t)ʃmən/ *noun*. Now *rare* or *obsolete*. Pl. **-men**. M17.
[App. a misreading of *treuchman* obsolete var. of TRUCHMAN.]
= TRUCHMAN.

†trenchment *noun*. *rare*. E17–E18.
[from TRENCH *verb* + -ER[1], or aphet. from ENTRENCHMENT.]
= ENTRENCHMENT 1.

trenchmore /ˈtrɛn(t)ʃmɔː/ *noun & adverb*. *obsolete* exc. *Hist.* M16.
[Origin unkn.]
► **A** *noun*. A kind of boisterous English country dance. M16.
► **†B** *adverb*. In a frisky or boisterous manner. L16–M17.

trench-plough /ˈtrɛn(t)ʃplaʊ/ *verb & noun*. Also ***-plow**. M18.
[from TRENCH *noun* or *verb* + PLOUGH *verb*.]
AGRICULTURE. ► **A** *verb trans. & intrans.* Plough to a depth of two furrows, bringing the lower soil to the surface; plough twice, turning the second furrow-slice on top of the first. M18.
► **B** *noun*. A plough designed or adjusted for trench-ploughing. E19.

trend /trɛnd/ *verb & noun*.
[Old English *trendan*, from Germanic base repr. also by Old English *trinda* round lump, ball, *ātrendlian* roll away: cf. TRENDLE, TRINDLE, TRUNDLE *noun*, *verb*.]
► **A** *verb*. **†1** *verb intrans.* Turn round, revolve, rotate, roll. OE–M17.
2 *verb trans.* Cause (a thing) to turn round; turn, roll, twist, (a thing). Long *obsolete* exc. as in sense 2b. ME. ▸**b** Wind (partly cleaned wool) in preparation for spinning. Cf. TRENDLE *noun* 5. *dial.* (now *rare*). L18.
3 *verb intrans.* Of land, a river, a current, etc.: turn in or take a (specified or contextually determined) direction; run, stretch, bend, (away). L16.
4 *verb intrans. fig.* Have or assume a general direction or tendency; move, be chiefly directed. M19.
> 📖 **3** J. R. GREEN Their path lay along the coast trending round to the west. T. HARDY The whole stream trended off in this new direction. K. ROBERTS The ground trended steadily upward. *Caves & Caving* Between the two faults are several cross faults .. trending NW/SE. **4** W. S. LANDOR The religion of blood .. will continue to trend northward. *Times* The risk of unemployment trending towards the million mark.

► **B** *noun*. **1** A rounded bend of a stream. *dial.* E17.
2 NAUTICAL. The part of the shank of an anchor where it thickens towards the crown. L18.
3 a The general direction taken by land, a river, a current, etc. L18. ▸**b** *fig. The* or a general course, tendency, or drift (of thought, fashion, behaviour, events, etc.); *esp.* a new or increasing tendency. Now also, a fashion. L19.
4 GEOLOGY. A geological formation which is a source of oil or gas. M20.
> 📖 **3a** C. KING Numerous ridges .. having a general north-east trend. *Scots Magazine* The .. coast with all its indentations was a difficulty, so the trend of the coastline had to suffice. **b** P. DALLY At times she seemed .. much improved .. but the overall trend was slowly downhill. J. FANE The trend of Rachel's thoughts was .. darkened by the death of Bobbety. A. HIGONNET She was .. joining the most advanced trends in painting.

Comb.: **trend analysis**: of (esp. statistical) data in order to detect or study any trend represented in them; **trend line** a line indicating the general course or tendency of something (as a geographical feature or a set of points on a graph); **trend-setter** a person who starts or establishes a trend, esp. in fashion; **trend-setting** *adjective* starting or establishing a trend, esp. in fashion; **trend-spotter** a person who observes or tries to predict new trends, esp. changes of fashion; **trend surface** a mathematically defined surface computed as a best fit to the sampled values of some parameter over an area of interest.
■ **trending** *verbal noun* the action of the verb; *esp.* (the fact of) turning in or taking a general (specified) direction: LME. **trendless** *adjective* (chiefly ECONOMICS) not exhibiting a definite trend or tendency M20.

Trendelenburg /trɛnˈdɛlənbəːɡ/ *noun*. L19.
[Friedrich *Trendelenburg* (1844–1924), German surgeon.]
MEDICINE. Used *attrib.* and in *possess.* to designate certain phenomena observed and medical procedures invented by Trendelenburg.
Trendelenburg position, **Trendelenburg's position** a position in which a patient lies supine on a tilted table or bed with the pelvis higher than the head, used for pelvic surgery and to treat shock. **Trendelenburg sign**, **Trendelenburg's sign** a positive sign in Trendelenburg's test of the hip. **Trendelenburg test**, **Trendelenburg's test** (*a*) a test for disorders of the hip-joint or gluteal muscles in which the patient stands on one leg and raises the other, dropping of the pelvis on the unsupported side being a positive sign; (*b*) a test in which the leg is raised to drain it of blood and then quickly lowered, rapid distension of the leg veins indicating incompetence of the valves.

trendle /ˈtrɛnd(ə)l/ *noun & verb*. *obsolete* exc. *dial.*
[Old English *trendel* = Middle Low German *trendel* round disc, Middle High German *trendel* ball, circle, from Germanic: see -LE[1]. Cf. TREND, TRINDLE, TRUNDLE *noun*, *verb*.]
► **A** *noun*. **†1** A circle, a ring, a coronet; a circular disc; a ball, a globe. OE–LME.
2 A wheel; *spec.* (*a*) the wheel of a wheelbarrow; (*b*) a lantern-wheel. ME.
3 Any of various round or rounded objects; *spec.* (*dial.*) a rounded tray, shallow tub, or trough. ME.
†4 A suspended hoop or wheel in a church, on which tapers were fixed to form a chandelier. LME–E16.
5 A bundle of partly cleaned wool wound up in preparation for spinning. Cf. TREND *verb* 2b. *dial.* E19.
▸**†B** *verb trans. & intrans.* (Cause to) roll or revolve. ME–L16.

trendoid /ˈtrɛndɔɪd/ *adjective & noun*. *colloq.* (orig. *US*). Chiefly *derog.* L20.
[from TREND(Y + -OID.]
(A person who is) extravagantly or indiscriminately trendy.

trendy /ˈtrɛndi/ *adjective & noun*. *colloq.* (freq. *derog.*) M20.
[from TREND *noun* + -Y[1].]
► **A** *adjective*. Fashionable, up to date; following or conforming to current fashionable trends. M20.
> 📖 *Melody Maker* He was into jazz long before it became trendy. *Times* Trendy middle-class aspirants and young street-wise Guardian readers.

► **B** *noun*. A trendy person. M20.
> 📖 *International Affairs* The vague and incoherent ideologies of the radical trendies.

■ **trendify** *verb trans.* make fashionable, give a fashionable appearance to M20. **trendily** *adverb* M20. **trendiness** *noun* M20. **trendyism** *noun* self-conscious fashionableness L20.

trental /ˈtrɛnt(ə)l/ *noun*. ME.
[Old French *trentel* or medieval Latin *trentalis*, ult. from Latin *triginta* thirty: see -AL[1].]
1 (Any of) a set of thirty masses offered for the repose of the soul of a dead person. Cf. TRICENARY *noun*, TRIGINTAL. *obsolete* exc. *Hist.* ME. ▸**b** *gen.* A set of thirty things. *rare*. Long *obsolete* exc. *dial.* E16.
2 (A commemoration held on) the thirtieth day after a burial. *arch. rare*. LME.

trente-et-quarante /trɑ̃tekarɑ̃ːt, trɒ̃teɪkaˈrɒ̃t/ *noun*. L17.
[French, lit. 'thirty-and-forty'.]
= ***rouge-et-noir*** s.v. ROUGE *noun*[1] & *adjective*.

Trentine /ˈtrɛntʌɪn/ *adjective*. *rare*. E19.
[from *Trent* (Italian *Trento*) a city in the Tyrol, NE Italy + -INE[1].]
= TRIDENTINE *adjective*.
■ Also **†Trentish** *adjective*: only in 17.

trepan /trɪˈpan/ *noun*[1]. LME.
[medieval Latin *trepanum* from Greek *trupanon* borer, from *trupan* pierce, bore, *trupē* hole.]
1 MEDICINE. A surgical instrument in the form of a crown-saw, for cutting out small pieces of bone, esp. from the skull. Cf. TREPHINE *noun* 1. Now chiefly *Hist.* LME.
2 MINING. A borer for sinking shafts. L19.

trepan /trɪˈpan/ *noun*[2]. Long *arch.* Orig. **†trapan**. M17.
[In sense 1 prob. from TRAP *noun*[1] or *verb*[2]. In sense 2 from TREPAN *verb*[2].]
1 A person who (for his or her own advantages) lures or tricks another into a disadvantageous or ruinous act or position. M17.
2 An act of entrapment; a stratagem, a trick; a trap, a snare. M17.
¶ Prob. orig. *Criminals' slang*.

trepan /trɪˈpan/ *verb*[1]. Infl. **-nn-**. LME.
[Old French *trépaner*, from *trépan* TREPAN *noun*[1].]
1 *verb trans. & intrans.* Operate on (a person) with a trepan; perforate (the skull) with a trepan. LME.
2 *verb trans.* ENGINEERING. Cut an annular groove or hole in (something) by means of a crown saw or other tool; make (a hole) thus, the core being removed as a solid piece. E20.
■ **trepaˈnation** *noun* (now *Hist.*) the operation of trepanning or perforating the skull LME. **trepanner** *noun*[2] (*a*) MEDICINE (*rare*) a person who operates with a trepan; (*b*) MINING a machine fitted with cutting-wheels for the automatic cutting and loading of coal along a longwall face: E18.

trepan /trɪˈpan/ *verb*[2] *trans.* Now *rare* or *obsolete*. Also **†trapan**. Infl. **-nn-**. M17.
[from TREPAN *noun*[2].]
1 Trap, ensnare, beguile, (a person). M17.
2 Lure, inveigle (*into* or *to* a place, course of action, etc.); deceitfully induce *to do* something. M17.
3 Trick, cheat, or swindle (a person) *out of* (a thing). M17.
■ **†trepanner** *noun*[2] M17–M19.

trepang /trɪˈpaŋ/ *noun*. L18.
[Malay *teripang*.]
= BÊCHE-DE-MER 1.
■ **trepanger** *noun* a person who fishes for trepang E20.

trephine /trɪˈfʌɪn, -ˈfiːn/ *noun & verb*. E17.
[from Latin *tres fines* three ends, app. alt. partly after TREPAN *noun*[1].]
MEDICINE. ► **A** *noun*. **1** An improved form of trepan with a transverse handle and a guiding centre-pin. E17.
2 = TREPHINATION. M20.
► **B** *verb trans. & intrans.* Operate (on) with a trephine. E19.
■ **trephiˈnation** *noun* the operation of trephining L19.

trepid /ˈtrɛpɪd/ *adjective*. *rare*. M17.
[Latin *trepidus* scared, alarmed.]
Trembling; agitated; fearful.
■ **treˈpidity** *noun* agitation, alarm, fearfulness E18. **trepidly** *adverb* L19.

trepidate /ˈtrɛpɪdeɪt/ *verb intrans.* *rare*. E17.
[Latin *trepidat-* pa. ppl stem of *trepidare*, formed as prec.: see -ATE[3].]
Tremble with fear or agitation.

■ **trepidant** *adjective* trepidating L19.

trepidation /trɛpɪˈdeɪʃ(ə)n/ *noun.* L15.
[Latin *trepidatio(n-)*, formed as prec.: see -ATION.]
1 Tremulous, vibratory, or rhythmic movement; oscillation, rocking; an instance of this. Also, involuntary trembling of the limbs; tremor. L15.
2 Tremulous agitation; confused hurry or alarm; mental perturbation. L15.
3 ASTRONOMY. A libration of the sphere of the fixed stars, added to the Ptolemaic system by the 10th-cent. Arab astronomer Thabet ben Korrah to account for phenomena, esp. precession, actually due to motion of the earth's axis. *obsolete* exc. *Hist.* M17.

> 1 M. MEYER He . . was invited to preach a sermon, which—with much trepidation . . —he did. R. M. WILSON I sat those exams. I wrote in hope and trepidation.

trepidatory /trɪˈpɪdət(ə)ri/ *adjective. rare.* L19.
[formed as TREPIDATE + -ORY[2].]
Of, pertaining to, or characterized by trepidation.

treponeme /ˈtrɛpəniːm/ *noun.* Also in mod. Latin form **-nema** /-ˈniːmə/, pl. **-nemata** /-ˈniːmətə/. E20.
[mod. Latin (see below), from Greek *trepein* turn + *nēma* thread.]
BIOLOGY & MEDICINE. An anaerobic spirochaete of the genus *Treponema*, parasitic or pathogenic in people and warm-blooded animals, including the causal agents of syphilis, yaws, and pinta.
■ **trepoˈnemal** *adjective* of, pertaining to, or caused by treponemes E20. **treponemaˈtosis** *noun*, pl. **-ˈtoses**, (a disease caused by) infection with treponemes E20. **treponemiˈcidal** *adjective* able to destroy treponemes M20.

très /trɛ, treɪ/ *adverb. colloq.* E19.
[French.]
Very. Usu. with ref. to a fashionable or modishly superior quality.

> N. BLAKE It's a sort of country club. Très snob. Très cad. *Publishers Weekly* A *très* cool modern kid.

tresaiel /trɪˈseɪ(ə)l/ *noun.* Long *obsolete* exc. *Hist.* Also **-aile**, **-ayle**. L15.
[Anglo-Norman (mod. French *trisaïeul*, from *tri-* TRI- + *aieul* AIEL), after BESAIEL.]
LAW. A great-great-grandfather.
writ of tresaiel LAW an action by a party based on the seisin of a great-great-grandfather for the recovery of land of which that party had been dispossessed.

tresance /trɪˈzɑːns/ *noun.* Also **-saunce** /-ˈzɔːns/. LME.
[medieval Latin *tresantia* a covered passage, esp. round a cloister: ult. origin unkn.]
ARCHITECTURE. A passage in or through a house; a corridor, a gallery.

tresayle *noun* var. of TRESAIEL.

tresette *noun* see TRESSETTE.

tresillo /treˈsiʎo/ *noun.* E19.
[Spanish, factitious dim. of *tres* three.]
The card-game ombre.

trespass /ˈtrɛspəs/ *noun.* ME.
[Old French *trespas* passing across etc. (mod. *trépas* death), formed as next.]
1 A transgression, an offence; a sin; a fault. *arch.* exc. as in sense 2. ME.
2 LAW. Formerly, an unlawful act; *esp.* any such act other than treason, felony, or misprision of either. Now *spec.* an unlawful act deliberately committed against the person or property of another, *esp.* wrongful entry on a person's land or property. ME.
3 *fig.* An encroachment, an intrusion. M18.

> 1 SHAKES. *Wint. T.* Be plainer with me; let me know my trespass. AV *Matt.* 6:14 If yee forgiue not men their trespasses, neither will your father forgiue your trespasses. 2 H. ALLEN He *might* be laying himself open to a technical charge of trespass by staying in the house. *City Limits* CND's . . mass trespass on to 3,000 acres of open moorland. ***trespass to person***, ***trespass to goods***, ***trespass to land***. **trespass on the case** (*obsolete* exc. *Hist.*) an action for trespass in which the damage alleged is not the immediate result of an unlawful act but a later consequence. 3 T. JEFFERSON I know the extent of this trespass on your tranquillity. GLADSTONE One trespass more I must make on your patience.

trespass /ˈtrɛspəs/ *verb.* ME.
[Old French *trespasser* pass beyond etc. (mod. *trépasser* die) from medieval Latin *transpassare*: see TRANS-, PASS *verb*.]
1 *verb intrans.* Transgress, offend; sin. Freq. foll. by *against*. *arch.* or *literary.* ME.
†**2** *verb trans.* **a** Commit (an offence), do (something wrong). LME–M17. ▸**b** Offend against, wrong, (a person). LME–M16. ▸**c** Disobey, violate, (a law etc.). LME–E17.
3 *verb intrans.* LAW. Commit a trespass; *spec.* wrongfully enter on a person's land or property. Freq. foll. by *on*, *upon*. LME.
4 *verb intrans. fig.* Make an unwarrantable claim, intrude, encroach, (*on* or *upon* a person's time, attention, patience, domain, etc.). M17.

> 1 WORDSWORTH I trespassed lately worse than ever. W. PLOMER We were to forgive those that trespass against us. 4 T. URQUHART I have trespassed a little upon the patience of the Reader. **trespass on a person's preserve** meddle in a person's affairs.

■ **trespasser** *noun* LME.

tress /trɛs/ *noun.* ME.
[Old & mod. French *tresse* (= Provençal *tressa*, Italian *treccia*, medieval Latin *tric(i)a*, *tricea*), perh. ult. from Greek *trikha* threefold.]
1 A long lock of human (esp. female) hair; in *pl.*, a woman's or girl's head of hair. ME. ▸**b** *spec.* A plait or braid of (esp. female) hair. Long *rare* or *obsolete.* ME.
†**2** A flat plait or braid (of interwoven threads, fibres, straw, etc.). L15–M16.

> 1 A. C. CLARKE Her long, dark hair . . hung in lustrous tresses. *fig.*: J. TRAPP The radiant tresses of the sun. ***lady's tresses***: see LADY *noun & adjective*. **b** SPENSER Her yellow golden heare Was . . in tresses wrought.

■ **tressy** *adjective* having, resembling, or adorned with tresses E17.

tress /trɛs/ *verb trans.* Now *rare* exc. as TRESSED. LME.
[Old & mod. French *tresser* = Italian *trecciare*, medieval Latin *tricare*: cf. prec.]
1 Arrange (hair) in tresses. LME.
2 Arrange (threads etc.) in braids. M19.

tressed /trɛst, *poet.* ˈtrɛsɪd/ *adjective.* LME.
[from TRESS *noun*, *verb*: see -ED[2], -ED[1].]
1 Having tresses (*lit.* & *fig.*). Freq. as 2nd elem. of comb. LME.
2 Of hair: arranged in tresses; braided. Long *rare* or *obsolete.* LME.

> 1 MILTON The Golden-tressed Sun.

tressel *noun* see TRESTLE.

tressette /treɪˈsɛt, trɛ-/ *noun.* Also ***tresette**. L18.
[Italian, from *tre* three + *sette* seven.]
An Italian card-game in which the 3 and 2 of each suit are the highest-ranking cards.

tressure /ˈtrɛʃə, ˈtrɛs(j)ʊə/ *noun.* Orig. †**tressour**. ME.
[Old French *tressour*, *tress(e)ure*, formed as TRESS *noun*: see -OUR, -URE.]
†**1** A ribbon, band, etc., worn round the head, esp. to secure the hair; a head-dress. ME–L15.
2 HERALDRY. A narrow orle, usu. borne double and flory. LME.
3 NUMISMATICS. An ornamental enclosure (circular or of several arches) containing a figure or distinctive device, formerly found on various gold and silver coins. M18.

trest /trɛst/ *noun. obsolete* exc. *Scot.* & *dial.* ME.
[Old French *treste* var. of *traste*, *trastre* from Latin *transtrum*: see next.]
1 = TRESTLE 1. ME.
2 = TRESTLE 2. *obsolete* exc. *dial.* L15.

trestle /ˈtrɛs(ə)l/ *noun.* Also (*obsolete* exc. as in sense 3) **tressel**. ME.
[Old French *trestel* (mod. *tréteau*) from Proto-Romance dim. of Latin *transtrum* beam: see -EL[2], -LE[2].]
1 A structure supporting a board, tabletop, etc., consisting of two frames fixed at an angle or hinged, or of a horizontal beam or bar with diverging (pairs of) legs; either of a pair of frames, (sets of) legs, etc., used to support a board so as to form a table; *spec.* (more fully ***trestle-table***) a table consisting of a board or boards laid on trestles or other supports. ME. ▸**b** An open framework with diagonal braces, used to support a bridge, viaduct, etc. L15. ▸**c** NAUTICAL. In full ***trestle-tree***. Either of a pair of pieces of timber horizontally fixed on a masthead or lower mast to support the topmast, cross-trees, etc. E17.
2 A tripod. Formerly also, a three-legged stool or seat. *obsolete* exc. *dial.* LME.
3 HERALDRY. (Usu. **tressel**.) A charge representing a low (usu. three-legged) stool or bench. E17.

> 1 T. WRIGHT The Anglo-Saxon table was formed . . by placing a board upon trestles. L. DAVIDSON Trestle tables containing tea urns and trays of sweetmeats. *fig.*: F. O'BRIEN She leant forward slightly, . . her chin on the trestle of her interlocking hands. **b** C. RYAN The engineers, utilizing the bridge's central trestle . . , spanned the canal.

Comb.: **trestle-bed** a movable bed supported on trestles; **trestle-board**: laid on trestles to form a table; **trestle-bridge**: supported on a trestle or trestles; ***trestle-table***: see sense 1 above; ***trestle-tree***: see sense 1c above; **trestle-work** = sense 1b above.

tret /trɛt/ *noun.* Now *Hist.* L15.
[Anglo-Norman, Old French, var. of *trait* draught: see TRAIT.]
COMMERCE. An allowance (usu. of 4 lb in 104 lb) formerly made to purchasers of various goods sold by weight, to compensate for waste during transportation. Cf. TARE *noun*[2] 1.
tare and tret: see TARE *noun*[2] 1.

trete *noun* var. of TREAT *noun*[1].

tretinoin /trəˈtɪnəʊɪn/ *noun.* L20.
[from *t-* of unkn. origin + RETINO(IC + -IN[1].]
PHARMACOLOGY. A preparation of retinoic acid, applied to the skin to treat acne and other disorders.

trevalli *noun* var. of TREVALLY *noun*[2].

trevally /trɪˈvali/ *noun*[1]. *obsolete* exc. *Scot.* & *dial.* M17.
[Perh. alt. of REVEILLE.]
†**1** A signal made by beating a drum. M17–L18.
2 A disturbance, a startling din. E19.

trevally /trɪˈvali/ *noun*[2]. *Austral.* & *NZ.* Also **-valli**. L19.
[App. alt. of CAVALLY (horse-mackerel).]
Any of several edible marine fishes, mainly of the family Carangidae. Cf. TURRUM.

trevat /ˈtrɛvət/ *noun. obsolete* exc. *Hist.* M19.
[Origin unkn.]
A sharp-bladed instrument formerly used to cut the loops forming the pile of hand-woven velvet carpets etc.

Trevira /trəˈvɪərə/ *noun.* M20.
[Origin unkn.]
(Proprietary name for) a type of polyester fibre; fabric made from this.

trevis *noun* var. of TRAVIS.

trews /truːz/ *noun pl.* M16.
[Irish *triús*, Gaelic *triubhas* (sing.): see TROUSE *noun*[2]. Cf. TROUSERS.]
1 Close-fitting trousers or breeches combined with stockings, formerly worn by Irishmen and Scottish Highlanders (*obsolete* exc. *Hist.*); a kind of tartan trouser worn by certain Scottish regiments. M16.
2 *gen.* Trousers; *spec.* close-fitting tartan trousers worn by women. M19.

trey /treɪ/ *noun.* Also **tray**. LME.
[Old French *trei(s)* (mod. *trois*) from Latin *tres* THREE.]
1 a The side of a die marked with three pips or spots; a throw which turns up this side. LME. ▸**b** CARDS. A three of any suit. L17.
2 Three of anything; a set of three; *spec.* (*US*) a three-dollar packet of a narcotic. Also (chiefly *Austral.* & *NZ*, now *Hist.*), a threepenny piece. *slang.* L19.
Comb.: **trey-bit** (*Austral.* & *NZ slang*, now *Hist.*), a threepenny piece.

TRF *abbreviation.*
BIOCHEMISTRY. Thyrotrophin-releasing factor.

TRH *abbreviation.*
1 Their Royal Highnesses.
2 BIOCHEMISTRY. Thyrotrophin-releasing hormone.

tri /trʌɪ/ *noun. colloq.* L20.
[Abbreviation.]
A trimaran.

tri- /trʌɪ/ *prefix.*
[Latin, Greek, combining form of Latin *tres* three, Greek *treis* three, *tris* thrice.]
Used in words adopted from Latin and Greek and in English formations modelled on these, and as a productive prefix, forming (*a*) adjectives (and derived nouns and adverbs) with the senses 'having, consisting of, or involving three', as ***tricuspid***, ***trilateral***, ***triune***, 'triply, in three ways', as ***triphibious***, ***tripinnate***, 'lasting for three, appearing every three, or (with resulting ambiguity) appearing three times in a', as ***triennial***, ***trimonthly***, ***tri-weekly***; (*b*) nouns with the sense 'triple, thing having or consisting of three', as ***tricycle***, ***trilogy***, ***triplane***; in chemical names indicating the presence of three atoms of an element or three similar radicals, as ***triacetate***, ***trichloride***, ***trinitrotoluene***; (*c*) verbs (and derivatives) with the sense 'into three', as ***trifurcate***, ***trisect***.
■ **triactor** *noun* (*Canad.*) a form of betting on racehorses in which triple success wins a big dividend L20. **triaˈllelic** *adjective* (GENETICS) having or involving three different alleles of a gene M20. **triˈapsal**, **triˈapsidal** *adjectives* having three apses M19. **tri-axle** *noun* a trailer or articulated lorry with three (rear) axles L20. **triˈbutyl** *adjective* (CHEMISTRY) having three butyl groups in the molecule; **tributyltin**, an organic radical, $(C_4H_9)_3Sn\cdot$, in which tetravalent tin is linked to three *n*-butyl groups; any compound containing this, some of which are used as pesticides esp. in paints and preservatives: M20. **tricarboˈxylic** *adjective* (CHEMISTRY) having three carboxyl groups in the molecule; ***tricarboxylic acid cycle***, = KREBS CYCLE: L19. **tricarˈpellary** *adjective* (BOTANY) consisting of or having three carpels L19. **trichloroaˈcetic**, **trichloracetic** *adjective* (CHEMISTRY etc.): ***trichloroacetic acid***, ***trichloracetic acid***, a toxic deliquescent crystalline acid, CCl_3COOH, used as an insecticide, antiseptic, and astringent; abbreviation *TCA*: L19. **trichloroˈethylene** *noun* (CHEMISTRY & PHARMACOLOGY) a liquid organochlorine compound, $CCl_2{=}CHCl$, used as a solvent, analgesic, and anaesthetic L19. **trichloroˈphenol** *noun* (CHEMISTRY etc.) each of six isomeric phenol derivatives having the formula $C_6H_2Cl_3(OH)$, used as insecticides, preservatives, and in the synthesis of various pesticides L19. **tricoˈlumnar** *adjective* having or occupying three columns M19. **triciontiˈnental** *adjective* embracing three continents M20. **triˈcornered** *adjective* having three corners E19. **triˈcresyl** *adjective* (CHEMISTRY) having three cresyl groups in the molecule;

tricresyl phosphate, a liquid, $(CH_3C_6H_4O)_3PO$, used as a fuel additive, plasticizer, and fire retardant (abbreviation ***TCP***): **L19.** **tri'dactyl** *adjective* having three fingers or toes **E19.** **tri'dactylous** *adjective* (now *rare*) = TRIDACTYL **E19.** **tri'facial** *adjective* (ANATOMY, now *rare*) = TRIGEMINAL **M19.** **tri'functional** *adjective* (CHEMISTRY) having three functional groups in the molecule **E20.** **tri'glyceride** *noun* (CHEMISTRY) an ester of glycerol in which three acid radicals combine with each glycerol molecule, examples of which are the main constituents of naturally occurring fats and oils **M19.** **trigynous** /'trɪdʒɪnəs/ *adjective* (BOTANY) having three pistils **L18.** **trihalo'methane** *noun* (CHEMISTRY) any of the compounds formed by substitution of halogen atoms for three of the hydrogen atoms of methane (also called ***haloform***) **M20.** **tri'hybrid** *adjective* (**a**) GENETICS of or pertaining to a hybrid that is heterozygous with respect to three independent genes; (**b**) involving or pertaining to a descent from three different races or types that interbred: **E20.** **tri'hydrate** *noun* (CHEMISTRY) a hydrate containing three moles of water per mole of the compound **M19.** **trihy'drated** *adjective* (CHEMISTRY) hydrated with three moles of water per mole of the compound **M19.** **tri'hydric** *adjective* (CHEMISTRY) (of an alcohol etc.) containing three hydroxyl groups **M19.** **triiodomethane** *noun* = IODOFORM **M20.** **triiodo'thyronine** *noun* (BIOCHEMISTRY) a thyroid hormone similar to thyroxine but having greater potency **M20.** **trijugate** *adjective* [Latin *jugum* yoke, pair] (BOTANY) having three pairs of leaflets **L19.** **tri'laminar** *adjective* (BIOLOGY) having or consisting of three layers **L19.** **tri-level** *adjective & noun* (*N. Amer.*) (**a**) *adjective* having or consisting of three levels; *esp.* (of a building) having three storeys or floors on three levels (cf. ***split-level*** s.v. SPLIT *ppl adjective*); (**b**) *noun* a tri-level building: **M20.** **tri'lineal** *adjective* (long *rare*) = TRILINEAR **E18.** **tri'lineate** *adjective* (ZOOLOGY) marked with three lines or streaks **E19.** **tri'locular** *adjective* (BOTANY & ZOOLOGY) having three cells or compartments **M18.** **trime'llitic** *adjective* (CHEMISTRY): ***trimellitic acid***, a colourless crystalline compound, $C_6H_3(COOH)_3$, 1,2,4-benzenetricarboxylic acid, obtained by the oxidation of pseudocumene **L19.** **tri'mesic** *adjective* (CHEMISTRY): ***trimesic acid***, a colourless crystalline compound, $C_6H_3(COOH)_3$, 1,3,5-benzenetricarboxylic acid **L19.** **tri-mix** *noun* a breathing mixture for deep-sea divers composed of nitrogen, helium, and oxygen **L20.** **tri'modal** *adjective* (chiefly STATISTICS) having three modes **E20.** **tri'monthly** *adjective* (**a**) occurring every three months; (**b**) lasting or extending over three months: **M19.** **trinitro'cellulose** *noun* cellulose nitrate, gun-cotton **L19.** **trinitro'phenol** *noun* (CHEMISTRY) a derivative of phenol in which three hydrogen atoms in the ring have been replaced by NO_2 groups; *esp.* picric acid: **M19.** **trinoctial** /-'nɒkʃ(ə)l/ *adjective* belonging to or lasting three nights **E17.** **tri'nodal** *adjective* having three nodes **M17.** **tri'nucleotide** *noun* (BIOCHEMISTRY) an oligonucleotide containing three nucleotides **E20.** **trionymal** /-'ɒnɪm(ə)l/ *adjective* (*rare*) having three names; *spec.* = TRINOMIAL *adjective* 2: **M17.** **tripa'rental** *adjective* (MICROBIOLOGY) involving or resulting from the simultaneous infection of a bacterium by three different bacteriophages **M20.** **tri'petalous** *adjective* (BOTANY) having three petals **E18.** **triphy'letic** *adjective* (BIOLOGY) derived from three different genetic stocks **E20.** **tri'radial** *adjective* = TRIRADIATE **L19.** **tri'radiate** *adjective* having or consisting of three rays; extending in three directions from a central point: **M19.** **tri'radius** *noun*, pl. **-radii** /-'reɪdɪʌɪ/, in dermatoglyphics, a point from which dermal ridges radiate in three directions at roughly equal angles **M20.** **tri'sepalous** *adjective* (BOTANY) having three sepals **M19.** **tri'septate** *adjective* having three septa or partitions **L19.** **tri'stearin** *noun* [STEARIN] CHEMISTRY the triglyceride formed by addition of three stearic acid residues to a molecule of glycerine, which is the chief constituent of tallow or suet **M19.** **tri'stylous** *adjective* (BOTANY) having three styles or kinds of style **L19.** **tri'substituted** *adjective* (CHEMISTRY) having three substituents in the molecule **E20.** **trisulcate** /trʌɪ'sʌlkət/ *adjective* having three branches, three-forked; BOTANY & ZOOLOGY marked or divided by three furrows or grooves: **E18.** **tri'ternate** *adjective* (BOTANY) biternate with the secondary divisions themselves being ternate **M18.** **tri'terpane** *noun* (CHEMISTRY) a terpane with the formula $C_{30}H_{60}$, analogous to the triterpenes **M20.** **tri'terpene** *noun* (CHEMISTRY) any of the group of terpenes of formula $C_{30}H_{48}$, found in plant gums and resins, or their derivatives **E20.** **tri'terpenoid** *adjective & noun* (CHEMISTRY) (designating) a triterpene or a derivative of one **M20.** **tritu'bercular** *adjective* = TRITUBERCULATE **L19.** **tritu'berculate** *adjective* (ZOOLOGY) (of a tooth) having three cusps; characterized by such teeth: **M19.**

triable /'trʌɪəb(ə)l/ *adjective.* **LME.**
[Anglo-Norman, formed as TRY *verb* + -ABLE.]
1 LAW. Of a case, issue, person, etc.: able to be tried in a court; liable to (a) judicial trial. **LME.**
2 Able to be attempted, tested, or put to the proof. **E17.**

triac /'trʌɪak/ *noun.* **M20.**
[from TRI(ODE + *ac* (= alternating current).]
ELECTRONICS. A three-electrode semiconductor device that will conduct in either direction when triggered by a positive or negative signal at the gate electrode.

triacetate /trʌɪ'asɪteɪt/ *noun.* **M19.**
[from TRI- + ACETATE.]
CHEMISTRY. †**1** A compound in which an acetate group was regarded as combined with three atoms of a base. Only in **M19.**
2 A compound containing three acetate groups in its molecule; *spec.* cellulose triacetate, containing the equivalent of three acetate groups for each glucose monomer; a fibre made from this. **L19.**

triacid /trʌɪ'asɪd/ *adjective & noun.* **M19.**
[from TRI- + ACID *noun.*]
▶ **A** *adjective.* **1** Of a base: able to neutralize three equivalents of a monobasic acid. Now *rare.* **M19.**
2 Designating a type of trichrome stain (see sense B. below). **L19.**
3 Of a triglyceride: containing three different acid radicals in its molecule. **M20.**
▶ **B** *noun.* A type of biological trichrome stain containing methyl green, fuchsine, and an orange dye. **L19.**

triaconta- /trʌɪə'kɒntə/ *combining form* of Greek *triakonta* thirty. Before a vowel **triacont-**.
■ **triacontahedral** /-'hiːdr(ə)l, -'hɛdr(ə)l/ *adjective* (of a crystal or solid figure) having thirty faces, usu. thirty rhombic faces **E19.** **triaconta'hedron** *noun*, pl. **-dra, -drons**, a solid figure or object with thirty plane faces **M20.** **triaconter** *noun* an ancient Greek galley with thirty oars **M19.**

triad /'trʌɪad/ *noun.* **M16.**
[French *triade* or late Latin *triad-*, *trias* from Greek *triad-*, *trias*, from *tri-* TRI-: see -AD[1].]
1 A group or set of three (persons, things, attributes, etc.); *spec.* (**a**) CHRISTIAN THEOLOGY the Trinity; (**b**) a Welsh form of literary composition characterized by an arrangement of subjects or statements in groups of three. **M16.**
2 In Pythagoreanism, the number three. **M17.**
3 MUSIC. A chord of three notes, consisting of a given note with the third and fifth above it. **M18.**
4 (Usu. **T-**.) Orig., a Chinese secret society formed in the early 18th cent., later having a large membership in southern China and various foreign countries (also more fully ***Triad Society***). Now also, (a member of) any of several Chinese secret societies in various countries, usu. involved in criminal activities. Freq. *attrib.* **E19.**
5 CHEMISTRY. Orig., a trivalent element or group. Now, a trimeric unit within a polymer. **M19.**

📖 **3** E. PROUT A chord . . containing a major third and an augmented fifth . . is called an augmented triad.

■ **tri'adic** *adjective* of, pertaining to, or constituting a triad; consisting of triads: **L18.** **tri'adically** *adverb* **M19.** **triadism** /'trʌɪədɪz(ə)m/ *noun* a triadic method, system, principle, or arrangement **M19.**

triadelphous /trʌɪə'dɛlfəs/ *adjective.* **E19.**
[from TRI- + Greek *adelphos* brother + -OUS.]
BOTANY. Of stamens: united by the filaments so as to form three groups. Of a plant: having the stamens so united.

triage /'trʌɪɪdʒ; *in senses A.2 & B. also* trɪ'ɑːʒ, *foreign* trijaːʒ/ *noun & verb.* **E18.**
[Old & mod. French, from *trier*: see TRY *verb*, -AGE.]
▶ **A** *noun.* **1** The action of sorting samples of a commodity according to quality. **E18.**
2 MEDICINE. The assignment of degrees of urgency of need in order to decide the order of treatment of a large number of injured or ill patients. **M20.** ▸**b** *gen.* Prioritization. **L20.**
▶ **B** *verb trans. & intrans.* Assign a degree of urgency of need to (a casualty); separate *out* by triage. **L20.**

triagonal /trʌɪ'ag(ə)n(ə)l/ *adjective.* **M17.**
[Erron. for TRIGONAL after *tetragonal*, *pentagonal*, etc.: see TRI-, -GON.]
Triangular.

trial /'trʌɪəl/ *noun.* **LME.**
[Anglo-Norman, or from medieval Latin *triallum*, from *trier*: see TRY *verb*, -AL[1].]
1 a LAW. (An) examination and determination of a cause by a judge or judicial tribunal; the procedure by which a court determines the guilt or innocence of an accused person. **LME.** ▸**b** Any of various other means of deciding a person's guilt or innocence, the rightness of a cause, etc.; *spec.* (*Hist.*) (**a**) = ***trial by battle*** s.v. BATTLE *noun*; (**b**) = ORDEAL 1. **LME.**
2 The action or process of testing (the quality of) a thing; an instance of this, a test, an experiment. Also, a method or procedure used to find a result, test a prediction, evaluate a hypothesis, etc.; experimental investigation or treatment. **L15.**
†**3 a** Evidence, proof. **M16–L18.** ▸**b** Investigation or examination (*of* a matter). Esp. in ***take trial of***, investigate, examine. Chiefly *Scot.* **M16–M17.**
4 a The fact or condition of being tried by suffering or temptation. **M16.** ▸†**b** (An) experience *of* something. Only in **17.** ▸**c** An event, experience, person, etc., by which a person's endurance, patience, or faith is put to the test; an affliction, a misfortune. **M18.**
5 An attempt (to do something); an endeavour. **E17.**
6 A sample specimen of a manufacture, material, etc., *esp.* one used as or in a test; *spec.* (POTTERY) a piece of clay used to test the progress of firing in a kiln. **E17.** ▸**b** A sieve, a screen for sifting. *obsolete* exc. *dial.* **E19.**
7 A test of a person's qualifications, knowledge, or academic attainments; an examination. Now also, an opportunity to prove one's worth. **L17.**
8 SPORT. **a** A match or competition to help selectors assess the abilities of players etc. eligible for a team. **E20.** ▸**b** *sing.* & *in pl.* A competition to test the abilities of motorcyclists (or, formerly, car-drivers) and their vehicles over long distances or rough terrain. **E20.** ▸**c** Any of various contests involving performances by horses, dogs, or other animals. **M20.**

📖 **1a** C. THIRLWALL He was brought to trial . . Theramenes . . became his accuser. H. HOWARD Murray's going to stand trial charged with murder one. **2** F. TEMPLE Science proceeds . . by trial of some theory as a working hypothesis. H. E. BATES I'll try it for a week . . I'll give it a trial. H. L. EDLIN Many trials of direct sowing of various kinds of tree have been carried out. *Lancet* Response to anti-depressants was judged . . on the basis of double-blind trials. **b** A. HARDING The Anglo-Saxons preferred trial by ordeal. **4a** MILTON That which purifies us is triall. **c** J. L. WATEN The trials of living in a strange land. J. SUTHERLAND It was a trial for Mary . . that . . Willie was her father's favourite. **5** W. CATHER After a dozen trials he succeeded in lighting the lantern. **6** DAVID POTTER Apart from the issued stamps, there are a number of trials in circulation.

Phrases: ***monkey trial***: see MONKEY *noun*. ***Nuremburg trials***: see NUREMBERG 2. **on trial** (**a**) (in the condition of) being tried by a court; (**b**) being tested; (**c**) to be chosen or retained only if found suitable or satisfactory. ***show trial***: see SHOW *noun*[1]. ***stand one's trial***: see STAND *verb*. ***take trial of***: see sense 3b above. **trial and error** repeated (usu. varied and unsystematic) attempts or experiments continued until successful. ***trial by battle***: see BATTLE *noun*. **trial by television**, **trial by the media** discussion of a case or controversy on television or in the media involving or implying accusations against a particular person. **trial of strength** a contest to decide which of two or more parties has the greater strength. ***trial of the pyx***: see PYX *noun* 2.

Comb.: **trial balance** in double entry bookkeeping, an addition of all the entries on each side of the ledger, to check that the sum of the debits balances that of the credits; **trial balloon** = BALLON D'ESSAI; **trial-bred** *adjective* (of a dog) bred to compete in trials; **trial court** LAW a court of first instance (as opp. to an appeal court); **trial eight** ROWING an eight-oared boat's provisional crew, from whom some members of the final eight may be chosen; ***trial heat***: see HEAT *noun* 11; **trial jury** US LAW a petty jury; **trial lawyer** US a lawyer practising in a trial court; **trial-piece** a thing, esp. a coin, made or taken as a test specimen; **trial run** a preliminary test of the performance of a new vessel, vehicle, procedure, etc.; **trial trench** *Archaeol.* an exploratory trench dug on a site.

trial /'trʌɪəl/ *adjective.* **L19.**
[from Latin *tri-* TRI- + -AL[1] after *dual*.]
GRAMMAR. Designating a form of nouns, verbs, etc., denoting three persons or things (with ref. to some languages of New Guinea and Polynesia).

trial /'trʌɪəl/ *verb.* Infl. **-ll-**, *-**l-**. **L20.**
[from the noun.]
1 *verb trans.* Test (a thing, esp. a new product). **L20.**
2 *verb intrans.* Perform in a specified manner in a test. *Austral.* **L20.**

trialism /'trʌɪəlɪz(ə)m/ *noun. rare.* **L19.**
[formed as TRIAL *adjective* + -AL[1] + -ISM, after *dualism*.]
1 The doctrine that the human being is a composite of three principles, esp. of body, soul, and spirit. **L19.**
2 A union of three States or countries. **E20.**

trialist /'trʌɪəlɪst/ *noun*[1]. **M20.**
[formed as prec.: see -IST.]
A person who advocates a union of three States or countries.

trialist /'trʌɪəlɪst/ *noun*[2]. Also **-ll-**. **M20.**
[from TRIAL *noun* + -IST.]
1 LAW. A person involved in a judicial trial. **M20.**
2 A person who plays or competes in a sports trial. **M20.**
3 MEDICINE. A person who takes part in clinical tests, trials of new drugs, etc. **L20.**

triality /trʌɪ'alɪti/ *noun.* **E16.**
[formed as TRIAL *adjective* after PLURALITY.]
†**1** ECCLESIASTICAL HISTORY. The holding of three benefices at once. **E16–M17.**
2 The condition or quality of being threefold. *rare.* **L19.**

triallist *noun* var. of TRIALIST *noun*[2].

trialogue /'trʌɪəlɒg/ *noun.* **M16.**
[Irreg. from TRI- + DI)ALOGUE *noun*, with prefix of the latter interpreted as DI-[2].]
A dialogue or colloquy between three people.

triamcinolone /trʌɪəm'sɪnələʊn/ *noun.* **M20.**
[Origin unkn.: *-olone* after *prednisolone*.]
PHARMACOLOGY. A synthetic steroid resembling prednisolone in effect but more potent as an anti-inflammatory agent.

trian /'trʌɪən/ *adjective.* **E19.**
[App. from Latin *tres*, *tria* three + -AN.]
HERALDRY. Three-quarter. Only in ***in trian aspect***, showing three-quarters of the body, facing partly forward.

triangle /'trʌɪaŋg(ə)l/ *noun.* **LME.**
[Old & mod. French, or Latin *triangulum* use as noun of neut. of *triangulus* three-cornered, formed as TRI- + *angulus* ANGLE *noun*[3].]
1 A figure (usu. a plane straight-sided figure) having three angles and three sides. **LME.** ▸**b** *fig.* A group or set of three; *esp.* a relationship of three people involving sexual rivalry. **E17.**
2 *gen.* A three-cornered object, marking, area, or space. **LME.**
3 (Usu. **T-**.) *The* constellation Triangulum. **LME.**
4 A drawing instrument in the form of a right-angled triangle made of wood, metal, plastic, etc. **LME.**

5 Chiefly NAUTICAL. A large tripod made of three poles or spars joined at the top and having a pulley for hoisting heavy weights. L17.
6 A percussion instrument consisting of a steel rod bent into a triangle and sounded by striking it with a small steel rod; a player on this in an orchestra etc. E19.
7 *Hist.* A tripod (orig. made of three halberds stuck in the ground and joined at the top) to which a prisoner or soldier was bound for flogging. Usu. in *pl.* E19.
8 ANGLING. A set of three hooks fastened together so that the barbs form a triangle. M19.
9 A small brownish Eurasian moth, *Heterogenea asella*, of oak and beech woods. Also ***triangle moth***. M19.
10 SNOOKER etc. A triangular wooden frame used to position the red balls before the start of play. L19.
11 A triangular reflective metal sign to warn vehicles on the road of a broken-down vehicle ahead. M20.

📖 **1** ***astronomical triangle***: see ASTRONOMICAL *adjective* 1. ***right triangle***: see RIGHT *adjective*. SPHERICAL ***triangle***. **triangle of forces** a triangle formed by three lines whose directions and magnitudes represent those of three forces in equilibrium acting at a point. **b** ***eternal triangle***: see ETERNAL *adjective* 2c. **2** M. KLINE The triangle formed by three mountain peaks. *Atlantic* A triangle of light from the streetlamp fell on my sheets. E. J. HOWARD Shrimps . . with thin triangles of toast. ***Bermuda Triangle***: see BERMUDA 3. **golden triangle** *the* area at the meeting-point of Myanmar (Burma), Laos, and Thailand, where much opium is grown. **in triangle** HERALDRY (of three or more charges) arranged in the form of a triangle. ***Pascal's triangle***: see PASCAL 1. **3** ***Southern Triangle***: see SOUTHERN *adjective*.

Comb.: **triangle inequality** MATH. the statement that the modulus of the sum of two quantities is less than or equal to the sum of their moduli (so called from the analogy with the distances between the vertices of a triangle); ***triangle moth***: see sense 9 above.
■ **triangled** *adjective* (now *rare*) †(*a*) triangular; †(*b*) arranged in a triangle; (*c*) HERALDRY divided into triangles by crossing lines: L15.

†triangle *adjective*. L15–E19.
[Latin *triangulus*: see prec.]
Triangular.

triangulable /trʌɪˈaŋɡjʊləb(ə)l/ *adjective*. M20.
[from TRIANGULATE *verb* + -ABLE.]
MATH. Of a topological space: capable of undergoing triangulation.

triangular /trʌɪˈaŋɡjʊlə/ *adjective* & *adverb*. M16.
[Late Latin *triangularis*, from Latin *triangulum*: see TRIANGLE *noun*, -AR[1].]
▶ **A** *adjective*. **1** Of or arranged in the form or shape of a triangle; three-cornered. M16.
2 Having three edges; having a cross-section in the form of a triangle; trihedral, triquetrous. E17. ▸**b** Of a solid: of which the faces are triangles. *rare*. E19.
3 Pertaining or relating to a triangle or to the construction of triangles. E18.
4 *fig.* Involving or taking place between three people or parties, three-sided. Also, constituting a set of three. E19.

📖 **1** O. MANNING The white triangular sails of the feluccas. **2** M. CONEY Sierro . . leaned the two top edges together and formed a triangular shelter. **3** **triangular number** any of the series of numbers (1, 3, 6, 10, 15, etc.) obtained by continued summation of the natural numbers 1, 2, 3, 4, 5, etc. **4** T. HARDY The triangular situation—himself—his wife—Lucy Savile. *Listener* The triangular co-operation of government, business and trade unions. **triangular trade** a multilateral system of trading in which a country pays for its imports from one country by its exports to another.

▶†**B** *adverb*. At the angular points of a triangle. E17–E18.
■ **triangu'larity** *noun* the quality or state of being triangular L17. **triangularly** *adverb* E17.

triangulate /trʌɪˈaŋɡjʊlət/ *adjective*. LME.
[medieval Latin *triangulatus* triangular, from Latin *triangulum*: see TRIANGLE *noun*, -ATE[2].]
Now chiefly ZOOLOGY. Having three angles, triangular; made up or composed of triangles; marked with triangles.
■ **triangulately** *adverb* in a triangulate manner; so as to form triangles: M19.

triangulate /trʌɪˈaŋɡjʊleɪt/ *verb*. M19.
[from Latin *triangulum* (see TRIANGLE *noun*) + -ATE[3].]
1 a *verb trans.* In surveying, navigation, etc., measure and map out (a region or territory) by triangulation; determine (a distance, altitude, etc.) in this way. M19. ▸**b** *verb intrans.* Perform triangulation. M19.
2 *verb trans. gen.* Mark out or divide into triangles. M19.
■ **triangulator** *noun* a person who triangulates something; an instrument used in triangulation: L19.

triangulated /trʌɪˈaŋɡjʊleɪtɪd/ *adjective*. E17.
[In sense 1 from TRIANGULATE *adjective*; in sense 2 from prec.: see -ED[1].]
1 = TRIANGULATE *adjective*. Now *rare* or *obsolete*. E17.
2 That has been triangulated. L19.

triangulation /trʌɪˌaŋɡjʊˈleɪʃ(ə)n/ *noun*. E19.
[formed as TRIANGULATE *verb*: see -ATION.]
1 In surveying, navigation, etc., the tracing and measurement of a series or network of triangles in order to determine the distances and relative positions of points spread over a territory or region, esp. by measuring the length of one side of each triangle and deducing its angles and the length of the other two sides by observation from this baseline, usu. with a theodolite; the result of such a survey. E19.
2 Division into triangles; *spec.* in MATH., division of a topological space into portions which are homoeomorphic with or analogous to the interior of a triangle; the result of such a process. L19.
1 attrib.: ***triangulation point***, ***triangulation station***, etc.

Triangulum /trʌɪˈaŋɡjʊləm/ *noun*. Also †**-us**. M16.
[Latin *triangulum* TRIANGLE *noun*.]
(The name of) a small constellation of the northern hemisphere between Andromeda and Aries; the Triangle.
Triangulum Australe /ɒˈstrɑːliː/ (the name of) a small constellation lying in the Milky Way near the South Pole; the Southern Triangle.

triannual /trʌɪˈanjʊəl/ *adjective*. *rare*. M17.
[from TRI- + ANNUAL *adjective*.]
= TRIENNIAL *adjective*.

triantelope /trʌɪˈantɪləʊp/ *noun*. *Austral.* M19.
[Popular alt. of TARANTULA.]
A huntsman spider.

triarch /ˈtrʌɪɑːk/ *adjective*. L19.
[from TRI- + Greek *arkhē* beginning.]
BOTANY. Of a vascular bundle: having three strands of xylem, formed from three points of origin.

triarchy /ˈtrʌɪɑːki/ *noun*. E17.
[from TRI- + -ARCHY, or Greek *triarkhia* triumvirate.]
1 A group of three districts or divisions of a country, each under its own ruler; *rare* a ruler of such a district or division. E17.
2 Government by three joint rulers; a triumvirate. M17.

trias /ˈtrʌɪəs/ *noun*. E17.
[Latin: see TRIAD. In sense 2 after German.]
1 The number three; a set of three, a triad. E17.
2 GEOLOGY. (Usu. **T-**.) A series of strata lying between the Jurassic and Permian systems (so called as divisible in German localities into three groups), represented in Britain esp. by the Upper New Red Sandstone. M19.

Triassic /trʌɪˈasɪk/ *adjective* & *noun*. M19.
[from prec. + -IC.]
GEOLOGY. ▶**A** *adjective*. Designating or pertaining to the first period of the Mesozoic era, following the Permian and preceding the Jurassic, characterized by the rise of ammonites, dinosaurs, and modern corals. M19.
▶ **B** *noun*. The Triassic period; the system of rocks dating from this time, the Trias. M19.

triathlon /trʌɪˈaθlɒn, -lən/ *noun*. L20.
[from TRI- + Greek *athlon* contest, after *decathlon* etc.]
An athletic or sporting contest in which competitors engage in three different events; *spec.* a race comprising three events performed consecutively, usu. swimming, cycling, and long-distance running.
■ **triathlete** *noun* a competitor in a triathlon L20.

triatic /trʌɪˈatɪk/ *adjective*. M19.
[App. from TRI-.]
NAUTICAL. ***triatic stay***, a stay attached horizontally to the top of the foremast and mainmast in a square-rigged ship, or to the two masts to which the signal halyards are fastened in other ships.

triatomic /trʌɪəˈtɒmɪk/ *adjective*. M19.
[from TRI- + ATOMIC *adjective*.]
CHEMISTRY. Containing three or more atoms; composed of molecules each containing three atoms. Formerly also, tribasic, trivalent.

triatomid /trʌɪˈatəmɪd/ *noun*. M20.
[mod. Latin *Triatomidae* family name (see below) from *Triatoma* genus name, formed as TRI- + Greek *tomos* cut (from the three joints in the antennae): see -ID[3].]
In full ***triatomid bug***. A bloodsucking assassin bug of the subfamily Triatominae (formerly family Triatomidae), which includes several vectors of disease.
■ **triatomine** *adjective* & *noun* of or pertaining to, a bug of, the subfamily Triatominae M20.

triaxial /trʌɪˈaksɪəl/ *adjective*. L19.
[from TRI- + AXIAL.]
Having or pertaining to three axes; occurring or responding in three (esp. mutually perpendicular) directions.
■ **triaxi'ality** *noun* triaxial nature L20. **triaxially** *adverb* L20.

For other words beginning with *tri-* see the entry for **tri-**

triazine /ˈtrʌɪəziːn, trʌɪˈaziːn, -zɪn/ *noun*. Also **-in** /-ɪn/. L19.
[from TRI- + AZO- + -INE[5], -IN[1].]
CHEMISTRY. Any compound whose molecule contains an unsaturated ring of three carbon and three nitrogen atoms. Freq. *attrib.*
triazine dye, ***triazine herbicide***, ***triazine nucleus***, ***triazine ring***, etc.

triazo- /trʌɪˈazəʊ, trʌɪˈeɪzəʊ/ *combining form*. Also as attrib. adjective **triazo**. L19.
[from TRI- + AZO-.]
CHEMISTRY. Forming names of compounds containing three atoms of nitrogen, esp. at adjacent positions in a ring, as ***triazobenzene***.

triazolam /trʌɪˈeɪzəlam, -ˈaz-/ *noun*. L20.
[from next + *-am* of unkn. origin.]
PHARMACOLOGY. A short-acting hypnotic drug of the benzodiazepine group, used to treat insomnia and as a sedative.

triazole /ˈtrʌɪəzəʊl, trʌɪˈazəʊl/ *noun*. L19.
[from TRI- + AZO- + -OLE[2].]
CHEMISTRY. Any compound whose molecule contains a ring of three nitrogen and two carbon atoms; *esp.* each of five isomeric compounds of formula $C_2H_3N_3$ containing such a ring with two double bonds.

Trib /trɪb/ *noun*. *colloq.* (chiefly *N. Amer.*). L19.
[Abbreviation of TRIBUNE *noun*[1].]
(A copy of) any of various N. American newspapers whose title contains the word 'Tribune'. Usu. with *the*.

tribade /ˈtrɪbəd/ *noun*. E17.
[French, or its source Latin *tribas*, *-ad-* from Greek *tribas*, from *tribein* rub.]
A lesbian.
■ **tribadism** *noun* (*a*) lesbianism; (*b*) a lesbian method of intercourse in which one partner lies on top of the other and simulates the movements of the male in heterosexual intercourse: E19.

tribal /ˈtrʌɪb(ə)l/ *adjective* & *noun*. M17.
[from TRIBE *noun* + -AL[1].]
▶ **A** *adjective*. **1** Of or pertaining to a tribe or tribes; characteristic of a tribe. M17.
2 *transf.* Characterized by the tendency to form groups or by strong group loyalty. M20.

📖 **1** R. GRAYSON The tribal instinct of the rich to protect themselves. S. WOODS A legal matter regarding tribal rights and territory. J. LE CARRÉ A delegation of West Africans in tribal costume. **2** G. GREER The tribal teenage situation.

▶ **B** *noun*. Chiefly in the Indian subcontinent: a member of a tribal community. Usu. in *pl.* M20.
■ **tribali'zation** *noun* the process of becoming tribalized L20. **tribalize** *verb trans.* unite into a tribal group or groups E20. **tribally** *adverb* L19.

tribalism /ˈtrʌɪbəlɪz(ə)m/ *noun*. L19.
[from prec. + -ISM.]
1 The condition of existing as a separate tribe or tribes; tribal organization. L19.
2 Loyalty to one's own particular tribe or social group. M20.
■ **tribalist** *noun* (*a*) *rare* a member of a tribe; (*b*) an advocate or practitioner of tribalism (TRIBALISM 2): L19. **triba'listic** *adjective* = TRIBAL *adjective* M20.

tribasic /trʌɪˈbeɪsɪk/ *adjective*. M19.
[from TRI- + BASIC *adjective*.]
CHEMISTRY. Of an acid: having three replaceable hydrogen atoms. Formerly also, trivalent.

tribe /trʌɪb/ *noun*. Also (earlier) †**tribu**. ME.
[Old & mod. French *tribu* or Latin *tribus* (sing. & pl.), perh. rel. to *tri-* three.]
1 A group of families, esp. of an ancient or indigenous people, claiming descent from a common ancestor, sharing a common culture, religion, dialect, etc., and usually occupying a specific geographical area and having a recognized leader. Orig. *spec.* (JEWISH HISTORY), each of the twelve divisions of the Israelites claiming descent from the twelve sons of Jacob. ME. ▸**b** A family with a recognized ancestry. LME.
2 a ROMAN HISTORY. Each of the political divisions of the Roman people (originally three, later thirty, ultimately thirty-five). M16. ▸**b** GREEK HISTORY. Each of the divisions of the ancient Greek people, originally on the basis of common ancestry, later forming a political unit; a phyle. L17. ▸**c** Any similar natural or political division of people. L17.
3 A set or number of people or things; *esp.* a set *of* people of a specified profession; *slang* a gang of criminals, delinquents, etc. Usu. *derog.* L16. ▸**b** In *pl.* Large numbers *of*. M19.
4 a TAXONOMY. A taxonomic grouping ranking next below a subfamily (formerly of variable rank); *loosely* a group or class of related animals or plants. M17. ▸**b** A class, a kind, a sort, (*of*). L17.

📖 **1** T. KENEALLY Tabidgi Jackie Smolders was . . of the . . Mungindi tribe. J. BARNES Here's this tribe of Indians, totally obscure. **b** LYTTON To what tribe of Camerons do you belong? **3** SWIFT Professors . . are . . worst qualified to explain their meanings to those, who are not of their tribe. BURKE The tribe of vulgar politicians are the lowest of our species. DAY LEWIS The church, he found . . filled with a whole tribe of tinkers. **b** *Time* Charter flights could not accommodate the tribes of ticket holders.

Phrases: ***idols of the tribe***: see IDOL *noun* 5b. ***Scheduled Tribe***: see SCHEDULED. **the Lost Tribes** *JEWISH HISTORY* the Ten Tribes after their deportation by Shalmaneser. **the Ten Tribes** *JEWISH HISTORY* the tribes of Israelites without Judah and Benjamin. **tribesman** a male (fellow) member of a tribe. **tribespeople** members of a tribe. **tribeswoman** a female (fellow) member of a tribe.

■ **tribeless** *adjective* belonging to no tribe E19. **tribelet** *noun* (*rare*) a small tribe M19. **tribeship** *noun* (*rare*) the condition or position of being a tribe (of a specified kind); the members of a tribe collectively: L18.

tribe /trʌɪb/ *verb trans. rare.* L17.
[from the noun.]
Classify in tribes; group in the same tribe *with*.

triblet /ˈtrɪblɪt/ *noun.* E17.
[French *triboulet*, of unkn. origin.]
A cylindrical rod or mandrel used in making nuts, rings, tubes, etc.

tribo- /ˈtrʌɪbəʊ, ˈtrɪbəʊ/ *combining form.*
[from Greek *tribos* rubbing: see -O-.]
Of or pertaining to rubbing or friction.
■ **triboeˈlectric** *adjective* of or pertaining to triboelectricity E20. **triboelecˈtricity** *noun* (the production of) electricity generated by friction L20. **triboeˌlectrifiˈcation** *noun* the production of triboelectricity M20. **tribolumiˈnescence** *noun* the emission of light from a material when rubbed, scratched, etc. L19. **tribolumiˈnescent** *adjective* exhibiting triboluminescence E20. **triboˈphysics** *noun* the physics of friction M20. **tribosphenic** /-ˈsfiːnɪk/ *adjective* [Greek *sphēn* wedge] (*ZOOLOGY*) of or pertaining to the basic modern mammalian dentition, in which the upper molars have three roots and bear a protocone and the lower molars have two roots and bear a talonid M20.

tribology /trʌɪˈbɒlədʒi/ *noun.* M20.
[from prec. + -LOGY.]
The branch of science and technology concerned with interacting surfaces in relative motion, and so with friction, wear, lubrication, and the design of bearings.
■ **triboˈlogical** *adjective* M20. **tribologist** *noun* M20.

tribometer /trʌɪˈbɒmɪtə/ *noun.* L18.
[French *tribomètre*, formed as TRIBO- + -METER.]
An instrument for measuring friction in sliding.

tribrach /ˈtrʌɪbrak, ˈtrɪ-/ *noun*¹. L16.
[Latin *tribrachys* from Greek *tribrakhus*, from *tri-* TRI- + *brakhus* short.]
PROSODY. A metrical foot consisting of three short syllables.
■ **triˈbrachic** *adjective* consisting of three short syllables; composed of tribrachs: M19.

tribrach /ˈtrʌɪbrak/ *noun*². L19.
[from TRI- + Greek *brakhiōn* arm.]
An object with three arms or branches; *esp.* a prehistoric flint implement of this form.
■ **triˈbrachial** *adjective* having three arms or branches L19.

†**tribu** *noun* var. of TRIBE *noun.*

tribual /ˈtrɪbjʊəl/ *adjective.* M17.
[from Latin *tribus* TRIBE *noun* + -AL¹.]
Of or pertaining to a tribe; tribal.

tribulage /ˈtrɪbjʊlɪdʒ/ *noun.* M16.
[medieval Latin *tribulagium*, from Latin *tribulum*: see TRIBULATION, -AGE.]
Hist. A type of poll tax formerly levied on each tin-miner in some of the stannaries.

tribulate /ˈtrɪbjʊleɪt/ *verb trans.* M17.
[Back-form. from next.]
Afflict; trouble greatly.

tribulation /trɪbjʊˈleɪʃ(ə)n/ *noun.* ME.
[Old & mod. French from ecclesiastical Latin *tribulatio(n-)*, from Latin *tribulare* press, oppress, afflict, from *tribulum* a board with sharp points on the underside, used in threshing, prob. from var. of stem of *terere* rub.]
1 A state of misery, great affliction, or oppression; a cause of this. ME. ▸†**b** A person who causes trouble. *rare* (Shakes.). Only in E17.
†**2** The state or condition of being held as a pledge. *slang.* M17–M18.

📖 **1** A. MAUPIN That . . depressed the matriarch more than all her other tribulations combined.

tribunal /trʌɪˈbjuːn(ə)l, trɪ-/ *adjective & noun.* LME.
[Old & mod. French, or Latin *tribunal(e)* raised platform for magistrates' seats, judgement-seat, from *tribunus* TRIBUNE *noun*¹: see -AL¹.]
▶ **A** *adjective.* **1** Designating a judgement-seat; pertaining to or authorized by a court of justice. LME.
†**2** Of or pertaining to a Roman tribune. *rare.* L16–L17.
▶ **B** *noun.* **I 1** A raised platform in a Roman basilica, on which the magistrates' seats were placed (*ROMAN ANTIQUITIES*); *transf.* a seat or bench for a judge or judges, a judgement-seat. LME.
2 A court of justice. L16. ▸**b** *fig.* Place of judgement or decision; judicial authority. M17.
3 A board appointed to adjudicate in some matter; *spec.* (in full ***tribunal of inquiry***) a board appointed by the Government to investigate a matter of public concern. E20.
3 industrial tribunal: arbitrating in disputes arising out of employment, such as complaints of unfair dismissal.
▶†**II 4** = TRIBUNE *noun*² 1, 3. M17–L18.

tribunate /ˈtrɪbjʊnət/ *noun.* M16.
[Latin *tribunatus*, from *tribunus* TRIBUNE *noun*¹: see -ATE¹.]
1 The office of tribune; tribuneship; government by tribunes. M16.
2 *FRENCH HISTORY.* A representative body of legislators established in 1800. E19.

tribune /ˈtrɪbjuːn/ *noun*¹. LME.
[Latin *tribunus* prob. orig. use as noun of adjective (sc. *magistratus*) 'magistrate of a tribe', from *tribus* TRIBE *noun.*]
1 *ROMAN HISTORY.* An ancient Roman official; *spec.* (***a***) any of several officials appointed to protect the interests and rights of the plebeians (also ***tribune of the people***); (***b***) (more fully ***military tribune***) a legionary officer. LME.
2 *transf. & fig.* An officer holding a position similar to that of a Roman tribune; a popular leader, a demagogue. L16.
■ **tribuneship** *noun* the office or position of a tribune; the term of this: M16.

tribune /ˈtrɪbjuːn/ *noun*². M17.
[French from Italian *tribuna* from medieval Latin *tribuna* alt. of Latin TRIBUNAL.]
1 A principal room or gallery in an Italian mansion; orig. *spec.* (**T-**), an octagonal hall in the Galleria degli Uffizi in Florence containing famous works of art. M17.
2 A raised platform; a dais, a rostrum; a bishop's throne. M18.
3 The apse of a basilica or basilican church containing a dais or a bishop's throne. L18.
4 A raised area or gallery with seats. M19.

Tribune group /ˈtrɪbjuːn gruːp/ *noun phr.* M20.
[from The *Tribune*, a radical left-wing Brit. journal.]
A group of Labour MPs advocating radical left-wing policies.
■ **Tribunite** *noun & adjective* of or pertaining to, a member of, the Tribune group L20.

tribunitian /trɪbjuːˈnɪʃ(ə)n/ *adjective.* Also **-ician**. M16.
[from Latin *tribunicius*, *-tius* + -AN.]
Of, pertaining to, or characteristic of a Roman tribune, or the office of tribune.
■ Also **tribunitial**, **-icial** *adjective* L16.

tributary /ˈtrɪbjʊt(ə)ri/ *adjective & noun.* LME.
[Latin *tributarius*, from *tributum*: see next, -ARY¹.]
▶ **A** *adjective.* **1** *Hist.* Required to pay or paying a tribute or tax. LME.
2 Offered or done as a tribute or mark of respect etc. *arch.* L16.
3 Subsidiary; *spec.* (of a stream or river) flowing into a larger river or a lake. E17.

📖 **1** BURKE As far independent as a tributary prince could be. **2** SHAKES. *Tit. A.* Lo, at this tomb my tributary tears I render. **3** K. GRAHAME Certain streams tributary to their own river.

▶ **B** *noun.* **1** *Hist.* A person paying tribute. LME.
2 *transf.* A stream or river flowing into a larger river or a lake. E19. ▸**b** A subsidiary thing. M19.

📖 **2** B. ENGLAND The main river ran along . . with two tributaries on the far side. F. FITZGERALD One of the Mekong tributaries flooded . . several provinces.

■ **tributarily** *adverb* M19. **tributariness** *noun* E18.

tribute /ˈtrɪbjuːt/ *noun & verb.* LME.
[Latin *tributum* use as noun of neut. of *tributus* pa. pple of *tribuere* assign, allot, grant, (lit. 'divide among the tribes'), from *tribus* TRIBE *noun.*]
▶ **A** *noun.* **1** *Hist.* **a** A payment made periodically by one State or ruler to another as a sign of dependence or submission or to ensure peace and protection; money or goods paid periodically by a subject to his sovereign or a vassal to his lord. LME. ▸**b** (An) obligation to pay this. LME.
2 *transf. & fig.* Something said, done, or given as a mark of respect or affection etc. L16. ▸**b** A thing attributable *to* or indicative of a praiseworthy quality etc. E20.
3 *MINING.* A proportion of ore raised, or its equivalent value, paid to a miner for his work, or to the owner of the mine or the land. L18.

📖 **1a** T. H. WHITE The Dictator of Rome . . had sent an embassy asking for tribute from Arthur. **b** ROBERT HALL His imperial fancy has laid all nature under tribute. **2** P. FITZGERALD He wore . . a . . peasant's blouse, a tribute to the memory of Lev Nikolaevich Tolstoy. *Times* Floral tributes following the passing away of . . Mr Jayant. **b** *Times* It is a tribute to the success of the Territorial experiment . . that these squadrons should have been chosen. **3 work on tribute** work under the system of paying or receiving certain proportions of the produce.

Comb.: **tribute-money**: paid as tribute.
▶ **B** *verb.* †**1** *verb intrans. & trans.* Pay (something) as tribute. *rare.* LME–M17.
2 *verb intrans. MINING.* Work on tribute. M19.
■ **tributor**, **-er** *noun* †(***a***) a person who pays tribute; (***b***) a miner who works on tribute: L15.

tricar /ˈtrʌɪkɑː/ *noun.* E20.
[from TRI- + CAR.]
A three-wheeled motor car.

tricast /ˈtrʌɪkɑːst/ *noun.* L20.
[from TRI- + FORE)CAST *noun.*]
A bet in which the punter forecasts the first three horses in a race in the correct order; = TRIFECTA.

trice /trʌɪs/ *noun.* LME.
[from the verb.]
Orig., a sharp pull, a tug. Long only *fig.*, the time taken for this, an instant, a moment. Chiefly & now only in ***in a trice***, instantly, without delay, in a very short time.

📖 J. R. ACKERLEY We were at Stratford in a trice. G. DALY He saw where he had gone wrong and fixed it in a trice.

trice /trʌɪs/ *verb trans.* LME.
[Middle Dutch *trīsen* (Dutch *trijsen* hoist) = Middle Low German *trīsen* rel. to Middle Dutch *trīse* windlass, pulley, of unkn. origin.]
†**1** Pull sharply; tug; snatch. LME–E17.
2 Chiefly *NAUTICAL.* Pull or haul with a rope; *spec.* haul *up* and secure with a rope or ropes. LME.

-trice /triːs/ *suffix* (not productive).
[French or Italian from Latin -TRIX.]
In fem. agent-nouns, as ***cantatrice***, ***directrice***, ***protectrice***, etc. Now usu. repl. by forms in *-tress* (see -OR, -ESS¹) or (*LAW*) -TRIX.

Tricel /ˈtrʌɪsɛl/ *noun.* Also **t-**. M20.
[from TRI(ACETATE + CEL(LULOSE *noun.*]
(Proprietary name for) a fibre and fabric made from cellulose triacetate.

tricenary /trʌɪˈsiːn(ə)ri/ *noun & adjective. rare.* L15.
[As noun from medieval Latin *tricenarium*; as adjective from Latin *tricenarius* of, pertaining to, or consisting of thirty, from *triceni* thirty each.]
▶ **A** *noun. ROMAN CATHOLIC CHURCH.* A series of masses said on thirty consecutive days. Cf. TRENTAL 1. L15.
▶ **B** *adjective.* Lasting thirty days. Long *rare* or *obsolete.* M17.

tricentenary /trʌɪsɛnˈtiːnəri, -ˈtɛn-, trʌɪˈsɛntɪn-/ *noun & adjective.* M19.
[from TRI- + CENTENARY.]
= TERCENTENARY.

tricentennial /trʌɪsɛnˈtɛnɪəl/ *noun & adjective.* L19.
[from TRI- + CENTENNIAL.]
= TERCENTENNIAL.

triceps /ˈtrʌɪsɛps/ *adjective & noun.* L16.
[Latin, formed as TRI- + *-ceps*, *caput* head.]
▶ **A** *adjective.* Three-headed. Now only *spec.*, (of a muscle) having three heads or points of attachment at one end. L16.
▶ **B** *noun.* Pl. same. A triceps muscle; *esp.* the extensor muscle of the back of the upper arm. E18.

triceratops /trʌɪˈsɛrətɒps/ *noun.* Pl. same. L19.
[mod. Latin (see below), from Greek *trikeratos* three-horned + *ōps* eye, face.]
A large quadrupedal herbivorous ornithischian dinosaur of the Cretaceous genus *Triceratops*, having a bony horn on the snout, two longer ones above the eyes, and a bony frill over the neck. Chiefly as mod. Latin genus name.

-trices *suffix* pl. of -TRICE, -TRIX.

trich /trɪk/ *noun. colloq.* L20.
[Abbreviation.]
= TRICHOMONIASIS (a).

trich- *combining form* see TRICHO-¹.

-trich /trɪk/ *suffix.*
[formed as TRICHO-¹.]
Forming nouns with the sense 'hair, hairs, hairlike structure', as ***gastrotrich***, ***peritrich***.

trichi /ˈtrɪtʃi/ *noun. arch. slang.* L19.
[Abbreviation.]
A Trichinopoli cigar.

trichiasis /trɪkɪˈeɪsɪs, trɪˈkʌɪəsɪs/ *noun.* M17.
[Late Latin from Greek *trikhiasis*, from *trikhian* be hairy: see -IASIS.]
MEDICINE. Irritation of the eyeball by inwardly turned eyelashes.

trichina /ˈtrɪkɪnə, trɪˈkʌɪnə/ *noun.* Pl. **-nae** /-niː/. M19.
[mod. Latin (see below), from Greek *trikhinos* of hair, from *trikh-*, *thrix* hair.]
A minute parasitic nematode worm of the genus *Trichinella* (formerly *Trichina*), esp. *Trichinella spiralis* of cold and temperate regions, which causes trichinosis.

For other words beginning with *tri-* see the entry for **tri-**

■ **trichinal** *adjective* of or pertaining to trichinae **M19.** **trichi'niasis** *noun* = TRICHINOSIS **M19.**

trichinelliasis /ˌtrɪkɪnəˈlʌɪəsɪs/ *noun.* **E20.**
[from mod. Latin *Trichinella* genus name + -IASIS.]
MEDICINE. = TRICHINOSIS.
■ Also **trichinellosis** *noun* **M20.**

Trichinopoli /trɪtʃɪˈnɒpəli/ *noun. arch.* **M19.**
[See below.]
Used *attrib.* to designate things, esp. cigars and jewellery, made in Tiruchirapalli (formerly Trichinopoli), a district and city in Tamil Nadu, India. Cf. TRICHI.

trichinosis /trɪkɪˈnəʊsɪs/ *noun.* Pl. **-noses** /-ˈnəʊsiːz/. **M19.**
[from TRICHINA + -OSIS.]
MEDICINE & VETERINARY MEDICINE. (A disease caused by) infection with trichinae, often from poorly cooked infected meat, whose larvae penetrate through the intestinal wall, migrate around the body, and encyst in muscular tissue, causing fever, pain, and stiffness.

trichite /ˈtrɪkʌɪt, ˈtrʌɪ-/ *noun.* **M19.**
[formed as TRICH(O-[1] + -ITE[1].]
A fine hairlike structure; *spec.* (**a**) *MINERALOGY* any of the minute dark hairlike crystallites occurring in some vitreous rocks; (**b**) *BIOLOGY* any of various filamentous organelles in certain ciliates and flagellates.
■ **trichitic** /-ˈkɪtɪk/ *adjective* **L19.**

tricho- /ˈtrɪkəʊ, ˈtrʌɪkəʊ/ *combining form*[1]. Before a vowel usu. **trich-**.
[from Greek *trikho-*, *trikh-*, combining stem of *thrix* hair: see -O-.]
Of, pertaining to, or resembling hair or hairs.
■ **tricho'bezoar** *noun* (*MEDICINE*) a concretion of hair in the stomach, a hair-ball **E20.** **trichocyst** *noun* (*BIOLOGY*) each of the minute rodlike structures containing a protrusible filament found near the surface of various ciliates etc. **M19.** **trichogen** /-dʒɛn/ *noun* (*ZOOLOGY*) a hypodermal cell in insects and other arthropods from which a hair arises **L19.** **tri'chogenous** *adjective* producing or promoting the growth of hair **M19.** **trichogyne** /-dʒʌɪn/ *noun* (*BOTANY*) a hairlike process from the female reproductive organ in certain algae, fungi, and lichens, which receives the male gamete **L19.** **tricho'monad** *noun* (*BIOLOGY*) a flagellate protozoan of the order Trichomonadida, having several flagella, typically parasitic and freq. pathogenic **M19.** **tricho'monal** *adjective* (chiefly *MEDICINE*) of, pertaining to, or caused by trichomonads **M20.** **tricho'monas** *noun* (**a**) = TRICHOMONAD; (**b**) = TRICHOMONIASIS: **M20.** **trichomoniasis** /-məˈnʌɪəsɪs/ *noun,* pl. **-niases** /-ˈnʌɪəsiːz/, *MEDICINE & VETERINARY MEDICINE* (a disease caused by) infection with trichomonads; *esp.* (**a**) a venereal disease of humans, chiefly women, caused by *Trichomonas vaginalis* and involving inflammation and discharge; (**b**) dysentery caused by *Trichomonas hominis* of the gut; (**c**) a sexually transmitted disease of cattle, caused by *Trichomonas foetus* and giving rise to abortion and sterility: **E20.** **tricho'phagia** *noun* = TRICHOPHAGY **E20.** **tri'chophagy** *noun* the persistent eating of or biting at one's own hair **M20.** **tricho'phobia** *noun* irrational fear of hair **L19.** **tricho'thallic** *adjective* (*BOTANY*) growing or taking place by means of intercalary cell division of the filament which forms the growing apex of an alga **L19.** **trichotillo'mania** *noun* [Greek *tillesthai* pull out (hair)] a compulsive desire to pull out one's hair **E20.** **trichotillo'maniac** *noun* a person with trichotillomania **M20.**

tricho- /ˈtrʌɪkəʊ, ˈtrɪkəʊ/ *combining form*[2].
[from Greek *trikha*, *trikhē* triply, in three, after DICHO-: see -O-.]
In three, as ***trichotomy***.

trichology /trɪˈkɒlədʒi, trʌɪ-/ *noun.* **M19.**
[from TRICHO-[1] + -LOGY.]
The branch of science that deals with the structure, functions, and diseases of the hair.
■ **tricho'logical** *adjective* **L19.** **trichologist** *noun* **L19.**

trichome /ˈtrʌɪkəʊm, ˈtrɪ-/ *noun.* **L19.**
[from Greek *trikhōma* growth of hair, from *trikhoun* cover with hair: see -OME.]
1 *BOTANY.* A hair, scale, prickle, or other outgrowth from the epidermis of a plant. Also, in certain bacteria, esp. cyanobacteria, a filament formed of closely linked cells. **L19.**
2 *ENTOMOLOGY.* An epidermal hair; *esp.* in myrmecophilous insects, a tuft of hairs near a gland producing a secretion attractive to ants. **E20.**

trichophyton /trɪkəˈfʌɪtɒn/ *noun.* Also Anglicized as **trichophyte** /ˈtrɪkəfʌɪt/. **M19.**
[mod. Latin (see below), formed as TRICHO-[1] + Greek *phuton* plant.]
A minute parasitic fungus of the genus *Trichophyton*, which infects the skin, hair, and nails; esp. *T. tonsurans*, which causes the disease ringworm, or *T. schoenleini*, which causes favus. Also *collect.*, this genus of fungi.
trichophyton fungus, ***trichophyton infection***, etc.
■ **trichophytic** /-ˈfɪtɪk/ *adjective* of or pertaining to a trichophyte **L19.** **trichophy'tosis** *noun* infection with trichophyton **L19.**

Trichoptera /trʌɪˈkɒpt(ə)rə/ *noun pl.* **E19.**
[mod. Latin, formed as TRICHO-[1] + Greek *pteron* wing: see -A[3].]
(Members of) an order of insects comprising the caddis-flies.
■ **trichopteran** *adjective & noun* (**a**) *adjective* = TRICHOPTEROUS; (**b**) *noun* a member of the order Trichoptera, a caddis-fly: **M19.** **trichopterous** *adjective* of, pertaining to, or characteristic of the Trichoptera **E19.**

trichord /ˈtrʌɪkɔːd/ *noun & adjective.* **L18.**
[Greek *trikhordos*, from *tri-* TRI- + *khordē* string (see CORD *noun*[1]).]
▶ **A** *noun.* A three-stringed lyre or lute. **L18.**
▶ **B** *adjective.* Designating a piano in which most of the keys have three strings each. **L18.**

trichothecene /trɪkəˈθiːsiːn, trʌɪ-/ *noun.* **L20.**
[from mod. Latin *Trichothecium* genus name of a fungus, formed as TRICHO-[1] + THECIUM: see -ENE.]
BIOCHEMISTRY. Any of a class of toxic sesquiterpenoids based on a tetracyclic ring system of formula $C_{15}H_{22}O_2$, mainly produced by certain fungi.
■ **trichothecin** /-kɪn, -sɪn/ *noun* a trichothecene ester produced by the mould *Trichothecium roseum* and toxic to some other fungi **M20.**

trichotomous /trʌɪˈkɒtəməs, trɪ-/ *adjective.* **E19.**
[from Greek *trikha* in three + *-tomos* cut: see TRICHO-[2], -OUS.]
1 *BOTANY.* Divided into three equal branches, each branch in each successive set being itself divided into three. **E19.**
2 Making three classes or categories. **M19.**
■ **trichotomously** *adverb* **M19.**

trichotomy /trʌɪˈkɒtəmi, trɪ-/ *noun.* **E17.**
[formed as TRICHO-[2] + -TOMY.]
Division (esp. sharply defined) into three parts, classes, or categories; an instance of this; *esp.* (*THEOLOGY*) division of human nature into body, soul, and spirit.
■ **tricho'tomic** *adjective* = TRICHOTOMOUS **L19.** **trichotomize** *verb trans. & intrans.* divide into three parts or categories **M17.**

trichroism /ˈtrʌɪkrəʊɪz(ə)m/ *noun.* **M19.**
[from Greek *trikhroos*, *trikhrous* three-coloured + -ISM.]
1 *CRYSTALLOGRAPHY & MINERALOGY.* Pleochroism resulting in the appearance of three different colours when viewed in three crystallographic directions. **M19.**
2 *ZOOLOGY.* The occurrence of three markedly distinct colour varieties of a species. *rare.* **L19.**
■ **tri'chroic** *adjective* exhibiting or pertaining to trichroism **L19.**

trichromasy /trʌɪˈkrəʊməsi/ *noun.* **E20.**
[from TRI- + -CHROMASY.]
OPHTHALMOLOGY. Trichromatic colour vision.

trichromat /ˈtrʌɪkrəmat/ *noun.* **E20.**
[Back-form. from next.]
OPHTHALMOLOGY. A person with trichromatic colour vision, esp. an anomalous form of it.

trichromatic /trʌɪkrəʊˈmatɪk/ *adjective.* **L19.**
[from TRI- + CHROMATIC.]
Having or pertaining to three colours; *spec.* of or pertaining to the perception of colours or their reproduction in printing, photography, etc., by the combination of images formed in three widely different single colours (as in normal colour vision).
■ **tri'chromatism** *noun* the quality or fact of being trichromatic; *spec.* = TRICHROMASY: **L19.**

trichrome /ˈtrʌɪkrəʊm/ *adjective.* **E20.**
[from TRI- + Greek *khrōma* colour.]
Trichromatic; *spec.* designating a stain and method of histological staining in which different tissues are stained in one of three different colours.

trichromic /trʌɪˈkrəʊmɪk/ *adjective.* **L19.**
[formed as prec. + -IC.]
= TRICHROMATIC.

trichuris /trɪˈkjʊərɪs/ *noun.* Pl. **-rides** /-rɪdiːz/. **E19.**
[mod. Latin (see below), from Greek *trikh-*, *thrix* hair + *oura* tail.]
ZOOLOGY & MEDICINE. A nematode of the genus *Trichuris*, which comprises slender worms several centimetres long that are intestinal parasites of humans and other vertebrates, esp. in the humid tropics; a whipworm. Now chiefly as mod. Latin genus name.
■ **trichu'riasis** /-rʌɪəsɪs/ *noun* infestation with *Trichuris trichuria* or similar nematodes which if heavy may cause pain, anaemia, and diarrhoea **E20.**

tricipital /trʌɪˈsɪpɪt(ə)l/ *adjective. rare.* **L19.**
[from TRICEPS, after *bicipital*.]
ANATOMY. = TRICEPS *adjective*.

trick /trɪk/ *noun & adjective.* **LME.**
[Old French *trique* dial. var. of *triche*, from *trichier* (mod. *tricher*) deceive, cheat, of unkn. origin. Cf. TREACHERY.]
▶ **A** *noun.* **I 1** An action or scheme undertaken to fool, outwit, or deceive; a ruse, a wile. **LME.** ▸**b** An optical or other illusion. **L16.**
2 †**a** A clever contrivance or invention. *rare.* **M16–E17.** ▸**b** A trinket, a bauble; in *pl.* (*US*), personal effects; *US & Austral. colloq.* a small or amusing person (esp. a child) or animal. **M16.**
3 A mischievous act; a prank; a practical joke. **L16.** ▸**b** A foolish or discreditable act. **L16.**
4 A clever or skilful expedient; a special technique; a knack or special way of doing something. **L16.** ▸**b** The art or faculty of doing something cleverly or skilfully. **E17.**
5 A feat of skill or dexterity; *transf.* an unusual action learned by an animal. **E17.** ▸**b** A robbery. Chiefly in ***turn a trick***, commit a successful robbery. *US slang.* **M19.** ▸**c** A voodoo spell cast on a person; an object used in casting such a spell. *US dial.* **L19.**

🕮 **1** J. T. STORY She also looked frightened . . . Just a trick to get her own way. *Company* Using baffling technical jargon is . . an old sales trick. **b** W. HORWOOD Was it, then, a trick of that strange light . . that made Boswell's fur . . brighter? **3** *Fast Forward* Our very latest joke and tricks catalogue . . so you can play some wicked pranks. **b** B. SCHULBERG You never find me going in for favors . . a sucker's trick. **4** A. G. GARDINER The trick of sawing wood is to work within your strength. S. BRETT He tried all his tricks, being sarcastic . . threatening (carefully) to resign. CLIVE JAMES I learned the trick of carrying nothing much except hand baggage. **b** SHAKES. *Cymb.* Nature prompts them in simple . . things, to prince it much Beyond the trick of others. **5** R. CAMPBELL Buffalo-drovers had a wonderful trick that I have seen nowhere else. A. S. NEILL They must not look on baby as a show piece to . . perform tricks when relatives come.

▶ **II 6** A fashion of dress. *arch.* **M16.**
7 A particular habit, way of acting; a habit; a characteristic practice, mannerism, or expression of the face or voice. **L16.**
8 Orig. *NAUTICAL*, the time allotted to a sailor on duty at the helm. Now *gen.* (chiefly *US*), any spell or stint of work or on duty. **M17.**
9 A prostitute's session with a client; a prostitute's client. *slang.* **E20.**

🕮 **7** B. FUSSELL The French trick of wrapping . . meat in paper to oven-poach it. QUILLER-COUCH He had a trick of half-closing his eyes when he looked at anything. **9** A. LURIE A girl like you . . could get at least a hundred a trick. B. TURNER I doubt there's one trick in twenty who isn't a married man.

▶ **III 10** *HERALDRY.* A sketch in pen and ink of a coat of arms. Chiefly in ***in trick***, sketched in pen and ink. **L16.**
▶ **IV 11** The cards contributed to a single round of card-play, usu. one from each player; such a round of play; a point gained from this. **L16.**
Phrases & comb.: **a trick worth two of that** a much better plan or expedient. ***bag of tricks***: see BAG *noun*. ***dirty trick***: see DIRTY *adjective*. ***do a disappearing trick***, ***do the disappearing trick***: see DISAPPEAR. **do the trick** accomplish one's purpose; achieve the required result. **how's tricks?** *colloq.* how are you? ***miss a trick***: see MISS *verb*[1]. ***odd trick***: see ODD *adjective*. ***quick trick***: see QUICK *adjective & adverb*. ***the whole bag of tricks***: see BAG *noun*. ***three-card trick***: see THREE *adjective & noun*. **trick or treat** (chiefly *N. Amer.*) a children's custom of calling at houses at Hallowe'en with the threat of pranks unless given a small gift of sweets etc. **trick-or-treating** (chiefly *N. Amer.*) the carrying out of this custom. **turn a trick** (**a**) *slang* (of a prostitute) have a session with a client; (**b**) see sense 5b above. **turn the trick** *US* = ***do the trick*** above.
▶ **B** *adjective.* **1** Intended or used to deceive or mystify or to create an illusion. **L19**
2 Stylish, fancy, smart. *colloq.* (orig. *US*). **M20.**
3 Unsound, unreliable. *N. Amer. colloq.* **M20.**

🕮 **1** P. MARSHALL A reflection . . in a trick mirror where . . features appear to thicken. *Time Out* The *Time Out* 1,000 resolutely failed to fall for our trick questions. **3** *Punch* He had this trick knee . . gave him hell.

Special collocations & comb.: **trick-cycling** (**a**) the action of performing tricks on a bicycle; (**b**) *slang* psychiatry. **trick cyclist** (**a**) a person who performs tricks on a bicycle, esp. in a circus; (**b**) *slang* a psychiatrist. **trick-frame** *adjective* designating a facility on a video recorder that enables frames to be quickly located, frozen, run in slow motion, etc. **trick photography** photography using various technical devices to create a visual illusion. **trick wheel** an auxiliary steering wheel on a ship.
■ **trickful** *adjective* (*rare*) full of tricks, tricky **L18.** **trickish** *adjective* = TRICKY *adjective* 1, 2 **E18.** **trickishly** *adverb* **E19.** **trickishness** *noun* **L18.** **trickless** *adjective* (chiefly *CARDS*) having no tricks **E20.**

trick /trɪk/ *verb.* **L15.**
[App. from prec.; in branch I perh. assoc. with French †*s'estriquer*, in branch II with Dutch *trekken* delineate.]
▶ **I 1** *verb trans.* Adorn, decorate, dress, esp. showily. Usu. foll. by *out*, *up*. **L15.**
†**2** *verb trans.* Arrange, adjust. Freq. in ***trick and trim***. **M16–E19.**

🕮 **1** J. RABAN Minarets . . tricked out with fairy-lights. *Far Eastern Economic Review* It's a . . provincial town tricked out like a big city.

▶ **II 3** *verb trans.* Sketch or draw in outline. Long only *spec.* (*HERALDRY*), draw (a coat of arms) in outline, with the tinctures denoted by initial letters or signs. **M16.**
▶ **III 4 a** *verb trans.* Deceive by a trick; fool; cheat. **L16.** ▸**b** Get or effect by trickery. *rare.* **M17.** ▸**c** Cheat *out of*; induce *into* by trickery. **L17.** ▸**d** Put a spell on (a person). *US dial.* **E19.**
5 *verb intrans.* Practise trickery, cheat. **L17.**
6 *verb intrans.* Play tricks or trifle *with*. **L19.**
7 Have casual sexual intercourse (*with*), esp. for money. *US slang.* **M20.**

🕮 **4** R. LAWLER I would've found out . . you couldn't trick me. G. R. TURNER Plants were tricked by the falsehoods of the weather and . . grew to extraordinary sizes. **c** C. PETERS Haggerty is tricked into marrying a girl . . after she had been . . made hideous by smallpox.

■ **tricking** *verbal noun* the action of the verb; an instance of this: M16. **trickment** *noun* (*rare*) (a) decoration, (an) adornment E17.

tricker /ˈtrɪkə/ *noun*[1]. M16.
[from TRICK *verb* + -ER[1].]
1 A person who plays tricks; a cheat; a practical joker. M16.
†**2** A person who arrays or artfully adorns something. M16–E17.
†**3** A person who tricks a coat of arms. L16–L17.

tricker *noun*[2] *& verb* see TRIGGER *noun*[1] *& verb*.

trickeration /trɪkəˈreɪʃ(ə)n/ *noun*. *US Black slang*. M20.
[from TRICKER(Y + -ATION.]
A trick, an expedient.

trickery /ˈtrɪk(ə)ri/ *noun*. E19.
[from TRICK *noun* + -ERY.]
The use of tricks; deception; an instance of this.

> 🕮 G. S. FRASER The riddle . . needs no verbal trickery . . it is a sad, familiar one. I. MURDOCH You imagine I am up to all kinds of trickery.

trickle /ˈtrɪk(ə)l/ *noun*. L16.
[from the verb.]
A slowly flowing drop; a thin halting stream (as) of liquid. Freq. foll. by *of*.

> 🕮 F. O'CONNOR Another trickle of people came out of the Odeon. C. MUNGOSHI Water . . flowed in a very thin trickle over . . pebbles. J. C. OATES A trickle of perspiration ran down her forehead. A. COHEN The trickle of political exiles . . had become a steady stream.

Comb.: **trickle-charge** *verb trans.* charge with a trickle charger; **trickle charger** ELECTRICITY a device for charging a storage battery at a low rate over a long period; **trickle irrigation** AGRICULTURE: involving the supply of a controlled restricted flow of water to a number of points in a cultivated area.
■ **tricklet** *noun* a small trickle L19.

trickle /ˈtrɪk(ə)l/ *verb*. ME.
[Imit.]
1 *verb intrans.* Flow or fall in successive drops; flow in a thin halting stream. ME. ▸**b** *transf. & fig.* Come or go slowly or gradually. E17.
2 *verb intrans.* Drip or run *with* tears, blood, etc. LME.
3 *verb trans.* Cause to flow in successive drops or a thin halting stream. E17. ▸**b** *transf. & fig.* Cause to come *out* slowly or gradually. M17. ▸**c** Esp. GOLF. Cause (a ball) to travel slowly over the ground. E20.

> 🕮 **1** V. BRITTAIN The tepid water trickled slowly into the bath. P. H. NEWBY Sweat trickled down his neck. I. MCEWAN He lifted a handful of sand and let it trickle on to his toes. **b** J. HELLER News of Green's . . bad behaviour . . usually trickles down to us. P. D. JAMES The first members of the congregation began to trickle in. **2** DICKENS His hand was trickling down with blood. **3** E. L. ORTIZ Float the rum . . by tilting the glass . . and trickling the rum down the side. **b** *Daily Telegraph* Leaks—news being trickled out ahead of the day when dealings begin.

Comb.: **trickle-down** *adjective* involving the gradual spreading of information etc. down through different ranks or groups of people.
■ **trickling** *noun* (*a*) the action of the verb; an instance of this; (*b*) a trickle: E17.

trickly /ˈtrɪkli/ *adjective*. *rare*. L19.
[from TRICKLE *noun* or *verb* + -Y[1].]
Of the nature of a trickle; trickling.

†**trick-madam** *noun*. E17–E18.
[French *trique-madame*, of uncertain origin. Cf. PRICK-MADAM, TRIP-MADAM.]
Any of several stonecrops formerly used in salads, esp. *Sedum reflexum* and *S. album*.

tricksome /ˈtrɪks(ə)m/ *adjective*. M17.
[from TRICK *noun* or *verb* + -SOME[1].]
1 = TRICKY *adjective* 1. M17.
2 Playful, sportive. E19.

trickster /ˈtrɪkstə/ *noun*. E18.
[from TRICK *noun* or *verb* + -STER.]
A person who practises trickery; a rogue, a cheat.
■ **trickstering** *noun* the action of a trickster, cheating E19.

tricksy /ˈtrɪksi/ *adjective*. M16.
[from TRICK *noun*, *verb* + -SY.]
1 Spruce, smart, fine. M16.
2 Given to playing tricks or practical jokes; mischievous, playful. L16.
3 = TRICKY *adjective* 1. M18.
4 = TRICKY *adjective* 2. M19.
■ **tricksily** *adverb* M19. **tricksiness** *noun* M16.

tricky /ˈtrɪki/ *adjective*. L18.
[from TRICK *noun* + -Y[1].]
1 Crafty, deceitful. L18.
2 Difficult; intricate; requiring care and adroitness. M19.
3 Skilled in performing clever tricks; resourceful, adroit. L19.

> 🕮 **1** E. EDWARDS The tricky and tortuous policy of Elizabeth's government. V. NABOKOV It might be a trap . . of his tricky opponent. **2** *Prima* The sleeves are trickier because you'll need to increase your stitches. *Practical Caravan* It was tricky finding somewhere to park. **3** *Essex Weekly News* His partner was the trickiest forward on the field. R. LYND He made such tricky use of the . . English climate as only a bowler of genius could do.

■ **trickily** *adverb* L19. **trickiness** *noun* E18.

triclad /ˈtrʌɪklad/ *adjective & noun*. L19.
[mod. Latin *Tricladida* (see below), formed as TRI- + Greek *klados* branch.]
ZOOLOGY. ▸**A** *noun*. Any member of the order Tricladida of turbellarian flatworms, characterized by having a main intestine with three branches. L19.
▸**B** *adjective*. Of, pertaining to, or designating this order. L19.

triclinia *noun* pl. of TRICLINIUM.

tricliniarch /trʌɪˈklɪnɪɑːk/ *noun*. *rare*. M17.
[Latin *tricliniarches*, formed as TRICLINIUM: see -ARCH.]
The master or host of a feast.

triclinic /trʌɪˈklɪnɪk/ *adjective*. M19.
[from TRI- + -*clinic* as in MONOCLINIC.]
CRYSTALLOGRAPHY. Of, pertaining to, or designating a crystal system referred to three unequal axes all obliquely inclined.

triclinium /trʌɪˈklɪnɪəm, -ˈklʌɪn-/ *noun*. Pl. **-ia** /-ɪə/. M17.
[Latin from Greek *triklinion* dim. of *triklinos* dining-room with three couches, from *tri-* TRI- + *klinē* couch, bed.]
ROMAN ANTIQUITIES. A couch, running round three sides of a table, on which to recline at meals. Also, a dining-room.

tricoccous /trʌɪˈkɒkəs/ *adjective*. E18.
[from TRI- + COCCUS + -OUS.]
BOTANY. (Of a fruit) composed of three carpels. Also, (of a plant) having a fruit of this kind.
■ Also (*rare*) **tricoccose** *adjective* L17.

tricolour /ˈtrɪkələ, ˈtrʌɪkʌlə/ *noun & adjective*. Also ***-color**. L18.
[French *tricolore* from late Latin *tricolor*, formed as TRI- + *color* COLOUR *noun*.]
▸**A** *noun*. **1** A flag of three colours; *esp.* the French national flag of blue, white, and red vertical stripes. L18. ▸**b** The green, white, and orange Irish Republican flag. M20.
2 A black, white, and tan dog. E20.
▸**B** *adjective*. **1** Having three colours. E19.
2 Using or pertaining to the use of the three primary colours. L19.

tricoloured /ˈtrʌɪkʌləd/ *adjective*. Also ***-colored**. L18.
[from TRI- + COLOURED.]
Having three colours.

triconodont /trʌɪˈkəʊnədɒnt/ *adjective & noun*. L19.
[mod. Latin *Triconodonta* (see below), from *Triconodon* genus name, from TRI- + Greek *kōnos* cone: see -ODON, -ODONT.]
ZOOLOGY. ▸**A** *adjective*. Of or pertaining to (an animal of) the extinct order Triconodonta of mainly Jurassic mammals characterized by molar teeth with three conical cusps arranged in a row. L19.
▸**B** *noun*. An animal of the order Triconodonta. M20.
■ **tricono'dontid** *adjective & noun* = TRICONODONT *adjective & noun* L19.

tricorn /ˈtrʌɪkɔːn/ *adjective & noun*. M18.
[French *tricorne* or Latin *tricornis* three-horned from TRI- + *cornu* horn.]
▸**A** *noun*. **1** An imaginary creature with three horns. M18.
2 A hat with the brim turned up on three sides. L19.
▸**B** *adjective*. Having three horns; (of a cocked hat) having the brim turned up on three sides. M19.

tricosane /ˈtrʌɪkəseɪn/ *noun*. L19.
[from TRI- + E)ICOSANE.]
CHEMISTRY. Any of a series of solid saturated hydrocarbons (alkanes) with the formula $C_{23}H_{48}$; *spec.* (also ***n*-tricosane**) the unbranched isomer, $CH_3(CH_2)_{21}CH_3$.

tricot /ˈtrɪkəʊ, ˈtriː-/ *noun*. L18.
[French, from *tricoter* knit.]
A fine warp knitted fabric made of a natural or man-made fibre, produced in any of various designs.

tricoteuse /trikɔtøːz/ *noun*. Pl. pronounced same. M19.
[French, from *tricoter* knit.]
FRENCH HISTORY. A woman who, during the French Revolution, sat and knitted at meetings of the Convention or at executions by guillotine.

Tricotine /ˈtrɪkətiːn/ *noun*. E20.
[from TRICOT + -INE[4].]
A worsted fabric with a double twill.
¶ Proprietary name in the US.

Tricouni /trʌɪˈkuːni/ *noun*. E20.
[App. from TRI- + CO- + UNI-.]
(Proprietary name for) a kind of climbing-boot nail with a serrated edge.

For other words beginning with *tri-* see the entry for **tri-**

tricrotic /trʌɪˈkrɒtɪk/ *adjective*. *rare*. L19.
[from TRI-, after *dicrotic*.]
PHYSIOLOGY. Of (a tracing of) the pulse: showing three undulations for each beat of the heart.
■ **'tricrotism** *noun* tricrotic condition L19.

tric-trac /ˈtrɪktrak/ *noun*. L17.
[French, from the clicking sound made by the pieces in the playing of the game.]
Hist. A form of backgammon.

tricuspid /trʌɪˈkʌspɪd/ *adjective & noun*. L17.
[from TRI- + Latin *cuspid-*, *cuspis* CUSP: see -ID[2].]
▸**A** *adjective*. Having three cusps or points; *spec.* designating or pertaining to the right atrio-ventricular valve of the heart. L17.
▸**B** *noun*. A tricuspid tooth, valve, etc. L19.

tricycle /ˈtrʌɪsɪk(ə)l/ *noun & verb*. E19.
[from TRI- + CYCLE *noun*.]
▸**A** *noun*. †**1** A three-wheeled coach. *rare*. Only in E19.
2 A vehicle with three wheels (two on an axle at the back and one at the front), driven by pedals in the same way as a bicycle. M19.
3 A three-wheeled motorized vehicle for a disabled person. L20.
Comb.: **tricycle landing-gear**, **tricycle undercarriage** AERONAUTICS: with three wheels.
▸**B** *verb intrans.* Ride a tricycle. L19.
■ **tricycler**, **tricyclist** *nouns* L19.

tricyclic /trʌɪˈsʌɪklɪk, -ˈsɪk-/ *adjective & noun*. L19.
[from TRI- + Greek *kuklos* circle + -IC.]
▸**A** *adjective*. Having three circles or rings; CHEMISTRY & PHARMACOLOGY having three usu. fused rings of atoms in the molecule. L19.
▸**B** *noun*. PHARMACOLOGY. A tricyclic antidepressant. L20.

tridacna /trʌɪˈdaknə, trɪ-/ *noun*. L18.
[mod. Latin (see below), from Greek *tridaknos* eaten at three bites, from *tri-* TRI- + *daknein* to bite.]
ZOOLOGY. (A shell of) any of several large tropical bivalve molluscs of the genus *Tridacna*, which includes the giant clam, *T. gigas*.

tridecane /ˈtrʌɪdɪkeɪn, trʌɪˈdɛkeɪn/ *noun*. L19.
[from Greek *tria* three + *deka* ten + -ANE. Cf. DECANE.]
CHEMISTRY. Any of a series of saturated hydrocarbons (alkanes) with the formula $C_{13}H_{28}$; *spec.* (also ***n*-tridecane**) the unbranched isomer, $CH_3(CH_2)_{11}CH_3$.
■ **trideca'noic** *adjective*. ***tridecanoic acid***: a colourless solid carboxylic acid, $CH_3(CH_2)_{11}COOH$ E20. **tridecyl** /ˈtrʌɪdɪsɪl/ *noun* a radical, $C_{13}H_{27}$·, derived from a tridecane M19. **tride'cylic**, **tride'coic** *adjectives* = TRIDECANOIC L19.

trident /ˈtrʌɪd(ə)nt/ *noun & adjective*. LME.
[Latin *trident-*, *-dens*, formed as TRI- + *dent-*, *dens* tooth.]
▸**A** *noun*. **1** An instrument or weapon with three prongs; *esp.* a three-pronged spear as the attribute of the sea-god Poseidon (Neptune) or of Britannia, or used by the retiarius in ancient Roman gladiatorial combats. LME.
2 GEOMETRY. A plane cubic curve resembling a three-pronged weapon. E18.
3 Anything resembling a trident in shape or configuration, as a piece of land with three promontories. M18.
4 (**T-**.) Any of a class of US nuclear-powered submarines designed to carry ballistic missiles (also ***Trident submarine***); a submarine-launched ballistic missile designed to be carried by such a submarine. L20.
▸**B** *adjective*. Having three prongs or forks; tridental. LME.
trident curve = sense A.2 above.
■ **tri'dental** *adjective* of, pertaining to, or of the nature of a trident; three-pronged, trifurcate: M17.

tridentate /trʌɪˈdɛnteɪt/ *adjective*. M18.
[from TRI- + Latin *dentatus* toothed: see -ATE[2].]
1 BOTANY & ZOOLOGY. Having three teeth or toothlike processes. M18.
2 CHEMISTRY. Of a ligand: forming three separate bonds, usu. with the same central atom. Of a molecule or complex: formed by such a ligand. E20.

tridented /trʌɪˈdɛntɪd, *in sense 2* ˈtrʌɪd(ə)ntɪd/ *adjective*. E17.
[formed as TRIDENT + -ED[2].]
1 Three-pronged; tridentate. E17.
2 Bearing a trident. E17.

Tridentine /trɪˈdɛntʌɪn, trʌɪ-/ *adjective & noun*. M16.
[medieval Latin *Tridentinus*, from *Tridentum* Trent (see below): see -INE[1].]
▸**A** *adjective*. Of or pertaining to the city of Trent in the Tyrol, or the Council of the Roman Catholic Church held there (1545–63). M16.
Tridentine mass the eucharistic liturgy used by the Roman Catholic Church from 1570 to 1964.
▸**B** *noun*. A person who accepts and conforms to the decrees of the Council of Trent; an orthodox or traditional Roman Catholic. M19.

tridimensional /trʌɪdɪˈmɛnʃ(ə)n(ə)l, -dʌɪ-/ *adjective*. M19.
[from TRI- + DIMENSIONAL.]
= *three-dimensional* s.v. THREE *adjective & noun*.
■ ˌtridimensioˈnality *noun* the quality of being of three dimensions L19. **tridimensionally** *adverb* E20.

Tridione /trʌɪˈdʌɪəʊn/ *noun*. M20.
[from TRI- + -DIONE.]
PHARMACOLOGY. (Proprietary name for) an analgesic and anticonvulsant drug related to oxazolidine.

tri-dominium /trʌɪdəˈmɪnɪəm/ *noun*. L19.
[mod. Latin, formed as TRI- + Latin *dominium* lordship, rule, DOMINION.]
The joint rule of three powers or States; *spec.* (*Hist.*) the former rule of Great Britain, Germany, and the United States in Samoa, and of Great Britain, Greece, and Turkey in Cyprus.

tridrachm /ˈtrʌɪdram/ *noun*. L18.
[Greek *tridrakhmon*, formed as TRI- + *drakhmē* DRACHM.]
GREEK ANTIQUITIES. A silver coin of ancient Greece, of the value of three drachmas.

triduan /ˈtrɪdjʊən, ˈtrʌɪ-/ *adjective*. LME.
[Latin *triduanus* from TRIDUUM: see -AN.]
Lasting for three days. Also, occurring every third day.

triduo /ˈtrɪdjʊəʊ, ˈtrʌɪ-/ *noun*. Pl. **-os**. M19.
[Italian & Spanish, from Latin TRIDUUM.]
ROMAN CATHOLIC CHURCH. A three days' prayer or festal celebration.

triduum /ˈtrɪdjʊəm, ˈtrʌɪ-/ *noun*. E18.
[Latin, use as noun of adjective (sc. *spatium* space), formed as TRI- + *dies* day.]
A period of three days; *esp.* (ROMAN CATHOLIC CHURCH) the last three days of Lent or the period from Maundy Thursday evening until the end of Holy Saturday. Also = prec.

tridymite /ˈtrɪdɪmʌɪt/ *noun*. M19.
[from Greek *tridumos*, from *tri-* TRI- + *-dumos*, as in *didumos* twin (with ref. to its compound forms consisting of three individual crystals): see -ITE[1].]
MINERALOGY. A high temperature form of quartz which occurs as thin hexagonal tabular crystals and is found in igneous rocks and stony meteorites.

trie *adjective* var. of TRY *adjective*.

triecious *adjective* see TRIOECIOUS.

tried /trʌɪd/ *ppl adjective*. ME.
[from TRY *verb* + -ED[1].]
1 Separated from the dross or refuse; (of a metal) purified, refined; (of fat) rendered, clarified; (of an egg-yolk) separated from the white; (of flour etc.) sifted, fine. Long *rare* or *obsolete*. ME.
†**2** Chosen, select, choice; excellent. LME–L16.
3 Proved or tested by experience or examination. LME.
3 tried and tested, **tried and true** proved reliable by experience.

tried *verb pa. t. & pple* of TRY *verb*.

†**triedral** *adjective & noun* var. of TRIHEDRAL.

triene /ˈtrʌɪiːn/ *noun*. E20.
[from TRI- + -ENE.]
CHEMISTRY. Any organic compound containing three double bonds between carbon atoms.

triennia *noun pl.* see TRIENNIUM.

triennial /trʌɪˈɛnɪəl/ *adjective & noun*. M16.
[Late Latin *triennis* of three years, *triennium* period of three years, formed as TRI- + *annus* year: see -AL[1].]
▶ **A** *adjective*. **1** Occurring every three years. M16.
2 Existing or lasting for three years; changed every three years. M17.
▶ **B** *noun*. **1** A period of three years; a triennium. M16.
2 An event recurring every three years; *spec.* the visitation by a bishop of his diocese every three years. M16.
■ ˌtrienniˈality *noun* (*rare*) E19. **triennially** *adverb* every three years; once in three years: L17.

triennium /trʌɪˈɛnɪəm/ *noun*. Pl. **-iums**, **-ia** /-ɪə/. M19.
[Latin, formed as TRI- + *annus* year.]
A space or period of three years.

trier /ˈtrʌɪə/ *noun*. ME.
[from TRY *verb* + -ER[1].]
1 A person who examines and determines a cause or question; a judge. ME.
2 A person who or thing which tests or proves something; a tester, a test. L15.
3 A person who or thing which separates some material from impurities. E16.
4 Either of two people appointed by a court of law to determine whether a challenge made to a juror is well founded. E16.
5 *Hist.* A member of the House of Lords sitting as a member of a jury at the trial of a peer for treason or felony. Usu. in *pl.* (also as ***Lords triers***). M16.
6 An umpire in sports or games. Now *dial.* E17.
7 ECCLESIASTICAL HISTORY. Any of a body of commissioners appointed in 1654 for the approbation of all public preachers and lecturers before their admission to benefices. M17.
8 a A thing devised to test quality. L18. ▸**b** A trying or difficult thing; a thing that tries one's patience. L18.
9 *Hist.* A member of a committee appointed by the monarch to determine to which court petitions should be referred, and if necessary to report them to the parliament. Usu. in *pl.* M19.
10 A person who tries or attempts to do something; a person who perseveres. L19.

trierarch /ˈtrʌɪərɑːk/ *noun*. M17.
[Latin *trierarchus* or Greek *triērarkhos*, *-arkhēs*, from *triērēs* trireme + -ARCH.]
GREEK HISTORY. The commander of a trireme. Also, a person charged with fitting out a trireme or galley.
■ trieˈrarchal, trieˈrarchic *adjectives* of or pertaining to a trierarch or trierarchs M19.

trierarchy /ˈtrʌɪərɑːki/ *noun*. M19.
[Greek *triērarkhia*, from *triērarkhos* TRIERARCH.]
GREEK HISTORY. The position or office of a trierarch; the equipment and maintenance of a trireme or other vessel; the system by which a fleet was thus maintained.

Triestine /triːˈɛstiːn/ *noun & adjective*. E20.
[*Trieste* a city and province in NE Italy: see -INE[1].]
▶ **A** *noun*. A native or inhabitant of Trieste. E20.
▶ **B** *adjective*. Of or pertaining to Trieste or its inhabitants. E20.

trieteric /trʌɪɪˈtɛrɪk/ *noun & adjective*. L16.
[Latin *trietericus* from Greek *trietērikos*, from *trietēris* a festival celebrated every third (i.e. alternate) year, formed as TRI- + *etos* year.]
ANTIQUITIES. ▶**A** *noun*. A festival, esp. of Bacchus, celebrated every alternate year. L16.
▶ **B** *adjective*. Taking place every alternate year, as the festivals of Bacchus and other gods. M17.

triethyl /trʌɪˈiːθʌɪl, -ˈɛθɪl/ *adjective*. M19.
[from TRI- + ETHYL.]
CHEMISTRY. Having three ethyl groups in the molecule.

triethylamine /trʌɪɪˈθʌɪləmiːn/ *noun*. M19.
[from prec. + AMINE.]
CHEMISTRY. A flammable liquid, $(C_2H_5)_3N$, with a strong ammoniacal odour.

trifa *noun & adjective* var. of TREFA.

trifarious /trʌɪˈfɛːrɪəs/ *adjective*. *rare*. M17.
[from Latin *trifarius*: see -IOUS.]
1 Of three sorts; facing three ways. M17.
2 BOTANY. Arranged in three rows. M19.

trifecta /trʌɪˈfɛktə/ *noun*. *N. Amer., Austral., & NZ*. M20.
[from TRI- + PER)FECTA.]
A method of betting in which the punter must pick the first three finishers of a race in the correct order.

triffid /ˈtrɪfɪd/ *noun*. M20.
[Word coined by John Wyndham (1903–69), Brit. writer, in his science-fiction novel *The Day of the Triffids* to refer to a race of locomotory stinging plants which threaten to overrun the world.]
A vigorous plant; *transf.* a thing that is invasive or rapid in development.

trifid /ˈtrʌɪfɪd/ *adjective*. In sense 3 also **trefid** /ˈtrɛfɪd/. M18.
[Latin *trifidus*, formed as TRI- + *fid-* stem of *findere* split.]
1 Chiefly BOTANY & ZOOLOGY. Divided into three parts by deep clefts or notches. M18.
2 *gen.* Divided into three parts; tripartite. *rare*. L19.
3 Designating an antique spoon with three notches splitting the end of the handle. L19.
2 Trifid Nebula ASTRONOMY an emission nebula in the constellation of Sagittarius which appears to be divided into three by lanes of dark matter.

trifle /ˈtrʌɪf(ə)l/ *noun*. ME.
[Old French *truf(f)le* by-form of *truf(f)e* deceit, gibe, corresp. to Italian *truffa*, Spanish, Portuguese *trufa*, of unkn. origin.]
†**1** A false or idle story told to deceive or amuse; a jest, a joke; a trivial or nonsensical saying. ME–L17.
2 a A matter of little value or importance; a trivial, paltry, or insignificant affair. ME. ▸†**b** A worthless person; a trifler. L15–E18.
3 A small article of little value; a toy, a trinket, a knick-knack. LME.
4 A literary work, piece of music, etc., that is light or trivial in style; a facetious composition; a bagatelle. L16.
5 a A small sum of money; a negligible payment. L16. ▸**b** *gen.* A small or insignificant amount. E18.
6 Orig., a dish composed of cream boiled with various ingredients. Now, a dessert of sponge cake (esp. flavoured with sherry or spirit) with custard, jelly, fruit, whipped cream, etc. L16.
7 A pewter of medium hardness; (in *pl.*) articles made of this. E17.

📖 **2a** HENRY MILLER Death . . was only an item, a trifle, in the history of his calamities. **3** A. BROOKNER I would come . . with flowers, or some little trifle—one always brought an offering. **5a** P. FITZGERALD His credit wasn't good enough to bear a little loss, a little trifle. **b a trifle** *adverb* to a small degree, a little; somewhat.

trifle /ˈtrʌɪf(ə)l/ *verb*. ME.
[Old French *truffler*, *truffer* make sport of, deceive = Italian *truffare*: cf. prec.]
†**1 a** *verb intrans.* Lie, cheat; mock, make fun. ME–E17. ▸**b** *verb trans.* Cheat, delude, fool; mock. *rare*. LME–M16.
2 *verb intrans.* Toy, play *with* an object; handle or finger a thing idly; fiddle, fidget *with*. LME.
3 a *verb intrans.* Dally, loiter; spend time idly; waste time. LME. ▸**b** *verb trans.* Spend (time) frivolously or idly; waste or fritter away (time). Now only foll. by *away*. M16.
4 *verb intrans.* Foll. by *with*: treat someone or something with a lack of seriousness or respect; dally, fool around. E16.
†**5** *verb trans.* Make a trifle of; make trivial or insignificant. *rare* (Shakes.). Only in E17.
6 a *verb intrans.* Act or speak in an idle or frivolous way, esp. in serious circumstances. M18. ▸**b** *verb trans.* Utter or pass in an idle or frivolous manner. *rare*. E19.

📖 **3a** H. JAMES I stayed, I dawdled, I trifled. **4** J. BARZUN Ability and achievement are too important . . to be . . trifled with.

■ **trifler** *noun* (*a*) a teller of false or frivolous stories, a joker; a worthless person; (*b*) a person who does not act seriously or earnestly; a time-waster, a frivolous person: LME. **trifling** *adjective* †(*a*) cheating, false; (*b*) frivolous, not serious; foolish; (*c*) of little importance, insignificant, petty: LME. **triflingly** *adverb* M16. **triflingness** *noun* L16.

trifluoperazine /ˌtrʌɪfluːəʊˈpɛrəziːn/ *noun*. M20.
[from TRI- + FLUO- + PI)PERAZINE.]
PHARMACOLOGY. An antipsychotic and sedative drug related to phenothiazine.

trifluralin /trʌɪˈflʊərəlɪn/ *noun*. M20.
[from TRI- + FLU(ORO- + *-alin* (perh. alt. of ANILINE).)]
CHEMISTRY & AGRICULTURE. A selective pre-emergence herbicide, $C_{13}H_{16}F_3N_3O_4$, which inhibits plant cell division.

trifocal /trʌɪˈfəʊk(ə)l/ *adjective & noun*. E19.
[from TRI- + FOCAL.]
▶ **A** *adjective*. †**1** Of spectacles: having three pairs of lenses in one frame. *rare*. Only in E19.
2 (Of a lens) having three parts with different focal lengths; (of spectacles) having such lenses. E20.
▶ **B** *noun*. A trifocal lens; (usu. in *pl.*) trifocal spectacles. L19.

trifold /ˈtrʌɪfəʊld/ *adjective*. L16.
[from TRI- + -FOLD.]
Triple, threefold.

trifoliate /trʌɪˈfəʊlɪət/ *adjective*. L17.
[from TRI- + FOLIATE *adjective*.]
BOTANY. (Of a leaf) consisting of three leaflets; (of a plant) having such leaves. Also *transf.*, having the form of such a leaf.
■ **trifoliated** *adjective* (*a*) BOTANY = TRIFOLIATE; (*b*) ARCHITECTURE having or consisting of trefoils: L17.

trifoliolate /trʌɪˈfəʊlɪələt/ *adjective*. E19.
[from TRI- + medieval Latin *foliolum* dim. of Latin *folium* leaf + -ATE[2].]
BOTANY. Consisting of three leaflets; having leaves of this form.

trifolium /trɪˈfəʊlɪəm, trʌɪ-/ *noun*. M16.
[Latin, formed as TRI- + *folium* leaf. Cf. TREFOIL.]
Any leguminous plant of the large genus *Trifolium*, characterized by trifoliate leaves; a clover, a trefoil; *spec.* crimson clover, *T. incarnatum*, once widely grown for fodder.

triforium /trʌɪˈfɔːrɪəm/ *noun*. Pl. **-ria** /-rɪə/. E18.
[Anglo-Latin, of unkn. origin.]
ARCHITECTURE. A gallery or arcade above the arches at the sides of the nave, choir, and sometimes transepts of some large churches, orig. *spec.* of Canterbury Cathedral.
■ **triforial** *adjective* of, pertaining to, or constituting a triforium M19.

triform /ˈtrʌɪfɔːm/ *adjective*. LME.
[Latin *triformis*, formed as TRI- + *forma* FORM *noun*.]
1 Having a triple form; combining three different forms; made in three parts. LME.
2 Existing or appearing in three different forms. E17.
■ Also **triformed** *adjective* M17.

trifurcate /*as adjective* trʌɪˈfəːkət, *as verb* ˈtrʌɪfəkeɪt/ *adjective & verb*. M19.
[from Latin *trifurcus* three-forked, formed as TRI- + *furca* FORK *noun*: see -ATE[2], -ATE[3].]
▶ **A** *adjective*. Divided into three branches like the prongs of a fork; three-forked, three-pronged, trichotomous. M19.
▶ **B** *verb intrans.* Divide or branch into three. L19.

■ **ˈtrifurcated** *adjective* = TRIFURCATE *adjective* E18. **trifurˈcation** *noun* L19.

trig /trɪg/ *noun*[1]. M17.
[from TRIG *verb*[1].]
A wedge or block for stopping the motion of a wheel or cask; *gen.* a brake.

trig /trɪg/ *noun*[2]. Now *dial.* M17.
[Origin unkn.]
A line traced, cut, or marked out on the ground, esp. as a boundary- or starting-line. Also, a shallow trench or ditch, a narrow path or track.

trig /trɪg/ *adjective*[1]. ME.
[Old Norse *tryggr* = Gothic *triggws* true, faithful: see TRUE *adjective*. Cf. TRIG *verb*[1].]
1 True, faithful; trustworthy, trusty. Now *Scot. & north.* ME.
2 Active, nimble, brisk, alert. *Scot.* L15.
3 Trim, tidy, neat; *esp.* (of a person) spruce, smart, well-dressed. Chiefly *arch.*, *Scot. & dial.* E16.
4 Orig., strong, sound, well. Later, firm, steady. *obsolete* exc. *Scot.* E18.
5 Prim, precise, exact. Freq. *derog. rare.* L18.
6 Full, distended, tightly stuffed. *dial.* E19.

🕮 **3** *Century Magazine* The stylish gait . . of the trig little body who wore them.

■ **trigly** *adverb* E18. **trigness** *noun* E19.

trig /trɪg/ *adjective*[2] & *noun*[3]. *colloq.* M19.
[Abbreviation.]
▶**A** *adjective.* Trigonometrical. Freq. in ***trig point***, ***trig station***. M19.
▶**B** *noun.* Trigonometry. L19.

trig /trɪg/ *verb*[1] *trans.* Infl. **-gg-**. L16.
[Origin uncertain: perh. from Old Norse *tryggja*, Old Danish *trygge* make firm or secure, from *tryggr*: see TRIG *adjective*[1].]
1 Make firm or fast; prevent from moving; *esp.* stop the motion of (a wheel or cask) with a wedge or block, brake. L16.
2 Support or shore up with a wedge; prop. Freq. foll. by *up*. E18.

trig /trɪg/ *verb*[2] *intrans. & trans.* Now *dial.* Infl. **-gg-**. L16.
[Origin unkn.]
Trot; walk quickly or briskly; trip; tramp.

trig /trɪg/ *verb*[3] *trans.* Infl. **-gg-**. M17.
[from TRIG *adjective*[1].]
1 Make full or distended; stuff tightly. *obsolete* exc. *dial.* M17.
2 Make trim, tidy or neat; *esp.* dress (a person) sprucely or smartly; rig *out* (usu. in *pass.*). Chiefly *arch.*, *Scot.*, *& dial.* L17.

trig /trɪg/ *verb*[4] *trans. & intrans.* Now *dial.* Infl. **-gg-**. E18.
[from TRIG *noun*[2].]
Trace, cut, or mark out a line, esp. a boundary- or starting-line, on (the ground); dig a shallow trench in (the ground).

trigamy /ˈtrɪgəmi/ *noun.* E17.
[Late Latin *trigamia* from Greek, from *trigamos*, from *tri-* TRI- + *gamos* marriage: see -Y[3].]
1 ECCLESIASTICAL LAW. Remarriage after the death of two spouses. Now *rare* or *obsolete.* E17.
2 The state of having three wives or husbands at once; the action of twice going through forms of marriage with other persons while a legal marriage is still in existence. Cf. BIGAMY. M17.
■ **trigamist** *noun* a trigamous person M17. **trigamous** *adjective* (*a*) BOTANY having male, female, and hermaphrodite flowers in the same head; (*b*) living in or involving trigamy: M19.

trigeminal /trʌɪˈdʒɛmɪn(ə)l/ *adjective & noun.* M19.
[formed as next + -AL[1].]
ANATOMY. ▶**A** *adjective.* Designating or pertaining to the fifth and largest pair of cranial nerves, which divide into three branches supplying the front half of the head. M19.
▶**B** *noun.* Either of the trigeminal nerves. L19.

trigeminus /trʌɪˈdʒɛmɪnəs/ *noun.* E18.
[Latin, from TRI- + *geminus* born at the same birth.]
ANATOMY. †**1** A muscle at the back of the neck. Only in E18.
2 The trigeminal nerve. L19.

trigenic /trʌɪˈdʒɛnɪk/ *adjective.* M19.
[from TRI- + Greek *genos* kind + -IC. In sense 1 with allus. to three substances used in making the acid; in sense 2 formed as GENIC.]
1 CHEMISTRY. ***trigenic acid***, a cyclic ethylidene derivative of biuret. M19.
2 GENETICS. Involving or controlled by three genes. M20.

trigesimal /trʌɪˈdʒɛsɪm(ə)l/ *adjective.* Long *rare* or *obsolete.* M17.
[from Latin *trigesimus* thirtieth + -AL[1].]
†**1** Thirtieth. Only in M17.
2 Consisting of or able to be divided into thirty equal parts. M17.

trigger /ˈtrɪgə/ *noun*[1] & *verb.* Also (earlier and *dial.*) **tricker**. E17.
[Dutch *trekker*, from *trekken* pull: see TREK *verb*, -ER[1].]
▶**A** *noun.* **1** A movable catch or lever for releasing a spring or catch and so setting off a mechanism; *spec.* (*a*) a catch for releasing the hammer of a gunlock on pressure by the finger (freq. in ***pull the trigger***); (*b*) a lever or snib for releasing the string of a crossbow. Also (*fig.*), an event, occurrence, etc., that sets off a chain reaction. E17.
2 ELECTRONICS. **a** A trigger circuit or trigger tube. M20. ▸**b** A momentary signal or change in signal level that causes a change of state in a trigger tube or other device. M20.
3 A fission bomb built into a fusion bomb in order to initiate the fusion reaction. M20.
4 An electronic device attached to a drum which causes sampled sounds to be played when the drumhead is struck. L20.

🕮 **1** C. S. FORESTER Randall . . squeezed the trigger, aimed and fired. T. HOOPER There must therefore be some trigger which initiates . . production. **quick on the trigger** quick to respond.

Comb.: **trigger area** PHYSIOLOGY & MEDICINE a sensitive area of the body, stimulation or irritation of which causes a specific effect in another part; **trigger circuit** ELECTRONICS a circuit that behaves like a trigger tube; a circuit for producing a trigger pulse; **trigger finger** (*a*) the forefinger of the right hand (as that with which the trigger of a gun is most easily pulled); (*b*) MEDICINE a defect of a finger joint, causing the finger to jerk or snap open when extended; **trigger fish** any of various deep-bodied fishes of the family Balistidae, in which the large first spine of the dorsal fin can only be depressed by releasing the second, and which are found mainly in inshore tropical waters; **trigger-hair** ZOOLOGY a fine hair or filament at the mouth of a nematocyst in some coelenterates, which operates like a trigger in emission of the stinging hair; **trigger-happiness** *colloq.* the state of being trigger-happy (*lit. & fig.*); **trigger-happy** *adjective* (*colloq.*) ready or eager to shoot on the least provocation (*lit. & fig.*); **trigger man** *slang* (chiefly *US*) a gunman; **trigger-plant** = STYLIDIUM; **trigger-point** (*a*) PHYSIOLOGY & MEDICINE = ***trigger area*** above; (*b*) *US* a price level at which price controls are imposed or re-imposed; **trigger price** *US* a minimum selling price for steel imported into the US, such that any steel imports below that price incur investigation to ensure that dumping is not taking place; **trigger pulse** ELECTRONICS a pulse that acts as a trigger (see sense 2b above); **trigger tube** ELECTRONICS a vacuum tube that has two operating states and changes rapidly from one to the other in response to a momentary application of, or change in, a signal.
▶**B** *verb.* **1** *verb trans.* Release the trigger of a mechanism; *esp.* fire (a gun etc.) by pressure on the trigger; *fig.* set (an action or process) in motion (freq. foll. by *off*); initiate, precipitate. Usu. in *pass.* M20.
2 ELECTRONICS. **a** *verb trans.* Initiate a change of state or a cycle of behaviour in (a device). M20. ▸**b** *verb intrans.* Of an electronic device: change state in response to a momentarily applied signal. M20.

🕮 **1** *New York* The Israeli invasion of Lebanon and the mass murder that triggered it. L. DEIGHTON Devices that fire . . pieces of metal and are triggered by anyone going near them.

■ **triggerable** *adjective* able to be triggered M20. **triggered** *adjective* provided with or activated by a trigger, that has been triggered M20. **triggerless** *adjective* without a trigger E19.

trigger /ˈtrɪgə/ *noun*[2]. L16.
[from TRIG *verb*[1] + -ER[1].]
1 A device or appliance for retarding or stopping the motion of a vehicle, a brake. Now *dial.* L16.
2 SHIPBUILDING. A support holding a dog-shore in position. Also, a dog-shore. M19.

trigintal /trʌɪˈdʒɪnt(ə)l/ *noun. obsolete* exc. *Hist.* L15.
[medieval Latin *trigintale*, from Latin *triginta* thirty: see -AL[1].]
= TRENTAL 1.

triglossia /trʌɪˈglɒsɪə/ *noun.* L20.
[from TRI- + DI)GLOSSIA.]
LINGUISTICS. The systematic use by a community of three different varieties or dialects of a language in different situations.

triglot /ˈtrʌɪglɒt/ *adjective & noun.* L19.
[from Greek *tri-* TRI- + *glōtta* tongue after *monoglot*, *polyglot*.]
▶**A** *adjective.* Written in three languages. L19.
▶**B** *noun.* **1** A book, esp. a Bible, in three languages. L19.
2 A person who knows three languages. L20.

triglyph /ˈtrʌɪglɪf/ *noun.* M16.
[Latin *triglyphus* from Greek *trigluphos*, from *tri-* TRI- + *gluphē* carving, GLYPH.]
ARCHITECTURE. A block or tablet with three vertical grooves alternating with metopes in a Doric frieze.
■ **triglyphed** *adjective* decorated with triglyphs M19. **triˈglyphic**, **triˈglyphical** *adjectives* of, pertaining to, or of the nature of a triglyph; decorated with triglyphs: M19.

trigon /ˈtrʌɪgɒn/ *noun.* Also (now only *US* in sense 5) **-one** /-əʊn/. M16.
[Latin *trigonum* from Greek *trigōnon* neut. of *trigōnos* three-cornered, from *tri-* TRI- + *gōnos* -GON. Cf. TRIGONE, TRIGONUM.]
1 ASTROLOGY. †**a** = TRINE *noun* 2. Only in M16. ▸**b** = TRIPLICITY 1a. Now *rare* or *obsolete.* L16.
†**2** A triangular instrument used in surveying. L16–E18.
3 A triangle; *esp.* an equilateral one. Now *rare* or *obsolete.* E17.
4 MUSIC. An ancient triangular lyre or harp. E18.
5 ZOOLOGY. A triangle formed by three cusps on the tribospheric upper molar tooth. L19.
■ **trigonid** /trʌɪˈgɒnɪd, trɪ-/ *noun* (ZOOLOGY) a triangle formed by three cusps on the tribosphenic lower molar tooth L19.

trigonal /ˈtrɪg(ə)n(ə)l/ *adjective.* L16.
[medieval Latin *trigonalis* triangular, from Latin *trigonum* triangle: see prec., -AL[1].]
1 **a** Of or pertaining to a triangle; triangular. L16. ▸**b** GEOMETRY. Having triangular faces; having the symmetry of an equilateral triangle; *spec.* (CRYSTALLOGRAPHY) of, pertaining to, or designating a crystal system referred to three equal axes separated by equal angles not right angles. L19. ▸**c** CHEMISTRY. Having three orbitals directed to the corners of an equilateral triangle. M20.
2 Triangular in cross-section. L16.
†**3** ASTROLOGY. Pertaining to or of the nature of a trigon. E–M17.
1b trigonal bipyramid a solid figure having the form of two triangular pyramids joined base to base. **trigonal quoin** a solid angle contained by three plane angles. **trigonal symmetry** the symmetry of a figure or body which coincides with its original position after rotation about an axis through an angle of 120° or 240°.
■ **trigonally** *adverb* L19.

trigone /trɪˈgəʊn, ˈtrʌɪgəʊn/ *noun.* L17.
[French from Latin *trigonum* TRIGON.]
1 See TRIGON. L17.
2 ANATOMY. A triangular region or tissue; *spec.* a triangular area at the base of the urinary bladder, between the openings of the ureters and urethra. M19.
■ **trigoˈnitis** *noun* (MEDICINE) inflammation of the trigone of the bladder E20.

trigonelline /trɪgəˈnɛliːn/ *noun.* L19.
[from mod. Latin *Trigonella* (see below) + -INE[5].]
CHEMISTRY. A betaine derived from nicotinic acid, found in the seeds of fenugreek and many other plants, including coffee beans.

trigonia /trʌɪˈgəʊnɪə/ *noun.* M19.
[mod. Latin (see below), formed as TRIGON + -IA[1].]
ZOOLOGY. (A shell of) any of various bivalve molluscs of the genus *Trigonia*, which have a triangular shell.

trigono- /ˈtrɪg(ə)nəʊ, trɪˈgəʊnəʊ/ *combining form.*
[from Greek *trigōnos* three-cornered, etc., neut. *trigōnon* as noun a triangle: see -O-.]
Trigonal, triangular.
■ **trigonoceˈphalic** *adjective* having a malformation of the skull caused by premature closing of the mediofrontal suture, in which the sides are flat and converge to an apex in front L19. **trigonoˈcephaly** *noun* trigonocephalic condition L19.

trigonometric /ˌtrɪg(ə)nə(ʊ)ˈmɛtrɪk/ *adjective.* E19.
[formed as next + -IC.]
= next.
trigonometric function MATH. a function of an angle, or of an abstract quantity, used in trigonometry, e.g. the sine, tangent, secant, etc.

trigonometrical /ˌtrɪg(ə)nə(ʊ)ˈmɛtrɪk(ə)l/ *adjective.* M17.
[from TRIGONOMETRY or mod. Latin *trigonometria* + -ICAL. Cf. mod. Latin *trigonometricus*.]
Of, pertaining to, or performed by trigonometry.
trigonometrical point, **trigonometrical station** SURVEYING a reference point on high ground used in triangulation and freq. marked by a pillar or other structure. **trigonometrical survey** a survey of a country or region performed by triangulation and trigonometrical calculation.
■ **trigonometrically** *adverb* M17.

trigonometry /trɪgəˈnɒmɪtri/ *noun.* E17.
[mod. Latin *trigonometria*, formed as prec. + -METRY.]
The branch of mathematics that deals with the relations between the sides and angles of triangles, esp. as expressed by the trigonometric functions, and including the theory of triangles, of angles, and of (elementary) singly periodic functions.
plane trigonometry: which deals with plane triangles and angles. **spherical trigonometry**: which deals with spherical triangles and angles.
■ **trigonometer** *noun* (*a*) any of various trigonometrical instruments; (*b*) an expert in trigonometry; *spec.* one engaged in trigonometrical survey: M18.

trigonon /trɪˈgəʊnɒn/ *noun. rare.* E18.
[Greek *trigōnon*: see TRIGON. Cf. TRIGONUM.]
MUSIC. = TRIGON 4.

trigonous /ˈtrɪg(ə)nəs/ *adjective.* E19.
[from Greek *trigōnos* (see TRIGON) + -OUS.]
Chiefly BOTANY. Triangular (esp. obtusely triangular) in cross-section. Cf. TRIQUETROUS.

trigonum /trɪˈgəʊnəm/ *noun.* E18.
[Latin: see TRIGON. Cf. TRIGONE.]
1 MUSIC. = TRIGON 4. E18.
2 ANATOMY. = TRIGONE 2. L19.

For other words beginning with *tri-* see the entry for **tri-**

trigram /ˈtrʌɪgram/ *noun*. E17.
[from TRI- + -GRAM. Cf. DIGRAM, MONOGRAM.]
1 A group of three letters, a trigraph; PSYCHOLOGY a (nonsense) word of three letters used in the study of learning or memory. E17.
2 A three-stroke figure or character; *spec.* each of eight figures composed of three whole or broken parallel lines, occurring with sixty-four hexagrams in the ancient Chinese text *I Ching*, and traditionally used for divination. E17.
3 GEOMETRY etc. A set of three lines; *spec.* the figure formed by three straight lines in one plane not intersecting in the same point. Also more generally, any figure composed of three elements. E17.
■ **trigraˈmmatic** *adjective* (*rare*) of, pertaining to, or of the nature of a trigram E19.

trigraph /ˈtrʌɪgrɑːf/ *noun*. M19.
[from TRI- + -GRAPH.]
A group of three letters, *esp.* one representing a single sound.

trihedral /trʌɪˈhiːdr(ə)l, -ˈhɛdr(ə)l/ *adjective & noun*. Also †**triedral**. L18.
[from Greek *tri-* TRI- + *hedra* base + -AL¹.]
▶ **A** *adjective*. Of a solid figure or body: having three sides or faces (in addition to the base or ends); bounded laterally by three surfaces; triangular in cross-section. L18.
trihedral angle, **trihedral quoin** a solid angle formed by three surfaces meeting at a point.
▶ **B** *noun*. GEOMETRY. A trihedral figure. E20.
■ **trihedron** *noun*, pl. **-dra**, **-drons**, = TRIHEDRAL *noun* E19.

trihemimeris /ˈtrʌɪhɪˌmɪmərɪs/ *noun*. *rare*. E18.
[mod. Latin, from Greek *tri-* TRI- + *hēmi-* half + *meros* part, *-merēs* -partite. Cf. HEPHTHEMIMER.]
CLASSICAL PROSODY. A group of three half-feet; the first part of a hexameter line preceding the caesura when this occurs in the middle of the second foot.
■ **triheˈmimeral** *adjective* L19.

†**trihemitone** *noun*. L17–M18.
[from TRI- + HEMITONE. Cf. DITONE.]
MUSIC. An interval containing three semitones or a tone and a semitone; *esp.* the Pythagorean minor third.

tri-jet /ˈtrʌɪdʒɛt/ *noun*. M20.
[from TRI- + JET *noun*².]
An aircraft powered by three jet engines.

trike /trʌɪk/ *noun & verb*. *colloq.* L19.
[Abbreviation of TRICYCLE.]
▶ **A** *noun*. **1** A tricycle. L19.
2 A kind of ultralight aircraft. L20.
▶ **B** *verb intrans.* Ride on a tricycle. L19.
■ **triker** *noun* a tricyclist E20.

trilateral /trʌɪˈlat(ə)r(ə)l/ *adjective & noun*. M17.
[from TRI- + LATERAL *adjective*.]
▶ **A** *adjective*. **1** Of, on, or with three sides; three-sided. M17.
2 Involving or shared by three States etc., esp. as parties to an agreement concerning trade and finance. M20.
▶ **B** *noun*. A three-sided figure; a triangle. M18.
■ **trilateralism** *noun* trilateral nature or condition L20. **trilateralist** *noun* an advocate or adherent of trilateralism L20. **trilateˈrality** *noun* (now *rare* or *obsolete*) trilateralism M19. **trilaterally** *adverb* M19. **trilateralness** *noun* (*rare*) E18.

trilateration /ˌtrʌɪlatəˈreɪʃ(ə)n/ *noun*. M20.
[from prec. + -ATION.]
SURVEYING. A method of surveying analogous to triangulation in which each triangle is determined by the measurement of all three sides.

trilby /ˈtrɪlbi/ *noun*. L19.
[The eponymous heroine of George du Maurier's novel (1894), an artist's model noted for her beautiful feet.]
1 The foot. *joc.* (now *rare* or *obsolete*). L19.
2 A soft felt hat with a narrow brim and indented crown, resembling that worn in the stage version of *Trilby*. Also ***trilby hat***. L19.

trilemma /trʌɪˈlɛmə/ *noun*. L17.
[from TRI- + DI)LEMMA.]
A choice between three (esp. unfavourable) options; LOGIC a syllogism with three conditional major premisses and a disjunctive minor premiss.

Trilene /ˈtrʌɪliːn/ *noun*. Also **t-**. M20.
[from TRI(CHLOROETHY)LENE.]
PHARMACOLOGY. (Proprietary name for) a medicinal grade of trichloroethylene, used as an analgesic and light anaesthetic.

trilinear /trʌɪˈlɪnɪə/ *adjective*. E18.
[from TRI- + LINEAR.]
GEOMETRY. Of, contained by, or having some relation to, three lines (curved or straight).
trilinear coordinate each of three coordinates determining a point in a plane by its distances measured in three fixed directions from three fixed straight lines forming a triangle (usu. in *pl.*).

trilingual /trʌɪˈlɪŋgw(ə)l/ *adjective*. M19.
[from Latin *trilinguis*, from TRI- + *lingua* tongue, + -AL¹.]
1 Written or inscribed in three languages; spoken in three languages. M19.
2 Able to speak three languages, esp. fluently. E20.
■ **trilingualism** *noun* ability to speak three languages, esp. fluently; the use of three languages: M20. **trilinguar** *adjective* (*rare*) †(*a*) uttered with three tongues; (*b*) trilingual: E19.

triliteral /trʌɪˈlɪt(ə)r(ə)l/ *adjective & noun*. M18.
[from TRI- + LITERAL *adjective*.]
▶ **A** *adjective*. Consisting of three letters; (of a Semitic language) having most roots with three consonants. M18.
▶ **B** *noun*. A triliteral word or root. E19.
■ **triliteralism** *noun* the characteristic use of triliterals, esp. in a Semitic language M19. **triliteˈrality** *noun* triliteral character, esp. of a Semitic language M19.

trilith /ˈtrʌɪlɪθ/ *noun*. Also (earlier) in Greek form **trilithon** /ˈtrʌɪlɪθ(ə)n/. M18.
[Greek *trilithon* use as noun of neut. of *trilithos*, from *tri-* TRI- + *lithos* stone.]
A prehistoric structure consisting of three large stones, esp. of two uprights and a lintel.
■ **triˈlithic**, **trilithonic** /-ˈθɒnɪk/ *adjectives* (*rare*) pertaining to or of the nature of a trilith M19.

trill /trɪl/ *noun*¹. M17.
[Italian *trillo*, †*triglio*, from *trillare* TRILL *verb*³. Cf. TRILLO.]
1 An ornament consisting of a tremulous utterance of a note or notes; a rapid alternation of sung or played notes a degree apart; a shake. M17.
2 *transf.* A tremulous high-pitched sound or succession of sounds, esp. in birdsong. L17.
3 Vibration of the tip of the tongue, or of another of the vocal organs, in the pronunciation of a consonant, esp. *r*; a consonant so pronounced. M19.

> 🕮 **1** *Opera Now* The trills, staccatos, scales and arpeggios of the coloratura specialist. **2** R. C. PRAED The trill and full chirrup of the chaffinch. **3** D. JONES Trills (e.g. rolled r) may also be classed among the simple sounds.

■ **trillet** *noun* (*rare*) a little or tiny trill M19.

trill *noun*² see THILL *noun*¹.

trill /trɪl/ *verb*¹. *arch.* ME.
[Perh. identical with next. Cf. DRILL *verb*².]
1 *verb intrans.* Of water, a brook, etc.: flow in a small continuous stream of constantly revolving water particles; purl. ME.
†**2** *verb intrans.* Fall or hang down in a flowing manner; stream, trail. LME–E17.
3 *verb trans.* Cause (water, a brook, etc.) to flow in a small continuous stream of constantly revolving water particles. L15.

trill /trɪl/ *verb*². Now *arch.*, *Scot.*, & *dial.* LME.
[Perh. rel. to Swedish *trilla*, Danish & Norwegian *trille* roll, trundle, wheel.]
1 *verb trans.* Turn (a thing) round, cause to revolve or rotate; *spec.* (*a*) twirl, twiddle, whirl, spin; (*b*) roll or bowl (a ball, hoop, etc.). LME.
†**2** *verb intrans.* Of a wheel, ball, etc.: revolve, spin, roll. M16–L17.

trill /trɪl/ *verb*³. M17.
[Italian *trillare*.]
1 *verb intrans.* Produce a trill by singing or playing; sound with a trill. M17.
2 *verb trans.* Utter or sing (a note, tune, etc.) with a trill. E18.
3 *verb trans.* Pronounce (a consonant, esp. *r*) with a trill; = ROLL *verb* 9b. M19.

> 🕮 **1** E. CAPERN And music trilled o'er moor and mead. B. HINES A skylark flew up, trilling as it climbed. **2** DICKENS The lark trilled out her happy song. H. ACTON Sentimental Victorian ballads which he trilled and warbled.

■ **triller** *noun* a person who trills L19. **trillingly** *adverb* in a trilling manner, with trilling L19.

trillibubs /ˈtrɪlɪbʌbz/ *noun pl.* *obsolete* exc. *dial.* E16.
[Origin unkn.]
Entrails, intestines.

trilling /ˈtrɪlɪŋ/ *noun*. M19.
[from TRI- + -LING¹, app. after Danish, Swedish *trilling*, Dutch *drieling*.]
1 Each of three children born at one birth; a triplet. Now *rare* or *obsolete*. M19.
2 CRYSTALLOGRAPHY. A crystal composed of three individuals, *esp.* a penetration twinning on a prism plane. L19.

trillion /ˈtrɪljən/ *noun & adjective*. L17.
[French, or Italian *trilione*, formed as MILLION by substitution of TRI-. Cf. BILLION.]
▶ **A** *noun*. Pl. same with specified number, **-s** when indefinite. Orig. (esp. in the UK), a million million million (10^{18}). Now usu. (orig. *US*), a million million (10^{12}; cf. BILLION). In *pl.* (*hyperbol.*), very large numbers (*of*). L17.
▶ **B** *adjective*. After article, possessive, etc.: a million (or a million million) times a million; *hyperbol.* a very great many. E20.

> 🕮 *New Yorker* About two trillion dollars' worth of insurance.

■ **trillionaire** /trɪljəˈnɛː/ *noun* [after *millionaire*] a person whose assets are worth at least a trillion pounds, dollars, etc. L19. **trillionth** *adjective & noun* (*a*) *adjective* one million (or million million) millionth; (*b*) *noun* a trillionth part, member of a series, etc.: M19.

trillium /ˈtrɪlɪəm/ *noun*. M19.
[mod. Latin (see below), app. alt. of Swedish *trilling* triplet, with ref. to the parts of the plant being in threes.]
Any of various N. American plants of the genus *Trillium*, of the lily family, related to herb Paris but bearing a whorl of three leaves at the summit of the stem and in the middle a solitary flower with three white or brightly coloured petals. Also called ***wake-robin***.

trillo /ˈtrɪləʊ/ *noun*. Now *rare*. Pl. **-os**. M17.
[Italian: see TRILL *noun*¹.]
MUSIC. = TRILL *noun*¹ 1.

trilobate /trʌɪˈləʊbeɪt/ *adjective*. L18.
[from TRI- + LOBATE.]
Having three lobes.
■ **trilobal** *adjective* trilobate; now *spec.* designating (artificial fibres having) a cross-section of this form L19. **triloˈbation** *noun* trilobate condition L19. **ˈtrilobe** *adjective* (*rare*) = TRILOBATE M20. **trilobed** *adjective* = TRILOBATE E19.

trilobite /ˈtrʌɪləbʌɪt, ˈtrɪ-/ *noun*. M19.
[mod. Latin *Trilobites* former group name, from Greek *tri-* TRI- + *lobos* lobe (of the ear etc.) + -ITE¹.]
PALAEONTOLOGY. Any of numerous extinct marine arthropods of the subphylum Trilobita, which had a body divided into an anterior solid cephalon, a segmented thorax or trunk, and a posterior pygidium, and which are found abundantly as fossils in Palaeozoic rocks.
■ **trilobitic** /-ˈbɪtɪk/ *adjective* pertaining to, of the nature of, or containing trilobites M19.

trilogy /ˈtrɪlədʒi/ *noun*. M17.
[Greek *trilogia*, from *tri-* TRI- + *logos*: see -LOGY.]
†**1** A speech or piece of writing consisting of three parts. *rare*. Only in M17.
2 A series or group of three related dramatic, literary, or operatic works; GREEK ANTIQUITIES a series of three connected tragedies for performance at the festival of Dionysus in ancient Athens. E19.
3 *transf.* & *fig.* A group or set of three related things. M19.

> 🕮 **2** G. B. SHAW The Rhine maidens in Wagner's Trilogy. **3** *Australian Business* Bob Hawke's trilogy of . . taxation, expenditure and the deficit.

trim /trɪm/ *noun*. L16.
[from TRIM *verb*.]
▶ **I** NAUTICAL & AERONAUTICS. **1** The state of being fully prepared for sailing (freq. in ***in good trim***, ***out of trim***, etc.). L16.
2 Adjustment of the balance of a ship by arrangement of the cargo etc. (freq. with specifying word, as *good*, *better*, *bad* etc.); the balance so achieved; adjustment of the sails to suit the wind. E17. ▸**b** The general appearance or look of a ship etc. *rare*. M18.
3 The degree of inclination of an aircraft or submarine to the horizontal. Also, the condition of static balance of the aerodynamic forces on an aircraft in straight flight; a device or action used to maintain such balance. E20.

> 🕮 **2** T. REID A ship requires a different trim for every variation of the . . wind. C. FRANCIS By pumping water . . sideways trim can be altered to eliminate list. **b** T. GRAY In gallant trim the gilded Vessel goes. **3** M. WOODHOUSE Yancy corrected trim We flew another mile. *attrib.*: M. HEBDEN Addams did a trim dive before he left.

▶ **II** *gen.* senses.
4 a Adornment, array; equipment, outfit; dress. L16. ▸†**b** A piece of personal adornment, an ornament; a style of dress. L16–L17. ▸**c** Ornament or decorative material, (a) trimming; (orig. *US*) ornamental additions or finishings to a vehicle, piece of furniture, etc.; *spec.* the upholstery or interior lining of a motor car. M17. ▸**d** A shop window display. *US*. L19. ▸**e** CINEMATOGRAPHY. A piece of film cut out during editing; *spec.* a very short piece cut out during the final editing stage. Orig. *US*. M20.
5 The action or an act of trimming a person's hair; the condition of being trimmed. E17.
6 Condition, state, or order, esp. of preparedness or fitness (freq. with specifying word). Freq. in ***in trim***, ***out of trim***. E17.
7 The nature, character, or manner of a person or thing. *arch.* E18.
8 A woman; sexual intercourse with a woman. *US slang*. M20.

> 🕮 **4a** SIR W. SCOTT Bucklaw, in bridegroom trim. *fig.*: W. COWPER Nature in her cultivated trim Dressed to his taste. **b** W. PENN Civil Affairs . . transacted under the different Liveries, or Trims of Religion. **c** *Time* The color of the trim on the wagon seats. *Annabel* Black . . belt with cream trim, £12.95. **5** *Hairdo Ideas* Visit your salon . . for a quick trim. **6** R. SUTCLIFF Sometimes I was . . not in good walking trim. **7** SIR W. SCOTT His wife knows his trim and . . the matter is quite certain. **8** E. LACY The broad isn't worth it, no trim is.

Comb.: **trim tab** (*a*) AERONAUTICS = ***trimming tab*** s.v. TRIMMING *noun*; (*b*) NAUTICAL a hinged tab or flap fitted to the trailing edge of a keel or rudder, or separately fitted at the stern, to facilitate steering.

trim /trɪm/ *adjective & adverb*. L15.
[from TRIM *verb*.]
▶ **A** *adjective*. **1** Neatly or smartly made, prepared, or arranged; neat and tidy in appearance or effect; spruce. L15.
2 In good condition or order; well arranged or equipped; NAUTICAL (of a ship) fully prepared for sailing; *gen.* sound, good, excellent. M16.

📖 **1** A. THWAITE His trim figure and his . . attractive stance. G. SWIFT Into the grounds of Ham House. Across the trim lawns. **2** POPE The vessel rides, . . In all her tackle trim to quit the shore. R. FRAME He liked to keep himself trim, in good shape.

▶ **B** *adverb*. Trimly. Now *rare* or *obsolete*. L15.
■ **trimly** *adverb* in a trim manner E16. **trimness** *noun* M16.

trim /trɪm/ *verb*. Infl. **-mm-**.
[Old English *trymman*, *trymian*. Branch II may be a different word.]
▶†**I 1 a** *verb trans*. Make firm or strong; give as security; arm or array (a force); arrange; encourage, exhort. Only in OE. ▸**b** *verb trans. & intrans*. Become pregnant with, conceive, give birth to, (a child). *rare*. Only in ME.
▶ **II 2** *verb trans*. Put into proper condition for some purpose or use; prepare, make ready; now chiefly *spec*. (*a*) *arch.* fit out (a ship etc.) for sea; (*b*) make (a lamp, fire, etc.) ready for use by removing burnt material and adding fresh fuel; cleanse or cut level (a wick). E16.
†**3** *verb trans*. Repair, restore, or put right (something broken, worn, or decayed). E16–L17.
†**4** *verb trans*. Provide *with* necessities; equip, supply. E16–M17.
5 *verb trans*. Dress (a person, oneself) neatly and smartly; dress *up*, deck *out*. E16. ▸**b** Decorate (a hat, clothing, etc.) with ribbons, lace, etc.; (of ribbons, lace, etc.) form the decorative finish of (a hat, clothing, etc.). M16.
6 *verb trans*. Beat, thrash. Also, rebuke sharply. Now *colloq. & dial.* E16.
7 *verb trans*. Cut away the irregular or unwanted parts of to reduce to a regular shape; cut away (irregular or unwanted parts) to reduce something to a regular shape; *spec.* (*a*) clip the unwanted or uneven ends of (the hair, nails, etc.); cut (the hair, nails, etc.), esp. to a required length; clip the unwanted or uneven ends of the hair, nails, etc., of (a person); (*b*) dub (a cock). M16. ▸**b** Cheat (a person) out of money; fleece. *arch. slang*. E17. ▸**c** Reduce the size, amount, or number of; reduce the profits or expenditure of. Orig. *US*. M20.
8 *verb trans*. NAUTICAL. Adjust the balance of (a ship) by arrangement of the cargo etc. L16. ▸**b** *verb trans. transf.* Adjust (a balance of power) between opposing sides. E19. ▸**c** *verb intrans*. Of a ship: undergo adjustment of the balance by arrangement of the cargo etc. M19.
9 *verb trans. & intrans*. NAUTICAL. Adjust (the sails) to suit the wind. Freq. foll. by *to*. E17.
10 *verb trans*. CARPENTRY. Bring (a piece of timber, etc.) to the required shape; (foll. by *in*) fit or frame (one piece) to or into another. L17.
11 *verb intrans*. Modify one's attitude in order to stand well with opposite parties; hold a middle course between opposing views; associate oneself with currently prevailing views, esp. for personal advancement. L17.
12 *verb trans*. Stow or arrange (coal or cargo) in a ship's hold. L18.
13 AERONAUTICS. **a** *verb trans*. Maintain or adjust the trim of (an aircraft). E20. ▸**b** *verb intrans*. Of an aircraft: undergo maintenance or adjustment of the trim. E20.

📖 **2** SHAKES. *Rich. II* He had not so trimm'd and dress'd his land As we this garden. J. S. BLACKIE Xerxes . . Trimmed vain fleets for thy undoing. **3** A. MUNDAY The repairing and trimming of this Church. **5** DRYDEN The Victim Ox . . Trimm'd with white Ribbons. **b** G. HUNTINGTON A hat trimmed with velvet pansies. G. NAYLOR Help me trim my Christmas tree. **6** SIR W. SCOTT How I trimmed them about . . hearkening behind the arras. P. G. WODEHOUSE Surely . . Rodney can trim a man with hay fever? **7** B. PYM His beard was newly trimmed. G. VIDAL A slave girl trimmed my toenails. *Woman's Journal* Trim the pork, removing the skin. **b** P. G. WODEHOUSE Some burgeoning scheme for trimming the investors. **c** *Times* Government was cutting back . . trimming benefits for the unemployed. **8** *Practical Boat Owner* To get the best out of a Canadian, it must be trimmed . . fore and aft. **b** JAS. MILL The balance among those powers might have been trimmed. **9** C. FRANCIS Sails had to be trimmed as the . . wind varied. *transf.*: *Daily Telegraph* Vanes which trim to get maximum power from whatever wind is around. *fig.*: L. STRACHEY Burghley, trimming his sails to the changing wind, thought it advisable . . to take the side of Essex.

■ **trimmed** *ppl adjective* (*a*) *gen.* that has been trimmed; (*b*) having a decorative finish (of a specified kind); (*c*) ***trimmed joist*** (CARPENTRY), a joist which is tenoned into a trimmer: M16. **trimmingly** *adverb* (*rare*) in a trimming manner E18.

trimaran /ˈtrʌɪmərən/ *noun*. M20.
[from TRI- + CATA)MARAN.]
A sailing boat with three hulls.

trimeprazine /trʌɪˈmɛprəziːn/ *noun*. M20.
[Prob. from TRIME(THYL + PR(OPYL + PHENOTHI)AZINE.]
PHARMACOLOGY. A drug derived from phenothiazine, used for its sedative and antihistamine properties.

trimer /ˈtrʌɪmə/ *noun*. M20.
[from TRI- + -MER.]
CHEMISTRY. A compound whose molecule is composed of three molecules of a monomer.
■ **triˈmeric** *adjective* of the nature of a trimer, consisting of a trimer or trimers M20. **trimeriˈzation** *noun* the formation of a trimer from smaller molecules M20.

trimerous /ˈtrɪm(ə)rəs, ˈtrʌɪ-/ *adjective*. E19.
[from Greek *trimerēs*, from *tri-* TRI- + *meros* part: see -OUS.]
1 Formed of three parts or segments; *spec.* (ENTOMOLOGY) (having tarsi etc.) consisting of three segments or joints. E19.
2 BOTANY. Of a flower: having the parts, esp. the petals or sepals, in threes. M19.

trimester /trʌɪˈmɛstə/ *noun*. E19.
[French *trimestre*, from Latin *trimestris*, formed as TRI- + *mensis* month. Cf. SEMESTER.]
A period or term of three months; *spec.* (*a*) MEDICINE one third of the length of a human pregnancy; (*b*) *N. Amer.* a three-month university or school term.

trimestral /trʌɪˈmɛstr(ə)l/ *adjective*. E17.
[from prec. + -AL[1]. Cf. next.]
Occurring every three months.
¶ Rare before E19.

trimestrial /trʌɪˈmɛstrɪəl/ *adjective*. L17.
[from Latin *trimestris* (see TRIMESTER) + -AL[1]. Cf. prec.]
Orig., consisting of or containing three months. Later, trimestral.

trimeter /ˈtrɪmɪtə, ˈtrʌɪ-/ *noun & adjective*. M16.
[Latin *trimetrus*, from Greek *trimetros*, from *tri-* TRI- + *metros* METRE *noun*[1].]
PROSODY. ▶**A** *noun*. A verse of three measures. M16.
▶ **B** *attrib.* or as *adjective*. Of or pertaining to a trimeter; (of a verse) consisting of three measures. E18.

trimethoprim /trʌɪˈmɛθə(ʊ)prɪm/ *noun*. M20.
[from TRIMETH(YL + O(XY- + P(Y)RIM(IDINE.]
PHARMACOLOGY. An antibiotic used esp. to treat malaria and respiratory and urinary infections (usu. in conjunction with a sulphonamide).

trimethyl /trʌɪˈmiːθʌɪl, -ˈmɛθɪl/ *adjective*. M19.
[from TRI- + METHYL.]
CHEMISTRY. Having three methyl groups in the molecule.
■ **trimethylamine** /trʌɪmɪˈθʌɪləmiːn/ *noun* a flammable gas, $(CH_3)_3N$, which has a fishy ammoniacal odour and is used in chemical manufacture M20. **triˈmethylene** *noun* = CYCLOPROPANE L19. ˌ**trimethylˈxanthine** *noun* any of the isomeric trimethyl derivatives of xanthine, *esp.* caffeine L20.

trimetric /trʌɪˈmɛtrɪk/ *adjective*. M19.
[Sense 1 from TRI- + Greek *metron* measure; sense 2 formed as TRIMETER: see -IC.]
1 CRYSTALLOGRAPHY. = ORTHORHOMBIC. M19.
2 PROSODY. Trimetrical. L19.

trimetrical /trɪˈmɛtrɪk(ə)l, trʌɪ-/ *adjective*. E19.
[formed as prec. + -AL[1].]
Having three parts; *spec.* in PROSODY, consisting of three measures.
Trimetrical Classic a Chinese elementary schoolbook written in lines of verse consisting of three characters each.

Trimetrogen /trʌɪˈmɛtrədʒ(ə)n/ *noun*. M20.
[from TRI- + *Metrogen* proprietary name in the US.]
Used *attrib.* with ref. to a technique in which aerial photographs are taken simultaneously by a camera pointing vertically downwards and two pointing obliquely in opposite directions.

trimmer /ˈtrɪmə/ *noun*. E16.
[from TRIM *verb* + -ER[1].]
†**1** A canopy. *rare*. E–M16.
2 A person who trims something; *spec.* a person who decorates a hat, clothing, etc., with ribbons, lace, etc. M16.
3 A thing which trims something; *spec.* an instrument for cutting away irregular or unwanted parts to reduce something to a regular shape. L16.
4 ARCHITECTURE. A short beam across an opening, as a stairwell or hearth, to carry the ends of truncated joists. M17.
5 A person who trims between opposing parties in politics etc.; a person who associates himself or herself with currently prevailing views, esp. for personal advancement; a time-server. L17.
6 A person who or thing which makes a powerful impression; *spec.* (*a*) a strongly worded message, rebuke, etc.; (*b*) (chiefly *Austral. & NZ*) a good or excellent person or thing. *colloq.* L18.
7 ANGLING. A float or fixed peg with a reel, attached to a line with baited hook, used on lakes and ponds for taking pike. L18.
8 a A person responsible for trimming the sails on a ship. Also more fully ***sail trimmer***. E19. ▸**b** A person employed to stow or arrange coal or cargo in a ship's hold; a mechanical contrivance for doing this. M19.
9 ELECTRONICS. A small adjustable capacitor usu. used for the fine adjustment of a larger capacitor to which it is connected. Also ***trimmer capacitor***, ***trimmer condenser***. M20.
10 AERONAUTICS. = ***trimming tab*** s.v. TRIMMING *noun*. M20.

trimming /ˈtrɪmɪŋ/ *noun*. E16.
[from TRIM *verb* + -ING[1].]
1 The action of TRIM *verb*; an instance of this. E16.
2 An ornamentation or decoration, esp. for a hat, clothing, etc. (freq. in *pl.*). E16.
3 In *pl.* Accessories, usual accompaniments, esp. of the main course of a meal (freq. in ***all the trimmings***). E17.
4 A beating, a thrashing; a sharp censure. L17.
5 In *pl.* Pieces cut off in trimming something; parings, cuttings, scraps. E19.
Comb.: **trimming gear** AERONAUTICS apparatus for altering the angle of the tailplane of an aircraft; **trimming-joist** ARCHITECTURE a joist into which the end of a trimmer is fitted; **trimming tab** AERONAUTICS an adjustable tab or aerofoil attached to a control surface, used to trim the aircraft in flight; **trimming tank** NAUTICAL a water tank in the bow or stern of a ship which is filled or emptied as the trim of the ship demands; **trimming wheel** AERONAUTICS a control wheel used to trim an aircraft by its action on the tailplane.

trimnasium /trɪmˈneɪzɪəm/ *noun*. Pl. **-iums**, **-ia** /-ɪə/. L20.
[from TRIM *adjective* + GYM)NASIUM.]
A type of gymnasium designed and equipped for keep-fit exercise.

trimoda necessitas /trʌɪmədə nɪˈsɛsɪtas, ˌtrɪmədɑː nɛˈkɛsɪtɑːs/ *noun phr.* Also †**trin-**. OE.
[Late Latin, from *trimoda* fem. of *trimodus* of three kinds, formed as TRI- + *modus* mode, manner, + *necessitas* necessity, obligation.]
LAW (now *Hist.*). The triple obligation on a land holder in pre-Norman England of rendering military service and contributing to the repair of fortresses and bridges.

trimoric /trʌɪˈmɒrɪk/ *adjective*. E20.
[from TRI- + MORA *noun*[1] + -IC.]
PROSODY. Containing three morae; having the length of three short syllables.

trimorphic /trʌɪˈmɔːfɪk/ *adjective*. M19.
[from Greek *trimorphos*, formed as TRI- + *morphē* form: see -IC.]
Of a plant, animal, or crystalline substance: existing in three distinct forms.
■ **trimorphism** *noun* trimorphic condition; occurrence in three different forms: M19. **trimorphous** *adjective* = TRIMORPHIC L19.

trimotor /ˈtrʌɪməʊtə/ *noun*. E20.
[from TRI- + MOTOR *noun*.]
An aeroplane fitted with three engines.
■ **tri-motored** *adjective* (of an aeroplane) fitted with three engines E20.

Trimphone /ˈtrɪmfəʊn/ *noun*. M20.
[from TRIM *adjective* + PHONE *noun*[2].]
(Proprietary name for) a type of lightweight telephone with a high-pitched vibratory ringing tone.

trim-tram /ˈtrɪmˈtram/ *noun, interjection, & adjective*. *obsolete* exc. *dial.* E16.
[Symbolic redupl. formation with vowel variation: prob. ult. from TRIM *adjective*. Cf. FLIMFLAM, WHIM-WHAM.]
▶ **A** *noun*. †**1** An inexpensive personal ornament; a pretty toy or trifle; a gewgaw. E16–M17.
†**2** An absurd or silly device or practice; an absurdity; a piece of nonsense. M16–E18.
3 A kind of shrimping net. Long *rare* or *obsolete*. L16.
4 A lich-gate. Also, a kissing-gate. *dial.* M19.
▶ **B** *interjection*. Expr. a desire for equal treatment for two parties, esp. in ***trim-tram, like master, like man***. Also, a meaningless refrain. Now *dial.* L16.
▶†**C** *attrib.* or as *adjective*. **1** Of like mind. Only in E17.
2 Trifling, absurd. M17–M18.

Trimurti /trɪˈmʊəti/ *noun*. Also **t-**. M19.
[Sanskrit, from *tri* three + *mūrti* form.]
1 HINDUISM. The gods Brahma, Vishnu, and Siva, conceived as aspects of one ultimate reality. M19.
2 A statue with three faces representing Brahma, Vishnu, and Siva. L19.

trin /trɪn/ *noun*. M19.
[Perh. from TRINE *noun* assim. to TWIN *noun*.]
= TRINE *noun* 3. Usu. in *pl.*

Trinacrian /trʌɪˈneɪkrɪən/ *adjective*. E17.
[from Latin *Trinacria* from Greek *Trinakria* Sicily, taken as from *tri-* TRI- + *akra* point, cape, but orig. *Thrinakiē* from *thrinax* trident: see -AN.]
Of Sicily, Sicilian. Also, three-pointed.
■ **trinacrite** /ˈtrɪnəkrʌɪt/ *noun* (GEOLOGY) a brown tuff with the composition of palagonite M19.

trinal /ˈtrʌɪn(ə)l/ *adjective & noun*. L15.
[medieval Latin *trinalis*, from Latin *trinus* threefold: see TRINE *adjective & noun*, -AL[1].]
▶ **A** *adjective*. **1** = TRINE *adjective* 1. L15.

2 GRAMMAR. Of a form or number: denoting three persons or things. *rare*. M19.
▶**B** *noun*. GRAMMAR. The trinal number; a trinal form or word. *rare*. L19.
■ **tri'nality** *noun* the quality of being trinal M19.

trinary /'trʌɪnəri/ *adjective & noun*. *rare*. L15.
[Late Latin *trinarius*, from Latin *trinus* threefold: see TRINE *adjective & noun*, -ARY[1].]
▶**A** *adjective*. Threefold, triple; ternary; MATH. of or designating a system of notation in which the base is 3. L15.
▶†**B** *noun*. = TRINE *noun* 1. L16–M17.

Trincomalee wood /ˌtrɪŋkə(ʊ)mə'liː wʊd/ *noun phr*. Also **-li**. M19.
[*Trincomalee*, a seaport of Sri Lanka.]
(The tough dark red timber of) a tree of the linden family, *Berrya cordifolia*, of southern India and Sri Lanka.

trindle /'trɪnd(ə)l/ *verb & noun*.
[Old English *tryndyl-* rel. to TRENDLE. Cf. TRUNDLE *noun, verb*.]
▶**A** *verb*. *obsolete* exc. *dial*.
†**1** *verb trans*. Make round. Only in OE.
2 *verb intrans*. Of a wheel, spindle, etc.: revolve, turn round. Of a ball etc.: roll along a surface. LME.
3 *verb trans*. Cause (a wheel etc.) to revolve; roll (a ball etc.) along a surface. L16.
▶**B** *noun*. **1** A wheel; esp. in a mill or on a wheelbarrow. *obsolete* exc. *dial*. ME.
2 A roll or coil of wax taper, used for light in medieval churches. *obsolete* exc. *Hist*. M16.
3 A pellet of sheep's or goat's dung. Also, a calf's guts. *dial*. E17.
4 BOOKBINDING. Each of a pair of flat shapers used to hold down the back of a book while the fore-edge is ploughed. E19.

trine /trʌɪn/ *adjective & noun*. LME.
[Old & mod. French, fem. of *trin* from Latin *trinus* threefold, from *tres, tria* THREE.]
▶**A** *adjective*. **1** Composed or consisting of three parts, threefold, triple. LME.
2 ASTROLOGY. Designating or pertaining to the aspect of two heavenly bodies a third part of the zodiac (120°) distant from each other; *fig*. favourable, benign. L15.
▶**B** *noun*. **1** A group of three, a trio, a triad; *spec*. (THEOLOGY) the Trinity. M16.
2 ASTROLOGY. A trine aspect. Freq. in ***in trine***. L16.
3 Each of three children or young animals born at one birth; a triplet. Usu. in *pl*. E17.

†**trine** *verb*[1]. LME–E19.
[Of Scandinavian origin: cf. Old Swedish *trina*, Norwegian *trine*.]
1 *verb intrans*. Go, march, step. Long *obsolete* exc. as below. LME–E19.
2 *verb intrans. & trans*. Die or execute by hanging. Also ***trine to the cheat***, ***trine to the nubbing-cheat***. *slang*. M16–E19.

trine /trʌɪn/ *verb*[2] *trans*. *rare*. L17.
[from TRINE *adjective* or *noun*.]
1 ASTROLOGY. Put or join in a trine aspect. L17.
2 Make a trine or triad of. M19.

tringle /'trɪŋg(ə)l/ *noun*. *rare*. L17.
[French.]
1 ARCHITECTURE. A small square moulding or ornament. L17.
2 A long slender rod, *esp*. a curtain-rod. Cf. TRANGLE. E18.

Trini /'trɪni/ *noun & adjective*. *W. Indies colloq*. M20.
[Abbreviation.]
= next.

Trinidadian /trɪnɪ'dadɪən, -'deɪdɪən/ *noun & adjective*. E20.
[from *Trinidad* (see below) + -IAN.]
▶**A** *noun*. A native or inhabitant of Trinidad, an island in the W. Indies. E20.
▶**B** *adjective*. Of or pertaining to Trinidad or its inhabitants. M20.

Trinidado /trɪnɪ'dɑːdəʊ/ *noun*. Long *arch*. L16.
[Spanish, adjective from *Trinidad* (see prec.).]
A kind of tobacco from Trinidad.

Trinitarian /trɪnɪ'tɛːrɪən/ *noun & adjective*. M16.
[from mod. Latin *trinitarius* (from Latin *trinitas* TRINITY): see -ARIAN.]
▶**A** *noun*. CHRISTIAN CHURCH.
1 †**a** A member of a sect having heretical views on the Trinity. M16–M17. ▸**b** A believer in the doctrine of the Trinity. E18.
2 *Hist*. A member of the religious order of the Holy Trinity, a Mathurin. E17.
▶**B** *adjective*. **I** CHRISTIAN CHURCH. **1** *Hist*. Belonging to the order of the Holy Trinity or Mathurins. E17.
2 Orig., holding heretical views on the Trinity. Now, of, pertaining to, or believing in the doctrine of the Trinity. M17.
▶**II** (**t-**.)
3 Composed or consisting of three parts; triple, threefold. E19.
■ **Trinitarianism** *noun* the doctrine of Trinitarians, Trinitarian belief L18.

trinitrin /trʌɪ'nʌɪtrɪn/ *noun*. Now *rare* or *obsolete*. M19.
[from next + -IN[1].]
CHEMISTRY. = NITROGLYCERINE.

trinitrotoluene /trʌɪˌnʌɪtrəʊ'tɒljʊiːn/ *noun*. E20.
[from TRI- + NITRO- + TOLUENE.]
Any of three isomeric nitro derivatives of toluene, $CH_3C_6H_2(NO_2)_3$, *esp*. the 2,4,6-isomer, used as a high explosive that is relatively insensitive to shock and can be conveniently melted. Abbreviation ***TNT***.
■ Also **trinitrotoluol** *noun* (now *rare*) E20.

trinity /'trɪnɪti/ *noun*. ME.
[Old & mod. French *trinité* corresp. to Provençal, Spanish *trinidad*, Italian *trinità* from Latin *trinitas*, from *trinus* trio, triad, TRINE *adjective & noun*: see -ITY.]
1 The state of being threefold or triple, threeness. *spec*. in CHRISTIAN THEOLOGY (**T-**), the existence of God in three persons. ME.
2 CHRISTIAN THEOLOGY. (**T-**.) *The* three persons or modes of being of the Godhead as conceived in orthodox Christian belief; the Father, Son, and Holy Spirit as constituting one God. Freq. in ***the Blessed Trinity***, ***the Holy Trinity***. ME. ▸**b** *ellipt*. The festival of the Holy Trinity; Trinity Sunday. ME.
3 A group or set of three persons or things, esp. as forming a unity; a triad, a trio. M16.

> 🕮 **2** R. HEBER God in three Persons, blessed Trinity! HERB ***Trinity***. **3** *Country Life* I watched with frantic admiration that trinity of great players. S. UNWIN Man was a trinity—hand, heart and brain.

Comb.: **Trinity Brethren** the members of Trinity House; **Trinity House** (a branch of) an association formerly having the official regulation of British shipping and now chiefly concerned with the licensing of pilots and the erection and maintenance of lighthouses, buoys, etc., on the coasts of England and Wales; **Trinity Sunday** the next Sunday after Whit Sunday; **Trinity term** a university etc. term beginning after Easter; a term or session of the High Court beginning after Easter.

trink /trɪŋk/ *noun*. Long *obsolete* exc. *Hist*. ME.
[Origin unkn.]
A kind of fixed fishing net formerly used esp. on the River Thames.
■ **trinkerman** *noun* a fisherman using a trink (freq. in *pl*., such people as a class) M16.

trinket /'trɪŋkɪt/ *noun*. M16.
[Origin unkn.]
†**1 a** A small article or tool. Usu. in *pl*., the equipment or paraphernalia associated with an occupation etc. M16–L18. ▸**b** A sweet or dainty article of food, a delicacy. L16–E19.
2 A small ornament, article of jewellery, etc., of little value, *esp*. one worn on the person. M16.

> 🕮 **2** L. GARFIELD A trinket that she wore on a chain round her neck . . a gold locket. *transf*.: SIR W. SCOTT Take them—they are to me valueless trinkets.

■ **trinketry** *noun* trinkets collectively E19.

†**trinket** *verb*[1] *intrans*. Chiefly *Scot*. M17–E19.
[Origin unkn.]
Have clandestine communications or underhand dealings, intrigue, (*with*).
■ †**trinketer** *noun* M17–E19.

trinket /'trɪŋkɪt/ *verb*[2] *trans*. *rare*. M19.
[from TRINKET *noun*.]
Deck or adorn with trinkets. Also foll. by *out*.

Trinkhalle /'trɪŋkhalə/ *noun*. L19.
[German, lit. 'drinking-hall'.]
A place at a spa where medicinal water is dispensed for drinking; a pump room. Also, an establishment at which alcoholic drink is served.

trinkle /'trɪŋk(ə)l/ *verb & noun*. *Scot. & dial*. LME.
[App. var. of TRICKLE *verb*.]
▶**A** *verb intrans*. Flow or fall drop by drop, trickle. LME.
▶**B** *noun*. A trickle. *Scot*. L19.

trinklement /'trɪŋk(ə)lm(ə)nt/ *noun*. Now *dial*. L16.
[Alt. of TRINKET *noun* + -MENT.]
Adornment; in *pl*., trinkets.

trinklet /'trɪŋklɪt/ *noun*. *rare*. M16.
[App. alt. of TRINKET *noun* after diminutives in -LET.]
†**1** A woman decked out with trinkets or finery. Only in M16.
2 A trinket. L19.

trinkum /'trɪŋkəm/ *noun*. Now *dial. & colloq*. M17.
[App. alt. of TRINKET *noun* with Latinized ending.]
A trinket.
■ Also **trinkum-trankum** /'trɪŋkəm 'traŋkəm/ *noun* L17.

trinocular /trɪ'nɒkjʊlə, trʌɪ-/ *adjective*. M20.
[from TRI-, after *binocular*.]
Of a microscope etc.: having provision for a camera as well as eyepieces for both eyes.

For other words beginning with *tri-* see the entry for **tri-**

trinomial /trʌɪ'nəʊmɪəl/ *noun & adjective*. L17.
[from TRI- after BINOMIAL.]
▶**A** *noun*. **1** MATH. An expression consisting of three terms connected by plus or minus signs. L17.
2 BIOLOGY. A trinomial taxonomic name. L19.
▶**B** *adjective*. **1** MATH. Consisting of three terms. E18.
2 BIOLOGY. Of a scientific name: consisting of three terms, esp. where the first is the name of the genus, the second that of the species, the third that of the subspecies or variety. Also, involving or characterized by such names. M19.
3 Of a married woman's name, esp. in the US: consisting of three elements, the forename, maiden name, and husband's surname. Of a woman: having such a name. M20.
■ **trinomialism** *noun* the trinomial system of nomenclature, the use of trinomial names L19. **trinomially** *adverb* by the use of trinomial names L19.

trinominal /trʌɪ'nɒmɪn(ə)l/ *adjective*. *rare*. L17.
[from TRI- + Latin *nominalis* NOMINAL.]
= TRINOMIAL *adjective*.

trio /'triːəʊ/ *noun*. Pl. **-os**. E18.
[Italian, from Latin *tres, tria* THREE after DUO.]
1 MUSIC. **a** A composition for three voices or instruments. Also, a group or company of three performers. E18. ▸**b** The central section of a minuet, scherzo, or march, freq. in a different key and style from the preceding and following main division. M19.
2 A group or set of three things or people. L18. ▸**b** CARDS. In piquet, a combination of three aces, kings, queens, jacks, or tens in one hand. L19.

> 🕮 **1a** O. KEEPNEWS The Art Tatum Trio, with . . Stewart on bass and . . Grimes on guitar. *Gramophone* The Divertimento for string trio in E flat. **2** V. BRITTAIN The third member of the devoted trio . . christened 'the Three Musketeers'. A. SCHROEDER A trio of youths trying to . . start an old Chevrolet.

Comb.: **trio-sonata** MUSIC a sonata written in three parts and freq. performed on four instruments.

triobol /'trʌɪəb(ə)l, trʌɪ'ɒb(ə)l/ *noun*. Also **triobolus** /trʌɪ'ɒbələs/, pl. **-li** /-lʌɪ, -liː/. M19.
[Greek *triōbolon*, from *tri-* TRI- + *obolos* OBOL.]
ANTIQUITIES. An ancient Greek coin of the value of three obols or half a drachma.

triode /'trʌɪəʊd/ *adjective & noun*. L19.
[from TRI- + -ODE[2].]
▶†**A** *adjective*. TELEGRAPHY. Permitting or involving the transmission of three signals simultaneously. Only in L19.
▶**B** *noun*. ELECTRONICS. A thermionic valve having three electrodes (also ***triode valve***). Also, an analogous semiconductor device with three terminals. E20.
Comb.: **triode-hexode**, **triode-pentode** a valve containing a triode and a hexode, pentode, in a single envelope, with separate anodes but a common cathode.

trioecious /trʌɪ'iːʃəs/ *adjective*. Also ***triec-**. M19.
[from TRI- + Greek *oikos* house + -OUS.]
BOTANY. Having male, female, and hermaphrodite parts on different plants.
■ **trioeciously** *adverb* L19.

triol /'trʌɪɒl/ *noun*. M20.
[from TRI- + -OL.]
CHEMISTRY. A trihydric alcohol.

triolet /'triːə(ʊ)lɛt, 'trʌɪəlɛt/ *noun*. M17.
[French, formed as TRIO: see -LET.]
A poem or stanza of eight usu. eight-syllabled lines rhyming *abaaabab*, the first line repeated as the fourth and seventh and the second as the eighth.

triology /trʌɪ'ɒlədʒi/ *noun*. M19.
[from TRI- + -OLOGY.]
A trilogy.

†**Triones** *noun pl*. LME–L18.
[Latin, pl. of *trio* plough-ox. Cf. SEPTENTRION.]
The seven principal stars in the constellation of the Great Bear or Plough.

triose /'trʌɪəʊz, -s/ *noun*. L19.
[from TRI- + -OSE[2].]
CHEMISTRY. Any monosaccharide sugar with three carbon atoms in its molecule. Formerly also, a trisaccharide.

trioxan /trʌɪ'ɒksan/ *noun*. Also **-ane** /-eɪn/. E20.
[from TRI- + OXY- + -AN, -ANE.]
CHEMISTRY. A cyclic trimer of formaldehyde obtained as colourless pliable crystals that are combustible and very volatile at room temperature.

trioxide /trʌɪ'ɒksʌɪd/ *noun*. M19.
[from TRI- + OXIDE.]
CHEMISTRY. Any oxide containing three atoms of oxygen in its molecule or empirical formula.

trip /trɪp/ *noun*[1]. ME.
[from the verb.]
▶**I 1** The action or an act of tripping a person by suddenly catching or entangling his or her foot. ME.

2 A mistake, a blunder; a slip, an inconsistency, an inaccuracy. **M16.**
3 A stumble or fall caused by catching or entangling one's foot against an object etc. **L16.**

📖 **1** H. BROOKE Gave a slight trip to his . . assailant, who instantly fell. **3** *Which?* Trips and falls cause nearly half of all accidents.

▸ **II 4** The action or an act of tripping or moving quickly and lightly; tripping gait; a nimble step, a skip. **ME.**
5 A journey or excursion, *esp.* one made repeatedly on a particular usu. short route or one taken for pleasure or health. **L17.** ▸**b** The catch or take of fish etc. obtained during a single voyage of a fishing boat. *N. Amer.* **M19.** ▸**c** *MINING.* A train of cars run in and out of a mine as a single unit. **E20.** ▸**d** *RACING.* The distance from start to finish of a race. **M20.**
6 A hallucinatory experience induced by a drug, esp. LSD; the period of this. *colloq.* **E20.** ▸**b** An experience, *esp.* a stimulating one. Also, an (illusory or self indulgent) activity or attitude. *slang.* **M20.**

📖 **4** SIR W. SCOTT He . . could . . hear the trip of a light female step. **5** J. A. FROUDE Two trips were required to transport the increased numbers. G. TINDALL Skiing trips always . . seemed to start at . . a traumatically early hour. P. ACKROYD He took off for a five-day trip to Paris. ***day trip***, ***round trip***, etc. **6** P. DICKINSON The high had turned itself into a bad trip. **b** *Melody Maker* The drums are bright shiny cab yellow . . . It's a trip. R. L. SIMON I shouldn't bother—politics was a sixties trip. *EGO-trip*.

▸ **III 7 a** A projecting part of a mechanism which comes briefly into contact with another part so as to cause or check some movement; a device which trips something. **E20.** ▸**b** A shutdown of a nuclear reactor initiated by an automatic safety system. **M20.**

Comb.: **trip-bucket** in Arabia, a bucket operated by a tripping device and pulled by animals, used for raising water from a well; **tripcock** a device on a train fitted to prevent the train passing a signal set at danger, by applying the brakes when engaged by a projection on the track; **trip-hammer** a massive machine-hammer operated by a tripping device, a tilt-hammer; **trip-hop** a style of dance music, usually slow in tempo, that combines elements of hip hop and dub reggae with softer, more ambient sounds; **tripmeter** an instrument used to record the distance travelled by a vehicle during a particular trip; **trip switch** *ELECTRICAL ENGINEERING* a switch for operating the tripping circuit of a circuit breaker.

trip /trɪp/ *noun*². **ME.**
[Origin unkn.]
1 A troop or company of people. *rare.* Long *obsolete* exc. *dial.* **ME.**
2 a A small flock of goats, sheep, etc. *obsolete* exc. *local.* **ME.** ▸**b** A small flock of wildfowl. **E19.**

trip /trɪp/ *noun*³. *obsolete* exc. *dial.* or *Hist.* **LME.**
[Origin unkn.]
A piece of cheese rind. Also, a kind of East Anglian curd cheese.

Trip /trɪp/ *noun*⁴. *slang.* **E20.**
[Abbreviation.]
= **TRIPOS** 2c.

trip /trɪp/ *verb.* Infl. **-pp-**. **LME.**
[Old French *trip(p)er*, *treper* = Provençal *trepar* from Middle Dutch *trippen* skip, hop, rel. to Old English *treppan* tread, trample.]
▸ **I 1** *a verb intrans. & trans.* (with *it*). Move, dance, or run with quick light steps; skip, caper, dance nimbly; *fig.* (of words, a rhythm, etc.) flow lightly and gracefully. **LME.** ▸**b** *verb intrans. & trans.* *ANGLING.* Touch lightly or brush (the bottom) with the bait. **L19.**
2 *verb trans.* **a** Cause to move or dance quickly and lightly. *rare.* **L16.** ▸**b** Perform (a dance) with a light lively step. *rare.* **E17.** ▸**c** Tread (ground etc.) quickly and lightly, dance nimbly on. **M18.**
3 a *verb intrans. & trans.* (with *it*). Make a trip or short excursion. (Foll. by *to* a place.) **M17.** ▸**b** *verb intrans.* *spec.* Travel through rough country by dog-sledge or canoe, esp. on a trading expedition. *Canad.* **E19.**
4 *verb intrans.* Experience hallucinations induced by a drug, esp. LSD; undergo a psychedelic trip. Also foll. by *out*. *colloq.* **M20.**

📖 **1a** *National Observer (US)* Watching a bevy of models trip gracefully down the runway. **2b** ***trip the light fantastic***: see **FANTASTIC** *adjective* 5b. **3** *Field* The managing director's wife . . likes the idea of tripping up to London for her shopping. **4** H. FERGUSON The bunch with whom I used to trip out and smoke pot.

▸ **II 5** *verb trans.* Cause to stumble or fall by suddenly catching or entangling the foot against an object etc. Freq. foll. by *up*. **LME.**
6 *verb intrans.* Strike the foot against something so as to stumble or fall; (of the tongue or speaker) stumble in articulation, falter in speaking. Freq. foll. by *on* or *over* an obstacle, *up*. **LME.** ▸**b** *WATCHMAKING.* Of an escape wheel: release itself from the pallet. **M19.**
7 a *verb intrans.* Make a mistake or blunder; fall into an inconsistency or error. **E16.** ▸**b** *verb trans.* Cause to make a mistake or blunder; detect in an inconsistency or error. **M16.**

📖 **5** *Idler Magazine* He thrust out his ski staff and tripped up his companion. M. HOCKING The floor was stone-flagged with rugs cast about here and there to trip the unwary. **6** J. MCGAHERN Tie your shoes or you'll trip. M. STOTT I tripped over an uneven paving stone. D. SHIELDS They trip over this *t*, fumble with that *f*. ***trip over oneself*** *colloq.* = ***fall over oneself*** (b) s.v. **FALL** *verb*. **7a** SWIFT Many endeavours to catch me tripping in some part of my story.

▸ **III 8** *NAUTICAL.* **a** *verb intrans.* Of an anchor: become released and raised from the bottom by means of a cable etc. **E17.** ▸**b** *verb trans.* Release and raise (an anchor) from the bottom thus. **M18.**
9 a *verb trans.* Tilt (a thing); *spec.* in *NAUTICAL*, turn (a yard etc.) from a horizontal to a vertical position for lowering. **M19.** ▸**b** *verb intrans.* Tilt, tip up; *spec.* in *NAUTICAL*, (of a ship's floor) be strained or twisted out of the horizontal. **M19.**
10 a *verb trans.* Release (a catch, lever, etc.) by contact with a projection; start (a mechanism) in this way. Also more widely, cause to start operating or responding by some simple change in external state or condition; *spec.* in *ELECTRONICS*, cause (a bistable device) to change from one stable state to the other; (foll. by *out*) disconnect electrically, esp. as an automatic action. **L19.** ▸**b** *verb intrans.* Of a mechanism etc.: undergo a sudden change of state, begin or (foll. by *out*) cease to operate. **M20.**
11 *verb trans.* *BOTANY.* Operate the pollination mechanism of (certain flowers) by disturbing the keel so that the anthers and style spring out of it. **E20.**

📖 **10a** P. THEROUX Any movement it detected caused a blink that tripped a signal and activated a beam.

tripack /ˈtrʌɪpak/ *noun.* **E20.**
[from **TRI-** + **PACK** *noun*.]
PHOTOGRAPHY. A set of three superimposed plates or films with different colour sensitivities and kept in contact, so that three separation negatives can be obtained at one exposure. Now usu. (in full ***integral tripack***), a film having three such emulsions on the one base.

tripalmitin /trʌɪˈpalmɪtɪn/ *noun.* **M19.**
[from **TRI-** + **PALMITIN**.]
CHEMISTRY. A naturally occurring triglyceride, $C_3H_5(C_{16}H_{31}O_2)_3$, found in palm oil and in many animal and vegetable fats and oils. Also called ***palmitin***.

tripart /ˈtrʌɪpɑːt/ *adjective.* *rare.* **L16.**
[from **TRI-** + **PART** *noun*.]
Tripartite, threefold.

triparted /trʌɪˈpɑːtɪd/ *adjective.* **LME.**
[from **TRI-** + **PARTED** *adjective*¹ or from Old French *triparti* or Latin *tripartitus*: see **TRIPARTITE**, **-ED**¹.]
Tripartite; *spec.* in *HERALDRY*, (of a cross) having each of the members consisting of three narrow bands with spaces between.

tripartisan /ˌtrʌɪpɑːtɪˈzan/ *adjective.* **M20.**
[from **TRI-** + **PARTISAN** *adjective*.]
Of, representing, or composed of members of three (political etc.) parties.

tripartism /trʌɪˈpɑːtɪz(ə)m/ *noun.* **M20.**
[from next + **-ISM**.]
1 Division into three political parties or other groups. **M20.**
2 A system involving representatives of three groups engaging in consultation, negotiation, or joint action; *spec.* a system of economic planning by representatives of government, employers, and trade unions. **M20.**

tripartite /trʌɪˈpɑːtʌɪt/ *adjective & noun.* **LME.**
[Latin *tripartitus* pa. pple of *tripartire*, formed as **TRI-** + **PARTITE**.]
▸ **A** *adjective.* **1** Divided into or consisting of three parts or kinds; involving or of the nature of division into three parts. **LME.**
2 Shared by or involving three parties; *spec.* (of an indenture) drawn up between three people and made in three copies. **LME.**
3 *BOTANY.* Divided into three segments almost to the base. **M18.**

📖 **1** J. GROSS His . . tripartite division of poetry into the Pure, the Ornate, the Grotesque. **2** B. VINE The tripartite discussion between Cosette, Ivor and Admetus.

▸ **B** *noun.* A tripartite book, document, treatise, etc. **L15.**
■ **tripartitely** *adverb* **E17.**

tripartition /trʌɪpɑːˈtɪʃ(ə)n/ *noun.* **M17.**
[Late Latin *tripartitio(n-)*, from *tripartire* divide into three: see prec., **-ION**.]
Division into three parts.

tripe /trʌɪp/ *noun.* **ME.**
[Old & mod. French = Provençal *tripa*, Italian *trippa*, of unkn. origin.]
▸ **I 1** *collect. sing.* & (now *rare*) in *pl.* The first or second stomach of a ruminant, esp. of a cow, prepared as food. Formerly also, the intestines of a pig or a fish regarded as food. **ME.**
2 *sing.* & in *pl.* A person's intestines, bowels, or guts; the paunch, the belly. *arch.* **LME.** ▸**b** A contemptible or repulsive person. *derog. arch.* **L16.**
3 Worthless material; rubbish, nonsense. *colloq.* **L17.**
1 ***black tripe***: see **BLACK** *adjective*. ***honeycomb tripe***: see **HONEYCOMB** *noun* 4. ***plain tripe***: see **PLAIN** *adjective*¹. ***rock tripe***: see **ROCK** *noun*¹.

▸†**II 4** Imitation velvet; velveteen, fustian. Also ***tripe of velvet***, ***tripe velvet***. **LME–E18.**

Comb.: **tripe-hound** *slang derog.* (*a*) an unpleasant or contemptible person; (*b*) a newspaper reporter; an informant; (*c*) a dog, *spec.* (*Austral. & NZ*) a sheepdog; ***tripe velvet***: see sense 4 above.
■ **tripelike** *adjective* resembling (that of) tripe **L19.** **tripery** *noun* a place for the preparation or sale of tripe **E17.** **tripey** *adjective* (*colloq.*) inferior, rubbishy, worthless **M20.**

triped /ˈtrʌɪpɛd/ *noun.* **E20.**
[Latin *triped-*, *tripes*, formed as **TRI-** + *ped-*, *pes* foot.]
A three-footed animal.

tripedal /trʌɪˈpiːd(ə)l/ *adjective.* *rare.* **E17.**
[Latin *tripedalis*, formed as prec. + **-AL**¹.]
Orig., three feet long. Now, having three feet, three-footed.

tripe de roche /trip də rɔʃ/ *noun phr.* *Canad.* **M18.**
[French.]
= ***rock tripe*** s.v. **ROCK** *noun*¹.

tripelennamine /trʌɪpəˈlɛnəmiːn/ *noun.* **M20.**
[from **TRI-** + **P**(**YRIDINE** + ***e(thy)len(edi)amine*** s.v. **ETHYLENE**.]
PHARMACOLOGY. An ethylenediamine derivative, $C_{16}H_{21}N_3$, used as an antihistamine drug.
¶ A proprietary name for this drug is **PYRIBENZAMINE**.

tripeptide /trʌɪˈpɛptʌɪd/ *noun.* **E20.**
[from **TRI-** + **PEPTONE** + **-IDE**.]
CHEMISTRY. Any peptide containing three amino-acid residues in its molecule.

tri-personal /trʌɪˈpəːs(ə)n(ə)l/ *adjective.* **M17.**
[from **TRI-** + **PERSON** *noun* + **-AL**¹.]
CHRISTIAN THEOLOGY. Of God: consisting of or existing in three persons. Also, of or pertaining to the three persons of God.
■ **tripersonalism** *noun* the doctrine or theory of God's three persons **L19.** **tripersonalist** *noun* an adherent or advocate of the doctrine of tripersonalism **M19.** **triperso'nality** *noun* the condition of being tripersonal, existence in three persons **M19.** **tripersonally** *adverb* **E20.**

triphane /ˈtrʌɪfeɪn/ *noun.* Now *rare.* **E19.**
[French from Greek *triphanēs* appearing threefold (with ref. to its cleavage).]
MINERALOGY. = **SPODUMENE**.

triphibian /trʌɪˈfɪbɪən/ *noun.* **M20.**
[from **TRI-** + **AM**)**PHIBIAN**.]
A person or thing capable of existing or operating in three different spheres, esp. on land, on water, and in the air.

triphibious /trʌɪˈfɪbɪəs/ *adjective.* **M20.**
[from **TRI-** + **AM**)**PHIBIOUS**.]
Capable of existing or operating in three different spheres, esp. on land, on water, and in the air; *spec.* of or pertaining to military operations involving land, sea, and air forces.
■ **triphibiously** *adverb* (*rare*) **L20.**

triphthong /ˈtrɪfθɒŋ/ *noun.* **M16.**
[French *triphtongue*, from *tri-* **TRI-**, after **DIPHTHONG**.]
A union of three vowels pronounced in one syllable. Also, a combination of three vowel characters representing the sound of a single vowel; a vocalic trigraph.
■ **triph'thongal** *adjective* of, pertaining to, or of the nature of a triphthong **M18.**

triphylite /ˈtrɪfɪlʌɪt/ *noun.* **M19.**
[from **TRI-** + Greek *phulē* tribe + **-ITE**¹ (as containing three metals).]
MINERALOGY. A greenish-grey or blue-green orthorhombic phosphate of lithium and iron often containing some magnesium and forming a series with lithiophilite.
■ Also †**triphyline** *noun*: only in **M19.**

tripinnate /trʌɪˈpɪneɪt/ *adjective.* **M18.**
[from **TRI-** + **PINNATE**.]
BOTANY. Of a bipinnate leaf: having the secondary divisions themselves pinnate.
■ **tripinnatifid** /-ˈnatɪfɪd/ *adjective* bipinnatifid with the secondary divisions themselves pinnatifid **M19.**

tripla /ˈtrɪplə/ *noun.* **M16.**
[Latin, fem. of *triplus* **TRIPLE** *adjective*.]
MUSIC. Triple proportion between one note and another; triple time or rhythm.

triplane /ˈtrʌɪpleɪn/ *noun.* **E20.**
[from **TRI-** + **PLANE** *noun*⁴.]
An aeroplane having three sets of wings, one above the other.

triplasian /trʌɪˈpleɪsɪən, -ʃ(ə)n/ *adjective.* *rare.* **L17.**
[from Greek *triplasios*: see **-IAN**.]
Threefold, triple.
■ Also **triplasic** /-ˈpleɪzɪk, -ˈplazɪk/ *adjective* **M19.**

For other words beginning with *tri-* see the entry for **tri-**

triple /ˈtrɪp(ə)l/ *noun*. LME.
[Use as noun of next. Cf. TREBLE *noun*.]
1 A threefold number, quantity, etc.; a thing consisting of three parts etc.; a set of three; an amount or quantity three times as great as another. LME.
2 †**a** *MUSIC*. Treble quality; a treble part or voice. L16–E17. ▸†**b** *MUSIC*. Triple measure or rhythm. L16–M18. ▸**c** (*CAMPANOLOGY*) in *pl.* Changes rung on seven bells in which three couples of bells change places in the order of ringing. L18. ▸**d** *BASEBALL*. A hit enabling the batter to reach third base. L19. ▸**e** *HORSE-RACING*. = TRIFECTA. L20. ▸**f** A drink of spirits of three times the standard measure. L20. ▸**g** A motorcycle with a three-cylinder engine. L20. ▸**h** In *pl.* A road train consisting of a lorry and three trailers. *colloq.* L20.

📖 **1** H. ANGELO To add more than triple to his income. JOYCE He pressed . . a triple of keys. **2d** *Chicago Tribune* He made in succession a single, double, triple, and home run. **f** R. RENDELL Guy fetched himself a drink, a very large brandy, a triple.

triple /ˈtrɪp(ə)l/ *adjective & adverb*. ME.
[Old & mod. French *triple* or Latin *triplus* from Greek *triplous*. Cf. TREBLE *adjective & adverb*.]
▶ **A** *adjective*. **1** Consisting of three members, things, layers, sets, etc.; threefold; involving three parties; existing or occurring three times or in three ways; of three kinds. ME.
2 Three times as much or many; of three times the, or three times *the*, measure, amount, or capacity; treble; *spec.* (of a drink of spirits) constituting three times the standard measure. M16.
†**3** That is one of three, third. *rare* (Shakes.). Only in E17.

📖 **1** G. GROTE The trireme . . with a triple bank of oars. H. JOLLY His triple immunization against whooping couch, diphtheria and tetanus. G. KEILLOR Our TV set . . was receiving triple and quadruple shadow images. *Spin* A triple-layer fudge cake. **2** W. RALEIGH Great conquests are won to repay the charges of Warre with triple interest. C. LUCAS The quantity should not be less than triple the weight of the solids consumed.

▶ **B** *adverb*. To three times the amount or extent; three times over, triply, thrice. E17.

📖 R. BENTLEY If we had double or triple as many. P. USTINOV The door was triple locked!

Special collocations & comb.: **triple-A** *Military slang* anti-aircraft artillery. **triple agent** = ***treble agent*** s.v. TREBLE *adjective & adverb*. **triple alliance** an alliance of three States, powers, groups, etc. **triple bond** *CHEMISTRY* three covalent bonds between the same two atoms. **triple century** a score or total of 300, esp. in cricket. **triple crown** (*a*) *ROMAN CATHOLIC CHURCH* the Pope's tiara; (*b*) the action of winning all three of a group of important events in horse-racing, rugby football, etc. **triple-decker** *noun & adjective* (designating) something with three decks or layers; *spec.* (designating) a sandwich consisting of three layers of bread and two layers of filling. ***triple harp***: see HARP *noun*. **triple-headed** *adjective* (*a*) having three heads, three-headed; (*b*) (of a train) pulled by three locomotives. **triple-header** (*a*) (chiefly *US*) a three-headed thing; a situation, occurrence, etc., having three aspects or involving three participants; (*b*) a train pulled by three locomotives; (*c*) *N. Amer.* a sporting event at which three consecutive matches are staged. **triple jump** an athletic exercise or contest comprising a hop, a step, and a jump. **triple play** *BASEBALL* an act or instance of putting out three runners in a row. **triple point** (*a*) *PHYSICS* the temperature and pressure at which the solid, liquid, and vapour phases of a pure substance can coexist in equilibrium; the point on a diagram representing this; an analogous point of equilibrium or stability between three phases of a system; (*b*) *GEOMETRY* a point common to three branches of a curve, or at which a curve has three tangents. **triple rhyme**: involving three syllables in each rhyming line. **triple salt** *CHEMISTRY* a salt which when crystalline is composed of three simple salts (which it usu. yields in solution) and has different properties from each. **triple-spaced** *adjective* typed or formatted so that two blank lines separate adjacent lines of text. **triple spacing**: in which two blank lines separate adjacent lines of (esp. typewritten) text. **triple-tail** a brownish fish of warm seas, *Lobotes surinamensis*, having the dorsal and anal fins extended into lobes resembling extra tail-fins. ***triple tiara***: see TIARA 2. **triple time** *MUSIC* (*a*) a rhythm with three beats in the bar; (*b*) a rhythm made three times as fast as the previous rhythm. **triple tonguing** *MUSIC*: in which alternate movements of the tongue are made (usu. as in sounding *ttk*) to facilitate rapid playing of a wind instrument. **triple tree** *arch. slang* a gallows. **triple vaccine** *MEDICINE* (*a*) a vaccine containing three strains of *Salmonella*, used against typhoid and paratyphoid; (*b*) a vaccine containing diphtheria and tetanus toxoids and killed whooping cough bacteria, administered in early childhood.
■ **tripleness** *noun* (*rare*) L19.

triple /ˈtrɪp(ə)l/ *verb*. LME.
[Late Latin *triplare*, from Latin *triplus* TRIPLE *adjective*. Cf. TREBLE *verb*.]
1 *verb trans.* Make three times as much or as many; multiply by three; make triple. LME. ▸**b** Fold in three thicknesses. *rare*. L16. ▸**c** Amount to three times as many or as much as. *rare*. L16.
2 *verb intrans.* Become three times as much as or as many. L18.
3 *verb intrans.* *BASEBALL*. Hit a triple. E20.

📖 **1** R. MERRY They force its tripled walls. A. STORR I would try to triple the price of alcohol. **2** *Times* The number of doctors in France has tripled in the past 20 years.

tripler /ˈtrɪplə/ *noun*. E20.
[from TRIPLE *verb* + -ER[1].]
ELECTRONICS. A device for producing an output whose frequency or whose voltage is three times that of the input.

triplet /ˈtrɪplɪt/ *noun*. M17.
[from TRIPLE *adjective* + -ET[1], after *doublet*.]
1 a A group of three successive lines of verse, esp. when rhyming together and of the same length. M17. ▸**b** Each of three children or animals born at one birth. Freq. in *pl.* L18. ▸**c** *MUSIC*. A group of three notes to be played in the time of two of the same time-value. E19. ▸**d** *ARCHITECTURE*. A group of three single-light windows. M19. ▸**e** *POKER*, in *pl.* Three cards of the same denomination. M19. ▸**f** *PHYSICS & CHEMISTRY*. A spectral multiplet composed of three lines or energy levels; an atomic or molecular state characterized by two unpaired electrons with parallel spins. L19. ▸**g** *PARTICLE PHYSICS*. A multiplet of three subatomic particles. M20.
2 *gen.* A set of three persons or things. M18.
f *LORENTZ* ***triplet***.
Comb.: **triplet code** *GENETICS* the standard version of the genetic code in which amino acids are specified by three successive nucleotides (a codon) in a nucleic acid molecule; **triplet lily** a plant of the south-western US, *Triteleia laxa* (family Amaryllidaceae), which is grown for its purple-blue tubular flowers (so called from the floral parts being arranged in threes).

triplex /ˈtrɪplɛks/ *noun, adjective, & verb*. LME.
[Latin *triplex*, *-plic-*, threefold, formed as TRI- + *plicare* fold.]
▶ **A** *noun*. †**1** *CHRISTIAN THEOLOGY*. The Trinity. *rare*. Only in LME.
2 (Usu. **T-**.) (Proprietary name for) a type of toughened or laminated glass for car windows etc., orig. consisting of two layers of glass sandwiching a layer of celluloid. E20.
3 An apartment or flat on three floors. Also, a building containing three self-contained apartments or flats; each of the flats etc. in such a building. Cf. DUPLEX *noun* 1. Chiefly *N. Amer.* M20.
▶ **B** *adjective*. Triple, threefold. E17.
▶ **C** *verb trans.* Provide or fit (equipment etc.) in triplicate so as to ensure reliability. L20.

triplicate /ˈtrɪplɪkət/ *adjective & noun*. LME.
[Latin *triplicat-* pa. ppl stem of *triplicare*, formed as prec.: see -ATE[2].]
▶ **A** *adjective*. Triple, consisting of three corresponding parts; existing in three copies or examples; being one of such copies etc. Also, tripled, consisting of three times the number or quantity. LME.

📖 H. BEVERIDGE A triplicate treaty by the British Government, the Maharajah, and Shah Shujah-ul-Moolk.

▶ **B** *noun*. Each of three things exactly alike, a third copy or corresponding part. L18.

📖 WELLINGTON I . . enclose the triplicate of a letter to the Governor of Bombay. J. E. TENNENT Not only a duplicate, but a triplicate of the . . relic were regarded with . . adoration. **in triplicate** in three exactly corresponding copies.

triplicate /ˈtrɪplɪkeɪt/ *verb trans.* E17.
[formed as prec. + -ATE[3].]
1 Multiply by three; triple. E17.
2 Make or be a third copy of, provide in triplicate; repeat a second time. M17.

triplication /trɪplɪˈkeɪʃ(ə)n/ *noun*. L16.
[Anglo-Norman *triplicacioun* or late Latin *triplicatio(n-)*, formed as prec.: see -ATION.]
1 *LAW* (now *Hist.*). A plaintiff's reply or surrejoinder to a defendant's rejoinder. Also occas., a rejoinder. L16.
2 The action or process of triplicating something; an instance of this; a triplicated thing. E17.

triplice /ˈtriːplɪtʃi/ *noun*. Also **T-**. L19.
[Italian = triple.]
An alliance of three States or powers; *spec.* (**T-**) that formed in 1882 between Germany, Austria-Hungary, and Italy against Russia and France.
■ **triplicist** /-sɪst/ *noun* a supporter of a triplice E20.

triplicity /trɪˈplɪsɪti/ *noun*. LME.
[Late Latin *triplicitas*, formed as TRIPLEX: see -ITY.]
1 a *ASTROLOGY*. Each of four sets of three signs of the zodiac (***airy triplicity***, ***earthy triplicity***, ***fiery triplicity***, ***water triplicity***), each sign being 120° distant from the other two. LME. ▸**b** A combination or group of three things or people, a trio. (Foll. by *of*.) L16.
2 The quality or state of being triple; threefold character, tripleness. M16.

triplo- /ˈtrɪpləʊ/ *combining form*.
[from Greek *triploos*, *triplous* threefold, triple: see -O-. Cf. DIPLO-.]
Triple.
■ **triploˈblastic** *adjective* [-BLAST] *ZOOLOGY* having an ectoderm, mesoderm, and endoderm, as in most animal groups other than coelenterates L19.

triploid /ˈtrɪplɔɪd/ *noun & adjective*. M18.
[from TRIPLO- + -OID. In senses A.2, B. prob. from TRI- + -PLOID after *diploid*.]
▶ **A** *noun*. †**1** *SURGERY*. A three-branched instrument used to raise depressed bones of the cranium. *rare*. Only in M18.
2 *BIOLOGY*. A triploid cell or organism. E20.
▶ **B** *adjective*. *BIOLOGY*. (Of a cell) containing three homologous sets of chromosomes; (of an individual) composed of diploid cells. E20.
■ **triploidy** *noun* (*BIOLOGY*) triploid condition E20.

triplum /ˈtrɪpləm/ *noun*. Pl. **-la** /-lə/. L18.
[medieval Latin, neut. of *triplus* TRIPLE *adjective*.]
MUSIC. In medieval polyphonic vocal music, the third and highest voice part. Also, a composition for three voices. Cf. TREBLE *noun* 1.

triply /trɪˈplʌɪ/ *verb & noun*. *obsolete* exc. *Hist.* E16.
[Old French *tripliquer*. Cf. DUPLY, QUADRUPLY *noun*.]
SCOTS LAW. ▶**A** *verb intrans.* Make a triply, reply to a defendant's rejoinder. E16.
▶ **B** *noun*. = TRIPLICATION 1. M16.

triply /ˈtrɪpli/ *adverb*. M17.
[from TRIPLE *adjective* + -LY[2].]
In a triple degree or manner; three times.

📖 M. R. MITFORD Heart-shaped and triply folded. *Essays in Criticism* Triply disqualified . . on grounds of class, nation and sex.

trip-madam /trɪpˈmadəm/ *noun*. L17.
[French *tripe-madame* alt. of earlier *trique-madame* TRICK-MADAM.]
= TRICK-MADAM.

tripod /ˈtrʌɪpɒd/ *noun & adjective*. E17.
[Latin *tripod-*, *tripus* from Greek *tripod-*, *tripous*, from *tri-* TRI- + *pod-*, *pous* foot.]
▶ **A** *noun*. **1** A three-legged stool, seat, or table; a utensil, pot, or cauldron resting on three legs; *CLASSICAL ANTIQUITIES* a similar ornamental vessel freq. presented as a prize or offering. Cf. TRIVET *noun* 2. E17.
2 *GREEK ANTIQUITIES*. A three-legged bronze altar at the shrine of Apollo at Delphi, on which the priestess sat to deliver oracles; the Delphic oracle; *gen.* an oracle. Cf. TRIVET *noun* 2b. E17.
3 A three-legged support; *spec.* a frame or stand with three usu. collapsible legs for supporting a camera, telescope, etc. E19.
4 *ANATOMY & ZOOLOGY*. A bone or other structure with three projections. *rare*. L19.
▶ **B** *adjective*. Having or resting on three feet, legs, or supports; three-footed, three-legged; of the form of a tripod. E18.
■ **tripodal** /ˈtrɪpəd(ə)l/ *adjective* = TRIPOD *adjective* L18.

tripody /ˈtrɪpədi/ *noun*. L19.
[from TRI- + DI)PODY.]
PROSODY. A measure or verse of three feet, a triple foot.

tripoli /ˈtrɪpəli/ *noun*. E17.
[French from *Tripoli*, either of two towns on the Mediterranean, one in Lebanon, the other the capital of Libya.]
1 = ***ROTTEN-stone***. E17.
2 A large, mild onion; the plant producing a bulb of this kind. Also ***tripoli onion***. E19.
1 ***tripoli polish***, ***tripoli powder***, ***tripoli stone***.

Tripoline /ˈtrɪpəliːn/ *adjective & noun*. L17.
[Senses A.1, B. from *Tripoli* in Libya; sense A.2 formed as prec.: see -INE[1].]
▶ **A** *adjective*. **1** Of or pertaining to Tripoli, the capital of Libya. L17.
2 (**t-**.) Of or pertaining to tripoli or rotten-stone. M18.
▶ **B** *noun*. A native or inhabitant of Tripoli. M19.

Tripolitan /trɪˈpɒlɪtən/ *adjective & noun*. L18.
[Italian *tripolitano*, or formed as next: see -AN.]
▶ **A** *adjective*. = TRIPOLINE *adjective* 1. Also = TRIPOLITANIAN *adjective*. L18.
▶ **B** *noun*. = TRIPOLITANIAN *noun*. L18.

Tripolitanian /trɪˌpɒlɪˈteɪnɪən/ *noun & adjective*. M20.
[from *Tripolitania* (see below) + -AN.]
▶ **A** *noun*. A native or inhabitant of Tripolitania, the region surrounding Tripoli in N. Africa. M20.
▶ **B** *adjective*. Of or pertaining to Tripolitania. M20.

Tripolye /trɪˈpɒljə/ *noun*. Also **-je**. E20.
[See below.]
Used ***attrib.*** to designate a neolithic culture in western Ukraine and eastern Romania during the late fourth and third millennia BC, typified by remains found at Tripolye, a village near Kiev, Ukraine.

tripos /ˈtrʌɪpɒs/ *noun*. L16.
[Alt. of Latin *tripus* TRIPOD.]
†**1** = TRIPOD *noun* 1, 2. L16–E19.
2 *Cambridge Univ.* **a** (**T-**.) A graduate appointed to make a humorous or satirical speech at commencement, while sitting on a three-legged stool. Cf. TERRAE FILIUS 2. *obsolete* exc. *Hist.* M17. ▸**b** A set of humorous verses published at commencement, orig. composed by the Tripos (also ***tripos verses***); the list of successful candidates for the

honours degree in mathematics, orig. printed on the back of these verses (also *tripos list*). *obsolete* exc. *Hist.* **M17.** ▸**c** (Freq. **T-**.) The final honours examination for the BA degree, orig. in mathematics but now in any subject. **M19.**

tripot /tripo/ *noun.* Pl. pronounced same. **M19.**
[French.]
In France: a gaming-house, a gambling-den.

tripotage /tripɔta:ʒ/ *noun.* **L18.**
[French.]
Underhand dealings, intrigue. Also (*rare*), pawing, handling, fingering.

trippage /ˈtrɪpɪdʒ/ *noun.* **M20.**
[from **TRIP** *noun*[1] + **-AGE**.]
The act or process of making a series of trips or short journeys over the same route; the number of such journeys made.

trippant /ˈtrɪp(ə)nt/ *adjective.* **M17.**
[Old French, pres. pple of *tripper* **TRIP** *verb*: see **-ANT**[1].]
HERALDRY. = **TRIPPING** *ppl adjective* 3. Usu. *postpositive.*

tripper /ˈtrɪpə/ *noun & verb.* **LME.**
[from **TRIP** *verb* + **-ER**[1].]
▶ **A** *noun.* **1** A person who moves with quick light steps. **LME.**
2 A person who or thing which stumbles or causes a person to stumble. **E17.**
3 A person who goes on a trip or short journey for pleasure. Freq. in *day-tripper*. **E19.**
4 An employee, esp. a tram conductor, paid by the trip or journey. *US.* **L19.**
5 *MECHANICS.* A device for tripping something; a trip. **L19.**
6 A person experiencing hallucinations induced by a drug, esp. LSD. *colloq.* **M20.**

🕮 **3** I. MURDOCH This rocky coast attracts . . no trippers with their 'kiddies'.

▶ **B** *verb intrans.* Go on a trip or excursion, behave like a tripper. *colloq. rare.* **M20.**
■ **tripperish** *adjective* (*colloq.*, freq. *derog.*) = **TRIPPERY** **M20.** **tripperishness** *noun* (*colloq.*, freq. *derog.*) **L19.** **trippery** *adjective* (*colloq.*, freq. *derog.*) of, pertaining to, or characterized by trippers, touristy **E20.** **trippist** *noun* (*colloq.*, *rare*) = **TRIPPER** *noun* 3 **L18.**

trippet /ˈtrɪpɪt/ *noun*[1]. **ME.**
[Sense 1 from Old French *tripo(u)t*; senses 2 & 3 from **TRIP** *noun*[1] or *verb* + **-ET**[1].]
†**1** An evil scheme; a malicious trick or plot. Only in **ME.**
†**2** An act of tripping someone up, a trip. **LME–E18.**
3 The tapered piece of wood used in tipcat; the game itself. *north.* **LME.**

trippet /ˈtrɪpɪt/ *noun*[2]. Now *north.* **M16.**
[Alt.]
A trivet.

tripping /ˈtrɪpɪŋ/ *adjective.* **M16.**
[from **TRIP** *verb* + **-ING**[2].]
1 Moving with quick light steps, nimble. **M16.**
2 Stumbling, erring, sinning. **M16.**
3 *HERALDRY.* Of a buck, stag, etc.: = **PASSANT** 2. **M16.**
4 *MECHANICS.* Of a device: that trips something. **L19.**
4 *tripping-circuit*, *tripping-lever*, etc.
■ **trippingly** *adverb* **LME.** **trippingness** *noun* **E19.**

tripple /ˈtrɪp(ə)l/ *noun. S. Afr.* **L19.**
[from **TRIPPLE** *verb*[2].]
A horse's gait, resembling the amble.

tripple /ˈtrɪp(ə)l/ *verb*[1] *intrans. obsolete* exc. *dial.* **E17.**
[Frequentative of **TRIP** *verb*: see **-LE**[3].]
Trip, move lightly; dance, skip.

tripple /ˈtrɪp(ə)l/ *verb*[2] *intrans. S. Afr.* **L19.**
[Dutch *trippelen*, from *trippen* trip, skip.]
Of a horse or rider: go at a tripple.
■ **trippler** *noun* **E20.**

trippy /ˈtrɪpi/ *adjective. colloq.* **M20.**
[from **TRIP** *noun*[1] + **-Y**[1].]
Of, pertaining to, or resembling a hallucinatory experience induced by a drug, esp. LSD; mind-expanding, psychedelic.

🕮 *New Age* Trippy music for meditation, massage . . and a relaxing environment.

■ **trippiness** *noun* **L20.**

tripsome /ˈtrɪps(ə)m/ *adjective.* Now *rare.* **M19.**
[from **TRIP** *noun*[1] or *verb* + **-SOME**[1].]
Characterized by tripping, nimble.
■ **tripsomely** *adverb* **E19.**

triptane /ˈtrɪpteɪn/ *noun.* **M20.**
[from **TRI-** + arbitrary *-p-* + **BUTANE**.]
A liquid branched paraffin used as a high-octane aviation fuel; trimethylbutane, $CH_3CH(CH_3)C(CH_3)_2CH_3$.

tripton /ˈtrɪptɒn/ *noun.* **M20.**
[German from Greek *tripton* neut. of *triptos* that which is rubbed or pounded, from *tribein* rub, pound: cf. **PLANKTON**.]
BIOLOGY & OCEANOGRAPHY. The non-living part of the fine particulate matter suspended in water. Cf. **SESTON**.

triptote /ˈtrɪptəʊt/ *noun & adjective.* **E17.**
[Latin *triptota* pl. from Greek *triptōta* neut. pl. from *triptōtos*, from *tri-* **TRI-** + *ptōtos* falling (*ptōsis* case). Cf. **DIPTOTE**.]
GRAMMAR. (A noun) having only three cases.

triptych /ˈtrɪptɪk/ *noun.* In sense 4 also **triptyque** /trɪpˈtiːk; *foreign* triptik (*pl. same*)/. **M18.**
[from **TRI-** + **DI)PTYCH**.]
1 a *ANTIQUITIES.* A set of three writing-tablets hinged or tied together. **M18.** ▸**b** A card made to fold in three divisions. **E20.**
2 A picture, relief carving, or set of such on three panels, usu. hinged vertically so as to allow the sides to fold over the central panel and freq. used as an altarpiece. Also, a set of three thematically connected paintings etc. hung together. **M19.**
3 a A set of three operas or pieces of music intended to be performed together. **E20.** ▸**b** *CINEMATOGRAPHY.* A sequence of film designed to be shown on a triple screen, using linked projectors. **L20.**
4 A customs permit (orig. in three sections) serving as a passport for a motor vehicle. **E20.**

tripudiate /trʌɪˈpjuːdɪeɪt/ *verb intrans.* Now *arch. rare.* **E17.**
[Latin *tripudiat-* pa. ppl stem of *tripudiare*, from *tripudium* dancing, a dance (prob. from *tri-* **TRI-** + *pod-*, *pous* foot): see **-ATE**[3].]
1 Dance or leap for joy or with excitement. **E17.**
2 Trample or stamp (*on*) in contempt or triumph. **L19.**
■ **tripudiant** *adjective* dancing; *fig.* exultant, triumphant: **E17.** **tripudiˈation** *noun* the action of dancing or leaping, esp. in joy or excitement **E17.** **tripudist** /ˈtrɪpjʊdɪst/ *noun* a person who tripudiates **M19.**

tripudium /trɪˈpjuːdɪəm/ *noun.* **E20.**
[Latin: see prec.]
ROMAN HISTORY. A ritual dance performed by the Salii or priests of Mars.

tripus /ˈtrʌɪpəs/ *noun.* **L17.**
[Latin: see **TRIPOD**.]
†**1 a** = **TRIPOS** 2a. *rare.* Only in **L17.** ▸**b** = **TRIPOD** *noun* 1. *rare.* Only in **L17.**
2 *ZOOLOGY.* In cyprinoid fishes, the last ossicle in the Weberian apparatus, touching the swim-bladder. **L19.**

trip-wire /ˈtrɪpwʌɪə/ *noun.* Also **tripwire**. **E20.**
[from **TRIP** *noun*[1] or *verb* + **WIRE** *noun*.]
1 A wire stretched close to the ground in order to trip up enemies, trespassers, etc., or operate a weapon or alarm. **E20.**
2 *fig.* A comparatively weak military force employed as a first line of defence, engagement with which will trigger the intervention of stronger forces. **M20.**

Trique /ˈtriːkeɪ/ *noun & adjective.* **L19.**
[Mixtecan.]
▶ **A** *noun.* Pl. **-s**, same.
1 An American Indian people of Oaxaca, Mexico. **L19.**
2 The Mixtecan language of this people. **E20.**
▶ **B** *adjective.* Of or pertaining to this people or their language. **E20.**

triquetra /trʌɪˈkwɛtrə, -ˈkwiːtrə/ *noun.* Pl. **-trae** /-triː/, **-tras**. **L16.**
[Latin, fem. of *triquetrus*: see **TRIQUETROUS**.]
Orig., a triangle. Now *spec.* a symmetrical triangular ornament formed of three interlaced arcs or lobes.

triquetral /trʌɪˈkwɛtr(ə)l, -ˈkwiːt-/ *adjective & noun.* **M17.**
[formed as next + **-AL**[1].]
▶ **A** *adjective.* = **TRIQUETROUS**. **M17.**
triquetral bone *ANATOMY* (*a*) a Wormian bone; (*b*) a carpal bone on the ulnar side of the wrist articulating with the pisiform bone.
▶ **B** *noun. ANATOMY.* A triquetral bone. **L20.**

triquetrous /trʌɪˈkwɛtrəs, -ˈkwiːt-/ *adjective.* **M17.**
[from Latin *triquetrus* three-cornered, triangular + **-OUS**.]
Three-sided, triangular; *esp.* (*BOTANY & ZOOLOGY*) triangular (*spec.* sharply triangular) in cross-section. Cf. **TRIGONOUS**.

trireme /ˈtrʌɪriːm/ *noun & adjective.* **L16.**
[Old & mod. French *trirème* or Latin *triremis*, formed as **TRI-** + *remus* oar.]
Hist. ▶**A** *noun.* A galley with three banks of oars. **L16.**
▶ **B** *adjective.* Of a galley: that is a trireme. **L17.**

tris /trɪs/ *noun.* **M20.**
[from the prefix, by abbreviation of systematic chemical names.]
CHEMISTRY. **1** A combustible compound, $(HOCH_2)_3CNH_2$, which forms a corrosive solution in water and is used as a buffer and emulsifying agent. Also *tris buffer*. **M20.**
2 An organophosphorus compound, $(Br_2C_3H_5)_3PO_4$, used as a flame retardant. **L20.**

tris- /trɪs/ *prefix.*
[Greek, from *tris* thrice.]
Thrice, threefold; *spec.* in *CHEMISTRY*, forming names of compounds containing three groups identically substituted or coordinated. Cf. **BIS-**, **TETRAKIS-**.
■ **trisazo** /trɪˈsazəʊ, trɪˈseɪzəʊ/ *adjective* containing three azo groups in the molecule **E20.** **trisoctaˈhedron** *noun*, pl. **-dra**, **-drons**, *GEOMETRY & CRYSTALLOGRAPHY* a solid figure having 24 faces, every three of which correspond to one face of an octahedron **M19.**

For other words beginning with *tri-* see the entry for **tri-**

trisaccharide /trʌɪˈsakərʌɪd/ *noun.* **E20.**
[from **TRI-** + **SACCHARIDE**.]
CHEMISTRY. Any sugar that consists of three monosaccharide residues linked together.

Trisagion /trɪˈsagɪən, -ˈseɪgɪən/ *noun.* Also in Latin form **-agium** /-eɪdʒɪəm/, pl. **-ia** /-ɪə/. **LME.**
[Greek (*to*) *trisagion* neut. of *trisagios* thrice holy, from *tris* thrice + *hagios* holy.]
CHRISTIAN CHURCH. The hymn beginning 'Holy God, Holy and mighty, Holy and immortal', sung esp. at the Little Entrance in the Orthodox Church. Also = **SANCTUS** 1.

trisect /trʌɪˈsɛkt/ *verb trans.* **L17.**
[from **TRI-** + Latin *sect-* pa. ppl stem of *secare* cut, after **BISECT**.]
Cut or divide into three (usu. equal) parts.
■ **trisection** *noun* division into three (equal) parts **M17.** **trisector** *noun* a person who or thing which trisects something **M19.**

triseme /ˈtrʌɪsiːm/ *noun.* **L19.**
[Greek *trisēmos*, from *tri* **TRI-** + *sēma* sign.]
CLASSICAL PROSODY. A foot consisting of three short syllables.

tri-service /trʌɪˈsəːvɪs/ *adjective.* **M20.**
[from **TRI-** + **SERVICE** *noun*[1].]
Of or pertaining to the three armed forces, Army, Navy, and Air Force.

trishaw /ˈtrʌɪʃɔː/ *noun.* **M20.**
[from **TRI-** + **RICK)SHAW**.]
A light three-wheeled pedalled vehicle used in the Far East, esp. as a taxi.

triskaidekaphobia /ˌtrɪskʌɪdɛkəˈfəʊbɪə/ *noun.* **E20.**
[from Greek *treiskaideka* thirteen + **-PHOBIA**.]
Fear of the number thirteen.

triskelion /trɪˈskɛlɪən/ *noun.* Also (earlier) **triskele** /ˈtrɪskiːl/, †**triskelos**. **M19.**
[Greek *tri* **TRI-** + *skelos* leg.]
A symbolic figure consisting of three legs or lines radiating from a common centre.

trismegistic /trɪsmɪˈgɪstɪk/ *adjective. rare.* **L17.**
[Latin *trismegistus* from Greek *trismegistos* lit. 'thrice-greatest', title of the Egyptian god, Hermes + **-IC**.]
Of, pertaining to, or characteristic of the Egyptian god, Hermes.

trismus /ˈtrɪzməs/ *noun.* **L17.**
[mod. Latin from Greek *trismos* = *trigmos* a scream, grinding.]
MEDICINE. Tonic spasm of the muscles in the neck and lower jaw, causing the mouth to remain tightly closed; tetanus characterized by this, lockjaw.

trisomic /trʌɪˈsəʊmɪk/ *adjective & noun.* **E20.**
[from **TRI-** + **-SOME**[3] + **-IC**.]
GENETICS. ▶**A** *adjective.* Of or pertaining to a trisome; exhibiting trisomy. **E20.**
▶ **B** *noun.* A trisomic cell or individual; a chromosome represented three times in a chromosomal complement. **E20.**
■ **ˈtrisome** *noun* = **TRISOMIC** *noun* **E20.** **trisomy** /ˈtrʌɪsəmi/ *noun* trisomic state; freq. with following numeral denoting the chromosome concerned, as *trisomy 21* (associated with Down's syndrome): **M20.**

trist /trɪst/ *noun*[1] *& verb.* Long *obsolete* exc. *dial.* **ME.**
[App. rel. to **TRUST** *noun*.]
▶ **A** *noun.* Trust; confidence, faith. **ME.**
▶ **B** *verb intrans. & trans.* Trust; have confidence or faith (in or that). **ME.**
■ **ˈtristy** *adjective* trusty, trustworthy **ME.**

†**trist** *noun*[2]. **ME–L15.**
[Old French *triste* or medieval Latin *trista*, *tristra*.]
An appointed place or station, esp. in hunting.

†**trist** *adjective* see **TRISTE**.

Tristanesque /trɪstəˈnɛsk/ *adjective.* **M20.**
[from *Tristan* hero of Wagner's opera, *Tristan und Isolde* (1865) + **-ESQUE**.]
Resembling the music of *Tristan und Isolde*; *esp.* characterized by tonal ambiguity and chromaticism.

Tristanian /trɪˈsteɪnɪən/ *noun & adjective.* **E20.**
[from *Tristan* da Cunha (see below) + **-IAN**.]
▶ **A** *noun.* A native or inhabitant of Tristan da Cunha, an island group in the S. Atlantic. **E20.**
▶ **B** *adjective.* Of or pertaining to Tristan da Cunha or its inhabitants. **M20.**

Tristanite /ˈtrɪstənʌɪt/ *noun.* **E20.**
[formed as prec. + **-ITE**[1].]
= **TRISTANIAN** *noun.*

triste /triːst/ *adjective.* Orig. Anglicized as †**trist**. **LME.**
[Old & mod. French from Latin *tristis*.]
1 Feeling or expressing sorrow; sad, melancholy; causing sorrow, lamentable. **LME.**
2 Not lively or cheerful; dull, dreary. **M18.**

🕮 **1** *New Yorker* This artist places the images of inherently sweet things . . in triste landscape settings. **2** O. HENRY The thrumming of lugubrious guitars added to the depression of the *triste* night.

tristesse /trɪˈstɛs/ *noun*. LME.
[Old French *tristesce* (mod. *tristesse*) from Latin *tristitia*, from *tristis*: see prec., -ESS[2].]
Sadness, sorrow; melancholy.

tristeza /trɪˈsteɪzə/ *noun*. E20.
[Portuguese, Spanish, lit. 'sadness', cogn. with prec.]
1 VETERINARY MEDICINE. In S. America, Texas fever of cattle. Now *rare*. E20.
2 AGRICULTURE. A viral disease affecting some citrus plants, causing yellowing of the leaves, stunting, and death. M20.

tristful /ˈtrɪs(t)fʊl, -f(ə)l/ *adjective*. *arch.* L15.
[from †*trist* var. of TRISTE + -FUL.]
Full of sadness or melancholy; sorrowful, doleful.
■ **tristfully** *adverb* M19. **tristfulness** *noun* E20.

tristich /ˈtrɪstɪk/ *noun*. E19.
[from TRI-, after DISTICH. Cf. Greek *tristikhia* set of three verses, from *tristikhos* three-rowed.]
PROSODY. A three-line poem or stanza.
■ **tristichic** /trɪˈstɪkɪk/ *adjective* consisting of or characterized by tristichs L19.

tristichous /ˈtrɪstɪkəs/ *adjective*. M19.
[from Greek *tristikhos* (see prec.) + -OUS.]
BOTANY. Of leaves: arranged alternately to form three vertical rows.

tristimulus /trʌɪˈstɪmjʊləs/ *noun*. Pl. **-li** /-lʌɪ, -liː/. M20.
[from TRI- + STIMULUS.]
OPTICS etc. Each of three reference colours (as red, green, and blue) which can be combined additively in specified proportions to produce any given colour. Usu. *attrib.*, as ***tristimulus specification***, ***tristimulus value***, etc.

tristubh /ˈtrɪʃtʊb/ *noun*. M19.
[Sanskrit *tristubh*.]
A Vedic metre of eleven syllables.

trisul /trɪˈʃuːl/ *noun*. Also **-la** /-lə/. L19.
[Sanskrit *triśūla* trident, from *tri-* three + *śūla* spit.]
A three-pointed figure emblematic of the Hindu god Siva; the same figure used as a Buddhist symbol.

trisyllabic /trʌɪsɪˈlabɪk/ *adjective*. M17.
[French *trissyllabique*, from Latin *trisyllabus* from Greek *trisullabos*, from TRI- + *sullabē* SYLLABLE *noun*: see -IC.]
Of a word or metrical foot: consisting of three syllables.
■ **trisyllabical** *adjective* M17. **trisyllabically** *adverb* M19.

trisyllable /trʌɪˈsɪləb(ə)l/ *noun & adjective*. L16.
[from TRI- + SYLLABLE *noun*. Cf. Latin *trisyllabus*, Greek *trisullabos* adjectives, French *trisyllabe*.]
▶ **A** *noun*. A word or metrical foot of three syllables. L16.
▶ **B** *adjective*. = TRISYLLABIC. *rare*. M18.

trit- *combining form* see TRITO-.

tritagonist /trʌɪˈtag(ə)nɪst, trɪ-/ *noun*. L19.
[Greek *tritagōnistēs*, from *tritos* third + *agōnistēs* AGONIST.]
The person of next importance to the deuteragonist in an ancient Greek drama.

tritanopia /trʌɪtəˈnəʊpɪə/ *noun*. E20.
[from TRIT(O- + AN-[5] + -OPIA.]
OPHTHALMOLOGY. A rare form of dichromatic colour-blindness marked by confusion of blues and greens.
■ **ˈtritanope** *noun* a person who has tritanopia E20. **tritanopic** *adjective* of, pertaining to, or exhibiting tritanopia E20.

tritaph /ˈtrʌɪtɑːf, -taf/ *noun*. *rare*. E20.
[from Greek *tri-* TRI- + *taphos* tomb.]
ARCHAEOLOGY. A group of three burial-chambers in a prehistoric tomb.

trite /ˈtrɪtiː/ *noun*. E17.
[Greek *tritē* fem. of *tritos* third.]
In ancient Greek music, the third note down in an upper tetrachord, immediately below the paranete.

trite /trʌɪt/ *adjective*. M16.
[Latin *tritus* pa. pple of *terere* rub.]
1 No longer novel or fresh; stale through constant use or repetition; hackneyed, commonplace. M16.
2 Physically worn away; well worn, frayed; (of a path) well-beaten. Now *rare*. L16.

> 🕮 **1** *Vanity Fair* Polke continues to use the deliberately trite images of his early paintings. J. TROLLOPE It's so trite to talk about being oneself, but it's what . . I truly feel.

■ **tritely** *adverb* L17. **triteness** *noun* E18. **tritical** /ˈtrɪtɪk(ə)l/ *adjective* (*joc.*) trite, commonplace E18. **tritish** *adjective* L18.

triternate /trʌɪˈtəːneɪt/ *adjective*. M18.
[from TRI- + TERNATE.]
BOTANY. Of a compound leaf: biternate with the secondary divisions themselves being ternate.

tritheism /ˈtrʌɪθiːɪz(ə)m/ *noun*. L17.
[from TRI- + THEISM *noun*[1].]
Belief in three gods; *esp.* (CHRISTIAN THEOLOGY) the doctrine of or belief in the three persons of the Trinity as three distinct gods.

tritheist /ˈtrʌɪθiːɪst/ *noun*. E17.
[from TRI- + THEIST.]
A believer in tritheism.
■ **tritheˈistic** *adjective* of, pertaining to, or believing in tritheism L17. **tritheˈistical** *adjective* = TRITHEISTIC E18.

tritheite /ˈtrʌɪθiːʌɪt/ *noun*. L16.
[Greek *tritheïtēs* from late Latin *tritheita*, from Greek *tri-* TRI- + *theos* god: see -ITE[1].]
= TRITHEIST.

trithing /ˈtrʌɪðɪŋ/ *noun*. Long *obsolete* exc. *Hist.* ME.
[Repr. unrecorded Old English form from Old Norse *þriðjungr* third part, from *þriði* THIRD *adjective*: see -ING[3].]
= RIDING *noun*[1] 1, 2.

tritiated /ˈtrɪtɪeɪtɪd, -ʃɪeɪtɪd/ *adjective*. M20.
[from TRITI(UM + -ATE[3] + -ED[2].]
CHEMISTRY. Containing tritium; having had an atom of ordinary hydrogen replaced by tritium, esp. as a radioactive label.
■ **tritiˈation** *noun* the introduction of tritium into a compound or molecule in place of ordinary hydrogen M20.

triticale /trɪtɪˈkeɪli/ *noun*. M20.
[mod. Latin, from genus names *Triti(cum* wheat + *Se)cale* rye.]
A hybrid between bread wheat, *Triticum aestivum*, and rye, *Secale cereale*.

tritium /ˈtrɪtɪəm/ *noun*. M20.
[from TRITO- + -IUM.]
CHEMISTRY. A radioactive heavy isotope of hydrogen, with two neutrons and a proton in the nucleus, which occurs naturally in minute amounts and is produced artificially for use in fusion reactors, as an isotopic label, etc. (symbols ^{3}H, T).
■ **tritide** *noun* a binary compound of tritium with a metal or radical M20.

trito- /ˈtrɪtəʊ, ˈtrʌɪtəʊ/ *combining form*. Before a vowel also **trit-**.
[Greek, from *tritos* third: see -O-.]
Forming words with the sense 'third, tertiary'. Cf. DEUTERO-.
■ **tritaˈnomalous** *adjective* pertaining to or exhibiting tritanomaly M20. **tritaˈnomaly** *noun* (OPHTHALMOLOGY) a rare form of anomalous trichromatism marked by a reduced sensitivity to blue M20. **tritoˈcerebral** *adjective* (ZOOLOGY) of or pertaining to the tritocerebrum E20. **tritoˈcerebrum** *noun* (ZOOLOGY) the third and hindmost segment of an insect's brain L19. **Trito-Iˈsaiah** *noun* the supposed later author of *Isaiah* 56–66 E20.

tritoma /ˈtrɪtəmə, trʌɪˈtəʊmə/ *noun*. E19.
[mod. Latin (see below), from Greek *tritomos* three-cleft (from the capsule splitting in three).]
Any plant of the former genus *Tritoma* (now *Kniphofia*); a red-hot poker. Cf. KNIPHOFIA.

Triton /ˈtrʌɪt(ə)n/ *noun*[1]. In sense 2 also **t-**. L16.
[Latin from Greek *Tritōn* a minor sea-god, son of Poseidon and Amphitrite in Greek mythol.; in sense 2 from former uses as mod. Latin genus name.]
1 CLASSICAL MYTHOLOGY. A mythical semi-human sea-monster; a merman. L16. ▸**b** *fig.* A person making their living from or otherwise connected with the sea. L16. ▸**c** A representation of a Triton; esp. in HERALDRY, a charge representing a Triton, usu. depicted as a man with a fish's tail carrying a trident and shell-trumpet. E17.
2 ZOOLOGY. **a** A tropical marine gastropod of the family Cymatiidae; the pointed spiral shell of such a gastropod, often strongly marked or sculpted. Also ***Triton shell***. L18. ▸**b** A newt. M19.
3 CHEMISTRY. (Proprietary name for) any of various synthetic organic surfactants used in detergents and emulsifiers. M20.
■ **Tritoness** *noun* (*rare*) a female Triton E17. **Tritonly** *adverb* (*rare*) like or in the manner of a Triton L16.

triton /ˈtrʌɪtɒn/ *noun*[2]. M20.
[from TRITIUM + -ON.]
PHYSICS. A subatomic particle composed of one proton and two neutrons, the nucleus of the tritium atom.

tritonality /trʌɪtəʊˈnalɪti/ *noun*. M20.
[from TRI- + TONALITY.]
MUSIC. The simultaneous use of three keys in a composition.

tritone /ˈtrʌɪtəʊn/ *noun*. E17.
[medieval Latin *tritonus* from Greek *tritonos*, from *tri-* TRI- + *tonos* TONE *noun*.]
MUSIC. An interval consisting of three whole tones; an augmented fourth, or its inversion, a diminished fifth.
■ **triˈtonal** *adjective* of or pertaining to a tritone M20.

trit-trot /ˈtrɪttrɒt/ *adjective & noun*. E19.
[Redupl. of TROT *noun*[1].]
(Making) the sound of trotting feet or hoofs.

triturate /ˈtrɪtjʊreɪt/ *noun*. L19.
[from next: see -ATE[2].]
A product of trituration; a pharmaceutical product in the form of a powder.

triturate /ˈtrɪtjʊreɪt/ *verb trans*. M18.
[Latin *triturat-* pa. ppl stem of *triturare* thresh corn, from *tritura* rubbing, threshing, from *trit-* pa. ppl stem of *terere* rub: see TRITE *adjective*, -URE, -ATE[3].]
1 Reduce to fine particles or powder by rubbing, crushing, or grinding; grind up, pulverize. Also, mix or dilute (solids, or a solid in a liquid) in this way. M18.
2 Chew, masticate, or grind (food) thoroughly. E19.
■ **triturable** *adjective* able to be triturated M17. **trituˈration** *noun* the action of triturating something; the state of being triturated something; *spec.* in PHARMACOLOGY, a preparation made by triturating something, esp. with lactose: M17. **triturator** *noun* an apparatus for triturating something M19.

†**triture** *noun*. E17.
[Latin *tritura*: see prec.]
1 Friction caused by a yoke. *rare*. Only in E17.
2 Trituration. M17–L18.

trityl /ˈtrʌɪtʌɪl, ˈtrɪt-, -tɪl/ *noun*. M19.
[from TRIT(O- + -YL.]
CHEMISTRY. †**1** = PROPYL. Only in M19.
2 The triphenylmethyl radical, $(C_6H_5)_3C\cdot$. Freq. in *comb.* M20.

triumfeminate /trʌɪʌmˈfɛmɪnət/ *noun*. *rare*. E18.
[from Latin *trium* genit. pl. of *tres* three + *femina* woman + -ATE[1], after TRIUMVIRATE.]
A governing body of three women.

triumph /ˈtrʌɪʌmf/ *noun*. LME.
[Old French *triumphe* (mod. *triomphe*) from Latin *triumphus*, earlier *triumpus*, prob. from Greek *thriambos* hymn to Bacchus. Cf. TRUMP *noun*[2].]
1 ROMAN HISTORY. The processional entrance of a victorious commander with his army and spoils into Rome. LME. ▸†**b** A public festivity, *esp.* one involving a procession; a spectacle, a pageant. E16–E19.
2 The action or fact of triumphing; the state of being victorious or successful (chiefly in ***in triumph***). Also, a great success or achievement; a supreme example *of* something. LME. ▸†**b** *transf.* The subject of triumph. *poet. rare*. Only in 17.
†**3** Pomp; splendour, magnificence. L15–E18.
†**4 a** = TRUMP *noun*[2] 1a. Only in 16. ▸**b** = TRUMP *noun*[2] 1b. E16–E17.
†**5** A trumpet blast declaring victory; a victorious or exultant shout. M16–E18.
6 Joy at victory or success; exultation, elation. L16.

> 🕮 **2** J. AGATE A revue of great beauty and a personal triumph for Beatrice Lilley. J. FRAME I thought Isabel's appliquéd giraffe a triumph of dressmaking. P. USTINOV I believe passionately in the final triumph of good. **6** C. DEXTER The high note of triumph in his voice as he reported his find.

Comb.: **triumph-gate** ROMAN HISTORY the gate through which a triumphal procession entered Rome.

triumph /ˈtrʌɪʌmf/ *verb*. L15.
[Old French *triumpher* (mod. *triompher*) from Latin *triumphare*, from *triumphus*: see prec.]
†**1** *verb intrans.* Be in a state of pomp or magnificence. L15–M16.
2 *verb intrans.* Be victorious or successful; gain a victory; prevail. Freq. foll. by *over*. E16. ▸†**b** *verb trans.* Prevail over; conquer. *poet.* E–M17.
3 *verb intrans.* ROMAN HISTORY. Celebrate a triumph. M16.
4 *verb intrans.* Rejoice at victory or success; exult *over* another. M16.

> 🕮 **2** N. ANNAN Stephen felt that he had triumphed over his nature. J. BARNES It was not virtue that triumphed, but strength. **4** SHAKES. *Lucr.* In great commanders grace and majesty you might behold, triumphing in their faces. S. T. WARNER Instead of triumphing over Mrs Ward's failure to catch a housekeeper, she mentioned . . Isa, who would . . take over.

■ **triumpher** *noun* (**a**) *Hist.* the celebrator of a Roman triumph; (**b**) *gen.* a victor, a conqueror: M16.

triumphal /trʌɪˈʌmf(ə)l/ *adjective & noun*. LME.
[Old French (mod. *triomphal*), or Latin *triumphalis*, from *triumphus* TRIUMPH *noun*: see -AL[1].]
▶ **A** *adjective*. **1** Of or pertaining to a triumph; celebrating or commemorating a triumph or victory. LME.
†**2** Victorious, triumphant. E16–E17.
1 triumphal arch an arch erected to commemorate a victory, esp. in battle.
▶†**B** *noun*. **1** = TRIUMPH *noun* 1b. L16–L17.
2 A token of triumph. *rare* (Milton). Only in L17.
■ **triumphally** *adverb* L19.

triumphalism /trʌɪˈʌmf(ə)lɪz(ə)m/ *noun*. M20.
[from prec. + -ISM.]
Extreme or ostentatious pride or excessive self-satisfaction at one's achievements or those of one's church etc.
■ **triumphalist** *adjective & noun* (**a**) *adjective* of or pertaining to triumphalism; (**b**) *noun* a person displaying triumphalism: M20. **triumphalistic** *adjective* = TRIUMPHALIST *adjective* M20.

triumphant /trʌɪˈʌmf(ə)nt/ *adjective & noun*. LME.
[Old French (mod. *triomphant*), or Latin *triumphant-*, *-ans* pres. pple of *triumphare* TRIUMPH *verb*: see -ANT[1].]
▶ **A** *adjective*. **1** That has achieved victory or success; conquering, victorious. LME. ▸†**b** *transf.* Obtained by conquest. *rare* (Shakes.). Only in L16.
†**2** Splendid; magnificent. L15–L17.
3 = TRIUMPHAL *adjective* 1. Now *rare*. M16.

For other words beginning with *tri-* see the entry for **tri-**

4 Rejoicing; exultant. L16.

1 H. J. LASKI To emerge triumphant from an ordeal where . . he should have failed. ***the Church triumphant***: see CHURCH *noun* 3. **4** ALDOUS HUXLEY His laugh was knowing and triumphant.

▶†**B** *noun.* A victor, a conqueror. M16–E19.

▪ **triumphancy** *noun* the state or quality of being triumphant L16. **triumphantly** *adverb* E16.

triumphator /ˈtrʌɪʌmfeɪtə/ *noun. rare.* LME.
[Latin, from *triumphare* TRIUMPH *verb*: see -OR.]
= TRIUMPHER.

triumvir /trʌɪˈʌmvə/ *noun.* Pl. **-virs**, **-viri** /-vɪrʌɪ, -vɪriː/. LME.
[Latin from *triumviri* pl., back-form. from *trium virorum* genit. pl. of *tres viri* three men.]
1 *ROMAN HISTORY.* Each of three public officers forming a committee overseeing any of the administrative departments. Also *spec.*, each member of the first or second triumvirate (see TRIUMVIRATE *noun* 1). LME.
2 *transf.* In *pl.* Any group of three persons or things in a joint position of power or authority. E17.
▪ **triumvirship** *noun* the position or office of triumvir L16. †**triumviry** *noun* = TRIUMVIRATE *noun* L16–M17.

triumviral /trʌɪˈʌmvɪr(ə)l/ *adjective.* L16.
[Latin *triumviralis*, from prec.: see -AL[1].]
Of or pertaining to a triumvir or a triumvirate.

triumvirate /trʌɪˈʌmvɪrət/ *noun & adjective.* L16.
[Latin *triumviratus*, from TRIUMVIR: see -ATE[1].]
▶**A** *noun.* **1** A group of three people in a joint position of power or authority; *spec.* (*ROMAN HISTORY*) the triumviri. Also, the office or function of (each of) such a group. Cf. TRIUMVIR 1. L16.
2 *transf.* A group of three notable or distinguished people or things. M17.
1 first triumvirate *ROMAN HISTORY* a coalition formed by Pompey, Caesar, and Crassus in 60 BC. **second triumvirate** *ROMAN HISTORY* a coalition formed by Caesar, Antony, and Lepidus in 43 BC.
▶**B** *adjective.* Of or pertaining to a triumvirate; that is a triumvirate. L16.

triune /ˈtrʌɪjuːn/ *noun & adjective.* E17.
[from TRI- + Latin *unus* one.]
▶**A** *noun.* A being that is three in one; *spec.* the Trinity. E17.
▶**B** *adjective.* Esp. of the Trinity: that is three in one. M17.
▪ **triˈunal** *adjective* (*poet.*, *rare*) = TRIUNE *adjective* E18.

triungulin /trʌɪˈʌŋgjʊlɪn/ *noun.* L19.
[from TRI- + Latin *ungula* claw + *-in* arbitrary suffix.]
ENTOMOLOGY. The small active first stage larva of various hypermetamorphic insects, esp. oil-beetles. Also ***triungulin larva***.

triunity /trʌɪˈjuːnɪti/ *noun.* E17.
[from TRIUNE + -ITY, or from TRI- + UNITY *noun*[1].]
1 A set or group of three in one; a thing that is three in one; *spec.* the Trinity. E17.
2 The state or condition of being three in one. M17.
▪ Also **triunion** *noun* (*rare*) M17.

trivalent /*esp. Chem.* trʌɪˈveɪlənt, *esp. Cytol.* ˈtrɪv-/ *adjective & noun.* M19.
[from TRI- + -VALENT.]
▶**A** *adjective.* **1** *CHEMISTRY.* Having a valency of three. M19.
2 *CYTOLOGY.* That is (part of) a trivalent. E20.
3 *IMMUNOLOGY.* Of a vaccine: giving immunity against three strains of an infective agent. M20.
▶**B** *noun. CYTOLOGY.* A multivalent consisting of three chromosomes. E20.
▪ **trivalence**, **trivalency** *nouns* the quality of being trivalent L19.

trivet /ˈtrɪvɪt/ *noun & adjective.* LME.
[Repr. Old English *trefet* of uncertain meaning from Latin *tripes*, *triped-* from *tri-* TRI- + *pes* foot, after Greek *tripous* TRIPOD.]
▶**A** *noun.* **1** A three-footed iron stand for a cooking pot, kettle, etc., placed over a fire; an iron bracket designed to hook on to the top bar of a grate for a similar purpose. Also *gen.*; a tripod; any stand or support with three or more legs. LME. ▸**b** *HERALDRY.* A charge representing such a three-footed stand. M16.
†**2** = TRIPOD *noun* 1. M16–L17. ▸**b** = TRIPOD *noun* 2. L16–M17.
1 as right as a trivet *colloq.* perfectly all right, esp. in perfectly good health.
▶**B** *adjective.* Three-footed; having three supports. L15.

trivia /ˈtrɪvɪə/ *noun pl.* E20.
[mod. Latin, pl. of TRIVIUM, infl. in sense by TRIVIAL.]
Trivialities, trifles; *spec.* unimportant factual information (as) used in the game of Trivial Pursuit (see TRIVIAL *adjective* 4).

Modern Maturity There's some trivia, some gossip, and a lot of straight talk in just four typewritten pages. ***attrib.***: *Independent* People who make a living out of trivia question machines.

trivial /ˈtrɪvɪəl/ *adjective & noun.* LME.
[Latin *trivialis*, from TRIVIUM: see -AL[1].]
▶**A** *adjective.* **I 1** *Hist.* Of a subject of study: belonging to the trivium. LME.
2 *ZOOLOGY.* Of or pertaining to the trivium of an echinoderm. *rare.* L19.
▶**II 3** Commonplace, ordinary, trite. Now *rare* exc. as passing into sense 4. L16.
4 Of small importance or value; trifling, slight; (of a person) concerned only with trifling or unimportant matters. L16. ▸**b** *MATH.* Of no significance or interest (e.g. because equal to zero); satisfying a given relation with every member of a set; *spec.* designating a subgroup that either contains only the identity element or is identical with the given group. E20.
5 *BIOLOGY.* **a** Designating a Latin name (the specific name or epithet) added to a genus name to distinguish the species. M18. ▸**b** Designating a name in ordinary as distinct from scientific use; popular, common, vernacular. E19.
6 *CHEMISTRY.* Of a chemical name: not systematic, but retained in use for reasons of convenience or tradition. Cf. SYSTEMATIC *adjective* 4. L19.

4 G. GORDON Indulging in trivial time-passing talk. *Times* It would make the public think that a seat-belt offence was trivial. **Trivial Pursuit** (proprietary name for) a board game in which players advance by answering general-knowledge questions in various subject areas.

▶**B** *noun.* **1** †**a** = TRIVIUM 1. *rare.* Only in LME. ▸**b** In *pl.* The three subjects of study constituting the trivium. *obsolete* exc. *Hist.* L15.
2 A triviality, a trifle. Usu. in *pl.* E18.
3 *BOTANY.* A specific epithet. Cf. sense A.5a above. E20.
▪ **trivialism** *noun* (*rare*) (a) triviality M19. **trivialist** *noun* (*rare*) (*a*) *Hist.* a student studying the trivium; (*b*) a person concerned with trivialities: E18. **triviˈality** *noun* (a thing of) trivial character or quality L16. **trivially** *adverb* L16. **trivialness** *noun* (now *rare*) triviality L17.

trivialize /ˈtrɪvɪəlʌɪz/ *verb trans.* Also **-ise**. M19.
[from TRIVIAL *adjective* + -IZE.]
Make trivial; reduce to (a) triviality.
▪ **triviaIiˈzation** *noun* M19. **trivializer** *noun* M20.

trivium /ˈtrɪvɪəm/ *noun.* E19.
[Latin = place where three ways meet, formed as TRI- + *via* way: see -IUM.]
1 *Hist.* In the Middle Ages, the lower division of a university course of study, comprising grammar, rhetoric, and logic. Cf. ART *noun*[1] 4, QUADRIVIUM. E19.
2 *ZOOLOGY.* The three anterior ambulacra of an echinoderm (ventral in a holothurian). Cf. BIVIUM. L19.

tri-weekly /trʌɪˈwiːkli/ *adverb, adjective, & noun.* M19.
[from TRI- + WEEKLY *adverb, adjective, & noun.*]
▶**A** *adverb.* Every three weeks; three times a week. M19.
▶**B** *adjective.* Occurring or appearing tri-weekly; *esp.* (of a periodical etc.) published three times a week. M19.
▶**C** *noun.* A tri-weekly periodical etc. M19.

-trix /trɪks/ *suffix.* Pl. **-trices** /-trɪˈsiːz/, **-trixes**.
[Repr. Latin fem. suffix corresp. to masc. *-tor*. Cf. -TRICE.]
Forming fem. agent-nouns. corresp. to masculine nouns in *-tor*, esp. in *LAW*, as ***executrix***, ***inheritrix***, ***testatrix***, etc., and in *GEOMETRY* (mod. Latin *linea* line (fem.) being understood), as ***directrix***, ***indicatrix***, ***quadratrix***, etc.

trizonal /trʌɪˈzəʊn(ə)l/ *adjective.* M20.
[from TRI- + ZONAL *adjective.*]
Of, pertaining to, or consisting of three zones; *spec.* (*Hist.*) of or pertaining to the British, French, and American zones of occupation in W. Germany after the war of 1939–45.

trizzie /ˈtrɪzi/ *noun. Austral. slang* (now *Hist.*). M20.
[Origin uncertain; perh. from TREY *noun* + -IE.]
A threepenny piece.

tRNA *abbreviation.*
BIOCHEMISTRY. Transfer RNA.

Troadic /trəʊˈadɪk/ *adjective.* M20.
[from Latin *Troad*, the region surrounding ancient Troy + -IC.]
Of or pertaining to ancient Troy and its surrounding regions.

troat /trəʊt/ *verb intrans.* E17.
[Origin uncertain: cf. Old French *trout*, *trut* interjection for urging on hunting dogs etc.]
= BELL *verb*[1] 1.

Trobriander /ˈtrəʊbrɪandə/ *noun.* E20.
[from *Trobriand* (see below) + -ER[1].]
A native or inhabitant of the Trobriand Islands in the Solomon Sea, now part of Papua New Guinea.

trocar /ˈtrəʊkɑː/ *noun.* E18.
[French *trocart*, also *trois-quarts*, from *trois* three + *carre* (Latin *quadra*) face of an instrument, so called from its triangular form.]
MEDICINE. A surgical instrument consisting of a shaft with a three-sided cutting point, enclosed in a cannula and used to introduce this into a body cavity for withdrawal of fluid, as in ascites etc.

trocha /ˈtrotʃa/ *noun.* Now *rare.* L19.
[Spanish.]
MILITARY. A strategic line of defences; a cordon.

trochaic /trə(ʊ)ˈkeɪɪk/ *adjective & noun.* L16.
[Latin *trochaicus* from Greek *trokhaikos* from *trokhaios*: see TROCHEE, -IC.]
PROSODY. ▶**A** *adjective.* Consisting of a trochee or trochees; characterized by the use of trochees; *spec.* (of a spondee) stressed on the first syllable. L16.
▶**B** *noun.* A trochee; a verse written in trochees. L17.
▪ **trochaical** *adjective* (*rare*) = TROCHAIC *adjective* M18.

trochal /ˈtrəʊk(ə)l/ *adjective.* M19.
[from Greek *trokhos* wheel + -AL[1].]
Chiefly *ZOOLOGY.* Resembling a wheel; wheel-shaped.
trochal disc a retractable disc on the head of a rotifer, bearing a crown of cilia and used for drawing in food or for propulsion.

trochanter /trəˈkantə/ *noun.* E17.
[French from Greek *trokhantēr* (in sense 1), from *trekhein* run.]
1 *ANATOMY & ZOOLOGY.* Any of several bony protuberances by which muscles are attached to the upper part of the thigh-bone. E17.
2 *ENTOMOLOGY.* The second segment of an insect's leg, between the coxa and the femur. E19.
▪ **trochanteral** *adjective* M20. **trochanˈteric** *adjective* of or pertaining to a trochanter or trochanters M19.

troche /ˈtrəʊkiː, trəʊʃ/ *noun.* L16.
[Alt. of TROCHISK.]
PHARMACOLOGY. A small usu. circular medicated tablet or lozenge, taken by mouth.

trochee /ˈtrəʊkiː/ *noun.* L16.
[Latin *trochaeus* from Greek *trokhaios* (*pous*) running (foot), from *trokhos*, from *trekhein* run.]
PROSODY. A foot consisting of one long followed by one short syllable, or one stressed followed by one unstressed syllable. Cf. CHOREE.
▪ **trocheize** *verb trans.* (*rare*) turn into a trochee, make trochaic M19.

trochi *noun pl.* see TROCHUS.

trochiform /ˈtrɒkɪfɔːm/ *adjective.* E19.
[from TROCHUS + -I- + -FORM.]
CONCHOLOGY. Having the form of a top-shell; conical with a flat base.

trochili *noun*[1], *noun*[2] pls. of TROCHILUS *noun*[1], *noun*[2].

trochilus /ˈtrɒkɪləs/ *noun*[1]. Pl. **-li** /-lʌɪ, -liː/. M16.
[Latin, app. same word as next.]
ARCHITECTURE. = SCOTIA.

trochilus /ˈtrɒkɪləs/ *noun*[2]. Pl. **-li** /-lʌɪ, -liː/. L16.
[Latin from Greek *trokhilos*, from *trekhein* run.]
1 A small Egyptian bird (perh. the crocodile bird *Pluvianus aegyptius*) said by ancient writers to pick the teeth of crocodiles. Formerly also, any of various small European birds, such as the wren and the water rail. L16.
2 A hummingbird. Now only as mod. Latin genus name of a Jamaican hummingbird. L17.

†**trochisk** *noun.* LME–M18.
[French *trochisque* from late Latin *trochiscus* from Greek *trokhiskos* small wheel, lozenge, pill, dim. of *trokhos* wheel.]
= TROCHE.

trochlea /ˈtrɒklɪə/ *noun.* Pl. **-eae** /-ɪiː/. L17.
[Latin: cf. Greek *trokhilia* sheave of a pulley.]
ANATOMY & ZOOLOGY. A structure or arrangement of parts resembling a pulley, with a smooth surface over which some other part, as a bone or tendon, slides; *spec.* (*a*) the groove at the lower end of the humerus, with which the ulna articulates at the elbow-joint; (*b*) the cartilaginous loop through which the superior oblique eye muscle passes.

trochlear /ˈtrɒklɪə/ *adjective.* L17.
[mod. Latin *trochlearis*, formed as prec.: see -AR[1].]
ANATOMY. Of or pertaining to a trochlea; forming a trochlea.
trochlear muscle the superior oblique muscle of the eye. **trochlear nerve** either of the fourth pair of cranial nerves, supplying the trochlear muscles.

trocho- /ˈtrɒkəʊ, ˈtrəʊkəʊ/ *combining form* of Greek *trokhos* wheel, disc: see -O-.
▪ **trochophore** *noun* (*ZOOLOGY*) = TROCHOSPHERE L19. **trochosphere** *noun* (*ZOOLOGY*) the planktonic larva of any of various invertebrates, including certain molluscs and polychaete worms, having a spheroidal body with a ring of cilia in front of the mouth L19.

trochoid /ˈtrəʊkɔɪd/ *noun & adjective.* E18.
[from Greek *trokhoeidēs* wheel-like, from *trokhos* wheel: see -OID.]
▶**A** *noun. GEOMETRY.* A curve traced by a point on or connected with a rolling circle. Now *spec.* a curve traced by a point on a radius of a circle rotating along a straight line or another circle. E18.
▶**B** *adjective.* **1** *CONCHOLOGY.* = TROCHIFORM. M19.
2 *ANATOMY.* Of a joint: in which one bone rotates freely around a central axis. M19.
3 *GEOMETRY.* Of the form of a trochoid. L19.

For other words beginning with *tri-* see the entry for **tri-**

trochoidal /trəˈkɔɪd(ə)l/ *adjective*. L18.
[formed as prec. + -AL¹.]
GEOMETRY. = TROCHOID *adjective* 3.

trochotron /ˈtrəʊkətrɒn, ˈtrɒk-/ *noun*. M20.
[from TROCHOID(AL) + -TRON.]
ELECTRONICS. A type of magnetron in which there are a number of anodes at different angular positions around the central cathode, with the electron beam able to be switched from one anode to another.

trochus /ˈtrəʊkəs, ˈtrɒkəs/ *noun*. Pl. **-chi** /-kʌɪ/, **-chuses**. E18.
[Latin from Greek *trokhos* wheel, from *trekhein* run.]
1 CLASSICAL HISTORY. A hoop used for play or exercise. E18.
2 ZOOLOGY. **a** A top-shell (also *trochus-shell*). Also *collect.*, this genus of gastropods. M18. ▸**b** The internal ring of cilia in the trochal organ of a rotifer. L19.

Trockenbeerenauslese /ˈtrɒkənbeːrənˌaʊsleːzə/ *noun*. Also **t-**. Pl. ***-sen*** /-zən/, ***-ses***. M20.
[German, from *trocken* dry + as BEERENAUSLESE.]
A sweet white wine of superior quality made (esp. in Germany) from selected individual grapes picked later than the general harvest and affected by noble rot.

troctolite /ˈtrɒktəlʌɪt/ *noun*. L19.
[German *Troktolit*, from Greek *troktēs* a marine fish (taken as 'trout'): see -LITE.]
GEOLOGY. A gabbro made up mainly of olivine and calcic plagioclase, with little pyroxene, often having a spotted appearance resembling a trout's back.

trod /trɒd/ *noun & verb*¹.
[Old English *trod* = Old Norse *troð* treading, trampling, from Old Norse *troða*, Gothic *trudan* tread. Cf. TREAD *verb*.]
▶ **A** *noun*. **1** A footprint, a footstep. Long *obsolete* exc. *Scot.* OE.
2 A footpath; a path used by animals. *dial.* L16.
3 The tread of a wheel. *dial.* L18.
▶ **B** *verb*. Infl. **-dd-**.
1 *verb trans.* Track, trace. Long *obsolete* exc *dial.* ME.
2 *verb intrans.* Pursue a path; tread, tramp. *US.* E20.

trod /trɒd/ *ppl adjective*. *arch.* L16.
[Abbreviation.]
= TRODDEN *ppl adjective*. Chiefly as 2nd elem. of comb., as ***down-trod***, ***well-trod***, etc.

trod *verb*² *pa. t. & pple*: see TREAD *verb*.

trodden /ˈtrɒd(ə)n/ *ppl adjective*. M16.
[pa. pple of TREAD *verb*.]
That has been trodden on or over; (of a path) formed by treading, beaten. Also as 2nd elem. of comb., as ***downtrodden*** etc.

trodden *verb* pa. pple: see TREAD *verb*.

trog /trɒg/ *noun*. *slang*. M20.
[Abbreviation of TROGLODYTE.]
1 A speleologist. *rare. Austral.* M20.
2 A contemptible person, *esp.* one belonging to a despised social group. M20.
3 An overhanging boulder or bluff providing shelter on a hillside. *NZ.* M20.

trog /trɒg/ *verb intrans.* *slang*. Infl. **-gg-**. L20.
[Origin uncertain; perh. blend of *trudge*, *trek*, *slog*, *jog*, etc.]
Walk heavily or laboriously, trudge. Also, walk casually, stroll.
📖 *Sunday Times* Charles had trogged all the way out to Gatwick.

troglo- /ˈtrɒgləʊ/ *combining form*.
[from Greek *trōglē* hole: see -O-.]
Chiefly ZOOLOGY. Of or pertaining to caves.
■ **trogloˈbion** *noun*, pl. **-bia**, an animal which lives exclusively in dark caves or underground caverns (usu. in *pl.*) E20. **trogloˈbiont** *noun* [-BIONT] = TROGLOBION E20. **troglobiˈotic**, **trogloˈbitic** *adjectives* cave-dwelling, esp. exclusively L20. **troglophil(e)** *noun* an animal which lives commonly but not exclusively in caves E20. **trogloxene** *noun* an animal which habitually visits caves E20.

troglodyte /ˈtrɒglədʌɪt/ *noun & adjective*. As noun orig. **†-dytan**. L15.
[Latin *troglodyta* from Greek *trōglodutēs* alt. of *trōgodutēs*, *-tai* an Ethiopian people, from *trōglē* hole.]
▶ **A** *noun*. **1** A member of a people, esp. in prehistoric times, inhabiting caves or dens; a cave-dweller. L15. ▸**b** *fig.* A person living in seclusion, a hermit. Also, a person regarded as living in (esp. wilful) ignorance; an unprogressive or old-fashioned person. M19.
2 An animal which lives in caves (or was formerly supposed to do so). M17.
📖 **1b** *Newsday* The troglodytes can no longer prevent a writer of such talents from reaching a large audience.
▶ **B** *adjective*. Troglodytic. E18.
■ **troglodytish** *adjective* resembling or characteristic of a troglodyte or troglodytes M19. **troglodytism** *noun* the state or condition of a troglodyte; the habit of living in caves: M19.

troglodytic /trɒgləˈdɪtɪk/ *adjective*. L16.
[Latin *troglodyticus* from Greek *trōglodutikos*, from *trōglodutēs*: see prec., -IC.]
1 Inhabited by troglodytes. L16.
2 Of or pertaining to troglodytes; that is a troglodyte, cave-dwelling. L17.
3 Resembling or characteristic of a troglodyte; unprogressive, old-fashioned. L19.
■ Also **troglodytical** *adjective* M19.

trogon /ˈtrəʊgɒn/ *noun*. L18.
[mod. Latin (see below), from Greek *trōgōn* pres. pple of *trōgein* gnaw.]
Any bird of the genus *Trogon* or the family Trogonidae, widely distributed in tropical and subtropical forests, esp. in the New World, and having a short thick bill and soft plumage of varied and often brilliant colour.

†Troian *noun & adjective* see TROJAN.

Troic /ˈtrəʊɪk/ *adjective*. *rare*. M19.
[Greek *trōïkos*, from *Trōs* the mythical founder of Troy.]
= TROJAN *adjective* 1.

troika /ˈtrɔɪkə/ *noun*. M19.
[Russian *troĭka*, from *troe* a set of three.]
1 A Russian vehicle drawn by three horses abreast; the team of horses for such a vehicle. M19.
2 A group of three people or things working together, esp. in an administrative or managerial capacity. M20.
📖 **2** *Economist* The usual African troika of war, pestilence and drought. *Independent* She . . suggested forming a troika comprised of Ronald Reagan, Mikhail Gorbachev and her good self to solve world problems.

troilism /ˈtrɔɪlɪz(ə)m/ *noun*. M20.
[Perh. from French *trois* three: see -ISM.]
Sexual activity involving three participants.
■ **troilist** *adjective* of or pertaining to troilism L20.

troilite /ˈtrəʊɪlʌɪt/ *noun*. M19.
[from Domenico *Troili*, 18th-cent. Italian scientist, who described a meteorite containing this mineral which fell in 1766: see -ITE¹.]
MINERALOGY. A non-magnetic hexagonal form of ferrous sulphide occurring in meteorites.

trois point /trwɑ pwɛ̃/ *noun phr.* M18.
[French.]
BACKGAMMON. The third point in from either end on a board.

Trojan /ˈtrəʊdʒ(ə)n/ *noun & adjective*. Orig. **†Troian**, **†-yan**. ME.
[Latin *Troianus*, from *Troia* Troy: see -AN.]
▶ **A** *noun*. **1** A native or inhabitant of the ancient city of Troy in Asia Minor. ME.
2 a A boon companion; a boisterous person; a person of dissolute habits. Long *rare* exc. as a familiar form of address to a person. Cf. GREEK *noun* 5. *arch.* L16. ▸**b** A person of great energy, courage, or endurance. Chiefly in ***like a Trojan***. M19.
3 ASTRONOMY. A Trojan asteroid. E20.
4 COMPUTING. = ***Trojan horse*** (c) below. L20.
▶ **B** *adjective*. **1** Of or pertaining to ancient Troy or its inhabitants. LME.
2 ASTRONOMY. Pertaining to or designating either of two groups of asteroids which orbit the sun at the same distance as Jupiter, at the Lagrangian points roughly 60 degrees ahead of it and behind it in the same orbit. E20.
1 Trojan horse (*a*) CLASSICAL HISTORY a hollow wooden statue of a horse in which the Greeks are said to have concealed themselves to enter Troy; (*b*) *fig.* a person, device, etc., deliberately set to bring about an enemy's downfall or to undermine from within; (*c*) COMPUTING a program that breaches the security of a computer system, esp. by ostensibly functioning as part of a legitimate program, in order to erase, corrupt, or remove data.

†troke *verb* see TRUCK *verb*¹.

troland /ˈtrəʊlənd/ *noun*. M20.
[from L. T. *Troland* (1889–1932), US physicist and psychologist, who introduced the unit in 1917 under the name of *photon*.]
OPTICS. A unit of retinal illumination, being the illumination produced by a surface with a luminance of one candela per square metre when the pupil has an area of one square millimetre.

troll /trəʊl, trɒl/ *noun*¹. LME.
[Swedish (Danish *trold*) from Old Norse, of unkn. origin. Cf. Danish *trylla*, *trylde*, Swedish *trolla* bewitch, charm, Old Norse *trolldómr* witchcraft.]
Orig. (*rare*), a witch, a sorceress. Now (in Scandinavian mythology), a member of a race of grotesque dwarfs (or, formerly, giants) usu. dwelling in caves or under bridges.

troll /trəʊl, trɒl/ *verb & noun*². Also (*Scot.*) **trow** /traʊ/. LME.
[Origin uncertain: cf. Old French *troller* (mod. *trôler*) quest, wander casually, Middle High German *trollen* stroll, toddle.]
▶ **A** *verb*. **I 1** *verb intrans.* Saunter, stroll, amble; *spec.* (*slang*) cruise in search of a sexual partner etc. LME.
2 *verb trans. & intrans.* Roll, spin; turn over or round repeatedly. Now *Scot.* LME.
▶ **II 3 †a** *verb trans.* Entice, allure. M16–L17. ▸**b** *verb intrans. & trans.* ANGLING. Fish by drawing bait along in the water; *Scot. & N. Amer.* trail a baited line behind a boat. Also *fig.*, move in an alluring manner; search *for* or for. E17.
📖 **3b** B. MACDONALD By trolling . . we caught silvers, king and dog salmon. *Atlantic* Nancy had been . . herself, . . trolling her scooped neckline under the eyes of Russell's friends.
▶**†III 4 a** *verb trans.* Pass or hand round. L16–E19. ▸**b** *verb intrans.* Circulate; be passed round. E17–E19.
5 *verb intrans. & trans.* (Cause to) roll or flow (*in*). L16–L17.
▶ **IV 6** *verb trans. & intrans.* Sing (*out*) heartily; sing or recite in a jovial or carefree manner. L16.
7 *verb intrans.* Sound out or be played in a jovial or carefree manner; *transf.* (of a tune) recur constantly to the mind. E17.
📖 **6** R. L. STEVENSON He trolled with ample lungs. J. BERRYMAN Troll me the sources of that Song . . by Blake.
▶ **V 8 a** *verb intrans.* Move nimbly; (of the tongue) wag. Long *arch.* E17. ▸**†b** *verb trans.* Wag (the tongue). *rare.* M17–M18.
Comb.: **trolling motor** *US* a low-powered motor suitable for a boat used in trolling for fish; **trolling pole** *N. Amer.* a horizontal pole on each side of a fishing boat to keep the lines clear of the propeller.
▶ **B** *noun*. **†1** A small wheel; *spec.* a reel on a fishing-rod. L16–L17.
2 = TROLLEY *noun* 1. *local.* M17.
3 ANGLING. **a** The method of trolling, esp. in fishing for pike etc. L17. ▸**b** A bait or line used in trolling. M19. ▸**c** COMPUTING. A message posted to a newsgroup with the intention of inciting flame mail in response. *slang.* L20.
4 The action or an act of trolling; *Scot.* a roll, a rotation. E18.
5 A song sung as a round. E19.
■ **troller** *noun* (*a*) a person who trolls, esp. in fishing; (*b*) *N. Amer.* a fishing boat used for trolling a line; (*c*) COMPUTING a person who posts a troll to a newsgroup: M17.

trolley /ˈtrɒli/ *noun & verb*. Also **trolly**. E19.
[Of dial. origin, prob. from TROLL *verb & noun*².]
▶ **A** *noun*. **1** Any of various kinds of low cart adapted for a specific purpose; *esp.* a street-barrow. *local.* E19.
2 A low truck, usu. without sides or ends, running on a railway, or a track in a factory etc. M19.
3 More fully ***trolley-wheel***. A grooved metallic pulley receiving current from an overhead electric wire and conveying this by a pole etc. to the motor of a trolley bus or trolley-car. Also *gen.*, any pulley running along an overhead track. L19. ▸**b** *ellipt.* A trolley-car (*US*). Also, a trolley bus. L19.
4 A small table, stand, or basket on wheels or castors for serving food, transporting shopping, luggage, etc.; *spec.* = SUPERMARKET ***trolley***. M20.
📖 **2** *Railway Magazine* Small service trollies, used . . on track maintenance . . to transport men and materials. **off one's trolley** *slang* crazy. **3b** B. MALAMUD On the trolley he watched the passers-by in the street.
Comb.: **trolley-bar** = *trolley-pole* below; **trolley bus** a trackless passenger vehicle powered from an overhead cable by using a trolley-wheel; **trolley-car** *US* an electric tram using a trolley-wheel; **trolley-head** a mounting at the end of a trolley-pole supporting the trolley-wheel; **trolleyman** the driver of a trolley bus or trolley-car; **trolley-pole** a hinged pole supporting the trolley-wheel, and conveying the current from an overhead cable to a trolley bus or trolley-car; **trolley shop** a cart containing goods for sale wheeled around a hospital etc.; ***trolley-wheel***: see sense 3 above; **trolley-wire** an overhead electric cable supplying current to a trolley bus or trolley-car.
▶ **B** *verb*. **1** *verb trans.* Convey by trolley. L19.
2 *verb intrans.* Travel or be conveyed by trolley. E20.
■ **trolleyful** *noun* as much or as many as a trolley will hold L19.

trollius /ˈtrɒlɪəs/ *noun*. Pl. same. L19.
[mod. Latin (see below), app. repr. German *Trollblume* globe-flower, app. from stem of *trollen* to roll, with ref. to the globular shape of the flowers.]
A globe-flower (genus *Trollius*), esp. of a kind grown for ornament.

†troll-madam *noun*. L16–E19.
[App. alt. of French *trou-madame* (from *trou* hole), by assoc. with TROLL *verb*.]
= TRUNK *noun* 16.

trollop /ˈtrɒləp/ *noun & verb*. As noun also **trollope**. E17.
[Origin unkn. Cf. TRULL.]
▶ **A** *noun*. **1** A slovenly or disreputable girl or woman; a slattern, a slut; a prostitute. E17.
2 A thing which hangs loosely and untidily; *esp.* a loose rag, a tatter. *Scot.* M19.
▶ **B** *verb intrans.* **1** Act or dress like a trollop; be slovenly; slouch. *colloq.* M19.
2 Hang loosely and untidily; draggle. *Scot.* L19.
📖 **1** SOUTHEY Barefooted women in their caps, trolloping through the streets.
■ **trollopee** *noun* (*Hist.*) a woman's loose informal robe worn in the 18th cent. M18. **trollopish** *adjective* M19. **trollopy** *adjective*

resembling or characteristic of (that of) a trollop; ungainly, slovenly: M18.

Trollopian /trɒˈləʊpɪən/ *adjective & noun.* M19.
[from *Trollope* (see below) + -IAN.]
▸ **A** *adjective.* **1** Of, pertaining to, or characteristic of the English novelist Frances Trollope (1780–1863) or her writing. M19.
2 Of, pertaining to, or characteristic of the English novelist Anthony Trollope (1815–82) or his writing. E20.
▸ **B** *noun.* A student or admirer of Anthony Trollope or his writing. E20.

trolly /ˈtrɒli/ *noun*¹. L17.
[Origin uncertain: cf. Flemish *tralje*, *traalje* trellis, lattice.]
1 A kind of lace with a gimp edging (also ***trolly lace***); the bobbin holding the gimp thread in making this lace. L17.
2 In *pl.* Knickers. *dial. & slang.* L19.

trolly *noun*² & *verb* var. of TROLLEY *noun & verb*.

trolly-lolly /ˈtrɒlɪlɒli/ *interjection.* Now *rare.* LME.
[Redupl. of TROLL *verb*.]
Used as a meaningless refrain in a song.

tromba marina /trɒmbə məˈriːnə/ *noun phr.* L18.
[Italian.]
= ***trumpet marine*** s.v. TRUMPET *noun*.

trombash /ˈtrɒmbaʃ/ *noun.* M19.
[Sudanic.]
In Sudan, a kind of boomerang.

Trombe /trɒmb, *foreign* trɔ̃b/ *noun.* L20.
[Felix *Trombe*, 20th-cent. French inventor.]
Used *attrib.* to designate a masonry wall of a kind designed by F. Trombe and J. Michel, having glass sheeting fixed a small distance in front of it to absorb solar radiation, and usu. ventilated internally to release the heat into the building.

trombenik /ˈtrɒmb(ə)nɪk/ *noun. US slang.* M20.
[Yiddish, from *tromba* trumpet, horn + -NIK.]
A boaster, a bragger; an idle or dissolute person.

trombiculid /trɒmˈbɪkjʊlɪd/ *adjective & noun.* M20.
[mod. Latin *Trombiculidae* (see below), from *Trombicula* genus name: see -ID³.]
▸ **A** *adjective.* Of, pertaining to, or designating the family Trombiculidae, which includes harvest-mites and other species having parasitic larvae which cause or transmit disease in humans and other mammals. M20.
▸ **B** *noun.* A mite of this family. M20.

trombone /trɒmˈbəʊn, *in sense A.2 foreign* tromˈboːne/ *noun & verb.* E18.
[French or Italian, from *tromba* TRUMP *noun*¹.]
▸ **A** *noun.* Pl. **-s**, (in sense 2) **-ni** /-ni/.
1 A large brass wind instrument consisting of a long tube with a slide to extend its length. E18. ▸**b** A player of a trombone. M19. ▸**c** An organ-stop with the quality of a trombone. M19.
2 *Hist.* = BLUNDERBUSS 1. M18.
3 An Australian variety of green or yellow pear-shaped pumpkin. M20.
▸ **B** *verb intrans.* Play the trombone; *transf.* make a sound like that of a trombone. Chiefly as ***tromboning*** *verbal noun.* M19.
■ **trombonist** *noun* = TROMBONE *noun* 1b L19. **trombony** *adjective* (*colloq.*) characterized by the use of trombones L19.

tromino /ˈtrɒmɪnəʊ/ *noun.* Pl. **-oes.** M20.
[from TR(I- + D)OMINO. Cf. PENTOMINO.]
Any planar shape formed by joining three identical squares by their edges.

trommel /ˈtrɒm(ə)l/ *noun. US.* L19.
[German = drum.]
MINING. A rotating cylindrical sieve or screen used for washing and sizing ores, coal, gravel, etc.

tromp /trɒmp/ *verb intrans. & trans.* Orig. & chiefly *US.* L19.
[Alt.]
= TRAMP *verb*.

trompe /trɒmp/ *noun.* E19.
[French = trumpet.]
An apparatus for producing a blast in a furnace by using falling water to displace air.

trompe l'oeil /trɔ̃p lœːj/ *noun phr.* Pl. ***trompe l'oeils*** (pronounced same). L19.
[French, lit. 'deceives the eye'.]
Deception of the eye; (an) optical illusion; *esp.* a painting or object intended to give an illusion of reality.

tron /trɒn/ *noun & verb.* ME.
[Old French *trone* from Latin *trutina* from Greek *trutanē* balance.]
▸ **A** *noun.* **1** *Hist.* A public weighing-machine for weighing produce in the market-place of a city or burgh; the post of this used as a pillory. *Scot. & north.* ME. ▸**b** *transf.* The place in a city etc. where the tron was set up; a market-place. Now *Hist.* exc. in place-names. *Scot.* E16.
2 In *pl.* A pair of scales. *north.* E19.

Comb.: **tron-pound** *Hist.* the pound of tron weight (see below), varying locally between 21 and 28 ounces; **tron weight** *Hist.* the standard of weight for produce weighed at the tron.
▸ **B** *verb trans.* Weigh at the tron. *Scot. & north.* E17.
■ **troner** *noun* (*Scot. & north., obsolete* exc. *Hist.*) an official overseeing the weighing of produce at the tron LME.

-tron /trɒn/ *suffix.*
[The ending of ELECTRON *noun*², (but cf. Greek *-tron* instr. suffix).]
PHYSICS. Forming names of (*a*) kinds of thermionic valve and other electron tubes, as ***ignitron***, ***pliotron***, etc.; (*b*) subatomic particles, as ***mesotron***, ***positron***, etc.; (*c*) devices and machines, esp. particle accelerators, as ***betatron***, ***cyclotron***, etc.

trona /ˈtrəʊnə/ *noun.* L18.
[Swedish from Arab. *naṭrūn* NATRON.]
MINERALOGY. A native hydrated double salt of sodium carbonate and sodium bicarbonate, occurring esp. as an evaporite. Also called ***urao***.

tronage /ˈtrəʊnɪdʒ/ *noun.* ME.
[Anglo-Norman: see TRON, -AGE.]
Hist. The weighing of produce at the tron; (the right of levying) a charge on goods so weighed.

tronc /trɒŋk/ *noun.* E20.
[French = collecting box.]
In a hotel or restaurant, a common fund into which tips and service charges are paid for distribution to the staff.

†**trone** *noun & verb* see THRONE *noun & verb*.

tronk /trɒŋk/ *noun.* L17.
[Afrikaans from Portuguese *tronco* trunk, the stocks, prison.]
Esp. in South Africa, a prison.

troolie /ˈtruːli/ *noun.* M18.
[Tupi *tururí*.]
The immense leaf of an Amazonian palm, *Manicaria saccifera*, often up to 9 m (30 ft) long and used for thatching. Also (more fully ***troolie palm***), the tree bearing this leaf.

troop /truːp/ *noun.* M16.
[French *troupe* back-form. from *troupeau* flock, herd, dim. of medieval Latin *troppus* herd, prob. of Germanic origin. In sense 5 perh. partly from TROOPER.]
1 An assembled company of people or animals, esp. of one kind; *spec.* (*a*) a body of soldiers; (*b*) a number of animals of one kind, esp. apes or monkeys, feeding or travelling together; (*c*) a great number (*of*); in *pl.*, lots (*of*); (*d*) a company of performers; = TROUPE *noun*. M16.
2 In *pl.* ▸**a** Armed forces; soldiers collectively. L16. ▸**b** The members of a mob or gang collectively. *US slang.* M20.
3 MILITARY. **a** A cavalry unit commanded by a captain. Also, a unit of artillery and armoured formation. L16. ▸**b** The command of a cavalry troop. *rare.* E19.
4 MILITARY. A call to assemble given by a drum; the assembly. L17.
5 A member of a troop of soldiers etc.; a soldier, a trooper. *colloq.* (chiefly MILITARY). M19.
6 A company of Scouts comprising three or more patrols. E20.

> 📖 **1** LYTTON In this troop . . rode many of the best blood of Spain. L. M. ALCOTT A goodly troop of young and old set forth to church. R. CAMPBELL A huge troop of baboons. **2a** F. FITZGERALD Fourteen thousand troops had sufficed to keep . . Vietnam under French rule. **3a** K. DOUGLAS He allotted me two tanks, as a troop. **b** WELLINGTON There is a troop vacant for purchase in the regiment of Life Guards. **4** S. JUDD Tony's beat of the troop was the signal for the soldiers to assemble.

Comb.: **troop-carrier** a large aircraft or armoured vehicle for transporting troops; **troop-carrying** *adjective* (of an aircraft) for transporting troops; **troop-horse** (*a*) a cavalry horse; †(*b*) horsemen for a troop collectively; **troop-ship** a ship for transporting troops.

troop /truːp/ *verb.* M16.
[from the noun.]
1 *verb intrans.* Gather (as) in a troop; assemble. M16. ▸**b** *verb intrans.* Associate *with.* L16. ▸**c** *verb trans.* Form (individuals, a regiment, etc.) into a troop or troops. L16.
2 *verb intrans.* Walk, go, march, or pass (as) in a troop. Freq. foll. by *in, out, off,* etc. M16.
3 *verb trans.* Show (regimental colours) ceremonially along ranks of soldiers, esp. at a public mounting of garrison guards. Freq. in ***trooping the colour(s)***. E19.

> 📖 **1** SHAKES. *Tit. A.* There will the lovely Roman ladies troop. BURKE Multitudes . . would . . troop about him. **b** J. R. LOWELL Descendants of Sabine pigeons . . trooping with noisy rooks. **2** MILTON Flocking shadows pale Troop to th'infernall jail. B. CASTLE Twenty officials troop in on these occasions. *Listener* We trooped off to the Sellafield Vista Point. **3** *Times* The colours of the 52nd will be trooped for the last time.

trooper /ˈtruːpə/ *noun.* M17.
[from TROOP *noun* + -ER¹.]
1 A private soldier in a cavalry or armoured unit. M17.
2 A horse ridden by a trooper; a cavalry horse. M17.
3 a A mounted policeman. *Austral.* M19. ▸**b** More fully ***State trooper***. A mobile State policeman. *US.* E20.
4 A troop-ship. L19.
5 A paratrooper. Orig. *US.* M20.
1 lie like a trooper tell lies constantly and flagrantly. **swear like a trooper** swear extensively and forcefully.

troopial *noun* var. of TROUPIAL.

troopie /ˈtruːpi/ *noun. S. Afr. colloq.* Also **troepie.** L20.
[from TROOP *noun* or TROOPER + -IE.]
A private soldier, *esp.* a national serviceman without rank.

troostite /ˈtruːstʌɪt/ *noun*¹. M19.
[from Prof. Gerard *Troost* (1776–1850), Dutch-born US geologist + -ITE¹.]
MINERALOGY. A variety of willemite with manganese replacing some of the zinc, occurring in reddish hexagonal crystals.

troostite /ˈtruːstʌɪt/ *noun*². E20.
[from Louis Joseph *Troost* (1825–1911), French chemist + -ITE¹.]
METALLURGY. A constituent of some hardened and tempered steels, consisting of a microscopic aggregate of ferrite and cementite.
■ **troostitic** /-ˈtɪtɪk/ *adjective* pertaining to, containing, or consisting of troostite E20.

tropaeolin /trəʊˈpiːəlɪn/ *noun.* Also †**-ine.** L19.
[from next + -IN¹.]
CHEMISTRY. Any of a group of orange and yellow sulphonate azo dyes, some of which are used as acid–base indicators.
tropaeolin D = METHYL *orange*.

tropaeolum /trəʊˈpiːələm/ *noun.* L18.
[mod. Latin (see below), dim. of Latin *tropaeum* TROPHY *noun*, with ref. to the resemblance of the leaf to a shield and the flower to a helmet.]
Any of various climbing or trailing S. American plants constituting the genus *Tropaeolum* (family Tropaeolaceae), with irregular spurred, often orange or yellow flowers, including the nasturtium, *T. majus*, and other ornamental plants.

tropane /ˈtrəʊpeɪn/ *noun.* Also **-an** /-an/. E20.
[formed as TROP(INE + -ANE, -AN.]
CHEMISTRY. A liquid saturated bicyclic tertiary amine, $C_8H_{15}N$, which is obtained from various plants.
Comb.: **tropane alkaloid** any of a class of alkaloids formally derived from tropane, many of which are esters of tropine, as atropine, cocaine, etc.

troparion /trəʊˈparɪɒn, -ˈpɛːrɪɒn/ *noun.* Pl. **-ia** /-ɪə/. M19.
[Greek, dim. of *tropos* TROPE.]
A short hymn or verse used in the liturgy of the Greek Orthodox Church.

tropary /ˈtrəʊp(ə)ri/ *noun.* Also **-ery.** LME.
[medieval Latin *troparium*, *-erium*, from Latin *tropus* TROPE *noun*: see -ARY¹.]
ECCLESIASTICAL HISTORY. = TROPER.

trope /trəʊp/ *noun & verb.* M16.
[Latin *tropus* figure of speech from Greek *tropos* turn, rel. to *trepein* to turn.]
▸ **A** *noun.* **1** RHETORIC. A figure of speech consisting in the use of a word or phrase in a sense other than that which is proper to it; *gen.* a figurative use of a word; figurative or metaphorical language. M16.
2 ECCLESIASTICAL HISTORY. A phrase, sentence, or verse introduced as a choral embellishment into part of the Mass or of the breviary office. M19.
3 PHILOSOPHY. An argument advanced by a sceptic. M19.
4 GEOMETRY. The reciprocal of a node on a curve or surface. *rare.* M19.
▸ **B** *verb trans.* ECCLESIASTICAL HISTORY. Introduce (a trope) as a choral embellishment; embellish with a trope or tropes; add as a trope to. Usu. in *pass.* L19.
■ **troping** *noun* (*rare*) †(*a*) figurative or metaphorical speech or conversation; (*b*) the composition or use of tropes (TROPE *noun* 2): L17.

troper /ˈtrəʊpə/ *noun.* LOE.
[medieval Latin *troperium*: see TROPARY.]
ECCLESIASTICAL HISTORY. A book containing tropes (TROPE *noun* 2). Also, a sequentiary.

tropery *noun* var. of TROPARY.

troph- *combining form* see TROPHO-.

trophaeum *noun* see TROPHY *noun*.

trophallaxis /trɒfəˈlaksɪs/ *noun.* E20.
[from TROPH- + Greek *allaxis* exchange.]
ENTOMOLOGY. The mutual exchange of food material etc. by adult social insects and their larvae.
■ **trophallactic** *adjective* E20.

trophi /ˈtrəʊfʌɪ, -fiː/ *noun pl.* E19.
[mod. Latin, pl. of *trophus*, from Greek *trophos* feeder, from *triphein* nourish.]
1 ENTOMOLOGY. The mouthparts of an insect. Now *rare.* E19.
2 ZOOLOGY. The masticatory jaws in the mastax of a rotifer. L19.

trophic /ˈtrɒfɪk/ *adjective.* L19.
[from Greek *trophikos*, from *trophē* nourishment: see -IC.]
1 BIOLOGY & MEDICINE. Of or pertaining to nutrition; *spec.* (of certain nerves and ganglia) concerned with or regulating the nutrition of the tissues. L19.
2 ECOLOGY. Of or pertaining to the feeding habits of, and the food relationship between, different types of organisms in the food cycle. M20.
3 PHYSIOLOGY. Of a hormone: stimulating the production of another specific hormone from an endocrine gland. M20.
2 trophic level any of a hierarchy of levels of an ecosystem, each consisting of organisms sharing the same function in the food chain and the same relationship to the primary producers.

-trophic /ˈtrəʊfɪk, ˈtrɒfɪk/ *suffix.*
[from prec.]
BIOLOGY & PHYSIOLOGY. **1** Forming adjectives with the senses 'characterized by nutrition (of a certain kind)', 'finding nourishment in', '*autotrophic*, *heterotrophic*; also 'controlled by', as *neurotrophic*.
2 Forming adjectives with the sense '(esp. of a hormone) maintaining or regulating (a gland, tissue, etc.)', as *gonadotrophic*, *sebotrophic*. Cf. -TROPIC.

trophied /ˈtrəʊfɪd/ *adjective.* E17.
[from TROPHY *noun*, *verb*: see -ED², -ED¹.]
1 Decorated or provided with a trophy or trophies. E17.
2 Formed into or constituting a trophy. E19.

tropho- /ˈtrɒfəʊ, ˈtrəʊfə/ *combining form* of Greek *trophē* nourishment, from *trephein* nourish: see -O-. Before a vowel also **troph-**.
■ **troˈphectoderm** *noun* (EMBRYOLOGY) = TROPHOBLAST M20. **trophectoˈdermal** *adjective* (EMBRYOLOGY) = TROPHOBLASTIC L20. **trophoˈbiont** *noun* [-BIONT] ENTOMOLOGY an insect etc. (e.g. an aphid) which produces a secretion used as food by a social insect which protects it (e.g. an ant) E20. **trophoblast** *noun* (EMBRYOLOGY & MEDICINE) a layer of cells or a membrane surrounding an embryo, which supplies it with nourishment and later forms most of the placenta L19. **trophoˈblastic** *adjective* (EMBRYOLOGY & MEDICINE) relating to or consisting of trophoblast L19. **trophoˈchromatin** *noun* (CYTOLOGY) (now *rare* or *obsolete*) chromatin which was formerly thought to be concerned only with the regulation of the metabolism and growth of the cell and not with its reproduction E20. **trophocyte** *noun* (BIOLOGY) any of various cells that provide nourishment for other cells, forming most of the fat-body in insects, or functioning as nurse cells etc. E20. **troˈphology** *noun* the branch of physiology that deals with nutrition L19. **trophoˈlytic** *adjective* (ECOLOGY) (of part of a lake) characterized by the decomposition of organic matter (opp. TROPHOGENIC 2) M20. **trophoˈnema** *noun*, pl. **-mata** /-mətə/, ZOOLOGY any of numerous glandular villi or filaments in the uterus of many viviparous selachian fishes, which supply nutrient to the embryos (usu. in *pl.*) L19. **trophoneuˈrosis** *noun*, pl. **-roses** /-ˈrəʊsiːz/, MEDICINE (now *rare*) any of a class of functional disorders due to derangement of the trophic action of the nerves M19. **trophoˈnucleus** *noun*, pl. **-nuclei**, ZOOLOGY = MACRONUCLEUS E20. **trophophore** *noun* (ZOOLOGY) any of the amoeboid nutritive cells in a sponge which give rise to gemmules L19. **trophoplasm** *noun* (*obsolete* exc. *Hist.*) undifferentiated protoplasm which was formerly believed to furnish nutriment to the idioplasm L19. **trophosome** *noun* (ZOOLOGY) (**a**) (now *rare*) the aggregate of nutritive zooids in a colonial hydrozoan; (**b**) a large mass of tissue in a pogonophoran which contains symbiotic bacteria: L19. **trophoˈtaxis** *noun* (ZOOLOGY) = TROPHOTROPISM L19. **trophotropic** /-ˈtrəʊpɪk, -ˈtrɒpɪk/ *adjective* (BIOLOGY) exhibiting or characterized by trophotropism L19. **trophotropism** /-ˈtrəʊp-/ *noun* (BIOLOGY) the movement of (a part of) an organism or cell in response to a food stimulus L19. **trophoˈzoite** *noun* (ZOOLOGY) a sporozoan in its growing stage, when it is absorbing nutrient from the host E20. **trophoˈzooid** *noun* (ZOOLOGY) = GASTROZOOID L19.

trophogenic /trɒfə(ʊ)ˈdʒɛnɪk, trəʊfə-/ *adjective.* E20.
[from TROPHO- + -GENIC.]
1 ENTOMOLOGY. Arising from feeding; *spec.* (of a caste in a social insect) originating by trophogeny. E20.
2 ECOLOGY. Of part of a lake: characterized by the photosynthetic production of oxygen and organic matter. Opp. TROPHOLYTIC. M20.
■ **troˈphogeny** *noun* (ENTOMOLOGY) the determination of a social insect's caste by differential feeding of the larvae E20.

Trophonian /trəˈfəʊnɪən/ *adjective. literary.* L18.
[from Latin *Trophonius*, Greek *Trophonios* (see below) + -AN.]
Of or pertaining to Trophonius, the deified legendary builder of the original temple of Apollo at Delphi, whose oracle in a Boeotian cave was said to affect those who entered with such awe that they never smiled again.

trophy /ˈtrəʊfi/ *noun.* Also (esp. in sense 1) in Latin form **trophaeum** /trəˈfiːəm/, pl. **-phaea** /-ˈfiːə/. L15.
[French *trophée* from Latin *trophaeum*, earlier *tropaeum* from Greek *tropaion* use as noun of neut. of *tropaios*, from *tropē* turning, putting to flight, defeat.]
1 CLASSICAL ANTIQUITIES. A structure consisting of the weapons etc. of a defeated army set up, orig. on the battlefield, as a memorial of victory. L15. ▸**b** A representation of such a memorial; (a representation of) an ornamental group of symbolic or typical objects arranged for display. M17.
2 a A thing taken in war, hunting, etc.; a spoil, a prize, *esp.* one kept or displayed as a memorial. E16. ▸**b** A thing serving as evidence of victory, bravery, strength, skill, etc.; *spec.* a cup or other decorative object awarded as a prize or memento of victory or success esp. in a sporting contest. M16.

> 📖 **1** GIBBON Alexander erected the Macedonian trophies on the banks of the Hyphasis. **b** M. W. MONTAGU A gilded trophy wreathed with flowers. **2a** F. TUOHY Such battered hunting trophies . . as a stuffed lynx and a frieze of roebuck antlers. **b** *Daily News* The presentation of a silver trophy to each corps.

Comb.: **trophy-money** (**a**) *Hist.* a county tax for incidental militia expenses; (**b**) = ***trophy tax*** below; **trophy tax** an annual payment made in the City of London to the City of London Territorial Army and Volunteer Reserve Association; **trophy wife** *colloq.* a young, attractive wife regarded as a status symbol for an older man.

trophy /ˈtrəʊfi/ *verb trans. arch.* L16.
[from the noun.]
†**1** Transform into a trophy. *rare*. Only in L16.
2 Give a trophy to, celebrate with a trophy; decorate with a trophy or trophies. Usu. in *pass.* M17.

-trophy /trəfi, trəʊfi/ *suffix.*
[formed as TROPHIC *adjective* + -Y³.]
Forming nouns corresp. to adjectives in -TROPHIC.

tropic /ˈtrɒpɪk/ *noun & adjective*¹. LME.
[Latin *tropicus* from Greek *tropikos* pertaining to the apparent turning of the sun at the solstice, tropical, from *tropē*: see TROPIC *adjective*³.]
▶**A** *noun.* **1** ASTRONOMY. †**a** = ***solstitial point*** s.v. SOLSTITIAL *noun*. LME–M17. ▸**b** Either of two circles of the celestial sphere parallel to, and 23° 26′ north and south of, the celestial equator, and touching the ecliptic at the solstitial points. E16. ▸**c** *fig.* A turning-point; a limit, a boundary. *arch.* M17.
2 a GEOGRAPHY. Either of two parallels of latitude on the earth's surface corresponding to the celestial circles, 23° 26′ north and south of the equator, being the boundaries of the torrid zone. E16. ▸**b** In *pl.* *The* region between (and about) these parallels; *the* torrid zone and parts immediately adjacent. M19.
Phrases: **tropic of Cancer** ASTRONOMY & GEOGRAPHY the tropic 23° 26′ north of the (celestial or terrestrial) equator. **tropic of Capricorn** ASTRONOMY & GEOGRAPHY the tropic 23° 26′ south of the (celestial or terrestrial) equator.
▶**B** *adjective.* †**1** ASTRONOMY. Connected with the sun's apparent turning back towards the equator at the solstices; pertaining to either or both of the tropics. M16–E18.
2 GEOGRAPHY etc. = TROPICAL 3. L18.
2 tropic bird each of three tropical sea birds of the genus *Phaethon* and family Phaethontidae, which have usu. white plumage marked with long black tail streamers and highly aerial habits.
■ **tropiˈcana** *noun pl.* [-ANA] things concerning or associated with tropical regions; objects from the tropics: M20.

tropic /ˈtrəʊpɪk/ *adjective*². L19.
[formed as TROPINE + -IC.]
CHEMISTRY. ***tropic acid***, an acid obtained from atropine by hydrolysis; 2-hydroxy-1-phenylpropanoic acid, $C_9H_{10}O_3$.

tropic /ˈtrəʊpɪk/ *adjective*³. E20.
[from Greek *tropē* turn, turning + -IC.]
1 BIOLOGY. Pertaining to, consisting of, or exhibiting tropism. E20.
2 PHYSIOLOGY. = TROPHIC 3. M20.

-tropic /ˈtrəʊpɪk, ˈtrɒpɪk/ *suffix.*
[formed as TROPIC *adjective*³.]
Forming adjectives with the senses: (**a**) (chiefly BIOLOGY) 'turning or attracted towards', as *geotropic*, *heliotropic*; (**b**) (chiefly CHEMISTRY & PHYSICS) 'turning, changing', as *enantiotropic*, *thixotropic*; (**c**) (chiefly PHYSIOLOGY) 'affecting', as *neurotropic*, *psychotropic*.
¶ In epithets of hormones used interchangeably with -TROPHIC 2.

tropical /ˈtrɒpɪk(ə)l/ *adjective & noun.* LME.
[formed as TROPIC *noun & adjective*¹: see -ICAL.]
▶**A** *adjective.* **1** ASTRONOMY. Pertaining or relating to either or both tropics. LME.
2 Pertaining to, involving, or of the nature of a trope or tropes; metaphorical, figurative. M16.
3 a GEOGRAPHY etc. Pertaining to, occurring in, characteristic of, or inhabiting the tropics; belonging to the torrid zone. L17. ▸**b** Of clothing, fabric, etc.: suitable for wearing or using in hot climates; lightweight and porous. Also more fully ***tropical weight***. L18. ▸**c** Resembling the tropics, esp. in climate; very hot; *fig.* passionate. M19.
1 tropical year the interval between two successive passages of the sun through the same solstitial (or equinoctial) point; the natural year as reckoned from one solstice (or equinox) to its next occurrence. **3a tropical cyclone** a localized, very intense cyclone that forms over tropical oceans with winds of hurricane force.
▶**B** *noun.* In *pl.* Tropical clothes (see sense A.3b above). M20.
■ **tropiˈcality** *noun* the state or condition of being tropical E20. **tropicaliˈzation** *noun* the process or state of being tropicalized M20. **tropicalize** *verb trans.* (**a**) make tropical; give a tropical character to; (**b**) make suitable for use under tropical conditions: L19. **tropically** *adverb* (**a**) in the manner of a trope; metaphorically, figuratively; (**b**) in a way characteristic of the tropics: M16.

tropicopolitan /ˌtrɒpɪkə(ʊ)ˈpɒlɪt(ə)n/ *adjective.* Now *rare*. L19.
[from TROPIC *noun & adjective*¹ after *cosmopolitan*.]
BOTANY & ZOOLOGY. Belonging to or inhabiting the whole of the tropics, or tropical regions generally.

tropine /ˈtrəʊpiːn, -pʌɪn/ *noun.* M19.
[from ATROPINE.]
CHEMISTRY. A bicyclic alkaloid, $C_8H_{15}ON$, of which atropine and many tropane alkaloids are derivatives.

tropism /ˈtrəʊpɪz(ə)m, ˈtrɒp-/ *noun.* L19.
[2nd elem. of HELIOTROPISM etc.]
BIOLOGY. The turning of (part of) an organism in a particular direction by growth, bending, or locomotion, in response to some special external stimulus. Cf. TAXIS 6.
■ **troˈpistic** *adjective* pertaining to or constituting tropism E20.

-tropism /ˈtrəʊpɪz(ə)m/ *suffix.*
[formed as TROPIC *adjective*³ + -ISM.]
Chiefly BIOLOGY & PHYSIOLOGY. Forming nouns corresp. to adjectives in -TROPIC. Cf. -TROPY.

tropo /ˈtrɒpəʊ, ˈtrəʊ-/ *noun.* M20.
[Abbreviation.]
TELECOMMUNICATIONS. = TROPOSCATTER.

tropo- /ˈtrəʊpəʊ, ˈtrɒpəʊ/ *combining form* of Greek *tropos* turning etc.: see TROPE, -O-.
■ **tropoˈcollagen** *noun* (BIOCHEMISTRY) the molecular constituent of collagen fibrils, formed of three supercoiled polypeptide chains M20. **tropomyosin** /-ˈmʌɪəsɪn/ *noun* (BIOCHEMISTRY) a protein related to myosin found together with troponin in the thin filaments of myofibrils, and involved in muscle contraction: M20. **troponin** *noun* (BIOCHEMISTRY) a globular protein complex which occurs with tropomyosin in the thin filaments of muscle tissue, and is involved in muscle contraction M20. **tropophyte** *noun* (BOTANY) a plant adapted to a seasonal climate, which forms resting buds in periods unsuitable to growth E20. **tropoˈtactic** *adjective* (ZOOLOGY) of or pertaining to tropotaxis M20. **tropoˈtaxis** *noun* (ZOOLOGY) a taxis in which an animal's movement is in response to the difference in stimulation of two symmetrically placed receptors M20.

tropology /trəˈpɒlədʒi/ *noun.* LME.
[Late Latin *tropologia* from Greek, from *tropos* TROPE *noun* + -O- + -LOGY.]
1 Figurative interpretation, esp. of the Scriptures to give moral guidance. LME.
2 A figure of speech, a metaphor; the figurative use of language. E16.
3 A treatise on tropes or figures of speech. M17.
■ **tropologic** /trɒpəˈlɒdʒɪk/ *adjective* tropological LME. **tropological** /trɒpəˈlɒdʒɪk(ə)l/ *adjective* of, pertaining to, or involving tropology E16. **tropoˈlogically** *adverb* M16.

tropolone /ˈtrɒpələʊn/ *noun.* M20.
[formed as TROPINE + -OL + -ONE.]
CHEMISTRY. A water-soluble enolic ketone, $C_7H_6O_2$, whose molecule is a seven-membered carbon ring. Also, any of a series of derivatives of this found in various plants, as colchicine and the thujaplicins.
■ **tropone** /ˈtrəʊp-/ *noun* a viscous hygroscopic oil, C_7H_6O, which is a cyclic aromatic ketone and of which tropolone is the hydroxylated derivative M20.

tropopause /ˈtrɒpəpɔːz, ˈtrəʊp-/ *noun.* E20.
[from TROPO(SPHERE + PAUSE *noun*.]
METEOROLOGY. The upper limit of the troposphere, separating it from the stratosphere, at which temperature ceases decreasing with height.

troposcatter /ˈtrɒpəʊskatə, ˈtrəʊpə-/ *noun.* M20.
[from TROPO(SPHERIC + SCATTER *noun*.]
TELECOMMUNICATIONS. The scattering of radio waves etc. by clouds and local variations in the troposphere, thus extending the range of radio communication.

troposphere /ˈtrɒpəsfɪə, ˈtrəʊp-/ *noun.* E20.
[from TROPO- + -SPHERE.]
METEOROLOGY. The lowest region of the atmosphere, extending to a height of between 8 and 18 km (5 and 11 miles) and marked by convection and a general decrease of temperature with height.
■ **tropoˈspheric** *adjective* of, pertaining to, or involving the troposphere; ***tropospheric scatter*** = TROPOSCATTER: M20.

troppo /ˈtrɒpəʊ/ *adjective. Austral. slang.* M20.
[from TROPIC *noun & adjective*¹ + -O.]
Mentally disturbed from exposure to a tropical climate; crazy, mad.

troppo /ˈtrɒpəʊ/ *adverb.* E20.
[Italian.]
MUSIC. In directions: too much.
MA NON TROPPO.

-tropy /ˈtrəpi, *occas.* ˈtrəʊpi/ *suffix.*
[formed as TROPIC *adjective*[3] + -Y[3].]
Chiefly CHEMISTRY & PHYSICS. Forming nouns corresp. to adjectives in -TROPIC. Cf. -TROPISM.

tropylium /trəˈpɪlɪəm/ *noun.* M20.
[from TROP(OLONE + -YL + -IUM.]
CHEMISTRY. The cation $C_7H_7^+$, consisting of a ring of seven =CH– groups. Usu. in *comb.*

trot /trɒt/ *noun*[1]. ME.
[Old & mod. French, from *troter*: see TROT *verb*. Branch II perh. a different word.]
▶ **I 1 a** A gait between walking and running; *spec.* (*a*) the gait of a horse or other quadruped, in which the legs move in diagonal pairs almost together, so that when moving fast all four feet are momentarily off the ground at once; (*b*) the gait of a person running at a moderate pace with short strides. ME. ▸**b** Orig., a journey or expedition on horseback. Later, an act or spell of trotting; a ride at this pace. *rare.* M17. ▸**c** The sound made by a trotting horse etc. M19.
2 A trotting-race. In *pl.* (*colloq.*, orig. *Austral. & NZ*), a series of trotting-races held at a fixed time on a regular course. M19.
3 A toddling child; a small or young animal. *arch. colloq.* M19.
4 A literal translation of a text used by students; a crib. *US slang.* L19.
5 A sequence, a succession, esp. in a game of chance; a run of luck (freq. with specifying word). *colloq.* (orig. *Austral.*). E20.

> 📖 **1** J. CLAVELL They were riding downhill in a quick, bone-jarring trot. G. TINDALL He set off at a trot up the path. **c** OUIDA The trot of the chargers . . had passed into silence. **2** SHERWOOD ANDERSON Mayer's bay stallion . . had won the two-fifteen trot at the fall races. **4** *Times Lit. Suppl.* The translations are rarely better than lame trots. **5** D. R. STUART He's had a damn good trot.

▶ **II 6** In full ***trot-line***. A long fishing-line lightly anchored or buoyed and supporting short lines with baited hooks. Also called ***trout-line***. M19.
7 NAUTICAL. A multiple mooring for small boats or yachts consisting of a base mooring laid in a straight line and supporting individual moorings at spaced intervals. E20.

Phrases: **on the trot** *colloq.* (*a*) continually busy; (*b*) in succession; (*c*) escaping, running away, absconding. **the trots** *slang* an attack of diarrhoea.
■ **trotty** *adjective* (*arch. colloq.*) of daintily small proportions; pleasing: L19.

trot /trɒt/ *noun*[2]. *arch. derog.* ME.
[Anglo-Norman *trote*, of unkn. origin. Cf. BAWDSTROT.]
An old woman; a hag.

Trot /trɒt/ *noun*[3] & *adjective. colloq.* (usu. *derog.*). M20.
[Abbreviation.]
= TROTSKYIST *noun & adjective*.

trot /trɒt/ *verb.* Infl. **-tt-**. LME.
[Old & mod. French *troter* (mod. *trotter*) from Proto-Romance, from Latin *trottare*, of Germanic origin. Branch II perh. a different word.]
▶ **I 1** *verb intrans.* Of a horse, person, etc.: proceed at the trot. LME.
2 *verb intrans.* Go or move quickly; go briskly or busily; walk, run. *colloq.* LME.
†**3** *verb trans.* Traverse or move over (as) at the trot. L16–M17.
4 *verb trans.* Cause (a horse, person, etc.) to proceed at the trot. L16. ▸**b** Make (a person) appear ridiculous; make a butt of (a person). Freq. foll. by *out*. *arch.* E19. ▸**c** Jog (a child) on one's knee. M19. ▸**d** Bid against (a person) for an item at auction to force up the price; make or accept a bid for (an item at auction) to force up the price. Also foll. by *up*. *slang.* M19. ▸**e** Conduct or escort (a person) *to* or *round* a place; keep company with (a woman), esp. regularly in a romantic or sexual relationship. Also foll. by *out*. *slang.* L19.

> 📖 **1** D. H. LAWRENCE Gerald Crich trotted up on a red Arab mare. W. MAXWELL The dog . . trots ahead importantly. **2** *Sunday Times* I may trot round to Portobello market for vegetables. W. TREVOR You trot along, my dear. I'll sit and watch the boats. **3** SHAKES. *Hen. V* My horse . . bounds from the earth . . he trots the air. **4** G. CARLETON He commanded William . . to trott the horses up and downe. P. THEROUX They . . tried to trot him through the woods. **e** H. S. MERRIMAN Perhaps you'll trot us round the works. *Baby* Parents who trot their children off to the doctor.

▶ **II 5 a** *verb trans. & intrans.* Fish with a trot-line. M19. ▸**b** *verb trans.* Cause (a trot-line or any of its baited hooks) to be carried downstream by the current. Also foll. by *down*. M20.

Phrases: **strong enough to trot a mouse on**, **thick enough to trot a mouse on**, etc., *dial.* (of liquid food or drink) particularly strong or thick. **trot out** (*a*) lead out and show off the paces of (a horse); (*b*) *colloq.* produce or introduce (a person, opinion, etc.) (as if) for inspection or approval, esp. tediously or repeatedly; (*c*) see senses 4b, e above.

Comb.: **trot-cosy** *Scot.* (now *Hist.*) a hooded cloak for cold-weather travel.
■ **trotting** *noun* (*a*) the action or an act of the verb; (*b*) racing for trotting horses pulling a two-wheeled vehicle and driver (freq. in ***trotting-race***): LME. **trotting** *adjective* (*a*) *gen.* that trots; (*b*) ***trotting horse***, a horse bred or trained for trotting, a trotter: LME.

troth /trəʊθ/ *noun & verb. arch.* ME.
[Var. of TRUTH *noun*.]
▶ **A** *noun.* **I 1** One's faith as pledged or plighted in a solemn agreement or undertaking; one's plighted word; the act of pledging one's faith, a promise, a covenant. Chiefly in ***pledge one's troth***, ***plight one's troth*** below. ME.

> 📖 **1** ALLAN RAMSAY Give me back my maiden-vow And . . my troth. LYTTON Gryffyth will never keep troth with the English.

▶ **II 2** = TRUTH *noun* II. Now *rare* or *obsolete*. ME.

> 📖 **2** S. RICHARDSON Troth, sir . . I never knew her peer. M. TWAIN In troth I might go yet farther.

Phrases: **by my troth**: expr. asseveration. **in troth** truly, really, indeed. **pledge one's troth**, **plight one's troth** pledge one's word esp. in marriage or betrothal.
▶ **B** *verb trans.* Pledge one's word to, esp. in marriage or betrothal. LME.

Comb.: **troth-plight** *noun, adjective, & verb* (*a*) *noun* the action or an act of pledging one's word esp. in marriage or betrothal; (a) betrothal; (*b*) *adjective* betrothed; (*c*) *verb trans.* = TROTH *verb*.
■ **trothful** *adjective* (*rare*) loyal, faithful; trustworthy, truthful: LME. **trothless** *adjective* (*a*) faithless, disloyal; †(*b*) false; untrustworthy: ME.

tro-tro /ˈtrəʊtrəʊ/ *noun.* Pl. same, **tro-tros**. L20.
[Prob. from Akan *tro* threepence, with ref. to the fare.]
In Ghana: a converted lorry or van used as a public conveyance, a minibus.

Trotskyism /ˈtrɒtskɪɪz(ə)m/ *noun.* E20.
[from Leon *Trotsky* (see below) + -ISM.]
The political or economic principles of the Russian revolutionary Leon Trotsky (1879–1940), who believed in the theory of continuing revolution rather than the more pragmatic ideas of State Communism generally accepted in the USSR in the post-Revolutionary era.
■ **Trotskyist** *noun & adjective* (*a*) *noun* a follower or supporter of Trotsky or Trotskyism; (*b*) *adjective* of, pertaining to, or characteristic of Trotskyists or Trotskyism: E20. **Trotskyite** *adjective & noun* (*a*) *adjective* = TROTSKYIST *adjective*; (*b*) *noun* = TROTSKYIST *noun*: E20.

trotter /ˈtrɒtə/ *noun.* ME.
[from TROT *verb* + -ER[1].]
1 An animal which trots; *spec.* a horse bred or trained for trotting. ME.
2 A foot; *spec.* (*a*) an animal's foot as food; (*b*) *joc.* a person's foot. Usu. in *pl.* LME.
3 A person who trots; *esp.* a person who moves or goes about briskly and constantly. *arch.* exc. in ***globe-trotter*** s.v. GLOBE *noun*. M16.

> 📖 **1** *Carriage Driving* The racing was . . geared for pacers and young trotters. **2** JOYCE A cold sheep's trotter sprinkled with . . pepper. J. HARVEY He had small quick feet, deft nimble trotters. **3** S. FOOTE That eternal trotter after all the . . girls of town.

trotteur /ˈtrɒtəː/ *noun.* E20.
[French, formed as TROTTOIR + *-eur* -OR.]
Hist. An ankle-length skirt, usu. flared at the back for ease of walking.

trottles *noun pl.* var. of TRATTLES.

trottoir /ˈtrɒtwɑː; *foreign* trɔtwaːr (*pl. same*)/ *noun.* L18.
[French, from *trotter* TROT *verb* + *-oir* -ORY[1].]
Esp. in France and French-speaking countries: a pavement.

trotyl /ˈtrəʊtɪl, -tʌɪl/ *noun.* E20.
[from TRINI)TROT(OLUENE + -YL.]
= TRINITROTOLUENE.

troubadour /ˈtruːbədɔː/ *noun.* E18.
[French from Provençal *trobador* (= Old French *troveor*), from *trobar* (= Old French *trover*) compose in verse, invent, find, ult. origin unkn. Cf. TROUVÈRE.]
1 *Hist.* Any of a class of French medieval lyric poets composing and singing in Provençal esp. on the themes of chivalry and courtly love, living in southern France, eastern Spain, and northern Italy, between the 11th and 13th cents.; a minstrel. E18.
2 A person who composes or sings verses or ballads; a singer, a poet. E19.
■ **troubadourish** *adjective* of, pertaining to, or resembling the work of a troubadour M19. **troubadourishly** *adverb* L19.

†**troublance** *noun.* LME–E19.
[Old French *trublance*, *troblance*, from *trubler*, *trobler* TROUBLE *verb* + -ANCE.]
The action of troubling or state of being troubled; disturbance; trouble, pain.

trouble /ˈtrʌb(ə)l/ *noun.* ME.
[Old French *truble*, *turble* (mod. *trouble*), formed as TROUBLE *verb*.]
1 Disturbance of the mind or feelings; worry, vexation; grief; perplexity; distress; difficulty; inconvenience, bother. Formerly also, harm, injury, offence. ME. ▸**b** An instance of this; a distressing or vexatious circumstance, occurrence, or experience; a difficulty, an inconvenience, a bother. E16. ▸**c** A person who or thing which causes affliction or distress; a source or occasion of worry or vexation. L16. ▸**d** Faulty functioning of a mechanism; a problem caused by this; *transf.* (a) difficulty within a personal relationship. Freq. with specifying word. E20.
2 Public disturbance, civil unrest or disorder; strife; an instance of this, a disturbance, an agitation (freq. in *pl.*). LME.
3 Effort or exertion, esp. in accomplishing or attempting something. LME.
4 Unpleasant, difficult, or embarrassing circumstances. Chiefly in ***ask for trouble***, ***get into trouble***, and other similar phrs. below. M16. ▸**b** The condition of a pregnant unmarried woman. Chiefly in ***in trouble***, ***get into trouble*** below. *colloq.* L19.
5 MINING. A dislocation in a stratum; a fault, *esp.* a small one. L17.
6 a A disease, a disorder, an illness. Now chiefly *Scot. & colloq.* E18. ▸**b** Childbirth, labour. Chiefly *dial. & euphem.* E19.

> 📖 **1** MILTON The trouble of thy thoughts this night . . Affects me equally. E. BLISHEN Their trouble sprang from poor articulation. *Economist* The . . government has caused trouble for this . . industry by raising its costs. **b** F. A. PALEY His troubles seemed at an end. A. MILLER The trouble with you kids is you *think* too much. A. MACRAE Other people have troubles too. **c** SHAKES. *Temp.* Alack, what trouble Was I then to you! **d** *Autocar* Spence . . pitted on lap 36 with sudden engine trouble. J. LE CARRÉ Bill was having girl trouble. **2** H. LATIMER It maketh trouble and rebellion in the realme. T. PARKER Aden, where soon after my arrival . . the troubles began. **3** J. WAIN He was willing to take a little trouble to influence Charles. D. EDEN Annabel had . . gone to a lot of trouble with the room. **6a** D. L. SAYERS Dr. Grainger diagnosed the trouble as acute gastritis. **b** M. GRAY He rode over . . to help . . Pink's wife in her trouble.

Phrases: **ask for trouble**, **look for trouble** *colloq.* invite unpleasantness or difficulty by one's actions, behaviour, etc.; behave rashly or indiscreetly. **be no trouble** cause no inconvenience etc. ***borrow trouble***: see BORROW *verb*[1]. **get into trouble** (*a*) *verb phr. intrans.* become involved in a matter likely to bring censure or punishment; (*b*) *verb phr. trans.* (*colloq.*) make (an unmarried girl or woman) pregnant. **in trouble** (*a*) involved in a matter likely to bring censure or punishment; (*b*) *colloq.* pregnant while unmarried. ***look for trouble***: see ***ask for trouble*** above. ***meet trouble halfway***: see MEET *verb*. ***save the trouble***: see SAVE *verb*. ***teething troubles***. **the Troubles** any of various rebellions, civil wars, and unrest in Ireland, *spec.* in 1919–23 and (in Northern Ireland) from 1968. **trouble and strife** *rhyming slang* (*a*) *rare* life; (*b*) a wife. **trouble at t' mill**, **trouble at the mill**, **trouble at mill** (chiefly *joc.*) an industrial dispute, as at a textile mill in the Midlands or north of England; any disagreement or problem at work, home, etc.

Comb.: **trouble lamp**, **trouble light** *N. Amer.*: for use in an emergency, esp. by a motorist carrying out roadside repairs; **troublemaker** a person who habitually causes trouble; **troublemaking** the action of causing trouble; **trouble man** *US* = ***troubleshooter*** (a) below; **troubleshoot** *verb* (*a*) *verb intrans.* act as a troubleshooter (freq. as ***troubleshooting*** *verbal noun & ppl adjective*); (*b*) *verb trans.* deal with (a problem etc.) as a troubleshooter; **troubleshooter** (orig. *US*) (*a*) a person who traces and corrects faults in machinery etc.; (*b*) a person who specializes in removing or solving difficulties; *esp.* a mediator in diplomatic or industrial affairs; **trouble spot** a place where difficulties frequently occur; a scene of (impending) conflict.
■ **troubleless** /-l-l-/ *adjective* (*rare*) M19.

trouble /ˈtrʌb(ə)l/ *verb.* ME.
[Old French *trubler*, *turbler* (mod. *troubler*), from Proto-Romance base also of Old & mod. French *trouble* adjective disturbed, turbid from Latin *turbidus* TURBID.]
▶ **I 1** *verb trans.* Disturb or agitate (water, air, etc.); *esp.* make (water etc.) turbid, dim, or cloudy by stirring. Now *arch. rare.* ME. ▸†**b** *verb intrans.* Of water, air, etc.: be or become disturbed or agitated; (of water etc.) grow turbid, dim, or cloudy. LME–M16.
2 *verb trans.* Interfere with, interrupt; hinder, mar. *arch.* ME.

> 📖 **1** AV *John* 5:4 An Angel went downe . . into the poole, and troubled the water. SHAKES. *Tam. Shr.* Like a fountain troubled—Muddy, ill-seeming, thick. **2** ADDISON Such who . . might . . trouble and pervert the course of justice.

▶ **II 3** *verb trans.* Disturb the mind or feelings of (a person); distress, grieve; worry, vex; perplex. Also foll. by *with*. ME. ▸**b** *verb trans.* Cause inconvenience to (a person) (freq. foll. by *with*, *to do*). Also, importune (a person) *for*. E16. ▸**c** *verb refl.* Take pains or exert oneself *to do*. E16.
4 *verb trans.* Do harm or injury to; molest, oppress. *arch.* ME. ▸**b** Of disease, illness, etc.: afflict; cause pain etc. to. Freq. in *pass.*, foll. by *with*. LME.
5 *verb intrans.* Be or become disturbed, distressed, or worried. LME. ▸**b** Exert oneself *to do*; be subjected to inconvenience or bother. L19.

📖 **3** Shakes. *Wint. T.* Take the boy to you; he so troubles me, 'Tis past enduring. G. W. Knight This . . troubles him . . planting a nightmare of unrest in his mind. D. Cusack The problem that has been troubling us all. **b** Steele I will not trouble you with more Letters. OED May I trouble you to pass the mustard? **c** Ld Macaulay The officer never troubles himself to ascertain whether the arms are in good order. **4** R. C. Singleton Swans . . Whom, swooping from . . the skies, Jove's bird was troubling. **b** Shakes. *Oth.* Being troubled with a raging tooth, I could not sleep. **5** J. McCarthy He . . allowed reform to go its way for him, and never troubled. S. Hill I am sorry . . . Don't trouble about this, please. **b** G. Greene Faults . . that he never troubled to amend.

■ **troubler** *noun* LME. **troubling** *verbal noun* the action of the verb; an instance of this: ME.

troubled /ˈtrʌb(ə)ld/ *adjective.* ME.
[from prec. + -ED[1].]
That has been troubled; *esp.* showing, experiencing, or affected by disturbance, anxiety, etc.

📖 O. Manning Guy, shaken by this mention of courtesy, raised troubled eyes. R. Lindner The sleep I managed to get . . was troubled. ***pour oil on troubled waters***: see POUR *verb* 1.

■ **troubledly** *adverb* (*rare*) L16. **troubledness** *noun* (*rare*) M16.

troublement /ˈtrʌb(ə)lm(ə)nt/ *noun.* Long *arch. rare.* L15.
[French, formed as TROUBLE *verb* + -MENT.]
The act of troubling; the condition of being troubled.

troublesome /ˈtrʌb(ə)ls(ə)m/ *adjective.* M16.
[from TROUBLE *noun* + -SOME[1].]
Full of, characterized by, or causing trouble; vexing, annoying.

📖 *Science News Letter* Phantom . . pains, a troublesome affliction in amputation cases. *She* I sagely advised my girlfriends about their many troublesome love affairs.

■ **troublesomely** *adverb* M16. **troublesomeness** *noun* M16.

troublous /ˈtrʌbləs/ *adjective. arch.* LME.
[Old French *troubleus*, formed as TROUBLE *noun* + -OUS.]
Full of troubles, troubled, agitated, disturbed. Also, causing trouble; troublesome.

📖 H. James Her troublous faculty of seeing everything in . . different lights. C. McCullough He guided the country through its most troublous of all times.

■ **troublously** *adverb* M16. **troublousness** *noun* LME.

trou-de-loup /trudəlu/ *noun.* Pl. ***trous-de-loup*** (pronounced same). L18.
[French, lit. 'wolf-pit'.]
FORTIFICATION. Any of a row of conical pits each with a central vertical pointed stake constructed in front of a fieldwork to hinder an enemy's advance. Usu. in *pl.*

trough /trɒf/ *noun & verb.*
[Old English *trog*, Old High German *troc* (Dutch *trog*, German *Trog*), Old Norse *trog*, from Germanic from Indo-European base also of TREE *noun*. Cf. TROW *noun*[2], TRUG *noun*[1].]
► **A** *noun.* **1** A long narrow open receptacle for water, animal feed, etc., usu. made of stone, metal, or plastic, and often constituting a fixture. Also, any receptacle of similar shape and function. Freq. with specifying word. OE. ▸**b** A person who drinks heavily. *arch. derog.* E17. ▸**c** An oblong vessel containing the water in which a grindstone runs; (the site of) a grindstone; a workman's compartment in a grindery. Now *rare* or *obsolete.* E18. ▸**d** An oblong box with divisions serving as the cells of a voltaic battery. Also ***trough battery***. Now *rare* or *obsolete.* E19. ▸**e** A place where food is provided, *spec.* a dining-table; a meal. *colloq.* E20.
2 = TROW *noun*[2]. *obsolete* exc. *dial.* OE.
3 A channel or pipe for conveying a liquid, esp. water; a conduit; a rainwater gutter under the eaves of a building (also ***eaves-trough***). LME.
4 A stone tomb or coffin. Formerly also, a flat gravestone. Now *dial.* L15.
5 A naturally occurring trough-shaped hollow; *spec.* (***a***) a river-bed, a river-valley; (***b***) PHYSICAL GEOGRAPHY a broad elongate depression or valley, a narrow syncline; (***c***) OCEANOGRAPHY an elongate depression of the sea floor; (***d***) a hollow between two wave crests; (***e***) METEOROLOGY an elongated region of lower barometric pressure. E16.
6 The lowest point of something; *spec.* (***a***) the lowest level of economic activity or prosperity; (***b***) a region around the minimum on a curve of a varying quantity. E20.

📖 **1** I. Wallace Pigs lined the troughs, jostling, squealing, eating their swill. R. Fraser Water . . brought specially from the trough in the centre of town. ***cattle-trough, drinking-trough, horse-trough***, etc. ***book-trough, dough-trough***, etc. **5** W. de la Mare In the trough of the billows. C. Embleton The great glacial troughs . . carved out to depths of . . thousands of metres. **6** *Opera Now* Rysanek's voice . . can plunge an octave . . into a trough of despair.

Phrases: ***pneumatic trough***: see PNEUMATIC *adjective* 4. **trough of the sea** *arch.* a hollow between two swells or waves.
Comb.: ***trough battery***: see sense 1d above; **trough fault** = GRABEN; **trough garden** a miniature garden comprising a group of small (esp. alpine) plants, in a stone troughlike container; **trough shell** (the shell of) any of various marine bivalve molluscs of the family Mactridae, which have thin shells with a triangular pit in the hinge.
► **B** *verb.* **1** *verb trans.* †**a** Provide with a trough or troughs. Only in M17. ▸**b** GEOLOGY. Form into a trough; make troughlike. M19. ▸**c** Dye, mould, or otherwise treat, in a trough. L19.
2 *verb intrans.* Feed (as) at a trough; feed greedily. *rare.* M18.
■ **troughful** *noun* as much or as many as a trough will hold L19. **troughing** *noun* troughs collectively; a set or system of troughs: E19. **troughlike** *adjective* resembling a trough M19. **troughy** *adjective* having a trough or troughs E19.

trounce /traʊns/ *verb*[1] *trans.* M16.
[Origin unkn.]
†**1** Afflict, distress; discomfit. M16–M17.
2 Beat, thrash, esp. as a punishment. M16.
3 Censure; rebuke or scold severely. E17.
4 Punish severely; (now *dial.*) punish by legal action or process; indict, sue. Also, get the better of, defeat heavily. M17.

📖 **2** W. Besant They were tied up . . and soundly trounced. **3** R. Gittings Trouncing the Government for suspending Habeas Corpus. **4** J. Howell How Rich. the first trounced her for murthuring the Jews. C. Connolly The disheartened Conservative party, after being trounced in the general election. *Athletics Today* Johnson trounced Lewis in last year's World Championships.

■ **trouncer** *noun* (***a***) a person who trounces someone or something; (***b***) (now *rare* or *obsolete*) an assistant to a carman, drayman, or lorry-driver: E17. **trouncing** *noun* the action or an act of the verb; an instance of this: M16.

trounce /trəʊns/ *verb*[2]. Chiefly *Scot.* M16.
[Var. of TRANCE *verb*[2].]
1 *verb intrans.* = TRANCE *verb*[2]. M16.
2 *verb trans.* Cause to move rapidly; cause to go. *rare.* E19.

troupe /truːp/ *noun.* E19.
[French = TROOP *noun*.]
A company of actors, acrobats, etc.

trouper /ˈtruːpə/ *noun.* L19.
[from prec. + -ER[1].]
1 A member of a troupe, an actor, an acrobat, etc. L19.
2 *transf.* A reliable, uncomplaining person; a staunch supporter or colleague. *colloq.* M20.

📖 **1** D. Rutherford A good trouper can still shimmy in her fifties. **2** *New York Post* She has been in great pain, but she has been a trouper.

troupial /ˈtruːpɪəl/ *noun.* Also **troopial**. E19.
[French *troupiale*, alt. (after *troupe* flock) of Amer. Spanish *turpial*, of Carib origin.]
Any of various American orioles of the family Icteridae; spec. *Icterus icterus* of S. America, which has orange and black plumage and yellow eyes.

trous-de-loup *noun* pl. of TROU-DE-LOUP.

trouse /traʊs/ *noun*[1] *& verb.* Long *dial.*
[Old English *trus* perh. from Old Norse *tros* rubbish, fallen leaves and twigs etc. used for burning (Norwegian *tros*, Swedish *trås*): ult. origin unkn.]
► **A** *noun.* Brushwood, cuttings from a hedge or copse. OE.
►†**B** *verb trans.* Cut (brushwood); trim cuttings from (a hedge or copse). *rare.* E16–L18.

trouse /truːz, traʊz/ *noun*[2]. *arch.* LME.
[Irish *triús* or Gaelic *triubhas* (sing.), ult. origin unkn. Cf. TREWS, TROUSERS.]
1 *sing.* & in *pl.* Orig., a close-fitting garment reaching from the waist to the knees, divided into two parts to cover the thighs and sometimes with stockings attached; *spec.* trews. Later, drawers, knee-breeches. LME.
†**2** In *pl.* Trousers. L17–E19.

trouser /ˈtraʊzə/ *verb trans. slang.* M19.
[from next.]
Put (money etc.) into one's trouser-pocket; appropriate, esp. dishonestly.

📖 G. Mitchell The butler . . trousered her five-pound note. *Nature* The room being dark, Wood adroitly trousered the prism.

trousers /ˈtraʊzəz/ *noun pl.* In attrib. use & in comb. usu. in sing. **trouser** (otherwise *rare*). E17.
[from TROUSE *noun*[2] after *drawers*. Cf. TREWS.]
†**1** = TROUSE *noun*[2] 1. E17–M19.
2 Orig., a loose-fitting garment covering the loins and legs. Now, an outer garment reaching from the waist usu. to the ankles, divided into two parts to cover the legs (freq. with specifying word). Also ***pair of trousers***. L17. ▸**b** *Hist.* Pantalettes. E19. ▸**c** The hair on the hind legs of a dog, esp. one of a long-coated breed. M20.

📖 **2** G. Orwell He was . . holding up his trousers with both hands as he ran. J. Trollope She wore a . . smock over wide blue trousers. ***Cossack trousers, Oxford trousers, Petersham trousers, Turkish trousers***, etc. ***long trousers***: see LONG *adjective*[1]. ***short trousers***: see SHORT *adjective*. ***striped trousers***. **b** J. Ashby-Sterry Girls . . in short frocks, frilled trousers, and broad blue sashes.

Phrases: **anything in trousers** *colloq.* any man, whether eligible, suitable, or not. **not in these trousers** *colloq.* certainly not. **with one's trousers down** *colloq.* = ***with one's*** PANTS ***down***. ***wear the trousers***: see WEAR *verb*[1].
Comb.: **trouser-clip** = ***bicycle clip*** s.v. BICYCLE *noun*; **trouser-cuff** the turn-up on a trouser-leg; **trouser-press** a device for pressing trouser-legs to produce a crease; **trouser-presser** (***a***) a person who irons trousers; (***b***) = ***trouser-press*** above; **trouser suit** a woman's suit of matching jacket or tunic and trousers; **trouser-suited** *adjective* wearing a trouser suit.
■ **trousered** *adjective* wearing or dressed in trousers L18. **trouserettes** *noun* (***a***) pantalettes; (***b***) short trousers: L19. **trousering** *noun* (***a***) any cloth suitable for trousers (freq. in *pl.*); (***b***) in *pl.*, trousers: M19. **trouserless** *adjective* M19. **trousies** *noun pl.* (*dial. & colloq.*) trousers L19.

trousseau /ˈtruːsəʊ/ *noun*[1]. Pl. **-s**, **-x** /-z/. ME.
[French, dim. of *trousse* TRUSS *noun*.]
1 Orig., a bundle; a package. Later, a bunch. Cf. TRUSSELL 1. Long *rare* or *obsolete.* ME.
2 The clothes etc. collected by a bride in preparation for her marriage. M19.

Trousseau /ˈtruːsəʊ, *foreign* truso/ *noun*[2]. L19.
[Armand *Trousseau* (1801–67), French physician.]
MEDICINE. ***Trousseau's phenomenon***, ***Trousseau's sign***, spasm of a muscle evoked by pressure on the nerve supplying it, as seen in cases of tetany.

trousseaux *noun pl.* see TROUSSEAU *noun*[1].

trout /traʊt/ *noun.* Pl. same, **-s**: see note below.
[Late Old English *truht* from late Latin *tructa*, from Greek *trōktēs* gnawer, a marine fish, from *trōgein* gnaw.]
1 A salmonid fish, *Salmo trutta*, which is found in most rivers and lakes in the temperate or colder parts of Europe, occurs also in migratory forms, and is greatly valued for its sporting and edible qualities. Also, the flesh of this fish as food. LOE. ▸**b** Any of various other salmonid fishes, esp. of the genera *Salmo* and *Salvelinus*. Usu. with specifying word. M19. ▸**c** Any of various fishes resembling the true trouts but not related to them, esp. (*US*) of the genus *Cynoscion* and family Sciaenidae. Usu. with specifying word. L19.
2 †**a** A confidential friend or servant. *slang.* M–L17. ▸**b** A woman, *esp.* an old or ill-tempered one. Orig. & chiefly in ***old trout***. *slang. derog.* L19.

📖 **1 *brown trout, lake trout, sea trout***, etc. **b *brook trout, bull trout, Dolly Varden trout, lake trout, rainbow trout, Sebago trout***, etc. **c *sea trout***.

Comb.: **trout-fly** (***a***) a mayfly; (***b***) an artificial fly for trout-fishing; **trout-lily** *US* a yellow-flowered dog's-tooth violet, *Erythronium americanum*, so called from its mottled leaves; **trout-line** (***a***) a line used in trout-fishing; (***b***) *US* = ***trot-line*** s.v. TROT *noun*[1] 6; **trout-perch** either of two small slender freshwater fishes constituting the genus *Percopsis* and family Percopsidae; spec. *P. omiscomaycus*, which is widely distributed across N. America.
¶ The pl. *-s* is now used only *techn.* to denote different species of trout.
■ **trouter** *noun* a person who fishes for trout, a trout-fisher E18. **troutful** *adjective* full of or having many trout M17. **trouting** *verbal noun* fishing for trout, trout-fishing L18. **troutless** *adjective* without trout M19. **troutlet** *noun* a small or young trout E19. **troutling** *noun* a troutlet M18. **trouty** *adjective* (***a***) full of trout, having many trout; (***b***) resembling a trout, *esp.* speckled like a trout: L17.

Trouton /ˈtraʊt(ə)n/ *noun.* L19.
[Frederick Thomas *Trouton* (1863–1922), Irish physicist.]
PHYSICS. ***Trouton's law***, ***Trouton's rule***, the observation that for many substances the latent heat of vaporization of one mole, divided by the absolute temperature of the boiling point, is a constant (***Trouton constant***, ***Trouton's constant***) equal to approximately 88 joules per kelvin.

trouvaille /truvɑːj/ *noun.* Pl. pronounced same. M19.
[French, from *trouver* to find.]
A lucky find; a windfall.

trouvère /truːˈvɛː, *foreign* truvɛːr (*pl. same*)/ *noun.* Also **-veur** /-ˈvəː, *foreign* -vœːr (*pl. same*)/. L18.
[Old French *trovere* (mod. *trouvère*, *trouveur*) from *troveor*, from *trover* (mod. *trouver* find) compose in verse, invent, find, ult. origin unkn. Cf. TROUBADOUR.]
Hist. Any of a class of French medieval epic poets composing esp. *chansons de geste* and fabliaux, living in northern France between the 11th and 14th cents.

trove /trəʊv/ *noun.* L19.
[from ***treasure trove*** s.v. TREASURE *noun*.]
A valuable find; a source of treasure; a store or reserve of valuable things.

trover /ˈtrəʊvə/ *noun.* L16.
[Anglo-Norman use as noun of Old French *trover* (mod. *trouver*): see TROUVÈRE, -ER[4].]
LAW. The action of finding and assuming possession of personal property (now *Hist.*, superseded by conversion (CONVERSION 8)). Also (in full ***action of trover***), a common-

law action to recover the value of personal property illegally converted by another to his or her own use.

trow /trəʊ/ *noun*[1]. Long *arch. rare.*
[Old English *trēow* (see TRUCE *noun*), *trūwa*, from Germanic base also of TROW *verb*[1]. Later directly from TROW *verb*[1]. Cf. TRUE *adjective, noun & adverb*.]
1 Belief; faith, trust. Formerly also, an assurance of faith or trust; a pledge, a covenant. OE.
†**2** Fancy, supposition. LME–M16.

trow /trəʊ, traʊ/ *noun*[2]. Long chiefly *local*. ME.
[Dial. var. of TROUGH *noun*.]
Any of various boats or barges used on coastal or river waters; *spec.* (*a*) a large flat-bottomed sailing barge; (*b*) a double canoe or boat used in spearing salmon; (*c*) a small flat-bottomed boat used in herring-fishing.
Comb.: **trowman** the master or captain of a trow.

trow /traʊ/ *noun*[3]. *Orkney & Shetland*. M17.
[Var. of TROLL *noun*[1].]
A troll.
■ **trowie** *adjective* of, pertaining to, or belonging to a troll L18.

trow /trəʊ/ *verb*[1]. *arch.* OE.
[Partly Old English *trēowian*, *trēowan*, from *trēow* (see TRUCE *noun*), partly Old English *trūwian*, from Germanic. Cf. TROW *noun*[1].]
1 *verb trans.* Trust, have confidence in. OE.
2 *verb intrans.* Believe or have confidence *in*; trust *to*. OE. ▸†**b** *verb trans.* Believe in (a doctrine etc.). ME–E16.
3 *verb trans.* Think, be of the opinion (*that*), suppose, imagine; feel sure of. OE.
†**4** *verb trans.* Prove to be true; vouch for. *rare*. OE–E17.
5 *verb trans.* Believe (a statement etc.); give credence to, accept as true or trustworthy. Formerly also, believe or suppose (a person or thing) *to be* or *to do*. ME.
†**6** *verb intrans.* Believe; hold a belief; have or exercise faith. ME–L16.
†**7** *verb trans.* Expect, hope. ME–E17.

> 3 COLERIDGE Why, this is strange, I trow! SIR W. SCOTT I trow he's a dealer in cattle. 5 W. MORRIS Men trowed his every word.

trow *verb*[2] & *noun*[4] see TROLL *verb & noun*[2].

trowel /ˈtraʊəl/ *noun*. ME.
[Old French *truele* (mod. *truelle*) from medieval Latin *truella* alt. of Latin *trulla* ladle, scoop, from *trua* skimmer, spoon.]
1 A small hand-held tool with a flat (occas. rounded) blade of metal, wood, etc., used to apply and spread mortar, cement, plaster, etc. ME.
2 A culinary ladle or slice of similar shape. *rare*. L18.
3 A small hand-held tool used in gardening, with a blade consisting of a curved semi-cylindrical scoop for lifting plants or earth. L18.
1 *lay it on with a trowel*: see LAY *verb*[1].
■ **trowelful** *noun* as much or as many as a trowel will hold L16.

trowel /ˈtraʊəl/ *verb trans.* Infl. **-ll-**, ***-l-**. L16.
[from the noun.]
1 Build *up* (as) with a trowel; form or mould with a trowel. Now *rare*. L16.
2 Dress (a surface) (as) with a trowel. M17.
3 Apply (mortar, cement, plaster, etc.) (as) with a trowel. L18.
■ **troweller** *noun* a person who uses a trowel E17.

troxidone /ˈtrɒksɪdəʊn/ *noun*. M20.
[from TR(I- + OX- + -ID(INE + -ONE, elems. of the systematic name.]
PHARMACOLOGY. An analgesic and anticonvulsant drug which is a derivative of oxazolidine.
¶ A proprietary name for this drug is TRIDIONE.

troy /trɔɪ/ *noun*. LME.
[Prob. from a weight used at the fair of *Troyes* in France.]
More fully ***troy weight***. A system of weights used for precious metals and gems, based on a pound of 12 ounces or 5,760 grains (0.3732 kg). Freq. *attrib.* or *postpositive*, as ***troy pound***, ***pound troy***.

†**Troyan** *noun & adjective* see TROJAN.

trs. *abbreviation*.
Transpose (letters, words, etc.).

truancy /ˈtruːənsi/ *noun*. L18.
[from next + -CY.]
The action or an act of playing truant.

truant /ˈtruːənt/ *noun & adjective*. ME.
[Old French (mod. *truand*) from Proto-Gallo-Romance, prob. of Celtic origin (cf. Welsh *truan* wretched (person), Gaelic *truaghan* Irish *truaghán* wretched).]
▸ **A** *noun*. †**1** A person begging through choice rather than necessity; an able-bodied beggar, an idle rogue. Also *gen.* as a term of abuse. ME–M17.
2 A child who stays away from school without permission or explanation; a person who goes absent from work or who shirks his or her duty. LME.

> 2 SHAKES. *1 Hen. IV* I have a truant been to chivalry. J. CALDER He was a frequent truant from classes. **play truant**, †**play the truant** stay away as a truant.

Comb.: **truant-inspector**, (*US*) **truant officer** a school attendance officer;
▸ **B** *adjective*. **1 a** That is a truant or plays truant; idle, lazy; shirking; wandering, straying. M16. ▸**b** Characterized or marked by truancy or idleness; befitting a truant or idler. E17.
†**2** Trivial, trite; vain. *rare*. L16–L17.

> 1a E. DARWIN Down the steep slopes He led . . The willing pathway, and the truant rill. J. C. OATES Mischievous as a truant schoolgirl. **b** SIR W. SCOTT My truant days . . in London having thrown me a little behind.

truant /ˈtruːənt/ *verb*. LME.
[from prec.]
†**1** *verb intrans.* Beg through choice rather than necessity, be an idle rogue. Only in LME.
2 *verb intrans.* Play truant, esp. from school; absent oneself from work; wander, stray. L16.
3 *verb trans.* Orig., waste or idle away (time). Now only *Scot. & dial.*, play truant from (school etc.). L16.

> 2 J. CROALL Bowles . . truanted from the England squad. *Times* Over a quarter of the fifth formers were . . truanting every day.

■ **truanting** *verbal noun* the action of the verb; an instance of this: LME. **truantism** *noun* (*rare*) truancy E19.

truantly /ˈtruːəntli/ *adjective & adverb*. Now *rare* or *obsolete*. L16.
[from TRUANT *noun*: see -LY[1], -LY[2].]
▸†**A** *adjective*. Having the qualities of a truant; characteristic of or befitting a truant. L16–L17.
▸ **B** *adverb*. In the manner of a truant. E19.

truantry /ˈtruːəntri/ *noun*. LME.
[French *truanderie*, from *truand* TRUANT *noun*: see -RY.]
†**1** Fraudulent begging. Only in LME.
2 Idleness, truancy; the practice or an act of playing truant. L15.

trub /trʌb/ *noun*. *obsolete* exc. *dial.* E17.
[App. abbreviation of TRUFFLE, or alt. of Latin TUBER.]
1 A short squat woman. Also (*derog.*), a slut; a slattern. E17.
2 A truffle. M17.

Trubenized /ˈtruːbənʌɪzd/ *adjective*. M20.
[from *Tru-* of unkn. origin + *Benjamin Liebowitz*, inventor of the process + -IZE + -ED[1].]
(Proprietary name.) Of clothing, esp. shirt collars: made durably stiff by a special process in manufacture.

Trubetzkoyan /truːbɛtˈskɔɪən/ *adjective*. M20.
[from *Trubetzkoy* (see below) + -AN.]
Of or pertaining to the Russian linguist Nikolai Sergeevich Trubetzkoy (1890–1938) or his phonological theory and methodology.

truce /truːs/ *noun*.
[Old English *trēowa* pl. (used as sing.) of *trēow* corresp. to Old Frisian *trouwe*, Old Saxon *treuwa*, Old High German *triuwa* (Dutch *trouw*, German *Treue*), Gothic *triggwa* covenant, from Germanic base also of TRUE *adjective*: cf. TROW *noun*[1], *verb*[1]. Mod. form from Middle English pl. with -s.]
†**1** = TROW *noun*[1] 1. Only in OE.
2 A temporary suspension of hostilities, usu. for a limited period, between warring factions or armies or between individuals in a private feud or quarrel; an armistice; an agreement or treaty effecting this. ME. ▸**b** Cessation or absence of hostilities without a time-limit; peace. Now *rare*. LME. ▸**c** A temporary pause or respite during a game. Also as *interjection*, calling for such a truce (cf. ***king's truce*** below). L19.
3 Respite or temporary freedom from something troublesome, painful, or oppressive. LME.

> 2 LYNDON B. JOHNSON An uneasy truce between the warring states prevailed until 1965. R. RENDELL The apparent truce or *détente* between him and Robin. **b** J. SYLVESTER Behold the peacefull Dove . . boading weal And truce with God. **3** MILTON Where he may . . find Truce to his restless thoughts.

Phrases: **a truce to**, **a truce with** *arch.* enough of, have done with. **call a truce**, **call truce** call for a truce. **day of truce** (*obsolete* exc. *Hist.*) (the day appointed for) a court held by the Wardens of the Marches (of England and Scotland), on which a truce was observed. ***flag of truce***: see FLAG *noun*[4]. **king's truce** *interjection* a call for a temporary pause or respite during a game (cf. sense 2c above). **truce of God** (*obsolete* exc. *Hist.*) a suspension of hostilities or feuds, ordered by the Church during certain days and seasons in medieval times. **truce to**, **truce with** *arch.* = ***a truce to*** above.
■ **truceless** *adjective* that is without truce or respite; unceasing in hostility: M17.

truce /truːs/ *verb*. Now *rare*. LME.
[from prec.]
1 *verb intrans.* Make a truce. LME.
†**2** *verb trans.* Bring to an end (as) by calling a truce; put an end to. E17–E18.

truchman /ˈtrʌtʃmən/ *noun*. Now *rare*. Pl. **-mans**, **-men**. L15.
[medieval Latin *turchemanus* (whence also French *trucheman*) from Arab. *tarjumān*, from *tarjama* translate. See also DRAGOMAN, TARGUM, TRENCHMAN.]
An interpreter.

trucial /ˈtruːʃ(ə)l/ *adjective*. Also T-. L19.
[from TRUCE *noun* + -IAL, app. after *fiducial*.]
Hist. Of, pertaining to, or bound by the maritime truce made in 1835 between the British Government and certain Arab sheikhs of the Oman peninsula. Freq. in ***Trucial States***.
¶ The truce was replaced by a permanent peace treaty in 1853, but the territories concerned were known as the Trucial States until they became the United Arab Emirates in 1971.

trucidation /truːsɪˈdeɪʃ(ə)n/ *noun*. *rare*. E17.
[Latin *trucidatio(n-)* noun of action from *trucidare* cut to pieces, slaughter.]
A cruel killing or murder; slaughter.

truck /trʌk/ *noun*[1]. ME.
[Perh. shortening of TRUCKLE *noun*.]
1 A small solid wooden wheel or roller; *spec.* (NAUTICAL, now *Hist.*) each of the wheels of a ship's gun-carriage. ME.
2 NAUTICAL. **a** A circular or square cap of wood at the top of a mast or flagstaff, usu. with small holes for halyards. E17. ▸**b** Any of the small wooden blocks through which the rope of a parrel is passed to prevent fraying. Also, a similar block lashed to the shrouds to form a guide for running rigging. E17.
3 A wheeled vehicle for carrying heavy weights; *spec.* (*a*) an open railway wagon for carrying freight; (*b*) a handcart; (*c*) a railway bogie; (*d*) a small two-wheeled barrow for moving sacks or other heavy packages. L18. ▸**b** A large strong motor vehicle for carrying goods, troops, etc., by road; a lorry. Orig. *US*. E20. ▸**c** An axle unit of a skateboard to which the wheels are attached. L20.
4 A dance popular esp. in the US in the 1930s and 1940s, similar to the jitterbug, and characterized by shuffling steps. *US*. M20.
3b *cattle truck*, ***dumper truck***, ***fork-lift truck***, ***pick-up truck***, ***utility truck***, etc.
Comb.: **truck camper** *N. Amer.* a type of camper mounted on a pick-up truck; **truck frame** *US* the frame of a railway bogie; **trucklot** *N. Amer.* a quantity of goods sufficient to fill a truck and sold at a cheap bulk rate; **truckman** a person who drives a truck; a trucker; **truckstop** (chiefly *US*) an establishment providing refreshments for truck-drivers and fuel and servicing for their trucks; **truck tractor** *US* a tractor used to pull a trailer or a number of trailers loaded with goods; **truck trailer** *US* a trailer designed to be drawn by a truck tractor or other motorized truck.
■ **truckful** *noun* as much or as many as a truck will hold M19. **truckie** *noun* (*Austral. & NZ colloq.*) a truck-driver, a trucker M20.

truck /trʌk/ *noun*[2]. M16.
[from TRUCK *verb*[2].]
1 The action or practice of bartering or of trading by exchange of commodities; an act or instance of this; a transaction, a deal. M16.
2 a *collect. sing.* & †in *pl.* Commodities for barter (*obsolete* exc. *US*). Also (now *Scot. & colloq.*), small miscellaneous items; odds and ends; trash, rubbish. M16. ▸**b** Market-garden produce; culinary vegetables. Also ***truck crop***. *N. Amer.* L18.
3 Social intercourse, communication, dealings. Chiefly in neg. contexts. E17. ▸**b** In *pl.* Small matters of business or work; odd jobs, errands, chores. *Scot. dial.* E19.
4 The payment of wages in kind or as vouchers rather than money; (more fully ***truck system***) the system or practice of such payment. Now chiefly *N. Amer.* M18.

> 1 A. TASMAN They indeavoured to begin a Truck or Merchandize with the yacht. *fig.*: M. ROBINSON My girl has money, my Lord has a title;—'tis a sort of truck. **2a** H. L. WILSON It's all nonsense . . , her saying all that truck helps to 'finish' me. **3 have no truck with** avoid dealing or contact with.

Comb.: ***truck crop***: see sense 2b above; **truck-house** US HISTORY a storehouse, *esp.* one used for trading with Indians; **truck-master** *Hist.* (*a*) *US* a person in charge of a truck-house; (*b*) an employer who used the truck system; **truck-shop** *Hist.* a shop at which vouchers given instead of wages may be exchanged for goods; **truck-store** (*a*) = ***truck-shop*** above; (*b*) *US* a greengrocer's shop; ***truck system***: see sense 4 above.

truck /trʌk/ *verb*[1]. Long *obsolete* exc. *dial.* Orig. †**troke**.
[Old English *trucian*, of unkn. origin.]
1 *verb intrans.* Fail; be wanting or lacking. OE.
†**2** *verb trans.* Deceive, beguile. Only in ME.

truck /trʌk/ *verb*[2]. ME.
[from unrecorded Anglo-Norman and Old French verbs (reflected in medieval Latin *trocare*), of unkn. origin.]
1 *verb trans.* Exchange (one thing) for or *for* another. (Foll. by *with* a person.) Now *rare* in *gen.* sense. ME.
2 *verb trans.* *spec.* Exchange (commodities) for profit; barter (goods) for or *for* other goods. (Foll. by *with* a person.) Formerly also, obtain (goods) by barter. ME. ▸**b** Barter away or *away*; *esp.* part with for a (usu. mercenary or unworthy) consideration. Also (now *rare* or *obsolete*), dispose of *to* a person by barter. M17.
3 *verb intrans.* Trade by exchange of commodities; barter, bargain, deal. (Foll. by *for* a commodity, *with* a person.) L16. ▸**b** *fig.* Have dealings or communication, be

on familiar terms. Formerly also, have sexual intercourse. (Foll. by *with*.) **E17.**
4 *verb intrans.* Walk about on trivial business; potter. *Scot.* **L18.**
5 *verb trans. & intrans.* Pay (an employee) in kind rather than in money; pay (an employee) according to the truck system. Now chiefly *N. Amer.* **L19.**

> 🕮 **1** G. Farquhar Despised! my honourable love trucked for a whore! **2** W. Cobbett My own stock being gone, I have trucked turnips for apples. **b** Defoe Liberty's too often truck'd for Gold. **3b** J. Dunning The Amish have built their own schools, so their kids won't have to truck with outsiders.

truck /trʌk/ *verb*[3]. **M18.**
[from **truck** *noun*[1].]
1 *verb trans.* Convey on or in a truck or trucks. **M18.**
2 *verb intrans.* Drive or take charge of a truck. *N. Amer. colloq.* **E20.**
3 *verb intrans.* Proceed; go; move, stroll. *N. Amer. slang.* **E20.**
4 *verb intrans.* CINEMATOGRAPHY. Track with a camera. **E20.**
5 *verb intrans.* Dance the truck. *US.* **M20.**

> 🕮 **1** *Sun (Baltimore)* The fighters are trucked in crated from cargo ships. *New Yorker* Janet rents a farmhouse in Monterey and trucks in antiques. **2** M. Machlin The private contractors who were trucking for Denali. **3** *Scootering* After trucking around . . we eventually settled down in an accommodating back-street bar. **keep on trucking** *N. Amer. slang*: expr. encouragement.

truckage /ˈtrʌkɪdʒ/ *noun.* **M19.**
[from **truck** *noun*[1] or *verb*[3] + **-age**.]
Conveyance of goods by truck or trucks; the cost of this; trucks collectively.

trucker /ˈtrʌkə/ *noun*[1]. **M16.**
[from **truck** *verb*[2], *noun*[2] + **-er**[1].]
1 A person who trucks or barters; a barterer, a bargainer; *Scot.* a pedlar. Formerly also (*derog.*), a haggler, a huckster, a trafficker. **M16.**
2 A person who grows truck or market-garden produce. *N. Amer.* **M19.**

trucker /ˈtrʌkə/ *noun*[2]. **M19.**
[from **truck** *noun*[1] + **-er**[1].]
1 A labourer who uses a truck or barrow to transport goods. **M19.**
2 A (long-distance) lorry-driver. Also, a firm or organization dealing in the long-distance carriage of goods by truck. Orig. *US.* **M20.**

trucking /ˈtrʌkɪŋ/ *verbal noun*[1]. **L16.**
[from **truck** *verb*[2] or *noun*[2] + **-ing**[1].]
1 The action of **truck** *verb*[2]; bartering, bargaining; dealings, intercourse; *spec.* (*Hist.*), the giving or receiving of wages in kind. Now *arch.* or *Scot.* **L16.**
2 The cultivation of truck or market-garden produce. *N. Amer.* **L19.**

trucking /ˈtrʌkɪŋ/ *verbal noun*[2]. **E19.**
[from **truck** *verb*[3] + **-ing**[1].]
1 The action of conveying goods by truck. Now *esp.* (orig. *US*), the conveyance of goods by means of a truck or other motor vehicle; lorry-driving. **E19.**
2 The action of dancing the truck. *US.* **M20.**
3 CINEMATOGRAPHY. The action of tracking with a camera. **M20.**

truckle /ˈtrʌk(ə)l/ *noun.* **LME.**
[Anglo-Norman *trocle* from Latin *trochlea* from Greek *trokhileia* sheaf of a pulley.]
1 A small grooved wheel in a pulley-block for a cord to run on; a pulley. **LME.**
2 A small roller or wheel placed under or attached to a heavy object to facilitate moving the object; a castor. Now *dial.* **LME.**
3 In full ***truckle-bed***. A low bed on truckles or castors, pushed under a larger bed for storage. **LME.**
4 A low-wheeled cart or wagon. Chiefly *Anglo-Irish & Canad.* **L17.**
5 A small barrel-shaped cheese. Also ***truckle cheese***. Orig. *dial.* **E19.**

truckle /ˈtrʌk(ə)l/ *verb.* **E17.**
[from *truckle*-bed: see prec.]
†**1** *verb intrans.* Sleep in a truckle-bed. (Foll. by *under*, *beneath*.) Only in **17.**
2 *verb intrans. fig.* Take a subordinate or inferior position; submit, give precedence. Now *esp.* yield obsequiously; act with servility. Usu. foll. by *to* a person, *for* a thing. **M17.** ▸**b** Give way timidly; quail, cower. **M19.**
3 *verb intrans. & trans.* Move (an object) on truckles or castors; trundle. *obsolete* exc. *Canad. dial.* **M17.**
4 *verb intrans.* Traffic or deal *with*. *rare.* **E19.**

> 🕮 **2** L. Auchincloss All my life I've had to truckle to the idea that you knew everything. *Times* Many Afrikaners accused him of . . truckling to foreigners.

■ **truckler** *noun* a person who truckles or yields obsequiously **E19.** **trucklingly** *adverb* in a truckling or obsequious manner **M19.**

trucks /trʌks/ *noun. obsolete* exc. *Hist.* **L17.**
[Italian *trucco*, Spanish *troco*.]
An early form of billiards, in which an ivory peg called the king was placed near one end of the table.

truckster /ˈtrʌkstə/ *noun. rare.* **M19.**
[from **truck** *verb*[2] + **-ster**.]
A low trader; a pedlar, a huckster.

truculence /ˈtrʌkjʊl(ə)ns/ *noun.* **E18.**
[Latin *truculentia*, formed as **truculent**: see **-ence**.]
The condition or quality of being truculent; aggressiveness, fierceness.
■ Also **truculency** *noun* **M16.**

truculent /ˈtrʌkjʊl(ə)nt/ *adjective.* **M16.**
[Latin *truculentus*, from *truc-*, *trux* fierce, savage: see **-ulent**.]
1 Characterized by or exhibiting ferocity or aggressiveness; fierce, savage; pugnacious, aggressive; aggressively defiant; (esp. of speech or writing) hostile, rude, scathing. **M16.**
2 Mean, low, mercenary. *rare.* **E19.**

> 🕮 **1** *Spectator* Dr. Inge . . an old *Evening Standard* war-horse, has . . some truculent things to say. V. Glendinning On top of the whiskies, the wine made her truculent. M. Meyer Tough and . . truculent young men who enjoyed getting into fist fights.

■ **truculently** *adverb* **M17.**

trudge /trʌdʒ/ *noun.* **L16.**
[from **trudge** *verb*[1]. Sense 1 is perh. a different word.]
†**1** A thrust; a push. Cf. **thrutch** *noun*. Only in **L16.**
2 A person who trudges or walks laboriously; a trudger. **M18.**
3 An act of trudging; a laborious steady walk. **M19.**

> 🕮 **3** A. Brookner He would . . begin the long trudge back.

¶ In sense 1, meaning is uncertain.

trudge /trʌdʒ/ *verb*[1]. **M16.**
[Origin unkn.]
1 *verb intrans. & trans.* (with *it*). Walk laboriously, or without energy or spirit, but steadily and persistently. **M16.** ▸**b** *verb intrans.* Go away, be off, depart. Now *rare.* **M16.**
2 *verb trans.* Perform (a journey) or travel over (a distance) by trudging. **M17.**

> 🕮 **1** T. S. Surr Give me your arm, we'll trudge it. J. G. Farrell He . . trudged out of the room with heavy steps. G. Tindall The very thought of . . trudging around in the snow is hell. **b** Sir W. Scott A banker has bought his house . . , and I fear he must trudge.

■ **trudger** *noun*[1] a person who trudges or walks laboriously **M19.**

trudge /trʌdʒ/ *verb*[2] *intrans.* **E20.**
[from next.]
Swim with a trudgen stroke.
■ **trudger** *noun*[2] a person who swims with a trudgen stroke **E20.**

trudgen /ˈtrʌdʒ(ə)n/ *noun.* **L19.**
[from John *Trudgen* (1852–1902), English swimmer.]
In full ***trudgen stroke***. A kind of swimming stroke similar to the crawl with an alternate overarm action and a scissors kick, first demonstrated by Trudgen in 1873.

true /truː/ *adjective, noun, & adverb.*
[Old English (*ġe*)*triewe*, *trēowe*, later *trȳwe* = Old Frisian *triuwe*, Old Saxon *triuwi*, Old High German (*gi*)*triuwi* (Dutch *getrouw*, German *treu*), Old Norse *tryggr*, Gothic *triggws*, from Germanic base also of **truce** *noun*. Cf. **trow** *noun*[1].]
▸ **A** *adjective.* **1** Steadfast in allegiance, loyal; faithful, constant. Now *arch.* exc. with *to*. **OE.** ▸**b** Reliable; trusty. Formerly also, sure, secure. *arch.* **ME.**
2 Honest, honourable, upright, virtuous; straightforward; sincere. Now chiefly as passing into senses 3b, 5a. **OE.**
3 Of a statement, report, etc.: consistent with fact; conforming with reality. **ME.** ▸**b** Of a person: speaking truly, telling the truth; truthful; trustworthy in statement. **ME.**
4 a Of the right kind, fitting, proper. Also, rightful, lawful, legitimate. Now *rare.* **LME.** ▸**b** Accurately or exactly positioned, fitted, or formed; correctly balanced or aligned. **LME.** ▸**c** Conforming to a standard, pattern, or rule; exact, precise; correct. Also, (of a note) exactly in tune. **M16.** ▸**d** Remaining constant to type; not subject to variation. *rare.* **M19.** ▸**e** Of a compass bearing: measured relative to true north. **M19.** ▸**f** Of the ground or other surface, esp. as prepared for cricket, bowls, etc.: level and smooth. **M19.** ▸**g** Of the wind: steady, uniform in direction and force. **L19.**
5 a Genuine; rightly answering to the description; authentic; not counterfeit, synthetic, spurious, or imaginary. **LME.** ▸**b** *techn.* Conforming to the accepted or typical character of the class or kind whose name it bears; properly or strictly so called. **LME.**

> 🕮 **1** Ld Berners Ye haue done as a trew subjet ought to do to his lorde. Sir W. Scott I will be true to my word. *Plays International* While most of the hard left writers . . have softened . . Bond remains resolutely true to the cause. **b** D. Greenwell To the rock the root adheres, in every fibre true. **2** Addison Good Men and true for a Petty Jury. **3** J. Bingham The fact was too true, and the charge too well-grounded, to be denied. T. Wells Reading a true confessions magazine. *Woman* I only wish it were true! **b** AV *Prov.* 14:25 A true witnesse delivereth soules: but a deceitfull witnesse speaketh lyes. **4a** Shakes. *Sonn.* Methinks no face so gracious is . . , No shape so true. **b** A. C. Clarke The thin thread of light . . climbed upward . . straight and true as a laser beam. *Ideal Home* A perfect fit even if your walls are not true. **c** J. Imison Clocks and watches . . so regulated as to measure true equal time. Tennyson One . . touch'd a jarring lyre at first, But ever strove to make it true. **5a** I. Murdoch This is deep true love and not a fantasy. *Q* A true maestro of the turntables.

▸ **B** *noun.* †**1** A faithful or loyal person. *rare.* **LME–M18.**
2 That which is true; *the* truth. *arch. rare.* **E19.**
3 Accurate position; exact alignment. Only in ***out of the true***, ***out of true*** below. **L19.**
▸ **C** *adverb.* **1** Faithfully. Formerly also, honestly; confidently. Long *non-standard.* **ME.**
2 In accordance with fact; truthfully. Also, certainly, without doubt, admittedly. **ME.**
3 a Exactly, accurately, correctly. **M16.** ▸**b** In agreement with the ancestral type; without variation. Chiefly in ***breed true***. **M19.**
4 Genuinely; authentically. *arch.* **L16.**

> 🕮 **2** *Athenaeum* If report speak true. *Lancashire Life* True, Blackburn has in recent years shown resilience. **3a** D. Bagley Instruments did not read true and there was no hope of getting a valid ground-sighting.

Phrases: **come true** be the case or be realized in actual experience; actually happen or transpire. ***hold true***: see **hold** *verb*. **it is true** certainly, admittedly; (as *interjection*) expr. agreement with or admitting the veracity of a statement etc. ***one of the truest***: see **one** *adjective, noun, & pronoun*. **out of the true**, **out of true** not accurately or exactly positioned or aligned; deviating from a standard, pattern or rule. ***ring true***: see **ring** *verb*[1]. ***show one's true colours***: see **colour** *noun*. **so — it isn't true** — to an almost incredible extent. ***too good to be true***: see **good** *adjective*. ***tried and true***: see **tried** *ppl adjective* 3. ***true as steel***: see **steel** *noun*[1]. **true for you** *Anglo-Irish* expr. assent to a remark made. **true to** consistent with, faithful to. **true to form** being or behaving as expected; faithful to all expectations. ***true to life***: see **life** *noun*. **true to type** = ***true to form*** above. ***twelve good men and true***: see **twelve** *adjective*.
Special collocations & comb.: **true bill** (now *Hist.* exc. *US*) a bill of indictment found by a grand jury to be supported by sufficient evidence to justify the hearing of a case. ***true blue***: see **blue** *adjective*. **true-born** *adjective* of genuine or legitimate birth; truly such by birth. **true-bred** *adjective* of a true or genuine breed; having or manifesting true breeding or education. **true bug** an insect of the order Hemiptera. **true–false** *adjective* (EDUCATION & PSYCHOLOGY) designating a type of test question designed to elicit either the response 'true' or 'false' (or another pair of opposites); characterizing a test that uses this technique. **true fly** an insect of the order Diptera. ***true grit***: see **grit** *noun*[1] 5. **true-hearted** *adjective* faithful, loyal; honest, sincere. **true-heartedness** loyalty, faithfulness; sincerity. ***true horizon***: see **horizon** *noun* 3. **true leaf** a foliage leaf of a plant, as opp. to a seed-leaf or cotyledon. **true left**, **true right** the side which is on the left, right, as one looks down from a hill or downstream. **true-metal** *adjective* like that of genuine metal; *fig.* genuine, authentic. ***true molar***: see **molar** *noun* 1. ***true north***. **truepenny** *arch.* a trusty or honest person. **true rib** ANATOMY any of the upper seven pairs of ribs, attached directly to the sternum. ***true right***: see ***true left*** above. ***true topaz***: see **topaz** *noun* 1.

true /truː/ *verb trans.* **M17.**
[from prec.]
†**1** Prove true, verify. *rare.* Only in **M17.**
2 Position, adjust, or form (a tool, manufactured item, wheel, etc.) accurately; bring into an exact position or form as according to a standard, pattern, or rule; balance; align. Freq. foll. by *up*. Cf. **truth** *verb* 4. **M19.**

> 🕮 **2** J. Wyndham Give him a hand with truing up a wheel. *Woodworking* True it up on a disc sander.

■ **truer** *noun* (*rare*) **L19.**

trueish /ˈtruːɪʃ/ *adjective.* Also (earlier, *rare*) **truish**. **M17.**
[from **true** *adjective* + **-ish**[1].]
Partly true, almost true.
¶ Rare before **L20.**

true-love /ˈtruːlʌv/ *noun.* **OE.**
[from **true** *adjective* + **love** *noun*.]
1 (Usu. **true love**.) Faithful love. **OE.**
2 The plant herb Paris, *Paris quadrifolia*, whose whorl of four leaves, with a single flower in the middle, suggests a true-love knot. **ME.**
3 A faithful lover; a sweetheart. **LME.**
†**4** An ornament or design symbolizing true love; *esp.* a true-love knot. **LME–L16.**
Comb.: **true-love knot** a kind of knot usu. with interlacing bows on each side symbolizing true love; a design in the shape of such a knot.
■ **true lover** *noun phr.* a true-love; (now *rare*) a person with a sincere regard for another; ***true lover's knot*** = ***true-love knot*** above: **LME.**

trueness /ˈtruːnɪs/ *noun*. OE.
[from TRUE *adjective* + -NESS.]
▸†I **1** Trust, confidence; object of trust. *rare*. Only in OE.
2 A truce. *rare*. Only in LME.
▸II **3** Faithfulness, loyalty. Now *rare*. ME.
4 Conformity with fact; truth; genuineness; authenticity. L16.
5 Conformity with a standard etc.; accuracy, exactitude. L16.

📖 **5** *Which?* A panel . . rated them for sharpness, trueness of colour.

truff /trʌf/ *verb trans. obsolete* exc. *Scot. & north.* LME.
[Old French *tru(f)fer* mock, deride, gibe at.]
1 Deceive, fool. LME–M17.
2 Obtain by deceit; steal, pilfer. E18.

truffle /ˈtrʌf(ə)l/ *noun & verb*. L16.
[Prob. from Dutch *truffel*, †*truffele* from French †*truffle* (now *truffe*), perh. ult. from popular Latin var. of Latin *tubera* pl. of TUBER.]
▸A *noun*. **1** Any of various underground fungi of the order Tuberales; *spec*. either of two strong-smelling edible fungi, *Tuber melanosporum* (more fully ***black truffle***, ***Périgord truffle***) and *Tuber magnatum* (more fully ***white truffle***), having a rough warty exterior, regarded as a great culinary delicacy and collected in France and northern Italy with the help of trained dogs or pigs. L16.
2 A usu. round sweet made of a mixture of chocolate and cream, freq. flavoured with rum, coffee, etc., and rolled in cocoa or coated with chocolate. E20.
Comb.: **truffle-dog**, **truffle-hound**, **truffle-pig**: trained to find truffles.
▸B *verb intrans*. Hunt or root for truffles. M20.

📖 *fig*.: *Times* The book is worth reading . . . You can truffle happily among the errors and the fantasy.

▪ **truffled** *adjective* cooked, garnished, or stuffed with truffles (fungi) M19.

trug /trʌg/ *noun*[1]. LME.
[Perh. dial. var. of TROUGH *noun*.]
1 A basin, *esp*. a shallow wooden milk-pan. Also (*north*.), a wooden coal-box. Now *arch. & dial*. LME.
2 A local measure for wheat, equal to two-thirds of a bushel. *obsolete* exc. *Hist*. L17.
3 A shallow oblong basket usu. made of wooden strips and chiefly used for carrying garden produce, flowers, etc. Also more fully ***trug-basket***. M19.
▪ **trugger** *noun* a person who makes trugs L16.

trug /trʌg/ *noun*[2]. *obsolete* exc. *dial*. L16.
[Perh. from Italian *trucca*.]
A prostitute; a disreputable or promiscuous woman.

truish *adjective* see TRUEISH.

truism /ˈtruːɪz(ə)m/ *noun*. E18.
[from TRUE *adjective* + -ISM.]
1 A self-evident or indisputable truth, *esp*. a trivial or hackneyed one. Also, a proposition that states nothing beyond what is implied in any of its terms. E18.
2 Truistic statement. *rare*. E19.

📖 **1** W. GOLDING The truism that money cannot be spent twice. *Vanity Fair* It is . . truism that art has become our secular faith.

truistic /trʊˈɪstɪk/ *adjective*. M19.
[from prec.: see -ISTIC.]
Having the character of a truism; trivially self-evident or indisputable.
▪ Also **truistical** *adjective* M19.

truite au bleu /trɥit o blø/ *noun phr*. Also (earlier) ***truite bleue***. E20.
[French, lit. 'trout in the blue'.]
A dish consisting of trout cooked with vinegar, which turns the fish blue.

trull /trʌl/ *noun*. *arch*. E16.
[German *Trulle*. Cf. TROLLOP.]
1 A prostitute; a disreputable or promiscuous woman. E16.
†**2** A girl, a lass. *rare*. M–L16.

trulli *noun* pl. of TRULLO.

†**trullization** *noun*. *rare*. M17–M18.
[Latin *trullissatio(n-)*, from *trullissare* to plaster, from *trulla* TROWEL *noun*: see -ATION.]
ARCHITECTURE. The action or practice of plastering, *esp*. the application of layers of mortar, gypsum, etc., to line the interior of a vault.

trullo /ˈtrullo/ *noun*. Pl. ***-lli*** /-lli/. E20.
[Italian.]
In Apulia in southern Italy, a small round house built of stone, with a conical roof.

truly /ˈtruːli/ *adverb*. OE.
[from TRUE *adjective*, *noun*, & *adverb* + -LY[2].]
1 a Faithfully, loyally, constantly. *arch*. OE. ▸†**b** Confidently. Also (*rare*), securely. ME–M16.
2 In accordance with fact or reality; truthfully. ME.
3 Genuinely, really, indeed; sincerely. Freq. used as emphatic affirmative. ME.
†**4** Honestly, honourably, uprightly. LME–M16.
5 a In accordance with a standard, pattern, or rule; exactly, precisely, correctly. LME. ▸**b** Rightly, duly; properly. Freq. in ***well and truly***, decisively, completely. LME. ▸†**c** Rightfully, legitimately. *rare*. LME–E17. ▸**d** Without crossbreeding; purely. Also, without variation from the ancestral type. M19.

📖 **2** GOLDSMITH An elegy that may truly be called tragical. *Field* It has been truly said that Crufts is . . a festival of the dog. **3** O. NASH I read the Mavis Gallant book; truly the most boringly unloveable heroine for years. *Apollo* They chose to erect a truly baroque monument. B. BETTELHEIM He is not truly in love. REALLY ***truly***. **yours truly** (*a*) a customary formula for closing a business or formal letter; (*b*) *joc*. myself. **5a** E. H. KNIGHT To make the spindle run truly. **b** H. ROSENTHAL I had been well and truly bitten by the opera bug. **c** SHAKES. *Wint. T.* His innocent babe truly begotten.

Truman doctrine /ˈtruːmən ˌdɒktrɪn/ *noun phr*. M20.
[Harry S. *Truman* (1884–1972), US President 1945–53.]
The principle first voiced by Truman in 1947 that the US should give support to those peoples or nations threatened by Communist aggression or attempted domination.
▪ **Truma'nesque** *adjective* of, pertaining to, or resembling Truman or his policies, esp. in being energetic, candid, or single-minded L20.

trumeau /truːˈməʊ/ *noun*. Pl. **-x** /-z/. L19.
[French, lit. 'calf of the leg'.]
1 A pier-glass. Also ***trumeau mirror***. L19.
2 ARCHITECTURE. A section of wall or a pillar between two openings, *esp*. a pillar supporting the middle of the tympanum of a church doorway. L19.

trump /trʌmp/ *noun*[1]. ME.
[Old French *trompe* (= Portuguese *tromba*, *trompa*, Spanish *trompa*, Italian *tromba*) from Frankish: prob. imit.]
1 A trumpet; a trumpet-blast; *fig*. a thing which or person who proclaims, celebrates, or summons loudly like a trumpet. *arch. & poet*. ME. ▸**b** A Jews' harp. Now *Scot. & north*. M16. ▸**c** A sound likened to that of a trumpet; *slang* an audible act of breaking wind. E19.
†**2** A trumpeter. *rare*. ME–L15.
†**3** A hollow tube or pipe; *esp*. the trunk of an elephant, the proboscis of an insect. *rare*. LME–M18.

📖 **1** T. GRAY Say we sound The trump of liberty. SIR W. SCOTT Louder yet . . Swells the high trump that wakes the dead! ***last trump***: see LAST *adverb*, *adjective*, & *noun*[5].

Comb.: **trump marine** = ***trumpet marine*** s.v. TRUMPET *noun*.

trump /trʌmp/ *noun*[2]. E16.
[Alt. of TRIUMPH *noun*.]
1 CARDS. **a** A playing-card of a suit ranking above the other three for the duration of a deal or game; (more fully ***trump card***) a card belonging to, or turned up to determine, such a suit. Also (in *pl*.), the suit determined, usu. by cutting or bidding, to rank above the other three during a deal or game. Cf. TRIUMPH *noun* 4a. E16. ▸†**b** = RUFF *noun*[2] 1. Cf. TRIUMPH *noun* 4b. E16–L18. ▸**c** An act of trumping; the taking of a trick with a trump card. M19.
2 †**a** *fig*. An obstruction, a hindrance. Chiefly in ***a trump in a person's way***. Only in 16. ▸**b** *fig*. An advantage; a fortunate or successful outcome, *esp*. one which is unexpected. Freq. in ***turn up trumps*** below. L16.
3 a An admirable, excellent, or reliable person. *colloq*. E19. ▸**b** A person in authority. *Austral. & NZ slang*. E20.

📖 **1a** POPE Let Spades be trumps! *Field* It was necessary to cash the . . queen of diamonds and lead another trump.

Phrases etc.: ***no-trump***, ***no trump(s)***: see NO *adjective*. **put a person to his or her trump(s)** (*a*) oblige a card-player to play out his or her trumps; (*b*) *fig*. reduce a person to his or her last resources. **turn up trumps** *colloq*. turn out better than expected; be very successful or helpful.
Comb.: **trump card** (*a*) see sense 1a above; (*b*) *colloq*. a valuable resource, *esp*. one's most valuable resource; an unexpected move to gain an advantage; **trump signal** BRIDGE & WHIST a call for trumps.

trump /trʌmp/ *verb*[1]. ME.
[Old & mod. French *tromper*, formed as TRUMP *noun*[1].]
1 *verb intrans*. Blow or sound a trumpet. Also foll. by *up*. *obsolete* exc. *Scot*. ME. ▸**b** Make a sound like a trumpet; *slang* break wind audibly. LME.
2 *verb trans*. Proclaim, celebrate, or praise (as) by the sound of a trumpet. Freq. foll. by *up*. Now *rare*. LME.
▪ **trumper** *noun* †(*a*) a trumpeter; (*b*) *slang* a person who breaks wind audibly: ME.

trump /trʌmp/ *verb*[2]. M16.
[from TRUMP *noun*[2].]
†**1 a** *verb trans*. Put (something) *in* a person's way as a hindrance or obstruction. M16–E17. ▸**b** *verb intrans*. Foll. by *in*: get in a person's way, obstruct or hinder a person. L16–M17.
2 CARDS. **a** *verb trans*. Play a trump; take a trick with a trump card. L16. ▸**b** *verb intrans*. Lay a trump on; defeat (a card or player) with a trump. L17.
3 *verb trans*. *fig*. Compel (a person) to use on his or her most valuable resource. Now *esp*. beat, surpass; gain an unexpected advantage over. L16.
4 *verb trans*. Foll. by *up*: ▸†**a** Put (a person) off *with*. *rare*. Only in M17. ▸†**b** Bring forward, allege. L17–L18. ▸**c** Fabricate or invent (an accusation, excuse, etc.). L17.
†**5** *verb trans*. Impose or foist (something) *upon* a person. L17–E18.

📖 **2b** DICKENS Miller ought to have trumped the diamond. **3** L. H. TRIBE A state's interest in the fetus completely trumps a woman's liberty. **4c** *Boardroom* He . . was arrested on a trumped up traffic offence.

†**trumpa** *noun*. *rare*. E17–M19.
[French †*trumpeau*, †*trumpo*.]
A sperm whale.

trumpery /ˈtrʌmp(ə)ri/ *noun & adjective*. LME.
[Old & mod. French *tromperie*, from *tromper* deceive, of unkn. origin: see -ERY.]
▸A *noun*. **1** Deceit, fraud, trickery; an instance of this. Long *rare* or *obsolete*. LME.
2 A worthless, useless or trifling article; *collect. sing*. or (*rare*) in *pl*., worthless stuff, rubbish, nonsense. LME. ▸†**b** *collect. sing*. & in *pl*. Religious practices, ceremonies, etc., regarded as superficial trappings or superstitious nonsense. *derog*. M16–E19. ▸**c** Showy clothing; worthless finery. E17. ▸**d** Weeds; garden refuse. *obsolete* exc. *dial*. M17. ▸**e** A worthless person, esp. a woman. *obsolete* exc. *dial*. M18.

📖 **2** H. L. PIOZZI A heap of trumpery fit to furnish out the shop of a . . pawnbroker. D. W. JERROLD I'd put an end to freemasonry and all such trumpery. THACKERAY Cupboards crammed with the . . relics and . . trumperies of a couple of generations. **b** C. LUCAS Reliques of saints, and such like holy trumpery.

▸B *attrib*. or as *adjective*. Of little or no value; trifling, rubbishy; showy but worthless; superficial; delusive. L16.

📖 M. ARNOLD The accents of a trumpery rhetorician. B. W. ALDISS The houses . . had been given over to trumpery schools of English.

trumpet /ˈtrʌmpɪt/ *noun*. ME.
[Old & mod. French *trompette* dim. of *trompe* TRUMP *noun*[1]: see -ET[1].]
1 A usu. brass wind instrument with a bright, powerful, and penetrating tone, consisting of a straight or curved cylindrical or conical tube (now usu. with valves and keys) and a flared bell, used for giving signals or fanfares or played esp. in a jazz band or an orchestra. Also, the sound of the instrument; trumpet-playing. ME.
2 A person who plays or sounds a trumpet; a trumpeter. LME.
3 *fig*. A person who or thing which proclaims, celebrates, or gives warning of something. LME.
4 An organ reed-stop of 8-ft pitch, resembling the trumpet in tone. Also ***trumpet stop***. M17.
5 A thing shaped like a trumpet; *spec*.: (*a*) a device for amplifying sound, as a horn of an early gramophone, an ear-trumpet, a speaking-trumpet, etc.; (*b*) (more fully ***trumpet-shell***) any shell from which a note can be produced by blowing; *spec*. a triton; (*c*) a trumpet-shaped flower or part of a flower; *spec*. the tubular corona of a daffodil; (*d*) METALLURGY a vertical tube with a bell mouth and a refractory lining, through which metal is poured into runners in uphill casting. L17.
6 A sound like that of a trumpet; the loud cry of certain animals, esp. the elephant. M19.

📖 **1** GIBBON The general's trumpet gave the signal of departure. O. KEEPNEWS Bebop pianists . . trying to imitate Dizzy's trumpet or Bird's alto. **3** STEELE He must in some Measure be the Trumpet of his Fame. *Daily Telegraph* Outbreaks of salmonella . . acting as trumpets on the road to self-destruction.

Phrases: ***blow one's own trumpet***: see BLOW *verb*[1]. ***drum-and-trumpet history***: see HISTORY *noun*. ***ear-trumpet***: see EAR *noun*[1]. **feast of trumpets** a Jewish autumn festival observed at the beginning of the month Tishri, characterized by the blowing of trumpets. **marine trumpet** = ***trumpet marine*** below. ***natural trumpet***: see NATURAL *adjective*. ***speaking-trumpet***: see SPEAKING *verbal noun*. **trumpet marine** a large obsolete single-stringed musical instrument, played with a bow and producing a sound resembling that of a trumpet (also called ***marine trumpet***, ***tromba marina***, ***trump marine***).
Comb.: **trumpet-bird** a manucode (bird of paradise) of New Guinea and northern Queensland, *Manucodia* (or *Phonygammus*) *keraudrenii*; **trumpet-call** (*a*) a call or summons to action sounded on a trumpet; (*b*) *fig*. something acting as a rousing or rallying call; **trumpet creeper** either of two climbing shrubs constituting the genus *Campsis* (family Bignoniaceae), with orange or red trumpet-shaped flowers, *C. radicans*, of the eastern US, and the Chinese *C. grandiflora*; **trumpet daffodil** HORTICULTURE any narcissus having a corona as long as the perianth segments; **trumpet-fish** any of various fishes having a long tubular snout, as a pipefish; *esp*. any of the small family Aulostomidae of tropical reefs and rocky inshore waters; **trumpet-flower** any of

various plants with large trumpet-shaped flowers; *esp.* the trumpet creeper, *Campsis radicans*, the yellow trumpet-tree, *Tecoma stans*, and any of several other plants of the family Bignoniaceae; **trumpet honeysuckle** an evergreen scarlet-flowered honeysuckle, *Lonicera sempervirens*, of the US; **trumpet hypha** BOTANY (in certain brown algae) a filament whose cells are broader and inflated at the ends; **trumpet-leaf** any of several kinds of pitcher-plant (genus *Sarracenia*), esp. *S. flava*, in which the leaves are erect and trumpet-shaped, not decumbent and pitcher-shaped; **trumpet-lily** (*a*) the arum lily, *Zantedeschia aethiopica*; (*b*) a Japanese lily, *Lilium longiflorum*, with fragrant white flowers; **trumpet-lug** ARCHAEOLOGY a type of tubular handle with expanded ends, found on British neolithic pottery; **trumpet major** the chief trumpeter of a band or regiment; **trumpet medium** a spiritualistic medium in whose seances a speaking-trumpet is used; **trumpet-mouth** (something resembling) the mouth or flared end of a trumpet; **trumpet-mouthed** *adjective* (*a*) loud-voiced; (*b*) having a wide opening like the flared end of a trumpet; **trumpet narcissus** HORTICULTURE = ***trumpet daffodil*** above; **trumpet pattern** in medieval art, a pattern consisting of two whorls joined by a curved line; **trumpet-pipe** (*a*) *Hist.* a type of musket; (*b*) a pipe of the trumpet stop in an organ; **trumpet seance** a spiritualistic seance in which a speaking-trumpet is used; **trumpet-shaped** *adjective* of the shape of a trumpet; *esp.* (BOTANY) tubular with one end dilated; ***trumpet-shell***: see sense 5(b) above; **trumpet-snail** a ram's-horn snail (see RAM *noun*[1]); **trumpet spiral** in Celtic art, a double spiral pattern resembling two trumpets joined at their wide ends; ***trumpet stop***: see sense 4 above; **trumpet style** JAZZ a style of piano-playing imitative of a trumpet; **trumpet-tongue** *verb trans.* (*poet. & rhet.*) proclaim loudly; **trumpet-tongued** *adjective* (*poet. & rhet.*) loud-voiced; **trumpet-tree** (*a*) a tropical American tree, *Cecropia peltata* (family Cecropiaceae), with hollow branches which are used to make wind instruments; (*b*) ***yellow trumpet-tree***, a tropical American shrub or small tree, *Tecoma stans* (family Bignoniaceae), with yellow trumpet-shaped flowers and pinnate leaves (also called ***yellow elder***); **trumpet-vine** = ***trumpet creeper*** above; **trumpet-weed** *N. Amer.* (*a*) a kind of joe-pye weed, *Eupatorium purpureum*, with hollow stems which children blow through like trumpets; (*b*) a N. American wild lettuce, *Lactuca canadensis*.

■ **trumpetless** *adjective* without a trumpet, without trumpeting E18. **trumpetry** *noun* trumpets collectively; trumpeting: M19. **trumpety** *adjective* (*colloq.*) having the sound or style of a trumpet, blaring: E19.

trumpet /ˈtrʌmpɪt/ *verb*. M16.
[from prec. or Old & mod. French *trompeter*.]
1 *verb intrans.* Play or sound a trumpet. M16. ▸**b** Esp. of an enraged elephant: make a sound as of a trumpet. E19.
2 *verb trans.* **a** *fig.* Announce or proclaim loudly as by the sound of a trumpet; celebrate, praise highly. Also foll. by *forth*. E17. ▸**b** Summon or denounce formally, or drive away, by the sound of a trumpet. Now *rare*. L17. ▸**c** Sound (a signal etc.) on a trumpet; utter with a sound like that of a trumpet. E18.

📖 **1b** N. BAWDEN Molly took a man's . . handkerchief out of . . her smock and trumpeted into it. **2a** *Yorkshire Post* The Government has been . . nervous about trumpeting . . achievements which have involved spending more money. G. DALY HUNT, the . . painter whose bachelor status had been trumpeted in the gossip columns. **c** S. HASSEL 'We ain't got no more irons, sir!' trumpets Tiny.

trumpeted /ˈtrʌmpɪtɪd/ *adjective*. E17.
[from TRUMPET *noun*, *verb*: see -ED[2], -ED[1].]
1 Sounded on a trumpet; *fig.* celebrated as with a trumpet, praised highly; proclaimed loudly. E17.
2 Provided (as) with a trumpet. M19.
3 Shaped like a trumpet; made with a flared end. L19.

trumpeter /ˈtrʌmpɪtə/ *noun*. L15.
[from TRUMPET *noun* or *verb* + -ER[1], or French *trompeteur*.]
1 A person who sounds or plays a trumpet; *spec.* a soldier in a cavalry regiment who gives signals with a trumpet. L15.
2 *fig.* A person who proclaims or praises something as by trumpeting. L16.
3 An animal which makes a trumpeting sound; *esp.* (*joc.*) a braying ass. M17.
4 Any of various birds having a loud note suggesting the sound of a trumpet; *esp.* (*a*) a particular variety of domestic pigeon; (*b*) each of three birds of the gruiform family Psophiidae, which are stout ground-dwelling birds of S. American forests; (*c*) = ***trumpeter swan*** below. E18.
5 †**a** = ***trumpet-fish*** s.v. TRUMPET *noun*. Only in M18. ▸**b** Any of several large edible marine fishes of the family Latridae, of Australasian waters, which grunt loudly when taken out of water. E19.

📖 **2** E. A. FREEMAN Osbert, Prior of Westminster, the special trumpeter of Eadward's renown.

Comb.: **trumpeter hornbill** a large black and white hornbill, *Ceratogymna bucinator*, of central and southern Africa; **trumpeter's muscle** = BUCCINATOR; **trumpeter swan** a large N. American wild swan, *Cygnus buccinator*, with a black bill.

trumpeting /ˈtrʌmpɪtɪŋ/ *noun*. M16.
[from TRUMPET *verb* + -ING[1].]
1 The action of TRUMPET *verb*; an instance of this. M16.
2 MINING. A channel or passageway made in a shaft by a partition of brickwork, boarding, etc., for ventilation or other purposes. M19.

trumph /trʌmf/ *noun*. *Scot. & north.* L18.
[Var.]
= TRUMP *noun*[2]. Chiefly in phrs. below.
play trumph about vie in achievements *with*. **what's trumph?** what is happening? what is the news?

truncage /ˈtrʌŋkɪdʒ/ *noun*. *rare*. L19.
[medieval Latin *truncagium*, from Latin *truncus* TRUNK *noun*: see -AGE.]
Hist. The provision of a tree-trunk for the sovereign's hearth, as a condition of tenure of certain lands.

truncal /ˈtrʌŋk(ə)l/ *adjective*. M19.
[from Latin *truncus* TRUNK *noun* + -AL[1].]
Of or pertaining to the trunk of a body or a tree, or that of a blood-vessel, nerve, etc.

truncate /ˈtrʌŋkeɪt/ *adjective*. L16.
[Latin *truncatus* pa. pple of *truncare*: see next, -ATE[2].]
1 *gen.* Cut short, mutilated. *obsolete* exc. as passing into sense 2. L16.
2 Chiefly BOTANY & ZOOLOGY. Ending abruptly as if cut off transversely. E18.
■ **truncately** *adverb* L16.

truncate /trʌŋˈkeɪt, ˈtrʌŋkeɪt/ *verb*. L15.
[Latin *truncat-* pa. ppl stem of *truncare* maim: see -ATE[3].]
1 *verb trans. gen.* Shorten or diminish by cutting off the top or end part of; cut short; mutilate. L15.
2 *verb trans. techn.* Make truncated; *spec.* in CRYSTALLOGRAPHY & GEOMETRY, replace (an edge or vertex) by a plane face, esp. so as to make equal angles with the adjacent faces. M18.
3 *verb trans. & intrans.* MATH. Cut short or approximate (a series etc.) by ignoring all the terms beyond a chosen term. E20.

📖 **1** A. BURGESS Lawrence wrote a remarkable amount in a life truncated by tuberculosis. *Time* The battle . . lasted long enough to give the allies time to truncate Iraq's military.

truncated /ˈtrʌŋkeɪtɪd, -ˈkeɪt-/ *adjective*. L15.
[from Latin *truncatus* (see prec.) + -ED[1], or from prec. + -ED[1].]
1 HERALDRY. Of a cross or tree: having the limbs or boughs cut off, so as not to extend to the boundaries of the shield; couped. L15.
2 *techn.* **a** (Of a figure or shape) having one end cut off by a transverse line or plane; (of a cone or pyramid) having the vertex cut off by a plane section, esp. parallel to the base. Also, (of an edge or vertex) cut off or replaced by a plane face, esp. one equally inclined to the adjacent faces; (of a crystal form or solid figure) having its edges or angles so cut off. E18. ▸**b** ARCHITECTURE. (Of a roof) terminating in a horizontal surface instead of a ridge or point; (of a column etc.) appearing as if the top has been cut off; shortened; terminating abruptly. E18. ▸**c** BOTANY & ZOOLOGY. = TRUNCATE *adjective* 2. M18. ▸**d** STATISTICS. Of a frequency distribution or sample: obtained by disregarding values of the variate greater or less than some chosen value. Of a variate: treated in this way. M20. ▸**e** Of soil: having lost the upper horizon(s) as a result of rapid erosion. M20.
3 *gen.* Shortened (as) by cutting off; (apparently) cut short; mutilated. M18.

📖 **2** ***truncated*** OCTAHEDRON. **3** H. BRODKEY The . . truncated kind of thought available to my thirteen-year-old intelligence. *New York Review of Books* Truncated arms and legs, the tragedies of nature augmented by the . . war.

truncation /trʌŋˈkeɪʃ(ə)n/ *noun*. LME.
[Late Latin *truncatio(n-)*, formed as TRUNCATE *verb*: see -ATION.]
1 *gen.* The action of truncating something; cutting short; mutilation; an instance of this. LME.
2 *techn.* The process of truncating something; the condition of being truncated; diminution by or as by cutting off an end or point, so that the object terminates in a straight edge or plane surface instead; *spec.* in CRYSTALLOGRAPHY, replacement of an edge or solid angle by a plane face, esp. one equally inclined to the adjacent faces. L18. ▸**b** STATISTICS. The cutting off of a frequency distribution at a certain value of the variate. M20. ▸**c** The loss or removal of the upper horizon(s) of a soil by erosion. M20. ▸**d** MATH. The cutting short of a numerical computation or expression before its natural end (if any). Usu. *attrib.* in ***truncation error***. M20.
3 The point at which or part where something is truncated. E19.

📖 **1** B. BRYSON English . . favors crisp truncations: IBM, laser, NATO. J. LE CARRÉ Death of their own natures . . could result from . . truncation of their natural feeling. **3** *Antique Collector* A . . wax portrait of Matthew Boulton . . signed on the truncation 'P. Rouw'.

truncature /ˈtrʌŋkətjʊə/ *noun*. Now *rare* or *obsolete*. E19.
[from TRUNCATE *verb* + -URE.]
= TRUNCATION 2.

trunch /trʌn(t)ʃ/ *adjective*. Now *dial.* L17.
[App. shortened from attrib. use of TRUNCHEON *noun*.]
Short and thick.
■ Also **trunched**, **trunchy** *adjectives* (*US, rare*) L18.

truncheon /ˈtrʌn(t)ʃ(ə)n/ *noun*. ME.
[Old French *tronchon* (mod. *tronçon*) repr. Proto-Romance noun from Latin *truncus* TRUNK *noun*.]
1 A piece broken or cut off, a fragment; *spec.* a fragment of a spear or lance. *arch.* ME. ▸**b** The shaft of a spear. *arch.* ME.
2 A short thick staff; a club, a cudgel. Now *esp.* a short club or cudgel carried by a police constable. ME.
3 †**a** The stem or trunk of a tree. *rare*. Only in LME. ▸**b** A length cut from a plant, *esp.* a thick cutting used for propagation. Now *rare*. L16.
†**4** A short thick-bodied intestinal worm, parasitic in horses. LME–M18.
5 A staff carried as a symbol of office or authority; a marshal's baton. L16.

📖 **1** R. L. STEVENSON A huge truncheon of wreck half buried in the sands. **2** *Warsaw Voice* The police . . responded with truncheons and water hoses. **5** LD MACAULAY The truncheon of a Marshal of France.

■ **truncheoned** *adjective* provided or armed with a truncheon M18. †**truncheoner** *noun* (*rare*, Shakes.) a person carrying a truncheon: only in E17.

truncheon /ˈtrʌn(t)ʃ(ə)n/ *verb trans*. L15.
[French *tronçonner*, from *tronçon* TRUNCHEON *noun*.]
1 †**a** Reduce to fragments, break in pieces, shatter. L15–E16. ▸**b** *spec.* Carve (an eel). Now *rare* or *obsolete*. L15.
2 Hit with a truncheon. L16.

truncus /ˈtrʌŋkəs/ *noun*. Pl. **-ci** /-kʌɪ/. L17.
[Latin: see TRUNK *noun*.]
ANATOMY. = TRUNK *noun* 5.

trundle /ˈtrʌnd(ə)l/ *noun*. See also TRUNNEL. M16.
[Parallel to TRENDLE *noun*, TRINDLE *noun*. Cf. TREND.]
1 A small wheel or roller; *esp.* a small sturdy wheel for supporting a heavy weight, as a castor. Now chiefly *dial.* M16. ▸**b** In the drawstop action of an organ, a roller with two arms by the rotation of which a slider is drawn or replaced. L19.
2 A device consisting of two discs turning on an axle, and connected by a series of parallel rods cylindrically arranged, which engage with the teeth of a cog-wheel; a lantern-wheel. Also ***trundle-wheel***. E17.
3 A low truck or carriage on small wheels. Now *rare*. M17.
4 An act of trundling or rolling (*lit. & fig.*); a push causing something to roll. Also (*dial.*), a departure (only in ***run one's trundle***, ***take one's trundle***, take oneself off, depart). L17.
5 An embroiderer's quill of gold thread; HERALDRY a charge representing such a quill. L18.

📖 **4** O. WISTER That station gone, our caboose took up again its easy trundle.

Comb.: **trundle-bed** a truckle-bed; **trundle-head** (*a*) (each of the discs of) a trundle (sense 2); (*b*) NAUTICAL the lower drumhead of a double capstan; **trundle-tail** *arch.* (*a*) a dog with a curly tail; (*b*) *derog.* a worthless or contemptible person; ***trundle-wheel***: see sense 2 above.

trundle /ˈtrʌnd(ə)l/ *verb*. L16.
[Parallel to TRENDLE *verb*, TRINDLE *verb*. Cf. TREND.]
1 **a** *verb trans.* Cause to roll along a surface; roll. L16. ▸**b** *verb intrans.* Move along a surface by rolling. E17. ▸**c** *verb trans. & intrans.* CRICKET. Bowl (the ball). *colloq.* M19.
2 **a** *verb intrans.* Move or roll on a wheel or wheels, esp. heavily or noisily. L17. ▸**b** *verb trans.* Push (a wheeled vehicle) along, esp. heavily or noisily. E19.
3 **a** *verb intrans.* Go or move, esp. heavily, noisily, or rapidly; go away; walk in a cumbersome manner. L17. ▸**b** *verb trans.* Carry or send off, dismiss. *rare*. L18.
4 *verb trans.* Twirl or spin (something held in the hand). M18.
5 *verb trans. & intrans.* Convey or travel in a wheeled vehicle. L18.

📖 **1b** D. WALCOTT The sawn trunks trundled down hillsides. **2a** J. TROLLOPE The shop van trundled out of Pitcombe. **b** P. SAYER An old man . . appeared, trundling a wheelchair. **3a** T. C. BOYLE Her mother trundled back and forth, rearranging the furniture. *Business* Classic Fame trundled in . . seventh of the 12 runners in last month's Derby. **4** H. J. POWELL The English workman attains the same result by trundling the glass during reheating. **5** A. WILSON I intend to call a cab and trundle you both off . . for . . luncheon. L. KENNEDY We trundled down the runway and headed up and over the . . warships.

■ **trundler** *noun* a person who or thing which trundles something; *spec.* in CRICKET (*colloq.*), a bowler: M17.

trunk /trʌŋk/ *noun*. LME.
[Old & mod. French *tronc* from Latin *truncus*. In branch III app. assoc. with TRUMP *noun*[1].]
▸ **I** **1** The main stem of a tree (as opp. to the roots and branches). LME.
2 The human body, or that of an animal, without the head and limbs, or considered apart from these; the torso. LME.

3 The main part of any structure or thing; *spec.* (*a*) ARCHITECTURE the shaft of a column; (*b*) the main part of the case of a long-case clock; (*c*) the main line or course of a river, transport system, etc. M16. ▸**b** [Back-form. from TRUNKING *noun*.] A long shift of driving a lorry along trunk roads; a spell of trunking. *colloq.* M20.

†**4** A dead body, a corpse. L16–E18.

5 ANATOMY. The main part of a blood-vessel, nerve, etc., from which its branches arise. E17.

6 TELEPHONY. In full ***trunk line***. A telephone line connecting two exchanges a long way apart or in different telephone areas; *US* a line connecting exchanges within the same area. Also, a line connecting selectors etc. of different rank within an exchange. L19. ▸**b** In *pl.* The operators who deal with trunk calls. *colloq.* L19.

📖 **3** *attrib.*: *Take Off* Flying the trunk New York–Los Angeles route.

▸ **II 7** A chest, a coffer, a box. *obsolete* in *gen.* sense. LME.

8 a *Hist.* A perforated floating box for keeping live fish in a pond etc. LME. ▸**b** A net or trap for lobster-catching. *Scot. & dial.* M19. ▸**c** An open box or case in which fresh fish are sold wholesale. L19.

9 a A large box, usu. with a hinged lid, for carrying clothes and other luggage when travelling. E17. ▸**b** The luggage compartment or boot of a motor vehicle. *N. Amer.* M20.

10 A boxed-in passageway for light, air, water, etc.; a shaft, a conduit. Now *esp.* an enclosed shaft or duct for cables or ventilation. E17. ▸**b** A chute through which coal is emptied from a wagon into a lighter etc. *dial.* E18. ▸**c** In a steam engine, a cylinder fitted in place of a piston-rod to allow lateral movement of a connecting-rod jointed directly to the piston. M19. ▸**d** NAUTICAL. A watertight shaft passing through the decks of a vessel, for loading, coaling, etc. M19. ▸**e** A floodgate or sluice controlling the flow of water into and out of rice-fields. *US.* M19. ▸**f** The watertight casing enclosing the centre-board of a sailing boat. L19.

11 MINING. A long shallow trough in which lead or tin ore is dressed. M17.

📖 **9a** A. EDEN My mother did the work . . , packing our trunks for school. A. N. WILSON Their boyhood toys, locked up in a trunk in the attic. **b** *attrib.*: A. TYLER He heard the Chevy's trunk lid clanging shut.

▸ **III** †**12** A cylindrical case for containing or discharging explosives, as the barrel of a mortar, the case of a rocket, etc. M16–L18.

†**13** A pipe used as a speaking-tube or ear-trumpet. M16–E18.

†**14** A hollow tube from which a dart or pellet is shot by blowing; a peashooter. M16–E19.

15 The mobile elongated snout of an elephant, containing the passages to the nostrils and also used in the manipulation of food, spraying of water for cooling, etc. Also, a flexible snout in other animals, such as the tapir etc. M16. ▸**b** Any of various long narrow usu. hollow parts of animals, as a heron's beak, an insect's proboscis etc. Now *rare* or *obsolete*. L16. ▸**c** A person's nose. *arch. slang.* L17.

16 In *pl.* A game resembling bagatelle, played esp. by women. Cf. TROLL-MADAM. *obsolete* exc. *dial.* L16.

▸ **IV 17** In *pl.* ▸†**a** = TRUNK-HOSE. L16–L17. ▸**b** Short breeches, esp. as formerly worn by actors over tights; knickerbockers. E19. ▸**c** Men's shorts worn for swimming, boxing, etc., either loose-fitting and extending to the mid-thigh or close-fitting with brief legs. Orig. *US.* L19. ▸**d** Men's underpants with short legs. M20.

📖 **17b** DICKENS Mr. Snodgrass in blue satin trunks and cloak. **c** P. SCOTT Except for a pair of swimming trunks he was naked.

Comb.: **trunkback** *US* = ***leatherback*** s.v. LEATHER *noun & adjective*; **trunk-band** a shallow box in the horizontal bellows of an organ to which the wind-trunk is attached; **trunk-breeches** *Hist.* = TRUNK-HOSE; **trunk call** a telephone call on a trunk line with charges made according to distance; **trunk dialling** = ***subscriber trunk dialling*** s.v. SUBSCRIBER 2b; **trunk-engine** an engine having a cylinder or trunk (see sense 10c above) in place of a piston-rod; **trunkfish** any of various tropical fishes of the family Ostraciontidae, having an angular body covered in hexagonal bony plates; a box-fish; **trunk line** (*a*) see sense 6 above; (*b*) a main railway route or line; (*c*) a large or main pipeline for oil or gas, *esp.* one from a production field to a refinery or terminal; **trunk main** a principal main for the conveyance of water etc., as distinct from the network of smaller mains which it feeds; **trunk-maker** a person who makes trunks or large boxes (formerly freq. with allus. to the use of the sheets of unsaleable books for lining trunks); **trunk murder** a murder after which the body is hidden in a trunk; **trunk murderer** a person who commits a murder and hides the body in a trunk; **trunk road** an important main road; †**trunk sleeve** (*rare*, Shakes.) a full puffed sleeve; **trunk-turtle** = ***leatherback (turtle)*** s.v. LEATHER *noun & adjective*; **trunk-work** *rare* secret or clandestine action (characterized by the perpetrator hiding in a trunk).

■ **trunkful** *noun* as much or as many as a trunk will hold E18. **trunkless** *adjective* having no trunk; *esp.* without a body: M17.

trunk /trʌŋk/ *verb*[1] *trans. obsolete* exc. as TRUNKED *ppl adjective*[1]. LME.
[Latin *truncare* TRUNCATE *verb*.]
Cut a part off from; cut short, truncate.

trunk /trʌŋk/ *verb*[2] *trans.* E17.
[from TRUNK *noun*.]

†**1** Shut up as in a trunk; imprison. *rare.* Only in E17.

2 MINING. Dress (lead or tin ore) by agitating it in water in a trunk or trough. M18.

3 Of an elephant: pick up or pull with the trunk. *rare.* E19.

4 Cover or enclose as with a casing. M19.

5 Make (a minor road) into a trunk road; upgrade and reclassify as a trunk road. M20.

trunked /trʌŋkt/ *ppl adjective*[1]. M16.
[from TRUNK *verb*[1] + -ED[1].]

1 Cut short, truncated; mutilated. *obsolete* exc. as in sense 2. M16.

2 HERALDRY. Truncated; *spec.* (*a*) couped; (*b*) caboshed. M16.

trunked /trʌŋkt/ *adjective*[2]. M17.
[In branch I from TRUNK *noun* + -ED[2]; in branch II from TRUNK *verb*[2] + -ED[1].]

▸ **I 1** Esp. of a tree: having a trunk (of a specified kind). M17. ▸**b** HERALDRY. Having the trunk of a tincture different from the rest of the tree. L17.

2 Of an animal: having a trunk. L18.

3 Wearing trunks or shorts. *rare.* E20.

1 ***hollow-trunked***, ***smooth-trunked***, ***straight-trunked***, etc.

▸ **II 4** MINING. Of lead or tin ore: dressed in a trunk or trough. *rare.* E19.

trunker /ˈtrʌŋkə/ *noun.* L19.
[from TRUNK *noun* or *verb*[2] + -ER[1].]

1 MINING. A person who dresses lead or tin ore in a trunk or trough. L19.

2 a A long-distance lorry-driver, *esp.* one who drives at night and is not responsible for loading or unloading his or her vehicle. M20. ▸**b** A lorry used for long journeys along trunk roads. M20.

trunk-hose /ˈtrʌŋkhəʊz/ *noun.* Pl. **-hose**, (*arch.*) **-hosen** /-ˈhəʊz(ə)n/. M17.
[from TRUNK *noun* or *verb*[1] + HOSE *noun*.]
Hist. Full baglike breeches extending to the upper thighs and sometimes padded with wool etc., worn over tights by men in the 16th and early 17th cents.

trunking /ˈtrʌŋkɪŋ/ *noun.* M19.
[from TRUNK *verb*[2] or *noun* + -ING[1].]

1 The action of TRUNK *verb*[2]. M19.

2 A system of ducts or trunks, esp. for cables or ventilation. M19.

3 TELEPHONY. The use or arrangement of trunk lines. L19.

4 The driving of lorries on long journeys along trunk roads. M20.

trunnel /ˈtrʌn(ə)l/ *noun.* E19.
[Dial. var. of TRUNDLE *noun*.]
= TRUNDLE *noun*. Chiefly in comb.

Comb.: **trunnel-head** *US* a circular plate or disc at the head of a coke-oven or in a furnace; **trunnel-hole** the aperture or throat of a puddling furnace in which a trunnel-head works.

trunnion /ˈtrʌnjən/ *noun.* E17.
[Old & mod. French *trognon* core of fruit, trunk of a tree, of unkn. origin.]

1 Either of a pair of cylindrical projections on opposite sides of a cannon or mortar, by which it is pivoted on its carriage. E17.

2 Either of any similar pair of opposing pins or pivots, on which a thing is supported; *spec.* in an oscillating steam engine, a hollow gudgeon on each side of the cylinder, on which it pivots and through which steam passes in and out. Also, a single projecting peg or pivot. E18.

†**trusion** *noun.* E17–E18.
[medieval Latin *trusio(n-)*, from Latin *trus-* pa. ppl stem of *trudere* push, thrust: see -ION.]

1 LAW. = INTRUSION 1. *rare.* Only in E17.

2 The action of pushing or thrusting. M17–E18.

truss /trʌs/ *noun & adjective.* ME.
[Old French *trusse*, *torse* (mod. *trousse*), formed as next.]

▸ **A** *noun.* **1** A collection of things bound or packed together; a bundle, a pack. Now chiefly *techn.* ME. ▸**b** A bundle of a definite weight; *spec.* (*a*) a bundle of old hay weighing 56 lb (approx. 25.5 kg); (*b*) a bundle of new hay weighing 60 lb (approx. 27.3 kg); (*c*) a bundle of straw weighing 36 lb (approx. 16.4 kg). L15.

2 NAUTICAL. A tackle or fitting securing the lower yards to the mast. Now *esp.* a heavy iron ring with a goose-neck used for this purpose. ME.

3 ARCHITECTURE. A large corbel or modillion supporting a cornice etc. E16. ▸**b** A framework, esp. of rafters, posts, and struts, supporting a roof, bridge, etc.; *spec.* a diagonal framework beneath the deck of a ship. M17.

†**4 a** A man's or woman's close-fitting jacket. M16–E17. ▸**b** In *pl.* = TROUSE *noun*[2] 1. L16–M17.

5 A surgical appliance used to provide even pressure on a hernia etc., now usu. consisting of a padded belt fitted with straps or springs. M16.

6 HORTICULTURE. A compact cluster of flowers growing on one stalk. L17.

Comb.: **truss-beam** (*a*) a beam forming part of a truss; (*b*) a beam or iron frame strengthened with struts etc. to form a truss; **truss-hoop**: used to compress the staves of a barrel into position; **truss-rod** a tie-rod forming part of a truss.

▸† **B** *adjective.* Neatly and compactly framed; tight, compact. L17–E19.

truss /trʌs/ *verb.* ME.
[Old French *trusser* (mod. *trousser*), medieval Latin *trossare*, prob. from late Latin *tors-* pa. ppl stem of Latin *torquere* twist. Cf. prec.]

1 *verb trans.* Tie in a bundle; pack tightly together or in a receptacle; *spec.* (NAUTICAL) furl (a sail). Also foll. by *up*. ME. ▸†**b** Load (an animal, ship, etc.) with a pack or packs. ME–L16. ▸†**c** Pack up and carry away; transport in a pack. Chiefly *Scot.* ME–M16.

2 a *verb intrans.* Of a person: pack or prepare for a journey. Long *obsolete* exc. *Scot.* ME. ▸**b** *verb intrans.* Leave, depart. Long *obsolete* exc. *Scot.* ME. ▸†**c** *verb trans.* Drive off, put to flight. *rare.* L15–L16.

3 *verb trans.* Bind or tie securely around or to something. Usu. foll. by *about*, *on*, *to*, etc. *arch.* ME. ▸**b** *spec.* Attach (hose) to a doublet by tying the points; tie (the doublet points); lace (a person) up in this way. *obsolete* exc. *Hist.* LME. ▸†**c** Insert closely, tuck. E16–M17.

4 *verb trans.* Wrap around with something, as clothing, a bandage, etc.; fasten or pin up (the hair); *transf.* dress (a person) elaborately or ostentatiously (usu. in *pass.*). Also foll. by *up*. ME. ▸†**b** Tighten up (a bell) on its stock. LME–E17. ▸**c** Compress the staves of (a barrel) into position with a hoop. M16.

5 *verb trans.* Of a bird of prey: seize or clutch (prey) in its talons. *arch.* exc. HERALDRY. L15.

6 *verb trans.* Fasten for execution on a gallows or cross, hang as a criminal. Usu. foll. by *up*. *arch.* M16.

7 *verb trans.* Tie or skewer the wings and legs of (a fowl etc.) to the body for cooking; *transf.* bind (the arms) close to a person's body so as to restrict movement; tie *up* (a person) in this way. E18.

8 *verb trans.* Support (a roof, bridge, etc.) with a truss or trusses. E19.

📖 **1** A. UTTLEY Tom cut and Dan trussed the hay and carried it to the barns. **4** LADY BIRD JOHNSON Mr. Dobie, all trussed up in white tie and tails. **7** B. HEAD Amazed neighbours found him . . still trussed up and gagged. *Cook's Magazine* Twine . . . you need it to truss poultry.

Comb.: **trussing hoop** = ***truss-hoop*** s.v. TRUSS *noun*; **trussing needle**: used to truss or tie up meat, poultry, etc.

■ **trussing** *noun* (*a*) the action of the verb; (*b*) material used for a supporting truss; a structure consisting of trusses: ME.

†**trussell** *noun.* LME.
[Old French *troussel* (mod. *trousseau*) dim. of *trousse*, formed as TRUSS *noun*.]

1 = TROUSEAU *noun*[1] 1. Only in LME.

2 A punch for impressing the upper side of a coin. L15–L19.

trusser /ˈtrʌsə/ *noun.* E16.
[from TRUSS *verb* + -ER[1].]

†**1** A binding, a bandage. E–M16.

2 A person who or thing which trusses something; *spec.* (*a*) a person employed in trussing poultry; (*b*) a person who or machine which trusses hay or straw. M16.

3 HORTICULTURE. A plant that produces trusses of blossom. Usu. with specifying word. M19.

📖 **3** *Garden* This . . Polyanthus . . is a noble trusser.

trust /trʌst/ *noun.* ME.
[Old Norse *traust*: see next. Cf. TRIST *noun*[1] & *verb*.]

1 Faith or confidence in the loyalty, strength, veracity, etc., of a person or thing; reliance on the truth of a statement etc. without examination. (Foll. by *in*, †*of*, †*to*.) ME. ▸**b** *transf.* A person who or thing which is trusted or relied on. *arch.* LME.

2 (A) confident expectation; (a) hope. LME.

3 a The state or condition of being entrusted to a person or body. Only in ***in trust***, †***on trust***. LME. ▸**b** The state or condition of being trusted or relied on; the state of being entrusted *with* something. Freq. in ***in trust***, ***under trust***. M16. ▸**c** The obligation or responsibility placed on a person who is trusted or relied on. M16. ▸**d** A duty, an office; a person or thing entrusted to someone. M17.

4 LAW. Confidence placed in a person by making him or her the nominal owner of property to be held or used for the benefit of another; a property or estate held in this way; the legal relationship between the nominal owner and the property. LME.

5 The quality of being trustworthy; trustiness. Now *rare*. LME.

6 = CREDIT *noun* 6. Chiefly in ***on trust***, ***upon trust***. L16.

7 *COMMERCE*. **a** A body of trustees; an organization or company managed by trustees. L19. ▸**b** An association of several companies in a particular area of business, organized to reduce or defeat competition, lessen mutual expenses, etc.; *esp.* one in which a central committee of trustees holds a majority or all of the stock and has a controlling vote in each company. L19.

> 🕮 **1** ALDOUS HUXLEY Afraid of taking decisions . . she had no trust in her own powers. **3a** G. PRIESTLAND The animals are in trust to us from our Creator. **b** F. WARNER We hold The precious centre of our Jewish faith In sacred trust for coming generations. **c** J. E. WORCESTER A breach of trust by one who has charge or management of money. **d** D. CUSACK I regard every girl who comes to my school as a sacred trust. **4** J. ROSSNER The family was wealthy and there were trusts from grandparents. **7a** *Money & Family Wealth* Like all ethical trusts, it avoids companies active in . . areas which . . investors would prefer to avoid.

Phrases: ***blind trust***: see BLIND *adjective*. **in trust** *LAW* held on the basis of trust; see also senses 3a, b above. ***labourer-in-trust***: see LABOURER 1. ***National Trust***: see NATIONAL *adjective*. **on trust** (*a*) (of a dog) obeying the command to trust (see TRUST *verb* 1 b); (*b*) on the basis of trust or confidence; ***take on trust*** accept or give credit to without investigation or evidence; (*c*) see senses 3a, 6 above. ***turnpike trust***: see TURNPIKE *noun* 4b. ***unit trust***: see UNIT *noun*[1] & *adjective*. **upon trust** = *on trust* (b) above.

Comb.: **trust-buster** *colloq.* (chiefly *US*) a person or agency employed to dissolve trusts; *spec.* (*US*) a government official responsible for the enforcement of legislation against trusts; **trust-busting** *verbal noun & ppl adjective colloq.* (chiefly *US*) (of or pertaining to) work or action against trusts; **trust company** a company formed to act as a trustee or to deal with trusts; **trust corporation** *LAW* a corporation empowered to act as a trustee; **trust deed** a deed of conveyance creating and setting out the conditions of a trust; **trust fund** a fund of money etc. held in trust; **trust-investment** (*a*) the investment of trust money; (*b*) a security in which trustees may legally invest trust money; **trust officer** *N. Amer.* an officer of a trust company; **trust-stock** stock in which trust funds may legally be invested; **Trust Territory** a territory under the trusteeship of the United Nations or a State designated by them.

■ **trustify** *verb trans.* (*COMMERCE*) make into a trust; form a trust of or in: E20. **trustless** *adjective* (now *rare*) (*a*) untrustworthy, unreliable, treacherous; (*b*) having no trust or confidence, distrustful: E16. **trustlessness** *noun* (*rare*) (*a*) untrustworthiness; (*b*) distrustfulness: E19.

trust /trʌst/ *verb*. ME.

[Old Norse *treysta*, assim. to TRUST *noun*.]

1 *verb intrans.* Have faith or confidence in the loyalty, strength, veracity, etc., of a person or thing; rely on a person or thing *to do*. Foll. by *in*, †*on*, *to*, †*upon*. ME. ▸**b** In *imper.* As an instruction to a dog: wait for a reward usu. in a begging position. M19.

2 *verb trans.* Commit or entrust to the safe-keeping of a person (foll. by *to*, *with*). Formerly also, put *in* a particular place for safe-keeping. *arch.* ME.

3 *verb trans.* Have faith or confidence in the loyalty, strength, veracity, etc., of; rely or depend on; have confidence in the ability of (a person) *to do*. ME.

4 *verb intrans.* Have faith or confidence *that* a thing is or will be the case. Also, confidently hope or expect *to do*. ME.

5 *verb trans.* Believe (a statement); rely on the veracity or evidence of (a person). LME.

6 *verb trans.* Foll. by *with*: give responsibility for, or allow to keep or use, in confidence of safety or proper care; entrust with confidential information etc. M16.

7 *verb trans. & intrans.* Give (a customer) credit *for* goods supplied. M16.

> 🕮 **1** J. BALDWIN She had only to endure and trust in God. J. UPDIKE The true . . creator of fiction . . trusts to memory and imagination. **2** MILTON Not wandring poor, but trusting all his wealth With God. **3** R. DAVIES Could Hannah be trusted not to spill the beans? *Bon Appetit* Chefs . . will . . learn to trust their own judgement rather than follow the next big trend. **4** E. WAUGH 'He asked *me* to go . . for the week-end,' said Flossie . . . 'Florence, I trust you refused?' C. BLACKWOOD She trusted that I had had a good train journey. **5** D. H. LAWRENCE Never trust the artist. Trust the tale. **6** K. LINES There was no one he could trust with his infant son. N. FARAH Could he trust him with these secrets?

Phrases: **not trust X as far as one can see him or her**, **not trust X as far as one can throw him or her** trust the specified person hardly or not at all. **trust X (to do a thing)!**, **trust you (to do a thing)!** it is characteristic or predictable for the specified person to act in such a way.

■ **trustable** *adjective* trustworthy E17. **truster** *noun* (*a*) a person who trusts; (*b*) *SCOTS LAW* a person who puts property in trust: M16.

Trustafarian /trʌstəˈfɛːrɪən/ *noun*. *colloq. derog.* L20.

[from *trust* fund (s.v. TRUST *noun*) + RASTAFARIAN.]

A wealthy young person who adopts an ethnic lifestyle and lives in or frequents a traditionally non-affluent area, e.g. the Notting Hill district of London.

trustee /trʌsˈtiː/ *noun & verb*. M17.

[from TRUST *verb* + -EE[1].]

▸ **A** *noun*. **1** *gen.* A person who is trusted or to whom a thing is entrusted. *obsolete* exc. as in sense 1b or passing into sense 3. M17. ▸**b** A prisoner given special privileges for good behaviour. Cf. TRUSTY *noun*. *US*. M20.

2 *LAW*. A person who has responsibility for controlling or administering property in trust (see TRUST *noun* 4); *COMMERCE* a member of the central committee of a trust (see TRUST *noun* 7a). Also *gen.*, any of a group of people appointed to manage the affairs of an institution etc. M17. ▸**b** A person to whom the property of a debtor is attached in a trustee process (see below). *US*. E19.

3 A person or body responsible for the preservation or administration of something; *spec.* a State made responsible for the government of a particular area by the United Nations. M17.

Comb.: **trustee bank** = *trustee savings bank* below; **trustee process** *US LAW* a judicial process by which the goods, effects, and credits of a debtor may be attached while in the hands of a third person; **trustee savings bank** a savings bank, formerly *spec.* one managed by unpaid trustees; **trustee security**, **trustee stock** = ***trust-stock*** s.v. TRUST *noun*.

▸ **B** *verb*. Pa. t. & pple **-teed**.

1 *verb trans.* Place in the hands of a trustee or trustees. E19.

2 *verb trans.* *US LAW*. ▸**a** Appoint as a trustee in a trustee process. L19. ▸**b** Attach (a debtor's effects etc.) to a third person. L19.

■ **trusteeship** *noun* (*a*) the office or function of a trustee; *spec.* the administration of a territory by a State designated by the United Nations; (*b*) a body of trustees: M18.

†trusten *verb*. Long *obsolete* exc. *dial.* ME–L19.

[from TRUST *verb* + -EN[5].]

= TRUST *verb*.

trustful /ˈtrʌs(t)fʊl, -f(ə)l/ *adjective*. L16.

[TRUST *noun* + -FUL.]

†**1** Trustworthy, trusty. L16–L18.

2 Full of or trust or confidence; not suspicious; trusting, confiding. M19.

■ **trustfully** *adverb* M19. **trustfulness** *noun* M19.

trustworthy /ˈtrʌs(t)wəːði/ *adjective*. E19.

[from TRUST *noun* + -WORTHY.]

Deserving of trust or confidence; reliable.

■ **trustworthily** *adverb* M19. **trustworthiness** *noun* E19.

trusty /ˈtrʌsti/ *adjective & noun*. ME.

[from TRUST *noun* + -Y[1].]

▸ **A** *adjective*. **1** Having or displaying trust; confident, assured. Now *rare*. ME.

2 Trustworthy; faithful, reliable; loyal. *arch.* (freq. *joc.*). ME. ▸**b** *spec.* Of a prisoner: granted special privileges for good behaviour. Orig. *US*. M19.

> 🕮 **2** W. MCILVANNEY With the trusty lance of my imagination, I shall challenge the dragons of our time.

▸ **B** *noun*. A trustworthy person or thing; *spec.* a prisoner granted special privileges for good behaviour (cf. TRUSTEE *noun* 1b). L16.

> 🕮 HENRY MILLER The old trusty who guarded the door.

■ **trustily** *adverb* ME. **trustiness** *noun* M16.

truth /truːθ/ *noun*. See also TROTH.

[Old English *triewþ*, *trēowþ* corresp. to Old High German *triuwida*, Old Norse (pl.) *trygðir* plighted faith, from TRUE *adjective*: see -TH[1].]

▸†**I 1** = TROTH *noun* 1. OE–E17.

▸ **II 2** The character of being, or disposition to be, true or steadfast in allegiance; faithfulness, loyalty, constancy. *arch. rare*. OE.

†**3** Faith, trust, confidence. Also, belief; a formula of belief, a creed. ME–L17.

4 Disposition to speak or act truly or sincerely; truthfulness, sincerity. Formerly also, honesty, honourableness, uprightness, virtue. ME.

5 Fact, facts; the matter or circumstance as it really is. ME. ▸†**b** The real thing, as distinguished from a representation or imitation; an antitype. M16–L18.

6 True statement; report or account consistent with fact or reality. Chiefly in ***say the truth***, ***speak the truth***, ***tell the truth*** below. LME. ▸**b** Mental apprehension of truth; knowledge. *rare*. M17. ▸**c** (Also **T-**.) A game in which players have to answer truthfully questions put by the others or, in some forms of the game, fulfil an alternative requirement. Also ***truth, dare, and promise***, ***truth game***, ***truth or dare***. M19.

7 a Religious belief or doctrine held to be true or orthodox; orthodoxy. LME. ▸**b** Conduct in accordance with the divine standard; spirituality of life and behaviour. LME.

8 What is true or real; reality; *spec.* spiritual reality as the subject of revelation or object of faith. LME.

9 A true statement; something held or accepted as true; a fixed or established principle. LME.

10 Conformity with fact; faithfulness to reality; genuineness; authenticity. LME. ▸**b** Accuracy of delineation or representation, esp. in art or literature; lifelike quality. Also (*ARCHITECTURE*), absence of pretence or imitation (as the use of paint or plaster to imitate stone etc.). E19.

11 Conformity with a standard, pattern, or rule; accuracy, precision, correctness; *esp.* accuracy of position or alignment. Freq. in ***out of truth*** below. LME.

> 🕮 **2** R. GRAFTON The king had alwayes known his truth and fidelitie towarde the crowne of Fraunce. **4** SHAKES. *Ven. & Ad.* Love is all truth: Lust full of forged lies. **5** L. H. TRIBE Solomon's wisdom lay not in splitting the baby but in using that suggestion . . to discover the truth. **6** M. ATWOOD What would I tell her about myself? The truth, or whatever would make me look good? **c** *Times* Carole . . stripped to her panties during a game of 'truth, dare and promise'. **7b** AV *John* 3:21 But hee that doeth trueth, commeth to the light, that his deeds may be made manifest, that they are wrought in God. **8** D. BREWSTER Truth has no greater enemy than its unwise defenders. B. W. ALDISS I'd rather face the truth about myself . . than deceive you. R. RHODES Science was a potential source of truth, however hard, unmediated by adults. **9** K. A. PORTER He . . spoke outright some scalding and awful truths. G. R. TURNER Differences in received and actual truths. **10** SHAKES. *Meas. for M.* She, having the truth of honour in her. *Hit Parader* At least a smidgen of truth in some of the rumours. **11** *Cycling* Upon the correct tensioning of the spokes . . depends the 'truth' of the wheel.

▸ **III 12** *PARTICLE PHYSICS*. = TOP *noun*[1] 22. Also = TOPNESS (b). L20.

Phrases: ***home truth***: see HOME *adjective*. **in truth** (chiefly *literary*) in fact; truly, really, indeed. ***logical truth***: see LOGICAL *adjective*. ***MOMENT of truth***. ***naked truth***: see NAKED *adjective*. **of a truth** *arch.* = *in truth* above. **out of truth** = *out of the true* s.v. TRUE *adjective, noun, & adverb*. ***ring of truth***: see RING *noun*[2]. **speak the truth**, **tell the truth**, (*arch.*) **say the truth** speak truly; report the matter honestly or as it really is. **to tell the truth**, **truth to tell** *adverbial* to be frank or honest. ***truth, dare, and promise***, ***truth or dare***: see sense 6c above.

Comb.: **truth-condition** *LOGIC* the condition under which a given proposition etc. is true; **truth drug** any of various drugs supposedly capable of inducing a person to tell the truth; **truth-function** *LOGIC* a function whose truth-value is dependent on the truth-value of its arguments; **truth-functional** *adjective* (*LOGIC*) of or pertaining to a truth-function; **truth-functionality** *LOGIC* the quality of being truth-functional; ***truth game***: see sense 6c above; **truth serum** a truth drug in the form of an injection; **truth set** *MATH. & LOGIC* the set of all elements that may be substituted in an expression of relationship without altering the truth of the expression; **truth squad** *US POLITICS* a group of people with the task of questioning the truth of statements made by members of an opposing party; **truth-table** *LOGIC* a tabular representation of the truth or falsity of a complex proposition as determined by the possible combinations of truth-values of its components; *COMPUTING* a table representing the outputs from all possible combinations of input; **truth-value** *LOGIC* the value of truth (or falsehood) assigned to a proposition, esp. in two-valued logic.

■ **truthy** *adjective* (chiefly *dial.*) characterized by truth; faithful; truthful: L18.

truth /truːθ/ *verb trans.* *rare*. ME.

[from prec. In sense 3 translating Greek *alētheuein* in *Ephesians* 4:15.]

†**1** Believe, trust. Only in ME.

†**2** = TROTH *verb*. Only in ME.

†**3** With *it*: Speak or deal truly. Only in M17.

4 = TRUE *verb* 2. L19.

truthful /ˈtruːθfʊl, -f(ə)l/ *adjective*. L16.

[from TRUTH *noun* + -FUL.]

1 Of a statement etc.: full of truth; sincere. *obsolete* exc. as passing into sense 2. L16.

2 Of a person: disposed to tell, or habitually telling, the truth; free from deceitfulness. L18.

3 Esp. of artistic or literary representation: characterized by truth; accurate, true to life; realistic, faithful. M19.

> 🕮 **2** V. WOOLF Being naturally truthful, he did not see the point of these exaggerations. J. TROLLOPE 'Do you remember . . ?' 'No. To be truthful, I don't.' **3** A. C. SWINBURNE There is none left . . whose bright and sweet invention is so fruitful, so truthful, . . as Mrs. Molesworth's. *Opera Now* I always want to know whether a production is truthful.

¶ Earlier in UNTRUTHFUL.

■ **truthfully** *adverb* M19. **truthfulness** *noun* M19.

truthless /ˈtruːθlɪs/ *adjective*. ME.

[from TRUTH *noun* + -LESS.]

†**1** Lacking faith; distrustful. *rare*. Only in ME.

2 Esp. of a statement: having no truth; untrue, false. LME.

†**3** Disloyal, perfidious. M16–E17.

4 Of a person: untruthful, deceitful; making false statements. *arch.* M16.

■ **truthlessness** *noun* M19.

truthlike /ˈtruːθlʌɪk/ *adjective*. Now *rare*. M16.

[formed as prec. + -LIKE.]

Like or resembling truth or the truth; having a degree of truthfulness. Formerly also, likely to be true, probable.

■ **truthlikeness** *noun* L16.

trutine /ˈtruːtiːn/ *noun.* Long *obsolete* exc. *Hist.* **M17.**
[Latin *trutina* = Greek *trutanē* balance, pair of scales.]
ASTROLOGY. ***trutine of Hermes***, a method of adjusting a horoscope by calculation of the time of a person's conception.

try /trʌɪ/ *noun.* **L15.**
[from the verb.]
▶ **I** †**1** A sieve. **L15–E19.**
▶ **II** †**2** *NAUTICAL.* The position of a ship when lying to. Only in ***at try***, ***a-try***. **M16–E18.**
3 *gen.* The action or an act of trying; an experiment or attempt at something; an endeavour. **E17.**
4 The state of wood when tried with a plane (see **TRY** *verb* 9). **L17.**
5 In *RUGBY FOOTBALL*, the act of touching the ball down behind the opposing goal-line, scoring points and entitling the scoring side to a kick at goal. In *AMER. FOOTBALL*, an attempt to score an extra point or points in various ways after a touchdown. **M19.**

📖 **3** W. GOLDING Even that was a lot to expect but it was worth a try. S. BELLOW A bad driver failing to back into a parking space—ten tries and no luck. B. BETTELHEIM A crisis . . convinced me to give psychoanalysis a try. **5** *Rugby World & Post* Desperate Welsh tackling prevented . . two certain French tries. ***pushover try***: see **PUSHOVER** 3.

Comb.: **try gun** a gun with adjustable stock used as a measure by a gun fitter; **try-pot** a pot for trying oil from blubber; **try-sail** *Naut.* a small strong fore-and-aft sail set on the mainmast or other mast of a ship in heavy weather; **try-square** a carpenter's square, usu. with one wooden and one metal limb; **tryworks** a furnace used for trying oil from blubber.

†**try** *adjective.* Also **trie**. **ME–L17.**
[Prob. from Old French *trié* pa. pple of *trier* (see next), or *trie* choice, élite.]
Choice, excellent, good; *spec.* (of a surface or angle) true, accurately level or flat.

try /trʌɪ/ *verb.* Pa. t. & pple **tried** /trʌɪd/. **ME.**
[Old French *trier* sift, pick out = Portuguese, Catalan *triar*, of unkn. origin.]
▶ **I** *verb trans.* **1** Set apart from another or others; distinguish; separate *out*. Formerly also, pick out, select. Long *arch.* **ME.** ▸†**b** Sift, strain; separate *out* by sifting or straining. **LME–L18.** ▸†**c** Separate (metal) from ore or dross by melting; refine, purify by fire. Also, remove (the dross or impurity) from metal by fire. Usu. foll. by *out*. **LME–L17.** ▸**d** Extract (oil) from blubber or fat by heating; melt down or render to obtain oil etc. Usu. foll. by *out*. **LME.**
2 †**a** Ascertain, discover; search or sift *out*. **ME–M18.** ▸**b** Determine the truth of (a matter), esp. in battle; settle (a quarrel) etc. in this way. Also foll. by *out*. Now *rare*. **M16.**
3 *LAW.* **a** Examine and decide (a case or issue) judicially; adjudicate, judge; *US* submit (a case) for trial. **ME.** ▸**b** Subject (a person) to trial. **M16.**
4 Test the truth, strength, soundness, etc., of by some action, put to the test, (freq. foll. by *out*); *spec.* test the degree of fastening of (a door, window, etc.). **ME.** ▸**b** Test (a person) to determine the truth of an assertion or belief about him or her. Freq. as ***try me***. **L20.**
5 Make an attempt at; make an effort to achieve or accomplish. **ME.**
6 Show or prove to be; demonstrate. Now *rare* or *obsolete*. **LME.**
7 Make severe demands on; strain the endurance or patience of. **M16.**
8 Test the effect or operation of; examine the effectiveness of a thing or action to produce a desired result. **M16.**
9 Smooth roughly planed wood with a plane to give an accurately flat surface. Freq. foll. by *up*. **L16.**
10 Attempt to find out or determine by experiment or effort. Now chiefly in ***try one's luck*** s.v. **LUCK** *noun*. **L16.**
†**11** Experience; undergo. Chiefly *poet.* **L16–M18.**

📖 **3a** W. MARCH A murder case which was being tried. **b** V. S. REID Flemming was arrested, tried, and executed. S. BEDFORD Antonia was arrested and tried for murder. **4** E. MITTELHOLZER He sat . . on the bed 'to try it out', as he put it. F. O'CONNOR He . . tried the front door. It was not locked. F. FORSYTH Each . . had been tried and tested in battle many times. **b** A. PRICE 'Maybe you won't like it, Oliver.' . . 'Try me.' **5** S. LEACOCK He . . tried the examination: and he . . failed. P. MARSHALL You begin to know . . how much you are capable of . . by daring to try something. **7** E. TAYLOR Don't work too hard, . . or try your eyes. P. ANGADI The twins are enough to try anyone's patience. **8** Q. CRISP First they tried religion, then drugs, then meditation and now hypnosis. *Bon Appetit* Try an Alsatian Gewurtztraminer . . to balance the spiciness of the dish.

▶ **II** *verb intrans.* †**12** *NAUTICAL.* Of a ship etc: lie to. **M16–M19.**
13 Foll. by *at*, *(out) for*: attempt to reach or obtain; apply or compete for. **M16.**
14 Make an effort to perform a specified action or act in a specified way; make an attempt at something understood; endeavour. (Foll. by *to do*, *(colloq.) and do*.) **M17.**
15 Search ground for game etc. *colloq.* **E19.**

📖 **13** M. ATWOOD I could try for a movie. P. FITZGERALD You oughtn't to try for the certificate. **14** E. BOWEN I'd love to try. E. J. HOWARD She tried unsuccessfully to free her ear-ring from the gauze ruffle. W. BAGEHOT The greatest mistake is trying to be more agreeable than you can be. A. BLEASDALE He has gone faster and faster to try and get away.

Phrases: ***try a fall***: see **FALL** *noun*[2]. **try anything once**: indicating willingness on the part of the speaker to attempt or experience something new. ***try a person's mettle***: see **METTLE** *noun*. **try back** search or cover ground a second time; retrace one's steps. ***try conclusions with***: see **CONCLUSION**. ***try for size***: see **SIZE** *noun*[1]. **try in** *DENTISTRY* place (a denture etc.) in the patient's mouth to test the fit. **try it on the dog** *colloq.* test the effect of a thing, esp. a play etc., on a person or group considered less important than the intended users or audience. **try it on (with)** *colloq.* (*a*) test the patience or endurance of (another); (*b*) attempt to outwit, deceive, or seduce (another person). ***try masteries***: see **MASTERY** 5. ***try me***: see sense 4b above. **try on** put on (a garment) to see if it fits or suits one. **try one's hand at** attempt for the first time; test one's ability or aptitude at. ***try one's luck***: see **LUCK** *noun*. ***try one's wings***: see **WING** *noun*.

Comb.: **try-in** *DENTISTRY* the experimental trial of a denture etc. in a patient's mouth; **trying-plane** a long heavy plane used after the jack-plane in squaring timber; **trying-pot** = ***try-pot*** s.v. **TRY** *noun*; **try-on** *colloq.* (*a*) an attempt to outwit or deceive another person; *transf.* the subject of such an attempt; (*b*) the action or an act of trying on a garment; **try-out** *colloq.* an experimental test of performance, popularity, etc.; a trial run or period; **try-your-strength**, **try-your-weight** *adjectives* designating a machine at a fair etc. which measures a person's strength or weight.

■ **trying** *adjective* (*a*) *rare* attempting, endeavouring; (*b*) that strains patience or endurance; annoying, vexatious: **L16.** **tryingly** *adverb* **M19.** **tryingness** *noun* **L19.**

†**trygon** *noun.* **M–L18.**
[Latin from Greek *trugōn* stingray, turtle-dove.]
A stingray.

tryma /ˈtrʌɪmə/ *noun.* **M19.**
[Greek *truma* hole, from *truein* rub down.]
BOTANY. A fruit (e.g. that of the walnut) resembling a drupe but with an ultimately dehiscent fleshy or fibrous exocarp and a stony endocarp.

trypaflavine /trɪpəˈfleɪviːn/ *noun.* **E20.**
[from **TRYPA(NOCIDE** + **FLAVINE.**]
PHARMACOLOGY. = **ACRIFLAVINE.**

trypan /ˈtrɪp(ə)n/ *noun.* **E20.**
[from **TRYPAN(OSOME.**]
BIOLOGY & PHARMACOLOGY. ***trypan blue***, ***trypan red***, either of two diazo dyes used as biological stains and formerly as drugs in the treatment of trypanosomiasis and other protozoan infections.

trypano- /ˈtrɪp(ə)nəʊ, trɪˈpanəʊ/ *combining form.*
[from **TRYPANO(SOME**: see **-O-**.]
Chiefly *MEDICINE.* Pertaining to trypanosomes.
■ **trypanoˈcidal** *adjective* fatal to trypanosomes **E20.** **tryˈpanocide** *noun* a trypanocidal agent **E20.** **trypaˈnolysis** *noun* destruction of trypanosomes **E20.** **trypanoˈlytic** *adjective* causing or connected with the destruction of trypanosomes **E20.**

trypanosoma /trɪp(ə)nəˈsəʊmə/ *noun.* **L19.**
[mod. Latin genus name, from Greek *trupanon* borer + *sōma* body.]
ZOOLOGY. = **TRYPANOSOME.** Now only as mod. Latin genus name.

trypanosome /ˈtrɪp(ə)nəsəʊm, trɪˈpanə-/ *noun.* **E20.**
[Anglicized from prec.]
ZOOLOGY & MEDICINE. A protozoan of the genus *Trypanosoma*, parasitic in the blood of humans and animals and transmitted by the bite of an insect vector. Also (in full ***trypanosome form***), (any trypanosomid at) a stage in its life cycle characterized by an elongated mononucleate form with a posterior flagellum and an undulating border.
■ **trypanoˈsomal** *adjective* of, pertaining to, or caused by trypanosomes **E20.** **trypanoˈsomic** *adjective* = **TRYPANOSOMAL** **E20.** **trypanoˈsomid** *adjective & noun* (pertaining to or designating) a member of the family Trypanosomidae, which comprises trypanosomes and related flagellate protozoans which have a trypanosome stage in their life cycle **M20.** **trypanoˈsomatid** *adjective & noun* [from mod. Latin *Trypanosomatidae* alternative family name] = **TRYPANOSOMID** *adjective & noun* **M20.**

trypanosomiasis /ˌtrɪp(ə)nəsəˈmʌɪəsɪs/ *noun.* Pl. **-ases** /-əsiːz/. **E20.**
[from prec. + **-IASIS.**]
MEDICINE. Any of several diseases caused by trypanosomal infection, *esp.* sleeping sickness and Chagas' disease.

tryparsamide /trɪˈpɑːsəmʌɪd/ *noun.* **E20.**
[from **TRYPANOSOMA** + **ARSENIC** *noun* + **AMIDE.**]
PHARMACOLOGY. An organic compound of arsenic, $C_8H_{10}AsN_2NaO_4$, used to treat trypanosomiasis and (formerly) syphilis of the central nervous system.

trypsin /ˈtrɪpsɪn/ *noun.* **L19.**
[App. from Greek *tripsis* friction, from *tribein* rub (because it was first obtained by rubbing down the pancreas with glycerine): see **-IN**[1].]
BIOLOGY. The chief digestive enzyme of the pancreatic juice, an endopeptidase which splits proteins into polypeptides.
■ **trypsinize** *verb trans.* (*BIOCHEMISTRY*) treat with trypsin (chiefly as ***trypsinized*** *ppl adjective*, ***trypsinizing*** *verbal noun*) **M20.** **trypsiniˈzation** *noun* (*BIOCHEMISTRY*) treatment with trypsin **M20.** **trypˈsinogen** *noun* the inactive form in which trypsin is secreted **L19.**

tryptamine /ˈtrɪptəmiːn/ *noun.* **E20.**
[from **TRYPTOPHAN** + **AMINE.**]
BIOCHEMISTRY. A heterocyclic amine, $C_8H_6NCH_2CH_2NH$, which is produced from tryptophan by decarboxylation and whose derivatives include serotinin.

tryptic /ˈtrɪptɪk/ *adjective.* **L19.**
[from **TRYPSIN** after *pepsin*/*peptik*.]
BIOCHEMISTRY & PHYSIOLOGY. Of or pertaining to trypsin.

tryptophan /ˈtrɪptəfan/ *noun.* Also **-ane** /-eɪn/. **L19.**
[from prec. + **-O-** + *-phan* (from Greek *phainein* appear).]
CHEMISTRY. An amino acid, $C_8H_6N{\cdot}CH_2CH(NH_2)COOH$, which occurs in proteins and is essential in the human diet; indole-α-aminopropionic acid.

tryst /trɪst/ *noun & verb. arch.* Orig. *Scot.* **LME.**
[Var. of **TRIST** *noun*[2].]
▶ **A** *noun.* **1** *gen.* A mutual appointment or agreement; a covenant. Now *rare* or *obsolete*. **LME.**
2 *spec.* An appointment, now esp. between lovers, to meet at a specified time and place; an appointed meeting or assembly, an assignation. **LME.** ▸**b** The time and place appointed for such a meeting. **LME.**
3 A market or fair, esp. for cattle. *Scot. & north.* **M16.**

📖 **2** CLIVE JAMES Those lonely roads on which lovers walk to make a tryst.

▶ **B** *verb.* **1** *verb intrans.* Make an agreement *with* a person; *esp.* arrange to meet *with* a person at an appointed time and place. Chiefly *Scot.* **LME.**
2 *verb trans.* Appoint (a time for a meeting etc.); arrange for, engage. Chiefly *Scot.* **L16.**
†**3** *verb intrans.* Negotiate *with*. *Scot.* **L16–M17.**
4 *verb trans.* Engage (a person) to do something, esp. to meet at an appointed place and time; agree to meet. Also, entice to a place. Chiefly *Scot.* **M17.**
5 *verb trans.* Come upon, befall; visit *with*. Chiefly *Scot.* **M17.**
†**6** *verb intrans.* Coincide in time *with*; concur. **L17–M18.**
7 *verb intrans.* Keep a tryst; meet at an appointed time and place. **M19.**

📖 **4** J. BUCHAN I was trysted with Haraldsen to walk to the . . end of the island. **5** SIR W. SCOTT Sair she's been trysted wi' misfortunes. **7** *Publishers Weekly* A lovely maple tree under which lovers will tryst.

¶ In sense A.2 only Scot. before **19.**
■ **tryster** *noun* a person who makes or keeps a tryst **M17.**

TS *abbreviation.*
1 Tough shit; tough situation; tough stuff. *US Military slang.*
2 Typescript.

tsaddik /ˈtsadɪk/ *noun.* Also **tz-**. Pl. **-im** /-ɪm/, **-s**. **L19.**
[Hebrew *ṣaddīq* just, righteous.]
In Judaism, a man of exemplary righteousness; a Hasidic spiritual leader or sage.

Tsakonian /tsəˈkəʊnɪən/ *noun & adjective.* **E20.**
[from *Tsakon* (see below) + **-IAN.**]
(Of or pertaining to) a modern Greek dialect spoken in Tsakon, an area in the eastern Peloponnese.

tsama *noun* var. of **TSAMMA.**

tsamba /ˈtsambə/ *noun.* **M19.**
[Tibetan.]
In Tibet, roasted and ground meal from maize or barley.

tsamma /ˈtsamə/ *noun.* Also **tsama**. **L19.**
[Nama *tsamã*.]
(The fruit of) a wild watermelon, *Citrullus lanatus*, native to parts of southern Africa.

tsantsa /ˈtsantsə/ *noun.* **E20.**
[Jivaro.]
A human head shrunk as a trophy by the Jivaros of Ecuador.

ts'ao shu /tsaʊ ˈʃuː/ *noun phr.* **L19.**
[Chinese *cǎoshū* (Wade–Giles *ts'ao shu*), from *cǎo* hasty + *shū* writing.]
In Chinese calligraphy, a cursive script developed during the Han dynasty.

tsar /zɑː, tsɑː/ *noun.* Also **czar**. Also (esp. in titles) with cap. initial. **M16.**
[Russian *tsar'*, Old Church Slavonic *cěsarĭ*, ult. repr. Latin **CAESAR**, prob. through Germanic. Spelling with *cz-* is not Slavonic.]
1 *Hist.* (The title of) the former emperor of Russia. Also, (the title of) any of certain Serbian rulers in the 14th cent.; (the title of) the 20th-cent. king of Bulgaria. **M16.**
2 *transf.* A person with great authority or power; a tyrant. **M19.**
■ **tsarate** *noun* = **TSARSHIP** **M19.** **tsardom** *noun* (*a*) the territory ruled by a tsar; (*b*) the office or power of a tsar: **M19.** **tsarian** *adjective* = **TSARISH** **E18.** **tsaricide** *noun* the murder or murderer of a tsar **L19.** **tsarish** *adjective* of or pertaining to a tsar; that is a tsar:

L17. **tsarism** *noun* a system of government centred on a tsar M19. **tsarist** *noun & adjective* (**a**) *noun* an advocate or supporter of tsarism; (**b**) *adjective* advocating or supporting tsarism: E20. **tsarlet** *noun* (*rare*) a petty tsar L19. **tsarship** *noun* the position or office of tsar M19.

tsarevich /ˈzɑːrɪvɪtʃ, tsɑːˈrjeɪvɪtʃ/ *noun*. Also **czar-**. Also (esp. in titles) with cap. initial. E18.
[Russian, formed as TSAR + patronymic *-evich*. Cf. CESAREWITCH.]
The eldest son of the former emperor of Russia; the (male) heir of a tsar.

tsarevna /zɑːˈrɛvnə, tsɑːˈrɛvnə/ *noun*. Also **czar-**. Also (esp. in titles) with cap. initial. L19.
[Russian.]
Hist. A daughter of a tsar.

tsarina /zɑːˈriːnə, tsɑːˈriːnə/ *noun*. Also **czar-**. Also (esp. in titles) with cap. initial. E18.
[Italian & Spanish *tzarina*, (*c*)*zarina*, French *tsarine*, *czarine*, from German *Zarin*, *Czarin* fem. of *Zar*, *Czar*.]
The wife of a tsar; *Hist.* (the title of) the former empress of Russia.

tsaritsa /zɑːˈrɪtsə, tsɑːˈrɪtsə/ *noun*. Also **czar-**. Also (esp. in titles) with cap. initial. L17.
[Russian.]
Hist. (The title of) the former empress of Russia.

tsatlee /ˈtsatliː/ *noun*. M19.
[Chinese *Qi Li*, the area of production, in Zhejiang province.]
A high-quality white raw silk produced in China esp. for export.

tsatske /ˈtsɒtskə/ *noun*. *US colloq.* Also **tchotchke** /ˈtʃɒtʃkə/. M20.
[Yiddish from Slavonic: cf. Russian *tsatska*.]
A trinket; *transf.* a pretty girl or woman.

Tschermak's molecule /ˈtʃəːmaks ˌmɒlɪkjuːl/ *noun phr.* Also **Tschermak molecule**. M20.
[from Gustav *Tschermak* (1836–1927), Austrian mineralogist.]
MINERALOGY. A pyroxene consisting of pure calcium aluminium aluminosilicate, either synthetic or regarded as a hypothetical component of natural pyroxenes. Also, the aluminium aluminosilicate part of this molecular structure.
■ **tschermakite** *noun* any of a series of monoclinic aluminium-rich amphiboles containing calcium and varying amounts of magnesium and ferrous iron; *esp.* the magnesium-rich end-member: M20.

tschinke /ˈtʃɪŋkə/ *noun*. Pl. **-kes**, **-ken** /-kən/. E20.
[German from *Cieszyn*, a town in Poland where it was developed.]
Hist. A light wheel-lock fowling rifle of the 17th cent., freq. with ornately decorated stock.

tsessebi /tsɛˈseɪbi/ *noun*. Also **-be**. M19.
[Setswana *tsessébe*, *-âbi*.]
A topi (antelope) of the nominate subspecies occurring in eastern and southern Africa. Also called ***bastard hartebeest***. Cf. SASSABY.

tsetse /ˈtsɛtsi, ˈtɛtsi/ *noun*. M19.
[Setswana.]
More fully ***tsetse-fly***. Any tabanid fly of the genus *Glossina*, native to tropical and southern Africa, which feeds on the blood of humans and other mammals with a needle-like proboscis, and transmits trypanosomiasis (sleeping sickness).

TSH *abbreviation*.
1 Their Serene Highnesses.
2 BIOCHEMISTRY. Thyroid-stimulating hormone.

T-shirt /ˈtiːʃəːt/ *noun*. Orig. *US*. Also **teeshirt**. E20.
[from T, T + SHIRT *noun*.]
A light short-sleeved casual garment, usu. of cotton with a round neck and no buttons, which forms a T-shape when spread out flat.
Phrases & comb.: ***been there, done that, bought the T-shirt***: see THERE. **T-shirt dress** a dress in the shape of a long T-shirt, worn loose or tied with a belt etc. at the waist.
■ **T-shirted** *adjective* wearing a T-shirt M20.

tsimmes *noun* var. of TZIMMES.

Tsimshian /ˈtʃɪmʃɪən/ *adjective & noun*. M19.
[Tsimshian *čamsián* lit. 'inside the Skeena River'.]
► **A** *adjective*. Of or pertaining to a Penutian people of the north Pacific coast or their language. M19.
► **B** *noun*. Pl. same.
1 A member of the Tsimshian people. L19.
2 The Penutian language of this people. E20.

Tsin *noun & adjective* var. of QIN.

tsine /tsʌɪn/ *noun*. L19.
[Burmese *saing*.]
= BANTENG.

Tsing *noun & adjective* var. of QING.

tsipouro /ˈtsɪpʊrəʊ/ *noun*. M20.
[mod. Greek.]
A rough Greek liquor resembling raki, sometimes flavoured with mastic gum.

tsitsith /ˈtsɪtsɪt/ *noun* (treated as *sing.* or *pl.*). Also **tzitzit(h)**. L17.
[Hebrew *ṣīṣīt*.]
The tassels on the corners of the Jewish tallith or prayer-shawl. Also, (the tassels on each corner of) a small tasselled rectangular garment with a large hole in the middle, worn under the shirt by orthodox male Jews.

tsk /tsk/ *interjection, noun, & verb*. Also redupl. **tsk tsk**. M20.
[Imit.]
► **A** *interjection & noun*. (A sound) expr. commiseration, disapproval, or irritation. M20.

📖 *Dandy* What's this? Tsk! You've spelled million as 'milion'.

► **B** *verb*. **1** *verb intrans.* Make this sound, express disapproval or irritation. M20.
2 *verb trans.* Say disapprovingly or in irritation, utter with a 'tsk'. M20.

Tsonga /ˈtsɒŋɡə/ *noun & adjective*. Also **Thonga** /ˈtɒŋɡə/. E20.
[Bantu.]
► **A** *noun*. Pl. same, **-s**.
1 The Bantu language spoken by the Shangaan of parts of South Africa and southern Mozambique (also called ***Shangaan***). E20.
2 A member of the Shangaan. M20.
► **B** *adjective*. Of, pertaining to, or designating this people or their language. E20.

Tsongdu /ˈtsɒŋduː/ *noun*. E20.
[Tibetan *t'sogs du* lit. 'an assembly meets'.]
The national assembly of Tibet.

tsores /ˈtsɒrəs/ *noun pl. US colloq.* Also **tsuris** /ˈtsʊrɪs/. E20.
[Yiddish, pl. of *tsore* trouble, woe, from Hebrew *ṣārāh*.]
Troubles, worries; (treated as *sing.*) trouble, worry.

tsotsi /ˈtsɒtsi/ *noun*. *S. Afr.* M20.
[Perh. from Nguni *-tsotsa* dress in exaggerated clothing.]
A thug, a hoodlum, *esp.* a member of a black African street gang wearing clothing of exaggerated cut. Cf. SKOLLY.

tsp. *abbreviation*.
Teaspoon(ful).

TSS *abbreviation*.
1 Toxic shock syndrome.
2 Typescripts.

tsu /tsuː/ *noun*. M20.
[Chinese *zū* (Wade–Giles *tsu*) ancestor, grandfather.]
ANTHROPOLOGY. A Chinese patrilineal kinship group.

tsuba /ˈtsuːba/ *noun*. Pl. same, **-s**. L19.
[Japanese.]
A Japanese sword-guard.

tsubo /ˈtsuːbəʊ/ *noun*. Pl. same, **-s**. E18.
[Japanese.]
A Japanese unit of area equal to approximately 3.31 sq. metres (3.95 sq. yards).

tsugi ashi /tsuːɡɪ ˈaʃi/ *noun phr.* M20.
[Japanese, from *tsugi* next, following + *ashi* foot.]
In judo and other martial arts, a method of moving in which the same foot always leads rather than both feet alternating.

tsuica /ˈtsuːɪkə/ *noun*. Also **tuica** /ˈtuːɪkə/. E20.
[Romanian *tuică*.]
A Romanian plum brandy.

Tsukahara /tsʊkəˈhɑːrə/ *noun*. L20.
[Mitsuo *Tsukahara* (b. 1947), Japanese gymnast who introduced the vault in international competition.]
GYMNASTICS. A vault consisting of a quarter- or half-turn on to the horse followed by one and a half somersaults off. Also ***Tsukahara vault***.

tsukemono /tsuːkiˈmoːno, -kɪˈməʊnəʊ/ *noun*. L19.
[Japanese, from *tsukeru* pickle + *mono* thing.]
A Japanese side dish of pickled vegetables, usu. served with rice.

tsukuri /tsʊˈkuːri/ *noun*. M20.
[Japanese.]
JUDO. A preparatory movement to facilitate the unbalancing of one's opponent.

tsun /tsʊn/ *noun*. M20.
[Chinese *zūn* (Wade–Giles *tsun*).]
A style of Chinese vessel, either wide-mouthed or animal-shaped.

tsunami /tsuːˈnɑːmi/ *noun*. Pl. **-s**, same. L19.
[Japanese, from *tsu* harbour + *nami* wave.]
A long high undulation or series of undulations of the surface of the sea caused by an earthquake or similar underwater disturbance, travelling at great speed and in shallow waters often building up enough height and force to flood the land. Also called ***seismic sea-wave***, ***tidal wave***.
■ **tsunamic** *adjective* of, pertaining to, or of the nature of a tsunami M20.

tsung /tsʊŋ/ *noun*. E20.
[Chinese *cóng* (Wade–Giles *ts'ung*).]
ARCHAEOLOGY. A Chinese ritual artefact, usu. of jade, consisting of a hollow cylinder with central rectangular casing, usu. thought to symbolize the fertility of the earth.

tsurikomi /tsuːrɪˈkəʊmi/ *noun*. E20.
[Japanese, from *tsuri* lifting + *komi* bringing or pushing in.]
JUDO. The technique of lifting and pulling one's opponent off balance during a throw.

tsuris *noun pl.* var. of TSORES.

tsutsugamushi /ˌtsuːtsuːɡəˈmʊʃi/ *noun*. E20.
[Japanese name of the mite which transmits the disease.]
MEDICINE. In full ***tsutsugamushi disease***. = ***scrub typhus*** s.v. SCRUB *noun*[1].
attrib.: ***tsutsugamushi fever***, ***tsutsugamushi mite***, etc.

tsutsumu /tsʊˈtsuːmuː/ *noun*. L20.
[Japanese = wrap.]
The Japanese art of wrapping items in an attractive and appropriate way.

Tswana /ˈtswɑːnə/ *noun & adjective*. In sense A.1 sing. also **Motswana** /mɒˈtswɑːnə/. M20.
[Bantu. Cf. BATSWANA, SETSWANA.]
► **A** *noun*. Pl. BATSWANA *noun*, **Tswana(s)**.
1 A member of a Bantu-speaking people inhabiting Botswana and parts of southern Africa. M20.
2 The language of this people, Setswana. M20.
► **B** *adjective*. Of or pertaining to the Batswana or their language. M20.

TT *abbreviation*.
1 Teetotal, teetotaller.
2 COMMERCE. Telegraphic transfer.
3 Tourist Trophy (race).
4 Tuberculin-tested.

TTF *abbreviation*.
Tetrathiafulvalene, a sulphur-containing organic compound having salts of very low resistivity.

TTL *abbreviation*.
1 PHOTOGRAPHY. Through-the-lens (metering).
2 ELECTRONICS. Transistor–transistor logic.

TU *abbreviation*.
Trade Union.

Tu. *abbreviation*.
Tuesday.

tuak /ˈtuːak/ *noun*. M19.
[Malay.]
A Malaysian or Indonesian palm wine or rice-wine.

tuan /tuːˈɑːn/ *noun*[1]. L18.
[Malay.]
In Malaysia and Indonesia: a master, a lord. Also used as a respectful form of address corresponding to ***Mr*** or ***sir***.

tuan /ˈtjuːən/ *noun*[2]. *Austral.* M19.
[Aboriginal.]
Orig., a flying phalanger. Now also, a phascogale.

Tuareg /ˈtwɑːrɛɡ/ *noun & adjective*. E19.
[Berber.]
► **A** *noun*. Pl. same, **-s**. A member of a nomadic people of the western and central Sahara; the Berber language of this people. E19.
► **B** *adjective*. Of or pertaining to this people or their language. E19.

tuart /ˈtuːət/ *noun*. Also †**tooart**. M19.
[Aboriginal *tuwart*.]
A eucalyptus of western Australia, *Eucalyptus gomphocephala*, which yields a hard durable timber.

tuatara /tuːəˈtɑːrə, tjuː-/ *noun*. L19.
[Maori, from *tua* on the back + *tara* spine.]
A large lizard-like reptile, *Sphenodon punctatum*, dark bronze green in colour with a row of yellow spines down its back, now found only on a few islands off New Zealand, and sometimes regarded as the sole living representative of an otherwise extinct order Rhynchocephalia.

tuath /ˈtʊə(h)/ *noun*. Pl. ***tuatha*** /ˈtʊəhə/. L17.
[Irish. See also TOGHE.]
IRISH HISTORY & MYTHOLOGY. A people, a tribe; the area inhabited by a people or tribe, a territory, a district. Earliest as below.
Tuatha Dé Danann /deɪ ˈdanən/ [= of Danann, the mother of the gods] in Irish mythology, a people who inhabited prehistoric Ireland.
¶ In independent historical use recorded in English from L19.

tub /tʌb/ *noun*[1]. ME.
[Prob. from Low Dutch (cf. Middle Low German, Middle Dutch *tubbe*, also Middle Flemish, Dutch *tobbe*), of unkn. origin.]
► **I 1** An open flat-bottomed container, usu. of greater width than height, made esp. of wooden staves and hoops and used for washing, bathing, planting, etc. ME.
►**b** Now only more fully ***sweating-tub***. A tub in which a

patient sweated as a treatment for venereal disease. *obsolete* exc. *Hist.* L16.

2 The amount contained in a tub, formerly used as a varying measure of capacity. E18.

3 A bath-tub; the action or an act of taking a bath. *colloq.* (now esp. *N. Amer.*). L18.

†**4** A small cask or keg of smuggled alcoholic liquor. *dial.* M19–E20.

5 A (usu. cardboard or plastic) carton in which food is sold; *spec.* such a carton containing a portion of ice-cream; the contents of such a tub. M20.

📖 **1** R. RAYNER She'd seen a jacuzzi tub spinning down the street after a particularly bad storm. *Garden Answers* Fruit can be grown to excellent effect in tubs. ***bath-tub, dolly-tub, peggy tub, sweating-tub, toby tub, washtub,*** etc. **3** A. LURIE Once in the tub among his boats and submarines, Freddy recovered. G. A. SHEEHAN The hot tub had soaked some of the pain out of my legs. **5** *Which?* Mrs. S. found a piece of metal in a tub of coleslaw. *attrib.*: *Food & Wine* Liquid vegetable oils are hardened . . to make stick and tub margarines.

▶ **II 6** A gurnard, *esp.* the brightly coloured *Trigla lucerna*. Also ***tub-fish, tub gurnard***. E17.

7 A slow clumsy ship; a short broad boat, *esp.* a stout roomy boat used for rowing practice. E17.

8 A pulpit, esp. of a Nonconformist minister. Also ***tub-pulpit***. *derog.* (now *rare*). M17.

9 a A small wheeled truck for carrying cut coal from the coalface. *Scot. & north.* M19. ▸**b** The lining of a pit-shaft. M19.

10 A fire engine. *US slang* (now *rare*). M19.

11 A short and fat person. *colloq.* L19.

12 A bus. Chiefly in ***work the tubs***, pick pockets on buses or at bus-stops. *slang.* E20.

📖 **7** A. PRICE What a rotten old tub the *Vengeful* was! **11** *Honey* Tall girls or tubs have to go shopping further afield.

Phrases: †**a tale of a tub** an apocryphal or incredible tale. **a tub for a whale** a diversion, *esp.* one created to escape a threatened danger. ***hot tub***: see HOT *adjective*. ***maidening tub***: see MAIDEN *verb* 2. ***Roman tub***: see ROMAN *adjective*. **throw a tub to a whale** create a diversion, esp. to escape a threatened danger. ***work the tubs***: see sense 12 above.

Comb.: **tub-bass** a bass stringed instrument made from a tub; **tubchair**: having solid arms continuous with a usu. semicircular back; ***tub-fish***: see sense 6 above; **tub garden**: containing plants grown in tubs; **tub-gig** *Hist.* = ***governess cart*** s.v. GOVERNESS *noun*; ***tub gurnard***: see sense 6 above; ***tub-pulpit***: see sense 8 above; **tub-size** *verb trans.* size (paper) in a tub or vat; size by hand; **tub-wheel** a horizontal water-wheel with spiral floats.

■ **tubber** *noun* (*a*) *dial.* a cooper; (*b*) *rare* a person who bathes in a tub: E19. **tubbish** *adjective* (*colloq.*) somewhat tubby M16. **tubful** *noun* as much as a tub will hold L18.

tub /tʌb/ *noun*². *slang.* L20.
[Abbreviation.]
= ***tubular tyre*** s.v. TUBULAR *adjective*.

tub /tʌb/ *verb*. Infl. **-bb-**. E17.
[from TUB *noun*¹.]

1 *verb trans.* Bathe or wash in a tub or bath. *colloq.* E17. ▸**b** *verb intrans.* Wash oneself in a tub or bath; take a bath. *colloq.* M19.

2 *verb trans.* Line (a pit-shaft) with a watertight casing; dam *back* or shut *off* (water) from a shaft in this way. E19.

3 *verb trans.* Put or pack in a tub; plant in a tub. Chiefly as ***tubbed*** *ppl adjective*. E19.

4 *verb trans. & intrans.* Coach (rowers) or practise rowing in a tub or practice boat. *slang.* L19.

📖 **3** J. HATTON A courtyard . . gay with tubbed laurel and tented tables.

■ **tubbable** *adjective* (*colloq.*) (of clothing) suitable for washing in a tub or washing machine E20. **tubbing** *noun* (*a*) the action of the verb; (*b*) the watertight casing used to line a pit-shaft: M17.

tub- *combining form* see TUBO-.

tuba /ˈtjuːbə/ *noun*¹. Pl. **tubas**, (sense 1b) **tubae** /ˈtjuːbiː/. LME.
[Italian from Latin.]

1 †**a** A trumpet. Only in LME. ▸**b** *ROMAN HISTORY.* A straight bronze war-trumpet. L19.

2 *MUSIC.* A large bass brass wind instrument of the saxhorn family played in a vertical position; a player of this instrument. M19. ▸**b** A high-pressure organ-stop producing a sound resembling that of a tuba. M19.

2 WAGNER TUBA.

tuba /tuːˈbɑː, ˈtuːbə/ *noun*². E18.
[Malay.]

1 The fermented sap of any of several palms, esp. the coconut palm, drunk as an arrack. E18.

2 In the Malay archipelago etc., any of several kinds of derris, esp. *Derris elliptica* and *D. malaccensis*, whose powdered roots are used to stupefy fish; a preparation of the roots of such a tree. M19.

tuba /ˈtuːbə/ *noun*³. E19.
[Arab. *ṭūbā*.]
In Islam, (the name of) a tree growing in paradise. Also ***tuba-tree***.

tubae *noun pl.* see TUBA *noun*¹.

tubage /ˈtjuːbɪdʒ/ *noun*. L19.
[French, formed as TUBE *noun*: see -AGE.]

1 *MEDICINE.* Intubation, esp. of the larynx. L19.

2 A tubular construction; tubing, a system of tubes. L19.

tubal /ˈtjuːb(ə)l/ *adjective*. M18.
[mod. Latin *tubalis*, from Latin *tubus* TUBE *noun*: see -AL¹.]

1 Tubular. *rare.* M18.

2 *ANATOMY & MEDICINE.* Of, pertaining to, or affecting the Fallopian tubes, the bronchial tubes, or the renal tubules. E19.

2 tubal ligation (sterilization by) ligation of the Fallopian tubes. **tubal pregnancy** ectopic pregnancy occurring in a Fallopian tube.

tubboe /ˈtʌbəʊ/ *noun*. M18.
[Perh. from a W. African lang.]
Each of the swellings or sores characteristic of yaws, esp. on the soles and palms.

tubby /ˈtʌbi/ *adjective*. E19.
[from TUB *noun*¹ + -Y¹.]

1 (Of a sound) dull or hollow, as that of a tub when struck; *spec.* (of a violin) lacking resonance. E19.

2 Tub-shaped; having a rounded outline and proportionately stout or broad; (of a person) short and fat. M19.

📖 **2** E. BEHR He was round-eyed, round-faced, on the tubby side.

■ **tubbily** *adverb* in a tubby manner; with an appearance of tubbiness: E20. **tubbiness** *noun* L19.

tube /tjuːb/ *noun & verb*. M17.
[French, or Latin *tubus* rel. to TUBA *noun*¹.]

▶ **A** *noun*. **I** Artificial.

1 A hollow (usu. cylindrical) rigid or flexible body, long in proportion to its diameter, *esp.* one for holding or conveying a liquid or fluid. M17. ▸**b** Material in tubular form; tubing. E19. ▸**c** *ellipt.* The inner tube of a bicycle tyre. E20.

2 An object or instrument in the form of or resembling a tube; *spec.* (*a*) *arch.* a telescope; (*b*) *colloq.* a telephone. M17. ▸**b** A cigarette. *slang.* M20.

3 a Formerly (*poet.*), a cannon. Now, (the barrel of) a rifle. M18. ▸**b** A small pipe containing explosive, inserted through the priming-hole of a cannon. L18. ▸**c** *ellipt.* A torpedo tube. L19.

4 A container in the form of or resembling a tube, as (*a*) a test-tube; (*b*) a soft metal or plastic cylinder sealed at one end and having a screw cap at the other, for holding a semi-liquid substance ready for use; (*c*) *Austral. slang* a bottle or can of beer. E19. ▸**b** A woman's close-fitting garment, freq. of simple design without darts or other tailoring; a tube dress, skirt, or top. M20.

5 *PHYSICS.* A sealed container, evacuated or gas-filled, containing two or more electrodes between which an electric current can be made to flow; *spec.* (*a*) a cathode-ray tube; (*b*) (chiefly *US*) a thermionic valve. M19. ▸**b** ***the tube***, television; the television set. M20.

6 A tube used for pneumatic dispatch. M19.

7 An underground tunnel or system of tunnels in which a railway runs; an underground railway system, *esp.* (freq. ***the Tube***) (proprietary name for) the system in London; a train running on such a system. M19.

8 *PHYSICS.* A tubular figure conceived as being formed by lines of force or action passing through every point of a closed curve. L19.

📖 **1** R. BOYLE The Mercury in the Tube fell down lower, about three inches. H. NORMAN He kicked aside cardboard tubes holding maps. **2** ***drainage tube, extension tube, photomultiplier tube, pitot tube, pressure tube, stomach tube,*** etc. ***down the tube(s)***: see DOWN *preposition*. **4** C. POTOK I . . found him sorting tubes of oil colors. V. GLENDINNING Martha never put the top back on the toothpaste tube. R. HILL Mow my lawn and then cool off with a tube of lager. ***boob tube***: see BOOB *noun*². **5** ***discharge tube, electron tube, vacuum tube,*** etc. **b** *attrib.*: *New Musical Express* Ready-made TV for people who like their tube time mental. ***boob tube***: see BOOB *noun*¹. **6** ***pneumatic tube***: see PNEUMATIC *adjective* 1. **7** *attrib.*: ***tube line, tube station, tube train,*** etc. **8** ***tube of flow, tube of force,*** etc.

▶ **II** Natural.

9 *ANATOMY & ZOOLOGY.* A hollow cylindrical vessel or organ in the body; a canal, a duct, a passage; *spec.* (in *pl.*, *colloq.*) the Fallopian tubes. M17. ▸**b** The penis. *slang.* E20.

10 A hollow cylindrical structure in a plant; *spec.* (*BOTANY*) the lower united portion of a gamopetalous corolla (more fully ***corolla-tube***) or gamosepalous calyx (more fully ***calyx-tube***). Also, a united circle of stamens. E18.

11 *transf.* Any of various tubular objects or formations of natural origin; *spec.* (*SURFING*) the hollow curve under the crest of a breaking wave. M19.

9 ***Eustachian tube, Fallopian tube, neural tube,*** etc. **10** ***pollen-tube, sieve tube,*** etc. **11** ***lava tube***.

Comb.: **tube curare**: kept or transported in bamboo tubes; **tube dress** a close-fitting clinging dress usu. made of elasticized material; **tube-dwelling** *adjective* (of an animal, esp. a marine worm) living, usu. permanently, in a tube which it constructs or secretes; **tube-feed** a meal, or nourishment, taken by tube-feeding; **tube-feeding** the feeding of a person (sometimes forcibly) by passing nourishment through a tube into the stomach; **tube-flower** a Malayan plant of the verbena family, *Clerodendrum indicum*, in which the corolla is funnel-shaped with a very long tube; **tube-foot** *ZOOLOGY* each of the numerous small flexible cylindrical organs by which an echinoderm collects food and moves, operated by internal water pressure; **tube-lift**: for conveying passengers between street-level and an underground railway; **tube-nosed** *adjective* (*ZOOLOGY*) having tubular nostrils; **tube shelter** an underground tube station used as an air-raid shelter; **tube skirt** a tight close-fitting skirt, usu. made from a single piece of knitted or elasticized material; **tube sock** an elasticized sock with no shaping for the heel; **tube steak** *US slang* a hot dog, a frankfurter; **tube top** a women's close-fitting elasticated top reaching from the waist to underarm level; **tube-well** (a well consisting of) an iron pipe with a solid steel point and lateral perforations near the end, which is driven into the earth until a water-bearing stratum is reached, when a suction pump is applied to the upper end; **tube-worm** a tube-dwelling worm.

▶ **B** *verb*. **1** *verb trans.* Equip or fit with a tube or tubes. E19.

2 *verb trans.* Enclose in a tube. M19.

3 *verb trans.* (with *it*) & *intrans.* Travel by tube. *colloq.* E20.

4 *verb trans. & intrans.* Fail; perform poorly (in). *US slang.* M20.

📖 **3** T. BEATTIE Jean went to London every day, commuting . . to Waterloo, and then tubing it to Bank.

■ **tubed** *adjective* having, equipped with, or resembling a tube or tubes, tubular E19. **tubeful** *noun* as much as a tube will hold L19. **tubeless** *adjective* M19. **tubelike** *adjective* resembling (that of) a tube M19.

tubectomy /tjuːˈbɛktəmi/ *noun*. E20.
[from TUBE *noun* + -ECTOMY.]
= SALPINGECTOMY.

tuber /ˈtjuːbə/ *noun*. Pl. **-s**, (in sense 2) **-bera** /-bərə/. M17.
[Latin = hump, swelling. Cf. TRUFFLE *noun & verb*.]

1 *BOTANY.* A much thickened underground part of a stem or rhizome (e.g. in the potato), which serves as a food reserve and bears buds from which new plants arise. Also = ***tuberous root*** s.v. TUBEROUS 2. M17.

2 *ANATOMY & MEDICINE.* A rounded swelling or protuberant part in the animal body. Chiefly in mod. Latin phrs. M17.

2 tuber cinereum /sɪˈnɪərɪəm/ [Latin *cinereus* ash-coloured] *ANATOMY* the part of the hypothalamus to which the pituitary gland is attached.

tuberation /tjuːbəˈreɪʃ(ə)n/ *noun*. *rare.* E18.
[from TUBER + -ATION.]
Formation of a tuber or tubers.

tubercle /ˈtjuːbək(ə)l/ *noun*. Also **-cule** /-kjuːl/. L16.
[Latin *tuberculum* dim. of TUBER: see -CLE, -CULE.]

1 *ANATOMY & ZOOLOGY.* A small rounded projection or protuberance, as on a bone, or on the surface of the body in various animals. L16.

2 *MEDICINE.* A small firm rounded swelling or nodule, now usu. *spec.* a nodular lesion in the lungs etc. characteristic of tuberculosis. Also (*arch.*), the disease tuberculosis. L16.

3 *BOTANY.* **a** A small tuber or tuberous root. E18. ▸**b** A small wart or swelling, e.g. on a perianth segment of a fruiting dock. E18.

Comb.: **tubercle bacillus** a bacillus which causes tuberculosis.

■ **tubercled** *adjective* having a tubercle or tubercles M18.

tubercula *noun* pl. of TUBERCULUM.

tubercular /tjʊˈbəːkjʊlə/ *adjective & noun*. L18.
[formed as prec. + -AR¹.]

▶ **A** *adjective*. **1** *MEDICINE.* Of, pertaining to, caused or characterized by, or affected with tubercles or tuberculosis; tuberculous. L18.

2 *BIOLOGY.* Of the form of a tubercle; having or covered with tubercles. E19.

▶ **B** *noun*. A person with tuberculosis. M20.

■ **tubercularize** *verb trans.* infect with tuberculosis L19. **tuberculariˈzation** *noun* infection with tuberculosis M19. **tubercularly** *adverb* (as) by tuberculosis L19.

tuberculate /tjʊˈbəːkjʊlət/ *adjective*. L18.
[formed as prec. + -ATE².]
BIOLOGY & MEDICINE. Having a tubercle or tubercles; characterized by or covered with tubercles.

■ Also **tuberculated** *adjective* L18.

tuberculation /tjʊˌbəːkjʊˈleɪʃ(ə)n/ *noun*. M19.
[formed as prec. + -ATION.]
BIOLOGY & MEDICINE. Formation of tubercles; the state of being tuberculate. Also, a growth of tubercles.

tubercule *noun* var. of TUBERCLE.

tuberculiform /tjʊˈbəːkjʊlɪfɔːm/ *adjective*. E19.
[from Latin *tuberculum* TUBERCLE: see -FORM.]
BIOLOGY. Having the form of a tubercle.

tuberculin /tjʊˈbəːkjʊlɪn/ *noun*. L19.
[formed as prec. + -IN¹.]
MEDICINE & VETERINARY MEDICINE. A sterile liquid protein extract prepared from cultures of tubercle bacillus, used in the diagnosis and (formerly) the treatment of tuberculosis.

Comb.: **tuberculin test** a test for infection with or immunity from tuberculosis performed by injection (usu. intradermal) of tuberculin; **tuberculin-tested** *adjective* that has undergone a tuberculin test.

tuberculize /tjʊˈbəːkjʊlʌɪz/ *verb*. Also **-ise**. **M19.**
[formed as prec. + **-IZE**.]
1 *verb trans.* Affect or infect with tubercle or tuberculosis. **M19.**
2 *verb intrans.* Become tuberculous. **M19.**
■ **tuberculiˈzation** *noun* infection with or formation of tubercles **M19.**

tuberculo- /tjʊˈbəːkjʊləʊ/ *combining form.*
[formed as prec. + **-O-**.]
Chiefly *MEDICINE*. Of, pertaining to, or involving tubercles or tuberculosis.
■ **tuberculo-ˈprotein** *noun* protein from tubercle bacilli, esp. as used in the tuberculin test **E20.** **tuberculoˈstatic** *adjective & noun* (*a*) *adjective* inhibiting the multiplication of the tubercle bacillus; (*b*) *noun* a tuberculostatic drug: **M20.**

tuberculoid /tjʊˈbəːkjʊlɔɪd/ *adjective.* **L19.**
[from Latin *tuberculum* **TUBERCLE** + **-OID**.]
1 *ZOOLOGY & MEDICINE.* = **TUBERCULIFORM**. **L19.**
2 *MEDICINE.* Designating one of the two principal forms of leprosy, characterized by a few well-defined lesions similar to those of tuberculosis, often with loss of feeling in the affected areas. **M20.**

tuberculoma /tjʊˌbəːkjʊˈləʊmə/ *noun.* Pl. **-mas**, **-mata** /-mətə/. Formerly also Anglicized as †**-ome**. **L19.**
[formed as prec. + **-OMA**.]
MEDICINE. A mass of soft material in the brain, lung, etc., resembling a tumour and caused by the tubercle bacillus.

tuberculose /tjʊˈbəːkjʊləʊs/ *adjective.* **M18.**
[formed as prec. + **-OSE**[1].]
ZOOLOGY & BOTANY. = **TUBERCULATE**.

tuberculosed /tjʊˈbəːkjʊləʊzd/ *adjective.* **L19.**
[from next + **-ED**[2].]
Affected with tuberculosis.

tuberculosis /tjʊˌbəːkjʊˈləʊsɪs/ *noun.* Pl. **-loses** /-ˈləʊsiːz/. **M19.**
[mod. Latin, from Latin *tuberculum* **TUBERCLE** + **-OSIS**.]
MEDICINE & VETERINARY MEDICINE. Orig., any disease characterized by the formation of tubercles. Now *spec.* a disease caused by the bacillus *Mycobacterium tuberculosis* (or, esp. in animals, by a related bacillus) and characterized by the formation of nodular lesions or tubercles in the tissues. Abbreviation ***TB***.
miliary tuberculosis: see **MILIARY** *adjective*[2] 2. **pulmonary tuberculosis**: characterized by primary infection of the lungs, with fever, night sweating, weight loss, and spitting of blood; also called ***consumption***, ***phthisis***.

tuberculous /tjʊˈbəːkjʊləs/ *adjective.* **M18.**
[from Latin *tuberculum* **TUBERCLE** + **-OUS**.]
1 *MEDICINE.* Pertaining to, produced by, affected with, or characterized by tubercles (*spec.* those of tuberculosis). **M18.**
†**2** *ZOOLOGY & BOTANY.* = **TUBERCULATE**. **E–M19.**

tuberculum /tjʊˈbəːkjʊləm/ *noun.* Pl. **-la** /-lə/. **L17.**
[Latin: see **TUBERCLE**.]
ANATOMY, MEDICINE, & ZOOLOGY. = **TUBERCLE**.

tuberiferous /tjuːbəˈrɪf(ə)rəs/ *adjective.* **M19.**
[from **TUBER** + **-I-** + **-FEROUS**.]
BOTANY. Producing or bearing tubers.

tuberiform /ˈtjuːbərɪfɔːm/ *adjective.* **E19.**
[from **TUBER** + **-I-** + **-FORM**.]
BIOLOGY & MEDICINE. Having the form of a tuber; (of a disease) characterized by growths of this form.

tuberization /tjuːbərʌɪˈzeɪʃ(ə)n/ *noun.* Also **-isation**. **E20.**
[from **TUBER** + **-IZE** + **-ATION**.]
BOTANY. Formation of tubers; transformation of a part of a plant into tubers.
■ **ˈtuberize** *verb intrans.* undergo tuberization **M20.**

tubero- /ˈtjuːbərəʊ/ *combining form.*
[from **TUBER**: see **-O-**.]
Chiefly *ANATOMY*. Of or pertaining to a tuber; *spec.* pertaining to the tuber cinereum and (some other part), as ***tubero-hypophyseal***, ***tubero-infundibular***, etc.

tuberose /ˈtjuːbərəʊz/ *noun.* Also (by confusion with **TUBE** *noun*, **ROSE** *noun*) **tube-rose** /ˈtjuːbrəʊz/. **M17.**
[Latin *tuberosa* specific epithet of the plant, fem. of *tuberosus* **TUBEROSE** *adjective*.]
1 A plant of the agave family, *Polianthes tuberosa*, with a tuberous root, cultivated for its waxy-white, funnel-shaped, very fragrant flowers. **M17.**
2 A perfume extracted from the flowers of this plant. **L17.**

tuberose /ˈtjuːbərəʊs/ *adjective.* **LME.**
[Latin *tuberosus*, from **TUBER**: see **-OSE**[1].]
= **TUBEROUS**.
tuberose sclerosis = ***tuberous sclerosis*** s.v. **TUBEROUS** 1.

tuberosity /tjuːbəˈrɒsɪti/ *noun.* **LME.**
[French *tubérosité* from medieval Latin *tuberositas*, from Latin *tuberosus*: see prec., **-OSITY**.]
1 The quality or condition of being tuberous. Now *rare* or *obsolete*. **LME.**
2 A tuberous formation or part, a protuberance, a swelling; *spec.* (*ANATOMY & ZOOLOGY*) a large irregular projection of a bone, usually serving for attachment of a muscle. **E17.**
2 *ISCHIAL* ***tuberosity***. ***tibial tuberosity***: see **TIBIAL** *adjective*.

tuberous /ˈtjuːb(ə)rəs/ *adjective.* **M17.**
[French *tubéreux* or Latin *tuberosus*, formed as **TUBER**: see **-OUS**.]
1 *BIOLOGY & MEDICINE* etc. Covered with or bearing several rounded swellings or projections; knobbed. Also (*MEDICINE*), characterized or affected by such swellings. **M17.**
2 *BOTANY.* **a** Of the nature of a tuber. Chiefly in ***tuberous root***, a root thickened so as to resemble a tuber, but bearing no buds (as in the dahlia). **M17.** ▸**b** Of a plant: having tubers or a tuberous root. **M17.**
1 tuberous sclerosis a rare hereditary disease, usu. fatal, characterized by small hard swellings on the brain, skin, and other organs, with diminished intelligence and epilepsy.
■ **tuberously** *adverb* **L19.** **tuberousness** *noun* **L17.**

tubi- /ˈtjuːbi/ *combining form.*
[from Latin *tubus* **TUBE**: see **-I-**. Cf. **TUBO-**.]
Of, pertaining to, or having a tube or tubular structure.
■ **tubicolar** /tjuːˈbɪkələ/ *adjective* (*ZOOLOGY*, now *rare*) = **TUBICOLOUS** **M19.** **tubicolous** /tjuːˈbɪkələs/ *adjective* (*ZOOLOGY*) inhabiting a tube, tube-dwelling **L19.** **tubifex** *noun* (more fully ***tubifex worm***) a red oligochaete (tubicifid) worm of the genus *Tubifex*, found in mud at the bottom of rivers or lakes and used as live food for aquarium fish **M20.** **tubificid** *adjective & noun* (*ZOOLOGY*) (*a*) *noun* an aquatic oligochaete worm of the family Tubificidae; (*b*) *adjective* of or pertaining to (a worm of) this family: **M20.** **tubiˈflorous** *adjective* (*BOTANY*) belonging to the former subfamily Tubiflorae of the composite family, in which some or all the florets are tubular **L19.** **tubiform** *adjective* having the form of a tube, tube-shaped, tubular **M18.** **tubipore** *noun* an organ-pipe coral **E19.**

tubing /ˈtjuːbɪŋ/ *noun.* **M19.**
[from **TUBE** + **-ING**[1].]
The action of **TUBE** *verb*; tubes collectively, a quantity of tubes; a length or piece of tube.

Tubist /ˈtjuːbɪst/ *adjective.* **E20.**
[from **TUBE** *noun* + **-IST**, after *cubist*.]
ART. Of painting: characterized by the use of tubular forms, esp. as developed by the French artist Fernand Léger (1881–1955).
■ **Tubism** *noun* the Tubist style or school of painting **M20.**

tubman /ˈtʌbmən/ *noun.* Pl. **-men**. **M17.**
[from **TUB** *noun*[1] + **MAN** *noun*.]
†**1** = **TUB-PREACHER**. Only in **M17.**
2 A barrister in the former Court of Exchequer who stood beside the postman, after whom he had precedence in motions except in Crown business. Cf. **POSTMAN** *noun*[2]. *obsolete* exc. *Hist.* **M18.**

tubo- /ˈtjuːbəʊ/ *combining form.* Before o also **tub-**.
[from Latin *tubus* **TUBE**: see **-O-**. Cf. **TUBI-**.]
1 *ZOOLOGY.* Tubular and —. Now *rare*.
2 *ANATOMY & MEDICINE.* Of or pertaining to a tube or tubes, esp. the Fallopian tubes (and another organ), as ***tubo-uterine***, ***tubovarian***.
■ **tuboˈcornual** *adjective* (*ANATOMY & MEDICINE*) of or pertaining to the Fallopian tubes and the cornua of the uterus; *spec.* designating an operation to reconnect a severed or occluded tube: **L20.** **tuboplasty** *noun* (*MEDICINE*) the surgical repair of one or both Fallopian tubes **M20.**

tubocurarine /tjuːbəʊˈkjʊərəriːn/ *noun.* **L19.**
[from **TUBO-** + **CURARE** + **-INE**[5].]
PHARMACOLOGY. An isoquinoline alkaloid, the active ingredient of tube curare, whose chloride is used as a muscle relaxant.

tub-preacher /ˈtʌbpriːtʃə/ *noun. obsolete* exc. *Hist.* **M17.**
[from **TUB** *noun*[1] + **PREACHER**.]
A person who preaches from a pulpit, *spec.* (*derog.*) a dissenting preacher or minister.

tubster /ˈtʌbstə/ *noun. slang. derog.* Now *rare* or *obsolete.* **L17.**
[from **TUB** *noun*[1] + **-STER**.]
= **TUB-PREACHER**.

tub-thumper /ˈtʌbθʌmpə/ *noun.* **M17.**
[from **TUB** *noun*[1] + **THUMPER**.]
1 Orig., a preacher who thumps the pulpit for emphasis. Now usu. (*gen.*), a violent or declamatory preacher or orator, a ranter. **M17.**
2 A cooper. *joc. dial.* **L19.**
■ **tub-thumping** *noun & adjective* (given to or characterized by) ranting oratory **L19.** **tub-thumpery** *noun* (*rare*) speech or behaviour characteristic of a tub-thumper **E20.**

tubular /ˈtjuːbjʊlə/ *adjective & noun.* **L17.**
[from Latin *tubulus* small tube: see **-AR**[1].]
▶ **A** *adjective.* **1** Tube-shaped; consisting of, made from, or having a tube or tubes. **L17.** ▸**b** *BOTANY.* (Of a corolla or calyx) having the lower part fused into a tube; *spec.* designating one of the two main types of floret in the flowerhead of a plant of the composite family (opp. ***ligulate***). **L18.** ▸**c** In *SURFING*, (of a wave) hollow, well-curved, and excellent for riding; *transf.*, wonderful, excellent. *slang* (chiefly *US*). **L20.**
2 *MEDICINE.* Of or involving tube-shaped organs or structures; *esp.* bronchial. **E19.** ▸**b** *OPHTHALMOLOGY.* Of, pertaining to, or designating a visual field restricted to a small area surrounding the fixation point. **E20.**
1 tubular bells *MUSIC* an orchestral instrument consisting of a row of vertically suspended metal tubes of different lengths struck with a hammer. **tubular bridge**: formed from a massive (usu. iron) tube or hollow beam through which traffic passes. **tubular tyre** a lightweight pneumatic tyre used esp. on racing bicycles, consisting of an inner tube completely encased within an outer covering cemented or otherwise attached to the wheel-rim (cf. **TUB** *noun*[2]). **2b tubular vision** tunnel vision.
▶ **B** *ellipt.* as *noun.* A tubular bridge, tyre, etc. **E19.**
■ **tubuˈlarity** *noun* the quality of being tubular **M18.** **tubularly** *adverb* **M19.**

tubularian /tjuːbjʊˈlɛːrɪən/ *adjective & noun.* **M19.**
[from mod. Latin *Tubularia* genus name, from Latin *tubulus* **TUBULE**: see **-ARIAN**.]
ZOOLOGY. (Of, pertaining to, or designating) a colonial hydroid of a type in which the polyps are of tubular form, protected by a perisarc, with naked hydranths.

tubulate /ˈtjuːbjʊlət/ *adjective.* **M18.**
[formed as next + **-ATE**[2].]
ZOOLOGY & BOTANY. Formed into or like a tube; tubular.

tubulated /ˈtjuːbjʊleɪtɪd/ *adjective.* **M17.**
[Latin *tubulatus*, from *tubulus* **TUBULE**: see **-ED**[2], **-ED**[1].]
1 Having a tube; *esp.* (of a chemical retort or receiver) having a short tube with a stopper through which substances can be introduced. **M17.**
2 Formed into or resembling a tube; tubular. **E18.**
■ **tubuˈlation** *noun* the process of making or becoming tubular **M17.** **tubulature** *noun* (*CHEMISTRY*) = **TUBULURE** **E19.**

tubule /ˈtjuːbjuːl/ *noun.* **L17.**
[Latin **TUBULUS**: see **-ULE**.]
A small tube; *esp.* a minute tubular structure in a living organism.
kidney tubule, ***microtubule***, ***renal tubule***, etc. **MALPIGHIAN** ***tubule***. ***seminiferous tubule***: see **SEMINIFEROUS** 2.

tubuli *noun* pl. of **TUBULUS**.

tubuli- /ˈtjuːbjʊli/ *combining form* of **TUBULE**: see **-I-**.
■ **tubuliˈdentate** *adjective & noun* (*ZOOLOGY*) of or pertaining to, an animal of, the order Tubulidentata of mammals having compound teeth traversed by parallel vertical tubules, comprising only the aardvark and its fossil relatives **E20.** **tubuliform** *adjective* having the form of a tubule, tubular **L18.**

tubulin /ˈtjuːbjʊlɪn/ *noun.* **M20.**
[from **TUBULE** + **-IN**[1].]
BIOCHEMISTRY. A protein that is the main constituent of microtubules.

tubulose /ˈtjuːbjʊləʊs/ *adjective.* Now *rare* or *obsolete.* **E18.**
[mod. Latin *tubulosus*, from Latin *tubulus* **TUBULE**: see **-OSE**[1].]
Tube-shaped.

tubulous /ˈtjuːbjʊləs/ *adjective.* **M17.**
[formed as prec. + **-OUS**.]
1 Tube-shaped. **M17.**
2 Containing or composed of tubes. *rare.* **M19.**

tubulure /ˈtjuːbjʊl(j)ʊə/ *noun.* **E19.**
[French, formed as **TUBULE** + **-URE**.]
CHEMISTRY. A short tube, or a projecting opening for receiving a tube, in a retort or receiver.

tubulus /ˈtjuːbjʊləs/ *noun.* Pl. **-li** /-lʌɪ, -liː/. **E19.**
[Latin, dim. of *tubus* **TUBE** *noun*: see **-ULE**.]
1 = **TUBULE**. **E19.**
2 = **TUBULURE**. **L19.**

TUC *abbreviation.*
Trades Union Congress.

Tucana /tʊˈkɑːnə/ *noun.* Also (earlier) **Tou-**. **M19.**
[mod. Latin, from **TOUCAN**.]
(The name of) a constellation of the southern hemisphere south of Grus and Phoenix; the Toucan.

tuchun /ˈtuːtʃʊn/ *noun.* **E20.**
[Chinese *dūjūn* (Wade–Giles *tuchun*), from *dū* govern + *jūn* military.]
Hist. In China: (the title of) a military leader, a warlord; *spec.* a provincial military governor.

tuck /tʌk/ *noun*[1]. **LME.**
[from **TUCK** *verb*[1].]
1 A fold or pleat in material, a garment, etc. Now chiefly *spec.*, a flattened usu. stitched fold (*esp.* any of several such) put in a garment to shorten or tighten it or for ornament. **LME.** ▸**b** A plait of hair. *rare.* Long *obsolete* exc. *Scot.* **E17.**
2 *NAUTICAL.* (The shape of) the part of a ship's hull where the bottom planks or plates terminate at the tuck-rail or tuck-plate. **E17.**
3 *ellipt.* = ***tuck-net*** below. **E17.**
4 A pull, a tug. *obsolete* exc. *dial.* **M17.**
5 a Usu. more fully ***tuck-in***, (earliest, now *rare*) ***tuck-out***. A hearty meal; a feast of delicacies. *colloq.* (orig. *slang*). **E19.**

▸**b** Food, eatables; *esp.* cakes, sweets, etc., eaten by children. *School slang.* **M19.** ▸**c** A hearty appetite for food. *dial.* **M19.**

6 a An act of pushing in the ends or edges of a thing to secure them in position. **M19.** ▸**b** A folding flap on one cover of a book, which is tucked into a band or the like on the other cover to keep the book closed. **L19.**

7 a In diving, gymnastics, etc.: (the adoption of) a tuck position. **M20.** ▸**b** In downhill skiing: a squatting position. **L20.**

Phrases: ***nip and tuck***: see NIP *noun*¹. ***TUMMY tuck***.

Comb.: **tuck box**: for storing sweets, cakes, etc., esp. at a boarding-school; **tuck-comb** *US* = *TUCKING-comb*; ***tuck-in***: see sense 5a above; **tuck-mill** (chiefly *dial.*, now *rare*) = *TUCKING-mill*; **tuck-net**, **tuck-seine** a small net for taking caught fish from a larger net; ***tuck-out***: see sense 5a above; **tuck-plate** NAUTICAL a curved plate of the hull of an iron ship where the stern-post is bolted to the transom-frame; **tuck-point** *verb trans.* point (brickwork) with coloured mortar so as to have a narrow groove which is filled with fine white lime putty allowed to project slightly; **tuck position** in diving, gymnastics, etc., a position with the thighs pulled close to the chest, the knees bent, and the hands clasped round the shins; **tuck-rail** NAUTICAL: forming a rabbet which caulks the butt-ends of the bottom planks in a ship's hull; ***tuck seine***: see ***tuck net*** above; **tuck shop** a small shop, usu. in or near a school, selling food (esp. sweets) to children; **tuck-stitch**: used in making a tuck.

tuck /tʌk/ *noun*². Now *arch.* & *dial.* Chiefly *Scot.* **LME.**
[from TUCK *verb*².]

†**1** A blast of a trumpet. *rare.* Only in **LME.**

2 A blow, a stroke, a tap. Chiefly in ***tuck of drum***. **L15.**

tuck /tʌk/ *noun*³. Now *arch.* or *Hist.* **E16.**
[Prob. from French dial. *étoc*, Old French, Provençal *estoc*, from Germanic, whence also German *Stock* stick.]

A slender straight thrusting sword, a rapier.

tuck /tʌk/ *verb*¹.
[Old English *tūcian*; later infl. by Middle Low German, Middle Dutch *tucken* draw, pull sharply or forcibly (= Old High German *zucchen*, German *zucken* twitch, snatch), from Germanic base rel. also to TUG *verb*.]

†**1** *verb trans.* Punish, chastise; ill-treat, torment. **OE–ME.**

†**2** *verb trans. fig.* Reprove, find fault with; upbraid, reproach. **ME–M17.**

3 *verb trans.* Formerly, tug at, pluck, pull. Now only *spec.* (*dial.*), pull the loose hay from the sides of (a new rick). **ME.**

4 *verb trans.* Dress or finish (woven cloth), stretch (woven cloth) on tenters. Now *local.* **LME.**

5 *verb trans.* Pull or gather (cloth, clothing, etc.) up in a fold or folds; gird up (a garment etc.). Freq. foll. by *up*. **LME.** ▸**b** Put a tuck or tucks in (material, a garment, etc.); shorten, tighten, or ornament with tucks. **E17.**

6 *verb trans.* **a** Pull or gather up and confine the loose garments of, gird *up* (a person). Usu. in *pass.* Now *rare* or *obsolete.* **LME.** ▸**b** Dress (an infant) up or *up* in short clothes. *dial.* **L19.** ▸**c** *fig.* Cramp or hamper by lack of space, time, or means. *colloq.* **L19.**

7 *verb trans.* Put or stow (an object) away, esp. in or into a specified (often concealed) place or in a specified way. Now also, hit (a ball) to the desired place. Freq. foll. by *away*. **L16.**

8 *verb trans.* Push in the edge or end of (something loose) so as to secure or confine it; *esp.* turn in the edges of (bedclothes) under a bed or its occupant. Freq. foll. by *in*. **M17.** ▸**b** Thrust in the edges of bedclothes around (a person). Foll. by *in*, *up*. **L17.**

9 *verb trans.* Hang (a criminal). Usu. foll. by *up*. *slang* (now *rare*). **L17.**

10 a *verb trans.* Consume, swallow, (food or drink), esp. in large quantities. Freq. foll. by *away*. **L18.** ▸**b** *verb intrans.* Feed heartily or greedily. Usu. foll. by *in*, *into*. *colloq.* **E19.**

11 *verb trans.* ANGLING. Take (fish) from a larger net by means of a tuck-net. **M19.**

> 📖 **5** DICKENS He tucked up his sleeves and squared his elbows. OUIDA The . . countrywoman tucked up her petticoats, and began to climb up the steep path. **7** E. WAUGH That . . cushion had been tucked under her arm. *Times* His low forehead, as he tucks the ball away. W. GOLDING Tucked away at the bottom of the yard . . was a forge. *Soldier of Fortune* Most are tucking away as much money as they can for retirement. **8** M. SPARK She tucked in the loose blanket. I. MCEWAN He took my napkin . . and tucked it into the front of my shirt. S. RADLEY Anne . . stood with her left hand tucked . . through the crook of his arm. D. PROFUMO Do tuck your shirt in. You look a mess. **b** M. WESLEY Laura hustled them back into bed, tucked them in. **10a** *Decanter* The last morsels of a sumptuous . . meal were tucked away.
> **b** J. BUCHAN I have never seen a company tuck in more resolutely to more substantial viands. P. L. FERMOR He gave me a feast . . , urging me to tuck in. D. LODGE They tucked into hot cakes and bacon.

Comb.: **tuck-away** *adjective* able to be tucked away; **tuck-in** *adjective* (of a blouse etc.) able to be tucked in.

tuck /tʌk/ *verb*². Chiefly *Scot.* **LME.**
[Old Northern French *toquer* touch, strike, north. form of *toucher* TOUCH *verb*.]

1 *verb trans.* & *intrans.* Beat, sound, (a drum). Long *obsolete* exc. *Scot. dial.* **LME.**

2 *verb intrans.* †**a** Of a drum: sound. **L15–M17.** ▸**b** Of the wind: blow in gusts. *dial.* **M19.**

tuckahoe /ˈtʌkəhəʊ/ *noun. US.* **E17.**
[Virginia Algonquian *tockawhoughe*.]

1 Any of various roots and other underground plant parts formerly eaten by N. American Indians, esp. in Virginia; *esp.* (*a*) the starchy rhizome of the arrow arum, *Peltandra virginica*; (*b*) the sclerotium of a bracket-fungus, *Poria cocos*. **E17.**

2 (**T-**.) A native or inhabitant of the lowlands of Virginia. *local.* **E19.**

tuckamore /ˈtʌkəmɔː/ *noun. Canad.* **M19.**
[from *tucka-* prob. regional pronunc. of *tucking* pres. pple of TUCK *verb*¹ + MORE *noun*¹.]

A stunted bush, esp. a spruce or juniper, with creeping roots and interlacing branches; dense scrub formed by such bushes.

tucked /tʌkt/ *ppl adjective.* **M16.**
[from TUCK *noun*¹, *verb*¹: see -ED², -ED¹.]

1 That has been tucked (*up*, *in*, or *away*); arranged in tucks; shortened or ornamented with tucks. **M16.**

2 *spec.* Of a person: hampered or cramped for lack of space, time, or means. *colloq.* **L19.**

3 In diving, gymnastics, etc.: drawn up into the tuck position; (performed) with the body in this position. **M20.**

1 tucked up (*a*) that has been tucked up; (*b*) *dial.* (of a dog or horse) having the flanks drawn in from hunger, fatigue, etc.; tired out, exhausted.

†**Tuckeh** *noun* & *adjective* see TEKKE *noun*² & *adjective*.

tucker /ˈtʌkə/ *noun.* **LME.**
[from TUCK *verb*¹ + -ER¹; in sense 3 perh. from TUCK *noun*¹.]

1 A person who tucks something; *esp.* (now *arch.* or *Hist.*) a person who fulls and dresses cloth, a fuller. **LME.**

2 A piece of lace, linen, etc., worn in or around the top of a bodice; a frill of lace worn round the neck. Now *Hist.* exc. in ***best bib and tucker*** (see BIB *noun* 1). **L17.**

3 Orig., the daily food supplies or rations of a gold-digger or station hand. Now usu. (*gen.*), food. *colloq.* (chiefly *Austral.* & *NZ*). **M19.**

4 NEEDLEWORK. A device in a sewing-machine for making tucks. **E20.**

3 earn one's tucker, **make one's tucker** earn just enough to pay for one's keep.

Comb.: **tucker-bag**, **tucker-box** (*colloq.*, chiefly *Austral.* & *NZ*) a container for food.

■ **tuckerless** *adjective* (*Austral.* & *NZ colloq.*) without food **E20.**

tucker /ˈtʌkə/ *verb*¹ *trans. N. Amer. colloq.* **M19.**
[from TUCK *verb*¹ + -ER⁵.]

Tire (*out*); weary. Esp. in ***tuckered out***, worn out, exhausted.

tucker /ˈtʌkə/ *verb*². *colloq.* (chiefly *Austral.* & *NZ*). **L19.**
[from the noun.]

1 *verb trans.* & *refl.* Supply with food. **L19.**

2 *verb intrans.* Eat; have a meal. **L19.**

tucket /ˈtʌkɪt/ *noun*¹. *arch.* **L16.**
[from TUCK *verb*²: see -ET¹.]

A flourish on a trumpet, esp. as a signal for troops to march.

tucket /ˈtʌkɪt/ *noun*². *US.* **M19.**
[Origin uncertain; perh. French *toquet* dim. of TOQUE.]

A small ear of maize in the unripe milky stage.

tucking /ˈtʌkɪŋ/ *noun.* **LME.**
[from TUCK *verb*¹ + -ING¹.]

1 The action of TUCK *verb*¹. **LME.**

2 The part of a garment that is tucked; a series of usu. stitched tucks in material or a garment. **L19.**

Comb.: **tucking-comb**: confining the hair; **tucking-mill** (*dial.* or *Hist.*) a fulling-mill.

tucktoo /tʌkˈtuː/ *noun.* **L19.**
[Burmese *tokté*, *taukte*: of imit. origin.]

In Myanmar (Burma), a large house lizard or gecko.

tuco-tuco /ˈtuːkəʊtuːkəʊ/ *noun.* Pl. **-os.** Also **tucutucu** /tuːkuːˈtuːkuː/. **M19.**
[Imit. of the call of some species.]

A ratlike gregarious burrowing rodent of the S. American genus *Ctenomys*.

tucum /ˈtuːkəm/ *noun.* **E17.**
[Tupi *tukũ*.]

A tropical S. American palm, *Astrocaryum vulgare*; the very tough fibre obtained from this palm.

tucuma /ˈtuːkəmə/ *noun.* **E19.**
[Tupi *tukumaa*.]

A Brazilian palm, *Astrocaryum tucuma*, which yields an edible oil-rich fruit and a fibre like that of the tucum.

tucutucu *noun* var. of TUCO-TUCO.

'tude /tjuːd/ *noun. N. Amer. slang.* **L20.**
[Abbreviation.]

Attitude; *esp.* a bad or negative disposition.

> 📖 *Entertainment Weekly* Armed with . . a don't-mess-with-me 'tude, Guns ['n' Roses] . . shoved their way to the front of the line.

-tude /tjuːd/ *suffix.* Also (see below) **-itude.**
[from or after French from Latin *-tudo*, *-tudin-*.]

Forming (usu. with intermediate **-I-**) abstract nouns, as *altitude*, *exactitude*, *fortitude*, *solitude*, etc.

Tudeh /ˈtuːdeɪ/ *noun.* **M20.**
[Persian, lit. 'mass'.]

In full ***Tudeh party***. The Communist Party of Iran.

Tudesco *noun* var. of TEDESCO *noun*².

Tudesque /tjuːˈdɛsk/ *adjective.* Now *rare* or *obsolete.* **E19.**
[French from Italian TEDESCO *adjective*.]

Esp. of the language: German.

Tudor /ˈtjuːdə/ *noun* & *adjective.* **M18.**
[Owen *Tudor* (see below).]

▶ **A** *noun.* **1** *Hist.* A member of the royal family descended from the union of the Welsh squire Owen Tudor (d.1461) and Henry V's widow Catherine of Valois; *spec.* any of the monarchs of England from Henry VII to Elizabeth I (1485–1603). **M18.**

2 A style of architecture prevalent under monarchs of the house of Tudor or (esp., more fully ***mock Tudor***) imitative of this, characterized particularly by half-timbering and appropriate decoration. **M20.** ▸**b** A house in this style. *N. Amer.* **M20.**

2 *Stockbroker's Tudor*, ***Stockbroker Tudor***: see STOCKBROKER.

▶ **B** *adjective.* **1** Of, characteristic of, or associated with (the period of) the Tudors, the royal family ruling England between 1485 and 1603. **L18.**

2 *spec.* Of, designating, or pertaining to, or (esp., more fully ***mock-Tudor***) imitative of, the prevalent architectural style of the Tudor period, characterized particularly by half-timbering and appropriate decoration. **E19.**

> 📖 **1 Tudor rose** (esp. in late Perpendicular decoration) a conventional usu. five-lobed figure of a rose, freq. depicting a red rose encircling a white one. **2** D. L. SAYERS A plateful of synthetic pastries in Ye Olde Worlde Tudor Tea-Shoppe.

■ **Tudoˈresque** *adjective* characteristic of the Tudor period; in or resembling the Tudor style: **M19.** **Tudorish** *adjective* = TUDORESQUE **M20.** **Tudorize** *verb trans.* make Tudor in form or character, *esp.* build or renovate in this style (chiefly as ***Tudorized*** *ppl adjective*.) **E20.** **Tudory** *noun* & *adjective* (freq. *joc.* & *derog.*) (*a*) *noun* Tudor architecture or decoration; (*b*) *adjective* imitative or suggestive of Tudor style: **M20.**

Tudorbethan /ˌtjuːdəˈbiːθ(ə)n/ *adjective.* **M20.**
[Blend of prec. and ELIZABETHAN. Cf. JACOBETHAN.]

Of (esp. architectural) design: imitative of Tudor and Elizabethan styles.

Tudric /ˈtjuːdrɪk/ *noun.* **E20.**
[App. a blend of TUDOR and CYMRIC.]

(Proprietary name for) a type of pewter.

tue /tjuː/ *noun.* **L19.**
[Abbreviation: cf. TEW-IRON.]

= TUYÈRE. Also more fully ***tue-iron***.

Tue. *abbreviation.* Also **Tues.**

Tuesday.

tuel *noun* var. of TEWEL.

Tuesday /ˈtjuːzdeɪ, -di/ *noun.*
[Old English *Tīwesdæg* = Old Frisian *Tiesdei*, Old High German *ziostag* (German dial. *Zistig*), Old Norse *tý(r)sdagr*, from genit. of *Tīw* (= Old High German *Zīo*, Old Norse *týr* a Teutonic god identified with Mars, from Germanic cognate of Latin *deus* god) + *dæg* DAY *noun*, translating Latin *dies Marti* day of Mars.]

▶ **A** *noun.* The third day of the week, following Monday. **OE.**

Hock Tuesday, ***Pancake Tuesday***, ***Shrove Tuesday***, etc. ***Super Tuesday***: see SUPER *adjective*.

▶ **B** *adverb.* On Tuesday. Now *colloq.* **ME.**

▶ **C** *attrib.* or as *adjective.* Of Tuesday; characteristic of Tuesday; taking place on Tuesday(s). **L15.**

■ **Tuesdays** *adverb* (*colloq.*) on Tuesdays, each Tuesday **M20.**

tufa /ˈtuːfə, ˈtjuːfə/ *noun.* **L18.**
[Italian, obsolete local var. of *tufo*, from late Latin *tofus*, TOPHUS. Cf. next.]

GEOLOGY. Orig., a friable porous stone formed of consolidated, often stratified material; tuff, tophus. Now usu. *spec.*, a soft porous calcium carbonate rock formed by deposition around mineral springs.

■ **tuˈfaceous** *adjective* of the nature or texture of tufa **E19.**

tuff /tʌf/ *noun.* **M16.**
[French *tuffe*, *tufle* from Italian *tufo*: see prec.]

GEOLOGY. A light porous cellular rock or tufa; now usu. *spec.*, one formed by the consolidation of volcanic ash etc.

■ **tuffaceous** /tʌˈfeɪʃəs/ *adjective* of the nature or texture of tuff **L19.**

tuff /tʌf/ *verb intrans. rare.* **M16.**
[Imit.]

Make a short explosive sound; puff.

📖 F. SWINNERTON His train's now tuffing in that long tunnel.

tuffet /ˈtʌfɪt/ *noun*. **M16**.
[Alt. of TUFT *noun*.]
1 A bunch of threads, grass, hair, etc., held or growing together at the base, a tuft. **M16**.
2 A hassock, a footstool. **L19**.
3 A hillock, a mound. **L19**.

tuffite /ˈtʌfʌɪt/ *noun*. **E20**.
[from TUFF *noun* + -ITE¹.]
GEOLOGY. A rock consisting of a mixture of pyroclastic and sedimentary material, esp. with pyroclasts predominant.

tuff-tuff /ˈtʌftʌf/ *noun*. *colloq*. **E20**.
[Alt. of TEUF-TEUF.]
A motor vehicle. As interjection also, repr. the repeated sound of gases escaping from the exhaust of a combustion engine.

tuft /tʌft/ *noun*. **LME**.
[Prob. from Old French *tof(f)e* (mod. *touffe*), of unkn. origin: for alt. of *-ff* to *-ft* see GRAFT *noun*². Cf. TOFF, TUFFET.]
1 a A bunch of small (usu. soft and flexible) things, as hairs, feathers, etc., fixed or attached at the base; *spec*. a tufted patch of hair on the head or chin. **LME**. ▸**b** BOTANY. A cluster of short-stalked flowers etc. growing from a common point; a (freq. dense or compact) cluster of vegetative shoots or stems growing from a common root. **E16**.
2 An ornamental tassel, esp. on a cap; *spec*. (now *Hist*.) the gold tassel formerly worn by titled Oxbridge undergraduates. **LME**. ▸**b** A person who wears a tuft; *spec*. (now *Hist*.) a titled Oxbridge undergraduate (*Univ. slang*). **M18**.
3 A clump of trees or bushes. **M16**.
4 ANATOMY. A small cluster or plexus of capillary blood-vessels; a glomerulus. **M19**.

📖 **1a** TENNYSON A light-green tuft of plumes she bore. R. P. JHABVALA He had shaved his head completely, leaving only the Hindu tuft on top. **branchial tuft**, **respiratory tuft** ZOOLOGY a small cluster of elongated gills. ***scent tuft***: see SCENT *noun*. **b** W. IRVING Picking his way . . through this . . forest; stepping from tuft to tuft of rushes and roots.

tuft /tʌft/ *verb*. **M16**.
[from prec.]
1 *verb trans*. Provide with a tuft or tufts. **M16**. ▸**b** Make regularly spaced depressions in by passing a thread through (a cushion, mattress, etc.). **L19**.
2 *verb intrans*. Form a tuft or tufts; grow in tufts. **L16**.
3 *verb trans*. & (*rare*) *intrans*. In stag-hunting: beat (a covert); drive (a deer) from cover by beating. **L16**.
▪ **tufter** *noun* (*a*) in stag-hunting, a hound trained to drive the deer out of cover; (*b*) a person who or machine which tufts mattresses, carpets, etc.: **M19**.

tuftaffeta /tʌfˈtafɪtə/ *noun* & *adjective*. Long *arch*. *rare*. Also **-ty** /-ti/. **L16**.
[from TUFT *noun* + TAFFETA.]
▶**A** *noun*. A kind of taffeta with a pile or nap arranged in tufts. **L16**.
▶**B** *attrib*. or as *adjective*. Made of or clothed in tuftaffeta; luxuriously dressed. **L16**.

tufted /ˈtʌftɪd/ *adjective*. **E17**.
[from TUFT *noun*, *verb*: see -ED², -ED¹.]
1 Having or decorated with a tuft or tufts. **E17**. ▸**b** Of a bird: having a tuft of feathers on the head; crested (esp. in the names of particular species). **M18**.
2 BOTANY. Bearing flowers in tufts or fascicles. **E17**.
3 Growing in a tuft or tufts; clustered. **M17**.
1b tufted duck a small Old World freshwater duck, *Aythya fuligula*, with a drooping crest on the back of the head and brownish plumage (glossy black with white sides in breeding males). **2 *tufted loosestrife***, ***tufted vetch***, etc. **tufted hair-grass** a coarse grass, *Deschampsia cespitosa*, esp. of clay soils; also called ***tussock grass***, ***windlestraw***.

tuft-hunter /ˈtʌfthʌntə/ *noun*. Now *rare* or *obsolete*. **M18**.
[from TUFT *noun* + HUNTER.]
A person who obsequiously courts the acquaintance of rich or titled people; a sycophant.
▪ **tuft-hunted** *adjective* sought after by tuft-hunters **M19**. **tuft-hunting** *noun* the behaviour characteristic of a tuft-hunter **L18**.

tufting /ˈtʌftɪŋ/ *noun*. **M16**.
[from TUFT *verb* + -ING¹.]
1 The action of TUFT *verb*. **M16**.
2 Tufts collectively; a mass of tufts. **L18**.
3 The process or result of using tufts in the making of carpets etc. **M20**.

tufty /ˈtʌfti/ *adjective*. **E17**.
[from TUFT *noun* + -Y¹.]
1 Full of tufts, having many tufts; covered or decorated with tufts. **E17**.
2 Forming a tuft or tufts; consisting of or growing in tufts. **E17**.
▪ **tuftily** *adverb* **M19**.

tug /tʌɡ/ *noun*¹. **LME**.
[from TUG *verb*.]
1 A pair of short chains attached to the hames in a horse's harness to connect the collar with the shafts (usu. in *pl*.); a trace; a short strap for keeping a harness in position; in *pl*., the loops of the back-strap which support the shafts. **LME**. ▸**b** MINING. The iron hoop of a corf. **L18**. ▸**c** A rope. *US*. **E19**.
2 An act or instance of tugging, *spec*. (*a*) a forcible, violent, or jerky pull; (*b*) a determined effort, a hard try. Now also, a sudden strong emotional feeling. **E16**.
3 A strenuous contest between two forces or persons. **M17**.
4 A wagon for pulling timber. *dial*. (now *rare* or *obsolete*). **E18**.
5 a A small stoutly built powerful boat used to tow larger vessels. **E19**. ▸**b** Any towing craft or vehicle, *esp*. an aircraft that tows a glider. **M20**.
6 At Eton College: a colleger (as opp. to an oppidan). Also, a hard-working pupil. *slang*. *derog*. **M19**.

📖 **2** I. MCEWAN She pulled her hands free, this time a decisive tug. *Scientific American* Initially circular orbits are perturbed into ellipses by gravitational tugs from passing . . moons. **3** *New Yorker* Much of Estonian history has been characterized by this tug between East and West. **tug of love** *colloq*. a dispute, usu. between parents, over the custody of a child. **tug of war** (*a*) a decisive contest, an intense struggle; (*b*) a trial of strength between two teams pulling against each other on a rope. **5a** A. COHEN The ship . . met the tug which guided it to its berth. **b** *Sailplane & Gliding* The 15 tugs gave . . launches up to 2000 ft to 108 gliders.

Comb.: **tug aircraft** a powered aircraft used to tow a glider; **tugboat** = sense 5a above; **tug-boating** *US* working on a tugboat; **tug pilot**: of a tug aircraft.

tug /tʌɡ/ *noun*². *Austral*. *slang*. **L19**.
[Origin unkn.]
A rogue, *esp*. a sharper.

tug /tʌɡ/ *adjective*. *School slang*. **L19**.
[Perh. rel. to TUG *noun*¹.]
Ordinary, commonplace.

tug /tʌɡ/ *verb*. Infl. **-gg-**. **ME**.
[from base also of TOW *verb*¹.]
▶**I** *verb intrans*. †**1** Tussle playfully or amorously. *rare*. Only in **ME**.
2 Pull, esp. with force or urgency; jerk; drag, haul. Freq. foll. by *at*. **ME**.
3 Contend, strive in opposition. Now *rare* or *obsolete*. **LME**.
4 Toil, struggle; go laboriously. **E17**.

📖 **2** J. L. WATEN One of the boys tugged at my coat. R. MACAULAY I have to tug on the reins. *fig*.: A. N. WILSON London, the old place tugged at his heart strings. **tug at the oar** row as a galley-slave; *fig*. toil unremittingly, do the drudging. **3** DRYDEN Fierce Ramirez . . Who tugged for empire with our warlike son. **4** J. G. HOLLAND To tug and tug all their lives to get money together. E. SIDGWICK He had . . tugged up one great boulevard . . and down another.

▶**II** *verb trans*. **5** Move by pulling forcibly; pull hard, jerk; drag, haul. **ME**.
6 Pull at with force; strain or haul at. **ME**. ▸†**b** Pull about roughly; maul. **ME–E18**.
7 Tow (a ship etc.) by means of a tugboat. **M19**.

📖 **5** LD MACAULAY Fifty pieces of ordnance . . each tugged by a long team of white oxen. P. LIVELY 'Come on!' cries Alice, tugging him into the road. *fig*.: R. INGALLS She was tugged in different directions. **6** : *tug the* LABOURING *oar*.

▪ **tugger** *noun* (*colloq*.) a person who tugs, esp. in a tug of war **E17**.

tuggle /ˈtʌɡ(ə)l/ *verb*. Long *obsolete* exc. *Scot*. **LME**.
[Frequent. from TUG *verb*: see -LE³.]
1 *verb trans*. Pull about roughly or jerkily. **LME**.
†**2** *verb intrans*. Struggle, toil. **M17–M18**.

tuggy *noun* var. of TOGGY.

tughra /ˈtʊɡrə/ *noun*. Also **toughra**, **tugra**. **M19**.
[Turkish *tuğra*.]
Hist. A Turkish ornamental monogram incorporating the name and title of the Sultan.

tugrik /ˈtuːɡriːk/ *noun*. **M20**.
[Mongolian.]
The basic monetary unit of Mongolia, equal to one hundred mongos.

†**tugwithe** *noun*. **E16–M18**.
[from TUG *noun*¹ or *verb* + WITHE *noun*.]
A withe formerly used to attach a swingletree to the head of a plough or to a harrow or cart.

tui /ˈtuːi/ *noun*. *NZ*. **M19**.
[Maori.]
A large honeyeater, *Prosthemadura novaeseelandiae*, native to New Zealand, having glossy bluish-black plumage with two white tufts at the throat. Also called ***parson-bird***.

tuile /twiːl; *in sense 2 also foreign* tɥil (*pl. same*)/ *noun*. In sense 1 also **-ll-**. **LME**.
[French, or from Old French *tieule* from Latin *tegula*: see TILE *noun*.]
1 *Hist*. In medieval armour, any of two or more steel plates hanging below or forming the lowest part of the tasses, and covering the front of the thighs. **LME**.
2 A thin curved biscuit, usu. made with almonds. **M20**.
▪ **tuiˈlette** *noun* (*Hist*.) in medieval armour, a small tuile **M19**.

Tuileries /ˈtwiːləri, *foreign* tɥilri/ *noun pl*. **E19**.
[A former palace in Paris, built on the site of an ancient tile-works: cf. prec.]
Hist. The royal or imperial family, court, or administration of France.

tuille *noun* see TUILE.

Tuinal /ˈt(j)uːɪnal, -əl/ *noun*. **M20**.
[Origin uncertain (perh. *tu* repr. *two* + IN *preposition*): *-al* after *Amytal*, *Seconal*, etc.]
PHARMACOLOGY. (Proprietary name for) a combination of two barbiturates, quinalbarbitone and amylobarbitone, used as a sedative and hypnotic.

tuism /ˈtjuːɪz(ə)m/ *noun*. *rare*. **L18**.
[from Latin *tu* thou, you + -ISM, after *egoism*, *egotism*.]
A form of expression involving the use of the pronoun *thou*; excessive use of such expressions. Also, an ethical theory which regards the interests of another person or persons as the foundation of morality (as opp. to ***egoism***).

tuition /tjuːˈɪʃ(ə)n/ *noun*. **LME**.
[Old French from Latin *tuitio(n-)* protection, from *tuit-* ppl stem of *tueri* watch, guard: see -ITION.]
†**1 a** The action of looking after or taking care of a person or thing; the condition of being taken care of; protection, defence, custody, care. **LME–L18**. ▸**b** *spec*. The position of a guardian in relation to a ward; guardianship. **L15–L17**.
2 The action, business, or function of a teacher; teaching, instruction, (esp. in return for a fee). **L16**. ▸**b** A fee or fees paid for tuition. Orig. *US*. **E19**.

📖 **2** GIBBON They pursued their studies . . under the tuition of the most skilful masters. J. LE CARRÉ He lectured a little and gave private tuition.

▪ **tuitional** *adjective* pertaining or relating to tuition **M19**. **tuitionary** *adjective* pertaining to tuition **E19**.

tuk-tuk /ˈtʊktʊk/ *noun*. *joc*. **M20**.
[Imit.]
In Thailand, a *samlor*.

tukul /ˈtʊk(ə)l/ *noun*. **E20**.
[African name.]
Esp. in Ethiopia: a dwelling with a thatched roof, shaped like a beehive.

tukutuku /tʊkʊˈtʊkʊ/ *noun*. *NZ*. **M20**.
[Maori.]
Ornamental lattice-work of toi-toi reeds interlaced with flax etc., used as wall panelling in Maori meeting-houses.

tularaemia /tjuːləˈriːmɪə/ *noun*. Also ***-rem-**. **E20**.
[from mod. Latin *tularensis* specific epithet (see below), from *Tulare* County, California: see -AEMIA.]
MEDICINE & VETERINARY MEDICINE. An acute infectious febrile disease of people and domestic animals showing variable symptoms and caused by the bacterium *Francisella tularensis*, endemic among wild rodents and rabbits esp. in N. America, and often transmitted by contact with these or by biting insects, esp. deer-flies. Also called ***rabbit fever***.
▪ **tularaemic** *adjective* **M20**.

tule /ˈtuːli/ *noun*. *US*. **M19**.
[Spanish from Nahuatl *tollin*, *tullin*. Cf. TOOLIES.]
Either of two species of bulrush, *Scirpus lacustris* and *S. acutus*, abundant in flooded marshy areas in south-western N. America, esp. in California; an area of low-lying ground dominated by such a plant.
Comb.: **tule fog** fog over low-lying ground; **tule wren** a variety of the marsh wren, *Cistothorus palustris*, which frequents the tules of California.

tulgey /ˈtʌldʒi/ *adjective*. **L19**.
[Nonsense word invented by Lewis Carroll.]
Orig. of a wood: thick, dense, and dark.

tulip /ˈtjuːlɪp/ *noun*. Also (earlier) †**tulipa**. **L16**.
[French †*tulipan*, *tulipe* from Turkish *tülbend* from Persian *dulband* TURBAN (with ref. to the shape of the expanded flower).]
1 Any of various bulbous plants constituting the genus *Tulipa*, of the lily family, with showy, erect, usu. solitary cup-shaped or bell-shaped flowers; *esp*. any ornamental spring-blooming plant of this genus, chiefly derived from *T. gesnerana*, introduced to Europe from Turkey in the 16th cent. Also, a flower of such a plant. **L16**. ▸**b** Usu. with specifying word: any of various plants resembling the tulip, esp. in their showy flowers. **L16**.
2 *fig*. A person who or thing which is showy or greatly admired. **M17**.

3 An explosive charge used to destroy a length of railway track. Now *Hist.* E20.
4 *ellipt.* = *tulip-glass* below. M20.
1 *Darwin tulip*, *parrot tulip*, *Rembrandt tulip*, etc. **b** *mariposa tulip*, *star tulip*, etc.
Comb.: **tulip break**, **tulip breaking** a virus disease of tulips, causing pale streaks and patches in dark-coloured flowers; **tulip fire** a fungus disease of tulips, producing speckled leaves and flowers; **tulip-glass** a drinking-glass with a bowl resembling a flowering tulip; **tulip poplar** = *tulip tree* below; **tulip-root** a disease of oats, characterized by a swelling at the base of the stem, caused by a nematode worm; **tulip tree** a tall tree of the eastern US, *Liriodendron tulipifera*, of the magnolia family, with large tulip-like greenish-yellow flowers variegated with orange, and three-lobed leaves with a notched or truncate apex; **tulip-wood** (*a*) the wood of the tulip tree; also called *American whitewood*; (*b*) any of various ornamental striped or variegated timbers; *esp.* that of the Australian tree *Harpullia pendula* (family Sapindaceae).
■ **tulip-like** *adjective* resembling (that of) a tulip E18 **tulipo'mania** *noun* an excessive fondness for valuable or unusual tulips, *esp.* (*Hist.*) that which prevailed in the Netherlands in the 17th cent. E18. **tulipo'maniac** *noun* a person affected by tulipomania M19.

†tulipan(t) *nouns & verbs* vars. of TURBAN.

tulle /t(j)uːl/ *noun & adjective.* E19.
[*Tulle*, a town in SW France where orig. made.]
▶**A 1** A fine soft silk bobbin-net used for women's dresses, veils, etc. E19.
2 *tulle gras* /grɑː/ [French = fatty], a gauze dressing for the skin impregnated with petroleum jelly. M20.
▶**B** *attrib.* or as *adjective.* Made of tulle. M19.

tullibee /'tʌlɪbiː/ *noun.* L18.
[Canad. French *toulibi*, ult. from Ojibwa.]
A whitefish, *Coregonus tullibee*, found in the Great Lakes of N. America.

tulp /təːlp/ *noun. S. Afr.* M19.
[Afrikaans from Dutch = TULIP.]
Any of various southern African plants of the iris family, esp. *Homeria breyniana* and (in full ***blue tulp***) *Moraea polystachya*, which bear showy flowers and are highly poisonous to stock.

tulsi /'tuːlsi:/ *noun.* L17.
[Hindi *tulsī*.]
In the Indian subcontinent, holy basil, *Ocimum sanctum*.

Tulu /'tuːluː/ *adjective & noun.* L19.
[Dravidian *tuḷu* the region where the language is spoken.]
(Of or pertaining to) a Dravidian language spoken in the Mangalore region of SW India.

tulwar /'tʌlwɑː/ *noun.* E19.
[Hindi *talvār* from Sanskrit *taravāri*.]
In the Indian subcontinent: a kind of sabre.

tum /tʌm/ *noun. colloq.* M19.
[Abbreviation. Cf. TUM-TUM *noun*⁴.]
= TUMMY.

tuman /tʊ'mɑːn/ *noun.* E19.
[Ult. from Persian *tūmān*: see TOMAN *noun*¹.]
†**1** A village in the region of Baluchistan. *rare.* Only in E19.
2 A Baluchi or Pathan tribe. E20.
■ **tuman'dar** *noun* a Baluchi or Pathan chief E20.

tumatakuru /'tuːmətəˌkʊruː/ *noun.* M19.
[Maori.]
= MATAGOURI.

tumbaga /tʊm'bɑːgə/ *noun.* Also **†tom-**, **-go** /-gəʊ/. E17.
[Spanish from Malay *tembaga* copper, brass: see TOMBAC.]
†**1** = TOMBAC. E17–L18.
2 Chiefly ARCHAEOLOGY. An alloy of gold and copper commonly used in pre-Columbian S. and Central America. M20.

tumbak /tuːm'bɑːk/ *noun.* Also **-ki** /-ki/. M19.
[Arab. *tunbāk* from French *tabac* tobacco.]
In Turkey, a coarse kind of tobacco imported from Iran and used esp. in a narghile.

tumble /'tʌmb(ə)l/ *noun.* M17.
[from the verb.]
1 Disorder, confusion, disturbance; an instance of this; a confused or tangled heap or mass. M17.
2 A sudden or headlong fall; an accidental fall. E18.
▶**b** A sign of recognition or acknowledgement, a response. *US slang.* E20.
3 A somersault or other acrobatic feat. *rare.* E19.
4 An act of sexual intercourse; a woman who is readily available for this. *slang.* E20.

📖 **1** *Westminster Gazette* The moorhen . . swimming out from the overhanging tumble of bush and bramble. **2a** *Daily Chronicle* A collision brought a tumble. S. MILLER From inside the house she could hear the tumble of Randall's bathwater. *fig.*: *Pall Mall Gazette* A terrible tumble in the price of . . oil. **4** A. BEATTIE A . . divorcée . . offering him a tumble.

Phrases etc.: **give a tumble** *slang* (*a*) *US* recognize or acknowledge (a person); (*b*) have sexual intercourse with (a person). ROUGH-AND-TUMBLE. **take a tumble** (*a*) have a sudden fall (*lit.* & *fig.*); (*b*) *slang* (foll. by *to*) suddenly become aware of the facts of one's situation.

tumble /'tʌmb(ə)l/ *verb.* ME.
[Middle Low German *tummelen* = Old High German *tumalōn* (German *tummeln*), frequentative from base of Old High German *tūmōn*, *tūmalōn* (German *taumeln*): see -LE³. Cf. Old English *tumbian* dance, Middle High German *tumben*, Old Norse *tumba* tumble.]
1 *verb intrans.* Perform leaps, somersaults, and other acrobatic feats. Formerly also, dance with posturing or contortions. ME.
2 *verb intrans.* **a** Fall or fall down, esp. suddenly, clumsily, or headlong; (of a stream) fall in a cataract. Also foll. by *down*, *over*. ME. ▶**b** Of a structure: fall in ruins or fragments; collapse. LME. ▶**c** Esp. of stocks: fall rapidly in value or amount. *slang.* L19.
3 *verb trans.* **a** Cause to fall or fall down suddenly or violently; throw down. ME. ▶**b** Pull down and destroy (a structure); demolish, reduce to ruins. LME.
4 a *verb intrans.* & *†refl.* Roll or toss about; throw oneself around restlessly. Also, wallow. LME. ▶**b** *verb intrans.* (Of a pigeon) repeatedly turn over backwards in flight; *transf.* (of a projectile) turn end over end in flight. L17. ▶**c** *verb intrans.* Of washing: be tossed about in a tumble-drier or washing machine. L20.
5 *verb trans.* Propel or drive headlong, or with a falling or rolling movement; throw roughly or forcibly; toss, pitch. E16.
6 *verb trans.* Cause to fall in a disordered manner or a confused heap. Also foll. by *down*, *in*, *out*, etc. M16.
7 *fig.* **a** *verb intrans.* Come upon by chance, blunder *into*, *on*, *upon*. M16. ▶**b** *verb intrans.* Perceive or grasp the meaning or hidden implication of an idea, circumstance, etc. Also foll. by *to*, *that*. *slang.* M19. ▶**c** *verb trans.* Detect, see through. *slang.* M20.
8 *verb intrans.* Move or rush in a headlong or blundering manner; proceed in disorderly haste. Also foll. by *into*, *out*, etc. Now *colloq.* L16.
9 *verb trans.* Look or search through, esp. roughly or hastily. Now *rare.* L16.
10 *verb trans.* Have sexual intercourse with. *slang.* E17.
11 *verb intrans.* Of the sides of a ship: incline or slope inwards above the widest point, batter. Usu. ***tumble home***. L17.
12 *verb trans.* Handle roughly; disorder, rumple; disarrange, pull about. E18.
13 *verb trans.* Clean or polish (castings, gems, etc.) in a tumbling-barrel. L19.

📖 **1** *Radio Times* She's utterly fearless and she can tumble really well. **2a** A. P. HERBERT Streams . . tumbling in tiny cascades to the watercress beds. K. VONNEGUT The staircase down which Marilee had tumbled. B. SIDHWA A tiny sparrow . . had tumbled from its nest. **b** J. RHYS These beautiful places are tumbling down because no one has cared for them. **c** P. P. READ Prices began to tumble first in New York and then Tokyo. **3a** BEVERLEY CLEARY One of the twine loops broke, tumbling Ramona to the sidewalk. **4a** DICKENS He was very restless . . and for some hours tossed and tumbled. **5** *Scientific American* The rats were briefly tumbled in a revolving drum. **6** H. F. TOZER He tumbled on to my plate . . half a dishful of mulberries. **7b** K. DOUGLAS And so on, for three or four times, till I tumbled to it. **8** H. JAMES I tumbled into bed. J. STEINBECK Her words tumbled out in a passion of communication. A. MASON The flood of ideas that tumbled into his brain. **10** J. I. M. STEWART Tumbling a strange woman on an apology for a bed. **12** SIR W. SCOTT The couch . . is tumbled like a stormy sea.

With adverbs in specialized senses: **tumble up** *slang* make haste, orig. (NAUTICAL) from below deck.
Comb.: **tumble-action** the tumbling action of a tumble-drier; **tumble-bug** (chiefly *US*) a dung-beetle; **tumble-drier** a machine for drying washing in a heated rotating drum; **tumble-dry** *verb trans.* & *intrans.* dry (washing) in a tumble-drier; **tumble-dung** = *tumble-bug* above; **tumble home** = TUMBLING *home*; **tumble-over** *noun & adjective* (*a*) *noun* an act of falling over; a toy so weighted that it always stays upright (cf. TUMBLER *noun* 5c); (*b*) *adjective* inclined to fall down, rickety, tottering; **tumble-up** a tumbler which sits upside down on the neck of a carafe; **tumbleweed** *N. Amer.* & *Austral.* any of various plants, esp. of arid regions, which in late summer are broken off and blown along by the wind in light globular rolling masses.

tumbledown /'tʌmb(ə)ldaʊn/ *adjective.* L18.
[from TUMBLE *verb* + DOWN *adverb*.]
†**1** Of a horse: that falls down habitually. *rare.* Only in L18.
2 Falling or fallen into ruin; dilapidated, ruinous. E19.

📖 **2** M. MEYER A ramshackle old house . . in tumbledown condition.

tumbler /'tʌmblə/ *noun.* ME.
[from TUMBLE *verb* + -ER¹.]
1 a An acrobat, *esp.* one who performs somersaults, leaps, etc. ME. ▶**b** A person who tumbles down or falls; *spec.* an inexperienced window-cleaner. *joc.* E20.
2 a A dog like a small greyhound, which tumbles and turns to attract its prey, formerly used to catch rabbits. *obsolete* exc. *Hist.* E16. ▶**†b** *transf.* A person who allures others into the hands of swindlers. *slang.* E17–L18.
3 a *techn.* A thing that rotates or acts as a pivot; *spec.* (*a*) a notched pivoted plate in a gunlock through which the mainspring acts on the hammer; (*b*) a pivoted piece in a lock which holds the bolt until lifted by a key; (*c*) a revolving barrel used in tanning skins; (*d*) a tumbling-barrel. M16. ▶**b** NAUTICAL. A device fitted on a mast, with a hook, ring, or swivel to which something may be attached. M19. ▶**c** More fully ***tumbler-drier***. = *tumble-drier* s.v. TUMBLE *verb.* M20.
†**4** A person who tosses things into confusion or disorder; a muddler. *rare.* L16–L17.
5 = TUMBREL 2, 2b. *slang & dial.* E17.
6 a A drinking-vessel, orig. having a rounded or pointed base, so that it could not stand upright unsupported. Now, a tapering cylindrical, or barrel-shaped, drinking-vessel, esp. made of glass, with a heavy flat base and no handle or foot. M17. ▶**b** The contents of a tumbler; a tumblerful. M19. ▶**c** A toy, usu. representing a grotesque squatting figure, with a weighted rounded base so that it rocks but always regains position when touched or pushed. *rare.* M19.
7 *Hist.* In the game of gleek, the six of trumps. L17.
†**8** A porpoise. L17–E19.
9 A variety of domestic pigeon which repeatedly turns over backwards in flight. Also ***tumbler pigeon***. L17.
10 A detached mass or piece of rock; a rolled stone or boulder. Now *dial.* M18.

📖 **1a** J. S. BLACKIE Expert tumblers in the circus. **3a** *Atlantic* He heard the stealthy tick of keys and tumblers. **6a** J. CAREW A tumbler of pale purple wine. M. KEANE Long . . tumblers, were for whisky-and-sodas. **9** P. CARTER Mr Black had all sorts of birds: rollers, tumblers, doves.

Comb.: **tumbler-cart** = sense 5 above; **tumbler-cup** a cup with a rounded base (cf. sense 6a above); ***tumbler-drier***: see sense 3c above; **tumbler-glass** = sense 6a above; ***tumbler pigeon***: see sense 9 above.
■ **tumblerful** *noun* as much as a tumbler will hold E19.

†tumblester *noun.* LME–M19.
[from prec. + -STER.]
A female tumbler or dancer; a dancing-girl.

tumblification /ˌtʌmblɪfɪ'keɪʃ(ə)n/ *noun. joc.* M19.
[Irreg. from TUMBLE *verb* + -FICATION.]
Tumbling, tossing; *esp.* the pitching and rolling of a ship in a storm.

tumbling /'tʌmblɪŋ/ *verbal noun & ppl adjective.* LME.
[from TUMBLE *verb* + -ING¹, -ING².]
▶**A** *noun.* The action of TUMBLE *verb*; an instance of this. LME.
▶**B** *adjective.* That tumbles. LME.
Special collocations & comb.: **tumbling-barrel** a revolving drum or other receptacle containing an abrasive substance, in which castings, gemstones, etc., are cleaned or polished by friction. **tumbling-bay** an outfall from a river, canal, or reservoir; the pool into which this flows. **tumbling-box** = ***tumbling-barrel*** above. **tumbling home** the inward inclination of the upper part of a ship's sides. **tumbling-mill** (*a*) *rare* a tumbling-barrel; (*b*) a sandblaster. **tumbling stone** a loose stone embedded in clay; a boulder (cf. TUMBLER 10).

tumbok lada /'tumbok ˌlada/ *noun phr.* M19.
[Malay, lit. 'pepper-crusher', from *tumbuk* thump, pound + *lada* pepper.]
A small Malayan dagger.

tumbrel /'tʌmbr(ə)l, -brɪl/ *noun.* Also **-bril**. ME.
[Old French *tomb-*, *tumberel* (mod. *tombereau*), in Anglo-Latin *tumb(e)rellus*, *-um*, from *tomber* to fall: see -EL². Cf. TUMBLE *verb.*]
1 An instrument of punishment, of uncertain early form, but from the 16th cent. usu. identified with a cucking-stool. ME.
2 An open cart which tilts backwards to empty out its load; *spec.* (*a*) a dung-cart; (*b*) *Hist.* a cart used to carry condemned prisoners to their execution, esp. to the guillotine during the French Revolution. LME. ▶**†b** *transf.* A light open carriage. L16–E19.
†**3** A flat-bottomed boat, a barge; *fig.* a drunkard, a person filled with alcoholic drink. LME–E18.
4 A square rack for holding fodder in a field or yard. *dial.* M17.
5 MILITARY. A two-wheeled covered cart for carrying ammunition, tools, etc. E18.

📖 **2** W. COWPER Like a slain deer, the tumbrel brings him home. *fig.*: J. KRANTZ I wish you'd been in that audience. I could hear the tumbrels coming for me.

tumbu /'tʊmbuː/ *noun.* L19.
[Mande.]
The larva of a fly, *Cordylobia anthropophaga*, of sub-Saharan Africa, which is a subcutaneous parasite of humans and animals. Also (in full ***tumbu fly***), the adult insect, a yellow fly with grey markings; also called ***mango fly***.
Comb.: **tumbu disease**, **tumbu sickness**, **tumbu fly disease**, **tumbu fly sickness**: caused by infestation with larvae of the tumbu fly.

Tumbuka /tʊmˈbuːkə/ *noun & adjective.* L19.
[Origin uncertain: in Tumbuka app. lit. 'be disembowelled'.]
▶ **A** *noun.* Pl. same.
1 A member of a group of Bantu-speaking peoples inhabiting the Nyika Plateau area of northern Malawi. L19.
2 Any of the Bantu languages of this people; the language group containing these languages. E20.
▶ **B** *attrib.* or as *adjective.* Of or pertaining to the Tumbuka or their language. M20.

tumefaction /tjuːmɪˈfakʃ(ə)n/ *noun.* LME.
[French *tuméfaction*, from Latin *tumefact-* pa. ppl stem of *tumefacere*: see next, -FACTION.]
1 The action of tumefying or state of being tumefied; swelling, swollen condition, esp. in a part of the body. LME.
2 A swollen part; a swelling, a tumour. E19.

tumefy /ˈtjuːmɪfʌɪ/ *verb.* L16.
[French *tuméfier* from Latin *tumefacere*, pass. *-fieri*, from *tumere* swell: see -FY.]
1 *verb trans.* Cause to swell; make tumid. L16. ▸**b** *fig.* Inflate or puff up, as with pride; make (language, literary style) turgid or bombastic. L17.
2 *verb intrans.* Swell, swell up, become tumid. E17.

📖 **1** W. LEWIS The tumefied face, the swollen and blackened eyes and lips. **b** J. MORIER Having tumefied himself and his possessions by . . a variety of heraldic insignia.

■ **tumefacient** /tjuːmɪˈfeɪʃ(ə)nt/ *adjective* (*rare*) tumefying, swelling L19.

tumesce /tjʊˈmɛs/ *verb intrans.* M20.
[Back-form. from next or from Latin *tumescere*: see TUMESCENT.]
= TUMEFY 2.

tumescence /tjʊˈmɛs(ə)ns/ *noun.* M19.
[from next: see -ENCE.]
The action of swelling up or becoming tumid; a tendency to tumidity; *spec.* (*a*) swelling in response to sexual stimulation; (*b*) GEOLOGY the swelling of a volcano due to accumulation of magma. Also, a tumid part, a swelling.

tumescent /tjʊˈmɛs(ə)nt/ *adjective.* M19.
[Latin *tumescent-* pres. ppl stem of *tumescere*, from *tumere* swell: see -ENT.]
Becoming tumid, swelling; somewhat tumid; *spec.* swelling in response to sexual stimulation.
■ **tumescently** *adverb* L20.

tumid /ˈtjuːmɪd/ *adjective.* M16.
[Latin *tumidus*, from *tumere* swell: see -ID¹.]
1 Esp. of a part of the body: swollen, inflated; protuberant, bulging. M16.
2 *fig.* Esp. of language or literary style: inflated, turgid, bombastic; *rare* pregnant or teeming *with*. M17.

📖 **1** G. ROLLESTON An orifice with prominent tumid lips.

■ **tumidly** *adverb* E19. **tumidness** *noun* L17.

tumidity /tjʊˈmɪdɪti/ *noun.* E18.
[Late Latin *tumiditas*, from *tumidus* TUMID: see -ITY.]
The quality or condition of being tumid; an instance of this, swollenness.

tummelberry /ˈtʌm(ə)lb(ə)ri/ *noun.* L20.
[from the River *Tummel* in Tayside, Scotland + BERRY *noun*¹.]
A dark purple soft fruit produced by crossing the tayberry with another hybrid of raspberry and blackberry, and introduced in Scotland in 1984; the plant bearing this fruit.

tummied /ˈtʌmɪd/ *adjective.* L20.
[from TUMMY + -ED².]
Having a stomach of a specified kind. Freq. as 2nd elem. of comb.
flat-tummied etc.

tummler /ˈtʊmlə/ *noun. colloq.* M20.
[Yiddish, from German *tummeln* stir.]
A person who causes things to happen, esp. by acting the clown, a prankster; *spec.* a professional entertainer in a hotel or the like.

tummy /ˈtʌmi/ *noun. colloq.* (orig. *nursery*). M19.
[Alt. of STOMACH *noun*. Cf. TUM.]
1 The stomach, the intestine; the abdomen. M19.
2 An abdominal pain or complaint; *spec.* (with preceding place-name) diarrhoea, sickness, etc., suffered by visitors to that place. L19.
Comb.: **tummy-ache** (an) abdominal pain; **tummy bug** (a germ causing) a stomach upset; **tummy-button** the navel; **tummy tuck** *colloq.* a surgical operation involving the removal of excess flesh from the abdomen, for cosmetic purposes.

tu-mo /ˈtjuːməʊ/ *noun.* L20.
[Chinese *dū mài* (Wade–Giles *tu mai*).]
In Chinese medical theory, the chief passage through which vital energy circulates, located in the spine.

tumor *noun* see TUMOUR.

tumoricidal /tjuːmərɪˈsʌɪd(ə)l/ *adjective.* M20.
[from Latin *tumor* TUMOUR + -I- + -CIDE + -AL¹.]
MEDICINE. Capable of destroying tumours.

tumorigenic /tjuːmərɪˈdʒɛnɪk/ *adjective.* M20.
[formed as prec. + -GENIC.]
MEDICINE. Capable of causing tumours.
■ **ˈtumorigen** *noun* a tumorigenic agent M20. **tumorigenesis** *noun* the production or formation of a tumour M20. **tumorigenicity** /-ˈnɪsɪti/ *noun* tumorigenic property M20.

tumorous /ˈtjuːm(ə)rəs/ *adjective.* M16.
[Late Latin *tumorosus*, formed as next + -OUS. In mod. use formed as next + -OUS.]
†**1** *gen.* Characterized by or causing swelling; swollen, bulging, tumid. M16–L17. ▸**b** *spec.* Of, pertaining to, or of the nature of a tumour, tumoural; affected with tumours. M19.
†**2** *fig.* Swelling or swollen with pride or passion; (of language, style, or manner) inflated, turgid. Only in 17.

tumour /ˈtjuːmə/ *noun.* Also ***tumor**. LME.
[Latin *tumor*, from *tumere* swell: see -OR.]
1 The action or an act of swelling; swollen condition. Now *rare.* LME.
2 a MEDICINE & BIOLOGY. An abnormal swelling or enlargement in any part of the body of an animal or plant; an excrescence. Now usu. *spec.*, a permanent swelling without inflammation, caused by excessive continued growth and proliferation of cells in a tissue, which may be either benign or malignant. LME. ▸**b** More widely, any part rising above or projecting beyond the general level or surface; a swelling. Now *rare* exc. as in sense 2a above. E17.
†**3** *fig.* **a** Swelling of passion, pride, etc.; the condition of being puffed up; haughtiness, arrogance, vain-glory; inflated pride or conceit. E17–L18. ▸**b** Turgidity of language, style, or manner; affected grandeur; bombast. M17–M19.
2 *brain tumour, Burkitt tumour, Pancoast's tumour, theca cell tumour*, etc.
Comb.: **tumour virus** a virus that induces tumours.
■ **tumoural** *adjective* (MEDICINE) of, pertaining to, or characteristic of a tumour M20. **tumour-like** *adjective* resembling (that of) a tumour L19.

tump /tʌmp/ *noun.* L16.
[Origin unkn.]
1 A hillock, a mound, a molehill, an anthill; a barrow, a tumulus. Chiefly *dial.* L16.
2 A heap, esp. of hay or stones. Chiefly *Scot. & dial.* L18.
3 A clump of trees, shrubs, or grass. *dial.* E19.
4 *fig.* Trivial writing, bad prose. E20.
■ **tumpy** *adjective* (of ground) humpy, hummocky E19.

tump /tʌmp/ *verb*¹. *Scot. & dial.* E18.
[from prec.]
Make a tump or mound about the root of a tree.

tump /tʌmp/ *verb*² *trans. US local.* M19.
[from TUMP-LINE.]
Drag or carry by means of a tump-line.

tump /tʌmp/ *verb*³ *trans. US dial. & colloq.* L19.
[Prob. repr. colloq. pronunc. of THUMP *verb*.]
Strike (a person) forcibly; pound, thump. Also, knock *down* or tip *over* roughly.

tump-line /ˈtʌmplʌɪn/ *noun. N. Amer.* L18.
[from (ult.) Algonquian *mat)tump* + LINE *noun*².]
A sling for carrying a load on the back, with a strap which passes round the forehead; this strap.

tump-tump /ˈtʌmptʌmp/ *noun.* E20.
[Imit.]
A short sound as of water slopping or a large ball being kicked.

tum-tum /ˈtʌmtʌm/ *noun*¹ & *verb.* Also **tum-ti-tum** /ˈtʌmtɪtʌm/ & other vars. M19.
[Imit.]
▶ **A** *noun.* A regular, esp. monotonous, strumming sound made by a stringed instrument or instruments being played. M19.
▶ **B** *verb intrans.* Infl. **-mm-**. Make such a sound, strum monotonously. M19.

tum-tum /ˈtʌmtʌm/ *noun*². M19.
[Origin unkn.]
In the Indian subcontinent: a light vehicle, a dogcart.

tum-tum /ˈtʌmtʌm/ *noun*³. *W. Indies.* M19.
[Origin unkn.]
A West Indian vegetable or fish dish.

tum-tum /ˈtʌmtʌm/ *noun*⁴. *nursery & joc.* M19.
[Redupl. of TUM *noun*.]
= TUMMY 1.

tumular /ˈtjuːmjʊlə/ *adjective.* E19.
[from Latin TUMULUS + -AR¹.]
Pertaining to or consisting of a mound or tumulus.

tumulary /ˈtjuːmjʊləri/ *adjective.* M18.
[formed as prec. + -ARY².]
Pertaining to or placed over a tomb; sepulchral.

tumulate /ˈtjuːmjʊleɪt/ *verb trans. rare.* E17.
[Latin *tumulat-* pa. ppl stem of *tumulare*, from TUMULUS: see -ATE³.]
Bury, entomb.
■ **tumuˈlation** *noun* (*rare*) burying, interment, esp. in a tumulus or grave-mound E17.

tumuli *noun pl.* see TUMULUS.

tumulous /ˈtjuːmjʊləs/ *adjective. rare.* E19.
[from TUMULUS + -OUS.]
Hilly, rounded. Also, forming a tumulus, tumular.

tumult /ˈtjuːmʌlt/ *noun & verb.* LME.
[Old & mod. French *tumulte* or Latin *tumultus* (cf. Sanskrit *tumula* tumult, noisy).]
▶ **A** *noun.* **1** Uproar or disturbance of a disorderly crowd; public disturbance, riotous behaviour. Also, an instance of this, a popular commotion, a riot. LME. ▸**b** A disorderly crowd. *rare.* E17.
2 *gen.* Commotion, agitation, disturbance; an instance of this, a confusing or turbulent action. M16.
3 *fig.* Disturbance or agitation of the mind or feelings; a conflict of emotions. M17.

📖 **1** C. THIRLWALL A tumult . . in which the populace set fire to Milo's house. *Christian Science Monitor* Traders who dominated the economy before the tumult started two decades ago, then fled or died. **2** W. COWPER Some . . are averse to noise And hate the tumult half the world enjoys. J. MCPHEE In the tumult that followed the explosion, marine limestone . . fell into the kimberlite and was preserved. **3** BURKE The wild tumult of joy that the news . . caused.

▶ **B** *verb.* **1** *verb intrans.* Make a tumult, commotion, or disturbance; riot. Now *rare.* L16.
2 *verb trans.* Agitate violently. E19.

tumultuary /tjʊˈmʌltjʊəri/ *adjective & noun.* LME.
[Latin *tumultuarius* of or belonging to hurry or tumult, (of troops) raised hastily, from *tumultus*: see prec., -ARY¹.]
▶ **A** *adjective.* **1** †**a** Of a fortification: hastily constructed. Only in LME. ▸**b** Hurriedly done; disorderly, confused; haphazard. E17.
2 Of troops: gathered in haste and disorder; irregular, undisciplined. Of warfare etc.: conducted by such troops, or in a disorganized way. L16.
3 Disposed to or characterized by tumult; tumultuous, turbulent. M17.

📖 **3** GEO. ELIOT Struggling with a tumultuary crowd of thoughts.

▶ **B** *noun.* In *pl.* Tumultuary troops or forces. *rare.* M17.

tumultuate /tjʊˈmʌltjʊeɪt/ *verb.* Now *rare.* E17.
[Latin *tumultuat-* pa. ppl stem of *tumultuari* make a bustle or disturbance, from *tumultus* TUMULT: see -ATE³.]
1 *verb intrans.* Stir up a tumult; make a disturbance or commotion; be or become tumultuous. E17.
2 *verb trans.* Make tumultuous; disorder or disturb violently. E17.

📖 **2** *Blackwood's Magazine* The feelings that tumultuate the heart of a father.

■ **tumultuˈation** *noun* (now *rare*) the action of making a tumult; a tumultuous state; commotion, disturbance, agitation: L15.

tumultuous /tjʊˈmʌltjʊəs/ *adjective.* M16.
[Old French (mod. *tumultueux*), or Latin *tumultus* TUMULT: see -OUS.]
1 Full of tumult or commotion; causing a tumult; disorderly, turbulent; uproarious. M16. ▸†**b** Tending to excite tumult; seditious. Only in 17.
2 Of an action or agent: irregular and violent; agitated, tempestuous. M17.
3 *fig.* Of an emotion or thought: disturbed, confused, turbulent. M17.

📖 **1** E. EDWARDS His house was beset by a tumultuous crowd. R. LOWELL A trying and tumultuous visit from my mother. J. MASSON Psychoanalysis . . cannot transform the tumultuous storm of human relationships into . . artificial calm. **2** E. K. KANE A roaring and tumultuous river.

■ **tumultuously** *adverb* M16. **tumultuousness** *noun* E17.

tumulus /ˈtjuːmjʊləs/ *noun.* Pl. **-li** /-lʌɪ, -liː/. LME.
[Latin, rel. to *tumere* swell.]
An ancient sepulchral mound, a barrow.

tun /tʌn/ *noun*¹. Also †**ton**, †**tonne**. See also TON *noun*¹.
[Old English *tunne* corresp. to Old Frisian, Middle Low German, Middle Dutch *tunne*, *tonne* (Dutch *ton*), Old High German *tunna* (German *Tonne*), late Old Norse *tunna*, from medieval Latin *tunna* (whence French *tonne* etc.), prob. of Gaulish origin.]
▶ **I 1** A large cask or barrel, used esp. for wine, ale, or beer. OE. ▸†**b** Any large vessel; a tub, a vat, a chest. ME–E17. ▸**c** BREWING. A brewer's vat for fermenting or mashing malt. E18.
2 A cask of a specific capacity; a unit of capacity for wine and other liquids, usually equal to 4 hogsheads (216 imperial gallons or 259.43 US gallons of beer, or 210 imperial gallons or 252 US gallons of wine). LME.
3 A chimney, *spec.* the part of a chimney that extends above the roof of a house. Now *dial.* LME.
4 A kind of cup or small drinking-vessel. M16.

📖 **1** K. A. PORTER The enormous old wine tuns, each with a name and a date. *fig.*: C. WAKE His enormous tun of a body. **2** T. PENNANT The well . . is found to fling out about twenty one tuns of water in a minute.

▶ **II** See TON *noun*[1].

Comb. & phrases: **tun-bellied** *adjective* (*arch.*) having a belly rounded like a tun; pot-bellied, corpulent; **tundish** (*a*) BREWING a shallow dish or other vessel with a tube at the base which fits into the bung-hole of a tun or cask, to form a kind of funnel; (*b*) *gen.* a funnel; (*c*) a broad, open container with one or more holes in the bottom, used as an intermediate reservoir in metal-founding, or in other industrial processes; **tun-pail** BREWING a kind of funnel or tundish; ***tun tight***: see TIGHT *adjective*.

■ **tunful** *noun* as much as will fill a tun ME.

tun /tʌn, tʊn/ *noun*[2]. Also (esp. as a title) **T-**. E19.
[Malay.]
Orig., a Malaysian hereditary title of respect or distinction of patrilineal descent, held by either sex. Now (since 1958), an honorary non-hereditary male title denoting membership of the Order of Chivalry for the Federation of Malaya. Also, a person who holds this title.

tun *noun*[3] var. of TOON *noun*[1].

tun /tʌn/ *verb trans.* Also †**tonne**. Infl. **-nn-**. ME.
[from TUN *noun*[1]. Cf. Anglo-Latin *tunnare* put into tuns.]
1 Put (wine etc.) into a tun or tuns, store in a tun or tuns. Also foll. by *up*, (rare) *in*. ME.
2 *fig.* Put or store as in a tun; *spec.* drink to excess. L15.

tuna /ˈtjuːnə/ *noun*[1]. M16.
[Spanish from Taino.]
A prickly pear; *esp.* (the edible purple fruit of) a tall-growing prickly pear, *Opuntia tuna*, native to Central America and the W. Indies.

tuna /ˈtʊnə/ *noun*[2]. M19.
[Maori.]
Either of two freshwater eels, *Anguilla dieffenbachii* and *A. australis*, found in New Zealand.

tuna /ˈtjuːnə/ *noun*[3]. Pl. same, **-s**. L19.
[Amer. Spanish, perh. rel. to Latin *thunnus*, *tunnus* tunny.]
1 Any of several large marine food and game-fishes of the family Scombridae, of the genera *Thunnus*, *Euthynnus*, *Katsuwonus*, and closely related genera, having a rounded body and pointed snout, and found in warm seas worldwide; *esp.* (more fully ***common tuna***, ***bluefin tuna***) the very large *Thunnus thynnus*. L19.
2 In full ***tuna fish***. The flesh of the tuna or tunny as food, usu. tinned in oil or brine. E20.

> 📖 **1** ***skipjack tuna***, ***striped tuna***, ***yellowfin tuna***, etc. **2** *attrib.*: SARA MAITLAND Phoebe . . made tuna fish sandwiches.

tunability /tjuːnəˈbɪlɪti/ *noun*. E20.
[from next: see -BILITY.]
The quality of being tunable, *spec.* ability to be varied in frequency and wavelength.

tunable /ˈtjuːnəb(ə)l/ *adjective*. Also **tuneable**. L15.
[from TUNE *noun* or *verb* + -ABLE.]
1 Tuneful, musical, melodious, harmonious. *arch.* L15.
2 Able to be tuned; *spec.* able to have the operating frequency and wavelength varied. E18.
■ **tunableness** *noun* M16. **tunably** *adverb* E16.

tunal /tjuːˈnɑːl/ *noun*. E17.
[Spanish, from TUNA *noun*[1]: see -AL[1].]
A grove or thicket of tunas or prickly pears.

Tunbridge /ˈtʌnbrɪdʒ/ *attrib. adjective*. Also (in sense 2) **Tonbridge**. M17.
[from (*Royal*) *Tunbridge Wells* or (in sense 2) *Tonbridge*, nearby towns in Kent.]
1 Designating water from the chalybeate spring at Tunbridge Wells. M17.
2 Designating wooden articles with a characteristic mosaic decoration, traditionally made in and about Tunbridge Wells and Tonbridge. Chiefly in ***Tunbridge ware***. L18.
3 ***Tunbridge filmy fern***, a European filmy fern, *Hymenophyllum tunbrigense*, first found on shady rocks near Tunbridge Wells. E19.

tunc /tʊŋk/ *noun*. Also **tunk**. M17.
[Welsh *twng*, *twnc*, rel. to *tyngu* swear an oath.]
WELSH HISTORY. A kind of customary rent or payment, similar to a chief-rent or quit-rent, formerly payable on certain lands in North Wales.

tund /tʌnd/ *verb*. M19.
[Latin *tundere* to beat.]
1 *verb trans.* At Winchester College, beat with a stick by way of punishment. *slang*. M19.
2 *verb trans.* & *intrans.* *gen.* Beat, thump. L19.

tundra /ˈtʌndrə/ *noun*. L16.
[Lappish.]
A vast, nearly level, treeless Arctic region usu. with a marshy surface and underlying permafrost.
Comb.: **tundra swan** an Arctic-breeding migratory swan, *Cygnus columbianus*, with a black and yellow bill, of which the Bewick's swan and the whistling swan are both races.

tune /tjuːn/ *noun*. LME.
[Unexpl. alt. of TONE *noun*. Cf. TOON *noun*[2].]
†**1** †**a** A (musical) sound or tone; *esp.* the sound of the voice. Cf. TONE *noun* 1. LME–M19. ▸**b** A particular intonation; pitch and cadence of speech. Cf. TONE *noun* 5a, b. L18.
2 a A rhythmical succession of musical tones produced by or composed for an instrument or voice; an air, a melody, with or without its accompanying harmony. LME. ▸**b** *spec.* A musical setting of a hymn or psalm, usually in four-part harmony, intended for use in public worship. LME. ▸**c** In full ***act-tune***. A piece of music played between the acts of a play. Cf. ENTR'ACTE. L19.
3 a The proper musical pitch or intonation; accordance of pitch, harmony. Chiefly in ***in tune***, ***out of tune***, below. LME. ▸**b** *transf.* Harmony or accordance of vibrations other than those of sound, esp. between a radio transmitter and receiver. E20. ▸**c** The process of tuning an engine etc. in order to improve its efficiency; the state of a mechanism with regard to its tuning. Cf. TUNE *verb* 3c. L20.
4 *fig.* Frame of mind; temper, mood, disposition. Cf. TONE *noun* 7. L16.

> 📖 **2a** DRYDEN The Tune I still retain, but not the Words. *Classic CD* The Minuet . . is a tune meant to be danced to. **4** T. CALVERT This is the tone and tune of men in distress.

Phrases etc.: ***act-tune***: see sense 2c above. **call the tune** be in control. **change one's tune** *fig.* change one's tone, opinion, attitude, etc. **in tune** (*a*) having the proper musical pitch or intonation; agreeing in pitch or harmony (*with*); (*b*) *fig.* harmonizing with or *with* one's company, surroundings, etc. **keep tune** stay in tune. **out of tune** (*a*) not having the proper musical pitch or intonation, unharmonious, discordant; (*b*) *fig.* clashing or not in keeping with or *with* one's company, surroundings, etc. ***pay the piper and call the tune***: see PAY *verb*[1]. ***signature tune***: see SIGNATURE *noun* 3d. ***sing a different tune***: see SING *verb*[1]. **the tune the cow died of**, **the tune the old cow died of** *joc.* a discordant and unmusical succession of sounds; a tedious badly played piece of music. **to some tune** to a considerable extent. **to the tune of** to the (considerable) amount or sum of.
■ **tunesome** *adjective* (*rare*) tuneful, melodious L19. **tunester** *noun* (chiefly *US*) a song-writer; a singer; a musician: E20.

tune /tjuːn/ *verb*. L15.
[from the noun.]
1 *verb intrans.* Give forth a musical sound; sound; sing. L15.
2 *verb trans.* **a** Express or sound (something) musically, sing; celebrate in music. (Cf. earlier ENTUNE 1.) *arch.* L15. ▸†**b** Set or start the tune for (a hymn etc. in public worship), as a precentor. M17–L19.
3 a *verb trans.* Adjust the tones of (a musical instrument) to a certain pitch, or for correct production of the required sounds; put in tune. (Cf. earlier ENTUNE 2.) E16. ▸**b** *verb trans.* Adapt (the voice, a song, etc.) to a particular tone or mood; modify the tones of for a particular purpose. L16. ▸**c** *verb trans.* Set or adjust for accurate working; *spec.* adjust (an engine etc.) or balance (mechanical parts) in order to increase efficiency or ensure smooth-running. E19. ▸**d** *verb trans.* Adapt or accord in respect of, or make responsive to, a particular quality, condition, or stimulus; *spec.* make (a radio receiver etc.) sensitive to a chosen signal frequency or wavelength, adjust (a device or component) by varying the operational frequency. L19. ▸**e** *verb intrans.* Of a radio etc.: be tuned. E20.
4 *verb trans. fig.* ▸**a** Bring into a proper or desirable condition; give a special tone or character to. M16. ▸**b** Bring into accord or harmony; attune, harmonize. L16. ▸**c** Adjust or adapt to a required or different purpose, situation, etc. L16.
5 *verb trans.* Produce music from, play on (an instrument, esp. a lyre). *poet.* E18.

> 📖 **3a** J. TYNDALL These two tuning-forks are tuned absolutely alike. A. BURGESS The piano . . never got tuned. **b** MILTON To sorrow must I tune my song. **c** *Hot Rod* Is there a way to tune these machines to reach even higher . . performance? **d** J. N. LOCKYER Ears are tuned to hear different sounds. *Physics Bulletin* The laser would not revolutionise spectroscopy until its operating wavelength could be tuned. *absol.*: *Satellite Times* Tune to one of the sports channels. **4b** A. BRINK Our bodies had become tuned to each other. **c** *Sunday Telegraph* A Budget tuned to the needs of the economy.

With adverbs in specialized senses: **tune in** (*a*) *verb phr. trans.* & *intrans.* tune a radio receiver etc. to (a particular station, wavelength, frequency, etc.) (foll. by *on*, *to*); (*b*) *verb phr. intrans.* (*fig.*) become mentally receptive to or aware of (foll. by *on*, *to*); (*c*) **tuned in** *adjective* (of a radio etc.) adjusted to a particular station, frequency, etc.; *fig.* in rapport with, in harmony with, (foll. by *on*, *to*); *colloq.* = ***switched-on*** s.v. SWITCHED 3; **tune off** *rare* (*a*) *verb phr. intrans.* get out of tune or adjustment; (*b*) *verb phr. trans.* = ***tune out*** below. **tune out** (*a*) *verb phr. trans.* eliminate reception of (a radio signal of a particular frequency) by tuning; (*b*) *verb phr. trans.* & *intrans.* (*fig.*) disregard (something); cease listening (to). **tune up** (*a*) *verb phr. intrans.* begin to play or sing; (*b*) *verb phr. trans.* & *intrans.* bring (an instrument or instruments) up to the proper or a uniform pitch; (*c*) *verb phr. trans.* bring up to the most efficient condition or working order.
Comb.: **tune-in** *US* (*a*) the state of being tuned to a particular radio or television station or channel; (*b*) the size of the audience for a station or channel; **tune-up** (orig. *US*) (*a*) the action, or an act, of tuning up; (*b*) SPORT an event that serves as a practice for a subsequent event.

tuneable *adjective* var. of TUNABLE.

tuneful /ˈtjuːnfʊl, -f(ə)l/ *adjective*. L16.
[from TUNE *noun* + -FUL.]
1 Musical, melodious, sweet-sounding. L16.
2 Producing musical sounds; performing or skilled in music. L16.
3 Relating or adapted to music. L17.
■ **tunefully** *adverb* M17. **tunefulness** *noun* L19.

tuneless /ˈtjuːnlɪs/ *adjective*. L16.
[from TUNE *noun* + -LESS.]
1 Untuneful, unmelodious, harsh-sounding. L16.
2 Having no song or sound; not making music; silent. E18.
■ **tunelessly** *adverb* E20. **tunelessness** *noun* L19.

tuner /ˈtjuːnə/ *noun*. L16.
[from TUNE *verb* + -ER[1].]
1 a A person who produces or utters musical sounds; a player, a singer. *arch.* L16. ▸†**b** A person who gives a particular (vocal) tone to something. *rare* (Shakes.). Only in L16.
2 A person who tunes a musical instrument, esp. a piano or organ. E19.
3 A device for varying the frequency to which a radio or television is tuned. Also, a separate unit for detecting and preamplifying a programme signal and supplying it to an audio amplifier. E20.
Comb.: **tuner-amplifier** a combined radio tuner and amplifier, a radio receiver. **tuner-timer** a device used with a video recorder to enable the pre-set automatic recording of selected programmes.

tunesmith /ˈtjuːnsmɪθ/ *noun*. *colloq.* (orig. *US*). E20.
[from TUNE *noun* + SMITH *noun*.]
A composer of popular music or songs; *derog.* a composer of unoriginal or trifling music.

tuney *adjective* var. of TUNY.

tung /tʌŋ/ *noun*. L19.
[Chinese *tóng* (Wade–Giles *t'ung*).]
1 Each of three trees of the genus *Aleurites*, of the spurge family, *A. fordii* and *A. montana*, native to China, and *A. montana*, of Japan, cultivated for the oil from their seeds. Also ***tung tree***. L19.
2 In full ***tung oil***. A drying oil extracted from seeds of the tung tree and used in inks, paints, and varnishes. Also called ***wood-oil***. E20.
Comb.: ***tung oil***: see sense 2 above; ***tung tree***: see sense 1 above; **tung-yu** /-juː/ [Chinese *yóu* oil] tung oil.

Tungan /ˈtʌŋgən, ˈtʊŋ-/ *noun & adjective*. L19.
[Chagatai *Döngan*.]
▶ **A** *noun*. Pl. **-s**, **-i** /-iː/. A member of a Muslim people of Chinese descent in China and Russian central Asia. L19.
▶ **B** *attrib.* or as *adjective*. Of or pertaining to the Tungans. E20.

Tungar /ˈtʌŋgɑː/ *noun*. E20.
[from TUNG(STEN + AR(GON.]
ELECTRONICS. A type of low-voltage discharge tube filled with argon and having a heated cathode of thoriated tungsten, used as a rectifier for currents of a few amperes.
¶ Proprietary name in the US.

tungstate /ˈtʌŋsteɪt/ *noun*. E19.
[from TUNGSTIC + -ATE[1].]
CHEMISTRY. A salt containing oxyanions of (hexavalent) tungsten; *esp.* a salt of the anion WO_4^{2-}.

tungsten /ˈtʌŋstən/ *noun*. L18.
[Swedish, from *tung* heavy + *sten* stone.]
†**1** MINERALOGY. = SCHEELITE. L18–E19.
2 A dense refractory steel-grey metal which is a chemical element of the transition series, atomic no. 74, present in scheelite, wolframite, and other minerals, and used esp. for the filaments of electric lamps, in steel alloys, etc. Also called ***wolfram***. (Symbol W.) L18.
Comb.: **tungsten carbide** either of two very hard black compounds of tungsten and carbon used in cutting tools, dies, abrasives, etc.

tungstenite /ˈtʌŋstənʌɪt/ *noun*. L18.
[from prec. + -ITE[1].]
MINERALOGY. †**1** Tungsten (the metal). Only in L18.
2 = SCHEELITE. L19.
3 A tungsten sulphide that occurs as both hexagonal and rhombohedral polytypes in dark grey scaly aggregates. E20.

tungstic /ˈtʌŋstɪk/ *adjective*. L18.
[from TUNGSTEN + -IC.]
CHEMISTRY. Of, pertaining to, or containing tungsten, esp. in the hexavalent state. Chiefly in ***tungstic acid***, a parent acid of tungstates; a hydrated form of tungsten trioxide obtained from acid solutions of tungstates.

tungstite /ˈtʌŋstʌɪt/ *noun*. M19.
[from TUNGST(EN + -ITE[1].]
MINERALOGY. A rare earthy yellow tungsten oxide, valuable as an indicator of tungsten ores.

tungstous /ˈtʌŋstəs/ *adjective. rare.* M19.
[from TUNGSTEN + -OUS, after *ferrous* etc.]
CHEMISTRY. Of, pertaining to, or containing tungsten in the tetravalent state. Cf. TUNGSTIC.

Tungus /ˈtʊŋʊs, tʊŋˈuːs/ *noun & adjective.* E17.
[Yakut.]
▶ **A** *noun.* Pl. same.
1 A member of a people of eastern Siberia. E17.
2 An Altaic language or group of languages related to Manchu, spoken in parts of Siberia. E19.
▶ **B** *attrib.* or as *adjective.* Of or pertaining to the Tungus or their language. L17.
¶ Cf. MANCHU-Tungus.
■ **Tungˈusian** *adjective & noun* (*a*) *adjective* = TUNGUS *adjective*; (*b*) *noun* = TUNGUS *noun*: E18. **Tungˈusic** *adjective & noun* (*a*) *adjective* = TUNGUS *adjective*; (*b*) *noun* = TUNGUS *noun* 2: M19.

tunhoof /ˈtʌnhuːf/ *noun.* Now *dial.* OE.
[from TUN *noun*[1] + *hove* as in *hayhove* s.v. HAY *noun*[2], from its use in brewing.]
Ground ivy, *Glechoma hederacea*.

tunic /ˈtjuːnɪk/ *noun.* OE.
[Old & mod. French *tunique* or its source Latin *tunica*. Cf. next.]
1 A loose garment resembling a shirt or gown, as worn in ancient Greece and Rome. Also, in medieval times, a garment resembling a coat over which a loose mantle or cloak was worn. OE.
2 a ANATOMY. = TUNICA *noun*[1] 1. LME. ▶**b** The integument of a part or organ in a plant; *spec.* in BOTANY, any loose membranous skin not formed from the epidermis. Also, any of the layers of a tunicate bulb. M18.
3 a A close-fitting short usu. plain coat, esp. worn as a part of police or military uniform. M17. ▶**b** A garment worn by women or girls, consisting of a bodice and upper skirt, drawn in at the waist, and worn over a longer skirt or trousers. Also, a kind of loose pleated dress drawn in at the waist. M18.
4 ECCLESIASTICAL. = TUNICLE 2. L17.
5 In full *tunic shirt*. A long loose-fitting shirt worn, esp. in the East, over trousers. L19.

> 📖 **3a** M. IGNATIEFF His regimental tunic was stained. **b** *Harpers & Queen* The perfect A-line dress worn as a tunic over the shortest straight skirt. **5** R. P. JHABVALA A prince in pearls, turban, and silk tunic.

■ **tunicked** *adjective* wearing a tunic, usu. of a specified kind M18. **tunicless** *adjective* without a tunic E20.

tunica /ˈtjuːnɪkə/ *noun*[1]. L17.
[Latin: see prec.]
1 ANATOMY. A membranous sheath enveloping or lining an organ. Chiefly in mod. Latin combs. L17.
2 BOTANY. The outer layer or layers of cells in an apical meristem, which divide anticlinically and contribute to surface growth. Cf. CORPUS 5. M20.
1 tunica adventitia /advenˈtɪʃə/ [mod. Latin = adventitious] an outer layer or sheath, esp. that of the wall of a blood-vessel. **tunica albuginea** /albjʊˈdʒɪnɪə/ [mod. Latin = albugineous] a white fibrous layer in the covering of the penis, testis, or ovary. **tunica intima** /ˈɪntɪmə/ [Latin = innermost] = INTIMA. **tunica media** [Latin = middle] a middle layer or sheath, esp. the middle layer in the wall of a blood-vessel. **tunica vaginalis** /vadʒɪˈnɑːlɪs/ [mod. Latin = forming a sheath] a serous membrane covering part of the testis and epididymis.

Tunica /ˈtjuːnɪkə/ *noun*[2] *& adjective.* Also †**Tonika**. E18.
[French *Tonika*, *Tounika*, perh. from Tunica *tóniku* the man.]
▶ **A** *noun.* Pl. same, **-s**.
1 A member of a N. American Indian people of the lower Mississippi valley. E18.
2 The language (now extinct) of this people. E20.
▶ **B** *attrib.* or as *adjective.* Of or pertaining to the Tunica or their language. L18.
■ **Tunican** *noun* a postulated language family having Tunica as the chief member E20.

tunicary /ˈtjuːnɪk(ə)ri/ *noun & adjective.* M19.
[from Latin *tunica* TUNIC + -ARY[1].]
▶†**A** *noun.* ZOOLOGY. A tunicate. M–L19.
▶ **B** *adjective.* MEDICINE. Of or pertaining to a tunica or membrane. E20.

tunicate /ˈtjuːnɪkeɪt/ *adjective & noun.* M18.
[Latin *tunicat-* pa. ppl stem of *tunicare* clothe with a tunic, from *tunica* TUNIC: see -ATE[1].]
▶ **A** *adjective.* Having or enclosed in a tunic or covering; BOTANY (of a bulb etc.) consisting of a series of concentric layers. Also *spec.* in ZOOLOGY, of, pertaining to, or characteristic of tunicates. M18.
▶ **B** *noun.* ZOOLOGY. Any of a group of marine animals, once regarded as molluscs but now classified as chordates in the subphylum Urochordata (or Tunicata), comprising the sea squirts or ascidians and related pelagic and sessile forms characterized by a pouchlike body with a tough leathery or rubbery outer coat, having a single or double aperture through which the water enters and leaves a central pharynx. M19.

tunicated /ˈtjuːnɪkeɪtɪd/ *adjective.* E17.
[formed as prec. + -ED[1].]
†**1** Wearing a coat or tunic. *rare.* Only in E17.
2 = TUNICATE *adjective.* M18.

tunicin /ˈtjuːnɪsɪn/ *noun.* M19.
[from TUNIC + -IN[1].]
BIOCHEMISTRY. A polysaccharide resembling cellulose which occurs in the outer coat of tunicates.

tunicle /ˈtjuːnɪk(ə)l/ *noun.* LME.
[Old French (alt. of *tunique*), or Latin *tunicula*, dim. of *tunica* TUNIC: see -CLE. Cf. TOURNIQUET.]
†**1** A small tunic; *fig.* a wrapping, a covering, an integument. LME–M18.
2 ECCLESIASTICAL. A short vestment worn by a subdeacon over the alb or (formerly) by a bishop between the alb and the dalmatic at celebrations of the Eucharist. LME.
3 An enclosing membrane; = TUNIC 2a. Long *arch. rare.* LME.

tuning /ˈtjuːnɪŋ/ *noun.* M16.
[from TUNE *verb* + -ING[1].]
The action of TUNE *verb*, an instance of this; *spec.* (*a*) the action or process of putting a musical instrument in tune; a system by which this is done; (*b*) the process of adjusting an engine or its parts in order to increase efficiency; (*c*) the adjustment of a transmitter or receiver to a particular signal frequency or wavelength; variation of the resonant frequency of an oscillatory circuit; the facility on a radio set etc. allowing reception of different stations, frequencies, or wavelengths.
Comb.: **tuning-cone** a hollow cone of wood or metal used for tuning the metal flue-pipes of an organ; ***tuning-fork***: see FORK *noun* 4; **tuning-hammer** a tuning-key used to drive in the wrest-pins in a piano; **tuning-key** a key used to turn the wrest-pins when tuning or fitting strings in a piano, harp, etc.; **tuning meter** a device which measures how accurately a radio receiver is tuned to a given frequency etc.; **tuning-peg**, **tuning-pin** any of the pegs round which the strings of a stringed instrument are passed, and which are turned to tune the instrument; a wrest-pin; **tuning-slide** a slide in a metal wind instrument, used to bring it into tune; **tuning-wire** a bent wire in a reed-pipe of an organ, used in tuning.

Tuniseen *noun & adjective* var. of TUNISINE.

Tunisian /tjuːˈnɪzɪən/ *noun & adjective.* E19.
[from *Tunis* or *Tunisia* (see below) + -IAN, -AN.]
▶ **A** *noun.* **1** A native or inhabitant of Tunisia, a country in N. Africa, or of Tunis, the capital of Tunisia or (*Hist.*) the former Barbary State which preceded Tunisia. E19.
2 The demotic speech of the Tunisians. E20.
▶ **B** *adjective.* Of or pertaining to Tunisia or Tunis. M19.

Tunisine /ˈtjuːnɪsiːn/ *noun & adjective.* Now *rare* or *obsolete.* Also **-een**. M17.
[from *Tunis* (see prec.) + -INE[1].]
▶ **A** *noun.* A native of Tunis, a city and former Barbary State of N. Africa; *esp.* a pirate from Tunis. M17.
▶ **B** *adjective.* Of or belonging to Tunis. M19.

tunk *noun* var. of TUNC.

Tunker *noun* var. of DUNKER *noun*[1].

tunket /ˈtʊŋkɪt/ *noun. US dial. & colloq.* L19.
[Origin unkn.]
In exclamatory phrs., as a substitute for *hell*, expr. anger, incredulity, surprise, etc., or merely emphatic.

tunku /ˈtʊŋkuː/ *noun.* Also (esp. in titles) **T-**. L18.
[Malay.]
A male title of rank in certain states of Western Malaysia; prince.

tunnage *noun* see TONNAGE *noun.*

tunnel /ˈtʌn(ə)l/ *noun.* LME.
[Old & mod. French *tonel* (mod. *tonneau* tun, cask), from *tonne* TUN *noun*[1]: see -EL[2]. Cf. TONEL.]
1 A net with a wide opening leading into a narrowing pipelike passage, for catching partridges, ducks, fish, etc. Now *rare* or *obsolete.* LME.
†**2 a** The shaft or flue of a chimney. LME–E19. ▶**b** *gen.* A pipe, a tube. M16–L19.
3 A funnel. *obsolete* exc. *dial.* E16.
4 A man-made underground passage, esp. through a hill or mountain, or under a river or road, usu. for a railway or road to pass through. Also, an underground passage in a mine etc. M18.
5 *transf.* **a** An underground passage dug by a burrowing animal. L19. ▶**b** A natural structure resembling a tunnel, *esp.* a canal or hollow groove in an organ of the body. L19. ▶**c** AERONAUTICS etc. = ***wind tunnel*** s.v. WIND *noun*[1]. E20. ▶**d** SPORT. A subway or covered passage by which players enter or leave the field of play. M20. ▶**e** A long narrow greenhouse or cloche, usu. made of polythene. M20.

> 📖 **4** *Saturday Review* A tunnel thirty miles long under the Channel. R. RAYMOND The vein has been attacked by various tunnels. J. C. OATES Like shouting in a tunnel, and all you hear . . is your own voice echoing back. S. HILL The train whistled . . running through a tunnel. **5a** W. HORWOOD The moles made their way by tunnel. **d** *Running* He ran off the track and straight out through the tunnel.

Phrases: **light at the end of the tunnel** *colloq.* a long-awaited sign that a period of hardship or adversity is nearing an end. **tunnel of love** a fairground amusement involving a romantic train- or boat-ride through a darkened tunnel.

Comb.: **tunnel-back** *local* a rear extension on a house, containing a scullery etc.; a house built in this style; **tunnel diode** ELECTRONICS a two-terminal semiconductor device, consisting of a heavily doped *p–n* junction, which has negative resistance at low voltage due to quantum-mechanical tunnelling and is used in high-speed switching; **tunnel effect** PHYSICS = TUNNELLING (c); **tunnel-head** (*a*) the top of a blast-furnace; (*b*) the limit of the construction of a tunnel; **tunnel house** = sense 5e above; **tunnel-kiln**: in which the items being fired are carried on trucks along a continuously-heated passage; **tunnel-net** = sense 1 above; **tunnel-pit**, **tunnel-shaft** a shaft sunk to the level of a tunnel; **tunnel-vault** = ***barrel vault*** s.v. BARREL *noun*; **tunnel vision** a condition in which there is a major loss of peripheral vision, or in which anything away from the centre of the field of view escapes attention; *fig.* inability to see more than a single or limited point of view; **tunnel-visioned** *adjective* having tunnel vision.
■ **tunnelist** *noun* (*rare*) a person who constructs a tunnel; *transf.* a burrowing animal L18. **tunnel-like** *adjective* resembling (that of) a tunnel M19.

tunnel /ˈtʌn(ə)l/ *verb.* Infl. **-ll-**, ***-l-**. L16.
[from prec.]
1 †**a** *verb trans.* Provide with a tunnel-net or a similar tubular passage. *rare.* Only in L16. ▶**b** *verb trans. & intrans.* Catch (partridges etc.) with a tunnel-net. L17.
†**2** *verb trans.* Form into or cause to resemble a tube or pipe. Only in E18.
3 a *verb intrans.* Make a tunnel; excavate a passage below ground or through some substance. (Foll. by *along*, *through*, etc.) L18. ▶**b** *verb trans.* Excavate as or by means of a tunnel; make (something, one's way) by boring or excavating. M19. ▶**c** *verb trans.* Make a tunnel or tunnels through. M19. ▶**d** *verb intrans.* PHYSICS. Of a subatomic particle: pass *through* a potential barrier by tunnelling. M20.

> 📖 **3a** D. ATTENBOROUGH Active burrowers, tunnelling through the mud. *Garden Answers* Maggots will be found tunneling in the roots. *fig.*: B. MUKHERJEE A sandy trail tunneled through . . mossy trees. **b** E. K. KANE The stream which tunnels its way out near the glacier-foot. **c** *Blackwood's Magazine* The cover warped and tunnelled by white ants.

■ **tunneller** *noun* (*a*) a person who catches partridges etc. with a tunnel-net (now *rare* or *obsolete*); (*b*) a person who excavates a tunnel; *transf.* a burrowing animal: E17. **tunnelling** *noun* (*a*) the action of the verb; (*b*) work on a tunnel; underground excavation, esp. for a road or railway; a tunnel, tunnels collectively; (*c*) PHYSICS a quantum-mechanical effect whereby a particle has a finite probability of passing a potential barrier even if it has less energy than the height of the barrier: L17.

tunner /ˈtʌnə/ *noun. obsolete* exc. *dial.* ME.
[from TUN *noun*[1] or *verb* + -ER[1].]
An instrument for tunning wine etc.; a person who tuns wine etc.
■ **tunnery** *noun* a place where wine etc. is tunned L18.

tunny /ˈtʌni/ *noun.* M16.
[Old & mod. French *thon* from Provençal *ton* = Italian *tonno* from Latin *thunnus* from Greek *thunnos*. The -y ending is unexplained.]
= TUNA *noun*[3] 1.
Comb.: **tunnyman** a boat used for tuna-fishing.
¶ Long the usual word in Britain, but now largely replaced by *tuna*, esp. for the larger commercial species.

tuny /ˈtjuːni/ *adjective. colloq.* Also **tuney**. L19.
[from TUNE *noun* + -Y[1].]
Melodious, tuneful.
■ **tuniness** *noun* (*rare*) E20.

tup /tʌp/ *noun.* Chiefly *Scot. & north.* ME.
[Origin unkn.]
1 A male sheep; a ram. ME.
2 *transf.* A man; *spec.* a cuckold. *derog.* M17.
3 A mallet used in paving; a weight or hammerhead used esp. in pile-driving. M19.

tup /tʌp/ *verb intrans. & trans.* Infl. **-pp-**. LME.
[from prec.]
Esp. of a ram: copulate (with).

> 📖 R. HILL He's tupped more typists . . than you've had hot dinners.

tupaiid /tʊˈpʌɪɪd/ *noun.* L19.
[mod. Latin *Tupaiidae* (see below), from *Tupaia* genus name, from Malay *tupai* squirrel: see -ID[3].]
A tree shrew of the family Tupaiidae (order Scandentia).

Tupamaro /tuːpəˈmɑːrəʊ/ *noun.* Pl. **-os**. M20.
[from *Tupac Amaru* I (d. 1571) and II (d. 1781), Inca leaders.]
A member of a left-wing urban guerrilla organization in Uruguay.

tupan /ˈtuːpan/ *noun.* E20.
[Chinese *dūbàn* (Wade–Giles *tu pan*).]
The civil governor of a Chinese province under the Republican regime.

tupelo /ˈtjuːpɪləʊ/ *noun. N. Amer.* Pl. **-os**. M18.
[from Creek *ito* tree + *opilwa* swamp.]
= NYSSA; *esp.* (*a*) (more fully ***tupelo gum***) *N. aquatica* of swamps in the south-eastern US; (*b*) the black gum, *N. sylvatica*. Also, the wood of these trees.

Tupi /ˈtuːpi/ *noun & adjective.* M19.
[Amer. Indian name.]
▶ **A** *noun.* Pl. same, **-s**.
1 A member of a S. American Indian people native to the Amazon valley. M19.
2 The language of this people, one of the main divisions of the Tupi-Guarani language family. L19.
▶ **B** *attrib.* or as *adjective.* Of or pertaining to the Tupi or their language. M19.
■ **Tupian** *noun & adjective* = TUPI E20.

Tupi-Guarani /ˌtuːpɪgwɑːrəˈniː/ *noun & adjective.* M19.
[from prec. + GUARANI.]
▶ **A** *noun.* Pl. same, **-s**.
1 A member of a S. American people of Tupi, Guarani, or other related stock. M19.
2 A S. American Indian language family, whose principal members are Tupi and Guarani. E20.
▶ **B** *attrib.* or as *adjective.* Of or pertaining to the Tupi-Guarani or Tupi-Guarani. E20.

tupik /ˈtuːpɪk/ *noun.* M19.
[Inupiaq *tupiq*.]
A hut or tent of skins used by Eskimos as a summer residence. Also called ***summer lodge***.

Tupinamba /tuːpɪˈnambə/ *noun & adjective.* E19.
[S. Amer. name, prob. formed as TUPI + unexpl. 2nd elem.]
▶ **A** *noun.* Pl. same, **-s**. A member of a group of extinct peoples of the coast of Brazil. E19.
▶ **B** *attrib.* or as *adjective.* Of or pertaining to the Tupinamba. M19.

-tuple /tjʊp(ə)l/ *suffix.*
[The ending of QUINTUPLE, OCTUPLE, etc.]
Chiefly MATH. Forming nouns and adjectives with preceding algebraic symbol with the sense '(an entity or set) consisting of as many parts or elements as indicated by the symbol', as ***n-tuple***.

tuplet /ˈtjuːplɪt/ *noun.* L20.
[Back-form. from the suffix.]
MATH. An entity or set with a given number of elements, a vector.

-tuplet /tjʊplət/ *suffix.*
[The ending of QUINTUPLET, OCTUPLET, etc.]
MATH. Forming nouns with preceding algebraic symbol denoting entities or sets consisting of as many parts or elements as indicated by the symbol, as ***n-tuplet***.

tuppence *noun*, **tuppen(n)y** *adjective & noun* vars. of TWOPENCE, TWOPENNY.

Tupperian /tʌˈpɪːrɪən/ *adjective.* M19.
[from Martin F. *Tupper* (1810–1899), English writer + -IAN.]
Of, belonging to, or in the style of Martin F. Tupper's *Proverbial Philosophy* (1838–42), a moralistic work popular in the 19th cent.
■ **'Tupperism** *noun* a saying or generalization characteristic of those in Tupper's *Proverbial Philosophy* L19.

Tupperware /ˈtʌpəwɛː/ *noun.* M20.
[from the *Tupper* Corporation, the US manufacturers + WARE *noun*².]
(Proprietary name for) a range of plastic containers for storing food, sold exclusively at specially held parties in private homes.

tupsee /ˈtʌpsiː/ *noun.* Also **topsy** /ˈtɒpsi/. M19.
[Hindi *tapsī* from Sanskrit *tapasvin* in sense 'name of a month'.]
In the Indian subcontinent, an edible estuarine fish of the threadfin family, of the genus *Polynemus*. Also ***tupsee-fish***. Also called ***mango-fish***.

tuque /tuːk/ *noun. Canad.* L19.
[Canad. French, from French TOQUE.]
A close-fitting knitted cap, *esp.* a knitted stocking cap sealed at both ends, one end being tucked into the other to form a cap.

tu quoque /tuː ˈkwəʊkwiː, tjuː, ˈkwɒkweɪ/ *noun phr.* L17.
[Latin, lit. 'thou also' = English slang 'you're another'.]
An argument which consists of turning an accusation back on the accuser.

attrib.: M. BERESFORD The *tu quoque* argument that other lords had also inherited enclosed lands.

tur /tʊə/ *noun.* L19.
[Russian.]
Either of two greyish-brown wild goats, *Capra caucasica* and *C. cylindricornis*, of the Caucasus.

turacin /ˈtjʊərəsɪn, ˈtʊə-/ *noun.* M19.
[from next + -IN¹.]
CHEMISTRY. A bright crimson pigment found in the wing-feathers of turacos, which is chemically a copper complex of a porphin derivative.

turaco /ˈtʊərəkəʊ/ *noun.* Also **tour-**. Pl. **-os**. M18.
[French *touraco*, from a W. African name.]
Any of numerous birds of the family Musophagidae, which typically have brilliant purple, green, and crimson plumage with a prominent crest and long tail, and are found in woodland in sub-Saharan Africa. Also called ***plantain-eater***.

Turanian /tjʊˈreɪnɪən/ *adjective & noun.* Now *rare.* L18.
[from Persian *Tūrān* the region north of the Oxus + -IAN.]
▶ **A** *adjective.* **1** Designating or pertaining to the non-Indo-European and non-Semitic languages of central Asia, formerly regarded as belonging to a single family, *esp.* Ural-Altaic. L18.
2 Of or pertaining to any of the central Asian peoples speaking these languages. M19.
▶ **B** *noun.* **1** A member of any of the Turanian peoples. L18.
2 The Turanian languages collectively. M19.

turanose /ˈtjʊərənəʊz, -s/ *noun.* L19.
[formed as TURANIAN (with ref. to the source of manna from which first prepared) + -OSE².]
CHEMISTRY. A disaccharide containing fructose and glucose units, formed by partial hydrolysis of melezitose.

turb /təːb/ *noun. obsolete* exc. *Hist.* ME.
[French *tourbe*, Old French *torbe* from Latin TURBA.]
A crowd, a swarm; a troop.

turba /ˈtʊəbə/ *noun.* Pl. **-bae** /-biː/. L19.
[Latin = crowd.]
MUSIC. The chorus in passion-plays and other religious oratorios in which crowds participate in the action.

turban /ˈtəːb(ə)n/ *noun & verb.* Also †**tulipan(t)** & other vars. M16.
[French †*tolliban*, †*tulban*, †*turbant*, Italian †*tolipano*, -*ante*, Spanish, Portuguese, Italian *turbante* from Turkish *tülbend* from Persian *dulband*. Cf. TULIP.]
▶ **A** *noun.* **1** A man's head-dress, consisting of a length of cotton or silk wrapped round the head or a cap, worn esp. by Muslims and Sikhs. M16.
2 Any headgear resembling this; *spec.* (*a*) *Hist.* a woman's head-dress consisting of material piled round the head, fashionable in the late 18th and early 19th cents.; (*b*) a woman's round brimless hat of swathed material; (*c*) a scarf, towel, etc., swathed round the head, esp. for protective purposes. E17.
3 ZOOLOGY. **a** The spire of a twisted univalve shell. Now *rare* or *obsolete.* L17. ▶**b** [by confusion with TURBO *noun*¹.] A mollusc of the genus *Turbo* or the family Turbinidae. Also ***turban shell***. L17.
4 ZOOLOGY. Any of several somewhat flattened regular echinoids, esp. of the genus *Cidaris*. Now *rare* or *obsolete.* E18.
5 More fully ***Turk's turban***, ***turban buttercup***. A double form of a chiefly scarlet-flowered buttercup, *Ranunculus asiaticus*, of the eastern Mediterranean, grown for ornament. M18.
Comb.: ***turban buttercup***: see sense 5 above; ***turban gourd*** = ***turban squash*** below; ***turban shell***: see sense 3b above; ***turban squash*** a variety of winter squash, *Cucurbita maxima*, in which the fleshy receptacle does not extend over the ovary, which therefore protrudes so as to suggest a turban; ***turban tumour*** MEDICINE a rare benign tumour, probably of sweat glands, that spreads over the scalp or thorax in grapelike clusters.
▶ **B** *verb trans.* **1** Envelop (as) with a turban. E19.
2 Wind (cloth) round the head in the form of a turban. M19.
■ **turbaned** *adjective* wearing a turban, provided with a turban L16. **turbanless** *adjective* without a turban M19. **turbanwise** *adverb* in the manner of a turban L19.

turbary /ˈtəːb(ə)ri/ *noun.* LME.
[Anglo-Norman *turberie*, Old French *tourberie* (medieval Latin *turbaria*), from *tourbe* TURF *noun*: see -ARY¹.]
1 (A tract of) land where peat may be dug for fuel; (a) peatbog, (a) peatmoss. Formerly also (*rare*), peat. LME.
2 LAW. The right to dig peat for fuel on a common or on another person's land. M16.
Comb.: ***turbary pig***, ***turbary sheep*** (an animal of) a prehistoric breed of domesticated pig, sheep, first found in turbaries in Swiss neolithic lake-dwellings and sometimes identified with certain surviving breeds.

turbeh /ˈtəːbeɪ, ˈtʊə-/ *noun.* L17.
[Turkish *türbe* from Arab. *turba* tomb, from base also of TORBA.]
A small building, resembling a mosque, erected over the tomb of a Muslim, esp. a person of sanctity or rank.

turbellarian /təːbɛˈlɛːrɪən/ *adjective & noun.* L19.
[mod. Latin *Turbellaria* (see below), from Latin *turbella* bustle, stir, dim. of *turba* crowd: see -ARY¹, -AN.]
ZOOLOGY. ▶**A** *adjective.* Of or pertaining to the class Turbellaria of mainly free-living flatworms of fresh or salt water or damp earth, having a ciliated body surface. L19.
▶ **B** *noun.* A worm of this class. L19.

turbid /ˈtəːbɪd/ *adjective.* LME.
[Latin *turbidus* full of confusion, muddy, etc., from *turba* crowd, disturbance: see -ID¹.]
1 *fig.* Characterized by or producing confusion or obscurity of thought, feeling, etc.; unclear. LME.
2 Esp. of liquid: cloudy or opaque with suspended matter; not clear; thick, dense. E17.

1 *Edinburgh Review* The turbid utterances and twisted language of Carlyle. **2** D. ATTENBOROUGH Rivers . . so full of rotting leaves that they are black and turbid. D. MADDEN She . . watched them fly . . pale against the turbid clouds.

■ **tur'bidity** *noun* turbid quality; ***turbidity current***, an underwater current flowing swiftly downslope owing to the weight of sediment it carries: L18. **turbidly** *adverb* (*rare*) E18. **turbidness** *noun* L17.

turbidimeter /təːbɪˈdɪmɪtə/ *noun.* Also **-dometer** /-ˈdɒmɪtə/. E20.
[from TURBIDITY + -IMETER, -OMETER.]
BIOLOGY & CHEMISTRY. An instrument for determining the turbidity of a liquid from the decrease in the intensity of a beam of light passing through it. Cf. NEPHELOMETER 2.
■ **turbidi'metric** *adjective* E20. **turbidi'metrically** *adverb* by turbidimetry E20. **turbidimetry** *noun* the use of a turbidimeter, esp. for the quantitative analysis of turbid solutions E20.

turbidite /ˈtəːbɪdʌɪt/ *noun.* M20.
[from TURBIDITY + -ITE¹.]
GEOLOGY. A sediment or rock deposited, or presumed to have been deposited, by a turbidity current.
■ **turbiditic** /-ˈdɪtɪk/ *adjective* L20.

turbidometer *noun* var. of TURBIDIMETER.

turbinal /ˈtəːbɪn(ə)l/ *adjective & noun.* L16.
[from Latin *turbin-*, *turbo* (see TURBO *noun*¹) + -AL¹.]
▶ **A** *adjective.* = TURBINATE *adjective.* L16.
▶ **B** *noun.* ANATOMY & ZOOLOGY. Each of three thin curved shelves of bone in the sides of the nasal cavity in humans and higher vertebrates, covered in mucous membrane; a turbinate bone. Also called ***scroll-bone***, ***nasal concha***. M19.

turbinate /ˈtəːbɪnət/ *adjective & noun.* M17.
[Latin *turbinatus*, formed as prec.: see -ATE².]
▶ **A** *adjective.* BIOLOGY. Resembling a spinning-top in shape, conical; in BOTANY, inversely conical; in ANATOMY, designating or pertaining to the turbinals of the nasal cavity. M17.
▶ **B** *noun.* **1** ZOOLOGY. A turbinate shell. *rare.* E19.
2 ANATOMY. A turbinate bone. L19.
■ Also **turbinated** *adjective* E17.

turbination /təːbɪˈneɪʃ(ə)n/ *noun.* E17.
[Latin *turbinatio(n-)*, from prec.: see -ATION.]
1 Orig., the action of making a thing top-shaped. Now only, turbinate form. E17.
†**2** The action of spinning like a top. M–L17.

turbine /ˈtəːbʌɪn, -ɪn/ *noun.* M19.
[French from Latin *turbin-*, *turbo*: see TURBO *noun*¹.]
Orig., a high-speed water-wheel, esp. a horizontal one driven by a column of water falling into its interior and escaping through oblique channels so as to impel the wheel in the opposite direction. Now, any rotary machine in which a revolving wheel, or a cylinder or disk bearing vanes, is driven by a flow of water, steam, gas, wind, etc., esp. to generate electrical power.
gas turbine, ***impulse turbine***, ***jet turbine***, ***pump-turbine***, ***reaction turbine***, ***shaft turbine***, ***steam turbine***, etc.
■ **turbined** *adjective* having or propelled by a turbine or turbines E20. **turbiner** *noun* a vessel driven by a turbine E20.

turbinectomy /təːbɪˈnɛktəmi/ *noun.* E20.
[from TURBINAL *noun* + -ECTOMY.]
Surgical excision of a turbinate bone or bones; an instance of this.

turbines *noun*¹, *noun*² pls. of TURBINE *noun*, TURBO *noun*¹.

turbiniform /təːˈbɪnɪfɔːm/ *adjective.* E19.
[from Latin *turbin-*, *turbo*: see TURBO *noun*¹, -I-, -FORM.]
ZOOLOGY. = TURBINATE *adjective.*

turbit /ˈtəːbɪt/ *noun.* L17.
[App. from Latin *turbo* (see TURBO *noun*¹), from its shape.]
A small fancy variety of the domestic pigeon, distinguished by a stout rounded build, a short beak, a ruffle or frill on the neck and breast, and a small crest.

†**turbith** *noun* var. of TURPETH.

turble *adjective & adverb* see TURRIBLE.

turbo /ˈtəːbəʊ/ *noun*¹. Pl. **-bines** /-bɪniːz/. M17.
[mod. Latin, from Latin *turbo*, *turbin-* spinning-top, whirlwind.]
A gastropod mollusc of the genus *Turbo* (family Turbinidae), having a regularly whorled spiral shell, with a rounded aperture and a calcareous operculum; *loosely* any member of the family Turbinidae.

turbo /ˈtəːbəʊ/ *noun*². *colloq.* Pl. **-os**. E20.
[Abbreviation.]
1 A turbine. E20.
2 = TURBOCHARGER. Also, a motor vehicle equipped with this device. M20.

turbo- /ˈtəːbəʊ/ *combining form.*
[from TURB(INE: see -O-.]
Consisting of a turbine; driven by or directly coupled to a turbine.
■ **turbocar** *noun* a motor car powered by a gas turbine M20. **turbo-compound** *adjective* designating a piston engine in which the exhaust gases drive a turbine coupled to the crank-

shaft M20. **turbodrill** *noun & verb* (OIL INDUSTRY) (*a*) *noun* a drill in which the drilling bit is rotated by a turbine situated next to it in the drilling string and driven by the upflow of mud; (*b*) *verb trans.* drill using a turbodrill: M20. **turbo-eˈlectric** *adjective* involving or employing electricity generated by means of a turbine E20. **turbofan** *noun* a fan connected to or driven by a turbine; *spec.* (AERONAUTICS) such a fan used to drive air around the exhaust gases of a jet engine to give additional thrust; (an aircraft powered by) an engine employing such a fan: E20. **turboˈgenerator** *noun* a large electricity generator driven by a steam turbine E20. **turbojet** *noun* (AERONAUTICS) (an aircraft having) a type of jet engine in which the jet gases also power a turbine-driven compressor for compressing the air drawn into the engine M20. **turboprop** *noun* (AERONAUTICS) (an aircraft having) a jet engine in which a turbine is used as in a turbojet and also to drive a propeller M20. **turbopump** *noun* a pump incorporating a small turbine to provide mechanical power, used esp. in aircraft and rockets E20. **turboramjet** *noun* (AERONAUTICS) any of a class of jet engine constructed either as a turbojet with provision for afterburning, or as a ramjet containing a turbojet which is shut down at high velocities M20. **turboshaft** *noun* a gas turbine engine in which the turbine drives a shaft other than a propeller shaft M20. **turboˈsupercharger** *noun* = TURBOCHARGER M20. **turbotrain** *noun* a train powered by a gas turbine M20.

turbocharger /ˈtəːbəʊtʃɑːdʒə/ *noun.* M20.
[Abbreviation of TURBOSUPERCHARGER.]
ENGINEERING. A supercharger driven by a turbine powered by the engine's exhaust gases.
■ **turbocharge** *verb trans.* equip with a turbocharger (chiefly as *turbocharged ppl adjective*) M20.

turbopause /ˈtəːbəʊpɔːz/ *noun.* M20.
[from TURBULENCE after *tropopause* etc.]
METEOROLOGY. The outer limit of a turbosphere, where the distribution of constituents is due equally to diffusion and turbulent mixing.

turbosphere /ˈtəːbəʊsfɪə/ *noun.* M20.
[from TURB(ULENCE + -O- + -SPHERE.]
METEOROLOGY. A region of a planetary atmosphere in which mixing occurs predominantly through turbulence.

turbostratic /təːbəʊˈstratɪk/ *adjective.* M20.
[from Latin *turbat-* pa. ppl stem of *turbare* disorder, disturb + -O- + STRATUM + -IC.]
PHYSICS. Of or pertaining to a material (esp. one allotrope of carbon) having a structure intermediate between amorphous and crystalline, consisting of stacked disordered layers.

turbot /ˈtəːbət/ *noun.* ME.
[Old French from Old Swedish *tornbut*, from *törn* THORN *noun* + *but* BUTT *noun*[1].]
1 A large speckled pale brown European flatfish, *Scophthalmus maximus*, having a broad scaleless diamond-shaped body covered with bony tubercles, valued for food; the flesh of this as food. ME.
2 Any of various other fishes resembling or related to the turbot; *spec.* (*a*) *Scot. & north.* the halibut; (*b*) *US* any of various large flatfishes; (*c*) (chiefly *W. Indies*) a trigger fish, esp. *Balistes vetula.* M16.

turbulence /ˈtəːbjʊləns/ *noun.* LME.
[Old & mod. French, or late Latin *turbulentia*, from *turbulentus*: see TURBULENT, -ENCE.]
1 Violent commotion or disturbance; disorderly or unruly character or conduct; an instance of this. LME.
2 Turbulent flow in a fluid, e.g. in the atmosphere, a body of moving water, etc. Cf. TURBULENT 3. E20.

> 🕮 **1** E. M. GOULBURN Think of Him as calm . . amidst the most furious agitations and turbulences of nature. M. PATTISON It required . . the personal influence of the king to check the turbulence of his . . followers. **2** H. NORMAN In the roughest turbulence he hummed a monotone as if to steady the plane.

■ Also **turbulency** *noun* (now *rare*) E17.

turbulent /ˈtəːbjʊlənt/ *adjective.* LME.
[Latin *turbulentus*, from *turba* crowd, *turbare* disturb, agitate: see -ULENT.]
1 Characterized by violent disturbance or commotion; violently disturbed or agitated. LME.
2 Causing disturbance or commotion; tumultuous, wild, unruly; having a violent or (formerly) disturbing effect. LME.
3 Of, pertaining to, or designating flow of a fluid in which the velocity at any point fluctuates irregularly and there is continual mixing rather than a steady or laminar flow pattern. Cf. TURBULENCE 2. L19.

> 🕮 **1** D. ACHESON Life with Ernie was . . turbulent, for his temper could build up . . suddenly. A. BRINK The peaceful evening brought . . rest to his turbulent thoughts. *Scots Magazine* The turbulent tides of the Pentland Firth. **2** R. C. TRENCH He expelled . . the crowd of turbulent mourners.

■ **turbulently** *adverb* E17.

turca *noun* var. of TURCO *noun*[1].

†**Turcism** *noun.* M16.
[from medieval Latin *Turcus* TURK *noun*[1] + -ISM. Cf. TURKISM.]
1 The religious system of the Turks; Islam. M16–E18.
2 Turkish principles and practice. L16–E18.

turco /ˈtəːkəʊ/ *noun*[1]. Pl. **-os**. Also **-ca** /-kə/. M19.
[Amer. Spanish from a S. American lang.]
A brown Chilean bird of the tapaculo family, *Pteroptochos megapodius.*

turco /ˈtəːkəʊ/ *noun*[2]. Also **T-**. Pl. **-os**. M19.
[Spanish, Portuguese, Italian = TURK *noun*[1].]
Hist. A member of a body of light infantry formed of Algerians in the French army; a Zouave.

Turco- /ˈtəːkəʊ/ *combining form.* Also **Turko-**.
[from medieval Latin *Turcus* TURK *noun*[1] + -O-.]
Forming adjective and noun combs. with the meaning 'Turkish; Turkish and —', as *Turco-American, Turco-Bulgarian, Turco-Tatar*, etc.
■ **Turcoˈcentric** *adjective* centred round Turkey and Turkish things M20. **Turˈcologist** *noun* an expert in or student of Turkish literature, art, etc. L19. **Turcophil(e)** *adjective & noun* (a person) who is friendly towards Turkey or fond of Turkey and Turkish things L19. **Turˈcophilism** *noun* Turcophile sentiments L19. **Turcophobe** *noun* a person who is affected with a dread or dislike of Turkey and Turkish things L19.

Turcoman *noun & adjective* var. of TURKOMAN.

turcopole /ˈtəːkəpəʊl/ *noun.* Now *Hist.* Also **T-**. E18.
[medieval Latin *Turcopolus, -pulus* from Byzantine Greek *Tourkopouloi* (pl.), from *Tourko-* TURK *noun*[1] + *pōlos* foal, child, applied to children of a Turkish or Saracen father and a Greek mother.]
A soldier of the Order of St John of Jerusalem with light weapons or armour.

turcopolier /ˈtəːkəpəlɪə/ *noun.* Now *Hist.* Also **T-**. L15.
[medieval Latin *turcopolerius, -arius*, from *Turcopolus*: see prec.]
The commander of the turcopoles of the order of St John of Jerusalem.

turd /təːd/ *noun.* Now *coarse slang.*
[Old English *tord* = Middle Dutch *tort, torde* (also in Old English *tordwifel*, Dutch †*tortwevel*, Old Norse *tordýfill* dung-beetle, lit. 'turd-weevil'), from Germanic. Cf. TREDDLE *noun*[1].]
1 A lump or piece of faeces. Also, faeces, excrement. OE.
2 A contemptible, obnoxious, or worthless person. Cf. SHIT *noun* 2. LME.

> 🕮 **2** G. KEILLOR Arlen, the little turd who tried to set the woods on fire.

■ **turdish** *adjective* M20.

turdine /ˈtəːdʌɪn/ *adjective.* L19.
[from Latin *turdus* thrush + -INE[1].]
Of, pertaining to, or characteristic of thrushes.

turdoid /ˈtəːdɔɪd/ *adjective.* L19.
[formed as prec. + -OID.]
Resembling a thrush.

tureen /tjʊˈriːn, tə-/ *noun.* M18.
[Alt. of TERRINE, perh. after *Turin* a city of N. Italy.]
A deep vessel (usu. oval) with a lid, from which soup is served. Also, a smaller vessel of similar shape for sauce or gravy.
■ **tureenful** *noun* as much as a tureen will hold L19.

turf /təːf/ *noun.* Pl. **turves** /təːvz/, **turfs**.
[Old English *turf* corresp. to Old Frisian, Old Saxon (Dutch) *turf* (Low German *torf*, German *Torf*), Old High German *zurba, zurf*, Old Norse *torf, torfa*, from Germanic, whence also medieval Latin *turba*, Old French *tourbe* (cf. TURBARY), from Indo-European base repr. also by Sanskrit *darbha* tuft of grass.]
1 The layer of grass etc. with earth and matted roots, forming the surface grassland; grass etc. with earth and matted roots cut from the ground. OE.
2 A piece of this cut from the ground; a sod. OE.
3 A slab of peat dug for use as (esp.) fuel; peat. Now chiefly *Anglo-Irish.* LME.
4 (Freq. **T-**.) *The* institution or practice of horse-racing; *the* grassy course over which this takes place. *colloq.* M18.
5 An area regarded as being under the control of a particular person or group, *one's* personal territory; *spec.* (*a*) the streets controlled by a (juvenile) street-gang; (*b*) the part of a city etc. within which a particular criminal or detective operates; (*c*) *fig.* a person's sphere of influence or activity. *slang* (orig. & chiefly *N. Amer.*). M20.

> 🕮 **1** SIR W. SCOTT Throwing stones, turf and other missiles. *Daily News* A low wall of turf and stones. P. SAYER I . . stood on the springy turf of the cliff-top. **2** *Nature* A wild hill-top . . had been unturfed, the turves and gorse being piled in heaps. **4 on the turf** (*a*) on the racecourse; (*b*) *slang* engaged in prostitution. **5** J. F. FIXX *Dogs* . . are assiduous defenders of turf. M. HOWARD Like any neighbourhood punk . . Manny is often afraid when he's not on his turf.

Comb.: **turf-accountant** a bookmaker; **turf-cutter** a person who digs peat, a spade for digging peat; **turf-line** a line formed from turf; *spec.* in an archaeological excavation, a layer of soil representing former grassland; **turfman** (chiefly *US*) a horse-racing enthusiast; **turf war** *colloq.* a dispute over territory or influence;
■ **turfdom** *noun* the horse-racing community, the world of horse-racing M19. **turfen** *adjective* made of or covered with turf L18. **turfite** *noun* a horse-racing enthusiast M19. **turfless** *adjective* without turf M18.

turf /təːf/ *verb trans.* Pa. t. & pple **turfed**, **turved** /təːvd/; pres. pple & verbal noun **turfing**, **turving** /ˈtəːvɪŋ/. LME.
[from the noun.]
1 Cover or lay with turf. Also, bury under the turf. LME.
2 Dig up or excavate (ground) for turf or peat. L18.
3 Throw a person etc. forcibly *out, off. colloq.* L19.

> 🕮 **1** *Amateur Gardening* Sow a lawn rather than turf it. **3** *Maclean's Magazine* The patients are turfed out of their group home.

■ **turfing** *verbal noun* the action of the verb; *turfing-iron*, a tool for raising turf: M17.

Turfanian /təːˈfeɪnɪən/ *noun.* M20.
[from *Turfan* in Chinese Turkestan + -IAN.]
The western dialect of Tocharian; Tocharian A.
■ Also **Turfan** /təːˈfɑːn/ *noun* M20.

turfy /ˈtəːfi/ *adjective.* M16.
[from TURF *noun* + -Y[1].]
1 Covered with or consisting of turf; grassy. M16.
2 Of the nature of or having much peat; peaty. M17.
3 Pertaining to or suggestive of horse-racing. *colloq.* M19.
■ **turfiness** *noun* E20.

Turgenevian /təːgɛˈnjɛvɪən/ *adjective.* E20.
[from *Turgenev* (see below) + -IAN.]
Of, pertaining to, or characteristic of the work of the Russian novelist and playwright Ivan Sergeevich Turgenev (1818–83).

turgent /ˈtəːdʒ(ə)nt/ *adjective.* Now *rare* or *obsolete.* LME.
[Latin *turgent-* pres. ppl stem of *turgere* swell: see -ENT.]
1 Physically swollen; distended. LME.
2 *fig.* Swollen with pride or conceit. Also, using inflated language. E17.
■ **turgency** *noun* M17.

turgescent /təːˈdʒɛs(ə)nt/ *adjective.* E18.
[Latin *turgescent-* pres. ppl stem of *turgescere* inceptive of *turgere*: see prec., -ESCENT.]
Becoming turgid; swelling.
■ **turgescence** *noun* M17. **turgescency** *noun* M17.

turgid /ˈtəːdʒɪd/ *adjective.* E17.
[Latin *turgidus*, from *turgere* to swell: see -ID[1].]
1 Swollen, distended. E17.
2 *fig.* Of language: inflated, bombastic. E18.

> 🕮 **2** A. STORR The clumsy turgid prose in which he struggles to express himself.

■ **turˈgidity** *noun* turgid condition or quality; an instance of this: M18. **turgidly** *adverb* M17. **turgidness** *noun* M18.

turgor /ˈtəːgə/ *noun.* L19.
[Late Latin, from *turgere* swell: see -OR.]
PHYSIOLOGY & BOTANY. **1** The normal swollen condition of the capillaries and smaller blood-vessels. L19.
2 A state of turgidity and consequent rigidity in a cell, as caused by the absorption of fluid. L19.

Turinese *adjective & noun* var. of TORINESE.

Turing /ˈtjʊərɪŋ/ *noun.* M20.
[A. M. *Turing* (1912–54), English mathematician.]
1 *Turing machine*, a hypothetical computing machine which scans and alters a linear array of symbols according to predetermined rules, devised by Turing in 1936 in connection with theories of computability. M20.
2 *Turing test*, a test for intelligence in computers, requiring that a human should be unable to distinguish the machine from another human using the replies to questions put to both. L20.

turion /ˈtjʊərɪən/ *noun.* Also (earlier) in Latin form †**turio**, pl. **-iones**. E18.
[French from Latin *turio.*]
BOTANY. **1** An underground bud or shoot from which an aerial stem arises. E18.
2 In certain aquatic plants, a kind of perennating bud which becomes detached and remains dormant at the bottom of the water. E20.

turismo /tjʊˈrɪzməʊ/ *noun.* E20.
[Spanish, Italian.]
Tourism as an industry or dedicated pursuit, esp. in Spain and Italy.

turista /tjʊˈrɪstə/ *noun.* L20.
[Spanish, lit. 'tourist'.]
Diarrhoea suffered by visitors to Mexico.

Turk /təːk/ *noun*[1]. LME.
[French *Turc*, Italian, Spanish, Portuguese *Turco*, medieval Latin *turcus*, Byzantine Greek *Tourkos*, Persian from Turkish *türk* a Turk (cf. Arab. *al-turk* (the) Turks), prob. ult. a Turkish name.]
1 Orig. (now *Hist.*), a Seljuk or Ottoman Turk (see sense 2 below); more widely, any subject of the Ottoman Sultan. Now, a native or inhabitant of modern Turkey; a person of Turkish descent. LME.
2 *Hist.* A member of an ancient and widely spread central Asian people, speaking Turkic languages, to which the Seljuks and Ottomans belonged. E16.
†**3** A Muslim. M16–M18.

4 A cruel, tyrannical person; a ferocious, wild, or unmanageable person. *derog.* & *racially offensive.* M16.
†**5** A human figure at which to practise shooting. M16–M17.
6 A horse of Arabian origin, = ARAB *noun* 2. Now *rare.* E17.
7 A Turkish cigarette. E20.
8 [Perh. rel. to Irish *torc* boar, hog.] A person of Irish birth or descent. *slang (derog.).* Chiefly *US.* E20.
Phrases: **little Turk** = *Young Turk* (c) below. **the Grand Turk**, **the Great Turk** *Hist.* the Ottoman Sultan. **the Turk** (*a*) Turks collectively, the Turkish power; (*b*) *Hist.* the Ottoman Sultan. *Turk's turban*: see TURBAN *noun* 5. †**turn Turk** become a Muslim. **Young Turk** (*a*) *Hist.* a member of a revolutionary party in Ottoman Turkey in the early 20th cent.; (*b*) *transf.* a young person eager for radical change to the established order; (*c*) (with lower-case initials) (*derog.* & *racially offensive*) a violent child or youth.
■ **Turkdom** *noun* the realm or domain of the Turks; Turkey: E20. **Turkery** *noun* †(*a*) the Turkish religious system; Islam; (*b*) Turks collectively: L16.

turk /tɜːk/ *noun*². Now *rare* or *obsolete.* E18.
[French *turc* app. rel. to Breton *teurec*, *teurg* tick.]
Any of various beetle larvae which cause damage to fruit trees.

Turkana /tɜːˈkɑːnə/ *noun & adjective.* E20.
[Nilotic.]
▶ **A** *noun.* Pl. same.
1 A member of an E. African people living between Lake Turkana (formerly Lake Rudolf) in NW Kenya and the Nile. E20.
2 The Nilotic language of the Turkana. E20.
▶ **B** *attrib.* or as *adjective.* Of or pertaining to the Turkana or their language. M20.

Turkey /ˈtɜːki/ *noun*¹. L15.
[A country in SW Asia and SE Europe between the Mediterranean and the Black Sea (formerly the centre of the Ottoman empire). Cf. next.]
1 *ellipt.* **a** = *Turkey stone* below. L15. ▸†**b** = *Turkey leather* below. E18–M19.
2 Used *attrib.* to designate things found in, made in, or associated with Turkey. L15.
2 Turkey carpet = *Turkish carpet* s.v. TURKISH *adjective.* **Turkey hone** = *Turkey stone* (b) below. **Turkey leather** leather which has been steeped in oil before the hair side is removed. **Turkey rug** = *Turkish rug* s.v. TURKISH *adjective.* **Turkey sponge** a superior grade of commercial sponge from the Mediterranean and Adriatic. **Turkey stone** (*a*) *arch.* a turquoise; (*b*) a hard fine-grained siliceous stone used for whetstones, orig. one imported from the eastern Mediterranean region, now usu. *spec.* novaculite; a whetstone made of this. **Turkey wheat** maize. **Turkey work** Turkish tapestry work; embroidery imitating this.

turkey /ˈtɜːki/ *noun*². M16.
[Short for TURKEYCOCK, TURKEYHEN, app. applied orig. (in these forms) to the guinea-fowl, a native of Africa imported through Turkey (see prec.), and then, by confusion of the two birds, to the American bird.]
1 A large stout game-bird of the pheasant family, *Meleagris gallopavo*, native to Mexico and the southern US but now widely domesticated, which has brownish variegated iridescent plumage and a bald head, with red wattles in the male, and is valued for its flesh. M16. ▸**b** The flesh of this bird, esp. the domestic variety, as food. L16.
†**2** The guinea-fowl. Only in M17.
3 With specifying word: any of various other large birds, e.g. (more fully ***native turkey***) the Australian bustard, *Choriotis australis.* E19.
4 A bag or holdall for a lumberjack's belongings; a holdall or bundle carried by an itinerant worker, vagrant, etc. *N. Amer.* & *Austral.* L19.
5 a A poor or unsuccessful film or theatrical production, a flop. More widely, anything disappointing or of little value; a stupid or inept person. *slang* (orig. *N. Amer.*). E20. ▸**b** = TURK *noun*¹ 8; *spec.* an Irish immigrant in the US. *slang (derog.).* M20.
Phrases etc.: ***brush-turkey***: see BRUSH *noun*¹. ***cold turkey***: see COLD *adjective.* **ocellated turkey** a small wild turkey of Central America, *Agriocharis ocellata.* ***plains turkey***, ***plain turkey***: see PLAIN *noun*¹. **talk turkey** (chiefly *N. Amer.*) (*a*) talk pleasantly or agreeably; (*b*) now usu., speak frankly and openly, talk hard facts. ***wild turkey***: see WILD *adjective, noun, & adverb.*
Comb.: **turkey-beard** a tall plant of the eastern US, *Xerophyllum asphodeloides*, of the lily family, with wiry root-leaves and a dense raceme of small white flowers; **turkey-berry** *W. Indies* = SUSUMBER; **turkey-blossom** *W. Indies* a yellow-flowered caltrop, *Tribulus cistoides*; **turkey-bush** an evergreen Australian shrub, *Myoporum deserti*, (family Myoporaceae), whose berries are eaten by the native turkey or Australian bustard; **turkey-buzzard** = *turkey vulture* below; **turkey-call** (*a*) the characteristic gobbling sound made by a turkey-cock; (*b*) an instrument for imitating this, used to decoy the wild turkey; **turkey-corn** a N. American bleeding heart, *Dicentra canadensis*, having tubers like grains of maize; also ***squirrel-corn***; **turkey-fat ore** a variety of smithsonite (zinc carbonate) coloured yellow by greenockite; **turkey-gnat** a small black fly of the genus *Simulium* which infests poultry in southern and western N. America; **turkey-merchant** *slang* a dealer in turkeys; **turkey-shoot** (*a*) a shooting-match in which the mark is a live turkey, or its head only; (*b*) *US colloq.* a situation, esp. in a war, in which the aggressor has an overwhelming advantage; **turkey-trot** *noun & verb* (*a*) *noun* a kind of ball-room dance originating in the US; a fast jogging trot supposed to resemble the gait of a turkey; (*b*) *verb intrans.* dance the turkey-trot; **turkey vulture** an American vulture, *Cathartes aura*, so called from its bare reddish head and neck and dark plumage.

turkeycock /ˈtɜːkɪkɒk/ *noun.* M16.
[from TURKEY *noun*² + COCK *noun*¹. In 16 synon. with *guinea-fowl*, the American bird being at first identified with or treated as a species of this. Cf. next.]
†**1** A male guinea-fowl, *Numida meleagris.* M16–E17.
2 A male turkey. L16. ▸**b** *fig.* A pompous or self-important person. E17.

turkeyhen /ˈtɜːkɪhɛn/ *noun.* M16.
[formed as prec. + HEN *noun.*]
†**1** A guinea-hen. M16–E17.
2 A female turkey. M16.

turkey oak /ˈtɜːki əʊk/ *noun phr.* In sense 2 usu. **T-.** E18.
[In sense 1 from TURKEY *noun*²; in sense 2 from TURKEY *noun*¹.]
1 Either of two oaks of the south-eastern US, *Quercus laevis* and *Q. falcata*, of dry sandy ground. E18.
2 An oak of central and southern Europe, *Q. cerris*, with scaly acorn-cups. E19.

Turkey red /ˈtɜːkɪ ˈrɛd/ *noun & adjectival phr.* E18.
[from TURKEY *noun*¹ + RED *noun, adjective.*]
1 *noun.* (A piece of) cotton cloth dyed with a brilliant red pigment obtained from madder or alizarin. E18.
2 *noun & adjective.* (Dyed with) this pigment; (of) the colour of this pigment. L18.
Comb.: **Turkey red oil** sulphonated castor oil, used esp. with alizarin to produce Turkey red.

Turki /ˈtɜːki/ *noun & adjective.* L18.
[Persian *turkī*, from *turk* TURK *noun*¹.]
▶ **A** *noun.* Pl. same, **-s**.
†**1** A horse of Arabian origin; = TURK *noun*¹ 6. Only in L18.
2 A member of a Turkic-speaking people. L18.
3 The Turkic languages, *esp.* those of central Asia, collectively. E19.
▶ **B** *attrib.* or as *adjective.* †**1** Turkish; (of a horse) Arabian. Only in E19.
2 Of or pertaining to the Turkic languages, esp. those of central Asia, or the peoples speaking them. M19.

Turkic /ˈtɜːkɪk/ *adjective & noun.* M19.
[from TURK *noun*¹ + -IC.]
▶ **A** *adjective.* Of, pertaining to, or designating a large group of Altaic languages including Turkish, Azerbaijani, Uigur, Kirghiz, Tatar, and Kazakh, or the peoples speaking these languages. M19.
▶ **B** *noun.* The Turkic languages collectively. L19.

Turkicize /ˈtɜːkɪsʌɪz/ *verb trans.* Also **-ise.** M20.
[from prec. + -IZE.]
Make Turkic or Turkish; Turkify.
■ **Turkiciˈzation** *noun* M20.

Turkify /ˈtɜːkɪfʌɪ/ *verb trans.* L17.
[from TURK *noun*¹ + -I- + -FY.]
Make Turkish in character.
■ **Turkifiˈcation** *noun* E20.

†**turkis(e)** *nouns & adjectives* see TURQUOISE.

Turkish /ˈtɜːkɪʃ/ *adjective & noun.* M16.
[from TURK *noun*¹ + -ISH¹.]
▶ **A** *adjective.* **1** Of or pertaining to the Turks or Turkey; *esp.* (now *Hist.*), Ottoman. M16. ▸**b** Of, pertaining to, or designating the Altaic language of the Turks; *spec.* the western Turkic language which is the official language of Turkey. Also more widely, = TURKIC *adjective.* L16.
2 Resembling the Turks; (regarded as) characteristic of the Turks. E17.
Special collocations: **Turkish bath** a hot-air or (*loosely*) steam bath followed by washing, massage, etc.; (in *sing.* or *pl.*) a building for this. **Turkish carpet**, **Turkish rug**: woven esp. in Turkey in a rich colour with a deep wool pile. **Turkish coffee** a strong black coffee served, usu. sweetened, with the grounds. **Turkish crescent** MUSIC a percussion instrument consisting of an inverted crescent from which hang a number of small bells which jingle (cf. ***pavillon chinois*** s.v. PAVILLON 2, ***jingling Johnny*** (a) s.v. JINGLE). ***Turkish Cypriot.*** **Turkish delight**: see DELIGHT *noun* 4. **Turkish music** MUSIC classical music involving the use of various percussion instruments as cymbals and triangle, introduced to western Europe in the 18th cent. ***Turkish rug***: see ***Turkish carpet*** above. **Turkish slipper** a soft heelless slipper with turned-up toe, a babouche. **Turkish tobacco** a strong dark variety of tobacco grown in eastern Europe. **Turkish towel**: made of cotton terry towelling. **Turkish trousers** baggy oriental pantaloons.
▶ **B** *noun.* **1** The Turkish language; *spec.* the western Turkic language which is the official language of Turkey. E17.
2 *ellipt.* The Turkish style; Turkish delight, coffee, tobacco, etc. L17.
■ **Turkishly** *adverb* in a Turkish way or manner E17. **Turkishness** *noun* Turkish quality or conduct; attraction to things Turkish: M16.

Turkism /ˈtɜːkɪz(ə)m/ *noun. rare.* L16.
[from TURK *noun*¹ + -ISM. Cf. earlier TURCISM.]
†**1** Islam. L16–M17.
2 Turkish principles, culture, etc. L19.

Turkize /ˈtɜːkʌɪz/ *verb.* Also **-ise.** L16.
[from TURK *noun*¹ + -IZE.]
1 *verb trans.* = TURKICIZE. L16.
2 *verb intrans.* Act like a Turk; formerly *spec.*, tyrannize over. Now *rare.* L16.

Turkman /ˈtɜːkmən/ *noun & adjective. rare.* L15.
[Partly from Persian *turkmān* (see TURKMEN); partly from TURK *noun*¹ + MAN *noun.* Cf. TURKOMAN.]
▶ **A** *noun.* **1** A Turkish person. L15.
2 = TURKMEN *noun* 1. Long *poet.* L17.
▶ **B** *attrib.* or as *adjective.* = TURKMEN *adjective.* L20.

Turkmen /ˈtɜːkmən/ *noun & adjective.* E20.
[(Persian *turkmān* from) Turkish *türkmen*, from *türk* Turk + *-man* prob. augm. suffix, also infl. by Russian *turkmen.* Cf. TURKOMAN.]
▶ **A** *noun.* Pl. **-s**, same.
1 A member of a group of Turkic peoples inhabiting the region east of the Caspian Sea and south of the Sea of Aral, now comprising Turkmenistan and parts of Iran and Afghanistan. E20.
2 The Turkic language of these peoples. M20.
▶ **B** *attrib.* or as *adjective.* Of or pertaining to the Turkmens, their language, or the region which they inhabit. E20.

Turko- *combining form* var. of TURCO-.

Turkoman /ˈtɜːkəʊmən/ *noun & adjective.* Also **Turc-.** E17.
[medieval Latin *Turcomannus*, French *turcoman*, from Persian *turkmān*: see TURKMEN. Cf. earlier TURKMAN.]
▶ **A** *noun.* Pl. **-s.**
1 = TURKMEN *noun* 1. E17.
2 = TURKMEN *noun* 2. L18.
3 A horse of Turkmen origin. M19.
4 A fabric resembling woven chenille. Also, = ***Turkoman carpet***, ***Turkoman rug*** below. L19.
▶ **B** *attrib.* or as *adjective.* = TURKMEN *adjective.* E17.
Turkoman carpet, **Turkoman rug**: soft and rich-coloured, made by Turkmens.

Turk's cap /ˈtɜːks ˈkap/ *noun phr.* L16.
[from TURK *noun*¹ + -'S¹ + CAP *noun*¹.]
†**1** The tulip. L16–E17.
2 Any of various lilies in which the perianth segments are rolled back; *spec.* (more fully ***Turk's cap lily***) the martagon lily, *Lilium martagon*, and the American swamp lily, *L. superbum.* L17.
3 A kind of cactus; = ***pope's head*** (a) s.v. POPE *noun*¹. M18.

Turk's head /ˈtɜːks ˈhɛd/ *noun phr.* L17.
[from TURK *noun*¹ + -'S¹ + HEAD *noun.*]
1 A kind of cactus; = ***pope's head*** (a) s.v. POPE *noun*¹. Chiefly *W. Indies.* L17.
2 NAUTICAL A knot made to form a stopper on the end of rope, resembling a turban in shape. M19.
3 A long-headed broom; = ***pope's head*** (b) s.v. POPE *noun*¹. M19.

turlough /ˈtʊələʊx/ *noun.* L17.
[Irish *turloch*, from *tur* dry + *loch* lake.]
In Ireland, a low-lying area on limestone which becomes flooded in wet weather through the welling up of groundwater from the rock.

Turlupin /ˈtɜːlʊpɪn/ *noun. rare.* M17.
[Old French from Latin *turlupinus*, of unkn. origin.]
Hist. A member of an extreme antinomian Christian sect of the 14th cent.

turm /tɜːm/ *noun.* Long *poet. rare.* L15.
[Old French *turme* or Latin *turma* troop, squadron.]
A body or band of people, esp. horsemen; *spec.* a troop of thirty or thirty-two horsemen.

turmeric /ˈtɜːmərɪk/ *noun.* Also (earlier) †**tarmaret** & other vars. LME.
[App. from French *terre mérite*, mod. Latin *terra merita* lit. 'deserving earth', perh. alt. of some oriental word: assim. to -IC.]
A pungent aromatic yellow powder used to flavour and colour curry powder and as the source of a yellow dye; the rhizome of a tropical Asian plant, *Curcuma longa*, of the ginger family, from which this is prepared. Also, the plant from which this is obtained.
Comb.: **turmeric paper** unsized paper tinged with a solution of turmeric, used as a test for alkalis.

turmoil /ˈtɜːmɔɪl/ *noun & verb.* E16.
[Origin unkn.]
▶ **A** *noun.* **1** A state of agitation or commotion; disturbance, tumult, trouble. E16.
†**2** Hard labour, toil. *rare.* M–L16.

> **1** J. GLASSCO My brain was in a turmoil of love and jealousy. M. FORSTER There was a war on and everything was in a state of turmoil.

▶ **B** *verb.* **1** *verb trans.* **a** Agitate, disturb; throw into commotion and confusion; trouble, worry, torment. Now *arch. rare.* E16. ▸**b** Disorder or distress physically. Now *arch. rare.* M16. ▸†**c** Drive or throw roughly or casually. L16–E17.

2 *verb intrans.* Be in turmoil, move agitatedly or restlessly. Now *arch. rare.* M16.

3 *verb intrans.* Toil, labour. Now *dial.* M16.

> **1a** J. CLAVELL Still turmoiled by his boundless joy at her reprieve. **2** D. DUNN Waves of the sea turmoil against the river's waters.

■ **turmoiler** *noun* (*rare*) a person who creates turmoil, a disturber L16.

turn /tə:n/ *noun.* ME.

[Partly from Anglo-Norman *t(o)urn* = Old French *torn* (mod. *tour*) from Latin *tornus* from Greek *tornos* lathe; partly from the verb. Cf. TOUR *noun*.]

▸**I** Rotation, and connected senses.

1 The action of turning about an axis; rotation. Now *rare.* ME.

2 An act of turning about an axis; a (total or partial) rotation or revolution. L15.

3 An object or apparatus (having a part) which turns or spins round; *spec.* (*a*) a watchmaker's lathe; (*b*) (*obsolete* exc. *dial.*) a spinning-wheel; (*c*) a revolving stand in a hatch. L15.

4 The gid. Also, an animal affected with this. Now *rare* or *obsolete.* E16.

5 The condition or manner of being twisted or convoluted; a single coil, twist, or whorl. M17.

6 An act of passing a rope etc. once round an object. M18.

7 MUSIC. A melodic ornament consisting of a group of three, four, or five notes, comprising the principal note and the note one degree above and/or below it. E19.

> **2** B. H. MALKIN Florence and her dowry . . were lost . . by a turn of the dice. J. RUSKIN In a few turns of the hands of the . . clock. **5** *Professional Photographer* The . . rings on the . . roller were made by applying a number of turns of masking tape.

▸**II** Change of direction or course, and connected senses.

8 An act or (*rare*) the action of turning aside from one's course; a deviation. ME.

9 An act of turning or facing another way; a change of direction. LME. ▸**b** CRICKET. The (intentional) deviation of a ball on pitching. E20.

10 A place at which a road, river, etc., changes direction; a bend; a turning. LME. ▸**b** The halfway point in a round of golf. L19.

11 †**a** A journey. LME–M18. ▸**b** = TOURN. *obsolete* exc. *Hist.* M17.

12 A short stroll or ride, esp. one following a circular route. L16.

13 The action or an act of changing, (an) alteration. Chiefly *spec.*, a change in circumstances or in the course of events, esp. for better or worse. L16. ▸**b** The transition period from one specified period of time to the next. Foll. by *of*. Chiefly in ***turn of the century***. M19.

14 An act of turning so as to face or go in the opposite direction; *spec.* a change of the tide from ebb to flow or from flow to ebb. M17. ▸**b** CARDS. The inversion of two cards in faro. M19.

15 PRINTING. Type turned wrong side up as a temporary substitute for a missing letter. *obsolete* exc. *Hist.* L19.

> **8** W. GREENER The woodcock . . its turn to right and left being most erratic. **9** G. J. WHYTE-MELVILLE The many turns and windings of his wearisome . . chase. **b** *Times* On a pitch giving slow turn there was no chance of Gloucestershire achieving this target. **10** P. D. JAMES Every turn . . of the overgrown garden path . . was so familiar. M. FORSTER The landing was gloomy on this turn of the stairs. **12** E. WHARTON She took a restless turn about the room. G. R. TURNER He took a turn round the lawns. **13** R. MACAULAY She felt aggrieved at the extraordinary turn things had taken. L. P. HARTLEY Her father's mental illness took a turn for the worse. J. CARTWRIGHT Life was taking a turn for the better. W. M. CLARKE The sudden turn in the autumn weather. **b** R. HOGGART Novels from . . the turn of the century. B. DUFFY The liberal tide . . sweeping Vienna at the turn of century. **14** H. WILLIAMSON The tide . . began to go out strongly at the turn. *Swimming Times* The men surfaced after the first turn.

▸**III** An action; a feeling.

16 A movement by a wrestler designed to achieve a fall. Long *obsolete* exc. *dial.* ME.

17 A trick, a wile, a stratagem. *obsolete* exc. *Scot. dial.* ME.

18 An act, a deed. Long only *spec.*, an act that does good or harm to another, a (*good*, *ill*, etc.) service. ME.

19 A spell of work; a task. Orig. *Scot.* Long *rare* exc. in ***do a hand's turn*** s.v. HAND *noun*. LME.

20 A spell or bout of activity. Now passing into sense 24. LME.

†**21** An event, an occurrence. (Not always distinguishable from sense 13.) L16–E18.

22 An attack of illness; *esp.* a momentary feeling of illness or nervous shock. M18.

> **18** W. SCHIRRA One turn I did for the . . team was to help perfect the spacesuit. B. PYM She had done Claudia a good turn in helping her to avoid somebody. **20** C. H. SPURGEON I like to see you run and I am glad to take a turn at it. **22** R. H. MORRIESON Having the sergeant with us . . must have given Mr Lynch a nasty turn. *New Yorker* When I looked again, there was no dog anywhere. Gave me quite a turn. S. TOWNSEND Mrs Harriman had a funny turn. N. LOWNDES He's had a bad turn and they've put him to bed.

▸**IV** Occasion, time.

†**23** The time at which something happens. Only in ME.

24 An opportunity or obligation to do something or to have something done, that comes successively to each of several persons or things. LME. ▸**b** A short performance on stage, *esp.* each of a number given by different performers in succession. E18. ▸**c** A period of work done by a group of people in succession, a shift. L18.

25 Requirement, need; purpose. *arch.* exc. in ***serve one's turn***, ***serve the turn*** s.v. SERVE *verb*[1]. L16.

> **24** C. CHAPLIN The basis of contention was . . whose turn it was to do the housework. G. GREENE He had to wait his turn at the counter. **b** F. FORSYTH The pair of them, standing on the threshold . . , looked like a comic turn. **c** *Daily Telegraph* A man doing a turn of 87 miles . . would get the . . drivers' basic rate.

▸**V** Abstract senses.

26 Character, style; *esp.* style of language; a variation or particular manner of linguistic expression, esp. for effect. Freq. in ***turn of phrase***. E17. ▸†**b** Form, mould, or cast of an object. E–M18.

27 Disposition; aptitude (usu. foll. by *for* or with specifying adjective). Formerly also, a characteristic. M17.

28 Direction, drift, trend. E18.

29 A particular construction or interpretation put upon an action, statement, etc. E18.

> **26** E. WHARTON The adroit feminine hand which should give the right turn to her correspondence. *Observer* He can take offence at the turn of a phrase. D. HOGAN Phineas became famous for his literary turn of phrase. **27** R. TRAVERS His religious turn of mind . . made him . . too serious for the other students. D. CECIL Humorous and with a turn for repartee. **28** J. COULTER I discovered what gave my thoughts a new turn. **29** J. AUSTEN You are giving it a turn which that gentleman did by no means intend.

▸**VI** Technical senses.

30 a A quantity of loose fish for sale. L17. ▸**b** A quantity or load of a commodity, esp. wood, being as much as can be carried by a person at one time. Chiefly *N. Amer.* L18.

31 COMMERCE. The difference between the buying and selling price of a stock; the profit made by this. M19.

Phrases: **at every turn** at every change of circumstance, at each new stage; continually. **by turns**, (*rare*) **by turn** one after another in regular succession; alternately. **call the turn** guess the order of the last three cards in the pack. ***do a hand's turn***: see HAND *noun*. ***do an ill turn to***: see ILL *adjective & adverb*. **done to a turn** cooked to exactly the right degree (orig. of a roast on a spit). **give a hare a turn** HUNTING (of a dog) make a hare veer off sharply in a different or the opposite direction. **in one's turn** when one's turn or opportunity comes. **in turn(s)** in due order of succession; successively, alternately. ***jump turn***: see JUMP *verb*. ***left turn***: see LEFT *adjective*. ***LODGING turn***. **on the turn** (*a*) changing; (*b*) (of food, esp. milk) going off; (*c*) at the turning point. **out of turn**, **out of one's turn** at a time when it is not one's turn; ***speak out of turn***, ***talk out of turn***, say more than one ought to say, speak inadvisedly or tactlessly. ***parallel turn***: see PARALLEL *adjective*. ***right turn***: see RIGHT *adjective*. ***round turn***: see ROUND *adjective*. ***serve one's turn***, ***serve the turn***: see SERVE *verb*[1]. **take it in turns** = ***take turns*** below. **take turns** act or work alternately or in succession. ***THREE-point turn***. **turn and turn about** alternately. ***turn of phrase***: see sense 26 above. ***turn of the century***: see sense 13b above. **turn of speed** ability to go fast when necessary. ***twists and turns***: see TWIST *noun*[1]. ***U-turn***: see U, U 2. ***walk a turn***: see WALK *verb*[1].

Comb.: **turns ratio** ELECTRICITY the ratio of the number of turns on the primary coil of a transformer to the number on the secondary, or vice versa.

turn /tə:n/ *verb.*

[Old English *tyrnan*, *turnian* from Latin *tornare* turn in a lathe, round off, from *tornus* lathe from Greek *tornos* lathe, circular movement; prob. reinforced from Old French *turner*, *torner* (mod. *tourner*), also from Latin.]

▸**I** Rotate, revolve; form or shape by rotation.

1 *verb trans. & intrans.* (Cause to) move round on an axis or about a centre; rotate, revolve. OE. ▸**b** *verb trans. & intrans.* (Cause to) move round or (esp.) partly round in this way, so as to open or close something. ME. ▸**c** *verb trans.* Perform (a somersault or cartwheel). M19.

2 *verb intrans.* Of time, life, etc.: revolve, whirl. Later esp. of the head: have a sensation as of whirling; be affected with giddiness; reel. OE.

3 *verb trans. & intrans.* Shape (wood, metal, etc., an object) esp. into a rounded form, by rotating it in a lathe against a cutting tool. ME. ▸**b** *verb trans.* Build (an arched or vaulted structure). E18. ▸**c** *verb trans.* KNITTING & LACE-MAKING. Shape (a curved part). L19.

4 *verb trans. gen.* Shape or form artistically or gracefully; *fig.* express elegantly, give an elegant form to (a composition etc.). E17.

5 *verb intrans.* Foll. by *on*, *upon*. ▸**a** Depend on, be determined by. M17. ▸**b** Be concerned with, involve, be about. E18.

> **1** W. COWPER Waters turning busy mills. G. GREENE He turned the heating wheel. A. CHRISTIE She turned the ring on her finger round and round. H. NORMAN A newly skinned beaver slowly turning over a fire. **b** KEATS The key turns, and the door upon its hinges groans. G. MANVILLE FENN She softly turned the handle of the door. J. MCGAHERN They'd . . place her in the wood. Quietly they'd turn the screws of the lid. **3** E. B. RAMSAY He . . taught us to saw, and to plane, and to turn. *Practical Woodworking* In turning these goblets I . . cut from the outside to the centre. **4** LEIGH HUNT The hand long, delicate, and well turned. J. UPDIKE Brief essays turned to oblige a friend. **5a** G. GREENE The whole story is made to turn on whether or not his hunt will be successful. D. FRASER The situation . . would . . ultimately turn on sea power. **b** T. HARDY The talk turned . . on the castle-competition.

▸**II** Change position or course.

6 a *verb intrans.* Change position by a rotary motion or movement through an angle. OE. ▸**b** Of a balance, or its beam: move up or down from the horizontal position. L16.

7 *verb trans.* Change the position of (an object, *arch.* oneself) by a rotary motion or movement through an angle. ME. ▸**b** *fig.* Consider (a matter) thoroughly; revolve *in the mind*. Now usu. foll. by *over*. E18. ▸**c** Twist (an ankle) out of position, esp. by landing awkwardly; sprain. M19.

8 *verb trans.* Give a curved or crooked form to; bend, twist; fold (now *rare* exc. in ***turn back***, ***turn down***, ***turn in***, ***turn up*** below); *spec.* bend back (a sharp edge) so as to make blunt or useless. ME. ▸**b** *verb intrans.* Of a sharp edge: become blunted by bending. L16.

9 *verb trans.* Change the course of; cause to take a new direction; divert, deflect. Now usu. foll. by *aside*. ME. ▸**b** *verb trans.* Check the course of. E17. ▸**c** *verb intrans. & trans.* CRICKET. Of a ball: change direction on pitching, break. Of a bowler or pitch: cause (a ball) to do this. L19.

10 *verb trans. fig.* Divert or deflect from a course of action, development, thought, etc. ME.

11 *verb trans.* **a** Transfer, hand over. Long *obsolete* exc. *dial.* ME. ▸**b** Cause (money or a commodity) to circulate. *arch.* E17.

12 *verb intrans.* Change course, so as to go in a different direction; deviate; (of the wind) shift. Usu. foll. by preposition. ME. ▸**b** NAUTICAL. Tack. M16. ▸**c** Of a road, line, etc.: bend, curve; branch off at an angle from a main road etc. M16.

13 *verb trans.* Alter one's course to get to the other side of, go round, (a corner etc.). L17. ▸**b** MILITARY. Pass round (an enemy's position, flank, etc.) so as to attack from the side or rear. M19. ▸**c** FOOTBALL etc. Get round (an opponent at close quarters) by forcing him or her to change direction. L20.

14 *verb trans.* Pass or get beyond (a specified age or time). E18.

> **6** SIR W. SCOTT Turning to the other side to enjoy his slumbers. TOLKIEN He lay tossing and turning and listening . . to the . . night-noises. **7** R. J. GRAVES He cannot be . . turned in bed, without having a tendency to faint. E. WELTY He had a small key . . and was turning it over and over in his fingers. **b** J. GALSWORTHY For the hundredth time . . he turned over this problem. K. ISHIGURO I watched them . . , turning over in my mind the news about Matsuda. **9** *Daily Telegraph* Miss Lansing smilingly turned aside all such speculation. **b** J. CLARE Spreading thorns that turn'd a summer shower. **10** E. M. FORSTER She turned the conversation to a less disturbing topic. J. MARQUAND No individual ever turned the stream of events from its course. **12** T. HARDY When they reached the turnpike-road she turned to the right. V. NABOKOV He turned into a side gallery. W. GOLDING He turned off what was already no major highway. A. DILLARD I turned down the row to my study. **13** LD MACAULAY Before Gama had turned the Cape. **14** R. LINDNER Soon after Mac had turned three he was taken to . . his grandfather's house. P. BAILEY I earned my first wages . . when I was just turned twelve.

▸**III** Reverse position or course.

15 *verb trans.* Reverse the position of; move so that the underside becomes the uppermost, or the back the front; invert; *spec.* (*a*) plough or dig (soil) so as to bring the under parts to the surface; (*b*) reverse (a page of a book) in order to read or write on the other side, or on the next page. ME. ▸**b** Alter or remake (a garment or esp. a sheet) by putting the worn outer side on the inside. L15. ▸**c** PRINTING. Set or print (a type or letter) upside down in letterpress printing, either accidentally or as a marker for a future change or correction to be made. Chiefly as TURNED *ppl adjective*. E18.

16 *verb trans.* Reverse the course of; cause to go in the opposite direction. Also foll. by *back*. ME.

17 *verb intrans.* Reverse one's or its course, begin to go in the opposite direction, (also foll. by *back*); *spec.* (of the tide) change from flood to ebb, or from ebb to flood. ME.

†**18** *verb intrans.* Go or come back. ME–L16. ▸**b** *verb trans.* Give or send back. L16–M17.

19 *verb trans.* Cause (the stomach) to be nauseated. M16. ▸**b** *verb intrans.* Of the stomach: be nauseated. E18.

📖 **15** C. M. Yonge He turned his horse, and was about to flee. J. Ruskin Her.. fine legerdemain in turning pancakes. S. Trott I prepared my vegetable garden.., fertilizing, turning the soil. B. Chatwin The girl was turning the leaves of an album. **b** Shakes. *Tam. Shr.* A pair of old breeches thrice turn'd. **16** J. Morley The man who turned the tide back. **17** *Times* Before the tide turned the water was.. rough in the Putney Reach. **19** A. Haley It turned his stomach to watch.. swine.. being butchered. **b** J. Gardner The smell of formaldehyde made his stomach turn.

▸**IV** Senses connected with II and III, with the direction or destination prominent.

20 a *verb trans.* Change the direction of; direct (esp. the eyes or face) another way. ME. ▸**b** *verb intrans.* & (*arch.*) *refl.* Change one's position so as to face in a different or the opposite direction. ME.

21 *verb trans. & intrans.* (Cause to) move so as to face or be directed towards or away from a specified (or implied) person or thing. ME. ▸†**b** *verb intrans.* Face (in a specified direction). *rare.* M16–E17.

22 *verb trans. & intrans.* (Cause to) go in a specified direction. Now chiefly of footsteps. ME.

23 *verb trans. fig.* Direct (one's thoughts, attention, etc.) *to* or *from*. ME.

24 *verb intrans.* & (now *rare*) *refl.* Direct one's thoughts, attention, etc., *to* or *from*; *spec.* (foll. by *to*) begin to consider or speak of something else. ME. ▸**b** *verb intrans.* Go *to* (a page, passage, etc., in a book) by turning the pages. M17. ▸**c** *verb intrans.* Apply oneself *to* or take up an occupation or pursuit. M17. ▸**d** *verb intrans.* Resort or have recourse *to*; appeal *to* for help etc. E19.

25 *verb trans.* †**a** Convert to or *to* a (different) religion. ME–L17. ▸**b** Induce or persuade (a person) to act as a spy or informer. M20.

26 *verb intrans.* **a** Adopt a different religion; be converted. *arch.* ME. ▸**b** Go over to another side or party. *arch.* ME. ▸**c** Become an informer. L20.

27 *verb trans.* Cause to recoil or have an adverse result *on*; use *against*. ME. ▸**b** *verb intrans.* Recoil or have an adverse result *on*. Now *rare* or *obsolete*. LME.

28 *verb trans.* Put *to* a specified use or purpose. ME. ▸**b** Set to work *on*. L18.

29 *verb intrans.* Become hostile towards (foll. by *against*, *on*, *upon*); attack (foll. by *on*, *upon*). LME. ▸**b** *verb trans.* Make hostile towards. Foll. by *against*. M19.

30 *verb trans.* Cause to go; send, drive. Usu. foll. by adverb. E16. ▸**b** Put or convey into a receptacle, esp. by inverting the containing vessel. L16.

📖 **20a** G. Greene She turned her head and stared in my direction. **b** G. Vidal I turned to go inside. Scott Fitzgerald She.. turned.. and sped back the way she had come. I. Murdoch Turning every now and then to look back at him. P. P. Read She.. smiled, turned and went down stairs. **21** E. Allen Others stand with their bodies turned away from the pitcher. G. Vidal Suddenly a spotlight was turned upon the stage. Lyndon B. Johnson I turned to John McCone and asked what his reports.. indicated. P. D. James Barbara Berowne turned on him her remarkable eyes. V. Glendinning Heads turned.. as he emerged from the lift. **23** J. Agee Never turning their attention from their work. A. J. Ayer Wittgenstein.. turned his attention to other pursuits. **24** M. Maartens She turned from the thought of scandal with impatience. C. P. Snow His thoughts turned to more cheerful themes. G. K. Wolfe Critics of fantasy would turn to myth as an appropriate narrative model. **b** K. S. Macquoid He took up a local paper and turned to the list of visitors. **d** A. Briggs She had to turn to Parliament for financial support. P. Mailloux Kafka's one close friend, the person he turned to in times of trouble. **27** T. Parks Two old disappointed people.. turning their frustrations on us. **b** G. Burnet The Dutch war had turned so fatally on the king. **28** Bacon Virgil, turning his pen to the advantage of his country. C. P. Snow He had foreseen the danger..: he had also forseen how to turn it to his own use. **29** M. Keane She could have turned on him and told him he didn't know what he was talking about. D. Athill I would suddenly turn against the very people who loved me. **b** D. G. Phillips 'You've turned him against me!' cried the girl. **30** F. Burney You will not.. turn me from your door. V. S. Reid He turns the goats and pigs into the open. **b** E. David When your spaghetti is ready,.. turn it into a big.. dish.

▸**V** Change, alter.

31 *verb trans. & intrans.* Change; make or become different; substitute (a thing) for something else of the same kind. Now *rare* exc. as in senses below. ME.

32 *verb trans. & intrans.* Foll. by *into*, *to*: change in nature, form, or condition; transform; convert. ME. ▸**b** *verb trans.* Translate *into* another language; put *into* another form of expression. Also, word differently. ME.

33 *verb intrans.* With adjective or noun compl.: become. ME. ▸**b** *verb trans.* With adjective or noun compl.: make, cause to become. *rare.* E17.

†**34** *verb intrans.* Foll. by *to*; lead to as a consequence; result in. ME–L18. ▸**b** *verb trans.* Result in trouble, harm, etc., for (a person). Foll. by *to*. ME–E17.

†**35** *verb trans.* Bring *into* a specified condition. LME–E17.

36 *verb trans.* Foll. by *into*, †*to*: make the subject of praise, mockery, etc. Now only in ***turn into ridicule***. LME.

37 a *verb trans.* Orig., curdle (milk). Later, cause (milk) to sour or go off. M16. ▸**b** *verb intrans.* Orig., curdle; later, (of food, esp. milk) go off. L16.

38 *verb intrans.* Of fruit, leaves, etc.: change colour. L16. ▸**b** *verb trans.* Change the colour of. L18.

📖 **31** Shakes. *Merch. V.* Some dear friend dead, else nothing.. Could turn so much the constitution Of any constant man. Pope Things change their titles, as our manners turn. M. Howard As soon as the weather turns they go down there. **32** E. M. Forster I turned the old kitchen into a hall. E. Waugh His anger softened and turned to shame. J. Barth Three of us turned into chronic alcoholics. R. J. Conley They can turn into owls or dogs or.. anything they want to. Anne Stevenson Fictional material suitable for turning into film scripts. **33** N. Shute The evening was turning chilly. H. McLeave Every time Lord Blye turned nasty.. her consumption of *petit fours*.. soared. I. Melchior Himmler had turned traitor! J. Barzun Georges Sorel, the engineer turned social theorist. H. Norman He's tall with hair that's turning grey. **b** Shakes. *Timon* It almost turns my dangerous nature mild. Pope That gay Free-thinker,.. What turns him now a stupid silent dunce? **34** Goldsmith Any general theory that shall turn to public benefit. **b** Shakes. *Coriol.* A word or two; The which shall turn you to no further harm. **37a** *fig.*: Defoe This.. turned the very blood within my veins. **b** L. Hellman The fish was turning,.. enough to make us carry it out to the street. W. Abish But there is milk. It's turned, Ulrich said. **38** M. Atwood It's.. September; the leaves are already turning.

Phrases: ***a worm will turn***: see WORM *noun*. **not know which way to turn**, **not know where to turn** be completely at a loss, be unsure how to act etc. ***not turn a hair***: see HAIR *noun*. ***turn a blind eye (to)***: see BLIND *adjective*. ***turn a deaf ear (to)***: see DEAF *adjective* 3. ***turn an honest penny***: see HONEST *adjective*. **turn a person's head**, **turn a person's brain** make a person conceited or mad. **turn a profit** *N. Amer.* make a profit. **turn bridle** turn one's horse and ride back. ***turn cat in pan***: see CAT *noun*[1]. **turn colour** (now *rare*) change colour; (of a person) become pale or red in the face. ***turn geese into swans***: see GOOSE *noun*. ***turn in one's grave***: see GRAVE *noun*[1] 1. ***turn inside out***: see INSIDE *noun* 2. ***turn into ridicule***: see sense 36 above. **turn loose** (*a*) set free (an animal) and allow to go where it will; *transf.* allow (a person) to go where, or do as, he or she will; (*b*) *US dial.* let go (of). **turn on a sixpence**, (*N. Amer.*) **turn on a dime** (of a motor vehicle) make a sharp turning, turn within a narrow radius, have a small turning-circle. ***turn one's back on***: see BACK *noun*[1]. ***turn one's coat***: see COAT *noun* 1. ***turn one's face to the wall***: see WALL *noun*[1]. ***turn one's girdle***: see GIRDLE *noun*[1] 1. ***turn one's hand to***: see HAND *noun*. ***turn on one's heel***: see HEEL *noun*[1]. ***turn on the heat***: see HEAT *noun* 15. ***turn over a new leaf***: see LEAF *noun*[1] 6. ***turn round one's finger***, ***turn round one's little finger***: see FINGER *noun*. ***turn sides to middle***: see SIDE *noun*. ***turn tail***: see TAIL *noun*[1]. ***turn the cat in the pan***: see CAT *noun*[1]. ***turn the corner***: see CORNER *noun* 2. ***turn the other cheek***: see CHEEK *noun*. ***turn the scale(s)***: see SCALE *noun*[1]. ***turn the screw(s)***: see SCREW *noun*[1]. ***turn the tables (on)***: see TABLE *noun*. **turn the tide** *fig.* reverse the trend of events. ***turn the trick***: see TRICK *noun*. ***turn to account***: see ***turn to good account*** below. ***turn to ashes***: see ASH *noun*[2]. **turn to good account**, **turn to account** make use of for one's profit or advantage. ***turn Turk***: see TURK *noun*[1]. ***turn turtle***: see TURTLE *noun*[2] 1. ***turn up one's nose at***: see NOSE *noun*. ***turn up one's toes***: see TOE *noun*. ***turn up trumps***: see TRUMP *noun*[2].

With adverbs in specialized senses: (See also Phrases above.) **turn about** †(*a*) rotate, revolve; (*b*) move so as to face or go in the opposite direction. **turn again** (*a*) (long *arch.*) face round the other way; †(*b*) return; go back; *fig.* revert. **turn around** (chiefly *N. Amer.*) = ***turn round*** below. **turn away** (*a*) turn to face another direction, avert (one's face); (*b*) divert, avert; (*c*) send away, dismiss; (*d*) refuse to accept, reject. **turn back** (*a*) (*obsolete* exc. *US*) send or give back; (*b*) come or go back; (*c*) fold back; (see also senses 16, 17 above). **turn down** (*a*) fold or bend down; *transf.* fold back the sheets etc. of (a bed); (*b*) admit of being folded down; (*c*) turn upside down, invert; (*d*) (*obsolete* exc. *US*) put down to a lower position in a class; (*e*) reject (a proposal, application, etc.); (*f*) put (game etc.) in a place to increase stocks; (*g*) reduce the volume of sound from (a radio etc.), or the intensity of heat or light from (a heater, cooker, lamp, etc.), by means of a knob; reduce the volume of (sound) or the intensity of (heat or light) in this way; reduce the temperature at which (food) is being cooked; (*h*) (of economic activity) decline, worsen. **turn in** (*a*) hand in or over; (*b*) give or produce (a performance or result of a specified kind); (*c*) *colloq.* abandon (a plan etc.); (*d*) AGRICULTURE dig or plough (weeds, manure, etc.) into the ground; (*e*) fold or bend inwards; (*f*) (cause to) point inwards; (*g*) *colloq.* (orig. NAUTICAL) go to bed in the evening. **turn off** (*a*) dismiss, *spec.* from employment; *Austral.* send (livestock) to market; (*b*) *slang* hang on a gallows; *joc.* marry; (*c*) deflect, divert; *spec.* divert attention from; (*d*) leave a main road or route to take a side-road etc.; (of a side-road) lead off from another road; (*e*) stop the flow of (water, gas, electricity, etc.) by means of a tap, switch, etc.; stop the operation of (an electrical device etc.) in this way; operate (a tap, switch, etc.) to achieve this; (*f*) *colloq.* repel; cause to lose interest; (*g*) = ***turn out*** (*e*) below; (*h*) (now *dial.*) (of food) go off; (*i*) *arch.* become. **turn on** (*a*) start the flow of (water, gas, electricity, etc.) by means of a tap, switch, etc.; start the operation of (an electrical device etc.) in this way; operate (a tap, switch, etc.) to achieve this; ***turn it on***, make a particular effort, esp. to be charming; (*b*) *colloq.* excite, interest; *esp.* arouse sexually; (*c*) *slang* intoxicate with or introduce to drugs; (*d*) *slang* become intoxicated with drugs; (foll. by *to*) become interested in. **turn out** (*a*) cause to go or come out; expel; MILITARY call (a guard) from the guardroom; (*b*) put (an animal) out to pasture or into the open; (*c*) empty out (the contents of a receptacle, room, etc.); clear out (a room etc.); empty (a pocket) to see the contents; (*d*) extinguish (an electric light etc.) by means of a switch etc.; (*e*) produce or manufacture, esp. rapidly; (*f*) dress, equip; (*g*) go or come out; *esp.* (of a crowd etc.) assemble, attend a meeting etc.; (*h*) *colloq.* get out of bed; †(*i*) *Austral. slang* become a bush-ranger; (*j*) (foll. by noun or adjective compl., *that*, *to be*) prove to be, result; (*k*) (cause to) point outwards. **turn out of** (*a*) expel or eject from; (*b*) empty out of (a vessel) by inverting it; (*c*) get out of. **turn over** (*a*) turn on to one side, or from one side to the other, or upside down; bring the under or reverse side (of) into view; (*b*) (cause to) fall over; (*c*) (of an engine etc.) start running; (*d*) cause (an engine etc.) to start running; (*e*) transfer the care of (a person or thing) *to*; *spec.* (*arch.*) transfer (an apprentice) to another master; (*f*) COMMERCE invest and realize; do business to the amount of; (*g*) *slang* ransack; (*h*) *colloq.* upset; affect with nausea; (*i*) PRINTING carry over (a letter, part of a word, etc.) to the next line; (*j*) N. AMER. SPORT lose possession of (the ball) to the opposing team; (*k*) *arch.* hang on a gallows; (see also sense 7b). **turn round** (*a*) (cause to) revolve on an axis or centre; (*b*) turn so as to face in the opposite direction; (*c*) *fig.* change to the opposite opinion etc.; (*d*) COMMERCE unload and reload (a ship, vehicle, etc.); (*e*) receive, process, and send out again; cause to progress through a system. **turn to** set to work. **turn up** (*a*) (cause to) point or bend upwards; (*b*) *arch.* turn upside down, invert; (*c*) increase the width of (a hem); shorten (a garment, or part of a garment) by increasing the width of the hem or by making a hem; (*d*) dig or plough (soil etc.) so as to bring the under parts to the surface; bring (something buried) to the surface by digging etc.; (*e*) turn (a card) face upwards; (*f*) *arch.* look up or refer to (a passage, book, etc.); (*g*) *colloq.* cause to gag or vomit; (*h*) increase the volume of sound from (a radio etc.), or the intensity of heat or light from (a heater, cooker, lamp, etc.), by means of a knob; increase the volume of (sound) or intensity of (heat or light) in this way; increase the temperature at which (food) is being cooked; (*i*) (now *slang*) set free, release; (*j*) (now *slang*) give up, renounce; (*k*) NAUTICAL summon (the crew) on deck; (*l*) NAUTICAL tack; (*m*) happen; present itself casually or unexpectedly; (of a person) put in an appearance, arrive; (*n*) be found; (*o*) discover, reveal; (*p*) (with compl.) produce, result in; †(*q*) be a prostitute.

With prepositions in specialized senses: **turn after** take after, resemble.

Comb.: **turnagain** †(*a*) a revolution; a deviation; (*b*) *rare* = ANTISTROPHE 2; **turn-and-bank**, **turn-and-slip** *adjectives & nouns* (AERONAUTICS) (designating) an indicator which shows a pilot the rate of turn and margin of error in banking; **turnaround** (chiefly *N. Amer.*) (*a*) = ***turn-round*** below; (*b*) a space for vehicles to turn round in, esp. at the end of a drive etc.; (*c*) a point in a team game at which the teams change ends; **turnaway** *noun & adjective* (*a*) *noun* the action or an act of turning away or deviating from a course etc.; (*b*) *adjective* (of a crowd) so large that part of it has to be turned away; **turn-beam** the drum of a windlass; **turn-bench** a watchmaker's portable lathe; **turn-bolt** a rotating bolt; **turn-bridge** a swing-bridge; **turnbroach** *arch.* a person employed to turn a spit, a turnspit; **turn-buckle** (*a*) a thin flat bar which pivots into a groove to fasten a window, shutter, etc.; (*b*) a device for tightly connecting parts of a metal rod or for coupling electric wires; (*c*) NAUTICAL a screw used for tightening rigging; **turn-button** a small pivoting bar on a frame etc., keeping something in place but allowing easy removal; **turn-cap** a revolving chimney top; **turncock** †(*a*) a stop-cock; (*b*) *Hist.* an official responsible for turning on the water from the mains to supply-pipes etc.; **turn-crowned** *adjective* (of a domestic pigeon) having the feathers on the crown reversed; **turn-furrow** the mould-board of a plough; **turn-in** (*a*) an edge of material that is folded inwards; *spec.* the part of a book's binding which shows along the edges of the inside covers; (*b*) an entrance, a drive; **turn indicator** (*a*) AERONAUTICS a device which indicates whether an aircraft is deviating from a straight course; (*b*) = INDICATOR 3c; **turn-mark** a buoy or boat round which yachts turn in racing; **turn-on** (*a*) the action or an act of causing something to start operation; (*b*) *colloq.* a person who or thing which causes (esp. sexual) arousal; **turn-pin** (*a*) a pivot; (*b*) a conical plug for stopping or enlarging the end of a pipe; **turn-plough** a plough with a mould-board; **turn-round** (*a*) the process of unloading and reloading a ship, vehicle, etc.; the time taken for this; (*b*) the process of receiving, processing, and sending out again; progress through a system; (*c*) the reversal of an opinion, trend, etc.; **turn-row** *US* a space at the side of a field where horses turn in ploughing, used as a path; **turn-screw** a screwdriver; **turn signal** *N. Amer.* = INDICATOR 3c; **turntable** (*a*) a circular revolving platform laid with rails connecting with adjacent tracks, for turning a railway locomotive or other vehicle; (*b*) a circular revolving plate on which a gramophone record is placed to be played; the unit housing this plate; (*c*) any similar revolving platform or stand; **turn-to** a tussle, a set-to; **turn-tree** = ***turn-beam*** above; **turn-under** the curving in of a carriage-body towards the bottom; **turnwrest plough**: in which the mould-board may be shifted from one side to the other at the end of each furrow, so that the furrow-slice is always thrown the same way.

■ **turnable** *adjective* (*rare*) able to be turned L15.

turnabout /ˈtəːnəbaʊt/ *noun.* L16.

[from ***turn about*** s.v. TURN *verb*.]

†**1** *The* gid. L16–E17.

†**2** An innovator. Only in M17.

3 A merry-go-round. *US.* L18.

4 A change or reversal of direction; *fig.* an abrupt change of opinion, policy, etc. M19.

5 A small steamer built so as to be able to turn quickly. *rare.* L19.

turnback /ˈtəːnbak/ *noun & adjective.* M19.

[from ***turn back*** s.v. TURN *verb*.]

▸**A** *noun.* **1** A part of a garment etc. which is folded back. M19.

2 The return of something borrowed or rented. M20.

▸**B** *attrib.* or as *adjective.* Esp. of a cuff: folded back. L19.

turncoat /ˈtəːnkəʊt/ *noun, adjective, & verb.* M16.
[from TURN *verb* + COAT *noun.*]
▶ **A** *noun.* **1** A person who changes sides in a conflict, dispute, etc. M16.
†**2** *transf.* Something that changes in appearance or colour. M16–E17.
▶ **B** *adjective.* Of, pertaining to, or that is a turncoat. L16.
▶ **C** *verb intrans.* Change sides in a conflict, dispute, etc. E17.

turn-down /ˈtəːndaʊn/ *adjective & noun.* M19.
[from *turn down* s.v. TURN *verb.*]
▶ **A** *adjective.* Esp. of a collar: that may be turned down. M19.
▶ **B** *noun.* **1** A part of something, esp. a garment, which is turned down. M19.
2 A rejection; a refusal. E20. ▸**b** A person who is rejected, esp. as unfit for military service. *US.* M20.
3 A downturn. M20.

turned /təːnd/ *ppl adjective.* ME.
[from TURN *verb* + -ED¹.]
†**1** Opposite, contrary. *rare.* Only in ME.
2 That has turned; that has been turned. Also foll. by adverb. LME.
†**3** Of a person, the mind, etc.: naturally adapted or suited to a specified occupation. Foll. by *for, to.* L17–M18.
4 Of a person: having a nature or disposition of a specified kind. *US colloq.* M20.

🕮 **2** E. PAUL Her legs were . . well turned below the knees. CLIVE JAMES Elegantly turned-out gentlemen . . on the esplanade. R. SCRUTON A little table-lamp of turned mahogany. S. HILL The . . turned-back covers of the . . bed. A. LEE A nurse with a turned-up nose. **3** SWIFT By nature turn'd to play the rake.

turnel /ˈtəːn(ə)l/ *noun. obsolete* exc. *dial.* L17.
[Origin unkn.]
A tub, esp. a shallow oval one.

turner /ˈtəːnə/ *noun*¹. ME.
[Old French *tornere, torneor* from late Latin *tornator,* from *tornare*: see TURN *verb,* -ER².]
▶ **I 1** A person who or thing which turns; *spec.* a person who turns wood etc. on a lathe; a potter, *esp.* one who finishes and smooths the ware before firing. ME.
†**2** (A bird of) a variety of domestic pigeon with a curved crest. L17–M18.
3 A seal between the immature and mature stages of development. *Canad. dial.* L19.
▶ **II** [German, from *turnen* perform gymnastic exercises from French *tourner.*]
4 *Hist.* A member of any of the gymnastic societies founded in Germany by F. L. Jahn (1778–1852). M19.

turner /ˈtəːnə/ *noun*². M17.
[Perh. alt. of TOURNOIS.]
Hist. = BODLE.

Turner /ˈtəːnə/ *noun*³. M19.
[from the surname *Turner* (see below).]
1 [James *Turner* (fl. 1781), English colour-maker.] Used *attrib.* and in *possess.* to designate a mineral yellow pigment (oxychloride of lead) patented by Turner. Now chiefly *Hist.* M19.
2 MEDICINE. [Henry Hubert *Turner* (1892–1970), US physician.] Used in *possess.* and (occas.) *attrib.* to designate a congenital syndrome affecting females in which the cells contain only one instead of two X chromosomes, characterized by developmental abnormalities including absence of ovaries, webbing of the neck, and shortness of stature. Also *ellipt.* as ***Turner's.*** M20.

Turneresque /təːnəˈrɛsk/ *adjective.* M19.
[from *Turner* (see below) + -ESQUE.]
Characteristic of the pictures of the English landscape painter Joseph Mallord William Turner (1775–1851).
■ **Turnerian** /təːˈnɪərɪən/ *adjective* = TURNERESQUE M19. ˈ**Turnerism** *noun* the style or school of Turner M19.

turnerite /ˈtəːnərʌɪt/ *noun.* E19.
[from Edward *Turner* (1798–1837), English chemist and mineralogist + -ITE¹.]
MINERALOGY. A variety of monazite occurring as golden crystals esp. associated with quartz.

turnery /ˈtəːn(ə)ri/ *noun.* M17.
[from TURNER *noun*¹ + -Y³.]
1 The art of the turner; the making of objects on a lathe. M17.
2 Orig., an object made on a lathe. Now *collect.,* objects made on a lathe. M17.
3 A turner's workshop. M19.

turning /ˈtəːnɪŋ/ *noun.* ME.
[from TURN *verb* + -ING¹.]
1 The action of TURN *verb*; an instance of this. Also foll. by adverb. ME.
2 *spec.* The use, or art of using, a lathe. LME. ▸**b** In *pl.* Chips or shavings from a lathe. E19.
3 A place where a road etc. turns or turns off; *esp.* a road that branches off another. LME.
4 A part of something folded over, a fold. M17.
5 A row of hay turned with a rake. *local.* L18.

🕮 **1** R. FRAME After a number of wrong turnings they found their bearings. *attrib.*: *Do-It-Yourself* Create a turning area so that you can drive in and out forwards. **2** *Practical Householder* For . . creative delight, few aspects of woodworking compare with turning.

Comb.: **turning-circle** the smallest circle within which a ship, motor vehicle, etc., can turn without reversing; ***turning-lathe***: see LATHE *noun*³ 1; **turning-mill** a horizontal lathe; **turning-pin** = *turn-pin* (a) s.v. TURN *verb*; **turning radius** the radius of a turning-circle; **turning-saw**: with a narrow blade for cutting a curve.

turning-point /ˈtəːnɪŋpɔɪnt/ *noun.* M19.
[from prec. + POINT *noun*¹.]
1 A point at which something turns or changes direction. M19.
2 *fig.* A point at which a decisive or important change takes place. M19.
3 SURVEYING. Each of the points from which readings are taken for successive positions of the level. M19.

🕮 **2** M. C. SMITH The siege of Leningrad was one of the . . turning points in human history. R. K. NARAYAN It . . could be a turning point in my career.

turnip /ˈtəːnɪp/ *noun & verb.* M16.
[from unkn. 1st elem. + NEEP. Cf. PARSNIP.]
▶ **A** *noun.* **1** The usu. white globular 'root' (the swollen hypocotyl) of a yellow-flowered cruciferous plant, *Brassica rapa,* long cultivated as a vegetable and as cattle-feed; the plant from which this is obtained. Also (with specifying word), (the similarly swollen edible part of) any of several other brassicas or plants of other families. M16.
2 A large thick old-fashioned watch. *arch. slang.* M19.
3 A dull stupid person. *colloq.* M19.
1 ***French turnip, Hungarian turnip, Indian turnip, prairie turnip, Swedish turnip,*** etc. ***get blood from a turnip, get blood out of a turnip***: see BLOOD *noun.*
Comb.: **turnip-cabbage** *arch.* = KOHLRABI; **turnip-flea, turnip flea-beetle** a minute shiny black jumping beetle of the genus *Phyllotreta,* which feeds on leaves of the turnip and other crucifers; **turnip-fly** (*a*) = *turnip-flea* above; (*b*) = *turnip sawfly* below; **turnip-ghost** a simulated ghost, with the head made from a turnip-lantern; **turnip greens** = *turnip-tops* below; **turnip-lantern** a hollowed-out turnip with holes cut in the side, used as a lantern esp. at Hallowe'en; **turnip moth** a noctuid moth, *Agrotis segetum,* whose caterpillar, the common cutworm, is a pest of root vegetables; **turnip sawfly** a sawfly, *Athalia rosae,* whose larvae feed on turnips; **turnip-tops** the leaves of a turnip eaten as a vegetable; **turnip-wood** any of several Australian timbers which smell like turnips when fresh, *esp.* that of *Dysoxylum mollissimum* (family Meliaceae).
▶ **B** *verb trans. rare.* Infl. **-p(p)-**.
1 Plant (land) with turnips. L18.
2 Feed or fatten (sheep) on turnips. L18.
■ **turniˈpology** *noun* (*derog., rare*) phrenology E19. **turnipy** *adjective* of or pertaining to a turnip or turnips; resembling (that of) a turnip: L18.

turnkey /ˈtəːnkiː/ *noun & adjective.* M17.
[from TURN *verb* + KEY *noun*¹.]
▶ **A** *noun.* **1** A jailer, *esp.* a subordinate one. M17.
†**2** A burglar's implement for turning from the outside a key left in a door. Also, an instrument for extracting teeth. Only in 19.
▶ **B** *adjective.* Of a contract etc.: providing for the supply of equipment etc. in a state ready for immediate use. M20.

turn-off /ˈtəːnɒf/ *adjective & noun.* L17.
[from *turn off* s.v. TURN *verb.*]
▶†**A** *adjective.* That turns or screws off. Only in L17.
▶ **B** *noun.* **1** A turning off a main road. L19.
2 The quantity of a finished product that is sold off; *spec.* the quantity of livestock sent to market; the sending of livestock to market. L19.
3 The action or an act of causing something to cease operation. M20.
4 A thing that repels a person or causes a loss of interest. *colloq.* L20.

🕮 **1** A. COOKE I drove along Sunset Boulevard . . and watched for the turn-off into North La Brea. M. WESLEY At the turn-off from the motorway she stopped. **2** *Meat Trades Journal* A disruption of livestock turn-off caused by wet weather. **3** *Globe & Mail (Toronto)* 'It's inconvenient . . ,' she said of the electricity turnoffs. **4** S. KITZINGER Chilblains or indigestion can . . be a turn-off. *Independent* The biggest turn-off for . . investment.

turnout /ˈtəːnaʊt/ *noun.* Also **turn-out**. L17.
[from *turn out* s.v. TURN *verb.*]
1 An act of turning or getting out; *spec.* a call to duty. L17.
2 A strike by a group of workers; a striker. *arch.* E19.
3 The number of people attending a meeting, voting in an election, etc. E19.
4 A siding in a railway; a passing place in a narrow road or canal. E19.
5 Style of equipment or outfit; a set of equipment, an outfit; *esp.* a carriage with its horse or horses, and other equipment. E19.
6 A clear-out. M19.
7 A place where animals may be turned out to graze. L19.
8 The quantity of goods produced in a given time; output. L19.

🕮 **1** R. CROMPTON William . . watched a practice 'turn out' at the fire station. **3** *Times* Council election turnouts rose . . in 1979. E. SEGAL There were always great turnouts for the school's athletic events. **5** G. STEIN Jem . . had a swell turn-out to drive in. *Your Horse* The turn-out and condition of the animals. A. POWELL An unsatisfactory boy . . , slovenly turnout, lack of cleanliness. **6** A. CHRISTIE We'll have a turn-out . . and throw most of those things away.

turnover /ˈtəːnəʊvə/ *noun & adjective.* Also **turn-over**. E17.
[from *turn over* s.v. TURN *verb.*]
▶ **A** *noun.* **1** (A part of) something which is turned or folded over, as the flap of an envelope, a leaf of a book, etc.; *spec.* a turn-down collar or neckband. E17. ▸**b** JOURNALISM. An article beginning in the last column of a page and continuing overleaf. L19. ▸**c** PRINTING. The last (usu. short) line of a paragraph; the part of a divided word carried over to the next line. M20.
2 The action or an act of turning over. M17. ▸**b** A break in play at the end of a side of a record. M20.
3 An apprentice whose indentures are transferred to another master on the retirement or failure of his original one. *arch.* M17.
4 A kind of sweet pastry made by folding a piece of pastry over on to itself, so as to enclose a (usu. fruit) filling. L18.
5 The total amount of money taken by a given time; the amount of goods produced and disposed of by a manufacturer; *transf.* the amount or number of anything dealt with, processed, etc. L19. ▸**b** The simultaneous synthesis and degradation of a substance in a living organism. M20. ▸**c** The number of employees joining and leaving a workforce. M20.
6 US SPORT. Loss of possession of the ball to the opposing team. M20.

🕮 **2** R. KIPLING Reversing into a following gale . . there is always risk of a turn-over. P. INCHBALD This address would be worth a turnover in connection with the . . burglary. **5** G. B. SHAW The sixpenny doctor, with his . . quick turnover of patients. P. FITZGERALD Paperbacks . . would have a rapid turnover. *Rail* These . . services . . produce an annual turnover of £45 million.

▶ **B** *adjective.* That turns or is turned over; having a part that is turned over. E17.

🕮 *Rugby World* Nylon socks in plain colours and turn-over tops.

Special collocations: **turnover article** = sense A.1b above. **turnover board** FOUNDING a flat board on which a flat-bottomed pattern stands while sand is packed round it. **turnover cartridge** a gramophone cartridge with a pivoted mounting for two styluses for use at different speeds.

turnpike /ˈtəːnpʌɪk/ *noun & verb.* LME.
[from TURN *verb* + PIKE *noun*¹.]
▶ **A** *noun.* **I 1** *Hist.* A spiked barrier fixed in or across a road or passage, as a defence against sudden attack. LME.
†**2** A turnstile. M16–M18.
†**3** A barrier across a stream allowing the water to flow, but obstructing cattle. Also, a lock on a navigable stream. E17–M18.
4 *Hist.* **a** A toll-gate. L17. ▸**b** A trust or committee responsible for the maintenance of a turnpike. Also ***turnpike trust.*** E18.
5 a *Hist.* A road on which a toll was collected at a toll-gate. Also ***turnpike road.*** M18. ▸**b** A motorway on which a toll is charged. *US.* M20.
6 A small cake used to raise bread. *US local.* M19.
▶ **II 7** A spiral staircase. *Scot.* E16.
Comb.: **turnpike gate** = sense 4a above; ***turnpike road***: see sense 5a above; **turnpike sailor** *arch.* a beggar in the guise of a distressed sailor; ***turnpike trust***: see sense 4b above.
▶ **B** *verb trans.* Erect turnpikes on (a road). L18.
■ **turnpiker** *noun* (*a*) a foot-traveller; (*b*) *arch.* = ***turnpike sailor*** above: E19.

turnsick /ˈtəːnsɪk/ *adjective & noun.* LME.
[from TURN *verb* + SICK *adjective.*]
▶†**A** *adjective.* Affected with vertigo; dizzy. LME–M17.
▶ **B** *noun.* †**1** Vertigo, dizziness. LME–L16.
2 A disease of domestic animals characterized by turning motions; *esp.* the gid. *dial.* M19.

turnsole /ˈtəːnsəʊl/ *noun.* Also **tournesol** /ˈtʊənsɒl/. LME.
[Old French *tournesole* (mod. *tournesol*) from Italian *tornasole* or Spanish *tornasol,* from Latin *tornare* TURN *verb* + *sol* sun.]
1 A violet-blue or purple substance obtained from the plant *Chrozophora tinctoria* (see sense 2) formerly much used for colouring jellies, confectionery, wines, etc., and as a pigment. LME. ▸**b** [app. by confusion in French.] = LITMUS. Now *rare* or *obsolete.* M19.

2 A plant whose flowers follow the sun or open and shut with the sun's motions; *esp.* (***a***) a Mediterranean plant of the spurge family, *Chrozophora tinctoria*, cultivated in the south of France for its colouring juice (see sense 1); (***b***) a heliotrope, esp. *Heliotropium europaeum*; †(***c***) the sunflower, *Helianthus annuus*. **L16.**

turnspit /ˈtəːnspɪt/ *noun.* **L16.**
[from **TURN** *verb* + **SPIT** *noun*[1].]
1 *Hist.* A dog kept to turn a roasting-spit by running on a treadmill connected with it; a servant whose job was to turn a roasting-spit. **L16.**
2 A roasting-jack (see **JACK** *noun*[1] 5). *rare.* **E17.**

turnstile /ˈtəːnstʌɪl/ *noun.* **LME.**
[from **TURN** *verb* + **STILE** *noun*[1].]
A gate for admission or exit, consisting of horizontally revolving arms fixed to a vertical post, orig. to prevent passage by riders etc., now to allow people on foot to pass through one by one.

turnstone /ˈtəːnstəʊn/ *noun.* **L17.**
[from **TURN** *verb* + **STONE** *noun*.]
A small widely distributed shore-bird with a short bill, *Arenaria interpres*, which turns over stones and seaweed to feed on small invertebrates found underneath. Also ***common turnstone***.
black turnstone a similar bird, *Arenaria melanocephala*, of Alaska and the western US. ***ruddy turnstone***: see **RUDDY** *adjective*.

turn-up /ˈtəːnʌp/ *noun & adjective.* **E17.**
[from ***turn up*** s.v. **TURN** *verb*.]
▶ **A** *noun.* †**1** A prostitute. *rare.* Only in **E17.**
2 A turned up part of something, esp. of a garment; *spec.* the lower turned up end of a trouser leg. **L17.**
3 The turning up of a particular card or die in a game; the card or die turned up. Now chiefly *fig.* (*colloq.*), an unexpected (esp. welcome) result or happening; a surprise. **E19.**
4 Orig. *spec.*, a boxing contest. Later *gen.*, a fight, a tussle; a row. *colloq.* **E19.**
5 The curve of the projecting lower jaw of a bulldog. **E20.**

> 🕮 **2** B. Malamud The trousers a little frayed at the turn-ups. **3** R. Pilcher 'I think it's . . very kind of you.' 'Well, that's a turn-up for the books; we thought you'd be livid.' *Autosport* I'm surprised to be . . in such a healthy championship position—it's a real turn-up. **4** J. B. Priestley We had a noisy and inconclusive turn-up . . at a production meeting.

▶ **B** *adjective.* That is turned up or turns up. **L17.**

turnverein /ˈtəːnvərʌɪn, -nfə-/ *noun.* **M19.**
[German, from *turnen* do gymnastic exercises + *Verein* society, club.]
In the US, a gymnastics club, orig. for German immigrants, on the model of those founded by Jahn (see **TURNER** *noun*[1] 4).

turpentine /ˈtəːp(ə)ntʌɪn/ *noun & verb.* **ME.**
[Old French *ter(e)bentine* from Latin *ter(e)benthina* (sc. *resina* resin), from *terebinthus* **TEREBINTH**: see **-INE**[1].]
▶ **A** *noun.* **1** Orig. (more fully ***Chian turpentine***) the sticky fragrant resin of the terebinth tree (see sense 2). Now (more fully ***crude turpentine***, ***gum turpentine***, ***turpentine gum***), any of various viscous oleoresins which exude from coniferous trees, esp. pines, and can be distilled to yield gum rosin and oil of turpentine. Freq. with specifying word. **ME.**
2 †**a** The fruit of the terebinth tree. Only in **M16.** ▸**b** The terebinth tree, *Pistacia terebinthus*; the related *P. palaestina*; any of various conifers and other trees yielding turpentine or a similar resin; *Austral.* the tree *Syncarpia glomulifera*, of the myrtle family. **L16.**
3 In full ***oil of turpentine***, ***spirits of turpentine***. A volatile essential oil with a pungent odour, obtained by the distillation of gum turpentine or pine wood, consisting chiefly of α-pinene and diterpene, and used chiefly as a solvent and paint thinner, and in medical liniments. Cf. **TURPS.** **L16.**
1 ***Strasbourg turpentine***, ***Venice turpentine***, etc.
Comb.: **turpentine beetle** a N. American scolytid beetle, *Dendroctonus valens*, which burrows under the bark of pines etc.; ***turpentine gum***: see sense 1 above; **turpentine oil** = sense 3 above; **Turpentine State** *US* the State of North Carolina; **turpentine still** an apparatus for distilling oil of turpentine from pine wood or crude turpentine; **turpentine substitute** any of various paint and varnish thinners derived from petroleum; **turpentine-tree** = sense 2b above; **turpentine weed** any of several plants exuding a resinous sap; *esp.* the prairie dock, *Silphium terebenthinaceum*.
▶ **B** *verb trans.* Treat with turpentine, apply turpentine to. **M18.**
■ **turpentiny** *adjective* covered with or containing turpentine, resembling turpentine in smell etc. **M18.**

turpeth /ˈtəːpɪθ/ *noun.* Also †**turbith**. **LME.**
[medieval Latin *turbit(h)um*, *turpetum*, from Persian *turbid* from Sanskrit *triputā*.]
1 A cathartic drug prepared from the root of a climbing plant of the Old World tropics, *Operculina turpethum*, of the bindweed family; the plant from which this is obtained. **LME.**
2 In full ***turpeth mineral***. Mercurous sulphate, Hg_2SO_4, a toxic yellow crystalline powder formerly used as an emetic and purgative. **E17.**

turpid /ˈtəːpɪd/ *adjective. literary. rare.* **E17.**
[Irreg. from Latin *turpis* + **-ID**[1], after *torpid*.]
Base, worthless; foul, filthy.
■ **turpidly** *adverb* **M19.**

turpitude /ˈtəːpɪtjuːd/ *noun. literary.* **L15.**
[French, or Latin *turpitudo*, *-din-*, from *turpis* base, disgraceful: see **-TUDE**.]
Baseness, vileness; depravity, wickedness; an instance of this.
moral turpitude: see **MORAL** *adjective*.
■ **turpiˈtudinous** *adjective* (*literary*) characterized by turpitude; base, depraved, wicked: **M20.**

turps /təːps/ *noun.* **E19.**
[Abbreviation.]
1 Oil of turpentine; *colloq.* turpentine substitute. **E19.**
2 Intoxicating liquor, *esp.* beer. *Austral. slang.* **M19.**

turquoise /ˈtəːkwɔɪz, -kwɑːz/ *noun & adjective.* Also †**turkis(e)** & other vars. **LME.**
[Old French *turqueise*, later *-quoise*, for *pierre turqueise* etc. 'Turkish stone'.]
▶ **A** *noun.* **1** A semiprecious stone, usu. opaque and of a sky-blue to blue-green colour, which is a triclinic mineral consisting of a basic hydrated phosphate of copper and aluminium. Also ***turquoise stone*** (cf. ***Turkey stone*** s.v. **TURKEY** *noun*[1]). **LME.**
2 A fossil tooth etc. coloured blue by copper salts. Also ***bone turquoise***. **L18.**
3 The colour of the stone turquoise; a bright rich greenish blue. Also more fully ***turquoise blue***. **E19.**

> 🕮 **3** *Edinburgh Review* The turquoise-tinted feathers of the Kingfisher.

▶ **B** *adjective.* Made of or resembling turquoise; of the colour turquoise. **L16.**

> 🕮 A. Carter I could see . . stucco villas . . , the turquoise flash of a swimming pool.

turr /təː/ *noun. Canad. dial.* **L18.**
[Prob. imit.]
= **MURRE.**

turr /təː/ *verb intrans. & trans.* Long *obsolete* exc. *dial.* **LME.**
[Origin unkn.]
Of a ram etc.: butt; push *down* by butting.

turret /ˈtʌrɪt/ *noun & verb.* **ME.**
[Old French *to(u)rete* dim. of *tur*, *to(u)r* **TOWER** *noun*[1]: see **-ET**[1].]
▶ **A** *noun.* **1** A small or subordinate tower, *esp.* one projecting (freq. at some height above the ground) from an angle of the walls of a castle etc. as a decorative addition. **ME.** ▸†**b** *fig.* Highest point or position, acme. **ME–L17.** ▸**c** *HERALDRY.* A small tower on top of a larger one. **M18.**
2 Any of various things resembling a turret; *spec.* †(***a***) a woman's tall head-dress; †(***b***) a tall chimney on a lamp; (***c***) *US* a raised central portion in the roof of a railway passenger carriage. **L15.**
3 †**a** A tall movable structure used in storming a fortified place, a tower. *rare.* **M16–E17.** ▸**b** A low flat usu. revolving tower or enclosure for a gun and gunner on a ship, tank, aircraft, etc. **M19.**
4 **a** An attachment to a lathe, drill, etc., holding various tools or bits and rotated to present the required tool etc. to the work. **L19.** ▸**b** *CINEMATOGRAPHY & TELEVISION.* = ***lens turret*** s.v. **LENS** *noun.* **M20.**

> 🕮 **1** D. Sweetman A . . castle with four turrets and a crenellated parapet.

Comb.: **turret lathe** = **CAPSTAN** ***lathe***; **turret shell** (the shell of) any of various marine gastropod molluscs of the families Turritellidae and Turridae, which have long slender pointed shells.
▶ **B** *verb trans.* Fit, fortify, or adorn (as) with a turret or turrets. **LME.**
■ **turreted** *adjective* (***a***) fitted with or having (something resembling) a turret or turrets; (***b***) (of a mollusc shell etc.) having a long pointed spire resembling a turret: **M16.** **turreting** *noun* (***a***) the action of the verb; (***b***) turrets collectively: **M19.**

turrible /ˈtʌrɪb(ə)l/ *adjective & adverb. dial.* (chiefly *US*). Also **turble** /ˈtəːb(ə)l/. **L19.**
[Repr. a pronunc.]
= **TERRIBLE** *adjective & adverb*.

turriform /ˈtʌrɪfɔːm/ *adjective.* **L19.**
[from Latin *turris* tower + **-FORM**.]
Tower-shaped.

turrited /ˈtʌrʌɪtɪd/ *adjective.* Now *rare* or *obsolete.* **M18.**
[from Latin *turritus* towered (from *turris* tower) + **-ED**[1].]
Esp. of a mollusc shell: turreted.

turron /tʊˈrɒn/ *noun.* Pl. **-es** /-ɪz/, **-s**. **E20.**
[Spanish *turrón*.]
A kind of Spanish confectionery resembling nougat, made from almonds and honey; a piece of this.

turrum /ˈtʌrəm/ *noun.* **M20.**
[Prob. from Aboriginal.]
Any of several large carangid game-fishes found off the north coast of Australia. Cf. **TREVALLY** *noun*[2].

turtle /ˈtəːt(ə)l/ *noun*[1] *& verb*[1].
[Old English *turtla*, *turtle* = Old High German *turtulo*, *-ula*; Old English also *turtur* partly from Old French *turtre* or Old Norse *turturi*; all from Latin *turtur* of imit. origin: for change of *r* to *l* cf. **PURPLE** *adjective & noun*.]
▶ **A** *noun.* **1** = **TURTLE-DOVE** 1. *arch. rare.* **OE.**
2 = **TURTLE-DOVE** 2. *arch. rare.* **LME.**
3 = **TURTLE-DOVE** 3. Usu. in *pl. rhyming slang.* **L19.**

> 🕮 **1** Coverdale *S. of S.* 11:12 The voice of the turtle is heard in our land. ***SEA turtle***.

▶†**B** *verb intrans. & trans.* (with *it*). Behave fondly and amorously. **E–M18.**
■ Also †**turtur** *noun* **OE–M17.**

turtle /ˈtəːt(ə)l/ *noun*[2] *& verb*[2]. **M16.**
[Perh. alt. of French *tortue* **TORTOISE**, or from Bermudian name.]
▶ **A** *noun.* **1** Any of several large marine chelonian reptiles which constitute the families Cheloniidae and Dermochelyidae, having a streamlined body, non-retractable head, and limbs modified as flippers (also ***sea turtle***). Also, any of various other, esp. freshwater, chelonians. **M16.** ▸**b** The flesh of various turtles used as food, esp. for soup. **M18.**
2 In full ***American turtle***. An early form of submarine. *obsolete* exc. *Hist.* **L18.**
3 *PRINTING.* A cylindrical surface on which to secure type or stereotypes on a rotary press. *obsolete* exc. *Hist.* **M19.**
4 *COMPUTING.* A directional cursor in a computer graphics system which can be instructed to move around a screen. **L20.**
1 ***box-turtle***, ***green turtle***, ***hawksbill turtle***, ***leatherback turtle***, ***loggerhead turtle***, ***snapping turtle***, ***soft-shell turtle***, etc. **turn turtle** (***a***) catch turtles by throwing them on their backs; (***b***) turn over, capsize, be upset. **b** ***mock turtle soup***: see **MOCK** *adjective*.
Comb.: **turtle-back** (***a***) the back of a turtle; (***b***) an arched structure over the deck of a steamer; an upper deck curving down at the sides to give protection from damage in a heavy sea; (***c***) *N. Amer.* (the lid of) a rounded projecting boot on a motor vehicle; (***d***) *ARCHAEOLOGY* a large stone flake of oval shape with a convex flaked dorsal surface; (***e***) a ridge or hill shaped like a turtle-shell; **turtle-backed** *adjective* having a back like a turtle's; fitted with a turtle-back; **turtle-crawl** (***a***) an enclosure in which to keep turtles; (***b***) the track of a turtle to and from its nest; **turtle-deck** = ***turtle-back*** (b), (c) above; **turtle-grass** a submerged marine flowering plant of the Caribbean, *Thalassia testudinum*, of the frogbit family, with long grasslike leaves; **turtlehead** a N. American plant of the figwort family, *Chelone glabra*, allied to *Pentstemon*, so called from the shape of the flower; **turtle-neck** (***a***) a high close-fitting neck or collar on a knitted garment, intermediate in height between a crew neck and a polo-neck; a jersey etc. having such a collar; (***b***) *US* = ***polo-neck*** s.v. **POLO** *noun*[1]; **turtle-necked** *adjective* (of a garment) having a turtle-neck; **turtle-shell** the shell of a turtle; tortoiseshell; **turtle-stone** septarium (from the resemblance of the markings in cross-section to tortoiseshell).
▶ **B** *verb.* **1** *verb intrans.* Fish for or catch turtles. Chiefly as ***turtling*** *verbal noun.* **M17.**
2 *verb trans.* Make mock turtle soup out of. *rare.* **M18.**
3 *verb trans. & intrans.* Turn over, capsize. **L19.**
■ **turtlet** *noun* a small or young turtle **M19.**

turtle-dove /ˈtəːt(ə)ldʌv/ *noun.* **ME.**
[from **TURTLE** *noun*[1] + **DOVE** *noun*. Cf. Old High German *turtulatuba* (German *Turteltaube*) = Middle Low German *torteldure*, Middle Swedish *turturdufva*.]
1 Any of several Old World doves of the genus *Streptopelia*, freq. having chestnut and pink plumage; esp. *S. turtur* of Eurasia and N. Africa, which has a purring call. **ME.**
2 *fig.* A very fond or amorous person, esp. a member of a couple; a beloved person. **M16.**
3 A glove. Usu. in *pl. rhyming slang.* **M19.**

turtler /ˈtəːtlə/ *noun.* **L17.**
[from **TURTLE** *noun*[2] + **-ER**[1].]
1 A person or vessel engaged in catching turtles. **L17.**
2 A seller of turtle-meat. *rare.* **M18.**

turved *verb pa. t. & pple*: see **TURF** *verb*.

turves *noun pl.* see **TURF** *noun*.

Turveydrop /ˈtəːvɪdrɒp/ *noun.* Now *rare.* **L19.**
[A character in Dickens's *Bleak House*.]
A person who poses as a perfect model of deportment.
■ **Turveyˈdropian** *adjective* reminiscent of a Turveydrop **L19.**

turving *pres. pple & verbal noun* see **TURF** *verb*.

Tuscan /ˈtʌsk(ə)n/ *noun & adjective.* **LME.**
[Old French (mod. *toscan*), Italian *toscano* from Latin *Tuscanus*, from *Tusci* pl. of *Tuscus* = *Etruscus* **ETRUSCAN**: see **-AN**.]
▶ **A** *noun.* **1** **a** = **ETRUSCAN** *noun* 1. **LME.** ▸**b** A native or inhabitant of medieval or modern Tuscany, a region of western Italy. **L16.**
2 The language of Tuscany, regarded as the classical form of Italian. **M16.**
3 The golden-yellow colour of Tuscan straw. **L19.**
4 *PRINTING.* A letterform with bifurcated or trifurcated serifs, used esp. in the early 19th cent. Now *Hist.* **L19.**

▶**B** *adjective*. **1** = ETRUSCAN *adjective* 1. E16.
2 Of or pertaining to medieval or modern Tuscany. E16.
3 *ARCHITECTURE*. Of or designating the simplest of the five classical orders, resembling the Doric but devoid of all ornament. M16.
4 Designating (a method of plaiting) the fine wheat straw grown in Tuscany for hats etc. Also, of the golden-yellow colour of this straw. M19.
■ **Tuscanism** *noun* Tuscan style or character; a Tuscan idiom or phrase: L16. **Tuscanize** *verb* (*a*) *verb intrans.* become Tuscan; adopt Tuscan habits, use Tuscan Italian; (*b*) *verb trans.* make Tuscan: E17.

Tuscarora /tʌskəˈrɔːrə/ *adjective & noun*. Pl. of noun **-s**, same. M17.
[Iroquois: cf. Oneida *taskalô:lę* traditionally interpreted as 'hemp-gatherer'.]
Of or pertaining to, a member of, an Iroquoian people orig. inhabiting Carolina and later upper New York State; (of) the language of this people.

tusche /ˈtʊʃə/ *noun*. L19.
[German, back-form. from *tuschen* from French *toucher* to touch.]
A greasy black composition, in liquid form or to be mixed with liquids, used for making lithographic drawings; lithographic drawing ink.

tush /tʌʃ/ *noun*[1].
[Old English *tusc*: see TUSK *noun*[1].]
1 = TUSK *noun*[1] 1. Now chiefly *arch.* & *dial.* OE. ▸**b** A canine tooth, esp. of a male horse. L15. ▸**c** A stunted tusk in some Indian elephants. M19.
2 = FIN *noun*[1] 5. *obsolete* exc. *dial.* M17.
3 *ARCHITECTURE*. A projecting course on which to bond an additional structure. Cf. TOOTHING 2b, TUSS. *rare*. E20.
■ **tushed** *adjective* having a tush or tushes, tusked LME.

tush /tʌʃ/ *noun*[2]. *arch.* M16.
[from the interjection.]
An utterance of 'tush'.

tush /tʊʃ/ *noun*[3]. *slang* (chiefly *N. Amer.*). M20.
[Abbreviation or dim. of TOKUS.]
The buttocks.

tush /tʌʃ/ *verb*[1] *intrans.* *arch.* M16.
[from the interjection.]
Say 'tush'; sneer or scoff *at*.

tush /tʊʃ, tʌʃ/ *verb*[2] *trans.* Orig. *dial.* M19.
[Origin unkn.]
Haul or drag (esp. a log) along the ground by means of attached chains etc.

tush /tʌʃ/ *interjection*. *arch.* LME.
[Natural exclam. Cf. PISH *interjection & noun*.]
Expr. impatience, scorn, or disgust.

> BARONESS ORCZY Tush, man, you talk nonsense.

■ **tushery** *noun* (*joc.*) conventional romantic writing characterized by excessive use of affected archaisms such as 'tush'; *gen.* sentimental or romanticizing writing: L19.

tusk /tʌsk/ *noun*[1].
[Old English *tux* (var. of *tusc* TUSH *noun*[1]) by metathesis = Old Frisian *tusk*, *tosk*.]
1 A long pointed tooth; *esp.* one specially developed so as to protrude from the closed mouth, as in the elephant, wild boar, walrus, etc. OE. ▸**b** A tusklike human tooth. LME. ▸**c** = TUSH *noun*[1] 1b. L16.
2 A projecting part or object resembling a tusk; *spec.* (*CARPENTRY*) a bevel or sloping shoulder on a tenon. L17.
Comb.: **tusk shell** (the shell of) a scaphopod mollusc.
■ **tuskless** *adjective* M19. **tusklike** *adjective* resembling a tusk or tusks L19.

tusk /tʌsk/ *noun*[2]. *obsolete* exc. *dial.* M16.
[Origin unkn.: cf. TUSSOCK.]
A tuft of hair, grass, etc.

tusk *noun*[3] see TORSK.

tusk /tʌsk/ *verb*. L15.
[from TUSK *noun*[1].]
1 *verb trans.* Carve (a barbel) into portions. Now *rare* or *obsolete*. L15.
2 *verb intrans.* †**a** Show the teeth. Only in E17. ▸**b** Use the tusks; tear or thrust with a tusk or tusks. E19.
3 *verb trans.* Gore, thrust at, or tear up with a tusk or tusks. E17.

tuskar /ˈtʌskə/ *noun*. Also **tusker**. E19.
[Old Norse *torfskeri*, from *torf* turf + *skera* cut, shear.]
An implement for cutting peat used in Orkney and Shetland.

tusked /tʌskt/ *adjective*. LME.
[from TUSK *noun*[1] + -ED[2].]
1 Having tusks (of a specified kind). LME.
2 *HERALDRY*. Having the tusks of a specified tincture different from that of the rest of the body. M17.

tusker /ˈtʌskə/ *noun*[1]. M19.
[formed as prec. + -ER[1].]
An animal, esp. an elephant or wild boar, having (esp. well-developed) tusks.

tusker *noun*[2] var. of TUSKAR.

tusky /ˈtʌski/ *adjective*. LME.
[from TUSK *noun*[1] + -Y[1].]
1 Characterized by (well-developed) tusks; tusked. Chiefly *poet.* LME.
2 Having projections like tusks. M19.

> **1** DRYDEN On Mountain tops to chace the tusky Boar.

tuss /tʌs/ *noun*. *obsolete* exc. *dial.* LME.
[Var. of TUSK *noun*[1].]
ARCHITECTURE. Each of a series of stones or bricks forming a projecting course for the continuance of building on the same alignment. Cf. TUSH *noun*[1] 3, TOOTHING 2b.

tussac *noun* see TUSSOCK.

tussah, **tusser** *nouns* see TUSSORE.

tussie-mussie *noun* var. of TUZZY-MUZZY.

tussilago /tʌsɪˈleɪɡəʊ/ *noun*. Now chiefly *Scot.* Orig. Anglicized as †**tussilage**. E16.
[Latin, from *tussis* cough, from its use to cure coughs.]
Any plant of or formerly included in the genus *Tussilago*, of the composite family; *spec.* coltsfoot, *T. farfara*.

tussive /ˈtʌsɪv/ *adjective*. M19.
[from Latin *tussis* cough + -IVE.]
Of, pertaining to, or caused by a cough.

tussle /ˈtʌs(ə)l/ *verb & noun*. LME.
[App. orig. Scot. & north., perh. from TOUSE: see -LE[3]. Cf. TOUSLE.]
▶**A** *verb*. **1** *verb trans.* Pull or push about roughly, hustle; engage in a scuffle with. Now *rare*. LME.
2 *verb intrans.* Struggle in a vigorous but confused or inconclusive way; engage in a scuffle *together* or *with*. M17.

> **2** *Running* Saleh and Dinsamo tussled for the lead between 35 and 40 km. J. TROLLOPE In the back seat . . the boys tussled mildly together.

▶**B** *noun*. A vigorous but confused or inconclusive struggle or conflict; a scuffle. E17.

> *Times* Tempers fray in tussle between home loan chiefs and Government. M. DIBDIN The bill, over which she and Jenny had a gentle tussle won by the younger woman.

tussock /ˈtʌsək/ *noun*. In sense 3 also **tussac**. M16.
[Prob. alt. of TUSK *noun*[2] assim. to words in -OCK.]
1 A tuft or clump of grass etc. forming a small hillock; (now *rare*) a tuft of leaves, hair, etc. M16.
2 More fully ***tussock moth***. Any of various moths of the family Lymantriidae, whose larvae have long dorsal tufts of hairs and are freq. pests of trees. E19.
3 = ***tussock grass*** (a), (b) below. E19.

> **1** K. M. E. MURRAY Jumping from tussock to tussock over a patch of bog.

Comb.: **tussock grass** any of various grasses forming (large) tussocks; *esp.* (*a*) a giant grass of the Falkland Islands, *Poa flabellata*; (*b*) *Austral.* & *NZ* (more fully ***serrated tussock grass***) an aggressive Chilean grass, *Nassella trichotoma*, a serious weed in pastures; (*c*) in Britain, tufted hair-grass, *Deschampsia cespitosa*; **tussock land** *Austral.* & *NZ* uncultivated grassland used for sheep-grazing; ***tussock moth***: see sense 2 above.
■ **tussocked** *adjective* covered with or formed into tussocks; covered with tussock grass: L18. **tussocker** *noun* (*NZ slang*) = SUNDOWNER 1 L19. **tussocky** *adjective* covered with, resembling, or forming tussocks M17.

tussore /ˈtʌsɔː, ˈtʌsə/ *noun*. Also **tusser**, ***tussah** /ˈtʌsə/. L16.
[Hindi *tasar*, *tasar* app. from Sanskrit *tasara* shuttle.]
1 A kind of strong coarse silk produced in India etc. by saturniid silkworms of the genus *Antheraea* (also ***tussore silk***); a garment, esp. a dress, made of this silk. Also (*US*), (a garment of) a fine corded cotton dress fabric. L16.
2 A silkworm producing tussore. L18.
Comb.: **tussore moth** any saturniid moth of the genus *Antheraea* whose larvae yield tussore; **tussore silkworm**, **tussore worm** (the larva of) a tussore moth.

†**tussy** *noun*. *rare*. M16–M17.
[Origin uncertain: cf. TUTTY *noun*[2], TUZZY-MUZZY.]
A cluster or bunch of flowers, leaves, etc.; an ornament of this form.

tut /tʌt/ *noun*[1]. E16.
[Origin unkn.]
1 Each of a number of objects used as bases in rounders or similar games. Also, stoolball, rounders, or a similar game (also ***tut-ball***). *local*. E16.
2 A small seat, cushion, or hassock of straw. *dial.* M16.

tut /tʌt/ *noun*[2]. *local*. L17.
[Origin unkn.]
MINING & AGRICULTURE. Piece-work. Also, unproductive work. Also ***tut-work***.

tut /tʌt/ *interjection, noun*[3], *& verb*. Freq. redupl. **tut-tut** /tʌtˈtʌt/, **tut tut**. E16.
[Natural exclam. As interjection freq. repr. the sound of a click of the tongue against the teeth.]
▶**A** *interjection*. Expr. impatience, annoyance, rebuke, disapproval, etc. E16.

> THACKERAY Tut, tut! . . let us hear no more of this nonsense.

▶**B** *noun*. An utterance of 'tut-tut'. L16.

> R. P. GRAVES To the accompaniment of shocked tut-tuts . . he made slighting references to . . Herbert Spencer.

▶**C** *verb*. Infl. **-tt-**.
1 *verb intrans.* Utter or exclaim 'tut-tut'. M19.
2 *verb trans.* Express disapproval of by exclaiming 'tut-tut'; say disapprovingly. L20.

> **1** O. MANNING Galpin tut-tutted at Yakimov's ignorance. **2** *Just Seventeen* 'Shocking, the prices in this place,' tutted the customer.

tutania /tjuːˈteɪnɪə/ *noun*. L18.
[from William *Tutin* (fl. 1770), English manufacturer + -IA[1].]
METALLURGY. An alloy similar to Britannia metal, used chiefly for domestic and decorative purposes.

tute /tjuːt/ *verb & noun*. *slang*. M16.
[Abbreviation.]
▶**A** *verb trans. & intrans.* = TUTOR *verb*. *rare*. M16.
▶**B** *noun*. = TUTORIAL *noun* 1. M20.
¶ Unrecorded between M16 and L19.

tutee /tjuːˈtiː/ *noun*. E20.
[from TUTOR *verb* + -EE[1].]
A student or pupil of a tutor.

tutelage /ˈtjuːtɪlɪdʒ/ *noun*. E17.
[from Latin *tutela* keeping, from *tut-*: see TUTOR, -AGE.]
1 Protection, care, guardianship; patronage. E17. ▸**b** Instruction, tuition. M19.
2 The condition or duration of being under protection or guardianship. M17.

> **1** *New Yorker* No . . solution worked—not colonial tutelage, . . not Bolshevism. **b** *Dance* She finished her studies . . under the tutelage of Ninella Kurgapkina, former prima ballerina.

tutelar /ˈtjuːtɪlə/ *adjective & noun*. E17.
[Late Latin *tutelaris* adjective & noun, formed as prec.: see -AR[1].]
▶**A** *adjective*. = TUTELARY *adjective*. E17.
▶**B** *noun*. A tutelar person, deity, saint, etc.; a guardian, a protector. E17.

tutelary /ˈtjuːtɪləri/ *adjective & noun*. E17.
[Latin *tutelarius* guardian, formed as prec.: see -ARY[1].]
▶**A** *adjective*. **1** Serving as a protector, guardian, or patron; *esp.* watching over a particular person, place, or thing. E17.
2 Of or pertaining to protection or a protector or guardian. M17.

> **1** C. BIGG The Lares, . . the little tutelary gods, who watched over . . the home. **2** R. FRASER They exchanged the tutelary influence of the gentle . . Maria for that of Miss Branwell.

▶**B** *noun*. = TUTELAR *noun*. M17.

tutenag /ˈtuːtɪnaɡ/ *noun*. E17.
[Portuguese *tutunaga*, *tutenaga* from Tamil *tuttunākam*; cf. Kannada *tuttu*, *tutte* copper sulphate, Sanskrit *nāga* tin, lead, ult. from Akkadian *anāku* tin.]
METALLURGY. A whitish alloy consisting chiefly of copper, zinc, and nickel, resembling nickel silver. Also (*rare*), spelter, zinc.

tutiorist /ˈtjuːʃɪərɪst/ *noun*. M19.
[from Latin *tutior* compar. of *tutus* safe, from *tut-*: see TUTOR, -IST.]
ROMAN CATHOLIC THEOLOGY. A person who holds that in cases of conscience the course of greater moral safety or certainty should be chosen. Cf. RIGORIST 2.
■ **tutiorism** *noun* the doctrine of tutiorists L19.

tut-mouthed /ˈtʌtmaʊðd/ *adjective*. *rare*. Now chiefly *Scot.* *dial.* Also **-mouth** /-maʊθ/. LME.
[from TOOT *verb*[1] + MOUTH *noun* + -ED[2].]
Having protruding lips or a projecting lower jaw.

tutor /ˈtjuːtə/ *noun & verb*. LME.
[Anglo-Norman, Old French *tutour* (mod. *tuteur*) or Latin *tutor*, from *tut-* pa. ppl stem of *tueri* watch, look after, protect: see -OR.]
▶**A** *noun*. †**1** A custodian, a keeper; a protector, a defender. LME–E17.
2 A person having custody of a ward, a guardian (now only *ROMAN & SCOTS LAW*). Also *spec.* (*SCOTS LAW*), the guardian, representative, and administrator of the estate of a person legally incapable. LME.
3 A privately employed teacher of an individual, *esp.* one in general charge of a pupil's education. LME.
4 A teacher in a university, college, etc., responsible for supervising orig. the general conduct and now usu. the academic work of an assigned student or students. E17.
5 A book of instruction in any subject, now esp. the playing of a musical instrument. M17.
6 In some English public schools: a senior appointed to help a junior's studies; a master responsible for the supervision of a particular pupil. L17.

3 R. GODDEN Samuel had engaged a tutor to coach .. his sons. 4 *Oxford Today* He became a Fellow of Oriel and tutor in law. ***moral tutor***: see MORAL *adjective*. ***senior tutor***: see SENIOR *adjective*.

▶**B** *verb*. **1** *verb trans.* Act as a tutor towards; teach or instruct (*in* a subject), esp. on an individual basis. L16.
2 *verb trans.* Instruct or train under discipline, school; discipline; restrain. Also, admonish, reprove. L16.
3 *verb trans.* Instruct (a person) in a course of action; *spec.* illicitly influence or tamper with (a witness or evidence). E17.
4 *verb intrans.* Study under a tutor. *US*. E20.

1 H. CARPENTER He began to tutor undergraduates in mathematics. *Modern Maturity* Retired professionals .. volunteer to tutor .. students who've failed. *absol.*: P. FITZGERALD Rooms .. in Jesus, where he tutored in experimental physics. 2 F. D. MAURICE Seneca .. had tutored himself to endure personal injuries. 3 C. BUTLER Emissaries were employed, witnesses tutored, .. and even torture applied.

■ **tutordom** *noun* (*rare*) = TUTORSHIP 1 M19. **tutorer** *noun* (*rare*) E18. **tutorhood** *noun* (*rare*) = TUTORSHIP 1 M18. **tutorize** *verb trans.* = TUTOR *verb* 1 E17. **tutorless** *adjective* E17. **tutorly** *adjective* (*rare*) of or pertaining to a tutor; resembling or befitting a tutor: E17. **tutress** *noun* = TUTORESS L16.

tutorage /ˈtjuːt(ə)rɪdʒ/ *noun*. E17.
[from TUTOR *noun* + -AGE.]
1 The office, authority, or action of a tutor; tutorial control, instruction, or supervision. E17. ▶**b** A tutor's post, a tutorship. L18.
†**2** The condition of being under a tutor's authority or control. *rare*. M17–M18.

tutoress /ˈtjuːt(ə)rɪs/ *noun*. E17.
[formed as prec. + -ESS¹.]
A female tutor, a governess; a female guardian.

tutorial /tjuːˈtɔːrɪəl/ *adjective & noun*. E18.
[from Latin *tutorius* (from TUTOR): see -IAL.]
▶**A** *adjective*. Of or pertaining to a tutor, guardian, or instructor; relating to tuition, esp. at a college etc. E18.
▶**B** *noun*. **1** A period of tuition given by a university etc. tutor to an individual pupil or a small group. E20.
2 Any period of tuition or training; a printed account or explanation of a subject intended for private study. L20.
■ **tutorially** *adverb* E19.

tutorship /ˈtjuːtəʃɪp/ *noun*. M16.
[from TUTOR *noun* + -SHIP.]
1 The position or office of a guardian or teacher. M16.
2 A post as a tutor, *spec.* in a university. E20.

tutory /ˈtjuːt(ə)ri/ *noun*. LME.
[formed as prec.: see -ORY².]
1 Guardianship, protection; *spec.* the custody of a ward. *obsolete* exc. LAW. LME.
†**2** Tuition, instruction. *rare*. L17–M18.

tutoyer /tʊˈtwɑːjeɪ/ *verb trans.* Infl. **tutoy-**, pa. t. also **-ered** /-eɪd/. L17.
[French, from the sing. pronoun *tu, toi, te*.]
In French, address with the singular and more familar pronoun *tu, toi, te* rather than the plural and more formal *vous*; *gen.* treat or address with familiarity.
■ **tutoiement** /tytwamɑ̃/ *noun* the action of addressing a person in this way E19. **tutoyant** /tytwajɑ̃/ *adjective* (*rare*) intimate, affectionate; suggesting a degree of familiarity sufficient to tutoyer a person: L19.

†**tutrix** *noun*. L15–E18.
[Latin, fem. of TUTOR: see -TRIX.]
= TUTORESS.

tutsan /ˈtʌts(ə)n/ *noun*. LME.
[Anglo-Norman †*tutsaine*, French *toute-saine*, from *toute* fem. of *tout* all + *saine* fem. of *sain* healthy.]
Any of several plants credited with healing properties: *esp.* (*a*) a St John's wort, *Hypericum androsaemum*, with large aromatic leaves and a berry-like fruit (also called ***shrubby St John's wort***); †(*b*) the chaste-tree, *Vitex agnus-castus*, formerly confused with this.

Tutsi /ˈtʊtsi/ *noun & adjective*. M20.
[Bantu.]
▶**A** *noun*. Pl. same, **-s**. = WATUSI *noun* 1. M20.
▶**B** *attrib.* or as *adjective*. = WATUSI *adjective*. M20.

tutti /ˈtʊti/ *adverb & noun*. E18.
[Italian, pl. of *tutto* all from Latin *totus*.]
MUSIC. ▶**A** *adverb*. A direction: with all the voices or instruments together. E18.
▶**B** *noun*. A passage to be played in this way. E19.

tutti-frutti /tuːtɪˈfruːti/ *noun*. Also **tutti frutti**, **Tutti Frutti**, (esp. sense 2) **Tutti-frutti**. M19.
[Italian = all fruits: cf. prec.]
1 A confection of mixed fruits; *spec.* a mixture of chopped preserved fruits, nuts, etc., used to flavour ice-cream; ice-cream so flavoured. M19.
2 (US proprietary name for) a chewing-gum with a mixed fruit flavouring. M19.

tutti quanti /ˈtutti ˈkwanti/ *noun phr*. L18.
[Italian.]
Everyone, everything; all the people or things of this or that kind.

tut-tut *interjection, noun, & verb* see TUT *interjection, noun*³, & *verb*.

tutty /ˈtʌti/ *noun*¹. ME.
[Old French *tutie* from medieval Latin *tutia* from Arab. *tūtiyā*.]
Crude zinc oxide obtained chiefly from the flues of zinc-smelting furnaces, formerly used medically in ointments etc., and now chiefly as a polishing powder.

tutty /ˈtʌti/ *noun*². Now *dial.* L16.
[Origin uncertain: cf. TUSSY, TUZZY-MUZZY.]
A nosegay, a posy; a cluster or bunch of flowers.

tutu /ˈtuːtuː/ *noun*¹. *NZ*. M19.
[Maori.]
An indigenous shrub, *Coriaria arborea* (family Coriariaceae), having black berries with poisonous seeds, which reputedly were freq. fatal to newly landed cattle but could be eaten safely by animals that had become gradually accustomed to their use.
eat one's tutu, **eat tutu** *slang* (*obsolete* exc. *Hist.*) become acclimatized to colonial life in New Zealand.

tutu /ˈtuːtuː/ *noun*². E20.
[French, childish alt. of *cucu* dim. of *cul* buttocks, bottom.]
A ballet dancer's skirt made up of layers of stiffened frills, very short and standing out from the legs (***classic tutu***) or reaching halfway between the knee and the ankle (***romantic tutu***).

tutulus /ˈtjuːtjʊləs/ *noun*. Pl. **-li** /-lʌɪ, -liː/. M18.
[Latin.]
ROMAN ANTIQUITIES. A head-dress formed by plaiting the hair in a cone above the forehead, worn esp. by a flamen and his wife.

Tuva /ˈtuːvə/ *noun & adjective*. M20.
[Republic in Outer Mongolia: see TUVINIAN.]
(Of, pertaining to, or designating) the Turkic language of the Tuvinians (see TUVINIAN).

Tuvaluan /tuːvəˈluːən, tuːˈvɑːluən/ *noun & adjective*. L20.
[from *Tuvalu* (see below) + -AN.]
▶**A** *noun*. A native or inhabitant of the State of Tuvalu (formerly the Ellice Islands) in the south Pacific. L20.
▶**B** *adjective*. Of or pertaining to Tuvalu. L20.

Tuvinian /tuːˈvɪnɪən/ *noun & adjective*. M20.
[from Russian *Tuvin-* adjective stem + -IAN.]
▶**A** *noun*. **1** A member of a pastoral Turkic-speaking people inhabiting the Tuva Autonomous Republic of Russia in Outer Mongolia. M20.
2 The Turkic language of this people. M20.
▶**B** *adjective*. Of or pertaining to the Tuvinians or their language. M20.

tu-whit /tʊˈwɪt/ *interjection, noun, & verb*. L16.
[Imit.]
▶**A** *interjection & noun*. (Repr.) the call or hoot of an owl (properly a tawny owl). Orig. & chiefly in ***tu-whit tu-whoo*** (see next). L16.
▶**B** *verb intrans.* Infl. **-tt-**. Of an owl (properly a tawny owl): utter its natural call or hoot. E20.

tu-whoo /tʊˈwuː/ *interjection, noun, & verb*. L16.
[Imit.]
▶**A** *interjection & noun*. (Repr.) the call or hoot of an owl (properly a tawny owl), esp. in response to a previous call. Orig. in ***tu-whit tu-whoo*** (see prec.). L16.
▶**B** *verb intrans.* Of an owl (properly a tawny owl): utter its natural call or hoot, esp. in response to a previous call. M19.

tux /tʌks/ *noun*. *colloq.* (chiefly *N. Amer.*). E20.
[Abbreviation.]
= next.

tuxedo /tʌkˈsiːdəʊ/ *noun*. Chiefly *N. Amer.* Pl. **-o(e)s**. L19.
[*Tuxedo* Park in New York, USA, site of a country club where the garment was first worn.]
A dinner jacket (also more fully ***tuxedo coat***, ***tuxedo jacket***). Also, a suit of clothes including this.
Comb.: **tuxedo sofa**, **tuxedo-style sofa**: having back and arms of the same height.
■ **tuxedoed** *adjective* wearing a tuxedo M20.

tuyère /twiːˈjɛː, tuː-/ *noun*. Also **tuyere**, **twyer** /ˈtwʌɪə/. L18.
[French, from *tuyau* pipe.]
METALLURGY. A nozzle through which the air is forced into a forge or furnace.

tuzzy-muzzy /ˈtʌzɪmʌzi/ *noun*. Also **tussie-mussie** /ˈtʌsɪmʌsi/. LME.
[Origin uncertain: cf. TUSSY, TUTTY *noun*².]
1 A bunch of flowers; a nosegay, a posy, a garland. LME.
2 The female genitals. *slang & dial.* E18.
¶ Sense 1 rare after E18 until revived in M20.

TV /tiːˈviː/ *noun*. M20.
[Abbreviation.]
1 = TELEVISION.
2 Transvestite. *colloq.* (chiefly *N. Amer.*).
Comb.: **TV dinner** a prepared frozen meal needing only to be heated, suitable for eating while watching television.

TVA *abbreviation*.
1 French *Taxe à la valeur ajoutée* value added tax, VAT.
2 Tennessee Valley Authority.

TVEI *abbreviation*.
Technical and Vocational Educational Initiative.

tvorog /ˈtvɔːrək/ *noun*. E20.
[Russian.]
A soft Russian cheese similar to cottage or curd cheese.

TVP *abbreviation*.
Textured vegetable protein (in foods made from vegetable but given a texture like that of meat).
¶ *TVP* is a proprietary name.

TWA *abbreviation*.
Hist. Trans World Airlines.

Twa /twɑː/ *noun*¹ & *adjective*¹. M19.
[Bantu = foreigner, outsider.]
▶**A** *noun*. Pl. same, **-s**; **Batwa** /ˈbatwɑː/. A member of a pygmy people inhabiting parts of Burundi, Rwanda, and the Congo (Zaire). M19.
▶**B** *attrib.* or as *adjective*. Of, pertaining to, or designating the Twa. M20.

twa *noun*² & *adjective*² see TWO.

twaa-grass /ˈtwɑːgrɑːs/ *noun*. *S. Afr.* Also **twa-grass** & other vars. M19.
[Perh. from Nama *toab* name of such grasses + GRASS *noun*.]
Any of several tall feathery grasses of the genus *Aristida* native to the Kalahari region, esp. *A. brevifolia*. Also called ***bushman grass***.

Twaddell /ˈtwɒd(ə)l/ *noun*. Also **Twaddle**, **t-**. M19.
[William *Twaddell* (d. *c* 1840), Scot. inventor.]
Now chiefly DYEING & POTTERY. Used *absol.* and *attrib.* to designate a form of hydrometer or hydrometric scale in which 200 degrees correspond to one unit of relative density, with that of distilled water defining the zero.

twaddle /ˈtwɒd(ə)l/ *noun*¹. L18.
[Alt. of TWATTLE *noun*, TWITTLE-TWATTLE.]
1 Senseless, silly, or dull talk, writing, or ideas; nonsense, rubbish. L18.
†**2** A speaker or writer of twaddle, a twaddler. E–M19.

1 F. TREVES Guided by .. experience, and not by the twaddle of theorists. G. DALY Georgie hated dinner parties; .. people talked twaddle and wasted one's time.

■ **twaddlesome** *adjective* full or of the nature of twaddle M19. **twaddling** *adjective* (*a*) having the character of twaddle; senseless, rubbishy; trifling, insignificant; (*b*) uttering or prone to talking twaddle: L18. **twaddly** *adjective* characterized by or of the nature of twaddle M19.

Twaddle *noun*² var. of TWADDELL.

twaddle /ˈtwɒd(ə)l/ *verb*¹. E19.
[from TWADDLE *noun*¹, or perh. alt. of TWATTLE *verb*.]
1 *verb intrans.* Utter twaddle; talk or write in a senseless, silly, or dull style. E19.
2 *verb trans.* Utter as twaddle; (foll. by *away*) spend or pass in empty talk. M19.
■ **twaddler** *noun* L18.

twaddle /twɒd(ə)l/ *verb*² *intrans.* Chiefly *dial.* E19.
[Origin uncertain: cf. WADDLE *verb*.]
Walk with a feeble uncertain gait.
Comb.: **twaddle-toed** *adjective* hobbling, waddling.

twa-grass *noun* var. of TWAA-GRASS.

twain /tweɪn/ *adjective, noun, & verb*. *arch.*
[Old English *twegen* (corresp. to Old Frisian, Old Saxon *twēne*, Old High German *zwēne* (arch. German *zween*)) nom. and accus. masc. of the numeral of which the fem. and neut. are repr. by TWO.]
▶**A** *adjective*. **1** One more than one, two; forming a pair, twin. Now usu. *postpositive* & chiefly *poet.* OE.
2 **a** Consisting of two parts or elements; double, twofold. *rare*. LME. ▶**b** *pred.* Separate, apart; estranged, at variance. L15.

1 J. KEBLE Five loaves hath he, And fishes twain. R. BUCHANAN Thy blue eyes twain stars. R. ELLIS Brothers twain has Gallus. 2b SHAKES. *Sonn.* We two must be twain, Although our undivided loves are one.

▶**B** *noun*. **1** Two persons or things identified contextually. OE. ▶**b** NAUTICAL (now *Hist.*). Two fathoms. Chiefly in ***mark twain***, the two fathom mark on a sounding-line. *US*. L18.
†**2** The abstract number two. LME–L15.
3 In *pl.* Twins. *dial.* L16.
4 A group of two; a pair, a couple. E17.

1 Sir W. Scott Pray him . . to tarry a day or twain. Tennyson The world may know You twain are reconciled. R. Kipling East is East, and West is West, and never the twain shall meet. **in twain** into two parts or pieces, in two, asunder.

▶†**C** *verb trans.* Part, divide, separate, scatter. ME–E20.

Twainian /ˈtweɪnɪən/ *adjective*. M20.
[from *Twain* (see below) + -IAN.]
Of, pertaining to, or characteristic of the American writer Mark Twain (S. L. Clemens, 1835–1910) or his work.

twaite /tweɪt/ *noun*. Also **twait**. E17.
[Origin unkn.]
An anadromous European fish of the herring family, *Alosa fallax*. Now usu. more fully ***twaite shad***.

Twana /ˈtwɑːnə/ *noun & adjective*. M19.
[Twana *tuwáduxq*.]
▶**A** *noun*. Pl. same, **-s**.
1 A member of a Salish people of western Washington. M19.
2 The language of this people. L19.
▶**B** *attrib.* or as *adjective*. Of or pertaining to the Twana or their language. L19.

twang /twaŋ/ *noun*[1] & *adverb*. M16.
[Imit.]
▶**A** *noun*. **1** A sharp fairly deep ringing sound, as made by suddenly plucking or releasing a string of a bow or musical instrument. M16. ▸**b** *transf. & fig.* Ringing sound or tone. M17.
2 A nasal quality of a person's voice; a nasal or other distinctive manner of pronunciation or intonation characteristic of the speech of an individual, area, country, etc. M17.
3 A ringing or resounding blow. *rare*. E18.
4 The action of twanging something; a sharp pluck, a tweak. Also (now chiefly *dial.*), a twinge, a sharp pang. E18.

1 F. Quarles The sprightly twang of the melodious Lute. A. S. Byatt She heard . . the twang of the springs on the sofa. **2** P. P. Read He . . spoke fluent English with an American twang.

▶**B** *adverb*. With a twang. M16.

M. Prior Twang goes the bow, my Girls, have at your hearts.

twang /twaŋ/ *noun*[2]. E17.
[Alt. of TANG *noun*[1], but freq. assoc. with prec.]
1 A slight usu. disagreeable flavour or odour (*of* something); an aftertaste, a taint. Cf. TANG *noun*[1] 3. E17.
2 *fig.* = TANG *noun*[1] 4. M17.

twang /twaŋ/ *noun*[3]. *Austral. slang*. Now *rare* or *obsolete*. L19.
[Var. of TWANKAY.]
Opium.

twang /twaŋ/ *verb*[1]. M16.
[Imit.: rel. to TWANG *noun*[1].]
1 *verb intrans.* Emit a twang or ringing sound; produce such a sound (as) by plucking a string or stringed instrument; (usu. *derog.*) play *on* a stringed instrument. M16.
2 *verb trans.* Cause to emit a twang; play on (a stringed instrument), pluck (a string); (usu. *derog.*) play (a tune) in this way. M16.
3 a *verb trans.* Pull or pluck (a bowstring) so as to shoot. E17. ▸**b** *verb trans.* Discharge (an arrow) with or as with a twang of the bowstring. M18. ▸**c** *verb intrans.* Of an arrow: leave the bowstring with a twang. L18.
†**4 a** *verb trans.* Utter with a sharp ringing tone. Cf. TANG *verb*[2] 2. *rare*. Only in E17. ▸**b** *verb intrans.* Speak. *rare*. Only in E17.
5 *verb intrans.* Speak with a nasal intonation or twang. *rare*. E17. ▸**b** *verb trans.* Utter or pronounce with a nasal or other twang. M18.

1 Dryden His bow twanged, and his arrows rattled as they flew. R. H. Dana The musicians were still there, . . scraping and twanging away. **2** H. D. Wolff Guitar players . . twanged a variety of airs. **3b** *Reader* An athletic man . . twanged an arrow . . against some object. **c** G. P. R. James The missile twanged away from the string. **5b** E. E. Saltus 'Now Becky,' twanged the ponderous person, 'what is your name?'

■ **twanger** *noun* (*a*) a person or thing which twangs; a person playing a stringed instrument; (*b*) *dial. & arch. slang* anything very large or fine of its kind: L16. **twanging** *noun* the action of the verb; the sound made by the twanged string(s) of a bow or musical instrument: M16. **twanging** *adjective* (*a*) that twangs; †(*b*) *slang* exceptionally fine or good: M16. **twangingly** *adverb* (*a*) in a twanging manner, with a twang; (*b*) *arch. slang* very well or successfully: E19.

twang /twaŋ/ *verb*[2]. *rare*. L17.
[from TWANG *noun*[2] or alt. of TANG *verb*[1].]
†**1** *verb trans.* Provide with a tang or point. Cf. TANG *verb*[1] 2. Only in L17.
2 *verb trans.* Cause (a sharp object) to pierce something. E19.
3 *verb intrans.* Smack or have a tang *of* something specified. E19.

twangle /ˈtwaŋg(ə)l/ *verb & noun*. M16.
[Dim. and frequentative of TWANG *verb*[1]: see -LE[3].]
▶**A** *verb*. **1** *verb intrans.* Twang lightly and continuously or frequently; jingle. M16.
2 *verb trans.* Twang (a stringed instrument) lightly; play on carelessly or unskilfully, strum; play (a tune) in this way. E17.
▶**B** *noun*. The action of twangling; an instance of this; a light and continuous or repeated twanging sound, a jingle. E19.
■ **twangler** *noun* L16.

twangy /ˈtwaŋi/ *adjective*. L19.
[from TWANG *noun*[1] + -Y[1].]
Having a twang, characterized by a twanging sound.

Philadelphia Inquirer Songs . . delivered with a powerful, twangy guitar attack. Anne Stevenson Sylvia rode up . . to ask in her twangy American accent for directions.

■ **twanginess** *noun* L19.

twank /twaŋk/ *verb trans. & intrans. dial.* E18.
[Imit.]
Strike with the open palm, spank; twang smartly.
■ **twanker** *noun* E19.

Twankay /ˈtwaŋkeɪ/ *noun*. M19.
[Chinese *Tongke*, *Tongkei*, etc., dial. vars. of *Túnxī* (Wade–Giles *T'un-hsi*), a city in Anhu province, China.]
In full ***Twankay tea***. A variety of green tea, properly that from the place so called (see above). Also, a blend of such tea with other varieties.

twat /twɒt, twat/ *noun*. M17.
[Origin unkn.]
1 The female genitals, the vulva. *coarse slang*. M17.
2 A stupid or unpleasant person. *coarse slang*. E20.
3 The buttocks. *US dial.* M20.

2 *Independent* An enormous . . benign old twat who blithered on endlessly.

twatchel /ˈtwatʃ(ə)l/ *noun*. *arch.* M17.
[Rel. to Old English *twæcce* in *angol-twæcce* earthworm (cf. ANGLE *noun*[1]).]
ANGLING. An earthworm.

twattle /ˈtwɒt(ə)l/ *verb & noun*. *obsolete* exc. *dial.* L16.
[Perh. alt. of TATTLE: cf. TWADDLE *noun*[1], *verb*[1], TWITTLE-TWATTLE.]
▶**A** *verb*. **1 a** *verb intrans.* Talk idly or trivially; chatter, babble. L16. ▸**b** *verb trans.* Utter or tell idly. L16.
2 *verb intrans.* Sound, make a noise. Chiefly as ***twattling*** *ppl adjective*. L16.
3 *verb trans.* Pat, fondle, pet. *dial.* L18.
▶**B** *noun*. Idle talk, chatter, babble. M17.
■ **twattler** *noun* L16.

tway /tweɪ/ *adjective & noun*. *arch.*
[Old English *twe* shortened from *twegen* TWAIN.]
▶**A** *adjective* (*attrib.* or (*poet.*) *postpositive*). = TWAIN *adjective* 1. OE.
▶**B** *noun*. **1** = TWAIN *noun* 1. ME.
2 = TWAIN *noun* 4. L18.
1 in tway, **into tway** = *in twain* s.v. TWAIN *noun* 1.

twayblade /ˈtweɪbleɪd/ *noun*. L16.
[from prec. + BLADE noun, translating medieval Latin *bifolium*.]
1 Any of various orchids constituting the genus *Listera*, with two nearly opposite broad stem-leaves and greenish flowers; esp. *L. ovata* (in full ***common twayblade***), of woods and grassland, and *L. cordata* (in full ***lesser twayblade***), of mountain moors. L16.
2 In N. America, any of various orchids of the genus *Liparis*, with two leaves springing from the root. E19.

tweak /twiːk/ *noun*[1]. E17.
[from the verb.]
1 An act of tweaking something; a sharp jerking pull; a twitch. E17.
2 A state of excitement or agitation (orig. & chiefly in ***in a tweak***). Also, an attack of illness, a sharp pain. *obsolete* exc. *dial.* L17.
3 An additional feature or embellishment (esp. on a motor vehicle); an optional extra. Also, a slight modification or adjustment made to improve the efficiency of a mechanism. *colloq.* L20.

1 A. Guinness She settled herself more comfortably . . giving a tweak to her . . beret. **3** *UnixWorld* Technology with some newly developed tweaks . . to help software developers.

†**tweak** *noun*[2]. *slang*. E17–E18.
[Perh. same word as prec.]
A prostitute. Also, a person who has dealings with prostitutes.

tweak /twiːk/ *verb trans.* E17.
[Prob. alt. of TWICK.]
1 Seize and pull sharply with a twisting movement; pull at with a jerk; twitch. E17.
2 Hit with a missile from a catapult. *arch. slang*. L19.
3 CRICKET. Of a bowler: impart spin to (the ball). *colloq.* M20.
4 Make fine adjustments to (a mechanism). M20.

1 W. Golding She reached forward . . and tweaked off my spectacles. J. Gathorne-Hardy The . . scream of annoyance which Helen gives when Nigel tweaks her hair. **4** *Rally Sport* To be competitive you need to tweak the turbo boost. *fig.*: *Precision Marketing* It's possible to access the data easily . . if they 'tweak' certain factors.

■ **tweaker** *noun* (*colloq.*) a person who or thing which tweaks something; *spec.* (*a*) a catapult; (*b*) CRICKET a bowler who imparts spin to the ball; a ball bowled with spin: L19.

†**twee** *noun*[1]. L17–L18.
[Aphet. from *etwee* var. of ETUI. Cf. TWEEZE *noun*.]
= TWEEZE *noun*.

twee /twiː/ *noun*[2]. E18.
[Imit.]
A shrill sound, *esp.* the chirp of a small bird.

twee /twiː/ *adjective*. *colloq.* E20.
[Repr. a childish pronunc. of *sweet*.]
Sweet, dainty, chic. Now chiefly *derog.*, affectedly dainty or quaint.

Independent We do not want Coniston to end up as another twee tourist village.

■ **tweely** *adverb* M20. **tweeness** *noun* M20.

tweed /twiːd/ *noun & adjective*. M19.
[Orig. a misreading of *tweel* Scot. var. of TWILL, infl. by assoc. with the River *Tweed*.]
▶**A** *noun*. **1** A rough-surfaced woollen cloth of varying texture, usu. of mixed flecked colours, orig. made in Scotland. M19.
2 A fabric or garment of this material. Usu. in *pl.* M19.

2 L. Kennedy Photographs show him in baggy tweeds . . usually with a dog at his side.

▶**B** *attrib.* or as *adjective*. Made of tweed. M19.
■ **tweeded** *adjective* wearing tweed E20.

Tweede Nuwejaar /ˈtwɪədə nyvəˈjɑːr/ *noun phr. S. Afr.* M20.
[Afrikaans, lit. 'second New Year'.]
The second of January, a public holiday in Cape Province, South Africa.

tweedle /ˈtwiːd(ə)l/ *verb*[1] & *noun*[1]. L17.
[Imit. Cf. TWEETLE, TWIDDLE *verb*[2].]
▶**A** *verb*. **1** *verb intrans.* Play on or *on* a high-pitched musical instrument or sing with a succession of shrill notes. Freq. *derog.* L17.
2 *verb trans.* Bring into some place or condition (as) by tweedling; wheedle, cajole. E18.

1 Day Lewis The double-mouthed pipe tweedles for addicts.

▶**B** *noun*. **1** The action or practice of tweedling; music. Now *rare* or *obsolete*. L18.
2 A sound of tweedling; a shrill note. M20.

tweedle /ˈtwiːd(ə)l/ *verb*[2] & *noun*[2]. E19.
[Var. of TWIDDLE *verb*[1] & *noun*. Sense A.2 may be a different word.]
▶**A** *verb trans.* **1** Twiddle (a thing). Also foll. by *round*. *rare*. E19.
2 Counterfeit, swindle, practise a confidence trick on. *Criminals' slang*. E20.
▶**B** *noun*. A counterfeit ring. Also, a swindle involving counterfeit goods; a fiddle, a racket. *Criminals' slang*. L19.
■ **tweedler** *noun* E20.

Tweedledee /twiːd(ə)lˈdiː/ *noun*. Also **t-**. E18.
[from TWEEDLE *verb*[1] + 2nd elem. repr. a note from a high-pitched musical instrument. Cf. TWEEDLEDUM.]
Either of a pair of virtually indistinguishable persons or things. Chiefly in ***Tweedledee and Tweedledum*** or ***Tweedledum and Tweedledee***.

Times Lit. Suppl. Darwin and Wallace were not Tweedledum and Tweedledee; they had different styles and careers.

¶ *Tweedle-dum* and *Tweedle-dee* orig. applied to the rival composers Handel and Bononcini in a 1725 satire by John Byrom, and were later popularized as twin characters in Lewis Carroll's *Through the Looking-Glass*.

tweedledee /twiːd(ə)lˈdiː/ *verb intrans. derog.* Pa. t. & pple **-deed**. M19.
[from the noun.]
Play or sing in a high-pitched tone, tweedle.

Tweedledum /twiːd(ə)lˈdʌm/ *noun*. Also **t-**. E18.
[from TWEEDLE *verb*[1] + 2nd elem. repr. a note from a low-pitched musical instrument. Cf. TWEEDLEDEE *noun*.]
Either of a pair of virtually indistinguishable persons or things. Chiefly in ***Tweedledee and Tweedledum***, ***Tweedledum and Tweedledee***.
¶ See note s.v. TWEEDLEDEE *noun*.

tweedy /ˈtwiːdi/ *adjective*. E20.
[from TWEED + -Y[1].]
Consisting of or relating to tweed cloth; characterized by or dressed in tweeds, esp. habitually; *fig.* characteristic of the country gentry, heartily informal.

📖 *Daily Telegraph* Miss Foster, . . a perfectly splendid, large and tweedy lady.

■ **tweedily** *adverb* M20. **tweediness** *noun* M20.

tweek /twiːk/ *noun.* M20.
[Imit.]
RADIO. A type of whistler heard as a short, high-pitched chirruping noise.

tweel *noun & verb* see TWILL.

Tween /twiːn/ *noun*[1]. M20.
[Origin unkn.]
BIOCHEMISTRY. (Proprietary name for) any of a class of derivatives of fatty acid esters of sorbitan, several of which are used as emulsifiers, solubilizers, and surfactants. Freq. with specifying numeral, as ***Tween 60***.

tween /ˈtwiːn/ *noun*[2]. *colloq.* (chiefly *N. Amer.*). L20.
[Abbreviation.]
= TWEEN-AGER.

'tween /twiːn/ *preposition. arch.* Also †**tween.** ME.
[Aphet. from BETWEEN. Cf. ATWEEN.]
Between.
Comb.: **'tween-decks** NAUTICAL the space between the decks of a ship.

tween-ager /ˈtwiːneɪdʒə/ *noun. colloq.* M20.
[Blend of 'TWEEN and TEENAGER.]
A person who is nearly, or has only just become, a teenager.
■ **tween-age** *noun & adjective* M20.

tweeny /ˈtwiːni/ *noun. colloq.* L19.
[from 'TWEEN + -Y[6].]
1 = BETWEEN-***maid***. *arch.* L19.
2 = TWEEN-AGER. L20.

tweet /twiːt/ *noun & verb.* M19.
[Imit.]
▶ **A** *noun.* The high-pitched chirp of a small bird. M19.
▶ **B** *verb.* **1** *verb trans.* Utter with a tweet. M19.
2 *verb intrans.* Utter a tweet. E20.

tweeter /ˈtwiːtə/ *noun.* M20.
[from TWEET *verb* + -ER[1].]
A small loudspeaker designed to reproduce high frequencies. Cf. WOOFER 2.

tweetle /ˈtwiːt(ə)l/ *verb intrans.* Orig. & chiefly *dial. rare.* M18.
[Alt. of TWEEDLE *verb*[1].]
Tweedle; make a succession of high-pitched sounds.

†**tweeze** *noun.* Only in 17.
[formed as TWEE *noun*[1] + -S[1].]
An etui; a case of surgical instruments.

tweeze /twiːz/ *verb trans.* M20.
[Back-form. from next.]
1 Grasp or pluck *out* with tweezers. M20.
2 Pluck (the eyebrows) with tweezers. M20.

tweezer /ˈtwiːzə/ *noun & verb.* M17.
[from TWEEZE *noun* + -ER[1].]
▶ **A** *noun.* **1** = TWEEZE *noun.* Freq. in *pl.* (also ***pair of tweezers***). Also more fully ***tweezer-case***. *obsolete* exc. *Hist.* M17.
2 In *pl.* exc. *attrib.* A small pair of pincers for taking up small objects, plucking out hairs, etc. Also ***pair of tweezers***. M17.

📖 **2** R. P. JHABVALA She held her tweezers in her hand and was plucking her eyebrows.

▶ **B** *verb.* **1** *verb intrans.* Use tweezers for taking up small objects, plucking out hairs, etc. E19.
2 *verb trans.* Pluck *out* with tweezers; pinch or pluck (as) with tweezers. M19.

twelfth /twɛlfθ/ *adjective & noun (ordinal numeral).*
[Old English *twelfta* = Old Frisian *twil(i)fta*, Middle Dutch *twalefde*, Old High German *zwelifto* (Dutch *twaalfde*, German *zwölfte*), Old Norse *tólfti*, from Germanic, from base of TWELVE, -TH[2].]
▶ **A** *adjective.* Next in order after the eleventh; that is number twelve in a series, (represented by 12th). OE.

📖 H. ROSE As early as the twelfth century. *Times* The twelfth anniversary of Togolese independence. **Twelfth Day** the sixth of January, the twelfth day after Christmas, the festival of the Epiphany. **twelfth man** a player selected as reserve to a cricket team. **Twelfth Night** (*a*) the evening of the fifth of January, preceding Twelfth Day, the eve of the Epiphany, formerly the last day of the Christmas festivities and observed as a time of merrymaking; (*b*) = ***Twelfth Day*** above. **twelfth part** *arch.* = sense B.2 below.

▶ **B** *noun.* **1** The twelfth person or thing of a category, series, etc., identified contextually, as day of the month, (following a proper name) person, esp. monarch or pope, of the specified name, etc. OE.
2 Each of twelve equal parts into which something is or may be divided, a fraction which when multiplied by twelve gives one, (= ***twelfth part*** above). M16.
3 MUSIC. An interval embracing twelve consecutive notes in the diatonic scale, equivalent to an octave and a fifth; a note a twelfth above another given note; a chord of two notes a twelfth apart. L16.

📖 **1** *Naval Chronicle* In the reign of Louis the Twelfth. D. A. LAMB On the twelfth of February. **the Twelfth** (*a*) (more fully ***glorious Twelfth***) the twelfth of August, on which the grouse-shooting season opens; (*b*) the twelfth of July, celebrated by upholders of Protestant supremacy in Ireland as the anniversary of William III's victory over James II at the Battle of the Boyne.

Comb.: Forming compound numerals with multiples of a hundred, as ***three-hundred-and-twelfth*** (*312th*) etc. Special combs., as **Twelfth-cake** *Hist.* a large cake for Twelfth Night celebrations.
■ **twelfthly** *adverb* in the twelfth place M16.

twelve /twɛlv/ *adjective & noun (cardinal numeral).*
[Old English *twelf*, inflected *twelfe* = Old Frisian *twel(e)f*, Old Saxon *twelif*, Old High German *zwelif* (Dutch *twaalf*, German *zwölf*), Old Norse *tólf*, Gothic *twalif*, from Germanic, prob. from base of TWO + base repr. also by ELEVEN.]
▶ **A** *adjective.* One more than eleven (a cardinal numeral represented by 12 in arabic numerals, xii, XII in roman). OE.

📖 DAY LEWIS My father remarried some twelve years later. P. FITZGERALD Lodgings and laundry cost him twelve shillings and fivepence a week. R. M. WILSON Twelve cigarettes left. ***the Twelve Tables***: see TABLE *noun*. **twelve good men and true** *arch. & joc.* the twelve members of a jury. **Twelve Tribes** *the* twelve tribes of ancient Israel.

▶ **B** *noun.* **1** Twelve persons or things identified contextually, as years of age, points, runs, etc., in a game, chances (in giving odds), minutes, inches, shillings (now *Hist.*), pence, etc. OE.
2 One more than eleven as an abstract number; the symbols or figures representing this (12 in arabic numerals, xii, XII in roman). OE.
3 The time of day at midnight or midday (on a clock, watch, etc., indicated by the numeral twelve displayed or pointed to). Also ***twelve o'clock***. LME.
4 The twelfth of a set or series with numbered members, the one designated twelve, (usu. ***number twelve***, or with specification, as ***book twelve***, ***chapter twelve***, etc.); a size etc. denoted by twelve, a shoe, garment, etc., of such a size, (also ***size twelve***). E16.
5 A set of twelve; a thing having a set of twelve as an essential or distinguishing feature; *spec.* (*a*) in *pl.*, twelve leaves to the sheet in a printed book; (*b*) an engine or motor vehicle with twelve cylinders. L16.
6 Each of a set of twelve; *spec.* (*a*) a plant-pot of which twelve are formed from a cast of clay; (*b*) a candle of which twelve constitute a pound in weight. E19.

📖 **1** AV 2 *Sam.* 2:15 Twelue of the seruants of Dauid. LD MACAULAY Manlius, eldest of the Twelve Who kept the Golden Shield. L. W. MEYNELL Baa-Lamb came home . . at the very agreeable odds of twelve to one. *Japan Times* Twelve survived, but none of the cases involved blood clots. **the Twelve** the twelve apostles. **2** OED Five twelves make sixty. **3** M. E. BRADDON The clock struck twelve. E. BOWEN It was twenty to twelve: extraordinary how one's mornings went! ***twelve noon***: see NOON *noun* 2. **4** J. RAZ This use of 'moral' is compatible with the one described in Chapter Twelve. **5** ***long twelves***: see LONG *adjective*[1].

Comb.: Forming compound numerals with multiples of a hundred, as *712* (read ***seven hundred and twelve***, US also ***seven hundred twelve***) etc. In dates used for one thousand two hundred, as *1260* (read ***twelve sixty***), ***twelve-nineties***, etc. With nouns + -ER[1] forming nouns with the sense 'something (identified contextually) being of or having twelve —s', as ***twelve-seater*** etc. Special combs., as **twelve-bore** a shotgun with a bore corresponding to the diameter of a round bullet of which twelve constitute a pound in weight; **twelve-gauge** *US* = ***twelve-bore*** above; **twelve-inch** a gramophone record twelve inches in diameter and played at 45 rpm; **twelvemonth** *arch.* a period of twelve months, a year; ***this time twelvemonth***, a year from now; **twelvemonthly** *adverb* (*arch.*) every twelve months, yearly, annually; **twelve-note**, **twelve-tone** *adjectives* (MUSIC) using the twelve notes of the chromatic scale on an equal basis without dependence on a key system; **twelvepence** (*a*) twelve pence, esp. of the old British currency before decimalization; †(*b*) a coin of this value, a shilling; **twelvepenny** *adjective & noun* (*a*) *adjective* worth or costing twelve pence; paying or receiving twelve pence; (*b*) *noun* (chiefly *Scot.*) = ***twelvepence*** (b) above; **twelve-pounder** a gun throwing a shot that weighs twelve pounds; **twelve-step program**, **twelve steps** a programme (containing twelve stages) designed by Alcoholics Anonymous to help people recover from alcoholism; any similar programme designed to help people recover from addiction; ***twelve-tone***: see ***twelve-note*** above; **twelve-toner** MUSIC a composer employing the twelve-tone technique.
■ **twelvefold** *adjective & adverb* (*a*) *adjective* twelve times as great or as numerous; having twelve parts, divisions, elements, or units; (*b*) *adverb* to twelve times the number or quantity: OE. **twelvemo** *noun* duodecimo E18. **twelver** *noun* †(*a*) *slang* a coin worth twelve pence; (*b*) (**T-**) a member of a Shiite sect acknowledging twelve as opp. to seven Imams or religious leaders (opp. *Sevener*): L17.

twentieth /ˈtwɛntɪɪθ/ *adjective & noun (ordinal numeral).*
[Old English *twentigoþa*, repl. in Middle English by forms from TWENTY + -TH[2].]
▶ **A** *adjective.* Next in order after the nineteenth, that is number twenty in a series, (represented by 20th). OE.

📖 *Saturday Review* 'Ferdinand the Bull' . . now in its twentieth edition. P. GASKELL During the first half of the twentieth century. **twentieth part** *arch.*= sense B.2 below.

▶ **B** *noun.* **1** The twentieth person or thing of a category, series, etc., identified contextually, as day of the month, (following a proper name) person, esp. monarch or pope, of the specified name, etc. OE.
2 Each of twenty equal parts into which something is or may be divided, a fraction which when multiplied by twenty gives one, (= ***twentieth part*** above). ME.
3 MUSIC. An interval embracing twenty consecutive notes in the diatonic scale; a note a twentieth above another given note; a chord of two notes a twentieth apart. E17.

📖 **1** *Dublin Review* The twentieth of October . . witnessed the destruction of the Ottoman fleet. H. K. MANN In the sixth century, as in the twentieth. **2** W. WOOD Nineteen twentieths of a Crown. *New Scientist* The wings are very narrow, only one-twentieth as wide as they are long.

Comb.: Forming compound numerals with multiples of a hundred, as ***four-hundred-and-twentieth*** (*420th*) etc., and (*arch.*) with numerals below ten, as ***three-and-twentieth*** etc. Special combs., as **twentieth-century** *adjective* (*spec.*) designating a method of diamond-cutting in which the stone has eighty facets.

twenty /ˈtwɛnti/ *adjective & noun (cardinal numeral).*
[Old English *twentig* = Old Frisian *twintich*, Old Saxon *twêntig*, Old High German *zweinzug* (German *zwanzig*), from Germanic, perh. from base of TWO: see -TY[2]. Cf. Old Norse *tuttugu*, Gothic *twai tigjus*.]
▶ **A** *adjective.* One more than nineteen (a cardinal numeral represented by 20 in arabic numerals, xx, XX in roman). OE.

📖 GOLDSMITH Feversham . . hanged up above twenty prisoners. J. TEY Miss Tuff had worn peter-pan collars . . for twenty years. R. PERRY The tape would automatically self-destruct after twenty minutes. **twenty questions** a parlour game in which a participant has twenty questions (answered by either 'yes' or 'no') to identify a chosen object.

▶ **B** *noun.* **1** Twenty persons or things identified contextually, as years of age, points, runs, etc., in a game, chances (in giving odds), minutes, inches, pence, etc. OE.
2 One more than nineteen as an abstract number; the symbols or figures representing this (20 in arabic numerals, xx, XX in roman). OE.
3 The twentieth of a set or series with numbered members, the one designated twenty, (usu. ***number twenty***, or with specification, as ***book twenty***, ***chapter twenty***, etc.); a size etc. denoted by twenty, a garment etc. of such a size, (also ***size twenty***). E16.
4 A set of twenty; a thing having a set of twenty as an essential or distinguishing feature; *spec.* (*a*) in *pl.*, twenty leaves to the sheet in a printed book; (*b*) a twenty-pound note; a twenty-dollar bill. M17.
5 In *pl.* The numbers from 20 to 29 inclusive, esp. denoting years of a century or units of a scale of temperature; *one's* years of life between the ages of 20 and 29. L19.
6 The location or position of a citizens' band radio operator. *slang.* L20.

📖 **1** *New Yorker* At twenty she was taking care . . of a tubercular half sister. D. FRY In English . . about twenty are the vowel phonemes. ***free, white, and over twenty-one***: see FREE *adjective*. ***top twenty***: see TOP *adjective*. **2** B. MATHER To count up to twenty. **4** *Daily Telegraph* The bank . . loaded fivers, tenners, and twenties into the wrong magazines. **5** L. TWINING A temperature in the twenties for some days. R. FRASER By Maria's twenties, Penzance had become a social centre in Cornwall. **roaring twenties** the decade of the 1920s (with ref. to its postwar buoyancy).

Comb.: Forming compound numerals (cardinal or ordinal) with numerals below ten, as ***twenty-nine*** (*29*), ***twenty-first*** (*21st*), etc., and (cardinals) with multiples of a hundred, as *220* (read ***two hundred and twenty***, US also ***two hundred twenty***), etc. With nouns + -ER[1] forming nouns with the sense 'something (identified contextually) being of or having twenty —s', as ***twenty-seater*** etc. Special combs., as **twenty-eight** a small yellow-collared Australian parrot, *Barnardius zonarius*, whose call resembles the words 'twenty-eight', *esp.* one of the race from SW Australia; **twenty-firster** *colloq.* (*a*) a twenty-first birthday (until 1970 in the UK a person's coming-of-age); a party to celebrate this; (*b*) a twenty-first birthday present; **twenty-five** (*a*) HOCKEY & (formerly) RUGBY FOOTBALL the line drawn across the ground twenty-five yards from each goal; the space enclosed by this; (*b*) an Irish card-game in which each trick counts five and the game is twenty-five; **twenty-four** (*a*) in *pl.*, twenty-four leaves to the sheet in a printed book; (*b*) a plant-pot of which twenty-four are formed from one cast of clay; (*c*) ***twenty-four carat***, (of gold) pure; *colloq.* thoroughgoing, unalloyed; genuine, trustworthy; (*d*) ***twenty-four-hour***, lasting or operating for twenty-four hours; of or pertaining to a system of time reckoning whereby the hours of the day are numbered from one to twenty-four; (*e*) ***twenty-four seven*** (usu. *24-7*) *colloq.* (orig. *US*), twenty-four hours a day, seven days a week; **twentyfourmo** the size of a book having twenty-four leaves to the sheet; **twenty-one** = VINGT-ET-UN; **twenty-pence piece** a cupro-nickel heptagonal coin worth twenty (new) pence, current in the UK from 1982; a similar coin of the Republic of Ireland; **Twenty-six Counties** *the* counties constituting the Republic of Ireland (cf. ***the Six Counties*** s.v. SIX *adjective*); ***twenty-SOMETHING***; **twenty-twenty**, **20|20** *OPHTHALMOLOGY* the Snellen fraction for normal visual acuity, expressed in feet; *colloq.* used *attrib.* to denote good eyesight; **twenty-two** a twenty-two calibre rifle.

■ **twentyfold** *adjective & adverb* (*a*) *adjective* twenty times as great or as numerous; having twenty parts, divisions, elements, or units; (*b*) *adverb* to twenty times the number or quantity: OE. **twentyish** *adjective* (*a*) about twenty (in age, measurements, etc.); (*b*) of, pertaining to, or characteristic of the 1920s; resembling or recalling the fashions etc. of the 1920s: E20. **twentymo** *noun* a size of book or paper in which each leaf is one-twentieth of a standard printing-sheet M19.

twerp /twəːp/ *noun. slang.* Also **twirp**. L19.
[Origin unkn.]
An objectionable or stupid person; an insignificant person, a nobody; a nincompoop.

📖 A. HOLLINGHURST That man is the most insufferable little twerp.

Twi /twiː, tʃwiː/ *noun & adjective.* L19.
[Kwa.]
▶ **A** *noun.* Pl. same.
1 One of two main varieties of Akan spoken in Ghana, the other being the mutually intelligible Fante. L19.
2 A member of a Twi-speaking people inhabiting Ghana. L20.
▶ **B** *attrib.* or as *adjective.* Of or pertaining to the Twi or their language. M20.

twi- /twʌɪ/ *prefix. arch.* Also **twy-**.
[Old English *twi-*, *twy-* = Old Frisian *twi-*, Old High German *zwi-*, Old Norse *tvi-* cogn. with Latin BI-, Greek DI-², Sanskrit *dvi-*, from base rel. to that of TWO.]
Forming words with the senses 'having two', as ***twi-headed***, ***twi-natured***; 'doubly', as ***twi-yoked***; 'twofold, double', as ***twi-circle***, ***twi-reason***; 'twice, a second time', as ***twi-born***.

■ **twifallow** *verb trans.* (now *dial.*) fallow (land) twice or for a second time M16.

twibill /ˈtwʌɪbɪl/ *noun.* Also **twybill**.
[Old English *twibil(l)*, *twibile*, from prec. + BILL *noun*¹, *noun*².]
†**1** A two-edged axe used for cutting mortises. OE–L17.
2 A double-bladed battleaxe. *arch.* LME.
3 Now *dial.* ▸**a** A mattock. LME. ▸**b** A reaping-hook, *esp.* one for beans and peas. M18.

twice /twʌɪs/ *adverb, noun, adjective, & verb.*
[Late Old English *twiges* from Old English *twige*, (earlier) *twig(e)a* = Old Frisian *twia*, Old Saxon *twio*, from base also of TWO: see -S³. Cf. THRICE.]
▶ **A** *adverb.* **1** For two (successive) times; on two occasions. Also, for a second time. LOE.
2 (Esp. before a numeral) two times in number, amount, or value. LOE.
3 In a twofold degree; doubly. ME.

📖 **1** *Times* To tax the owners of property twice over in respect of the same thing. J. MITCHELL Jumbo's succeeded in making me perjure myself twice. G. BATTISCOMBE She was twice crossed in love. ***ONCE or twice***. ***think twice (about)***: see THINK *verb*². **2** *Saturday Review* Twice one makes two. **3** T. HOOK Which . . makes beauty doubly winning, and talent twice bewitching. ***cousin twice removed***: see COUSIN *noun*.

▶ **B** *noun pl.* Two occasions, two times. Chiefly in ***at twice***. Now *rare.* L15.

📖 HOR. WALPOLE I have written this at twice. T. COBB Lady Kitty's demeanour the last twice they had met.

▶ **C** *adjective.* Performed, occurring, given, etc., two times; twofold, double. Now *rare.* L16.

📖 MRS H. WARD Twice meat was forbidden and twice pudding allowed.

▶ **D** *verb trans.* Make twice as much or as many, double; do twice as much as. *rare.* M17.

Comb.: **twice-born** *adjective* that has been born twice; born again, regenerate; **twice-laid** *adjective* (chiefly *NAUTICAL*) (of rope) made from the strands of old rope; *transf.* made from old or used material; **twice-told** *adjective* (*a*) counted or reckoned twice; twice as much as; (*b*) narrated or related twice.

■ **twicer** *noun* (*slang*) (*a*) a person who does something twice; (*b*) *rare* something of twice the usual force or value; (*c*) a crook, a cheat; a deceitful or cunning person: L17.

twick /twɪk/ *verb trans.* Long *obsolete* exc. *dial.*
[Old English *twiććian* from Germanic base also of TWITCH *verb*¹.]
Pull sharply or suddenly; twitch.

twiddle /ˈtwɪd(ə)l/ *verb*¹ *& noun.* M16.
[App. imit., after *twirl*, *twist*, and *fiddle*, *piddle*. Cf. TWEEDLE *verb*².]
▶ **A** *verb.* **1** *verb intrans.* Occupy oneself busily with trivial matters; trifle. Now *rare.* M16.
2 *verb trans. & intrans.* (with *at* or *with*). Cause to rotate lightly or delicately with the fingers; twirl; adjust or bring into some place or condition in this way. Also, play with idly or absently. L17.
3 *verb intrans.* Move twirlingly or aimlessly. E19.

📖 **2** A. RANSOME The weed began to twist as if someone were twiddling the other end of it. V. WOOLF He twiddled the cross on his watchchain. J. WINTERSON A radiogram . . with . . a fat Bakelite knob to twiddle for the stations. **twiddle one's thumbs** make one's thumbs rotate round each other; *fig.* have nothing to do, be idle. **3** THACKERAY A few wretched little vessels are twiddling up and down.

▶ **B** *noun.* An act of twiddling; a twirl, a twist. Also, a twirled mark or sign. L18.

📖 P. G. WODEHOUSE One twiddle of a tap and the whole thing becomes a fountain.

■ **twiddler** *noun* M19. **twiddling** *noun* (*a*) the action of the verb; an instance of this; (*b*) ***twiddling line*** (*NAUTICAL*), orig., a light line used to steady or secure the wheel; now, a line attached to the compass-box for freeing the card when caught: M19.

twiddle /ˈtwɪd(ə)l/ *verb*² *intrans.* M19.
[Imit., or alt. of TWEEDLE *verb*¹ after prec.]
Twitter, warble; play on an instrument, talk, etc., triflingly or carelessly.

twiddle-twaddle /ˈtwɪd(ə)ltwɒd(ə)l/ *noun.* L18.
[Alt. & redupl. of TWADDLE *noun*¹. Cf. TWITTLE-TWATTLE.]
Idle talk, foolish chatter.

twiddly /ˈtwɪdli/ *adjective.* E20.
[from TWIDDLE *verb*¹ + -Y¹.]
That twiddles; characterized by twiddling.
twiddly bit a fancy or intricate embellishment; a detail.

twiffler /ˈtwɪflə/ *noun.* Now *Hist.* L18.
[Dutch *twijfelaar*, from *twijfelen* be unsure, vacillate.]
A plate or shallow dish intermediate in size between a dessert plate and a dinner plate.

twifold /ˈtwʌɪfəʊld/ *adjective & adverb. arch.* Also **twy-**. OE.
[from TWI- + -FOLD.]
▶ **A** *adjective.* **1** Twofold, double. OE.
†**2** *fig.* Deceitful, insincere. Also, irresolute. OE–ME.
▶ **B** *adverb.* In two parts; in two ways, doubly. *rare.* ME.

twig /twɪɡ/ *noun*¹.
[Old English (late Northumbrian) *twigge* rel. to *twiġ*, *twī* corresp. to Old Danish *tvige* fork, Middle Low German *twich*, *twigh* (Dutch *twijg*), Old High German *zwīg* (German *Zweig*), ult. from Germanic from Indo-European base also of TWAIN, TWIN *adjective & noun*, TWINE *noun & adjective*, TWO.]
1 A slender shoot growing from a branch or stem; a small branch or shoot of a tree or shrub; *spec.* †(*a*) *rare* such shoots collectively as the material for basket-making; †(*b*) = ***lime-twig*** (a) s.v. LIME *noun*¹; (*c*) *arch.* in *pl.*, the twigs forming a birch-rod. OE. ▸**b** A stout stick. Also, a dowsing-rod. *dial.* M19.
2 *ANATOMY.* A small branch of a blood-vessel or nerve. L16.

📖 **1** ANTHONY HUXLEY A great mass of leaves is produced on slender, whippy twigs. A. CARTER He showed me how to . . weave osier twigs into baskets. ***hop the twig***: see HOP *verb*¹.

Comb.: **twig-blight** *US* blight affecting a plant's twigs; *esp.* a disease of apple and quince trees caused by the pear-blight bacterium *Micrococcus amylovorus*; **twig-borer** *US* any of various larval or adult insects which bore into the twigs of trees; **twig-gall** an abnormal enlargement of a twig, due to the action of insects, fungi, or bacteria; **twig-girdler** *US* an American beetle, *Oncideres cingulata*, which lays its eggs in the tips of twigs and then removes a ring of bark below the eggs; **twig-pruner** *US* an American longhorn beetle, *Elaphidionoides villosus*, whose larvae mine down the centre of hardwood twigs.

■ **twiggage** *noun* (*rare*) twigs collectively E20. **twiggen** *adjective* (*arch.*) made of or with twigs M16. **twiggery** *noun* twigs collectively E20. **twigginess** *noun* the condition or quality of being twiggy E20. **twiggy** *adjective* (*a*) resembling a twig; slender; †(*b*) made of twigs; (*c*) full of or having many twigs; bushy, shrubby: M16. **twiglet** *noun* (*a*) a little twig; (*b*) (**T-**) (proprietary name for) a crisp savoury snack in the shape of a twig: M19.

twig /twɪɡ/ *noun*². *arch. slang.* E19.
[Origin unkn.]
Style, fashion; condition, state. Freq. in ***in twig***, ***in prime twig***, ***in good twig***.

twig /twɪɡ/ *verb*¹ *trans. obsolete* exc. *dial.* Infl. **-gg-**. M16.
[from TWIG *noun*¹.]
1 Beat with or as with a twig; *fig.* rebuke. M16.
2 Orig., make with twigs. Later, provide with twigs. Chiefly as **TWIGGED** *adjective.* M17.

twig /twɪɡ/ *verb*² *intrans. obsolete* exc. *dial. rare.* Infl. **-gg-**. L16.
[Origin unkn.]
Do something vigorously or strenuously.

twig /twɪɡ/ *verb*³ *trans. & intrans.* Now *dial.* Infl. **-gg-**. E18.
[Origin unkn.]
†**1** Break in two, break off. *slang.* Only in E18.
2 Pull, pluck, twitch. M18.

twig /twɪɡ/ *verb*⁴. *colloq.* Infl. **-gg-**. M18.
[Origin unkn.]
1 *verb trans.* Look at, observe; perceive; recognize. M18.
2 *verb trans. & intrans.* Understand, grasp the meaning or nature of (something). E19.

📖 **1** J. T. HEWLETT Oblige me by twigging that trio. **2** J. WAIN My mother had twigged that this was the best. J. FOWLES Sarah had twigged Mrs Poultenay, and she was soon . . adept at handling her.

twigged /twɪɡd/ *adjective.* M17.
[from TWIG *noun*¹, *verb*¹: see -ED², -ED¹.]
Provided with or bearing twigs. Formerly also, made with twigs.

twilight /ˈtwʌɪlʌɪt/ *noun & adjective.* LME.
[from TWI- + LIGHT *noun*.]
▶ **A** *noun.* **1** The soft glowing light from the sky when the sun is below the horizon, esp. in the evening; the period of this, the time between daylight and darkness. Also *transf.*, a faint light resembling twilight; partial illumination. LME.
2 *fig.* An intermediate condition or period; a condition or period of decline or destruction. Also, a state of imperfect knowledge or understanding. L16.

📖 **1** KEATS The faded moon Made a dim, silver twilight. J. WYNDHAM Just enough of the twilight left for me to see his grin. A. BURGESS It was twilight The electric lights came on in the ward. **2** H. F. TOZER The minor deities . . live in a dim twilight of popular belief. ALAN BENNETT Stuck on some deserted aerodrome in the twilight of Empire for two years. **twilight of the gods** [translating Old Norse *ragna rökr*: see RAGNAROK] *SCANDINAVIAN MYTHOLOGY* the destruction of the gods and of the world in conflict with the powers of evil (cf. GÖTTERDÄMMERUNG).

▶ **B** *attrib.* or as *adjective.* Of, pertaining to, or resembling twilight; characteristic of twilight; done or occurring in twilight. M17.

📖 S. WYNTER This twilight time was when ghosts walked. P. SAYER I would doze in some twilight state that was neither sleep nor waking. *Independent* Born during the twilight years of Queen Victoria's reign.

Comb. & special collocations: **twilight area** = ***twilight zone*** (a) below; **twilight home** (*a*) a residential home for the elderly; (*b*) = ***twilight house*** below; **twilight house** a house in a twilight zone; **twilight housing** housing in a twilight zone; **twilight night** *BASEBALL* = TWI-NIGHT; **twilight shift** a shift worked between the day shift and the night shift; **twilight sleep** a state of amnesia and partial analgesia induced by drugs, esp. by the administration of morphine and scopolamine to lessen the pains of childbirth; a similar state resulting from certain psychological disorders etc.; **twilight world** a shadowy region; a world characterized by uncertainty, obscurity, or decline; **twilight zone** (*a*) an urban area that is becoming dilapidated; (*b*) any physical or conceptual area that is undefined or intermediate; (*c*) [with ref. to the US television series *The Twilight Zone* (first broadcast 1959)] a sphere of experience in which mysterious or supernatural events occur; (*d*) the lowest level of the ocean to which light can penetrate.

■ **twilightless** *adjective* L19. **twilighty** *adjective* resembling twilight M19.

twilight /ˈtwʌɪlʌɪt/ *verb trans. literary.* Pa. t. & pple **-lighted**; pa. pple also **-lit**. E19.
[from the noun.]
Light imperfectly or faintly; make twilit.

twilit /ˈtwʌɪlɪt/ *adjective.* M19.
[pa. pple of prec.]
Lit (as) by twilight.

📖 R. C. SHERRIFF The room is cool and twilit, because big elms shade it. *Times* A downgraded man . . surrounded by twilit personalities.

twilit *verb* see TWILIGHT *verb.*

twill /twɪl/ *noun & verb.* Also (*Scot.*) **tweel** /twiːl/. ME.
[Scot. & north. var. of TWILLY *noun*¹.]
▶ **A** *noun.* **1** A woven fabric with a surface of diagonal parallel ridges, produced by passing the weft threads over one and under two or more threads of the warp, instead of over and under in regular succession. ME.
2 The method or process of weaving this fabric; the characteristic appearance of this fabric. L18.
1 ***eight-leaf twill***: see LEAF *noun*¹ 12.
▶ **B** *verb trans.* Weave (fabric) with a surface of parallel diagonal ridges. Orig. & chiefly as ***twilled*** *ppl adjective.* ME.

■ **twilling** *noun* (*a*) the action or process of the verb; (*b*) a twilled fabric or texture: E18.

twilly /ˈtwɪli/ *noun*¹ *& adjective.*
[Old English *twili* = Old High German *zwilīh* (German *zwillich*), from TWI- + base of Latin *licium* thrum, thread after Latin *bilic-*, *bilix* two-threaded. Sense 2 may be a different word.]
†**1** Twilled (cloth etc.); (designating) a twilled cloth etc. OE–E18.
2 ***twilly hole***, a central hole in a wattle hurdle for the insertion of a pole on which several hurdles may be carried simultaneously. OE.

twilly /ˈtwɪli/ *noun*² *& verb.* M19.
[Alt. of WILLY *noun*¹.]
▶ **A** *noun.* = WILLY *noun*¹ 3. M19.
▶ **B** *verb trans.* Pass (cotton etc.) through a twilly. L19.

twin /twɪn/ *adjective & noun.*
[Late Old English *twinn*, earlier *ġetwinn* adjective & noun, corresp. to Old Norse *tvinnr*, *tvennr* twofold, double, from Germanic base also of TWI-.]
▶ **A** *adjective.* **I 1** Consisting of two; twofold, double. Long *obsolete* exc. as passing into branch II. LOE.
†**2** Two; both. Only in ME.
▶ **II 3** That is a twin (sense B.1 below); (of a child or animal) born at the same birth as one other sibling. LME.

4 a Forming a closely related or associated, or similar or equal, pair or couple. L16. ▸**b** Composed of or having two associated, or closely related or similar or equal, parts or constituents; consisting of two joined in one. L16. ▸**c** *BOTANY & ZOOLOGY.* Growing or occurring in pairs; geminate. E19.

5 Forming one of a pair or couple; closely related to or associated with another. E17.

> 📖 **3** W. C. L. MARTIN Every twin female . . is not necessarily barren, even when the other calf is a male. C. MORLEY His twin daughters, Alma and Sophie. **4a** SHAKES. *Twel. N.* An apple cleft in two is not more twin than these two creatures. D. LEAVITT They shaved together at twin sinks in the bathroom. **b** D. W. THOMPSON In some twin eggs a thin partition of white intervenes to prevent the yolks mixing. **5** J. C. LOUDON Having in a twin volume treated of Gardening as an Art of Design and Taste.

▸ **B** *noun.* **1** Either of two children or animals born at the same birth, a child or animal born at the same birth as one other sibling. ME. ▸**b** (Usu. **T-**.) In *pl. The* constellation and zodiacal sign Gemini. LME. ▸**c** Each of three triplets. Usu. in *pl. dial.* E17.

†**2** ***in twin, on twin***, in or into two parts or divisions; in twain, in two, apart, asunder. ME–M16.

3 Either of two closely related or associated, or similar or equal, persons or things; a counterpart. M16.

4 a A pair of twin children or animals; a pair, a couple, a brace. *obsolete* exc. *dial.* M16. ▸**b** An agricultural implement with two rows of teeth, for breaking up ploughed land and clearing it of weeds. *dial.* M19.

5 *CRYSTALLOGRAPHY.* A composite crystal consisting of two (usu. equal and similar) crystals having reversed, rotated, or shifted positions with respect to each other, united along a plane or interpenetrating. Also, a composite crystal consisting of more than two. Also ***twin crystal***. M19.

6 *ellipt.* A twin bed, a twin-bedded room, a twin-engined aircraft, etc. E20.

> 📖 **1** *Annual Register* He and his twin, Jean Fèlix. *Punch* Mrs Potter has given birth to healthy twins. ***fraternal twin***: see FRATERNAL *adjective*. ***identical twin***: see IDENTICAL *adjective* 3. ***Siamese twin***: see SIAMESE *adjective*. **3** P. SCOTT I sat in one armchair, he in its twin. M. L. KING The inseparable twin of racial injustice was economic injustice. ***terrible twins***: see TERRIBLE *adjective* 2b. **5** ***glide twin***: see GLIDE *verb*. ***mechanical twin***: see MECHANICAL *adjective*. ***multiple twin***: see MULTIPLE *adjective*. ***PENETRATION twin***. **6** *Economist* The cheapest single room . . will cost £22 a night . . . The cheapest twin will cost £28.

Special collocations & comb.: **twin bed** either of a pair of matching single beds. **twin-bedded** *adjective* (of a room) furnished wth twin beds. **twin-bill** *BASEBALL* = ***double header*** (c) s.v. DOUBLE *adjective & adverb*. **twin-birth** the birth of twins; *arch.* a pair of twins (chiefly *fig.*). **twin-born** *adjective* (*arch.*) born a twin; (of a child or animal) born at the same birth as one other sibling. **twin brother** a male twin, a brother born at the same birth as one other sibling. **twin carburettor** either of a pair of carburettors in the same engine. **twin city** (*a*) *N. Amer.* either of two neighbouring cities lying close together; *spec.* in *pl.*, St Paul and Minneapolis in the US, and (*Hist.*) Fort William and Port Arthur in Canada; (*b*) a city which has been twinned with another (TWIN *verb* 3a). ***twin crystal***: see sense 5 above. **twin double** *RACING* a system of betting in which the winners of four successive races must be selected. **twin-engined** *adjective* (of an aircraft etc.) having two engines. **twin float** either of a pair of floats on a seaplane (usu. in *pl.*). **twinflower** the linnaea, *Linnaea borealis*. **twin-jet** *adjective & noun* (*AERONAUTICS*) (*a*) *adjective* (of an aircraft) having two jet engines; (*b*) *noun* a twin-jet aircraft. **twin lamb disease** pregnancy toxaemia in sheep, apparently caused by malnutrition. **twin-law** *CRYSTALLOGRAPHY* the law expressing the relation of components of a twin crystal. **twinleaf** a N. American woodland plant of the barberry family, *Jeffersonia diphylla*, the leaves of which are divided in two almost to the base. **twin-lens** *adjective* (of a camera) having two identical sets of lenses, either for taking stereoscopic pictures, or with one forming an image for viewing and the other an image to be photographed. **twin-pair** a pair of things precisely similar and equal. **twin paradox** *PHYSICS* in relativity theory, the conclusion that if one of a pair of twins makes a long journey at near the speed of light and then returns, he or she will have aged less than the twin who remains behind. **twin plate** plate glass ground and polished on both sides at once in the manufacturing process. **twin prime** *MATH.* either of a pair of prime numbers whose difference is 2. **twin-screw** *adjective & noun* (*a*) *adjective* having twin screws; *spec.* (of a ship) having two screw propellers on separate shafts rotating in opposite directions, to counteract the tendency to lateral vibration; (*b*) *noun* a twin-screw ship. **twin set** a woman's matching jumper and cardigan. **twin sister** a female twin, a sister born at the same birth as one other sibling. **twin soul** *literary* a kindred spirit. **twin species** *BIOLOGY* two species which are morphologically identical but reproductively distinct. **twin-spot**, **twin-spotted** *adjectives* (esp. of a moth) having pairs of spots on the wings. **twin town** a town which has been twinned with another (TWIN *verb* 3a). **twin-tub** *adjective & noun* (*a*) *adjective* (of a washing machine) having two separate top-loading drums, one for washing and the other for spin-drying; (*b*) *noun* a twin-tub washing machine.

■ **twinhood** *noun* = TWINSHIP L19. **twinling** *noun* (long *dial.*) = TWIN *noun* 1 ME. **twinly** *adverb* (*rare*) to an equal extent, doubly; in an identical degree: E20. **twinship** *noun* the condition of being twin or a twin; the relation of a twin or twins: L17.

twin /twɪn/ *verb*. Infl. **-nn-**. ME.
[from prec.]

▸ **I** *obsolete* exc. *Scot.* **1** *verb trans.* Separate, sever, divide; deprive *of*. Formerly also (*rare*), part with. ME.

2 *verb intrans.* Split, separate, divide; part (†*from*, *with*). Formerly also, depart, go away. ME.

> 📖 **1** *Fraser's Magazine* Ah, my cruel cruel step-dame, who hath twinn'd our love for aye. **2** S. RUTHERFORD We should never twin again.

▸ **II 3 a** *verb trans.* Couple, join, unite; combine (two things or persons) closely or intimately; *spec.* establish official links between (two towns or cities, esp. in different countries) for the purposes of friendship and cultural exchange (usu. in *pass.*). LME. ▸**b** *verb intrans.* Be coupled, join, unite; (of two things or persons) be combined closely or intimately; *spec.* (of a town or city) be or become twinned *with* (another). E17. ▸**c** *verb trans.* In *pass.* *CRYSTALLOGRAPHY.* Of two crystals: be united according to some definite law to form a twin crystal; undergo twinning. M19.

4 *verb intrans.* & †*trans.* Give birth to (two children or animals) at one time; bear (twins). L16. ▸**b** *verb intrans.* Be born at the same birth *with*; be the twin brother or sister of another. Now *rare* or *obsolete*. E17.

5 *verb trans.* Be or provide a counterpart to; match, parallel. Chiefly *poet.* E17.

6 *verb trans.* Break up or clear (land) with a twin (TWIN *noun* 4b). *dial.* M19.

> 📖 **3a** TENNYSON Still we moved Together, twinn'd as horse's ear and eye. *Harrogate Advertiser* Harrogate was the first town in the country to be twinned with a French town—Luchon. **b** E. BENLOWES Wealth twins with fear. *Guardian* 30 British councils have twinned with towns in the Third World. **4** T. HARDY Two more ewes have twinned. **b** SHAKES. *Oth.* Though he had twinn'd with me, both at a birth. **5** J. R. LOWELL O'erhead the balanced hen-hawk slides, Twinned in the river's heaven below.

twindle /ˈtwɪnd(ə)l/ *noun*. Long *dial.* E16.
[App. from alt. of TWIN *noun* + -LE^1.]
= TWIN *noun* 1.

twine /twʌɪn/ *noun & adjective*.
[Old English *twin*, *twigin* linen = Dutch *twijn* twine, twist, from Germanic base of TWI-.]

1 Thread or string made of two or more twisted strands; now *spec.* strong thread or string made of the twisted strands of hemp, cotton, etc., used esp. for sewing coarse materials, tying or holding things together, etc. Also, a piece of this. OE.

2 A twined or twisted object or part; *spec.* (*a*) a twining or trailing plant stem or spray; (*b*) a fold; a coil; a twist in the course of something; (*c*) a tangle, an interlacing (chiefly *fig.*). L16.

3 The action or an act of twining, an instance of this; *spec.* (now *rare* or *obsolete*) an embrace. E17.

> 📖 **1** H. NORMAN Attach balloons to the porch ceiling with twine. J. TROLLOPE To buy seeds and brown garden twine. ***settler's twine***: see SETTLER 2. **2** MARVELL Bind me, ye woodbines, in your 'twines. E. PEACOCK As full of twines as a sheep-track. **3** J. MARSTON Clipping the strumpet with luxurious twines. BROWNING Vain each twist and twine Those lithe limbs try.

Comb.: **twine-spinner** a person who spins twine; **twine-spinning** the action or process of spinning twine.

twine /twʌɪn/ *verb*^{1}. ME.
[from the noun.]

▸ **I** *verb trans.* **1** Twist together (two or more strands) to form a thread or string; twist (one strand) *with* another; form (thread or string) by twisting together two or more strands; *gen.* combine or make compact by twisting. ME. ▸**b** *transf.* Form (a garland etc.) by interlacing; weave, wreathe, interlock; entwine (*together*). E17.

2 Cause (one thing) to encircle or embrace another; coil or wind (a thing) *about* or *around* another. LME.

3 *refl.* Encircle, embrace, coil or wind *round* or *about*. Also, proceed in a winding manner, move sinuously. M16.

4 Turn (a thing) *about*, *away*, *round*, etc.; twist, wring; get *off* or *out* by twisting. Now *dial.* L16.

5 Embrace or encircle (one thing) *in* or *with* another; *esp.* garland (a person's brow). Also, (of a plant etc.) grow over or round in a twisting or winding manner. E17.

> 📖 **1** C. KINGSLEY We'll twine a double strong halter for the Captain. RIDER HAGGARD To twine little threads into a rope. **b** M. PRIOR I'll twine fresh Garlands for Alexis' Brows. T. WILLIAMS Stanley and Stella twine arms as they follow. **2** SHAKES. *Coriol.* Let me twine Mine arms about that body. E. DARWIN Round the white circlet . . A Serpent twines his scaly length. A. BROOKNER Watching her twine a blue scarf around her hair. **3** SIR W. SCOTT The snake . . twines himself through the grass. *fig.*: C. LAMB Awful ideas . . twined themselves about his presence. **4** S. WESLEY The iron latch of my door was twined off. **5** POPE Let wreaths of triumph now my temples twine. D. HOGAN Patsy had twined my neck in a scarlet tie.

▸ **II** *verb intrans.* **6** Coil or wind, esp. *about*, *over*, or *round* something; (of a plant) grow in a twisting or spiral manner; *spec.* become twisted together in growing; grow in spiral convolutions. ME.

†**7** (Of a weapon) twist or turn aside; (of timber) be contorted or irregular in formation. *rare.* LME–E17.

8 Extend or proceed in a winding manner; meander; (of a snake etc.) move sinuously. M16.

9 Contort the body; writhe, wriggle, squirm. Now *Scot.* & *dial.* M17.

> 📖 **6** J. MASEFIELD The vetches have twined about his bones. R. INGALLS The string of pearls that twined through the pile of stacked braids. **8** P. H. GOSSE Sea-worms twined over the mud. J. BUCHAN The little brown river . . twined to the sea.

■ **twiner** *noun* a person who or thing which twines; *spec.* (*a*) a person or machine which twines thread; (*b*) a plant which grows twiningly: E17. **twiningly** *adverb* (*rare*) in a twining manner M18.

twine /twʌɪn/ *verb*^{2} *intrans. & trans. Scot.* E17.
[Var. of TWIN *verb*.]
Separate, part; = TWIN *verb* I.

twing /twɪŋ/ *noun*. Long *obsolete* exc. *dial.* E17.
[Origin unkn.]
A small red spider supposed to be injurious to cattle.

twinge /twɪn(d)ʒ/ *noun*. M16.
[from the verb.]

†**1** An act of tweaking or pinching a person or thing; a tweak, a pinch. M16–L17.

2 A sharp pain, *esp.* one that is momentary and local. E17.

3 *fig.* A sharp mental pain; a pang *of* shame, remorse, sorrow, etc. E17.

4 An earwig. *dial.* L18.

5 A twist, a turn. *rare.* M19.

> 📖 **1** R. L'ESTRANGE A Master that gives you so many Blows, and Twinges by the Ears. **2** C. MACKENZIE A twinge of rheumatism made his face contract with pain. V. S. PRITCHETT He had nearly broken his back: he often got twinges there even now. **3** K. WATERHOUSE I felt a twinge of alarm. S. FREEDMAN Businesses named with homesick twinges.

■ **twingy** *adjective* (*rare*) experiencing twinges, esp. habitually M19.

twinge /twɪn(d)ʒ/ *verb*. Pres. pple **twingeing**, **twinging**. OE.
[Old English *twengan* = Middle Low German *twengen*, Old High German *zwengen*, from Germanic base also of Middle High German *zwange* tongs, *zwangen* pinch, Old High German *zwangōn*, *zwengen*.]

1 *verb trans.* Tweak, pinch. Long *obsolete* exc. *dial.* OE.

2 *verb trans. & intrans.* (Cause to) experience a twinge (*lit.* & *fig.*). M17.

> 📖 **2** GEO. ELIOT I've a twinging knee. D. BALLANTYNE That familiar scary feeling twinged his inside.

twingle /ˈtwɪŋg(ə)l/ *verb intrans.* Long *obsolete* exc. *Scot.* & *dial.* *rare.* M17.
[Prob. imit. Cf. next.]
Twist, twine, wriggle, writhe.

twingle-twangle /twɪŋg(ə)lˈtwaŋg(ə)l/ *noun & verb. derog.* *rare.* M17.
[Redupl. of TWANGLE with vowel variation. Cf. JINGLE-JANGLE, next.]
▸ **A** *noun*. = next. M17.
▸ **B** *verb trans.* Play (a harp etc.) with a twingle-twangle. E20.

twing-twang /twɪŋˈtwaŋ/ *noun. derog. rare.* M18.
[Redupl. of TWANG *noun*^{1} with vowel variation. Cf. prec.]
A continuous or repeated resonant sound made by a harp or other stringed instrument.

twi-night /ˈtwʌɪnʌɪt/ *noun. N. Amer.* M20.
[from TWI(LIGHT *noun & adjective* + NIGHT *noun*.]
BASEBALL. An event consisting of two successive games or matches between the same opponents, beginning in daylight and concluded in the evening by artificial light. Freq. *attrib.*

■ Also **twi-nighter** *noun* M20.

twink /twɪŋk/ *noun*^{1}. LME.
[from TWINK *verb*^{1}.]

1 = TWINKLE *noun* 1. Now only in ***in a twink***, in an instant. LME.

2 A glint, a sparkle. *rare.* M19.

twink /twɪŋk/ *noun*^{2}. *dial.* E19.
[Imit.]
The chaffinch.

twink /twɪŋk/ *verb*^{1} *intrans.* ME.
[Corresp. to Middle High German *zwinken* (cf. German *zwinkern* blink, wink, twinkle) from Germanic base also of TWINKLE *verb*^{1}.]

†**1** Wink, blink. ME–L17.

2 Twinkle, sparkle. M17.

twink /twɪŋk/ *verb*^{2} *trans.* Now *dial.* M18.
[Origin unkn.]
Chastise, punish.

twinkie /ˈtwɪŋki/ *noun. US slang* (usu. *derog.*). Also **-ky**. L20.
[Prob. rel. to TWINK *noun*[1], *verb*[1], TWINKLE *noun*, *verb*[1]: see -IE.]
A male homosexual; an effeminate man.

Twinkie defence /ˈtwɪŋki dɪˈfɛns/ *noun phr. US colloq.* Also ***Twinkie defense**. L20.
[from proprietary name for a brand of finger-shaped sponge cake with a creamy filling.]
A legal defence of diminished responsibility in which irregular behaviour is attributed to an unbalanced diet of convenience food.

twinkle /ˈtwɪŋk(ə)l/ *noun*. M16.
[from next.]
1 A winking of the eye; a wink, a blink; the time taken by this; a twinkling. Now chiefly in ***in a twinkle***, ***in the twinkle of an eye*** below. M16. ▸**b** A slight rapid movement; a twitch, a quiver. M18.
2 A brief or intermittent gleam of light; a sparkle, a scintillation; a glimmer. M17.
3 A form of one-step danced to slow Blues music. E20.

🕮 **1** SIR W. SCOTT An occasional convulsive sigh, or twinkle of the eyelid. **b** G. CHEYNE Now and then an uncertain Twitch or Twinkle in the Pulse. **2** G. MEREDITH Seeing . . Our household's twinkle of light Through spruce-boughs. V. SACKVILLE-WEST A twinkle in his eye as though . . enjoying a secret joke.

Phrases: ***a twinkle in one's eye***: see EYE *noun*. **in a twinkle**, **in the twinkle of an eye** in an instant.
Comb.: **twinkle roll** AERONAUTICS an aerobatic manoeuvre in which the two outside members of a three-aircraft formation simultaneously perform an individual roll; **twinkle-toed** *adjective* light-footed, nimble; (of a dance) quick, requiring agility; **twinkletoes** *colloq.* (a name for) a person who is nimble and quick on their feet.

twinkle /ˈtwɪŋk(ə)l/ *verb*[1].
[Old English *twinclian*, from Germanic base also of TWINK *verb*[1]: see -LE[3].]
1 a *verb intrans.* Shine with brief or intermittent gleams of light; sparkle; glimmer; look with twinkling eyes (*at*). OE. ▸**b** *verb trans.* Emit (gleams of light) briefly or intermittently. M16. ▸**c** *verb trans.* Guide or light *to* a place by brief or intermittent gleams of light (*poet.*). Also, communicate (a message etc.) by this means. L17.
2 *verb intrans.* & *trans.* Blink or wink (the eyes) quickly, voluntarily or involuntarily. *arch.* ME.
3 *verb intrans.* Appear and disappear in quick succession, flicker; move rapidly to and fro; (esp. of the feet) move lightly and rapidly. E17. ▸**b** *verb trans.* Move (a thing) rapidly to and fro; move (the feet) lightly and rapidly. M19.
4 *verb intrans.* Dance the twinkle (TWINKLE *noun* 3). *rare.* E20.

🕮 **1a** A. GUINNESS His bright, little, blue Welsh eyes twinkled at me. *Scots Magazine* Frost had set in and stars were twinkling. **b** G. MEREDITH A broad fire that twinkled branchy beams through an east hill-orchard. **c** DRYDEN The star of love That twinkles you to fair Almeyda's bed. **2** SIR W. SCOTT He was observed to twinkle with his eyelids. N. HAWTHORNE Phoebe took leave . . twinkling her eyelids to shake off a dewdrop. **3** C. KINGSLEY Her feet twinkled past each other so fast, that you could not see which was foremost.

▪ **twinkler** *noun* a person or thing which twinkles; *spec.* (*a*) *rare* a person who winks; (*b*) a thing which shines with brief or intermittent gleams of light: LME. **twinkling** *noun* (*a*) the action of the verb; an instance of this; a brief or intermittent gleam of light; (*b*) ***in a twinkling***, ***in the twinkling of an eye***, in an instant: ME. **twinklingly** *adverb* in a twinkling manner M16.

twinkle /ˈtwɪŋk(ə)l/ *verb*[2] *intrans. rare.* ME.
[Imit.]
= TINKLE *verb* 2.

twinkly /ˈtwɪŋkli/ *adjective*. L19.
[from TWINKLE *noun* or *verb*[1]: see -Y[1].]
That twinkles, esp. habitually; given to twinkling.

🕮 T. O'BRIEN A twinkly night sky. *fig.*: J. GASH That tickled him into a twinkly humour.

twinky *noun* var. of TWINKIE.

twinned /twɪnd, *poet.* ˈtwɪnɪd/ *adjective*. E17.
[from TWIN *noun*, *verb*: see -ED[2], -ED[1].]
1 Born two at one birth; twin. *arch.* E17.
2 a (Of two things or persons) closely related or associated; *spec.* (of a town or city) officially linked *with* another, esp. in a different country, for the purposes of friendship and cultural exchange. E17. ▸**b** Of crystals: formed into a twin (TWIN *noun* 5). L19.

twinning /ˈtwɪnɪŋ/ *noun*. ME.
[from TWIN *verb* + -ING[1].]
†**1** Parting, separation. *Scot.* ME–L16.
2 Giving birth to two children or animals at a birth; the bearing of twins. L16.
3 Coupling, close union or combination; *spec.* (*a*) CRYSTALLOGRAPHY the union of two crystals to form a twin (TWIN *noun* 5); (*b*) the official linking of one town or city with or *with* another, esp. in a different country, for the purposes of friendship and cultural exchange. M19.

twinter /ˈtwɪntə/ *noun & adjective*. Now *Scot.* & *north.* LME.
[Blend of TWO *adjective* and WINTER *noun*. Cf. THRINTER.]
▸**A** *noun*. A two-year-old cow, ox, horse, or sheep. LME.
▸**B** *adjective*. Of a cow, sheep, etc.: of two winters, two years old. M16.

twiny /ˈtwʌɪni/ *adjective. rare.* E17.
[from TWINE *noun*, *verb*[1]: see -Y[1].]
That twines, esp. habitually; given to twining. Also, of the nature of or resembling twine.

†**twire** *noun. slang.* L17–E18.
[from the verb.]
A glance, a leer.

twire /twʌɪə/ *verb intrans.* Now *arch.* & *dial.* M16.
[Origin unkn., but corresp. in form to Middle High German (mod. German Bavarian dial.) *zwieren* blink, peer.]
1 Look covertly; look through a narrow gap; peer; peep. M16.
2 Orig., wink. Later, (of a star etc.) twinkle. E17.

twirk /twəːk/ *verb trans.* Long *rare* or *obsolete* exc. *Scot.* L16.
[App. from same stem as TWIRL *verb*.]
Twist (a moustache etc.); = TWIRL *verb* 3.

twirl /twəːl/ *noun*. L16.
[from the verb.]
1 The action or an act of twirling; the condition of being twirled; a rapid whirling or spinning; a spin, a whirl. L16.
2 A thing that twirls or spins, as a reel, a winch, or a cylinder; a twirled shape or object, as a whorl of a shell, a flourish made by a pen, or a cake in the shape of a spiral. L17. ▸**b** A skeleton key; = TWIRLER 2. *Criminals' slang.* L19.
3 A prison warder. *slang.* L19.

🕮 **1** DICKENS He performed . . spins and twirls. E. FERBER Pinky tossed his big Stetson with an expert twirl. ***twist and twirl***: see TWIST *noun*[2].

twirl /twəːl/ *verb*. L16.
[Prob. alt. (by assoc. with *whirl*) of *tirl* obsolete metath. alt. of TRILL *verb*[2].]
1 *verb intrans.* Rotate rapidly, spin; be whirled round; turn *round* quickly so as to be facing or pointing in the opposite direction. Also *fig.*, (of the mind or head) be in a whirl, be confused or giddy. L16.
2 *verb trans.* Cause to rotate or spin; turn (an object) round rapidly; turn round and round in the hands; spin between the finger and thumb etc. Also *spec.*, manipulate a baton as leader of a marching band (chiefly as ***twirling*** *verbal noun*). E17. ▸**b** Shake out or sprinkle (as) by twirling a mop. *rare.* M18. ▸**c** Turn (one's fingers or thumbs) round and round, esp. in a purposeless way. Chiefly in ***twirl one's thumbs***. L18.
3 *verb trans.* Twist (threads, hair, a moustache, etc.) into a spiral. E17.
4 *verb trans.* Move or hurl with a rapid or violent turning motion; tumble. Now *rare.* M17.
5 *verb intrans.* Form coils, curl. *rare.* E18.

🕮 **1** M. MACHLIN Deirdre . . twirled thoughtfully in the swivel chair. C. DEXTER She twirled round on the points of her . . court shoes. D. HOGAN Tornadoes twirled over cornfields here. **2** W. SOYINKA He twirled the glass stem between his fingers. L. ELLMANN I twirled the cookie packet in the air to reseal it. **3** R. RAYNER A woman, alone, twirling strands of blonde hair. **4** R. HERRICK Carouse, Till Liber Pater twirles the house About your eares. **5** THACKERAY The monster's hideous tail . . writhing and twirling.

twirler /ˈtwəːlə/ *noun*. E19.
[from prec. + -ER[1].]
1 A person or thing which twirls; *spec.* (*N. Amer.*) a person who twirls a baton as leader of a marching band; a drum major or drum majorette. E19.
2 A skeleton key; = TWIRL *noun* 2b. *Criminals' slang.* E20.

twirligig /ˈtwəːlɪgɪg/ *noun*. E20.
[from TWIRL *verb* after WHIRLIGIG.]
A twirly pattern; a whirligig.

twirly /ˈtwəːli/ *adjective*. M17.
[from TWIRL *noun* + -Y[1].]
Full of or characterized by twirls, spirals, or curves.

🕮 N. GORDIMER The house had a twirly wrought-iron gate.

twirp *noun* var. of TWERP.

twisel /ˈtwɪs(ə)l, ˈtwɪz(ə)l/ *noun & adjective*. Also **twissel** /ˈtwɪs(ə)l/.
[Old English *twisla* = Old High German *zwisila* (Middle High German *zwisel*, German *Zwiesel*), from TWI-.]
▸**A** *noun*. A point or part at which something divides into branches; a fork. *obsolete* exc. *dial.* OE.
▸**B** *attrib.* or as *adjective*. Double, twofold. Only in comb. *obsolete* exc. *poet.* OE.

twist /twɪst/ *noun*[1].
[Old English *-twist* (in combs.) from Germanic, prob. ult. from base also of TWIN *adjective* & *noun*, TWINE *noun* & *adjective*; partly directly from the verb.]
▸**I** †**1** A divided object or part. Only as 2nd elem. of comb. *rare.* Only in OE.
†**2 a** The flat part of a hinge, fastened on a door or gate, and turning on a hook or pintle fixed in the post. ME–E19. ▸**b** A twig; a branch. LME–E17.
3 The part of something at which it divides or branches; *spec.* the point at which the legs join the body in sheep or cattle, (*arch.*) the human crotch. LME. ▸†**b** A main beam of wood, a girder. E18–E19.

🕮 **3** R. L. STEVENSON If I had my hand under your twist I would send you flying.

▸**II 4** Thread or cord made by winding together strands of hemp, silk, wool, cotton, etc. Freq. with specifying word. M16. ▸**b** *spec.* Strong warp yarn made of strands of cotton twisted together during spinning (also ***twist yarn***); fine strong silk thread used by tailors etc. E19.
5 *fig.* Something likened to a twist or thread; *esp.* †(***a***) the continuation or course of life (cf. THREAD *noun* 7); (***b***) a tenuous support on which something depends; (***c***) a means of tracing one's way; (***d***) the composition of something formed as by spinning. M16.
6 A thing formed by twisting, spinning, or plaiting; *spec.* (***a***) a small bag or wrapper of twisted paper, a screw; (***b***) NAUTICAL each of the strands making up a rope. L16.
7 A drink consisting of a mixture of two different spirits or other ingredients, as gin and brandy etc. L17.
8 Tobacco made into a thick cord; a piece of this. L18.
9 A small loaf made of one or more twisted rolls of dough; a small bread roll in the form of a twist. M19.
10 A curled piece of lemon etc. peel used to flavour a drink. M20.

🕮 **4** ***cotton twist***, ***gold twist***, ***silk twist***, etc. **5** J. FORD 'Tis in my power to cut off The twist thy life is spun by. **6** R. GODDEN Her dark hair was piled in elaborate twists on the top of her head. M. WARNER He held out the newspaper twist of seeds and nuts. T. C. BOYLE Meg . . made the pasta salad—bow-tie twists. **10** M. CHABON Glasses of . . something ginger or clear with a twist.

▸**III 11** The action or an act of twisting (as) on an axis; the condition of being twisted; rotary motion; (a) spin. L16. ▸**b** A dance characterized by twisting movements of the body; *spec.* a dance of this kind popular in the early 1960s. Also, music for such a dance. L19.
12 An irregular bend; a kink. Also, a tangle, as of a yarn or thread. Chiefly *fig.* E17.
13 *spec.* **a** CRICKET & TENNIS etc. Lateral spin imparted to the ball in striking or delivery, causing it to curve in flight; a stroke or shot by which such spin is given; the action or skill of twisting the ball; a ball to which such spin has been imparted. L17. ▸**b** PHYSICS. Movement both parallel to and around an axis (as in the motion of a screw); the velocity of such movement. L19.
14 The amount or direction of twisting given to the strands of a rope (*rare*); the degree of twisting given to yarn in spinning. E18.
15 a The condition of being twisted spirally; the amount or degree of this; *spec.* the angle of torsion. Also, a spirally twisted object or shape; a spiral line or pattern; *spec.* the rifling in the bore of a gun. E18. ▸**b** A spiral ornament in the stem of a wineglass; a wineglass with this kind of stem. Freq. with specifying word. L19. ▸**c** MECHANICS. Twisting strain or force; torque. L19. ▸**d** *fig.* A means or opportunity of applying coercion; a hold. *slang.* L19. ▸**e** Cheating, swindling, dishonesty; an instance of this. Freq. in ***on the twist***. *slang.* M20.
16 A hearty appetite. *slang.* L18.
17 A turning aside, a deviation; a point or place at which a road changes direction; a bend, a turning. Also *fig.*, a change of circumstances or fortune. Freq. in ***twists and turns*** below. L18.
18 *fig.* **a** An eccentric inclination or attitude; *esp.* a peculiar mental turn or bent; an intellectual or moral bias; a craze. E19. ▸**b** A corruption or misrepresentation of meaning; a phonetic distortion. M19. ▸**c** An unexpected development of events, esp. in a work of fiction; a departure from the norm. M20.
19 A screwing up or contortion of the body or features. Also, a strain or wrench of a limb or joint. M19.

🕮 **11** A. YOUNG Grasping the leaves of the plants, and taking them off with a twist. *Gay Times* They impressed everyone with their spins, twists, . . and tap dancing. *fig.*: D. LEAVITT The final twist of the knife that those who cured should also be stricken. **12** *Westminster Gazette* The twists into which some consciences have got tangled. **15a** *Target Gun* Rifling is offered in 178mm to 305mm twist to suit SS109 or M193 ammunition types. **b** ***air-twist***, ***colour twist***, ***opaque twist***, etc. **17** D. HOGAN A . . jaunt on . . a motorbike around twists by the sea. *Gamut* A strange twist of fate. **18a** DICKENS If in a mind so beautiful any moral twist . . could be found. **b** *Motor Boat & Yachting* A faint Stateside twist to his accent. **c** B. SCHULBERG A comedy with a helluva twist in it. *Taste* We have taken traditional Indian dishes . . and given them an interesting twist. **19** A. TYLER Something fierce about him—maybe the twist of his mouth.

Phrases: ***French twist***: see FRENCH *adjective*. **get in a twist** become confused or muddled. ***get one's knickers in a twist***: see KNICKERS 2. ***on the twist***: see sense 15e above. **out of twist** free from twisting or torsion. **round the twist** = ***round the bend*** s.v.

BEND *noun*^{3}. **twists and turns** intricate or convoluted dealings or circumstances; ins and outs.

Comb.: **twist barrel** a gun barrel formed of a spirally twisted strip or strips of iron; **twist-drill**: with a twisted body like that of an auger; **twist grip** a control operated manually by twisting, *spec.* one serving as a handgrip for operating the throttle on a motorcycle or scooter, or changing the gears on a bicycle; **twist knot** a figure-of-eight knot, repeated or continued so as to form a kind of plait; **twist-lock** a locking device for securing freight containers to the trailers on which they are transported; **twist-off** *noun & adjective* (*a*) *noun* (OIL INDUSTRY) a breaking off of a rotary drill pipe due to torsional strain; (*b*) *adjective* (of a lid, cap, etc.) that may be removed manually by twisting; **twist pile** *noun & adjective* (designating) a carpet or rug with a tightly curled pile, as opp. to a shag pile; **twist tie** a small strip of plastic-covered wire, twisted around the neck of a plastic bag as a closure; *twist yarn*: see sense 4b above.

twist /twɪst/ *noun*^{2}. *slang* (chiefly *US*). Freq. *derog.* E20.
[Rhyming slang.]
More fully *twist and twirl*. A girl, a young woman.

twist /twɪst/ *verb*. ME.
[from (the same root as) the noun.]
▶ **I** †**1** *verb intrans.* Divide into branches; branch. *rare.* Only in ME.
2 *verb trans.* †**a** Detach, take away. Only in LME. ▶**b** Prune, clip. *obsolete* exc. *dial.* L15.
▶ **II 3** *verb trans.* Wrench out of place or shape with a turning action, wring; *esp.* sprain (a limb etc.). Formerly also *fig.*, torment, harass. LME. ▶**b** In *pass.* Be hanged. Now chiefly in *twist in the wind* below. *slang.* E18.
4 *verb trans.* Force, pull, or wrench in a specified direction with a turning motion. Freq. foll. by *off*. LME.
5 *verb intrans. & trans.* Eat heartily. Also foll. by *down*. *slang.* L17.
6 *verb trans.* Give a spiral form to; bend or coil spirally. M18. ▶**b** *verb intrans.* Take a spiral form. L19.
7 a *verb trans. & intrans.* Screw up or contort (the features etc.). L18. ▶**b** *verb trans.* Corrupt or misrepresent the meaning of; force a meaning from. E19.
8 a *verb trans.* Cheat, swindle. *slang.* E20. ▶**b** *verb trans. & intrans.* Induce (a person) to change an insurance policy from one company to another. Chiefly as *twisting verbal noun*. Orig. & chiefly *US*. E20.

📖 **3** J. BUCHAN Able to twist one of their necks before they downed me. *fig.*: S. DESHPANDE The thought of living without him had twisted my insides. **4** B. MOORE The . . man caught Dillon's arm, twisting it up into the small of his back. *Food & Wine* Separate the heads from the tails by twisting off the heads. **6** D. H. LAWRENCE She sat on in silence . . , her fingers twisting her handkerchief. **7a** S. MIDDLETON Her face twisted into gravity, as if she had suddenly tasted something bitter. **b** B. EMECHETA Anybody could twist what He said to suit his own interpretation.

▶ **III 9** *verb trans.* Wind together or spin (strands of hemp, wool, cotton, etc.) into a thread or cord; form (a thread or cord) by winding or spinning the strands. L15. ▶**b** Plait, weave. L16.
10 *verb trans.* Join or unite by twining or interweaving; entwine. Freq. foll. by *together, with*. M16. ▶**b** *fig.* Combine, connect, or associate intimately, like strands in a cord. Also, entangle, mix up; confuse. L16.
11 *verb trans.* Wind or coil (a thread etc.) around something; encircle (an object) with or as with a thread etc. Freq. foll. by *round*. L16.
12 *verb intrans. & refl.* Pass or move in a tortuous manner; coil or wind *about* or *round*; penetrate *into* something with a winding movement or action. M17.

📖 **9** *fig.*: SHAKES. *Much Ado* Was't not to this end That thou began'st to twist so fine a story? **b** H. BROOKE To twist the garland of your blessedness. **10** M. FARADAY Twist together five or six folds of steel harpsichord wire. **b** DRYDEN Pity your own, or pity our Estate; Nor twist our Fortunes with your sinking Fate. SUSAN WARNER The question . . was inextricably twisted up with the other question. **11** BEVERLEY CLEARY Twisting a lock of hair around her finger. **12** G. CUPPLES Flowers . . twisting in thick snaky coils close up the stems. J. RUSKIN Weeds . . have twisted themselves into its crannies.

▶ **IV 13** *verb intrans.* Rotate, revolve; turn so as to face another way. L17. ▶**b** *verb intrans.* In pontoon, request, deal, or be dealt a card face upwards. E20.
14 *verb trans.* Cause to rotate (as) on an axis; change the form, position, or aspect, of (something) by rotating or turning. L18. ▶**b** *verb trans.* Impart lateral spin to (the ball) in cricket, billiards, etc.; cause (the ball) to rotate while following a curved trajectory. E19. ▶**c** *verb intrans.* Dance the twist. M20.
15 *verb intrans.* Take a curved course, wind; proceed with frequent turns; turn and proceed in a new direction. E19.

📖 **13** J. WAINWRIGHT Barker . . twisted in his chair to view the newcomers. **14** R. INGALLS Raymond twisted his head around and smiled. M. KEANE He looked away . . to twist the knobs on the wireless. **15** M. HOCKING A sunken lane which twisted down, wooded hills rising steeply to one side.

Phrases: **twist a person's arm** *colloq.* coerce or persuade a person to do something, esp. by exerting moral pressure. **twist in** *Hist.* initiate or swear in as a member or associate of the Luddites. **twist in the wind** *fig.* be left in an exposed or humiliating position. **twist one's fingers** turn one's fingers about nervously. *twist round one's finger*, *twist round one's little finger*: see FINGER *noun*. *twist the knife*: see KNIFE *noun*. **twist the lion's tail** *US* provoke the resentment of the British. **twist a person's tail** annoy or provoke a person.
■ **twistable** *adjective* able to be twisted M19. **twistingly** *adverb* in a twisting manner M18.

twisted /ˈtwɪstɪd/ *adjective*. LME.
[from prec. + -ED^{1}.]
1 That has been twisted; *esp.* spun or wound together. LME.
2 Wrenched or pulled out of shape; contorted (as) by twisting; tangled, confused; tortuous; BOTANY having a spiral or helical curvature. E18.
3 Esp. of a person: emotionally or mentally unbalanced; neurotic; perverted. Also foll. by *up*. E20.

📖 **1** T. MCGUANE A twisted wire snaffle and draw reins. **2** M. HOCKING Light slanted on twisted branches. *Skin Diver* The twisted wreckage now rests in 60 feet of water. *fig.*: *New Orleans Review* The devices of rhetoric, twisted and confusing or resisting shape themselves. **3** W. HORWOOD He . . grunted to himself with some kind of twisted satisfaction. C. STOLL You've been all twisted up over this hacker—a break will do you good. *Interview* A very adolescent, stunted, twisted sexuality.

Special collocations: **twisted pair** a pair of insulated conductors twisted about each other, as in a flex, or (in TELEPHONY) by alternating their positions on successive telegraph poles. **twisted pillar** ARCHITECTURE a pillar having the appearance of being spirally twisted or consisting of two shafts intertwined. **twisted-stalk** any of several N. American and Asian plants of the genus *Streptopus*, of the lily family, bearing bell-shaped flowers on bent or twisted stalks.
■ **twistedly** *adverb* E20.

twister /ˈtwɪstə/ *noun*. L15.
[from TWIST *verb* + -ER^{1}.]
†**1** A person who prunes or clips trees. *rare.* Only in L15.
2 A person who or device which spins thread, cord, etc.; a machine for spinning yarn or twisting ropes. L16. ▶**b** A wheel, tourniquet, or other device by which torsional force is applied. M19.
3 †**a** A twisting or twining shoot. *rare.* Only in L18. ▶**b** A person who turns this way and that (chiefly *fig.*); *esp.* a dishonest person, a swindler. *colloq.* M19. ▶**c** CRICKET & TENNIS etc. A ball to which twist or lateral spin has been imparted. M19. ▶**d** A grossly exaggerated tale; a lie. *Nautical slang.* M19. ▶**e** A tornado; a waterspout. *N. Amer. colloq.* L19. ▶**f** A key. *US slang.* M20. ▶**g** A twitch, a loop of cord attached to a stick for restraining a horse (see TWITCH *noun*^{1} 1b). *US.* M20. ▶**h** A person who dances the twist. M20.
4 A person or thing causing contortion, confusion, or astonishment; *esp.* something extremely astonishing or staggering (*slang*). Also (*colloq. & dial.*), a blow causing the victim to twist or writhe. M19.
5 A girder. *rare.* L19.
6 An insurance salesperson or agent who induces a holder to change his or her policy from one company to another. Orig. *US.* E20.
7 An intravenous injection of a narcotic drug, esp. a combined dose of heroin or morphine and cocaine. *US slang.* M20.
8 COMPUTING. = TWISTOR 1. L20.
Comb.: **twister's cramp** MEDICINE (now *rare*) pain in the hands or fingers produced by repeated twisting or wringing movements.

twister /ˈtwɪstə/ *verb*. Now *dial.* E17.
[formed as prec. + -ER^{5}.]
†**1** *verb trans. & intrans.* Twist or spin (thread etc.). Only in 17.
2 *verb intrans.* Wind, meander. *dial.* E19.
■ †**twisterer** *noun* (*rare*) a spinner: only in E18.

twisteroo /twɪstəˈruː/ *noun*. *colloq.* M20.
[from TWIST *noun*^{1} + -EROO.]
(A narrative with) an unexpected twist or development.

twistical /ˈtwɪstɪk(ə)l/ *adjective*. *colloq.* E19.
[Irreg. from TWIST *noun*^{1} + -ICAL.]
Somewhat twisted or crooked; *fig.* not straightforward; devious.

twistification /ˌtwɪstɪfɪˈkeɪʃ(ə)n/ *noun*. *rare* (chiefly *US*). M19.
[from TWIST *verb* + -FICATION.]
An act of twisting; a twisted object or part.

twistify /ˈtwɪstɪfʌɪ/ *verb trans.* *US dial. & colloq.* M19.
[from TWISTY + -FY.]
Make twisty (*lit. & fig.*); twist.

twistle /ˈtwɪs(ə)l/ *noun*. *Scot.* L18.
[Cf. next, TWIZZLE *noun*.]
A twist, a wrench.

twistle /ˈtwɪs(ə)l/ *verb trans.* *Scot. & dial.* L18.
[App. from TWIST *verb* + -LE^{3}. Cf. TWIZZLE *verb*.]
Twist, twirl; screw.

twistor /ˈtwɪstə/ *noun*. M20.
[from TWIST *verb* + -OR.]
1 COMPUTING. A non-volatile memory element consisting of an insulated copper wire wound helically round with a wire of readily magnetized material. Freq. *attrib.* in *twistor memory*. Also called *twister*. M20.
2 PHYSICS. A type of spinor used in some descriptions of space–time. M20.

twisty /ˈtwɪsti/ *adjective*. M19.
[from TWIST *noun*^{1}, *verb* + -Y^{1}.]
1 Full of twists or turns; characterized by twisting or winding; *fig.* dishonest, devious, not straightforward. M19.
2 Twisted (physically or mentally). *rare.* E20.

📖 **1** D. LODGE Driving along some twisty coastal road. D. FRANCIS You're a twisty bastard . . . You'd lie as soon as spit. **2** *Interview* The director of the . . perversely life-affirming scare comedy *Near Dark* . . isn't twisty herself.

■ **twistiness** *noun* E20.

twit /twɪt/ *noun*^{1}. E16.
[formed as TWIT *verb*.]
1 An act of twitting; a (good-humoured or teasing) censure or reproach; a taunt. Now *rare.* E16.
2 A person given to twitting; *dial.* a talebearer. E18.
3 A foolish, stupid, or ineffectual person. *colloq.* M20.

📖 **3** *Esquire* Some pompous twit whom most people privately dismiss.

twit /twɪt/ *noun*^{2}. *rare.* E19.
[Origin unkn. Cf. TWITTER *noun*^{3}, *verb*^{2}.]
A fault or entanglement in a thread, which hinders the process of spinning or weaving.
■ **twitty** *adjective* full of or containing twits L19.

twit /twɪt/ *verb*. Earlier †**a-**. Infl. **-tt-**. OE.
[formed as AT *preposition* + WITE *verb*. Aphet. form not recorded until M16.]
1 *verb trans.* Find fault with, censure, reproach, (a person), esp. in a good-humoured or teasing way; taunt. Freq. foll. by *about, for, with*. OE.
2 *verb trans.* (†with *it*). Condemn as a fault, reprove, rebuke, (an act etc.); disparage. Now *rare.* L16.
3 *verb intrans.* Tell tales; blab. Now *dial.* M17.

📖 **1** D. H. ROBINSON His waxed moustache that Phyllis twitted him about. A. BISHOP He . . twitted her for her feminist ideals.

■ **twittingly** *adverb* (*rare*) in a twitting manner L17.

twit /twɪt/ *interjection & noun*^{3}. Freq. redupl. **twit-twit**. L16.
[Imit.]
†**1** (Repr.) the cry of an owl. *rare.* Only in L16.
2 (Repr.) the shrill chirp or tweet of a small bird. E19.

twitch /twɪtʃ/ *noun*^{1}. LME.
[from TWITCH *verb*^{1}.]
1 †**a** *sing.* & in *pl.* Forceps, tweezers. *rare.* LME–L16. ▶**b** A noose, a loop; *spec.* a loop of cord attached to a stick, used to restrain a horse during shoeing etc., by twisting the stick to tighten the loop around the animal's upper lip. E17.
2 An act of twitching; a sudden sharp pull or tug; a jerk. E16.
3 A sudden sharp pain; a pang or twinge, esp. of emotion or conscience. M16.
4 MINING. A point in, or a part of, a vein of ore where it is compressed or narrowed. M17.
5 A sudden involuntary contraction or movement of a muscle etc., esp. of nervous origin; a convulsive or spasmodic jerk or quiver. E18.
6 An occasion or instance of (obsessive) bird-watching; *spec.* an expedition made by a twitcher or bird-watcher to see a rare bird, a gathering of bird-watchers in response to a reported sighting. *slang.* L20.

📖 **2** K. MANSFIELD She gave the bedclothes such a twitch that both her feet became uncovered. **3** J. GALSWORTHY Jon felt a twitch of compassion for the young idiot. **5** G. SWIFT Henry . . comes home . . a mass of twitches, trembles, shakes and jitters. L. NKOSI Not really a smile, but a simple twitch of the lips.

twitch /twɪtʃ/ *noun*^{2}. L16.
[Alt. of QUITCH.]
Couch grass, *Elytrigia repens*. Also *twitch-grass*.

twitch /twɪtʃ/ *verb*^{1}. ME.
[Corresp. to Low German *twikken*, Old High German *gizwickan*, Middle & mod. High German *zwicken*, from Germanic, repr. also by Old English *twiċċian* pluck, TWICK.]
1 *verb intrans.* Pull or jerk sharply; give a sudden sharp pull or tug *at*. ME.
2 *verb trans.* Give a sudden sharp pull at; take suddenly or with a jerk; snatch *away, from*, etc. Also (now *rare*), pluck (the strings of a musical instrument). Freq. with prepositions or adverbs. ME. ▶**b** Snatch by way of

robbery or theft. Now *rare*. E17. ▸**c** Pull (logs) along the ground with a chain. M19.

3 *verb trans.* Pinch and pluck at (as) with pincers or tweezers, nip; hurt or pain in this way. Now chiefly *dial.* LME.

4 *verb trans.* Orig., (esp. of a horse) draw *up* (a limb etc.) sharply or with a jerk. Now, move (part of the body etc.) spasmodically or convulsively. E16.

5 *verb intrans.* Orig. (*rare*), proceed in a jerking or irregular way. Now, (of the muscles, limbs, etc.) make jerky or spasmodic involuntary movements; contract convulsively. L16. ▸**b** *verb intrans.* Of a motor vehicle etc.: judder slightly or veer momentarily sideways, esp. when travelling at high speed. Also foll. by *out*. *colloq.* L20.

6 *verb trans.* **a** Draw tight by means of a cord etc.; tie or fasten tightly or firmly. Also, tie or fasten (a cord etc.) tightly. Now *dial.* E17. ▸**b** Castrate (a horse) by means of a cord looped over the testicles and drawn tight. Also, restrain (a horse) by means of a twitch or noose around the lips (see TWITCH *noun*[1] 1b). M19.

7 *verb intrans.* MINING. Of a vein of ore: become compressed or narrowed; run *out*. E18.

8 a *verb intrans.* Watch for or spot rare birds, esp. obsessively. Cf. TWITCHER 4. *slang.* L20. ▸**b** *verb trans.* Make a sighting of (a rare bird). *slang.* L20.

📖 **1** E. WHARTON Fidgeting, twitching at her draperies . . when people were noticing her. **2** V. WOOLF She twitched her husband's sleeve. P. D. JAMES She leaned forward to twitch another grape from the bunch. **3** *fig.*: D. W. JERROLD [He] was twitched by a momentary surprise, but directly recovered himself. **4** J. C. OATES Lodestar held his ground, . . twitching his nostrils. **5** G. VIDAL His mouth was twitching from the strain. A. CARTER Its paws would twitch as it chased rabbits in its sleep. **6a** W. LAW Her Stays which her Mother had ordered to be twitch'd so strait.

■ **twitched** *ppl adjective* (**a**) that has (been) twitched; (**b**) *slang* twitchy, irritable: L19.

twitch /twɪtʃ/ *verb*[2]. *dial.* L18.
[from TWITCH *noun*[2].]
1 *verb intrans.* Gather and destroy twitch or couch grass. L18.
2 *verb trans.* Clear (land) of twitch. *rare.* L19.

twitchel /ˈtwɪtʃ(ə)l/ *noun. dial.* Also **twitchen**.
[Old English *twycene, twicen*. Cf. TWITTEN.]
†**1** A fork in a road, a forked way. OE–ME.
2 A narrow lane; a narrow passage between walls or hedges. LME.

twitcher /ˈtwɪtʃə/ *noun.* L16.
[from TWITCH *verb*[1] + -ER[1].]
1 An instrument for plucking or pinching something; *spec.* †(**a**) an instrument for clinching a ring through a pig's nose; †(**b**) in *pl.*, tweezers; (**c**) in *pl.* (*dial.*), pincers. L16.
2 A person who or thing which moves jerkily or spasmodically. *rare.* L18.
3 That which causes twitching; a severe blow; an acute pain. *dial.* E19.
4 A bird-watcher whose main aim is to collect sightings of rare birds. *slang.* L20.

twitchety /ˈtwɪtʃɪti/ *adjective.* M19.
[from TWITCH *verb*[1], *noun*[1] after *crotchety, fidgety*, etc.]
Twitchy, nervous (*colloq.*); (of a thing) moving back and forth.

twitchy /ˈtwɪtʃi/ *adjective*[1]. *rare.* M17.
[from TWITCH *noun*[2] + -Y[1].]
Full of or infested with twitch or couch grass; made of twitch.

twitchy /ˈtwɪtʃi/ *adjective*[2]. M18.
[from TWITCH *verb*[1] + -Y[1].]
1 MINING. Of a vein of ore: compressed, narrowed. M18.
2 Characterized by twitching; having a tendency to twitch; nervous, fidgety; irritable. M19. ▸**b** Of a motor vehicle etc.: tending to judder slightly or veer momentarily sideways, esp. at high speed; that handles unstably or unpredictably. *colloq.* L20.

📖 **2** J. COLE Those with marginal seats are inevitably more twitchy as the election draws nearer. R. F. HOBSON He became less twitchy, less scared of people.

■ **twitchily** *adverb* in a twitchy manner; nervously: M20. **twitchiness** *noun* the state or condition of being twitchy; nervousness, irritability: M20.

twite /twʌɪt/ *noun.* M16.
[Imit. of the bird's call.]
A small Eurasian moorland finch, *Acanthis flavirostris*, resembling the linnet.

twitten /ˈtwɪt(ə)n/ *noun. dial.* E19.
[Perh. rel. to Low German *twiete* alley, lane. Cf. TWITCHEL.]
A narrow path or passage between two walls or hedges.

twitter /ˈtwɪtə/ *noun*[1]. L16.
[from TWIT *verb* + -ER[1].]
A person who twits or reproaches someone (long *rare*); *dial.* a talebearer.

twitter /ˈtwɪtə/ *noun*[2]. L17.
[from TWITTER *verb*[1].]
1 A state of tremulous excitement or agitation. Now *colloq.* L17. ▸**b** A suppressed laugh, a titter; a fit of laughter. *dial.* M18.
2 The action or an act of twittering; light tremulous chirping; a twittering sound; (trivial or idle) chatter. M19.

📖 **1** P. G. WODEHOUSE The dazed feeling passed off, leaving me all of a twitter. **2** B. HEAD To listen to the twitter of birds. *Sunday Correspondent* Between high conversation and low comedy—'drawing-room twitter and the banana skin'.

twitter /ˈtwɪtə/ *noun*[3]. *Scot. & north.* E18.
[Origin unkn. Cf. TWIT *noun*[2], TWITTER *verb*[2].]
A thin part of unevenly spun yarn. Also, an entanglement; a complication.

twitter /twɪtə/ *noun*[4]. Long *obsolete* exc. *dial.* L19.
[Var. of QUITTER *noun*[1].]
= QUITTER *noun*[1] 2. Also more fully ***twitter-bone***.

twitter /ˈtwɪtə/ *verb*[1]. LME.
[Imit.: see -ER[5].]
1 *verb intrans.* Of a bird: utter a succession of light tremulous sounds; chirp continuously with a tremulous effect. Of a person: make a sound similar to this; talk rapidly in a tremulous voice; chatter, esp. in an idle or trivial manner. LME.
2 *verb trans.* Utter or express by twittering. LME.
3 *verb intrans.* Move tremulously, tremble or quiver, esp. with excitement or agitation. Formerly also, hanker *after*. Now chiefly *Scot. & dial.* E17. ▸**b** *verb trans.* Move (a thing) tremulously; twiddle (the fingers). *rare* (chiefly *Scot.*). M19.
4 *verb intrans.* Laugh in a suppressed way, titter. *dial.* L17.
5 *verb trans.* Bring into a specified condition by twittering. *rare.* M19.

📖 **1** *Slimming* Twittering on and on . . until I finally gabbled to a stop. *Raritan* She talked to me . . in her skeptically hoarse, twittering English. **2** A. PILLING 'Henry's quite a *trendy* name these days,' Miss Bingham twittered faintly. **3** R. L. STEVENSON I was . . twittering with cold.

■ **twitteˈration** *noun* (*colloq.*, *rare*) = TWITTER *noun*[2] 1 E19. **twitterer** *noun* M19. **twitteringly** *adverb* (*rare*) in a twittering manner M19.

twitter /ˈtwɪtə/ *verb*[2] *trans. Scot. & north.* L17.
[Origin unkn. Cf. TWIT *noun*[2], TWITTER *noun*[3].]
Spin or twist (yarn) unevenly.

twitter /ˈtwɪtə/ *verb*[3] *trans. rare* (now *dial.*). M18.
[from TWIT *verb* + -ER[5].]
Reproach, twit; tease.

twittery /ˈtwɪt(ə)ri/ *adjective.* L19.
[from TWITTER *noun*[2], *verb*[1] + -Y[1].]
Apt to twitter or tremble; tremulous, shaky.

†**twittle** *verb trans. rare.* L16–L18.
[App. alt. of TITTLE *verb*[1]. Cf. next.]
Utter or express idly; babble; twitter.

†**twittle-twattle** *noun.* M16–E18.
[App. alt. of TITTLE-TATTLE. Cf. TWATTLE.]
Idle talk, tittle-tattle.

twit-twit *interjection & noun* see TWIT *interjection & noun*[3].

'twixt /twɪkst/ *preposition. arch. & dial.* Also †**twixt**. ME.
[Aphet.]
= BETWIXT *preposition.*

twizzle /ˈtwɪz(ə)l/ *noun.* Chiefly *dial.* M19.
[Prob. from next. Cf. TWISTLE *noun.*]
1 A twist, a turn; a change of direction. M19.
2 In a spinning-machine, the eye of a flyer. L19.

twizzle /ˈtwɪz(ə)l/ *verb. dial. & colloq.* L18.
[App. an imit. formation suggested by TWIST *verb*. Cf. TWISTLE *verb.*]
1 *verb trans.* Twirl, twist; turn round; form by twisting. L18.
2 *verb intrans.* Rotate rapidly, spin, twirl. E19.

two /tuː/ *adjective & noun (cardinal numeral).* Also (*Scot.*) **twa** /twɑː/.
[Old English *twā* fem., *twā, tū* neut. = Old Frisian *twā*, Old Saxon *twā, twō*, Old High German *zwā, zwō*, Old Norse *tvær*, Gothic *twōs*, cogn. with Greek, Latin *duo*, Sanskrit *dvau* masc., *dve* fem. and neut.]
▸ **A** *adjective.* **1** One more than one (a cardinal numeral represented by 2 in arabic numerals, ii, II in roman). OE.
2 Of a pair of people, things, etc.: different from one another, distinct. L16.

📖 **1** SOUTHEY The two best ships in the navy. J. STEINBECK Two ropes, one tied to a . . stone and one to a basket. DAY LEWIS My first two years, in the house where I was born. *Interview* A rap group from Los Angeles that has sold two million albums. ***as like as two peas***: see PEA *noun*[1] 1. ***between two fires***: see FIRE *noun*. ***crazy as a two-bob watch***: see WATCH *noun*. ***have two left feet***: see LEFT *adjective* 2. ***have two strings to one's bow***: see STRING *noun*. ***in two ticks***: see TICK *noun*[3] 4. **in two twos** *colloq.* = ***in two ticks*** s.v. TICK *noun*[3] 4. **in two ups** *Austral.* = ***in two ticks*** s.v. TICK *noun*[3] 4. ***kill two birds with one stone***: see BIRD *noun*. ***lesser of two evils***: see EVIL *noun*[1]. ***not have two pennies to rub together***: see RUB *verb*. ***no two ways about it***: see WAY *noun*. ***two bites at the cherry***: see CHERRY *noun* 1. ***two cheers***: see CHEER *noun*[1] 7. ***two figures***: see FIGURE *noun*. **two fingers** a coarse gesture of contempt in which the index and second fingers are made into a V-sign. ***two jumps ahead***: see JUMP *noun*[1]. **two natures** CHRISTIAN THEOLOGY the divine and human natures united in Christ. **two or three** an indefinite or inconsequential number of; a few. ***two pair (of stairs)***: see PAIR *noun*[1]. **two parts** two out of three equal parts; two-thirds. **two times** (now chiefly *Scot. & dial.*) twice. ***walking on two legs, walking with two legs***: see WALKING *noun*. **2** G. S. STREET Gerald in town and Gerald in the country were two people. ***be in two minds***: see MIND *noun*[1]. ***fall between two stools***: see STOOL *noun* 2b. ***the beast with two backs***: see BEAST *noun*. ***the two cultures***: see CULTURE *noun* 6. ***two nations***: see NATION *noun*[1]. ***two sides of a shield***: see SHIELD *noun*[1].

▸ **B** *noun.* **1** Two persons or things identified contextually, as parts or divisions, years of age, points, runs, etc., in a game, chances (in giving odds), minutes, inches, shillings (now *Hist.*), pence, etc. OE.
2 One more than one as an abstract number; the symbol(s) or figure(s) representing this (2 in arabic numerals, ii, II in roman); a figure shaped like 2. OE.
3 The time of day two hours after midnight or midday (on a clock, watch, etc., indicated by the numeral two displayed or pointed to). Also **two o'clock**. LME.
4 A set of two; a thing having a set of two as an essential or distinguishing feature; *spec.* (**a**) a playing-card, domino, or face of a die marked with two pips or spots; (**b**) a unit of two soldiers in a military drill, formed when executing a wheeling movement; (**c**) CRICKET a hit for which two runs are scored. LME.
5 The second of a set or series with numbered members, the one designated two, (usu. ***number two***, or with specification, as ***book two***, ***chapter two***, etc.); a size etc. denoted by two, a shoe, glove, garment, etc., of such a size (also ***size two***). E16.
6 Either of a set of two; *spec.* a large plant-pot of which two are formed from one cast of clay. E19.

📖 **1** C. P. SNOW The other two were talking cheerfully. **a — or two** one or two —s; a few —s (***bring down a peg or two***, ***take down a peg or two***: see PEG *noun*[1] 2). ***a trick worth two of that***: see TRICK *noun*. **in two** (**a**) into or in two parts or pieces; †(**b**) so as to be separate the one from the other; apart. ***know a thing or two***: see KNOW *verb*. **that makes two of us** *colloq.* that is true of me also. ***two a penny***: see PENNY *noun*. **two by two**, **two and two** in pairs; two at a time. **two can play at that game** another person's behaviour can be copied to that person's disadvantage. **2 put two and two together** make an (esp. obvious) inference or conclusion from the known facts. **two and two make four** a typically obvious or undeniable statement. **3** WORDSWORTH The minster-clock has just struck two. **4** L. GARFIELD The congregation began to come out, at first in ones and twos. **twos and threes** a children's chasing game for six or more players. **two-up and two-down**, **two-up two-down** a house with two reception rooms downstairs and two bedrooms upstairs. **5** ***number two***: see NUMBER *noun*. ***Radio Two***: see RADIO *noun* 3.

Comb.: Forming compound cardinal numerals with multiples of ten from twenty to ninety, as ***thirty-two***, (*arch.*) ***two-and-thirty***, etc., and (*arch.*) their corresponding ordinals as. ***two-and-thirtieth*** etc., and with multiples of a hundred, as **302** (read ***three hundred and two***, US also ***three hundred two***) etc. With nouns + -ER[1] forming nouns with the sense 'something (identified contextually) being of or having two —s', as ***two-seater***, ***two-wheeler***, etc. Special combs., as **two-address** *adjective* (COMPUTING) having two addresses; **two-and-eight** *rhyming slang* a state of agitation; ***two-backed beast***: see BEAST *noun*; **two-bagger** BASEBALL a hit enabling the batter to reach second base safely; **two-bill** = TWIBILL; **two-bit** *adjective* (*N. Amer.*) (**a**) of the value of a quarter of a dollar; (**b**) *colloq.* cheap, petty, worthless; small-time; **two-body** *adjective* (PHYSICS) involving or pertaining to two objects or particles; **two-bottle** *adjective* (of a person) capable of drinking two bottles of wine at a sitting; **two-by-four** *noun & adjective* (**a**) *noun* (orig. *US*) a length of timber measuring 2 inches by 4 in cross-section; (**b**) *adjective* (*US*) small, insignificant; **two-cent** *adjective* (*US*) (**a**) of the value of two cents; (**b**) *colloq.* = ***two-bit*** (b) above; **two-China(s)** *adjective* (*US* POLITICS) designating a proposal or policy for admitting to the United Nations representatives of both Communist China and Taiwan; **two-coat** *adjective* requiring two coats of plaster, paint, etc.; **two-cycle** *adjective* = ***two-stroke*** (a) below; **two-decker** *noun & adjective* (designating) a thing with two main decks, layers, or divisions; *spec.* (designating) a warship with two gun-decks; **two-dimensional** *adjective* (**a**) having or appearing to have length and breadth but no depth; (**b**) *fig.* lacking depth or substance; shallow, superficial; **two-dimensionality** two-dimensional quality; **two dimensionally** *adverb* in a two-dimensional manner, in terms of two dimensions; **two-eared** *adjective* having two ears; *esp.* (of a cup etc.) two-handled; **two-edged** *adjective* (**a**) having two edges; *esp.* (of a sword, axe, etc.) having two cutting edges; (*b*) *fig.* equally damaging to a user or opponent; (of a compliment etc.) cutting both ways, double-edged; **two-egg** *adjective* = DIZYGOTIC; **two-ended** *adjective* having two ends (*spec.* with different properties, as a magnet); **two-eyed** *adjective* having two eyes; involving or adapted for the use of both eyes; ***two-eyed stance*** CRICKET, a batting stance in which the batsman turns the head to face the oncoming ball as far as possible, whilst keeping the left shoulder on the line of the ball; **two-faced** *adjective* (*a*) having two faces; (*b*) *fig.* deceitful, insincere; **two-facedness** *rare* the quality of being two-faced; **two-field** *adjective* denoting a system of agriculture in which two fields are cropped and fallowed alternately; **two-fisted** *adjective* (*a*) *dial.* & *colloq.* awkward with the hands, clumsy; (*b*) *US colloq.* tough, aggressive; hearty, vigorous; (*c*) TENNIS (of a ground stroke) played with both hands on the racket; **two-foot** *adjective* †(*a*) two-footed; (*b*) measuring two feet in length, breadth, etc.; **two-footed** *adjective* (*a*) having two feet; biped; (*b*) (of a footballer) able to kick equally well with either foot; **two-forked** *adjective* having two forks, branches, or prongs; bifurcate; dichotomous; **two-four** *adjective* & *noun* (designating) time or rhythm with two crotchets in a bar; **two-hand** *adjective* (*obsolete* exc. *Scot.*) two-handed; **two-headed** *adjective* (*a*) (represented as) having two heads; (*b*) having two leaders or rulers; **two-holer** *N. Amer.* a water-closet or lavatory accommodating two people; **two-horse** *adjective* (*a*) (of a cart, plough, etc.) drawn or used with two horses; (*b*) (of a race or other contest) in which only two of the competitors or participants are likely winners; **two-leaf** *adjective* (*rare*) = ***two-leaved*** below; **two-leaved** *adjective* having or consisting of two leaves; (of a table etc.) having two hinged or folding parts; **two-legged** *adjective* having two legs; ***two-legged mare***: see MARE *noun*¹; **two-line** *adjective* having, consisting of, or marked with two lines; *spec.* (*a*) PRINTING (of a capital letter) extending to the depth of two lines of text; (*b*) ***two-line whip***, a notice, underlined twice to indicate less urgency than a three-line whip, requesting the members of Parliament of a particular party to attend a parliamentary vote; the discipline of such a notice; **two-lined** *adjective* (*rare*) having or consisting of two lines, two-line; **two-lipped** *adjective* having two lips; BOTANY (of a corolla, calyx, etc.) having its limb fused into two unequal lobes, the upper of which projects over the lower like a lip; **two-meal** *adjective* (*a*) (now *dial.*) (of cheese) made from a blend of milk from two separate meals or milkings; (*b*) of or involving two meals a day; **two-old-cat** *US* a form of baseball similar to one-old-cat, but played with two batters; **two-one** (a graduate having) an upper-second-class degree; **two-part** *adjective* (MUSIC) composed for two parts or voices; **two-piece** *adjective* & *noun* (*a*) *adjective* consisting of two matching items, as a suite of furniture or suit of clothes; (*b*) *noun* a two-piece suit; a bikini; a two-piece suite; **two-piecer** *US* a two-piece suit or swimming costume; **two-pipe** *adjective* (*a*) (of a hot-water central heating system) in which a flow pipe supplies the radiators and a separate return pipe receives water from them; (*b*) (of a plumbing system) that uses separate pipes from sinks, toilets, etc., to convey waste to the sewer; **two-platoon (system)** AMER. FOOTBALL the system of training and playing two separate offensive and defensive units; ***two-pot screamer***: see SCREAMER 1; **two-pronged** *adjective* having two prongs or projecting points (***two-pronged bristletail***: see ***bristletail*** s.v. BRISTLE *noun*); **two-revolution** *adjective* (PRINTING) designating a cylinder press in which the impression cylinder rotates continuously, alternately printing and delivering sheets as the forme moves to and fro; **two-rowed** *adjective* having two rows; ***two-rowed barley***, a barley, *Hordeum distichon*, having two longitudinal rows of fertile spikelets (now the usual form in cultivation); **two-shear** *adjective* & *noun* (*a*) *adjective* (of a sheep) that has been shorn twice; (*b*) *noun* a two-shear sheep; the time or age of the second shearing; **two-shoes** (in full ***goody two-shoes***) (a name for) a child (the nickname of the girl heroine of the *History of Little Goody Two-shoes* (1766)); **two-shot** a cinema or television shot of two people together; **two-sided** *adjective* (*a*) having two sides, bilateral; (*b*) *fig.* having two parts or aspects, controversial; **two-spot** *US* (*a*) a two-pipped playing-card, a deuce; (*b*) *Hist.* a two-dollar banknote; (*c*) an insignificant or worthless person; (*d*) a two-year prison sentence; **two-star** *adjective* & *noun* (*a*) *adjective* given two stars in a grading system in which this denotes the next standard up from the lowest, as a hotel, restaurant, grade of petrol, etc.; having or designating a military rank distinguished by two stars on the shoulder-piece of the uniform; (*b*) *noun* something, esp. petrol, given a two-star grading; **two-state** *adjective* capable of existing in either of two states or conditions; **two-step** *noun*, *verb*, & *adjective* (*a*) *noun* a round dance for couples characterized by sliding steps in duple rhythm; a piece of music for this dance; (***Aztec two-step***: see AZTEC *adjective*; ***military two-step***: see MILITARY *adjective*); (*b*) *verb intrans.* dance a two-step; (*c*) *adjective* having or consisting of two successive actions or stages; **two-sticker** *colloq.* a two-masted ship; ***two-striper***: see STRIPER 1; **two-stroke** *adjective* & *noun* (*a*) *adjective* (of an engine) working mechanically by means of a repeated reciprocal movement, in and out or up and down; (of a vehicle) having an internal-combustion engine in which the power cycle is completed in one up and down stroke of a piston; (*b*) *noun* a two-stroke engine or vehicle; **two-suiter** (*a*) BRIDGE a hand with two suits strong enough to bid; (*b*) (orig. *US*) a suitcase designed to hold two suits and accessories; **two-tailed** *adjective* (*a*) having two tails; (*b*) STATISTICS (of a test) that tests for deviation from the null hypothesis in both directions; **two-teeth** *adjective* & *noun* (now *rare*) = ***two-tooth*** below; **two-thirds** *noun* & *adjective* (*a*) *noun* two of the three equal parts into which a thing is or may be divided; (*b*) *adjective* consisting of two-thirds of something; measuring two-thirds of something identified contextually; (of a garment) being two-thirds of the normal length; **two-time** *adjective* & *verb* (*colloq.*, orig. *US*) (*a*) *adjective* characterized by something that has happened or been done twice; (*b*) *verb trans.* & *intrans.* deceive or be unfaithful to (esp. a spouse or lover); swindle, double-cross (a person); **two-timer** a person who is unfaithful or deceitful; **two-tone**, **two-toned** *adjectives* (*a*) in two colours or two shades of the same colour; (*b*) being or emitting two sounds, usu. alternately at intervals; **two-tongued** *adjective* (now *rare*) (*a*) having two tongues; (*b*) *fig.* double-tongued, deceitful; **two-tooth** *adjective* & *noun* (now *Austral.* & *NZ*) (designating) a sheep between one and two years old with two full-grown permanent teeth; **two-two** (*a*) *adjective* designating (ammunition for) a gun of .22 calibre; (*b*) *noun* a gun of .22 calibre; (a graduate having) a lower second-class degree; **two-up** *noun* & *adverb* (*a*) *noun* (*Austral.* & *NZ*) a gambling game played by tossing two coins, bets being laid on the showing of two heads or two tails; (*b*) *adverb* (*rare*) two at a time, two together; **two-valued** *adjective* (chiefly LOGIC) capable of taking one or other of only two values; characterized by the usual two truth-values, i.e. truth and falsity; **two-yearling** (now *rare* or *obsolete*) an animal of two years old.

■ **twoer** *noun* (*colloq.*) something consisting of or counted as two, as a hit at cricket for which two runs are scored L19. **twofold** *adjective*, *adverb*, & *noun* (*a*) *adjective* twice as great or as numerous; having two parts, divisions, elements, or units; double, dual (*lit.* & *fig.*); (of yarn) consisting of two yarns twisted into one; *Scot.* folded or bent double; (*b*) *adverb* to twice the number or quantity, doubly; (chiefly *Scot.*) so as to be folded or doubled, esp. from age; (*c*) *noun* (*rare*) a twofold yarn: OE. **twofoldly** *adverb* in a twofold manner, doubly ME. **twofoldness** *noun* the fact, quality, or condition of being two in number or twofold, duality E19. **twoness** *noun* the fact or condition of being two; duality: M17. **twosome** *noun* & *adjective* (orig. *Scot.*) (*a*) *noun* a set of two persons or things, *esp.* a pair of lovers; a game, dance, etc., for two people; (*b*) *adjective* (chiefly *Scot.*) consisting of two, for two; *esp.* (of a dance) performed by two people together: LME.

twoc /twɒk/ *verb trans. slang.* Infl. **-cc-**, **-ck-**. L20.
[from *TWOC*, acronym from *taking without owner's consent*, orig. used by UK police.]
Steal (a car). Usu. in *pass.* or as ***twoccing*** *verbal noun.*

🕮 J. GOODWIN I've got a criminal record. Nothing major: twocking, credit cards—serves the dopey fuckers right.

■ **twoccer** *noun* a person who steals a car L20.

twofer /ˈtuːfə/ *noun. US colloq.* L19.
[Repr. a pronunc. of *two for* (one): see prec., FOR *preposition.*]
1 A cigar sold at two for a quarter; *loosely* any cheap cigar. L19.
2 A coupon entitling a person to buy two tickets for a specified theatre show for the price of one. M20.
3 Any two items (regarded as being) obtained for the price of one; *spec.* a woman from a racial minority appointed to a post, the appointment being seen as satisfying the requirements of both racial and sexual equality of opportunity. M20.

two-handed /tuːˈhandɪd, *esp. attrib.* ˈtuːhandɪd/ *adjective & adverb.* LME.
[from TWO *adjective* + HAND *noun* + -ED².]
▶ **A** *adjective.* **1** Requiring the use of both hands; (of a sword etc.) wielded with both hands. LME.
2 Involving two people; *spec.* (*a*) (of a saw etc.) worked by two people; (*b*) (of a card-game etc.) for two players; (*c*) (of a play) for two actors. L16.
3 Big, bulky; strapping. *colloq.* (now *rare* or *obsolete*). L17.
4 Having two hands. *rare.* M19.
5 Using both hands equally well, ambidextrous; handy, efficient. Chiefly *Scot.* M19.
6 Generous, open-handed. *US colloq.* E20.
▶ **B** *adverb.* Two-handedly. L20.
■ **two-handedly** *adverb* with or in both hands E20. **two-handedness** *noun* the state of being two-handed L19. **two-hander** *noun* (*a*) a two-handed sword; (*b*) a play for two actors: L19.

twopence /ˈtʌp(ə)ns/ *noun.* Also **tuppence**. LME.
[from TWO *adjective* + PENCE.]
1 A British silver coin worth two old pennies; a half-groat (since 1662 coined only as Maundy money) (*obsolete* exc. *Hist.*); a copper coin of this value issued in the reign of George III (*obsolete* exc. *Hist.*). Also, since 1968, a coin worth two (new) pence. LME.
2 Two pence, esp. of the old British currency before decimalization. L15.
3 A very small amount. Freq. in neg. contexts. L17.
Phrases: **for twopence** very easily, with the slightest encouragement. **herb twopence** = CREEPING *Jenny*. **not care twopence** not care at all.
Comb.: **twopence coloured** *adjective* cheap and gaudy (from the price of coloured prints of characters for toy theatres sold in the early 19th cent., as opp. to black and white ones sold for one penny).
¶ Post-decimalization sense of the coin usu. two words and pronounced /tuː ˈpɛns/.

twopenn'orth *noun* var. of TWOPENNYWORTH.

twopenny /ˈtʌp(ə)ni/ *adjective & noun.* Also **tuppen(n)y**. LME.
[from TWO *adjective* + PENNY.]
▶ **A** *adjective.* **1** Worth or costing twopence or two (new) pence. LME.
2 *fig.* Paltry, trifling, worthless. Freq. in ***(not) care a twopenny damn***, ***(not) care a twopenny hang***, ***(not) give a twopenny damn***, ***(not) give a twopenny hang***. M16.

🕮 **2** G. GREENE Wealth! one smiles at the word in the face of that twopenny interior.

▶ **B** *ellipt.* as *noun.* **1** *Hist.* **a** Twopenny ale. Latterly *Scot.* E18. ▶**b** The twopenny post; a letter sent by this service. E19.
2 A twopenny piece; the sum of twopence. *rare.* M18.
3 As a term of endearment to a child or woman: dearest, darling. M19.
4 [Abbreviation of *twopenny loaf of bread.*] The head. *rhyming slang.* M19.
Special collocations & comb.: **twopenny ale**, **twopenny beer** *Hist.* a quality of ale originally sold at twopence per quart; in Scotland, at twopence a Scotch pint (3 imperial pints). **twopenny-halfpenny** *adjective* (*a*) worth twopence-halfpenny; (*b*) cheap, insignificant. **twopenny library** *Hist.* a lending library, usu. operated from a shop, from which a book could be borrowed for twopence a week. **twopenny piece** a coin worth twopence or two (new) pence. **twopenny post** *Hist.* (designating) a postal service operating in London (1801–1839) by which letters etc. were conveyed at an ordinary charge of twopence each. **twopenny upright** *slang* a prostitute.

twopennyworth /ˈtʌp(ə)nɪwəθ, -wəːθ/ *noun.* Also **twopenn'orth** /tuːˈpɛnəθ/. M19.
[from prec. + WORTH *noun*¹.]
As much as is worth or costs twopence; *fig.* a paltry or insignificant amount.
add one's twopennyworth, **put in one's twopennyworth** *colloq.* contribute one's opinion.

twos /tuːz/ *verb intrans. US colloq.* E20.
[from TWO *noun.*]
Keep company with a person of the opposite sex. Chiefly as ***twosing*** *verbal noun.*

'twould *verb* see IT *pronoun.*

two-way /ˈtuːweɪ, tuːˈweɪ/ *adjective & noun.* L16.
[from TWO *adjective* + WAY *noun.*]
▶ **A** *adjective.* **1** Having or involving two ways, roads, or channels; situated where two ways meet. Now *esp.*, (of a tap) permitting fluid etc. to flow in either of two channels or directions. L16. ▶**b** Of a plug or adaptor: capable of accommodating two plugs at the same time. E20. ▶**c** Of a loudspeaker: having two separate drive units for different frequency ranges. M20.
2 Extending in two directions or dimensions; having two modes of variation. L19.
3 Of a switch, wiring, etc.: permitting a current to be switched on or off at either of two points. L19.
4 a Involving or permitting communication in two directions; (of a radio) capable of both transmitting and receiving signals; (of traffic etc.) moving in two esp. opposite directions. E20. ▶**b** Of an arrangement, relationship, etc.: involving two participants; involving reciprocal action or responsibility. M20. ▶**c** ***two-way mirror***, a panel of glass which can be seen through from one side and is a mirror on the other. M20.
2 two-way stretch (designating) a garment, esp. a corset or girdle, capable of stretching in both length and width. **4b two-way street** *fig.* a situation of mutual action; something that works both ways.
▶ **B** *ellipt.* as *noun.* A two-way radio. M20.

TWT *abbreviation.*
Travelling-wave tube.

twy- *prefix* var. of TWI-.

twybill *noun* var. of TWIBILL.

twyer *noun* var. of TUYÈRE.

twyfold *adjective & adverb* var. of TWIFOLD.

TX *abbreviation.*
Texas.

-ty /ti/ *suffix*¹ (not productive).
[Old French *-te(t)* (mod. *-té*) from Latin *-itat-*, *-itas*. In many cases superseded by -ITY.]
Forming nouns of quality or condition (or instances of it), as ***admiralty***, ***bounty***, ***cruelty***, ***faculty***, ***honesty***, ***plenty***, ***puberty***, ***safety***, ***subtlety***, ***temporalty***.

-ty /ti/ *suffix*² (not productive).
[Old English *-tig* corresp. to Old Frisian *-tich*, Old Saxon *-tig* (Dutch *-tig*), Old High German *-zug* (German *-zig*), and Old Norse *tigr*, Gothic *tigus* ten.]
Forming cardinal numerals from 20 to 90 (in Old English to 120), denoting 'so many tens', as ***eighty***, ***forty***, ***sixty***, ***twenty***.

Tyburn /ˈtʌɪbəːn/ *adjective.* LME.
[A place in London, near the site of Marble Arch, where public hangings were held *c* 1300–1783.]
Hist. Of or pertaining to Tyburn or a public hanging. Chiefly in collocations (see below).
Tyburn ticket *slang* a certificate formerly granted to a person who secured a criminal's conviction, exempting the holder from all parochial duties in the parish where the offence was committed. **Tyburn tree** *slang* the gallows.

Tyburnian /tʌɪˈbəːnɪən/ *adjective. arch.* M19.
[from *Tyburnia* (see below): see -IAN.]
Of or pertaining to Tyburnia, former name for a residential district near the site of Tyburn.

tychism /ˈtʌɪkɪz(ə)m/ *noun.* L19.
[from Greek *tukhē* chance + -ISM.]
PHILOSOPHY. The theory that objective account must be taken of the element of chance in philosophical etc. reasoning.

tycho- /ˈtʌɪkəʊ/ *combining form*.
[from Greek *tukhē* fortune, chance: see **-O-**.]
Chiefly BIOLOGY. Exceptional; occasional.
■ **tychopartheno'genesis** *noun* exceptional or occasional parthenogenesis E20. **tychopo'tamic** *adjective* (of algae, plankton, etc.) occasionally or exceptionally occurring in or near rivers E20.

Tychonian /tʌɪˈkəʊnɪən/ *noun & adjective*. M17.
[formed as next + **-IAN**.]
Hist. ▶**A** *noun*. An advocate of the Tychonic theory. *rare*. M17.
▶**B** *adjective*. = next. E18.

Tychonic /tʌɪˈkɒnɪk/ *adjective*. L17.
[from *Tychon-* stem of the Latinized form of the name of *Tycho* (Danish *Tyge*) Brahe (see below) + **-IC**.]
Of or pertaining to the Danish astronomer Tycho Brahe (1546–1601); designating or pertaining to his theory that the planets revolve around the sun, which revolves around the earth.

tycoon /tʌɪˈkuːn/ *noun*. M19.
[Japanese *taikun* great lord or prince, from Chinese *dà* great + *jūn* prince.]
1 *Hist.* A title applied by foreigners to the shogun of Japan in power between 1857 and 1868. M19.
2 A business magnate. M19.

📖 **2** A. BROOKNER They will become tycoons, captains of industry. K. VONNEGUT An American artist made as much money as many movie stars and tycoons.

■ **tycoonery** *noun* (*a*) the practice of a tycoon or tycoons; (*b*) a group of tycoons: M20. **tycoonish** *adjective* characteristic of a tycoon M20. **tycoonship** *noun* the status or position of a tycoon; the fact of being a tycoon: M20.

tye /tʌɪ/ *noun*[1] & *verb*[1]. *obsolete* exc. *dial.* Also **tie**.
[Old English *tēag*, *tēah*, of unkn. origin.]
▶**A** *noun*. **I** †**1** A small box for valuables. OE–M16.
2 a MINING. A deep trough for collecting the dross and refuse in washing ore. M16. ▸**b** A pit from which turf or peat is dug. M19.
3 The stuffed case forming a mattress or pillow. E17.
▶**II 4** An enclosed piece of land. Also, a large common. OE.
▶**B** *verb trans.* MINING. Separate (the ore) from the dross or refuse using a deep trough. M18.

tye *noun*[2] see **TIE** *noun*[1].

†**tye** *verb*[2] var. of **TIE** *verb*[1].

tyee /ˈtʌiː/ *noun*. Also **tyhee**. L18.
[Chinook Jargon, from Nootka *taːyiː* elder brother, senior.]
1 A chief; a person of distinction. *N. Amer. slang*. L18.
2 The Chinook salmon, *Oncorhynchus tshawytscha*. Also ***tyee salmon***. E20.

tyer *noun*[1] var. of **TIRE** *noun*[4].

tyer *noun*[2] var. of **TIER** *noun*[2].

tyg /tɪɡ/ *noun*. Also **tig**. M19.
[Origin unkn.]
Hist. A drinking-cup with two or more handles, *esp.* one of the 17th and 18th cents.

tyger *noun* see **TIGER** *noun*.

tyhee *noun* var. of **TYEE**.

tying /ˈtʌɪɪŋ/ *noun*. L15.
[from **TIE** *verb*[1] + **-ING**[1].]
1 The action of **TIE** *verb*[1]; an instance of this. L15.
2 A thing used for tying; a binding; a tie. Now *rare* or *obsolete*. L15.

tying *verb pres. pple*: see **TIE** *verb*[1].

tyke /tʌɪk/ *noun*. Also **tike**. LME.
[Old Norse *tík* bitch (Norwegian *tik* bitch, vixen); cf. Middle Low German *tike* bitch.]
1 A dog; *esp.* a mongrel. LME.
2 An unpleasant, ill-mannered, or coarse man. LME.
3 In full ***Yorkshire tyke***. A Yorkshireman. *slang*. L17.
4 A child, *esp.* a small boy. L19.
5 [Alt. of **TAIG**.] A Roman Catholic. *Austral. & NZ slang* (*derog.* & *offensive*). E20.

📖 **2** R. RENDELL Wexford tried to imagine . . this shifty tyke and Knighton meeting. **3** *Darts Player* A quietly spoken Tyke from East of the Pennines. **4** A. HOLLINGHURST The ferocious, broken-nosed little tyke who captained the . . gang.

■ **tykish** *adjective* characteristic of a tyke L19. **tykishness** *noun* M19.

tykhana /tʌɪˈkɑːnə/ *noun*. M19.
[Persian & Urdu *tahkāna*, from *tah* bottom + *kāna(h)* chamber.]
In the Indian subcontinent, an underground chamber in which to shelter during hot weather.

tyl- *combining form* see **TYLO-**.

tyle *verb* see **TILE** *verb*.

tyled *ppl adjective* see **TILED**.

Tylenol /ˈtʌɪlənɒl/ *noun*. *N. Amer.* M20.
[Origin unkn.]
PHARMACOLOGY. (Proprietary name for) paracetamol.

tyler *noun* see **TILER**.

tylo- /ˈtʌɪləʊ/ *combining form*. Before a vowel also **tyl-**.
[from Greek *tulos* knob or *tulē* callus, cushion: see **-O-**.]
Chiefly ZOOLOGY & MEDICINE. A knob, a callus, a swelling, a lump.
■ **ty'lectomy** *noun* (now *rare*) (an instance of) surgical excision of a lump or swelling, esp. a cancerous one L20. **tylopod** *adjective* & *noun* (*a*) *adjective* of or pertaining to the suborder Tylopoda of ruminants having pads on the digits instead of hoofs, comprising the camels and llamas (family Camelidae); (*b*) *noun* a member of the suborder Tylopoda: L19.

Tylorian /tʌɪˈlɔːrɪən/ *adjective*. M20.
[from *Tylor* (see below) + **-IAN**.]
Of, pertaining to, or designating the theories of the English anthropologist Sir Edward Tylor (1832–1917), esp. that concerning the evolutionary development of human culture.
■ Also **Tylorean** *adjective* M20.

tylose /ˈtʌɪləʊs/ *noun*[1]. L19.
[French from Greek *tulōsis*: see **TYLOSIS**.]
BOTANY. In woody tissue, a bladder-like intrusive outgrowth from a parenchyma cell into an adjacent tracheary vessel.

Tylose /ˈtʌɪləʊs/ *noun*[2]. M20.
[Origin unkn.: see **-OSE**[2].]
CHEMISTRY. (Proprietary name for) any of various esters or ethers of cellulose, esp. the methyl ether, used as a medium in pharmaceuticals and cosmetics.

tylosin /ˈtʌɪlə(ʊ)sɪn/ *noun*. M20.
[Origin unkn.: see **-IN**[1].]
VETERINARY MEDICINE. A macrolide antibiotic, $C_{46}H_{77}NO_{17}$, produced by various strains of *Streptomyces* and used esp. to treat respiratory infections in animals.

tylosis /tʌɪˈləʊsɪs/ *noun*. Pl. **-loses** /-ˈləʊsiːz/. L19.
[In sense 1 mod. Latin from Greek *tulōsis* formation of a callus: see **TYLO-**, **-OSIS**. In sense 2 prob. false sing. of *tyloses* pl. of **TYLOSE** *noun*[1].]
1 MEDICINE. The development of a callus on the skin; a callosity. Also *spec.*, (*a*) (more fully ***tylosis ciliaris***) an inflammation of the eyelids with thickening and hardening of their edges; (*b*) (more fully ***tylosis linguae***) = **LEUCOPLAKIA**. L19.
2 BOTANY. = **TYLOSE** *noun*[1]. Now *rare*. L19.
■ **tylotic** /-ˈlɒtɪk/ *adjective* (MEDICINE) of, pertaining to, or affected with tylosis L19.

tymbal *noun* var. of **TIMBAL**.

tymber *noun & verb* var. of **TIMBRE** *noun*[2] & *verb*.

tymp /tɪmp/ *noun*. M17.
[App. abbreviation of next.]
1 The mouth of the hearth of a blast-furnace, through which the molten metal passes, formed by a masonry arch and a stone or water-cooled metal block. M17.
2 MINING. A horizontal timber roof-support in a coalmine. L19.

tympan /ˈtɪmpən/ *noun*.
[Old English *timpana* from Latin **TYMPANUM**; later reinforced by Old & mod. French *tympan*.]
1 a A drum; a similar percussion instrument, as a tambourine. *arch.* OE. ▸**b** [Irish *tiompán*.] An ancient Irish stringed instrument played with a bow. LME.
†**2** ANATOMY & ZOOLOGY. = **TYMPANUM** 2. M16–E18.
3 PRINTING. A frame covered with taut material, into which a smaller similarly covered frame is fitted, with packing of cloth or paper between the two surfaces, interposed between the platen and the paper to be printed in order to cushion and equalize the pressure; the taut material covering such a frame (also ***tympan sheet***). L16. ▸**b** A tense membrane or thin plate in any mechanical apparatus. L19.
4 ARCHITECTURE. = **TYMPANUM** 3. E18.

tympan- *combining form* see **TYMPANO-**.

tympana *noun pl.* see **TYMPANUM**.

tympanal /ˈtɪmpən(ə)l/ *adjective & noun*. E19.
[formed as **TYMPANIC** + **-AL**[1].]
ANATOMY & ZOOLOGY. ▶**A** *adjective*. = **TYMPANIC** *adjective* 1. E19.
▶**B** *noun*. = **TYMPANIC** *noun*. L19.

tympani *noun pl.* var. of **TIMPANI**.

tympanic /tɪmˈpanɪk/ *adjective & noun*. E19.
[from **TYMPAN(UM** + **-IC**.]
▶**A** *adjective*. **1** ANATOMY & ZOOLOGY. Of, pertaining to, or connected with the tympanum or the eardrum; of the nature of a tympanum. E19.
2 Pertaining to or resembling a drum; MEDICINE tympanitic. *rare*. L19.
3 Of or pertaining to an architectural tympanum. E20.
1 tympanic bone in mammals, a bone of annular or tubular form supporting the eardrum and surrounding part of the external auditory meatus, in the adult forming part of the temporal bone; in lower vertebrates, any of several bones supposed to be homologous with this, esp. the quadrate. **tympanic cavity** the cavity of the middle ear. **tympanic membrane** the eardrum.
▶**B** *noun*. A tympanic bone. M19.

tympaniform /tɪmˈpanɪfɔːm, ˈtɪmpənɪ-/ *adjective*. M19.
[from **TYMPAN(UM** + **-I-** + **-FORM**.]
Chiefly ZOOLOGY. Having the form of a drum or (usu.) of a drumhead; *spec.* designating certain membranes in the bronchi of birds.

tympanist /ˈtɪmpənɪst/ *noun*[1]. *rare*. E17.
[from **TYMPAN** + **-IST**.]
A person who plays a tympan.

tympanist *noun*[2] var. of **TIMPANIST**.

tympanites /tɪmpəˈnʌɪtiːz/ *noun*. LME.
[Late Latin from Greek *tumpanitēs*, from *tumpanon* **TYMPANUM**.]
MEDICINE. Severe distension of the abdomen by gas in the intestine, so that it gives a hollow sound on percussion; meteorism.

tympanitic /tɪmpəˈnɪtɪk/ *adjective*. M19.
[from Latin *tympaniticus*, formed as prec.: see **-IC**.]
1 Of, pertaining to, or characteristic of tympanites; ***tympanitic note***, ***tympanitic resonance***, ***tympanitic sound***, a resonant sound produced by percussion of a distended abdomen or other abnormally hollow organ. M19.
2 Giving a tympanitic sound; affected with tympanites. E20.

tympanitis /tɪmpəˈnʌɪtɪs/ *noun*. L18.
[In sense 1 alt. of **TYMPANITES**; in sense 2 from **TYMPANUM**: see **-ITIS**.]
MEDICINE. **1** = **TYMPANITES**. L18.
2 Inflammation of the eardrum; myringitis. M19.

tympano- /ˈtɪmpənəʊ, tɪmˈpanəʊ/ *combining form* of **TYMPANUM**: see **-O-**. Before a vowel **tympan-**. Cf. **MYRINGO-**.
■ **tympanogram** *noun* a graphical record of pressure changes obtained in tympanometry M20. **tympano'metric** *adjective* of or pertaining to tympanometry L20. **tympa'nometry** *noun* the measurement, for diagnostic purposes, of changes in the compliance of the tympanic membrane as the air pressure is altered in the passage of the external ear M20. **tympanoplasty** *noun* = **MYRINGOPLASTY** M20. **tympa'notomy** *noun* (*rare*) = **MYRINGOTOMY** E20.

tympanum /ˈtɪmpənəm/ *noun*. Pl. **-nums**, **-na** /-nə/. E16.
[Latin from Greek *tumpanon* drum, from nasalized var. of base of *tuptein* strike.]
†**1** MEDICINE. = **TYMPANITES**. *rare*. Only in E16.
2 ANATOMY & ZOOLOGY. The tympanic membrane or eardrum; (the cavity of) the middle ear. Also, a membrane in any animal which is thought to form part of a hearing organ. E17. ▸**b** ORNITHOLOGY. Either of the two inflatable air-sacs at the sides of the neck in certain birds, such as grouse. Also, a bony labyrinth at the base of the trachea in certain diving ducks, having resonant membranes in its walls. *rare*. L19.
3 ARCHITECTURE. **a** The die or dado of a pedestal. M17. ▸**b** A vertical recessed area within a pediment; a similar area over a door between the lintel and the arch; a carving on this. L17.
4 A drum, *esp.* a hand drum of ancient Greece and Rome. Also, a drumhead. *arch.* L17.
5 A kind of wheel (originally drum-shaped) with curved radial partitions, used for raising water from a stream. L19.

tympany /ˈtɪmpəni/ *noun*. LME.
[Greek *tumpanias*, from *tumpanon* **TYMPANUM**.]
1 = **TYMPANUM** 4. Long *arch.* LME.
2 a MEDICINE & (now chiefly) VETERINARY MEDICINE. = **TYMPANITES**. Formerly with *the*. E16. ▸†**b** *transf.* Any swelling or rounded form, *esp.* that of the abdomen in pregnancy. L16–E18.
3 *fig.* A condition of being inflated with pride, conceit, etc.; an excess *of* pride etc.; inflated style, bombast. Now *rare* or *obsolete*. L16.
4 ARCHITECTURE. = **TYMPANUM** 3b. *Scot.* M18.

Tyndall /ˈtɪnd(ə)l/ *noun*. E20.
[John *Tyndall*, English physicist (1820–1893).]
Used *attrib.* with ref. to the effect of Rayleigh scattering of a beam of light by small particles, esp. the blue colour that results, as in a clear sky, a cloud of tobacco smoke, etc.
Tyndall blue, ***Tyndall cone***, ***Tyndall effect***, ***Tyndall scattering***, etc. **Tyndall meter** an instrument that makes use of the Tyndall effect for measuring the turbidity or concentration of aerosols and suspensions.

tyndallization /ˌtɪndəlʌɪˈzeɪʃ(ə)n/ *noun*. Also **-isation**. L19.
[from John *Tyndall* (see prec.) + **-IZATION**.]
A method of sterilization in which time is allowed between repeated heatings for bacteria to develop; fractional or intermittent sterilization.
■ **'tyndallize** *verb trans.* sterilize by this process E20.

tyne *verb*[1], *verb*[2] vars. of **TINE** *verb*[1], *verb*[2].

Tynesider /ˈtʌɪnsʌɪdə/ *noun*. **L19**.
[from *Tyneside* (see below) + **-ER**[1].]
A native or inhabitant of Tyneside, the area adjacent to the River Tyne in NE England, *spec.* of the city of Newcastle-upon-Tyne.

Tynwald /ˈtɪnw(ə)ld/ *noun*. **LME**.
[Old Norse *þingvǫllr* (genit. *-vallar*) place of assembly, from *þing* assembly, **THING** *noun*[2] + *vǫllr* field, level ground.]
The Parliament of the Isle of Man; an annual assembly of this at which the laws which have been enacted are proclaimed to the people.

typ- *combining form* see **TYPO-**.

type /tʌɪp/ *noun & adjective*. **L15**.
[Latin *typus* from Greek *tupos* blow, impression, image, figure, from base of *tuptein* strike, beat.]
▶ **A** *noun*. **I 1** That by which something is symbolized; a symbol; *spec.* (*THEOLOGY*) a foreshadowing in the Old Testament of a person or event of the Christian dispensation. Correl. to ***antitype***. **L15**.
2 †**a** A figure or picture of something. *rare*. **M16–L18**. ▸**b** A device on either side of a coin or medal. **L18**.
3 A distinguishing mark. *rare*. **L16**.
4 a *MEDICINE*. The characteristic form of a fever, esp. the period of an intermittent fever. Now *rare* or *obsolete*. **E17**. ▸**b** *gen.* The general form, structure, or character distinguishing a particular group or class of things; *transf.* (esp. *ART*) a pattern or model after which something is made. **M19**.
5 A class of people or things distinguished by common essential characteristics; a kind, a sort. **M19**.
6 a A person or thing showing the characteristic qualities of a class; a representative specimen; *spec.* a person or thing exemplifying the ideal characteristics *of* a class, *the* perfect specimen *of* something. **M19**. ▸**b** A person of a particular (specified or contextually implied) character; (with *possess.*) the sort of person to whom one is attracted. *colloq.* **E20**.

📖 **1** N. FRYE Salvation out of water is connected with the . . dolphin, a conventional type of Christ. **3** SHAKES. *3 Hen. VI* Thy father bears the type of King of Naples. **4b** J. H. PARKER The original type of all Christian churches is . . the Roman Basilica. **5** K. VONNEGUT The . . ice we skate upon . . is only one of several types of ice. C. MUNGOSHI Your type always comes back for money! M. BERGMANN Three types: the erotic, the narcissistic, and the obsessional. *Which?* Some types of accidents (such as falls . .) can happen . . in the home. *New Scientist* A new type of jet engine which spins a multibladed propeller. **6a** F. W. ROBERTSON Arnold of Rugby is the type of English action. **b** G. DURRELL Apart from anything else, the girl was not my type. D. EDEN That young woman didn't look the spinster type. D. E. WESTLAKE Three army types were there . . tall, fat, khaki-uniformed. A. MACRAE He's just the type to have herpes.

▶ **II** *techn.* **7** *TYPOGRAPHY*. A character for printing, originally a metal casting from a matrix, reproducing a punch on which a letter or other character was engraved; such pieces, collectively, *spec.* with reference to size or design. **E18**. ▸**b** The printed characters produced by type collectively. Formerly also, a printed character. **L18**.
8 *BIOLOGY & MINERALOGY* etc. A general plan of structure characterizing a group of animals, plants, minerals, etc.; a group or division of animals, etc., having a common form or structure. **M19**.
9 *BIOLOGY*. A species or genus which is taken to exhibit best the essential characters of its species, genus, family, etc. (cf. ***type species***, ***type genus*** below). **M19**. ▸**b** *spec.* The essential element making valid the scientific name of a new species etc.; usu. (in full ***type specimen***), the specimen, or one of the specimens, from which it was originally described. Cf. ***holotype***, ***lectotype***, ***syntype***, etc. **L19**.
10 *LINGUISTICS*. A class of observed linguistic units, as a phoneme, sentence, etc. Cf. **TOKEN** *noun* 1d. **E20**.

📖 **7** V. LEE Musical types had . . been invented by an Italian. L. WOOLF I bought . . Caslon Old Face Titling type . . for printing the covers. **b** J. RUSKIN Here it is in full type, for it is worth careful reading.

▶ **B** *adjective*. **1** As 2nd elem. of comb.: having the characteristics of; resembling; functioning like. **L19**.
2 Type of, kind of. *US colloq.* **M20**.

📖 **1** *Chicago Tribune* A J. R. Ewing-type villain. *Which?* Convenience-type dishes.

Phrases: ***font of type***: see **FONT** *noun*[2] 2. ***ideal type***: see **IDEAL** *adjective*. ***Moon's type***, ***Moon type***: see **MOON** *noun*[2]. ***movable type***: see **MOVABLE** *adjective* 3. ***revert to type***: see **REVERT** *verb* 6b. ***script type***: see **SCRIPT** *noun*[1] 2b. ***small type***: see **SMALL** *adjective*. ***strong silent type***: see **SILENT** *adjective*. ***true to type***: see **TRUE** *adjective, noun, & adverb*. ***wild type***: see **WILD** *adjective, noun, & adverb*.
Comb.: **type A** (a person of) a personality type characterized by ambition, impatience, and aggressive competitiveness, thought to be particularly susceptible to stress (cf. ***type B*** below); **type approval** confirmation that a new piece of equipment meets its required specifications; **type area** (*a*) the part of a page occupied by print; (*b*) = ***type site*** below; **type B** (a person of) a personality type characterized as easy-going and thought to have low susceptibility to stress (cf. ***type A*** above); **type-ball** = ***golf ball*** (b) s.v. **GOLF** *noun*; **type-bar** in a typewriter, each of the bars carrying the type; **type basket** the assembly of type-bars in a typewriter; **type-cylinder**: on which the type or plates are fastened in a rotary printing-press; **typeface** (*a*) a set of printing types, or of letters etc. otherwise printed, in a particular design; (*b*) the inked part of type; the impression made by this; **type facsimile** a copy of a piece of printing which is either a page-for-page copy using type as close as possible to the original or a faithful photographic reproduction; **type-fallacy** *LOGIC* the fallacy of including amongst the members of a type something belonging to another type; **type-form** a typical or representative form; **type-genus** a genus taken to exemplify best the essential characters of the family to which it belongs; *esp.* the genus from which the name of the family is taken; **type-high** *adjective & adverb* (*a*) *adjective* of the standard height of type (now 0.918 inch, 23.32 mm); (*b*) *adverb* as high as the type; **type-holder** an apparatus for holding type, used in stamping or lettering books; **type-lever**: by which a type or character is impressed; **type locality** (*a*) *BIOLOGY* the place in which a type specimen was found; (*b*) = ***type site*** below; **type-metal** an alloy of lead and antimony, sometimes with tin or copper, used for casting printing-types; **type-psychology** psychological study or theory based on the classification of people by type of personality or physique; **typescript** *noun & verb* (*a*) *noun* a typewritten document (*spec.* a literary composition), esp. for a printer; (*b*) *verb trans.* record in typescript; **typeset** *verb trans.* (*PRINTING*) set (a text) in type, prepare for printing (chiefly as ***typesetting*** *verbal noun*); **typesetter** *PRINTING* (*a*) a compositor; (*b*) a composing-machine; **type site** *ARCHAEOLOGY, GEOLOGY*, etc.: where objects regarded as defining the characteristics of a culture, stratigraphic level, etc., are found; **type species** *BIOLOGY* orig., a species taken to exemplify best the characteristics of its genus; now *spec.* the species on which the genus is based and with which the genus name remains associated during any taxonomic revision; **type specimen** (*a*) see sense 9b above; (*b*) a printed sheet or book showing the variety of typefaces a printer or manufacturer has available; **type test**: conducted to determine whether a new piece of equipment meets its specifications; **type-wheel**: with raised characters on its outer edge.
■ **typal** *adjective* (*a*) of the nature of or serving as a type; typical; (*b*) pertaining to a type or symbol; symbolic: **M19**.

type /tʌɪp/ *verb*[1]. **L16**.
[from the noun.]
1 *verb trans.* **a** *THEOLOGY*. Foreshadow as a type. **L16**. ▸**b** Be a symbol of; symbolize. **M19**.
2 *verb trans.* Be an example of; = **TYPIFY** 2. *rare*. **E17**.
3 *verb trans.* Reproduce by means of type; print. *rare*. **M18**.
4 *verb trans. & intrans.* Write with a typewriter. Also foll. by *out*, *up*. **L19**.
5 *verb trans.* Assign to a particular type; classify; *esp.* in *BIOLOGY & MEDICINE*, determine the type to which (blood, tissue, etc.) belongs. **E20**.
6 *verb trans.* = **TYPECAST** 2. **M20**.

📖 **4** G. GREENE Mrs Smith typed for him on a portable Corona. A. BURGESS Two cassettes were full and he went . . to type it all out. ANNE STEVENSON Aurelia Plath sat . . typing up her daughter's stories.

■ **typer** *noun* (*arch.*) = **TYPEWRITER** 1 **L19**.

†**type** *verb*[2] see **TIP** *verb*[2].

-type /tʌɪp/ *suffix*.
[Repr. French *-type*, Latin *-typus*, Greek *-tupos*, from base of *tuptein* beat, strike.]
1 Forming nouns denoting a model or specimen (in *TAXONOMY* a type specimen), as ***antitype***, ***archetype***, ***lectotype***, ***prototype***.
2 Forming nouns denoting a method of printing, or a block, plate, or impression produced by this, as ***collotype***, ***daguerreotype***, ***electrotype***, ***stereotype***.

typecast /ˈtʌɪpkɑːst/ *verb trans*. Pa. t. & pple **-cast**. **M19**.
[from **TYPE** *noun* + **CAST** *verb*.]
1 Form into type for printing. Chiefly as ***typecasting*** *verbal noun*. **M19**.
2 Assign (an actor or actress) repeatedly to the same type of part, esp. one in character; *transf.* regard as a stereotype. Chiefly as ***typecast*** *ppl adjective*. **E20**.

typed /tʌɪpt/ *adjective*. **M19**.
[from **TYPE** *noun*, *verb*[1]: see **-ED**[2], **-ED**[1].]
1 Of or pertaining to a (specified) type; having a certain character. **M19**.
2 That is typed; *esp.* written with a typewriter. **M19**.

typewrite /ˈtʌɪprʌɪt/ *verb trans. & intrans.* Now *formal*. Pa. t. **-wrote** /-rəʊt/; pa. pple **-written** /-rɪt(ə)n/. **L19**.
[Back-form. from next.]
= **TYPE** *verb*[1] 4.

typewriter /ˈtʌɪprʌɪtə/ *noun*. **M19**.
[from **TYPE** *noun* + **WRITER**.]
1 A machine for writing in characters like those used in printing, having keys which when pressed one at a time cause a type mounted on a bar or ball to strike a sheet of paper on a roller, through an inked ribbon. **M19**.
2 = **TYPIST** 2. *arch.* **L19**.
3 A machine-gun. *slang*. **E20**.
1 ***electronic typewriter***: see **ELECTRONIC** *adjective*.

typewritten /ˈtʌɪpwrɪt(ə)n/ *ppl adjective*. **L19**.
[pa. pple of **TYPEWRITE**.]
Written with a typewriter, typed.

typewritten *verb*, **typewrote** *verb* see **TYPEWRITE**.

typey /ˈtʌɪpi/ *adjective*. **M20**.
[from **TYPE** *noun* + **-Y**[1].]
Of a domestic animal: exhibiting (esp. perfectly) the distinctive characteristics of the breed.

typha /ˈtʌɪfə/ *noun*. **M16**.
[mod. Latin (see below), from Greek *tuphē*.]
Any of various aquatic plants constituting the genus *Typha* (family Typhaceae), which includes the common reed-mace or bulrush, *T. latifolia*.

typhlitis /tɪˈflʌɪtɪs/ *noun*. *arch.* **M19**.
[from Greek *tuphlon* the caecum or 'blind gut' (use as noun of neut. of *tuphlos* blind) + **-ITIS**.]
MEDICINE. Inflammation of the caecum (often including that of the appendix).

typhlosole /ˈtɪfləsəʊl, ˈtʌɪf-/ *noun*. **M19**.
[Irreg. from Greek *tuphlos* blind + *sōlēn* channel, pipe.]
ZOOLOGY. In various animals, a ridge or fold extending along the inner wall of the intestine, increasing its area and partly dividing its lumen, as in lampreys and earthworms.

typho- /ˈtʌɪfəʊ/ *combining form* of **TYPHOID** or of **TYPHUS**: see **-O-**.
¶ Now little used owing to ambiguity of sense.
■ **typhoˈgenic** *adjective* producing typhus or typhoid fever **E20**.

†**Typhoean** *adjective*. *rare* (Milton). Only in **M17**.
[from Latin *Typhoeus*, another name for *Typhon* (see **TYPHON** *noun*[2]) + **-AN**.]
Characteristic of Typhoeus or Typhon; violent.

typhoid /ˈtʌɪfɔɪd/ *adjective & noun*. **E19**.
[from **TYPHUS** + **-OID**.]
▶ **A** *adjective*. *MEDICINE*.
1 Resembling or characteristic of typhus; designating or exhibiting symptoms like those of typhus, esp. a state of delirious stupor in certain fevers. *obsolete* exc. *Hist.* **E19**.
2 Of or pertaining to, characteristic of, or affected with typhoid fever. **L19**.
Special collocations: **Typhoid Mary** [nickname of Mary Mallon (d. 1938), Irish-born cook who transmitted typhoid fever in the US] a person who transmits a disease widely without showing its symptoms; *fig.* a transmitter of undesirable opinions, sentiments, etc. **typhoid fever** a severe infectious fever caused by the bacterium *Salmonella typhi*, involving a rash, myalgia and sometimes delirium and intestinal inflammation (formerly thought a variety of typhus); also (with paratyphoid) called ***enteric fever***.
▶ **B** *noun*. *MEDICINE*.
1 = ***typhoid fever*** above. **M19**.
2 A case of typhoid; a patient with typhoid. *colloq.* **L19**.
■ **tyˈphoidal** *adjective* (now *rare* or *obsolete*) = **TYPHOID** *adjective* 2 **L19**.

typhomania /tʌɪfə(ʊ)ˈmeɪnɪə/ *noun*. Now *rare* or *obsolete*. **L17**.
[mod. Latin from Greek *tuphōmania*, from *tuphos* **TYPHUS** + **-MANIA** (by later writers taken as **TYPHO-** + **-MANIA**).]
MEDICINE. A delirious stupor occurring in typhus and other fevers.

typhon /ˈtʌɪfɒn/ *noun*[1]. Now *rare* or *obsolete*. **M16**.
[Greek *tuphōn*; later infl. by **TYPHOON**. Cf. next.]
A whirlwind, a tornado; a hurricane.

Typhon /ˈtʌɪfɒn/ *noun*[2]. **L16**.
[Latin from Greek *Tuphōn*, name of a mythological hundred-headed fire-breathing monster, believed to raise hurricanes and whirlwinds; also, another name for the Egyptian god Set. Cf. prec.]
A fire-breathing monster like Typhon; a powerful or violent person or thing.
■ **Typhonian** /tʌɪˈfəʊnɪən/ *adjective* = **TYPHONIC** *adjective*[2] **M19**.

typhonic /tʌɪˈfɒnɪk/ *adjective*[1]. **M19**.
[from **TYPHON** *noun*[1] + **-IC**; later from **TYPHOON**.]
Of the nature or force of a whirlwind or a typhoon; *fig.* tempestuous.

Typhonic /tʌɪˈfɒnɪk/ *adjective*[2]. **L19**.
[from **TYPHON** *noun*[2] + **-IC**.]
Of, pertaining to, or representing the Greek mythological monster Typhon or the Egyptian god Set.

typhoon /tʌɪˈfuːn/ *noun*. **L16**.
[Partly from Portuguese *tufão* from Urdu *ṭūfān* hurricane, tornado, from Arab., perh. from Greek *tuphōn* (see **TYPHON** *noun*[1]); partly from Chinese dial. *tai fung* big wind, from Chinese *dà* big + *fēng* wind.]
A violent storm occurring in or around the Indian subcontinent; *esp.* a tropical cyclone occurring in the region of the Indian or western Pacific oceans.
■ **typhoonish** *adjective* resembling or portending a typhoon **L19**.

typhous /ˈtʌɪfəs/ *adjective*. Now *rare*. **E19**.
[from **TYPHUS** + **-OUS**.]
MEDICINE. Of, pertaining to, or having the character of typhus.

typhus /ˈtʌɪfəs/ *noun.* M17.
[In sense 1 from late Latin; in sense 2 from Greek *tuphos* smoke, vapour, stupor, from *tuphein* to smoke.]
†**1** Pride, conceit. Only in M17.
2 Any of a group of acute infectious fevers caused by rickettsiae, often transmitted by lice or fleas, and characterized by a purple rash, headaches, and usu. delirium; *esp.* the classical epidemic form, transmitted by lice. Also ***typhus fever***. Also called ***spotted fever***. L18.
2 ***epidemic typhus***, ***marine typhus***, ***scrub typhus***, etc.

typic /ˈtɪpɪk/ *adjective.* E17.
[French *typique* from late Latin *typicus* from Greek *tupikos* typical, from *tupos* TYPE *noun*: see -IC.]
1 Symbolic; = TYPICAL *adjective* 1. E17.
2 Of a fever: conforming to a particular type (TYPE *noun* 4a); intermittent, periodic. Now *rare* or *obsolete*. E17.

📖 **1** *Literature & Theology* The . . figurative structures of 'The Displaced Person' depend on . . recurring typic images.

typical /ˈtɪpɪk(ə)l/ *adjective.* E17.
[medieval Latin *typicalis* from late Latin *typicus*: see prec., -AL[1].]
1 Symbolic; = TYPIC *adjective* 1. E17.
2 Typographical. Now *rare* or *obsolete*. L18.
3 Serving as a characteristic example; representative. M19. ▸**b** BIOLOGY. That is the type of the genus, family, etc. M19. ▸**c** MEDICINE. Of a fever: = TYPIC *adjective* 2. Now *rare* or *obsolete*. M19.
4 Characteristic *of* or serving to distinguish a type. Also, conforming to expected (esp. undesirable) behaviour, attitudes, etc. M19.

📖 **3** G. BATTISCOMBE Gabriele remained indelibly Italian, a typical Neopolitan. *She* A typical day started with breakfast of cold, lumpy porridge. **4** J. BRAINE It struck me as typical of my father-in-law that he hadn't sent anyone to meet me. M. GIROUARD Its mixture of symmetry and irregularity was . . typical of the 'Queen Anne' movement.

▪ **typiˈcality** *noun* = TYPICALNESS M19. **typically** *adverb* (*a*) symbolically; (*b*) representatively; characteristically: E17. **typicalness** *noun* the quality of being typical, *esp.* symbolic character M17.

typify /ˈtɪpɪfʌɪ/ *verb trans.* M17.
[from Latin *typus* TYPE *noun*: see -FY.]
1 Represent by a symbol; serve as a symbol of; symbolize. M17.
2 Be a representative example of; embody the essential characters of. M19.
3 TAXONOMY. Designate or identify the type of specimen of (a species etc.). M20.

📖 **1** F. BOWEN A Syllogism . . is appropriately typified by a triangle. **2** E. WHARTON Gertrude . . typified the mediocre and the ineffectual. H. CARPENTER Benjamin Franklin . . in many ways typified the founding fathers of the USA.

▪ **typifiˈcation** *noun* (*a*) the action of typifying something; (*b*) that which typifies something: E19. **typifier** *noun* (*rare*) M19.

typist /ˈtʌɪpɪst/ *noun.* M19.
[from TYPE *noun* + -IST.]
1 A printer, a compositor. *rare*. M19.
2 A person who types or uses a typewriter, esp. as a profession. L19.

typo /ˈtʌɪpəʊ/ *noun. colloq.* Pl. **-os**. E19.
[Abbreviation.]
1 A typographer; *spec.* a compositor. E19.
2 A typographical error. E19.

📖 **2** *Times Lit. Suppl.* Since few proof-readers are perfect, a typo here and there is easily forgiven.

typo- /ˈtʌɪpəʊ, ˈtɪpəʊ/ *combining form.* Before a vowel **typ-**.
[from Greek *tupos* TYPE *noun* + -O-.]
Forming words with the senses 'of or pertaining to (printing) type', 'of a type'.
▪ **typoliˈthography** *noun* a process in which impressions from type are reproduced by lithography E19. **typophil(e)** *noun* a person who is fond of or interested in typography L19. **typoscript** *noun* (*arch.*) a typescript L19.

typograph /ˈtʌɪpəgrɑːf/ *noun. arch.* M18.
[formed as next: see prec., -GRAPH.]
A typographer; a typographist. Formerly also, a kind of typesetting machine.

typographer /tʌɪˈpɒgrəfə/ *noun.* M16.
[French *typographe* or mod. Latin *typographus*, formed as TYPO- + -GRAPHER.]
1 A person skilled in typography; a printer. M16.
2 = TYPEWRITER 1. *rare. obsolete* exc. *Hist.* E19.
3 Any of several bark beetles which make markings in the bark of trees likened to print, *esp.* the spruce bark beetle, *Ips typographus*. Also ***typographer bark beetle***, ***typographer beetle***. M19.

typographical /tʌɪpəˈgrafɪk(ə)l/ *adjective.* L16.
[from mod. Latin *typographicus* + -AL[1].]
1 Of or pertaining to typography or printing. L16.
2 Produced by typography; printed. E19.
▪ **typographic** *adjective* = TYPOGRAPHICAL L18. **typographica** *noun pl.* (*rare*) [-A[3]] examples of fine printing M20. **typographically** *adverb* M18.

typography /tʌɪˈpɒgrəfi/ *noun.* E17.
[French *typographie* or mod. Latin *typographia*, formed as TYPO- + -GRAPHY.]
1 The art or practice of printing. E17.
2 The process of printing; *spec.* the process of setting and arranging types and printing from them; the style and appearance of printed matter. L17.

📖 **1** F. H. A. SCRIVENER The first fruit of typography, the beautiful Latin Bible known as Cardinal Mazarin's. **2** *Library* Its typography echoes the classical elegance of the publications of Pushkin's time.

▪ **typographist** *noun* (*rare*) an expert in or student of typography M19.

typology /tʌɪˈpɒlədʒi/ *noun.* M19.
[from TYPO- + -LOGY.]
1 The branch of religion that deals with (esp. biblical) symbolic representation; *transf.* symbolism. M19.
2 The branch of knowledge that deals with classes with common characteristics; (a) classification esp. of human behaviour or characteristics according to type. L19.
▪ **typoˈlogical** *adjective* of or pertaining to typology M19. **typoˈlogically** *adverb* by means of or according to typology L19. **typologist** *noun* M19. **typologize** *verb trans. & intrans.* interpret or classify (things) typologically L19.

typothetae /tʌɪˈpɒθɪtiː, tʌɪpəˈθiːtiː/ *noun pl.* E19.
[mod. Latin, formed as TYPO- + Greek *thetos*, from *tithenai* set, place.]
Master printers collectively; *spec.* the members of a N. American association of master printers.

tyramine /ˈtʌɪrəmiːn/ *noun.* E20.
[from TYROSINE + AMINE.]
BIOCHEMISTRY. A tyrosine derivative occurring naturally in cheese and other foods, having sympathomimetic properties and capable of causing dangerously high blood pressure in people taking a monoamine oxidase inhibitor; 2-(*p*-hydroxyphenyl)ethylamine, $HOC_6H_4CH_2CH_2NH_2$.

tyranness /ˈtʌɪrənɪs/ *noun.* LME.
[from Latin *tyrannus* TYRANT + -ESS[1].]
A female tyrant.

tyrannic /tɪˈranɪk/ *adjective. arch.* L15.
[formed as next: see -IC.]
= next.

tyrannical /tɪˈranɪk(ə)l, tʌɪ-/ *adjective.* M16.
[Old & mod. French *tyrannique* from Latin *tyrannicus* from Greek *turannikos*, from *turannos* TYRANT: see -AL[1], -ICAL.]
1 Of or pertaining to a tyrant; despotic; arbitrary. M16.
2 Characteristic of a tyrant; despotically harsh, cruel, or oppressive. M16.

📖 **1** C. THIRLWALL Miletus, after the overthrow of a tyrannical dynasty, was split into two factions. **2** J. MORSE His conduct in Poland was . . tyrannical and oppressive. A. STEVENS A tyrannical father, who . . made terrifying scenes whenever he was thwarted.

▪ †**tyrannial** *adjective* = TYRANNICAL M17–L18. **tyrannically** *adverb* (*a*) in a tyrannical manner; †(*b*) *colloq.* exceedingly; violently: M16. **tyrannicalness** *noun* (*rare*) M17.

tyrannicide /tɪˈranɪsʌɪd/ *noun.* M17.
[French, from (in sense 1) Latin *tyrannicidium*, (in sense 2) Latin *tyrannicida*, from *tyrannus*: see TYRANT, -CIDE.]
1 The killing of a tyrant. M17.
2 A person who kills a tyrant. M17.
▪ **tyranniˈcidal** *adjective* E19.

tyrannis /tɪˈranɪs/ *noun.* L19.
[Latin from Greek *turannis* rule of a despot.]
GREEK HISTORY. = TYRANNY 1.

tyrannize /ˈtɪrənʌɪz/ *verb.* Also **-ise**. L15.
[Old & mod. French *tyranniser*, from *tyran* TYRANT: see -IZE.]
1 *verb intrans.* Rule oppressively or cruelly; exercise power or control oppressively or cruelly. (Foll. by *over*.) L15.
2 *verb trans.* Rule, control, or behave towards oppressively or cruelly. M16.
3 *verb intrans.* Chiefly *Hist.* Be an absolute ruler; exercise absolute rule. (Foll. by *over*.) L16. ▸†**b** *verb trans.* Exercise absolute rule in or over. L16–L18.

📖 **1** G. STEINER Fascism tyrannizes through contempt of man. C. PETERS Capricious, card-playing old women who tyrannize over . . young men. **2** G. DALY The mighty art critic was reduced to a dutiful little boy tyrannized by his mother.

▪ **tyrannizer** *noun* a tyrant L16.

tyrannosaur /tɪˈranəsɔː, tʌɪ-/ *noun.* Also (earlier) **-saurus** /-ˈsɔːrəs/, pl. **-ri** /-rʌɪ/, **-ruses**. E20.
[mod. Latin *Tyrannosaurus* (see below), from Greek *turannos* TYRANT: see -SAUR.]
A huge bipedal carnivorous saurischian dinosaur of the Upper Cretaceous, *Tyrannosaurus rex*, having powerful hind legs and jaws, a large tail, and small clawlike front legs, known from N. American fossils. Also *fig.*, a powerful or ruthless person, organization, etc.

tyrannous /ˈtɪr(ə)nəs/ *adjective.* LME.
[from Latin *tyrannus* TYRANT + -OUS.]
Tyrannical; *fig.* severe, overpowering.
▪ **tyrannously** *adverb* LME. **tyrannousness** *noun* (*rare*) L19.

tyranny /ˈtɪr(ə)ni/ *noun.* LME.
[Old & mod. French *tyrannie* from late Latin *tyrannia*, from Latin *tyrannus* TYRANT: see -Y[3].]
1 Chiefly GREEK HISTORY. Rule by a tyrant or usurper; a period of this; a State under such rule. LME. ▸**b** *gen.* Absolute sovereignty. *rare*. M17.
2 Cruel or oppressive government or rule. LME.
3 Arbitrary or oppressive exercise of power, cruel or oppressive action or behaviour; an instance of this. LME.
4 Violent or lawless action. Long *rare* or *obsolete*. L15.

📖 **2** C. V. WEDGWOOD The result would be a military tyranny under Cromwell. M. ROBINSON A laissez-faire government can practice tyranny by default. **3** A. G. GARDINER Women submit to . . incredible tyrannies of fashion without a murmur. G. DALY His unwillingness to exhibit was a courageous refusal to give in to the tyranny of the Royal Academy.

tyrant /ˈtʌɪr(ə)nt/ *noun, adjective, & verb.* ME.
[Old French *tyrant*, *tiran* (mod. *tyran*) from Latin *tyrannus* from Greek *turannos*: see -ANT[2].]
▶ **A** *noun.* **1** Chiefly GREEK HISTORY. A person who seizes absolute power in a State without legal right; an absolute ruler; a usurper. ME.
†**2** A ruler, a governor. ME–M18.
3 A cruel or oppressive ruler. ME.
4 Any person exercising power or authority cruelly or oppressively. ME. ▸†**b** A cruel, violent, or wicked person. LME–L16.
5 More fully ***tyrant-flycatcher***. Any member of the family Tyrannidae of New World flycatchers, *esp.* any of the genus *Tyrannus* noted for driving off any other bird approaching its nest. Also ***tyrant-bird***, ***tyrant-shrike***. M18.

📖 **1** R. L. FOX The Hellespont where he ruled as local tyrant. **3** J. A. MICHENER Tiberius was succeeded by the even worse tyrant Caligula. **4** H. T. LANE If a child has been harshly treated, it will become a dominating tyrant in its games. J. BRAINE You try to boss everyone. You're a bully and a tyrant.

▶ **B** *adjective.* That is a tyrant; tyrannical. Long only *attrib.*, & now usu. taken as noun. ME.

📖 P. J. BAILEY Those basest few who thought to win The tyrant monster's favour.

▶†**C** *verb intrans. & trans.* (with *it*). Tyrannize. L16–M17.
▪ **tyrantess** *noun* (*rare*) a female tyrant L19. **tyrantship** *noun* (*rare*) the condition of being a tyrant; tyranny: LME.

tyre /ˈtʌɪə/ *noun & verb.* Also ***tire**. See also TIRE *noun*[2], *verb*[4]. L15.
[Var. of TIRE *noun*[2].]
▶ **A** *noun.* **I** †**1** See TIRE *noun*[2]. L15.
▶ **II 2** A continuous circular band of iron or steel placed round the wheel of a vehicle (esp. a locomotive) to strengthen it. L18.
3 A rubber covering, usu. inflated, placed round a wheel to form a soft contact with the road. L19.
4 *transf.* Any circle or roll of soft cushiony material; *spec.* a roll of fat round a part of the body, a spare tyre. M20.

📖 **3** ***balloon tyre***: see BALLOON *noun*. ***flat tyre***: see FLAT *adjective*. ***pneumatic tyre***: see PNEUMATIC *adjective* 1. ***side-wall tyre***: see SIDE-WALL 2. ***spare tyre***: see SPARE *adjective*. ***tubular tyre***: see TUBULAR *adjective* 1. **4** B. HINES She crumpled her sweater into a tyre and eased her head through the hole. M. GEE Wendy had grown huge; blubber-armed, tyres on her throat.

Comb.: **tyre-cement**: for fixing or repairing rubber tyres; **tyre chain**: fastened to a tyre to prevent skidding on snow or ice; **tyre gauge** a portable device for measuring the air pressure in a tyre; **tyre-iron** *N. Amer.* a steel lever for removing tyres from wheel-rims.
▶ **B** *verb trans.* **I 1** See TIRE *verb*[4]. L15.
▶ **II 2** Provide (a vehicle) with a tyre or tyres. L19.
¶ From the 17th cent. to the 19th cent. *tire* was the current form in both US and British English; in the 19th cent. *tyre* was reintroduced in British English.
▪ **tyred** *adjective* provided with a tyre or tyres; having a tyre or tyres of a specified kind: L19. **tyreless** *adjective* having no tyres L19.

Tyrian /ˈtɪrɪən/ *noun & adjective.* ME.
[from Latin *Tyrius* (from *Tyrus* Tyre) + -AN.]
▶ **A** *noun.* A native or inhabitant of Tyre, an ancient Phoenician city and commercial port. ME.
▶ **B** *adjective.* Of, pertaining to, or made in Tyre. LME.
Tyrian purple: see PURPLE *noun* 1.

tyro *noun* var. of TIRO.

tyrocidin /tʌɪrəˈsʌɪdɪn/ *noun.* Also **-ine** /-iːn/. M20.
[from mod. Latin *Tyrothrix* (see TYROTHRICIN) + -CIDE + -IN[1], -INE[5].]
PHARMACOLOGY. Any of various cyclic decapeptide antibiotics obtained from the bacterium *Bacillus brevis* and active esp. against Gram-positive bacteria. Cf. TYROTHRICIN.

tyrocinium *noun* var. of TIROCINIUM.

Tyrode /ˈtʌɪrəʊd/ *noun.* E20.
[M. V. *Tyrode* (1878–1930), US pharmacologist.]
MEDICINE & PHYSIOLOGY. ***Tyrode's solution***, ***Tyrode solution***, ***Tyrode's medium***, a physiological saline solution used to irrigate tissue and in laboratory work. Also *ellipt.* as ***Tyrode's***.

tyroglyphid /tʌɪrəˈglɪfɪd/ *adjective & noun.* E20.
[mod. Latin *Tyroglyphidae* (see below), from *Tyroglyphus* genus name, from Greek *turos* cheese + *gluphein* carve: see -ID[3].]
ZOOLOGY. ▶**A** *adjective.* Of, pertaining to, or designating the family Tyroglyphidae, which includes cheese-mites and house-mites. E20.
▶**B** *noun.* A mite of this family. E20.

Tyrolean /tɪrəˈliːən, tɪˈrəʊlɪən/ *adjective & noun.* E19.
[from the *Tyrol* (see below) + -EAN.]
▶**A** *adjective.* Of or pertaining to the Alpine region comprising parts of Austria and northern Italy or the Austrian province of the Tyrol. E19.
Tyrolean hat a soft felt hat with a brim turned up at the sides and usu. a feather cockade.
▶**B** *noun.* A native or inhabitant of the Tyrol. E19.
■ ˈ**Tyroler** *adjective & noun* [German] (**a**) *adjective* = TYROLEAN *adjective*; (**b**) *noun* = TYROLEAN *noun*; also, the dialect of German spoken in the Tyrol: L19. **Tyroˈlese** *adjective & noun* (pl. of noun same) = TYROLEAN E19.

tyromancy /ˈtʌɪrəmansi/ *noun. rare.* M17.
[French *tyromantie*, from Greek *turos* cheese: see -MANCY.]
Divination by watching cheese coagulate.

tyrosinaemia /tʌɪrəsɪˈniːmɪə/ *noun.* Also ***-nemia**. M20.
[from TYROSINE + -AEMIA.]
MEDICINE. A defect of metabolism marked by abnormally large amounts of tyrosine and its metabolites in the blood and urine, and tending to cause damage to the liver and kidneys, or to the eyes and skin.

tyrosinase /ˈtʌɪrəsɪneɪz, tʌɪˈrɒs-/ *noun.* L19.
[from next + -ASE.]
BIOCHEMISTRY. A copper-containing enzyme found in many plants and animals which catalyses the formation of quinones from phenols and polyphenols (as melanin from tyrosine).

tyrosine /ˈtʌɪrəsiːn/ *noun.* M19.
[Irreg. from Greek *turos* cheese + -INE[5].]
CHEMISTRY. A hydrophilic amino acid widely present in proteins and a metabolic precursor of several important substances, including adrenalin, thyroxine, and melanin; 3-(*p*-hydroxyphenyl)alanine, $C_6H_4(OH)CH_2\text{-}CH(NH_2)COOH$.

tyrosinemia *noun* see TYROSINAEMIA.

tyrosinosis /tʌɪrəsɪˈnəʊsɪs/ *noun.* Pl. **-noses** /-ˈnəʊsiːz/. M20.
[from prec. + -OSIS.]
MEDICINE. A rare defect of tyrosine metabolism in which there is increased excretion of oxidation products of tyrosine but no liver or kidney damage. Also (now *rare*) = TYROSINAEMIA.

tyrothricin /tʌɪrəˈθrʌɪsɪn, -ˈθrɪsɪn/ *noun.* M20.
[from mod. Latin *Tyrothrix* former genus name of a bacterium (from Greek *turos* cheese + *thrix* hair) + -IN[1].]
PHARMACOLOGY. An antibacterial preparation of gramicidin and tyrocidin which is used externally and in lozenges in the treatment of skin and mouth infections.

Tyrrhenian /tɪˈriːnɪən/ *adjective & noun.* M16.
[from Latin *Tyrrhenus* of or pertaining to the Etruscans, or *Tyrrhenia* Etruria: see -AN, -IAN.]
▶**A** *adjective.* Of or pertaining to (the people of) ancient Etruria; Etruscan. M16.
Tyrrhenian Sea the sea lying between the mainland of Italy and the islands of Corsica, Sardinia, and Sicily.
▶**B** *noun.* An Etruscan. E17.
■ Also ˈ**Tyrrhene** *adjective & noun* LME.

Tyrtaean /təːˈtiːən/ *adjective.* L19.
[from *Tyrtaeus* (see below) + -AN.]
Pertaining to or in the style of Tyrtaeus, a Greek poet of the 7th cent. BC, who composed martial songs.

Tyson /ˈtʌɪs(ə)n/ *noun.* L19.
[Edward Tyson (1650–1708) English anatomist.]
ANATOMY. ***Tyson's glands***, ***glands of Tyson***, the sebaceous glands of the prepuce.
■ **Tysonian** /tʌɪˈsəʊnɪən/ *adjective*: ***Tysonian glands***, Tyson's glands L19.

tystie /ˈtʌɪsti, ˈtiːsti/ *noun.* Chiefly *Scot.* Also **teistie** & other vars. L18.
[Of Norse origin: cf. Norn *täisti*, Old Norse *þeisti*, Norwegian *teist(e)*.]
The black guillemot, *Cepphus grylle*.

tyuyamunite /tjuːjəˈmuːnʌɪt/ *noun.* E20.
[from *Tyuya Muyun*, a village near Osh in Kyrgyzstan, central Asia: see -ITE[1].]
MINERALOGY. A hydrated calcium uranyl vanadate, occurring as soft yellowish orthorhombic crystals and mined for its uranium content.

tzatziki /tsatˈsiːki/ *noun.* M20.
[mod. Greek, from Turkish *cacık*.]
A Greek side dish made with yoghurt, cucumber, garlic, and sometimes mint.

tzedaka /tseˈdɔka/ *noun.* Also ***-kah***. M20.
[Hebrew *ṣĕdāqāh* righteousness.]
The obligation to help fellow Jews; *gen.* charity.

Tzeltal /tselˈtɑːl, ˈtseltɑːl; s-/ *adjective & noun.* Also **Tzen-** /ˈtsen-/. M19.
[Spanish, one of the three regions of the Mexican State of Chiapas, as divided by the Spanish; ult. origin unkn.]
▶**A** *adjective.* Of or pertaining to an American Indian people inhabiting parts of southern Mexico, or their language. M19.
▶**B** *noun.* Pl. same, **-s**, **-es** /-ɪz/. A member of this people; the Mayan language of this people. L19.

tzigane /tsɪˈgɑːn/ *noun & adjective.* M18.
[French from Hungarian †*czigany*, *cigány*.]
▶**A** *noun.* A Hungarian Gypsy. M18.
▶**B** *adjective.* That is a tzigane; consisting of tziganes; characteristic of the tziganes or esp. their music. L19.

tzimmes /ˈtsɪməs/ *noun.* Also **ts-**, **-mis**. Pl. same. L19.
[Yiddish *tsimes*, of unkn. origin.]
A Jewish stew of sweetened vegetables or vegetables and fruit, sometimes with meat; *fig.* a fuss, a confusion.

tzitzit(h) *nouns* vars. of TSITSITH.

tzolkin /ˈtsɔːlkɪn, s-/ *noun.* M20.
[Maya.]
The cycle of two hundred and sixty days constituting a year in the Mayan sacred calendar.

Tzotzil /ˈtsəʊtsɪl, tsəʊtˈsɪl; s-/ *noun & adjective.* L19.
[Spanish from Tzotzil *soćil* bat people.]
▶**A** *noun.* Pl. same, **-s**, **-es** /-ɪz/.
1 A member of an American Indian people inhabiting parts of southern Mexico. L19.
2 The Mayan language of this people. E20.
▶**B** *attrib.* or as *adjective.* Of or pertaining to the Tzotzil or their language. E20.

Tz'u Chou /tsuː ˈtʃəʊ/ *adjective & noun.* E20.
[Chinese *Cizhou* (Wade–Giles *Tz'u-Chou*), a district in NE China.]
(Designating) pottery made at Tz'u Chou, or in similar styles elsewhere, from the Sui dynasty onwards.

Uu

U, u /juː/.
The twenty-first letter of the modern English alphabet and the twentieth of the ancient Roman one, a differentiated form of the letter V. Latin manuscripts written in capitals have V only, but other Latin manuscripts also have a modified form of this, resembling u. Both forms occur in Old English manuscripts: capital V represents either V or U, and the modified form usually represents the vowel u. In Middle English the symbols u and v both occur, but without formal distinction of use. During the 16th cent. continental printers began to distinguish lower case u as the vowel symbol and v as the consonant symbol, and by the mid 17th cent. this was also the case in English. Capital V continued to be used for both V and U into the 17th cent., but in the course of that century it was replaced, for the vowel, by capital U. From about 1700 the regular forms have been U u for the vowel, and V v for the consonant. However, many dictionaries etc. continued into the 19th cent. to give items beginning with u or v in a single alphabetic sequence. In Old English the vowel u was sounded either short or long. In Middle English short u remained while long u was replaced in spelling by ou, adopted from French spelling. Also borrowed at this time were the sounds of long and short French u, pronounced with lip-rounding. In mod. English the Old English short u has normally become /ʌ/, though /ʊ/ remains in some words after a labial (***bull***, ***full***, ***put***). The Old English long u has normally become /aʊ/, written ou or ow (***thou***, ***town***). The long u from French and Latin has become /juː, jʊə/, as in ***huge***, ***cure***, with reduction to /uː, ʊə/ after *s* (= /ʃ/, /ʒ/) and *r*, as in ***sure***, ***brute***, ***jury***, and more widely in American usage. U is often silent after *g* (***guard***, ***guess***) and has the value of *w* after *q* (***queen***, ***quick***) and in some words after g and *s* (***anguish***, ***suave***). Pl. **U's**, **Us**.
▸ **I 1** The letter and its sound. ▸**b** = YOU *pronoun.* Cf. IOU. *informal* (chiefly *commercial*).
2 The shape of the letter.
2 U-bend (a part of) a pipe, esp. a waste pipe, shaped like a U. **U-shaped** *adjective* having a shape or a cross-section like a U. **U-turn** a turning round of a vehicle etc. to face the opposite direction; *fig.* a reversal of policy or opinion. **U-valley** a valley with a U-shaped cross-section, esp. as a result of glacial erosion.
▸ **II** Symbolical uses.
3 Used to denote serial order; applied e.g. to the twenty-first (or often the twentieth, either I or J being omitted) group or section, sheet of a book, etc.
4 (Cap. U.) A coefficient representing the rate at which heat is lost through a structure, expressed in B.t.u. per hour per square foot per degree Fahrenheit, or watts per square metre per degree Celsius. Also ***U factor***, ***U value***.
5 ***U.P.*** /juːˈpiː/ [spelling pronunc. of UP *adverb*[2]], over, finished, beyond remedy. *slang.*
6 PHYSICS. [German *ungerade* odd.] (Usu. italic *u.*) Designating functions, esp. wave functions, which change sign on inversion through the origin, and atomic states etc. represented by such functions. Cf. **G**, G 8.
7 PHYSICS. ***U-process***, ***u-process***, = UMKLAPP PROCESS.
▸ **III 8** Abbrevs.: (A small selection only is given here. Those all in caps. or small caps. also occur with a full stop after each letter; some of those all in caps. also occur (i) with initial cap. only, (ii) in small caps.) **U** = universal (in a film censorship classification); university; (CHEMISTRY) uranium. **u** (PARTICLE PHYSICS) = up.

U /uː, juː/ *noun*[1]. M20.
[Burmese.]
In Myanmar (Burma), a title of respect before a man's name.

U /juː/ *adjective & noun*[2]. M20.
[Abbreviation of *upper-class*. Cf. NON-U.]
▸ **A** *adjective.* Upper-class; supposedly characteristic of the upper class; (esp. of linguistic usage) fashionable, proper. M20.
▸ **B** *noun.* Upper-class people or characteristics collectively. M20.

UAE *abbreviation.*
United Arab Emirates.

uakari /wəˈkɑːri/ *noun.* M19.
[Tupi.]
Each of three short-tailed cebid monkeys of the genus *Cacajao*, found in the Amazon basin; *esp.* (more fully ***red uakari***) *C. rubicundus*, which has a naked red face and shaggy reddish fur.

-ual /jʊəl/ *suffix.*
[Repr. late Latin *-ualis*, *-uale*.]
Forming adjectives with the sense 'of the kind of, pertaining to', from Latin nouns with stems in *-u-*, as ***accentual***, ***eventual*** (Latin *accentus*, *eventus*), or from Latin adjectives in *-uus*, as ***individual*** (medieval Latin *individualis*, from Latin. *individuus*). See also -AL[1].

UAP *abbreviation.*
United Australia Party.

UAR *abbreviation.*
United Arab Republic.

UAW *abbreviation.* Also **UAWA**. *US.*
United Automobile Workers (of America).

ubac /ˈjuːbak/ *noun.* M20.
[French (orig. dial.), app. from Latin *opacus* shady.]
GEOGRAPHY. A hill or mountain slope which receives little sunshine, esp. one facing north. Opp. ADRET.

U-bahn /ˈuːbaːn, ˈjuː-/ *noun.* M20.
[German, from *U* abbreviation of *Untergrund* underground + *Bahn* railway.]
The underground railway in various major cities of Germany and Austria.

Ubaid /ʊˈbʌɪd/ *adjective.* M20.
[The tell Al *'Ubaid* near Ur in the Euphrates valley.]
ARCHAEOLOGY. Designating or pertaining to a culture thought to have flourished throughout Mesopotamia in the fifth millennium BC.

Ubangi /juːˈbaŋgi, uː-/ *adjective & noun.* E20.
[A river between the Central African Republic and the Democratic Republic of Congo (Zaire).]
▸ **A** *adjective.* Of, pertaining to, or designating a group of peoples inhabiting the Ubangi region of central Africa, certain women of whom wear ornamental plates that distend their upper lips. E20.
▸ **B** *noun.* Pl. same, **-s**. A member of one of these peoples. M20.

📖 S. BELLOW Carnival sideshows with . . their bearded ladies and Ubangis with platter lips.

uber- /ˈuːbə, *foreign* yːbər/ *combining form.* Also **über-**. L20.
[German *über* over.]
Forming colloq. nouns (on the pattern of ÜBERMENSCH) denoting the ultimate or supreme person or thing of a particular kind, as ***uberbabe***, ***ubergeek***, ***ubermodel***.

über alles /yːbər ˈaləs/ *adjectival & adverbial phr.* M20.
[German, from *über* over + *alles* all.]
Above all else.

Überfremdung /yːbərˈfrɛmdʊŋ/ *noun.* M20.
[German, from *überfremden* give foreign character to (from *über* over + *fremd* foreign) + *-ung* -ING[1].]
The admission or presence of too many foreigners.

überhaupt /yːbərˈhaʊpt/ *adverb.* L19.
[German, from *über* over + *Haupt* head, (in compounds) main.]
In general, (taken) as a whole; par excellence.

Übermensch /ˈyːbərmɛnʃ/ *noun.* Pl. **-en** /-ən/. L19.
[German, back-form. from *übermenschlich* superhuman, from *über* over + *menschlich* human, from *Mensch* person.]
= SUPERMAN.
■ ***übermenschlich*** /ˈyːbərmɛnʃlɪç/ *adjective* [see above] superior; like a superman, superhuman: E20. ***Übermenschlichkeit*** /ˈyːbərˌmɛnʃlɪçkaɪt/ *noun* [German *Menschlichkeit* humanity] the quality of a superman, superhumanity M20.

uberous /ˈjuːb(ə)rəs/ *adjective.* Now *rare.* E17.
[from Latin *uber* rich, fruitful, from *uber* udder: see -OUS.]
1 Of an animal or the breast: supplying milk or nourishment in abundance. E17.
†**2** Of a place: richly productive; fertile. E–M17.
3 Abundant, copious, full. M17.

uberrima fides /juːˌbɛrɪmə ˈfʌɪdiːz/ *noun phr.* M19.
[Latin.]
LAW. The utmost good faith.

uberty /ˈjuːbəti/ *noun.* Now *rare.* LME.
[Old French *uberté* or Latin *ubertus*, formed as UBEROUS: see -TY[1].]
Rich growth, fertility; abundance.

†**ubi** *noun.* E17–M18.
[from Latin = where.]
Place, position; location.

ubication /juːbɪˈkeɪʃ(ə)n/ *noun.* M17.
[medieval Latin *ubicatio(n-)* whereness, from *ubicare* situate, from Latin *ubi* where: see -ATION.]
The condition or fact of being in a certain place or position; location.

ubicity /juːˈbɪsɪti/ *noun. rare.* E20.
[from Latin *ubi*: see prec., -ICITY.]
Whereabouts.

ubiety /juːˈbʌɪɪti/ *noun.* L17.
[medieval Latin *ubietas*, from Latin *ubi* where: see -ITY.]
The fact or condition of being in a definite place; local relationship; whereness.

ubiquarian /juːbɪˈkwɛːrɪən/ *noun & adjective.* M18.
[from Latin *ubique* everywhere + -ARIAN.]
▸ **A** *noun.* †**1** In *pl.* (The name of) a society or club that existed in the 18th cent. Only in M18.
2 A person who goes everywhere. *rare.* M18.
▸ **B** *adjective.* Existing or found everywhere; ubiquitous. M18.

ubiquinone /juːˈbɪkwɪnəʊn/ *noun.* M20.
[Blend of UBIQUITOUS and QUINONE.]
BIOCHEMISTRY. Any of a class of substituted quinones which act as electron-transfer agents in cell respiration.

†**ubiquious** *adjective. rare.* M17–M19.
[formed as UBIQUARIAN + -IOUS.]
Ubiquitous.

Ubiquist /ˈjuːbɪkwɪst/ *noun. rare.* M17.
[French *ubiquiste*, formed as UBIQUARIAN: see -IST.]
CHRISTIAN CHURCH. = UBIQUITARIAN *noun* 2.

ubiquitarian /juːˌbɪkwɪˈtɛːrɪən/ *noun & adjective.* In senses A.2, B.1 usu. **U-**. M17.
[formed as next: see -ARIAN.]
▸ **A** *noun.* †**1** = UBIQUITARY *noun* 1. M17–M18.
2 CHRISTIAN CHURCH. A person, esp. a Lutheran, who believes that Christ's body is everywhere present at all times. M17.
▸ **B** *adjective.* **1** CHRISTIAN CHURCH. Pertaining to or believing in the doctrine of the Ubiquitarians. M17.
2 Ubiquitous. *rare.* M17.
■ **ubiquitarianism** *noun* (CHRISTIAN CHURCH) = UBIQUITISM L19.

ubiquitary /juːˈbɪkwɪt(ə)ri/ *noun & adjective.* Also (esp. in senses A.2, B.1) **U-**. L16.
[mod. Latin *ubiquitarius*, formed as UBIQUARIAN: see -ARY[1].]
▸ **A** *noun.* **1** A person or thing that is or can be everywhere at once. Now *rare.* L16. ▸†**b** A clergyman having no settled benefice but taking duty anywhere. Only in M17.
†**2** CHRISTIAN CHURCH. = UBIQUITARIAN *noun* 2. L16–E18.
▸ **B** *adjective.* †**1** CHRISTIAN CHURCH. = UBIQUITARIAN *adjective* 1. L16–E17.
2 Ubiquitous. E17.
3 Very widespread, extensive. *rare.* M17.

ubiquitin /juːˈbɪkwɪtɪn/ *noun.* L20.
[from UBIQUITOUS + -IN[1].]
BIOCHEMISTRY. A single-chain polypeptide involved in the destruction of defective and superfluous proteins, and found in all eukaryotic organisms with little variation.
■ **ubiquitinate** *verb trans.* bind ubiquitin to L20. **ubiquiti'nation** *noun* the process of ubiquitinating something L20.

Ubiquitism /juːˈbɪkwɪtɪz(ə)m/ *noun.* E17.
[from UBIQUITY + -ISM.]
CHRISTIAN CHURCH. The doctrine of the omnipresence of Christ's body.

ubiquitous /juːˈbɪkwɪtəs/ *adjective.* M19.
[from next + -OUS.]
Present, appearing, or found everywhere; omnipresent.

📖 *Time* Scrooge and Tiny Tim are almost as ubiquitous as Santa Claus. *Guardian* The offices are bland and pleasant, with ubiquitous bland furnishings.

■ **ubiquitously** *adverb* M19. **ubiquitousness** *noun* L19.

ubiquity /juːˈbɪkwɪti/ *noun.* Also (in sense 1) **U-**. L16.
[mod. Latin *ubiquitas*, formed as UBIQUARIAN: see -ITY.]
1 CHRISTIAN CHURCH. The omnipresence of Christ or his body. L16.
2 The ability to be everywhere or in all places at the same time. E17.

ubi sunt /ʊbɪ ˈsʊnt/ *attrib. adjectival phr.* E20.
[Latin = 'where are', the opening words or refrain of certain medieval Latin works.]
LITERARY CRITICISM. Designating or characterizing a literary theme or passage lamenting the mutability of things.

ubity /ˈjuːbɪti/ *noun. rare.* E17.
[from Latin *ubi* where + -TY[1].]
Place, locality.

-uble /əb(ə)l/ *suffix* (not productive).
[French from Latin *-ubilis* adjectival suffix, the form taken by the suffix *-bilis* (see **-BLE**) when added to verbs in *-vere*, as *solubilis* **SOLUBLE** from *solvere*, *volubilis* **VOLUBLE** from *volvere*.]
Forming adjectives with the senses 'able to be', as ***soluble***, and 'able to', as ***voluble***. Cf. **-ABLE**, **-IBLE**.

U-boat /ˈjuːbəʊt/ *noun*. **E20**.
[German *U-Boot*, abbreviation of *Unterseeboot* lit. 'undersea boat'.]
A (German) submarine.

UBR *abbreviation*.
Uniform business rate, a flat-rate tax levied on business properties in England and Wales since April 1990 in place of rates.

Ubykh /ˈuːbɪx/ *noun & adjective*. **M20**.
[Circassian *wəbəχ*, prob. through Russian.]
(Of or pertaining to) an almost extinct NW Caucasian language, now spoken only in Turkey.

UC *abbreviation*.
University College.

u.c. *abbreviation*.
Upper case.

UCATT *abbreviation*.
Union of Construction, Allied Trades, and Technicians.

UCCA /ˈʌkə/ *abbreviation*.
Universities Central Council on Admissions.

UCD *abbreviation*.
University College, Dublin.

Uchee *noun* var. of **YUCHI**.

uchimata /ʊtʃɪˈmɑːtə/ *noun*. **E20**.
[Japanese, from *uchi* inside, interior + *mata* thigh.]
JUDO. An inner-thigh throw made with one's leg braced between those of one's opponent.

uchiwa /ˈuːtʃiwa/ *noun*. Pl. same. **L19**.
[Japanese.]
A flat Japanese fan that does not fold.

uckers /ˈʌkəz/ *noun*. **M20**.
[Origin unkn.]
A board game resembling ludo, played in the Navy.

ucky /ˈʌki/ *adjective*. *colloq*. Also **ukky**. **M20**.
[Cf. **YUCKY** *adjective*.]
Sticky and dirty; disgusting.

UCL *abbreviation*.
University College London.

UCLA *abbreviation*.
University of California at Los Angeles.

UCW *abbreviation*.
Union of Communication Workers.

UDA *abbreviation*.
Ulster Defence Association.

udad *noun* var. of **AOUDAD**.

udal /ˈjuːd(ə)l/ *noun*. Also **odal** /ˈəʊd(ə)l/. **L15**.
[Norwegian, Swedish *odal*, Danish *odel*, from Old Norse *óðal* property held by inheritance = Old Saxon *ōþil*, Old High German *uodal*, from Germanic, whence also Old English *æþele* **ATHEL**.]
Chiefly *Hist*. A form of freehold tenure requiring no service or acknowledgement of a superior, characteristic of Orkney and Shetland and formerly practised by other Scandinavian and early Germanic peoples; land held in this way. Usu. *attrib*.

> *attrib*.: G. BARRY These udal or allodial lands are directly opposed to fees or feus. SIR W. SCOTT The wide Udal possessions of their father . . were divided betwixt the brothers.

¶ The usual form in Orkney and Shetland is *udal*.
■ **udaller** *noun* a tenant of land by udal right **M17**.

udarnik /uˈdarnɪk/ *noun*. Pl. **-i** /-i/. **M20**.
[Russian.]
A member of a shock-brigade in the former USSR.

udatta /ʊˈdɑːtə/ *noun*. **M19**.
[Sanskrit *udātta* raised.]
The tone of the accented or main syllable of a word in Vedic Sanskrit. Cf. **ANUDATTA**, **SVARITA**.

UDC *abbreviation*.
Hist. Urban District Council.

udder /ˈʌdə/ *noun*.
[Old English *ūder* = Old Frisian, Old Saxon, Middle Low German, Middle Dutch *ūder* (Dutch *uier*, *uijer*), Old High German *ūtar* (German *Euter*), from West Germanic.]
1 A pendulous baggy organ, provided with two or more teats or nipples, in which the milk is produced in certain female ungulate mammals. **OE**.
2 An animal's teat. Usu. in *pl. poet. rare*. **L16**.
3 In *pl*. A woman's breasts. *rare*. **E18**.

> **1** V. WOOD How lovely, fresh milk straight from the udder.

■ **uddered** *adjective* †(*a*) suckled; (*b*) having an udder or udders: **L16**. **udderful** *adjective & noun* (*rare*) (*a*) *adjective* having a full udder; (*b*) *noun* as much (milk) as an udder will hold: **L19**.

uddiyana /ʊdɪˈjɑːnə/ *noun*. **M20**.
[Sanskrit *uddiyāna* rising.]
A physical exercise in yoga, involving contraction of the abdominal muscles and raising of the diaphragm.

ude-garami /ˌuːdɪgəˈrɑːmi/ *noun*. **M20**.
[Japanese, from *ude* arm + *karami* entwinement, lock.]
JUDO. An armlock applied to the arm of one's opponent bent at the elbow.

ude-gatame /ˌuːdɪgəˈtɑːmi/ *noun*. **M20**.
[Japanese *udegatame*, formed as prec. + *katame* lock, hold.]
JUDO. An armlock applied to the straight arm of one's opponent.

†udge *verb trans*. **L16–E17**.
[Repr. a supposed Welsh pronunc.]
Judge.

UDI *abbreviation*.
Unilateral declaration of independence.

Udi /ˈuːdiː/ *noun & adjective*. **M20**.
[Udi.]
(Of or pertaining to) an almost extinct NE Caucasian language of Dagestan.

UDM *abbreviation*.
Union of Democratic Mineworkers.

Udmurt /ˈʊdmʊət/ *noun & adjective*. **M20**.
[Russian from Udmurt *Ud murt*, from *Ud* the region of Vyatsk + *murt* man. Cf. **VOTYAK**.]
▶ **A** *noun*. Pl. same, **-s**.
1 A member of a Finno-Ugrian people inhabiting the Ural mountain region of the Udmurt Republic of Russia. **M20**.
2 The Finno-Ugric language of this people. **M20**.
▶ **B** *attrib*. or as *adjective*. Of or pertaining to the Udmurts or their language. **M20**.
¶ Now the official name (in place of *Votyak*).

udometer /juːˈdɒmɪtə/ *noun*. **E19**.
[French *udomètre*, from Latin *udus* wet: see **-OMETER**.]
A rain-gauge.

udon /ˈuːdɒn/ *noun*. **E20**.
[Japanese.]
In Japanese cookery: a thick strip of pasta made from wheat flour; pasta in this form.

UDR *abbreviation*.
Hist. Ulster Defence Regiment.

†Uds *noun*. Also **Ud's**, **Udz**. **E17–M19**.
[Alt. of **GOD** *noun*: see **-'S**[1]. Cf. **OD** *noun*[1], **GAWD**.]
God's: chiefly as interjection & in exclamatory phrs. corresponding to those s.v. **GOD** *noun* 5.
Udsbud, ***Udsfoot***, ***Udzooks***, etc.

Uduk /ˈʊdʊk/ *noun & adjective*. **E20**.
[Perh. from (*Jebel*) *Uduk*, a hill in the area inhabited by this people.]
▶ **A** *noun*. Pl. same, **-s**.
1 A member of a people inhabiting the Upper Nile region of Sudan. **E20**.
2 The language of this people. **M20**.
▶ **B** *adjective*. Of or pertaining to this people or their language. **M20**.

†Udz *noun* var. of **UDS**.

UEFA /juːˈeɪfə, -ˈiːfə/ *abbreviation*.
Union of European Football Associations.

U-ey /ˈjuːi/ *noun*. *slang* (chiefly *Austral*.). **L20**.
[from U, U + **-Y**[6].]
A U-turn.

UF *abbreviation*.
1 United Free (Church, of Scotland); also, a member of this.
2 Urea-formaldehyde.

ufer /ˈjuːfə/ *noun*. **M18**.
[Alt. of **JUFFER**.]
A piece of timber from 4 to 7 inches (10 to 18 cm) in diameter and over 20 feet (6.1 m) long.

UFF *abbreviation*.
Ulster Freedom Fighters.

uff /ʌf/ *interjection*. **E20**.
[Imit.]
Expr. exertion, weariness, relief, etc.

uffish /ˈʌfɪʃ/ *adjective*. **L19**.
[Alt.]
= **HUFFISH**.

UFO /ˈjuːfəʊ, juːɛfˈəʊ/ *noun*. Also **ufo**. Pl. **UFOs**, **ufos**. **M20**.
[Acronym.]
An unidentified flying object; a flying saucer.

> *Raritan* In contemporary America . . hundreds of people claim to have been abducted by aliens from UFOs.

■ **UF'Oish** *adjective* (*rare*) characteristic of a UFO **L20**.

ufology /juːˈfɒlədʒi/ *noun*. **M20**.
[from prec. + **-LOGY**.]
The branch of knowledge that deals with UFOs.
■ **ufo'logical** *adjective* **M20**. **ufologist** *noun* **M20**.

UFOnaut /ˈjuːfəʊnɔːt/ *noun*. Also **ufonaut**. **L20**.
[from UFO + *-naut*, after *aeronaut*, *astronaut*, etc.]
A being who travels in a UFO; an extraterrestrial.

ug /ʌg/ *verb*. *obsolete* exc. *Scot*. & *dial*. Infl. **-gg-**. **ME**.
[Old Norse *ugga* fear, dread, apprehend.]
1 *verb intrans*. & *trans*. Feel or fill with dread, loathing, or disgust. **ME**.
2 *verb trans*. Abhor, loathe, detest. **ME**.

ugali /uːˈgɑːli/ *noun*. **L20**.
[Kiswahili.]
A type of maize porridge eaten in east and central Africa.

Uganda /juːˈgandə/ *noun*. **E20**.
[See below.]
Used ***attrib***. to designate people or things from or associated with Uganda, a country in E. Africa.
Uganda Asian = ***Ugandan Asian*** s.v. **UGANDAN** *adjective* 1. **Uganda kob** a large brown race of the kob, *Kobus kob*, found in parts of Uganda.

Ugandan /juːˈgandən/ *adjective & noun*. **M20**.
[from prec. + **-AN**.]
▶ **A** *adjective*. **1** Of or pertaining to Uganda or its people. **M20**.
2 *euphem*. Sexual. **L20**.
1 Ugandan Asian an Asian, esp. from India or Pakistan, resident or formerly resident in Uganda.
▶ **B** *noun*. A native or inhabitant of Uganda. **M20**.
¶ In sense A.2 popularized by the British satirical magazine *Private Eye*.
■ **Ugandani'zation** *noun* in Uganda, the replacement of settlers and Asians by Ugandan Africans in government posts, the civil service, etc. **M20**.

Ugaritic /uːgəˈrɪtɪk/ *noun & adjective*. **M20**.
[from *Ugarit*, an ancient city in northern Syria + **-IC**.]
▶ **A** *noun*. A pre-Phoenician Semitic language examples of which were first discovered at the site of Ugarit in 1929. **M20**.
▶ **B** *adjective*. Of or pertaining to this language. **M20**.

UGC *abbreviation*.
Hist. University Grants Committee.

ugg /ʌg/ *adjective*. *Austral*. *colloq*. **M20**.
[Perh. abbreviation of **UGLY** *adjective*.]
ugg boot, a kind of soft sheepskin boot.

ugglesome /ˈʌg(ə)ls(ə)m/ *adjective*. Now *rare*. **M16**.
[Prob. from **UG** or **UGLY** + **-SOME**[1]. Cf. **UGSOME**.]
Fearful, horrible, gruesome.

ugh /ʊh, ʌh, əː, ʊx, ʌg/ *interjection & noun*. **M18**.
[Imit.]
▶ **A** *interjection*. **1** Expr. the inarticulate sound of a hollow cough or grunt. **M18**.
2 Expr. disgust, dislike, or revulsion. **M19**.

> **2** A. LAMBERT Ugh, she thought, how horrid! and shut her eyes firmly.

▶ **B** *noun*. An inarticulate sound resembling a hollow cough or grunt. **M19**.

Ugli /ˈʌgli/ *noun*. Also **u-**. Pl. **-is**, **-ies**. **M20**.
[Alt. of **UGLY** *adjective*.]
(Proprietary name for) a mottled green and yellow hybrid citrus fruit first produced in Jamaica, a form of tangelo.

uglify /ˈʌglɪfʌɪ/ *verb trans*. **L16**.
[from **UGLY** *adjective* + **-FY**.]
Make ugly or repulsive in appearance; disfigure.

> M. AMIS He got a real kick out of . . looking for new ways to uglify the home.

■ **uglifi'cation** *noun* (*a*) the action or process of making something ugly; (*b*) an ugly feature of something: **E19**. **uglifier** *noun* a person who uglifies something **M19**.

ugliness /ˈʌglɪnɪs/ *noun*. **ME**.
[from **UGLY** *adjective* + **-NESS**.]
†**1** Horror, dread, loathing. Only in **ME**. ▸**b** A cause of horror or loathing. Only in **L16**.
2 The state of being ugly to look at; repulsiveness or marked unpleasantness of appearance. **ME**. ▸**b** An ugly thing or feature. **M18**.
3 Moral repulsiveness; disgusting wickedness. **E17**.

> **2** G. DALY He worried that his age and ugliness would repulse her. **3** A. MACLAREN The Bible tells the shameful history in all its naked ugliness.

ugly /ˈʌgli/ *adjective, adverb, noun, & verb*. As adjective also †**ougly**. **ME**.
[Old Norse *uggligr* be feared, from *ugga* **UG**: see **-LY**[1]. Cf. **UGSOME**.]
▶ **A** *adjective*. **1** Having an appearance which causes dread or horror; frightful, horrible, esp. through deformity or squalor. *obsolete* exc. as passing into sense 4. **ME**.
†**2** Of an event, time, sound, etc.: dreadful, terrible. **ME–E18**.
3 a Morally repulsive; base, vile. **ME**. ▸**b** Offensive to refined taste or good feelings; disagreeable, unpleasant.

E17. ▸c Causing disquiet or discomfort; problematic, awkward. M17.

4 Offensive or repulsive to the eye; of markedly disagreeable or unpleasant appearance. LME.

5 Offensive to the sense of smell or taste; noisome, nasty. LME.

6 a Hazardous, perilous. *rare.* M17. ▸b Suggestive of trouble or danger. M17. ▸c Of the weather, sea, etc.: threatening, dangerously rough. M18.

7 Cross, angry, ill-tempered. L17.

> 1 MILTON O sight Of terrour, foul and ugly to behold, .. how horrible to feel! 3b J. L. WATEN He began to shout ugly and hateful words. J. C. OATES He's crooning obscene words .. and making ugly twisting gestures at his crotch. c DISRAELI A horse which he was endeavouring to cure of some ugly tricks. *Fly Rod & Reel* Here are ugly answers, about water rights, overcrowding, pollution. 4 J. FRAME A motorbike accident had broken his nose and battered his teeth and he was ugly. A. N. WILSON The main school buildings, lumpish and ugly. *Here's Health* The ugly ulcer .. had been preceded by raw red sores all over her hands. ***raise its ugly head***: see RAISE *verb*. ***rear its ugly head***: see REAR *verb*[1] 10. 6b J. REED An ugly crowd had gathered around, abusing the patrol. c A. W. KINGLAKE An ugly black sky above, and an angry sea beneath. 7 B. HEAD He found the lady in an ugly stamping rage.

Special collocations: **Ugly American** [with allus. to the title of a book by Lederer and Burdick] an American who behaves offensively abroad. **ugly customer** a person, animal, etc., who is likely to cause trouble or be difficult to deal with. **ugly duckling** [with allus. to a tale by Hans Andersen of a cygnet in a brood of ducks] a young person who shows no promise at all of the beauty, success, etc., that will eventually come with maturity.

▸B *adverb.* Horribly, terribly; offensively, repulsively. LME.

▸C *noun.* 1 An ugly person, animal, etc. Cf. also PLUG-UGLY. (*rare* before M18.) LME.

2 *Hist.* A kind of protective brim or shade attached to the front of a lady's bonnet. M19.

3 ***the uglies***, depression, bad temper. *slang.* M19.

> 1 WILBUR SMITH We never sleep next to a cooking-fire, it can attract the uglies.

▸D *verb trans.* Make ugly, uglify. Also foll. by *up*. M18.

■ **uglily** *adverb* ME.

Ugrian /ˈuːgrɪən, ˈjuː-/ *adjective & noun.* M19.
[formed as next: see -AN, -IAN.]
▸A *adjective.* = UGRIC *adjective.* M19.
▸B *noun.* 1 A person of Ugric stock. M19.
2 = UGRIC *noun.* M19.

Ugric /ˈuːgrɪk, ˈjuː-/ *adjective & noun.* M19.
[from Russian *Ugry*, a people living east of the Urals: see -IC.]
▸A *adjective.* Of or pertaining to the eastern branch of the Finnic peoples (which includes the Magyars) or the group of Finno-Ugric languages that includes Hungarian and Ob-Ugrian. M19.
▸B *noun.* The Ugric group of languages. L19.

Ugro- /ˈuːgrəʊ, ˈjuː-/ *combining form.* M19.
[from UGR(IAN + -O-.]
Ugrian and —, as ***Ugro-Altaic***, ***Ugro-Finn***, ***Ugro-Finnish***, ***Ugro-Slavonic***, etc.

ugsome /ˈʌgs(ə)m/ *adjective.* Chiefly *Scot. & north.* LME.
[from UG + -SOME[1].]
Horrible, horrid, loathsome.
¶ App. revived by Sir Walter Scott in 19.
■ **ugsomely** *adverb* (*rare*) LME. **ugsomeness** *noun* †(*a*) loathing; (*b*) loathsomeness, ugliness: LME.

uguisu /uːˈgwiːzuː/ *noun.* L19.
[Japanese.]
The Japanese warbler *Cettia diphone*, which has delicate olive green plumage.

uh /ʌ/ *adjective.* *US Black English.* L19.
[Repr. a pronunc.]
= A *adjective.*

uh /ʌh, ʌ/ *interjection.* E17.
[Imit.: cf. UGH.]
1 Expr. an inarticulate sound, such as that produced in coughing. E17.
2 Expr. hesitation; = ER *interjection.* *N. Amer.* M20.
3 = EH 3. L20.

UHF *abbreviation.*
Ultrahigh frequency.

uh-huh /ˈʌhʌ/ *interjection & adverb.* *colloq.* E20.
[Imit.]
Expr. affirmation, assent, or a non-committal response to a question or remark; yes.

uhlan /ˈuːlɑːn, ˈjuː-; ʊˈlɑːn/ *noun.* Also **hulan** /ˈh(j)uːlən/. M18.
[French *uhlan*, German *U(h)lan* from Polish *ulan*, *hulan* from Turkish *oğlan* youth, servant.]
Hist. A type of cavalryman or lancer in certain European armies, esp. that of Poland or (later) Germany.

uh-oh /ˈʌˌəʊ/ *interjection.* L20.
[Imit.]
Expr. alarm, dismay, or realization of a difficulty.

> *Premiere* Uh-oh, this isn't going to be easy.

UHT *abbreviation.*
1 Ultra heat treated (esp. of milk, for long keeping).
2 Ultrahigh temperature.

uht-song /ˈuːtsɒŋ/ *noun.*
[Old English *ūhtsang*, from *ūhte* early morning, the part of night just before daybreak + *sang* SONG *noun*[1].]
ECCLESIASTICAL HISTORY. In pre-Conquest England, the ecclesiastical office (nocturns, matins) celebrated just before daybreak.

uh-uh /ˈʌʌ, ʌˈʌ/ *interjection & adverb.* *colloq.* (chiefly *N. Amer.*). Also **huh-uh** /ˈhʌʌ, hʌˈʌ/. E20.
[Imit.]
Expr. a negative response to a question or remark; no.

Uhuru /ʊˈhuːruː/ *noun.* M20.
[Kiswahili = freedom.]
National independence of an African country, *spec.* Kenya.

Uigur /ˈwiːgʊə/ *adjective & noun.* Also **Uighur**. M18.
[Eastern Turkic.]
▸A *adjective.* Of or pertaining to a Turkic people of NW China. M18.
▸B *noun.* 1 A member of this people. L18.
2 The Turkic language of this people. M19.
■ **Uiˈgurean** *adjective* = UIGUR *adjective* L18. **Uiˈgurian** *adjective* = UIGUR *adjective* L19.

UIL *abbreviation.*
United Irish League.

uillean pipe /ˈɪlɪn ˈpʌɪp/ *noun phr.* E20.
[Irish *píob uilleann*, from *píob* PIPE *noun*[1] + *uilleann* genit. sing. of *uille* elbow. Cf. earlier UNION PIPE.]
sing. & (usu.) in *pl.* A form of bagpipe in which the bag is inflated by bellows worked by the elbow; Irish bagpipes.

uintaite /juːˈɪntʌɪt/ *noun.* Also **uintahite**. L19.
[from *Uinta(h)* Mountains, Utah, USA + -ITE[1].]
MINERALOGY. A brittle lustrous black variety of asphaltite used in the manufacture of paints and inks.
¶ A proprietary name for this mineral is GILSONITE.

uintathere /juːˈɪntəθɪə/ *noun.* L19.
[from mod. Latin *Uintatherium* (see below), formed as prec. + Greek *thērion* wild animal.]
PALAEONTOLOGY. An animal of the extinct genus *Uintatherium* or the extinct order Dinocerata containing it, which included large hoofed herbivorous mammals with greatly elongated upper canines whose remains are found in Asia and N. America.

Uitlander /ˈeɪtlandə, ˈɔɪt-, *foreign* ˈœytlandər/ *noun.* *S. Afr.* L19.
[Afrikaans, from Dutch *uit* OUT *adjective* + *land* LAND *noun*[1]: see -ER[1].]
A foreigner, an alien; *spec.* a British person who went to South Africa before the Boer War of 1899–1902.

ujamaa /ʊdʒaˈmɑː/ *noun.* M20.
[Kiswahili = consanguinity, brotherhood, from *jamaa* family from Arab. *jamāʿa* group (of people), community.]
A kind of socialism introduced in Tanzania by President Nyerere in the 1960s, in which self-help village cooperatives were established.

uji /ˈʊdʒi/ *noun.* Pl. same. L19.
[Japanese.]
In feudal and pre-feudal Japan, a name indicating to which ancestral family the bearer belonged; a patriarchal lineage group of all those with the same *uji*.

ujigami /ʊdʒɪˈgɑːmi/ *noun.* Pl. same. L19.
[Japanese, from prec. + *kami* god.]
In feudal and pre-feudal Japan, the ancestral deity of an *uji*, or (later) the tutelary deity of a particular village or area.

UK *abbreviation.*
United Kingdom.

UKAEA *abbreviation.*
United Kingdom Atomic Energy Authority.

ukase /juːˈkeɪz/ *noun.* E18.
[Russian *ukaz* ordinance, edict, from *ukazat'* show, order, decree.]
1 A decree or edict, having legal force, issued by the tsarist Russian government. E18.
2 *gen.* Any proclamation or decree; an order, an arbitrary command. E19.

> 2 W. A. PERCY Mother .. used to correct my manners, issue ukases on conduct.

uke /juːk/ *noun*[1]. *colloq.* E20.
[Abbreviation.]
= UKULELE.

uke /ˈuːkeɪ/ *noun*[2]. M20.
[Japanese, from *ukeru* receive, be passive, defend.]
In judo and other martial arts, the person who is held, thrown, etc., the person on the defensive.

ukeke /uːˈkeɪkeɪ/ *noun.* L19.
[Hawaiian *'ūkēkē*.]
A Hawaiian stringed instrument consisting of a strip of wood with two or three strings that are played with the fingers and mouth.

ukelele *noun* var. of UKULELE.

ukemi /ˈuːkemi/ *noun.* M20.
[Japanese, from UKE *noun*[2] + *mi* body.]
JUDO etc. The art of falling safely.

ukha /ʊˈxa/ *noun.* Also ***oukha***. E20.
[Russian.]
A Russian fish soup.

uki /ˈuːki/ *noun.* E20.
[Japanese = floating.]
JUDO. Used in the names of various techniques involving a controlled throw in which the opponent's feet and body leave the ground.
Comb.: **uki-gatame** /gaˈtameɪ/ [Japanese *katame* to lock, hold] a ground hold applied after an opponent has been thrown; **uki-otoshi** /ɒˈtɒʃi/ [Japanese = dropping] a throw made using only the hand.

ukiyo-e /ukijoˈjeː, ˌuːkɪjəʊˈjeɪ/ *noun.* L19.
[Japanese, from *ukiyo* fleeting world (from *uku* float, go by fleetingly + *yo* world) + *e* picture.]
A Japanese art-form in which everyday subjects are treated simply in woodblock prints or paintings; a work in this art-form.

ukky *adjective* var. of UCKY.

Ukrainian /juːˈkreɪnɪən/ *noun & adjective.* E19.
[from *Ukraine* (see below) from Russian †*ukraina* frontier regions, from *u* at + *kraĭ* edge: see -IAN.]
▸A *noun.* 1 A native or inhabitant of Ukraine, a country of eastern Europe bordering the Black Sea (formerly a republic of the USSR). E19.
2 The Slavonic language spoken in Ukraine. L19.
▸B *adjective.* Of or pertaining to Ukraine. E19.

ukulele /juːkəˈleɪli/ *noun.* Also **uke-**. L19.
[Hawaiian, lit. 'jumping flea'.]
A small four-stringed guitar originating in Hawaii but developed from an earlier Portuguese instrument.

ulama *noun* var. of ULEMA.

-ular /jʊlə/ *suffix.*
[Latin *ularis*, from dim. suffix *-ul-* + *-aris* -AR[1].]
Forming adjectives from nouns, either as adaptations of Latin, medieval Latin, or mod. Latin forms, as ***angular***, ***secular***, etc., or formed in English from Latin nouns, as ***corpuscular***, ***globular***, etc. When both the simple noun and its diminutive exist in English, as ***gland***, and ***glandule***, the adjective in *-ular* is usu. associated with the former.

ulcer /ˈʌlsə/ *noun & verb.* LME.
[Latin *ulcer-*, *ulcus* rel. to Greek *helkos* wound, sore.]
▸A *noun.* 1 *MEDICINE.* A defect of continuity in the epithelium covering a surface, esp. when forming a defined crater. LME. ▸b An ulcerative condition. E17.
2 *fig.* A corroding or corrupting influence; a moral blemish. L16.
▸B *verb trans. & intrans.* Make or become ulcerous (*lit. & fig.*); = ULCERATE *verb.* Now *rare.* LME.
■ **ulcered** *adjective* = ULCERATED LME.

†ulcerate *ppl adjective.* LME–E18.
[Latin *ulceratus* pa. pple of *ulcerare*: see next.]
Ulcerated, ulcerous.

ulcerate /ˈʌlsəreɪt/ *verb.* LME.
[Latin *ulcerat-* pa. ppl stem of *ulcerare*, from *ulcus*: see ULCER, -ATE[3].]
1 *verb intrans.* Form an ulcer; break out into ulcers. LME.
2 *verb trans.* Cause ulcers in or on. Now *rare.* LME.
3 *verb trans. fig.* Affect as with an ulcer; damage, erode, infect. M17.

> 3 *Times Lit. Suppl.* The rash of abominable little villas .. that ulcerates the slopes of Arthur's seat.

■ **ulcerated** *ppl adjective* afflicted with or characterized by an ulcer or ulcers M16.

ulceration /ʌlsəˈreɪʃ(ə)n/ *noun.* LME.
[from Latin *ulceratio(n-)*, formed as prec.: see -ATION.]
MEDICINE. 1 The process or state of forming ulcers; an ulcerated condition. LME.
2 An ulcer, a group of ulcers. Now *rare.* LME.

ulcerative /ˈʌlsəreɪtɪv, -ətɪv/ *adjective.* LME.
[from ULCERATE *verb* + -IVE.]
MEDICINE. †1 = ULCEROGENIC. LME–E19.
2 Of the nature of ulceration; accompanied or caused by ulceration. E19.

ulcerogenic /ʌls(ə)rə(ʊ)ˈdʒɛnɪk/ *adjective.* M20.
[from ULCER + -O- + -GENIC.]
MEDICINE. Causing ulceration.

ulcerous /ˈʌls(ə)rəs/ *adjective.* LME.
[from Latin *ulcerosus*, formed as ULCER: see -OUS.]
1 Ulcerated. LME.
2 Of the nature of an ulcer. L16.
3 Produced by ulcers. M17.

ule *noun* var. of **HULE**.

-ule /juːl/ *suffix*.
[Repr. Latin dim. ending *-ulus*, *-ula*, *-ulum*.]
Forming dim. nouns, chiefly from corresp. Latin forms, as ***capsule***, ***globule***, ***nodule***, ***pustule***, etc., and occas. as mod. formations, as ***faunule***. The Latin ending *-ula* is retained in some (esp. technical) words, as ***blastula***, ***campanula***, ***scrofula***.

ulema /ˈʊləmə, ˈuːlɪmə, uːləˈmɑː/ *noun*. Also **ulama** /ˈʊləmə, uːləˈmɑː/. **L17.**
[Arab. (Turkish, Persian) *ʿulamā* pl. of *ʿālim*, *ʿalim* learned, from *ʿalima* have (religious) knowledge.]
1 *collect.* & in *pl.* The members of a Muslim society or country who are recognized as having specialist knowledge of Islamic sacred law and theology; *spec.* (*Hist.*) such a body in the Ottoman Empire. **L17.**
2 A person who belongs to the *ulema*. **M19.**

ulendo /ʊˈlɛndəʊ/ *noun*. Pl. **-os**. **E20.**
[Nyanja.]
In central Africa: a trek, a safari.

-ulent /jʊlənt/ *suffix*.
[Latin *-ulentus*.]
Forming adjectives, usu. with the sense 'full of, having much', many of which are direct adoptions from Latin, as ***fraudulent***, ***opulent***, ***truculent***, etc., and others of which are later additions from medieval or mod. Latin or direct formations on Latin stems, as ***flocculent***, ***muculent***, etc.

ulexite /ˈjuːlɛksʌɪt/ *noun*. **M19.**
[from G. L. *Ulex* (d. 1883), German chemist + **-ITE**¹.]
MINERALOGY. A triclinic hydrated borate of sodium and calcium, occurring on alkali flats as rounded loose-textured masses of very fine white crystals, and used as a source of borax.

uliginal /juːˈlɪdʒ(ɪ)n(ə)l/ *adjective*. **M19.**
[from Latin *uligin-* (see **ULIGINOUS**) + **-AL**¹.]
BOTANY. Growing in bogs or wet peaty ground.

uliginose /juːˈlɪdʒɪnəʊs/ *adjective*. *rare*. **LME.**
[formed as next: see **-OSE**¹.]
†**1** = **ULIGINOUS** *adjective* 2. Only in **LME.**
2 *BOTANY.* = **ULIGINAL**. **M19.**

uliginous /juːˈlɪdʒɪnəs/ *adjective*. **L16.**
[from Latin *uliginosus*, from *uligin-*, *uligo* moisture, or directly from *uligin-*: see **-OUS**.]
1 Of a watery, slimy, or oozy nature. **L16.**
2 Of a place or of soil: soaked through with water or moisture; water-logged; marshy, swampy. **E17.**

ullage /ˈʌlɪdʒ/ *noun & verb*. **LME.**
[Anglo-Norman *ulliage* (cf. Anglo-Latin *oillagium*, *ull-*) = Old French *eull(i)age* (French *ouillage*), from *euillier* (French *ouiller*) fill (a barrel) (cf. Anglo-Latin *oillare*) from Proto-Gallo-Romance verb from Latin *oculus* eye, used in the sense of bung-hole: see **-AGE**.]
▶ **A** *noun*. **1** The amount of wine etc. by which a cask or bottle falls short of being full after leakage, evaporation, or use. **LME.** ▸**b** The part of a fuel tank in a vehicle, esp. a rocket, not filled with fuel; the capacity of this part. **M20.**
2 a The amount of wine etc. remaining in a cask after leakage, evaporation, and use. **M19.** ▸**b** The dregs remaining in a glass etc. *slang*. **L19.**
3 *transf.* A useless or worthless member of a ship's crew. *Nautical slang*. **E20.**

> 🕮 **1** F. MARRYAT I held the bottle up to the candle to ascertain the ullage. **on ullage** (of a cask etc.) not full; partly used.

Comb.: **ullage rocket** *ASTRONAUTICS* an auxiliary rocket used in weightless conditions to provide sufficient acceleration to force a liquid propellant to the end of its tank and ensure a continuous fuel supply.
▶ **B** *verb trans.* **1** Calculate the amount of ullage in (a cask). **M18.**
2 Reduce or increase the level in (a cask etc.) **L19.**
■ **ullaged** *adjective* (*a*) (of a cask or bottle) not full; (*b*) (of wine) affected in quality by ullage: **M16.**

ullagone /ˈʌləgəʊn, ʌləˈgəʊn/ *noun*. *Anglo-Irish*. **E19.**
[Irish *olagón*, *olo-*, *olagán*, of imit. origin.]
A cry of lamentation, a wail. Also as *interjection*.

ulli *noun* var. of **HULE**.

'ullo *interjection* see **HULLO**.

ulmin /ˈʌlmɪn/ *noun*. **E19.**
[Latin *ulmus* elm + **-IN**¹.]
†**1** A substance which exudes from the inner bark of elm and some other trees. **E–M19.**
2 A dark brown or black amorphous degradation product of wood or plant matter, which is an early stage of conversion to coal, and is also synthesized artificially from sugars etc. **M19.**
■ **ulmic** *adjective* (now *rare* or *obsolete*): **ulmic acid** = **ULMIN** **M19.**

ulmo /ˈʌlməʊ/ *noun*. Pl. **-os**. **M20.**
[(S. Amer.) Spanish.]
A Chilean eucryphia tree, *Eucryphia cordifolia*, sometimes cultivated as an ornamental; the hard wood of this tree.

ULMS *abbreviation*.
Underwater long-range missile system.

ulna /ˈʌlnə/ *noun*. Pl. **ulnae** /ˈʌlniː/. **LME.**
[Latin, rel. to Greek *ōlenē* and Old English *eln* **ELL** *noun*¹.]
ANATOMY. **1** Orig., the humerus. Now, the larger and inner of the two bones of the forearm, extending from the elbow to the wrist. **LME.**
2 The corresponding bone of a vertebrate's foreleg or a bird's wing. **M19.**

ulnage /ˈʌlnɪdʒ/ *noun*. *obsolete* exc. *Hist.* **LME.**
[medieval Latin *ullnagium*, formed as prec. after Old French *alnage* **AULNAGE**.]
= **AULNAGE**.
■ **ulnager** *noun* = **AULNAGER** **M18.**

ulnar /ˈʌlnə/ *adjective & noun*. **M18.**
[from **ULNA** + **-AR**¹.]
ANATOMY. ▶**A** *adjective*. Of, pertaining to, or associated with the ulna; *spec.* situated on the inner (little finger) side of the forearm. **M18.**
ulnar artery, ***ulnar nerve***, ***ulnar vein***, etc.
▶ **B** *noun*. An ulnar nerve, artery, etc. **L19.**

-ulose /jʊləʊz, -s/ *suffix*¹.
[Repr. Latin *-ulosus*, formed by adding *-osus* (see **-OSE**¹) to nouns in *-ulus*, *-ula*, *-ulum*.]
Forming adjectives with the sense 'full of, having', either directly from Latin words in *-ulosus*, as ***fistulose***, ***glandulose***, ***nebulose***, etc., or as later formations on (words from) Latin stems, as ***granulose***, ***nodulose***, ***rugolose***, etc. Many of these have corresp. forms in *-ulous* and are usu. either obsolete variants of these, or introduced later in order to convey the common distinction between words in *-ose* and *-ous*.

-ulose /jʊləʊz; *in a few words* -s/ *suffix*².
[from **LAEV)ULOSE**. Cf. **-OSE**².]
BIOCHEMISTRY. Forming the systematic names of ketoses from the names of the corresponding aldoses, esp. ketoses having the carbonyl group at the second carbon atom, as ***ribulose***, ***sedoheptulose***, ***xylulose***.

ulotrichous /juːˈlɒtrɪkəs/ *adjective*. **M19.**
[from Greek *oulos* crisp + **-TRICH** + **-OUS**.]
ANTHROPOLOGY. Having hair that is naturally tightly curled; (of hair) curled in this way.
■ **ulotrichy** *noun* the state or condition of being ulotrichous **E20.**

-ulous /jʊləs/ *suffix*.
[Repr. Latin *-ulosus*, *-ulus*.]
Forming adjectives with the sense 'full of, having', either from Latin words in *-ulosus*, as ***calculous***, ***fabulous***, ***populous***, etc. (many of which also have corresp. forms in *-ulose*), or from Latin words in *-ulus*, as ***credulous***, ***garrulous***, ***pendulous***, ***sedulous***, etc.

ulpan /ulˈpan/ *noun*. Pl. ***ulpanim*** /ulpaˈniːm/. **M20.**
[mod. Hebrew *ʾulpān*, from Aramaic *allēp* teach.]
An intensive course in the Hebrew language, orig. for immigrants to the State of Israel; a centre providing such a course; *transf.* any intensive language course.

Ulster /ˈʌlstə/ *noun*. **M16.**
[A former province of Ireland comprising the present Northern Ireland and the counties of Cavan, Donegal, and Monaghan.]
1 *HERALDRY.* (The title of) the former King of Arms for Ireland, whose duties now fall upon the Norroy and Ulster King of Arms. **M16.**
2 (Also **u-**.) A long loose overcoat of rough cloth, freq. with a belt and a detachable hood or shoulder cape. **L19.**

> 🕮 **1** *Norroy and Ulster*. **2** W. MARSHALL An expert resplendent in a long Ulster and beaten-up tweed hat.

Comb.: **Ulsterman**, **Ulsterwoman** a male, female, native or inhabitant of Ulster or Northern Ireland.
■ **Ulsteri'zation** *noun* the policy of replacing British security forces in Northern Ireland by Northern Irish ones **L20.**

ult /ʌlt/ *adjective*. Also **ult.** (point). **M18.**
[Abbreviation.]
= **ULTIMO** 2.

ulterior /ʌlˈtɪərɪə/ *adjective*. **M17.**
[Latin = further, more distant. Cf. **-IOR**.]
1 a Beyond what is immediate or present; coming later; further, future. **M17.** ▸**b** Beyond what is openly stated or evident; intentionally concealed or kept in the background. **M18.**
2 Situated beyond a point or boundary; more remote in position. **E18.**

> 🕮 **1a** J. A. FROUDE The request was only preparatory to ulterior measures. **b** D. DEVINE He cast round for ulterior motives. Was she . . making a pass at him?

■ **ulteri'ority** *noun* (*rare*) (*a*) an ulterior thing or matter; (*b*) remoteness: **E19.** **ulteriorly** *adverb* later, afterwards **E19.**

ultima /ˈʌltɪmə/ *noun*. **E20.**
[Latin, fem. of *ultimus* last.]
LINGUISTICS. The last syllable of a word.
ultima Thule: see **THULE** 1b.

ultimacy /ˈʌltɪməsi/ *noun*. **M19.**
[from **ULTIMATE** *adjective & noun*: see **-ACY**.]
The quality or state of being ultimate.

ultima ratio /ˌʌltɪmə ˈreɪʃɪəʊ/ *noun phr.* **M19.**
[Latin.]
The final sanction.

ultimata *noun pl.* see **ULTIMATUM** *noun*.

ultimate /ˈʌltɪmət/ *adjective & noun*. **M17.**
[Late Latin *ultimatus* pa. pple of *ultimare* come to an end, from Latin *ultimus* last, final: see **-ATE**².]
▶ **A** *adjective*. **1** Of an aim, intention, resolve, etc.: beyond all others, final, absolute. **M17.**
2 Coming at the end of a process, course of action, etc.; occurring last in a succession or series. **M17.** ▸**b** *spec.* Falling on the last syllable of a word. **E18.**
3 a Beyond which no advance can be made; fundamental, primary. **M17.** ▸**b** Pertaining to or designating the smallest components or particles of matter. Now *rare*. **E19.**
4 Constituting a result or conclusion; eventual, resultant. **L18.**
5 Designating the maximum possible strength, resistance, etc., of an object, beyond which it breaks. **M19.**

> 🕮 **1** WELLINGTON I consented to wait till then for their ultimate decision. *Science* Most discussions of the population crisis lead . . to zero population growth as the ultimate goal. **2a** E. MIALL Ultimate success will require union, patience, persevering energy. *Insight* The ultimate responsibility for the violence lies with the Soviet president. W. STYRON In depression, this faith in deliverance, in ultimate restoration, is absent. **3a** J. GILBERT The ultimate law of moral agents must be the will of God. *Correspondent* A clown performs the ultimate English joke. He drops his trousers. *New Scientist* The endless feeds, chaotic nights and ultimate lunacy of taking triplets out on reins. **4** P. L. FERMOR To my ultimate discomfiture but immediate delight.

Special collocations & phrases: ***in the ultimate analysis***: see **ANALYSIS** 1. **ultimate Frisbee** *US* a form of the game of Frisbee, played in teams. **ultimate ratio** *MATH.* the limiting ratio between two variable quantities which simultaneously approach definite fixed values or limits.
▶ **B** *noun*. **1** The final point or result; the end, the conclusion. **L17.** ▸**b** ***the ultimate***, the best that can be achieved or imagined; the last word (*in*). **M20.**
2 The point at which investigation or analysis stops; a final or fundamental fact or principle. **E18.**

> 🕮 **1b** *Times* A friend of mine had the ultimate in embarrassing experiences. **2** *Daily Telegraph* If, in the ultimate, young people cannot be dissuaded from experimenting.

■ **ultimately** *adverb* **M17.** **ultimateness** *noun* **L19.** **ultimative** *adjective* (*rare*) that tends to produce some final result **L19.**

ultimate /ˈʌltɪmeɪt/ *verb*¹ *trans. & intrans.* **E19.**
[from prec.: see **-ATE**³.]
Bring or come to an end; finish.

ultimate /ˈʌltɪmeɪt/ *verb*² *trans. rare*. **L19.**
[Back-form. from **ULTIMATUM** *verb*.]
= **ULTIMATUM** *verb*.

ultimation /ʌltɪˈmeɪʃ(ə)n/ *noun*. **L18.**
[from **ULTIMATE** *adjective & noun* or late Latin *ultimat-* pa. ppl stem of *ultimare*: see **ULTIMATE** *adjective & noun*, **-ATION**.]
The action or process of bringing to an ultimate result; final issue or development.
■ **ultimatization** *noun* **L19.**

ultimatory /ʌltɪˈmeɪt(ə)ri/ *adjective*. *rare*. **E20.**
[from **ULTIMATE** *adjective* + **-ORY**².]
Having the character of an ultimatum.

ultimatum /ʌltɪˈmeɪtəm/ *noun & verb*. **M18.**
[Use as noun of neut. of late Latin *ultimatus* in the medieval Latin senses 'final, completed': see **ULTIMATE** *adjective & noun*.]
▶ **A** *noun*. Pl. **-matums**, **-mata** /-ˈmeɪtə/.
1 The final terms presented by one party in a dispute etc. to another, the rejection of which could cause a breakdown in relations, a declaration of war, an end of cooperation, etc. **M18.**
2 The final point, the extreme limit; an ultimate end or aim. (Foll. by *of*.) **M18.**
3 A primary element beyond which advance or analysis is impossible; something fundamental. **M19.**

> 🕮 **1** E. SIMPSON The editors . . , losing patience, issued an ultimatum. D. A. THOMAS Gensoul . . rejected the ultimatum and . . Somerville's ships opened fire. **2** E. PARSONS To be married was still the ultimatum of her wishes.

▶ **B** *verb trans.* Present with an ultimatum. *rare*. **L19.**

ultimity /ʌlˈtɪmɪti/ *noun*. *rare*. **E17.**
[from Latin *ultimus* furthest + **-ITY**.]
The final point or last stage of something.

ultimo /ˈʌltɪməʊ/ *adjective.* L16.
[Latin (sc. *die* or *mense*) abl. sing. masc. of *ultimus* last, final.]
†**1** Designating the last day (of a specified month). L16–L17.
2 Of last month. Freq. written ULT, ULTO. E17.

> **2** G. WASHINGTON I was very glad to receive your letter of the 31st ultimo.

ultimobranchial /ˌʌltɪməʊˈbraŋkɪəl/ *adjective.* E20.
[from Latin *ultimus* last, final + -O- + BRANCHIAL, with ref. to the development of the gland from the most posterior pharyngeal pouches.]
ANATOMY & ZOOLOGY. Designating a gland in the neck which in many lower vertebrates regulates the calcium level in the body, but in humans and several higher vertebrates is absorbed into the thyroid during embryonic life.

ultimogeniture /ˌʌltɪməʊˈdʒɛnɪtʃə/ *noun.* L19.
[formed as prec. after PRIMOGENITURE.]
The right of the youngest child of a family to succeed or to inherit property or title (as in borough-English).

†**ultion** *noun. rare.* M16–E20.
[Latin *ultio(n-)*, from *ulcisci* avenge: see -ION.]
Vengeance, revenge.

Ultisol /ˈʌltɪsɒl/ *noun.* M20.
[from ULTI(MATE *adjective* + -SOL.]
SOIL SCIENCE. A highly weathered, leached, red or reddish-yellow acid soil marked by a clay-rich B horizon and found in warm humid climates.

ulto /ˈʌltəʊ/ *adjective.* Also **ulto.** (point). L18.
[Abbreviation.]
= ULTIMO 2.

Ultonian /ʌlˈtəʊnɪən/ *adjective & noun.* M18.
[from medieval Latin *Ultonia* Ulster, from Old Irish *Ult-* stem of *Ulaidh* men of Ulster: see -IAN.]
▶**A** *adjective.* Of or belonging to Ulster. M18.
▶**B** *noun.* A native or inhabitant of Ulster. L18.

ultra /ˈʌltrə/ *adjective & noun.* E19.
[Independent use of ULTRA-, orig. as an abbreviation of French *ultra-royaliste.*]
▶**A** *adjective.* **1** Ultra-royalist (esp. with ref. to early 19th-cent. France). *obsolete* exc. *Hist.* E19.
2 Of a person or party: holding extreme views in politics or other matters of opinion. Also, expressive of extreme views. E19.
3 Going beyond what is usual or ordinary; excessive, extreme; *esp.* (*colloq.*) representing the extreme of fashion; *loosely* marvellous. E19.

> **3** P. G. WODEHOUSE In came April, looking extraordinarily ultra in some filmy stuff.

▶**B** *noun.* **1** An ultra-royalist (in France). *obsolete* exc. *Hist.* E19.
2 A person who holds extreme opinions, esp. in religion or politics; an extremist. E19.
3 A person who goes to the extreme of fashion. Now *rare.* E19.
4 A long-distance run of great length, *esp.* one longer than a marathon. *colloq.* L20.

> **2** *Time* In everything that he finds displeasing .. the ultra sees evidence of Communist plots.

ultra /ˈʌltrə/ *preposition. rare.* L19.
[Latin.]
Lying beyond.
ultra crepidam /ˈkrɛpɪdam/ [see ULTRACREPIDARIAN] on matters beyond a person's knowledge.
¶ Earlier in ULTRA VIRES.

ultra- /ˈʌltrə/ *prefix.*
[Repr. Latin *ultra* beyond, in late and medieval Latin used as prefix Sense (d) app. originated in French *ultra-révolutionnaire* and *ultra-royaliste.*]
Used in a few words adopted from Latin and as a freely productive prefix, with the senses (*a*) 'lying spatially beyond or on the other side of', as ***ultramontane*** etc. (cf. TRANS-); (*b*) 'going beyond, surpassing, transcending the limits of', as ***ultra-human***, ***ultra-natural***, etc.; (*c*) 'exceeding in quantity, number, scale, minuteness, etc.', as ***ultracentrifuge***, ***ultramicroscopic***, etc.; (*d*) 'of or in an extreme or excessive degree', as ***ultra-conservative***, ***ultra-cool***, ***ultra-leftist***, ***ultra-modern***, ***ultra-nationalist***, ***ultra-Orthodox***, ***ultra-Protestantism***, ***ultra-rapid***, ***ultra-strict***, etc.
■ **ultraˈbasic** *adjective & noun* (*GEOLOGY*) (pertaining to or designating) an igneous rock having a silica content that is lower than that of the basic rocks, esp. less than 45 per cent by weight L19. **ultrafiche** *noun* a microfiche in which the linear reduction of the image size is of the order of 100 or more; documentary material of this kind: L20. **ultraˈfidian** *adjective* [Latin *fides* faith] going beyond mere faith, blindly credulous M19. **ultraˈfidianism** *noun* (*rare*) ultrafidian belief E19. **ultraˈhigh** *adjective* exceedingly high; *spec.* (of a radio frequency) in the range 300 to 3,000 megahertz: M20. **Ultraˈlente** *noun* [LENTE] *MEDICINE* (US proprietary name for) a form of insulin that remains active long after introduction into the body M20. **ultraˈmafic** *adjective & noun* (*GEOLOGY*) (pertaining to or designating) an igneous rock composed chiefly of mafic minerals M20. **ultra-ˈmarathon** *noun* a race over a distance longer than that of a marathon L20. **ultra-ˈred** *adjective & noun* (now *rare* or *obsolete*) = INFRARED L19. **ultra-ˈroyalist** *noun & adjective* (of or pertaining to) an extreme royalist, esp. in early 19th-cent. France E19. **ultra-ˈshort** *adjective* extremely short (in length or duration); *spec.* (of radio waves) having a wavelength significantly shorter than that of the usual short waves, esp. shorter than 10 metres (i.e. of a VHF frequency above 30 MHz): E20. **ultraˈstable** *adjective* stable against all subsequent disturbances, even those not taken into account in the design of the system M20. **ultraˈthin** *adjective* extremely thin; *spec.* in *BIOLOGY,* (of a section) cut with an ultramicrotome: M20.

ultracentrifugal /ˌʌltrəsɛnˈtrɪfjʊg(ə)l, -ˈsɛntrɪfjuːg(ə)l, -ˈfjuː-/ *adjective.* M20.
[from next + -AL[1].]
Of, pertaining to, or involving, an ultracentrifuge.
■ **ultracentrifugally** *adverb* M20.

ultracentrifuge /ʌltrəˈsɛntrɪfjuːdʒ/ *noun & verb.* E20.
[from ULTRA- + CENTRIFUGE.]
▶**A** *noun.* A very fast centrifuge used to separate small particles and large molecules in a liquid and to determine their sedimentation rate (and hence their size). E20.
▶**B** *verb trans.* Spin in an ultracentrifuge. M20.
■ ˌ**ultracentrifuˈgation** *noun* the action or process of ultracentrifuging something M20.

ultracold /ʌltrəˈkəʊld/ *noun & adjective.* M20.
[from ULTRA- + COLD *adjective.*]
▶**A** *noun.* Extreme coldness. M20.
▶**B** *adjective. NUCLEAR PHYSICS.* Of a neutron: having an energy of the order of 10^{-7} eV or less. M20.

ultracrepidarian /ˌʌltrəkrɛpɪˈdɛːrɪən/ *adjective & noun. literary.* E19.
[from Latin (*ne sutor*) *ultra crepidam* (let the cobbler not go) beyond his last: see -ARIAN.]
▶**A** *adjective.* Going beyond one's proper province; giving opinions on matters beyond one's knowledge. E19.
▶**B** *noun.* An ultracrepidarian person; an ignorant or presumptuous critic. E19.
■ **ultracrepidarianism** *noun* = ULTRACREPIDATION L19. **ultraˈcrepidate** *verb intrans.* venture beyond one's scope E19. **ultracrepidation** *noun* the action or fact of criticizing ignorantly E19.

ultradian /ʌlˈtreɪdɪən/ *adjective.* M20.
[from ULTRA- + *-dian*, after CIRCADIAN.]
PHYSIOLOGY. Of a rhythm or cycle: having a frequency higher than circadian, i.e. of a period shorter than a day (but longer than an hour). Cf. INFRADIAN.

ultrafiltration /ˌʌltrəfɪlˈtreɪʃ(ə)n/ *noun.* E20.
[from ULTRA- + FILTRATION.]
Chiefly *BIOLOGY.* Filtration through a medium sufficiently fine to retain colloidal particles, viruses, or large molecules.
■ ˈ**ultrafilter** *noun & verb* (*a*) *noun* a medium or membrane used for ultrafiltration; (*b*) *verb trans.* subject to ultrafiltration: E20. **ultraˈfilterable** *adjective* capable of passing through an ultrafilter E20. **ultraˈfiltrate** *noun* (a) liquid that has passed through during ultrafiltration E20.

ultraism /ˈʌltrəɪz(ə)m/ *noun.* E19.
[from ULTRA *adjective* + -ISM.]
1 The fact or an instance of holding extreme opinions. E19.
2 (U-.) A Spanish and Latin American expressionist movement characterized by the rejection of traditional literary forms in favour of free verse and radical imagery. M20.
■ **ultraist** *noun* (*a*) a person who holds extreme opinions, an extremist; (*b*) (U-) an adherent or practitioner of Ultraism: M19. **ultraˈistic** *adjective* M19.

ultralight /*as adjective* ʌltrəˈlʌɪt, *as noun* ˈʌltrəlʌɪt/ *adjective & noun.* L20.
[from ULTRA- + LIGHT *adjective*[1].]
▶**A** *adjective.* Extremely lightweight; *spec.* designating a small inexpensive usu. one-seater aircraft whose fuselage is an open framework without an enclosed cockpit, capable of soaring or of low-speed powered flight. L20.
▶**B** *noun.* An ultralight aircraft. L20.

ultramarine /ʌltrəməˈriːn, ˈʌlt-/ *adjective & noun.* L16.
[Italian †*oltramarino* (mod. *oltre-*) in *azzurro oltramarino* lit. 'azure from overseas', later assim. to medieval Latin *ultramarinus*, from Latin *ultra* beyond + *mare* sea: see -INE[1].]
▶**A** *adjective.* **1** Situated beyond the sea. Now *rare.* L16.
2 ***ultramarine blue***, = senses B.1, 2 below. L17.
3 Of the colour ultramarine (see senses B.1, 2 below). L18.

> **3** J. BARTH Her mother's ultramarine eyes.

▶**B** *noun.* **1** Orig., a pigment of various shades of blue, orig. made from imported lapis lazuli. Now also (more fully ***French ultramarine***), a brilliant deep blue pigment made in imitation of this from powdered fired clay, sodium carbonate, sulphur, and resin. L16. ▸**b** With specifying word.: a pigment derived from or chemically similar to ultramarine but of another colour. E18.
2 A blue colour like that of the pigment. L17.

ultrametric /ʌltrəˈmɛtrɪk/ *adjective & noun.* M20.
[from ULTRA- + METRIC *noun*[1] & *adjective*[1].]
MATH. ▶**A** *adjective.* Pertaining to or designating a metric according to which the distance between two points must be less than or equal to the greater of the two distances between either of these points and any third point. M20.
▶**B** *noun.* A metric of this kind. L20.

ultramicro- /ʌltrəˈmʌɪkrəʊ/ *prefix.* Also as attrib. adjective **ultramicro**. M20.
[from ULTRA- + MICRO-.]
CHEMISTRY. Designating or pertaining to chemical analysis or research involving very minute quantities (of the order of a few micrograms or less), as ***ultramicroanalysis***, ***ultramicrochemical*** *adjective*, ***ultramicro method***, etc.

ultramicroscope /ʌltrəˈmʌɪkrəskəʊp/ *noun.* E20.
[from ULTRA- + MICROSCOPE.]
An optical microscope used to detect particles smaller than the wavelength of light by illuminating them at an angle and observing the light scattered by the Tyndall effect against a dark background.
■ **ultramiˈcroscopy** *noun* E20.

ultramicroscopic /ˌʌltrəmʌɪkrəˈskɒpɪk/ *adjective.* L19.
[from ULTRA- + MICROSCOPIC.]
Of such minute size as to be invisible or indistinct under an ordinary light microscope; of or pertaining to the use of an ultramicroscope.
■ **ultramicroscopical** *adjective* = ULTRAMICROSCOPIC E20. **ultramicroscopically** *adverb* E20.

ultramicrotome /ʌltrəˈmʌɪkrətəʊm/ *noun.* M20.
[from ULTRA- + MICROTOME *noun.*]
A microtome for cutting sections thin enough for electron microscopy (typically about 300 nanometres thick).
■ **ultramicrotomed** *adjective* sectioned with an ultramicrotome L20. **ultramicrotomy** /-ˈkrɒtəmi/ *noun* the practice or technique of using an ultramicrotome M20.

ultramontane /ʌltrəˈmɒnteɪn/ *noun & adjective.* L16.
[medieval Latin *ultramontanus*, formed as ULTRA- + *mont-*, *mons* mountain: see -ANE.]
▶**A** *noun.* **1** *CHRISTIAN CHURCH.* **a** A representative of the Roman Catholic Church north of the Alps, as opp. to the Italian clergy. Now *rare.* L16. ▸**b** = ULTRAMONTANIST *noun.* E19.
2 *gen.* A native or inhabitant of a country beyond a mountain range, esp. north of the Alps. Now *rare.* E17.
▶**B** *adjective.* **1 a** Of or pertaining to the countries or peoples north of the Alps. Now *rare.* E17. ▸**b** *CHRISTIAN CHURCH.* Orig., pertaining to or characteristic of the Italian party in the Roman Catholic Church. Now usu., advocating papal authority. E18. ▸**c** *transf.* Extremely strict, conservative, or reactionary in views. L19.
2 *gen.* Situated beyond a mountain range; pertaining to a region beyond a mountain range. *rare.* L18.

> **1b** E. B. PUSEY The old Ultramontane doctrine of the inerrancy of the Pope.

¶ In senses A.1a and B.1a the word is used from the point of view of Italy, in senses A.1b and B.1b from that of France and northern Europe.

ultramontanism /ʌltrəˈmɒntənɪz(ə)m/ *noun.* E19.
[French *ultramontanisme*, formed as prec.: see -ISM.]
The principles and practice of the ultramontane party in the Roman Catholic Church; the advocacy of papal authority.

ultramontanist /ʌltrəˈmɒntənɪst/ *noun & adjective.* E19.
[from ULTRAMONTANE + -IST.]
ROMAN CATHOLIC CHURCH. ▶**A** *noun.* A supporter of ultramontane principles and doctrines; an advocate of papal authority. E19.
▶**B** *adjective.* Of or pertaining to ultramontanists or ultramontanism. M19.

ultramundane /ʌltrəˈmʌndeɪn/ *noun & adjective.* M16.
[Latin *ultramundanus*, formed as ULTRA- + *mundus* world: see -ANE.]
▶†**A** *noun.* In *pl.* Matters beyond the physical world; metaphysics. Only in M16.
▶**B** *adjective.* Lying beyond the physical world or outside the solar system. M17.

ultrasaurus /ˈʌltrəsɔːrəs/ *noun.* L20.
[mod. Latin genus name, formed as ULTRA- + Greek *sauros* lizard.]
An enormously tall and heavy late Jurassic dinosaur related to brachiosaurus, known from only a few bones.

ultrasonic /ʌltrəˈsɒnɪk/ *adjective.* E20.
[from ULTRA- + SONIC.]
1 Designating sound waves and vibrations with a frequency above the range of human hearing (i.e. greater than 15–20 kHz); pertaining to or involving such waves, esp. in devices and techniques which make use of their reflection. E20.
2 Designating speeds above that of sound; supersonic. *rare.* M20.

■ **ultrasonically** *adverb* at an ultrasonic frequency; by means of ultrasound: M20.

ultrasonication /ˌʌltrəsɒnɪˈkeɪʃ(ə)n/ *noun*. M20.
[from ULTRA- + SONICATION.]
= SONICATION.
■ **ultraˈsonicate** *verb trans*. = SONICATE *verb* M20.

ultrasonics /ʌltrəˈsɒnɪks/ *noun pl*. E20.
[from ULTRASONIC: see -ICS.]
1 Ultrasonic waves; ultrasound. E20.
2 Treated as *sing*. The branch of science and technology concerned with the study and use of ultrasonic waves. M20.

ultrasonography /ʌltrəsəˈnɒgrəfi/ *noun*. M20.
[from ULTRA- (in *ultrasound*) + SONO- + -GRAPHY.]
MEDICINE. A technique employing echoes of ultrasound pulses to delineate objects or areas of different density in the body, esp. for diagnostic purposes.
■ **ultraˈsonogram** *noun* an image obtained by ultrasonography M20. **ultraˈsonograph** *noun* an apparatus for producing ultrasonograms L20. **ultrasonographer** *noun* a specialist in or practitioner of ultrasonography L20.

ultrasound /ˈʌltrəsaʊnd/ *noun*. E20.
[from ULTRA- + SOUND *noun*².]
Sound or vibrations of an ultrasonic frequency. Also, ultrasonic techniques.

attrib.: *Observer* During an ultrasound scan, sound waves bounced off the unborn baby produce an image.

ultrastructure /ˈʌltrəstrʌktʃə/ *noun*. M20.
[from ULTRA- + STRUCTURE *noun*.]
BIOLOGY. Fine structure not visible with an optical microscope.
■ **ultraˈstructural** *adjective* of or pertaining to ultrastructure M20. **ultraˈstructurally** *adverb* with regard to ultrastructure L20.

Ultrasuede /ˈʌltrəsweɪd/ *noun*. *N. Amer*. L20.
[from ULTRA- + SUEDE.]
(Proprietary name for) a synthetic non-woven fabric resembling suede; a garment made of this.

ultraviolation /ˌʌltrəvʌɪəˈleɪʃ(ə)n/ *noun*. *slang*. L20.
[from ULTRAVIOLET + -ATION (with joc. ref. to VIOLATION).]
Irradiation with ultraviolet light.
■ **ultraˈviolate** *verb trans*. irradiate with ultraviolet light L20.

ultraviolet /ʌltrəˈvʌɪələt/ *adjective* & *noun*. M19.
[from ULTRA- + VIOLET *noun*, *adjective*.]
▶ **A** *adjective*. **1** Designating electromagnetic radiation with a wavelength shorter than that of violet light (about 420 nm) but (in mod. use) longer than that of the longest X-rays (of the order of 4 to 40 nm). M19.
2 Involving or pertaining to ultraviolet radiation or its use; producing or sensitive to ultraviolet radiation. E20.

1 J. GALSWORTHY They talk about these ultra-violet rays. Plain sunshine used to be good enough. **2** *ultraviolet filter*, *ultraviolet irradiation*, *ultraviolet lamp*, etc. **ultraviolet catastrophe** *PHYSICS* a rapid increase that the Rayleigh–Jeans law predicts should occur in the radiation emitted by a black body at successively shorter wavelengths (where the law in fact becomes invalid).

▶ **B** *noun*. The ultraviolet part of the spectrum; ultraviolet radiation. L19.
the far ultraviolet, **the near ultraviolet** the part of the ultraviolet far from, close to, the visible spectrum.

ultra vires /ʌltrə ˈvʌɪriːz, ʊltrɑː ˈviːreɪz/ *adverbial phr*. L18.
[Latin = beyond the powers.]
Chiefly *LAW*. Beyond the powers or legal authority of a corporation or person. Opp. INTRA VIRES.

ultreya /ulˈtreja, ʊlˈtreɪə/ *noun*. M20.
[Spanish, app. recalling the medieval cry *(E)ultreya* 'onward!', 'forward!' in the hymn sung by pilgrims to Compostela.]
ROMAN CATHOLIC CHURCH. A regular discussion group held by participants in a *cursillo*.

ultroneous /ʌlˈtrəʊnɪəs/ *adjective*. M17.
[from Latin *ultroneus*, from *ultro* of one's own accord: see -OUS.]
1 Made, offered, etc., of one's own accord; spontaneous, voluntary. M17.
2 *SCOTS LAW*. Of a witness: offering testimony without being cited. Now *rare*. E18.
■ **ultroneously** *adverb* E17. **ultroneousness** *noun* (*rare*) E17.

ulu /ˈuːluː/ *noun*¹. Also **ooloo**. M19.
[Inupiaq.]
An Eskimo woman's short-handled knife with a broad crescent-shaped blade.

ulu /ˈuːluː/ *noun*². L19.
[Malay *(h)ulu* head, upper part.]
The up-river interior part of the Malay peninsula; the jungle of this region.

ululant /ˈjuːljʊlənt, ˈʌl-/ *adjective*. M19.
[formed as next: see -ANT¹.]
Having the character of ululation; ululating, howling.
■ **ululance** *noun* (*rare*) ululation M20.

ululate /ˈjuːljʊleɪt, ˈʌl-/ *verb intrans*. E17.
[Latin *ululat-* pa. ppl stem of *ululare* howl, of imit. origin (cf. ULULU): see -ATE³.]
(Orig. of an animal) howl, hoot, wail; lament loudly; make a high wavering sound with the voice and tongue, expressing grief, joy, etc.
■ **uluˈlatory** *adjective* = ULULANT M19.

ululation /juːljʊˈleɪʃ(ə)n, ʌl-/ *noun*. L16.
[formed as prec. + -ATION.]
The action of ululating; a cry, howl, or other sound so produced.

ululu /uːlʊˈluː/ *noun*. M19.
[Imit. Cf. Irish *liúgh* shout, cry, and ULULATE, WHILLALOO.]
A wailing or ululating cry, *esp*. a lament.

ulva /ˈʌlvə/ *noun*. M18.
[Latin = sedge.]
A seaweed of the genus *Ulva*, which includes sea lettuce, *U. lactuca*.

ulvospinel /ˌʌlvəʊspɪˈnɛl/ *noun*. Also **ulvö-**. M20.
[from the *Ulvö* Islands, Sweden + SPINEL.]
MINERALOGY. A ferrous titanate of the spinel group, often occurring as lamellae in magnetite.

Ulyssean /juːˈlɪsɪən/ *adjective*. E17.
[from Latin *Ulysses* (= Greek *Odusseus*) king of Ithaca and hero of Homer's *Odyssey*: see -EAN.]
Of or pertaining to Ulysses; *esp*. characteristic of or resembling Ulysses in craftiness or deceit, or in extensive wanderings; Odyssean.
¶ In poet. use sometimes pronounced /juːlɪˈsiːən/.

Ulysses /juːˈlɪsiːz, ˈjuːlɪsiːz/ *noun*. E17.
[Latin: see prec.]
A traveller, an adventurer. Occas. also, a crafty and clever schemer.

um /əm/ *pronoun*¹. Now *dial*. Also **'um**. E17.
[Alt. of 'EM *pronoun*.]
Them.

um /əm/ *pronoun*². *dial*. Also **'um**. E19.
[Repr. a pronunc.]
Him.

um /(ə)m/ *interjection*, *noun*, & *verb*. E17.
[Natural exclam. Cf. MM.]
▶ **A** *interjection*. **1** = ER *interjection*. E17.
2 Expr. an indistinct murmur of assent or interrogation. (*rare* before 20.) E17.
▶ **B** *noun*. An utterance of this sound. E20.
▶ **C** *verb intrans*. Infl. **-mm-**. Make this sound. M20.

umami /uːˈmɑːmi/ *noun*. L20.
[Japanese, lit. 'deliciousness'.]
A category of taste in food, corresponding to the flavour of glutamates, esp. monosodium glutamate; this flavour.
¶ Some scientists believe that umami constitutes a fifth basic taste, in addition to sweet, sour, salt, and bitter.

U-matic /juːˈmatɪk/ *noun*. L20.
[from *U* (from the shape of the path followed by the tape around the drum and heads of the machine) + -MATIC.]
(Proprietary name for) a system for recording and playing audio-visual material and videos, mainly restricted to professional use.

Umayyad /ʊˈmʌɪjad/ *adjective* & *noun*. Also **Ommayyad** & other vars. M18.
[from *Umayya* (see below).]
▶ **A** *adjective*. Of or pertaining to a Muslim dynasty descended from Umayya (a cousin of Muhammad's grandfather and ancestor of one of the principal clans of the Koreish), which ruled the Islamic world from 660 (or 661) to 750 and Moorish Spain from 756 to 1031. M18.
▶ **B** *noun*. A member of this dynasty. M18.

Umbanda /ʊmˈbandə/ *noun*. M20.
[Portuguese from Bantu.]
A syncretistic Brazilian folk religion combining elements of macumba, Roman Catholicism, and S. American Indian practices and beliefs.
■ **Umbanˈdista** *noun* an adherent of Umbanda M20.

umbel /ˈʌmb(ə)l/ *noun*. L16.
[French †*umbelle* (mod. *ombelle*) or Latin UMBELLA: see -EL².]
1 *BOTANY*. An inflorescence (often flat-topped) whose stalks or rays all spring from a common centre, like the spokes of an umbrella. L16.
2 *ZOOLOGY*. A similar arrangement of parts in an animal. *rare*. L19.
1 compound umbel: in which the rays of the umbel at the top of the stem are themselves each terminated by another, smaller umbel. **partial umbel**, **secondary umbel** any of the smaller umbels which terminate the primary rays of a compound umbel.

umbella /ʌmˈbɛlə/ *noun*. Pl. **-llae** /-liː/, **-llas**. L17.
[Latin = parasol, dim. of *umbra* shade, shadow: see -ELLA.]
1 *BOTANY*. = UMBEL 1. Now *rare*. L17.
2 *ZOOLOGY*. = UMBRELLA *noun* 3b. *rare*. M19.

umbellate /ˈʌmbəleɪt, -lət/ *adjective*. M18.
[from UMBELLA + -ATE².]
BOTANY. Arranged in or bearing an umbel or umbels.
■ **umbellated** *adjective* (now *rare*) = UMBELLATE L17. **umbellately** *adverb* L19.

umbelled /ˈʌmb(ə)ld/ *adjective*. L18.
[from UMBEL + -ED².]
BOTANY. = UMBELLATE.

umbellet /ˈʌmb(ə)lɪt/ *noun*. Now chiefly *US*. L18.
[from UMBEL + -LET.]
BOTANY. = UMBELLULE.

umbellifer /ʌmˈbɛlɪfə/ *noun*. E18.
[French †*umbellifère* (mod. *ombell-*), from Latin UMBELLA (French *ombelle*): see -FER.]
BOTANY. An umbelliferous plant.

umbelliferous /ʌmbɛˈlɪf(ə)rəs/ *adjective*. M17.
[from Latin UMBELLA + -I- + -FEROUS.]
Belonging to the plant family Umbelliferae (also called Apiaceae), which includes carrot, parsley, celery, and dill, and most members of which have their flowers arranged in umbels; produced by or pertaining to plants of this family.

umbelliform /ʌmˈbɛlɪfɔːm/ *adjective*. *rare*. L19.
[from Latin UMBELLA + -I- + -FORM.]
BOTANY. Having the form of an umbel.

umbellule /ʌmˈbɛljuːl/ *noun*. L18.
[mod. Latin *umbellula* dim. of UMBELLA: see -ULE.]
BOTANY. = ***partial umbel*** s.v. UMBEL 1.

umber /ˈʌmbə/ *noun*¹. Long *obsolete* exc. *dial*. Also †**oumer**. ME.
[from Old French *umbre*, (also mod.) *ombre*, or Latin *umbra* shade, shadow. Cf. UMBER *verb*¹.]
1 Shade, shadow, (*lit*. & *fig*.). ME. ▸†**b** The shadow of the pointer on a sundial or quadrant. Only in LME. ▸†**c** A reflection. Only in LME.
†**2** The visor of a helmet. Cf. UMBREL, UMBRERE. LME–E17.

umber /ˈʌmbə/ *noun*². L15.
[Old French *umbre*, (also mod.) *ombre*, orig. *umbre de mer*, *umbre de rivière*, from Latin *umbra* (app. the maigre): cf. German *Umberfish*, Dutch *ombervis*): perh. same word as prec. Cf. UMBRA *noun*².]
The grayling (fish), *Thymallus thymallus*.

umber /ˈʌmbə/ *noun*³ & *adjective*. M16.
[French (*terre d'*)*ombre* or Italian (*terra di*) *ombra*, from Latin *umbra* UMBER *noun*¹ or *Umbra* fem. of *Umber* UMBRIAN.]
▶ **A** *noun*. **1** A red-brown earth containing iron and manganese oxides and darker than ochre and sienna, used to make various pigments. Also, any of these pigments; the colour of these. M16.
2 Any of several geometrid moths with dark brown wings or markings. M19.
1 *BURNT* **umber**. *raw* **umber**: see RAW *adjective*. **2** ***barred umber***, ***mottled umber***, ***scarce umber***, etc.
▶ **B** *attrib*. or as *adjective*. Of the colour umber; dark brown. Also, dark, dusky. E19.

umber /ˈʌmbə/ *verb*¹ *trans*. Chiefly *poet*. & *dial*. Also (*dial*.) **oumer** /ˈaʊmə, ˈuːm-/. LME.
[Old French *umbrer*, *ombrer*, from Latin *umbrare*, from *umbra*: see UMBER *noun*¹.]
Shade, protect.

umber /ˈʌmbə/ *verb*² *trans*. L16.
[from UMBER *noun*³.]
Stain or paint with umber; make a dark brown colour.

umbery /ˈʌmb(ə)ri/ *adjective*. M19.
[from UMBER *noun*³ & *adjective* + -Y¹.]
Of the colour of umber; dark brownish.

†**umbethink** *verb* see UNBETHINK.

umbilic /ʌmˈbɪlɪk/ *adjective* & *noun*. L16.
[Obsolete French (now *ombilic*), or directly from Latin UMBILICUS.]
▶ **A** *adjective*. = UMBILICAL *adjective*. *rare*. L16.
▶ **B** *noun*. †**1** The centre, the middle point or part; the navel. L16–M17.
2 *MATH*. An umbilical point on a surface. M19.

umbilical /ʌmˈbɪlɪk(ə)l, ʌmbɪˈlʌɪk(ə)l/ *adjective* & *noun*. M16.
[Obsolete French (now *ombilical*), formed as prec.: see -AL¹.]
▶ **A** *adjective*. **1** Of or pertaining to the umbilicus or navel. M16. ▸**b** *CONCHOLOGY*. Possessing, pertaining to, or of the nature of an umbilicus. M18.
2 *MATH*. †**a** ***umbilical point***, a focal point. Only in E18. ▸**b** Designating or pertaining to a point on a surface where the curvature is zero or spherical (i.e. the curvature in all directions is equal). M19.
3 Occupying a central point or position. Now *rare*. M18.
4 Resembling or acting as an umbilical cord; connecting a person or device to a source of essential supplies, services, etc. M20.

1 ***umbilical artery***, ***umbilical hernia***, ***umbilical vein***, etc. **4** *New Scientist* The Buggy is connected to a BBC computer by an umbilical cable. ***umbilical connection***, ***umbilical pipe***, etc.

Special collocations: **umbilical cord** (*a*) *ANATOMY* & *ZOOLOGY* the flexible cordlike structure by which a human or other mammalian foetus is attached to the placenta and through which it is nourished; (*b*) ZOOLOGY a similar cord connecting a bird or reptile embryo to the yolk-sac in the egg; (*c*) BOTANY (now *rare* or *obsolete*) the funicle of a seed; (*d*) *fig.* a cable, pipe, or similar linking device by which electrical power or other essential services and supplies are transferred, e.g. between a guided missile and its launcher, an astronaut and a spacecraft, a deep-sea diver and the surface, etc.

▶ **B** *noun*. **1** ANATOMY. In *pl.* The umbilical blood-vessels. *rare*. L18.

2 An umbilical connection, pipe, line, etc. M20.

■ **umbilically** *adverb* by means of an umbilicus, or an umbilical cord or connection; as regards, or as if attached by, an umbilical connection: E19. **umbilicar** *adjective* of or pertaining to an umbilicus or (MATH.) an umbilical point M19.

umbilicate /ʌmˈbɪlɪkət/ *adjective*. L17.
[from UMBILICUS + -ATE[2].]
Chiefly BOTANY & ZOOLOGY. Resembling a navel; having a navel or umbilicus.
■ Also **umbilicated** *adjective* (now chiefly MEDICINE) L17.

umbilication /ˌʌmbɪlɪˈkeɪʃ(ə)n/ *noun*. L19.
[from next + -ATION.]
MEDICINE. A central depression on the upper part of a rounded swelling or vesicle; the condition of having such a depression.

umbilicus /ʌmˈbɪlɪkəs, ʌmbɪˈlʌɪkəs/ *noun*. Pl. **-ci** /-sʌɪ/, **-cuses**. L17.
[Latin, from base of UMBO, rel. to Greek *omphalos* and Indo-European base of NAVEL.]
1 ANATOMY. = NAVEL 1. L17. ▸**b** BOTANY. The scar on a seed marking its separation from the placenta; the hilum. Now *rare*. M19.
2 MATH. †**a** A focus of an ellipse. Only in E18. ▸**b** An umbilical point. M19.
3 A small usu. central depression or hole suggestive of a navel; *esp.* (*a*) ORNITHOLOGY either of the holes at each end of the hollow shaft of a feather; (*b*) CONCHOLOGY a central hole between the whorls of a coiled shell with no solid columella; (*c*) BOTANY (in some foliose lichens) a single central holdfast attaching the thallus to the substrate. E19.

umbles /ˈʌmb(ə)lz/ *noun pl. arch.* LME.
[Alt. of NUMBLES.]
Entrails; *spec.* the offal of an animal, esp. a deer.
Comb.: **umble pie** a pie made with umbles.

umbo /ˈʌmbəʊ/ *noun*. Pl. **umbones** /ʌmˈbəʊniːz/, **umbos**. E18.
[Latin = shield-boss, knob.]
1 The boss of a shield. E18.
2 A rounded or conical projection or knob, esp. in the centre of a rounded natural structure; *spec.* (*a*) ZOOLOGY the central tip or highest point of a univalve shell, or of each valve of a bivalve shell; (*b*) BOTANY a central swelling on the pileus of a fungus above the stipe; (*c*) ANATOMY the central projection of the inner surface of the eardrum, attached to the malleus. M18.
■ **umbonal** *adjective* of, pertaining to, or associated with an umbo; of the nature of an umbo: M19. **umbonate** *adjective* (chiefly BOTANY) formed into or having an umbo or knob E19.

umbone /ˈʌmbəʊn/ *noun*. E17.
[Latin *umbon-* stem of UMBO.]
†**1** BOTANY. A pistil, a style. E17–E18.
2 ZOOLOGY. = UMBO 2(a). *rare*. M19.

umbones *noun pl.* see UMBO.

umboth /ˈʌmbɒθ, -bəd/ *noun*. Chiefly *Orkney & Shetland*. Long *obsolete* exc. *Hist.* LME.
[Old Norse *umboð* (Norn *ombod*, *ombuth*, Norwegian, Swedish, Danish *ombud*) agency, office, administration, from *boð* command.]
1 A form of teind or land tax, orig. payable to an agent of the Bishop of Orkney. Also ***umboth duty***, ***umboth tithe***. LME.
†**2** Agency, part (in affairs). Only in E16.
Comb.: ***umboth duty***: see sense 1 above; †**umbothman**, †**umbothsman** [Old Norse *umboðsmann*, nom. *-maðr*: cf. OMBUDSMAN] an agent, a procurator; ***umboth tithe***: see sense 1 above.

umbra /ˈʌmbrə/ *noun*[1]. Pl. **-bras**, **-brae** /-briː/. L16.
[Latin = shadow, shade.]
1 A phantom, a ghost, a spectre. L16.
2 A shadow. Chiefly *techn.*, the wholly shaded inner part of a shadow (contrasted with the penumbra) when the light is from a source of some size; *esp.* (ASTRONOMY) that of the shadow cast by the moon or the earth in an eclipse. M17. ▸**b** The dark core (or, formerly, the penumbra) of a sunspot. L18.
3 An inseparable companion, a hanger-on. L17.

umbra /ˈʌmbrə/ *noun*[2]. *rare*. E17.
[Latin: see UMBER *noun*[2].]
†**1** = UMBER *noun*[2]. E17–M18.
2 Any of several European marine sciaenid fishes, esp. *Umbrina cirrosa* of the Mediterranean. Also, a mud minnow, *esp.* one of the genus *Umbra*. M18.

umbracious /ʌmˈbreɪʃəs/ *adjective*. *rare*. M17.
[Irreg. from Latin *umbra* shadow + -ACIOUS.]
Shady, umbrageous.

umbrae *noun pl.* see UMBRA *noun*[1].

umbrage /ˈʌmbrɪdʒ/ *noun*. LME.
[Old French (mod. *ombrage*), from Latin *umbra* shadow: see -AGE.]
†**1** Shade, shadow, (*lit.* & *fig.*). LME–M18.
2 *spec.* Shade or shadow cast by trees etc. Also, the foliage of a tree etc. as giving shade. Now *literary*. M16.
3 A shadowy appearance or indication; a semblance, an outline; a glimmering *of* something. Now *rare*. E17.
†**4** A slight suspicion (*of* a matter). E17–M18. ▸**b** A reason or ground for suspicion, or for an opinion. M17–M18.
†**5 a** Shelter, protection. Freq. in ***under the umbrage of***. E17–L18. ▸**b** A pretext, a pretence. Freq. in ***under the umbrage of***. M17–M18.
6 Displeasure, annoyance, offence; a sense of injury. Freq. in ***give umbrage (to)***, ***take umbrage (at)***. E17.

> 🕮 **1** L. WOMOCK Clouds and Umbrages that did eclipse and darken the glory of the Gospel. **2** M. E. BRADDON Two figures are seated . . beneath the umbrage of an ancient thorn. **4b** L. CLARKE There is not the least umbrage for such a conjecture . . in the scripture. **5a** R. FRANCK I left . . to seek Umbrage in the City of London. **b** BOLINGBROKE A Struggle for personal Power, under the Pretence and Umbrage of Principle. **6** H. ROGERS The sermon . . gave great umbrage to the parliamentary party. Y. MENUHIN Despite . . the umbrage discernible on the faces of the newsmen, I persisted. J. M. MCPHERSON Catholic immigrants . . who took umbrage at . . Protestant efforts to reform their drinking habits.

umbrage /ˈʌmbrɪdʒ/ *verb trans*. M17.
[from prec. or French *ombrag(i)er*, †*umbrag(i)er*, from *ombrage*: see prec.]
1 Shade, shadow; *fig.* overshadow. Usu. in *pass.* M17.
†**2 a** Colour over, disguise. *rare*. Only in L17. ▸**b** Give a pretext or ground for. *rare*. Only in L17.
3 Offend, displease. *rare*. L19.

umbrageous /ʌmˈbreɪdʒəs/ *adjective*. L16.
[Old & mod. French *ombrageux*, from *ombrage* (see UMBRAGE *noun*), or directly from UMBRAGE *noun* + -OUS.]
1 a Forming or giving shade. L16. ▸**b** Shaded by trees etc; dark, overshadowed; shadowy. E17.
2 Of a person etc.: suspicious, jealous; apt or disposed to take offence. E17.
†**3** Obscure, dubious. Only in M17.
■ **umbrageously** *adverb* M17. **umbrageousness** *noun* E17.

umbral /ˈʌmbr(ə)l/ *adjective*. M19.
[from UMBRA *noun*[1] + -AL[1].]
Of or pertaining to an umbra or umbras.

umbratile /ˈʌmbrətʌɪl, -tɪl/ *adjective & noun*. L16.
[Latin *umbratilis* keeping in the shade, formed as UMBRA *noun*[1]: see -ILE.]
▶ **A** *adjective*. **1** †**a** Of a person's life: spent indoors. Only in L16. ▸**b** Carried on in retirement or seclusion; of an academic or theoretical nature; (of a person) reclusive, retiring. M17.
2 Of, pertaining to, or resembling a shadow or shadows; of a shadowy nature, unsubstantial, unreal. Now *rare* or *obsolete*. M17.
3 Giving shade, shady. *rare*. M17.
▶ **B** *noun*. A person who spends his or her time in the shade. *rare*. L19.

umbre /ˈʌmbə/ *noun*. L18.
[from Latin *umbra* or French *ombre*, after UMBER *noun*[3] and mod. Latin *umbretta* (see UMBRETTE).]
= HAMMERHEAD 4.

†**umbrel** *noun*. LME–M16.
[Old French *ombrel* shade.]
The visor of a helmet. Cf. UMBER *noun*[1] 2, UMBRERE.

umbrella /ʌmˈbrɛlə/ *noun & adjective*. As noun also †**-ello**, pl. **-o(e)s**. E17.
[Italian *ombrella*, *ombrello*, dims. of *ombra*, formed as UMBRA *noun*[1] after Latin *umbella* UMBEL.]
▶ **A** *noun*. **1** A light hand-held device carried as protection against rain or strong sun, consisting of a usu. circular canopy of fabric supported on a central stick; *esp.* one in which the fabric is mounted on a metal frame that can be collapsed to make a cylindrical shape. E17.
2 *fig.* †**a** A means of shelter or protection. E17–M18. ▸†**b** A screen, a disguise. E–M17. ▸**c** MILITARY. A screen of fighter aircraft or of anti-aircraft artillery. M20.
3 a BOTANY. A part of a plant resembling an outspread umbrella. M17. ▸**b** ZOOLOGY. The gelatinous convex disc or bell-shaped structure of a jellyfish or other medusoid animal, which it contracts and expands to move through the water. M19.
†**4** A sun-blind, a window awning. L17–E18.
5 A structure resembling an open umbrella in shape or purpose. L17. ▸**b** A parachute. *US Military slang*. M20.
6 Authority, protection, means of defence; a controlling or unifying agency; a general or all-embracing term. Freq. in ***under the umbrella***. M20.
6 ***nuclear umbrella***: see NUCLEAR *adjective*.

▶ **B** *attrib.* or as *adjective*. Acting as an overall coordinating or unifying agency; covering or protecting a number of things; (of a word, name, etc.) covering a number of meanings or concepts; general, catch-all. M20.
Comb.: **umbrella bird** any of several S. American cotingas of the genus *Cephalopterus*, which have a black radiating crest over their head; **umbrella body** = ***umbrella organization*** below; **umbrella bridge** a temporary raised traffic lane with ramp approaches, used to allow construction work underneath; **umbrella field** CRICKET an arrangement of close fieldsmen spread in a cordon on both sides of the wicket; **umbrella fund** a type of investment fund in which investment can be easily transferred between a range of different portfolios; **umbrella organization** an organization which represents and supports separate member bodies; **umbrella pine** (*a*) the stone pine, *Pinus pinea*; (*b*) a tall Japanese evergreen conifer, *Sciadopitys verticillata*, with whorls of double needles in the axils of scale leaves; **umbrella plant** (*a*) a Californian plant of boggy places, *Darmera peltophylla*, of the saxifrage family, with large peltate leaves; (*b*) a house-plant, *Cyperus involucratus*, of the sedge family, with a whorl of radiating bracts at the top of the stem; **umbrella stand** a stand for holding closed umbrellas in an upright position; **umbrella tree** any of various trees with whorls of radiating leaves, *esp.* (*a*) a N. American magnolia, *Magnolia tripetala*; (*b*) an Australian tree, *Schefflera actinophylla*, of the ivy family, grown as a house-plant.
■ **umbrellaed** /-ləd/ *adjective* protected or covered as by an umbrella; provided with an umbrella or umbrellas: E19. **umbrellaless** *adjective* M19. **umbrella-like** *adjective* resembling an open umbrella L18.

†**umbrere** *noun*. Also **umbriere**. LME–M17.
[App. Anglo-Norman, formed as UMBER *noun*[1]: see -ER[2]. Cf. Anglo-Latin (*viserium*) *umbrarium* (visor) shading the face.]
The visor of a helmet. Cf. UMBER *noun*[1] 2, UMBREL.

umbrette /ʌmˈbrɛt/ *noun*. Now *rare*. L19.
[mod. Latin *umbretta* specific epithet, formed as UMBRA *noun*[1] + *-etta* -ET[1].]
= HAMMERHEAD 4. Cf. UMBRE.

Umbrian /ˈʌmbrɪən/ *noun & adjective*. E17.
[from Latin *Umber* or *Umbria* + -IAN, -AN.]
▶ **A** *noun*. **1** A native or inhabitant of Umbria, a province of central Italy; *esp.* a member of the Italic people inhabiting this region in pre-Roman times. E17.
2 The extinct Italic language of the ancient Umbrians. M19.
3 A painter of the Umbrian school. M19.
▶ **B** *adjective*. **1** Of or pertaining to ancient Umbria, its inhabitants, or their language. E17.
2 Of or pertaining to medieval or modern Umbria or its inhabitants. M19.
2 Umbrian School a school of Italian Renaissance painting to which Raphael and Perugino belonged.
■ **Umbro-** *combining form* [-O-] Umbrian and —: M19.

†**umbriere** *noun* var. of UMBRERE.

umbriferous /ʌmˈbrɪf(ə)rəs/ *adjective*. E17.
[from Latin *umbrifer*, formed as UMBRA *noun*[1]: see -FEROUS.]
Giving shade.

umbril /ˈʌmbrɪl/ *noun*. E19.
[Alt. of UMBREL.]
Hist. A part of a helmet projecting above the eyes. Also, the visor of a helmet.

umbrose /ʌmˈbrəʊs/ *adjective*. *rare*. LME.
[Latin *umbrosus*, formed as UMBER *noun*[1]: see -OSE[1].]
= next.

umbrous /ˈʌmbrəs/ *adjective*. L15.
[Old French *umbreux*, (also mod.) *ombreux*, formed as prec., or directly from the Latin: see -OUS.]
Shady, shadowed.

umfaan /ˈʊmfɑːn/ *noun*. *S. Afr. offensive*. M19.
[Zulu *umFana* small boy.]
A young African boy, *esp.* one employed in domestic service.

umfundisi /ʊmˈfʊndɪsi, ʊmfʊnˈdiːzi/ *noun*. *S. Afr.* E19.
[Xhosa, Zulu *umFundisi*.]
A teacher, a minister, a missionary. Also used as a respectful form of address.

Umgangssprache /ˈʊmgaŋsˌʃpraːxə/ *noun*. Pl. **-chen** /-xən/. M20.
[German = colloquial speech.]
LINGUISTICS. The vernacular language between standard and dialect speech customarily used in a linguistic community.

umiak /ˈuːmɪak/ *noun*. Also **-aq**, **oomiak**. M18.
[Inupiaq *umiaq*.]
A large Eskimo canoe with a wooden frame covered in skins, *esp.* one paddled by women.

Umklapp process /ˈʊmklap ˌprəʊsɛs/ *noun phr.* Also **U-**. M20.
[German *Umklappprozess*, from *umklappen* turn down, turn over + *Prozess* process.]
PHYSICS. An interaction between phonons, or phonons and electrons, in a crystal lattice in which total momentum is not conserved, and the momentum of the initial excitations is reversed. Abbreviation ***U-process***, ***u-process***.

umlaut /ˈʊmlaʊt/ *noun & verb.* **M19.**
[German, from *um-* about + *Laut* sound.]
▶ **A** *noun.* **1** *PHILOLOGY.* Vowel change arising historically by partial assimilation to an adjacent sound, usu. a vowel or semivowel in a following syllable (often now lost), as in German *Mann, Männer*, or English *man, men*. Also called ***mutation, vowel mutation***. **M19.**
2 A diacritical sign (¨) placed over a vowel, esp. in Germanic languages, to indicate such a change. **M20.**
▶ **B** *verb. PHILOLOGY.*
1 *verb trans.* Modify (a form or sound) by (an) umlaut. **M19.**
2 *verb intrans.* Undergo such modification. **L20.**

umma /ˈʊmə/ *noun.* **L19.**
[Arab. = people, community, nation.]
The Muslim community, orig. founded by Muhammad at Medina, comprising individuals bound to one another predominantly by religious ties.

ump /ʌmp/ *noun. slang* (chiefly *N. Amer.*). Also **umps** /ʌmps/. **E20.**
[Abbreviation.]
An umpire, *esp.* in baseball.

umph *noun* var. of **OOMPH**.

umph /(ə)mf/ *interjection & verb.* **M16.**
[Natural exclam. Cf. **HUMPH, MPH.**]
▶ **A** *interjection.* Expr. hesitation, dissatisfaction, or disapproval. **M16.**
▶ **B** *verb intrans.* Utter the sound 'umph'. **L19.**

umpire /ˈʌmpʌɪə/ *noun & verb.* As noun orig. †**noumpere**. **LME.**
[from Old French *nonper*, from *non-* **NON-** + *per, pair* **PEER** *noun*[1], with loss of initial *n* through misdivision as in *adder, apron.*]
▶ **A** *noun.* **1** A person who decides between disputants or contending parties and whose decision is usually accepted as final; an arbitrator. **LME.** ▸**b** A thing which serves to decide or settle a matter. **L16.** ▸†**c** A thing which stands between others, connecting or separating them. **L16–E17.**
2 *LAW.* A third person called upon to decide a matter submitted to arbitrators who cannot agree. **LME.**
3 In various games and sports (e.g. cricket, tennis, and baseball), a person to whose decision all doubtful points are referred during play and who sees that the rules are kept. **E18.**

> 🕮 **1** LD MACAULAY He already saw himself, in imagination, the umpire of Europe. **3** J. SYMONS The ball sailed high into the air . . . The umpire signalled a six.

▶ **B** *verb.* †**1** *verb trans.* Appoint (a person to an office) by virtue of being an arbitrator. *rare.* Only in **L16.**
†**2** *verb trans.* Act as umpire between or for (persons etc.). *rare.* **E–M17.**
3 *verb trans.* **a** Settle or decide (a matter in dispute) as umpire or like an umpire. **E17.** ▸**b** Supervise (a game or contest) in the capacity of umpire. **M19.**
4 *verb intrans.* Act as umpire. Also foll. by *between.* **E17.**
■ **umpirage** *noun* the action of umpiring; the position or power of an umpire; the decision of an umpire: **L15.** **umpireship** *noun* the position or office of umpire; umpirage: **M16.** **umpiress** *noun* a female umpire **E17.**

umps *noun* var. of **UMP**.

umpteen /ʌm(p)ˈtiːn, ˈʌm(p)tiːn/ *adjective & noun. colloq.* Also **umteen**. **E20.**
[formed as next + **-TEEN**, after *thirteen, fourteen*, etc.]
▶ **A** *adjective.* Of an indefinite number; many, several, a lot of (freq. with connotation of wearisome repetition). **E20.**

> 🕮 J. KELMAN I had told them umpteen times never to go there.

▶ **B** *noun.* An indefinite number in the abstract; a particular member at an unspecified or indeterminate position in a series. **E20.**

> 🕮 A. PRICE A potential offender against section umpteen of the Road Traffic Act.

■ **umpteenth** *adjective* **E20.**

umpty /ˈʌm(p)ti/ *noun & adjective*[1]. *colloq.* **L19.**
[Joc. formation after cardinal numerals *twenty, thirty*, etc., perh. orig. after military slang repr. of the dash in Morse code.]
▶ **A** *noun.* An indefinite number, usu. fairly large. **L19.**
▶ **B** *adjective.* Of an indefinite, usu. fairly large, number. **E20.**
Comb.: Forming combs. in imitation of compound numerals (cardinal and ordinal), as ***umpty-nine, umpty-seventh***, etc. **umpty-ump** *adjective & noun* (of) an indefinite largish number.
■ **umptieth** *adjective* **E20.**

umpty /ˈʌm(p)ti/ *adjective*[2]. *colloq.* **M20.**
[Origin unkn.]
Of a person, a place, a circumstance: unpleasant.

umquhile /ˈʌmhwʌɪl/ *adverb & adjective.* Long *arch.* (chiefly *Scot.*). Also (earlier) **umwhile**. **ME.**
[Repr. Old English *ymb hwīle* about while (respelt with Scot. and north. *-quh-* for *-wh-*).]
▶ **A** *adverb.* †**1** At times; sometimes. **ME–M16.**
†**2** At some later time; by and by. *rare.* **LME–E16.**
3 At one time, formerly. **LME.**
▶ **B** *adjective.* Former, erstwhile. **LME.**

umrah /ˈʊmrə/ *noun.* **E19.**
[Arab. *ʿumra.*]
A lesser pilgrimage to Mecca made independently of or at the same time as the hajj, and consisting of a number of devotional rituals performed within the city.

umtagati *noun* var. of **UMTHAKATHI**.

umteen *adjective & noun* var. of **UMPTEEN**.

umthakathi /ʊmtaˈgati/ *noun. S. Afr.* Also **umtagati**. **L19.**
[Nguni.]
A (supposed) worker of witchcraft and evil.

UMTS *abbreviation.*
Universal Mobile Telephone System.

umu /ˈʊmʊ/ *noun.* Chiefly *NZ.* **M19.**
[Maori.]
= **HANGI**.

Umwelt /ˈʊmvɛlt/ *noun.* Pl. **-en** /-ən/. **M20.**
[German = environment.]
The outer world as it affects and is perceived by the organisms inhabiting it; the environment.

umwhile *adverb & adjective* see **UMQUHILE**.

umzimbeet /ʊmzɪmˈbiːt/ *noun.* Also **-bete** /-ˈbɛti/ & other vars. **L19.**
[Zulu *umSimbithi* ironwood.]
The hard heavy wood of a southern African leguminous tree, *Millettia grandis*, which bears clusters of pink or purple flowers; the tree yielding this wood.

UN *abbreviation.*
United Nations.

un /ən/ *pers. pronoun*[1]. Now *dial.* Also **'un**, (earlier) †**hin(e)**.
[Old English *hi(e)ne* accus. of **HE** *pronoun.*]
= **HIM** *pronoun* 1, 1b.

un /ən/ *pronoun*[2]. *dial. & colloq.* Also **'un**. **E19.**
[Alt.]
= **ONE** *noun & pronoun* 1–3.
a good 'un: see **GOOD** *adjective.* ***Pink 'Un***: see **PINK** *adjective*[2]. ***red 'un***: see **RED** *adjective.* ***young 'un***: see **YOUNG** *adjective & noun.*

un- /ʌn/ *prefix*[1].
[Old English *un-* = Old Saxon, Old High German, Gothic *un-*, Old Norse *ú-, ó-*, corresp. to Old Irish *in-, an-*, Latin **IN-**[3], Greek **AN-**[5], **A-**[10], Sanskrit *an-, a-*, from Indo-European ablaut var. of base of *ne* not.]
1 Prefixed to adjectives, ppl adjectives, and nouns (esp. abstract nouns) to express negation or privation, as ***uneducated, unfair, unhappiness, unnourishing, unrest***; sometimes expressing a reversal of sense, as ***unselfish, unsociable*** (in such cases a simple neg. is expressed using **NON-**). ▸**b** Prefixed to verbs in ppl form as ***untouching***. Chiefly *Scot.*
2 Forming parasynthetic adjectives from a noun + *-ed*, with the sense 'not having (what is denoted by the noun)', as ***unbranched, unjointed***. ▸**b** Forming parasynthetic adjectives from verbal phrs., as ***uncalled-for, unget-at-able, unlived-in***.
3 Forming adverbs in *-ly*, either by addition of *un-* to an adverb in *-ly* or by addition of *-ly* to an adjective in *un-*, as ***unmercifully, unprofessionally***.
†**4** Redundantly prefixed to adjectives in *-less* as ***unmerciless, unrestless***.
¶ Now little used with short simple adjectives of native origin (e.g. *broad, glad*) where the neg. is expressed by another word; and usu. avoided where a Latin form in *in-, im-*, etc. (see **IN-**[3]) is well established, though it alternated with these in early mod. English (cf. ***unaccessible, unaccurate, unapplicable***). Otherwise the number of words that can be formed with this prefix is potentially as large as the number of adjectives in use: only a selection can be included here (in this article or in the alphabetical sequence following).
■ **unaˈbbreviated** *adjective* **L18.** **unaˈbiding** *adjective* not abiding or enduring **LME.** **unaˈbolished** *adjective* **L16.** **unaˈbraded** *adjective* **E19.** **unˈabrogated** *adjective* **M16.** **unabˈsolved** *adjective* **E17.** **unabˈsorbable** *adjective* **E19.** **unabˈsorbed** *adjective* **M18.** **unaˈbused** *adjective* **M17.** **unacaˈdemic** *adjective* not academic, *esp.* not scholarly or theoretical **M19.** **unacˈcelerated** *adjective* **L18.** **unacˈcented** *adjective* not accented or stressed; not emphasized: **L16.** **unacˈcentuated** *adjective* **E18.** **unaccéptaˈbility** *noun* **L18.** **unacˈcepted** *adjective* not accepted; rejected: **E17.** †**unaccessible** *adjective* inaccessible **L16–M18.** **unaˈcclaimed** *adjective* **E20.** **unaˈcclimated** *adjective* unacclimatized **M19.** **unaˈcclimatized** *adjective* not acclimatized **M19.** **unaˈccordant** *adjective* = **INACCORDANT** **LME.** †**unaccording** *adjective* = **INACCORDANT** **LME–M18.** **unaˈccredited** *adjective* **E19.** †**unaccurate** *adjective* inaccurate **M17–E18.** †**unaccurately** *adverb* **L17–E18.** †**unaccurateness** *noun* inaccuracy **M17–E18.** **unaccursed** /-ˈkəːsɪd, -ˈkəːst/, **-st** /-st/ *adjective* (*arch.*) **L17.** **unaˈchievable** *adjective* **M17.** **unaˈchieved** *adjective* **E17.** **unˈaching** *adjective* **E17.** **unaˈcquirable** *adjective* **M17.** **unaˈcquired** *adjective* not acquired; unattained; innate: **M17.** **unˈactorish** *adjective* **L20.** **unˈactressy** *adjective* **L20.** **unˈactuated** *adjective* not actuated or motivated (*by*) **M17.** **unaˈddicted** *adjective* **L16.** **unaˈddressed** *adjective* not addressed, lacking an address **L18.** **unaˈdept** *noun & adjective* (**a**) *noun* a person who is not an adept; (**b**) *adjective* not adept or proficient: **M18.** **unˈadjectived** *adjective* not having or qualified by an adjective **E19.** **unaˈdjourned** *adjective* **M17.** **unadˈministered** *adjective* (esp. *LAW*) not administered **L16.** **unadˈmonished** *adjective* **L16.** **unaˈdoptable** *adjective* **M19.** **unaˈdored** *adjective* **E17.** **unaˈdoring** *adjective* **M18.** **unadˈvanced** *adjective* not advanced or promoted; not pushed forward: **LME.** **unˈaerated** *adjective* **L18.** **unˈaffable** *adjective* **E17.** **unaˈffectionate** *adjective* **L16.** **unaˈffianced** *adjective* **M18.** **unaˈffiliated** *adjective* **M19.** **unaˈffixed** *adjective* **E17.** **unaˈfflicted** *adjective* **L16.** **unaˈffordable** *adjective* **E19.** **unaˈffronted** *adjective* (**a**) not affronted or insulted; (**b**) not confronted or faced: **M18.** **unˈageing** *adjective* **M19.** **unˈaggravated** *adjective* **M18.** **unˈaggregated** *adjective* **L19.** **unˈaimed** *adjective* not aimed (*at*) **M17.** **unˈaired** *adjective* †(**a**) *rare* untravelled; (**b**) not aired: **E17.** **unaˈkin** *adjective* **M19.** **unaˈlarmed** *adjective* **M18.** **unaˈlarming** *adjective* **M18.** **unˈalcoholized** *adjective* (*rare*) **L18.** **unaˈlert** *adjective* **E19.** **unˈalienated** *adjective* **L18.** **unaˈligned** *adjective* (**a**) not physically aligned; (**b**) politically non-aligned: **M20.** **unaˈlike** *adjective* different; not alike: **M20.** **unaˈllayed** *adjective* **E16.** **unaˈlliable** *adjective* (*rare*) **M18.** **unaˈllied** *adjective* (**a**) not allied or related (*to*); (**b**) having no allies: **M17.** **unˈallocated** *adjective* **M19.** **unaˈllotted** *adjective* **L18.** **unaˈllowable** *adjective* **M16.** **unaˈllowed** *adjective* **M17.** **unaˈlluring** *adjective* **L18.** **unalphaˈbetic** *adjective* **L19.** **unaˈmalgamated** *adjective* **E19.** **unaˈmazed** *adjective* **L16.** **unamˈbivalent** *adjective* **L20.** **unamˈbivalently** *adverb* **L20.** **unaˈmenable** *adjective* **L18.** **unaˈmendable** *adjective* **LME.** **unaˈmended** *adjective* **LME.** **unˈamorous** *adjective* (*rare*) **M17.** **unˈamplified** *adjective* **E20.** **unaˈmusable** *adjective* **E19.** **unaˈmused** *adjective* **M18.** **unaˈmusing** *adjective* **L18.** **un,analysaˈbility** *noun* **M20.** **unanaˈlysable** *adjective* **E19.** **unˈanalysed** *adjective* **M17.** **unanaˈlytic** *adjective* **M19.** **unanaˈlytical** *adjective* **M19.** **unanˈgelic** *adjective* **E18.** **unˈanimated** *adjective* **L17.** **unaˈnnexed** *adjective* **M19.** **unaˈnnihilated** *adjective* **L18.** **unˈannotated** *adjective* **M19.** **unaˈnnoyed** *adjective* **LME.** **unaˈnnulled** *adjective* (*rare*) **L16.** **unaˈnointed** *adjective* **M17.** **unanˈticipated** *adjective* **L18.** **unˈanxious** *adjective* **M18.** **unˈanxiously** *adverb* **M18.** **unapoloˈgetic** *adjective* **M19.** **unapoloˈgetically** *adverb* **M20.** **unaˈppalled** *adjective* **L16.** **unaˈpparelled** *adjective* (*arch.*) unclothed, not apparelled **E17.** **unaˈpparent** *adjective* **M16.** **unaˈpplauded** *adjective* **M18.** **unaˈpplied** *adjective* not applied **M16.** **unaˈppointable** *adjective* not able to be appointed **M17.** **unaˈppointed** *adjective* (**a**) *gen.* not appointed; (**b**) not provided with necessities; not equipped: **M16.** **unaˈppreciable** *adjective* inappreciable **E19.** **unaˈppreciated** *adjective* not appreciated or valued; not properly estimated: **E19.** **unaˈppreciative** *adjective* **M19.** **unappreˈhended** *adjective* (**a**) not grasped by the senses or the intellect; (**b**) not arrested: **L16.** †**unapprehensible** *adjective* inapprehensible **E17–M18.** **unappreˈhensive** *adjective* inapprehensive **E17.** **unappreˈhensiveness** *noun* inapprehensiveness **M17.** **unaˈpprised** *adjective* not apprised (*of*) **E18.** **unaˈppropriate** *adjective* (now *rare*) (**a**) unappropriated; (**b**) inappropriate: **M18.** **unaˈppropriated** *adjective* (**a**) not allocated or assigned; (**b**) not taken into possession by someone: **M18.** **unaˈpproved** *adjective* †(**a**) not shown to be skilled; not demonstrated; unproved; (**b**) not approved or sanctioned: **LME.** **unarchiˈtectural** *adjective* (**a**) not in accordance with the principles of architecture; (**b**) not skilled in architecture: **M19.** **unˈarguable** *adjective* **L19.** **unˈarguably** *adverb* **E20.** **unˈargued** *adjective* (now *rare*) **E17.** **unarguˈmentative** *adjective* **E18.** **unarguˈmentatively** *adverb* **M19.** **unarithˈmetic** *adjective* (*rare*) **L18.** **unarithˈmetical** *adjective* **L17.** **unˈarmoured** *adjective* **M19.** **unaˈrraigned** *adjective* **L16.** **unaˈrranged** *adjective* **L18.** **unaˈrrayed** *adjective* **ME.** **unaˈrrested** *adjective* (**a**) not apprehended; (**b**) not stopped or checked: **LME.** **unaˈrresting** *adjective* not arresting; *esp.* uninteresting, dull: **E20.** **unaˈrrestingly** *adverb* in an unarresting manner **L20.** **unaˈrrived** *adjective* not arrived (*lit.* & *fig.*) **E17.** **unˈartful** *adjective* (*arch.*) (**a**) not artificial or contrived; artless; (**b**) unskilful, clumsy; inartistic: **M17.** **unˈartfully** *adverb* (*arch.*) in an unartful manner **E18.** **unarˈticulate** *adjective* (*rare*) †(**a**) = **INARTICULATE** 2; (**b**) = **INARTICULATE** 1: **E17.** **unarˈticulated** *adjective* (**a**) not articulated; *spec.* not clearly pronounced or uttered, not distinct; (**b**) not jointed or hinged: **L17.** **unartiˈficial** *adjective* (**a**) (now *rare* or *obsolete*) unskilful, inartistic, clumsy; (**b**) not artificial; simple, natural: **L16.** **unartiˈficially** *adverb* in an unartificial manner **L16.** **unarˈtistic** *adjective* **M19.** **unarˈtistically** *adverb* **M20.** **unaˈscendable** *adjective* **E17.** **unaˈscended** *adjective* **E19.** **unascerˈtained** *adjective* †(**a**) not informed or apprised, not guaranteed; (**b**) not ascertained or known: **E17.** **unˈaskable** *adjective* not able to be asked **M19.** **unˈasked** *adjective* (**a**) not requested or invited; (**b**) not asked *for*; not made the subject of a request: **ME.** **unˈasking** *adjective* not asking or requesting **E18.** **unˈaspirated** *adjective* **L18.** **unaˈspiring** *adjective* **E18.** **unaˈspiringness** *noun* **L17.** **unaˈssaultable** *adjective* **L16.** **unaˈssaulted** *adjective* **E17.** **unaˈssayed** *adjective* **LME.** **unaˈssignable** *adjective* **L17.** **unaˈssigned** *adjective* **L15.** **unaˈssimilable** *adjective* **L19.** **unaˈssimilated** *adjective* **M18.** **unaˈssisted** *adjective* **E17.** **unaˈssociable** *adjective* (*rare*) **L18.** **unaˈssociated** *adjective* **E18.** **unaˈssoiled** *adjective* (*arch.*) (**a**) not assoiled; not absolved from sin; †(**b**) *rare* not settled; undecided: **LME.** **unaˈssorted** *adjective* **L18.** **unaˈssuageable** *adjective* **E17.** **unaˈssuaged** *adjective* **M17.** **unaˈstonished** *adjective* **M16.** **unathˈletic** *adjective* **M18.** **unathˈletically** *adverb* **E20.** **unatmosˈpheric** *adjective* **E20.** **unatmosˈpherically** *adverb* **L20.** **unaˈtonable** *adjective* †(**a**) *rare* not accordant; (**b**) not reconcilable; (**c**) not able to be atoned for or expiated: **M17.** **unaˈtoned** *adjective* (**a**) not atoned for or expiated; †(**b**) not reconciled: **E18.** **unaˈttackable** *adjective* **E18.** **unaˈttacked** *adjective* **M17.** **unaˈttemptable** *adjective* **M17.** **unaˈttempted** *adjective* **M16.** †**unattentive** *adjective* = **INATTENTIVE** 1 **E16–L18.** **unaˈttenuated** *adjective* **E18.** **unaˈttested** *adjective* **M17.** **unaˈttired** *adjective* not attired, unclothed **LME.** **unaˈttributable** *adjective* **E19.** **unaˈttributably** *adverb* **L20.** **unaˈttributed** *adjective* **L20.** **unaˈttributively** *adverb* not attributively; without an attributed or acknowledged source: **L20.** **unaˈttuned** *adjective* **L18.** †**unaudible** *adjective* inaudible **E17–L18.** **unˈaudited** *adjective* **E19.** **unaugˈmentable** *adjective* (*rare*) **M19.** **unaugˈmented** *adjective* **M16.** **unauˈspicious** *adjective* (long *rare* or *obsolete*) inauspicious **E17.** **unaˈvenged** *adjective* **L15.** **unaˈvertable** *adjective* = **UNAVERTIBLE** **E19.** **unaˈverted** *adjective* **M18.** **unaˈvertible** *adjective* **L19.**

unaˈwaked *adjective* (*arch.*) unawakened M17. **unaˈwakened** *adjective* E18. **unˈawed** *adjective* not awed or awestruck (*by*) L17. **unˈawful** *adjective* (*arch.*) †(*a*) not full of awe; (*b*) not inspiring or causing awe: E17. **unˈbadged** *adjective* not bearing a badge L19. **unˈbaffled** *adjective* L18. **unˈbailable** *adjective* E17. **unˈbaked** *adjective* not baked; not prepared by baking: M16. **unˈballasted** *adjective* not ballasted; *fig.* not steadied or supported by serious principles or qualities: M17. **unˈbanded** *adjective* (long *rare*) not provided with a band or bands; not banded: L16. **unˈbanished** *adjective* M16. **unˈbanked** *adjective*[1] not banked up L18. **unˈbanked** *adjective*[2] (of money etc.) not banked M20. **unˈbarbered** *adjective* M19. **unˈbathed** *adjective* L16. **unˈbattered** *adjective* E17. **unˈbearded** *adjective* M16. **unˈbearing** *adjective* unfertile, unproductive, barren OE. **unbeˈclouded** *adjective* E18. **unbeˈdimmed** *adjective* M19. **unbeˈfriended** *adjective* E17. **unˈbegged** *adjective* L16. **unbeˈheld** *adjective* (chiefly *poet.*) not beheld, unseen M17. **unbeˈholden** *adjective* (*a*) not under an obligation (*to*); independent; (*b*) = UNBEHELD: L17. **unˈbeing** *noun* (*literary*) absence or lack of being; non-existence: LME. **unbeˈloved** *adjective* L16. **unbeˈmoaned** *adjective* (*arch.*) not bemoaned or lamented E17. **unˈbeneficed** *adjective* not endowed or invested with a benefice E17. **unbeneˈficial** *adjective* E17. **unˈbenefited** *adjective* not having benefited, unimproved M18. **unbeˈnevolent** *adjective* L17. **unbeˈnign** *adjective* not kindly or gentle; unfavourable: M17. **unbeˈqueathed** *adjective* L15. **unbeˈreft** *adjective* E17. **unbeˈsieged** *adjective* E17. **unbeˈsought** *adjective* (*arch.*) not besought M17. **unbeˈspoken** *adjective* not bespoken; not ordered or requested: L17. **unbeˈstowed** *adjective* M16. **unbeˈthought** *adverb & adjective* (now *dial.*) (*a*) *adverb* without premeditation, unintentionally; (*b*) *adjective* unpremeditated: M16. **unbeˈtrayed** *adjective* L16. **unbeˈtrothed** *adjective* L16. **unˈbetterable** *adjective* not able to be improved E19. **unˈbettered** *adjective* unimproved E17. **unˈbevelled** *adjective* L16. **unbeˈwailed** *adjective* (*arch.*) unlamented, unregretted L16. **unbeˈwildered** *adjective* E19. **unˈbiblical** *adjective* E19. **unˈbid** *adjective* (*poet.*) (*a*) = UNBIDDEN *adjective*; †(*b*) (*rare*, Spenser) unprayed for: LME. **unˈbiddable** *adjective* not biddable or docile; obstinate; disobedient: E19. **unˈbidden** *adjective* not asked or invited; not commanded: OE. **unˈbigged** *adjective* (now *Scot.*) (*a*) unbuilt; (*b*) not built upon: ME. **unˈbigoted** *adjective* not bigoted; tolerant: E18. **unbioˈlogical** *adjective* (*a*) not in accord with the findings of biology; (*b*) not occurring in nature: M20. **unˈbirthday** *noun* (chiefly *joc.*) any day except a person's birthday L19. **unˈbishoped** *adjective* (long *rare*) not blessed or confirmed by a bishop OE. **unˈbitted** *adjective* not provided with a bit; unbridled, unrestrained: L16. **unˈbitten** *adjective* L18. **unˈblanched** *adjective* not blanched; unbleached; (esp. of almonds) unpeeled: LME. **unˈblasted** *adjective* L16. **unˈblazoned** *adjective* (*arch.*) L18. **unˈbleached** *adjective* M16. **unˈblenched** *adjective* (*a*) not turned aside; unaverted, unflinching; (*b*) *poet. rare* unstained, untarnished: M17. **unˈblenching** *adjective* not turning aside, unflinching M19. **unˈblended** *adjective* ME. **unˈblighted** *adjective* not blighted, unmarred L18. **unˈblinded** *adjective* (*a*) not blinded or deprived of sight; *fig.* not deluded or deceived; (*b*) not provided with or covered by a window-blind: E17. **unˈblissful** *adjective* not blissful, unhappy ME. **unˈblooded** *adjective* (*a*) *arch.* = UNBLOODIED; (*b*) (of an animal) not of a good breed, not thoroughbred: L18. **unˈbloodied** *adjective* not bloody or stained with blood L16. **unˈbloomed** *adjective* (orig. *Scot.*, now *rare*) not bearing blooms E16. **unˈblossomed** *adjective* E17. **unˈblotted** *adjective* not blotted; unstained, untarnished: M16. †**unblowed** *adjective* (*rare*, Shakes.) = UNBLOWN *adjective* 1: only in E17. **unˈblunted** *adjective* not blunted or dulled L16. **unˈblurred** *adjective* E19. **unˈboastful** *adjective* M18. **unˈbobbed** *adjective* E20. **unˈbold** *adjective* (long *obsolete* exc. *Scot.*, now *rare*) not bold; timid, bashful; backward: OE. **unˈbonded** *adjective* L19. **unˈboned** *adjective* (*a*) not furnished with (a) bone, boneless; (*b*) (of meat, fish, etc.) not having the bones removed: E17. **unˈbonneted** *adjective* not wearing a hat or bonnet; with the head uncovered, esp. as a mark of respect: E17. **unˈbonny** *adjective* (*Scot. & dial.*) ugly, unsightly M19. **unˈbooked** *adjective* (*a*) *literary* not entered in a book or list; unrecorded; (*b*) (of a performer) not engaged; (of a seat etc.) not reserved: L16. **unˈbookish** *adjective* not bookish or studious; unlearned: E17. **unˈbored** *adjective* not bored into or through L16. **unˈboring** *adjective* not boring, interesting M19. **unˈborne** *adjective* (*rare*) not carried *away*; not borne *out* or sustained: L15. **unˈborrowed** *adjective* not borrowed or adopted; native, inherent, original: M17. **unˈbothered** *adjective* not bothered, unconcerned E20. **unˈbottomed** *adjective* (*a*) bottomless; (*b*) unsupported, unfounded: E17. **unˈbought** *adjective* not bought; unpurchased: OE. **unˈbowdlerized** *adjective* L19. **unˈbowed** *adjective* not bowed or bent LME. **unˈboyish** *adjective* M19. **unˈbraided** *adjective* †(*a*) *rare* untarnished, undamaged; (*b*) not braided or plaited: E17. **unˈbranched** *adjective* not having or divided into branches M17. **unˈbranded** *adjective* M17. **unˈbrave** *adjective* not brave L17. **unˈbreachable** *adjective* not able to be breached M19. **unˈbreached** *adjective* L19. **unˈbreakable** *adjective* L15. **unˈbreakfasted** *adjective* not having had breakfast M17. **unˈbreeched** *adjective* (*arch.*) not wearing breeches E17. **unˈbridled** *adjective* not wearing a bridle; *fig.* unrestrained, unchecked: LME. **unˈbriefed** *adjective* not briefed, *esp.* not thoroughly instructed or informed L19. **unˈbright** *adjective* not bright, dim E16. **un-ˈBritish** *adjective* not British, *esp.* uncharacteristic of Great Britain or its inhabitants M18. **unˈbroached** *adjective* (esp. of a cask) not broached, unopened L17. **unˈbrookable** *adjective* (chiefly *Scot.*) unendurable, intolerable M17. **unˈbrought** *adjective* (*arch.*) not brought E16. **unˈbruised** *adjective* LME. **unˈbrushed** *adjective* not brushed; *fig.* uncouth, rugged: M17. **unˈbudded** *adjective* E19. **unˈbudgeable** *adjective* M20. **unˈbulky** *adjective* L17. **unˈbumptious** *adjective* not bumptious; unassertive, unassuming: M19. **unbureauˈcratic** *adjective* L20. **unˈburiable** *adjective* M19. **unˈburied** *adjective* OE. **unˈburnable** *adjective* not able to be burned L19. **unˈburning** *adjective* not burning L15. **unˈburnished** *adjective* L17. **unˈburst** *adjective* not burst; *spec.* (of computer printout) not separated along the perforated edges: L18. **unˈburstable** *adjective* not able to be burst L19. **unˈbusinesslike** *adjective* E19. **unˈbusy** *adjective* not busy; quiet: M18. **unˈbuttered** *adjective* not spread or coated with butter L16. **unˈbuttressed** *adjective* not supported or strengthened with a buttress M19. **unˈcabled** *adjective* not provided with or secured by a cable or cables L18. **unˈcaged** *adjective* not enclosed or confined in a cage M18. **unˈcalcified** *adjective* M19. **unˈcalcined** *adjective* E17. **unˈcalculated** *adjective* not calculated or estimated, unexpected E19. **unˈcalculating** *adjective* M19. **unˈcalm** *adjective* E19. **unˈcancellable** *adjective* E17. **unˈcancelled** *adjective* M16. **unˈcandour** *noun* lack of candour; partiality, bias: L19. **unˈcanopied** *adjective* E17. **unˈcanvassed** *adjective* L18. **uncaˈpacious** *adjective* M17. **unˈcaptious** *adjective* (*rare*) not captious M17. **unˈcaptured** *adjective* not (yet) captured L19. **unˈcared-for** *adjective* not cared for or looked after; disregarded, neglected: L16. **unˈcarpeted** *adjective* not covered or provided with a carpet E19. **unˈcarried** *adjective* not carried or transported L16. **unˈcarved** *adjective* L16. **unˈcashed** *adjective* (esp. of a cheque) not yet cashed L19. **unˈcast** *adjective* LME. **unˈcastable** *adjective* (of an actor) not able to be cast (*as* or *in* a role etc.) L20. **unˈcastigated** *adjective* not castigated; unchastised: M17. **unˈcatalogued** *adjective* M19. **unˈcatalysed** *adjective* M20. **unˈcatchable** *adjective* not able to be caught E19. **unˈcatechized** *adjective* not formally instructed or examined in Christian religion (as) with a catechism E17. **unˈcategorizable** *adjective* not able to be categorized M20. **unˈcaught** *adjective* not (yet) caught ME. **unˈcaused** *adjective* having no cause; not created: E17. **unˈcautious** *adjective* incautious L20. **unˈceiled** *adjective* (*arch.*) not having an inner roof; (of a roof) not plastered or lined: E19. **unˈceilinged** *adjective* not having a ceiling M19. **unceˈlestial** *adjective* M17. **unceˈmented** *adjective* not united (as) with cement; not cohering: E18. **unˈcensored** *adjective* L19. **uncenˈsorious** *adjective* E18. **unˈcensurable** *adjective* not able to be censured or reproved M17. **unˈcensured** *adjective* not censured or reproved L16. **unˈcentral** *adjective* not central; marginal, peripheral: L18. **uncerˈtificated** *adjective* (esp. of a teacher) not certificated M19. **unˈcertitude** *noun* = INCERTITUDE M16. **unˈchalked** *adjective* L18. **unˈchambered** *adjective* (esp. ARCHAEOLOGY) M17. **unˈchannelled**, *-eled *adjective* E17. **unˈchanted** *adjective* L18. **unˈchaperoned** *adjective* not accompanied by a chaperon M19. **unˈcharred** *adjective* L18. **unˈchary** *adjective* E17. **unˈchastened** *adjective* M17. **unchasˈtised** *adjective* LME. **unˈchewed** *adjective* M17. **unˈchid** *adjective* (*literary*) unrebuked M19. **unˈchidden** *adjective* (*arch.*) unrebuked L15. **unˈchilled** *adjective* L18. **unˈchipped** *adjective* M17. **unˈchiselled** *adjective* L18. **unˈchoosing** *adjective* (now *rare*) not exercising choice, undiscriminating L16. **unˈchopped** *adjective* M17. **unˈchosen** *adjective* E16. **unˈcicatrized** *adjective* not healed by scarring L18. **unˈciliated** *adjective* M19. **unˈcinctured** *adjective* (*poet.*) not wearing a girdle or belt L18. **unˈcircular** *adjective* L18. **unˈclarified** *adjective* (esp. of a liquid) not clarified L16. **unˈclarity** *adjective* lack of clarity, esp. clarity of expression M20. **unˈclashing** *adjective* M17. **unˈcleavable** *adjective* M19. **unˈcleaved** *adjective* L19. †**unclement** *adjective* inclement L16–M18. **unˈclerical** *adjective* not appropriate to or characteristic of a member of the clergy M18. **unˈclerkly** *adjective* L19. **unˈclever** *adjective* L18. **unˈclotted** *adjective* L18. **unˈcloven** *adjective* E17. **unˈclubbable** *adjective & noun* (a person) that is not clubbable M18. **unˈclued** *adjective* lacking a clue (in a crossword) L20. **unˈcluttered** *adjective* not cluttered; austere, simple: E20. **uncoˈagulable** *adjective* M17. **uncoˈagulated** *adjective* L18. **unˈcoded** *adjective* E20. **uncoˈerced** *adjective* L18. **unˈcoffined** *adjective* not enclosed in a coffin M17. **unˈcognizable** *adjective* E18. **uncognosciˈbility** *noun* E19. **uncogˈnoscible** *adjective* E19. **uncoˈllated** *adjective* L18. **uncoˈllectable** *adjective* E20. **unˈcolonized** *adjective* M19. **uncoˈmmendable** *adjective* E16. **uncoˈmmendably** *adverb* L16. **unˈcommenting** *adjective* occurring or done without comment L19. **uncoˈmmercial** *adjective* not commercial; contrary to commercial principles: M18. **uncoˈmmissioned** *adjective* M17. **uncoˈmmixed** *adjective* (*arch.*) E17. **unˈcommonplace** *adjective* E19. **uncomˈpacted** *adjective* M17. **uncomˈpassionate** *adjective* lacking compassion, unfeeling L16. **uncomˈpelled** *adjective* LME. **uncomˈpelling** *adjective* L20. **uncomˈpetitive** *adjective* L19. **uncomˈpetitiveness** *noun* M20. **uncomˈplaisant** *adjective* (now *rare*) L17. **unˈcomplex** *adjective* E18. **unˈcomplexed** *adjective* (CHEMISTRY) not combined in a complex M20. **uncomˈpliant** *adjective* M17. **uncompliˈmentary** *adjective* not complimentary; insulting: M19. **uncomˈplying** *adjective* not compliant, unaccommodating M17. **uncomˈpressed** *adjective* M17. **uncomˈputable** *adjective* L17. **unconˈciliatory** *adjective* not conciliatory; not showing a spirit of conciliation: L18. †**unconclusive** *adjective* inconclusive M17–E18. **unconˈdemned** *adjective* not condemned, *esp.* not pronounced to be at fault or guilty E16. **uncondeˈscending** *adjective* M17. **unconˈducive** *adjective* not conducive *to* M17. **unˈconfidence** *noun* (*rare*) uncertainty M17. **unˈconfident** *adjective* not confident, uncertain M17. **unconfiˈdential** *adjective* L18. **unconˈflicting** *adjective* L19. **unconˈfounded** *adjective* not confounded, *esp.* not mixed or confused M16. **unconˈfronted** *adjective* M17. **unconˈfutable** *adjective* M17. **unconˈfuted** *adjective* (now *rare* or *obsolete*) E17. **unˈconjugal** *adjective* M17. **unˈconjugated** *adjective* E20. †**unconniving** *adjective* (*rare*, Milton): only in L17. **unconˈsecutive** *adjective* E20. **unconˈsented** *adjective* (now *rare*) not consented (*to*) M17. **unconˈsenting** *adjective* L17. **unconˈservative** *adjective* L19. **unconˈsigned** *adjective* (*rare*) M17. **unconˈsolidated** *adjective* E19. **unˈconsonant** *adjective* inconsonant M16. **unconˈspicuous** *adjective* inconspicuous E19. **unˈconstancy** *noun* (now *rare*) inconstancy M16. †**unconstant** *adjective* inconstant, *esp.* unfaithful in love or marriage L15–M18. †**unconstantly** *adverb* inconstantly M16–E18. **unconˈstricted** *adjective* L20. **unconˈstruable** *adjective* M19. **unconˈstructive** *adjective* M19. **unconˈtactable** *adjective* L20. †**uncontemned** *adjective* (*rare*) not contemned E–M17. **unˈcontemplated** *adjective* not contemplated, *esp.* not considered or taken into account E18. **unconˈtemporary** *adjective* M19. **unconˈtentious** *adjective* not contentious, not causing contention E19. **unˈcontrite** *adjective* not contrite, not showing contrition LME. **unconˈtrived** *adjective* not contrived, not artificial E17. **unconˈvenient** *adjective* (*obsolete* exc. *dial.*) inconvenient LME. **unconˈversable** *adjective* (now *rare* or *obsolete*) unfit or unsuitable for social converse L16. **unconˈversant** *adjective* not conversant *with* or *in* L17. **unconˈversion** *noun* the state or condition of being unconverted, esp. to a particular belief, opinion, or religious faith M19. **unconˈveyed** *adjective* LME. **unconˈvicted** *adjective* L17. **unˈcooked** *adjective* not cooked; raw: M19. **unˈcool** *adjective* not cool; *colloq.* not stylish or fashionable, out of date: M20. **unˈcooled** *adjective* not cooled; warm, hot: E16. **unˈcoped** *adjective* not coped or dealt competently *with* L16. **unˈcopyrightable** *adjective* E20. **unˈcopyrighted** *adjective* M19. **unˈcordial** *adjective* †(*a*) uncongenial (*Scot.*); (*b*) not cordial; lacking in warmth: LME. **unˈcoroneted** *adjective* not wearing a coronet; not ennobled: E19. **unˈcorrelated** *adjective* L19. **uncorreˈspondent** *adjective* (now *rare*) not corresponding M17. **uncorreˈsponding** *adjective* E19. **unˈcorrigible** *adjective* (now *rare*) incorrigible LME. **uncoˈrroborated** *adjective* (esp. of evidence) not corroborated, unsupported L18. **uncoˈrroded** *adjective* L17. **unˈcorseted** *adjective* M19. **unˈcosted** *adjective* not costed; without the cost having been determined: L20. **unˈcostly** *adjective* inexpensive M17. **unˈcountenanced** *adjective* L18. **uncouˈrageous** *adjective* L19. **unˈcoursed** *adjective* (of masonry) not laid or set in courses E19. **unˈcourted** *adjective* (now *rare* or *obsolete*) L18. **unˈcourtierlike** *adjective* L18. **unˈcourtlike** *adjective* (now *rare*) M17. **unˈcoveted** *adjective* M18. **unˈcovetous** *adjective* LME. **unˈcowed** *adjective* L19. **unˈcramped** *adjective* not cramped or affected by cramp; unrestricted: L18. **unˈcreased** *adjective* L19. **unˈcreaturely** *adjective* not characteristic of or proper to creatures M17. **unˈcrested** *adjective* not decorated or provided with a crest; lacking a crest: M17. **unˈcriminal** *adjective* M19. **unˈcrippled** *adjective* L18. †**uncrooked** *adjective* not crooked; straight; honest: E17–L18. **unˈcrowded** *adjective* not crowded; not subjected to crowding: E18. †**uncrudded** *adjective* (*rare*, Spenser) uncurdled: only in L16. **unˈcruel** *adjective* (*arch.*) E17. **unˈcrumbled** *adjective* L18. **unˈcuckolded** *adjective* (*rare*) not made a cuckold of E17. **unˈculled** *adjective* M17. †**unculpable** *adjective* not culpable or blameworthy; blameless: LME–M18. **unculiˈvation** *noun* (*rare*) lack of cultivation or culture L18. **unˈcurdled** *adjective* L18. **unˈcurious** *adjective* (now *rare*) incurious; lacking curiosity; unremarkable: L16. **unˈcuriously** *adverb* (now *rare*) L15. **unˈcurrent** *adjective* (now *rare*) not current; now *esp.* (of money) not in circulation: E17. **unˈcurried** *adjective* (of a horse) not curried, ungroomed E17. **uncurˈtailed** *adjective* M18. **unˈcushioned** *adjective* (of a seat) not provided with a cushion or cushions L18. **unˈdamageable** *adjective* M17. **unˈdamaged** *adjective* M17. **unˈdamnified** *adjective* (long *rare* or *obsolete*) undamaged L16. **unˈdared** *adjective* not dared L16. **unˈdaring** *adjective* not daring, unadventurous E17. **unˈdarkened** *adjective* not darkened M18. **unˈdarned** *adjective* not having a darn or darns; not yet darned: L18. **unˈdaubed** *adjective* M17. **unˈdazed** *adjective* M18. **unˈdazzled** *adjective* not dazzled E17. **unˈdazzling** *adjective* E17. **unˈdealt** *adjective* †(*a*) *rare* undivided; (*b*) not dealt *with*: ME. **undeˈbarred** *adjective* L16. **undeˈbased** *adjective* M18. **undeˈbated** *adjective* E17. **undeˈbauched** *adjective* M17. **undeˈclarable** *adjective* LME. **undeˈclared** *adjective* E16. **undeˈclinable** *adjective* (now *rare* or *obsolete*) indeclinable M16. **undeˈclined** *adjective* (GRAMMAR) having no inflections E16. **undecomˈposable** *adjective* indecomposable E19. **undecomˈposed** *adjective* M18. **undecomˈpounded** *adjective* L18. **unˈdecorated** *adjective* M18. **unˈdecorative** *adjective* L19. **undeˈcorticated** *adjective* L19. **unˈdedicated** *adjective* M17. †**undeeded** *adjective* (*rare*, Shakes.) having performed no deeds: only in E17. **unˈdeemed** *adjective* †(*a*) not judged or condemned; (*b*) unimagined: ME. **unˈdeep** *adjective & noun* †(*a*) *adjective* not deep; (*b*) *noun* (*rare*) a shallow place: OE. **unˈdefaced** *adjective* (*a*) not disfigured or marred; (*b*) not blotted out or obliterated: LME. **undeˈfeatable** *adjective* M17. **undeˈfeated** *adjective* E19. †**undefied** *adjective* not challenged to combat or battle L16–L17. **unˈdefinite** *adjective* indefinite L16. **undeˈflected** *adjective* M19. **undeˈflowered** *adjective* M16. **undeˈformable** *adjective* L20. **undeˈformed** *adjective* L17. **undeˈfrayed** *adjective* E17. **undeˈgassed** *adjective* M20. **undeˈgraded** *adjective* E19. **undeˈjected** *adjective* E17. **undeˈliberate** *adjective* E16. **unˈdeliberated** *adjective* L17. **undeˈluded** *adjective* M18. **unˈdelved** *adjective* not delved or dug; not excavated: E17. **undeˈmolished** *adjective* L16. **undeˈnatured** *adjective* M20. **unˈdenizened** *adjective* not naturalized M17. **undeˈnoted** *adjective* M19. **undeˈnounced** *adjective* L18. **undeˈparting** *adjective* L16. **undeˈplored** *adjective* E17. **undeˈpraved** *adjective* (*a*) not morally depraved or corrupted; (*b*) (long *rare*) (of a text) not vitiated: M17. **undeˈpreciated** *adjective* (of money) not depreciated E19. **undeˈpressed** *adjective* (*a*) not dejected or dispirited; (*b*) not pressed down; not flattened or hollowed: L17. **undeˈprived** *adjective* not deprived M16. **undeˈrided** *adjective* (*rare*) E17. **undeˈrivative** *adjective* M17. **undeˈscried** *adjective* L16. **undeˈscriptive** *adjective* M18. **unˈdesecrated** *adjective* (*rare*) M19. **undeˈsert** *noun* (*rare*) unworthiness; lack of merit, excellence, or worth: L16. **undeˈserted** *adjective* L18. **unˈdesignated** *adjective* L18. **undeˈsire** *noun* (*rare*) lack of desire L19. **undeˈspairing** *adjective* M18. **undeˈspoiled** *adjective* M19. **unˈdestined** *adjective* (*rare*) not destined or predetermined E19. **undeˈstructible** *adjective* (*rare*) indestructible L18. **unˈdetailed** *adjective* not detailed; lacking detail: M19. **undeˈterred** *adjective* not deterred; not inhibited or discouraged *by* fear, doubt, etc.: E17. **unˈdevious** *adjective* not devious; direct; straightforward: L18. **undeˈvised** *adjective* (*a*) LAW not assigned by will; (*b*) not planned or intended: M18. **undeˈvoured** *adjective* not devoured; uneaten: M17. **unˈdewy** *adjective* (long *rare* or *obsolete*) not dewy LME. **unˈdextrous** *adjective* L17. **undiagˈnosable** *adjective* E20. **unˈdiagnosed** *adjective* M19. **undicˈtated** *adjective* not dictated or prescribed; not forced or compulsory: L18. **unˈdieted** *adjective* M17. **unˈdifferenced** *adjective* (chiefly HERALDRY) not differenced M19. **unˈdiligent** *adjective* M16. **unˈdiligently** *adverb* M17. **unˈdimmed** *adjective* E18. **unˈdimpled** *adjective* L18. **unˈdined** *adjective* that has not been given dinner E16. **unˈdinted** *adjective* E17. **undisˈarmed** *adjective* M17. **undisˈbanded** *adjective* M17. **undisˈcoloured** *adjective* M17. **undisˈcomfited** *adjective* LME. **undisconˈtinued** *adjective* E17. **undisˈcording** *adjective* (now *rare* or *obsolete*) not discordant E17. **undisˈcourageable** *adjective* L16. **undisˈcouraged** *adjective* E17. **undisˈcursive** *adjective* M17. **undiˈseased** *adjective* LME. **undisˈfigured** *adjective* E18. **undisˈgraced** *adjective* M18. **undisˈhonoured** *adjective* L16. **unˈdislocated** *adjective* L19. **undisˈlodged** *adjective* M19. **undisˈmantled** *adjective* M19. **undiˈspersed** *adjective* L16. **undisˈplaced** *adjective* E19. **undisˈproved** *adjective* L16. **undisˈquieted** *adjective* LME. **undiˈssected** *adjective* M19. **unˈdissipated** *adjective* M17. **undiˈssociated** *adjective* (CHEMISTRY) (of a molecule) whole, not split into oppositely charged ions L19.

undis'tempered adjective L16. **undi'stilled** adjective E17. **undi'storted** adjective M17. **undi'straught** adjective L18. **undi'stressed** adjective L16. **undis'trustful** adjective M17. **undi'versified** adjective L17. **undi'vulged** adjective E17. **undoctri'naire** adjective M20. **un'doffed** adjective LME. **un'donnish** adjective M19. **un'doomed** adjective L18. **un'dotted** adjective M19. **un'dowered** adjective (arch.) without a dowry or gift E19. **un'dreaded** adjective M16. **un'dreading** adjective M18. **un'dried** adjective LME. **un'drilled** adjective M19. **un'drivable** adjective L19. **un'driven** adjective E17. **un'drooping** adjective M18. **un'drowned** adjective L16. **un'drugged** adjective M19. **un'drunk** adjective E17. **un'drunken** adjective (rare) OE. **un'dug** adjective M17. **un'dull** adjective LME. **un'dulled** adjective M19. **un'dunged** adjective LME. **un'durable** adjective LME. **un'dyed** adjective M16. **un'dyked** adjective E17. **undy'namic** adjective M20. **un'eager** adjective E19. **un'eared** adjective (arch.) unploughed, untilled OE. **un'earnest** adjective M16. **unecclesi'astical** adjective M19. **unecclesi'astically** adverb M18. **un'echoing** adjective E19. **une'clipsed** adjective M17. **un'edible** adjective inedible L19. **un'edited** adjective E19. **une'ffaceable** adjective E17. **une'ffaced** adjective L17. **une'ffected** adjective L16. **unego'istic** adjective M20. **unego'tistic** adjective M20. **une'laborate** adjective not elaborate; not complicated or ornate; not minutely careful or painstaking: M17. **une'laborated** adjective E19. **une'lastic** adjective E18. **une'lated** adjective E18. **un'elbowed** adjective not elbowed or pushed M18. **une'lectric** adjective L19. **une'lectrified** adjective M18. **un'elegant** adjective (now rare) inelegant L16. **†unelegantly** adverb E17–M18. **un'elevated** adjective not elevated or exalted E17. **†uneligible** adjective ineligible L17–L18. **un'eloquent** adjective M16. **un'eloquently** adverb E17. **une'mancipated** adjective L18. **une'masculated** adjective L18. **unem'banked** adjective L18. **unem'battled** adjective (rare) not having battlements E17. **unem'bellished** adjective M17. **unem'bezzled** adjective M16. **unem'bittered** adjective E18. **unem'bodied** adjective M17. **unem'braced** adjective not embraced or kissed L18. **unem'broidered** adjective (esp. of a narrative) not embroidered M17. **unem'broiled** adjective not embroiled or involved M18. **unem'phatic** adjective E19. **unem'phatically** adverb M19. **unem'pirical** adjective M19. **un'emptiable** adjective (rare) inexhaustible L16. **un'emptied** adjective E17. **unen'acted** adjective (of a bill, law, etc.) not enacted E19. **une'namoured** adjective L18. **unen'chanted** adjective M17. **unen'closed** adjective L17. **unen'compassed** adjective L18. **unen'countered** adjective E19. **unen'couraged** adjective L18. **unen'couraging** adjective M19. **unen'dangered** adjective M17. **unen'dorsed** adjective L17. **unen'dowed** adjective M17. **unen'dued** adjective not endued with a quality, ability, etc. M17. **unener'getic** adjective E19. **unen'feebled** adjective M17. **unen'franchised** adjective L18. **un-'English** adjective M17. **un-'Englishness** noun M20. **unen'hanced** adjective M20. **unen'larged** adjective M18. **unen'livened** adjective L17. **une'nnobled** adjective L18. **unen'riched** adjective E18. **unen'rolled** adjective M19. **unen'tailed** adjective (esp. of an estate) not entailed E18. **unen'thralled** adjective M17. **unen'ticed** adjective L18. **unen'ticing** adjective E20. **unen'titled** adjective M18. **une'numerated** adjective L18. **une'piscopal** adjective not episcopal; not befitting a bishop: M17. **unequi'librated** adjective M19. **une'quipped** adjective L18. **un'equitable** adjective M17. **une'radicated** adjective that has not been eradicated M19. **une'rotic** adjective M20. **un'errable** adjective (long rare or obsolete) = INERRABLE E17. **un'errancy** noun (rare) inerrancy M17. **une'rupted** adjective L18. **une'scapable** adjective inescapable E17. **une'scorted** adjective L18. **une'spied** adjective LME. **une'ssayed** adjective unattempted, untried M17. **une'stablished** adjective M17. **une'steemed** adjective M16. **un'ethical** adjective L19. **un'ethically** adverb E20. **unetymo'logical** adjective not in accordance with etymology L19. **uneu'phonious** adjective L19. **uneu'phoniously** adverb L19. **un-Euro'pean** adjective M19. **une'vaporated** adjective E19. **un'evidenced** adjective not attested or justified M19. **†unevitable** adjective = INEVITABLE adjective LME–E18. **une'volved** adjective L18. **une'xact** adjective = INEXACT M18. **une'xacting** adjective not exacting, undemanding M19. **une'xaggerated** adjective L18. **une'xalted** adjective E17. **une'xampled** adjective unprecedented, unparalleled E17. **un'excavated** adjective L18. **unex'celled** adjective not excelled, unsurpassed L18. **unex'cepted** adjective (a) exceptionless, without exception; †(b) rare not protested at: E17. **unex'ceptional** adjective (a) (now rare) = UNEXCEPTIONABLE; (b) (now rare) admitting of no exception; (c) not exceptional, ordinary: L18. **unex'ceptionally** adverb (a) without exception; (b) in an unexceptional manner: M19. **un'excised** adjective[1] [EXCISE verb[2]] not subject or subjected to an excise M18. **unex'cised** adjective[2] [EXCISE verb[1]] not excised or cut out L19. **unexcita'bility** noun the quality of being unexcitable L19. **unex'citable** adjective not easily excited M19. **unex'cited** adjective (a) not mentally excited or stirred; (b) not affected by outside influence: M18. **unex'citing** adjective not exciting, esp. uninteresting, dull M19. **un'executable** adjective impossible to execute, esp. impossible to put into effect E18. **un'executed** adjective not executed, esp. not carried out or put into effect LME. **une'xemplary** adjective †(a) unexampled, unprecedented; (b) not exemplary: M17. **une'xemplified** adjective (a) unexampled, unprecedented; (b) not appearing in any example or instance: M17. **une'xerted** adjective (esp. of a faculty) unused, unpractised L17. **une'xhibited** adjective L18. **un'exhilarating** adjective E19. **une'xistence** noun = NON-EXISTENCE L16. **une'xistent** adjective (now rare or obsolete) = NON-EXISTENT adjective L17. **une'xisting** adjective non-existent L18. **un'exorcised** adjective M18. **une'xotic** adjective M20. **unex'panded** adjective that has not (been) expanded M17. **unex'panding** adjective not expanding E20. **unex'pansive** adjective M19. **†unexpedient** adjective = INEXPEDIENT LME–M18. **unex'peditated** adjective (now rare or obsolete) L16. **unex'pended** adjective not spent or consumed L16. **unex'pensive** adjective M17. **unex'perimented** adjective †(a) inexperienced, unskilled; (b) not tested or known by experiment: L16. **†unexpert** adjective = INEXPERT adjective LME–L18. **un'expiated** adjective L17. **unex'pired** adjective (of a lease, period of time, etc.) that has not expired L16. **unex'plainable** adjective inexplicable E18. **unex'plainably** adverb L19. **unex'plained** adjective M17. **unex'planatory** adjective that does not provide an explanation E19. **unex'plicable** adjective †(a) indescribable; (b) inexplicable: M16. **unex'plicit** adjective not explicit, esp. vague, ambiguous L18. **unex'plicitly** adverb M19. **unex'ploded** adjective L19. **unex'ploitable** adjective E20. **unex'ploited** adjective L19. **unex'plored** adjective L17. **unex'plosive** adjective E19. **unex'portable** adjective E19. **unex'posed** adjective L17. **unex'poundable** adjective E17. **unex'pounded** adjective M17. **unex'pugnable** adjective (now rare) = INEXPUGNABLE LME. **un'expurgated** adjective (esp. of a text) not expurgated, complete L19. **unex'tended** adjective not extended or stretched out; spec. not occupying space: M17. **unex'tenuated** adjective L18. **unex'tinct** adjective (chiefly fig.) unextinguished E17. **unex'tinguishable** adjective M17. **unex'tinguished** adjective L16. **un'extirpated** adjective M17. **unex'tracted** adjective M17. **un'extricable** adjective (rare) M17. **un'eyed** adjective (poet.) unobserved, unperceived E17. **un'faceable** adjective (a) (dial., rare) irrational, indefensible; (b) that cannot be faced or confronted: E19. **'unfact** noun (a) a false statement, an untruth; (b) POLITICS a fact which is officially denied or disregarded: L19. **un'fain** adjective (long arch. & dial.) ME. **un'fainting** adjective not growing faint or flagging, tireless E17. **un'fallen** adjective M17. **un'fallible** adjective (long rare) infallible L15. **un'fallowed** adjective (long rare or obsolete) E17. **un'famed** adjective not well-known or famous E17. **un'famous** adjective (long rare) (a) not famous; †(b) infamous: LME. **unfa'natical** adjective E19. **un'fancied** adjective not fancied; esp. (a) arch. not imagined or conceived; (b) (of a racehorse etc.) not thought likely to win: M17. **un'fanned** adjective not fanned or kindled M17. **unfan'tastic** adjective L18. **un'farced** adjective E18. **un'farrant** adjective (obsolete exc. Scot.) unattractive, unpleasant E16. **un'fast** adjective (now rare or obsolete) not firm or secure OE. **unfa'stidious** adjective E19. **unfa'stidiously** adverb E20. **un'fathered** adjective (a) having no (known or acknowledged) father, illegitimate; (b) of obscure or unknown origin: L16. **un'fatherliness** noun M19. **un'fatherly** adjective not befitting a father E17. **un'faulty** adjective M16. **un'feathered** adjective featherless (cf. UNFEATHER) E16. **un'featured** adjective without (good) features L17. **un'fecundated** adjective L18. **un'fed** adjective not fed (lit. & fig.) ME. **un'feed** adjective not paid a fee E17. **unfe'licitous** adjective E19. **un'felled** adjective (esp. of a tree) not felled M16. **un'fellowed** adjective L16. **un'felt** adjective L16. **un'fenced** adjective (a) unprotected; (b) not fenced round: M16. **un'festive** adjective M19. **un'fighting** adjective L17. **un'filed** adjective[1] (long obsolete exc. dial.) [FILE verb[1]] undefiled, unfouled ME. **un'filed** adjective[2] [FILE verb[2]] (a) not reduced or smoothed by filing; (b) fig. unpolished, rude: L16. **un'filed** adjective[3] [FILE verb[3]] (of a document etc.) not arranged (as) in a file; not filed away: L16. **un'filleted** adjective E19. **un'filtered** adjective L19. **un'findable** adjective LME. **un'fine** adjective (now rare or obsolete) not fine LME. **un'fined** adjective (of wine etc.) not fined or cleared L15. **un'fingered** adjective (a) rare fingerless; (b) not touched with the fingers, unhandled: E17. **un'flagging** adjective tireless, persistent E18. **un'flaggingly** adverb M19. **un'flanked** adjective (MILITARY) not guarded or defended on the flank M16. **un'flattened** adjective L18. **un'flattered** adjective L16. **un'flattering** adjective L16. **un'flatteringly** adverb L19. **un'flavoured** adjective M19. **un'flawed** adjective not flawed or cracked M17. **un'flecked** adjective not flecked or dappled M19. **un'fleshly** adjective spiritual, immaterial M19. **un'flickering** adjective M19. **un'flinching** adjective E18. **un'flinchingly** adverb M19. **un'flooded** adjective L20. **un'floored** adjective E19. **un'flourishing** adjective L18. **un'flown** adjective that has not flown or been flown L18. **un'fluctuating** adjective E18. **un'flurried** adjective M19. **un'flushed** adjective [FLUSH verb[1]] M18. **un'fluted** adjective not having grooves or flutes M19. **un'flyable** adjective unable to be flown; unsuitable for flying: L20. **un'focused** adjective L19. **†unfoiled** adjective not coated or backed with foil M17–M18. **un'folded** adjective[1] (of a sheep) not enclosed in a fold L16. **un'folded** adjective[2] not folded or arranged in folds L17. **un'foliaged** adjective L18. **un'foliated** adjective (ARCHITECTURE) not foliated M19. **un'followed** adjective E16. **un'fond** adjective E19. **un'foolish** adjective E17. **un'footed** adjective untrodden E19. **unfor'bid** adjective (arch.) = UNFORBIDDEN M17. **unfor'bidden** adjective M16. **un'fordable** adjective E17. **unfore'boding** adjective E18. **unfore'knowable** adjective impossible to know in advance, unforeseeable L17. **unfore'known** adjective M17. **unfore'thought** adjective E17. **unfore'told** adjective M19. **unfore'warned** adjective M17. **un'forgeable** adjective unable to be forged or counterfeited M19. **un'forged** adjective not forged, esp. genuine LME. **un'formal** adjective = INFORMAL LME. **un'formalized** adjective M19. **un'formatted** adjective M20. **un'formidable** adjective M17. **un'formulated** adjective M19. **unfor'saken** adjective M17. **un'fortified** adjective E16. **unfossi'liferous** adjective M19. **un'fossilized** adjective M19. **un'fought** adjective LME. **un'foughten** adjective (long arch.) unfought LME. **un'fouled** adjective not fouled, undefiled LME. **un'found** adjective L16. **un'fractionated** adjective M20. **un'fractured** adjective not fractured or broken M18. **un'franchised** adjective unenfranchised M17. **un'franked** adjective (of a letter, parcel, etc.) not franked M18. **un-'French** adjective E19. **†unfrequency** noun = INFREQUENCY E17–M19. **un'frequent** adjective (now rare) E17. **unfre'quented** adjective (of a place) not frequented L16. **un'frequently** adverb (now rare) M17. **un'fretted** adjective (a) not eaten or worn away; (b) not distressed or worried: L16. **un'frighted** adjective E17. **un'frightened** adjective L17. **un'frosted** adjective not affected by frost L18. **un'fructed** adjective (HERALDRY) L17. **un'fructuous** adjective (long obsolete exc. fig., now rare) unfruitful LME. **un'frugal** adjective E17. **un'frustrable** adjective (rare) E18. **un'fuelled** adjective not supplied with fuel L17. **un'fumed** adjective (rare) that has not (been) fumed M17. **un'functional** adjective L19. **un'funded** adjective (esp. of a debt) not funded L18. **un'furred** adjective (rare) not lined, trimmed, or provided with fur LME. **un'furrowed** adjective M16. **un'fused** adjective[1] [FUSE verb[1]] not fused, melted, or joined L18. **un'fused** adjective[2] [FUSE verb[2]] not provided with a fuse L19. **un'galled** adjective L16. **un'gardened** adjective not cultivated as a garden E17. **un'garmented** adjective (chiefly poet.) undressed, unclothed L18. **un'garrisoned** adjective not occupied by a garrison M17. **un'gartered** adjective L16. **un'gated** adjective M20. **un'gaudy** adjective not gaudy or garish L18. **un'gauged** adjective not gauged or measured; unevaluated: M18. **un'gay** adjective M20. **un'gazed** adjective (poet.) not gazed at or upon E19. **unge'latinizable** adjective (rare) E19. **un'generalizable** adjective M19. **un'generated** adjective E17. **ungene'rosity** noun ungenerousness, meanness M18. **un'generous** adjective not generous or magnanimous; illiberal, mean: M17. **un'generously** adverb E18. **un'generousness** noun M18. **†ungenitured** adjective (rare, Shakes.) impotent: only in E17. **un'genuine** adjective M17. **un'genuineness** noun M19. **ungeo'metrical** adjective (long rare) L16. **un-'German** adjective not German; esp. uncharacteristic of Germans or Germany: M19. **un'germinated** adjective L19. **unget-'at-able** adjective (colloq.) inaccessible, unreachable M19. **un'gettable** adjective that cannot be got; unattainable: M16. **un'ghostly** adjective (a) arch. unspiritual; (b) not of or pertaining to or resembling a ghost: E16. **un'giddy** adjective E17. **un'gimmicky** adjective M20. **un'girdled** adjective not surrounded (as) with a girdle; not wearing a girdle: L16. **un'girthed** adjective not surrounded or secured (as) by a girth E17. **un'glaciated** adjective not covered with, or not modified by, glaciers or ice sheets L19. **un'glad** adjective not glad; unhappy, sorry: OE. **un'gladly** adverb ME. **un'glamorous** adjective M20. **un'glazed** adjective not glazed L16. **un'gleaned** adjective not gleaned, uncollected L18. **un'glittering** adjective E19. **un'glorified** adjective not glorified LME. **un'glorious** adjective (now rare or obsolete) = INGLORIOUS adjective LME. **un'glossed** adjective[1] (a) poet. not glazed or glossy; (b) not veiled, not glossed over: E19. **un'glossed** adjective[2] (of a word or text) not provided with a gloss or glosses M19. **un'gloved** adjective not wearing a glove or gloves E17. **un'glutted** adjective not glutted or replete; ungratified: E19. **un'gnawed** adjective M19. **un'goaded** adjective L18. **un'godlike** adjective M17. **un'golden** adjective not golden; ungilded: M20. **un'gone** adjective not (yet) gone or departed L15. **†ungored** adjective (rare, Shakes.) not gored or pierced: only in E17. **un'gorged** adjective not gorged, not satiated E18. **un'gospelled** adjective (rare) not believing in or having been taught the gospel L17. **un'gowned** adjective not wearing a gown E17. **un'graded** adjective not graded; not divided according to grades: M19. **un'grafted** adjective (esp. of a plant) not grafted M17. **un'graithed** adjective (obsolete exc. dial.) not ready, not prepared; not equipped: ME. **un'granted** adjective not granted or conferred; not given a grant: L16. **un'grassed** adjective not sown or covered with grass M19. **un'gratified** adjective E17. **un'graven** adjective not engraved or carved LME. **un'grazed** adjective E20. **un-'Grecian** adjective un-Greek; esp. (of a nose) not Grecian in outline: L18. **un'greedy** adjective M20. **un'greeted** adjective not greeted or saluted; not welcomed: E17. **ungre'garious** adjective E19. **un'grieved** adjective not grieved; not accompanied by grieving: L17. **un'gritted** adjective (esp. of an icy road etc.) not gritted L20. **un'groomed** adjective not groomed; (of appearance etc.) not carefully attended to: E19. **un'grooved** adjective having no groove or grooves M20. **unguaran'teed** adjective not guaranteed; unsecured: M19. **un'guerdoned** adjective (now arch. & poet.) unrewarded, uncompensated LME. **un'gutted** adjective (esp. of a fish) not gutted E18. **un'gyved** adjective (arch.) unfettered, unshackled E17. **unha'bitual** adjective not habitual; not customary: M19. **unha'bituated** adjective not habitual; unaccustomed to: L18. **un'had** adjective (long obsolete exc. north.) not obtained LME. **un'hailed** adjective (chiefly poet.) not hailed or saluted; not given recognition: E18. **un'haltered** adjective not haltered M20. **un'harboured** adjective (rare, poet.) having or providing no shelter LME. **un'harrowed** adjective not harrowed; esp. (of ground) not broken up L16. **un'hassled** adjective L20. **un'hatted** adjective not wearing a hat M19. **un'hazarded** adjective not hazarded; not staked or risked: L16. **un'hazardous** adjective L17. **un'healable** adjective incapable of being healed; incurable: LME. **un'healed** adjective not (yet) healed ME. **un'heated** adjective not heated or warmed L17. **un'heavenly** adjective M18. **un'hedged** adjective not hedged or fenced M17. **un'held** adjective E17. **un'-Hellenized**, **un'hellenized** adjective E20. **un'heralded** adjective not heralded; unannounced: M19. **un'herded** adjective (esp. of sheep, cattle, etc.) not herded L18. **un'heritable** adjective (a) rare unable to inherit; (b) not inheritable: M16. **un'hip** adjective (slang) unaware of current fashions M20. **un'hired** adjective E17. **un'hit** adjective not hit or struck E16. **un'hollowed** adjective not made hollow E17. **un'homed** adjective not provided with a home; homeless: E19. **un'honoured** adjective not honoured or revered E16. **un'hooded** adjective not wearing or covered by a hood L16. **un'hoodwinked** adjective not hoodwinked; not deluded or deceived: M17. **un'hopped** adjective not hopped; esp. (of a drink) not made or flavoured with hops: E18. **un'horned** adjective (esp. of an animal) not having a horn or horns LME. **un'hosed** adjective (long obsolete exc. poet.) not wearing hose ME. **un'hospitable** adjective = INHOSPITABLE adjective E17. **un'hostile** adjective not hostile (to) E18. **un'hydrolysed** adjective (CHEMISTRY) that has not undergone hydrolysis M20. **un'hymned** adjective (a) not celebrated in a hymn; (b) not accompanied by a hymn or hymns: M19. **unhypo'critical** adjective M19. **unhy'sterical** adjective not hysterical; calm: L19. **uni'dea'd** adjective not having an idea, lacking in ideas M18. **unidio'matic** adjective E19. **uni'dolatrous** adjective M19. **unig'nited** adjective L18. **unig'norable** adjective unable to be ignored; that demands attention: M20. **unig'norably** adverb in a way that cannot be ignored M20. **uni'lluminated** adjective L16. **uni'lluminating** adjective L19. **uni'llumined** adjective L18. **uni'llusioned** adjective having no illusions M20. **un'illustrated** adjective not illustrated, without illustrations L18. **uni'llustrative** adjective not illustrative or explanatory E19. **un'imaged** adjective without a form or image (lit. & fig.) M17. **unim'bued** adjective L18. **un'imitable** adjective (now rare or obsolete) L16. **un'imitated** adjective E17. **un'imitative** adjective E19. **uni'mmediate** adjective E19. **uni'mmediately** adverb E19. **uni'mmersed** adjective L18. **uni'mmortal** adjective M17. **uni'mmortalized** adjective L18. **unim'paired** adjective L16. **unim'parted** adjective M17. **unim'passioned** adjective M18. **unim'perious** adjective L18. **un'implicated** adjective E19. **unim'plored** adjective not implored or asked for M17. **unim'portunate** adjective M18. **unim'portuned** adjective E17. **unim'pugned** adjective L18. **unim'pulsive** adjective L18. **unin'carnate** adjective L17. **unin'censed** adjective L16. **uninci'dental** adjective L18. **unin'cisive** adjective L19. **unin'cited** adjective M17. **unin'cluded** adjective L18. **unin'creasable** adjective M17. **unin'creased** adjective L18. **un'incubated** adjective M19. **unin'debted** adjective L17.

For other words beginning with *un-* see the entry for **un-**[2] and the main alphabetic sequence of entries

unˈindexed *adjective* M19. **un-ˈIndian** *adjective* not characteristic of the inhabitants of India M19. **unˈindicated** *adjective* L18. **uninˈdicted** *adjective* L18. **uninˈdulged** *adjective* L18. **uninˈdulgent** *adjective* M18. **uninˈdustrialized** *adjective* M20. **uninˈdustrious** *adjective* L16. **uninˈfested** *adjective* L17. **uninˈfringed** *adjective* E17. **uninˈgenious** *adjective* (*a*) not ingenuous; (*b*) not ingenious, lacking in ingenuity: M17. **uninˈheritable** *adjective* †(*a*) incapable of inheriting; (*b*) incapable of being inherited: E17. **uninˈhumed** *adjective* E17. **uninˈjectable** *adjective* M19. **uninˈjected** *adjective* M20. **unˈinnocence** *noun* (*rare*) want of innocence L16. **unˈinnocent** *adjective* L19. **uniˈnoculated** *adjective* L18. **uninˈquired** *adjective* not inquired *after, into* E18. **uninˈquiring** *adjective* E19. **uninˈquisitive** *adjective* E17. **uninˈscribed** *adjective* E18. **uninˈspected** *adjective* L18. **uninˈsulted** *adjective* M18. **unˈintegrated** *adjective* M19. **uninterˈcepted** *adjective* M17. **uninterˈmixed** *adjective* L16. **uninˈterpretable** *adjective* E17. **uninˈterpreted** *adjective* M17. **uninˈterred** *adjective* M17. **uninˈterrogated** *adjective* E19. **unˈintimate** *adjective* E20. **uninˈtimidated** *adjective* M18. **uninˈtoxicating** *adjective* L18. **unintroˈduced** *adjective* M18. **uniˈnured** *adjective* M17. **uninˈvaded** *adjective* M17. **uninˈverted** *adjective* M18. **uninˈvested** *adjective* L18. **uninˈvestigable** *adjective* L17. **uninˈvestigated** *adjective* E19. **uninˈvoked** *adjective* E18. **uninˈvolved** *adjective* L18. **unionized** /ʌnˈʌɪənʌɪzd/ *adjective* not ionized E20. **un-ˈIrish** *adjective* not characteristic of the Irish E19. **unˈironed** *adjective* not fitted with iron; not bound in irons; (of clothes etc.) not pressed or smoothed with an iron: LME. **uniˈrradiated** *adjective* E19. **unˈirrigated** *adjective* M19. **unˈirritated** *adjective* (*rare*) M17. **unˈirritating** *adjective* L18. **un-Isˈlamic** *adjective* not characteristic of Islam, not in accordance with Islamic principles M20. **unˈissued** *adjective* M17. **uniˈtalicized** *adjective* L19. **unˈjacketed** *adjective* E20. **unˈjaded** *adjective* L18. **unˈjarring** *adjective* E17. **unˈjaundiced** *adjective* L18. **unˈjealous** *adjective* L17. **un-ˈJewish** *adjective* not characteristic of the Jews; not in accordance with Jewish principles: E19. **unˈjolly** *adjective* L18. **unˈjolted** *adjective* L18. **unˈjudged** *adjective* M17. **unˈjuicy** *adjective* E18. **unˈkeeled** *adjective* (*a*) (of water) not sailed upon; (*b*) not having a keel: E19. **unˈkerchiefed** *adjective* not wearing or covered by a kerchief L18. **unˈkilled** *adjective* not killed, still alive M16. **unˈkilned** *adjective* (*rare*) M17. **unˈkindled** *adjective* E16. **unˈkindred** *adjective* not kindred, not allied in nature or properties E18. **unˈkinkable** *adjective* incapable of being kinked or twisted M20. **unˈkissed** *adjective* not kissed; without being kissed: LME. **unˈknowledgeable** *adjective* (*a*) *rare* unknowable; (*b*) not knowledgeable, ill-informed: E20. **unˈkosher** *adjective* E20. **unlaˈborious** *adjective* M17. **unˈlacquered** *adjective* L18. **unˈladylike** *adjective* E19. **unˈlamed** *adjective* (*rare*) not crippled L15. **unlaˈmented** *adjective* L16. **unˈlanded** *adjective* not possessed of land L15. **unˈlasting** *adjective* (*rare*) L16. **unˈlaudable** *adjective* M16. **unˈlaunched** *adjective* L18. **unˈlaundered** *adjective* L19. **unˈleached** *adjective* not leached or subjected to percolation E19. **unˈleafed** *adjective* (of a tree etc.) not leafed, without leaves M19. **unˈleal** *adjective* (*arch.*) unfaithful, disloyal, dishonest ME. **unˈlearnable** *adjective* M19. **unˈleased** *adjective* not held or let on lease; not having a lease E18. **unˈlectured** *adjective* not lectured to or on L16. **unˈlegal** *adjective* M17. **unleˈnited** *adjective* (PHONETICS) not lenited M20. **unˈlessened** *adjective* M18. **unˈlessoned** *adjective* not taught or lessoned M16. **unˈlevied** *adjective* (now *rare*) LME. **unˈliable** *adjective* (now *rare*) E17. **unˈliberated** *adjective* M19. **unˈliftable** *adjective* L18. **unˈlifted** *adjective* L18. **unˈlineal** *adjective* L16. **unˈliteral** *adjective* (*rare*) M19. **unˈliterally** *adverb* M18. **unˈliterariness** *noun* M20. **unˈliterary** *adjective* E19. **unˈliterate** *adjective* †(*a*) illiterate; (*b*) not interested in reading or literature, unliterary: M16. **unˈlittered** *adjective* M18. **unliˈturgical** *adjective* M19. **unloˈcatable** *adjective* L19. **unloˈcated** *adjective* M18. **unlocoˈmotive** *adjective* (*rare*) not inclined to travel E19. **unˈlogical** *adjective* illogical, not involving logic M17. **unˈlonely** *adjective* M20. **unˈlopped** *adjective* L16. **unˈloverlike** *adjective* L18. **unˈlovesome** *adjective* (*obsolete* exc. *Scot.*) not lovesome ME. **unˈloyal** *adjective* L16. **unˈlubricated** *adjective* L18. **unˈlucid** *adjective* M19. **unˈlucrative** *adjective* L18. **unˈluminous** *adjective* L18. **unˈlustrous** *adjective* E18. **unluˈxuriant** *adjective* E18. **unluˈxurious** *adjective* E18. **unmaˈcadamized** *adjective* M19. **unmagˈnetic** *adjective* E19. **unˈmagnetized** *adjective* M19. **unˈmailable** *adjective* (*US*) L19. **unˈmaimed** *adjective* L15. **unmaˈlicious** *adjective* E17. **unmaˈliciously** *adverb* L19. **unmaˈlignant** *adjective* (*rare*) M17. **unˈmalted** *adjective* M17. **unˈmangled** *adjective* not mutilated or disfigured M16. **unˈmanifest** *adjective* = UNMANIFESTED M16. **unˈmanifested** *adjective* not revealed or evident L17. **unmanuˈfactured** *adjective* E18. **unmanuˈmitted** *adjective* not released from slavery or bondage M17. **unmaˈnured** *adjective* (*a*) (of land) uncultivated, untilled; (*b*) not provided or enriched with manure: L16. **unˈmapped** *adjective* E19. **unˈmarketable** *adjective* M17. **unˈmarred** *adjective* not marred or ruined ME. **unˈmartial** *adjective* not martial, unwarlike E17. **unˈmartyred** *adjective* L16. **unˈmasterable** *adjective* (*rare*) E17. **unˈmastered** *adjective* M16. **unˈmasticated** *adjective* E19. **unˈmated** *adjective* (*a*) unmatched, unrivalled; (*b*) without a mate or partner: E17. **unmaˈterial** *adjective* immaterial LME. **unmaˈternal** *adjective* E19. **unmatheˈmatical** *adjective* E18. **unmaˈtriculated** *adjective* M17. **unmaˈtured** *adjective* not yet matured LME. **unˈmediated** *adjective* M17. **unˈmedical** *adjective* E19. **unˈmeditated** *adjective* (now *rare*) E17. **unˈmeditative** *adjective* M19. **unˈmellowed** *adjective* L16. **unˈmenaced** *adjective* L18. **unˈmerchantable** *adjective* E17. **unˈmerged** *adjective* E19. **unˈmetalled** *adjective* (esp. of a road) not metalled M19. **unmeˈtallic** *adjective* M18. **unmetaˈmorphosed** *adjective* E17. **unmetaˈphysical** *adjective* L17. **unˈmeted** *adjective* unmeasured M19. **unˈmetered** *adjective* not measured by means of a meter; not provided with a meter: E20. **unˈmetrical** *adjective* not composed in or conforming to metre L18. **unˈmighty** *adjective* (long *arch.*) without might or strength; weak, feeble, powerless: OE. **unˈmild** *adjective* (long *arch.*) not mild or gentle; harsh, rough, unkind: OE. **unˈmilked** *adjective* M17. **unˈmilled** *adjective* M16. **unˈmined** *adjective* not extracted by mining M19. **unˈmineralized** *adjective* M19. **unˈmingled** *adjective* not mingled or mixed M16. **unˈmingling** *adjective* M17. **unˈminished** *adjective* (*arch.*) not diminished M16. **unminiˈsterial** *adjective* E18. **unˈminted** *adjective* E17. **unˈminuted** *adjective* L18. **unmiˈraculous** *adjective* M18. **unˈmirthful** *adjective* E19. **unˈmirthfully** *adverb* L19. **unˈmiscible** *adjective* immiscible L18. **unmisˈgiving** *adjective* without misgivings or uncertainty L17. **unmisˈgivingly** *adverb* M19. **unmisˈtrusting** *adjective* L16. **unˈmitred** *adjective* L17. **unˈmoaned** *adjective* not moaned for, unlamented M16. **unˈmocked** *adjective* M17. **unˈmockingly** *adverb* L19. **unˈmodern** *adjective* not modern, traditional M18. **unˈmodernized** *adjective* not modernized, retaining original features L18. **unˈmodish** *adjective* unfashionable M17. **unˈmodulated** *adjective* E19. **unˈmoist** *adjective* E17. **unˈmoistened** *adjective* E17. **unˈmollified** *adjective* E17. **unˈmolten** *adjective* (*arch.*) not melted E16. **unmoˈmentous** *adjective* E19. **unmoˈnastic** *adjective* M19. **unˈmoneyed** *adjective* L17. **unmoˈnopolized** *adjective* M18. **unˈmoored** *adjective* not moored, *esp.* freely floating or flying L17. **unˈmortal** *adjective* (now *rare*) immortal M16. **unˈmortared** *adjective* not fixed or joined with mortar M17. **unˈmortgaged** *adjective* M17. **unˈmortified** *adjective* LME. **unˈmortifiedness** *noun* M17. **un-Moˈsaic** *adjective* not pertaining to Moses or his writings M17. **unˈmotivated** *adjective* E20. **unˈmotived** *adjective* L18. **unˈmourned** *adjective* not mourned or lamented M17. **unˈmowed** *adjective* M18. **unˈmown** *adjective* M16. **unˈmuddied** *adjective* M17. **unˈmurdered** *adjective* L16. **unˈmuscled** *adjective* M18. **unˈmuscular** *adjective* E19. **unˈmutilated** *adjective* L18. **unˈmyelinated** *adjective* E20. **unmyˈsterious** *adjective* M18. **unˈnapped** *adjective* (of cloth) without a nap E17. **unˈnational** *adjective* M18. **unˈneat** *adjective* M17. **unˈneatness** *noun* M19. **unneˈcessitated** *adjective* M17. **unˈneutral** *adjective* L18. **unˈneutralized** *adjective* M18. **unˈnimble** *adjective* M16. **unˈnimbly** *adverb* E17. **unˈnotched** *adjective* M16. **unˈnoteworthy** *adjective* L19. **unˈnotified** *adjective* L18. **unˈnurtured** *adjective* M16. **unnuˈtritious** *adjective* M19. **unˈnutritive** *adjective* L18. **unoˈbedient** *adjective* LME. **unoˈbeyed** *adjective* L16. **unobˈjective** *adjective* M19. **unobˈnoxious** *adjective* E17. **unobˈscured** *adjective* M17. **unobˈsequious** *adjective* L18. **unobˈsequiousness** *noun* M17. **unˈobstinate** *adjective* M17. **unˈobvious** *adjective* M17. **unˈobviously** *adverb* M20. **unˈobviousness** *noun* M20. **unˈoffered** *adjective* E16. **unˈofficered** *adjective* M17. **unˈofficerlike** *adjective* E19. **unoˈfficious** *adjective* E17. **unˈoften** *adverb* (*rare*) (with neg.) infrequently, seldom M18. **unˈoiled** *adjective* E18. **unˈoperable** *adjective* †(*a*) not able to be done; (*b*) MEDICINE inoperable: M17. **unˈoperated** *adjective* (chiefly MEDICINE) not having been operated on or *on* E19. **unˈoperating** *adjective* E18. †**unoperative** *adjective* inoperative M17–E19. **unoˈppressed** *adjective* L16. **unoˈppressive** *adjective* M17. **unˈordinary** *adjective* M16. **unorˈganic** *adjective* E19. **unoriˈental** *adjective* E19. **unˈoriented** *adjective* M20. **unˈossified** *adjective* E18. **unoverˈlooked** *adjective* M20. **unoverˈthrown** *adjective* M16. †**unowed** *adjective* *rare* (Shakes.) unowned: only in L16. **unˈowned** *adjective* (*a*) not possessed as property, without an owner or possessor; (*b*) unacknowledged, unadmitted: E17. **unˈoxidized** *adjective* E19. **unˈoxygenated** *adjective* L18. **unˈpaced** *adjective* L18. **unpaˈcific** *adjective* L18. **unˈpacified** *adjective* L16. **unˈpacifiedly** *adverb* M18. **unˈpackaged** *adjective* not made into or enclosed in a package M20. **unˈpadlocked** *adjective* L17. **unˈpagan** *adjective* E17. **unˈpaged** *adjective* with pages not numbered L19. **unˈpaired** *adjective* not arranged in pairs; not forming one of a pair: L16. **unˈpalled** *adjective* not palled or jaded M18. **unˈpalliated** *adjective* L18. **unˈpalpable** *adjective* (now *rare*) impalpable M16. **unˈpalsied** *adjective* L18. **unˈpampered** *adjective* L18. **unˈparagoned** *adjective* (now *arch.* or *poet.*) unequalled, matchless E17. **unˈparalyzed** *adjective* M19. **unˈparcelled** *adjective* L18. **unˈpared** *adjective* ME. **unˈparented** *adjective*[1] having no (known or acknowledged) parent L19. **unˈparriable** *adjective* not able to be parried E19. **unˈparted** *adjective* M16. **unparˈticipated** *adjective* (now *rare*) L17. **unparˈticipating** *adjective* L18. **unˈpastoral** *adjective* L18. **unˈpatched** *adjective* L18. **unˈpatentable** *adjective* M19. **unˈpatented** *adjective* E18. **unˈpathed** *adjective* pathless E17. **unpaˈthetic** *adjective* L18. **unˈpatronized** *adjective* E17. **unˈpausing** *adjective* M19. **unˈpausingly** *adverb* L19. **unpaˈvilioned** *adjective* L18. **unˈpawned** *adjective* M17. **unpeˈdantic** *adjective* L18. **unˈpedigreed** *adjective* E19. **unˈpeered** *adjective* unequalled, unrivalled E17. **unˈpenitent** *adjective* M16. **unˈpensioned** *adjective* E18. **unˈpent** *adjective* E19. **unˈpeppered** *adjective* M17. **unˈperforated** *adjective* L17. **unˈperfumed** *adjective* E18. **unˈperilous** *adjective* E17. **unˈperjured** *adjective* L17. **unˈpermanency** *noun* M19. **unˈpermanent** *adjective* M17. **unperˈmissible** *adjective* L18. **unperˈmitted** *adjective* L16. **unperˈsonified** *adjective* L18. **unperˈspicuous** *adjective* L18. **unˈpestered** *adjective* L16. **unˈpetticoated** *adjective* E19. **unphoˈnetic** *adjective* M19. **unˈphoney** *adjective* (*colloq.*) genuine M20. **unˈphotographed** *adjective* E20. **unˈphrased** *adjective* not expressed in phrases or words; not phrased as music: M17. **unˈpickled** *adjective* E17. **unˈpigmented** *adjective* lacking pigment L19. **unˈpillowed** *adjective* not provided with a pillow M17. **unˈpiloted** *adjective* (of a ship etc.) lacking a pilot L18. †**unpinked** *adjective* (*rare*, Shakes.) not pinked or pierced: only in L16. **unˈplagued** *adjective* M16. **unˈplain** *adjective* (long *rare*) LME. **unˈplaned** *adjective* L18. **unˈplastered** *adjective* not covered with plaster M17. **unˈplastic** *adjective* (*a*) unable to be shaped or moulded; (*b*) *rare* not made of plastic: L18. **unˈplasticized** *adjective* M20. **un-Plaˈtonic**, **unplaˈtonic** *adjective* M18. **unˈplausible** *adjective* implausible L16. **unˈplausibly** *adverb* M18. †**unplausive** *adjective* (*rare*, Shakes.) unapproving: only in E17. **unˈpleadable** *adjective* †(*a*) *rare* on which legal pleadings are not allowed; (*b*) unable to be pleaded or urged: M16. **unˈpleated** *adjective* E17. **unˈpledged** *adjective* E17. **unˈploughed**, *-**plowed** *adjective* L16. **unˈplucked** *adjective* M16. **unˈplundered** *adjective* M17. **unˈpolarized** *adjective* E19. **unpoˈlemical** *adjective* M20. **unpoˈliceable** *adjective* L20. **unpoˈliced** *adjective* L18. **unˈpollarded** *adjective* M19. **unˈpolymerized** *adjective* L19. **unˈpompous** *adjective* M19. **unpornoˈgraphic** *adjective* M20. **unporˈtentous** *adjective* E19. **unˈposed** *adjective* (esp. of a picture) not posed M20. **unˈposh** *adjective* (*colloq.*) L20. †**unpossessing** *adjective* (*rare*, Shakes.): only in E17. **unˈposted** *adjective* (chiefly MILITARY) not appointed to a post or command L18. **unpotable** /-ˈpəʊt-/ *adjective* undrinkable M19. **unpreˈcarious** *adjective* E18. **unˈprecious** *adjective* (*rare*) L16. **unpreˈcipitated** *adjective* M17. **unˈprefaced** *adjective* L18. **unˈpregnant** *adjective* E17. **unpreˈlatical** *adjective* M17. **unpreˈoccupied** *adjective* L18. **unˈprescient** *adjective* M19. **unpreˈscribed** *adjective* M17. **unpreˈsentable** *adjective* E19. **unpreˈsented** *adjective* E16. **unpreˈserved** *adjective* M17. **unˈpressurized** *adjective* M20. **unˈprickly** *adjective* M17. **unˈprimed** *adjective*[1] that has not been primed L18. **unˈprimed** *adjective*[2] not having a prime as a superscript L19. **unˈprimitive** *adjective* not primitive; of later development: E18. **unˈprinceliness** *noun* unprincely character M19. **unˈprincely** *adjective* not princely; not befitting or characteristic of a prince: M16. **unˈprivileged** *adjective* L16. **unˈprobed** *adjective* L18. **unproˈclaimed** *adjective* M17. **unproˈcurable** *adjective* unobtainable E17. **unproˈfaned** *adjective* M17. **unˈprogrammable** *adjective* unable to be programmed L20. **unˈprogrammed** *adjective* M20. **unproˈjected** *adjective* (now *rare*) not (yet) thought of M17. **unproleˈtarian** *adjective* M20. **unproˈlific** *adjective* L17. **unˈpromulgated** *adjective* L18. **unˈprone** *adjective* not predisposed or inclined *to do* E17. **unˈpropertied** *adjective* L18. **unproˈphetic** *adjective* E18. **unˈprosecuted** *adjective* M17. **unˈprostituted** *adjective* E18. **unproˈvisioned** *adjective* L18. **unpruˈdential** *adjective* M17. **unˈpublic** *adjective* M17. **unˈpublicized** *adjective* M20. **unˈpuckered** *adjective* L18. **unpugˈnacious** *adjective* M20. **unˈpulled** *adjective* LME. **unˈpulverized** *adjective* L18. **unˈpumped** *adjective* not provided with a pump; not extracted with a pump: M17. **unˈpuncturable** *adjective* L19. **unˈpurchasable** *adjective* E17. **unˈpurchased** *adjective* LME. **unˈpurified** *adjective* L16. **unˈpuritan** *adjective* not puritanical; not like that of the Puritans: M20. **unpuriˈtanical** *adjective* not puritanical E20. **unˈpurposed** *adjective* having no purpose L16. **unpurˈsued** *adjective* LME. **unˈpushy** *adjective* (*colloq.*) M20. **unˈputrefied** *adjective* L16. **unˈquailed** *adjective* undaunted L16. **unˈquailing** *adjective* that does not quail M19. **unˈquantifiable** *adjective* L19. **unˈquantified** *adjective* M19. **unˈquarrelsome** *adjective* M19. **unˈquarried** *adjective* L18. **unˈquelled** *adjective* LME. **unˈquick** *adjective* (*rare*) (*a*) lifeless, dead; (*b*) not fast, lively, or active: LME. **unˈquickened** *adjective* E17. **unˈquivering** *adjective* E19. **unˈraced** *adjective* not having taken part in a race M20. **unˈrailed** *adjective* L18. **unˈraised** *adjective* E16. **unˈrallied** *adjective* M17. **unˈransacked** *adjective* E16. **unˈransomed** *adjective* M16. **unˈraptured** *adjective* M18. **unˈrateable** *adjective* E17. **unˈrated** *adjective* not rated; not having received a rating or assessment; *colloq.* not highly esteemed: M17. **unˈratified** *adjective* E17. **unˈrationed** *adjective* E20. **unˈrattled** *adjective* (*colloq.*) not flustered or alarmed M20. **unˈravaged** *adjective* L18. **unˈravished** *adjective* E17. **unˈrazored** *adjective* unshaven M17. **unreˈacted** *adjective* (CHEMISTRY) that has not reacted M20. **unreˈactive** *adjective* (esp. of a substance) not reactive, inert M20. **unreacˈtivity** *noun* unreactive quality, lack of reactivity M20. **unˈreaped** *adjective* not (yet) reaped L16. **unreˈbellious** *adjective* L16. **unreˈbukeable** *adjective* M16. **unreˈbuked** *adjective* LME. **unreˈciprocated** *adjective* M19. **unreˈcited** *adjective* (long *rare*) not told or recounted L15. **unrecoˈllected** *adjective* M18. **unˈrecompensed** *adjective* LME. **unreˈcounted** *adjective* (long *rare*) L15. †**unrecuring** *adjective* (*rare*, Shakes.) not admitting of recovery: only in L16. **unˈreferenced** *adjective* lacking a reference L19. **unreˈfracted** *adjective* M17. **unreˈfrained** *adjective* (now *rare*) M16. **unreˈfrigerated** *adjective* M20. **unreˈfusable** *adjective* L17. **unreˈfusing** *adjective* L16. **unreˈfutable** *adjective* L16. **unreˈfuted** *adjective* L16. **unreˈgainable** *adjective* M17. **unˈregal** *adjective* E17. **unˈregimented** *adjective* L17. **unˈregistered** *adjective* E17. **unreˈgretted** *adjective* L17. **unˈregular** *adjective* (chiefly *dial.*) E17. **unˈregulated** *adjective* E18. **unreˈjectable** *adjective* E19. **unreˈjected** *adjective* M18. **unreˈjoiced** *adjective* E19. **unreˈjoicing** *adjective* E18. **unreˈlinquished** *adjective* L18. **unreˈlished** *adjective* L16. **unreˈluctant** *adjective* M18. **unreˈluctantly** *adverb* M17. **unreˈmaining** *adjective* E19. **unˈremedied** *adjective* LME. **unˈrendered** *adjective* not rendered; (of fat) not melted; (of stone or brickwork) without a coating of plaster: L18. **unreˈnormalizable** *adjective* not permitting of renormalization M20. **unreˈnowned** *adjective* without renown or fame L16. **unˈrent** *adjective* not torn or lacerated L16. **unreˈpaid** *adjective* not repaid M17. **unreˈpayable** *adjective* E18. **unreˈpelled** *adjective* L18. **unreˈplenished** *adjective* M16. **unreˈpressed** *adjective* L16. **unreˈprinted** *adjective* L19. **unreˈpublican** *adjective* L19. **unreˈpugnant** *adjective* L16. **unreˈpulsive** *adjective* M19. **unˈreputable** *adjective* (long *rare*) not reputable L17. **unreˈquested** *adjective* not requested or asked for L16. **unˈrequisite** *adjective* not requisite or necessary L16. **unreˈscinded** *adjective* E18. **unˈrescued** *adjective* (*rare*) LME. **unreˈsembling** *adjective* L16. **unreˈsigned** *adjective* M17. **unreˈsilient** *adjective* M20. **unrespirable** /ʌnˈrɛspɪrəb(ə)l, -rɪˈspʌɪrəb(ə)l/ *adjective* E19. **unˈrespited** *adjective* L16. **unreˈsponsible** *adjective* †(*a*) lacking substance or standing; (*b*) irresponsible: M17. **unreˈstored** *adjective* LME. **unreˈtaliated** *adjective* L17. **unreˈtarded** *adjective* E17. **unreˈtentive** *adjective* M18. **unˈreticent** *adjective* L19. **unreˈtouched** *adjective* not retouched or touched up L19. **unreˈtractable** *adjective* E17. **unreˈtracted** *adjective* not retracted or withdrawn M17. **unreˈtrieved** *adjective* L19. **unˈretted** *adjective* (of flax etc.) not yet softened by soaking M19. **unreˈversed** *adjective* LME. **unreˈviewable** *adjective* M20. **unreˈviewed** *adjective* L18. **unreˈvised** *adjective* not revised, in an original form L18. **unreˈvoked** *adjective* not revoked or annulled; still in force: L15. **unrevoˈlutionary** *adjective* L20. **unrheˈtorical** *adjective* L18. **unˈribbed** *adjective* L18. **unˈrich** *adjective* not rich L19. **unˈringed** *adjective* (*a*) (of a pig, bull, etc.) not provided with a nose-ring; (*b*) (of a bird) not fitted with a ring on one or both legs: E16. **unˈrinsed** *adjective* M17. **unˈrippled** *adjective* E19. **unˈrisen** *adjective* L18. **unrituaˈlistic** *adjective* L19. **unˈriven** *adjective* not riven; not split or torn apart: LME. **unˈroasted** *adjective* LME. **unˈrobbed** *adjective* LME. **unroˈbust** *adjective* L18. **unˈrocked** *adjective* L15. **un-ˈRoman** *adjective* not Roman L17. **unˈromanized** *adjective* not romanized; not brought under the influence of the Roman Catholic Church: L18. **unˈrouged** *adjective* M19. **unˈrough** *adjective* not rough; *spec.* not rough-chinned, unbearded: LME. **unˈroughened** *adjective* L18. **unˈrousable** *adjective* not able to be roused L19. **unˈroused** *adjective* E19. **unˈrouted** *adjective* not routed; not dispelled or forced to retreat: E17. **unˈrubbed** *adjective* LME. **unˈrummaged** *adjective* †(*a*) (of a ship) not kept in order, esp. in the hold; (*b*) not searched or investigated thoroughly: L16. **un'rumpled** *adjective* M17. **un'rung** *adjective* = UNRINGED (a) M16. **un'ruptured** *adjective* L18. **un'rusted** *adjective* M17. **un'ruth** *noun* (now *arch.*) lack of pity or compassion, ruthlessness LME. **unsacer'dotal** *adjective* M19. **un'sackable** *adjective* not dismissible L20. **un'sacked** *adjective* not plundered L16. **unsacra'mental** *adjective* M19. **un'sacred** *adjective* not sacred, profane E17. **un'sacrificed** *adjective* M19. **un'sailed** *adjective* not sailed over or navigated L16. **un'sained** *adjective* (now *arch.* & *dial.*) ME. **un'salaried** *adjective* M19. **un'salt** *adjective* not salty or treated with salt LME. **un'salted** *adjective* LME. **unsa'lubrious** *adjective* L18. **un'salutary** *adjective* L18. **unsa'luted** *adjective* M16. **un'salvable** *adjective* not salvable, irredeemable E17. **un'salvageable** *adjective* M20. **un'sampled** *adjective* (*rare*) †(*a*) unexampled; (*b*) untried: M17. **un'sanctioned** *adjective* not sanctioned or ratified L18. **un'sandalled** *adjective* (of a foot) not sandalled L18. **un'sane** *adjective* (*rare*) †(*a*) unhealthy; (*b*) = INSANE: L17. **un'sanguine** *adjective* not sanguine or optimistic E18. **un'sanitary** *adjective* L19. **un'sated** *adjective* L17. **un'saturable** *adjective* (*rare*) M16. **†unsaught** *noun* discord, dissension LOE–E18. **un'sawn** *adjective* L16. **un-'Saxon** *adjective* M19. **un'scalped** *adjective* E18. **un'scandalized** *adjective* L18. **un'scandalous** *adjective* E17. **un'scared** *adjective* M18. **un'scarred** *adjective* L16. **un'scathed** *adjective* uninjured, unharmed LME. **un'scattered** *adjective* M16. **un'scented** *adjective* L18. **un'sceptical** *adjective* E19. **un'scheduled** *adjective* not planned or scheduled L19. **unscho'lastic** *adjective* L17. **un'scissored** *adjective* (long *rare* or *obsolete*) E17. **un'scorched** *adjective* not scorched or burnt E17. **un'scored** *adjective* L16. **un'scorned** *adjective* LME. **un'scoured** *adjective* not scoured or cleansed LME. **un'scourged** *adjective* LME. **un'scraped** *adjective* E18. **un'scribbled** *adjective* (*rare*) not scribbled on E17. **un'scripted** *adjective* (of a speech etc.) delivered or made without a prepared script; not contained in a script: M20. **un'scrubbed** *adjective* L19. **un'scrutable** *adjective* (*rare*) = INSCRUTABLE LME. **un'scrutinized** *adjective* E18. **un'sculptured** *adjective* E19. **un'seamanlike** *adjective* E18. **un'seared** *adjective* not made sear, unwithered L16. **un'seaworthiness** *noun* E19. **un'seaworthy** *adjective* E19. **un'seconded** *adjective* L16. **un'secret** *adjective* (long *rare*) L16. **unsec'tarian** *adjective* M19. **†unsecure** *adjective* insecure M17–E18. **unse'cured** *adjective* (esp. of a loan) not secured L18. **unse'duced** *adjective* M16. **unse'ductive** *adjective* L18. **un'seeking** *adjective* L16. **unseg'mented** *adjective* (chiefly ZOOLOGY) M19. **un'segregated** *adjective* E20. **unself-'knowing** *adjective* (*rare*) M17. **un'self-seeking** *adjective* M20. **unsen'sational** *adjective* M19. **unsen'sationally** *adverb* E20. **un'sentenced** *adjective* E16. **unsen'tentious** *adjective* M19. **un'sentient** *adjective* M18. **un'sentinelled** *adjective* not provided with a sentinel E19. **†unseparable** *adjective* inseparable LME–M18. **un'separated** *adjective* M16. **un'sepulchred** *adjective* not provided with a tomb, unburied E17. **un'sepultured** *adjective* unburied M19. **unse'questered** *adjective* M17. **unse'rene** *adjective* M17. **un'servile** *adjective* E18. **un'sewered** *adjective* lacking sewers M19. **un'shaded** *adjective* M17. **un-Shake'spearian** *adjective* M19. **un'shared** *adjective* [SHARE *verb*²] not shared (with or by another or others) E17. **un'shatterable** *adjective* that cannot be shattered E20. **un'shattered** *adjective* M17. **un'shaved** *adjective* = UNSHAVEN M17. **un'shaven** *adjective* not shaved, *esp.* (of a person, beard, etc.) not shaven LME. **un'sheared** *adjective* not sheared or shorn E18. **un'shed** *adjective* (*a*) (esp. of blood or tears) not shed or poured out; †(*b*) (*rare*, Spenser) unparted: LME. **un'sheltered** *adjective* L16. **un'sheltering** *adjective* that does not provide shelter E17. **un'shent** *adjective* (*arch.*) [SHEND *verb*] uninjured, undamaged, unspoiled ME. **un'shielded** *adjective* not protected (by or as by a shield) E18. **un'shingled** *adjective* (of a house, roof, etc.) not shingled E17. **un'shining** *adjective* L17. **un'shiny** *adjective* M20. **un'shivered** *adjective* (*rare*) not shivered or smashed into fragments L16. **un'shook** *adjective* (*obsolete* or *arch.*) = UNSHAKEN M17. **un'shorn** *adjective* ME. **un'shortened** *adjective* M18. **un'shovelled** *adjective* not shovelled or dug L18. **un'showered** *adjective* (*rare*, *poet.*) not dampened by showers E17. **un'showy** *adjective* M19. **un'shrived** *adjective* (now *rare* or *obsolete*) = UNSHRIVEN L18. **un'shriven** *adjective* [SHRIVE] not shriven ME. **†unshrubbed** *adjective* (*rare*, Shakes.) not set with shrubs: only in E17. **un'shuffled** *adjective* (of playing-cards) not shuffled L18. **un'shunnable** *adjective* E17. **†unshunned** *adjective* (*rare*) inevitable E–M17. **un'shy** *adjective* (esp. of a person) not shy M18. **un'sighing** *adjective* M18. **un'signatured** *adjective* not provided with or identified by a signature E19. **un'signifying** *adjective* M17. **un'signposted** *adjective* M20. **unsi'licified** *adjective* L19. **un'silly** *adjective* not silly; sensible: M20. **un'silvered** *adjective* not covered with or coloured silver; *esp.* (of glass) not silvered on the back: L18. **un'singable** *adjective* that cannot be sung; unsuitable for singing: L19. **un'singed** *adjective* not singed; untouched by fire: L16. **un'sinister** *adjective* M20. **un'sinning** *adjective* not committing or involving sin; not constituting a sin: LME. **†unsisting** *adjective* (*rare*, Shakes.) unshifting: only in E17. **un'skiable** *adjective* M20. **un'skimmed** *adjective* M17. **un'slain** *adjective* (*arch.*) not killed or slaughtered ME. **un'slaughtered** *adjective* not (yet) slaughtered E18. **un'sliced** *adjective* (esp. of food) not sliced; not cut into slices: L19. **un'slothful** *adjective* M17. **un'slowed** *adjective* not slowed down M20. **un'slumbering** *adjective* (*literary*) = UNSLEEPING E18. **un'smashed** *adjective* M20. **un'smeared** *adjective* M17. **un'smelted** *adjective* E19. **un'smirched** *adjective* not smirched or soiled; untainted: E17. **un'smitten** *adjective* (now *arch.* & *poet.*) not smitten or struck down; not strongly affected by something: ME. **un'smutched** *adjective* not smudged or blackened; unstained: E19. **un'snubbable** *adjective* unable to be snubbed or rebuffed M19. **un'snuffed** *adjective* not snuffed or extinguished E19. **un'soaped** *adjective* not soaped; unwashed: M19. **unsocio'logical** *adjective* M20. **un'socketed** *adjective* not placed in or fitted with a socket M20. **un'soft** *adjective* not soft; hard, rough: ME. **un'softened** *adjective* M17. **un'soiled** *adjective* not soiled or dirtied; untarnished: LME. **un'solaced** *adjective* given no solace L18. **un'soldered** *adjective* not united or fastened with solder M17. **un'soluble** *adjective* = INSOLUBLE *adjective* M16. **un'sonlike** *adjective* M17. **un'sonorous** *adjective* not sonorous or resonant; (of language etc.) not grand, unimposing: E18. **un'sordid** *adjective* M19. **un'sorry** *adjective* M20. **un'sorted** *adjective* not sorted; *esp.* not arranged or classified: M16. **un'soured** *adjective* E17. **un'sparkling** *adjective* L18. **un'spawned** *adjective* E19. **un'specialized** *adjective* L19. **unspe'cific** *adjective* not specific; general, inexact: E19. **un'specified** *adjective* not specified; not named explicitly: E17. **un'specked** *adjective* not specked or speckled L18. **un'speckled** *adjective* L16. **un'spectacled** *adjective* not provided with or wearing spectacles L18. **unspec'tacular** *adjective* E20. **un'speculative** *adjective* not based on or characterized by speculation M17. **un'spiced** *adjective* not flavoured with spices; not spicy or piquant: M17. **un'spied** *adjective* (chiefly *poet.*) unseen, unobserved LME. **un'spirited** *adjective* having no or little spirit; spiritless, lethargic: E17. **un'spliced** *adjective* (esp. of a gene or gene fragment) that has not been spliced M19. **un'splinterable** *adjective* E20. **un'split** *adjective* M17. **un'splittable** *adjective* E20. **unspon'taneous** *adjective* not spontaneous; premeditated, laboured: L18. **un'sported** *adjective* (*arch.*) (of a door) open, not closed L19. **un'sprayed** *adjective* not sprayed, esp. with a chemical or chemicals L19. **un'spread** *adjective* not spread (out) L16. **un'springy** *adjective* L17. **un'sprinkled** *adjective* not sprinkled with water etc.; *spec.* unbaptized: M17. **un'spun** *adjective* not spun; not formed or prepared by spinning: M16. **un'squandered** *adjective* L18. **un'squeamish** *adjective* L19. **un'squeezed** *adjective* L17. **un'squelched** *adjective* (ELECTRONICS) designating or pertaining to a signal that has not been subjected to the action of a squelch circuit M20. **un'stacked** *adjective* L18. **un'staffed** *adjective* not provided with staff; operating without staff: M20. **un'stagy** *adjective* not stagy; not overly theatrical or affected: L19. **un'staled** *adjective* not made or grown stale L19. **un'stalked** *adjective* having no stalk or stalks L19. **un'standardized** *adjective* E20. **un'starched** *adjective* not starched; *fig.* not stiff or formal: E19. **un'startled** *adjective* M17. **un'stately** *adjective* M19. **un'statesmanlike** *adjective* L18. **un'staunch** *adjective* E17. **un'steeped** *adjective* not steeped or soaked, unsaturated E17. **un'stereotyped** *adjective* M20. **un'sterile** *adjective* M20. **un'sterilized** *adjective* E20. **un'stifled** *adjective* not stifled or smothered; unconstrained: M18. **un'stigmatized** *adjective* L18. **un'stockinged** *adjective* not wearing a stocking or stockings L18. **un'stolen** *adjective* M16. **un'stooping** *adjective* not stooping, upright L16. **un'stout** *adjective* (now *rare*) not stout or sturdy M16. **un'straitened** *adjective* M17. **un'strange** *adjective* (chiefly *literary*) not strange; familiar: LME. **unstra'tegic** *adjective* M19. **un'stratified** *adjective* not stratified; not arranged in strata or layers: E19. **un'streaked** *adjective* M19. **un'streamlined** *adjective* M20. **un'strenuous** *adjective* L19. **un'stretched** *adjective* M17. **un'striated** *adjective* L19. **un'stricken** *adjective* not stricken or struck M16. **un'striped** *adjective* M19. **un'stripped** *adjective* not stripped; not removed by stripping: L17. **un'strong** *adjective* (*obsolete* exc. *dial.*) not strong; feeble, weak: OE. **un'struck** *adjective* E17. **un'structured** *adjective* not structured; informal: M20. **un'struggling** *adjective* E19. **un'studded** *adjective* E20. **un'stung** *adjective* E17. **un'stylish** *adjective* M19. **un'stylishly** *adverb* M20. **un'stylishness** *noun* L19. **un'subjugated** *adjective* L18. **un'sublimated** *adjective* E20. **unsub'limed** *adjective* (*rare*) LME. **unsub'merged** *adjective* L19. **unsub'mitting** *adjective* not submitting; refusing to yield: M18. **†unsubordinate** *adjective* insubordinate M17–E18. **unsu'borned** *adjective* (now *rare* or *obsolete*) M17. **unsub'scribed** *adjective* L16. **unsub'scribing** *adjective* L18. **un'subsidized** *adjective* not subsidized; not supported by subsidy: M18. **un'substanced** *adjective* (long *rare* or *obsolete*) not substanced; not made substantial: M17. **un'substituted** *adjective* (CHEMISTRY) (of an atom or group) that has not been substituted by another; (of a compound) that has not had certain atoms or groups substituted by others: E20. **unsub'verted** *adjective* L18. **unsuc'ceeded** *adjective* (*rare*) not succeeded; without a successor or a successive event: M17. **un'succoured** *adjective* not succoured; unprotected; unassisted: LME. **un'sucked** *adjective* (*rare*) M17. **un'sued** *adjective* (now *poet.*, *rare*) not sued; *esp.* (of a person) not appealed *to*, (of a thing) not appealed *for*: L16. **†unsuffered** *adjective* (*rare*) not suffered; unendured: M16–L18. **un'suffering** *adjective* †(*a*) *rare* impatient, not long-suffering; (*b*) not suffering: M16. **unsu'fficed** *adjective* (now *rare*) not sufficed; unsatisfied: L16. **un'suffixed** *adjective* (GRAMMAR) without a suffix M20. **un'sugared** *adjective* L16. **unsu'ggestive** *adjective* not suggestive; unevocative *of*: L18. **un'suiting** *adjective* (*arch. rare*) not suiting; unsuitable; not fitting: L16. **un'summed** *adjective* not summed up; uncounted: LME. **un'summoned** *adjective* L15. **un'sunk** *adjective* ME. **un'sunny** *adjective* M19. **†unsuperable** *adjective* insuperable LME–L18. **un'supercharged** *adjective* E20. **unsu'perfluous** *adjective* L16. **unsuper'seded** *adjective* L18. **unsuper'stitious** *adjective* M17. **un'supervised** *adjective* L19. **un'supped** *adjective* (*arch. rare*) without having supped; supperless: LME. **unsu'pportive** *adjective* L20. **†unsured** *adjective* (*rare*) unconfirmed; unguaranteed, unsecured: LME–L16. **un'surfaced** *adjective* M20. **un'surgical** *adjective* E19. **unsur'mised** *adjective* L18. **unsur'prised** *adjective* L18. **unsur'prising** *adjective* L17. **unsur'prisingly** *adverb* M20. **unsu'rrendered** *adjective* L18. **unsu'rrounded** *adjective* E19. **unsur'veyed** *adjective* M16. **un'suspect** *adjective* (chiefly *Scot.*, now *rare*) not suspect; dependable; trustworthy: LME. **unsu'spended** *adjective* E18. **un'swallowable** *adjective* L19. **un'swallowed** *adjective* LME. **un'sweepable** *adjective* (*rare*) M19. **un'swinging** *adjective* M20. **un'swollen** *adjective* L16. **unsy'llabic** *adjective* not syllabic; not forming or constituting a syllable: M19. **un'syllabled** *adjective* not formed into or uttered in syllables L16. **unsym'bolic** *adjective* L19. **unsy'mmetrical** *adjective* M18. **unsy'mmetrically** *adverb* M18. **un'sympathizing** *adjective* M18. **un'sympathy** *noun* (*rare*) lack of sympathy M19. **un'syncopated** *adjective* L19. **un'tactful** *adjective* M19. **un'tagged** *adjective* M16. **un'tailed** *adjective* (*a*) not provided with a tail; (*b*) deprived of a tail: E17. **un'talented** *adjective* M18. **un'talkative** *adjective* M18. **un'talked** *adjective* not talked *of* or *about* L16. **un'tampered** *adjective* not tampered (*with*) L17. **un'tangible** *adjective* (*rare*) intangible L18. **un'tanned** *adjective* not tanned; not subjected to tanning; not brown from exposure to the sun: M16. **un'tapered** *adjective* (*rare*) L18. **un'tarred** *adjective* not smeared or covered with tar L16. **un'tasked** *adjective* not having been assigned a task L18. **un'tasted** *adjective* †(*a*) untouched; (*b*) not tasted; not (yet) sampled (*lit.* & *fig.*): LME. **un'tasteful** *adjective* E17. **un'tearable** *adjective* that cannot be torn M17. **un'technical** *adjective* M19. **un'technically** *adverb* E19. **†untemperateness** *noun* (*a*) distempered or disturbed condition of the bodily humours; (*b*) intemperateness: LME–M18. **un'tended** *adjective* not tended or looked after; neglected: L16. **un'tendered** *adjective* (long *rare*) not offered E17. **un'tense** *adjective* M20. **un'tented** *adjective*¹ (*arch.*) (of a wound) unprobed, undressed E17. **un'tented** *adjective*² (*obsolete* exc. *Scot.*) unheeded, unregarded L18. **un'tented** *adjective*³ (*rare*) not provided with a tent or tents L19. **un'tenty** *adjective* (*Scot.*) careless, heedless E19. **un'tenured** *adjective* M20. **un'terraced** *adjective* (esp. of a slope) not terraced L19. **unte'rrific** *adjective* not terrific or terrifying L18. **unthe'atrical** *adjective* M18. **unthe'matic** *adjective* (esp. of a verb) not thematic L19. **untheo'logical** *adjective* M17. **untheo'retical** *adjective* L18. **un'thickened** *adjective* L18. **un'thinned** *adjective* M17. **un'thrashed** *adjective* (*a*) = UNTHRESHED; (*b*) *rare* not thrashed or beaten: E18. **un'threshed** *adjective* (of corn etc.) not threshed M16. **un'thronged** *adjective* not thronged, uncrowded M17. **un'thrown** *adjective* not thrown *away*, *out*, etc.; not disconcerted: M16. **un'thumbed** *adjective* not thumbed; *esp.* (of a book etc.) not showing signs of use: L18. **un'thwarted** *adjective* L18. **un'ticketed** *adjective* L18. **un'tight** *adjective* (now *rare*) not tight, *esp.* not watertight E17. **un'tiled** *adjective* (now *rare*) not covered with tiles (cf. UNTILE) LME. **un'tinctured** *adjective* (chiefly *fig.*) not tinctured; untinged or unaffected *by* or *with*: M18. **un'tinged** *adjective* M17. **un'tinned** *adjective* L18. **un'tinted** *adjective* M19. **un'tipped** *adjective*¹ not provided with a tip; *esp.* (of a cigarette) not having a filter tip: L17. **un'tipped** *adjective*² not given a gratuity M19. **un'toasted** *adjective* M18. **unto'gether** *adjective* (*colloq.*) not well organized, lacking self-possession M20. **un'toiled** *adjective* †(*a*) untilled, uncultivated; (*b*) not subjected to or overcome by toil; (*c*) not toiled *for*, got without toil: L16. **un'toiling** *adjective* M18. **un'tongued** *adjective* without a tongue, tongueless L16. **un'toothsome** *adjective* unpleasant in taste; unpalatable, disagreeable: M16. **untor'mented** *adjective* LME. **un'torn** *adjective* LME. **un'touristy** *adjective* M20. **un'tracked** *adjective* (*a*) without a track or path, trackless; (*b*) not tracked or traced, not followed up: E17. **un'tradable, -eable** *adjective* unable to be traded or sold; not admitting of trade: M20. **un'traded** *adjective* (*a*) (long *rare*) unskilled, inexperienced, unfamiliar; †(*b*) not customary, unhackneyed; (*c*) not traded or dealt in: M16. **untra'ditional** *adjective* M20. **untra'ditionally** *adverb* L20. **un'tragic** *adjective* M19. **un'trammelled** *adjective* L18. **un'trampled** *adjective* M17. **un'tranquil** *adjective* E19. **untranscen'dental** *adjective* M19. **untrans'ferable** *adjective* M17. **untrans'formable** *adjective* L16. **untrans'formed** *adjective* L18. **untrans'missible** *adjective* L16. **untrans'mitted** *adjective* L18. **untrans'mutable** *adjective* LME. **untrans'muted** *adjective* M17. **untrans'parent** *adjective* L16. **untrans'planted** *adjective* M17. **untrans'portable** *adjective* E17. **untrans'ported** *adjective* M16. **untransub'stantiated** *adjective* L17. **un'travellable** *adjective* unable to be travelled over or traversed M17. **un'travelled** *adjective* (*a*) that has not travelled; (*b*) not travelled over or traversed: L16. **untra'versable** *adjective* unable to be traversed M19. **untra'versed** *adjective* E19. **un'trembling** *adjective* not trembling; *fig.* fearless: L16. **un'tremblingly** *adverb* without trembling M19. **un'tremulous** *adjective* E19. **un'trenched** *adjective* E19. **un'trended** *adjective* (*dial.*, now *rare*) (of wool) not trended or wound LME. **un'trendy** *adjective* (*colloq.*) unfashionable M20. **un'tressed** *adjective* (of hair) not arranged in tresses, loose, dishevelled LME. **un'trilled** *adjective* not pronounced with a trill M19. **un'trite** *adjective* L18. **un'trumpeted** *adjective* not trumpeted, *spec.* not praised or proclaimed loudly L18. **un'tumbled** *adjective* L17. **untu'multuous** *adjective* M18. **un'turbaned** *adjective* L18. **un'twinned** *adjective* not forming a twin crystal L19. **un'typable** *adjective* (MEDICINE & BIOLOGY) that cannot be assigned to a specific type M20. **un'unionized** *adjective* L20. **unu'nitable** *adjective* L17. **unu'nited** *adjective* L16. **unup'braided** *adjective* L17. **unup'braiding** *adjective* L18. **unup'braidingly** *adverb* E18. **unup'lifted** *adjective* E19. **un'urged** *adjective* not urged or incited to a course of action; (of an idea etc.) not thrust or pressed on a person: L16. **un'urgent** *adjective* M20. **un'urned** *adjective* not buried or placed in an urn, unburied M19. **un'ushered** *adjective* M17. **unutili'tarian** *adjective* E20. **un'utilized** *adjective* M19. **un'vaccinated** *adjective* L19. **un'vamped** *adjective* not served up as if new M17. **un'vanquishable** *adjective* LME. **un'vanquished** *adjective* LME. **un'vaulted** *adjective* L16. **un'veined** *adjective* E19. **un'venerable** *adjective* E17. **un'venged** *adjective* (*arch.*) LME. **un'vented** *adjective* without a vent or outlet E17. **un'ventilated** *adjective*(*a*) not provided with means of ventilation; (*b*) not discussed: E18. **un'ventured** *adjective* E17. **un'venturous** *adjective* M19. **un'verbalizable** *adjective* M20. **un'verbalized** *adjective* E20. **un'verdant** *adjective* M17. **un'verifiable** *adjective* M19. **un'verified** *adjective* E19. **un'vetted** *adjective* M20. **un'vexed** *adjective* LME. **unvia'bility** *noun* L20. **un'viable** *adjective* M20. **unvic'torious** *adjective* E17. **un'viewed** *adjective* L16. **un'vigilant** *adjective* E17. **un'vindicated** *adjective* M17. **unvin'dictive** *adjective* M19. **un'vintaged** *adjective* M19. **un'violable** *adjective* M16. **†unviolably** *adverb* M16–M17. **un'violated** *adjective* M16. **un'violent** *adjective* M20. **†unvisible** *adjective* LME–L16. **†unvisibleness** *noun* LME–E18. **†unvisibly** *adverb*: only in E17. **un'visitable** *adjective* incapable of or unsuitable for visiting; unfit to be visited: M17. **un'visited** *adjective* not visited L15. **un'vital** *adjective* M17. **un'vitiated** *adjective* M17. **unvitri'fiable** *adjective* M18. **un'vitrified** *adjective* L18. **un'volatile** *adjective* (*rare*) = INVOLATILE 2 E19. **un'voluntary** *adjective* (now *rare* or *obsolete*) L16. **un'vouched** *adjective* not guaranteed by evidence; not vouched *for*: L18. **unvouch'safed** *adjective* not vouchsafed M17. **un'vowed** *adjective* not bound by or performed on account of a vow L16. **un'vowelled** *adjective* lacking vowels E17. **un'voyageable** *adjective* (*literary*) unable to be voyaged or travelled over M17. **un'voyaged** *adjective* (*literary*) not travelled or voyaged over E19. **un'vulcanized** *adjective* L19. **un'vulgar** *adjective* †(*a*) uncommon, unusual; refined, rare; (*b*) free from vulgarity: L16. **un'vulgarly** *adverb* (*rare*) E17. **un'vulnerable** *adjective* (*rare*) E17. **un'waked** *adjective* not awoken LME. **un'wakened** *adjective* E17. **un'walkable** *adjective* unfit for walking in or on; not traversed by walking; incapable of walking: E19. **un'walked** *adjective* not made to walk; not traversed by walking: E17. **un'walking** *adjective* L18. **un'walled** *adjective* not provided with or defended

For other words beginning with *un-* see the entry for **un-**² and the main alphabetic sequence of entries

by a wall LME. **unˈwandered** *adjective* (of land etc.) untraversed; (of a person) untravelled: M17. **unˈwandering** *adjective* M16. **unˈwaning** *adjective* E19. **unˈwanton** *adjective* E17. **unˈwarded** *adjective* (*arch.*) unguarded, undefended LME. **unˈwarlike** *adjective* L16. **unˈwarlikeness** *noun* M19. **unˈwarmed** *adjective* not warmed, chilly E17. **unˈwarming** *adjective* M18. **unˈwarned** *adjective* OE. **unˈwasted** *adjective* not wasted, consumed, or squandered; undevastated: ME. **unˈwasting** *adjective* (now *literary*) not wasting, not being consumed: LME. **unˈwaving** *adjective* E18. **unˈwaxed** *adjective* not treated or covered with wax LME. **unˈweakened** *adjective* M17. **unˈweal** *noun* (*arch.*) unhappiness, distress ME. **unˈwealth** *noun* (*rare*) lack of prosperity ME. **unˈwealthy** *adjective* LME. **unˈweaned** *adjective* L16. **unˈweaponed** *adjective* unarmed ME. **unˈwearable** *adjective* L18. **unˈweathered** *adjective* L18. **unˈwedgeable** *adjective* (*rare*) that cannot be split by a wedge, uncleavable, (chiefly *fig.*, with allus. to Shakes. *Meas. for M.* II.ii.116) E17. **unˈweeded** *adjective* not cleared of weeds E17. **unˈweened** *adjective* (*arch.*) not thought of, imagined, or expected LME. **unˈweft** *adjective* (*rare*) unwoven M19. **unˈwelded** *adjective* L18. **unˈwept** *adjective* (**a**) not wept for, unlamented; (**b**) (of tears) unshed: L16. **unˈwhipped** *adjective*(**a**) not punished (as) by whipping; (**b**) POLITICS not subject to or directed by a party whip: E17. **unˈwhisperables** *noun pl.* (*arch. colloq.*) trousers M19. **unˈwhispered** *adjective* E19. **unˈwhitened** *adjective* M19. **unˈwhitewashed** *adjective* L18. **unˈwifely** *adjective* M19. **unˈwily** *adjective* ME. **unˈwindowed** *adjective* windowless E19. **unˈwinged** *adjective* wingless E17. **unˈwinnable** *adjective* M16. **unˈwinnowed** *adjective* M16. **unˈwistful** *adjective* L18. **unwithˈstood** *adjective* L16. **unˈwitnessed** *adjective* LME. **unˈwon** *adjective* not won or earned; *spec.* (of a woman) not successfully wooed L16. **unˈwooded** *adjective* not wooded, treeless E17. **unˈwooed** *adjective* (now *literary*) not wooed or courted L16. **unˈwordable** *adjective* impossible to express in words M17. **unˈworded** *adjective* not expressed in words M19. **unˈwormed** *adjective* (of an animal or person) that has not had parasitic worms removed E17. **unˈworried** *adjective* L18. **unˈwoven** *adjective* LME. **unˈwrathful** *adjective* (long *rare*) M16. **unˈwreaked** *adjective* unrequited, unavenged L16. **unˈwrecked** *adjective* M18. **unˈwrested** *adjective* not wrested or strained M17. **unˈwritable** *adjective* L18. **unˈwronged** *adjective* L16. **unˈyeaned** *adjective* that has not been born or given birth L18. **unˈyouthful** *adjective* M19. **unˈzealous** *adjective* M17.

un- /ʌn/ *prefix*[2].
[Old English *un-*, *on-* = Old Saxon *ant-*, Old High German *ant-*, *int-*, Gothic *and-*.]
Forming verbs (mostly trans.) and derived ppl adjectives.

1 Prefixed to verbs, expr. reversal or cancellation of an action or process, as ***unbuckle***, ***unlock***.

2 Prefixed to nouns & verbs, expr. removal or deprivation, as ***unclothe***, ***unleash***, ***unmask***. ▸**b** Expr. freeing or releasing, as ***unburden***, ***untether***.

3 Prefixed to nouns, expr. removal or extraction from a place or receptacle, as ***undock***, ***unearth***.

4 Expr. the withdrawal or reversal of a property or status: prefixed to adjectives, as ***unlevel***, ***unround***, and to nouns, as ***unman***, ***unqueen***; freq. (esp. with nouns) with suffix *-ify* or *-ize*, as ***unglorify***, ***unjustify***, ***unhumanize***, ***unnaturalize***.

5 Redundantly prefixed to verbs, as ***unloose***, ***unstrip***. *rare*.

¶ In some adjectives, esp. those in *-ed*, both UN-[1] and UN-[2] can be understood (e.g. ***unbodied***, ***untailed***).

■ **unˈanchor** *verb* (**a**) *verb trans.* free (a ship) from being anchored; *fig.* release *oneself* from an anchorage; (**b**) *verb intrans.* (of a ship) be or become unanchored; draw up the anchor: LME. **unˈban** *verb trans.* remove a ban from (a person, political group, etc.); formally rescind an official order of exclusion or prohibition from: M20. **unˈbandage** *verb trans.* remove a bandage from M19. **unˈbarbarize** *verb trans.* make less barbarous; civilize: M17. **unˈbare** *verb trans.* (now *rare*) lay bare, expose to view M16. **unbeˈnumb** *verb trans.* free from numbness L16. †**unbeˈspeak** *verb trans.* countermand; cancel an order or request for: M17–M18. **unbeˈwitch** *verb trans.* free from witchcraft, disenchant L16. **unˈbishop** *verb trans.* (long *rare*) remove from the office of bishop L16. **unˈbit** *verb trans.* (now *rare*) free (a horse) from the bit M16. **unˈbitt** *verb trans.* (NAUTICAL) uncoil or unfasten (a cable) from the bitts M18. **unˈblind** *verb trans.* (**a**) free from blindness; *spec.* cause (a test or experiment) to be no longer blind; (**b**) *literary* = UNBLINDFOLD: L16. **unˈblindfold** *verb trans.* remove a blindfold from LME. **unˈbonnet** *verb* (**a**) *verb intrans.* & *refl.* remove one's hat or bonnet, esp. as a mark of respect; (**b**) *verb trans.* remove a bonnet from: E19. **unˈbottle** *verb trans.* extract or release (as) from a bottle E19. **unˈbox** *verb trans.* take out of a box E17. **unˈbraid** *verb trans.* untie (a braid); undo the braids of: E19. **unˈbran** *verb trans.* remove the bran from M19. **unˈbreech** *verb trans.* (**a**) remove the breeching from (a cannon etc.); (**b**) *arch.* strip (a person) of breeches: M16. **unˈbrick** *verb trans.* remove bricks from; open up by this action: L16. **unˈbridle** *verb trans.* remove the bridle from; *fig.* free from restraint: LME. **unˈbrother** *verb trans.* break brotherhood with; deprive of being a brother: M17. **unˈbudget** *verb trans.* (now *rare* or *obsolete*) disclose, reveal E17. **unˈcage** *verb trans.* release from a cage; *fig.* free from constraint, liberate: E17. †**unˈcape** *verb intrans.* (*rare*, Shakes.) uncover: only in L16. **unˈcardinal** *verb trans.* (now *rare*) remove from the office of cardinal M17. **unˈcart** *verb trans.* remove or unload from a cart M17. **unˈcastle** *verb trans.* (*arch.*) drive out of a castle E17. **unˈcellar** *verb trans.* (*rare*) remove (wine) from a cellar E17. **unceˈment** *verb trans.* cause to break apart (as) by removing cement; sever, disjoin: M17. **unˈcharnel** *verb trans.* remove from a charnel E19. **unˈcinch** *verb trans.* unfasten (a saddle-girth, a pack, etc.) from a horse L19. **unˈcipher** *verb trans.* (*arch.*) decipher L16. **unˈclamp** *verb trans.* E19. **unˈclay** *verb trans.* remove the clay from M17. **unˈclutch** *verb trans.* release from one's clutch M17. **unˈclutter** *verb trans.* make free of clutter M20. **uncoˈllegiate** *verb trans.* deprive of the status of a collegiate church or parish M19. †**unˈcolted** *adjective* (*rare*, Shakes.) deprived of a horse: only in L16. **unˈcomment** *verb trans.* (COMPUTING) change (a piece of text within a program) from being a comment to being part of the program run by the computer L20. **unconˈvince** *verb trans.* (*rare*) change or negate the conviction or belief of E19. **unˈcowl** *verb trans.* uncover; remove the cowl or covering from: E17. **unˈcramp** *verb trans.* & *intrans.* make or become less cramped or affected by cramp M19. **unˈcrest** *verb trans.* remove the crest or top from E17. **unˈcrinkle** *verb* (**a**) *verb intrans.* lose crinkles, become less crinkled; (**b**) *verb trans.* remove crinkles from: E20. **unˈdam** *verb trans.* release from a dam L17. **unˈdarken** *verb trans.* dispel the darkness from, make light L16. **unˈdazzle** *verb intrans.* (*rare*) become restored to an undazzled state E17. **unˈdeaf** *verb trans.* (*rare*) restore hearing to L16. **undeˈcree** *verb trans.* reverse a decree on M17. **unˈdeify** *verb trans.* deprive of the status or qualities of a deity M17. **undeˈlete** *verb trans.* cancel the deletion of L20. **unˈdevil** *verb trans.* free from demoniacal possession M17. **unˈdig** *verb trans.* exhume or open again by digging M17. **unˈdouble** *verb trans.* & *intrans.* make or become unfolded, straighten E17. **unˈduke** *verb trans.* (*rare*) remove the dignity or office of a duke from E17. **unˈface** *verb trans.* expose the face of E17. **unˈfather** *verb trans.* deprive of a father L16. **unˈfeather** *verb trans.* strip (a bird, nest, etc.) of feathers L15. **unˈfool** *verb trans.* disabuse, undeceive, (a person) (long *rare* or *obsolete*) L16. **unˈfrenchify** *verb trans.* (*rare*) L16. **unˈgag** *verb trans.* remove a gag from E18. **unˈgarter** *verb trans.* remove a garter from L16. **unˈgirth** *verb trans.* undo a girth from; release by undoing a girth: L16. **unˈglobe** *verb trans.* (*rare*) make no longer spherical E17. **unˈglorify** *verb trans.* divest of glory or radiance M18. **unˈglove** *verb trans.* & *intrans.* remove a glove or gloves (from) LME. **unˈgod** *verb trans.* remove the status or attributes of a god from; undeify: E17. **unˈgoddess** *verb trans.* undeify (a goddess) M18. **unˈgrave** *verb trans.* (*literary*) remove from a grave; disinter: M17. **unˈgroup** *verb trans.* (COMPUTING) separate (items) from a group formed within a word-processing or graphics package L20. **unˈgyve** *verb trans.* (*arch.*) unfetter, unshackle M16. **unˈhalter** *verb trans.* remove a halter from L16. **unˈharbour** *verb trans.* dislodge (a deer) from a covert L16. **unˈhasp** *verb trans.* free (as) from a hasp or catch; unfasten: ME. **unˈhat** *verb intrans.* remove one's hat, esp. as a mark of respect L16. **unˈhive** *verb trans.* turn out of a hive E18. **unˈhoard** *verb trans.* (now *rare*) take or bring out of a hoard M17. **unˈholster** *verb trans.* remove (a gun) from a holster L20. **unˈhood** *verb trans.* remove a hood or covering from L16. **unˈhoop** *verb trans.* (long *rare*) remove a hoop or hoops from E17. **unˈjam** *verb trans.* free from being jammed L18. **unˈkey** *verb trans.* †(**a**) remove the keystone from (an arch); (**b**) unfasten by means of a pin, wedge, etc.; (**c**) *rare* unlock with a key: M18. **unˈkingdomed** *adjective* (*rare*) deprived of a kingdom E17. **unˈkiss** *verb trans.* (long *rare*) cancel by means of a kiss M16. **unˈleaf** *verb trans.* strip (a tree etc.) of leaves L16. **unˈleash** *verb trans.* free from a leash or restraint; set free in order to pursue or attack: L17. **unˈleave** *verb trans.* = UNLEAF *verb* L16. **unˈliver** *verb trans.* (now *rare* or *obsolete*) discharge (a ship or cargo) M17. **unˈlivery** *noun* (now *rare* or *obsolete*) discharge of a ship or cargo E19. **unˈlodge** *verb trans.* (now *rare*) dislodge; drive from a lodging or resting-place: M16. **unˈmesh** *verb trans.* undo the meshes of; free from meshes: E19. **unˈmonarch** *verb trans.* (**a**) deprive of a monarch; (**b**) remove the dignity and position of monarch from: M17. **unˈnest** *verb trans.* remove or unsettle from a nest or place LME. **unˈpedestal** *verb trans.* remove from a pedestal (*lit.* & *fig.*) E19. **unˈperch** *verb trans.* dislodge from a perch L16. **unˈpile** *verb trans.* demolish (a pile); remove from a pile: E17. **unˈpocket** *verb trans.* take out of a pocket E17. †**unˈqualitied** *adjective* (*rare*, Shakes.) deprived of qualities: only in E17. †**unˈquilt** *verb trans.* (*rare*) uncover, unbind E–M17. **unˈray** *verb trans.* (now *dial.*) divest of clothes, undress, strip L15. **unˈreeve** *verb trans.* withdraw (a rope etc.) from being reeved E17. **unˈrind** *verb trans.* strip (a tree etc.) of rind or bark LME. **unˈsack** *verb trans.* take out of a sack LME. **unˈscabbard** *verb trans.* remove from the scabbard E17. **unˈscottify** *verb trans.* (*rare*) L18. **unˈseam** *verb trans.* undo the seam or seams of (a garment etc.); rip up: L16. **unˈshawl** *verb intrans.* take off one's shawl E19. **unˈshelve** *verb trans.* remove from a shelf E19. **unˈsiphon** *verb trans.* prevent from functioning as a siphon L19. **unˈslate** *verb trans.* remove the slates from L16. **unˈslave** *verb trans.* (chiefly *poet.*, now *rare*) free from slavery E17. **unˈsleeve** *verb trans.* (long *arch.*) remove or roll up the sleeve of L16. **unˈslough** *verb trans.* (*slang*) unlock, unfasten M19. **unˈsluice** *verb trans.* (chiefly *poet.*) release (as) from a sluice; allow to flow: E17. **unˈsnare** *verb trans.* release from a snare M16. **unˈsnarl** *verb trans.* disentangle M16. **unˈsneck** *verb trans.* & *intrans.* (orig. *Scot.* & *north.*) unlatch L18. **unˈsnib** *verb trans.* unfasten (a catch); open (a door etc.) by this action: E20. **unˈsocket** *verb trans.* remove from a socket E18. **unˈsolder** *verb trans.* undo the soldering of; *fig.* dissolve: M16. **unˈsole** *verb trans.* remove the sole or soles from L16. **unˈson** *verb trans.* deprive of the status or character of a son M17. **unˈspan** *verb trans.* & *intrans.* (now *rare*) unyoke or unharness (a horse etc.) from a vehicle M17. **unˈspar** *verb trans.* unbar or unbolt (a door etc.) ME. **unˈspin** *verb trans.* untwist (a spun thread etc.); unravel: L16. **unˈspit** *verb trans.* remove from a spit L16. **unˈstack** *verb trans.* remove or dismantle from a stack or pile M19. **unˈstall** *verb* (AERONAUTICS) (**a**) *verb intrans.* (of an aircraft) recover from a stall; (**b**) *verb trans.* cause (an aircraft) to recover from a stall: E20. **unˈsteek** *verb trans.* (*obsolete* exc. *Scot.* & *north.*) undo, unfasten, open ME. **unˈstep** *verb trans.* (NAUTICAL) detach (a mast) from a step M19. **unˈsting** *verb trans.* remove the sting from E17. **unˈstow** *verb trans.* remove stowed articles from (a ship's hold etc.) E18. **unˈstrap** *verb trans.* undo the strap or straps of; unfasten by this action: E19. **unˈstretch** *verb trans.* & *intrans.* relax, slacken E17. **unˈstrike** *verb trans.* (FALCONRY) draw the strings of (a hawk's hood) to facilitate removal E17. **unˈstrip** *verb trans.* (now *dial.* *rare*) strip L16. **unˈswaddle** *verb trans.* (**a**) take (a child) out of swaddling-clothes; (**b**) unwrap or unwind the bandages or garments from: L16. **unˈswathe** *verb trans.* free from a swathe or swathes; unwrap: LME. **unˈswell** *verb intrans.* (now *rare*) recover from a swollen state LME. **unˈtangle** *verb trans.* (**a**) free from a tangled state; (**b**) release from entanglement: M16. **unˈtape** *verb trans.* remove tape from, free from being taped M20. **unˈtense** *verb trans.* & *intrans.* make or become less tense or rigid; relax: L20. **unˈtent** *verb* (long *rare* or *obsolete*) (**a**) *verb trans.* take out of a tent; (**b**) *verb intrans.* remove tents from a camp: E17. **unˈthrone** *verb trans.* dethrone E17. **unˈtighten** *verb trans.* (*rare*) loosen L18. **unˈtile** *verb trans.* (now *rare*) strip (a roof etc.) of tiles LME. **unˈtranquillize** *verb trans.* L19. **unˈtreasure** *verb trans.* (*arch. rare*) rob or empty of or *of* treasure E17. **unˈtripe** *verb trans.* (now *rare*) disembowel E17. **unˈvote** *verb trans.* (**a**) reverse or annul by revoting; (**b**) deprive *of* by voting: M17. **unˈweave** *verb trans.* disentangle, unravel M16. **unˈwheeled** *adjective* (of a chariot etc.) bereft of a wheel or wheels M17. **unˈwhig** *verb trans.* (now *rare* or *obsolete*) divest of the character or opinions of a Whig E19. **unˈwinter** *verb intrans.* & *trans.* lose, or divest of, the qualities of winter E17. †**unˈwit** *verb trans.* (*rare*, Shakes.) deprive of wit or wits: only in E17. **unˈwitch** *verb trans.* (*arch.*) = UNBEWITCH L16. **unˈwoman** *verb trans.* deprive of the (typical) qualities or status of a woman E17. **unˈworld** *verb trans.* deprive of the qualities or character of a world; undo: M17. **unˈwreathe** *verb trans.* disentwine, untwist L16.

un- /ʌn/ *prefix*[3].
[from Latin *unus* one.]
Forming proposed name of chemical elements with atomic numbers greater than 100, as *unnilquadium* (element 104), *unnilpentium* (element 105), etc.
¶ Such names use a conventional series of word-forming elems., as *-nil-* zero, *-quad-* four, *-pent-* five, etc.

UNA *abbreviation.*
United Nations Association.

Una /ˈjuːnə/ *noun.* L19.
[Name of an early boat of this kind.]
In full ***Una boat***. A catboat.

unabashed /ʌnəˈbaʃt/ *adjective.* L16.
[from UN-[1] + *abashed* pa. pple of ABASH.]
Not abashed; undaunted; not disconcerted.
■ **unabashable** *adjective* M19. **unabashedly** *adverb* L19. **unabashedness** *noun* E20.

unabated /ʌnəˈbeɪtɪd/ *adjective.* E17.
[from UN-[1] + *abated* pa. pple of ABATE *verb*[1].]
Not abated; undiminished.

📖 T. HARDY The dancing progressed with unabated spirit. A. S. BYATT The storm continued unabated for three or four days.

■ **unabatable** *adjective* L18. **unabatedly** *adverb* E19. **unabating** *adjective* L18.

unability /ʌnəˈbɪlɪti/ *noun. arch.* LME.
[from UN-[1] + ABILITY, after Old French *inhabilité* or medieval Latin *inhabilitas*.]
Inability.

unable /ʌnˈeɪb(ə)l/ *adjective.* LME.
[from UN-[1] + ABLE *adjective*, after Old & mod. French *inhabile* or Latin *inhabilis*.]
1 Chiefly of a person: not having ability or power. Foll. by *to do*, †*for*, †*to*. LME.
2 (Of a person) lacking ability in some respect, incompetent; (of a faculty, action, etc.) inefficient, ineffectual. LME.
3 Of a person or (formerly) a thing: unfit, unsuited; incapable. Long *obsolete* exc. *Scot.*, foll. by *for*. LME.
†**4** Impossible. LME–M16.
5 Lacking in physical ability or strength; weak, feeble. Now *Scot.* L16.

📖 **1** G. GREENE Mr Ford is unable to write narrative. A. S. BYATT He has . . tried to make her speak of it, and has always been unable. **2** GOLDSMITH No hopes of succour from such unable protectors.

■ †**unableness** *noun* inability, incapacity; disability: LME–E18. †**unably** *adverb* in an unable or incapable manner LME–E18.

unable /ʌnˈeɪb(ə)l/ *verb trans.* Long *rare*. LME.
[from UN-[2] + ABLE *adjective*, or from prec.]
Make unable or unfit (*to do*); incapacitate, disable.

unabridged /ʌnəˈbrɪdʒd/ *adjective* & *noun.* L16.
[from UN-[1] + *abridged* pa. pple of ABRIDGE.]
▸**A** *adjective.* Esp. of a dictionary or other book: not abridged or shortened; complete. L16.
▸**B** *noun.* An unabridged dictionary. M19.
■ **unabridgeable** *adjective* E19.

unacceptable /ʌnəkˈsɛptəb(ə)l/ *adjective* & *noun.* L15.
[from UN-[1] + ACCEPTABLE.]
▸**A** *adjective.* Not acceptable. L15.

📖 G. BOYCOTT Jackman was unacceptable to the Guyana government and would be asked to leave.

▸**B** *noun.* An unacceptable thing; that which is unacceptable. E19.
■ **unacceptableness** *noun* M17. **unacceptably** *adverb* M17.

unaccommodated /ʌnəˈkɒmədeɪtɪd/ *adjective.* E17.
[from UN-[1] + *accommodated* pa. pple of ACCOMMODATE *verb*.]
Not accommodated; not possessed *of*, not provided *with*.
■ **unaccommodating** *adjective* not accommodating, not obliging L18.

unaccompanied /ʌnəˈkʌmpənɪd/ *adjective.* M16.
[from UN-[1] + *accompanied* pa. pple of ACCOMPANY.]
1 Not accompanied or attended; having no companion. (Foll. by *by*, *with*.) M16.
2 Lacking instrumental accompaniment. E19.

unaccomplished /ʌnəˈkʌmplɪʃt, -ˈkɒm-/ *adjective*. E16.
[from UN-[1] + ACCOMPLISHED.]
1 Not accomplished or achieved; uncompleted. E16.
2 Of a person: not socially or intellectually accomplished. E18.
■ **unaccomplishable** *adjective* L17.

unaccountable /ʌnəˈkaʊntəb(ə)l/ *adjective & noun*. M17.
[from UN-[1] + ACCOUNTABLE.]
▶**A** *adjective*. **1 a** Unable to be explained; inexplicable. M17. ▸**b** Of a person: difficult to make out; of a strange or puzzling disposition. E18.
2 Not liable to be called to account; irresponsible. M17.
†**3** Incalculable; uncountable. L17–E18.
▶**B** *noun*. **1** An unaccountable person. M18.
2 An unaccountable thing or event. L18.
■ **unaccountaˈbility** *noun* E18. **unaccountableness** *noun* L17. **unaccountably** *adverb* †(*a*) irresponsibly; (*b*) inexplicably: L17.

unaccounted /ʌnəˈkaʊntɪd/ *adjective*. L16.
[from UN-[1] + *accounted* pa. pple of ACCOUNT *verb*.]
1 †**a** Not taken account *of*. *rare*. Only in L16. ▸**b** Not accounted *for*. L18.
2 Of which no account is given. L17.

📖 **1b** *Guardian* Unable to estimate how many . . cheques were unaccounted for.

unaccused /ʌnəˈkjuːzd/ *adjective*. E16.
[from UN-[1] + ACCUSED.]
Not accused.
■ **unaccusable** *adjective* L16.

unaccustomed /ʌnəˈkʌstəmd/ *adjective*. E16.
[from UN-[1] + ACCUSTOMED.]
1 Not customary; unfamiliar, unusual. E16.
2 Not accustomed or used (*to* a thing). E17.

📖 **1** D. H. LAWRENCE The unaccustomed sound of the old piano startled me. **2** A. T. ELLIS Having been twice a wife . . she was unaccustomed to being single. *Guardian* Negative tactics had been forced on the Egyptians . . unaccustomed as they were to public battering.

■ **unaccustomedly** *adverb* M17. **unaccustomedness** *noun* E17.

unacknowledged /ʌnəkˈnɒlɪdʒd/ *adjective*. L16.
[from UN-[1] + ACKNOWLEDGED.]
Not acknowledged.
■ **unackowledging** *adjective* (now *rare*) ungrateful L16.

una corda /uːnə ˈkɔːdə/ *adverbial & adjectival phr*. M19.
[Italian = one string.]
MUSIC. A direction: using the soft pedal of the piano. Cf. TRE CORDE.

unacquainted /ʌnəˈkweɪntɪd/ *adjective*. E16.
[from UN-[1] + ACQUAINTED.]
†**1** Of another person: not personally known to one. Of a thing: unknown, unfamiliar, strange, unusual. E16–L17.
2 Of a person or (*rare*) a thing: having no acquaintance *with* something. Formerly also foll. by *in*, *of*, *to*. M16. ▸**b** *absol*. Inexperienced; ignorant. Also, unaware *that*. Now *rare* or *obsolete*. L16.
3 (Of a person): not having acquaintance *with* another; (of two or more people) not mutually acquainted. M17.

📖 **2** CARLYLE A Peasant unacquainted with botanical Physiology.

■ **unacquaint** *adjective* (chiefly *Scot*.) unacquainted L16. **unacquaintance** *noun* the fact or state of being unacquainted L16. **unacquaintedness** *noun* E17.

unactable /ʌnˈaktəb(ə)l/ *adjective*. E19.
[from UN-[1] + ACTABLE.]
Unable to be acted (on the stage); unsuitable for dramatic representation.
■ **unactaˈbility** *noun* E20.

unacted /ʌnˈaktɪd/ *adjective*. L16.
[from UN-[1] + *acted* pa. pple of ACT *verb*.]
1 Not carried out in action; not done. *arch*. L16.
2 Not performed on the stage. M19.

unactive /ʌnˈaktɪv/ *adjective*. L16.
[from UN-[1] + ACTIVE.]
†**1** Habitually or naturally inactive; indisposed or unable to act; sluggish, lazy. L16–M18.
2 Not active at a particular time; quiescent; characterized by an absence of activity. Now *rare*. L16.
■ †**unactivity** *noun* inactivity M17–M18.

unadapted /ʌnəˈdaptɪd/ *adjective*. L18.
[from UN-[1] + *adapted* pa. pple of ADAPT.]
Not adapted; not suited (*to*).
■ **unadaptaˈbility** *noun* the state or quality of not being adaptable E19. **unadaptable** *adjective* not adaptable L19. **unadaptive** *adjective* not adaptive M19.

unadjacent /ʌnəˈdʒeɪs(ə)nt/ *adjective*. M20.
[from UN-[1] + ADJACENT.]
Not adjacent.
not unadjacent to *colloq*. in the region of, approximately.

unadjusted /ʌnəˈdʒʌstɪd/ *adjective*. L18.
[from UN-[1] + *adjusted* pa. pple of ADJUST.]
Not adjusted.

unadmired /ʌnədˈmʌɪəd/ *adjective*. E18.
[from UN-[1] + *admired* pa. pple of ADMIRE.]
Not admired.
■ **unˈadmirable** *adjective* M19. **unadmiring** *adjective* M19.

unadmitted /ʌnədˈmɪtɪd/ *adjective*. E17.
[from UN-[1] + *admitted* pa. pple of ADMIT.]
1 Not allowed to enter. E17.
2 Unacknowledged, unconfessed. L19.

unadopted /ʌnəˈdɒptɪd/ *adjective*. M17.
[from UN-[1] + *adopted* pa. pple of ADOPT.]
Not adopted; (of a road, sewer, etc.) not taken over for maintenance by the local authority.

unadorned /ʌnəˈdɔːnd/ *adjective*. M17.
[from UN-[1] + *adorned* pa. pple of ADORN *verb*.]
Not adorned, not embellished.

📖 H. HALLAM Speeches in this tragedy are . . long, the style unadorned.

unadulterated /ʌnəˈdʌltəreɪtɪd/ *adjective*. L17.
[from UN-[1] + *adulterated* pa. pple of ADULTERATE *verb*.]
1 Not adulterated; pure; concentrated. L17.
2 Complete, sheer, utter. E19.

📖 **1** D. WILLIAMS Pure food . . unadulterated by mechanical or chemical intervention. **2** F. T. BULLEN The change of the monsoon . . is beastliness unadulterated.

■ **unadulterate** *adjective* (*arch*.) = UNADULTERATED M17. **unadulteratedly** *adverb* L19.

unadventurous /ʌnədˈvɛntʃ(ə)rəs/ *adjective*. L17.
[from UN-[1] + ADVENTUROUS.]
Not adventurous; timid.
■ **unadventurously** *adverb* E20. **unadventurousness** *noun* E20.

unadvertised /ʌnˈadvətʌɪzd/ *adjective*. LME.
[from UN-[1] + *advertised* pa. pple of ADVERTISE.]
†**1** Not notified or warned; uninformed (*of* something). LME–M17.
2 Not publicly announced or made known. (*rare* before M19.) E17.

unadvisable /ʌnədˈvʌɪzəb(ə)l/ *adjective*. L17.
[from UN-[1] + ADVISABLE.]
1 Of a person: not open to advice; obstinate. L17.
2 Of a thing: = INADVISABLE. M18.
■ **unadvisableness** *noun* L18. **unadvisably** *adverb* E18.

unadvised /ʌnədˈvʌɪzd/ *adjective & adverb*. ME.
[from UN-[1] + ADVISED.]
▶**A** *adjective*. **1** (Of acts, words, etc.) done or spoken without due consideration; ill-advised; (of a person, conduct, character, etc.) imprudent, indiscreet, thoughtless. ME. ▸**b** Not having consulted *with* another; not having been consulted *with*. L16.
2 Not having had advice. M19.
▶**B** *adverb*. †**1** Without warning; unexpectedly. LME–L15.
2 Without consideration or reflection. LME–E17.
■ **unadvisedly** /-zɪdli/ *adverb* ME. **unadvisedness** /-zɪdnɪs/ *noun* LME.

unaesthetic /ʌniːsˈθɛtɪk, -nɛs-/ *adjective*. Also ***unes-**. M19.
[from UN-[1] + AESTHETIC *adjective*.]
Not aesthetic; lacking in aesthetic taste.

unaffected /ʌnəˈfɛktɪd/ *adjective*. L16.
[from UN-[1] + AFFECTED.]
▶**I 1** Not adopted or assumed; free from affectation or artificiality; genuine, sincere. L16. ▸**b** Of a person: not affected in manner; unpretentious. L17.

📖 **1** R. C. HUTCHINSON An unaffected pleasure in her brother-in-law's return. **b** C. PETERS She was unaffected and natural, qualities he . . admired.

▶**II 2** Not influenced in mind or feeling; untouched, unmoved. L16.
3 Not attacked by disease. L18.
4 Not acted on or altered *by* an agent or influence. M19.

📖 **2** M. M. SHERWOOD The old man was quite unaffected, and looked quite stupid. **4** *Lancet* The patient was patch-tested . . and . . the control patch remained unaffected. P. ACKROYD The street . . could not have been entirely unaffected by the closeness of the city.

■ **unaffectedly** *adverb* M17. **unaffectedness** *noun* †(*a*) indifference; (*b*) freedom from affectation: L17. †**unaffectible** *adjective* unable to be affected L17–M19. **unaffecting** *adjective* †(*a*) free from affectation; (*b*) not affecting, not influencing: E17.

unaffied /ʌnəˈfʌɪd/ *adjective*. *arch*. E16.
[from UN-[1] + *affied* pa. pple of AFFY.]
Not affianced.

unaffrighted /ʌnəˈfrʌɪtɪd/ *adjective*. *arch. & poet*. L16.
[from UN-[1] + AFFRIGHTED.]
Unfrightened.

unafraid /ʌnəˈfreɪd/ *adjective*. LME.
[from UN-[1] + AFRAID.]
Not afraid; undaunted, undismayed. (Foll. by *of*.)

unaggressive /ʌnəˈgrɛsɪv/ *adjective*. M19.
[from UN-[1] + AGGRESSIVE.]
Not aggressive.
■ **unaggressively** *adverb* L19. **unaggressiveness** *noun* L19.

unagitated /ʌnˈadʒɪteɪtɪd/ *adjective*. M17.
[from UN-[1] + *agitated* pa. pple of AGITATE *verb*.]
1 Not physically moved or disturbed. M17.
2 Not perturbed or excited in the mind or feelings. L18.
■ **unagitatedly** *adverb* L19.

unagreeable /ʌnəˈgriːəb(ə)l/ *adjective*. Now *rare*. LME.
[from UN-[1] + AGREEABLE *adjective*.]
1 Not agreeable or pleasing; not to one's liking or taste; uncongenial. LME.
†**2** Unconformable or unsuitable *to*, inconsistent or incongruous *with*. M16–E18.
■ †**unagreeableness** *noun*: only in M17. **unagreeably** *adverb* †(*a*) inconsistently; (*b*) unpleasantly, disagreeably: M16.

unaided /ʌnˈeɪdɪd/ *adjective*. L16.
[from UN-[1] + *aided* pa. pple of AID *verb*.]
Not aided; unassisted, without help.

📖 A. C. CLARKE The tiny 'bricks' of H_2O were too small to be visible to the unaided sense.

■ **unaidable** /ʌnˈeɪdəb(ə)l/ *adjective* that cannot be aided M17. **unaidedly** *adverb* M19.

unaker /ˈjuːnəkə/ *noun*. *obsolete* exc. *Hist*. M18.
[Perh. from Cherokee *u:né:ka* white.]
An American china clay of Virginia and N. Carolina imported and used in early Bow porcelain.

unal /ˈjuːn(ə)l/ *adjective*. *rare*. E18.
[from Latin *unus* one + -AL[1].]
Single; that is one only; based on unity.

unalienable /ʌnˈeɪlɪənəb(ə)l/ *adjective*. E17.
[from UN-[1] + ALIENABLE.]
= INALIENABLE.
■ **unalienably** *adverb* E18.

unalist /ˈjuːn(ə)lɪst/ *noun*. *rare*. M18.
[from (the same roof as) UNAL *adjective* + -IST after *dualist*, *pluralist*.]
†**1** A holder of only one benefice. Only in M18.
2 A person who believes in one supreme God, a monist. L19.
■ **unalism** *noun* the beliefs or practices of unalists L19.

unalive /ʌnəˈlʌɪv/ *adjective*. E19.
[from UN-[1] + ALIVE.]
1 Not fully susceptible or aware *to*. E19.
2 Lacking in vitality; not living. E20.

unalleviated /ʌnəˈliːvɪeɪtɪd/ *adjective*. M18.
[from UN-[1] + *alleviated* pa. pple of ALLEVIATE.]
Not alleviated, relentless.
■ **unaˈlleviable** *adjective* not able to be alleviated E19.

unalloyed /ʌnəˈlɔɪd/ *adjective*. M17.
[from UN-[1] + *alloyed* pa. pple of ALLOY *verb*.]
Not alloyed, pure; *fig*. complete, utter.

📖 P. L. FERMOR They have left a memory of complete and unalloyed bliss.

unalterable /ʌnˈɔːlt(ə)rəb(ə)l/ *adjective*. L16.
[from UN-[1] + ALTERABLE.]
Not alterable, not able to be altered or changed.

📖 P. GARDINER His commitment to Christianity was by now fixed and unalterable.

■ **unalteraˈbility** *noun* M19. **unalterableness** *noun* E17. **unalterably** *adverb* M17. **unaltered** *adjective* not altered; *spec*. (of an animal) not castrated or spayed: M16. **unaltering** *adjective* not altering, unchanging E19.

unambiguous /ʌnamˈbɪgjʊəs/ *adjective*. M18.
[from UN-[1] + AMBIGUOUS.]
Not ambiguous, clear or definite in meaning.
■ **unambiˈguity** *noun* M19. **unambiguously** *adverb* L18.

unambitious /ʌnamˈbɪʃəs/ *adjective*. E17.
[from UN-[1] + AMBITIOUS.]
Not ambitious; without ambition.
■ **unambitiously** *adverb* M18. **unambitiousness** *noun* M18.

un-American /ʌnəˈmɛrɪk(ə)n/ *adjective*. E19.
[from UN-[1] + AMERICAN.]
Not in accordance with American characteristics; contrary to the ideals and interests of the US.
■ **un-Americanism** *noun* E20. **un-Americanized** *adjective* not Americanized L19.

Unami /ʊˈnɑːmi/ *noun & adjective*. M18.
[Algonquian.]
▶**A** *noun*. Pl. same.
1 A member of a branch of the Delawares. M18.
2 The Algonquian language of this people. M19.
▶**B** *attrib*. or as *adjective*. Of or pertaining to the Unami or their language. E20.

unamiable /ʌnˈeɪmɪəb(ə)l/ *adjective*. L15.
[from UN-[1] + AMIABLE.]
Not amiable.
■ **unamiaˈbility** *noun* E19. **unamiableness** *noun* E17. **unamiably** *adverb* M19.

For other words beginning with *un-* see the entries for **un-**[1], **un-**[2]

unanalogous /ʌnəˈnaləɡəs/ *adjective.* L18.
[from UN-^{1} + ANALOGOUS.]
Not analogous.
■ **unanaˈlogical** *adjective* M18.

unaneled /ʌnəˈniːld/ *adjective. arch.* E17.
[from UN-^{1} + *aneled* pa. pple of ANELE *verb.*]
Not anointed; not having received extreme unction.

Unani /juːˈnɑːni/ *adjective.* Also **Yunani**. E20.
[Arab. *Yūnānī* lit. 'Greek'.]
Designating or pertaining to the Western medical tradition. Opp. AYURVEDIC.

unanimism /juːˈnanɪmɪz(ə)m/ *noun.* M20.
[French *unanimisme*, from *unanime* unanimous: see -ISM.]
A French poetic movement of the early 20th cent., emphasizing the submersion of the poet in the group consciousness and characterized by simple diction, absence of rhyme, and strongly accented rhythms.
■ Also ˈ**unanism** *noun* E20.

unanimist /juːˈnanɪmɪst/ *noun & adjective.* E20.
[French *unanimiste*, formed as prec.: see -IST.]
▶ **A** *noun.* An adherent of unanimism. E20.
▶ **B** *attrib.* or as *adjective.* Of or pertaining to unanimists or unanimism. E20.

unanimity /juːnəˈnɪmɪti/ *noun.* LME.
[Old & mod. French *unanimité* or Latin *unanimitas*, from *unanimus*: see next, -ITY.]
The state of being unanimous; an instance of this. Also foll. by *of*.

F. W. FARRAR Animated by a sublime unanimity of purpose. GLADSTONE Parliament, upon that question, would speak with unanimity.

unanimous /juːˈnanɪməs/ *adjective.* E17.
[from Latin *unanimus*, (late) *unanimis*, from *unus* one + *animus* spirit, mind: see -OUS.]
1 Of one mind or opinion; all in agreement. E17.
2 Held, given, or undertaken by general agreement or consent. L17.

1 P. G. WODEHOUSE What the Press . . was unanimous in describing as a well-earned sentence. **2** N. MAILER To impose the death penalty it does require a unanimous vote of all twelve of you.

■ **unanimously** *adverb* E17. **unanimousness** *noun* (*rare*) L18.

unannealed /ʌnəˈniːld/ *adjective.* M18.
[from UN-^{1} + *annealed* pa. pple of ANNEAL *verb.*]
Untempered (*lit. & fig.*).

unannounced /ʌnəˈnaʊnst/ *adjective.* L18.
[from UN-^{1} + *announced* pa. pple of ANNOUNCE *verb.*]
Not announced; without warning.

M. FLANAGAN I had given my solemn oath never again to show up unannounced.

unanswerable /ʌnˈɑːns(ə)rəb(ə)l/ *adjective.* E17.
[from UN-^{1} + ANSWERABLE.]
†**1** Not corresponding (*to*); dissimilar. Only in 17.
2 Not able to be answered. E17.
3 Not liable to answer; not responsible *for. rare.* L19.

2 M. KEANE A question . . she avoided . . because she found it so unanswerable.

■ **unansweraˈbility** *noun* M19. **unanswerableness** *noun* †(*a*) the inability to answer or be responsive (*to*); (*b*) the state or condition of being unanswerable: E17. **unanswerably** *adverb* L16. **unanswered** *adjective* not answered LME. **unanswering** *adjective* not answering E17.

unapostolic /ˌʌnapəˈstɒlɪk/ *adjective.* L17.
[from UN-^{1} + APOSTOLIC.]
Contrary to apostolic custom; not having apostolic authority.
■ **unapostolically** *adverb* in an unapostolic manner M19.

unappealable /ʌnəˈpiːləb(ə)l/ *adjective.* M17.
[from UN-^{1} + APPEALABLE.]
Chiefly LAW. Not able to be appealed against.

GLADSTONE The judgments of this Pope . . are unappealable and irreversible.

■ **unappealableness** *noun* (*rare*) M17. **unappealably** *adverb* M19. **unappealed** *ppl adjective* (LAW) (of a judgement etc.) not appealed against, uncontested (also foll. by *from*) L19.

unappealing /ʌnəˈpiːlɪŋ/ *adjective.* M19.
[UN-^{1} + UNAPPEALING.]
Not appealing; *esp.* not attractive or pleasing.

J. RABAN Opening his lips to disclose an unappealing collection of gunmetal fillings.

■ **unappealingly** *adverb* L20.

unappeasable /ʌnəˈpiːzəb(ə)l/ *adjective.* M16.
[from UN-^{1} + APPEASABLE.]
Not appeasable.
■ **unappeasableness** *noun* E17. **unappeasably** *adverb* M17. **unappeased** *adjective* not appeased L16.

unappetizing /ʌnˈapɪtʌɪzɪŋ/ *adjective.* Also **-ising**. L19.
[from UN-^{1} + APPETIZING.]
Not appetizing.
■ **unappetizingly** *adverb* M20.

†**unapplicable** *adjective.* M17–M18.
[from UN-^{1} + APPLICABLE.]
Inapplicable.

unapproachable /ʌnəˈprəʊtʃəb(ə)l/ *adjective & noun.* L16.
[from UN-^{1} + APPROACHABLE.]
▶ **A** Not approachable; remote, inaccessible (*lit. & fig.*). L16.

F. W. FARRAR Districts in which the heat was so intense that they were unapproachable. JULIETTE HUXLEY He could be aloof, fastidious and unapproachable.

▶ **B** *absol.* as *noun.* **the unapproachable**, the person who or thing which is unapproachable. E19.
■ **unapproachaˈbility** *noun* M19. **unapproachableness** *noun* E18. **unapproachably** *adverb* E19.

unapproached /ʌnəˈprəʊtʃt/ *adjective.* M17.
[from UN-^{1} + *approached* pa. pple of APPROACH *verb.*]
Not approached (*lit. & fig.*).

unapropos /ˌʌnaprəˈpəʊ, ʌnˈaprəpəʊ/ *adjective & adverb.* M19.
[from UN-^{1} + APROPOS.]
▶ **A** *adjective.* Not apropos; irrelevant; inappropriate. M19.
▶ **B** *adverb.* In an unapropos manner; irrelevantly, inappropriately. M20.

unapt /ʌnˈapt/ *adjective.* LME.
[from UN-^{1} + APT.]
1 Not suited, fitted, adapted, or prepared (*for*, *to do*). Long *arch.* LME.
2 Not suitable, appropriate, or apposite. M16.
3 Not habitually liable, customarily disposed, likely, or prone, *to do*. L16.

1 E. GAYTON Guests . . very unapt to sleep anywhere but in their own houses. W. COWPER I shall prove of little force Hereafter, and for manly feats unapt. **2** *Observer* The language of cruelty, kindness and compassion is unapt. **3** SIR W. SCOTT A mind which was unapt to apprehend danger. J. T. MICKLETHWAITE Of little creative power, but not unapt to take up ideas suggested to them.

■ **unaptly** *adverb* M16. **unaptness** *noun* M16.

unarch /ʌnˈɑːtʃ/ *verb trans. & intrans. rare.* L16.
[from UN-^{2} + ARCH *verb*^{1}.]
Uncurve; straighten.

unarched /ʌnˈɑːtʃt/ *adjective. rare.* M17.
[from UN-^{1} + ARCH *noun*^{1}, *verb*^{1}: see -ED^{2}, -ED^{1}.]
Not covered over or provided with an arch or arches.

unarm /ʌnˈɑːm/ *verb trans.* ME.
[from UN-^{2} + ARM *verb*^{1}.]
1 Free (a person, oneself) of armour; assist (a person) to disarm. ME.
†**2 a** Deprive of arms, weapons, etc.; remove arms, weapons, etc., from. M16–M17. ▸**b** Make (a weapon) harmless. *rare.* Only in E18.

unarmed /ʌnˈɑːmd/ *adjective.* ME.
[from UN-^{1} + ARMED *adjective*^{1}.]
Not armed; without armour or weapons (*lit. & fig.*); *spec.* (*a*) (of an animal) not having horns, claws, etc.; †(*b*) (of a magnet) not provided with an armature; (*c*) (of a plant) not having prickles, thorns, etc.

R. L. STEVENSON Observing Gray to be unarmed, I handed him my cutlass. **unarmed combat** any of various modes of combat in which weapons are not used.

unary /ˈjuːnəri/ *adjective.* E20.
[from Latin *unus* one + -ARY^{1}, after BINARY, TERNARY.]
Consisting of or involving a single component or element.

unashamed /ʌnəˈʃeɪmd/ *adjective.* E17.
[from UN-^{1} + ASHAMED.]
Not ashamed, not feeling or showing guilt or embarrassment; blatant, bold.

Times Lit. Suppl. As an unashamed Mediterranean male, he is suitably misogynistic.

■ **unashamedly** /-mɪdli/ *adverb* E20. **unashamedness** /-mɪdnɪs/ *noun* L19.

unassailable /ʌnəˈseɪləb(ə)l/ *adjective.* L16.
[from UN-^{1} + ASSAILABLE.]
Not assailable (*lit. & fig.*); impregnable.

J. C. OATES His rank as full professor is unassailable. P. LOMAS The recent critiques . . of the hitherto unassailable Lacan.

■ **unassailaˈbility** *noun* E20. **unassailableness** *noun* M19. **unassailably** *adverb* L19. **unassailed** *adjective* L16.

unassertive /ʌnəˈsəːtɪv/ *adjective.* M19.
[from UN-^{1} + ASSERTIVE.]
Not assertive; not forthcoming or positive, reticent.

T. TANNER Fanny is timid, silent, unassertive, shrinking and excessively vulnerable.

■ **unasserted** *adjective* M19. **unassertively** *adverb* L20. **unassertiveness** *noun* M20.

unassuming /ʌnəˈsjuːmɪŋ/ *adjective.* E18.
[from UN-^{1} + ASSUMING.]
Not assuming; not pretentious or arrogant, modest.

W. BOYD An unassuming single-storey stone building.

■ **unassumed** *adjective* E19. **unassumingly** *adverb* E20. **unassumingness** *noun* M18.

unassured /ʌnəˈʃʊəd/ *adjective.* LME.
[from UN-^{1} + ASSURED *ppl adjective.*]
1 Orig., not safe; insecure. Later, not made safe, not guaranteed. LME.
2 Not self-possessed or confident. LME.
3 Not certain or sure (*of*). L15.

unattached /ʌnəˈtatʃt/ *adjective.* L15.
[from UN-^{1} + *attached* pa. pple of ATTACH *verb.*]
†**1** LAW. Not arrested or seized by authority. L15–M17.
2 Not attached, esp. to a particular body, organization, etc. Freq. foll. by *to*. L18.
3 Not engaged or married. L19.
2 unattached participle = DANGLING *participle*.
■ **unattachedness** *noun* M20.

unattainable /ʌnəˈteɪnəb(ə)l/ *adjective & noun.* M17.
[from UN-^{1} + ATTAINABLE.]
▶ **A** *adjective.* Not attainable. M17.
▶ **B** *noun.* **1** An unattainable thing. *rare.* M17.
2 With *the*: that which is unattainable. M19.
■ **unattainableness** *noun* L17. **unattainably** *adverb* L19.

unattained /ʌnəˈteɪnd/ *adjective & noun.* E17.
[from UN-^{1} + *attained* pa. pple of ATTAIN *verb.*]
▶ **A** *adjective.* †**1** Untouched, unaffected. Only in E17.
2 Not attained or reached. L17.
▶ **B** *noun.* With *the*: that which is not attained. M19.

unattaint /ʌnəˈteɪnt/ *adjective. arch.* M17.
[from UN-^{1} + ATTAINT *pa. pple & ppl adjective.*]
†**1** = UNATTAINTED 2. Only in M17.
2 = UNATTAINTED 1. M19.

unattainted /ʌnəˈteɪntɪd/ *adjective.* L16.
[from UN-^{1} + *attainted* pa. pple of ATTAINT *verb.*]
1 Not tainted or sullied; free from blemish. L16.
2 Not convicted or attainted in law. Cf. earlier UNATTAINT 1. L18.

unattended /ʌnəˈtɛndɪd/ *adjective.* E17.
[from UN-^{1} + *attended* pa. pple of ATTEND *verb.*]
1 Not accompanied, alone, with no one in attendance. E17.
2 Foll. by *by* or *with*: not occurring with or as a result of a specified thing, circumstance, etc. L17.
3 Not made the object of one's attention, concern, etc.; not dealt with. Freq. foll. by *to*. E18.

unattractive /ʌnəˈtraktɪv/ *adjective.* E19.
[from UN-^{1} + ATTRACTIVE.]
Not attractive; *esp.* not pleasing or alluring.

E. BOWEN In grumbling about his niece . . he was presenting himself in a most unattractive light.

■ **unattracted** *adjective* not attracted E18. **unattractively** *adverb* M19. **unattractiveness** *noun* M19.

unau /ˈjuːnɔː/ *noun.* L18.
[French from Tupi *unáu*.]
The two-toed sloth, *Choloepus didactylus*.

unauthentic /ʌnɔːˈθɛntɪk/ *adjective.* M17.
[from UN-^{1} + AUTHENTIC.]
Not authentic.
■ **unauthentically** *adverb* E17. **unauthenˈticity** *noun* L18.

unauthenticated /ʌnɔːˈθɛntɪkeɪtɪd/ *adjective.* L18.
[from UN-^{1} + *authenticated* pa. pple of AUTHENTICATE.]
Not authenticated.

unauthorised *adjective* var. of UNAUTHORIZED.

unauthoritative /ʌnɔːˈθɒrɪtətɪv, -teɪtɪv/ *adjective.* M17.
[from UN-^{1} + AUTHORITATIVE.]
Not authoritative.
■ **unauthoritatively** *adverb* (long *rare* or *obsolete*) M17. **unauthoritativeness** *noun* (*rare*) E19.

unauthorized /ʌnˈɔːθərʌɪzd/ *adjective.* Also **-ised**. L16.
[from UN-^{1} + AUTHORIZED.]
Not authorized.
■ **unauthorizedly** *adverb* M19.

unavailable /ʌnəˈveɪləb(ə)l/ *adjective.* M16.
[from UN-^{1} + AVAILABLE.]
1 Unavailing; ineffectual. *arch.* M16.
2 Not available; not able to be used or turned to account. M19.
■ **unavailaˈbility** *noun* M19. **unavailableness** *noun* M16. **unavailably** *adverb* M19.

unavailing /ʌnəˈveɪlɪŋ/ *adjective.* L17.
[from UN-^{1} + AVAILING.]
Not availing; achieving nothing, ineffectual.

R. LINDNER This time his pleas were unavailing.

■ **unavailingly** *adverb* M18.

una voce /juːneɪ ˈvəʊsiː, uːnə ˈvəʊkeɪ/ *adverbial phr.* M16.
[from Latin *una* abl. sing. fem. of *unus* one + *voce* abl. sing. of *vox* voice.]
With one voice; unanimously.

For other words beginning with *un-* see the entries for **un-**^{1}, **un-**^{2}

unavoidable /ʌnəˈvɔɪdəb(ə)l/ *adjective.* L16.
[from UN-[1] + AVOIDABLE.]
Not avoidable; inevitable.

R. CARVER He was dying, it was as . . unavoidable as that. F. KAPLAN The unavoidable youthful anxieties, particularly . . his separation from his mother.

■ **unavoidaˈbility** *noun* M19. **unavoidableness** *noun* L16. **unavoidably** *adverb* E17. **unaˈvoided** *adjective* (*a*) not avoided or escaped; †(*b*) *rare* unavoidable; inevitable: M16.

unavowed /ʌnəˈvaʊd/ *adjective.* L18.
[from UN-[1] + *avowed* pa. pple of AVOW *verb*[1].]
Not avowed.
■ **unaˈvowable** *adjective* not avowable L18. **unavowedly** /-ɪdli/ *adverb* M19.

unaware /ʌnəˈwɛː/ *adverb & adjective.* L16.
[from UN-[1] + AWARE. Cf. earlier UNWARE.]
▶ **A** *adverb.* Unawares; inadvertently, unintentionally; unexpectedly, suddenly. L16.

SHAKES. *Ven. & Ad.* As one that unaware Hath dropp'd a precious jewel in the flood. KEATS Long have I sought for rest, and, unaware, Behold I find it!

Phrases: **at unaware** *arch.* = **at unawares** s.v. UNAWARES *adverb.*
▶ **B** *adjective.* **1** Ignorant or not aware (*of, that*). E18.
2 Reckless; lacking caution; unwary. Later also, insensitive, unperceptive. E19.

1 K. ISHIGURO I am not unaware of this viewpoint.

■ **unawareness** *noun* M19.

unawares /ʌnəˈwɛːz/ *adverb & adjective.* M16.
[from (the same root as) prec. + -s[3]. Cf. earlier UNWARES.]
▶ **A** *adverb.* **1** Without being aware; inadvertently; unintentionally. Also, without being noticed; unobserved. M16.
2 Without intimation or warning; unexpectedly, suddenly. M16.

1 J. BENTHAM So great a master having fallen unawares into an error. **2** R. FULLER The curious word popped out unawares.

Phrases: **at unawares** *arch.* unexpectedly, suddenly; unobserved; inadvertently, unintentionally. **catch unawares**, **take unawares** catch or take unprepared or off guard, surprise.
▶ **B** *adjective.* †**1** Ignorant or not aware *of*. Only in M16.
2 Unknown, unperceived, unrealized. Also foll. by *to*, †*of*. Now *rare* or *obsolete*. M16.

unbacked /ʌnˈbakt/ *adjective.* L16.
[from UN-[1] + BACK *noun*[1], *verb*: see -ED[2], -ED[1].]
Not backed; *spec.* (*a*) (of a horse) unmounted, unridden; not broken in; (*b*) not supported or endorsed; (*c*) (of a racehorse etc.) not betted on; (*d*) not provided with a back or backing.
■ **unbackable** *adjective* not able to be backed E20.

unbag /ʌnˈbag/ *verb trans.* Infl. **-gg-**. E17.
[from UN-[2] + BAG *noun.*]
Take out of or release from a bag.

unbait /ʌnˈbeɪt/ *verb trans. rare.* L16.
[from UN-[2] + BAIT *noun*[1].]
Remove bait from (a hook, snare, etc.).

unbaited /ʌnˈbeɪtɪd/ *ppl adjective.* E16.
[from UN-[1] + *baited* pa. pple of BAIT *verb*[1]. In sense 2 perh. also from BAIT *noun*[1] + -ED[2].]
1 Of a chained or confined animal: not baited by dogs. E16.
2 Of a hook, snare, etc.: not provided with bait. L19.

unbalance /ʌnˈbal(ə)ns/ *noun.* L19.
[from UN-[1] + BALANCE *noun.*]
Lack of balance; (esp. mental) instability.

unbalance /ʌnˈbal(ə)ns/ *verb trans.* L16.
[from UN-[2] + BALANCE *verb.*]
†**1** Remove ballast from (a ship). *rare*. Only in L16.
2 Throw (a person or thing) off balance; upset the physical or mental balance of. M19.

2 C. CONRAN Excessive use of herbs and spices unbalances a dish—usually irreparably.

unbalanced /ʌnˈbal(ə)nst/ *adjective.* M17.
[from UN-[1] + BALANCED.]
Not balanced; *esp.* (of a person etc.) mentally unstable or deranged.

unbank /ʌnˈbaŋk/ *verb trans.* M19.
[from UN-[2] + BANK *verb*[1].]
Free from the confines of a bank or banks (*lit.* & *fig.*); clear (a fire) of banked-up matter.

unbankable /ʌnˈbaŋkəb(ə)l/ *adjective.* M19.
[from UN-[1] + BANKABLE.]
Of money etc.: not bankable.

unbaptise *verb*, **unbaptised** *adjective* vars. of UNBAPTIZE, UNBAPTIZED.

unbaptize /ʌnbapˈtʌɪz/ *verb trans.* Also **-ise**. E17.
[from UN-[2] + BAPTIZE.]
Divest (a person) of the effect of baptism.

unbaptized /ʌnbapˈtʌɪzd/ *adjective.* Also **-ised**. LME.
[from UN-[1] + *baptized* pa. pple of BAPTIZE *verb.*]
Not baptized.

unbar /ʌnˈbɑː/ *verb trans.* Infl. **-rr-**. ME.
[from UN-[2] + BAR *verb.*]
Remove a bar or bars from (a door, gate, etc.); unfasten, unlock, open.

†**unbarbed** *adjective*[1]. M16–E17.
[from UN-[1] + BARBED *adjective*[2].]
= UNBARDED.

unbarbed /ʌnˈbɑːbd/ *adjective*[2]. M19.
[from UN-[1] + BARBED *adjective*[1].]
Not provided with a barb or barbs.

unbarded /ʌnˈbɑːdɪd/ *adjective.* L16.
[from UN-[1] + *barded* pa. pple of BARD *verb.*]
Hist. Not barded (BARD *verb* 1).

unbark /ʌnˈbɑːk/ *verb*[1] *trans.* M16.
[from UN-[2] + BARK *noun*[2].]
Deprive or strip (a tree) of bark.

unbark /ʌnˈbɑːk/ *verb*[2] *trans. obsolete* exc. *dial.* M16.
[from UN-[2] + BARK *noun*[3].]
Disembark.

unbarked /ʌnˈbɑːkt/ *adjective.* M16.
[from UN-[1] + *barked* pa. pple of BARK *verb*[2].]
†**1** Not treated with bark; untanned. Only in M16.
2 Not stripped of bark. M19.

unbarred /ʌnˈbɑːd/ *adjective.* M16.
[from UN-[1] + BARRED.]
Not barred; *spec.* (*a*) (of a harbour) not obstructed by a sandbank; (*b*) not secured or shut with a bar or bars; (*c*) LAW not excluded or blocked by objection; (*d*) MUSIC not marked off by bars.

unbarrel /ʌnˈbar(ə)l/ *verb trans.* Infl. **-ll-**, ***-l-**. E17.
[from UN-[2] + BARREL *noun.*]
Remove from or take out of a barrel.

unbarrelled /ʌnˈbar(ə)ld/ *adjective. rare.* Also ***-eled**. L15.
[from UN-[1] + *barrelled* pa. pple of BARREL *verb.*]
Not placed or stored in a barrel or barrels.

unbashful /ʌnˈbaʃfʊl, -f(ə)l/ *adjective.* Chiefly *literary.* M16.
[from UN-[1] + BASHFUL.]
Not bashful.
■ **unbashfully** *adverb* L18. **unbashfulness** *noun* E17.

unbated /ʌnˈbeɪtɪd/ *adjective. arch.* L16.
[from UN-[1] + *bated* pa. pple of BATE *verb*[2].]
1 Unabated, undiminished. L16.
2 Of a sword etc.: not blunted. E17.

unbe /ʌnˈbiː/ *verb*[1] *intrans. rare.* Only in inf. & as pa. pple **unbeen** /ʌnˈbiːn/. LME.
[from UN-[1] + BE.]
Lack being; be non-existent.

unbe /ʌnˈbiː/ *verb*[2] *trans. rare.* Only in inf. E17.
[from UN-[2] + BE.]
Deprive of being; make non-existent.

unbearable /ʌnˈbɛːrəb(ə)l/ *adjective.* LME.
[from UN-[1] + BEARABLE.]
Not bearable; unendurable, intolerable.

J. GATHORNE-HARDY Suicide . . a straightforward reaction to unbearable stress.

■ **unbearableness** *noun* M18. **unbearably** *adverb* E19.

unbeatable /ʌnˈbiːtəb(ə)l/ *adjective.* L19.
[from UN-[1] + BEAT *verb*[1] + -ABLE.]
Not able to be beaten; *esp.* that cannot be surpassed or defeated, excelling.
■ **unbeatably** *adverb* E20.

unbeaten /ʌnˈbiːt(ə)n/ *adjective.* ME.
[from UN-[1] + BEATEN.]
Not beaten; *esp.* not surpassed or defeated; CRICKET not out.

unbeauteous /ʌnˈbjuːtɪəs/ *adjective. literary.* M17.
[from UN-[1] + BEAUTEOUS.]
Unbeautiful.
■ **unbeauteousness** *noun* (*rare*) L19.

unbeautified /ʌnˈbjuːtɪfʌɪd/ *ppl adjective.* E17.
[from UN-[1] + *beautified* pa. pple of BEAUTIFY.]
Not beautified.

unbeautiful /ʌnˈbjuːtɪfʊl, -f(ə)l/ *adjective.* L15.
[from UN-[1] + BEAUTIFUL.]
Not beautiful, ugly.
■ **unbeautifully** *adverb* M19. **unbeautifulness** *noun* (*rare*) E18.

unbeautify /ʌnˈbjuːtɪfʌɪ/ *verb trans.* L16.
[from UN-[2] + BEAUTIFY.]
Make unbeautiful.

unbecome /ʌnbɪˈkʌm/ *verb trans. literary.* Pa. t. (*rare*) **unbecame** /ʌnbɪˈkeɪm/; pa. pple (*rare*) **unbecome**. E17.
[from UN-[1] + BECOME or back-form. from next.]
Not become or suit; be unbecoming to. Chiefly in neg. contexts.

unbecoming /ʌnbɪˈkʌmɪŋ/ *adjective.* L16.
[from UN-[1] + BECOMING *adjective.*]
Not becoming or befitting; unsuitable; indecorous. Also foll. by *to*, *for*.

R. B. SHERIDAN Very unbecoming in you to want to have the last word with your Mamma. A. TYLER An unbecoming pale blue swimsuit that exposed her thin, limp legs.

■ **unbecomingly** *adverb* M17. **unbecomingness** *noun* M17.

unbed /ʌnˈbɛd/ *verb trans.* Infl. **-dd-**. E17.
[from UN-[2] + BED *noun.*]
Remove from a bed.

unbedded /ʌnˈbɛdɪd/ *adjective.* M19.
[from UN-[1] + *bedded* pa. pple of BED *verb.*]
Not bedded; *spec.* in GEOLOGY, not stratified in beds.

unbefitting /ʌnbɪˈfɪtɪŋ/ *adjective.* L16.
[from UN-[1] + BEFITTING.]
Not befitting; unsuitable.
■ **unbefittingly** *adverb* L19. **unbefittingness** *noun* M19.

unbeget /ʌnbɪˈgɛt/ *verb trans. arch.* Pa. t. (*rare*) **-got** /-ˈgɒt/, (*arch.*) **-gat** /-ˈgat/; pres. pple **-getting**; pa. pple **-gotten** /-ˈgɒt(ə)n/. L16.
[from UN-[2] + BEGET.]
Annul or undo the begetting of.

unbeginning /ʌnbɪˈgɪnɪŋ/ *adjective.* L16.
[from UN-[1] + *beginning* p. pple of BEGIN *verb.*]
Not having a beginning.
■ **unbeginningly** *adverb* L17. **unbeginningness** *noun* M19.

unbegot *verb pa. t.*: see UNBEGET.

unbegotten /ʌnbɪˈgɒt(ə)n/ *adjective.* L15.
[from UN-[1] + *begotten* pa. pple of BEGET.]
Not begotten.
■ **unbegot** *adjective* (*arch.*) unbegotten L16. **unbegottenly** *adverb* M18. **unbegottenness** /-n-n-/ *noun* M17.

unbegotten *verb* pa. pple: see UNBEGET.

unbeguile /ʌnbɪˈgʌɪl/ *verb trans.* Long *arch. rare.* E17.
[from UN-[2] + BEGUILE *verb.*]
Undeceive.

unbeguiled /ʌnbɪˈgʌɪld/ *adjective.* M16.
[from UN-[1] + *beguiled* pa. pple of BEGUILE *verb.*]
Not beguiled.

unbegun /ʌnbɪˈgʌn/ *ppl adjective.* OE.
[from UN-[1] + *begun* pa. pple of BEGIN.]
1 Not having a beginning; ever existent. OE.
2 Not yet begun; not commenced. M16.

unbeknown /ʌnbɪˈnəʊn/ *pred. adjective & adverb.* M17.
[from UN-[1] + *beknown* pa. pple of BEKNOW.]
1 Foll. by *to*: ▶**a** Without the knowledge of. M17. ▶**b** Unacquainted with. M19.
2 Without its being known; unrecognized. E19.

1a C. WARWICK Unbeknown to Peter, part of the financial arrangements proved to be unsoundly based. **2** A. E. HOUSMAN My love rose up so early And stole out unbeknown.

unbeknownst /ʌnbɪˈnəʊnst/ *pred. adjective & adverb.* M19.
[from prec. + *-st* after *amidst*, *amongst*, etc.]
1 Foll. by *to*: = UNBEKNOWN 1a. M19.
2 a Unknowingly. *rare.* M19. ▶**b** = UNBEKNOWN 2. L19.

1 A. BROOKNER Mr. Markus . . unbeknownst to her, is watching her. **2b** JOYCE And we to be there, mavrone, and you to be unbeknownst.

unbelief /ʌnbɪˈliːf/ *noun.* ME.
[from UN-[1] + BELIEF.]
Absence or lack of belief, esp. of religious faith; disbelief, incredulity. Also, an instance of this.

AV *Mark* 9:24 Lord, I beleeue, helpe thou mine vnbeliefe. *Longman's Magazine* I had received the news with contemptuous unbelief.

unbelievable /ʌnbɪliːvəb(ə)l/ *adjective.* M16.
[from UN-[1] + BELIEVABLE.]
Not believable; incredible.

J. GATHORNE-HARDY Some of the new modern drugs are unbelievable by my standard of twenty years ago. A. BURGESS The more outrageous, because unbelievable, the better.

■ **unbelievaˈbility** *noun* M19. **unbelievableness** *noun* E20. **unbelievably** *adverb* M19.

unbelieve /ʌnbɪˈliːv/ *verb*[1] *trans. & intrans.* M16.
[from UN-[1] + BELIEVE.]
Not believe in (esp., a particular religion); disbelieve. Freq. as ***unbelieving*** *ppl adjective.*
■ **unbelieved** *adjective* †(*a*) unbelieving; †(*b*) unbelievable, incredible; (*c*) not believed; disbelieved: ME. **unbeliever** *noun* a person who does not believe, esp. in a particular religion, an infidel E16. **unbelieving** *verbal noun* the action of not believing; disbelief; an instance of this: LME. **unbelievingly** *adverb* in an unbelieving manner L17. **unbelievingness** *noun* the state or condition of being unbelieving M16.

unbelieve /ʌnbɪˈliːv/ *verb*[2] *trans.* E17.
[from UN-[2] + BELIEVE.]
Give up belief in; discard or abandon (belief, esp. religious faith).

unbelt /ʌnˈbɛlt/ *verb trans.* L15.
[from UN-[2] + BELT *verb*.]
Release or unfasten the belt of. Also, detach or remove (a sword etc.) by unfastening the belt.
¶ Rare before E19.

unbelted /ʌnˈbɛltɪd/ *adjective.* E19.
[from UN-[1] + BELTED.]
Not wearing or fastened by a belt, esp. a seat belt.

unbend /ʌnˈbɛnd/ *verb.* Infl. as BEND *verb*; pa. t. & pple usu. **unbent** /ʌnˈbɛnt/. ME.
[from UN-[2] + BEND *verb*.]
1 *verb trans.* Release (a bow) from tension; unstring. ME. ▸**b** Relax (the brow) from a frown. E18.
2 *verb trans. & intrans. fig.* Relax (one's mind, manner, etc.) from strain or severity; make or become affable or genial. L16.
†**3** Slacken; weaken. E17–M19.
4 *verb trans.* NAUTICAL. Unfasten (a sail) from a yard or stay; cast (a cable) loose; untie (a rope). E17.
5 *verb trans. & intrans.* Straighten from a bent or curved position. M17.

> 🕮 **2** D. H. LAWRENCE Dr Mitchell was beginning to expand. With Alvina he quite unbent. D. DUNNETT He was snooty, and she felt challenged to try and unbend him.

unbended /ʌnˈbɛndɪd/ *adjective.* M17.
[from UN-[1] + *bended* pa. pple of BEND *verb*.]
Not bent.

unbending /ʌnˈbɛndɪŋ/ *adjective.* L17.
[from UN-[1] + *bending* pres. pple of BEND *verb*.]
1 Not giving way, unyielding, inflexible. L17.
2 Not curving, remaining upright or erect. E18.
■ **unbendable** *adjective* L18. **unbendingly** *adverb* M19. **unbendingness** *noun* E19.

unbent /ʌnˈbɛnt/ *adjective.* ME.
[from UN-[1] + BENT *adjective*.]
1 Not submissive or subservient. ME.
2 Not curved or bowed. L16.

unbent *verb pa. t. & pple*: see UNBEND.

unberufen /ʊnbəˈruːfən/ *interjection.* M19.
[German = unauthorized, gratuitous.]
Touch wood! (to avert ill luck).

unbeseem /ˌʌnbɪˈsiːm/ *verb trans. arch.* L16.
[from UN-[1] + BESEEM.]
1 Be unseemly for or unbecoming to; be inappropriate for or to, not befit. Usu. *impers.* in ***it unbeseems*** etc. L16.
2 Fail in; fall short of. E19.
■ **unbeseeming** *adjective* unseemly, inappropiate; unbecoming: L16. **unbeseemingly** *adverb* E17. **unbeseemingness** *noun* E17. **unbeseemly** *adjective* (*rare*) unseemly M17.

unbethink /ʌnbɪˈθɪŋk/ *verb trans.* Long *obsolete* exc. *dial.* Also (earlier) †**um-**; (*dial.*) **on-** /ɒn-/. Pa. t. & pple **-thought** /-ˈθɔːt/. ME.
[from reduced form of Old English *ymb(e)*-around, about, Old Norse *umb-* (cogn. with German *um-*) + BETHINK.]
†**1** With obj. clause Think about, consider; remember *how, that*, etc. ME–E16.
2 Bethink (oneself); call to mind. (Foll. by obj. clause or *of, on*.) LME.

> 🕮 **2** E. GASKELL If I could only onbethink me what they would like.

unbiased /ʌnˈbʌɪəst/ *adjective.* Also **-biassed**. E17.
[from UN-[1] + BIASED.]
Not biased; unprejudiced, impartial.

> 🕮 *Times Educ. Suppl.* Accurate . . unbiased information had not always been . . available or accessible.

■ **unbiasedly** *adverb* L17. **unbiasedness** *noun* M17.

unbind /ʌnˈbʌɪnd/ *verb trans.* Infl. as BIND *verb*; pa. t. & pple usu. **unbound** /ʌnˈbaʊnd/.
[Old English *unbindan*, formed as UN-[2] + BIND *verb*. Cf. next.]
1 Release (as) from a bond or binding; free from restraint. OE. ▸**b** Set (a person) free by this action; deliver. Formerly also *spec.*, absolve from sin. OE. ▸**c** *transf.* Loosen, open up or out. L16.
2 Undo (a bond etc.); unfasten, unwind. OE. ▸**b** *fig.* Dissolve, undo, destroy. ME.

> 🕮 **1** SIR W. SCOTT He unbound his horse from the tree. **b** SHELLEY They bore me to a cavern in the hill . . and unbound me there. **2** T. F. POWYS The clergyman . . unbound the wire.

unbinding /ʌnˈbʌɪndɪŋ/ *adjective.* E17.
[from UN-[1] + BINDING *ppl adjective*. Cf. prec.]
Not binding; invalid.

unblameable /ʌnˈbleɪməb(ə)l/ *adjective.* Also **unblamable**. M16.
[from UN-[1] + BLAMEABLE.]
Not deserving blame; blameless, irreproachable.
■ **unblameably** *adverb* M16. **unblamed** *adjective* not blamed; uncensured: ME.

unblemished /ʌnˈblɛmɪʃt/ *adjective.* ME.
[from UN-[1] + *blemished* pa. pple of BLEMISH *verb*.]
Having no physical or moral blemish or stain; untarnished, spotless; undefiled.

> 🕮 GEO. ELIOT Mr Irwine was in the witness-box, telling of Hetty's unblemished character. S. HILL Thea's round face shone, fresh and unblemished.

■ **unblemishable** *adjective* unable to be blemished; unstainable: E17.

unbless /ʌnˈblɛs/ *verb trans.* Chiefly *poet.* E17.
[from UN-[2] + BLESS *verb*[1].]
Remove a blessing from, deprive of happiness.

unblessed /ʌnˈblɛsɪd/, *esp. pred.* ʌnˈblɛst/ *adjective & noun.* Also (now chiefly *poet.*) **unblest** /ʌnˈblɛst/. ME.
[from UN-[1] + BLESSED *adjective*.]
▸ **A** *adjective.* **1** Not formally blessed, unconsecrated; deprived of or excluded from a blessing or benediction. ME.
2 Not blessed in fortune; unfortunate, wretched. Also, not favoured *by* or *with* something. ME.
3 Unhallowed, unholy; evil, malignant. ME.

> 🕮 **1** M. CABLE To a Russian emigré the home would be unblessed without the shrine. **2** DICKENS Gaslights flared in the shops with a haggard and unblest air. **3** COLERIDGE I had vowed . . To clear yon wood from thing unblest.

▸ **B** *absol.* as *noun.* Those who are not blessed; *esp. the* souls not in paradise. *rare.* E19.
■ **unblessedness** *noun* M16.

unblinking /ʌnˈblɪŋkɪŋ/ *adjective.* E20.
[from UN-[1] + BLINKING *adjective*.]
Not blinking; steadfast, unflinching; stolid.

> 🕮 G. MCINNES The unblinking stare of the lizard on the sun-baked rock.

■ **unblinkable** *adjective* unable to be ignored, unavoidable M20. **unblinkingly** *adverb* M19.

unblock /ʌnˈblɒk/ *verb.* E17.
[from UN-[2] + BLOCK *verb*.]
1 *verb trans.* Remove an obstruction from; open up, clear. E17.
2 *verb trans. & intrans.* CARDS. Ensure the later unobstructed play of (a suit) by playing a high card. L19.

unbloody /ʌnˈblʌdi/ *adjective.* M16.
[from UN-[1] + BLOODY *adjective*.]
1 Not involving or characterized by bloodshed. M16.
2 Not stained with blood. L16.
3 Not bloodthirsty. M17.

> 🕮 **1** C. KINGSLEY I have offered . . the unbloody sacrifice to Him who will perhaps require . . a bloody one. **2** D. B. HUGHES Clean hands . . unbloody, ungrimed.

■ **unbloodily** *adverb* M16. **unbloodiness** *noun* M19.

unblown /ʌnˈbləʊn/ *adjective.* L16.
[from UN-[1] + *blown* pa. pple of BLOW *verb*[1], *verb*[2].]
1 Of a flower: not yet in bloom, unopened. *arch.* L16.
2 Of a wind instrument: not sounded. E17.
3 Not blown by the wind. M17.

unblushing /ʌnˈblʌʃɪŋ/ *adjective.* L16.
[from UN-[1] + *blushing* pres. pple of BLUSH *verb*.]
1 Not blushing or reddening. L16.
2 Unashamed, unabashed; immodest, shameless. M18.
■ **unblushingly** *adverb* M18.

unbodied /ʌnˈbɒdɪd/ *adjective.* E16.
[from UN-[1], UN-[2] + BODIED.]
1 Having no body; removed from the body, disembodied. E16.
2 Not having material form; incorporeal. E17.
■ **unbodily** *adjective* incorporeal LME.

unbody /ʌnˈbɒdi/ *verb.* LME.
[from UN-[2] + BODY *verb*.]
†**1** *verb intrans.* Leave the body. *rare.* Only in LME.
2 *verb trans.* = DISEMBODY 1. Long *rare* or *obsolete.* LME.

unboiled /ʌnˈbɔɪld/ *noun & adjective.* L16.
[from UN-[1] + BOILED *adjective*.]
▸†**A** *absol.* as *noun.* That which is not boiled. *rare.* Only in L16.
▸ **B** *adjective.* Not boiled. E17.

unbolt /ʌnˈbəʊlt/ *verb.* L15.
[from UN-[2] + BOLT *verb*[2].]
1 *verb intrans.* Of a door: open or unfasten by having the bolt withdrawn. L15.
2 *verb trans. & intrans.* Draw back the bolt of (a door etc.); unfasten (a door etc.) in this way. L16.

> 🕮 **2** B. CHATWIN The . . man unbolted . . the immense baroque doors of the Church.

unbolted /ʌnˈbəʊltɪd/ *adjective*[1]. L16.
[from UN-[1], UN-[2] + *bolted* pa. pple of BOLT *verb*[2].]
Not secured with a bolt, unfastened by the withdrawal of a bolt; not fastened together with a bolt or bolts.

unbolted /ʌnˈbəʊltɪd/ *adjective*[2]. L16.
[from UN-[1] + *bolted* pa. pple of BOLT *verb*[1].]
Unsifted.

unboot /ʌnˈbuːt/ *verb.* L16.
[from UN-[2] + BOOT *verb*[2].]
1 *verb trans.* Take the boots off (a person). L16.
2 *verb intrans.* Take off one's boots. E19.

unborn /ʌnˈbɔːn/ *adjective & noun.* OE.
[from UN-[1] + BORN *ppl adjective*.]
▸ **A** *adjective.* **1** Not yet born; *spec.* (of a child) still in the womb; *fig.* not yet begun or in existence. OE.
2 Not having been born; never to be brought into existence. Chiefly *pred.* ME.

> 🕮 **1** I. WATTS Nations unborn, and ages unbegun. *New Internationalist* Genetic testing had revealed her unborn child had cystic fibrosis.

▸ **B** *absol.* as *noun.* Those who or that which is unborn. E19.

> 🕮 *Here's Health* Deaths . . occurring mainly in the elderly . . and the unborn.

unbosom /ʌnˈbʊz(ə)m/ *verb.* L16.
[from UN-[2] + BOSOM *verb*.]
1 *verb trans.* Give vent to; disclose, reveal, confess. L16. ▸**b** *verb trans.* Disclose to the eye. *poet.* E17.
2 *verb intrans. & refl.* Disclose or reveal one's thoughts, secrets, etc. E17.

> 🕮 **1** W. S. MAUGHAM I have unbosomed my soul. **2** C. DEXTER Charles . . needed to unbosom himself to his brother about some delicate . . relationship. L. WHISTLER He loitered . . with some worry to confide, and never did. Unbosoming no longer came easy.

unbound /ʌnˈbaʊnd/ *adjective*[1]. OE.
[from UN-[1] + BOUND *adjective*[2].]
1 Not bound or tied up; *fig.* unconfined, unconstrained. OE.
2 Not fastened round with a band etc. M16. ▸**b** Of a book etc.: not having a binding; having paper covers. M16.
3 CHEMISTRY & PHYSICS. (Of a substance) in a free state; (of an electron etc.) free, not bound to an atom or molecule etc. E20.
4 LINGUISTICS. = FREE *adjective* 24b. M20.

†**unbound** *adjective*[2]. L16–E18.
[from UN-[1] + BOUND *verb*[1].]
= UNBOUNDED 1.

unbound *verb pa. t. & pple*: see UNBIND.

unbounded /ʌnˈbaʊndɪd/ *adjective.* L16.
[from UN-[1] + BOUNDED *adjective*[1].]
1 Not bounded; not subject to bounds or limits; *fig.* unrestrained, unchecked, uncontrolled. L16.
2 LINGUISTICS. = FREE *adjective* 24b. M20.

> 🕮 **1** A. S. EDDINGTON Finite but unbounded space. D. F. CHESHIRE At the first enthusiasm was unbounded.

■ **unboundable** *adjective* unable to be bounded or limited; unrestrainable: E17. **unboundedly** *adverb* E17. **unboundedness** *noun* M17.

†**unbowel** *verb trans.* Infl. **-l(l)-**. M16.
[from UN-[2] + BOWEL *verb*.]
1 Disembowel. M16–E18.
2 *fig.* Empty of contents; open up; disclose, uncover. L16–L18.

unbowelled /ʌnˈbaʊəld/ *adjective. arch.* Also ***-eled**. L16.
[from UN-[1] + BOWELLED.]
Having no bowels; *fig.* unaffectionate, pitiless.

unbrace /ʌnˈbreɪs/ *verb.* LME.
[from UN-[2] + BRACE *verb*[1].]
1 *verb intrans. & refl.* Undo the braces or fastenings of one's clothing or armour. Long *rare* or *obsolete.* LME.
2 *verb trans.* Carve (a duck). *obsolete* exc. *Hist.* LME.
3 *verb trans.* **a** Loosen or undo (a band, clasp, etc.). Chiefly *poet.* Long *rare.* LME. ▸**b** Remove a brace or fastening from; loosen or set free by this action; *fig.* free from tension or restraint, relax. L16.
4 *verb intrans.* Become loose or lax. L17.

unbraced /ʌnˈbreɪst/ *adjective.* E16.
[from UN-[1] + *braced* pa. pple of BRACE *verb*[1].]
1 With clothing unfastened or loose. E16.
2 Not made tense or firm; loose, relaxed. E17.
3 Not braced or supported (*by* something). E19.

unbreathed /ʌnˈbriːðd/ *adjective.* L16.
[from UN-[1] + *breathed* pa. pple of BREATHE.]
†**1** Unexercised; unpractised. L16–M17.
2 Not breathed (*upon*); not respired. E19. ▸**b** Not uttered or whispered. E19.
3 Not out of breath. *arch.* E20.

> 🕮 **2** P. D. JAMES The melancholy, unbreathed atmosphere of a seldom-visited country house drawing room. **3** R. KIPLING Kim's messenger dropped from the steep pasture as unbreathed as when she had set out.

■ **unbreathable** *adjective* not able to be breathed M19. **unbreathing** *adjective* not breathing, holding the breath; *fig.* without pause: E18.

unbred /ʌn'brɛd/ *adjective.* L16.
[from UN-[1] + BRED *adjective.*]
†**1** Unborn. *rare* (Shakes.). Only in L16.
2 Ill-bred, unmannerly. E17. ▸**b** Not trained *in* or for a specified occupation. Long *rare.* L17.

unbribed /ʌn'brʌɪbd/ *adjective.* E17.
[from UN-[1] + *bribed* pa. pple of BRIBE *verb.*]
1 Not offered or given a bribe; not corrupted by bribery. E17.
2 Not purchased or obtained by bribery. M17.
■ **un'bribable** *adjective* not bribable M17.

unbridgeable /ʌn'brɪdʒəb(ə)l/ *adjective.* L18.
[from UN-[1] + BRIDGEABLE.]
Not able to be bridged.
■ **unbridged** *adjective* not bridged E19.

unbroken /ʌn'brəʊk(ə)n/ *adjective.* Also (*arch.*) **unbroke** /ʌn'brəʊk/. ME.
[from UN-[1] + BROKEN.]
1 Not broken or fractured; intact; unviolated. ME. ▸**b** Of ground: not broken up by digging etc. L16.
2 Not interrupted or disturbed; continuous. LME.
3 Not crushed in health or spirit; not subdued or weakened. E16. ▸**b** Of a horse etc.: not broken in; untamed. M16.

> 📖 **1** R. MACAULAY When the ordered frame of things was still unbroken. **3** *Lancet* An unbroken sleep of nine hours. E. WAUGH The jungle stretched unbroken to the sea.

■ **unbrokenly** *adverb* M19. **unbrokenness** /-n-n-/ *noun* M19.

unbrotherly /ʌn'brʌðəli/ *adjective & adverb.* L16.
[from UN-[1] + BROTHERLY.]
▸**A** *adjective.* Not brotherly; unkind, unaffectionate. L16.
▸†**B** *adverb.* In an unbrotherly manner. L16–M17.
■ **unbrotherlike** *adjective* = UNBROTHERLY *adjective* L16. **unbrotherliness** *noun* M17.

unbuckle /ʌn'bʌk(ə)l/ *verb.* LME.
[from UN-[2] + BUCKLE *verb.* Cf. next.]
1 *verb trans.* Unfasten the buckle of (a shoe, belt, etc.); undo or release by this action. LME.
2 *verb intrans. & refl.* Undo the buckle or buckles of one's belt, clothing, etc. L16.

> 📖 **1** K. HULME The boy . . unbuckles a sandal. **2** D. FRANCIS The passengers yawned and unbuckled themselves. T. BARLING Carradine unbuckled and went aft.

unbuckled /ʌn'bʌk(ə)ld/ *adjective.* L15.
[from UN-[1] + *buckled* pa. pple of BUCKLE *verb.* Cf. prec.]
Not buckled; with the buckle not fastened.

unbuild /ʌn'bɪld/ *verb trans.* Infl. as BUILD *verb*; pa. t. & pple usu. **unbuilt** /ʌn'bɪlt/. E17.
[from UN-[2] + BUILD *verb.*]
Pull down, destroy, demolish.

unbuilded /ʌn'bɪldɪd/ *adjective.* Long *arch.* E16.
[from UN-[1] + *builded* pa. pple of BUILD *verb.*]
= UNBUILT *adjective.*

unbuilt /ʌn'bɪlt/ *adjective.* LME.
[from UN-[1] + BUILT *ppl adjective.*]
1 Not (yet) built or erected. LME.
2 Of land: not built *on* or *upon.* M17.

unbuilt *verb pa. t. & pple*: see UNBUILD.

unbundle /ʌn'bʌnd(ə)l/ *verb trans.* E17.
[from UN-[2] + BUNDLE *verb.*]
1 Unpack; remove from a bundle. E17.
2 Market or price (goods or services) separately rather than collectively. M20.
3 COMMERCE. Split (a company or conglomerate) into its constituent businesses or assets prior to reorganization or selling off. L20.
■ **unbundler** *noun* a person who unbundles a company etc.; an asset-stripper: L20.

unbung /ʌn'bʌŋ/ *verb trans.* E17.
[from UN-[2] + BUNG *verb*[1].]
Take the bung out of; unblock.

unbunged /ʌn'bʌŋd/ *adjective.* M18.
[from UN-[1] + *bunged* pa. pple of BUNG *verb*[1].]
Not stopped with a bung.

unburden /ʌn'bəːd(ə)n/ *verb trans.* Also (*arch.*) **unburthen** /ʌn'bəːð(ə)n/. M16.
[from UN-[2] + BURDEN *verb.* Cf. next.]
1 Remove a burden from; unload, disencumber; relieve (*of*). M16. ▸**b** *refl.* Disclose one's secrets, emotions, etc.; confess. L16.
2 Get rid of, discharge; disclose, reveal. L16.

> 📖 **1** B. EMECHETA Who else was there for the students to unburden their souls to? G. DALY Edith could never unburden herself of such weighty baggage. **b** P. SCOTT He wanted to confess aloud, unburden himself. **2** SHAKES. *Merch. V.* From your love I have a warranty To unburden all my plots and purposes.

unburdened /ʌn'bəːd(ə)nd/ *adjective.* E17.
[from UN-[1] + *burdened* pa. pple of BURDEN *verb.* Cf. prec.]
Not burdened or encumbered.

> 📖 J. DUNN A rare spirit, elusive, unburdened by responsibility.

unburn /ʌn'bəːn/ *verb trans.* Pa. t. & pple **-burned, -burnt** /-'bəːnt/. E19.
[from UN-[2] + BURN *verb.*]
Restore from the effects of burning.

unburnt /ʌn'bəːnt/ *adjective.* Also **unburned** /ʌn'bəːnt, -'bəːnd/. ME.
[from UN-[1] + BURNT.]
Not burnt or consumed by fire; not charred or scorched.

unburrow /ʌn'bʌrəʊ/ *verb.* M18.
[from UN-[2] + BURROW *verb.*]
1 *verb intrans.* Come out (as) from a burrow. M18.
2 *verb trans.* Drive from a burrow. M18.

unburthen *verb* see UNBURDEN.

unbury /ʌn'bɛri/ *verb trans.* LME.
[from UN-[2] + BURY *verb.*]
1 Disinter; remove from the ground after burial. LME.
2 *fig.* Recall from oblivion or obscurity etc.; unearth, uncover. E17.

> 📖 **2** M. TREVOR It's a mistake to unbury the past.

unbutton /ʌn'bʌt(ə)n/ *verb.* ME.
[from UN-[2] + BUTTON *verb.* Cf. next.]
1 *verb trans.* Unfasten (a button or buttons); undo the buttons on (a garment); undo the buttons on the clothing of (a person); *fig.* relax, free from tension or formality. ME.
2 *verb intrans.* Undo the buttons on one's clothing; *fig.* relax, become communicative. E17.

> 📖 **1** W. BOYD The boy started to unbutton his shirt. **2** N. STREATFEILD She definitely unbuttoned about her letters.

unbuttoned /ʌn'bʌt(ə)nd/ *adjective.* L16.
[from UN-[1] + BUTTONED. Cf. prec.]
1 Not having a button or buttons. L16.
2 Not fastened with buttons; with the buttons of one's clothing unfastened; *fig.* communicative, unrestrained, informal. L16.

> 📖 **1** A. PRICE They were fencing with unbuttoned foils. **2** J. UPDIKE A book so unbuttoned in manner, so dishevelled in content.

uncalendar /ʌn'kalɪndə/ *verb trans. rare.* M17.
[from UN-[2] + CALENDAR *verb.*]
Remove from a calendar or roll.

uncalendared /ʌn'kalɪndəd/ *adjective. rare.* M19.
[from UN-[1] + *calendared* pa. pple of CALENDAR *verb.*]
Not registered or entered in a calendar.

uncalled /ʌn'kɔːld/ *adjective.* LME.
[from UN-[1] + *called* pa. pple of CALL *verb.*]
Not called or summoned; not invited; *spec.* (of capital) not called up.
uncalled-for not asked for or requested; unnecessary, unjustified, impertinent.

uncandid /ʌn'kandɪd/ *adjective.* L17.
[from UN-[1] + CANDID *adjective.*]
Not candid or frank; disingenuous.
■ **uncandidly** *adverb* E19. **uncandidness** *noun* L17.

uncanny /ʌn'kani/ *adjective.* L16.
[from UN-[1] + CANNY *adjective.*]
1 Of, pertaining to, or associated with the supernatural or occult; baleful, malignant; malicious. Orig. *Scot.* L16.
2 Careless, incautious. *Scot. & north.* M17.
3 Unpleasantly severe or hard. *Scot.* M18.
4 Unreliable, untrustworthy; dangerous, unsafe. *Scot. & north.* L18.
5 Seemingly supernatural; uncomfortably strange or unfamiliar, weird; of an unsettling accuracy, intensity, etc. M19.

> 📖 **5** N. ANNAN Stephen had such uncanny powers of sympathy. M. IGNATIEFF The quiet was uncanny; water running in a gutter . . but no cars, no voices.

■ **uncannily** *adverb* E19. **uncanniness** *noun* M19.

uncanonical /ʌnkə'nɒnɪk(ə)l/ *adjective.* M17.
[from UN-[1] + CANONICAL *adjective.*]
Not canonical; not standard or accepted.
■ **uncanonically** *adverb* E18.

uncanonise *verb*, **-ised** *adjective* vars. of UNCANONIZE, UNCANONIZED.

uncanonize /ʌn'kanənʌɪz/ *verb trans.* Also **-ise**. E17.
[from UN-[2] + CANON *noun*[1] + -IZE.]
1 Remove from the canon of saints. E17.
2 Reject from a collection of authoritative writings, esp. the scriptural canon. E18.

uncanonized /ʌn'kanənʌɪzd/ *adjective.* Also **-ised**. M16.
[from UN-[1] + *canonized* pa. pple of CANONIZE.]
1 Not included in the scriptural canon. M16.
2 Of a saint: not formally recognized. M17.

uncap /ʌn'kap/ *verb.* Infl. **-pp-**. M16.
[from UN-[2] + CAP *noun*[1], *verb*[1].]
1 *verb trans. & intrans.* Remove a cap from (the head or another person). M16.
2 *verb trans.* Remove the cap or covering from; *fig.* reveal; release (an emotion etc.). L17. ▸**b** Remove the upper limit or restriction on the value of (a currency). L20.

> 📖 **1** L. MANTELL Lance uncapped, crisp fair hair gleaming. **2** D. B. HUGHES The girl uncapped the Coke bottle. *Chicago Tribune* Top diplomats . . prefer to uncap their pique in icy words and stern facades.

†**uncapable** *adjective.* L16.
[from UN-[1] + CAPABLE.]
1 = INCAPABLE *adjective* 2. L16–E18.
2 = INCAPABLE *adjective* 3. L16–M18.
3 = INCAPABLE *adjective* 4. L16–E19.
4 = INCAPABLE *adjective* 5. L16–E18.
5 = INCAPABLE *adjective* 6. E17–M18.
6 = INCAPABLE *adjective* 1. E17–E18.
■ †**uncapableness** *noun* E17–E18.

uncapped /ʌn'kapt/ *adjective.* M16.
[from UN-[1] + *capped* pa. pple of CAP *verb*[1].]
Not wearing or having a cap; uncovered; *spec.* never having been selected as a member of a national sports team.

uncareful /ʌn'kɛːfʊl, -f(ə)l/ *adjective.* Now *rare.* M16.
[from UN-[1] + CAREFUL *adjective.*]
1 Not careful or caring; careless, inattentive; (foll. by *of, for*) unconcerned about. M16.
2 Free from care or anxiety; untroubled. M17.

uncaring /ʌn'kɛːrɪŋ/ *adjective.* L18.
[from UN-[1] + *caring* pres. pple of CARE *verb.*]
Not caring or compassionate; disinterested, unconcerned.
■ **uncaringly** *adverb* M19. **uncaringness** *noun* M20.

uncase /ʌn'keɪs/ *verb.* L16.
[from UN-[2] + CASE *verb.*]
1 †**a** *verb trans.* Skin, flay. L16–E18. ▸**b** *verb trans. & intrans.* Strip; undress. *arch.* L16.
2 *verb trans.* Remove from a case or cover; remove the casing from. L16. ▸**b** *fig.* Uncover, lay bare; expose to view. L16.

> 📖 **2** *Field & Stream* I uncased a rifle.

uncastrated /ʌnka'streɪtɪd, ʌn'kastreɪtɪd/ *adjective.* E18.
[from UN-[1] + *castrated* pa. pple of CASTRATE *verb.*]
1 Not castrated; ungelded. E18.
2 Unexpurgated. M18.

uncatholic /ʌn'kaθ(ə)lɪk/ *adjective.* Also **un-Catholic**. E17.
[from UN-[1] + CATHOLIC.]
Not catholic or Catholic.

uncatholicize /ʌnkə'θɒlɪsʌɪz/ *verb trans.* Also **-ise**. E19.
[from UN-[2] + CATHOLIC + -IZE.]
Make no longer catholic or Catholic.

unceasing /ʌn'siːsɪŋ/ *adjective.* LME.
[from UN-[1] + *ceasing* pres. pple of CEASE *verb.*]
Not ceasing; incessant, continuous.

> 📖 K. VONNEGUT Their unceasing demands for more and more pay and fringe benefits.

■ **unceasingly** *adverb* ME. **unceasingsness** *noun* E18.

uncelebrated /ʌn'sɛlɪbreɪtɪd/ *adjective.* M17.
[from UN-[1] + CELEBRATED.]
1 Not observed or commemorated with ceremonies, festivities, etc. M17.
2 Not famous or renowned. M18.

> 📖 **2** A. DESAI The true poet . . sat huddled and silent, ignored and uncelebrated.

uncenter *verb*, **uncentered** *adjective* see UNCENTRE etc.

uncentre /ʌn'sɛntə/ *verb trans.* Also ***uncenter**. E17.
[from UN-[2] + CENTRE *verb.*]
Remove or sever *from* a centre.

uncentred /ʌn'sɛntəd/ *adjective.* Also ***uncentered**. M17.
[from UN-[1] + *centred* pa. pple of CENTRE *verb.*]
Not having a (fixed) centre.

> 📖 W. GADDIS The uncentred pools behind the thick lenses.

unceremonious /ˌʌnsɛrɪ'məʊnɪəs/ *adjective.* L16.
[from UN-[1] + CEREMONIOUS.]
Lacking ceremony or formality; (of a person etc.) acting without ceremony; abrupt.
■ **unceremoniously** *adverb* M17. **unceremoniousness** *noun* E19.

uncertain /ʌn'səːt(ə)n, -tɪn/ *adjective.* ME.
[from UN-[1] + CERTAIN *adjective.*]
1 Not determined or fixed; liable to change, variable, erratic; (of a person) changeable, capricious. ME.

2 About which one cannot be certain, unreliable; (of a path etc.) not clearly leading to a certain goal or destination. ME.

3 a Not known with certainty; not established beyond doubt. ME. ▸**b** Without clear meaning; ambiguous. LME. ▸**c** Not clearly identified, located, or determined; (of something seen) not clearly defined or outlined. E17.

4 a Of a person: doubtful; not fully confident or assured *of* something. Also foll. by subord. clause LME. ▸**b** Not directed to a definite end. LME.

📖 **1** S. JOHNSON A duty of very uncertain extent. J. McCOSH There is nothing so uncertain as .. human destiny. R. K. NARAYAN He was a man of uncertain temper and one could not .. guess how he would react. **2** A. S. BYATT It was uncertain ground, a kind of morass. **3a** *EMBO Journal* Their biological role remains uncertain. **b** AV *1 Cor.* 14:8 If the trumpet give an vncertaine sound, who shall prepare himselfe to the battell? **in no uncertain terms** emphatically, very clearly indeed. **c** M. INNES A bit chilly .. for a lady of uncertain years. **4a** M. FORSTER She stood .. on the landing uncertain what to do.

▪ **uncertainly** *adverb* (*a*) without definite knowledge, doubtfully; (*b*) in a variable manner; by chance; (*c*) without definite result, course, or aim: LME. **uncertainness** /-n-n-/ *noun* (*arch. rare*) E17.

uncertainty /ʌnˈsəːt(ə)nti, -tnti/ *noun.* LME.
[from UN-¹ + CERTAINTY.]

1 The quality or state of being uncertain; doubtfulness; hesitation, irresolution. LME.

2 a A doubtful point. LME. ▸**b** A thing of which the occurrence, outcome, etc., is uncertain. E17.

3 SCIENCE. The amount of variation in a numerical result that is consistent with observation. M19.

Phrases: **uncertainty principle** PHYSICS the principle that certain pairs of observables (e.g. the momentum and position of a particle) cannot both be precisely determined at the same time, and that the product of the uncertainties of these quantities cannot be less than $h/4\pi$ (h = Planck's constant); also ***Heisenberg uncertainty principle***, ***Heisenberg's uncertainty principle***.

uncertified /ʌnˈsəːtɪfʌɪd/ *adjective.* M16.
[from UN-¹ + *certified* pa. pple of CERTIFY.]

1 Not made certain in mind; not assured. Now *rare.* M16.

2 Not attested as certain; not guaranteed by certification. L17.

3 Not certified insane. L19.

▪ **uncertifiable** *adjective* M20.

uncessant /ʌnˈsɛs(ə)nt/ *adjective.* Long *rare.* M16.
[from UN-¹ + Latin *cessant-*: see INCESSANT.]
= INCESSANT.

unchain /ʌnˈtʃeɪn/ *verb trans.* L16.
[from UN-² + CHAIN *noun, verb.*]
Set free from a chain or chains; remove the chain(s) from; *gen.* liberate.

📖 DICKENS Cautiously unchaining the door before she opened it.

unchained /ʌnˈtʃeɪnd/ *adjective.* M17.
[from UN-¹ + CHAINED.]
Not chained; *esp.* not fastened or attached by chains.
▪ **unchainable** *adjective* M19.

unchallengeable /ʌnˈtʃalɪn(d)ʒəb(ə)l/ *adjective.* E17.
[from UN-¹ + CHALLENGEABLE.]
Not challengeable; unassailable.
▪ **unchallengeably** *adverb* E19. **unchallenged** *adjective* M17.

unchancy /ʌnˈtʃɑːnsi/ *adjective.* Chiefly *Scot.* M16.
[from UN-¹ + CHANCY.]

1 Ill-fated, inauspicious; unlucky. M16.

2 Dangerous, hazardous; not safe to meddle with. L18.

📖 **1** S. WEYMAN 'Tis a cold, damp, unchancy place you've chosen.

unchangeable /ʌnˈtʃeɪndʒəb(ə)l/ *adjective.* ME.
[from UN-¹ + CHANGEABLE *adjective.*]
Incapable of changing or being changed; immutable, invariable.
▪ **unchangeaˈbility** *noun* LME. **unchangeableness** *noun* M16. **unchangeably** *adverb* ME.

unchanged /ʌnˈtʃeɪndʒd/ *adjective.* LME.
[from UN-¹ + *changed* pa. pple of CHANGE *verb.*]
Unaltered.
▪ **unchanging** *adjective* L16. **unchangingly** *adverb* LME. **unchangingness** *noun* L19.

uncharacteristic /ˌʌnkarəktəˈrɪstɪk/ *adjective.* M18.
[from UN-¹ + CHARACTERISTIC *adjective.*]
Not characteristic (*of*).
▪ **uncharacteristically** *adverb* M18. **unˈcharacterized** *adjective* E18.

uncharge /ʌnˈtʃɑːdʒ/ *verb trans.* Now *rare.* ME.
[from UN-² + CHARGE *verb.*]

†**1 a** Free from a charge or burden. Only in ME. ▸**b** Acquit of guilt. *rare* (Shakes.). Only in E17.

2 Unload (a gun or, formerly, a ship). ME.

uncharged /ʌnˈtʃɑːdʒd/ *adjective.* LME.
[from UN-¹ + CHARGED.]

†**1** Not called on; unsummoned. LME–M16.

2 Not burdened (*with* something). L15.

3 That has not been or is not charged. L16.

4 HERALDRY. Not bearing a charge. E17.

5 Not made the subject of a criminal or financial charge. E17.

📖 **3** H. M. ROSENBERG Although uncharged, the neutron has an intrinsic magnetic moment. *Financial Times* The interrogation of an uncharged police prisoner. **5** *Economist* Sanction .. to take from the club uncharged property valued at £275,000. *Los Angeles Times* Hubbell could have considered the uncharged crime when he sentenced Jensen.

uncharitable /ʌnˈtʃarɪtəb(ə)l/ *adjective.* LME.
[from UN-¹ + CHARITABLE.]
Not charitable; showing or proceeding from a lack of charity; censorious, severe in judgement.

📖 M. WESLEY Edith allowed herself .. uncharitable criticisms when she thought of Rose's neglectful parents.

▪ **uncharitableness** *noun* M16. **uncharitably** *adverb* LME. **uncharity** *noun* lack of charity M16.

uncharm /ʌnˈtʃɑːm/ *verb trans.* L16.
[from UN-² + CHARM *verb*¹.]

1 Deprive of magical powers; nullify the efficacy of (a charm). L16.

2 Free from enchantment. E17.

uncharmed /ʌnˈtʃɑːmd/ *adjective.* L16.
[from UN-¹ + CHARMED.]

1 Not subject to a charm; not invested with charm; not delighted. L16.

2 PARTICLE PHYSICS. Not having the property of charm. L20.

▪ **uncharming** *adjective* not attractive or delightful L17.

uncharted /ʌnˈtʃɑːtɪd/ *adjective.* M19.
[from UN-¹ + *charted* pa. pple of CHART *verb.*]
Of which there is no map or chart; not shown on a map or chart; *fig.* unexplored, not previously reached.

📖 *Edinburgh Review* In tracking the Siberian coast .., many uncharted islands were discovered. *Nature* Scientific misconduct investigations were .. uncharted territory.

unchartered /ʌnˈtʃɑːtəd/ *adjective.* E19.
[from UN-¹ + CHARTERED.]

1 Not provided with a charter; not formally privileged or constituted. E19.

2 Not authorized as by a charter; irregular, lawless. E19.

unchaste /ʌnˈtʃeɪst/ *adjective.* LME.
[from UN-¹ + CHASTE *adjective.*]
Not chaste; impure, lascivious.
▪ **unchastely** *adverb* LME. **unchasteness** *noun* M16. **unchastity** *noun* LME.

unchecked /ʌnˈtʃɛkt/ *adjective.* LME.
[from UN-¹ + CHECKED *adjective*².]

1 Not repressed; freely allowed, unrestrained. Also, not tested or investigated. LME.

†**2** Of a report: uncontradicted. L16–E17.

▪ †**uncheck** *verb trans.* (*rare*, Shakes.) fail to check: only in E17. **uncheckable** *adjective* unable to be checked, restrained, or tested M18.

uncheckered *adjective* var. of UNCHEQUERED.

uncheerful /ʌnˈtʃɪəfʊl, -f(ə)l/ *adjective.* LME.
[from UN-¹ + CHEERFUL.]

1 Not enlivening or gladdening; cheerless. LME.

2 Not cheerful; in low spirits, gloomy. M16.

▪ **uncheered** *adjective* L18. **uncheerfully** *adverb* E17. **uncheerfulness** *noun* E17. **uncheering** *adjective* L18. **uncheery** *adjective* M18.

unchequered /ʌnˈtʃɛkəd/ *adjective.* Also **uncheckered**. L18.
[from UN-¹ + CHEQUERED.]
Not spoiled by discreditable or unhappy episodes.

uncherished /ʌnˈtʃɛrɪʃt/ *adjective.* ME.
[from UN-¹ + *cherished* pa. pple of CHERISH.]
Not cherished.
¶ Not recorded between ME and L18.

unchild /ʌnˈtʃʌɪld/ *verb trans.* E17.
[from UN-² + CHILD *noun.*]

1 Make childless. E17.

2 Deprive of the status of a child or of the qualities peculiar to childhood. E17.

unchilded /ʌnˈtʃʌɪldɪd/ *adjective.* E17.
[from prec. + -ED¹ or from UN-¹ + CHILD *noun* + -ED².]
Deprived of or lacking children; childless.

unchildish /ʌnˈtʃʌɪldɪʃ/ *adjective.* L16.
[from UN-¹ + CHILDISH.]
Not childish.
▪ **unchildlike** *adjective* M19.

unchinked /ʌnˈtʃɪnkt/ *adjective.* E19.
[from UN-¹ + *chinked* pa. pple of CHINK *verb*².]
Having unstopped holes, gaps, or cracks.

unchivalrous /ʌnˈʃɪv(ə)lrəs/ *adjective.* M19.
[from UN-¹ + CHIVALROUS.]
Not chivalrous; bad-mannered, discourteous.
▪ **unchivalric** *adjective* unchivalrous M19. **unchivalrously** *adverb* M19. **unchivalry** *noun* lack of chivalry, discourtesy M19.

unchoke /ʌnˈtʃəʊk/ *verb trans.* L16.
[from UN-² + CHOKE *verb.*]
Make no longer choked, unblock.

unchoked /ʌnˈtʃəʊkt/ *adjective.* M19.
[from UN-¹ + *choked* pa. pple of CHOKE *verb.*]
Not choked or blocked.

unchristen /ʌnˈkrɪs(ə)n/ *verb trans.* L16.
[from UN-² + CHRISTEN *verb.*]

1 Reverse the christening of; deprive of the name given at christening. L16.

†**2** = UNCHRISTIANIZE. M17–E18.

unchristened /ʌnˈkrɪs(ə)nd/ *adjective.* ME.
[from UN-¹ + *christened* pa. pple of CHRISTEN *verb.*]

1 Not baptized; not converted to Christianity. ME.

2 Having no name. M19.

unchristian /ʌnˈkrɪstʃ(ə)n, -tɪən/ *adjective.* M16.
[from UN-¹ + CHRISTIAN *adjective.*]

1 Of a person, community, etc.: not professing Christianity; devoid of Christian principles or feeling. M16.

2 Of an action, institution, etc.: at variance with Christian principles, *esp.* uncaring, selfish; unbecoming a Christian. L16. ▸**b** Objectionable; unnatural. M17.

▪ **unchristiˈanity** *noun* M17. **unchristianlike** *adjective & adverb* E17. **unchristianly** *adjective* = UNCHRISTIAN *adjective* M17. **unchristianly** *adverb* in an unchristian manner M16.

†**unchristian** *verb trans.* M17–E18.
[from UN-² + CHRISTIAN *adjective.*]
= UNCHRISTIANIZE.

unchristianise *verb*, **unchristianised** *adjective* vars. of UNCHRISTIANIZE, UNCHRISTIANIZED.

unchristianize /ʌnˈkrɪstʃənʌɪz, -tɪən-/ *verb trans.* Also **-ise**. M17.
[from UN-² + CHRISTIAN *adjective* + -IZE.]
Deprive of the character or status of a Christian; make unchristian.

unchristianized /ʌnˈkrɪstʃənʌɪzd, -tɪən-/ *adjective.* Also **-ised**. L18.
[from UN-¹ + *Christianized* pa. pple of CHRISTIANIZE.]
Not converted to Christianity.

un-Christlike /ʌnˈkrʌɪs(t)lʌɪk/ *adjective.* M19.
[from UN-¹ + CHRISTLIKE.]
Not Christlike.
▪ **unchristly** *adjective* L19.

unchronicled /ʌnˈkrɒnɪk(ə)ld/ *adjective.* L16.
[from UN-¹ + *chronicled* pa. pple of CHRONICLE *verb.*]
Not chronicled, unrecorded.

unchronological /ˌʌnkrɒnəˈlɒdʒɪk(ə)l/ *adjective.* M18.
[from UN-¹ + CHRONOLOGICAL.]

1 Not arranged in order of time; not in accordance with chronology. M18.

2 Of a person: not skilled in or not observing chronology. E19.

unchurch /ʌnˈtʃəːtʃ/ *verb trans.* E17.
[from UN-² + CHURCH *noun.*]

1 Remove or exclude from membership of or participation in a church; excommunicate. E17.

2 Divest of the character of a church; deprive of the possession of a church. M17.

unchurched /ʌnˈtʃəːtʃt/ *adjective.* L17.
[In sense 1 from prec. + -ED¹; in sense 2 from UN-¹ + CHURCH *noun* + -ED².]

1 Excluded from membership of or participation in a church. L17.

2 Not belonging to or connected with a church. L19.

📖 **2** *absol.*: *Christianity Today* Evangelization of the unchurched is not the priority it should be.

unchurchly /ʌnˈtʃəːtʃli/ *adjective.* E19.
[from UN-¹ + CHURCHLY.]
Not churchly; not belonging to, befitting, or characteristic of a church.
▪ **unchurchlike** *adjective* M17.

unci *noun* pl. of UNCUS.

uncia /ˈʌnsɪə/ *noun.* Pl. **-iae** /-iːiː/. L17.
[Latin: see OUNCE *noun*¹.]

†**1** MATH. A numerical coefficient of a term of a polynomial. L17–M18.

2 ROMAN ANTIQUITIES. A copper coin, orig. equal in value to a twelfth of an as. M19.

uncial /ˈʌnsɪəl/ *adjective & noun.* M17.
[Latin *uncialis*, formed as prec.: see -AL¹. In sense A.2 after late Latin *unciales litterae*.]

▸ **A** *adjective.* **1 a** Pertaining to an inch or an ounce. M17. ▸**b** Based on a duodecimal division; divided into twelve equal parts. M19.

2 (Of letters or writing) having the large rounded unjoined forms characteristic of Greek and Latin manuscripts of the 4th to the 18th cents. (from which modern capitals are derived); written, cut, etc., in such characters. L17.
▶**B** *noun.* **1** An uncial letter. L18.
2 An uncial manuscript or style of writing. L19.
■ **uncially** *adverb* †(*a*) *rare* in uncial measurement; (*b*) in uncial letters: M17.

unciform /ˈʌnsɪfɔːm/ *adjective & noun.* M18.
[from Latin UNCUS + -I- + -FORM.]
ANATOMY. ▶**A** *adjective.* = UNCINATE *adjective*; *spec.* designating the hamate bone of the wrist. M18.
▶**B** *noun.* The hamate bone. M19.

uncinariasis /ˌʌnsɪnəˈrʌɪəsɪs/ *noun.* Pl. **-ases** /-əsiːz/. E20.
[from mod. Latin *Uncinaria* name of a genus of hookworms + -IASIS.]
MEDICINE. = ANCYLOSTOMIASIS.

uncinate /ˈʌnsɪnət, -eɪt/ *adjective & noun.* M18.
[Latin *uncinatus*, formed as next: see -ATE[1], -ATE[2].]
▶**A** *adjective.* **1** Hooked; hook-shaped. M18.
2 *MEDICINE.* Involving or affecting the uncinate gyrus. Also, designating a type of epileptic fit in which hallucinatory sensations of taste and smell are experienced. L19.
1 uncinate gyrus *ANATOMY & ZOOLOGY* the hook-shaped anterior part of the hippocampus involved in the perception of olfactory stimuli.
▶**B** *noun. ZOOLOGY.* An uncinate process. L19.
■ **uncinated** *adjective* = UNCINATE *adjective* 1 M18.

uncinus /ʌnˈsʌɪnəs/ *noun.* Pl. **-ni** /-nʌɪ, -niː/. M19.
[Latin, formed as UNCUS + *-inus* -INE[1].]
ZOOLOGY. A hook-shaped part or process; *esp.* a hooklike tooth of a mollusc.

uncirculated /ʌnˈsəːkjʊleɪtɪd/ *adjective.* L18.
[from UN-[1] + *circulated* pa. pple of CIRCULATE.]
That has not circulated; *spec.* (of a coin or note) that has never been in circulation, mint.

uncircumcised /ʌnˈsəːkəmsʌɪzd/ *adjective.* LME.
[from UN-[1] + *circumcised* pa. pple of CIRCUMCISE.]
1 Not circumcised. LME.
2 *fig.* Not spiritually chastened or purified; irreligious; heathen. *arch.* LME.
■ ˌ**uncircumˈcision** *noun* E16.

uncircumscribed /ʌnˈsəːkəmskrʌɪbd/ *adjective.* E17.
[from UN-[1] + *circumscribed* pa. pple of CIRCUMSCRIBE.]
Not circumscribed.
■ ˌ**uncircumˈscribable** *adjective* E17.

uncircumspect /ʌnˈsəːkəmspɛkt/ *adjective.* E16.
[from UN-[1] + CIRCUMSPECT.]
Not circumspect; imprudent, unwary; (of an action etc.) not marked by circumspection, incautious.
■ ˌ**uncircumˈspection** *noun* L16.

uncircumstanced /ʌnˈsəːkəmstɑːnst/ *adjective.* L17.
[from UN-[1] + *circumstanced* pa. pple of CIRCUMSTANCE *verb.*]
Not justified or supported by circumstances.

uncircumstantial /ˌʌnsəːkəmˈstanʃ(ə)l/ *adjective.* M17.
[from UN-[1] + CIRCUMSTANTIAL.]
Not circumstantial.

uncited /ʌnˈsʌɪtɪd/ *adjective.* L16.
[from UN-[1] + *cited* pa. pple of CITE.]
1 Not quoted or mentioned. L16.
†**2** Not called or summoned. L16–M17.

uncivic /ʌnˈsɪvɪk/ *adjective.* L18.
[from UN-[1] + CIVIC.]
Not civic.

uncivil /ʌnˈsɪv(ə)l, -vɪl/ *adjective.* M16.
[from UN-[1] + CIVIL *adjective.*]
1 Uncivilized, barbarous; unrefined. Now *rare.* M16.
†**2 a** Undeveloped, primitive. L16–M17. ▶**b** Not responsive to cultivation. L17–M18.
3 Discourteous, impolite; lacking in manners. L16.
†**4** Not seemly; indecorous. L16–L17.
5 Not in accordance with civic unity; contrary to civil well-being. Now *rare.* L16.

🕮 **3** M. INNES I said I'd arrive in time for luncheon, and it seems uncivil to be late.

■ **unciˈvility** *noun* L16. **uncivilly** *adverb* L16.

uncivilise *verb*, **uncivilised** *adjective* vars. of UNCIVILIZE, UNCIVILIZED.

uncivilize /ʌnˈsɪvɪlʌɪz/ *verb trans.* Also **-ise.** E17.
[from UN-[2] + CIVILIZE.]
Deprive of civil, civilized, or civic character; decivilize.

uncivilized /ʌnˈsɪvɪlʌɪzd/ *adjective.* Also **-ised.** E17.
[from UN-[1] + CIVILIZED.]
Not civilized; barbarous, rough, uncultured.
■ **uncivilizable** *adjective* L19. **uncivili'zation** *noun* lack of civilization E19.

unclad /ʌnˈklad/ *adjective.* Now chiefly *arch. & formal.* LME.
[from UN-[1] + *clad* pa. pple of CLOTHE.]
Not clad; undressed, naked.

unclad /ʌnˈklad/ *verb trans.* Long *arch. & poet.* Infl. **-dd-.** L15.
[from UN-[2] + CLAD *verb*[2]. Cf. CLAD *verb*[1].]
Remove the clothes of.

unclaimed /ʌnˈkleɪmd/ *adjective.* E17.
[from UN-[1] + *claimed* pa. pple of CLAIM *verb.*]
Not claimed.
unclaimed layaway: see LAYAWAY 2b.

unclasp /ʌnˈklɑːsp/ *verb.* M16.
[from UN-[2] + CLASP *verb.*]
1 *verb trans.* Unfasten the clasp or clasps of. M16. ▶†**b** *fig.* Open up, display. L16–M17.
2 *verb trans. & intrans.* Loosen the grasp or grip of (one's hand etc.). E17.

unclasped /ʌnˈklɑːspt/ *adjective.* E17.
[Partly from UN-[1] + *clasped* pa. pple of CLASP *verb*, partly from prec. + -ED[1].]
Having the clasp undone or not fastened.

unclassed /ʌnˈklɑːst/ *adjective.* L18.
[from UN-[1] + *classed* pa. pple of CLASS *verb.*]
Not classed; unclassified.

unclassical /ʌnˈklasɪk(ə)l/ *adjective.* E18.
[from UN-[1] + CLASSICAL.]
Not classical.
■ **unclassic** *adjective* E18. **unclassically** *adverb* L18.

unclassified /ʌnˈklasɪfʌɪd/ *adjective.* M19.
[from UN-[1] + *classified* pa. pple of CLASSIFY.]
Not classified; *spec.* (*a*) not classified as secret; (*b*) (of a road) not classified by the Department of Transport, minor.
■ **unclassifiable** *adjective* M19.

uncle /ˈʌŋk(ə)l/ *noun & verb.* ME.
[Anglo-Norman *uncle*, Old & mod. French *oncle* from late Latin *aunculus* alt. of *avunculus* maternal uncle.]
▶**A** *noun.* **I 1** The brother of one's father or mother; an aunt's husband. (Used as a form of address by a nephew or niece.) ME.
2 Used as a form of address or mode of reference to a man other than an uncle, esp. an elderly man or (by a child) a male family friend. L18. ▶**b** *Hist.* A male announcer or storyteller for children's radio programmes. E20.
3 A male friend or lover of a child's mother. M20.
4 A person regarded as having the kindly protective qualities traditionally associated with an uncle; a benevolent adviser, protector, or patron. M20.
▶**II 5** A pawnbroker. *slang.* M18.
6 [Ellipt. for *Uncle Sam* below.] (The members of) a federal agency of the US. *US colloq.* M19.
Phrases & comb.: ***Bob's your uncle***: see BOB *noun*[5]. **cry uncle**, **holler uncle**, **say uncle** *N. Amer. colloq.* acknowledge defeat, cry for mercy. ***Dutch uncle***: see DUTCH *adjective.* ***holler uncle***, ***say uncle***: see ***cry uncle*** above. **Uncle Ned** *rhyming slang* (*a*) a bed; (*b*) the head. **Uncle Sam** *colloq.* the government (or people) of the US. **Uncle Tom Cobley (and all)** [the last of a long list of people in the song *Widecombe Fair*] *colloq.* a whole lot of people. ***Welsh uncle***: see WELSH *adjective.*
▶**B** *verb trans.* Address as uncle. L16.
■ **uncleship** *noun* the state or condition of being an uncle; the relationship of an uncle: M18.

-uncle /ˈʌŋk(ə)l/ *suffix.*
[Repr. Old French *-uncle* (*-oncle*) and ult. Latin *-unculus*, *-uncula*.]
Forming nouns, usu. dims., as ***carbuncle***, ***peduncle***. Cf. -CULE.

unclean /ʌnˈkliːn/ *adjective.* OE.
[from UN-[1] + CLEAN *adjective.*]
1 Morally impure; unchaste; defiled. OE.
2 (Of an animal) regarded as impure, unfit to be eaten; *gen.* ceremonially impure. ME.
3 Not physically clean; dirty, filthy, foul. ME.

🕮 **1** E. BLAIR She wished he wouldn't stare at her—it made her feel unclean.

Special collocations: **unclean spirit** a wicked spirit; a demon.
■ **uncleaned** *adjective* M19. **uncleanness** /-n-n-/ *noun* OE.

uncleanly /ʌnˈklɛnli/ *adjective.* Now *arch. & formal.* OE.
[from UN-[1] + CLEANLY *adjective.*]
= UNCLEAN.
■ **uncleanliness** *noun* E16.

uncleanly /ʌnˈkliːnli/ *adverb.* OE.
[from UNCLEAN + -LY[1], or from UN-[1] + CLEANLY *adverb.*]
In an unclean manner.

uncleanse /ʌnˈklɛnz/ *verb trans.* L16.
[from UN-[2] + CLEANSE.]
Make or declare unclean.

uncleansed /ʌnˈklɛnzd/ *adjective.* OE.
[from UN-[1] + *cleansed* pa. pple of CLEANSE.]
Not cleansed.

unclear /ʌnˈklɪə/ *adjective.* ME.
[from UN-[1] + CLEAR *adjective.*]
1 Not easy to understand; obscure. ME.
2 Not clear in understanding, perception, or statement; confused; (of a person) uncertain or doubtful about something. LME.
†**3** Not free from fault or blame. LME–E17.
4 Not easy to see through. Long *rare.* LME.

🕮 **1** *Harper's Magazine* Whether this boosted his morale or irked him is unclear. *Times Educ. Suppl.* It is unclear how much notice he took of civil servants. **2** J. PAGET I am unclear as to their . . names.

■ **unclearly** *adverb* M19. **unclearness** *noun* M17.

uncleared /ʌnˈklɪəd/ *adjective.* M17.
[from UN-[1] + *cleared* pa. pple of CLEAR *verb.*]
1 Of a debt etc.: not settled, undischarged. Of a cheque: that has not been cleared. M17.
2 Not freed from the imputation of guilt. E18.
3 Not cleared of obstructions or unwanted objects; *spec.* (of land) not cleared of trees. M18.
4 Not explained or clarified. E19.

🕮 **3** V. CANNING Jean sat at the uncleared breakfast table.

unclench /ʌnˈklɛn(t)ʃ/ *verb.* LME.
[from UN-[2] + CLENCH *verb.* Cf. UNCLINCH.]
†**1** *verb trans.* **a** Unfasten (bars). *rare.* Only in LME. ▶**b** Unclinch (a nail etc.). L18–E19.
2 a *verb trans.* Cause (a grip) to relax; force open (a clenched hand); relax (one's grip). L18. ▶**b** *verb intrans.* Of the hand: relax from a clenched state. E20.
3 *verb trans.* Loosen from a grasp or hold. M19.

Uncle Tom /ʌŋk(ə)l ˈtɒm/ *noun, adjective, & verb. derog.* M19.
[The hero of H. B. Stowe's novel *Uncle Tom's Cabin* (1851–2).]
▶**A** *noun.* A black man who is submissively loyal or servile to white people; anyone regarded as betraying his or her cultural or social allegiance. Cf. TOM *noun*[1] 1e. M19.

🕮 *New Yorker* He attacked Foster and Stokes as the Uncle Toms of the gay movement.

▶**B** *adjective.* Designating or characteristic of an Uncle Tom. M20.

🕮 G. GREENE The African University . . where Uncle Tom professors . . produce dangerous students.

▶**C** *verb intrans. & trans.* (with *it*). Infl. **-mm-.** Act in a manner characteristic of an Uncle Tom. M20.
■ **Uncle Tommery** *noun* Uncle Tom behaviour L20. **Uncle Tommish** *adjective* somewhat like (that of) an Uncle Tom M20. **Uncle Tommism** *noun* = UNCLE TOMMERY M20.

unclew /ʌnˈkluː/ *verb trans.* Also **unclue** (pres. pple & verbal noun **-clueing**). E17.
[from UN-[2] + CLEW *verb.*]
1 Unwind, undo; *fig.* ruin. E17.
2 *NAUTICAL.* Let down the lower ends of (a sail); clew down. M19.

unclimbable /ʌnˈklʌɪməb(ə)l/ *adjective.* M16.
[from UN-[1] + CLIMBABLE.]
Not climbable.
¶ Rare before L19.
■ **unclimbed** *adjective* L18.

unclinch /ʌnˈklɪn(t)ʃ/ *verb trans. & intrans.* L16.
[from UN-[2] + CLINCH *verb.* Cf. UNCLENCH.]
1 Unclench (the hands, fists, etc.). L16.
2 Unfasten by removing clinched nails etc.; straighten and remove (a clinched nail etc.). L17.
3 Make (an argument etc.) less conclusive. L19.

uncling /ʌnˈklɪŋ/ *verb.* Long *rare.* Pa. t. & pple **-clung** /-ˈklʌŋ/. M17.
[from UN-[2] + CLING *verb.*]
1 *verb intrans.* Loosen hold. M17.
2 *verb trans.* Loosen from clinging; release from a grip. E18.

unclip /ʌnˈklɪp/ *verb trans.* Infl. **-pp-.** L16.
[from UN-[2] + CLIP *verb*[1].]
†**1** Release from an embrace. Only in L16.
2 Release from being fastened or held with a clip. M20.

unclipped /ʌnˈklɪpt/ *adjective.* Also (*arch.*) **-clipt.** LME.
[from UN-[1] + *clipped* pa. pple of CLIP *verb*[1].]
1 Not clipped or cut. LME.
2 Not fastened or held with a clip. E20.

uncloak /ʌnˈkləʊk/ *verb.* L16.
[from UN-[2] + CLOAK.]
1 *verb trans.* Remove a cloak from. Chiefly *refl.* L16. ▶**b** *verb intrans.* Take off one's cloak. M19.
2 *verb trans. fig.* Expose, reveal. M17.

uncloaked /ʌnˈkləʊkt/ *adjective.* M16.
[from UN-[1] + *cloaked* pa. pple of CLOAK.]
Not provided with or covered by a cloak; *fig.* manifest, visible.

unclog /ʌnˈklɒg/ *verb trans.* Infl. **-gg-.** E17.
[from UN-[2] + CLOG *verb.*]
Free from a hindrance or encumbrance; unblock.

unclogged /ʌnˈklɒgd/ *adjective.* M16.
[from UN-[1] + *clogged* pa. pple of CLOG *verb.*]
Not clogged or hampered; clear, unblocked.

uncloister /ʌnˈklɔɪstə/ *verb trans.* E17.
[from UN-[2] + CLOISTER *verb.*]
Release or remove from a cloister; set free, liberate.

uncloistered /ʌnˈklɔɪstəd/ *adjective.* E17.
[Partly from prec. + -ED[1], partly from UN-[1] + CLOISTERED.]
That has been released or removed from a cloister; not shut up (as) in a cloister; not organized as a cloister.

unclose /ʌnˈkləʊz/ *verb.* ME.
[from UN-[2] + CLOSE *verb.*]
1 *verb trans.* Make open; cause to open. ME. ▸**b** *fig.* Disclose, make known, reveal. Long *rare.* ME.
2 *verb intrans.* Become open. LME.
†**3** *verb trans.* = DISCLOSE *verb* 2b. L15–L16.

unclosed /ʌnˈkləʊzd/ *adjective.* LME.
[from UN-[1] + CLOSED.]
1 Not closed; open. LME.
†**2** Not enclosed. LME–M16.
■ **unclosable** *adjective* E19.

unclothe /ʌnˈkləʊð/ *verb trans.* ME.
[from UN-[2] + CLOTHE.]
1 Remove the clothes from; undress. ME.
2 Strip of leaves or vegetation. E17.
3 Remove a cloth or cloths from. E17.

unclothed /ʌnˈkləʊðd/ *adjective.* LME.
[from UN-[1] + *clothed* pa. pple of CLOTHE.]
1 Not covered with clothes; bare, naked. LME.
2 Not covered with a cloth or cloths. M19.

uncloud /ʌnˈklaʊd/ *verb.* L16.
[from UN-[2] + CLOUD *verb.*]
1 *verb trans.* Clear or free from clouds. Chiefly *fig.*, free from obscurity or gloom, make clear. L16.
2 *verb intrans.* Become clear. L19.

unclouded /ʌnˈklaʊdɪd/ *adjective.* L16.
[from UN-[1] + *clouded* pa. pple of CLOUD *verb.*]
Not obscured or darkened; nor troubled or marred by anything.

> S. BUTLER Days which, if not quite unclouded, were . . very happy ones. G. WILL Minds unclouded by ignorance.

■ **uncloudedly** *adverb* E19. **uncloudedness** *noun* M17. **uncloudy** *adjective* M17.

uncloyed /ʌnˈklɔɪd/ *adjective.* M16.
[from UN-[1] + *cloyed* pa. pple of CLOY.]
†**1** Unhurt, uninjured. Only in M16.
2 Not cloyed or surfeited. E17.
■ **uncloying** *adjective* L18.

unclue *verb* var. of UNCLEW.

unco /ˈʌŋkə/ *adjective, adverb, & noun. Scot. & north.* LME.
[Alt. of UNCOUTH.]
▸**A** *adjective.* **1** Unknown, strange; unusual. LME. ▸**b** Weird, uncanny. E19.
2 Remarkable, great, large. E18.
▸**B** *adverb.* Extremely, remarkably, very. E18.
the unco guid /gɪd/ those who are professedly strict in matters of morals and religion.
▸**C** *noun.* Pl. **uncos**.
1 A strange or unusual thing; a piece of news. Usu. in *pl.* L18.
2 A stranger. L18.

uncoat /ʌnˈkəʊt/ *verb trans.* L16.
[from UN-[2] + COAT.]
Remove a coat or coating from.

uncoated /ʌnˈkəʊtɪd/ *adjective.* M17.
[from UN-[1] + COATED.]
Not covered with a coating of some substance.

uncock /ʌnˈkɒk/ *verb trans. & intrans.* L16.
[from UN-[2] + COCK *verb*[1].]
†**1** Take (the match) out of the cock of a matchlock gun. L16–M17.
2 Lower the cock of (a firearm) in order to prevent accidental discharge. E19.

uncocked /ʌnˈkɒkt/ *adjective.* E18.
[from UN-[1] + *cocked* pa. pple of COCK *verb*[1].]
Of a hat: not having the brim cocked or turned up.

uncoil /ʌnˈkɔɪl/ *verb.* E18.
[from UN-[2] + COIL *verb.*]
1 *verb trans.* Unwind; take out of a coiled state. E18.
2 *verb intrans.* Become uncoiled. M19.

uncoined /ʌnˈkɔɪnd/ *adjective.* LME.
[from UN-[1] + *coined* pa. pple of COIN *verb*[1].]
Not coined, not made into coinage; used as money without being coined.

uncollected /ʌnkəˈlɛktɪd/ *adjective.* E17.
[from UN-[1] + COLLECTED.]
1 Not collected in one's thoughts, not self-possessed. E17.
2 Not gathered together or gathered up. M18.

uncoloured /ʌnˈkʌləd/ *adjective.* Also ***uncolored**. M16.
[from UN-[1] + COLOURED.]
1 Having no colour, not having been coloured. M16.
2 *fig.* **a** Having no specious or deceptive appearance or quality; not influenced *by* something. L16. ▸**b** Plain, simple; not exaggerated. M19.

uncombed /ʌnˈkəʊmd/ *adjective.* M16.
[from UN-[1] + *combed* pa. pple of COMB *verb.*]
(Of hair) not made tidy with a comb; (of a person) having uncombed hair; (of wool) not dressed with a comb.

uncombine /ʌnkəmˈbʌɪn/ *verb trans.* L16.
[from UN-[2] + COMBINE *verb*[1].]
Separate.

uncombined /ʌnkəmˈbʌɪnd/ *adjective.* E17.
[from UN-[1] + COMBINED.]
Not combined; CHEMISTRY (of an element) not combined in a compound.
■ **uncombinable** *adjective* L18.

†**uncome** *noun.* M16–L17.
[Prob. var. of ONCOME. Cf. ANCOME, INCOME *noun*[2].]
= INCOME *noun*[2].

uncome-at-able /ʌnkʌmˈatəb(ə)l/ *adjective. colloq.* L17.
[from UN-[1] + *come at* s.v. COME *verb* + -ABLE, or UN-[1] + *come-at-able* s.v. COME *verb.*]
Inaccessible; unattainable.

uncomely /ʌnˈkʌmli/ *adjective.* ME.
[from UN-[1] + COMELY.]
1 Not pleasing to the moral sense; unbecoming, improper, unseemly. ME.
2 Not pleasing to the eye; unattractive. ME.
■ **uncomelily** *adverb* (now *rare* or *obsolete*) LME. **uncomeliness** *noun* M16.

uncomfortable /ʌnˈkʌmf(ə)təb(ə)l/ *adjective.* LME.
[from UN-[1] + COMFORTABLE *adjective.*]
1 Causing or involving discomfort. LME.
†**2** Inconsolable. L16–M17.
3 Feeling discomfort; uneasy. L18.

> **1** C. HARMAN New York was extremely humid and uncomfortable. ***lead a person an uncomfortable life***: see LEAD *verb*[1]. **3** M. ROBERTS She pushed that thought away, it made her uncomfortable.

■ **uncomfortableness** *noun* M17. **uncomfortably** *adverb* LME. **uncomforted** *adjective* M16.

uncomfy /ʌnˈkʌmfi/ *adjective. colloq.* L19.
[from UN-[1] + COMFY.]
Uncomfortable.

uncommanded /ʌnkəˈmɑːndɪd/ *adjective.* LME.
[from UN-[1] + *commanded* pa. pple of COMMAND *verb.*]
1 Not commanded to be done or observed. LME.
2 Not commanded to do something. M16.
3 Not dominated or overlooked (*by*). L17.

uncommitted /ʌnkəˈmɪtɪd/ *adjective & noun.* LME.
[from UN-[1] + COMMITTED.]
▸**A** *adjective.* **1** Not entrusted or delegated. LME.
2 Not done. L16.
3 Not dedicated to any particular cause or group. E19.
▸**B** *noun.* The people who are uncommitted. M20.

uncommon /ʌnˈkɒmən/ *adjective & adverb.* M16.
[from UN-[1] + COMMON *adjective & adverb.*]
▸**A** *adjective.* †**1** Not possessed in common. *rare.* Only in M16.
2 Not commonly (to be) met with; not of ordinary occurrence; unusual, rare; exceptional in kind or quality. E17.
3 Unusual in amount, extent, or degree; remarkably great. E18.

> **2** G. BERKELEY Nor is it an uncommon thing to behold ignorance and zeal united in men. F. HOYLE Such globules are not uncommon in the Milky Way. M. WARNER Tommaso had uncommon eyes, neither blue nor grey. **3** J. A. FROUDE He was a man of uncommon power.

▸**B** *adverb.* Uncommonly. *arch. & dial.* L18.
■ **uncommonly** *adverb* in an uncommon degree; unusually; ***not uncommonly***, not rarely, fairly often: M18. **uncommonness** /-n-n-/ *noun* E18.

uncommunicative /ʌnkəˈmjuːnɪkətɪv/ *adjective.* L17.
[from UN-[1] + COMMUNICATIVE.]
Not communicative; not inclined to conversation, taciturn.
■ **uncommunicable** *adjective* = INCOMMUNICABLE 2, 3 LME. **uncommunicated** *adjective* L16. **uncommunicating** *adjective* M17. **uncommunicativeness** *noun* M18.

uncompanied /ʌnˈkʌmpənɪd/ *adjective. arch.* M16.
[from UN-[1] + *companied* pa. pple of COMPANY *verb.*]
Unaccompanied.

uncompanioned /ʌnkəmˈpanjənd/ *adjective.* E17.
[from UN-[1] + COMPANIONED.]
†**1** Unmatched, unequalled. Only in E17.
2 Having no companion; unaccompanied by any other (person or thing); characterized by the absence of a companion. E19.

> **2** J. WILSON His hours of uncompanioned darkness.

■ **uncompanionable** *adjective* not companionable, unsociable E17.

uncomparable /ʌnˈkɒmp(ə)rəb(ə)l/ *adjective.* LME.
[from UN-[1] + COMPARABLE.]
1 = INCOMPARABLE *adjective* 1. *arch.* LME.
2 = INCOMPARABLE *adjective* 2. E19.
■ **uncomˈpared** *adjective* L16.

uncompensated /ʌnˈkɒmpɛnseɪtɪd/ *adjective.* L18.
[from UN-[1] + *compensated* pa. pple of COMPENSATE.]
1 Accompanied by no compensating gain or good. L18.
2 Not balanced or made up for. L18.
3 Unrecompensed; not financially reimbursed or remunerated. M19.

uncomplaining /ʌnkəmˈpleɪnɪŋ/ *adjective.* M18.
[from UN-[1] + *complaining* pres. pple of COMPLAIN *verb.*]
Not given to complaining; resigned.
■ **uncomplained** *adjective* (long *rare*) not having been complained *of* M17. **uncomplainingly** *adverb* M19. **uncomplainingness** *noun* M19.

†**uncomplete** *adjective.* LME–E18.
[from UN-[1] + COMPLETE *adjective.*]
Incomplete.

uncompleted /ʌnkəmˈpliːtɪd/ *adjective.* E16.
[from UN-[1] + *completed* pa. pple of COMPLETE *verb.*]
Not completed.

uncomplicated /ʌnˈkɒmplɪkeɪtɪd/ *adjective.* L18.
[from UN-[1] + COMPLICATED.]
Not complicated; simple, straightforward.

uncomposed /ʌnkəmˈpəʊzd/ *adjective.* L16.
[from UN-[1] + COMPOSED.]
1 Not composite. Long *rare* or *obsolete.* L16.
2 Not put together in proper form. L16.
3 Not reduced to an orderly state; disordered, excited; disorderly. Long *rare* or *obsolete.* E17.
4 Not resolved or settled. Long *rare* or *obsolete.* M17.

uncompounded /ʌnkəmˈpaʊndɪd/ *adjective.* L16.
[from UN-[1] + COMPOUNDED.]
Not compounded; not made up of various elements; unmixed.
■ **uncompoundedly** *adverb* E17. **uncompoundedness** *noun* M17.

uncomprehending /ˌʌnkɒmprɪˈhɛndɪŋ/ *adjective.* M19.
[from UN-[1] + *comprehending* pres. pple of COMPREHEND.]
Lacking understanding.
■ **uncomprehend** *verb intrans.* (*rare*) fail to understand E17. **uncomprehended** *adjective* L16. **uncomprehendingly** *adverb* M19.

†**uncomprehensible** *adjective.* LME–M18.
[from UN-[1] + COMPREHENSIBLE.]
Incomprehensible.

uncomprehension /ˌʌnkɒmprɪˈhɛnʃ(ə)n/ *noun.* M19.
[from UN-[1] + COMPREHENSION.]
Incomprehension.
■ **uncomprehensive** *adjective* †(*a*) *rare* (Shakes.) incomprehensible; (*b*) not sufficiently comprehensive: E17.

uncompromising /ʌnˈkɒmprəmʌɪzɪŋ/ *adjective.* E19.
[from UN-[1] + *compromising* pres. pple of COMPROMISE *verb.*]
Unwilling to compromise; arising from or showing an unwillingness to compromise; unyielding, stubborn; relentless, direct, outspoken.

> J. ROSENBERG An uncompromising search for truth.

■ **uncompromised** *adjective* L18. **uncompromisingly** *adverb* M19. **uncompromisingness** *noun* M19.

unconcealed /ʌnkənˈsiːld/ *adjective.* L18.
[from UN-[1] + *concealed* pa. pple of CONCEAL.]
Not concealed or hidden; obvious.
■ **unconcealable** *adjective* E19.

unconceited /ʌnkənˈsiːtɪd/ *adjective. rare.* L18.
[from UN-[1] + CONCEITED.]
Not conceited or vain.
■ **unconceitedly** *adverb* E19.

unconceivable /ʌnkənˈsiːvəb(ə)l/ *adjective.* Now *rare.* E17.
[from UN-[1] + CONCEIVABLE.]
Inconceivable.
■ **unconceivableness** *noun* E17. **unconceivably** *adverb* M17.

unconceived /ʌnkənˈsiːvd/ *adjective.* LME.
[from UN-[1] + *conceived* pa. pple of CONCEIVE.]
1 Not conceived or thought of; unimagined. LME.
2 Not brought into being; not properly formed or developed. *rare.* L16.
■ **unconceiving** *adjective* (now *rare*) not comprehending or understanding; dull-witted: L16.

unconcern /ʌnkənˈsəːn/ *noun.* E18.
[from UN-[1] + CONCERN *noun.*]
Lack of concern or solicitude; indifference, equanimity.

unconcerned /ʌnkənˈsəːnd/ *adjective.* M17.
[from UN-[1] + CONCERNED.]
1 Lacking concern or interest; indifferent, unmoved. Freq. foll. by *about*, *at.* M17.
2 Not anxious; free from solicitude; untroubled. M17.
3 Not favouring one party over another; disinterested, impartial. Now *rare.* M17.

4 Not involved *with* or *in*, having no part or share *in*. Now *rare*. M17.

> 1 R. S. SURTEES He saw Soapey Sponge's preparations for departure with an unconcerned air. **4** MILTON The Morn, All unconcern'd with our unrest.

■ **unconcernedly** /-nɪdli/ *adverb* M17. **unconcernedness** /-nɪdnɪs/ *noun* M17.

unconcerning /ʌnkənˈsəːnɪŋ/ *adjective*. Now *rare*. E17.
[from UN-¹ + CONCERNING *ppl adjective*.]
Not of concern to or affecting one; unconnected with one's affairs or interests; unimportant, irrelevant.

unconcernment /ʌnkənˈsəːnm(ə)nt/ *noun*. M17.
[from UN-¹ + CONCERNMENT.]
The fact of not concerning oneself; unconcern.

unconcerted /ʌnkənˈsəːtɪd/ *adjective*. L16.
[from UN-¹ + CONCERTED.]
Not concerted or coordinated; disunited in action or intention.

unconcluded /ʌnkənˈkluːdɪd/ *adjective*. M16.
[from UN-¹ + *concluded* pa. pple of CONCLUDE.]
Not concluded; unfinished; undecided.
■ **unconcludable** *adjective* M17.

unconcocted /ʌnkənˈkɒktɪd/ *adjective*. Now *rare*. E17.
[from UN-¹ + *concocted* pa. pple of CONCOCT.]
1 Of food etc.: not digested in the stomach. E17.
2 *fig.* Not properly devised, prepared, or elaborated. E17.
3 Not brought to a proper state or condition; unripe, immature. M17.

uncondensed /ʌnkənˈdɛnst/ *adjective*. E18.
[from UN-¹ + *condensed* pa. pple of CONDENSE *verb*.]
Not condensed.
■ **uncondensable** *adjective* L18.

unconditional /ʌnkənˈdɪʃ(ə)n(ə)l/ *adjective*. M17.
[from UN-¹ + CONDITIONAL *adjective*.]
Not limited by or subject to conditions; absolute, complete.

> *Times* The [hijackers'] surrender was 'unconditional'. A. STEVENS Her love is absolute and largely unconditional.

■ **unconditio'nality** *noun* the state or quality of being unconditional E18. **unconditionally** *adverb* M17. **unconditionalness** *noun* (*rare*) = UNCONDITIONALITY M19.

unconditionate /ʌnkənˈdɪʃ(ə)nət/ *adjective*. Now *rare*. M17.
[from UN-¹ + CONDITIONATE *adjective*.]
Not subject to or limited by conditions; unconditional.
■ **unconditionately** *adverb* L17.

unconditioned /ʌnkənˈdɪʃ(ə)nd/ *adjective*. M17.
[from UN-¹ + CONDITIONED.]
1 Not subject to conditions, unconditional. M17.
2 Not dependent on an antecedent condition; not determined by conditioning, innate. L18.
3 PHILOSOPHY. Not subject to the conditions of finite existence and cognition. E19.

> 1 P. J. BAILEY Who thus pour forth Unmeasured, Unconditioned, your divine Riches. **2** **unconditioned reflex** an inborn, instinctual reflex response. **3** *absol.*: W. HAMILTON The Unconditioned, that which is inconceivable or incogitable.

■ **unconditionedness** *noun* M19.

unconfessed /ʌnkənˈfɛst/ *adjective*. LME.
[from UN-¹ + *confessed* pa. pple of CONFESS.]
1 Not confessed or declared; unacknowledged. LME. ▸**b** Of a person: having his or her character or identity concealed. M18.
2 Not having confessed one's sins; unshriven. E17.

unconfine /ʌnkənˈfʌɪn/ *verb trans*. Chiefly *poet*. M17.
[from UN-² + CONFINE *verb*.]
Release from constraint; give free rein to.

unconfined /ʌnkənˈfʌɪnd/ *adjective*. E17.
[from UN-¹ + CONFINED.]
1 Not restricted in respect of freedom of action. E17. ▸**b** Unlimited, boundless. E17.
2 Not shut up or enclosed; not secured or kept in place. M17.

> 1 J. P. NEALE The eye roams unconfined over the . . plains of Shropshire. **2** H. MARTINEAU Her hair [was] unconfined by any cap.

■ **unconfinable** *adjective* L16. **unconfinedly** /-nɪdli/ *adverb* M17. **unconfinedness** /-nɪdnɪs/ *noun* L17.

unconfirm /ʌnkənˈfəːm/ *verb trans*. *rare*. M16.
[from UN-² + CONFIRM.]
Disestablish; make less secure or settled.

unconfirmed /ʌnkənˈfəːmd/ *adjective*. M16.
[from UN-¹ + CONFIRMED.]
1 Not having received the rite of confirmation. M16.
2 Not strengthened; not yet made firm or sure. Now *rare*. L16. ▸†**b** Uninstructed, ignorant. *rare* (Shakes.). Only in L16.
3 Not ratified or sanctioned (*rare*); not supported or verified by further evidence; uncorroborated. M17.

> 2 SOUTHEY His faith, yet unconfirm'd, Determined to prompt action. **3** C. ACHEBE There were unconfirmed rumours of unrest.

†**unconform** *adjective*. M17.
[from UN-¹ + CONFORM *adjective*.]
1 Not conformed *to*. Only in M17.
2 = NONCONFORM *adjective*. M–L17.

unconformable /ʌnkənˈfɔːməb(ə)l/ *adjective*. L16.
[from UN-¹ + CONFORMABLE.]
1 Not conformable or correspondent (*to*); (of a person) unwilling to conform. L16.
2 *spec.* Chiefly *Hist.* Not conforming to the usages of the Church of England. (Foll. by *to*.) E17.
3 GEOLOGY. Showing unconformity to older underlying rocks. (Foll. by *to*.) E19.
■ **unconforma'bility** *noun* (chiefly GEOLOGY) the state or quality of being unconformable M19. **unconformably** *adverb* (GEOLOGY) in an unconformable manner or position M19.

unconformed /ʌnkənˈfɔːmd/ *adjective*. M17.
[from UN-¹ + *conformed* pa. pple of CONFORM *verb*.]
†**1** Not conforming; nonconformist. M–L17.
2 GEOLOGY. = UNCONFORMABLE 3. Now *rare*. M19.
■ **unconforming** *adjective* M17.

unconformity /ʌnkənˈfɔːmɪti/ *noun*. L16.
[from UN-¹ + CONFORMITY.]
1 Lack of conformity (*to*). L16.
†**2** = NONCONFORMITY 1. M–L17.
3 GEOLOGY. A large break in the geological record, observable as the overlying of rocks by younger rocks which would not normally succeed them directly and which may have a different direction or plane of stratification. E19. ▸**b** An instance of this; the surface of contact between two groups of unconformable strata. M19.

unconfused /ʌnkənˈfjuːzd/ *adjective*. E17.
[from UN-¹ + CONFUSED.]
Not confused; unmixed, unmingled; ordered.
■ **unconfusable** *adjective* M20. **unconfusedly** /-zɪdli/ *adverb* (now *rare* or *obsolete*) M17.

uncongeal /ʌnkənˈdʒiːl/ *verb trans. & intrans*. L16.
[from UN-² + CONGEAL.]
Unfreeze; thaw.

uncongealed /ʌnkənˈdʒiːld/ *adjective*. M17.
[from UN-¹ + *congealed* pa. pple of CONGEAL.]
Not congealed; not coagulated or frozen.
■ **uncongealable** *adjective* E17.

uncongenial /ʌnkənˈdʒiːnɪəl/ *adjective & adverb*. L18.
[from UN-¹ + CONGENIAL.]
▸ **A** *adjective*. **1** Not having the same disposition or character, not kindred. L18.
2 Unsuited to the nature of anything. L18.
3 Not agreeable; not to one's taste or inclination. (Foll. by *to*, *with*.) L18.

> 1 W. BLACK Refusing to habor such uncongenial guests. **2** J. A. SYMONDS Into the Æolian style Anacreon introduced a new and uncongenial element. **3** N. SYMINGTON She pitied me being forced to do something that I would find so uncongenial.

▸†**B** *adverb*. At variance *with*. L18–E19.
■ **uncongeni'ality** *noun* E19.

unconjectured /ʌnkənˈdʒɛktʃəd/ *adjective*. M17.
[from UN-¹ + *conjectured* pa. pple of CONJECTURE *verb*.]
Not conjectured.
■ **unconjecturable** *adjective* E19.

unconnected /ʌnkəˈnɛktɪd/ *adjective*. M18.
[from UN-¹ + CONNECTED.]
1 Not connected or associated; not physically joined. (Foll. by *to*, *with*.) M18.
2 Characterized by a lack of connection; incohesive. M18.
3 Disconnected; not joined in order or sequence. L18.
4 Not related by family ties etc. E19.

> 1 J. BRAINE *Not* entirely unconnected with the Chairman of the Finance Committee. **2** J. FANE The so-called Ruins are . . just some unconnected flint walls. **3** F. E. GRETTON I simply record unconnected anecdotes and disjointed facts.

■ **unconnectedly** *adverb* L18. **unconnectedness** *noun* L18.

unconnection /ʌnkəˈnɛkʃ(ə)n/ *noun*. M18.
[from UN-¹ + CONNECTION.]
The state or fact of being unconnected.

unconquerable /ʌnˈkɒŋk(ə)rəb(ə)l/ *adjective*. L16.
[from UN-¹ + CONQUERABLE.]
1 That cannot be overcome or defeated by conquest or force (*lit.* & *fig.*); invincible. L16.
2 Unable to be mastered or brought under control; insuperable. M17.

> 1 A. RADCLIFFE He fought with unconquerable audacity and fierceness. BOSW. SMITH Hannibal was still . . unconquered, and, as far as they knew, unconquerable. **2** J. BEATTIE Check'd by . . poverty's unconquerable bar. J. KLEIN Language which aroused in me an unconquerable aversion.

■ **unconquerableness** *noun* M17. **unconquerably** *adverb* M17.

unconquered /ʌnˈkɒŋkəd/ *ppl adjective*. M16.
[from UN-¹ + *conquered* pa. pple of CONQUER *verb*.]
Not conquered or defeated.

> *Spectator* Saint Elias, . . the still unconquered peak of Alaska. G. WILL Hungary flung its unconquered consciousness in the face of the totalitarian state.

unconscientious /ˌʌnkɒnʃɪˈɛnʃəs/ *adjective*. L18.
[from UN-¹ + CONSCIENTIOUS.]
Not conscientious; not scrupulous or careful.
■ **unconscientiously** *adverb* M17. **unconscientiousness** *noun* M19.

unconscionable /ʌnˈkɒnʃ(ə)nəb(ə)l/ *adjective & adverb*. M16.
[from UN-¹ + CONSCIONABLE.]
▸ **A** *adjective*. **1** Showing no regard for conscience; not in accordance with what is right or reasonable. M16. ▸**b** Unreasonably excessive. L16. ▸**c** As an intensive: egregious, blatant. L16.
2 Having no conscience; not controlled by conscience; unscrupulous. Also (*derog.*) used as an intensive. L16.

> 1 *New York Times* Dropping a bomb on an occupied row house was unconscionable. **b** K. MOORE He . . occupied the bathroom for an unconscionable period. **c** R. NORTH A due Reward of unconscionable Cheating. **2** MRS ALEXANDER What an unconscionable old slave-holder!

▸ **B** *adverb*. Unconscionably, excessively. Now *colloq*. L16.
■ **unconsciona'bility** *noun* (chiefly US LAW) = UNCONSCIONABLENESS E20. **unconscionableness** *noun* the quality or state of being unconscionable; unscrupulousness, unreasonableness: E17. **unconscionably** *adverb* L16.

unconscious /ʌnˈkɒnʃəs/ *adjective & noun*. E18.
[from UN-¹ + CONSCIOUS.]
▸ **A** *adjective*. **1** Not conscious or knowing within oneself; unaware. (Foll. by *of*, *that*.) E18.
2 Not having, manifesting, or characterized by the faculty of consciousness. E18. ▸**b** Temporarily devoid of consciousness. E19.
3 Of a quality, emotion, etc.: not realized as existing in oneself; of which one is unaware. E19.
4 Of an action etc.: performed without conscious awareness; unintentional; not deliberate or planned. E19.
5 PSYCHOLOGY. Designating mental processes of which a person is not aware but which have a powerful effect on his or her attitudes and behaviour; *spec.* in Freudian theory, designating processes activated by desires, fears, or memories which are unacceptable to the conscious mind and so repressed. Also, designating that part of the mind or psyche in which such processes operate. E20.

> 1 E. WAUGH Quite unconscious of the alarm he had caused. **2b** C. PHILLIPS Three KGB men . . were kicking him unconscious. **3** K. A. PORTER Children with unconscious cruelty try to train their pets to eat at table. **4** *Economist* The PLF described the raid, with unconscious irony, as 'a military lesson' for Israel. ***unconscious cerebration***: see CEREBRATION.

▸ **B** *noun*. PSYCHOLOGY. *The* unconscious mind. L19.
collective unconscious: see COLLECTIVE *adjective* 4.
■ **unconsciously** *adverb* E18. **unconsciousness** *noun* M18.

unconsecrate /ʌnˈkɒnsɪkrət/ *adjective*. *arch*. E16.
[from UN-¹ + CONSECRATE *adjective*.]
Unconsecrated.

unconsecrate /ʌnˈkɒnsɪkreɪt/ *verb trans*. Now *rare* or *obsolete*. L16.
[from UN-² + CONSECRATE *verb*.]
Make unconsecrated; desecrate.

unconsecrated /ʌnˈkɒnsɪkreɪtɪd/ *adjective*. L16.
[from UN-¹ + CONSECRATED.]
Not consecrated.

unconsequential /ˌʌnkɒnsɪˈkwɛnʃ(ə)l/ *adjective*. M18.
[from UN-¹ + CONSEQUENTIAL.]
1 Not consequential; not following as an effect or logical inference. M18.
2 Of no consequence; inconsequential, insignificant. L18.

unconsidered /ʌnkənˈsɪdəd/ *adjective*. L16.
[from UN-¹ + CONSIDERED.]
1 Not considered or thought of; not taken into account; disregarded. L16.
2 Not done with or characterized by consideration or mature reflection; unpremeditated, immediate. L19.

> 1 M. R. MITFORD The gift of some unconsidered trifles. G. HUNTINGTON At no time could he tempt her into saying a single unconsidered word.

■ **unconsiderable** *adjective* inconsiderable M17. **unconsidering** *adjective* M17.

unconsolable /ʌnkən'səʊləb(ə)l/ *adjective*. E17.
[from UN-¹ + CONSOLABLE.]
Not able to be consoled; inconsolable.
■ **unconsolably** *adverb* L19.

unconsoled /ʌnkən'səʊld/ *adjective*. E19.
[from UN-¹ + *consoled* pa. pple of CONSOLE *verb*.]
Not consoled, uncomforted.

unconstitutional /ˌʌnkɒnstɪ'tjuːʃ(ə)n(ə)l/ *adjective*. M18.
[from UN-¹ + CONSTITUTIONAL *adjective*.]
1 Not in harmony with or authorized by the constitution of a State etc.; at variance with the recognized principles of a State or with procedural rules. M18.
2 Not inherent in, or in accordance with, a person's constitution. *rare*. L18.

> 📖 **1** LD MACAULAY The Declaration of Indulgence was unconstitutional. *New York Times* A . . judge has held Virginia's law against cross burning to be unconstitutional.

■ **unconstitutionalism** *noun* M20. **unconstitutionality** /-'nalɪti/ *noun* L18. **unconstitutionally** *adverb* L18.

unconstrained /ʌnkən'streɪnd/ *adjective*. LME.
[from UN-¹ + CONSTRAINED.]
1 Not constrained or compelled; not acting under compulsion; without constraint, free; unrestrained. LME.
2 Free from embarrassment; natural. E18.

> 📖 **1** F. W. FARRAR The intercourse which the prisoner could hold with any who came to visit him was unconstrained. **2** L. STERNE He looked frank,—unconstrained.

■ **unconstrainable** *adjective* (*rare*) M17. **unconstrainedly** /-nɪdli/ *adverb* M16.

unconstraint /ʌnkən'streɪnt/ *noun*. E18.
[from UN-¹ + CONSTRAINT.]
The state or quality of being unconstrained; freedom from constraint.

unconstructed /ʌnkən'strʌktɪd/ *adjective*. Chiefly *N. Amer.* L20.
[from UN-¹ + *constructed* pa. pple of CONSTRUCT *verb*.]
Of a garment: made with little or no interfacing or other material which would give definition to its shape; designed to fit loosely or easily rather than to emphasize structure. Also, designating this style of design.

unconsulted /ʌnkən'sʌltɪd/ *adjective*. M16.
[from UN-¹ + *consulted* pa. pple of CONSULT *verb*.]
†**1** Uncounselled, unadvised. *rare*. Only in M16.
2 Not consulted (*with*) or referred to. E17.
■ **unconsultable** *adjective* M19. **unconsulting** *adjective* (*rare*) L16.

unconsumed /ʌnkən'sjuːmd/ *adjective*. M16.
[from UN-¹ + CONSUMED.]
Not consumed.
■ **unconsumable** *adjective* L16. **unconsuming** *adjective* E17.

unconsummate /ʌnkən'sʌmət, ʌn'kɒnsəmət/ *adjective*. *arch*. E17.
[from UN-¹ + CONSUMMATE *adjective*.]
Not completed or fully accomplished; unconsummated.

unconsummated /ʌn'kɒnsəmeɪtɪd, -sjʊ-/ *adjective*. E19.
[from UN-¹ + *consummated* pa. pple of CONSUMMATE *verb*.]
Not consummated.

uncontained /ʌnkən'teɪnd/ *adjective*. E17.
[from UN-¹ + CONTAINED.]
Not contained, not restrained or reserved.
■ **uncontainable** *adjective* E17.

uncontaminate /ʌnkən'tamɪnət/ *adjective*. *arch*. L17.
[from UN-¹ + *contaminate* arch. pa. pple of CONTAMINATE.]
Uncontaminated.

uncontaminated /ʌnkən'tamɪneɪtɪd/ *adjective*. E17.
[from UN-¹ + *contaminated* pa. pple of CONTAMINATE.]
Not contaminated; pure, unpolluted.

uncontent /ʌnkən'tɛnt/ *adjective*. *arch*. E16.
[from UN-¹ + CONTENT *pred. adjective*.]
Not contented.

uncontented /ʌnkən'tɛntɪd/ *adjective*. M16.
[from UN-¹ + CONTENTED.]
Not contented; unsatisfied.

uncontested /ʌnkən'tɛstɪd/ *adjective*. L17.
[from UN-¹ + *contested* pa. pple of CONTEST *verb*.]
Not contested; *esp*. unchallenged, undisputed.
■ **uncontestable** *adjective* L17. **uncontestedly** *adverb* L17.

uncontracted /ʌnkən'traktɪd/ *adjective*. E16.
[from UN-¹ + CONTRACTED.]
†**1** Not engaged to be married. E16–E17.
2 Not subjected to contraction; not shortened or condensed. M18.

uncontradicted /ˌʌnkɒntrə'dɪktɪd/ *adjective*. E17.
[from UN-¹ + *contradicted* pa. pple of CONTRADICT.]
Not contradicted, not opposed or denied.
■ **uncontradictable** *adjective* E18. **uncontradictably** *adverb* M19.

uncontrol /ʌnkən'trəʊl/ *noun*. *rare*. M19.
[from UN-¹ + CONTROL *noun*.]
The state of being uncontrolled.

uncontrollable /ʌnkən'trəʊləb(ə)l/ *adjective & noun*. Also †**-controul-**. L16.
[from UN-¹ + CONTROLLABLE.]
▶ **A** *adjective*. †**1** Incontrovertible, indisputable, irrefutable. L16–M18.
2 Not subject to control from a higher authority; absolute. L16.
3 That cannot be controlled or restrained. M17.

> 📖 **2** M. EDGEWORTH She had an uncontroulable right to marry as she thought proper. **3** C. THUBRON A burst of uncontrollable merriment.

▶ **B** *noun*. A person who or thing (esp. a factor) which is uncontrollable or unpredictable. L20.
■ **uncontrolla'bility** *noun* E20. **uncontrollableness** *noun* M17. **uncontrollably** *adverb* E17.

uncontrolled /ʌnkən'trəʊld/ *adjective*. Also †**-controul-**. E16.
[from UN-¹ + *controlled* pa. pple of CONTROL *verb*.]
1 Not subjected to control; unrestrained, unregulated, unchecked. E16.
†**2** Not called in question; undisputed. M16–M18.

> 📖 **1** G. WILL The insistent . . prompting of uncontrolled memory. *Reader's Digest* The well began to 'kick'—meaning it was beginning to flow uncontrolled. **2** SWIFT The most uncontrouled and universally agreed maxim.

■ **uncontrolledly** /-lɪdli/ *adverb* L16.

uncontroversial /ˌʌnkɒntrə'vəːʃ(ə)l/ *adjective*. M19.
[from UN-¹ + CONTROVERSIAL.]
Not controversial.
■ **uncontroversially** *adverb* M19.

uncontroverted /ʌn'kɒntrəvəːtɪd, ˌʌnkɒntrə'vəːtɪd/ *adjective*. M17.
[from UN-¹ + *controverted* pa. pple of CONTROVERT.]
Not controverted; not subjected to contention or debate.
■ **uncontrovertedly** *adverb* (*rare*) M17. **uncontrovertible** *adjective* M17. **uncontrovertibly** *adverb* M18.

unconventional /ʌnkən'vɛnʃ(ə)n(ə)l/ *adjective*. M19.
[from UN-¹ + CONVENTIONAL *adjective*.]
Not limited or bound by convention or custom; diverging from accepted standards or models, unusual, unorthodox. Also, (of weapons, warfare, etc.) nuclear.

> 📖 M. MEYER The unconventional manner of the two girls offended the . . conservative . . Scandinavian community. *Nation* 'Unconventional' weapons of mass destruction.

■ **unconventionalism** *noun* M19. **unconventionality** /-'nalɪti/ *noun* the quality or state of being unconventional; an unconventional thing or practice: M19. **unconventionally** *adverb* E20.

unconvert /ʌnkən'vəːt/ *verb trans*. *rare*. M17.
[from UN-² + CONVERT *verb*.]
Change in character or function. Also, reverse or undo the conversion of.

unconverted /ʌnkən'vəːtɪd/ *adjective*. M17.
[from UN-¹ + CONVERTED.]
Not converted; *esp*. that has not adopted, or been brought over to, a religious faith; not changed from one faith or opinion to another.
■ **unconvertible** *adjective* L17.

unconvinced /ʌnkən'vɪnst/ *adjective*. M17.
[from UN-¹ + *convinced* pa. pple of CONVINCE.]
†**1** Undisproved, unrefuted. *rare*. Only in M17.
2 Not convinced or persuaded (*of*). L17.
■ **unconvincible** *adjective* M18.

unconvincing /ʌnkən'vɪnsɪŋ/ *adjective*. M17.
[from UN-¹ + CONVINCING.]
Not convincing, unable to convince; (of an excuse, attempt, etc.) feeble, unimpressive, half-hearted.
■ **unconvincingly** *adverb* L19.

uncooperative /ʌnkəʊ'ɒp(ə)rətɪv/ *adjective*. M20.
[from UN-¹ + COOPERATIVE *adjective*.]
Not cooperative; not willing to cooperate.
■ **uncooperatively** *adverb* L20.

uncoordinated /ʌnkəʊ'ɔːdɪneɪtɪd/ *adjective*. L19.
[from UN-¹ + *coordinated* pa. pple of COORDINATE *verb*.]
Not coordinated; not functioning in the proper order; (of a person's movements etc.) lacking coordination.

uncopied /ʌn'kɒpɪd/ *adjective*. M18.
[from UN-¹ + *copied* pa. pple of COPY *verb*¹.]
Not copied.
■ **uncopiable** *adjective* M19.

uncord /ʌn'kɔːd/ *verb trans*. LME.
[from UN-² + CORD *verb*¹.]
Unstring (a bow) (long *rare* or *obsolete*); remove the cord or cords from.

uncork /ʌn'kɔːk/ *verb trans*. E18.
[from UN-² + CORK *verb*¹.]
1 Draw the cork from (a bottle etc.). E18.
2 Release as from a bottle; allow (feelings etc.) to be vented. M18.

> 📖 **2** J. BARTH A squall . . spun across the Bay like an uncork genie.

uncorked /ʌn'kɔːkd/ *adjective*. L18.
[UN-¹ + CORKED.]
Not fitted or stopped with a cork; (of a bottle etc.) having the cork removed.

uncorrect /ʌnkə'rɛkt/ *adjective*. Now *rare* or *obsolete*. E16.
[from UN-¹ + CORRECT *adjective*.]
†**1** Uncorrected. E–M16.
2 Incorrect. M16.
■ **uncorrectable** *adjective* M16.

uncorrected /ʌnkə'rɛktɪd/ *adjective*. LME.
[from UN-¹ + *corrected* pa. pple of CORRECT *verb*.]
Not corrected. Now *esp*. (of an error etc.) not put right or revised, unamended.

uncorrupt /ʌnkə'rʌpt/ *adjective*. LME.
[from UN-¹ + CORRUPT *adjective*.]
= UNCORRUPTED.
■ **uncorruptly** *adverb* (now *rare*) M16. **uncorruptness** *noun* (now *rare*) L16.

uncorrupted /ʌnkə'rʌptɪd/ *adjective*. LME.
[from UN-¹ + *corrupted* pa. pple of CORRUPT *verb*.]
1 Of organic matter: not decayed or decomposed. LME.
2 Of a person, personal attribute, or action: not morally corrupted, unspoilt, honourable; not influenced by bribes. M16.
3 Unadulterated; now *esp*. (of a language or text) pure, correct. M16.

> 📖 **2** W. S. MAUGHAM The noble savage, uncorrupted by the vices of civilization.

■ **uncorruptedly** *adverb* L16. **uncorruptedness** *noun* E17.

uncorruptible /ʌnkə'rʌptɪb(ə)l/ *adjective*. LME.
[from UN-¹ + CORRUPTIBLE.]
Incorruptible.

uncorruption /ʌnkə'rʌpʃ(ə)n/ *noun*. Now *rare*. LME.
[from UN-¹ + CORRUPTION.]
Absence of corruption; moral purity; integrity.

uncouch /ʌn'kaʊtʃ/ *verb*. *arch*. *rare*. LME.
[from UN-² + COUCH *verb*.]
†**1** *verb trans*. Raise up from a couch or bed. LME–E17.
2 †**a** *verb trans*. Drive (an animal) out of its lair. M16–E17.
▸**b** *verb intrans*. Of an animal: emerge from its lair. M19.

uncounselled /ʌn'kaʊns(ə)ld/ *adjective*. Also ***-eled**. LME.
[from UN-¹ + *counselled* pa. pple of COUNSEL *verb*.]
Not counselled, not having been advised.
■ **uncounsellable** *adjective* (now *rare*) (of a person) not open to counsel L16.

uncountable /ʌn'kaʊntəb(ə)l/ *adjective & noun*. LME.
[from UN-¹ + COUNTABLE.]
▶ **A** *adjective*. †**1** Not liable to be called to account; unaccountable. Only in LME.
2 Not able to be counted; innumerable; *spec*. in MATH., infinite and incapable of being put into a one-to-one correspondence with the integers (cf. DENUMERABLE). L16.
3 Inestimable, immense. M19.
4 GRAMMAR. Of a noun: that cannot form a plural or be used with an indefinite article. E20.

> 📖 **2** A. TUTUOLA Uncountable people . . used to come to . . greet him. **3** CARLYLE Which has been of uncountable advantage to Brandenburg.

▶ **B** *noun*. GRAMMAR. An uncountable noun or its referent. E20.
■ **uncounta'bility** *noun* the property of being uncountable M20. **uncountably** *adverb* L16.

uncounted /ʌn'kaʊntɪd/ *adjective*. L15.
[from UN-¹ + *counted* pa. pple of COUNT *verb*.]
Not counted or countable; innumerable.

uncounterfeit /ʌn'kaʊntəfɪt, -fiːt/ *adjective*. M16.
[from UN-¹ + COUNTERFEIT *adjective*.]
Not counterfeit; genuine; unfeigned.

uncounterfeit /ʌn'kaʊntəfɪt, -fiːt/ *verb trans*. Long *rare*. L16.
[from UN-² + COUNTERFEIT *verb*.]
Represent in a genuine or unfeigned manner.

uncouple /ʌn'kʌp(ə)l/ *verb*. ME.
[from UN-² + COUPLE *verb*.]
1 *verb trans*. & †*intrans*. Release (hunting dogs) from being fastened together in couples; unleash for the chase. ME.
2 *verb trans*. Unfasten, disconnect, detach; *spec*. release (railway vehicles) from couplings. M16.

3 *verb trans.* SCIENCE. Make independent or separate *from*; decouple. M20.
4 *verb intrans.* Of a couple: separate at the end of a relationship. *colloq.* M20.

📖 **2** *Guardian* Smith . . began the effort to uncouple the party from blame for the dispute. **3 uncoupling agent** BIOCHEMISTRY an uncoupler.

■ **uncoupler** *noun* a thing which uncouples something; *spec.* in BIOCHEMISTRY, an agent that causes the uncoupling of oxidative phosphorylation: E18.

uncoupled /ʌnˈkʌp(ə)ld/ *adjective.* LME.
[from UN-¹ + COUPLED.]
1 Not coupled or joined; left detached or separate. LME.
2 PHYSICS. Not physically interacting; decoupled. M20.

uncourteous /ʌnˈkəːtjəs/ *adjective.* ME.
[from UN-¹ + COURTEOUS.]
Not showing courtesy; lacking in courtesy; discourteous.
■ **uncourteously** *adverb* ME. **uncourteousness** *noun* M16.

uncourtly /ʌnˈkɔːtli/ *adjective.* L16.
[from UN-¹ + COURTLY *adjective.*]
1 Not adapted or suited to a royal court; *esp.* not sufficiently polished or refined, discourteous, ill-mannered. L16.
2 Not subservient to or seeking to please a royal court. E18.
■ **uncourtliness** *noun* (now *rare*) M17.

uncouth /ʌnˈkuːθ/ *adjective & noun.* OE.
[from UN-¹ + COUTH. See also UNCO, UNQUOTH.]
▶ **A** *adjective.* †**1** Unknown; not certainly known, uncertain. OE–M17.
2 Unfamiliar, unaccustomed; with which one is not acquainted. *arch.* OE.
3 Unusual, uncommon; strange; astonishing. Now *rare.* OE. ▸†**b** Alien or foreign *to. rare.* LME–L17.
†**4** Unknowing, ignorant. *rare.* ME–E17.
†**5** Of a repellent, unpleasant, or distasteful character. LME–L18. ▸†**b** Unseemly, indecorous. *rare.* L16–M17.
6 Of an unfamiliar or strange appearance or form; *esp.* odd, awkward, or clumsy in shape or bearing. *arch.* E16.
7 Of a place: unfrequented; desolate, wild, rugged. Also (of one's surroundings etc.), unpleasant, uncomfortable. *arch.* M16.
8 Of language, style, etc.: clumsy; lacking sophistication or delicacy. L17.
9 Of a person, a person's manner, appearance, etc.: lacking refinement or grace; uncultured, ill-mannered; rough. M18.

📖 **2** MILTON I Toild out my uncouth passage. **3** G. HARRIS The uncouth, unaccustomed spectacle presented by the Highlanders. **6** R. FORD The ponies of Gallicia, although ugly and uncouth, are admirably suited to the . . hilly country. **7** JOHN MORGAN The Ruins of . . stately Buildings . . in uncouth Mountains. **8** J. R. LOWELL Bad sense, uncouth metre, or false grammar. **9** M. HOLROYD Uncouth to the point of rudeness.

▶ **B** *noun.* †**1** An unknown person; a stranger. Only in ME.
2 In *pl.* Things not commonly known; news. Now *dial.* E16.
■ **uncouthie** *adjective* (*Scot.*) dreary; uncomfortable; unfriendly: M18. **uncouthly** *adverb* OE. **uncouthness** *noun* LME. **uncouthsome** *adjective* (*rare*) unfavourable, unpleasant: L17.

uncovenant /ʌnˈkʌv(ə)nənt/ *verb trans.* M17.
[from UN-² + COVENANT *verb.*]
Release or disengage (a person, oneself) from a covenant.

uncovenanted /ʌnˈkʌv(ə)nəntɪd/ *adjective.* M17.
[from UN-¹ + COVENANTED.]
1 Not promised by or based on a covenant, esp. a covenant with God. Also (*rare*), lying outside of God's covenant. M17.
2 Not sanctioned by or in accordance with a covenant or agreement. E18.
3 Of a person: not bound by a covenant; *spec.* (*Hist.*) not covenanted (see COVENANTED 2). L18.

uncover /ʌnˈkʌvə/ *verb.* LME.
[from UN-² + COVER *verb*².]
1 *verb trans.* Expose to view by the removal of some covering thing or matter; remove a cover or covering from. Formerly also, remove the roof from (a house etc.). LME. ▸**b** Unclothe (part of the body). LME. ▸**c** Drive (a fox) out of cover. E19.
2 *verb trans.* Disclose, bring to light, make known. LME.
3 *verb trans. & intrans.* Remove one's hat from (the head), esp. as a mark of respect or courtesy. *arch.* M16.
4 *verb trans.* MILITARY. Expose (part of a division etc.) by the moving or manoeuvring of troops; leave unprotected by withdrawal of troops. L18.

📖 **1** G. DANIEL Excavations . . uncovered a dozen villas. *absol.*: *Food & Wine* Uncover, sprinkle in . . vinegar and cook to reduce slightly. **b** B. JOWETT Uncover your chest . . that I may have a better view. **2** R. STRANGE Truth . . is uncovered only in relationship with the divine. *Voice of the Arab World* Our quarterly publication . . will endeavour to uncover facts that . . propagandists seek to hide.

uncovered /ʌnˈkʌvəd/ *adjective.* LME.
[from UN-¹ + COVERED.]
1 Of a house etc.: unroofed, open to the sky. LME.
2 Unclothed; bare. LME. ▸**b** Not wearing a hat, bareheaded. LME.
3 Having no covering; left exposed; not covered *by* or *with* something. M16.
4 Not protected or screened by another or others. L18.
5 Not covered by insurance. L19.

uncovery /ʌnˈkʌv(ə)ri/ *noun.* M20.
[from UNCOVER after *discovery, recovery,* etc.: see -ERY.]
The action of uncovering or bringing something to light.

uncracked /ʌnˈkrakt/ *adjective.* L16.
[from UN-¹ + CRACKED.]
Not cracked; unbroken; sound.
■ **uncracka'bility** *noun* the quality of being uncrackable E20. **uncrackable** *adjective* unable to be cracked M20.

uncreate /ʌnkriːˈeɪt/ *adjective. arch.* M16.
[from UN-¹ + CREATE *adjective.*]
Uncreated.

uncreate /ʌnkriːˈeɪt/ *verb trans.* Chiefly *literary.* M17.
[from UN-² + CREATE *verb.*]
Undo the creation of; unmake; destroy.

uncreated /ʌnkriːˈeɪtɪd/ *adjective.* M16.
[from UN-¹ + *created* pa. pple of CREATE *verb.*]
1 Not brought into existence by a divine act of creation; of a self-existent or eternal nature. M16.
2 Not created; not made or brought into being. E17.

📖 **1** J. L. ESPOSITO For Muslims, the Quran is . . the eternal, uncreated, literal word of God.

■ **uncreatable** *adjective* M19. **uncreatedness** *noun* M17.

uncreative /ʌnkriːˈeɪtɪv/ *adjective.* M19.
[from UN-¹ + CREATIVE.]
Not creative; uninventive; unimaginative.

📖 K. A. PORTER To dissect music . . to listen to it is the . . snobbism of uncreative people.

uncredited /ʌnˈkrɛdɪtɪd/ *adjective.* L16.
[from UN-¹ + *credited* pa. pple of CREDIT *verb.*]
Not credited; *esp.* not acknowledged or ascribed.

📖 *New Yorker* Short, who is uncredited, plays the tiny role of Nick's agent.

■ **uncreditable** *adjective* discreditable; disreputable: M17.

uncritical /ʌnˈkrɪtɪk(ə)l/ *adjective.* M17.
[from UN-¹ + CRITICAL.]
1 Not critical; lacking in judgement; not given to censure. (Foll. by *of.*) M17.
2 Showing lack of critical exactness; not in accordance with the principles of criticism. M19.

📖 **1** T. TANNER It does not follow that her work is uncritical of her society. J. TROLLOPE A bottomless well of woolly uncritical forgiveness.

■ **uncritically** *adverb* E19.

uncriticized /ʌnˈkrɪtɪsʌɪzd/ *adjective.* Also **-ised.** M19.
[from UN-¹ + *criticized* pa. pple of CRITICIZE.]
Not criticized; not subjected to criticism or censure.
■ **uncriticizable** *adjective* M19.

uncropped /ʌnˈkrɒpt/ *adjective.* E17.
[from UN-¹ + *cropped* pa. pple of CROP *verb.*]
1 (Of grass etc.) not eaten by animals; (of a plant, fruit, etc.) not picked. E17.
2 Of the ears, hair, etc.: not cropped or cut; left uncut. E19.
3 Of land: left fallow, not used for growing crops. M19.

uncross /ʌnˈkrɒs/ *verb trans.* L16.
[from UN-² + CROSS *verb.*]
Take out of or change back from a crossed position.

📖 V. WOOLF Some relaxed their fingers; and others uncrossed their legs.

uncrossed /ʌnˈkrɒst/ *adjective.* M16.
[from UN-¹ + *crossed* pa. pple of CROSS *verb.*]
1 Not wearing or invested with a cross. M16.
†**2** Not crossed out or cancelled. Only in 17.
3 Not thwarted or opposed. M17.
4 Of a cheque: not crossed with two parallel lines to indicate that it must be paid into a bank account. L19.
■ **uncrossable** *adjective* L17.

uncrown /ʌnˈkraʊn/ *verb trans.* ME.
[from UN-² + CROWN *verb*¹.]
1 Take the crown from (a monarch); deprive of royalty; deprive of a ruling position. ME.
2 Remove a crown from (the head); divest *of* a crown. Long *rare.* L16. ▸**b** *fig.* Uncover; display. *rare.* M19.

uncrowned /ʌnˈkraʊnd/ *adjective.* LME.
[from UN-¹ + CROWNED.]
†**1** Untonsured. Only in LME.
2 Not consummated or perfected. *rare.* E17.
3 a Not invested with a crown. M17. ▸**b** Having the status or authority (as) of a ruler but not formally acknowledged as such. E20.

📖 **3b** S. WOODS The uncrowned King of the diamond smugglers.

uncrumple /ʌnˈkrʌmp(ə)l/ *verb.* E17.
[from UN-² + CRUMPLE *verb.*]
1 *verb trans.* Remove the crumples from; straighten; smooth out. E17.
2 *verb intrans.* Become free from crumples. M19.

uncrumpled /ʌnˈkrʌmp(ə)ld/ *adjective.* M19.
[from UN-¹ + CRUMPLED.]
Not crumpled; without creases.

uncrushed /ʌnˈkrʌʃt/ *adjective.* E17.
[from UN-¹ + *crushed* pa. pple of CRUSH *verb.*]
Not crushed; not creased; *fig.* not subdued or overwhelmed.
■ **uncrushable** *adjective* not crushable; (of a fabric, garment, etc.) crease-resistant: E19.

uncrystallized /ʌnˈkrɪst(ə)lʌɪzd/ *adjective.* Also **-ised.** M18.
[from UN-¹ + *crystallized* pa. pple of CRYSTALLIZE.]
Not crystallized.
■ **uncrystallizable** *adjective* L18.

UNCSTD *abbreviation.*
United Nations Conference on Science and Technology for Development.

UNCTAD /ˈʌŋktad/ *abbreviation.*
United Nations Conference on Trade and Development.

unction /ˈʌŋ(k)ʃ(ə)n/ *noun.* LME.
[Latin *unctio(n-)*, from *unct-* pa. ppl stem of *ung(u)ere* smear: see -ION.]
1 The action or an act of anointing a person or thing with oil as a religious rite. Also, the sacrament of extreme unction. LME.
2 The action or an act of anointing a person with oil as a symbol of investiture in an office or position of rank, esp. that of a monarch. LME.
3 *fig.* A spiritual influence (esp. that of the Holy Spirit) acting on a person. LME. ▸**b** (The manifestation of) intense spiritual emotion; a manner suggestive of religious earnestness. Now freq. *derog.*, simulated or self-satisfied religious earnestness or spiritual emotion. L17. ▸**c** *transf.* A manner of speech or address showing appreciation or enjoyment of a subject or situation; gusto. E19.
4 The action of anointing or rubbing something or someone with an unguent or ointment for medical purposes. LME.
5 An unguent, an ointment. LME. ▸**b** *fig.* A soothing influence, a salve. E17.

📖 **1** *extreme unction*: see EXTREME *adjective* 3. **3b** J. R. LOWELL That clerical unction which . . easily degenerates into greasiness. **c** L. STRACHEY Mr. Scott replied with such vigour and unction . . that not a Dean was unconvinced. **5b** L. OLIVIER These tender venturings into the blessed unction of sex were gifts to me. FLATTERING *unction.*

■ **unctional** *adjective* (*rare*) full of spiritual unction; deeply religious: M19.

†**unctious** *adjective.* L15–M18.
[Var. of UNCTUOUS by substitution of -IOUS, prob. after UNCTION.]
Unctuous; oily, greasy.

unctuosity /ʌŋktjʊˈɒsɪti/ *noun.* LME.
[medieval Latin *unctuositas*, formed as next: see -ITY.]
1 Unctuousness; oiliness, greasiness. LME.
2 *fig.* Unctuous religiosity; oiliness in behaviour or tone. L19.

unctuous /ˈʌŋktjʊəs/ *adjective.* See also UNCTIOUS. LME.
[medieval Latin *unctuosus*, from Latin *unctus*, from *unct-*: see UNCTION, -OUS.]
1 Of the nature or quality of an unguent or ointment; *gen.* oily, greasy. LME. ▸**b** Of meat: greasy, fatty, rich. *arch.* LME. ▸**c** Characterized by the presence of oil or fat; fat, plump. M17.
2 Of ground or soil: of a soft adhesive nature; rich. Now *rare.* M16.
3 Now chiefly of a mineral: having a greasy or soapy feel. M17.
4 Characterized by spiritual unction, esp. of a simulated or self-satisfied nature. Now *esp.* unpleasantly flattering; oily; characterized by obsequious charm. M18.

📖 **1** *Art & Artists* He painted . . in rich unctuous pigment. P. V. PRICE Anything spicy, piquant or unctuous, such as stuffed eggs, can dull . . the palate. **4** S. LEWIS His voice had changed from rasping efficiency to an unctuous familiarity with . . the Almighty. W. STYRON Growing ever more servile and unctuous as I became older, always the crafty flatterer.

■ **unctuously** *adverb* in an unctuous or oily manner; obsequiously: M19. **unctuousness** *noun* the quality or state of being unctuous LME.

uncultivable /ʌnˈkʌltɪvəb(ə)l/ *adjective.* M17.
[from UN-¹ + CULTIVABLE.]
Unable to be cultivated.
■ **uncultivaˈbility** *noun* (*rare*) L19.

†**uncultivate** *adjective.* M17–L18.
[from UN-¹ + medieval Latin *cultivat-* pa. ppl stem of *cultivare* CULTIVATE: see -ATE².]
Uncultivated.

uncultivated /ʌnˈkʌltɪveɪtɪd/ *adjective.* M17.
[from UN-¹ + *cultivated* pa. pple of CULTIVATE.]
1 Of a person, his or her mind, etc.: not improved by education or training. M17. ▸**b** Of a nation, an age, etc.: uncultured, uncivilized. E18.
2 Of land: not cultivated; unprepared or unused for cultivation. L17. ▸**b** Of a plant: not produced or improved by cultivation; growing untended or wild. L17.
3 Not attended to or practised; not fostered or developed. L17.

📖 **1** J. CARLYLE He was a coarse, uncultivated man. **3** H. HALLAM A comic writer . . in the same vein of uncultivated genius.

unculture /ʌnˈkʌltʃə/ *noun.* E17.
[from UN-¹ + CULTURE *noun.*]
Lack of culture or cultivation.

uncultured /ʌnˈkʌltʃəd/ *adjective.* M16.
[from UN-¹ + CULTURED.]
1 Of ground, a plant, etc.: not cultivated; not subjected to or produced by cultivation. M16.
2 *fig.* Not developed or improved by education or training; not possessed of culture; unrefined. L18.

📖 **2** F. BURNEY Those who unite native hardness with uncultured minds and manners.

■ **unculturable** *adjective* (*rare*) unable to be cultured or cultivated M19.

uncumber /ʌnˈkʌmbə/ *verb trans.* Now *rare.* LME.
[from UN-² + CUMBER *verb.*]
Free from encumbrance; disencumber.

uncumbered /ʌnˈkʌmbəd/ *adjective.* M16.
[from UN-¹ + *cumbered* pa. pple of CUMBER *verb.*]
Not encumbered.

uncunning /ʌnˈkʌnɪŋ/ *adjective.* ME.
[from UN-¹ + CUNNING *adjective.*]
Not cunning. Now *esp.* not deceitful or crafty, straightforward; unskilful.
■ **uncunningly** *adverb* (now *rare*) ME.

uncurb /ʌnˈkəːb/ *verb trans.* L16.
[from UN-² + CURB *verb*¹.]
Remove a curb or curbs from; free from restraint.

uncurbed /ʌnˈkəːbd/ *adjective.* L16.
[from UN-¹ + *curbed* pa. pple of CURB *verb*¹.]
Not curbed; (of a horse) free from a curb; *fig.* unchecked, unrestrained.

📖 W. H. DIXON Uncurbed by scruple, she gave orders to employ material force.

■ †**uncurbable** *adjective* (*rare*, Shakes.): only in E17.

uncured /ʌnˈkjʊəd/ *adjective.* LME.
[from UN-¹ + *cured* pa. pple of CURE *verb.*]
1 Not healed or restored to health; (of an illness etc.) not remedied. LME.
2 Of meat, fish, etc.: not prepared for keeping by salting, drying, etc. E17.
■ **uncurable** *adjective* (now *rare* or *obsolete*) incurable ME.

uncurl /ʌnˈkəːl/ *verb trans. & intrans.* L16.
[from UN-² + CURL *verb.*]
Unfold or cause to unfold from a curled form or an incurved posture; straighten out; unwind.

📖 THACKERAY A . . servant, . . on the box beside the fat coachman, uncurled his bandy legs.

uncurled /ʌnˈkəːld/ *adjective.* L16.
[from UN-¹ + CURLED.]
1 Of hair: not formed into or growing in curls. L16.
2 Not in a curled or coiled form or posture; uncoiled; unwound. L16.
■ **uncurling** *adjective* E18.

uncurse /ʌnˈkəːs/ *verb trans. rare.* L16.
[from UN-² + CURSE *verb.*]
Release from a curse; remove a curse from.

uncursed /ʌnˈkəːst/ *adjective.* Also †**uncurst**. E17.
[from UN-¹ + CURSED.]
Not cursed; not damned; not deserving of or under a curse.

uncurtain /ʌnˈkəːt(ə)n/ *verb trans.* E17.
[from UN-² + CURTAIN *noun, verb.*]
Remove a curtain or curtains from; disclose, reveal. Chiefly *fig.*

uncurtained /ʌnˈkəːt(ə)nd/ *adjective.* L18.
[from UN-¹ + *curtained* pa. pple of CURTAIN *verb.*]
Not curtained.

uncus /ˈʌŋkəs/ *noun.* Pl. **unci** /ˈʌnsʌɪ/. E19.
[Latin = hook.]
ZOOLOGY & ANATOMY. A hook or hooklike process or structure.

uncustomary /ʌnˈkʌstəm(ə)ri/ *adjective.* M17.
[from UN-¹ + CUSTOMARY *adjective.*]
Not according to custom; not commonly or habitually done; unusual.

📖 *Times Lit. Suppl.* How one's pen fairly glides with uncustomary speed over the paper.

■ **uncustomarily** *adverb* E20.

uncustomed /ʌnˈkʌstəmd/ *adjective.* LME.
[from UN-¹ + *customed* pa. pple of CUSTOM *verb.*]
1 On which no customs duty has been paid. Also, not liable to customs duty. LME.
2 Unaccustomed *to* something. *arch.* E16.
3 Not customary; unusual. *arch.* M16.

📖 **1** E. DYSON Odgson, whose office stock of uncustomed whisky never ran short. **2** J. S. BLACKIE They show like moles uncustomed to the light.

■ **uncustomable** *adjective* (now *rare* or *obsolete*) LME.

uncut /ʌnˈkʌt/ *adjective.* LME.
[from UN-¹ + CUT *ppl adjective.*]
1 Not cut; not having received a cut or cuts; that has not been subjected to cutting; not cut down or off; not mown or trimmed. LME.
2 Of a stone, esp. a diamond: not shaped by cutting. Also, (of a pile fabric) having the pile-loops intact. L16.
3 Of a book: not having the leaves cut open; with untrimmed margins. E19.
4 Of a book, film, etc.: not curtailed or shortened; complete; without excisions. Also, uncensored. L19.
5 Of alcohol, a drug, etc.: undiluted, unadulterated. M20.

📖 **1** *New Age Journal* The city said it would allow uncut grass as part of 'nature preserves'. L. GRANT-ADAMSON His hair was uncut and straggled . . around a grimy face. **2** W. J. BURLEY The uncut-moquette armchairs. **4** *Guardian* 'Ulysses' is due to be shown uncut at the Academy Cinema. **5** H. WAUGH Gorman took another sip of uncut bourbon.

■ **uncuttable** *adjective* M20.

unda maris /ʌndə ˈmɑːrɪs/ *noun phr.* E19.
[Latin, lit. 'wave of the sea'.]
MUSIC. A type of organ-stop, usually consisting of two ranks of pipes, one of which is tuned slightly sharp or flat, together producing a slowly undulating tone.

undamned /ʌnˈdamd/ *adjective.* LME.
[from UN-¹ + DAMNED *adjective.*]
Not damned.

undamped /ʌnˈdam(p)t/ *adjective.* M18.
[from UN-¹ + *damped* pa. pple of DAMP *verb.*]
1 Of a person, hopes, etc.: not discouraged or checked; undepressed. M18.
2 Of a vibration, oscillation, wave, etc.: not damped. L19.

undangerous /ʌnˈdeɪn(d)ʒ(ə)rəs/ *adjective.* E18.
[from UN-¹ + DANGEROUS.]
Not dangerous.
■ **undangered** *adjective* (*rare*) not endangered LME. **undangerousness** *noun* E19.

undashed /ʌnˈdaʃt/ *adjective.* E17.
[from UN-¹ + *dashed* pa. pple of DASH *verb*¹.]
1 Undaunted. E17.
2 Not qualified *with* or diluted *by* something. E19.

undated /ˈʌndeɪtɪd/ *adjective*¹. Now *rare* or *obsolete.* L15.
[from medieval Latin *undatus*, from Latin *unda* wave: see -ED¹.]
1 HERALDRY. Wavy. L15.
2 BOTANY & ZOOLOGY. Having wavy markings; waved. L18.

undated /ʌnˈdeɪtɪd/ *adjective*². L16.
[from UN-¹ + *dated* pa. pple of DATE *verb.*]
Not provided or marked with a date.

undation /ʌnˈdeɪʃ(ə)n/ *noun.* M17.
[Late Latin *undatio(n-)*, from Latin *undare* rise in waves, from *unda* wave: see -ATION. In sense 2 from Dutch *undatie (theorie).*]
†**1** *gen.* A waving; an undulation. *rare.* Only in M17.
2 *undation theory*, (GEOLOGY) a theory that selective internal heating of the earth's mantle causes large wavelike folds to appear in the crust. M19.

undaunted /ʌnˈdɔːntɪd/ *adjective.* LME.
[from UN-¹ + *daunted* pa. pple of DAUNT *verb.*]
†**1** (Of a horse) not broken in; *transf.* unbridled, unrestrained. LME–L17.
2 Not daunted; not discouraged or intimidated. LME.

📖 **2** J. BARTH Wallace could no longer be heard, but nevertheless he continued undaunted. *Times Educ. Suppl.* Shocked but undaunted by her first three sorties touring orphanages and schools for the deaf.

■ **undauntable** *adjective* unable to be daunted, dauntless E16. **undauntedly** *adverb* L16. **undauntedness** *noun* L16.

undead /ʌnˈdɛd/ *adjective & noun.* LME.
[from UN-¹ + DEAD *adjective.*]
▸ **A** *adjective.* Not dead; alive. Now *esp.*, (of a supernatural being, esp. a vampire) technically dead but still animate. LME.

📖 *Dragon Magazine* Undead creatures . . appear cold (blue) and can only be seen dimly.

▸ **B** *noun.* An undead being (*rare*); *collect.* those who are undead. L19.
■ **undeadened** *adjective* E19.

undear /ʌnˈdɪə/ *adjective.* OE.
[from UN-¹ + DEAR *adjective*¹.]
†**1** Not high in worth or value. OE–ME.
2 Not regarded with affection. LME.
¶ Not recorded between LME and M18.

undeca- /ʌnˈdɛkə/ *combining form.* Before a vowel **undec-**.
[Latin *undecim* eleven.]
Used with the sense 'having eleven'; *esp.* in names of molecules that contain eleven atoms of carbon or a second element.
■ **undecagon** *noun* (GEOMETRY) a polygon with eleven sides E18. **undecane** *noun* (CHEMISTRY) any of a series of saturated hydrocarbons (alkanes) with the formula $C_{11}H_{24}$; *spec.* (also ***n*-undecane**) the unbranched isomer $CH_3(CH_2)_9CH_3$: L19. **undecaˈpeptide** *noun* (BIOCHEMISTRY) any polypeptide composed of eleven amino-acid residues M20. **undecylenic** /-dɛsɪˈliːɪk/ *adjective*: ***undecylenic acid*** (CHEMISTRY), a yellow water-insoluble carboxylic acid, $CH_2{=}CH(CH_2)_8COOH$, which is used as an antifungal agent and in perfumery L19.

undecayed /ʌndɪˈkeɪd/ *adjective.* E16.
[from UN-¹ + *decayed* pa. pple of DECAY *verb.*]
1 Not reduced in quality or condition. E16.
2 Not fallen into ruin or disrepair; not rotten. M17.
■ **undecayable** *adjective* M16. **undecaying** *adjective* L16.

undeceitful /ʌndɪˈsiːtfʊl, -f(ə)l/ *adjective.* L16.
[from UN-¹ + DECEITFUL.]
Not deceitful.

undeceive /ʌndɪˈsiːv/ *verb trans.* L16.
[from UN-² + DECEIVE.]
Free (a person) from a misconception, deception, or error; disabuse. (Foll. by *of*.)
■ **undeceiver** *noun* M17.

undeceived /ʌndɪˈsiːvd/ *adjective.* LME.
[from UN-¹ + *deceived* pa. pple of DECEIVE.]
Not deceived.
■ **undeceivable** *adjective* †(*a*) incapable of deceiving someone; (*b*) unable to be deceived: M16.

undecent /ʌnˈdiːs(ə)nt/ *adjective.* M16.
[from UN-¹ + DECENT.]
1 = INDECENT 1. *arch.* M16.
2 = INDECENT 3. *obsolete* exc. *dial.* M16.
†**3** = INDECENT 2. Only in 17.
■ **undecency** *noun* (now *rare* or *obsolete*) = INDECENCY 1 L16. †**undecently** *adverb* M16–E18.

undeception /ʌndɪˈsɛpʃ(ə)n/ *noun.* L17.
[from UN-² + DECEPTION.]
The action of undeceiving someone; the fact of being undeceived.
■ **undeceptive** *adjective* M19.

undecidable /ʌndɪˈsʌɪdəb(ə)l/ *adjective & noun.* M17.
[from UN-¹ + DECIDABLE.]
▸ **A** *adjective.* **1** Unable to be decided. M17.
2 MATH. & LOGIC. Of a proposition etc.: unable to be either proved or disproved (within a given formal system). M20.
▸ **B** *noun.* That which is undecidable. M20.
■ **undecidaˈbility** *noun* M20.

undecide /ʌndɪˈsʌɪd/ *verb trans. & intrans. rare.* E17.
[from UN-² + DECIDE.]
Change or reverse a decision on (something).

undecided /ʌndɪˈsʌɪdɪd/ *adjective & noun.* M16.
[from UN-¹ + DECIDED.]
▸ **A** *adjective.* **1** Not (yet) decided; not settled or certain. M16. ▸**b** Of an opinion etc.: not definite. E19. ▸**c** COURSING. Not decided between the competing dogs. M19.
2 Hesitating, irresolute. L18.

📖 **1** J. NICHOLSON This point . . remains in a very undecided state. **2** D. HAMMETT Dorothy . . was in the doorway, undecided whether to come in or run off.

▸ **B** *noun.* **1** COURSING. An undecided course. L19.
2 An undecided person, a person yet to decide on something. M20.
■ **undecidedly** *adverb* M19. **undecidedness** *noun* L19.

undecipher /ʌndɪˈsʌɪfə/ *verb trans.* M17.
[from UN-² + DECIPHER *verb.*]
Decipher.

undecipherable /ʌndɪˈsʌɪf(ə)rəb(ə)l/ *adjective.* M18.
[from UN-¹ + DECIPHERABLE.]
Indecipherable.
▪ **undecipheraˈbility** *noun* L19. **undecipherably** *adverb* M19. **undeciphered** *adjective* M17.

undecisive /ʌndɪˈsʌɪsɪv/ *adjective.* Now *rare.* M17.
[from UN-¹ + DECISIVE.]
1 = INDECISIVE 1. M17.
2 = INDECISIVE 2. L18.
▪ **undecision** *noun* indecision E17. **undecisively** *adverb* L18. **undecisiveness** *noun* L18.

†**undeck** *verb trans.* Only in L16.
[from UN-² + DECK *verb.*]
Remove the adornment from.

undecked /ʌnˈdɛkt/ *adjective.* L16.
[from UN-¹ + *decked* pa. pple of DECK *verb.*]
1 Not adorned. L16.
2 Not provided with a deck or decks. M18.

undee /ˈʌndeɪ/ *adjective.* Also **undé(e)**. E16.
[Old French *undé(e)* (mod. *ondé(e)*), from *unde, onde* wave: see -EE¹. See also UNDY.]
HERALDRY. Having the form of waves; wavy, waved. Cf. WATERY 8.

undefended /ʌndɪˈfɛndɪd/ *adjective.* LME.
[from UN-¹ + *defended* pa. pple of DEFEND.]
†**1** Not forbidden. LME–L16.
2 Unprotected. M16.
3 *LAW.* **a** Not represented by a legal counsel. E17. ▸**b** Against which no defence is presented. L19.
▪ **undefendable** *adjective* (*a*) (of a place) that cannot be defended; (*b*) (of a person) defenceless: M20. **undefending** *adjective* M17. **undefensible** *adjective* indefensible E16.

undefiled /ʌndɪˈfʌɪld/ *adjective.* LME.
[from UN-¹ + *defiled* pa. pple of DEFILE *verb*¹.]
Not defiled; *esp.* pure.
▪ **undefiledly** *adverb* M16. **undefiledness** *noun* L16.

undefined /ʌndɪˈfʌɪnd/ *adjective.* E17.
[from UN-¹ + *defined* pa. pple of DEFINE.]
Not defined; not clearly marked; indefinite.
▪ **undefinable** *adjective* not definable L17. **undefinableness** *noun* E18. **undefinably** *adverb* L18. **undefinedly** /-nɪdli/ *adverb* E19. **undefinedness** *noun* M19.

undegenerate /ʌndɪˈdʒɛn(ə)rət/ *adjective.* M18.
[from UN-¹ + DEGENERATE *adjective.*]
Not degenerate; not debased or degraded; showing no deterioration.
▪ **undegenerated** *adjective* L18. **undegenerating** *adjective* (now *rare*) E17.

undelayed /ʌndɪˈleɪd/ *adjective.* LME.
[from UN-¹ + *delayed* pa. pple of DELAY *verb*¹.]
Not delayed or deferred; immediate.
▪ **undelayable** *adjective* (*rare*) E17. **undelaying** *adjective* L18.

†**undelible** *adjective.* M16–M18.
[from UN-¹ + DELIBLE.]
Indelible.

undelightful /ʌndɪˈlʌɪtfʊl, -f(ə)l/ *adjective.* L16.
[from UN-¹ + DELIGHTFUL.]
Not delightful; unpleasant.
▪ **undelight** *noun* (*poet.*) lack of delight E19. **undelighted** *adjective* M17. **undelightfully** *adverb* M18. **undelighting** *adjective* (*a*) taking no delight (*in*); (*b*) giving no delight: L16.

undelivered /ʌndɪˈlɪvəd/ *adjective.* L15.
[from UN-¹ + *delivered* pa. pple of DELIVER *verb.*]
1 Not handed over to another's possession or keeping; *esp.* (of mail) not distributed. L15.
2 Not set free or released. E16.
3 Of a child: not yet born. L16.
4 Of a woman: not yet having given birth. L18.
▪ **undeliverable** *adjective* M19.

undemanding /ʌndɪˈmɑːndɪŋ/ *adjective.* M20.
[from UN-¹ + DEMANDING.]
Not demanding; easy to satisfy; not exacting or difficult.
▪ **undemanded** *adjective* E16. **undemandingness** *noun* M20.

undemocratic /ˌʌndɛməˈkratɪk/ *adjective.* M19.
[from UN-¹ + DEMOCRATIC *adjective.*]
Not democratic.
▪ **undemocratically** *adverb* M19.

undemonstrated /ʌnˈdɛmənstreɪtɪd/ *adjective.* M17.
[from UN-¹ + *demonstrated* pa. pple of DEMONSTRATE *verb.*]
Not demonstrated.
▪ **undeˈmonstrable** *adjective* L16.

undemonstrative /ʌndɪˈmɒnstrətɪv/ *adjective.* M19.
[from UN-¹ + DEMONSTRATIVE *adjective.*]
Not given to or characterized by open expression of feelings etc.; reserved.

> A. LAMBERT Touched by this evidence of emotion and concern from her undemonstrative child.

▪ **undemonstratively** *adverb* M19. **undemonstrativeness** *noun* M19.

undeniable /ʌndɪˈnʌɪəb(ə)l/ *adjective.* M16.
[from UN-¹ + DENIABLE.]
1 Unable to be refuted; indisputable, certain. M16. ▸**b** Of a witness: irrefragable. E17.
2 Unable to be refused. Now *rare.* M16.
3 Not open to objection; excellent. L18.

> **1** P. LOMAS Although speech is of undeniable importance, it constitutes only one aspect of our dealings with people. **2** S. MIDDLETON 'Can I come round to see you, Alice?' The appeal in the voice was undeniable. **3** H. MITCHELL His public character is undeniable.

▪ **undeniableness** *noun* M17. **undeniably** *adverb* M17. **undenied** *adjective* E17.

undenominated /ʌndɪˈnɒmɪneɪtɪd/ *adjective.* L19.
[from UN-¹ + *denominated* pa. pple of DENOMINATE.]
1 Lacking a name or designation. L19.
2 Of a postage stamp: having no value specified on it. L20.

undenominational /ˌʌndɪnɒmɪˈneɪʃ(ə)n(ə)l/ *adjective.* L19.
[from UN-¹ + DENOMINATIONAL.]
Not denominational; *esp.* (of education, a school, etc.) non-sectarian.
▪ **undenominationalism** *noun* L19. **undenominationalist** *noun* L19. **undenominationally** *adverb* E20.

undependable /ʌndɪˈpɛndəb(ə)l/ *adjective.* M19.
[from UN-¹ + DEPENDABLE.]
Not to be depended on; unreliable.
▪ **undependaˈbility** *noun* M20. **undepending** *adjective* (long *rare*) (*a*) not depending *on* something; (*b*) not dependent; independent: M17.

under /ˈʌndə/ *noun. rare.* E17.
[In sense 1 from UNDER *adverb*; in sense 2 abbreviation.]
1 A low or inferior state. Only in ***be at a great under***. *obsolete* exc. *dial.* E17.
2 In *pl.* Underclothes. *colloq.* M18.

under /ˈʌndə/ *adjective.* ME.
[from UNDER-, detached from compounds on the analogy of OVER *adjective.*]
1 Having a lower place or position; lying underneath or at a lower level. ME.
2 a Lying underneath so as to be covered. M16. ▸**b** Of a surface: facing downwards. M18. ▸**c** Of sound: low, subdued. E19.
3 Inferior, subordinate. L16.
4 Below the proper standard, amount, etc. L17.

> **1** A. URE The upper stopcock is closed, and the under is opened. **2a** AV *2 Esd.* 12:19 Eight small vnder feathers sticking to her wings. **3** R. C. LEHMANN The . . servants . . going in batches to the pantomime—at least, the under ones. **4** H. BRACKEN 'Tis best to begin rather with an under than over Dose.

¶ Usu. *attrib.*; in all senses exc. 1, now usu. joined to the following noun (cf. UNDER-).

under /ˈʌndə/ *adverb.*
[Old English *under*: see next.]
1 Below, down below, beneath. OE. ▸**b** Lower down on a page etc. Usu. in *comb.* LME. ▸**c** Of the sun etc.: below the horizon; set. L15. ▸**d** Under water; submerged. M19.
2 In or into a position or state of subjection. ME.
3 Less in number or amount; lower in price. Long *rare* or *obsolete.* L16.
4 In or into a state of unconsciousness. Also, under the influence of alcohol. *colloq.* M20.

> **1** SHELLEY I wield the flail of the lashing hail, And whiten the green plains under. A. B. SOYER Saw the rib bones asunder . . ; pass your knife under. **2** EVELYN The King keeps them under by an army of 40,000 men.

Phrases: ***down under***: see DOWN *adverb.* ***get out from under*** *colloq.* escape from a dangerous or awkward situation. ***six feet under***: see SIX *adjective.* ***under-and-over*** *adjective & noun* = ***over-and-under*** s.v. OVER *adverb.*

under /ˈʌndə/ *preposition.*
[Old English *under* = Old Frisian *under*, Old Saxon *undar* (Dutch *onder*), Old High German *untar* (German *unter*), Old Norse *undir*, Gothic *undar* from Germanic base from Indo-European compar. formation (cf. Sanskrit *adhara* (adjective) lower, *adhas* below).]
▸**I 1** In or to a position lower than; so as to have (the sun etc.) overhead; (immediately) beneath or below; so as to be covered or sheltered by; *transf.* in the service or support of that symbolized by (a flag etc.). OE. ▸**b** Below the surface of (the earth or water); in or through (a liquid). OE. ▸**c** While being ridden by. OE.
2 Covered by, enveloped in; within, on the inside of. OE.
3 At the foot of, by the side of, close to. Freq. with implication of shelter. OE.
4 Powered by (sail, steam, etc.). OE.
5 Planted with (a crop); stocked with (a type of livestock). M16.
6 During the period of ascendancy of (a star, zodiacal sign, etc.). L16.

> **1** D. ABSE The apple tree under which I made a grave for the frog. M. FRAYN He . . pulled the suitcases out from under the bed. A. CARTER A . . napkin was tucked under his chin. W. J. TURNER Under a grey October sky. I. MURDOCH Under the canopy of the leaves the air was hot. A. PRICE He felt the smooth, thick paper under his fingers. V. S. PRITCHETT The sea had tunnelled under the rock. **b** M. KEANE Being held under the bath water till she drowned. **c** STEELE Lord Galway had his Horse shot under him. **2** T. HARDY A buff petticoat worn under a puce gown. G. GREENE The rain ran down under my macintosh collar. S. TOWNSEND I would lie in bed under the blankets. **3** E. BOWEN Two avenues . . meet . . under the front steps. DYLAN THOMAS We . . Who live our lives under Milk Wood. A. PRICE This marvellous . . old house under the downs. **4** A. GARVE I went through the Sound under engine . . left the boat at Oban. **5** *Geographical Magazine* The upland . . remains under forest and pasture.

▸**II 7** In an inferior or subordinate position or capacity to; below in rank or standing. OE.
8 Subject to the authority, control, direction, or guidance of; *spec.* (*a*) led or commanded by; (*b*) being treated by (a doctor); (*c*) *MUSIC* conducted by. OE. ▸**b** During the reign or administration of; during (a reign, government, etc.). Cf. sense 20 below. OE. ▸**c** Beneath the rule or domination of; subject to. Long *rare* or *obsolete.* OE.
9 Subject to (authority, control, direction, etc.); liable to the risk of incurring. OE. ▸**b** Undergoing, in the process of. M16. ▸**c** *MATH.* On performance of or with respect to (an operation). E20.
10 Controlled, restrained, or bound by. OE.
11 Afflicted, oppressed, or affected by; while suffering from or affected by. ME.

> **7** ADDISON It was too great an Honour for any Man under a Duke. C. LAMB Deputy, under Evans, was Thomas Tame. R. S. SURTEES A maid of all work, and a girl under her. **8** K. H. DIGBY He studied under Albert at Cologne. LD MACAULAY He . . had fought bravely under Monmouth. **b** F. TUOHY Businessmen who had made their fortunes under the last dictatorship. *Guardian* Its view of England under Thatcher. **9** *Times* A proclamation ordering the tribes to join him under pain of death. T. HARDY Joiners . . under her directions enclosed the recess with a . . door. G. GREENE I am under orders . . . I am doing my duty. I. MURDOCH Statements whose falsity would have been clear under the lightest scrutiny. *Which?* A service call . . should be free if your oven is still under guarantee. **b** R. BANKS A huge pool-and-pavilion complex under construction. *Times Lit. Suppl.* Fogelin's book is the . . sharpest of those under review. *Which?* An EC directive, currently under discussion. **c** *Encycl. Brit.* Some properties are not preserved under projection. **10** *Guardian* The suspect was . . under heavy guard. **11** A. WHITE Your own personality . . breaks down under the strain of doing the work of two. *Practical Health* A small operation, usually done under general anaesthetic.

▸**III 12 a** In the form of, as. *arch.* OE. ▸**b** In the guise of. ME. ▸**c** Called or known by, having, with, (a specified name or title); with authorship indicated by (a specified name). M17.
13 Included or classified in (a group, category, etc.); in the section or article of a book etc. with (a specified heading). OE. ▸**b** *GEOMETRY.* Of a size or extent determined by (a line or angle). Now *rare.* L16.
14 Protected by, in the safety of. OE.
15 In a state or condition of; having regard to, taking account of, (circumstances, conditions). ME.
16 a Authorized or attested by. *arch.* ME. ▸**b** In accordance with. L18.

> **12a** GOLDSMITH Some insects continue under the form of an aurelia not above ten days. **b** E. B. PUSEY The Body and Blood of Christ, under the Bread and Wine. **c** A. WHITE The article . . was published . . under the title of 'Smoking Flax'. *Atlantic* The entry under 'Indians, American', is about twenty pages long. **14** L. URIS It crossed into Austria under the personal protection of a sympathetic . . commander. **15** A. BAIN The physical state of a muscle under contraction. M. KEANE That would have been the height of absurdity, under the circumstances. G. GREENE A nation in mourning rather than . . under arms. **16b** *Times* Bankers . . risk jail sentences . . under a new offence of laundering.

▸**IV 17** Unworthy of, beneath. Long *rare* or *obsolete.* OE.
18 Less than (a specified number or amount); at or for a lower cost than. Also placed after a statement of size, price, etc., in ***and under, or under***. LME. ▸**b** In less time than (that specified). M17.
19 Below (a certain standard). E17.

> **18** R. MACAULAY The speakers were all girls under thirty. G. GREENE Pete's mother was a little under five feet tall.

▸**V** †**20** During (a period of time or an activity). Also with demonstr. pronoun Cf. sense 8b above. OE–M17.
Phrases: (A selection of cross-refs. only is included: see esp. other nouns.) ***under age***: see AGE *noun* 2. ***under a mistake***: see MISTAKE *noun.* ***under a person's nose, under a person's very nose***: see NOSE *noun.* ***under bare poles***: see POLE *noun*¹ 1c. ***under correction***: see CORRECTION 1. ***under cover to***: see COVER *noun*¹. ***under hand***: see HAND *noun.* ***under lock and key***: see LOCK *noun*². ***under night*** *Scot.* during the night, by night. ***under*** OBSERVATION. ***under one*** (*obsolete* exc. *dial.*) together, at one time. ***under one roof***: see ROOF *noun.* ***under one's arm***: see ARM *noun*¹. ***under one's belt***: see BELT *noun.* ***under one's*** BREATH. ***under one's hand***: see HAND *noun.* ***under protest***: see PROTEST *noun* 3b. ***under sentence of***: see

SENTENCE noun 2. ***under separate cover***: see COVER noun[1]. ***under the heel of***: see HEEL noun[1]. ***under the plough***: see PLOUGH noun 3. ***under the rose***: see ROSE noun. ***under the same roof***: see ROOF noun. ***under the sun***: see SUN noun[1]. ***under the table***: see TABLE noun. ***under the weather***: see WEATHER noun. ***under way***: see WAY noun.

under- /ˈʌndə/ *combining form.*

[Repr. UNDER adverb, preposition. In early use translating Latin SUB-.]

Prefixed to verbs, nouns, adjectives, & adverbs in various relations and with various senses, esp. indicating (*a*) position or motion below or beneath; (*b*) inferiority, subjection, subordination; (*c*) lesser amount or degree; (*d*) insufficiency, inadequacy, incompleteness.

■ **underˈact** *verb trans. & intrans.* act (a part) inadequately or with excessive restraint E17. **under-action** *noun* (*rare*) (*a*) subordinate or subsidiary action in a dramatic plot; (*b*) insufficient action: L17. **underˈactive** *adjective* showing or marked by underactivity M20. **underacˈtivity** *noun* diminished or insufficient activity M20. **under-actor** *noun* a subordinate actor or protagonist E18. **under-agent** *noun* a deputy or subordinate agent L17. **underˈarch** *verb trans.* (*rare*) support (as) with an arch E17. **underbark** *adjective* (of a measurement) taken after the bark has been removed from a log E20. **underˈbear** *verb trans.* (now *rare*) (*a*) suffer, endure; (*b*) support; †(*c*) (*rare*, Shakes.) in *pass.*, be trimmmed or edged round the lower part: OE. **underˈbearer** *noun* (now *dial.* & *US*) a pallbearer E18. **underbearing** *adjective* (*rare*) unassuming E19. **underbed** *noun & adjective* (*a*) *noun* (now *rare*) a bed under another bed; (*b*) *adjective* (of a drawer etc.) situated under a bed: M17. **underbevelling** *noun* bevelling on the inside of a timber frame M18. **underˈbill** *verb trans.* (*US*) bill or enter (goods) at less than the actual amount or value L19. **underbit** *noun* (*US*) an earmark made on the lower part of an animal's ear M19. **underbite** *noun* [after OVERBITE] (in non-technical use) the projection of the lower jaw or the lower incisors beyond the upper L20. **underˈbitted** *adjective* (*north.*) (of an animal) earmarked on the lower part of the ear M16. **underblanket** *noun* a blanket (now esp. an electric blanket) laid under the bottom sheet, as opp. to one used as a covering E19. **underboard** *adverb* (*long arch.*) †(*a*) under the table; (*b*) secretly; not openly or honestly: M16. **underbodice** *noun* a bodice worn under another L19. **underbonnet** *adjective & adverb* (situated or occurring) under the bonnet of a motor vehicle M20. **underboss** *noun* a boss's deputy, esp. in the Mafia or another criminal organization M20. **underbough** *noun* a lower branch of a tree E16. **underbreath** *noun & adjective* (*a*) *noun* a whisper; (*b*) *adjective* whispered: M19. **underbridge** *noun* a bridge spanning an opening beneath a road or railway E19. **underbrim** *noun* (a trimming or lining attached to) the underside of the brim of a hat E20. **underˈbuild** *verb trans.* build under so as to strengthen or support, underpin E17. **under-builder** *noun* an assistant or subordinate builder M17. **underˈburn** *verb trans.* burn insufficiently M19. **underbush** *noun* undergrowth M19. **under-butler** *noun* an assistant butler E17. **undercap** *noun* (long *obsolete* exc. *Scot.*) a cap worn under another M16. **undercard** *noun* (BOXING) a contest placed second on the billing M20. **undercart** *noun* (*colloq.*) = UNDERCARRIAGE 2 M20. **underˈcarve** *verb trans.* cut away from below or behind E20. **underˈcharacterize** *verb trans.* depict or play with insufficient characterization or subtlety M20. **underchosen** *adjective* designating members of a sociometric group who are chosen less than the average number of times M20. **underˈclad** *adjective* (*arch.*) insufficiently clothed E17. **underclass** *noun* a subordinate social class; *spec.* a class of people excluded by poverty and unemployment from any opportunity offered by society: E20. **underclassman** *noun* (*US*) a sophomore, a freshman L19. **underclay** *noun* a bed of clay under a stratum, now *spec.* under a coal seam M17. **under-clerk** *noun* an assistant or subordinate clerk LME. **undercliff** *noun* a terrace or lower cliff formed by a landslip E19. **undercling** *noun & verb* (MOUNTAINEERING) (*a*) *noun* a handhold which faces down the rock face; (*b*) *verb intrans.* climb using such handholds: L20. **undercloak** *noun* (BUILDING) the lower of two layers of material used to form a watertight covering L19. **underˈclub** *verb refl. & intrans.* (GOLF) select for (oneself) a club which will not, in the normal course of events, strike the ball the required distance E20. **undercolour** *noun & verb* (*a*) *noun* a colour under another; (*b*) *verb trans.* colour lightly or less strongly (*lit.* & *fig.*) (chiefly as ***undercoloured*** *ppl adjective*): E17. **underconˈsumption** *noun* consumption exceeded by production or supply L19. **underconˈsumptionist** *noun & adjective* (*a*) *noun* an advocate of an economic theory of underconsumption; (*b*) *adjective* of or pertaining to underconsumption or underconsumptionists: M20. **underˈcook** *verb trans.* cook too little or for too short a time M19. **under-cook** *noun* a subordinate cook L16. **underˈcool** *verb* (*a*) *verb trans. & intrans.* supercool (freq. as ***undercooled*** *ppl adjective*, ***undercooling*** *verbal noun*); (*b*) *verb trans.* cool insufficiently: L19. **undercount** *noun* an incomplete enumeration; *spec.* the amount by which the number enumerated in a census falls short of the actual number in the group: M20. **underˈcount** *verb trans.* make an undercount of (chiefly as ***undercounting*** *verbal noun*) M20. **undercovering** *noun* a covering under another, an undercoat L15. **undercovert** *noun* (*a*) a covert of undergrowth; (*b*) any of the small close feathers on the underside of a bird's wing or tail: E19. †**undercraft** *noun* (*a*) hidden or secret craft or cunning; (*b*) a sly underhand trick: LME–M18. **underˈcreep** *verb* (*obsolete* exc. *dial.*) (*a*) *verb intrans.* creep in; (*b*) *verb trans.* creep under (a thing); *fig.* subvert secretly; outdo by cunning: LME. †**undercrest** *verb trans.* support as on a crest: only in E17. **undercrust** *noun* a crust or layer beneath another E18. **undercup** *noun* the lower section or underside of a brassière cup M20. **underˈdamp** *verb trans.* damp (a physical system) incompletely, so as to allow only a few oscillations after a single disturbance: M20. **underdamper** *noun* a damper placed below a hammer in an upright piano L19. **underdeck** *noun* the lower deck of a ship E19. **under-devil** *noun* (*rare*) a subordinate devil M17. **underdifferentiˈation** *noun* (LINGUISTICS) incomplete differentiation of phonemic elements, esp. in loanwords from a language in which certain phonemic distinctions do not correspond to those in the receiving language M20. **underdip** *adjective* (MINING) lying below the level of the bottom of the engine-pit M19. **underdiˈspersed** *adjective* (ECOLOGY) exhibiting underdispersion M20. **underdiˈspersion** *noun* (ECOLOGY) a greater evenness in the distribution of individuals than would be expected on purely statistical grounds M20. **underˈdoctored** *adjective* insufficiently supplied with doctors; short of doctors M20. **underˈdot** *verb trans.* mark with a dot or dots beneath (chiefly as ***underdotted*** *ppl adjective*) L19. **underdrain** *noun* an underground drain E19. **underˈdrain** *verb trans.* drain by means of underground trenches (freq. as ***underdraining*** *verbal noun*) E19. **underdrainage** *noun* underground drainage E19. **underdrift** *noun* an undercurrent (*lit.* & *fig.*) M19. **underdrive** *noun* a speed-reducing gear in a motor vehicle which may be used in addition to the ordinary gears to provide an additional set of gear ratios E20. **underearth** *noun* (*a*) the earth or soil lying under the surface soil; MINING the layer of clay etc. under a coal-seam; (*b*) the regions below the earth: E17. **underearth** *adjective* (*arch.*) subterranean, underground L16. **underedge** *noun* the lower edge of something, *spec.* the inside- or bottom edge of a cricket bat L17. **underˈeducate** *verb trans.* educate to an insufficient degree or for an insufficient length of time (chiefly as ***undereducated*** *ppl adjective*) M19. **under-eduˈcation** *noun* education to an insufficient degree or for an insufficient length of time L20. **underˈemphasis** *noun* an insufficient degree of emphasis E20. **underˈemphasize** *verb trans.* emphasize insufficiently M20. **underemˈploy** *verb trans.* provide insufficient employment for (chiefly as ***underemployed*** *ppl adjective*) E20. **underface** *noun* (*poet.*) the lower part of the face M19. **under-falconer** *noun* (chiefly *Hist.*) a subordinate falconer M17. **underfall** *noun* a foothill M19. **under-farmer** *noun* a subordinate farmer, a tenant farmer E17. **underfeature** *noun* a minor feature in a landscape; a slight elevation: L19. **underfelt** *noun* felt for an underlay, esp. beneath a carpet L19. †**underfiend** *noun* a fiend from the regions beneath the earth: only in E17. **under-flame** *noun* (*arch.*, *rare*) a lesser or lower flame M17. **underfloor** *adjective* occurring or situated below floor level, operating below the surface of the floor, (freq. in ***underfloor heating***) L19. **underˈfloor** *verb trans.* provide with a floor, form a floor to L18. **underframe** *noun* (*a*) the substructure of a railway carriage or motor vehicle; (*b*) the framework supporting a chair seat or tabletop: M19. **underframing** *noun* an underframe M19. **underfug** *noun* (*School slang*) an undervest; underpants: E20. **underfunction** *noun & verb* (MEDICINE) (*a*) *noun* = HYPOFUNCTION *noun*; (*b*) *verb intrans.* exhibit underfunction; have a diminished capacity for acting and responding: M20. **underˈfund** *verb trans.* provide insufficient funding for (chiefly as ***underfunded*** *ppl adjective*) L20. **underˈfunding** *noun* insufficient funding M20. **underfur** *noun* an inner layer of shorter fur or down underlying an animal's outer fur L19. **under-gardener** *noun* a subordinate gardener L17. **undergarment** *noun* a garment worn under others, an article of underclothing M16. **undergear** *noun* (*a*) *rare* underclothing; (*b*) the chassis of a caravan: L19. **underˈgird** *verb trans.* †(*a*) gather up (a garment) from below with a belt etc.; (*b*) make secure underneath, *fig.* strengthen, support, (orig. with allus. to *Acts* 27:17): LME **under-god** *noun* a subordinate or minor god L16. **undergrass** *noun* (*rare*) a grass beneath a tree etc.; grass forming an underlayer: M19. **undergrip** *noun* (*a*) GYMNASTICS a hold in which the hands pass beneath the horizontal bar, with the palms facing the gymnast; (*b*) MOUNTAINEERING = UNDERHOLD (b): E20. **under-grove** *noun* (*literary*) a lower or lesser grove M18. **undergrowl** *noun* a low growl, a growl in an undertone M19. **underhair** *noun* (*a*) the shorter hair in a tress or lock of hair; (*b*) ZOOLOGY = UNDERFUR: M20. **underhammer** *noun* a mechanism in a piano regulating the adjustment of a hopper M19. **under-hangman** *noun* (*rare*) a subordinate or lesser hangman E17. **under-head** *noun* (*a*) a subordinate or lesser official; †(*b*) a person of inferior intelligence: L16. **underheaven** *noun* (*poet.*, *rare*) the region below the heavens, the earth L16. **underˈhew** *verb trans.* (*rare*) †(*a*) undercut, undermine; (*b*) *US* fell (timber) so that it contains less than the proper number of cubic feet: E16. **underˈhive** *verb trans.* (long *rare* or *obsolete*) place (bees) in too small a hive M17. **underhold** *noun* (*a*) a hold in wrestling in which the arms are below those of one's opponent; (*b*) a hold in mountaineering in which the hand grasps a downturned edge or point from beneath with the palm upwards, used esp. to maintain balance (also called ***undergrip***): L19. **underˈhole** *verb trans. & intrans.* (*rare*) †(*a*) undermine; (*b*) MINING (*US*) undercut: LME. **underˈhonest** *adjective* (*rare*) less than honest, dishonest E17. **underˈhorsed** *adjective* having a horse or horses inadequate to one's needs or means M19. **under-housemaid** *noun* a subordinate housemaid L18. **underinˈsurance** *noun* insurance of goods, property, etc., at less than the real value L19. **underinˈsure** *verb trans. & intrans.* insure (goods, property, etc.) at less than the real value L19. **underinˈvest** *verb trans. & intrans.* fail to invest (money, resources, etc.) to a sufficient level L20. **underinˈvestment** *noun* the underinvesting of money, resources, etc. M20. **underjaw** *noun* (now *rare*) the lower jaw, the mandible L17. **underjawed** *adjective* having an underhung lower jaw L18. **underkeel** *noun* (*US*, now *rare* or *obsolete*) a notch on the underside of an animal's ear as a mark of ownership L17. †**underkeep** *verb trans.* (*rare*, Spenser) keep under or in subjection: only in L16. **under-keeper** *noun* (*a*) an assistant keeper of a forest, park, etc.; a subordinate or assistant gamekeeper; (*b*) (now *rare*) a subordinate custodian or warder: E16. **under-king** *noun* (*obsolete* exc. *Hist.*) a king subordinate to other rulers having the title of king OE. **under-kingdom** *noun* (*obsolete* exc. *Hist.*) The realm of an under-king; a subordinate kingdom: L16. **under-labourer** *noun* a subordinate or assistant labourer M17. **underland** *noun* (chiefly *literary*) a land lying under or below another L19. **underlap** *noun* (*a*) *rare* the fact or state of underlapping something; (*b*) WARP KNITTING the lateral movements of the guide bar made on the side of the needle remote from the hook; (*c*) a thing which underlaps another; *esp.* a piece of material extending beneath another fold or pleat: L19. **underˈlap** *verb trans.* lie or be situated so as to extend beneath and be covered by part of (a thing) M19. **underlead** *noun* (BRIDGE) the lead of a low card in a suit of which a higher card is held by the player M20. **underˈlead** *verb trans.* (BRIDGE) lead with a card of lower value than (another card of the suit held) M20. **underleaf** *noun* (*a*) a variety of cider apple; (*b*) the underside of a leaf; a lower leaf: E18. **underlease** *noun* a sublease E18. **underˈlease** *verb trans.* sublease (property) E19. **underleather** *noun* a piece of leather forming the lower part of something; *esp.* the leather sole of a shoe: ME. **underlessee** *noun* a person holding property under a sublease M18. **underˈlet** *verb trans.* (*a*) let at less than the true value; (*b*) sublet: L17. **underlever** *noun & adjective* (operated by) a lever behind the trigger-guard on a rifle L19. **underlid** *noun* a lower lid; *spec.* the lower eyelid E17. **underlife** *noun* a life beneath the surface or on a lower level (*lit.* & *fig.*) M19. **underlift** *noun* upward movement from below M19. **underlight** *noun* (*rare*) (*a*) light from below; (*b*) insufficient light: E17. **underˈlimbed** *adjective* (esp. of a horse) having legs too slender in proportion to the body L17. **underlinen** *noun* underclothing, esp. made of linen M19. **underlip** *noun* (*a*) the lower lip; (*b*) MUSIC an indentation in the foot of an organ-pipe: M17. **underload** *noun* an occurrence or state of not being loaded to capacity M20. **underˈloaded** *adjective* not loaded or burdened to capacity; *spec.* in PHYSICAL GEOGRAPHY (of a stream), carrying less than the maximum amount of sediment and eroding down into the bed: L19. **underlook** *noun* a covert look or glance E19. **underˈlook** *verb trans.* (*a*) look at or inspect from beneath, look up at; (*b*) fail to see or observe by looking too low: LME. **under-looker** *noun* a subordinate overseer, esp. in a specified industry L19. **under-lord** *noun* a lord subordinate to other lords or rulers; a person in authority below another: E20. **under-lordship** *noun* (*rare*) the position or authority of an under-lord M20. **underlout** *noun* (long *obsolete* exc. *dial.*) an underling ME. **under-manager** *noun* a manager subordinate to another manager M18. **under-marshal** *noun* a subordinate or deputy marshal L17. **undermass** *noun* (GEOLOGY) an older, deformed body of rock overlain by younger, undeformed strata M20. **underˈmasted** *ppl adjective* (of a ship) provided with too low or too light a mast or masts L16. **under-master** *noun* (*a*) a subordinate instructor; *spec.* in a school, a master subordinate to a headmaster; (*b*) *rare* a subordinate director or supervisor: LME. **undermeaning** *noun* an underlying meaning M19. **underˈmeasure** *verb trans.* (*rare*) measure or calculate insufficiently or below the correct amount L17. **underˈmodulate** *verb trans.* & *intrans.* (ELECTRONICS) subject to, cause, or suffer undermodulation M20. **undermoduˈlation** *noun* (ELECTRONICS) insufficient amplitude modulation that fails to make full use of the available capacity of a transmitter or medium or results in too weak a signal M20. **undernote** *noun* a subdued note; an undertone, a suggestion: E19. **underˈnourished** *adjective* insufficiently nourished, esp. over a sustained period; in a state of semi-starvation: E20. **underˈnourishment** *noun* the state or condition of being undernourished E20. **underoccuˈpation** *noun* the state or condition of underoccupying a house etc. M20. **underˈoccupy** *verb trans.* (*a*) occupy (a house etc.) without using the available accommodation to full capacity; (*b*) provide insufficient occupation for: M20. **under-officer** *noun* a sub-officer LME. **underˈofficered** *adjective* insufficiently staffed or provided with officers M19. **under-ˈofficered** *adjective* staffed by or provided with under-officers M19. **underpaint** *noun* a layer of paint subsequently overlaid by another coat or finish, an underpainting M20. **underpainting** *noun* (the application of) a layer of paint subsequently overlaid by another coat or finish; a painting underlying a finished work: M19. **underpan** *noun* a protective metal covering fitted beneath the engine, clutch, and transmission of a motor vehicle E20. **underpants** *noun pl.* (in attrib. use usu. **underpant**) an undergarment covering the lower part of the body and part of the legs, esp. as worn by men and boys; short knickers, briefs: M20. **underpart** *noun* (*a*) a lower part or portion; *spec.* a part of the underside of an animal's body (usu. in *pl.*); (*b*) a minor or secondary role or part, esp. in a play; a person playing such a part; (*c*) a subdivision: M17. **underˈparted** *adjective* (*rare*) (of an actor) having too easy a part to play L19. **underˈpeep** *verb* (*rare*) (*a*) *verb trans.* peep under (a thing); (*b*) *verb intrans.* peep from under a thing: E17. **underˈpeopled** *adjective* having too few people, underpopulated L17. **underpetticoat** *noun* (chiefly *Hist.*) a petticoat, worn esp. to show beneath a dress E17. **underpitch** *adjective* (ARCHITECTURE) designating a groin or system of groining in which two cylindrical vaults of differing vertical heights intersect L19. **underˈpitched** *adjective* †(*a*) (of a roof) having too low a pitch; not sufficiently steep; (*b*) CRICKET (of a ball) not pitched far enough in bowling, short: L17. **underplate** *verb trans.* (GEOLOGY) underlie; *spec.* form a layer on the underside of (an existing stratum); deposit (rock etc.) as such a layer: L20. **under-plot** *noun* (*a*) a subordinate plot in a play etc., a sub-plot; (*b*) *arch.* an underhand scheme or trick: M17. **underˈpole** *verb trans.* (*rare*) (*a*) provide (hops or a hop-ground) with too short a pole or poles; (*b*) METALLURGY fail to pole (copper) adequately in refining, so that insufficient oxide is removed: E18. **underˈpopulated** *adjective* having an insufficient or very small population L20. **underpopuˈlation** *noun* the state of being underpopulated E20. **underˈpraise** *verb trans.* praise insufficiently L17. **underˈprint** *verb trans.* †(*a*) print or stamp from below or on the underside; (*b*) print (an engraving or photograph) with insufficient depth of tone: L16. **underˈprivilege** *noun* the state of being underprivileged; lack of the normal standard of living or rights in a society: M20. **underˈprivileged** *adjective & noun* (*a*) *adjective* possessing or enjoying too few privileges; *spec.* lacking the normal standard of living or rights in a society; (*b*) *noun* (*collect. pl.*) *the* class of underprivileged people: L19. **underˈprize** *verb trans.* prize too little; undervalue: L16. **underproˈduce** *verb trans. & intrans.* produce less of (a commodity) than is usual or required M20. **underproˈduction** *noun* production of less of a commodity than is usual or required M19. **underproducˈtivity** *noun* inadequate productivity L20. **underproˈportioned** *adjective* not adequately proportioned L17. **underˈqualified** *adjective* insufficiently qualified, esp. for a particular job etc. E17. **underˈquote** *verb trans.* (*a*) quote a lower price than (a person); (*b*) quote a lower price than others for (goods etc.): L19. **underˈread** *verb* (*a*) *verb trans.* read (a measurement etc.) as lower than that actually registered; (*b*) *verb intrans.* (of a gauge, dial, etc.) show a reading lower than the true one; (*c*) *verb trans.* (of the reading public) read (an author, a book, etc.) with less than normal frequency: M20. **underreamer** *noun* a drilling bit on an oil rig used to drill a hole below the casing, of sufficient size for the casing to be lowered further E20. **underˈreckon** *verb trans.* (now *rare*) underestimate E17. **underreˈcord** *verb trans.* (*a*) make too few recordings of (a work or performer) (usu. in *pass.*);

(*b*) record (sound) using too low a signal, so that playback is distorted; (*c*) record (data, information, etc.) insufficiently or inadequately: M20. **underre'hearsal** *noun* insufficient rehearsal of a play, piece of music, etc., for performance E20. **underre'hearsed** *adjective* (of a play, piece of music, performer, etc.) insufficiently rehearsed for performance M20. **underre'port** *verb trans.* fail to report (news, data, etc.) fully (freq. as ***underreported*** *ppl adjective*) M20. **under'represent** *verb trans.* provide with inadequate or insufficient representation (freq. as ***underrepresented*** *ppl adjective*) L19. **underre'source** *verb trans.* provide insufficient resources for (chiefly as ***underresourced*** *ppl adjective*) L20. **under'ride** *verb trans.* (*a*) *rare* form the basis on which (something) occurs; (*b*) GEOLOGY (of a mass of rock, water, etc.) move underneath (another mass): M20. **under'ring** *verb trans. & intrans.* (of a till operator) record too low a price for (a purchase) on a cash register, esp. intentionally so as to keep the excess money; record (a price) incorrectly in this way: L20. **under'ripe** *adjective* (of fruit etc.) insufficiently ripe E18. **under'roast** *verb trans.* roast insufficiently L16. **underrobe** *noun* (*arch.*) a robe worn underneath another garment E18. **underroof** *noun* (now only *poet.*) a tester for a bed; a canopy: E17. †**underrower** *noun* each of the apostles, regarded as being subordinate rowers in the vessel of which Christ is the pilot (usu. in *pl.*) M17–L18. **under'ruff** *verb & noun* (BRIDGE) (*a*) *verb intrans.* undertrump; (*b*) *noun* the action of undertrumping, an instance of this: M20. **under'saturated** *adjective* not saturated, falling short of being saturated; PETROGRAPHY (of a rock or magma) in which there is insufficient free silica or other (specified) oxide to saturate all the bases present; MINERALOGY (of a mineral) unable to form in the presence of free silica: M19. **undersatu'ration** *noun* the property of being undersaturated E20. **under-school** *noun* (*Hist.*) a lower or junior school E17. †**underscriber** *noun* a subscriber to a document L17–L18. **under-servant** *noun* a subordinate servant M16. **under'serve** *verb trans.* †(*a*) be subservient to; (*b*) serve insufficiently; make inadequate provision for: E17. **under-service** *noun* (now *rare* or *obsolete*) service of an inferior kind; service as an under-servant: L16. **undersettle** *noun* (*obsolete* exc. *Hist.*) a person who occupies (part of) a house owned by another; a subtenant: ME. **under'sexed** *adjective* having a lesser degree of sexual desire than the average; lacking in sexual feelings or desire: M20. **under-sexton** *noun* (now *rare*) a subordinate sexton LME. **undersheet** *noun* a sheet (to be) placed beneath another L19. **under-shepherd** *noun* a subordinate shepherd M17. **under-sheriff** *noun* a sheriff's deputy LME. **undershirt** *noun* an undergarment worn beneath a shirt; (chiefly *N. Amer.*) a vest: M17. **under'shore** *verb trans.* prop up with a shore or shores; support or strengthen (*lit. & fig.*): LME. **undershrub** *noun* a small or low-growing shrub; *spec.* in BOTANY, a subshrub: L16. **undersketching** *noun* (ART) preliminary sketching left beneath (and visible through) the finished surface of a painting or drawing M20. **underskin** *noun* (*rare*) an inner skin or layer M17. **under-skinker** *noun* †(*a*) a subordinate skinker or tapster; (*b*) NAUTICAL (now *rare* or *obsolete*) an assistant to the purser's steward: L16. **underskirt** *noun* a skirt worn under another; a petticoat: M19. **undersky** *noun* (chiefly *poet.*) the region of air just beneath the sky; a low layer of cloud: M19. **undersleeve** *noun* a sleeve, esp. one of light material, worn below another M16. **under'slept** *adjective* having had insufficient sleep; suffering from or characterized by lack of sleep: M20. **underslung** *adjective* (*a*) (of a vehicle chassis) hanging lower than the axles; (*b*) *gen.* that is suspended underneath something or supported from above: E20. **undersoil** *noun* subsoil E18. **undersong** *noun* (chiefly *poet.*) (*a*) a subordinate or subdued song or strain, *esp.* one serving as an accompaniment or refrain to another; (*b*) *fig.* an underlying meaning; an undertone: L16. **undersort** *noun* (*obsolete* exc. *dial.*) the common people M17. **undersound** *noun* (*rare*) a sound which is heard beneath another sound M19. **underspin** *noun* a backward spin on a ball causing it to stop quickly or bounce backwards after contact with a surface E20. **under'spread** *verb trans.* (*rare*) spread below or underneath E17. **understair(s)** *noun & adjective* (a space) under a staircase E17. **under-steward** *noun* (now *rare* or *obsolete*) a deputy steward LME. **under'stimulate** *verb trans.* subject to understimulation (chiefly as ***understimulated*** *ppl adjective.*) L20. **understimu'lation** *noun* an insufficiency of either intellectual or sensory stimulation M20. **understock** *noun* = ***rootstock*** (b) s.v. ROOT *noun*[1] M20. **under'stock** *verb trans.* stock (a farm etc.) insufficiently (chiefly as ***understocked*** *ppl adjective*) L17. †**understocking** *noun* a stocking worn underneath another (usu. in *pl.*) E17–M18. **understorey** *noun* (ECOLOGY) the (layer of) vegetation growing beneath the main canopy of a forest M20. **understratum** *noun* an underlying stratum or layer; a substratum: M18. **understream** *noun* a stream flowing beneath another; an undercurrent: M19. **under'strike** *verb trans.* †(*a*) *rare* let down (the sails of a ship); (*b*) strike (from) below: E17. **undersucking** *adjective* (*rare*) (*a*) sucking from below; (*b*) sucking down: E17. **undersurface** *noun* the lower or under surface M18. **underswell** *noun* (chiefly *fig.*) a swell below the surface; an undercurrent: M19. **under'tax** *verb trans.* tax insufficiently (chiefly as ***undertaxed*** *ppl adjective*) E18. **under-teacher** *noun* (now *rare*) a deputy or subordinate teacher L16. **underthrust** *noun* (GEOLOGY) an instance of underthrusting; a fault at which this has taken place: L19. **under'thrust** *verb trans.* (GEOLOGY) (of a mass of rock) be forced underneath (another mass) L19. **undertide** *noun* an underlying tide or flow, an undercurrent, (chiefly *fig.*) M19. **under'tie** *verb trans.* (*rare*) (*a*) tie (something) beneath; tie beneath (something); (*b*) ANGLING tie (the wings of a fly) so as to cover the point of the hook: M16. **under'tip** *verb trans.* give an inadequate or insufficient gratuity to L20. **under-treasurer** *noun* a deputy treasurer; *spec.* (*Hist.*) the officer immediately subordinate to the Lord High Treasurer of England: LME. **under'trial** *noun* in the Indian subcontinent, a person held in custody awaiting trial M20. **undertrick** *noun* (BRIDGE) a trick by which the declarer falls short of his or her contract E20. **under'trump** *verb trans. & intrans.* (CARDS) play a lower trump than (another player) M19. **undertunic** *noun* a tunic worn beneath other clothing E19. **underturf** *adjective* (now *rare* or *obsolete*) (of earth or soil) situated or found below the turf L17. **undervalu'ation** *noun* the action or an act of undervaluing E17. **undervalue** *noun* †(*a*) *rare* insufficiency in worth; (*b*) value or estimate below the worth of a thing: E17. **under'value** *verb trans.* †(*a*) rate as inferior in value *to*; (*b*) underestimate the value or worth of; (*c*) appreciate insufficiently; (*d*) reduce or diminish in value or worth; devalue: L16. **under'valuer** *noun* a person who undervalues something: M17. **under-vassal** *noun* (*obsolete* exc. *Hist.*) a subordinate vassal L16. **undervest** *noun* an undergarment worn on the upper part of the body; a vest: E19. **under-viewer** *noun* (MINING) an under-looker L19. **undervoice** *noun* (*rare*) an undertone; an underlying voice (*lit. & fig.*): E19. **undervoltage** *noun & adjective* (ELECTRICITY) (*a*) *noun* a voltage less than that required to operate a device efficiently; (*b*) *adjective* designating a shunt release which opens or closes a circuit when the voltage drops below a pre-determined value: M20. **undervote** *noun* (*US*) a ballot paper or vote not counted because of unclear marking by the voter L20. **underwaistcoat** *noun* a waistcoat worn beneath a coat or jacket M18. **under-warden** *noun* a deputy or subordinate warden LME. **underwave** *noun* (chiefly *poet.*) an underlying wave M19. **underwear** *noun* underclothes L19. **under'wind** *verb trans.* wind (a thing) insufficiently; BIOCHEMISTRY wind (a helical molecule, esp. DNA) less tightly than normal (freq. as ***underwinding*** *verbal noun*, ***underwound*** *ppl adjective*) L20. **underwire** *noun* (*a*) a wire or other support stitched into the underside of each cup of a brassière to uplift or shape the breast (freq. *attrib.*); the material used for this; (*b*) a brassière with such support: L20. **underwired** *adjective* (of a bra) having an underwire M20. **underwit** *noun* (long *rare*) †(*a*) a poor or inferior kind of wit; (*b*) a stupid or foolish person, an imbecile: M17. **under'witted** *adjective* (long *rare*) stupid, foolish; imbecile: L17. **underwood** *noun* (*a*) small trees, shrubs, etc., growing beneath higher timber trees; (*b*) a quantity, area, or particular kind of this undergrowth: ME. **underwool** *noun* (*a*) *rare* wool used to make underwear; woollen underclothes; (*b*) a layer of wool lying beneath the outer layer on an animal: E20. **under-worker** *noun* an assistant or subordinate worker E18. **under-workman** *noun* (now *rare* or *obsolete*) an assistant or subordinate workman E17.

underabundance /ʌndərəˈbʌnd(ə)ns/ *noun.* L20.
[from UNDER- + ABUNDANCE.]
Too little a quantity; a deficiency.
■ **underabundant** *adjective* L20.

underachiever /ʌndərəˈtʃiːvə/ *noun.* M20.
[from UNDER- + ACHIEVER.]
A person who achieves less than is expected or predicted (e.g. on the basis of intelligence tests).
■ **underachieve** *verb intrans.* achieve less than is expected or predicted M20. **underachievement** *noun* M20.

underage /ʌndərˈeɪdʒ, *attrib.* ˈʌndəreɪdʒ/ *adjective & noun.* L16.
[from UNDER- + AGE *noun.*]
▶ **A** *adjective.* **1** That is under a certain age or limit of age; too young. L16.
2 Of an activity: carried on by a person below the legal age for the activity. L20.

> 🕮 **1** *Daily Express* Guilty of sex with an underage girl. N. HINTON There were more people than jobs and, anyway, he was under-age. **2** *New York Times* Advertising is not causing underage drinking.

▶†**B** *noun.* The time during which a person is underage. E–M17.

underarm /ˈʌndərɑːm/ *adjective, adverb, & noun.* E19.
[from UNDER- + ARM *noun*[1].]
▶ **A** *adjective.* **1** (Of a throw, a delivery in cricket, a serve in tennis, etc.) performed with the hand lower than the level of the shoulders; (of a person) using such an action in throwing, bowling, or serving. E19.
2 Designating a swimming stroke made with the arm below the level of the body. E20.
3 DRESSMAKING. Of a seam: that edges the lower half of the armhole of a garment, or that joins the underside of a sleeve. E20.
4 Of a bag or case: carried under the arm. E20.
5 Of or for the armpit. M20.
▶ **B** *adverb.* With an underarm action. E20.
▶ **C** *noun.* The armpit. M20.

underback /ˈʌndəbak/ *noun.* Also **-beck** /-bɛk/. M17.
[from UNDER- + BACK *noun*[2].]
BREWING. A tub placed below the mash-tub to collect the raw wort discharged from this.

underbelly /ˈʌndəbɛli/ *noun.* E17.
[from UNDER- + BELLY *noun.*]
1 The underside of an animal; *transf.* the underside of a motor vehicle. Cf. UNDERBODY 2, 3b. E17.
2 *fig.* An area vulnerable to attack; an inferior or concealed part of something. M20.

> 🕮 **1** *attrib.*: *Off Road & 4 Wheel Drive* The impressive underbelly clearance of Land Rovers.

underbid /*as verb* ʌndəˈbɪd, *as noun* ˈʌndəbɪd/ *verb & noun.* L16.
[from UNDER- + BID *verb.*]
▶ **A** *verb.* Infl. **-dd-**. Pa. t. & pple **-bid**.
†**1** *verb trans.* Undervalue. L16–M17.
2 *verb intrans.* Make too low an offer. E17.
3 *verb trans.* Make a lower bid than; *spec.* offer goods, services, etc., at a lower price than; undercut. L17.
4 *verb trans. & intrans.* BRIDGE. Bid less on (a hand) than is justified. E20.
▶ **B** *noun.* BRIDGE. An invalid bid of a number of tricks insufficient to surpass the previous bid (*rare*); a bid that is lower than is justified by one's cards. E20.
■ **underbidder** *noun* L19.

underbody /ˈʌndəbɒdi/ *noun.* E17.
[from UNDER- + BODY *noun.*]
1 †**a** The lower part of a woman's dress. *rare.* Only in E17. ▸**b** An undergarment for the upper body. *US dial.* L19.
2 The underside of an animal's body. L19.
3 a The part of a ship's hull which is below the waterline. L19. ▸**b** The underside of a motor vehicle. E20.

underbred /*as adjective* ʌndəˈbrɛd, *as noun* ˈʌndəbrɛd/ *adjective & noun.* M17.
[from UNDER- + BRED *adjective.*]
▶ **A** *adjective.* **1** Ill-bred; vulgar. M17.
2 Of an animal: not pure bred. L19.
▶ **B** *noun.* An underbred animal or person. E19.
■ **underbreeding** *noun* inferior upbringing L17.

underbrush /ˈʌndəbrʌʃ/ *noun & verb.* Orig. & chiefly *N. Amer.* L18.
[from UNDER- + BRUSH *noun*[1].]
▶ **A** *noun.* Shrubs and small trees forming the undergrowth in a forest. L18.
▶ **B** *verb trans. & intrans.* Clear (land) of underbrush. E19.

undercapitalize /ʌndəˈkapɪt(ə)lʌɪz/ *verb trans.* Also **-ise**. M20.
[from UNDER- + CAPITALIZE.]
Provide (a business etc.) with insufficient capital to achieve a desired result; estimate the capital of (a business) at too low an amount. Chiefly as ***undercapitalized*** *ppl adjective.*

undercarriage /ˈʌndəkarɪdʒ/ *noun.* L18.
[from UNDER- + CARRIAGE.]
1 The supporting frame under the body of a vehicle. L18.
2 The wheeled structure beneath an aircraft (usu. retracted when not in use) which receives the impact on landing and supports the aircraft on the ground. E20.

undercast /ˈʌndəkɑːst/ *noun.* L19.
[from UNDER- + CAST *noun*[1].]
MINING. An air passage under a road or the floor of a mine; the lower of two underground air passages which cross each other.

undercast /ʌndəˈkɑːst/ *verb trans.* Pa. t. & pple **-cast**. ME.
[from UNDER- + CAST *verb.*]
†**1** Cast down; subdue. ME–E17.
2 Allot (a part) to an inadequate actor; cast (an actor) in an insufficient role. E19.

undercharge /ˈʌndətʃɑːdʒ/ *noun.* M19.
[from UNDER- + CHARGE *noun.*]
A charge (of money, electricity, etc.) that is too little; an instance of undercharging.

undercharge /ʌndəˈtʃɑːdʒ/ *verb trans.* M17.
[from UNDER- + CHARGE *verb.*]
1 Charge (a person) a price that is too low; charge too low a price for (a thing). M17.
2 Give less than a full or adequate charge to (an electric battery etc.). L18.

> 🕮 **1** A. LIVINGSTONE Lou had increasing financial problems yet . . she often undercharged her patients.

underclothe /ˈʌndəkləʊð/ *verb trans. rare.* M19.
[Back-form. from UNDERCLOTHES.]
Provide with underclothes.

underclothed /ʌndəˈkləʊðd/ *adjective.* L19.
[from UNDER- + *clothed* pa. pple of CLOTHE.]
Insufficiently clothed.

underclothes /ˈʌndəkləʊðz, -kləʊz/ *noun pl.* M19.
[from UNDER- + CLOTHES.]
Clothes worn under others, esp. next to the skin; underwear.
■ **underclothing** /ˈʌndəkləʊðɪŋ/ *noun* underclothes collectively M19.

undercoat /ˈʌndəkəʊt/ *noun & verb.* E17.
[from UNDER- + COAT *noun.*]
▶ **A** *noun.* **1** †**a** A woman's underskirt; a petticoat. E17–M19. ▸**b** A coat worn under another. M17.
2 An animal's underfur. M19.
3 a A preliminary layer or layers of paint under the finishing coat; the paint used for this. L19. ▸**b** = UNDERSEAL *noun.* M20.
▶ **B** *verb trans.* Apply an undercoat of paint to; underseal. Chiefly as ***undercoated*** *ppl adjective*, ***undercoating*** *verbal noun.* E20.

undercorrect /ʌndəkəˈrɛkt/ *verb.* M19.
[from UNDER- + CORRECT *verb.*]
1 *verb trans.* Correct (a lens) insufficiently, so that aberration is still present. M19.
2 *verb trans. & intrans.* Make an insufficient correction to or in (a thing). M20.
■ **undercorrection** *noun* (an) insufficient correction E20.

undercover /ʌndəˈkʌvə, *esp. attrib.* ˈʌndə-/ *adjective & noun.* M19.
[from UNDER- + COVER *noun*¹.]
▶ **A** *adjective.* **1** Situated or occurring under cover; sheltered. M19.
2 *fig.* Operating or conducted in secret within a community or organization, esp. for the purposes of investigation or espionage; surreptitious, covert. E20.

> **1** *News Chronicle* A good fun-fair and some under-cover amusements. **2** N. MAILER When a patrolman, Nielsen did some under-cover work in narcotics. J. AIKEN She was conducting an undercover romance.

▶ **B** *noun.* An undercover agent. *slang.* M20.

undercroft /ˈʌndəkrɒft/ *noun.* LME.
[from UNDER- + CROFT *noun*².]
The crypt of a church; an underground vault or chamber.

undercure /*as verb* ʌndəˈkjʊə, *as noun* ˈʌndəkjʊə/ *verb & noun.* E20.
[from UNDER- + CURE *verb, noun*¹.]
▶ **A** *verb trans.* Cure (plastic or rubber) for less than the optimal period. E20.
▶ **B** *noun.* The process or result of undercuring plastic or rubber; an instance of this. E20.

undercurrent /ˈʌndəkʌr(ə)nt/ *noun & adjective.* L17.
[from UNDER- + CURRENT *noun.*]
▶ **A** *noun.* **1** A current below the surface or at a lower level. L17.
2 *fig.* A suppressed or underlying activity, force, feeling, etc. L18.

> **1** C. LYELL The descending water sinks down and forms an under-current. **2** C. WARWICK Deeper issues . . created an undercurrent of tension.

▶ **B** *attrib.* or as *adjective.* Of or pertaining to an undercurrent; concealed, hidden; suppressed. *rare.* M19.

undercut /*as verb* ʌndəˈkʌt, *as noun* ˈʌndəkʌt/ *verb & noun.* LME.
[from UNDER- + CUT *verb, noun*².]
▶ **A** *verb trans.* Infl. **-tt-**. Pa. t. & pple **-cut**.
†**1** Cut down or off. *rare.* Only in LME.
2 Cut away (material) at a lower level; *spec.* (*a*) cut away the part behind to leave (a carved design etc.) in relief; (*b*) MINING cut away the lower part of (a vein of ore or a face of coal); obtain (coal etc.) in this way. L16. ▸**b** Form by cutting away material at a lower level; *spec.* in MOUNTAINEERING, cut (a handhold) from below, esp. to maintain balance while climbing (freq. as **undercut** *ppl adjective*). M20.
3 In golf, strike (a ball) below the centre, causing it to rise high. In tennis, slice down on (a ball) below the centre, imparting backspin (freq. as **undercut** *ppl adjective*). L19.
4 Work for lower wages or payment than; sell at lower prices than. L19.
5 *fig.* Make unstable or less firm, undermine. M20.

> **2** *Hair Flair* For this dramatic shape the hair was undercut very short through the back and sides. **b** W. UNSWORTH An undercut hold is one that is upside down. **4** *Which?* Superstores which negotiate bulk buys . . can often undercut smaller shops. **5** L. GORDON The wry, derisive note . . undercuts the posturing of Saint Narcissus. R. HAYMAN Undercutting all his gestures towards healthy living by starving himself of sleep.

▶ **B** *noun.* **1** The underside of a sirloin. M19.
2 A cut at a lower level; *spec.* (*a*) a notch in a tree-trunk on the side towards which it is intended to fall; (*b*) a horizontal cut at the base of a tooth cavity, esp. to secure a filling; (*c*) MINING a cut under a vein of ore or a face of coal. L19.
3 A space formed by the removal or absence of material from the lower part of something. E20.
4 A projection on a pattern corresponding to an undercut portion of the mould. E20.
5 SPORT. Underspin; a stroke or shot which imparts this to the ball. E20.
■ **undercutter** *noun* L19.

underdetermine /ʌndədɪˈtəːmɪn/ *verb trans.* M20.
[from UNDER- + DETERMINE.]
Determine or account for with fewer conditions than are necessary; in *pass.*, have fewer determining factors than the minimum necessary.
■ **underdetermiˈnation** *noun* M20.

underdeveloped /ʌndədɪˈvɛləpt/ *adjective.* L19.
[from UNDER- + DEVELOPED.]
1 Not fully developed, immature; *spec.* in PHOTOGRAPHY, not developed sufficiently to give a normal image. L19.
2 Of, pertaining to, or designating a country etc. below its potential economic level. M20.
■ **underdevelopment** *noun* L19.

underdiagnosis /ˌʌndədʌɪəgˈnəʊsɪs/ *noun.* M20.
[from UNDER- + DIAGNOSIS.]
MEDICINE. Failure, on a significant scale, to recognize or correctly diagnose all the cases of a disease examined.
■ **underdiagnose** *verb trans.* L20.

underdo /ʌndəˈduː/ *verb.* Infl. as DO *verb*; pa. t. usu. **-did** /-ˈdɪd/, pa. pple usu. **-done** /-ˈdʌn/. E17.
[from UNDER- + DO *verb.*]
1 *verb intrans.* Do less than is requisite or necessary. Now *rare.* E17.
2 *verb trans.* Do (a thing) inadequately or incompletely; *esp.* cook (food) insufficiently or lightly (chiefly as UNDERDONE *adjective*). E18.

underdog /ˈʌndədɒg/ *noun.* Orig. *US.* L19.
[from UNDER- + DOG *noun.*]
The dog or (now usu.) person in the process of losing or defeated in a fight or contest; a person who is in a state of inferiority or subjection.
■ **underdogger** *noun* a person who supports the underdog in a fight or contest L20. **underˈdoggery** *noun* the state or condition of being an underdog M20.

underdone /ʌndəˈdʌn, *attrib.* ˈʌndə-/ *adjective.* L17.
[pa. pple of UNDERDO.]
Not adequately or completely done; *esp.* (of food) insufficiently or lightly cooked.

underdone *verb pa. pple*: see UNDERDO.

underdose /*as verb* ʌndəˈdəʊs, *as noun* ˈʌndədəʊs/ *verb & noun.* M18.
[from UNDER- + DOSE *verb, noun.*]
▶ **A** *verb trans.* Give (medicine etc.) in too small a dose; give too small a dose to. M18.
▶ **B** *noun.* A dose of medicine etc. that is too small. E19.

underdraw /ʌndəˈdrɔː/ *verb trans.* Pa. t. **-drew** /-ˈdruː/; pa. pple **-drawn** /-ˈdrɔːn/. L18.
[from UNDER- + DRAW *verb.*]
1 Mark (text etc.) with a line drawn underneath. L18.
2 Apply an inner layer to (a roof, floor, etc.), esp. for insulation. L18.
3 Represent or depict inadequately. M19.
4 Draw money from (one's bank account) so as to leave a reserve. L19.

underdrawing /ˈʌndədrɔːɪŋ/ *noun.* M20.
[from UNDER- + DRAWING *noun.*]
A preliminary sketch, subsequently covered by layers of paint.

underdrawn *verb pa. pple* of UNDERDRAW.

underdress /ˈʌndədrɛs/ *noun.* L18.
[from UNDER- + DRESS *noun.*]
1 Underclothes; a set of underclothing. *arch.* L18.
2 Chiefly *Hist.* A dress that can be worn under another dress; part of a dress made to look like an underdress. E19.

underdress /ʌndəˈdrɛs/ *verb trans. & intrans.* E20.
[from UNDER- + DRESS *verb.*]
Dress with too little display or formality; dress too lightly.

> L. DEIGHTON Lots of women in long dresses. I felt underdressed.

underdrew *verb pa. t.* of UNDERDRAW.

underemployment /ʌndərɪmˈplɔɪm(ə)nt/ *noun.* E20.
[from UNDER- + EMPLOYMENT.]
A situation in which the number of people unemployed exceeds the number of vacancies for jobs, producing a labour surplus.

underestimate /*as verb* ʌndərˈɛstɪmeɪt, *as noun* ʌndərˈɛstɪmət/ *verb & noun.* E19.
[from UNDER- + ESTIMATE *verb, noun.*]
▶ **A** *verb trans.* Attribute too low an estimated value to; have too low an opinion of, undervalue. E19.

> P. ACKROYD It would be wrong to underestimate the bonds between Eliot and Vivien.

▶ **B** *noun.* An estimate that is too low. E19.

> J. K. JEROME It would take quite ten minutes, we thought. That was an under-estimate.

underexpose /ʌndərɪkˈspəʊz, -rɛk-/ *verb trans. & intrans.* M19.
[from UNDER- + EXPOSE.]
Expose too little; *spec.* (*a*) PHOTOGRAPHY use too short an exposure or too narrow an aperture with (a film or plate) or when taking (a photograph), resulting in a darkened picture; (*b*) expose too little to the public eye.
■ **underexposure** *noun* L19

underfeed /ʌndəˈfiːd/ *verb trans.* Pa. t. & pple **-fed** /-ˈfɛd/. M17.
[from UNDER- + FEED *verb*¹.]
Feed or nourish insufficiently.

underfeet *adverb* see UNDERFOOT.

underfill /*as noun* ˈʌndəfɪl, *as verb* ʌndəˈfɪl/ *noun & verb.* E20.
[from UNDER- + FILL *verb*, after *overfill*.]
▶ **A** *noun.* METALLURGY. An insufficiency of metal to fill the aperture between rolls, the impression of a die, etc., so that the desired shape is not taken; a bar etc. that is too small for the rolling it is to undergo. E20.
▶ **B** *verb trans.* Fill incompletely or inadequately. M20.

underfilling /ʌndəˈfɪlɪŋ/ *noun.* E17.
[In sense 1 from UNDER- + FILLING *noun*; in sense 2 from prec. + -ING¹.]
†**1** ARCHITECTURE. The substructure of a building. Only in E17.
2 METALLURGY. The action or result of causing an underfill. M20.

underfit /ˈʌndəfɪt/ *adjective.* E20.
[from UNDER- + FIT *noun*³, after *misfit*.]
PHYSICAL GEOGRAPHY. Designating or pertaining to a stream which, on the basis of its present-day flow, would have eroded a smaller valley than it has done. Cf. MISFIT *adjective* 2, OVERFIT.
■ **underˈfitness** *noun* E20.

underflow /ˈʌndəfləʊ/ *noun.* M19.
[from UNDER- + FLOW *noun*¹.]
1 An undercurrent (*lit.* & *fig.*). M19.
2 The (horizontal) flow of water through the ground, *spec.* underneath a river-bed. L19.
3 COMPUTING. The generation of a number that is too small to be represented in the device meant to store it. M20.

underflow /*in sense* 1 ʌndəˈfləʊ; *in sense* 2 *usu.* ˈʌndəfləʊ/ *verb.* OE.
[from UNDER- + FLOW *verb.*]
1 *verb trans. & intrans.* Flow under or beneath (something). *rare.* OE.
2 *verb intrans.* COMPUTING. Of the result of an arithmetical operation: become too small for the device meant to store it. M20.

underfocus /ˈʌndəfəʊkəs, ʌndəˈfəʊkəs/ *verb & noun.* M20.
[from UNDER- + FOCUS *verb.*]
▶ **A** *verb trans.* Infl. **-s-**, **-ss-**. Focus (the beam of an electron microscope) to a point somewhat short of the specimen. Chiefly as **underfocused** *ppl adjective*, **underfocusing** *verbal noun.* M20.
▶ **B** *noun.* The situation in which the beam of an electron microscope is underfocused. L20.

†**underfong** *verb trans. (inf. & pres.).* ME.
[from UNDER- + var. of FANG *verb*¹.]
1 Come to have or possess; accept. ME–L16.
2 Receive (a person); admit to one's friendship or society. ME–M16.
3 Take in hand, undertake. ME–E16.
4 Seduce, entrap, overcome. L16–E17.
5 Surround, enclose. *rare.* Only in L16.

underfoot /ʌndəˈfʊt/ *adverb, adjective, & noun.* As adverb also (*arch.*) **-feet** /-ˈfiːt/. ME.
[from UNDER- + FOOT *noun.*]
▶ **A** *adverb.* **1** Beneath one's foot or feet; on the ground. ME. ▸**b** NAUTICAL. Under a ship's bottom; *spec.* (of an anchor) directly under the forefoot. M17. ▸**c** Down below; underneath; underground. M19.
2 *fig.* In or to a state of subjection or inferiority. ME.
†**3** Below the real or current value. L16–M17.
4 About one's feet, constantly present, so as to obstruct or inconvenience a person. *colloq.* L19.

> **1** P. PEARCE Underfoot the earth was soft. B. BAINBRIDGE A length of threadbare ribbon . . was trodden underfoot. **c** CARLYLE The obscure sojourn of demons . . is underfoot. **2** G. MEREDITH Not he the man to have pity of women underfoot! **4** M. DICKENS The house was full of dogs, getting underfoot, jostling for the best place.

▶ **B** *adjective.* **1** Lying beneath one's foot or feet; *spec.* in regard to the going in horse-racing. L16.
2 *fig.* Inferior, abject, low, downtrodden. L16.
▶ **C** *noun.* The surface of the ground at the foot of a tree. *rare.* E20.
■ **underfooting** *noun* (*a*) the ground underfoot, esp. with regard to its condition for walking, riding, etc.; (*b*) *Anglo-Irish* a method of turf-cutting in which vertical cuts are made: M20.

undergang /ʌndəˈgaŋ/ *verb trans. (inf. & pres.).* Long *obsolete* exc. *dial.* OE.
[from UNDER- + GANG *verb*¹.]
Undergo.

underglaze /ˈʌndəgleɪz/ *noun & adjective.* L19.
[from UNDER- + GLAZE *noun.*]
▶ **A** *noun.* A glaze applied before another, *spec.* in CERAMICS, to form a glazed surface for decoration over which a second glaze is applied. Also, printed or painted decoration done on porcelain etc. before application of a glaze. Cf. OVERGLAZE *noun.* L19.
▶ **B** *adjective.* Of, pertaining to, or suitable for an underglaze. L19.

undergo /ʌndəˈgəʊ/ *verb trans.* Infl. as **GO** *verb*; pa. t. usu. **-went** /-ˈwɛnt/, pa. pple usu. **-gone** /-ˈgɒn/. **OE.**
[from **UNDER-** + **GO** *verb*.]
†**1** Undermine. Chiefly *fig.* **OE–M17.**
2 †**a** Be willing *to do*; accept, admit. *rare.* Only in **ME.** ▸**b** Be subject to, serve. Now *rare* or *obsolete.* **L16.**
†**3** Go or pass under. **ME–E17.**
†**4** Occupy oneself with; get knowledge of. Only in **ME.**
5 Endure, suffer, go through. **ME.** ▸†**b** Carry (a burden etc.). **LME–M17.**
6 Be subjected to; experience; pass through. **ME.** ▸†**b** Partake of, enjoy. *rare.* Only in **E17.**
†**7** Be called by, assume, (a name). **ME–E19.**
8 Undertake (a task etc.). Now *rare.* **LME.** ▸†**b** Discharge (an office). **E17–E18.**

📖 **1** D. ROGERS Lest thou shouldest undergo thy selfe in purchasing the pearle. **2b** BROWNING The new metre is admirable . . . So have you made our language undergo you. **3** G. CHAPMAN Better my shoulders underwent the earth, than thy decease. **5** H. MARTINEAU His fine spirit was broken by the anxieties he had undergone. V. WOOLF She need not undergo that degradation. **b** H. PHILLIPS Equality in the loss . . , that so the burden may be the more easily undergone. **6** D. MELTZER She suffered a sudden illness and underwent surgery. M. MARRIN Scientific tests the paintings had undergone in the United States. **b** SHAKES. *Meas. for M.* If any in Vienna be of worth To undergo such ample grace, and honour. **7** B. H. MALKIN A large ape, which underwent the name of Cupid. **8** T. STANLEY Him a perfect Agent we may call, Who first considers what he undergoes. **b** S. PEPYS [He is] a very young man to undergo that place.

undergrad /ʌndəˈgrad/ *noun. colloq.* **E19.**
[Abbreviation Cf. **GRAD** *noun*¹, **POSTGRAD.**]
An undergraduate.

undergraduacy /ʌndəˈgradjʊəsi/ *noun. rare.* **E20.**
[from next: see **-ACY.**]
The position or status of an undergraduate.

undergraduate /ʌndəˈgradjʊət/ *noun & adjective.* **M17.**
[from **UNDER-** + **GRADUATE** *noun & adjective.*]
▶**A** *noun.* A student at a university who has not yet taken a first degree; *transf. & fig.* a person who is not yet an expert (*in*). **M17.**
▶**B** *attrib.* or as *adjective.* †**1** Of lower degree; of lesser importance. Only in **M17.**
2 Having the position or status of an undergraduate; that is an undergraduate. **L17.**
3 Of or belonging to an undergraduate; characteristic of undergraduates. **M19.**
4 Consisting of undergraduates. **M19.**
▪ **undergraduateship** *noun* the position or status of an undergraduate **E19.** **undergraduatish** *adjective* characteristic of an undergraduate; somewhat like an undergraduate: **E20.**

undergraduette /ʌndəˌgradjʊˈɛt/ *noun. joc.* **E20.**
[from prec.: see **-ETTE.**]
A female undergraduate.

underground /ˈʌndəgraʊnd/ *noun, adjective, & verb.* **L16.**
[from the adverb.]
▶**A** *noun.* **1** The region below the earth; the underworld. Also, an underground space or passage. **L16.**
2 Underlying ground or soil; subsoil. Also, ground lying at a lower level or below trees. **E19.**
3 (Also **U-**.) An underground railway. **M19.**
4 *fig.* A secret group, movement, or activity, *esp.* one aiming to subvert an established order or a ruling power. Also, a subculture seeking to provide radical alternatives to the socially accepted or established mode. **M20.**

📖 **1** T. KYD Come we for this from depth of vnder ground? **2** M. O. W. OLIPHANT The mossy underground beneath the firs. **3** S. BRETT The Underground slowly took him back into central London. **4** C. HOPE He . . joined the political underground.

▶**B** *adjective.* **1** Situated, existing, or occurring underground or under the earth; belonging to the underworld; subterranean. **E17.** ▸**b** To be worn or used underground. **E19.**
2 *fig.* **a** Hidden, concealed, secret; not open or public. **L17.** ▸**b** Of, pertaining to, or designating a secret group, movement, or activity, esp. one aiming to subvert an established order or a ruling power. Also, of or pertaining to a subculture seeking to provide radical alternatives to the socially accepted or established mode; unconventional, experimental. **M20.**

📖 **1** S. BARING-GOULD The underground folk seek union with human beings. D. ADAMS A . . hitherto undetected underground river lying far beneath the surface. **b** F. HUME They arrayed themselves in underground garments. **2a** J. KEBLE There may be an unseen, underground unity. **b** G. BRENAN People suspected of Underground activity had been arrested. *Listener* His plays and other writings circulate only in underground editions.

Special collocations: **underground economy** *N. Amer.* = **black economy** s.v. **BLACK** *adjective.* **underground mutton** *Austral. slang* a rabbit; rabbit meat. **underground railroad**, **underground railway** (*a*) a railway running under the surface of the ground, esp. beneath the streets and buildings of a city; (*b*) *US HISTORY* the secret system by which slaves were enabled to escape to the Free States and Canada.
▶**C** *verb trans.* Lay (electricity or telephone cables) below ground level. **L19.**
▪ **undergrounder** *noun* an underground person **L19.**

underground /ʌndəˈgraʊnd/ *adverb.* **LME.**
[from **UNDER-** + **GROUND** *noun.*]
1 Beneath the surface of the ground. **LME.**
2 *fig.* **a** In secrecy or concealment; in a hidden or obscure manner. **M17.** ▸**b** Into hiding or secret activity, esp. aiming to subvert an established order or a ruling power. **M20.**

📖 **1** TENNYSON Then sprang the happier day from underground. A. J. CRONIN Andrew had been underground before, he was used to the . . Drineffy mines. **2a** SHAFTESBURY In Philosophical Disputes, 'tis not allowable to work underground. **b** G. GREENE To radio London that we were breaking off and then go underground.

undergrown /ʌndəˈgrəʊn/ *ppl adjective.* **LME.**
[from **UNDER-** + **GROWN.**]
1 Not fully grown or developed. **LME.**
†**2** Showing signs of puberty. *rare.* Only in **E17.**
3 Provided with an undergrowth, esp. of a specified kind. **L19.**

undergrowth /ˈʌndəgrəʊθ/ *noun.* **E17.**
[from **UNDER-** + **GROWTH** *noun.*]
1 A dense growth of plants or bushes, esp. under tall trees; brushwood, underwood. **E17.** ▸**b** An undergrown stem of flax, wheat, etc. **M18.**
2 Underfur, underhair. *rare.* **M17.**
3 Growth that is insufficient or too slow; an instance of this. **L19.**

underhand /ˈʌndəhand/ *adjective & noun.* **M16.**
[from the adverb.]
▶**A** *adjective.* **1 a** *ARCHERY.* Aimed with the target sighted below the bow hand. *rare.* **M16.** ▸**b** Executed with the hands below shoulder-level, underarm; *spec.* in *CRICKET*, (of bowling) performed with the hand held under the ball and lower than the shoulder or (formerly) the elbow; (of a person) using such an action in bowling. **E18.**
2 Secret, clandestine, surreptitious; not above-board or straightforward. Also (*arch.*), not open or obvious; unobtrusive; quiet. **L16.**
3 Held in or operated by the hand. Now *rare* or *obsolete.* **E18.**
4 *MINING.* Worked from above downwards. **L19.**

📖 **2** SHAKES. *A.Y.L.* I had . . notice of my brother's purpose . . and have by underhand means laboured to dissuade him. E. A. FREEMAN Their influence must have been exercised in a purely underhand way. A. FRASER Parliamentary leaders were . . aware of the underhand nature of their king. **3** J. ABERCROMBIE Ridge out melons in underhand glasses.

▶**B** *noun.* **1** An underhand ball; underhand bowling. **M19.**
2 *The* position of inferiority. *rare.* **L19.**

underhand /ʌndəˈhand/ *adverb.* **OE.**
[from **UNDER-** + **HAND** *noun.*]
†**1 a** In or into subjection; under rule or command; in one's possession or power. **OE–ME.** ▸**b** In hand. **LME–L17.**
2 In a secret, covert, or clandestine manner; by secret, deceptive, or crafty means. **LME.**
3 a Beneath or below the hand; *spec.* (*a*) *ARCHERY* (*rare*) with the target sighted below the bow hand; †(*b*) with a coffin carried slung from rings instead of on the bearers' shoulders. **E16.** ▸**b** With the hand held under or below the object which it grasps; *CRICKET* (with ref. to bowling) with the hand held under the ball and lower than the shoulder, underarm. **E19.**

📖 **3b** B. HINES He . . lobbed it . . underhand at the bedroom window. **3** D. NEAL His Majesty was underhand preparing for war.

underhanded /*as adverb* ʌndəˈhandɪd, *as adjective* ˈʌndəhandɪd/ *adverb & adjective.* **E19.**
[from **UNDERHAND** *adjective* + **-ED**².]
▶**A** *adverb.* **1** = **UNDERHAND** *adverb* 2. **E19.**
2 = **UNDERHAND** *adverb* 3b. *rare.* **E19.**
▶**B** *adjective.* **1** = **UNDERHAND** *adjective* 2. **E19.**
2 Underpopulated; undermanned. **M19.**
3 Undersized. *dial.* **M19.**
4 Placed or printed below. **L19.**
▪ **underhandedly** *adverb* **E19.** **underhandedness** *noun* **L19.**

underhang /ˈʌndəhaŋ/ *noun. rare.* **E20.**
[from **UNDER-** + **HANG** *noun.*]
The fact of being underhung; the extent to which something is underhung.

underhanging /ˈʌndəhaŋɪŋ/ *noun.* **M19.**
[from **UNDER-** + **HANGING** *noun.*]
Projection of the lower jaw beyond the upper jaw.

underhanging /ˈʌndəhaŋɪŋ/ *adjective.* **M19.**
[from **UNDER-** + **HANGING** *adjective.*]
Having an underhung lower jaw.

underhung /ˈʌndəhʌŋ, ʌndəˈhʌŋ/ *adjective.* **L17.**
[from **UNDER-** + **HUNG** *adjective.*]
1 Having the lower jaw projecting beyond the upper jaw. **L17.** ▸**b** (Of the lower jaw) projecting beyond the upper jaw. **E19.**
2 Supported from below; *spec.* (of a sliding door) moving on a rail placed below it. *rare.* **M19.**

underived /ʌndɪˈrʌɪvd/ *ppl adjective.* **E17.**
[from **UN-**¹ + *derived* pa. pple of **DERIVE.**]
Not derived *from* a source; primary, original.
▪ **underivable** *adjective* **M17.** **underivedly** *adverb* **M17.** **underivedness** *noun* **M19.**

underkill /ˈʌndəkɪl/ *noun. colloq.* (orig. *US*). **M20.**
[from **UNDER-** + **KILL** *noun*¹ after *overkill*.]
Insufficient killing; *spec.* the amount by which destruction by a nuclear weapon falls short of that required for victory or annihilation, or the capacity for such destruction.

underlaid *verb pa. t. & pple* of **UNDERLAY** *verb*¹.

underlain *verb pa. pple* of **UNDERLIE** *verb.*

underlay /ˈʌndəleɪ/ *noun.* **L16.**
[from next.]
†**1** Subjunction. Only in **L16.**
2 a An additional piece placed beneath something; *spec.* †(*a*) a piece added to the sole or heel of a shoe; (*b*) a cylinder of straw or wood placed underneath a beehive to increase capacity; (*c*) *PRINTING* a piece of paper or cardboard placed under type or blocks to raise these to the required level. **E17.** ▸**b** A layer underlying another; a substratum; *spec.* material laid under a carpet or mattress for protection and support; a sheet of this. **L19.**
3 *MINING.* The inclination of a mineral vein, fault, etc., from the vertical or horizontal. **M19.**
4 *EARLY MUSIC.* The placing of the text of a song etc. in relation to music. **M20.**

📖 **2b** *fig.*: H. GUNTRIP The schizoid underlay in hysteria.

underlay /ʌndəˈleɪ/ *verb*¹. Pa. t. & pple **-laid** /-ˈleɪd/. **OE.**
[from **UNDER-** + **LAY** *verb*¹.]
1 *verb trans.* Provide (a thing) with an underlay, esp. for protection and support or to give added height. Also foll. by *with*. **OE.**
†**2** *verb trans.* Place (a thing) under or beneath another. **OE–L17.**
3 *verb trans.* = **UNDERLIE** *verb* 3, 3b. **L16.**
4 *verb intrans. MINING.* = **UNDERLIE** *verb* 5. **E18.**
5 *verb trans. EARLY MUSIC.* Place (the text of a song etc.) in relation to the music. **M20.**

📖 **1** R. EDEN They vnderlaye them with grasse. *Athenaeum* Underlaying the sea with electric wires. **3** M. DRABBLE The courage . . that underlaid the nonsense.

▪ **ˈunderlayment** *noun* (*US*) carpet underlay; material laid beneath roofing-tiles etc.: **M20.**

underlay *verb*² *pa. t.* of **UNDERLIE** *verb.*

underlayer /ˈʌndəleɪə/ *noun*¹. **ME.**
[from **UNDERLAY** *verb*¹ + **-ER**¹.]
†**1** An underlying part or thing; a base, a support. **ME–L18.**
†**2** A cobbler. Only in **L17.**
3 *MINING.* A perpendicular shaft sunk to cut a lode at a required depth. **M19.**

underlayer /ˈʌndəleɪə/ *noun*². **L19.**
[from **UNDER-** + **LAYER** *noun.*]
A lower layer; a substratum.

underlie /ˈʌndəlʌɪ/ *noun.* **L18.**
[from **UNDER-** + **LIE** *noun*².]
MINING. = **UNDERLAY** *noun* 3.

underlie /ʌndəˈlʌɪ/ *verb.* Pa. t. **-lay** /-ˈleɪ/, pres. pple **-lying** /-ˈlʌɪɪŋ/, pa. pple **-lain** /-ˈleɪn/. **OE.**
[from **UNDER-** + **LIE** *verb*¹.]
†**1** *verb trans.* Be subject or subordinate to (a person or thing); submit to or be controlled by. **OE–L16.**
2 *verb trans.* Be subjected to or undergo (esp. a punishment, penalty, or accusation). Now chiefly *Scot.* **OE.**
3 *verb trans.* Lie or be situated under or beneath (a stratum etc.). **L16.** ▸**b** *fig.* Form a basis or foundation to; exist beneath the superficial aspect of. **M19.**
†**4** *verb intrans.* Lie below ground; be buried. **M17–M18.**
5 *verb intrans. MINING.* Of a mineral vein, fault, etc., incline from the vertical or horizontal, slope. **L18.**

📖 **2** J. W. DONALDSON He underlies also the graver charge of intentional misrepresentation. **3b** K. CLARK Some drama of light and shade must underlie all landscape compositions. E. BOWEN The manners she had taught him were underlain by hostility to strangers. **4** R. HERRICK She . . for this dead which under-lies, Wept out her heart.

▪ **ˈunderlier** *noun* (*rare*) (*a*) a thing which underlies (another); (*b*) *MINING* a shaft which intersects with and follows the inclination of a mineral vein: **M16.**

For other words beginning with *under-* see the entries for **under-**

underline /ˈʌndəlʌɪn/ *noun*. L19.
[from UNDER- + LINE *noun*².]
1 The line of the lower part of an animal's body. L19.
2 A line drawn below a printed or written word, phrase, etc., esp. for emphasis or to indicate italic or other special type. L19.
3 A line at the bottom of a playbill announcing the next production. L19.
4 The caption below an illustration in a book, newspaper, etc. E20.

underline /ʌndəˈlʌɪn/ *verb*¹ *trans*. M16.
[from UNDER- + LINE *verb*¹.]
Provide with an underlining; form an underlining to (see UNDERLINING *noun*¹).

underline /ʌndəˈlʌɪn/ *verb*² *trans*. M16.
[from UNDER- + LINE *verb*².]
1 a Draw a line below (a word, phrase, etc.), esp. for emphasis or to indicate italic or other special type. M16. ▸**b** *fig*. Emphasize, stress. L19.
2 Announce (the next production) by an underline on a playbill. E19.

📖 **1a** B. BAINBRIDGE Underlining certain words as if they were significant. G. SWIFT The typescripts—annotated and underlined with red ink. **b** M. MEYER The incident . . underlines a problem which Ibsen was to face for the whole of his career. ANTHONY SMITH Dr William Gooddy then further underlined his point.

■ **underlineation** /ˌʌndəlɪnɪˈeɪʃ(ə)n/ *noun* the action or result of underlining something E19.

underling /ˈʌndəlɪŋ/ *noun & adjective*. ME.
[from UNDER- + -LING¹. Cf. OVERLING.]
▶ **A** *noun*. **1** A subordinate. Freq. *derog*. ME.
2 A low-growing branch, plant, etc.; an undersized or weak plant, animal, etc. Now *dial*. L17.

📖 **1** J. P. HENNESSY Trollope's manner to his underlings was aggressive and off-hand. R. DAVIES Words and expressions that did not . . mark me as an underling.

▶ **B** *attrib*. or as *adjective*. **1** Subordinate (*to*); of or pertaining to an underling. Freq. *derog*. LME.
2 Of a plant, animal, etc.: undersized, weak; (of a branch, plant, etc.) low-growing. Now *dial*. E18.

underlining /ˈʌndəlʌɪnɪŋ/ *noun*¹. L16.
[from UNDER- + LINING *noun*¹.]
A lining placed under something; the inner lining of a garment.

underlining /ʌndəˈlʌɪnɪŋ/ *noun*². M19.
[from UNDERLINE *verb*² + -ING¹.]
The action or process of underlining a word, phrase, etc., esp. for emphasis or to indicate italic or other special type; a result of this, an underline.

†**underly** *adjective*. *rare*. M17.
[from UNDER *adverb* + -LY¹.]
1 Subordinate; inferior. M–L17.
2 In a poor state of health. Only in E18.

underlying /ʌndəˈlʌɪɪŋ/ *ppl adjective*. LME.
[from UNDERLIE *verb* + -ING².]
1 Lying under or beneath the surface; that underlies something. Chiefly *fig*., not openly present. LME.
2 LINGUISTICS. Designating a representation of a sentence or other linguistic unit which differs from the actual form and from which the latter is derived. M20.

📖 **1** J. M. MURRY The underlying thought throughout that passage . . is intimately connected with Shakespeare. P. KAVANAGH Changes took place . . on the surface of their lives but the underlying material remained . . the same.

■ **underlyingly** *adverb* L20.

underlying *verb pres. pple* of UNDERLIE *verb*.

underman /ˈʌndəmən, *in sense 2* -man/ *noun*. Pl. **-men**. ME.
[from UNDER- + MAN *noun*.]
1 A man inferior or subordinate to others. Long *rare* exc. as passing into sense 2. ME.
2 A person of inferior power or ability; a subhuman person. (Cf. OVERMAN *noun* 4.) E20.
3 A subordinate member of a body of workers, esp. platelayers. E20.

underman /ʌndəˈman/ *verb trans*. Infl. **-nn-**. M19.
[from UNDER- + MAN *verb*.]
Fail to provide with enough men or (now esp.) with enough workers. Chiefly as ***undermanned*** *ppl adjective*, ***undermanning*** *verbal noun*.

undermatch /ʌndəˈmatʃ/ *verb & noun*. *arch*. L16.
[from UNDER- + MATCH *verb*¹.]
▶ **A** *verb trans*. †**1** Undervalue by comparison. Only in L16.
2 Unite or give in marriage to a person of lesser rank or status. M17.
†**3** Be less than a match for, be inferior to. Chiefly as ***undermatched*** *ppl adjective*. M17–M18.
▶†**B** *noun*. A person who or thing which is less than a match for another. M17–M18.

undermentioned /ʌndəˈmɛnʃ(ə)nd, *esp. attrib*. ˈʌndəmɛnʃ(ə)nd/ *adjective*. M17.
[from UNDER- + *mentioned* pa. pple of MENTION *verb*.]
Mentioned at a later point in a book, legal document, etc.

undermine /ˈʌndəmʌɪn/ *noun*. *rare*. L16.
[In branch I from UNDER- + MINE *noun*, in branch II from next.]
▶†**I 1** An underground excavation. L16–E17.
2 A submerged mine. Only in L17.
▶ **II 3** An undermining movement. L19.

undermine /ʌndəˈmʌɪn/ *verb trans*. ME.
[from UNDER- + MINE *verb*, prob. after Middle Dutch *ondermineren* (cf. Dutch *ondermijnen*).]
1 Dig or excavate beneath, make a passage or mine under (a wall etc.), esp. as a military operation; sap. ME.
2 *transf*. **a** Of a river, stream, etc.: work under and wash away the base or foundation of (land etc.). LME. ▸**b** Of an animal: burrow under or in; destroy the foundations of (land etc.) through burrowing. E16. ▸**c** MEDICINE. Erode beneath the surface. L19.
3 *fig*. **a** Work secretly or stealthily against (a person etc.); overthrow or supplant (formerly also persuade or win over) by subtle or underhand means. LME. ▸**b** Weaken, injure, destroy, or ruin (reputation, authority, belief, etc.) surreptitiously or insidiously. M16. ▸**c** Weaken or destroy (the health or constitution) by degrees; sap. E19.

📖 **1** F. MARRYAT We must under-mine the gate . . ; we must pull up the pavement until we can creep under. *absol*.: P. HOLLAND Necessarie it is . . to undermine a great way by candle-light . . under the mountains. **2a** C. E. S. NORTON The prisoned streamlet . . undermining all the creviced bank. **3a** DRYDEN She undermin'd my Soul With Tears. LD MACAULAY Those who had . . undermined him began to struggle for the fragments of his power. **b** D. ACHESON New ideas . . undermined the old ways and old loyalties. H. MACMILLAN Nasser's humiliating defeat . . undermined the Egyptian dictator's strength and influence. **c** B. GUEST Her normal work schedule . . would undermine the healthiest of constitutions.

■ **underminer** *noun* E16. **underminingly** *adverb* in an undermining manner L16.

undermost /ˈʌndəməʊst/ *adjective & adverb*. M16.
[from UNDER *adverb* + -MOST.]
▶ **A** *adjective*. Holding the lowest place or position. M16.
▶ **B** *adverb*. In the lowest place or position, underneath. E17.

undern /ˈʌndən/ *noun*. Long *arch*. & *dial*.
[Old English = Old Frisian *unde(r)n*, Old Saxon *undorn*, *undern*, Old High German *untorn*, *untarn* (Dutch dial. *onder*, German dial. *Untern*, *Undern*, *Unnern*), Old Norse *undorn*, *undarn*, Gothic *undaurn-* (in *undaurnimats*), from Germanic formation meaning 'morning' or 'midday', prob. ult. from base of UNDER *preposition*.]
1 The third hour of the day; the time at or about nine o'clock in the morning; ECCLESIASTICAL terce. OE.
†**2** The sixth hour of the day; midday. ME–L15.
3 The afternoon, the evening. L15.
4 A snack or light meal, *esp*. one taken in the afternoon. L17.

undernamed /ʌndəˈneɪmd, *attrib*. ˈʌndəneɪmd/ *adjective*. L16.
[from UNDER- + *named* pa. pple of NAME *verb*.]
Named or specified at a later point in a book, document, etc.

📖 *absol*.: *Satellite Times* You are hereby cordially invited to join the undernamed.

underneath /ʌndəˈniːθ/ *preposition, adverb, noun, & adjective*.
[Old English *underneoþan*, from UNDER *preposition, adverb* + *neoþan* beneath.]
▶ **A** *preposition*. **1** At or to a place or level lower than or down below; directly beneath or covered by (esp. an outer garment). OE.
2 In subordination or subjection to; under the power or control of. *arch*. LME.
†**3** Less than. LME–E16.

📖 **1** SHELLEY Underneath thy feet writhe Faith . . and mortal Melancholy. M. SARTON Daff was, underneath a highly cultivated crusty exterior, horribly sensitive. D. SHIELDS With . . his chest protector underneath his blue uniform. *Which?* Put a slide underneath the lens. **2** N. BACON A man underneath many Passions. SHELLEY Philosophy, thou canst not even Compel their causes underneath thy yoke.

▶ **B** *adverb*. **1** Down below; at a lower place or level; directly beneath or covered by something, esp. an outer garment. OE.
2 On the underside; on the lower surface or part. L18.

📖 **1** P. SAYER I . . dislodged a stone with my foot. Underneath was a toad. V. GLENDINNING The lemon mousse . . had separated out, fluff on the top and stiff jelly underneath. **2** W. WITHERING Leaves . . with little scales and fringed appendages underneath.

▶ **C** *noun*. That which is underneath; the lower surface or side. L17.

📖 E. TAYLOR It . . began to lick the pink underneath of a paw.

▶ **D** *adjective*. **1** Underhand; secret. *rare*. M18.
2 Situated underneath; lower. L19.

📖 **2** E. WILSON When one shape overlaps another, lay the underneath one down first.

undern-time /ˈʌndəntʌɪm/ *noun*. Long *arch*. & *dial*. OE.
[from UNDERN + TIME *noun*.]
= UNDERN 1, 2.

underpaid *verb pa. t. & pple* of UNDERPAY *verb*.

underpass /ˈʌndəpɑːs/ *noun*. Orig. *US*. E20.
[from UNDER- + PASS *noun*¹.]
A (section of) road providing passage beneath another road or a railway; a subway.

underpay /*as verb* ʌndəˈpeɪ, *as noun* ˈʌndəpeɪ/ *verb & noun*. E19.
[from UNDER- + PAY *verb*¹, *noun*.]
▶ **A** *verb trans*. Pa. t. & pple **-paid** /-ˈpeɪd/. Pay less than what is due or deserved to (a person etc.) or for (a service etc.). Freq. as ***underpaid*** *ppl adjective*. E19.
▶ **B** *noun*. Payment less than what is due or deserved to a person etc. or for a service etc. M19.
■ **underpayment** *noun* M19.

underperform /ʌndəpəˈfɔːm/ *verb*. L20.
[from UNDER- + PERFORM.]
1 *verb intrans*. Perform below expectation; *esp*. (of an investment) be less profitable than expected. L20.
2 *verb trans*. Perform less well than; *esp*. (of an investment) be less profitable than. L20.
■ **underperformance** *noun* L20. **underperformer** *noun* L20.

underpin /ʌndəˈpɪn/ *verb trans*. Infl. **-nn-**. E16.
[from UNDER- + PIN *verb*.]
Support or strengthen (a building etc.) from beneath, *spec*. by laying a solid foundation below ground level, or by substituting stronger or more solid for weaker or softer materials; *fig*. support, corroborate.

📖 *Nature* The large Subject Index . . does not adequately underpin the guidebook function. *New York Review of Books* Similar convictions underpinned the expansionist policy of . . other Democratic leaders.

■ **underpinning** *noun* (*a*) the action of the verb; (*b*) a thing which underpins something, *esp*. the materials or structure used for giving support to or strengthening a building etc. from beneath; (*c*) *fig*. a support, a prop; *US slang* (*sing*. & (usu.) in *pl*.) the legs: LME.

underplant /ʌndəˈplɑːnt/ *verb trans*. OE.
[from UNDER- + PLANT *verb*.]
†**1** Supplant. *rare*. OE–L16.
2 Plant or cultivate the ground about (a tall plant) with smaller ones. Freq. foll. by *with*. L19.
■ ˈ**underplanting** *noun* (*a*) the action of the verb; an instance of this; *spec*. in FORESTRY, the process of growing shade-bearing trees among taller ones which they may eventually replace; (*b*) a plant etc. grown by underplanting: E20.

underplay /ʌndəˈpleɪ/ *verb*. M18.
[from UNDER- + PLAY *verb*.]
†**1** *verb refl*. Play chess etc. below one's ability. Only in M18.
2 *verb intrans*. Play a low rather than a high card of a suit held. M19.
3 *verb intrans*. & *trans*. THEATRICAL. Underact; perform with deliberate restraint. L19.
4 *verb trans*. Play down the importance of; present less emphatically than usual. M20.

underprice /*as noun* ˈʌndəprʌɪs, *as verb* ʌndəˈprʌɪs/ *noun & verb*. E17.
[from UNDER- + PRICE *noun, verb*.]
▶ **A** *noun*. A price below the standard or usual price; an inadequate payment. E17.
▶ **B** *verb trans*. **1** Price (a commodity) lower than what is usual or appropriate. M18.
2 Undercut (a person etc.) in price. L19.

underprop /*as verb* ʌndəˈprɒp, *as noun* ˈʌndəprɒp/ *verb & noun*. E16.
[from UNDER- + PROP *verb, noun*¹.]
▶ **A** *verb trans*. Infl. **-pp-**.
1 Sustain, support, maintain. E16.
2 Support with a prop or props; keep firm or upright with some form of material support. M16.
3 Form a prop or support to. L16.
▶ **B** *noun*. A prop or support placed under a thing; a thing which underprops something (*lit*. & *fig*.). L16.
■ **underpropper** *noun* M16. **underpropping** *noun* (*a*) the action or an act of the verb; (*b*) an underprop: L16.

underran *verb pa. t.* of UNDERRUN *verb*.

underrate /ˈʌndəreɪt/ *noun*. Long *rare* or *obsolete*. M17.
[from UNDER- + RATE *noun*¹.]
A rate lower than the true or standard one.

underrate /ʌndəˈreɪt/ *verb trans*. L16.
[from UNDER- + RATE *verb*¹.]
Rate or assess at too low a value or worth; have too low an opinion of; undervalue, underestimate.

underrun /ˈʌndərʌn/ *noun*. L19.
[Partly from UNDER- + RUN *noun*; partly from next.]
1 An undercurrent. L19.
2 (An instance of) underrunning; the extent to which a radio or TV programme etc. underruns. M20.
3 The action of running under something, *spec.* (of a vehicle) under the back of a large vehicle in front. Chiefly *attrib.* M20.
Comb.: **underrun bar**, **underrun bumper**, etc., a guard attached to the back of a large-wheeled vehicle to prevent other vehicles running underneath.

underrun /ʌndəˈrʌn/ *verb*. Infl. as RUN *verb*; pa. t. **-ran** /-ˈran/, pa. pple usu. **-run**. M16.
[from UNDER- + RUN *verb*.]
1 *verb trans.* NAUTICAL. Overhaul or examine (a cable etc.) on the underside, esp. by drawing a boat along under it. M16. ▸**b** Pull in (a net or trawl) in order to clear the net of the catch and reset it. L19.
2 *verb trans.* Run, flow, or pass beneath. L16.
3 *verb intrans.* Of a radio or TV programme etc.: run or extend for less than the allotted time or limit. M20.
4 *verb intrans.* Of a car: run under a larger vehicle in front. L20.

underrunner /ˈʌndərʌnə/ *noun*. L19.
[from UNDER- + RUNNER.]
1 TYPOGRAPHY. A continuation of marginal notes run at the foot of the page in a similar manner to a footnote. Usu. in *pl.* L19.
2 CRICKET. A batsman who makes too few runs for his hits. *rare.* E20.
3 A subterranean stream. *NZ.* E20.

underscore /ˈʌndəskɔː/ *noun*. E20.
[from UNDER- + SCORE *noun*.]
A line drawn below a word etc.; an instance of underlining; this facility on a typewriter etc.

underscore /ʌndəˈskɔː/ *verb trans.* L18.
[from UNDER- + SCORE *verb*.]
1 Draw a line beneath; underline. L18.
2 Emphasize, stress, reinforce. L19.

📖 **2** *Toronto Star* The report . . underscores the common complaint made by several groups.

underscrub /ˈʌndəskrʌb/ *noun & verb*. E19.
[from UNDER- + SCRUB *noun*[1].]
▸ **A** *noun*. **1** An undergrown or insignificant person. *arch. slang.* E19.
2 Undergrowth; brushwood. L19.
▸ **B** *verb intrans.* Infl. **-bb-**. Cut back underscrub. Chiefly as ***underscrubbing*** *verbal noun*. *NZ.* M20.

undersea /*as adjective* ˈʌndəsiː, *as adverb* ʌndəˈsiː/ *adjective & adverb*. E17.
[from UNDER- + SEA.]
▸ **A** *adjective*. **1** Situated or lying below the sea or the surface of the sea; submarine. E17.
2 Intended for use below the surface of the sea. E20.
▸ **B** *adverb*. Below the sea or its surface. Now only *poet.* L17.

underseal /ˈʌndəsiːl/ *noun*. M20.
[from UNDER- + SEAL *noun*[2].]
(US proprietary name for a brand of) waterproofing material used as a protective coating on the underbodies of motor vehicles.

underseal /ˈʌndəsiːl/ *verb trans.* M20.
[from UNDER- + SEAL *verb*[1].]
Coat (the underbody of a motor vehicle) with waterproof material, esp. to protect against rust.

under-secretary /ʌndəˈsɛkrət(ə)ri/ *noun*. L17.
[from UNDER- + SECRETARY *noun*.]
A subordinate official, *esp.* a junior minister or a senior civil servant.
parliamentary under-secretary: see PARLIAMENTARY *adjective*. ***Permanent Under-secretary***: see PERMANENT *adjective*.
▪ **under-secretaryship** *noun* L17.

undersell /ʌndəˈsɛl/ *verb trans.* Pa. t. & pple **-sold** /-ˈsəʊld/. E17.
[from UNDER- + SELL *verb*.]
1 Sell at a lower price than (another person); cut out (another seller) by selling at a lower rate. E17.
2 Sell (a commodity) at less than the real value. M17.

📖 **1** JAS. ROBERTSON The price of labour will become so enormous that we shall . . be undersold in every market. **2** *fig.*: *Notes & Queries* The rather ordinary language undersells an ingenious idea.

▪ **underseller** *noun* M19.

underset /ˈʌndəsɛt/ *noun*. E16.
[from UNDER- + SET *noun*[1]. In sense 1 abbreviation of UNDERSETTLE.]
†**1** A subtenant; = UNDERSETTLE. *Scot. rare.* Only in E16.
2 MINING. A lower vein of ore. *rare.* M18.
3 NAUTICAL. An undercurrent in a bay caused by the counterflow of water against an onshore wind. E19.

underset /ʌndəˈsɛt/ *verb trans.* Infl. **-tt-**. Pa. t. & pple **-set**. ME.
[from UNDER- + SET *verb*[1].]
1 Support or strengthen by means of a post, prop, etc., placed beneath; prop up. ME. ▸†**b** Serve as a support to. *rare.* ME–E17.
2 Set or place (a thing) under something else. ME.
3 *fig.* Support, sustain, provide foundation for. LME.
4 Sublet. *rare.* E19.

📖 **1** G. W. FRANCIS The Custom House . . was underset . . , a new foundation having been made to it. **2** E. GLANVILLE While Miles pressed the rock forward, Hans kept it from swinging back by undersetting a stone. **3** L. MORRIS The archetypes which underset the world With one broad perfect Law.

▪ **undersetting** *noun* (*a*) the action of the verb; (*b*) a support, a prop; a supporting or sustaining structure (*lit.* & *fig.*): LME.

undershoot /ˈʌndəʃuːt/ *noun*. M20.
[from the verb.]
The action or result of undershooting; *spec.* (*a*) ECONOMICS an underspend; (*b*) ELECTRONICS a small variation in signal immediately before or after, and in the opposite direction to, a sudden (larger) change.

undershoot /ʌndəˈʃuːt/ *verb*. Infl. as SHOOT *verb*; pa. t. & pple usu. **-shot** /-ˈʃɒt/. M17.
[from UNDER- + SHOOT *verb*.]
1 *verb trans. & intrans.* Shoot a missile etc. short of or below (a target); *fig.* (esp. of financial performance) fall short of or fail to reach (a target). M17.
2 *verb trans. & intrans.* Of an aircraft or pilot: fail to reach (a designated landing-point) while attempting to land; land short of (a runway etc.). E20.

📖 **1** *Century Magazine* The sportsman of unsteady nerve . . is apt to undershoot. *Times* The public sector borrowing requirement . . undershot the Government's original estimate.

undershot /ˈʌndəʃɒt/ *adjective*. E17.
[from UNDER- + SHOT *ppl adjective*.]
1 Of a water-wheel: driven by the weight of a flow of water passing under rather than over the wheel. E17.
2 Having the lower jaw or teeth projecting beyond the upper; underhung. L19.

undershot *verb pa. t. & pple*: see UNDERSHOOT *verb*.

underside /ˈʌndəsʌɪd/ *noun*. L17.
[from UNDER- + SIDE *noun*.]
The under or lower side or surface.

📖 M. HUNTER The . . young child, to whom the underside of a table may be a dark cave. *fig.*: GEO. ELIOT Comfort, which is the under-side . . of all pleasure.

Comb.: **underside-couching** EMBROIDERY: in which the couched thread is drawn through the fabric to the underside by each of the couching stitches.

undersign /ʌndəˈsʌɪn/ *verb trans.* Long *rare.* L16.
[from UNDER- + SIGN *verb*.]
Sign one's name below (a piece of writing).

undersigned /ʌndəˈsʌɪnd, *attrib.* ˈʌndəsʌɪnd/ *adjective*. M17.
[from UNDER- + SIGNED *adjective*[2].]
Whose signature is appended below.

📖 *absol.*: SYD. SMITH We, the undersigned, being clergymen of the Church of England.

undersize /ˈʌndəsʌɪz/ *noun & adjective*. L18.
[from UNDER- + SIZE *noun*[1].]
▸ **A** *noun*. A size less than the proper or usual size. Long *rare.* L18.
▸ **B** *adjective*. Of less than the usual size; undersized. E19.

undersized /ʌndəˈsʌɪzd, *attrib.* ˈʌndəsʌɪzd/ *adjective*. M17.
[from UNDER- + SIZED.]
†**1** Inadequately employed. Only in M17.
2 Of less than the proper or usual size. E18.

undersold *verb pa. t. & pple* of UNDERSELL.

undersow /ʌndəˈsəʊ/ *verb trans.* Pa. t. **-sowed** /-ˈsəʊd/; pa. pple **-sowed**, **-sown** /-ˈsəʊn/. M17.
[from UNDER- + SOW *verb*[1].]
†**1** Sow too little seed on (a piece of ground). *rare.* Only in M17.
2 Sow (a later-growing crop) on land already seeded with another crop. Also, sow land already seeded with (one crop) *with* a second, later-growing crop. M20.

underspend /*as verb* ʌndəˈspɛnd, *as noun* ˈʌndəspɛnd/ *verb & noun*. M17.
[from UNDER- + SPEND *verb*.]
▸ **A** *verb*. Pa. t. & pple **-spent** /-ˈspɛnt/.
†**1** *verb trans.* Consume less food or drink than. *rare.* Only in M17.
2 a *verb trans.* Spend less than (a specified amount or budget). L19. ▸**b** *verb intrans. & refl.* Spend too little. L19.
▸ **B** *noun*. The action of underspending a budget etc.; an instance of this. Also, an amount by which a budget etc. is underspent. L20.

understaff /ʌndəˈstɑːf/ *verb trans.* L19.
[from UNDER- + STAFF *verb*.]
Provide (a business, institution, etc.) with insufficient staff. Now chiefly as ***understaffed*** *ppl adjective*.
▪ **understaffing** *noun* M20.

understand /ʌndəˈstand/ *verb*. Pa. t. & pple **-stood** /-ˈstʊd/.
[Old English *understandan* = Old Frisian *understonda*, Old Norse (as a foreign word) *undirstanda*, formed as UNDER- + STAND *verb*.]
▸ **I** *verb trans.* **1** Perceive the meaning or explanation of; grasp the idea of. Also, have a sympathetic awareness of the character or nature of (a person). OE. ▸**b** Be conversant or familiar with, have mastery of, (a subject, skill, etc.); be able to practise or deal with competently. ME. ▸†**c** *verb refl.* Know one's place, know how to conduct oneself properly. E17–M18.
2 Be sufficiently acquainted with (a language) to be able to interpret the meaning of the words employed. OE. ▸**b** Grasp the meaning of the words or gestures used by (a person). ME.
3 Have a clear grasp of; realize fully. Usu. foll. by obj. clause OE. ▸†**b** Ascertain the substance of (a document etc.) by perusal and consideration. LME–E16.
4 Learn or gain knowledge of, esp. from information received; (now chiefly) accept as true without positive knowledge or certainty; believe, assume (usu. foll. by obj. clause or, passing into *verb intrans.*, parenthetically). OE. ▸**b** Grasp as an established fact or principle; regard as settled or implied without specific mention. OE.
5 Take, explain, or view in a specified way; construe. Also foll. by *by*, *of*. OE.
†**6** Give heed to, attend to. OE–LME.
7 Stand under. Formerly also, support, assist; prop up. Now *arch. rare.* ME.
8 Recognize or regard as present in thought or conception, though not expressed; supply (a word) mentally, imagine. Now chiefly as ***understood*** *ppl adjective*. LME.

📖 **1** J. CONRAD Only then . . I understood the loneliness of the man in charge. A. T. ELLIS She had considered Ronald's contribution . . scholarly and enlightening, although she hadn't understood it. **b** E. WAUGH An old man . . who understood the workings of the water system. **2** J. RABAN A Syrian taxi driver kindly pretended . . to understand my Arabic. **b** *Times Educ. Suppl.* Pupils may still be understood despite an imperfect accent. **3** G. DALY Having teetered back and forth . . , he finally understood that he had to stay put. **4** SIR W. SCOTT They understood it was his wish to observe incognito. H. S. MERRIMAN Mr. Wade . . was, he understood, distantly related to the mother. P. FUSSELL It was understood that a man fulfilled his combat obligation . . if he served a fixed term. **b** MILTON Warr then, Warr Open or understood must be resolv'd. **5** J. W. WARTER I do not . . know how Miss Bremer . . intended these words to be understood. J. RUSKIN We do not understand by this . . the mere making of money. **8** F. L. BARCLAY 'Present company excepted' is always understood . . when sweeping generalities are being made.

▸ **II** *verb intrans.* **9** Have comprehension or understanding (in general or in a particular matter). Freq. foll. by *about*. OE.
†**10** Have knowledge or information, learn, *of* something. ME–M17.

📖 **9** V. S. REID Puzzle-marks 'twixt her eyes tells me she does no' understand. L. P. HARTLEY With Harold, to understand was often to look glum.

Phrases: ***give to understand***: see GIVE *verb*. ***(if) you understand what I mean***: see MEAN *verb*[1]. **understand each other** (*a*) know each other's views or feelings; (*b*) be in agreement or collusion. ***you must understand***: see MUST *aux. verb*[1].

understandable /ʌndəˈstandəb(ə)l/ *adjective*. LME.
[from prec. + -ABLE.]
†**1** Able to understand; capable of understanding. LME–M17.
2 That can be understood; intelligible. LME.

📖 **2** G. VIDAL She approached the . . subject with understandable caution. A. S. DALE Browning was not a metaphysical philosopher, understandable only to the elite.

▪ **understandaˈbility** *noun* M20. **understandably** *adverb* for understandable reasons; in a manner that can be understood: E20.

understander /ʌndəˈstandə/ *noun*. LME.
[from (the same root as) UNDERSTAND + -ER[1].]
1 A person who understands; a person who has knowledge or comprehension of something. LME.
†**2** A leg, a foot. Also, a boot, a shoe. *rare.* L16–M18.
3 A spectator standing on the ground or pit of a theatre; a groundling. *obsolete* exc. *Hist.* M17.
4 A supporter, an upholder (*of*). *poet. rare.* L19.

understanding /ʌndəˈstandɪŋ/ *noun*. OE.
[from UNDERSTAND + -ING[1].]
1 Power or ability to understand; (the) intellect, *the* faculty of comprehending and reasoning; intelligence. OE. ▸†**b** Mind, purpose, intent. *rare.* LME–M16.
†**2** Signification, meaning. ME–E18.
3 A person's intellectual ability or reasoning faculty. LME.

4 †**a** Intelligence, information. L15–L16. ▸**b** Comprehension *of* something; an individual's perception or judgement of a situation. M16.
5 *slang.* In *pl.* ▸**a** Footwear, as boots or shoes. L18. ▸**b** Legs; feet. E19.
6 A mutual arrangement or agreement; something agreed on, esp. informally. E19.
7 Sympathetic awareness; tolerance; empathy. M20.

> 🕮 **1** MILTON For Understanding rul'd not, and the Will Heard not her lore. R. SCRUTON Hirsch is . . compelled to distinguish interpretation from understanding. A. DILLARD Anthropologist . . Lienhardt describes the animistic understanding of the Dinka tribe. **3** SIR W. SCOTT The idea of parting . . never once occurred to the simplicity of his understanding. **4b** B. BETTELHEIM The central concern informing Trilling's understanding and appreciation of literature. **6** T. MCGUANE They bought the house . . with the understanding that Mrs Callahan . . could have a day in the house alone. B. DUFFY Between them . . was the tacit understanding that each would speak appreciatively . . about the other. **7** A. WALKER To ask your understanding and forgiveness seems corniness personified.

Phrases: **a good understanding**, †**a right understanding** amicable or cordial relations between people; harmony of feeling. **of understanding** intelligent, capable of judging with knowledge.

understanding /ʌndəˈstandɪŋ/ *adjective.* ME.
[formed as prec. + -ING².]
1 a Having the faculty of understanding; having knowledge and (good) judgement; intelligent. ME. ▸†**b** Knowledgeable or possessing judgement *in* (a matter etc.). E17–M18.
2 Of the mind etc.: having intelligence; intellectual. Now *rare.* LME.
3 Of a person etc.: displaying sympathetic awareness or tolerance; of a forgiving nature. E20.
▪ **understandingly** *adverb* ME.

understate /ʌndəˈsteɪt/ *verb.* E19.
[from UNDER- + STATE *verb.*]
1 *verb trans.* State or express (esp. a case, argument, etc.) in unduly restrained terms; represent as being less than is actually the case. E19.
2 *verb intrans.* Make an understatement. E19.

> 🕮 **1** *Economist* These figures may well understate the truth.

▪ **understater** *noun* M20.

understated /ʌndəˈsteɪtɪd/ *adjective.* M20.
[from UNDER- + STATED.]
1 That understates the actual facts; stated or expressed in unduly restrained terms. M20.
2 Of clothes, a person's appearance, etc.: restrained in style or colour; not showy. M20.

> 🕮 **1** J. LE CARRÉ The . . room where every understated word had the authority of an engraved tablet. **2** *L.A. Style* Simple dressing—understated yet strong clothes in subdued colors.

▪ **understatedly** *adverb* L20.

understatement /ʌndəˈsteɪtm(ə)nt, ˈʌndə-/ *noun.* L18.
[from UNDER- + STATEMENT *noun.*]
1 The action of understating; an instance of this. L18.
2 The quality of being understated or restrained in style of dress or appearance. M20.

understeer /ˈʌndəstɪə/ *verb & noun.* L16.
[from UNDER- + STEER *verb*¹.]
▸ **A** *verb.* †**1** *verb trans.* Steer under (something). *rare.* Only in L16.
2 *verb intrans.* Of a motor vehicle: (have a tendency to) turn less sharply than intended by the driver. M20.
▸ **B** *noun.* A tendency in a motor vehicle to understeer. M20.

understood *verb pa. t. & pple* of UNDERSTAND.

understrapper /ˈʌndəstrapə/ *noun.* E18.
[from UNDER- + STRAPPER.]
An underling; a subordinate; an assistant. Cf. STRAPPER 4.
▪ **understrapping** *adjective* of a subordinate or inferior character or standing M18.

understudy /ˈʌndəstʌdi/ *verb & noun.* L19.
[from UNDER- + STUDY *verb.*]
▸ **A** *verb.* **1** *verb trans.* Study or prepare for (a role etc.) in order to be able to take the place of a principal actor or actress or cover for a person's absence if necessary. L19.
2 *verb trans.* Act as an understudy to (esp. a principal actor or actress). L19.
3 *verb intrans.* Act as an understudy. E20.

> 🕮 **2** *Daily Telegraph* An opening for a man or woman to understudy the present Manager.

▸ **B** *noun.* An actor or actress who studies a principal performer's part in order to be able to take it if required; a person who takes on another's role or duties in order to cover for the other's absence. L19.

undersubscribe /ʌndəsəbˈskrʌɪb/ *verb.* M16.
[from UNDER- + SUBSCRIBE.]
†**1** *verb intrans.* Subscribe to a document. *Scot.* M16–L18.
2 *verb trans.* Subscribe for less than the available quantity of (shares, places, a commodity, etc.). Chiefly as ***undersubscribed*** *ppl adjective.* L20.
▪ †**undersubscriber** *noun* (*Scot.*) a person subscribing to a document L17–L18.

undertake /ʌndəˈteɪk/ *verb.* Pa. t. **-took** /-ˈtʊk/; pa. pple **-taken** /-ˈteɪk(ə)n/. ME.
[from UNDER- + TAKE *verb*, superseding Old English *underfōn* (cf. FANG *verb*¹) and *underniman* (cf. NIM *verb*).]
▸ **I** *verb trans.* †**1 a** Take by stealth, entrap; seize on. ME–L15. ▸**b** Rebuke, chide. LME–L17.
†**2** Accept, receive. ME–L17. ▸**b** Receive into the mind; hear. ME–L16.
†**3** Understand. ME–E16.
4 Take on (an obligation, duty, task, etc.); commit oneself to perform; begin (an undertaking, enterprise, etc.). Freq. foll. by *to do.* ME. ▸**b** Give a formal promise or pledge *that*; guarantee, affirm; venture to assert. LME. ▸†**c** Be surety for. *rare* (Shakes.). Only in L16.
5 Take in charge; accept the duty of attending to or looking after. Now *rare.* ME. ▸†**b** Engage in combat with. L15–M17. ▸†**c** Take in hand to deal with (a person). Only in 17.
†**6** Assume (another's name, appearance, etc.). L16–E17.
7 Conduct the funeral of. *rare.* E20.

> 🕮 **4** E. J. HOWARD If one undertook marriage and fatherhood, one's first responsibilities lay there. J. I. M. STEWART I undertook to take Junkin to call on Talbert. *Literary Review* Although he was a carver rather than a sculptor, he did undertake . . commissions for funerary monuments. **b** *Times* The . . representatives undertook that there would be no further . . stoppages. **I dare undertake**, **I undertake** *arch.* I promise, I guarantee; I may venture to assert. **5** H. S. MERRIMAN It fell to Hilda's lot to undertake the Frenchman.

▸ **II** *verb intrans.* †**8** Enter on, or commit oneself to, an enterprise. LME–M17.
†**9** Give a pledge or promise; enter into a formal agreement. L15–L17.
10 Become surety, or make oneself answerable or responsible, *for* a person etc. *arch.* M16. ▸**b** Engage oneself in a promise *for.* E18.
11 Carry on the business of a funeral undertaker. *colloq. rare.* L19.

> 🕮 **10** J. ARBUTHNOT She . . undertook for her brother John's good behaviour.

▪ ˈ**undertaking** *ppl adjective* (now *rare* or *obsolete*) †(*a*) ready to undertake an enterprise, task, etc., esp. one involving some danger or risk; (*b*) prepared to act as publishers; (*c*) pledged, bound by promise: LME.

undertaker /ˈʌndəteɪkə; *in sense 2 also* -ˈteɪkə/ *noun.* LME.
[from prec. + -ER¹.]
†**1** A person who aids or assists someone; a helper. LME–M17.
2 A person who undertakes a task or enterprise. LME. ▸†**b** A person who takes up a challenge. *rare* (Shakes.). Only in E17.
3 *Hist.* **a** A person who undertook to hold crown lands in Ireland in the 16th and 17th cents. L16. ▸**b** A person who in the reigns of the first three Stuart kings of England undertook to procure particular legislation, esp. to obtain supplies from the House of Commons if the King would grant some concession. E17. ▸**c** Any of the Lowland Scots who attempted to colonize the Island of Lewis towards the end of the 16th cent. E19.
4 A person who undertakes to carry out work or business for another; a contractor. Formerly also, a collector of taxes. Now *rare.* E17.
5 †**a** A person who engages in the serious study of a subject or science. Only in 17. ▸**b** A person who embarks on, or invests in, a business venture. Now *rare.* E17. ▸†**c** A person who undertakes the preparation of a literary work. L17–E19. ▸†**d** A book publisher. L17–E19. ▸†**e** A producer of an opera or play; a manager, an impresario. E–M18.
†**6** A person who acts as surety *for* another. Formerly also *spec.*, a baptismal sponsor. E17–E18.
7 A person whose business is to make arrangements for funerals. L17.

undertaking /ʌndəˈteɪkɪŋ; *in sense 3* ˈʌn-/ *noun.* LME.
[from UNDERTAKE + -ING¹.]
1 †**a** Enterprise, energy. Only in LME. ▸**b** An action, task, etc., undertaken or begun; an enterprise. LME. ▸**c** The action of beginning or taking on an enterprise, task, etc. E17.
2 A pledge, a promise; a guarantee. LME.
3 The business or occupation of a funeral undertaker. M19.

> 🕮 **1b** B. MAGEE The radical reconstruction of society is a huge undertaking. **2** J. RATHBONE He . . nodded at my undertaking to follow his wishes in everything.

undertenant /ˈʌndətɛnənt/ *noun.* M16.
[from UNDER- + TENANT *noun.*]
A subtenant.
▪ **undertenancy** *noun* the status, right, or holding of an undertenant M18.

underthing /ˈʌndəθɪŋ/ *noun.* E17.
[from UNDER- + THING *noun*¹.]
†**1** A lower or inferior creature or thing. Only in E17.
2 In *pl.* Underclothes. *colloq.* M19.

underthink /ʌndəˈθɪŋk/ *verb. rare.* Pa. t. & pple **-thought** /-ˈθɔːt/. E17.
[from UNDER- + THINK *verb*².]
†**1** *verb trans.* Think too little of, underestimate. Only in E17.
†**2** *verb intrans.* Think insufficiently. Only in E18.
3 *verb trans.* Penetrate under by thinking. L19.

underthought /ˈʌndəθɔːt/ *noun.* E17.
[from UNDER- + THOUGHT *noun*¹.]
(An) underlying or subconscious thought.

underthought *verb pa. t. & pple* of UNDERTHINK.

undertone /ˈʌndətəʊn/ *noun & verb.* M18.
[from UNDER- + TONE *noun.*]
▸ **A** *noun.* **1** A low or subdued tone; a murmured or quiet utterance; a low sound. M18.
2 *fig.* **a** An underlying or implicit element or quality; an undercurrent of feeling. M19. ▸**b** A subdued or underlying tone of colour. L19. ▸**c** *STOCK EXCHANGE.* The general basis of exchange or market dealings in any stock or commodity. L19.

> 🕮 **1** C. CHAPLIN Men who worked hard in a darkened shed and spoke softly in undertones. **2a** C. CONRAN The flavour of the garlic . . in the background . . adds subtle undertones to the dish. G. WILL Brinkley's book has an understandable undertone of melancholy.

▸ **B** *verb trans.* Accompany as an undertone; express in an undertone. E19.

undertoned /ʌndəˈtəʊnd/ *adjective.* E19.
[from UNDER- + TONED.]
Defective in tone.

undertook *verb pa. t.* of UNDERTAKE.

undertow /ˈʌndətəʊ/ *noun.* E19.
[from UNDER- + TOW *noun*³.]
A current below the surface of the sea, moving in a contrary direction to that of the surface current.

> 🕮 *fig.*: J. WAINWRIGHT A meal in which the undertow of hatred made even surface politeness portentous.

undertread /ˈʌndətrɛd/ *noun.* M20.
[from UNDER- + TREAD *noun.*]
A layer of reinforcement in a rubber tyre.

undertread /ʌndəˈtrɛd/ *verb trans.* Now *arch. rare.* Infl. as TREAD *verb*; pa. t. usu. **-trod** /-ˈtrɒd/, pa. pple **-trodden** /-ˈtrɒd(ə)n/, **-trod**. E16.
[from UNDER- + TREAD *verb.*]
Tread under foot; subdue, subjugate.

undertreat /ʌndəˈtriːt/ *verb trans.* E18.
[from UNDER- + TREAT *verb.*]
Orig., treat with too little respect. Now, provide (a patient, disease, etc.) with insufficient medical treatment to effect a complete cure.
▪ **undertreatment** *noun* insufficient medical treatment to provide a patient, disease, etc., with a complete cure L20.

undertrod, **undertrodden** *verbs* see UNDERTREAD *verb.*

underuse /ʌndəˈjuːs/ *noun.* M20.
[from UNDER- + USE *noun.*]
Insufficient use of a facility, resources, etc.; use below the optimum level or frequency.

underuse /ʌndəˈjuːz/ *verb trans.* M20.
[from UNDER- + USE *verb.*]
Make insufficient use of (a facility, resources, etc.); use below the optimum level or frequency.

underutilize /ʌndəˈjuːtɪlʌɪz/ *verb trans.* Also **-ise**. M20.
[from UNDER- + UTILIZE.]
Underuse.
▪ ˌ**underutiliˈzation** *noun* M20.

underwater /ˈʌndəwɔːtə/ *noun.* Now chiefly *Scot.* M17.
[from UNDER- + WATER *noun.*]
1 Water below the surface of the ground. M17.
2 Water entering a vessel from beneath. *rare.* M17.

underwater /ʌndəˈwɔːtə, *attrib. adjective* ˈʌndəwɔːtə/ *adjective & adverb.* L16.
[Attrib. use of **under water** s.v. WATER *noun.*]
▸ **A** *adjective.* **1** Situated, happening, carried out, etc., under water. L16.
2 *spec.* Of a ship: situated below the water-line. L19.
▸ **B** *adverb.* = **under water** s.v. WATER *noun.* M20.

underway /ʌndəˈweɪ/ *adverb.* Also (earlier) **under way**. M18.
[Dutch *onderweg*, from *onder* under, in the course of + *weg* way.]
1 *NAUTICAL.* Of a vessel: in motion; having begun to move through the water. M18.

2 Of a process, project, activity, etc.: having been instigated, in progress, being done or carried out. Also, (of a person) having started doing something. **E19.**

📖 **2** *She* When divorce proceedings were already underway.

underweight /*as noun* ˈʌndəweɪt, *as adjective* ʌndəˈweɪt/ *noun & adjective.* **L17.**
[from UNDER- + WEIGHT *noun.*]
▸ **A** *noun.* **1** Insufficient weight; deficiency in weight. **L17.**
2 a An underweight person. **L19.** ▸**b** The condition of weighing less than is normal or desirable for one's height and build. **M20.**
▸ **B** *adjective.* Not sufficiently heavy, lacking in weight; *spec.* (of a person) weighing less than is normal or desirable for one's height and build. **L19.**

📖 *fig.*: *Times* With many institutional investors still underweight, the price is set to move up.

underwent *verb* see UNDERGO.

underwhelm /ʌndəˈwɛlm/ *verb trans. joc.* **M20.**
[from UNDER- + WHELM *verb*, after OVERWHELM *verb.*]
Leave unimpressed, arouse little or no interest in.

📖 *Dance* The Bolshoi's . . season left much of the dance press distinctly underwhelmed.

underwing /ˈʌndəwɪŋ/ *noun & adjective.* **M16.**
[from UNDER- + WING *noun.*]
▸ **A** *noun.* **1 a** A wing placed under, or partly covered by, another; *spec.* in ENTOMOLOGY, the hindwing of an insect. **M16.** ▸**b** The underside of a bird's wing. **M20.**
2 ENTOMOLOGY. Any of various noctuid moths with distinctively coloured hindwings, esp. of the genera *Noctua* and *Catocala*. Also more fully ***underwing moth***. Usu. with specifying word. **M18.**
2 ***orange underwing, red underwing, yellow underwing***, etc.
▸ **B** *attrib.* or as *adjective.* (Of a bird) situated beneath the wings; (of an aeroplane) located or occurring beneath the wing or wings. **L19.**

underwork /ˈʌndəwəːk/ *noun.* **E17.**
[from UNDER- + WORK *noun.*]
†**1** An undercurrent. *rare.* Only in **E17.**
2 A structure placed under or supporting something; a substructure. **E17.**
3 †**a** Work done at lower rates. *rare.* Only in **E17.** ▸**b** Subordinate or inferior work. **M17.** ▸**c** Underhand or secret work. *rare.* **E19.**

underwork /ʌndəˈwəːk/ *verb.* **E16.**
[from UNDER- + WORK *verb.*]
1 a *verb intrans.* Work secretly; take clandestine measures. Now *rare* or *obsolete.* **E16.** ▸†**b** *verb trans.* Work against secretly; seek to overthrow. **L16–M17.**
2 †**a** *verb trans.* Work on insufficiently; leave unfinished. Only in **L17.** ▸**b** *verb intrans.* Do too little work. **M19.** ▸**c** *verb trans.* Impose too little work on. **L19.**
†**3** *verb trans.* Work for lower wages than (another). *rare.* **L17–E18.**
■ **underworking** *noun* (an) action of a secret or unapparent nature **E17.**

underworld /ˈʌndəwəːld/ *noun.* **E17.**
[from UNDER- + WORLD *noun.*]
1 The sublunary or terrestrial world. Chiefly *poet.* **E17.**
2 a The mythical abode of the dead, imagined as being under the earth. **E17.** ▸**b** A region below the surface of the earth; a subterranean or underlying area. *rare.* **L19.**
3 The antipodes. **M19.**
4 A sphere or region (regarded as) lying below the ordinary one. Also, a lower, or the lowest, stratum of society etc.; *spec.* the community of criminals or of organized crime; this community's inhabitants collectively. **M19.**

📖 **4** F. T. BULLEN The begrimed . . toilers . . in the underworld of engines and boilers. *attrib.*: *San Diego* A playwright . . solicits underworld figures to back his latest play.

■ **underworldling** *noun* (*rare*) a member of an underworld **E20.** **underworldly** *adjective* belonging to or suggestive of the criminal underworld **L20.**

underwrite /ʌndəˈrʌɪt, *in branch I also* ˈʌndərʌɪt/ *verb.* Pa. t. **-wrote** /-ˈrəʊt/; pa. pple **-written** /-ˈrɪt(ə)n/. **LME.**
[from UNDER- + WRITE *verb*, after Latin *subscribere.*]
▸ **I 1** *verb trans.* **a** Write (words, figures, etc.) below something, esp. after other written matter. **LME.** ▸†**b** Write or subscribe (one's name) to a document etc. **M16–L18.**
2 †**a** *verb trans.* Subscribe (a document) with one's name. **M16–M18.** ▸**b** *verb trans.* Sign and accept liability under (a policy of esp. marine insurance); accept (liability) in this way. **E17.** ▸**c** *verb intrans.* Practise (marine) insurance. **L18.**
3 *verb trans.* Subscribe to (a decision, statement, etc.); agree to or confirm by signature. Also *fig.*, support or reinforce (an idea, quality, etc.); lend support to (a party etc.). **E17.**
4 *verb trans.* †**a** Guarantee to contribute (a certain sum of money etc.). **E17–E18.** ▸**b** Agree to take up in a new company or new issue (a certain number of shares) if not applied for by the public. **L19.** ▸**c** Support (a company etc.) by a guarantee of funds. Also *transf.*, guarantee by military or other power. **L19.**
5 *verb trans.* †**a** Undertake or guarantee in writing *to do.* **E–M17.** ▸**b** Guarantee or promise *that. rare.* **M19.**

📖 **3** *Listener* We must not always find ourselves underwriting the regimes of yesterday. B. GUEST Given a handsome sum . . which would underwrite the publishing venture.

▸ **II 6** *verb trans.* Describe insufficiently fully or completely. *rare.* **E18.**
7 *verb refl.* Fall short of (one's capabilities) in writing. *rare.* **M18.**
■ **underwriting** *verbal noun* (*a*) the action of the verb; (*b*) *spec.* the action or practice of (marine) insurance; the business of an underwriter: **L16.**

underwriter /ˈʌndərʌɪtə/ *noun.* **E17.**
[from prec. + -ER¹.]
†**1** A subscriber to, or shareholder in, a mercantile venture. Only in **E17.**
2 A person who underwrites an insurance policy; *spec.* a person who carries on an insurance business, esp. of shipping. **E17.**
†**3** A subordinate writer or clerk. *rare.* **M17–E18.**
4 A person who agrees to take up a certain number of company shares in the event of the issue being undersubscribed by the public. **L19.**

underwritten *verb pa. pple* of UNDERWRITE.

underwrote *verb pa. t.* of UNDERWRITE.

undescended /ʌndɪˈsɛndɪd/ *adjective.* **E18.**
[from UN-¹ + *descended* pa. pple of DESCEND.]
1 Of a person: not in the line of descent. Long *rare.* **E18.**
2 MEDICINE. Of a testis: that has not descended into the scrotum from its foetal position in the abdominal cavity. **L19.**
■ **undescendable** *adjective* (*rare*) unable to be descended; down which a person may not go: **L19.**

undescribable /ʌndɪˈskrʌɪbəb(ə)l/ *adjective.* **E18.**
[from UN-¹ + DESCRIBABLE.]
Indescribable; that cannot be described or is beyond description.
■ **undescribably** *adverb* **L18.**

undescribed /ʌndɪˈskrʌɪbd/ *adjective.* **L16.**
[from UN-¹ + *described* pa. pple of DESCRIBE.]
1 Not described; not portrayed in words; not given a detailed account of. **L16.**
2 Not marked off or delineated. *rare.* **M19.**

undeserve /ʌndɪˈzəːv/ *verb trans.* **LME.**
[from UN-¹ + DESERVE.]
Fail to deserve; be unworthy of having.
■ †**undeserver** *noun* **L16–E18.**

undeserved /ʌndɪˈzəːvd/ *adjective.* **LME.**
[from UN-¹ + DESERVED.]
†**1** Without having deserved it; undeserving. **LME–L16.**
2 Not deserved or merited (as a reward or punishment). **LME.**
■ **undeservedly** /-vɪdli/ *adverb* unworthily; unjustly; in an unmerited degree: **M16.** **undeservedness** /-vɪdnɪs/ *noun* the quality of being undeserved; lack of deservedness: **E17.**

undeserving /ʌndɪˈzəːvɪŋ/ *noun.* Now *rare.* **L16.**
[from UN-¹ + DESERVING *verbal noun.*]
Unworthiness; lack of desert or merit.

undeserving /ʌndɪˈzəːvɪŋ/ *adjective.* **M16.**
[from UN-¹ + DESERVING *adjective.*]
1 Not deserving reward, praise, etc.; unworthy. Also foll. by *of.* **M16.**
2 Not deserving punishment etc.; innocent. **L16.**
†**3** Undeserved, unmerited. *rare* (Shakes.). Only in **L16.**
■ **undeservingly** *adverb* **M16.**

undesigned /ʌndɪˈzʌɪnd/ *adjective.* **M17.**
[from UN-¹ + DESIGNED.]
Not designed or intended; unintentional.
■ **undesignedly** /-nɪdli/ *adverb* **L17.** **undesigning** *adjective* (*rare*) †(*a*) not designing or planning; (*b*) having no ulterior or selfish designs; free from designing or artful motives: **L17.**

undesirable /ʌndɪˈzʌɪərəb(ə)l/ *adjective & noun.* **M17.**
[from UN-¹ + DESIRABLE.]
▸ **A** *adjective.* Not to be desired; objectionable. **M17.**
undesirable discharge *US* discharge from military service under less than honourable conditions but without a court martial.
▸ **B** *noun.* An undesirable person or thing. **L19.**
■ **undesiraˈbility** *noun* **L19.** **undesirableness** *noun* **L17.** **undesirably** *adverb* **L19.**

undesired /ʌndɪˈzʌɪəd/ *adjective.* **L15.**
[from UN-¹ + DESIRED.]
†**1** Not asked or requested; uninvited. **L15–M17.**
2 Not desired or wished for; unsought. **L16.**
■ **undesiring** *adjective* not desiring; lacking desire: **L17.**

undesirous /ʌndɪˈzʌɪərəs/ *adjective.* **M17.**
[from UN-¹ + DESIROUS.]
Not desirous. Usu. foll. by *of.*

undestroyed /ʌndɪˈstrɔɪd/ *adjective.* **LME.**
[from UN-¹ + *destroyed* pa. pple of DESTROY.]
Not destroyed; intact; preserved; still in existence.
■ **undestroyable** *adjective* **LME.**

undetached /ʌndɪˈtatʃt/ *adjective.* **L18.**
[from UN-¹ + DETACHED.]
Not detached.
■ **undetachable** *adjective* **L19.**

undetected /ʌndɪˈtɛktɪd/ *adjective.* **L16.**
[from UN-¹ + *detected* pa. pple of DETECT.]
Not detected; undiscovered.

undeterminable /ʌndɪˈtəːmɪnəb(ə)l/ *adjective.* **L16.**
[from UN-¹ + DETERMINABLE *adjective.*]
†**1** Incapable of being terminated; unending. **L16–E17.**
2 = INDETERMINABLE 3, 3b. **L16.**
3 That cannot be limited in range etc.; = INDETERMINABLE 1. Long *rare.* **M17.**

undeterminate /ʌndɪˈtəːmɪnət/ *adjective.* Now *rare.* **E17.**
[from UN-¹ + DETERMINATE *adjective.*]
Indeterminate.

undetermined /ʌndɪˈtəːmɪnd/ *adjective.* **LME.**
[from UN-¹ + DETERMINED.]
1 Not authoritatively decided or settled; not brought to a decisive conclusion. **LME.** ▸**b** Not yet fixed; still subject to alteration or uncertainty. **M17.**
2 Doubtful; not certainly known or identified. **L16.**
3 Of indefinite meaning or application. **L16.**
4 Not restrained within limits. **E17.**
5 Not determined or fixed in respect of character, action, etc. **L17.**
6 Undecided, irresolute. **E18.**

📖 **2** *Journal of Musicology* Its probable assembly from two . . sketchbooks . . at an undetermined time. **4** SHELLEY The mountains are wide and wild, and the whole scenery broad and undetermined. **5** ADDISON False Modesty . . is only a general undetermined Instinct. **6** G. BORROW We were undetermined . . with respect to where we should go.

undeveloped /ʌndɪˈvɛləpt/ *adjective.* **M18.**
[from UN-¹ + DEVELOPED.]
That has not developed or been developed.

undeviated /ʌnˈdiːvɪeɪtɪd/ *adjective. rare.* **L19.**
[from UN-¹ + *deviated* pa. pple of DEVIATE *verb.*]
Not deviated or deviant.

undeviating /ʌnˈdiːvɪeɪtɪŋ/ *adjective.* **M18.**
[from UN-¹ + *deviating* pres. pple of DEVIATE *verb.*]
Showing no deviation; maintaining the same course; steady, constant.
■ **undeviatingly** *adverb* **E19.**

undevout /ʌndɪˈvaʊt/ *adjective.* **LME.**
[from UN-¹ + DEVOUT *adjective.*]
Not devout, *esp.* lacking in religious spirit.
■ **undevoutly** *adverb* **ME.**

undid *verb pa. t.* of UNDO.

undies /ˈʌndɪz/ *noun pl. colloq.* **E20.**
[Abbreviation of *underclothes* or *-garments*, prob. after *frillies*.]
Articles of underwear, esp. of a girl or woman.

undifferentiated /ˌʌndɪfəˈrɛnʃɪeɪtɪd/ *adjective.* **M19.**
[from UN-¹ + *differentiated* pa. pple of DIFFERENTIATE *verb.*]
Not differentiated or distinguished; without distinguishing features; amorphous.

📖 G. GREENE They were . . undifferentiated like birds of the same plumage.

undigested /ʌndɪˈdʒɛstɪd, -dʌɪ-/ *adjective.* **E16.**
[from UN-¹ + *disgested* pa. pple of DIGEST *verb.*]
1 Not brought to a mature or proper condition by natural physical change. Now *rare* or *obsolete.* **E16.**
2 Of food etc.: not digested in the stomach. **L16.**
3 Of information, ideas, etc.: not properly arranged or considered; chaotic, confused. **L16.**
■ **undigestible** *adjective* (*rare*) indigestible **E17.**

undight /ʌnˈdʌɪt/ *verb trans.* Pa. pple **undight**. **LME.**
[from UN-² + DIGHT.]
1 Divest of clothing, armour, etc.; unclothe, strip, disarray. (Foll. by *of.*) Now only (*arch.* or *dial.*) as ***undight ppl adjective.*** **LME.**
†**2** Unfasten, undo; unclench, open. **L16–M17.**

undignified /ʌnˈdɪgnɪfʌɪd/ *adjective.* **L17.**
[from UN-¹ + DIGNIFIED.]
†**1** Of clergy: not ranking as a dignitary. **L17–M19.**
2 Not dignified *by* or *with* something; undistinguished. **E18.**
3 Lacking in dignity of manner etc. **L18.**

📖 **3** P. BROWN A man unduly preoccupied with his body was an undignified sight.

■ **undignifiedly** *adverb* **M19.**

undignify /ʌnˈdɪgnɪfʌɪ/ *verb trans.* **E18.**
[from UN-² + DIGNIFY.]
Make undignified.

undiluted /ʌndʌɪˈluːtɪd/ *adjective.* M17.
[from UN-[1] + *diluted* pa. pple of DILUTE *verb.*]
Not diluted or weakened.

> JONATHAN ROSS He drank a very large undiluted whisky. *Guardian* He had demonstrated . . undiluted contempt for green politics.

■ **undilutedly** *adverb* L20.

undiminished /ʌndɪˈmɪnɪʃt/ *adjective.* L16.
[from UN-[1] + *diminished* pa. pple of DIMINISH.]
Not diminished, reduced, or lessened.

> S. WEINTRAUB Her interest in masculine good looks remained undiminished.

■ **undiminishable** *adjective* M17. **undiminishableness** *noun* M17. **undiminishing** *adjective* not diminishing L19.

undine /ˈʌndiːn/ *noun.* Also **ondine** /ˈɒndiːn/. E19.
[mod. Latin *undina*, *undena* from Latin *unda* wave: see -INE[1].]
1 A female water-spirit, a nymph. E19.
2 OPHTHALMOLOGY. A small bulbous flask with a tapered spout, used to irrigate the eye. E20.
■ **un'dinal** *adjective* of, pertaining to, or characteristic of undines (water-sprites) L19.

Unding /ˈʊndɪŋ/ *noun.* M20.
[German = absurdity.]
A non-existent thing, a vague abstraction, a concept having no properties.

Undinism /ˈʌndiːnɪz(ə)m/ *noun.* E20.
[from UNDINE + -ISM.]
PSYCHOLOGY. The arousal of sexual thoughts by water, esp. urine and urination; urolagnia.

undiplomatic /ˌʌndɪpləˈmatɪk/ *adjective.* M19.
[from UN-[1] + DIPLOMATIC *adjective.*]
Not diplomatic; *spec.* tactless, unsubtle.
■ **undiplomatically** *adverb* M20.

undipped /ʌnˈdɪpt/ *adjective.* Also †**-dipt**. M17.
[from UN-[1] + *dipped* pa. pple of DIP *verb.*]
1 Not dipped in a liquid etc. M17. ▸**b** *spec.* Unbaptized. L17.
2 Of (the beams of) a vehicle's headlights: not lowered. M20.

undirected /ʌndɪˈrɛktɪd, -dʌɪ-/ *adjective.* L16.
[from UN-[1] + *directed* pa. pple of DIRECT *verb.*]
Not directed, aimed, or guided.

> A. N. WILSON He had . . an undirected, if intense, desire to write.

†**undiscernable** *adjective* see UNDISCERNIBLE.

undiscerned /ʌndɪˈsəːnd/ *adjective.* E16.
[from UN-[1] + *discerned* pa. pple of DISCERN.]
Not discerned.
■ **undiscernedly** *adverb* M17.

undiscernible /ʌndɪˈsəːnɪb(ə)l/ *adjective.* Also (earlier) †**-able**. L16.
[from UN-[1] + DISCERNIBLE.]
= INDISCERNIBLE *adjective*
■ **undiscernibleness** *noun* M17. **undiscernibly** *adverb* L16.

undiscerning /ʌndɪˈsəːnɪŋ/ *adjective & noun.* L16.
[from UN-[1] + DISCERNING.]
▶ **A** *adjective.* Not discerning, lacking discernment; *spec.* lacking good judgement, insight, or taste. L16.
▶ **B** *noun.* Lack of discernment. Now *rare.* E18.
■ **undiscerningly** *adverb* E18.

undischarged /ʌndɪsˈtʃɑːdʒd/ *adjective.* L16.
[from UN-[1] + *discharged* pa. pple of DISCHARGE *verb.*]
Esp. of a debt or a bankrupt: not discharged.
■ **undischargeable** *adjective* (*rare*) L16.

undisciplined /ʌnˈdɪsɪplɪnd/ *adjective.* LME.
[from UN-[1] + *disciplined* pa. pple of DISCIPLINE *verb.*]
Not subjected or submissive to discipline, lacking discipline, untrained.
■ **undisciplinable** *adjective* unable to be disciplined M17. **undiscipline** *noun* indiscipline E19. **undisciplinedness** *noun* M17.

undisclosed /ʌndɪsˈkləʊzd/ *adjective.* L16.
[from UN-[1] + DISCLOSED.]
1 Not revealed or made known; of concealed identity, nature, or amount. L16.
2 Of a young bird etc.: unhatched. Now *rare* or *obsolete.* L16.

> **1** *Independent* The family . . was awarded undisclosed damages at the High Court.

undiscovered /ʌndɪˈskʌvəd/ *adjective.* M16.
[from UN-[1] + *discovered* pa. pple of DISCOVER.]
Not discovered, found, or revealed; unobserved, undetected.

> SHAKES. *Haml.* The undiscover'd country, from whose bourn No traveller returns. DEFOE A little cape which kept us perfectly undiscovered.

■ **undiscoverable** *adjective* M17. **undiscoverableness** *noun* (*rare*) M17. **undiscoverably** *adverb* M17.

†**undiscreet** *adjective.* ME–L17.
[from UN-[1] + DISCREET.]
= INDISCREET *adjective*[1].
■ †**undiscreetly** *adverb* LME–E18. †**undiscreetness** *noun* M16–M17.

undiscriminated /ʌndɪˈskrɪmɪneɪtɪd/ *adjective.* M18.
[from UN-[1] + *discriminated* pa. pple of DISCRIMINATE *verb.*]
Not discriminated between or *against.*

undiscriminating /ʌndɪˈskrɪmɪneɪtɪŋ/ *adjective.* L18.
[from UN-[1] + DISCRIMINATING.]
Not discriminating; not perceiving or making distinctions with sensitivity, lacking judgement, undiscerning.
■ **undiscriminatingly** *adverb* L19. **undiscriminatingness** *noun* M19.

undiscussed /ʌndɪˈskʌst/ *adjective.* ME.
[from UN-[1] + *discussed* pa. pple of DISCUSS *verb.*]
Not discussed.
■ **undiscussable** *adjective* M19.

undisguise /ʌndɪsˈɡʌɪz/ *noun.* E19.
[from UN-[1] + DISGUISE *noun.*]
Lack of disguise; openness, candour.

undisguise /ʌndɪsˈɡʌɪz/ *verb trans.* M17.
[from UN-[2] + DISGUISE *verb.*]
Strip of or free from a disguise.

undisguised /ʌndɪsˈɡʌɪzd/ *adjective.* L15.
[from UN-[1] + *disguised* pa. pple of DISGUISE *verb.*]
Not disguised or concealed; open; candid.

> I. MCEWAN The drinkers . . watched him with undisguised curiosity.

■ **undisguisable** *adjective* L17. **undisguisedly** /-zɪdli/ *adverb* E17. **undisguisedness** *noun* E19.

undismayed /ʌndɪsˈmeɪd/ *adjective.* E17.
[from UN-[1] + *dismayed* pa. pple of DISMAY *verb.*]
Not dismayed or discouraged.
■ **undismayable** *adjective* L16.

undispatched /ʌndɪˈspatʃt/ *adjective.* L16.
[from UN-[1] + *dispatched* pa. pple of DISPATCH *verb.*]
Not dispatched.
■ **undispatchable** *adjective* M19.

undispelled /ʌndɪˈspɛld/ *adjective.* M19.
[from UN-[1] + *dispelled* pa. pple of DISPEL.]
Not dispelled.
■ **undispellable** *adjective* M19.

undispensed /ʌndɪˈspɛnst/ *adjective.* ME.
[from UN-[1] + *dispensed* pa. pple of DISPENSE *verb.*]
Not dispensed; *spec.* not absolved or released by dispensation.
■ **undispensable** *adjective* (long *rare*) indispensable M16.

†**undispose** *verb trans.* LME–L18.
[from UN-[1] + DISPOSE *verb.*]
Indispose.

undisposed /ʌndɪˈspəʊzd/ *adjective.* LME.
[from UN-[1] + DISPOSED.]
1 = INDISPOSED. LME.
2 a Not assigned or put to a purpose. L15. ▸**b** Not disposed *of.* E17.

undisputed /ʌndɪˈspjuːtɪd/ *adjective.* L16.
[from UN-[1] + *disputed* pa. pple of DISPUTE *verb.*]
1 Not disputed or argued *with. rare.* L16.
2 Not disputed or called into question. E17.

> **2** B. CHATWIN The Rabbi Loew had been the undisputed leader of Prague Jewry.

■ **undisputable** *adjective* (now *rare*) indisputable L16. **undisputably** *adverb* (now *rare*) E18. **undisputedly** *adverb* L18.

undissembled /ʌndɪˈsɛmb(ə)ld/ *adjective.* M17.
[from UN-[1] + *dissembled* pa. pple of DISSEMBLE *verb*[1].]
1 Not feigned or pretended; genuine. M17.
2 Not disguised or concealed; evident. L17.
■ **undissembling** *adjective* not dissembling E17. **undissemblingly** *adverb* L16.

undissolved /ʌndɪˈzɒlvd/ *adjective.* M16.
[from UN-[1] + *dissolved* pa. pple of DISSOLVE *verb.*]
Not dissolved.
■ **undissolvable** *adjective* E17. **undissolving** *adjective* not dissolving E18.

undistinct /ʌndɪˈstɪŋkt/ *adjective.* LME.
[from UN-[1] + DISTINCT *adjective.*]
1 = INDISTINCT *adjective* 1. LME.
†**2** = INDISTINCT *adjective* 2. M16–M17.
■ †**undistinctly** *adverb* M16–E18.

undistinctive /ʌndɪˈstɪŋktɪv/ *adjective.* M19.
[from UN-[1] + DISTINCTIVE *adjective.*]
Not distinctive.

undistinguishable /ʌndɪˈstɪŋɡwɪʃəb(ə)l/ *adjective.* L16.
[from UN-[1] + DISTINGUISHABLE.]
1 = INDISTINGUISHABLE 2. L16.
2 = INDISTINGUISHABLE 1. L17.
■ **undistinguishableness** *noun* E18. **undistinguishably** *adverb* L17.

undistinguished /ʌndɪˈstɪŋɡwɪʃt/ *adjective.* L16.
[from UN-[1] + *distinguished* pa. pple of DISTINGUISH.]
1 Not separated or kept distinct. L16. ▸**b** In which no distinction is or can be made. Now *rare.* E17. ▸**c** Not distinguished *from* or *by* something. E17.
2 a Indistinct, confused. Now *rare.* L16. ▸**b** Not clearly perceived or discerned. E19.
3 Lacking distinction, not noted or elevated above others, mediocre. E17.

> **3** I. MURDOCH His undistinguished career as a schoolmaster. D. LODGE An undistinguished modern building situated . . next to a petrol station.

undistinguishing /ʌndɪˈstɪŋɡwɪʃɪŋ/ *adjective.* L16.
[from UN-[1] + *distinguishing* pres. pple of DISTINGUISH.]
Making no distinction; undiscriminating, lacking judgement; indiscriminate.
■ **undistinguishingly** *adverb* M17.

undistracted /ʌndɪˈstraktɪd/ *adjective.* M17.
[from UN-[1] + DISTRACTED.]
1 Not diverted or interrupted by other occupations, interests, etc.; undisturbed. M17.
2 Not drawn aside or away *from* something. M19.
■ **undistractedly** *adverb* M17. **undistractedness** *noun* M17.

undistributed /ʌndɪˈstrɪbjuːtɪd/ *adjective.* L15.
[from UN-[1] + *distributed* pa. pple of DISTRIBUTE.]
Not distributed.
undistributed middle LOGIC a fallacy resulting from the failure of the middle term of a syllogism to refer to all the members of a class in at least one premiss.

undisturbed /ʌndɪˈstəːbd/ *adjective.* E17.
[from UN-[1] + DISTURBED.]
Not disturbed, interfered with, or anxious; tranquil, quiet.
■ **undisturbable** *adjective* L16. **undisturbedly** /-bɪdli/ *adverb* M17. **undisturbedness** *noun* M17. **undisturbing** *adjective* not causing disturbance E17.

undiverted /ʌndʌɪˈvəːtɪd/ *adjective.* M17.
[from UN-[1] + *diverted* pa. pple of DIVERT.]
1 Not turned aside. M17.
2 Not entertained or amused. L18.
■ **undivertible** *adjective* unable to be diverted M19. **undivertibly** *adverb* M19. **undiverting** *adjective* not diverting or entertaining L17.

undivided /ʌndɪˈvʌɪdɪd/ *adjective.* LME.
[from UN-[1] + *divided* pa. pple of DIVIDE *verb.*]
1 Not divided or broken into parts. LME.
2 Not separated or parted; not divided by disagreement etc. LME.
3 a Not divided between persons, not shared, not held jointly or in common. M16. ▸**b** Not shared by others; confined to one person. M19.
4 Not divided between different objects; concentrated, whole, entire. M18.

> **4** E. K. KANE The object which seemed to usurp the undivided attention of our party.

■ **undividable** *adjective* (now *rare*) indivisible M16. **undividably** *adverb* (*rare*) E17. **undividedly** *adverb* M16. **undividedness** *noun* L19.

undivine /ʌndɪˈvʌɪn/ *adjective.* L17.
[from UN-[1] + DIVINE *adjective.*]
Not divine.
■ **undivinely** *adverb* E17.

undivined /ʌndɪˈvʌɪnd/ *adjective.* M19.
[from UN-[1] + *divined* pa. pple of DIVINE *verb.*]
Not divined or guessed at.
■ **undivinable** *adjective* E17.

undivisible /ʌndɪˈvɪzɪb(ə)l/ *adjective.* LME.
[from UN-[1] + DIVISIBLE.]
Indivisible.

undivorced /ʌndɪˈvɔːst/ *adjective.* M18.
[from UN-[1] + *divorced* pa. pple of DIVORCE *verb.*]
Not divorced.
■ **undivorceable** *adjective* E19.

undo /ʌnˈduː/ *verb.* Pres. indic. 3 sing. **undoes** /ʌnˈdʌz/; pa. t. **undid** /ʌnˈdɪd/; pa. pple **undone** /ʌnˈdʌn/.
[Old English *undōn* = Old Frisian *un(d)dua*, Middle Dutch *ontdoen*, Old High German *intuon*: see UN-[2], DO *verb.*]
▶ **I 1** *verb trans.* Loosen the fastenings of (a door, garment, package, etc.) so as to open or remove. OE.
†**2** *verb trans.* Open (the mouth or eyes). OE–LME.
3 *verb trans.* Loosen or unfasten (a button, knot, catch, etc.) by untying or by releasing from a fixed position; unfix. OE. ▸**b** Unfasten the clothing of (a person). M17.
†**4** *verb trans.* Release or free from a bond, bandage, covering, etc.; unbind. OE–E16.
†**5** *verb intrans.* Come apart; open; become unfastened. OE–M16.
†**6** *verb trans.* **a** Remove, take away; detach, cut off. ME–E16. ▸**b** Cut up (an animal). ME–L15. ▸**c** Cut open; open with a knife. LME–L17.

1 L. PARR She undid the gate, and held it half open. I. MURDOCH Marcus . . undid Patrick's pyjama jacket and started to pull it off. 3 W. MORRIS She . . turned the box round . . undid The clasp, and fearfully raised up the lid. E. BOWEN Lois undid the top buttons of her mackintosh.

▶ **II 7** *verb trans.* Reduce to the condition of not having happened or been done; reverse the doing of so as to restore the original form or condition; annul, cancel, rescind. OE.

8 a *verb trans.* Destroy, do away with; harm or injure seriously. OE. ▸**b** Ruin the prospects, reputation, or morals of; cause the downfall of. LME.

9 *verb trans.* Explain, interpret, expound. Now *rare*. ME.

7 GEO. ELIOT She liked to insist that work done without her orders should be undone from beginning to end. A. J. P. TAYLOR An attempt to undo the trades disputes act of 1927. C. BRAYFIELD What's been done can't be undone now. **8a** T. S. ELIOT I had not thought death had undone so many. **b** W. LEWIS Some men are undone by women and some by wine.

undoable /ʌnˈduːəb(ə)l/ *adjective*. M19.
[from UN-¹ + DOABLE.]
Unable to be done, impracticable, impossible.

undock /ʌnˈdɒk/ *verb*. M18.
[from UN-² + DOCK *verb*².]
1 *verb trans.* Take (a ship) out of a dock; *spec.* launch. M18.
2 *verb trans. & intrans.* Separate (a spacecraft) from another in space. M20.

undocked /ʌnˈdɒkt/ *adjective*. L17.
[from UN-¹ + *docked* pa. pple of DOCK *verb*¹.]
Not docked or reduced; without the hair, tail, etc., having been cut short.

undoctor /ʌnˈdɒktə/ *verb trans. rare*. L16.
[from UN-² + DOCTOR *verb*.]
Remove the status of doctor from.

undoctored /ʌnˈdɒktəd/ *adjective*. E19.
[from UN-¹ + *doctored* pa. pple of DOCTOR *verb*.]
Not doctored or altered. Also, lacking the status of doctor.

undocumented /ʌnˈdɒkjʊmɛntɪd/ *adjective*. L19.
[from UN-¹ + *documented* pa. pple of DOCUMENT *verb*.]
That has not been documented; not proved by or recorded in documents; *US* not having the appropriate legal document or licence.

undoer /ʌnˈduːə/ *noun*¹. LME.
[from UNDO + -ER¹.]
A person who or thing which undoes something or someone; *esp.* a destroyer, a ruiner.

undoer /ʌnˈduːə/ *noun*². *rare*. E17.
[from UN-¹ + DOER.]
A person who does not act or do something.

undoes *verb* see UNDO.

undogmatic /ʌndɒgˈmatɪk/ *adjective*. M19.
[from UN-¹ + DOGMATIC *adjective*.]
Not dogmatic.
■ **undogmatical** *adjective* undogmatic M19. **undogmatically** *adverb* E20. **undogmaticism** *noun* lack of dogma L19.

undoing /ʌnˈduːɪŋ/ *noun*. ME.
[from UNDO + -ING¹.]
1 Exposition, interpretation. Now *rare*. ME.
2 The action of opening, unfastening, or loosening something. LME.
3 The action of destroying, ruining, or causing the downfall of a person or thing; the state or fact of being destroyed etc.; ruin, destruction, downfall; an instance of this. Freq. with *possess*. LME.
4 A cause of ruin, destruction, or downfall. LME.
5 The action of reversing or annulling something done, decided, etc. LME. ▸**b** PSYCHOANALYSIS. The obsessive repetition of a ritualistic action as if to undo or allay guilt arising from some previous event, action, or attitude, or to signify that it never happened, usu. a symptom of obsessional neurosis. E20.

3 THACKERAY He was not the first that has . . brought about his own undoing. 4 E. JOHNSON The financial imprudence that had been his father's undoing.

undoing /ʌnˈduːɪŋ/ *adjective*. Now *rare*. M17.
[from UNDO *verb* + -ING².]
Ruinous, destructive.

undomestic /ʌndəˈmɛstɪk/ *adjective*. M18.
[from UN-¹ + DOMESTIC *adjective*.]
1 Not fond of or pertaining to home life or duties. M18.
2 Unlike a home, lacking the character of a home. L18.

undomesticate /ʌndəˈmɛstɪkeɪt/ *verb trans*. M18.
[from UN-² + DOMESTICATE *verb*.]
Make undomestic.

undomesticated /ʌndəˈmɛstɪkeɪtɪd/ *adjective*. M19.
[from UN-¹ + *domesticated* pa. pple of DOMESTICATE *verb*.]
Not domesticated.

undone /ʌnˈdʌn/ *adjective*¹. ME.
[from UN-¹ + DONE *ppl adjective*.]
Not done; unaccomplished, uneffected; incomplete.

D. FRANCIS Undone work still sitting reproachfully in heaps.

undone /ʌnˈdʌn/ *adjective*². ME.
[pa. pple of UNDO.]
1 Ruined, destroyed; reversed, annulled. ME.
2 Unfastened, untied, loosened. ME.

1 P. A. MOTTEUX He has spoiled me. I am undone.

■ **undoneness** *noun* M19.

undone *verb* pa. pple of UNDO.

undoubted /ʌnˈdaʊtɪd/ *adjective*. LME.
[from UN-¹ + *doubted* pa. pple of DOUBT *verb*.]
Not doubted, not regarded as doubtful; definite, indubitable.

J. W. CLARK Relics of undoubted authenticity. C. WARWICK His undoubted success and rapidly spreading fame.

■ **undoubtable** *adjective* that cannot be doubted, indubitable LME.

undoubtedly /ʌnˈdaʊtɪdli/ *adverb*. LME.
[from prec. + -LY².]
1 Without or beyond any doubt; indubitably, certainly, definitely. LME.
†**2** So as to remove or reject all doubt; positively, decidedly. E16–M17.

1 G. P. R. JAMES He was . . undoubtedly a man of much courage. *Oxford Today* Undoubtedly financial constraints . . have played a role.

undoubtful /ʌnˈdaʊtfʊl, -f(ə)l/ *adjective*. LME.
[from UN-¹ + DOUBTFUL.]
†**1** Not mixed with or qualified by doubt; firm, sure. LME–E17.
2 Not doubted, undoubted, certain. M16.
3 Not feeling doubt; certain (*of* something). E17.
■ **undoubtfully** *adverb* (*rare*) E17. **undoubtfulness** *noun* (*rare*) E17.

undoubting /ʌnˈdaʊtɪŋ/ *adjective*. LME.
[from UN-¹ + DOUBTING.]
†**1** Undoubted. *Scot.* LME–M16.
2 Having no doubts, confident. M18.
■ **undoubtingly** *adverb* LME. **undoubtingness** *noun* (*rare*) M19.

UNDP *abbreviation*.
United Nations Development Programme.

undrained /ʌnˈdreɪnd/ *adjective*. L16.
[from UN-¹ + *drained* pa. pple of DRAIN *verb*.]
Not drained, exhausted, or emptied of water.
■ **undrainable** *adjective* (*a*) unable to be drained dry, inexhaustible; (*b*) unable to be drained or emptied of water: E17.

undramatic /ʌndrəˈmatɪk/ *adjective*. M18.
[from UN-¹ + DRAMATIC.]
Not in the form of or suitable for drama; not dramatic; unimpressive, moderate, understated.
■ **undramatical** *adjective* (*rare*) = UNDRAMATIC E19. **undramatically** *adverb* E19.

undrape /ʌnˈdreɪp/ *verb trans*. M19.
[from UN-² + DRAPE *verb*.]
Remove the drapery or clothing from, uncover.

undraped /ʌnˈdreɪpt/ *adjective*. E19.
[from UN-¹ + *draped* pa. pple of DRAPE *verb*.]
Not draped, not covered with drapery; (esp. in ART) nude, naked.

A. B. JAMESON Eve . . is the only undraped figure . . allowable in sacred art.

undraperied /ʌnˈdreɪp(ə)rɪd/ *adjective*. E19.
[from UN-¹ + *draperied* pa. pple of DRAPERY *verb*.]
Not covered with drapery.

undraw /ʌnˈdrɔː/ *verb*. Pa. t. **undrew** /ʌnˈdruː/; pa. pple **undrawn** /ʌnˈdrɔːn/. LME.
[from UN-² + DRAW *verb*.]
†**1** *verb trans.* Draw out, withdraw. Only in LME.
2 *verb trans.* Draw back (esp. a curtain); unfasten by pulling. L17.
3 *verb intrans.* Move back on being pulled. L18.

undrawn /ʌnˈdrɔːn/ *adjective*¹. E16.
[from UN-¹ + DRAWN.]
†**1** That has never drawn a plough. Only in E16.
2 Not drawn; *esp.* (of curtains etc.) open, not drawn across the window. M16.
■ **undrawable** *adjective* M19.

undrawn /ʌnˈdrɔːn/ *adjective*². M18.
[pa. pple of UNDRAW.]
Drawn back, withdrawn.

undrawn *verb* pa. pple of UNDRAW.

undreamed /ʌnˈdriːmd, -ˈdrɛmt/ *adjective*. Also **undreamt** /ʌnˈdrɛmt/. E17.
[from UN-¹ + *dreamed* pa. pple of DREAM *verb*.]
Not even dreamed of, not imagined or thought of; completely unexpected but (esp.) very pleasing. Freq. foll. by *of*.

T. MOORE A light Leading to undreamt happiness. *Q* As '80s technology zoomed ahead . . the camera . . discovered undreamed-of abilities.

■ **undreamable** *adjective* E20.

undress /ʌnˈdrɛs, *esp. as adjective* ˈʌndrɛs/ *noun & adjective*. L17.
[from UN-¹ + DRESS *noun*.]
▶ **A** *noun*. Partial or incomplete dress; (a set of) casual or informal clothing; the state of being casually or only partially dressed or of being naked; MILITARY (a set of) uniform or clothing worn on ordinary rather than ceremonial occasions (opp. ***full dress***). L17.

A. MAUPIN Sun-worshippers in varying stages of undress. *Oxford Times* I thought . . that Folies Bergeres undress had come to the Tower Ballroom. *fig.*: G. DAWSON History shows us people in full dress, biography shows them in undress.

▶ **B** *adjective*. Chiefly MILITARY. Constituting or pertaining to an undress, worn when in undress. L18.

undress /ʌnˈdrɛs/ *verb*. L15.
[from UN-² + DRESS *verb*.]
†**1** Undo (esp. the hair). L15–M17.
2 *verb trans.* Remove the clothes from (a person, oneself). L16.
3 *verb intrans.* Take off one's clothes. E17. ▸**b** *verb trans.* Dress scantily or lightly. Chiefly *joc.* E19.
4 *verb trans.* Remove the dressing from (a wound). M17.

2 R. BUCHANAN We must undress the child at once and put him to bed. *fig.*: J. LE CARRÉ She felt the policemen's eyes undress her.

■ **undressable** *adjective* (esp. of a doll) that can be undressed L20. **undresser** *noun* (*rare*) E17.

undressed /ʌnˈdrɛst/ *adjective*. LME.
[from UN-¹ + *dressed* pa. pple of DRESS *verb*.]
1 That has not been dressed; (of the hair) not combed and styled; (of cloth, leather, stone, etc.) not treated or prepared for use; (of food) without a dressing, plain. LME.
2 Not or no longer clothed, partly or wholly naked. E17. ▸**b** Not properly or fully dressed, wearing undress or informal dress. E17. ▸**c** *transf.* Not requiring formal or full dress. L18.

2 C. BERNHEIMER Despite her being partly undressed she seems neither vulnerable nor deliberately provocative. D. STEEL He walked into the bathroom and got undressed.

undrew *verb pa. t.* of UNDRAW.

undrinkable /ʌnˈdrɪŋkəb(ə)l/ *adjective*. E17.
[from UN-¹ + DRINKABLE.]
Unable to be drunk, not suitable for drinking.
■ **undrinkably** *adverb* L19.

UNDRO *abbreviation*.
United Nations Disaster Relief Office.

und so weiter /ʊnt zo ˈvaɪtər/ *adverbial phr.* L19.
[German.]
And so forth.

undub /ʌnˈdʌb/ *verb trans. slang*. Now *rare* or *obsolete*. Infl. **-bb-**. M18.
[from UN-² + DUB *verb*³.]
Unlock, unfasten, or open (a door etc.).

undubbed /ʌnˈdʌbd/ *adjective*¹. E17.
[from UN-¹ + *dubbed* pa. pple of DUB *verb*¹.]
1 Not invested with a dignity or title. E17.
2 Of a cock: not having the comb and wattles removed. M19.

undubbed /ʌnˈdʌbd/ *adjective*². M20.
[from UN-¹ + *dubbed* pa. pple of DUB *verb*⁵.]
Of a film, recording, etc.: not dubbed.

undubitable /ʌnˈdjuːbɪtəb(ə)l/ *adjective*. Now *rare*. M17.
[from UN-¹ + DUBITABLE.]
Indubitable.
■ **undubitably** *adverb* M17. **undubitate** *adjective* (long *arch.*) undoubted, indubitable L15.

undue /ʌnˈdjuː/ *adjective*. LME.
[from UN-¹ + DUE *adjective*, after Old & mod. French *indu*.]
1 Not owing or payable. Now *rare*. LME.
2 That ought not to be or to be done; inappropriate, unsuitable, improper; unrightful, unjustifiable. LME.
3 Going beyond what is warranted or natural; excessive, disproportionate. LME.

2 B. JOWETT The undue awarding of honours is the ruin of states. **undue influence** LAW: whereby a person enters into a transaction without exercising an independent judgement or under pressure. 3 *Insight* Weaknesses in this thesis have . . been noted, such as his undue emphasis on frontier settlement.

undulant /ˈʌndjʊlənt/ *adjective*. M19.
[from UNDULATE *verb*, perh. after French *ondulant*: see -ANT[1].]
Rising and falling like waves, undulating, fluctuating.
undulant fever MEDICINE brucellosis in humans, which can lead to chronic intermittent fever and chiefly affects the reticuloendothelial system.
■ **undulancy** *noun* (*rare*) wavelike motion E20.

undular /ˈʌndjʊlə/ *adjective*. M18.
[formed as prec.: see -AR[1].]
†**1** Wavy, undulating. M18–E19.
2 Designating a type of hydraulic jump consisting of a number of waves of diminishing size trailing downstream, with little difference in the water-levels on either side of them. M20.

undulate /ˈʌndjʊlət/ *adjective*. M17.
[formed as next: see -ATE[2].]
Chiefly BOTANY & ZOOLOGY. Having a wavy surface or edge.
■ **undulately** *adverb* (*rare*) L19.

undulate /ˈʌndjʊleɪt/ *verb*. M17.
[Prob. from late Latin *undulatus* waved, from *undula* from Latin *unda* wave: see -ULE, -ATE[3].]
1 *verb intrans.* Have a wavelike motion, move with a smooth regular rising and falling; fluctuate; have a wavy or rippling form or outline. M17.
2 *verb trans.* Cause to move like waves, give a smooth regular rising and falling motion to; cause to fluctuate; give a wavy or rippling form or outline to. M17.

> 🕮 **1** *New York Times* A couple of . . girls swiveled and undulated to the disco-beat. T. CAPOTE Perry undulated between half-awake stupors and sickly sweat-drenched sleep. I. MURDOCH A hill from which . . the road, undulating straight onward, was visible. **2** L. NIVEN He undulated his legs and torso to move the blanket in waves.

undulated /ˈʌndjʊleɪtɪd/ *adjective*. E17.
[from prec. + -ED[1].]
1 Formed into a waved surface or outline; arranged in a series of wavelike curves; undulating. E17.
2 Marked with a rippling pattern, having wavy markings. M17.

undulating /ˈʌndjʊleɪtɪŋ/ *adjective*. E18.
[formed as prec. + -ING[2].]
1 Rising and falling in or like waves, having a wavelike motion; fluctuating. E18.
2 Having a wavy or rippling form or surface, gently rising and falling in outline. L18.

> 🕮 **1** A. MOOREHEAD The pelicans, with their curious undulating flight—a series of upward flaps and a down-glide. **2** H. MELVILLE The land rolled away in bright hillsides, . . warm and undulating. I. MURDOCH A very simple hat with an undulating brim of . . pale yellow voile.

■ **undulatingly** *adverb* L18.

undulation /ʌndjʊˈleɪʃ(ə)n/ *noun*. M17.
[mod. Latin *undulatio(n-)*, formed as UNDULATE *verb*: see -ATION.]
1 The action or fact of undulating or fluctuating; an instance of this; (a) wavelike motion. M17. ▸**b** A wavelike motion of the air, electromagnetic radiation, etc., as in the passage of sound or light. M17.
2 A wavelike curve; a series of these; (a) smooth and regular rise and fall of form or outline. L17.

> 🕮 **1** R. CHURCH The delicious undulation of the lapping water. **2** H. STURGIS The green undulations of an English park.

■ **undulationist** *noun* (*obsolete* exc. *Hist.*) a person who supports the undulatory theory of light M19.

undulator /ˈʌndjʊleɪtə/ *noun*. E20.
[from UNDULATE *verb* + -OR.]
1 TELEGRAPHY. A pen recorder for recording Morse signals. E20.
2 PHYSICS. A device in which a beam of particles is made to describe a sinusoidal path (and so emit radiation), by using a series of transverse electric or magnetic fields of alternating polarity. M20.

undulatory /ˈʌndjʊlət(ə)ri/ *adjective*. E18.
[formed as prec. + -ORY[2].]
Of undulating motion or form, characterized by undulation; wavy, rippled.
undulatory hypothesis, **undulatory theory** (*obsolete* exc. *Hist.*) the theory that light consists of an undulatory movement of an elastic medium pervading space.

undulose /ˈʌndjʊləʊs, -ləʊz/ *adjective*. L19.
[formed as next + -OSE[1].]
Chiefly GEOLOGY. Designating extinction of polarized light that occurs in strips which move across the field of view of a microscope as the stage holding a specimen is turned. Chiefly in ***undulose extinction***.

undulous /ˈʌndjʊləs/ *adjective*. E18.
[from UNDULATE *verb* or UNDULATION + -OUS, after *populate*, *population*, *populous*.]
Of an undulating nature.
■ **undulously** *adverb* E20.

unduly /ʌnˈdjuːli/ *adverb*. LME.
[from UN-[1] + DULY.]
1 Without due cause or justification; unrightfully, improperly, unjustifiably. LME.
2 More than is warranted or natural; excessively, disproportionately. L18.

> 🕮 **1** E. B. BROWNING Malvern hills, for mountains counted Not unduly, loom a-row. **2** E. WAUGH It is natural to the literary mind to be unduly observant of the choice of words. D. CECIL These anxieties did not seem to have worried him unduly.

undust /ʌnˈdʌst/ *verb trans.* E17.
[from UN-[2] + DUST *noun*.]
Free from dust, wipe clean.

undusted /ʌnˈdʌstɪd/ *adjective*. M17.
[from UN-[1] + *dusted* pa. pple of DUST *verb*.]
1 Not sprinkled with dust or powder. M17.
2 Not freed from dust, left dusty. M19.

undutiful /ʌnˈdjuːtɪfʊl, -f(ə)l/ *adjective*. L16.
[from UN-[1] + DUTIFUL.]
Not dutiful, contrary to or lacking dutifulness.
■ **unduteous** *adjective* (*arch.*) undutiful L16. **undutifully** *adverb* L16. **undutifulness** *noun* M16.

undy /ˈʌndi/ *adjective*. L16.
[Anglicized from UNDEE: see -Y[5].]
HERALDRY. Wavy.

undying /ʌnˈdʌɪɪŋ/ *adjective*. ME.
[from UN-[1] + DYING *ppl adjective*[2].]
That does not die, immortal; eternal, never-ending.

> 🕮 E. BLAIR They had sworn undying love.

■ **undyingly** *adverb* L19. **undyingness** *noun* M19.

unearned /ʌnˈəːnd/ *adjective*. ME.
[from UN-[1] + *earned* pa. pple of EARN *verb*[1].]
1 Not earned by merit or desert, undeserved. ME.
2 Not earned by labour, not worked for. M17.
2 unearned income (an) income from property, interest payments, etc., as opp. to a salary, wages, or fees. **unearned increment** an increase in the value of land or property without labour or expenditure on the part of the owner.

unearth /ʌnˈəːθ/ *verb trans.* LME.
[from UN-[2] + EARTH *noun*[1].]
1 Dig out of the earth; disclose by the removal of earth. LME. ▸**b** Drive (a fox etc.) out of an earth or burrow. E17.
2 Discover by investigation or searching or when rummaging, bring to light. E19.

> 🕮 **1** *Independent* Excavations have unearthed the remains of a gateway. **2** R. L. STEVENSON Long John Silver unearthed a very competent man for a mate. J. GATHORNE-HARDY Byron's . . biographer seems to have been the first to unearth the facts.

unearthed /ʌnˈəːθt/ *adjective*. E16.
[from UN-[1] + *earthed* pa. pple of EARTH *verb*.]
Not (esp. electrically) earthed.

unearthly /ʌnˈəːθli/ *adjective*. E17.
[from UN-[1] + EARTHLY.]
1 Not earthly or terrestrial; exalted, sublime; celestial. E17.
2 Supernatural, ghostly; mysterious, sinister. E19.
3 Not appropriate to anything earthly; absurdly early or inconvenient. *colloq.* M19.

> 🕮 **2** DICKENS A strange unearthly figure, whom Gabriel felt . . was no being of this world. C. GEIKIE Suddenly an unearthly sound broke from one side, a sort of screech. **3** *Sunday Times* In the Army I often had to get up at an unearthly hour.

■ **unearthliness** *noun* M19.

unease /ʌnˈiːz/ *noun*. ME.
[from UN-[1] + EASE *noun*.]
Want or lack of ease, uneasiness; discomfort, distress, anxiety.

> 🕮 *Guardian* This kind of story creates a sense of unease in parents.

■ **uneaseful** *adjective* (*arch.*) not giving ease or comfort, uncomfortable E16. **uneasefulness** *noun* (long *rare*) M17.

unease /ʌnˈiːz/ *verb trans.* Long *arch.* LME.
[from UN-[2] + EASE *noun*.]
Make uneasy or uncomfortable; trouble, distress.

uneasy /ʌnˈiːzi/ *adjective*. ME.
[from UN-[1] + EASY *adjective*.]
1 a Producing physical discomfort, not conducive to ease or comfort. ME. ▸†**b** Causing mental discomfort; unpleasant, disagreeable. Freq. foll. by *to*. L15–L18. ▸**c** Characterized by or suggesting unease or discomfort. E16.
2 †**a** Of a road etc.: difficult to traverse. ME–M18. ▸**b** Not easy or simple, difficult. Now *rare*. LME.
†**3** Of a person: troublesome, annoying, unaccommodating, (*to* another). LME–M18.
4 Uncomfortable or disturbed in mind or body; anxious, apprehensive; (of an animal) restless, unsettled. LME.

> 🕮 **1c** G. ANSON That uneasy and suffocating sensation. L. H. TRIBE The tension in this uneasy alliance. **2b** SIR W. SCOTT 'The road will be uneasy to find', answered Gurth. **4** *Daily Telegraph* They are profoundly uneasy about actively assisting a suicide. N. WILLIAMS The first sight of the coffin made Henry feel distinctly uneasy.

■ **uneasily** *adverb* ME. **uneasiness** *noun* LME.

uneatable /ʌnˈiːtəb(ə)l/ *adjective*. E17.
[from UN-[1] + EATABLE *adjective*.]
Not able or fit to be eaten, not edible.

> 🕮 C. HARKNESS As in all English institutions, the food was uneatable.

■ **uneatableness** *noun* M19.

uneaten /ʌnˈiːt(ə)n/ *adjective*. ME.
[from UN-[1] + *eaten* pa. pple of EAT *verb*.]
Not (yet) eaten.

uneath /ʌnˈiːθ/ *adjective & adverb*. *arch.*
[Old English *unēaþe*, from UN-[1] + *ēaþe* EATH.]
▸ **A** *adjective*. Difficult, hard, troublesome. OE.
▸ **B** *adverb*. **1** Not easily, (only) with difficulty; scarcely, hardly, barely. OE. ▸†**b** Almost. *rare*. L16–E17.
†**2 a** Reluctantly, unwillingly. OE–LME. ▸**b** In difficult circumstances, in hardship. Only in L16.
†**3** With no intervening time; no sooner than; only just. OE–M16.
■ †**uneaths** *adverb* ME–M17.

uneconomic /ˌʌniːkəˈnɒmɪk, ˌʌnɛk-/ *adjective*. E20.
[from UN-[1] + ECONOMIC *adjective*.]
Not economic; unprofitable; not or scarcely able to be operated etc. at a profit.

> 🕮 A. T. ELLIS He had sold his livestock when the smallholding had proved uneconomic.

uneconomical /ˌʌniːkəˈnɒmɪk(ə)l, ˌʌnɛkə-/ *adjective*. E19.
[from UN-[1] + ECONOMICAL.]
Not economical; wasteful, not sparing or thrifty.
■ **uneconomicalness** *noun* E19.

uneconomically /ˌʌniːkəˈnɒmɪk(ə)li, ˌʌnɛk-/ *adverb*. L19.
[from UNECONOMIC or UNECONOMICAL + -LY[2].]
In an uneconomic or uneconomical way; unprofitably; wastefully.

unedge /ʌnˈɛdʒ/ *verb trans.* L15.
[from UN-[2] + EDGE *verb*.]
Take the edge off, blunt.

unedged /ʌnˈɛdʒd/ *adjective*. L18.
[from UN-[1] + EDGED.]
Not edged; lacking a cutting edge.

unedifying /ʌnˈɛdɪfʌɪɪŋ/ *adjective*. M17.
[from UN-[1] + EDIFYING.]
Not edifying; *esp.* not instructive or morally improving; degrading, sordid.

> 🕮 N. F. DIXON The unedifying sight of a bored schoolboy . . pulling the wings off flies.

■ **unedified** *adjective* not edified or instructed E17. **unedifyingly** *adverb* M19.

uneducable /ʌnˈɛdʒʊkəb(ə)l, -djʊ-/ *adjective*. L19.
[from UN-[1] + EDUCABLE.]
Unable to be educated, unteachable.
■ Also **unedu'catable** *adjective* M20.

uneducate /ʌnˈɛdʒʊkət, -djʊ-/ *adjective*. *obsolete* exc. *Scot.* L16.
[from UN-[1] + *educate* obsolete & Scot. pa. pple of EDUCATE.]
Uneducated.

uneducate /ʌnˈɛdʒʊkeɪt, -djʊ-/ *verb trans.* M19.
[from UN-[2] + EDUCATE.]
Make uneducated.

uneducated /ʌnˈɛdʒʊkeɪtɪd, -djʊ-/ *adjective*. L16.
[from UN-[1] + *educated* pa. pple of EDUCATE.]
Not educated.

> 🕮 I. MURDOCH The people who came to the Mission were uneducated, some of them illiterate.

■ **uneducatedness** *noun* E19.

UNEF *abbreviation*.
United Nations Emergency Force.

unelectable /ʌnɪˈlɛktəb(ə)l/ *adjective*. M20.
[from UN-[1] + ELECTABLE.]
Not electable; *esp.* (of a candidate, party, etc.) associated with or holding views likely to bring defeat at an election.
■ **unelecta'bility** *noun* L20.

unelected /ʌnɪˈlɛktɪd/ *adjective*. L16.
[from UN-[1] + *elected* pa. pple of ELECT *verb*.]
Not elected.

> 🕮 *Guardian* It has no local government, only an unelected development corporation.

unembarrassed /ʌnɪmˈbarəst, -ɛm-/ *adjective*. E18.
[from UN-[1] + EMBARRASSED.]
Not embarrassed; unconstrained.
■ **unembarrassable** *adjective* impossible to embarrass L20.

For other words beginning with *un-* see the entries for **un-**[1], **un-**[2]

unemotional /ʌnɪˈməʊʃ(ə)n(ə)l/ *adjective*. L19.
[from UN-[1] + EMOTIONAL.]
Not emotional; lacking emotion.
■ **unemotionally** *adverb* L19.

unemployable /ʌnɪmˈplɔɪəb(ə)l, -ɛm-/ *adjective & noun*. L19.
[from UN-[1] + EMPLOYABLE.]
► **A** *adjective*. Unfitted for paid employment. L19.
► **B** *noun*. An unemployable person. E20.
■ **unemployaˈbility** *noun* E20.

unemployed /ʌnɪmˈplɔɪd, -ɛm-/ *adjective & noun*. As adjective also †**unim-**. E17.
[from UN-[1] + *employed* pa. pple of EMPLOY *verb*.]
► **A** *adjective*. **1** Not made use of, usu. for a particular purpose. E17.
2 Not engaged in any occupation; idle; out of paid employment, redundant. M17.
► **B** *absol*. as *noun*. (*The*) unemployed people. Now also (*rare*), an unemployed person. L18.

📖 LYNDON B. JOHNSON Jobs were plentiful, but the unemployed were incapable of filling them. *Daily Telegraph* Young unemployeds can lose their rights to grants when taking up full-time education.

unemployment /ʌnɪmˈplɔɪm(ə)nt, -ɛm-/ *noun*. L19.
[from UN-[1] + EMPLOYMENT.]
1 The state or condition of being unemployed; the extent of this in a country, region, etc., *esp*. the number or percentage of unemployed people. L19.
2 *ellipt*. = ***unemployment benefit*** below. L20.

📖 **1** M. FOOT We were faced . . with . . a hideous rise in unemployment. *STRUCTURAL* ***unemployment***.

Comb.: **unemployment benefit** a payment made to an unemployed person by the State or (in the US) a trade union.

unencumbered /ʌnɪnˈkʌmbəd, ʌnɛn-/ *adjective*. Also †**unin-**. E18.
[from UN-[1] + *encumbered* pa. pple of ENCUMBER *verb*.]
Not encumbered, free; *spec*. (*LAW*) (of an estate) free of any liabilities.

📖 M. PLOWMAN Dialectical materialists, unencumbered by any ethical humbug.

■ **unencumbering** *adjective* that does not encumber or hamper a person E19.

unendeared /ʌnɪnˈdɪəd, ʌnɛn-/ *adjective*. *rare*. Orig. †**unindeard**. M17.
[from UN-[1] + *endeared* pa. pple of ENDEAR.]
Not endeared.
■ **unendearing** *adjective* not endearing E20.

unended /ʌnˈɛndɪd/ *adjective*. ME.
[from UN-[1] + *ended* pa. pple of END *verb*[1].]
1 Not made to end or stop; limitless, infinite. Long *rare* or *obsolete*. ME.
2 Not concluded; unfinished, incomplete. LME.

unending /ʌnˈɛndɪŋ/ *adjective*. M17.
[from UN-[1] + ENDING *ppl adjective*.]
Endless.
■ **unendingly** *adverb* L17. **unendingness** *noun* L19.

unendurable /ʌnɪnˈdjʊərəb(ə)l/ *adjective*. Orig. †**unin-**. M17.
[from UN-[1] + ENDURABLE.]
†**1** Intolerant *of*. *rare*. Only in M17.
2 Not endurable; insufferable. E19.
■ **unenduraˈbility** *noun* M19. **unendurableness** *noun* L19. **unendurably** *adverb* in an unendurable manner or degree M19. **unenduring** *adjective* L18.

unenforceable /ʌnɪnˈfɔːsəb(ə)l, ʌnɛn-/ *adjective*. M19.
[from UN-[1] + ENFORCEABLE.]
Of a law, claim, contract, etc.: that cannot be enforced.
■ **unenforceaˈbility** *noun* M20.

unenforced /ʌnɪnˈfɔːst, ʌnɛn-/ *adjective*. Also (earlier) †**unin-**. E17.
[from UN-[1] + *enforced* pa. pple of ENFORCE *verb*.]
Not enforced.

unengaged /ʌnɪnˈɡeɪdʒd, ʌnɛn-/ *adjective*. M17.
[from UN-[1] + ENGAGED.]
1 Not bound or committed, esp. by a pledge or promise; *spec*. not engaged to marry. M17.
2 Not hired. M17.
3 Not occupied or busy (*in* an activity). E18.
■ **unengaging** *adjective* not engaging, unattractive M18.

unenjoyed /ʌnɪnˈdʒɔɪd, ʌnɛn-/ *adjective*. Also (earlier) †**unin-**. M17.
[from UN-[1] + *enjoyed* pa. pple of ENJOY.]
Not enjoyed.

unenjoying /ʌnɪnˈdʒɔɪɪŋ, ʌnɛn-/ *adjective*. L17.
[from UN-[1] + *enjoying* pres. pple of ENJOY.]
Not able or disposed to find enjoyment; unhappy.
■ **unenjoyable** *adjective* not enjoyable L18.

unenlightened /ʌnɪnˈlʌɪt(ə)nd, ʌnɛn-/ *adjective*. M17.
[from UN-[1] + *enlightened* pa. pple of ENLIGHTEN.]
1 Not enlightened; not illuminated (*lit. & fig*.); uninformed. M17.
2 Characterized by lack of enlightenment. L18.
■ **unenlightening** *adjective* that produces no enlightenment M18. **unenlightenment** *noun* lack of enlightenment M20.

unentangle /ʌnɪnˈtaŋɡ(ə)l, ʌnɛn-/ *verb trans*. E17.
[from UN-[2] + ENTANGLE.]
Disentangle.

unentangled /ʌnɪnˈtaŋɡ(ə)ld, ʌnɛn-/ *adjective*. L16.
[from UN-[1] + *entangled* pa. pple of ENTANGLE.]
Not entangled.

unentered /ʌnˈɛntəd/ *adjective*. L15.
[from UN-[1] + *entered* pa. pple of ENTER *verb*.]
1 Not recorded as an entry in an account-book etc. L15.
†**2** Not initiated *in* a subject. M16–M17.
3 *SCOTS LAW*. Not formally admitted. E18.
4 Of a hound: not yet put into a pack. L18.
5 Not gone into; not penetrated. L18.
■ **unenterable** *adjective* (of a place etc.) that cannot be entered M17.

unenterprising /ʌnˈɛntəprʌɪzɪŋ/ *adjective*. L18.
[from UN-[1] + ENTERPRISING.]
Not enterprising; lacking initiative or resourcefulness.
■ **unenterprisingly** *adverb* M19.

unentertained /ˌʌnɛntəˈteɪnd/ *adjective*. E17.
[from UN-[1] + *entertained* pa. pple of ENTERTAIN *verb*.]
Not entertained or amused.
■ **unentertaining** *adjective* not entertaining, unamusing, dull L17. **unentertainingly** *adverb* M19.

unenthusiastic /ˌʌnɪnθjuːzɪˈastɪk, ˌʌnɛn-/ *adjective*. E19.
[from UN-[1] + ENTHUSIASTIC *adjective*.]
Not enthusiastic.
■ **unenˈthused** *adjective* (of a person) unenthusiastic M20. **unenthusiastically** *adverb* E20.

unenvied /ʌnˈɛnvɪd/ *adjective*. LME.
[In sense 1 from UN-[1] + ENVY *noun* + -ED[2]; in sense 2 from UN-[1] + *envied* pa. pple of ENVY *verb*[1].]
†**1** Not mixed with envy. Only in LME.
2 Not envied. E17.
■ **unenviable** *adjective* M17. **unenviably** *adverb* M19.

unenvious /ʌnˈɛnvɪəs/ *adjective*. M17.
[from UN-[1] + ENVIOUS.]
Not envious; not feeling or showing envy.
■ **unenviously** *adverb* E17.

UNEP *abbreviation*.
United Nations Environment Programme.

unequable /ʌnˈɛkwəb(ə)l/ *adjective*. L17.
[from UN-[1] + EQUABLE.]
Not equable.
■ **unequably** *adverb* M19.

unequal /ʌnˈiːkw(ə)l/ *adjective & adverb*. M16.
[from UN-[1] + EQUAL *adjective*.]
► **A** *adjective*. **1** Not equal in amount, size, value, etc. M16. ►**b** Of a whole number: odd, not even. *rare*. L17.
2 Varying, variable; inconsistent. M16. ►**b** *spec*. Of a surface: uneven, undulating. *arch*. E17.
†**3** Of a person, act, etc.: inequitable, unjust. M16–M18.
4 Of a contest, conflict, treaty, etc.: not evenly balanced; lacking equal advantage to all parties; not uniform in effect or operation. M16.
5 Inadequate in ability, resources, etc. Now only foll. by *to*. L16.

📖 **4** P. ROSE People would think the match unequal, with all the advantages on her side. **5** A. BROOKNER He would be unequal to the task of being Toto's father.

► **B** *adverb*. Unequally. Long *rare*. E17.

📖 SHAKES. *Haml*. Unequal match'd, Pyrrhus at Priam drives.

■ **unequalable** *adjective* that cannot be equalled M17. **uneˈquality** *noun* inequality M16. **unequalized** *adjective* L16. **unequalled** *adjective* superior to all others E17. **unequally** *adverb* (**a**) in an unequal manner, not equally; †(**b**) (*rare*, Spenser) unjustly: M16. **unequalness** *noun* (**a**) the quality or condition of being unequal; †(**b**) lack of equity, unfairness: M16.

unequals /ʌnˈiːkw(ə)lz/ *noun pl*. E17.
[from UN-[1] + EQUAL *noun* + -S[1].]
Persons who or things which are unequal.

unequivocable /ʌnɪˈkwɪvəkəb(ə)l/ *adjective*. E20.
[Irreg. from UN-[1] + EQUIVOC(AL *adjective* + -ABLE.]
= next.
■ **unequivocably** *adverb* E20.

unequivocal /ʌnɪˈkwɪvək(ə)l/ *adjective*. L18.
[from UN-[1] + EQUIVOCAL *adjective*.]
Not equivocal; plain, unmistakable.
■ **unequivocally** *adverb* E18. **unequivocalness** *noun* M19.

unerring /ʌnˈəːrɪŋ/ *adjective*. E17.
[from UN-[1] + *erring* pres. pple of ERR.]
1 Not missing the intended target; certain, sure. E17.
2 That makes no mistake; true. M17.
■ **unerringly** *adverb* M17. **unerringness** *noun* L17.

uneschewable /ʌnɪsˈtʃuːəb(ə)l, ʌnɛs-/ *adjective*. LME.
[from UN-[1] + ESCHEW + -ABLE.]
That cannot be eschewed; inescapable.

UNESCO /juːˈnɛskəʊ/ *abbreviation*.
United Nations Educational, Scientific, and Cultural Organization.

unessence /ʌnˈɛs(ə)ns/ *verb trans*. Now *rare* or *obsolete*. M17.
[from UN-[2] + ESSENCE *noun*.]
Deprive of essential properties or attributes.

unessential /ʌnɪˈsɛnʃ(ə)l/ *adjective & noun*. M17.
[from UN-[1] + ESSENTIAL: cf. INESSENTIAL.]
► **A** *adjective*. **1** Possessing no essence or substance; immaterial. M17.
2 Not pertaining to or affecting the essence of a matter; dispensable, relatively unimportant. M17.
► **B** *noun*. An unessential thing, part, or feature. Usu. in *pl*. E19.
■ **unessentially** *adverb* M19.

unevangelical /ˌʌniːvanˈdʒɛlɪk(ə)l/ *adjective*. M17.
[from UN-[1] + EVANGELICAL *adjective*.]
Not in accordance with the Christian gospel, not Evangelical.
■ **unevangelized** /ʌnɪˈvan(d)ʒ(ə)lʌɪzd/ *adjective* not evangelized L18.

uneven /ʌnˈiːv(ə)n/ *adjective*.
[Old English *unefen*, from UN-[1] + EVEN *adjective*.]
1 Unequal; not completely or exactly corresponding or matched. OE. ►**b** Of a whole number: odd. Of a thing or things: making up or marked by an odd number. LME.
2 Not smooth or level; irregular, inconsistent, variable; not uniform. ME.
3 Of an act, dealings, or (formerly) a person: unequitable, unfair. LME.
4 Not straight or parallel. *arch*. LME.

📖 **1** SPENSER They traueld an vneuen payre, . . A saluage man matcht with a Ladie fayre. R. BOYLE Two pipes of Glass very uneven in length. **2** SHAKES. *Meas. for M*. In most uneven and distracted manner. His actions show much like to madness. W. GOLDING A chair that rocked slightly on an uneven floor. *Daily Telegraph* The writing is uneven, often degenerating into the novelettish.

■ **unevenly** *adverb* LME. **unevenness** /-n-n-/ *noun* (**a**) the quality or state of being uneven; (**b**) an instance of this, *esp*. an uneven place, part, or feature: LME.

uneventful /ʌnɪˈvɛntfʊl, -f(ə)l/ *adjective*. E19.
[from UN-[1] + EVENTFUL.]
Not eventful.
■ **uneventfully** *adverb* M19. **uneventfulness** *noun* L19.

unexamined /ʌnɪɡˈzamɪnd, ʌnɛɡ-/ *adjective*. L15.
[from UN-[1] + *examined* pa. pple of EXAMINE *verb*.]
Not examined.
■ **unexaminable** *adjective* not examinable M17. **unexamining** *adjective* incurious, uncritical E17.

unexceptionable /ʌnɪkˈsɛpʃ(ə)nəb(ə)l, ʌnɛk-/ *adjective*. E17.
[from UN-[1] + EXCEPTIONABLE.]
To whom or to which no exception can be taken; perfectly satisfactory or adequate.

📖 *Times Lit. Suppl*. The definition seems innocuous enough, indeed, unexceptionable at first reading. J. AIKEN A . . good-looking man—height, air, address, all were unexceptionable.

■ **ˌunexceptionaˈbility** *noun* M19. **unexceptionableness** *noun* M17. **unexceptionably** *adverb* (**a**) in an unexceptionable manner; (**b**) without exception: M17.

unexclusive /ʌnɪkˈskluːsɪv, ʌnɛk-/ *adjective*. E19.
[from UN-[1] + EXCLUSIVE *adjective*.]
Not exclusive.
■ **unexclusively** *adverb* E19. **unexclusiveness** *noun* E19.

unexercised /ʌnˈɛksəsʌɪzd/ *adjective*. LME.
[from UN-[1] + *exercised* pa. pple of EXERCISE *verb*.]
1 Not made use of, unused; not put into practice. LME.
2 Of a person: not prepared by training or practice; untrained. LME.
3 Not taking exercise; remaining inactive or unmoved. M16.

unexhausted /ʌnɪɡˈzɔːstɪd, ʌnɛɡ-/ *adjective*. E17.
[from UN-[1] + *exhausted* pa. pple of EXHAUST *verb*.]
1 Not used up, expended, or brought to an end. E17.
2 Not emptied or drained. M17.
■ **unexhaustible** *adjective* (now *rare* or *obsolete*) = INEXHAUSTIBLE L16.

unexpected /ʌnɪkˈspɛktɪd, ʌnɛk-/ *adjective*. L16.
[from UN-[1] + EXPECTED.]
Not expected; surprising.
■ **unexpectable** *adjective* not able to be expected L16. **unexpectant** *adjective* not expectant E19. **unexpectedly** *adverb* L16. **unexpectedness** *noun* E17.

unexperienced /ʌnɪkˈspɪərɪənst, ʌnɛk-/ *adjective*. M16.
[from UN-[1] + EXPERIENCED.]
1 Not having experience; inexperienced (*in*). M16.
2 Not (previously) known by experience. L17.
■ †**unexperience** *noun* = INEXPERIENCE E17–M18. **unexperienceable** *adjective* impossible to experience E20. **unexperiencedness** *noun* (*rare*) M17. †**unexperient** *adjective* (*rare*) inexperienced L16–M18.

unexpressed /ʌnɪkˈsprɛst, ʌnɛk-/ *adjective.* M16.
[from UN-¹ + *expressed* pa. pple of EXPRESS *verb*¹.]
Not expressed or made known; implicit.
■ †**unexpressable** *adjective* = INEXPRESSIBLE *adjective* M16–M18. **unexpressible** *adjective* (now *rare*) = INEXPRESSIBLE *adjective* E17. †**unexpressibly** *adverb* M17–E18.

unexpressive /ʌnɪkˈsprɛsɪv, ʌnɛk-/ *adjective.* E17.
[from UN-¹ + EXPRESSIVE: cf. INEXPRESSIVE.]
†**1** = INEXPRESSIBLE. E–M17.
2 = INEXPRESSIVE 2. M18.

unfading /ʌnˈfeɪdɪŋ/ *adjective.* M17.
[from UN-¹ + FADING.]
That does not fade, never-fading, (*lit.* & *fig.*).
■ **unfadable** *adjective* (*rare*) not liable to fade E17. **unfaded** *adjective* M16. **unfadingly** *adverb* L17. **unfadingness** *noun* M17.

unfailing /ʌnˈfeɪlɪŋ/ *adjective.* LME.
[from UN-¹ + *failing* pres. pple of FAIL *verb.*]
Not failing; *spec.* (**a**) never-ending, unceasing, constant, continual; (**b**) never running short; (**c**) infallible, certain, absolutely reliable.
📖 M. ROBERTS Impractically dressed . . because of her unfailing optimism about the weather. S. HASTINGS His . . unfailing politeness made him much admired.
■ **unfailable** *adjective* (long *rare* or *obsolete*) not liable to fail or prove false, reliable LME. **unfailably** *adverb* (long *rare*) M16. **unfailingly** *adverb* in all cases or circumstances, without fail LME. **unfailingness** *noun* E17.

unfair /ʌnˈfɛː/ *adjective.*
[Old English *unfæger*, from UN-¹ + FAIR *adjective.*]
†**1** Not pleasing to the sight; ugly. OE–M17.
2 Not equitable, unjust; not according to the rules, partial. Freq. foll. by *to*. L17.
3 Of a wind: unfavourable. E19.
📖 **2** J. BUTLER Opportunity to an unfair mind of explaining away . . that evidence. *Economist* The unfair competition between law-abiding and tax-evading firms. J. MCPHEE Locking the land up is unfair to future generations.
■ **unfairly** *adverb* L17. **unfairness** *noun* L17.

†**unfair** *verb trans. rare* (Shakes.). Only in L16.
[from UN-² + FAIR *verb.*]
Deprive of fairness or beauty.

unfaith /ˈʌnfeɪθ/ *noun.* LME.
[from UN-¹ + FAITH *noun.*]
Lack of (esp. religious) faith, disbelief.

unfaithful /ʌnˈfeɪθfʊl, -f(ə)l/ *adjective.* ME.
[from UN-¹ + FAITHFUL *adjective.*]
1 Not having religious faith; unbelieving. ME.
2 Not keeping good faith, disloyal; behaving treacherously; *spec.* adulterous, not faithful (*to* a sexual partner). LME.
3 Of conduct: not honest or upright. M16.
4 Of a translation, interpretation, etc.: not true to the original; incorrect, inaccurate. L17.
📖 **2** TENNYSON With quiet eyes unfaithful to the truth. *Best* She's recently split up with him for the second time because he was unfaithful. **3** T. OTWAY I might think with Justice most severely Of this unfaithful dealing with your Brother.
■ **unfaithfully** *adverb* ME. **unfaithfulness** *noun* LME.

unfalsified /ʌnˈfɔːlsɪfʌɪd, -ˈfɒl-/ *adjective.* L17.
[from UN-¹ + *falsified* pa. pple of FALSIFY.]
Not falsified.
■ ˌ**unfalsiˈfiable** *adjective* impossible to falsify M20.

unfaltering /ʌnˈfɔːlt(ə)rɪŋ, -ˈfɒl-/ *adjective.* E18.
[from UN-¹ + *faltering* pres. pple of FALTER *verb*¹.]
That does not falter; steady, resolute.
■ **unfalteringly** *adverb* M17.

unfamiliar /ʌnfəˈmɪlɪə/ *adjective.* L16.
[from UN-¹ + FAMILIAR *adjective.*]
Not familiar; *esp.* (**a**) not known or recognized from prior acquaintance; (**b**) unusual; (**c**) (of a person) not well acquainted *with* (a thing, idea, etc.).
■ ˌ**unfamiliˈarity** *noun* M18. **unfamiliarized** *adjective* L18. **unfamiliarly** *adverb* L19.

unfashion /ʌnˈfaʃ(ə)n/ *noun. rare.* E19.
[from UN-¹ + FASHION *noun.*]
Unfashionableness.

unfashion /ʌnˈfaʃ(ə)n/ *verb trans.* Long *rare.* M16.
[from UN-² + FASHION *noun, verb.*]
Unmake, destroy; deform, change the nature of.

unfashionable /ʌnˈfaʃ(ə)nəb(ə)l/ *adjective & noun.* M16.
[from UN-¹ + FASHIONABLE.]
▶**A** *adjective.* †**1** **a** Impossible to fashion or shape. M16–E17. ▸**b** Badly formed, misshapen. L16–M17.
2 Not following or in accordance with current fashion or styles. M17.
▶**B** *noun pl.* Unfashionable people. *rare.* E19.
■ **unˌfashionaˈbility** *noun* L20. **unfashionableness** *noun* L17. **unfashionably** *adverb* E17.

unfashioned /ʌnˈfaʃ(ə)nd/ *adjective.* L15.
[from UN-¹ + FASHIONED.]
1 Not given or made into (a specific) form or shape. L15.
†**2** Not refined, elegant, or fashionable. E17–E19.

unfasten /ʌnˈfɑːs(ə)n/ *verb.* ME.
[from UN-² + FASTEN *verb.*]
1 *verb trans.* **a** Deprive of firmness or fixity; make loose. ME. ▸**b** Detach, undo, release. LME.
2 *verb intrans.* Become detached or loose; open. ME.
📖 **1a** *absol.*: SHAKES. *2 Hen. IV* Plucking to unfix an enemy, He doth unfasten so and shake a friend. **b** A. NIN He playfully unfastened the first button of her blouse.

unfastened /ʌnˈfɑːs(ə)nd/ *adjective.* L16.
[from UN-¹ + *fastened* pa. pple of FASTEN *verb.*]
That has not been fastened; that has been loosened, opened, or detached.

unfathomable /ʌnˈfað(ə)məb(ə)l/ *adjective.* E17.
[from UN-¹ + FATHOMABLE.]
Impossible to measure the depth of or fully comprehend; inscrutable; immeasurable, vast. Chiefly *fig.*
📖 ADDISON Sounding the unfathomable Depths of fate. THACKERAY her eyes . . shone with . . mystery unfathomable. M. E. BRADDON Boulevards stretching into unfathomable distance.
■ **unˌfathomaˈbility** *noun* (*rare*) M19. **unfathomableness** *noun* L17. **unfathomably** *adverb* to an unfathomable degree or extent L17. **unfathomed** *adjective* (**a**) of unmeasured depth (*lit.* & *fig.*); (**b**) not fully explored or comprehended: E17.

unfatiguable /ʌnfəˈtiːgəb(ə)l/ *adjective.* Also (earlier) **-fatigable** /-ˈfatɪgəb(ə)l/. M16.
[from UN-¹ + FATIGUABLE.]
Indefatigable; not easily tired out.

unfatigued /ʌnfəˈtiːgd/ *adjective.* E18.
[from UN-¹ + *fatigued* pa. pple of FATIGUE *verb.*]
Not tired.
■ **unfatiguing** *adjective* not tiring or strenuous E19.

unfavorable *adjective* see UNFAVOURABLE.

unfavorite *adjective* see UNFAVOURITE.

unfavourable /ʌnˈfeɪv(ə)rəb(ə)l/ *adjective.* Also ***-vor-**. M16.
[from UN-¹ + FAVOURABLE.]
1 Not favourable; *spec.* (**a**) ill-disposed, hostile; (**b**) adverse, unpropitious. M16.
2 Of features or appearance: ill-favoured. L18.
■ **unfavourableness** *noun* M18. **unfavourably** *adverb* LME. **unfavoured** *adjective* not favoured, treated kindly, or preferred LME.

unfavourite /ʌnˈfeɪv(ə)rɪt/ *adjective.* Also ***-vor-**. M20.
[from UN-¹ + FAVOURITE *adjective.*]
Least favourite; most disliked.

unfazed /ʌnˈfeɪzd/ *adjective.* Orig. *US.* Also (earlier) **unphased**. M19.
[from UN-¹ + *fazed* pa. pple of FAZE *verb*¹.]
Not disconcerted; unperturbed.
■ **unfazable**, **-eable** *adjective* not able to be fazed, imperturbable L20.

unfeared /ʌnˈfɪəd/ *adjective.* LME.
[from UN-¹ + FEARED.]
†**1** Not frightened or dismayed. LME–E17.
2 Not regarded with fear. E17.
■ **unfearful** *adjective* having no fear, fearless LME. **unfearing** *adjective* fearless L18.

unfeasible /ʌnˈfiːzɪb(ə)l/ *adjective.* LME.
[from UN-¹ + FEASIBLE.]
= INFEASIBLE.
■ **unfeasiˈbility** *noun* M17. **unfeasibly** *adverb* M20.

unfeeling /ʌnˈfiːlɪŋ/ *noun. rare.* E17.
[from UN-¹ + FEELING *noun.*]
Lack of feeling; an instance of this.

unfeeling /ʌnˈfiːlɪŋ/ *adjective.* LOE.
[from UN-¹ + FEELING *adjective.*]
1 Having no feeling or sensation, insensible. LOE.
2 Not sensitive to or concerned about the feelings of others; harsh, unsympathetic. L16.
📖 **1** W. COWPER [He] pressed his lips to the pale and unfeeling lips. **2** SIR W. SCOTT I was neither a false lover nor an unfeeling son. A. N. WILSON Sent away from home . . to a school run on harshly unfeeling lines.
■ **unfeelingly** *adverb* LME. **unfeelingness** *noun* LME.

unfeigned /ʌnˈfeɪnd/ *adjective.* LME.
[from UN-¹ + *feigned* pa. pple of FEIGN.]
Not feigned; sincere, genuine, honest.
■ **unfeignedly** /-nɪdli/ *adverb* E16. **unfeignedness** /-nɪdnɪs/ *noun* (long *rare* or *obsolete*) the state or quality of being unfeigned M16. **unfeigning** *adjective* = UNFEIGNED LME.

unfeminine /ʌnˈfɛmɪnɪn/ *adjective.* M18.
[from UN-¹ + FEMININE *adjective.*]
Not characteristically feminine; not (regarded as) suitable or appropriate for a woman.
📖 *Guardian* The myth that physics is somehow unfeminine.
■ **unfemiˈninity** *noun* L20. **unfeminist** *adjective* not characteristic of a feminist E20.

unfermented /ʌnfəˈmɛntɪd, -fɜːˈm-/ *adjective.* M17.
[from UN-¹ + *fermented* pa. pple of FERMENT *verb.*]
That has not (been) fermented.
■ **unfermentable** *adjective* M19.

unfertile /ʌnˈfɜːtʌɪl/ *adjective.* L16.
[from UN-¹ + FERTILE.]
Infertile, unproductive.
■ **unfertilized** *adjective* not fertilized L18.

unfetter /ʌnˈfɛtə/ *verb trans.* ME.
[from UN-² + FETTER *noun, verb.*]
Release (as) from fetters.

unfettered /ʌnˈfɛtəd/ *adjective.* E17.
[from UN-¹ + *fettered* pa. pple of FETTER *verb.*]
Not restrained by fetters; *fig.* unrestrained, unrestricted.
📖 W. H. PRESCOTT A people accustomed from infancy to the unfettered exercise of their faculties.

unfigured /ʌnˈfɪgəd/ *adjective.* L16.
[from UN-¹ + FIGURED.]
1 Not expressed in or using figurative language. L16.
2 Not marked with a numerical figure or figures. L16.
3 Not previously represented by a figure or figures. E19.
4 LOGIC. Of a syllogism: not belonging to any of the standard figures. M19.

unfilial /ʌnˈfɪlɪəl/ *adjective.* E17.
[from UN-¹ + FILIAL.]
Not befitting a son or daughter.
■ **unfilially** *adverb* M19.

unfilled /ʌnˈfɪld/ *adjective.* LME.
[from UN-¹ + FILLED.]
†**1** Unfulfilled. *rare.* LME–M17.
2 Not filled (*up*), less than full; left vacant, empty, or unsatisfied. LME.
■ **unfillable** *adjective* (now *rare*) ME.

unfilm /ʌnˈfɪlm/ *verb trans. poet. rare.* M19.
[from UN-² + FILM *noun, verb.*]
Remove a film from (a person's eyes).

unfilmable /ʌnˈfɪlməb(ə)l/ *adjective.* E20.
[from UN-¹ + FILMABLE.]
Not suitable for making into a cinema or television film.

unfinished /ʌnˈfɪnɪʃt/ *adjective.* M16.
[from UN-¹ + FINISHED.]
Not finished; incomplete.
■ **unfinishable** *adjective* M18. **unfinishedness** *noun* (*rare*) L19.

unfired /ʌnˈfʌɪəd/ *adjective.* L16.
[from UN-¹ + *fired* pa. pple of FIRE *verb.*]
1 Not ignited or set on fire. L16.
2 Not subjected to the action or effect of fire. L18.
3 Of a gun, bullet, etc.: not discharged by firing. L19.

unfirm /ʌnˈfɜːm/ *adjective.* L16.
[from UN-¹ + FIRM *adjective*: cf. INFIRM *adjective.*]
1 Of a loose or soft consistency; not solid or compact in structure. L16.
†**2** Unsteady, flighty. *rare* (Shakes.). Only in E17.
3 Not firmly placed or fixed; insecure; unstable, unsteady. L17.
■ **unfirmly** *adverb* M17. **unfirmness** *noun* M16.

unfished /ʌnˈfɪʃt/ *adjective.* M19.
[from UN-¹ + *fished* pa. pple of FISH *verb*¹.]
Of a stretch of water etc.: not fished.
■ **unfishable** *adjective* L19.

unfit /ʌnˈfɪt/ *adjective & noun.* LME.
[from UN-¹ + FIT *adjective.*]
▶**A** *adjective.* Compar. & superl. **-tt-**.
1 Of a thing: not fit, proper, or suitable (*for*, *to do*, *to be done*). Of a person etc.: not fitted, qualified, or worthy (*to do*, *for*); incompetent. LME.
2 Not physically fit. (Foll. by *for*, *to do*.) M17.
📖 **1** G. BERKELEY Monsters, utterly unfit for human society. LD MACAULAY One man might fill a post for which he was unfit. A. SILLITOE The houses . . were condemned as unfit to live in.
▶**B** *noun.* A person whose mental or physical health falls below a desired standard. *rare.* E20.
■ **unfitly** *adverb* inappropriately, unsuitably M16. **unfitness** *noun* L16. **unfitted** *adjective* (**a**) unfit, unsuitable (*for*, *to do*); (**b**) not equipped or provided with fittings: L16. **unfittedness** *noun* (*rare*) unsuitability M17. **unfitting** *adjective* not fitting or suitable; unbecoming, improper: LME. **unfittingly** *adverb* LME. **unfitty** *adjective* (*rare*, long *obsolete* exc. *dial.*) not fitty, unfit E17.

unfit /ʌnˈfɪt/ *verb trans.* Infl. **-tt-**. E17.
[from UN-² + FIT *verb*¹.]
Make unfit or unsuitable. Usu. foll. by *for*.

unfix /ʌnˈfɪks/ *verb.* L16.
[from UN-² + FIX *verb.*]
1 *verb trans.* Loosen or release from a fixed state or position; detach, undo. L16.
2 *verb trans. fig.* Unsettle; make uncertain or doubtful. M17.

3 *verb intrans.* Become unfixed. *rare.* M19.

> 2 LD MACAULAY The shock which . . overturned his early prejudices had . . unfixed all his opinions.

unfixed /ʌnˈfɪkst/ *adjective.* L16.
[from UN-[1] + FIXED.]
1 Not fixed in place or position; loose, free. L16.
2 *fig.* Unsettled, uncertain; fluctuating, variable. M17.
■ **unfixedness** /-sɪdnɪs/ *noun* M17.

unflappable /ʌnˈflapəb(ə)l/ *adjective. colloq.* M20.
[from UN-[1] + FLAP *noun or verb* + -ABLE.]
Imperturbable; *esp.* not liable to panic or become flustered under pressure.
■ **unflappaˈbility** *noun* M20. **unflappably** *adverb* M20.

†unfledge *verb trans. rare.* L16–E19.
[from UN-[2] + FLEDGE *verb.*]
Remove the feathers from (a bird etc.).

unfledged /ʌnˈflɛdʒd/ *adjective.* L16.
[from UN-[1] + FLEDGED.]
1 Not yet fledged (*lit. & fig.*); undeveloped; inexperienced. L16.
2 Pertaining to or characteristic of youth and inexperience. L16.

> 1 E. SITWELL The unfledged thoughts within my brain / sing in their sad and wintry nest. 2 SHAKES. *Wint. T.* In those unfledg'd days was my wife a girl.

unflesh /ʌnˈflɛʃ/ *verb trans.* L16.
[from UN-[2] + FLESH *verb.*]
Strip of flesh.

unfleshed /ʌnˈflɛʃt/ *adjective.* M16.
[from UN-[1] + *fleshed* pa. pple of FLESH *verb.*]
(Esp. of a hound) that has not yet tasted flesh; *fig.* (esp. of a person) untried, inexperienced.

unfold /ʌnˈfəʊld/ *verb*[1]. OE.
[from UN-[2] + FOLD *verb*[1].]
► **I** *verb trans.* **1** Open the fold or folds of; spread or straighten out, expand. OE. ▸**b** Part (the lips etc.); open or undo (a gate, door, etc.). Now *rare.* ME.
2 Reveal (a thought, idea, mystery, etc.); explain, make clear. OE.
3 Lay open to view; show, display. LME.
4 Unwrap. *rare.* M16.

> 1 F. W. FARRAR Would some new rosebud . . unfold itself among them? M. WARNER Davide took up his razor, unfolded the blade from its sheath. *fig.*: G. HERBERT Unfold thy forehead gather'd into frowns. **b** SOUTHEY The gates of iron, by no human arm Unfolded, turning on their hinges slow. 2 SHAKES. *Haml.* Nay, answer me. Stand and unfold yourself. M. A. CAWS I would prefer to see this endeavour as explicating or unfolding . . each subject. 3 H. I. JENKINSON When the . . journey is accomplished a lovely prospect is unfolded. *fig.*: C. PETERS The book . . unfolds Ireland to the reader.

► **II** *verb intrans.* **5** Open up or out; spread out; expand, develop; become clear. ME.

> 5 W. ROBERTSON The queen's scheme began gradually to unfold. E. H. SEARS A system of infinite truth, which is to unfold through the ages. M. HOCKING Crocuses were already unfolding in flower borders.

■ **unfolder** *noun* E17. **unfoldment** *noun* the process of unfolding M19.

unfold /ʌnˈfəʊld/ *verb*[2] *trans.* M16.
[from UN-[2] + FOLD *noun*[1] or *verb*[2].]
Release (sheep) from a fold or folds.

unforced /ʌnˈfɔːst/ *adjective.* L16.
[from UN-[1] + FORCED.]
1 Not compelled or constrained; not caused by force of circumstances. L16.
2 Not strained; not produced by or involving (strenuous) effort; easy, natural. E17.

> 1 DRYDEN Why thus, unforced, should we so tamely yield? 2 ADDISON This is one of Ovid's finished stories. The transition to it is proper and unforced.

■ **unforcedly** /ʌnˈfɔːsɪdli/ *adverb* M17. **unforcible** *adjective* lacking force or power L16. **unforcibly** *adverb* M19.

unforeseeing /ʌnfɔːˈsiːɪŋ/ *adjective.* E17.
[from UN-[1] + *foreseeing* pres. pple of FORESEE.]
Not foreseeing; not exercising foresight.
■ **unforeseeable** *adjective* L17. **unforeseeingly** *adverb* E17.

unforeseen /ʌnfɔːˈsiːn/ *adjective.* LME.
[from UN-[1] + *foreseen* pa. pple of FORESEE.]
That has not been foreseen.

> *Elle* Sudden unforeseen events that can turn your world upside down.

†unforeskinned *adjective. rare* (Milton). Only in L17.
[from UN-[1] or UN-[2] + FORESKIN: see -ED[2], -ED[1].]
Circumcised.

unforfeited /ʌnˈfɔːfɪtɪd/ *adjective. rare.* L16.
[from UN-[1] + *forfeited* pa. pple of FORFEIT *verb.*]
Not forfeited.
■ **†unforfeit** *adjective* = UNFORFEITED M17. **unforfeitable** *adjective* not forfeitable M17.

unforgettable /ʌnfəˈɡɛtəb(ə)l/ *adjective.* E19.
[from UN-[1] + FORGETTABLE.]
That cannot be forgotten; memorable, wonderful.
■ **unforgetful** *adjective* (*rare*) not forgetful M17. **unforgettably** *adverb* L19.

unforgivable /ʌnfəˈɡɪvəb(ə)l/ *adjective.* Also **-giveable.** M16.
[from UN-[1] + FORGIVABLE.]
Not forgivable.
■ **unforgivably** *adverb* L19.

unforgiven /ʌnfəˈɡɪv(ə)n/ *adjective.* LME.
[from UN-[1] + *forgiven* pa. pple of FORGIVE.]
†**1** *SCOTS LAW.* Without remission. LME–E17.
2 Not forgiven. M16.

unforgiving /ʌnfəˈɡɪvɪŋ/ *adjective.* E18.
[from UN-[1] + *forgiving* pres. pple of FORGIVE.]
Not forgiving.
■ **unforgiveness** *noun* = UNFORGIVINGNESS E17. **unforgivingly** *adverb* L19. **unforgivingness** *noun* M18.

unforgotten /ʌnfəˈɡɒt(ə)n/ *adjective.* E19.
[from UN-[1] + *forgotten* pa. pple of FORGET *verb.*]
Not forgotten.
■ Also **unforgot** *adjective* (*arch.*) M17.

unform /ʌnˈfɔːm/ *verb trans.* E17.
[from UN-[2] + FORM *noun* or *verb*[1].]
Divest of (a) form; make shapeless.

unformed /ʌnˈfɔːmd/ *adjective.* ME.
[from UN-[1] + *formed* pa. pple of FORM *verb*[1].]
1 a Not having or given a regular or definite form, shapeless. ME. ▸**b** Not (well or properly) developed; crude. L17.
2 Not formed or made; uncreated. ME.

> 1a S. HILL The face . . had somehow become a child's face again, soft, unformed. **b** L. NKOSI A very curious incident . . left a deep impression on my young and unformed mind.

unforthcoming /ʌnfɔːθˈkʌmɪŋ/ *adjective.* E20.
[from UN-[1] + FORTHCOMING *ppl adjective.*]
Of a person: not forthcoming, reticent, disinclined to be responsive.

unfortunate /ʌnˈfɔːtʃ(ə)nət/ *adjective & noun.* LME.
[from UN-[1] + FORTUNATE *adjective & noun.*]
► **A** *adjective.* **1** Esp. of a person: not favoured by fortune; suffering misfortune; unlucky, unhappy. LME. ▸**b** Of a woman: engaged in prostitution. *arch.* L18.
2 Disastrous, inauspicious. Also, untoward, regrettable. M16.

> 1 W. ROBERTSON Late next morning . . the fate of the unfortunate prince was known. *Independent* If you are unfortunate enough to make a loss . . you can claim a special relief. 2 *Mind* It is unfortunate that many . . Analysts have been too literal-minded. F. L. ALLEN Unfortunate publicity had a tendency to rock the boat. E. O'BRIEN A new pullover, a most unfortunate colour, like piccalilli.

► **B** *noun.* **1** An unfortunate person. L17.
2 *spec.* A prostitute. *arch.* E19.
■ **†unfortunable** *adjective* unfortunate E16–E18. **unfortunately** *adverb* (**a**) in an unfortunate manner; unhappily, unluckily; (**b**) (modifying a sentence) it is unfortunate that: E16. **unfortunateness** *noun* M16. **unfortune** *noun* (*arch.*) misfortune, bad luck LME.

unfounded /ʌnˈfaʊndɪd/ *adjective.* M17.
[from UN-[1] + FOUNDED.]
Having no foundation or basis. Chiefly *fig.*

> *Premiere* Her concerns about being typecast in . . urban films seem to be unfounded.

■ **unfoundedly** *adverb* E19. **unfoundedness** *noun* L20.

UNFPA *abbreviation.*
United Nations Fund for Population Activities.

unframe /ʌnˈfreɪm/ *verb trans.* Long *rare* or *obsolete.* ME.
[from UN-[2] + FRAME *verb.*]
†**1** Distress, trouble. Only in ME.
2 Take to pieces; destroy. M16.
3 Throw into confusion or disorder. L16.

> 2 *fig.*: R. SOUTH Sin has unframed the fabrick of the whole man.

unframed /ʌnˈfreɪmd/ *adjective.* M16.
[from UN-[1] + FRAMED.]
1 Not formed, moulded, or fashioned. Long *rare* or *obsolete.* M16.
2 Esp. of a picture: not set in a frame. E18.

unfraught /ʌnˈfrɔːt/ *adjective. rare.* L16.
[from UN-[1] + FRAUGHT *adjective.*]
Not fraught (*with*).

†unfraught *verb trans.* M16–L18.
[from UN-[2] + FRAUGHT *noun* or *verb.*]
Unload, discharge.

unfree /ʌnˈfriː/ *adjective.* ME.
[from UN-[1] + FREE *adjective.*]
†**1** Ignoble, base. *rare.* Only in ME.
2 Characterized by lack of freedom; deprived of liberty. LME. ▸**b** *spec.* Not holding the position of a freeman of a corporation, city, etc. Long *arch.* LME.

> 2 *Times* The use of criminal law against dissidents in unfree countries. B. MALAMUD It's marriage . . . I feel boxed in, unfree. *Times Lit. Suppl.* Many . . infer from physicalism that the will is unfree.

■ **unfreed** *adjective* not freed, *esp.* imprisoned M16. **unfreedom** *noun* lack of freedom LME. **unfreeman** *noun* (*arch.*) a person who is not a freeman of a corporation etc. LME.

unfreeze /ʌnˈfriːz/ *verb.* Infl. as FREEZE *verb*; pa. t. **-froze** /-ˈfrəʊz/; pa. pple usu. **-frozen** /-ˈfrəʊz(ə)n/. L16.
[from UN-[2] + FREEZE *verb.*]
1 *verb trans.* Cause to thaw (*lit. & fig.*). L16. ▸**b** Make (assets, credits, etc.) realizable; remove restrictions or rigid control from (wages, prices, etc.). M20.
2 *verb intrans.* Thaw (*lit. & fig.*). M17.

> 1 G. K. CHESTERTON Laughter . . unfreezes pride and unwinds secrecy. J. GARDNER He had unfrozen a quiche, cooked last week. **b** *Time* Leaders agreed . . to unfreeze the aid package for Israel. 2 *Scotsman* The atmosphere unfroze; . . even the hotel people became polite and gentle.

unfresh /ʌnˈfrɛʃ/ *adjective.* M19.
[from UN-[1] + FRESH *adjective.*]
Not fresh.
■ **unfreshness** *noun* L19.

unfriend /ʌnˈfrɛnd, ˈʌn-/ *noun.* ME.
[from UN-[1] + FRIEND *noun.*]
A person who is not a friend or on friendly terms; an enemy.
■ **unˈfriendship** *noun* (*arch.*) unfriendliness, enmity ME.

unfriended /ʌnˈfrɛndɪd/ *adjective.* Now *literary.* E16.
[from UN-[1] + FRIENDED.]
Without friends; friendless.

unfriendly /ʌnˈfrɛndli/ *adjective & noun.* LME.
[from UN-[1] + FRIENDLY *adjective & noun.*]
► **A** *adjective.* Not friendly; inimical, hostile; not favourable (*to*). LME.

> R. W. CHURCH His . . suspicious, but probably not unfriendly relative. A. F. DOUGLAS-HOME If in that arid and unfriendly land a man was parted from his mount, he perished. R. ELLMANN André Raffalovich, an unfriendly witness, says that Wilde boasted.

► **B** *noun.* An unfriendly person or thing; *spec.* an enemy. *colloq.* (chiefly *US*). L20.
■ **unfriendliness** *noun* L17.

unfriendly /ʌnˈfrɛndli/ *adverb.* Now *rare.* OE.
[from UN-[1] + FRIENDLY *adjective* or *adverb.*]
In an unfriendly manner.

unfrock /ʌnˈfrɒk/ *verb trans.* M17.
[from UN-[2] + FROCK.]
Defrock; deprive of priestly function or office.

unfroze *verb pa. t.* of UNFREEZE.

unfrozen /ʌnˈfrəʊz(ə)n/ *adjective.* L16.
[from UN-[1] + FROZEN *adjective.*]
Not frozen.

unfrozen *verb pa. pple*: see UNFREEZE.

unfruitful /ʌnˈfruːtfʊl, -f(ə)l/ *adjective.* LME.
[from UN-[1] + FRUITFUL.]
1 Not bearing offspring, barren; *fig.* unprofitable, unrewarding. LME.
2 (Of a tree) not bearing fruit; (of soil, a season, etc.) unfertile, unproductive. LME.
■ **unfruitfully** *adverb* LME. **unfruitfulness** *noun* M16.

unfulfilled /ʌnfʊlˈfɪld/ *adjective.* LME.
[from UN-[1] + *fulfilled* pa. pple of FULFIL.]
Not fulfilled; not carried out or brought to completion.
■ **unfulfillable** *adjective* impossible to fulfil M20. **unfulfilling** *adjective* that does not fulfil or satisfy a person E19. **unfulfilment** *noun* (*rare*) failure (of a prophecy) to be fulfilled M19.

unfunny /ʌnˈfʌni/ *adjective.* M19.
[from UN-[1] + FUNNY *adjective.*]
Not funny or amusing (though intended to be).
■ **unfunnily** *adverb* M20. **unfunniness** *noun* E20.

unfurl /ʌnˈfəːl/ *verb.* M17.
[from UN-[2] + FURL *verb.*]
1 *verb trans.* Spread out (a flag or sail) to the wind. Now also, open out (a fan, umbrella, etc.). M17.
2 *verb intrans.* Open to the wind; become spread out. E19.

> 1 *fig.*: R. CAMPBELL One or two whose love is not unfurled Like a salutation banner to the world. 2 C. PATMORE As to the breeze a flag unfurls My spirit expanded.

■ **unfurlable** *adjective* (*rare*) M19.

unfurnish /ʌnˈfəːnɪʃ/ *verb trans.* L16.
[from UN-[2] + FURNISH *verb.*]
1 Divest (a place etc.) of men or defences. Also foll. by *of.* Long *rare.* L16.

2 Divest of furniture; remove the furnishings from. L16.
†3 Deprive (a person) *of* a thing. L16–M17.

📖 1 W. F. P. NAPIER English troops should, without unfurnishing Lisbon, co-operate for the relief of Oporto. 3 SHAKES. *Wint. T.* Thy speeches Will bring me to consider that which may Unfurnish me of reason.

unfurnished /ʌnˈfəːnɪʃt/ *adjective.* M16.
[from UN-¹ + *furnished* pa. pple of FURNISH *verb.*]
1 Not provided, equipped, or prepared. Also foll. by *with*, (arch.) *of*. M16.
2 Of a house, flat, etc.: not provided with furniture; *spec.* not furnished by the landlord or letter. L16.

📖 1 W. COWPER All the tricks, . . To fill the void of an unfurnished brain. C. LAMB Nor am I so unfurnished . . Of practicable schemes. J. BADCOCK The sight-hole . . is still unfurnished with a glass of any sort.

unfussy /ʌnˈfʌsi/ *adjective.* E19.
[from UN-¹ + FUSSY.]
Not fussy, not excessively concerned with trivial matters.
■ **unfussily** *adverb* M20.

ungain /ʌnˈgeɪn/ *noun. Long arch. rare.* ME.
[from UN-¹ + GAIN *noun*¹.]
Detriment, loss.

ungain /ʌnˈgeɪn/ *adjective. obsolete* exc. *dial.* LME.
[from UN-¹ + GAIN *adjective.*]
1 Of a path etc.: indirect; roundabout. LME.
2 Unpleasant, disagreeable. LME.
3 Inconvenient, troublesome, difficult. LME.
4 Unskilled, incompetent; clumsy, ungainly. LME.

ungainful /ʌnˈgeɪnfʊl, -f(ə)l/ *adjective.* L16.
[from UN-¹ + GAINFUL.]
Not gainful; (of employment) unpaid, badly paid.
■ **ungainfully** *adverb* L16.

ungainly /ʌnˈgeɪnli/ *adjective.* E17.
[from UN-¹ + GAINLY *adjective.*]
Awkward, clumsy, ungraceful.

📖 C. EASTON An overgrown, somewhat ungainly schoolgirl. INA TAYLOR Deafness which necessitated her carrying . . an ungainly ear-trumpet.

■ **ungainliness** *noun* M18.

ungainly /ʌnˈgeɪnli/ *adverb.* ME.
[from UN-¹ + GAINLY *adverb.*]
†1 Threateningly, terribly. *rare.* Only in ME.
†2 Improperly; unsuitably. LME–M16.
3 In an ungainly manner; awkwardly, clumsily. M17.

ungainsayable /ʌngeɪnˈseɪəb(ə)l/ *adjective.* E17.
[from UN-¹ + GAINSAY *verb* + -ABLE.]
Undeniable, irrefutable.

📖 R. GRAVES My pleasure in your feet and hair Is ungainsayable.

■ **ungainsayably** *adverb* M17.

ungallant /ʌnˈgal(ə)nt, ʌngəˈlant/ *adjective.* E18.
[from UN-¹ + GALLANT *adjective.*]
Not gallant; unchivalrous, discourteous.
■ **ungallantly** *adverb* M19. **ungallantry** /-ˈgaləntri/ *noun* ungallant or unchivalrous behaviour E18.

ungarbled /ʌnˈgɑːb(ə)ld/ *adjective.* LME.
[from UN-¹ + *garbled* pa. pple of GARBLE *verb.*]
1 Not cleansed or sifted; not selected or sorted out. Now *rare.* LME.
2 Of a statement, story, etc.: clearly and correctly presented; not mutilated or distorted. E18.

ungarnish /ʌnˈgɑːnɪʃ/ *verb trans.* M16.
[from UN-² + GARNISH *verb.*]
Remove the garnish from.

ungarnished /ʌnˈgɑːnɪʃt/ *adjective.* LME.
[from UN-¹ + GARNISHED.]
Having no garnish; unembellished, unadorned.

ungathered /ʌnˈgaðəd/ *adjective.* LME.
[from UN-¹ + *gathered* pa. pple of GATHER *verb.*]
1 Not gathered or brought together; uncollected. LME.
▸b Of a flower, fruit, etc.: not picked or harvested. L16.
2 Not drawn up by a thread. E17.

ungave *verb pa. t.* of UNGIVE.

ungear /ʌnˈgɪə/ *verb trans.* E17.
[from UN-² + GEAR *noun & verb.*]
1 Unharness. Now *dial.* & *N. Amer.* E17.
2 Disconnect or undo the gearing of. E19.

ungeared /ʌnˈgɪəd/ *adjective.* E16.
[from UN-¹ + GEARED.]
Not having gears or gearing. Also, ill-equipped.

ungelded /ʌnˈgɛldɪd/ *adjective.* Also (now *rare*) **ungelt**. LME.
[from UN-¹ + *gelded* pa. pple of GELD *verb*¹.]
Not gelded; uncastrated.

ungenial /ʌnˈdʒiːnɪəl/ *adjective.* E18.
[from UN-¹ + GENIAL *adjective*¹.]
1 Not conducive to growth; *esp.* (of climate etc.) cold, wet; raw. E18.
2 Not agreeable or suited *to* a person. L18.
3 Not jovial, kindly, or sociable. L18.

📖 1 *Washington Post* The first wet, ungenial summer night. 3 *Washington Post* He began to grow . . unpopular, branded as 'unsociable, ungenial, and morose.'

■ **ungenially** *adverb* E19.

ungenteel /ʌndʒɛnˈtiːl/ *adjective.* M17.
[from UN-¹ + GENTEEL.]
Not genteel.
■ **ungenteelly** *adverb* M17. **ungenteelness** *noun* E18.

ungentle /ʌnˈdʒɛnt(ə)l/ *adjective.* LME.
[from UN-¹ + GENTLE *adjective.*]
†1 Of a person, a person's birth, family, etc.: not noble or distinguished. LME–L17.
2 (Of a person) not of noble character; (of an action etc.) inappropriate to a person of gentle birth; unchivalrous, discourteous. *arch.* LME.
3 Not gentle in action, effect, or degree; not mild or benign in disposition; rough, harsh, cruel. LME.

📖 2 R. MACAULAY Poor clothes and manners and ungentle outlook. 3 J. KEBLE Jesus in His babes abiding Shames our cold ungentle ways. LD MACAULAY His temper, naturally ungentle, had been exasperated by his domestic vexations.

■ **ungentleness** *noun* LME. **ungently** *adverb* LME.

ungentleman /ʌnˈdʒɛnt(ə)lmən/ *verb trans. Long rare.* L17.
[from UN-² + GENTLEMAN.]
Deprive of the status or character of a gentleman.

ungentlemanlike /ʌnˈdʒɛnt(ə)lmənlʌɪk/ *adjective & adverb.* L16.
[from UN-¹ + GENTLEMANLIKE.]
▶ **A** *adjective.* = UNGENTLEMANLY *adjective.* L16.
▶ **B** *adverb.* Not in the manner of a gentleman. Now *rare.* M17.

ungentlemanly /ʌnˈdʒɛnt(ə)lmənli/ *adjective & adverb.* M16.
[from UN-¹ + GENTLEMANLY.]
▶ **A** *adjective.* Not gentlemanly; not resembling or appropriate to a gentleman. M16.

📖 D. L. SAYERS It's very ungentlemanly to commit suicide without leaving a note.

▶ **B** *adverb.* Not as befits a gentleman. Now *rare.* L16.
■ **ungentlemanliness** *noun* E19.

unget /ʌnˈgɛt/ *verb trans. rare.* Infl. as GET *verb*; pa. t. usu. **-got** /-ˈgɒt/, pa. pple usu. **-got**, ***-gotten** /-ˈgɒt(ə)n/. L18.
[from UN-² + GET *verb.*]
Cause to be unbegotten. Also, give up possession of.

ungifted /ʌnˈgɪftɪd/ *adjective.* M17.
[from UN-¹ + GIFTED.]
1 Having no exceptional talents or gifts; (foll. by *with*) not possessing a specified talent. M17.
2 Having received no gifts. *poet.* M17.

📖 1 *Washington Post* The ungifted Americans who had . . played at Miami.

ungild /ʌnˈgɪld/ *verb trans.* Pa. t. & pple **ungilded**, **ungilt** /ʌnˈgɪlt/. L16.
[from UN-² + GILD *verb*¹.]
Remove gilding from.

ungilded /ʌnˈgɪldɪd/ *adjective.* L17.
[from UN-¹ + GILDED.]
Not gilded; not covered (as) with gilding.
■ Also **ungilt** *adjective* LME.

ungilded *verb*, **ungilt** *verb pa. t. & pple*: see UNGILD.

ungird /ʌnˈgəːd/ *verb trans.* Pa. t. & pple **ungirded**, **ungirt** /ʌnˈgəːt/. OE.
[from UN-² + GIRD *verb*¹.]
1 Undo a belt, girdle, or girth from. OE.
2 Release or take off by undoing a belt, girdle, or girth. L15.

ungirded /ʌnˈgəːdɪd/ *adjective.* Orig. †**ungird**. LME.
[from UN-¹ + *girded* pa. pple of GIRD *verb*¹.]
= next.

ungirt /ʌnˈgəːt/ *adjective.* ME.
[from UN-¹ + *girt* pa. pple of GIRD *verb*¹.]
Not wearing or fastened with a belt or girdle; *fig.* undisciplined, unprepared.

📖 R. W. EMERSON Our later generation appears ungirt, frivolous. E. BOWEN Long . . curtains that hung down ungirt beside the window.

ungirt *verb pa. t. & pple*: see UNGIRD.

ungive /ʌnˈgɪv/ *verb intrans. obsolete* exc. *dial.* Pa. t. **ungave** /ʌnˈgeɪv/; pa. pple **ungiven** /ʌnˈgɪv(ə)n/. E16.
[from UN-² + GIVE *verb.*]
Give way, relax; slacken.

ungiven /ʌnˈgɪv(ə)n/ *adjective.* ME.
[from UN-¹ + GIVEN.]
1 Not given or bestowed. Formerly *spec.*, not given in marriage. ME.
2 Not partial or prone *to* something. *rare.* L19.

ungiven *verb pa. pple* of UNGIVE.

ungiving /ʌnˈgɪvɪŋ/ *adjective.* L17.
[from UN-¹ + *giving* pres. pple of GIVE *verb.*]
Not giving; not inclined to give.

unglue /ʌnˈgluː/ *verb.* Pres. pple & verbal noun **unglu(e)ing**. M16.
[from UN-² + GLUE *verb.*]
1 *verb trans.* Separate or loosen (things glued together); *transf.* open (the eyes) after sleep. M16. ▸**b** *fig.* Detach (*from*); separate, dissolve. E17.
2 *verb intrans.* Lose cohesion; become detached. L17.

📖 1 SWIFT She stretches, gapes, unglues her eyes. **b** H. CAINE Unless we unglue ourselves from the vanities which imperil our existence.

unglued /ʌnˈgluːd/ *adjective.* E17.
[from UN-¹ + *glued* pa. pple of GLUE *verb.*]
Having no glue, unstuck; *fig.* confused, incoherent. Chiefly in ***become unglued***, ***come unglued***.

ungodly /ʌnˈgɒdli/ *adjective.* E16.
[from UN-¹ + GODLY *adjective.*]
1 Not observant of or in accordance with divine will or law; irreligious, impious. E16. ▸**b** Of the stomach: insatiable, greedy. Now *rare* or *obsolete.* M18.
2 Outrageous, dreadful. *colloq.* L19.

📖 1 V. GLENDINNING His sport was disapproved of . . as frivolous and ungodly. 2 R. FULLER I was frightened of her . . criticism of my being up at such an ungodly hour.

■ **ungodlily** *adverb* (now *rare*) L16. **ungodliness** *noun* E16.

ungodly /ʌnˈgɒdli/ *adverb.* E16.
[from UN-¹ + GODLY *adverb.*]
In an ungodly manner; *colloq.* (chiefly *US*) outrageously, dreadfully.

📖 G. NAYLOR This place was ungodly hot.

ungood /ʌnˈgʊd/ *adjective & noun.* OE.
[from UN-¹ + GOOD *noun, adjective.*]
▶ **A** *adjective.* Not good; evil, bad; wicked. OE.

📖 *New York Review of Books* We . . see ourselves as ungood, . . so we are attracted to descriptions of naughtiness.

▶ **B** *noun.* That which is not good; evil. ME.
¶ Not recorded between L16 and L19.

ungot *verb pa. t. & pple*: see UNGET *verb.*

ungotten /ʌnˈgɒt(ə)n/ *ppl adjective.* Also †**ungot**. LME.
[from UN-¹ + GOTTEN *ppl adjective.*]
†1 Unbegotten. LME–L16.
2 Not acquired, obtained, or won. M16.

ungotten *verb pa. pple*: see UNGET.

ungovernable /ʌnˈgʌv(ə)nəb(ə)l/ *adjective.* L17.
[from UN-¹ + GOVERNABLE.]
That cannot be governed; uncontrollable.

📖 C. THUBRON Ungovernable fits of violence. P. P. READ It irked them to submit . . . They were by nature . . almost ungovernable.

■ **ungoverna'bility** *noun* M20. **ungovernableness** *noun* (now *rare*) L17. **ungovernably** *adverb* L17. **ungoverned** *adjective* not governed, uncontrolled L16.

ungraceful /ʌnˈgreɪsfʊl, -f(ə)l/ *adjective.* M17.
[from UN-¹ + GRACEFUL.]
Not graceful; clumsy.

📖 DICKENS A sullen, cumbrous, ungraceful, unshiplike leviathan. J. MCCARTHY His gestures were angular and ungraceful.

■ **ungrace** *noun* (*rare*) lack of grace LME. **ungraced** *adjective* not graced (*by* or *with*) L16. **ungracefully** *adverb* M17. **ungracefulness** *noun* M17.

ungracious /ʌnˈgreɪʃəs/ *adjective.* ME.
[from UN-¹ + GRACIOUS.]
†1 Not possessing or characterized by divine grace; ungodly, unrighteous, reprobate. ME–E19.
†2 Unfortunate, unlucky, unfavourable. LME–M17.
†3 Rude; unmannerly. M16–E17.
4 Not finding favour; unacceptable; disagreeable, unpleasant. *arch.* L16.
5 Not graceful or elegant; unattractive. M17.
6 Not kindly or congenial; not beneficent to others; discourteous. M18.

📖 5 R. RENDELL Ungracious living was evinced by . . doorbells, seven in an eight-roomed house. 6 E. WAUGH It is an ungracious habit to praise one thing while disparaging another.

■ **ungraciously** *adverb* ME. **ungraciousness** *noun* E16.

ungraduated /ʌnˈgradʒʊeɪtɪd, -djʊ-/ *adjective.* L18.
[from UN-¹ + GRADUATED.]
1 That has not graduated from a course of education or training. L18.
2 Not arranged or marked in grades or gradations. M19.

ungrammatical /ʌngrəˈmatɪk(ə)l/ *adjective.* M17.
[from UN-¹ + GRAMMATICAL.]
1 Not in accordance with the rules of grammar. M17.
2 *transf.* Not conforming to the rules or method of an art or science. M19.

1 R. M. DIXON 'I don't know why to go' is ungrammatical. **2** *Listener* His harmony is often ungrammatical.

■ **ungrammatiˈcality** *noun* M20. **ungrammatically** *adverb* E18. **ungrammaticalness** *noun* (now *rare*) L17.

ungraspable /ʌnˈgrɑːspəb(ə)l/ *adjective.* M18.
[from UN-¹ + GRASPABLE.]
That cannot be grasped; incomprehensible.

Times Lit. Suppl. The past is elusive and truth ungraspable.

■ **ungrasped** *adjective* not grasped, uncomprehended M18.

ungrate /ʌnˈgreɪt/ *noun & adjective.* LME.
[from UN-¹ + GRATE *adjective.*]
▶†**A** *noun.* = INGRATE *noun.* LME–E18.
▶**B** *adjective.* **1** Ungrateful. Cf. INGRATE *adjective* 2. *obsolete* exc. *Scot.* M16.
†**2** = INGRATE *adjective* 3. M16–M17.

ungrateful /ʌnˈgreɪtfʊl, -f(ə)l/ *adjective.* M16.
[from UN-¹ + GRATEFUL.]
1 Not feeling or showing gratitude; (of an action etc.) showing lack of gratitude. M16. ▶**b** *transf.* Of soil etc.: not responding to cultivation. *arch.* L17.
2 Unpleasant, disagreeable, distasteful. L16.

1 A. LAMBERT You're a thoroughly ungrateful little girl. After all the trouble we've been to. **2** J. GALSWORTHY The world was the most ungrateful place anybody could live in.

■ **ungratefully** *adverb* L16. **ungratefulness** *noun* L16.

ungreased /ʌnˈgriːst, -iːzd/ *adjective.* LME.
[from UN-¹ + *greased* pa. pple of GREASE *verb.*]
Not greased; unsoiled, unlubricated.
■ **ungreasy** *adjective* not greasy M20.

un-Greek /ʌnˈgriːk/ *noun & adjective.* M16.
[from UN-¹ + GREEK *noun & adjective.*]
▶**A** *noun.* A person who is not a Greek. Long *rare* or *obsolete.* M16.
▶**B** *adjective.* Not Greek; *esp.* not in accordance with Greek character, ideas, etc. M19.

ungreen /ʌnˈgriːn/ *adjective.* LME.
[from UN-¹ + GREEN *adjective.*]
1 Not green; lacking greenery. LME.
2 Harmful to the environment; not ecologically acceptable. L20.

1 E. B. BROWNING Her vales, ungreen Where steps of man have been!

ungrew *verb pa. t.*: see UNGROW.

unground /ʌnˈgraʊnd/ *adjective.* L15.
[from UN-¹ + GROUND *ppl adjective.*]
1 Not reduced to fine particles by grinding or crushing. L15.
2 Not shaped, sharpened, or polished by grinding. E17.

ungrounded /ʌnˈgraʊndɪd/ *adjective.* LME.
[from UN-¹ + GROUNDED.]
1 Not based or established *in* something. Also, (of an aircraft etc.) no longer grounded. LME.
2 Having no basis or justification; unfounded, groundless. LME.
3 Not thoroughly instructed or proficient *in* a subject etc. LME.
4 ELECTRICITY. Not grounded or earthed. M20.
■ **ungroundedness** *noun* E17.

ungrow /ʌnˈgrəʊ/ *verb intrans.* Long *rare.* Infl. as GROW *verb*; pa. t. usu. **ungrew** /ʌnˈgruː/, pa. pple usu. **ungrown** /ʌnˈgrəʊn/. L16.
[from UN-² + GROW *verb.*]
Grow smaller, esp. (ZOOLOGY) in the process of metamorphosis to an adult.

ungrown /ʌnˈgrəʊn/ *adjective.* L16.
[from UN-¹ + GROWN.]
Not yet fully grown; immature.
■ **ungrown-up** /ˈʌngrəʊnʌp, ʌngrəʊnˈʌp/ *adjective* not grown-up; immature: M20.

ungrown *verb pa. pple*: see UNGROW.

ungrudged /ʌnˈgrʌdʒd/ *adjective.* M17.
[from UN-¹ + *grudged* pa. pple of GRUDGE *verb.*]
Not grudged; given, granted, or allowed willingly.
■ **ungrudging** *adjective* not grudging L18. **ungrudgingly** *adverb* M17.

ungual /ˈʌŋgw(ə)l/ *adjective & noun.* Also †**ungueal**. M19.
[from Latin *unguis* nail + -AL¹.]
▶**A** *adjective.* **1** Chiefly ANATOMY & MEDICINE. Of, pertaining to, resembling, or affecting a fingernail or toenail. M19.
2 ZOOLOGY. Of or pertaining to an animal's claw or hoof. Also (*rare*), horny. L19.
1 †**ungual bone** (*a*) = *ungual phalanx* below; (*b*) = *lacrimal bone* s.v. LACHRYMAL *adjective.* **ungual phalanx** the terminal phalanx of a finger or toe.
▶**B** *noun.* An ungual phalanx or bone; a nail, hoof, or claw. M20.

unguard /ʌnˈgɑːd/ *verb trans.* L16.
[from UN-² + GUARD *verb.*]
†**1** Remove an ornamental trimming from. *rare.* Only in L16.
2 Remove a guard or defence from; expose to attack. M18. ▶**b** CARDS. Place (a high card) at risk of capture by discarding a lower protecting card. M19.

unguarded /ʌnˈgɑːdɪd/ *adjective.* L16.
[from UN-¹ + GUARDED.]
1 Not protected by a guard or sentry; undefended, open to attack, etc. L16. ▶**b** *transf.* CHESS & CARDS. Not protected by other pieces or cards. L17.
2 Not on one's guard; (of speech, behaviour, time, etc.) incautious, thoughtless, revealing. M17.
3 Not provided with a protective screen or other safety device. L18.

1 J. CONRAD This is now an unguarded spot. **2** L. NKOSI At such an unguarded moment I might be moved into making rash disclosures. A. LAMBERT All were relaxed, unguarded faces . . away from the scrutiny of the girls.

■ **unguardedly** *adverb* E18. **unguardedness** *noun* E19.

†**ungueal** *adjective & noun* var. of UNGUAL.

unguent /ˈʌŋgwənt/ *noun, verb, & adjective.* LME.
[Latin *unguentum*, from *unguere* anoint.]
▶**A** *noun.* A substance, esp. a perfumed oil, used as an ointment or lubricant; (a) salve. LME.
▶**B** *verb trans.* Apply (an) unguent to; anoint. M17.
▶**C** *adjective.* That is an unguent; *fig.* unctuous in manner. *rare.* E20.
■ **unguentous** *adjective* (*rare*) of the nature of (an) unguent; oily, greasy: M17.

unguentarium /ʌŋgwənˈtɛːrɪəm/ *noun.* Pl. **-ria** /-rɪə/. M19.
[Latin, use as noun of neut. of *unguentarius*: see next, -ARIUM.]
ARCHAEOLOGY. A vessel for holding perfumed oil or unguent.

unguentary /ˈʌŋgwənt(ə)ri/ *noun & adjective.* LME.
[Latin *unguentarius*, formed as UNGUENT: see -ARY¹.]
▶**A** *noun.* Now *rare.*
1 A producer of or trader in perfumed unguents or ointment. LME.
2 = UNGUENTARIUM. E20.
▶**B** *adjective.* Of, pertaining to, or used with unguents; *fig.* unctuous. M17.

Time His tongue utters unguentary lies.

■ **unguenˈtarian** *noun* (*rare*) = UNGUENTARY *noun* 1 M17.

ungues *noun* pl. of UNGUIS.

unguessed /ʌnˈgɛst/ *adjective.* LME.
[from UN-¹ + *guessed* pa. pple of GUESS *verb.*]
1 Unexpected, unanticipated. Long *rare* or *obsolete.* LME.
2 Not solved or known by guessing. L16. ▶**b** Not guessed *at*; unimagined. M18.

2 *Pilot* An explanation of its mysterious and once unseen and unguessed processes. **b** *New York Review of Books* Perhaps . . he withdrew into some unguessed at wilderness to re-examine his art.

■ **unˈguessable** *adjective* that cannot be guessed (at); unimaginable: M19.

†**unguicle** *noun.* M17–L18.
[Latin *unguiculus* dim. of UNGUIS.]
BOTANY. A part of a leaf or petal resembling a nail or claw.

unguiculate /ʌŋˈgwɪkjʊlət/ *adjective & noun.* E19.
[mod. Latin *unguiculatus*, from Latin *unguiculus* fingernail, toenail, dim. of UNGUIS: see -CULE, -ATE².]
▶**A** *adjective.* **1** BOTANY. Of a petal: having a narrow tapering lower part; clawed. E19.
2 ZOOLOGY. **a** Of a limb, foot, or digit: ending in or bearing one or more claws or nails. E19. ▶**b** Of an organ or part: having the form of a nail or claw, clawlike. E19. ▶**c** Of a mammal: having nails or claws. Cf. UNGULATE *adjective* 2. M19.
▶**B** *noun.* An unguiculate mammal. M19.
■ **unguiculated** *adjective* (now *rare*) = UNGUICULATE *adjective* 2 M18.

unguided /ʌnˈgʌɪdɪd/ *adjective.* L16.
[from UN-¹ + *guided* pa. pple of GUIDE *verb.*]
Not guided in a particular path or direction; undirected, uncontrolled.

G. GREENE Better . . they should believe they still had the true time . . than trust to their unguided guesses.

■ **unguidable** *adjective* not able to be guided E19. **unguidedly** *adverb* M17.

unguiform /ˈʌŋgwɪfɔːm/ *adjective.* E18.
[from UNGUIS + -I- + -FORM.]
Having the form of a nail or claw; claw-shaped.

unguilty /ʌnˈgɪlti/ *adjective.* OE.
[from UN-¹ + GUILTY *adjective.*]
1 Not guilty (*of*); guiltless; innocent. OE.
†**2** Not culpable or criminal. L16–M17.
■ **unguiltily** *adverb* M17.

unguis /ˈʌŋgwɪs/ *noun.* Pl. **-gues** /-gwiːz/. L17.
[Latin = nail, claw.]
†**1** = ONYX 3. L17–E18.
2 BOTANY. The narrow lower part of a petal; the claw. Opp. *lamina.* E18.
3 ZOOLOGY. A nail or claw. L18.

ungula /ˈʌŋgjʊlə/ *noun.* Pl. **-lae** /-liː/. LME.
[Latin = claw, hoof, from UNGUIS: see -ULE.]
†**1** = ONYCHA. Only in LME.
†**2** = ONYX *noun* 3. LME–L17.
3 GEOMETRY. An obliquely truncated cone or cylinder. Now *rare* or *obsolete.* E18.

ungulate /ˈʌŋgjʊlət, -leɪt/ *adjective & noun.* E19.
[Late Latin *ungulatus*, from UNGULA: see -ATE².]
Chiefly ZOOLOGY. ▶**A** *adjective.* **1** Having the form of a hoof; hoof-shaped. E19.
2 Of a mammal: having hoofs; belonging to a group of mammals (formerly the order Ungulata) characterized by hoofs. Cf. UNGUICULATE *adjective* 2C. M19.
▶**B** *noun.* An ungulate mammal. M19.
■ **ungulated** *adjective* (now *rare*) = UNGULATE *adjective* 2 E19.

unguled /ˈʌŋgjuːld/ *adjective.* L16.
[from UNGULA: see -ED².]
HERALDRY. Of an animal: with hoofs of a different tincture from the body.

unguligrade /ˈʌŋgjʊlɪgreɪd/ *adjective.* M19.
[formed as UNGULA + -I- + Latin *-gradus* walking.]
ZOOLOGY. Walking on hoofs or other modifications of the tips of the digits.

ungum /ʌnˈgʌm/ *verb trans.* Infl. **-mm-**. L16.
[from UN-² + GUM *verb*¹.]
Free (as) from gum or from being gummed.

ungummed /ʌnˈgʌmd/ *adjective.* L18.
[from UN-¹ + GUMMED *adjective*¹.]
Not gummed; not treated with gum.

unhabile /ʌnˈhabɪl/ *adjective. obsolete* exc. SCOTS LAW. M16.
[from UN-¹ + HABILE.]
Unfit, unable; unqualified; SCOTS LAW (of a witness) inadmissible. Cf. INHABILE.

unhabited /ʌnˈhabɪtɪd/ *adjective.* Now *rare.* L15.
[from UN-¹ + *habited* pa. pple of HABIT *verb.*]
Uninhabited.
■ **unhabitable** *adjective* uninhabitable LME.

unhacked /ʌnˈhakt/ *adjective. rare* (Shakes.). L16.
[from UN-¹ + *hacked* pa. pple of HACK *verb*¹.]
Not hacked or cut.

SHAKES. *John* With unhacked swords and helmets all unbruis'd.

unhackneyed /ʌnˈhaknɪd/ *adjective.* M18.
[from UN-¹ + HACKNEYED.]
1 Not habituated; inexperienced *in.* M18.
2 Not made to seem trite or commonplace through familiarity or overuse. E19.

1 SIR W. SCOTT One unhackneyed in the ways of intrigue. **2** *Gramophone* The all-too-familiar Op. 9 No. 2 is made to sound unhackneyed.

unhair /ʌnˈhɛː/ *verb* LME.
[from UN-² + HAIR *noun, verb.*]
1 *verb trans.* Remove the hair from (a person's head); make bald. LME. ▶**b** TANNING. Remove the hair from (a hide). M19.
2 *verb intrans.* TANNING. Of a hide: have the hair removed. M19.

unhaired /ʌnˈhɛːd/ *adjective. rare* (Shakes.). L16.
[from UN-¹ + HAIRED.]
Hairless, beardless.

unhallow /ʌnˈhaləʊ/ *verb trans.* M16.
[from UN-² + HALLOW *verb*¹.]
Remove the holy or sacred character of; secularize; profane.

unhallowed /ʌnˈhaləʊd/ *adjective.* OE.
[from UN-¹ + *hallowed* pa. pple of HALLOW *verb*¹.]
1 Not formally hallowed or consecrated. OE.
2 Not of a hallowed or sacred character; unholy, profane. L16.

unhamper /ʌnˈhampə/ *verb trans.* Now *rare.* **M17.**
[from UN-^{2} + HAMPER *verb*^{1}.]
Free of obstruction or restraint; set free, release.

unhampered /ʌnˈhampəd/ *adjective.* **L17.**
[from UN-^{1} + *hampered* pa. pple of HAMPER *verb*^{1}.]
Not hampered; unimpeded.

> J. ROSENBERG A quiet superiority, attained through greater knowledge, unhampered by fear or scepticism.

unhand /ʌnˈhand/ *verb trans. arch. & joc.* **E17.**
[from UN-^{2} + HAND *verb*.]
Take one's hands off (a person); release from one's grasp.

> M. TWAIN Unhand me, thou foolish creature. A. T. ELLIS She had grown too sympathetic towards him to demand that he unhand her.

unhandled /ʌnˈhand(ə)ld/ *adjective.* **M16.**
[from UN-^{1} + *handled* pa. pple of HANDLE *verb*^{1}.]
1 Of a horse etc.: not broken in; untamed. **M16.**
2 Not dealt with or treated. **E17.**
3 Not touched or felt with the hand. **M17.**

unhandsome /ʌnˈhans(ə)m/ *adjective.* **M16.**
[from UN-^{1} + HANDSOME *adjective*.]
1 Not handsome in appearance; plain, unattractive. **M16.**
2 Unhandy, inconvenient, troublesome. Long *obsolete* exc. *dial.* **M16.**
†**3** Inexpert, unskilful. *rare* (Shakes.). Only in **E17.**
4 Not fitting or proper; unbecoming; not generous, mean. **M17.**
■ **unhandsomely** *adverb* **M16.** **unhandsomeness** *noun* **M16.**

unhandy /ʌnˈhandi/ *adjective.* **M17.**
[from UN-^{1} + HANDY.]
1 Not convenient to handle or use; awkward, clumsy. **M17.**
2 Not skilful with the hands; not dexterous. **M17.**

> **1** A. DUGGAN Guards, wearing armour of an antique fashion and carrying unhandy spears and swords. **2** B. COTTLE I have only once been on a little . . boat, being unhandy at things like this.

■ **unhandily** *adverb* **E18.** **unhandiness** *noun* **E18.**

unhang /ʌnˈhaŋ/ *verb trans.* Infl. as HANG *verb*; pa. t. & pple usu. **unhung** /ʌnˈhʌŋ/. **LME.**
[from UN-^{2} + HANG *verb*.]
Take down from a hanging position; NAUTICAL unship (a rudder).

unhanged /ʌnˈhaŋd/ *adjective.* **LME.**
[from UN-^{1} + *hanged* pa. pple of HANG *verb*. Cf. UNHUNG *adjective*.]
Not (yet) executed by hanging.

unhappen /ʌnˈhap(ə)n/ *verb.* **E19.**
[from UN-^{2} + HAPPEN *verb*.]
1 *verb intrans.* Of an occurrence: be reversed; become as though never having happened. **E19.**
2 *verb trans.* Cause not to have happened. **L20.**

> **1** A. D. T. WHITNEY Had I been letting things happen that couldn't unhappen any more, ever? **2** I. MURDOCH These things did happen. Keeping them secret isn't going to unhappen them.

unhappily /ʌnˈhapɪli/ *adverb.* **LME.**
[from UN-^{1} + HAPPILY.]
1 By misfortune or mischance; unfortunately; regrettably. Freq. modifying a sentence. **LME.**
2 With bad fortune or outcome; infelicitously; miserably, wretchedly. *arch.* exc. as passing into sense 4. **LME.** ▸**b** Unsuccessfully. Formerly also, inappropriately. **M16.** ▸†**c** With an unpleasant degree of accuracy etc. **L16–E17.**
†**3** Mischievously, maliciously. **E16–M17.** ▸†**b** Unfavourably. *rare* (Shakes.). Only in **E17.**
4 Not characterized by or involving happiness or pleasure. **L17.**

> **1** *Scientific American* Unhappily, Professor Lindenmayer died before the book was completed. **2** W. COWPER If, unhappily deceiv'd, I dream. **c** SHAKES. *Haml.* There might be thought, Though nothing sure, yet much unhappily. **4** B. PYM 'It said Old Gold on the tin,' said Julian unhappily. E. S. PERSON Falling in love later in life can provide unhappily married spouses with . . solace.

unhappiness /ʌnˈhapɪnɪs/ *noun.* **L15.**
[from UN-^{1} + HAPPINESS.]
1 The state or condition of being unhappy; discontent; misery; an instance of this. **L15.**
2 Misfortune, mishap; an instance of this. Now *rare.* **L15.**
†**3** Evil; mischief. **L15–E17.**

> **1** A. LAMBERT I shall die of unhappiness here. **2** TENNYSON I . . here lie thrown by whom I know not, all thro' mere unhappiness.

unhappy /ʌnˈhapi/ *adjective.* **ME.**
[from UN-^{1} + HAPPY *adjective*.]
1 Of an event, circumstance, place, etc. (formerly also of a person): causing or associated with misfortune or trouble. **ME.** ▸†**b** Mischievous; malicious, evil. **L15–L17.**
2 Not favoured or marked by good fortune; unfortunate, ill-fated. Now *esp.*, not happy with one's circumstances; miserable, wretched; (foll. by *with*) dissatisfied, not pleased. Also foll. by *in*. **LME.** ▸**b** Unsuccessful; infelicitous; inappropriate. **M17.**

> **1** J. G. LOCKHART He had an unhappy propensity to drinking. A. N. WILSON One of those unhappy strokes Providence deals out to the virtuous. **2** J. BARZUN The unhappy projectors of these visions, some of whom were to pay . . with their lives. M. WARNER You were disappointed not to see him, but not yet unhappy. *Which?* If you are unhappy with the service provided by a bank, you can complain to the . . Ombudsman. **b** S. JOHNSON His imitation of Horace on Lucilius is not inelegant or unhappy.

unhappy /ʌnˈhapi/ *verb trans.* Long *arch.* **L16.**
[from UN-^{2} + HAPPY *verb*.]
Make unhappy.

unharassed /ʌnˈharəst, ʌnhəˈrast/ *adjective.* **L18.**
[from UN-^{1} + *harassed* pa. pple of HARASS *verb*.]
Not harassed; untroubled.

unharden /ʌnˈhɑːd(ə)n/ *verb trans.* **M16.**
[from UN-^{2} + HARDEN *verb*.]
Remove or lessen the hardness of; soften (*lit. & fig.*).

unhardened /ʌnˈhɑːd(ə)nd/ *adjective.* **L16.**
[from UN-^{1} + *hardened* pa. pple of HARDEN *verb*.]
Not hardened or made hard (*lit. & fig.*).

unhardy /ʌnˈhɑːdi/ *adjective.* **LME.**
[from UN-^{1} + HARDY *adjective*.]
Not hardy; not vigorous or robust.
■ **unhardiness** *noun* **E17.**

unharmed /ʌnˈhɑːmd/ *adjective* (usu. *pred.*). **ME.**
[from UN-^{1} + *harmed* pa. pple of HARM *verb*.]
Not harmed; uninjured, undamaged.
■ **unharmful** *adjective* not harmful; harmless: **M16.** **unharmfully** *adverb* **L19.** **unharming** *adjective* (chiefly *literary*) causing no harm **L18.**

unharmonious /ʌnhɑːˈməʊnɪəs/ *adjective.* **M17.**
[from UN-^{1} + HARMONIOUS.]
1 Not harmonious in sound; untuneful, unmelodious. **M17.**
2 Not showing harmony or agreement; not cordial. **M17.**
■ **unharmoniously** *adverb* **L18.** **unharmonized** *adjective* not harmonized (*with*) **E19.**

unharness /ʌnˈhɑːnɪs/ *verb trans.* **LME.**
[from UN-^{2} + HARNESS *verb*.]
1 Remove armour from. Long *arch.* **LME.**
2 Free (a horse etc.) from harness; unyoke. **E17.**

unharnessed /ʌnˈhɑːnɪst/ *adjective.* **LME.**
[from UN-^{1} + HARNESSED.]
1 Not armed or wearing armour. Long *arch.* **LME.**
2 Not put in harness; (of a river etc.) not utilized for motive power. **E17.**

unharvested /ʌnˈhɑːvɪstɪd/ *adjective.* **M19.**
[from UN-^{1} + *harvested* pa. pple of HARVEST *verb*.]
1 Of land etc.: from which no harvest is taken. **M19.**
2 Of grain etc: not reaped and brought in. **L19.**

unhaste /ʌnˈheɪst/ *noun.* **L19.**
[from UN-^{1} + HASTE *noun*.]
Lack of haste.
■ **unhasting** *adjective* (*arch.*) not hastening; unhurrying: **M19.** **unhasty** *adjective* not hasty, unhurried **L16.**

unhatched /ʌnˈhatʃt/ *adjective*^{1}. **E17.**
[from UN-^{1} + *hatched* pa. pple of HATCH *verb*^{1}.]
(Of an egg, young bird, etc.) not yet hatched; *fig.* (of a plot etc.) not yet devised.

†**unhatched** *adjective*^{2}. *rare* (Shakes.). Only in **E17.**
[from UN-^{1} + *hatched* pa. pple of HATCH *verb*^{2}.]
Unmarked; unstained.

unhaunted /ʌnˈhɔːntɪd/ *adjective.* **LME.**
[from UN-^{1} + HAUNTED.]
1 Not frequented; uninhabited; lonely, solitary. **LME.**
2 Not haunted by a ghost etc. **E19.**

UNHCR *abbreviation.*
United Nations High Commission for Refugees.

unhead /ʌnˈhɛd/ *verb trans.* **LME.**
[from UN-^{2} + HEAD *verb*.]
1 Behead (a person). Long *arch.* **LME.**
2 Remove the top or end of. **E17.**

unheaded /ʌnˈhɛdɪd/ *adjective.* **L16.**
[from UN-^{1} + HEADED.]
Having no head (*arch. & poet.*); without a (written or printed) heading.

unheal *verb* var. of UNHELE.

unhealth /ʌnˈhɛlθ/ *noun.* **OE.**
[from UN-^{1} + HEALTH.]
Lack of good health; poor health.
■ **unhealthful** *adjective* not healthful; unhealthy: **L16.** **unhealthfully** *adverb* **L17.** **unhealthfulness** *noun* **L16.** **unhealthsome** *adjective* (now *rare*) (**a**) unwholesome; (**b**) unhealthy: **M16.**

unhealthy /ʌnˈhɛlθi/ *adjective.* **L16.**
[from UN-^{1} + HEALTHY.]
1 Harmful or not conducive to health; insalubrious; unwholesome. **L16.** ▸**b** Dangerous to life. *slang.* **E20.**
2 Not possessing or indicative of good health; weak, sickly. **E17.** ▸**b** MEDICINE. Not in a sound or healthy condition; diseased, infected. **E17.**
3 *fig.* Having bad or unpleasant effects; detrimental; imprudent. **E19.**

> **1** J. CAREW The over-heated room had a stale unhealthy smell. *Guardian* Junk food at lunch-times and unhealthy snacks at breaks. **2** D. SIMPSON She . . looked hot, her plump cheeks mottled an unhealthy shade of red. *Insight* This practice increases the population of unhealthy dogs . . for sale. **3** G. PALEY We . . often quarrelled, accusing other children of unhealthy aggression.

■ **unhealthily** *adverb* **M17.** **unhealthiness** *noun* **M17.**

unhear /ʌnˈhɪə/ *verb trans. rare.* Pa. t. & pple **unheard** /ʌnˈhəːd/. **ME.**
[from UN-^{2} + HEAR.]
Not hear; refuse to hear.

unheard /ʌnˈhəːd/ *adjective.* **ME.**
[from UN-^{1} + *heard* pa. pple of HEAR.]
1 Not perceived with the ear. **ME.** ▸**b** Of a person: not heard in a court of law etc.; not listened to. **L16.**
2 Not previously heard of; unknown, strange. Chiefly as ***unheard-of***. **LME.**

> **1** E. WAUGH The ocean, which lay unseen, unheard behind the scrubby foothills. **2** P. MEDAWAR Viruses were unrecognized, hormones were unheard of.

■ **unhearable** *adjective* (*rare*) inaudible **L15.** **unhearing** *adjective* not hearing, deaf **L18.**

unheart /ʌnˈhɑːt/ *verb trans. arch.* **L16.**
[from UN-^{2} + HEART *verb*.]
Dishearten.

unhearty /ʌnˈhɑːti/ *adjective.* **LME.**
[from UN-^{1} + HEARTY *adjective*.]
†**1** Faint-hearted; not bold. **LME–L15.**
2 Not hearty or genial. **L16.**
3 Listless, dispirited; in poor condition. *Scot.* (now *dial.*). **L17.**
■ **unheartsome** *adjective* (*Scot. & north.*) melancholy, cheerless **M17.**

unheeded /ʌnˈhiːdɪd/ *adjective.* **E17.**
[from UN-^{1} + *heeded* pa. pple of HEED *verb*.]
Not heeded; unnoticed, disregarded.
■ **unheedful** *adjective* heedless **L16.** **unheedfully** *adverb* (*rare*, Shakes.) **L16.** **unheedfulness** *noun* **L16.** †**unheedily** *adverb* heedlessly **L16–E18.** **unheeding** *adjective* not heeding; heedless or inattentive: **M18.** **unheedingly** *adverb* **L18.** **unheedy** *adjective* (long *rare* exc. *poet.*) heedless **L16.**

unheimlich /ʊnˈhaɪmlɪç/ *adjective.* **L19.**
[German.]
Uncanny, weird.

unhele /ʌnˈhiːl/ *verb trans. obsolete* exc. *dial.* Also **unheal**.
[Old English *unhelan*, from UN-^{2} + HELE *verb*.]
Uncover, expose; *spec.* strip of covering, esp. roofing material.

unhelm /ʌnˈhɛlm/ *verb refl. & trans. arch.* **LME.**
[from UN-^{2} + HELM *verb*^{1}.]
Remove a helmet from (oneself or another).

unhelmed /ʌnˈhɛlmd/ *adjective. arch.* **L15.**
[from UN-^{1} + HELMED.]
Not wearing a helmet; having had a helmet removed.

unhelp /ʌnˈhɛlp/ *verb trans. rare* (now *literary*). **L16.**
[from UN-^{2} + HELP *verb*.]
Deprive of help; hinder.

unhelped /ʌnˈhɛlpt/ *adjective.* **LME.**
[from UN-^{1} + *helped* pa. pple of HELP *verb*.]
Not helped; unaided.
■ **unhelpable** *adjective* not able to be helped **L19.** **unhelping** *adjective* not helping **E17.** **unhelpless** *adjective* (long *rare*) helpless **L17.**

unhelpful /ʌnˈhɛlpfʊl, -f(ə)l/ *adjective.* **L16.**
[from UN-^{1} + HELPFUL.]
Not giving or productive of help; unprofitable; not useful.
■ **unhelpfully** *adverb* **L19.** **unhelpfulness** *noun* **E17.**

unhemmed /ʌnˈhɛmd/ *adjective.* **LME.**
[from UN-^{1} + *hemmed* pa. pple of HEM *verb*^{1}.]
1 Not enclosed or confined. Long *rare.* **LME.**
2 Of a garment or piece of cloth: not having a hem. **M16.**

unheroic /ʌnhɪˈrəʊɪk/ *adjective.* M18.
[from UN-[1] + HEROIC *adjective.*]
Not heroic.
■ **un-ˈhero** *noun* an unheroic person; a person not resembling a conventional hero: M20. **unheroical** *adjective* unheroic M17. **unheroically** *adverb* M19. **unheroism** /ʌnˈhɛrəʊɪz(ə)m/ *noun* (*rare*) lack of heroism M19.

unhesitating /ʌnˈhɛzɪteɪtɪŋ/ *adjective.* M18.
[from UN-[1] + *hesitating* pres. pple of HESITATE.]
Not hesitating; confident; prompt.
■ **unhesitatingly** *adverb* E19.

unhewn /ʌnˈhjuːn/ *adjective.* LME.
[from UN-[1] + *hewn* pa. pple of HEW *verb.*]
1 Not chopped or cut with a weapon. LME.
2 Not formed or shaped by hewing; *fig.* rough, rugged. M17.

unhid *verb pa. t.* of UNHIDE.

unhidden /ʌnˈhɪd(ə)n/ *adjective.* L16.
[from UN-[1] + HIDDEN *ppl adjective.*]
Not hidden or concealed; open to view.
■ **unhideable** *adjective* unable to be hidden or concealed E17.

unhide /ʌnˈhʌɪd/ *verb trans.* Infl. as HIDE *verb*[1]; pa. t. **unhid** /ʌnˈhɪd/, pa. pple usu. **unhidden** /ʌnˈhɪd(ə)n/. ME.
[from UN-[2] + HIDE *verb*[1].]
Make open to view; disclose, reveal.

unhindered /ʌnˈhɪndəd/ *adjective.* E17.
[from UN-[1] + *hindered* pa. pple of HINDER *verb.*]
Not hindered or obstructed; unimpeded.
■ **unhinderable** *adjective* unable to be hindered or obstructed L17.

unhinge /ʌnˈhɪn(d)ʒ/ *verb trans.* Pres. pple & verbal noun **unhing(e)ing.** E17.
[from UN-[2] + HINGE *verb.*]
1 Take (a door etc.) off the hinges; remove the hinges from; *transf.* unlock, open. E17.
2 Unsettle, unbalance; disorder in mind etc.; throw into confusion. E17.
3 Detach or separate *from* something; dislodge. M17.

> 🕮 **2** *National Observer (US)* We are unhinging some old concepts. S. CHITTY The break with Jean seems to have unhinged her and she stole twenty francs.

■ **unhingement** *noun* the action or an act of unhinging; the fact of being or becoming unhinged: E19.

unhinged /ʌnˈhɪn(d)ʒd/ *adjective.* E18.
[pa. pple of UNHINGE: see -ED[1].]
1 Unsettled, unbalanced; mentally disordered; confused. E18.
2 Having the hinges removed; taken off the hinges. E19.

unhistorical /ʌnhɪˈstɒrɪk(ə)l/ *adjective.* E17.
[from UN-[1] + HISTORICAL.]
Not historical; not based on or in accordance with history.

> 🕮 F. KERMODE Pilate . . is already in the gospel accounts being given an unhistorical character.

■ **unhistoric** *adjective* not historic or historical M19. **unhistorically** *adverb* M19.

unhitch /ʌnˈhɪtʃ/ *verb trans.* E17.
[from UN-[2] + HITCH *verb.*]
Detach or release from a hitched state; unhook, unfasten; *spec.* unharness (a horse etc.).

unholpen /ʌnˈhəʊlp(ə)n/ *adjective.* Long *arch. & US dial.* LME.
[from UN-[1] + *holpen* arch. & US dial. pa. pple of HELP *verb.*]
Not helped; unaided, unassisted.

> 🕮 M. TWAIN She did climb to that eminence by her own unholpen merit.

unholy /ʌnˈhəʊli/ *adjective & noun.*
[Old English *unhālig*, formed as UN-[1] + HOLY *adjective.*]
▶ **A** *adjective.* **1** Not holy; impious, profane, wicked. OE.
2 Awful, dreadful, outrageous. *colloq.* M19.

> 🕮 **1** SHELLEY Unholy men, Feasting like fiends upon the infidel dead. ***unholy alliance*** an (esp. political) alliance between unlikely or incongruous parties (cf. ***Holy Alliance*** s.v. HOLY *adjective*). **2** L. ERDRICH She began to beat on the . . iron bedstead, . . making an unholy racket.

▶ **B** *absol.* as *noun.* **1** *pl. The* people who are unholy, as a class. E16.
2 An unholy person or thing. M19.
■ **unholily** *adverb* M16. **unholiness** *noun* M16.

unhomelike /ʌnˈhəʊmlʌɪk/ *adjective.* M19.
[from UN-[1] + HOMELIKE.]
Unlike home; not homely.

> 🕮 L. T. MEADE The unpacked trunk . . gave it a very unhomelike feel.

■ **unhomeliness** *noun* lack of homeliness or cosiness LME. **unhomely** *adjective* not homely; not cosy, formal: L19.

unhomogeneous /ˌʌnhɒmə(ʊ)ˈdʒiːnɪəs, -ˈdʒɛn-, ˌʌnhəʊm-/ *adjective.* E19.
[from UN-[1] + HOMOGENEOUS.]
Not homogeneous; incongruous, dissimilar.
■ **unhomogeˈneity** *noun* M19. **unhoˈmogenized** *adjective* M20.

unhonest /ʌnˈɒnɪst/ *adjective. arch.* exc. *Scot. & dial.* ME.
[from UN-[1] + HONEST *adjective.* Cf. DISHONEST *adjective.*]
1 Physically or morally objectionable; ugly, vile. ME. ▸**b** Unseemly, improper. LME.
2 a Disreputable; immoral; lewd. ME. ▸**b** Dishonourable, discreditable. LME.
3 Dishonest. M16.
■ **unhonestly** *adverb* LME. **unhonesty** *noun* absence or lack of honesty; dishonesty: LME

unhook /ʌnˈhʊk/ *verb trans.* E17.
[from UN-[2] + HOOK *verb.*]
1 Remove from a hook or hooks; detach or free (as) from a hook. E17.
2 Undo the hooks of (a garment etc.); unfasten by this action. M19.
3 Disengage from a hooked or curved position. M19.

> 🕮 **1** C. PHILLIPS Michael unhooked his clothes from behind the door. **3** DICKENS As she said it, she unhooked her arm.

unhooked /ʌnˈhʊkt/ *adjective.* E17.
[from UN-[1] + HOOKED.]
Not hooked; having no hook or hooks.

unhope /ʌnˈhəʊp/ *noun.* Long *obsolete* exc. *poet.* ME.
[from UN-[1] + HOPE *noun*[1].]
Lack of hope; despair.

> 🕮 T. HARDY But death will not appal One who, past doubtings all, Waits in unhope.

unhoped /ʌnˈhəʊpt/ *adjective & adverb.* LME.
[from UN-[1] + *hoped* pa. pple of HOPE *verb.*]
▶ **A** *adjective.* †**1** Unexpected, unforeseen. LME–L17.
2 Not anticipated with desire; not hoped *for.* Now chiefly as ***unhoped-for.*** LME.

> 🕮 **2** D. ACHESON A young man to whom had come this unhoped-for bonanza.

▶ **B** *adverb.* Unexpectedly; beyond expectation. *poet. arch.* M17.

> 🕮 SIR W. SCOTT Redeem'd, unhoped, from desperate strife.

■ **unhopedly** *adverb* (*rare*) E17. **unhoping** *adjective* not hoping; unhopeful, despondent: E17.

unhopeful /ʌnˈhəʊpfʊl, -f(ə)l/ *adjective.* LME.
[from UN-[1] + HOPEFUL.]
1 Not inspiring hope; unpromising. LME.
2 Not feeling or entertaining hope; despondent. M19.

> 🕮 **1** T. S. ELIOT A situation . . as unhopeful as that of today. **2** CARLYLE Jobst . . finding all very anarchic, grew unhopeful.

■ **unhopefully** *adverb* M19.

unhorse /ʌnˈhɔːs/ *verb trans.* LME.
[from UN-[2] + HORSE *verb.*]
1 Throw or drag from a horse, esp. in battle; (of a horse) throw (a rider). LME. ▸**b** *fig.* Dislodge, overthrow. *arch.* L16.
2 Take or steal a horse from. *rare.* LME.
3 Unharness a horse or horses from. M17.

> 🕮 **1** R. BARBER If you unhorse your opponent, offer to fight him with swords. **b** SIR W. SCOTT Thou hast unhorsed me with that very word.

unhouse /ʌnˈhaʊz/ *verb trans.* LME.
[from UN-[2] + HOUSE *verb*[1].]
Turn out of a house or dwelling; make homeless.

unhoused /ʌnˈhaʊzd/ *adjective.* L16.
[from UN-[1] + *housed* pa. pple of HOUSE *verb*[1].]
†**1** Of land: not occupied by houses. *rare.* L16–E17.
2 Not provided with or living in a house; homeless. E17.

unhouseled /ʌnˈhaʊz(ə)ld/ *adjective.* Now *literary* (after Shakes.). M16.
[from UN-[1] + *houseled* pa. pple of HOUSEL *verb.*]
Not having received the Eucharist.

> 🕮 SHAKES. *Haml.* Cut off . . in my sin, Unhous'led disappointed, unanel'd.

unhulled /ʌnˈhʌld/ *adjective.* L16.
[In sense 1 from UN-[1] + HULL *noun*[1] + -ED[2]; in sense 2 from UN-[1] + *hulled* pa. pple of HULL *verb*[1].]
1 Not having a hull or husk. L16.
2 Not having the husk removed; unshelled. L19.

unhuman /ʌnˈhjuːmən/ *adjective.* M16.
[from UN-[1] + HUMAN *adjective.*]
1 = INHUMAN *adjective* 1. M16.
2 Superhuman. L18.
3 Not of, pertaining to, or characteristic of humankind. M19.

> 🕮 **1** *Oxford Diocesan Magazine* Laws whose object is to protect the unhuman apparatus behind that State façade. **3** F. WELDON A pendant . . round his neck . . nestled in grey, wiry, unhuman hairs.

■ **unhumanly** *adverb* inhumanly L16.

unhumanise *verb*, **-ised** *adjective* vars. of UNHUMANIZE, UNHUMANIZED.

unhumanize /ʌnˈhjuːmənʌɪz/ *verb trans.* Also **-ise.** M18.
[from UN-[2] + HUMANIZE.]
Deprive of human character or qualities; make inhuman or callous.

> 🕮 N. HAWTHORNE That cold tendency . . appeared to have gone far towards unhumanizing my heart.

unhumanized /ʌnˈhjuːmənʌɪzd/ *adjective.* Also **-ised.** L18.
[from UN-[1] + *humanized* pa. pple of HUMANIZE.]
Not (yet) humanized or made human.

> 🕮 J. HILTON There were such places still . . on earth—distant, inaccessible, as yet unhumanised.

unhumble /ʌnˈhʌmb(ə)l/ *adjective.* E17.
[from UN-[1] + HUMBLE *adjective*[1].]
Not humble or deferential.
■ **unhumbled** *adjective* not humbled or abased E17.

unhumorous /ʌnˈhjuːm(ə)rəs/ *adjective.* L19.
[from UN-[1] + HUMOROUS.]
Not humorous; humourless.

> 🕮 D. FRANCIS An obstinate jaw and unhumorous eyes.

■ **unhumorously** *adverb* M18.

unhung /ʌnˈhʌŋ/ *adjective.* M17.
[from UN-[1] + *hung* pa. pple of HANG *verb.* Cf. UNHANGED.]
▶ **I 1** Not provided or decorated with hangings. M17.
2 Not hung up for exhibition etc. L19.
▶ **II 3** = UNHANGED. L18.

unhung *verb pa. t. & pple*: see UNHANG.

unh-unh /ˈʌ̃ʌ̃/ *interjection.* M20.
[Natural exclam.]
Expr. negation or denial.

> 🕮 M. MCCARTHY Gus shook his head. 'Unh-unh', he said.

unhunted /ʌnˈhʌntɪd/ *adjective.* L16.
[from UN-[1] + HUNTED *adjective.*]
1 Of an area: not hunted or scoured for game etc. L16.
2 Not hunted or pursued. M17.
■ **unhuntable** *adjective* M19.

unhurried /ʌnˈhʌrɪd/ *adjective.* L18.
[from UN-[1] + HURRIED.]
Not hurried or rushed; not hasty.

> 🕮 O. MANNING Kites, roused from sleep, floated up . . in unhurried flight.

■ **unhurriedly** *adverb* L19. **unhurrying** *adjective* not hurrying or rushing L18.

unhurt /ʌnˈhəːt/ *adjective.* Also (long *obsolete* exc. *dial.*) **unhurted** /ʌnˈhəːtɪd/. ME.
[from UN-[1] + *hurt* pa. pple of HURT *verb.*]
Not hurt; unharmed, uninjured.
■ **unhurtful** *adjective* causing no hurt; not harmful or injurious: M16. **unhurting** *adjective* †(*a*) *Scot. rare* not violating an oath; (*b*) not causing hurt or pain: L16.

unhusbanded /ʌnˈhʌzbəndɪd/ *adjective. arch.* M16.
[from UN-[1] + *husbanded* pa. pple of HUSBAND *verb.*]
1 Of ground etc.: untilled, uncultivated. M16.
2 Not provided with a husband. L18.

unhusk /ʌnˈhʌsk/ *verb trans.* L16.
[from UN-[2] + HUSK *noun*[1].]
Strip of the husk or shell; *fig.* lay open, expose.

unhusked /ʌnˈhʌskt/ *adjective.* M18.
[from UN-[1] + *husked* pa. pple of HUSK *verb*[1].]
Not having the husk removed; unshelled.

unhygienic /ˌʌnhʌɪˈdʒiːnɪk/ *adjective.* L19.
[from UN-[1] + HYGIENIC.]
Not hygienic or conducive to health; unclean and insanitary.
■ **unhygienically** *adverb* in an unhygienic manner M19.

unhyphenated /ʌnˈhʌɪfəneɪtɪd/ *adjective.* M20.
[from UN-[1] + HYPHENATED.]
1 Not joined by or written with a hyphen. M20.
2 Not designated by a hyphenated term; undivided in political or cultural allegiance. Cf. HYPHENATED *ppl adjective* (b). *N. Amer.* L20.

> 🕮 **1** *American Speech* Some unhyphenated terms comprising two words have only the first capitalized. **2** *Washington Post* Unhyphenated Democrats . . have a brand-new patron saint.

uni /ˈjuːni/ *noun. colloq.* L19.
[Abbreviation.]
= UNIVERSITY *noun* 1. Cf. UNIV.

For other words beginning with *un-* and *uni-* see the entries for **un-**[1], **un-**[2], and **uni-**

uni- /ˈjuːni/ *combining form*.
[Latin, combining form of *unus* one, a single.]
Used in words with the senses 'one, single', 'having, consisting of, characterized by, etc., one'. Orig. occurring in words adopted from French or Latin, as ***unanimity***, ***unicorn***, ***unison***, ***universe***, etc., and in words adapted from or modelled on Latin compounds, as ***univocal***. Later forming many words including, by analogy with other numerical prefixes, ***unifold***, ***unipresent***, etc., and by the 19th cent. freely productive in the formation of *spec.* scientific and technical (esp. *BOTANY & ZOOLOGY*) words, freq. after mod. Latin formations, as ***unicellular***, ***unilabiate***, or from French terms, or in combination with English forms or words, sometimes in place of Greek MONO-.
■ **uniˈalgal** *adjective* (*BOTANY*) derived from a single algal cell E20. **uniˈaxal** *adjective* (now *rare* or *obsolete*) = UNIAXIAL 1 E19. **uniˈcapsular** *adjective* (*BOTANY*) having the carpels united into a single capsule E18. **unicell** *noun* (*BOTANY*) a unicellular plant L19. **unicelled** *adjective* (*BIOLOGY*) unicellular L19. **uniˈcentral** *adjective* pertaining to, arising from, or having a single centre M19. **uniˈclinal** *adjective* (*GEOLOGY*) †(*a*) = MONOCLINAL *adjective* 2; (*b*) = HOMOCLINAL: M19. **unicode** *noun* (now *rare*) (a message in) a telegraphic code in which one word or set of letters represents a sentence or phrase L19. **uniˈcolorate** *adjective* (*rare*) unicolorous M17. **uniˈcolorous** *adjective* having only one colour; uniform in colour: M17. **uniˈcoloured** *adjective* unicolorous E19. **uniˈcursal** *adjective* (*MATH.*) designating a curve or surface which is closed and can be drawn or swept out in a single movement M19. **uniˈcuspid** *adjective & noun* (*a*) *adjective* having a single cusp or point; (*b*) *noun* a unicuspid tooth: L19. **uniˈdentate** *adjective* (*a*) *ZOOLOGY & BOTANY* having a single toothlike serration; (*b*) *CHEMISTRY* = MONODENTATE: E19. **unidiˈmensional** *adjective* of one dimension L19. **unidimensioˈnality** *noun* the fact of having only one dimension M20. **uniface** *adjective* (of a coin etc.) having one side blank or unfinished L19. **uniˈfacial** *adjective & noun* (*a*) *adjective* pertaining to or having one face; *ARCHAEOLOGY* (of a flint etc.), worked on one face only (cf. BIFACIAL); (*b*) *noun* (*ARCHAEOLOGY*) a unifacial stone tool: M19. **uniˈfilar** *adjective* designating or having a moving part suspended by a single thread or wire M19. **uniˈfilarly** *adverb* (*BIOCHEMISTRY*) in a single strand of a DNA duplex L20. **uniˈflagellate** *adjective* (*ZOOLOGY*) (of a protozoan) having one flagellum L19. **uniˈflorous** *adjective* (*BOTANY*) bearing only one flower M18. **uniflow** *adjective & noun* (*a*) *adjective* involving flow in one direction only; *esp.* designating or pertaining to a steam or internal-combustion engine in which steam or waste gases flow directly through the cylinder in one direction; (*b*) *noun* a uniflow engine: E20. **uniˈfoliate** *adjective* (*BOTANY*) = UNIFOLIOLATE M19. **uniˈfoliolate** *adjective* (*BOTANY*) (of a compound leaf) reduced to one leaflet; (of a plant) characterized by leaves of this kind: M19. **uniˈgeniture** *noun* (*a*) *THEOLOGY* the fact of being the only-begotten Son; (*b*) the fact of being an only child; the practice of having only one child: M17. **uniˈjugate** *adjective* (*BOTANY*) having one pair of leaflets M19. **unijunction** *noun* (*ELECTRONICS*) a negative resistance device consisting of a rectifying *p–n* junction in the middle of a length of semiconducting material that has an ohmic contact at each end, used as a switching element M20. **uniˈlabiate** *adjective* (chiefly *BOTANY*, of a corolla or calyx) one-lipped E19. **unilaˈmellar** *adjective* having one lamella, lamina, or layer L19. **uniˈlinear** *adjective* affecting or involving one line; unilineal: M19. **uniˈliteral** *adjective* using or consisting of only one letter E19. **uniˈlobar** *adjective* (*ZOOLOGY & MEDICINE*) pertaining to, affecting, or having one lobe L19. **uniˈlobular** *adjective* (*MEDICINE*) pertaining to or affecting single lobules L19. **uniˈlocular** *adjective* (*BIOLOGY & MEDICINE*) having, consisting of, or characterized by only one loculus or cavity; one-celled: M18. **uniˈmodular** *adjective* (*MATH.*) having a determinant whose value is 1 M19. **uniˈnodal** *adjective* having one node or nodal point M19. **uniˈnuclear**, **uniˈnucleate**, **uniˈnucleated** *adjectives* = MONONUCLEAR *adjective* L19. **uniˈovular** *adjective* (*BIOLOGY*) = MONOZYGOTIC *adjective* E20. **uniˈpartite** *adjective* consisting of or involving a single part L19. **uniˈpersonal** *adjective* comprising or existing as a single person or individual E19. **uniˈpivot** *adjective* (*ELECTRICITY*) designating or having a moving-coil system balanced on a single pivot E20. **uniˈplanar** *adjective* (*MATH. & MECHANICS*) pertaining to, situated in, or operating in one plane M19. **uˈniplicate** *adjective* having a single fold M19. **unipole** *noun* = MONOPOLE *noun*² 2 M20. **uniˈprocessor** *adjective & noun* (*COMPUTING*) (*a*) *adjective* designating a system with only one processor; (*b*) *noun* a uniprocessor system; each of the constituent processors of a multiprocessor: M20. **uniˈramous** *adjective* (*ZOOLOGY*) having or consisting of a single ramus or branch L19. **uniseg'mental** *adjective* pertaining to or consisting of one segment L20. **uniselector** *noun* (*TELEPHONY & ELECTRICITY*) a single-motion switch which has a wiper that rotates in one plane only M20. **uniseptate** *adjective* (*BOTANY*) having a single septum M19. **uniˈseriate** *adjective* (*BOTANY & ZOOLOGY*) = UNISERIAL M19. **uniˈvallate** *adjective* (*ARCHAEOLOGY*) having a single encircling rampart M20. **uniˈvariant** *adjective* (*PHYSICAL CHEMISTRY*) (of a chemical system) having one degree of freedom L19. **uniˈvariate** *adjective* (*STATISTICS*) involving or having one variate E20.

Uniate /ˈjuːnɪeɪt/ *noun & adjective*. Also **Uniat** /ˈjuːnɪat, -ət/. M19.
[Russian *uniat* from *uniya* union from Latin *unio* UNION *noun*².]
▶ **A** *noun*. A member of a Church in eastern Europe or the Near East which acknowledges papal supremacy but retains its own liturgy etc. M19.
▶ **B** *attrib.* or as *adjective*. Designating or pertaining to such a Church. M19.
■ **Uniatism** *noun* the form of Christianity practised by Uniates; the adoption by Uniates of Catholic doctrines: M20.

uniaxial /juːnɪˈaksɪəl/ *adjective*. E19.
[from UNI- + AXIAL.]
1 *OPTICS & CRYSTALLOGRAPHY*. Having one optic axis. E19.
2 Characterized by one axis of alignment or action. M20.
■ **uniaxially** *adverb* E20.

unibody /ˈjuːnɪbɒdi/ *noun*. Also **uni-body**. M20.
[from UNI- + BODY *noun*.]
A single moulded unit forming both the bodywork and chassis of a vehicle. Freq. *attrib.*

†**unic** *adjective & noun* see UNIQUE.

unica *noun* pl. of UNICUM.

unicameral /juːnɪˈkam(ə)r(ə)l/ *adjective*. M19.
[from UNI- + medieval Latin *cameralis* belonging to a chamber: see CAMERAL.]
Of a parliamentary system: having or characterized by one legislative chamber.
■ **unicameralism** *noun* the system of having only one legislative chamber E20. **unicameralist** *noun* an advocate of unicameralism L19. **unicamerally** *adverb* M20.

UNICEF /ˈjuːnɪsɛf/ *abbreviation*.
United Nations International Children's Emergency Fund (now officially United Nations Children's Fund).

unicellular /juːnɪˈsɛljʊlə/ *adjective*. M19.
[from UNI- + CELLULAR.]
BIOLOGY. **1** Of protozoans, certain algae, etc.: consisting of a single cell. M19.
2 Of an evolutionary or developmental stage: characterized by the formation or presence of a single cell or cells. M19.
■ **unicelluˈlarity** *noun* unicellular condition or formation L19.

unicist /ˈjuːnɪsɪst/ *noun*. E19.
[from Latin *unicus* one and only (see UNIQUE) + -IST.]
1 A believer in the unicity of the Godhead. E19.
2 *MEDICINE*. A supporter of the theory of unicity. *obsolete* exc. *Hist.* L19.

unicity /juːˈnɪsɪti/ *noun*. L17.
[Perh. from medieval Latin *unicitas* var. of *unitas* (see UNITY *noun*¹) or formed as prec.: see -ITY.]
1 The fact of being or consisting of one; oneness. L17.
▶**b** *MEDICINE*. The theory that venereal diseases are caused by only one kind of micro-organism. *obsolete* exc. *Hist.* M19.
2 The fact or quality of being unique; uniqueness. M19.

unicorn /ˈjuːnɪkɔːn/ *noun*. ME.
[Old & mod. French *unicorne* from Latin *unicornis* one-horned, unicorn, from *unus* one + *cornu* horn, repr. Greek *monokerōs*; in early biblical translations, *unicorn* repr. Latin *unicornis*, *rhinoceros*, translating Hebrew *rĕ'ēm* wild ox.]
1 A mythical animal with the body of a horse and a single straight horn projecting from its forehead. ME.
†**2** A one-horned rhinoceros. LME–L17.
3 A representation of a unicorn, esp. (*HERALDRY*) with the head, neck, and body of a horse, the legs of a deer, the tail of a lion, and a long spiralled horn growing from its forehead, occurring *spec.* as a charge or supporter of the Royal Arms of Great Britain (or Scotland). LME.
4 The designation of one of the pursuivants of the court of the Lyon King of Arms. *Scot.* LME.
5 A Scottish gold coin worth 18 shillings Scots current in the 15th and 16th cents., so called from the unicorn stamped on its obverse. *Hist.* L15.
6 The narwhal. Also more fully ***unicorn whale***. Now *rare*. M17.
7 (Usu. **U-**.) The minor constellation Monoceros. L18.
8 A carriage, coach, etc., drawn by three horses, two abreast and one in front. Now usu., a team of three horses so arranged. L18.

📖 **1** T. H. WHITE A unicorn is a magic animal, and only a maiden can catch it. **8** *Carriage Driving* Team entries . . comprised two fours, three unicorns and a three-abreast.

Comb.: **unicorn auk** the rhinoceros auklet, *Cerorhinca monocerata*; **unicorn beetle** a rhinoceros beetle; **unicorn bird** the horned screamer, *Anhima cornuta*; **unicorn-fish** (*a*) (now *rare*) the narwhal; (*b*) any of various fishes bearing a spike or projection on the head; *esp.* a surgeonfish of the genus *Naso*; a file-fish of the genus *Aluterus*; **unicorn-plant** any of several N. American plants, esp. *Proboscidea louisianica* (family Pedaliaceae), the capsule of which terminates in a long curved beak; **unicorn-root** *US* either of two plants with roots having medicinal uses, the blazing star, *Aletris farinosa*, and the devil's bit, *Chamaelirium luteum*; **unicorn shell** (the shell of) any of various marine gastropod molluscs of the genus *Acanthina* (family Thaididae), which bear a stout tooth at the end of the outer lip and are found off the west coast of America; **unicorn's horn** (*a*) a horn supposedly obtained from a unicorn, but actually from a rhinoceros, narwhal, or other animal, freq. made into a drinking cup and said to prevent poisoning; †(*b*) the material of such a horn used medicinally; *unicorn whale*: see sense 6 above.

unicum /ˈjuːnɪkəm/ *noun*. Pl. **-ca** /-kə/. L19.
[Latin, neut. sing. of *unicus* UNIQUE.]
A unique example, specimen, or thing.

unicycle /ˈjuːnɪsʌɪk(ə)l/ *noun & verb*. M19.
[from UNI- + CYCLE *noun*, *verb*.]
▶ **A** *noun*. A cycle with only one wheel, esp. as used by acrobats or for gymnastic displays. M19.
▶ **B** *verb intrans.* Ride on a unicycle. L20.
■ **unicyclist** *noun* a person who rides on a unicycle L19.

unideal /ʌnʌɪˈdɪəl, -ˈdiːəl/ *adjective*. M18.
[from UN-¹ + IDEAL *adjective*.]
†**1 a** Expressing or conveying no idea. M–L18. ▶**b** Lacking in ideas. M18–E19.
2 Having or following no ideal. M18.
3 Not marked by idealism. M19.

unidentified /ʌnʌɪˈdɛntɪfʌɪd/ *adjective*. M19.
[from UN-¹ + *identified* pa. pple of IDENTIFY.]
That has not been identified. Esp. in ***unidentified flying object***, ***unidentified object*** (cf. UFO).
■ **uniˈdentifiable** *adjective* E20. **uniˈdentifiably** *adverb* M20.

unidirectional /juːnɪdɪˈrɛkʃ(ə)n(ə)l, juːnɪdʌɪ-/ *adjective*. L19.
[from UNI- + DIRECTIONAL.]
Moving or having movement in one direction; operating in one direction only.
■ **unidirectioˈnality** *noun* M20. **unidirectionally** *adverb* M20.

UNIDO *abbreviation*.
United Nations Industrial Development Organization.

unific /juːˈnɪfɪk/ *adjective*. L18.
[from UNIFY after *pacify*, *pacific*, etc.: see -FIC.]
That unifies or unites; producing unity.

unification /juːnɪfɪˈkeɪʃ(ə)n/ *noun*. M19.
[from UNIFY + -FICATION, perh. after French *unification*.]
The action or an instance of unifying or uniting; the state of being unified.
Comb.: **Unification Church** an evangelistic religious and political organization founded in 1954 in Korea by Sun Myung Moon (cf. MOONIE).
■ **unificationist** *noun & adjective* (*a*) *noun* an advocate of unification; *spec.* a member of the Unification Church; (*b*) *adjective* of or relating to unification or to the Unification Church: E20. **unificatory** *adjective* tending to unify L19.

unified /ˈjuːnɪfʌɪd/ *ppl adjective*. M19.
[from UNIFY + -ED¹.]
That is or has been made into one from separate parts; united, consolidated.
unified field theory, **unified theory**, **grand unified field theory**, **grand unified theory** *PHYSICS* a field theory that describes two or more of the four interactions previously described by separate theories.

uniform /ˈjuːnɪfɔːm/ *noun*. E17.
[After French *uniforme* use as noun of adjective.]
▶†**I 1** *in uniform*, in one body or group. Only in E17.
▶ **II 2 a** The distinctive clothing of uniform cut, fabric, and colour worn by all members of an armed force or, more widely, by the members of any civilian association or distinct body of people, to which the clothing is recognized as belonging. M18. ▶**b** A single outfit of this kind. Formerly also (in *pl.*), the separate garments composing this. L18. ▶**c** *transf.* The particular style of dress or appearance characteristic of a specific group of people. M20.
3 A person wearing a uniform. *rare*. L18.

📖 **2a** C. POTOK Our team had no particular uniform, and each of us wore whatever he wished. H. KISSINGER Wearing the uniform of a French brigadier general. *Times Educ. Suppl.* School traditionalism—a uniform, a house system . . and pennants. ***full-dress uniform***: see FULL *adjective*. **c** A. GHOSH Our usual student uniform of kurta and crumpled trousers.

■ **uniformless** *adjective* lacking or not wearing uniform M19.

uniform /ˈjuːnɪfɔːm/ *adjective*. M16.
[Old & mod. French *uniforme* or Latin *uniformis*, from *unus* UNI- + *forma* FORM *noun*. In sense 5b attrib. use of UNIFORM *noun*.]
1 Of one unchanging form, character, or kind; that is or stays the same in different places or circumstances, or at different times. M16. ▶**b** Of a person: unchanging in conduct, opinion, etc., consistent. Of disposition: consistent, unvaried, equable. M16.
2 Having the same appearance throughout; showing little or no diversity of form or dimensions; having a plain or unbroken surface or exterior. M16.
3 Constant in speed or dimension. M16.
4 Of the same form, character, or kind as another or others; conforming to one standard, rule, or pattern; alike, similar. M16. ▶†**b** In agreement with, matching with. Foll. by *to*. L16–E18.
5 Of clothing or dress: of the same pattern, colour, and fabric across a body of people. M18. ▶**b** *attrib.* Forming (part of) a uniform. Also, (of a person) wearing a uniform. E19.

📖 **1** T. HEGGEN 'You need an aspirin,' was his uniform diagnosis. *Discover* DNA is not a uniform helix, but a varied piece of architecture. J. LE CARRÉ Gdansk hotels are of a uniform frightfulness. **2** C. DARWIN The face of nature remains uniform for long periods of time. **3** W. WITHERING Branches of a uniform breadth. M. F. MAURY The flow of heat from the sun is held to be uniform. **4** DICKENS There is not . . any uniform Edition of his books. *Business Traveller* A uniform package of amenities at a choice of . . hotels.

■ **uniforˈmation** *noun* (*rare*) reduction to uniformity L18. **uniformly** *adverb* in a uniform manner, with uniformity LME. **uniformness** *noun* L16.

uniform /ˈjuːnɪfɔːm/ *verb trans.* L16.
[from UNIFORM *noun, adjective*.]
†**1** Make conformable *to*. Only in L16.
2 Make (a number of people or things) uniform or alike; bring to uniformity. L17.
3 Clothe in uniform. Freq. as ***uniformed*** *ppl adjective*. E19.

> 📖 **3** ALDOUS HUXLEY The British Freemen are uniformed in green.

uniformal /juːnɪˈfɔːm(ə)l/ *adjective*. L16.
[from UNIFORM *adjective* + -AL¹.]
Uniform.
▪ **uniformalize** *verb trans.* (*rare*) make uniform; reduce to uniformity: E19. **uniformally** *adverb* (*rare*) L16.

uniformise *verb* var. of UNIFORMIZE.

uniformitarian /ˌjuːnɪfɔːmɪˈtɛːrɪən/ *noun & adjective*. M19.
[from next + -ARIAN.]
Chiefly GEOLOGY. ▶**A** *noun*. A person who supports the theory that natural processes and phenomena have always been and still are due to causes or forces operating continuously and with uniformity (cf. CATASTROPHIST). M19.
▶**B** *adjective*. Of or pertaining to uniformitarians or uniformitarianism. M19.
▪ **uniformitarianism** *noun* the principles or doctrines held by uniformitarians M19.

uniformity /juːnɪˈfɔːmɪti/ *noun*. LME.
[Old & mod. French *uniformité* or late Latin *uniformitas*, from Latin *uniformis*: see UNIFORM *adjective*, -ITY.]
1 The fact or condition of having the same form or character as another or others; conformity amongst several things, parts, etc.; *spec.* conformity of several things etc. to one standard, esp. in matters of religion. LME. ▸**b** An instance of this; a uniform state or condition. M16.
2 The condition of having or existing in only one form or character; consistency or sameness at all times or in all circumstances. Freq. foll. by *of*. L16.
3 Similarity of appearance, design, style, constituent parts, etc.; freedom from or lack of variety or diversity. Also (*spec.*), wearisome sameness, monotony. E17. ▸**b** An instance of this. M17.

> 📖 **1** M. WARNOCK The system of public examinations . . ensures . . a reasonable degree of uniformity. *Parents* There seems to be no uniformity in the size of clothes. **Act of Uniformity** ENGLISH HISTORY each of four Acts of Parliament securing uniformity in public worship and in the use and acceptance of the *Book of Common Prayer*, *esp.* that of May 1662. **2** W. PALEY The uniformity of plan observable in the universe. **3** W. HOGARTH Variety is more pleasing than uniformity. **b** B. RUSSELL The business of science is to find uniformities, such as the laws of motion.

uniformize /ˈjuːnɪfɔːmʌɪz/ *verb trans.* Also **-ise**. M19.
[from UNIFORM *adjective* + -IZE.]
1 Make uniform; reduce to a uniform system. *rare*. M19.
2 MATH. Transform (an equation or expression) so that each variable is expressed as a single-valued function of a new parameter; parametrize. L19.
▪ **uniformiˈzation** *noun* L19.

unify /ˈjuːnɪfʌɪ/ *verb trans.* E16.
[Old & mod. French *unifier* or late Latin *unificare*: see UNI-, -FY.]
Make, form into, or cause to become one; reduce to unity or uniformity.

> 📖 *Islamic Quarterly* A unifying note which binds the community together. *Word* Paprotté . . seeks to unify the opposing views. *New York Review of Books* A Disraelian 'one nation' conservatism that would unify all classes.

▪ **unifiable** *adjective* able to be unified or united L19. **unifier** *noun* M19.

unilateral /juːnɪˈlat(ə)r(ə)l/ *adjective*. E19.
[from UNI- + LATERAL.]
1 BOTANY & ZOOLOGY. Turned to one side; *esp.* arranged or having flowers on one side only of the axis of an inflorescence. E19.
2 a Performed by or affecting only one person or party. E19. ▸**b** *spec.* in LAW. Of an obligation etc.: entered on by one party, esp. with no reciprocal obligation from any other; binding or imposed on one party only. E19.
3 Concerned with or relating to only one side of a subject; one-sided. M19.
4 Chiefly BIOLOGY & MEDICINE. Relating to, occurring on, or affecting only one side of a thing, esp. of the body, the brain, an organ, etc. M19.
5 PHONETICS. Of a speech sound: made with partial closure of the air passage so that breath flows on one side of the obstruction only. M19.
6 Of a line of descent or succession: through ancestors of one side or one sex only. L19.
7 MATH. (Of a surface) having only one side; (of an equation, limit, etc.) lying or evaluated on only one side. L19.
8 Of the parking of vehicles: restricted to one side of a street. M20.

> 📖 **2a** *Time* It was a unilateral action rather than an agreement negotiated with the Iraquis. **unilateral disarmament** disarmament (in recent use, esp. of nuclear weapons) by one State, irrespective of whether others take similar action. **3** J. MORLEY A unilateral view of the social contract . . omits the element of reciprocity.

▪ **unilateˈrality** *noun* the quality or character of being unilateral M19. **unilaterally** *adverb* M19.

unilateralisation *noun* var. of UNILATERALIZATION.

unilateralism /juːnɪˈlat(ə)r(ə)lɪz(ə)m/ *noun*. E20.
[from prec. + -ISM.]
Unilaterality, unilateral state; *spec.* (***a***) = ***unilateral disarmament*** s.v. UNILATERAL 2a; (***b***) *US* the pursuit of a foreign policy without (regard to the views of) allies.

> 📖 *Independent* The . . revamped Labour Party . . with socialism and unilateralism banished to the shadows.

unilateralist /juːnɪˈlat(ə)r(ə)lɪst/ *noun & adjective*. E20.
[formed as prec. + -IST.]
▶**A** *noun*. A person who favours or adopts a policy of unilateral disarmament. E20.
▶**B** *adjective*. Of or pertaining to unilateral disarmament or unilateralists. M20.

unilateralization /juːnɪˌlat(ə)r(ə)lʌɪˈzeɪʃ(ə)n/ *noun*. Also **-isation**. M20.
[from UNILATERAL *adjective* + -IZATION.]
ELECTRONICS. Neutralization, esp. of resistive as well as reactive feedback.
▪ **uniˈlateralized** *adjective* subjected to unilateralization M20.

unilineal /juːnɪˈlɪnɪəl/ *adjective*. M20.
[from UNI- + LINEAL *adjective*.]
1 ANTHROPOLOGY. Designating or pertaining to a kinship system in which relationships, succession, etc., are established through either the father's or the mother's line. M20.
2 Of an evolution, theory, progression, etc.: following a single line of development or reasoning. M20.
▪ **unilinealism** *noun* adherence to unilineal views M20. **unilineally** *adverb* M20.

unilingual /juːnɪˈlɪŋgw(ə)l/ *adjective & noun*. M19.
[from UNI- + LINGUAL.]
▶**A** *adjective*. = MONOLINGUAL *adjective* 1. M19.
▶**B** *noun*. = MONOLINGUAL *noun*. M20.
▪ **unilingually** *adverb* L20.

unimaginable /ʌnɪˈmadʒɪnəb(ə)l/ *adjective*. E17.
[from UN-¹ + IMAGINABLE.]
Incapable of being imagined; inconceivable, incomprehensible.
▪ **unimaginableness** *noun* M17. **unimaginably** *adverb* M17. **unimaginary** *adjective* not imaginary E17.

unimaginative /ʌnɪˈmadʒɪnətɪv/ *adjective*. E19.
[from UN-¹ + IMAGINATIVE.]
Not imaginative; lacking in imagination.
▪ **unimaginatively** *adverb* L19. **unimaginativeness** *noun* M19.

unimagined /ʌnɪˈmadʒɪnd/ *adjective*. M16.
[from UN-¹ + *imagined* pa. pple of IMAGINE.]
Not imagined.

unimer /ˈjuːnɪmə/ *noun*. M20.
[from UNI- + -MER.]
Chiefly BIOCHEMISTRY. Each of the single molecules (usu. macromolecules) that go to make up a multimeric aggregation.

unimmergible /ʌnɪˈməːdʒɪb(ə)l/ *adjective*. E19.
[from UN-¹ + IMMERGE + -IBLE.]
Insubmergible.

unimodal /juːnɪˈməʊd(ə)l/ *adjective*. E20.
[from UNI- + MODAL *adjective*.]
Chiefly STATISTICS. Having one mode.
▪ **unimoˈdality** *noun* M20.

unimolecular /ˌjuːnɪməˈlɛkjʊlə/ *adjective*. E20.
[from UNI- + MOLECULAR.]
CHEMISTRY. **1** Of a reaction: †(***a***) of order one (ORDER *noun* 10d); (***b***) having a molecularity of one; involving the fragmentation or internal transformation of a single molecule in the rate-determining step. Cf. MONOMOLECULAR 1. E20.
2 = MONOMOLECULAR 2. E20.
▪ **unimolecularly** *adverb* E20.

unimpeachable /ʌnɪmˈpiːtʃəb(ə)l/ *adjective*. L18.
[from UN-¹ + IMPEACHABLE.]
Not impeachable.
▪ **unimpeachaˈbility** *noun* M19. **unimpeachableness** *noun* E19. **unimpeachably** *adverb* E19.

unimpeached /ʌnɪmˈpiːtʃt/ *adjective*. LME.
[from UN-¹ + *impeached* pa. pple of IMPEACH *verb*.]
†**1** Not impeded or hindered. Only in LME.
2 Not assailed, accused, or called in question. L16.

unimpeded /ʌnɪmˈpiːdɪd/ *adjective*. M18.
[from UN-¹ + *impeded* pa. pple of IMPEDE *verb*.]
Not impeded.
▪ **unimpededly** *adverb* M19.

†**unimployed** *adjective* see UNEMPLOYED.

unimportant /ʌnɪmˈpɔːt(ə)nt/ *adjective*. E18.
[from UN-¹ + IMPORTANT.]
1 Unassuming, modest. *rare*. E18.
2 Of no importance or moment. M18.
▪ **unimportance** *noun* M18.

unimposing /ʌnɪmˈpəʊzɪŋ/ *adjective*. M18.
[from UN-¹ + IMPOSING.]
†**1** Not burdensome or oppressive. Only in M18.
2 Unimpressive. E19.
▪ **unimposingly** *adverb* L19.

unimpregnated /ʌnˈɪmprɛgneɪtɪd, ʌnɪmˈprɛg-/ *adjective*. M18.
[from UN-¹ + *impregnated* pa. pple of IMPREGNATE *verb*.]
1 Not made pregnant or fruitful. M18.
2 Not impregnated (*with*). L18.

unimpressed /ʌnɪmˈprɛst/ *adjective*. M18.
[from UN-¹ + *impressed* pa. pple of IMPRESS *verb*¹.]
Not impressed.

> 📖 *Independent* Share traders remain unimpressed by Nigel Lawson's . . speech.

unimpressible /ʌnɪmˈprɛsɪb(ə)l/ *adjective*. E19.
[from UN-¹ + IMPRESSIBLE.]
Not impressible.
▪ **unimpressiˈbility** *noun* E19. **unimpressibleness** *noun* M19.

unimpressionable /ʌnɪmˈprɛʃ(ə)nəb(ə)l/ *adjective*. M19.
[from UN-¹ + IMPRESSIONABLE.]
Not impressionable.

unimpressive /ʌnɪmˈprɛsɪv/ *adjective*. L18.
[from UN-¹ + IMPRESSIVE.]
Not impressive.
▪ **unimpressively** *adverb* M19. **unimpressiveness** *noun* E19.

unimprisoned /ʌnɪmˈprɪz(ə)nd/ *adjective*. M17.
[from UN-¹, UN-² + *imprisoned* pa. pple of IMPRISON.]
Not imprisoned; released from prison.

unimprovable /ʌnɪmˈpruːvəb(ə)l/ *adjective*. M17.
[from UN-¹ + IMPROVABLE *adjective*².]
Not improvable.
▪ **unimprovaˈbility** *noun* E19.

†**unimproved** *adjective*¹. Only in E17.
[from UN-¹ + *improved* pa. pple of IMPROVE *verb*¹.]
Unreproved, uncensured.

unimproved /ʌnɪmˈpruːvd/ *adjective*². M17.
[from UN-¹ + *improved* pa. pple of IMPROVE *verb*².]
1 Not made better. M17.
2 Not turned to use; not taken advantage of. L18.

> 📖 **1** R. BOLDREWOOD A cheap unimproved property. J. PURSEGLOVE Only 100 acres of fine unimproved pasture survives.

unimproving /ʌnɪmˈpruːvɪŋ/ *ppl adjective*. M18.
[from UN-¹ + *improving* pres. pple of IMPROVE *verb*².]
Not improving; *spec.* not edifying.

unincorporate /ʌnɪnˈkɔːp(ə)rət/ *adjective*. E19.
[from UN-¹ + INCORPORATE *adjective*².]
1 Not having a bodily form; unembodied. *rare*. E19.
2 = UNINCORPORATED 2. L19.

unincorporated /ʌnɪnˈkɔːpəreɪtɪd/ *adjective*. E18.
[from UN-¹ + *incorporated* pa. pple of INCORPORATE *verb*.]
1 Not incorporated or united *with*. E18.
2 Not formed into a corporation. E19.

> 📖 **2** T. LUNDBERG An unincorporated business can be set up almost instantly.

†**unincumbered** *adjective* var. of UNENCUMBERED.

†**unindeard** *adjective* see UNENDEARED.

unindented /ʌnɪnˈdɛntɪd/ *adjective*. M18.
[from UN-¹ + INDENTED *ppl adjective*.]
1 Not marked with indentations. M18.
2 Of type or writing: set up without indention. E20.

unindifferent /ʌnɪnˈdɪf(ə)r(ə)nt/ *adjective*. M16.
[from UN-¹ + INDIFFERENT.]
†**1** Unequal, unfavourable. Only in M16.
2 a Of a person: not impartial or fair-minded; prejudiced. *arch.* L16. ▸†**b** Of an action etc.: lacking in impartiality. L16–E17.
▪ **unindifference** *noun* lack of impartiality M17. **unindifferency** *noun* (*arch.*) = UNINDIFFERENCE L16.

unindividual /ˌʌnɪndɪˈvɪdjʊəl/ *adjective*. E19.
[from UN-¹ + INDIVIDUAL.]
Not individual.
▪ **unindividualized** *adjective* M19.

unindurable *adjective* see UNENDURABLE.

unineme /ˈjuːnɪniːm/ *adjective*. M20.
[from UNI- + Greek *nēma* thread.]
CYTOLOGY. (Of a chromatid) containing a single duplex of DNA; designating or pertaining to the hypothesis that this is the normal content of a chromatid.
▪ **uniˈnemic** *adjective* containing a single duplex of DNA L20. **uninemy** *noun* the state of containing one duplex of DNA per chromatid L20.

uninfected /ʌnɪnˈfɛktɪd/ *adjective.* E17.
[from UN-[1] + *infected* pa. pple of INFECT *verb*.]
1 Not infected or tainted with moral corruption. E17.
2 Not infected or contaminated with disease-causing agents. E17.
■ **uninfectious** *adjective* M18.

uninfeft /ʌnɪnˈfɛft/ *adjective.* M19.
[from UN-[1] + INFEFT.]
SCOTS LAW. Not infefted.

uninflamed /ʌnɪnˈfleɪmd/ *adjective.* E17.
[from UN-[1] + *inflamed* pa. pple of INFLAME *verb*.]
1 Not set on fire. E17.
2 *fig.* Not emotionally roused. E18.
3 MEDICINE. Not affected by inflammation. L18.

uninflammable /ʌnɪnˈflaməb(ə)l/ *adjective.* M17.
[from UN-[1] + INFLAMMABLE.]
Not inflammable.
■ **uninflammaˈbility** *noun* E19.

uninflected /ʌnɪnˈflɛktɪd/ *adjective.* E18.
[from UN-[1] + INFLECTED.]
1 Not bent or deflected; not changing or varying. E18.
2 GRAMMAR. (Of a case, form, or language) not exhibiting or characterized by inflection. L19.

uninfluenced /ʌnˈɪnflʊənst/ *adjective.* M18.
[from UN-[1] + *influenced* pa. pple of INFLUENCE *verb*.]
Not influenced or affected (*by*).

uninfluential /ˌʌnɪnflʊˈɛnʃ(ə)l/ *adjective.* M17.
[from UN-[1] + INFLUENTIAL.]
Having little or no influence.

†**uninforced** *adjective* see UNENFORCED.

uninformed /ʌnɪnˈfɔːmd/ *adjective.* L16.
[from UN-[1] + INFORMED.]
1 Not informed or instructed; unacquainted with the facts. L16. ▸**b** Uneducated, ignorant. M17.
2 Not animated or inspired. Now *rare*. E18.

📖 **1** J. S. C. ABBOTT Uninformed as to its contents.

■ **uninformative** *adjective* not informative, giving little information M19. **uninformatively** *adverb* M20. **uninforming** *adjective* E18.

uninhabitable /ʌnɪnˈhabɪtəb(ə)l/ *adjective.* LME.
[from UN-[1] + INHABITABLE *adjective*[2].]
Not inhabitable, unsuitable for habitation.
■ **uninhabitableness** *noun* M17.

uninhabited /ʌnɪnˈhabɪtɪd/ *adjective.* L16.
[from UN-[1] + INHABITED.]
Not inhabited.

📖 J. CONRAD These uninhabited islets basking in the sun.

■ **uninhabitedness** *noun* M17.

uninhibited /ʌnɪnˈhɪbɪtɪd/ *adjective.* L19.
[from UN-[1] + INHIBITED.]
Not inhibited; unrestrained.
■ **uninhibitedly** *adverb* M20. **uninhibitedness** *noun* M20.

uninitiated /ʌnɪˈnɪʃɪeɪtɪd/ *noun & adjective.* L17.
[from UN-[1] + INITIATED.]
▶**A** *noun pl. The* people who are not initiated as a class. L17.
▶**B** *adjective.* Not initiated. E19.
■ **uninitiate** *adjective* = UNINITIATED *adjective* E19. **uninitiˈation** *noun* lack of initiation M19.

†**uninjoyed** *adjective* see UNENJOYED.

uninjured /ʌnˈɪndʒəd/ *adjective.* L16.
[from UN-[1] + INJURED.]
Without injury, unhurt.
■ **uninˈjurious** *adjective* E19.

uninomial /juːnɪˈnəʊmɪəl/ *adjective & noun.* L19.
[from UNI- + *-nomial* after *binomial*.]
TAXONOMY. ▶**A** *adjective.* Designating, pertaining to, or using names consisting of a single word in the classification of living organisms. L19.
▶**B** *noun.* A uninomial name. L19.

uninominal /juːnɪˈnɒmɪn(ə)l/ *adjective.* L19.
[French: see UNI-, NOMINAL.]
1 Of an electoral system etc.: in which one member is elected by each constituency. L19.
2 = UNINOMIAL *adjective.* L19.

uninspired /ʌnɪnˈspʌɪəd/ *adjective.* L17.
[from UN-[1] + INSPIRED.]
Not inspired; *spec.* (of rhetoric etc.) commonplace.
■ **uninspiring** *adjective* not inspiring E19. **uninspiringly** *adverb* E20.

uninstall /ˈʌnɪnstɔːl/ *verb & noun.* L18.
[from UN-[2] + INSTALL *verb*[1].]
▶**A** *verb trans.* **1** As *uninstalled ppl adjective*: not installed. *rare.* L18.
2 COMPUTING. Remove (an application or file) from a computer. L20.
▶**B** *noun.* COMPUTING. The action of uninstalling an application or file. Usu. *attrib.* L20.
■ **uninˈstaller** *noun* (COMPUTING) a utility program which uninstalls files or applications L20.

uninstructed /ʌnɪnˈstrʌktɪd/ *ppl adjective.* L16.
[from UN-[1] + *instructed* pa. pple of INSTRUCT.]
Not instructed or informed; unenlightened, ignorant.
■ **uninstructedness** *noun* M19. **uninstructing** *adjective* (now *rare*) uninstructive M17. **uninstructive** *adjective* not instructive M17.

uninsulate /ʌnˈɪnsjʊleɪt/ *verb trans.* M19.
[from UN-[2] + INSULATE *verb*.]
Deprive of insulation.

uninsulated /ʌnˈɪnsjʊleɪtɪd/ *ppl adjective.* L18.
[from UN-[1] + *insulated* pa. pple of INSULATE *verb*.]
Not insulated.

uninsured /ʌnɪnˈʃʊəd/ *adjective.* L18.
[from UN-[1] + *insured* pa. pple of INSURE.]
Not insured.
■ **uninsurable** *adjective* M19.

unintellectual /ˌʌnɪntɪˈlɛktjʊ(ə)l/ *adjective.* L17.
[from UN-[1] + INTELLECTUAL.]
†**1** Without intellect, unintelligent. Only in L17.
2 a Not intellectually developed; dull. E19. ▸**b** Marked by lack of intellect. E19.
■ **unintellectuˈality** *noun* M19. **unintellectually** *adverb* M19.

unintelligent /ʌnɪnˈtɛlɪdʒ(ə)nt/ *adjective.* E17.
[from UN-[1] + INTELLIGENT.]
1 Having no knowledge or understanding *of* something. *rare.* E17.
2 Devoid of intelligence. M17.
3 Deficient in intelligence or intellect; dull, stupid. L17.

📖 **2** E. B. PUSEY Time . . the most spiritual of the unintelligent creatures of God. **3** F. L. OLMSTED The company were . . rude and unintelligent.

■ **unintelligence** *noun* M17. **unintelligently** *adverb* M18.

unintelligible /ʌnɪnˈtɛlɪdʒɪb(ə)l/ *adjective & noun.* E17.
[from UN-[1] + INTELLIGIBLE.]
▶**A** *adjective.* Not intelligible; incapable of being understood. E17.

📖 G. GREENE He began to talk . . so fast that the words were almost unintelligible.

▶**B** *absol.* as *noun.* An unintelligible thing. M19.
■ **unintelligiˈbility** *noun* M17. **unintelligibleness** *noun* E17. **unintelligibly** *adverb* M17.

unintended /ʌnɪnˈtɛndɪd/ *adjective.* M17.
[from UN-[1] + INTENDED.]
Not intended, unintentional.
■ **unintendedly** *adverb* L18.

unintentional /ʌnɪnˈtɛnʃ(ə)n(ə)l/ *adjective.* L18.
[from UN-[1] + INTENTIONAL.]
Not intentional.
■ **unintentionally** *adverb* M18.

uninterested /ʌnˈɪnt(ə)rɪstɪd/ *ppl adjective.* M17.
[from UN-[1] + INTERESTED.]
†**1** Impartial, disinterested. M17–M18.
2 Unconcerned, indifferent. L18.
■ **uninterest** *noun* lack of interest, indifference L19. **uninterestedly** *adverb* L19. **uninterestedness** *noun* L17.

uninteresting /ʌnˈɪnt(ə)rɪstɪŋ/ *adjective.* M18.
[from UN-[1] + INTERESTING.]
Not interesting.
■ **uninterestingness** *noun* L18. **uninterestingly** *adverb* L18.

unintermitted /ˌʌnɪntəˈmɪtɪd/ *adjective.* E17.
[from UN-[1] + *intermitted* pa. pple of INTERMIT.]
Not intermitted; ceaseless, uninterrupted.
■ **unintermittedly** *adverb* L17.

unintermittent /ˌʌnɪntəˈmɪt(ə)nt/ *adjective.* M19.
[from UN-[1] + INTERMITTENT.]
Not intermittent; continuous.
■ **unintermittently** *adverb* L19.

unintermitting /ˌʌnɪntəˈmɪtɪŋ/ *adjective.* M17.
[from UN-[1] + *intermitting* pres. pple of INTERMIT.]
Not intermitting, continuous.
■ **unintermittingly** *adverb* L18.

uninterrupted /ˌʌnɪntəˈrʌptɪd/ *adjective.* E17.
[from UN-[1] + INTERRUPTED.]
Not interrupted or broken; continuous; unbroken.

📖 B. HARTE The dwellings were . . uninterrupted by shops. J. MCCARTHY His career was one of uninterrupted success.

■ **uninterruptaˈbility** *noun* uninterruptable quality M20. **uninterruptable** *adjective* = UNINTERRUPTIBLE L20. **uninterruptedly** *adverb* M17. **uninterruptedness** *noun* M17. **uninterruptible** *adjective* not interruptible L17. **uninterruption** *noun* M17.

unintuitive /ʌnɪnˈtjuːɪtɪv/ *adjective.* M19.
[from UN-[1] + INTUITIVE.]
Not intuitive.
■ **unintuitively** *adverb* E20.

uninvented /ʌnɪnˈvɛntɪd/ *adjective.* E17.
[from UN-[1] + *invented* pa. pple of INVENT.]
Not invented.

uninventive /ʌnɪnˈvɛntɪv/ *adjective.* L18.
[from UN-[1] + INVENTIVE.]
Not inventive.
■ **uninventively** *adverb* M19. **uninventiveness** *noun* M19.

uninvite /ʌnɪnˈvʌɪt/ *verb trans.* M17.
[from UN-[2] or UN-[1] + INVITE *verb*.]
Cancel or omit the invitation of (a person).

uninvited /ʌnɪnˈvʌɪtɪd/ *adjective.* L16.
[from UN-[1] + INVITED.]
Not invited.
■ **uninvitedly** *adverb* M17. **uninviting** *adjective* not inviting L17.

unio /ˈjuːnɪəʊ/ *noun.* Pl. **-os**. E19.
[mod. Latin (see below), from Latin = single large pearl: see UNION *noun*[1].]
ZOOLOGY. (The shell of) any of various freshwater mussels of the genus *Unio* and related genera of the family Unionidae, esp. one yielding pearls; a river mussel, a pearl mussel.

uniocular /juːnɪˈɒkjʊlə/ *adjective.* M19.
[from UNI- + OCULAR. Cf. medieval Latin *unioculus*.]
1 Characterized by the use of one eye. *rare.* M19.
2 Of, pertaining to, or affecting one eye. Cf. MONOCULAR *adjective* 2. L19.

union /ˈjuːnjən, -ɪən/ *noun*[1]. *arch.* ME.
[Latin *unio(n-)*: see next. Cf. ONION *noun*.]
A large good quality pearl of great value, *esp.* one which is supposed to occur singly.

union /ˈjuːnjən, -ɪən/ *noun*[2]. LME.
[Old & mod. French, or ecclesiastical Latin *unio(n-)* the number one, unity, from Latin *unus* one: see -ION.]
1 a The action or an instance of joining or uniting one thing to another or others, or two or more things together, to form a single complete body or unit; the state of being so united. LME. ▸**b** The joining together of separate physical parts; *spec.* (**a**) SURGERY the growing together and healing of the parts of a broken bone, sides of a wound, etc.; (**b**) sexual conjunction, copulation. L15. ▸**c** The action of uniting or state of being united into one political body; *esp.* (*the Union*) the uniting of the English and Scottish crowns in 1603, of the English and Scottish parliaments in 1707, or of the parliaments of Great Britain and Ireland in 1801. M16.
2 a The uniting together of the different parts or individuals of a nation, people, etc., to produce agreement or concord; the condition resulting from this, harmony, unity. LME. ▸**b** ART. Harmony of colour, design, etc. E18.
3 The joining of two people in matrimony; (a) marriage. LME.
4 SCOTS LAW (now *Hist.*). The uniting into one tenantry of lands or tenements which are not contiguous. E16.
5 a ECCLESIASTICAL. The uniting or combination of two or more churches or benefices into one. E16. ▸**b** *Hist.* A number of parishes united for the administration of the poor laws; an area so formed and administered. Also (in full *Union House*, *Union Workhouse*), a workhouse set up by such a group of parishes. M19.
†**6** The quality of being one in number; oneness. E16–M17.
7 a That which is united or combined into one; a body or whole formed by the combination of separate parts or things. M17. ▸**b** (Also **U-**.) A body of people or States united for a common purpose; a league, a society. Now *esp.* = TRADE UNION. M17. ▸**c** (Freq. **U-**.) *spec.* A political unit consisting of a number of States, provinces, etc., united into one legislative confederacy; *esp.* the United States, the United Kingdom, South Africa, and (formerly) the USSR. Also *spec.* (US HISTORY), the Northern States which remained as one body in the Union during the American Civil War, as opp. to the Southern States which attempted secession. L18. ▸**d** In the Indian subcontinent: a local administrative unit comprising several rural villages. L19.
8 A thing which unites or connects one thing to another; *spec.* a joint or coupling for pipes etc. L17.
9 a A Union flag, a Union Jack. M18. ▸**b** A part of a flag, usu. the upper corner beside the staff, with a device (esp. a Union Jack) indicating union. E19.
10 (**U-**.) A general social club and debating society at some universities and colleges (orig. at Oxford and Cambridge). Also, the buildings or accommodation of such a society. M19.
11 A textile fabric made of two or more yarns, esp. cotton and linen or silk; in *pl.*, kinds of goods or fabrics so woven. M19.
12 MATH. The set that comprises all the elements (and no others) contained in any of two or more given sets; the operation of forming such a set. M20.

For other words beginning with *un-* and *uni-* see the entries for **un-**[1], **un-**[2], and **uni-**

📖 **1a** E. MIALL The union of church and state. *Which?* The . . member states . . hope to achieve monetary union. ***hypostatic union***: see HYPOSTATIC *adjective*. **b** I. KENNEDY Sex . . has always been recognized as the union of man and woman. **c** A. J. P. TAYLOR A proposal for indissoluble union of the two countries. *Independent* Chancellor Kohl's . . commitment to union . . within the European Community. *Guardian* A . . treaty for a union of sovereign states. **2a** SIR W. SCOTT Thanks . . to God, who has restored union to my family. A. STEVENS The ring was a magic gift, a symbol of union. **b** G. MURRAY Lautrec achieved a union of Naturalism and abstraction. **3** J. GALSWORTHY The brutality of a union without love. **7b** W. FALCONER Where Dangers grow and hostile unions rise. *Independent* Unions are seeking a £25-a-week rise, management is offering £17. *Times Educ. Suppl.* The union . . may ballot for industrial action. *World Magazine* Artists . . have to belong to the Union to exhibit. ***craft union***, ***credit union***, ***Mothers' Union***, ***Postal Union***, ***print union***, etc. **c** J. R. LOWELL The South will come back to the Union. P. BARR At that time Colorado . . was an untamed territory outside the Union. ***State of the Union message***: see STATE *noun*. **10** A. F. DOUGLAS-HOME Contentious characters came to the Union or the Carlton or Canning Clubs. E. HEATH An active part in university politics, both in the Conservative Association and the Union.

Comb.: **union-basher** *colloq.* a person who engages in union bashing; **union-bashing** *colloq.* active opposition to trade unions and their rights; **union catalogue** a catalogue of the combined holdings of several libraries; **union down** *adverb* (of the hoisting of a flag) in an inverted position, with the union in the lower corner, indicating distress or mourning; **union dye** a dye which works on the two materials of a union cloth, esp. cotton and wool, at the same time; **Union flag** the national flag or ensign of Great Britain or (later) the United Kingdom, introduced to symbolize the union of the English and Scottish crowns and formed by combining the crosses of St George, St Andrew, and St Patrick; **Union Jack** (*a*) orig. & properly, a small British Union flag flown as the jack of a ship; later & now usu., a Union flag of any size or adaptation, regarded as the national flag of the United Kingdom; a representation of this; (*b*) *US* (**u- j-**) a jack consisting of the union from the national flag; ***Union House***: see sense 5b above; **union joint** a joint for pipes etc.; **union list** a union catalogue, *esp.* one giving details of periodical holdings in several libraries; **union nut** a nut used with a screw to join two parts together; **union rustic** a European noctuid moth, *Apamea pabulatricula*, which has greyish-white wings with distinctive dark markings; **union screw** a screw fitting for joining pipes etc.; **union shop** a shop, factory, trade, etc., in which employees must belong to or join a trade union; **union suit** (chiefly *N. Amer.*) a single undergarment for the body and legs; combinations; **union-wide** *adjective* that involves the whole of a trade union (movement); ***Union Workhouse***: see sense 5b above.

■ **unional** *adjective* of or pertaining to (esp. political and legislative) union or a union L19. **Uni'onic** *adjective* of or pertaining to a university or college Union M19.

Union Corse /ynjɔ̃ kɔrs/ *noun phr.* M20.
[French, lit. 'Corsican union'.]
A Corsican criminal organization operating in France and elsewhere.

Unione Siciliana /u'njoːne sitʃi'ljaːna/ *noun phr.* E20.
[Italian, lit. 'Sicilian union'.]
A Sicilian criminal organization operating in Italy and the US. Cf. MAFIA.

unionise *verb* var. of UNIONIZE.

unionism /'juːnjənɪz(ə)m, -ɪən-/ *noun*. Also **U-**. M19.
[from UNION *noun*² + -ISM.]
The principle or policy of union; combination into one body as a system of social or political organization; advocacy of this; *spec.* (*a*) *US* advocacy of or adherence to a legislative union among States; (*b*) loyalty to or advocacy of the principles or views of the Unionist party of Great Britain and Ireland. Also *ellipt.* = TRADE-UNIONISM.

📖 A. J. P. TAYLOR A new unionism, aiming at compromise or even partnership. *Independent* The Northern Ireland Office's change of direction eased the pressure on Unionism.

unionist /'juːnjənɪst, -ɪən-/ *noun & adjective*. Also **U-**. L18.
[formed as prec. + -IST.]
▶ **A** *noun*. **1** An adherent of or believer in unionism as a system of social or political organization; *esp.* one who supports the existence of a legislative union. L18. ▸**b** A supporter or advocate of the Union of the United States of America; *esp.* (*Hist.*) one who opposed secession during the American Civil War of 1861–5. *US*. M19. ▸**c** A member of a British political party formed in 1886 which supported maintenance of the parliamentary union between Great Britain and Ireland; an opponent of Home Rule, orig. for Ireland and later for Northern Ireland. Also, a member of a political party in Northern Ireland supporting union with Great Britain. L19.
2 A member of a trade union; a trade-unionist. Also, an advocate of trade unions. M19.
3 A person who advocates the union of churches or congregations. M19.
1c ***Liberal Unionist***: see LIBERAL *adjective*.
▶ **B** *attrib.* or as *adjective*. **1** Of, pertaining to, or supporting a legislative union, esp. that between Great Britain and (Northern) Ireland. E19. ▸**b** Of or belonging to a political party supporting unionism between (Northern) Ireland and Great Britain. L19.
2 Of or belonging to trade-unionism or trade-unionists. L19.

■ **unio'nistic** *adjective* of or relating to unionists; advocating or supporting union or unionism: M19.

unionize /'juːnjənʌɪz, -ɪən-/ *verb*. Also **-ise**. M19.
[from UNION *noun*² + -IZE.]
1 *verb trans.* **a** Form into a union. *rare* in *gen.* sense. M19. ▸**b** *spec.* Bring under trade-union rules or organization; cause (a person) to join a trade union. L19.
2 *verb intrans.* Become unionized; join or constitute a trade union. M20.

📖 **1b** *European Sociological Review* About half the labor force is presently unionized. **2** S. BRILL The women . . seemed . . unsure about taking the bold step of unionizing.

■ **unioni'zation** *noun* L19.

union pipe /'juːnjən 'pʌɪp/ *noun phr.* M19.
[Perh. from Irish *píob uilleann* (see UILLEAN PIPE) with assim. to UNION *noun*².]
sing. & (usu.) in *pl.* Uillean pipes.

uniparental /juːnɪpə'rɛnt(ə)l/ *adjective*. E20.
[from UNI- + PARENTAL.]
BIOLOGY. Of, pertaining to, or derived from, one parent.
■ **uniparentally** *adverb* M20.

uniparous /juː'nɪp(ə)rəs/ *adjective*. M17.
[from mod. Latin *uniparus*: see UNI-, -PAROUS.]
1 *ZOOLOGY.* Pertaining to or characterized by giving birth to only one young at a single birth. M17.
2 *BOTANY.* Of a cyme: developing only one lateral branch at each node; monochasial. M19.

uniped /'juːnɪpɛd/ *noun & adjective*. E19.
[from UNI- + Latin *ped-*, *pes* foot.]
▶ **A** *noun*. A person or creature having only one foot or leg. E19.
▶ **B** *adjective*. Having only one foot or leg. M19.

unipod /'juːnɪpɒd/ *noun*. M20.
[from UNI- + Greek *pod-*, *pous* foot, after TRIPOD.]
PHOTOGRAPHY. A one-legged support for a camera etc.; a monopod.

unipolar /juːnɪ'pəʊlə/ *adjective*. E19.
[from UNI- + POLAR.]
1 *ELECTRICITY.* **a** Produced by or proceeding from one magnetic pole; exhibiting one kind of polarity. E19. ▸**b** Of apparatus: having or operating by means of one magnetic pole; involving or operating by means of unipolar induction. L19.
2 *BIOLOGY.* Of nerve cells etc.: having one pole or process. M19.
3 *ELECTRONICS.* Of a transistor etc.: involving conduction by charge carriers of a single polarity. M20.
4 *PSYCHIATRY.* Of a psychiatric disorder: characterized by either depressive or (more rarely) manic episodes but not both. M20.
1a unipolar induction electrical induction in which a continuous direct current is produced in a conductor joining a magnetic pole and equator by the rotation of either the conductor or the magnet.
■ **unipo'larity** *noun* the condition or quality of being unipolar L19. **unipolarly** *adverb* E20.

unipotent /juːnɪ'pəʊt(ə)nt/ *adjective*. M20.
[from UNI- + POTENT *adjective*² & *noun*².]
1 *MATH.* (Of a semigroup) having only one idempotent element; (of a matrix or linear transformation) having the single eigenvalue 1. M20.
2 *MEDICINE & BIOLOGY.* Of an immature cell: capable of giving rise to only one type of cell or tissue. L20.

unique /juː'niːk/ *adjective & noun*. Also (earlier) †**unic**. E17.
[French, formerly †*unic* masc. from Latin *unicus* one and only, alone of its kind, from *unus* one: see -IC.]
▶ **A** *adjective*. **1** Of which there is only one; single, sole, solitary. E17.
2 That is, or who is, the only one of a kind; having no like or equal; unparalleled, unrivalled, esp. in excellence. Now also *loosely*, unusual, remarkable. E17.

📖 **1** J. HOWELL He hath lost . . his unic Son in the very flower of his age. R. COBB That unique specimen: an Irishman who turned his back on history. **2** *Here's Health* Health remedies unique to Oriental traditional medicine.

▶ **B** *noun*. **1** A thing (formerly esp. a coin or medal) of which there is only one example or copy. E18.
2 A person or thing which stands alone and is without equal or parallel, esp. in excellence. M18.

📖 **2** W. COWPER He is . . quite an unique in this country.

¶ The sense 'unusual' is often regarded as incorrect.
■ **uniquely** *adverb* E19. **uniqueness** *noun* E19. **u'niquity** *noun* uniqueness L18.

unireme /'juːnɪriːm/ *noun*. L17.
[from UNI- + Latin *remus* oar, after *quadrireme*, *trireme*, etc.]
A galley having one bank of oars.

uniserial /juːnɪ'sɪərɪəl/ *adjective*. M19.
[from UNI- + SERIAL *adjective* & *noun*.]
Chiefly *BOTANY & ZOOLOGY.* Arranged in or consisting of one series or row; characterized by this form or arrangement.
■ **uniserially** *adverb* L19.

unisex /'juːnɪsɛks/ *adjective & noun*. M20.
[from UNI- + SEX *noun*.]
▶ **A** *adjective*. Designed to be suitable for both sexes; sexually indeterminate or neutral. M20.

📖 *Times Lit. Suppl.* Student actors, all with cropped hair . . and dressed in unisex denims.

▶ **B** *noun*. A state or condition in which people dress and behave in a sexually indistinguishable way. M20.

unisexual /juːnɪ'sɛksjʊəl, -ʃʊəl/ *adjective & noun*. E19.
[from UNI- + SEXUAL.]
▶ **A** *adjective*. **1 a** *BOTANY.* Of a flower: having stamens only or pistils only but not both. Of a plant: having flowers of this kind. E19. ▸**b** *ZOOLOGY.* Of one sex; having the reproductive organs of only one sex. M19.
2 Pertaining or restricted to one sex. L19.
3 = UNISEX *adjective*. M20.
▶ **B** *noun*. *BOTANY & ZOOLOGY.* A unisexual organism or inflorescence. L19.
■ **unisexu'ality** *noun* (a) unisexual state or condition M19. **unisexually** *adverb* L19.

unison /'juːnɪs(ə)n/ *noun & adjective*. LME.
[Old French (mod. *unisson*), or late Latin *unisonus* of the same sound, from Latin *unus* one + *sonus* SOUND *noun*².]
▶ **A** *noun*. **1** *MUSIC & ACOUSTICS.* Identity in pitch of two or more sounds or notes; the relation of two notes of the same pitch regarded as a musical interval; the sounding of notes or melodies at the same pitch, or at pitches one or more octaves apart, by different voices or instruments together; also *transf.*, a single note of the same pitch as another or taken as a starting-point for measuring an interval. LME.
2 A single unvaried tone; a monotone. *rare*. E17.
3 *fig.* **a** A thing perfectly agreeing or responding harmoniously with another. Now *rare* or *obsolete*. M17. ▸**b** Perfect agreement; concord, harmony. M17.
4 A combination of concordant sounds; a united utterance. E19.

📖 **1** W. MASON The stupendous effect both of unison and harmony. *Independent* The men . . intone in a single unison with a rich accompaniment. **3a** COLERIDGE Make the intellectual faith a fair analogon or unison of the vital faith. **b** KEATS That unison of sense Which marries sweet sound with the grace of form.

Phrases: **in unison** *adjectival & adverbial phr.* in agreement or harmony; harmonious(ly); together, as one; (*lit.* & *fig.*).
Comb.: **unison string** a string tuned to the same pitch as another, or to a pitch an octave higher, and meant to be sounded with it; **unison-tuning** the tuning of the strings of an instrument in unison.
▶ **B** *adjective*. †**1** Sounding at once or together. Only in L16. ▸**b** *fig.* In complete agreement; unanimous, concordant. M17–M18. ▸**c** Concordant or consonant *to* something. E–M18.
2 *MUSIC & ACOUSTICS.* Identical in pitch; singing, sounding, etc., in unison. E17.

📖 **2** *Guardian* A trumpeter brought up to play unison passages alongside Charlie Parker.

■ **u'nisonal** *adjective* (*MUSIC*) = UNISONOUS *adjective* 1 E18. **u'nisonally** *adverb* in unison L19. **u'nisonance** *noun* (*rare*) agreement or identity of sounds E18. **u'nisonant** *adjective* of the same pitch or sound, unisonous; *fig.* concordant, harmonious: E19.

unisonous /juː'nɪs(ə)nəs/ *adjective*. L18.
[from late Latin *unisonus* UNISON + -OUS.]
1 *MUSIC.* Of the same pitch for different voices or instruments; composed or performed in unison or in octaves, and not in parts. L18.
2 *fig.* Showing agreement or harmony of character or nature; concordant. E19.

unit /'juːnɪt/ *noun*¹ *& adjective*. L16.
[from Latin *unus*, prob. after DIGIT. Cf. earlier UNITY *noun*¹.]
▶ **A** *noun*. **I 1** *MATH.* **a** The quantity of one considered as an undivided whole and the basis of all numbers. Also (now *rare* or *obsolete*), a number exactly divisible by one, a whole number, an integer. L16. ▸**b** In *pl.* The rightmost digit of a whole number in decimal notation, representing an integer less than ten; the equivalent digit in other scales of numerical notation. L17. ▸†**c** (Without article.) The numeral one; = UNITY *noun*¹ 1b. E18–E19.
2 A quantity adopted as a basis or standard of measurement in terms of which other quantities may be expressed. M18. ▸**b** A substance adopted as a standard for the measurement of relative density, atomic weight, etc. E19. ▸**c** A specific quantity used in measuring and charging for a commodity or service; *esp.* one kilowatt-hour of mains electricity. L19. ▸**d** A measure of educational attainment comprising a specific number of hours of study in a course, a number of which are required to be completed for matriculation etc. Also

course unit. Cf. CREDIT *noun* 11. Orig. *US*. L19. ▸**e** *PHARMACOLOGY*. The amount of a drug, antibiotic, etc., required to produce a specific effect, used esp. as a measure of the biological activity of an impure substance. L19. ▸**f** *COMMERCE*. The smallest measure of investment in a unit trust. M20. ▸**g** A measure of the alcohol content of a drink equivalent to 9 grams of absolute alcohol (roughly corresponding to half a pint of beer or a measure of spirits). L20.

🕮 **1b** *Engineering* Three tubes count the hundreds, tens and units respectively. **2** ***astronomical unit, atomic mass unit, Svedberg unit, thermal unit***, etc.

▶ **II 3** An individual thing, person, or group regarded as single and complete, esp. for the purposes of calculation; each of the (smallest) separate individuals or groups into which a complex whole may be analysed. E17.

4 A subdivision of a larger military grouping. L19.

5 A group of buildings, wards, etc., in or connected with a hospital; *spec*. one providing care in a specified field. L19.

6 A piece of (esp. storage) furniture which may be fitted with other pieces to form a larger system, or which is made of smaller complementary parts. E20.

7 A private residence forming one of several in a large building or group of buildings; a flat. Also ***home unit***. *N. Amer., Austral., & NZ*. M20.

8 A group of people having a particular (specified) role in an organization or team; a device with a specified function forming part of a complex mechanism. M20.

9 A motor vehicle, *esp*. one having both engine and haulage sections in a single body; *spec*. (*NZ*) a suburban train. M20.

🕮 **3** SAKI A group of speakers of whom Henry Greech had been an impatient unit. A. WILSON Individuals against State tyranny, the unit against the monopoly. F. ASTAIRE The show traveled intact as a unit. *Making Music* Which one has the career? The band as a 'unit' or you as a musician? ***social unit***: see SOCIAL *adjective*. **4** G. F. KENNAN The retention of the expected Czech units . . as part of the Allied occupying force. C. RYAN The unit of 544 men now approaching was hand-picked, every soldier a veteran. **5** *Nature* An active research programme . . carried out . . with the renal unit. *Nursery World* A partial hearing unit attached to their local school. **6** *Home Finder* Fully-fitted kitchens with high-quality units. **8** *Birds Magazine* Natural history film units around the world.

Phrases: **unit of account** a monetary unit in which accounts are kept.

▶ **B** *attrib*. or as *adjective*. **1** Of, pertaining to, or equivalent to (that of) a unit; forming a unit. M19.

2 Having the individual existence of a unit; individual. *rare*. L19.

Special collocations & comb.: **unit cell** *CRYSTALLOGRAPHY* the smallest structural unit having the overall symmetry of a crystal, which by repetition in three dimensions gives the entire lattice. **unit character** *GENETICS* a character inherited according to Mendelian laws, esp. one controlled by a single pair of alleles; also formerly, the alleles themselves. **unit cost** the cost of producing one item of manufacture. **unit-factor** *GENETICS* (*obsolete* exc. *Hist*.) = GENE. **unit-holder** a person holding securities in a unit trust. **unit-linked** *adjective* (designating a life assurance policy) in which part of the premium is invested in a unit trust. **unit load** a package of goods arranged for shipment etc. as a single unit, to facilitate handling. **unit matrix** *MATH*. = ***identity matrix*** s.v. IDENTITY. **unit membrane** *BIOLOGY* a lipoprotein membrane composed of two electron-dense layers enclosing a less dense layer, found enclosing many cells and cell organelles. **unit price** the price charged for each unit of goods supplied. **unit train** *N. Amer*. a train transporting a single commodity at a special rate between two points. **unit trust** a trust company whose business is managing investments on behalf of investors, the investors' holding being in the form of units that represent a certain fraction of the value of the investments and are issued by and bought back by the managers. **unit vector** *MATH*. a vector which has a magnitude of one.

unit *noun*[2] var. of UNITE *noun*.

UNITA /juːˈniːtə/ *abbreviation*.

Portuguese *União Nacional por Independência Total de Angola* National Union for the Total Independence of Angola.

unital /ˈjuːnɪt(ə)l/ *adjective*. M19.

[from UNIT *noun*[1] or UNITY *noun*[1]: see -AL[1].]

Producing unity; of the nature of a unit.

UNITAR *abbreviation*.

United Nations Institute for Training and Research.

unitard /ˈjuːnɪtɑːd/ *noun*. M20.

[from UNI- + LEO)TARD.]

A tight-fitting one-piece garment of stretchable fabric which covers the body from neck to feet.

Unitarian /juːnɪˈtɛːrɪən/ *noun & adjective*. L17.

[from mod. Latin *unitarius*, from Latin *unitas* unity: see -ARIAN.]

▶ **A** *noun*. **1** *THEOLOGY*. A person who believes that God is not a Trinity, but one person (cf. TRINITARIAN); *spec*. a member of a Christian religious body maintaining this. Later also, a member of any of various Christian and non-Christian sects advocating freedom from formal dogma and emphasizing the value of love and the goodness of human nature. L17. ▸**b** Any non-Christian monotheist, *esp*. a Muslim. E18.

2 An adherent or advocate of any theory or system based on unity or on a single (political, spiritual, etc.) unit. L17.

▶ **B** *adjective*. Of, pertaining to, or characteristic of the Unitarians; that is a Unitarian. L17.

■ **Unitarianism** *noun* Unitarian doctrine, belief, or theory L17.

unitarist /ˈjuːnɪt(ə)rɪst/ *noun*. M19.

[from next + -IST.]

An advocate of a unitary system of government.

■ **unitarism** *noun* E20.

unitary /ˈjuːnɪt(ə)ri/ *adjective*. E19.

[from UNIT *noun*[1] or UNITY *noun*[1]: see -ARY[1].]

†**1** *CRYSTALLOGRAPHY*. Of a crystal form: derived from a primary form by decrement of one row of molecules. Only in E19.

2 Of, pertaining to, characterized by, or based on unity; *spec*. of or pertaining to a system of government in which the powers of the separate constituent parts are vested in a central body (cf. FEDERAL *adjective* 2). M19. ▸**b** *PHILOSOPHY*. Of or pertaining to unity of being or existence. M19.

3 Of the nature of a unit; having the separate existence or individual character of a unit. M19.

4 Of or pertaining to a unit or units; *spec*. (*Hist*.) designating a chemical theory in which molecules are regarded as units. M19.

5 *MATH. & PHYSICS*. Pertaining to or based on (mathematical) unity. L19.

🕮 **2** I. ASIMOV The apparent strength and actual weakness of a unitary, centralised government. *Times* One man one vote in a unitary system. **unitary authority**, **unitary council** (in some parts of the UK) a single administrative division of local government established in place of a two-tier system of local councils. **3** C. RYCROFT His theories, so far from constituting a unitary, fixed structure . . are . . a collection of miscellaneous ideas. *Classic & Sportscar* The steel body is based on a unitary Kadett platform. **5** **unitary group** the group of all square unitary matrices of a given size. **unitary matrix** a matrix which, when multiplied by the transpose of its complex conjugate, gives the identity matrix. **unitary symmetry** the symmetry of a unimodular unitary group as used to relate the properties of different subatomic particles.

■ **unitarily** *adverb* in a unitary manner E20. **uniˈtarity** *noun* the property of being unitary M20.

unite /ˈjuːnʌɪt, juːˈnʌɪt/ *noun*. Also **unit** /ˈjuːnɪt/, (long *arch*.) **unity** /ˈjuːnɪti/. E17.

[from *unite* obsolete pa. pple of next.]

Hist. An English gold coin first struck in the reign of James I and equivalent to 20 or 22 shillings. Cf. JACOBUS.

unite /juːˈnʌɪt/ *verb*. Pa. t. & pple **united**, (earlier) †**unite**. See also UNITED. LME.

[Latin *unit-* pa. ppl stem of *unire* join together, from *unus* one.]

1 *verb trans. & intrans*. Put or come together to form a single unit or mass; make or become one; combine; join together, fuse. LME. ▸**b** *verb trans*. Join or clasp (hands), esp. as part of a wedding ceremony. E17.

2 *verb trans. & intrans*. Join together by a common interest, feeling, etc., or for a common purpose or action. (Foll. by *in*, *to do*.) M16.

3 *verb trans. & intrans*. Join in marriage. E18.

4 *verb trans*. Possess or exhibit (qualities, esp. opposite ones) in combination. L18.

🕮 **1** C. THIRLWALL The forces of Greece . . had been united. A. MEADOWS The tubes . . sometimes . . dividing and uniting again. J. REED To unite all the anti-Bolshevik elements in one huge organization. I. MURDOCH The Sikh . . happily united with his fellow males. **2** *Philadelphia Inquirer* If we can unite, we can win. C. WARWICK People, says Ustinov, are united by their doubts but divided by their convictions. **4** J. FERRIAR D'Aubigné's style . . unites the severe and the ludicrous.

■ **unitable** *adjective* able to be united M17. **uniter** *noun* L16. **uniting** *verbal noun* the action of the verb; an instance of this; (a) union: M16.

united /juːˈnʌɪtɪd/ *adjective & noun*. M16.

[from UNITE *verb* + -ED[1].]

▶ **A** *adjective*. **1** That has united or been united. M16.

2 a Of, pertaining to, or produced by two or more persons or things in union; joint. L16. ▸**b** Constituted by or resulting from the union of two or more parts. Freq. in the titles of churches, societies, etc. (see special collocations below) and in the names of football clubs. L17.

†**3** Forming or conferring union. *rare* (Shakes.). Only in L16.

🕮 **1** M. BRADBURY They were united souls, of an ambience, sharing a single cause. **2a** R. PEEL The united voice of King, Lords, and Commons.

Special collocations: **United Brethren** *ECCLESIASTICAL* the Moravians. **United Free Church** a Scottish Church formed in 1900 by amalgamation of the Free Church of Scotland and the United Presbyterian Church. **United Kingdom** the kingdom of Great Britain (*Hist*.), (after 1801) of Great Britain and Ireland (*Hist*.), (since 1922) of Great Britain and Northern Ireland (in official use also ***United Kingdom of Great Britain and Northern Ireland***). **United Nations (Organization)** orig. (*Hist*.), the Allied nations who united against the Axis powers in the war of 1939–45; later, a supranational peace-seeking organization of these and many other States (cf. ***League of Nations*** s.v. LEAGUE *noun*[2]). **United Presbyterian Church**: see PRESBYTERIAN *adjective*. **United Provinces** *Hist*. (*a*) the seven provinces united in 1579 and forming the basis of the kingdom of the Netherlands; (*b*) an Indian administrative division formed by the union of Agra and Oudh, now called Uttar Pradesh. **United Reformed Church** a Church formed in 1972 from the English Presbyterian and Congregational Churches.

▶ **B** *ellipt*. as *noun* (treated as *pl*.). (**U-**.) Any of various football clubs having 'United' in their name. *colloq*. L19.

🕮 L. GOLDING United's match next week, away, against Aston Villa.

■ **unitedly** *adverb* E17. **unitedness** *noun* M17.

United States /juːˌnʌɪtɪd ˈsteɪts/ *noun phr. pl*. (treated as *sing*. or *pl*.). E17.

[from prec. + STATE *noun* + -S[1].]

1 = ***United Provinces*** (a) s.v. UNITED *adjective*. *obsolete* exc. *Hist*. E17.

2 A federal republic of 50 States (orig. 13, formed after the American War of Independence), mostly in N. America and including Alaska and Hawaii. Also more fully ***United States of America***. L18. ▸**b** American English. L19.

3 *gen*. Any (hypothetical or actual) union of the States of a specified geographical area into a political federation. M19.

Comb.: **United Statesman** *noun* a male citizen or inhabitant of the United States of America.

■ **United-Stateser** *noun* a citizen or inhabitant of the United States of America E20.

unition /juːˈnɪʃ(ə)n/ *noun*. Now *rare*. LME.

[Late Latin *unitio(n-)*, from *unit-*: see UNITE *verb*, -ION.]

The action of uniting; the fact or condition of being united. Now only with ref. to abstract or spiritual union.

unitise *verb* var. of UNITIZE.

unitive /ˈjuːnɪtɪv/ *adjective*. LME.

[Late Latin *unitivus*, from *unit-*: see UNITE *verb*, -IVE.]

1 *CHRISTIAN THEOLOGY*. Having the quality of uniting spiritually to God. LME.

2 *gen*. Having the effect of uniting; characterized by or involving union. E16.

🕮 **1** *Church Times* God's unitive purpose of love. **unitive life**, **unitive way** the third and final stage of spiritual advancement. **2** *Times* Eros was the . . unitive principle that brought coherence to the discordant elements of Chaos.

■ **unitively** *adverb* L17. **unitiveness** *noun* M17.

unitize /ˈjuːnɪtʌɪz/ *verb trans*. Also **-ise**. M19.

[from UNIT *noun*[1] + -IZE.]

1 Form into a unit; unite, make one. M19.

2 Package (cargo) into unit loads; palletize. M20.

3 Convert (an investment trust) into a unit trust. L20.

■ **unitiˈzation** *noun* (*a*) the action or process of unitizing; (*b*) the joint development of a petroleum source which straddles territory controlled by several companies: M20.

unity /ˈjuːnɪti/ *noun*[1]. ME.

[Old & mod. French *unité* from Latin *unitas*, from *unus* one: see -ITY.]

▶ **I 1** The fact, quality, or condition of being or consisting of one in number; oneness. ME. ▸**b** *MATH*. (Without article.) The smallest whole number, the numeral one; the quality of being the numeral one. LME. ▸**c** A quantity or magnitude taken as equivalent to one for the purpose of calculation, measurement, or comparison; *loosely* a thing or substance with a property so taken. E18.

†**2** = UNIT *noun*[1] 1a. LME–M19.

3 A single or individual thing. L16.

🕮 **1** I. WATTS The Unity and Spirituality of the Godhead. **b** T. H. HUXLEY The ratio of the . . transverse to the . . longitudinal diameter of a skull, the latter measurement being taken as unity. **3** CARLYLE The clear view of it as an indivisible Unity.

▶ **II 4** The quality or condition of agreeing or being one in feeling, opinion, purpose, or action; agreement, concord, harmony. ME.

5 The fact of uniting or being united into one body or whole; union. LME. ▸**b** A group formed by union; *esp*. (**U-**) = ***United Brethren*** s.v. UNITED. L18.

6 The quality or fact of being one body or whole, esp. as made up of two or more parts. Also, a thing forming a complex whole. LME. ▸**b** Due interconnection and coherence of the parts of which a literary or artistic work etc. is composed. E18.

7 Equality, identity, esp. of various conditions pertaining to each tenant in a joint tenancy. E17.

8 *THEATRICAL*. Each of the three dramatic principles requiring limitation of the supposed time of a play to that occupied in acting it or to a single day (more fully ***unity of time***), use of one scene throughout (more fully

unity of place), and concentration on the development of a single plot (more fully ***unity of action***). M17.

📖 **4** H. H. MILMAN Religious unity must have contributed . . to . . national unity. GEO. ELIOT The possession of this child would give unity to her life. M. L. KING Man and God, made one in a marvellous unity of purpose. P. WARNER England and Scotland . . were near a form of unity and friendship. **5** JULIA HAMILTON They have approved the unity of the legislative power in one branch. **6** E. WILSON I have never yet . . combined in a living unity so many apparently discordant threads. **b** R. FRY Unity of some kind is necessary for our . . contemplation of the work of art as a whole.

unity *noun*² see UNITE *noun*.

Univ /ˈjuːnɪv/ *noun*. Also **Univ.** (point). M16.
[Abbreviation.]
= UNIVERSITY 1.

univalent /juːnɪˈveɪl(ə)nt, *esp.* CYTOLOGY juːˈnɪvəl(ə)nt/ *adjective & noun*. M19.
[from UNI- + -VALENT.]
▶ **A** *adjective*. **1** CHEMISTRY. = MONOVALENT 1. M19.
2 CYTOLOGY. Of or pertaining to a univalent. L19.
3 IMMUNOLOGY. = MONOVALENT 2b. M20.
▶ **B** *noun*. CYTOLOGY. A chromosome which remains unpaired during meiosis. E20.
■ **univalence**, **uniˈvalency** *nouns* L19.

univalve /ˈjuːnɪvalv/ *adjective & noun*. M17.
[from UNI- + VALVE *noun*.]
▶ **A** *adjective*. Chiefly ZOOLOGY. Having one valve or part; *spec.* (of a mollusc) having a shell in one piece. M17.
▶ **B** *noun*. ZOOLOGY. A univalve mollusc, esp. one of the class Gastropoda. M17.

universal /juːnɪˈvəːs(ə)l/ *adjective & noun*. LME.
[Old & mod. French *universel*, †*-sal*, or Latin *universalis*, from *universus*: see UNIVERSE, -AL¹.]
▶ **A** *adjective*. **1** Including, affecting or involving, done, made, etc., by all people or things, or all individuals in a particular (specified or implied) group or class. LME. ▸**b** *spec.* (Of a rule, law, etc.) applicable in all cases; LOGIC (of a proposition) in which something is asserted of the whole of a class (opp. ***particular***). M16. ▸**c** Of a language (esp. an artificial one) etc.: (intended to be) used or understood everywhere. M17. ▸**d** Chiefly SCOTS LAW. Of or in respect of the whole of an estate or property. M17.
2 Of or pertaining to the universe in general or (occas.) all nature. Chiefly *poet. & rhet.* LME.
3 = CATHOLIC *adjective* 2. L15.
4 Constituting or regarded as a complete whole; entire. Now *rare*. L15.
5 a Educated or learned in many subjects; having a wide range of experience, interests, or activities; widely accomplished. E16. ▸**b** Not limited to a particular type of work etc. M17. ▸**c** Covering or applicable to all or a great variety of subjects etc. M17.
†**6** Of motion or action: constant, continual. *rare*. L16–E17.
7 Of a tool, machine, etc.: adjustable to or appropriate for all requirements; not restricted to a single purpose, position, etc. L17.

📖 **1** E. A. FREEMAN The English visitors were the objects of universal . . admiration. D. H. LAWRENCE It was universal in the district, and therefore unnoticed. D. J. ENRIGHT Death is universal, and not a fate reserved for you or me. **b** B. MAGEE Whether or not singular statements were empirically verifiable, universal statements such as scientific laws were certainly not. **2** R. I. WILBERFORCE The Universal Mind which pervades all things. **4** C. DARWIN I care not what the universal world says. **5** SMOLLETT He sets up for an universal man, because he has a small tincture of every science.

Special collocations: **universal agent**: empowered to do all that can be delegated. †**universal arithmetic** algebra. **Universal Aunt** (*Hist.*) an employee of a company providing all types of domestic assistance. **universal bishop** *Hist.* (a title of) the Pope. **universal compass**: with legs that may be extended for large circles. **universal coupling** = ***universal joint*** below. **universal donor** MEDICINE a person of blood group O, whose blood can theoretically be given to recipients belonging to any blood group of the ABO system. **universal gas constant** = ***gas constant*** s.v. GAS *noun*¹. **universal grammar** LINGUISTICS: composed of rules applicable to all natural languages or of principles believed to be genetically inherited. **universal indicator** CHEMISTRY a mixture of dyes that changes colour gradually over a range of pH and is used (esp. as indicator paper) in testing for acids and alkalis. **universal joint** a joint which permits free movement in any direction of the parts joined, *spec.* one which can transmit rotary power by a shaft at any angle. **universal maid** a maid of all work. **universal quantifier** LOGIC: referring to all the members of a universe or class. **universal recipient** MEDICINE a person of blood group AB, who can theoretically receive blood from donors of any blood group in the ABO system. **universal serial bus** COMPUTING a standard form of connector used to link peripheral devices to a computer. **universal set** STATISTICS & LOGIC = UNIVERSE 4. **universal suffrage** a suffrage extending to all people (formerly, only all men) over a certain age, with minor exceptions. **universal time** Greenwich Mean Time. ***universal tincture***: see TINCTURE *noun* 4a. ***universal veil***: see VEIL *noun* 7.
▶ **B** *noun*. **1** *The* whole of something (specified or implied); *spec.* (LOGIC & PHILOSOPHY) *the* whole class or genus, as distinct from the individuals comprising it. LME.
2 LOGIC & PHILOSOPHY. A universal proposition; a term or concept of general application; a nature or essence signified by a general term. Usu. in *pl.* M16.
3 That which is universal; a person or thing having universal power, currency, etc. M16.
†**4** The universe. M16–E17.
†**5** A medicine affecting the whole body. M–L17.
6 LINGUISTICS. A fundamental rule or feature found generally in natural languages. M20.
■ **univerˈsalian** *adjective* (*rare*) universalistic M19. **universally** *adverb* (*a*) in a universal manner; in every case or instance, without exception; by, to, among, etc., all people or things; †(*b*) so as to affect every part of something specified or implied, all over: LME. **universalness** *noun* M16.

universalise *verb* var. of UNIVERSALIZE.

universalism /juːnɪˈvəːs(ə)lɪz(ə)m/ *noun*. E19.
[from prec. + -ISM.]
1 The fact or quality of being learned in many subjects or of having a wide range of interests etc. E19.
2 CHRISTIAN THEOLOGY. The doctrine that all people will eventually be saved. E19.
3 The fact or condition of being universal in character or scope. M19.
4 SOCIOLOGY & ECONOMICS. A system based on generally applicable rules and principles. M20.

universalist /juːnɪˈvəːs(ə)lɪst/ *noun & adjective*. E17.
[formed as prec. + -IST.]
▶ **A** *noun*. **1** CHRISTIAN THEOLOGY. Orig., an adherent of the doctrine that redemption is available to all people. Later, an adherent of the doctrine of universalism; *spec.* (**U-**) a member of a US sect holding this doctrine. E17.
2 A person who is learned in many subjects or who has a wide range of interests etc. E18.
3 A person advocating loyalty to and concern for others without regard to national allegiances. M20.
▶ **B** *adjective*. Universalistic. E19.
■ **universaˈlistic** *adjective* (*a*) CHRISTIAN THEOLOGY of, pertaining to, or characteristic of the Universalists; (*b*) (inclined to be) universal in scope or character: M19.

universality /juːnɪvəːˈsalɪti/ *noun*. LME.
[Old & mod. French *universalité* or late Latin *universalitas*, from Latin *universalis*: see UNIVERSAL, -ITY.]
▶ **I 1** The fact or quality of being universal. LME.
2 *spec.* The extension of a religion, esp. Roman Catholicism, to all people. Now *rare* or *obsolete*. M16.
3 The fact of having a large acquaintance of or of people. Now *rare*. L18.
▶ **II 4 a** The whole *of* a group of people or things, humankind, etc. Cf. UNIVERSITY 2a. *arch.* M16. ▸†**b** People in general. Only in 17.
†**5** A general statement or description, a generality. Usu. in *pl.* L16–M17.
†**6** A collective whole, as distinct from its composite parts. L16–M17.

universalize /juːnɪˈvəːs(ə)lʌɪz/ *verb trans*. Also **-ise**. M17.
[from UNIVERSAL *adjective* + -IZE.]
1 Make universal; give a universal character to; apply or extend to all the members of a class. M17.
2 Bring into universal use; extend over the whole of an area. E19.
■ **universalizaˈbility** *noun* the quality of being universalizable M20. **universaˈlizable** *adjective* (chiefly PHILOSOPHY) that can be made universal; capable of universal application: M20. **universaˈlizably** *adverb* M20. **universaliˈzation** *noun* the action or an act of universalizing; the process of becoming universal: L18. **universalizer** *noun* M19.

universe /ˈjuːnɪvəːs/ *noun*. LME.
[Old & mod. French *univers* or Latin *universum* the whole world, use as noun of neut. of *universus* all taken together, lit. 'turned into one', formed as UNI- + *versus* pa. pple of *vertere* turn.]
†**1** ***in universe***, of universal application. Only in LME.
2 ***the universe***, all existing matter, space, and other phenomena regarded collectively and esp. as constituting a systematic or ordered whole; this regarded as created by a divine agency; the creation; the cosmos. L16. ▸**b** *fig.* A domain or sphere characterized by a particular (specified) quality or activity; a sphere of activity, existence, interest, etc. M17. ▸**c** PHYSICS. Any of a class of entities of which the known universe is considered to be a member. Formerly also (in full ***island universe***), a distinct stellar system, a galaxy. L19.
3 The world, esp. as the scene of human existence or activity; *transf.* humankind in general. M17.
4 STATISTICS & LOGIC. All the objects or items under consideration. Also (LOGIC) ***universe of discourse***. M19.

📖 **2** P. DAVIES The universe is full of distinct, well-separated galaxies. ***expanding universe***: see EXPANDING *adjective*. **b** E. M. FORSTER Her two daughters came to grief—to the worst grief known to Miss Austen's universe. P. KURTH Life in a bitter universe of imputation and doubt. *Television Week* There are now two television universes—cable and non-cable.

universitas /juːnɪˈvəːsɪtɑːs/ *noun*. M18.
[Latin: see next.]
SCOTS LAW. The whole (*of* an estate or inheritance).

university /juːnɪˈvəːsɪti/ *noun*. ME.
[Old & mod. French *université* from Latin *universitas* the whole, the whole number (of), the universe, (later, in legal use) society, guild, corporation), from *universus*: see UNIVERSE, -ITY.]
▶ **I 1** Orig., a corporation of teachers and students formed for the purpose of giving and receiving instruction in a fixed range of subjects at a level beyond that provided at a school. Later, an institution of higher education, offering courses and research facilities in mainly non-vocational subjects and having acknowledged powers and privileges, esp. that of conferring degrees. ME. ▸**b** *collect.* The members of a university; the buildings, colleges, etc., belonging to or occupied by a university. ME. ▸**c** Without article: some university, known or unknown; attendance at a university. M19.
2 a = UNIVERSALITY 4a. Long *arch.* LME. ▸†**b** All people or things, everything. LME–E17. ▸†**c** The universe. L15–M17.
†**3 a** ***your university***: used in an official document as a form of address to a specific group of people. LME–L16. ▸**b** A group of people, *esp.* one forming a corporate body. L15–L17.
1 ***open university***: see OPEN *adjective*. **university of life** the experience of life regarded as a means of instruction. **university of the air** an organization providing a course of higher education partly through radio and television broadcasts; *spec.* (***University of the Air***) the Open University. **University of the Third Age** an organization providing courses of (higher) education for retired or elderly people.
▶ **II** †**4** The fact or quality of including, affecting or involving the whole of something; universality. *rare*. M16–L17.
Comb.: **university college** a college affiliated to a university, *spec.* one which is not or was not empowered to grant degrees; ***university extension***: see EXTENSION 3b; **university member** *Hist.* a member of the House of Commons representing a university or a group of universities.
■ **universiˈtarian** *adjective* of, pertaining to, or characteristic of a university M19.

univocal /juːnɪˈvəʊk(ə)l, juːˈnɪvək(ə)l/ *adjective & noun*. M16.
[Late Latin *univocus* having one meaning, formed as UNI- + *voc-*, *vox* VOICE *noun*: see -AL¹.]
▶ **A** *adjective*. †**1** Chiefly MEDICINE. Of a symptom, sign, etc.: signifying one thing; certain or unmistakable in significance. M16–L18.
2 Now chiefly LOGIC. Of a term or word: having only one proper meaning; capable of only one single interpretation; unambiguous. Opp. EQUIVOCAL *adjective* 2. L16.
†**3** Uniform, homogeneous. E17–E18.
†**4** Made, uttered, etc., (as) with one voice; unanimous. E17–M18.
†**5** Of, pertaining to, or characteristic of things of the same name, order, or species. M17–E19.
▶ **B** *noun*. A univocal term or word. L17.
■ **univoˈcality** *noun* M20. **univocally** *adverb* (*a*) with only one meaning; unambiguously; (*b*) by members of the same species; regularly, normally; (*c*) *rare* unanimously: L16.

univocalic /juːnɪvəˈkalɪk/ *adjective & noun*. M19.
[from UNI- + VOCALIC.]
▶ **A** *adjective*. Of poetry or prose: composed using only one of the vowels. M19.
▶ **B** *noun*. A piece of univocalic writing. L20.

univoltine /juːnɪˈvɒltʌɪn/ *adjective*. L19.
[French *univoltin*, from Italian *volta* time: see UNI-, -INE¹.]
Of an insect (esp. a silkworm moth): producing only one brood a year.

Unix /ˈjuːnɪks/ *noun*. Also **u-**. L20.
[from UNI- + *-ix* repr. -ICS.]
COMPUTING. (Proprietary name for) a portable multi-user operating system.

unjoin /ʌnˈdʒɔɪn/ *verb trans*. ME.
[from UN-² + JOIN *verb*.]
1 Detach from being joined; sever, separate. ME.
2 Separate the parts of; take apart. ME.

unjoined /ʌnˈdʒɔɪnd/ *adjective*. M16.
[from UN-¹ + *joined* pa. pple of JOIN *verb*.]
Not joined.

unjoint /ʌnˈdʒɔɪnt/ *verb trans*. LME.
[from UN-² + JOINT *verb*.]
1 Disjoint, dislocate (*lit. & fig.*). LME.
†**2** Carve (a cooked bird). LME–E19.

unjointed /ʌnˈdʒɔɪntɪd/ *adjective*. L16.
[from UN-¹ + JOINTED.]
1 Lacking due connection or coherence; disjointed. L16.
2 Not provided with or having joints. L17.

unjoyful /ʌnˈdʒɔɪfʊl, -f(ə)l/ *adjective*. ME.
[from UN-¹ + JOYFUL.]
Not joyful.
■ **unjoyfully** *adverb* M16. **unjoyous** *adjective* M17.

unjudicial /ʌndʒuːˈdɪʃ(ə)l/ *adjective*. L16.
[from UN-¹ + JUDICIAL.]
Not judicial.
■ **unjudicially** *adverb* E17. **unjudicious** *adjective* (now *rare* or *obsolete*) injudicious E17.

unjust /ʌn'dʒʌst/ *adjective.* LME.
[from UN-¹ + JUST *adjective.*]
1 Not impartial in one's dealings; not in accordance with the principles of moral right or of equity; unfair. LME.
2 Not faithful or honourable in one's social relations; dishonest. (Foll. by *of, to.*) Now *rare.* L15.
†**3** Improper; incorrect. M16–E18.

1 W. COWPER He saw his people . . avaricious, arrogant, unjust. J. D. SUTHERLAND He felt this punishment was extremely unjust. **2** GOLDSMITH Nothing could have ever made me unjust to my promise.

■ **unjustice** *noun* (*obsolete* exc. *Scot.*) injustice LME. **unjustly** *adverb* LME. **unjustness** *noun* LME.

unjustifiable /ʌn'dʒʌstɪfʌɪəb(ə)l/ *adjective.* M17.
[from UN-¹ + JUSTIFIABLE.]
Not justifiable, indefensible.
■ **unjustifiableness** *noun* M17. **unjustifiably** *adverb* M18.

unjustified /ʌn'dʒʌstɪfʌɪd/ *adjective.* ME.
[from UN-¹ + *justified* pa. pple of JUSTIFY.]
†**1** Not punished or sentenced. ME–L16.
2 THEOLOGY. Not made or reckoned righteous. LME.
3 Not made exact. Now *spec.* in TYPOGRAPHY etc., not having the type adjusted to fill up the line; (of text) having a ragged edge to the right. L17.
4 Unwarranted. L17.

unk /ʌŋk/ *noun. nursery & colloq.* M20.
[Abbreviation.]
= UNKIE.

unkard, unked, *adjectives* vars. of UNKID.

unkeen /ʌn'kiːn/ *adjective.* M20.
[from UN-¹ + KEEN *adjective.*]
Not keen, not eager or interested; unenthusiastic, unwilling.

unkempt /ʌn'kɛm(p)t/ *adjective.* Also (earlier, *obsolete* exc. *dial.*) **-kembed** /-kɛmd/. LME.
[from UN-¹ + KEMPT *adjective.*]
1 (Of hair or wool) uncombed, untrimmed; *transf.* dishevelled, untidy, of neglected appearance. LME.
†**2** *fig.* Of language: inelegant, unrefined; rude. LME–E17.

1 F. NORRIS The unkempt room . . had not been cleaned for days. W. C. WILLIAMS The unkempt straggling / hair of the old man. *Sunday Post (Glasgow)* The . . verges and banks are looking . . unkempt and untidy, with long grass.

■ **unkemptly** *adverb* M20. **unkemptness** *noun* L19.

unkenned /ʌn'kɛnd/ *adjective.* Also **-kent** /-kɛnt/. Chiefly & now only *Scot. & north.* ME.
[from UN-¹ + *kenned* pa. pple of KEN *verb.*]
1 Unknown; strange. ME.
2 Unperceived; unexplored. L15.

unkennel /ʌn'kɛn(ə)l/ *verb.* Infl. **-ll-**, *-**l-**. L16.
[from UN-² + KENNEL *verb.*]
1 *verb trans.* Dislodge (a fox) from an earth. L16. ▸**b** *verb intrans.* Of a fox: come out of an earth. M18.
2 *verb trans. fig.* Drive out from a place or position; bring to light. E17.
3 *verb trans.* Let (a pack of hounds) out of a kennel. E17.

unkent *adjective* var. of UNKENNED.

unkept /ʌn'kɛpt/ *adjective.* ME.
[from UN-¹ + KEPT *ppl adjective.*]
1 Not looked after or tended; neglected. ME. ▸**b** Unguarded, undefended. Long *rare* or *obsolete.* LME.
2 Of a promise, law, etc.: not observed; disregarded. LME.

unkid /'ʌŋkɪd/ *adjective.* Long *dial.* Also **-kard** /-kəd/, **-ked.** ME.
[from UN-¹ + KID *adjective.*]
1 Not made known; unknown, unfamiliar. ME.
2 Awkward or troublesome through being unknown or unfamiliar. M17.
3 Lonely, dismal. E18.
4 Unpleasant, unnatural, eerie. E19.
■ **unkedness** *noun* (*rare*) L18.

unkie /'ʌŋki/ *noun. nursery & colloq.* Also **-ky**; (esp. in names) **U-**. E20.
[from UNCLE after AUNTIE: see -IE.]
Uncle.

unkillable /ʌn'kɪləb(ə)l/ *adjective.* L19.
[from UN-¹ + KILLABLE.]
Unable to be killed.
■ **unkilla'bility** *noun* M19. **unkilled** *adjective* not killed, still alive M16.

unkind /ʌn'kʌɪnd/ *adjective.* ME.
[from UN-¹ + KIND *adjective.*]
†**1** Strange, foreign. Only in ME.
2 Of the weather or climate: not mild or pleasant; unseasonable. Now *arch. & dial.* ME. ▸†**b** Contrary to the usual course of nature. LME–E17. ▸**c** Naturally bad (*for*); unfavourable, unsuitable; *esp.* (of land etc.) not favourable to growth, poor; (of an animal or plant) not thriving. Also foll. by *to.* Now *dial.* LME.
†**3** Lacking in natural gratitude, ungrateful; lacking in filial affection or respect, undutiful. ME–M17. ▸**b** Vile, wicked, villainous. ME–E17.
†**4** Not according to (the laws of) nature, unnatural; *esp.* unnaturally wicked or cruel. ME–M17.
5 Not having or displaying a gentle, sympathetic, or benevolent disposition; not showing consideration for others; harsh, cruel. LME.

5 SHAKES. *Haml.* Rich gifts wax poor when givers prove unkind. W. PLOMER She . . was never heard to . . say an unkind word.

unkindly /ʌn'kʌɪndli/ *adjective.* ME.
[from UN-¹ + KINDLY *adjective.*]
1 = UNKIND 2. Also, not properly developed. Now *dial.* ME. ▸†**b** Prejudicial to health. LME–E19.
†**2** = UNKIND 4. ME–M17. ▸**b** Lacking natural affection. *rare.* L15–L16.
3 = UNKIND 5. E19.
■ **unkindliness** *noun* LME.

unkindly /ʌn'kʌɪndli/ *adverb.* ME.
[from UN-¹ + KINDLY *adverb*, or UNKIND + -LY².]
†**1** Not in accordance with (the laws of) nature, unnaturally; with unnatural wickedness or cruelty. ME–E17. ▸**b** Improperly, unjustly; ungratefully. LME–L16.
2 †**a** Unsuitably. *rare.* Only in ME. ▸†**b** Contrary to the usual course of nature; uncharacteristically. LME–M18. ▸**c** Badly, unsuccessfully. M18.
3 In an unkind manner; unsympathetically, inconsiderately; with a lack of affection. LME.
4 With dissatisfaction or resentment. Freq. in ***take unkindly***. M16.

unkindness /ʌn'kʌɪn(d)nɪs/ *noun.* ME.
[from UN-¹ + KINDNESS, or UNKIND + -NESS.]
†**1** Unnatural conduct; absence of natural affection. ME–L16.
†**2** Ingratitude. ME–E17.
3 The quality or habit of being unkind; unkind behaviour; an instance of this, an unkind act. LME.
4 Ill will, enmity, hostility. Now *rare* or *obsolete.* LME.
5 A flock of ravens. *rare.* LME.

unking /ʌn'kɪŋ/ *verb trans.* M16.
[from UN-² + KING *noun.*]
1 Deprive of the position of king, dethrone, depose; *refl.* abdicate. M16.
2 Deprive (a country) of a king. M17.

unkinged /ʌn'kɪŋd/ *adjective.* M19.
[from UN-¹ + *kinged* pa. pple of KING *verb.*]
Not raised to the dignity of king.

unkingly /ʌn'kɪŋli/ *adjective.* E17.
[from UN-¹ + KINGLY.]
Not befitting a king; not having the character or quality of a king.
■ **unkinglike** *adjective* E17.

unkink /ʌn'kɪŋk/ *verb.* L19.
[from UN-² + KINK *verb*².]
1 *verb trans.* Remove the kinks from, straighten. L19.
2 *verb intrans.* Lose the kinks, become straight. L20.

unknew *verb pa. t.* of UNKNOW *verb*¹, *verb*².

unknight /ʌn'nʌɪt/ *verb trans.* E17.
[from UN-² + KNIGHT *verb.*]
Divest of a knighthood.

unknightly /ʌn'nʌɪtli/ *adjective. poet.* LME.
[from UN-¹ + KNIGHTLY *adjective.*]
1 Not befitting a (medieval) knight. LME.
2 Not having the qualities of a (medieval) knight. L16.
■ **unknighted** *adjective* not knighted M17.

unknightly /ʌn'nʌɪtli/ *adverb. poet.* LME.
[from UN-¹ + KNIGHTLY *adverb.*]
In an unknightly manner.

unknit /ʌn'nɪt/ *adjective.* E17.
[from UN-¹ + *knit* pa. pple of KNIT *verb.*]
Not closely united.

unknit /ʌn'nɪt/ *verb.* Infl. **-tt-**. Pa. t. & pple **unknitted**, **unknit.** OE.
[from UN-² + KNIT *verb.*]
1 *verb trans.* Untie (a knot etc.). OE. ▸**b** *verb intrans.* Of a knot etc.: become untied. L16.
2 *verb trans. & intrans. fig.* Separate, disunite, dissolve; weaken. LME.
3 *verb trans. & intrans.* Smooth out (knitted brows). Of knitted brows: become smoothed out. *rare.* L16.

unknot /ʌn'nɒt/ *verb trans.* Infl. **-tt-**. L16.
[from UN-² + KNOT *verb.*]
Untie the knot in, remove the knot from.

unknotted /ʌn'nɒtɪd/ *adjective.* M17.
[from UN-¹ + KNOTTED.]
Not knotted.

unknow /ʌn'nəʊ/ *verb*¹ *trans. arch.* Pa. t. **unknew** /ʌn'njuː/; pa. pple **unknown** /ʌn'nəʊn/. LME.
[from UN-¹ + KNOW *verb.*]
1 Not to know (something); fail to recognize or perceive. LME.
†**2** Be ignorant or unaware *that.* LME–E18.

unknow /ʌn'nəʊ/ *verb*² *trans.* Pa. t. **unknew** /ʌn'njuː/, pa. pple **unknown** /ʌn'nəʊn/. L16.
[from UN-² + KNOW *verb.*]
Cease to know, forget, (something previously known).

P. WENTWORTH Whether he believed her or not, he couldn't unknow what she had told him.

unknowable /ʌn'nəʊəb(ə)l/ *adjective & noun.* LME.
[from UN-¹ + KNOWABLE.]
▶ **A** *adjective.* Unable to be known. LME.

K. VONNEGUT God is unknowable, but nature is explaining herself all the time.

▶ **B** *noun.* **1** An unknowable thing. E18.
2 ***the unknowable***: that which cannot be known; (**U-**) the postulated absolute or ultimate reality. E19.

2 N. SYMINGTON They felt in touch with the mysterious, the unknowable in man.

■ **unknowa'bility** *noun* M19. **unknowableness** *noun* M17.

unknowing /ʌn'nəʊɪŋ/ *noun.* ME.
[from UN-¹ + KNOWING *noun.*]
Ignorance. Esp. in ***cloud of unknowing***.
¶ Obsolete after 17; revived in 20.

unknowing /ʌn'nəʊɪŋ/ *adjective & adverb.* ME.
[from UN-¹ + KNOWING *adjective.*]
▶ **A** *adjective.* **1** Not knowing; not having knowledge, ignorant, (of). Also foll. by *of, that.* ME.
2 Without the knowledge of, unbeknown *to. obsolete* exc. *dial.* LME.

1 S. RICHARDSON They were all working for me . . unknowing that they did so. GOLDSMITH Mankind wanders, unknowing his way. E. A. FREEMAN He laid his hand on the chest, while still unknowing of all that was in it. *Dirt Bike* Imparting your vast knowledge upon my unknowing brain.

▶ **B** *adverb.* Unknowingly. LME.
■ **unknowingly** *adverb* without knowledge, ignorantly; unintentionally: ME. **unknowingness** *noun* L15.

unknown /ʌn'nəʊn/ *adjective & noun.* ME.
[from UN-¹ + KNOWN *adjective & noun.*]
▶ **A** *adjective.* **1** Not known, not generally recognized, unfamiliar. ME.
†**2** Ignorant (*of*); unskilled *in.* ME–M17.
3 Foll. by *to*, (arch.) *of*: without the knowledge of, unbeknown to. LME.

1 J. F. LEHMANN Contributions arrived . . from quite unknown writers. I. MURDOCH Fleeing for reasons unknown from her husband. **3** F. SWINNERTON Unknown to Simon, Vera was . . in conversation with Morrison.

Special collocations: ***unknown country***: see COUNTRY *noun*. **unknown quantity** a person, thing, or quantity whose nature, significance, value, etc., cannot be determined. **Unknown Soldier**, **Unknown Warrior** an unidentified representative member of a country's armed forces killed in war, given burial with special honours in a national memorial.
▶ **B** *noun.* **1** An unknown person or thing. L16.
2 ***the unknown***, that which is unknown. M17.
3 MATH. An unknown quantity. E19.

1 M. GOWING He acknowledged the unknowns in the situation. A. HIGONNET Manet in 1860 was still a young unknown.

■ **unknownness** /-n-n-/ *noun* E17.

unknown *verb* pa. pple of UNKNOW *verb*¹, *verb*².

unk-unk /'ʌŋkʌŋk/ *noun. US slang.* L20.
[Repr. pronunc. of two first syllables of *unknown unknown*.]
A factor of which the existence, as well as the nature, is not yet known; *loosely*, an unknown person or thing.

unky *noun* var. of UNKIE.

unlabelled /ʌn'leɪb(ə)ld/ *adjective.* Also *-**eled.** E19.
[from UN-¹ + LABELLED.]
Not labelled; *spec.* (BIOLOGY & CHEMISTRY) not made recognizable by isotopic, fluorescent, or other labelling (see LABEL *verb* 2).

unlaboured /ʌn'leɪbəd/ *adjective.* Also *-**labored.** LME.
[from UN-¹ + LABOURED.]
†**1** Not brought on by study. Only in LME.
2 Of land: unworked, uncultivated. L15.
3 **a** Not subjected to labour or physical work. L16. ▸**b** Not obtained or effected by labour; *esp.* accomplished in an easy or natural manner. M17.
■ **unlabouring** *adjective* E17.

unlace /ʌn'leɪs/ *verb trans.* ME.
[from UN-² + LACE *verb.*]
1 Undo the lace or laces of; unfasten or loosen in this way. ME. ▸**b** NAUTICAL. Undo and remove (the bonnet) from the foot of a sail. M17.

2 Free or relieve by undoing a lace or laces. ME. †**3** Cut up or carve (esp. a rabbit). LME–L18. **4** *fig.* **a** Undo, destroy. LME. ▸†**b** Disclose, reveal. M–L16.

📖 **1** R. C. HUTCHINSON He unlaced and took off her shoes. **2** J. VANBRUGH Unlace me, or I shall swoon. **4a** *New Quarterly (Canada)* It's the unquiet deaths that unlace minds.

unlaced /ʌnˈleɪst/ *adjective.* LME.
[from prec. or from UN-¹ + *laced* pa. pple of LACE *verb*: see -ED¹.]
Having a lace or laces undone or slackened; without a lace or laces.

unlade /ʌnˈleɪd/ *verb.* Pa. pple **unladen** /ʌnˈleɪd(ə)n/, **unladed**. LME.
[from UN-² + LADE *verb*.]
1 *verb trans.* Unload (a horse, a vehicle, etc.); take the cargo out of (a ship). LME. ▸**b** Disburden, relieve by the removal of something. Chiefly *fig.* L16. **2** *verb trans.* Discharge (a cargo etc.) from a ship. LME. ▸**b** Discharge or get rid of (a burden etc.). Chiefly *fig.* L16. **3** *verb intrans.* Discharge a cargo or cargoes. M16. ▸**b** Discharge a burden etc. E17.

📖 **1a** C. KINGSLEY Canoes drawn up to be unladen. **2a** *Harper's Magazine* All cargoes must be unladed between sunrise and sunset.

unladen /ʌnˈleɪd(ə)n/ *ppl adjective.* E19.
[from UN-¹ + LADEN.]
Not laden, not loaded.
unladen weight the weight of a vehicle etc. when not loaded with goods etc.

unlaid /ʌnˈleɪd/ *adjective.* LME.
[from UN-¹ + *laid* pa. pple of LAY *verb*¹.]
Not laid; not placed, set, etc.; *spec.* (**a**) (of a spirit) not laid by exorcism; (**b**) (of a woman) not having had sexual intercourse, esp. with a particular person (*slang*).

unlaid *verb pa. t. & pple* of UNLAY.

unlanguaged /ʌnˈlaŋgwɪdʒd/ *adjective.* M17.
[from UN-¹ + LANGUAGED.]
1 Not gifted with speech. M17. **2** Not expressed in articulate speech. M19.

unlap /ʌnˈlap/ *verb trans.* Now *rare.* Infl. **-pp-**. LME.
[from UN-² + LAP *verb*².]
Uncover, unwrap, unfold.

unlash /ʌnˈlaʃ/ *verb trans.* M18.
[from UN-² + LASH *verb*².]
Release by undoing a lashing; unfasten, untie.

unlatch /ʌnˈlatʃ/ *verb*¹ *trans. & intrans. rare.* L16.
[from UN-² + LATCH(ET *noun*¹ 2.]
Unlace (a shoe).

unlatch /ʌnˈlatʃ/ *verb*². M17.
[from UN-² + LATCH *verb*².]
1 *verb trans.* Undo the latch or catch of (a door etc.); unfasten in this way. M17. **2** *verb intrans.* Of a gate etc.: open by being unlatched. L19.

📖 **1** *New Yorker* If I had to ask him how to unlatch the seat belt.

unlatched /ʌnˈlatʃt/ *adjective.* L19.
[from UN-¹ + *latched* pa. pple of LATCH *verb*².]
Not fastened by a latch.

un-Latin /ʌnˈlatɪn/ *adjective.* L17.
[from UN-¹ + LATIN *adjective & noun*.]
†**1** Not knowing Latin. Only in L17. **2** Not characteristic of Latin or a Latin person. M19.
■ **unlatined** *adjective (rare)* not knowing Latin L16.

unlaw /ˈʌnlɔː/ *noun.*
[Old English *unlagu* = Old Norse *úlǫg*: see UN-¹, LAW *noun*¹.]
1 Illegal action; illegality. OE. ▸†**b** An evil custom or habit. Only in ME. †**2** A fine, an amercement; a penalty. *Scot.* LME–M18.
¶ In sense 1 revived in 19.

unlaw /ʌnˈlɔː/ *verb.* LME.
[from prec. or from UN-² + LAW *noun*¹ or *verb*.]
†**1** *verb trans. & intrans.* Fine, amerce. *Scot.* LME–M18. **2** *verb trans.* Annul (a law). *rare.* M17.

unlawed /ʌnˈlɔːd/ *adjective.* L16.
[from UN-¹ + *lawed* pa. pple of LAW *verb*.]
Illegal.

unlawful /ʌnˈlɔːfʊl, -f(ə)l/ *adjective.* ME.
[from UN-¹ + LAWFUL.]
1 Against the law; illegal. ME. ▸**b** Of offspring: illegitimate. E17. **2** Of a person: not obeying the law; acting illegally. LME. **3** Contrary to moral standards. L15. **4** Contrary to a rule; irregular. *rare.* E18.

📖 **1** F. W. FARRAR A fresh edict . . declared Christianity to be an unlawful religion. *Guardian* He told the jury murder was unlawful killing. **3** S. JOHNSON The allurements of unlawful pleasure.

Phrases: **unlawful assembly** a meeting likely to cause a breach of the peace or to endanger the public. ***unlawful homicide***: see HOMICIDE *noun*.
■ **unlawfully** *adverb* ME. **unlawfulness** *noun* L15.

unlawyer-like /ʌnˈlɔːjəlʌɪk, -ˈlɔɪə-/ *adjective.* E19.
[from UN-¹ + LAWYER-LIKE.]
Not like (the practice of) a lawyer.

unlay /ʌnˈleɪ/ *verb trans.* Pa. t. & pple **unlaid** /ʌnˈleɪd/. E18.
[from UN-² + LAY *verb*¹.]
Untwist (a rope) into separate strands.

unlead /ʌnˈlɛd/ *verb trans.* L16.
[from UN-² + LEAD *verb*².]
Divest or strip of lead.

unleaded /ʌnˈlɛdɪd/ *adjective.* E17.
[from UN-¹ + LEADED.]
1 Not weighted, covered, or provided with lead. E17. **2** PRINTING. Not spaced (as) with leads. E19. **3** Of petrol etc.: without added lead. M20.

📖 **3** *ellipt.*: *Investors Chronicle* Unleaded goes down by 3.6p a gallon.

unleared /ʌnˈlɪəd/ *adjective.* *obsolete* exc. *dial.*
[Old English *unlǣred* = Old Norse *ulærðr*: see UN-¹, LERE *verb*.]
Unlearned, untaught; ignorant.

unlearn /ʌnˈləːn/ *verb.* Infl. as LEARN *verb*; pa. t. & pple usu. **unlearned** /ʌnˈləːnd/, **unlearnt** /ʌnˈləːnt/. LME.
[from UN-² + LEARN.]
1 *verb trans. & intrans.* Discard (a thing) from knowledge or memory; give up knowledge of (a thing). LME. **2** *verb trans.* Unteach. M17.

📖 **1** J. BRYCE The habits of centuries were not to be unlearned in a few years. J. VAN DE WETERING You are still young. You can unlearn a lot.

unlearned /ʌnˈləːnd, -ˈləːnɪd/ *adjective & noun.* Also in sense A.3 **unlearnt** /ʌnˈləːnt/. LME.
[from UN-¹ + LEARNED.]
▸ **A** *adjective.* **1** Not (well) educated; untaught; ignorant. Also, characterized by a lack of learning. LME. **2** Not skilled *in* something. M16. **3** Not acquired by learning. Now *rare.* M16.

📖 **1** W. D. WHITNEY The unlearned speech of the lower orders.

▸ **B** *absol.* as *noun pl.* *The* people who have no learning, as a class. LME.
■ **unlearnedly** *adverb* M16. **unlearnedness** *noun* M16.

unleavened /ʌnˈlɛv(ə)nd/ *adjective.* M16.
[from UN-¹ + *leavened* pa. pple of LEAVEN *verb*.]
Not leavened; made without yeast or other raising agent.

📖 J. M. GOOD Toasted bread, and unleavened biscuits. *fig.*: A. LAMBERT Painstaking hard work quite unleavened by inspiration.

unled /ʌnˈlɛd/ *adjective.* M16.
[from UN-¹ + *led* pa. pple of LEAD *verb*¹.]
1 Of a crop: not carried in. *Scot. & dial. rare.* M16. **2** Not led; unconducted, unguided. E17.

unless /ʌnˈlɛs/ *preposition, conjunction, & noun.* Orig. in sense A.1 two words. LME.
[from IN *preposition*, ON *preposition* + LESS *adjective* or *noun*, orig. two words which coalesced into one, *onless*, the 1st elem. of which was assim. through lack of stress to UN-¹.]
▸ **A** *preposition.* †**1** On a less or lower condition, requirement, etc., *than.* LME–L15. **2** †**a** In conjunction phr. ***unless than***, ***unless that***: except if, if . . not (cf. sense B.2 below). LME–L16. ▸**b** Except for, with the exception of. Now *rare.* M16.

📖 **2b** J. MORSE Unless the Swedish part . . the Laplanders can be said to be under no regular government.

▸ **B** *conjunction.* †**1** Lest. Only in 16. **2** Used before a statement expressing a case in which an exception to a preceding statement may or will exist; except if, if . . not. E16.

📖 **2** J. CONRAD The man . . never spoke unless addressed. M. KEANE She never goes there unless she's expressly bidden. D. JONES We should . . stick to that pronunciation unless and until we find another . . whose speech . . is more characteristic. E. FROMM We are headed for economic catastrophe unless we radically change our social system. W. BRONK Unless to you, to whom should I praise love?

▸ **C** *noun.* An utterance or instance of 'unless'; a reservation, a proviso. M19.

unlet /ʌnˈlɛt/ *adjective.* LME.
[from UN-¹ + *let* pa. pple of LET *verb*¹.]
Not let or rented out.
■ **unlettable** *adjective* M19.

unlettered /ʌnˈlɛtəd/ *adjective.* ME.
[from UN-¹ + LETTERED.]
1 Not instructed in letters; not (well) educated; illiterate. ME. ▸**b** Pertaining to or characterized by ignorance of letters. L16. **2** Not expressed in or marked with letters. M17.

📖 **1** B. BRYSON Primitive unlettered warriors from the barbaric fringes of the Roman empire. **b** G. CHALMERS An upright stone still forms the unlettered memorial of his odious end.

■ **unletteredness** *noun (rare)* M17.

unlevel /ʌnˈlɛv(ə)l/ *adjective.* L16.
[from UN-¹ + LEVEL *adjective*.]
Not level, uneven.
■ **unlevelled** *adjective* not made level E17. **unlevelness** *noun* L18.

unlevel /ʌnˈlɛv(ə)l/ *verb trans.* Infl. **-ll-**, ***-l-**. L16.
[from UN-² + LEVEL *verb*¹.]
Make uneven or no longer level.

unlicensed /ʌnˈlʌɪs(ə)nst/ *adjective.* E17.
[from UN-¹ + LICENSED.]
1 Not licensed; *spec.* (of a person or organization) not officially authorized or permitted, esp. by formal licence, to do something, as practise an occupation, sell, etc. E17. **2** Free from requiring a licence. *rare.* M17.

📖 **1** J. R. MCCULLOCH A fine . . rigorously exacted from unlicensed dealers. *Harpers & Queen* The club . . is unlicensed and you have to bring your own drink. *Independent* Unlicensed public entertainments that led to gross noise disturbances.

unlicked /ʌnˈlɪkt/ *adjective.* L16.
[from UN-¹ + *licked* pa. pple of LICK *verb*.]
Not licked into shape; not made presentable; unfinished, rough, crude.

unlid /ʌnˈlɪd/ *verb trans.* Infl. **-dd-**. ME.
[from UN-² + LID *verb*.]
Remove the lid from, uncover.

unlidded /ʌnˈlɪdɪd/ *adjective.* E19.
[from UN-¹ + LIDDED.]
Not provided or covered with a lid.

unlight /ʌnˈlʌɪt/ *verb intrans.* Now *dial.* E17.
[from UN-² + LIGHT *verb*¹.]
Alight, dismount.

unlighted /ʌnˈlʌɪtɪd/ *adjective.* L17.
[from UN-¹ + *lighted* pa. pple of LIGHT *verb*².]
1 Not set on fire; unkindled. L17. **2** Not lit up or illuminated; not provided with light. L18.

unlightened /ʌnˈlʌɪt(ə)nd/ *adjective.* L16.
[from UN-¹ + *lightened* pa. pple of LIGHTEN *verb*².]
†**1** Unenlightened. L16–E17. **2** Not lit up; dark; unlit. M17.

unlightsome /ʌnˈlʌɪts(ə)m/ *adjective.* Now *rare.* L16.
[from UN-¹ + LIGHTSOME *adjective*².]
Without (proper) light; dark, gloomy.

unlikable *adjective* var. of UNLIKEABLE.

unlike /ʌnˈlʌɪk/ *adjective, preposition, & noun.* ME.
[Perh. orig. alt. of Old Norse *úlíkr*, *úglíkr* = Old English *ungelīc*. Later from UN-¹ + LIKE *adjective, preposition, adverb, & conjunction*.]
▸ **A** *adjective.* **1** Not like or resembling, different from, or dissimilar to, some other person or thing. Also (*arch.*) foll. by *to*. ME. ▸**b** Not like each other; different, mutually dissimilar. LME. **2** Presenting points of difference or dissimilarity; not uniform; unequal. Now *rare.* LME. **3** *pred.* Unlikely, improbable. Foll. by subord. clause, *to do*. Now *arch. & dial.* LME.

📖 **1b** H. JAMES Utterly unlike in temper and tone, they neither thought nor felt . . together.

▸ **B** *preposition.* (Retaining an adjectival character and able to be qualified by adverbs of degree and compared.)
1 Not like or resembling, different from, dissimilar to. Orig. with dat. obj. ME. ▸**b** Uncharacteristic of (a person). E20. **2** In a manner differing from. L16.

📖 **1** J. CALDER A man wholly unlike anyone Fanny or Belle had met before. **b** D. H. LAWRENCE It is so unlike him, to be whistling . . , when any of us is around. **2** A. CARTER Unlike the rest, Uncle Philip did not smile at the camera.

▸ **C** *noun.* **1** A person differing from another or others. ME. **2** In *pl.* Dissimilar things or people. E17.

unlike /ʌnˈlʌɪk/ *adverb & conjunction.* ME.
[from UN-¹ + LIKE *preposition, adjective, adverb, & conjunction*.]
▸ **A** *adverb.* †**1** Unevenly, unequally. Only in ME. **2** Differently, diversely. Long *rare.* LME. †**3** Improbably; unlikely. M–L16.

📖 **2** *Nature* Pairs of unlike charged residues.

▸ **B** *conjunction.* Not in the same way as, not as. L20.

📖 *Esquire* Unlike at the Ritz, it is served without ice and a slice.

unlikeable /ʌnˈlʌɪkəb(ə)l/ *adjective.* Also **unlikable**. M19.
[from UN-[1] + LIKEABLE.]
Not likeable.

unlikely /ʌnˈlʌɪkli/ *adjective, adverb, & noun.* LME.
[from UN-[1] + LIKELY.]
▸ **A** *adjective.* **1 a** Not likely to happen; improbable (*that*). LME. ▸**b** Not likely to succeed or to be suitable; unpromising. M16. ▸**c** Not likely to be true; implausible. L16.
2 Not expected or likely *to do* something. LME.
3 †**a** Unsuitable, unfit. LME–L16. ▸**b** Unseemly, unbecoming; objectionable. *obsolete* exc. *dial.* LME.

> 🕮 **1a** J. BUCHAN He thought it unlikely that Allins would be at the Station Hotel. **b** G. LAVINGTON He cures Diseases . . with unlikely Remedies. G. GREENE They sprang up like mushrooms overnight in the most unlikely places. **c** E. A. FREEMAN The presence of Matilda . . at such a time is in itself unlikely. H. BRODKEY I put my hands on the window and stared at the wild, slanting, unlikely marvels. **2** S. HOOD He was unlikely to remember much about the evening before. A. CRAIG I . . wanted her approval, and . . was unlikely ever to merit it.

▸ **B** *adverb.* Improbably. LME.
▸ **C** *noun.* An unlikely person. M19.
■ **unlikelihood** *noun* †(*a*) unlikeness, dissimilarity; (*b*) the state or fact of being unlikely; an instance of this: L15. **unlikeliness** *noun* LME.

unlikeness /ʌnˈlʌɪknɪs/ *noun.* ME.
[from UN-[1] + LIKENESS.]
†**1** Strangeness. Only in ME.
2 Absence of likeness or resemblance; dissimilarity. LME. ▸**b** An instance of this. M17.
3 A bad or poor likeness. E18.

unliking /ʌnˈlʌɪkɪŋ/ *noun.* LME.
[from UN-[1] + LIKING.]
Absence of liking; dislike. Formerly also, dissatisfaction.

unlimber /ʌnˈlɪmbə/ *verb.* E19.
[from UN-[2] + LIMBER *noun*[1].]
MILITARY. **1** *verb trans.* Free (a gun) from its limber prior to bringing it into action. E19.
2 *verb intrans.* Detach and withdraw the limber from a gun. E19.

unlime /ʌnˈlʌɪm/ *verb trans. rare.* ME.
[from UN-[2] + LIME *verb*[1].]
†**1** Detach, separate. Only in ME.
2 Free (a dressed hide) from lime. L19.

unlimed /ʌnˈlʌɪmd/ *adjective. rare.* E17.
[from UN-[1] + *limed* pa. pple of LIME *verb*[1].]
1 Not smeared or clogged with birdlime. Chiefly *fig.* E17.
2 Not dressed or treated with lime. M18.

unlimited /ʌnˈlɪmɪtɪd/ *adjective.* LME.
[from UN-[1] + *limited* pa. pple of LIMIT *verb.*]
Without limit, unrestricted, esp. in amount, extent, or degree; *spec.* (*a*) MATH. (of a problem) having an infinite number of solutions; (*b*) (of a hydroplane) having no limit placed on its engine capacity.

> 🕮 A. MARSH-CALDWELL My confidence in his talents and energy is unlimited. J. C. CALHOUN A government of unlimited powers.

■ **unlimitable** *adjective* (now *rare*) E17. **unlimitedly** *adverb* E17. **unlimitedness** *noun* M17.

unline /ʌnlʌɪn/ *verb. rare.* E17.
[from UN-[2] + LINE *verb*[1].]
1 *verb trans.* Remove the lining from. E17.
2 *verb intrans.* Separate as a lining. M19.

unlined /ʌnˈlʌɪnd/ *adjective*[1]. E16.
[from UN-[1] + LINED *adjective*[1].]
Not provided with a lining.

unlined /ʌnˈlʌɪnd/ *adjective*[2]. M19.
[from UN-[1] + LINED *adjective*[2].]
(Of paper etc.) not marked with lines; (of a face etc.) without wrinkles.

unlink /ʌnˈlɪŋk/ *verb.* L16.
[from UN-[2] + LINK *verb*[1].]
1 a *verb trans. & intrans.* Detach or release (something) by undoing a link or chain. L16. ▸**b** *verb trans.* Undo the links of (a chain etc.). E17.
2 *verb intrans.* Part; become detached or no longer linked. M17.

> 🕮 **2** W. GILPIN We travelled amicably, arm in arm . . we had not one occasion to unlink.

unlinked /ʌnˈlɪŋkt/ *adjective.* E19.
[from UN-[1] + LINKED.]
Not linked or connected; separate, distinct.

unliquefied /ʌnˈlɪkwɪfʌɪd/ *adjective. rare.* E18.
[from UN-[1] + LIQUEFIED.]
Not liquefied.

unliquid /ʌnˈlɪkwɪd/ *adjective.* M16.
[from UN-[1] + LIQUID.]
1 Not liquid, solid. M16.
2 (Of assets etc.) not in cash, not easily convertible into cash, illiquid. E19.

unliquidated /ʌnˈlɪkwɪdeɪtɪd/ *adjective.* M18.
[from UN-[1] + *liquidated* pa. pple of LIQUIDATE *verb.*]
1 Not cleared or paid off. M18.
†**2** Not made clear or distinct. L18–E19.

unlisted /ʌnˈlɪstɪd/ *adjective.* M17.
[from UN-[1] + LISTED *adjective*[2].]
Not placed or included on a list; *spec.* (*a*) STOCK EXCHANGE orig., designating securities not dealt in on the Stock Exchange; now, designating a securities market in small companies admitted for trading on the Stock Exchange but not bound by the rules for listed securities; (*b*) (chiefly *N. Amer.*) (of a telephone or telephone number) ex-directory.

unlistenable /ʌnˈlɪs(ə)nəb(ə)l/ *adjective.* L20.
[from UN-[1] + LISTENABLE.]
Impossible or unbearable to listen to or *to.*
■ **unlistenaˈbility** *noun* M20.

unlistening /ʌnˈlɪs(ə)nɪŋ/ *adjective.* M18.
[from UN-[1] + *listening* pres. pple of LISTEN *verb.*]
Not listening, unhearing.
■ **unlistened** *adjective* unheard; not listened *to*: L18.

unlit /ʌnˈlɪt/ *adjective.* M19.
[from UN-[1] + LIT *ppl adjective.*]
Not lit.

> 🕮 W. GARNER An unlit cigarette between his fingers. *Independent* She had been raped in an unlit lay-by.

unlivable /ʌnˈlɪvəb(ə)l/ *adjective.* Also **unliveable**. M19.
[from UN-[1] + LIVEABLE.]
1 That cannot be lived. M19.
2 That cannot be lived in or *in*; uninhabitable. M19.

unlive /ʌnˈlɪv/ *verb trans.* L16.
[from UN-[2] + LIVE *verb.*]
†**1** Deprive of life. L16–E18.
2 Reverse or annul the living of (past life or experience). E17.

> 🕮 **2** M. LOWRY If only he could unlive the past two months.

unliveable *adjective* var. of UNLIVABLE.

unlived /ʌnˈlɪvd/ *adjective.* M19.
[from UN-[1] + *lived* pa. pple of LIVE *verb.*]
Not really or fully lived.
Comb.: **unlived-in** uninhabited; unused by the inhabitants; not homely or comfortable.

unlively /ʌnˈlʌɪvli/ *adjective.* M16.
[from UN-[1] + LIVELY *adjective.*]
†**1** Unliving, lifeless. Only in M16.
2 Not lively or animated; dull. E17.

unliving /ʌnˈlɪvɪŋ/ *adjective.* LME.
[from UN-[1] + LIVING *adjective.*]
Not living or alive, lifeless.

unload /ʌnˈləʊd/ *verb.* E16.
[from UN-[2] + LOAD *verb.*]
1 a *verb trans. & intrans.* Take off or remove (a load) from a vehicle etc.; discharge (a cargo). E16. ▸**b** *verb trans.* Discharge the cargo from (a ship or aircraft). L16. ▸**c** *verb trans.* Discharge or pour (a liquid). *rare.* E17.
2 *fig.* **a** *verb trans.* Give vent to or express (feelings, problems, etc.); communicate (information etc.) to another. Also foll. by *on.* L16. ▸**b** *verb intrans.* Confide in someone, divulge information, etc. Also foll. by *on.* L19.
3 a *verb trans. & refl.* Free, relieve, or divest of a load or burden; clear of or *of* something weighty L16. ▸**b** *verb trans.* Relieve by evacuation. Chiefly MEDICINE. M17.
4 *verb trans.* †**a** Discharge, fire (artillery etc.). E17–M18. ▸**b** Remove the charge from (a firearm, cartridge, etc.). E18.
5 *verb trans.* Get rid of or dispose of (esp. something undesirable) freq. by sale. Also foll. by *on.* L19.
6 *verb trans.* Deliver (a blow or series of blows) forcefully. L20.

> 🕮 **1a** G. VIDAL The guard on the dock helped the boatmen unload groceries. J. GRADY The loudspeaker was blaring about the arrival of . . Flight 409, now unloading. **b** *Pilot* Loading and unloading the 707 required great care. **2a** A. MAUPIN Michael unloaded his rodeo experiences on an ever-indulgent Ned. **3a** C. ACHEBE Some of them used the occasion to unload themselves of other grievances. **4b** STEELE A Pistol which he knew he had unloaded. **5** *Time* Many a landlord . . has already unloaded a building, at a fat price, on his tenants. *Times* One nervous seller unloaded two million shares.

■ **unloader** *noun* a person who or thing which unloads E17.

unloaden /ʌnˈləʊd(ə)n/ *verb trans. obsolete* exc. *dial.* M16.
[from UN-[2] + LOADEN *verb*[1].]
Unload.

unlocal /ʌnˈləʊk(ə)l/ *adjective.* M19.
[from UN-[1] + LOCAL *adjective.*]
Not local.
■ **unˈlocalizable** *adjective* unable to be localized M19. **unlocalized** *adjective* E19.

unlock /ʌnˈlɒk/ *verb.* LME.
[from UN-[2] + LOCK *verb*[1].]
▸ **I** *verb trans.* **1** Undo the lock of (a door, box, etc.); make capable of opening by this means. LME.
2 a Set free, esp. by undoing a lock; *fig.* release, allow to come forth. LME. ▸**b** Release (thoughts, emotions, etc.) from the mind; (cause to) reveal thoughts etc. from (the mind). M16. ▸**c** Explain, provide a key to (something obscure). M17.
3 a (Cause to) open by physical action; separate, part. L16. ▸**b** Undo, unfasten. E17. ▸**c** Release from immobility. M18.

> 🕮 **1** C. BRONTË I knelt down at and unlocked a trunk. L. GRANT-ADAMSON She unlocked the french windows and went out. **2a** *Times* The most appropriate way to unlock the group's vast . . wealth. **b** GEO. ELIOT I know you have a key to unlock hearts. **c** *Economist* Such research could help unlock the mysteries of the mass extinction. **3a** J. TYNDALL The discharge seemed to unlock the clouds above us.

▸ **II** *verb intrans.* **4** Become unlocked. L15.
5 Undo the lock of a door etc. L20.

> 🕮 **4** *Farmers Weekly* Front freewheeling hubs lock or unlock automatically.

unlockable /ʌnˈlɒkəb(ə)l/ *adjective.* M20.
[from UN-[1] + LOCKABLE.]
Not able to be locked.

unlocked /ʌnˈlɒkt/ *adjective.* E17.
[from UN-[1] + LOCKED *adjective*[2].]
Not locked (up).

unlooked /ʌnˈlʊkt/ *adjective.* ME.
[from UN-[1] + *looked* pa. pple of LOOK *verb.*]
†**1** Not attended to; neglected. Only in ME.
2 Not looked at, on, to, etc.; unheeded, unexamined. Foll. by *at, on, to,* etc. E16.
3 Not looked for; unexpected, unanticipated. Foll. by *for.* Formerly also without *for.* M16.

> 🕮 **2** R. A. VAUGHAN The wares lay unlooked at and untouched. **3** BOSW. SMITH Elated by an unlooked-for victory.

unloop /ʌnˈluːp/ *verb trans.* L16.
[from UN-[2] + LOOP *noun*[2] or *verb*[1].]
Unfasten by removing or undoing a loop.

unlooped /ʌnˈluːpt/ *adjective.* E18.
[from UN-[1] + LOOPED *adjective*[1].]
Not looped.

unloose /ʌnˈluːs/ *verb.* LME.
[from UN-[2] + LOOSE *verb.*]
1 *verb trans.* Slacken the tension or firmness of (a part of the body, one's hold, etc.). LME.
2 *verb trans.* **a** Set free, release (*lit. & fig.*). LME. ▸**b** Undo, unfasten. LME.
3 *verb trans.* Detach, so as to get rid of or remove. L15.
4 *verb intrans.* Become loose or unfastened. *rare.* L16.

> 🕮 **1** L. RITCHIE He found it impossible to unloose her arms from his neck.

unloosen /ʌnˈluːs(ə)n/ *verb trans.* LME.
[from UN-[2] + LOOSEN.]
= UNLOOSE *verb.*

unlord /ʌnˈlɔːd/ *verb trans.* L16.
[from UN-[2] + LORD *verb.*]
Deprive of the rank of lord.

unlorded /ʌnˈlɔːdɪd/ *adjective.* M17.
[from UN-[1] + *lorded* pa. pple of LORD *verb.*]
Not having the rank of a lord.

unlordly /ʌnˈlɔːdli/ *adjective.* L16.
[from UN-[1] + LORDLY *adjective.*]
Not lordly.

unlosable /ʌnˈluːzəb(ə)l/ *adjective.* Also **unloseable**. M17.
[from UN-[1] + LOSABLE.]
Not losable.

unlost /ʌnˈlɒst/ *adjective.* E16.
[from UN-[1] + LOST *adjective.*]
Not lost.

unlovable /ʌnˈlʌvəb(ə)l/ *adjective.* Also **unloveable**. L16.
[from UN-[1] + LOVABLE.]
Not lovable.
■ **unlovableness** *noun* M20.

unlove /ʌnˈlʌv/ *noun.* E17.
[from UN-[1] + LOVE *noun.*]
Absence of love.

unlove /ʌnˈlʌv/ *verb trans.* LME.
[from UN-[2] + LOVE *verb.*]
Cease to love (a person etc.).

unloveable *adjective* var. of UNLOVABLE.

unloved /ʌnˈlʌvd/ *adjective*. LME.
[from UN-¹ + *loved* pa. pple of LOVE *verb*.]
1 Not loved or cared for; unrequited in love. LME.
†**2** Not pursued or felt as love. *rare* (Shakes.). Only in E17.

unlovely /ʌnˈlʌvli/ *adjective*. LME.
[from UN-¹ + LOVELY *adjective*.]
Not attractive; unpleasant, ugly.
■ **unloveliness** *noun* L16.

unloving /ʌnˈlʌvɪŋ/ *adjective*. LME.
[from UN-¹ + LOVING *adjective*.]
Not loving.
■ **unlovingly** *adverb* E16. **unlovingness** *noun* L16.

unluck /ʌnˈlʌk/ *noun*. L18.
[from UN-¹ + LUCK *noun*.]
Bad luck, ill luck.

unlucky /ʌnˈlʌki/ *adjective*. M16.
[from UN-¹ + LUCKY *adjective*.]
1 Marked by misfortune or failure; unfortunate. M16.
2 Boding misfortune; ill-omened, inauspicious. M16.
3 Having ill luck; experiencing misfortune. M16.
4 Bringing ill luck; mischievous, harmful. L16.

🕮 **1** ADDISON This unlucky Accident happened to me in a Company of Ladies. **2** C. FRANCIS It's unlucky to sail on a Friday.

■ **unluckily** *adverb* M16. **unluckiness** *noun* M16.

unlusty /ʌnˈlʌsti/ *adjective*. *obsolete* exc. *dial*. ME.
[from UN-¹ + LUSTY.]
1 Slothful, lazy; dull, listless. ME.
2 Unwieldy; very fat. *dial*. L19.

unlute /ʌnˈluːt/ *verb trans*. M17.
[from UN-² + LUTE *verb*². Cf. LUTE *noun*².]
Remove the lute or seal from (a container etc.).

unmade /ʌnˈmeɪd/ *adjective*. ME.
[from UN-¹ + MADE *ppl adjective*.]
1 Not made, not yet made. Also foll. by *up*. ME.
2 Existing without having been made; uncreated but existent. ME.

🕮 **1** S. RANSOME The bed had been slept in and left unmade. M. FRENCH Their plain, unmade-up faces. *Country Walking* The track joins an un-made lane.

unmade *verb pa. t. & pple* of UNMAKE.

unmaid /ʌnˈmeɪd/ *verb trans*. M17.
[from UN-² + MAID *noun*.]
= UNMAIDEN.

unmaiden /ʌnˈmeɪd(ə)n/ *verb trans*. L16.
[from UN-² + MAIDEN *noun*.]
Deprive of maidenhood; deflower.

unmaidenly /ʌnˈmeɪd(ə)nli/ *adjective*. M17.
[from UN-¹ + MAIDENLY *adjective*.]
Not befitting or characteristic of a maiden.
■ **unmaidenliness** *noun* L19.

unmaintainable /ʌnmeɪnˈteɪnəb(ə)l/ *adjective*. E17.
[from UN-¹ + MAINTAINABLE.]
Not maintainable.
■ **unmaintained** *adjective* L17.

unmakable /ʌnˈmeɪkəb(ə)l/ *adjective*. Also **unmakeable**. L17.
[from UN-¹ + MAKABLE.]
Not makable.

unmake /ʌnˈmeɪk/ *verb trans*. Pa. t. & pple **unmade** /ʌnˈmeɪd/. LME.
[from UN-² + MAKE *verb*.]
1 Reverse or undo the making of; reduce again to an unmade condition. LME.
2 a Deprive of a particular rank or station; depose. L15. ▸**b** Deprive of a certain character or quality; alter in nature. E17.
3 Undo; ruin, destroy. L15.
4 Annul. L19.

🕮 **1** J. RAZ Parliament . . can make and unmake any law.

■ **unmaker** *noun* LME.

unmakeable *adjective* var. of UNMAKABLE.

unmalleable /ʌnˈmalɪəb(ə)l/ *adjective*. E17.
[from UN-¹ + MALLEABLE.]
Not malleable.
■ **unmalleaˈbility** *noun* L19.

unman /ʌnˈman/ *noun*. *rare*. Pl. **unmen** /ʌnˈmɛn/. LME.
[from UN-¹ + MAN *noun*.]
A person below the status of a man. Also, a monster.

unman /ʌnˈman/ *verb trans*. Infl. **-nn-**. L16.
[from UN-² + MAN *verb*.]
1 Deprive of the attributes of a man or a human; remove from the category of humans; *spec*. (now *rare*) degrade, bestialize. L16.
2 Deprive of supposed manly qualities, as self-control, courage, etc.; weaken, discourage. L16.
3 Deprive of virility; emasculate. L17.
4 Deprive (a ship, fleet, etc.) of men. L17.

🕮 **1** R. SHIRRA The first ungods him; the other unmans him. **2** *Vanity Fair* Sitting in the dock awaiting a sentence . . will unman the stoutest heart.

unmanacle /ʌnˈmanək(ə)l/ *verb trans*. L16.
[from UN-² + MANACLE.]
Free from manacles.

unmanacled /ʌnˈmanək(ə)ld/ *adjective*. E18.
[from UN-¹ + *manacled* pa. pple of MANACLE *verb*.]
Lacking a manacle or manacles.

unmanageable /ʌnˈmanɪdʒəb(ə)l/ *adjective*. E17.
[from UN-¹ + MANAGEABLE.]
Unable to be (easily) governed or controlled; unable to be properly handled or manipulated.

🕮 F. KING A difficult situation had . . become totally unmanageable.

■ **unmanageableness** *noun* M17. **unmanageably** *adverb* E19. **unmanaged** *adjective* not controlled or regulated E17.

unmanfully /ʌnˈmanfʊli, -f(ə)li/ *adverb*. LME.
[from UN-¹ + MANFULLY.]
Not manfully, uncourageously.

unmanlike /ʌnˈmanlʌɪk/ *adjective & adverb*. L16.
[from UN-¹ + MANLIKE.]
▶ **A** *adjective*. **1** Below the level of manly conduct towards others; brutal, inhuman. L16.
2 Inappropriate to a man or men. L16.
3 = UNMANLY *adjective*. L16.
▶ **B** *adverb*. = UNMANFULLY. E17.

unmanly /ʌnˈmanli/ *adjective*. LME.
[from UN-¹ + MANLY *adjective*.]
Not manly; *spec*. (**a**) not human, not befitting a human; (**b**) not courageous, weak, effeminate.

🕮 LD MACAULAY Hatred, which showed itself by unmanly outrages to defenceless captives. P. LEWIS To dilute hard liquor . . was . . unmanly.

■ **unmanliness** *noun* E17.

unmanly /ʌnˈmanli/ *adverb*. Now *rare*. LME.
[from UN-¹ + MANLY *adverb*.]
1 Dishonourably; treacherously. LME.
2 Inhumanely. L15.

unmanned /ʌnˈmand/ *adjective*¹. M16.
[from UN-¹ + MANNED *ppl adjective*.]
1 Not manned; without a person or people; *spec*. (of an aircraft or spacecraft) without a human crew. M16. ▸**b** Unsupported by a person or people. E17.
2 Esp. of a hawk: not trained or broken in. L16.

🕮 **1** A. TOFFLER The third nation to send an unmanned spacecraft to the moon.

unmanned /ʌnˈmand/ *adjective*². L17.
[from UNMAN *verb* + -ED¹.]
Deprived of courage; made weak or emotional.

🕮 B. HEAD I . . stand unmanned, drained of strength and will.

unmannered /ʌnˈmanəd/ *adjective*. LME.
[from UN-¹ + MANNERED.]
†**1** Not regulated or moderated. Only in LME.
2 Not having or showing good manners; ill-mannered, rude. L16.
3 Free from artificial manners. E19.

🕮 **2** SIR W. SCOTT This awkward, ill-dressed, unmannered dowdy.

unmannerly /ʌnˈmanəli/ *adjective*. LME.
[from UN-¹ + MANNERLY *adjective*.]
1 Of a person: devoid of good manners; impolite, rude. LME.
2 Of conduct, speech, etc.: showing a lack of good manners. LME.
■ **unmannerliness** *noun* L16.

unmannerly /ʌnˈmanəli/ *adverb*. ME.
[from UN-¹ + MANNERLY *adverb*.]
In an unmannerly fashion; impolitely, rudely.

unmantle /ʌnˈmant(ə)l/ *verb trans*. L16.
[from UN-² + MANTLE *noun*.]
1 Divest of a mantle or covering. L16.
2 Divest of furnishings. *rare*. E19.

unmarked /ʌnˈmɑːkt/ *adjective*. LME.
[from UN-¹ + *marked* pa. pple of MARK *verb*. Cf. MARKED.]
1 a Having no visible or distinguishing mark; (left) without a mark. LME. ▸**b** Not marked off or out, not distinguished or characterized (*by*). L18.
2 Unnoticed, unobserved. M16.
3 LINGUISTICS. Of a form, entity, etc. in a binary pair: not marked (see MARKED *adjective* 3). M20.

🕮 **1a** M. MITCHELL Thousands in unmarked graves. *City Limits* An unmarked police van pulled up.

■ **unmarkedness** /-kɪd-/ *noun* (LINGUISTICS) the quality of being unmarked L20.

unmarriageable /ʌnˈmarɪdʒəb(ə)l/ *adjective*. L18.
[from UN-¹ + MARRIAGEABLE.]
Not marriageable.

unmarried /ʌnˈmarɪd/ *adjective & noun*. ME.
[from UN-¹ + MARRIED.]
▶ **A** *adjective*. Not married, unwedded; single. ME.
▶ **B** *absol*. as *noun*. An unmarried person; *collect*. (*sing*. & in *pl*.), *the* class of unmarried people. M16.
■ **unmarriedness** *noun* M20.

unmarry /ʌnˈmari/ *verb*. M16.
[from UN-² + MARRY *verb*.]
1 *verb trans*. Dissolve the marriage of; divorce. M16.
2 *verb intrans*. Free oneself from marriage. M17.

unmasculine /ʌnˈmaskjʊlɪn/ *adjective*. M17.
[from UN-¹ + MASCULINE.]
Not masculine.

unmask /ʌnˈmɑːsk/ *verb*. L16.
[from UN-² + MASK *verb*².]
1 *verb trans*. Free (the face) from a mask; remove a mask or covering from. Also *fig*., reveal the true character of, expose. L16.
2 *verb intrans*. Remove one's mask. Also *fig*., display one's true character. E17.
3 *verb trans*. MILITARY. Reveal, make clear; *spec*. reveal the presence of (a gun or battery) by opening fire. M18.

🕮 **1** *Independent* Unmasked as the villain, the employer came to a violent end.

■ **unmasker** *noun* M17.

unmasked /ʌnˈmɑːskt/ *adjective*. L16.
[from UN-¹ + MASKED.]
Not masked.

unmatchable /ʌnˈmatʃəb(ə)l/ *adjective*. M16.
[from UN-¹ + MATCHABLE.]
1 Incapable of being matched, equalled, or rivalled; incomparable, matchless. M16.
2 To which nothing corresponding or properly matching can be found. E19.
■ **unmatchably** *adverb* E17.

unmatched /ʌnˈmatʃt/ *adjective*. L16.
[from UN-¹ + *matched* pa. pple of MATCH *verb*¹.]
1 Not matched or equalled; matchless; unrivalled. L16.
2 Not provided with something equal or alike. M17.
■ **unmatching** *adjective* unalike M20.

unmeaning /ʌnˈmiːnɪŋ/ *adjective*. L17.
[from UN-¹ + MEANING *adjective*.]
1 a Of features etc.: expressionless, vacant, unintelligent. L17. ▸**b** Of a person: having no serious aim or purpose. M18.
2 Having no meaning or significance; meaningless. E18.
■ **unmeaningly** *adverb* L18. **unmeaningness** *noun* L18.

unmeant /ʌnˈmɛnt/ *adjective*. M17.
[from UN-¹ + *meant* pa. pple of MEAN *verb*¹.]
Not meant or intended.

unmeasurable /ʌnˈmɛʒ(ə)rəb(ə)l/ *adjective, adverb, & noun*. LME.
[from UN-¹ + MEASURABLE.]
▶ **A** *adjective*. Incapable of being measured; immense, inordinate, vast. LME.
▶ **B** *adverb*. = UNMEASURABLY *adverb*. Long *rare*. LME.
▶ **C** *noun*. An unmeasurable thing. *rare*. M17.
■ †**unmeasurableness** *noun* M16–M18. **unmeasurably** *adverb* excessively, extremely LME.

unmeasure /ʌnˈmɛʒə/ *noun*. Long *rare* or *obsolete*. ME.
[from UN-¹ + MEASURE *noun*.]
†**1** Lack of measure; excess. ME–L16.
2 An improper or illegal measure. E19.

unmeasured /ʌnˈmɛʒəd/ *adjective*. LME.
[from UN-¹ + MEASURED.]
1 Not limited or known by measurement; immense. LME.
2 Immoderate, unrestrained. LME.
3 PROSODY. Not composed of measured syllables. E17.
†**4** Not doled *out* by measure. *rare* (Milton). Only in M17.

🕮 **1** J. SMEATON The unmeasured violence of the sea. **2** H. HALLAM The unmeasured eulogies he bestows upon him.

■ **unmeasuredness** *noun* (*rare*) LME.

unmechanical /ʌnmɪˈkanɪk(ə)l/ *adjective*. L17.
[from UN-¹ + MECHANICAL.]
Not mechanical.
■ Also **unmechanic** *adjective* L17.

unmechanized /ʌnˈmɛk(ə)nʌɪzd/ *adjective*. Also **-ised**. E19.
[from UN-¹ + *mechanized* pa. pple of MECHANIZE.]
Not mechanized.

unmeddled /ʌnˈmɛd(ə)ld/ *adjective*. LME.
[from UN-¹ + *meddled* pa. pple of MEDDLE.]
†**1** Unmixed. LME–L16.
2 Not meddled or interfered *with*. M16.

■ **unmeddlesome** *adjective* not given to meddling M19. **unmeddling** *adjective* not inclined to meddle (*with*) E17.

unmeek /ʌnˈmiːk/ *adjective*. ME.
[from UN-[1] + MEEK *adjective*.]
Not meek or gentle. Formerly also, unkind, cruel.
■ **unmeekness** *noun* LME.

unmeet /ʌnˈmiːt/ *adjective*. *arch.* OE.
[from UN-[1] + MEET *adjective*.]
†**1** Excessive in size or amount; immense; immoderate. OE–L15.
†**2** Unequal; unevenly matched. ME–M18.
†**3** Remote. LME–L15.
4 Unfitting, unsuitable, improper. (Foll. by *for*, *to do*.) LME.
5 Unfit or unsuited for a purpose. (Foll. by *for*, †*to*, *to do*.) E16.

> **4** W. MORRIS Humble words, unmeet For a great King. **5** W. ROW Mr Blair was now infirm and unmeet for travel.

■ **unmeetly** *adverb* ME. **unmeetness** *noun* L16.

unmeetable /ʌnˈmiːtəb(ə)l/ *adjective*. M19.
[from UN-[1] + MEET *verb* + -ABLE.]
Unable to meet or be met.

unmelodious /ʌnmɪˈləʊdɪəs/ *adjective*. M17.
[from UN-[1] + MELODIOUS.]
Not melodious, discordant.
■ **unmelodic** *adjective* unmelodious M19. **unmelodiously** *adverb* M19.

unmelted /ʌnˈmɛltɪd/ *adjective*. M16.
[from UN-[1] + *melted* pa. pple of MELT *verb*.]
Not melted.
■ **unmelting** *adjective* M18.

unmemorable /ʌnˈmɛm(ə)rəb(ə)l/ *adjective*. L16.
[from UN-[1] + MEMORABLE *adjective*.]
Not memorable.
■ **unmemorably** *adverb* L20. **unmemoried** *adjective* (*a*) forgotten; (*b*) without a memory: M19.

unmendable /ʌnˈmɛndəb(ə)l/ *adjective*. L16.
[from UN-[1] + MENDABLE.]
Not mendable.
■ **unmended** *adjective* L18.

unmentionable /ʌnˈmɛnʃ(ə)nəb(ə)l/ *noun & adjective*. E19.
[from UN-[1] + MENTIONABLE.]
▶ **A** *noun*. **1** In *pl.* Trousers (*arch. colloq.*); (chiefly *joc.*) underwear, esp. women's. E19.
2 A person who or thing which cannot or should not be mentioned. Usu. in *pl.* E20.

> **1** S. C. HALL The priest's unmentionables drying on a hedge.

▶ **B** *adjective*. That cannot or should not be mentioned. M19.

> J. D. SUTHERLAND Sexuality and its aura of guilt and sin were almost unmentionable.

■ **unmentionaˈbility** *noun* (*a*) *arch.* in *pl.*, trousers, underpants; (*b*) the fact of being unmentionable: M19. **unmentionableness** *noun* L19. **unmentionably** *adverb* L19.

unmentioned /ʌnˈmɛnʃ(ə)nd/ *adjective*. M16.
[from UN-[1] + *mentioned* pa. pple of MENTION *verb*.]
Not mentioned.

unmercenary /ʌnˈməːsɪn(ə)ri/ *adjective*. M17.
[from UN-[1] + MERCENARY *adjective*.]
Not mercenary.
■ **unmercenariness** *noun* M19.

unmerciful /ʌnˈməːsɪfʊl, -f(ə)l/ *adjective*. LME.
[from UN-[1] + MERCIFUL.]
1 Merciless; showing no mercy. LME.
2 Unsparing; excessive in amount etc. E18.
■ **unmercifully** *adverb* M16. **unmercifulness** *noun* M16.

unmeritable /ʌnˈmɛrɪtəb(ə)l/ *adjective*. L16.
[from UN-[1] + MERITABLE.]
Unable to claim merit.

unmerited /ʌnˈmɛrɪtɪd/ *adjective*. E17.
[from UN-[1] + *merited* pa. pple of MERIT *verb*.]
Not merited, undeserved.
■ **unmeritedly** *adverb* L18. **unmeriting** *adjective* undeserving L16. **unmeriˈtorious** *adjective* L16.

unmerry /ʌnˈmɛri/ *adjective*. Long *rare*. OE.
[from UN-[1] + MERRY *adjective*.]
Not merry.

unmet /ʌnˈmɛt/ *adjective*. E17.
[from UN-[1] + *met* pa. pple of MEET *verb*.]
Orig., unencountered. Now usu., (of a demand, goal, etc.) unfulfilled, unachieved.

unmetaphorical /ˌʌnmɛtəˈfɒrɪk(ə)l/ *adjective*. M18.
[from UN-[1] + METAPHORICAL.]
Not metaphorical.
■ **unmetaphorically** *adverb* E19.

unmethodical /ʌnmɪˈθɒdɪk(ə)l/ *adjective*. E17.
[from UN-[1] + METHODICAL.]
Not methodical.
■ **unmethodically** *adverb* M17. **unmethodized** *adjective* not reduced to method L17.

unmilitary /ʌnˈmɪlɪt(ə)ri/ *adjective*. L18.
[from UN-[1] + MILITARY *adjective*.]
1 Not in accordance with military practice; not conforming to military standards. L18.
2 Not belonging to or characteristic of the military profession. E19.
■ **unmilitarily** *adverb* M19.

unminded /ʌnˈmʌɪndɪd/ *adjective*. E16.
[from UN-[1] + *minded* pa. pple of MIND *verb*.]
†**1** Unmentioned, not borne in mind. Only in 16.
2 Unheeded, unregarded. M16. ▶**b** Left unnoticed, overlooked. L17.

unmindful /ʌnˈmʌɪndfʊl, -f(ə)l/ *adjective*. LME.
[from UN-[1] + MINDFUL.]
Not mindful; careless, heedless; *rare* not inclined or intending. Usu. foll. by *of*, *that*, *to do*.

> *Ecologist* Industry has . . pursued short-term economic goals, uncaring or unmindful of harm to workers.

■ **unmindfully** *adverb* M18. **unmindfulness** *noun* M16.

unmissable /ʌnˈmɪsəb(ə)l/ *adjective*. M20.
[from UN-[1] + MISSABLE.]
That cannot or should not be missed.

> *Observer* One unmissable part of her daily routine. *Daily Telegraph* Valerie Kaye's unmissable documentary . . set mainly in California.

unmissed /ʌnˈmɪst/ *adjective*. LME.
[from UN-[1] + *missed* pa. pple of MISS *verb*[1].]
Not missed.

> SIR W. SCOTT Of comfort there was little, and, being unknown, it was unmissed.

unmistakable /ʌnmɪˈsteɪkəb(ə)l/ *adjective*. M17.
[from UN-[1] + MISTAKABLE.]
That cannot be mistaken, confused, or doubted; clear, certain, obvious.

> I. MURDOCH The restless unmistakable shrugging movements of someone who is about to rise and depart. JULIA HAMILTON An envelope addressed to her . . : Gerard's unmistakable handwriting.

■ **unmistakaˈbility** *noun* E20. **unmistakableness** *noun* M19. **unmistakably** *adverb* M19.

unmistaken /ʌnmɪˈsteɪk(ə)n/ *adjective*. M18.
[from UN-[1] + MISTAKEN.]
Not mistaken; right, correct.

unmitigated /ʌnˈmɪtɪgeɪtɪd/ *adjective*. L16.
[from UN-[1] + *mitigated* pa. pple of MITIGATE.]
1 Not softened, not lessened in severity or intensity. L16.
2 Not modified or toned down; absolute, unqualified. M19.

> **1** J. AUSTEN The unmitigated glare of day. **2** A. J. P. TAYLOR War still seemed to him an unmitigated disaster.

■ **unmitigable** *adjective* unable to be mitigated E17. **unmitigably** *adverb* M19. **unmitigatedly** *adverb* M19.

unmix /ʌnˈmɪks/ *verb*. M16.
[from UN-[2] + MIX *verb*.]
1 *verb trans.* Make unmixed, separate. M16.
2 *verb intrans.* Become unmixed or separate. M20.
■ **unmixing** *verbal noun* the action of the verb; *spec.* the process by which the components of a mixture separate: E20.

unmixed /ʌnˈmɪkst/ *adjective*. E16.
[from UN-[1] + MIXED.]
Not mixed; pure.

> R. MAY No human being's motives are really unmixed . . but rather are complex blendings. W. PLOMER A kind of wisdom not unmixed with disillusionment and resignation. **unmixed blessing** a thing having advantages and no disadvantages (freq. with neg.).

■ **unmixable** *adjective* M18. **unmixableness** *noun* L19. **unmixedly** *adverb* M17. **unmixedness** *noun* E17.

unmodified /ʌnˈmɒdɪfʌɪd/ *adjective*. L18.
[from UN-[1] + *modified* pa. pple of MODIFY.]
Not modified, in an unchanged condition.
■ **unmodifiable** *adjective* E19. **unmodifiableness** *noun* L19.

unmolested /ʌnməˈlɛstɪd/ *adjective*. M16.
[from UN-[1] + *molested* pa. pple of MOLEST *verb*.]
Not molested, left in peace.
■ †**unmolest** *adjective* unmolested M16–L18. **unmolestedly** *adverb* M17. **unmolesting** *adjective* not molesting a person etc. L18.

unmoor /ʌnˈmʊə, -ˈmɔː/ *verb*. L15.
[from UN-[2] + MOOR *verb*.]
1 *verb trans.* Release the moorings of (a vessel), free from moorings. Formerly also, weigh all but one anchor of (a vessel). L15.
2 *verb intrans.* Cast off moorings. E17.

unmoral /ʌnˈmɒr(ə)l/ *adjective*. M19.
[from UN-[1] + MORAL *adjective*.]
Non-moral; not influenced by moral considerations, not concerned with morality.
■ **unmoˈrality** *noun* the condition of being unmoral M19. **unmoralized** *adjective* [UN-[2], UN-[1]] (*a*) made unmoral; (*b*) not concerned with morality: M17. **unmorally** *adverb* L20. **unmoralness** *noun* (*rare*) M17.

unmothered /ʌnˈmʌðəd/ *adjective*. E17.
[from UN-[2], UN-[1] + *mothered* pa. pple of MOTHER *verb*[1].]
1 Deprived of motherly feelings. E17.
2 Deprived of or without a mother. M19.

unmotherly /ʌnˈmʌðəli/ *adjective*. L16.
[from UN-[1] + MOTHERLY *adjective*.]
Not motherly, unlike a mother.
■ **unmotherliness** *noun* E20.

†**unmotherly** *adverb*. Only in LME.
[from UN-[1] + MOTHERLY *adverb*.]
In an unmotherly way, unkindly.

unmould /ʌnˈməʊld/ *verb*. E17.
[from UN-[2] + MOULD *verb*[1].]
1 *verb trans.* **a** Destroy the mould or form of. E17. ▶**b** Take out of a mould. L19.
2 *verb intrans.* Lose form or shape. M19.

unmoulded /ʌnˈməʊldɪd/ *adjective*. E17.
[from UN-[1] + MOULDED *adjective*[2].]
Not moulded or shaped.

unmount /ʌnˈmaʊnt/ *verb*. L17.
[from UN-[2] + MOUNT *verb*.]
1 *verb trans.* Unfix and take down or remove. L17.
2 *verb trans. & intrans.* Dismount (from). L18.

unmounted /ʌnˈmaʊntɪd/ *adjective*. L16.
[from UN-[1] + MOUNTED.]
1 Not mounted on a horse etc. L16.
2 Of a cannon: not placed on a carriage. E17.
3 Not fixed on a mount for use or display. L19.
■ **unmountable** *adjective* M16.

unmovable /ʌnˈmuːvəb(ə)l/ *adjective & noun*. Also **-moveable**. LME.
[from UN-[1] + MOVABLE.]
▶ **A** *adjective*. **1** = IMMOVABLE *adjective* 1. Now *rare*. LME.
2 = IMMOVABLE *adjective* 2. LME.
†**3** *LAW*. = IMMOVABLE *adjective* 3. LME–E17.
▶ **B** *noun*. †**1** *LAW*. In *pl.* Immovable property. M–L16.
2 An immovable thing. L19.
■ **unmovableness** *noun* LME. **unmovably** *adverb* LME.

unmoved /ʌnˈmuːvd/ *adjective*. LME.
[from UN-[1] + *moved* pa. pple of MOVE *verb*.]
1 Unaffected by emotion or excitement; impassive; collected, calm. LME.
2 Not changed in position, remaining fixed or steady; not changed in one's purpose. LME.

> **1** D. M. THOMAS Lisa pleaded, cried; but the men were unmoved. **2** CLARENDON He found the Duke unmoved by . . the considerations . . he had to offer.

■ **unmovedly** /-vɪdli/ *adverb* E17.

unmoving /ʌnˈmuːvɪŋ/ *adjective*. LME.
[from UN-[1] + MOVING *adjective*.]
1 Not moving, devoid of motion. LME.
2 Unaffecting, stirring no feeling. L17.
■ **unmovingly** *adverb* L18.

unmuffle /ʌnˈmʌf(ə)l/ *verb*. E17.
[from UN-[2] + MUFFLE *verb*.]
1 *verb trans.* Remove a muffler from (a face, bell, drum, etc.), free from something muffling or concealing. E17.
2 *verb intrans.* Remove or cast off a muffling. *rare*. M17.

unmurmuring /ʌnˈməːm(ə)rɪŋ/ *adjective*. L18.
[from UN-[1] + *murmuring* pres. pple of MURMUR *verb*.]
Not murmuring; *spec.* not complaining.
■ **unmurmuringly** *adverb* M19.

unmusical /ʌnˈmjuːzɪk(ə)l/ *adjective*. E17.
[from UN-[1] + MUSICAL *adjective*.]
1 Not pleasing to the ear; unmelodious, harsh. E17.
2 Not musically skilled or gifted; not appreciative of music. M17.
3 Not based on musical principles. L18.

> **1** *Quarterly Review* The not unmusical roar of the Falls. **2** *Psychology Today* With keyboards . . even a decidedly unmusical teenager can get involved with music.

■ **unmusiˈcality** *noun* L19. **unmusically** *adverb* E17. **unmusicalness** *noun* L17.

unmuzzle /ʌnˈmʌz(ə)l/ *verb trans.* E17.
[from UN-[2] + MUZZLE *verb*[1].]
Free (a dog etc.) from a muzzle, remove the muzzle from; *fig.* relieve of an obligation to remain silent.

> *Globe & Mail (Toronto)* They have unmuzzled the press.

unmuzzled /ʌnˈmʌz(ə)ld/ *adjective*. E17.
[from UN-[1], UN-[2] + MUZZLED *adjective*[1].]
Not muzzled, freed from a muzzle.

unnail /ʌnˈneɪl/ *verb trans.* ME.
[from UN-[2] + NAIL *verb*.]
Detach or unfasten by the removal of nails.

unnailed /ʌnˈneɪld/ *adjective.* E17.
[from UN-¹ + *nailed* pa. pple of NAIL *verb.*]
Not fastened or fixed with nails.

unnameable /ʌnˈneɪməb(ə)l/ *adjective.* Also **-namable**. E17.
[from UN-¹ + NAMEABLE.]
Unable to be named; *esp.* too bad, hideous, etc., to be named or adequately described.

📖 J. DUNN Force the cupboard door shut—particularly if it bulged with dark unnameable shapes. J. HALPERIN A veteran . . dies of some . . unnameable disease.

■ **unnameaˈbility** *noun* M19.

unnamed /ʌnˈneɪmd/ *adjective.* E16.
[from UN-¹ + *named* pa. pple of NAME *verb.*]
1 Not mentioned or specified by name. E16.
2 Not having a name, nameless. E17.

📖 **1** *Guardian* A statement from an unnamed PLO official in Tunis. **2** *Garden News* A new but yet unnamed African violet.

unnatural /ʌnˈnatʃ(ə)r(ə)l/ *adjective.* LME.
[from UN-¹ + NATURAL *adjective.*]
1 Not in accordance with the physical nature of humans or animals; contrary to the usual course of nature. LME. ▸**b** Abnormal; monstrous. E16. ▸**c** Without natural qualities or characteristics; artificial; stilted, affected. M18.
2 Contrary to or lacking natural feelings or moral standards; *esp.* excessively cruel or wicked. L15.
3 At variance with what is usual, or expected; unusual, strange. L16.

📖 **1** R. C. HUTCHINSON Regarding snow in the English way as an unnatural visitation. C. BERNHEIMER To prefer perverse and unnatural pleasures to the more banal fulfillments of conjugal love. *Guardian* Genetic engineering is often presented as producing unnatural hybrids. G. MURRAY The unnatural contortions of the dancers. **c** LYTTON You perceive all people timid, stiff, unnatural, and ill at ease. H. JAMES The young woman with . . hair of an unnatural yellow. **2** SIR W. SCOTT The unnatural child, who thinks of a stranger's captivity before a parent's. **3** ALAN BENNETT That really is unnatural George is . . besotted with his mother-in-law.

■ **unnaturalism** *noun* the quality or fact of being unnatural M18. **unnatuˈrality** *noun* (*rare*) (*a*) unnatural feeling or conduct; (*b*) *Scot.* imbecility, weak-mindedness: M16. **unnaturally** *adverb* L15. **unnaturalness** *noun* M16.

unnaturalise *verb*, **-ised** *adjective* vars. of UNNATURALIZE, UNNATURALIZED.

unnaturalize /ʌnˈnatʃ(ə)r(ə)lʌɪz/ *verb trans.* Also **-ise**. E17.
[from UN-² + NATURALIZE.]
1 Deprive of natural character; make unnatural in disposition. E17.
2 Deprive of the status or privileges of a native-born subject. L17.
3 Make unnatural or artificial. M18.

unnaturalized /ʌnˈnatʃ(ə)r(ə)lʌɪzd/ *adjective.* Also **-ised**. E17.
[from UN-¹ + *naturalized* pa. pple of NATURALIZE.]
Not naturalized or given the status and privileges of a native-born subject.
■ **unnaturalizable** *adjective* M19.

unnature /ʌnˈneɪtʃə/ *verb trans.* Now *rare.* L16.
[from UN-² + NATURE *verb.*]
Deprive of a particular or individual nature; make unnatural.

unnavigable /ʌnˈnavɪgəb(ə)l/ *adjective.* L16.
[from UN-¹ + NAVIGABLE.]
1 Of a river or sea: unable to be sailed on or over, not allowing a vessel passage. L16.
2 Of a vessel: unable to be sailed, unseaworthy. M18.
■ **unnavigaˈbility** *noun* M19. **unnavigated** *adjective* not navigated L18.

†unnealed *adjective.* M16–L18.
[from UN-¹ + *nealed* pa. pple of NEAL.]
Of pottery etc.: not fired or glazed.

†unneath *preposition.* M17–M19.
[Contr.]
Underneath, beneath.

unnecessary /ʌnˈnɛsəs(ə)ri/ *adjective & noun.* M16.
[from UN-¹ + NECESSARY.]
▸**A** *adjective.* **1** Not necessary or requisite, needless; redundant; more than is necessary, excessive. Freq. foll. by *for, to, to do.* M16.
†**2** Not requiring much. *rare* (Shakes.). Only in E17.

📖 **1** SIR W. SCOTT Ringing the dinner-bell—a most unnecessary ceremony for assembling three persons. *Motor Trend* This aerodynamic . . 2-seater will eschew all unnecessary frills. *Guardian* New navigational aids made it unnecessary for many ships . . to use pilots. A. S. BYATT Mother Superior . . believed dusty papers were an unnecessary waste of space. **come over all unnecessary**, **go all unnecessary** *colloq.* become affected with emotion or (esp. sexual) excitement.

▸**B** *noun.* An unnecessary thing. Usu. in *pl.* M16.

📖 D. FRANCIS Jack and Flora . . never wasted good cash on unnecessaries.

■ **unnecessarily** *adverb* L16. **unnecessariness** *noun* E17. **unneˈcessitated** *adjective* M17.

unneeded /ʌnˈniːdɪd/ *adjective.* M19.
[from UN-¹ + *needed* pa. pple of NEED *verb.*]
Not needed.

unneedful /ʌnˈniːdfʊl, -f(ə)l/ *adjective.* LME.
[from UN-¹ + NEEDFUL *adjective.*]
1 Unnecessary, not required. LME.
2 Not being in need *of* something. L19.
■ **unneedfully** *adverb* M17. **unneedy** /ʌnˈniːdi/ *adjective* LME.

unneighbourly /ʌnˈneɪbəli/ *adverb & adjective.* Also ***-bor-**. M16.
[from UN-¹ + NEIGHBOURLY.]
▸**A** *adverb.* In an unneighbourly way. *rare.* M16.
▸**B** *adjective.* Not neighbourly, unfriendly, unsociable. L16.
■ **unneighboured** *adjective* M17. **unneighbourliness** *noun* M17.

unnerve /ʌnˈnəːv/ *verb trans.* E17.
[from UN-² + NERVE *verb.*]
1 Deprive of strength, render physically weak. E17.
2 Deprive of resolution or courage, destroy the confidence of; disquiet, disturb. E18.

📖 **2** O. MANNING She was unnerved by the glimmer of the headstones. I. MURDOCH The unnerving silence of the place. J. DUNN Something in her uncompromisingly clear gaze unnerved him.

■ **unnervingly** *adverb* in an unnerving manner, disquietingly M20.

unnoble /ʌnˈnəʊb(ə)l/ *adjective & noun.* Now *rare.* LME.
[from UN-¹ + NOBLE.]
▸**A** *adjective.* **1** Not distinguished by rank or birth. LME.
†**2** Of a thing: undistinguished, common, mean. LME–M17.
3 Not noble in disposition, ignoble. LME.
▸**B** *absol.* as *noun. The* unnoble people. LME.

unnoted /ʌnˈnəʊtɪd/ *adjective.* M16.
[from UN-¹ + NOTED.]
1 Not noticed or observed. M16.
2 Not specially noted or observed; undistinguished, obscure. L16.
3 Lacking musical notes or a score. *rare.* M19.
■ **unˈnotable** *adjective* E16.

unnoticed /ʌnˈnəʊtɪst/ *adjective.* E18.
[from UN-¹ + *noticed* pa. pple of NOTICE *verb.*]
Not noticed or observed.
■ **unnoticeable** *adjective* L18. **unnoticeableness** *noun* L19. **unnoticeably** *adverb* L19. **unnoticing** *adjective* L18.

unnourishing /ʌnˈnʌrɪʃɪŋ/ *adjective.* E17.
[from UN-¹ + NOURISHING *adjective.*]
Not nourishing or sustaining.
■ **unnourishable** *adjective* L16. **unnourished** *adjective* E17.

unnumbered /ʌnˈnʌmbəd/ *adjective.* LME.
[from UN-¹ + *numbered* pa. pple of NUMBER *verb.*]
1 Not numbered or reckoned up, uncounted; innumerable. LME.
2 Not included in an enumeration; not marked or provided with a number. M16.
■ **unnumberable** *adjective* innumerable ME.

UNO /ˈjuːnəʊ/ *abbreviation.*
United Nations Organization.

unobjectionable /ʌnəbˈdʒɛkʃ(ə)nəb(ə)l/ *adjective.* L18.
[from UN-¹ + OBJECTIONABLE.]
Not objectionable; acceptable, inoffensive, unexceptionable.

📖 M. E. BRADDON His conduct was unobjectionable. D. M. THOMAS Other poems . . were unobjectionable, except in aesthetic terms.

■ **unobjected** *adjective* not objected *to* M18. **unobjectible** *adjective* unobjectionable M18. **unobjectionableness** *noun* L19. **unobjectionably** *adverb* E19.

unobliging /ʌnəˈblʌɪdʒɪŋ/ *adjective.* L19.
[from UN-¹ + OBLIGING.]
Not obliging; unhelpful, uncooperative, unaccommodating.

📖 H. HERMAN An uncivil, unobliging, ugly young brute.

■ **unobliged** *adjective* not obliged to do something; not made obligatory or necessary: M17. **unobligingly** *adverb* M20. **unobligingness** *noun* M17.

unobliterated /ʌnəˈblɪtəreɪtɪd/ *adjective.* M17.
[from UN-¹ + *obliterated* pa. pple of OBLITERATE *verb.*]
Not obliterated or obscured.
■ **unobliterable** *adjective* M17. **unobliteratable** *adjective* M19.

unobservable /ʌnəbˈzəːvəb(ə)l/ *adjective & noun.* M17.
[from UN-¹ + OBSERVABLE.]
▸**A** *adjective.* **1** Unable to be observed; imperceptible, unnoticeable. M17.
†**2** Undeserving of notice or remark. M–L17.
▸**B** *noun.* In *pl.* Things unable to be observed. M20.
■ **unobservaˈbility** *noun* M20.

unobservant /ʌnəbˈzəːv(ə)nt/ *adjective.* E17.
[from UN-¹ + OBSERVANT *adjective.*]
†**1** Unattentive in service. Only in E17.
2 Not observant; not taking notice, unperceptive. M17.
■ **unobservance** *noun* lack of observance M17. **unobservantly** *adverb* M19.

unobserved /ʌnəbˈzəːvd/ *adjective.* E17.
[from UN-¹ + *observed* pa. pple of OBSERVE.]
Not observed; unperceived, unnoticed.

📖 F. BURNEY This was not unobserved by Edgar. S. LEE Day had unobserved stolen upon them.

■ **unobservedly** /-vɪdli/ *adverb* M17. **unobserving** *adjective* L17.

unobstructed /ʌnəbˈstrʌktɪd/ *adjective.* M17.
[from UN-¹ + *obstructed* pa. pple of OBSTRUCT.]
Not obstructed, clear.

📖 S. PARKINSON The eye having an unobstructed view through the hole.

■ **unobstructedly** *adverb* E19. **unobstructive** *adjective* E18.

unobtainable /ʌnəbˈteɪnəb(ə)l/ *adjective.* L18.
[from UN-¹ + OBTAINABLE.]
Not obtainable.

📖 E. WAUGH When they tried to ring him up they were told the number was 'unobtainable'. *Guardian* The part is unobtainable in Yugoslavia.

■ **unobtained** *adjective* not obtained L16.

unobtrusive /ʌnəbˈtruːsɪv/ *adjective.* M18.
[from UN-¹ + OBTRUSIVE.]
Not obtrusive, not unduly or unpleasantly noticeable or prominent, not making oneself noticed.
■ **unobtrusively** *adverb* L18. **unobtrusiveness** *noun* L18.

unoccupied /ʌnˈɒkjʊpʌɪd/ *adjective.* LME.
[from UN-¹ + *occupied* pa. pple of OCCUPY.]
Not occupied; not engaged in any work or activity, idle; not taken up or used; not occupied by inhabitants, empty.

📖 E. B. WHITE Buildings stand unoccupied for most of the year. A. J. P. TAYLOR The Germans moved into unoccupied France. A. BROOKNER They looked expectant, unoccupied, ready for diversion.

■ **unoccupancy** *noun* the state of being unoccupied M19.

unoffending /ʌnəˈfɛndɪŋ/ *adjective.* M16.
[from UN-¹ + OFFENDING.]
Not offending; harmless, innocent, inoffensive.

📖 SIR W. SCOTT Who . . could have thought of harming a creature so simple, and so unoffending?

■ **unoffendable** *adjective* M19. **unoffended** *adjective* L15. **unoffendedly** *adverb* M19. **†unoffensive** *adjective* E17–M18. **†unoffensively** *adverb*: only in E17.

unofficial /ʌnəˈfɪʃ(ə)l/ *adjective & noun.* L18.
[from UN-¹ + OFFICIAL *adjective.*]
▸**A** *adjective.* **1** Not officially authorized or confirmed, not having an official character. L18.
2 Not holding an official position, not acting in an official capacity; not characteristic of officials. E19.

📖 **1** *Guardian* Unofficial estimates suggest price rises may reach 220 per cent this month. *transf.*: R. BROOKE Unkempt about those hedges blows An English unofficial rose. **unofficial strike**: not duly called or endorsed by the relevant union. **2** A. J. P. TAYLOR He . . often relies more on 'unofficial' advisers than on members of his cabinet. **unofficial member** = *private member* s.v. PRIVATE *adjective.*

▸**B** *noun.* A person who is not an official. L19.
■ **unofficially** *adverb* M19.

unopened /ʌnˈəʊp(ə)nd/ *adjective.* E17.
[from UN-¹ + *opened* pa. pple of OPEN *verb.*]
Not opened; left closed or shut, remaining sealed.

📖 DICKENS A book . . unopened on a shelf. *Zigzag* An unopened Christmas present bottle of Glenfiddich.

■ **unopen** *adjective* not open; *esp.* narrow-minded: E19. **unopenable** *adjective* M19. **unopening** *adjective* not opening M18.

unopposable /ʌnəˈpəʊzəb(ə)l/ *adjective.* M17.
[from UN-¹ + OPPOSE *verb* + -ABLE.]
Not opposable.

unopposed /ʌnəˈpəʊzd/ *adjective.* M17.
[from UN-¹ + OPPOSED.]
Not opposed; without opposition, unchallenged.

📖 A. J. P. TAYLOR The Germans took over Denmark unopposed. *Guardian* The Lords gave an unopposed third reading to the Australian Constitution . . Bill.

unordain /ʌnɔːˈdeɪn/ *verb trans.* ME.
[from UN-² + ORDAIN.]
Make unordained.

unordained /ʌnɔːˈdeɪnd/ *adjective.* ME.
[from UN-¹ + *ordained* pa. pple of ORDAIN.]
†**1** Not regulated or controlled. Only in ME.
2 Not ecclesiastically ordained. M17.
3 Not appointed or decreed. E19.

unorder /ʌnˈɔːdə/ *verb trans.* LME.
[from UN-² + ORDER *verb*.]
Recall an order for (a thing), countermand.

unordered /ʌnˈɔːdəd/ *adjective.* LME.
[from UN-¹ + ORDERED.]
†**1** Not belonging to a religious order; not properly ordained. LME–E17.
2 Not put in order, unarranged. L15. ▸**b** LINGUISTICS. Of rules: not requiring to be applied in a particular order. M20.
†**3** Not observing due order, disorderly. L16–E17.
4 Not ordered, commanded, or commissioned. L19.

unorderly /ʌnˈɔːdəli/ *adverb & adjective.* Now *rare.* LME.
[from UN-¹ + ORDERLY *adverb, adjective*.]
▸ **A** *adverb.* Not in an orderly manner, without fixed sequence or arrangement, irregularly. LME.
▸ **B** *adjective.* **1** Not in conformity with good order, irregular. L15. ▸**b** Disorderly. L16.
2 Not observing due order or arrangement; disordered, confused. L16.

unorganized /ʌnˈɔːg(ə)nʌɪzd/ *adjective.* Also **-ised.** L17.
[from UN-¹ + ORGANIZED.]
Not organized; not brought into an organized state; not formed into an orderly or regulated whole; *spec.* not represented by or formed into a trade union, (of a company) not having or recognizing such a union.
■ **unorganizable** *adjective* M19. **unorganizedness** *noun* M17.

unoriginal /ʌnəˈrɪdʒɪn(ə)l/ *adjective & noun.* M17.
[from UN-¹ + ORIGINAL.]
▸ **A** *adjective.* **1** Having no origin, uncreated. M17.
2 Not original, lacking originality; derivative; second-hand. L18.

> 📖 **2** *Guardian* Western sounds reproduced . . by talented and entirely unoriginal local bands.

▸ **B** *noun.* A person lacking originality. M19.
■ **unorigiˈnality** *noun* L18. **unoriginally** *adverb* M20.

unoriginate /ʌnəˈrɪdʒɪnət/ *adjective & noun.* E18.
[from UN-¹ + *originate* obsolete pa. pple of ORIGINATE.]
▸ **A** *adjective.* = next. E18.
▸ **B** *noun.* An unoriginated being. E18.
■ **unoriginately** *adverb* E18. **unoriginateness** *noun* E18.

unoriginated /ʌnəˈrɪdʒɪneɪtɪd/ *adjective.* L17.
[from UN-¹ + *originated* pa. pple of ORIGINATE.]
Not originated; having no origin, uncreated.
■ **unoriginatedness** *noun* M19.

unornamental /ˌʌnɔːnəˈmɛnt(ə)l/ *adjective.* M18.
[from UN-¹ + ORNAMENTAL.]
Not ornamental or decorative.
■ **unornamentally** *adverb* L19.

unornamented /ʌnˈɔːnəmɛntɪd/ *adjective.* L17.
[from UN-¹ + *ornamented* pa. pple of ORNAMENT *verb*.]
Not ornamented, plain.

unorthodox /ʌnˈɔːθədɒks/ *adjective.* M17.
[from UN-¹ + ORTHODOX *adjective*.]
Not orthodox; not in accordance with accepted opinion or usage; unconventional, unusual.

> 📖 A. THWAITE *Gosse* . . for all his unorthodox background, succeeded in becoming part of the establishment. *Guardian* One of the cameramen crawling about the floor for unorthodox shots.

■ **unorthodoxly** *adverb* M20. **unorthodoxy** *noun* the quality or character of being unorthodox; an unorthodox opinion, practice, feature, etc.: E18.

unostentatious /ˌʌnɒstɛnˈteɪʃəs/ *adjective.* M18.
[from UN-¹ + OSTENTATIOUS.]
Not ostentatious or showy; discreet, unpretentious.
■ **unostentatiously** *adverb* L18. **unostentatiousness** *noun* M19.

unpack /ʌnˈpak/ *verb.* L15.
[from UN-² + PACK *verb*¹.]
1 a *verb trans. & intrans.* Undo or open and remove the contents of (a bag, case, pack, etc.); *fig.* analyse into component elements. L15. ▸**b** *verb trans.* Unpack a bag etc. of (a person, oneself). L18.
2 *verb trans.* Take (a thing) out of a bag etc. L16.
3 *verb trans.* Remove a pack or load from (a horse, carriage, etc.). L16.
4 *verb trans.* COMPUTING. Convert (an item of stored data) *into* a less compressed form; retrieve data from (a record). M20.

> 📖 **1a** E. BOWEN A spare-room . . in which an overnight bag has been unpacked hastily. J. HIGGINS You can unpack and tidy up here while I'm having my bath. A. DAVIES Let us try to unpack this question. **b** H. GRANVILLE The Bessboroughs have been unpacked about a couple of hours.
> **2** R. P. JHABVALA I unpacked the sandwiches I had brought.

■ **unpacker** *noun* M18.

unpacked /ʌnˈpakt/ *adjective.* L15.
[from UN-¹ + PACKED *ppl adjective*¹.]
1 Not made up in or put into a pack. L15.
2 Not taken out of a pack or bag. *rare.* E18.

unpaid /ʌnˈpeɪd/ *adjective.* LME.
[from UN-¹ + *paid* pa. pple of PAY *verb*¹.]
1 Of a person: to whom payment has not been made, not receiving payment. LME.
2 Of a sum of money: not given in payment. Of a debt or bill: not discharged or cleared by payment. LME.
3 Of work, an item, etc.: not paid for or *for.* LME.

> 📖 **1** *Times Educ. Suppl.* Most of their work is carried out by unpaid volunteers. *absol.*: **the Great Unpaid, the Unpaid** the class of unpaid magistrates and justices.
> **3** J. SUTHERLAND Two . . removal men came to take back the unpaid-for piano. *Guardian* Years of unpaid charity work.

unpainful /ʌnˈpeɪnfʊl, -f(ə)l/ *adjective.* LME.
[from UN-¹ + PAINFUL.]
†**1** Not subject to pain. Only in LME.
2 Not causing or involving pain or discomfort. LME.
3 Marked or characterized by absence of pain. M19.
■ **unpained** *adjective* LME.

unpaint /ʌnˈpeɪnt/ *verb trans.* E17.
[from UN-² + PAINT *verb*.]
1 Free from paint. E17.
2 Obliterate (something painted), paint out. E18.

unpaintable /ʌnˈpeɪntəb(ə)l/ *adjective.* M19.
[from UN-¹ + PAINT *verb* + -ABLE.]
Unable to be painted.
■ **unpaintaˈbility** *noun* L19. **unpaintableness** *noun* L19.

unpainted /ʌnˈpeɪntɪd/ *adjective.* M16.
[from UN-¹ + PAINTED.]
Not painted.

unpalatable /ʌnˈpalətəb(ə)l/ *adjective.* L17.
[from UN-¹ + PALATABLE.]
1 Not agreeable to the palate, not pleasant in taste. L17.
2 Of an idea, suggestion, etc.: unpleasant, distasteful, disagreeable. E18.

> 📖 **2** H. GUNTRIP This unpalatable truth, that we do not succeed very well in growing up. M. IGNATIEFF The regime of Nicholas II was increasingly unpalatable to liberals.

■ **unpalataˈbility** *noun* M20. **unpalatableness** *noun* E19. **unpalatably** *adverb* L19.

unpaper /ʌnˈpeɪpə/ *verb trans.* E18.
[from UN-² + PAPER *verb*.]
Remove paper from; *esp.* strip of a paper covering.

unpapered /ʌnˈpeɪpəd/ *adjective.* L18.
[from UN-¹ + *papered* pa. pple of PAPER *verb*.]
Not covered with paper; *esp.* not decorated with wallpaper.

unparadise /ʌnˈparədʌɪs/ *verb trans.* Now *arch. & poet.* L16.
[from UN-² + PARADISE *noun* or *verb*.]
1 Turn out of or expel from paradise. L16.
2 Deprive of the character of paradise. M17.

unparalleled /ʌnˈparəlɛld/ *adjective.* L16.
[from UN-¹ + *paralleled* pa. pple of PARALLEL *verb*.]
Having no parallel or equal; unsurpassed, unequalled; unprecedented.

> 📖 R. GRAVES A crime unparalleled in the history of Rome. *Listener* An international recession of unparalleled severity. *Daily Telegraph* The view, especially from the tower, is unparalleled.

■ **unparallel** *adjective* not parallel M17. **unparallelable** *adjective* M17. **unparalleledly** *adverb* M19. **unparalleledness** *noun* M17. **unparallelness** *noun* E18.

unpardonable /ʌnˈpɑːd(ə)nəb(ə)l/ *adjective.* E16.
[from UN-¹ + PARDONABLE.]
That cannot be pardoned, unforgivable; (of a fault, crime, etc.) very serious.

> 📖 M. E. BRADDON There was nothing unpardonable in Miss Bridgeman's plainness. *Times* The priggism of intellectual pretension is the one unpardonable sin.

■ **unpardonableness** *noun* M17. **unpardonably** *adverb* M17. **unpardoned** *adjective* M16. **unpardoning** *adjective* M17.

unparliamentary /ˌʌnpɑːləˈmɛnt(ə)ri/ *adjective.* E17.
[from UN-¹ + PARLIAMENTARY *adjective*.]
Contrary to proper parliamentary usage; (of language) impermissible in parliament, abusive, foul.
■ **unparliamentarily** *adverb* E18. **unparliamentariness** *noun* M17.

unpartial /ʌnˈpɑːʃ(ə)l/ *adjective.* L16.
[from UN-¹ + PARTIAL *adjective*.]
1 †**a** Impartial, unbiased, fair. L16–M17. ▸**b** Free from inclination or fondness. M19.
2 Unrestricted, ample. *rare.* L18.
■ †**unpartially** *adverb* L16–M17. †**unpartialness** *noun*: only in M17.

unpass /ʌnˈpɑːs/ *verb trans. rare.* E17.
[from UN-² + PASS *verb*.]
Repeal or revoke (a law etc.).

unpassable /ʌnˈpɑːsəb(ə)l/ *adjective.* M16.
[from UN-¹ + PASSABLE.]
1 = IMPASSABLE 1. Now *dial.* M16.
2 Unable to be transcended or exceeded. L16.
3 Of money: unable to be passed or circulated. M17.
■ **unpassed** *adjective* not passed; *esp.* not traversed or crossed: M16. **unpassing** *adjective* not passing; *esp.* never-ending, eternal: L16.

unpassionate /ʌnˈpaʃ(ə)nət/ *adjective.* Now *rare.* L16.
[from UN-¹ + PASSIONATE *adjective*.]
Not passionate; not easily swayed by passion or strong emotion; calm, self-possessed.
■ **unpassionately** *adverb* M17. **unpassionateness** *noun* E17. **unpassioned** *adjective* unpassionate E17.

unpasteurized /ʌnˈpɑːstʃərʌɪzd, -tjərʌɪzd, ʌnˈpas-/ *adjective.* Also **-ised.** E20.
[from UN-¹ + *pasteurized* pa. pple of PASTEURIZE.]
Not pasteurized.

unpastured /ʌnˈpɑːstʃəd/ *adjective.* M16.
[from UN-¹ + *pastured* pa. pple of PASTURE *verb*.]
1 Not led to pasture, unfed. M16.
2 Not used for pasture. E19.
■ **unpasturable** *adjective* L18.

unpatient /ʌnˈpeɪʃ(ə)nt/ *adjective.* Now *dial.* LME.
[from UN-¹ + PATIENT *adjective*.]
Impatient.
■ †**unpatience** *noun* LME–M17. †**unpatiently** *adverb* LME–E17.

unpatriotic /ˌʌnpatrɪˈɒtɪk, ˌʌnpeɪt-/ *adjective.* L18.
[from UN-¹ + PATRIOTIC.]
Not patriotic.
■ **unpatriotically** *adverb* L18. **unˈpatriotism** *noun* L19.

unpatterned /ʌnˈpat(ə)nd/ *adjective.* E17.
[from UN-¹ + *patterned* pa. pple of PATTERN *verb*.]
1 Unexampled, unequalled. *arch.* E17.
2 Not decorated with a pattern. L19.
3 Not formed or cast into a pattern. M20.

unpave /ʌnˈpeɪv/ *verb trans.* L16.
[from UN-² + PAVE *verb*.]
Lift or remove the paving of (a street etc.).

unpaved /ʌnˈpeɪvd/ *adjective.* M16.
[from UN-¹ + *paved* pa. pple of PAVE *verb*.]
Not paved.

†**unpay** *verb trans. rare* (Shakes.). Only in L16.
[from UN-² + PAY *verb*¹.]
Undo, make good.

unpayable /ʌnˈpeɪəb(ə)l/ *adjective.* LME.
[from UN-¹ + PAYABLE.]
1 Of a debt, person, etc.: unable to be paid. LME.
2 Incapable of paying or making a profit, unremunerative. L19.
■ **unpaying** *adjective* not paying L17.

unpeace /ʌnˈpiːs/ *noun. arch.* ME.
[from UN-¹ + PEACE *noun*.]
Absence of peace; dissension, strife.

unpeaceable /ʌnˈpiːsəb(ə)l/ *adjective.* Now *rare.* E16.
[from UN-¹ + PEACEABLE.]
1 Not disposed to peace; contentious, argumentative. E16.
2 Characterized by lack of peace or quiet. M16.
■ **unpeaceableness** *noun* L15. **unpeaceably** *adverb* M17.

unpeaceful /ʌnˈpiːsfʊl, -f(ə)l/ *adjective.* M16.
[from UN-¹ + PEACEFUL.]
Not peaceful.

unpeel /ʌnˈpiːl/ *verb trans.* E20.
[from UN-² + PEEL *verb*¹.]
Remove peel from, peel.

unpeeled /ʌnˈpiːld/ *adjective.* L16.
[from UN-¹ + PEELED.]
Not peeled.

unpeg /ʌnˈpɛg/ *verb trans.* Infl. **-gg-.** E17.
[from UN-² + PEG *verb*.]
Unfasten by the removal of a peg or pegs; *fig.* cease to fix or stabilize (currency, stock, a price, etc.).

unpen /ʌnˈpɛn/ *verb trans.* Infl. **-nn-.** L16.
[from UN-² + PEN *verb*¹.]
Release from a pen or enclosure, cease to confine.

unpenetrated /ʌnˈpɛnɪtreɪtɪd/ *adjective.* L18.
[from UN-¹ + *penetrated* pa. pple of PENETRATE.]
Not penetrated.
■ **unpenetrable** *adjective* LME. **unpenetrating** *adjective* M18.

unpeople /ˈʌnpiːp(ə)l/ *noun pl.* M20.
[from UN-¹ + PEOPLE *noun*.]
1 Persons excluded from 'the people' as a political grouping. M20.
2 Unpersons. M20.

unpeople /ʌnˈpiːp(ə)l/ *verb trans.* M16.
[from UN-² + PEOPLE *verb*.]
Empty of people, depopulate.

For other words beginning with *un-* see the entries for **un-¹**, **un-²**

unpeopled /ʌnˈpiːp(ə)ld/ *adjective*. L16.
[from UN-¹ + *peopled* pa. pple of PEOPLE *verb*.]
Not populated, uninhabited, without people.

unperceived /ʌnpəˈsiːvd/ *adjective*. ME.
[from UN-¹ + *perceived* pa. pple of PERCEIVE.]
Not perceived; without being perceived or noticed, unnoticed, unobserved.
■ **unperceivable** *adjective* imperceptible LME. **unperceivably** *adverb* LME. **unperceivedly** *adverb* M17. **unperceiving** *adjective* E17.

unperceptive /ʌnpəˈsɛptɪv/ *adjective*. L17.
[from UN-¹ + PERCEPTIVE.]
Not perceptive.
■ **unperceptible** *adjective* (long *rare*) LME. **unperceptively** *adverb* L20. **unperceptiveness** *noun* L20.

unperfect /ʌnˈpəːfɪkt/ *adjective*. Now *rare*. ME.
[from UN-¹ + PERFECT *adjective*.]
1 a = IMPERFECT *adjective* 1. ME. ▸**b** = IMPERFECT *adjective* 4. LME.
2 = IMPERFECT *adjective* 2. LME.
■ **unperfectly** *adverb* LME. **unperfectness** *noun* ME.

unperfected /ʌnpəˈfɛktɪd/ *adjective*. E16.
[from UN-¹ + *perfected* pa. pple of PERFECT *verb*.]
Not perfected.

unperformed /ʌnpəˈfɔːmd/ *adjective*. LME.
[from UN-¹ + *performed* pa. pple of PERFORM.]
Not performed.

> *Guardian* Music, poems, stories, sketches and songs—all new and previously unperformed.

■ **unperformable** *adjective* unable to be performed; (esp. of music etc.) too difficult or complex to be performed properly: L17. **unperforming** *adjective* L17.

unperished /ʌnˈpɛrɪʃt/ *adjective*. LME.
[from UN-¹ + *perished* pa. pple of PERISH *verb*.]
Not perished; undecayed, not rotted; alive, not dead.
■ **unperishable** *adjective* M16. **unperishableness** *noun* M17. **unperishing** *adjective* M16.

unperplex /ʌnpəˈplɛks/ *verb trans*. M17.
[from UN-² + PERPLEX *verb*.]
Make unperplexed, enlighten.

unperplexed /ʌnpəˈplɛkst/ *adjective*. M16.
[from UN-¹ + PERPLEXED.]
1 Not puzzled or confused. M16.
2 Not involved or intricate. M17.

unperson /ˈʌnpəːs(ə)n/ *noun & verb*. M20.
[from UN-¹ + PERSON *noun*.]
▸**A** *noun*. A person whose existence is denied or ignored and whose name is removed from public records, usu. for political misdemeanour; *gen*. an ignored or forgotten person. M20.

> G. ORWELL Syme was not only dead, he was abolished, an *unperson*.

▸**B** *verb trans*. Make into an unperson. Chiefly as **unpersoned** *ppl adjective*. M20.

unpersuadable /ʌnpəˈsweɪdəb(ə)l/ *adjective*. L16.
[from UN-¹ + PERSUADABLE.]
†**1** Not removable by persuasion. Only in L16.
2 Not able to be persuaded, obstinate. E17.
■ **unpersuadableness** *noun* E17. **unpersuadably** *adverb* M20.

unpersuaded /ʌnpəˈsweɪdɪd/ *adjective*. M16.
[from UN-¹ + *persuaded* pa. pple of PERSUADE.]
Not persuaded, unconvinced.

unpersuasive /ʌnpəˈsweɪsɪv/ *adjective*. M18.
[from UN-¹ + PERSUASIVE.]
Not persuasive, unconvincing.
■ **unpersuasively** *adverb* M19.

unperturbed /ʌnpəˈtəːbd/ *adjective*. LME.
[from UN-¹ + PERTURBED.]
Not perturbed; PHYSICS not subjected to perturbation.

> O. MANNING 'I wouldn't worry,' David said in his usual unperturbed tone.

■ **unperturbedly** /-bɪdli/ *adverb* M20. **unperturbedness** *noun* L17.

unpervert /ʌnpəˈvəːt/ *verb trans*. M17.
[from UN-² + PERVERT *verb*.]
Make unperverted.

unperverted /ʌnpəˈvəːtɪd/ *adjective*. M17.
[from UN-¹ + PERVERTED.]
Not perverted.

unpetrified /ʌnˈpɛtrɪfʌɪd/ *adjective*. M17.
[from UN-¹ + *petrified* pa. pple of PETRIFY.]
Not petrified; not turned to stone.

unpetrify /ʌnˈpɛtrɪfʌɪ/ *verb trans*. E19.
[from UN-² + PETRIFY.]
Make unpetrified. Chiefly *fig*.

unphased *adjective* see UNFAZED.

unphilosophical /ˌʌnfɪləˈsɒfɪk(ə)l/ *adjective*. M17.
[from UN-¹ + PHILOSOPHICAL.]
Not philosophical; *esp*. not in accordance with philosophy.
■ **unphilosophic** *adjective* = UNPHILOSOPHICAL E18. **unphilosophically** *adverb* L17.

unphilosophize /ʌnfɪˈlɒsəfʌɪz/ *verb trans*. *rare*. Also **-ise**. E18.
[from UN-² + PHILOSOPHIZE.]
Bring (a person) out of a philosophical state, make unphilosophical.

unphysical /ʌnˈfɪzɪk(ə)l/ *adjective*. L16.
[from UN-¹ + PHYSICAL.]
Not physical; *esp*. not consonant with the laws or principles of physics; not corresponding to a physically possible situation.

> *Nature* The unphysical shape of peak 7.. argues against its identification as a real γ-ray line.

■ **unphysically** *adverb* L18.

unphysiological /ˌʌnfɪzɪəˈlɒdʒɪk(ə)l/ *adjective*. L18.
[from UN-¹ + PHYSIOLOGICAL.]
Not characteristic of normal physiological functions or conditions; not consonant with physiology.

> *Science Journal* Unphysiological doses of cortisone.

■ **unphysiologic** *adjective* (chiefly *US*) M20. **unphysiologically** *adverb* M20.

unpick /ʌnˈpɪk/ *verb trans*. LME.
[from UN-² + PICK *verb*¹.]
†**1** Pick (a lock); undo (a door) in this way. LME–M17.
2 Undo the sewing of (a garment etc.); take out (stitches), undo (knitting). L18.
3 Extricate (one thing) *from* another by picking. L20.

> **2** *fig*.: G. GREENE His lawyer's mind began to unpick the threads of the case. **3** J. M. COETZEE I unpick his fingers from my arm.

unpickable /ʌnˈpɪkəb(ə)l/ *adjective*. E17.
[from UN-¹ + PICKABLE.]
Unable to be picked.

unpicked /ʌnˈpɪkt/ *adjective*. L16.
[from UN-¹ + PICKED *adjective*².]
1 Not picked out or selected. L16.
2 Not gathered or plucked. L16.
3 Not unfastened; not rifled or robbed. Now *rare*. L16.

unpickupable /ʌnpɪkˈʌpəb(ə)l/ *adjective*. *colloq*. L20.
[from UN-¹ + *pick up* s.v. PICK *verb*¹ + -ABLE.]
Of a book: so dull or difficult that one has no interest in resuming reading it. Cf. UNPUTDOWNABLE.

unpicturable /ʌnˈpɪktʃ(ə)rəb(ə)l/ *adjective*. M19.
[from UN-¹ + PICTURABLE.]
Unable to be pictured or imagined.
■ **unpictura'bility** *noun* L19.

unpicturesque /ˌʌnpɪktʃəˈrɛsk/ *adjective*. L18.
[from UN-¹ + PICTURESQUE.]
Not picturesque.
■ **unpicturesquely** *adverb* M19. **unpicturesqueness** *noun* M19.

unpierced /ʌnˈpɪəst/ *adjective*. L16.
[from UN-¹ + PIERCED.]
Not pierced.
■ **unpierceable** *adjective* L15.

unpin /ʌnˈpɪn/ *verb trans*. Infl. **-nn-**. ME.
[from UN-² + PIN *verb*.]
1 Unbolt (a door). ME.
2 Remove a pin or peg from; unfasten, detach, or remove in this way. L16. ▸**b** Undo the dress of (a woman) by the removal of pins. E17.
3 CHESS. Release (a man that has been pinned). L19.

> **2** F. BRITTEN The balance sping has.. to be unpinned every time the balance staff is removed. M. ROBERTS We unpin our hats.

un-pin-downable /ʌnpɪnˈdaʊnəb(ə)l/ *adjective*. M20.
[from UN-¹ + *pin down* s.v. PIN *verb* + -ABLE.]
Unable to be pinned down or defined.

unpinned /ʌnˈpɪnd/ *adjective*. LME.
[from UN-¹, UN-² + PINNED.]
Not fastened with a pin or pins.

unpiteous /ʌnˈpɪtɪəs/ *adjective*. *arch*. LME.
[from UN-¹ + PITEOUS.]
1 Pitiless, unmerciful. LME.
†**2** Impious, wicked. Only in LME.
■ **unpiteously** *adverb* LME.

unpitiable /ʌnˈpɪtɪəb(ə)l/ *adjective*. M17.
[from UN-¹ + PITIABLE.]
Undeserving of pity; not arousing pity.
■ **unpitiably** *adverb* E19. **unpitied** *adjective* L16.

unpitiful /ʌnˈpɪtɪfʊl, -f(ə)l/ *adjective*. Long *rare*. LME.
[from UN-¹ + PITIFUL.]
Pitiless.
■ **unpitifully** *adverb* L16. **unpitifulness** *noun* E16.

unpitying /ʌnˈpɪtɪɪŋ/ *adjective*. E17.
[from UN-¹ + PITYING.]
Showing no pity.
■ **unpityingly** *adverb* M18.

unplacable /ʌnˈplakəb(ə)l/ *adjective*. Long *rare*. M16.
[from UN-¹ + PLACABLE.]
Implacable.

unplace /ʌnˈpleɪs/ *verb trans*. Now *rare*. M16.
[from UN-² + PLACE *noun*¹.]
Displace.

unplaced /ʌnˈpleɪst/ *adjective*. E16.
[from UN-¹ + *placed* pa. pple of PLACE *verb*.]
1 Not assigned to or set in a definite place. E16. ▸**b** RACING. Not finishing among the first three (or four) in a race. M19.
2 Not appointed to a post or office. M16.
■ **unplaceable** *adjective* M20.

unplait /ʌnˈplat/ *verb trans*. LME.
[from UN-² + PLAIT.]
Release (hair) from a plait, take out a plait or plaits from.

unplaited /ʌnˈplatɪd/ *adjective*. M17.
[from UN-¹ + PLAITED.]
Not plaited.

unplank /ʌnˈplaŋk/ *verb trans*. M17.
[from UN-² + PLANK *noun*, *verb*.]
Remove planks from.

unplanked /ʌnˈplaŋkt/ *adjective*. M17.
[from UN-¹ + *planked* pa. pple of PLANK *verb*.]
Having no planks.

unplanned /ʌnˈpland/ *adjective*. E20.
[from UN-¹ + PLANNED.]
Not planned.

unplanted /ʌnˈplɑːntɪd/ *adjective*. LME.
[from UN-¹ + *planted* pa. pple of PLANT *verb*.]
1 Not set in the ground; growing without having been planted. LME. ▸**b** Of ground: not set with plants. L18.
2 Of land: not occupied or colonized; not developed by cultivation. E17.
■ **unplantable** *adjective* L17.

unplayable /ʌnˈpleɪəb(ə)l/ *adjective*. M19.
[from UN-¹ + PLAYABLE.]
Unable to be played (on); *spec*. (of a ball) unable to be struck or returned.
■ **unplayably** *adverb* M20. **unplayed** *adjective* L18. **unplaying** *adjective* (*rare*) L19.

unpleasant /ʌnˈplɛz(ə)nt/ *adjective*. LME.
[from UN-¹ + PLEASANT *adjective*.]
1 Not pleasant; displeasing, disagreeable. LME.
2 Not entertaining or amusing. Long *rare* or *obsolete*. E18.

> **1** G. VIDAL Not really bad pains: just unpleasant sensations. I. MURDOCH He had always told them the truth, however unpleasant. ***an unpleasant quarter of an hour***: see QUARTER *noun*.

■ **unpleasantish** *adjective* E19. **unpleasantly** *adverb* M16. **unpleasantness** *noun* unpleasant quality; an unpleasant event, remark, etc. (***the late unpleasantness*** (US HISTORY), the American Civil War): M16. **unpleasantry** *noun* an unfriendly or impolite remark; (an) unpleasantness: M19.

unpleasing /ʌnˈpliːzɪŋ/ *adjective*. LME.
[from UN-¹ + PLEASING *adjective*.]
Not pleasing; unpleasant.
■ **unpleasable** *adjective* M16. **unpleased** *adjective* displeased LME. **unpleasingly** *adverb* L16. **unpleasingness** *noun* (now *rare*) E17.

unpleasurable /ʌnˈplɛʒ(ə)rəb(ə)l/ *adjective*. M18.
[from UN-¹ + PLEASURABLE.]
Not pleasurable.
■ **unpleasurably** *adverb* E19.

unpleasure /ʌnˈplɛʒə/ *noun*. L18.
[from UN-¹ + PLEASURE *noun*.]
1 (An) unpleasantness; displeasure. L18.
2 PSYCHOANALYSIS. The sense of inner pain, discomfort, or anxiety which results from the blocking of an instinctual impulse by the ego. E20.

unpliable /ʌnˈplʌɪəb(ə)l/ *adjective*. LME.
[from UN-¹ + PLIABLE.]
1 Obstinate, stubborn. LME.
2 Stiff, difficult to bend; not adaptable. E17.
■ **unpliableness** *noun* (now *rare*) M17.

unpliant /ʌnˈplʌɪənt/ *adjective*. M16.
[from UN-¹ + PLIANT.]
1 = UNPLIABLE 2. M16.
2 = UNPLIABLE 1. M17.
■ **unpliancy** *noun* M18.

unplug /ʌnˈplʌg/ *verb trans*. Infl. **-gg-**. L18.
[from UN-² + PLUG *noun*, *verb*.]
1 Unblock, unstop. L18.
2 Disconnect (an electrical appliance) by removing its plug from a socket; remove (a plug) from a socket. L19.

> **1** K. REISZ One of the furnacemen is unplugging the tap hole with an iron tapping bar. **2** A. GLYN Mr Jackson unplugged the television and turned out the lights.

■ **unplugged** *adjective* (***a***) having no stopper, open; (***b***) (of an electric device) having its plug removed from the socket; (***c***) (of a musical performance or recording) using acoustic instruments rather than electric ones: L19.

unplumbed /ʌnˈplʌmd/ *adjective.* E17.
[from UN-¹ + *plumbed* pa. pple of PLUMB *verb*.]
Not plumbed. Chiefly *fig.*, not fully explored or understood.
■ **unplumbable** *adjective* E20.

unplume /ʌnˈpluːm/ *verb trans.* L16.
[from UN-² + PLUME *noun, verb*.]
1 Strip of plumes or feathers. L16.
2 Deprive of distinction, prestige, etc. Now *rare.* E17.

unplumed /ʌnˈpluːmd/ *adjective.* L16.
[from UN-¹ + PLUMED.]
Having no plumes or feathers.

unpoetic /ʌnpəʊˈɛtɪk/ *adjective.* E17.
[from UN-¹ + POETIC.]
Not poetic.
■ **unpoetical** *adjective* M18. **unpoetically** *adverb* L17.

unpointed /ʌnˈpɔɪntɪd/ *adjective.* M16.
[from UN-¹ + POINTED.]
1 Not pointed *at*; (of brickwork) not pointed. M16.
2 Having no point or points; *spec.* (*a*) (of written Hebrew etc.) having no vowel-points or similar marks; (*b*) (of a sword etc.) having a blunt end rather than a sharp point; (*c*) unpunctuated. L16.

unpoise /ʌnˈpɔɪz/ *verb trans. poet. & literary.* E18.
[from UN-² + POISE *verb*.]
Unbalance.

unpoised /ʌnˈpɔɪzd/ *adjective. poet. & literary.* L16.
[from UN-¹ + POISED.]
Unbalanced.

unpoison /ʌnˈpɔɪz(ə)n/ *verb trans.* L16.
[from UN-² + POISON *noun, verb*.]
Remove poison from; *esp.* clear (the mind) of poisonous ideas.

unpoisoned /ʌnˈpɔɪz(ə)nd/ *adjective.* L18.
[from UN-¹ + *poisoned* pa. pple of POISON *verb*.]
Not poisoned.

unpolicied /ʌnˈpɒlɪsɪd/ *adjective.* Long *rare.* E17.
[from UN-¹ + *policied*, partly pa. pple of POLICY *verb*, partly from POLICY *noun*¹ + -ED².]
Unorganized. Also, having no policy.

unpolish /ʌnˈpɒlɪʃ/ *verb trans.* L16.
[from UN-² + POLISH *noun*¹, *verb*.]
Remove the polish from.

unpolished /ʌnˈpɒlɪʃt/ *adjective.* LME.
[from UN-¹ + *polished* pa. pple of POLISH *verb*.]
1 Not made smooth or bright by polishing. LME.
2 Inelegant in respect of style, language, etc.; not refined in behaviour; uncultured; crude. L15.

> 📖 **2** GIBBON The unpolished wives of the barbarians. F. W. FARRAR It cannot be Chrysippus; the Greek is too modern, and too unpolished.

■ **unpolishable** *adjective* L17.

unpolite /ʌnpəˈlʌɪt/ *adjective.* M17.
[from UN-¹ + POLITE.]
†**1** = IMPOLITE 1 *rare.* M17–E18.
2 = IMPOLITE 2. E18.
†**3** Unfashionable, inelegant. E–M18.
■ **unpolitely** *adverb* M18. **unpoliteness** *noun* E18.

unpolitic /ʌnˈpɒlɪtɪk/ *adjective.* M16.
[from UN-¹ + POLITIC *adjective*.]
Impolitic.
■ †**unpoliticly** *adverb* L16–M18.

unpolitical /ʌnpəˈlɪtɪk(ə)l/ *adjective.* M17.
[from UN-¹ + POLITICAL.]
Not political; not concerned or dealing with politics.

> 📖 *Independent* Such totally unpolitical charities as the Samaritans.

■ **unpolitically** *adverb* M20.

unpolled /ʌnˈpəʊld/ *adjective.* M17.
[from UN-¹ + *polled* pa. pple of POLL *verb*.]
1 Uncut, unshorn. *rare.* M17.
2 Not having voted at an election; not having had one's views etc. sought in an opinion poll. E19.

unpolluted /ʌnpəˈluːtɪd/ *adjective.* L16.
[from UN-¹ + POLLUTED.]
Not polluted.

unpope /ʌnˈpəʊp/ *verb trans.* M16.
[from UN-² + POPE *noun*¹.]
Deprive of the position of pope, depose from the papacy; deprive of a pope.

unpopular /ʌnˈpɒpjʊlə/ *adjective.* M17.
[from UN-¹ + POPULAR.]
Not popular; not liked by the public or by people in general.
■ **unpopuˈlarity** *noun* M18. **unpopularly** *adverb* L19.

unpopularize /ʌnˈpɒpjʊlərʌɪz/ *verb trans.* Also **-ise.** M19.
[from prec. + -IZE.]
Make unpopular.

unpopulate /ʌnˈpɒpjʊleɪt/ *verb trans.* M17.
[from UN-² + POPULATE *verb*.]
Depopulate.

unpopulated /ʌnˈpɒpjʊleɪtɪd/ *adjective.* L19.
[from UN-¹ + *populated* pa. pple of POPULATE *verb*.]
Not populated, having no inhabitants.

unpopulous /ʌnˈpɒpjʊləs/ *adjective.* L18.
[from UN-¹ + POPULOUS.]
Not populous; thinly populated.

unportable /ʌnˈpɔːtəb(ə)l/ *adjective.* LME.
[from UN-¹ + PORTABLE.]
†**1** Unbearable, intolerable. LME–E17.
2 Too heavy or bulky to carry. LME.

unportioned /ʌnˈpɔːʃ(ə)nd/ *adjective.* M18.
[from UN-¹ + *portioned* pa. pple of PORTION *verb*.]
Having no dowry to bring to a prospective husband.

unpossessed /ʌnpəˈzɛst/ *adjective.* L16.
[from UN-¹ + POSSESSED.]
1 Not possessed or owned; unoccupied. L16.
†**2** Unprejudiced. L16–L17.
3 Not in possession *of* something. L18.

unpossible /ʌnˈpɒsɪb(ə)l/ *adjective.* Now *dial.* LME.
[from UN-¹ + POSSIBLE.]
Impossible.
¶ Very common until 17.
■ **unpossiˈbility** *noun* E17.

unpowdered /ʌnˈpaʊdəd/ *adjective.* LME.
[from UN-¹ + *powdered* pa. pple of POWDER *verb*¹.]
†**1** Not sprinkled with salt. LME–E17.
2 *Hist.* Not whitened with hair-powder. M18.
3 Not wearing face-powder; having no face-powder. E20.

unpower /ʌnˈpaʊə/ *noun.* Long *obsolete* exc. *dial.* LME.
[from UN-¹ + POWER *noun*.]
Lack of power; inability; weakness; helplessness.

unpowered /ʌnˈpaʊəd/ *adjective.* M20.
[from UN-¹ + POWERED.]
Having or involving no fuel-burning source of power for propulsion.

unpowerful /ʌnˈpaʊəfʊl, -f(ə)l/ *adjective. rare.* E17.
[from UN-¹ + POWERFUL.]
Not powerful; weak.

unpracticable /ʌnˈpraktɪkəb(ə)l/ *adjective.* M17.
[from UN-¹ + PRACTICABLE.]
Impracticable.
■ **unpracticableness** *noun* M17.

unpractical /ʌnˈpraktɪk(ə)l/ *adjective.* M17.
[from UN-¹ + PRACTICAL.]
Not practical; *esp.* (of a person) having little practical skill.
■ **unpractiˈcality** *noun* L19. **unpractically** *adverb* L19. **unpracticalness** *noun* M19.

unpractised /ʌnˈpraktɪst/ *adjective.* Also *****-iced.** M16.
[from UN-¹ + PRACTISED.]
1 Not familiarized or skilled by practice; inexperienced, inexpert. (Foll. by *in*.) M16.
2 Not put into practice; untried. M16. ▸†**b** Not previously travelled, untraversed. E17–L18.

unpraise /ʌnˈpreɪz/ *verb trans.* Long *rare.* LME.
[from UN-² + PRAISE *verb*.]
= DISPRAISE *verb* 1a, 2.

unpraised /ʌnˈpreɪzd/ *adjective.* LME.
[from UN-¹ + *praised* pa. pple of PRAISE *verb*.]
Not praised.
■ **unpraisable** *adjective* (*a*) *rare* unable to be praised; †(*b*) unable to be appraised or valued: L15. **unpraiseworthy** *adjective* (*rare*) L16.

unpray /ʌnˈpreɪ/ *verb trans.* E17.
[from UN-² + PRAY *verb*.]
Retract or cancel the effect of (a prayer).

unprayed /ʌnˈpreɪd/ *adjective.* LME.
[from UN-¹ + *prayed* pa. pple of PRAY *verb*.]
1 Of a person: not entreated; unasked; uninvited. LME.
2 Not prayed *for.* M16.

unpreach /ʌnˈpriːtʃ/ *verb trans.* L17.
[from UN-² + PREACH *verb*.]
Retract or deny the contents of (preaching).

unpreaching /ʌnˈpriːtʃɪŋ/ *adjective.* M16.
[from UN-¹ + *preaching* pres. pple of PREACH *verb*.]
1 Omitting or neglecting to preach; characterized by absence of preaching. M16.
†**2** *spec.* Not undertaking the duty of preaching; merely reading church services. L16–E18.

unprecedented /ʌnˈprɛsɪdɛntɪd/ *adjective.* E17.
[from UN-¹ + PRECEDENTED.]
Having no precedent, unparalleled; that has not previously occurred.

> 📖 A. E. STEVENSON We are entering an age of abundance unprecedented in history.

■ **unprecedentedly** *adverb* E19. **unprecedentedness** *noun* L17.

unprecise /ʌnprɪˈsʌɪs/ *adjective.* L18.
[from UN-¹ + PRECISE *adjective*.]
Imprecise.

†**unpredict** *verb intrans. rare* (Milton). Only in L17.
[from UN-² + PREDICT *verb*.]
Of a prediction: fail to come true.

unpredictable /ʌnprɪˈdɪktəb(ə)l/ *adjective & noun.* M19.
[from UN-¹ + PREDICTABLE.]
▸ **A** *adjective.* Unable to be predicted. M19.
▸ **B** *noun.* An unpredictable thing. M20.
■ **unpredictaˈbility** *noun* E20. **unpredictableness** *noun* M20. **unpredictably** *adverb* M20. **unpredicted** *adjective* unforeseen M20.

unpreferred /ʌnprɪˈfəːd/ *adjective.* L15.
[from UN-¹ + PREFERRED.]
†**1** Not advanced or promoted. L15–L17.
2 Not regarded with preference. L19.

unprejudiced /ʌnˈprɛdʒʊdɪst/ *adjective.* E17.
[from UN-¹ + PREJUDICED.]
†**1** Not affected prejudicially. Only in E17.
2 Free from prejudice. E17.
■ **unprejudicedly** *adverb* L17. **unprejudicedness** *noun* L17.

unpremeditated /ʌnpriːˈmɛdɪteɪtɪd/ *adjective.* L16.
[from UN-¹ + PREMEDITATED.]
Not premeditated; unplanned; unintentional.
■ **unpremeditate** *adjective* (*arch.*) = UNPREMEDITATED M16. **unpremeditatedly** *adverb* L18. **unpremeditatedness** *noun* E19. †**unpremeditately** *adverb* unpremeditatedly L17–M18. **unpremediˈtation** *noun* E19.

unprepare /ʌnprɪˈpɛː/ *verb trans. rare.* L16.
[from UN-² + PREPARE *verb*.]
†**1** Undo the preparation of. Only in L16.
2 Make unprepared or unsuited, unfit. M17.

unprepared /ʌnprɪˈpɛːd/ *adjective.* M16.
[from UN-¹ + *prepared* pa. pple of PREPARE *verb*.]
1 Of a person: not in a state of preparation; not ready; *spec.* not prepared for death. (Foll. by *for*.) M16.
2 Not made ready; left, introduced, taken, etc., without special preparation. L16.

> 📖 **1** GOLDSMITH A heavy shower of rain. I was unprepared; but they . . had large coats. JOSEPH PARKER He came back . . glowing, and totally unprepared for the reaction he received. **2** *Independent* No skiing at all in Pamporovo: the . . pistes were left unprepared.

■ **unprepaˈration** *noun* (*rare*) unpreparedness E17. **unpreparedly** /-rɪdli/ *adverb* E17. **unpreparedness** *noun* the state of being unprepared E17.

unprepossessing /ˌʌnpriːpəˈzɛsɪŋ/ *adjective.* E19.
[from UN-¹ + PREPOSSESSING.]
Not prepossessing; unattractive.

> 📖 T. DREISER A broken nose . . gave to him a most unprepossessing, almost sinister, look.

■ **unprepossessed** *adjective* not prepossessed; not predisposed: M17.

unpressed /ʌnˈprɛst/ *adjective*¹. M16.
[from UN-¹ + *pressed* pa. pple of PRESS *verb*¹.]
1 Not pressed or squeezed; not subjected to pressure; (of a garment) not ironed. M16.
2 Not obtained by pressing. M17.

unpressed /ʌnˈprɛst/ *adjective*². E17.
[from UN-¹ + *pressed* pa. pple of PRESS *verb*².]
Not pressed into service; unconstrained.

unpresuming /ʌnprɪˈzjuːmɪŋ/ *adjective.* L18.
[from UN-¹ + PRESUMING.]
Not presumptuous; modest, unassuming.
■ **unpresumptuous** *adjective* E18. **unpresumptuously** *adverb* M19.

unpretending /ʌnprɪˈtɛndɪŋ/ *adjective.* L17.
[from UN-¹ + PRETENDING.]
Unpretentious, unassuming. Also, real, genuine.
■ **unpretendingly** *adverb* E19. **unpretendingness** *noun* E18.

unpretentious /ʌnprɪˈtɛnʃəs/ *adjective.* M19.
[from UN-¹ + PRETENTIOUS.]
Not pretentious; modest, simple.

> 📖 DAY LEWIS It is an unpretentious building, but has . . a certain romantic charm.

■ **unpretentiously** *adverb* M19. **unpretentiousness** *noun* M19.

unpretty /ʌnˈprɪti/ *adjective.* L18.
[from UN-¹ + PRETTY *adjective*.]
Not pretty; unattractive.
■ **unprettily** *adverb* E20. **unprettiness** *noun* L17.

unprevailing /ʌnprɪˈveɪlɪŋ/ *adjective & adverb.* E17.
[from UN-¹ + PREVAILING.]
▸ **A** *adjective.* **1** Ineffective, unsuccessful. E17.
2 Not prevalent or usual. *rare.* M19.
▸ **B** *adverb.* Ineffectively, vainly. Now *poet.* M17.

unpreventable /ʌnprɪˈvɛntəb(ə)l/ *adjective*. E17.
[from UN-¹ + PREVENTABLE.]
Not preventable; unavoidable.
■ **unpreventably** *adverb* M17. **unprevented** *adjective* L16. **unpreventible** *adjective* L17.

unpriced /ʌnˈprʌɪst/ *adjective*. M19.
[from UN-¹ + PRICED.]
1 Beyond price; priceless. *poet.* M19.
2 Not having a price fixed, marked, or stated. L19.

unpricked /ʌnˈprɪkt/ *adjective*. L16.
[from UN-¹ + PRICKED.]
1 Not marked with dots; (of a Hebrew text) unpointed. Long *rare* or *obsolete*. L16.
2 Not subjected to pricking; unpunctured. E17.

unpriest /ʌnˈpriːst/ *verb trans*. M16.
[from UN-² + PRIEST.]
Deprive of the character or position of priest.

unpriestly /ʌnˈpriːstli/ *adjective*. M16.
[from UN-¹ + PRIESTLY *adjective*.]
Not priestly; not befitting or characteristic of a priest.

unprincipled /ʌnˈprɪnsɪp(ə)ld/ *adjective*. M17.
[from UN-¹ + PRINCIPLED.]
1 Lacking sound or honourable principles of conduct. M17. ▸**b** Based on or exhibiting a lack of principle. L18.
†**2** Not instructed or grounded *in* something. Only in M17.

> 🕮 **1** W. PERRIAM He's an unprincipled self-seeker out for the main chance. **b** E. A. FREEMAN The ambition of Philip the Good was quite . . unprincipled.

■ **unprincipledness** *noun* E19.

unprintable /ʌnˈprɪntəb(ə)l/ *noun & adjective*. M19.
[from UN-¹ + PRINTABLE.]
▶**A** *noun*. In *pl.* Trousers; = UNMENTIONABLE *noun* 1. *arch. colloq.* M19.
▶**B** *adjective*. Unable to be printed; *esp.* not fit to be printed because too indecent, libellous, or blasphemous. L19.

> 🕮 D. BAGLEY His report was unfavourable . . his remarks were unprintable. *Amateur Photographer* Again my negs were so dense as to be almost unprintable.

■ **unprintably** *adverb* M20. **unprinted** *adjective* M16.

unprison /ʌnˈprɪz(ə)n/ *verb trans*. Now *rare*. LME.
[from UN-² + PRISON.]
Free from prison.

unprized /ʌnˈprʌɪzd/ *adjective*. LME.
[from UN-¹ + *prized* pa. pple of PRIZE *verb*¹.]
†**1** Unpriced; of which the price has not been fixed. Only in LME.
2 Not prized or valued. L16.
■ †**unprizeable** *adjective* (*a*) of little value; (*b*) beyond all price, of great value: LME–M17.

†**unprobable** *adjective*. M16–L17.
[from UN-¹ + PROBABLE.]
Unprovable. Also, improbable.

unprobably /ʌnˈprɒbəbli/ *adverb*. E17.
[from UN-¹ + PROBABLY.]
†**1** Without good reason. E17–E18.
2 Without high probability. E17.

unproblematic /ˌʌnprɒbləˈmatɪk/ *adjective*. L17.
[from UN-¹ + PROBLEMATIC.]
Not problematic; presenting no problems, straightforward.
■ **unproblematical** *adjective* = UNPROBLEMATIC L18. **unproblematically** *adverb* M20.

unproblematize /ʌnˈprɒbləmətʌɪz/ *verb trans*. Also **-ise**. L20.
[from UN-² + PROBLEMATIZE.]
Treat or accept as unproblematic.

unprocessed /ʌnˈprəʊsɛst/ *adjective*. M16.
[from UN-¹ + *processed* pa. pple of PROCESS *verb*¹.]
Esp. of food or raw materials: not processed.
¶ Rare before M20.

unproducible /ʌnprəˈdjuːsɪb(ə)l/ *adjective*. E19.
[from UN-¹ + PRODUCIBLE.]
Not producible; *spec.* (of a book, play, etc.) impracticable to produce for publication or performance; unworthy of production.
■ **unproduceable** *adjective* = UNPRODUCIBLE E19. **unproduced** *adjective* L15.

unproductive /ʌnprəˈdʌktɪv/ *adjective*. M18.
[from UN-¹ + PRODUCTIVE.]
Not productive (*of*); *esp.* not materially productive; not yielding crops, minerals, etc.
■ **unproductively** *adverb* E19. **unproductiveness** *noun* E19.

unprofessed /ʌnprəˈfɛst/ *adjective*. LME.
[from UN-¹ + PROFESSED.]
Not professed; not acknowledged or declared.

unprofessional /ʌnprəˈfɛʃ(ə)n(ə)l/ *adjective & noun*. E19.
[from UN-¹ + PROFESSIONAL.]
▶**A** *adjective*. **1** Contrary to professional standards of conduct. E19.
2 Not belonging to a profession; amateur. E19.
▶**B** *noun*. A person who is not professionally qualified. M19.
■ **unprofessionalism** *noun* M20. **unprofessionally** *adverb* M19.

unprofit /ʌnˈprɒfɪt/ *noun*. Long *rare*. LME.
[from UN-¹ + PROFIT *noun*.]
Absence of profit or benefit.

unprofitable /ʌnˈprɒfɪtəb(ə)l/ *adjective*. ME.
[from UN-¹ + PROFITABLE.]
Not profitable.
■ **unprofitableness** *noun* E16. **unprofitably** *adverb* LME. **unprofited** *adjective* (*a*) that has not profited or benefited; (*b*) that has not been taken advantage of or *of*: E17. **unprofiting** *adjective* that derives no advantage or benefit E17.

UNPROFOR /ˈʌnprəʊfɔː/ *abbreviation*.
UN Protection Force, a multinational peace-keeping force administrated by the United Nations.

unprogressive /ʌnprəˈgrɛsɪv/ *adjective*. L18.
[from UN-¹ + PROGRESSIVE.]
Not progressive.
■ **unprogressively** *adverb* L19. **unprogressiveness** *noun* E19.

unpromise /ʌnˈprɒmɪs/ *verb intrans. & trans. arch.* L16.
[from UN-² + PROMISE *verb*.]
Break or withdraw (a promise); break a promise to (a person).

unpromising /ʌnˈprɒmɪsɪŋ/ *adjective*. M17.
[from UN-¹ + PROMISING.]
Not likely to turn out well; not affording much hope.

> 🕮 J. CALDER Rarely can a marriage have taken place in more difficult or unpromising circumstances.

■ **unpromised** *adjective* E16. **unpromisingly** *adverb* M19. **unpromisingness** *noun* (*rare*) M17.

unprompted /ʌnˈprɒm(p)tɪd/ *adjective & adverb*. M17.
[from UN-¹ + *prompted* pa. pple of PROMPT *verb*.]
▶**A** *adjective*. Not prompted; spontaneous. M17.

> 🕮 *Independent* More than 10 per cent of heads 'made unprompted complaints'.

▶**B** *adverb*. Without prompting; spontaneously. M18.

> 🕮 *Economist* 'He is the Arab hero,' enthused one passer-by . . unprompted.

unpronounced /ʌnprəˈnaʊnst/ *adjective*. E17.
[from UN-¹ + PRONOUNCED.]
1 Unspoken; not articulated. E17.
2 Not prominent or distinct. M19.
■ **unpronounceable** *adjective* unable to be pronounced or articulated; too difficult to say: M19. **unpronounceably** *adverb* L20.

unprop /ʌnˈprɒp/ *verb trans*. Infl. **-pp-**. E17.
[from UN-² + PROP *verb*.]
Remove a prop or props from.

unproper /ʌnˈprɒpə/ *adjective*. LME.
[from UN-¹ + PROPER.]
†**1** = IMPROPER *adjective* 1. LME–M17.
2 = IMPROPER *adjective* 2. Now *dial.* LME.
†**3** Not peculiar to an individual; general, common. *rare* (Shakes.). Only in E17.
4 = IMPROPER *adjective* 3. *rare*. M19.

unpropitious /ʌnprəˈpɪʃəs/ *adjective*. L17.
[from UN-¹ + PROPITIOUS.]
Not propitious, not boding well; (of weather, an occasion, etc.) unfavourable, untimely.

> 🕮 T. HARDY The season was unpropitious for accidental encounters with her out of doors. S. CHITTY William John, for all his unpropitious origins, brought the family into the professional classes.

■ **unpropitiously** *adverb* E17. **unpropitiousness** *noun* (*rare*) M19.

unproportional /ʌnprəˈpɔːʃ(ə)n(ə)l/ *adjective*. E18.
[from UN-¹ + PROPORTIONAL.]
Not proportional.

unproportionate /ʌnprəˈpɔːʃ(ə)nət/ *adjective*. Now *rare*. L16.
[from UN-¹ + PROPORTIONATE *adjective*.]
Disproportionate, unproportioned.
■ †**unproportionable** *adjective* disproportionate L16–M18. †**unproportionably** *adverb* M16–E19. **unproportionately** *adverb* L19. **unproportionateness** *noun* LME.

unproportioned /ʌnprəˈpɔːʃ(ə)nd/ *adjective*. L16.
[from UN-¹ + PROPORTIONED.]
Disproportionate (*to*).

unpropped /ʌnˈprɒpt/ *adjective*. E17.
[from UN-¹ + *propped* pa. pple of PROP *verb*.]
Not propped, having no prop or support.

unprosperous /ʌnˈprɒsp(ə)rəs/ *adjective*. L16.
[from UN-¹ + PROSPEROUS.]
Not prosperous.
■ **unprosˈperity** *noun* E17. **unprosperously** *adverb* M17. **unprosperousness** *noun* (now *rare*) M17.

unprotected /ʌnprəˈtɛktɪd/ *adjective*. L16.
[from UN-¹ + *protected* pa. pple of PROTECT.]
1 Lacking protection. L16.
2 Of sexual intercourse: performed without a condom or other contraceptive. L20.
■ **unprotectedly** *adverb* E19. **unprotectedness** *noun* L19.

unprotestant /ʌnˈprɒtɪst(ə)nt/ *adjective*. M19.
[from UN-¹ + PROTESTANT.]
Not characteristic of or compatible with Protestantism.

unprotestantize /ʌnˈprɒtɪst(ə)ntʌɪz/ *verb trans*. Also **-ise**. M19.
[from UN-² + PROTESTANT + -IZE.]
Deprive of a Protestant character; make less Protestant.

unprotesting /ʌnprəˈtɛstɪŋ/ *adjective*. L19.
[from UN-¹ + *protesting* pres. pple of PROTEST *verb*.]
Making no protest; done without a protest.
■ **unprotestingly** *adverb* M20.

unproud /ʌnˈpraʊd/ *adjective*. L16.
[from UN-¹ + PROUD.]
Not proud. Freq. with neg. in litotes.

> 🕮 A. L. ROWSE My father grew not unproud . . of his son's bookish inclinations.

unprovable /ʌnˈpruːvəb(ə)l/ *adjective*. Also **unproveable**. LME.
[from UN-¹ + PROVABLE.]
Unable to be proved; not susceptible to proof.

> 🕮 A. STORR Many of Melanie Klein's concepts remain unproven and unprovable.

■ **unprovability** *noun* L19. **unprovableness** *noun* L19.

unproved /ʌnˈpruːvd/ *adjective*. LME.
[from UN-¹ + PROVED *adjective*. Cf. next.]
†**1** Untried, untested. LME–L16.
2 Not shown to be true or genuine. M16.

unproven /ʌnˈpruːv(ə)n, -ˈprəʊv-/ *adjective*. Orig. *Scot.* M16.
[from UN-¹ + PROVEN *adjective*. Cf. prec.]
= UNPROVED 2.

unprovide /ʌnprəˈvʌɪd/ *verb trans. rare*. M16.
[from UN-² + PROVIDE.]
Leave unprovided; unsettle, unhinge, (the mind).

unprovided /ʌnprəˈvʌɪdɪd/ *adjective*. LME.
[from UN-¹ + PROVIDED.]
1 Not in a state of readiness; unprepared. Now *rare*. LME.
2 Not provided, supplied, or equipped. (Foll. by *with*, †*of*; *for* a person etc.) E16.
3 Against which provision has not (or cannot) be made; unforeseen. E16.
4 Not provided for or *for*. L16.

> 🕮 **2** H. BROOKE Since you will go, you must not go unprovided. *Daily Mail* This Department is . . unprovided with many of the safeguards it has itself demanded. **3** A. ALISON The unprovided expenditure of the year. **4** E. HARDWICK Old oxen left behind, totally unprovided for.

■ **unprovidedly** *adverb* M16. **unprovidedness** *noun* M17.

†**unprovident** *adjective*. L16–M17.
[from UN-¹ + PROVIDENT.]
Improvident.
■ †**unprovidently** *adverb* E17–E19.

unprovocative /ʌnprəˈvɒkətɪv/ *adjective*. E19.
[from UN-¹ + PROVOCATIVE.]
Not provocative.

†**unprovoke** *verb trans. rare* (Shakes.). Only in E17.
[from UN-² + PROVOKE.]
Inhibit.

unprovoked /ʌnprəˈvəʊkt/ *adjective*. L16.
[from UN-¹ + PROVOKED.]
Done, occurring, or acting without provocation.

> 🕮 *New York Times* This attack was entirely unprovoked.

■ **unprovokable** *adjective* E19. **unprovokedly** /-kɪdli/ *adverb* M17. **unprovokedness** *noun* M19. **unprovoking** *adjective* E18.

unpruned /ʌnˈpruːnd/ *adjective*. L16.
[from UN-¹ + *pruned* pa. pple of PRUNE *verb*².]
Not pruned, not trimmed by cutting or lopping.

unpublished /ʌnˈpʌblɪʃt/ *adjective*. E17.
[from UN-¹ + *published* pa. pple of PUBLISH.]
1 Not made generally known; not divulged or disclosed. E17.
2 Not publicly issued in print. L17. ▸**b** Of an author: having had no writings published. M20.
■ **unpublishable** *adjective* unsuitable for publication E19. **unpublishably** *adverb* M19.

unpunctual /ʌnˈpʌŋ(k)tʃʊəl, -tjʊəl/ *adjective*. M18.
[from UN-¹ + PUNCTUAL.]
Poor at observing an appointed time or times.
■ **unpunctuˈality** *noun* E19.

unpunctuated /ʌnˈpʌŋ(k)tʃʊeɪtɪd, -tjʊ-/ *adjective*. **M19**.
[from UN-[1] + *punctuated* pa. pple of PUNCTUATE *verb*.]
Lacking punctuation.

unpunished /ʌnˈpʌnɪʃt/ *adjective*. **ME**.
[from UN-[1] + *punished* pa. pple of PUNISH.]
Not punished; without punishment.
■ **unpunishable** *adjective* **M16**. **unpunishably** *adverb* **M17**.

†**unpure** *adjective*. **LME**.
[from UN-[1] + PURE *adjective*.]
1 Morally impure. **LME–M18**.
2 Not physically pure or clean. **LME–M17**.

unpurged /ʌnˈpəːdʒd/ *adjective*. **LME**.
[from UN-[1] + *purged* pa. pple of PURGE *verb*.]
1 Not cleansed or freed from baser elements. **LME**.
2 Not freed or cleared from wrongdoing, accusation, etc. **M16**.
3 Not removed or got rid of. **E17**.

unpurse /ʌnˈpəːs/ *verb*. **LME**.
[from UN-[2] + PURSE *noun*, *verb*.]
1 *verb trans.* Take (money) out of a purse; spend. Long *rare*. **LME**.
2 *verb trans. & intrans.* Relax from a pursed state. **L19**.

†**unpurveyed** *adjective*. **ME**.
[from UN-[1] + *purveyed* pa. pple of PURVEY *verb*.]
1 Of a person: not provided or equipped. Foll. by *of*. **ME–L16**.
2 Not prepared, not ready. **LME–L16**.
3 Unforeseen, unexpected. **LME–L15**.

unput /ʌnˈpʊt/ *adjective*. **LME**.
[from UN-[1] + *put* pa. pple of PUT *verb*[1].]
That has not been put (*on*, *out*, etc.).
■ **unputˈdownable** *adjective* (*colloq.*) (of a book) so engrossing that one cannot stop reading it **M20**.

unqualified /ʌnˈkwɒlɪfʌɪd/ *adjective*. **M16**.
[from UN-[1] + QUALIFIED.]
1 Not qualified, fitted, or competent; not having the necessary qualifications. (Foll. by *for*, *to do*.) **M16**.
2 Not modified, limited, or restricted. **L18**.

📖 **1** GIBBON Dominions which they were unqualified to govern. **2** W. STYRON Depression is much too complex . . for unqualified conclusions to be drawn from the experience of one individual.

■ **unqualifiable** *adjective* **M18**. **unqualifiedly** *adverb* without qualification; unreservedly: **M19**. **unqualifiedness** *noun* (now *rare*) **M17**.

unqualify /ʌnˈkwɒlɪfʌɪ/ *verb trans.* Now *rare*. **M17**.
[from UN-[2] + QUALIFY.]
Disqualify.

unqueen /ʌnˈkwiːn/ *verb trans.* **L16**.
[from UN-[2] + QUEEN *noun*.]
Deprive of the position of queen.

unqueenly /ʌnˈkwiːnli/ *adjective*. **M19**.
[from UN-[1] + QUEENLY *adjective*.]
Not resembling or befitting a queen.

unquenchable /ʌnˈkwɛn(t)ʃəb(ə)l/ *adjective*. **LME**.
[from UN-[1] + QUENCH *verb* + -ABLE.]
Of fire, thirst, desire, etc.: unable to be quenched, inextinguishable, unsuppressible.
¶ Recorded much earlier than QUENCHABLE.
■ **unquenchably** *adverb* **E17**.

unquenched /ʌnˈkwɛn(t)ʃt/ *adjective*. **ME**.
[from UN-[1] + *quenched* pa. pple of QUENCH *verb*.]
1 Of fire, thirst, desire, etc.: unextinguished, unsuppressed. **ME**.
†**2** Of lime: unslaked. **LME–M17**.

unquestionable /ʌnˈkwɛstʃ(ə)nəb(ə)l/ *adjective & noun*. **E17**.
[from UN-[1] + QUESTIONABLE.]
▶ **A** *adjective*. **1** Having an assured character or position; unexceptionable. **E17**.
2 Not submitting or liable to question. *rare*. **E17**.
3 Unable to be doubted or disputed; indisputable, certain. **M17**.

📖 **1** J. CORBET The Reformation in England, for its Legality and Orderliness, is unquestionable. **3** A. N. WILSON It is unquestionable that Mrs Moore was a demanding companion.

▶ **B** *noun*. An unquestionable fact or truth. *rare*. **M17**.
■ **unquestionaˈbility** *noun* **M19**. **unquestionableness** *noun* **E18**. **unquestionably** *adverb* without or beyond question, indisputably, certainly **M17**.

unquestioned /ʌnˈkwɛstʃ(ə)nd/ *adjective*. **E17**.
[from UN-[1] + *questioned* pa. pple of QUESTION *verb*.]
1 Of a person: not subjected to questioning, not interrogated. **E17**.
2 Not inquired into, unexamined. **E17**.
3 Not called into question; undisputed, definite, certain. **E17**.

unquestioning /ʌnˈkwɛstʃ(ə)nɪŋ/ *adjective*. **E19**.
[from UN-[1] + *questioning* pres. pple of QUESTION *verb*.]
Asking no questions; performed or accepted without asking questions.

📖 A. MARSH-CALDWELL Unquestioning obedience to the authority of his superiors.

■ **unquestioningly** *adverb* **M19**. **unquestioningness** *noun* **L19**.

unquiet /ʌnˈkwʌɪət/ *adjective & noun*. **LME**.
[from UN-[1] + QUIET *adjective*, *noun*.]
▶ **A** *adjective*. **1** Not disposed to be quiet or inactive; restless, agitated. **LME**.
2 Uneasy, perturbed, anxious. **LME**.
3 Marked by unrest, commotion, or disorder. **E16**.

📖 **1** J. FORBES Restless and unquiet spirits. **2** T. C. WOLFE He paused . . and an old unquiet feeling . . stirred in his heart. **3** B. DUFFY Jesus . . bade Peter . . walk to him across the unquiet water.

▶ **B** *noun*. Lack of quiet or peace; disturbance. **M16**.
■ **unquietly** *adverb* without being or keeping quiet, restlessly, uneasily **E16**. **unquietness** *noun* the condition or fact of being unquiet; restlessness, disturbance, agitation: **E16**.

unquote /ʌnˈkwəʊt/ *verb intrans.* (*imper.*) & *interjection*. **M20**.
[from UN-[2] + QUOTE *verb*.]
Used in dictation, reading aloud, etc., to indicate or imply the presence of closing quotation marks. Cf. QUOTE *verb* 4C.

📖 P. USTINOV He expressed the personal opinion that the picture was quote great for America unquote.

unquoted /ʌnˈkwəʊtɪd/ *adjective*. **E19**.
[from UN-[1] + *quoted* pa. pple of QUOTE *verb*.]
Not quoted, esp. on the Stock Exchange.
■ ˌ**unquotaˈbility** *adjective* the quality of being unquotable **E20**. **unquotable** *adjective* unable to be quoted **M19**.

unquoth /ʌnˈkwəʊθ/ *adjective*. *obsolete* exc. *dial.* **M16**.
[Alt.]
= UNCOUTH.

unrake /ʌnˈreɪk/ *verb trans.* **LME**.
[from UN-[2] + RAKE *verb*[2].]
Uncover or expose by raking.

unraked /ʌnˈreɪkt/ *adjective*. **L16**.
[from UN-[1] + *raked* pa. pple of RAKE *verb*[2].]
Not raked, not smoothed or gathered with a rake.

unravel /ʌnˈrav(ə)l/ *verb*. Infl. **-ll-**, ***-l-**. **E17**.
[from UN-[2] + RAVEL *verb*.]
1 *verb trans.* Cause to be no longer ravelled, tangled, or intertwined, disentangle; unweave or undo (a fabric, esp. a knitted one). **E17**.
†**2** *verb trans.* Reverse, annul. **M17–M18**.
3 *verb trans.* Investigate and solve (a mystery etc.); make plain or obvious, reveal, disclose. **M17**.
4 *verb intrans.* Become undone, disentangled, or unravelled. **M17**.

📖 **1** P. G. WODEHOUSE Too impatient to unravel the tangled knot, he had cut it. **3** *Guardian* Scientists have for years been trying to unravel the mysteries of ageing. **4** S. CISNEROS Pull one string and the whole cloth unravels.

■ **unravellable** *adjective* unable to be unravelled **M19**. **unraveller** *noun* **E18**. **unravelling** *noun* the action of the verb; an instance of this: **E17**. **unravelment** *noun* the action or process of unravelling; an instance of this: **L18**.

unreachable /ʌnˈriːtʃəb(ə)l/ *adjective*. **L16**.
[from UN-[1] + REACHABLE.]
Not reachable, beyond reach.
■ **unreachableness** *noun* **E20**. **unreachably** *adverb* **L19**. **unˈreached** *adjective* **E17**.

unread /ʌnˈrɛd/ *adjective*. **LME**.
[from UN-[1] + READ *adjective*.]
1 Not read. **LME**.
2 Not instructed (*in*) by reading, not well-read. **E17**.

unread /ʌnˈriːd/ *verb trans.* Pa. t. & pple **unread** /ʌnˈrɛd/. **M16**.
[from UN-[2] + READ *verb*.]
Undo the reading of.

unreadable /ʌnˈriːdəb(ə)l/ *adjective*. **E19**.
[from UN-[1] + READABLE.]
1 Too dull or too difficult to read. **E19**.
2 Illegible. **M19**.
3 Of a facial expression, a remark, etc.: inscrutable, uninterpretable. **M19**.

📖 **2** J. JOHNSTON There are upstanding crosses and leaning ones, some moss-covered with the inscriptions almost unreadable. **3** J. CONRAD He . . dragged the veil off, unmasking a still, unreadable face.

■ **unreadaˈbility** *noun* **L19**. **unreadableness** *noun* **L18**. **unreadably** *adverb* **L18**. **unreading** *adjective* not reading **E19**.

unready /ʌnˈrɛdi/ *adjective*[1]. **ME**.
[from UN-[1] + READY *adjective*. Cf. next.]
1 Not ready, unprepared. (Foll. by *for*, *to do*, *with*.) **ME**.
2 Not properly dressed; in dishabille. *obsolete* exc. *dial.* **L16**.
3 Not quick or prompt in action; hesitating, slow. **L16**.
■ **unreadily** *adverb* **L16**. **unreadiness** *noun* **E16**.

unready /ʌnˈrɛdi/ *adjective*[2]. **L16**.
[Later form of UNREDY, after prec.]
= REDELESS *adjective*
¶ Only used as an epithet of Ethelred II (d. 1016), and freq. regarded as a use of UNREADY *adjective*[1] 1 or 3.

unreal /ʌnˈrɪəl/ *adjective*. **E17**.
[from UN-[1] + REAL *adjective*[2].]
1 Not real; imaginary, illusory. **E17**.
2 Incredible, amazing, remarkable. Chiefly *N. Amer. & Austral. slang*. **M20**.
■ **unreˈality** *noun* absence or lack of reality; an instance of this: **M18**. **unrealness** *noun* unreality **M19**.

unrealisable *adjective*, **unrealise** *verb*, **unrealised** *adjective* vars. of UNREALIZABLE *adjective* etc.

unrealism /ʌnˈrɪəlɪz(ə)m/ *noun*. **M19**.
[from UN-[1] + REALISM.]
Absence or lack of realism.

unrealist /ʌnˈrɪəlɪst/ *noun & adjective*. **M20**.
[from UN-[1] + REALIST.]
▶ **A** *noun*. A person who is not a realist. **M20**.
▶ **B** *adjective*. Not realistic or realist. **M20**.
■ **unreaˈlistic** *adjective* not realistic **M19**. **unreaˈlistically** *adverb* **M20**.

unrealizable /ʌnˈrɪəlʌɪzəb(ə)l/ *adjective*. Also **-isable**. **M19**.
[from UN-[1] + REALIZABLE.]
Unable to be realized.

unrealize /ʌnˈrɪəlʌɪz/ *verb trans.* Also **-ise**. **E19**.
[from UN-[2] + REALIZE.]
Make unreal; deprive of reality.

unrealized /ʌnˈrɪəlʌɪzd/ *adjective*. Also **-ised**. **L18**.
[from UN-[1] + *realized* pa. pple of REALIZE *verb*.]
Not realized.

📖 E. JOHNSON The gleaming hopes of his earlier career were largely unrealized.

unreally /ʌnˈrɪəli/ *adverb*. **M19**.
[from UN-[1] + REALLY.]
In an unreal way.

📖 A. N. WILSON It was a beautifully, unreally happy first term.

unreason /ʌnˈriːz(ə)n/ *noun*. **ME**.
[from UN-[1] + REASON *noun*[1].]
†**1** Unreasonable action or intention; injustice, impropriety. **ME–E17**.
2 Absence of reason; inability to act or think reasonably. **E19**.
3 A thing which is against or without reason. **M19**.
Phrases: **Abbot of Unreason**, **Abbot Unreason** SCOTTISH HISTORY a person elected as the leading character in Christmas revelries mocking the Church and ecclesiastical establishments.
■ **unreasoned** *adjective* (*a*) devoid of reason; (*b*) not developed by reasoning: **L16**.

unreason /ʌnˈriːz(ə)n/ *verb trans.* Now *rare*. **M17**.
[from UN-[2] + REASON *verb*.]
1 Disprove, refute. **M17**.
2 Deprive of reason. **L17**.

unreasonable /ʌnˈriːz(ə)nəb(ə)l/ *adjective*. **ME**.
[from UN-[1] + REASONABLE.]
1 Not endowed with reason; irrational. *rare*. **ME**.
2 Not based on or acting in accordance with reason or good sense. **ME**.
3 Going beyond what is reasonable or equitable; excessive. **LME**.

📖 **2** SIR W. SCOTT He was capricious, unreasonable, peremptory, and inconsistent. MRS ALEXANDER A vague, unreasonable anxiety about Elsie haunted him. **3** LD MACAULAY He had to wait a most unreasonable time for a judgment.

■ **unreasonableness** *noun* **M16**. **unreasonably** *adverb* (*a*) in an unreasonable manner; (*b*) to an unreasonable extent: **LME**.

unreasoning /ʌnˈriːz(ə)nɪŋ/ *adjective*. **M18**.
[from UN-[1] + *reasoning* pres. pple of REASON *verb*.]
Not reasoning.
■ **unreasoningly** *adverb* **M19**.

unrebated /ʌnrɪˈbeɪtɪd/ *adjective*. **L16**.
[from UN-[1] + *rebated* pa. pple of REBATE *verb*[1].]
†**1** Unblunted; undulled. **L16–M18**.
2 Not subject to rebate or deduction. *rare*. **L19**.

unrebutted /ʌnrɪˈbʌtɪd/ *adjective*. **LME**.
[from UN-[1] + *rebutted* pa. pple of REBUT *verb*.]
†**1** Not repulsed or driven back. **LME–E16**.
2 Not disproved or refuted. *rare*. **L19**.

unrecalled /ʌnrɪˈkɔːld/ *adjective*. **E17**.
[from UN-[1] + *recalled* pa. pple of RECALL *verb*.]
Not called or brought back; *esp.* not brought back to mind.
■ **unrecallable** *adjective* **E17**. **unrecalling** *adjective* (*rare*) **L16**.

unreceived /ʌnrɪˈsiːvd/ *adjective.* M16.
[from UN-[1] + *received* pa. pple of RECEIVE *verb.*]
Not received.
■ **unreceivable** *adjective* unable to be received E17.

unreceptive /ʌnrɪˈsɛptɪv/ *adjective.* L18.
[from UN-[1] + RECEPTIVE.]
Not receptive.
■ **unrecepˈtivity** *noun* (*rare*) M19.

unrecked /ʌnˈrɛkt/ *adjective. arch.* E19.
[from UN-[1] + *recked* pa. pple of RECK *verb.*]
Unheeded, unregarded. Also foll. by *of.*

unreckoned /ʌnˈrɛk(ə)nd/ *adjective.* ME.
[from UN-[1] + *reckoned* pa. pple of RECKON *verb.*]
Not calculated, not taken into account.
■ **unreckonable** *adjective* (*rare*) unable to be reckoned M19.

unreclaimable /ʌnrɪˈkleɪməb(ə)l/ *adjective.* Long *rare.* L16.
[from UN-[1] + RECLAIMABLE.]
Unable to be reclaimed or reformed.

unreclaimed /ʌnrɪˈkleɪmd/ *adjective.* L15.
[from UN-[1] + *reclaimed* pa. pple of RECLAIM *verb.*]
†**1** Not summoned to return. Only in L15.
2 Not reclaimed from error or wrongdoing; unreformed. E17.
3 Untamed; uncultivated; wild. E17.

unrecognisable, **unrecognised** *adjectives* vars. of UNRECOGNIZABLE, UNRECOGNIZED.

unrecognizable /ʌnˈrɛkəgnʌɪzəb(ə)l/ *adjective.* Also **-isable.** E19.
[from UN-[1] + RECOGNIZABLE.]
Unable to be recognized.

> *Washington Post* His face would twist itself and become unrecognizable with anger.

■ **unrecognizableness** *noun* L19. **unrecognizably** *adverb* L19.

unrecognized /ʌnˈrɛkəgnʌɪzd/ *adjective.* Also **-ised.** L18.
[from UN-[1] + *recognized* pa. pple of RECOGNIZE *verb*[1].]
Not recognized.
■ **unrecogˈnition** *noun* lack of recognition M19. **unrecognizing** *adjective* E19.

unrecommended /ʌnrɛkəˈmɛndɪd/ *adjective.* M16.
[from UN-[1] + *recommended* pa. pple of RECOMMEND *verb.*]
Not recommended.
■ **unrecommendable** *adjective* (*rare*) M19.

unreconciled /ʌnˈrɛk(ə)nsʌɪld/ *adjective.* LME.
[from UN-[1] + *reconciled* pa. pple of RECONCILE *verb.*]
Not reconciled.
■ **unreconcilable** *adjective* (now *rare*) L16. †**unreconciliable** *adjective* unreconcilable L16–E17.

unreconstructed /ˌʌnriːkənˈstrʌktɪd/ *adjective.* M19.
[from UN-[1] + *reconstructed* pa. pple of RECONSTRUCT.]
Not reconstructed, not rebuilt. Also *spec.*, not reconciled or converted to a current political orthodoxy; *US HISTORY* not reconciled to the outcome of the American Civil War.

unrecorded /ʌnrɪˈkɔːdɪd/ *adjective.* L16.
[from UN-[1] + *recorded* pa. pple of RECORD *verb.*]
Not recorded.
■ **unrecordable** *adjective* L19.

unrecoverable /ʌnrɪˈkʌv(ə)rəb(ə)l/ *adjective.* LME.
[from UN-[1] + RECOVERABLE.]
1 That cannot be recovered; completely lost. LME.
2 From which no recovery is possible; past remedy. LME.

unrecovered /ʌnrɪˈkʌvəd/ *adjective.* E17.
[from UN-[1] + *recovered* pa. pple of RECOVER *verb*[1].]
1 From which no recovery is or has been made. Now *rare.* E17.
2 Not recovered or regained. L17.
3 Not having recovered (*from* something). M18.

> **2** *Daily News* A telegram . . states that the body of Fowler is unrecovered.

unrecruitable /ʌnrɪˈkruːtəb(ə)l/ *adjective.* Also (earlier) †**-ible.** M17.
[from UN-[1] + RECRUITABLE. See -IBLE.]
†**1** Not capable of recruiting. Only in M17.
2 Not able to be recruited. L18.
¶ Form with *-able* recorded from L18.

unrecruited /ʌnrɪˈkruːtɪd/ *adjective.* M17.
[from UN-[1] + *recruited* pa. pple of RECRUIT *verb.*]
Not recruited.

†**unrecruitible** *adjective* see UNRECRUITABLE.

unrectified /ʌnˈrɛktɪfʌɪd/ *adjective.* M17.
[from UN-[1] + RECTIFIED.]
1 Not corrected or amended. M17.
2 Not purified or refined. M17.

unredeemed /ʌnrɪˈdiːmd/ *adjective.* E16.
[from UN-[1] + *redeemed* pa. pple of REDEEM *verb.*]
†**1** Unretrieved, unremedied. Only in E16.
2 Not spiritually redeemed; unsaved. M16.
3 Not recovered or released by purchase etc. M16.
4 Not relieved *by* or by something good; unmitigated. E19.
5 Not performed or realized. E19.

> **3** *Daily News* An average loss to the pawnbroker on these unredeemed pledges. **4** W. ROSCOE A man so totally unredeemed by a single virtue.

■ **unredeemable** *adjective* unable to be redeemed L16. **unredeemably** *adverb* M20.

unredressed /ʌnrɪˈdrɛst/ *adjective.* M16.
[from UN-[1] + *redressed* pa. pple of REDRESS *verb.*]
Not redressed.
■ **unredressable** *adjective* (long *rare*) E17.

unreduced /ʌnrɪˈdjuːst/ *adjective.* L16.
[from UN-[1] + REDUCED.]
†**1** Not annulled or repealed. *Scot.* L16–M17.
2 Not brought down or lessened in strength, complexity, etc. L17. ▸**b** *PHONETICS.* Of a vowel sound etc.: not reduced, articulated fully, given its strong or full form. M20.
3 *MEDICINE.* Not restored to a normal state or position. M18.
4 Not dissolved or comminuted. L18.
■ **unreducible** *adjective* irreducible M17.

unredy /ʌnˈrɛdi/ *adjective.* Long *obsolete* exc. *Hist.* LME.
[from UN-[1] + REDE *noun* + -Y[1]. Cf. UNREADY *adjective*[2].]
= REDELESS.
¶ Only used as an epithet of Ethelred II (d. 1016).

unreel /ʌnˈriːl/ *verb.* M16.
[from UN-[2] + REEL *verb.*]
1 *verb trans.* Unwind from a reel or skein. Chiefly *fig.* M16.
2 *verb intrans.* Become unwound. L19.
3 Chiefly *US.* ▸**a** *verb intrans.* Of a film: wind from one reel to another during projection; be shown. M20. ▸**b** *verb trans.* Project (a film). L20.

> **3a** *Washington Post* Cleffi's suspicions . . unreeled like a horror movie.

unreelable /ʌnˈriːləb(ə)l/ *adjective.* E17.
[from UN-[1] + REELABLE.]
Not reelable.

unrefined /ʌnrɪˈfʌɪnd/ *adjective.* L16.
[from UN-[1] + REFINED.]
1 Not refined in manners, feelings, or speech. L16.
2 Not freed from impurities or extraneous matter. L16.

> **2** T. NEWTE Rocksalt in the raw and unrefined state.

unreflected /ʌnrɪˈflɛktɪd/ *adjective.* E17.
[from UN-[1] + *reflected* pa. pple of REFLECT *verb.*]
Not reflected; not thought over or about (foll. by *on*, *upon*); not returned by reflection.

unreflecting /ʌnrɪˈflɛktɪŋ/ *adjective.* M17.
[from UN-[1] + *reflecting* pres. pple of REFLECT *verb.*]
Not reflecting, not given to reflective or meditative thought.

> T. HARDY Taken . . by surprise, . . she yielded to his embrace with unreflecting inevitableness.

■ **unreflectingly** *adverb* L17. **unreflectingness** *noun* E19. **unreflective** *adjective* M19.

unreformable /ʌnrɪˈfɔːməb(ə)l/ *adjective.* L16.
[from UN-[1] + REFORMABLE.]
1 Unable to be reformed or amended. L16.
2 Unable to be re-cast or altered. E17.

unreformed /ʌnrɪˈfɔːmd/ *adjective.* E16.
[from UN-[1] + REFORMED.]
1 Not reformed; *esp.* not morally, politically, or socially improved or amended. E16.
2 Not affected by the Reformation. L18.

> **1** J. PURSEGLOVE The administration of drainage remains to this day substantially unreformed.

■ **unreformedness** *noun* E17.

unrefreshed /ʌnrɪˈfrɛʃt/ *adjective.* M18.
[from UN-[1] + *refreshed* pa. pple of REFRESH *verb.*]
Not refreshed.
■ **unrefreshing** *adjective* E19.

unregarded /ʌnrɪˈgɑːdɪd/ *adjective.* M16.
[from UN-[1] + *regarded* pa. pple of REGARD *verb.*]
Not regarded or respected. (Foll. by *by.*)

> ROBERT MORRIS Architecture is so unregarded by our modern Builders.

■ **unregard** *noun* lack of regard M17. **unregardful** *adjective* L16. **unregarding** *adjective* L16.

unregenerate /ʌnrɪˈdʒɛn(ə)rət, -ˈdʒɛnəreɪt/ *adjective & noun.* L16.
[from UN-[1] + REGENERATE *ppl adjective & noun.*]
▶ **A** *adjective.* Not regenerate; inveterately bad or wrong. L16.

> A. T. ELLIS The professor was an unregenerate chaser of skirt.

▶ **B** *noun.* An unregenerate person; *the* unregenerate people collectively. E17.
■ **unregenerable** *adjective* M20. **unregeneracy** *noun* the state of being unregenerate E17. **unregenerated** *adjective* L16. **unregenerately** *adverb* E20. **unregeneˈration** *noun* lack of (esp. moral or spiritual) regeneration E17.

unrehearsed /ʌnrɪˈhəːst/ *adjective.* LME.
[from UN-[1] + *rehearsed* pa. pple of REHEARSE *verb.*]
1 Not related or mentioned; untold. LME.
2 Not previously practised. M19.

unrein /ʌnˈreɪn/ *verb trans.* E17.
[from UN-[2] + REIN *verb.*]
Cease to check or control; allow to go unchecked.

unreined /ʌnˈreɪnd/ *adjective.* E17.
[from UN-[1] + *reined* pa. pple of REIN *verb.*]
Unchecked, uncontrolled. Also, without reins.

unrelated /ʌnrɪˈleɪtɪd/ *adjective.* E17.
[from UN-[1] + RELATED.]
1 Not narrated or told. *rare.* E17.
2 Having no connection or common link. E17.
3 Not connected by blood or marriage; *BIOLOGY* not sharing a recent common ancestor. E17.

> **2** BURKE Detached and unrelated offences.

■ **unreˈlatable** *adjective* E17. **unrelatedness** *noun* M19.

unrelative /ʌnˈrɛlətɪv/ *adjective.* M18.
[from UN-[1] + RELATIVE *adjective.*]
Not relative.

unrelaxed /ʌnrɪˈlakst/ *adjective.* E16.
[from UN-[1] + RELAXED.]
Not relaxed.
■ **unrelaxing** *adjective* L18.

unreleased /ʌnrɪˈliːst/ *adjective.* LME.
[from UN-[1] + *released* pa. pple of RELEASE *verb.*]
Not released; *esp.* (of a film, record, etc.) not (yet) available to the public.

unrelenting /ʌnrɪˈlɛntɪŋ/ *adjective.* L16.
[from UN-[1] + *relenting* pres. pple of RELENT *verb.*]
Not softening or yielding; *esp.* not giving way to kindness or compassion; unmerciful, unabating, relentless.

> C. M. YONGE I don't think you can be very unrelenting when you see . . how altered he is. N. S. MOMADAY The grim, unrelenting advance of the U.S. Cavalry. A. LAMBERT The heat outside was unrelenting.

■ **unrelented** *adjective* unrelaxed L17. **unrelentingly** *adverb* M17. **unrelentingness** *noun* E18.

unreliable /ʌnrɪˈlʌɪəb(ə)l/ *adjective.* M19.
[from UN-[1] + RELIABLE.]
Not reliable; inconsistent, erratic.
■ **unreliaˈbility** *noun* E19. **unreliableness** *noun* M19. **unreliably** *adverb* E20.

unrelieved /ʌnrɪˈliːvd/ *adjective.* M16.
[from UN-[1] + *relieved* pa. pple of RELIEVE *verb.*]
1 Not freed from some obligation. Long *rare* or *obsolete.* M16.
2 Not provided with relief; not aided or assisted. M16.
3 Not freed from monotony or depression; not diversified or varied (*by* something). M18.

> **3** A. T. ELLIS We all wear unrelieved black like a funeral procession.

■ **unrelievable** *adjective* L16. **unrelievedly** *adverb* L19.

unreligious /ʌnrɪˈlɪdʒəs/ *adjective.* LME.
[from UN-[1] + RELIGIOUS.]
1 Irreligious. LME.
2 Not connected or concerned with religion. M19.
■ **unreligiously** *adverb* L15.

unremarkable /ʌnrɪˈmɑːkəb(ə)l/ *adjective.* E17.
[from UN-[1] + REMARKABLE.]
Unworthy of remark; not notable or striking; uninteresting.
■ **unremarkably** *adverb* M20. **unremarked** *adjective* L18.

unremember /ʌnrɪˈmɛmbə/ *verb trans.* L15.
[from UN-[2] + REMEMBER *verb.*]
Fail or omit to remember, forget.

unrememberable /ʌnrɪˈmɛmb(ə)rəb(ə)l/ *adjective.* E19.
[from UN-[1] + REMEMBERABLE.]
Not able to be remembered, not memorable.

unremembered /ʌnrɪˈmɛmbəd/ *adjective.* LME.
[from UN-[1] + *remembered* pa. pple of REMEMBER.]
Not borne in mind; forgotten.
■ **unremembrance** *noun* (a) lack of remembrance or recollection LME.

unremitted /ʌnrɪˈmɪtɪd/ *adjective.* M17.
[from UN-[1] + *remitted* pa. pple of REMIT *verb.*]
1 Not pardoned or cancelled. Long *rare.* M17.
2 Continuous, unremitting; not allowed to slacken or fall off. E18.
■ **unremittedly** *adverb* L18. **unremittent** *adjective* unremitting L19.

unremitting /ʌnrɪˈmɪtɪŋ/ *adjective.* E18.
[from UN-¹ + *remitting* pres. pple of REMIT *verb.*]
Never relaxing or slackening; continuing with the same force; incessant.
■ **unremittingly** *adverb* incessantly, continually L18. **unremittingness** *noun* E19.

unremorseful /ʌnrɪˈmɔːsfʊl, -f(ə)l/ *adjective.* E17.
[from UN-¹ + REMORSEFUL.]
Not remorseful.
■ **unremorsefully** *adverb* M19.

unremoved /ʌnrɪˈmuːvd/ *adjective.* LME.
[from UN-¹ + *removed* pa. pple of REMOVE *verb.*]
1 Not got rid of or done away with. LME.
2 Not moved or shifted in place. LME.
3 Fixed in place; firmly stationed. M16.
> 📖 **2** CARLYLE Bodies of Swiss lie piled there; naked, unremoved till the second day. **3** J. A. SYMONDS The mountain stands for ever unremoved.

■ **unremovable** *adjective* †(**a**) unable to be moved; fixed, steady; (**b**) unable to be removed, irremovable: LME.

unremunerated /ʌnrɪˈmjuːnəreɪtɪd/ *adjective.* L18.
[from UN-¹ + *remunerated* pa. pple of REMUNERATE.]
Not remunerated.

unremunerative /ʌnrɪˈmjuːn(ə)rətɪv/ *adjective.* M19.
[from UN-¹ + REMUNERATIVE.]
Not remunerative; bringing no or insufficient profit or income.
■ **unremuneratively** *adverb* E20. **unremunerativeness** *noun* E20.

unrenewable /ʌnrɪˈnjuːəb(ə)l/ *adjective.* M16.
[from UN-¹ + RENEWABLE.]
Not renewable, unable to be renewed.
■ **unrenewed** *adjective* L16.

unrenounced /ʌnrɪˈnaʊnst/ *adjective.* M19.
[from UN-¹ + *renounced* pa. pple of RENOUNCE *verb.*]
Not renounced.
■ **unrenounceable** *adjective* M19.

unrepair /ʌnrɪˈpɛː/ *noun. arch.* M19.
[from UN-¹ + REPAIR *noun*².]
Lack of repair; disrepair.

unrepaired /ʌnrɪˈpɛːd/ *adjective.* E16.
[from UN-¹ + *repaired* pa. pple of REPAIR *verb*².]
Not repaired.
■ **unrepairable** *adjective* E17.

unrepassable /ʌnrɪˈpɑːsəb(ə)l/ *adjective.* E17.
[from UN-¹ + RE- + PASSABLE.]
Unable to be passed again, irrepassable.

unrepealed /ʌnrɪˈpiːld/ *adjective.* L15.
[from UN-¹ + *repealed* pa. pple of REPEAL *verb.*]
Not repealed.
■ **unrepealable** *adjective* E17.

unrepeatable /ʌnrɪˈpiːtəb(ə)l/ *adjective.* M19.
[from UN-¹ + REPEATABLE.]
1 Unable to be uttered again, *esp.* too coarse to be repeated. M19.
2 Unable to be done or made again, not renewable. L19.
> 📖 **1** *Punch* An account of his most infamous exploits in unrepeatable language. **2** A. PRICE An unrepeatable opportunity to establish his credentials.

■ **unrepeataˈbility** *noun* L20.

unrepeated /ʌnrɪˈpiːtɪd/ *adjective.* L16.
[from UN-¹ + REPEATED.]
1 Not recounted or uttered again. L16.
2 Not renewed. L18.

unrepentant /ʌnrɪˈpɛntənt/ *adjective.* LME.
[from UN-¹ + REPENTANT.]
Not repentant, impenitent.
■ **unrepentance** *noun* lack of repentance; an instance of this: LME. **unrepentantly** *adverb* LME.

unrepented /ʌnrɪˈpɛntɪd/ *adjective.* L16.
[from UN-¹ + *repented* pa. pple of REPENT *verb.*]
Not repented (*of* or †*for*).
■ **unrepenting** *adjective* unrepentant L16.

unrepining /ʌnrɪˈpʌɪnɪŋ/ *adjective.* M17.
[from UN-¹ + *repining* pres. pple of REPINE *verb.*]
Not repining.
■ **unrepiningly** *adverb* E17.

unreplaceable /ʌnrɪˈpleɪsəb(ə)l/ *adjective.* E19.
[from UN-¹ + REPLACEABLE.]
Not replaceable, irreplaceable.
■ **unreplaced** *adjective* L19.

unreplying /ʌnrɪˈplʌɪɪŋ/ *adjective.* L18.
[from UN-¹ + *replying* pres. pple of REPLY *verb.*]
Not replying.
■ **unreplied** *adjective* E19.

unreported /ʌnrɪˈpɔːtɪd/ *adjective.* E17.
[from UN-¹ + *reported* pa. pple of REPORT *verb.*]
Not reported.
■ **unreportable** *adjective* E17.

unreposing /ʌnrɪˈpəʊzɪŋ/ *adjective.* E19.
[from UN-¹ + *reposing* pres. pple of REPOSE *verb*².]
Not resting, constantly active.
■ **unrepose** *noun* lack of repose; exertion, activity: M19.

unrepresentative /ˌʌnrɛprɪˈzɛntətɪv/ *adjective.* M19.
[from UN-¹ + REPRESENTATIVE.]
Not representative.
■ **unrepresentativeness** *noun* M20.

unrepresented /ˌʌnrɛprɪˈzɛntɪd/ *ppl adjective.* L17.
[from UN-¹ + *represented* pa. pple of REPRESENT.]
Not represented.
■ **unrepresentable** *adjective* M19.

unreprieved /ʌnrɪˈpriːvd/ *adjective.* M17.
[from UN-¹ + *reprieved* pa. pple of REPRIEVE *verb*¹.]
Not reprieved.
■ **unreprievable** *adjective* (now *rare*) L16.

unreproachable /ʌnrɪˈprəʊtʃəb(ə)l/ *adjective.* Now *rare.* E17.
[from UN-¹ + REPROACHABLE.]
Not reproachable, irreproachable.

unreproached /ʌnrɪˈprəʊtʃt/ *adjective.* M17.
[from UN-¹ + *reproached* pa. pple of REPROACH *verb.*]
Not reproached.
■ **unreproachful** *adjective* E18. **unreproaching** *adjective* M18.

unreproducible /ˌʌnriːprəˈdjuːsɪb(ə)l/ *adjective.* L19.
[from UN-¹ + REPRODUCIBLE.]
Not reproducible.
■ **unreproductive** /-ˈdʌktɪv/ *adjective* not reproductive M20.

unreproved /ʌnrɪˈpruːvd/ *adjective.* LME.
[from UN-¹ + *reproved* pa. pple of REPROVE *verb.*]
Not reproved.
■ **unreprovable** *adjective* (now *rare*) not able to be reproved, irreproachable LME.

unrequired /ʌnrɪˈkwʌɪəd/ *adjective.* LME.
[from UN-¹ + REQUIRED.]
1 Of a person: not requested or asked; without being asked. LME.
2 Of a thing: unasked for, unsought. E16.

unrequited /ʌnrɪˈkwʌɪtɪd/ *adjective.* M16.
[from UN-¹ + *requited* pa. pple of REQUITE *verb.*]
Esp. of love: not returned or requited.
■ **unrequitable** *adjective* (now *rare*) L16. **unrequitedly** *adverb* M19. **unrequitedness** *noun* M17.

unresentful /ʌnrɪˈzɛntfʊl, -f(ə)l/ *adjective.* L18.
[from UN-¹ + RESENTFUL.]
Not resentful.
■ **unresented** *adjective* E18. **unresentfully** *adverb* M19. **unresenting** *adjective* E18.

unreserve /ʌnrɪˈzəːv/ *noun.* M18.
[from UN-¹ + RESERVE *noun.*]
Lack of reserve; frankness.

unreserved /ʌnrɪˈzəːvd/ *adjective.* M16.
[from UN-¹ + RESERVED.]
1 Unrestricted, unlimited, absolute. M16.
2 Free from reserve; frank, open. E18.
3 Not set apart for a particular purpose; not booked in advance. M19.
> 📖 **2** JOHN BOYLE Her manners were . . easy, and unreserved. **3** *Daily Telegraph* Spectators would clamber over the unreserved seats towards the front row.

■ **unreservedly** /-vɪdli/ *adverb* M17. **unreservedness** /-vɪdnɪs/ *noun* M17.

unresisted /ʌnrɪˈzɪstɪd/ *adjective.* E16.
[from UN-¹ + *resisted* pa. pple of RESIST *verb.*]
Not resisted; not meeting with resistance. Formerly also, irresistible.
■ **unresistable** *adjective* (now *rare*) irresistible L16. **unresistance** *noun* (now *rare*) M17. **unresistedly** *adverb* L17. **unresistible** *adjective* (now *rare*) irresistible E17.

unresisting /ʌnrɪˈzɪstɪŋ/ *adjective.* E17.
[from UN-¹ + *resisting* pres. pple of RESIST *verb.*]
Not resisting.
> 📖 P. BARKER The knife slid in easily, through unresisting plastic.

■ **unresistingly** *adverb* L18. **unresistingness** *noun* E20.

unresolvable /ʌnrɪˈzɒlvəb(ə)l/ *adjective.* E17.
[from UN-¹ + RESOLVABLE.]
Of a problem, conflict, etc.: unable to be resolved.

unresolve /ʌnrɪˈzɒlv/ *noun.* L17.
[from UN-¹ + RESOLVE *noun.*]
Lack of resolve.

unresolve /ʌnrɪˈzɒlv/ *verb trans. & intrans.* E17.
[from UN-² + RESOLVE *verb.*]
Reverse a decision about (something).

unresolved /ʌnrɪˈzɒlvd/ *ppl adjective.* L16.
[from UN-¹ + RESOLVED.]
1 Of a question etc.: undetermined, undecided, unsolved. L16.
2 a Uncertain how to act; irresolute. L16. ▸**b** Uncertain in opinion; undecided. L16.
3 Not broken up or dissolved. E19.
■ **unresolvedness** *noun* the state of being unresolved, irresolution E17.

unrespectable /ʌnrɪˈspɛktəb(ə)l/ *adjective.* M18.
[from UN-¹ + RESPECTABLE.]
Not respectable.
■ **unrespectaˈbility** *noun* M19.

unrespected /ʌnrɪˈspɛktɪd/ *adjective.* L16.
[from UN-¹ + *respected* pa. pple of RESPECT *verb.*]
†**1** Unregarded, unnoticed. L16–M17.
2 Not held in respect or regard. L16.
> 📖 **2** SIR W. SCOTT I am . . an unrespected exile.

■ **unrespecting** *adjective* L16.

unrespectful /ʌnrɪˈspɛktfʊl, -f(ə)l/ *adjective.* E17.
[from UN-¹ + RESPECTFUL.]
Lacking in respect; disrespectful.
■ **unrespectfully** *adverb* (now *rare*) M17.

unrespective /ʌnrɪˈspɛktɪv/ *adjective.* L16.
[from UN-¹ + RESPECTIVE *adjective.*]
†**1** Inattentive, heedless. L16–M17.
2 Making no distinction; undiscriminating. E17.
†**3** Disrespectful, rude. E–M17.

unresponsive /ʌnrɪˈspɒnsɪv/ *adjective.* M17.
[from UN-¹ + RESPONSIVE.]
1 Unable to reply, speechless. Long *rare.* M17.
2 Not responsive; irresponsive. L18.
■ **unresponsively** *adverb* L19. **unresponsiveness** *noun* L19.

unrest /ʌnˈrɛst/ *noun.* ME.
[from UN-¹ + REST *noun*¹.]
Lack of rest. Also, disturbance, trouble, agitation.
> 📖 *Times* Full employment, high wages, and no industrial unrest.

unrest /ʌnˈrɛst/ *verb trans.* Long *rare.* LME.
[from UN-² + REST *verb*¹.]
Disturb, trouble.

unrestful /ʌnˈrɛstfʊl, -f(ə)l/ *adjective.* LME.
[from UN-¹ + RESTFUL.]
Restless, stirring, unquiet; marked by lack of rest or quiet, not restful.
■ **unrested** *adjective* (**a**) not laid to rest; (**b**) not refreshed by rest: E17. **unrestfully** *adverb* L15.

unresting /ʌnˈrɛstɪŋ/ *adjective.* L16.
[from UN-¹ + RESTING *ppl adjective.*]
Not resting.
■ **unrestingly** *adverb* M19. **unrestingness** *noun* M19.

unrestrainable /ʌnrɪˈstreɪnəb(ə)l/ *adjective.* LME.
[from UN-¹ + RESTRAINABLE.]
Not restrainable.
■ **unrestrainably** *adverb* E17.

unrestrained /ʌnrɪˈstreɪnd/ *adjective.* L16.
[from UN-¹ + RESTRAINED.]
1 Not restrained or restricted; not kept in check or under control. L16.
2 Free from restraint of manner; easy, natural. M19.
> 📖 **1** F. BURNEY Her tears . . flowed fast from unrestrained delight. *British Medical Journal* Unrestrained front seat occupants showed a higher incidence of serious injury. **2** J. A. FROUDE His letters . . are simple, easy, and unrestrained.

■ **unrestrainedly** /-nɪdli/ *adverb* M17. **unrestrainedness** /-nɪdnɪs/ *noun* L18. **unrestraint** *noun* E19.

unrestricted /ʌnrɪˈstrɪktɪd/ *adjective.* M18.
[from UN-¹ + RESTRICTED.]
Not restricted.
■ **unrestrictedly** *adverb* M19. **unrestrictedness** *noun* M19.

unretired /ʌnrɪˈtʌɪəd/ *adjective.* M17.
[from UN-¹, UN-² + RETIRED.]
Orig., not receded or retired. Now usu., not or no longer retired from work or employment.

unreturnable /ʌnrɪˈtəːnəb(ə)l/ *adjective.* E16.
[from UN-¹ + RETURNABLE.]
†**1** Admitting of no return. E16–M17.
2 Unable to be returned. M18.
■ **unreturnably** *adverb* (now *rare*) E16.

unreturned /ʌnrɪˈtəːnd/ *adjective.* L16.
[from UN-¹ + RETURNED.]
1 Not having returned or been returned. L16.
2 Not reciprocated or responded to. M17.
> 📖 **2** M. E. BRADDON She knows that her affection is unreturned, unappreciated.

■ **unreturning** *adjective* E17.

unrevealed /ʌnrɪˈviːld/ *adjective.* E16.
[from UN-¹ + *revealed* pa. pple of REVEAL *verb.*]
Not revealed; secret.
■ **unrevealable** *adjective* E17. **unrevealing** *adjective* E17.

unrevenged /ʌnrɪˈvɛn(d)ʒd/ *adjective.* M16.
[from UN-¹ + *revenged* pa. pple of REVENGE *verb.*]
Not revenged.
■ **unrevenging** *adjective* L16.

unreverenced /ʌnˈrɛv(ə)rənst/ *adjective.* LME.
[from UN-^{1} + *reverenced* pa. pple of REVERENCE *verb*.]
Not reverenced.
■ **unreverence** *noun* †(*a*) lack of reverence; irreverence; (*b*) ***your unreverence*** (*rare, joc.*), a disrespectful form of address, opp. REVERENCE *noun* 4: LME.

unreverent /ʌnˈrɛv(ə)r(ə)nt/ *adjective.* LME.
[from UN-^{1} + REVERENT.]
Irreverent.
■ **unreverend** *adjective* †(*a*) irreverent; (*b*) unworthy of reverence: M16. **unreverently** *adverb* (long *rare*) LME.

unrevived /ʌnrɪˈvʌɪvd/ *adjective.* M17.
[from UN-^{1} + *revived* pa. pple of REVIVE.]
Not revived.
■ **unrevivable** *adjective* E19.

unrewarded /ʌnrɪˈwɔːdɪd/ *adjective.* LME.
[from UN-^{1} + *rewarded* pa. pple of REWARD *verb*.]
1 Not rewarded; unrequited. LME.
2 Unpunished. E17.

unrewarding /ʌnrɪˈwɔːdɪŋ/ *adjective.* M17.
[from UN-^{1} + REWARDING.]
Not rewarding.

unrhymed /ʌnˈrʌɪmd/ *adjective.* E19.
[from UN-^{1} + *rhymed* pa. pple of RHYME *verb*.]
Not rhymed, without rhyme.

unrhythmical /ʌnˈrɪðmɪk(ə)l/ *adjective.* L18.
[from UN-^{1} + RHYTHMICAL.]
Not rhythmical.
■ **unrhythmic** *adjective* (*rare*) L19. **unrhythmically** *adverb* E20.

unridable /ʌnˈrʌɪdəb(ə)l/ *adjective.* Also **unrideable**. L19.
[from UN-^{1} + RIDABLE.]
Not ridable.

unridden /ʌnˈrɪd(ə)n/ *adjective.* L16.
[from UN-^{1} + RIDDEN *adjective*.]
Esp. of a horse: not ridden, not broken-in.

unriddle /ʌnˈrɪd(ə)l/ *verb trans.* L16.
[from UN-^{2} + RIDDLE *verb*^{1}.]
Solve or explain (a mystery etc.).
■ **unriddler** *noun* M17.

unrideable *adjective* var. of UNRIDABLE.

unrifled /ʌnˈrʌɪf(ə)ld/ *adjective*^{1}. E17.
[from UN-^{1} + RIFLED *adjective*^{1}.]
Not plundered or ransacked. Formerly also, not disordered.

unrifled /ʌnˈrʌɪf(ə)ld/ *adjective*^{2}. M19.
[from UN-^{1} + RIFLED *adjective*^{2}.]
Of a gun: not rifled.

unrig /ʌnˈrɪg/ *verb.* Infl. **-gg-**. L16.
[from UN-^{2} + RIG *verb*^{2}.]
1 *verb trans.* Divest (a ship) of all its rigging. L16. ▸**b** *verb intrans.* Remove or take down rigging. M17.
2 *verb trans. transf.* Undress. Now *dial.* L16.

unrigged /ʌnˈrɪgd/ *adjective.* L16.
[from prec. + -ED^1 or from UN-^{1} + *rigged* pa. pple of RIG *verb*^{2}.]
Divested of rigging; not provided with rigging.

unright /ʌnˈrʌɪt/ *noun.* Long *arch.* OE.
[from UN-^{1} + RIGHT *noun*^{1}.]
1 Wrong, wrongdoing, iniquity. Also, an instance of this. OE.
2 Unfairness, injustice. OE.

unright /ʌnˈrʌɪt/ *adjective.* Now *Scot.* or *arch.* OE.
[from UN-^{1} + RIGHT *adjective*.]
Not right or equitable; improper, unfair, wrong.

unrighteous /ʌnˈrʌɪtʃəs/ *adjective.* OE.
[from UN-^{1} + RIGHTEOUS.]
Not righteous or upright; unjust, wicked.
■ **unrighteously** *adverb* OE. **unrighteousness** *noun* OE.

unrightful /ʌnˈrʌɪtfʊl, -f(ə)l/ *adjective.* Now *rare.* ME.
[from UN-^{1} + RIGHTFUL.]
Unrighteous, unjust, wrong; not rightful.
■ **unrightfully** *adverb* ME. **unrightfulness** *noun* ME.

unrightly /ʌnˈrʌɪtli/ *adverb.* Now *rare.* OE.
[from UN-^{1} + RIGHTLY.]
Not rightfully; unfairly, wrongly.

unrimed /ʌnˈrʌɪmd/ *adjective.* L18.
[from UN-^{1} + RIMED.]
= UNRHYMED.

unrip /ʌnˈrɪp/ *verb trans.* Infl. **-pp-**. E16.
[from UN-^{2} + RIP *verb*^{1}.]
1 Strip (a house or roof) of tiles, slates, etc. Now *dial.* E16.
2 a Lay open or detach by ripping. M16. ▸†**b** Break (a seal); open (a sealed document). L16–M17.
3 *fig.* †**a** Bring suddenly or violently to light or notice. L16–M17. ▸**b** Open up; disclose, make known. Now *rare.* L16.

> 🕮 **2a** M. E. BRADDON He . . carefully unripped a part of one of the seams in the waistcoat. **3b** J. M. BARRIE Unrip your plan, Captain.

unripe /ʌnˈrʌɪp/ *adjective.* OE.
[from UN-^{1} + RIPE *adjective*.]
†**1** Of death: untimely, premature. OE–M17.
2 Immature; not (yet) fully developed. ME.
3 Of fruit etc.: not (yet) ready for harvesting or eating, not fully grown. ME.
■ **unripely** *adverb* L16. **unripened** *adjective* not (yet) ripened L16. **unripeness** *noun* ME.

unrivalled /ʌnˈrʌɪv(ə)ld/ *adjective.* Also *-**aled**. L16.
[from UN-^{1} + *rivalled* pa. pple of RIVAL *verb*.]
Having no rival or equal; peerless.

> 🕮 *Rhythm* The fluency of his double-bass drum work is unrivalled.

unrivet /ʌnˈrɪvɪt/ *verb trans.* Infl. **-t-**, **-tt-**. L16.
[from UN-^{2} + RIVET *verb*.]
1 Undo, unfasten, or detach by the removal of rivets. L16.
2 *fig.* Loosen, relax, undo, detach. E17.

> 🕮 **2** E. S. SHEPPARD Before I had spoken or even unriveted my gaze.

unroadworthy /ʌnˈrəʊdwəːði/ *adjective.* M20.
[from UN-^{1} + ROADWORTHY.]
Not roadworthy.

unrobe /ʌnˈrəʊb/ *verb trans. & intrans.* L16.
[from UN-^{2} + ROBE *noun*^{1} or *verb*.]
Divest of or take off a robe or robes; disrobe.

unrobed /ʌnˈrəʊbd/ *adjective.* L18.
[from UN-^{1} + *robed* pa. pple of ROBE *verb*.]
Not wearing a robe, disrobed.

unroll /ʌnˈrəʊl/ *verb.* LME.
[from UN-^{2} + ROLL *verb*.]
1 *verb trans.* Open out from a rolled-up state; display or be displayed in this form. LME.
2 *verb intrans.* Become unrolled. L16.
†**3** *verb trans.* Remove from a roll or list. *rare* (Shakes.). Only in E17.

> 🕮 **1** SIR W. SCOTT The mist . . unrolled itself upon brook, glade, and tarn. B. HEAD They unrolled their blankets and prepared their beds. J. HIGGINS Carter in the dark room . . gently unrolled the film. **2** *fig.: Independent* The action unrolls over 40 years.

unromantic /ʌnrə(ʊ)ˈmantɪk/ *adjective.* M18.
[from UN-^{1} + ROMANTIC *adjective*.]
Not romantic.
■ **unromantically** *adverb* in an unromantic manner M19.

unroof /ʌnˈruːf/ *verb trans.* M16.
[from UN-^{2} + ROOF *noun*.]
Remove the roof from.

unroofed /ʌnˈruːft/ *adjective.* E19.
[from UN-^{1} + ROOFED.]
Not provided with a roof; not roofed in.

unroost /ʌnˈruːst/ *verb.* L16.
[from UN-^{2} + ROOST *noun*^{1} or *verb*.]
1 *verb trans.* Dislodge from a roost or perch. Also *fig.*, dislodge from or drive out of a place. L16.
2 *verb intrans.* Leave a roost; *fig.* rise from bed. E17.

unroot /ʌnˈruːt/ *verb.* LME.
[from UN-^{2} + ROOT *verb*^{1}.]
1 *verb trans.* Pull or dig up by the roots, uproot; *fig.* eradicate, remove altogether. LME.
2 *verb intrans.* Become uprooted. *rare.* E17.

unrooted /ʌnˈruːtɪd/ *adjective.* M16.
[from UN-^{1} + ROOTED.]
1 Not rooted out; not uprooted. Foll. by *out.* M16.
2 Not provided with roots. M17.

unrope /ʌnˈrəʊp/ *verb.* L19.
[from UN-^{2} + ROPE *verb*.]
1 *verb trans.* Detach by undoing a rope. L19.
2 *verb intrans. & refl.* MOUNTAINEERING. Detach oneself from a rope. L19.

unroped /ʌnˈrəʊpt/ *adjective.* L19.
[from UN-^{1} + *roped* pa. pple of ROPE *verb*.]
Not tied with rope; (of climbers) not connected with rope.

unrotted /ʌnˈrɒtɪd/ *adjective.* LME.
[from UN-^{1} + *rotted* pa. pple of ROT *verb*.]
Not rotted.
■ **unrotten** *adjective* (now *rare*) L16.

unround /ʌnˈraʊnd/ *adjective.* L16.
[from UN-^{1} + ROUND *adjective*.]
Not round.

unround /ʌnˈraʊnd/ *verb trans.* E17.
[from UN-^{2} + ROUND *verb*^{2}.]
Remove or reduce the roundness of; make no longer round; *spec.* (PHONETICS) reduce or eliminate the rounding of the lips when enunciating (a vowel etc.).

unrounded /ʌnˈraʊndɪd/ *adjective.* E16.
[from UN-^{1} + ROUNDED *adjective*.]
Not rounded; *spec.* (PHONETICS) (of a vowel etc.) enunciated with the lips not rounded.

unroyal /ʌnˈrɔɪəl/ *adjective.* L16.
[from UN-^{1} + ROYAL *adjective*.]
1 Not befitting a king or queen. L16.
2 Not of royal rank or birth. E17.
■ **unroyally** *adverb* L18.

UNRRA /ˈʌnrə/ *abbreviation.*
United Nations Relief and Rehabilitation Administration.

unruffle /ʌnˈrʌf(ə)l/ *verb.* L17.
[from UN-^{2} + RUFFLE *verb*^{1}.]
1 *verb intrans.* Become smooth or tranquil. L17.
2 *verb trans.* Restore to smoothness or tranquillity from a ruffled state. E19.

unruffled /ʌnˈrʌf(ə)ld/ *adjective.* M17.
[from UN-^{1} + *ruffled* pa. pple of RUFFLE *verb*^{1}.]
1 Not affected by violent feeling; not agitated or disturbed; calm, unmoved. M17.
2 Not physically ruffled or made rough; not disarranged or untidied. E18.
■ **unrufflable** *adjective* L20. **unruffledness** *noun* M19.

unruined /ʌnˈruːɪnd/ *adjective.* E17.
[from UN-^{1} + *ruined* pa. pple of RUIN *verb*.]
Not ruined.
■ **unruinable** *adjective* (now *rare*) L17.

unrule /ʌnˈruːl/ *noun. arch. rare.* LME.
[from UN-^{1} + RULE *noun*.]
Lack of rule or government.
¶ Revived by Sir Walter Scott in 19.

unruled /ʌnˈruːld/ *adjective.* LME.
[from UN-^{1} + *ruled* pa. pple of RULE *verb*.]
1 Not ruled or governed; ungoverned, disorderly. LME.
2 Not having ruled lines. L19.
■ **unrulable** *adjective* not able to be ruled L17.

unruly /ʌnˈruːli/ *adjective & noun.* LME.
[from UN-^{1} + RULY.]
▸**A** *adjective.* **1** Not easily controlled or disciplined; ungovernable; disorderly. LME. ▸**b** Characterized by disorder or disquiet. LME.
†**2** Severe, incurable. L16–E17.
3 Stormy, tempestuous; impetuous. Now *rare.* L16.

> 🕮 **1** P. COLQUHOUN It is impracticable to control their unruly passions. P. KAVANAGH Some of the boys got unruly and did what they liked.

▸**B** *noun.* An unruly person; *collect. pl.*, *the* class of unruly people. E17.
■ †**unruliment** *noun* (*rare*, Spenser) unruliness: only in L16. **unruliness** *noun* M16.

UNRWA /ˈʌnrɑː/ *abbreviation.*
United Nations Relief and Works Agency.

unsaddle /ʌnˈsad(ə)l/ *verb trans.* LME.
[from UN-^{2} + SADDLE *noun* or *verb*.]
1 Remove the saddle from (a horse etc.). LME.
2 Dislodge (a person) from a saddle. LME.

unsaddled /ʌnˈsad(ə)ld/ *adjective.* E17.
[from UN-^{1} + *saddled* pa. pple of SADDLE *verb*.]
Not saddled.

unsafe /ʌnˈseɪf/ *adjective.* L16.
[from UN-^{1} + SAFE *adjective*.]
1 Not safe, dangerous. L16.
2 Unreliable; *spec.* (LAW) (of a verdict, conviction, etc.) likely to constitute a miscarriage of justice. E17.
Special collocations: **unsafe sex**: engaged in by people who have not taken precautions to protect themselves against sexually transmitted diseases such as Aids.
■ **unsafely** *adverb* E17. **unsafeness** *noun* L17. **unsafety** *noun* lack of safety, danger E17.

unsaid /ʌnˈsɛd/ *pred. adjective.* OE.
[from UN-^{1} + SAID *adjective*.]
Not said or uttered.

unsaid *verb pa. t. & pple*: see UNSAY.

unsaint /ʌnˈseɪnt/ *verb trans.* L16.
[from UN-^{2} + SAINT *verb*.]
Deprive of or cause to lose saintly character or status.

unsaintly /ʌnˈseɪntli/ *adjective.* M17.
[from UN-^{1} + SAINTLY.]
Not saintly or virtuous.
■ **unsainted** *adjective* not sanctified or canonized M17. **unsaintlike** *adjective* L17.

unsaleable /ʌnˈseɪləb(ə)l/ *adjective.* Also **unsalable**. M16.
[from UN-^{1} + SALEABLE.]
Not saleable.
■ **unsaleability** *noun* L19. **unsaleableness** *noun* E18.

unsanctified /ʌnˈsaŋktɪfʌɪd/ *adjective.* L16.
[from UN-^{1} + SANCTIFIED.]
Not sanctified or made holy.

unsanctify /ʌnˈsaŋktɪfʌɪ/ *verb trans.* L16.
[from UN-^{2} + SANCTIFY.]
Make unholy, profane.

unsatiable /ʌnˈseɪʃəb(ə)l/ *adjective.* Long *rare.* LME.
[from UN-^{1} + SATIABLE.]
Not satiable, insatiable.
■ **unsatiableness** *noun* M16. **unsatiate** *adjective* insatiate E16. **unsatiated** *adjective* not satiated E18.

unsatisfactory /ˌʌnsatɪsˈfakt(ə)ri/ *adjective.* M17.
[from UN-^{1} + SATISFACTORY.]
Not satisfactory.
■ **unsatisfaction** *noun* lack of satisfaction M17. **unsatisfactorily** *adverb* M17. **unsatisfactoriness** *noun* M17.

unsatisfied /ʌnˈsatɪsfʌɪd/ *adjective.* LME.
[from UN-^{1} + *satisfied* pa. pple of SATISFY.]
Not satisfied.
■ **unsatisfiable** *adjective* M16. **unsatisfiedness** *noun* M17.

unsatisfying /ʌnˈsatɪsfʌɪɪŋ/ *adjective.* M17.
[from UN-^{1} + *satisfying* pres. pple of SATISFY.]
Unsatisfactory; that fails to give satisfaction or contentment.
■ **unsatisfyingly** *adverb* M17. **unsatisfyingness** *noun* M17.

unsaturate /ʌnˈsatʃʊrət, -tjʊrət/ *noun.* M20.
[from UN-^{1} + SATURATE *noun.*]
CHEMISTRY. Any unsaturated compound; *esp.* an unsaturated fatty acid. Cf. POLYUNSATURATE.

unsaturated /ʌnˈsatʃʊreɪtɪd, -tjʊr-/ *adjective.* M18.
[from UN-^{1} + SATURATED *ppl adjective.*]
Not saturated; *spec.* in CHEMISTRY (of an organic compound etc.) having one or more multiple bonds (cf. SATURATED 2).
■ **unsatuˈration** *noun* (CHEMISTRY) the condition of an organic compound etc. of having one or more multiple bonds L19.

unsavable /ʌnˈseɪvəb(ə)l/ *adjective.* Also **unsaveable.** M17.
[from UN-^{1} + SAVABLE.]
Esp. THEOLOGY. Not savable.

unsaved /ʌnˈseɪvd/ *adjective.* M17.
[from UN-^{1} + *saved* pa. pple of SAVE *verb.*]
Esp. in THEOLOGY: not saved.

unsavoury /ʌnˈseɪv(ə)ri/ *adjective.* Also ***unsavory.** ME.
[from UN-^{1} + SAVOURY *adjective.*]
†**1** Having no taste or savour; insipid. ME–L18. ▸**b** Having no scent. M16–E18.
2 a Unpleasant or disagreeable to the taste, smell, or refined feelings; disgusting, distasteful. LME. ▸**b** Morally objectionable or offensive; having an unpleasant or disagreeable character. LME.

📖 **2a** W. COWPER The pent-up breath of an unsav'ry throng. **b** B. WEBB The unsavoury element in Parliamentary life is the intense competition for the limelight.

■ **unsavoured** *adjective* having no savour; unsavoury: LME. **unsavourily** *adverb* LME. **unsavouriness** *noun* LME.

unsaw *verb pa. t.* of UNSEE.

unsay /ʌnˈseɪ/ *verb.* Infl. as SAY *verb*^{1}; pa. t. & pple usu. **unsaid** /ʌnˈsɛd/. LME.
[from UN-^{2} + SAY *verb*^{1}.]
†**1** *verb trans.* Deny. Only in LME.
2 a *verb trans.* Withdraw, retract, (a statement etc.). L15. ▸**b** *verb intrans.* Withdraw or retract what one has said. L16.
■ **unsayable** *adjective* L19.

unscalable /ʌnˈskeɪləb(ə)l/ *adjective.* L16.
[from UN-^{1} + SCALABLE.]
That cannot be scaled or climbed, not scalable.

📖 *Nature* The almost unscalable crag on which Stirling Castle stands.

unscale /ʌnˈskeɪl/ *verb trans.* E16.
[from UN-^{2} + SCALE *noun*^{3}.]
Remove the scales from.

unscaled /ʌnˈskeɪld/ *adjective*^{1}. E19.
[from UN-^{1} + SCALED *adjective*^{1}.]
Not covered with scales.

unscaled /ʌnˈskeɪld/ *adjective*^{2}. E19.
[from UN-^{1} + *scaled* pa. pple of SCALE *verb*^{2}.]
Not (yet) climbed.

unscanned /ʌnˈskand/ *adjective.* L16.
[from UN-^{1} + *scanned* pa. pple of SCAN *verb.*]
Not scanned, unobserved.
■ **unscannable** *adjective* (esp. of verse) not able to be scanned E19.

unscepter *verb*, **-tered** *adjective* see UNSCEPTRE, UNSCEPTRED.

unsceptre /ʌnˈsɛptə/ *verb trans.* Also ***-ter.** L16.
[from UN-^{2} + SCEPTRE *noun.*]
Deprive of a sceptre.

unsceptred /ʌnˈsɛptəd/ *adjective.* Also ***-tered.** M18.
[from UN-^{1}, UN-^{2} + SCEPTRED.]
Having no sceptre; deprived of a sceptre.

unscholarly /ʌnˈskɒləli/ *adjective.* L18.
[from UN-^{1} + SCHOLARLY *adjective.*]
Not scholarly; deficient in scholarship.

📖 G. SAYER He thought Eliot's . . criticism superficial and unscholarly.

■ **unscholarlike** *adjective* unscholarly, not befitting a scholar E17.

unschool /ʌnˈskuːl/ *verb trans. arch.* E19.
[from UN-^{2} + SCHOOL *verb*^{1}.]
Deprive of teaching, unteach.

unschooled /ʌnˈskuːld/ *adjective.* L16.
[from UN-^{1} + *schooled* pa. pple of SCHOOL *verb*^{1}.]
1 Uneducated, untaught. L16. ▸**b** *spec.* Not sent to school. M19.
2 Untrained, undisciplined. L16. ▸**b** Not made artificial by education; natural, spontaneous. E19.

📖 **2** M. E. BRADDON A generous . . nature . . but unschooled and unchastened as yet. **b** M. ARNOLD The artless, unschooled perception of a child.

unscience /ˈʌnsʌɪəns/ *noun.* LME.
[from UN-^{1} + SCIENCE.]
Lack of knowledge (now *rare* or *obsolete*); unscientific thinking, pseudo-science.

unscientific /ˌʌnsʌɪənˈtɪfɪk/ *adjective.* L18.
[from UN-^{1} + SCIENTIFIC *adjective.*]
Not in accordance with scientific principles; not familiar with science.
■ **unscientifically** *adverb* L18.

unscramble /ʌnˈskramb(ə)l/ *verb trans.* E20.
[from UN-^{2} + SCRAMBLE *verb.*]
1 Reverse the process of scrambling (eggs). E20.
2 Put into or restore to order; make sense of, render intelligible, (anything muddled or intricate); disentangle (*lit.* & *fig.*); separate into constituent parts; *spec.* restore (a scrambled signal), interpret (a scrambled message). E20.

📖 **1** R. H. TAWNEY The discovery of the sage who observed that it is not possible to unscramble eggs. **2** *Listener* When the Conservatives returned to office . . they didn't unscramble the National Health Service. P. THEROUX A coded message on his company screen . . . He unscrambled it.

■ **unscrambler** *noun* a device for unscrambling scrambled messages or signals M20.

unscratched /ʌnˈskratʃt/ *adjective.* L16.
[from UN-^{1} + SCRATCHED.]
Not scratched.
■ **unscratchable** *adjective* M20.

unscreened /ʌnˈskriːnd/ *adjective.* M17.
[from UN-^{1} + *screened* pa. pple of SCREEN *verb.*]
1 Not protected, covered, or provided with a screen. M17.
2 a Not passed through a screen; unsifted. M19. ▸**b** Not investigated or checked, esp. for security or medical problems. L20.
3 Of a film etc.: not (previously) shown on a screen. L20.

unscrew /ʌnˈskruː/ *verb.* E17.
[from UN-^{2} + SCREW *verb.*]
1 *verb trans.* Slacken, unfasten, open, or detach by turning a screw or screws; loosen (a screw) by turning. E17.
2 *verb intrans.* Be slackened, loosened, removed, or removable by turning a screw or screws; (of a screw) be loosened or removed by turning. E19.

unscriptural /ʌnˈskrɪptʃ(ə)r(ə)l/ *adjective.* M17.
[from UN-^{1} + SCRIPTURAL.]
Not scriptural, *esp.* contrary to the teaching of Scripture.
■ **unscripturally** *adverb* L17.

unscrupulous /ʌnˈskruːpjʊləs/ *adjective.* E19.
[from UN-^{1} + SCRUPULOUS.]
Unprincipled; having or displaying no scruples.

📖 *Scientific American* An unscrupulous . . landlord in a slum-house area. *Spectator* Until Maupertuis' death . . Voltaire did not relent in his flood of unmerciful, unscrupulous . . ridicule.

■ **unscrupulously** *adverb* M19. **unscrupulousness** *noun* E19.

unseal /ʌnˈsiːl/ *verb trans.* OE.
[from UN-^{2} + SEAL *noun*^{2}, *verb*^{1}.]
1 Remove a seal from, break the seal of, open, (a letter, container, etc.). OE.
2 *fig.* Free from some constraining influence, allow free action to; *spec.* free from the necessity of remaining closed. L16.
3 Disclose, reveal, (a mystery etc.). *rare.* M17.

📖 **2** R. W. EMERSON Why when mirth unseals all tongues Should mine alone be dumb?

unsealed /ʌnˈsiːld/ *adjective.* LME.
[from UN-^{1} + SEALED.]
1 Not stamped, marked, or closed with a seal; lacking a seal. LME.
2 *fig.* Not formally confirmed or ratified. E17.
3 Of a road: not surfaced with bitumen or the like; untarred. Chiefly *Austral.* & *NZ.* M20.

unsearchable /ʌnˈsəːtʃəb(ə)l/ *adjective.* LME.
[from UN-^{1} + SEARCHABLE.]
Inscrutable; unable to be fully comprehended.

📖 S. JOHNSON The unsearchable will of the Supreme Being.

■ **unsearchableness** *noun* E17. **unsearchably** *adverb* E18. **unsearched** *adjective* not searched or examined E16.

unseason /ʌnˈsiːz(ə)n/ *verb trans.* Long *rare* or *obsolete.* L16.
[from UN-^{2} + SEASON *verb.*]
Deprive of seasoning or relish. Chiefly *fig.*

unseasonable /ʌnˈsiːz(ə)nəb(ə)l/ *adjective.* LME.
[from UN-^{1} + SEASONABLE.]
1 Untimely, inopportune; (esp. of a time) unsuitable, unreasonable. LME.
2 Of fish etc.: not in season. LME. ▸†**b** Not properly matured or seasoned, unseasoned. LME–M16.
3 (Of weather) not appropriate or usual for the season of the year; (of a day etc.) marked by such weather. E16.

📖 **3** P. MARSHALL The week-long, unseasonable rain.

■ **unseasonableness** *noun* E16. **unseasonably** *adverb* in an unseasonable manner; at an unsuitable time: L16. **unseasonal** *adjective* not typical of or appropriate to the time or season M20. **unseasonally** *adverb* M20.

unseasoned /ʌnˈsiːz(ə)nd/ *adjective.* L16.
[from UN-^{1} + *seasoned* pa. pple of SEASON *verb.*]
1 Of food: not seasoned. L16.
†**2** Unseasonable. L16–L18.
3 Not matured by growth or time; not habituated by time or experience. E17.

unseat /ʌnˈsiːt/ *verb trans.* L16.
[from UN-^{2} + SEAT *noun.*]
1 Dislodge from a seat, esp. one on horseback. L16.
2 Remove from some position or office. E17. ▸**b** *spec.* POLITICS. Deprive (a Member of Parliament etc.) of a seat, esp. by electoral victory. M19.

unseated /ʌnˈsiːtɪd/ *adjective.* M17.
[from UN-^{1} + *seated* pa. pple of SEAT *verb.*]
†**1** Of land: unsettled, unoccupied. *US.* M17–L19.
2 Not seated; not provided with a seat. L18.

unsecular /ʌnˈsɛkjʊlə/ *adjective.* M19.
[from UN-^{1} + SECULAR *adjective.*]
Not secular or worldly.

unsecularize /ʌnˈsɛkjʊlərʌɪz/ *verb trans.* Also **-ise.** E19.
[from UN-^{2} + SECULARIZE.]
Make unsecular; remove from lay control.

unsee /ʌnˈsiː/ *verb trans. rare.* Pa. t. **unsaw** /ʌnˈsɔː/; pa. pple **unseen** /ʌnˈsiːn/. LME.
[from UN-^{1} or UN-^{2} + SEE *verb.*]
Avoid seeing; leave or make unseen.

unseeded /ʌnˈsiːdɪd/ *adjective.* L18.
[from UN-^{1} + SEEDED.]
1 Unsown. L18.
2 SPORT (esp. TENNIS). Not seeded. M20.

unseeing /ʌnˈsiːɪŋ/ *adjective.* ME.
[from UN-^{1} + SEEING *ppl adjective.*]
†**1** Unseen, invisible. *rare.* Only in ME.
2 Not seeing, unobservant; blind. L16.

📖 **2** SOUTHEY I sat in silence, . . unheeding and unseeing all Around me. T. HARDY She might have been in a trance, her eyes open, yet unseeing.

■ **unseeable** *adjective* invisible LME. **unseeingly** *adverb* blindly, without seeing L19.

†**unseel** *verb trans.* M16.
[from UN-^{2} + SEEL *verb*^{1}.]
Chiefly FALCONRY. **1** Unstitch (the eyes of a hawk etc.); *fig.* open. M16–M17.
2 Unsew or uncover the eyes of (a hawk etc.). M16–E18.

unseely /ʌnˈsiːli/ *adjective.* Now *arch. rare.* OE.
[from UN-^{1} + SEELY.]
†**1** Unfortunate, miserable, wretched; deserving pity. OE–M16.
2 Bringing misfortune on oneself or others; mischievous, harmful; wicked. OE.
3 Causing, involving, or accompanied by, misfortune or unhappiness. OE.

†**unseem** *verb intrans. rare* (Shakes.). Only in L16.
[from UN-^{1} + SEEM *verb.*]
Seem not *to.*

unseeming /ʌnˈsiːmɪŋ/ *adjective.* ME.
[from UN-^{1} + *seeming* pres. pple of SEEM *verb.*]
†**1 a** Unbecoming, unseemly. ME–M17. ▸**b** Unsuitable for (a person). L16–E18.
2 Unapparent. *rare.* E20.
■ **unseemingly** *adverb* (*rare*) unbecomingly E17.

unseemly /ʌnˈsiːmli/ *adjective.* ME.
[from UN-^{1} + SEEMLY *adjective.*]
1 Unbecoming, unfitting; improper; indecent. ME.
2 Not comely or handsome. ME.

📖 **1** D. CECIL The middle-aged man drunk is an unseemly spectacle. E. PAWEL Her mother died. Her father remarried with unseemly haste.

■ **unseemliness** *noun* LME.

unseemly /ʌnˈsiːmli/ *adverb*. LME.
[from UN-^{1} + SEEMLY *adverb*.]
In an unseemly manner.

unseen /ʌnˈsiːn/ *adjective & noun*. ME.
[from UN-^{1} + SEEN.]
▸ **A** *adjective*. **1** Not seen; unperceived, invisible. ME.
2 Not seen before; *esp.* unfamiliar, strange, unknown. ME. ▸**b** Of a passage for translation: not previously read or prepared. L19.
†**3** Unskilled, inexperienced. Only in 17.

📖 **1** T. GRAY Full many a flower is born to blush unseen. A. STEVENS An unseen hand operating mysteriously behind the scenes. ***unsight unseen***: see UNSIGHT *adjective*.

▸ **B** *noun*. An unseen passage for translation; a translation of such a passage. L19.

📖 *Times* Time which could be used for teaching computer science . . was taken up by Latin unseens.

unseen *verb* pa. pple of UNSEE.

†**unseize** *verb trans*. L16–E18.
[from UN-^{2} + SEIZE *verb*.]
Cause (esp. a hawk) to release something held; remove (an object) from the grip of something.

unseized /ʌnˈsiːzd/ *adjective*. LME.
[from UN-^{1} + SEIZED *adjective*.]
Not seized.
■ **unseizable** *adjective* that cannot be seized or grasped E18.

unseldom /ʌnˈsɛldəm/ *adverb*. M17.
[from UN-^{1} + SELDOM *adverb*.]
not unseldom, often, not infrequently.

unselect /ʌnsɪˈlɛkt/ *adjective*. E19.
[from UN-^{1} + SELECT *adjective*.]
Not select.
■ **unselected** *adjective* not selected; random, randomly picked out: M20. **unselective** *adjective* not selective or discriminating M20. **unselectively** *adverb* E20.

unself /ʌnˈsɛlf/ *verb trans*. M17.
[from UN-^{2} + SELF *noun*.]
Deny, destroy, act contrary to the character of, (oneself, one's nature, etc.).

unselfconscious /ʌnsɛlfˈkɒnʃəs/ *adjective*. M19.
[from UN-^{1} + SELF-CONSCIOUS.]
Not self-conscious.
■ **unselfconsciously** *adverb* E20. **unselfconsciousness** *noun* M19.

unselfish /ʌnˈsɛlfɪʃ/ *adjective*. L17.
[from UN-^{1} + SELFISH.]
Not selfish; mindful of the needs, interests, etc., of others.

📖 HUGH WALPOLE Your aunt's so unselfish, she'd do herself out of anything.

■ **unselfishly** *adverb* M19. **unselfishness** *noun* E19.

unsell /ʌnˈsɛl/ *verb trans*. Orig. *US*. Pa. t. & pple **unsold** /ʌnˈsəʊld/. M20.
[from UN-^{2} + SELL *verb*.]
Dissuade a person from belief in the value or desirability of (a commodity, idea, etc.), discommend; *spec.* (also foll. by *on*) dissuade a person from buying (a commodity).

unsellable /ʌnˈsɛləb(ə)l/ *adjective*. L20.
[from UN-^{1} + SELLABLE.]
That cannot be sold, *esp.* that no one wants to buy.
■ **unselling** *adjective* (esp. of a book) that does not sell E18.

†**unseminared** *adjective*. *rare* (Shakes.). Only in E17.
[Perh. from UN-^{2} + Latin *seminar-* (see SEMINARY *noun*^{1}, *adjective & noun*^{2}) + -ED^1.]
Castrated.

unsense /ʌnˈsɛns/ *verb trans*. E17.
[from UN-^{2} + SENSE *noun*.]
Make (a person) insensible.

unsensed /ʌnˈsɛnst/ *adjective*. M17.
[from UN-^{1} + (partly) SENSE *noun* + -ED^2, (partly) *sensed* pa. pple of SENSE *verb*.]
Orig., senseless, meaningless. Later, not sensed or perceived.

unsensible /ʌnˈsɛnsɪb(ə)l/ *adjective*. LME.
[from UN-^{1} + SENSIBLE *adjective*.]
1 Insensible. Long *rare*. LME.
2 Lacking sense or intelligence; foolish, irrational. LME.

📖 **2** *Times Lit. Suppl.* Other manifestations of fear of AIDS are unsensible and counter-productive.

■ †**unsensibleness** *noun* M16–M18. **unsensitive** *adjective* insensitive E17. **unsensitized** *adjective* not sensitized L19.

unsensual /ʌnˈsɛnsjʊəl, -ʃʊəl/ *adjective*. M19.
[from UN-^{1} + SENSUAL *adjective*.]
Not sensual.
■ **unsensuous** *adjective* not sensuous M19.

unsensualize /ʌnˈsɛnsjʊəlʌɪz, -ʃʊəl-/ *verb trans*. Also **-ise**. L18.
[from UN-^{2} + SENSUALIZE.]
Make unsensual.

unsent /ʌnˈsɛnt/ *adjective*. LME.
[from UN-^{1} + *sent* pa. pple of SEND *verb*^{1}.]
1 Unsummoned, not sent *for*. LME.
2 Not sent or dispatched. M16.

unsentimental /ˌʌnsɛntɪˈmɛnt(ə)l/ *adjective*. M18.
[from UN-^{1} + SENTIMENTAL.]
Not sentimental.
■ **unsentimenˈtality** *noun* E19. **unsentimentally** *adverb* E19.

unsentimentalize /ˌʌnsɛntɪˈmɛnt(ə)lʌɪz/ *verb trans*. Also **-ise**. E19.
[from UN-^{2} + SENTIMENTALIZE.]
Make unsentimental; treat unsentimentally.

unserious /ʌnˈsɪərɪəs/ *adjective*. M17.
[from UN-^{1} + SERIOUS.]
Not serious, light-hearted.
■ **unseriously** *adverb* L20. **unseriousness** *noun* L17.

unserved /ʌnˈsəːvd/ *adjective*. ME.
[from UN-^{1} + *served* pa. pple of SERVE *verb*^{1}.]
1 Esp. of a person: not served; not attended or ministered to. ME.
2 a *LAW*. Of a writ, summons, etc.: not officially delivered to a person. LME. ▸**b** *SCOTS LAW* (now *Hist.*). Not formally declared heir to an estate, not served. L15.

📖 **1** R. HEATHCOTE His boy . . sent away unserved a customer. H. MARTINEAU Conscience awakes . . to the cry of unserved humanity.

unserviceable /ʌnˈsəːvɪsəb(ə)l/ *adjective*. M16.
[from UN-^{1} + SERVICEABLE.]
1 Of a thing: not able to be used for an appropriate purpose; unusable, unfit for use. M16.
2 Of a person: unable or failing to be useful or of service; *spec.* unfit for military service. L16.
■ **unserviceaˈbility** *noun* L19. **unserviceableness** *noun* E17.

unset /ʌnˈsɛt/ *adjective*. LME.
[from UN-^{1} + SET *verb*^{1}.]
1 Not set, arranged, or put in position; *spec.* †(***a***) (of a time or place) not prearranged; (***b***) (of a jewel) not placed in a setting, unmounted. LME.
2 a Not placed in the ground to grow; not planted. Formerly also, not transplanted. LME. ▸**b** Not provided with plants. L16.
3 Not assigned or allocated (*to* a person); unlet. L15.
■ **unsetting** *adjective* †(***a***) *rare* unseemly, unfitting; (***b***) (chiefly *poet.*) not going beneath the horizon, not setting: M16.

unset /ʌnˈsɛt/ *verb trans*. Infl. **-tt-**. Pa. t. & pple **unset**. E17.
[from UN-^{2} + SET *verb*^{1}.]
Put out of place or position; undo or cancel the setting of (anything).

unsettle /ʌnˈsɛt(ə)l/ *verb*. L16.
[from UN-^{2} + SETTLE *verb*.]
1 *verb trans*. Undo from a fixed position; unfix, loosen. Now *rare* or *obsolete*. L16.
2 *verb intrans*. Become unsettled. E17.
3 *verb trans*. Force out of a settled condition; disturb, discompose, disconcert; deprive of fixity or quiet. M17.

📖 **1** KEATS He . . strives . . to unsettle and wield A Jovian thunderbolt. **2** SHAKES. *Lear* His wits begin t'unsettle. **3** LD MACAULAY This theory, though intended to strengthen the foundations of government, altogether unsettles them. *Spectator* His mind had been unsettled by his peril. M. PAFFARD A major effect of the theory of evolution . . was to unsettle the Victorian confidence in . . 'progress'.

unsettled /ʌnˈsɛt(ə)ld/ *adjective*. L16.
[from UN-^{1} + SETTLED.]
1 Not (yet) settled, peaceful, or firmly established; restless, unstable; undecided, unresolved, open to change or further discussion. L16. ▸**b** Of weather: changeable, variable. E18.
2 Disturbed in thought or feeling; disconcerted, discomposed; nervous; *occas.* mentally unbalanced. E17.
3 a Of an estate etc.: not assigned by will. L17. ▸**b** Of a debt, bill, etc.: undischarged, unpaid. E19.
4 Not occupied by settlers. E18.

📖 **1** T. INNES The Francs . . a people unsettled, roving up and down. R. BURNS In an unsettled state, at home, I would only dissipate my little fortune. J. RUSKIN I haven't made up my mind . . and there are several other points . . yet unsettled.

■ **unsettledly** *adverb* L16. **unsettledness** *noun* E17. **unsettlement** *noun* M17.

unsevered /ʌnˈsɛvəd/ *adjective*. LME.
[from UN-^{1} + *severed* pa. pple of SEVER.]
Not severed.
■ **unseverable** *adjective* †(***a***) *rare* not able to be diverted; (***b***) inseparable, not severable: LME.

unsew /ʌnˈsəʊ/ *verb trans*. Pa. t. **unsewed** /ʌnˈsəʊd/; pa. pple **unsewed**, **unsewn** /ʌnˈsəʊn/. ME.
[from UN-^{2} + SEW *verb*^{1}.]
1 Undo the sewing of, remove the stitches from, (a garment etc.). ME.
2 Unwrap, uncover, or set free by removing stitches. LME.

unsewn /ʌnˈsəʊn/ *adjective*. M17.
[from UN-^{1} + *sewn* pa. pple of SEW *verb*^{1}.]
Not sewn; *spec.* = PERFECT *adjective* 16.
■ **unsewed** *adjective* not sewn (*up*, *together*, etc.) ME.

unsex /ʌnˈsɛks/ *verb trans*. E17.
[from UN-^{2} + SEX *noun*.]
Deprive of gender, sexuality, or the typical qualities of one or other sex.

unsexed /ʌnˈsɛkst/ *adjective*. L18.
[from prec., or from UN-^{1} + SEX *noun*: see -ED^1, -ED^2.]
That has been unsexed; lacking sexuality or the typical qualities of one or other sex.

unsexual /ʌnˈsɛksjʊəl, -ʃʊəl/ *adjective*. E19.
[from UN-^{1} + SEXUAL.]
Not sexual.
■ **unsexy** *adjective* not sexy (*lit.* & *fig.*) M20.

unshackle /ʌnˈʃak(ə)l/ *verb trans*. L16.
[from UN-^{2} + SHACKLE *noun*^{1}.]
1 Release from a shackle or shackles; *fig.* set free. L16.
2 *NAUTICAL*. Remove a shackle from (a chain etc.). M19.

unshackled /ʌnˈʃak(ə)ld/ *adjective*. L18.
[from UN-^{1} + *shackled* pa. pple of SHACKLE *verb*^{1}.]
Not shackled; free.

unshadow /ʌnˈʃadəʊ/ *verb trans*. M16.
[from UN-^{2} + SHADOW *noun* or *verb*.]
Free from a shadow or shadows; *fig.* disclose, reveal.

unshadowed /ʌnˈʃadəʊd/ *adjective*. L16.
[from UN-^{1} + *shadowed* pa. pple of SHADOW *verb*.]
Not covered or darkened by a shadow or shadows.

📖 *fig.*: J. CHEEVER Eberhart, whose plain, healthy, and unshadowed mind amazes me.

unshakeable /ʌnˈʃeɪkəb(ə)l/ *adjective*. Also **unshakable**. E17.
[from UN-^{1} + SHAKEABLE.]
That cannot be shaken; steadfast, firm, resolute.
■ **unshakeaˈbility** *noun* E20. **unshakeably** *adverb* M19.

unshaken /ʌnˈʃeɪk(ə)n/ *adjective*. LME.
[from UN-^{1} + *shaken* pa. pple of SHAKE *verb*.]
1 a Not shaken or agitated. LME. ▸**b** Not moved from a firm position or state; unweakened; steadfast, steady. M16.
2 Not shivered or cracked. *rare*. L16.

📖 **1b** STEELE A firm and unshaken Expectation of another Life. J. DUNN Fry remained unshaken by the broadsides directed against him.

■ †**unshaked** *adjective* L16–M17. **unshakenly** *adverb* L19.

unshamed /ʌnˈʃeɪmd/ *adjective*. LME.
[from UN-^{1} + *shamed* pa. pple of SHAME *verb*.]
Not put to shame; unashamed.

unshapable /ʌnˈʃeɪpəb(ə)l/ *adjective*. *rare*. Also **unshapeable**. M17.
[from UN-^{1} + SHAPABLE.]
Not shapable, *esp.* having no definite shape, shapeless.

unshape /ʌnˈʃeɪp/ *verb trans*. *rare*. LME.
[from UN-^{2} + SHAPE *noun*^{1} or *verb*.]
Deform, destroy.

unshapeable *adjective* var. of UNSHAPABLE.

unshaped /ʌnˈʃeɪpt/ *adjective*. L16.
[from UN-^{1} + *shaped* pa. pple of SHAPE *verb*.]
Not shaped; shapeless, ill-formed; unfinished.

📖 WORDSWORTH The unshaped half-human thoughts Which solitary Nature feeds.

■ **unshapen** *adjective* (*arch.*) ME.

unshapely /ʌnˈʃeɪpli/ *adjective*. ME.
[from UN-^{1} + SHAPELY.]
Not shapely.
■ **unshapeliness** *noun* M18.

unsharp /ʌnˈʃɑːp/ *adjective*. E17.
[from UN-^{1} + SHARP *adjective*.]
Not sharp, *esp.* (*PHOTOGRAPHY*) not well-defined, fuzzy.
■ **unsharpened** *adjective* not sharpened E17. **unsharpness** *noun* (*PHOTOGRAPHY*) M20.

unsheathe /ʌnˈʃiːð/ *verb trans*. LME.
[from UN-^{2} + SHEATHE.]
Draw (a knife, sword, etc.) out of a sheath or scabbard; remove (as) from a sheath or covering.
unsheathe the sword begin hostilities or slaughter.

unsheathed /ʌnˈʃiːðd/ *adjective*. LME.
[from UN-¹, UN-² + SHEATHED.]
1 Of a weapon: drawn from a sheath or scabbard; not placed or replaced in a sheath or scabbard. LME.
2 Not protected (as) by a sheath or covering. L17.

unshell /ʌnˈʃɛl/ *verb trans*. L16.
[from UN-² + SHELL *noun*.]
Extract (a nut etc.) from the shell, remove the shell or husk from. Now chiefly as ***unshelled*** *ppl adjective*.

unshelled /ʌnˈʃɛld/ *adjective*. L16.
[from UN-¹ + SHELLED.]
Not taken out of the shell or husk, not having the shell or husk removed.

unshewn *adjective* see UNSHOWN.

unshift /ˈʌnʃɪft/ *verb intrans*. M20.
[from UN-² + SHIFT *noun*.]
Release or cancel the shift key on a keyboard.

unshiftable /ʌnˈʃɪftəb(ə)l/ *adjective*. E17.
[from UN-¹ + SHIFTABLE.]
†**1** Unable to help oneself. E–M17.
2 That cannot be shifted; immovable. L19.
■ **unshifted** *adjective* not shifted; (of a keyboard character, symbol etc.) obtained without the use of the shift key: M17.

unship /ʌnˈʃɪp/ *verb*. Infl. **-pp-**. LME.
[from UN-² + SHIP *verb*.]
1 *verb trans*. Take off or disembark from a ship. LME.
2 a *verb trans*. Detach or remove from a fixed place or position. Orig. & chiefly NAUTICAL. L16. ▸**b** *verb intrans*. Be detachable; become detached. M19.
3 *verb trans*. Unbalance, upset; *spec*. unseat (a rider). E19.

> 🕮 **2** B. ENGLAND MacConnachie unshipped the single oar. W. HAGGARD Got your cameras unshipped in case you have to jump?

unshipped /ʌnˈʃɪpt/ *adjective*. E18.
[from UN-¹ + *shipped* pa. pple of SHIP *verb*.]
Not provided with a ship.

unshirted /ʌnˈʃəːtɪd/ *adjective*. *US slang*. M20.
[from UN-¹ + *shirted* pa. pple of SHIRT *verb*.]
unshirted hell, serious trouble, a bad time.

unshocked /ʌnˈʃɒkt/ *adjective*. E18.
[from UN-¹ + *shocked* pa. pple of SHOCK *verb*².]
Not shocked.
■ **unshockaˈbility** *noun* the condition of being unshockable L20. **unshockable** *adjective* impossible to shock, horrify, or disgust E20. **unshockably** *adverb* L20.

unshod /ʌnˈʃɒd/ *adjective*. OE.
[from UN-¹ + *shod* pa. pple of SHOE *verb*.]
Lacking a shoe or shoes; not shod; not wearing shoes, barefooted.
¶ Recorded earlier than SHOD *adjective*.
■ **unshodden** *adjective* (*arch*.) unshod M19.

unshoe /ʌnˈʃuː/ *verb trans*. Pa. t. & pple **unshod** /ʌnˈʃɒd/, (*rare*) **unshoed** /ʌnˈʃuːd/; pres. pple & verbal noun **unshoeing**. LME.
[from UN-² + SHOE *noun*.]
Remove a shoe or shoes from; deprive of shoes.
Comb.: **unshoe-the-horse** (*obsolete* exc. *dial*.) the fern moonwort, *Botrychium lunaria*, formerly reputed to draw the horseshoes off horses treading on it.

unshoed /ʌnˈʃuːd/ *adjective*. LME.
[from UN-¹ + SHOED.]
= UNSHOD.

unshot /ʌnˈʃɒt/ *adjective*. M16.
[from UN-¹ + SHOT *ppl adjective*.]
1 (Of a gun etc.) not fired or let off; not shot (*at*). M16.
2 Of grain etc.: that has not sprouted. M19.

unshoulder /ʌnˈʃəʊldə/ *verb*. L16.
[from UN-² + SHOULDER *noun* or *verb*.]
†**1** *verb intrans*. Dislocate a shoulder-joint. *rare*. Only in L16.
2 *verb trans*. Remove (a weapon, pack, etc.) from the shoulder or shoulders. E17.

unshout /ʌnˈʃaʊt/ *verb trans*. *rare*. E17.
[from UN-² + SHOUT *verb*.]
Undo or cancel by shouting.

> 🕮 SHAKES. *Coriol*. Unshout the noise that banish'd Marcius.

unshown /ʌnˈʃəʊn/ *adjective*. Also (*arch*.) **unshewn**. E17.
[from UN-¹ + *shown* pa. pple of SHOW *verb*.]
Not shown or revealed; hidden.

unshrine /ʌnˈʃrʌɪn/ *verb trans*. Now *rare* or *obsolete*. L16.
[from UN-² + SHRINE *noun* or *verb*.]
Remove or expel from a shrine.

unshrined /ʌnˈʃrʌɪnd/ *adjective*. Long *rare* or *obsolete*. ME.
[from UN-¹ + *shrined* pa. pple of SHRINE *verb*.]
Not enshrined; unburied.

unshrinkable /ʌnˈʃrɪŋkəb(ə)l/ *adjective*. L19.
[from UN-¹ + SHRINKABLE.]
Of fabric etc.: not liable to shrink.
■ **unshrinkaˈbility** *noun* M20.

unshrinking /ʌnˈʃrɪŋkɪŋ/ *adjective*. E17.
[from UN-¹ + *shrinking* pres. pple of SHRINK *verb*.]
Not shrinking back; unyielding, fearless, unhesitating.
■ **unshrinkingly** *adverb* E19.

unshroud /ʌnˈʃraʊd/ *verb trans*. L16.
[from UN-² + SHROUD *noun*¹ or *verb*¹.]
Remove a shroud from; *fig*. uncover, expose.

unshrouded /ʌnˈʃraʊdɪd/ *adjective*. LME.
[from UN-¹ + *shrouded* pa. pple of SHROUD *verb*¹.]
Not wrapped in or covered (as) with a shroud.

unshut /ʌnˈʃʌt/ *adjective*. LME.
[from UN-¹ + *shut* pa. pple of SHUT *verb*.]
Opened, unclosed; not shut.

unshut /ʌnˈʃʌt/ *verb*. Now *rare*. Infl. **-tt-**. Pa. t. & pple **unshut**. ME.
[from UN-² + SHUT *verb*.]
1 a *verb trans*. Open, unlock, (a door etc.). ME. ▸**b** *verb intrans*. Of a door, lock, etc.: open. LME.
2 *verb trans*. Unharness (a horse). *dial*. E19.

unshutter /ʌnˈʃʌtə/ *verb trans*. M19.
[from UN-² + SHUTTER *noun* or *verb*.]
Open or remove the shutters of (a window etc.).

unshuttered /ʌnˈʃʌtəd/ *adjective*. M19.
[from UN-¹ + *shuttered* pa. pple of SHUTTER *verb*.]
Not (yet) shuttered.

unsicker /ʌnˈsɪkə/ *adjective*. *obsolete* exc. *Scot*. ME.
[from UN-¹ + SICKER *adjective*.]
Uncertain; unsafe; insecure.

unsifted /ʌnˈsɪftɪd/ *adjective*. L16.
[from UN-¹ + *sifted* pa. pple of SIFT *verb*.]
1 Not passed through a sieve; unstrained. L16.
2 Not examined closely; unscrutinized. E17.

unsight /ˈʌnsʌɪt/ *noun*. *literary*. *rare*. LME.
[from UN-¹ + SIGHT *noun*.]
Blindness.

> 🕮 T. HARDY In vain do I urge my unsight To conceive my lost prize.

†**unsight** *adjective*. E17–E19.
[Prob. var. of UNSIGHTED *adjective*¹.]
unsight unseen, without inspection or examination.

unsight /ʌnˈsʌɪt/ *verb trans*. E17.
[from UN-² + SIGHT *noun*, *verb*.]
1 Blind. *poet*. E17.
2 Cause to lose sight of something; SPORT deprive (a player or official) of a clear view. Usu. in *pass*. E19.

unsighted /ʌnˈsʌɪtɪd/ *adjective*¹. L16.
[from UN-¹ + *sighted* pa. pple of SIGHT *verb*. Cf. UNSIGHT *adjective*.]
Not seen, unseen; unexamined; unperceived.
■ **unˈsightable** *adjective* unable to be sighted or seen LME.

unsighted /ʌnˈsʌɪtɪd/ *adjective*². L19.
[from UN-¹ + SIGHTED.]
1 Not provided with a sight or sights. L19.
2 Lacking the power of sight; blind. L20.

> 🕮 **2** *Nature* The text does not reveal how unsighted subjects fare with this prosthesis.

unsightly /ʌnˈsʌɪtli/ *adjective*. LME.
[from UN-¹ + SIGHTLY *adjective*.]
Not pleasing to the eye; ugly.

> 🕮 E. FIGES Crying always made my nose unsightly.

■ **unsightliness** *noun* E17.

unsigned /ʌnˈsʌɪnd/ *adjective*¹. L16.
[from UN-¹ + SIGNED *adjective*².]
Not signed; not identified or authorized by a signature; not contracted for employment etc.

unsigned /ʌnˈsʌɪnd/ *adjective*². M20.
[from UN-¹ + SIGNED *adjective*¹.]
Not provided with a sign; *spec*. (MATH. & COMPUTING) (of a number) not having a plus or minus sign, or a bit representing this.

unsilenced /ʌnˈsʌɪlənst/ *adjective*. E17.
[from UN-¹ + *silenced* pa. pple of SILENCE *verb*.]
Not silenced.
■ **unsilenceable** *adjective* L17.

unsimilar /ʌnˈsɪmɪlə/ *adjective*. M18.
[from UN-¹ + SIMILAR *adjective*.]
Unlike, not resembling. Chiefly in ***not unsimilar (to)***.

unsimple /ʌnˈsɪmp(ə)l/ *adjective*. M16.
[from UN-¹ + SIMPLE *adjective*.]
Not simple; complex.
■ **unsimplify** *verb trans*. make less simple; state in a more complex form: M19.

unsin /ʌnˈsɪn/ *verb trans*. Infl. **-nn-**. E17.
[from UN-² + SIN *noun*¹, *verb*.]
1 Annul (a sin) by subsequent action. E17.
2 Absolve (a person) from sin. *arch*. E17.
3 Maintain or prove to be not sinful. L17.

> 🕮 **1** BROWNING The proper process of unsinning sin Is to begin well-doing.

unsincere /ʌnsɪnˈsɪə/ *adjective*. Long *rare* or *obsolete*. L16.
[from UN-¹ + SINCERE.]
1 = INSINCERE *adjective*. L16.
†**2** Not pure, adulterated; not genuine. M17–E18.
■ †**unsincerity** *noun* = INSINCERITY M17–E18.

unsinew /ʌnˈsɪnjuː/ *verb trans*. L16.
[from UN-² + SINEW *verb*.]
Weaken the sinews of; *fig*. enfeeble; enervate.

unsinewed /ʌnˈsɪnjuːd/ *adjective*. M16.
[from UN-¹ + SINEWED.]
Having no sinews; not sinewy or strong; feeble.

unsinful /ʌnˈsɪnfʊl, -f(ə)l/ *noun & adjective*. L15.
[from UN-¹ + SINFUL.]
▸†**A** *noun*. A person who is free from sin, an innocent. Only in L15.
▸ **B** *adjective*. Not sinful; not committing or involving sin. L16.
■ **unsinfully** *adverb* LME.

unsinkable /ʌnˈsɪŋkəb(ə)l/ *adjective*. M17.
[from UN-¹ + SINKABLE.]
Esp. of a ship: unable to be sunk or submerged.
■ **unsinkaˈbility** *noun* M19. **unˈsinking** *adjective* not sinking; not subsiding: E18.

unsisterly /ʌnˈsɪstəli/ *adjective*. M18.
[from UN-¹ + SISTERLY *adjective*.]
Not sisterly; *esp*. not characteristic of or befitting a sister.

> 🕮 S. KAYE-SMITH She complained . . that Susan did not come to see her—'I call it unsisterly'.

unsizeable /ʌnˈsʌɪzəb(ə)l/ *adjective*. Also **unsizable**. M17.
[from UN-¹ + SIZEABLE.]
†**1** Unequal in size; of the wrong or inexact size. M17–E18.
†**2** Oversized; outsize. L17–M18.
3 Not fully grown; immature. M18.

unsized /ʌnˈsʌɪzd/ *adjective*¹. E17.
[from UN-¹ + *sized* pa. pple of SIZE *verb*¹.]
†**1** Underweight. *rare*. Only in E17.
2 Not made to an exact size or fit; not sorted by size. E18.

unsized /ʌnˈsʌɪzd/ *adjective*². L18.
[from UN-¹ + *sized* pa. pple of SIZE *verb*².]
Not covered, prepared, or stiffened with size.

unskilful /ʌnˈskɪlfʊl, -f(ə)l/ *adjective*. Also ***-skill-**. ME.
[from UN-¹ + SKILFUL.]
†**1** Unreasonable, improper. ME–L15. ▸**b** Undiscerning; unwise, foolish. *rare*. ME–M16.
†**2** Foll. by *of*: ignorant of; unfamiliar with. M16–M17.
3 Lacking or showing a lack of skill; inexpert (*at*); clumsy. M16.

> 🕮 **3** C. LAMB His wounds by unskilful treatment had been brought to a dangerous crisis. THACKERAY He was not unskilful at this kind of exercise.

■ **unskilfully** *adverb* ME. **unskilfulness** *noun* LME.

unskill /ˈʌnskɪl/ *noun*. Long *arch*. ME.
[from UN-¹ + SKILL *noun*.]
†**1** Improper or foolish conduct; folly; wrongdoing. ME–L15. ▸**b** Lack of reason; irrationality. LME–L15.
2 Lack of skill; inexpertness. Formerly also, ignorance (*of* a thing). M16.

unskilled /ʌnˈskɪld/ *adjective*. L16.
[from UN-¹ + SKILLED.]
1 Lacking skill or special training; inexpert; untrained. Also foll. by *in*, †*of*. L16.
2 Not requiring skill or special training; produced without skill or special training. M19.

> 🕮 **1** M. O. W. OLIPHANT A watchful readiness evident to the most unskilled eye. *Atlantic* Work . . routine enough for unskilled workers to do. **2** E. L. DOCTOROW These guys . . with their toolboxes and employment records all wanting the same dumb unskilled jobs I put in for.

unskillful *adjective* see UNSKILFUL.

unskin /ʌnˈskɪn/ *verb trans*. Infl. **-nn-**. L16.
[from UN-² + SKIN *noun*.]
Remove the skin from; skin, flay.

unskinned /ʌnˈskɪnd/ *adjective*. L19.
[from UN-¹ + *skinned* pa. pple of SKIN *verb*.]
Not having the skin removed.

unslacked /ʌnˈslakt/ *adjective*. L16.
[from UN-¹ + *slacked* pa. pple of SLACK *verb*.]
1 Unslackened. Chiefly *literary*. L16.
2 = UNSLAKED 1. M17.
3 = UNSLAKED 2. L18.
■ **unslackened** *adjective* not slackened or loosened; not reduced in force or intensity: L18. **unslackening** *adjective* not slackening M18.

unslakable /ʌnˈsleɪkəb(ə)l/ *adjective*. Also **unslakeable**. E19.
[from UN-¹ + SLAKE *verb*¹ + -ABLE.]
Unable to be slaked, unquenchable.

unslaked /ʌnˈsleɪkt/ *adjective.* L16.
[from UN-^{1} + *slaked* pa. pple of SLAKE *verb*^{1}.]
1 Of lime: not slaked. L16.
2 (Of thirst etc.) not slaked or quenched; *fig.* not appeased or satisfied. L17.

> 📖 **2** P. GAY To treat life as a tragicomedy of unslaked desire and perilous consummations.

unsleeping /ʌnˈsliːpɪŋ/ *adjective.* E17.
[from UN-^{1} + SLEEPING *ppl adjective.*]
Not or never sleeping; *fig.* vigilant, alert, attentive.

> 📖 E. LONGFORD Her great intelligence, exceptional memory and unsleeping sympathies.

■ **unsleepingly** *adverb* L19.

unslept /ʌnˈslɛpt/ *adjective.* L15.
[from UN-^{1} + *slept* pa. pple of SLEEP *verb.*]
1 Not having slept. L15.
2 Of a bed etc.: not slept *in.* M19.

> 📖 **1** D. DUNNETT She looked unslept and rather cross.

unsling /ʌnˈslɪŋ/ *verb trans.* Pa. t. & pple **unslung** /ʌnˈslʌŋ/. M17.
[from UN-^{2} + SLING *verb.*]
Remove from a sling; take down or release from a slung or suspended position.

> 📖 M. DUFFY He unslung his duffel bag.

unslip /ʌnˈslɪp/ *verb trans.* Infl. **-pp-**. E17.
[from UN-^{2} + SLIP *verb*^{1}.]
Set free; release; unleash.

unslippery /ʌnˈslɪp(ə)ri/ *adjective.* L19.
[from UN-^{1} + SLIPPERY.]
Not slippery.
■ **unslipping** *adjective* not slipping E17.

unslung *verb pa. t. & pple* of UNSLING.

unsmart /ʌnˈsmɑːt/ *adjective.* L15.
[from UN-^{1} + SMART *adjective.*]
Not smart; unstylish; not clever.

> 📖 *Listener* Forest Hill, on the unsmart edge of Blackheath.

■ **unsmartly** *adverb* L20.

unsmelled /ʌnˈsmɛld/ *adjective.* Also **unsmelt** /ʌnˈsmɛlt/. L18.
[from UN-^{1} + *smelled, smelt* pa. pples of SMELL *verb.*]
Not smelled; (of an odour) not perceived.

unsmiling /ʌnˈsmʌɪlɪŋ/ *adjective.* E19.
[from UN-^{1} + SMILING.]
Not smiling; not accompanied by a smile or smiles.

> 📖 A. LAMBERT She waited, her concentration fixed and her face unsmiling. G. MCCAUGHREAN He had an unsmiling, melancholy face, as if preoccupied with some distant sadness.

■ **unsmilingly** *adverb* L19.

unsmokable /ʌnˈsməʊkəb(ə)l/ *adjective.* Also **unsmokeable.** L19.
[from UN-^{1} + SMOKABLE.]
Not able to be smoked, not smokable.

unsmoked /ʌnˈsməʊkt/ *adjective.* M17.
[from UN-^{1} + SMOKED.]
1 Not exposed to smoke; *esp.* (of food) not cured by smoking. M17.
2 Not consumed by smoking. M18.

> 📖 **2** C. MCCARRY She snuffed out the cigarette, three-fourths of it unsmoked.

■ **unsmoking** *adjective* M16.

unsmooth /ʌnˈsmuːð/ *adjective.* L16.
[from UN-^{1} + SMOOTH *adjective.*]
Not smooth; rough, harsh; uneven.

> 📖 *Scientific American* An unsmooth surface such as a .. tablecloth.

unsmooth /ʌnˈsmuːð/ *verb trans.* E17.
[from UN-^{2} + SMOOTH *verb.*]
Make no longer smooth; ruffle, crease, wrinkle.

unsmoothed /ʌnˈsmuːðd/ *adjective.* E17.
[from UN-^{1} + *smoothed* pa. pple of SMOOTH *verb.*]
Not smoothed; left rough, uneven, or irregular.
■ **unsmoothable** *adjective* M19.

unsmothered /ʌnˈsmʌðəd/ *adjective.* M19.
[from UN-^{1} + *smothered* pa. pple of SMOTHER *verb.*]
Not smothered; not stifled or repressed.
■ **unsmotherable** *adjective* E17.

unsnap /ʌnˈsnap/ *verb.* Infl. **-pp-**. M19.
[from UN-^{2} + SNAP *verb.*]
1 *verb trans.* Undo a snap or snaps on; unfasten or release by such an action. M19.
2 *verb intrans.* Give way with a snapping sound. M19.

> 📖 **1** J. HELLER The other was .. busy .. trying to unsnap her stockings. T. TRYON He unsnapped the case of crocodile leatherette. **2** JAYNE PHILLIPS Billy heard the leather straps unsnap.

unsnapped /ʌnˈsnapt/ *adjective.* M19.
[from UN-^{1} + *snapped* pa. pple of SNAP *verb.*]
Not having snapped or given way; unbroken.

unsober /ʌnˈsəʊbə/ *adjective.* LME.
[from UN-^{1} + SOBER *adjective.*]
†**1** Uncontrolled, immoderate. LME–L17.
2 Not solemn or staid. M16.
3 Drunk; drunken. E17.
■ **unsoberly** *adverb* (long *rare*) LME. **unsoberness** *noun* M16.

unsociable /ʌnˈsəʊʃəb(ə)l/ *adjective.* L16.
[from UN-^{1} + SOCIABLE *adjective.*]
1 Not sociable or companionable; unfriendly; disliking or disinclined to seek the company of others. L16.
2 Incompatible, incongruous. E17.
3 Devoid of or precluding social intercourse. M17.

> 📖 **1** S. PLATH Trees .. screened it from view, which was considered unsociable in our community. A. S. BYATT Emily was .. unsociable, had made .. no effort to fit in. **3** H. MANN Florence is the most unsociable place ... One must either be alone or in a crowd. **unsociable hours** = *UNSOCIAL hours.*

■ **unsociaˈbility** *noun* the state of being unsociable; unsociable character, behaviour, etc.: M18. **unsociableness** *noun* E17. **unsociably** *adverb* M17.

unsocial /ʌnˈsəʊʃ(ə)l/ *adjective.* M18.
[from UN-^{1} + SOCIAL *adjective.*]
Not suitable for or seeking society; not conforming to normal social behaviour, conditions, etc.; antisocial.

> 📖 R. MACAULAY The dream of some different life .. in unsocial aloneness. C. S. LEWIS Once we killed bad men: now we liquidate unsocial elements. **unsocial hours** socially inconvenient working hours; hours outside the normal working day.

■ **unsocialist** *noun & adjective* (a person who is) not socialist L19. **unsociˈality** *noun* unsocial character or behaviour M19. **unsocialized** *adjective* not socialized M20. **unsocially** *adverb* M17.

unsodden /ʌnˈsɒd(ə)n/ *adjective.* LOE.
[from UN-^{1} + SODDEN *adjective*^{1}.]
1 Unboiled; uncooked. Long *rare* or *obsolete.* LOE.
2 Not sodden or soaked through. E19.

unsold /ʌnˈsəʊld/ *adjective.* LME.
[from UN-^{1} + *sold* pa. pple of SELL *verb.*]
Not sold; *esp.* not disposed of by sale.

> 📖 *Sunday Express* If the picture is unsold, the auctioneers are bound to pay up. *Which?* Airlines offload unsold seats to specialist ticket agents at discounted prices.

unsold *verb pa. t. & pple* of UNSELL.

unsoldier /ʌnˈsəʊldʒə/ *verb trans.* Now *rare.* E17.
[from UN-^{2} + SOLDIER *noun.*]
Cause not to resemble or be a soldier.

unsoldiered /ʌnˈsəʊldʒəd/ *adjective.* E17.
[from UN-^{1} + SOLDIER *noun* + -ED^{2}.]
Not containing or accompanied by soldiers.
■ **unsoldierlike** *adjective* unsoldierly L16. **unsoldierly** *adjective* inappropriate to or not befitting a soldier; not having the qualities of a soldier: L16.

unsolemn /ʌnˈsɒləm/ *adjective.* LME.
[from UN-^{1} + SOLEMN.]
†**1** Uncelebrated. *rare.* Only in LME.
2 Not solemn; lacking in gravity. M16.
3 LAW. Of a will: informal. L16.

unsolicited /ʌnsəˈlɪsɪtɪd/ *adjective.* L16.
[from UN-^{1} + *solicited* pa. pple of SOLICIT *verb.*]
1 Of a person: unasked; uninvited. L16.
2 Not asked for; given or done voluntarily; *spec.* (of a manuscript) sent to a publisher without having been requested. L17.

> 📖 **1** T. H. HUXLEY He had been .. civil enough to sign my certificate—unsolicited. **2** J. SUTHERLAND A hundred times as many unsolicited manuscript novels as they could .. publish. *Which?* Unsolicited calls, whether by phone or on your doorstep, are banned.

■ **unsolicitedly** *adverb* E19.

unsolicitous /ʌnsəˈlɪsɪtəs/ *adjective.* M17.
[from UN-^{1} + SOLICITOUS.]
Not solicitous, not showing care or concern.

unsolid /ʌnˈsɒlɪd/ *adjective.* L16.
[from UN-^{1} + SOLID *adjective.*]
Not solid; unsound.

> 📖 J. S. MILL The breaking up of the great unsolid structure which Charlemagne had raised.

■ **unsoˈlidity** *noun* lack of solidity M18.

unsolvable /ʌnˈsɒlvəb(ə)l/ *adjective.* M17.
[from UN-^{1} + SOLVABLE.]
†**1** Insolvent. *rare.* Only in M17.
2 That cannot be solved; insoluble. E19.
■ **unsolvaˈbility** *noun* M20. **unsolvableness** *noun* L19. **unsolved** *adjective* not solved; unresolved, unanswered: M17.

unsonsy /ʌnˈsɒnsi/ *adjective. Scot., Anglo-Irish, & north.* M16.
[from UN-^{1} + SONSY.]
1 Unlucky, hapless; ill-omened. M16.
2 Not handsome; unattractive, plain. *rare.* L19.

unsoothing /ʌnˈsuːðɪŋ/ *adjective.* M19.
[from UN-^{1} + SOOTHING *adjective.*]
Not soothing or calming; unsettling.
■ **unˈsoothed** *adjective* M17.

unsophistical /ʌnsəˈfɪstɪk(ə)l/ *adjective.* M18.
[from UN-^{1} + SOPHISTICAL.]
†**1** Unsophisticated. *rare.* Only in M18.
2 Not sophistic. L18.

unsophisticated /ʌnsəˈfɪstɪkeɪtɪd/ *adjective.* M17.
[from UN-^{1} + SOPHISTICATED.]
1 Unmixed, unadulterated, pure. M17.
2 Not altered or falsified; uncorrupted, genuine. M17.
3 Not experienced or worldly, natural, artless, ingenuous, naive; not involving advanced or refined methods or concepts, uncomplicated, basic. M17.

> 📖 **3** C. MACKENZIE He was .. unsophisticated enough to be impressed at hearing a woman called a poetess. *Nature* Telephone supplies .. tend to be unsophisticated in computer technology.

■ **unsophisticate** *adjective* unsophisticated E17. **unsophisticatedly** *adverb* L20. **unsophisticatedness** *noun* M19. **unsophistiˈcation** *noun* lack of sophistication E19.

unsought /ʌnˈsɔːt/ *adjective.* ME.
[from UN-^{1} + *sought* pa. pple of SEEK *verb.*]
1 Not searched for or sought after; not obtained by searching. ME.
2 †**a** Unassailed. *rare.* Only in ME. ▸**b** Unasked; uninvited. L15.
3 Unexamined, unexplored; untried. Now *rare* or *obsolete.* LME.

> 📖 **1** G. GREENE It was for these moments of unsought revelation that the Assistant Commissioner lived.

unsoul /ʌnˈsəʊl/ *verb trans. arch.* M17.
[from UN-^{2} + SOUL *noun.*]
Remove the soul from; *fig.* cause to lose spirit or courage.

unsouled /ʌnˈsəʊld/ *adjective.* LME.
[from UN-^{1} + *souled* pa. pple of SOUL *verb.*]
Not having a soul.

unsound /ʌnˈsaʊnd/ *adjective.* ME.
[from UN-^{1} + SOUND *adjective.*]
1 Not physically sound; unwell, unhealthy, diseased. Formerly also, wounded, injured. ME.
2 Morally corrupt; wicked, evil. ME.
3 Not mentally sound; insane. M16.
4 Unwholesome, unhealthy. L16.
5 Not based on well-grounded principles; fallacious, erroneous. Now also, unapproved, unorthodox, heretical. L16. ▸**b** Of a person: not holding sound opinions or beliefs, not reliable. L16.
6 Not solid or firm; weak, rotten; *fig.* insecure, unreliable. L16.
7 Of sleep: broken, disturbed. L16.

> 📖 **1** *Blackwood's Magazine* They were fit young schoolboys and we were unsound in wind and full of beer. **2** C. LAMB Took a pleasure in exposing the unsound and rotten parts of human nature. **3** T. S. ELIOT Unhesitatingly render a verdict of suicide while of unsound mind. **5** C. MCWILLIAM The gum is made from the feet of cows .. and is therefore ideologically unsound. *Essays in Criticism* Prediction is an unsound gridding of past patterns of event upon the future. **b** R. DAVIES Thomas was unsound, if not actually a crook. **6** E. F. BENSON You make out that the very foundations of our life are unsound.

■ **unsoundly** *adverb* †(***a***) harmfully; (***b***) in an unsound manner: ME. **unsoundness** *noun* L16.

unsounded /ʌnˈsaʊndɪd/ *adjective*^{1}. M16.
[from UN-^{1} + *sounded* pa. pple of SOUND *verb*^{1}.]
Not expressed or pronounced; not made to sound.

unsounded /ʌnˈsaʊndɪd/ *adjective*^{2}. L16.
[from UN-^{1} + *sounded* pa. pple of SOUND *verb*^{2}.]
Not sounded or tested as to depth etc.; unfathomed (*lit.* & *fig.*).
■ **unsoundable** *adjective* unable to be sounded; unfathomable: E17.

unsown /ʌnˈsəʊn/ *adjective.* LME.
[from UN-^{1} + *sown* pa. pple of SOW *verb*^{1}.]
Not sown; growing without having been sown.

unsparing /ʌnˈspɛːrɪŋ/ *adjective.* L16.
[from UN-^{1} + SPARING *adjective.*]
1 Merciless; unrelenting. L16.
2 Not niggardly; liberal, lavish, profuse. M17.

> 📖 **1** *Times Lit. Suppl.* A splendidly unsparing attack on .. a life that, it seems, cannot bring anything but unfulfilment. **2** LD MACAULAY Unsparing devotion .. and singleness of eye.

■ **unspareable** *adjective* (*rare*) †(***a***) unavoidable; (***b***) not able to be spared, unaffordable, indispensable: LME. **unspared** *adjective* ME. **unsparingly** *adverb* L15. **unsparingness** *noun* E19.

unspeakable /ʌnˈspiːkəb(ə)l/ *adjective & noun.* LME.
[from UN-^{1} + SPEAKABLE.]
▸ **A** *adjective.* **1** That cannot be expressed in words; inexpressible, indescribable, ineffable. LME.

2 *spec.* Indescribably bad or objectionable. Also (now *rare*), indescribably good or enjoyable. LME.
3 That may not be spoken (about); unmentionable. M16.
4 Unwilling or unable to speak. *US.* L19.

📖 **1** J. McDougall The psychic representation of . . unspeakable terror. **2** F. Weldon For a mother to leave her children . . was an unspeakable thing to do. M. Ignatieff The journey had been unspeakable, bumper to bumper on the country roads. **3** A. Stevens The . . taboo which rendered all sexual experience unspeakable.

▸ **B** *noun.* An unspeakable person or thing. E19.

📖 E. M. Forster I'm an unspeakable of the Oscar Wilde sort.

■ **unspeakaˈbility** *noun* (*rare*) M19. **unspeakableness** *noun* L16. **unspeakably** *adverb* LME. **unspeaking** *adjective* (*a*) not speaking; unable to speak; †(*b*) *rare* unspeakable, ineffable: OE.

unsped /ʌnˈspɛd/ *adjective.* Long *arch.* ME.
[from UN-¹ + *sped* pa. pple of SPEED *verb.*]
1 Not successfully accomplished or performed. ME.
2 Of a person: not having succeeded or prospered in a venture. LME.

unspell /ʌnˈspɛl/ *verb trans.* E17.
[from UN-² + SPELL *verb*⁴.]
1 Undo or dissolve (a spell). E17.
2 Free (as) from a spell. M17.

unspelled /ʌnˈspɛld/ *adjective.* L17.
[from UN-¹ + *spelled* pa. pple of SPELL *verb*⁴.]
Not charmed or bewitched (as) with a spell.

unspent /ʌnˈspɛnt/ *adjective.* LME.
[from UN-¹ + SPENT *adjective.*]
1 Not expended; unused. LME.
2 Not consumed or exhausted; not at an end, not over. E17.

📖 **1** A. Desai Money was unexpectedly found unspent and a water cooler bought.

unsphere /ʌnˈsfɪə/ *verb trans.* Chiefly *poet.* L16.
[from UN-² + SPHERE *noun.*]
Remove (a celestial body etc.) from its sphere; *fig.* free from confinement, release.

unspike /ʌnˈspʌɪk/ *verb trans.* L17.
[from UN-² + SPIKE *verb*¹.]
Unplug (a cannon etc.) by removing a spike.

unspiked /ʌnˈspʌɪkt/ *adjective.* E20.
[from UN-¹ + *spiked* pa. pple of SPIKE *verb*¹.]
Not spiked.

📖 *New Yorker* Unspiked punch, coffee . . and mints were served.

unspilled /ʌnˈspɪld/ *adjective.* Also **unspilt** /ʌnˈspɪlt/. L16.
[from UN-¹ + *spilled, spilt* pa. pples of SPILL *verb.*]
Not spilled.
■ **unspillable** *adjective* (of a container) from which the contents cannot be spilled L19.

unspiritual /ʌnˈspɪrɪtjʊəl/ *adjective.* M17.
[from UN-¹ + SPIRITUAL *adjective.*]
Not spiritual; earthly, worldly.
■ **unspirituˈality** *noun* lack of spirituality M19. **unspiritualize** *verb trans.* remove spiritual character or qualities from; make unspiritual: E18. **unspiritually** *adverb* L19. **unspiritualness** *noun* M17.

unspoil /ʌnˈspɔɪl/ *verb trans.* L18.
[from UN-² + SPOIL *verb.*]
Restore from a spoiled state or condition.

unspoiled /ʌnˈspɔɪld/ *adjective.* Also **unspoilt** /ʌnˈspɔɪlt/. L15.
[from UN-¹ + *spoiled, spoilt* pa. pples of SPOIL *verb.*]
1 Not despoiled or plundered. *arch.* L15.
2 Not spoiled; *esp.* not deteriorated in character or value. M18.

📖 **2** G. Greene She plays a showgirl, oh so generous and unspoilt. *Smithsonian* Millions of acres of pristine and unspoiled back country.

■ **unspoilable** *adjective* M19.

unspoken /ʌnˈspəʊk(ə)n/ *adjective.* LME.
[from UN-¹ + SPOKEN *ppl adjective.*]
1 Not spoken *of.* Long *rare.* LME.
2 Not expressed in speech, unsaid; undeclared, unmentioned. LME.
3 *Scot.* **a** Without having spoken. *rare.* L16. ▸**b** Not spoken over; collected or used in silence. *obsolete* exc. *Hist.* E19.
4 Not spoken *to*; not addressed. E17.

📖 **2** E. Figes It was an unspoken thing between them. P. Casement The most important communication from a patient is unspoken. **4** A. Trollope She had sat the whole evening through . . not speaking and unspoken to.

unspool /ʌnˈspuːl/ *verb.* M20.
[from UN-² + SPOOL *verb.*]
1 *verb trans. & intrans.* Unwind (as) from a spool. M20.
2 CINEMATOGRAPHY. **a** *verb trans.* Project or screen (a film). M20. ▸**b** *verb intrans.* Of a film: be projected or screened. L20.

📖 **1** S. Plath The spindling rivulets Unspool and spend themselves. **2a** *Daily Telegraph* 'Napoleon' is . . longer than when it was first unspooled . . at 4 hours 50 minutes. **b** *Premiere* The ten o'clock show of *Batman* . . has over an hour yet to unspool.

unsporting /ʌnˈspɔːtɪŋ/ *adjective.* M19.
[from UN-¹ + SPORTING *adjective.*]
Not sporting; not fair or generous.

📖 V. G. Kiernan Also regarded as unsporting was the hair-trigger which permitted a steadier . . fire.

unsportsmanlike /ʌnˈspɔːtsmənlʌɪk/ *adjective.* M18.
[from UN-¹ + SPORTSMANLIKE.]
Not sportsmanlike; dishonourable, unseemly.

📖 P. Goodman High pressure advertising has been . . denounced . . as giving kids an unsportsmanlike taste for publicity.

unspotted /ʌnˈspɒtɪd/ *adjective.* LME.
[from UN-¹ + SPOTTED.]
1 Not marked or decorated with spots; not stained with spots. LME.
2 *fig.* Not morally stained; unblemished, pure. LME.

📖 **2** J. Priestley A being of unspotted purity. G. Crabbe A heart unspotted, and a life unblamed.

■ **unspottable** *adjective* unable to be spotted or seen E18. **unspottedly** *adverb* L16. **unspottedness** *noun* L16.

unsprang *verb pa. t.*: see UNSPRING.

unspring /ʌnˈsprɪŋ/ *verb.* Pa. t. **unsprang** /ʌnˈspraŋ/, ***unsprung** /ʌnˈsprʌŋ/; pa. pple **unsprung**. ME.
[from UN-² + SPRING *verb*¹.]
†**1** *verb intrans.* Spring open. *rare.* Only in ME.
2 *verb trans.* Release (a mechanism) by the action of a spring. E19.

unsprung /ʌnˈsprʌŋ/ *adjective.* E20.
[from UN-¹ + SPRUNG *ppl adjective*².]
Not provided with a spring or springs; (of a floor) not suspended above a subfloor.

unsprung *verb pa. t. & pple*: see UNSPRING.

unspurred /ʌnˈspəːd/ *adjective.* M17.
[from UN-¹ + *spurred* pa. pple of SPUR *verb.*]
Not urged on (as) by a spur or spurs.

unsquare /ʌnˈskwɛː/ *verb trans. & intrans.* E17.
[from UN-² + SQUARE *verb.*]
(Cause to) lose squareness of form or structure.

unsquared /ʌnˈskwɛːd/ *adjective.* M16.
[from UN-¹ + *squared* pa. pple of SQUARE *verb.*]
Not squared, *esp.* not made square in form or cross-section.

unstable /ʌnˈsteɪb(ə)l/ *adjective.* ME.
[from UN-¹ + STABLE *adjective.*]
1 a Not keeping to one place; shifting in position; not stationary. ME. ▸**b** Not firmly fixed in place; easily displaced or overbalanced; liable to give way or shift. LME. ▸**c** Of movement: unsteady. Now *rare.* M16. ▸**d** Not firm or solid; insecure. Long *rare.* M16.
2 Of a person: not stable in character; liable to sudden changes in mood; vacillating, fickle, changeable. ME.
3 Not stable or constant in composition or nature; not firmly established; apt to change, variable. ME. ▸**b** Of a physical system, chemical compound, isotope, subatomic particle, etc.: readily or spontaneously disintegrating, decomposing or decaying. M19.

📖 **1a** T. Herbert Sands . . so light and vnstable, that the high wayes are neuer certaine. **b** *unstable* EQUILIBRIUM. **2** J. Gardner Downay . . is unstable He . . can only bring harm to any resistance movement. **3** P. Carey They didn't know about . . his unstable home life. A. Munro The man is . . younger than Isobel and . . the relationship is periodically 'unstable'. **b** *New Yorker* Someone would knowingly choose to live on . . a pile of unstable munitions.

■ **unstaˈbility** *noun* (now *rare*) instability LME. **unstabilized** *adjective* M20. **unstableness** *noun* (now *rare*) instability ME. **unstably** *adverb* LME.

unstaid /ʌnˈsteɪd/ *adjective. arch.* Also †**unstayed**. See also UNSTAYED *adjective*¹. M16.
[from UN-¹ + STAID *adjective.*]
▸ **I 1** Not staid in character or conduct. M16.
2 Of a person, belief, institution, etc.: changeable, unstable, unsettled. M16.
3 Unrestrained, unregulated. L16.

📖 **2** A. Hill While roving thus uncenter'd and unstaid. **3** Spenser To the gay gardins his vnstaid desire Him wholly caried. Shakes. *Rich. II* Will the King come, that I may breathe my last In wholesome counsel to his unstaid youth?

▸ **II** See UNSTAYED *adjective*¹.

■ **unstaidness** *noun* M16.

unstained /ʌnˈsteɪnd/ *adjective.* M16.
[from UN-¹ + *stained* pa. pple of STAIN *verb.* Cf. STAINED.]
1 Not stained; not coloured or discoloured; spotless, clean. M16.
2 *fig.* Not defiled or tainted in reputation, character, etc.; pure. L16.

📖 **1** J. Conrad The sky . . was a benign immensity of unstained light. O. Lancaster An 'artist designed' table of unstained oak. **2** Mrs H. Wood He was proud of his . . unstained name.

■ **unstainable** *adjective* L16.

unstamped /ʌnˈstampt/ *adjective.* L16.
[from UN-¹ + *stamped* pa. pple of STAMP *verb.*]
1 Not crushed by stamping. L16.
2 Not marked by stamping; not having an official stamp. E17.
3 Not having a postage stamp or stamps affixed. L19.

Unstan /ˈʌnstən/ *adjective.* M20.
[The site of a chambered tomb on Mainland, Orkney.]
Designating a type of early neolithic pottery originally found on Mainland, Orkney.

unstanchable /ʌnˈstɑːn(t)ʃəb(ə)l, -ˈstɔːn(t)ʃ-/ *adjective.* Also **unstaunchable** /-ˈstɔːn(t)ʃ-/. LME.
[from UN-¹ + STANCH *verb* + -ABLE.]
1 Unable to be stopped or restricted in flow. LME.
2 Unquenchable; insatiable. LME.

📖 **1** D. Peterley I suspect unstaunchable wounds.

■ **unstanched** *adjective* (*a*) not stopped or restricted; unsatisfied, unsated; (*b*) (long *rare*) not made staunch or watertight: LME.

unstarred /ʌnˈstɑːd/ *adjective.* M19.
[from UN-¹ + STARRED.]
Not starred; not marked or decorated with a star or stars.
unstarred question: asked in the House of Lords with the intention of raising a debate.

unstarted /ʌnˈstɑːtɪd/ *adjective.* M17.
[from UN-¹ + *started* pa. pple of START *verb.*]
1 Unstartled. Long *rare* or *obsolete.* M17.
2 Not started or begun. L19.

unstate /ʌnˈsteɪt/ *verb trans.* Long *arch.* L16.
[from UN-² + STATE *noun.*]
Deprive of status, rank, or position.

unstated /ʌnˈsteɪtɪd/ *adjective.* M19.
[from UN-¹ + *stated* pa. pple of STATE *verb.* Cf. STATED.]
Not stated or declared.
■ **unstatable** *adjective* unable to be stated or declared L19.

unstatutable /ʌnˈstatjʊtəb(ə)l/ *adjective.* M17.
[from UN-¹ + STATUTABLE.]
Not statutable; contrary to a statute or statutes.
■ **unstatutably** *adverb* L17.

unstaunchable *adjective* var. of UNSTANCHABLE.

unstayed /ʌnˈsteɪd/ *adjective*¹. *arch.* Also †**unstaid**. See also UNSTAID. E17.
[from UN-¹ + *stayed* pa. pple of STAY *verb*¹.]
▸ **I** †**1** See UNSTAID. E17.
▸ **II 2** Not stayed or stopped; unhindered, unimpeded. E17.
■ **unstayable** *adjective* M17. **unstaying** *adjective* not stopping or pausing E17.

unstayed /ʌnˈsteɪd/ *adjective*². Long *arch.* L16.
[from UN-¹ + *stayed* pa. pple of STAY *verb*².]
Unsupported, unstrengthened.

unsteadfast /ʌnˈstɛdfɑːst, -fəst/ *adjective.* ME.
[from UN-¹ + STEADFAST *adjective.*]
1 Not steadfast in belief, loyalty, etc.; inconstant, fickle, wavering. ME.
2 Unsettled or unstable in character; not firmly established; changeable. Long *rare.* ME.
3 Not securely fixed in position; not firm; unsteady, insecure. *obsolete* exc. *literary.* ME.

📖 **1** Longfellow The oscillation of a mind Unsteadfast. **3** Wordsworth Desolation stalks, afraid, Unsteadfast.

■ **unsteadfastness** *noun* ME.

unsteady /ʌnˈstɛdi/ *adjective.* L16.
[from UN-¹ + STEADY *adjective.*]
1 Not steady in position; liable to give way or overbalance; not firm or secure. L16.
2 Not steady or constant in character, behaviour, etc.; fluctuating, fickle, wavering. L16.
3 Not steady or regular in movement, pitch, etc.; uneven. L17.

📖 **1** G. Santayana Their raft was far too unsteady for standing on. K. Crossley-Holland Still rather unsteady on his feet, Odin lurched across the room. **2** R. K. Narayan He was unsteady—sometimes he announced . . his indifference to money, next minute he'd suddenly show . . miserliness. **3** R. Fuller His lower lip and voice became unsteady, and I saw tears brim his eyes.

■ **unsteadily** *adverb* M16. **unsteadiness** *noun* E17.

unsteady /ʌnˈstɛdi/ *verb trans.* M16.
[from UN-² + STEADY *adjective*.]
Make unsteady.

R. L. STEVENSON I ran to fetch it; but I was . . unsteadied . . and I broke one glass.

unsteel /ʌnˈstiːl/ *verb trans. literary.* M18.
[from UN-² + STEEL *noun*¹.]
Remove strength or determination from; enervate, enfeeble.

S. RICHARDSON Why then should this enervating pity unsteel my foolish heart?

unsteeled /ʌnˈstiːld/ *adjective.* M18.
[from UN-¹ + STEELED.]
Not (yet) steeled or strengthened; unfortified.

M. BEERBOHM Not unsteeled against the shock of a bereavement.

unstick /ˈʌnstɪk/ *noun. colloq.* M20.
[from the verb.]
AERONAUTICS. The moment of take-off.

unstick /ʌnˈstɪk/ *verb.* Infl. as STICK *verb*¹; pa. t. & pple usu. **unstuck** /ʌnˈstʌk/. E18.
[from UN-² + STICK *verb*¹.]
1 *verb trans.* Cause to become unstuck; separate (a thing that is stuck to another thing). E18.
2 *colloq.* **a** *verb intrans.* Of an aircraft: take off. E20. ▸**b** *verb trans.* Cause (an aircraft) to take off. E20.

1 P. BOWLES She unstuck the lighted candle from the chest. S. PLATH Behind the concrete bunkers Two lovers unstick themselves.

Phrases: **come unstuck** (*a*) *fig.* (*colloq.*) come to grief, fail; (*b*) (of an aircraft) take off. **get unstuck** = *come unstuck* (b) above.

unstiffen /ʌnˈstɪf(ə)n/ *verb trans. & intrans.* E17.
[from UN-² + STIFFEN *verb*.]
(Cause to) lose stiffness; loosen, relax.

unstiffened /ʌnˈstɪf(ə)nd/ *adjective.* L16.
[from UN-¹ + *stiffened* pa. pple of STIFFEN *verb*.]
Not stiffened; flexible, supple.

unstill /ʌnˈstɪl/ *adjective.* M18.
[from UN-¹ + STILL *adjective*.]
Not (keeping) still; restless, unsettled.
■ **unstilled** *adjective* not stilled or quietened; unallayed: M17. **unstillness** *noun* M19.

unstimulated /ʌnˈstɪmjʊleɪtɪd/ *adjective.* L18.
[from UN-¹ + *stimulated* pa. pple of STIMULATE *verb*.]
Not stimulated or aroused.
■ **unstimulating** *adjective* M19.

unstinted /ʌnˈstɪntɪd/ *adjective.* L15.
[from UN-¹ + *stinted* pa. pple of STINT *verb*.]
Not stinted; not given sparingly or meanly; unrestrained, liberal.

T. HARDY The genial thumping of the town band, renowned for its unstinted use of the drum-stick. A. SILLITOE I'd given my unstinted loyalty for twenty years.

■ **unstintedly** *adverb* M19. **unstinting** *adjective* †(*a*) *rare* unceasing; (*b*) unsparing, lavish: LME. **unstintingly** *adverb* M19.

unstirred /ʌnˈstəːd/ *adjective.* ME.
[from UN-¹ + *stirred* pa. pple of STIR *verb*.]
Not stirred or agitated; unmoved, unaroused.

J. RUSKIN Glassy pools, upon which the drinking cattle cast an unstirred image. H. JAMES Ways and means . . had hitherto left his fancy unstirred.

■ **unstirrable** *adjective* unable to be stirred ME. **unstirring** *adjective* (*a*) *rare* not causing to stir or move; (*b*) not stirring or moving; inactive, quiet: LME.

unstitch /ʌnˈstɪtʃ/ *verb trans.* M16.
[from UN-² + STITCH *verb*¹.]
Undo the stitches of; detach or separate by this action; *fig.* dismantle, disassemble.

Money & Family Wealth The Government is unstitching SERPS and encouraging younger people . . to be self-supporting.

unstitched /ʌnˈstɪtʃt/ *adjective.* L16.
[from UN-¹ + *stitched* pa. pple of STITCH *verb*¹.]
Not stitched; unsewn; *fig.* unattached, disconnected.

P. G. WODEHOUSE Do you mean to tell me that the thing became unstitched?

unstock /ʌnˈstɒk/ *verb trans.* M16.
[from UN-² + STOCK *noun*¹, *verb*¹.]
1 a Remove (a ship) from the stocks. Now *rare.* M16. ▸**b** Remove the stock from (a gun etc.). E18.
2 Remove a stock or supply of goods, animals, etc., from. M17.

unstocked /ʌnˈstɒkt/ *adjective.* LME.
[from UN-¹ + STOCKED.]
1 Of a gun: not fitted with a stock. LME.
2 Not provided with a stock of goods, animals, etc. M17.

unstop /ʌnˈstɒp/ *verb.* Pa. t. & pple **unstopped**, †**unstopt**; pres. pple & verbal noun **unstopping**. LME.
[from UN-² + STOP *verb*.]
1 *verb trans.* Free from obstruction; remove a stop or stopper from; unblock, open. LME.
2 *verb intrans.* Become opened or unblocked; unclog. LME.
3 *verb intrans.* Restart after having stopped. M19.

1 R. HILL Unstopping a decanter with his left hand. **2** M. BRADBURY The traffic jam unstops. Howard lets out the clutch. **3** R. H. DANA They were . . stopping and unstopping . . and fishing for three hours.

unstoppable /ʌnˈstɒpəb(ə)l/ *adjective.* M19.
[from UN-¹ + STOPPABLE.]
Unable to be stopped; that cannot be prevented.

Times Strating shot in an unstoppable goal. R. RAYNER I had come to California on an unstoppable impulse.

■ **unstoppaˈbility** *noun* M20. **unstoppably** *adverb* M20.

unstopped /ʌnˈstɒpt/ *adjective.* Also †**unstopt**. LME.
[from UN-¹ + *stopped* pa. pple of STOP *verb*.]
1 Not stopped up or closed. LME.
2 Not stopped or hindered; unchecked. E17.
3 PHONETICS. Of a sound: formed without closure of the vocal tract. Cf. STOP *noun*² 17b. L19.

unstopper /ʌnˈstɒpə/ *verb trans.* M19.
[from UN-² + STOPPER *verb*.]
Remove the stopper from.

unstoppered /ʌnˈstɒpəd/ *adjective.* M19.
[from UN-¹ + *stoppered* pa. pple of STOPPER *verb*.]
Not provided with or closed with a stopper.

†**unstopt** *adjective, verb* see UNSTOPPED, UNSTOP.

unstored /ʌnˈstɔːd/ *adjective.* E17.
[from UN-¹ + *stored* pa. pple of STORE *verb*.]
Not supplied with a store or stores; unprovided *with* something.

unstoried /ʌnˈstɔːrɪd/ *adjective.* L18.
[from UN-¹ + STORIED *adjective*¹.]
Not inscribed with historical or legendary scenes; not celebrated in legend or stories.

unstraight /ʌnˈstreɪt/ *adjective.* M17.
[from UN-¹ + STRAIGHT *adjective*¹.]
Not straight; deviating, indirect.
■ **unstraightened** *adjective* not made straight M19. **unstraightforward** /ʌnstreɪtˈfɔːwəd/ *adjective* not straightforward; indirect, complicated: L19.

unstrain /ʌnˈstreɪn/ *verb trans.* E17.
[from UN-² + STRAIN *verb*¹.]
Free from strain or tension; relax.

unstrained /ʌnˈstreɪnd/ *adjective.* ME.
[from UN-¹ + STRAINED.]
1 Not subjected to strain; free from tension, relaxed. Now also, not injured by overuse or excessive demands. ME.
2 Not passed through a strainer; not refined by straining. LME.
3 Not forced or produced by deliberate effort. L16.

unstream /ʌnˈstriːm/ *verb trans. & intrans.* M20.
[from UN-² + STREAM *verb*.]
EDUCATION. End the practice of streaming in (a school).

unstreamed /ʌnˈstriːmd/ *ppl adjective.* M20.
[from UN-¹ + STREAM *verb* + -ED¹.]
EDUCATION. Not streamed; (of school classes, children, etc.) not arranged in streams.

unstrengthen /ʌnˈstrɛŋθ(ə)n, -ŋkθ(ə)n/ *verb trans.* L16.
[from UN-² + STRENGTHEN *verb*.]
Deprive of strength; weaken.

unstrengthened /ʌnˈstrɛŋθ(ə)nd, -ŋkθ(ə)nd/ *adjective.* L16.
[from UN-¹ + *strengthened* pa. pple of STRENGTHEN *verb*.]
Not strengthened; unfortified.

unstress /ˈʌnstrɛs/ *noun.* M20.
[from UN-¹ + STRESS *noun*.]
PHONETICS. Absence of stress; the pronunciation of a syllable etc. without stress.

unstressed /ʌnˈstrɛst/ *adjective.* L19.
[from UN-¹ + STRESSED.]
Not affected by or showing signs of stress; (of a word, syllable, etc.) not pronounced with stress, unemphasized.
■ **unstressful** *adjective* M20.

unstring /ʌnˈstrɪŋ/ *verb.* Infl. as STRING *verb*; pa. t. & pple usu. **unstrung** /ʌnˈstrʌŋ/. L16.
[from UN-² + STRING *verb*. See also UNSTRUNG *adjective*.]
1 *verb trans.* Relax or remove the string or strings of (a bow, musical instrument, etc.). L16. ▸**b** *verbt & intrans. spec.* Undo the strings of (a purse); give out money (from). Now *rare.* L17.
2 *verb trans.* Detach from a string. L17.
3 a *verb trans.* Weaken or disorder (the nerves etc.); unnerve, enervate. Freq. as ***unstrung*** *ppl adjective.* L17. ▸**b** *verb intrans.* Of the nerves: relax, weaken. E20.

1 POPE His golden lyre Demodocus unstrung. **b** GEO. ELIOT My father wasn't quite so ready to unstring as some . . I know of. **2** GIBBON Unstringing the beads from the rosary of antiquity. **3** A. POWELL He was . . shaken, certainly more unstrung than Henchman after his fall. M. FLANAGAN My mind is unstrung. **b** T. HARDY My nerves unstring, . . my flesh grows weak.

unstringed /ʌnˈstrɪŋd/ *adjective.* Now *rare.* L16.
[from UN-¹ + STRINGED *adjective*.]
Not having a string or strings; not stringed. Also, not strung.

unstrung /ʌnˈstrʌŋ/ *adjective.* M17.
[from UN-¹ + *strung* pa. pple of STRING *verb*.]
Of a bow, musical instrument, etc.: not strung.

unstrung *verb pa. t. & pple*: see UNSTRING.

unstuck *verb pa. t. & pple*: see UNSTICK *verb*.

unstudied /ʌnˈstʌdɪd/ *adjective.* LME.
[from UN-¹ + STUDIED.]
1 Of a subject: not studied or learned. LME.
2 Of a person: not learned; not skilled or practised (*in* a subject). M17.
3 Not the result of deliberate effort or intention; not laboured or artificial. M17.

2 N. HAWTHORNE The young stranger . . was not unstudied in the great poem of his country. **3** *Daily Chronicle* It was an unstudied utterance which came straight from the heart.

■ **unstudiedly** *adverb* L20. **unstudious** *adjective* M17.

unstuff /ʌnˈstʌf/ *verb trans.* LME.
[from UN-² + STUFF *verb*¹.]
Remove stuffing from; empty out, unload; unblock.

unstuffed /ʌnˈstʌft/ *adjective.* L15.
[from UN-¹ + STUFFED.]
Not stuffed (up); not containing stuffing.

New York Times Early spring . . brought crisp weather, dry sidewalks and unstuffed nose.

■ **unstuffy** *adjective* not stuffy; informal, casual: E20.

unsubdued /ʌnsəbˈdjuːd/ *adjective.* L16.
[from UN-¹ + SUBDUED.]
Not subdued; still active, forceful, or intense.
■ **unsubduable** *adjective* E17. **unsubduedness** *noun* M17.

unsubject /ʌnˈsʌbdʒɪkt/ *adjective.* LME.
[from UN-¹ + SUBJECT *adjective*.]
Not subject; *esp.* not susceptible *to* a condition, influence, etc.

unsubjected /ʌnsəbˈdʒɛktɪd/ *adjective.* LME.
[from UN-¹ + *subjected* pa. pple of SUBJECT *verb*.]
Not subjected; not subjugated, subordinate, or made submissive *to* a person or thing.

unsubmissive /ʌnsəbˈmɪsɪv/ *adjective.* M17.
[from UN-¹ + SUBMISSIVE.]
Not submissive; not disposed to submit.
■ **unsubmissively** *adverb* (*rare*) M19. **unsubmissiveness** *noun* (*rare*) M19.

unsubstantial /ʌnsəbˈstanʃ(ə)l/ *adjective.* LME.
[from UN-¹ + SUBSTANTIAL *adjective*.]
1 Having no basis or foundation in fact. LME.
2 Having no material substance; lacking in substance or solidity. L16.

2 E. R. EDDISON His hand passed through branch and leaves as though they were unsubstantial as a moonbeam.

■ ˌ**unsubstantiˈality** *noun* M19. **unsubstantially** *adverb* E16.

unsubstantiate /ʌnsəbˈstanʃɪeɪt/ *verb trans.* L18.
[from UN-² + SUBSTANTIATE.]
Deprive of substance; make unsubstantial.

unsubstantiated /ʌnsəbˈstanʃɪeɪtɪd/ *adjective.* L18.
[from UN-¹ + *substantiated* pa. pple of SUBSTANTIATE.]
Not substantiated; *esp.* (of a claim, rumour, etc.), not substantiated by evidence or fact.

unsubtle /ʌnˈsʌt(ə)l/ *adjective.* LME.
[from UN-¹ + SUBTLE.]
Not subtle; obvious; clumsy.
■ **unsubtly** *adverb* M20.

unsuccess /ʌnsəkˈsɛs/ *noun.* L16.
[from UN-¹ + SUCCESS.]
Lack of success, failure; an instance of this.

A. MOTION His own poems . . register the certainty of unsuccess, loneliness and death.

unsuccessful /ʌnsəkˈsɛsfʊl, -f(ə)l/ *adjective.* E17.
[from UN-¹ + SUCCESSFUL.]
Not successful, not resulting in or attaining success.
■ **unsuccessfully** *adverb* M17. **unsuccessfulness** *noun* E17.

unsuccessive /ʌnsəkˈsɛsɪv/ *adjective.* Now *rare* or *obsolete.* E17.
[from UN-¹ + SUCCESSIVE.]
†**1** Unsuccessful. Only in E17.
2 Not characterized by or involving succession. M17.

unsufferable /ʌnˈsʌf(ə)rəb(ə)l/ *adjective & adverb.* Now *rare* or *obsolete.* ME.
[from UN-¹ + SUFFERABLE.]
▶ **A** *adjective.* **1** That cannot be tolerated or endured; insufferable. ME.
2 Too intense or severe to be borne without discomfort; causing pain or grief; unbearable. ME.
1 SWIFT The.. unsufferable cant of taking all occasions to disparage the heathen philosophers. POPE Unsufferable wrong Cries to the Gods. **2** S. PURCHAS The high ridges.. are vnsufferable for cold. DEFOE The unsufferable Torment of the Swellings.
▶†**B** *adverb.* = UNSUFFERABLY. LME–L17.
■ †**unsufferableness** *noun* LME–L17. †**unsufferably** *adverb* intolerably, unbearably; insufferably: LME–M18.

unsufficient /ʌnsəˈfɪʃ(ə)nt/ *adjective.* Long *obsolete* exc. *Scot. rare.* LME.
[from UN-¹ + SUFFICIENT *adjective.*]
Insufficient.
■ **unsufficiently** *adverb* LME. **unsufficientness** *noun* M16.

unsuit /ʌnˈs(j)uːt/ *verb trans.* M17.
[from UN-² + SUIT *verb.*]
1 Be at variance with. Long *rare.* M17.
2 Make unsuitable. M19.
2 J. DUNN The life of a don and a cleric (for which his agnosticism unsuited him).

unsuitable /ʌnˈsuːtəb(ə)l, -ˈsjuːt-/ *adjective.* L16.
[from UN-¹ + SUITABLE.]
Not suitable; *esp.* not appropriate *to* or fitted *for* a person, thing, purpose, etc.
B. LOPEZ Leather boots.. were completely unsuitable as arctic footwear. A. LURIE It was still believed in.. progressive circles that fairy tales were unsuitable for children.
■ **unsuitaˈbility** *noun* E19. **unsuitableness** *noun* L16. **unsuitably** *adverb* E17.

unsuited /ʌnˈsuːtɪd, ʌnˈsjuːt-/ *adjective.* L16.
[from UN-¹ + *suited* pa. pple of SUIT *verb.*]
†**1** Not sued *for. rare.* Only in L16.
2 Not suited; not adapted *to*; inappropriate; unfit *for.* L16.
2 JOHN ROGERS I.. am eminently unsuited to be a mother.

unsullied /ʌnˈsʌlɪd/ *adjective.* L16.
[from UN-¹ + *sullied* pa. pple of SULLY *verb.*]
Not sullied; pure; undefiled; untarnished.
P. D. JAMES His city firm.. had enjoyed an unsullied reputation for over two hundred years.
■ **unsulliable** *adjective* (*rare*) M18.

unsung /ʌnˈsʌŋ/ *adjective.* LME.
[from UN-¹ + *sung* pa. pple of SING *verb*¹.]
1 Not sung; not uttered by singing. LME.
2 Not celebrated in or by song; unrecognized. M17.
2 *Publishers Weekly* The unsung heroes behind the scenes who.. get little press coverage.

unsunned /ʌnˈsʌnd/ *adjective.* E17.
[from UN-¹ + *sunned* pa. pple of SUN *verb.*]
Not penetrated or reached by sunlight; not exposed to, illuminated, or affected by the sun; *fig.* not made public.
SHAKES. *Cymb.* I thought her As chaste as unsunn'd snow. COLERIDGE That branchless ash, Unsunn'd and damp. D. H. LAWRENCE A white, unsunned body was fishy and unhealthy.

unsupplied /ʌnsəˈplʌɪd/ *adjective.* Now *rare.* L16.
[from UN-¹ + *supplied* pa. pple of SUPPLY *verb*¹.]
1 Not supplied or provided with something. Freq. foll. by *with.* L16.
2 (Of a deficiency etc.) not made up; (of a want etc.) not met or satisfied. E17.
1 S. JOHNSON The town was.. unsupplied with almost everything necessary for supporting a siege. **2** V. KNOX Nor is the loss of a Goldsmith's.. strain unsupplied by a Cowper.
■ **unsuppliable** *adjective* (now *rare*) M17.

unsupportable /ʌnsəˈpɔːtəb(ə)l/ *adjective.* L16.
[from UN-¹ + SUPPORTABLE.]
1 Too objectionable or distressing to be endured; unendurable, intolerable. L16.
2 Indefensible; unjustifiable. E18.
1 D. BREWSTER A heat.. unsupportable by the spectators. **2** *Times* The present overregulated system of air transport was quite unsupportable.
■ **unsupportably** *adverb* M17.

unsupported /ʌnsəˈpɔːtɪd/ *adjective.* LME.
[from UN-¹ + *supported* pa. pple of SUPPORT *verb.*]
1 Not given backing or assistance. Also, unsubstantiated; not corroborated. Freq. foll. by *by.* LME.
2 Not physically supported or held up. M17.
3 PHYSICS. Of (the decay of) a radioactive substance: not maintained at a constant level by the decay of a parent nuclide. M20.
1 J. MASSON Her claim, unsupported by any evidence, is that Jung acted correctly. *She* Women friends who.. had inadvertently become unsupported single working mothers. **2** P. FRANCIS This leaves the original roof of the magma chamber unsupported, so it falls in.
■ **unsupportedly** *adverb* M19. **unsupportedness** *noun* (*rare*) L19.

unsupposed /ʌnsəˈpəʊzd/ *adverb & adjective. rare.* LME.
[from UN-¹ + SUPPOSED.]
▶†**A** *adverb.* Unexpectedly. Only in LME.
▶ **B** *adjective.* Not supposed or imagined. LME.
■ **unsupposable** *adjective* L15.

unsuppressed /ʌnsəˈprɛst/ *adjective.* E17.
[from UN-¹ + *suppressed* pa. pple of SUPPRESS.]
Not suppressed or subdued; unrestrained.
■ **unsuppressible** *adjective* (*rare*) M17.

unsure /ʌnˈʃʊə/ *adjective.* LME.
[from UN-¹ + SURE *adjective.*]
1 Not safe against attack or mishap; exposed to danger or risk. *obsolete* exc. *dial.* LME. ▸**b** Not affording or conducive to safety; unsafe, unstable. Now *rare.* LME.
2 Marked or characterized by uncertainty; dependent on chance or accident; precarious. Now *rare.* LME.
3 Not to be trusted or relied on; unreliable, untrustworthy. Now *rare.* LME.
4 Subject to doubt or question; not fixed or certain; doubtful. LME.
5 Esp. of a person: lacking assurance or confidence; not sure *of*; not knowing *whether* etc. LME.
6 Marked or characterized by lack of sureness; faltering; irresolute. M17.
1b BURKE Utterly unsafe to touch, and unsure to stand on. **2** J. DUNCOMBE Whose houses are as unsure a possession, as if they were built with cards. **3** R. L. STEVENSON Keep an eye on Sir Daniel; he is unsure. **4** R. CARPENTER The speedy approach of death, sure in the end, vnsure in the time. **5** R. G. MYERS Researchers.. are often unsure of themselves. They need reinforcement from colleagues. JOHN ROGERS Clare stood.. as if unsure whether to come in or go out.
■ **unsurely** *adverb* LME. **unsureness** *noun* LME. **unsurety** *noun* (long *rare*) LME.

unsurmountable /ʌnsəˈmaʊntəb(ə)l/ *adjective.* E17.
[from UN-¹ + SURMOUNTABLE.]
1 That cannot be surpassed or exceeded. Long *rare.* E17.
2 That cannot be surmounted or overcome; insurmountable. E18.

unsurpassable /ʌnsəˈpɑːsəb(ə)l/ *adjective.* E17.
[from UN-¹ + SURPASSABLE.]
Not surpassable; unable to be surpassed in quality, degree, etc.
■ **unsurpassably** *adverb* M19.

unsurpassed /ʌnsəˈpɑːst/ *adjective.* L18.
[from UN-¹ + *surpassed* pa. pple of SURPASS.]
Not surpassed; matchless.

unsusceptible /ʌnsəˈsɛptɪb(ə)l/ *adjective.* L17.
[from UN-¹ + SUSCEPTIBLE *adjective.*]
†**1** Unable to receive and retain. Only in L17.
2 Not susceptible; insusceptible. M18.
2 LD MACAULAY His serene intellect, singularly unsusceptible of enthusiasm.
■ **unsusceptiˈbility** *noun* L18.

unsuspected /ʌnsəˈspɛktɪd/ *adjective.* L15.
[from UN-¹ + SUSPECTED.]
1 Not thought to exist or to be such; not imagined possible or likely. L15.
2 Not suspected; not regarded with suspicion. E16.
1 SHAKES. *Rich. III* That ignoble traitor, The dangerous and unsuspected Hastings. A. LURIE People we.. overlook have unsuspected powers. **2** COLERIDGE I had.. stolen unnotic'd on them, And unsuspected.. heard the whole.
■ **unsuspectable** *adjective* M17. **unsuspectedly** *adverb* M17. **unsuspectedness** *noun* (long *rare* or *obsolete*) M17.

unsuspecting /ʌnsəˈspɛktɪŋ/ *adjective.* L16.
[from UN-¹ + *suspecting* pres. pple of SUSPECT *verb.*]
Not suspecting; not harbouring any suspicion.
J. B. MORTON Deceived.. into thinking the bird harmless, the unsuspecting victim makes friendly overtures.
■ **unsuspectingly** *adverb* M17. **unsuspectingness** *noun* E19.

unsuspicion /ʌnsəˈspɪʃ(ə)n/ *noun. rare.* L18.
[from UN-¹ + SUSPICION *noun.*]
Lack of suspicion or suspiciousness.

unsuspicious /ʌnsəˈspɪʃəs/ *adjective.* L16.
[from UN-¹ + SUSPICIOUS.]
Not suspicious; not inviting suspicion; not disposed to suspect.
■ **unsuspiciously** *adverb* E19. **unsuspiciousness** *noun* E19.

unsustained /ʌnsəˈsteɪnd/ *adjective.* M17.
[from UN-¹ + SUSTAINED.]
Not sustained; *esp.* not supported materially or as valid, correct, etc.
■ **unsustainaˈbility** *noun* the quality of not being sustainable L20. **unsustainable** *adjective* L17. **unsustainably** *adverb* M20. **unsustaining** *adjective* not sustaining; (of food) not nutritious: E19.

unswayed /ʌnˈsweɪd/ *adjective.* L16.
[from UN-¹ + *swayed* pa. pple of SWAY *verb.*]
†**1** Unwielded; uncontrolled. *rare* (Shakes.). Only in L16.
2 Uninfluenced, unaffected. E17.
3 Unmoved, unstirred. *rare.* M19.
■ **unswayable** *adjective* unable to be influenced E17.

unswear /ʌnˈswɛː/ *verb trans. & intrans.* Pa. t. **unswore** /ʌnˈswɔː/; pa. pple **unsworn** /ʌnˈswɔːn/. L16.
[from UN-² + SWEAR *verb.*]
Retract (something sworn or asserted).

unsweet /ʌnˈswiːt/ *adjective.* OE.
[from UN-¹ + SWEET *adjective.*]
1 Unpleasant, disagreeable, unattractive. OE.
2 a Not sweet or pleasant to the taste; sour. Now *rare.* LME. ▸**b** Not smelling sweetly. L15. ▸**c** Unpleasant to the ear; discordant. L16.
1 B. MALAMUD The not unsweet remembrance of past triumphs. **2c** MRS H. WARD A little laugh, which.. was not unsweet.

unsweeten /ʌnˈswiːt(ə)n/ *verb trans.* Long *rare.* E17.
[from UN-² + SWEETEN.]
Make sour; take the sweetness from (*lit.* & *fig.*).

unsweetened /ʌnˈswiːt(ə)nd/ *adjective & noun.* E19.
[from UN-¹ + *sweetened* pa. pple of SWEETEN.]
▶ **A** *adjective.* Not sweetened. E19.
▶ **B** *ellipt.* as *noun.* Unsweetened gin. *colloq.* (now *rare*). L19.

unswept /ʌnˈswɛpt/ *adjective.* L16.
[from UN-¹ + SWEPT *adjective.*]
1 That has not been swept. L16.
2 AERONAUTICS. Of the wing of an aircraft: not swept-back, not having sweepback or sweep-forward. M20.

unswerving /ʌnˈswəːvɪŋ/ *adjective.* L17.
[from UN-¹ + *swerving* pres. pple of SWERVE *verb.*]
Not turning aside; steady, constant; unwavering in one's loyalty etc.
■ **unswervingly** *adverb* E19.

unswore *verb pa. t.* of UNSWEAR.

unsworn /ʌnˈswɔːn/ *adjective.* E16.
[from UN-¹ + SWORN *adjective.*]
1 Of a person: not subjected to or bound by an oath. E16.
2 Not confirmed by or sworn as an oath. E17.

unsworn *verb pa. pple* of UNSWEAR.

unsympathetic /ˌʌnsɪmpəˈθɛtɪk/ *adjective.* E19.
[from UN-¹ + SYMPATHETIC *adjective.*]
Not sympathetic; not capable of feeling sympathy; not in sympathy with a person or thing.
J. CALDER Deep divisions with his family, who were unsympathetic towards his liaison with Fanny. *Which?* Unsympathetic improvements [to a house] could actually *reduce* value.
■ **unsympathetically** *adverb* M19.

unsystematic /ˌʌnsɪstəˈmatɪk/ *adjective.* L18.
[from UN-¹ + SYSTEMATIC *adjective.*]
Not systematic; not organized or conducted according to a system.
■ **unsystematically** *adverb* M18.

unsystematized /ʌnˈsɪstəmətʌɪzd/ *adjective.* Also **-ised**. M19.
[from UN-¹ + *systematized* pa. pple of SYSTEMATIZE.]
Not systematized.
■ **unsystematizable** *adjective* L18.

untack /ʌnˈtak/ *verb*¹ *trans.* M17.
[from UN-² + TACK *verb*¹.]
1 Take apart, break up. Long *rare* or *obsolete.* M17.
2 Detach, esp. by removing tacks. M17.

untack /ʌnˈtak/ *verb*² *trans.* M20.
[from UN-² + TACK *noun*⁶.]
Remove the saddle and bridle from (a horse).

untackle /ʌnˈtak(ə)l/ *verb trans.* M16.
[from UN-² + TACKLE *verb.*]
1 Strip (a ship) of tackle. Now *rare.* M16.
2 Unharness (a horse). L16.
3 Free from tackling; unfasten. E20.

untainted /ʌnˈteɪntɪd/ *adjective.* L16.
[from UN-¹ + TAINTED.]
†**1** Not attainted. *rare* (Shakes.). Only in L16. ▸**b** Not dishonoured. *rare.* Only in E17.
2 Not tainted; not affected by a taint; unblemished. Freq. foll. by *by.* L16.
2 A. PRICE Youth, untainted by experience. *Health Shopper* Foods grown in a safe, untainted environment.
■ **untaintable** *adjective* E17. **untaintedness** *noun* (*rare*) M17.

For other words beginning with *un-* see the entries for **un-¹**, **un-²**

untaken /ʌnˈteɪk(ə)n/ *adjective*. ME.
[from UN-¹ + *taken* pa. pple of TAKE *verb*.]
1 Not taken by force; uncaptured. ME.
2 *gen.* Not taken; not taken *from, away, up*, etc. LME.

📖 **2** T. MALLON Diaries that contain the . . revenges untaken.

■ **untakable** *adjective* (*rare*) unable to be taken, esp. by force M17.

untamable *adjective* var. of UNTAMEABLE.

untame /ʌnˈteɪm/ *adjective*. Now *rare*. LME.
[from UN-¹ + TAME *adjective*.]
Not tame or gentle; wild.
■ **untameness** *noun* E18.

untameable /ʌnˈteɪməb(ə)l/ *adjective*. Also **untamable**. M16.
[from UN-¹ + TAMEABLE.]
Not tameable.
■ **untameableness** *noun* M17.

untamed /ʌnˈteɪmd/ *adjective*. ME.
[from UN-¹ + *tamed* pa. pple of TAME *verb*¹.]
Not tamed; wild; unsubdued.

untapped /ʌnˈtapt/ *adjective*. L18.
[from UN-¹ + *tapped* pa. pple of TAP *verb*¹.]
Not (yet) tapped; unexploited; (of a telephone etc.) free from listening devices.

📖 A. S. BYATT Ellen was raging with . . untapped talent. *Soviet Life* The Caspian oil-bearing region is only one of our untapped large reservoirs.

■ **untappable** *adjective* E20.

untarnished /ʌnˈtɑːnɪʃt/ *adjective*. M18.
[from UN-¹ + *tarnished* pa. pple of TARNISH *verb*.]
Not tarnished; lustrous; unsullied.
■ **untarnishable** *adjective* L19.

untaught /ʌnˈtɔːt/ *adjective*. ME.
[from UN-¹ + TAUGHT *adjective*¹.]
1 Not trained by teaching; uninstructed; ignorant. ME.
2 Not imparted or acquired by teaching; natural, spontaneous. LME.

📖 **1** C. BRONTË Wholly untaught, with faculties quite torpid. **2** STEELE I have a . . pretty untaught Step in Dancing.

untaught *verb pa. t. & pple* of UNTEACH.

untaxed /ʌnˈtakst/ *adjective*. LME.
[from UN-¹ + TAXED.]
†**1** Unassailed; unchallenged. LME–L17.
2 Not required to pay taxes. LME. ▸**b** Of money or a commodity: not subject to taxation; that has not had tax paid on it. M19.
■ **untaxable** *adjective* †(**a**) that cannot be accused of an offence etc.; (**b**) not liable or subject to taxation: E17.

unteach /ʌnˈtiːtʃ/ *verb*. Pa. t. & pple **untaught** /ʌnˈtɔːt/. M16.
[from UN-² + TEACH *verb*.]
1 *verb trans.* Cause (a person) to forget or discard previous knowledge. Also with double obj. M16.
2 *verb intrans.* Undo previous knowledge or teaching. M16.
3 *verb trans.* Expel from the mind (something known or taught) by instilling with different knowledge or training. M16.

📖 **1** R. BOYLE The Reading of the Bible untaught them the Purity of the Roman Language.

unteachable /ʌnˈtiːtʃəb(ə)l/ *adjective*. L15.
[from UN-¹ + TEACHABLE.]
1 Not able to be taught; not receptive to instruction. L15.
2 That cannot be imparted by teaching. M17.
■ **unteachableness** *noun* E17.

untellable /ʌnˈtɛləb(ə)l/ *adjective*. LME.
[from UN-¹ + TELLABLE.]
Unspeakable, unutterable; indescribable.
¶ Not recorded between M16 and M19.
■ **untellably** *adverb* LME.

untelling /ʌnˈtɛlɪŋ/ *adjective*. *Scot., north., & US dial.* ME.
[from UN-¹ + TELLING *adjective*.]
1 Innumerable, countless. ME.
2 Untellable. E19.

untempered /ʌnˈtɛmpəd/ *adjective*. LME.
[from UN-¹ + TEMPERED.]
1 Unregulated; not moderated or controlled; (freq. foll. by *by*) unmodified. LME.
2 Of lime or mortar: not properly mixed and prepared. LME.
3 Of metal etc.: not brought to the required degree of hardness. E19.

📖 **1** A. TAN The darkness within, where untempered passions lie. A. N. WILSON These . . abhor murder, dishonesty . . ruthless 'justice' untempered by mercy.

■ †**untempering** *adjective* (*rare*, Shakes.) not ingratiating: only in L16.

untempted /ʌnˈtɛm(p)tɪd/ *adjective*. E17.
[from UN-¹ + *tempted* pa. pple of TEMPT.]
1 Not tempted; not subjected to temptation. E17.
2 Not due to or resulting from temptation or enticement. *rare*. M18.
■ **untemptable** *adjective* E19.

untempting /ʌnˈtɛm(p)tɪŋ/ *adjective*. E19.
[from UN-¹ + TEMPTING *adjective*.]
Not tempting; unattractive, uninviting.
■ **untemptingly** *adverb* M19.

untenable /ʌnˈtɛnəb(ə)l/ *adjective*. M17.
[from UN-¹ + TENABLE.]
1 Not able to be defended (*lit. & fig.*). M17.
2 Not able to be occupied; (of an office, position, etc.) not able to be possessed or enjoyed. L17.

📖 **1** D. FRASER He believed the Axis position in North Africa untenable. L. H. TRIBE The traditional immunity of women from prosecution for abortion would be untenable.

■ **untenaˈbility** *noun* M17. **untenableness** *noun* M19. **untenably** *adverb* L20.

untenant /ʌnˈtɛnənt/ *verb trans*. E17.
[from UN-² + TENANT *verb*.]
1 Dislodge from a dwelling. *rare*. E17.
2 Deprive (a house, land, etc.) of a tenant or tenants. M17.
3 Depart from, leave. *rare*. L18.

untenanted /ʌnˈtɛnəntɪd/ *adjective*. L17.
[from UN-¹ + *tenanted* pa. pple of TENANT *verb*.]
Not occupied by a tenant or tenants.
■ **untenantable** *adjective* not tenantable; unfit for occupation: M17.

untender /ʌnˈtɛndə/ *adjective*. E17.
[from UN-¹ + TENDER *adjective*.]
1 Not tender in dealing with others; insensitive, unkind. E17.
†**2** Not having a tender conscience; lacking in religious susceptibility. M17–E19.
3 Not immature. *rare*. L19.
■ **untenderly** *adverb* LME. **untenderness** *noun* M17.

Untergang /ˈʊntərgaŋ/ *noun*. M20.
[German = decline, downfall.]
An irreversible decline, esp. leading to the destruction of culture or civilization.

Untermensch /ˈʊntərmɛnʃ/ *noun*. Pl. ***-en*** /-ən/. M20.
[German.]
Esp. in Nazi Germany, a person regarded or classified as racially inferior.

unterminated /ʌnˈtəːmɪneɪtɪd/ *adjective*. L18.
[from UN-¹ + *terminated* pa. pple of TERMINATE *verb*.]
Not terminated; unlimited.
■ **unterminating** *adjective* (*rare*) E19.

Unteroffizier /ˈʊntərɔfiˌtsiːr/ *noun*. Pl. ***-e*** /-ə/. E20.
[German.]
MILITARY. In Germany and German-speaking countries, a non-commissioned officer.

unterrified /ʌnˈtɛrɪfʌɪd/ *adjective*. E17.
[from UN-¹ + *terrified* pa. pple of TERRIFY.]
Not terrified or frightened.
■ **unterrifying** *adjective* L17.

untested /ʌnˈtɛstɪd/ *adjective*. L18.
[from UN-¹ + *tested* pa. pple of TEST *verb*².]
Not tested or proved; not put to the test.
■ **untestable** *adjective* E20.

untether /ʌnˈtɛðə/ *verb trans*. L18.
[from UN-² + TETHER *verb*.]
Release from a tether.

untethered /ʌnˈtɛðəd/ *adjective*. E19.
[from UN-¹ + *tethered* pa. pple of TETHER *verb*.]
Not tethered.

unthanked /ʌnˈθaŋkt/ *adjective*. M16.
[from UN-¹ + *thanked* pa. pple of THANK *verb*.]
Not thanked; unacknowledged.

unthankful /ʌnˈθaŋkfʊl, -f(ə)l/ *adjective*. ME.
[from UN-¹ + THANKFUL.]
1 Not giving thanks; not feeling or showing appreciation. Also foll. by *for* (a thing), *to* (a person). ME.
2 Not earning thanks or gratitude; unappreciated, thankless. LME.
3 Characterized by ingratitude. Long *rare* or *obsolete*. E17.

📖 **1** R. C. SINGLETON Unconscious of events, and for escape Unthankful. **2** B. LEIGH Dull, unthankful work . . redeemed by the affectionate sauce of our patients.

■ **unthankfully** *adverb* ungratefully LME. **unthankfulness** *noun* ingratitude L15.

unthatch /ʌnˈθatʃ/ *verb trans*. L17.
[from UN-² + THATCH *verb*.]
Strip of thatch.

unthatched /ʌnˈθatʃt/ *adjective*. L16.
[from UN-¹ + THATCHED.]
Not covered with thatch.

unthaw /ʌnˈθɔː/ *verb trans. & intrans*. Now *dial. & N. Amer.* L16.
[from UN-² + THAW *verb*.]
Melt, thaw.

unthawed /ʌnˈθɔːd/ *adjective*. L16.
[from UN-¹ + *thawed* pa. pple of THAW *verb*.]
Not thawed; remaining frozen.

unthink /ˈʌnθɪŋk/ *noun*. M20.
[from UN-¹ + THINK *noun*.]
Acceptance (of an idea etc.) without due thought; failure to use logical reasoning.

unthink /ʌnˈθɪŋk/ *verb trans*. Pa. t. & pple **unthought** /ʌnˈθɔːt/. L15.
[from UN-² + THINK *verb*².]
Forget; remove from thought; cancel out or reverse by a mental effort.

📖 J. R. ILLINGWORTH There is no question of the inevitableness of this conclusion. . . we cannot unthink it.

unthinkable /ʌnˈθɪŋkəb(ə)l/ *adjective & noun*. LME.
[from UN-¹ + THINK *verb*² + -ABLE.]
▶ **A** *adjective*. Unable to be imagined or grasped by the mind; *colloq.* highly unlikely or undesirable. LME.

📖 *Westminster Gazette* Cool glades of unthinkable beauty. C. TOMALIN Behaviour which would have been unthinkable a generation earlier.

▶ **B** *absol.* as *noun*. That which is unthinkable; an unthinkable thing. L19.

📖 B. DUFFY Wittgenstein did the unthinkable when he declined the emperor's offer to ennoble the Wittgenstein family.

■ **unthinkaˈbility** *noun* M19. **unthinkableness** *noun* E20. **unthinkably** *adverb* E16.

unthinking /ʌnˈθɪŋkɪŋ/ *adjective*. L17.
[from UN-¹ + THINKING *ppl adjective*.]
Not thinking; characterized by thoughtlessness or absence of thought.

📖 LYTTON The unthinking and lavish idolatry you manifest. F. SPALDING Individualism . . has liberated artists from unthinking adoption of fashionable styles.

■ **unthinkingly** *adverb* without thought; unintentionally: E18. **unthinkingness** *noun* L17.

unthought /ʌnˈθɔːt/ *noun*. M19.
[from UN-¹ + THOUGHT *noun*¹.]
Thoughtlessness; lack of due consideration or reflection; unthinkingness.

📖 N. BAGNALL Political jargon . . can . . induce a dangerous state of unthought.

unthought /ʌnˈθɔːt/ *adjective*. M16.
[from UN-¹ + *thought* pa. pple of THINK *verb*².]
1 Not thought (of). Freq. foll. by *of*, *out*. M16.
†**2** Not regarded in a certain (specified or implied) way. Chiefly with adjective compl. L16–E19.
3 Unimagined; not formed in thought. M17.

📖 **1** *Computer Bulletin* Personal computing . . crystallising many un-thought-of applications. **3** A. PRICE The recollection of what Wimpey had said died unthought.

unthought *verb pa. t. & pple* of UNTHINK *verb*.

unthoughtful /ʌnˈθɔːtfʊl, -f(ə)l/ *adjective*. LME.
[from UN-¹ + THOUGHTFUL.]
Not thoughtful; unthinking, thoughtless; unmindful *of*.
■ **unthoughtfully** *adverb* E18. **unthoughtfulness** *noun* M17.

unthread /ʌnˈθrɛd/ *verb trans*. L16.
[from UN-² + THREAD *verb*.]
Take the thread out of (a needle etc.). Also, find one's way out of (a narrow or obstructed passage etc.).

unthreaded /ʌnˈθrɛdɪd/ *adjective*. L16.
[from UN-¹ + THREADED.]
Not threaded.

unthreatened /ʌnˈθrɛt(ə)nd/ *adjective*. M17.
[from UN-¹ + THREATENED.]
Not threatened; not endangered.
■ **unthreatening** *adjective* not threatening; safe: E20.

unthrift /ʌnˈθrɪft/ *noun & adjective*. Now *arch. rare*. ME.
[from UN-¹ + THRIFT *noun*¹.]
▶ **A** *noun*. †**1** A fault, a foolish action. Only in ME.
2 An unthrifty, dissolute, or profligate person; a spendthrift. ME.
3 Lack of thrift or economy; neglect of thriving or doing well. Formerly also, dissolute behaviour, profligacy, impropriety. LME.
▶ **B** *adjective*. Profligate, spendthrift. M16.

†**unthriftihead** *noun*. *rare* (Spenser). Only in L16.
[from UN-¹ + THRIFTY + -HEAD.]
Thriftlessness.

unthrifty /ʌnˈθrɪfti/ *adjective*. LME.
[from UN-¹ + THRIFTY.]
1 Not profitable or serviceable; leading to no advantage; tending to ineffectual use or harm. *arch.* LME.

2 Not flourishing physically; lacking vigour or promise in growth. LME. ▸†**b** Characterized by lack of prosperity. LME–M16.

†**3** Dissolute in conduct; unchaste, profligate. LME–L16.

4 Not thrifty, economical, or frugal; wasteful, extravagant, spendthrift. M16. ▸†**b** Prodigal or lavish *of* something; unsparing. E17–E18.

■ **unthriftily** *adverb* LME. **unthriftiness** *noun* LME.

†**unthrive** *verb*. Pa. t. **unthrove**, **unthrived**; pa. pple **unthriven**, **unthrived**. LME.
[from UN-² + THRIVE *verb*.]
1 *verb intrans.* Fail to thrive; be unprosperous. LME–E18.
2 *verb trans.* Make unprosperous. *rare*. Only in M16.

unthriven /ʌnˈθrɪv(ə)n/ *adjective*. Now *Scot.* L17.
[from UN-¹ + *thriven* pa. pple of THRIVE *verb*.]
Characterized by a failure to thrive or flourish; physically underdeveloped or weak.

†**unthriven** *verb pa. pple*: see UNTHRIVE.

unthriving /ʌnˈθrʌɪvɪŋ/ *adjective*. ME.
[from UN-¹ + *thriving* pres. pple of THRIVE *verb*.]
†**1** Not doing well; lacking merit or excellence; unworthy. Only in ME.
2 Not thriving or growing vigorously; not prospering or flourishing. E17.
3 Leading to no gain or profit; unprofitable. Long *rare* or *obsolete*. E17.

†**unthrove** *verb pa. t.*: see UNTHRIVE.

untidy /ʌnˈtʌɪdi/ *adjective*. ME.
[from UN-¹ + TIDY *adjective*.]
†**1** Untimely, unseasonable; unsuitable, unseemly. ME–M17.
2 Not neat or orderly; not methodically or neatly arranged. ME.

📖 **2** A. TYLER One of her spring-cleaning attacks that . . made the house seem untidier than before.

■ **untidily** *adverb* LME. **untidiness** *noun* L18.

untidy /ʌnˈtʌɪdi/ *verb trans.* L19.
[from UN-² + TIDY *verb*.]
Make untidy.

untie /ʌnˈtʌɪ/ *verb*. Pa. t. & pple **untied** /ʌnˈtʌɪd/; pres. pple **untying** /ʌnˈtʌɪɪŋ/, **untieing**. OE.
[from UN-² + TIE *verb*¹.]
1 *verb trans.* Release or detach by undoing a cord or similar fastening. OE. ▸**b** Free from a confining or encircling cord or fastening; unfasten the cords of (a package etc.). OE.
2 *verb trans.* Undo or unfasten (a cord, knot, etc.). L16. ▸**b** *fig.* Solve (a difficulty). Chiefly with *(Gordian) knot* (see GORDIAN *adjective* 1, KNOT *noun*¹ 9). L16. ▸**c** *fig.* Dissolve or loosen (a bond, esp. of a relationship). E17.
3 *verb intrans.* Become loosened or untied. Long *rare* or *obsolete*. L16.

📖 **1** POPE I climbed my vessel's lofty side; my train obeyed me, and the ship unty'd. *fig.*: SHAKES. *Macb.* Though you untie the winds and let them fight Against the churches. **2** C. RAYNER She stood there untying her . . straw bonnet. **b** L. STERNE That is cutting the knot . . instead of untying it.

untied /ʌnˈtʌɪd/ *adjective*. LME.
[from UN-¹ + TIED *adjective*¹.]
1 Not tied. LME.
†**2** Unloosed. *rare* (Shakes.). Only in E17.

until /ənˈtɪl/ *preposition & conjunction*. ME.
[from Old Norse *und* (only in *unz*, *undz* = *und es* till that) corresp. to Old English, Old Frisian, Old Saxon *und*, Gothic *untē* up to, as far as + TILL *preposition & conjunction*, the meaning thus being duplicated. Cf. 'TIL.]
▶ **A** *preposition*. **1** = TILL *preposition* 1. Now only *Scot. & north.* ME. ▸†**b** In contact with; against. Long only *Scot. & north.* LME–E19.
†**2** To (the person or thing towards whom or which an action, statement, etc., is directed). Long only *Scot.* ME–L18.
3 = TILL *preposition* 2a. Freq. with adverb or adverbial phr. of time. ME.
†**4** Up to (a given number); amounting or extending to. *rare*. LME–L16.
5 Before (a specified time). L19.

📖 **1** SPENSER He hastned them vntill. R. HAKLUYT Staires . . ascending vp vntill the midst of the pillers. SIR W. SCOTT The Laird . . had devoted his leisure untill tillage and agriculture. **2** J. FISHER He shal be a comforter vntyl vs. **3** D. H. LAWRENCE Walter Morel lay in bed . . until nearly dinner-time. D. ABSE No more school . . not until Monday. *New York Times* Known until now as Ulms, has been renamed the Trident. *Q* Bob . . doesn't re-emerge until the following afternoon. **up until**: see UP *adverb*¹.

▶ **B** *conjunction*. **1** = TILL *conjunction* 1. Formerly also foll. by *that*. ME.
2 So long or so far that; so that eventually. LME.
3 Before the time that; before. E17.

📖 **1** *Cook's Magazine* Heat sugar, butter . . and water over medium heat until the syrup thickens. F. TUOHY If only she'd wait until we got a bit more settled. **2** C. THIRLWALL The flames . . spread . . until almost the whole island was left bare. A. BROOKNER He could not let them have the run of the place until they took root there. **3** J. HOWELL 'Tis held . . incivility for maidens to drink wine untill they are married. J. RUSKIN Not permitted . . to enter the life room until they had mastered drawing from . . casts.

¶ As *conjunction* in freq. use from E19.

untilled /ʌnˈtɪld/ *adjective*. ME.
[from UN-¹ + *tilled* pa. pple of TILL *verb*¹.]
Esp. of land: not tilled or cultivated.
■ **untillable** *adjective* E18.

untimber /ʌnˈtɪmbə/ *verb trans.* Long *rare*. E17.
[from UN-² + TIMBER *verb*.]
Strip of timber; destroy the timber or timbers of.

untimbered /ʌnˈtɪmbəd/ *adjective*. E17.
[from UN-¹ + TIMBERED.]
1 Not constructed or provided with timbers; unsound. Chiefly *fig.* E17.
2 Not wooded. E19.

untimed /ʌnˈtʌɪmd/ *adjective*. L18.
[from UN-¹ + *timed* pa. pple of TIME *verb*.]
Not timed.

untimely /ʌnˈtʌɪmli/ *adjective*. ME.
[from UN-¹ + TIMELY *adjective*.]
1 Inopportune, ill-timed. ME.
2 Coming before the proper or natural time; (esp. of death) premature; (*poet.*) unripened, immature. M16.
3 Unseasonable (in respect of the time of year). L16.

📖 **1** J. GALSWORTHY She regarded her aunt's untimely visit in the light of a personal injury. **2** G. BERKELEY Drinkers . . bringing on the untimely symptoms of old age. D. JUDD King Lear rails against the untimely death of his daughter Cordelia. **3** S. BEDFORD In April . . one of those untimely heat waves had struck London.

■ **untimeliness** *noun* L16.

untimely /ʌnˈtʌɪmli/ *adverb*. *arch.* ME.
[from UN-¹ + TIMELY *adverb*.]
1 At an unsuitable time; unseasonably, inopportunely. ME.
2 Before the proper or natural time; prematurely. L16.

📖 **1** SIR W. SCOTT To avenge the deed expelling Thee untimely from thy dwelling. **2** E. B. PUSEY Melancthon . . prolonged the conference, only lest he should seem to break it off untimely.

untimeous /ʌnˈtʌɪməs/ *adjective*. Chiefly *Scot.* LME.
[from UN-¹ + TIMEOUS *adjective*.]
1 = UNTIMELY *adjective* 1, 3. LME.
2 = UNTIMELY *adjective* 2. M16.
■ **untimeously** *adverb* E16.

untine /ʌnˈtʌɪn/ *verb trans.* Long *obsolete* exc. *dial.* OE.
[from UN-² + TINE *verb*¹.]
1 Open. OE.
2 Separate, sever. L15.

untire /ʌnˈtʌɪə/ *verb trans. rare*. L17.
[from UN-² + TIRE *verb*¹.]
Free from being tired; rest.

untired /ʌnˈtʌɪəd/ *adjective*. L16.
[from UN-¹ + TIRED.]
Not tired or exhausted; unwearied. Also foll. by *by*, *with*.
■ **untirable** *adjective* tireless, indefatigable E17.

untiring /ʌnˈtʌɪərɪŋ/ *adjective*. E19.
[from UN-¹ + TIRING *adjective*.]
Tireless, indefatigable.
■ **untiringly** *adverb* M19.

untithed /ʌnˈtʌɪðd/ *adjective*. E17.
[from UN-¹ + *tithed* pa. pple of TITHE *verb*.]
1 On which no tithe is paid or imposed. E17.
2 Not receiving tithes. *rare*. E19.
■ **untithable** *adjective* (*rare*) not subject to the payment of tithes L18.

untitle /ʌnˈtʌɪt(ə)l/ *verb trans. rare*. L16.
[from UN-² + TITLE *verb*.]
Deprive of a title; remove or omit the title from.

untitled /ʌnˈtʌɪt(ə)ld/ *adjective*. E17.
[from UN-¹ + *titled* pa. pple of TITLE *verb*.]
†**1** Unentitled; having no right (to rule). *rare* (Shakes.). Only in E17.
2 Not having a title; unnamed. E17.
3 Not distinguished by a title of rank, office, etc. L18.

📖 **2** J. C. OATES Bosch's untitled triptych in the Prado Museum. **3** J. CONRAD All the men of whom the nation is proud . . knights all, titled and untitled.

unto /ˈʌntʊ/ *preposition & conjunction*. Chiefly *arch.* & *literary*. ME.
[from UNTIL *preposition* with TO *preposition* replacing northern equivalent TILL *preposition*.]
▶ **A** *preposition*. **I** Introducing a noun or pronoun.
1 Expr. a spatial or local relation: = TO *preposition* 1a, b, c, e. ME.
2 Expr. a temporal relationship. Cf. TO *preposition* 2. ▸**a** Until, till. Also, indicating regular recurrence within specified units of time, as ***day unto day***. ME. ▸**b** After a neg.: before. Now *rare*. LME.
3 Expr. the relation of purpose, destination, result, resulting condition or status: = TO *preposition* 3. ME.
4 Expr. a limit in extent, amount, or degree: = TO *preposition* 4a, b. ME.
5 Expr. addition, attachment, accompaniment, or possession. ▸**a** = TO *preposition* 5b. ME. ▸**b** = TO *preposition* 5c. LME. ▸**c** By way of increase to; in addition to; with, besides. Cf. TO *preposition* 5a. E16.
6 Expr. relation to a standard or to a stated term or point: = TO *preposition* 6a, c, d, e. ME.
7 Expr. the relation to a specified object of speech, action, etc.: = TO *preposition* 7a, b, c, d. ME.
8 Repr. an original dative: = TO *preposition* 8c, d, e. ME.

📖 **1** SHAKES. *Hen. V* Once more unto the breach, dear friends. GOLDSMITH A strong haven, with walls reaching unto the city. WORDSWORTH In that very place My Lady first took me unto her grace. R. ALLAN The hope . . to press thee Unto my fond bosom. **2a** I. MACLAREN Doctor Manley . . praises Kate unto this day. **3** SHAKES. *Mids. N. D.* He hath turn'd a heaven unto a hell! WORDSWORTH The prison, unto which we doom ourselves. **4** SIR T. BROWNE The whole world perished unto eight persons before the floud. M. FORSTER He had been . . very ill, nigh unto death. **5a** D. G. ROSSETTI Still some golden hair Unto his shoulder clinging, since the last Embrace. **6** TENNYSON All thy passions, match'd with mine, Are as moonlight unto sunlight. M. FORSTER I am like unto a leper . . with all faces turned against me. **7** *Oxford Today* Sing Praise and thanksgiving unto God our king. **8** AV *Matt.* 22:21 Render therefore unto Caesar the things which are Caesar's. *Proverb*: Do unto others as you would they should do unto you. **unto oneself** set aside from or unconnected with others, in and of oneself. ***be a law unto oneself***: see LAW *noun*¹.

▶†**II** Introducing an infinitive.
9 = TO *preposition* 9. LME–L15.
▶ **B** *conjunction*. Until. ME–L16.

untold /ʌnˈtəʊld/ *adjective*. OE.
[from UN-¹ + TOLD *ppl adjective*.]
†**1** Not enumerated or reckoned; not counted out or paid; unspecified. OE–E17.
2 Not related or recounted. ME.
3 Not (able to be) counted or measured; immense, vast, countless. LME.
4 Not informed of a fact etc. *rare*. L16.

📖 **2** *Face* No event, however boring, is left untold. **3** J. H. NEWMAN All the untold riches of his treasury. T. W. HIGGINSON It had also cost the Americans untold suffering.

untomb /ʌnˈtuːm/ *verb trans.* L16.
[from UN-² + TOMB.]
Disentomb, unearth, (*lit.* & *fig.*).

untombed /ʌnˈtuːmd/ *adjective*. M16.
[from UN-¹ + *tombed* pa. pple of TOMB *verb*.]
Not placed in a tomb, without a grave, unburied.

untone /ʌnˈtəʊn/ *verb trans.* E19.
[from UN-² + TONE *verb*.]
Deprive of tone.

untoned /ʌnˈtəʊnd/ *adjective*. E19.
[from UN-¹ + TONED.]
Not toned; lacking tone or shade.

untouchable /ʌnˈtʌtʃəb(ə)l/ *adjective & noun*. M16.
[from UN-¹ + TOUCHABLE.]
▶ **A** *adjective*. **1** Unable to be touched; immaterial; beyond the reach of touch. M16. ▸**b** *fig.* Unmatchable, unrivalled. M19.
2 That may not be touched; *spec.* that cannot legally be interfered with or used. E17.
3 Too bad, unpleasant, or defiling to touch; *spec.* of or belonging to the Hindu caste of untouchables. L19.

📖 **1b** E. H. YATES In his day untouchable as a romantic actor. **2** P. ACKROYD She had . . become something of a sacred and untouchable object. *Economist* Incompetent as they were, their jobs were untouchable.

▶ **B** *noun*. An untouchable person; *spec.* (in the Indian subcontinent), a member of a hereditary Hindu caste held to defile members of higher castes on contact. Cf. HARIJAN. Freq. in *pl.* E20.

¶ Use of the term and practice of its accompanying social restrictions were declared illegal under the Indian constitution in 1949 and the Pakistani one in 1953.

■ **untoucha'bility** *noun* the quality or state of being untouchable; the social practice of having a caste of untouchables: E20. **untouchableness** *noun* E20. **untouchably** *adverb* E20.

untouched /ʌnˈtʌtʃt/ *adjective*. LME.
[from UN-¹ + TOUCHED.]
▶ **I 1** Not touched by the hands, another body, etc.; not handled. LME. ▸**b** Not approached, crossed, or traversed. E17.

2 Not affected physically, esp. in a harmful way; undamaged, unhurt, uninjured. LME. ▸**b** Not having had (a) sexual experience. LME. ▸**c** Not used or consumed, left intact; *esp.* untasted. M16.
3 Not modified, altered, or treated; free from influence or corruption. L16.
4 Not affected emotionally, unmoved. E17.
5 Not equalled in quality, unmatched, unparalleled. M18.
6 Not entered on, not begun. L19.

1 SIR W. SCOTT Untouch'd, the harp began to ring. **2** C. W. C. OMAN The plague had left the rest of Greece almost untouched. *Guardian* His violin miraculously untouched by his backward leap. **3** *Oxford Today* The landscape is . . rich in archaeological remains and has been virtually untouched. **4** M. FORSTER Timothy . . said he had not been untouched by Miss Elizabeth's plight. **5** *San Diego* Attained a stature untouched by any of his fellows at the Kirov Opera.

▸ **II 7** Not discussed, not treated in writing or speech. LME.
■ **untouchedness** *noun* L19.

untouching /ʌnˈtʌtʃɪŋ/ *adjective.* E17.
[from UN-¹ + TOUCHING *adjective*.]
1 Not touching something. E17. ▸**b** Not having contact. E19.
2 Having no emotional effect, unaffecting. M18.
■ **untouchingly** *adverb* M19.

untoward /ʌntəˈwɔːd, ʌnˈtəʊəd/ *adjective.* E16.
[from UN-¹ + TOWARD *adjective*.]
†**1** Disinclined or unwilling *for*, *to*, or *to do* something. E16–M17. ▸†**b** Lacking proficiency or aptitude, inept. *rare.* M–L16.
2 a Difficult to manage, awkward to deal with; intractable, unruly, perverse. E16. ▸†**b** Clumsy, ungainly, ungraceful. L16–L18.
3 Characterized by or involving misfortune; unlucky, unfortunate. L16.
4 Unfavourable, unpropitious. E17.
5 Unseemly, improper. E17.

3 A. CARTER The . . parade passed off without any untoward occurrence.

■ **untowardness** *noun* LME.

untowardly /ʌntəˈwɔːdli, -ˈtəʊəd-/ *adjective.* Now *rare.* L15.
[from UN-¹ + TOWARDLY *adjective*.]
1 = UNTOWARD *adjective* 5. L15.
2 = UNTOWARD *adjective* 2a. Also, awkward, clumsy. M16.
3 = UNTOWARD *adjective* 4. M18.
■ **untowardliness** *noun* L16.

untowardly /ʌntəˈwɔːdli, -ˈtəʊəd-/ *adverb.* M16.
[from UNTOWARD + -LY².]
In an untoward manner.

untraceable /ʌnˈtreɪsəb(ə)l/ *adjective.* M17.
[from UN-¹ + TRACEABLE.]
Unable to be traced.
■ **untraceableness** *noun* M19. **untraceably** *adverb* L19. **untraced** *adjective* not traced M17.

untractable /ʌnˈtraktəb(ə)l/ *adjective.* Now *rare.* M16.
[from UN-¹ + TRACTABLE.]
1 = INTRACTABLE 2. M16.
2 = INTRACTABLE 1. E17.
■ **untractaˈbility** *noun* L18. **untractableness** *noun* L16.

untrained /ʌnˈtreɪnd/ *adjective.* M16.
[from UN-¹ + TRAINED *ppl adjective*².]
Not trained; uninstructed, undisciplined, unskilled.
■ **untrainable** *adjective* M19.

untranslatable /ʌntransˈleɪtəb(ə)l, ʌntrɑː-, -zˈleɪt-/ *adjective.* M17.
[from UN-¹ + TRANSLATABLE.]
Unable to be translated (satisfactorily).

Guardian That brand of lovable pathos best summed up by the untranslatable Yiddish adjective nebbish.

■ **untranslataˈbility** *noun* M19. **untranslatableness** *noun* E19. **untranslatably** *adverb* M19. **untranslated** *adjective* not translated M16.

untrapped /ʌnˈtrapt/ *adjective.* M17.
[from UN-¹ + (sense 1) *trapped* pa. pple of TRAP *verb*², (sense 2) TRAP *noun*¹: see -ED¹, -ED².]
1 Not trapped, confined, or ensnared. M17.
2 Of a drain or sink: not fitted with a trap. M19.

untread /ʌnˈtrɛd/ *verb trans.* Infl. as TREAD *verb*; pa. t. usu. **-trod** /-ˈtrɒd/, pa. pple **-trodden** /-ˈtrɒd(ə)n/, **-trod**. L16.
[from UN-² + TREAD *verb*.]
Retrace (steps, a path, etc.).

untreated /ʌnˈtriːtɪd/ *adjective.* LME.
[from UN-¹ + *treated* pa. pple of TREAT *verb*.]
Not treated.

New Statesman Cells which, if left untreated, will . . develop into invasive cancer. *Guardian* Pipes which dump untreated sewage at . . the low tide mark.

■ **untreatable** *adjective* †(*a*) intractable, unmanageable; (*b*) unable to be treated, not curable by medical treatment: LME. **untreatableness** *noun* L17.

untried /ʌnˈtrʌɪd/ *adjective.* E16.
[from UN-¹ + TRIED *ppl adjective*.]
1 Not tried, proved, or tested; inexperienced. Also, not attempted. E16.
2 Not yet tried by a judge. E17.

1 H. JAMES She was young, untried, nervous. P. ACKROYD His hitherto untried powers of observation were growing . . stronger.

untrim /ʌnˈtrɪm/ *adjective. rare.* L16.
[from UN-¹ + TRIM *adjective*.]
Not trim, untidy.

untrim /ʌnˈtrɪm/ *verb trans.* Infl. **-mm-**. L16.
[from UN-² + TRIM *verb*.]
1 Deprive of neatness, make untidy; strip of trim or ornament. L16.
2 Unbalance. L19.

untrimmed /ʌnˈtrɪmd/ *adjective.* M16.
[from UN-¹ + *trimmed* pa. pple of TRIM *verb*.]
1 Not made neat; not decorated or ornamented with trimming. M16.
2 Not trimmed or cut to shape. E17.
3 Not properly balanced. M18.
■ **untrimmable** *adjective* unable to be trimmed M19. **untrimmedness** *noun* L19.

untrodden /ʌnˈtrɒd(ə)n/ *adjective.* ME.
[from UN-¹ + TRODDEN *ppl adjective*.]
Not trodden or stepped on, untraversed; unexplored.

GOLDSMITH Those untrodden forests . . which formerly covered the . . country.

■ Also **unˈtrod** *adjective* L16.

untroubled /ʌnˈtrʌb(ə)ld/ *adjective.* LME.
[from UN-¹ + TROUBLED.]
Not troubled or disturbed (*lit.* & *fig.*); tranquil, calm, undisturbed.

R. BOLDREWOOD Untroubled by care or consuming anxiety. *Yours* Enjoy untroubled refreshing sleep and . . rest.

untroublesome /ʌnˈtrʌb(ə)ls(ə)m/ *adjective.* M18.
[from UN-¹ + TROUBLESOME.]
Not troublesome.
■ **untroublesomeness** *noun* L19.

untrue /ʌnˈtruː/ *adjective & adverb.* OE.
[from UN-¹ + TRUE *adjective* & *adverb*.]
▸ **A** *adjective.* **1** Of a person: unfaithful, faithless, disloyal. Freq. foll. by *to*. OE.
2 Deviating from a standard, not straight or direct, inexact. ME. ▸**b** Not genuine; improper, imperfect. M16.
3 Contrary to fact; false, erroneous. LME.
4 Dishonest; unfair, unjust. LME.
▸ **B** *adverb.* Untruly. ME.
■ **untrueness** *noun* ME. **untruly** *adverb* OE.

untruism /ʌnˈtruːɪz(ə)m/ *noun.* M19.
[from UNTRUE *adjective* after *truism*.]
1 An untruth. M19.
2 That which is untrue. M19.

untruss /ʌnˈtrʌs/ *verb.* ME.
[from UN-² + TRUSS *verb*.]
1 *verb trans.* Free from a pack or burden. *rare.* ME.
2 *verb trans.* Unfasten, undo, (a pack, trussed fowl, etc.); free from fastening. LME.
3 a *verb trans.* Undo or unfasten the garments of (a person). M16. ▸**b** *verb trans.* & *intrans. spec.* Undo (a fastening or point of a garment); unfasten (one's lower garments). *obsolete* exc. *Hist.* L16.

untrust /ʌnˈtrʌst/ *noun.* Now *rare.* ME.
[from UN-¹ + TRUST *noun*.]
1 Unbelief, distrust. ME.
†**2** Untrustworthiness. LME–L16.

untrusted /ʌnˈtrʌstɪd/ *adjective.* M16.
[from UN-¹ + *trusted* pa. pple of TRUST *verb*.]
Not trusted.
■ **untrustable** *adjective* unable to be trusted M19. **untrustful** *adjective* not trustful M16. **untrusting** *adjective* not trusting M19.

untrustworthy /ʌnˈtrʌstwəːði/ *adjective.* M19.
[from UN-¹ + TRUSTWORTHY.]
Not trustworthy, unreliable, not to be trusted.
■ **untrustworthiness** *noun* E19. **untrusty** *adjective* (*arch.*) untrustworthy LME.

untruth /ʌnˈtruːθ/ *noun.* OE.
[from UN-¹ + TRUTH *noun*.]
1 Unfaithfulness, disloyalty. Long *arch.* OE.
2 a The state of being untrue; falsehood, falsity. LME. ▸**b** A falsehood, a false or incorrect statement. LME.
3 Inexactness. M19.

2b L. BARBER I always hoped . . an editor would sue *her* for libel, for saying that he printed untruths.

untruthful /ʌnˈtruːθfʊl, -f(ə)l/ *adjective.* LME.
[from UN-¹ + TRUTHFUL.]
†**1** Lacking religious faith, unbelieving. Only in LME.
2 Not truthful; untrue. M19.
■ **untruthfully** *adverb* M19. **untruthfulness** *noun* M19.

untuck /ʌnˈtʌk/ *verb trans.* E17.
[from UN-² + TUCK *verb*¹.]
Free or loosen (a person, bedclothes, etc.) from being tucked up or in.

untucked /ʌnˈtʌkt/ *adjective.* LME.
[from UN-¹ + *tucked* pa. pple of TUCK *verb*¹.]
Not tucked up; loose. Formerly *spec.*, (of cloth) not stretched or tentered.

untunable /ʌnˈtjuːnəb(ə)l/ *adjective.* Also **untuneable**. M16.
[from UN-¹ + TUNABLE.]
1 Not tuneful, unmelodious. M16.
2 Unable to be tuned. E19.
3 Not appreciative of music. M19.
■ **untunableness** *noun* E17. **untunably** *adverb* E16.

untune /ʌnˈtjuːn/ *verb trans.* L16.
[from UN-² + TUNE *verb*.]
Put out of tune; make discordant or unmelodious; *fig.* disorder, discompose.

untuneable *adjective* var. of UNTUNABLE.

untuned /ʌnˈtjuːnd/ *ppl adjective.* M16.
[from prec. + -ED¹, or from UN-¹ + *tuned* pa. pple of TUNE *verb*.]
1 Not tuned; not in tune, discordant, unmelodious; *fig.* not in harmony or concord, disordered. M16.
2 Of an electronic device, radio, etc.: not tuned to any one frequency, able to deal with signals of a wide range of frequencies. E20.

untuneful /ʌnˈtjuːnfʊl, -f(ə)l/ *adjective.* E18.
[from UN-¹ + TUNEFUL.]
Not tuneful; discordant, unmelodious.
■ **untunefully** *adverb* L19. **untunefulness** *noun* L19.

unturn /ʌnˈtəːn/ *verb trans.* & *intrans.* E19.
[from UN-² + TURN *verb*.]
Turn in the opposite direction, reverse.

unturned /ʌnˈtəːnd/ *adjective.* M16.
[from UN-¹ + TURNED.]
1 Not turned over, round, away, or back. M16.
2 Not shaped by turning. E19.
1 *leave no stone unturned*: see STONE *noun*.
■ **unturnable** *adjective* M19. **unturning** *adjective* (*a*) not turning round, not revolving; (*b*) not turning back or aside, undeviating: L16.

untutored /ʌnˈtjuːtəd/ *adjective.* L16.
[from UN-¹ + *tutored* pa. pple of TUTOR *verb*.]
1 Uneducated, untaught; simple, unsophisticated; (of a thing) not produced or formed as the result of education or training. L16.
2 Not subject to a tutor or tutors. *rare.* M17.

untwine /ʌnˈtwʌɪn/ *verb.* LME.
[from UN-² + TWINE *verb*¹.]
1 *verb trans.* Undo from a twined state, untwist. LME. ▸**b** *fig.* Dissolve, undo, destroy. Now *rare.* LME.
2 *verb trans.* Loosen, detach, or release by untwining. M16.
3 *verb intrans.* Become untwined or undone. L16.

1 P. BARKER Sharon clung onto her until Brenda untwined her arms.

untwist /ʌnˈtwɪst/ *verb.* M16.
[from UN-² + TWIST *verb*.]
1 *verb trans.* Open or undo from a twisted or spiralled state; untwine, disentangle. M16. ▸**b** *fig.* Dissolve, undo, destroy. Now *rare.* E17.
†**2** *verb trans.* Expound, make plain. L16–L18.
3 *verb intrans.* Become untwined. L16.
4 *verb trans.* Loosen, detach, or release by untwisting. M17.

1 COLERIDGE Cutting the knot which it cannot untwist. **4** JAYNE PHILLIPS Danner untwisted bottle tops.

■ **untwisting** *noun* the action of the verb; the result of this; in *pl.*, untwisted fibres or threads: L16.

untwisted /ʌnˈtwɪstɪd/ *adjective.* L16.
[from UN-¹ + TWISTED.]
Not twisted or twined.
■ **untwistable** *adjective* unable to be twisted E19.

untying *verb pres. pple* of UNTIE.

untypical /ʌnˈtɪpɪk(ə)l/ *adjective.* M19.
[from UN-¹ + TYPICAL.]
Not typical, unusual.

Guardian 1987–8 with its higher . . inflation rate . . was an untypical year.

■ **untypically** *adverb* M20.

unum necessarium /juːnəm nɛsɪˈsɛːrɪəm/ *noun phr.* M20.
[mod. Latin, from late Latin (Vulgate) *unum est necessarium* one thing is necessary (Luke 10:42).]
The one or only necessary thing, the essential element.

ununderstandable /ˌʌnʌndəˈstandəb(ə)l/ *adjective.* M17.
[from UN-[1] + UNDERSTANDABLE.]
Not understandable, incomprehensible.
■ **ununderstandably** *adverb* (*rare*) LME. **ununderstanding** *adjective* not understanding, uncomprehending E17. **ununderstood** *adjective* not understood M17.

ununiform /ʌnˈjuːnɪfɔːm/ *adjective.* M17.
[from UN-[1] + UNIFORM *adjective.*]
Not uniform, consistent, or unvarying.
■ **ˌununiˈformity** *noun* M18. **ununiformly** *adverb* M17. **ununiformness** *noun* E18.

ununiformed /ʌnˈjuːnɪfɔːmd/ *adjective.* M19.
[from UN-[1] + *uniformed* pa. pple of UNIFORM *verb.*]
Not uniformed, not wearing uniform.

unuse /ʌnˈjuːs/ *noun.* E17.
[from UN-[1] + USE *noun.*]
Lack of use.

unused /*in sense 1* ʌnˈjuːst, *in senses 2 & 3* ʌnˈjuːzd/ *adjective.* ME.
[from UN-[1] + *used* pa. pple of USE *verb.*]
1 Unaccustomed (*to*, *to doing*, (arch.) *to do*). ME.
2 Not in use. Also, never having been used. LME.
3 Not customary, unusual, unwonted. *arch.* E16.

> 🕮 **1** E. BLUNDEN Unused to going without sleep, I felt very weary. **2** M. ROBERTS Their . . unused dormitories had been converted into a hostel. **3** W. MORRIS Strange dainty things they are, Of unused savour.

■ **unusable** *adjective* not usable E19. **unusedness** *noun* L16.

unuseful /ʌnˈjuːsfʊl, -f(ə)l/ *adjective.* L16.
[F. UN-[1] + USEFUL.]
Not useful, unprofitable, useless.
■ **unusefully** *adverb* E17. **unusefulness** *noun* L17.

unusual /ʌnˈjuːʒʊəl/ *adjective.* L16.
[from UN-[1] + USUAL *adjective.*]
Not usual; contrary to or different from what is usual or expected; uncommon, exceptional, unconventional.

> 🕮 I. MURDOCH He had . . long flowing . . hair at a time when this was unusual. A. PILLING It was a mild . . night, unusual for mid December. E. BLAIR Unusual name, Natasha, I've never heard it before.

■ **unusuˈality** *noun* L18. **unusually** *adverb* in an unusual manner, to an unusual extent E17. **unusualness** *noun* L16.

unutterable /ʌnˈʌt(ə)rəb(ə)l/ *adjective & noun.* L16.
[from UN-[1] + UTTERABLE.]
▶ **A** *adjective.* **1** Too great, bad, intense, etc., to describe; inexpressible, indescribable; very great. L16.
2a That may not be uttered or spoken. M17. ▸**b** Unable to be uttered, unpronounceable. M19.

> 🕮 **1** R. SUTCLIFF You are an unutterable nuisance, but I suppose you must have your own way. E. LONGFORD He clasped Frank's hand with a look of unutterable sympathy.

▶ **B** *noun.* **1** An unutterable thing. L18.
2 In *pl.* Trousers; = UNMENTIONABLE *noun* 1. *arch. colloq.* M19.
■ **unutteraˈbility** *noun* M19. **unutterableness** *noun* L17. **unutterably** *adverb* inexpressibly, indescribably, very greatly E17. **unuttered** *adjective* †(*a*) not traded or sold; (*b*) not uttered or spoken: LME.

unvaluable /ʌnˈvaljʊ(ə)b(ə)l/ *adjective.* Now *rare.* M16.
[from UN-[1] + VALUABLE *adjective.*]
†**1** = INVALUABLE 1. M16–E18.
2 = INVALUABLE 2. E17.

unvalued /ʌnˈvaljuːd/ *adjective.* L16.
[from UN-[1] + VALUED.]
1 a Unable to be valued, extremely great or valuable, priceless. Now *rare.* L16. ▸**b** Not having been valued. E19.
2 Not regarded as valuable. E17.

unvariable /ʌnˈvɛːrɪəb(ə)l/ *adjective.* Now *rare.* LME.
[from UN-[1] + VARIABLE *adjective.*]
Not variable, invariable.
■ **unvariableness** *noun* E17. **unvariably** *adverb* M18.

unvaried /ʌnˈvɛːrɪd/ *adjective.* L16.
[from UN-[1] + VARIED.]
Not varied; consistent, monotonous.
■ **unvariedly** *adverb* L18.

unvarnished /ʌnˈvɑːnɪʃt/ *adjective.* E17.
[from UN-[1] + VARNISHED.]
1 Of a statement, person, etc.: unembellished, plain and simple, direct; unsophisticated, unpolished. E17.
2 Not covered with varnish. M18.

> 🕮 **1** C. MACLEOD If you want the unvarnished truth, I married you because Mother forced me to.

■ **unvarnishedly** *adverb* E19.

unvarying /ʌnˈvɛːrɪɪŋ/ *adjective.* L17.
[from UN-[1] + *varying* pa. pple of VARY *verb.*]
Not varying, consistent, monotonous.
■ **unvaryingly** *adverb* E19. **unvaryingness** *noun* M19.

unveil /ʌnˈveɪl/ *verb.* LME.
[from UN-[2] + VEIL *verb*[1].]
1 *verb trans.* Free (the eyes etc.) from a veil or covering to give clearer sight. Now *rare.* LME.
2 *verb trans.* Uncover or display (as) by removing a veil or covering; *fig.* make publicly known, reveal, disclose. LME. ▸**b** *spec.* Remove the covering from (a statue etc.) as part of the ceremony of the first public display; *transf. & fig.* reveal to the public as a new product etc. M19.
3 *verb intrans.* Become free from a veil or covering; remove one's veil. M17.

> 🕮 **2** B. PYM The mysteries of secret societies were to be unveiled. I. MURDOCH They're going to have the bell veiled, and unveil it at the Abbey gate. **b** *Times* Fashion Designer Pierre Cardin . . unveiled three new creations at a London showing. LYNDON B. JOHNSON I went to Mexico City . . to unveil a statue of Abraham Lincoln. *Guardian* The group unveil their plans for a buy-out of British Aerospace.

■ **unveiled** *ppl adjective* not covered or veiled, not concealed or secret, open E17. **unveiledly** /-lɪdli/ *adverb* M17. **unveiledness** *noun* E20. **unveiler** *noun* L17. **unveiling** *verbal noun* the action of the verb; an instance of this; *spec.* an occasion or ceremony revealing a new product etc. to the public: E17.

unvendible /ʌnˈvɛndɪb(ə)l/ *adjective.* Also **-able**. M17.
[from UN-[1] + VENDIBLE.]
Unable or unfit to be sold, unsaleable.
■ **unvendibleness** *noun* E17.

unvenom /ʌnˈvɛnəm/ *verb trans.* E17.
[from UN-[2] + VENOM *verb.*]
Deprive of venom.

unvenomous /ʌnˈvɛnəməs/ *adjective.* M17.
[from UN-[1] + VENOMOUS.]
Not venomous or poisonous.
■ **unvenomed** *adjective* without venom, not poisonous LME.

unveracious /ʌnvəˈreɪʃəs/ *adjective.* M19.
[from UN-[1] + VERACIOUS.]
Chiefly *formal.* Not veracious or truthful.
■ **unveraciously** *adverb* E20. **unveracity** *noun* lack of veracity M19.

unversed /ʌnˈvəːst/ *adjective*[1]. M17.
[from UN-[1] + *versed* pa. pple of VERSE *verb*[1].]
Not versified, not expressed in verse.
■ Also **unversified** *adjective* L18.

unversed /ʌnˈvəːst/ *adjective*[2]. L17.
[from UN-[1] + VERSED.]
Inexperienced *in* something.

> 🕮 W. CAMDEN A young man raw and unversed in military matters.

unvest /ʌnˈvɛst/ *verb.* E17.
[from UN-[2] + VEST *verb.*]
1 *verb trans.* Divest, strip. E17.
2 *verb intrans. & refl.* Remove one's ecclesiastical vestments. M18.

unvirtuous /ʌnˈvəːtjʊəs, -tʃʊəs/ *adjective.* LME.
[from UN-[1] + VIRTUOUS.]
Not virtuous.
■ **unvirtue** *noun* (*rare*) lack of virtue; a fault: M19. **unvirtuously** *adverb* L15. **unvirtuousness** *noun* M19.

unvisor /ʌnˈvʌɪzə/ *verb trans.* Long *rare.* L16.
[from UN-[2] + VISOR *noun or verb.*]
Strip of a visor; unmask.
■ Also **unvizard** *verb trans.* (long *arch.*) E17.

unvisored /ʌnˈvʌɪzəd/ *adjective.* Also **unvizored**. E19.
[from UN-[1] + VISORED.]
Not wearing a visor; not masked.

unvocal /ʌnˈvəʊk(ə)l/ *adjective.* L18.
[from UN-[1] + VOCAL *adjective.*]
Not vocal.
■ **unvocalized** *adjective* M19.

unvoice /ʌnˈvɔɪs/ *verb trans.* M17.
[from UN-[2] + VOICE *verb.*]
Deprive of voice; *spec.* in PHONETICS, utter with breath in place of voice.

unvoiced /ʌnˈvɔɪst/ *adjective.* LME.
[from UN-[1] + VOICED.]
Not spoken or expressed; PHONETICS not voiced.

unwaged /ʌnˈweɪdʒd/ *adjective.* M16.
[from UN-[1] + WAGED.]
(Of work) not recompensed with wages, unpaid; (of a person) not receiving a wage; out of work; doing unpaid work.

> 🕮 *Guardian* Unwaged work by women contributes to national wealth. *absol.*: *Times* A community centre for the unwaged.

unwanted /ʌnˈwɒntɪd/ *adjective.* L17.
[from UN-[1] + WANTED *adjective.*]
Not wanted or desired; without value, surplus.

> 🕮 J. DUNN Virginia . . felt the outsider: unwanted, left behind, disregarded. *Guardian* Unwanted pregnancies have played havoc with Polish society.

■ **unwantedness** *noun* M20.

unware /ʌnˈwɛː/ *adjective, noun, & adverb.* Long *arch.* OE.
[from UN-[1] + WARE *adjective.*]
▶ **A** *adjective.* **1** Unwary, incautious; not on one's guard. OE.
2 Unaware, ignorant. Foll. by *of*, *that*. LME.
3 Unexpected, unforeseen. LME.
4 Unknown. Foll. by *to*. LME.
▶ **B** *noun.* ***at unware***, ***in unware***, ***on unware***, unawares, unexpectedly. OE.
▶ **C** *adverb.* **1** = UNWARES 1. OE.
2 = UNWARES 2. LME.
■ †**unwarely** *adverb* (*a*) incautiously, without taking heed; (*b*) without warning, unexpectedly: OE–L16. **unwareness** *noun* unwariness, lack of caution LME.

unwares /ʌnˈwɛːz/ *adverb.* Long *arch.* LOE.
[from prec. + -S[3]. Cf. UNAWARES.]
1 Without warning; unexpectedly, suddenly. LOE.
2 Unknowingly, in ignorance; unintentionally, innocently. LME.

unwarp /ʌnˈwɔːp/ *verb trans.* M17.
[from UN-[2] + WARP *verb.*]
Uncoil, straighten out; free from prejudice.

unwarped /ʌnˈwɔːpt/ *adjective.* M18.
[from UN-[1] + *warped* pa. pple of WARP *verb.*]
Not warped.

unwarranted /ʌnˈwɒr(ə)ntɪd/ *adjective.* L16.
[from UN-[1] + WARRANTED.]
Not warranted; unauthorized; unjustified.

> 🕮 J. GARDNER His fury seemed . . inexplicable, unwarranted by anything Henry had said.

■ **unwarrantaˈbility** *noun* unwarrantable quality M19. **unwarrantable** *adjective* not warrantable; unjustifiable, indefensible, inexcusable; HUNTING (of a deer) too young to be hunted: E17. **unwarrantableness** *noun* M17. **unwarrantably** *adverb* M17. **unwarrantedly** *adverb* L19.

unwary /ʌnˈwɛːri/ *adjective.* L16.
[from UN-[1] + WARY *adjective.*]
1 Not wary; careless, unguarded, incautious; not aware *of* possible danger etc. L16.
†**2** Unexpected. *rare* (Spenser). Only in L16.

> 🕮 **1** P. FRANCIS Unwary spectators are sometimes injured by the explosions. *absol.*: *Guardian* The courts should . . protect the unwary from possible error.

■ **unwarily** *adverb* †(*a*) without warning, unexpectedly; (*b*) incautiously; inadvertently: M16. **unwariness** *noun* M16.

unwashed /ʌnˈwɒʃt/ *adjective & noun.* LME.
[from UN-[1] + WASHED.]
▶ **A** *adjective.* **1** Not washed, not cleaned by washing. LME.
2 Of a person: not having washed, not usually washed or clean. L16.
3 Not washed *off* or *out*. E17.
▶ **B** *absol.* as *noun pl.* *The* lower classes; *the* majority, *the* mass, *the* rabble. Also ***the great unwashed***. *colloq.* (freq. *joc.*). M19.
■ **unwashable** *adjective* M19. **unwashedness** *noun* L19. **unwashen** *adjective* (*arch.*) unwashed OE.

unwatched /ʌnˈwɒtʃt/ *adjective.* LME.
[from UN-[1] + *watched* pa. pple of WATCH *verb.*]
Not watched.
■ **unwatchable** *adjective* not fit or able to be watched L19.

unwatchful /ʌnˈwɒtʃfʊl, -f(ə)l/ *adjective.* E17.
[from UN-[1] + WATCHFUL.]
Not watchful.
■ **unwatchfully** *adverb* M19. **unwatchfulness** *noun* E17.

unwater /ʌnˈwɔːtə/ *verb trans.* M17.
[from UN-[2] + WATER *verb.*]
Drain of water, carry off water from, (esp. a mine).

unwatered /ʌnˈwɔːtəd/ *adjective.* LME.
[from UN-[1] + WATERED.]
Not watered; not sprinkled or moistened with water; not mixed with water, undiluted; not provided with a supply of water, waterless.
■ **unwatery** *adjective* not supplied with or containing water OE.

unwavering /ʌnˈweɪv(ə)rɪŋ/ *adjective.* L16.
[from UN-[1] + WAVERING.]
Not wavering, hesitating, or fluctuating; resolute, steadfast.

> 🕮 J. A. FROUDE An unwavering pursuit of a single policy. C. BRAYFIELD His mother delivered an unwavering glare of disapproval.

■ **unwaveringly** *adverb* M19.

unwearied /ʌnˈwɪərɪd/ *adjective*. ME.
[from UN-[1] + *wearied* pa. pple of WEARY *verb*.]
1 Not wearied or tired; never becoming weary, indefatigable. ME.
2 Unabating, unremitting. M16.
■ **unweariable** *adjective* impossible to tire or weary; indefatigable, unremitting: M16. **unweariably** *adverb* E17. **unweariedly** *adverb* M17. **unweariedness** *noun* E17.

unweary /ʌnˈwɪəri/ *adjective*. OE.
[from UN-[1] + WEARY *adjective*.]
Not weary (*of*); unwearied.
■ **unweariness** *noun* E17.

unwearying /ʌnˈwɪərɪɪŋ/ *adjective*. E17.
[from UN-[1] + *wearying* pres. pple of WEARY *verb*.]
1 That does not grow weary; persistent, unremitting, untiring. E17.
2 Not causing or producing weariness. L18.
■ **unwearyingly** *adverb* M19.

unweb /ʌnˈwɛb/ *verb trans. rare*. Infl. **-bb-**. L19.
[from UN-[2] + WEB *verb*.]
Unweave.

unwebbed /ʌnˈwɛbd/ *adjective*. M18.
[from UN-[1] + WEBBED.]
Esp. of a bird's feet: not webbed.

unwedded /ʌnˈwɛdɪd/ *adjective*. ME.
[from UN-[1] + WEDDED.]
1 Unmarried. ME.
2 Free from or occurring outside marriage. E19.

> 🕮 **2** H. H. MILMAN The saintly quiet of the unwedded state.

■ **unwed** *adjective* = UNWEDDED E16. **unweddedness** *noun* (*rare*) M19.

unweeting /ʌnˈwiːtɪŋ/ *adjective*. *arch*. ME.
[from UN-[1] + *weeting* pres. pple of WEET *verb*[1].]
1 = UNWITTING *adjective* 1. ME.
†**2** = UNWITTING *adjective* 2. LME–L16.
†**3** Ignorant, uninformed, unlearned. L15–E18.

> 🕮 **1** SPENSER He stood aloofe, unweeting what to doe. W. SOMERVILLE Joyous he scents The rich Repast, unweeting of the Death That lurks within.

■ **unweetingly** *adverb* (*a*) unknowingly, unconsciously; †(*b*) unbeknown to any other person: LME.

unweighed /ʌnˈweɪd/ *adjective*. LME.
[from UN-[1] + WEIGHED.]
1 Of goods etc.: not weighed. LME.
2 Not deliberately considered or pondered; hasty. L16.
■ **unweighable** *adjective* E20. †**unweighing** *adjective* (*rare*, Shakes.) thoughtless, inconsiderate: only in E17.

unweight /ʌnˈweɪt/ *verb trans*. M20.
[Back-form. from next.]
SKIING. Shift the weight from, cease to press heavily on, (a ski etc.).

unweighted /ʌnˈweɪtɪd/ *adjective*. L19.
[from UN-[1] + *weighted* pa. pple of WEIGHT *verb*.]
Not weighted.

unwelcome /ʌnˈwɛlkəm/ *adjective, verb, & noun*. ME.
[from UN-[1] + WELCOME *adjective*.]
▶ **A** *adjective*. Not welcome or acceptable; unpleasing. ME.
▶ **B** *verb trans*. Receive without cordiality, treat as unwelcome. Chiefly as ***unwelcomed*** *ppl adjective*. M16.
▶ **C** *noun*. Unwelcomeness. E17.
■ **unwelcomely** *adverb* M17. **unwelcomeness** *noun* L17. **unwelcoming** *adjective* (*a*) not cordial or friendly; (*b*) such as to make a person (esp. a visitor) uncomfortable: M19.

unwell /ʌnˈwɛl/ *adjective*. ME.
[from UN-[1] + WELL *adjective*.]
1 Not well or in good health; somewhat ill; indisposed. ME.
2 *spec*. Having a menstrual period. *euphem*. M19.
■ **unwellness** *noun* M17.

unwemmed /ʌnˈwɛmd/ *adjective*. Long *arch. & dial. rare*. OE.
[from UN-[1] + *wemmed* pa. pple of WEM *verb*.]
1 Pure, immaculate. OE. ▸**b** Not physically spotted or stained. ME.
†**2** Not hurt, injured, or scarred. Only in ME.

> 🕮 **1** J. ADDIS A love unwemmed, guiltless of attaint.

unwet /ʌnˈwɛt/ *adjective*. LME.
[from UN-[1] + WET *adjective*.]
Not wet or moistened.
■ **unwettable** *adjective* not wettable M20. **unwetted** *adjective* not wetted M17.

unwholesome /ʌnˈhəʊls(ə)m/ *adjective*. ME.
[from UN-[1] + WHOLESOME *adjective*.]
1 Not beneficial or conducive to physical, mental, or moral health; not promoting well-being; harmful. ME. ▸**b** *spec*. Of climate, air, etc.: unhealthy, unsalubrious. M16.
2 a Of a person: of dubious morals, character, etc.; morally tainted. LME. ▸**b** Not sound in health; diseased, sick. M17. ▸**c** Unhealthy-looking. M19.
3 Impaired; defective. *rare* (Shakes.). Only in E17.

> 🕮 **1** G. HARRIS The walls were not dry, but very damp and unwholesome. G. BANCROFT Sick . . and enfeebled by unwholesome diet. *Times* Proclaimed deep concern at the unwholesome exploitation of sex by certain newspapers. **2b** THACKERAY An unwholesome little Miss of seven years of age. **c** C. BRONTË Large and stout . . with a dingy and unwholesome skin. **3** SHAKES. *Oth*. Prithee bear some charity to my wit; do not think it so unwholesome.

■ **unwholesomely** *adverb* LME. **unwholesomeness** *noun* LME.

unwieldiness /ʌnˈwiːldɪnɪs/ *noun*. LME.
[from next + -NESS.]
†**1** The state or condition of being weak or feeble; infirmity. LME–M18.
2 The state or condition of being unwieldy. L16.

unwieldy /ʌnˈwiːldi/ *adjective*. Also **unwieldly** /ʌnˈwiːldli/. LME.
[from UN-[1] + WIELDY.]
†**1** (Of a person, the body, etc.) lacking strength, too weak or feeble; infirm; (of age etc.) characterized or attended by weakness or infirmity. LME–L17.
2 Indisposed to submit to guidance or command; restive, recalcitrant. E16.
3 Of a person or animal: moving ungracefully or with difficulty; lacking litheness or flexibility; awkward, clumsy. M16. ▸**b** Characterized by clumsy massiveness or awkward shape. L16. ▸**c** Clumsily or awkwardly expressed or performed. M17.
4 Difficult to wield, control, or manage, esp. owing to size, shape, or weight; unmanageable. M16.

> 🕮 **1** T. FULLER The weilding of his sword hath not made him unweildie to do any other work. DRYDEN With'ring time the taste destroyes With sickness and unwieldy years. **3** A. BROOKNER She took a bath, feeling as unwieldy as an invalid. **b** W. HOGARTH Elephants and whales please us with their unwieldy greatness. **c** J. THOMSON The broad Monsters . . flounce, and tumble in unwieldy joy. **4** H. LAWRENCE The weapon would be too heavy, to unweildy for us to use. R. P. JHABVALA Our committee . . should not be so large as to be unwieldy. *Publishers Weekly* An unwieldy patchwork of other books' chapters. *fig*.: D. J. ENRIGHT Much of his verse is laboured and unwieldy.

■ **unwieldily** *adverb* clumsily, awkwardly E17.

unwig /ʌnˈwɪɡ/ *verb trans*. Infl. **-gg-**. E19.
[from UN-[2] + WIG *noun*[3].]
Divest of a wig.

unwigged /ʌnˈwɪɡd/ *adjective*. M19.
[from UN-[1] + WIGGED.]
Not wearing or covered with a wig.

unwilful /ʌnˈwɪlfʊl, -f(ə)l/ *adjective*. Long *rare*. Also ***unwillful**. LME.
[from UN-[1] + WILFUL.]
1 Involuntary; unintentional. LME.
2 Not wilful, obstinate, or perverse. *rare*. L16.

unwill /ʌnˈwɪl/ *noun*. L19.
[from UN-[1] + WILL *noun*[1].]
1 The fact or condition of being displeased or offended; displeasure. L19.
2 Lack of will or purpose. L19.

unwill /ʌnˈwɪl/ *verb trans*. M17.
[from UN-[2] + WILL *verb*[2].]
1 Reverse or go back on (a desire, intention, or resolution). M17.
2 LAW. Revoke or annul (a will, testamentary provision, etc.). M17.
3 Deprive (a person) of will or will-power. *rare*. M19.

unwillful *adjective* see UNWILFUL.

unwilling /ʌnˈwɪlɪŋ/ *adjective*. OE.
[from UN-[1] + WILLING *adjective*.]
†**1** Not intending or desiring (to do a particular thing). OE–ME.
2 Not inclined, willing, or ready; averse, reluctant, loath. Also foll. by *to* also *do, that*. OE.
†**3** Involuntary; unintentional; unwilled. M16–L17.
4 Performed, manifested, expressed, or avowed reluctantly or unwillingly. E17.

> 🕮 **2** J. BRYCE A racially distinct body of unwilling subjects . . included within a State. *Time* Shelter . . for those whose families are either unwilling or unable to care for them. *fig*.: T. GRAY Command the Winds, and tame th' unwilling Deep. **3** SHAKES. *Tam. Shr*. Patience, I pray you; 'twas a fault unwilling. **4** LD MACAULAY That sagacity . . which had . . extorted the unwilling admiration of his enemies.

■ **unwilled** *adjective* not willed or intended, involuntary M16. **unwillingly** *adverb* LME. **unwillingness** *noun* L16.

†**unwilly** *adjective*. ME.
[from UN-[1] + WILLY *adjective*.]
1 Unwilling (*to do*); averse. ME–L15.
2 Illiberal. *Scot. rare*. Only in M19.

unwind /ʌnˈwaɪnd/ *verb*. Infl. as WIND *verb*[1]; pa. t. & pple usu. **unwound** /ʌnˈwaʊnd/. ME.
[from UN-[2] + WIND *verb*[1].]
1 *verb trans*. Wind off, draw out, or detach (a thing that has been wound); undo, slacken, or unravel by winding; untwine, untwist. ME. ▸**b** Cause to uncoil. E17. ▸**c** *fig*. Relieve from tension or anxiety, cause to relax. *colloq*. M20.
2 †**a** *verb refl*. Free or extricate (oneself) from an entanglement, difficulty, etc. M16–E18. ▸**b** *verb trans*. Wind off, undo, or unravel a wrapping, bandaging, thread, or covering round (a thing); unwrap. L16.
3 *verb intrans*. **a** Of a thing that has been wound: work loose, uncoil; become drawn out, untwisted, or free. M17. ▸**b** *fig*. Obtain relief from tension or anxiety; relax. *colloq*. M20.
4 *verb trans*. Open up, trace to an outlet or end. E18.

> 🕮 **1** M. SINCLAIR As she unwound her ball of wool it rolled out of her lap. I. MCEWAN Unwound the mooring rope from a bollard. *fig*.: S. E. WHITE There's an awful lot of red-tape to unwind. **3b** J. FANE To unwind . . after her parties and all she put into them. **4** L. STERNE The fifth act . . terminates in unwinding the labyrinth.

■ **unwinding** *verbal noun* the action of the verb; an instance of this: E17.

unwinking /ʌnˈwɪŋkɪŋ/ *adjective*. L18.
[from UN-[1] + *winking* pres. pple of WINK *verb*[1].]
1 (Of a look etc.) marked by absence of winking; (of attention, vigilance, etc.) ceaseless, never relaxing. L18.
2 Not winking; never closing the eyes. E19.
■ **unwinkingly** *adverb* M19.

unwiped /ʌnˈwaɪpt/ *adjective*. E17.
[from UN-[1] + WIPED.]
Not wiped.
■ **unwipeable** *adjective* E20.

unwisdom /ʌnˈwɪzdəm/ *noun*. OE.
[from UN-[1] + WISDOM.]
1 Lack or absence of wisdom; folly, ignorance, stupidity; imprudence. OE.
2 An instance of this; an unwise act. ME.
¶ Rare between 16 and 19.

unwise /ʌnˈwaɪz/ *adjective & noun*. OE.
[from UN-[1] + WISE *adjective*.]
▶ **A** *adjective*. **1** Of a person etc.: lacking or deficient in (practical) wisdom, discretion, or prudence; foolish. OE.
2 Of an act, attitude, behaviour, etc.: not marked or prompted by (practical) wisdom; characterized by lack of sound judgement; injudicious. LME.
†**3** Out of one's senses; mad. LME–L15.

> 🕮 **1** MILTON A nation . . unwise in thir counsels. **2** J. TROLLOPE He . . took a third and unwise glass of whisky. A. HIGONNET It would have been unwise to ignore the evidence of his popular support.

▶ **B** *noun*. Pl. same. An unwise person. OE.
■ **unwisely** *adverb* OE. **unwiseness** *noun* ME.

unwish /ʌnˈwɪʃ/ *verb trans*. L16.
[from UN-[2] + WISH *verb*.]
1 Retract, cancel, abrogate, (a wish, choice, etc.). L16.
2 a Annihilate by wishing; wish away. L16. ▸**b** Wish or desire (a circumstance or thing) not to be. E17.

> 🕮 **1** C. M. YONGE Never was a more absurd wish . . unwish it forthwith.

unwished /ʌnˈwɪʃt/ *adjective*. L16.
[from UN-[1] + WISHED.]
Not wished (*for*), desired, or asked for; *spec*. unwelcome, unpleasing.
■ **unwishful** *adjective* not wishful L18. **unwishing** *adjective* free from desire or wishes M18.

unwist /ʌnˈwɪst/ *adjective & adverb*. *arch*. LME.
[from UN-[1] + *wist* pa. pple of WIT *verb*.]
▶ **A** *adjective*. †**1** Unknown (*to* or *by* a person). Also foll. by *of*. LME–M19.
†**2** Unaware (*of* a thing); not knowing. LME–L16.
3 Not recognized; strange. M18.
▶†**B** *adverb*. Without (a specified fact) being known. LME–L16.

unwithdrawn /ʌnwɪðˈdrɔːn/ *adjective*. E19.
[from UN-[1] + WITHDRAWN.]
Not withdrawn, drawn back, or retracted.
■ †**unwithdrawing** *adjective* (*rare*) that does not hold back, generous M17–M18.

unwithered /ʌnˈwɪðəd/ *adjective*. L16.
[from UN-[1] + *withered* pa. pple of WITHER *verb*.]
Not withered; still vigorous or fresh.
■ **unwithering** *adjective* that does not wither or fade M18.

unwitting /ʌnˈwɪtɪŋ/ *adjective & adverb*. OE.
[from UN-[1] + *witting* pres. pple of WIT *verb*.]
▶ **A** *adjective*. **1** Not knowing, unaware, unconscious, (*of*); unheeding, not realizing. OE.
†**2** Without the knowledge *of*, unbeknown *to*. ME–M17.
3 Performed unwittingly; unintentional. E19.
▶ **B** *adverb*. Unwittingly. OE.
¶ Rare between 16 and 19.
■ **unwittingly** *adverb* not knowingly or intentionally; unconsciously, inadvertently: LME. **unwittingness** *noun* †(*a*) ignorance; (*b*) lack of self-awareness, unconsciousness: ME.

unwitty /ʌnˈwɪti/ *adjective.* OE.
[from UN-¹ + WITTY.]
1 Of a person or mind: deficient in wit or intelligence; ignorant, foolish. Now *rare* or *obsolete.* OE.
†**2** Of an act etc.: characterized by lack of knowledge; senseless. ME–L16.
3 Not witty or amusing. M17.
■ **unwittily** *adverb* †(*a*) ignorantly, unwisely; (*b*) in a manner that is not witty or amusing: LME.

unwive /ʌnˈwʌɪv/ *verb trans.* E17.
[from UN-² + WIVE.]
Deprive of a wife.

unwived /ʌnˈwʌɪvd/ *adjective.* L16.
[from UN-¹ + *wived* pa. pple of WIVE.]
Wifeless.

unwomanly /ʌnˈwʊmənli/ *adverb & adjective.* LME.
[from UN-¹ + WOMANLY *adverb, adjective.*]
► **A** *adverb.* In an unwomanly manner. LME.
► **B** *adjective.* **1** Of behaviour: not (regarded as) characteristic of or befitting a woman. E16.
2 Of a woman: lacking the qualities traditionally associated with women; mannish. M19.
¶ Rare between 16 and 19.
■ **unwomanlike** *adjective* not womanlike M17. **unwomanliness** *noun* M19.

unwonted /ʌnˈwəʊntɪd/ *adjective.* M16.
[from UN-¹ + WONTED.]
1 Not customary or habitual; unusual, not commonly encountered; infrequent. M16.
2 Unused *to*; unaccustomed (*to*). Orig. foll. by *to do.* L16.

📖 **1** C. BRONTË New rules and un-wonted tasks. C. DEXTER Was there an unwonted note of tetchiness in Conrad's voice?

■ **unwont** *adjective* (now *rare* or *obsolete*) = UNWONTED LME. **unwontedly** *adverb* M17. **unwontedness** *noun* L16.

unwork /ʌnˈwəːk/ *verb trans. rare.* Pa. t. & pple **unwrought** /ʌnˈrɔːt/. M16.
[from UN-² + WORK *verb.*]
†**1** Detach (a person) *from* a thing. Only in M16.
†**2** Spoil, destroy. Only in L16.
3 Release from an intertwined condition. M17.
4 Undo, restore to a former condition. E18.

unworkable /ʌnˈwəːkəb(ə)l/ *adjective.* M19.
[from UN-¹ + WORKABLE.]
Not workable or operable; unmanageable, uncontrollable; impracticable.
■ **unworkaˈbility** *noun* L19. **unworkableness** *noun* L19. **unworkably** *adverb* E20.

unworked /ʌnˈwəːkt/ *adjective.* M17.
[from UN-¹ + WORKED. See also UNWROUGHT *adjective.*]
1 Orig., of a mine, shaft, etc.: not worked. Now also (*fig.*), not exploited or turned to account. M17.
2 Not wrought into shape; not worked on. M18.
■ **unworking** *adjective* (esp. of a person) that does not or will not work L17.

unworkmanlike /ʌnˈwəːkmənlʌɪk/ *adjective.* M17.
[from UN-¹ + WORKMANLIKE *adjective.*]
Not workmanlike; *spec.* badly done or made.
■ Also (earlier) **unworkmanly** *adjective* M16.

unworldly /ʌnˈwəːldli/ *adjective.* E18.
[from UN-¹ + WORLDLY *adjective.*]
1 Transcending or exceeding what is usually found or experienced; = OTHERWORLDLY 1. E18.
2 Of a person: actuated by spiritual motives; spiritual. E19.

📖 **1** T. AIRD Sequestered they in love's unworldly dream. **2** B. HILTON Death was thought to be a lesser calamity than debt, and not only by unworldly clerics.

■ **unworldliness** *noun* E19.

unworn /ʌnˈwɔːn/ *adjective.* L16.
[from UN-¹ + WORN *adjective.*]
1 Not worn (out) or damaged by use, weather, etc. L16.
▸**b** Pristine, fresh. M18.
2 Of a garment etc.: not (yet) worn or put on. L18.

📖 **1b** BURKE In the morning of our days, when the senses are unworn and tender.

unworshipful /ʌnˈwəːʃɪpfʊl, -f(ə)l/ *adjective.* LME.
[from UN-¹ + WORSHIPFUL *adjective.*]
1 Unworthy or devoid of esteem or honour. Now *rare* or *obsolete.* LME.
2 Characterized by lack of a spirit of worship. M19.
■ **unworshipped** *adjective* not worshipped, not revered LME.

unworth /ˈʌnwəːθ/ *noun.* ME.
[from UN-¹ + WORTH *noun*¹.]
†**1** Lack of merit or claim to reward. *rare.* Only in ME.
2 Lack or absence of worth or value. M19.

📖 **2** J. RUSKIN Nature and Heaven command you . . to discern worth from unworth in everything.

unworth /ʌnˈwəːθ/ *adjective.* OE.
[from UN-¹ + WORTH *adjective.* Re-formed in 16.]
†**1** Lacking (sufficient) worth; unworthy, worthless, contemptible. OE–L18.
2 Not worthy of (something). L16.

📖 **2** MILTON Many things . . not ordinary, nor unworth the noting. J. R. LOWELL You . . may deem it not unworth your while to review it.

unworthy /ʌnˈwəːði/ *adjective, noun, & adverb.* ME.
[from UN-¹ + WORTHY *adjective.*]
► **A** *adjective.* **1** Lacking worth, worthless; having little or no merit or value; *spec.* (of a person) despicable, contemptible. ME. ▸**b** Disreputable; harmful to reputation; unseemly, discreditable. L17.
2 Having or possessing insufficient merit, excellence, or worth; not deserving. Usu. foll. by *of, to do.* ME. ▸**b** Inferior to what is merited or deserved; reprehensible, base. E16.
3 Of treatment, fortune, etc.: undeserved, unwarranted, unmerited; worse than deserved. LME.
4 Not worthy of or befitting the character, standing, or ability of or *of* (a person etc.); not worthy or deserving *of* notice etc. M17.

📖 **1** J. WOODALL Unworthy imposters under the names of Surgeons. SHELLEY These limbs, the unworthy temple of Thy spirit. **b** WORDSWORTH I suspect unworthy tales Have reached his ears. W. BESANT She repressed her indignation at this unworthy suggestion. **2** POPE Curs'd is the man, . . Unworthy property, unworthy light, . . who delights in war. W. COWPER Nature pines, Abandon'd, as unworthy of our love. R. POLLOK Unworthy is your servant To stand in presence of the King. J. DUNN She seemed surprised by . . happiness . . . She felt in some profound sense unworthy of it. **b** E. STILLINGFLEET Far be such unworthy thoughts from our apprehension of a Deity. **4** POPE Unmanly pride, Unworthy the high race from which we came. J. A. THOMSON He must be a bold man who will declare . . Nature's beckonings to be unworthy of attention. M. ARLEN This disorderly kind of life is unworthy of you.

► **B** *noun.* An unworthy person. Opp. ***worthy.*** E17.
► **C** *adverb.* Unworthily, in a manner unworthy *of* or (*rare*) of. M17.
■ **unworthily** *adverb* in an unworthy manner, state, or condition ME. **unworthiness** *noun* (*a*) the quality or condition of being unworthy, lack of worth or merit; (*b*) an instance of this: ME.

unwound /ʌnˈwaʊnd/ *adjective.* M17.
[from UN-¹ + *wound* pa. pple of WIND *verb*¹.]
Not wound (up).

unwound *verb pa. t. & pple*: see UNWIND.

unwounded /ʌnˈwuːndɪd/ *adjective.* OE.
[from UN-¹ + WOUNDED.]
Not wounded; unhurt.
■ **unwoundable** *adjective* E17.

unwrap /ʌnˈrap/ *verb.* Infl. **-pp-**. LME.
[from UN-² + WRAP *verb.*]
► **I** *verb trans.* **1** Remove the wrapping from; open or uncover by or as by removing a wrapping. Also, unwind, unroll. LME.
2 *fig.* Unfold, reveal, disclose. LME.
3 Release, free, deliver. M16.

📖 **2** *Daily Star* The Chancellor seems certain to unwrap an austerity package in his first Budget.

► **II** *verb intrans.* **4** Become unwrapped. M19.
¶ Rare between 16 and 19.

unwrapped /ʌnˈrapt/ *adjective.* L16.
[from UN-¹ + *wrapped* pa. pple of WRAP *verb.*]
Not wrapped (up).

unwrinkle /ʌnˈrɪŋk(ə)l/ *verb trans.* L16.
[from UN-² + WRINKLE *verb* or *noun*¹.]
Free from wrinkles; smooth.

unwrinkled /ʌnˈrɪŋk(ə)ld/ *adjective.* L16.
[from UN-¹ + WRINKLED.]
Esp. of the face or forehead: not wrinkled.

unwrite /ʌnˈrʌɪt/ *verb trans.* Infl. as WRITE *verb*; pa. t. usu. **-wrote** /-ˈrəʊt/, pa. pple usu. **-written** /-ˈrɪt(ə)n/. L16.
[from UN-² + WRITE *verb.*]
Cancel, annul, or rescind (something written).

unwritten /ʌnˈrɪt(ə)n/ *adjective.* LME.
[from UN-¹ + WRITTEN *adjective.*]
1 Not written (down) or recorded in print; *spec.* (*a*) orally transmitted; (*b*) (of a law, constitution, etc.) not promulgated in a written code, statute, or document; (*c*) (of a convention etc.) not expressed in words, implicit. LME.
2 Not written on or *on.* M16.

📖 **1** N. HAWTHORNE Diseases unwritten in medical books. A. MACVICAR The unwritten law that priests and journalists have a right to protect their sources. A. BROOKNER Conforming to this unwritten and indeed unspoken rule.

unwritten *verb*, **unwrote** *verb* see UNWRITE.

unwrought /ʌnˈrɔːt/ *adjective.* LME.
[from UN-¹ + WROUGHT *adjective.* See also UNWORKED.]
1 Not made, done, or performed; not formed or fashioned by being worked on; *spec.* (*a*) (of a material) still in a crude, raw, or natural state; (*b*) (esp. of a metal) not hammered into shape or worked into a finished condition. LME.
2 Of land, a mine, etc.: not worked. Now chiefly *dial.* E17. ▸**b** Of coal: not dug or mined. L18.

📖 **1** W. WOOD Every Country which . . returns us unwrought Materials to be manufactured here. SHELLEY Love's work was left unwrought—no brood . . took wing. H. SCHLIEMANN A wall of unwrought stones. **2** *fig.*: N. HAWTHORNE Treasures of wit and wisdom . . in the unwrought mines of human thought.

unwrought *verb pa. t. & pple* of UNWORK.

unwrung /ʌnˈrʌŋ/ *adjective.* E17.
[from UN-¹ + *wrung* pa. pple of WRING *verb.*]
Not wrung. Chiefly *fig.* in ***one's withers are unwrung***, ***one's withers remain unwrung***, etc. (with allus. to Shakes.).

📖 SHAKES. *Haml.* It touches us not. Let the galled jade wince, our withers are unwrung.

unyielding /ʌnˈjiːldɪŋ/ *adjective.* L16.
[from UN-¹ + YIELDING.]
1 Not yielding to force or pressure; *spec.* (*a*) (of a person etc.) unwilling to give way, firm, obstinate; (*b*) (of a substance, material, etc.) stiff, hard. Also foll. by *to.* L16.
2 Of an attitude etc.: characterized by firmness or obstinacy. L17.
■ **unyieldingly** *adverb* L19. **unyieldingness** *noun* E17.

unyoke /ʌnˈjəʊk/ *verb.* OE.
[from UN-² + YOKE *noun*¹, *verb.*]
► **I** *verb trans.* **1** Release (an animal) from a yoke or harness. OE. ▸**b** Disconnect, unlink. L16.
2 *fig.* Liberate, deliver from oppression. LME.

📖 **2** N. WHITING When British Isles . . From sad oppression had unyok'd their necks. MILTON The property of Truth is, . . to unyoke and set free the . . spirits of a Nation.

► **II** *verb intrans.* **3** **a** Unyoke an animal. Now *rare* or *obsolete.* L16. ▸**b** *fig.* Cease from labour. L16.

unyoked /ʌnˈjəʊkt/ *adjective*¹. L16.
[from UN-¹ + YOKED.]
Not provided with, subject to, or wearing a yoke.

📖 *fig.*: SHAKES. *1 Hen. IV* The unyok'd humour of your idleness.

unyoked /ʌnˈjəʊkt/ *adjective*². E18.
[pa. pple of UNYOKE.]
Set free from the yoke.

📖 W. WHITEHEAD The . . Swain . . at evening led His unyok'd heifers to the common stream.

unzip /ʌnˈzɪp/ *verb.* Infl. **-pp-**. M20.
[from UN-² + ZIP *verb.*]
1 *verb trans.* Unfasten the zip of (a garment etc., the wearer of a garment); unfasten (a zip). M20.
2 *verb intrans.* Open or separate (as) by means of a zip. L20.
3 *verb trans.* COMPUTING. Decompress (a file) that has previously been zipped. Cf. ZIP *verb* 5. L20.
■ **unzipper** *verb trans.* = UNZIP *verb* 1 M20.

unzipped /ʌnˈzɪpt/ *adjective.* M20.
[from UN-¹ + *zipped* pa. pple of ZIP *verb.*]
Having the zip unfastened; not zipped up.
■ Also **unzippered** *adjective* M20.

unzoned /ʌnˈzəʊnd/ *adjective.* M17.
[from UN-¹ + ZONED *adjective.*]
†**1** MYTHOLOGY. Of a god: not restricted to a particular region of the celestial sphere. Only in M17.
2 Not wearing a belt or girdle. E18.

uomo universale /ˈwɔːmo univerˈsaːle/ *noun phr.* Pl. ***uomini universali*** /woːˈmini univerˈsaːli/. M20.
[Italian, lit. 'universal man'.]
A man who excels in the major fields of learning and action. Cf. *RENAISSANCE man.*

-uous /ˈjuːəs/ *suffix.*
[Repr. Latin *-uosus*, Anglo-Norman, Old French *-uous, uos* (French *-ueux*): cf. -IOUS, -OUS.]
Forming adjectives from or after Latin or French, with the sense 'characterized by, of the nature of, consisting of, having much or many', as ***ambiguous***, ***portentous***, ***tempestuous***, ***tortuous***.

UP *abbreviation.*
1 United Party, *spec.* of South Africa.
2 United Presbyterian.
3 United Press.
4 Uttar Pradesh (formerly United Provinces, of Agra and Oudh, India).

up /ʌp/ *noun.* M16.
[from UP *adjective*¹, *adverb*¹, *adverb*² & *adjective*².]
1 *gen.* A person who or thing which is up. *rare.* M16.
2 An ascent (*lit.* & *fig.*); *esp.* a spell of prosperity or good fortune; a success. Chiefly in ***ups and downs***, alternate periods of good and bad fortune. M17. ▸**b** A feeling or period of mental stimulation or excitement. *US colloq.* M20.

3 In football at Winchester College, a forward. *slang.* M19.
4 A prospective customer. *US slang.* M20.
5 = UPPER *noun*². Usu. in *pl. slang.* M20.

> 📖 **2** CONAN DOYLE I've had ups in my life, and I've had downs. **b** *New York Times* Shapes . . in colors you can get an up from.

Phrases: **in two ups**: see TWO *adjective* 1. **on the up-and-up** (*a*) (orig. & chiefly *N. Amer.*) honest(ly), straightforward(ly); (*b*) steadily improving; prospering, successful.

up /ʌp/ *attrib. adjective*¹. Compar. UPPER *adjective*, superl. UPMOST, UPPERMOST. ME.
[from UP *adverb*¹, *adverb*² & *adjective*².]
1 Living up-country. Also, situated on high ground. Long *rare* or *obsolete*. ME.
2 (Of a train or coach) travelling towards the capital or principal terminus; (of a line or platform) used by such a train. L18.
3 (Of a drink) effervescing, effervescent; *fig.* cheerful, vivacious. E19.
4 Directed upwards; ascending. M19.
5 Esp. of a patient: not confined to bed. *colloq.* M20.
6 PARTICLE PHYSICS. Designating a quark associated with a charge of ⅔. Cf. DOWN *adjective* 5. L20.

> 📖 **2** O. S. NOCK The up W.R. 8.30 a.m. Plymouth–Paddington express. **4** E. GLYN That up look under the eyelashes was the affair of the devil! M. CARREL The man . . slammed the gate and punched the 'Up' button.

up /ʌp/ *verb*. Infl. **-pp-**. M16.
[from UP *adverb*¹, *adjective*².]
▶ **I** *verb trans.* **1** Take up and mark (a swan, esp. on the River Thames) with a mark of ownership. Long chiefly in **swan-upping** s.v. SWAN *noun*. M16.
†**2** Form or compose *of* something. *rare.* Only in M17.
†**3** With *it*: move upwards. *rare.* Only in M18.
4 Lift or put up; *esp.* raise (a weapon etc.), preparatory to use. L19.
5 NAUTICAL. Place (the helm or tiller) so as to carry the rudder to windward. Also, pull in (a trawl-net). L19.
6 Raise in value or status; *spec.* (*a*) CARDS raise (a bid, stake, etc.); (*b*) *colloq.* increase (a price, production, etc.); (*c*) *colloq.* promote (a person) to a higher rank or position. E20.

> 📖 **4** J. MARQUAND Sitting in front of her mirror, upping her hair. D. NORDEN Everybody was uttering cheers and upping their glasses. **6** D. JOHNSON They were upping my voltage. G. NAYLOR Them developers upped the price.

▶ **II** *verb intrans.* **7** Rise to one's feet; get up from a sitting or recumbent posture; get out of bed. Now chiefly *fig.* (*colloq.*), begin, esp. abruptly or boldly, to say or do something (usu. foll. by *and*). M17.
8 Foll. by *with*: ▸**a** Disclose or relate (a story etc.). *rare.* Only in E18. ▸**b** Lift or pick up; *esp.* raise (a weapon etc.) preparatory to use. *colloq.* M18. ▸**c** NAUTICAL. Place (the helm or tiller) so as to carry the rudder to leeward. M19.
9 Move upwards; rise, ascend. E19.

> 📖 **7** C. H. SORLEY Suddenly the division ups and marches to Aldershot. A. SILLITOE Suddenly upping and saying he was getting married, without having mentioned . . it before. P. MARSHALL She just ups and leaves, ruining the trip. **8b** H. NEWLAND Had he upped with his pilgrim-staff and broken the man's heretical head.

up /ʌp/ *adverb*¹.
[Old English *up*, *upp* = Old Frisian *up*, *op*, Old Saxon *up* (Dutch *op*), Old Norse *upp*, rel. to Old High German *ūf* (German *auf*), from Germanic base of UP *adverb*² & *adjective*². Cf. UP *adjective*¹.]
▶ **I** Denoting motion or direction in space.
1 To or towards a higher point or place; in an ascending direction; from a lower to a higher position; *spec.* (of the hands) towards or above shoulder-level. OE. ▸**b** So as to invert relative position; *esp.* so as to have a particular surface of a card or coin facing upwards. ME.
2 Towards a point overhead; away from the surface of the earth; into the air. OE. ▸**b** To a height above the ground or other specified surface; *spec.* (*a*) on to the back of a horse etc.; (*b*) NAUTICAL to or towards the masthead. OE. ▸**c** So as to be suspended at a height; into a hanging position. OE.
3 From a point below to a point above; *spec.* (*a*) from beneath the horizon to the line of sight; (*b*) from below the level of the earth, water, etc., to the surface; so as to detach or remove something from a fixed place in the ground etc.; (*c*) from the stomach into, or out at, the mouth. OE.
4 a So as to extend or rise to a higher point or level, esp. above the surface of the ground. OE. ▸**b** So as to become distended; so as to form a heap or pile. ME.
5 Into an upright position, esp. from a sitting, stooping, kneeling, or recumbent posture, or a fallen position; *spec.* out of bed. OE.
6 a To a higher level or altitude by gradual ascent, esp. in contact with a surface; *spec.* upstairs, esp. to bed. OE. ▸**b** To a place regarded as higher in position; e.g. towards the source of a river, against the current; NAUTICAL against the wind; from the country to the capital; to university. OE.
7 So as to direct the sight to a higher point or level. OE.

> 📖 **1** AV *Job* 10:15 *If* I be righteous, *yet* will I not lift vp my head. J. B. PRIESTLEY 'I do,' said Mrs. Joe firmly, holding up her hand. *New Yorker* He picked up a cardboard box. M. ROBERTS The priest's mouth works up and down in a frenzy. **b** *Times* He turned up the Knave of Clubs. **2** SHAKES. *Ven. & Ad.* Here the gentle lark . . mounts up on high. AV *Acts* 1:9 Hee was taken vp, and a cloud receiued him out of their sight. **b** W. DAMPIER Having fine handsome weather, we got up our Yard again. J. N. MCILWRAITH He might not have managed to mount had not Gib been at hand to give him 'a leg up'. **3** MILTON Living Creatures . . out of the ground up rose. J. THOMSON The welcome Sun, just verging up. W. E. SHUCKARD A . . prodigious quantity of the common mustard plant shot up. *Daily Chronicle* Half a dozen great trees were torn up by the roots. **dig up**, **grub up**, etc. **4a** R. J. FARRER Towering up into the sky from its plinth of hills. A. K. LOBECK A . . *driblet cone* may be built up 10 to 12 feet above the ground. **rise up**, **soar up**, etc. **b** P. KEITH The vessels . . swell up into a bunch. **earth up**, **puff up**, **swell up**, **throw up**, etc. **5** E. TOPSELL The tayle is very long . . turning vp like a Vipers tayle. A. MAUPIN We get up at some godawful hour of the morning. J. KOSINSKI Gaufridi was interrupted by the departure of the Soviet Ambassador. Everyone stood up. **help up**, **sit up**, etc. **6a** COLERIDGE The moving Moon went up the sky . . Softly she was going up. GOLDSMITH More company below, sir . . shall I shew them up? **b** J. HATTON The voyage up . . is done in a canoe. P. FITZGERALD He was known to drive up to London to work. **7** I. MURDOCH I stepped back . . and looked up at the house.

▶ **II** *transf.* & *fig.* **8** From a lower to a higher status in respect of position, rank, reputation, etc. OE.
9 a To a higher spiritual or moral level or object. OE. ▸**b** To a state of greater cheerfulness, confidence, resolution, etc. ME. ▸**c** Into a state of activity, commotion, excitement, etc. ME. ▸**d** To or at a greater or higher speed, rate, amount, etc. M16.
10 So as to cause sound to be heard or to increase in volume; so as to increase in degree or intensity. OE.
11 To or towards maturity, proficiency, etc. OE.
12 a Into existence, prominence, vogue, or currency; so as to appear or prevail. OE. ▸**b** To the notice or consideration of some higher authority; *spec.* (*a*) before a judge, magistrate, etc.; (*b*) from the House of Commons to the House of Lords. OE. ▸**c** So as to divulge, reveal, or disclose something, esp. as a charge or accusation. L16.
13 Into the hands or possession of another; so as to relinquish, abandon, or forsake someone or something. OE.
14 Into a receptacle or place of storage, as for security, convenience, or use when required. ME.
15 Into the position or state of being open (orig. by the raising of a gate, barrier, etc.). ME.
16 To or towards a state of completion, finality, or order. ME.
17 By way of summation or enumeration; to a final or total sum or amount. ME.
18 a So as to cover or envelop. ME. ▸**b** Into a close or compact form or condition; so as to be confined or secured. LME. ▸**c** Into a closed or enclosed state; so as to be shut or restrained. L15.
19 Into one's possession, charge, custody, etc. ME.
20 Into an open or loose condition of surface; so as to sever or separate something, esp. into many parts, fragments, or pieces. LME.
21 a Into a state of union, conjunction, or combination; so as to bring something together. LME. ▸**b** So as to supply deficiencies, defects, etc. M16.
22 a To or towards a person, place, or point; so as to approach or arrive. LME. ▸**b** To or into later life. M16. ▸**c** So as to find, come upon, overtake, or keep on the track of. E17.
23 To a stop or halt. E17.

> 📖 **8** J. R. LOWELL A preacher-up of Nature. CLIVE JAMES Not yet fully famous but plainly on her way up. M. AMIS Generally speaking, he has gone up in my estimation. **9a** W. BEVERIDGE A good while before we can get up our hearts from earth to heaven. **b** S. BARING-GOULD I really could not pluck up courage to do so. W. S. MAUGHAM It does one good to hear conversation like that . . it brightens one up. **c** E. STILLINGFLEET To work up a heated . . Imagination to the Fancy of Raptures. SHELLEY Their sounds . . Rouse up the astonished air. **d** H. KINGSLEY Whipping up his horse, he drove there. E. GLYN Carry had better hurry up and get that house in Park Street. **10** R. K. SMITH Why didn't you speak up when we were discussing the question? I. MURDOCH Speak up, please, I cannot hear you. W. CORLETT It is colder . . I must turn up the central heating. **11** F. A. KEMBLE As soon as they begin to grow up. **12a** A. CRICHTON Sabellians, Valentinians, and a host of obscurer sects, all rose up. A. GRIFFITHS The difficulty of providing funds cropped up. W. S. MAUGHAM The white shirt . . threw up his sunburned, weather-beaten face. L. BRUCE He . . had the real estate guy draw up the papers. **b** *Fraser's Magazine* The writ went up to the Lords. W. E. COLLINSON Touts are often had up before the courts. **c** J. GILMOUR If his two companions in accusation would not own up. **13** *Times* He gave himself up at Clacton-on-Sea. **14** SHAKES. *Oth.* Keep up your bright swords, for the dew will rust them. *Punch* This plan to store up the dead at minus two hundred degrees C. **15** *Temple Bar* She hastily threw up the window. O. MANNING The shops were opening up and people coming out. **16** W. S. GILBERT I polished up the handle of the big front door. L. VAN DER POST Gobbling up tangles of serpents like spaghetti. W. S. MAUGHAM I shall finish up as the wife of the local M.P. B. W. ALDISS Ernest sold up and retired. **cash up**, **clean up**, **clear up**, **eat up**, **sweep up**, etc. **17** B. JOWETT All my years when added up are many. W. S. MAUGHAM We must find someone else to make up the pat-ball set. *New Scientist* A simple way would be . . to count up the number of carbon atoms. **18a** T. HARDY She presently emerged, muffled up like a nun. **b** A. SOMERVILLE He was tied up. S. D. GROSS The limbs are drawn up as in acute enteritis. **bind up**, **fold up**, **roll up**, etc. **c** LD MACAULAY The Jacobites . . were forced to shut themselves up in their houses. **dam up**, **pent up**, etc. **19** M. EDGEWORTH One of his boys was taken up amongst the rioters. **20** THOMAS HUGHES Engaged in tearing up old newspapers . . into small pieces. **break up**, **plough up**, etc. **chop up**, **cut up**, etc. **21a** *Fraser's Magazine* Some smart magazine papers, bound up in a volume called *Pelham*. *Times Lit. Suppl.* Breton collected up some of his shorter pieces. **b** S. CHAPLIN Afterwards we'll fill up with some fish and chips. P. WRIGHT To make up the required number of hours for the week. **22a** DICKENS He would have rode boldly up, and dashed in among these villains. R. KIPLING An' the dawn comes up like thunder outa China 'crost the Bay. **b** WORDSWORTH I from my Childhood up Had known him. **23** P. G. WODEHOUSE What more likely than that he should have fetched up in Hollywood. **draw up**, **pull up**, etc.

▶ **III 24** With ellipsis of verb of action (esp. *get*, *stand*), *imper.*, & after aux. verbs. ME.

> 📖 **24** WORDSWORTH Up! up! my Friend, and quit your books. SIR W. SCOTT 'Up, Guards, and at them,' cried the Duke of Wellington. S. BECKETT Up the Republic!

Phrases: **up** NORTH. **up till** (*a*) *arch.* so as to reach, against; (*b*) = **up until** below. **up to** (*a*) as high or as far as; (*b*) up towards; upwards in the direction of; (*c*) so as to reach or arrive at; (*d*) = **up until** below; (*e*) so as to reach or attain by deliberate action; (*f*) so as to reach by progression or gradual ascent; (*g*) as many or as much as; including all below (a specified number etc.); (*h*) **lead up to** (Bridge), lead in a manner which allows (a particular card or suit) to be played from the third or fourth hand. **up to date** *adverbial & adjectival phr.* (*a*) *adverbial phr.* right up to the present time or the time of writing; (*b*) *adjectival phr.* (also (*attrib.*) **up-to-date**) meeting or in accordance with the latest requirements, knowledge, or fashions; modern, contemporary. **up-to-dateness** the quality of being up to date. **up to the minute** *adverbial & adjectival phr.* (*a*) *adverbial & adjectival phr.* right up to the present time; (*b*) *adjectival phr.* (also (esp. *attrib.*) **up-to-the-minute**) as up to date as possible, completely modern. **up until** throughout or during the (whole) time until. **up with** so as to reach.

Comb.: **up-and-over** *adjective* (of a door, esp. of a garage) opened by being raised and pushed back into a horizontal position; **up-and-under** RUGBY FOOTBALL a high kick intended to give the kicker and other team members time to reach the point where the ball will come down.

up /ʌp/ *adverb*² & (after *be* or other copula) *pred. adjective*². Compar. UPPER *adjective*, superl. UPMOST, UPPERMOST.
[Old English *uppe* = Old Frisian, Old Saxon *uppa*, Old Norse *uppi*, from Germanic base of UP *adverb*¹. Cf. UP *adjective*¹.]
▶ **I** Denoting position in space.
1 a At some distance above the ground or earth; high in the air. OE. ▸**b** Of the sun, moon, etc.: above the horizon; risen. OE.
2 On high or higher ground; (further) inland. Formerly also, on shore; on land. OE.
3 In an elevated position; at some distance above a usual or natural level; *spec.* (*a*) (of an adjustable, esp. sliding, device or part) raised; (*b*) *colloq.* (esp. of a jockey) on horseback; riding; (*c*) (of a woman's hair) worn fastened on top of or at the back of the head instead of hanging down, formerly indicating entry into adult society; (*d*) upstairs. OE.
4 Of a gate, door, etc.: open. *obsolete* exc. *Scot.* ME.
5 In an upright position; *spec.* (*a*) on one's feet, standing; (*b*) erected, built; (*c*) BASEBALL at bat. ME.
6 a Of a river, tide, etc.: in flood, (running) high. LME. ▸**b** Back out of the stomach, throat, or mouth. L16. ▸**c** On or above the surface of the water; above ground. M19.
7 a Out of bed; risen; not yet gone to bed. LME. ▸**b** Of game: roused, started. E17.
8 Towards a place or position; forward; advanced in place; *spec.* (*a*) further away from the mouth towards the source of a river, the inner part of a bay, etc.; (*b*) at or in the capital from the country; (*c*) *colloq.* in residence at university etc.; (*d*) (of a hound, huntsman, etc.) keeping pace with, or present at the death of, a hunted animal. E17.
9 Facing upward, uppermost. L17.
10 Of a crop: out of the ground, harvested and in store. M19.
11 Of a road etc.: with the surface broken or removed, esp. while under repair. L19.

> 📖 **1a** SHAKES. *Rich. II* Mount, mount, my soul! thy seat is up on high. F. HOYLE All this is going on not more than fifty miles up. **b** TOLKIEN The moon was up and was shining into the clearing. **2** SIR W. SCOTT The Red Pool . . lies up towards

the hills. L. GOLDING The Sakais of Malaya, who live up in the hills. **3** S. PEPYS In my Lord's roome . . where all the Judges' pictures hung up. JOYCE A dead cert for the Gold cup? . . Sceptre with O. Madden up. A. MAUPIN The landlady's hair was up in curlers. **5** BUNYAN Not able without staggering to stand up under it. DICKENS Members arrive . . to report that 'The Chancellor of the Exchequer's up.' G. A. SALA Tall potato-sacks, propped up in dark corners. **6a** DEFOE The tide was up. **c** J. RUSKIN The soldanella . . distinguished for its hurry to be up in the spring. **7a** G. VIDAL I've been up since seven. **8** A. TROLLOPE You'll be up in London . . next month. *Daily Telegraph* The Princess's party was not up at either kill. C. HARMAN He was still up at Cambridge with a scholarship to read history. **11** *Times* Finding a way round the many places where the road is up.

▶ **II** *fig.* **12 a** Actively stirring or moving about, roused; *spec.* (**a**) in a state of tumult or insurrection; in rebellion; (**b**) in a state of agitation, excitement, exaltation, or confidence; *colloq.* in a state of emotional or nervous stimulation. ME. ▸**b** Ready *for*. *colloq.* L19.

13 In a prevalent or continuing state (freq. in ***hold up***, ***keep up***). Formerly also, in power, in force. ME. ▸**b** Much or widely spoken of. *arch.* E17. ▸**c** Occurring, esp. as a special, unusual, or undesirable event; taking place, going on. *colloq.* M19. ▸**d** Of food or drink: ready, served. *colloq.* M20.

14 a Of a period of time: completed, ended, expired, over. LME. ▸**b** Of an assembly: risen; adjourned. M17. ▸**c** At the number or limit agreed upon as the winning score in a game. Also, (of a score) for each side, as the total for each side for the time being. M17. ▸**d** Having reached or attained a fruitless or undesired end. Freq. in ***the game is up*** s.v. GAME *noun*. L18.

15 a Higher in the ascending scale in respect of position, rank, fortune, etc.; in a position of affluence or influence. E16. ▸**b** In a state of increased power, force, strength, or vigour; ready for action; *spec.* (COMPUTING) running and available for use. Freq. in ***up and running***. M16. ▸**c** At a higher value, price, etc.; *arch.* advanced *in* years. M16. ▸**d** In advance of a competitor by so many points etc. L19.

16 On a charge before a magistrate etc.; in court. E20.

12a LD MACAULAY The hue and cry was raised . . the whole country was up. DICKENS Up one minute and down the next; now in spirits . . now in despondency. A. LANG My blood was up; no man shall call Allan . . a liar. J. RIDLEY The men of Beverley were up, and a formidable rising had gained control. **b** *Rolling Stone* I'm definitely up for trying again. **13c** E. REVELEY He seemed . . a bit sleepy and George wondered what was up. G. SWIFT You're quiet. What's up? **d** J. PORTER Grub's up! . . Them as wants forks can fetch 'em! **14a** J. S. WINTER His leave was nearly up. *Truck & Driver* When his driving time was up he carried on home. **b** J. HATTON There was much bustle of departing travellers. Parliament was up. **15b** *Computing* British Steel's giant private packet-switched network is up—and running successfully. **c** J. TEY Did I tell you that paraffin is up a penny, dear? D. J. ENRIGHT Artichokes are being burnt in France, / to keep the price up. **d** *Times* They were two up at the third hole.

Phrases etc.: ***it is all up with someone***, ***it is all up with something***: see ALL UP 1. ***not up to much***, ***thumbs up***: see THUMB *noun*. ***two-up and two-down***, ***two-up two-down***: see TWO *noun* 4. **up against** (**a**) close to, in contact with; ***up against the wall***: see WALL *noun*[1]; (**b**) *colloq.* (orig. *US*) faced or confronted by; ***up against it***, in great difficulties. **up and about** active, moving about; no longer in bed (esp. after an illness). **up and doing** busy and active. **up at** attending (a specified college or university). **up for** available for or being considered for (office etc.); ***up for grabs***: see GRAB *noun*[2]. **up in** *colloq.* = ***up on*** below. ***up in arms***: see ARM *noun*[2]. ***up NORTH***. **up on** *colloq.* well-informed or instructed in a subject, work, etc. (freq. with qualifying adverb). **up there** (**a**) above the earth, in heaven; (**b**) *colloq.* up on a level *with* something highly rated. **up to** (**a**) capable of or fit for; possessing a thorough knowledge of; *colloq.* a match for; (**b**) equal to, not more than; on a level with; (**c**) occupied or busy with; doing; planning; (**d**) *colloq.* (orig. *US*) obligatory, incumbent on; (**e**) ***be up to*** (*School slang*), be tutored by. **up top** (**a**) *Military slang* above decks; (of an aircraft) in the sky; (**b**) in a position of authority or influence; (**c**) in the brain, in terms of mental capacity; in terms of bust measurement; (esp. in ***not much up top***). **up with** (**a**) on a level with; (**b**) (now *dial.*) even with; quits with; (**c**) *colloq.* the matter with, wrong with.

■ **upness** *noun* the quality of being up (chiefly as 2nd elem. of comb., in ***grown-upness***, ***one-upness***, etc.) L19.

†up *preposition*[1].

[Old English *uppan*, *uppon* = Old Frisian *uppa* (*oppa*), Old Saxon *uppan* (cf. also Old High German *ūf(f)an* (Middle High German *uffen*)): see UP *adverb*[1]. Repl. in 16 by UP *preposition*[2].]

▶ **I** Denoting motion or direction in space.

1 On, upon; so as to reach or be on by ascent. OE–LME.

2 In attack on; in active opposition to. OE–LME.

▶ **II** Denoting position in space.

3 On, upon; so as to be suspended from or supported on; on the bank or brink of; close beside. OE–L16. ▸**b** On penalty of. OE–L15.

4 In respect of, in accordance with; by (chance etc.); concerning. ME–E16.

5 More than; above. Only in ME.

3b up land in the country as opp. to the town.

▶ **III** In respect of time.

6 After (a specified time); at (a stated time). OE–ME.

¶ Early forms distinct from UPON *preposition*.

up /ʌp/ *preposition*[2]. E16.

[from UP *adverb*[1] by ellipsis of *against*, *along*, etc. Repl. UP *preposition*[1] in 16.]

▶ **I** Denoting or implying movement.

1 Upwards along, through, or into; so as to ascend; from the bottom to the top of. E16. ▸**b** Extending upwards on. L16. ▸**c** Up into (a room etc.). *US local.* L18. ▸**d** Of a man: having sexual intercourse with. *coarse slang.* M20.

2 Towards the source of (a river etc.) from the mouth. E16.

3 Towards the inner or upper end of; into or towards the interior of. Also, along towards the other end of (a street, passage, shore, etc.). L16.

4 In a direction contrary to; against. E17.

1 G. GREENE Walking up a long staircase to meet Maurice at the top. D. ABSE When we were half-way up the hill. A. CARTER A coal fire . . thrust yellow flames up the chimney. **c** S. HALE Louise . . carrying some new pails up garret. **2** LD MACAULAY The Dutch fleet sailed up the Thames. G. HOUSEHOLD After the Severn bore has passed up river. **3** SPENSER They passing in Went up the hall. G. GREENE As you go up Maiden Lane. **4** T. D'URFEY The Fox has broke Covert . . she runs up the Wind.

▶ **II** Denoting location.

5 At or in a higher or more remote part of. M17. ▸**b** Up in (a room etc.). *US.* M19. ▸**c** At (a specified place). *colloq.* & *dial.* M20.

6 At the top of; at some distance up on or in. M17.

5 S. PEPYS Nova Scotia . . hath a river 300 miles up the country. SIR W. SCOTT Far up the lake, 'twere safest land. J. K. BAXTER My father . . Is up a ladder plucking down . . clusters Of passion fruit. **b** R. FROST We asked was there anything Up attic that we'd ever want again. **c** M. SPARK Collie Gould up the Elephant with young Leslie. **6** T. MOORE Alone in my chambers, up two pairs of stairs, Trinity College. TENNYSON We that day had been Up Snowdon.

Phrases: ***lead up the garden (path)***: see LEAD *verb*[1]. ***up a tree***: see TREE *noun*. ***up hill and down dale***: see HILL *noun*. ***up the creek***: see CREEK *noun*[1]. ***up the line***: see LINE *noun*[2]. ***up the pole***: see POLE *noun*[1] 1. ***up the river***: see RIVER *noun*[1]. ***up the spout***: see SPOUT *noun*. ***up the stick***: see STICK *noun*[1]. ***up the Straits***: see STRAIT *noun*[1]. ***up the wall***: see WALL *noun*[1]. **up yours** *coarse slang*: expr. contemptuous rejection.

up- /ʌp/ *prefix.*

[Repr. UP *adverb*[1], *adverb*[2], *preposition*[2].]

Prefixed to nouns, adjectives, and verbs, in various relations and in various senses, esp. indicating (**a**) position above, at a higher level (of), or nearer the interior or source (of), as ***upland***, ***upheartened***, ***upside***; (**b**) motion or direction up, upwards, to a higher level (of), or nearer towards the interior or source (of), as ***upcurved***, ***update***, ***upheave***, ***upswing***.

■ **up-anchor** *verb intrans.* (NAUTICAL) weigh anchor L19. **upbank** *adverb* (*rare* exc. *north.*) uphill M18. **up'bear** *verb trans.* (*arch.*) bear up, support, sustain (*lit.* & *fig.*); raise, exalt: ME. **up'bind** *verb trans.* (*arch.*) bind up L16. **up'blown** *adjective* (*arch.*) blown up; *esp.* inflated, puffed up: L16. **up'boil** *verb intrans.* (*literary*) boil up (*lit.* & *fig.*) LME. **upbound** *adjective* & *adverb* (*US*) going upstream L19. **†upbounden** *adjective* tied up LME–L16. **upbow** *noun* (MUSIC) a stroke in which a bow is drawn across a string from the tip to the heel L19. **'upbreak** *noun* (*obsolete* exc. *Scot.*) (**a**) an eruption, an outburst; (**b**) a breaking-up, a dissolution: M19. **up'break** *verb* †(**a**) *verb intrans.* (*rare*) begin to speak; (**b**) *verb trans.* (now *poet.*) break up; break open; (**c**) *verb intrans.* (*poet.*) force or make a way upwards or to the surface: ME. **up'breathe** *verb trans.* (*poet.*) send up as a breath E17. **up'bristled** *adjective* (*rare*) bristled up E17. **up'brushed** *adjective* brushed upwards M19. **up'bubble** *verb intrans.* (*literary*) bubble up M19. **up'build** *verb trans.* build up (*lit.* & *fig.*) E16. **up'builder** *noun* a person who upbuilds something M19. **up'buoy** *verb trans.* (*literary*) buoy up M17. **upburst** *noun* an upward outburst or outbreak M19. **up'burst** *verb* (**a**) *verb trans.* (*rare*, Spenser) burst open (a door); (**b**) *verb intrans.* burst upwards: L16. **up-card** *noun* (*US*) a playing-card turned face up on the table; *esp.* (in rummy) the top card of the waste-heap: M20. **up'catch** *verb trans.* (*poet.*) catch up (usu. in *pass.*) M16. **up-'channel** *adverb* & *adjective* (moving, leading, etc.) towards the upper end of a channel L19. **†upcheer** *verb trans.* (*rare*) cheer up, encourage: only in L16. **up-'choked** *adjective* (*Scot.*) choked up L18. **upchuck** *verb intrans.* & *trans.* (*N. Amer. slang*) vomit M20. **up'climb** *verb intrans.* & *trans.* (*arch.*) climb up; ascend: M16. **up'close** *verb trans.* & *intrans.* (*arch.*) close up LME. **upcoast** *adjective* & *adverb* (situated or extending) further up the coast L19. **up'curl** *verb trans.* & *intrans.* curl up E19. **upcurrent** *noun* a rising current of air or water E20. **upcurved** *adjective* curved upwards L19. **upcut** *noun* (ENGINEERING) a cut made by a cutter rotating so that the teeth are moving upwards when cutting M20. **up'dart** *verb intrans.* (*literary*) dart upwards E18. **up-dip** *adjective* & *adverb* (GEOLOGY) (situated or occurring) in a direction upwards along the dip E20. **up-do** *noun* (*colloq.*, orig. & chiefly *US*) a hairstyle in which the hair is swept up and fastened away from the face and neck M20. **updoming** *noun* (GEOLOGY) the upward expansion of a rock mass into a dome shape M20. **updraught**, ***updraft** *noun* †(**a**) *rare* = INDRAUGHT 2; (**b**) an ascending current of air: LME. **up'draw** *verb trans.* (**a**) *rare* pull out of the ground; (**b**) (now *poet.*) draw upwards: ME. **up'dry** *verb trans.* (*arch.*) dry up (usu. in *pass.*) LME. **up'fill** *verb trans.* (now *rare*) fill up LME. **up'filling** *noun* (now *rare*) the action or an act of filling something up; a thing which fills something up: E19. **upflung** *adjective* (*literary*) flung upwards E19. **upfold** *noun* (GEOLOGY) an anticline E20. **up'fold** *verb trans.* (*arch.*) fold up, fold together ME. **upfurled** *adjective* (*literary*) furled up E19. **upgang** *noun* (*obsolete* exc. *Scot.* & *north.*) (**a**) the action of ascending; ascension; (**b**) an ascent, an upward path or way: OE. **up'gather** *verb trans.* (*literary*) gather up, collect L16. **up'gaze** *verb intrans.* (*literary*) gaze upwards E19. **upglide** *noun* (PHONETICS) a glide from a relatively low tone to a higher one M20. **up'go** *verb intrans.* (now *arch.* & *Scot.*) go up; ascend, mount: ME. **up'grow** *verb intrans.* (*literary*) grow up (*lit.* & *fig.*) LME. **upgrowth** *noun* the process or result of growing up; an instance of this; *spec.* a raised growth or process: M19. **uphand** *adjective* operated or performed with the hand raised L17. **up'hang** *verb* (*arch.*) (**a**) *verb intrans.* hang on high; (**b**) *verb trans.* hang up, suspend: ME. **uphaul** *noun* a rope used for hauling up a boat's sail or centreboard E20. **up'heap** *verb trans.* accumulate or pile up (now chiefly as ***upheaped*** *ppl adjective*) LME. **up'hearted** *adjective* (*rare*) in good spirits, not downhearted M19. **†uphoard** *verb trans.* hoard up L16–M17. **uphoisted** *adjective* hoisted upwards M18. **up'hurl** *verb trans.* (*arch.*) hurl up, throw upwards L16. **up'knit** *verb trans.* (*rare*) knit or join together L16. **up'lay** *verb trans.* (*arch.*) lay or store up L16. **upleap** *noun* (**a**) an upward leap or spring; (**b**) MINING a fault resembling an upthrow: L19. **up'leap** *verb intrans.* (now *poet.*) leap or spring up or upwards ME. **up'led** *adjective* (*poet.*, *rare*) led up M17. **uplight** *noun* = UPLIGHTER L20. **uplighter** *noun* a light placed or designed to throw illumination upwards M20. **uplink** *noun* a communication link for transmissions from the earth to a satellite, weather balloon, etc. M20. **upload** *verb trans.* (COMPUTING) transfer (software or data) to a larger machine L20. **†uplock** *verb trans.* lock up L16–L17. **uplong** *preposition*, *noun*, & *adjective* †(**a**) *preposition* up along; (**b**) *noun* a strengthening bar extending along the sail of a windmill; (**c**) *adjective* (*arch.*) extending upwards: M18. **uplying** *adjective* situated or lying on high ground; upland: L19. **up'mount** *verb intrans.* & *trans.* (*arch.*) (cause to) mount up M16. **up-'pent** *adjective* (*arch.*) pent up E17. **up-'piled** *adjective* (*poet.*) piled up E17. **up-pricked** *adjective* (*rare*) (esp. of an animal's ears) pricked up L16. **up-push** *noun* (*rare*) a pushing upwards E20. **up-putting** *noun* (*Scot.*) †(**a**) the action or an act of putting something up; (**b**) accommodation, lodging: E16. **up'rend** *verb trans.* (*rare*) pull or tear up, uproot E20. **uproused** *adjective* (*poet.*) roused or stirred up L16. **up'send** *verb trans.* send up, discharge upwards M17. **upshift** *noun* & *verb* (chiefly *US*) (**a**) *noun* a movement upwards, esp. in a device; *spec.* a change to a higher gear in a motor vehicle; (**b**) *verb intrans.* change into a higher gear in a motor vehicle: M19. **upsize** *verb trans.* & *intrans.* increase the size, extent, or complexity of (something); undergo such an increase: L20. **up'skill** *verb trans.* (**a**) reskill; (**b**) increase or enhance the skill required in (a job): L20. **up'soar** *verb intrans.* (*poet.*) soar upwards L16. **up'speak** *verb intrans.* (*poet.*) speak up, begin to speak E19. **up'startle** *verb trans.* (*poet.*) startle up, cause to stand up by startling E19. **up'stay** *verb trans.* (*poet.*) hold up, prop up; *fig.* sustain, support: L16. **up'steer** *verb trans.* (now *dial.*) stir up, throw into turmoil or disorder M16. **upstir** *noun* (now *dial.*) a disturbance, a commotion M16. **upstirring** *noun* the action of stirring up a person or thing; stimulation, incitement, encouragement: E17. **upstirring** *adjective* stimulating, rousing M18. **up-street** *adverb* (*colloq.* & *dial.*) up the street; in, into, towards the higher part of a town: E19. **upstretched** *adjective* stretched upwards M16. **up-stroke** *noun* (**a**) *dial.* an upshot, a conclusion; (**b**) a stroke delivered upwards; the upward stroke of a pen etc.; (**c**) PHYSIOLOGY the part of a nerve impulse at which the action potential becomes more positive: E19. **up'swallow** *verb trans.* (*poet.*) swallow up L16. **up'swarm** *verb trans.* (*rare*) swarm up or over L16. **up'swell** *verb* (**a**) *verb intrans.* swell up; rise up as by swelling; (**b**) *verb trans.* increase the volume or amount of (as) by swelling: LME. **up'tear** *verb trans.* pull up by the roots, tear out L16. **up'tie** *verb trans.* (*poet.*) tie, bind, or fasten up LME. **uptilted** *adjective* tilted upwards M19. **uptime** *noun* time when a computer or similar device is operating or able to function M20. **up'torn** *adjective* torn up L16. **up'toss** *verb trans.* toss up E19. **up'tower** *verb intrans.* (*poet.*) tower above or over M19. **up'trained** *adjective* (*poet.*) trained M16. **uptrend** *noun* (chiefly *US*) an upward tendency; *spec.* (ECONOMICS) a rise in value over a period of time: E20. **upvaluation** *noun* (ECONOMICS) a revaluation upwards, esp. of one currency in relation to others on a common standard M20. **upvalue** *verb trans.* raise the value of (a currency etc.) on a scale M20. **up'waft** *verb trans.* (*poet.*, *rare*) waft upwards M18. **up'wake** *verb intrans.* & *trans.* (*rare*) wake up ME. **upwarp** *noun* (GEOLOGY) a gentle extensive elevation of the earth's surface E20. **upwarping** *noun* (GEOLOGY) the local raising of the earth's surface to form an upwarp M20. **up'wash** *noun* (**a**) *rare* a wash of a wave up a beach; (**b**) AERONAUTICS the upward deflection of an air-stream by an aerofoil: E20. **up'well** *verb intrans.* well up; (*spec.* of liquid, esp. seawater) surge upwards: L19. **upwelling** *verbal noun* a welling upwards; *spec.* the rising of cold water from the bottom of the sea, often bringing with it a renewed source of nutrients; the water that has risen in this way: M19. **up'whirled** *adjective* (*poet.*) whirled upwards M17. **up'wing** *verb intrans.* & *trans.* (*poet.*, *rare*) soar or fly up or above L19. **up'wound** *adjective* wound up L16.

up-a-daisy /ʌpəˈdeɪzi/ *interjection.* Now *arch.* & *dial.* E18.

[from UP *adverb*[1] + extended form of *a-day* (cf. LACKADAISY). Cf. UPSY-DAISY.]

= UPSY-DAISY.

upanayana /ʊpəˈnʌɪənə/ *noun.* E19.

[Sanskrit, from *upa* towards + *nayana* leading, bringing (from *nī-* to lead).]

An initiation ceremony for Hindu boys of the three higher castes between the ages of eight and sixteen, involving investiture with the sacred thread.

up-and-coming /ʌp(ə)nˈkʌmɪŋ/ *adjective. colloq.* M19.

[from UP *adverb*[2] + AND *conjunction*[1] + COMING *adjective*.]

1 Active, alert, energetic. *US.* M19.

2 Esp. of a person: promising, making progress, likely to succeed. E20.

2 H. CARPENTER The ingenious framework . . was the work of the up and coming engineer Monsieur Eiffel. *Match Fishing* The young up and coming anglers in the south want to win things.

■ **up-and-comer** *noun* an up-and-coming person M20. **up-and-comingness** *noun* L19.

up and down /ʌp (ə)n ˈdaʊn/ *adverbial, prepositional, adjectival, & noun phr.* As adjective also **up-and-down**. ME.
[from UP *adverb*[1], *adverb*[2] + AND *conjunction*[1] + DOWN *adverb*.]
▶ **A** *adverbial & pred. adjectival phr.* **1** Alternately upwards and downwards, on or to a higher and lower level or plane; *fig.* changeable, unstable; *colloq.* (of a person) in varying health or spirits, alternately elated and depressed. ME.
2 Here and there; to and fro; backward and forward; in every direction. ME.
3 Here and there; in various places throughout a district, country, etc. ME.
4 Upside down; topsy-turvy. Long *dial.* ME.
5 In or into a vertical position; vertically. LME.
6 In every respect; entirely, thoroughly, completely. Now *dial.* M16.
7 (Acting in) a straightforward or blunt manner. *colloq.* (chiefly *US*). M19.

> 🕮 **1** C. S. LEWIS Mrs. Moore is up and down; very liable . . to fits of jealousy. A. WILSON Looking Terence up and down, he added, 'A little training . . would soon give you the physique needed.' *Lydney (Glos.) Observer* His health had been up and down since he left the pit in 1959. **2** G. VIDAL Priests strolled up and down. *Rail* Locomotives . . spend long periods of time . . just shunting up and down. **3** E. BUDGELL With several Ribbons stuck up and down in it. BROWNING Brother Lippo's doings, up and down, You know them? **4** MILTON This is the Pharisee up and down, 'I am not as other men are'.

▶ **B** *prepositional phr.* **1** Backward and forward in; to and fro along or on. LME.
2 Here and there in or on; in various places throughout. L16.
3 On or to a higher and lower level or plane in or on. M17.

> 🕮 **1** STEELE Strolling up and down the Walks in the Temple. **2** LD MACAULAY Early in August hints . . were whispered up and down London. *Gardener* Drought has caused problems for gardeners up and down the country.

▶ **C** *attrib. adjective.* **1** Of movement or action: directed or occurring alternately upwards and downwards or to or on a higher and lower level or plane; characterized by such movement or action. E17. ▸**b** Chiefly NAUTICAL. Adapted or used for hauling up and down. L18.
2 a Perpendicular; very steep. E18. ▸**b** Direct, straightforward. *colloq.* (chiefly *US*). M19.
3 a Having an uneven or irregular surface; consisting of ups and downs; undulating. L18. ▸**b** *fig.* Changeable, variable; *colloq.* (of a person) subject to changing moods, alternately elated and depressed. E20.
4 Taking place to and fro or backward and forward; spent in moving about. E19.
5 Of a fist-fight: continuing after one of the combatants is knocked down. M19.
6 Of or pertaining to up trains and down trains. L19.

> 🕮 **1** G. PALEY I hummed a little up-and-down tune. **2** C. FIENNES Such up and down steep hills. **b** H. KEMELMAN I want a straight up-and-down vote without discussion. **3b** *Listener* Dalton had an up-and-down relationship with Crossman. **4** M. R. MITFORD She has, in the course of an up-and-down life, met with . . many authors. G. A. SALA The perpetual up-and-down flowing of the crowd.

▶ **D** *noun phr.* Pl. **ups and downs**.
1 An up-and-down movement; a variation or alternation of condition, circumstance, quality, etc. Also foll. by *of*. Usu. in *pl.* M17.
2 An irregularly undulating surface, lineation, etc.; an undulation. Usu. in *pl.* L17.

> 🕮 **1** J. R. LOWELL The regular up and down of the pentameter churn. J. CAREY Thackeray's life was punctuated by wild ups-and-downs of fortune. M. FRENCH Discussing the ups and downs of the market. **2** W. COBBETT The ups and downs of sea in a heavy swell.

▪ **up-and-downer** *noun* (*slang*) an up-and-down fight; a violent quarrel: E20.

Upanishad /uːˈpanɪʃad/ *noun.* E19.
[Sanskrit *upaniṣad*, from *upa* near + *ni-ṣad* sit down.]
Each of a series of Sanskrit religious and philosophical treatises concluding the exposition of the Vedas.
▪ **Upaniˈshadic** *adjective* of or pertaining to the Upanishads E20.

uparch /ʌpˈɑːtʃ/ *verb trans.* L19.
[from UP- + ARCH *verb*[1].]
GEOLOGY. Raise (strata etc.) to form a broad dome or anticline.
▪ **uparching** *noun* (*a*) the action of the verb; (*b*) the structure produced by uparching: E20.

upas /ˈuːpəs/ *noun.* L18.
[Malay (*pohun*) *upas* poison.]
1 A poisonous Javanese tree, *Antiaris toxicaria*, of the mulberry family, formerly reputed to destroy all animal life in its vicinity. Also ***upas tree***. L18. ▸**b** *fig.* A deadly or highly destructive influence. E19.
2 The poisonous latex of this and similar trees, used as an arrow poison. E19.

upbeat /ˈʌpbiːt/ *noun & adjective.* M19.
[from UP- + BEAT *noun*[1].]
▶ **A** *noun.* **1** MUSIC. An unaccented beat *esp.* that before the downbeat. M19.
2 PROSODY. An anacrusis. Also, an arsis, a stressed syllable. L19.
3 *fig.* An optimistic or positive mood, development etc.; a pleasant occurrence. M20.
▶ **B** *adjective.* Cheerful; optimistic, positive; lively, vigorous. *colloq.* (orig. *US*). M20.

> 🕮 A. HAILEY Delighted to share some upbeat, inspirational news for a change. *Investors Chronicle* Lonhro has meanwhile tannoyed to anyone who'll listen its upbeat view of its trading prospects.

†**upbraid** *noun.* ME–L17.
[from UP- + BRAID *noun* (cf. next). Cf. UPBRAY *noun*.]
(A) reproach, (a) reproof; (a) slander.

upbraid /ʌpˈbreɪd/ *verb.*
[Late Old English *upbrēdan*, perh. after unrecorded Old Norse verb from *upp-* UP- + *bregða* BRAID *verb*[1]. Cf. BRAID *verb*[2], UPBRAY *verb*.]
▶ **I** †**1** *verb trans.* Bring forward or attribute (a matter) as a ground for censure or reproach. (Foll. by *against*, *to*.) LOE–E18.
2 *verb trans.* Censure, find fault with; *esp.* chide or reproach (a person). (Foll. by *for*, *with*.) ME.
3 *verb intrans.* Censure, find fault; *esp.* speak chidingly or reproachfully to a person. ME.

> 🕮 **1** W. GOUGE This is not upbraided to David as a crime. **2** S. RICHARDSON Mr. Clerimont then upbraids her Guilt. R. LINDNER She . . upbraided me almost daily for my 'coldness'. S. J. PERELMAN My wife objects to cigar fumes in the bath, she's constantly upbraiding me. **3** M. MITCHELL Scarlett glared at her, too tired to rail, too tired to upbraid.

▶ **II** †**4** *verb intrans.* Cast, pull, or set up. Only in ME.
†**5** *verb intrans.* Come out of a faint; start up, spring up. LME–E16.
6 a *verb intrans.* Of food: be regurgitated. Now *dial.* M16. ▸**b** *verb trans.* Of food: cause indigestion in, nauseate. Now *dial.* L16.
▪ **upbraider** *noun* (now *rare*) L16. **upbraiding** *verbal noun* the action of the verb; an instance of this, a reproach, a reproof: ME. **upbraidingly** *adverb* in an upbraiding manner L16.

†**upbray** *noun. rare* (Spenser). Only in L16.
[Alt. Cf. next.]
= UPBRAID *noun*.

upbray /ʌpˈbreɪ/ *verb trans. obsolete* exc. *dial.* L16.
[Alt. Cf. prec.]
= UPBRAID *verb* 1, 2.

upbring /ʌpˈbrɪŋ/ *verb trans.* Long *arch. & dial.* Pa. t. & pple **upbrought** /ʌpˈbrɔːt/. ME.
[from UP- + BRING.]
Bring up; *esp.* rear, educate. Freq. as ***upbrought*** *ppl adjective.*

upbringing /ˈʌpbrɪŋɪŋ/ *noun.* L15.
[from prec. + -ING[1].]
†**1** Building. Only in L15.
2 The bringing up of a child; the fact of being brought up as a child; the manner of this, education. Also, an instance of this. E16.

> 🕮 **2** M. T. TSUANG A control group . . chosen as having similar upbringings . . was examined. A. N. WILSON Given her background and upbringing . . she would take the notion of the religious life seriously.

upbrought *verb pa. t. & pple* of UPBRING.

up-by /ˈʌpbʌɪ/ *adverb. Scot. & north.* M18.
[from UP- + BY *adverb*.]
Up there; up at or to a particular place.

UPC *abbreviation.*
1 Uganda People's Congress.
2 Universal product code.

upcast /*as verb* ʌpˈkɑːst, *as noun* ˈʌpkɑːst/ *verb & noun.* ME.
[from UP- + CAST *verb*, *noun*[1].]
▶ **A** *verb trans.* Pa. t. & pple **upcast**.
†**1** Utter loudly. Only in ME.
2 Cast or throw upwards. LME. ▸**b** Utter as a reproach. *Scot. & north.* E19.
3 Direct (a look, the eyes, etc.) upwards. Long only as ***upcast*** *ppl adjective.* LME.
†**4** Throw or force open (a gate etc.). *Scot.* LME–M16.
▶ **B** *noun.* **1** (A mass of) soil or other material thrown up in digging, ploughing, etc. M16.
2 A chance, an accident. *rare.* E17. ▸**b** An upset. *Scot.* E19.
3 A reproach, a taunt; a ground or occasion of this. *Scot. & north.* E17.
4 MINING & GEOLOGY. = UPTHROW *noun* 1a. L18.
5 MINING. A ventilating shaft through which air leaves a mine. Also ***upcast shaft***. M19.
6 The action or an act of casting or throwing something upwards. L19.

upcome /*as verb* ʌpˈkʌm, *as noun* ˈʌpkʌm/ *verb & noun.* OE.
[from UP- + COME *verb*.]
▶ **A** *verb intrans.* Pa. t. (*rare*) **upcame** /ʌpˈkeɪm/, pa. pple (*rare*) **upcome**. Come up, ascend. Now chiefly as UPCOMING. OE.
▶ **B** *noun.* Chiefly *Scot.*
1 (A) way up, (an) ascent. *rare.* LME.
2 A person's outward appearance. Now *rare* or *obsolete.* E17.
3 The final or decisive point. E19.
4 A result; a yield. L19.

upcoming /ʌpˈkʌmɪŋ/ *adjective.* M19.
[from prec. + -ING[2].]
That is coming up; *spec.* (chiefly *N. Amer.*) that is about to happen; forthcoming.

> 🕮 *Times* STC was also hurt by City trepidation about upcoming profit results.

upconverter /ˈʌpkənvəːtə/ *noun.* M20.
[from UP- + CONVERTER.]
ELECTRONICS. A device that converts a signal to a higher frequency.
▪ **upconversion** *noun* conversion (of a signal) to a higher frequency, esp. in television reception M20. **upconvert** *verb trans.* subject to upconversion M20.

up-country /*as noun* ˈʌpkʌntri, *as adjective & adverb also* ʌpˈkʌntri/ *noun, adjective, & adverb.* L17.
[from UP- + COUNTRY.]
▶ **A** *noun.* Orig., an upland or inland district. Later, the or *the* interior or inland part of a country. L17.

> 🕮 L. NKOSI I can see it all . . the beach . . the sweating pink-faced tourists from upcountry.

▶ **B** *adjective.* Of, pertaining to, or situated in the interior of a country, inland. E19.

> 🕮 *Sun* Planning to resell them at a huge profit to some up-country bandit chief.

▶ **C** *adverb.* Towards the interior of a country, inland. E19.

> 🕮 E. WAUGH He . . travelled upcountry as far as the Venezuelan border.

update /*as verb* ʌpˈdeɪt, *as noun* ˈʌpdeɪt/ *verb & noun.* Orig. *US.* M20.
[from UP- + DATE *verb*.]
▶ **A** *verb trans.* Bring up to date. M20.

> 🕮 *Sunday Times* I'll update myself . . and emerge as a real Seventies mum. A. BLOND A lexicographic set-up deep in computers for updating dictionaries. S. BELLOW He has been updating his research material.

▶ **B** *noun.* The action or an act of updating someone or something; the result of this; an updated version of something; a report or account containing the latest or current information on something. *colloq.* M20.

> 🕮 D. DELILLO We listened to news updates on the radio. *Games Review* The game is probably due for an update next year. *attrib.*: *Word Ways* Supplemented by update lists which the computer . . generates.

▪ **updatable** *adjective* L20. **updater** *noun* (chiefly COMPUTING) (*a*) = UPDATE *noun*; (*b*) a person who or thing which updates something; *spec.* a computer program etc. which provides updates: M20.

up-end /ʌpˈɛnd/ *verb.* Orig. *dial.* E19.
[from UP- + END *noun*.]
1 *verb trans.* Set (something) on its end; turn end upwards. E19.
2 *verb intrans.* Rise up on end; *spec.* (of a duck etc.) dip the head below water and raise the tail into the air, when feeding in shallow water. L19.
3 *verb intrans.* OIL INDUSTRY. Manoeuvre an offshore oil platform into an upright position. Only as ***up-ending*** *verbal noun.* L20.

> 🕮 **1** R. D. LAING He . . disarranged and upended the beds. P. LIVELY He upends the bottle into her glass. **2** *New Scientist* It had a beak like a swan and it could probably up-end in water.

upfield /*as adverb* ʌpˈfiːld, ˈʌp-; *as adjective* ˈʌpfiːld/ *adverb & adjective.* M20.
[from UP- + FIELD *noun*.]
▶ **A** *adverb.* **1** SPORT. In or to a position nearer to the opponents' end of a football etc. field. M20.
2 CHEMISTRY & PHYSICS. In a direction corresponding to increasing field strength. M20.
▶ **B** *adjective.* **1** SPORT. Directed into or occurring in a position nearer to the opponents' end of a football etc. field. M20.
2 CHEMISTRY & PHYSICS. Situated or occurring in the direction of increasing field strength. M20.

upfloor /ˈʌpflɔː/ *noun.* OE.
[from UP- + FLOOR *noun*.]
Orig., an upper floor or room. Now only *spec.*, a triforium.
¶ Not recorded between OE and L19.

For other words beginning with *up-* see the entry for **up-**

upfront /ʌp'frʌnt, 'ʌp-/ *adverb & adjective. colloq.* (orig. *US*). Also **up-front**, **up front**. M20.
[from UP- + FRONT *noun.*]
▶**A** *adverb.* At the front, in front, prominently; openly, frankly; (of payment) in advance, initially. M20.

> 🕮 *Times* If.. officials are saying this kind of thing, they ought to have the guts to say it up front. *Hair Flair* Create lots of interest up-front with clever use of gel.

▶**B** *adjective.* **1** That is in the forefront, prominent; open, frank; (of a payment) made in advance, initial. M20.
2 *spec.* Of a control switch etc.: located at the front of something for easy access. Chiefly *US.* L20.

> 🕮 **1** *Landscape* Two young surveyors.. charge a £500 up-front fee to cover travel costs. *Daily Telegraph* British Aerospace.. had now become more vocal and up-front.

upgrade /*as noun & adverb* 'ʌpgreɪd, *as verb* ʌp'greɪd/ *noun, adverb, & verb.* Orig. *US.* L19.
[from UP- + GRADE *noun, verb.*]
▶**A** *noun.* **1** An upward slope or incline. Now chiefly in ***on the upgrade*** below. L19.
2 The action or an act of upgrading something. Also, an upgraded version of something; an upgraded piece of equipment, machinery, etc. L20.
3 A thing which upgrades something; *spec.* an additional feature or enhancement. *US.* L20.

> 🕮 **1** K. SANBORN I have no taste for overtaking runaway mules on a steep and interminable upgrade. **2** *Times* ISC upgrade lifts shares. *Which Micro?* Upgrade to 86B brings twin double density disks. *Nature* As with any new software *Mathematica* is not without bugs, so upgrades are essential.

Phrases: **on the upgrade** (*a*) ascending, rising; (*b*) improving.
▶**B** *adverb.* Uphill. *US.* L19.
▶**C** *verb.* **1** *verb trans.* Raise to a higher standard or level; *spec.* (*a*) increase the grade or status of (a job); raise (an employee) to a higher grade or rank; (*b*) improve or enhance (machinery, equipment, etc.), esp. by adding or replacing components. E20.
2 *verb intrans.* Upgrade (a person or thing). M20.

> 🕮 **1** *Which Micro?* A 16-bit computer.. can be upgraded to IBM compatibility. R. P. JHABVALA The area of Earl's Court where they lived together was.. being upgraded. M. STANTON He is upgraded to work exclusively as a neurologist. **2** *Times* The man.. advised me to buy a standard fare and upgrade on the train.

▪ **upgrada'bility** *noun* ability to be upgraded L20. **upgradable** *adjective* able to be upgraded L20. **upgra'dation** *noun* the raising or improvement of grade, status, etc.; upgrading; an instance of this: L20. **upgrader** *noun* L20.

Uphaliday /ʌp'halɪdeɪ/ *noun. Scot.* L15.
[from UP- + var. of HOLIDAY *noun.* Cf. UPHELLY-.]
Epiphany as the end of the Christmas holiday.

upheaval /ʌp'hiːv(ə)l/ *noun.* M19.
[from next + -AL¹.]
1 GEOLOGY. = UPLIFT *noun* 1b. M19.
2 *fig.* A sudden or violent change or disruption. M19.
3 *gen.* The action or an act of heaving up; an instance of this. L19.

> 🕮 **2** A. T. ELLIS Unfamiliar with the current upheavals in the Roman Church. H. CARPENTER Soon will come a major upheaval in the form of war or revolution.

upheave /ʌp'hiːv/ *verb.* ME.
[from UP- + HEAVE *verb.*]
1 *verb trans.* Orig., exalt. Later, heave or lift up (something), esp. forcibly. ME.
2 *verb intrans.* Rise up; be lifted up. M17.

> 🕮 **1** BROWNING While Hebron upheaves The dawn.. on his shoulder. E. BOWEN Since the twentieth century opened, no Western European capital had been.. upheaved by internal strife. **2** *Scribner's Magazine* Along the west it upheaves into the fine Valles range.

▪ **upheavement** *noun* the action or process of upheaving; the fact of being upheaved M19. **upheaver** *noun* L16. **upheaving** *verbal noun* the action of the verb; an instance of this: M19.

upheld *verb pa. t. & pple*: see UPHOLD.

Uphelly- /ʌp'hɛli/ *combining form. Scot.* M16.
[Var. of abbreviation of UPHALIDAY.]
Of Epiphany as the end of the Christmas holiday.
▪ **Up-Helly-Aa** /ˌʌphɛlɪ'ɑː/ *noun* (*a*) = UPHALIDAY; (*b*) an annual festival held at Lerwick in the Shetland Islands, celebrated as the revival of a traditional midwinter fire-festival: L19.

uphill /*as noun & attrib. adjective* 'ʌphɪl, *as adverb & pred. adjective* ʌp'hɪl/ *noun, adverb, & adjective.* M16.
[from UP- + HILL *noun.*]
▶**A** *noun.* **1** The upward slope of a hill; an ascent, an incline, *esp.* a steep one. M16.
†**2** In *pl.* False dice which give high numbers. *slang.* L17–E19.

> 🕮 **1** *Dirt Bike* The slow rpm build-up hurt our lap time.. on a long uphill.

▶**B** *adverb & adjective.* **I** *adverb* & (after *be* or other copula) *pred. adjective.* **1** Up a slope, esp. of a hill; in an ascending direction; on an incline, upwards; *fig.* in a situation of difficulty or involving hard work. E17.
2 To or on the upper side *of. rare.* E20.

> 🕮 **1** O. MANNING A road wound uphill. J. BUCHAN I pushed uphill among the trees.

▶**II** *attrib. adjective.* **3** Situated or occurring up a slope, esp. of a hill; elevated. E17.
4 Sloping or ascending upwards, esp. steeply; *fig.* arduous, difficult; *rare* contending against difficulties. E17.

> 🕮 **3** O. HEYWOOD My last and best journey will be to the up-hill city. K. M. WELLS The uphill clatter of farmer Jim's manure-spreader. **4** R. COBDEN We had an up-hill battle, but we succeeded. *Discovery* The slight sinking feeling experienced by pedestrian members.. when faced by the considerable uphill trudge. *Guardian* On the uphill road to Villard-de-Lans. J. DIDION It's uphill work making you laugh.

▪ **uphillward** *adverb & adjective* (*a*) *adverb* in an uphill direction; (*b*) *adjective* uphill: M17.

uphold /ʌp'həʊld/ *verb trans.* Infl. as HOLD *verb*; pa. t. & pple usu. **upheld** /ʌp'hɛld/. ME.
[from UP- + HOLD *verb.*]
1 Hold up, support, sustain, (*lit. & fig.*); maintain unimpaired and intact. ME.
2 Orig., provide or perform regularly. Later, keep in a proper state of repair; provide with food etc. Now *Scot. & dial.* ME.
3 Raise or lift up; direct upwards. *arch.* LME.
4 Support by advocacy or assent, esp. against objection or criticism; confirm or maintain (a decision, judgement, etc.); give countenance to (a person, practice, etc.). L15. ▸**b** Maintain (a statement), warrant (a fact). Now chiefly *Scot. & north.* M16.

> 🕮 **1** R. C. HUTCHINSON A fierceness which would uphold him in his struggle. E. WAUGH The manager.. manfully upheld the integrity of British hotel-keeping. D. PARKER The center-table was upheld by.. three carved figures. **2** *Westminster Gazette* He was also bound by a covenant in the lease to 'uphold' the premises. **3** F. W. FARRAR They upheld their clenched hands.. to plead for mercy. **4** J. MARTINEAU This plea.. upholds a practice essentially unjust. H. JAMES Vermont, which she boldly upheld as the real heart of New England. *Sun (Baltimore)* The.. Court of Appeals upheld today a lower court decision. **b** C. M. YONGE He always upheld that you acted for his good.

upholder /ʌp'həʊldə/ *noun.* ME.
[from prec. + -ER¹.]
1 a An upholsterer (now only as a guild-name). Formerly also, a dealer in small wares or secondhand goods. ME. ▸†**b** An undertaker. E18–E20.
2 A person who or thing which upholds someone or something. LME.

> 🕮 **1** *Times* The Lord Mayor.. attended the annual dinner of the Upholders' Company. **2** J. WOODALL Wheat flower.. is the principall naturall upholder of the life and health of man. H. CARPENTER I was an upholder of the old stern doctrines.

†**upholster** *noun.* LME.
[formed as prec. + -STER.]
1 An upholsterer. LME–M18.
2 *spec.* A maker of or dealer in beds and bedding. M16–L17.

upholster /ʌp'həʊlstə, -'hɒl-/ *verb.* Orig. *US.* M19.
[Back-form. from UPHOLSTERER or UPHOLSTERY.]
1 *verb intrans.* Do upholstery work. *rare.* M19.
2 *verb trans.* Provide (as) with upholstery. M19.
▪ **upholstered** *adjective* provided (as) with upholstery; ***well-upholstered*** (joc.), (of a person) fat: M19.

upholsterer /ʌp'həʊlst(ə)rə, -'hɒl-/ *noun.* E17.
[Expanded form of UPHOLSTER *noun*: see -ER¹. Cf. *panterer* etc.]
A person who makes, repairs, or deals in articles of furniture covered with textile fabrics and stuffed with padding, springs, etc.; a person who upholsters furniture, esp. professionally.
▪ **upholstress** *noun* (*rare*) a female upholsterer M19.

upholstery /ʌp'həʊlst(ə)ri, -'hɒl-/ *noun.* M17.
[formed as prec.: see -ERY.]
The textile fabrics, padding, springs, etc., used in the covering and stuffing of furniture; an upholsterer's work.

uphroe /'juːfrəʊ/ *noun.* Also **eu-**. M17.
[Dutch *juffrouw* lit. 'maiden', from *jong* young + *vrouw* woman. Cf. JUFFER, UFER, YUFFROUW.]
NAUTICAL. A wooden or brass rod or bar pierced at intervals with holes through which small lines can be run to hold in place an awning or stays.

up Jenkins /ʌp 'dʒɛŋkɪnz/ *noun phr.* L19.
[from UP *adverb*¹ + the surname *Jenkins*.]
A parlour game in which an object concealed in a player's hand must be detected by a player on the opposing side. Cf. ***tip-it*** s.v. TIP *verb*⁴.

upkeep /'ʌpkiːp/ *noun.* L19.
[from UP- + KEEP *noun.*]
Maintenance in good condition or repair; the cost or means of this.

upkeep /ʌp'kiːp/ *verb trans.* Pa. t. & pple **upkept** /ʌp'kɛpt/. LME.
[from UP- + KEEP *verb.* In sense 2 infl. by the noun.]
†**1** Support. Only in LME.
2 Maintain in good condition or repair. Orig. & chiefly as ***upkeeping*** *verbal noun.* L19.

upland /'ʌplənd/ *noun & adjective.* OE.
[from UP- + LAND *noun*¹.]
▶**A** *noun.* **I 1** *sing.* & in *pl.* The parts of a country outside the towns; the rural districts. Long *arch. rare.* OE.
▶**II 2** (An area or stretch of) high, hilly, or mountainous country; (chiefly *local & US*) high as opp. to low-lying ground, ground above flood-level, a stretch of this. M16.
3 The interior or inland part of a country; an area or stretch of this. *arch.* L16.
4 *ellipt.* In *pl.* Upland cotton. M19.

> 🕮 **2** M. HALE The Downs or Uplands of Cammington in Huntingdonshire. C. MERIVALE They had.. gained the open upland of swamp and moor. G. BRENAN Dry uplands planted with unpromising soil.

▶**B** *attrib.* or as *adjective.* †**I 1** Living out in the country; rustic, rural. LME–L17.
▶**II 2** Of or pertaining to the interior or inland part of a country; situated, living, or occurring inland. L16.
3 Of, pertaining, or belonging to high, hilly, or mountainous country or (chiefly *local & US*) high as opp. to low-lying ground; situated, living, or occurring on high ground. E17. ▸**b** Flowing from high to low ground. *rare.* M17.

> 🕮 **2** ROBERT JOHNSON The vpland townes are fairer and richer, then those.. nearer the sea. **3** LYTTON The twin green hills.. with the upland park and chase. *Times* The 59 species breeding in upland woods.

Special collocations: **upland cotton** any of various esp. medium- and short-stapled forms of cotton, chiefly derived from *Gossypium hirsutum* var. *latifolium*, which are grown in the US (orig. named in contrast with ***sea-island cotton***). **upland plover**, **upland sandpiper** a N. American sandpiper, *Bartramia longicauda*, which breeds on upland fields etc.
▪ **uplander** *noun* a native or inhabitant of an upland part or district L17.

uplandish /ʌp'landɪʃ/ *adjective & noun.* Now *rare.* ME.
[from prec. + -ISH¹.]
▶**A** *adjective.* †**1** = UPLAND *adjective* 1. ME–M17.
2 = UPLAND *adjective* 2. ME.
†**3** = UPLAND *adjective* 3. M16–E17.
†**4** Outlandish, foreign. Only in E17.
▶†**B** *noun.* (A) foreign language. Only in L16.

uplift /*as verb* ʌp'lɪft, *as noun* 'ʌplɪft/ *verb & noun.* ME.
[from UP- + LIFT *verb, noun*².]
▶**A** *verb trans.* Pa. pple **-lifted**, (*arch.*) **-lift**.
1 Lift up, raise; GEOLOGY raise (part of the earth's surface). Freq. as ***uplifted*** *ppl adjective.* ME.
2 *fig.* **a** Raise in rank, honour, or estimation. Now *rare.* ME. ▸**b** Elevate or stimulate morally, emotionally, or spiritually. Also (now *Scot. & dial.*), make proud. Freq. as ***uplifted*** *ppl adjective.* LME.
3 a Collect or levy (a rent etc.); draw (wages). *Scot.* L15. ▸**b** *gen.* Collect, pick up; *spec.* (of public transport) take up (passengers). Chiefly *Scot.* M20.
4 Utter (a prayer, cry, etc.); make (the voice) heard. E19.
5 Increase (a price, wages, etc.). M20.

> 🕮 **1** N. HAWTHORNE The boy uplifted his axe. *Spectator* Some internal force has up-lifted the earth's crust. P. NORMAN The daisy faces uplifted to see him fly past. **2a** SHAKES. *Cymb.* Your low-laid son our godhead will uplift. E. B. PUSEY He uplifts ordinary things, that they too should be sacred. **b** P. H. GIBBS Excited and uplifted by a tremendous surge of patriotism. U. HOLDEN Mamma would be singing for soldiers, uplifting their morale. **3b** S. JAY The objective is to uplift the message without being detected. *Freight Guide* Foreign carriers willing to uplift cargo from India. **4** R. W. EMERSON New flowerets bring, new prayers uplift. J. CONRAD The fellow.. was moved to uplift his voice ... and he trolled out in Castilian that song you know.

▶**B** *noun.* **1** The action or an act of uplifting something; the fact of being uplifted; an instance of this. M19. ▸**b** *spec.* in GEOLOGY. (A) raising of a part of the earth's surface. M19.
2 *fig.* A morally, emotionally, or spiritually uplifting effect, result, or influence. L19.
3 Support from a garment that raises part of the body, esp. the breasts; (a part of) a garment giving such support. E20.
4 An increase in price, wages, etc. M20.

For other words beginning with *up-* see the entry for **up-**

📖 **1** G. E. HUTCHINSON A remnant of an old surface that escaped the general Pleistocene uplift. **2** J. G. HOLLAND What an uplift he gave to the life to which he ministered. ROSEMARY MANNING The day school was . . full of moral platitudes and uplift. **3** *Housewife* The bra that gives a natural uplift. **4** *Times* The negative slope of the yield curve only makes the bills self-financing via capital uplift.

Comb.: **uplift bra**, **uplift brassière**: designed to support and raise the breasts.

■ **uplifter** *noun* †(*a*) *Scot.* a collector of rents etc.; (*b*) *gen.* a person who or thing which uplifts something (*lit. & fig.*); *N. Amer.* a person engaged in social reform: **E20**. **uplifting** *verbal noun* the action of the verb; an instance of this: **LME**. **upliftment** *noun* the action or process of improving esp. economic or social conditions; the result of this: **E20**.

uplook /*as verb* ʌpˈlʊk, *as noun* ˈʌplʊk/ *verb & noun. arch.* **ME**.
[from **UP-** + **LOOK** *verb*, *noun*.]
▸**A** *verb intrans.* Look upwards. **ME**.
▸**B** *noun.* An upward look or glance. **M19**.
■ **uplooker** *noun* **L16**.

upmanship /ˈʌpmənʃɪp/ *noun. colloq.* **M20**.
[Abbreviation.]
= ***one-upmanship*** s.v. **ONE** *adjective, noun, & pronoun*.

up-market /*as adjective* ˈʌpmɑːkɪt, *as adverb & verb* ʌpˈmɑːkɪt/ *adjective & adverb.* **L20**.
[from **UP-** + **MARKET** *noun*.]
▸**A** *adjective.* Of, pertaining to, or suitable for the more expensive or affluent end of the market; dearer; of superior quality. **L20**.
▸**B** *adverb.* Towards the more expensive or affluent end of the market. **L20**.
▸**C** *verb trans.* Make (a product) up-market. **L20**.

upmost /ˈʌpməʊst/ *adverb & adjective.* **LME**.
[from **UP** *adjective*¹, *adverb*² & *adjective*² + **-MOST**. Cf. **UPPERMOST**.]
Furthest up, uppermost.

upon /əˈpɒn/ *adverb.* Long *arch.* **ME**.
[from the preposition.]
1 †**a** On something indicated or specified; in or to a position on a surface or object. **ME–L16**. ▸**b** Of clothing etc.: on the body. **LME**. ▸†**c** In a direction towards something indicated or specified. **LME–L16**.
†**2** Thereafter, thereupon. **LME–E17**.

upon /əˈpɒn/ *preposition.* **ME**.
[from **UP** *adverb*¹, *adverb*² + **ON** *preposition*, after Old Norse *upp á* (Old Swedish *up a*, *uppa*, Swedish *på*, Norwegian, Danish *paa*).]
1 Of position: = **ON** *preposition* I. **ME**. ▸†**b** = **OVER** *preposition* 10. **LME–M16**. ▸**c** By means of, with. Now *dial.* **LME**. ▸†**d** = **IN** *preposition* 8. *rare.* **E17–M18**.
2 Of time, or action implying time: = **ON** *preposition* II. **ME**.
3 Of order, arrangement, manner, or state: = **ON** *preposition* III. **ME**. ▸†**b** From, of, (an illness, injury, privation, etc.). **LME–L17**. ▸†**c** At (an expense, cost, etc.). **LME–E18**. ▸†**d** On condition of. **E16–M17**. ▸†**e** Out of, from, (a specified material). **M16–L17**.
4 Of motion, direction, or relation: = **ON** *preposition* IV; *spec.* (*a*) denoting cumulative addition or repetition; (*b*) (of a season, event, etc.) into proximity, approaching, arrived; (preferred to *on* in these senses). **ME**. ▸†**b** From the possession of (a person), esp. by force. **ME–M18**. ▸†**c** Among, between, (a number of people etc.). **L15–L16**. ▸**d** To (a person) in marriage or (formerly) by descent. *obsolete* exc. *Scot.* **L15**.

📖 **1** W. LAUD He hath constantly resided upon his episcopal houses. DEFOE A tract of land . . seated upon some navigable river. W. THOMSON An island bordering upon Istria. BOSWELL I intended to have printed it upon . . an English letter. SHELLEY Pestilence, And Panic, shall wage war upon our side! V. WOOLF Drawn blinds, and upon them a curious pattern. E. WAUGH A familiar cry . . Mr Salter had heard it upon upon the lips of countless distressed colleagues. T. HARDY Upon the door was a neglected brass plate. I. MURDOCH The road led downhill with the rose nursery upon the left. **c** SHAKES. *Mids. N. D.* To die upon the hand I love so well. **2** SHAKES. *Meas. for M.* Upon the heavy middle of the night. E. GRIFFITH I wrote upon the instant but . . cannot recollect what I said. KEATS Upon a Sabbath-day it fell. E. R. EDDISON It was now upon mid July. JOCELYN BROOKE 'How long you been out, then?' he asked. 'Two years—just upon'. E. BOWEN Upon there seeming to be no answer, he had turned and gone out. ***ONCE upon a time.*** **3** SHAKES. *A.Y.L.* It was upon this fashion bequeathed me by will. R. BENTLEY He order'd every man upon the pain of death to bring in all the money he had. BOSWELL Security being taken upon the property. J. AUSTEN Depend upon it, . . I will visit them all. SOUTHEY The fate of the continent was upon the hazard. TENNYSON When you want me, sound upon the bugle-horn. *Chambers's Journal* Upon the most insubstantial of pretexts. DICKENS He was never absent . . unless upon an errand. C. H. SPURGEON The leaves are just upon the turn, and the fall . . close at hand. *Law Times* A commission . . upon the sums received. **b** A. TELFAIR Which frightened him so much, that he fell sick upon it. **4** SHAKES. *L.L.L.* Advance your standards, and upon them, lords. AV *Exod.* 7:17 I will smite with the rod . . vpon the waters. J. STRYPE After the entrance of Queen Elizabeth upon her government. ADDISON A young Fellow . . sent upon a long Voyage. *Fraser's Magazine* O'Connell is bent upon the disruption of the British empire. TENNYSON To lift the woman's fall'n divinity Upon an even pedestal. J. PAYNE A deadly terror got A sudden hold upon her. T. HARDY He . . asked upon whom were the Baronet's suspicions directed. R. MACAULAY An inadequate meal . . upon which to face so trying a day. V. WOOLF She flung herself upon him, went into raptures. M. KEANE He shut the window upon the . . bark of a fox. G. VIDAL The eyes were turned upon me. I. MURDOCH He had seen the coffin . . and heard the earth fall upon it. R. SUTCLIFF We learned verse upon verse of Macaulay's *Lays of Ancient Rome*. **b** E. O'BRIEN Winter was almost upon them. J. BRAMHALL Whatsoever the Popes of Rome gained upon us. **d** R. L. STEVENSON She was married . . upon my Uncle Robin.

¶ In many contexts (though not in *spec.* meanings of sense 4), *upon* is now considered more formal than *on*.

upper /ˈʌpə/ *noun*¹. **L18**.
[from **UPPER** *adjective*.]
1 The part of a boot or shoe above the sole. Freq. in *pl.* **L18**.
2 *ellipt.* **a** An upper jaw, plate of artificial teeth, etc. **L19**. ▸**b** An upper deck, storey, berth, etc. **M20**.
3 A log or piece of sawed lumber of superior grade. *US.* **L19**.
4 a A pupil of the upper school. *School slang.* **E20**. ▸**b** An upper-class person. *colloq.* **M20**.
1a on one's uppers *colloq.* in poor or reduced circumstances, extremely short of money.

upper /ˈʌpə/ *noun*². *slang* (orig. *US*). **M20**.
[from **UP** *verb* + **-ER**¹.]
A drug, esp. an amphetamine pill, with a stimulant or euphoric effect. Cf. **UP** *noun* 5.

upper /ˈʌpə/ *adjective.* **ME**.
[from **UP** *adjective*¹, *adjective*² + **-ER**³. Cf. Middle Dutch *upper* (Dutch *opper*), Low German *upper*.]
▸**I** *lit.* **1** Of, pertaining to, or occupying a higher or more elevated site or position; *spec.* (*a*) (of part of a region) situated on high or higher ground, further inland or to the north; (*b*) (of part of a river etc.) that is nearer to the source or further from the sea; (*c*) that is higher in altitude; (*d*) (of a storey, floor, etc.) that occupies or constitutes the higher or highest part of a building. **ME**. ▸**b** Furthest removed from the door or entrance; innermost. Chiefly in ***upper end***. **L16**.
2 Situated above another of the same; (of part of the gut) situated closer to the mouth; (of a side, surface, etc.) lying above the corresponding lower side, surface, etc. **LME**.
3 a Of a garment etc.: worn above or outside another; outer. **E16**. ▸**b** Designating the section of a stocking above the knee. Only in ***upper-stock***. *obsolete* exc. *Hist.* **M16**. ▸**c** Of (part of) a garment: covering (part of) the body above the waist. **L16**.
4 Occurring, taking place in, or directed towards a higher or the highest position. Freq. in ***upper-cut*** below. **E17**.
5 a Of or pertaining to the earth's surface; lying above the lower regions. Chiefly *poet.* **M17**. ▸**b** *GEOLOGY & ARCHAEOLOGY.* (Freq. **U-**.) Designating a younger, and hence usu. shallower, part of a stratigraphic division, archaeological deposit, etc., or the period in which it was formed or deposited. **L17**.

📖 **1** I. WATTS They . . bless the Mansions of the upper Skies. K. BONFIGLIOLI Penthouse flats in Upper Brook Street. W. BOYD Government House, with its . . half-timbered upper floor. ***Upper California***, ***Upper Canada***, ***Upper Danube***, ***Upper Egypt***, etc. **b** SIR W. SCOTT The walls of this upper end of the hall. **2** J. J. SEIDEL Bellows . . consist first of an upper and under board. I. MURDOCH Wearing, on his now visible upper half, a . . corduroy jacket. ***stiff upper lip***: see **STIFF** *adjective*. **5** MILTON Those . . had left their charge, Flown to the upper World. BYRON He's dead—and upper earth with him has done; He's buried.

▸**II** *fig.* **6** Of, pertaining to, or occupying a higher or the highest position, station, or rank; superior in authority, influence, etc. **ME**.
7 Of a better quality; superior. *literary.* **L16**.
8 Of or pertaining to more advanced studies. Freq. in ***upper school*** below. **E17**.
9 *MUSIC.* Constituting or producing a higher tone or note. **M19**.

📖 **6** J. AUSTEN Her upper-housemaid and laundry-maid. CARLYLE The best-informed Upper-Circles.

Special collocations & comb.: **upper air** (now *rare*), **upper atmosphere** the upper part of the earth's atmosphere; now *spec.* that above the troposphere. ***upper case***: see **CASE** *noun*² 6. **Upper Chamber** = ***Upper House*** below. ***Upper Chinook***: see **CHINOOK** 1. **upper circle** the tier of seats in a theatre etc. above the dress circle. **upper-class** *adjective* of, pertaining to, or characteristic of the upper class. **upper class(es)** (the members of) the highest class of society, *esp.* the aristocracy. **upperclassman** *US* a junior or senior high school or college student. **upper crust** (*a*) the top crust of a loaf; †(*b*) the exterior or surface layer of the earth; (*c*) *colloq.* the aristocracy. **upper-crusty** *adjective* (*colloq.*) aristocratic, socially superior. **upper-cut** *noun* (*a*) a short upward blow, esp. to the chin, delivered with the arm bent; (*b*) *BRIDGE* a strategy by which the defender tries to promote a trump card in his or her partner's hand by forcing the declarer to overtrump a ruff. **upper-cut** *verb* (*a*) *verb trans. & intrans.* hit (a person) with an upper-cut; (*b*) *verb intrans. & trans.* (*BRIDGE*) (of the defender) employ an upper-cut to force (the declarer) to overtrump a ruff. **upper deck** a deck in a ship, bus, etc., situated above the lower deck, *esp.* the topmost one. **upper dog** *rare* [after *underdog*] the victorious party in a contest; a person in a superior or dominant position. **upper fourth**, **upper fifth**, etc., an upper division of a fourth, fifth, etc., form in a secondary school. **upper hand** (*a*) dominance, control, mastery (freq. in ***gain the upper hand***, ***get the upper hand***); (*b*) *the* place of honour (freq. in ***give the upper hand***, ***take the upper hand***). **Upper House** one of the houses of a legislature consisting of two houses, usu. the smaller and less representative (sometimes unelected) one, often dealing with legislation after the Lower House; *esp.* the House of Lords. ***upper jaw***: see **JAW** *noun*¹ 1. **upper leather** (*a*) = **UPPER** *noun*¹ 1; (*b*) leather from which the upper of a boot, shoe, etc., is or may be made. **upper-middle** *ellipt.* a member of the upper middle class (usu. in *pl.*). **upper-middlebrow** *noun & adjective* (a person) claiming to be or regarded as intellectually or culturally between the middlebrow and the highbrow. **upper middle class(es)** (the members of) the class of society between the upper and the middle class. **upper-middle-class** *adjective* of, pertaining to, or characteristic of the upper middle class. ***upper pastern(-bone)***: see **PASTERN** 2c. **upper regions** (*a*) heaven as opp. to earth; (*b*) the sky. **upper school** (*a*) in a secondary school, (the pupils in) the fifth and sixth forms; (*b*) a secondary school for children aged from about fourteen upwards, usu. following on a middle school. **upper second** an upper division of a second-class honours degree. **upper sixth** an upper division of a sixth form in a secondary school. ***upper storey***. **upper ten (thousand)** *colloq.* the upper classes; the aristocracy. **uppertendom** (*colloq.*, chiefly *US*) = ***upper ten*** above. **upperwing** *ENTOMOLOGY* = **FOREWING**; ***orange upperwing***: see **ORANGE** *noun & adjective*¹. **upper works** (*a*) *NAUTICAL* the part of a ship above the main deck; (*b*) *slang* the head; a person's mental abilities. ***upper yield point***: see ***yield point*** s.v. **YIELD** *verb*.
¶ Freq. opp. **LOWER** *adjective*.

upper /ˈʌpə/ *adverb.* Long *rare.* **LME**.
[from **UP** *adverb*¹, *adverb*²: see **-ER**³.]
To or in a higher or more elevated place or position; higher, further up.

upperest /ˈʌp(ə)rɪst/ *adjective.* Long *rare.* **ME**.
[from **UPPER** *adjective* + **-EST**¹.]
Uppermost.

uppermost /ˈʌpəməʊst/ *adjective, adverb, & noun.* **LME**.
[from **UPPER** *adjective* + **-MOST**. Cf. **UP** *adjective*¹, *adjective*², **UPMOST**.]
▸**A** *adjective.* **1 a** Outermost; external. Now *rare.* **LME**. ▸**b** Occupying the highest or most elevated position or place; topmost; (of part of a river etc.) that is nearest to the source or furthest from the sea. **L15**.
2 *fig.* Highest in respect of rank, importance, influence, authority, etc.; predominant, supreme. **L17**.

📖 **1a** J. MAPLET The Adder . . casteth off yearley his uppermost skin or coate. **b** AV *Luke* 11:43 Woe vnto you Pharisees: for ye loue the vppermost seats in the Synagogues. J. A. BROWN There had been . . Paleolithic implements on this uppermost floor. **2** LD MACAULAY The politician whose practice was always to be on the side which was uppermost. H. JAMES Her uppermost feeling in regard to them was . . cold scorn.

▸**B** *adverb.* In or to the uppermost position (*lit. & fig.*). **LME**.

📖 J. WESLEY Lie with that Ear uppermost. WORDSWORTH We . . saw . . generous love . . Uppermost in the midst of fiercest strife. R. OWEN It is not East-West comradeship which will be uppermost in Russian minds.

▸†**C** *noun.* A person who or thing which is uppermost; *esp.* the highest part of something. **LME–M18**.

Upper Voltan /ʌpə ˈvɒltən/ *adjectival & noun phr.* **L20**.
[from *Upper Volta* (see below) + **-AN**.]
Hist. (A native or inhabitant) of Burkina Faso in W. Africa when it was known as Upper Volta. Cf. **BURKINAN**, **VOLTAIC** *adjective*².

uppie /ˈʌpi/ *noun. slang.* **M20**.
[from **UPPER** *noun*²: see **-Y**⁶, **-IE**.]
= **UPPER** *noun*². Usu. in *pl.*

upping /ˈʌpɪŋ/ *noun.* **M16**.
[from **UP** *verb* + **-ING**¹.]
1 The action of **UP** *verb*. **M16**.
2 The end or upshot of a matter. *dial.* **E19**.
Comb.: **upping-block**, **upping-stock** (now *rare*) a horse-block, a mounting block.

uppish /ˈʌpɪʃ/ *adjective.* **L17**.
[from **UP** *adverb*² & *adjective*² + **-ISH**¹.]
†**1** Plentifully supplied with money. Only in **L17**.
2 Orig., elated; in high spirits. Later, self-assertive, arrogant; (*obsolete* exc. *dial.*) ready to take offence, short-tempered. **E18**.
3 Pretentious, affectedly superior, putting on airs. **M18**.
4 Slightly elevated or directed upwards. (*lit. & fig.*) **L18**.

📖 **2** G. B. SHAW I don't like selfish uppish domineering people. **3** L. GORDON Plain Hester Fitzjohn turns down handsome Roger Buckdale under the influence of her uppish family. **4** *Times* An uppish stroke off the last ball of Goodwin's opening over.

■ **uppishly** *adverb* **E20**. **uppishness** *noun* **E18**.

For other words beginning with *up-* see the entry for **up-**

uppity /ˈʌpɪti/ *adjective. colloq.* L19.
[Fanciful from UP *adverb*[1]: see -Y[1].]
Above oneself, self-important, uppish.
▪ **uppitiness** *noun* M20.

upraise /*as verb* ʌpˈreɪz, *as noun* ˈʌpreɪz/ *verb & noun.* ME.
[from UP- + RAISE *verb*.]
▶ **A** *verb trans.* †**1** Raise from the dead. ME–M16.
2 †**a** Praise, extol. ME–L16. ▸**b** Raise to a higher level, lift up, elevate; direct upwards. Freq. as ***upraised*** *ppl adjective.* ME. ▸**c** Raise the spirits of; assist, encourage, cheer. ME. ▸†**d** Excite or rouse (a feeling, emotion, etc.). *rare.* L16–M17.
3 Erect, set up, build. Long *rare.* ME.

📖 **2b** R. GARNETT Worshippers upraise pale consternated looks. H. G. DE LISSER A dozen . . men rushed forward . . with upraised machetes. **c** MILTON He . . thus with peaceful words uprais'd her soon.

▶ **B** *noun.* A sloping mining shaft excavated from the lower end upwards. *US.* L19.

uprate /ʌpˈreɪt/ *verb trans.* M20.
[from UP- + RATE *verb*[1].]
Raise to a higher standard, upgrade; increase the value or performance of.

📖 *National Observer (US)* Its engines have been uprated to produce more power. *Times* Child benefit is unlikely to be uprated fully in line with inflation.

uprava /uˈpraːva/ *noun.* L19.
[Russian = authority.]
Hist. In Imperial Russia, the executive board of a municipal council.

uprear /ʌpˈrɪə/ *verb.* ME.
[from UP- + REAR *verb*[1].]
1 *verb trans.* Raise up, elevate, erect. ME. ▸**b** Raise in dignity, exalt. Long *poet.* LME.
2 *verb trans.* Bring up, tend in growing. Long *rare.* ME.
3 *verb trans.* Rouse, stir up, excite, (an emotion etc.). Now *rare.* L15.
4 *verb intrans.* Rise up. *rare.* E19.

uprest /ʌpˈrɛst/ *noun. rare.* E17.
[Var. of UPRIST *noun*.]
The action or an act of rising up.

upright /ˈʌprʌɪt, ʌpˈrʌɪt/ *adjective, verb, adverb, & noun.*
[Old English *upriht* corresp. to Old Frisian *upriuht*, Middle & mod. Dutch *oprecht*, Old High German *ūfreht* (German *aufrecht*), Old Norse *upréttr*: see UP *adverb*[1], -RIGHT.]
▶ **A** *adjective.* **I** *lit.* **1** Erect on end or on the feet, vertical, perpendicular; not leaning over or inclined. OE. ▸**b** Designating a device or structure designed to be used in a vertical or upright position; *spec.* (of a piano, harpsichord, etc.) having vertical strings. L18. ▸**c** Of a picture, book, etc.: greater in height than in width. L19.
†**2** Lying flat at full length, on the back with the face upwards, supine. Chiefly in ***lie upright***. OE–E17.
3 Characterized by a vertical position or bearing; erect in carriage. LME. ▸**b** Of a vagrant: big, strong, sturdy. Chiefly in ***upright-man***. *slang.* Now *rare* or *obsolete.* M16.
4 = PERPENDICULAR *adjective* 2c. *rare.* L16.
5 Taking place in a vertical direction; upward. Now *rare.* M17.

📖 **1** V. WOOLF The thousand white stones, some slanting, others upright, the decayed wreaths. F. HOYLE They reared up . . on their hind limbs and began to walk upright. I. MCEWAN Mary woke with a shout . . and sat upright in bed. B. CORNWELL The Captain held his sword blade upright, almost at the salute. *She* The seat will keep your child upright and prevent him from tipping over. **b** ***upright bass***, ***upright chair***, ***upright freezer***, etc. **3** G. THORNE Hibbert was an upright, soldierly-looking man.

▶ **II** *fig.* †**6** **a** True, undoubted, rightful. *Scot.* Only in L15. ▸**b** In good condition, in proper order, correct. E16–M17. ▸**c** Plain, straightforward, unambiguous. L16–E17.
7 Strictly honest or honourable, having integrity, morally good. M16.
8 Stable, equable; *dial.* sound in health. *rare.* M16.

📖 **7** *Face* Tidy suburban gardens . . soda-bar, drive-in and upright American values. *Guardian* The life . . of upright and upstanding English soldier Clive Candy.

▶ **B** *verb trans.* Raise or restore to an upright or vertical position; erect, right. LME.

📖 P. D. JAMES One of the stacked chairs had been uprighted.

▶ **C** *adverb.* **1** = UPRIGHTLY 1. E16.
2 In a vertical direction, vertically upwards. L16.
3 Independently, on one's own means. *dial.* E19.
▶ **D** *noun.* †**1** **a** A vertical front, face, or plane. M16–E18. ▸**b** = ELEVATION 5. E17–M19.
2 An upright or vertical position, the perpendicular. L17.
3 A post, rod, etc., fixed or standing upright, esp. as a structural support; *spec.* in FOOTBALL, a goalpost. L17. ▸**b** An upright piano. M19. ▸**c** BASKET-MAKING. A plane used for shaving skeins to a required width. M19. ▸**d** A crossword clue or answer intended to fill spaces along a vertical line of the frame. E20.

📖 **2** P. FITZGERALD The Master . . gently raised himself to the upright. **3** *Glasgow Herald* Barr . . had little difficulty in placing the ball between the uprights. J. FOWLES One huge crossbeam supported on three uprights.

Phrases: ***twopenny upright***: see TWOPENNY *adjective* 1.

uprighteousness /ʌpˈrʌɪtʃəsnɪs/ *noun. arch.* M16.
[from UPRIGHT *adjective* after ***righteousness***.]
The quality of being upright or honourable.
▪ †**uprighteously** *adverb* (*rare*, Shakes.) honourably: only in E17.

uprightly /ˈʌprʌɪtli/ *adverb.* M16.
[from UPRIGHT *adjective* + -LY[2].]
1 Honourably, honestly. M16. ▸†**b** Candidly, straightforwardly. M16–M17.
2 In an upright position; vertically, perpendicularly. E17.

uprightness /ˈʌprʌɪtnɪs/ *noun.* M16.
[formed as prec. + -NESS.]
1 The state or condition of being honest, honourable, or morally good; integrity. M16.
2 The state or condition of being erect or vertical. M17.

uprisal /ʌpˈrʌɪz(ə)l/ *noun. rare.* L19.
[from UPRISE *verb* + -AL[1].]
The action or an act of rising up.

uprise /ʌpˈrʌɪz, *as noun also* ˈʌprʌɪz/ *verb & noun.* Now *poet.* ME.
[from UP- + RISE *verb, noun*.]
▶ **A** *verb intrans.* Infl. as RISE *verb*; pa. t. **uprose** /ʌpˈrəʊz/, pa. pple usu. **uprisen** /ʌpˈrɪz(ə)n/.
1 Rise to one's feet, assume a standing posture. ME. ▸**b** Rise from bed, get up. ME.
2 Of the sun: rise, come up. ME.
3 Rise from the dead. ME. ▸**b** Come up from the underworld. M16.
4 Ascend to a higher level; rise into view or hearing. ME. ▸**b** Become erect, stand on end. L18.
5 Come into existence or notice, arise. L15.
▶ **B** *noun.* †**1** Resurrection. Only in ME.
2 **a** The rising of the sun; dawn. L15. ▸†**b** The action of rising from bed. Only in M17. ▸**c** The action of rising to a higher level; ascent; the beginning of an ascent; an ascending shaft in a mine. L17.
3 **a** Ascent to power or dignity; rise to wealth or importance. E19. ▸**b** The action of coming into existence or notice. E19.

uprising /ʌpˈrʌɪzɪŋ; *in sense 4* ˈʌprʌɪz-/ *noun.* ME.
[from UP- + RISING *noun*.]
1 The action or an act of rising or uprising; (now *rare*) resurrection. ME.
2 Improvement in position or circumstances, advancement. LME.
3 A slope, an ascent; a swelling; a welling-up. L16.
4 A rising against authority etc., an insurrection, a revolt. L16.

📖 **4** M. PATTISON The great communistic uprising under Wat Tyler in 1381.

▪ **upriser** *noun* LME.

†**uprist** *noun.* See also UPREST. ME.
[from UPRISE: see -T[1].]
1 Rising from the dead; resurrection. Only in ME.
2 The rising of the sun. ME–E17.

uprist /ʌpˈrɪst/ *adjective. pseudo-arch.* L16.
[Alt. of *uprisen* pa. pple of UPRISE: see -T[3].]
Risen up.

up-river /*as adjective* ˈʌprɪvə, *as adverb* ʌpˈrɪvə/ *adjective & adverb.* L18.
[from UP- + RIVER *noun*[1].]
▶ **A** *adjective.* Situated or occurring further up or nearer the source of a river; leading or directed towards the source of a river. L18.
▶ **B** *adverb.* Towards or in the direction of the source of a river. M19.

uproar /ˈʌprɔː/ *noun & verb.* E16.
[Middle Dutch *uproer* (mod. *op-*), Middle Low German *uprōr*, from *op-* UP- + *roer* confusion: see ROAR *noun*[2]. In sense 2 assoc. with ROAR *noun*[1].]
▶ **A** *noun.* **1** (A state of) tumult or commotion; a violent disturbance; (a) sustained protest, (an) expression of outrage; (now *rare*) a popular rising, a revolt. E16.
2 Noisy confusion, noise of shouting or tumult. M16.

📖 **1** *Face* The desecration of the cave . . caused an uproar. *Guardian* The Parliamentary Labour Party has been in uproar. **2** E. WAUGH 'Silence!' shouted Paul above the uproar. R. CAMPBELL The most deafening . . uproar of clanging laughter.

▶ **B** *verb.* **1** *verb trans.* Throw into confusion. *rare.* E17.
2 *verb intrans.* Make an uproar. *rare.* M19.

uproarious /ʌpˈrɔːrɪəs/ *adjective.* E19.
[from UPROAR *noun* + -IOUS.]
1 (Given to) making an uproar. E19.
2 Characterized by or involving uproar; violent; very noisy. Also, provoking loud laughter, very amusing. E19.

📖 **2** E. P. THOMPSON Food riots were sometimes uproarious. W. SHEED The narrator's throwaway lines, and Salinger's own uproarious imitation of Esmé.

▪ **uproariously** *adverb* M19. **uproariousness** *noun* M19.

uproll /*as verb* ʌpˈrəʊl, *as noun* ˈʌprəʊl/ *verb & noun.* Now *rare.* E16.
[from UP- + ROLL *verb, noun*[2].]
▶ **A** *verb.* **1** *verb trans.* Push upwards by rolling. E16. ▸**b** Roll or wind up. E17.
2 *verb intrans.* Become concentrated by rolling, form a roll. E19.
▶ **B** *noun.* A rolling movement upwards. *rare.* L19.

uproot /ʌpˈruːt/ *verb*[1] *trans.* L16.
[from UP- + ROOT *verb*[1].]
1 Remove (an immaterial thing) forcibly, eradicate, exterminate; displace (a person) from an accustomed location or home. L16.
2 Tear (a tree or plant) up by the roots; remove from a fixed position. M17.
3 *verb intrans.* Move away from one's accustomed location or home. M20.

📖 **1** *Daily News* A system of tipping had prevailed . . which he would endeavour to uproot. *Daily Telegraph* She uprooted the family from Kent . . and went to farthest Pembrokeshire. **2** J. MORSE Storms and hurricanes uproot trees. *Athenaeum* In the chancel . . rests the uprooted headstone of Dr. Thoroton.

▪ **uprootal** *noun* = UPROOTING M19. **uprootedness** *noun* the state of being uprooted E20. **uprooter** *noun* E19. **uprooting** *verbal noun* the action of the verb; an instance of this: L18.

uproot /ʌpˈruːt/ *verb*[2] *trans.* E18.
[from UP- + ROOT *verb*[2].]
Of an animal: grub up, extract by rooting in the ground.

uprose *verb pa. t.* of UPRISE *verb*.

uprush /*as verb* ʌpˈrʌʃ, *as noun* ˈʌprʌʃ/ *verb & noun.* E19.
[from UP- + RUSH *verb*[2], *noun*[2].]
▶ **A** *verb intrans.* Rush up. *poet.* E19.
▶ **B** *noun.* An upward rush or flow of or *of* something; a surge *of* emotion, ideas, etc. L19.

UPS *abbreviation.*
Uninterruptible power supply.

ups-a-daisy *interjection* var. of UPSY-DAISY.

upsaddle /ˈʌpsad(ə)l/ *verb intrans. S. Afr.* M19.
[Dutch *opzadelen*, from *op-* UP- + *zadelen* SADDLE *verb*.]
Saddle a horse.

upsara *noun* var. of APSARA.

upscale /ˈʌpskeɪl/ *adjective. N. Amer.* M20.
[from UP- + SCALE *noun*[4].]
At the higher end of the social scale; of a high quality; up-market.

upset /ˈʌpsɛt/ *noun.* In sense 3c usu. **-tt**. LME.
[from the verb, or from UP- + SET *noun*[1].]
†**1** An insurrection, a revolt. *Scot.* Only in LME.
2 *Hist.* The action of setting up in business on one's own or of becoming a freeman in a particular trade; the sum paid to the guild when doing so. *Scot. & north.* LME.
3 †**a** A curved part of a bridle-bit, fitting over the tongue of the horse. L16–E18. ▸**b** MINING. A working-place driven upwards following the course of the seam. M18. ▸**c** BASKET-MAKING. The first section of waling, which sets the stakes firmly in place. E20.
4 = UPSHOT *noun* 4. *dial.* E19.
5 A gloss, a translation; a rough draft. E19.
6 **a** An overturning of a vehicle, vessel, etc.; the fact of being overturned. E19. ▸**b** A disruption or rejection *of* an idea, plan, etc. Now also, a surprising result in a sporting match etc. E19. ▸**c** A condition of being distressed, angered, or offended; a physical, esp. digestive, disturbance. M19. ▸**d** A quarrel, a misunderstanding. L19.

📖 **6a** B. HALL When an upset was . . inevitable, the horses slackened their pace. C. B. MANSFIELD The Major . . was afraid of the . . consequences of an upset of the canoe. **b** *Manchester Examiner* The result was a complete upset of all the predictions of the prophets. *Guardian* The defeat of Liverpool in one of the FA Cup final's greatest upsets. **c** *She* The emotional upset of having to bath a previously fastidious mother. ***stomach upset***: see STOMACH *noun*.

upset /ʌpˈsɛt, ˈʌpsɛt/ *adjective.* LME.
[pa. pple of UPSET *verb*.]
1 Set up, erected, raised. Long *obsolete* exc. *Scot.* LME.
2 Overturned, capsized. M19.
3 Angry, unhappy, discomposed, troubled, distressed, offended; physically disordered, *spec.* having disturbed digestion. M19.

📖 **3** H. ROBBINS Big parties make me nervous. All day my stomach is upset thinking about it. *Essentials* When we split up, I was very upset.

Special collocations: **upset price** the lowest acceptable selling price of a property in an auction etc., a reserve price.

upset /ʌp'sɛt/ *verb*. In sense 1d usu. **-tt**. Infl. **-tt-**. Pa. t. & pple **-set**, (in sense 1d) **-setted**. LME.
[from UP- + SET *verb*[1].]
1 *verb trans.* †**a** Set up, raise, erect; establish in position or power. LME–E17. ▸**b** Force back the end of (a metal bar etc.) by hammering or beating, esp. when heated. L17. ▸**c** AGRICULTURE. Ridge up. M18. ▸**d** BASKET-MAKING. Bend upwards (a stake) plaited into the base of a basket to form part of the frame for the side. Also, form the upsett of (a basket). L19.
2 *verb trans.* †**a** Make good, make up for; get over or recover from (a loss etc.). *Scot.* E16–E19. ▸**b** Restore to good or the usual condition. *obsolete* exc. *dial.* M17.
3 *verb intrans.* Be overturned or capsized. L18.
4 *verb trans.* Overturn, capsize; knock over. L18. ▸**b** *fig.* Disrupt, undo. E19.
5 *verb trans.* **a** Disturb the composure of; make unhappy or angry; trouble, distress, offend. E19. ▸**b** Disorder physically; *spec.* disturb the digestion of. M19.

📖 **3** T. KNIGHT If the horses had not run so fast we should not have upset. **4** *Pall Mall Gazette* A fishing-boat was upset by a squall . . and its three occupants perished. JO GRIMOND He ordered tea, which he upset . . all over his desk. **b** G. GREENE He continues . . to upset all our notions of what a novel's form should be. **5a** D. MADDEN Don't cry so . . try not to upset yourself. C. BRAYFIELD Cruelty to animals upset Victoria.

■ **upsettable** *adjective* L19.

upsett *noun, verb* see UPSET *noun, verb*.

upsetter /ʌp'sɛtə/ *noun*. E16.
[from prec. + -ER[1].]
†**1** A person setting up as a worker. *Scot.* Only in E16.
†**2** *Scot.* **a** A person posting a placard. Only in E16. ▸**b** A founder, an establisher. L16–E18.
†**3** A support, a prop. *Scot.* E–M17.
4 A person who or thing which upsets, overturns, or disturbs someone or something. M19.

upsetting /ʌp'sɛtɪŋ/ *noun*. LME.
[from UPSET *verb* + -ING[1].]
The action of UPSET *verb*; the fact or condition of being upset; an instance of this.

upsetting /ʌp'sɛtɪŋ/ *adjective*. E19.
[from UPSET *verb* + -ING[2].]
1 Unduly aspiring or forward, presumptuous. *Scot.* E19.
2 Disruptive; disturbing, distressing. L19.
■ **upsettingly** *adverb* E20. **upsettingness** *noun* E20

upshoot /*as verb* ʌp'ʃu:t, *as noun* 'ʌpʃu:t/ *verb & noun*. L16.
[from UP- + SHOOT *verb, noun*[1].]
▸**A** *verb*. Pa. t. & pple (*rare*) **upshot** /ʌp'ʃɒt/, pa. pple also **upshotten** /ʌp'ʃɒt(ə)n/.
1 *verb intrans.* Spring or grow up. *poet.* L16.
2 *verb trans.* Send or raise up. *poet.* E19.
▸**B** *noun*. **1** = UPSHOT 4. *obsolete* exc. *dial.* L16.
2 The action of shooting up; a result of this; an upward rush (*of* something). M19.

upshot /'ʌpʃɒt/ *noun*. M16.
[from UP- + SHOT *noun*[1].]
1 A final shot in an archery match. Formerly freq. *fig.*, a closing or parting shot. M16.
†**2** A mark or end aimed at. L16–M18.
3 †**a** An end, a conclusion, a termination. L16–M17. ▸**b** The extreme limit. M17.
4 The final or eventual outcome or conclusion (*of* a course of action, an argument, etc.); a result, a consequence. E17.

📖 **4** G. BROWN The upshot was that . . he chose to resign. P. L. FERMOR As the upshot of all this, I was asked to stay. R. S. WOOLHOUSE The upshot of Berkeley's theory is relatively easy to grasp. **in the upshot** in the end, at last.

upshot *verb*, **upshotten** *verb* see UPSHOOT.

upsidaisy *interjection* var. of UPSY-DAISY.

upside /'ʌpsʌɪd/ *noun, adjective, & preposition*. E17.
[from UP- + SIDE *noun*.]
▸**A** *noun*. **1** The upper side or surface (*of* a thing); the upper half or part. E17.
2 An upward movement or trend of share prices etc., a potential for rising in value; a positive aspect. M20.
▸**B** *attrib.* or as *adjective*. (Having potential for) rising in value; positive in aspect. M20.
▸**C** *preposition*. On, against. Only in ***upside one's head***, ***upside the head***. *N. Amer. slang.* L20.
go upside a person's head strike a person on the head, attack or fight a person.

upside down /ʌpsʌɪd 'daʊn/ *adverbial & adjectival phr.* ME.
[Orig. *up so down*, perh. with *so* meaning 'as if'.]
▸**A** *adverbial phr.* So that the upper part or surface becomes the under or lower; in or into an inverted position; *fig.* in or into a state of reversal or total disorder. ME.

📖 H. SECOMBE She felt that her world was being turned upside down. M. SPUFFORD Felt-tip pens work by capillary action, so I could write upside-down. S. TOWNSEND We turned the house upside down looking for my birth certificate.

▸**B** *adjectival phr.* Also (*attrib.*) **upside-down**. Turned or positioned upside down; inverted, overturned; *fig.* reversed, totally disordered. M19.

📖 DENNIS POTTER A proprietor . . started to put the chairs upside down on the swabbed tables. J. LE CARRÉ The upside down bats dangling from the roof. M. FORSTER The house was upside down in preparation for the exodus to the country. **upside-down cake** a sponge cake baked with fruit in syrup at the bottom, and inverted for serving. **upside-down catfish** a small African freshwater catfish, *Synodontis nigriventris*, that habitually swims upside down, enabling it to browse on algae on the undersides of floating leaves.

■ **upside downward(s)** *adverbial phr.* = UPSIDE DOWN *adverbial phr.* E17.

upsides /'ʌpsʌɪdz/ *adverb*. *colloq. & dial.* E18.
[from UPSIDE + -S[3].]
1 Even, equal, or quits *with* a person, esp. by retaliation or successful rivalry. E18.
2 On a level *with*; alongside *of*. L19.

upsilon /ʌp'sʌɪlən, ju:p-; 'ʊpsɪlɒn, 'ju:p-/ *noun*. M17.
[Greek *u psilon* simple or slender u, from *psilos* slender, with ref. to the need to distinguish upsilon from the diphthong οι, with which upsilon shared a pronunciation in late Greek.]
1 The twentieth letter (Υ, υ) of the Greek alphabet. M17.
2 PARTICLE PHYSICS. A meson with a mass of about 9.4 GeV that is thought to consist of a *b* quark and its antiquark. Also ***upsilon particle***. L20.

upsitting /ʌp'sɪtɪŋ/ *noun*. L16.
[from UP- + SITTING *noun*.]
1 The occasion of a woman's first sitting up to receive company after giving birth. *obsolete* exc. *dial.* L16.
†**2** The fact of sitting up again after an illness. M17–M18.
3 S. AFR. HISTORY The custom of *opsitting* (see OPSIT). M19.

upslope /'ʌpsləʊp/ *noun, adjective, & adverb*. E20.
[from UP- + SLOPE *noun*[1].]
▸**A** *noun*. An upward slope; rising ground. E20.
▸**B** *adjective*. Caused by, occurring, or acting on an upward slope; ascending. M20.
upslope fog METEOROLOGY fog formed on the windward side of high ground by moist air rising until its saturation point is reached.
▸**C** *adverb*. At or towards a higher point on a slope. M20.

upsprang *verb pa. t.*: see UPSPRING *verb*.

upspring /'ʌpsprɪŋ/ *noun & adjective*. *arch.* OE.
[from UP- + SPRING *noun*[1].]
▸**A** *noun*. †**1** Rising *of* the sun; dawn *of* day. OE–M16.
2 The action of springing up into existence; beginning of growth or development; origin. OE.
†**3** A lively kind of dance. E–M17.
▸†**B** *adjective*. Upstart; newly arisen or come in. Also, lively. L16–E17.

upspring /ʌp'sprɪŋ/ *verb intrans.* *arch.* Infl. as SPRING *verb*[1]; pa. t. usu. **upsprang** /ʌp'spraŋ/, pa. pple **upsprung** /ʌp'sprʌŋ/. OE.
[from UP- + SPRING *verb*[1].]
1 Of a plant etc.: spring up, grow. OE. ▸**b** *fig.* Arise, come into being. LME.
2 Rise, ascend; spring or leap upwards; start to one's feet. LME.

upstage /ʌp'steɪdʒ/ *verb trans.* E20.
[from the adverb.]
Move upstage of so as to make (an actor or actress) face away from the audience; *fig.* divert attention from (another person) to oneself, outshine, treat snobbishly.

📖 A. T. ELLIS A . . bit-part actor . . trying to upstage the principals. *Guardian* Provincial doctors who felt upstaged by the snooty medical royal colleges in London.

■ **upstager** *noun* M20.

upstage /ʌp'steɪdʒ, *as adjective also* 'ʌpsteɪdʒ/ *adverb, adjective, & noun*. L19.
[from UP- + STAGE *noun*.]
▸**A** *adverb*. At or in the direction of the back of a theatre stage, on the part of the stage furthest from the audience; *fig.* in a superior or aloof manner, snobbishly. L19.
▸**B** *adjective*. Situated or occurring at or towards the rear of the stage; *fig.* superior or aloof in manner, snobbish. E20.
▸**C** *noun*. The back of the stage. M20.

For other words beginning with *up-* see the entry for **up-**

upstairs /ʌp'stɛ:z, *as adjective* 'ʌpstɛ:z/ *adverb, adjective, & noun*. L16.
[from UP- + STAIR + -S[1].]
▸**A** *adverb*. **1** Up the stairs; to or on the upper floor or floors of a house etc. L16. ▸**b** *transf.* Chiefly *Hist.* In the private rather than servants' quarters of a household. M20.
2 a To or in a more influential position or higher authority. L17. ▸**b** AERONAUTICS. In or up into the air; in flight. E20. ▸**c** Mentally, in the head, with reference to mental capacity. Chiefly in phrs. *slang*. M20.

📖 **1** M. SINCLAIR Upstairs in her bed she still heard Aunt Lavvy's . . voice. M. KEANE She went upstairs to her bedroom. **b** D. CARNEGIE She sometimes made it for the servants, but no one ate it upstairs. **2a** ***kick a person upstairs***: see KICK *verb*[1]. **send a bill upstairs** refer a bill for its committee stage from the floor of the House of Commons to a standing committee. **the Man Upstairs** *US slang* God. **c** *People* A little nutter who had . . not too much upstairs.

▸**B** *adjective*. Also **-stair** /-stɛ:/.
1 Situated or occurring upstairs; of or pertaining to the upper floor or floors of a house etc. L18.
2 *transf.* Chiefly *Hist.* Of, pertaining to, or characteristic of life in the private quarters of a household; refined, genteel, privileged. M20.

📖 **1** *Times Lit. Suppl.* A young woman, writing alone in the upstairs room.

▸**C** *noun*. An upper floor, or floors, of a house etc.; *transf.* a person or persons living on an upper floor. L19.

📖 A. LURIE You should see the upstairs, too.

upstand /*as verb* ʌp'stand, *as noun* 'ʌpstand/ *verb & noun*. ME.
[from UP- + STAND *verb, noun*[1]. Cf. next.]
▸**A** *verb intrans.* Pa. t. & pple **upstood** /ʌp'stʊd/.
1 Stand erect or upright. Long *rare*. ME.
2 Rise to one's feet, stand up. Chiefly *poet.* ME.
▸**B** *noun*. An upstanding thing, an upright structure or part; *spec.* a turned-up edge of a flat surface or sheeting, esp. in a roof space where it meets the wall. M19.
■ **upstander** *noun* a person who or thing which stands up or erect; *spec.* either of two upright posts on a sledge: M17.

upstanding /ʌp'standɪŋ/ *adjective*. LOE.
[from UP- + STAND *verb* + -ING[2]. Cf. prec.]
1 Standing up, erect, on one's feet. LOE.
2 Remaining in good or the same condition, intact. *north.* LME.
3 a Of an animal (esp. a horse) or a person: having an erect carriage, of noble bearing, strong and healthy. M19. ▸**b** Of a person: honest, honourable, decent; responsible. M19.

📖 **1 be upstanding!**: directing people present in a lawcourt etc. to stand up. **3b** A. MAUPIN Still some decent upstanding young men left in the world.

upstare /ʌp'stɛ:/ *verb intrans.* *rare*. L16.
[from UP- + STARE *verb*.]
1 Of hair: stand on end. Chiefly as ***upstaring*** *ppl adjective*. *poet.* L16.
2 Gaze upwards. Chiefly as ***upstaring*** *ppl adjective*. M19.

upstart /'ʌpstɑ:t/ *noun & adjective*. M16.
[from the verb.]
▸**A** *noun*. **1** A person newly or suddenly risen to prominence or in social position, *esp.* one regarded as behaving arrogantly or as lacking appropriate qualifications or accomplishments; a parvenu. M16.
2 a An upward start or spring. *obsolete* exc. *poet.* M17. ▸**b** GYMNASTICS. A series of movements on the parallel or asymmetric bars by which a gymnast swings to a position in which the body is supported by the arms above the bar, esp. at the start of a routine. E20.
3 A stick forming a support for a thatched roof. *Scot.* M18.

📖 **1** J. CARY The . . people are too proud to bear the rule of a foreign upstart. A. WEST Time . . for this young upstart from below stairs to be taught a lesson.

▸**B** *adjective*. **1** Of a thing: recently come into existence or notice, new, novel. M16.
2 Of a person etc.: that is an upstart; characteristic of upstarts. M16.
†**3** Rising on end. *rare* (Spenser). Only in L16.

📖 **1** BOSW. SMITH The upstart naval power of Rome. **2** E. P. THOMPSON The upstart *nouveau riche*, fattened by the war.

upstart /ʌp'stɑ:t/ *verb*. Now *poet.* ME.
[from UP- + START *verb*.]
1 *verb intrans.* Start or spring up; *esp.* spring to one's feet. ME. ▸**b** Of the hair: rise on end. E16. ▸**c** Spring up by growth; come into existence. L16. ▸**d** Rise suddenly into view. L19.
2 *verb trans.* Cause to start or spring up. L19.

upstate /ˈʌpsteɪt/ *adverb, adjective, & noun. US.* **E20.**
[from UP- + STATE *noun*.]
▶ **A** *adverb.* **1** In or to the part of a State remote from the large cities, esp. the northern part. **E20.**
2 In prison. *slang.* **M20.**
▶ **B** *adjective.* Of, pertaining to, or characteristic of an area upstate; situated upstate, rural. **E20.**

📖 M. CHABON Cleveland's family's summer house in upstate New York.

▶ **C** *noun.* The upstate region of a State, a rural area. **M20.**
■ **upstater** *noun* a person who comes from or lives upstate **M20.**

upstood *verb pa. t. & pple* of UPSTAND *verb.*

upstream /*as adv* ʌpˈstriːm, *as adjective* ˈʌpstriːm/ *adverb & adjective.* **L17.**
[from UP- + STREAM *noun*.]
▶ **A** *adverb.* **1** In the direction contrary to the flow of a river or stream, further up or along a stream. **L17.**
2 In the oil and gas industries: at or towards the source of production; *spec.* at a stage in the process of extraction and production before the raw material is ready for refining. **L20.**
3 *BIOLOGY.* Towards that part of a sequence of genetic material where transcription takes place earlier than at a given point. Opp. DOWNSTREAM *adverb* 2. **L20.**
▶ **B** *adjective.* **1** Situated or occurring further upstream. **E19.**
2 Pertaining to the stages in the production of oil and gas before the raw material is ready for refining. **M20.**

upsurge /ˈʌpsəːdʒ/ *noun.* **E20.**
[from UP- + SURGE *noun*.]
An upward surge; *spec.* (**a**) a sudden rise or increase of feeling; (**b**) an uprising, an insurrection; (**c**) a sharp rise in economic activity, demand, or prices; (**d**) a rapid growth in number or size.

📖 *Face* A big fundamentalist upsurge has stuck women back in the kitchen. *Guardian* There has been an upsurge in violent crime. *Times Educ. Suppl.* The recent upsurge of interest . . is encouraging.

■ Also **upˈsurgence** *noun* **M20.**

upsweep /ˈʌpswiːp/ *noun.* **L19.**
[from UP- + SWEEP *noun*.]
1 An upward movement in a long sweeping curve; a raising or lifting up. **L19.**
2 An upswept hairstyle. **M20.**

upswept /ˈʌpswɛpt/ *adjective.* **L18.**
[from UP- + SWEPT *adjective*.]
1 Cleared or thrown up by sweeping. **L18.**
2 Having an upward sweep, curved upwards; *spec.* (of hair) brushed or combed up towards the top of the head, swept-up. **M20.**

upswing /ˈʌpswɪŋ/ *noun.* **E20.**
[from UP- + SWING *noun*[1].]
1 *GOLF.* = ***back-swing*** s.v. BACK-. *rare.* **E20.**
2 (A period marked by) an upward trend, esp. in economic conditions. **M20.**

†**upsy** *preposition, noun, & adverb. slang.* **L16.**
[Dutch *op zijn* lit. 'on his, her, or its', as in *op zijn Vriesch* in Frisian fashion.]
▶ **A** *preposition.* In the — fashion; after the manner of. Chiefly in ***upsy Dutch***, ***upsy Friese***, (of drinking) deeply, heavily, to excess. **L16–E18.**
▶ **B** *noun.* ***upsy Friese***, a manner of drinking or carousing. **L16–E17.**
▶ **C** *adverb.* Extremely, very. **M–L17.**

upsy-daisy /ʌpsɪˈdeɪzi, ʌpsə-/ *interjection. colloq.* Also **oops-a-daisy** /uːpsəˈdeɪzi/, **ups-a-daisy**, **upsidaisy**. **M19.**
[Alt. of UP-A-DAISY. Cf. WHOOPS.]
Expr. encouragement to a child being lifted or being helped up after falling.

upta *adjective* var. of UPTER.

uptake /*as verb* ʌpˈteɪk, *as noun* ˈʌpteɪk/ *verb & noun.* **ME.**
[from UP- + TAKE *verb, noun*.]
▶ **A** *verb trans.* Pa. t. **uptook** /ʌpˈtʊk/; pa. pple **uptaken** /ʌpˈteɪk(ə)n/.
†**1** Perform or pursue (a flight) upwards. **ME–E18.**
2 Pick or take up; raise, lift. Long *rare. arch.* **ME.** ▸†**b** *fig.* Relieve from distress, take into one's care or protection. **ME–M16.**
†**3** Take possession of, occupy. **LME–E16.**
†**4** Reprove, rebuke. Long *obsolete* exc. *Scot. rare.* **LME.**
5 Obtain or exact by way of tax, contribution, or payment; levy. *Scot.* **LME.**
6 Comprehend, understand. *Scot. & north.* **E17.**
▶ **B** *noun.* **1** The action of or capacity for understanding; comprehension. Chiefly in ***quick in the uptake***, ***quick on the uptake***, ***slow in the uptake***, ***slow on the uptake***. Orig. *Scot.* **E19.**
2 The part between the smoke-box and the bottom of the funnel of a steamship's boiler. **M19.**
3 A ventilating shaft. **L19.**
4 An upward draught or current of air. **L19.**
5 *PHYSIOLOGY & BIOCHEMISTRY.* Absorption or incorporation *of* something by a living system. **M20.**
6 Positive response to a promotion, offer, etc.; use of an available facility or service; the extent of this. Cf. TAKE-UP 2(c). **L20.**

📖 **1** A. SILLITOE In the morning he could be . . impossibly slow on the uptake. **5** *Independent* Insulin regulates the uptake of sugar by all the body cells and tissues.

■ **uptaken** *adjective* (*obsolete* exc. *dial.*) taken up, captivated, or charmed *with* something **E17.** **uptaker** *noun* (*Scot.*) (**a**) a person who uptakes a person or thing; (**b**) = PRECENTOR: **ME.**

uptalk /ˈʌptɔːk/ *noun.* **L20.**
[from UP- + TALK *noun*.]
A manner of speaking in which declarative sentences are uttered with rising intonation at the end, as if they were questions.

📖 *Guardian* You know what uptalk is? You know, like, where they don't end a sentence and they keep talking like this?

up-tempo /ʌpˈtɛmpəʊ/ *adjective & adverb.* Also **uptempo**. **M20.**
[from UP- + TEMPO *noun*[1].]
MUSIC. At or having a fast tempo.

upter /ˈʌptə/ *adjective. Austral. slang.* Also **upta**. **E20.**
[Prob. a corruption of ***up to putty*** s.v. PUTTY *noun*.]
Bad, worthless, useless.

upthrew *verb pa. t.*: see UPTHROW *verb.*

upthrow /ˈʌpθrəʊ/ *noun.* **E19.**
[from the verb.]
1 *GEOLOGY.* **a** The upward movement of strata on one side of a fault; the extent of this. **E19.** ▸**b** = UPTHRUST *noun* 1a. **E19.**
2 *gen.* The action or an instance of throwing or casting something upwards; a thing thrown up, a manifestation. **M19.**

upthrow /ʌpˈθrəʊ/ *verb trans.* Chiefly *poet.* Infl. as THROW *verb*; pa. t. usu. **upthrew** /ʌpˈθruː/, pa. pple usu. **upthrown** /ʌpˈθrəʊn/. **E17.**
[from UP- + THROW *verb*.]
Throw or cast upwards, toss or fling up.

upthrust /ˈʌpθrʌst/ *noun.* **M19.**
[from UP- + THRUST *noun*.]
1 *GEOLOGY.* **a** The action of thrusting or fact of being thrust upwards, esp. by volcanic action. **M19.** ▸**b** = UPTHROW *noun* 1a. **M20.**
2 The upward force that a liquid exerts on a body floating in it. **E20.**

upthrust /ʌpˈθrʌst/ *adjective.* **M19.**
[from UP- + ***thrust*** pa. pple of THRUST *verb*.]
That has been thrust upwards.
■ **upthrusting** *noun* the action or an act of thrusting upwards **E20.** **upthrusting** *adjective* that thrusts upwards **M20.**

uptick /ˈʌptɪk/ *noun.* Chiefly *US.* **L20.**
[from UP- + TICK *noun*[3].]
An increase, *esp.* a small one.

uptight /ʌpˈtʌɪt, ˈʌptʌɪt/ *adjective.* **M20.**
[from UP- + TIGHT *adjective*.]
1 Nervously tense or angry, unwarrantedly worried, inhibited; overly formal or correct, strait-laced, rigidly conventional. *colloq.* **M20.**
2 Excellent, fine. *slang* (chiefly *US*). **M20.**
3 Short or out of money, penniless. *US slang.* **M20.**

📖 **1** F. POHL We just sleep wherever is convenient, and nobody gets uptight about it. G. NAYLOR Why are you always so uptight about sex or men? *New Statesman* Blacks are more *natural* than uptight whites.

■ **uptightness** *noun* **M20.**

uptook *verb* pa. pple of UPTAKE *verb.*

uptown /ˈʌptaʊn/ *adverb, adjective, & noun.* Chiefly *N. Amer.* **E19.**
[from UP- + TOWN *noun*.]
▶ **A** *adverb.* In or into the upper or more prosperous or residential part of a town or city. **E19.**

📖 D. STEEL Oliver lived uptown, in an apartment . . on East 79th Street. M. AMIS He would drive me uptown twenty blocks.

▶ **B** *adjective.* Situated, directed, or occurring uptown; pertaining to or characteristic of such an area; *transf.* sophisticated, prosperous, elegant. **M19.**

📖 *Times* A clean-cut, middle-class uptown young man. *Guardian* The Peachtree club, in uptown Atlanta.

▶ **C** *noun.* The uptown part of a town or city. **M20.**

📖 J. GORES High-rollers from uptown out for a night of slumming.

For other words beginning with *up-* see the entry for **up-**

■ **uptowner** *noun* an inhabitant of an uptown area **E20.**

upturn /ˈʌptəːn/ *noun.* **M19.**
[from UP- + TURN *noun*.]
1 An upturned part. **M19.** ▸**b** *spec.* A turn-up of a trouser leg etc. *rare.* **E20.**
2 A social upheaval. **M19.**
3 An improvement or upward turn, esp. in economic conditions; a rise in rate or value. **M20.**

📖 **3** *Daily Telegraph* An imminent upturn in the economy. *Guardian* An upturn in bookings for local tours.

upturn /ʌpˈtəːn/ *verb.* **ME.**
[from UP- + TURN *verb*.]
†**1** *verb trans.* Overthrow, cause to fall. Only in **ME.**
2 *verb trans.* Turn up; turn over or upside down, invert. Freq. as ***upturned*** *ppl adjective.* **M16.**
3 *verb trans.* Direct or cast (the eye, face, etc.) upwards. Freq. as ***upturned*** *ppl adjective.* **L16.**
4 *verb intrans.* Turn upwards; *esp.* curve upwards at the end (chiefly as ***upturned*** *ppl adjective*). **E19.**

📖 **2** MILTON Boreas and Caecus . . rend the Woods and Seas upturn. J. LE CARRÉ The prisoner's mess tin is upturned and its contents spilt. *Guardian* You could sit on an upturned washtub. **3** T. HARDY He leant back . . and with upturned face made observations on the stars. **4** BYRON Laid on thy lap, his eyes to thee upturn. C. BRAYFIELD Her mother had a cute, sharp, upturned little nose.

■ **upturner** *noun* **L19.** **upturning** *verbal noun* the action of the verb; an instance of this: **M19.**

UPU *abbreviation.*
Universal Postal Union.

uPVC *abbreviation.*
Unplasticized polyvinyl chloride, a rigid, chemically resistant form of PVC used for pipework, window frames, etc.

upward /ˈʌpwəd/ *adverb, preposition, adjective, & noun.*
[Old English *upweard*, from UP *adverb*[1] + -WARD.]
▶ **A** *adverb.* **1** = UPWARDS *adverb* 1. **OE.**
2 = UPWARDS *adverb* 4a. **OE.** ▸**b** = UPWARDS *adverb* 4b. **E16.**
3 = UPWARDS *adverb* 3. **ME.**
4 a = UPWARDS *adverb* 2a. **M16.** ▸**b** ***upward of*** = UPWARDS *adverb* 2b. **E17.**
▶†**B** *preposition.* Up; along the line of ascent of. *rare.* **L15–E19.**
▶ **C** *adjective.* **1** Directed, moving, extended, pointing, leading, etc., towards what is above; inclined upward. **L16.**
2 Lying or situated above; higher. *rare.* **E17.**

📖 **1** I. MURDOCH The gentle yet . . strong upward tilt of the nose. P. FRANCIS The cloud ceases its swift upward expansion, spreading out horizontally. *Engineer* A continued upward trend in order levels.

Special collocations & comb. (of adjective & adverb): **upward compatibility** *COMPUTING* a property of software and hardware by virtue of which software written for a machine can be used on a more capable one. **upward-compatible** *adjective* (*COMPUTING*) exhibiting upward compatibility. **upward mobility** movement from a lower to a higher social or professional level.
▶ **D** *noun. rare.*
†**1** The top part; the crown, the summit. Only in **E17.**
2 Upward movement. **L19.**
■ **upwardly** *adverb* in an upward direction, upwards (***upwardly mobile***: see MOBILE *adjective* 4) **E19.** **upwardness** *noun* (**a**) tendency to rise upwards; the quality of suggesting upward movement; (**b**) *rare* the quality of being upward, relative altitude: **E17.**

upwards /ˈʌpwədz/ *adverb & preposition.*
[Old English *up(p)weardes*, from prec.: see -WARDS.]
▶ **A** *adverb.* **1** Towards a higher place or position; towards what is above; with an ascending motion or tendency. **OE.**
2 a To a higher aggregate, figure, or amount; somewhat more than a specified number, value, size, etc. Freq in ***and upwards***, ***or upwards***. **E16.** ▸**b** ***upwards of***, somewhat more than a specified number etc. **E18.**
3 Towards something which is higher in order, larger, superior, or more important or valuable. (Cf. earlier UPWARD *adverb* 3.) **M16.**
4 (Cf. earlier UPWARD *adverb* 2.) ▸**a** Backwards in time, into the past. **M17.** ▸**b** To or into later life. **E19.**

📖 **1** SHAKES. *Much Ado* She shall be buried with her face upwards. R. HAKLUYT These men goe naked from the girdle vpwardes. H. F. TOZER We followed this stream upwards. G. GREENE A tiny pillar of smoke fumed upwards in the grate. I. MCEWAN Mary massaged his back, upwards from the base of his spine. E. BLAIR 'Steep hill this', Nevil commented as they trudged upwards. **2a** *Daily Chronicle* Worth as much as £30 and upwards. P. KAVANAGH Although he was only thirty-four . . he looked anything from fifty upwards. **b** B. BAINBRIDGE I am medical superintendent . . and have been so upwards of ten years. **3** *Guardian* Takeover speculation has been helping to push prices upwards.

▶†**B** *preposition.* = UPWARD *preposition. rare.* Only in **E17.**

upwind /ʌp'wʌɪnd/ *verb*. Long *rare*. Pa. t. & pple **upwound** /ʌp'waʊnd/. ME.
[from UP- + WIND *verb*¹.]
†**1 a** *verb intrans.* Fly up. Only in ME. ▶†**b** *verb trans.* Perform or pursue (a flight) upwards. Only in ME.
†**2** *verb trans.* Finish up, complete. Only in LME.
3 *verb trans.* Wind, coil, or roll up (a thing); raise or hoist by winding. M16.
4 *verb intrans.* Become coiled up. E17.
5 *verb intrans.* Wind upwards. L19.

upwind /ʌp'wɪnd/ *adverb & adjective*. Also as two words. M19.
[from UP- + WIND *noun*¹.]
▶ **A** *adverb*. Contrary to or against the direction of the wind, into the wind. M19.

H. GREEN To prospect for a site to place the pigsties, up wind of course. *Practical Boat Owner* By lashing the helm over to head upwind, I managed to get her to self-steer.

▶ **B** *adjective*. Occurring or situated upwind. M20.

upwith /'ʌpwɪθ/ *adjective, adverb, preposition, & noun*. Chiefly *Scot.* Now *rare*. L15.
[from UP- + WITH *preposition & adverb*.]
▶ **A** *adjective*. Having an upward inclination or slope; rising. L15.
▶ **B** *adverb*. In an upward course or direction, upwards. E16.
▶ **C** *preposition*. Up along the course of. E16.
▶ **D** *noun*. Upward course. E16.

upwound *verb pa. t. & pple* of UPWIND *verb*.

upya /'ʌpjə/ *interjection*. *slang* (chiefly *Austral.*). Also **upyer**. M20.
[Corrupt.]
= ***up yours*** s.v. UP *preposition*².

ur /ə:/ *interjection & noun*. M19.
[Imit.]
(Expr.) the inarticulate sound made by a speaker who hesitates or is uncertain what to say. Cf. ER.

ur- /ʊə/ *combining form*. M19.
[German.]
Forming words with the sense 'primitive, original, earliest'.

Literature & Theology The arche-type, or ur-type, of biblical displacement is the Fall.

urachus /'jʊərəkəs/ *noun*. E17.
[mod. Latin from Greek *ourakhos*.]
ANATOMY. A foetal canal that connects the bladder with the allantois, usu. persisting in the adult as a ligament between the bladder and the umbilicus.
■ **urachal** *adjective* L19.

uracil /'jʊərəsɪl/ *noun*. L19.
[Perh. from UR(EA + AC(ETIC + -IL.]
BIOCHEMISTRY. A derivative of pyrimidine which is one of the bases of RNA (replaced by thymine in DNA); 2,6-dioxytetrahydropyrimidine, $C_4H_4N_2O_2$.

uraei *noun* pl. of URAEUS.

uraemia /jʊ'ri:mɪə/ *noun*. Also ***uremia**. M19.
[mod. Latin, from Greek *ouron* + *aima* blood.]
MEDICINE. A raised level of nitrogenous waste compounds (orig. *spec.* urea) in the blood, normally excreted by the kidneys, which results in nausea, drowsiness, etc.
■ **uraemic** *adjective* of or pertaining to, marked or characterized by, uraemia; (of a person) affected by uraemia: M19.

uraeus /jʊ'ri:əs/ *noun*. Pl. **uraei** /jʊ'ri:ʌɪ/. M19.
[mod. Latin from Greek *ouraios* (perh. from *oura* tail), repr. Egyptian word for 'cobra'.]
EGYPTOLOGY. A representation of the sacred asp or snake, symbolizing supreme power, esp. worn on the headdresses of ancient Egyptian divinities and sovereigns.

ural /'jʊərəl/ *noun*. Now *rare*. L19.
[from UR(ETHANE + CHLOR)AL.]
PHARMACOLOGY. A preparation of chloral hydrate and urethane, used as a hypnotic.

Ural /'jʊər(ə)l/ *adjective*. L18.
[The *Ural* Mountains, forming the north-eastern boundary of Europe with Asia.]
Pertaining to, characteristic of, or found in the Urals.
Ural-Altaic *adjective & noun* (*a*) *adjective* of or pertaining to the region including the Ural and Altaic Mountains (in central Asia), its inhabitants, or their languages, formerly believed to constitute a single family; (*b*) *noun* (*Hist.*) a supposed language family of eastern Europe and northern Asia comprising the Uralic and Altaic subfamilies. **Ural owl** a large round-headed Eurasian owl, *Strix uralensis*, which is found in open woodland and cultivated country from Norway and the Balkans to Japan.

urali *noun* var. of URARI.

Uralian /jʊ'reɪlɪən/ *adjective*. L18.
[from URAL *adjective* + -IAN.]
Of, pertaining to, or inhabiting the area of the Urals.

Uralic /jʊ'ralɪk/ *noun & adjective*. M19.
[formed as prec. + -IC.]
▶ **A** *noun*. A language family comprising Finno-Ugric and Samoyed. M19.
▶ **B** *adjective*. Of or pertaining to the Urals or the inhabitants of the surrounding area; of or pertaining to Uralic. L19.

uralite /'jʊər(ə)lʌɪt/ *noun*¹. M19.
[from URAL *adjective* + -ITE¹.]
MINERALOGY. A green fibrous variety of amphibole, esp. hornblende, which occurs in altered rocks and is derived from primary pyroxene.
■ **ura'litic** *adjective* containing or consisting of uralite M19.

Uralite /'jʊər(ə)lʌɪt/ *noun*². L19.
[Origin unkn.]
(Proprietary name for) an asbestos-based prefabricated building material.

uralitization /ˌjʊər(ə)lɪtʌɪ'zeɪʃ(ə)n/ *noun*. Also **-isation**. L19.
[from URALITE *noun*¹ + -IZATION.]
PETROGRAPHY. The alteration of a pyroxene, esp. augite, to form an amphibole, esp. hornblende.
■ **uralitized** *adjective* that has been subjected to uralitization E20.

uralium /jʊ'reɪlɪəm/ *noun*. Now *rare*. L19.
[from URAL *noun* + -IUM.]
PHARMACOLOGY. = URAL *noun*.

Uralo- /jʊ'reɪləʊ/ *combining form*. M19.
[from URAL *adjective* + -O-.]
Forming adjectives and nouns with the sense 'Ural or Uralic and —', as ***Uralo-Altaic***, ***Uralo-Caspian***, ***Uralo-Finnic***.

uramil /jʊ'ramɪl/ *noun*. M19.
[formed as UR(EA + AM(MONIA + *-il* -YL.]
CHEMISTRY. A crystalline derivative, $C_4H_5O_3N_3$, of barbituric acid which is obtained from alloxan and other derivatives of uric acid; 5-aminobarbituric acid.

uran- *combining form* see URANO-².

ura-nage /'u:ranagi/ *noun*. E20.
[Japanese, from *ura* back, underside + *nage* throw.]
JUDO. A throw executed by rolling backwards to the floor to pull an opponent over the left shoulder.

uranate /'jʊərəneɪt/ *noun*. M19.
[from URANIC *adjective*² + -ATE¹.]
CHEMISTRY. A salt containing oxyanions of uranium.

Urania /jʊ'reɪnɪə/ *noun*. E17.
[Latin (the muse of astronomy) from Greek *Ourania* fem. of *ouranios* heavenly, spiritual, from *ouranos* heaven.]
In titles, a book or poem dealing with celestial or astronomical themes.

Uranian /jʊ'reɪnɪən/ *adjective*¹ *& noun*¹. Now *arch.* or *literary*. E17.
[formed as prec. + -AN. Cf. URNING.]
▶ **A** *adjective*. **1** Of, pertaining to, or befitting heaven; celestial, heavenly. Also as an epithet of Venus or Aphrodite. E17. ▶**b** [with allus. to a ref. to Aphrodite in Plato's *Symposium*.] Homosexual. L19.
2 Of, pertaining to, or dedicated to Urania, the muse of astronomy; pertaining to astronomy, astronomical. M17.

1 SHELLEY Sculptures of divine workmanship . . the earthly image of Uranian love. TENNYSON O'er his . . head Uranian Venus hung. **b** P. FUSSELL The poem's Uranian leanings.

▶ **B** *noun*. A homosexual. E20.
■ **Uranianism** *noun* homosexuality E20.

Uranian /jʊ'reɪnɪən/ *adjective*² *& noun*². M19.
[from URANUS + -IAN.]
▶ **A** *adjective*. Of or pertaining to the planet Uranus. M19.
▶ **B** *noun*. An (imaginary or hypothetical) inhabitant of the planet Uranus. L19.

uranic /jʊ'ranɪk/ *adjective*¹. *rare*. M19.
[from Latin *uranus* from Greek *ouranos* heaven + -IC.]
Astronomical; celestial.

uranic /jʊ'ranɪk/ *adjective*². M19.
[from URANIUM + -IC.]
CHEMISTRY. Of or containing uranium, esp. in one of its higher valencies.

uraniferous /jʊərə'nɪf(ə)rəs/ *adjective*. E20.
[from URANO-² + -I- + -FEROUS.]
Containing or yielding uranium.

uraninite /jʊ'ranɪnʌɪt/ *noun*. L19.
[from URANO-² + -IN¹ + -ITE¹.]
MINERALOGY. A black, brown, or grey cubic mineral which consists mainly of uranium dioxide, is found most frequently in botryoidal form as pitchblende, and is the major ore of uranium.

uranism /'jʊər(ə)nɪz(ə)m/ *noun*. *rare*. L19.
[German *uranismus*, from Greek *ouranios* heavenly, spiritual. Cf. URNING.]
Homosexuality.
■ **uranist** *noun* a homosexual L19.

uranite /'jʊər(ə)nʌɪt/ *noun*. L18.
[from URANO-² + -ITE¹.]
†**1** CHEMISTRY. = URANIUM. L18–E19.
2 MINERALOGY. Any of a group of tetragonal uranium-containing minerals of the autunite and torbernite type. E19.
■ **uranitic** /-'nɪtɪk/ *adjective* (now *rare*) of, pertaining to, or containing uranite or uranium L18.

uranium /jʊ'reɪnɪəm/ *noun*. L18.
[from URANUS + -IUM.]
A heavy radioactive metallic chemical element of the actinide series, atomic no. 92, which occurs in pitchblende and other ores, and is important as fissile material in nuclear reactors and weapons. (Symbol U.)
Comb.: **uranium bomb** an atomic bomb in which uranium is the fissile material; **uranium lead** the isotope lead-206; **uranium-lead** *adjective* designating a method of isotopic dating and the results obtained with it, based on measurement of the relative amounts in rock of uranium-238 and -235 and of their ultimate decay products lead-206 and -207; **uranium series** the series of isotopes produced by the radioactive decay of uranium-238, each member resulting from the decay of the previous one.

urano- /'jʊər(ə)nəʊ/ *combining form*¹.
[from Greek *ouranos* sky, heavens, roof of the mouth: see -O-.]
1 Forming words with the sense 'pertaining to the sky or heavens'.
2 MEDICINE. Forming words with the sense 'pertaining to the palate'.
■ **ura'nology** *noun* (now *rare* or *obsolete*) (a treatise on) astronomy M18. **urano'logical** *adjective* (now *rare* or *obsolete*) astronomical E19. **urano'metria** *noun* = URANOMETRY L19. **ura'nometry** *noun* a treatise showing the relative positions, distances, and magnitudes of celestial objects, esp. stars; the measurement of these: E18. **urano'plastic** *adjective* (MEDICINE) of or pertaining to uranoplasty L19. **uranoplasty** *noun* (MEDICINE) (an instance of) plastic surgery of the hard palate M19. **ura'noscopus** *noun* (ZOOLOGY) the stargazer (fish) (now chiefly as mod. Latin genus name) L16.

urano- /'jʊər(ə)nəʊ/ *combining form*². Before a vowel **uran-**.
[from URANIUM: see -O-.]
Forming words with the sense 'containing, composed of, or having the structure of uranium'.
■ **uranophane** *noun* a radioactive orthorhombic secondary mineral, which is a hydrated calcium uranyl silicate occurring as minute yellow crystals M19. **urano'thorite** *noun* a form of thorite containing uranium L19. **uranotile** *noun* = URANOPHANE L19.

uranography /jʊərə'nɒgrəfi/ *noun*. Now *rare*. Also †**ouran-**. M17.
[from Greek *ouranographia*: see URANO-¹, -GRAPHY.]
†**1** A description of heaven. *rare*. M17–E18.
2 The branch of science that deals with the description and mapping of the night sky; a description or delineation of the stars etc. L17.
■ **uranographer** *noun* L17. **urano'graphic** *adjective* E18. **urano'graphical** *adjective* M19.

uranous /'jʊər(ə)nəs/ *adjective*. M19.
[from URANIUM + -OUS.]
CHEMISTRY. Of or containing trivalent uranium.

Uranus /'jʊər(ə)nəs, jʊ'reɪnəs/ *noun*. E19.
[Latin from Greek *Ouranos*, husband of Gaea (Earth) and father of Kronos (Saturn).]
The seventh planet in order of distance from the sun, a greenish-blue gas giant whose orbit lies between those of Saturn and Neptune.

uranyl /'jʊər(ə)nʌɪl, -nɪl/ *noun*. M19.
[from URANIUM + -YL.]
CHEMISTRY. The radical :UO_2, present in some compounds of uranium. Usu. in *comb.*

urao /ʊ'rɑ:əʊ/ *noun*. M19.
[S. Amer. Spanish.]
MINERALOGY. = TRONA.

urari /ʊ'rɑ:ri/ *noun*. Now *rare*. Also **urali**, **oorali** /-ɑ:li/. M19.
[from Carib word repr. also by CURARE, WOURALI.]
= CURARE.

Urartian /ʊ'rɑ:tɪən/ *noun & adjective*. M20.
[from *Urartu* (see below) + -IAN.]
▶ **A** *noun*. **1** A native or inhabitant of the ancient kingdom of Urartu in eastern Anatolia. M20.
2 The language of Urartu, related to Hurrian. M20.
▶ **B** *adjective*. Of or pertaining to the Urartians or their language. Cf. KHALDIAN, VANNIC. M20.

urate /'jʊəreɪt/ *noun*. E19.
[from URIC + -ATE¹.]
CHEMISTRY. A salt or ester of uric acid.
■ **ura'taemia** *noun* (MEDICINE) the presence of urates in the blood L19. **uratic** /jʊ'ratɪk/ *adjective* (chiefly MEDICINE) of, pertaining to, or containing a urates L19.

urban /'ə:b(ə)n/ *adjective & noun*. E17.
[Latin *urbanus*, from *urb-*, *urbs* city: see -AN.]
▶ **A** *adjective*. **1** Of, pertaining to, or constituting a city or town; occurring in or characteristic of a city or town. E17.

2 a Having authority or jurisdiction over a city or town. M17. ▸**b** Resident in a city or town. M19.

🕮 **1** A. B. GIAMATTI The suburbs, that under-city that is neither urban nor rural. A. WALKER His culture .. , black urban street culture. **2b** *New Internationalist* Housing and access to land for the urban poor.

Special collocations: **urban blight**: see BLIGHT *noun* 3b. **urban district** *Hist.* in the UK, a group of urban communities governed by an elected council. **urban drift** the gradual migration of a population into urban areas. **urban guerrilla** a terrorist operating in an urban area. **urban legend**, **urban myth** an entertaining story or piece of information of uncertain origin that is circulated as though true. **urban renewal** slum clearance and redevelopment in a city or town. **urban sprawl** the uncontrolled expansion of urban areas.

▸ **B** *noun*. = URBANITE. Now *rare* or *obsolete*. L19.

■ **urbanism** *noun* urban life or character; urbanization: L19. **urbanite** *noun* a resident of a city or town L19.

urbane /əːˈbeɪn/ *adjective*. M16.

[Old & mod. French *urbain(e)*, or Latin *urbanus*: see prec., -ANE.]

1 = URBAN *adjective*. *arch.* M16.

2 Having the qualities or characteristics associated with town or city life; *esp.* elegant and refined in manners, courteous, suave, sophisticated. E17. ▸**b** Refined in expression; elegantly expressed. E19.

🕮 **1** WORDSWORTH Raising .. savage life To rustic, and the rustic to urbane. **2** T. FERRIS Galileo was an urbane gentleman who loved wine.

■ **urbanely** *adverb* E19. **urbaneness** *noun* E18.

Urbanist /ˈəːb(ə)nɪst/ *noun*[1]. E16.

[from papal name *Urban* (see below) + -IST.]

1 A supporter of Pope Urban VI (1378–89), the opponent of antipope Clement VII. *rare.* E16.

2 A Franciscan nun of the branch of the order of St Clare which followed the mitigated rule laid down by Pope Urban IV in 1264. L17.

urbanist /ˈəːb(ə)nɪst/ *noun*[2]. M20.

[from URBAN + -IST.]

An expert in or advocate of town planning.

■ **urbaˈnistic** *adjective* of or pertaining to town planning M20.

urbanity /əːˈbanɪti/ *noun*. M16.

[Old & mod. French *urbanité*, or Latin *urbanitas*, formed as URBAN: see -ITY.]

1 The character or quality of being urbane; courtesy, refinement, or elegance of manner etc. M16. ▸**b** In *pl.* Civilities, courtesies. M17.

†**2** Pleasant or witty conversation; sophisticated wit. M16–L17.

3 The state, condition, or character of a town or city; urban life. M16.

🕮 **1** SIR W. SCOTT The gentleness and urbanity of his .. manners. A. B. GIAMATTI Urbanity .. may seem too smooth, too slick, but we .. recognize in it a political gift. **3** R. CAPELL Men from the mountains .. come down .. for their first taste of urbanity.

urbanize /ˈəːb(ə)nʌɪz/ *verb*. Also **-ise**. M17.

[from URBAN + -IZE.]

1 *verb trans.* Make urbane; civilize. Now *rare* or *obsolete*. M17.

2 *verb trans.* & *intrans.* Make or become urban in character or appearance; develop into an urban area; (cause to) lose rural character or quality. L19.

3 *verb trans.* Accustom to urban life. Chiefly as ***urbanized*** *ppl adjective*. M20.

🕮 **2** *Daily Telegraph* A legendary place, once filled with mystery .. , has been urbanised into a municipal park. *Times Lit. Suppl.* An urbanizing society clinging to rural values. **3** J. ADDAMS The Italian woman .. became urbanized, .. and thus the habits of her entire family were modified.

■ **urbaniˈzation** *noun* L19.

urbanology /əːbəˈnɒlədʒi/ *noun*. M20.

[from URBAN + -OLOGY.]

The branch of knowledge that deals with urban areas and urban life.

■ **urbanologist** *noun* M20.

urbic /ˈəːbɪk/ *adjective*. *rare*. M17.

[Latin *urbicus*, from *urb-*, *urbs* city.]

†**1** = SUBURBICARIAN. Only in M17.

2 = URBAN *adjective* 1. M19.

†**urbicary** *adjective*. L17–E18.

[Latin *urbicarius*, formed as prec. Cf. SUBURBICARIAN.]

= SUBURBICARIAN.

urbicide /ˈəːbɪsʌɪd/ *noun*. M20.

[from Latin *urb-*, *urbs* city + -CIDE.]

The destruction of (the character of) a city.

urbiculture /ˈəːbɪkʌltʃə/ *noun*. M20.

[formed as prec. + CULTURE *noun*.]

1 The development or cultivation of urban areas and urban life. M20.

2 = RURBANIZATION. M20.

urbi et orbi /əːbɪ ɛt ˈɔːbi/ *adverbial phr.* M19.

[Latin.]

(Of a papal proclamation etc.) to the city (of Rome) and to the world; *transf.* for general information or acceptance, to everyone.

Urbino /əːˈbiːnəʊ/ *adjective*. L19.

[City in Le Marche province, Italy.]

Designating (an item of) majolica made in Urbino from the 15th to the 17th cents.

urbs /əːbz/ *noun*. M20.

[Latin = city.]

The city, esp. as a symbol of harsh or busy modern life.

🕮 A. B. GIAMATTI To be of the *urbs*, to be urbane, is to be political and .. civilised.

URC *abbreviation*.

United Reformed Church.

urceolate /ˈəːsɪələt/ *adjective*. M18.

[formed as next + -ATE[2].]

Chiefly BOTANY & ZOOLOGY. **1** Pitcher-shaped; having a cylindrical or globular body contracted at the mouth. M18.

2 Provided with or contained in an urceolus. *rare*. L19.

■ Also **urceolated** *adjective* (ZOOLOGY, *rare*) M18.

urceolus /əːˈsiːələs/ *noun*. Pl. **-li** /-lʌɪ, -liː/. M19.

[Latin, dim. of *urceus* pitcher.]

BOTANY & ZOOLOGY. A pitcher-shaped sheath or structure, as the tube in which some rotifers live.

urchin /ˈəːtʃɪn/ *noun* & *adjective*. ME.

[Old Northern French *herichon* var. of Old French *heriçon* (mod. *hérisson*, dial. *hérichon*, *hurchon*), from Proto-Romance, from Latin *hericius* late form of *ericius* hedgehog. Cf. HURCHEON.]

▸ **A** *noun*. **1** A hedgehog. *arch.* ME. ▸†**b** A goblin; an elf. L16–E17.

2 *transf.* †**a** A porcupine. *rare*. Only in LME. ▸**b** A sea urchin. E17.

3 a A mischievous child or youth; a brat; *spec.* (*poet.*) Cupid. LME. ▸**b** A young boy or girl, *esp.* one poorly or raggedly dressed. M16.

4 A physically deformed person; a hunchback. Now *dial.* E16.

🕮 **3a** SWIFT The urchin .. Took aim, and shot with all his strength. **b** S. RUSHDIE An urchin who had spent eleven years in the gutter.

▸ **B** *adjective*. That is an urchin; of, pertaining to, or resembling an urchin. M16.

Comb. & special collocations: †**urchin crowfoot** the corn buttercup, *Ranunculus arvensis* (cf. HEDGEHOG 5); **urchin cut** a short ragged style of haircut; **urchin fish** the porcupine fish.

■ **urchinly** *adjective* of the nature of or resembling an urchin M17.

urdee /ˈəːdeɪ/ *adjective*. In sense 2 also Anglicized as **urdy** /ˈəːdi/. M16.

[Origin unkn.]

HERALDRY. **1** Of a cross: pointed at the extremities. M16.

2 Of a bend or line: deflected or broken into a series of parallel projections. L17.

Urdu /ˈʊəduː, ˈəːduː/ *noun* & *adjective*. L18.

[Persian & Urdu (*zabān i*) *urdū* (language of the) camp, from Persian *urdū* from Turkish *ordu* camp (see HORDE).]

▸ **A** *noun*. An Indo-Aryan language closely related to Hindi with an admixture of Persian and Arabic words, now the official language of Pakistan. Formerly also = HINDUSTANI *noun* 1. L18.

▸ **B** *adjective*. Of or pertaining to Urdu. M19.

urdy *adjective* see URDEE.

ure /jʊə/ *noun*[1]. Long *arch.* LME.

[Anglo-Norman = Old French *e(u)vre*, *uevre* (mod. OEUVRE), from Latin OPERA *noun*[1].]

Custom, habit; practice, use. Chiefly in ***in ure***, in or into use, practice, or effect.

ure /jʊə, əː/ *noun*[2]. *obsolete* exc. *Hist.* E16.

[Old Norwegian *øyrir* (Norwegian *øyre*, *øre*) = Middle & mod. Swedish *öre*, (M)Da. *øre*, Old Norse (Icelandic) *eyrir*, from Latin *aureus* gold solidus. Cf. ORA *noun*[1].]

In Orkney and Shetland, an eighth of a Norse mark, equivalent to an ounce of silver; a piece of land assessed to this value for feu duty (also ***ure of land***).

†**ure** *noun*[3]. M16–M17.

[(Old French) formed as URUS.]

= AUROCHS.

-ure /jʊə/ *suffix*.

[Repr. Old & mod. French *-ure* from Latin *-ura*.]

1 Forming nouns from or after French or Latin denoting action, process, or result, as ***censure***, ***closure***, ***picture***, ***scripture***; nouns of function or office, as ***judicature***, ***prefecture***; collective nouns, as ***legislature***, ***nature***.

2 Used to Anglicize French nouns in ***-ir***, ***-or***, ***-our***, etc., as ***pleasure***, ***treasure***, ***velure***.

urea /jʊˈriːə, ˈjʊərɪə/ *noun*. E19.

[French *urée* (with Latinized ending) from Greek *ouron* URINE or *ourein* urinate.]

1 CHEMISTRY. A soluble crystalline compound, $CO(NH_2)_2$, which is the main nitrogenous breakdown product of protein metabolism in mammals and some other animals, is excreted in their urine, and has numerous industrial uses. Also called ***carbamide***. E19.

2 A urea-formaldehyde plastic or resin. M20.

Comb.: **urea cycle** BIOCHEMISTRY a cyclic metabolic pathway by which urea is formed in the liver; **urea-formaldehyde** *adjective* & *noun* (pertaining to or designating) a plastic, resin, or foam made by condensation of urea with formaldehyde, used esp. in cavity insulation; **urea resin** a synthetic resin derived from urea; a urea-formaldehyde resin.

■ **ureal** *adjective* (now *rare*) M19. **ureˈameter** *noun* = UREOMETER L19. **urease** *noun* (BIOCHEMISTRY) an enzyme produced by certain bacteria and plants, which breaks down urea into carbon dioxide and ammonia L19.

ureaplasma /jʊərɪəˈplazmə/ *noun*. L20.

[mod. Latin *Ureaplasma* (see below), formed as UREA + PLASMA.]

BIOLOGY. Any of several micro-organisms of the genus *Ureaplasma*, which are related to the mycoplasmas and are characterized by the ability to metabolize urea.

Urecholine /jʊərɪˈkəʊliːn, -ɪn/ *noun*. M20.

[from UREA + CHOLINE.]

PHARMACOLOGY. A quaternary ammonium compound, $C_7H_{17}ClN_2O_2$, used as a parasympathomimetic agent to stimulate bowel or bladder muscle activity.

¶ Proprietary name in the US.

uredia *noun* pl. of UREDIUM.

uredines *noun* pl. of UREDO.

uredinia *noun* pl. of UREDINIUM.

urediniospore /jʊərɪˈdɪnɪəspɔː/ *noun*. E20.

[from next + -O- + SPORE. Cf. UREDIOSPORE, UREDOSPORE.]

MYCOLOGY. In the life cycle of a rust fungus, any of the one-celled, freq. reddish, spores which develop on a host plant in the summer and are rapidly spread by the wind to infect other plants. Cf. TELIOSPORE.

uredinium /jʊərɪˈdɪnɪəm/ *noun*. Pl. **-nia** /-nɪə/. E20.

[from Latin *uredin-*, UREDO + *-ium*.]

MYCOLOGY. A sorus or pustule in which urediniospores are formed.

■ **uredinial** *adjective* E20.

uredium /jʊˈriːdɪəm/ *noun*. Pl. **-dia** /-dɪə/. M20.

[mod. Latin, from Latin UREDO.]

MYCOLOGY. = UREDINIUM.

■ **uredial** *adjective* M20. **urediospore** *noun* = UREDINIOSPORE M20.

uredo /jʊˈriːdəʊ/ *noun*. Pl. **-dines** /-dɪniːz/. E18.

[Latin, from *urere* to burn.]

MYCOLOGY. **1** Blight caused by a rust fungus. *rare*. E18.

2 Any of various rust fungi producing or known only from urediniospores, formerly regarded as forming a distinct genus *Uredo*. E18.

■ **uredoˈsorus** *noun*, pl. **-ri** /-rʌɪ/, = UREDINIUM E20. **uredospore** *noun* = UREDINIOSPORE L19.

ureide /ˈjʊərɪʌɪd/ *noun*. Also †**-id**. M19.

[from UREA + -IDE.]

CHEMISTRY. Any of various (often cyclic) acyl derivatives of urea.

ureilite /ˈjʊərɪlʌɪt/ *noun*. E20.

[from Novo-*Urei*, a village near Penza, Russia + -LITE.]

GEOLOGY. Any of a group of calcium-poor achondrite meteorites that consist mainly of olivine and pigeonite.

uremia *noun* see URAEMIA.

urent /ˈjʊər(ə)nt/ *adjective*. *rare*. M17.

[Latin *urent-* pres. ppl stem of *urere* to burn: see -ENT. Cf. Italian, Spanish *urente*.]

Burning; causing a burning sensation.

ureo- /ˈjʊərɪəʊ/ *combining form* of UREA: see -O-.

■ **ureˈometer** *noun* (MEDICINE & CHEMISTRY) an apparatus for determining the concentration of urea in a liquid L19. **ureotelic** /-ˈtɛlɪk/ *adjective* (BIOCHEMISTRY) (of an animal or its metabolism) producing nitrogenous waste chiefly in the form of urea E20.

ure-ox /ˈjʊərɒks/ *noun*. E17.

[formed as UROCHS.]

= AUROCHS. Cf. UROCHS, URUS.

-uret /jʊərɛt/ *suffix* (no longer productive).

[mod. Latin *-uretum*, *-oretum*.]

CHEMISTRY. Forming names of simple compounds of an element with another element or a radical, as ***carburet***, ***sulphuret***, etc. Cf. BIURET.

¶ Now replaced by -IDE.

ureter /jʊˈriːtə, ˈjʊərɪtə/ *noun*. L16.

[French *urétère* or mod. Latin *ureter* from Greek *ourētēr*, from *ourein* urinate, from *ouron* urine.]

ANATOMY. Either of two tubes which convey urine from the pelvis of the kidney to the bladder; a urinary duct.

■ **uˈreteral** *adjective* = URETERIC L19. **ureˈteric** *adjective* pertaining to, affecting, or occurring in a ureter or ureters E19.

uretero- /jʊˈriːt(ə)rəʊ/ *combining form* of URETER: see -O-. Before a vowel also **ureter-**. Chiefly MEDICINE.

■ **ureteˈrectomy** *noun* (an instance of) the surgical removal of a ureter L19. **ureteˈritis** *noun* inflammation of a ureter E19.

ureterocele *noun* an outward protrusion of the wall of a ureter **E20.** **urete'rography** *noun* radiography of the ureters after they have been injected with a radio-opaque fluid **E20.** **ureteroli'thotomy** *noun* (an instance of) the surgical removal of a stone from a ureter **L19.** **ureterosigmoi'dostomy** *noun* (an instance of) a surgical operation to implant the ureters into the sigmoid flexure of the colon **M20.** **urete'rostomy** *noun* (an instance of) the surgical creation of an opening from a ureter to the external skin surface **E20.** **urete'rotomy** *noun* (an instance of) a surgical incision into a ureter **L19.**

urethane /'jʊərɪθeɪm, jʊ'rɛθeɪm/ *noun*. Also †**-than**. **M19.**
[formed as UREA + ETHANE.]
1 CHEMISTRY. An ester of carbamic acid; *spec.* ethyl carbamate, $CO(NH_2)OC_2H_5$, a toxic compound formerly used as an anaesthetic. Cf. CARBAMATE. **M19.**
2 = POLYURETHANE. **M20.**

urethra /jʊ'riːθrə/ *noun*. **M17.**
[Late Latin from Greek *ourēthra*, from *ourein* urinate.]
ANATOMY. The tube or canal through which urine is conveyed out of the body from the bladder, and which in the male also conveys semen.
■ **urethral** *adjective* of or pertaining to, connected with, or affecting the urethra; adapted for operating on the urethra: **M19.**

urethro- /jʊ'riːθrəʊ/ *combining form* of URETHRA: see -O-. Before a vowel also **urethr-**. Chiefly MEDICINE.
■ **ure'thritis** *noun* (MEDICINE) inflammation of the urethra **E19.** **urethrogram** *noun* (*a*) (now *rare*) a recording made by a urethrometer; (*b*) a photograph made by urethrography: **L19.** **ure'thrography** *noun* radiography of the urethra after it has been injected with a radio-opaque fluid **M20.** **ure'thrometer** *noun* (now *rare*) a device for measuring the lumen of the urethra **L19.** **urethroscope** *noun* an instrument for the visual examination of the urethra **M19.** **urethro'scopic** *adjective* of, pertaining to, or by means of urethroscopy **L19.** **ure'throscopy** *noun* examination of the urethra using a urethroscope **L19.** **urethrotome** *noun* a surgical instrument for use in urethrotomy **M19.** **ure'throtomy** *noun* (an instance of) a surgical operation to cut a stricture in the urethra **M19.**

uretic /jʊ'rɛtɪk/ *adjective*. Now *rare*. **M19.**
[Late Latin *ureticus* from Greek *ourētikos*, from *ourein* urinate.]
Chiefly MEDICINE. Of or pertaining to the urine. Formerly also, diuretic.

Urfirnis /'ʊəfəːnɪs/ *noun & adjective*. **E20.**
[German, from UR- + *firnis* varnish, veneer.]
GREEK ARCHAEOLOGY. (Designating) an early form of Greek pottery characterized by the use of dark lustrous paint.

urge /əːdʒ/ *verb & noun*. **M16.**
[Latin *urgere* press, drive, compel.]
▶ **A** *verb*. **I 1** *verb trans.* Present or state earnestly or insistently in argument, justification, or defence. (Foll. by *on*, *upon*, etc., a person.) **M16.**
2 *verb trans.* Advocate or recommend (a course of action, *that*, etc.) eagerly or insistently. **L16.**

> 🕮 **1** G. STEINER Let me urge the point . . . The implied differentiation is of the essence. **2** R. GITTINGS The doctor urged that his brother should be sent for. *Times Educ. Suppl.* The tape message will explain safe practice rather than urge abstinence.

▶ **II 3** *verb trans.* Entreat earnestly or persistently (*to do*); incite or impel strongly. Also foll. by *on*. **M16.** ▶†**b** Charge or accuse strongly. Usu. foll. by *with*. **L16–E18.**
4 *verb trans.* Put (esp. excessive) pressure on; strain. *arch.* **L16.**

> 🕮 **3** D. JACOBSON I urged Amnon to commit the crime. **4** SIR W. SCOTT Do not urge my patience with mockery.

▶ **III 5** *verb trans.* Force to advance or accelerate; press, push; drive forcibly in a particular direction; force or press (one's way etc.). Freq. foll. by *forward*, *on*, *towards*, *up*, etc. **M16.**
6 *verb trans.* Provoke, excite; intensify. Now *rare*. **L16.** ▶**b** Anger; annoy. Now *dial.* **L16.**
7 *verb trans.* Use or work vigorously. *poet.* **L17.**

> 🕮 **5** SCOTT FITZGERALD The fresh flow from one end urged its way towards the drain. G. GREENE He urged Mrs Wilcox towards the door with a friendly . . hand. J. M. COETZEE Though I urge it on, my horse is too weak to raise more than a shambling trot. R. K. NARAYAN He urged and bullied the goats. **7** SHELLEY Urge The strokes of the inexorable scourge.

▶ **IV 8** *verb intrans.* Plead or entreat earnestly (*for*). Now *rare*. **L16.**
9 *verb intrans.* Press or push forward; hasten *along*, *on*, etc. Now *rare*. **E17.**
10 *verb intrans.* Act as an incentive or stimulus (*to do*). Long *rare* exc. *poet.* **M17.**

> 🕮 **8** GOLDSMITH The tribunes . . began . . to urge for the removal. **10** POPE The combat urges, and my soul's on fire.

▶ **B** *noun*. The action of urging a person or thing; the fact of being urged; an eager desire or strong impulse (*to do*). **E17.**

> 🕮 G. ORWELL The urge to shout filthy words . . was . . strong. I. MURDOCH A young composer . . is psycholanalysed and then finds that his creative urge is gone.

urgence /'əːdʒ(ə)ns/ *noun*. *arch.* **L16.**
[French, or formed as URGENT: see -ENCE.]
1 = URGENCY 2. **L16.**
2 = URGENCY 1. **E17.**
3 Speed; haste. **E17.**
4 = URGENCY 3. **L19.**

urgency /'əːdʒ(ə)nsi/ *noun*. **M16.**
[formed as next: see -ENCY.]
1 The state, condition, or fact of being urgent; pressing necessity; imperativeness. **M16.** ▶**b** An instance of this; a pressing or urgent need. **M17.**
2 (An) earnest or pressing entreaty; (an) importunity, (an) insistence. **E17.**
3 (A) driving or stimulating force or quality; (a) strong impulse or incitement. **E19.**

urgent /'əːdʒ(ə)nt/ *adjective*. **L15.**
[Old & mod. French from Latin *urgent-* pres. ppl stem of *urgere* URGE *verb*: see -ENT.]
1 Demanding or requiring prompt action or attention; pressing. **L15.** ▶**b** Of a statement etc.: expressing a need for prompt action or attention. **E17.**
2 Strongly stimulating or exciting; compelling, driving. **M16.**
3 Moving with great force or impetus. Formerly also *spec.*, (of time) passing quickly, pressing. Chiefly *poet.* **M16.**
4 Pressing in demand; importunate, insistent. Also foll. by *for*, *on*, *that*. **M16.** ▶**b** Having an eager wish or desire *to do*. **M18.**
†**5** Oppressive; severe. **M16–L17.**

> 🕮 **1** I. MURDOCH But it's urgent, it's a matter of days and hours. *Peace News* The Guaymi example . . the most urgent illustration of the unacceptable face of RTZ. **b** C. S. FORESTER Hornblower walked over to him with an urgent request . . . 'My parole expires in ten minutes, sir'. J. MAY If life's force is still urgent within you, . . . you should remain here. **4** O. MANNING The urgent advocacy made Clarence sit up, sobered. *Oxford Diocesan Magazine* The APMs are urgent that their ministry should be fully understood.

■ **urgently** *adverb* **E16.** **urgentness** *noun* (long *rare* or *obsolete*) urgency **L16.**

urger /'əːdʒə/ *noun*. **L16.**
[from URGE *verb* + -ER[1].]
1 A person who urges or incites someone or something. **L16.** ▶**b** A person who obtains money dishonestly, esp. as a racing tipster. *Austral. slang.* **E20.**
2 An instigator or advocate *of* something. Now *rare*. **L16.**

urgicenter /'əːdʒɪsɛntə/ *noun*. *US*. **L20.**
[from URG(ENT + CENTRE *noun*, after *Surgicenter*.]
A clinic providing immediate outpatient treatment for minor ailments or injuries. Cf. EMERGICENTER.

Urheimat /'uːrhaɪmaːt/ *noun*. **M20.**
[German, from UR- + *Heimat* home, homeland.]
The place of origin of a people or language.

URI *abbreviation*.
Upper respiratory (tract) infection.

uri *noun pl.* see URUS.

-uria /'jʊərɪə/ *suffix*.
[Late Latin from Greek *-ouria*, from *ouron* urine.]
MEDICINE. Forming nouns denoting abnormal conditions of urine production, composition, etc., or disorders characterized by these, as ***dysuria***, ***glycosuria***, ***polyuria***, etc.

Uriah Heep /jʊˌrʌɪə 'hiːp/ *noun*. **L19.**
[A character in Dickens's *David Copperfield* (1850).]
A person who feigns excessive humility.
■ **Uriah Heepish** *adjective* reminiscent of Uriah Heep; hypocritically humble: **E20.**

urial /'ʊərɪəl/ *noun*. Also (earlier) †**oorial**. **M19.**
[Panjabi *ūrial*.]
A wild sheep, *Ovis vignei*, that has a reddish coat and long curved horns, found in central Asia from Kashmir to Iran and Turkestan.

uric /'jʊərɪk/ *adjective*. **L18.**
[formed as URINE + -IC.]
Chiefly BIOCHEMISTRY. Of, pertaining to, or derived from urine.
uric acid an almost insoluble bicyclic acid, 2,6,8-trioxypurine, $C_5H_4N_4O_3$, which is the end-product of purine metabolism in primates and carnivores, is excreted in their urine, and is the main nitrogenous excretory product in birds, reptiles, and insects. †**uric oxide** = XANTHINE.
■ **'uricaci,daemia** *noun* (MEDICINE, now *rare*) = HYPERURICAEMIA **L19.** **uri'caemia** *noun* (MEDICINE) = HYPERURICAEMIA **M19.** **uricaemic** *adjective* (MEDICINE) = HYPERURICAEMIC **E20.** **uricase** *noun* (BIOCHEMISTRY) an enzyme which promotes the conversion of uric acid into allantoin, found in certain insects and most mammals **E20.** **urico'suric** *adjective* (MEDICINE) causing or characterized by an increased excretion of uric acid or urate in the urine **M20.** **urico'telic** *adjective* (BIOCHEMISTRY) (of an animal or its metabolism) producing nitrogenous waste chiefly in the form of uric acid or urates rather than urea **E20.**

-uric /'jʊərɪk/ *suffix*.
[from -URIA + -IC.]
MEDICINE. Forming adjectives corresponding to nouns in *-uria*, as ***dysuric***, ***glycosuric***, ***polyuric***, etc.

uridine /'jʊərɪdiːn/ *noun*. **E20.**
[from UR(ACIL + -IDINE.]
BIOCHEMISTRY. A nucleoside containing uracil linked to ribose, obtained by partial hydrolysis of RNA.

uridrosis /jʊərɪ'drəʊsɪs/ *noun*. **M19.**
[from Greek *ouron* urine + *idron* sweat: see -OSIS.]
MEDICINE. The excretion of excessive amounts of urea in the sweat.

uridylic /jʊərɪ'dɪlɪk/ *adjective*. **M20.**
[from URIDINE + -YL + -IC.]
BIOCHEMISTRY. ***uridylic acid***, a nucleotide composed of a phosphoric acid ester of uridine, present in RNA.

Urim /'jʊərɪm/ *noun*. **M16.**
[Hebrew *'ūrīm* pl. of *'ōr*.]
One of the two objects of a now unknown nature worn on the breastplate of a Jewish high priest. Chiefly in ***Urim and Thummim***. Cf. THUMMIM.

urinal /jʊ'rʌɪn(ə)l, 'jʊərɪn(ə)l/ *noun*. **ME.**
[Old & mod. French from late Latin use as noun of neut. of *urinalis* urinary, from Latin *urina* URINE: see -AL[1].]
†**1** A glass vessel for the medical examination or inspection of urine. **ME–M19.**
†**2** ALCHEMY. A glass phial for solutions etc. **LME–M18.**
3 *gen.* A receptacle for urine; a chamber-pot. **LME.**
4 A container for receiving and holding urine worn by a person with urinary incontinence. **M19.**
5 A sanitary fitting, esp. against a wall, for men to urinate into; a public lavatory containing several of these. **M19.**

> 🕮 **5** B. HINES The copper pipe across the top of the urinals began to dribble.

urinal /jʊ'rʌɪn(ə)l, 'jʊərɪn(ə)l/ *adjective*. Now *rare* or *obsolete*. **M16.**
[French from late Latin *urinalis*: see prec.]
1 Of, pertaining to, or characteristic of urine. **M16.**
2 Of or pertaining to the secretion and discharge of urine. **E17.**

urinalysis /jʊərɪ'nalɪsɪs/ *noun*. Pl. **-lyses** /-lɪsiːz/. **L19.**
[Blend of URINE + ANALYSIS.]
Chiefly MEDICINE. Analysis of urine by physical, chemical, and microscopical means to test for the presence of disease, drugs, etc.; an instance of this.

urinant /'jʊərɪnənt/ *adjective*. **L17.**
[Latin *urinant-* pres. ppl stem of *urinari* dive: see -ANT[1].]
HERALDRY. Of a fish etc.: with head downward and tail erect.

urinary /'jʊərɪn(ə)ri/ *adjective*. **L16.**
[from Latin *urina* URINE + -ARY[1].]
1 Of or pertaining to urine, or the secretion and discharge of urine. **L16.**
2 Consisting of, containing, or contained in urine. **E17.**
3 Of, pertaining to, affecting, or occurring in the urinary system or organs. **L18.**
Special collocations: ***urinary bladder***: see BLADDER 1a. ***urinary meatus***: see MEATUS 2. **urinary system** ANATOMY the system of organs and structures concerned with the excretion and discharge of urine, comprising (in mammals) the kidneys, ureters, bladder, and urethra. **urinary tract** (chiefly MEDICINE) the series of channels by which the urine passes from the pelvis of the kidney to the urinary meatus.

urinate /'jʊərɪneɪt/ *verb*. **L16.**
[from medieval Latin *urinat-* pa. ppl stem of *urinare*, from Latin *urina* URINE: see -ATE[3].]
1 *verb intrans.* Discharge urine, make water, micturate. **L16.**
2 *verb trans.* **a** Wet or saturate (something) with urine. Now *rare*. **M18.** ▶**b** Pass (blood etc.) with or after the manner of urine. **E20.**
■ **uri'nation** *noun* the action of passing water; micturition: **L16.**

urine /'jʊərɪn, 'jʊərʌɪn/ *noun & verb*. **ME.**
[Old & mod. French from Latin *urina* rel. to Greek *ouron*. As verb perh. from French *uriner* from medieval Latin *urinare* urinate.]
▶ **A** *noun*. The pale yellow fluid containing waste products filtered from the blood by the kidneys in higher vertebrates, stored in the bladder, and discharged at intervals through the urethra. Also, a type or sample of urine. **ME.**
Comb.: **urine mark** *noun* (ZOOLOGY) a scent mark consisting of urine; **urine-mark** *verb intrans.* (ZOOLOGY) (of a mammal) scent-mark using urine.
▶†**B** *verb intrans.* Urinate. **L16–E19.**

uriniferous /jʊərɪ'nɪf(ə)rəs/ *adjective*. **M18.**
[from URINE *noun* + -I- + -FEROUS.]
ANATOMY & ZOOLOGY. That conveys or secretes urine.
uriniferous tubule any of the long fine convoluted tubules conveying urine from the Bowman's capsules to the collecting ducts in the vertebrate kidney.

urino- /'jʊərɪnəʊ/ *combining form* of Latin *urina* URINE *noun*: see -O-. Chiefly MEDICINE.

■ **uri'nologist** *noun* (now *rare* or *obsolete*) = UROLOGIST L19. **uri'nology** *noun* (now *rare* or *obsolete*) = UROLOGY 2 M19. **urinomancy** *noun* (*Hist.*) diagnosis based on examination of the urine E20. **uri'nometer** *noun* a device or hydrometer for measuring the relative density of urine M20. **uri'noscopy** *noun* (now *rare* or *obsolete*) = UROSCOPY M19.

urinogenital /jʊərɪnəʊˈdʒɛnɪt(ə)l, jʊˌrʌɪnəʊ-/ *adjective*. M19.
[from URINO- + GENITAL *adjective*.]
Of, pertaining to, or affecting both the urinary and the genital organs; genito-urinary, urogenital.

urinoir /yrinwaːr/ *noun*. Pl. pronounced same. M20.
[French.]
A public urinal (in France).

urinous /ˈjʊərɪnəs/ *adjective*. M17.
[from URINE *noun* + -OUS.]
1 Of, pertaining to, consisting of, or derived from urine. M17.
2 Characteristic of or resembling urine. L17.
3 Marked by the presence or prevalence of urine. L18.

urisk /ˈuːrɪsk/ *noun*. E19.
[Gaelic *ùruisg*.]
In Scottish Highland folklore, a supernatural creature haunting mountain streams and other lonely places.

urkingdom /ˈʊəkɪŋdəm/ *noun*. L20.
[from UR- + KINGDOM.]
TAXONOMY. Each of three primary divisions above the level of kingdom which have been proposed for the grouping of all living organisms (usu. as archaebacteria, eubacteria, and eukaryotes).

URL *abbreviation*.
Uniform (or universal) resource locator, the address of a World Wide Web page.

urlar /ˈʊələ/ *noun*. L19.
[Gaelic *ùrlar* ground, floor.]
MUSIC. The ground theme in a pibroch.

urn /əːn/ *noun & verb*[1]. LME.
[Latin *urna* rel. to *urceus* pitcher.]
▶ **A** *noun*. **1** A vessel or vase, usu. with rounded or oviform body and circular base, used to store the ashes of the cremated dead. Also *transf.* (chiefly *poet.*), a tomb, a grave. LME.
2 ROMAN ANTIQUITIES. A vessel for holding tokens used in casting lots, voting, etc. E16.
3 A rounded or oviform vessel for carrying water or other liquid; a water-pitcher. E17. ▸**b** (**U-**.) The constellation of Aquarius. Long *rare* or *obsolete*. M17. ▸**c** The source of a river; a spring (with allus. to the artistic representation of river gods etc. holding urns). *poet.* E18.
4 An ornamental sculpture representing an urn. M17.
5 A large metal container, fitted with a tap, in which tea, coffee, etc., is made and kept hot or water for making tea etc. is boiled and kept. L18.
6 a BOTANY. The spore capsule of a moss. M19. ▸**b** ZOOLOGY. An urn-shaped process or part. L19.
1 CINERARY *urn*. *funeral urn*: see FUNERAL *adjective* 1. **5 coffee urn**, **tea-urn**.
Comb.: **urnfield** *noun & adjective* (ARCHAEOLOGY) (*a*) *noun* a cemetery of individual graves containing cinerary urns, found esp. in central Europe after 1300 BC; (*b*) *adjective* designating a people etc. characterized by this method of burial.
▶ **B** *verb trans.* = INURN. E17.
■ **urnal** *adjective* (long *rare* or *obsolete*) = URNED (b) L16. **urned** *adjective* (*a*) placed or buried in an urn; (*b*) containing or effected in a cinerary urn: E17. **urnful** *noun* (*rare*) as much as an urn will hold E19.

urn *verb*[2] see RUN *verb*.

Urnes /əːˈnɛs/ *adjective*. M20.
[Town in W. Norway, the site of an 11th-cent. church in this style.]
Designating a style of late Viking decorative art, characterized by the use of animal motifs and complex interlacing.

urning /ˈəːnɪŋ/ *noun*. Now *rare*. L19.
[German, formed as URANIA. Cf. URANIAN *adjective*[1] & *noun*[1], URANISM.]
A homosexual. Cf. URANIAN *noun*[1].

uro- /ˈjʊərəʊ/ *combining form*[1].
[from Greek *ouron* urine: see -O-.]
BIOCHEMISTRY & MEDICINE etc. Forming words with the sense 'pertaining to, present in, or derived from urine'.
■ **urochlo'ralic** *adjective*: **urochloralic acid**, a metabolite formed in the body after chloral has been administered L19. **urochrome** *noun* (CHEMISTRY) an amorphous yellow pigment found in urine M19. **uro'daeum** *noun*, pl. **-daea**, ZOOLOGY the part of the cloaca into which the urinary ducts open L19. **urody'namic** *adjective* of or pertaining to urodynamics M20. **urody'namics** *noun* the branch of medicine that deals with the containment and flow of urine in the body M20. **uro'gastrone** *noun* (BIOCHEMISTRY) any of various closely related polypeptides which retard gastric secretion and motor activity and occur in the urine M20. **uro'kinase** *noun* (BIOCHEMISTRY & PHARMACOLOGY) an enzyme which catalyses the conversion of plasminogen to plasmin, used to treat blood clots M20. **uro'lagnia** *noun* [Greek *lagneia* lust] PSYCHOLOGY sexual pleasure derived from the sight or thought of urination E20. **uro'lagnic** *adjective* (PSYCHOLOGY) of or pertaining to urolagnia E20. **uroli'thiasis** *noun* lithiasis in the bladder or urinary tract M19. **uro'philia** *noun* obsessive interest in urine and urination; urolagnia: M20. **uropoietic** /-pɔɪˈɛtɪk/ *adjective* of or pertaining to the secretion of urine L18. **uro'porphyrin** *noun* (BIOCHEMISTRY) any of a group of porphyrins, occurring esp. in the urine during certain types of porphyria, in which each of the pyrrole rings has one acetate and one propionate side-chain E20. **uroporphy'rinogen** *noun* (BIOCHEMISTRY) any porphyrinogen in which the pyrrole rings have side-chains as in a uroporphyrin E20. **u'roscopy** *noun* (now *rare*) examination of the urine; *esp.* the former practice of diagnosis by simple inspection of the urine: M17. **uro'thelial** *adjective* of, pertaining to, or consisting of urothelium L20. **uro'thelium** *noun* the epithelium of the urinary tract, esp. that of the bladder M20. **urotoxic** *adjective* (now *rare*) of or pertaining to the toxicity or toxic constituents of the urine L19. **urotoxy** *noun* (now *rare* or *obsolete*) the toxicity of the urine; a unit used to express this: L19. **uro'tropine** *noun* = HEXAMETHYLENETETRAMINE L19. **uro'xanic** *adjective*: ***uroxanic acid*** (CHEMISTRY), an acid, $C_5H_8N_4O_6$, obtained by oxidation of uric acid in alkaline solution M19. **uro'xanthin** *noun* (CHEMISTRY) = INDICAN 2 M19.

uro- /ˈjʊərəʊ/ *combining form*[2].
[from Greek *oura* tail: see -O-.]
ANATOMY & ZOOLOGY. Forming words with the sense 'pertaining to or designating a posterior or caudal part, region, or process'.
■ **uropod** *noun* (ZOOLOGY) (*a*) any abdominal appendage of a crustacean; (*b*) *spec.* each of the sixth and last pair of abdominal appendages of malacostracans, forming part of the tail fan in lobsters etc.: L19. **urostyle** *noun* (ZOOLOGY) the posterior unsegmented portion of the vertebral column in certain lower vertebrates, esp. anuran amphibians L19.

urobilin /jʊərə(ʊ)ˈbʌɪlɪn/ *noun*. Also †**-ine**. L19.
[from URO-[1] + Latin *bilis* bile: see -IN[1].]
BIOCHEMISTRY. Any of several brown bile pigments formed from urobilinogen and excreted chiefly in the faeces.
■ **urobi'linogen** *noun* any of several colourless tetrapyrrole compounds produced by the reduction of bilirubin, esp. by bacterial action in the gut L19. **urobilinu'ria** *noun* (MEDICINE) an abnormal condition of the urine characterized by an excess of urobilin L19.

uroboros /jʊərəʊˈbɒrəs/ *noun*. Also **ouro-**. M20.
[Greek (*drakōn*) *ouroboros*, *ourēboros* (snake) devouring its tail.]
A usu. circular symbol depicting a snake (or occas. dragon) swallowing its tail, as an emblem of wholeness or infinity.
■ **uroboric** *adjective* of, pertaining to, or resembling a uroboros M20.

urochord /ˈjʊərəkɔːd/ *noun*. L19.
[from URO-[2] + CHORD *noun*[2].]
ZOOLOGY. **1** The notochord of tunicates, corresponding to the primordial spinal column in vertebrates. L19.
2 = UROCHORDATE *noun*. L19.

urochordate /jʊərə(ʊ)ˈkɔːdeɪt/ *adjective & noun*. L19.
[formed as prec. + -ATE[1].]
ZOOLOGY. ▶**A** *adjective*. Possessing a urochord; *spec.* of, pertaining to, or designating a chordate of the subphylum Urochordata, which comprises the tunicates. L19.
▶ **B** *noun*. A member of this subphylum, a tunicate. L19.

urochs /ˈuːrɒks, ˈjʊə-/ *noun*. M19.
[German, var. of *Auerochs* AUROCHS.]
= AUROCHS. Cf. URE-OX, URUS.

urodele /ˈjʊərədiːl/ *noun & adjective*. M19.
[from French *urodèle* or mod. Latin *Urodela*, from Greek *oura* URO-[2] + *dēlos* evident.]
ZOOLOGY. ▶**A** *noun*. A member of the order Urodela, which comprises the tailed amphibians; a newt, a salamander. M19.
▶ **B** *adjective*. Of, pertaining to, or belonging to this order. L19.
■ **uro'delan** *noun* = URODELE *noun* L19. **uro'delous** *adjective* = URODELE *adjective* M19.

urogenital /jʊərəʊˈdʒɛnɪt(ə)l/ *adjective*. M19.
[from URO-[1] + GENITAL *adjective*.]
ANATOMY & ZOOLOGY. = URINOGENITAL.

urography /jʊˈrɒgrəfi/ *noun*. E20.
[from URO-[1] + -GRAPHY.]
MEDICINE. Radiography of the urinary tract after it has been injected with a radio-opaque fluid.
■ **uro'graphic** *adjective* of or pertaining to urography E20. **urogram** *noun* a radiograph of the urinary tract E20.

urology /jʊˈrɒlədʒi/ *noun*. M18.
[from URO-[1] + -LOGY.]
†**1** A treatise or discourse on urine. Only in M18.
2 The branch of medicine that deals with disorders of the kidney and urinary tract. M19.
■ **uro'logic** *adjective* = UROLOGICAL L19. **uro'logical** *adjective* pertaining to or dealing with urology M19. **urologist** *noun* a student of or expert in urology L19.

uronic /jʊˈrɒnɪk/ *adjective*. E20.
[from URO-[1] + -n- + -IC, or from GLYC)URONIC.]
CHEMISTRY. ***uronic acid***, any derivative of a monosaccharide in which a $\cdot CH_2OH$ group has been oxidized to a $\cdot COOH$ group.

uroo *noun* var. of EURO *noun*[1].

uropygium /jʊərəˈpɪdʒɪəm/ *noun*. L18.
[medieval Latin from Greek *ouropugion*: see URO-[2].]
ZOOLOGY. The rump of a bird, supporting the tail feathers.
■ **uropygial** *adjective* pertaining to or situated on the rump; ***uropygial gland*** = ***oil-gland*** s.v. OIL *noun*: L19.

urs /ʊəs/ *noun*. M19.
[Arab. *'urs* lit. 'wedding, wedding feast'.]
Esp. in the Indian subcontinent, a ceremony celebrating the anniversary of the death of a Muslim saint.

Ursa /ˈəːsə/ *noun*. OE.
[Latin = (female) bear, the Great Bear.]
More fully ***Ursa Major***. (The name of) a conspicuous constellation of the northern hemisphere that contains the Plough; the Great Bear. Also, the Plough itself.
Ursa Minor (the name of) the constellation that includes the polestar; the Little Bear.

ursal /ˈəːs(ə)l/ *adjective*. M19.
[from Latin *ursus* bear + -AL[1]]
Resembling or characteristic of a bear or bears; bearish.

Urschleim /ˈuːrʃlaɪm/ *noun*. E20.
[German, from UR- + *Schleim* slime.]
BIOLOGY (now *Hist.*). The earliest form of life, conceived as amorphous protoplasm.

ursid /ˈəːsɪd/ *noun & adjective*. L19.
[mod. Latin *Ursidae* (see below), from Latin *ursus* bear: see -ID[3].]
ZOOLOGY. ▶**A** *noun*. A mammal of the family Ursidae, which comprises the bears; a bear. L19.
▶ **B** *adjective*. Of, pertaining to, or designating this family. E20.

ursine /ˈəːsʌɪn, -ɪn/ *adjective*. M16.
[Latin *ursinus* from *ursus* bear: see -INE[1].]
Of or pertaining to a bear or bears; characteristic of or resembling (that of) a bear; bearlike, bearish.

> 🕮 *New Yorker* Scheller . . has brown hair and a beard and is chummy in an ursine way. *Daily Telegraph* Sooty, the ursine glove puppet. **ursine baboon** = CHACMA. **ursine dasyure** = DEVIL *noun* 5(c). **ursine howler** the red howler (monkey), *Alouatta seniculus*, of S. America. **ursine seal** = ***fur-seal*** s.v. FUR *noun*[1]. **ursine sloth** = ***sloth bear*** s.v. SLOTH *noun*.

ursinia /əːˈsɪnɪə/ *noun*. E20.
[mod. Latin (see below), from John *Ursinus* (1608–66), German botanist + -IA[1].]
Any of various southern African plants constituting the genus *Ursinia*, of the composite family, grown for their daisy-like flowers.

urson /ˈəːs(ə)n/ *noun*. L18.
[French *ourson*, dim. of *ours* bear.]
The N. American porcupine, *Erethizon dorsatum*.

Ursprache /ˈuːrʃpraːxə/ *noun*. Pl. **-en** /-ən/. E20.
[German, from UR- + *Sprache* speech.]
= PROTO-LANGUAGE.

Ursuline /ˈəːsjʊlʌɪn, -lɪn/ *noun & adjective*. L17.
[from St *Ursula* the founder's patron saint, + -INE[1].]
▶ **A** *noun*. A nun of an Augustinian order founded by St Angela in 1535, esp. for teaching girls and nursing the sick. L17.
▶ **B** *adjective*. Of, pertaining to, or designating this religious order. M18.

Urtext /ˈuːrtɛkst/ *noun*. Pl. **-e** /-ə/. M20.
[German, from UR- + *Text* text (ult. from Latin *textus*).]
An original or the earliest version of a text.

urtica /ˈəːtɪkə/ *noun*. L17.
[Latin, from *urere* burn.]
1 Any plant of the genus *Urtica* (family Urticaceae); a stinging nettle. L17.
†**2** ZOOLOGY. = ***SEA-nettle***. *rare*. L17–M18.
■ **urti'caceous** *adjective* of or pertaining to the family Urticaceae M19.

urticant /ˈəːtɪk(ə)nt/ *adjective*. L19.
[medieval Latin *urticant-* pres. ppl stem of *urticare* URTICATE *verb*: see -ANT[1].]
Adapted for stinging; that stings or irritates.

urticaria /əːtɪˈkɛːrɪə/ *noun*. L18.
[from URTICA + -r- + -IA[1].]
MEDICINE. Nettle-rash; any other skin rash that resembles this.
■ **urticarial** *adjective* of, pertaining to, or characteristic of urticaria L19. **urticarious** *adjective* (now *rare*) = URTICARIAL M19.

urticate /ˈəːtɪkeɪt/ *adjective*. *rare*. L19.
[formed as next: see -ATE[2].]
MEDICINE. Presenting the appearance of urticaria.

urticate /ˈəːtɪkeɪt/ *verb.* M19.
[medieval Latin *urticat-* pa. pple of *urticare* sting, from Latin *urtica* nettle: see -ATE³.]
1 *verb intrans. & trans.* Sting, prick; prickle; *fig.* irritate, nettle. M19.
2 *verb trans.* Beat with nettles; *gen.* flagellate. M19.
■ **urticated** *ppl adjective* (MEDICINE, *rare*) = URTICATE *adjective* L20.

urtication /əːtɪˈkeɪʃ(ə)n/ *noun.* M17.
[medieval Latin *urticatio(n-)*, formed as prec.: see -ATION.]
1 The action or an act of urticating or stinging. M17.
2 A stinging or pricking sensation. M19.

urtite /ˈəːtʌɪt/ *noun.* L19.
[from Lujaur-*Urt* (now Lovozero), a lake in the Kola peninsula, Russia: see -ITE¹.]
GEOLOGY. A light-coloured plutonic rock of the ijolite series, composed chiefly of nephelite and containing some mafic minerals.

urubu /ʊrʊˈbuː/ *noun & adjective.* Also **U-**. L17.
[Tupi *urubú*.]
▶ **A** *noun.* Pl. **-s**, (esp. in sense 2) same.
1 The American black vulture, *Coragyps atratus.* L17.
2 (**U-**.) A member of a S. American Indian people inhabiting parts of NE Brazil; the Tupi-Guarani language of this people. M20.
▶ **B** *adjective.* (**U-**.) Of, pertaining to, or designating the Urubu or their language. M20.

urucu /ʊrʊˈkuː/ *noun.* E17.
[Portuguese from Tupi-Guarani *urucú* body paint.]
= ROUCOU.

urucuri /ʊrʊˈkʊəri/ *noun.* Also **ouricury** /ʊərɪˈkʊəri/. M19.
[Portuguese from Tupi *urikúri*.]
Any of several large Brazilian palm trees; esp. *Attalea excelsa*, which has large oily nuts.

Uruguayan /jʊərəˈgwʌɪən, (j)ʊr-/ *adjective & noun.* M19.
[from *Uruguay* (see below) + -AN.]
▶ **A** *adjective.* Of, pertaining to, or characteristic of Uruguay, a republic in S. America, or its inhabitants. M19.
▶ **B** *noun.* A native or inhabitant of Uruguay. M19.

Uruk /ˈʊrʊk/ *adjective.* M20.
[A city in ancient Iraq.]
ARCHAEOLOGY. Designating or pertaining to a culture thought to have flourished, primarily in southern Mesopotamia, in the fourth millenium BC.

urus /ˈjʊərəs/ *noun.* Pl. **uri** /ˈjʊəri/, **uruses**. E17.
[Latin from Greek *ouros*. Cf. AUROCHS.]
ZOOLOGY. **1** The aurochs, *Bos primigenius.* Cf. URE-OX, UROCHS. E17.
2 Any of various other extinct oxen. E19.

urushi /ʊˈruːʃi/ *noun.* E18.
[Japanese.]
The lacquer-tree, *Rhus verniciflua*. Also, Japanese lacquer, obtained from this tree.
■ **urushiol** *noun* (CHEMISTRY) an oily phenolic liquid causing skin irritation, which is the toxic principle of poison ivy and other plants, and the main constituent of Japanese lacquer E20.

US *abbreviation.*
1 Under-Secretary.
2 United States (of America). Also (*colloq.*) **US of A**.
3 Also **U/S**. Unserviceable.

us /ʌs, *unstressed* (ə)s/ *pers. pronoun, 1 pl. objective (accus. & dat.).* Also (*colloq.*) **'s** /(ə)s/.
[Old English *ūs* = Old Frisian, Old Saxon *ūs*, Middle & mod. Dutch *ons*, Old & mod. High German *uns*, Old Norse *oss*, Gothic *uns*, from Germanic, from Indo-European (cf. Sanskrit *nas*).]
1 Objective (direct & indirect) of WE *pronoun*: the speakers or writers themselves. OE. ▸**b** Ourselves. Now *arch. & dial.* exc. *US colloq.* OE. ▸**c** Our ship, our vessel, our organization, etc. E17. ▸**d** Me; to me. Now *dial. & colloq.* E19.
2 Subjective: we. In standard use esp. pred. after *be* & after *as, than*. Now *colloq. & dial.* L15.

> 🕮 **1** R. KIPLING It cost us our ship. E. WAUGH Can't think what they want *us* here for. E. BOWEN Your father works hard to keep us. I. MURDOCH There are two of us and only one of him. M. AMIS If *you're* insecure, what hope is there for us poor mortals? **b** SHAKES. *A.Y.L.* Come, shall we go and kill us venison? R. BROOKE We flung us on the windy hill. *Saturday Evening Post* Let's go and wake us up a preacher. **c** TENNYSON And the rest they came aboard us. **d** M. E. WILKINS Giv us a kiss. **2** N. MARSH Hand over thik rapper . . . Us'll take the edge off of it. *Zigzag* Us kids just wanted to play.

Phrases: ***that makes two of us***: see TWO *noun* 1. ***them and us***, ***us and them***: see THEM *pronoun* 1. ***us lot***: see LOT *noun*. ***with us***: see WITH *preposition* 17.
■ **us-ness** *noun* (*joc. & colloq.*) the fact of being us E20. **usward** *adverb* (*arch.*) towards us, in our direction LME.

U/S *abbreviation.*
Unserviceable.

USA *abbreviation.*
1 United States of America.
2 United States Army. *US.*

USAAF *abbreviation.*
Hist. United States Army Air Forces.

usable /ˈjuːzəb(ə)l/ *adjective.* Also **useable**. LME.
[from USE *verb* + -ABLE.]
Able to be used, admitting of use.

> 🕮 *Nature* A possible method for storing very large amounts of useable energy. HUGH THOMAS The line between Hüttledorf-Hacking and St Pölten was only usable on a single track.

■ **usaˈbility** *noun* M19. **usableness** *noun* L19.

USAF *abbreviation.*
United States Air Force.

usage /ˈjuːsɪdʒ/ *noun.* ME.
[Old & mod. French, formed as USE *noun* + -AGE.]
1 Habitual or customary practice or procedure, esp. as creating a right, obligation, or standard; an instance of this, an established custom or habit. ME. ▸**b** A right of way. *local.* E19.
2 Usual conduct or behaviour; an instance of this. Long *rare* or *obsolete.* ME.
3 The action of using something; the fact of being used; use, employment. LME. ▸**b** The amount or quantity used; the rate at which something is used. M20.
4 Treatment of a person or thing; mode of dealing with or being dealt with. Freq. with specifying word. Also foll. by *of.* M16.
5 *spec.* Established or customary use in a language of words, expressions, constructions, etc.; an instance of this. Freq. with specifying word. L17.

> 🕮 **1** G. F. MACLEAR Adamnan was won over from the Celtic to the Catholic usage. E. TEMPLETON It is always a bad sign when ceremony and usage are discarded. P. FUSSELL A way which does not make an enemy of the usages of the past. **the Usages** ECCLESIASTICAL HISTORY the four Eucharistic practices revived in the rite introduced by some nonjuring clergy in 1719. **3** *Fraser's Magazine* The usage of hops was entirely unknown to the ancient Gauls. *Organic Gardening* Pesticide usage most readily calls to mind . . damage to the environment. U. HOLDEN She fingered her seed pearls . . . Usage improved pearls. **4** EVELYN He . . was . . displeas'd at the usage we received. P. WRIGHT The barbarous usage of those poor people. **5** K. M. E. MURRAY The history of a word in its changing usage from century to century. *Dictionaries* The prefatory notes to the volumes of the *DAE* offer taxonomies of American usages.

■ **usageaster** *noun* (*derog.*, orig. *US*) [after *poetaster*] an inferior critic of language usage, esp. one with conservative or pedantic views on correctness L20. **usager** *noun* †(*a*) LAW (*rare*) a person who has the usufruct of something; (*b*) ECCLESIASTICAL HISTORY a member of the section of nonjurors who in 1719 accepted the newly drawn-up Eucharistic rite including the four Usages: L16.

usance /ˈjuːz(ə)ns/ *noun.* LME.
[Old French from Proto-Romance (medieval Latin *usantia, -cia*), from base of USE *verb*: see -ANCE.]
1 Habitual, usual, or customary practice or behaviour; an instance of this. Also = USAGE 3. *arch.* LME.
2 The time allowed by commercial usage or law for the payment of (esp. foreign) bills of exchange. Orig. in †***at usance***. L15.
3 †**a** The practice or fact of lending or borrowing money at interest. *rare.* L16–E17. ▸**b** = INTEREST *noun* 10. *arch.* L16.

USB *abbreviation.*
COMPUTING. Universal serial bus.

USC *abbreviation.*
Ulster Special Constabulary.

USD *abbreviation.*
United States dollar.

USDA *abbreviation.*
United States Department of Agriculture.

USDAW /ˈʌzdɔː/ *abbreviation.*
Union of Shop, Distributive, and Allied Workers.

use /juːs/ *noun.* ME.
[Old & mod. French *us* from Latin *usus* use, usage, from *us-*: see next.]
▶ **I** Act of using, fact of being used.
1 *gen.* The action of using something; the fact or state of being used; application or conversion to some purpose. ME. ▸**b** Employment or maintenance of a person for sexual intercourse (*arch.*); utilization of an animal for breeding purposes (freq. in ***in use, into use***). M16. ▸**c** The action of using something as food, drink, a drug, etc.; the fact of being so used; (regular) consumption. L16.
2 LAW (now *Hist.*). The holding of land or other property by one person for the profit or benefit of another. Also, a trust vested in a person holding land or other property of which another received or was entitled to the profits or benefits. Freq. in ***in use, to use***. L15.
3 **a** Premium on money lent to another; interest, usury. Freq. in ***pay use, at use, to use***. Now *arch. & dial.* M16. ▸**b** The fact of using money borrowed or lent at a premium. E17.

> 🕮 **1** DRYDEN All other Themes that careless Minds invite, Are worn with Use. *Essex Review* A handworked chaff-box was in almost daily use on every large farm. *Guardian* Their deliberate use of murder and plastic bombs. **b** ALAN ROSS His step-mother desired the use of his body. **c** N. ROBINSON The Patient should be exhorted not to leave off the Use of the Bark too soon. *Times* The use of amphetamine drugs in sport. **2** W. BLACKSTONE Possession of the soil being vested in one man, and the use, or profit thereof, in another. **3a** *fig.*: W. COWPER Human life Is but a loan to be repaid with use.

▶ **II** Habit of using.
4 Habitual, usual, or common practice; custom, usage, esp. of a particular country, community, etc.; an instance of this. ME.
5 The opportunity, right, or power of using something, *esp.* the exercise of a particular faculty or ability. ME.
6 ECCLESIASTICAL. The ritual and liturgy of a church, diocese, etc. (freq. in ***Sarum use***). Also, a customary form of religious observance or service. ME.
7 Habituation, practice. *arch.* LME.

> 🕮 **4** HOBBES Long Use obtaineth the authority of a Law. J. OZELL Metellus Pius commanded them . . according to the Use of those Days. SHELLEY She knows not yet the uses of the world. **5** E. ROOSEVELT The use of his hands and arms came back completely . . but his legs remained useless. R. J. CONLEY The Nation owned all the land, and citizens had the use of it. K. VONNEGUT He lost the use of his right hand. **6** D. ROCK Almost the whole of the Salisbury Use had been printed while this country was . . Catholic. C. MACKENZIE It was the use at St. Chad's to say Compline by candlelight. **7** SHELLEY Should the offender live? . . and make, by use, His crime Thine . . element.

▶ **III** Manner of using.
8 Manner or mode of using, employing, or utilizing something; an instance of this. Freq. with specifying word. ME.

> 🕮 **8** *Medical & Physical Journal* The result of the advantageous use of that remedy. SHELLEY A weapon in the hand of God To a just use. G. SWIFT I was taught the . . use of a camera.

▶ **IV** Purpose served by the thing used.
9 A purpose, an object, an end. Freq. with specifying word. ME. ▸†**b** A part of a sermon or homily devoted to the practical application of doctrine. M17–E19. ▸**c** A slab of metal welded for a particular purpose. L18.
10 LAW. The advantage *of* a specified person or persons in respect of profit or benefit derived from land or other property. LME.
11 Ability to be used, esp. for a particular purpose; usefulness; advantage. Freq. in ***of no use, of little use***, etc. LME.
12 Office; function; service. E16.
13 Need or occasion for using or employing something; necessity, demand, exigency. Freq. in ***have no use for*** below. E17.

> 🕮 **9** SWIFT I had the tallow . . for greasing my boat, and other uses. D. FRANCIS There was . . an armchair of sorts, visitors for the use of. **11** MILTON God made two great Lights, great for thir use To Man. T. HARDY Is there any use in saying what can do no good? *Language* A consideration of the taxonomic phonemes of a language may be of use. **12** W. LAW Things may, and must differ in their use. A. T. THOMSON The use of the sand . . is to prevent the amber . . from passing over into the receiver. **13** SHAKES. *Oth.* Give it me . . I have use for it. M. SINCLAIR He had no longer any use for his wheel-chair.

Phrases: ***definition in use***: see DEFINITION 2. **for the use of** to be used by a specified person etc. **have no use for** (*a*) be unable to find a use for; (*b*) *colloq.* dislike or be impatient with. ***ill use***: see ILL *adjective & adverb*. **make use of** (*a*) employ, utilize; (*b*) benefit from. **use and wont** established custom.
Comb.: **use immunity** *US* LAW immunity from prosecution on the basis of testimony given under compulsion; **use-life** useful life; **use-money** (now *dial.*) = sense 3a above.

use /juːz, *in branch IV* juːs/ *verb.* Pa. t. & pple **used** /juːzd, *in branch IV* juːst/. Informal abbreviated forms **usen't** /ˈjuːs(ə)nt/ = *used not*, **useter** /ˈjuːstə/ = *used to*. ME.
[Old & mod. French *user* †employ (now *user de*), consume, wear out from Proto-Romance from Latin *us-* pa. ppl stem of *uti*.]
▶ **I** **1** *verb trans.* Celebrate or observe (a rite, custom, etc.); follow as a custom or usage. *arch.* ME.
†**2** *verb trans.* Observe or comply with (a law, rule, etc.). ME–E17.
3 *verb trans.* †**a** Follow (a particular course of life); carry on (an occupation, profession, etc.); discharge the functions of (an office). ME–E19. ▸**b** Spend or pass (a period of time) in a certain way. *obsolete* exc. as passing into sense 7. LME. ▸†**c** Frequent the company of (a person). LME–L16.
4 *verb trans.* Take part or engage in (a game, activity, etc.). Now *rare.* ME.
5 *verb trans.* Pursue (some course of action); do, perform. Now *rare.* ME.
6 *verb trans.* Put into practice or operation, esp. towards or against others. LME.

📖 **2** TINDALE 1 *Tim.* 1:8 We knowe that the lawe is god, yf a man vse it lawfully. **3a** AV 1 *Tim.* 3:10 Then let them vse the office of a Deacon. SIR W. SCOTT I am determined to turn honest man, and use this life no longer. **4** T. BRIDGES Use War abroad, at home use Peace. S. WILLIAMS He uses no exercise. **6** MILTON The like severity no doubt was us'd. SHELLEY Tell me all, what poisonous Power Ye use against me.

▶ **II 7** *verb trans.* Make use of (a thing), esp. for a particular end or purpose; utilize, turn to account. **ME.** ▸**b** Wear (a garment etc.). *arch.* **LME.** ▸†**c** Work, till, occupy, (land, ground, etc.). **L16–M18.**

8 *verb trans.* Cause (an implement, instrument, etc.) to work, esp. for a particular purpose; manipulate, operate. **ME.**

9 *verb trans.* Take as food, drink, etc.; consume by eating or drinking; *esp.* take (alcohol, narcotics, etc.) regularly or habitually. Formerly also *spec.*, receive (the eucharist). **ME.**

10 *verb intrans.* †**a** Foll. by *of*, *with*: make use of or employ something. **LME–E18.** ▸**b** Esp. of a drug addict: take drugs. *slang.* **M20.**

11 *verb trans.* Employ or make use of (a person, animal, etc.) in a specified function or capacity; *esp.* (now *arch. & dial.*) have sexual intercourse with. Now also, take advantage of, manipulate, (a person). **LME.**

12 *verb trans.* Expend or consume (a commodity etc.) by employment. **LME.**

📖 **7** R. GRAVES I won Livilla by using my brains. G. F. NEWMAN What d'you use for money when buying up these mansions? R. W. CLARK Radioisotopes were . . to be used for removing the growths of physical disease. **8** SHAKES. *Merch. V.* Good Launcelot Gobbo, use your legs . . run away. AV *Jer.* 23:31 I *am* against the prophets . . that vse their tongues. I. MURDOCH He showed Dora the little instrument he used to make the sound. **9** S. PURCHAS They drinke not wine, nor vse vinegar. *Fortune* They . . don't now use drugs. **11** R. SCOT Manie are so bewitched that they cannot use their owne wives. MILTON Were not his purpose To use him further yet in some great service. **12** H. GLASSE A Cook that used six Pounds of Butter to fry twelve Eggs.

▶ **III 13** *verb trans.* Speak or write in (a language); say or utter (words, phrases, etc.). **ME.**

14 *verb trans.* Resort to (a place) frequently or habitually; frequent. Now *rare.* **LME.** ▸**b** *verb intrans.* Go frequently or customarily to a place or person, frequent a place (now *dial. & US*). Formerly also, associate or cohabit *with* a person, live in or at a place. **LME.**

15 *verb trans.* **a** *refl.* Orig., resort, repair. Later, behave, conduct oneself, esp. in a specified manner. Now *arch. & Scot.* **LME.** ▸**b** Deal with or behave towards (a person or thing) in a specified way, treat. **LME.**

📖 **13** J. WILKINS The Language used in Denmark. LYTTON Thou usest plain language, my friend. ANTHONY SMITH A fast talker uses three words a second. **14** H. SLOANE It uses more the low sandy inland parts than the plovers. **15a** E. HERBERT He used himself more like a Fellow . . than like a Subject. **b** L. STERNE 'Tis . . using him worse than a German. A. W. KINGLAKE They won France. They used her hard.

▶ **IV 16** *verb trans.* Habituate, accustom, inure. Now chiefly in ***be used to***, ***be used to doing***, (*arch.*) ***be used to do***. **ME.**

17 *verb intrans.* Be accustomed *to do*. Now only in pa. ***used***, (in emphatic, neg., & interrog. contexts) ***did use***, (informal) ***did used***. **ME.** ▸**b** Do a thing customarily; be wont to do. Now *literary.* **LME.**

18 *verb intrans.* †**a** Behave in a specified manner. *rare.* **ME–L16.** ▸**b** Accustom oneself or become accustomed *to* something. *Scot.* **M19.**

📖 **16** EVELYN Nor were they used of old to be read in churches. SIR W. SCOTT He wanted to use her by degrees to live without meat. LEIGH HUNT She was used to leave cares Without. THACKERAY A person . . used to making sacrifices. G. GREENE Our guests were . . used to eating badly at home. **17** E. FARJEON Mama, did you use to be a flirt? M. SINCLAIR *The Spectator* is not what it used to be in my father's time. E. WAUGH He always used to take a leading part. **b** BROWNING Die at good old age as grand men use.

Phrases etc.: **be able to use** *colloq.* be in need of, be in a position to benefit from, want (chiefly in ***I could use***, ***they could use***, etc.). ***ill-use***: see **ILL** *adjective & adverb.* ***use a sledgehammer to crack a nut***: see **SLEDGEHAMMER** *noun.* **use-by date**: marked on the packaging of (esp. perishable) foods to indicate the latest recommended date of use. **use the sea**, †**use the seas** *arch.* be a sailor. **use up** (*a*) consume (a commodity or stock) completely; exhaust the supply of; (*b*) *colloq.* exhaust with fatigue, overwork, etc., overtire, (chiefly as ***used up*** *ppl adjective*); (*c*) find a use for (something left over).

■ **used** *attrib. adjective* (*a*) usual, wonted, customary; now only *Scot.* in ***used and wont***, usual or customary, according to use and custom; (*b*) that is or has been made use of; utilized; *spec.* (of a vehicle etc.) second-hand; (of paper currency) not in mint condition; (*c*) (now only *Scot.*) experienced *in*; expert: **LME.** †**usedly** *adverb* commonly: only in **M16.** **usedness** *noun* **L17.**

useable *adjective* var. of **USABLE.**

used-to-be /ˈjuːstəbiː/ *noun. colloq.* **M19.**
[from *used* pa. t. of **USE** *verb* + **TO** *preposition* + **BE.**]
A person whose time of popularity or efficiency is past. Also (*US*) = **EX** *noun.*

useful /ˈjuːsfʊl, -f(ə)l/ *adjective & noun.* **L16.**
[from **USE** *noun* + **-FUL.** Cf. earlier **USEFULNESS.**]
▶ **A** *adjective.* **1** Of use for a purpose; serviceable; producing or able to produce good results, advantageous, beneficial. Also (*colloq.*), reasonably effective or successful. **L16.**

2 Designating an odd-job man. *Austral. colloq.* **M19.**

📖 **1** R. MACAULAY How useful he was helping in the garden. N. STACEY A useful school sportsman . . got into the first eleven at most sports at Dartmouth. A. N. WILSON A most useful addition to the Society's list of titles. **make oneself useful** perform useful services, be helpful. **useful load** the maximum load that can be carried by an aircraft etc. in addition to its own unladen weight.

▶ **B** *noun.* †**1** A useful article. *rare.* Only in **M17.**

2 An odd-job man. *Austral. colloq.* **L19.**

■ **usefully** *adverb* **M17.** **usefulness** *noun* †(*a*) *rare* the advantage or benefit *of* a place etc.; (*b*) the state or condition of being useful; *rare* an instance of this, a benefit, an advantage: **L15.**

useless /ˈjuːslɪs/ *adjective.* **L16.**
[from **USE** *noun* + **-LESS.**]
Of no use; serving no purpose; not producing or able to produce good results. Also (*colloq.*), incompetent; inefficient; feebly ineffectual.

📖 E. LANGLEY We were too late; it was useless to look for work. G. GREENE Useless objects known . . as doilies. W. PERRIAM Some bloody useless girl . . who doesn't know our system.

■ **uselessly** *adverb* **E17.** **uselessness** *noun* **M17.**

usen't *verb* see **USE** *verb.*

user /ˈjuːzə/ *noun*¹. **LME.**
[from **USE** *verb* + **-ER**¹.]
1 A person who or thing which uses something; *spec.* (*a*) (orig. *US*) a person who takes drugs, a drug addict; (*b*) a person or organization making use of a computer or system (freq. in ***user-definable***, ***user-friendly***, etc., below); (*c*) *colloq.* a person who manipulates others for personal advantage. **LME.**

†**2** A person who puts a writ etc. in force or execution. *Scot.* **L16–M17.**

Comb. (chiefly **COMPUTING**): **user-definable** *adjective* having a function or meaning that can be specified and varied by a user; **user-defined** *adjective* that has been specified or varied by a user; **user-friendliness** the state or condition of being user-friendly; **user-friendly** *adjective* (of a machine or system) designed with the needs of users in mind; *transf.* easy to use; **user-hostile** *adjective* (of a machine or system) not user-friendly; not designed with the needs of users in mind; **user interface** the means by which a person is enabled to use a computer; **username** **COMPUTING** an identification used by a person with access to a computer network; **user-orientated**, **user-oriented** *adjectives* designed with the user's convenience given priority; **user-programmable** *adjective* able to be programmed or assigned a function by the user; **user-unfriendliness** the state or condition of being user-unfriendly; **user-unfriendly** *adjective* = ***user-hostile*** above.

■ **usership** *noun* (*a*) the fact or condition of being a user; (*b*) the users of a product, service, etc., collectively, the body of users: **M20.**

user /ˈjuːzə/ *noun*². **M19.**
[from **ABUSER** *noun*², **NON-USER**, or directly as prec. + **-ER**⁴.]
LAW. Continued use, exercise, or enjoyment of a right, etc.; presumptive right arising from use.

useter *verb* see **USE** *verb.*

ush /ʌʃ/ *verb. dial. & colloq.* **E19.**
[Back-form. from **USHER** *noun.*]
†**1** *verb trans.* Guide, escort, lead. Only in **E19.**

2 *verb intrans.* Act as usher at a wedding. *US.* **L19.**

ushabti /uːˈʃabti/ *noun.* Pl. **-tiu** /-tɪuː/, **-tis.** **L19.**
[Egyptian *wšbty* answerer, repl. *šwbt(y)* **SHAWABTI.** Cf. **SHABTI.**]
EGYPTOLOGY. A figurine of a dead person, made of faience, stone, wood, etc., and placed with the body in the tomb to substitute for the dead person in any work required in the afterlife. Also ***ushabti-figure***.

Ushak /ˈʊʃak/ *noun.* **E20.**
[A town in western Turkey.]
A type of antique rug made at Ushak and woven with the Ghiordes knot.

usher /ˈʌʃə/ *noun & verb.* **LME.**
[Anglo-Norman *usser* = Old French *ussier*, *uissier* (mod. *huissier*) from medieval Latin *ustiarius* from Latin *ostiarius* doorkeeper, from *ostium* door + *-arius* **-ER**².]
▶ **A** *noun.* **1** An official or servant in charge of the door and of admitting people to a hall, chamber, etc.; a doorkeeper, esp. in a court of justice; a person who shows people to their seats in a hall, theatre, cinema, etc. Also, an official in a court of justice in England and Wales whose functions include swearing in jurors and witnesses and keeping order. **LME.** ▸**b** *spec.* A person who performs the functions of an usher at a wedding. Orig. *US.* **L19.**

2 An officer of a court, household, etc., with the duty of walking before a person of high rank. Also a chamberlain. **E16.** ▸†**b** A male attendant on a lady. **E17–E19.**

3 An assistant to a schoolmaster or head-teacher; an assistant master, a teacher. *arch.* **E16.** ▸†**b** An assistant fencing-master. **M16–M18.**

4 A person sent in advance of another, esp. a higher dignitary or personage; a precursor, a forerunner; *transf. & fig.* a sign *of* some approaching person or thing. **M16.** ▸**b** **ENTOMOLOGY.** Any of several European geometrid moths that appear in early spring, *esp.* (in full ***spring usher***) *Agriopis leucophaearia*, the males of which have pale wings with blackish-brown markings, and the females vestigial wings. **E19.**

📖 **1b** J. O'HARA She was being a bridesmaid and he an usher at a wedding.

▶ **B** *verb.* **1** *verb trans.* Act as an usher to; show *in*; guide *into*, *out of*, etc.; *arch.* precede, be the forerunner of. **L16.**

2 *verb intrans.* Act as an usher, now esp. in a theatre or cinema or at a wedding. **E17.**

📖 **1** BYRON The day . . has broken. What a night Hath usher'd it! H. STURGIS They were ushered into a little sanctum. G. GREENE The man-servant . . ushered in another visitor. *fig.*: A. BRIGGS The year 1851 . . ushered in a period of agricultural prosperity.

■ **usherdom** *noun* the position, office, or status of an usher **M19.** **usherer** *noun* an usher **L16.** **usherless** *adjective* (*arch.*) without an usher **L16.** **ushership** *noun* the office, position, or function of an usher; an appointment as an usher: **L16.**

usherette /ʌʃəˈrɛt/ *noun.* **E20.**
[from **USHER** *noun* + **-ETTE.**]
A female usher, esp. in a cinema or theatre.

USIA *abbreviation.*
United States Information Agency.

usine /juːˈziːn/ *noun.* **L18.**
[French = factory, (in early use) water-mill.]
†**1** Material used or suitable for a furnace or foundry. Only in **L18.**

2 A factory; *esp.* a West Indian sugar factory. **M19.**

usitative /ˈjuːzɪtətɪv/ *adjective. rare.* **M19.**
[from Latin *usitat-* pa. ppl stem of *usitari* use often: see **-ATIVE.**]
GRAMMAR. That denotes customary action.

USM *abbreviation.* **STOCK EXCHANGE.**
Unlisted securities market.

USN *abbreviation.*
United States Navy.

usnea /ˈʌsnɪə/ *noun.* Pl. **-eae** /-ɪiː/, **-eas.** **L16.**
[medieval & mod. Latin from Arab. & Persian *ušna* moss, lichen.]
Any of numerous epiphytic fruticose lichens constituting the genus *Usnea*, often forming grey pendulous masses on trees.

usnic /ˈʌznɪk/ *adjective.* **M19.**
[from prec. + **-IC.**]
CHEMISTRY. ***usnic acid***, a yellow tricyclic crystalline solid, $C_{18}H_{16}O_7$, which is present in many lichens and is used as an antibiotic.

■ **usnin** *noun* usnic acid **M19.**

USO *abbreviation. US.*
United Service Organization.

Usonan /juːˈsəʊnən/ *noun. rare.* **M20.**
[from initial letters of United States of North America + **-AN**, perh. infl. by Esperanto *Usono* United States of America.]
= **USONIAN** *noun* 1.

Usonian /juːˈsəʊnɪən/ *noun & adjective.* **E20.**
[from *US* abbreviation of United States + *-onian*, after *Arizonian*, *Devonian*, etc. Cf. prec.]
▶ **A** *noun.* **1** A native or inhabitant of the United States. **E20.**

2 **ARCHITECTURE.** A Usonian house. **M20.**

▶ **B** *adjective.* Of or pertaining to the United States; **ARCHITECTURE** designating (the style of) buildings designed in the 1930s by Frank Lloyd Wright, characterized by inexpensive construction and flat roofs. **M20.**

USP *abbreviation.*
United States Pharmacopeia.

†**usque** *noun. Scot.* See also **WHISKY** *noun*¹. **E–M18.**
[Abbreviation of **USQUEBAUGH.**]
Whisky.

usque ad nauseam /ˌʌskweɪ ad ˈnɔːzɪam, -sɪəm/ *adverbial phr. rare.* **E17.**
[Latin, lit. 'right up to sickness'.]
= **AD NAUSEAM.**

usquebaugh /ˈʌskwɪbɔː/ *noun.* Chiefly *Scot. & Anglo-Irish.* **L16.**
[Gaelic *uisge beatha* water of life, from *uisge* water + *beatha* life.]
Whisky.

USS *abbreviation.*
United States Ship.

USSR *abbreviation.*
Hist. Union of Soviet Socialist Republics.

ustad /ʊsˈtɑːd/ *noun.* E20.
[Persian & Urdu *ustād*.]
In the Indian subcontinent and Middle Eastern countries, a master, esp. of music.

Ustashi /uːˈstɑːʃi/ *noun pl.* Also **-si** /-zi/, **-sha** /-ʃə/, **-se** /-zi/, **-she** /-ʃi/. M20.
[Serbo-Croat. *Ustaše* insurgent rebels.]
Chiefly *Hist.* Supporters of Croatian nationalism and separatism holding power in Croatia in German-occupied Yugoslavia 1941–5; (treated as *sing.*) the party and movement of the Ustashi.

ustilago /ʌstɪˈleɪɡəʊ/ *noun.* Pl. **-lagines** /-ˈleɪdʒɪniːz/. L16.
[mod. Latin use of late Latin = a kind of thistle, by assoc. with Latin *ustilare*, *ustulare* scorch (see USTULATION), with ref. to the blackened appearance of smutted plants.]
BOTANY. Smut on wheat, oats, or other cereal grasses. Also *spec.*, any smut fungus of the genus *Ustilago*.
■ **ustilagineous** /ʌstɪləˈdʒɪnɪəs/ *adjective* of or pertaining to the genus *Ustilago* or the order Ustilaginales L19. **ustilaginous** /ʌstɪˈladʒɪnəs/ *adjective* = USTILAGINEOUS M19.

†ustion *noun.* M16.
[Old & mod. French from Latin *ustio(n-)*, from *ust-*: see next, -ION.]
1 The action of burning; the fact of being burnt; *MEDICINE* cauterization. M16–E19.
2 *fig.* Libidinous desire, lust. *rare.* M16–E17.

ustulation /ʌstjʊˈleɪʃ(ə)n/ *noun.* M17.
[Late Latin *ustulatio(n-)*, from *ustulat-* pa. ppl stem of *ustulare* burn, scorch, sear, from *ust-* pa. ppl stem of *urere* burn: see -ATION. Cf. prec.]
1 The action of burning; the fact of being burnt; *spec.* roasting. M17.
†2 *fig.* = USTION 2. *rare.* Only in M17.

usual /ˈjuːʒʊəl/ *adjective & noun.* LME.
[Old French *usual*, (also mod.) *usuel* or late Latin *usualis*, from Latin *usus* USE *noun*: see -AL¹.]
▶ **A** *adjective.* **1** Commonly or customarily observed or practised; having general currency, validity, or force; current, prevalent. LME.
2 Ordinarily used; constantly or customarily employed, esp. in a specified capacity; ordinary. LME.
3 That ordinarily happens, occurs, or is to be found; such as is commonly met with or observed in ordinary practice or experience. Freq. foll. by *to*, *to do*. L16.

> 🕮 **1** I. MURDOCH She was expected at Pimlico again, according to their usual arrangement. N. GORDIMER He gave the usual flourish of a dirty rag over the windscreen. **2** OED Our usual postman did not come to-day. C. HART The most usual method is notching with a spade or mattock. **3** J. CONRAD The usual noises refilled the place. *Mind* It is usual to ascribe to Bradley a coherence theory of truth.

Phrases: ***as per usual***, ***as usual***: see AS *adverb* etc. ***BUSINESS as usual***. ***than usual*** than is or was customary or habitual. ***the usual channels***: see CHANNEL *noun*¹ 9. ***the usual warning***: see WARNING *noun*.
▶ **B** *absol.* as *noun.* Following *the*, *my*, etc.: what is usual, customary, or habitual; *colloq.* a person's usual drink etc. L18.
■ **usually** *adverb* (*a*) in a usual or customary manner; (*b*) (esp. modifying a sentence) as a rule, generally speaking: LME. **usualness** *noun* M17.

usuary /ˈjuːzjʊəri/ *noun.* L19.
[Late Latin *usuarius* from Latin *usus* USE *noun*: see -ARY¹.]
ROMAN LAW. A person who has the use but not the income or ownership of a thing.

usucapient /juːzjʊˈkeɪpɪənt/ *noun.* L19.
[Latin *usucapient-* pres. ppl stem of *usucapere*: see next, -ENT.]
ROMAN & SCOTS LAW. A person who has acquired or claims a title or right to property by usucapion.

usucapion /juːzjʊˈkeɪpɪən/ *noun.* E17.
[French, or Latin *usucapio(n-)*, from *usucapere* acquire ownership by prescription, from *usu* abl. of *usus* USE *noun* + *capere* take, seize: see -ION.]
ROMAN & SCOTS LAW. The acquisition of a title or right to property by uninterrupted possession for a prescribed term. Cf. USUCAPTION.
■ **usucapionary** *adjective* (*rare*) L19.

usucapt /ˈjuːzjʊkapt/ *verb trans. & intrans.* L19.
[Latin *usucapt-* pa. ppl stem of *usucapere* (see prec.), or back-form. from next.]
ROMAN & SCOTS LAW. Acquire a title or right to (property) by usucapion.
■ **usucaptable**, **usucaptible** *adjectives* able to be held by usucapion L19. **usucaptor** *noun* a person who has acquired a title or right to property by usucapion L19.

usucaption /juːzjʊˈkapʃ(ə)n/ *noun.* M17.
[Latin *usucaptio(n-)*, formed as prec.: see -ION.]
ROMAN & SCOTS LAW. = USUCAPION.

usufruct /ˈjuːzjʊfrʌkt/ *noun & verb.* E17.
[Latin *usufructus* from *usus (et) fructus*, *usus fructus(que)* use (and) enjoyment, from *usus* USE *noun* + *fructus* FRUIT *noun*.]
▶ **A** *noun.* **1** *ROMAN & SCOTS LAW.* The right of enjoying the use of and income from another's property without destroying, damaging, or diminishing the property. E17.
2 *gen.* Use, enjoyment, or profitable possession (*of*). E19.
▶ **B** *verb trans.* *ROMAN & SCOTS LAW.* Hold (property) in usufruct. L19.

usufructuary /juːzjʊˈfrʌktjʊəri/ *noun & adjective.* E17.
[Latin *usufructuarius*, formed as prec.: see -ARY¹.]
▶ **A** *noun.* **1** *ROMAN & SCOTS LAW.* A person who holds property in usufruct. E17.
2 *gen.* A person who has the use, enjoyment, or profitable possession of or *of* something. E17.
▶ **B** *adjective.* *ROMAN & SCOTS LAW.* Of or pertaining to usufruct; of the nature of usufruct. E18.

†usufruit *noun.* L15–E18.
[Old & mod. French, formed as USUFRUCT.]
= USUFRUCT *noun* 1.

†usure *noun & verb.* ME.
[Old & mod. French: see next.]
▶ **A** *noun.* = USURY 1. ME–E17.
▶ **B** *verb.* **1** *verb intrans.* Practise usury, lend money at interest. ME–M16.
2 *verb trans.* Lend (money) at interest. *rare.* Only in E17.
■ **†usuring** *adjective* (*a*) practising or given to usury; usurious; (*b*) *rare* expecting ample return or increase; causing cost without return: L16–E18. **†usurous** *adjective* (*rare*) = USURIOUS E17–L18.

usurer /ˈjuːʒ(ə)rə/ *noun.* ME.
[Anglo-Norman *usurer*, Old French *usureor*, (also mod.) *usurier* from *usure* from Latin *usura* USURY: see -ER².]
A person who practises usury; a moneylender, esp. one charging an excessive rate of interest.
■ **usuress** *noun* (*rare*) a female usurer M17.

usurious /juːˈʒʊərɪəs, juːˈzj-/ *adjective.* E17.
[from USURY: see -IOUS.]
1 Characterized by, of the nature of, or involving usury; (esp. of interest) taken or charged by usury, exorbitant, excessive. E17.
2 Practising usury; taking or charging excessive interest. E17. ▸**b** Characteristic of a usurer. E18.
■ **usuriously** *adverb* L17. **usuriousness** *noun* (*rare*) E18.

usurp /jʊˈzəːp, jʊˈsəːp/ *verb.* ME.
[Old & mod. French *usurper* from Latin *usurpare* seize for use.]
▶ **I** *verb trans.* **1** Appropriate (a right, prerogative, etc.) wrongfully; *esp.* seize or assume (another's position or authority) by force. ME.
2 Supplant or oust (a person), esp. from a position of influence or authority. ME.
3 Take possession of (land etc.) unlawfully; assume the rule or control of by force. LME.
†4 Get possession of by trickery or violence; steal. LME–M17.
5 Make use of unlawfully; use wrongly; assume or claim (a name or title), esp. without right. Also, borrow or appropriate (a word etc.) from another language, source, etc. *arch.* LME.
†6 Practise or inflict (injury, cruelty, etc.); impose (a penalty etc.) *on*. *rare.* LME–L17.

> 🕮 **1** SHELLEY The almighty Fiend Whose name usurps thy honours. C. THIRLWALL Cleon . . did not wish to usurp the functions of Nicias. **2** F. FITZGERALD Young modern leadership . . was necessary to usurp the corrupt traditionalists. *Times* Sultan . . al Said . . usurped his father in 1970. **3** M. PRIOR The three Kingdoms You Usurped. G. SWIFT They started to usurp the television and establish special claims over it. **5** DRYDEN The noble Arimant usurp'd my name. W. HAMILTON Latin terms . . were very rarely usurped in their present psychological meaning.

▶ **II** *verb intrans.* **†7** Claim or presume *to be* or *to do*. LME–E16.
8 Be a usurper; *esp.* rule or exercise authority as a usurper. Now *rare.* LME.
9 Practise usurpation *on* or *upon*; *esp.* encroach *on* another's rights, privileges, territory, etc.; infringe gradually *on* another's position or authority. L15.
†10 Take possession *of* by usurpation. *rare.* E16–E17.

> 🕮 **8** W. HABINGTON The house of Lancaster usurping against Edward. **9** H. BROOKE When any of the three estates have usurped upon the others.

Phrases: **usurp the place of** take the place of (chiefly *fig.*).
■ **usurping** *noun* the action or an act of the verb; an instance of this; (a) usurpation: E16. **usurpingly** *adverb* in a usurping manner L16.

usurpation /juːzəːˈpeɪʃ(ə)n, juːs-/ *noun.* LME.
[Old & mod. French, or Latin *usurpatio(n-)*, from *usurpat-* pa. ppl stem of *usurpare*: see prec., -ATION.]
1 The action or an act of usurping a person or thing; an instance of this; *esp.* (a) wrongful seizure of another's position or authority. LME. ▸**b** Usurpatory rule or power. Freq. in ***the usurpation*** (*arch.*, *derog.*), the rule of the Commonwealth in England between 1649 and 1660. Now *rare.* M17.
2 *ECCLESIASTICAL LAW.* The action on the part of a stranger of dispossessing a lawful patron of the right of presenting a cleric to a benefice. E17.
■ **uˈsurpative** *adjective* of the nature of or characterized by usurpation, usurping L18. **uˈsurpatory** *adjective* = USURPATIVE M19. **usurpature** *noun* (*poet.*) usurpation M19.

usurped /jʊˈzəːpt, jʊˈsəːpt/ *ppl adjective.* LME.
[from USURP + -ED¹.]
1 That has been usurped. LME. ▸**b** Marked or characterized by usurpation. LME. ▸**†c** Used or borrowed unjustly. Also, false, counterfeit. *rare.* M16–L17.
†2 Of a person etc.: that has usurped another's position or authority, usurping. M16–L18.

usurper /jʊˈzəːpə, jʊˈsəːpə/ *noun.* LME.
[from USURP + -ER¹.]
A person who usurps someone or something; *esp.* a person who unlawfully seizes another's position or authority.

> 🕮 GIBBON The reign of the usurper was short and turbulent. J. BERMAN Hindley sees Heathcliff as the usurper of his father's affections.

■ **usurpress** (*noun* (*rare*) a female usurper M17.

usury /ˈjuːʒ(ə)ri/ *noun.* ME.
[Anglo-Norman (=(O)Fr. *usure*), or medieval Latin *usuria* from Latin *usura*, from *usus* USE *noun*: see -Y³. Cf. USURE.]
1 The fact or practice of lending money at interest, esp. at an exorbitant, excessive, or illegal rate; interest on money lent, esp. at such a rate. Formerly also (*rare*), profit made by lending money. Freq. in ***at usury***, ***on usury***. ME. ▸**†b** An instance of usury. Usu. in *pl.* Only in E17.
†2 Increase, augmentation; advantage. L16–E17.
1 with usury with interest (*lit.* & *fig.*).

UT *abbreviation.*
1 Universal Time.
2 Utah. *US.*

ut /ʊt, ʌt/ *noun.* ME.
[Latin, the lowest of the series *ut*, *re*, *mi*, *fa*, *sol*, *la* the initial syllables of each half-line, and *si* the initial letters of the closing words *Sancte Iohannes* (St John), of a stanza of the Latin office hymn for the Nativity of St John Baptist. Cf. GAMUT.]
MUSIC. In medieval music, the first note in Guido d'Arezzo's hexachords. Now = DOH.
¶ Cf. RAY *noun*³, MI *noun*, FAH, SOL *noun*¹, LAH, SI.

uta /ˈjuːtə/ *noun.* Pl. same. M19.
[Japanese = poem, song.]
A Japanese poem; *spec.* = TANKA *noun*².

Utahan /ˈjuːtɔːən, ˈjuːtɑːən/ *noun.* Also **Utahn**. M19.
[from *Utah* (see below) + -AN.]
A native or inhabitant of the State of Utah in the west central US.

Utahraptor /ˈjuːtɑraptə/ *noun.* L20.
[Mod.Latin (genus name), from *Utah* (see prec.), where the remains of this dinosaur were found + Latin RAPTOR *noun*¹.]
A very large dromaeosaurid dinosaur of the Lower Cretaceous period, perhaps up to seven metres in height.

utas /ˈjuːtas/ *noun.* ME.
[Contr. of *utaves* pl. of *utave* var. of OCTAVE, or of Old French *outaves* from Latin *octavas (dies)* accus. pl. of *octava (dies)* eighth day: see OCTAVE.]
ECCLESIASTICAL HISTORY. = OCTAVE *noun* 1.

Ute /juːt/ *noun*¹ & *adjective.* Also (earlier) **Utah** /ˈjuːtɔː, -tɑː/. E19.
[(Abbreviation of) Spanish *Yuta* an unidentified Amer. Indian lang. Cf. PAIUTE.]
▶ **A** *noun.* Pl. same, **-s**.
1 A member of a Shoshonean people inhabiting parts of Colorado, Utah, and New Mexico. E19.
2 The language of this people. L19.
▶ **B** *adjective.* Of or pertaining to the Ute or their language. M19.

ute /juːt/ *noun*². *colloq.* (chiefly *Austral.* & *NZ*). M20.
[Abbreviation.]
= UTILITY *noun* 4b.

utensil /juːˈtɛns(ə)l/ *noun.* LME.
[Old French *utensile* (mod. *ustensile*) from medieval Latin *utensile* use as noun of Latin *utensilis* fit for use, useful (*utensilia* noun pl., implements), from *uti* use.]
†1 *collect. sing.* Vessels or instruments for domestic use. Chiefly *Scot.* LME–M16.
2 An implement, vessel, or article, *esp.* one for domestic use. L15.
3 **†a** A part of the human frame serving a special purpose. *rare.* Only in 17. ▸**b** A person made use of, a useful person. *rare.* L17.
4 A sacred vessel, furnishing, etc., belonging to or used in a church etc. M17.
5 A chamber-pot. Chiefly in ***chamber utensil***. L17.

> 🕮 **2** J. H. BURN The Bantu in Africa . . use cooking utensils of iron.

uteri *noun* pl. of UTERUS.

uterine /ˈjuːtərɪn, -ʌɪn/ *adjective*. LME.
[In sense 1 from late Latin *uterinus*, from Latin *uterus* + *-inus* -INE[1]; in sense 2 from UTERUS + -INE[1].]
1 Born of the same mother but not the same father; related by blood through the mother; pertaining to those so related. Opp. ***consanguineous***. LME.
2 Chiefly MEDICINE. Of or pertaining to the uterus or womb; *esp.* (***a***) (of a part, vessel, etc.) situated in or connected with the uterus; (***b***) occurring in or affecting the uterus. E17.
1 brother uterine, **uterine brother**: see BROTHER *noun*. **2 uterine tube** (chiefly ZOOLOGY & VETERINARY MEDICINE) = *FALLOPIAN tube*.

utero- /ˈjuːt(ə)rəʊ/ *combining form*.
[from Latin UTERUS: see -O-.]
ANATOMY & MEDICINE. Forming words with the sense 'of or pertaining to the uterus or womb (and)'.
■ **utero-geˈstation** *noun* the progressive development of the embryo in the uterus from conception until birth L18. **uteropla'cental** *adjective* pertaining to or supplying the uterus and the placenta M19. **utero-ˈsacral** *adjective* pertaining to or connecting the uterus and the sacrum M19. **uteˈrotomy** *noun* (an instance of) surgical incision of the uterus, hysterotomy M19. **utero-ˈtubal** *adjective* pertaining to (the junction between) the uterus and the Fallopian tubes M20. **uterovaˈginal** *adjective* pertaining to or connecting the uterus and the vagina L19. **uteroˈvesical** *adjective* pertaining to or affecting the uterus and the bladder E19.

uterus /ˈjuːt(ə)rəs/ *noun*. Pl. **-ri** /-rʌɪ/, (*occas.*) **-ruses**. LME.
[Latin.]
1 The organ in female therian mammals in which the embryo develops and is nourished until birth, and which is usu. paired (except in primates); the womb. LME. ▸**b** In some other vertebrates and certain invertebrates, an enlarged part of the oviduct in which the eggs (or young) develop. M18.
2 MYCOLOGY. The peridium of a gasteromycetous fungus. E19.

utile /ˈjuːtɪli/ *noun*. M20.
[mod. Latin specific epithet (see below): see UTILE *adjective*.]
The wood resembling mahogany of a large W. African forest tree, *Entandrophragma utile* (family Meliaceae); the tree from which this is obtained.

utile /ˈjuːtɪl/ *adjective*. Now *rare*. L15.
[Old & mod. French from Latin *utilis*, from *uti* use: see -ILE.]
Useful, profitable, advantageous.

Utilidor /juːˈtɪlɪdɔː/ *noun*. *Canad*. M20.
[from UTILITY + *-dor* (from Greek. *dōron* gift), after *humidor*. Cf. THERMIDOR.]
(Proprietary name for) a system of enclosed conduits used esp. for carrying water and sewerage in regions of permafrost.

utilise *verb* var. of UTILIZE.

utilitarian /jʊˌtɪlɪˈtɛːrɪən/ *noun & adjective*. L18.
[from UTILITY + -ARIAN.]
▶ **A** *noun*. An adherent or advocate of the doctrine of utilitarianism. Also, a person devoted to mere utility or material benefit. L18.
▶ **B** *adjective*. **1** Of, pertaining to, or characterized by the doctrine of utilitarianism; holding or advocating such a doctrine. E19.
2 Of or pertaining to utility or material benefit; designed to be practically useful rather than attractive; severely practical, functional. M19.
■ **utilitarianize** *verb trans*. (*rare*) make utilitarian M19. **utilitarianly** *adverb* L19.

utilitarianism /jʊˌtɪlɪˈtɛːrɪənɪz(ə)m/ *noun*. E19.
[from prec. + -ISM.]
The doctrine that actions are right if they are useful or for the benefit of a majority; *spec.* in PHILOSOPHY, the doctrine that the greatest good of the greatest number should be the guiding principle of conduct.

utility /juːˈtɪlɪti/ *noun & adjective*. LME.
[Old & mod. French *utilité* from Latin *utilitas*, from *utilis* useful, from *uti* use: see -ITY.]
▶ **A** *noun*. **1** The condition, quality, or fact of being useful or beneficial; usefulness, profit; serviceability, practicality. LME. ▸**b** PHILOSOPHY. The ability or capacity of a person or thing to satisfy the needs or wants of the majority. M18. ▸**c** MATH. In game theory, (a measure of) that which is sought to be maximized in any situation involving a choice. L19.
†**2** The quality of being advantageous or profitable; profit, advantage, use. LME–M18.
3 a A useful, advantageous, or profitable thing. Usu. in *pl.* L15. ▸**b** ECONOMICS. A thing able to satisfy human needs or wants. M19. ▸**c** In full ***public utility***. A service, as electricity, water, etc., essential to the community; a company providing such a service or supply, usu. controlled by a nationalized or private monopoly and subject to public regulation. Also (in *pl.*), shares in such a company. Chiefly *N. Amer.* E20.
4 *ellipt.* **a** = ***utility actor*** below. Also, the role of a utility actor, the taking of any small part. E19. ▸**b** = ***utility vehicle*** below. Chiefly *Austral. & NZ*. M20. ▸**c** COMPUTING. A program for carrying out a routine function. L20.

📖 **1** A. S. BYATT She was a 'superfluous person', 'Of no utility' in this world. *Guardian* The PLO accepted the diplomatic utility of this.

▶ **B** *attrib.* or as *adjective*. Made or serving for utility, useful; severely practical and standardized, functional rather than attractive; useful in various ways, versatile. M19.
Special collocations: **utility actor**: taking the smallest speaking parts in a play. **utility area** = *utility room* below. **utility curve** a graph of a utility function. **utility function** a mathematical function which ranks alternatives according to their utility to an individual. **utility man** (*a*) = *utility actor* above; (*b*) *US* = *utility player* below. **utility player** FOOTBALL etc.: capable of playing in various positions. **utility pole** (chiefly *N. Amer.*) a telegraph pole. **utility program** = sense A.4c above. **utility room**: equipped with domestic appliances such as a washing machine, freezer, boiler, etc. **utility routine** = sense A.4c above. **utility truck**, **utility vehicle**: designed to carry both passengers and goods.

utilize /ˈjuːtɪlʌɪz/ *verb trans*. Also **-ise**. E19.
[French *utiliser* from Italian *utilizzare*, from *utile*: see UTILE *adjective*, -IZE.]
Make practical use of, use effectively, turn to account.

📖 E. R. PITMAN Her services could not be utilized for missions.

■ **utilizable** *adjective* able to be utilized L19. **utiliˈzation** *noun* the action of utilizing something; the fact of being utilized; ***utilization factor***, the proportion of a given resource or output which is being used or is available for use: M19. **utilizer** *noun* L19.

uti possidetis /juːtʌɪ pɒsɪˈdiːtɪs, -ˈdeɪtɪs/ *noun phr.* L17.
[Late Latin = as you possess.]
LAW. A principle whereby property or territory not expressly disposed of in a treaty remains in the hands of the party holding it at the end of hostilities.

utmost /ˈʌtməʊst/ *adjective & noun*.
[Old English *ūt(e)mest*, formed as OUT *adverb* + as -MOST.]
▶ **A** *adjective*. **1** Situated furthest from the inside or centre, most remote in position, outermost. OE. ▸**b** Furthest extended; greatest in extent, length, or measure. E18.
2 Of the largest amount or number; greatest in degree, most extreme, ultimate. ME.
3 Latest in order or time; last, final. Now *rare*. LME.

📖 **1** TENNYSON Knights of utmost North and West. **2** J. BUCHAN I assure you it's a matter of the utmost importance. INA TAYLOR Mary Ann was treated with the utmost consideration.

▶ **B** *noun*. Usu. with *the* exc. in sense 2b.
1 That which is outermost or most remote; the furthest part or limit *of* an extent or area. *arch.* OE.
2 a That which is greatest in degree, amount, or extent; the extreme limit, the ultimate degree, (*of* something). Freq. in ***at the utmost***, ***to the utmost***. L15. ▸**b** W. possess.: the greatest or best of one's ability or power. E17.
3 The end, finish, or issue *of* something. E17.

📖 **2a** T. REID The utmost which the human faculties can attain. H. READ Their real strength is tried to the utmost. P. KAVANAGH They had filled a day to the utmost of two men's capacity. **b do one's utmost** do one's best, do all that one can.

Uto-Aztecan /juːtəʊˈaztɛk(ə)n/ *noun & adjective*. L19.
[from UTE *noun*[1] & *adjective* + -O- + AZTECAN.]
(Of, pertaining to, or designating) a language family of Central America and western N. America.
■ Also **Uto-Aztec** *adjective & noun* M20.

Utopia /juːˈtəʊpɪə/ *noun*. Also **u-**. M16.
[mod. Latin = no-place (from Greek *ou* not + *topos* place: see -IA[1]), title of a book by Sir Thomas More (1477–1535).]
1 An imaginary or hypothetical place or state of things considered to be perfect; a condition of ideal (esp. social) perfection. M16. ▸**b** An imaginary distant region or country. Now *rare* or *obsolete*. E17.
2 An impossibly ideal scheme, esp. for social improvement. M18.

📖 **1** G. B. SHAW In the imagination . . England is a Utopia in which everything and everybody is 'free'. L. STARKE A first tiny, faltering step on the road to our Green utopia.

■ **Utopiast** *noun* (*rare*) = UTOPIAN *noun* 2 M19.

Utopian /juːˈtəʊpɪən/ *adjective & noun*. Also **u-**. M16.
[mod. Latin *Utopianus*, formed as prec.: see -AN.]
▶ **A** *adjective*. **1** Of, pertaining to, or characteristic of a Utopia; advocating or constituting an ideally perfect state; impossibly ideal, visionary, idealistic. M16.
†**2** Having no known location, existing nowhere. *rare*. Only in 17.

📖 **1** *Courier-Mail (Brisbane)* If God's laws were followed, we would have a Utopian world. C. BRAYFIELD Your theory is just a Utopian daydream. **utopian socialism**: achieved by the moral persuasion of capitalists to surrender the means of production peacefully to the people.

▶ **B** *noun*. **1** A native or inhabitant of a Utopia. M16.
2 A conceiver or advocate of Utopian schemes; an idealistic social reformer, a visionary. L19.
■ **Utopianism** *noun* †(*a*) a Utopian idea or condition; (*b*) Utopian thought, beliefs, or aims: M17. **Utopianist** *noun* = UTOPIAN *noun* 2 M19. **Utopianize** *verb* (*a*) *verb trans.* make Utopian, form a Utopia out of; (*b*) *verb intrans.* conceive Utopian schemes: M19. **Utopianizer** *noun* M19. **utopianly** *adverb* M20. **utopic** *adjective* (*rare*) = UTOPIAN *adjective* 1 M20. **utopical** *adjective* (*rare*) = UTOPIAN *adjective* 1 E17. **ˈUtopism** *noun* = UTOPIANISM (b) L19. **ˈUtopist** *noun* = UTOPIAN *noun* 2 M19.

utopiate /juːˈtəʊpɪeɪt/ *noun*. M20.
[Blend of UTOPIA and OPIATE *noun*.]
A drug which induces fantasies of a Utopian existence; a euphoriant.

Utraquism /ˈjuːtrəkwɪz(ə)m/ *noun*. Also **u-**. M19.
[formed as next + -ISM.]
1 ECCLESIASTICAL HISTORY. The doctrine or beliefs of the Utraquists. M19.
2 The use of two languages on an equal footing. *rare*. L19.

Utraquist /ˈjuːtrəkwɪst/ *noun & adjective*. Also **u-**. M19.
[mod. Latin *Utraquista*, from Latin *utraque* each, both, esp. as in phr. *sub utraque specie* under each kind: see -IST.]
▶ **A** *noun*. **1** ECCLESIASTICAL HISTORY. = CALIXTINE. M19.
2 A user or speaker of both or two languages. *rare*. E20.
▶ **B** *adjective*. **1** ECCLESIASTICAL HISTORY. Of, pertaining to, or characteristic of the Utraquists. M19.
2 Speaking or using both or two languages. *rare*. M19.
■ **utraquistic** *adjective* = UTRAQUIST *adjective* 1 L19.

Utrecht /ˈjuːtrɛkt/ *noun*. L15.
[A town and province in the Netherlands.]
Used *attrib.* to designate things made in or associated with Utrecht.
Utrecht velvet a strong thick kind of plush used in upholstering furniture etc.

utricle /ˈjuːtrɪk(ə)l/ *noun*. M18.
[French *utricule* or Latin UTRICULUS.]
1 BOTANY. Any of various small bladder-like structures; *esp.* (***a***) a one-seeded indehiscent fruit with a thin inflated fruit, as in the goosefoot family; (***b***) = PERIGYNIUM 1; (***c***) any of the bladder-like appendages of a bladderwort. M18.
2 ANATOMY & ZOOLOGY. A small cell, sac, or bladder-like process; *spec.* the larger of the two divisions of the membranous labyrinth of the inner ear. E19.

utricular /juːˈtrɪkjʊlə/ *adjective*[1]. M18.
[from UTRICULUS + -AR[1].]
Of the nature of or resembling a utricle; composed of utricles.

utricular /juːˈtrɪkjʊlə/ *adjective*[2]. E19.
[from Latin *utriculus* dim. of UTERUS: see -AR[1].]
MEDICINE. Of or pertaining to the uterus or abdomen; uterine.

utricularia /jʊˌtrɪkjʊˈlɛːrɪə/ *noun*. Pl. **-riae** /-rɪiː/, **-rias**. L18.
[mod. Latin (see below), from Latin UTRICULUS.]
Any of various carnivorous, usu. aquatic, plants constituting the genus *Utricularia* (family Lentibulariaceae); a bladderwort.

utriculi *noun* pl. of UTRICULUS.

utriculoplasty /juːˈtrɪkjʊlə(ʊ)ˌplasti/ *noun*. E20.
[formed as UTRICULAR *adjective*[2] + -O- + -PLASTY.]
MEDICINE. (An instance of) a surgical operation to reduce the size of the uterus by removing part of the uterine wall.

utriculus /juːˈtrɪkjʊləs/ *noun*. Pl. **-li** /-lʌɪ, -liː/. M18.
[Latin, dim. of *uter* leather bottle or bag: see -CULE.]
1 BOTANY. = UTRICLE 1. M18.
2 ANATOMY. The utricle of the ear. M19.

utrum /ˈjuːtrəm/ *noun*. *obsolete* exc. *Hist.* ME.
[Anglo-Norman, Anglo-Latin = Latin *utrum* neut. sing. of *uter* which, whether.]
LAW. A writ authorizing the holding of an assize to decide the status of a property. Chiefly in ***assize of utrum***.

ut supra /ʊt ˈsuːprə/ *adverbial phr.* LME.
[Latin, from *ut* as + SUPRA.]
In a book etc.: as previously, as before, as above. Freq. abbreviated to ***ut sup.***

utter /ˈʌtə/ *adjective*.
[Old English *ūter(r)a*, *uttra* compar. formed on *ūt* OUT *adverb* (see -ER[3]), corresp. to Old Frisian *utt(e)ra*, *ūtera*, Middle Dutch *ūtere* (Dutch *uiter-*), Old High German *ūzaro* (German *äusser*): for shortening of *ū* cf. *udder*.]
▶ **I 1** = OUTER *adjective* 1. Now *poet.* OE.
†**2** = OUTER *adjective* 2. OE–LME.
†**3** = OUTWARD *adjective* 2. ME–L16.
▶ **II 4** Extreme, absolute; complete, entire, total. LME. ▸**b** Of an answer, decision, etc.: given without reserve or qualification, decisive, definite. Long *rare*. LME.

📖 4 SIR W. SCOTT They blew out their lights . . and left the knight in utter darkness. R. L. STEVENSON At first the silence of the night was utter. *Guardian* The general mood is one of complete and utter despair.

utter /ˈʌtə/ *verb.* LME.
[Middle Dutch *ūteren* (Dutch *uiteren*) drive away, speak, show, make known = Old Frisian *ūt(r)ia*, Middle Low German *ūtern*, assim. to UTTER *adjective*.]
▸ **I** †**1** *verb trans.* Put (goods etc.) on the market, offer for sale, sell. LME–E19.
2 *verb trans.* **a** Put (money etc.) into circulation; *esp.* fraudulently pass or circulate (forged notes or coins) as legal tender. L15. ▸**b** Issue by way of publication, publish. *arch. rare.* M16.
3 *verb trans.* **a** Send out; *esp.* give out from a store. *rare.* E16. ▸**b** Put, thrust, or shoot out; discharge, emit. Now *dial.* M16.
▸ **II 4** *verb trans.* Send out as a sound, emit audibly; give expression to (an emotion etc.). LME.
5 *verb trans.* Speak or say (words, speech, a sentence, etc.); express (a subject, one's thoughts, etc.) in spoken or (occas.) written words. Also with direct speech or subord. clause as object. LME. ▸**b** *refl.* Express oneself in words. E17.
†**6** *verb trans.* **a** Disclose or reveal (something unknown, secret, or hidden). LME–L17. ▸**b** Make the character or identity of (a person etc.) known. Only in 16. ▸**c** Show, display; bring to light. M–L16.
7 *verb intrans.* **a** Exercise the faculty of speech, speak. LME. ▸**b** Of words etc.: be spoken. L18.

📖 4 B. TARKINGTON Fanny found her voice, and uttered a long, loud cry. **5** E. W. LANE If, at my grave, you utter my name. J. CONRAD The Editor uttered slowly—'You will be a rich man.' I. MURDOCH We sit together for hours, sometimes without uttering a word.

■ **utteraˈbility** *noun* (*rare*) the quality or condition of being utterable M19. **utterable** *adjective* †(*a*) able to be sold; (*b*) able to be uttered or expressed in words: L16. **utterer** *noun* E16.

†**utter** *adverb.*
[Old English *ūt(t)or*, *ūtter* compar. of *ūt* OUT *adverb* (see -ER³), corresp. to Middle Low German *uter* (German *äusser*), Old Norse *ūtarr*.]
1 Further out, away, or apart; out, outside. OE–E16.
2 Utterly, quite, altogether. E17–E19.

utterance /ˈʌt(ə)r(ə)ns/ *noun*¹. LME.
[from UTTER *verb* + -ANCE.]
†**1** The disposal of goods etc. by sale. LME–M17.
2 a The action or an act of uttering with the voice; vocal expression (*of* something); speaking, speech. LME. ▸**b** The faculty or power of speech; a person's manner of speaking. L15.
3 That which is uttered or expressed in words; a spoken or occas. written statement or expression; an articulated sound. LME. ▸**b** LINGUISTICS. An uninterrupted chain of words uttered by a speaker; a sentence as uttered on a particular occasion. M20.
†**4** The action of issuing something from a store. *rare.* L15–M18.

📖 **2a** J. WILKINS The utterance of articulate sounds. S. AUSTIN These protests were only the utterance of the feeling that France yielded to force. GEO. ELIOT The Squire was purple with anger . . and found utterance difficult. **b** F. BURNEY All utterance seemed denied her. DICKENS A deep, gruff, husky utterance. **3** B. BRYSON The utterances of children are overwhelmingly statements.

utterance /ˈʌt(ə)r(ə)ns/ *noun*². Now *arch.* or *literary.* LME.
[Old French *oultrance*, (also mod.) OUTRANCE, with assim. to UTTER *adjective*: see -ANCE.]
A degree of severity or intensity surpassing bounds or going beyond measure; immoderate force or violence, excess. Now only in phrs. (see below).
†**at the utterance**, †**at utterance** with the greatest energy, with the utmost force or violence. †**bring to utterance**, †**put to utterance** overcome completely, bring to ruin, put to death. **to the utterance** to an extreme degree; to the death, to the bitter end.

utterest /ˈʌt(ə)rɪst/ *adjective & noun.* ME.
[Superl. of UTTER *adjective*: see -EST¹.]
▸ **A** *adjective.* **I** †**1** = UTMOST *adjective* 1. ME–L15.
2 = UTMOST *adjective* 2. Now *rare.* LME.
▸ **II** †**3** = UTMOST *adjective* 3. LME–L15.
4 Of a person: that is such to a superlative degree, most complete, greatest. L16.
▸ **B** *noun.* †**1** = UTMOST *noun* 1. Only in ME.
2 = UTMOST *noun* 2a. Now only in ***to the utterest***. LME.

utterless /ˈʌtəlɪs/ *adjective.* M17.
[from UTTER *verb* + -LESS.]
1 Unable to be uttered, unutterable. Chiefly *poet.* M17. ▸**b** Unable to be expressed or described, inexpressible. Chiefly *poet.* M19.
2 Incapable of utterance, speechless. *rare.* M19.

utterly /ˈʌtəli/ *adverb.* ME.
[from UTTER *adjective* + -LY².]
†**1** Without reserve or qualification; sincerely, truly. ME–M16.
2 To an extreme or absolute degree; completely, entirely, totally. LME.

📖 **2** J. TYNDALL It would be utterly destroyed before reaching the bottom. I. MURDOCH Geoffrey . . so utterly belonged to her accustomed world. G. GREENE I am utterly incapable of reading instructions of a technical nature.

uttermost /ˈʌtəməʊst/ *adjective & noun.* ME.
[formed as prec. + -MOST. Cf. OUTERMOST.]
▸ **A** *adjective.* **1** = UTMOST *adjective* 1. *arch.* ME.
2 = UTMOST *adjective* 2. ME.
3 a = UTMOST *adjective* 3. Long *rare.* LME. ▸**b** Last of a series, store, etc. Chiefly in ***uttermost farthing***. Long *rare.* M16.
▸ **B** *noun.* **1** = UTMOST *noun* 1. *arch.* ME.
2 = UTMOST *noun* 2a. *obsolete* exc. in ***to the uttermost***. LME.
†**3 a** = UTMOST *noun* 3. *rare.* L15–L16. ▸**b** The extreme or furthest limit in time. *rare* (Shakes.). Only in E17.

utterness /ˈʌtənɪs/ *noun.* E19.
[formed as prec. + -NESS.]
The condition or quality of being utter, absolute, or complete.

utu /ˈʊtʊ/ *noun. NZ.* E19.
[Maori.]
Recompense, revenge, or payment for injury or harm received.

UUC *abbreviation.*
Ulster Unionist Council.

UV *abbreviation.*
Ultraviolet (radiation).

UVA *abbreviation.*
Ultraviolet A (i.e. of the longest wavelengths, greater than about 320 nanometres).

uva /ˈjuːvə/ *noun.* Pl. **uvae** /ˈjuːviː/. L17.
[Latin.]
1 BOTANY. A grape, a raisin; a grapelike fruit. *rare* (chiefly in Dicts.). L17.
2 *uva ursi* /ˈəːsʌɪ/, the bearberry, *Arctostaphylos uva-ursi*; (an infusion of) the leaves of this plant. Now *rare.* M18.

uvala /ˈuːvələ/ *noun.* E20.
[Serbo-Croat = hollow, depression.]
PHYSICAL GEOGRAPHY. A large depression in the ground surface occurring in karstic regions, resulting from the collapse of an underground watercourse.

uvarovite /uːˈvarəvʌɪt/ *noun.* M19.
[from Count Sergei Semenovich *Uvarov* (1785–1855), Russian statesman + -ITE¹.]
MINERALOGY. An emerald green variety of garnet.

UVB *abbreviation.*
Ultraviolet B (i.e. of intermediate wavelengths, about 280–320 nanometres).

UVC *abbreviation.*
Ultraviolet C (i.e. of the shortest wavelengths, less than about 280 nanometres).

uvea /ˈjuːvɪə/ *noun.* LME.
[medieval Latin, from Latin UVA.]
ANATOMY. †**1** The choroid layer of the eye. LME–L18.
2 A pigmented layer which is the middle vascular coat of the eye, composed of the choroid, iris, and ciliary body. Also called ***uveal tract***. M18.
■ **uveal** *adjective* pertaining or belonging to, consisting of, or affecting the uvea; ***uveal tract*** = UVEA 2: M17. **uveˈitis** *noun* (MEDICINE) inflammation of the uvea M19.

uveoparotid /ˌjuːvɪəʊpəˈrɒtɪd/ *adjective.* E20.
[from UVEA + -O- + PAROTID.]
MEDICINE. Affecting or involving the uvea and the parotid gland.
uveoparotid fever = UVEOPAROTITIS.
■ **uveoparoˈtitis** *noun* inflammation of the uvea and the parotid, a common manifestation of sarcoidosis E20.

uver /ˈʌvə/ *adjective.* Now *dial.* OE.
[Var. of OVER *adjective*.]
That is higher in position, upper.
uver hand the upper hand.
■ **uvermost** *adjective* uppermost, highest M16.

UVF *abbreviation.*
Ulster Volunteer Force.

uvula /ˈjuːvjʊlə/ *noun.* LME.
[Late Latin, dim. of Latin UVA: see -ULE.]
ANATOMY. **1** A fleshy projection hanging from the rear margin of the soft palate in man and some other primates. Also ***palatine uvula***. LME.
2 Any of several other pendent fleshy masses; *esp.* (more fully ***uvula of the bladder***) a rounded eminence in the bladder at the apex of the trigone, projecting into the urethral orifice. M19.
Comb.: **uvula trill** PHONETICS a consonantal trilling sound made by vibrating the uvula.
■ **uvuˈlatomy** *noun* (MEDICINE) (an instance of) a surgical operation to cut or excise the uvula L19. **uvuˈlitis** *noun* (MEDICINE) inflammation of the uvula M19. **uvuˈlotomy** *noun* (MEDICINE) = UVULATOMY L19.

uvular /ˈjuːvjʊlə/ *adjective & noun.* E18.
[from prec. + -AR¹.]
▸ **A** *adjective.* †**1** MEDICINE. Of a drug etc.: used in disorders of the uvula. Only in E18.
2 ANATOMY. Of a part or structure: associated with the uvula. M19.
3 PHONETICS. Of a consonantal sound: produced by vibration of the uvula. L19.
▸ **B** *noun.* PHONETICS. A uvular consonant. L19.
■ **uvularly** *adverb* with a thick obstructed utterance M19.

uvularia /juːvjʊˈlɛːrɪə/ *noun.* E18.
[mod. Latin (see below), from late Latin UVULA, app. with ref. to the pendulous flowers.]
†**1** A southern European shrub, *Ruscus hypoglossum*, related to butcher's broom. *rare.* Only in E18.
2 Any plant of the N. American genus *Uvularia*; = ***bellwort*** s.v. BELL *noun*¹. E19.

uxorial /ʌkˈsɔːrɪəl/ *adjective.* E19.
[from Latin *uxor* wife: see -IAL. In sense 2 alt. of UXORIOUS.]
1 Of or pertaining to a wife or wives. E19.
2 = UXORIOUS *adjective* 2. M19.
■ **uxoriˈality** *noun* the condition of being a wife, wifehood M19.

uxoricide /ʌkˈsɔːrɪsʌɪd/ *noun.* M19.
[formed as prec. + -CIDE.]
1 A man who murders his wife. M19.
2 The murder of one's wife. M19.
■ **uxoriˈcidal** *adjective* of, pertaining to, or tending to uxoricide L19.

uxorilocal /ˌʌksɒrɪˈləʊk(ə)l/ *adjective.* M20.
[formed as prec. + LOCAL *adjective*.]
Designating or pertaining to a pattern of marriage in which a couple settles in the wife's home or community.
■ **uxorilocally** *adverb* M20.

uxorious /ʌkˈsɔːrɪəs/ *adjective.* L16.
[Latin *uxoriosus* (from *uxor* wife): see -OUS.]
1 Greatly or excessively fond of one's wife, doting. L16.
2 Of behaviour etc.: marked or characterized by such fondness. E17.

📖 **1** A. BROOKNER He had always impressed me as home-loving and uxorious. S. TUROW Dixon was uxorious. He . . loved to see her pampered and expensively dressed.

■ **uxoriously** *adverb* M17. **uxoriousness** *noun* E17.

Uzbek /ˈʊzbɛk, ˈʌz-/ *noun & adjective.* E17.
[Turkish, Uzbek *özbek*, perh. through Persian or Russian *uzbek*.]
▸ **A** *noun.* Pl. **-s**, same. A member of a Turkic people of central Asia, forming the basic population of Uzbekistan and also living in Afghanistan; the language of this people. E17.
▸ **B** *adjective.* Of or pertaining to this people or their language. M19.

Uzi /ˈuːzi/ *noun.* M20.
[from the Israeli army officer Uziel Gal, designer of the gun.]
An Israeli type of submachine gun. Also ***Uzi submachine gun***.

Vv

V, v /viː/.
The twenty-second letter of the modern English alphabet and the twentieth of the ancient Roman one, of which U is a differentiated form. Orig. an adoption of the early Greek vowel-symbol V, now also represented by U and Y, it also represented in Latin a semi-vocalic sound /w/ (corresp. to the Greek digamma) which gradually changed to a bilabial /β/ and later a labiodental /v/ consonant. English use of V first became established in Middle English under French influence, but without a formal distinction of use from U, with which it continued to share the functions of representing both a vowel and a consonant until about 1700 (see **U, U**) before being regularly distinguished as the consonant. The sound now normally represented by the letter is a voiced labiodental fricative consonant. Pl. **V's**, **Vs**. See also **VEE**.
▶ **I 1** The letter and its sound.
2 The shape of the letter.
2 V aerial, **V antenna** an aerial in which the conductors form a large horizontal V that transmits principally along its axis. ***V antenna***: see ***V aerial*** above. **V belt** a belt which is V-shaped in cross-section in order to give better traction on a pulley. **V-block** a metal block with a V-shaped recess cut in it to hold a cylindrical object while it is being worked on. **V-eight**, **V-8** a V-engine with eight cylinders; a motor vehicle with such an engine. **V-engine** an internal-combustion engine with the cylinders arranged in two rows at an angle to each other, forming a V-shaped cross-section. **V-moth** a geometrid moth, *Semiothisa wauaria*, which has a dark V-shaped mark on the pale forewing. **V-neck** (a pullover or other garment with) a neckline in the shape of a V. **V-pug** a small geometrid moth, *Chloroclystis v-ata*, which has a V-shaped mark on the forewing. **V-shaped** *adjective* having a shape or a cross-section like the letter V. **V-six**, **V-6** a V-engine with six cylinders; a motor vehicle with such an engine. **V-thread** a screw thread which is V-shaped in profile.
▶ **II** Symbolical uses.
3 Used to denote serial order; applied e.g. to the twenty-second (or often the twenty-first, either I or J being omitted) group or section, sheet of a book, etc. ▸**b** ***V-agent***, any of a group of organophosphorus nerve gases having anticholinesterase activity; ***VX***, a liquid V-agent produced esp. by the US in the 1960s.
4 The roman numeral for five.
5 PARTICLE PHYSICS. (Cap. V.) Any of a group of heavy unstable particles, now identified as hyperons and kaons, that produce characteristic V-shaped tracks when they decay. *obsolete exc. Hist.*
▶ **III 6** Abbrevs.: **V** = (*US*) a five-dollar note; (CHEMISTRY) vanadium; [German] *Vergeltungswaffe* reprisal weapon (esp. in ***V-1***, a type of German flying bomb used in the war of 1939–45, ***V-2***, a type of German rocket-powered missile used in the war of 1939–45); (ECCLESIASTICAL) versicle; victory; volt. **v.** = verb; verse; verso; versus; very; *vide*. **v** = velocity; volume.

V /viː/ *verb intrans.* Pa. t. & pple **V-ed**, pres. pple **V-ing**. E20.
[from prec.]
Of geese: fly in a formation shaped like a horizontal V.

VA *abbreviation.*
1 (Order of) Victoria and Albert.
2 Veteran's administration. *US.*
3 Vicar Apostolic.
4 Vice admiral.
5 Also **Va.** Virginia.
6 Visual acuity.

Vaad Leumi /ˈvaːaːd ləˈuːmiː/ *noun phr.* E20.
[Hebrew *wa'ad* committee + *lĕ'ummī* national.]
Hist. A national committee of Palestinian Jews, serving as their people's official representative during the period of the British Mandate from 1920 to 1948.

vaalhaai /ˈfɑːlhʌɪ/ *noun. S. Afr.* M20.
[Afrikaans, from Dutch *vaal* pale, tawny + *haai* shark.]
The tope or soupfin shark, *Galeorhinus galeus*.

vaaljapie /ˈfɑːljɑːpiː/ *noun. S. Afr.* M20.
[Afrikaans, lit. 'tawny Jake', from Dutch *vaal* pale + *japie* dim. of male forename *Jaap* from *Jakob* Jacob.]
Rough young wine, cheap or inferior wine.

Vaalpens /ˈfɑːlpɛns/ *noun. S. Afr. colloq.* Pl. same. L19.
[Afrikaans, formed as prec. + *pens* paunch, belly.]
A Transvaaler.

vaatjie /ˈfʌɪki, -tʃi/ *noun. S. Afr.* Also **vatje**. M19.
[Afrikaans, from *vaat* vat + *-tjie* dim. suffix.]
A small cask for carrying water or wine; a soldier's canteen.

va banque /va bɑ̃ːk/ *interjection.* M20.
[French, lit. 'go bank'.]
In baccarat: expr. a player's willingness to bet against the banker's whole stake. Cf. **BANCO**.

vac /vak/ *noun*¹. *colloq.* E18.
[Abbreviation of **VACATION** *noun*.]
The period between terms (esp. of a university).

📖 K. Tynan I shall be in London for the first week of the vac.

vac /vak/ *verb & noun*². *colloq.* M20.
[Abbreviation.]
▶ **A** *verb trans. & intrans.* Infl. **-c(c)-**. Vacuum. M20.
▶ **B** *noun.* A vacuum cleaner. L20.

vacance /ˈveɪk(ə)ns/ *noun.* Chiefly *Scot.* Now *rare.* M16.
[Latin *vacantia*: see next, **-ANCE**.]
†**1** A period without a ruler or laws. Only in M16.
2 = **VACATION** *noun* 2. M16.
†**3** Leisure, relaxation. E17–M18.

vacancy /ˈveɪk(ə)nsi/ *noun.* L16.
[from next, or from late Latin *vacantia*, from *vacant-*: see next, **-ANCY**.]
1 *sing.* & in *pl.* = **VACATION** *noun* 2. *arch.* L16.
†**2** Temporary freedom from or cessation of business, work, etc.; leisure, free time. Also, an instance of this, *spec.* a period of leisure or free time. L16–L18.
3 The state or condition of being free from business, work, etc.; idleness; inactivity. Also foll. by *from*. Now *rare* or *obsolete.* E17.
4 a The fact or condition of a position, office, etc., being or falling vacant; an instance of this; a vacant position, office, etc. E17. ▸**b** An available room in a hotel, guest-house, etc. M20.
5 Empty space. E17.
6 a An unfilled or unoccupied space; a gap, an opening. M17. ▸**b** Absence or lack of something. *rare.* M17. ▸**c** CRYSTALLOGRAPHY. A defect in a crystal lattice consisting of the absence of an atom or ion from a position where there should be one. M20.
7 a The state of being empty or unoccupied; emptiness. L18. ▸**b** Lack of intelligence; inanity; mental vacuity. M19.

📖 **2a** S. Patrick He did not find so much vacancy as his heart desired for private Prayer. **4a** W. Blackstone The vacancy of the throne was precedent to their meeting without any royal summons. P. Fitzgerald Do stop asking Daisy all these questions . . . You might be interviewing her for a vacancy. P. Lively There's a vacancy at the moment. It's a question of the right man coming along. **b** *attrib.*: R. Macdonald The first motel . . was decorated with a vacancy sign. **5** B. Emecheta They would sit there for hours . . staring into vacancy. **6a** N. Hawthorne This great arch . . with the lofty vacancy beneath it. **7a** Sir W. Scott Quentin felt a strange vacancy and chillness of the heart.

vacant /ˈveɪk(ə)nt/ *adjective & noun.* ME.
[Old & mod. French from Latin *vacant-* pres. ppl stem of *vacare*: see **VACATE**, **-ANT**¹. Reintroduced in 16 directly from Latin.]
▶ **A** *adjective.* **1** Of a benefice, office, position, etc.: not (yet) filled or occupied. ME. ▸†**b** Of goods: having no owner. *rare.* M16–M18.
2 a Containing no objects; empty. LME. ▸**b** (Of land, a house, etc.) uninhabited, untenanted; (of a place, space, room, etc.) not occupied or in use. E16. ▸**c** Characterized by the absence of life, activity, etc. L18.
3 Devoid or destitute of, entirely free from or lacking, something. Foll. by *of*. LME. ▸†**b** Empty-handed; destitute. *rare.* LME–L16.
4 a Of time: free of or *from* business, an occupation, etc.; devoted to leisure. Now *rare* or *obsolete.* M16. ▸†**b** Of a person: free of or *from* (normal) work or duties; having little or nothing to do. E17–L18. ▸**c** Characterized by or proceeding from leisure or idleness; undisturbed by business or work. E17. ▸**d** Free to devote oneself *to* an aim etc. Also, (of a thing) open *to* an influence etc. Now *rare* or *obsolete.* M17.
5 Of the mind or brain: not occupied in thought or reflection. L16. ▸†**b** Free from care or anxiety. *rare.* M17–E18.
6 Characterized by or exhibiting a lack of attention, intelligence, or thought; empty-headed, unthinking; expressionless, meaningless; inane. E18.

📖 **1** H. J. Laski An unconstitutional Parliament thereupon declared the throne vacant. ***situations vacant***: see **SITUATION**. **2b** F. M. Ford The head waiter piloted him . . to a vacant table. W. S. Churchill To grant a charter for settling vacant lands. M. Spark Placed in rooms . . while waiting for an Embassy flat to fall vacant. **vacant possession** the right of a purchaser to exclusive use of a property or premises on completion of the sale. **c** W. Cowper Amid the stillness of the vacant night. **3** S. Patrick Select friends, vacant of business, . . met together at one table. **4c** R. W. Chambers An idle and vacant life . . is not . . a happy one. **d** S. Johnson When the heart is vacant to every fresh . . delight. **6** V. Woolf Rhoda's face, mooning, vacant.

▶†**B** *noun. rare.*
1 A vacant estate. *Scot.* Only in L15.
2 A person who is temporarily unemployed or out of office. Only in E17.
3 In *pl.* A vacation. Only in M17.
4 A vacant space, a vacuum. *poet.* Only in E18.
■ **vacantly** *adverb* E17.

vacat /ˈveɪkat/ *noun.* Now *rare* or *obsolete.* L16.
[Latin, 3rd person sing. pres. indic. of *vacare*: see next. Cf. **VACATUR**.]
LAW. An annulment, an abrogation.

vacate /vəˈkeɪt, veɪˈkeɪt/ *verb.* M17.
[Latin *vacat-* pa. ppl stem of *vacare* be empty or unoccupied: see **-ATE**³.]
▶ **I** *verb trans.* **1 a** Make void in law; deprive of legal authority or validity; annul, cancel. M17. ▸**b** *transf.* Deprive of force or efficacy; make inoperative, meaningless, or useless. Now *rare* or *obsolete.* M17. ▸**c** Remove or withdraw (something). *rare.* M18.
2 Make (a post or position) vacant; deprive of an occupant or holder. L17. ▸**b** Leave (an office, position, etc.) vacant by death, resignation, or retirement. M19.
3 Leave, cease to occupy, (a place, seat, house, etc.). L18.

📖 **1a** Ld Macaulay A bill vacating all grants of Crown property. **2** E. A. Freeman The throne which, when it was vacated, was filled by Hadrian. **3** P. H. Johnson A guest had vacated the room . . that morning. W. Trevor Vacated his chair and sat on the piano stool. *fig.*: R. H. Tawney Ground . . vacated by the Christian moralist is quickly occupied by theorists of another order.

▶ **II** *verb intrans.* **4** Give up an office or position; retire. E19.
5 Take a holiday or vacation. *US.* M19.
■ **vacatable** *adjective* L19.

vacation /vəˈkeɪʃ(ə)n, veɪ-/ *noun & verb.* LME.
[Old & mod. French, or from Latin *vacatio(n-)*, formed as prec.: see **-ATION**.]
▶ **A** *noun.* **1 a** Freedom or rest from or *from* an occupation, work, etc. LME. ▸†**b** Leisure for, or devoted to, some special purpose. LME–M17. ▸†**c** Absence from duty or one's usual post. LME–L16.
2 A fixed period of formal suspension of work or other activity; *esp.* a period of the year when lawcourts, universities, or schools are closed. LME. ▸**b** (A) holiday; a break from one's regular work. Chiefly *N. Amer.* L19.
†**3** Chiefly ECCLESIASTICAL. The fact of a position or office being or falling vacant; the duration of a vacancy. LME–E18.
4 †**a** A state or period characterized by the absence *of* a thing, activity, etc. M16–E18. ▸**b** A state or period of inactivity. M17.
5 A time of freedom or respite (*from* something). E17.
6 The action of vacating a house, position, etc. M19.

📖 **2** A. S. Byatt Anna should have come home for the Christmas vacation. ***long vacation***: see **LONG** *adjective*¹. **b** A. K. Green She went away for a short vacation. S. Brill He received five weeks paid vacation each year. **5** C. Cotton Giving himself a vacation from the hardships of War. **6** W. C. Russell Ignorant of the true reason of old Mrs. Ransome's sudden vacation of the house.

Comb.: **vacation home** *US* a house used for holidays or at weekends; **vacation job** paid employment for a student during a vacation from a university, polytechnic, etc.; **vacation land** *US* an area providing attractions for holiday-makers.
▶ **B** *verb intrans.* Take a vacation or holiday. L19.
■ **vacationer** *noun* (*a*) (orig. & chiefly *N. Amer.*) a holiday-maker; (*b*) a student on vacation: L19. **vacationist** *noun* (orig. & chiefly *US*) a holiday-maker L19.

vacatur /veɪˈkeɪtʊə/ *noun. rare.* L17.
[Latin, 3rd person sing. pres. indic. pass. of *vacare*: see **VACATE**. Cf. **VACAT**.]
LAW. An annulment, a setting aside.

vaccary /ˈvakəri/ *noun. obsolete* exc. *Hist.* L15.
[medieval Latin *vaccaria*, from *vacca* cow: see -ARY[1].]
A place where cows are kept or pastured; a dairy farm.

vaccinal /ˈvaksɪn(ə)l, vakˈsʌɪn(ə)l/ *adjective.* L19.
[from VACCINE + -AL[1]; in sense 2 from VACCINIA.]
MEDICINE. **1** Of or pertaining to vaccine or vaccination. Now *rare* or *obsolete.* L19.
2 Of or pertaining to vaccinia (cowpox); vaccinial. *rare.* E20.

vaccinate /ˈvaksɪneɪt/ *verb.* E19.
[from VACCINE + -ATE[3].]
1 *verb trans.* MEDICINE. Inoculate (a person etc.) with a vaccine, orig. *spec.*, with that of vaccinia (cowpox) or a related virus as a protection against smallpox. E19.
2 *verb intrans.* MEDICINE. Perform or practise vaccination. M19.
3 *verb trans.* COMPUTING. Provide (a computer) with a vaccine program. L20.
▪ **vaccinator** *noun* (*a*) a person who performs, practises, or advocates vaccination; (*b*) (now *rare*) an instrument used in performing vaccination: E19.

vaccination /vaksɪˈneɪʃ(ə)n/ *noun.* E19.
[from prec. + -ION: see -ATION.]
1 MEDICINE. The inoculation of an individual with a vaccine in order to induce or increase immunity; orig. *spec.*, inoculation with a preparation of vaccinia etc. as a protection against smallpox. E19.
2 COMPUTING. The operation of a vaccine program. L20.

vaccine /ˈvaksiːn, -ɪn/ *adjective & noun.* L18.
[Latin *vaccinus* (as used in mod. Latin *variolae vaccinus* cowpox, *virus vaccinus* cowpox vaccine), from *vacca* cow: see -INE[1].]
▶ **A** *adjective* (now *rare*).
1 MEDICINE. Designating, appearing in, or characteristic of the disease of cowpox; designating or pertaining to the causative agent of cowpox. L18.
2 Of, or pertaining to, or derived from cows. E19.
▶ **B** *noun.* **1** MEDICINE. A preparation of the causative agent of a disease, its products, or a synthetic substitute, that has been specially treated for use in vaccination; orig. *spec.*, a preparation of vaccinia (cowpox) for inoculation against smallpox. E19.
2 COMPUTING. A program designed to protect a computer system from the effect of destructive software such as a virus. Also ***vaccine program.*** L20.
1 ***Hib vaccine, Sabin vaccine, Salk vaccine,*** etc. ***triple vaccine***: see TRIPLE *adjective & adverb.*
Special collocations & comb.: **vaccine damage** harm, esp. serious, caused by a vaccine. **vaccine-damaged** *adjective* subjected to vaccine damage. **vaccine disease** = ***cowpox*** s.v. COW *noun*[1]. **vaccine lymph, vaccine matter** an extract containing the causative agent of cowpox, formerly employed in vaccination. ***vaccine program***: see sense B.2 above. **vaccine therapy** treatment of a disease with an appropriate vaccine.

vaccinee /vaksɪˈniː/ *noun.* L19.
[from VACCIN(ATE + -EE[1].]
MEDICINE. A person who is or has been vaccinated.

vaccinia /vakˈsɪnɪə/ *noun.* E19.
[mod. Latin from Latin *vaccinus*: see VACCINE, -IA[1].]
MEDICINE. Cowpox.
▪ **vaccinial** *adjective* L19.

vaccinist /ˈvaksɪnɪst/ *noun.* Now *rare.* M19.
[from VACCINE + -IST.]
MEDICINE. A vaccinator; a supporter or advocate of vaccination.

vaccinium /vakˈsɪnɪəm/ *noun.* L18.
[mod. Latin use as genus name of Latin = bilberry.]
Any of various dwarf evergreen moorland shrubs constituting the genus *Vaccinium*, of the heath family, which includes bilberries and blueberries.

vaccinoid /ˈvaksɪnɔɪd/ *adjective.* L19.
[from VACCINE or VACCINIA + -OID.]
MEDICINE. Esp. of a local vaccination reaction: resembling a vaccinia (cowpox) infection.

vaccy *noun* var. of VACKY.

vacherin /vaʃrɛ̃/ *noun.* M20.
[French.]
1 A soft French or Swiss cheese made from cow's milk. M20.
2 A dessert of a meringue shell filled with whipped cream, fruit, etc. M20.

vacillant /ˈvasɪl(ə)nt/ *adjective.* E16.
[Latin *vacillant-* pres. ppl stem of *vacillare*: see next, -ANT[1].]
Uncertain, hesitating, wavering.
▪ **vacillancy** *noun* (long *rare* or *obsolete*) vacillation M17.

vacillate /ˈvasɪleɪt/ *verb intrans.* L16.
[Latin *vacillat-* pa. ppl stem of *vacillare* sway, totter: see -ATE[3].]
1 a Swing or sway unsteadily; be in unstable equilibrium, oscillate; stagger. L16. ▸**b** Vary; fluctuate. M19.
2 Alternate or waver between different opinions, options, actions, etc.; be indecisive. E17.

🕮 **1b** I. D'ISRAELI The fate of books vacillates with the fancies of book-lovers. **2** J. RUSKIN He may pause . . and tremble, but he must not vacillate. J. GARDNER She vacillated between stony silence and intense, nervous chatter.

▪ **vacillator** *noun* a person who vacillates or wavers L19. **vacillatory** *adjective* (*a*) marked by vacillation; (*b*) (of a person) tending to vacillate: M18.

vacillation /vasɪˈleɪʃ(ə)n/ *noun.* LME.
[Latin *vacillatio(n-)*, formed as prec.: see -ATION.]
1 The action or habit of wavering between opinions, options, etc.; hesitation, indecision. Now also, an instance of this. LME.
2 The action of swaying or swinging unsteadily to and fro; an instance of this. M17.

vacky /ˈvaki/ *noun. colloq.* (now *Hist.*). Also **-ccy, -kky.** M20.
[Abbreviation from EVACUEE: see -Y[6].]
An evacuee, *esp.* a child evacuated from the city to the country at the beginning of the 1939–45 war.

vacua *noun pl.* see VACUUM *noun.*

†**vacuate** *verb trans.* L16–M18.
[Latin *vacuat-* pa. ppl stem of *vacuare*, from *vacuus* empty: see -ATE[3].]
= EVACUATE 1, 3, 5.

†**vacuation** *noun.* M16.
[Late Latin *vacuatio(n-)*, formed as prec.: see -ATION.]
1 A hollow part. *rare.* Only in M16.
2 = EVACUATION 1. L16–E18.
3 Emptiness. *rare.* E–M17.

†**vacuefy** *verb intrans. & trans. rare.* E18–E19.
[from VACUUM *noun* after Latin *vacuefacere* make empty.]
Produce a vacuum (in).

vacuist /ˈvakjʊɪst/ *noun.* Long *obsolete* exc. *Hist.* M17.
[mod. Latin *vacuista*, from Latin VACUUM: see -IST.]
An adherent of the theory that a space empty of matter can exist in nature. Opp. PLENIST.

vacuity /vəˈkjuːɪti/ *noun.* M16.
[Old & mod. French *vacuité*, or from Latin *vacuitas*, from *vacuus* empty: see -ITY.]
▶ **I 1** An empty or vacant space within something; *spec.* (*a*) a vacuum; (*b*) a small hollow cavity in a solid body; (*c*) a space left in or forming part of a composite structure. M16. ▸**b** A gap or open space between or among things. *rare.* M17. ▸**c** An empty space due to the absence or disappearance of a person or thing habitually present. M17.
2 *fig.* An emptiness, a void, a blank. M17.
3 An empty or inane thing; something without meaning or value. M17.

🕮 **1** H. HAMMOND The earth . . sinks down and fills up the vacuities. G. ROLLESTON By a vacuity in the skull walls for the blood to pass out.

▶ **II 4** Absolute emptiness of space; complete absence of (solid or liquid) matter. M16. ▸**b** Emptiness due to the absence or disappearance of a person or thing habitually present. M17. ▸**c** The fact of being unfilled or unoccupied. M17.
5 Complete absence of ideas; vacancy of or *of* mind, thought, etc. L16.
6 Complete absence or lack *of* something. Formerly also, freedom or exemption *from* something. E17.
7 Orig., leisure *for* some pursuit. Later, lack of occupation; idleness. E17.
8 *fig.* The quality or fact of being empty, emptiness. E17.

vacuole /ˈvakjʊəʊl/ *noun.* M19.
[French from Latin *vacuolus*, dim. of *vacuus* empty: see -OLE[1].]
Chiefly BIOLOGY. A small cavity or vesicle in organic tissue; *esp.* a membrane-bound space containing fluid in the cytoplasm of a cell.
▪ **vacuolar** /-kjʊələ/ *adjective* of, pertaining to, or of the nature of a vacuole or vacuoles M19. **vacuolate** *adjective* = VACUOLATED L19. **vacuolated** *adjective* rendered vacuolar; modified or altered by vacuolation: M19. **vacuolating** *adjective* (MEDICINE) that vacuolates; ***vacuolating agent, vacuolating virus***, a papovavirus which is capable of causing tumours in animals and animal tissue cultures (also called ***SV 40***); a virus related to this: M20. **vacuoˈlation** *noun* the formation of vacuoles; the state of being vacuolated: M19. **vacuoliˈzation** *noun* = VACUOLATION L19. **vacuolized** *adjective* (*rare*) = VACUOLATED E20.

vacuome /ˈvakjʊəʊm/ *noun.* E20.
[French, from Latin *vacuus* empty: see -OME.]
CYTOLOGY. Orig., the inclusions of a plant cell collectively. Now, the membrane-bound spaces of a plant cell, excluding the mitochondria and plastids.

vacuous /ˈvakjʊəs/ *adjective.* M17.
[from Latin *vacuus* empty, void: see -OUS.]
1 Empty of matter; containing nothing solid, tangible, or visible. M17. ▸**b** Empty of air or gas; containing a vacuum. Now *rare.* M17.
2 Devoid of ideas; unintelligent; expressionless. M19.
3 Devoid of content or substance; meaningless. L19.
4 Idle, indolent; not profitably occupied. L19.

🕮 **2** P. L. FERMOR Subsiding in a vacuous and contented trance. J. HELLER Muriel's vacuous teen-age daughter finally terminated her conceited prattling. **3** *Times* The original ideals have been . . submerged beneath mountains of paper and vacuous talk. *Look Now* Success in doing something you don't enjoy is very vacuous.

▪ **vacuously** *adverb* M19. **vacuousness** *noun* M17.

vacuum /ˈvakjʊəm/ *noun & verb.* M16.
[mod. Latin, use as noun of neut. sing. of Latin *vacuus* empty.]
▶ **A** *noun.* Pl. **vacuums**, (exc. in sense 4) **vacua** /ˈvakjʊə/.
1 Emptiness of space; space unoccupied by matter. Now *rare* or *obsolete.* M16.
2 An empty space or place (*lit.* & *fig.*); *spec.* (a place, situation, etc., marked by) an absence of the usual, former, or expected contents. L16.
3 a A space entirely empty of matter. E17. ▸**b** A space from which air or other gas has been completely or partly removed by a pump etc. Also, the degree of exhaustion of gas within this. M17.
4 A vacuum cleaner (see below). *colloq.* (orig. *US*). E20.
Comb.: **vacuum abortion** = ***vacuum aspiration*** below; **vacuum activity** ZOOLOGY the performance of an innate pattern of behaviour without the appropriate releasing stimulus; a pattern of behaviour so performed; **vacuum aspiration** MEDICINE a method of induced abortion in which the contents of the uterus are removed by suction through a tube passed into it via the vagina; **vacuum bottle** = ***vacuum flask*** below; **vacuum brake**: operated by negative pressure caused by the condensation of steam or the exhaustion of air; **vacuum chamber**: designed to be emptied of air; **vacuum-clean** *verb trans.* = VACUUM *verb* 1; **vacuum cleaner** an electrical appliance for removing dust from carpets, other flooring, soft furnishings, etc., by suction; **vacuum deposition** deposition of a substance by allowing it to condense from the vapour state in what is otherwise a vacuum; **vacuum distillation** distillation of a liquid under reduced pressure, enabling it to boil at a much lower temperature than normal; **vacuum extraction** MEDICINE the application of suction to a baby's head to assist its birth; **vacuum extractor** MEDICINE a cup-shaped appliance for achieving vacuum extraction; **vacuum-fitted** *adjective* (of a railway car) fitted with a vacuum brake; **vacuum flask** a vessel with a double wall enclosing a vacuum so that liquid in the inner receptacle retains its temperature; **vacuum fluctuation** PHYSICS a fluctuation in field strength in a nominally field-free vacuum, occurring in consequence of the quantization of any radiation field; **vacuum forming** a type of thermoforming in which a vacuum is used to draw the plastic into the mould; **vacuum gauge**: for measuring the pressure remaining after the production of a vacuum; **vacuum grease** a grease which because of its low vapour pressure is suitable for sealing joints in a vacuum apparatus; **vacuum-pack** *verb trans.* pack (something) in a vacuumized container, seal (a vacuumized container), (chiefly as ***vacuum-packed*** *ppl adjective*); **vacuum packaging** (*a*) the action of vacuum-packing something; (*b*) the vacuumized container used for this; **vacuum polarization** PHYSICS the spontaneous appearance and disappearance of electron-positron pairs in a vacuum; **vacuum pump**: for evacuating a container of air or other gas; **vacuum-tight** *adjective* airtight; **vacuum tube** (*a*) an evacuated tube or pipe, *esp.* one along which vehicles or other objects can be propelled by allowing air to enter behind them; (*b*) a sealed glass tube containing a near-vacuum for the free passage of electric current; *spec.* one used as a thermionic valve; **vacuum wax** = ***vacuum grease*** above.
▶ **B** *verb.* **1** *verb trans. & intrans.* Clean (a room, carpet, etc.) or remove (dust etc.) with a vacuum cleaner. Orig. *US.* E20.
2 *verb trans.* Subject to a medical procedure involving a vacuum (e.g. vacuum aspiration, liposuction). *colloq.* L20.
▪ **vacuumize** *verb trans.* create a vacuum in (something); seal (a container from which air has been evacuated): E20.

VAD *abbreviation.*
(A member of a) Voluntary Aid Detachment.

vade /veɪd/ *verb intrans.* Long *arch. rare.* L15.
[Var. of FADE *verb.*]
†**1** Of a colour, flower, etc.: fade. L15–M17.
2 *fig.* Pass away, vanish; decay, perish. L15.
▪ **vading** *adjective* †(*a*) that fades; (*b*) fleeting, transient: M16.

†**vadelet** *noun.* Orig. **vadelict.** L16–M19.
[Anglo-Latin *vadelectus* from Anglo-Norman *vadlet* var. of Old French *vaslet*, *varlet*: see VALET *noun*, VARLET.]
A servant, a serving-man.

vade-mecum /vɑːdɪˈmeɪkəm, veɪdɪˈmiːkəm/ *noun.* E17.
[French from mod. Latin use as noun of Latin *vade mecum* go with me.]
1 A small book or manual carried on one's person for ready reference; a handbook, a guidebook. E17.
2 Anything useful commonly carried about or kept available for use by a person. M17.

vadiation /veɪdɪˈeɪʃ(ə)n/ *noun.* Now *rare* or *obsolete.* M18.
[medieval Latin *vadiatio(n-)*, from *vadiat-* pa. ppl stem of *vadiare* give security: see -ATION.]
LAW. The action of requiring or giving a surety or pledge.

vadose /ˈveɪdəʊs, -z/ *adjective.* L19.
[Latin *vadosus*, from *vadum* shallow piece of water: see -OSE[1].]
PHYSICAL GEOGRAPHY. Pertaining to or designating underground water above the water-table. Cf. PHREATIC 1.

vae /vʌɪ/ *noun*. M16.
[Latin = alas.]
†**1** A denunciation; a curse, a woe. M16–M17.
2 *vae victis* /ˈvɪktɪs/ [= woe to the conquered], (a cry noting or calling for) the humiliation of the vanquished by their conquerors. Orig. & chiefly as *interjection*. E17.

> **2** S. BELLOW Life is hard. *Vae victis!* The wretched must suffer.

va-et-vient /va e vjɛ̃/ *noun*. E20.
[French, lit. 'goes-and-comes'.]
Coming and going, toing and froing; exchange; bandying (of argument).

†**vafrous** *adjective*. M16–E18.
[from Latin *vafer*: see -OUS.]
Sly, cunning, crafty, shifty.

vag /vag/ *noun & verb*. *N. Amer. & Austral. slang*. M19.
[Abbreviation.]
▶**A** *noun*. A vagrant; vagrancy. M19.

> S. KING I've been travelling around but I'm not a vag. **on the vag** on a charge of vagrancy.

▶**B** *verb trans*. Infl. **-gg-**. Charge with vagrancy; treat as a vagrant. L19.

vagabond /ˈvagəbɒnd/ *noun & adjective*. ME.
[Old & mod. French, or from Latin *vagabundus*, from *vagari* wander: cf. VAGRANT.]
▶**A** *noun*. **1** Orig., a criminal. Later, a disreputable, idle, or worthless person; a rascal, a rogue. ME.
2 A homeless person who wanders about from place to place; *spec*. an itinerant beggar, a tramp, a vagrant. L15. ▸**b** A nomad. *rare*. M18.
3 More fully ***vagabond hat***. = SLOUCH *noun* 3. E20.

> **1** D. PAE What are you lying there for, you lazy vagabond? **2 vagabond's disease, vagabond's skin** a dark leather-like condition of the skin caused by long-term scratching and exposure.

▶**B** *adjective*. **1** Roaming or wandering from place to place without settled habitation; leading a wandering life; nomadic. LME. ▸**b** Of, pertaining to, or characteristic of a homeless wanderer. L16.
2 *fig*. Roving, straying; not subject to control or restraint. LME.
3 Leading an unsettled, irregular, or disreputable life; good-for-nothing, worthless; dissolute. L15.

> **2** F. QUARLES My heart is . . a vagabond and unstable heart.

■ **Vagaˈbondia** *noun* (*US*) the realm or world of vagabonds L19. **vagaˈbondical** *adjective* (*rare*) roaming, wandering; vagabondish: L16. **vagabondish** *adjective* pertaining to, characteristic of, or resembling a vagabond or vagabonds E19. **vagabondism** *noun* = VAGABONDAGE 1 E19. **vagabondize** *verb intrans*. & (now *rare* or *obsolete*) *trans*. (with *it*) live or wander as or like a vagabond; roam or travel in a free, idle, or unconventional manner: E17. **vagabondry** *noun* (now *rare*) = VAGABONDAGE 1 M16.

vagabond /ˈvagəbɒnd/ *verb intrans*. & *trans*. (with *it*). L16.
[from VAGABOND *noun*.]
Roam or wander (*about*) as or like a vagabond or vagrant. Freq. as ***vagabonding*** *ppl adjective*.

vagabondage /ˈvagəbɒndɪdʒ/ *noun*. E19.
[French, or from VAGABOND *noun* + -AGE.]
1 The state, condition, or character of a vagabond; life or conduct characteristic of a vagabond; idle or unconventional wandering or travelling. E19.
2 Vagabonds collectively. *rare*. M19.

vagal /ˈveɪg(ə)l/ *adjective*. M19.
[from VAGUS + -AL[1].]
ANATOMY & MEDICINE. Designating, of, or pertaining to the vagus nerve; affecting the vagus nerve.
■ **vagally** *adverb* by, or by means of, the vagus nerve M20.

vagancy /ˈveɪg(ə)nsi/ *noun*. *rare*. M17.
[from next: see -ANCY.]
Wandering, strolling; an instance of this.

†**vagant** *adjective*. LME.
[Old French *vaga(u)nt*, or from Latin *vagant-* pres. ppl stem of *vagari* wander: see -ANT[1].]
1 Wandering, roaming, or travelling from place to place; having no settled home. LME–L16.
2 Devious, erratic. *rare*. LME–E18.

vagantes /vəˈganti:z, -teɪz/ *noun pl*. E20.
[Latin, nom. pl. of *vagans* pres. pple of *vagari* wander.]
Itinerant medieval scholar monks.

vagarious /vəˈgɛ:rɪəs/ *adjective*. L18.
[from VAGARY *noun*.]
†**1** Variable, inconstant, changing. Only in L18.
2 Marked or characterized by vagaries; erratic. E19.
3 Wandering, roving. L19.

vagary /ˈveɪg(ə)ri/ *verb & noun*. L16.
[Latin *vagari* wander, roam.]
▶†**A** *verb intrans*. Wander, roam. L16–L18.
▶**B** *noun*. †**1** A wandering or devious journey or tour; an excursion, a ramble. L16–E19.
†**2** An act of wandering or straying from the subject under consideration; a digression. L16–M18.
3 A departure from regular or usual norms of conduct or propriety; a frolic, a prank. Now *rare* or *obsolete* exc. as passing into sense 4. L16.
4 A capricious, outlandish, or eccentric act or notion; a caprice, a whim. Freq. foll. by *of*. E17.

> **4** G. H. NAPHEYS To follow the vagaries of fashion. L. AUCHINCLOSS Kitty shrugged as if the vagaries of the male sex were beyond her.

†**vagation** *noun*. ME–E18.
[Latin *vagatio(n-)*, from *vagari* wander: see -ATION.]
The action of wandering or departing from the proper or regular course (*lit. & fig.*); an instance of this.

vagi *noun* pl. of VAGUS.

vagile /ˈveɪdʒʌɪl, ˈvadʒ-, ˈveɪg-/ *adjective*. E20.
[from Latin *vagus* wandering, straying + -ILE.]
BIOLOGY. Of an organism or group of organisms: having the ability to disperse or be dispersed in a given environment.
■ **vagility** /vəˈdʒɪlɪti/ *noun* the quality of being vagile M20.

vagina /vəˈdʒʌɪnə/ *noun*. Pl. **-nas**, **-nae** /-ni:/. L17.
[Latin = sheath, scabbard.]
1 a ANATOMY. A canal leading from the vulva to the cervix of the uterus in women and most female mammals. L17. ▸**b** ZOOLOGY. An analogous canal in some invertebrates. E19.
2 †**a** ZOOLOGY. A part or structure serving as or resembling a sheath; a theca. E18–E19. ▸**b** BOTANY. = SHEATH *noun*[1] 2(b). E18.
1 vagina dentata /dɛnˈtɑ:tə/ the motif or theme of a vagina equipped with teeth which occurs in myth, folklore, and fantasy, and is said to symbolize fear of castration, the dangers of sexual intercourse, of birth or rebirth, etc.

vaginal /vəˈdʒʌɪn(ə)l, ˈvadʒɪn(ə)l/ *adjective*. E18.
[from prec. + -AL[1].]
1 a ANATOMY. Of the nature of, or having the form or function of, a sheath; *spec*. pertaining to the tunica vaginalis. E18. ▸**b** BOTANY. Pertaining to the sheath of a leaf etc. M19.
2 a Of, pertaining to, or affecting the vagina. E19. ▸**b** MEDICINE. Of a surgical instrument: used in dealing with or operating on the vagina. L19.
2a vaginal plug ZOOLOGY a secretion which blocks the vagina of some rodents and insectivores after mating.
■ **vaˈginally** *adverb* via the vagina E20.

vaginant /ˈvadʒɪnənt/ *adjective*. M18.
[mod. Latin *vaginant-*, from Latin VAGINA: see -ANT[1].]
BOTANY. Forming a vagina round the stem; sheathing.

vaginate /ˈvadʒɪneɪt/ *adjective*. *rare*. M19.
[from VAGINA + -ATE[2].]
Enclosed in a sheath or vagina.
■ Also †**vaginated** *adjective* L17–M19.

vaginismus /vadʒɪˈnɪzməs/ *noun*. M19.
[mod. Latin, from VAGINA: see -ISM.]
MEDICINE. Painful spasmodic contraction of the vagina in response to physical contact or pressure (esp. in sexual intercourse).

vaginitis /vadʒɪˈnʌɪtɪs/ *noun*. M19.
[formed as prec. + -ITIS.]
MEDICINE. Inflammation of the vagina.

vaginoplasty /vəˈdʒʌɪnə(ʊ)plasti/ *noun*. M20.
[from VAGIN(A + -O- + -PLASTY.]
MEDICINE. (An instance of) the creation of a vagina by plastic surgery.

vaginula /vəˈdʒɪnjʊlə/ *noun*. Pl. **-lae** /-li:/. M19.
[mod. Latin, dim. of VAGINA: see -ULE.]
Chiefly BOTANY. A little sheath; *esp*. (in certain mosses) the enlarged lower half of the archegonium, which forms a sheath round the base of the seta.

vagitus /vəˈdʒʌɪtəs/ *noun*. M17.
[Latin, from *vagire* utter cries of distress, wail.]
A cry, a wail, *spec*. that of a newborn child.

vagolytic /veɪgə(ʊ)ˈlɪtɪk/ *adjective & noun*. M20.
[from VAGUS + -O- + -LYTIC.]
MEDICINE. ▶**A** *adjective*. Acting to disrupt or impede the activity of the vagus nerve. M20.
▶**B** *noun*. A vagolytic agent. M20.

vagotomy /veɪˈgɒtəmi/ *noun*. E20.
[from VAGUS + -O- + -TOMY.]
MEDICINE & PHYSIOLOGY. (An instance of) a surgical operation in which the vagus nerve is cut, either as a research technique or as a means of reducing the rate of gastric secretion.
■ **vagotomized** *adjective* that has been subjected to vagotomy M20.

vagotonia /veɪgəˈtəʊnɪə/ *noun*. E20.
[formed as prec. + Greek *tonos* TONE *noun* + -IA[1].]
PHYSIOLOGY. The state or condition in which there is increased influence of the parasympathetic nervous system and increased excitability of the vagus nerve. Cf. SYMPATHICOTONIA.
■ **vagotonic** /-ˈtɒnɪk/ *adjective* displaying or promoting vagotonia E20. **vaˈgotony** *noun* = VAGOTONIA L20.

vagous /ˈveɪgəs/ *adjective*. Long *rare*. M17.
[from Latin *vagus* (see VAGUE *adjective*) + -OUS.]
Vagrant, vague; *esp*. (**a**) not kept within reasonable bounds, inordinate; (**b**) irregular, unsettled, wandering.

vagrancy /ˈveɪgr(ə)nsi/ *noun*. M17.
[from VAGRANT *adjective*: see -ANCY.]
1 Mental wandering, vacillation, or digression; an instance of this. M17.
2 The state, condition, or action of roaming or wandering from place to place; an instance of this. L17. ▸**b** *spec*. Idle wandering with no settled home, job, or obvious means of support; the life or behaviour characteristic of a vagrant. E18.
■ Also **vagrance** *noun* (*rare*) M18.

vagrant /ˈveɪgr(ə)nt/ *noun & adjective*. LME.
[Anglo-Norman *vagrant*, *vagraunt(e)*, perh. alt. of *wakerant*, *wa(l)crant* by assoc. with Old & mod. French *vaguer*, Latin *vagari* wander: see -ANT[1].]
▶**A** *noun*. **1** A person with no settled home or regular work who wanders from place to place, subsisting by begging or other unlawful means (chiefly LAW); a tramp, a vagabond. LME.
2 A person who roams about or leads a wandering life; a rover. L16.
3 ORNITHOLOGY. A bird which has strayed or been blown beyond its usual range. E20.
▶**B** *adjective*. **1** Living illegally in vagrancy; being an itinerant beggar. LME.
2 *fig*. Wandering, roving; inconstant, unsettled, wayward. E16.
3 Leading a wandering or nomadic life; ranging or roaming from place to place. Later also *transf*., (of a plant etc.) rambling, straggling. M16.
4 Of, pertaining to, or characteristic of a vagrant or wanderer. L16.
5 Of a thing: not fixed or stationary; moving, esp. unpredictably. L16.
■ **vagrantize** *verb trans*. (*rare*) †(**a**) arrest as a vagrant; (**b**) reduce to the condition of a vagrant: L18. **vagrantly** *adverb* as a vagrant; in a vagrant or wandering manner: M16.

vagrom /ˈveɪgrəm/ *adjective*. *arch*. L16.
[Alt. of VAGRANT *adjective*.]
Vagrant, vagabond, wandering, (with allus. to Shakes. *Much Ado*).

vague /vag/ *noun*[1]. Pl. pronounced same. M20.
[French, lit. 'wave'.]
A movement, a trend. Cf. NOUVELLE VAGUE.

vague /veɪg/ *adjective*, *noun*[2], & *adverb*. M16.
[French, or from Latin *vagus* wandering, inconstant, uncertain.]
▶**A** *adjective*. **1** Of a statement etc.: couched in general, indefinite, or imprecise terms; deficient in details or particulars. M16. ▸**b** Of the Egyptian month or year: beginning at varying seasons; movable, shifting. M17.
2 Of language, a word, etc.: imprecise; of uncertain or ill-defined meaning. L17.
3 Of an idea, notion, feeling, sensation, etc.: lacking in definiteness, difficult to formulate; unclear, indistinct. E18.
4 Lacking physical definiteness of form or outline; indistinctly seen or perceived; formless, shadowy. E19.
5 Of a person, the mind, etc.: unable to think clearly or precisely; indefinite or inexact in thought, expression, or understanding. E19.

> **4** R. DAVIES Naked, but decently vague about the crotch. **5** F. BRANSTON He was a bit vague about the specifics.

▶**B** *noun*. *The* vague aspect or consideration of things; *the* indefinite expanse *of* something. M19.
in the vague in a vague state, uncertain; without entering into details, in general.
▶**C** *adverb*. Vaguely; indistinctly. Chiefly in comb. *poet*. M19.
■ **vagueness** *noun* the quality or condition of being vague; an instance of this: L18. **vaguish** *adjective* somewhat vague E19.

vague /veɪg/ *verb intrans*. Chiefly *Scot*. Now *rare*. LME.
[Latin *vagari* wander.]
Wander; roam idly or as a vagrant.

vaguely /ˈveɪgli/ *adverb*. L18.
[from VAGUE *adjective* + -LY[2].]
1 In a vague, indefinite, or imprecise manner; to a slight but indeterminate degree; in vague terms. L18. ▸**b** Dimly, obscurely, indistinctly. L19.
2 Without attention or concentration; idly, vacantly. E19.

1 LD MACAULAY A motion .. so vaguely worded that it could hardly be said to mean any thing. K. VONNEGUT I was vaguely ill, still a little drunk. **b** E. WAUGH Binoculars which she remembered vaguely having lent to the scout-master. **2** SIR W. SCOTT Listening vaguely to what the magistrate was saying.

vagus /ˈveɪɡəs/ *noun.* Pl. **vagi** /ˈveɪdʒʌɪ/. **M19.**
[Latin = wandering, straying.]
ANATOMY. In full ***vagus nerve***. Either of the tenth pair of cranial nerves, which supply the upper digestive tract and the organs of the chest cavity and abdomen.

vahana /ˈvɑːhənə/ *noun.* Also **-han** /-hən/. **E19.**
[Sanskrit *vāhana* lit. 'conveyance.']
INDIAN MYTHOLOGY. The mount or vehicle of a god.

vahine /vaˈhine, vɑːˈhiːni/ *noun.* **M20.**
[Tahitian: cf. WAHINE.]
A Tahitian woman or wife.

Vai /vʌɪ/ *noun & adjective.* Also **Vei**. **M19.**
[Vai.]
▶ **A** *noun.* Pl. same, **-s**.
1 A member of a people of the southern coasts of Liberia and Sierra Leone. **M19.**
2 The language of this people. **M20.**
▶ **B** *attrib.* or as *adjective.* Of or pertaining to the Vai or their language. **M19.**

†**vaik** *verb* var. of VAKE.

vail /veɪl/ *noun*¹. Now *arch. & dial.* **LME.**
[from VAIL *verb*¹. Cf. AVAIL *noun*.]
▶ **I** **1** †**a** Advantage, benefit, profit. **LME–M16.** ▶**b** Advance, progress. *dial.* **M19.**
†**2** Value, worth; account, estimation. *Scot.* **L15–M16.**
▶ **II** †**3** = PERQUISITE 3. Usu. in *pl.* **LME–M19.** ▶**b** A gift in the nature of a bribe. **L17.**
4 In *pl.* Leftover materials or scraps customarily appropriated by a servant, worker, etc. Cf. PERQUISITE 3b. Now *rare* or *obsolete.* **L16.**
5 In *pl.* & (*rare*) *sing.* A gratuity for services rendered, a tip; *spec.* one given to the servants of a house by a departing guest. **E17.**

†**vail** *noun*². *rare* (Shakes.). Only in **E17.**
[from VAIL *verb*².]
The going down or setting *of* the sun.

†**vail** *verb*¹. **ME.**
[Old French *vail-* tonic stem of *valoir* be of value, from Latin *valere* be strong, powerful, or of value. Cf. AVAIL *verb*.]
1 *verb intrans.* Be of use, service, value, or profit (*to* a person etc., (with impers. *it*) *to do*). Usu. in neg. & interrog. contexts. **ME–E17.**
2 *verb trans.* Be of use, advantage, or benefit to, assist or help, (a person etc.) Freq. with impers. *it* (foll. by *that*, *to do*). **ME–E19.**

vail /veɪl/ *verb*². *arch.* Orig. †**vale**. **ME.**
[Aphet. from AVALE.]
▶ **I** *verb trans.* **1** Cause or allow to go down or drop; *esp.* lower (a weapon or banner, the eyes or head, a sail, etc.) as a sign of submission or respect. **ME.**
2 Take off (one's hat, crown, plumes, etc.) as a sign of submission or respect. **LME.**
3 *fig.* Humble, yield, (one's pride, heart, courage, etc.); submit or subject (one thing) *to* (another). **L16.**

1 F. QUARLES What dire disaster bred This change, that thus she vails her golden head? J. KEBLE Go .. teach proud Science where to vail her brow. **2 vail bonnet, vail one's bonnet, vail the bonnet** *fig.* show respect or submission, acknowledge defeat or inferiority. **3** JOSEPH HALL No reason why you should vail your owne just advantage to another mans excesse.

▶ **II** *verb intrans.* †**4** Fall (*down*); descend. **LME–E17.**
†**5** NAUTICAL. Lower the sail. **E16–M17.**
6 Of a hat: be taken off as a sign of submission or respect. *rare.* **M16.**
7 Take off one's hat (*to* a person etc.) as a sign of respect. **L16.**
8 *fig.* Submit, yield, or give way *to*. **E17.** ▶**b** Do homage *to* a person. *rare* (Shakes.). Only in **E17.**

8 L. MURRAY They all vail to the English idiom, and scruple not to acknowledge its superiority.

vain /veɪn/ *adjective & noun.* **ME.**
[Old & mod. French *vain(e)* from Latin *vanus* empty, without substance.]
▶ **A** *adjective.* **1** Devoid of real value, worth, or significance; idle, unprofitable, useless; ineffectual; fruitless, futile. **ME.**
†**2** Empty, vacant, void. **LME–M16.**
3 Of a person: lacking sense or wisdom; foolish, thoughtless; of an idle or futile disposition. Now *rare* or *obsolete.* **LME.**
4 Having an excessively high opinion of one's own appearance, abilities, worth, etc.; delighting in or desirous of attracting the admiration of others; conceited, proud. Also foll. by *of*. **LME.**

1 J. RUSKIN All literature, art, and science are vain .. if they do not enable you to be glad. D. M. FRAME It is .. vain to try to be other than we are. *New York Review of Books* The vain attempts of feminist critics to prove there is a .. 'women's language'. **3** SHAKES. *Com. Err.* This I think, there's no man is so vain That would refuse so fair an offer'd chain. **4** E. TEMPLETON I am still vain enough to be pleased when my theories are confirmed. J. HARVEY He evidently exercised and was vain of his figure.

Phrases: †**for vain** (*rare*, Shakes.) in vain, for nothing. **in vain** to no effect or purpose; ineffectually, uselessly. ***labour in vain***: see LABOUR *noun.* **take a person's name in vain** use a person's name (formerly esp. that of God) lightly or profanely; mention or speak of a person casually or irreverently.
▶ †**B** *noun.* **1** Vanity; a vain thing. **ME–M18.**
2 Emptiness, vacant space. *rare.* **LME–E16.**

1 O. FELTHAM The power of the Gospel, in crying down the vains of men.

■ **vainful** *adjective* (*obsolete* exc. *dial.*) vain, unprofitable, useless **E16. vainly** *adverb* in a vain futile manner; in vain: **LME. vainness** /-n-n-/ *noun* the state or condition of being vain; futility, ineffectiveness, uselessness; (now *rare*) vanity, conceit: **LME.**

vainglorious /veɪnˈɡlɔːrɪəs/ *adjective.* **LME.**
[from VAINGLORY *noun*, after Old French *vaneglorieus*, medieval Latin *vanagloriosus* (*vaniglorius*).]
1 Filled with, given to, or indulging in, vainglory; inordinately boastful or proud of one's own abilities, worth, etc.; excessively and ostentatiously vain. Formerly foll. by *of*. **LME.**
2 Characterized by or indicative of vainglory. **M16.**

1 B. TARKINGTON He was vainglorious in his triumph. **2** R. L. STEVENSON Admirals were full of heroic superstitions, and had a strutting and vainglorious style of fight.

■ **vaingloriously** *adverb* **M16. vaingloriousness** *noun* **M16.**

vainglory /veɪnˈɡlɔːri/ *noun & verb.* **ME.**
[from VAIN *adjective* + GLORY *noun* after Old & mod. French *vaine gloire*, Latin *vana gloria*.]
▶ **A** *noun.* **1** Glory or renown that is vain or worthless; inordinate pride in one's abilities, worth, etc.; excessive vanity or boastfulness. **ME.**
†**2** A vainglorious thing, action, etc. *rare.* **LME–E18.**

1 A. WILSON His apprehensions of disaster brought on by overreaching and vainglory. **2** SHAKES. *Timon* What needs these feasts, pomps, and vainglories?

▶ **B** *verb. rare.*
†**1** *verb refl.* Praise (oneself) unduly. Only in **M17.**
2 *verb intrans.* Indulge in vainglory. **L19.**

vair /vɛː/ *noun.* **ME.**
[Old & mod. French, from Latin *varius*: see VARIOUS.]
1 Fur obtained from a variety of red squirrel with grey back and white belly, much used in the 13th and 14th cents. as a trimming or lining for garments. Now *arch.* or *Hist.* **ME.**
2 A weasel, a stoat. Now *dial.* **LME.**
3 HERALDRY. One of the two chief furs, consisting of small angular bell- and cup-shaped figures, usu. of the two tinctures azure and argent, placed alternately so as to fill the space concerned. Cf. ERMINE *noun* 3, VAIRY 1. **M16.**

vairy /ˈvɛːri/ *adjective & noun.* Also †**varr(e)y**. **L15.**
[Old French, formed as prec. + -Y⁵.]
1 HERALDRY. (A fur) filled with figures like those of vair, esp. when of tinctures other than azure and argent. **L15.**
2 (Trimmed or lined with) vair (the fur). *rare.* **E18.**

Vaishnava /ˈvʌɪʃnəvə/ *noun & adjective.* **L18.**
[Sanskrit *vaiṣṇava* relating to Vishnu; a worshipper or follower of Vishnu.]
HINDUISM. ▶**A** *noun.* A member of one of the principal Hindu sects, devoted to the worship of the god Vishnu as the supreme being. **L18.**
▶ **B** *adjective.* Of or pertaining to this Hindu sect. **L19.**
■ **Vaishnavism** *noun* = VISHNUISM **L19. Vaishnavite** *adjective* of or pertaining to Vaishnavas or Vishnuism **E20.**

Vaisya /ˈvʌɪʃjə/ *noun.* Also **Vaishya**. **M17.**
[Sanskrit *vaiśya* peasant, tradesman.]
A member of the third of the four main Hindu castes.

vaivode /ˈveɪvəʊd/ *noun.* **M16.**
[(mod. Latin *vayvoda* or French *vayvode*) ult. from Hungarian *vajvoda* (now *vajda*) from Slavonic base also of VOIVODE. Cf. WAYWODE.]
= VOIVODE.

vajra /ˈvʌdʒrə/ *noun.* **L18.**
[Sanskrit.]
HINDUISM & BUDDHISM. (A representation of) a thunderbolt or mythical weapon, *esp.* one wielded by the god Indra.

†**vake** *verb intrans.* Chiefly *Scot.* Also **vaik**. **LME.**
[Latin *vacare* be empty.]
1 Of an office or position, esp. an ecclesiastical benefice: become or fall vacant; remain vacant or unfilled. **LME–E18.**
2 Of a person: have time or leisure for engaging in an activity; be occupied or busy. Freq. foll. by *for*, *(up)on*. **LME–E17.** ▶**b** Be free *from* an activity or occupation. **L15–L16.**

vakeel /vəˈkiːl/ *noun. Indian subcontinent.* Also **vakil**. **E17.**
[Persian & Urdu *wakīl*, Turkish *vakīl* from Arab. *wakīl*.]
1 An agent, a representative, esp. of a person of political importance; a minister, an envoy, an ambassador. **E17.**
2 An attorney, a barrister; a pleader in the lawcourts. **L18.**

vakky *noun* var. of VACKY.

Val /val/ *noun. colloq.* (orig. *US*). **L19.**
[Abbreviation.]
In full ***Val lace***. = ***VALENCIENNES lace***.

Valaisan /vaˈleɪz(ə)n/ *noun & adjective.* **L18.**
[from *Valais* a French-speaking canton in SW Switzerland + -AN: cf. next.]
▶ **A** *noun.* A native or inhabitant of Valais. **L18.**
▶ **B** *adjective.* Of or pertaining to Valais or its people. **L20.**

Valaisian /vaˈleɪzɪən/ *noun & adjective.* **M19.**
[formed as prec. + -IAN.]
= prec.

valance /ˈval(ə)ns/ *noun & verb.* As noun also **-lence**. **LME.**
[Perh. Anglo-Norman, from *valer* aphet. from Old & mod. French *avaler*: see AVALE, -ANCE; perh. from use as noun of pl. of pres. pple of *valer*.]
▶ **A** *noun.* **1** A vertical hanging drapery attached lengthways to a canopy, altar-cloth, etc. **LME.**
2 *spec.* **a** A border of drapery hanging round the canopy of a bed; now *esp.*, a short curtain around the frame of a bedstead serving to screen the space underneath. **LME.** ▶**b** A pelmet. **E18.**
3 a A border or edging of velvet, leather, wood, etc. **L17.** ▶**b** A flap attached to a head-dress, esp. as a protection against the sun. *rare.* **L18.** ▶**c** A protective panel extending below the basic chassis construction of a motor vehicle. **M20.**
▶ **B** *verb trans. rare.* Provide, drape, or fringe (as) with a valance. **M19.**

valanced /ˈval(ə)nst/ *adjective.* **LME.**
[from VALANCE *noun* + -ED².]
1 Provided or draped with a valance. **LME.**
2 *transf.* Fringed with hair. **E17.**

Val-A-Pak *noun* see VALPACK.

Valdepeñas /valdɪˈpenjəs, *foreign* baldeˈpeɲas/ *noun.* **M19.**
[See below.]
A red or dry white wine from the district of Valdepeñas in the province of La Mancha, southern Spain.

Valdez Principles /valˈdiːz ˈprɪnsɪp(ə)lz/ *noun phr. pl.* **L20.**
[The Exxon *Valdez*, an oil tanker which ran aground off the Alaskan coast in 1989, causing considerable environmental damage.]
A set of guidelines drawn up in 1989, designed to regulate and monitor the conduct of corporations in matters relating to the environment.

vale /veɪl/ *noun*¹. Now *arch.* or *poet.* exc. in place-names. **ME.**
[Old & mod. French *val* from Latin *valles*, *vallis*: cf. VALLEY.]
1 A valley, *esp.* one which is comparatively wide and flat. **ME.**
2 *fig.* The world in general, esp. as regarded as a place or time of suffering or trouble; the world regarded as the scene of one's earthly existence. Freq. foll. by *of*. **LME.**

1 WORDSWORTH A slumber seems to steal O'er vale, and mountain. DAY LEWIS Haunted by the rainshine of orchards in the vale of Evesham. ***lily of the vale***: see LILY *noun.* **2** SHAKES. *2 Hen. VI* Great is his comfort in this earthly vale Although by his sight his sin be multiplied. **the vale of years** *literary* the declining years of a person's life; old age. **vale of tears** *literary* the world or one's earthly existence regarded as a place of sorrow or trouble (also ***valley of tears***).

Comb.: **vale-lily** *poet.* lily of the valley.

†**vale** *verb* see VAIL *verb*².

vale /ˈvɑːleɪ/ *interjection & noun*². **M16.**
[Latin, imper. of *valere* be strong or well.]
▶ **A** *interjection.* Farewell; goodbye. **M16.**
▶ **B** *noun.* A written or spoken farewell; a goodbye. **L16.**

valediction /valɪˈdɪkʃ(ə)n/ *noun.* **M17.**
[from Latin *vale* (see VALE *interjection & noun*²) or *valedict-* pa. ppl stem of *valedicere* say 'vale', after BENEDICTION: see -ION.]
1 The action of saying farewell; an instance of this; a farewell. **M17.**
2 A statement, address, etc., made at (or by way of) leave-taking or saying farewell. **M17.**

1 R. MACAULAY A gesture of dignified valediction before departure into the unknown.

valedictory /valɪˈdɪkt(ə)ri/ *adjective & noun.* **M17.**
[from prec. + -ORY².]
▶ **A** *adjective.* **1** Spoken or delivered on taking farewell; of the nature of a valediction. **M17.**
2 Performed or done by way of valediction. **E19.**

2 B. CHATWIN It was Utz who had arranged .. this valedictory breakfast.

▸**B** *noun*. **1** An oration or farewell address usu. given by the highest-ranking member of a graduating class at a N. American high school, college, or university. **L18.**

2 A valedictory statement or address made on leaving a position, person, etc. **L19.**

■ **valedictorian** /-ˈtɔːrɪən/ *noun* (*N. Amer.*) a student who delivers a valedictory **M18.** **valedictorily** *adverb* (*rare*) **M19.**

valence /ˈveɪləns/ *noun*[1]. **LME.**
[Var. of VALENCY: see -ENCE.]
†**1** An extract or preparation (*of* a herb) used in medicine. Only in **LME.**
†**2** Valour, courage; valiance. *rare*. Only in **E17.**
3 *CHEMISTRY & PHYSICS*. = VALENCY 2. Now usu. *attrib.* & in *comb.* **L19.**
4 *PSYCHOLOGY*. Emotional force or significance, *spec.* the extent to which an individual is attracted or repelled by an object, event, or person. **E20.**
5 *LINGUISTICS*. = VALENCY 3. **M20.**
Comb.: **valence band** *CHEMISTRY & PHYSICS* the energy band that contains the valence electrons in a solid and is the highest filled or partly filled band; **valence bond** *CHEMISTRY & PHYSICS* orig., a chemical bond thought of in terms of atomic valencies; now, one described in terms of individual valence electrons rather than molecular orbitals; **valence electron** *CHEMISTRY & PHYSICS* any of the electrons of an atom that are involved when it forms a bond with another atom, i.e. those in the outer shell; **valence grammar** *LINGUISTICS* = *VALENCY grammar*; **valence quark** *PARTICLE PHYSICS* any quark whose presence as a constituent of a particle contributes towards the spectroscopic properties of that particle; **valence shell** *CHEMISTRY & PHYSICS* the outer shell of an atom, containing the valency electrons.

valence *noun*[2] var. of VALANCE *noun*.

Valencia /vəˈlɛnsɪə/ *noun*. **L18.**
[A province, town, and former kingdom of eastern Spain.]
▸**I 1** Used *attrib.* to designate things originating from or associated with Valencia. **L18.**
Valencia almond, *Valencia raisin*, etc. **Valencia orange** a late-ripening variety of sweet orange.
▸**II 2** (Also **v-**.) A mixed fabric mainly used for livery waistcoats, with a worsted weft and a silk or cotton warp, and usu. striped. Also, a lightweight twilled English suit and dress fabric made of woollen (or wool and silk) yarns. **M19.**
3 *ellipt.* **a** A Valencia almond or raisin; a type of raisin similar to that from Valencia. **M19.** ▸**b** A Valencia orange. **L19.**
■ **Valencian** *noun* & *adjective* (*a*) *noun* a native or inhabitant of Valencia; the Catalan dialect of Valencia; (*b*) *adjective* of or pertaining to Valencia or the Valencians: **M18.**

Valenciennes /vaˌlɒnsɪˈɛn, valɑ̃sjɛn/ *noun*. **E18.**
[A town in NE France.]
A variety of fine bobbin lace originally made at Valenciennes in the 17th and 18th cents. (also more fully *Valenciennes lace*); a ruffle or trimming made of this lace.

valency /ˈveɪl(ə)nsi/ *noun*. **E17.**
[Latin *valentia* power, competence, from *valere* be powerful: see -ENCY.]
†**1** Might, power, strength. Only in Dicts. **E–M17.**
2 *CHEMISTRY*. The power or capacity of an atom or group to combine with or displace other atoms or groups in the formation of compounds, equivalent to the number of hydrogen atoms that it could combine with or displace; a unit of this. Cf. VALENCE *noun*[1] 3. **M19.** ▸**b** *IMMUNOLOGY*. The combining power of an antibody (i.e. the number of binding sites). **M20.**
3 *LINGUISTICS*. The power of a grammatical element, esp. a verb, to govern other elements in the same sentence; *spec.* the number of noun phrases with which a verb combines in some relation. **L20.**
Comb.: **valency dictionary**: setting out the syntactic and collocational patterns of words; **valency electron** *PHYSICS* = *valence electron* s.v. VALENCE *noun*[1]; **valency grammar** *LINGUISTICS* a syntactic system by which verbs have particular valencies.

valenki /ˈvalənki/ *noun pl.* **M20.**
[Russian, pl. of *valenok*, *valenka* felt boot.]
Felt boots of a kind worn in Russia.

valent /ˈveɪl(ə)nt/ *noun*. **M18.**
[Latin, 3rd person pl. pres. indic. of *valere* be of worth.]
SCOTS LAW (now *Hist.*). The value or worth of an estate or a piece of land. Chiefly as below.
Comb.: **valent clause** the clause in a retour of special service in which the old and new extent of the lands are specified.

-valent /ˈveɪl(ə)nt/ *suffix*.
[from Latin *valent-* pres. ppl stem of *valere* be strong: see -ENT.]
1 Esp. *CHEMISTRY & IMMUNOLOGY*. Forming adjectives with the sense 'having a valency of the specified number', as ***monovalent***, ***divalent***, ***multivalent***; ***univalent***, ***bivalent***, ***polyvalent***.
2 *CYTOLOGY*. Forming adjectives and nouns with the sense '(a meiotic structure) composed of the specified number of chromosomes' as ***univalent***, ***bivalent***, ***quadrivalent***.
¶ Although the suffix is of Latin origin, the Greek-derived porefixes (*mono-*, *di-*, etc.) are now more usual in *Chem.* than the Latin ones (*uni-*, *bi-*, etc.).

†**valentia** *noun*. *rare*. **L17–E19.**
[Spanish *venencia* from *avenencia* agreement, from *avenir* come to (Latin *advenire*).]
= VALINCHE.

†**Valentide** *noun*. *rare* (Spenser). Only in **L16.**
[from VALENTINE *noun* + TIDE *noun*.]
St Valentine's day; the time of year when this festival falls.

valentine /ˈvaləntʌɪn/ *noun* & *verb*. **LME.**
[Old & mod. French *Valentin* from Latin *Valentinus* name of either of two Italian saints whose festival falls on 14 February.]
▸**A** *noun*. **1** ***St Valentine's day***, ***Valentine's day***, 14 February (traditionally associated with the choosing of sweethearts and the mating of birds). ***St Valentine's eve*** (*arch.*), the eve of St Valentine's day. **LME.**
2 A person chosen (formerly also drawn by lot) on St Valentine's day, as a sweetheart or special friend. **LME.** ▸†**b** God or one of the Saints chosen as a patron by a worshipper. **LME–M17.**
3 †**a** A folded paper bearing the name of a person to be drawn as a valentine. **M16–L18.** ▸**b** A gift sent to one's chosen sweetheart or friend on St Valentine's day. Now chiefly *US*. **E17.** ▸**c** A letter or (now esp.) a card, usu. with verses or other words of a romantic or light-hearted nature, sent (often anonymously) on St Valentine's day as a token of love or affection. Also ***valentine card***. **E19.**

🕮 **2** O. NASH No thrill of premonition . . Foreshadowed the appearance Of my only valentine.

▸**B** *verb*. **1** *verb trans.* & *intrans.* Of a bird: sing to (a mate). *poet. rare*. **M19.**
2 *verb intrans.* Of children: go from house to house on St Valentine's Day soliciting small gifts. Chiefly as ***valentining*** *verbal noun*. *dial.* **M19.**

Valentinian /valənˈtɪnɪən/ *noun* & *adjective*. **LME.**
[ecclesiastical Latin *Valentinianus*, from *Valentinus* (see below) + -IAN.]
▸**A** *noun*. A follower of the Egyptian heresiarch Valentinus (fl. AD 150), founder of a Gnostic sect. **LME.**
▸**B** *adjective*. Of or pertaining to the Valentinians or their doctrine. **L16.**
■ **Valentinianism** *noun* (*rare*) the Valentinian doctrine **L19.**

Valentino /valənˈtiːnəʊ/ *noun* & *adjective*. **E20.**
[Rudolph *Valentino* (Rodolfo Guglielmi di Valentino, 1895–1926), Italian-born American film star noted for his roles as a romantic and dashing lover.]
▸**A** *noun*. Pl. **-os**. Orig., a gigolo. Now, a man having the sort of romantic good looks associated with Rudolph Valentino. **E20.**
▸**B** *attrib.* or as *adjective*. Designating looks, actions, etc., associated with or characteristic of the roles played by Rudolph Valentino. **M20.**

valeraldehyde /valəˈraldɪhʌɪd/ *noun*. **M19.**
[from VALERIC + ALDEHYDE.]
CHEMISTRY. A flammable liquid, $CH_3(CH_2)_3CHO$, which has an unpleasant odour and is produced by the oxidation of amyl alcohol.

valerian /vəˈlɪərɪən/ *noun*. **LME.**
[Old & mod. French *valériane* from medieval Latin *valeriana* (sc. *herba* plant), app. fem. sing. of Latin adjective *Valerianus*, from the personal name *Valerius*: see -IAN.]
1 Any of various plants constituting the genus *Valeriana* (family Valerianaceae), with small tubular mostly white or pink flowers in terminal cymes and strong-smelling roots; *esp.* (more fully ***common valerian***, ***wild valerian***) *V. officinalis*, the chief source of the drug valerian (see sense 2). Also (more fully ***red valerian***, ***spur valerian***), a related Mediterranean plant, *Centranthus ruber*, differing in its spurred corolla-tube, which is grown for its red, pink, or white flowers and is widely naturalized. **LME.**
2 *MEDICINE*. A bitter-tasting drug derived from the rootstocks of *Valeriana officinalis* and other species, used as a sedative and antispasmodic. **L18.**

🕮 **1** C. LAMB No less pleased than . . cats . . when they purr over a new-found sprig of valerian. ***garden valerian***: see GARDEN *noun*. ***Greek valerian***: see GREEK *noun* & *adjective*.

■ **valeria'naceous** *adjective* of or pertaining to the Valerianaceae or valerian family **M19.** **valerianate** *noun* (*CHEMISTRY*, now *rare* or *obsolete*) = VALERATE **M19.** **valeri'anic** *adjective* (*CHEMISTRY*, now *rare* or *obsolete*) = VALERIC **M19.**

valeric /vəˈlɛrɪk/ *adjective*. **M19.**
[from VALER(IAN + -IC.]
CHEMISTRY. Derived or obtained from valerian.
valeric acid pentanoic acid.
■ **'valerate** *noun* a salt or ester of valeric acid **M19.** **'valeryl** *noun* the radical of valeric acid, $CH_3(CH_2)_3CO\cdot$ **M19.**

valet /ˈvalɪt, ˈvaleɪ/ *noun* & *verb*. **L15.**
[Old & mod. French, (also †*vaslet*, †*varlet* VARLET), ult. rel. to VASSAL *noun*.]
▸**A** *noun*. **1** *MILITARY*. A footman acting as attendant or servant to a horseman. Now *rare* or *obsolete*. **L15.**
2 A man's personal (usu. male) attendant, responsible for his or her master's clothes, appearance, etc. Now also, a hotel employee performing similar duties for guests. **M16.**
3 A rack on which clothing may be hung to retain its shape. Chiefly *US*. **M20.**
Comb.: **valet-park** *verb trans.* (*N. Amer.*) park (a motor vehicle) on behalf of a restaurant patron; **valet parking** *N. Amer.* a service provided at a restaurant etc., in which an attendant parks patrons' motor vehicles.
▸**B** *verb*. **1** *verb trans.* & *intrans.* Act as a valet (to). **M19.**
2 *verb trans.* Look after (clothes etc.). **M20.**
3 *verb trans.* Clean (a motor vehicle). **L20.**

🕮 **1** D. WELCH He valeted Charles perfectly, putting out . . shirt, trousers, coat, waistcoat and tie.

■ **valetry** /-lɪtri/ *noun* valets collectively; the office or post of valet; the quality of a valet: **E19.**

valeta *noun* var. of VELETA.

valet-de-chambre /valɛ də ʃɑ̃ːbr, ˌvaleɪ də ˈʃɒmbrə/ *noun*. Pl. ***valets-de-chambre*** (pronounced same). **M17.**
[French, lit. 'chamber-valet'.]
= VALET *noun* 2.

valet-de-place /valɛ də plas, ˌvaleɪ də ˈplas/ *noun*. Now *rare*. Pl. ***valets-de-place*** (pronounced same). **M18.**
[French, lit. 'place-servant'.]
A guide, esp. for tourists.

valets-de-chambre, ***valets-de-place*** *nouns* pls. of VALET-DE-CHAMBRE, VALET-DE-PLACE.

valetudinarian /ˌvalɪtjuːdɪˈnɛːrɪən/ *noun* & *adjective*. **E18.**
[formed as next + -IAN: see -ARIAN.]
▸**A** *noun*. A person in poor or indifferent health, *esp.* a person who is constantly or unduly concerned with his or her own health; an invalid. **E18.**
▸**B** *adjective*. = VALETUDINARY *adjective*. **E18.**
■ **valetudinarianism** *noun* the condition of a valetudinarian; tendency to be in poor health or to be unduly concerned about one's health: **E19.** †**valetudinarious** *adjective* having poor health; valetudinary: **M17–E18.**

valetudinary /valɪˈtjuːdɪn(ə)ri/ *adjective* & *noun*. **L16.**
[Latin *valetudinarius* in ill health, from *valetudo*, *-din-* state of health, from *valere* be strong or well: see -ARY[1]. Sense B.2 after medieval Latin *valetudinarium*.]
▸**A** *adjective*. **1** In poor or indifferent health; infirm, delicate; constantly or unduly concerned with one's health. **L16.**
2 Characterized by poor or indifferent health. **E17.**
▸**B** *noun*. †**1** An infirmary, a hospital. *rare*. Only in **17.**
2 A valetudinarian. **L18.**

valgus /ˈvalgəs/ *noun* & *adjective*. **E19.**
[Latin = knock-kneed.]
MEDICINE. ▸**A** *noun*. Any deformity of a limb joint which causes a distal bone or bones to be displaced obliquely outwards (orig. inwards), as in knock-knee and some forms of club-foot. Cf. VARUS *noun*[2]. **E19.**
GENU ***valgum***. *TALIPES* ***valgus***.
▸**B** *attrib.* or as *adjective*. Pertaining to or affected with such a deformity. **L19.**

Valhalla /valˈhalə/ *noun*. **L17.**
[mod. Latin from Old Norse *Valhǫll-*, *-hǫll*, from *valr* those slain in battle (= Old English *wæl*, Old Saxon, Old High German *wal*) + *hǫll* HALL *noun*. Cf. VALKYRIE.]
1 In Scandinavian mythology, the hall in which the souls of those who have died in battle feast with Odin for eternity. **L17.**
2 *transf.* & *fig.* A place or sphere assigned to a person or thing worthy of special honour. Also, paradise; a place or state of perfect bliss. **M19.**

vali /vaˈliː/ *noun*. **M18.**
[Turkish from Arab. *al-wālī* WALI: cf. VILAYET.]
A civil governor of a Turkish province or vilayet.

valiance /ˈvalɪəns/ *noun*. *arch.* **LME.**
[Anglo-Norman = Old & mod. French *vaillance*, from *vaillant*: see VALIANT, -ANCE.]
1 Bravery, valour. **LME.**
2 A valiant act or deed; a feat of valour or bravery. **L15.**

valiancy /ˈvalɪənsi/ *noun*. **L15.**
[from prec. + -ANCY.]
1 = VALIANCE 1. *arch.* **L15.**
†**2** = VALIANCE 2. *rare*. Only in **E17.**

valiant /ˈvalɪənt/ *adjective* & *noun*. **ME.**
[Anglo-Norman *valiaunt*, Old French *vailant*, (also mod.) *vaillant*, from Proto-Romance, from Latin *valent-* pres. ppl stem of *valere* be strong: see VAIL *verb*[1], -ANT[1].]
▸**A** *adjective*. **1** Of a person: stalwart or robust *of* body etc. Now only (*dial.*), stout, well-built. **ME.** ▸†**b** Of a thing: strong, firm. **M16–E17.** ▸†**c** Having a strong smell or taste. **E–M17.**
2 Brave, courageous, bold, esp. on the field of battle or in combat. Formerly foll. by *of*. **ME.**
3 Characterized by or performed with valour or courage. **ME.**
†**4** Worth (a specified sum); rich *in* (goods or property). *rare*. **L16–E17.**

📖 **1 valiant beggar** (*obsolete* exc. *Hist.*) a sturdy beggar. ***valiant trencherman***: see TRENCHERMAN 1. **2** N. MONSARRAT The valiant Knights of St. Elmo.. held onto their fort with matchless bravery. G. MCCAUGHREAN The officers set off .. through avalanches and mudslides, the valiant Miss Amelia riding .. behind. **3** A. THWAITE Two-year-old Sylvia making valiant attempts to open the .. door unassisted.

► **B** *noun.* A valiant, brave, or courageous person. **L16.**

📖 *Westminster Gazette* Valiants .. who, when they cannot drive, will tramp over the dreary marshes.

■ **valiantly** *adverb* **L15.** †**valiantness** *noun* **L15–M18.**

valid /ˈvalɪd/ *adjective.* **L16.**
[French *valide* or Latin *validus* strong, from *valere* be strong: see -ID[1]. Cf. earlier INVALID *adjective*[1].]
1 Possessing legal authority; executed with the proper formalities; legally acceptable or binding. **L16.** ▸**b** ECCLESIASTICAL. Of a sacrament: correctly performed and (esp. in the case of baptism) not needing to be repeated. **L17.**
2 Of an argument, assertion, objection, etc.: well-founded and applicable; sound, defensible. **M17.** ▸**b** *gen.* Effective; having some force, pertinency, or value. **M17.**
3 Of a thing: strong, powerful. *arch.* **M17.**
4 Of a person: sound or robust in body; healthy. *arch.* **M17.**

📖 **1** W. S. JEVONS According to law, .. many .. documents are not legally valid unless they be stamped. *Amiga Computing* A Eurocheque book .. means you can write a cheque valid in any currency in Europe. **2** M. MITCHELL I admit that you have valid ground for suspicion. *Health Now* Armed with your statistics about .. rain forests I could have made some very valid points. **3** *Cornhill Magazine* In addition to the strong jaws .. there are three exceedingly valid hooks. **4** G. A. SALA When he was a valid man he may have had many a boxing bout.

■ **validly** *adverb* so as to be valid; with validity: **M17.** **validness** *noun* (*rare*) validity **E18.**

validate /ˈvalɪdeɪt/ *verb trans.* **M17.**
[medieval Latin *validat-* pa. ppl stem of *validare* render (legally) valid, from Latin *validus*: see prec., -ATE[3].]
1 Make or declare legally valid; confirm the validity of (an act, contract, deed, etc.); legalize. **M17.**
2 a Lend force or validity to; confirm; ratify; substantiate. **L18.** ▸**b** COMPUTING etc. Examine (data etc.) for incorrectness or bias; confirm or test the suitability of (a system, program, etc.). **M20.**

📖 **1** A. ALISON Royal sanction .. required to validate the acts of the legislature. **2a** *Gamut* This fraud .. could .. have been an attempt to validate someone's theory of the evolutionary process. *Nursing Times* If a course is validated, it is officially .. approved for a specified period.

■ **vali'dation** *noun* **M17.** **validator** *noun* a person who or thing which confirms the validity of something **M20.**

validity /vəˈlɪdɪti/ *noun.* **M16.**
[French *validité* or late Latin *validitas*, from Latin *validus*: see VALID, -ITY.]
1 The quality of being (esp. legally) valid. **M16.**
2 Robustness, physical strength; physical capacity. Now *rare* or *obsolete.* **L16.**
3 Value, worth; efficacy. *obsolete* exc. as passing into sense 1. **L16.**
†**4** In *pl.* Valid powers or capacities. **L16–E17.**

📖 **1** M. SPARK Having the validity of his marriage examined by the ecclesiastical lawyers. A. STEVENS He will deny the validity of your suggestion. **3** J. SMEATON The most certain index of the validity of a limestone for Aquatic Buildings.

Comb.: **validity check** COMPUTING a check that data items conform to coding requirements.

valiha /vaˈliː/ *noun.* **L19.**
[Malagasy.]
A kind of zither made of bamboo, regarded as the national instrument of Madagascar.

valinche /vəˈlɪn(t)ʃ/ *noun.* Also **valinch**, **-cher** /-(t)ʃə/, ***vellinch**. **E19.**
[Alt. of earlier VALENTIA.]
A long tubular instrument for drawing a sample from a cask through the bung-hole.

valine /ˈveɪliːn/ *noun.* **E20.**
[from VAL(ERIANIC + -INE[5].]
BIOCHEMISTRY. A hydrophobic amino acid, $(CH_3)_2CH\text{-}CH(NH_2)COOH$, which occurs in proteins and is essential in the human diet; α-aminoisovaleric acid.

valinomycin /ˌvalɪnə(ʊ)ˈmʌɪsɪn/ *noun.* **M20.**
[from prec. + -O- + -MYCIN.]
PHARMACOLOGY. A dodecapeptide obtained from the bacterium *Streptomyces fulvissimus*, which has antibiotic activity against Gram-positive bacteria and is used experimentally.

valise /vəˈliːz/ *noun.* **E17.**
[French from Italian *valigia* corresp. to medieval Latin *valesia*, of unkn. origin.]
1 A travelling case or portmanteau, now usu. made of leather and of a size suitable for carrying by hand, formerly also for strapping to a horse's saddle. Now chiefly *US.* **E17.**
2 MILITARY. A soldier's cloth or leather kitbag. **M19.**

Valium /ˈvalɪəm/ *noun.* Also **v-**. **M20.**
[Origin unkn.]
PHARMACOLOGY. (Proprietary name for) the drug diazepam; a tablet of this.
■ **Valiumed** *adjective* affected by taking Valium **L20.**

Valkyrie /valˈkɪəri, ˈvalkɪri/ *noun.* **M18.**
[Old Norse *Valkyrja* lit. 'chooser of the slain', from *valr* those slain in battle (see VALHALLA) + *-kyrja* chooser, ult. from *kjósa* CHOOSE.]
In Scandinavian mythology, each of Odin's twelve handmaidens who hovered over battlefields and conducted the fallen warriors of their choice to Valhalla. Cf. WALKYRIE.

📖 *transf.*: S. SPENDER She was very tall .. with blonde hair loose over her shoulders, quite the collegiate Valkyrie.

■ **Val'kyrian** *adjective* of or pertaining to a Valkyrie or the Valkyries **M19.**

vallar /ˈvalə/ *adjective.* Also (the usual form in HERALDRY) **vallary** /ˈvaləri/. **M16.**
[Latin *vallaris*, from *vallum* or *vallus* rampart.]
In ROMAN ANTIQUITIES. = MURAL *adjective* 1. Now only HERALDRY in ***vallar crown***, ***crown vallar***, a circlet heightened by (usu. eight) vair-shaped points resembling a rampart or palisade.

vallate /ˈvaleɪt, -lət/ *adjective.* **L19.**
[Latin *vallatus* pa. pple of *vallare*: see next, -ATE[2].]
Surrounded by a wall or rampart; (ANATOMY & ZOOLOGY) having a raised outer edge.
vallate papilla ANATOMY a circumvallate papilla.

vallation /vaˈleɪʃ(ə)n/ *noun. rare.* **M17.**
[Late Latin *vallatio(n-)*, from Latin *vallat-* pa. ppl stem of *vallare* circumvallate, from *vallum* rampart: see -ATION.]
A bank of earth raised as a defence or protection; an earthwork or fortification of this nature.

vallecula /vaˈlɛkjʊlə/ *noun.* Pl. **-lae** /-liː/. **M19.**
[Late Latin var. of Latin *vallicula* dim. of *valles*, *vallis* VALLEY: see -CULE.]
1 ANATOMY. A furrow, a fissure, a fossa, *spec.* = ***vallecula epiglottica*** below. **M19.**
2 BOTANY. Any of the furrows between the primary ridges in the fruit of an umbelliferous plant. **M19.**
1 vallecula cerebelli /sɛrɪˈbɛlʌɪ/ ANATOMY a longitudinal hollow between the hemispheres of the cerebellum. **vallecula epiglottica** /ɛpɪˈglɒtɪkə/ ANATOMY a furrow between the median and lateral glosso-epiglottic folds on each side.
■ **vallecular** *adjective* of or relating to grooves or valleculae; ***vallecular canal*** (BOTANY), any of the intercellular spaces in the cortex of a horsetail, each corresponding to a groove in the stem: **L19.**

valley /ˈvali/ *noun & verb.* **ME.**
[Anglo-Norman *valey*, Old French *valée* (mod. *vallée*) from Proto-Romance, from Latin *valles*, *vallis*: see VALE *noun*[1], -Y[5].]
► **A** *noun.* **1** A low, usu. elongated, area more or less enclosed by hills or high ground and typically having a river or stream flowing through it. **ME.** ▸**b** The extensive tract of land drained by a single large river system. **L18.**
2 *fig.* A place or period of peacefulness, calm, sorrow, trouble, etc. Freq. in ***valley of tears*** below, ***the valley of the shadow of death*** s.v. SHADOW *noun*. **LME.**
3 *transf.* **a** Any depression or hollow resembling a valley; *esp.* a trough between two wave crests. **E17.** ▸**b** A region of a graph which is shaped like a valley; a set of low values of a varying quantity which would form such a region if plotted as a graph. **M20.**
4 BUILDING. The depressed angle formed by the junction of two sloping sides of a roof, or by the slope of a roof and a wall; a tile used to roof this angle. **L17.**
5 ANATOMY. = VALLECULA 1. **M19.**

📖 **1** C. LYELL The valley of Kingsclere .. is about five miles long and two in breadth. F. HOYLE Rivers by themselves cut deep V-shaped valleys in a mountainous topography. *attrib.*: K. VONNEGUT The other valley people .. go to Rochester .. looking for any kind of work. **2** F. W. ROBERTSON Be content with the quiet valleys of existence. **3a** R. L. STEVENSON The *Good Hope* swooped dizzily down into the valley of the rollers. **4** attrib.: ***valley-board***, ***valley gutter***, ***valley rafter***, etc.

Phrases: ***hanging valley***: see HANGING *adjective*. LACED ***valley***. ***lily of the valley***: see LILY *noun*. ***Murray Valley encephalitis***, ***Murray Valley fever***: see MURRAY *noun*[2] 2. ***pocket valley***: see POCKET *noun & adjective*. SAN JOAQUIN VALLEY FEVER. ***Silicon Valley***: see SILICON. ***swept valley***: see SWEPT *adjective*. ***the valley of the shadow of death***: see SHADOW *noun*. ***U-valley***: see U, U 2. ***valley of tears*** = ***vale of tears*** s.v. VALE *noun*[1] 2.
Comb.: **valley fever** *US* = COCCIDIOIDOMYCOSIS; **Valley Girl** *noun & adjective* (*US*) (of or pertaining to) a fashionable and affluent teenage girl from San Fernando Valley in southern California; (of or pertaining to) Valspeak; **valley lily** (chiefly *poet.*) the lily of the valley, *Convallaria majalis*; **valley tan** *US* a kind of whiskey produced in Salt Lake Valley, Utah; **valley train** PHYSICAL GEOGRAPHY a deposit of glacial outwash along a valley bottom.
► **B** *verb.* **1** *verb intrans.* Form a depression resembling a valley. *rare.* **M16.**
2 *verb trans.* Make a valley or valleys in, furrow. Formerly also (*rare*), adjoin as a valley. **M17.**
■ **valleyed** *adjective* (*rare*) situated in a valley **LME.** **valleyful** *noun* (*rare*) as much or as many as a valley can hold **L19.** **Valleyspeak** *noun* (*US*) = VALSPEAK **L20.**

Vallhund /ˈvalhʊnd/ *noun.* **M20.**
[Swedish = shepherd dog, from *vall* pasture + *hund* dog.]
(An animal of) a sturdy short-coated breed of dog, resembling and related to the Pembrokeshire corgi, and used as a herding dog in Sweden. Also ***Swedish Vallhund***.

Valliscaulian /valɪsˈkɔːlɪən/ *noun & adjective.* **L19.**
[from Latin *Vallis Caulium* Val des Choux (see below) + -IAN.]
► **A** *noun.* A member of an order of ascetic monks, forming a branch of the Benedictines, founded at Val des Choux in Scotland in 1193. **L19.**
► **B** *adjective.* Of or belonging to the Valliscaulians or their order. **L19.**

vallisneria /valɪsˈnɪərɪə/ *noun.* **L18.**
[mod. Latin (see below), from Antonio *Vallisneri* (1661–1730), Italian physician and naturalist: see -IA[1].]
Any of several aquatic plants of tropical and warm temperate regions constituting the genus *Vallisneria*, having long narrow straplike leaves and often planted in ponds and aquaria. Cf. ***tape-grass*** s.v. TAPE *noun*.

Vallombrosan /valəmˈbrəʊs(ə)n/ *adjective & noun.* **M19.**
[from *Vallombrosa* near Florence, Italy + -AN.]
► **A** *adjective.* Designating or belonging to a strictly contemplative Benedictine order established at Vallombrosa in the 11th cent. by St John Gualberto (d.1073). **M19.**
► **B** *noun.* A member of this order. **L19.**

vallota /vaˈləʊtə/ *noun.* **M19.**
[mod. Latin (see below), from Antoine *Vallot* (1594–1671), French botanist.]
An ornamental plant of the former genus *Vallota*, the Scarborough lily, *Cyrtanthus elatus* (formerly ***Vallota speciosa***).

vallum /ˈvaləm/ *noun.* **E17.**
[Latin collect. from *vallus* stake, palisade.]
1 A defensive wall or rampart of earth, sods, or stone; *esp.* one constructed by the Romans in northern England and central Scotland. **E17.**
2 ARCHAEOLOGY. A palisaded bank or rampart, formed of the earth dug up from the ditch or fosse around a Roman military camp. **E19.**

valonia /vaˈləʊnɪə/ *noun.* **E18.**
[Italian *vallonia* from mod.Greek †*balania* pl. of †*balani* (from Greek *balanos*) acorn.]
1 The large acorn-cups and acorns of an oak of the eastern Mediterranean, *Quercus macrolepis*, much used in tanning, dyeing, etc. **E18.**
2 In full ***valonia oak***. The oak from which these acorns are obtained. **E19.**

valor *noun* see VALOUR.

valorisation *noun*, **valorise** *verb* vars. of VALORIZATION, VALORIZE.

valorization /valərʌɪˈzeɪʃ(ə)n/ *noun.* Also **-isation**. **E20.**
[French *valorisation*, formed as next + -IZATION.]
The action or process of fixing the price or value of a commodity etc. by artificial means, esp. by government intervention. Also *gen.*, the action of giving validity to something; an instance of making something valid.

📖 J. P. FARRELL A Victorian protest against the Romantic valorizations of tragedy.

valorize /ˈvalərʌɪz/ *verb trans.* Also **-ise**. **E20.**
[French *valoriser*, from *valeur* value: see -IZE.]
Raise or fix the price or value of (a commodity etc.) by artificial means; *gen.* give validity to, make valid.

📖 P. ROSE Mainstream feminism has tended to valorize sexual fulfillment.

valorous /ˈval(ə)rəs/ *adjective.* **L15.**
[Old French *valerous* (mod. *valeureux*) or medieval Latin *valorosus* valiant, valuable, from late Latin *valor*: see next, -OUS.]
1 (Of a person) having or showing valour; valiant, courageous, bold; (of an action etc.) characterized by valour. **L15.**
†**2** Having value, worth, or merit; valuable. *rare.* **L16–E17.**

📖 **1** WELLINGTON The whole universe will acknowledge those valorous efforts. W. STYRON Hero of the Republic, valorous recipient of the Croix de Guerre.

■ **valorously** *adverb* **L16.** **valorousness** *noun* **E18.**

valour /ˈvalə/ *noun.* Also ***-or**. **ME.**
[Old French *valour* (mod. *valeur* value) from late Latin *valor*, from *valere* be strong: see -OUR, -OR.]
► **I** †**1** Worth or importance deriving from personal qualities or rank; worth or worthiness in respect of prowess in arms or battle. **ME–L16.**
2 The quality of character which enables a person to face danger with boldness or fortitude; courage, bravery, esp. in battle. **L16.**

3 A brave or valorous person. Also (chiefly *iron.*) as a title. *arch.* E17.

📖 **2** J. MORLEY Revealed the valour and godliness of Puritanism. *New York Review of Books* Such military virtues as blind obedience and battlefield valor. **3** C. KINGSLEY How . . came your valour thither?

▶†**II 4** Worth or merit of a thing as regards utility, desirability, etc. Cf. VALUE *noun* 5. ME–M17.
5 The value of a thing; the amount in money etc. that something is worth. ME–E19.
6 The duration, amount, extent, etc., *of* (so much). *rare.* E17–E19.
7 = POWER *noun* 11, 12. L17–E19.

📖 **4** R. CARPENTER We compare his works being of infinite valour with our works. **5** P. HOLLAND Send presents . . to the valour of two thousand Asses.

valpack /ˈvalpak/ *noun. US.* Also (earlier and as US proprietary name) **Val-A-Pak** /ˈvaləpak/. M20.
[Perh. from VAL(ISE + PACK *noun*.]
A type of soft zip-up travel bag.

Valpolicella /ˌvalpɒlɪˈtʃɛlə/ *noun.* E20.
[*Val Policella*, a valley in the western Veneto, Italy.]
A red or rosé wine made in the Val Policella district.

valproic /valˈprəʊɪk/ *adjective.* L20.
[from VAL(ERIC + PRO(PYL + -IC.]
PHARMACOLOGY. ***valpoic acid***, a branched-chain fatty acid, $C_7H_{15}COOH$; 2-propylpentanoic acid.
■ **ˈvalproate** *noun* (a salt or ester of) valproic acid, esp. the sodium salt, which is an anticonvulsant drug given orally in cases of epilepsy L20.

Valsalva /valˈsalvə/ *noun.* L19.
[Antonio Maria *Valsalva* (1666–1723), Italian anatomist.]
MEDICINE. **1** More fully ***Valsalva manoeuvre***, ***Valsalva experiment***, ***Valsalva's manoeuvre***, ***Valsalva's experiment***. An attempt made to exhale air while the nostrils and mouth, or the glottis, are closed, so as to increase pressure in the middle ear and the chest. L19.
2 Used *attrib.* and in *possess.* to designate various anatomical structures, esp. in the ear. L19.
■ **Valsalvan** *adjective* L19.

valse /vɑːls, vɔːls/ *noun.* L18.
[French from German *Walzer* WALTZ *noun*.]
A waltz; a piece of music for this dance or in its rhythm.

valse /vɑːls, vɔːls/ *verb intrans.* L19.
[from prec. or French *valser*.]
Dance the valse.

Valspeak /ˈvalspiːk/ *noun. US.* L20.
[Contr. of VALLEYSPEAK, from the San Fernando *Valley* (see below) + -SPEAK.]
A variety of slang originating among teenage girls in the San Fernando Valley of southern California and characterized by the use of filler words such as *like* and *totally* and a limited group of adjectives expressing approval or disapproval.

📖 *People* In pure, uncut Valspeak, Moon laments . . 'Like my mother like makes me do the dishes. It's like so *gross*.'

valuable /ˈvaljʊb(ə)l/ *adjective & noun.* L16.
[from VALUE *verb* + -ABLE. Cf. earlier UNVALUABLE.]
▶ **A** *adjective.* **1** Of material or monetary value; capable of commanding a high price; precious. L16.
†**2** Able to be valued. *rare.* Only in 17.
3 Having considerable importance or worth; of great use or benefit; having qualities which confer value. M17.
▶†**b** Of a person: entitled to consideration or distinction; estimable. M17–E19.

📖 **1** *Daily Star* Conmen . . tricking the elderly into handing over valuable heirlooms—for peanuts. **valuable consideration** LAW a consideration deemed to be valuable in a legal sense. **3** S. WYNTER If you could spare me some of your valuable time to grant me some meaningful advice. H. BASCOM This man is going to be valuable to us. He is a hunter. *Independent* They put . . Horne into the right-back position, . . depriving them of his valuable midfield industry.

▶ **B** *noun.* A valuable article or thing; *esp.* a small item of personal property. Usu. in *pl.* L18.

📖 R. C. HUTCHINSON I've put some of my valuables in the bank.

■ **valuableness** *noun* valuable quality; worth, importance: L17. **valuably** *adverb* (*a*) in a valuable manner, so as to be valuable or highly useful; †(*b*) *rare* with equivalence of value: E17.

valuate /ˈvaljʊeɪt/ *verb trans.* Chiefly *US.* L19.
[Back-form. from next.]
Estimate the value of; appraise.

📖 *New York Times* Ethics is not only an attempt to valuate the consequences of behavior. It must also be concerned about . . motivation.

valuation /valjʊˈeɪʃ(ə)n/ *noun.* E16.
[from VALUE *verb* + -ATION.]
1 a The action of estimating or fixing the monetary value of something, esp. by a professional valuator; an instance of this. E16. ▶**b** Estimated monetary value; worth or price, esp. as estimated by a professional valuator. M17.
†**2 a** Value or worth, esp. of a material nature. M16–M17. ▶**b** *spec.* Current value (of money). M16–L18.
3 (An) appraisal or estimation of something in respect of excellence or merit. M16.

📖 **1a** *Independent* Rating valuation (putting a rateable value on a property) falls on the Inland Revenue. attrib.: ***valuation law***, ***valuation officer***, ***valuation report***, etc. **b** *Guardian* An attempt to force down Wednesday's £800,000 valuation of the player. **3** P. TILLICH The Christian valuation of the individual soul as eternally significant. G. STEINER In painting and sculpture . . valuation . . lies in the work itself.

■ **valuational** *adjective* L19.

valuative /ˈvaljʊətɪv/ *adjective. rare.* M16.
[formed as prec. + -ATIVE.]
Expressive of value.

valuator /ˈvaljʊeɪtə/ *noun.* M18.
[from VALUATION + -OR: see -ATOR.]
A person who makes valuations, esp. in a professional or formal capacity.

value /ˈvaljuː/ *noun.* ME.
[Old French, fem. pa. ppl formation from *valoir* be worth from Latin *valere* be strong, be worth.]
▶**I 1 a** That amount of a commodity, medium of exchange, etc., considered to be an equivalent for something else; a fair or satisfactory equivalent or return. Freq. in ***value for money*** below. ME. ▶**b** Orig., a standard of valuation or exchange; an amount or sum reckoned in terms of this. Later (now *US*), a thing regarded as worth having. LME.
2 The material or monetary worth of a thing; the amount of money, goods, etc., for which a thing can be exchanged or traded. ME.
3 The extent or amount *of* a specified standard or measure of length, quantity, etc. Now *dial.* E17.

📖 **1a** R. DAHL Liquorice Bootlaces. At two for a penny they were the best value in the shop. *Illustrated London News* The . . court awarded the salvors less than a seventh of the value of the ship and her cargo. **2** M. PATTISON A fireproof chamber for the muniments and jewels of especial value. A. TOFFLER No hard evidence . . that the government was orchestrating . . moves in the value of the currency. *Dancing Times* Vouchers to the value of £50.00 per annum which reduce the price of . . tickets.

▶**II** †**4** = VALOUR 1, 2. ME–M17.
5 The worth, usefulness, or importance of a thing; relative merit or status according to the estimated desirability or utility of a thing. LME. ▶†**b** Estimate or opinion *of*, regard or liking *for*, a person or thing. M17–E19. ▶**c** In *pl.* The principles or moral standards of a person or social group; the generally accepted or personally held judgement of what is valuable and important in life. E20. ▶**d** The quality of a thing considered in respect of its ability to serve a specified purpose or cause an effect. E20.
6 a The number or amount represented by a mathematical term or expression; SCIENCE the numerical measure of a quantity; a number denoting magnitude on some conventional scale. M16. ▶**b** MUSIC. The relative length or duration of a sound signified by a note. M17. ▶**c** The relative rank or importance of a playing-card, counter, etc., according to the conventions of the game; the amount at which each (or each set) is reckoned in counting the score. L17. ▶**d** ART & PHOTOGRAPHY. Due or proper emphasis; relative tone of colour in each distinct section of a picture; a part characterized by a particular tone. L18. ▶**e** PHONETICS. The quality or tone of a speech sound; the sound represented by a letter. L19. ▶**f** That quality of a colour, corresponding to tone or reflectance, which when assigned a numerical value according to its degree of lightness or brilliance can be used in combination with hue and chroma to identify the colour uniquely. Cf. MUNSELL. E20.

📖 **5** *Country Life* Grape bottles similar to the pair sold . . are of no less decorative value. *She* The greatest discovery I made was the enormous value of women friends. **c** ISAIAH BERLIN Crumbling values and the dissolution of the fixed standards . . of our civilization. **d** G. BUTLER Ezra could see . . that he had news value. ***nuisance value***, ***sentimental value***, etc. **6e** B. BRYSON The long vowel sounds . . changed their values . . moving forward and upward in the mouth.

Phrases: ***absolute value***: see ABSOLUTE *adjective* 10. **good value** *colloq.* entertaining; worthy of interest; repaying one's efforts or attentions. **of value** valuable. ***present value***: see PRESENT *adjective*. ***rateable value***: see RATEABLE 2. **set a high value on**, **set a lower value on**, etc., estimate or judge the (relative) worth or importance of. ***tactile value***: see TACTILE *adjective* 2a. ***U value***: see U, U 4. **value for money** (designating) actual or perceived equivalence between worth and expenditure, (of or pertaining to) something well worth the money spent.
Comb.: **value added** *noun & adjective* (*a*) *noun* (ECONOMICS) the amount by which the value of an article is increased at each stage of its production, exclusive of the cost of the materials and bought-in parts and services; ***value added tax***, a tax on the amount by which the value of an article has been increased at each stage of its production or distribution (abbreviation *VAT*); (*b*) *adjective* (of food, goods, etc.) having features or ingredients added to a basic line or model to enhance the profit margin for the producer, retailer, etc.; (*c*) ***value-added reseller***, a distributor who resells goods, esp. computer software and hardware, either in a modified or customized form or with an added package of goods and services such as installation or maintenance; **value analysis** the systematic and critical assessment by an organization of design and costs in relation to realized value; **value analyst** a person who undertakes a value analysis; **value calling** BRIDGE a system of estimating bids which takes into account the scoring values of the suits; **value engineering** the modification of designs and systems according to value analysis; **value-free** *adjective* free from criteria imposed by subjective values or standards; purely objective; **value judgement** a judgement predicating merit or demerit of its subject; **value-laden**, **value-loaded** *adjectives* weighted or biased in favour of certain values; **value-neutral** *adjective* involving no value judgements, value-free; **value-orientation** the direction given to a person's attitudes and thinking by his or her beliefs or standards; **value-system** any set of connected or interdependent values; **value theory** (*a*) ECONOMICS the Marxist labour theory of value; (*b*) PHILOSOPHY axiology.
■ **valueless** *adjective* (*a*) having no value, worthless; (*b*) *rare* priceless, invaluable: L16. **valuelessness** *noun* M19. **valuer** *noun* a person who estimates or assesses values, esp. professionally L16.

value /ˈvaljuː/ *verb trans.* L15.
[from the noun.]
▶**I 1** Estimate or appraise as being worth a specified sum or amount. Freq. foll. by *at*. L15.
2 Estimate the value of; appraise, esp. professionally. E16.
3 Estimate or regard as having a certain value or worth. Now *rare.* L16.

📖 **1** H. BROOKE The appraisers . . valued the same to four pounds. *Sunday Correspondent* A consignment of hawksbill turtleshell . . valued at 6.5m yen . . was imported from the Cayman Islands. **2** J. MORLEY Voltaire got his bill back, and the jewels were to be duly valued. *Guardian* The basis on which the industry will be valued for . . privatisation. **3** SHAKES. *3 Hen. VI* The Queen is valued thirty thousand strong. J. LEONI The Cypress is valu'd almost equal with the Spice Trees.

▶**II 4** Consider of worth or importance; have a high opinion of; esteem. M16.
5 Have a value of (a certain amount or quantity). Formerly also, equal in value; be worth. M16.
6 Take account or notice of; be concerned about; care about. Only in neg. contexts. Now *rare.* L16.
†**7** Give greater value to; raise the estimation of. *rare.* Only in 17.
8 *refl.* Pride or congratulate oneself *on* or *upon*; take credit to or think highly of oneself *for*. M17.

📖 **4** A. J. TOYNBEE Spain must have valued this minor possession . . , or she would not have built the . . fortifications. B. RUBENS He valued his own privacy sufficiently to have respect for someone else's. D. HURD She valued her independence. **5** T. HERBERT An English shilling values twentie two pice. **6** DEFOE People infected . . valued not who they injur'd. **8** J. L. MOTLEY The learned Doctor valued himself upon his logic.

valued /ˈvaljuːd/ *ppl adjective.* L16.
[from prec. + -ED[1].]
1 Estimated, appraised; to which a definite value has been assigned. L16. ▶†**b** In which value is indicated. *rare* (Shakes.). Only in E17.
2 Held in high regard; highly appreciated. M17.

📖 **1 valued policy** an insurance policy in which a special amount, estimated and agreed in advance when the policy is issued, is payable in the event of a valid claim being made, whatever the actual value of the claim may be. **2** B. FUSSELL The head was also a valued part of soused pig. *Sphere* Rappart . . remained a valued friend for years.

valuta /vəˈljuːtə, -ˈluː-/ *noun.* L19.
[Italian = value.]
The value of one currency in respect of its exchange rate with another; a currency considered in this way.

valva /ˈvalvə/ *noun.* Pl. **-vae** /-viː/. E19.
[Latin: see VALVE *noun*.]
ENTOMOLOGY. = VALVE *noun* 4.

valval /ˈvalv(ə)l/ *adjective.* L19.
[from VALVE *noun* + -AL[1].]
Chiefly BOTANY. (Esp. with ref. to the valves of a diatom) = VALVAR.

valvar /ˈvalvə/ *adjective.* M19.
[from VALVE *noun* + -AR[1].]
Chiefly MEDICINE & BOTANY. Pertaining to or affecting a valve or valves; consisting of or containing a valve or valves.

valvassor *noun* var. of VAVASOUR.

valvate /ˈvalveɪt/ *adjective.* E19.
[Latin *valvatus* having folding doors, from *valva* VALVE *noun*, or from VALVE *noun* + -ATE[2].]
BOTANY. (Of sepals or petals, esp. in bud) meeting at the edges but not overlapping. Also, characterized by this arrangement of sepals or petals.

valve /valv/ *noun*. LME.
[Latin *valva* leaf of a door (usu. pl. *valvae* a folding door).]
▶ I 1 a Each of the leaves of a folding door; either of the halves of a double door. *arch.* LME. ▸b A door regulating the flow of water in a lock or sluice. Now *rare*. L18.
2 ZOOLOGY. Either of the halves of the hinged shell of a bivalve mollusc, brachiopod, etc.; any of the parts of the compound shell of a barnacle etc. M17.
3 BOTANY. a Each of the halves or sections into which a dry fruit (esp. a pod or capsule) or an anther dehisces. M18. ▸b Either of the overlapping halves of the cell wall of a diatom. M19.
4 ENTOMOLOGY. Any of various (usu. paired) plates or lobes, esp. associated with the genitals; a valvula. E19.
▶ II 5 ANATOMY & ZOOLOGY etc. ▸a A membranous fold in a hollow organ or tubular structure of the circulatory system, digestive tract, etc., which automatically closes to prevent the reflux of blood or other contents. E17. ▸b A similar part or structure serving to close or protect an aperture, as in the ear, throat, etc. E19.
6 MECHANICS. A device in a pipe or aperture that controls the passage of air, steam, water, etc.; *esp.* one acting automatically by yielding to pressure in one direction only. M17.
7 MUSIC. A device for extending the range of pitch of a brass instrument by increasing or decreasing the effective length of the tube. L19.
8 ELECTRONICS. = THERMIONIC *valve*. E20.
9 A move in a chess problem which opens one line while simultaneously shutting off another. M20.
Comb.: **valve gear** the mechanism that controls the opening and closing of the cylinder valves in a steam engine or internal-combustion engine; **valve head** MECHANICS the part of a lift valve that is lifted off the valve aperture to open the valve; **valve train** MECHANICS in an internal-combustion engine, the gearing and linkages by which the crankshaft is caused to open and close a valve at the proper time.
■ **valveless** *adjective* M19. **valvelet** *noun* (*rare*) a small valve, a valvule L18. **valviform** *adjective* (ZOOLOGY) valve-shaped E19.

valve /valv/ *verb*. *rare*. M19.
[from the noun.]
1 *verb trans.* Provide with a valve or valves; govern or check by a valve or similar device. M19.
2 *verb intrans.* Make use of a valve or valves; *spec.* in ballooning, open a valve in order to descend. E20.
3 *verb trans.* Discharge gas from (a balloon etc.) by opening a valve; (foll. by *off*) discharge (gas) thus. E20.

valved /valvd/ *adjective*. L17.
[from VALVE *noun* + -ED².]
Having a valve or valves; (as 2nd elem. of comb.) having valves of a specified kind or number.
many valved, *poppet-valved*, *two-valved*, etc.

valvifer /ˈvalvɪfə/ *noun*. E20.
[from Latin *valva* VALVE *noun* + -I- + -FER.]
ENTOMOLOGY. A modified limb joint (usu. paired) in some female insects, forming a basal plate of the ovipositor and bearing a valvula.

valving /ˈvalvɪŋ/ *noun*. M20.
[from VALVE *noun*, *verb* + -ING¹.]
A system or arrangement of valves; valves collectively. Also (*rare*), operation, esp. opening and shutting, in the manner of a valve.

valvotomy /valˈvɒtəmi/ *noun*. E20.
[from VALVE *noun* + -O- + -TOMY.]
MEDICINE. (An instance of) a surgical operation in which an incision is made into a (narrowed) valve, esp. of the heart.

valvula /ˈvalvjʊlə/ *noun*. Pl. **-lae** /-liː/. E17.
[mod. Latin, dim. of Latin *valva*: see VALVE *noun*, -ULE.]
1 ANATOMY. A valve or valvule. Usu. with Latin specifying word. E17.
2 ENTOMOLOGY. An elongated bladelike process attached to the coxa or valvifer of some female insects, forming part of the ovipositor; a valve. E20.
■ **valvular** *adjective* (chiefly MEDICINE & BOTANY) of, relating to, or affecting a valve or valves, *esp.* the valves of the heart; functioning as a valve: L18. **valvuˈlitis** *noun* (MEDICINE) inflammation of one or more valves, esp. of the heart L19. **valvuloplasty** *noun* (MEDICINE) (an instance of) the surgical repair of a valve, esp. of the heart M20. **valvuˈlotomy** *noun* (MEDICINE) = VALVOTOMY E20.

valvule /ˈvalvjuːl/ *noun*. M18.
[Anglicized from prec., or from French *valvule*.]
BIOLOGY & ANATOMY. A small valve. Formerly *spec.*, the palea of a grass floret.

vambrace /ˈvambreɪs/ *noun*. ME.
[Anglo-Norman *vauntbras* aphet. from Old French *avantbras*, from *avant* before + *bras* arm. Cf. VAMPLATE, VANTBRACE.]
Hist. A piece of armour for the arm, esp. the forearm.
■ **vambraced** *adjective* (HERALDRY) (of an arm) covered in armour E17.

vamoose /vəˈmuːs/ *verb*. *colloq.* (orig. *US*). Also **vamose** /vəˈməʊs/. M19.
[Spanish *vamos* let us go.]
1 *verb intrans.* Depart, make off, go away. Freq. in *imper.* M19.
2 *verb trans.* Decamp or disappear from; leave hurriedly. Freq. in ***vamoose the ranch***. *US*. M19.

vamp /vamp/ *noun*¹. ME.
[Aphet. from Old French *avantpié* (mod. *avantpied*), from *avant* before + *pié* foot.]
1 The part of a stocking which covers the foot and ankle. Also, a short stocking, a sock. Long *dial.* ME.
2 The part of a boot or shoe covering the front of the foot. M17.

vamp /vamp/ *noun*². L19.
[from VAMP *verb*¹.]
1 Anything vamped, patched up, or refurbished; a patchwork. L19.
2 An improvised musical accompaniment. L19.

vamp /vamp/ *noun*³. E20.
[Abbreviation of VAMPIRE *noun*.]
A woman who uses sexual attraction to exploit men; an unscrupulous flirt, a seductress.

vamp /vamp/ *verb*¹. L16.
[from VAMP *noun*¹.]
▶ I 1 *verb trans.* Provide or fit with a (new) vamp; mend or repair (as) with patches; refurbish, renovate, restore. Freq. foll. by *up*. L16.
2 *verb trans.* Make or produce (as) by patching; compile, put together, (a book, composition, etc.) out of old materials; serve up (something old) as new by addition or alteration. Freq. foll. by *up*. Also (foll. by *up*), fabricate. M17. ▸†b Presumptuously represent (a person) as or *as* something. M17–L18.
3 *verb trans.* MUSIC. Improvise (an accompaniment, tune, etc.). L18. ▸b *verb intrans.* Improvise an accompaniment. Also more widely, extemporize, ad lib. L19.

📖 1 DISRAELI Old furniture . . re-burnished and vamped up. 2 G. A. SALA I have vamped up my description of the function from accounts which I have read.

▶ II 4 a *verb intrans.* Make one's way on foot; tramp, trudge. Now *dial.* M17. ▸b *verb trans.* Tramp (the streets). *rare*. L19.

vamp /vamp/ *verb*². E20.
[from VAMP *noun*³.]
1 *verb intrans.* Behave seductively; act as a vamp. E20.
2 *verb trans.* Act as a vamp towards; attract and exploit (a man, occas. a woman). E20.
3 *verb trans.* & *intrans.* Persecute, harass, or intimidate (a person); attack (a person) physically. Also *spec.*, arrest (a person). *Black slang* (chiefly *US*). L20.

📖 2 L. M. MONTGOMERY Don't try to vamp me, woman. I've paid you all the compliments I'm going to.

vamper /ˈvampə/ *noun*. L17.
[from VAMP *verb*¹ + -ER¹.]
†1 A stocking. *slang*. Only in Dicts. Only in L17.
2 A person who vamps or renovates something. Also foll. by *up*. E18.
3 A person who improvises music, esp. piano accompaniments. L19.

vampire /ˈvampʌɪə/ *noun* & *verb*. As noun also (*arch.*) **-yre**. M18.
[French *vampire* or German *Vampir* from Serbo-Croat *vampir*: cf. Russian *upyr'*, Polish *upiór*, Czech *upír*, etc.]
▶ A *noun*. 1 A ghost, monster, or reanimated corpse supposed to leave its grave at night to suck the blood of sleeping people, often represented as a human figure with long pointed canine teeth. M18.
2 A person who preys ruthlessly on others. Cf. VAMP *noun*³. M18.
3 ZOOLOGY. a Any of various tropical (chiefly S. American) bats of the family Desmodontidae, which have sharp incisors for piercing flesh, and lap the blood of large mammals. Also ***vampire bat***. L18. ▸b Any of various venomous or bloodsucking creatures. *rare*. M19.
4 THEATRICAL. A small double-leaved spring trapdoor, used for sudden disappearances from the stage. Also more fully ***vampire trap***. L19.

📖 2 *attrib.*: R. LEHMANN Why should this vampire family so prey on her? **3a false vampire** any member of the family Megadermatidae of large, mainly insectivorous bats of Africa, SE Asia, and Australia.

▶ B *verb trans.* Assail or prey on like a vampire. M19.
■ **vampiredom** *noun* the state of being a vampire (sense 1) M20. **vampiric** /-ˈpɪrɪk/ *adjective* of or pertaining to vampires; of the nature of or characteristic of a vampire, or (occas.) of a vamp (VAMP *noun*³): M19. **vamˈpirical** *adjective* = VAMPIRIC M20. **vamˈpirically** *adverb* L20. **vampirine** *adjective* (*rare*) = VAMPIRIC E20. **vampirish** *adjective* = VAMPIRIC L19. **vampirism** *noun* (*a*) belief in the existence of vampires (sense 1); (*b*) the practices of a vampire: L18. **vampirize** *verb* (*a*) *verb intrans.* act as a vampire; (*b*) *verb trans.* = VAMPIRE *verb*: E19.

vampish /ˈvampɪʃ/ *adjective*. E20.
[from VAMP *noun*³ + -ISH¹.]
Suggestive or characteristic of a vamp; of the nature of a vamp.

📖 J. WILSON Her crêpe dress, low-cut and forties style, very vampish and sexy.

■ **vampishness** *noun* E20.

vamplate /ˈvampleɪt/ *noun*. ME.
[Anglo-Norman *vauntplate*, from *vaunt-* var. of *vant-* aphet. from *avant* before + *plate* PLATE *noun*. Cf. VAMBRACE.]
Hist. A circular plate fixed on a spear or lance to protect the hand, esp. in tilting.

vampy /ˈvampi/ *adjective*. M20.
[from VAMP *noun*³ + -Y¹.]
That is a vamp; vampish.
■ **vampiness** *noun* E20.

vampyre *noun* see VAMPIRE.

van /van/ *noun*¹. LME.
[Dial. var. of FAN *noun*¹, prob. reinforced by Old & mod. French *van* or Latin *vannus*. Cf. VANE, WAN *noun*¹.]
1 A winnowing basket or shovel; = FAN *noun*¹ 1a. Now *arch.* & *dial.* LME. ▸b A shovel used for lifting charcoal or testing ore. M17. ▸c A process of testing ore on a shovel; the amount of metal obtained by this test. L18.
2 A thing resembling a fan; *esp.* a wing. Chiefly *poet.* LME.
3 A sail of a windmill. M19.

📖 2 T. S. ELIOT No longer wings to fly but merely vans to beat the air.

van /van/ *noun*². E17.
[Abbreviation of VANGUARD.]
1 The foremost part of a company of people etc. moving or prepared to move forwards; the foremost position; *fig.* the forefront. E17. ▸b *spec.* The foremost division or detachment of a military or naval force when (set in order for) advancing. M17.
2 The front part of something. *rare*. E18.

📖 1 W. S. CHURCHILL In the eighth century . . England had claims to stand in the van of Western culture. ***lead the van***: see LEAD *verb*¹.

van /van/ *noun*³. E19.
[Abbreviation of CARAVAN *noun*.]
1 a Orig., a covered wagon used chiefly to carry goods, opening from behind. Now usu., a motor vehicle smaller than a lorry having the rear part given over to space for goods, luggage, etc., and usu. enclosed with no (side) windows. Also, a similar vehicle, larger than a car, for carrying passengers. E19. ▸b A caravan, esp. as used by gypsies or travellers. M19.
2 A railway carriage for mail, luggage, or for the use of the guard. M19.
1a *camper van*, *delivery van*, *furniture van*, *pantechnicon van*, *police van*, *prison van*, etc. 2 *brake van*, *guard's van*, *luggage-van*, etc.
Comb.: **van pool** *US* an arrangement for sharing a van provided by an employer to transport employees to work; a group of people with such an arrangement; **van-pool** *verb intrans.* (*US*) form or join a van pool; **van-pooler** *US* a member of a van pool.

van /van/ *noun*⁴. L19.
[Welsh *fan* mutated form of *ban* height, occurring in place-names in Wales.]
A Welsh hill or summit.

van /van/ *noun*⁵. *slang*. E20.
[Abbreviation.]
= ADVANTAGE *noun* 5.

van /van/ *verb*¹ *trans.* Infl. **-nn-**. ME.
[Var. of FAN *verb*: cf. VAN *noun*¹.]
†1 Winnow with a fan. ME–E18.
2 = FAN *verb* 3, 3b, 4. *rare*. E17.
3 Separate and test (ore) by washing on a van or shovel. L17.

van /van/ *verb*² *trans.* *rare*. Infl. **-nn-**. M19.
[from VAN *noun*².]
Go in the van of, lead.

van /van/ *verb*³. Infl. **-nn-**. M19.
[from VAN *noun*³.]
1 *verb trans.* Convey or carry in a van. M19.
2 *verb intrans.* Travel in a van. M20.

📖 1 M. C. SELF The horse being vanned will need to be blanketed.

vanadinite /vəˈnadɪnʌɪt/ *noun*. M19.
[from next + *-in-* + -ITE¹.]
MINERALOGY. A secondary mineral associated with lead ores and consisting of vanadate and chloride of lead, crystallizing as reddish or brownish-orange hexagonal prisms.

vanadium /vəˈneɪdɪəm/ *noun*. M19.
[mod. Latin from Old Norse *Vanadis* name of the Scandinavian goddess Freyja + -IUM.]
A hard grey chemical element, atomic no. 23, which is one of the transition metals and is used in small quantities to strengthen steels. (Symbol V.)
■ **vanadate** /ˈvanədeɪt/ *noun* a salt containing oxyanions of vanadium M19. **vanadian** *adjective* (MINERALOGY) having a constituent element partly replaced by vanadium M20. **vanadiate** *noun* (now *rare* or *obsolete*) = VANADATE M19. **vanadic** /vəˈnadɪk, vəˈneɪdɪk/

adjective derived from or containing vanadium, esp. in its higher (trivalent) oxidation state **M19. vanadious** *adjective* (now *rare* or *obsolete*) = VANADOUS **M19. vanadous** /ˈvanədəs/ *adjective* of or containing vanadium, esp. in the lower oxidation (divalent) state **M19. vanadyl** /ˈvanədʌɪl, -dɪl/ *noun* †(**a**) vanadium dioxide; (**b**) the divalent cation VO^{2+} (freq. *attrib.*): **M19**.

Van Allen belt /van ˈalən bɛlt/ *noun phr.* **M20.**
[from James A. *Van Allen* (b. 1914), US physicist.]
More fully ***Van Allen radiation belt***. Either of two regions partly surrounding the earth at heights of several thousand kilometres, containing intense radiation and high-energy charged particles trapped by the earth's magnetic field; a similar region around another planet.

vanaspati /vəˈnʌspəti/ *noun.* **M20.**
[Sanskrit *vanas-pati* lit. 'lord of the wood, lord of plants'.]
A hydrogenated vegetable oil used in India.

Vanbrughian /vanˈbruːɪən/ *adjective.* **M20.**
[from *Vanbrugh* (see below) + -IAN.]
Of, pertaining to, or characteristic of the architecture, landscaping, or plays of Sir John Vanbrugh (1664–1726).

vance-roof /ˈvɑːnsruːf/ *noun.* Chiefly *dial.* **L16.**
[Aphet. from ADVANCE *verb* + ROOF *noun*.]
In East Anglia, a garret.

vancomycin /vaŋkəˈmʌɪsɪn/ *noun.* **M20.**
[from *vanco-* of unkn. origin + -MYCIN.]
PHARMACOLOGY. A glycopeptide antibiotic produced by the actinomycete *Streptomyces orientalis* and active against most Gram-positive bacteria.

vancourier /ˈvankʊrɪə/ *noun. arch.* **L16.**
[Var. of VAUNT-COURIER.]
= AVANT-COURIER. Now chiefly *fig.*

vanda /ˈvandə/ *noun.* **E19.**
[mod. Latin (see below), from Sanskrit *vandā*.]
Any of various epiphytic orchids constituting the genus *Vanda* and native to tropical Asia, cultivated for their showy flowers.

V. & A. *abbreviation.*
Victoria and Albert Museum (in London).

vandal /ˈvand(ə)l/ *noun & adjective.* In senses A.1, B.1 **V-**.
[Old English *Wendlas* pl., Old High German *Wentil-* in personal names (German *Wandale*), Old Norse *Vendill*, from Germanic. Reintroduced in 16 from Latin *Vandalus*, from Germanic.]
► **A** *noun.* **1** *Hist.* A member of a Germanic people who in the 4th and 5th cents. invaded parts of western Europe, esp. Gaul and Spain, and finally migrated to N. Africa, sacking Rome on a marauding expedition in 455. Usu. in *pl.* **OE.**
2 A person who acts like a barbarian; a wilful or ignorant destroyer of property, or of anything beautiful, venerable, or worthy of preservation. **M17.**
► **B** *adjective.* **1** *Hist.* Of or pertaining to the Vandals or a Vandal. **E17.**
2 Wilfully, ignorantly, or ruthlessly destructive, esp. of things of beauty or historic interest; barbarous, rude, uncultured. **E18.**
3 Characterized by vandalism or lack of culture; vandalistic. **M18.**
■ **vandalish** *adjective* (*rare*) vandalistic, vandalic **M19.**

vandalic /vanˈdalɪk/ *adjective.* Also (esp. in sense 2) **V-**. **M17.**
[Latin *Vandalicus*, from *Vandalus* VANDAL *noun*.]
1 Characteristic of or resembling (that of) a vandal or vandals; barbarously or ignorantly destructive; vandalistic. **M17.**
2 *Hist.* Of, pertaining to, or designating the Vandals. **E18.**

vandalise *verb* var. of VANDALIZE.

vandalism /ˈvand(ə)lɪz(ə)m/ *noun.* **L18.**
[French *vandalisme*, formed as VANDAL: see -ISM.]
Wilful or malicious destruction or damage to works of art or other property; *loosely* barbarous, ignorant, or inartistic construction, alteration, or treatment. Also, an instance of this.
> 🕮 *Times* The worst examples of concrete vandalism and massive motorway intrusion. B. PYM It wasn't safe to leave a church open, what with thefts and vandalism.

■ **vandaˈlistic** *adjective* characterized by or given to vandalism **M19. vandaˈlistically** *adverb* **E20.**

vandalize /ˈvand(ə)lʌɪz/ *verb trans.* Also **-ise**. **E19.**
[from VANDAL *noun* + -IZE.]
Deal with or treat in a vandalistic manner; wilfully damage or destroy. Also *Hist.* (*rare*), make Vandal with respect to culture.
■ **vandaliˈzation** *noun* (**a**) the action of vandalizing or barbarizing something; (**b**) an act of vandalism: **E19.**

van de Graaff /van də ˈgrɑːf/ *noun.* **M20.**
[R. J. *van de Graaff* (1901–67), US physicist.]
1 In full ***van de Graaff generator***. A machine for generating electrostatic charge by means of a vertical endless belt which collects charge from a voltage source and carries it up to the inside of a large insulated metal dome, where a high voltage is produced. **M20.**
2 A particle accelerator based on such a machine. Also more fully ***van de Graaff accelerator***. **M20.**

Vandemonian /vandɪˈməʊnɪən/ *adjective & noun. Hist.* Also (earlier) **-die-**. **M19.**
[from *Van Diemen's* Land, former name (1642–1855) of Tasmania (after A. Van Diemen (1593–1645), governor of the Dutch East Indies), prob. after PANDEMONIUM: see -IAN.]
► **A** *adjective.* Of, belonging to, or inhabiting Tasmania; *esp.* of or connected with the 19th-cent. penal colony there. **M19.**
► **B** *noun.* A non-Aboriginal inhabitant of Tasmania; a former convict from Tasmania. **M19.**

Van der Hum /van də ˈhʌm/ *noun.* **M19.**
[Origin uncertain: perh. a personal name.]
A S. African brandy-based liqueur made with naartjies.

van der Waals /van də ˈvɑːls, ˈwɑːls/ *noun.* **L19.**
[Johannes *van der Waals* (1837–1923), Dutch physicist.]
Used *attrib.* and in *possess.* to designate (**a**) a form of the gas equation allowing for intermolecular attraction and finite molecular size, $(P + a/V^2)(V - b) = RT$ (where P = pressure, V = volume, R = the gas constant, T = absolute temperature, and a and b are constants); (**b**) short-range attractive forces between uncharged molecules, arising from interaction between actual or induced electric dipole moments.
van der Waals' equation; ***van der Waals attraction***, ***van der Waals cohesion***, ***van der Waals force***, etc.

Vandiemonian *adjective & noun* see VANDEMONIAN.

vandola /vanˈdəʊlə/ *noun.* **L20.**
[Spanish (now *bandola*): cf. BANDORE *noun*[1], MANDOLA.]
MUSIC. A Spanish instrument of the mandolin family.

Vandyke /vanˈdʌɪk/ *noun & adjective.* Also **v-**; in sense A.4 also **Van Dyke**. **M18.**
[Sir Anthony *Vandyke* (Anglicized spelling of Van Dyck), Flemish painter (1599–1641).]
► **A** *noun.* **1** A broad lace or linen collar, neckerchief, etc., with an edge deeply cut into large points (in imitation of a style freq. depicted in portraits by Van Dyck), fashionable in the 18th cent. **M18.**
2 Each of a number of large deep-cut points on the border or fringe of lace, cloth, etc. Usu. in *pl.* **E19.**
3 A notched, deeply indented, or zigzag border or edging. **M19.**
4 A beard cut to a V-shaped point. Also more fully ***Vandyke beard***. **L19.**
► **B** *attrib.* or as *adjective.* (**V-**.) Designating things associated with Van Dyck or his paintings; *esp.* having a border with large points. **L19.**
Vandyke beard: see sense A.4 above. **Vandyke brown** (**a**) a deep rich brown colour; (**b**) *spec.* an impermanent deep brown pigment containing organic matter, now disused.

vandyke /vanˈdʌɪk/ *verb.* **E19.**
[from prec.]
1 *verb trans.* Cut, shape, or edge (material) with deep angular indentations. Chiefly as ***vandyked*** *ppl adjective.* **E19.**
†**2** *verb intrans.* Proceed in an irregular zigzag manner; take a zigzag course. **E–M19.**

vane /veɪn/ *noun.* **LME.**
[Dial. var. of FANE *noun*[1]. Cf. VAN *noun*[1].]
1 A revolving plate or flat pointer of metal, usu. ornamental, fixed on a church spire or other high place to show the direction of the wind; a weathercock. Also ***weather-vane***. **LME.** ►**b** NAUTICAL. A piece of bunting or metal sheeting fixed to a masthead on a ship to show the direction of the wind. **E18.**
†**2** A metal plate in the form of a flag or banner bearing a coat of arms. Only in **16.**
3 a A sail of a windmill or wind-pump. Also, each of either flaps forming one of these. **L16.** ►**b** The flat part on either side of the shaft of a feather. **E18.** ►**c** *gen.* A broad projection attached to an axis or wheel so as to act on or be acted on by a current of air or liquid, as a blade of a propeller, turbine, etc. Also, a broad flat projecting surface designed to guide the motion of a projectile, as a feather on an arrow, a fin on a torpedo, etc. **E19.** ►**d** A revolving fan or flywheel. *rare.* **E19.**
4 The sight in a quadrant or other surveying instrument. **L16.**
> 🕮 **3a** *Scots Magazine* Regulate the sail speed by opening the vanes should the wind gust suddenly. **c** T. PYNCHON They . . switched over to vanes made of graphite, brought the yaw oscillation down to five degrees or so.

■ **vaned** *adjective* having a vane or vanes, esp. of a specified type **L19.**

vanessa /vəˈnɛsə/ *noun.* **M19.**
[Female forename coined by Jonathan Swift for Esther *Van*homrigh, adopted as mod. Latin (see below).]
A butterfly of the genus *Vanessa*, as the red admiral, ***Vanessa atalanta***. Now chiefly as mod. Latin genus name.

vanessid /vəˈnɛsɪd/ *adjective & noun.* **E20.**
[from prec. + -ID[3].]
ENTOMOLOGY. (Of, pertaining to, or designating) any of a group of brightly coloured butterflies including those now or formerly of the genus *Vanessa*, once placed in a family Vanessidae and now usu. regarded as nymphalids, including admirals, tortoiseshells, etc.

vanette /vaˈnɛt/ *noun.* **E20.**
[from VAN *noun*[3] + -ETTE.]
A small van.

vang /vaŋ/ *noun.* **M18.**
[Var. of FANG *noun*[1].]
NAUTICAL. A tackle used for steadying a fore-and-aft sail by preventing the boom from gybing, consisting of two ropes running from the end of the gaff to the rail on each side.

vanga /ˈvaŋgə/ *noun.* **M19.**
[mod. Latin (see below) from Latin, lit. 'mattock' (because of the shape of the bill).]
In full ***vanga shrike***. Any of various shrike-like songbirds of the genus *Vanga* or the family Vangidae, native to Madagascar.

Van Gelder /van ˈgɛldə/ *noun.* **L19.**
[Name of a Dutch paper-maker.]
In full ***Van Gelder paper***. A fine handmade paper with deckle edges.

vanguard /ˈvangɑːd/ *noun.* Also †**vantguard**. **LME.**
[Aphet. from Old & mod. French *avant-garde*, †*avangarde*, from *avant* before + *garde* GUARD *noun*. Cf. AVANT-GARDE, VAN *noun*[2].]
► **I 1** MILITARY. The foremost division of an army or fleet. Cf. VAN *noun*[2] 1b. **LME.**
2 (Those at) the forefront of political, cultural, or artistic development; the leaders of a movement, opinion, etc. **M19.**
3 The élite party cadre which, according to Lenin, would be used to organize the masses as a revolutionary force and to give effect to Communist planning. **E20.**
► **II 4** A variety of peach. **L18.**
■ **vanguardism** *noun* the quality of being in the vanguard of a political, cultural, or artistic movement **M20. vanguardist** *noun* a person in the vanguard of a political, cultural, or artistic movement **M20.**

vanilla /vəˈnɪlə/ *noun & adjective.* **M17.**
[Spanish *vainilla* dim. of *vaina* sheath, from Latin VAGINA: assim. to French *vanille*.]
► **A** *noun.* **1** The pod of an orchid of the genus *Vanilla* (see sense 2 below), esp. *V. fragrans*. Also ***vanilla bean***, ***vanilla pod***. **M17.**
2 Any of various tropical climbing epiphytic orchids constituting the genus *Vanilla*; esp. ***Vanilla fragrans***, native to Central America. **M17.**
3 A fragrant substance obtained from dried vanilla pods or synthesized, used to flavour chocolate, ice-cream, etc., and in perfumery; (more fully ***vanilla essence***) a concentrated extract of this. **E18.** ►**b** (A) vanilla-flavoured ice-cream. **M20.**
► **B** *attrib.* or as *adjective.* Vanilla-flavoured; of the colour of vanilla ice-cream, white or off-white; *fig.* ordinary, plain, unexciting, without extras. **M19.**
> 🕮 T. CLANCY Loiselle was vanilla . . good in everything but a non-specialist.

Comb. & special collocations: ***vanilla bean***: see sense A.1 above; ***vanilla essence***: see sense A.3 above; **vanilla ice(-cream)** (an) ice-cream flavoured with vanilla essence; **vanilla plant** (**a**) = sense A.2 above; (**b**) a plant of the composite family, *Trilisa odoratissima*, of the south-eastern US, with vanilla-scented leaves; ***vanilla pod***: see sense A.1 above; **vanilla sugar**: having absorbed the flavour of vanilla pods.

vanillaed /vəˈnɪləd/ *adjective.* **M20.**
[from prec. + -ED[2].]
Having vanilla added; vanilla-flavoured. Also *fig.*, made ordinary or unexciting.

vanille /vəˈniːl/ *noun & adjective. arch. rare.* **M19.**
[French from Spanish *vainilla*: see VANILLA.]
► **A** *noun.* = VANILLA *noun* 3. **M19.**
► **B** *adjective.* = VANILLA *adjective.* **M19.**

vanillin /vəˈnɪlɪn/ *noun.* **M19.**
[from VANILLA + -IN[1].]
CHEMISTRY. A sweet-smelling crystalline aldehyde which is the chief essential constituent of vanilla, used in flavourings, perfumes, and pharmaceuticals and in chemical synthesis; 3-methoxy-4-hydroxybenzaldehyde, $CH_3OC_6H_3(OH)CHO$.
■ **vanillic** *adjective* derived from or related to vanillin; ***vanillic acid***, a carboxylic acid, $CH_3OC_6H_3(OH)COOH$, formed by oxidation of vanillin: **M19. vanillyl** /ˈvanɪlʌɪl, -ɪl/ *noun* (CHEMISTRY & BIOCHEMISTRY) the radical $CH_3OC_6H_3(OH)CH=$ **L19.**

vanillon /vəˈnɪlɒn/ *noun.* **L19.**
[French, from VANILLE.]
An inferior variety of vanilla, usu. consisting of large pods from uncultivated plants.

vanish /ˈvanɪʃ/ *noun. rare.* M17.
[from the verb.]
Disappearance; vanishment.

vanish /ˈvanɪʃ/ *verb.* ME.
[Aphet. from Old French *e(s)vaniss-* lengthened stem of *e(s)vanir*, from Proto-Romance from Latin *evanescere* EVANESCE: see -ISH². Cf. EVANISH.]
1 *verb intrans.* Disappear from view, depart out of sight; become invisible, esp. rapidly and mysteriously; become untraceable. Also (now *rare*) foll. by *away.* ME.
2 *verb intrans.* Disappear by coming to an end or ceasing to exist. Also foll. by *away.* ME. ▸**b** MATH. Of a function, quality, etc.: become zero. E18.
3 *verb trans.* Cause to disappear; remove from sight. Now *colloq.* LME.

📖 **1** J. I. M. STEWART She got into her car . . and vanished in the direction of the Berkshire Downs. I. MCEWAN The street vanished into total darkness. P. ACKROYD He needed to vanish from the gaze of his . . creditors. **2** L. CARROLL In the midst of his laughter and glee He had softly and suddenly vanished away. *Guardian* The farmer sees his profits vanish. A. LAMBERT Jamie was so bitter . . that soon most people's tolerance vanished.

Phrases: **vanishing cream** a cream that leaves no visible trace when rubbed into the skin. **vanishing-point** (*a*) the point towards which parallel receding lines viewed in perspective appear to converge; (*b*) the point at which something vanishes; the state of complete disappearance of something. ***vanish into smoke***: see SMOKE *noun*. ***vanish into the woodwork***. ***vanish into thin air***: see THIN *adjective, adverb, & noun*.

■ **vanisher** *noun* a person or thing which vanishes or disappears M19. **vanishingly** *adverb* in such a manner or to such a degree as almost to become invisible, non-existent, or negligible L19. **vanishment** *noun* the action of vanishing or disappearing; the state of having vanished: M19.

Vanist /ˈveɪnɪst/ *noun.* M17.
[from Sir Henry Vane (1613–62), English parliamentarian, Puritan, and governor of Massachusetts (1636–7) + -IST.]
Hist. An antinomian, *spec.* of a 17th-cent. New England sect.

vanitas /ˈvanɪtɑːs/ *noun.* M16.
[Latin: see VANITY.]
1 In full ***vanitas vanitatum*** /vanɪˈtɑːtəm/ [late Latin (Vulgate) *Ecclesiastes* 1:2]. Vanity of vanities, futility. Freq. as an exclam. of disillusionment or pessimism. M16.
2 ART. (Usu. **V-**.) A still-life painting of a 17th-cent. Dutch genre incorporating symbols of mortality or mutability. E20.

Vanitory /ˈvanɪt(ə)ri/ *noun.* Orig. *US.* Also **v-**. M20.
[from VANITY + -ORY¹, after *lavatory*.]
(Proprietary name for) a vanity unit. Also ***Vanitory unit***.

vanitous /ˈvanɪtəs/ *adjective. rare.* E20.
[from French *vaniteux*, or from next: see -OUS.]
= VAIN *adjective* 4.
■ **vanitously** *adverb* M20.

vanity /ˈvanɪti/ *noun.* ME.
[Old & mod. French *vanité* from Latin *vanitas*, from *vanus* VAIN *adjective*: see -ITY.]
1 That which is vain, futile, or worthless; that which is of no value or profit; vain and unprofitable conduct or use of time. *arch.* ME.
2 The quality of being vain or worthless; the futility or worthlessness *of* something. *arch.* ME. ▸†**b** The quality of being foolish or in error. LME–M17.
3 The quality of being personally vain; self-conceit and desire for admiration. ME. ▸**b** An instance of this, an occasion for being vain. Now *rare.* E18. ▸**c** A thing of which one is vain. Also (*slang*), a person's favourite alcoholic drink. M19.
4 A vain, idle, or worthless thing; a thing or action of no value. ME. ▸†**b** An idle tale or matter; a worthless or unfounded idea or statement. ME–L19.
†**5** The state of being void or empty; emptiness, inanity. *rare.* LME–L16.
6 = COMPACT *noun*² 2. Now *rare* or *obsolete.* E20.
7 a = ***vanity table*** below. M20. ▸**b** = ***vanity unit*** below. *N. Amer.* M20.

📖 **1** AV *Eccles.* 1:14 All *is* vanitie, and vexation of spirit. **2** E. B. PUSEY The vanity of the resistance of the kings of Judah. **3** K. GRAHAME Your songs are all conceit and boasting and vanity. **c** W. STYRON Her golden hair had always been her most reassuring physical vanity. **7a** A. BEATTIE Sitting . . in front of an Art Deco vanity that her grandmother had given her.

Comb.: **vanity bag**, **vanity-box**, **vanity-case** a small handbag, box, case, fitted with a mirror and powder-puff; **vanity basin** a wash-basin for a vanity unit; ***vanity-box***, ***vanity-case***: see ***vanity bag*** above; **Vanity Fair** [orig. with allus. to Bunyan's *Pilgrim's Progress* (1678)] a place or scene where all is frivolity, idle amusement, and empty show; the world or a part of it so regarded; **vanity licence plate** = ***vanity number plate*** below; **vanity mirror** (*a*) a small make-up mirror, esp. as a fitting in a motor vehicle; (*b*) a dressing-table mirror; **vanity number plate**, **vanity plate** *N. Amer.* a vehicle licence plate bearing a distinctive or personalized combination of letters, numbers, or both; **vanity press**, **vanity publisher** (orig. *US*) a publisher who publishes only at the author's expense; **vanity publishing**: at the author's expense through a printer or a vanity publisher; **vanity set** (*a*) a set of cosmetics or toiletries; (*b*) *US* a matching bath and vanity unit; **vanity table** a dressing-table; **vanity unit** a unit comprising a wash-basin set into a flat top with cupboards beneath.

Van John /van ˈdʒɒn/ *noun. slang.* E19.
[Alt. of VINGT-ET-UN.]
= PONTOON *noun*² 1.

vanner /ˈvanə/ *noun*¹. M16.
[from VAN *noun*¹, *verb*¹ + -ER¹.]
1 A person who winnows with a fan. *rare.* M16.
2 In full ***wind-vanner***. The kestrel. Cf. FANNER *noun* 4. M17.
3 MINING. **a** A person who tests the quality of ore by washing it on a shovel. L17. ▸**b** An apparatus for separating minerals from the gangue. L19.

vanner /ˈvanə/ *noun*². L19.
[from VAN *noun*³ + -ER¹.]
1 A light cart-horse suitable for drawing a small van. L19.
2 An owner or operator of a van; *esp.* a person who uses a van for recreation. *N. Amer.* L20.

Vannetais /ˈvanteɪ, *foreign* vantɛ/ *noun & adjective.* M20.
[French, from *Vannes* (see below).]
(Designating or pertaining to) a dialect of Breton spoken in the region of Vannes in Brittany.

Vannic /ˈvanɪk/ *noun & adjective.* L19.
[from Lake *Van* in eastern Turkey, centre of ancient Urartu + -IC.]
▸**A** *noun.* = URARTIAN *noun* 2. L19.
▸**B** *adjective.* = URARTIAN *adjective.* L19.

vanquish /ˈvaŋkwɪʃ/ *verb.* Now *literary.* ME.
[from Old French *vencus* pa. pple, *venquis* pa. t. of *veintre*, *vaintre* (mod. *vaincre*), from Latin *vincere* conquer, with 1st syll. alt. by assoc. with later Old & mod. French *vain-* and ending assim. to -ISH².]
▸**I** *verb trans.* **1** Overcome or defeat (an opponent or enemy) in conflict or battle. ME. ▸**b** *fig.* Overcome by spiritual power. LME. ▸†**c** Expel or banish *from* a place. M16–E17.
2 Overcome (a person) by some means other than physical conflict. LME.
3 Subdue, suppress, put an end to, (a feeling, state of things, etc.). LME.
†**4** Win or gain (a battle or other contest). LME–M16.
▸**II** *verb intrans.* **5** Be victorious; gain victory. LME.
■ **vanquishable** *adjective* (earlier in UNVANQUISHABLE) M16. **vanquisher** *noun* a conqueror, a subduer LME. **vanquishment** *noun* the action of vanquishing or overcoming someone or something L16.

Vansittartism /vanˈsɪtɑːtɪz(ə)m, -tət-/ *noun.* M20.
[from Sir Robert (later Lord) *Vansittart* (1881–1957), English diplomat + -ISM.]
The foreign policy advocated by Vansittart, esp. with regard to the demilitarization of Germany.
■ **Vansittartite** *adjective & noun* (pertaining to or characteristic of) a supporter of the policy of Vansittart M20.

vantage /ˈvɑːntɪdʒ/ *noun.* ME.
[Anglo-Norman, aphet. from Old French *avantage* ADVANTAGE *noun*: see -AGE.]
1 Advantage, benefit, gain; profit. Long *arch.* ME. ▸†**b** A perquisite. LME–M16.
2 Advantage or superiority in a contest. Also, a position or opportunity likely to give superiority; *esp.* = ***vantage-point*** below. ME.
†**3 a** A greater amount *of* something. Only in LME. ▸**b** An additional amount. E16–E18.
†**4** An advantage; a position or state of superiority. Freq. foll. by *at*, *for*. LME–M17. ▸**b** An opportunity, a chance. L16–E17.
5 TENNIS. = ADVANTAGE *noun* 5. L19.

📖 **2** LD MACAULAY To retreat till he should reach some spot where he might have the vantage of ground. L. M. MONTGOMERY Mrs Rachel could . . see them from her window vantage. **4b** SHAKES. *Cymb.* When shall we hear from him? Be assur'd, madam, With his next vantage.

Phrases: †**and a vantage**, †**and the vantage** and more. **at vantage** *arch.* at a disadvantage (i.e. at the other's advantage). ***coign of vantage***: see COIGN *noun* 1. †**for the vantage** in addition. **place of vantage**, **point of vantage** = ***vantage-point*** below. †**to the vantage** in addition. †**with a vantage**, †**with the vantage** and more.
Comb.: **vantage-ground** a position of advantage as regards defence or attack; **vantage-point** (*a*) a place affording a good view or prospect; (*b*) the point from which a scene is viewed.

vantage /ˈvɑːntɪdʒ/ *verb.* LME.
[from the noun.]
1 *verb trans.* Profit or benefit (a person). Long *arch.* LME.
†**2** *verb intrans.* Make a gain or profit. Only in M16.

vantbrace /ˈvantbreɪs/ *noun.* LME.
[Anglo-Norman *vauntbras*: see VAMBRACE.]
Hist. = VAMBRACE.

†**vantguard** *noun* var. of VANGUARD.

van't Hoff /vant ˈhɒf/ *noun.* L19.
[J. H. *van 't Hoff* (1852–1911), Dutch chemist.]
CHEMISTRY. Used *attrib.* and in *possess.* to designate rules and hypotheses concerning (*a*) stereochemical properties of molecules; (*b*) the osmotic pressure of solutes in solution; (*c*) the thermodynamics of chemical reactions.

†**vantward** *noun* see VAWARD.

Vanuatuan /vanwəˈtuːən/ *adjective & noun.* L20.
[from *Vanuatu* (see below) + -AN.]
▸**A** *adjective.* Of or pertaining to Vanuatu in the western Pacific (formerly the Condominium of the New Hebrides) or any of its constituent islands. L20.
▸**B** *noun.* A native or inhabitant of Vanuatu. L20.

vanward *noun* see VAWARD.

vanward /ˈvanwəd/ *adjective & adverb. literary.* E19.
[from VAN *noun*² + -WARD.]
▸**A** *adjective.* Situated in the van, at the front. E19.
▸**B** *adverb.* Towards or in the front; *to* the front; forward. E19.

vapid /ˈvapɪd/ *adjective.* M17.
[Latin *vapidus* savourless, insipid: see -ID¹. In sense 2 app. assoc. with VAPOUR *noun*.]
1 Of a drink etc.: lacking in flavour, flat, insipid. M17. ▸**b** Of taste or flavour: disagreeably bland, insipid. L17. ▸†**c** MEDICINE. Of the blood: devoid of vigour, weak. L17–M19.
†**2** Vaporous. M–L17.
3 *fig.* Devoid of animation, zest, or interest; dull, flat, lifeless, insipid. M18.

📖 **3** H. DAVID Tuneful but vapid musical comedies.

■ **vaˈpidity** *noun* (*a*) the fact or quality of being vapid; (*b*) a vapid remark, idea, feature, etc.: E18. **vapidly** *adverb* M19. **vapidness** *noun* E18.

vapography /veɪˈpɒɡrəfi/ *noun.* Now *rare* or *obsolete.* L19.
[from VAPO(UR *noun* + -GRAPHY.]
The effect of vapours on photographic plates or other sensitized material.

vapor *noun*, *verb* see VAPOUR *noun*, *verb*.

vaporable /ˈveɪp(ə)rəb(ə)l/ *adjective.* LME.
[from medieval Latin *vaporabilis*, from Latin *vaporare* emit steam or vapour, from *vapor* steam: see VAPOUR *noun*, -ABLE.]
1 Able to be converted into vapour; vaporizable. LME.
†**2** Capable of converting substances into vapour. Only in LME.
■ **vaporaˈbility** *noun* M19.

†**vaporation** *noun.* LME–E18.
[Latin *vaporatio(n-)* noun of action from *vaporare*: see prec., -ATION.]
Evaporation; occas., fumigation.

vaporer *noun* see VAPOURER.

vaporetto /vapəˈrɛtəʊ/ *noun.* Pl. **-tti** /-ti/, **-ttos**. E20.
[Italian = small steamboat, dim. of *vapore* from Latin *vapor* steam: see VAPOUR *noun*.]
In Venice, a canal boat (orig. a steamboat, now a motor-boat) used for public transport.

vaporific /veɪpəˈrɪfɪk, vap-/ *adjective.* L18.
[from VAPOUR *noun* + -I- + -FIC.]
1 Pertaining to, connected with, or causing vapour or vaporization. L18.
2 Vaporous. Now *rare.* L18.

vaporiform /ˈveɪp(ə)rɪfɔːm/ *adjective.* M19.
[from VAPOUR *noun* + -I- + -FORM.]
In the form of vapour.

vaporimeter /veɪpəˈrɪmɪtə/ *noun.* L19.
[formed as prec. + -METER.]
PHYSICS & CHEMISTRY. An instrument for measuring the volatility of oils by heating them in an air current.

vaporise *verb*, **vaporiser** *noun* vars. of VAPORIZE, VAPORIZER.

vaporish *adjective* see VAPOURISH.

vaporize /ˈveɪpərʌɪz/ *verb.* Also **-ise**, **vapour-**. M17.
[from VAPOUR *noun* + -IZE.]
1 *verb trans.* Convert into smoke. *rare.* M17.
2 *verb trans.* Convert into vapour; *fig.* eliminate, destroy utterly; cause to vanish. E19.
3 *verb intrans.* Give off a vapour; become vaporous; *fig.* (*rare*) vanish. E19.
4 *verb trans.* Spray with fine particles of liquid. *rare.* E20.
5 *verb intrans.* = VAPOUR *verb* 5. L20.

📖 **2** *Independent* Using the crude euphemisms of cartoon combat, he writes of 'vaporising' . . Argentines. *Nature* When a comet approaches the Sun, the outer surface is vapourized and blown away.

■ **vaporizable** *adjective* E19. **vaporiˈzation** *noun* the action or process of converting something, or of being converted, into vapour L18.

vaporizer /ˈveɪpərʌɪzə/ *noun.* Also **-iser**. M19.
[from prec. + -ER¹.]
A device that vaporizes substances, esp. for medicinal inhalation.

vaporograph /ˈveɪp(ə)rəgrɑːf/ *noun. rare.* E20.
[from VAPOUR *noun* + -O- + -GRAPH.]
An image produced by vapography.

†**vaporose** *adjective. rare.* LME–M18.
[from Latin *vaporosus*, from *vapor*: see VAPOUR *noun*, -OSE[1].]
Vaporous; easily vaporizing.

vaporous /ˈveɪp(ə)rəs/ *adjective.* LME.
[from late Latin *vaporus* or Latin *vaporosus* (see prec.), or in later use from VAPOUR *noun*: see -OUS.]
†**1 a** *MEDICINE.* Of the nature of a supposed emanation from an internal organ or substance in the body. Cf. VAPOUR *noun* 3a. LME–M17. ▸**b** Esp. of food: emitting or exuding vapour or a strong aroma; provoking supposed unhealthy exhalations. M16–M18.
2 Of or designating the form, nature, or consistency of vapour; characterized by vapour or (*loosely*) moistness. LME. ▸**b** Of a fabric or garment: gauzy, filmy. M19.
3 Filled with vapour, thick or dim with vapour; foggy, misty; covered or hidden by vapour. Now chiefly *literary.* LME.
4 Of a person etc.: inclined to be fanciful or vague. Of an idea, a statement, etc.: fanciful, vague, insubstantial. E17.

> 📖 **1a** SIR T. BROWNE The brain doth . . suffer from vaporous ascensions from the stomach. **2** B. UNSWORTH Outside there was a thin vaporous mist in the air. **3** W. PETTY Holland is a Level Country, . . moist and vaporous. **4** J. LE CARRÉ I decided to take an official tone . . : no half promises, no vaporous reassurances for me.

■ **vapoˈrosity** *noun* vaporous quality LME. **vaporously** *adverb* L19. **vaporousness** *noun* E17.

vapory *adjective* see VAPOURY.

vapour /ˈveɪpə/ *noun.* Also ***-or.** LME.
[Old & mod. French *vapeur*, †*vapour* or Latin *vapor* steam, heat: see -OUR.]
1 Matter in the form of a tenuous fluid, either as a gas or as a suspension of minute droplets, esp. as produced by the action of heat on moisture. LME.
2 A substance in the form of a gas or of a suspension of minute droplets; *spec.* a fluid that fills a space like a gas but, being below its critical temperature, can be liquefied by pressure alone. Also *loosely* (chiefly *poet.*), smoke; a smoky substance emitted from burning material. LME. ▸**b** A mist or damp cloud rising by natural causes from the ground or from some damp place. LME. ▸**c** *fig.* Something insubstantial or worthless. LME.
3 In *pl.* ▸**a** *MEDICINE.* The unhealthy exhalations supposed to be developed in the organs of the body (esp. the stomach). *arch.* LME. ▸**b** A condition of ill health supposed to be caused by such exhalations, as depression, hypochondria, etc. (*arch.*). Now chiefly *joc.*, (an attack of) nervousness, indignant rage, etc.; hysterics. Freq. with *the*, now esp. in ***a fit of the vapours.*** M17.
4 A fantastic idea; a foolish boast. Now *rare.* E17.

> 📖 **1** U. LE GUIN They could see each other's breath, faint vapour in the steadily growing moonlight. **2** S. RUSHDIE He inhaled vapours from crushed boiled eucalyptus leaves. **3b** *Times* A four-letter word is surely not enough to give anyone . . the vapours.

Comb.: **vapour barrier** a thin layer of material, often polythene sheeting, impermeable to water vapour and used to insulate buildings, waterproof clothing, etc.; **vapour-bath** = ***steam bath*** s.v. STEAM *noun*; **vapour density** the density of a gas or vapour relative to that of hydrogen at the same pressure and temperature; **vapour lock** an interruption in the flow of a liquid through a pipe (esp. a fuel line) as a result of its vaporization; **vapour pressure** the pressure exerted by a vapour in contact with its liquid or solid form; **vapour-proof** *adjective* impervious to vapour; **vapour tension** = ***vapour pressure*** above; **vapour trail** a trail of condensed water vapour in the wake of an aircraft or rocket at high altitude, seen as a white streak against the sky (also called ***condensation trail***); **vapourware** *slang* computer software that as yet exists only in the plans or publicity material of its developers.
■ **vapourless** *adjective* free from vapour; *esp.* (of wind or the sky) dry, cloudless: M19.

vapour /ˈveɪpə/ *verb.* Also ***-or.** LME.
[from the noun Sense 1 may reflect Latin *vaporare* emit vapour or steam.]
1 *verb intrans.* Rise as vapour; be emitted or diffused in the form of vapour. (Foll. by *up*, *out*.) Now *rare.* LME. ▸**b** Evaporate *away*, be dissipated in the form of vapour. Now *rare.* M16. ▸**c** Pass or be dissolved *into* a moist or vaporous state. *rare.* M16.
2 *verb trans.* **a** Cause to rise *up* or up in the form of vapour. Now *rare.* LME. ▸**b** Convert to vapour; cause to evaporate *away*; drive *out* in the form of vapour. Now *rare.* LME.
3 †**a** *verb trans.* Emit or discharge in the form of vapour. Foll. by *out*, *up*. LME–M17. ▸**b** *verb intrans.* Emit vapour. Long *rare.* M16.
4 *verb trans.* Expose to the effect of vapour; treat with vapour; obscure with vapour. *rare.* M16.
5 *verb intrans.* Use empty or insubstantial language; talk or write vacuously, grandiloquently, or boastingly; bluster. E17. ▸**b** *verb trans.* Declare or assert in a boasting or grandiloquent manner. M17.
6 *verb intrans.* Act in a boasting or ostentatious manner; show off; swagger. M17.
7 a *verb trans.* Give (a person) the vapours; depress, bore. Now *rare.* L18. ▸**b** *verb intrans.* Get the vapours. *rare.* E19.

> 📖 **1** H. E. BATES I could see his breath and my own vapouring . . in the freezing air. **3b** S. HEANEY The supervisor rustled past, sibilant, vapouring into his breviary. **5** J. CAREY Vapouring on about the days of his youth.

■ **vapoured** *adjective* (now *rare*) †(*a*) filled with or formed from moisture; (*b*) affected with the vapours, suffering from depression or low spirits: M16. **vapouring** *verbal noun* †(*a*) evaporation; (*b*) grandiloquent or boastful speech or action; an instance of this, a piece of vain talk or imagination: LME.

vapourer /ˈveɪp(ə)rə/ *noun.* In sense 1 also ***-orer.** M17.
[from VAPOUR *verb* + -ER[1].]
1 A person who vapours; a boastful, grandiloquent, or vacuous talker. M17.
2 In full ***vapourer moth.*** A European day-flying moth of the genus *Orgyia*, the females of which are wingless and the larvae very hairy, *esp.* the red-brown *O. antiqua.* M17.

vapourise *verb* var. of VAPORIZE.

vapourish /ˈveɪpərɪʃ/ *adjective.* Also ***vapor-.** M17.
[from VAPOUR *noun* + -ISH[1].]
1 Of the nature of vapour; dimmed or obscured by vapour; vapoury. M17.
2 Of or pertaining to the vapours; inclined to depression or nervous afflictions. *arch.* E18.

> 📖 **1** E. GLASGOW In the early part of the night there was a vapourish moon. **2** S. RICHARDSON I am in the depth of vapourish despondency.

■ **vapourishness** *noun* M18.

vapourize *verb* var. of VAPORIZE.

vapoury /ˈveɪp(ə)ri/ *adjective.* Also ***-ory.** L16.
[from VAPOUR *noun* + -Y[1].]
1 Of the nature or consistency of vapour; composed of or caused by vapour; characterized by vapour. L16. ▸**b** *fig.* Insubstantial, indefinite, vague. E19.
2 = VAPOURISH 2. *rare.* L18.
3 Dimmed or obscured by vapour. E19.

vappa /ˈvapə/ *noun.* Now *rare* or *obsolete.* E17.
[Latin.]
Flat or sour wine.

vapulate /ˈvapjʊleɪt/ *verb. rare.* E17.
[Latin *vapulat-* pa. ppl stem of *vapulare* be beaten: see -ATE[3].]
1 *verb trans.* Beat, strike. E17.
2 *verb intrans.* **a** Undergo a flogging. L18. ▸**b** Administer a flogging. E19.
■ **vapuˈlation** *noun* a beating, a flogging M17.

vaquero /vəˈkɛːrəʊ/ *noun.* Pl. **-os.** E19.
[Spanish, from *vaca* cow. Cf. Portuguese *vaqueiro.*]
In Spanish-speaking parts of America: a cowboy, a cowherd; a cattle-driver.

VAR *abbreviation.*
Value-added reseller.

var /vɑː/ *noun. Canad.* L18.
[Dial. var. of FIR.]
The balsam fir, *Abies balsamea.*

var. *abbreviation.*
1 Variant.
2 Variety.

vara /ˈvɑːrə/ *noun.* L17.
[Spanish, Portuguese = rod, yardstick from Latin = forked pole, trestle, from *varus* bent.]
1 A linear measure used in Spain, Portugal, and Latin America, of varying length but usu. about 84 cm (33 inches). L17.
2 *BULLFIGHTING.* A long spiked lance used by a picador. M20.

varactor /vəˈraktə/ *noun.* M20.
[from *var(iable re)actor.*]
ELECTRONICS. A semiconductor diode with a variable capacitance dependent on the applied voltage. Also ***varactor diode.***

†**varan** *noun* see VARANUS.

Varangian /vəˈrandʒɪən/ *noun & adjective.* L18.
[from medieval Latin *Varangus* from medieval Greek *baraggos*, through Slavonic langs. from Old Norse *Væringi* (pl. *Væringjar*), prob. from *vár* (pl. *várar*) pledge: see -IAN.]
Hist. ▸**A** *noun.* **1** Any of the Scandinavian rovers who in the 9th and 10th cents. overran parts of Russia and reached Constantinople; a member of the Varangian Guard (see below). L18.
2 The language spoken by these people. *rare.* M19.
▸**B** *adjective.* Of or pertaining to the Varangians; composed of Varangians. L18.
Varangian Guard the bodyguard of the later Byzantine emperors, formed of Varangians (latterly including Anglo-Saxons).

varanian /vəˈreɪnɪən/ *noun & adjective.* Now *rare.* M19.
[from mod. Latin VARANUS + -IAN.]
ZOOLOGY. ▸**A** *noun.* = VARANID *noun.* M19.
▸**B** *adjective.* Of, pertaining to, or characteristic of varanids or monitor lizards. M19.

varanid /vəˈranɪd/ *noun & adjective.* L19.
[from mod. Latin *Varanidae*: see next, -ID[3].]
ZOOLOGY. ▸**A** *noun.* A lizard of the family Varanidae, a monitor lizard. L19.
▸**B** *adjective.* Of, pertaining to, or designating (a lizard of) the family Varanidae. M20.

varanus /ˈvarənəs/ *noun.* Also (earlier) †**varan.** M19.
[mod. Latin (see below), from Arab. *waran*, var. of *waral* monitor lizard. Cf. French. *varan.*]
A lizard of the genus *Varanus.* Also more widely, any monitor lizard. Now chiefly as mod. Latin genus name.

vardapet *noun* var. of VARTABED.

†**vardingale** *noun* var. of FARTHINGALE.

vardo /ˈvɑːdəʊ/ *noun.* Orig. *slang.* Pl. **-os.** Also **varda** /ˈvɑːdə/. E19.
[Romany.]
A waggon. Now *spec.* a Gypsy caravan.

vardy /ˈvɑːdi/ *noun.* Now *dial. rare.* M18.
[Colloq. or dial. var. of VERDICT *noun.*]
Opinion, judgement, verdict.

varec /ˈvarɛk/ *noun.* Now chiefly *dial.* Also **-ch.** L17.
[French. Cf. VRAIC, WRACK *noun*[2].]
Seaweed. Also *spec.* = KELP.

vargueño /vɑːˈgeɪnjəʊ/ *noun.* Pl. **-os.** E20.
[Spanish *bargueño*, *vargueño* adjective of Bargas, a village near Toledo, the former place of manufacture.]
A kind of cabinet made in Spain in the 16th and 17th cents., with numerous small compartments and drawers behind a fall-front which opens out to form a writing surface.

vari /ˈvɑːri/ *noun*[1]. L18.
[from Malagasy *varikandana* or *varianda.*]
The ruffed lemur, *Varecia variegata.*

†**vari** *noun*[2] pl. of VARUS *noun*[1].

vari- /ˈvɛːri/ *combining form* of VARIABLE *adjective*, VARIOUS *adjective*: see -I-.
■ **varihued** *adjective* of various hues, varicoloured E20. **vari-sized** *adjective* of various sizes M20.

variability /ˌvɛːrɪəˈbɪlɪti/ *noun.* L18.
[from next + -ITY.]
The fact or quality of being variable in some respect; tendency towards or capacity for variation or change.

variable /ˈvɛːrɪəb(ə)l/ *adjective & noun.* LME.
[Old & mod. French, or from Latin *variabilis*, from *variare*: see VARY *verb*, -ABLE.]
▸**A** *adjective.* **1** Varying or liable to vary in state or quality; mutable, changeable, fluctuating, uncertain. LME.
2 Of a person: apt to change from one opinion or course of action to another; inconstant, fickle, unreliable. Now *rare.* LME.
†**3** Of different kinds or degrees; diverse, various. LME–E17.
4 Of the weather etc.: liable to vary in temperature or character; changeable; (of wind, a current, etc.) tending to change in direction, shifting. L15.
†**5** Of land: of varying ownership; debatable. Only in M16.
6 That may be varied, changed, or modified; alterable; (of a gear) designed to give varying speeds. L16.
7 Liable to vary in size, number, amount, or degree; (of a quantity or number) liable to vary, having various values in different instances or at different times. E17. ▸**b** *ECONOMICS.* Of a cost: varying with output. M20.
8 Of a star: that varies periodically in actual or perceived brightness. L18.
9 *BIOLOGY.* **a** In names of animals and plants: of a form or colour which varies considerably between individuals, or at different seasons. L18. ▸**b** Liable to deviate from a typical form, or to occur in different forms; tending to change in structure etc. M19.

> 📖 **1** J. D. SUTHERLAND His general health remained variable with occasional febrile states. **6** *Guardian* After six months, the . . mortgage reverts to the society's variable base rate. *Practical Woodworking* Variable speed is . . better if you are . . cutting a variety of materials. **7** ALAN JOHNSON Its strength is more variable than that of a more homogeneous material. *Independent* Awards can be for highly variable amounts. **9b** A. R. WALLACE From such a variable species . . more new species may arise.

▸**B** *noun.* **1** *SCIENCE.* A quantity or force which during a calculation or investigation is assumed to vary or be capable of varying in value. E19. ▸**b** *COMPUTING.* A data item that may take on more than one value during or between programs and is stored in a particular designated area of memory; the area of memory itself; (more fully ***variable name***) the name referring to such an item or location. **M19.** ▸**c** *LOGIC.* A symbol whose referend is not specified, though the range of possible referends usually is. **E20.**

2 a Chiefly *NAUTICAL.* A variable or shifting wind; *spec.* in *pl.*, the region between the NE and SE trade winds. **M19.** ▸**b** *ASTRONOMY.* A variable star. **M19.**

3 *gen.* A thing which is liable to vary or change; a changeable factor, feature, or element. **M19.**

> 🕮 **2a** C. DARWIN The 'variables' which are so common in the Equatorial regions. **3** *Independent* The conclusions implied are . . inaccurate because they pick on one variable only.

■ **variableness** *noun* **LME.** **variably** *adverb* **L16.**

Variac /ˈvɛːrɪak/ *noun.* **M20.**
[from VARI(ABLE *adjective* + *-ac* perh. repr. *alternating current*.]
ELECTRICITY. (Proprietary name for) a type of autotransformer in which the ratio of the input and output voltages can be varied.

varia lectio /ˌvɛːrɪə ˈlɛktɪəʊ/ *noun phr.* Pl. ***variae lectiones*** /ˌvɛːrɪʌɪ lɛktɪˈəʊniːz/. **M17.**
[Latin.]
A variant reading in a text.

variance /ˈvɛːrɪəns/ *noun.* **ME.**
[Old French from Latin *variantia*, from *variare* VARY *verb*: see -ANCE.]
1 The fact or state of undergoing change or alteration; tendency to vary or become different. **ME.** ▸†**b** Inconstancy (of a person). **LME–E16.**
2 The fact or quality of differing; difference, divergence, discrepancy. Freq. in ***at variance***, inconsistent, incompatible, (foll. by *with*, occas. *to*). **LME.**
3 The state or fact of disagreeing or quarrelling; enmity, dissension, contention, debate. Freq. in ***at variance***, in disagreement, in conflict, (foll. by *with*, *from*). **LME.** ▸**b** Opposition or antagonism *to* something. *rare.* **M19.**
4 A disagreement, a quarrel, a dispute, formerly *esp.* one leading to legal action between parties. Now *rare* or *obsolete*. **LME.**
5 A difference, a discrepancy, esp. (*LAW*) between two statements or documents. **LME.** ▸**b** *US LAW.* An official dispensation, esp. from a building regulation. **E20.**
6 The fact of changing or varying *from* a state, opinion, etc.; an instance of this. Long *rare*. **LME.**
7 a *STATISTICS.* A measure of the variation of a set of quantities from the mean, equal to the square of the standard deviation. **E20.** ▸**b** *ECONOMICS.* The difference between actual and expected costs, profits, output, etc. **M20.**

> 🕮 **1** SIR T. BROWNE It being reasonable for every man to vary his opinion according to the variance of his reason. **2** O. SACKS The patient . . maintains a set of . . attitudes wholly at variance with the realities of her position. *Fremdsprachen* Variances in linguistic . . matters became criteria for discrimination. *Oxford News* A party . . too dictatorial to allow a variance of opinion within its ranks. **3** J. AGATE I find myself at variance with New York opinion.

Phrases: ***at variance***: see senses 2, 3 above. †**in variance** (*a*) forming a subject of debate, contention, or legal action; (*b*) = ***at variance*** (see sense 3 above).

variant /ˈvɛːrɪənt/ *adjective & noun.* **LME.**
[Old & mod. French, pres. pple of *varier* VARY *verb*: see -ANT[1].]
▶ **A** *adjective.* **1** Of a person: changeable in disposition or purpose; inconstant, fickle. (Foll. by *of*, *in*.) Now *rare*. **LME.** ▸†**b** Dissentient, disagreeing. Only in **LME.**
2 Of a thing: exhibiting variation or change; tending to vary or alter; not remaining uniform, variable. Now *rare*. **LME.**
3 Exhibiting difference or variety; varied, diverse, various. **LME.**
4 Differing or discrepant from something else; varying or diverging from the norm. (Foll. by *from*, †*to*.) **LME.**

> 🕮 **4** F. W. FARRAR Instances of variant readings in the Hebrew. OED The variant spelling *prophesy* is . . now confined to the verb.

▶ **B** *noun.* **1** A form or version of something differing in some respect from other forms of the same thing. (Foll. by *of*, occas. *on*.) **M19.**
2 *spec.* An alternative reading in a text; *esp.* a textual variation in two or more copies of a (printed) work. **M19.**

> 🕮 **1** *Times* A debased and impoverished variant of the real thing. *Heredity* Genetic variants . . coexist . . within a single interbreeding population. G. JONES Beowulf's fight with the dragon is merely a variant on his fight with . . Grendel.

variate /ˈvɛːrɪət/ *noun.* **L19.**
[from Latin *variatus* pa. pple of *variare* VARY *verb*: see -ATE[1].]
STATISTICS. A quantity or attribute having a numerical value for each member of a population; *esp.* one for which the values occur according to a frequency distribution. Formerly also, an observed value of such a quantity or attribute.

†**variate** *verb.* **M16.**
[Latin *variat-* pa. ppl stem of *variare* VARY *verb*: see -ATE[3].]
1 *verb trans.* Produce a modification or variation in (something); alter, cause to change, make various. **M16–M19.**
2 *verb intrans.* Vary, be variable or various. Only in **L16.**

variation /vɛːrɪˈeɪʃ(ə)n/ *noun.* **LME.**
[Old & mod. French, or directly from Latin *variatio(n-)*, formed as prec.: see -ATION.]
▶ **I** *gen.* **1** Difference, divergence, or discrepancy between two or more things or people; variance, conflict; an instance of this. Long *obsolete* exc. as passing into sense 3. **LME.**
†**2 a** Uncertainty, doubt. Only in **L15.** ▸**b** Inconstancy. **E–M16.**
3 The fact of varying in condition, character, degree, etc., over time or distance, or among a number of instances; the fact of undergoing change or alteration, esp. within certain limits; the degree or amount of this. **E16.**
4 An instance of varying or changing; a change in something, esp. within certain limits; a difference due to some change or alteration. **E17.**
5 A deviation or departure *from* something. **M17.**
6 The action or an act of making some change or alteration, esp. (*LAW*) in the terms of an order, trust, contract, etc. **E18.**
7 A different or distinct form or version of something; a variety, a variant; *CHESS* a particular line of play. Freq. foll. by *of* or (passing into *transf.* use of sense 12a) *on*. **M19.**

> 🕮 **3** ALAN JOHNSON Variation in wall thickness . . is typical of hollow cast-iron columns. *Independent* Temporary workers to cope with seasonal variation in demand. **4** T. H. HUXLEY In different specimens . . the lava exhibits great variations. B. BRYSON Minute variations in speech . . along the eastern seaboard. **5** W. CRUISE He did not . . make any variation from what was then determined. **6** *Independent* The first defendant sought a variation of the injunction. ***deed of variation***, ***variation order***, etc.

▶ **II** *spec.* **8** The (amount of) deviation of a compass needle etc. from the true north and south line; the angular difference between magnetic north and true north. Also more fully ***variation of the compass***, †***variation of the lodestone***, ***variation of the needle***. Cf. DECLINATION 4c. **LME.**
9 The change in the length of the mercury in the tube of a barometer, thermometer, etc.; the extent or range of this. **E18.**
10 *ASTRONOMY.* A deviation of a celestial object from its mean orbit or motion; *esp.* the libration of the moon. **E18.**
11 *MATH.* †**a** = PERMUTATION 3a. Only in **E18.** ▸†**b** = COMBINATION 3a. Only in **E18.** ▸**c** Change in a function or functions of an equation due to an indefinitely small increase or decrease in the value of the constants. **M18.** ▸**d** The amount by which some quantity changes in value; *esp.* the change in a function when there is a small change in the variables or constituent functions of the function. **E19.** ▸**e** The difference between the values of a function at either end of a subinterval; the sum of such differences for all the non-overlapping subintervals into which a given interval is divided; the upper bound (if any) of this sum when all possible modes of subdividing the interval are considered. **E20.**
12 a *MUSIC.* A version of a theme modified in melody, rhythm, harmony, or ornamentation, so as to present it in a new but still recognizable form; each of a set of versions of a theme so modified; in *pl.* (now *rare*), the embellishments added to a simple air to give variety on repetition. Also, the musical technique of so modifying a theme. Usu. foll. by *on* (a theme). **E19.** ▸**b** *BALLET.* A solo dance. **E20.**
13 *BIOLOGY.* Divergence, esp. genetic or heritable divergence, in the structure, character, or function of (part of) an organism from that considered typical of or usual in the species or group. Also, the fact or occurrence of an organism in more than one (esp. genetically) distinct form. **M19.** ▸**b** A slight departure or divergence from a typical or original form; a (heritable) change in an organism. **M19.**

> 🕮 **12a** *Guardian* Marvellously weighted accompanying chords in the fifth Trout variation. *transf.*: *Modern Painters* Minor variations on the themes and techniques of the French Impressionists. *fig.*: D. EDEN Her devious husband . . thought out new variations on the theme of burglary. **13** R. DAWKINS Darwinian selection has to have genetic variation to work on.

Phrases: **calculus of variations** *MATH.* a form of calculus applied to expressions or functions in which the law relating the quantities is liable to variation, esp. to find what relation between the variables makes an integral a maximum or a minimum. ***elegant variation***: see ELEGANT 2.

Comb.: **variation method** *PHYSICS* a method for finding an approximate solution to Schrödinger's equation by varying the trial solutions to find which gives the lowest value for the energy and is therefore closest to the true solution; **variation principle** *PHYSICS* the principle (employed in the variation method) that the energy corresponding to an arbitrary wave function cannot be less than the actual lowest energy of the system under consideration.

variational /vɛːrɪˈeɪʃ(ə)n(ə)l/ *adjective.* **L19.**
[from prec. + -AL[1].]
Chiefly *SCIENCE.* Of or pertaining to variation: marked or characterized by variation.
■ **variationally** *adverb* **M20.**

variationist /vɛːrɪˈeɪʃ(ə)nɪst/ *noun & adjective.* **E20.**
[formed as prec. + -IST.]
▶ **A** *noun.* **1** A person who practises variation or introduces variety in something; *esp.* a person who composes musical variations. **E20.**
2 *LINGUISTICS.* A person who studies variations in usage among different speakers of the same language. **L20.**
▶ **B** *adjective.* Of or pertaining to the study of linguistic variation. **L20.**

variative /ˈvɛːrɪətɪv/ *adjective. rare.* **L19.**
[from VARY *verb* + -ATIVE.]
Variational.

variator /ˈvɛːrɪeɪtə/ *noun.* **M18.**
[In sense 1 mod. Latin (cf. VARY *verb* 8b); in sense 2 from VARIATION: see VARIATE *verb*, -ATOR.]
1 At Oxford University, an orator who made a satirical speech at the annual degree ceremony. *obsolete* exc. *Hist.* **M18.**
2 A device which permits or compensates for variation. **L19.**

varicap /ˈvɛːrɪkap/ *noun.* **M20.**
[from *vari(able cap(acitance.*]
ELECTRONICS. = VARACTOR. Also ***varicap diode***.

variceal /varɪˈsiːəl/ *adjective.* **M20.**
[from Latin *varic-*, VARIX, after *corneal*, *laryngeal*, etc.]
MEDICINE. Of, pertaining to, or involving a varix.

varicella /varɪˈsɛlə/ *noun.* **L18.**
[mod. Latin, irreg. from VARIOLA + -ELLA.]
MEDICINE. Chickenpox; the virus causing this (also ***varicella zoster***).
■ **varicellar** *adjective* = VARICELLOUS **L19.** **varicellous** *adjective* of, pertaining to, affected with, or of the nature of varicella (chickenpox) **E19.**

varices *noun* pl. of VARIX.

variciform /vəˈrɪsɪfɔːm/ *adjective. rare.* **M19.**
[from Latin *varic-*, VARIX + -I- + -FORM.]
Resembling a varicose vein.

varicocele /ˈvarɪkəsiːl/ *noun.* **M18.**
[from Latin *varic-*, VARIX + -O- + -CELE.]
MEDICINE. (The condition characterized by) a clump of dilated veins in the spermatic cord, sometimes associated with a low sperm count.
■ **varicoceˈlectomy** *noun* surgical correction of a varicocele **L19.**

varicoloured /ˈvɛːrɪkʌləd/ *adjective.* Also ***-colored**. **M17.**
[from VARI- + COLOURED *adjective*.]
Of various or different colours; variegated in colour; *fig.* different, diverse.

varicose /ˈvarɪkəʊs, varɪˈkəʊs/ *adjective.* **LME.**
[Latin *varicosus*, from *varic-*, VARIX: see -OSE[1].]
1 *MEDICINE.* Esp. of a vein: abnormally swollen or distended and tortuous; affected with or characterized by such swelling. **LME.**
2 *ZOOLOGY & BOTANY.* Unusually enlarged or swollen; resembling a varicose vein. **E19.**
3 Of an appliance: designed or used for the treatment of varicose veins. **M19.**
1 varicose veins (the condition characterized by) veins which have become abnormally distended, esp. in the superficial parts of the legs.
■ **varicosed** *adjective* abnormally swollen; *esp.* affected by varicose veins: **L19.**

varicosity /varɪˈkɒsɪti/ *noun.* **M19.**
[from prec. + -ITY.]
1 An irregular or abnormal swelling or distension, esp. in a vessel or fibre. **M19.**
2 The state or condition of being varicose or abnormally swollen; an instance of this. Also, the state of having varicose veins; a varicose vein. **L19.**

†**varicous** *adjective.* **L16–L18.**
[French *variqueux* or Latin *varicosus* VARICOSE: see -OUS.]
Varicose.

varied /ˈvɛːrɪd/ *ppl adjective.* **LME.**
[from VARY *verb* + -ED[1].]
1 Varicoloured, variegated (esp. in the names of birds and animals). **LME.**
2 Differing from one another; of different or various sorts or kinds. **L16.**
3 Marked by variation or variety; occurring in different forms or qualities; undergoing or having undergone variation. **M18.**

📖 **1** *varied* SITTELLA. **varied thrush** a migratory thrush, *Ixoreus naevia*, of northern and western N. America, which has orange and black or brown underparts, with the back slate-blue in the male and grey-brown in the female. **2** SHAKES. *Tit. A.* Sweet varied notes, enchanting every ear! P. G. WODEHOUSE Varied methods . . of borrowing money. **3** G. P. R. JAMES The path she followed was like a varied but a pleasant life. W. STYRON Varied weather—hot days, then oddly cool, damp days.

■ **variedly** *adverb* in a varied manner, diversely E19. **variedness** *noun* (*rare*) L19.

variegate /ˈvɛːrɪgeɪt, ˈvɛːrɪə-/ *verb trans.* M17.
[Latin *variegat-* pa. ppl stem of *variegare* make varied, from *varius* VARIOUS: see -ATE[3].]
1 Diversify; give variety to; enliven with differences or changes. M17. ▸**b** *esp.* Make varied in colour or appearance; mark with irregular patches or streaks of different colours or appearance. E18.
2 Vary by change or alteration. *rare.* L17.
■ **variegator** *noun* (*rare*) a person who or thing which variegates something L19.

variegated /ˈvɛːrɪgeɪtɪd, ˈvɛːrɪə-/ *ppl adjective.* M17.
[from prec. + -ED[1].]
1 Marked with irregular patches or streaks of a different colour; exhibiting diverse colours. Freq. in BOTANY, having the leaves edged, patterned, etc., with a colour other than green. M17. ▸**b** Of colour: characterized by variegation. M17.
2 Marked or characterized by variety; of a varied character, form, or nature; diverse. M17.
3 Varied or diversified (in colour, appearance, etc.) *with* something. L17.
4 Produced by variation; variant. *rare.* L19.

📖 **1** T. FULLER Tulips . . variegated, with stripes of divers colours. *Practical Gardening* Variegated box can look very interesting in winter with heathers. **variegated thistle** (chiefly *NZ*) the milk-thistle, *Silybum marianum*, a naturalized European weed. **2** SARA MAITLAND Lisa's many and variegated attempts to get her, Phoebe, to take herself seriously.

variegation /vɛːrɪˈgeɪʃ(ə)n, vɛːrɪə-/ *noun.* M17.
[formed as prec.: see -ATION.]
1 The condition or quality of being variegated or varied in colour; the process or fact of variegating something; *spec.* in BOTANY, the presence of patches of different-coloured tissue in the leaves, petals, or other parts of a plant (freq. inherited or due to viral infection). M17. ▸**b** A variegated marking. Usu. in *pl.* M17.
2 The action or process of diversifying or making something varied in character; an instance of this. M17. ▸†**b** Alternation *of* (one thing with another). Only in L18.

varier /ˈvɛːrɪə/ *noun. rare.* LME.
[from VARY *verb* + -ER[1].]
†**1** A slanderer. Only in LME.
†**2** = PREVARICATOR 4. E–M17.
3 A person who varies or dissents *from* something. M19.

varietal /vəˈrʌɪət(ə)l/ *adjective & noun.* M19.
[from VARIETY + -AL[1].]
▶ **A** *adjective.* **1** BIOLOGY & MINERALOGY. Of, pertaining to, characteristic of, or forming a distinct variety of organism or mineral. M19.
2 (Of wine) made from a single designated variety of grape; of or pertaining to such wine. Orig. *US.* M20.
▶ **B** *noun.* A wine made from a single designated variety of grape. Orig. *US.* M20.
■ **varietally** *adverb* in respect of varietal qualities; as a distinct variety: L19.

varietist /vəˈrʌɪətɪst/ *noun & adjective.* E20.
[from next + -IST.]
▶ **A** *noun.* A person of unusual or varied habits etc.; a person who seeks variety, esp. in sexual partners. E20.
▶ **B** *attrib.* or as *adjective.* Of, pertaining to, or characteristic of a varietist. M20.
■ **varietism** *noun* the practices of a varietist E20.

variety /vəˈrʌɪəti/ *noun.* L15.
[Old & mod. French *variété* or Latin *varietas*, from *varius* VARIOUS + -(i)tas -ITY.]
†**1 a** Variation or change of fortune. L15–E17. ▸**b** Tendency to change one's mind; fickleness. M–L16. ▸**c** Dissension, division. Only in M16.
†**2** The fact or quality of being varied in colour; variegation. *rare.* L15–E17.
3 The fact, quality, or condition of being varied; (a) diversity of nature or character; absence of monotony, sameness, or uniformity. L15. ▸**b** In *pl.* A series or succession of different forms, conditions, etc.; variations. E17.
4 A number *of* things, qualities, etc., different or distinct in character; a varied assemblage, number, or quantity *of* something. Formerly also without article. Treated as *sing.* or (occas.) *pl.* L15.
5 Difference or discrepancy between two or more things, or in the same thing at different times. M16.
6 A different form *of* some thing, quality, or condition; a thing which differs or varies from others of the same class or kind; a kind, a sort. E17. ▸**b** BIOLOGY. A taxonomic grouping ranking next below a subspecies (where present) or species, whose members differ from others of the same subspecies or species in minor but permanent or heritable characters (cf. FORM *noun* 4d, SUBSPECIES); the organisms which compose such a grouping. Also, a plant or animal which varies in some trivial respect from its immediate parent or type. E17. ▸**c** PHILATELY. (A stamp belonging to) a set or group of postage stamps differing slightly from others of the same issue in colour, paper, etc., esp. as a result of a deliberate action during production. M19.
7 Theatrical or music hall entertainment of a light and varied character, including songs, dances, comedy acts, etc.; such entertainment presented on radio or television. E20.

📖 **3** R. INGALLS Her work at the studios was . . full of variety. J. UPDIKE I loved it all . . its social and ethnic variety. *Proverb:* Variety is the spice of life. ***requisite variety***: see REQUISITE *adjective.* **4** *Independent* Diverse programmes . . to appeal to a wide variety of tastes. *Antique Collector* A variety of colourful and spectacular styles. **6** *Economist* Czech communism would be different from the Russian variety. *Independent* More varieties of Turkish delight than you ever thought existed. **b** M. KRAMER The preponderant grape in sherry is the Palomino variety. **7** attrib.: ***variety artist***, ***variety performance***, ***variety show***, ***variety theatre***, etc.

Comb.: **variety meats** *N. Amer.* offal; **variety shop**, **variety store** (chiefly *N. Amer.*) a shop selling many kinds of small items.

varifocal /vɛːrɪˈfəʊk(ə)l/ *adjective & noun.* M20.
[from VARI- + FOCAL.]
▶ **A** *adjective.* **1** Having a focal length that can be varied. M20.
2 OPHTHALMOLOGY. Having an infinite number of focusing distances for near, intermediate, and far vision; omnifocal. L20.
▶ **B** *noun.* OPHTHALMOLOGY. A varifocal lens. L20.

variform /ˈvɛːrɪfɔːm/ *adjective.* M17.
[from VARI- + -FORM.]
Of various forms; varied or different in form.
■ **variformed** *adjective* (*rare*) = VARIFORM L16. **variˈformity** *noun* (*rare*) variety or diversity of form E18. **variformly** *adverb* L19.

†**varify** *verb trans.* E17–M18.
[from Latin *varius* VARIOUS + -FY.]
Make varied, vary, variegate.

varimax /ˈvɛːrɪmaks/ *noun.* M20.
[from VARI(ANCE + MAX(IMUM.]
STATISTICS. A method of factor analysis in which uncorrelated factors are sought by a rotation that maximizes the variance of the factor loadings.

Varinas /vəˈriːnas/ *noun.* Now *rare* or *obsolete.* M18.
[A town in Venezuela.]
A kind of tobacco. Also ***Varinas tobacco***.

vario /ˈvɛːrɪəʊ/ *noun. colloq.* Pl. **-os**. M20.
[Abbreviation.]
= VARIOMETER 3.

variola /vəˈrʌɪələ/ *noun.* L18.
[Late Latin = pustule, pock, from Latin *varius* VARIOUS.]
MEDICINE & VETERINARY MEDICINE. Smallpox.
variola major a severe form of smallpox. **variola minor** a less severe form of smallpox.
■ **variolar** *adjective* of, pertaining to, or resembling (that of) variola M19.

variolate /ˈvɛːrɪəleɪt/ *verb trans.* L18.
[from prec. + -ATE[3].]
MEDICINE (now *Hist.*). Infect with variola; inoculate with the variola or smallpox virus.
■ **varioˈlation** *noun* E19. **variolist** *noun* (now *Hist.*) an advocate of variolation (esp. in preference to vaccination) L18.

variole /ˈvɛːrɪəʊl/ *noun.* LME.
[formed as VARIOLA: see -OLE[1].]
1 A thing resembling a smallpox pustule or scar in appearance or formation; a shallow pit. LME.
2 GEOLOGY. A small spherical mass in a variolite. L19.
¶ Not recorded between LME and E19.

variolite /ˈvɛːrɪəlʌɪt/ *noun.* L18.
[from VARIOLA + -ITE[1].]
GEOLOGY. A fine-grained igneous rock, usu. basaltic, containing small spherical inclusions roughly the size of a pea which give its eroded surfaces a pock-marked appearance.
■ **variolitic** /-ˈlɪtɪk/ *adjective* of or designating the texture characteristic of variolite M19.

varioloid /ˈvɛːrɪəlɔɪd/ *adjective & noun.* Now *rare.* E19.
[from VARIOLA + -OID.]
MEDICINE. ▶**A** *adjective.* Resembling variola or smallpox; like that of variola. E19.
▶ **B** *noun.* A modified or mild form of variola; variola minor. E19.

variolous /vəˈrʌɪələs/ *adjective.* Now *rare.* M17.
[from VARIOLA + -OUS.]
1 Of a person: affected with smallpox. M17.
2 Of the nature of or resembling (that of) variola or smallpox; of, pertaining to, or characteristic of variola. L17.

variometer /vɛːrɪˈɒmɪtə/ *noun.* L19.
[from VARI- + -OMETER.]
1 An instrument for measuring variations in the intensity of the earth's magnetic field. L19.
2 ELECTRICITY. An inductor whose total inductance can be varied by altering the relative position of two coaxial coils connected in series, or by permeability tuning, and so usable to tune a circuit. E20.
3 An instrument for indicating the rate of climb or descent of an aircraft. E20.

variorum /vɛːrɪˈɔːrəm/ *noun & adjective.* E18.
[Latin, lit. 'of various (people)', genit. pl. of *varius* VARIOUS, esp. in phr. *editio cum notis variorum* edition with the notes of various (commentators).]
▶ **A** *noun.* **1 a** An edition, esp. of the complete works of a classical author, containing the notes of various commentators or editors. Also ***variorum edition***. E18. ▸**b** An edition, usu. of an author's complete works, containing variant readings from manuscripts or earlier editions. Also ***variorum edition***. M20.
2 Variation; (a) novelty; a source of variety. Also, an unnecessary decoration or flourish. *Scot.* L18.
▶ **B** *attrib.* or as *adjective.* Of, pertaining to, or designating a variorum; (of matter in a book etc.) obtained or collected from various sources. Also, (of a reading in a text) variant. E18.

various /ˈvɛːrɪəs/ *adjective & adverb.* LME.
[from Latin *varius* changing, diverse, variegated: see -OUS.]
▶ **A** *adjective.* **I 1** Varied in colour; varicoloured, variegated. Chiefly *poet.* LME.
2 Characterized by variation or variety of attributes or properties; having or showing (several) different characters or qualities; varied in nature or character. LME. ▸†**b** Causing variation or difference. Only in M17.
3 Exhibiting variety or versatility in knowledge, works, interests, or capabilities. Long *rare.* E17.
4 Of varied appearance; presenting different aspects at different times or places. M17.
5 Exhibiting variety of subject or topic; concerned with many different subjects or themes. L17.
6 Displaying or including a variety of people or objects. M18.

📖 **1** W. WILKIE With flow'rs of gold and various plumage crown'd. **2** D. LARDNER The velocity of rivers is very various. *New Scientist* Pigs and sheep generally are . . hybrids, . . though sheep are still various. **3** *Daily Telegraph* The heir to the throne . . is a rather various fellow. **4** MILTON The Earth outstretcht immense, a prospect wide And various. **5** THACKERAY One whose conversation was so various, easy, and delightful. **6** B. HEAD A various assortment of dried leaves . . and berries.

▶ **II** †**7** Subject to variation or change; variable, changing. M16–L18. ▸**b** Going in different directions. *rare.* E17–E18. ▸**c** Marked by changes of fortune. *rare.* Only in M18.
†**8** Of a person: changeable in character; inconstant, fickle. Also, changeable or vacillatory in opinions or views. M17–E19.

📖 **7** M. HALE Discoveries which make evident this various state of the Globe. **8** SWIFT Various in his nature, and . . under the power of the present persuader.

▶ **III 9 a** With pl. noun. Different from one another; of different kinds or sorts. Passing into sense A.10. M16. ▸**b** With sing. noun Distinct, particular, different, individual. Freq. preceded by *each* or *every.* E18.
10 In weakened sense: several, many, more than one. L17.

📖 **9a** B. W. ALDISS Some speak out for various religions. *Scientific American* A planned succession of various crops . . on one field. **b** LONGFELLOW Each pursued The promptings of his various mood. **various reading** a variant reading in a version of a text. **10** C. DEXTER For various reasons the pair . . had never . . considered having children. A. THWAITE He and Edmund were to work . . on various projects. I. COLEGATE The opinions of various people who had known him.

▶ **B** *adverb.* Variously. Usu. in *comb.*, as ***various-coloured***, ***various-priced***, etc. Chiefly *poet.* M17.

variously /ˈvɛːrɪəsli/ *adverb.* E17.
[from prec. + -LY[2].]
In a various manner; in various or different ways; differently, diversely; at different times; in various or different places or contexts.

variousness /ˈvɛːrɪəsnɪs/ *noun.* LME.
[formed as prec. + -NESS.]
1 Variety of character or nature; varied condition or quality. LME.
†**2** Changeableness, inconstancy, variability. E–M17.
†**3** Difference, variance. E–M17.

For other words beginning with *vari-* see the entry for **vari-**

variphone /ˈvɛːrɪfəʊn/ *noun.* M20.
[from VARI- + PHONE *noun*[1].]
LINGUISTICS. A set of two or more sounds used interchangeably by the same speaker in the same phonetic context.

Variscan /vəˈrɪsk(ə)n/ *adjective.* E20.
[from Latin *Varisci*, name of a Germanic tribe + -AN.]
GEOLOGY. Of, pertaining to, or designating a mountain system formerly extending from southern Ireland and Britain through central France and Germany to southern Poland, and the orogeny that gave rise to it during late Palaeozoic times.

variscite /ˈvarɪsʌɪt, -skʌɪt/ *noun.* M19.
[from medieval Latin *Variscia* a region of eastern Germany, from Latin *Varisci*: see prec., -ITE[1].]
MINERALOGY. An orthorhombic hydrated aluminium phosphate which occurs as green translucent or colourless fine-grained masses, crusts, and nodules.

varistor /vɛːˈrɪstə/ *noun.* M20.
[from VAR(IABLE *adjective* + RES)ISTOR.]
ELECTRICITY. A resistor, esp. a semiconductor diode, whose resistance varies non-linearly with the applied voltage.

varix /ˈvɛːrɪks/ *noun.* Pl. **varices** /ˈvɛːrɪsiːz/. LME.
[Latin.]
1 *MEDICINE.* An abnormal dilatation or enlargement of a blood-vessel, usu. a vein, esp. accompanied by tortuous development; a varicose vein. LME. ▸**b** The presence of such dilated vessels, regarded as a specific condition. Now *rare.* E19.
2 *CONCHOLOGY.* A ridge on the surface of a shell marking a former position of the aperture. E19.

varlet /ˈvɑːlɪt/ *noun.* LME.
[Old French, var. of *vaslet*, *vadlet*, VALET.]
1 A man or boy acting as an attendant or servant; a menial, a groom. *arch.* LME. ▸**b** *spec.* An attendant on a knight or other person of military importance. Now *Hist.* L15. ▸†**c** = SERGEANT 7. L16–M17.
†**2** The jack in cards. E16–E17.
3 A person of a mean or unprincipled disposition; a rogue, a rascal. Also used as a (mock) contemptuous form of address. Now *arch.* or *joc.* M16.
■ **varletess** *noun* (*rare*) a female varlet M18. **varletry** *noun* varlets collectively; a number or crowd of attendants or of rogues: E17. †**varletto** *noun* (*rare*, Shakes.) = VARLET 3: only in L16.

varment /ˈvɑːm(ə)nt/ *noun*[1] & *adjective.* Also **-int** /-ɪnt/. E19.
[Perh. from next with allus. to the proverbial characteristics of the fox.]
▸†**A** *noun.* A knowing person; *esp.* a knowledgeable amateur sportsman. Also, a smart person, a swell. *slang.* E–M19.
▸**B** *adjective.* †**1** Smart, well-dressed; dashing. *slang.* E–M19.
2 Knowing, clever, cunning. Cf. VARMINTY. *colloq.* (now *dial.*). E19.

varment *noun*[2] var. of VARMINT *noun*[1].

varmint /ˈvɑːmɪnt/ *noun*[1]. *dial.* & *N. Amer. colloq.* Also **-ent** /-(ə)nt/. M16.
[Alt. of VERMIN with parasitic *t*.]
1 a *collect.* Vermin. M16. ▸**b** A wild animal, esp. of a kind considered harmful, objectionable, or destructive to game; *spec.* a fox. M16.
2 An objectionable or troublesome person or persons; a mischievous child, *esp.* a boy. L18.
■ **varminty** *adjective* suggestive of or resembling a varmint; sharp, cunning: M19.

varmint *noun*[2] var. of VARMENT *noun*[1].

varna /ˈvɑːnə, ˈvɑː/ *noun.* M19.
[Sanskrit *varna* lit. 'appearance, aspect, colour'.]
Each of the four original castes of Hindu society; the system or basis of this division.

varnish /ˈvɑːnɪʃ/ *noun.* Also †**ver-**. ME.
[Old & mod. French *vernis* from medieval Latin *veronix*, *-ic-* fragrant resin, sandarac, or medieval Greek *berenikē*, prob. from the town *Berenice* in Cyrenaica. In branch III from the verb.]
▸**I 1** Resin dissolved in a liquid (usu. an oil or spirit) and used for spreading over a surface to form a hard shiny transparent coating for protection or ornament. Formerly also, dry resin for making this. ME. ▸**b** A particular preparation of this kind. M17. ▸**c** A preparation of this kind spread on a surface; a coating or surface so formed. M17.
2 A medical or cosmetic preparation resembling a varnish, for application to the skin. *rare.* L16. ▸**b** = *nail varnish* s.v. NAIL *noun.* M20.
3 A preparation of boiled oil (or other substances) used in the making of printers' ink. Now *rare.* E19.
4 A resinous deposit formed in engines by the oxidation of fuel and lubricating oils. M20.

> 📖 **1** A. S. BYATT Portraits . . blackened by . . thickened varnish. **b** *Which?* External varnishes which give a transparent finish are . . not as durable. **c** *Nature* The varnish on a Stradivarius violin. *transf.*: SIR W. SCOTT A black varnish of soot. **2b** *Country Living* By the 1920's . . pink varnish had become . . part of good grooming.

▸**II** *fig.* **5** An external appearance or display of some quality without underlying reality; (a) superficial gloss, (an) outward show; (a) pretence. Cf. VENEER *noun* 4. Freq. foll. by *of.* M16.
6 A means of embellishment or adornment; a beautifying or improving quality or feature. Also, a quality like that of varnish; shine, glossiness, brilliancy. L16.

> 📖 **5** T. FULLER Truth may be discovered under the varnish of his scoffing wit. **6** N. HAWTHORNE A . . rainy day takes the varnish off the scenery.

▸**III 7** An act of varnishing; an application of varnish. E17.

Phrases: desert varnish: see DESERT *noun*[2]. **Japan varnish** = *Japan lacquer* s.v. LACQUER *noun* 3. *LITHOGRAPHIC varnish. nail varnish*: see NAIL *noun. spirit varnish*: see SPIRIT *noun.*

Comb.: **varnish sumac** the Japanese lacquer-tree, *Rhus vernicifera*; **varnish-tree** any of various trees yielding resinous substances used in varnishes.

■ **varnishy** *adjective* characterized by varnish; suggestive or reminiscent of varnish: L19.

varnish /ˈvɑːnɪʃ/ *verb.* LME.
[Old French *verniss(i)er*, *-ic(i)er*, from *vernis*: see prec., -ISH[2].]
▸**I** *verb trans.* **1** Paint *over* or coat with varnish; overlay with a thin coating of varnish. LME. ▸**b** Give a bright or glossy appearance as if with varnish. Chiefly *poet.* LME.
2 Embellish, adorn; improve, furbish *up.* Now passing into sense 3. LME.
3 Cover or overlay with a specious or deceptive appearance; gloss *over*, disguise. L16.

> 📖 **1** *Notes & Queries* Receipt for varnishing the binding of old books. E. O'BRIEN His fingernails looked as though they had been varnished a tinted ivory. **3** SYD. SMITH He may . . varnish it over by simulated gaiety. *Independent* The white minority government . . varnishing over . . the rougher edges of its racist rule.

▸**II** *verb intrans.* **4** Apply varnish to something. L16.
■ **varnished** *adjective* coated with varnish; having a glossy appearance like that of varnish: M16. **varnisher** *noun* a person who varnishes something; *spec.* a person who makes a business or trade of varnishing: L16. **varnishing** *noun* (*a*) the action of the verb; the application of varnish; (*b*) (more fully *varnishing day*) = VERNISSAGE: E16.

varoom *noun, interjection,* & *verb* var. of VROOM.

†**varrey** *adjective* & *noun* var. of VAIRY.

varroa /ˈvarəʊə/ *noun.* L20.
[mod. Latin (see below), from *Varro* (see next), app. with allus. to his work on bee-keeping, + -A[1].]
A small mite, *Varroa jacobsoni*, which is a fatal parasite of the honeybee in the Far East and has spread to other parts in modern times; infection with this mite.

Varronian /vaˈrəʊnɪən/ *adjective.* L17.
[Latin *Varronianus*, from *Varro(n-)* (see below): see -IAN.]
Of, pertaining to, or characteristic of the Roman author Marcus Terentius Varro (116–27 BC); *esp.* (of a play by Plautus) admitted as genuine by Varro.

†**varry** *adjective* & *noun* var. of VAIRY.

varsal /ˈvɑːs(ə)l/ *adjective* & *adverb.* Chiefly *colloq.* & *dial.* (now *rare*). Also **'varsal**. L17.
[Abbreviation of UNIVERSAL *adjective.* Cf. VERSAL *adjective*[2].]
▸**A** *adjective.* **1** Universal, whole. Only in ***in the varsal world***. L17.
2 Single, individual. *rare.* M18.

> 📖 **1** SWIFT I believe there is not such another in the varsal world. **2** SIR W. SCOTT Every varsal soul in the family were gone to bed.

▸**B** *adverb.* Extremely, vastly. *rare.* E19.

varsity /ˈvɑːsɪti/ *noun* & *adjective. colloq.* Also (*arch.*) **'varsity**. M17.
[Abbreviation (with spelling repr. arch. pronunc.) of UNIVERSITY.]
▸**A** *noun.* **1** University. Now chiefly *joc.* or *arch.* M17.
2 A sports team which represents a university, college, etc., *spec.* a first team. Chiefly *N. Amer.* L19.
▸**B** *attrib.* or as *adjective.* Esp. of a sporting event, team, etc.: of or pertaining to a university, college, etc.; *spec.* (*N. Amer.*) designating a university etc. first team. L19.
varsity match a sporting contest between universities, colleges, etc.; *esp.* the annual rugby football match between Oxford and Cambridge Universities.

Varsovian /vɑːˈsəʊvɪən/ *noun* & *adjective.* M18.
[from medieval Latin *Varsovia* Warsaw (Polish *Warszawa*), perh. through French *varsovien* (see next): see -IAN.]
▸**A** *noun.* A native or inhabitant of Warsaw in Poland. M18.
▸**B** *adjective.* Of or pertaining to Warsaw. M18.

varsovienne /vɑːˌsəʊvɪˈɛn/ *noun.* Also in Italian form **-viana** /-vɪˈɑːnə/. M19.
[French, fem. of *varsovien* VARSOVIAN *adjective* from *Varsovie* Warsaw.]
Hist. A dance of French origin resembling a slow mazurka, popular in the 19th cent.

For other words beginning with *vari-* see the entry for **vari-**

vartabed /ˈvɑːtəbɛd/ *noun.* Also **vardapet** /ˈvɑːdəpɛt/ & other vars. E18.
[Armenian.]
CHRISTIAN CHURCH. A member of an order of celibate priests in the Armenian Church.

†**varus** *noun*[1]. Pl. **vari**. M18–M19.
[Latin = pimple.]
MEDICINE. A hard suppurating pimple.

varus /ˈvɛːrəs, ˈvɑːrəs/ *noun*[2] & *adjective.* E19.
[Latin = bow-legged.]
MEDICINE. (Designating or pertaining to) any deformity of a limb joint which causes a distal bone or bones to be displaced obliquely inwards, as in bow-legs and some forms of club-foot. Formerly also (by confusion) = VALGUS.
GENU varum. TALIPES varus.

varve /vɑːv/ *noun.* E20.
[Swedish = layer, turn.]
PHYSICAL GEOGRAPHY. A pair of thin layers of clay and silt of contrasting colour and texture which represent the deposit of a single year (summer and winter) in still water at some time in the past (esp. in a lake formed by a retreating ice sheet).
■ **varved** *adjective* characterized by varves E20.

varvel /ˈvɑːv(ə)l/ *noun.* Also (earlier) †**vervil**. M16.
[Old & mod. French *vervelle*, †*varvelle*, syncopated from *vertevelle* from dim. of late Latin *vertibulum* joint, from *vertere* turn: see -EL[2].]
FALCONRY. A metal ring (freq. of silver with the owner's name engraved on it) attached to the end of a hawk's jess and serving to connect it with the leash.
■ **varvelled** *adjective* (*rare*) provided with varvels M17.

vary /ˈvɛːri/ *noun.* E17.
[from the verb.]
A variation. Formerly also, a hesitation, a vacillation.

vary /ˈvɛːri/ *verb.* ME.
[Old & mod. French *varier* or Latin *variare*, from *varius* VARIOUS.]
▸**I** *verb trans.* **1** Cause to change or alter; introduce changes or alterations into (something); modify. Also, introduce variety into, make varied. ME. ▸†**b** Change the grammatical form of (a word). Only in M17. ▸**c** Arrange in a varied manner; occupy in a manner characterized by variety or variation. L17.
†**2** Express in different words; extemporize. L16–L17.
†**3** Set at variance. Only in L18.

> 📖 **1** CONAN DOYLE My professional charges are upon a fixed scale . . I do not vary them. W. CATHER He was a man who did not vary his formulae or his manners. M. MITCHELL They had fried eggs . . and fried ham . . to vary the monotony of the yams.

▸**II** *verb intrans.* **4** Undergo change or alteration; pass from one condition, state, etc., to another, esp. frequently or readily within certain limits. Freq. foll. by *from, between.* LME.
5 Differ or diverge *from* something else. LME. ▸**b** Of a compass: deviate from true north. *rare.* M17.
6 Of a person: differ or diverge in practice or observance (*from* some standard); deviate. LME. ▸**b** Wander in mind; rave. *Scot.* Now *rare.* E16.
†**7** Differ in what is stated; give a different or divergent account; (freq. foll. by *from* another or each other). In later use, depart *from* an author by some change of statement. LME–E19.
†**8** Differ in opinion, disagree (*about, for, in,* or *of* some matter); dissent *from* another; quarrel (*with*). LME–M17. ▸**b** At Oxford University: act as variator. L17–M18.
9 a Change or alter in conduct. Now *rare* or *obsolete.* L15. ▸**b** Move in different ways or directions. *rare.* M17.
10 Be inconsistent in one's statements; introduce a difference or discrepancy. Now *rare.* M16.

> 📖 **4** G. GREENE My price varied from twenty to fifty pounds. JO GRIMOND My powers of speaking French vary from day to day. **5** *Law Times* This edition varies very little from its predecessor.

■ **varying** *ppl adjective* that varies; exhibiting variety or variation; *varying hare* (*a*) = MOUNTAIN *hare*; (*b*) = ARCTIC *hare* (a): ME. **varyingly** *adverb* M19.

várzea /ˈvɑːzɪə/ *noun.* E20.
[Portuguese, lit. 'meadow, plain'.]
(An area of) periodically flooded land in Brazil, as the alluvial plains bordering the Amazon.

vas /vas/ *noun.* Pl. **vasa** /ˈveɪsə/. L16.
[Latin = vessel.]
ANATOMY, BOTANY, & ZOOLOGY. A duct or vessel by which fluid is conveyed; *ellipt.* the vas deferens (see below). Chiefly in mod. Latin phrs.
vas deferens /ˈdɛfərɛnz/, pl. **vasa deferentia** /dɛfəˈrɛnʃɪə/, [medieval Latin: see DEFERENT *adjective*[1]] *ANATOMY* the spermatic duct which runs from the testicle to the urethra. **vas vasorum** /veɪˈsɔːrəm/, pl. **vasa vasorum**, [genit. pl. of Latin *vas* vessel] *ANATOMY* each of the very small arteries that supply nutrients to the walls of larger blood-vessels.
■ **vasal** /ˈveɪs(ə)l/ *adjective* L19.

vasa /ˈveɪsə, ˈveɪzə/ *noun*[1]. E19.
[Malagasy *vaza*.]
In full ***vasa parrot***. A black parrot, *Coracopsis vasa*, of Madagascar and neighbouring islands.

vasa *noun*[2] pl. of VAS.

VASCAR *abbreviation*.
Visual average speed computer and recorder.

vascula *noun pl.* see VASCULUM.

vascular /ˈvaskjʊlə/ *adjective*. L17.
[mod. Latin *vascularis*, from Latin *vasculum* dim. of VAS: see -AR[1].]
1 *BOTANY*. Pertaining to or designating the plant tissues (xylem and phloem) which conduct water and nutrients in all flowering plants, ferns, and fern allies; characterized by the presence of such tissues. L17.
2 *ANATOMY, MEDICINE, & ZOOLOGY*. Of, pertaining to, or of the nature of a vessel or vessels, esp. those which carry blood; (well) provided with blood-vessels. E18. ▸**b** Of or affecting the vascular system. M19.
Special collocations & comb.: **vascular bundle** *BOTANY* a strand of vascular tissue in the stem or leaves of a vascular plant, each usu. having phloem on the outside and xylem on the inside. ***vascular cryptogam***. **vascular cylinder** *BOTANY* = STELE 2. **vascular plant** a plant characterized by the presence of vascular tissue. **vascular system** (*a*) the system of vascular tissues in a plant; (*b*) the (heart and) blood-vessels collectively. **vascular wilt (disease)** wilt disease involving the vascular system of a plant; *spec.* = ***Panama disease*** s.v. PANAMA 1.
■ **vascuˈlarity** *noun* vascular form or condition L18. **vasculariˈzation** *noun* conversion to a vascular condition; development of vascular tissue: E19. **vascularize** *verb trans.* make vascular; *esp.* provide with blood-vessels (chiefly as ***vascularized*** *ppl adjective*): L19. **vascularly** *adverb* as regards vessels; by means of vessels: L19.

vasculature /ˈvaskjʊlətʃə/ *noun*. M20.
[from prec. after *musculature*.]
ANATOMY. The vascular system and its arrangement in (a part of) the body.

vasculitis /vaskjʊˈlʌɪtɪs/ *noun*. Pl. **-litides** /-ˈlʌɪtɪdiːz/, **-litises**. E20.
[from Latin *vasculum*: see VASCULAR, -ITIS.]
MEDICINE. An inflammatory reaction in the wall of a blood-vessel; a condition characterized by such reactions.
■ **vasculitic** /-ˈlɪtɪk/ *adjective* of the nature of or characteristic of vasculitis L20.

vasculotoxic /ˌvaskjʊlə(ʊ)ˈtɒksɪk/ *adjective*. M20.
[formed as prec. + -O- + TOXIC *adjective*.]
PHYSIOLOGY. Affecting the vessels of the body adversely.
■ **vasculotoxicity** /-tɒkˈsɪsɪti/ *noun* vasculotoxic quality or effect L20.

vasculum /ˈvaskjʊləm/ *noun*. Pl. **-la** /-lə/, **-lums**. L18.
[Latin, dim. of VAS: see -CULE.]
A botanist's collecting box, usu. a flattened cylindrical metal case with a lengthwise opening, carried by a shoulder-strap.

vase /vɑːz/ *noun*. LME.
[French from Latin *vas* vessel.]
1 An open vessel, usu. of some depth and often circular in cross-section, made from earthenware, china, glass, metal, etc., and used as an ornament or a container, esp. for flowers. LME. ▸**b** An object, esp. an architectural ornament, having the form of a vase or urn; a cup-shaped whorl of petals, leaves, etc. E18.
†**2** *ARCHITECTURE*. = BELL *noun*[1] 3C. M16–M18.
1 ***mandarin vase***, ***rouleau vase***, ***stirrup-vase***, ***sugar vase***, etc.
Comb.: **vase carpet** an oriental (esp. Persian) carpet with a pattern incorporating a stylized vase of flowers.
■ **vased** *adjective* (*rare*) furnished or ornamented with vases E19. **vaseful** *noun* as much or as many as a vase will hold M19.

vasectomy /vəˈsɛktəmi/ *noun*. L19.
[from VAS + -ECTOMY.]
Surgical excision of part of a vas deferens; ligation of one or (usu.) both vasa deferentia, esp. as a means of sterilization. Also, an instance of this.
■ **vasectomize** *verb trans.* perform vasectomy on E20.

Vaseline /ˈvasɪliːn/ *noun & verb*. Also **v-**. L19.
[Irreg. from German *Wasser* water + Greek *elaion* oil + -INE[5].]
▶ **A** *noun*. **1** (Proprietary name for) a kind of petroleum jelly. L19.
2 The greenish-yellow colour of Vaseline; glassware of this colour (also ***Vaseline glass***). M20.
▶ **B** *verb trans.* Lubricate or rub with Vaseline. L19.

vasiform /ˈveɪzɪfɔːm/ *adjective*. M19.
[from Latin *vasi-*, VAS + -FORM.]
Chiefly *ZOOLOGY & BOTANY*. **1** Having the form of a duct or blood-vessel; tubular. M19.
2 Shaped like a vase. M19.

vaso- /ˈveɪzəʊ, ˈveɪsəʊ/ *combining form*.
[from Latin VAS + -O-.]
PHYSIOLOGY & MEDICINE. Of, pertaining to, or involving a vessel or vessels; *spec.* of, pertaining to, or involving blood-vessels.
■ **vasoconstricting** *adjective* = VASOCONSTRICTIVE E20. **vasoconstriction** *noun* narrowing of blood-vessels L19. **vasoconˈstrictive** *adjective* causing or promoting vasoconstriction L19. **vasoconstrictor** *noun* a vasoconstrictive nerve, substance, etc. L19. **vasodeˈpressor** *adjective & noun* (a drug) that causes vasodilation M20. **vasodilaˈtation** *noun* = VASODILATION L19. **vasodilating** *adjective* = VASODILATORY M20. **vasodiˈlation** *noun* widening or dilatation of blood-vessels E20. **vasodilator** *noun* a nerve, substance, etc., which causes or promotes vasodilation L19. **vasodiˈlatory** *adjective* acting as a vasodilator M20. **vasospasm** *noun* sudden constriction of a blood vessel, reducing its diameter and flow rate E20. **vasoˈspastic** *adjective* of, relating to, or involving vasospasm M20. **vasoˈvagal** *adjective* involving the vagus nerve and the vascular system; ***vasovagal attack***, a temporary fall in blood pressure, with pallor, fainting, sweating, and nausea, caused by overactivity of the vagus nerve esp. during stress: E20. **vasovaˈsostomy** *noun* an operation to reverse a vasectomy by rejoining the cut ends of the vas deferens M20.

vasoactive /veɪzəʊˈaktɪv/ *adjective*. M20.
[from VASO- + ACTIVE *adjective*.]
PHYSIOLOGY. Of a substance: affecting the physiological state of blood-vessels; *esp.* causing or promoting vasoconstriction or vasodilation.
vasoactive intestinal polypeptide, **vasoactive intestinal peptide** a polypeptide of twenty-eight amino acids which is a neurotransmitter found esp. in the brain and gastrointestinal tract; abbreviation ***VIP***.
■ **vasoacˈtivity** *noun* vasoactive power M20.

vasomotor /ˈveɪzəʊməʊtə/ *adjective & noun*. M19.
[from VASO- + MOTOR *noun & adjective*.]
PHYSIOLOGY. ▶**A** *adjective*. **1** Esp. of a nerve or ganglion: acting on the walls of blood-vessels to produce vasoconstriction or vasodilation and thus regulate the flow of blood. M19.
2 Affecting or originating in the vasomotor nerves or ganglia. L19.
▶ **B** *noun*. A vasomotor nerve. L19.
■ **vasoˈmotion** *noun* constriction and dilatation of blood-vessels M20. **vasomoˈtorial** *adjective* of or pertaining to vasomotor nerves L19. **vasomoˈtorially** *adverb* under the control of vasomotor nerves E20.

vasopressin /veɪzəʊˈpresɪn/ *noun*. E20.
[formed as next + -IN[1].]
PHYSIOLOGY. A polypeptide pituitary hormone in humans and other mammals which promotes the retention of water by the kidneys and when given in large quantities raises the blood pressure by vasoconstriction. Also called ***antidiuretic hormone*** (***ADH***).

vasopressor /veɪzəʊˈpresə/ *adjective & noun*. E20.
[from VASO- + PRESSOR.]
PHARMACOLOGY. ▶**A** *adjective*. Causing the constriction of blood-vessels. E20.
▶ **B** *noun*. A drug with this effect. E20.

vasquine /vaˈskiːn, vɑː-/ *noun*. *Scot.* Long *arch. rare*. M16.
[French, obsolete var. of BASQUINE.]
A petticoat.

vassal /ˈvas(ə)l/ *noun & adjective*. LME.
[Old & mod. French from medieval Latin *vassallus* manservant, retainer, of Celtic origin, the related form *vassus* (see VAVASOUR) corresp. to Gaulish *-vassus* in personal names, Breton *goaz*, Welsh *gwas*, Irish *foss*.]
▶ **A** *noun*. **1** *Hist.* In the feudal system, a person holding lands from a superior on condition of homage and allegiance; a feudatory; a tenant in fee. LME.
2 A person holding a position similar or comparable to that of a feudal vassal; *esp.* (*arch.*) a humble servant or subordinate, a person devoted to the service of another. L15. ▸**b** A person who is completely subject to some influence. Foll. by *of*, *to*. *arch.* E17.
3 A base or abject person; a slave. *arch.* E16.
1 great vassal a vassal who held land directly from the monarch. REAR-VASSAL.
▶ **B** *adjective*. **1** *Hist.* Of, pertaining to, or characteristic of a vassal. L16.
2 Having the status or character of a vassal; subordinate, subject, (*to*). Chiefly *fig.* *arch.* L16.
■ **vassaldom** *noun* (*rare*) = VASSALAGE 3 L19. **vassaless** *noun* (*rare*) a female vassal L16. **vassalic** /vaˈsalɪk/ *adjective* (*rare*) of or pertaining to vassals or vassalage; feudal: L19. **vassalize** *verb trans.* (now *rare*) = VASSAL *verb* L16. **vassalship** *noun* (*rare*) = VASSALAGE 3 L16.

vassal /ˈvas(ə)l/ *verb trans.* Long *rare*. Infl. **-ll-**. E17.
[from the noun.]
1 Reduce to the position of a vassal; subdue, subjugate. Esp. as ***vassalled*** *ppl adjective*. E17.
2 Make subject or subordinate *to* some thing or person. E17.

vassalage /ˈvas(ə)lɪdʒ/ *noun*. ME.
[Old French (mod. *vasselage*), from VASSAL *noun*: see -AGE.]
1 Action befitting a good vassal; courageous or spirited action; prowess in battle or in some difficult enterprise. Long *arch. rare*. ME. ▸†**b** A brave or chivalrous act; a noble or gallant exploit. ME–M17.
2 †**a** The position or authority of a superior in relation to a vassal. LME–L17. ▸**b** *Hist.* An estate held by a vassal. *rare*. M19.
3 The state or condition of a vassal; subordination, homage, or allegiance characteristic of or resembling that of a vassal; *arch.* subjection, subordination, servitude; service. Freq. foll. by *to* (a person or persons). L16. ▸**b** Subjection or subservience *to* some influence, esp. of a detrimental kind. *arch.* E17.
4 Chiefly *Hist.* A body or assemblage of vassals. E19.

vassalry /ˈvas(ə)lri/ *noun*. LME.
[from VASSAL *noun* + -RY.]
Chiefly *Hist.* **1** = VASSALAGE 4. LME.
†**2** = VASSALAGE 3. L16–E17.

vast /vɑːst/ *noun*. E17.
[from the adjective.]
1 A vast or immense space. (Foll. by *of*.) Chiefly *poet. & rhet.* E17.
2 A very great number or amount *of*. *dial.* L18.

> 🕮 **1** MILTON Through the vast of Heav'n It sounded. R. L. STEVENSON The sky was one vast of blue.

vast /vɑːst/ *adjective & adverb*. LME.
[Latin *vastus* void, immense.]
▶ **A** *adjective*. **1** Of very great or large dimensions or size; huge, immense, enormous. LME.
2 Very great or substantial in amount, quantity, or number. LME.
3 Of great or immense extent or area; extensive, far-stretching. L16.
4 Of the mind etc.: unusually large or comprehensive in grasp or aims. Now *rare*. E17.
5 In weakened sense: great, large, considerable. Esp. in ***the vast majority***, by far the greater part (freq. *hyperbol.* or *rhet.*). Formerly also as a mere intensive. L17.

> 🕮 **1** T. HARDY What a vast gulf lay between that lady and himself. V. WOOLF The heron . . stretches its vast wings. **2** O. MANNING He and his girl-friend have got vast sums salted away abroad. W. S. BURROUGHS Fat lady . . comes out . . supporting her vast weight on two canes. I. ASIMOV The possibilities may not be infinite, but they would be so vast that they might as well be. **3** O. MANNING The vast emptiness of the desert. D. W. WINNICOTT The field is so vast that specialization . . is inevitable. **5** JOSEPH STRUTT They shot with vast precision. *Times* The vast majority of trade unionists were . . in favour of democratic practices.

▶ **B** *adverb*. Vastly. Long *obsolete* exc. *dial.* L17.

'vast /vɑːst/ *interjection*. Also **vast**. M19.
[Aphet.]
= AVAST.

vastation /vaˈsteɪʃ(ə)n/ *noun*. Now *literary* or *formal*. M16.
[Latin *vastatio(n-)*, from *vastat-* pa. ppl stem of *vastare* lay waste, from *vastus* VAST *adjective*: see -ATION.]
1 The action or an act of devastating or destroying something. M16.
2 The fact or condition of being devastated or laid waste. L16.
3 The action of purifying a thing or person by the destruction of evil qualities or elements; spiritual purgation. M19.

vastidity /vɑːˈstɪdɪti/ *noun*. *rare*. E17.
[Irreg. var. of VASTITY, after words in *-idity*.]
Vastness.

> 🕮 SHAKES. *Meas. for M.* A restraint, Though all the world's vastidity you had, To a determined scope.

vastitude /ˈvɑːstɪtjuːd/ *noun*. M16.
[Latin *vastitudo*, from *vastus* VAST *adjective*: see -TUDE.]
†**1** Devastation; laying waste. Only in M16.
2 The quality of being vast; immensity; *hyperbol.* unusual largeness. E17.
3 A vast extent or space. M19.

vastity /ˈvɑːstɪti/ *noun*. Now *rare*. M16.
[Latin *vastitas*, from *vastus*: see prec., -ITY.]
†**1** The fact or quality of being desolate, waste, or empty. M16–M17.
2 The quality of being vast or immense; vastness, vastitude. E17.
†**3** A vast or immense space. *rare*. Only in M17.

vastly /ˈvɑːs(t)li/ *adverb*. L16.
[from VAST *adjective* + -LY[2].]
1 In a waste or desolate manner. *rare*. L16.
2 Immensely; to a very great extent or degree. M17.
3 In weakened sense: exceedingly, extremely, very. M17.

vastness /ˈvɑːs(t)nɪs/ *noun*. L16.
[from VAST *adjective* + -NESS.]
†**1** Desolation; waste. *rare*. L16–M17.
2 The quality of being vast; immensity. L16.
3 A vast or immense space. L17.

vastrap /ˈfastrap/ *noun*. E20.
[Afrikaans, from *vas* firm(ly) (Dutch *vast*) + *trap* step.]
A lively South African folk-dance; a piece of music for this dance.

vasty /ˈvɑːsti/ *adjective*. Now *arch.* or *literary*. L16.
[from VAST *adjective* + -Y[1].]
Vast, immense; *fig.* grand.

> 🕮 SHAKES. *1 Hen. IV* I can call spirits from the vasty deep.

■ **vastily** *adverb* M19.

vat /vat/ *noun*[1]. ME.
[Southern and western var. of FAT *noun*[1].]
1 A tub, tank, cask, or other large vessel used to hold a liquid, esp. fermenting beer, chemical preparations for dyeing or tanning, etc. ME.
2 A cask, barrel, or other vessel for holding or storing dry goods. Formerly, a measure of capacity for coal. ME.
3 DYEING. A dyeing liquor that contains a reduced vat dye. Usu. with specifying word. M18.
Comb.: **vat dye**, **vat dyestuff** a water-insoluble dye that is applied as an alkaline solution of a soluble leuco-form, the colour being obtained by oxidation; **vat-man** PAPER-MAKING a workman who lifts the pulp from the vat and moulds the sheets of paper.
■ **vatful** *noun* as much or as many as a vat will hold M17.

VAT /viːeɪˈtiː, vat/ *noun*[2]. Also **vat**. M20.
[Abbreviation.]
= ***value added tax*** s.v. VALUE *noun*.
Comb.: **VATman** *colloq.* a Customs and Excise officer who deals with VAT; *the* Customs and Excise department dealing with VAT.
■ **VATable** *adjective* (*colloq.*) liable to VAT L20.

vat /vat/ *verb trans.* Infl. **-tt-**. L18.
[from VAT *noun*[1].]
1 Place or store in a vat. L18.
2 Immerse in a dyeing solution or vat. L19.

VATC *abbreviation. Austral.*
Victorian Amateur Turf Club.

Vater /ˈfaːtə/ *noun*. M19.
[Abraham *Vater* (1684–1751), German anatomist.]
ANATOMY. Used in *possess.* to designate various structures in the body.
Vater's ampulla a dilatation formed by the joining of the common bile duct and the pancreatic duct before they enter the duodenum. **Vater's corpuscle** a lamellated or Pacinian corpuscle. **Vater's papilla** a small elevation in the lumen of the duodenum where the combined bile and pancreatic duct enters it.

Vaterland /ˈfaːtərlant/ *noun*. M19.
[German.]
Germany as the fatherland.

vates /ˈveɪtiːz/ *noun*. Pl. same. E17.
[Latin = seer, poet, rel. to Greek *ouateis* OVATE *noun*[1]. Cf. EUHAGES.]
1 A poet, *esp.* one divinely inspired; a prophet-poet. E17.
2 *Hist. pl.* = EUHAGES. E18.

vatic /ˈvatɪk/ *adjective*. Now *formal* or *literary*. E17.
[from Latin VATES + -IC.]
Pertaining to or characteristic of a seer; prophetic, inspired.
■ **vatically** *adverb* (*rare*) M17.

Vatican /ˈvatɪk(ə)n/ *noun & adjective*. M16.
[French, or Latin *Vaticanus* (sc. *collis* hill, *mons* mountain): see -AN.]
▸**A** *noun*. **1** (Now always with *the*.) The palace and official residence of the Pope on the Vatican Hill in Rome. Now also, the papal authorities or system; the Papacy. M16.
2 The Vatican galleries or library; the artistic or literary treasures preserved in them. E17.
▸**B** *attrib.* or as *adjective*. Of or pertaining to the Vatican or its library. M17.
Comb. & special collocations: **Vatican City** the State established by the Lateran Treaty of 1929, comprising the area immediately surrounding the Vatican Palace in Rome and headed by the Pope; **Vatican Council** any of several ecumenical councils of the Roman Catholic Church which met in the Vatican; *spec.* that of 1869–70, which proclaimed the infallibility of the Pope, or (more fully ***Second Vatican Council***) that of 1962–5, noted for the introduction of the vernacular for the Mass and other reforms; **Vatican roulette** *colloq.* the rhythm method of birth control, as permitted by the Roman Catholic Church; **Vatican II** *colloq.* the Second Vatican Council.
■ **Vaticanism** *noun* the tenet of absolute papal infallibility or supremacy as declared by the first Vatican Council L19. **Vaticanist** *noun & adjective* (*a*) *noun* a supporter of the Vatican or of Vaticanism; (*b*) *adjective* pertaining to Vaticanism or its adherents: M19. **Vaticanize** *verb trans.* subject to the authority of the Vatican; imbue with Vaticanism: L19. **Vaticaˈnologist** *noun* (*colloq.*) an expert on or student of the Vatican L20. **Vaticaˈnology** *noun* (*colloq.*) the branch of knowledge that deals with the history and policies of the Vatican L20.

vaticinal /vəˈtɪsɪn(ə)l/ *adjective*. Now *formal* or *literary*. L16.
[from Latin *vaticinus* prophetic, from *vaticinari*: see next, -AL[1].]
Of the nature of or characterized by vaticination; prophetic, vatic.

vaticinate /vəˈtɪsɪneɪt/ *verb intrans. & trans.* Now *formal* or *literary*. E17.
[Latin *vaticinat-* pa. ppl stem of *vaticinari* prophesy, from VATES: see -ATE[3].]
Foretell (an event) by prophetic inspiration.
■ **vaticiˈnation** *noun* (*a*) a prediction of an oracular or inspired nature; (*b*) the action or power of making prophecies: E17. **vaticinator** *noun* (now *rare* or *obsolete*) M17. **vaticiˈnatory** *adjective* vaticinal, prophetic L19.

Vatinian /vəˈtɪnɪən/ *adjective*. Long *rare*. E17.
[Latin *Vatinianus*, from P. *Vatinius* Roman tribune 59 BC, a person intensely hated: see -IAN.]
Of hatred: bitter, intense.

vatje *noun* var. of VAATJIE.

vatu /ˈvatuː/ *noun*. Pl. same. L20.
[Bislama, prob. alt. of *Vanuatu*.]
The basic monetary unit of Vanuatu, equal to 100 centimes.

vau /vɔː/ *noun*. LME.
[Late Latin from Hebrew = VAV.]
In the Hebrew alphabet, the letter waw. Also, the Greek digamma.

vauclusian /vɔːˈkluːzɪən/ *adjective*. M20.
[from Fontaine de *Vaucluse* in southern France: see -IAN.]
PHYSICAL GEOGRAPHY. Designating a type of spring occurring in karstic regions, in which the water is forced out under artesian pressure.

vaude /vɔːd, vəʊd/ *noun. N. Amer. colloq.* M20.
[Abbreviation.]
Vaudeville; a vaudeville theatre. Freq. *attrib.*

Vaudese /ˈvəʊdiːz/ *noun pl. & adjective*. L18.
[Alt.: see -ESE.]
= VAUDOIS *noun*[1] *& adjective*[1].

vaudeville /ˈvɔːdəvɪl, ˈvəʊd-/ *noun*. M18.
[French, earlier *vau* (pl. *vaux*) *de ville*, *vau de vire*, and in full *chanson du Vau de Vire* song of the valley of Vire (in Normandy, NW France).]
1 A satirical or topical song; *spec.* one sung on the stage. Now *rare*. M18.
2 A light stage play or comedy with interspersed songs. Also, such plays as a genre; *US* variety theatre, music hall. Freq. *attrib.* E19.
■ **vaudeˈvillian** *noun & adjective* (chiefly *US*) (*a*) *noun* a performer in vaudeville; (*b*) *adjective* of or pertaining to vaudeville: E20. **vaudevillist** *noun* a writer of vaudevilles M19.

Vaudois /ˈvəʊdwɑː, *foreign* vodwa/ *noun*[1] *& adjective*[1]. M16.
[French, repr. medieval Latin *Valdensis*: see WALDENSES.]
ECCLESIASTICAL HISTORY. ▸**A** *noun pl.* The Waldensians. M16.
▸**B** *adjective*. Waldensian. M19.

Vaudois /ˈvəʊdwɑː, *foreign* vodwa/ *noun*[2] *& adjective*[2]. M19.
[French, from *Vaud* (see below).]
▸**A** *noun*. Pl. same.
1 A native or inhabitant of the Swiss canton of Vaud. M19.
2 The French dialect spoken in Vaud. L19.
▸**B** *adjective*. Of or pertaining to Vaud or its dialect. L19.

†**vaudoo** *noun & verb* see VOODOO.

vault /vɔːlt/ *noun*[1]. ME.
[Old French *voute*, *vaute* (mod. *voûte*) from Proto-Romance alt. of Latin *voluta* use as noun of pa. pple fem. of *volvere* to roll, to turn.]
1 ARCHITECTURE. A continuous arch, or a series of arches (often radiating from a central point or line), used to form a roof over a space in the interior of a building; an arched roof or ceiling. ME. ▸**b** An arching structure or covering resembling a vault; *esp.* (more fully ***heavenly vault***, ***vault of heaven***) that formed by the sky (chiefly *poet.*). LME. ▸**c** ANATOMY. Any of several domed or arched structures. L16.
2 An enclosed space covered with an arched roof; *spec.* (*a*) a burial chamber, usu. wholly or partly underground; (*b*) an underground room or part of a building of this form for holding valuables, storing wine, etc.; †(*c*) the crypt of a church. ME.
†**3 a** A covered drain or sewer. LME–L17. ▸**b** A privy, a lavatory. E17–E19.
4 A natural cavern or overarched space. M16.
5 The inner portion of a steel furnace. Now *rare*. E19.

> 🕮 **1b** E. F. BENSON Above in the velvet vault the stars burned hot. **2** J. G. BLAINE From customs, an increasing revenue was . . enriching the Government vaults. V. SACKVILLE-WEST Your coffin will be borne to the family vault on a farm cart.

vault /vɔːlt/ *noun*[2]. L16.
[from VAULT *verb*[2].]
An act of vaulting; a leap, a spring. Formerly *spec.*, a hart's springing upon the female in copulation.
pole-vault: see POLE *noun*[1].

vault /vɔːlt/ *verb*[1]. LME.
[Old French *vouter* (mod. *voûter*), from *voute* VAULT *noun*[1].]
1 *verb trans.* Construct or cover in with a vault or arched roof. Also foll. by *over*. LME. ▸**b** Of a thing: cover like a vault; overarch. M17.
2 *verb trans.* Bend, arch, or construct in the form of a vault. M16.
3 *verb intrans.* Curve in the form of a vault. E19.

> 🕮 **2** J. BRYCE Looking . . across the vast expanse, with the wide blue sky vaulted over it. **3** *Scientific American* The ceiling [of a cave] vaults to . . twice that height inside.

vault /vɔːlt/ *verb*[2]. M16.
[Old French *volter*, *voulter* turn (a horse), gambol, leap from Proto-Romance frequentative of Latin *volvere* to roll: assim. to VAULT *verb*[1].]
1 *verb trans.* **a** Mount (a horse) by leaping. *rare*. M16. ▸**b** Get over (an obstacle) by a vault. L19.
2 *verb intrans.* Spring, leap; *spec.* leap with the hand or hands resting on the obstacle to be surmounted, or with the aid of a pole. Cf. VOLT *verb*[1] 3. M16.
†**3** *verb trans. & intrans.* Leap on (a female) in copulation. L16–E18.
4 *verb intrans. & trans. fig.* Rise or cause to rise in a short time to a much higher rank or position, a greater amount, etc. Foll. by *to*, *into*. E19.

> 🕮 **1b** *Auckland Star* The teenage attacker . . vaulted the counter and ran off up the street. **2** C. ISHERWOOD Bounding to meet me, he vaulted over the low railing. **4** *National Observer (US)* Nadia Comaneci's electrifying gymnastics performances vaulted her from obscurity to world-wide renown. *Waterloo (Ontario) Chronicle* The contract . . will . . see the average wage of a carrier vault to $13.40 per hour.

■ **vaulter** *noun* M16.

vaultage /ˈvɔːltɪdʒ/ *noun*. L16.
[from VAULT *noun*[1] + -AGE.]
A vaulted area; a series of vaults.

vaulted /ˈvɔːltɪd/ *adjective*. LME.
[from VAULT *noun*[1], *verb*[1]: see -ED[2], -ED[1].]
1 Provided with vaulting; covered by an arched roof. LME.
2 Having the form of a vault; arched, rounded. M16.

vaulting /ˈvɔːltɪŋ/ *noun*[1]. LME.
[from VAULT *noun*[1], *verb*[1] + -ING[1].]
1 The action of VAULT *verb*[1]. LME.
2 The work or structure forming a vault; an example or instance of this. E16.
2 fan vaulting: see FAN *noun*[1].

vaulting /ˈvɔːltɪŋ/ *verbal noun*[2]. M16.
[from VAULT *verb*[2] + -ING[1].]
The action of leaping over an obstacle with a vault, esp. as a gymnastic exercise.
Comb.: **vaulting horse** a wooden block to be vaulted over by gymnasts; †**vaulting-house** a brothel.

vaulting /ˈvɔːltɪŋ/ *ppl adjective*. L16.
[from VAULT *verb*[2] + -ING[2].]
That vaults or leaps. Freq. *fig.*
■ **vaultingly** *adverb* L19.

vaulty /ˈvɔːlti/ *adjective*. M16.
[from VAULT *noun*[1] + -Y[1].]
Having the arching form of a vault.

vaumure /vɔːˈmʊə/ *noun*. *obsolete* exc. *Hist.* L15.
[Aphet. alt. of French *avant-mur*, from *avant-* before, forward + *mur* wall.]
An outer wall or earthwork thrown out in front of the main fortifications.

†**vaunce** *verb trans. & intrans.* ME–E17.
[Aphet.]
= ADVANCE *verb*.

vaunt /vɔːnt/ *noun*[1]. Now *arch.* or *literary*. LME.
[Aphet. from AVAUNT *noun*[1].]
1 Boasting, bragging; boastful or vainglorious speech. LME.
2 A boastful assertion; a boast, a brag. L16.
3 A subject of boasting. *rare*. L18.

> 🕮 **1** W. H. PRESCOTT With all the vaunt and insolent port of a conqueror. **2** *Times Lit. Suppl.* Symon's letters . . are full of vaunts about sex.

Phrases: **make a vaunt**, **make vaunt** (now *rare*) boast, brag, (*of*).

†**vaunt** *noun*[2]. L16–E17.
[Repr. *vaunt-* in VAUNT-COURIER etc.]
A front part or portion; *esp.* the vanguard of an army.

vaunt /vɔːnt/ *verb*. Now *arch.* or *literary*. LME.
[Anglo-Norman *vaunter*, Old & mod. French *vanter* from late Latin *vanitare* frequentative of *vanare* speak empty words, from *vanus* vain, empty: partly aphet. from AVAUNT *verb*[1].]
1 *verb intrans.* Use boastful or vainglorious language; brag. (Foll. by †*in*, *of*, †*on*.) Now *rare*. LME.
2 *verb refl.* **a** Boast, brag, (*of*). Also with adjective compl. LME. ▸†**b** Bear oneself proudly or vaingloriously. L16–M17.
3 *verb trans.* Extol boastfully, brag of (a thing); claim boastfully *that*. Freq. as ***vaunted*** *ppl adjective*. E16. ▸†**b** Proclaim or display proudly. Only in L16.

> 🕮 **1** BOSWELL He did not vaunt of his new dignity. **2b** AV 1 *Cor.* 13:4 Charitie vaunteth not it selfe, is not puffed up. **3** J. H. NEWMAN Attila vaunted that the grass never grew again after his horse's hoof. C. THUBRON The vaunted equality of Russian women is a mirage.

■ **vaunter** *noun* LME. **vaunting** *noun* the action of the verb; an instance of this, a boast: LME. **vaunting** *adjective* boastful, ostentatious L16. **vauntingly** *adverb* L16.

vaunt-courier /ˈvɔːntkʊrɪə/ *noun.* Now *arch.* or *Hist.* **M16.**
[Aphet. formed as AVANT-COURIER. Cf. VANCOURIER.]
= AVANT-COURIER. Now chiefly *fig.*

vauntery /ˈvɔːnt(ə)ri/ *noun.* Now *rare* or *obsolete.* **L15.**
[Old & mod. French *vanterie*, from *vanter* VAUNT *verb*, or in later use from VAUNT *verb* + -ERY.]
Boastful speech; ostentatious display.

vauntful /ˈvɔːntfʊl, -f(ə)l/ *adjective. arch.* **L16.**
[from VAUNT *noun*¹ + -FUL.]
Boastful.

vauntlay /ˈvɔːntleɪ/ *noun. arch.* **L15.**
[from *vaunt-* as in VAUNT-COURIER + *-lay* as in RELAY *noun.*]
In a hunt, the releasing of fresh hounds before the first hounds have come up; a set of hounds so released. Cf. RELAY *noun* 1.

vaunty /ˈvɔːnti/ *adjective.* Chiefly *Scot. & dial.* **E18.**
[from VAUNT *noun*¹ + -Y¹.]
Boastful, vain.

vaurien /vorjɛ̃/ *noun.* Now *rare.* Also ***vaut-rien***. Pl. pronounced same. **L18.**
[French, from *vaut* 3 sing. pres. indic. of *valoir* be worth + *rien* nothing.]
A worthless person, a good-for-nothing.

Vauxhall /ˈvɒks(h)ɔːl/ *noun & adjective.* **M18.**
[A district of London on the south bank of the River Thames, site of *Vauxhall* Gardens, public gardens closed in 1859, and *Vauxhall* Glassworks, active in the late 17th and the 18th cents.]
▶ **A** *noun. Hist.* A fashionable public garden resembling Vauxhall Gardens. **M18.**
▶ **B** *adjective.* **1** Characteristic of or associated with Vauxhall Gardens. Now only in ***Vauxhall lamp***, ***Vauxhall light***, an ornamental lantern holding a candle, used in outdoor illuminations. **E19.**
2 Designating antique plate glass, esp. mirrors, believed to have been made at Vauxhall Glassworks. **M19.**

vav /vav/ *noun.* See also WAW *noun*³. **E19.**
[Hebrew *vāv*. Cf. VAU.]
= WAW *noun*³.

vavasory /ˈvavəs(ə)ri/ *noun.* **E17.**
[Old French *vavas(s)orie*, *va(u)vasserie*, or medieval Latin *vavas(s)oria*, from *vavas(s)or*: see next.]
Hist. The estate of a vavasour.

vavasour /ˈvavəsʊə/ *noun.* Also **valvassor** /ˈvalvəsə/, **vavassor**, & other vars. **ME.**
[Old French *vavas(s)our* (mod. *vavasseur*) from medieval Latin *vavas(s)or*, perh. from *vassus vassorum* vassal of vassals. Cf. VASSAL *noun.*]
Hist. A person holding his lands not directly from the crown but from a vassal of the crown (esp. a baron); a subvassal.

vaward /ˈvɑːwɔd, ˈvaʊəd/ *noun. arch.* Orig. †**vantward**. Also (long *arch.*) **vanward** /ˈvanwəd/. **LME.**
[Aphet. from Anglo-Norman *avantwarde* var. of Old French *avant-guarde* AVANT-GARDE.]
1 *MILITARY.* = VANGUARD 1. **LME.**
2 *fig.* The early part. **L16.**
📖 **2** SHAKES. *2 Hen. IV* We that are in the vaward of our youth.

VC *abbreviation.*
1 Vice-Chairman.
2 Vice-Chancellor.
3 Vice-Consul.
4 Victoria Cross.
5 Viet Cong.

VCH *abbreviation.*
Victoria County History (or Histories).

V-chip /ˈviːtʃɪp/ *noun.* **L20.**
[from V(IEWER + CHIP *noun*¹; the *V* is now usu. interpreted as the initial letter of VIOLENCE.]
A device installed in a TV set or receiver that can be programmed by the user to block or scramble any TV programme that contains an undesirable level of violence, sex, or bad language (as indicated by a code inserted into the signal by the broadcaster).

vCJD *abbreviation.*
Variant Creutzfeldt–Jakob disease.

VCO *abbreviation.*
Viceroy's Commissioned Officer.

VCR *abbreviation.*
Videocassette recorder.

VCT *abbreviation.*
Venture capital trust.

VD *abbreviation*¹.
1 Venereal disease.
2 *Hist.* Volunteer Decoration.

vd *abbreviation*².
Various dates.

V-Day *abbreviation.*
Victory Day, esp. with ref. to the allied victory in the war of 1939–45.

VDL *abbreviation.*
Van Diemen's Land.

VDQS *abbreviation.*
French *vin délimité de qualité supérieure* a wine of superior quality from amongst the wines of a limited area.

VDT *abbreviation.*
Video (or visual) display terminal.

VDU *abbreviation.*
Video (or visual) display unit.

VE *abbreviation.*
Victory in Europe, i.e. the victory of the Allied forces over Germany in the war of 1939–45; chiefly in ***VE Day***, the date of Germany's surrender (8 May 1945).

veal /viːl/ *noun & verb.* **ME.**
[Anglo-Norman *vel*, *veel* = Old French nom. *veiaus*, oblique *veel* (mod. *veau*) from Latin *vitellus* dim. of *vitulus* calf.]
▶ **A** *noun.* **1** The flesh of a calf as food. **ME.**
2 A calf, esp. as killed for food or intended for this purpose. Now *rare.* **ME.**
▶ **B** *verb trans.* Raise (a calf) for use as veal. **M19.**
Comb.: **veal calf** (*a*) = sense 2 above; (*b*) a variety of leather; **veal crate** a partitioned area with restricted light and space in which a calf is reared for slaughter so as to ensure the whiteness of the meat.
■ **vealer** *noun* (chiefly *Austral.* & *NZ*) a veal calf **E20.** **vealy** *adjective* resembling veal or a calf; *fig.* characterized by youthful immaturity: **M18.**

vease /viːz/ *noun.* Now *dial.* **LME.**
[Southern var. of FEEZE *noun.*]
A rush, an impetus; a run before a leap.

Veblenian /vəˈbliːnɪən/ *adjective & noun.* **M20.**
[from Thorstein *Veblen* (1857–1929), US economist and social scientist + -IAN.]
▶ **A** *adjective.* Of or pertaining to the work of Veblen, esp. the ideas (as of conspicuous consumption) expounded in his book *Theory of the Leisure Class* (1899). **M20.**
▶ **B** *noun.* An adherent of Veblenian ideas. **L20.**

vecchio /ˈvɛkɪəʊ/ *noun. rare.* **M16.**
[Italian.]
An old man.

Vectian /ˈvɛktɪən/ *adjective.* **L19.**
[from Latin *Vectis* Isle of Wight, England + -IAN.]
GEOLOGY. Of or pertaining to the Isle of Wight or the Lower Greensand strata exposed there; now *spec.* designating a province comprising the Isle of Wight and part of the Dorset coast.

vectigal /ˈvɛktɪɡ(ə)l, vɛkˈtʌɪɡ(ə)l/ *noun. obsolete* exc. *ROMAN HISTORY.* **M16.**
[Latin.]
Tribute, tax, or rent paid to a superior or to the State.

vectis /ˈvɛktɪs/ *noun.* **M17.**
[Latin.]
†**1** A lever. **M–L17.**
2 *MEDICINE.* Any surgical instrument used as a lever; *esp.* (*a*) one used during childbirth to free the head of the child; (*b*) one used to extract the lens of the eye. **L18.**

vectitation /vɛktɪˈteɪʃ(ə)n/ *noun. rare.* **M17.**
[from Latin *vectitare* frequentative of *vectare* carry, convey: see -ATION.]
The action of conveying something (frequently); the fact of being conveyed.

vector /ˈvɛktə/ *noun.* **E18.**
[Latin = carrier, traveller, rider, from *vect-* pa. ppl stem of *vehere* carry, convey: see -OR.]
†**1** *ASTRONOMY.* = ***radius vector*** s.v. RADIUS *noun.* Only in 18.
2 a *MATH.* A quantity having direction as well as magnitude, denoted by a line drawn from its original to its final position. Cf. SCALAR *noun.* **M19.** ▸**b** *MATH.* An ordered set of two or more numbers (interpretable as the coordinates of a point); a matrix with one row or one column. Also, any element of a vector space. **E20.** ▸**c** *AERONAUTICS.* A course to be taken by an aircraft, or steered by a pilot. **M20.** ▸**d** *COMPUTING.* A sequence of consecutive locations in memory; a series of items occupying such a sequence and identified within it by means of one subscript; *spec.* one serving as the address to which a program must jump when interrupted, and supplied by the source of the interruption. **M20.**
3 a *MEDICINE & BIOLOGY.* An organism, esp. an insect or other arthropod, which causes the transmission of a pathogen or parasite from one animal or plant to another; a carrier of a disease. **E20.** ▸**b** *GENETICS.* A bacteriophage which transfers genetic material from one bacterium to another; a phage or plasmid used to transfer extraneous DNA into a cell. **M20.**
📖 **2a** **axial vector** = PSEUDOVECTOR *noun.* **polar vector** a vector which changes sign when the signs of all its components are changed. **c** *fig.*: L. DURRELL I was on a different vector, hunting for other qualities. **3a** *fig.*: M. CICCONE Music is the main vector of celebrity.
Comb.: **vector address** *COMPUTING* an address specified by an interrupt vector; **vector-borne** *adjective* (of a disease or pathogen) transmitted or carried by a vector; **vector boson** *PARTICLE PHYSICS* a boson with a spin of 1, *esp.* each of three heavy bosons (two *W*s and a *Z*) that are mediators of the weak interaction; **vector field** *MATH.* a field defined at each point by a vector quantity; a map from a space to a space of two or more dimensions; **vector function** *MATH.* a function whose value is a vector quantity; **vector potential** *PHYSICS* a potential function that is a vector function (see POTENTIAL *noun* 4); **vector processor** *COMPUTING* a processor that is able to process sequences of data with a single instruction; **vector product** *MATH.* a vector function of two vectors, (a_1, a_2, a_3) of length a and (b_1, b_2, b_3) of length b, equal to $(a_2b_3 - a_3b_2, a_3b_1 - a_1b_3, a_1b_2 - a_2b_1)$, representing a vector at right angles to them both and of magnitude $ab \sin\theta$ (where θ is the angle between them); **vector space** *MATH.* a group whose elements can be combined with each other and with the elements of a scalar field as vectors can, addition within the group being commutative and associative, and multiplication by a scalar being distributive and associative; **vector triple product** *MATH.* a vector function of three three-vectors equal to the vector product of one of them with the vector product of the other two, i.e. $\mathbf{a} \times (\mathbf{b} \times \mathbf{c})$.

vector /ˈvɛktə/ *verb trans.* **M20.**
[from the noun.]
Chiefly *AERONAUTICS.* Guide (an aircraft) to a desired point, esp. from the ground by means of radar; *gen.* direct, esp. towards a destination, change the direction of.
📖 K. AMIS Brenda's tone was warm but the warmth was firmly vectored on her friend.
■ **vectoring** *verbal noun* (*a*) the action of the verb; (*b*) *COMPUTING* the provision or use of interrupt vectors: **M20.**

vectorcardiogram /vɛktəˈkɑːdɪəɡram/ *noun.* **M20.**
[from VECTOR *noun* + CARDIOGRAM.]
MEDICINE. An electrocardiogram that represents the directions as well as the magnitudes of electric currents in the heart.
■ **vectorcardiˈography** *noun* the practice or technique of obtaining and interpreting vectorcardiograms **M20.**

vectored /ˈvɛktəd/ *adjective.* **M20.**
[from VECTOR *verb*, *noun* + -ED¹, -ED².]
1 That is or can be aligned in a particular direction. **M20.**
2 *COMPUTING.* Of a facility for interrupting a program: supplying the address to which the program must jump when it is interrupted. **M20.**
1 vectored thrust *AERONAUTICS* engine thrust which can be altered in direction in order to steer an aircraft.

vectorial /vɛkˈtɔːrɪəl/ *adjective.* **E18.**
[from VECTOR *noun* (or Latin *vectorius*) + -IAL.]
†**1** Capable of carrying or conveying something. Only in **E18.**
2 *MATH.* Of, pertaining to, or connected with a vector or radius vector. **L19.**
3 *MEDICINE.* Of or pertaining to the ability to act as a vector of a disease. **M20.**
4 Esp. *BIOCHEMISTRY.* Occurring or operating in one direction only, or in a particular direction. **M20.**
■ **vectorially** *adverb* as a vector or vectors **L19.**

vectorize /ˈvɛkt(ə)rʌɪz/ *verb trans.* Also **-ise**. **L20.**
[from VECTOR *noun* + -IZE.]
Chiefly *COMPUTING.* Represent as or transform into a vector.
■ **vectoriˈzation** *noun* the action or process of vectorizing **L20.**

vectorscope /ˈvɛktəskəʊp/ *noun.* **M20.**
[from VECTOR *noun* + -SCOPE.]
ELECTRONICS. An oscilloscope used to analyse the phase and amplitude relationships in colour television signals.

VED *abbreviation.*
Vehicle excise duty.

Veda /ˈveɪdə, ˈviːdə/ *noun.* **M18.**
[Sanskrit *veda* (sacred) knowledge, sacred book, ult. from Indo-European base meaning 'know' repr. also in WIT *verb.*]
The sacred knowledge of Hinduism handed down in four (orig. three) collections, of which the oldest and principal is the Rig-veda. Also, any of the collections of which the Veda is composed.

vedalia /vɪˈdeɪlɪə/ *noun.* Also **V-**. **L19.**
[mod. Latin former genus name, of unkn. origin.]
ENTOMOLOGY. An Australian ladybird, *Rodolia cardinalis*, which has been imported into California and elsewhere to control scale insects.

Vedanta /vɪˈdɑːntə, -ˈdaː-, vɛ-/ *noun.* **L18.**
[Sanskrit *vedānta*, from *veda* VEDA + *anta* end.]
A leading system of Hindu (esp. monistic) philosophy, based on the Upanishads.
■ **Vedantic** *adjective* **L19.** **Vedantism** *noun* **M19.** **Vedantist** *noun* **M19.**

Vedda /ˈvɛdə/ *noun.* Also **-ah**. **L17.**
[Sinhalese *vädda* archer, hunter.]
A member of an aboriginal people inhabiting the forests of Sri Lanka. Cf. YAKKHA 2.

Veddoid /ˈvɛdɔɪd/ *adjective & noun.* **M20.**
[from VEDD(A + -OID.]
ANTHROPOLOGY. ▶**A** *adjective.* Belonging or pertaining to a southern Asian division of humankind typified by the Veddas and characterized by very dark skin, short stature, and wavy hair. **M20.**
▶**B** *noun.* A person of Veddoid physical type. **M20.**

vedette /vɪˈdɛt/ *noun.* Also (now *rare*) **vi-**. **L17.**
[French from Italian *vedetta*, alt. (after *vedere* see) of southern Italian *veletta*, perh. from Spanish *vela* watch, from *velar* keep watch from Latin *vigilare*.]
1 MILITARY. A mounted sentry placed in advance of an army's outposts to observe the movements of the enemy; a scout. **L17.**
2 In full ***vedette boat***. A small vessel used for scouting purposes in naval warfare. Also *gen.*, a small motor launch or patrol-boat. **L19.**
3 A leading star of stage or screen. **M20.**

Vedic /ˈveɪdɪk, ˈviː-/ *adjective & noun.* **M19.**
[French *védique* or German *vedisch*, formed as VEDA: see -IC.]
▶**A** *adjective.* Of, pertaining to, or contemporary with the Vedas. **M19.**
Special collocations: **Vedic religion** the ancient religion which was the precursor of Hinduism and was brought to India by the Aryan peoples entering from Persia *c* 2000–1200 BC.
▶**B** *noun.* The language of the Vedas, an early form of Sanskrit. **M19.**

Vedism /ˈveɪdɪz(ə)m, ˈviː-/ *noun.* **L19.**
[from VEDA + -ISM.]
The system of religious beliefs and practices contained in the Vedas.
■ **Vedist** *noun* a follower or student of Vedism **L19.**

vedro /vɛˈdrəʊ, *foreign* vjiˈdro/ *noun.* Pl. **-os**. **M18.**
[Russian, lit. 'pail'.]
A Russian liquid measure equal to approx. 12.3 litres (2.7 gallons).

veduta /veˈduːta/ *noun.* Pl. ***-te*** /-te/. **E20.**
[Italian = a view, from *vedere* see.]
In Italian art: a detailed, factually accurate landscape, usu. a townscape showing buildings of interest.
veduta ideata /ideˈaːta/, pl. ***ideate*** /ideˈaːte/, a realistically drawn but imaginary landscape.
■ ***vedutista*** /veduˈtista/ *noun*, pl. ***-sti*** /-sti/, a painter of *vedute* **M20.**

vee /viː/ *noun.* **L19.**
[Repr. pronunc. of *V*, *v* as the letter's name.]
The letter V, v; a thing shaped like a V.
Comb.: **vee engine** an engine with two (lines of) cylinders inclined so as to form a V.
■ **veed** *adjective* V-shaped **M20.**

veeboer /ˈfɪəbʊə/ *noun.* *S. Afr.* **E19.**
[Afrikaans, from *vee* cattle from Dutch (see FEE *noun*^{1}) + BOER.]
Chiefly *Hist.* A livestock farmer.

veejay /viːˈdʒeɪ/ *noun.* *slang* (chiefly *US*). **L20.**
[Repr. pronunc. of abbreviation VJ, after DEEJAY.]
A video jockey.

veena /ˈviːnə/ *noun.* Also **vina**. **L18.**
[Sanskrit & Hindi *vīṇā*.]
In the Indian subcontinent, a plucked musical instrument with a gourd at one or either end of a fretted finger-board and seven strings.

veep /viːp/ *noun.* *US colloq.* **M20.**
[from the initials *VP*.]
A vice-president.

veer /vɪə/ *noun.* **E17.**
[from VEER *verb*^{2}.]
1 An act of veering; a change of direction. **E17.**
2 AMER. FOOTBALL. An offensive play using a modified T-formation with a split backfield, which allows the quarterback the option of passing to the full-back, pitching to a running-back, or running with the ball. **L20.**

> 📖 **1** M. SAWYER I was forced to make a violent veer toilet-wards.

veer /vɪə/ *verb*^{1}. **LME.**
[Middle & mod. Dutch *vieren* let out, slacken = Old High German *fiaren*, *fieren* give direction to.]
NAUTICAL. **1** *verb trans.* Let out gradually (a line or rope, now usu. an anchor cable or a hawser); pay out. Now freq. with *out*. **LME.**
2 *verb trans.* Allow (a boat, buoy, etc.) to drift further off by letting out a line attached to it. Usu. with *away*, *out*. **M16.**
†**3** *verb intrans.* Of a ship: sail with the sheet let out. Only in 17.
Phrases: **veer and haul** alternately pay out and haul on a cable, in order to obtain extra pull on it.

veer /vɪə/ *verb*^{2}. **L16.**
[Old & mod. French *virer* = Spanish *virar*, Italian *virare*, perh. from Proto-Romance alt. of Latin *gyrare* GYRATE *verb*.]
1 *verb intrans.* Of the wind: change direction; *spec.* (***a***) shift in a clockwise direction (opp. BACK *verb* 11); (***b***) NAUTICAL (more fully ***veer aft***), shift to a direction nearer the stern of a boat (opp. ***haul forward***). **L16.**
2 *verb intrans.* NAUTICAL. Of a ship or its crew: change course, *spec.* in such a way that the head is turned away from the wind. Opp. TACK *verb*^{1} 7. Now *rare* in techn. use (repl. by WEAR *verb*^{2}). **E17.**
3 *verb intrans. gen.* Turn aside from a course; change direction, esp. suddenly or uncontrollably. Freq. *fig.* **M17.**
4 *verb trans.* Turn (a thing) from one course or direction to another, esp. suddenly. **M17.**

> 📖 **1** *Scotsman* Wind moderate, north-westerly, veering north-easterly. **3** T. O'BRIEN We veered off the road, through clumps of trees. P. LARKIN Wilfred . . as an adolescent veered from 'too high spirits' to depression. R. BERTHOUD Moore's work . . was to veer increasingly towards abstraction. **4** R. BRADBURY He veered the car wildly . . down the road.

■ †**veerable** *adjective* (of the wind) tending to veer; changeable: **L17–M18.** **veering** *verbal noun* the action of changing course or direction; an instance of this: **E17.**

veer *verb*^{3} var. of FEER.

veery /ˈvɪəri/ *noun.* **M19.**
[Perh. imit.]
A N. American thrush, *Catharus fuscescens*, that inhabits dense woodlands and thickets.

veg /vɛdʒ/ *noun.* *colloq.* Pl. same, **veges**. **L19.**
[Abbreviation.]
= VEGETABLE *noun* 2.

> 📖 *Bookseller* Sunday lunch (though not . . roast beef and two veg).

veg /vɛdʒ/ *verb intrans.* *slang* (chiefly *N. Amer.*). Infl. **-gg-**. **L20.**
[Abbreviation of VEGETATE.]
Do nothing, vegetate; *spec.* relax in a passive or mindless manner, esp. by watching television. Freq. foll. by *out*.

> 📖 *Vanity Fair* Vegging out in front of the tube can sometimes be therapeutic.

vega /ˈveɪɡə/ *noun.* **M17.**
[Spanish & Catalan *vega* = Portuguese *veiga*.]
1 In Spain and Spanish America, an extensive, usu. fertile and grass-covered, plain or valley. **M17.**
2 In Cuba, a tobacco field. **L19.**

vegan /ˈviːɡ(ə)n/ *noun & adjective.* **M20.**
[from VEG(ETABLE + -AN.]
▶**A** *noun.* A person who abstains from all food of animal origin, and avoids the use of animal products in other forms, e.g. the wearing of silk or wool. **M20.**
▶**B** *attrib.* or as *adjective.* Pertaining to vegans or veganism; based on the principles of vegans. **M20.**
■ **veˈganic** *adjective* designating a system of organic farming or horticulture which avoids the use of animal products **L20.** **veganism** *noun* the beliefs or practice of vegans **M20.**

Veganin /ˈvɛdʒənɪn/ *noun.* Also **v-**. **E20.**
[Invented word.]
PHARMACOLOGY. (Proprietary name for) a mixture of aspirin, paracetamol, and codeine phosphate, used as an analgesic.

Vegeburger /ˈvɛdʒɪbəːɡə/ *noun.* Also **v-**. **L20.**
[from VEGE(TABLE *noun* + BURGER.]
(Proprietary name for) a savoury cake resembling a hamburger but made with vegetable protein, soya, etc., instead of meat.

vegeculture /ˈvɛdʒɪkʌltʃə/ *noun.* **E20.**
[from VEGE(TABLE *noun* + CULTURE *noun*, after *agriculture*.]
The cultivation of vegetables.
■ **vegecultural** *adjective* **M20.**

Vegemite /ˈvɛdʒɪmʌɪt/ *noun.* *Austral. & NZ.* Also **v-**. **E20.**
[from VEGE(TABLE *noun* + *-mite*, after *marmite*.]
(Proprietary name for) a type of savoury spread made from concentrated yeast extract.

vegetabilise *verb* var. of VEGETABLIZE.

vegetability /ˌvɛdʒɪtəˈbɪlɪti, vɛdʒtə-/ *noun.* **LME.**
[medieval Latin *vegetabilitas* from late Latin *vegetabilis* VEGETABLE *adjective*.]
†**1** A vegetable organism. *rare.* Only in **LME.**
2 Vegetable quality or nature. **M17.**

vegetabilize *verb* var. of VEGETABLIZE.

vegetable /ˈvɛdʒɪtəb(ə)l, ˈvɛdʒtə-/ *adjective & noun.* **LME.**
[Old French (mod. *végétable*) or late Latin *vegetabilis* animating, vivifying, from Latin *vegetare*: see VEGETATE, -ABLE.]
▶**A** *adjective* (not now always distinguishable from the noun used *attrib.*).
†**1** Living and growing as a plant. **LME–L17.**
2 Of, pertaining to, or derived from a plant or plants; having the nature or characteristics of a plant; consisting of plants. Freq. opp. ***animal***, ***mineral***. **L16.**
3 Of existence etc.: uneventful, monotonous. Also, unresponsive to external stimuli. **M19.**

> 📖 **1** *fig.*: MARVELL My vegetable love should grow Vaster than empires and more slow. **2** W. A. MILLER The insoluble pectose contained in the vegetable tissue. F. H. A. SCRIVENER The ancient ink was purely vegetable, without any metallic base. ***vegetable dye***, ***vegetable fibre***, ***vegetable tissue***, etc. **3** J. S. C. ABBOTT The . . peasantry, weary of a merely vegetable life, were glad of any . . excitement.

▶**B** *noun.* **1** Any member of the plant kingdom; in *pl.*, plants collectively, vegetation. *arch.* **L16.**
2 Any cultivated (usu. herbaceous) plant of which any part, esp. the leaves or root, is eaten in savoury dishes, freq. with meat or fish; such a plant prepared for the table. Cf. FRUIT *noun* 2. **M18.**
3 *fig.* A person who lacks animation or leads a monotonous life. Also, a person deprived by brain damage etc. of normal intellectual life or response to stimuli. **E20.**

> 📖 **2** B. JOWETT Cabbages or any other vegetables which are fit for boiling. attrib.: ***vegetable garden***, ***vegetable knife***, ***vegetable soup***, etc. **3** J. DAWSON I'm going to go on working . . . Tony . . would hate a wife who was just a vegetable. B. CASTLE Pray she will die with dignity and not be reduced by a stroke into a vegetable.

Special collocations & comb.: ***vegetable butter***: see BUTTER *noun*^{1} 2. **vegetable caterpillar** = AWHETO. ***vegetable ivory***: see IVORY *noun*. **vegetable kingdom** plants collectively, as forming one of the three traditional divisions of the natural world. ***vegetable marrow***: see MARROW *noun*^{1} 5. ***vegetable oyster***: see OYSTER *noun*. ***vegetable parchment***: see PARCHMENT *noun* 1b. **vegetable sheep** *NZ* an upland plant of the composite family, *Raoulia eximia*, which forms grey cushions suggestive of sheep from a distance. **vegetable spaghetti** a type of vegetable marrow in which the flesh separates into strands resembling spaghetti; the flesh of such a marrow. **vegetable sponge** = LOOFAH. **vegetable sulphur** a flammable powder made from clubmoss spores, used in the manufacture of fireworks. **vegetable wax** a waxlike exudation from any of certain plants, e.g. the sumac.

vegetablize /ˈvɛdʒɪtəblʌɪz, ˈvɛdʒtə-/ *verb trans.* Also **-ise**, **-bil-** /-bɪl-, -b(ə)l-/. **M19.**
[from VEGETABLE + -IZE.]
1 Convert into a vegetable substance. *rare.* **M19.**
2 Make unresponsive to external stimuli, turn (a person) into a vegetable. **L20.**

vegetal /ˈvɛdʒɪt(ə)l/ *adjective & noun.* **LME.**
[medieval Latin *vegetalis*, from Latin *vegetare*: see VEGETATE, -AL^{1}.]
▶**A** *adjective.* **1** = VEGETABLE *adjective* 1, 2. Now usu. opp. ***animal***. **LME.**
2 Characterized by the faculty of growth but not of sensation or reason. Freq. opp. ***sensible***, ***rational***. Cf. VEGETATIVE *adjective* 1. Now *Hist.* **E17.**
3 EMBRYOLOGY. Designating or pertaining to that pole of the ovum or embryo that contains the less active cytoplasm, and freq. most of the yolk, in the early stages of development. Opp. ***animal***. **E20.**

> 📖 **1** H. SPENCER Phenomena of animal and vegetal life. J. S. HUXLEY The vegetal cover of the valley.

▶**B** *noun.* = VEGETABLE *noun* 1. *arch.* **L16.**
¶ Rare after **M17** until revived in **M19** by Herbert Spencer.
■ **vegetally** *adverb* **L20.**

vegetant /ˈvɛdʒɪt(ə)nt/ *adjective.* Now *rare.* **E16.**
[Latin *vegetant-* pres. ppl stem of *vegetare*: see VEGETATE, -ANT^{1}.]
1 = VEGETABLE *adjective* 1, 2. **E16.**
†**2** Animating, vivifying. *rare.* **E16–E17.**

vegetarian /vɛdʒɪˈtɛːrɪən/ *noun & adjective.* **M19.**
[Irreg. from VEGETABLE + -ARIAN.]
▶**A** *noun.* A person who on principle abstains from animal food; *esp.* one who avoids meat but will consume dairy produce and eggs and sometimes also fish (cf. VEGAN *noun*). **M19.**
▶**B** *adjective.* Living wholly or largely on vegetables or plants; (of diet) consisting wholly or largely of vegetables or plants; *esp.* of or pertaining to vegetarians or vegetarianism. **M19.**
■ **vegetarianism** *noun* the principles or practice of vegetarians **M19.**

vegetate /ˈvɛdʒɪteɪt/ *verb.* **E17.**
[Latin *vegetat-* pa. ppl stem of *vegetare* animate, enliven, from *vegetus* active, from *vegere* be active: see -ATE^{3}.]
1 *verb intrans.* Of a plant, seed, etc.: exercise vegetative functions; grow, sprout. **E17.** ▸**b** *transf.* Increase as if by vegetable growth, present the appearance of vegetable growth. **M18.**
†**2** *verb trans.* Stimulate growth in; animate, quicken. **E17–E19.**
3 *verb intrans. fig.* Lead an uneventful, monotonous, or empty existence; stagnate. **M18.**
4 *verb trans.* In *pass.* Be covered or provided with vegetation or plant life (esp. of a specified kind). **L19.**

> 📖 **1** J. MORSE Naturalists have observed that ore in swamps . . vegetates and increases. **3** W. IRVING The vast empire of China . . has vegetated through a succession of drowsy ages. B. WEBB I may simply . . vegetate here with garden, wireless and quiet reading. **4** G. E. HUTCHINSON A shallow richly vegetated lake.

vegetation /vɛdʒɪˈteɪʃ(ə)n/ *noun*. **M16**.
[Latin *vegetatio(n-)* in medieval Latin sense 'power of growth' etc., formed as prec.: see -ATION.]
▶ **I** Abstract senses.
1 The process of vegetating; the faculty of growth possessed by plants and seeds. **M16**.
†**2** *transf.* The production of a plantlike formation. **E18–M19**.
3 *fig.* Uneventful, monotonous, or empty existence; stagnation. **M18**.
▶ **II** Concrete senses.
4 †**a** A vegetable form or growth; a plant. **L17–E18**. ▸**b** A plantlike growth or formation due to chemical action. **L18**. ▸**c** MEDICINE. An abnormal excrescence; *esp.* (in endocarditis) one forming on the membrane of the heart valves. **M19**.
5 Plants collectively, *esp.* those dominating a particular area or habitat; plant cover. **M18**.

📖 **5** C. DARWIN Large spaces of the tropical lowlands were clothed with a mingled tropical and temperate vegetation.

▪ **vegetational** *adjective* pertaining to or characterized by vegetation or plant cover **E20**. **vegetationally** *adverb* as regards plant cover **L20**. **vegetationless** *adjective* devoid of plant cover **M19**.

vegetative /ˈvɛdʒɪtətɪv, -teɪtɪv/ *adjective & noun*. **LME**.
[Old & mod. French *végétatif*, *-ive* or medieval Latin *vegetativus*, formed as VEGETATE: see -IVE.]
▶ **A** *adjective*. **1** Of, pertaining to, or concerned with vegetable growth; having the faculty of growing as a plant. Orig. (now *Hist.*) = VEGETAL *adjective* 2. **LME**. ▸**b** BIOLOGY. Concerned with growth, feeding, etc., rather than sexual reproduction. Cf. ***vegetative reproduction*** below. **M19**. ▸**c** MICROBIOLOGY. Pertaining to or designating a stage in the replication of a virus at which non-infective viral components are synthesized and assembled within the host cell prior to its lysis. **M20**.
2 Of soil etc.: causing or able to promote vegetable growth. **L16**.
3 Consisting of plants. **L17**.
4 *fig.* Characterized by lack of intellectual activity, responsiveness to stimuli, etc. **E19**.

📖 **1** R. BARCKLEY There are three kindes of life: vegetative or increasing which is in plants; sensitive which is in beasts; rationall or reasonable which is in men. S. HAUGHTON The Europasian Forest is characterized by a pretty uniform temperature during the vegetative season. **2** ANTHONY SMITH The lush, vegetative heat of Africa's coastal belt. **3** ISAAC TAYLOR The living world, vegetative and animal. **4** *Nature* Critically ill patients, such as those in vegetative coma.

Special collocations: **vegetative cell**: that is actively growing, not forming spores. **vegetative pole** EMBRYOLOGY vegetal pole (see VEGETAL *adjective* 3). **vegetative reproduction**: taking place asexually (i.e. by means of rhizomes, bulbs, runners, etc.) and not by seed.
▶†**B** *noun*. An organism capable of growth and development but devoid of sensation or thought (cf. VEGETAL *adjective* 2); *spec.* a plant. **E17–M18**.

📖 O. FELTHAM Even Plants, which are but Vegetatives, will not grow in Caues, where . . Air is barred.

▪ **vegetatively** *adverb* in a vegetative manner; *esp.* by vegetative reproduction rather than by seed: **L19**. **vegetativeness** *noun* **E18**.

vegete /vɪˈdʒiːt/ *adjective*. Now *rare*. **M17**.
[Latin *vegetus*: see VEGETATE.]
1 Of a person, his or her looks, faculties, etc.: healthy and active or vigorous. **M17**.
2 Of a plant or its parts: growing strongly. **M17**.

📖 **1** J. GRANGER His body was firm and erect, and his faculties lively and vegete.

vegetive /ˈvɛdʒɪtɪv/ *adjective & noun*. Now *rare*. **E16**.
[Reduced form of VEGETATIVE *adjective*, after Latin *vegetare* or *vegetus*.]
▶ **A** *adjective*. **1** = VEGETATIVE *adjective* 1. **E16**.
2 = VEGETATIVE *adjective* 4. **L19**.
▶ **B** *noun*. = VEGETATIVE *noun*, VEGETABLE *noun* 1, 2. **E17**.

vegetivorous /vɛdʒəˈtɪv(ə)rəs/ *adjective*. **M19**.
[Irreg. from *veget-* stem of VEGETABLE *noun* after *herbivorous* etc.]
Feeding on plants.

veggie /ˈvɛdʒi/ *noun & adjective*. *colloq*. Also **veggy**, **vegie**. **M20**.
[Abbreviation.]
1 (A) vegetable. **M20**.
2 (A) vegetarian. **L20**.

Vegliote /vɛˈljɒt/ *noun & adjective*. Also **-ot**. **E20**.
[from *Veglia* (see below) + -OTE.]
(Of or pertaining to) an extinct dialect of Dalmatian, formerly spoken on the island of Veglia (now Krk) off the Dalmatian coast.

vehemence /ˈviːɪm(ə)ns/ *noun*. **LME**.
[French *véhémence* from Latin *vehementia*: see next, -ENCE.]
1 Powerful or excessive passion; fervour of feeling, expression, or action; passionate force or excitement. **LME**. ▸**b** An instance of this. Long *rare*. **M18**.
2 Great physical force or violence. **L15**.
3 Intensity or strength *of* smell or colour. *rare*. **M16**.

📖 **1** A. SETON He threw himself into whatever aspect of his life was uppermost with single-minded vehemence. R. FULLER As the amount of drink taken . . increased, so did the vehemence of his accusations. **2** L. M. MONTGOMERY The door . . had been shut with . . vehemence.

vehemency /ˈviːɪm(ə)nsi/ *noun*. Now *rare*. **L15**.
[Latin *vehementia*, from *vehement-*, *-ens*: see next, -ENCY.]
†**1** = VEHEMENCE 2. **L15–M17**.
2 = VEHEMENCE 1, 1b. **M16**.
3 Intensity or severity of pain, illness, cold, heat, etc. **M16**.

📖 **3** R. CARPENTER No man ever endured such rage, and vehemencie of pain.

vehement /ˈviːɪm(ə)nt/ *adjective*. **LME**.
[Old & mod. French *véhément* or Latin *vehement-*, *-ens* impetuous, violent, perh. from unrecorded adjective meaning 'deprived of mind' alt. by assoc. with *vehere* carry.]
1 Of pain, illness, heat, cold, etc.: intense, severe; reaching a high intensity. Now *rare* or *obsolete*. **LME**.
2 Of the wind, rain, etc.: blowing or falling with intensity or violence. *arch*. **L15**.
3 Of an action: characterized by or performed with exceptional force or violence. **L15**.
4 †**a** Strong in taste; (of a medicine etc.) powerful in operative effect. **L15–M17**. ▸**b** Of colour, light, etc.: vivid, intensely bright. *rare*. **M17**.
5 Esp. of an utterance: very forcibly or passionately expressed; caused by or indicative of strong feeling or excitement. **L15**.
6 Of debate, conflict, etc.: impassioned, heated; bitter. **L15**.
7 Of suspicion or likelihood: very firm, well-founded. Formerly also, (of a proof etc.) cogent; powerfully convincing. *arch*. **E16**.
8 Of thoughts, feelings, etc.: extremely powerful or deep; fervent, passionate; (of anger) violent or intense. **E16**.
9 Of a person, a person's character, etc.: acting, or tending to act, in a passionate or forceful manner. **M16**.

📖 **1** C. BUTLER The Snow . . causeth them . . to fall, and with his vehement cold to rise no more. **2** JOHN MORGAN Succeeding vehement Deluges of Rain. **3** D. M. THOMAS 'No, no!' She gave her red curls a vehement shake. 'I'm good for him.' **5** *Guardian* She brushes him aside with a vehement tirade about the mortgaging of the house. **8** G. STEINER The sculptures of Michelangelo . . may, at first, have been provocations to . . vehement distaste. **9** C. FORBES 'For God's sake!' Newman was unusually vehement . . 'He's innocent.'

▪ **vehemently** *adverb* in a vehement, violent, or forceful manner; fervently, passionately; (now *rare*) to an intense degree: **L15**.

vehicle /ˈviːɪk(ə)l/ *noun & verb*. **E17**.
[French *véhicule* or Latin VEHICULUM, from *vehere* carry.]
▶ **A** *noun*. **1** A substance, esp. a liquid, which facilitates the application or use of another substance mixed with it or dissolved in it; *spec.* (*a*) PHARMACOLOGY an inactive medium in which strong or unpalatable drugs are administered, or which is used to give bulk to a medicine; (*b*) PAINTING the fluid (either the medium or the diluent or a mixture of both) in which pigment is suspended for use. **E17**.
2 A thing serving as a means of transmitting, conveying, or embodying something; an instrument, a medium; a channel. **E17**. ▸**b** *spec.* in COMMERCE. A privately controlled company through which an individual or organization conducts a particular kind of business, esp. investment. **L20**.
3 A means or medium for conveying ideas or impressions; a medium of expression or utterance. Freq. foll. by *for*, *of*. **M17**. ▸**b** The literal meaning of the word or words used in a metaphor, as distinct from the metaphor's subject. Opp. ***tenor***. **M20**.
4 A material embodiment, or other shape or form, in which something spiritual appears or is manifested. **M17**.
5 A means of conveyance, usu. with wheels, for transporting people, goods, etc.; a car, cart, truck, carriage, sledge, etc. **M17**. ▸**b** Any means of carriage or transport; a receptacle in which something is placed in order to be moved. **L17**. ▸**c** A space rocket in relation to its payload. **M20**.
6 *fig.* A song, play, film, etc., that is intended or serves to display the leading actor or performer to the best advantage. **M19**.

📖 **2** J. MOORE If the water . . be the vehicle of this disease. J. MORSE They viewed the tea as a vehicle of an unconstitutional tax. M. C. GERALD Three major vehicles of therapy: prayers, surgery, and drugs. **3** G. M. TREVELYAN The language had changed—from a vehicle of poetry . . to a vehicle of science. H. CARPENTER A children's book can be the perfect vehicle for an adult's most . . private concerns. *Times Lit. Suppl.* She is . . only a vehicle to represent an aspect of the Indian scene. **5** JO GRIMOND Rolls-Royce armoured cars—superb vehicles. RECREATIONAL ***vehicle***. ***utility vehicle***: see UTILITY *adjective*. **b** A. MACLEAN The cable-car was a twelve-passenger vehicle. **6** *Q* Moonwalker . . the Michael Jackson vehicle was rolling to . . the best cinema grosses.

Comb.: **vehicle-mile** a distance of one mile travelled by one vehicle, used as a statistical unit; **vehicle mine** a land-mine designed to destroy vehicles; **vehicle registration document** a motor vehicle's logbook (see LOGBOOK 2).
▶ **B** *verb trans*. Place or convey in a vehicle. Chiefly as ***vehicled*** *ppl adjective*. **E18**.

vehicular /vɪˈhɪkjʊlə/ *adjective*. **E17**.
[Late Latin *vehicularis*, from Latin *vehiculum* VEHICLE: see -AR[1].]
1 Of or pertaining to a vehicle or vehicles; made or conducted by means of a vehicle or vehicles. **E17**. ▸**b** Of the nature of or serving as a vehicle. **E19**.
†**2** Appearing in or manifested by a vehicle or particular shape or form. *rare*. **M17–L18**.

📖 **1** *Lydney (Glos.) Observer* Construction of a new vehicular access, The Cottage, Hinders Lane. *New York Times* A street sport . . enjoyed wherever there is . . pavement without vehicular traffic. **b** R. W. EMERSON All language is vehicular and transitive, and is good . . for conveyance.

▪ **vehicularly** *adverb* (*rare*) **E19**.

vehiculate /vɪˈhɪkjʊleɪt/ *verb*. *rare*. **M17**.
[from Latin *vehiculum* VEHICLE + -ATE[3].]
1 *verb trans*. Carry or convey (as) in a vehicle. Chiefly *fig*. **M17**.
2 *verb intrans*. Travel or drive in a vehicle. **M17**.
▪ **vehicuˈlation** *noun* conveyance by means of a vehicle or vehicles; vehicular activity or traffic: **M19**. **vehiculatory** *adjective* vehicular **M19**.

†**vehiculum** *noun*. Pl. **-la**. **E17–L18**.
[Latin: see VEHICLE.]
= VEHICLE *noun* 1, 2, 4, 5.

Vehme /ˈveɪmə, *foreign* ˈfeːmə/ *noun*. Also **Fehm**. **E19**.
[Early mod. German (now *Fe(h)me*), Middle High German *veme*, *veime* judgement, punishment.]
Hist. = VEHMGERICHT.
▪ **Vehmic** *adjective* of or pertaining to the Vehmgericht **E19**.

Vehmgericht /ˈveɪmgərɪkt, *foreign* ˈfeːmgərɪçt/ *noun*. Also **F-**. Pl. **-e** /-ə/. **E19**.
[German (now *Fe(h)mgericht*), from *Vehm-* (see prec.) + *Gericht* court, tribunal, rel. to *recht* RIGHT *noun*[1].]
Hist. A German system of secret judicial tribunals prevailing esp. in Westphalia from the end of the 12th to the middle of the 16th cent.; such a tribunal.

Vei *noun & adjective* var. of VAI.

veigle /ˈviːg(ə)l/ *verb trans*. Now *dial*. **M18**.
[Aphet.]
Inveigle.

veil /veɪl/ *noun*. **ME**.
[Anglo-Norman *veil(e)* = Old French *voil(e)* (mod. *voile*) masc. veil, fem. sail, from Latin *vela* pl. sails and *velum* sing. sail, curtain, veil. See also VELE.]
1 A piece of linen or other fabric forming part of a nun's head-dress, and worn so as to drape the head and shoulders. **ME**.
2 A piece of thin, light, or transparent fabric (now usu. attached to a hat or other head-dress) worn, esp. by women, over the head or face for concealment or to protect the face from the sun, dust, etc. **ME**. ▸**b** ROMAN CATHOLIC CHURCH. = ***humeral veil*** s.v. HUMERAL 3. **L18**.
3 A piece of cloth serving as a curtain, awning, or hanging; *spec.* (*a*) JEWISH ANTIQUITIES the piece of precious cloth separating the sanctuary from the body of the Temple or the Tabernacle; (*b*) ECCLESIASTICAL a curtain hung between the altar and the choir, esp. during Lent (now only in the Orthodox Church). **ME**.
4 A piece of silk or other fabric used as a covering, *spec.* (ECCLESIASTICAL) to drape a crucifix, picture, etc., esp. during Lent, or to cover the chalice. **LME**.
5 *fig.* A thing which conceals, covers, or hides; a disguise, an obscuring medium or influence; a pretext. Also foll. by *of*. **LME**.
6 †**a** A slight tinge or colouring. *rare*. Only in **M17**. ▸**b** MUSIC. A slight lack of clarity in the voice. **L19**. ▸**c** PHOTOGRAPHY. Slight fogging. **L19**.
7 BIOLOGY. A membranous covering or structure. Freq. in MYCOLOGY, a membrane which is attached to the immature fruiting body of certain types of agaric and ruptures in the course of development, either (more fully ***universal veil***) one enclosing the whole fruiting body, or (more fully ***partial veil***) one joining the edges of the pileus to the stalk. **M18**. ▸**b** = CAUL *noun*[1] 3c. *dial*. **M19**.

📖 **1 take the veil** become a nun; enter a convent or nunnery. **the veil** the life of a nun. **2** C. G. SELIGMAN In this veil the men live and sleep. *Atlantic* Her navy hat with velvet band And net veil down. **3 behind the veil**, **beyond the veil**, **within the veil** in the unknown state of being after death. **5** J. C. POWYS The valley . . covered with an undulating veil of blue-purple mist. T. BENN Preparations must be kept behind the tightest veil of secrecy. G. NAYLOR The poison of reality . . scraped the veil from her eyes. **cast a veil over**, **draw a veil over**, **throw a veil over** hide or conceal, avoid discussing or dealing with, keep from public knowledge.

■ **veilless** /-l-l-/ *adjective* (*a*) having no veil; unprotected by a veil; (*b*) *transf.* unshaded, unclouded: E19.

veil /veɪl/ *verb*[1]. LME.
[from prec.]
1 *verb trans.* Cover (as) with a veil; conceal or hide by means of a veil; envelop or screen as or in the manner of a veil; serve as a veil to. Freq. as VEILED *adjective*. LME. ▸**b** *verb intrans.* Put on or wear a veil. E18. ▸**c** *verb refl.* Hide, cover, or wreathe oneself or itself *in* something. Chiefly *fig.* L18.
2 *verb trans.* Confer the veil of a nun on; admit into the religious life as a nun. *arch.* LME.
3 *verb trans. fig.* Conceal (some immaterial thing, condition, quality, etc.) from full knowledge or perception; treat so as to disguise or obscure; hide the real nature or meaning of. Freq. as VEILED *adjective*. M16.
4 *verb trans.* Make less distinct or apparent; soften, tone down. *rare.* M19.
5 *verb intrans.* PHOTOGRAPHY. Become dark or fogged. Now *rare.* L19.

📖 **1** W. COWPER His robe . . o'er his head Ulysses drew, behind its ample folds Veiling his face. A. RADCLIFFE The clouds . . veiling the sun. M. DE LA ROCHE The upper windows were veiled by a coating of frost. **c** A. BROOKNER The sun . . is beginning to veil itself . . in greyish mist. **3** M. EDWARDES 'Give away' pay awards, thinly . . veiled as productivity deals. *Guardian* I have . . veiled my identity behind an initial.

veil *verb*[2] var. of VAIL *verb*[2].

veiled /veɪld/ *adjective*. LME.
[from VEIL *noun*, *verb*[1]: see -ED[2], -ED[1].]
1 Concealed, screened, or hidden, as if by a veil; obscure. LME. ▸**b** *fig.* Disguised; not openly declared, expressed, or stated. L19.
2 Having, covered with, or wearing, a veil. L16.
3 †**a** Of sight: dim, indistinct. *rare.* Only in M17. ▸**b** Of sound, the voice, etc.: lacking clarity, muffled. M19.

📖 **1** A. MAUPIN This playful reference to her veiled past. **b** *Spy* When . . interviewed . . he made certain veiled threats against the publisher.

■ **veiledly** /-lɪdli/ *adverb* L19. **veiledness** *noun* L19.

veiling /ˈveɪlɪŋ/ *noun*. LME.
[formed as prec. + -ING[1].]
1 A thing serving as a veil, cover, or screen; a veil, a curtain. LME.
2 The action of VEIL *verb*[1]; now *esp.* the action or fact of becoming dim, indistinct, or fogged; dimness or indistinctness of appearance. L16.
3 Light gauzy fabric used for veils. L19.
3 *nun's veiling*: see NUN *noun*[1].

veillée /vɛje/ *noun*. Pl. pronounced same. L19.
[French, lit. 'vigil, wake', from *veiller* stay awake, keep watch.]
In French-speaking rural areas: a traditional evening social gathering of a family or community, often with singing, dancing, etc.

veilleuse /vɛjøːz/ *noun*. Pl. pronounced same. E19.
[French.]
A small and usually highly decorated night-light or night-lamp. Also, a small decorative bedside food-warmer, usu. with an enclosed burner under a bowl or teapot, and made of pottery or porcelain so as to give out some light.

vein /veɪn/ *noun*. ME.
[Old & mod. French *veine* from Latin *vena*.]
▸ **I 1** Orig., any blood-vessel. Now usu., any of the thin-walled tubes forming part of the system of vessels by which (usu. deoxygenated) blood is conveyed back to the heart from all parts of the body. ME.
2 †**a** A sap-vessel in a plant. LME–E16. ▸**b** BOTANY. A (slender) vascular bundle in a leaf, bract, etc.; *esp.* one that divides or branches (cf. NERVE *noun* 2). E16. ▸**c** ENTOMOLOGY. Any of the hardened branching tubes that form the framework of an insect's wing, consisting of extensions of the tracheal system. E19.
3 †**a** A narrow stripe of a different colour or material on a garment. *Scot.* Only in M16. ▸**b** A marking suggestive of a vein; *esp.* an irregular streak or stripe of a different colour in marble, cheese, wood, cloth, etc. M17. ▸**c** A streak or seam of a different material or texture from the main substance. M17.

📖 **1** N. HAWTHORNE There is Anglo-Saxon blood in her veins. A. PATON Angry veins stood out on the great bull neck. ***jugular vein***, ***portal vein***, etc. ***varicose veins***: see VARICOSE 1. **3b** B. SILLIMAN Delicate veins with which the surface is covered. ***statuary vein***: see STATUARY *adjective* 3.

▸ **II 4** A small natural underground channel through which water flows; a flow of water through such a channel. ME.
5 GEOLOGY & MINING. A deposit of minerals etc. having an extended or ramifying course under ground; a seam, a lode; *spec.* a tabular deposit of minerals (esp. metallic ore) occupying a rock fracture. LME.
6 †**a** A strip or limited stretch of ground or soil having a particular character or quality. M16–E19. ▸**b** A channel or lane of water; *esp.* one on ice or between ice floes. E17. ▸**c** A narrow track in which a current of wind moves. Now *rare.* L18.

📖 **5** T. KENEALLY The jungle ridges had prodigal veins of quartz.

▸ **III** *fig.* **7** A strain *of* some quality traceable in personal character or behaviour, in a discourse or writing, etc. M16. ▸**b** A line or course *of* thought etc.; a source *of* information. E18.
†**8 a** The tenor or general character *of* something. Only in M16. ▸†**b** A kind or species. *rare.* M16–M17.
9 A particular, individual, or characteristic style of language or expression. M16.
10 Personal character or disposition; a particular character trait; a mood. M16.
11 An innate tendency towards or a special aptitude or capacity for the production of literary or artistic work; a particular talent. *arch.* M16.
†**12 a** A habit, a practice. L16–E18. ▸**b** An inclination or desire towards something specified. L16–L17.

📖 **7** O. NASH Beneath this . . careless nonsense, there lies a vein of wisdom. **9** V. WOOLF Wrote letters to *The Times* in a jocular vein. J. BRAINE We would have continued in this vein for some time, becoming more and more outrageous. **10** SHELLEY You have a sly, equivocating vein. *Philadelphia Inquirer* Rockwood Museum . . has . . planned entertainment in a frankly old-fashioned vein for a weekend festival. **11** J. G. LOCKHART His . . addiction to verse, and the rebuke which his vein received from the Apothecary's . . wife. **12a** SWIFT It is become an impertinent vein . . to hunt after . . a good sermon.

Phrases: **fluid vein** a separate flow of blood in a larger vein. **in the vein** in a suitable mood (for something).
Comb.: **vein-banding** (designating a virus causing) a symptom of certain plant diseases in which there is a change of colour along the main veins of the leaves; **vein-gold** gold occurring in a vein or veins; **veinstone** stone or earthy matter composing a vein and containing metallic ore, gangue; a portion or variety of this; **vein-stuff** (now *rare*) = ***veinstone*** above.

■ **veinless** *adjective* (esp. of a leaf) having no veins L18. **veinlike** *adjective* resembling a vein or veins E20.

vein /veɪn/ *verb trans.* E16.
[from prec.]
1 †**a** Ornament (a garment etc.) with narrow stripes of differently coloured material. *Scot.* E16–M17. ▸**b** Decorate with coloured, incised, or impressed markings suggestive of veins. L17.
2 Of a thing: spread over or suffuse (something) (as) with veins. Chiefly *fig.* L17.

📖 **1b** A. MOTION The dark-green leaves were veined with yellow. **2** HENRY MILLER All objects animate or inanimate . . are veined with ineradicable traits.

veinal /ˈveɪn(ə)l/ *adjective*. *rare.* M19.
[from VEIN *noun* + -AL[1].]
= VENOUS 1.

veined /veɪnd/ *adjective*. E16.
[from VEIN *noun*, *verb*: see -ED[2], -ED[1].]
1 Having or marked with a vein or veins. E16.
2 Marked or decorated *with* something suggestive of veins. E17.

📖 **1** S. MILLER Her lashless blue-veined eyelid. **2** E. A. FLOYER Blue and purple marble veined with white.

veiner /ˈveɪnə/ *noun*. *rare.* M19.
[formed as prec. + -ER[1].]
1 A person who decorates something with veins or veinlike markings. M19.
2 In wood-carving, a small V-shaped tool used for making veins in leaves. L19.

veining /ˈveɪnɪŋ/ *noun*. L17.
[from VEIN *noun*, *verb* + -ING[1].]
1 The action or process of decorating something with veinlike markings; *spec.* (NEEDLEWORK) the operation of making veinlike patterns, esp. on muslin; the result of this work. L17.
2 A pattern of veins or streaks; a veined appearance or structure. E19.

veinlet /ˈveɪnlɪt/ *noun*. M19.
[from VEIN *noun* + -LET.]
A small or minor vein; *esp.* (BOTANY) a branch or subdivision of a vein or venule.

veinous /ˈveɪnəs/ *adjective*. LME.
[from VEIN *noun* + -OUS.]
1 Supplied or traversed by, or consisting of, veins. LME.
2 Having large or prominent veins. M19.

veinule *noun* see VENULE.

veinulet /ˈveɪnjʊlɪt/ *noun*. *rare.* M17.
[from VEIN *noun*: cf. VEINLET, VENULE.]
A small vein; a branch of a veinlet.

veiny /ˈveɪni/ *adjective*. LME.
[from VEIN *noun* + -Y[1].]
Full of or traversed by veins; having prominent veins; marked by veins or streaks of colour.
■ **veininess** *noun* M18.

veitchberry /ˈviːtʃbəri/ *noun*. E20.
[from *Veitch*, surname of a family of nurserymen + BERRY *noun*[1].]
A soft fruit resembling a mulberry, first produced in 1925 by crossing the raspberry and a kind of blackberry; the plant bearing this fruit.

Vela /ˈviːlə/ *noun*[1]. M19.
[Latin *vela* pl. of VELUM.]
(The name of) a constellation of the southern hemisphere, lying partly in the Milky Way between Carina and Pyxis and orig. part of Argo; the Sails.

vela *noun*[2] pl. of VELUM.

velamen /vɪˈleɪmən/ *noun*. Pl. **-lamina** /-ˈlamɪnə/. L19.
[Latin, = covering, from *velare* to cover, to veil.]
1 BOTANY. An outer layer of empty cells found in the aerial roots of various monocotyledons (esp. epiphytic orchids and aroids). L19.
2 ANATOMY. = VELUM 1. L19.
■ **vela'mentous** *adjective* of the nature of a membrane or membranous covering L19.

velar /ˈviːlə/ *adjective & noun*. E18.
[Latin *velaris*, from VELUM: see -AR[1].]
▸ **A** *adjective*. **1** ARCHITECTURE. Of a dome or cupola: having a surface resembling a sail, usu. terminated by four or more walls. E18.
2 PHONETICS. Of a sound: articulated with the back of the tongue against or near the soft palate. L19.
3 ZOOLOGY. Of or pertaining to a velum. L19.
▸ **B** *noun*. PHONETICS. A velar sound. L19.
■ **velaric** /-ˈlarɪk/ *adjective* (PHONETICS) produced or characterized by a velar articulation M20. **velarity** /-ˈlarɪti/ *noun* (PHONETICS) velar quality M20.

velaria *noun* pl. of VELARIUM.

velarise *verb* var. of VELARIZE.

velarium /vɪˈlɛːrɪəm/ *noun*. Pl. **-ria** /-rɪə/. M19.
[Latin = awning, sail, from VELUM: see -ARIUM.]
A large awning used to cover a theatre or amphitheatre as a protection against the weather, esp. in ancient Rome.

velarize /ˈviːlərʌɪz/ *verb trans.* Also **-ise**. E20.
[from VELAR + -IZE.]
PHONETICS. Make velar; articulate or supplement the articulation of (a sound, esp. a consonant) by raising the tongue to or towards the soft palate.
■ **velari'zation** *noun* E20.

velate /ˈviːlət/ *adjective*. M19.
[from VELUM + -ATE[2].]
Chiefly ZOOLOGY. Having a velum.
■ Also **velated** *adjective* M19.

Velcro /ˈvɛlkrəʊ/ *noun*. M20.
[from French *vel(ours cro(ché* hooked velvet.]
(Proprietary name for) a fastener for clothes etc. consisting of two strips of nylon fabric, one strip with a coarse mesh surface and the other having hooks, which adhere when pressed together.

📖 *attrib.*: *Ski* The boot has . . a . . two-position Velcro strap.

■ **Velcroed** *adjective* provided with Velcro; fastened by Velcro: L20.

veld /vɛlt/ *noun*. *S. Afr.* Also **veldt**. L18.
[Afrikaans from Dutch = field.]
Unenclosed country; open grassland. Freq. with specifying word.
bushveld: see BUSH *noun*[1]. ***sour veld***: see SOUR *adjective* ***sweet-veld***: see SWEET *adjective & adverb*.
Comb.: **veld-cornet** = ***field-cornet*** s.v. FIELD *noun & adjective*; **veld-craft** skill in matters pertaining to survival on the veld; **veld-kos(t)** /kɒs(t)/ [Dutch *kost* food] wild roots, bulbs, etc., eaten for survival on the veld; **veldman** a person possessing veld-craft; **veld pig** the warthog, *Phacochoerus aethiopicus*; **veld rat** any of several rats that occur on the veld, esp. of the genera *Aethomys* and *Rhabdomys*; **veld sickness** a condition of cattle etc. brought from the veld, due to poor nutrition; **veldsman** = ***veldman*** above; **veld sores** a skin eruption, probably due to dietary deficiency.

veldskoen /ˈfɛltskʊn, ˈfɛls-/ *noun*. E19.
[Afrikaans = field-shoe, ult. by assim. to VELD of earlier *velschoen*, from *fel* skin, FELL *noun*[1] + *schoen* shoe.]
Formerly, a light shoe made of untanned hide. Now, a strong but usu. soft leather or suede boot or shoe for walking etc.

veldt *noun* var. of VELD.

veldt-marshal *noun* var. of VELT-MARSHAL.

†**vele** *noun*. Only in L16.
[Var. of VEIL *noun* after Italian, Spanish *velo*, Latin VELUM.]
A veil, a covering.

velella /vɛˈlɛlə/ *noun.* Pl. same, **-llas**, **-llae** /-liː/. M19.
[mod. Latin (see below), from Latin *velum* sail.]
ZOOLOGY. Any of several chondrophores of the genus *Velella*, which have a flat oval float and a vertical sail.

veleta /vəˈliːtə/ *noun.* Also **val-**. E20.
[Spanish = weather-vane.]
An old-time round dance for couples in triple time, faster than a waltz and with partners side by side.

velic /ˈviːlɪk/ *noun & adjective.* M20.
[from VEL(UM + -IC.]
PHONETICS. (Of or pertaining to) the upper part of the velum facing the nasopharynx, which, when the velum is raised or lowered, closes or opens the nasal passage to produce an oral or a nasal sound respectively.

veliger /ˈviːlɪdʒə/ *noun & adjective.* L19.
[from VELUM + -I- + Latin *-ger* bearing.]
ZOOLOGY. ▶**A** *noun.* The free-swimming larva of a mollusc, which has a ciliated velum or swimming membrane. L19.
▶**B** *adjective.* Pertaining to or designating this stage of a mollusc's development. L19.
■ **veˈligerous** *adjective* (of certain larval forms) bearing a velum L19.

Velikovskianism /vɛlɪˈkɒfskɪənɪz(ə)m/ *noun.* L20.
[from Immanuel *Velikovsky* (1895–1979), Russian-born psychologist + -IAN + -ISM.]
The (controversial) theories of cosmology and history propounded by Velikovsky, based on the hypothesis that other planets have approached close to the earth in historical times.
■ **Velikovskian** *adjective* of or pertaining to Velikovskianism L20. **Velikovskyism** *noun* = VELIKOVSKIANISM L20. **Velikovskyite** *noun* an adherent of Velikovskianism L20.

velitation /vɛlɪˈteɪʃ(ə)n/ *noun. arch. rare.* E17.
[Latin *velitatio(n-)*, from *velitari* to skirmish, from *veles*: see next, -ATION.]
1 A slight or preliminary encounter with an enemy; a skirmish. E17.
2 *fig.* A verbal skirmish; a controversy or debate not carried to extremes. E17.

velites /ˈviːlɪtiːz/ *noun pl.* E17.
[Latin, pl. of *veles* skirmisher.]
ROMAN HISTORY. Light-armed infantry employed as skirmishers in the Roman armies.

vell /vɛl/ *noun.* Chiefly *dial.* E18.
[Origin unkn.]
The abomasum of a calf, used to provide rennet for cheese-making.

velleity /vɛˈliːɪti/ *noun.* Chiefly *literary.* E17.
[medieval Latin *velleitas*, from Latin *velle* wish, will: see -ITY.]
1 The least or a low degree of volition, unaccompanied by any effort or advance towards action or realization. E17.
2 A mere wish; a slight inclination without accompanying action or effort. Also foll. by *for, of, towards, to do,* etc. M17.

> 📖 **1** A. TUCKER Velleity can scarce be called a power, for a power which never operates is no power. **2** *New Left Review* This . . outlook is a recurrent velleity of the Party, rather than a permanent set of convictions.

vellicate /ˈvɛlɪkeɪt/ *verb.* Now *rare* or *obsolete.* E17.
[Latin *vellicat-* pa. ppl stem of *vellicare* frequentative of *vellere* pluck: see -ATE[3].]
1 *verb trans.* Act on or affect so as to irritate; tickle; *esp.* (of a medicinal substance etc.) act as an irritant or stimulant on (a part of the body). E17.
†**2** *verb trans. fig.* Carp at; criticize adversely. *rare.* M–L17.
3 *verb intrans.* Twitch; contract or move convulsively. *rare.* L17.

vellication /vɛlɪˈkeɪʃ(ə)n/ *noun.* Now *rare* or *obsolete.* E17.
[Latin *vellicatio(n-)*, formed as prec.: see -ATION.]
1 The action or process of irritating or tickling. E17.
2 An instance of this; a twitching or convulsive movement, esp. of a muscle or other part of the body. M17.

vellinch *noun* see VALINCHE.

vellon /vɛˈjəʊn/ *noun.* L17.
[Spanish *vellón* from French BILLON.]
A copper and silver alloy used in Spanish coinage.

vellum /ˈvɛləm/ *noun.* LME.
[Old & mod. French *vélin*, from Old French *veel* VEAL *noun* + *-in* -INE[4]. For the change of final *n* to *m* cf. *pilgrim, venom*.]
1 A fine kind of parchment prepared from the skin of a calf, lamb, or kid and used for writing, painting, or bookbinding. Also, any superior quality of parchment; an imitation of this, *esp.* a thick high-quality writing-paper. LME.
2 A piece or sheet of vellum; a manuscript or testimonial written on this material. LME.

> 📖 **1** ***Japanese vellum***: see JAPANESE *adjective.* ***NORMANDY vellum.*** **2** *Shetland Times* The lifeboat mechanic . . received a vellum for his part in the . . rescue.

■ **vellumy** *adjective* (*rare*) relating to or resembling vellum M19.

velly /ˈvɛli/ *adverb. joc.* L19.
[Repr. a supposed Chinese pronunc.]
Very.

vel non /vɛl ˈnəʊn/ *adverbial phr.* Chiefly *US.* L19.
[Latin.]
LAW. Or not; or the lack thereof. Usu. following a noun.
¶ Often regarded as superfluous.

velocimeter /vɛləˈsɪmɪtə/ *noun.* M19.
[from Latin *veloc-*, *velox* swift + -I- + -METER.]
An instrument or device for measuring the speed or velocity of engines, vessels, projectiles, etc.
■ **velocimetry** *noun* the measurement of speed, esp. speed of flow, by special techniques M20.

velocious /vɪˈləʊʃəs/ *adjective. arch. rare.* L17.
[formed as prec. + -IOUS.]
Rapid; fast.

velocipede /vɪˈlɒsɪpiːd/ *noun.* E19.
[French *vélocipède*, from Latin *veloc-*, *velox* (see next) + *ped-*, *pes* foot.]
1 *Hist.* An early form of bicycle propelled by the pressure of the rider's feet on the ground. E19.
2 *transf.* A swift-moving person or vehicle. E19.
3 Any early form of bicycle or tricycle propelled by the pressure of the rider's feet on pedals (now *Hist.*). Also (*US*), a child's tricycle. M19.
■ **velocipedist** *noun* [French *vélocipédiste*] a person who rides a velocipede E19.

velociraptor /vɪˈlɒsɪraptə/ *noun.* M20.
[mod. Latin *Velociraptor* genus name, from Latin *veloci-*, *velox* swift, rapid + RAPTOR *noun*[1].]
PALAEONTOLOGY. A small carnivorous dinosaur of the Cretaceous period having a single large curved claw on each hind foot.

velocity /vɪˈlɒsɪti/ *noun.* LME.
[Old & mod. French *vélocité* or Latin *velocitas*, from *veloc-*, *velox* swift, rapid: see -ITY.]
1 Rapidity of motion, operation, or action; swiftness, speed. LME.
2 Relative speed; the measure of the rate of motion. M17. ▸**b** ECONOMICS. The rate at which money changes hands; the rate of spending in an economy. E20.
3 Speed together with direction of travel, as a vector quantity; the measure of the rate of motion of an object in a given direction. M19.

> 📖 **1** A. POWELL Henchman . . moved with almost startling velocity on aluminium shoulder-crutches. **2** ***escape velocity***, ***muzzle velocity***, ***seismic velocity***, ***terminal velocity***, etc. **3** ***angular velocity***, ***radial velocity***, etc.

Comb.: **velocity head** the velocity pressure of a fluid expressed in terms of the height from which the fluid would have to fall to attain the velocity exerting this pressure; **velocity microphone** a microphone whose diaphragm is freely exposed to the air on both sides and so responds to the particle velocity within a sound wave rather than the pressure; **velocity modulation** ELECTRONICS variation of the velocity of an electron beam by alternate acceleration and retardation in a high-frequency electric field, as in some cathode-ray tubes; **velocity potential** a scalar function of position such that its space derivatives at any point are the components of the fluid velocity at that point; **velocity pressure** that part of the total pressure exerted by a fluid which is due to the velocity it possesses; **velocity profile** (a diagram of) the variation in velocity along a line at right angles to the general direction of flow.

velodrome /ˈvɛlədrəʊm/ *noun.* L19.
[French *vélodrome*, from *vélo* bicycle (abbreviation of *vélocipède* VELOCIPEDE) + *-drome* -DROME.]
A special place or building with a usu. banked track for cycle-racing etc.

velodyne /ˈvɛlə(ʊ)dʌɪn, ˈviːlə(ʊ)-/ *noun.* M20.
[from Latin *velox* swift + Greek *dunamis* force.]
ELECTRICITY. A device in which the output of a tachogenerator is fed back so as to keep the rotational speed of a shaft proportional to an applied voltage.

velometer /vɛˈlɒmɪtə/ *noun.* L19.
[Contr. of VELOCIMETER.]
†**1** A governor for a marine steam engine. Only in L19.
2 An instrument for measuring the speed of air, or of an aircraft through the air. E20.

velopharyngeal /ˌviːləʊfəˈrɪndʒɪəl/ *adjective.* M20.
[from VELUM + -O- + PHARYNGEAL.]
Of or pertaining to the soft palate and the pharynx.

velour /vəˈlʊə/ *noun & adjective.* Also **velours**. E18.
[French *velours* velvet from Old French *velour*, *velous* from Latin *villosus* hairy from *villus* hair. Cf. VELURE, VELVET *noun & adjective.*]
▶**A** *noun.* **1** A silk or velvet pad for smoothing hats. E18.
2 Any of various plush or pile fabrics similar to velvet and used for hats, garments, upholstery, etc. Also (*arch.*), a hat of this fabric. L18.
2 ***patte de velour***: see PATTE 1.
▶**B** *attrib.* or as *adjective.* Made of velour. E19.

velouté /vəˈluːteɪ/ *noun.* M19.
[French = velvety.]
More fully ***velouté sauce***. A rich white sauce made with chicken, veal, or fish stock, and often thickened with cream and egg-yolks.

veltheimia /vɛltˈhʌɪmɪə/ *noun.* E19.
[mod. Latin (see below), from August Ferdinand, Graf von *Veltheim* (1741–1801), German patron of botany + -IA[1].]
Either of two ornamental South African plants constituting the genus *Veltheimia*, of the lily family, with long straplike leaves and dense spikes of pink or purple flowers.

velt-marshal /ˈvɛltmɑːʃ(ə)l/ *noun. obsolete* exc. *Hist.* Also **veldt-**. E18.
[German *Feld-Marschall*, with spelling of 1st elem. infl. by Low German or Dutch.]
A (German or Dutch) field-marshal.

velum /ˈviːləm/ *noun.* Pl. **vela** /ˈviːlə/. M18.
[Latin = sail, curtain, veil.]
1 ANATOMY. A membrane or membranous structure; *esp.* (*a*) the soft palate; (*b*) either of two membranes extending from the vermis of the brain; (*c*) a triangular fold of the pia mater lying between the third ventricle and the fornix of the brain. M18.
2 A screen, a curtain, a protection; *spec.* a velarium. L18.
3 ZOOLOGY. A membrane or membranous integument, esp. in certain molluscs, medusae, or other invertebrates. E19.
4 BOTANY. A membranous structure or covering; *esp.* (MYCOLOGY) = VEIL *noun* 7. M19.

velure /vɛˈl(j)ʊə/ *noun & adjective.* Now *rare.* L16.
[Old French *velour*, *velous* (mod. *velours*): see -URE. Cf. VELOUR.]
▶**A** *noun.* **1** Velvet; velour. L16.
2 = VELOUR 1. L19.
▶**B** *attrib.* or as *adjective.* Made of velvet or velour. E17.

velutinous /vɛˈljuːtɪnəs/ *adjective.* E19.
[Perh. from Italian *vellutino* in same sense, from *velluto* velvet.]
Resembling velvet. Chiefly BOTANY, having a dense covering of short soft hairs.

velveret /ˈvɛlv(ə)rɪt/ *noun & adjective.* Now *rare.* M18.
[Irreg. from next.]
(Made of) a variety of fustian with a velvet surface.

velvet /ˈvɛlvɪt/ *noun & adjective.* ME.
[Old French *veluotte*, from *velu* velvety from medieval Latin *villutus*, from Latin *villus* hair.]
▶**A** *noun.* **1** A soft closely woven fabric of silk, cotton, etc., with a short dense pile. ME. ▸**b** A piece of this fabric. LME. ▸**c** A garment, esp. a dress, made of velvet. M19. ▸**d** Gain, profit, winnings. Freq. in ***to the velvet***, to the good. *slang.* E20.
2 The soft downy skin which covers a deer's antler while in the growing stage. LME.
3 A surface, substance, etc., resembling velvet in appearance or softness of texture. L16.

> 📖 **1** *fig.*: E. B. WHITE A line as smooth as velvet to the ear. **c** D. BARNES A tight-fitting velvet with buttons all down the front. **3** T. GRAY The velvet of her paws.

Phrases: ***black velvet***: see BLACK *adjective.* **in velvet** (of a deer) having the antlers covered with velvet. **on velvet** *slang* in a position of ease or advantage; in an advantageous or prosperous condition. ***Utrecht velvet***.
▶**B** *attrib.* or as *adjective.* **1** Made of velvet. ME.
2 Resembling velvet in texture; soft, smooth, velvety. L16.

> 📖 **1** A. CRAIG She tied a black velvet ribbon round her throat. **2** B. NEIL The [car] door . . shut . . with the velvet click of expensive machinery.

Comb. & special collocations: **velvet ant** any of various mutillid wasps which have a velvety appearance and wingless females; **velvet bean** a climbing bean with densely hairy pods, *Mucuna deeringiana*, grown as a fodder plant in tropical and subtropical regions; **velvet carpet** a cut-pile carpet similar to Wilton; **velvet copper ore** cyanotrichite; **velvet crab** = ***velvet swimming crab*** below; **velvet-dock** common mullein; **velvet duck** = ***velvet scoter*** below; **velvet fiddler crab** = ***velvet swimming crab*** below; **velvetfish** a small Australian fish, *Aploactisoma milesii*, which is covered with velvety papillae and is frequent in shallow coastal waters; **velvet glove** an appearance of urbanity and gentleness, *esp.* one masking firmness or inflexibility (cf. ***iron hand in a velvet glove*** s.v. IRON *adjective*); **velvet grass** *N. Amer.* Yorkshire fog, *Holcus lanatus*; †**velvet-guard** a trimming of velvet; a wearer of such trimmings; **velvet-leaf** any of several plants with soft velvety leaves; *esp.* the Indian mallow, *Abutilon theophrasti*, and the false pareira *Cissampelos pareira*; **velvet-painting** the art of painting on velvet using diluted semi-transparent colours; **velvet-pile** *adjective & noun* (*a*) *adjective* having a pile like that of velvet; (*b*) *noun* a carpet or fabric of this kind; **velvet revolution** [translating Czech *sametová revoluce*] a non-violent political revolution, *esp.* one in which a totalitarian regime is replaced; *spec.* the sequence of events in Czechoslovakia which led to the ending of communist rule in late 1989; **velvet sauce** = VELOUTÉ; **velvet scoter** a holarctic scoter, *Melanitta fusca*, which is black with a white wing patch; **velvet sponge** a soft flat commercial sponge which is a form of *Hippospongia equina* found in the Caribbean area; **velvet sumac**

stag-horn sumac, *Rhus hirta*; **velvet swimming crab** any of several swimming crabs which have the carapace covered with fine hair; esp. *Liocarcinus puber*, which is common on rocky coasts of the N. Atlantic; **velvet-worm** = ONYCHOPHORAN *noun*.
■ **velveted** *adjective* covered with velvet or a velvety substance; dressed in velvet: E17.

velvet /ˈvɛlvɪt/ *verb. rare.* E17.
[from prec.]
†**1** *verb intrans.* Imitate velvet in painting. Only in E17.
2 *verb trans.* Make like velvet; cover (as) with velvet. M19.

velveteen /vɛlvɪˈtiːn/ *noun & adjective.* L18.
[from VELVET *noun* + -EEN[1].]
▶ **A** *noun.* **1** A cotton fabric with a pile resembling velvet. L18.
2 A garment of velveteen; in *pl.*, trousers or knickerbockers made of velveteen, *transf.* a gamekeeper [as wearing velveteen clothes]. M19.
▶ **B** *attrib.* or as *adjective.* Made of velveteen. E19.

velveting /ˈvɛlvɪtɪŋ/ *noun. rare.* E18.
[from VELVET *noun* + -ING[1].]
†**1** The nap or pile of velvet. Only in E18.
2 Velvet as a commercial fabric; velvet in the piece; *esp.* (in *pl.*) velvet goods. L19.

velvety /ˈvɛlvɪti/ *adjective.* LME.
[from VELVET *noun* + -Y[1].]
1 Having the smooth and soft appearance or texture of velvet; smooth and soft to the taste. LME. ▸**b** Of colour: having an intensity, sheen, etc. like velvet. E19.
2 Characteristic of velvet; resembling velvet; *fig.* soft, smooth, gentle. M19.

> 🕮 **1** L. COLWIN The fat green leaves looked moist and velvety. **b** *Gardener* Close-packed, cinnamon-orange flowers in velvety rust-red calyces. **2** D. HALL Their odor is . . wave upon wave of velvety sensuous sweetness. M. STRAND Look at the night, the velvety, fragrant night.

■ **velvetiness** *noun* L19.

Ven. *abbreviation.*
Venerable (as a title etc.).

vena /ˈviːnə/ *noun.* Pl. **venae** /ˈviːniː/. LME.
[Latin.]
ANATOMY & ZOOLOGY. A vein. Usu. with specifying word.
vena cava /ˈkeɪvə/, pl. **venae cavae** /-viː/, [Latin = hollow] each of three large veins that return blood to the heart in higher vertebrates.

venal /ˈviːn(ə)l/ *adjective*[1]. Now *rare.* E17.
[from VENA + -AL[1].]
ANATOMY. = VENOUS.

venal /ˈviːn(ə)l/ *adjective*[2]. M17.
[Latin *venalis*, from *venum* something sold or for sale: see -AL[1].]
1 a Put on sale or available for purchase as an article of merchandise. Also, associated or connected with sale or purchase. *arch.* M17. ▸**b** Of support, favour, etc.: obtainable for a price; ready to be given in return for some reward regardless of higher principles. M17. ▸**c** Of an office, post, privilege, etc.: open to acquisition by bribery, instead of being conferred on grounds of merit or regarded as above bargaining for. L17.
2 Of a person: able to be bribed; ready to lend support or exert influence for purely mercenary considerations. L17.
3 Of conduct etc.: associated with bribery or unprincipled bargaining; subject to mercenary or corrupt influences. E18.

> 🕮 **1a** *Saturday Review* Figs . . might be venal at the nearest stall. **b** J. BRYCE As the Senate is smaller . . the vote of each member . . fetches, when venal, a higher price. **c** J. MENDHAM The Venal Indulgences and pardons of the Church of Rome. **2** K. AMIS A venal city official in some corruption-disclosing American classic. **3** C. BERNHEIMER Venal practices became so widespread . . that almost any woman . . might contemplate selling herself.

■ **venally** *adverb* M18. †**venalness** *noun*: only in E18.

venality /vɪˈnalɪti/ *noun.* E17.
[French *vénalité* or late Latin *venalitas*, from Latin *venalis* VENAL *adjective*[2]: see -ITY.]
1 The quality or fact of being for sale. *rare.* E17.
2 The quality of being venal or open to bribery; readiness to lend support in return for reward; prostitution of principles for mercenary considerations. L17.

> 🕮 **2** P. USTINOV With . . consumerism, and its attendant venality, a spy had . . become a freelance professional.

venatic /vɪˈnatɪk/ *adjective.* M17.
[Latin *venaticus*, from *venat-* pa. ppl stem of *venari* hunt: see -ATIC.]
Of, pertaining to, or used in, the hunting of animals.
■ **venatically** *adverb* L19.

venation /vɪˈneɪʃ(ə)n/ *noun*[1]. Now *rare* or *obsolete.* LME.
[Latin *venatio(n-)*, formed as prec.: see -ATION.]
The action or occupation of hunting animals.

venation /vɪˈneɪʃ(ə)n/ *noun*[2]. M17.
[from Latin *vena* vein + -ATION.]
†**1** The arrangement or structure of sap-vessels in a plant. *rare.* Only in M17.
2 *BOTANY & ENTOMOLOGY.* The arrangement of veins in the leaves of a plant or the wings of an insect. M17.

†**venator** *noun. rare.* M17–M19.
[Latin, from *venat-*: see VENATIC, -OR.]
A hunter, a huntsman.

venatorial /vɛnəˈtɔːrɪəl/ *adjective. rare.* M19.
[from Latin *venatorius*, from *venat-*: see VENATIC, -AL[1].]
1 Connected with hunting. M19.
2 Addicted to hunting. L19.

vend /vɛnd/ *noun.* E17.
[from next.]
1 Sale; an act or opportunity of vending. E17.
2 *spec.* Sale of coals from a colliery; the total amount sold during a certain period. E18.

vend /vɛnd/ *verb.* E17.
[Old & mod. French *vendre* or Latin *vendere* sell, from *venum* (see VENAL *adjective*[2]) + *-dere* var. of *dare* give. Cf. VENT *verb*[2].]
1 *verb intrans.* Be sold; find a market or purchaser. Now *rare* or *obsolete.* E17.
2 *verb trans.* Sell; offer for sale. M17.
3 *verb trans. fig.* Give utterance to, advance, (an opinion etc.). M17.

> 🕮 **1** B. FRANKLIN If our manufactures are too dear they will not vend abroad. **2** B. DUFFY A man . . vending sticky cakes and ices. **vending-machine** an automatic machine which, on the insertion of a coin or token, dispenses small goods such as sweets or cigarettes. **3** P. T. FORSYTH He is not free to vend in his pulpit . . an eccentric individualism.

Venda /ˈvɛndə/ *noun & adjective.* E20.
[Bantu.]
▶ **A** *noun.* Pl. same, **-s**.
1 A member of a Bantu-speaking people inhabiting north-eastern Transvaal and southern Zimbabwe. E20.
2 The Bantu language of this people. E20.
▶ **B** *adjective.* Of or pertaining to the Venda or their language. E20.

vendable /ˈvɛndəb(ə)l/ *adjective.* Now *rare.* LME.
[Old & mod. French, from *vendre* VEND *verb*: see -ABLE. In mod. use directly from VEND *verb.*]
= VENDIBLE.

vendace /ˈvɛndɪs/ *noun.* M18.
[Old French *vendese, -oise* (mod. *vandoise*) from Gaulish word rel. to Old Irish *find*, Welsh *gwyn* white.]
A form of a freshwater whitefish, *Coregonus albula*, found in Loch Maben in Scotland and in two lakes in the English Lake District. Cf. POLLAN.

vendange /vɑ̃dɑ̃ʒ/ *noun.* Pl. pronounced same. M18.
[Old & mod. French: see VINTAGE *noun & adjective.* Cf. VENDEMMIA, VENDIMIA.]
In France: the grape-harvest; the vintage or grapes harvested; a particular vintage of wine.
■ ***vendangeur*** /vɑ̃dɑ̃ʒœːr *(pl. same)*/ *noun* a grape-picker L19.

Vendean /vɛnˈdiːən/ *noun & adjective.* L18.
[French *vendéen*, from *La Vendée* (see below) + -AN.]
▶ **A** *noun.* An inhabitant of the Vendée (*La Vendée*), a maritime department in western France, esp. one who took part in the insurrection of 1793 against the Republic. L18.
▶ **B** *adjective.* Of or pertaining to the Vendée or its inhabitants, esp. in connection with the insurrection of 1793. L18.

vendee /vɛnˈdiː/ *noun.* M16.
[from VEND *verb* + -EE[1].]
The person to whom a thing is sold; the purchaser; *spec.* (*LAW*) the buying party in a sale, esp. of property. Opp. VENDOR.

Vendemiaire /vɛnˌdɛmɪˈɛː/ *noun.* Also ***Vendémiaire*** /vãdemjɛːr/. L18.
[French, from Latin *vindemia* (see VINTAGE *noun & adjective*) + *-aire* -ARY[1].]
Hist. The first month of the French Republican calendar (introduced 1793), extending from 22 September to 21 October.

vendemmia /venˈdemmja/ *noun.* Pl. ***-ie*** /-ie/. E19.
[Italian from Latin *vindemia*: see VINTAGE *noun & adjective.* Cf. VENDANGE, VENDIMIA.]
In Italy: the grape-harvest; the vintage or grapes harvested; a particular vintage of wine.

vender /ˈvɛndə/ *noun.* E17.
[from VEND *verb* + -ER[1]. Cf. VENDOR.]
1 A person who sells something; a seller. E17.
2 A person who advances an opinion etc. *rare.* E19.

vendetta /vɛnˈdɛtə/ *noun.* M19.
[Italian from Latin *vindicta* vengeance.]
1 A blood feud in which the family of a murdered person seeks vengeance on the murderer or the murderer's family, esp. as customary in Corsica and Sicily. M19.
2 A similar blood feud, or prosecution of private revenge. Also, a prolonged bitter quarrel with or campaign against a person etc. M19.

> 🕮 **2** *Sun* The dramatic moment when . . Danny Kaye almost cops it in a horrific bombing vendetta. *Guardian* He embarked on a furious vendetta to close the magazine down.

■ **vendettist** *noun* a person who takes part in or pursues a vendetta E20.

vendeuse /vɑ̃døːz/ *noun.* Pl. pronounced same. E20.
[French, from *vendre* sell.]
A saleswoman; *spec.* one employed in a fashion house.

vendible /ˈvɛndɪb(ə)l/ *adjective & noun.* LME.
[Latin *vendibilis*, from *vendere* VEND *verb*: see -IBLE.]
▶ **A** *adjective.* **1** Able to be vended or sold; saleable, marketable. LME. ▸†**b** = VENAL *adjective*[2] 1b, c. L16–L18. ▸†**c** = VENAL *adjective*[2] 2. E–M17.
†**2** Available for purchase; = VENAL *adjective*[2] 1a. M16–M18.
†**3** *fig.* Current, accepted, acceptable. *rare.* M–L17.
▶ **B** *noun.* A thing that is saleable or offered for sale. L17.
■ **vendiˈbility** *noun* M17.

vendimia /venˈdimja/ *noun.* M20.
[Spanish from Latin *vindemia*: see VINTAGE *noun & adjective.* Cf. VENDANGE, VENDEMMIA.]
In Spain: the grape-harvest; the vintage or grapes harvested; a particular vintage of wine. Also, a festival celebrating the vintage.

venditation /vɛndɪˈteɪʃ(ə)n/ *noun.* E17.
[Latin *venditatio(n-)*, from *venditat-* pa. ppl stem of *venditare* frequentative of *vendere* VEND *verb*: see -ATION.]
†**1** The action of putting forward or displaying something in a favourable or ostentatious manner. E–M17.
2 The action of offering for sale. *rare.* M19.

vendition /vɛnˈdɪʃ(ə)n/ *noun.* M16.
[Latin *venditio(n-)*, from *vendit-* pa. ppl stem of *vendere* VEND *verb*: see -ITION.]
In *ROMAN LAW* (now *Hist.*), sale in a contract of sale (correl. to EMPTION); *gen.* the action of selling.

venditive /ˈvɛndɪtɪv/ *adjective.* Long *rare.* M17.
[from Latin *vendit-* (see prec.) + -IVE.]
Of a person: ready to be of service for purely mercenary considerations.

vendor /ˈvɛndə, *in sense 1 also* ˈvɛndɔː/ *noun.* L16.
[Anglo-Norman *vendor, -dour* (mod. French *vendeur*), formed as VEND *verb*; see -OR.]
1 A person who sells something; *esp.* (*LAW*) the seller in a sale of property or land (opp. VENDEE). L16.
2 A vending-machine. L19.
Comb.: **vendor placing** *FINANCE* a type of placing used as a method of financing a takeover in which the purchasing company issues its own shares to the vending company as payment, with the prearranged agreement that these shares are then placed with investors in exchange for cash.

vendue /vɛnˈdjuː/ *noun. US & W. Indies.* L17.
[Dutch *vendu*, †*vendue* from Old & mod. French (now dial.) *vendue* sale, from *vendre* VEND *verb.*]
A public sale; an auction.

Venedotian /vɛnɪˈdəʊʃ(ə)n/ *adjective. rare.* M19.
[from medieval Latin *Venedotia* North Wales + -AN.]
Of or pertaining to North Wales.

veneer /vɪˈnɪə/ *noun.* E18.
[German *Furnier, Fournier*: see next and VENEERING.]
1 Any of the thin layers or slips of fine or decorative wood or other facing material applied or bonded to another coarser material, esp. wood. Also, any of the layers of wood used to form plywood. E18.
2 Material prepared for use in veneering, or applied to a surface by this or a similar process. M18.
3 *ENTOMOLOGY.* Any of several small European pyralid moths, esp. of the genera *Acentria* and *Nomophila*. E19.
4 *fig.* A misleading outward appearance of an attractive or commendable quality. Freq. foll. by *of.* M19.
5 *DENTISTRY.* In full ***veneer crown***. A crown in which the restoration is placed over the prepared surface of a natural crown. E20.

> 🕮 **2** *Country Homes* Such selected wood veneers as . . Limed Oak and Black or White Ash. **4** ALDOUS HUXLEY A veneer of jaunty self-confidence thinly concealed his nervousness. S. BRETT Her voice had . . lost its elocuted veneer.

veneer /vɪˈnɪə/ *verb trans.* Also †**fineer**. E18.
[German *furnieren* from Old & mod. French *fournir* FURNISH *verb.*]
1 Apply or bond (thin layers of wood or other veneer) to a surface. E18.
2 Face with veneer; apply veneer to (a surface, furniture, etc.). M18.
3 *fig.* Disguise (an unpleasant quality or character) with an outwardly attractive or commendable appearance. Usu. foll. by *with.* M19.

> 🕮 **2** *Antique Collector* A . . fine satinwood veneered corner cabinet. **3** HOLME LEE Another lady of neglected education, whom . . Elizabeth was veneering with thin plates of knowledge.

veneering /vɪˈnɪərɪŋ/ *noun.* E18.
[German *Furnierung, Fournierung*, formed as prec. + -ING¹.]
1 The action or process of VENEER *verb* 1, 2; the result obtained by this process. E18.
2 Wood or other material used as veneer; a facing of this. L18.
3 *fig.* The action of disguising something unpleasant with an outwardly attractive or commendable appearance; an instance of this. Also, a misleadingly attractive outward appearance; = VENEER *noun* 4. E19.

venefic /vɛˈnɛfɪk/ *adjective. arch. rare.* M17.
[Latin *veneficus*, from *venenum* poison: see -FIC.]
Practising or dealing in poisoning; acting by poison; poisonous.
■ †**venefical** *adjective* (*a*) venefic; (*b*) practising or associated with malignant sorcery or witchcraft: L16–E18.

veneficious /vɛnɪˈfɪʃəs/ *adjective. arch. rare.* M17.
[from Latin *veneficium*, from *veneficus*: see VENEFIC, -IOUS.]
Venefic; venefical.

venencia /veˈnenθja/ *noun.* L19.
[Spanish: see VALINCHE.]
A cylindrical metal tube on a long flexible handle, used to draw a sample of sherry from a cask.

venenose /ˈvɛnənəʊs/ *adjective.* Now *rare.* L17.
[Late Latin *venenosus*, from Latin *venenum* poison: see -OSE¹.]
Poisonous, venomous.
■ Also **venene** *adjective* (now *rare* or *obsolete*) M17.

venepuncture /ˈvɛnɪˌpʌŋ(k)tʃə, ˈviːnɪ-/ *noun.* Also **veni-**. E20.
[from Latin *vena* vein + PUNCTURE *noun*.]
MEDICINE. (An instance of) the puncture of a vein with a hypodermic needle, to withdraw blood or for intravenous injection.

venerable /ˈvɛn(ə)rəb(ə)l/ *adjective & noun.* LME.
[Old & mod. French *vénérable* or Latin *venerabilis*, from *venerari* VENERATE: see -ABLE.]
▶ **A** *adjective.* **1** (Of a person) worthy of being venerated or highly respected on account of character, position, achievements, etc.; (of a person, a person's features, attributes, etc.) commanding veneration due to a combination of age, personal qualities, and dignity of appearance. LME. ▸**b** CHRISTIAN CHURCH. Used as a title; now *spec.* (*a*) as the title of an archdeacon in the Church of England; (*b*) ROMAN CATHOLIC CHURCH as the title of a deceased person who has attained the first degree of canonization. LME.
2 Of a thing: worthy of veneration; deserving respect on account of distinguished qualities or associations; to be regarded with religious reverence. LME. ▸**b** Likely to inspire feelings of veneration; impressive, august. Now *rare.* E17.
3 Worthy of veneration on account of age or antiquity; made impressive by the appearance of age. E17. ▸**b** Ancient, old. L18.
†**4** Giving evidence of veneration; reverent, reverential. E17–E18.

> 🕮 **1** SIR W. SCOTT He wore a breast-plate, over which descended a grey beard of venerable length. *Literary Review* A venerable Columbia philosopher . . who also happens to be a . . rabbi. C. WARWICK This robust character . . lived to the venerable age of 108. **2** E. H. JONES Hardy . . had not intended in *Jude the Obscure* to attack venerable institutions. **3** DICKENS The nuns' house, a venerable brick edifice. **b** C. BRONTË Rows of venerable chairs, high-backed and narrow.

▶ **B** *noun.* A venerable person; an ecclesiastic with the title 'Venerable'. M18.
■ **veneraˈbility** *noun* M17. **venerableness** *noun* venerability L17. **venerably** *adverb* E17.

veneral /ˈvɛn(ə)r(ə)l/ *adjective.* L15.
[medieval Latin *veneralis*, from *vener-*, *venus* love: see -AL¹.]
†**1** = VENEREAL *adjective* 1. L15–E17.
2 = VENEREAL *adjective* 2a. Long *rare.* M17.

venerate /ˈvɛnəreɪt/ *verb trans.* E17.
[Latin *venerat-* pa. ppl stem of *venerari* adore, revere: see -ATE³.]
1 Regard with deep respect; revere on account of sanctity, character, etc. E17.
2 Pay honour to (something) by an act of obeisance. *rare.* M19.

> 🕮 **1** A. BRIGGS The law itself was venerated even if . . not always obeyed or enforced. *Vanity Fair* Venerated English actors Michael Redgrave and Rachel Kempson.

■ **venerative** *adjective* (*rare*) of the nature of or inclined to veneration E19. **venerator** *noun* M17.

veneration /vɛnəˈreɪʃ(ə)n/ *noun.* LME.
[Old & mod. French *vénération* or Latin *veneratio(n-)*, formed as prec.: see -ATION.]
1 A feeling of deep respect; reverence for a person or thing. Freq. in ***have in veneration***, ***hold in veneration***. LME.
2 The action or an act of showing respect or reverence. M16.
3 The fact or condition of being venerated. E17.

> 🕮 **1** DISRAELI The Reformation began to diminish the veneration for the Latin language. A. CRAIG My mother had been head girl . . and was still remembered with tremulous veneration. **2** P. ACKROYD The veneration of relics seemed . . another kind of theatre. **3** T. HERBERT Claudian observes there was scarce any Tree that had not its veneration.

venereal /vɪˈnɪərɪəl/ *adjective & noun.* LME.
[from Latin *venereus*, from *vener-*, *venus* love + -AL¹.]
▶ **A** *adjective.* **1** Of, pertaining to, or associated with sexual desire or intercourse. LME.
2 a (Of a disease etc.) acquired during sexual intercourse, or of a type usu. transmitted in this way; symptomatic of or associated with such a disease. M17. ▸**b** Of a person: infected with or having a venereal disease. *rare.* L17.
3 ASTROLOGY. Born under or affected by the planet Venus. Also, having the qualities associated with the goddess Venus; *esp.* inclined to be lascivious; devoted to lust. *arch. rare.* M17.

> 🕮 **1** J. NORRIS Sensual pleasure, especially that eminent species of it which we call venereal.

▶ **B** *noun.* **1** A person with venereal disease. *rare.* L18.
2 Venereal disease. *rare.* E19.
■ **venereally** *adverb* (*a*) by sexual intercourse; (*b*) *rare* with venereal disease: M20.

Venerean /vɪˈnɪərɪ(ə)n/ *adjective.* Also **v-**. M16.
[formed as prec. + -AN.]
†**1** Of, pertaining to, or connected with Venus. Cf. VENEREAL *adjective* 3. M16–L17.
2 = VENEREAL *adjective* 1. Long *rare.* M16.

venereology /vɪˌnɪərɪˈɒlədʒi/ *noun.* L19.
[formed as prec. + -O- + -LOGY.]
MEDICINE. The branch of medicine that deals with venereal diseases.
■ **venereoˈlogical** *adjective* M20. **venereologist** *noun* an expert in or student of venereology M20.

†**venereous** *adjective.* LME.
[formed as VENEREAL + -OUS.]
1 Devoted to or desirous of sexual enjoyment; libidinous, lustful. Cf. VENEREAL *adjective* 3. LME–E18.
2 = VENEREAL *adjective* 1. L15–L18.
3 Exciting or stimulating sexual desire. Only in 17.

venerer /ˈvɛn(ə)rə/ *noun. arch. rare.* M19.
[from VENERY *noun*¹ + -ER¹.]
A huntsman.

†**venerial** *adjective.* M16.
[from Latin *venerius*, from *vener-*: see VENEREAL, -IAL.]
1 = VENEREAL *adjective* 1. M16–M17.
2 = VENEREAL *adjective* 3. L16–M17.
3 Of or pertaining to (esp. the cure of) venereal disease. E–M18.

Venerian /vɪˈnɪərɪən/ *adjective & noun.* Long *rare.* Also **v-**. LME.
[formed as prec. + -IAN.]
▶ **A** *adjective.* **1** = VENEREAL *adjective* 3. LME.
†**2** = VENEREAL *adjective* 1. LME–E17.
▶†**B** *noun.* A person born under or affected by the planet Venus. LME–E17.

†**venerious** *adjective.* L15.
[from Latin *venerius*, formed as next: see -IOUS.]
1 = VENEREOUS 1. L15–E18.
2 = VENEREAL *adjective* 1. M16–M17.

venerous /ˈvɛn(ə)rəs/ *adjective.* Now *rare.* M16.
[from Latin *vener-*: see VENEREAL, -OUS.]
†**1** = VENEREAL *adjective* 1. M16–M17.
2 Lustful; inclined to lasciviousness. Cf. VENEREAL *adjective* 3. L16.
†**3** = VENEREOUS *adjective* 3. L16–M17.

venery /ˈvɛn(ə)ri/ *noun*¹. *arch.* ME.
[Old & mod. French *vénerie*, from *vener* to hunt, from Proto-Romance from Latin *venari*: see -ERY.]
1 The practice or sport of hunting; the chase. ME.
†**2** Wild animals hunted as game. ME–M17.

> 🕮 **1** T. H. WHITE That's the way to chase a beast of venery.

venery /ˈvɛn(ə)ri/ *noun*². *arch.* LME.
[medieval Latin *veneria*, from Latin *vener-*: see VENEREAL, -Y³.]
The practice or pursuit of sexual pleasure; sexual indulgence.

venesection /vɛnɪˈsɛkʃ(ə)n, viːnɪ-/ *noun.* M17.
[medieval Latin *venae sectio* cutting of a vein: see VENA, SECTION *noun*.]
MEDICINE. (An instance of) the surgical operation of cutting or opening a vein; phlebotomy; the former practice of this as a remedy.
■ **venesector** *noun* †(*a*) a blood-letter; (*b*) a phlebotomist: L19.

Veneti /ˈvɛnɛtiː/ *noun pl.* E17.
[Latin.]
Hist. **1** A people of ancient Italy inhabiting the area of Venetia around the head of the Adriatic from *c* 1000 BC, allied to Rome following the second Punic War of 218–201 BC. E17.
2 A Celtic people of ancient Brittany conquered by Julius Caesar in 57 BC. M17.

Venetian /vɪˈniːʃ(ə)n/ *noun & adjective.* Also **v-**. LME.
[Old French *Venicien* (mod. *Vénitien*): later assim. to medieval Latin *Venetianus*, from Latin *Venetia* Venice, a city (formerly also a medieval republic) in NE Italy (Italian *Venezia*): see -IAN.]
▶ **A** *noun.* **1** A native or inhabitant of Venice. Also (*rare*), a member of the Veneti. LME. ▸**b** The Italian dialect spoken in Venice. L16.
2 In *pl.* Hose or breeches of a particular fashion originating in Venice. *obsolete* exc. *Hist.* L16.
3 *Hist.* A sequin or gold coin of Venice, as current in India and adjacent countries. L17.
4 A closely-woven cloth with a fine twilled surface, used as a suiting or dress material. E18.
5 *ellipt.* †**a** A Venetian window. M–L18. ▸**b** A venetian blind. E19. ▸**c** Each of the tapes joining the slats of a venetian blind. Usu. in *pl.* L19.
6 = DOMINO *noun* 1. *rare.* L19.
▶ **B** *adjective.* Of, pertaining to, or associated with the city of Venice. Also (*rare*), of or pertaining to the Veneti. M16.
Venetian blind an adjustable window-blind consisting of narrow horizontal slats joined together by vertical tapes which allow the angle of the slats to be varied, thereby controlling the amount of light excluded. **Venetian blue** a rich turquoise or cobalt blue. **Venetian carpet** a durable type of carpet woven so that the warp conceals the weft, and usu. having a striped pattern. **Venetian chalk** a white compact talc used for marking cloth. **Venetian cloth** = sense A.4 above. **Venetian door**: with side-lights on either side for lighting an entrance-hall. **Venetian glass** delicate decorative glassware originally made at Murano near Venice. **Venetian lace** any of various types of lace originally made in or associated with Venice, as reticella, guipure needlepoint, etc. **Venetian red** (*a*) a reddish pigment of ferric oxides; (*b*) a strong reddish brown. **Venetian School** (*a*) a school of painting, noted for its mastery of colouring, which originated in Venice in the 15th cent. and reached its climax with artists such as Titian in the 16th; (*b*) a school of Italian architecture originating in Venice in the early 16th cent. and characterized by its richness of decorative detail, lightness, and elegance. **Venetian shutter**: constructed on the same principle as a venetian blind. **Venetian sumac** the smoke plant, *Cotinus coggygria*. **Venetian swell** MUSIC an organ swell with the soundboard covered by an inner lid with adjustable louvres similar to a Venetian shutter. ***Venetian whisk***: see WHISK *noun*¹ 2c. **Venetian window** a composite window with three separate openings, the central one being arched and taller than the others.
■ **venetianed** *adjective* (of a window, house, etc.) having venetian blinds M19. **Venetianly** *adverb* (*rare*) M19.

Venetic /vɪˈnɛtɪk/ *adjective & noun.* L19.
[from Latin VENETI or *Venetia* Venice + -IC.]
▶ **A** *adjective.* Of or pertaining to the Veneti, their country, or their language, or the modern province of Venice. L19.
▶ **B** *noun.* The language of the Veneti. E20.

Venezuelan /vɛnɪˈzweɪlən/ *adjective & noun.* E19.
[from *Venezuela* (see below) + -AN.]
▶ **A** *noun.* A native or inhabitant of Venezuela, a republic on the north coast of S. America. E19.
▶ **B** *adjective.* Of or pertaining to Venezuela or the Venezuelans. E19.

venge /vɛn(d)ʒ/ *verb. arch.* ME.
[Old & mod. French †*vengier*, *venger*, from Latin *vindicare* VINDICATE.]
1 *verb trans.* = AVENGE *verb* 1. ME.
†**2** *verb intrans.* = AVENGE *verb* 2. ME–L15.

> 🕮 **1** A. KOESTLER Every error . . venges itself unto the seventh generation.

■ †**vengeously** *adverb* (*rare*) violently, viciously L16–E19. **venger** *noun* = AVENGER ME.

vengeable /ˈvɛn(d)ʒəb(ə)l/ *adjective & adverb. obsolete* exc. *Scot. arch.* LME.
[Anglo-Norman *vengable*, formed as VENGE: see -ABLE.]
▶ **A** *adjective.* **1** = VENGEFUL 1, 2. LME.
2 Extreme, severe, intense. M16.
▶ **B** *adverb.* Extremely, intensely. M16.
■ **vengeably** *adverb* (long *arch.*) LME.

vengeance /ˈvɛn(d)ʒ(ə)ns/ *noun & adverb.* ME.
[Old & mod. French, from *venger* VENGE: see -ANCE.]
▶ **A** *noun.* The action or an act of avenging oneself or another; (an) infliction of injury or punishment in retribution for wrong to oneself or another. Freq. in ***take vengeance for***, ***take vengeance on***. ME.

> 🕮 SHAKES. *Cymb.* If you Should have ta'en vengeance on my faults, I never Had liv'd. K. CROSSLEY-HOLLAND They swore vengeance and began to prepare for war.

Phrases: **a vengeance on**, **vengeance on** *arch.* expr. hatred of or anger towards. **what a vengeance?**, **what the vengeance?** (*obsolete* exc. *Scot. arch.*): used as an intensive expr. annoyance, anger, amazement, etc. **with a vengeance** †(*a*) with a curse or malediction; (*b*) with great force or violence; in an extreme degree.
▶†**B** *adverb.* Extremely, intensely. M16–E18.

vengeful /ˈvɛn(d)ʒfʊl, -f(ə)l/ *adjective*. L16.
[from VENGE + -FUL, after *revengeful*.]
1 Of a person: wanting or inclined to take vengeance; vindictive. L16. ▸**b** Of a weapon, hand, etc.: used to inflict vengeance. *poet.* L16.
2 Of an action etc.: characterized or prompted by vengeance. M17.

🕮 **1** *Newsweek* They find some of his young outriders unruly, undisciplined and vengeful. **b** SHAKES. *2 Hen. VI* But here's a vengeful sword, rusted with ease.

■ **vengefully** *adverb* M19. **vengefulness** *noun* E18.

†**vengement** *noun*. ME–L16.
[Old French, formed as VENGE: see -MENT.]
Vengeance.

venial /ˈviːnɪəl/ *adjective & noun*. ME.
[Old French (mod. *véniel*) from late Latin *venialis*, from *venia* forgiveness: see -AL¹.]
▸**A** *adjective*. **1** That may be pardoned or forgiven; not grave or heinous; light; CHRISTIAN THEOLOGY (of sin) not entailing damnation (opp. ***deadly*** or ***mortal***). ME.
2 That may be excused or overlooked; unimportant, trivial. L16.
†**3** Allowable, permissible; blameless. *poet. rare.* L16–E18.

🕮 **1** J. YEATS Our own laws . . punished forgery and even more venial crimes with death. B. MASON Quarrelling on Christmas Day! as though on any other day these sins were venial. **2** SIR W. SCOTT This is a venial error compared to that of our ancestors.

▸**B** *noun*. A venial sin or offence; an excusable error. Long *rare* or *obsolete*. LME.
■ **veniˈality** *noun* (long *rare*) the state or condition of being venial E17. **venially** *adverb* ME. **venialness** *noun* (*rare*) E18.

Venice /ˈvɛnɪs/ *noun*. LME.
[A city in NE Italy.]
Used *attrib.* to designate things from or associated with Venice.
Venice glass a very fine glass orig. produced at Murano, near Venice; an article made of this, *esp.* a drinking-glass. †**Venice treacle** PHARMACOLOGY an electuary composed of many ingredients, supposed to possess universal alexipharmic and preservative properties. **Venice turpentine** a mixture of gum rosin and oil of turpentine; *spec.* a yellowish-green oleoresin obtained from the European larch.

venidium /vɛˈnɪdɪəm/ *noun*. M20.
[mod. Latin (see below), from Latin *vena* vein, with ref. to the ribbed achenes of some species.]
Any of various South African plants of the composite family constituting the former genus *Venidium* (now included in *Arctotis*), with yellow or orange daisy-like flowers; *esp.* = ***Cape daisy*** s.v. CAPE *noun*¹.

venipuncture *noun* var. of VENEPUNCTURE.

venire /vɪˈnʌɪri:/ *noun*. M17.
[Latin = come. In sense 1 ellipt. for next.]
1 LAW (now *Hist.*). = VENIRE FACIAS 1. M17.
2 US LAW. A panel of people available for jury service. M20.
1 ***venire de novo*** /diː ˈnəʊvəʊ/ a writ ordering a new trial after a mistrial.
Comb.: ***venireman***, ***veniremember*** US a member of a jury summoned by judicial writ.

venire facias /vɪˌnʌɪri: ˈfeɪʃɪas/ *noun phr.* LME.
[Latin, lit. 'make or cause to come'.]
LAW. **1** A judicial writ directing a sheriff to summon a jury. Now *Hist.* exc. *US*. LME.
†**2** A writ issuing a summons to appear before a court. LME–M18.

venison /ˈvɛnɪs(ə)n, ˈvɛnɪz(ə)n/ *noun*. ME.
[Old French *veneso(u)n*, *venison* (mod. *venaison*) formed as VENATION *noun*¹: see -ISON.]
1 The flesh of game or *of* a specified animal used as food; now *spec.* the flesh of deer used as food. ME.
2 *arch.* **a** An animal hunted as game, *esp.* a deer. ME. ▸**b** *collect.* Animals hunted as game. ME.
†**3** The practice or sport of hunting game. *rare.* LME–E16.

🕮 **1** *Food & Wine* A well-seasoned rich game terrine of pheasant, partridge, venison and hare. *attrib.*: ***venison pie***, ***venison sausage***, ***venison steak***, etc.

Venite /vɪˈnʌɪti:/ *noun*. ME.
[Latin = come (imper.), the first word of the psalm (see below).]
CHRISTIAN CHURCH. Psalm 95 (94 in the Vulgate) used as a canticle at matins; a musical setting of this. Cf. INVITATORY *adjective* 1.

Venizelist /vɛnɪˈzeɪlɪst/ *adjective & noun*. E20.
[from *Venizelos* (see below) + -IST.]
▸**A** *adjective*. Of, pertaining to, or supporting the Greek statesman Eleutherios Venizelos (1864–1936), or his policies. E20.
▸**B** *noun*. A supporter or adherent of Venizelos or his policies. E20.

Venn diagram /ˈvɛn ˌdʌɪəgram/ *noun phr.* E20.
[John *Venn* (1834–1923), English logician.]
A group of circles, representing logical sets, that may or may not intersect according as those sets do or do not have elements in common.

vennel /ˈvɛn(ə)l/ *noun*. LME.
[Old French *venel(l)e*, *vanelle* (mod. *venelle*), from medieval Latin *venella* dim. of Latin *vena* vein.]
1 A narrow lane or passage between buildings; an alley. Chiefly *Scot.*, *Anglo-Irish*, & *north.* LME.
2 A drain, a gutter; a sewer. *Scot. & north.* LME.

veno- /ˈviːnəʊ, ˈvɛnəʊ/ *combining form*.
[from Latin *vena* VEIN *noun*: see -O-.]
ANATOMY & MEDICINE. Forming words relating to the venous system.
■ **venoclysis** /-ˈklʌɪsɪs/ *noun* [Greek *klusis* washing] the introduction of fluid into the circulation by an intravenous drip E20. **venoconsˈtriction** *noun* constriction of a vein M20. **venoˈcclusive** *adjective* pertaining to the occlusion of veins; *spec.* designating a tropical disease characterized by this: M20. **venospasm** *noun* sudden, transient contraction of a vein M20. **venoˈstasis** *noun* a reduction (induced or spontaneous) in the flow of venous blood from a part of the body M20.

venography /vɪˈnɒgrəfi/ *noun*. M20.
[from prec. + -GRAPHY.]
MEDICINE. Radiography of a vein after injection of a radio-opaque fluid.
■ **venoˈgraphic**, **venoˈgraphical** *adjectives* of or pertaining to venography M20. **venoˈgraphically** *adverb* in a venographic way, with respect to venography M20. **venogram** *noun* a radiograph of a vein M20.

venom /ˈvɛnəm/ *noun, adjective, & verb*. ME.
[Old & mod. French †*venim*, *venin*, from Proto-Romance alt. (after Latin words in *-imen*) of Latin *venenum* potion, drug, poison. For the change of final *n* to *m* cf. *pilgrim*.]
▸**A** *noun*. **1** A poisonous fluid secreted by certain snakes, spiders, scorpions, etc. and usu. injected by them into other animals by means of a bite or sting. ME.
2 Poison, esp. as administered to or drunk by a person; any poisonous or noxious substance, preparation, or property; a microbial toxin. Now *rare* or *obsolete*. ME.
3 *fig.* Malignant or malicious character or quality; virulent feeling, language, behaviour, etc.; malice, spite. Also, an instance of this. ME. ▸**b** A malicious or spiteful person or animal. *obsolete* exc. *Scot. & dial.* L16.
4 A (type of) poison or toxin. LME.
†**5** A dye. *rare.* LME–M16.

🕮 **3** V. NABOKOV The thick venom of envy began squirting at me. S. BRETT 'Sod the lot of them!' said Alex Household with sudden venom.

▸**B** *adjective*. Venomous. Long *obsolete* exc. *dial.* ME.
▸**C** *verb trans.* = ENVENOM *verb*. Now *arch. & dial.* ME.
■ **venomer** *noun* (*arch. rare*) a poisoner M17. **venomness** *noun* (now *rare*) venomousness M16. **venomsome** *adjective* (long *obsolete* exc. *dial.*) venomous M17. **venomy** *adjective* (long *rare* exc. *dial.*) venomous, malignant LME.

venomed /ˈvɛnəmd/ *adjective*. LME.
[from VENOM *noun*, *verb*: see -ED², -ED¹.]
1 = VENOMOUS 1, 2, 3. Chiefly *literary.* LME.
2 Covered or impregnated with venom; poisoned. E17.

🕮 **2** R. WEST You find out everybody's vulnerable point and you shoot arrows at it, sharp, venomed arrows.

venomous /ˈvɛnəməs/ *adjective*. ME.
[Old & mod. French *venimeux*, formed as VENOM, after late Latin *venenosus* from *venenum*: see VENOM, -OUS.]
1 Containing, consisting of, or accompanied by venom; poisonous, deadly or injurious because of this. ME. ▸†**b** Of a wound etc.: poisonous; septic, festering. LME–L18. ▸†**c** = VENOMED 2. LME–M17. ▸**d** Harmful *to* a person or thing. *rare.* Only in 17.
2 *fig.* Malignant, malicious; virulent; spiteful. Formerly also, morally or spiritually corrupting; pernicious. ME.
3 Of animals, *esp.* certain snakes, or their parts: secreting venom; capable of injecting venom by means of a bite or sting, or of inflicting poisonous wounds in this way. LME.
4 Of, pertaining to, or characteristic of venom. LME.

🕮 **1** K. A. PORTER Doctor Nelson shot a venomous, emerald colored fluid into my arm. **d** SHAKES. *Coriol.* Thy tears are salter than a younger man's And venomous to thine eyes. **2** A. MACLEAN The once beautiful green eyes were venomous. **4** M. R. MITFORD It has a fine venomous smell.

■ **venomously** *adverb* LME. **venomousness** *noun* E16.

venose /ˈviːnəʊs/ *adjective*. M17.
[Latin *venosus*, from *vena* vein: see -OSE¹.]
Chiefly BOTANY & ENTOMOLOGY. Having numerous branched veins.
■ **venosity** /viːˈnɒsɪti/ *noun* (MEDICINE) (of the blood etc.) the state of being venous M19.

venous /ˈviːnəs/ *adjective*. E17.
[from Latin *venosus*, or *vena* vein + -OUS.]
1 Covered with or full of veins; BOTANY = VENOSE. E17.
2 ANATOMY & PHYSIOLOGY. Of, pertaining to, or of the nature of a vein; consisting or composed of veins. E17. ▸**b** Of blood: deoxygenated and of a dusky red colour (opp. ARTERIAL). L17.
2 venous system the system of veins by which deoxygenated blood is conveyed from the various parts of the body back to the lungs and heart.

vent /vɛnt/ *noun*¹. LME.
[Alt. of FENT *noun*.]
1 An opening or slit in a garment, esp. in the lower edge of the back of a coat or skirt. LME.
2 = CRENEL *noun*. Long *obsolete* exc. *Hist.* LME.

vent /vɛnt/ *noun*². LME.
[Partly from French = wind; partly after French *évent*, from *éventer*: see AVENTAIL.]
▸**I** †**1** A wind. *rare.* LME–L16.
†**2** = SCENT *noun* 2a. *rare.* L16–E18.
3 The surfacing of an otter, beaver, etc., for air; an instance of this. M17.
▸**II 4** Orig., an anus. Later also, the vulva of a female mammal. Now only, the anus or cloaca of an animal, esp. of a bird or a lower vertebrate. LME.
5 An opening or duct for the escape or emission of air, smoke, liquid, etc. (also ***vent-hole***); *gen.* an outlet, an exit. LME. ▸**b** GEOLOGY. An opening in the ground through which volcanic materials are emitted; the funnel or pipe of a volcano. E17. ▸**c** The flue of a chimney. Chiefly *Scot.* M18. ▸**d** An aperture in the enclosure of a loudspeaker. M20.
6 An aperture, a hole, *esp.* one used to provide ventilation or light (also ***vent-hole***); a fissure, a crack; *spec.* any of the finger-holes in a wind instrument. M16. ▸**b** The touch-hole of a gun or cannon. M17.

🕮 **5** *Which?* The spout, and lid vents, should keep steam away from the hand. **6** DRYDEN Th' industrious Kind . . contrive To stop the Vents and Crannies of their Hive.

▸**III 7** The action or an act of discharging something; (an) emission. *rare.* E16.
8 The action or an act of escaping or exiting from a confined space; (a) means or opportunity to do this; (an) issue, (an) outlet. Chiefly in ***find a vent***, ***find vent***, ***give vent (to)***. M16. ▸**b** = WINDAGE *noun* 1. M17.
9 *fig.* The release or expression of (esp. repressed) emotion, energy, etc.; (a) means or opportunity for this. Now chiefly in ***give vent to***, give expression or free play to; relieve (an emotion etc.) in this way. E17. ▸**b** A thing serving as an outlet for an emotion, energy, etc. M17.

🕮 **7** SHAKES. *Ven. & Ad.* Free vent of words love's fire doth assuage. **8** J. C. LOUDON In order to give vent to the rising sap. J. TYNDALL The smoke found ample vent through the holes. **9** W. LEWIS Paul . . gave vent . . to a burst of stylised belly-jeers. R. HEILBRONER Aspects of the conditioning process that find their vent in . . obedience and . . capacity for identification. **b** H. READ Art becomes a vent or safety-valve through which . . distress is restored to equilibrium.

Phrases: **full vent** to the greatest possible degree or extent. **give vent to**: see senses 8, 9 above. †**make vent of** (*rare*, Shakes.) speak of. **take vent** (of news etc.) become known, be divulged.
Comb.: ***vent-hole***: see senses 5, 6 above; ***vent-peg*** a small peg for plugging the vent-hole of a cask.
■ **vented** *adjective* provided with a vent or vents M20.

vent /vɛnt/ *noun*³. Now *arch. & dial.* M16.
[Old & mod. French *vente* from Proto-Romance from *vendita* fem. pa. pple of Latin *vendere* VEND *verb*.]
1 The action of selling or fact of being sold as goods. Also, (an) opportunity for selling or being sold; (a) market, (an) outlet. Freq. in ***find vent***, ***have vent***. M16.
†**2** An inn, a tavern; a hostel. L16–E17.

vent /vɛnt/ *noun*⁴. *slang.* L19.
[Abbreviation.]
= VENTRILOQUIST.

vent /vɛnt/ *verb*¹. LME.
[Prob. aphet. from Old French *aventer* var. of *esventer* (mod. *éventer*): see AVENTAIL.]
▸**I 1** *verb trans.* Provide with a vent or outlet for gas, steam, etc.; make a vent or air-hole in (a cask etc.). LME. ▸**b** *fig.* Relieve of emotion; unburden (one's heart etc.). *literary.* E17. ▸**c** Provide (a gun) with a vent. E19.
2 *verb intrans. & refl.* Of a thing: find or make a vent or outlet; discharge its force; pass *away*, *out*, etc. M16. ▸**b** Of an emotion, quality, etc.: be expressed; show (itself) *in* something. M17.
3 *verb trans. & intrans.* Discharge or expel (liquid, smoke, etc.); drain or clear (of) unwanted material by this action. L16. ▸†**b** *verb trans.* Of a person or animal: expel, discharge, or evacuate (urine, faeces, etc.). E17–M19.
4 *verb trans. fig.* ▸**a** Give vent or free expression to (an emotion etc.); subject another to (one's anger etc.), esp. without cause (also foll. by *on*, *upon*). L16. ▸**b** Make known or public; say openly. Also (chiefly *poet.*), give out (a groan, sigh, etc.). E17.
5 *verb trans.* Distribute, circulate; *spec.* put (coins) into circulation. *obsolete* exc. *Scot.* Now *rare.* E17.

📖 **1** J. C. Rich Molds may be vented to permit the ready escape of air from undercuts. **2** S. Brett The wind . . from the Urals vented itself against the . . Winter Gardens. *Ecologist* 'Underground' testing of nuclear weapons—tests which regularly vent into the atmosphere. **b** H. Reed This cheerfulness has vented itself in his playful poetry. **3** *Which?* The Table shows where the drier vents from. **4** C. Harman Sylvia had managed to vent some of her spleen by being sardonic. *Village Voice* Years with the Agency have taught George Bush to vent his anger on small targets. **b** *Times Lit. Suppl.* Ritual exclamations of outrage . . are vented.

▶ **II** †**6 a** *verb intrans.* Of an animal: sniff the air, esp. to pick up a scent. **M16–M17.** ▸**b** *verb trans.* Smell, sniff. *rare.* **M17.**
†**7** *verb trans.* Of an animal: pick up the scent of. **L16–M18.**
†**8** *verb trans.* Lift *up* to admit air. *rare* (Spenser). Only in **L16.**
9 a *verb intrans.* Of an otter, beaver, etc.: surface for air. **L16.** ▸†**b** *verb trans.* Force (an otter or beaver) to surface for air. **L16–L17.**
■ **venting** *noun* the action or an act of the verb; *spec.* the escape into the atmosphere of radioactive dust and debris from an underground nuclear explosion or a defective reactor **LME.**

vent /vɛnt/ *verb*[2]. *obsolete* exc. *dial.* **L15.**
[formed as **VENT** *noun*[3].]
1 *verb trans.* Sell (goods). Formerly also foll. by *away, off*, etc. **L15.**
†**2** *verb intrans.* Of goods: be sold; sell (*well* etc.). Only in **17.**

venta /ˈventa/ *noun.* **E17.**
[Spanish.]
In Spain: a hostel, an inn.

ventage /ˈvɛntɪdʒ/ *noun.* **E17.**
[from **VENT** *noun*[2] + **-AGE.**]
1 Any of the finger-holes in a wind instrument. **E17.**
2 A small vent or aperture, esp. for air. *rare.* **E17.**

ventail /ˈvɛnteɪl/ *noun.* **ME.**
[Old French *ventail(le)*, from *vent* wind from Latin *ventus*: see **-AL**[1].]
Hist. **1** A piece of protective armour for the neck. **ME.**
2 Orig., the lower movable front of a helmet. Later, the whole movable front of a helmet, including the visor. Cf. **AVENTAIL. LME.**

ventana /venˈtana/ *noun.* **L17.**
[Spanish.]
In Spain: a window.

venter /ˈvɛntə/ *noun*[1]. **M16.**
[(In branch I from law French for Old & mod. French *ventre* from) Latin *venter* belly.]
▶ **I 1** Chiefly **LAW.** Each of two or more women bearing children by the same man. Chiefly in ***by venter.*** Now *rare.* **M16.** ▸†**b** With preceding ordinal numeral: a woman's marriage. **E–M18.**
2 The womb; *transf.* a person's mother. Long *rare* or *obsolete.* **L16.** ▸†**b** A birth, a delivery. **M17–E18.**
3 *BOTANY.* The enlarged basal part of an archegonium, where the egg cell develops. **L19.**
▶ **II** †**4** Any of the three chief body cavities containing viscera, consisting of the abdomen, thorax, and head. Usu. in *pl.* or with specifying word. **E17–L18.**
5 †**a** Any of the four stomachs of a ruminant. **E17–E18.** ▸**b** *ZOOLOGY.* The abdomen, the belly; the underside of an animal. **E18.**
6 *ANATOMY.* †**a** The thicker part of a muscle. **E17–E18.** ▸**b** The concave surface of a bone. **M19.**

venter /ˈvɛntə/ *noun*[2]. **E17.**
[from **VENT** *verb*[1] + **-ER**[1].]
A person who gives vent to malicious or objectionable statements, opinions, etc.

ventiduct /ˈvɛntɪdʌkt/ *noun.* **E17.**
[from Latin *ventus* wind + **-I-** + Latin *ductus* **DUCT** *noun*.]
A duct allowing the passage of air or steam; *esp.* a ventilating duct or shaft in a building.

ventifact /ˈvɛntɪfakt/ *noun.* **E20.**
[formed as prec. + **-I-** + *factus* pa. pple of *facere* make, after *artefact*.]
A faceted stone shaped by wind-blown sand.

ventil /ˈvɛntɪl/ *noun.* **L19.**
[German from Italian *ventile* from medieval Latin = sluice.]
MUSIC. **1** Any of the shutters regulating the airflow in an organ. **L19.**
2 Any of the valves in a wind instrument. **L19.**

ventilate /ˈvɛntɪleɪt/ *verb trans.* **LME.**
[Latin *ventilat-* pa. ppl stem of *ventilare* brandish, fan, winnow, agitate (in late Latin = discuss, air a subject) from *ventus* wind: see **-ATE**[3].]
▶ **I 1** Winnow (grain etc.). Formerly also, winnow away, scatter. **LME.**
†**2** Fan or kindle (a flame etc.); *fig.* inflame, arouse. **E17–M18.**
†**3** Set (air) in motion to refresh someone. **M17–L18.**
4 a Aerate or oxygenate (the blood) during respiration. Now *rare* or *obsolete.* **M17.** ▸**b** *gen.* Expose to fresh air to maintain in or restore to good condition. **M18.** ▸**c** Supply air or oxygen to (the lungs or respiratory system), naturally or artificially. **E20.**
5 Of air: blow upon or through so as to purify or freshen. **L17.**
6 Provide with a vent or opening to the air. **E18.** ▸**b** Shoot; kill by shooting. *slang.* **L19.**
7 Provide with a supply of fresh air; cause air to circulate freely in to maintain a fresh atmosphere. Freq. as ***ventilated ppl adjective.*** **M18.**

📖 **4b** *Cook's Magazine* Garlic should be ventilated during storage. **6b** C. Egleton Pray he doesn't kill somebody . . because he's talking about ventilating people. **7** K. M. E. Murray The school room . . was ill ventilated owing to the low ceiling.

▶ **II 8** Submit (a question, topic, etc.) to public consideration or debate; discuss or examine openly. **L15.**
9 Express or air (an opinion etc.); make known or public. Also, give vent to (an emotion etc.). **M16.**

📖 **8** D. Cusack When a matter concerns the whole school, it should be ventilated thoroughly. **9** M. Moffatt Real racism . . could only be ventilated with very close friends.

■ **ventilative** *adjective* of, pertaining to, or producing ventilation **L18.**

ventilation /vɛntɪˈleɪʃ(ə)n/ *noun.* **LME.**
[Old & mod. French, or from Latin *ventilatio(n-)*, formed as prec.: see **-ION.**]
1 †**a** A movement or current of air; a breeze. **LME–M18.** ▸**b** Circulation or free passage of air. **E17.**
2 The action of fanning, blowing upon, or exposing to the open air to refresh, cool, etc. Formerly also, the winnowing of grain etc. **E16.**
3 †**a** Oxygenation of the blood during respiration. **E17–E19.** ▸**b** The supply of fresh air or oxygen to the lungs or respiratory system by natural or artificial respiration. **L19.**
4 The submission of a matter to public consideration or debate; open discussion or examination of a question, topic, etc. **E17.**
5 The provision of a supply of fresh air to a room, building, etc.; the means or method of achieving this. **M17.**

📖 **2** J. Hersey Your salmon needs a little ventilation . . I propose that we . . give it the night air. **4** C. V. Stanford A Parliamentary White-paper . . marks a . . step forward in the ventilation of the question. **5** *Architects' Journal* Adequate ventilation in these roofs cannot be provided by eaves ventilators alone. *Garden Answers* To grow alpines in pans you'll need . . additional side ventilation. attrib.: ***ventilation duct, ventilation fan, ventilation shaft***, etc.

ventilator /ˈvɛntɪleɪtə/ *noun.* **E18.**
[from **VENTILATE** + **-OR.**]
1 A person who or thing which provides ventilation. **E18.**
2 A device, esp. a fan fixed in a wall opening, for extracting warm air from a room and replacing it with fresh air. Also, an opening or duct providing a supply of fresh air to a room etc. **M18.** ▸**b** *Hist.* = ***Ladies' Gallery*** s.v. **LADY** *noun & adjective.* **E19.** ▸**c** *NAUTICAL.* = ***windsail*** (b) s.v. **WIND** *noun*[1]. **M19.** ▸**d** *MEDICINE.* An apparatus for artificially maintaining respiration, esp. in an unconscious or paralysed person. **M20.**

ventilatory /ˈvɛntɪlət(ə)ri/ *adjective.* **M19.**
[from **VENTILATE** + **-ORY**[2].]
†**1** Esp. of a hat: provided with ventilation. *rare.* Only in **M19.**
2 *MEDICINE.* Of, pertaining to, or serving for ventilation of the lungs or respiratory system. **M20.**

Ventile /ˈvɛntʌɪl, -tɪl/ *noun.* Also **v-. M20.**
[Prob. back-form. from **VENTILATE.**]
(Proprietary name for) a closely woven water-repellent cotton fabric.

Ventolin /ˈvɛntəlɪn/ *noun.* **M20.**
[Perh. after **VENTILATE.**]
PHARMACOLOGY. (Proprietary name for) the drug salbutamol.

†**ventose** *noun*[1]. **LME–E18.**
[Old & mod. French †*ventose, ventouse* from late Latin *ventosa* use as noun of fem. of Latin *ventosus*: see **VENTOSE** *adjective*.]
A type of cupping-glass.

Ventose /vɒ̃ˈtəʊz/ *noun*[2]. Also ***Ventôse*** /vɑ̃toz/. **E19.**
[French, formed as next.]
Hist. The sixth month of the French Republican calendar (introduced 1793), extending from 19 February to 20 March.

ventose /ˈvɛntəʊs/ *adjective. rare.* **LME.**
[Latin *ventosus*, from *ventus* wind: see **-OSE**[1].]
Windy; flatulent.
■ **ventoseness** *noun* **LME.**

ventosity /vɛnˈtɒsɪti/ *noun.* **LME.**
[Old & mod. French *ventosité*, or late Latin *ventositas*, formed as **VENTOSE** *adjective*: see **-ITY.**]
†**1** *MEDICINE.* The state of having the stomach or other part of the digestive tract filled with wind; flatulence. **LME–M18.** ▸**b** In *pl.* Gases generated in the stomach or bowels; attacks of flatulence. **LME–M17.** ▸**c** The quality in things that produces flatulence. Only in **E19.**
†**2** A blast or puff of wind; *esp.* a belch. **E16–E18.**
3 The state or condition of being windy; windiness. Now only *fig.*, (a) pompous conceit. **M16.**

ventouse /ˈvɛntuːs; *foreign* vɑ̃tuːz (*pl. same*)/ *noun.* **M20.**
[French, orig. 'cupping-glass': see **VENTOSE** *noun*[1].]
MEDICINE. A vacuum extractor.

ventrad /ˈvɛntrad/ *adverb.* **M19.**
[from Latin *ventr-*, *venter* abdomen + **-AD**[3].]
ANATOMY & ZOOLOGY. Towards the ventral side.

ventral /ˈvɛntr(ə)l/ *adjective & noun.* **LME.**
[from **VENTER** *noun*[1] + **-AL**[1].]
▶ **A** *adjective.* **1** Of or pertaining to the abdomen; situated or occurring in the region of the abdomen or the underside of the body. **LME.**
2 *ANATOMY & ZOOLOGY.* Situated on, pertaining to, or designating the part of a structure that faces to the front or the underside, or is the lower, inner, or concave part. **M19.**
3 *BOTANY.* Pertaining to or designating the adaxial or inner surface of a carpel etc., or the surface of a thallus closest to the substrate (i.e. the lower side). **M19.**
4 *AERONAUTICS.* Situated on or inside the belly of an aircraft. **M20.**
▶ **B** *noun.* A ventral fin. **M19.**
■ **ventrally** *adverb* in a ventral position or direction; on or towards the underside: **L19.**

ventre à terre /vɑ̃tr a tɛːr/ *adverbial phr.* **M19.**
[French, lit. 'belly to the ground'.]
1 Of an animal, esp. a horse: represented in a painting etc. with legs stretched out in line with the belly; moving at full speed. **M19.**
2 Lying on the stomach; prone. **M20.**

ventricle /ˈvɛntrɪk(ə)l/ *noun.* **LME.**
[Latin **VENTRICULUS**: see **-CLE.**]
ANATOMY & ZOOLOGY. **1** Either of the two muscular lower chambers of the heart (in some animals, a single chamber), which pump the blood to the arteries and through the body. **LME.**
2 Each of four fluid-filled cavities in the brain, formed by enlargements of the central canal of the spinal cord. **LME.**
3 †**a** = **VENTRICULUS** 1a, b. **L16–E19.** ▸**b** *ENTOMOLOGY.* = **VENTRICULUS** 1c. Now *rare.* **L17.**
4 Orig., any small hollow or cavity in an animal body. Now *spec.* the recess or space on each side of the larynx between the vertibular folds and the vocal cords; a laryngeal pouch or sac. **L16.**

ventricose /ˈvɛntrɪkəʊs/ *adjective.* **M18.**
[medieval or mod. Latin alt. of Latin *ventriosus* pot-bellied, from *ventr-*, *venter* belly, perh. infl. by **VENTRICULUS**: see **-OSE**[1].]
1 *BOTANY & ZOOLOGY.* Swelling out in the middle; strongly convex, esp. on one side. **M18.**
2 Of a person: big-bellied. **M19.**
■ **ventriˈcosity** *noun* (*ZOOLOGY*) convexity, degree of swelling; the ratio of breadth to length: **M19.** **ventricous** *adjective* (*rare*) = **VENTRICOSE E18.**

ventricular /vɛnˈtrɪkjʊlə/ *adjective.* **E19.**
[from **VENTRICULUS** + **-AR**[1].]
Chiefly *ANATOMY & MEDICINE.* **1** Of or pertaining to the stomach; abdominal, gastric. Now *rare* or *obsolete.* **E19.**
2 Of, pertaining to, forming part of, or affecting a ventricle. **M19.**
3 *ZOOLOGY.* Of the nature of a ventricle. **M19.**

ventricule /ˈvɛntrɪkjuːl/ *noun. rare.* **LME.**
[Old French from Latin **VENTRICULUS.**]
ANATOMY & ZOOLOGY. = **VENTRICLE.**

ventriculi *noun* pl. of **VENTRICULUS.**

ventriculite /vɛnˈtrɪkjʊlʌɪt/ *noun.* **E19.**
[from mod. Latin *Ventriculites* (see below), from Latin **VENTRICULUS**: see **-ITE**[1].]
PALAEONTOLOGY. A vase-shaped fossil sponge of the genus *Ventriculites* or a related genus.

ventriculitis /vɛnˌtrɪkjʊˈlʌɪtɪs/ *noun.* **E20.**
[from **VENTRICULUS** + **-ITIS.**]
MEDICINE. Inflammation of the lining of the ventricles of the brain.

ventriculography /vɛnˌtrɪkjʊˈlɒɡrəfi/ *noun.* **E20.**
[from **VENTRICULUS** + **-O-** + **-GRAPHY.**]
MEDICINE. Radiography of the ventricles of the brain with the cerebral fluid replaced by air or some other radio-opaque medium. Cf. **PNEUMOENCEPHALOGRAPHY.**
■ **venˌtriculoˈgraphic** *adjective* of or pertaining to ventriculography **M20.** **venˈtriculogram** *noun* a radiograph of the ventricles of the brain **E20.**

ventriculus /vɛnˈtrɪkjʊləs/ *noun.* Pl. **-li** /-lʌɪ, -liː/. **E18.**
[Latin, dim. of *ventr-*, *venter* belly: see **-CULE.**]
ANATOMY & ZOOLOGY. **1 a** The stomach of a mammal. Now *rare.* **E18.** ▸**b** The gizzard or stomach of a bird or a lower

vertebrate. L19. ▸**c** The midgut of an insect; the stomach of other arthropods etc. L19.
†**2** = VENTRICLE 1. Only in L18.
3 The body cavity of a sponge. L19.
▪ **ventriculo'atrial** *adjective* (MEDICINE) involving or connecting a ventricle (usu. of the brain) and the atrium of the heart M20. **ventriculo,perito'neal** *adjective* (MEDICINE) involving or connecting a ventricle of the brain and the peritoneum E20.

ventriloque /ˈvɛntrɪləʊk/ *noun & adjective*. As noun also (earlier) in Latin form †**-quus**, pl. **-qui**. L16.
[Latin *ventriloquus*, from *ventr-*, *venter* belly + *loqui* speak.]
▸†**A** *noun*. A ventriloquist. L16–M18.
▸**B** *adjective*. Ventriloquial. *rare*. E19.

ventriloquial /vɛntrɪˈləʊkwɪəl/ *adjective*. E19.
[from VENTRILOQUY + -AL¹.]
1 Of or pertaining to ventriloquism. E19.
2 Of a sound: (resembling that) produced by ventriloquism. M19.
▪ **ventriloquially** *adverb* L19.

ventriloquise *verb* var. of VENTRILOQUIZE.

ventriloquism /vɛnˈtrɪləkwɪz(ə)m/ *noun*. L18.
[from VENTRILOQUY + -ISM.]
1 The art or practice of speaking or producing sounds so that they seem to proceed from a source other than the speaker. L18. ▸**b** A sound produced in this way. M19.
2 The fact or appearance of speaking from the abdomen, esp. through supposed spiritual possession. E19.

ventriloquist /vɛnˈtrɪləkwɪst/ *noun*. M17.
[from VENTRILOQUY + -IST.]
1 Orig., a person speaking or appearing to speak from the abdomen, esp. due to supposed spiritual possession. Later, a practitioner of or expert in ventriloquism, esp. as a form of public entertainment. M17.
2 A bird or mammal with a ventriloquial call or voice. E19.
▪ **ventrilo'quistic** *adjective* (**a**) using or practising ventriloquism; (**b**) = VENTRILOQUIAL: M19.

ventriloquize /vɛnˈtrɪləkwʌɪz/ *verb*. Also **-ise**. E19.
[from VENTRILOQUY + -IZE.]
1 *verb intrans*. Use or practise ventriloquism; speak or produce sounds (as) by ventriloquism. E19.
2 *verb trans*. Say or express (as) by ventriloquism. M19.

📖 **1** THACKERAY The Strand Theatre where a Signor Benesontag . . was ventriloquizing. **2** W. H. AUDEN The Void desires . . you for its creature, / a doll through whom it may ventriloquize / its vast resentment.

ventriloquous /vɛnˈtrɪləkwəs/ *adjective*. E18.
[formed as VENTRILOQUE + -OUS.]
1 = VENTRILOQUISTIC (a). Long *rare* or *obsolete*. E18.
2 = VENTRILOQUIAL 2. M18.

†**ventriloquus** *noun* see VENTRILOQUE.

ventriloquy /vɛnˈtrɪləkwi/ *noun*. L16.
[mod. Latin *ventriloquium*, formed as VENTRILOQUE: see -Y³.]
Ventriloquism (both senses).

ventripotent /vɛnˈtrɪpət(ə)nt/ *adjective*. *literary*. Now *rare*. E17.
[French from medieval Latin *ventripotens*, from *ventr-*, *venter* belly + as POTENT *adjective*².]
1 Having a large abdomen; big-bellied. E17.
2 Having a voracious appetite; gluttonous. E19.

ventro- /ˈvɛntrəʊ/ *combining form*.
[formed as Latin VENTER *noun*¹ + -O-.]
The underside or abdomen and (what is denoted by the 2nd elem.).
▪ **ventro'lateral** *adjective* of, pertaining to, or involving the ventral and lateral surfaces M19. **ventro'laterally** *adverb* in a ventrolateral direction L19. **ventro'medial** *adjective* both ventral and medial; situated towards the median line and the ventral surface: E20. **ventro'medially** *adverb* in a ventromedial direction M20.

venture /ˈvɛntʃə/ *noun*. LME.
[Aphet. from ADVENTURE *noun* (partly taken as *a venture*).]
1 a *gen*. = ADVENTURE *noun* 1. *rare*. Long *obsolete* exc. *Scot*. LME. ▸†**b** (A) favourable chance or opportunity. E–M17.
†**2** = ADVENTURE *noun* 3. M16–E19.
3 An act or occasion of undertaking something without assurance of success; a risky or daring attempt or enterprise. M16.
4 A business enterprise involving considerable risk; a commercial speculation. L16. ▸**b** A thing risked in a commercial speculation. L16.
†**5** A prostitute. *rare* (Shakes.). Only in E17.

📖 **3** G. MEREDITH On her great venture, Man, Earth gazes. C. CONNOLLY She wanted her venture to be a success. **4** R. INGALLS If the idea could be turned into a commercial venture, it might make millions. **b** R. LLOYD The consequence has Æsop told, He lost his venture, sheep and gold.

Phrases: **at a venture** at random, without previous or due consideration. ***joint venture***: see JOINT *adjective*. †**put to a venture**, †**put to the venture** hazard, risk.

Comb.: **venture capital** = *risk capital* s.v. RISK *noun*; **venture capitalism** the system or practice of business investment based on venture capital; **venture capitalist** a supplier of venture capital for investment; **Venture Scout** a member of the Scout Association (of a branch which in 1967 replaced the Rover Scouts) aged between 16 and 20.

venture /ˈvɛntʃə/ *verb*. LME.
[Aphet. from ADVENTURE *verb*.]
▸**I** *verb trans*. **1** Risk the loss of or injury to, esp. in pursuit of some advantage or gain; hazard, stake. Freq. foll. by *for, in, on, to do*. LME. ▸**b** *refl*. Risk (oneself); expose (oneself) to danger or harm. *arch*. Usu. foll. by *in, with*, etc. L16.
2 Risk sending or moving elsewhere (foll. by *into, to*, etc.); risk entrusting *with* another person. Now *rare*. L16.

📖 **1** C. KINGSLEY His whole fortune is ventured in an expedition. *Proverb*: Nothing venture, nothing gain. **b** R. B. SHERIDAN Dare you venture yourself alone with me? **2** SWIFT They might be lost or spoiled, if I ventured them out of my possession.

▸**II** *verb intrans*. **3** †**a** Foll. by *on, upon*: dare to approach or attack (a person or animal). E16–M17. ▸**b** Foll. by *at, on, upon*: undertake (a risky course of action) without assurance of success; dare to attempt or engage in (something involving risk). Also make an attempt *at*, guess *at*. M16.
4 Undertake a journey, esp. one involving risk or chance; dare to go or proceed (foll. by *back, on, to*, etc.); dare to go *out*, esp. outdoors. M16.
5 Run or take risks; dare. M16.
6 Presume or be audacious enough *to do*. M16.

📖 **3b** D. H. LAWRENCE She would venture very gingerly on that experiment. **4** G. GREENE None of the girls had ventured out . . from their homes. J. N. ISBISTER The precariousness of those who venture into new uncharted areas. **5** H. H. FURNESS In emending Shakespeare's text . . those who know the most, venture the least. **6** A. J. AYER He dominated the discussion, and no one ventured to contradict him.

▸**III** *verb trans*. **7** Accept or encounter the dangers of; brave. Now *rare* exc. as passing into sense 8. M16. ▸**b** Risk trusting or confiding in (a person). Now *rare* or *obsolete*. L18.
8 Dare to attempt or undertake; risk the experience or result of. L16. ▸**b** Dare to put forward (an opinion, suggestion, etc.); express tentatively or with presumption. M17.

📖 **8** H. ROTH At Luter, he never ventured a glance. F. POHL He'd ventured oyster stew, and loved it. **b** S. SASSOON I ventured 'Ages since we met,' and tried My candid smile of friendship. C. MACKENZIE We shall not venture an opinion on this vexed question.

▪ **venturer** *noun* a person who ventures; an adventurer; *spec*. (*Hist*.) a person who undertakes or shares in a trading venture: M16.

venturesome /ˈvɛntʃəs(ə)m/ *adjective*. M17.
[from VENTURE *noun*, *verb* + -SOME¹.]
1 Characterized by or involving risk; hazardous, risky. M17.
2 Inclined to venture or take risks; characterized by the taking of risks; bold, daring, adventurous. L17.

📖 **2** *Time* The Manhattan Theatre Club . . fresh drama under . . venturesome leadership. *International Business Week* Venturesome insurers . . developed the skills to handle new, tough risks.

▪ **venturesomely** *adverb* E18. **venturesomeness** *noun* E18.

Venturi /vɛnˈtjʊəri/ *noun*. L19.
[Giovanni Battista *Venturi* (1746–1822), Italian physicist.]
Used ***attrib***. and ***absol***. to designate a short constriction in a tube between two longer tapered portions, producing a drop in pressure in a fluid flowing through the constriction which may be used to determine the rate of flow or used as a source of suction, devices having this form, and the effect involved.

venturous /ˈvɛntʃ(ə)rəs/ *adjective*. M16.
[Aphet. from ADVENTUROUS, after VENTURE *noun*, *verb*.]
1 = VENTURESOME 2. M16.
2 = VENTURESOME 1. L16.
3 Full of adventure; adventurous. *arch*. E19.
▪ **venturously** *adverb* M16. **venturousness** *noun* L16.

venue /ˈvɛnjuː/ *noun*. See also VENY. ME.
[Old & mod. French, use as noun of fem. pa. pple of *venir* come from Latin *venire*.]
†**1 a** A sally in order to assault someone, an attack. *rare*. Only in ME. ▸†**b** = VENY 1. L16–M17. ▸†**c** = VENY 2. L16–E19.
2 a LAW (now *Hist*.). The county, district, or locality within which a cause must be tried and a jury gathered (orig. the neighbourhood of the crime etc.). M16. ▸**b** The scene of a real or supposed action or event. M19. ▸**c** An appointed meeting-place, esp. for a sporting match or competition; a site or building for a theatrical, musical, etc., performance or event; a rendezvous. M19.

📖 **2c** *City Limits* He . . promoted the pub as a soul, rock and punk venue. *Guardian* They . . suggested Geneva or Paris as a venue for initial discussions. S. MIDDLETON I'll decide on the date of the wedding . . . You can choose the venue.

venule /ˈvɛnjuːl/ *noun*. Also (*rare*) **vein-**. M19.
[Latin *venula* dim. of *vena* vein: see -ULE.]
A small or minor vein: (**a**) BOTANY & ENTOMOLOGY any of the branches of a vein in a leaf or an insect's wing; (**b**) ANATOMY any of the small vessels which collect blood from the capillaries.

Venus /ˈviːnəs/ *noun*. OE.
[Latin.]
▸**I 1 a** MYTHOLOGY. The Roman goddess of beauty and (esp. sexual) love; the corresponding Greek goddess Aphrodite; the love goddess of any other culture. OE. ▸**b** A representation, esp. a statue or image, of Venus. LME. ▸**c** ARCHAEOLOGY. An upper palaeolithic human figurine, often female and often distinguished by exaggerated breasts, belly, and buttocks. E20.
2 Sexual love or desire; amorous activity or influence; lust. Now *poet. & literary*. LME.
†**3** A quality or characteristic exciting love; a charm, an attractive feature. M16–E18.
4 A beautiful or attractive woman. Chiefly *poet. & literary*. L16.

📖 **1b** L. GRANT-ADAMSON Another Venus, Botticelli's *Venus with Mars*. **4** *Harpers & Queen* Clare Mosely, a Venus in furs.

▸**II 5** The second planet in order of distance from the sun, whose orbit lies between those of Mercury and the earth. Cf. MORNING STAR 1, *EVENING star*. ME.
†**6** ALCHEMY. The metal copper. LME–L18.
†**7** HERALDRY. The tincture vert in the fanciful blazon of arms of sovereign princes. L16–E18.
8 The highest or most favourable throw in playing with huckle-bones. Long *arch*. E17.
9 ZOOLOGY. (The shell of) any of numerous rounded bivalve molluscs of the genus *Venus* or the family Veneridae. Also ***Venus clam*** (chiefly *US*). L18.
Comb. & phrases: **mount of Venus** = MONS VENERIS; ***Venus clam***: see sense 9 above; **Venus figure**, **Venus figurine** = sense 1c above; ***Venus fly-trap***: see FLY-TRAP 1; **Venus' hair** the maidenhair fern *Adiantum capillus-veneris*; **Venus hairstone** MINERALOGY rutilated quartz; **Venus's basin**, **Venus bath** the wild teasel, *Dipsacus fullonum*, so called from the hollow formed by the connate leaves; **Venus's comb** the plant shepherd's needle, *Scandix pecten-veneris*; **Venus's flower basket** ZOOLOGY any of several deep-water glass sponges of the genus *Euplectella*, which have a rigid lattice skeleton; ***Venus's fly-trap***: see FLY-TRAP 1; **Venus's girdle** ZOOLOGY any of several transparent ctenophores of the genus *Cestus*, which have a very long ribbon-like body and occur in warmer seas; **Venus's hairstone** MINERALOGY rutilated quartz; **Venus shell** = sense 9 above; **Venus's looking-glass** either of two plants of the genus *Legousia*, of the bellflower family, *L. speculum-veneris*, a Continental plant grown for its round violet-blue flowers, and *L. hybrida*, a plant found as a cornfield weed in England; **Venus's navelwort** (**a**) = *navelwort* s.v. NAVEL; (**b**) any of several small ornamental plants of the genus *Omphalodes*, of the borage family, esp. *O. linifolia*; **Venus's pride** *US* the plant bluets, *Hedyotis caerulea*.

Venusberg /ˈviːnəsbəːg/ *noun*. M19.
[German = mountain of Venus.]
In German legend, *the* court of Venus; *transf*. any environment characterized primarily by sensual pleasure.
▪ **Venusbergian** *adjective* of, pertaining to, or characteristic of the Venusberg L19.

Venusian /vɪˈnjuːsɪən/ *noun & adjective*¹. L19.
[from VENUS + -IAN.]
▸**A** *noun*. **1** A supposed inhabitant of the planet Venus; the language spoken by such a being. L19.
2 ASTROLOGY. A person supposedly subject to the influence of the planet Venus. *rare*. M20.
▸**B** *adjective*. **1** Of, pertaining to, or characteristic of the planet Venus or its supposed inhabitants. L19.
2 ASTROLOGY. Designating or pertaining to the movement or influence of the planet Venus. *rare*. E20.

Venusian /vɪˈnjuːsɪən/ *adjective*². *rare*. E17.
[from *Venusia* an ancient town in southern Italy and birthplace of Horace + -AN.]
Of or pertaining to the Roman poet Horace (65–8 BC), Horatian.

venust /vɛˈnʌst/ *adjective*. Long *arch*. E16.
[Latin *venustus*, formed as VENUS.]
Handsome, beautiful; elegant, graceful.

venville /ˈvɛnvɪl/ *noun*. LME.
[Origin unkn.]
A special form of tenure obtaining in parishes adjoining Dartmoor, by which the tenants enjoy certain privileges in the use of the moor. Chiefly in ***in venville***.

veny /ˈvɛni/ *noun*. *obsolete* exc. *dial*. L16.
[Var. of VENUE.]
1 A hit or thrust in fencing; a wound or blow with a weapon; *fig*. a sharp retort, a witty remark. L16.
2 A bout or turn of fencing. L16.

Veps /vɛps/ *noun & adjective.* Also (earlier, now *rare*) **Vesp** /vɛsp/. **M19.**
[Russian from Vepsian *Vepsa* Veps.]
▶ **A** *noun.* Pl. **Veps**, (now *rare*) **Vesps**.
1 A member of a Finnic people living in the region of Lake Onega in NW Russia. **M19.**
2 The Finno-Ugric language of this people, Vepsian. **M20.**
▶ **B** *adjective.* Of or pertaining to the Veps or their language. **M19.**
■ **Vepsic** *noun & adjective* (*rare*) Vepsian **L19.**

Vepsian /ˈvɛpsɪən/ *noun & adjective.* Also (earlier, now *rare*) **W-**. **E20.**
[formed as prec. + -IAN.]
▶ **A** *noun.* **1** = VEPS *noun* 1. *rare.* **E20.**
2 The Finno-Ugric language of the Veps. **E20.**
▶ **B** *adjective.* Of or pertaining to Vepsian. **M20.**

vera causa /vɛːrə ˈkaʊzə/ *noun phr.* Pl. ***verae causae*** /vɛːriː ˈkaʊziː/. **M19.**
[Latin = real cause.]
PHILOSOPHY. A true cause which brings about an effect as a minimum independent agency.

veracious /vəˈreɪʃəs/ *adjective.* Chiefly *formal.* **L17.**
[from Latin *verac-*, *verax*, from *verus* true: see -ACIOUS.]
1 Habitually speaking or disposed to speak the truth; truthful, honest. **L17.**
2 Of a statement etc.: conforming to truth or honesty; true, accurate. **L18.**
3 That estimates or judges truly or correctly. *rare.* **M19.**

🕮 **1** DICKENS The testimony of the two veracious and competent witnesses. **2** S. JOHNSON Is not my soul laid open in these veracious pages?

■ **veraciously** *adverb* **E19.** **veraciousness** *noun* **M19.**

veracity /vəˈrasɪti/ *noun.* **E17.**
[French *véracité* or medieval Latin *veracitas*, formed as prec.: see -ACITY.]
1 The quality or character of speaking the truth; truthful disposition; truthfulness, honesty, trustworthiness. **E17.**
2 Correspondence with truth or facts; correctness, accuracy. **M18.**
3 A truthful statement; a truth. *rare.* **M19.**

🕮 **1** *Guardian* Evidence which casts real doubt on the reliability or veracity of . . officers responsible for . . interrogations. **2** D. JACOBSON I have no irrefutable evidence . . of the veracity of the tale.

vera copula /vɛːrə ˈkɒpjʊlə/ *noun phr.* **M19.**
[Latin = true union.]
LAW. Sexual intercourse with erection and penetration.

verae causae *noun phr.* pl. of VERA CAUSA.

veranda /vəˈrandə/ *noun.* Also **-dah**; †**viranda**, **-do** (pl. **-os**). **E18.**
[Portuguese *varanda* prob. from Hindi *varaṇḍā* from Sanskrit *varaṇḍa* partition, gallery.]
1 A usu. roofed open portico or gallery extending along a wall of a house or building. **E18.**
2 A roof or canopy extending over the pavement outside a shop or business establishment. *Austral. & NZ.* **M19.**
■ **verandaed** *adjective* provided with a veranda or verandas **E19.**

verapamil /vəˈrapəmɪl/ *noun.* **M20.**
[from V(AL)ER(IC + AM(INO- + NITR)IL(E, elems. of the systematic name, with inserted *p*.]
PHARMACOLOGY. A bicyclic drug, $C_{27}H_{38}N_2O_4$, that is used to treat angina pectoris and cardiac arrhythmias.

veratric /vəˈratrɪk/ *adjective.* **M19.**
[from next + -IC.]
CHEMISTRY. ***veratric acid***, a cyclic carboxylic acid, $(CH_3O)_2C_6H_3COOH$, which is present in veratrums.
■ **veratria** /vəˈreɪtrɪə/ *noun* (now *rare*) = VERATRINE **E19.** **veratridine** *noun* a toxic yellowish-white amorphous alkaloid, $C_{36}H_{51}NO_{11}$, which is present in the seeds of veratrums and sabadilla and has anti-hypertensive properties, but is now used chiefly for experimental purposes **E20.** ˈ**veratrine**, **-in** *noun* a toxic mixture of alkaloids present in the seeds of veratrums and sabadilla, formerly used to relieve neuralgia and rheumatism **E19.** ˈ**veratrole**, **-ol** *noun* a colourless aromatic oil or solid, $C_6H_4(OCH_3)_2$, produced from catechol and used as an antiseptic **M19.**

veratrum /vəˈreɪtrəm/ *noun.* **L16.**
[Latin.]
Any of various tall acrid plants constituting the genus *Veratrum*, of the lily family, which have broad leaves and clustered greenish or whitish flowers (also called ***false hellebore***); *esp.* the European white hellebore, *Veratrum album*, and the N. American *V. viride*. Also, the poisonous rhizome of any of these plants.

verb /vəːb/ *noun & verb.* **LME.**
[Old & mod. French *verbe* or Latin *verbum* word, verb.]
GRAMMAR. ▶ **A** *noun.* A word used to indicate the occurrence or performance of an action or the existence of a state or condition, freq. connecting the subject of a sentence with the rest of the predicate. (One of the parts of speech.) **LME.**
active verb, ***auxiliary verb***, ***compound verb***, ***passive verb***, ***phrasal verb***, etc. ***action of a verb***: see ACTION *noun*. ***verb of incomplete predication***: see PREDICATION 2.
▶ **B** *verb trans.* Make into or use as a verb, verbify (a noun etc.). **M20.**
■ **verbless** *adjective* **M19.**

verbage /ˈvəːbɪdʒ/ *noun. rare.* **L18.**
[Alt.]
= VERBIAGE.

verbal /ˈvəːb(ə)l/ *adjective, noun, & verb.* **L15.**
[Old & mod. French, or late Latin *verbalis*, from Latin *verbum*: see VERB, -AL[1].]
▶ **A** *adjective.* **1 a** Of a person: dealing with or using words, esp. rather than things or realities. **L15.** ▸**b** Using many words; talkative, verbose; articulate. **E17.**
2 Of or pertaining to words; consisting or composed of words; of the nature of a word. **M16.**
3 GRAMMAR. Of, pertaining to, or derived from a verb; of the nature of a verb. **M16.**
4 Expressed or conveyed by speech rather than writing; oral. **L16.**
5 Concerned with, consisting of, or involving words only rather than things or realities. **E17.**
6 Corresponding word for word; literal. **E17.**

🕮 **1a** *She* Alcoholic parents; verbal abusers; and sexual abusers. **b** SARA MAITLAND He was ebullient, excitable, verbal, and passionate. **2** P. ACKROYD He had a remarkable memory, both verbal and visual. *Guardian* Children's verbal and reasoning skills. D. HIGHSMITH Punished with slaps, missed meals or verbal assaults. ***verbal action***: see ACTION *noun*. **verbal adjective** an adjective formed from a verb, though not necessarily constituting an inflection, and usu. closely related to it in meaning. **verbal conditioning** PSYCHOLOGY the reinforcing of certain verbal responses with the object of establishing the use of particular words or ways of speaking. **verbal diarrhoea** *colloq.* a tendency to talk too much, extreme verbosity. ***verbal*** INSPIRATION. **3** W. D. WHITNEY The plural verbal inflection. **verbal noun** GRAMMAR a noun formed as an inflection of a verb and partly sharing its constructions. **4** B. T. WASHINGTON A written or a verbal request from their parents. **5** B. JOWETT Opposition between these two modes of speaking is rather verbal than real. **6** F. W. FARRAR The sacred writers never aim at verbal accuracy in their quotations.

▶ **B** *noun.* **1** GRAMMAR. **a** A deverbal noun or other part of speech. *arch.* **M16.** ▸**b** A word or phrase functioning as a verb. **M20.**
2 A verbal statement, esp. a damaging admission, alleged to have been made by a suspected criminal and offered as evidence by the prosecution. *slang.* **M20.**
3 *sing.* & (usu.) in *pl.* Insults, abuse, invective. *slang.* **L20.**
4 In *pl.* Words spoken or sung; *esp.* the words of a song; the dialogue of a film. *colloq.* **L20.**
▶ **C** *verb trans.* Infl. **-ll-**, ***-l-**. Attribute a damaging admission to (a suspected criminal). *colloq.* **M20.**
■ **verbalism** *noun* (*a*) a verbal expression, a word; (*b*) predominance of or concentration on the merely verbal over reality or meaning; minute attention to words, verbal criticism: **L18.** **verbalist** *noun* (*a*) a person dealing in or concentrating on mere words rather than reality or meaning; (*b*) a person skilled in the use or knowledge of words: **E17.** **verbaˈlistic** *adjective* of, pertaining to, or characterized by verbalism **M20.** **verbaˈlistically** *adverb* **M20.** **verˈbality** *noun* (*a*) the quality of being merely verbal, that consisting of mere words; (*b*) in *pl.*, verbal expressions or phrases: **M17.** **verbally** *adverb* **L16.**

verbalize /ˈvəːb(ə)lʌɪz/ *verb.* Also **-ise**. **E17.**
[French *verbaliser*, or from VERBAL *adjective* + -IZE.]
1 *verb intrans.* Use many words, be verbose. **E17.**
2 *verb trans.* Make (a noun etc.) into a verb. **M17.**
3 *verb trans.* Express in words. **L19.**
■ **verbalizaˈbility** *noun* **M20.** **verbalizable** *adjective* able to be verbalized **M20.** **verbaliˈzation** *noun* (*a*) the action of verbalizing something; the fact of being verbalized; (*b*) a verbal expression or statement: **M19.** **verbalizer** *noun* a person who verbalizes; *spec.* a person who registers stimuli or thoughts mentally in verbal terms rather than in visual images. **M20.**

verbascum /vəːˈbaskəm/ *noun.* **M16.**
[Latin.]
Any plant of the genus *Verbascum*, of the figwort family, *esp.* one grown for ornament; a mullein.

verbatim /vəːˈbeɪtɪm/ *adverb, adjective, & noun.* **L15.**
[medieval Latin, from Latin *verbum* word. Cf. LITERATIM.]
▶ **A** *adverb.* **1** Word for word; in exactly the same words. **L15.**
†**2** In so many words; exactly, precisely. **E16–M17.**

🕮 **1** J. SYMONS His ability to read a piece of prose once, and then repeat it almost verbatim.

▶ **B** *adjective.* Corresponding with or following an original word for word. **M18.**

🕮 *Guardian* Give a verbatim report . . rather than a distorted interpretation.

▶ **C** *noun.* A full or word-for-word report of a speech etc. **L19.**

verbena /vəˈbiːnə/ *noun.* Pl. **-nas**, in sense 1 usu. **-nae** /-niː/. Also (*rare*) Anglicized as **verbene** /ˈvəːbiːn/. **M16.**
[Latin (usu. in pl.), in sense 2 repr. medieval Latin uses (= Latin *verbenaca*). Cf. VERVAIN.]
1 ROMAN ANTIQUITIES. In *pl.* The leafy boughs of certain aromatic trees and shrubs, used in religious ceremonies. **M16.**
2 Any of numerous chiefly N. and S. American plants constituting the genus *Verbena* (family Verbenaceae), which have spikes or clusters of tubular flowers; *esp.* any of those (esp. *V. hybrida*) grown for their fragrant colourful flowers, much used as bedding annuals. **M16.**
3 A perfume obtained from the leaves of lemon verbena. **M19.**
1 ***lemon verbena***: see LEMON *noun*[1]. ***sand-verbena***: see SAND *noun*.
■ **verbeˈnaceous** *adjective* of or pertaining to the Verbenaceae or verbena family **L19.**

verberant /ˈvəːb(ə)r(ə)nt/ *adjective.* **L19.**
[Latin *verberant-* pres. ppl stem of *verberare*: see next, -ANT[1].]
Reverberant.

verberate /ˈvəːbəreɪt/ *verb.* **L16.**
[Latin *verberat-* pa. ppl stem of *verberare* beat, flay, from *verber* a lash, a whip: see -ATE[3].]
1 *verb trans.* **a** Strike so as to produce a sound. *rare.* **L16.** ▸**b** Beat or strike so as to cause pain, esp. as punishment. **E17.**
2 *verb intrans.* Vibrate, quiver. **M18.**

verberation /vəːbəˈreɪʃ(ə)n/ *noun.* **E17.**
[Latin *verberatio(n-)*, formed as prec.: see -ATION.]
1 The action of beating or striking something so as to produce sound; the fact of being so struck; percussion. **E17.**
2 The action of beating or striking a person to cause pain, esp. as punishment. Also, a blow, a lash. **E18.**

verbiage /ˈvəːbɪɪdʒ/ *noun.* **E18.**
[French, from †*verbeier* chatter, from *verbe* word: see -AGE. See also VERBAGE.]
1 Superfluous abundance of words, tedious prose without much meaning; excessive wordiness, verbosity. **E18.**
2 Diction, wording, verbal expression. Now *rare.* **E19.**

verbicide /ˈvəːbɪsʌɪd/ *noun.* **M19.**
[from Latin *verbum* word + -I- + -CIDE.]
1 A person who mutilates or destroys a word. **M19.**
2 The destruction or perversion of a word's sense or meaning. **M19.**
■ **verbiˈcidal** *adjective* tending or liable to destroy or pervert a word's sense or meaning **L20.**

verbid /ˈvəːbɪd/ *noun.* **E20.**
[from VERB *noun* + -ID[2].]
GRAMMAR. A word, as an infinitive, gerund, or participle, having some verbal characteristics but not being a finite verb.

verbify /ˈvəːbɪfʌɪ/ *verb trans.* **E19.**
[formed as prec. + -I- + -FY.]
Make into or use as a verb.
■ **verbifiˈcation** *noun* **L19.**

verbigerate /vəˈbɪdʒəreɪt/ *verb intrans.* Now *rare.* **M17.**
[Latin *verbigerat-* pa. ppl stem of *verbigerare* chat, from *verbum* word + *gerere* carry on: see -ATE[3].]
†**1** Speak, talk. Only in **M17.**
2 MEDICINE. Go on repeating the same word or phrase in a meaningless fashion, esp. as a symptom of mental illness or brain disease. **L19.**
■ **verbigeˈration** *noun* (MEDICINE) **L19.**

verbose /vəːˈbəʊs/ *adjective.* **L17.**
[Latin *verbosus*, from *verbum* word: see -OSE[1].]
Expressed in or using an unnecessary number of words; wordy, long-winded.
■ **verbosely** *adverb* **L18.** **verboseness** *noun* **E18.**

verbosity /vəːˈbɒsɪti/ *noun.* **M16.**
[Latin *verbositas*, formed as prec.: see -ITY.]
The state or quality of being verbose; superfluity of words, wordiness, long-windedness.

verboten /fɛrˈboːtən/ *adjective.* **E20.**
[German.]
Forbidden, not allowed.

verb. sap. /vəːb ˈsap/ *interjection.* Also ***verbum sap.*** /vəːbəm ˈsap/. **E19.**
[Abbreviation of Latin *verbum sapienti sat est* a word is sufficient for a wise person.]
Used to imply that further explanation of or comment on a statement or situation is unnecessary.

verbum sat /vəːbəm 'sat/ *interjection*. M17.
[Latin, formed as prec. or shortening of *verbum sat est* a word is enough.]
Used to imply that further explanation of or comment on a statement or situation is unnecessary or inadvisable.

verd /vəːd/ *noun*. LME.
[Obsolete French, from Latin *viridis* green. Cf. VERT *noun*[1], VERD-ANTIQUE.]
1 †**a** *HERALDRY*. The tincture vert. Only in LME. ▸**b** The colour green. *poet.* E20.
†**2** Verdancy, freshness. Only in E17.
†**3** Forest greenery. Only in M17.
†**4** = ***greenstone*** (a) s.v. GREEN *adjective*. Only in L18.

verdad /ver'ðað/ *interjection & adverb*. E20.
[Spanish, lit. 'truth'.]
Indeed, truly, surely. Freq. interrog.

verdant /'vəːd(ə)nt/ *adjective*. L16.
[Perh. from Old French *verdeant* pres. pple of *verdoier* (mod. *-oyer*) = Italian *verdeggiare* be green ult. from Latin *viridis* green: see -ANT[1].]
1 Of vegetation, grass, etc.: green in colour, lush, fresh-looking. L16.
2 Green with vegetation, characterized by lush greenery. L16.
3 Of a person: inexperienced, gullible, naive. Cf. GREEN *adjective* 7. E19.

📖 **1** *Punch* To tread the verdant sward. **2** B. LOPEZ The verdant, fertile valley of the Thomsen River.

■ **verdancy** *noun* the quality, condition, or character of being verdant; greenness; naivety, inexperience: M17. **verdantly** *adverb* E19. **verdantness** *noun* (*rare*) E18.

verd-antique /vəːdan'tiːk/ *noun & adjective*. M18.
[French †*verd* (now *vert*) *antique*: see VERT *noun*[1], ANTIQUE. Cf. VERD.]
▸**A 1** An ornamental variety of marble, consisting chiefly of serpentine mixed with calcite and dolomite. M18.
2 A greenish patina or incrustation on brass or copper; verdigris. M19.
3 More fully ***oriental verd-antique***, ***verd-antique porphyry***. = ***greenstone*** (a) s.v. GREEN *adjective*. M19.
▸**B** *attrib.* or as *adjective*. Made or consisting of verd-antique. E19.
■ ***verde antico*** /'verde 'antiko/ *noun phr.* [Italian] = VERD-ANTIQUE *noun* 1 M18.

Verdea /vəː'deɪə, *foreign* ver'deːa/ *noun*. E17.
[Italian, from *verde* green.]
A white grape grown near Florence in Italy; the wine made from this grape.

Verdelho /vəː'dɛljuː, -ljəʊ/ *noun*. Also **v-**. E19.
[Portuguese.]
A white grape orig. grown in Madeira, now also in Portugal, Sicily, Australia, and South Africa; a medium Madeira made from this grape.

verderer /'vəːd(ə)rə/ *noun*. Now chiefly *arch.* or *Hist.* Also **-urer**. M16.
[Anglo-Norman, extended form (see -ER[1]) of *verder* = Old & mod. French *verdier* ult. from Latin *viridis* green: see VERT *noun*[1], -ER[2].]
A judicial officer of the royal forests.
■ †**verder** *noun* (*rare*) = VERDERER ME–E18. **verderership** *noun* the position or office of verderer E17.

verdet /'vəːdɛt/ *noun*. *arch.* M16.
[Old French, dim. of VERD. Cf. Provençal, Catalan *verdet*, Spanish, Portuguese *verdete*, Italian *verdetto*.]
CHEMISTRY. An acetate of copper; *esp.* = ***crystallized*** VERDIGRIS.

Verdian /'vɛːdɪən/ *adjective & noun*. M20.
[from *Verdi* (see below) + -AN.]
▸**A** *adjective*. Of, pertaining to, or characteristic of the Italian composer Giuseppe Verdi (1813–1901) or his music. M20.
▸**B** *noun*. An admirer of Verdi; an exponent of the music of Verdi. M20.

Verdicchio /vəː'diːkɪəʊ, *foreign* ver'dikkio/ *noun*. M20.
[Italian.]
A white grape grown in the Marche region of Italy; the dry white wine made from this grape.

verdict /'vəːdɪkt/ *noun & verb*. ME.
[Anglo-Norman *verdit* = Old French *veirdit*, *voir-*, from *veir*, *voir* (from Latin *verum* true) + *dit* (from Latin *dictum* saying, speech, use as noun of neut. pa. pple of *dicere* say): see VERY *adjective & adverb*.]
▸**A** *noun*. **1** *LAW*. A decision or finding, usu. of a jury, in a civil or criminal cause or in a coroner's court on an issue submitted. ME.
2 *transf.* & *fig.* A judgement, conclusion, or opinion expressed on some matter or subject. LME.

📖 **1** F. WELDON The jury was out for two days and brought back a verdict of guilty. *Guardian* The Oxfordshire coroner . . recorded a verdict of accidental death. ***majority verdict***, ***partial verdict***, ***party verdict***, ***sealed verdict***, ***special verdict***, etc. **open verdict** a verdict of a coroner's jury affirming the commission of a crime or the occurrence of a suspicious death but not specifying the criminal or cause. **2** O. NASH I'm naturally anxious to know your verdict on me. *Daily Telegraph* 400 tasters were recruited at random to give their verdict.

▸**B** *verb*. **1** *verb trans.* Pass judgement on, pronounce a verdict or opinion concerning. *rare.* L16.
2 *verb intrans.* Pronounce a verdict or sentence *against* something. *rare.* L19.
■ **verdictive** *noun* (*LINGUISTICS*, *rare*) a performative utterance consisting in the delivering of a verdict M20.

verdigris /'vəːdɪgriː, -griːs/ *noun*. Also †**-grease**. ME.
[Old French *verte-gres*, earlier *vert de Grece* (mod. *vert-de-gris*) lit. 'green of Greece': see VERT *noun*[1].]
Orig., basic copper acetate, formed as minute pale green or bright blue crystals by the action of acetic acid on copper, and used as a paint pigment, mordant, and fungicide (also ***verdigris blue***, ***verdigris green***). Now more usu., basic copper carbonate, formed esp. by atmospheric corrosion as a greenish or bluish patina or incrustation on exposed copper, brass, and bronze (also called ***aerugo***).
crystallized verdigris normal copper acetate, formed as greenish-blue crystals by the action of acetic acid on copper oxide, used as a pesticide and pigment, and in the manufacture of Paris green.
Comb.: **verdigris agaric**, **verdigris toadstool** a basidiomycetous fungus, *Stropharia aeruginosa*, with a slimy blue-green cap.
■ **verdigrised** *adjective* coated or tainted with verdigris M19.

verdin /'vəːdɪn/ *noun*. L19.
[French = yellowhammer.]
A small songbird of the penduline tit family, *Auriparus flaviceps*, which has a grey body and yellow head, and is found in south-western N. America.

verdite /'vəːdʌɪt/ *noun*. E20.
[formed as VERD(URE + -ITE[1].]
GEOLOGY. A deep green ornamental metamorphic rock, which consists of fuchsite with grains of rutile and occurs in southern Africa.

verditer /'vəːdɪtə/ *noun & adjective*. E16.
[from Old French *verd de terre* (mod. *vert de terre*) lit. 'green of the earth'. Cf. VERDIGRIS, VERT *noun*[1].]
▸**A** *noun*. **1** A light blue or bluish-green pigment, usu. prepared by adding chalk or whiting to a solution of copper nitrate, used in making crayons and as a water-colour. E16.
2 In full ***verditer blue***, ***verditer green***. The blue or greenish colour characteristic of verditer. M16.
▸**B** *attrib.* or as *adjective*. Of the colour verditer; light blue or bluish-green. M19.

verdomde /fər'dɔmdə/ *adjective*. *S. Afr. slang*. Also ***-doemde***, ***-domd***. M19.
[Afrikaans from Dutch *verdoemd*.]
Damned, infernal, cursed.

†**verdour** *noun*. *rare*. E16–E19.
[Old French, from *verd* green: see VERT *noun*[1], -OUR.]
= VERDERER.

verdoy /'vəːdɔɪ/ *noun & adjective*. M16.
[French *verdoyé* pa. pple of *verdoyer*, from Old French *verd* green: see VERT *noun*[1].]
▸†**A** *noun*. = VERDURE 3. Only in M16.
▸**B** *adjective*. *HERALDRY*. Of a bordure: charged with leaves, flowers, and fruit. M16.

verdure /'vəːdjə, -juə/ *noun*. LME.
[Old & mod. French, from Old French *verd* green: see VERT *noun*[1], -URE.]
▸**I 1** The fresh green colour characteristic of flourishing vegetation; greenness; a shade or tint of this green. LME.
2 Green vegetation, grass, or foliage, esp. when lush and flourishing; greenery. LME. ▸†**b** In *pl.* Green plants or herbs. L15–E18.
3 A rich tapestry ornamented with representations of trees or other vegetation. Now *Hist.* E16.
▸**II** †**4 a** Agreeable freshness or sharpness of taste in fruit or liquor. Also, taste, savour. LME–M17. ▸**b** Tartness or unpleasantness of taste. E16–E17.
†**5** Smell, odour. E16–E18.
6 *fig.* Fresh or flourishing condition. L16.
■ **verdured** *adjective* covered with verdure or vegetation L15. **verdureless** *adjective* (chiefly *literary*) lacking verdure or vegetation, bare, bleak E19.

verdurer *noun* var. of VERDERER.

verdurous /'vəːdjərəs/ *adjective*. E17.
[from prec. + -OUS.]
1 Rich in or covered with verdure; lushly green. E17.
2 Of, pertaining to, or characteristic of verdure; consisting or composed of verdure. M17.
■ **verdurousness** *noun* (*rare*) M19.

verecund /'vɛrɪkʌnd/ *adjective*. *rare*. M16.
[Latin *verecundus*, from *vereri* revere, fear.]
Modest, bashful; shy, coy.
■ **vere'cundity** *noun* E18. **verecundness** *noun* E18.

Verel /'vɪər(ə)l/ *noun*. M20.
[Invented word.]
(Proprietary name for) a synthetic acrylic fibre.

Verfremdung /fɛr'frɛmdʊŋ/ *noun*. M20.
[German.]
Chiefly *THEATRICAL*. Distancing, alienation, esp. of a theatrical audience. Also ***Verfremdungseffekt*** /fɛr'frɛmdʊŋsɛˌfɛkt/ [= effect].

vergaloo /vəːgə'luː/ *noun*. *US*. E19.
[Alt. of VIRGOULEUSE, prob. taken as pl.]
A variety of pear, the white doyenné.

verge /vəːdʒ/ *noun*. See also VIRGE. LME.
[Old & mod. French from Latin *virga* rod.]
▸**I 1 a** The penis. *arch. rare.* LME. ▸**b** *ZOOLOGY*. The male intromittent organ of certain invertebrates. Now *rare* or *obsolete*. L18.
†**2** *ARCHITECTURE*. The shaft of a column; a small ornamental shaft. *rare.* Only in LME.
3 A rod, a wand, *esp.* one carried before a bishop, dean, etc., as a symbol of office. LME.
4 *HOROLOGY*. **a** The spindle or arbor of an escapement, esp. a verge escapement. E18. ▸**b** In full ***verge watch***. A watch fitted with a verge escapement. L18.
▸**II 5 a** The edge, border, or margin *of* something limited in size or extent. Now *rare*. LME. ▸†**b** A brim, a rim; a circle of metal etc. M16–E18. ▸**c** *ARCHITECTURE*. An edge of tiling projecting over a gable. M19.
6 The edge, border, or margin *of* something extensive; the utmost limit *of* something. L16. ▸**b** *fig.* The end *of* life. M18. ▸**c** *fig.* The horizon. *poet.* E19.
7 The brink *of* something towards which there is progress or tendency; the point just before which something begins or happens. Chiefly in ***on the verge of***, ***to the verge of***. E17.
8 A limiting or bounding belt or strip; *spec.* a grass edging of a road, path, flower-bed, etc. Freq. in ***grass verge***. M17.

📖 **6** W. IRVING In the centre . . yawned the mouth of the pit. Sanchica ventured to the verge and peeped in. LD MACAULAY South of Leeds, on the verge of a wild moorland tract. **7** G. MACDONALD I had driven Catherine . . to the verge of suicide. J. F. DULLES To get to the verge without getting into the war. *Guardian* On the verge of securing some real political power. **8** C. FORBES He stopped the car on the grass verge of the . . road.

▸**III 9** ***the Verge (of the Court)***, the area extending to a distance of twelve miles from the royal court, under the jurisdiction of the Lord High Steward, and in the 18th cent. freq. denoting the precincts of Whitehall as a place of sanctuary. Freq. in ***within the Verge***. *obsolete* exc. *Hist.* E16.
10 The bounds, limits, or precincts *of* a particular place. Formerly also *fig.*, the range, sphere, or scope *of* something; all that within a category, jurisdiction, etc. Chiefly in ***in the verge***, ***out of the verge***, ***within the verge***. L16.
11 The space within a boundary (*lit.* & *fig.*); room, scope. Freq. foll. by *for*, *to*. L17.

📖 **10** SWIFT In . . dispute about certain Walks . . , whether they are in the Verge of God or the Devil. D. HUME She should be beheaded within the verge of the Tower. **11** M. PATTISON Not giving verge enough for the sweep of his soaring conception.

Comb.: **verge-board** *ARCHITECTURE* = ***bargeboard*** s.v. BARGE-; **verge escapement** *HOROLOGY* an early form of escapement used orig. in pendulum clocks in which two pallets engage with a crown wheel; a modification of this with an ordinary escape wheel in old clocks and watches.

verge /vəːdʒ/ *verb*[1]. E17.
[from the noun.]
1 *verb trans.* Provide *with* a specified kind of verge or border; edge, bound, limit. Freq. in *pass.* E17. ▸**b** Pass along the verge or edge of, skirt. *rare.* L19.
2 *verb intrans.* Foll. by *on* or *upon*: be contiguous or adjacent to, lie on the verge of; border on a state or condition. L18.

📖 **2** *Listener* Official explanations often verge on the farcical. A. BROOKNER The sort of teasing that verges on cruelty.

verge /vəːdʒ/ *verb*[2] *intrans.* E17.
[Latin *vergere* bend, incline.]
1 Of the sun: descend towards the horizon, sink. E17.
2 Move, esp. downwards; diverge. Also, extend, lie, stretch. M17.
3 Incline, tend, or draw near *to* or *towards* a state or condition. M17. ▸**b** Pass or undergo gradual transition *into* something else. M18. ▸**c** Pass or approximate in shade *to* a specified colour. E19.

📖 **3** C. THIRLWALL When the reign of Demetrius was verging to its close.

verge /vəːdʒ/ *verb*³ *intrans.* E20.
[Back-form. from VERGER.]
Act as a verger, be a verger.

vergée /ˈvəːʒeɪ/ *noun.* M19.
[Anglo-Norman, from French *terre vergée* measured land.]
In the Channel Islands, a measure of land, equal to 4/9 acre (approx. 0.180 hectare) in Jersey and 2/5 (approx. 0.162 hectare) in Guernsey.

vergence /ˈvəːdʒ(ə)ns/ *noun.* E20.
[In sense 1 extracted from CONVERGENCE, DIVERGENCE, etc.; in sense 2 after German *Vergenz*: cf. VERGE *verb*², -ENCE.]
1 OPHTHALMOLOGY. The simultaneous movement of the eyes towards or away from each other, as when they focus on a point that is nearer or further away. E20.
2 GEOLOGY. The direction in which a fold is inclined or overturned. M20.
Comb.: **vergence angle** OPHTHALMOLOGY (a measure of) the degree of convergence (or divergence) of the eyes.

vergency /ˈvəːdʒ(ə)nsi/ *noun*¹. M17.
[from VERGE *verb*² + -ENCY.]
†**1** The action or fact of verging or inclining *to* or *towards* a state or condition; tendency, leaning; an instance of this. M17–E18.
2 The fact or condition of being inclined towards an object or in a direction. M17. ▸**b** OPTICS. (A measure of) the degree of convergence or divergence of light rays. Now *rare* or *obsolete.* M19.

vergency /ˈvəːdʒ(ə)nsi/ *noun*². *rare.* E19.
[from VERGE *verb*¹ + -ENCY.]
The action or fact of verging or bordering *on* something.

verger /ˈvəːdʒə/ *noun.* Also (now *rare*) **virger**. ME.
[Anglo-Norman = Anglo-Latin *virgarius*, formed as VERGE *noun*: see -ER².]
1 An official who carries a rod or similar symbol of office before a bishop, dean, etc. ME.
2 An official in a church who acts as caretaker and attendant. E18.
▪ **vergeress** *noun* (*rare*) a female verger or church caretaker L19. **vergerless** *adjective* unaccompanied by or without a verger L19. **vergership** *noun* the office or position of verger L15.

Vergilian *adjective & noun* var. of VIRGILIAN.

verglas /ˈvɛːglɑː/ *noun.* E19.
[French, from *verre* glass + †*glas* (now *glace*) ice.]
A glassy coating of ice formed on the ground or an exposed surface by rain freezing on impact or the refreezing of thawed ice.

vergobret /ˈvəːgəbrɛt/ *noun.* M16.
[Latin *vergobretus*, of Gaulish origin.]
Hist. The chief magistrate among the ancient Aedui of Gaul.

veridical /vɪˈrɪdɪk(ə)l/ *adjective.* Now chiefly *formal.* M17.
[from Latin *veridicus*, from *verum* truth + *dic-* stem of *dicere* speak: see -AL¹.]
1 Speaking or telling the truth, truthful; true or faithful to an original. M17.
2 PSYCHOLOGY. Of a perception, hallucination, etc.: coincident with, corresponding to, or representing real events or people. Now *rare.* L19.
▪ **veridic** *adjective* (*rare*) veridical L19. **veridiˈcality** *noun* the quality of being veridical, truthfulness E20. **veridically** *adverb* M19. **veridicalness** *noun* E18. **veriˈdicity** *noun* veridicality M20.

verifiable /ˈvɛrɪfʌɪəb(ə)l/ *adjective.* L16.
[from VERIFY + -ABLE.]
Able to be verified or proved to be true; authentic, accurate, real.
▪ **verifiaˈbility** *noun* the fact of being verifiable; PHILOSOPHY the fact of being capable of verification through empirical experience: L19. **verifiableness** *noun* L19. **verifiably** *adverb* L20.

verification /ˌvɛrɪfɪˈkeɪʃ(ə)n/ *noun.* E16.
[Old & mod. French *vérification* or medieval Latin *verificatio(n-)*, from *verificat-* pa. ppl stem of *verificare*: see VERIFY, -ATION.]
1 The action of demonstrating or proving something to be true by evidence or testimony; formal assertion of truth. Now *rare.* E16.
2 Demonstration of truth or correctness by facts or circumstances. M16.
3 The action of establishing or testing the accuracy or correctness of something, esp. by investigation or by comparison of data etc; an instance of this; *spec.* (*a*) PHILOSOPHY the action or process of verifying a proposition or sentence through empirical experience (freq. in ***verification principle***); (*b*) the action or process of verifying procedures laid down in weapons limitation agreements. E17.
4 Ratification. L18.
▪ **verificationism** *noun* (PHILOSOPHY) the philosophical doctrine or principles associated with verification M20. **verificationist** *adjective & noun* (PHILOSOPHY) (*a*) *adjective* of, pertaining to, or supporting verificationism; (*b*) *noun* an adherent or supporter of verificationism: M20. **veriˈficatory** *adjective* that verifies something, of the nature of a verification M19.

verify /ˈvɛrɪfʌɪ/ *verb trans.* ME.
[Old & mod. French *vérifier* from medieval Latin *verificare*, from Latin *verus* true: see -FY.]
1 a LAW. Support (a statement) by evidence or testimony; testify or affirm formally or on oath; append an affidavit to (pleadings). Also foll. by *that.* ME. ▸**b** *gen.* Assert or affirm to be true or certain. Now *rare.* E16. ▸†**c** Support or back up by testimony. *rare* (Shakes.). Only in E17.
2 Show to be true or correct by demonstration or evidence; confirm the truth or authenticity of; substantiate. Also foll. by *that.* LME.
3 Of an event, person, etc.: bear out, fulfil, or prove true (a prediction, promise, etc.). LME.
4 Ascertain or test the accuracy or correctness of, esp. by examination or by comparison of data etc.; check or establish by investigation. Also foll. by *that, whether.* E16.
5 Cause to appear true or authentic. *rare.* L16.

> 📖 **2** D. SIMPSON My husband was at home for lunch . . a neighbour of ours can verify that. **3** *Scientific American* Hertz verified his prediction by detecting electromagnetic waves in space. **4** K. M. E. MURRAY Documentary evidence had been examined afresh and quotations from manuscripts verified. A. MAUPIN I have verified for certain that she and the children weren't among the dead.

▪ **verifier** *noun* (*a*) a person who or thing which verifies something; (*b*) *spec.* a keyboard device for checking whether a card or paper tape is correctly punched by indicating any discrepancy when it is inserted and the data on it keyed a second time: M17.

verily /ˈvɛrɪli/ *adverb. arch.* ME.
[from VERY *adjective* + -LY², after Old French *verrai(e)ment* (mod. *vraiment*), Anglo-Norman *veirement* = Old French *voirement*.]
In truth or fact; really, truly; indeed, certainly.

> 📖 R. KIPLING And verily it is not a good thing to live in the East. W. JAMES Verily you are the stuff of which world-changers are made!

verisimilar /vɛrɪˈsɪmɪlə/ *adjective.* L17.
[from Latin *verisimilis*, *veri similis* like the truth, from *veri* genit. sing. of *verus* true + *similis* like: see -AR¹.]
Appearing true or real; realistic, probable.
▪ **verisimilarly** *adverb* M19. **verisimilous** *adjective* (now *rare*) verisimilar M17.

verisimilitude /ˌvɛrɪsɪˈmɪlɪtjuːd/ *noun.* E17.
[Latin *verisimilitudo*, *veri similitudo*, formed as prec.: see -TUDE.]
1 The appearance of being true or real; likeness or resemblance to truth, reality, or fact; realistic quality; probability. E17.
2 A statement etc. having the mere appearance or show of being true or factual, an apparent truth. L18.

> 📖 **1** A. STORR A born journalist who made . . use of the experience of others . . to lend verisimilitude to his books.

verism /ˈvɪərɪz(ə)m/ *noun.* L19.
[formed as VERIST + -ISM.]
The style of the verists, realism or naturalism in literature or art. Cf. VERISMO, VÉRITÉ.

verismo /vɛˈrɪzməʊ/ *noun.* E20.
[Italian, formed as prec.]
Realism or naturalism in the arts, esp. with ref. to late-19th-cent. Italian opera. Cf. VERISM.

verist /ˈvɪərɪst/ *noun.* L19.
[from Latin *verum* or Italian *vero* true + -IST.]
An advocate or practitioner of strict realism or naturalism in literature or art; a realist, a naturalist.
▪ **veˈristic** *adjective* of or pertaining to verists or verism, realistic, naturalistic L19.

veritable /ˈvɛrɪtəb(ə)l/ *adjective.* LME.
[Old & mod. French *véritable*, from *vérité*: see next, -ABLE.]
1 Of a statement etc.: not false, true. Now *rare* or *obsolete.* LME. ▸†**b** Of a person: speaking the truth, truthful. LME–L16.
2 Genuine, real, actual; correctly or properly so called. M17.

> 📖 **2** F. EXLEY She looked about fourteen, a veritable Lolita. A. MAUPIN The room was a veritable jungle of greenery and flowers.

¶ App. obsolete by L17; revived in E19.
▪ **veritableness** *noun* M17. **veritably** *adverb* L15.

vérité /verite/ *noun.* M20.
[French = truth.]
Realism or naturalism, esp. in cinema, radio, and television; documentary method. Cf. CINÉMA-VÉRITÉ, VERISM.

verity /ˈvɛrɪti/ *noun.* LME.
[Old & mod. French *vérité* repl. Old French *verté* from Latin *veritas*, from *verus* true: see -ITY.]
1 (The) truth; conformity to fact or reality; the true or real facts or circumstances. LME. ▸†**b** The exact wording and meaning of the original Hebrew or Greek text of the Bible. M16–L18. ▸**c** The actuality or reality *of* something. M17.
2 A true statement, doctrine, etc., a truth, *esp.* one of fundamental import; an established fact, a reality. LME.
3 Truthfulness, veracity, sincerity. Now *rare* or *obsolete.* LME.

> 📖 **1** B. FRANKLIN A volume denying the verity of my experiments. **in verity** *arch.* truly, really, in fact. **2** J. LOCKE Propositions that are once true, must needs be eternal Verities. M. PUZO He was really opening Janelle's eyes to the verities of life. *New York Times* The verities of this great Christian feast.

verjuice /ˈvəːdʒuːs/ *noun & verb.* ME.
[Old French *vertjus*, (also mod.) *verjus*, from *vert* green + *jus* juice: see VERT *noun*¹, JUICE *noun*.]
▶ **A** *noun.* **1** An acid liquor obtained from crab-apples, sour grapes, etc., formerly used in cooking and medicine. ME.
2 *fig.* Something acid or sour; bitter feelings or thoughts. L16.
▶ **B** *verb trans.* Embitter, make sour. Chiefly as ***verjuiced*** *ppl adjective. rare.* M19.

verkrampte /ferˈkramptə/ *adjective & noun. S. Afr.* Also (as pred. adjective) ***verkramp*** /ferˈkramp/. M20.
[Afrikaans = narrow, cramped.]
▶ **A** *adjective.* Politically or socially conservative or reactionary, esp. in racial matters. M20.
▶ **B** *noun.* Such a conservative or reactionary person. M20.
¶ Cf. VERLIGTE.

Verlainesque /vɛːleɪˈnɛsk/ *adjective.* L19.
[from *Verlaine* (see below) + -ESQUE.]
Of, pertaining to, or characteristic of the French poet Paul Verlaine (1844–96) or his work.

verligte /ferˈlɪxtə/ *adjective & noun. S. Afr.* Also (as pred. adjective) ***-lig*** /-ˈlɪx/. M20.
[Afrikaans = enlightened.]
▶ **A** *adjective.* Progressive, enlightened, esp. in racial matters. M20.
▶ **B** *noun.* Such a progressive or enlightened person. M20.
¶ Cf. VERKRAMPTE.

vermeil /ˈvəːmeɪl, -mɪl/ *adjective & noun.* Also †**vermil(e)**. LME.
[Old & mod. French: see VERMILION *noun & adjective.* Cf. VERMIL *verb.*]
▶ **A** *adjective.* **1** Of a bright scarlet colour or tint; vermilion. Chiefly *poet.* LME.
2 Coated with silver gilt or gilt bronze. M19.
▶ **B** *noun.* **1** The colour vermilion. Chiefly *poet.* L16. ▸†**b** *transf.* Blood. *poet. rare.* L16–E19.
2 An orange-red garnet. L18.
3 Silver gilt; gilt bronze. M19.

vermes /ˈvəːmiːz/ *noun pl.* (treated as *sing.* or *pl.*). E18.
[Latin, pl. of *vermis* worm.]
†**1** MEDICINE. Worms (the condition). E18–E19.
2 ZOOLOGY. (Usu. **V-**.) (Members of) any of various former groups comprising all or most of the wormlike invertebrates. *obsolete* exc. *Hist.* L18.

vermetid /vəːˈmiːtɪd/ *noun.* M19.
[mod. Latin *Vermetidae* (see below), from *Vermetus* genus name, from Latin VERMES: see -ID³.]
ZOOLOGY. Any of various marine gastropod molluscs of the family Vermetidae, which have shells consisting of a long loosely coiled tube.

vermi- /ˈvəːmi/ *combining form* of Latin *vermis* worm: see -I-.
▪ **vermicide** *noun* (MEDICINE) = ANTHELMINTIC *noun* M19.

vermian /ˈvəːmɪən/ *adjective.* L19.
[from VERMES or VERMIS + -IAN.]
1 Of, pertaining to, or characteristic of worms; wormlike. L19.
2 ANATOMY. Of or pertaining to the vermis of the cerebellum. E20.

vermicelli /vəːmɪˈ(t)sɛli/ *noun.* M17.
[Italian, pl. of *vermicello* dim. of *verme* worm from Latin *vermis*.]
Pasta in the form of long slender threads, often added to soups; an Italian dish consisting largely of this and usu. a sauce. Now also (*transf.*), shreds of chocolate used as cake decoration etc.

vermicle /ˈvəːmɪk(ə)l/ *noun.* LME.
[Latin *vermiculus*: see VERMICULE, -CLE.]
†**1** Red or scarlet wool or yarn. *rare.* Only in LME.
2 = VERMICULE. M17.

vermicular /vəˈmɪkjʊlə/ *adjective.* M17.
[medieval Latin *vermicularis*, formed as VERMICULE: see -AR¹.]
1 PHYSIOLOGY. †**a** Of blood: appearing to contain small worms. *rare.* Only in M17. ▸**b** Of motion: resembling that of a worm; *spec.* = PERISTALTIC. Now *rare.* L17.
2 Having a sinuous or wormlike shape; resembling a worm in form. Also, consisting of or characterized by wavy outlines or markings. L17.
3 Of, pertaining to, or characteristic of a worm or worms; involving or produced by worms. E18.
4 Of the nature of a worm. L18.
5 MEDICINE. Of a disease: caused by (esp. intestinal) worms. L18.

vermiculate /vəˈmɪkjʊlət/ *adjective.* E17.
[Latin *vermiculatus* pa. pple of *vermiculari* be full of worms, from *vermiculus*: see VERMICULE, -ATE².]
Wormeaten; vermicular; tortuous, sinuous. Chiefly *fig.*

vermiculated /vəˈmɪkjʊleɪtɪd/ *adjective.* E17.
[formed as prec.: see -ED¹.]
1 Wormeaten; covered or ornamented with markings like those made by burrowing worms; covered with fine wavy lines. E17. ▸**b** ARCHITECTURE. Of rusticated masonry: carved or moulded with shallow wavy grooves to represent the tracks of worms. L18.
2 Of mosaic work: wrought, ornamented, or inlaid so as to resemble the sinuous movements or tracks of worms. M17.
3 Of a bird: marked *with* sinuous or wavy lines of a specified colour. L19.

vermiculation /vəmɪkjʊˈleɪʃ(ə)n/ *noun.* E17.
[Latin *vermiculatio(n-)*, formed as VERMICULATE *adjective*: see -ATION.]
1 The fact or condition of being infested with or eaten by worms. Long *obsolete* exc. *fig.* E17.
†**2** PHYSIOLOGY. = PERISTALSIS. M17–E18.
3 A sinuous boring or marking made by, or resembling the track of, a worm. Usu. in *pl.* L17. ▸**b** Vermiculated marking or ornamentation; a pattern of fine wavy lines. M19.

vermicule /ˈvəːmɪkjuːl/ *noun.* Also (earlier) in Latin form †**vermiculus**, pl. **-li**. L17.
[Latin *vermiculus* dim. of *vermis* worm: see -CULE.]
Chiefly MEDICINE. A small worm, maggot, or grub. Also, a wormlike structure.

vermiculite /vəˈmɪkjʊlʌɪt/ *noun.* E19.
[from Latin *vermiculari* (see VERMICULATE) + -ITE¹.]
1 MINERALOGY. Any of a group of hydrated silicates resulting from the alteration of biotite and ultrabasic rocks; *spec.* a monoclinic aluminosilicate of magnesium occurring as platy yellow or brown crystals or foliated scales. E19.
2 Flakes of this mineral used as a moisture-holding medium for plant growth or a protective covering for bulbs etc., or as a loose insulating material or a lightweight additive to concrete. M20.

vermiculous /vəˈmɪkjʊləs/ *adjective. rare.* LME.
[from late Latin *verminculosus*, formed as VERMICULE: see -OUS.]
†**1** = VERMICULAR 1b. Only in LME.
†**2** Full of worms. Only in L17.
3 Of, pertaining to, or resembling worms or grubs. E19.
4 MEDICINE. Infested with worms; accompanied or marked by the discharge of worms. E19.
5 Having a wormeaten appearance. M19.
■ **vermiculose** *adjective* (long *rare* or *obsolete*) infested with worms; wormlike: LME.

vermiculture /ˈvəːmɪkʌltʃə/ *noun.* L20.
[from VERMI- + CULTURE *noun.*]
The cultivation of earthworms, esp. in order to utilize them in the conversion of organic waste into fertilizer.

†**vermiculus** *noun* see VERMICULE.

vermiform /ˈvəːmɪfɔːm/ *adjective.* M18.
[from VERMI- + -FORM.]
1 Having the form of a worm; long, thin, and more or less cylindrical. M18.
2 ZOOLOGY. Of, pertaining to, or characteristic of a worm; resembling (that of) a worm. M19.
1 vermiform appendix: see APPENDIX *noun* 4. **vermiform process** = VERMIS *cerebelli*.

vermifuge /ˈvəːmɪfjuːdʒ/ *adjective & noun.* L17.
[VERMI- + -FUGE.]
MEDICINE. ▸**A** *adjective.* Causing the expulsion or destruction of intestinal worms; anthelmintic. L17.
▸**B** *noun.* A drug or agent having the property of expelling intestinal worms; an anthelmintic. E18.
■ **vermifugal** /-ˈfjuːg(ə)l/ *adjective* = VERMIFUGE *adjective* M19.

†**vermil** *adjective & noun* var. of VERMEIL.

vermil /ˈvəːmɪl/ *verb trans.* Chiefly *poet.* Now *rare* or *obsolete.* Infl. **-l(l)-**. L16.
[Prob. from VERMEIL *adjective*, infl. by VERMILION *noun & adjective.*]
Colour (*over*) or stain with or as with vermilion.

†**vermile** *adjective & noun* var. of VERMEIL.

vermilion /vəˈmɪljən/ *noun & adjective.* Also **-ll-**. ME.
[Old French *vermeillon*, from *vermeil* from Latin *vermiculus* dim. of *vermis* worm.]
▸**A** *noun.* **1** Cinnabar, *esp.* powdered cinnabar, used as a brilliant scarlet pigment. Also, any of various red earths and artificial pigments resembling this. ME. ▸**b** A fabric dyed with vermilion. *rare.* M17.
2 The colour of this pigment; a brilliant red or scarlet. LME.
▸**B** *adjective.* Of the colour vermilion; brilliant red, scarlet. LME.
■ **vermilioˈnette** *noun* a substitute for the pigment vermilion, consisting of eosin or a similar dye L19. **vermilionize** *verb trans.* (*rare*) = VERMILION *verb* M19.

vermilion /vəˈmɪljən/ *verb trans.* Also **-ll-**. E17.
[from the noun.]
Colour or paint (as) with vermilion; put vermilion on; make vermilion. Also (*arch.* or *poet.*) foll. by *over.*

†**vermily** *noun. rare* (Spenser). Only in L16.
[Irreg. from *vermile* obsolete var. of VERMEIL.]
Vermilion.

vermin /ˈvəːmɪn/ *noun.* ME.
[Old French, ult. from Latin *vermis* worm. See also VARMINT *noun*¹.]
1 *collect.* Orig., reptiles, snakes, or other animals regarded as harmful or objectionable. Now *spec.* (*a*) mammals or birds injurious to game, crops, etc.; (*b*) harmful insects, worms, etc., *esp.* those which infest or are parasitic on people, animals, and plants. ME.
2a A kind or class of animals or insects regarded as verminous. LME. ▸†**b** An animal or insect of this kind. LME–E19.
3 *collect.* Vile, objectionable, or despicable people. M16. ▸**b** An individual of this type. L16.

> 🕮 **1** C. DARWIN The stock of.. grouse.. on any large estate depends chiefly on the destruction of vermin. C. STEAD Sam has cyanide.. that's what they kill vermin with. E. JONG Rats scurried nearby and Vermin crawl'd. **2a** A. TUCKER Diseases.. proceeding from an imperceptible vermin swarming within us. A. EDEN Rats.. in the trenches.. this being our first experience of these vermin. **b** SIR W. SCOTT Each sly vermin.. That baulks the snare, yet battens on the cheese.

■ **vermined** *adjective* (*rare*) infested with vermin M19. **verminer** *noun* (*rare*) a destroyer of vermin E17. **verˈminicide** *noun* a preparation for killing parasites E20.

verminate /ˈvəːmɪneɪt/ *verb intrans. rare.* L17.
[Latin *verminat-* pa. ppl stem of *verminare* have worms, from *vermis* worm: see -ATE³.]
Breed or become infested with parasites. Chiefly as ***verminating** ppl adjective.*

vermination /vəːmɪˈneɪʃ(ə)n/ *noun.* Now *rare* or *obsolete.* E17.
[Latin *verminatio(n-)*, formed as prec.: see -ATION.]
†**1** The breeding, growth, or production of (esp. parasitic) vermin. E17–E18.
2 The fact of being infested with parasites; a disease due to this. E19.

verminous /ˈvəːmɪnəs/ *adjective.* E17.
[Old French (mod. *vermineux*) or Latin *verminosus*, from *vermis* worm: see -OUS.]
1 Of the nature of vermin; resembling vermin in character, harmful, vile, despicable. E17.
2 Infested with vermin, esp. lice, fleas, etc.; foul or offensive because of this. M17.
3 a MEDICINE. Of a disease etc.: caused by, due to, or characterized by the presence of parasites or intestinal worms. M17. ▸**b** Of a person: subject to parasites or intestinal worms. M19.
3a verminous bronchitis = HUSK *noun*² 1.

vermiparous /vəːˈmɪp(ə)rəs/ *adjective. rare.* M17.
[from VERMI- + -PAROUS.]
1 Producing young, or produced as young, in the form of maggots or larvae. M17.
2 Carrying verminous parasites. M19.

vermis /ˈvəːmɪs/ *noun.* L19.
[Latin = worm.]
ANATOMY. A wormlike structure; *esp.* (more fully ***vermis cerebelli*** /serɪˈbɛlʌɪ/) the median part of the cerebellum, between the two hemispheres (also called ***vermiform process***).

vermivorous /vəːˈmɪv(ə)rəs/ *adjective.* Now *rare.* E18.
[from VERMI- + -VOROUS.]
Feeding on worms, grubs, or insect pests.

Vermont /vəˈmɒnt/ *noun.* L19.
[A State in the north-eastern US.]
In full ***Vermont merino***. (An animal of) a variety of merino sheep with exaggerated skin folds.

Vermonter /vəˈmɒntə/ *noun.* L18.
[from prec. + -ER¹.]
A native or inhabitant of the State of Vermont in the US.

Vermontese /vəːmɒnˈtiːz/ *noun & adjective.* L18.
[formed as prec. + -ESE.]
▸**A** *noun.* Pl. same. A Vermonter. L18.
▸**B** *adjective.* Of or pertaining to the State of Vermont. L18.

Vermoral /ˈvəːmɒr(ə)l/ *noun.* E20.
[App. from V. *Vermorel*, the French manufacturer.]
Hist. In the war of 1914–18, a type of sprayer producing a fine spray of water to absorb residual poison gas.

vermouth /ˈvəːməθ, vəˈmuːθ/ *noun.* E19.
[French *vermout* from German *Wermut* wormwood.]
Wine flavoured with aromatic herbs (orig. wormwood), usu. drunk as an aperitif; a glass or drink of this.
French vermouth: see FRENCH *adjective.* ***Italian vermouth***: see ITALIAN *adjective.*

vernaccia /vəˈnatʃə/ *noun.* E19.
[Italian: cf. VERNAGE.]
A strong (usu. dry white) wine produced in the San Gimignano area of Italy and in Sardinia; the grape from which this is made.

vernacular /vəˈnakjʊlə/ *adjective & noun.* E17.
[Latin *vernaculus* native, indigenous, domestic, from *verna* home-born slave: see -AR¹.]
▸**A** *adjective.* **1** Of a person: using the native language or dialect of a country or district. E17.
2 Of a language or dialect: spoken as a mother tongue by the people of a particular country or district, not learned or imposed as a second language. M17.
3 a Of a composition, literary work, etc.: written or spoken in the native language of a particular country or people. M17. ▸**b** Of a word etc.: of, pertaining to, or forming part of the native language. E18. ▸**c** Connected or concerned with the native language. M19.
4 Of an artistic form or feature: native or peculiar to a particular country or locality; *esp.* (of architecture) consisting of or concerned with domestic and functional rather than monumental buildings. M19.

> 🕮 **1** E. A. FREEMAN The vernacular poet more kindly helps us to the real names. **2** G. DOWNES The congregation here being chiefly peasants,.. a sermon was delivered in the vernacular dialect. H. B. STOWE A speech in that.. slang dialect which was vernacular with them. **3a** J. H. BLUNT Vernacular prayer-books had.. been long known in England. B. PYM That rather dreadful vernacular Mass. **b** V. KNOX Brown.. preferred polysyllabic expressions.. from.. ancient Rome, to his vernacular vocabulary. **4** M. GIROUARD Vernacular farm buildings or modest.. town houses.

▸**B** *noun.* **1** The native language or dialect of a particular country or district; the informal, colloquial, or distinctive speech of a people or community. Now also, homely speech. L17.
2 A native or indigenous language; a mother tongue. E18.
3 The jargon or idiom *of* a particular profession, trade, etc. L19.
4 A vernacular style of building. E20.

> 🕮 **1** A. H. SAYCE A child can learn as readily the vernacular of Canton as the language of London. C. ACHEBE Speeches made in vernacular were liable to be distorted.. in the press. J. MCPHEE In the vernacular of the river people, hunting.. is known as 'getting your meat'. **3** *Rolling Stone* A note.. explains, in the vernacular of the military, that the report has been 'sanitized'. **4** M. GIROUARD Buildings in which Gothic merged into farmhouse vernacular.

■ **vernacularism** *noun* a vernacular word, idiom, or mode of expression M19. **vernacularist** *noun* an advocate or user of vernacular language or dialect M19. **vernacuˈlarity** *noun* the fact of belonging or adhering to the vernacular or native language M19. **vernacularly** *adverb* in conformity with the vernacular manner; in the vernacular: E19.

vernacularize /vəˈnakjʊlərʌɪz/ *verb trans.* Also **-ise**. E19.
[from prec. + -IZE.]
Translate into the native speech of a people; make vernacular.
■ **vernaculariˈzation** *noun* (*a*) the process of becoming vernacular or native to a language; (*b*) the historical process whereby a language learned by a community becomes its mother tongue: L19.

vernage /ˈvəːnɪdʒ/ *noun.* Long *obsolete* exc. *Hist.* LME.
[Old French from Italian VERNACCIA.]
A strong sweet kind of Italian white wine. Cf. VERNACCIA.

vernal /ˈvəːn(ə)l/ *adjective & noun.* M16.
[Latin *vernalis*, from *vernus* of the spring, from *ver* spring: see -AL¹.]
▸**A** *adjective.* **1** Coming, appearing, or occurring in spring. M16. ▸**b** *spec.* Of a flower, plant, etc.: appearing, coming up, or flowering in springtime. L17.
2 Of, pertaining to, or appropriate to (the season of) spring. E17. ▸**b** *fig.* Suggestive of spring; having the mildness or freshness of spring; early, youthful. L18.

> 🕮 **1 vernal equinox** the point in time at which the sun crosses the celestial equator in a southerly direction (approx. 21 March), or, in the southern hemisphere, in a northerly direction (approx. 22 September). **b vernal grass** an early-flowering Eurasian pasture grass, *Anthoxanthum odoratum*, smelling of coumarin; also more fully ***sweet vernal grass***, ***sweet-scented vernal grass***. **2b** SOUTHEY Late in beauty's vernal bloom. *Antiquaries Journal* The.. vernal years of a.. prehistorian.

▸**B** *noun.* †**1** The spring. Only in M17.
2 More fully ***sweet vernal***, ***sweet-scented vernal***. Vernal grass. L18.
■ **verˈnality** *noun* (*rare*) †(*a*) the springtime *of* something; (*b*) the quality of being vernal: M17. **vernally** *adverb* E18.

vernalize /ˈvəːn(ə)lʌɪz/ *verb trans.* Also **-ise**. **M19.**
[from **VERNAL** *adjective* + **-IZE**.]
1 Make vernal or springlike. *rare.* **M19.**
2 Subject (seeds etc.) to the process of vernalization (see below). **M20.**
■ **vernaliˈzation** *noun* [translating Russian *yarovizatsiya*] the technique of exposing seeds etc. to cold temperatures during germination in order to speed up flowering **M20.**

†vernant *adjective.* **LME–M19.**
[Old French from Latin *vernant-* pres. ppl stem of *vernare*: see next, **-ANT**[1].]
Flourishing or growing (as) in spring.

vernation /vəːˈneɪʃ(ə)n/ *noun.* **L18.**
[Latin *vernatio(n-)* a snake's sloughing of its skin in spring, from *vernare* show springtime growth, from *vernus*: see **VERNAL**, **-ATION**.]
1 *BOTANY.* The arrangement of bud scales or young leaves in a bud. Cf. **AESTIVATION** 2, **PTYXIS**. **L18.**
2 Plant growth, as characteristic of spring. Now *rare* or *obsolete*. **E19.**

Verné /ˈvɛːneɪ/ *noun.* Also **Verneh**. **E20.**
[Origin unkn.]
(In full ***Verné rug***, ***Verné kilim***) a Caucasian pileless rug or kilim; (in full ***Verné rug***) an Anatolian brocaded rug.

Vernean /ˈvəːnɪən/ *adjective.* **M20.**
[from *Verne* (see below): see **-AN**.]
Of, pertaining to, or characteristic of the science fiction of the French author Jules Verne (1828–1905).

Verneh *adjective* var. of **VERNÉ**.

Verner's Law /ˈvɛːnəz lɔː, ˈvəːnəz/ *noun phr.* **L19.**
[Karl Adolph *Verner* (1846–96), Danish philologist.]
PHILOLOGY. A law of phonetic change stating that voiceless fricatives in Germanic predicted by Grimm's Law were voiced if the preceding syllable in the corresponding Indo-European word was unaccented.

Verneuil /vəːˈnɔɪ, *foreign* vɛrnœːj/ *noun.* **E20.**
[August V. L. *Verneuil* (1856–1913), French chemist.]
Used *attrib.* with ref. to a technique for producing artificial rubies.

verneuk /fəˈnjəːk/ *verb trans. S. Afr. slang.* **L19.**
[Dutch *verneuken.*]
Cheat, swindle, trick.
■ **verneuker** *noun* **E20.** **verneukery** *noun* cheating, swindling, trickery **L19.**

vernicle /ˈvəːnɪk(ə)l/ *noun.* **ME.**
[Old French, alt. (with parasitic *l*) of *vernique*, (also mod.) *véronique* from medieval Latin **VERONICA**: see **-CLE**.]
= **VERONICA** 2.

vernier /ˈvəːnɪə/ *noun.* **M18.**
[Pierre *Vernier* (1580–1637), French mathematician.]
1 In full ***vernier scale***. A short movable scale used on various measuring and positioning instruments, by which fractional readings may be obtained from the divisions of an adjacent graduated scale. **M18.**
2 *ASTRONAUTICS.* In full ***vernier rocket***. = **THRUSTER** 3a. **M20.**

†vernile *adjective. rare.* **E17–M19.**
[Latin *vernilis*, from *verna* home-born slave: see **-ILE**.]
Servile, slavish.
■ **†vernility** *noun* servility, slavishness **E17–L18.**

†vernish *noun* var. of **VARNISH** *noun.*

vernis martin /vɛːniː ˈmɑːtan, *foreign* vɛrni martɛ̃/ *noun & adjectival phr.* **L19.**
[French, from *vernis* varnish + family name *Martin* of French brothers noted for using the lacquer.]
▶ **A** *noun phr.* A lacquer or varnish imitating oriental lacquer, used in the 18th cent. **L19.**
▶ **B** *adjectival phr.* Finished in vernis martin. **L19.**

vernissage /vɛrnisaːʒ/ *noun.* Pl. pronounced same. **E20.**
[French, lit. 'varnishing'.]
Orig., a day before an exhibition of paintings on which exhibitors could retouch and varnish pictures already hung. Now usu., a private view of paintings before public exhibition. Cf. **VARNISHING** (b).

vernix /ˈvəːnɪks/ *noun.* **L16.**
[medieval Latin, var. of *veronix*: see **VARNISH** *noun.*]
†1 Varnish. *rare.* Only in **L16.**
2 *MEDICINE.* In full ***vernix caseosa*** /keɪsɪˈəʊsə/ [from Latin *caseus* cheese]. A greasy deposit covering the skin of a baby at birth. **M19.**

verocytotoxin /vɪərə(ʊ)ˈsʌɪtə(ʊ)tɒksɪn/ *noun.* **L20.**
[from *Vero* (of unkn. origin, denoting a line of cell cultures from a green monkey) + **CYTOTOXIN**.]
BIOCHEMISTRY. Any of a group of cytotoxins produced by some strains of *Escherichia coli*, which can cause haemorrhagic diarrhoea and haemolytic uraemia in humans.
■ Also **ˈverotoxin** *noun* = **VEROCYTOTOXIN L20.**

Verona /vɪˈrəʊnə/ *noun.* **E18.**
[A city in northern Italy.]
Used *attrib.* to designate articles, esp. pigments, found or produced in, or associated with Verona or its surrounding district.

veronal /ˈvɛrən(ə)l/ *noun.* **E20.**
[from *Verona* (see prec.) + **-AL**[2].]
PHARMACOLOGY. = **BARBITONE**.

Veronese /vɛrəˈniːz/ *noun & adjective.* **L17.**
[Italian: see **VERONA** + **-ESE**.]
▶ **A** *noun.* Pl. same. A native or inhabitant of Verona in northern Italy. **L17.**
▶ **B** *adjective.* Of or pertaining to Verona or its inhabitants. **M18.**

veronica /vəˈrɒnɪkə/ *noun.* **E16.**
[In branch II from St *Veronica*. In branch I from medieval Latin, perh. alt. of Greek *berenikion*.]
▶ **I 1** A plant of the genus *Veronica*, a speedwell. Also, a plant of the genus *Hebe*, formerly included in the genus *Veronica*; *esp.* one of those grown for ornament. **E16.**
▶ **II 2** (**V-**.) The impression of the face of Jesus believed by some to be miraculously made on a head-cloth with which St Veronica wiped his face as he went to his crucifixion; *the* cloth used for this. Also, a devotional representation of Jesus' face; an ornament or token bearing this as worn by pilgrims. Cf. **VERNICLE**. **L17.**
3 *BULLFIGHTING.* A movement in which a matador swings the cape in a slow circle round himself away from the charging bull. **M19.**

veronique /vɛrəˈniːk, *foreign* verɔnik/ *noun & adjective.* As adjective usu. **Vé-**. **E17.**
[French *Véronique* Veronica: see prec.]
▶ **A** *noun.* **†1** The (supposed) imprint of Jesus' face on St Veronica's head-cloth. Cf. **VERONICA** 2. *rare.* **E17–E19.**
2 *BULLFIGHTING.* = **VERONICA** 3. **M20.**
▶ **B** *postpositive adjective. COOKERY.* Designating a dish, esp. of fish or chicken, prepared or garnished with grapes. **E20.**

verre /vɛːr, vəː/ *noun.* **LME.**
[Old & mod. French from Latin *vitrum*.]
1 Glass. Long *obsolete* exc. in phrs. below. **LME.**
†2 A glass vessel, esp. for drinking; a glass. **LME–M16.**
1 ***pâte de verre***: see **PÂTE** 3. ***verre églomisé***: see **ÉGLOMISÉ** *adjective.*

Verreaux's eagle /ˈvɛrəʊz ˌiːɡ(ə)l/ *noun phr.* Also **Verreaux eagle** /ˈvɛrəʊ/. **M19.**
[from Jules *Verreaux* (1807–73), French naturalist.]
A large mainly black eagle, *Aquila verreauxii*, found in eastern and southern Africa.

verrel /ˈvɛr(ə)l/ *noun. obsolete* exc. *dial.* **LME.**
[Old French *virelle*, *virol* (mod. *virole*) from Latin *viriola* dim. of *viriae* bracelets: cf. **FERRULE**, **VIRL**.]
A ferrule.

Verrocchiesque /vɛˌrɒkɪˈɛsk/ *adjective.* **M20.**
[from *Verrocchio* (see below) + **-ESQUE**.]
Suggestive of or resembling the works of the Florentine painter and sculptor Andrea del Verrocchio (1435–88).

verruca /vɛˈruːkə/ *noun.* Pl. **-cae** /-siː, -kiː/, **-cas**. **LME.**
[Latin = wart, excrescence on a precious stone.]
1 A wart; *esp.* a contagious wart on the sole of the foot. **LME.**
2 *BOTANY & ZOOLOGY.* A wartlike formation or outgrowth. **LME.**
■ **ˈverrucated** *adjective* (*ZOOLOGY*) having or covered with warty growths **E18.** **verruciform** *adjective* wart-shaped **M19.**

verrucose /vɛˈruːkəʊs, vɛˈruːkəʊs/ *adjective.* **L17.**
[Latin *verrucosus*, formed as prec.: see **-OSE**[1].]
BOTANY & ZOOLOGY. Having or covered with verrucae or wartlike excrescences or swellings.

verrucous /vɛˈruːkəs, ˈvɛrʊkəs/ *adjective.* **M17.**
[formed as prec.: see **-OUS**.]
1 = **VERRUCOSE**. *rare* (only in Dicts.). **M17.**
2 *MEDICINE.* Of the nature of a wart or warts; characterized by the formation of warts. **E18.**

verruculose /vɛˈruːkjʊləʊs/ *adjective. rare.* **M19.**
[from **VERRUCA** + **-ULOSE**[1].]
BOTANY & ZOOLOGY. Covered with minute wartlike excrescences.

verruga /vɛˈruːɡə/ *noun.* **L19.**
[Spanish = wart, from Latin **VERRUCA**.]
MEDICINE. More fully ***verruga peruana*** /pɛrʊˈɑːnə/, ***verruga peruviana*** /pəruːvɪˈɑːnə/ [mod. Latin = of Peru]. The second, chronic stage of a form of bartonellosis, characterized by wartlike skin lesions. Cf. **OROYA FEVER**.

†verry *adjective & noun.* **LME–L18.**
[Alt. of *varry* obsolete var. of **VAIRY**.]
HERALDRY. = **VAIRY** 1.

vers /vəːs/ *noun.* **E20.**
[Abbreviation.]
MATH. Versed sine (of).

†versability *noun.* **L17.**
[from Latin *versabilis* changeable, from *versare*: see **VERSE** *verb*[2], **-ITY**.]
1 = **VERSATILITY** 2. **L17–L18.**
2 Aptness or readiness to be changed or turned (round). **E–M18.**

Versailles /vɛːˈsʌɪ/ *noun.* **M18.**
[See below.]
1 A building similar in style or splendour to Versailles, a French royal hunting-lodge to the south-west of Paris enlarged into a palace by Louis XIV in the 17th cent. **M18.**
2 (The site of) the peace conference held at Versailles at the conclusion of the war of 1914–18; the resulting treaty signed there in 1919. **E20.**

📖 **1** R. KIPLING Jeypore Palace may be called the Versailles of India. **2** *attrib.*: G. B. SHAW The Versailles Treaty by which Germany was . . kept in a condition of . . military inferiority.

versal /ˈvəːs(ə)l/ *noun & adjective*[1]. **M17.**
[from Latin *vers-* pa. ppl stem of *vertere* turn, infl. by **VERSE** *noun*: see **-AL**[1].]
▶ **A** *noun.* **†1** = **VERSIFICATION** 3. *rare.* Only in **M17.**
2 A versal letter. **L19.**
▶ **B** *adjective.* Designating a special style of ornate capital letter used at the beginning of a verse, paragraph, etc., esp. in an illuminated manuscript (chiefly *Hist.*); designating a capital built up by inking between pen strokes and having serifs in the form of long thin straight lines. **L19.**

†versal *adjective*[2]. Chiefly *colloq.* **L16.**
[Abbreviation of **UNIVERSAL** *adjective*: cf. **VARSAL**.]
1 Universal; whole. Esp. in ***versal world*** (after Shakes.). **L16–L18.**
2 Single, individual. *rare.* Only in **E18.**

📖 **1** SHAKES. *Rom. & Jul.* She looks as pale as any clout in the versal world.

versant /ˈvəːs(ə)nt/ *noun.* **M19.**
[French, use as noun of pres. pple of *verser*: see **VERSE** *verb*[2], **-ANT**[1].]
The slope, side, or descent of a mountain or mountain chain; the general slope of an area or region.

versant /ˈvəːs(ə)nt/ *adjective.* Now *rare.* **LME.**
[Latin *versant-* pres. ppl stem of *versare*: see **VERSATILE**, **-ANT**[1].]
1 Concerned, anxious, or busy *about*, occupied or engaged *in* or *with*, (something). **LME.**
2 a Skilled, versed, or experienced *in* (a subject, practice, etc.). **E18.** ▸**b** Conversant, familiar, or intimately acquainted *with* (a subject or person). **L18.**

versatile /ˈvəːsətʌɪl/ *adjective.* **E17.**
[French, or Latin *versatilis*, from *versat-* pa. ppl stem of *versare* frequentative of *vertere* turn: see **-ATILE**.]
1 Characterized by inconstancy or fluctuation; variable, changeable. *arch.* **E17.**
2 Of a person, a person's mind, etc.: turning easily or readily from one subject, pursuit, or task to another; showing facility or aptitude in varied subjects; many-sided. Now also, (of a garment, product, device, etc.) having many uses; varied in application. **M17.** ▸**b** Of a person: bisexual. *slang.* **M20.**
3 a Chiefly *ZOOLOGY.* Able to be turned round (as) on a pivot or hinge; that may be turned different ways. Now *rare.* **M17.** ▸**b** *BOTANY.* Of an anther: attached near its middle on a filament and capable of moving freely. **M18.**

📖 **1** BURKE The versatile tenderness which marks the . . capricious feelings of the populace. **2** THACKERAY The . . versatile genius who has touched on almost every subject of literature. *Bon Appetit* A versatile . . filling for tostadas, tacos, or burritos. *Practical Householder* The jigsaw is one of the most versatile . . power tools going.

¶ In sense 2 rare before **L18.**
■ **versatilely** *adverb* **M17.** **versatileness** *noun* **M17.**

versatility /vəːsəˈtɪlɪti/ *noun.* **M18.**
[French *versatilité*, or from prec. + **-ITY**.]
1 The condition or quality of being changeable, fickle, or inconstant in character or behaviour; the tendency or liability to inconstancy in opinion or action. **M18.**
2 The ability to turn easily from one subject, pursuit, or task to another; facility in or aptitude for varied subjects; many-sidedness. **L18.**
3 Diversity of nature or character; variety of application. **E19.**

📖 **1** DISRAELI We . . condemn their versatility of principles as arising from dishonest motives. **2** SIR W. SCOTT His versatility and freedom from prejudices of every kind. C. C. FELTON The splendid versatility of poetical genius . . displayed by Goethe. **3** R. W. CHURCH The inexhaustible versatility of the English tongue. *Financial Times* Products which sell on their quality and versatility rather than on price.

†versation *noun.* **M17–M19.**
[Latin *versatio(n-)*, from *versat-* pa. ppl stem of *versare*: see **VERSATILE**, **-ATION**.]
An act of turning over or backwards and forwards.

vers de société /vɛr də sɔsjete/ *noun phr.* **L18.**
[French, lit. 'verse of society'.]
Verse treating topics provided by polite society in a light, often witty style.

vers d'occasion /vɛr dɔkazjɔ̃/ *noun phr.* M19.
[French.]
Light verse written for a special occasion.

verse /vəːs/ *noun.*
[Old English *fers* corresp. to Old Frisian *fers*, Middle Low German, Old High German (Dutch, German), Old Norse *vers*, from Latin *versus* turn of the plough, furrow, line, row, line of writing, from *vers-* pa. ppl stem of *vertere* turn; in Middle English reinforced by or re-formed from Old & mod. French *vers*, from same Latin source.]
▶ **I 1** A sequence of words arranged according to (particular) natural or recognized rules of prosody and forming a complete metrical line; each of the lines of a poem or piece of versification. (In *pl.* freq. merging into sense 2.) OE.
2 A small number of metrical lines constituting a distinct group; *spec.* (**a**) a stanza; (**b**) MUSIC a passage of an anthem etc. for solo voice; (**c**) in a modern popular song, a sequence of lines leading into the chorus or separating one chorus from another. ME.
3 Metrical composition, form, or structure; metrical language or speech, poetry. ME.
4 A body of metrical work or poetry considered as a whole; *spec.* the poetry of a particular author. L16.

> **1** E. ELSTOB The Saxon Verses consist of three, four, five, six, seven, eight, or more syllables. J. WARTON Like Ovid's Fasti, in hexameter and pentameter verses. ***half verse, heroic verse, long verse, Sotadic verse***, etc. ***cap verses***: see CAP *verb*¹ 4a. ***copy of verses***: see COPY *noun*¹. **2** DICKENS A ballad in four verses. *Melody Maker* Wonder charges through the verse and builds up into the . . chorus. ***tripos verses***: see TRIPOS 2b. **3** R. S. THOMAS Declaiming verse To the sharp prompting of the harp. V. NABOKOV The several translations into English . . have been attempts to render 'Eugene Onegin' in verse. G. S. FRASER Shakespeare . . uses great verse in his plays when he needs it. ***Alexandrine verse, elegiac verse, free verse, heroic verse, hexameter verse, Leonine verse, long verse, Saturnian verse***, etc. ***blank verse***: see BLANK *adjective*. ***concrete verse***: see CONCRETE *adjective*. ***PROJECTIVE verse***.

▶ **II 5** CHRISTIAN CHURCH. = VERSICLE 1. OE.
†**6** A clause, a sentence; *spec.* an article of the Creed. OE–M16.
7 a Any of the sections of a biblical psalm or canticle corresponding to the compound unit (usu. a couplet) of Hebrew poetry. *obsolete* exc. as passing into sense b below. ME. ▸**b** *gen.* Any of the short numbered divisions into which a chapter of the Bible (or other scripture) is divided. M16.

> **7b** W. LAW Religion . . is to be found in almost every verse of Scripture. E. ABBOTT The New Testament divided into our present verses. ***chapter and verse***: see CHAPTER *noun*.

Attrib. & comb.: In the sense 'composed or written in, consisting of, verse', as ***verse drama, verse epistle, verse epitaph, verse letter, verse play, verse translation***, etc. Special combs., as **verse anthem** an anthem with alternating sections for choir and soloists; **versecraft** the craft of, or skill in, writing verse; **versemaker** a poet, a versifier; **verseman** a person who writes verse; *esp.* a minor poet, a versifier; **versemonger** a versifier, *esp.* a poetaster.
■ **verseless** *adjective* lacking verse or poetry; (*rare*) unable to versify: M18. **verselet** *noun* a short verse or poem M19.

verse /vəːs/ *verb*¹. OE.
[from the noun.]
1 *verb intrans.* & (occas.) *trans.* (with *it*). Compose or make verses; versify. OE.
2 *verb trans.* Tell in verse; turn into verse; write, recount, or celebrate in verse. LME.

> **1** G. MEREDITH He began to verse extemporaneously in her ear. **2** SHAKES. *Mids. N. D.* Versing love To amorous Phillida.

■ **verser** *noun* a writer of verse, a versifier E17.

verse /vəːs/ *verb*² *trans.* E16.
[Old & mod. French *verser*, or Latin *versare*: see VERSATILE. In sense 4 app. back-form. from VERSED.]
†**1** Pour *out* (the voice). *rare*. Only in E16.
†**2** Overturn, upset. *rare*. Only in M16.
†**3** Turn over (an object of study or thought). E–M17.
4 Instruct, make versed, *in* something. Now usu. *refl.* Cf. VERSED. L17.

> **4** R. F. HORTON A feeling which grows . . the more I verse myself in His commandments.

versed /vəːst/ *adjective.* E17.
[French *versé*, or Latin *versatus* pa. pple of *versari* stay, be situated, be occupied or engaged, pass. of *versare*: see VERSATILE, -ED¹.]
Experienced, practised, or skilled in (a subject, matter, art, etc.); conversant with or knowledgeable about; expert, skilful. Usu. foll. by *in*.

> H. WOUK Torpedoes, a topic Henry was well versed in. M. HOLROYD An intelligent . . draughtsman, deeply versed in Rembrandt.

versed sine /vəːst 'sʌɪn/ *noun phr.* L16.
[translating mod. Latin *sinus versus*, from Latin *sinus* SINE + *versus* turned, pa. pple of *vertere* turn: see -ED¹.]
1 MATH. Orig., the length of the part of a radius between the foot of the line orig. called a 'sine' and the end of the corresponding arc. Now, the ratio of this line to the radius; the quantity obtained by subtracting the cosine from unity. Abbreviation ***vers, versin***. Cf. VERSINE. L16.
2 ENGINEERING. The rise of an arch of a bridge. M19.

Versene /'vəːsiːn/ *noun.* Also **v-**. M20.
[Origin unkn.]
CHEMISTRY. (Proprietary name for) a preparation containing EDTA or similar chelating agent, used esp. as a water-softener.

verset /'vəːsɪt/ *noun.* ME.
[Old & mod. French, from *vers*: see VERSE *noun*, -ET¹.]
Orig. (*obsolete* exc. *Hist.*), = VERSICLE 1. Later, a short verse, esp. from the Bible; a short piece of verse. Now also (MUSIC), a short prelude or interlude for organ.

versical /'vəːsɪk(ə)l/ *adjective. rare.* M19.
[from VERSE *noun* + -ICAL, after *poetical, metrical*.]
Of, pertaining to, or composed in verse.

versicle /'vəːsɪk(ə)l/ *noun.* ME.
[Old & mod. French *versicule*, or Latin *versiculus* dim. of *versus*: see VERSE *noun*, -CLE.]
1 CHRISTIAN CHURCH. A short sentence (usu. from the Bible, esp. the Psalms) said or sung antiphonally in a liturgy; *esp.* one said or sung by the officiant and followed by the response of the congregation. Also (in *pl.*), a set of these sentences with their accompanying responses. ME.
2 A little verse; *spec.* †(**a**) a short clause or sentence; = VERSE *noun* 6; (**b**) a single metrical line; (**c**) any of the subdivisions of a Hebrew verse. L15.
■ **versicular** /vəː'sɪkjʊlə/ *adjective* of, pertaining to, or consisting of (esp. biblical) versicles or verses E19.

versicolour /'vəːsɪkʌlə/ *adjective.* Now *rare.* E17.
[formed as next.]
= next.

versicoloured /'vəːsɪkʌləd/ *adjective.* E18.
[Latin *versicolor*, from *versus* pa. pple of *vertere* turn + *color*: see COLOUR *noun*, -ED².]
Changing or varying in colour; iridescent. Also, of various colours, variegated.

versicule /'vəːsɪkjuːl/ *noun. rare.* L15.
[formed as VERSICLE: see -CULE.]
A versicle; a short verse or poem.

versiculus /və'sɪkjʊləs/ *noun.* Pl. **-li** /-lʌɪ, -liː/. Now *rare.* M18.
[Latin: see VERSICLE.]
A versicle.

versification /ˌvəːsɪfɪ'keɪʃ(ə)n/ *noun.* E17.
[Latin *versificatio(n-)*, from *versificat-* pa. ppl stem of *versificare*: see VERSIFY, -FICATION.]
1 The action, art, or practice of composing verse. E17.
2 The metrical form or style of a poem; the structure of poetry or verse; measure, metre. L17.
3 A poetical or metrical version *of* something. E19.
■ **ver'sifical** *adjective* (long *arch. rare*) of or pertaining to versification M16. '**versificator** *noun* (now *rare*) a poet, a versifier E17. '**versificatory** *adjective* (*rare*) of or pertaining to the art of versification E18.

versify /'vəːsɪfʌɪ/ *verb.* LME.
[Old & mod. French *versifier* from Latin *versificare*, from *versus*: see VERSE *noun*, -FY.]
1 *verb intrans.* Compose verse; write poetry. LME.
2 *verb trans.* Narrate, recount, or treat in verse. LME.
3 *verb trans.* Turn (prose) into verse; translate, rewrite, or express in verse. M18.

> **2** GOLDSMITH The silly poet runs home to versify the disaster.

■ **versifier** *noun* a person who versifies; *spec.* a writer of poor verse, a poetaster: ME.

versin /'vəːsɪn/ *noun.* E19.
[Abbreviation.]
MATH. Versed sine (of).

versine /'vəːsʌɪn/ *noun.* M20.
[Abbreviation.]
MATH. = VERSED SINE 1.

version /'vəːʃ(ə)n/ *noun & verb.* LME.
[Old & mod. French from Latin *versio(n-)*, from *vers-* pa. ppl stem of *vertere* turn: see -ION.]
▶ **A** *noun.* **I** †**1** The action of overthrowing something. Only in LME.
2 An act or instance of turning something. Now only *spec.* (MEDICINE), the operation of manually turning a foetus so as to facilitate birth. E17.
3 Conversion, transformation. Long *rare* or *obsolete*. E17.
2 PODALIC *version*.
▶ **II 4** A rendering of a text, word, passage, etc., from one language into another, a translation; *spec.* (**a**) a book or work, esp. the Bible, in a particular translation; (**b**) a piece of translation, esp. as a scholastic exercise. LME.
5 An account, report, or view of a matter from the standpoint of a particular person, party, etc., *esp.* one that is partial, incomplete, or lacking authority. L18.
6 A particular form or variant of something; *spec.* a particular edition or draft of a work. M19.

> **4** J. HOWELL Things translated . . lose of their primative vigor . . unless a paraphrasticall version be permitted. ***Authorized Version, King James Version, Revised Standard Version***, etc. **5** H. WOUK His version of events . . can scarcely be taken at face value. A. FRASER The . . well-known incident is recounted in various different versions. **6** M. BANTON The Creoles . . developed a distinctive dialect version of . . English. M. FONTEYN Bournonville staged his own version of *La Sylphide*. C. WARWICK To select material for inclusion in the final version. *Flight International* Updated versions of its . . helicopter engines.

▶ **B** *verb trans.* Translate. M18.
■ **versional** *adjective* of or pertaining to a translation (esp. of the Bible) L19. **versionist** *noun* a translator L18.

vers libre /vɛr libr/ *noun phr.* Pl. ***vers libres*** (pronounced same). E20.
[French, lit. 'free verse'.]
Unrhymed verse which disregards the traditional rules of prosody; an example of this.
■ ***vers-libriste*** /vɛrlibrist (*pl.* same)/ *noun* a writer of *vers libre* E20.

verso /'vəːsəʊ/ *noun.* Pl. **-os**. M19.
[Latin *verso* (sc. *folio*) = (the leaf) being turned, abl. sing. neut. of *versus* pa. pple of *vertere* turn.]
1 The left-hand page of an open book; the back of a leaf in a manuscript or printed book, as opp. to the front or recto. M19.
2 The reverse side, esp. of a coin or medal. L19.

Versöhnung /fɛr'zøːnʊŋ/ *noun.* Pl. ***-en*** /-ən/. M19.
[German = conciliation, propitiation.]
A reconciliation of opposites.

versor /'vəːsə/ *noun.* M17.
[Latin *vers-* pa. ppl stem of *vertere* turn: see -OR.]
†**1** The needle of a compass. *rare*. Only in M17.
2 MATH. In quaternions, an operator which changes the direction of a vector without altering its length. M19.

verst /vəːst/ *noun.* M16.
[Russian *versta*, partly through German *Werst* and French *verste*.]
A Russian measure of length equal to approx. 1.07 km (0.66 miles).

Verstandesmensch /fɛr'ʃtandəsmɛnʃ/ *noun.* Pl. ***-en*** /-ən/. L19.
[German.]
A matter-of-fact person; a realist.

Verstehen /fɛr'ʃteːən/ *noun.* M20.
[German = understanding, comprehension.]
(The use of empathy in) the sociological or historical understanding of human action and behaviour.
■ ***verstehende*** /fɛr'ʃteːəndə/ *adjective* [pres. pple of *verstehen* comprehend] (of sociological thought) employing *Verstehen* M20.

versus /'vəːsəs/ *preposition.* LME.
[medieval Latin use of Latin *versus* towards, in sense of *adversus* against.]
Against, in opposition to. Esp. in legal or sporting contexts. Abbreviation ***v.***, ***vs.***

versute /və'sjuːt, 'vəːsjuːt/ *adjective.* Long *rare.* LME.
[Latin *versutus*, from *vers-* pa. ppl stem of *vertere* turn.]
Orig. (*rare*), unpredictable. Later, cunning, crafty, wily.
■ **versuteness** *noun* L17.

vert /vəːt/ *noun*¹ & *adjective.* LME.
[Old & mod. French from Latin *viridis* green, rel. to *virere* be green. Cf. VERD, VERDITER.]
▶ **A** *noun.* **1** Green vegetation growing in a wood or forest and capable of serving as cover for deer; the trees and timber of a forest. Now *arch.* or *Hist.* LME. ▸**b** The right to cut green trees or shrubs in a forest. *arch.* M17.
2 A green colour or pigment. Now only (HERALDRY), the tincture green. L15.

> **1** W. B. STONEHOUSE A royal demesne . . covered with vert, and well stocked with deer. **nether vert** the shrubs or shrubbery of a forest. **over vert** the trees of a forest. **special vert** any vegetation in a forest bearing fruit on which deer can feed.

▶ **B** *adjective.* HERALDRY. Of the tincture green. LME.

> T. H. WHITE A chevron gules, between three thistles vert.

vert /vəːt/ *noun*². Now *rare* or *obsolete.* M19.
[Aphet. from CONVERT *noun*.]
ECCLESIASTICAL. A convert, esp. to Roman Catholicism.

vert /vəːt/ *verb*¹ *trans. rare. obsolete* exc. MEDICINE. L15.
[Latin *vertere* turn.]
Orig., reverse. Later, turn (something) in a particular direction; turn or twist (something) out of the normal position.

vert /vəːt/ *verb*² *intrans.* Now *rare.* L19.
[from VERT *noun*².]
ECCLESIASTICAL. Become a convert, esp. to Roman Catholicism.

vertant /ˈvəːt(ə)nt/ *adjective*. Long *rare*. L17.
[French, from Latin *vertent-* pres. ppl stem of *vertere* turn.]
HERALDRY. Bending, curving.

vertebr- *combining form* see VERTEBRO-.

vertebra /ˈvəːtɪbrə/ *noun*. Pl. **-brae** /-breɪ, -briː/. E17.
[Latin, from *vertere* turn.]
1 ANATOMY & ZOOLOGY. Any of the bony joints or segments composing the spinal column in man and other vertebrates. E17.
2 In *pl. The* spinal column. E17.
3 ZOOLOGY & PALAEONTOLOGY. Any of the segments or ossicles of the arms of brittle-stars and other ophiuroid echinoderms. E18.
1 *caudal vertebra*, *cervical vertebra*, *lumbar vertebra*, *sacral vertebra*, *thoracic vertebra*, etc.

vertebral /ˈvəːtɪbr(ə)l/ *adjective & noun*. L17.
[mod. Latin *vertebralis*, from prec.: see -AL¹.]
▶ **A** *adjective*. **1** Of or pertaining to the vertebrae; situated in, on, or near the vertebrae. L17.
2 Composed of vertebrae. E19.
3 ZOOLOGY. = VERTEBRATE *adjective* 1. Now *rare*. E19.
4 ZOOLOGY. Designating the ossicles which form the vertebrae of ophiuroid echinoderms. L19.
2 vertebral column = *spinal column* s.v. SPINAL *adjective*.
▶ **B** *noun*. **1** A vertebral artery or vein. E18.
2 ZOOLOGY. Any of the row of dorsal scutes in the midline of the carapace of a tortoise or turtle. L19.

Vertebrata /vəːtɪˈbrɑːtə/ *noun pl*. Also **v-**. E19.
[mod. Latin from Latin, neut. pl. of *vertebratus*: see next.]
ZOOLOGY. (Members of) a subphylum of the phylum Chordata including all vertebrate animals.

vertebrate /ˈvəːtɪbrət/ *adjective & noun*. E19.
[Latin *vertebratus* jointed, articulated, formed as VERTEBRA: see -ATE¹, -ATE².]
▶ **A** *adjective*. **1** ZOOLOGY. Of or belonging to the subphylum Vertebrata, which comprises chordate animals with a bony or cartilaginous skeleton, skull, and spinal column, and includes fishes, amphibians, reptiles, birds, and mammals. E19.
2 Of, pertaining to, characteristic of, or found in a backboned animal or animals. M19.
3 *fig*. Of a literary text etc.: characterized by strength or coherence. L19.
▶ **B** *noun*. An animal of the subphylum Vertebrata; a vertebrate animal. E19.
■ **vertebrated** *adjective* (now *rare* or *obsolete*) (*a*) = VERTEBRATE *adjective* 1; (*b*) consisting of or provided with vertebrae: E19.

vertebrate /ˈvəːtɪbreɪt/ *verb trans*. Now *rare*. L19.
[from prec.: see -ATE³.]
Connect or join in a similar way to vertebrae. Usu. in *pass*.

vertebration /vəːtɪˈbreɪʃ(ə)n/ *noun*. L19.
[from VERTEBRA + -ATION.]
1 Vertebral formation; division into segments like those of the spinal column. L19.
2 *fig*. Strength, backbone. *rare*. L19.

†**vertebre** *noun*. M16.
[French *vertèbre* from Latin VERTEBRA.]
1 The rounded top of the thigh bone. Only in M16.
2 = VERTEBRA 1. L16–M19.

vertebro- /ˈvəːtɪbrəʊ/ *combining form* of VERTEBRA: see -O-. Before a vowel also **vertebr-**. Forming terms in ANATOMY.
■ **vertebrarˈterial** *adjective* of or pertaining to the vertebral artery L19. **vertebroˈbasilar** *adjective* of, pertaining to, or involving the vertebral and basilar arteries M20.

vertex /ˈvəːtɛks/ *noun*. Pl. **vertices** /ˈvəːtɪsiːz/, **vertexes**. LME.
[Latin = whirl, vortex, crown of the head, highest point, from *vertere* turn.]
1 a ANATOMY & ZOOLOGY. The crown or top of the head or skull; *spec*. in humans, the part lying between the occiput and the sinciput. LME. ▶**b** ENTOMOLOGY. The top of the head of an insect, between the eyes and the occipital suture. E19.
2 a GEOMETRY. The point opposite to the base of a (plane or solid) figure; the point in a curve or surface at which the axis meets it; an angular point of a triangle, polygon, etc. L16. ▶**b** OPTICS. The point where the optic axis intersects the surface of a lens. E18. ▶**c** ASTRONOMY. The point on the limb of a celestial object where it is intersected by a circle passing through the zenith and the centre of the object. Now also, the point to which a group of stars appears to converge, or from which a shower of meteors appears to radiate. L19. ▶**d** MATH. A junction of two or more lines in a network or graph; a node. M20.
3 The point in the sky vertically overhead, or directly above a given place; the zenith. M17.
4 The top or highest point of a thing; *spec*. (*a*) the summit of a hill; (*b*) the crown of an arch. M17.
Comb.: **vertex presentation** MEDICINE a presentation in which the vertex of the foetus lies nearest to the cervix as labour begins.

vertical /ˈvəːtɪk(ə)l/ *adjective & noun*. M16.
[French, or late Latin *verticalis*, from Latin *vertex*: see VERTEX, -AL¹.]
▶ **A** *adjective*. **1** Of, pertaining to, situated at, or passing through the vertex or zenith; occupying a position in the sky directly overhead or above a given place or point. M16.
2 Placed, extending, moving, or operating at right angles to a horizontal plane; perpendicular; upright. E18.
3 BOTANY & ZOOLOGY. Having a position at right angles to the plane of the axis, body, or supporting surface; pointing directly upwards or downwards. L18.
4 ZOOLOGY & ANATOMY. Of, pertaining to, situated on, or affecting the vertex of the head. E19.
5 MUSIC. Pertaining to or involving the relationship between notes sounded simultaneously (rather than successively); harmonic or chordal as opp. to melodic. L19.
6 Pertaining to or involving the different levels of a hierarchy or progression; *spec*. (*a*) involving successive stages in the production of a particular class of goods; (*b*) involving upward or downward social or economic mobility. E20.
7 Pertaining to or designating an aerial photograph taken looking vertically downwards. E20.

> 🕮 **2** C. DARWIN We give a vertical nod of approval. S. H. VINES The adaptation of the Virginian Creeper to climbing up vertical walls. N. SHERRY A storm burst and there was a vertical wall of water all day.

Special collocations: **vertical angle** MATH. (*a*) the angle opposite the base of a triangle or polygon; (*b*) (*pl*.) each of the pairs of opposite angles made by two intersecting straight lines. **vertical circle** an azimuth circle. **vertical fin** ZOOLOGY = *median fin* s.v. MEDIAN *adjective*² 1. **vertical integration** integration of firms engaged in successive stages in the production of goods. **vertical keel** NAUTICAL: formed from plating resting vertically on the inner side of a plate keel, and supporting the keelson. **vertical market**: comprising all the potential purchasers in a particular occupation or industry. **vertical plane** a plane at right angles to the horizontal. †**vertical point** (*a*) = VERTEX 3; (*b*) *fig*. the culminating point, the peak of perfection. **vertical proliferation** the increase in the number, kinds, or power of the nuclear weapons of a State which already possesses such weapons. **vertical take-off** the take-off of an aircraft directly upwards. **vertical tasting** a tasting in order of year of several different vintages of a particular wine. **vertical thinking** deductive reasoning (opp. *lateral thinking*).
▶ **B** *noun*. †**1** *fig*. A high point; a zenith. E–M17.
2 A vertical circle, line, or plane. M17.
3 A vertical aerial photograph. E20.
Phrases: **out of the vertical** not vertical, deviating from the perpendicular. *prime vertical*: see PRIME *adjective*.
¶ In many senses opp. *horizontal*.
■ **vertic** *adjective* (*poet*., now *rare* or *obsolete*) (esp. of the sun) overhead, vertical E17. **verticalism** *noun* (*rare*, ARCHITECTURE) the condition or quality of being vertical, vertical position M19. **vertiˈcality** *noun* (*a*) the fact of the sun or other celestial object being at the vertex or zenith; (*b*) the condition or quality of being vertical or perpendicular; vertical position: L16. **verticaliˈzation** *noun* the action or result of making something vertical M20. **verticalize** *verb trans*. make vertical M20. **vertically** *adverb* M17.

vertices *noun pl*. see VERTEX.

verticil /ˈvəːtɪsɪl/ *noun*. Also (earlier) **-cel** /-s(ə)l/. E18.
[Latin VERTICILLUS.]
†**1** A kind of glass bead used as a bobbin. *rare*. Only in E18.
2 BOTANY & ZOOLOGY. A set of three or more similar organs arising at the same point on an axis; a whorl. L18.

verticillaster /ˌvəːtɪsɪˈlastə/ *noun*. M19.
[mod. Latin, from Latin VERTICILLUS + -ASTER.]
BOTANY. A kind of false whorl characteristic of inflorescences of the labiate family, formed by the confluence of several almost sessile opposite cymes.

verticillate /vəːtɪˈsɪlət, vəˈtɪsɪlət/ *adjective*. M17.
[from VERTICILLUS + -ATE².]
BOTANY & ZOOLOGY. **1** Having leaves, flowers, setae, etc., arranged in whorls. M17.
2 Of leaves, flowers, setae, etc.: arranged in whorls. L18.
3 Characterized by verticillation. M19.
■ **verˈticillated** *adjective* (now *rare*) = VERTICILLATE L17. **vertici̍ˈllation** *noun* the formation of verticils; a verticillate form or structure, a verticil: M19.

verticilli *noun* pl. of VERTICILLUS.

verticillium /vəːtɪˈsɪlɪəm/ *noun*. E20.
[mod. Latin (see below), from Latin VERTICILL(US + -IUM.]
Any of various hyphomycetous fungi constituting the genus *Verticillium*, some of which, esp. *V. albo-atrum* and *V. dahliae*, cause wilt in garden plants.

verticillus /vəːtɪˈsɪləs/ *noun*. Pl. **-cilli** /-ˈsɪlʌɪ/. M18.
[Latin = whorl of a spindle, dim. of VERTEX.]
BOTANY. = VERTICIL 2.

verticity /vəːˈtɪsɪti/ *noun*. Now *rare* or *obsolete*. E17.
[mod. Latin *verticitas*, from Latin *vertic-* stem of *vertex*: see VERTEX, -ITY.]
1 The faculty (of a magnetic needle etc.) of turning towards a vertex or pole; magnetization; an instance of this. E17.
2 The power of turning or revolving; rotation, revolution. M17.

vertiginous /vəːˈtɪdʒɪnəs/ *adjective*. E17.
[Latin *vertiginosus*, formed as next: see -OUS.]
1 Of a person, the head, etc.: affected by or suffering from vertigo or giddiness; dizzy. E17. ▶**b** Of the nature of, pertaining to, or characterized by vertigo. E17.
2 *fig*. Unstable or unsettled in opinions etc.; inconstant, changeable; characterized by rapid change. E17.
3 Liable to cause vertigo or dizziness; inducing giddiness. M17.
4 Of motion: rotatory. M17.

> 🕮 **2** C. LAMBERT This . . speeding up in technical experiment gives a . . vertiginous quality to the Impressionist period. **3** *Time* Trees are . . thick on the vertiginous mountain slopes. J. BRIGGS Going up into the vertiginous mountains. **4** S. JOHNSON That vertiginous motion, with which we are carried round by the diurnal revolution of the earth.

■ †**vertiginate** *verb intrans*. turn round, spin, or rush dizzily M18–M19. **vertiginously** *adverb* M18. **vertiginousness** *noun* L16.

vertigo /ˈvəːtɪgəʊ/ *noun*. Pl. **-os**. LME.
[Latin *vertigo*, *-gin-* whirling about, giddiness, from *vertere* turn.]
1 MEDICINE. A sensation of whirling motion, tending to result in a loss of balance and sometimes of consciousness; giddiness, dizziness. LME.
2 *fig*. A disordered state of mind or things. M17.

> 🕮 **2** W. S. JEVONS That . . intellectual vertigo which often attacks writers on the currency. M. IGNATIEFF She realised, with a sudden sense of vertigo, that she had never deceived her family before.

Vertisol /ˈvəːtɪsɒl/ *noun*. M20.
[from VERTICAL + -SOL.]
SOIL SCIENCE. A clayey soil with little organic matter found in regions having distinct wet and dry seasons, characterized by deep wide cracks when dry and an uneven surface.

vertu *noun* var. of VIRTU.

verumontanum /ˌvɛrʊmɒnˈteɪnəm/ *noun*. Now *rare*. E18.
[Latin, from *veru* spit + *montanum* neut. of *montanus* hilly.]
ANATOMY. A rounded prominence in the wall of the male urethra, where the ejaculatory ducts enter it.

vervain /ˈvəːveɪn/ *noun*. LME.
[Old & mod. French *verveine* from Latin VERBENA.]
BOTANY. **1** A European and British plant of roadsides etc., *Verbena officinalis* (family Verbenaceae), with wiry stems and spikes of small lilac flowers. Also (now *rare*), with specifying word, any of various other plants of the genus *Verbena*. LME.
2 = VERBENA 2. M16.
Comb.: **vervain hummingbird** a minute green and white hummingbird, *Mellisuga minima*, which is found in Jamaica and Hispaniola.

verve /vəːv/ *noun*. L17.
[Old & mod. French = vigour (formerly also = form of expression, empty chatter, whim), from Latin *verba* pl. of *verbum* word.]
1 Special bent or talent in writing. Now *rare* or *obsolete*. L17.
2 Enthusiasm, vigour, or spirit, esp. in artistic or literary work or in sport; style, energy. E19.

> 🕮 **2** V. BROME An intellectual dynamism which injected tremendous verve into their talk. *Guardian* Organising . . wonderful events with the chutzpah and verve of a showman. *Times Educ. Suppl*. The story . . was told with considerable power and verve.

vervet /ˈvəːvɪt/ *noun*. L19.
[French, of unkn. origin.]
The common African savannah monkey, *Cercopithecus aethiops*; *spec*. one of a variable black-faced race found in southern and eastern Africa. Cf. *green monkey* s.v. GREEN *adjective*, GRIVET.

†**vervil** *noun* see VARVEL.

very /ˈvɛri/ *adjective*¹ & *adverb*. ME.
[Old French *ver(r)ai* (mod. *vrai*) from Proto-Gallo-Romance, ult. from Latin *verus* true: ending assim. to -Y¹.]
▶ **A** *adjective*. **1** Properly so called, truly entitled to the name or designation; real, genuine. *arch*. ME.
2 †**a** Truthful; sure, reliable. ME–E16. ▶**b** Of truth: exact, simple, actual. *arch*. LME.
†**3** Exact or precise as opp. to approximate. ME–M17.
4 So called in the fullest sense, possessing all the essential qualities of that specified; complete, absolute. Freq. in *superl*. *arch*. LME.
†**5** Of a friend etc.: faithful, sincere, staunch. LME–L17.
†**6** Esp. of a person: rightful, lawful, legitimate. LME–E17.

7 As an intensive emphasizing identity, significance, or extreme degree, usu. with *that*, *the*, or *this*: exact, actual, that is truly such. **LME.**

8 That is neither more nor less than that denoted or specified by the noun; exactly that specified; sheer; mere. **LME.**

📖 **1** *Book of Common Prayer* Very God of very God. W. MORRIS Half dead with very death still drawing nigh. **4** *Science News* This truth seems to be known to the veriest child. A. MILLER A very ape would weep at such calamity. **7** CARLYLE We do not . . see what is passing under our very eyes. C. KINGSLEY I said it, I said it. Those were my very words. T. HARDY He adores the very ground she walks on. M. FORSTER She had this very day been ordered back to England. *Guardian* Lyle kept the best for the very end. **8** LD MACAULAY The sailors mutinied from very hunger.

▶**B** *adverb.* †**1** Truly, really, genuinely; truthfully. **LME–L16.**

2 Modifying an adjective or adverb: in a high degree, to a great extent; exceedingly, extremely, greatly. **LME.** ▸**b** Modifying a noun or proper name used adjectively: extremely reminiscent of or appropriate for. *colloq.* **M20.**

3 As an intensive with a superl. or emphasizing absolute identity or difference: in the fullest sense, most completely or absolutely. **L15.**

†**4** With adverbs of time, place, or manner: exactly, precisely, just. **M16–M17.**

📖 **2** G. W. DASENT Her foot is very swollen. D. LODGE That was quick! Thank you very much. J. MCGAHERN She was very fond of the boy. A. N. WILSON Roger knew Greece very well, and loved it. **b** *Listener* The total effect is very Kirov; it has more in common with the Leningrad *Cinderella*. **3** L. STERNE In the very next page. LD MACAULAY Three of the very richest subjects in England. T. MITCHELL The very opposite word was . . expected. A. MAUPIN You guys are going to have your very own tent.

Phrases: ***all very well***: see WELL *adjective*. ***in very deed***: see DEED *noun*. ***in very sooth***: see SOOTH *noun*. **not very** (*a*) in a low degree; (*b*) far from being. ***the same very***: see SAME *adjective*. ***the very idea!***: see IDEA. ***the very nick of time***: see NICK *noun*¹. ***the very same***: see SAME *adjective*. **the very thing** the thing exactly suitable or required. ***under a person's very nose***: see NOSE *noun*. **very good**: expr. assent, approval, or acquiescence. **very high frequency** designating radio waves of frequency *c* 30–300 MHz and wavelength *c* 1–10 metres; abbreviation *VHF*. ***Very Reverend***: see REVEREND. **very well** = *very good* above.

Very /ˈvɛri, ˈvɪəri/ *adjective*². **E20.**
[Edward W. *Very* (1847–1910), US naval officer.]
Designating a type of coloured pyrotechnic flare projected from a special pistol for signalling or temporarily illuminating an area.
Very light, *Very pistol*, etc.

Vesak /ˈvɛsak/ *noun.* Also **W-**; (esp. as month) **Visākha** /vɪˈsɑːkə/. **L18.**
[Sinhalese *vesak* from Pali *vesākha* from Sanskrit *vaiśākha* the month April–May, from *viśākhā* a constellation, from *vi* apart + *śākhā* branch.]
An important Buddhist festival commemorating the birth, enlightenment, and death of the Buddha; the month (April–May) during which this is observed on the day of the full moon.

vesalian /vɪˈseɪlɪən/ *adjective.* Also **V-**. **L19.**
[from Andreas *Vesalius* (1514–64), Belgian anatomist + -AN.]
1 ANATOMY. Designating any of several structures named in honour of Vesalius, esp. various sesamoid bones. **L19.**
2 Connected with anatomical researches. **L19.**

vesania /vɪˈseɪnɪə/ *noun.* Now *rare* or *obsolete*. **E19.**
[Latin, from *vesanus* mad, from *ve-* not + *sanus* sane.]
MEDICINE. Full mental illness marked by mania, melancholia, paranoia, or dementia.

vesica /ˈvɛsɪkə, ˈviː-/ *noun.* Pl. **-cae** /-kiː/. **M17.**
[Latin = bladder, blister.]
1 ANATOMY. A bladder. Usu. with Latin specifying word. *rare.* **M17.**
2 In full ***vesica piscis*** /ˈpɪskɪs/, ***vesica piscium*** /ˈpɪskɪʌm/ [Latin = fish's or fishes' bladder]. A pointed oval figure used as an architectural feature and as an aureole enclosing figures of Christ, the Virgin, etc., in medieval painting and sculpture. **E19.**

vesical /ˈvɛsɪk(ə)l, ˈviː-/ *adjective.* **L18.**
[from prec. + -AL¹.]
1 Of, pertaining or connected to, or formed in the urinary bladder. **L18.** ▸**b** MEDICINE. Affecting or occurring in the urinary bladder. **M19.**
2 Having the form of a vesica piscis; of a pointed oval shape. **M19.**

vesicant /ˈvɛsɪk(ə)nt, ˈviː-/ *adjective & noun.* **LME.**
[from late Latin *vesicant-*, *-ans*, pres. pple of *vesicare*: see next, -ANT¹.]
▶**A** *adjective.* Causing, or efficacious in producing, blisters; vesicatory. **LME.**
▶**B** *noun.* A substance which produces blisters on the skin; formerly *esp.* (MEDICINE) a sharp irritating ointment, plaster, etc. Now also, such a substance as used in chemical warfare. **M17.**

vesicate /ˈvɛsɪkeɪt, ˈviː-/ *verb.* **M17.**
[from late Latin *vesicat-*, pa. ppl stem of *vesicare* form pustules, from VESICA: see -ATE³.]
Chiefly MEDICINE. **1** *verb trans.* Cause to rise in a blister or blisters; raise blisters on (the skin etc.). **M17.**
2 *verb intrans.* Produce blisters; become blistered. **E19.**

vesication /vɛsɪˈkeɪʃ(ə)n, ˈviː-/ *noun.* **LME.**
[medieval Latin *vesicatio(n-)* formation of pustules, formed as prec.: see -ION.]
MEDICINE. **1** The formation or development of blisters; the action or fact of blistering. **LME.**
2 The result of blistering; one or more blisters. **M16.**

vesicatory /ˈvɛsɪkeɪt(ə)ri, vɛˈsɪkət(ə)ri, ˈviː-/ *noun & adjective.* **E17.**
[prob. from prec.: see -ORY².]
MEDICINE. ▶**A** *noun.* A vesicant. Now *rare.* **E17.**
▶**B** *adjective.* Of the nature of a vesicant; capable of or characterized by raising blisters. **E17.**

vesicle /ˈvɛsɪk(ə)l, ˈviː-/ *noun.* **L16.**
[French *vésicule* or Latin *vesicula* dim. of VESICA: see -ULE.]
1 a ANATOMY & ZOOLOGY. A small fluid-filled bladder or sac within the body; an alveolus of the lung; a small cyst. Freq. with specifying word. **L16.** ▸**b** BOTANY. An air-filled swelling in a plant structure (e.g. the thallus of a seaweed). **L17.**
2 PHYSICS. A minute bubble or spherule of liquid or vapour, esp. any of those composing a cloud or fog. **M18.** ▸**b** GEOLOGY. A small spherical or oval cavity produced by the presence of bubbles of gas or vapour in volcanic rocks. **E19.**
3 MEDICINE. A small rounded elevation of the skin containing serous fluid; a blister. **L18.**
1a ***GRAAFIAN vesicle***. ***optic vesicle***: see OPTIC *adjective*. ***POLIAN vesicle***. ***PURKINJEAN vesicle***. ***seminal vesicle***: see SEMINAL *adjective*.

vesico- /ˈvɛsɪkəʊ, ˈviː-/ *combining form.*
[from VESICA + -O-.]
ANATOMY & MEDICINE. **1** Forming adjectives with the sense 'vesical and —'.
2 = VESICULO-.
■ **vesicoˈpustular** *adjective* = VESICULOPUSTULAR **E20.** **vesicouˈreteral** *adjective* = VESICOURETERIC **E20.** **vesicoureˈteric** *adjective* of or pertaining to the bladder and the ureters; *spec.* designating a reflux of urine back into the ureters: **M20.** **vesicoˈuterine** *adjective* of or pertaining to the bladder and the uterus **M19.** **vesicovaˈginal** *adjective* of or pertaining to the bladder and the vagina **M19.**

vesicula /vɪˈsɪkjʊlə/ *noun.* Pl. **-lae** /-liː/. **E18.**
[Latin, dim. of VESICA: see -CULE.]
= VESICLE. Usu. in *pl.*

vesicular /vɪˈsɪkjʊlə/ *adjective.* **E18.**
[from prec. + -AR¹.]
1 Having the form or structure of a vesicle; bladder-like. **E18.**
2 Characterized by the presence of vesicles; composed of parts having the form of vesicles. **E18.**
3 MEDICINE. **a** Characterized by the formation or presence of vesicles on the skin. **E19.** ▸**b** Affecting or connected with the vesicles or alveoli of the lungs. **E19.**
4 ZOOLOGY. Designating parasitic worms that spend part of the life cycle contained in a cyst. **M19.**
3a ***SWINE vesicular disease***.
■ **vesicuˈlarity** *noun* (GEOLOGY) vesicular condition **E20.**

vesiculate /vɪˈsɪkjʊlət, -leɪt/ *adjective.* **E19.**
[from VESICULA + -ATE².]
= VESICULATED *adjective*.

vesiculate /vɪˈsɪkjʊleɪt/ *verb.* **M19.**
[Back-form. from next.]
1 *verb trans.* Make vesicular or full of small cavities. *rare.* **M19.**
2 *verb intrans.* Become vesicular; develop vesicles. **L19.**

vesiculated /vɪˈsɪkʊleɪtɪd/ *adjective.* **E18.**
[formed as VESICULATE *adjective* + -ED¹.]
Containing or covered with vesicles or small cavities; of the nature of a vesicle.

vesiculation /vɪˌsɪkjʊˈleɪʃ(ə)n/ *noun.* **L19.**
[from VESICULA + -ATION.]
MEDICINE & GEOLOGY. The formation of vesicles; a vesicular condition.

vesiculitis /vɪˌsɪkjʊˈlʌɪtɪs/ *noun.* **M19.**
[from VESICULA + -ITIS.]
MEDICINE. Inflammation of a vesicle, esp. of the seminal vesicles.

vesiculo- /vɪˈsɪkjʊləʊ/ *combining form.*
[from VESICULA + -O-.]
Chiefly MEDICINE. Forming adjectives with the sense 'vesicular and —'.
■ **vesiculoˈbullous** *adjective* characterized by or involving both vesicles and bullae **E20.** **vesiculoˈpustular** *adjective* characterized by or involving both vesicles and pustules **E20.**

vesiculose /vɪˈsɪkjʊləʊs/ *adjective.* **E19.**
[Latin *vesiculosus* full of blisters: see VESICULA + -OSE¹.]
Chiefly ENTOMOLOGY. Full of vesicles; vesicular.

Vesp *noun & adjective* see VEPS.

Vespa /ˈvɛspə/ *noun.* **M20.**
[Italian = wasp, hornet.]
(Proprietary name for) an Italian make of motor scooter.

vespasienne /vɛspazjɛn/ *noun.* Pl. pronounced same. **E20.**
[French, abbreviation of *colonne vespasienne* Vespasian column (the Roman emperor Vespasian introduced a tax on public lavatories).]
In France, a public lavatory.
■ Also ***vespasian*** /vɛsˈpeɪʒ(ə)n/ *noun* [Anglicization] **M20.**

vesper /ˈvɛspə/ *noun.* **LME.**
[Partly from Latin = evening star, evening, corresp. to Greek *hesperos* HESPERUS; partly from Old French *vespres* (mod. *vêpres*) from ecclesiastical Latin *vesperas* accus. pl. of Latin *vespera* evening, after *matutinas* matins (see MATIN *noun*).]
1 a (**V-**.) The evening star, Hesperus. *poet. & rhet.* **LME.** ▸**b** (An) evening. *poet.* Now *rare.* **E17.**
2 ECCLESIASTICAL. In *pl.* (occas. treated as *sing.*) & *sing.* The sixth of the daytime canonical hours of prayer, orig. appointed for the early evening; the office appointed for this hour. Also, evensong. **L15.** ▸**b** *transf.* In *pl.* The evening song of a bird. *poet.* **L17.** ▸**c** In *pl.* Evening prayers or devotions. *poet.* **E19.**
†**3 a** At Oxford and Cambridge universities, (the day of) the public disputations immediately preceding the inception or commencement of a Bachelor of Arts. **L16–E18.** ▸**b** CHRISTIAN THEOLOGY. The eve of a festival or *of* Jesus' crucifixion. Only in **17.**
4 In full ***vesper bell***. A bell rung to signal vespers. **L18.**
2 ***Sicilian vespers***: see SICILIAN *adjective*.
Comb.: **vesper mouse** any of various large-eared mice of the genus *Calomys*, found in grassland and scrub in southern S. America; **vesper sparrow** a small bird, *Pooecetes gramineus* (family Emberizidae), with streaked brown plumage, found in open country in N. America and known for its evening song.

vesperal /ˈvɛsp(ə)r(ə)l/ *adjective & noun.* **E17.**
[French *vespéral*, from Latin *vespera* (see prec.) + *-al* -AL¹.]
▶**A** *adjective.* Of or pertaining to evening, vespertine. Also, of or pertaining to vespers. **E17.**
▶**B** *noun.* ECCLESIASTICAL. An office-book containing the psalms, canticles, anthems, etc., with their musical settings, used at vespers. **M19.**

vespertilian /vɛspəˈtɪlɪən/ *adjective.* **L19.**
[from Latin *vespertilio* bat (formed as VESPER) + -AN.]
Resembling (that of) a bat. Chiefly *fig.*

vespertilionid /ˌvɛspətɪlɪˈəʊnɪd/ *adjective & noun.* **L19.**
[mod. Latin *Vespertilionidae* (see below), from *Vespertilio* genus name, formed as prec.: see -ID³.]
ZOOLOGY. ▶**A** *adjective.* Of or belonging to the family Vespertilionidae, which comprises many typical insectivorous bats and includes the common European species. **L19.**
▶**B** *noun.* A bat of this family. **M20.**

vespertine /ˈvɛspətʌɪn, -tɪn/ *adjective.* **LME.**
[Latin *vespertinus*, formed as VESPER: see -INE¹.]
1 Of, pertaining to, or occurring in the evening; ZOOLOGY (of an animal) appearing or especially active in the evening. **LME.**
2 ASTRONOMY & ASTROLOGY. Of a star, planet, etc.: setting at or just after sunset. Now *rare* or *obsolete*. **E17.**
■ Also **vesperˈtinal** *adjective* **M19.**

vespiary /ˈvɛspɪəri/ *noun. rare.* **E19.**
[Irreg. from Latin *vespa* wasp, after *apiary*.]
A wasps' nest.

vespine /ˈvɛspʌɪn/ *adjective.* Now *rare.* **M19.**
[formed as next + -INE¹.]
Of or pertaining to wasps.

vespoid /ˈvɛspɔɪd/ *adjective.* **E19.**
[from Latin *vespa* wasp + -OID, or from mod. Latin *Vespoidea* (see below).]
ENTOMOLOGY. Resembling (that of) a wasp; *spec.* of or belonging to the hymenopteran superfamily Vespoidea, which comprises the typical wasps.

vessel /ˈvɛs(ə)l/ *noun*¹ *& verb.* **ME.**
[Anglo-Norman *vessel(e)* = Old French *vaissel*, Old & mod. French *vaisselle* (mod. *vaisseau* vessel, vase, ship) from late Latin *vascellum* small vase dim. of *vas*: see VASE, -EL².]
▶**A** *noun.* **1** *collect. sing.* Dishes or utensils for domestic or table use; *spec.* these made of gold or silver, plate. Long *obsolete* exc. *dial.* **ME.**
2 A hollow container or receptacle for a liquid etc., *esp.* a domestic or table utensil, as a cup, bottle, pot, bowl, or dish. **ME.**
3 A person regarded as the embodiment or exponent of a quality etc. Freq. foll. by *of*. Chiefly in biblical allusions. Now *arch. & joc.* **ME.** ▸†**b** In biblical use, a means, an agency. **ME–E17.** ▸†**c** The body, esp. as the receptacle of the soul. **LME–E18.**
4 A ship or boat, now usu. one of larger size; a craft. **ME.** ▸**b** An airship; a hovercraft. **E20.**
5 a ANATOMY & ZOOLOGY. Any of the canals, ducts, or tubes in which the body fluids (esp. blood) are circulated. **LME.** ▸**b** BOTANY. Any of the tubular structures in the vascular

system of a plant, which serve to conduct water and mineral nutrients from the root. Cf. ***vessel element*** below. L17.

📖 **2 *drinking-vessel*, *kitchen vessel***, etc. **3** H. CHAPONE They might . . prove . . chosen vessels to promote the honour of God. SIR W. SCOTT Nature . . grieves that so goodly a form should be a vessel of perdition. ***the weaker vessel***: see WEAK *adjective*. **4 *fishing vessel*, *merchant vessel*, *naval vessel*, *sailing vessel***, etc.

Comb.: **vessel element** any of the special tracheary elements which, joined end to end and forming a continuous structure through the absorption of the end walls, form a vessel (cf. TRACHEID).

► **B** *verb trans.* Infl. **-ll-**. Put or enclose (a liquid etc.) in a vessel or container. Now *rare* or *obsolete*. LME.

■ **vesselful** *noun* as much or as many as a vessel will hold M19.

vessel /ˈvɛs(ə)l/ *noun*[2]. Chiefly *local*. Now *rare*. L18.
[Origin unkn.]
In full ***vessel of paper***. A slip of paper, *esp.* an eighth of a sheet of foolscap.

vest /vɛst/ *noun*. E17.
[French *veste* garment from Italian from Latin *vestis* clothing, garment.]
1 A loose outer garment worn esp. in ancient times or in the East; a robe, a gown. Now chiefly *arch. & poet.* E17.
2 An ecclesiastical vestment. *rare*. M17.
3 a Orig. (now *Hist.*), a man's long sleeveless garment worn under a coat. Later (now *N. Amer. & Austral.*), a man's waistcoat. M17. ▸**b** A usu. sleeveless or short-sleeved undergarment for the upper part of the body; a similar sleeveless garment worn as a casual top. E19. ▸**c** A part of a woman's dress bodice, consisting of a collar and front. Also, a usu. V-shaped insert, usu. of contrasting material or colour, to fill the opening at the neck of a woman's dress. L19. ▸**d** A short sleeveless jacket. *N. Amer.* E20. ▸**e** An athlete's singlet; this denoting membership of a representative athletics team. L20.

Comb.: **vest-pocket** *noun & adjective* (chiefly *N. Amer.*) (**a**) *noun* a pocket in a vest or waistcoat; (**b**) *adjective* small enough to fit into a vest pocket, very small of its kind.

■ **vesting** *noun* (a) cloth or material for making vests or waistcoats E19. **vestless** *adjective* L19.

vest /vɛst/ *verb*. See also VESTED *ppl adjective*[1]. LME.
[Orig. pa. pple, from Old French *vestu* pa. pple of *vestir* (mod. *vêtir*) clothe, †invest from Latin *vestir* clothe, (in medieval Latin) put in possession, invest, from *vestis* VEST *noun*.]
1 *verb trans.* Bestow or confer (property, authority, power, etc.) on a person or persons. Usu. in *pass.* & foll. by *in*. Cf. INVEST 3b. LME.
2 *verb trans.* Place or establish (a person etc.) *in* full or legal possession or occupation of property, authority, power, etc.; endow formally or legally *with*. Usu. in *pass.* Cf. INVEST 3. LME.
3 *verb intrans.* Of property, a right, etc., pass into the possession of a person. (Foll. by *in*.) L16.
4 *verb trans.* Dress or clothe (a person) in a robe or garment, esp. as a formal act or ceremony. Of a garment: clothe or cover (a person). Cf. INVEST 1. (Earlier as VESTED *ppl adjective*[1] 1.) Now chiefly *literary*. L16. ▸**b** ECCLESIASTICAL. Drape or cover (an altar). M19.
5 *verb intrans. & refl.* Dress or clothe oneself, esp. in ecclesiastical vestments. M17.
6 *verb trans.* = INVEST 6. Now *rare* or *obsolete*. E18.

📖 **1** R. S. WOOLHOUSE Absolute power vested in the hands of a supreme authority. *She* His attractiveness is vested in something other than an . . abstract maleness. **2** H. H. WILSON The Indian Government was vested with the power of sovereignty. **4** CLARENDON The Speaker . . vested him with a rich purple Velvet Robe.

vesta /ˈvɛstə/ *noun*. M19.
[Latin *Vesta*, the Roman goddess of the hearth and household, corresp. to Greek *Hestia* identical with *hestia* hearth, house, household.]
Hist. A kind of short wooden or wax match.

vestal /ˈvɛst(ə)l/ *adjective & noun*. LME.
[Latin *vestalis*, formed as prec.: see -AL[1].]
► **A** *adjective*. **1** ROMAN HISTORY. Of a virgin: serving the goddess Vesta as a priestess. LME.
2 Of or pertaining to the Roman goddess Vesta; (of fire etc.) sacred, constantly burning. LME.
3 Of, pertaining to, or characteristic of a vestal virgin; chaste, pure, virginal. L16.
► **B** *noun*. **1** ROMAN HISTORY. In full ***vestal virgin***. Each of the virgin priestesses of the goddess Vesta, vowed to chastity, who had the duty of keeping the sacred fire burning on the goddess's altar. LME.
2 A virgin; a chaste woman; a nun. L16.

vested /ˈvɛstɪd/ *ppl adjective*[1]. E16.
[from VEST *verb* + -ED[1].]
1 Dressed or clothed, esp. in ecclesiastical vestments. E16.
2 Secured or settled in the possession of or assigned to a person etc. Freq. in ***vested interest*** below. M18.
2 vested interest (**a**) LAW an interest, usu. in land or money held in trust, recognized as already belonging to a person etc., as opp. to rights that he or she may acquire in the future; (**b**) a personal interest in a state of affairs, usu. with an expectation of gain; a person or group having such an interest (usu. in *pl.*).

vested /ˈvɛstɪd/ *adjective*[2]. Chiefly *N. Amer.* L20.
[from VEST *noun* + -ED[2].]
Of a suit: three-piece, having a waistcoat.

vestee /vɛˈstiː/ *noun*[1]. *rare*. L19.
[from VEST *verb* + -EE[1].]
LAW. A person vested with a right, property, etc.

vestee /vɛˈstiː/ *noun*[2]. Chiefly *N. Amer.* E20.
[from VEST *noun* + -EE[2].]
= VEST *noun* 3a, c. Also = DICKY *noun* 4a.

vestiarian /vɛstɪˈɛːrɪən/ *adjective*. L18.
[from VESTIARY + -IAN.]
1 Of or pertaining to clothing or dress. *rare*. L18.
2 Of or pertaining to ecclesiastical vestments or their use. M19.

vestiary /ˈvɛstɪəri/ *noun & adjective*. ME.
[As noun from Old French *vestiarie*, (also mod.) *vestiaire* from Latin *vestiarium* clothes-chest, wardrobe (in medieval Latin = vestry) use as noun of *vestiarius*, from *vestis* clothes, clothing. As adjective from Latin *vestiarius*: see -ARY[1].]
► **A** *noun*. **1** A vestry of a church. Now *rare* or *obsolete*. ME.
2 A room or building, esp. in a monastery or large establishment, for keeping clothes; a robing-room; a cloakroom. LME.
► **B** *adjective*. Of or pertaining to clothes or dress. E17.

vestibula *noun* pl. of VESTIBULUM.

vestibular /vɛˈstɪbjʊlə/ *adjective*. M19.
[from next + -AR[1].]
Of or pertaining to a vestibule; resembling or serving as a vestibule; *spec.* in ANATOMY, of or pertaining to the vestibule of the ear or its function as an organ of balance.
vestibular fold either of two folds of mucous membrane situated in the larynx above the vocal cords. **vestibular membrane** a thin membrane in the inner ear separating the scala vestibuli from the central duct of the cochlea; also called ***Reissner's membrane***. **vestibular nerve** a branch of the vestibulocochlear nerve conveying information about orientation and posture.

vestibule /ˈvɛstɪbjuːl/ *noun & verb*. E17.
[French (perh. from Italian *vestibulo*) or Latin *vestibulum*.]
► **A** *noun*. **1 a** ANTIQUITIES. The enclosed or partially enclosed space in front of the main entrance of a Roman or Greek house or building. E17. ▸**b** An antechamber or hall next to the outer door of a building or house; an entrance-hall, a lobby; a porch of a church etc. M18. ▸**c** An enclosed passage communicating between two railway carriages (chiefly *US*). Also, the area at either end of a railway carriage, usu. separated by a door from the seating. L19.
2 ANATOMY & ZOOLOGY. Any of various cavities or hollows forming an approach or entrance to a passage or canal; *esp.* (**a**) the bony cavity which forms the central portion of the labyrinth of the ear, between the tympanum and the internal auditory canal; (**b**) in the female, the space in the vulva into which both the urethra and vagina open; (**c**) the part of the mouth between the teeth and the lips; (**d**) a depression in the body wall of a ciliate protozoan, into which food is taken for ingestion. E18.
► **B** *verb trans.* Provide (a railway carriage) with vestibules; link by means of vestibules. Freq. as ***vestibuled*** *ppl adjective*. Chiefly *US*. L19.

vestibulo- /vɛˈstɪbjʊləʊ/ *combining form*.
[from Latin *vestibulum* VESTIBULE + -O-.]
ANATOMY & PHYSIOLOGY. Forming chiefly adjectives with the sense 'vestibular and —'.
■ **vestibuloˈauditory** *adjective* involving the vestibules and hearing M20. **vestibulocereˈbellar** *adjective* designating a tract of nerves running from the vestibular nucleus of the brain to the cerebellum M20. **vestibuloˈcochlear** *adjective* designating or pertaining to the eighth pair of cranial nerves, which supply the inner ears, dividing into the vestibular and cochlear nerves M20. **vestibulo-ˈocular** *adjective* involving both the vestibular and the oculomotor nerves; *esp.* designating the reflex by which balance is maintained when the visual field is in motion: E20. **vestibuloˈspinal** *adjective* designating a tract of nerves in the spinal cord that originate in the vestibular nucleus of the brain L19.

vestibulum /vɛˈstɪbjʊləm/ *noun*. Pl. **-la** /-lə/. M17.
[Latin: see VESTIBULE.]
1 = VESTIBULE *noun* 1a, b. M17.
2 ANATOMY & ZOOLOGY. = VESTIBULE *noun* 2. E18.

†vestigate *verb intrans. & trans. rare*. M16–L18.
[Latin *vestigat-* pa. ppl stem of *vestigare* track, trace, investigate: see -ATE[3].]
Investigate.

vestige /ˈvɛstɪdʒ/ *noun*. LME.
[French from Latin *vestigium* sole of the foot, footprint, trace.]
1 a A mark, trace, or visible sign of something no longer present or in existence; a piece of evidence, an indication; a surviving remnant. Usu. foll. by *of*. LME. ▸**b** A small or slight amount; a particle, a scrap. Usu. foll. by *of*. LME. ▸**c** BIOLOGY. A surviving trace *of* some part which formerly existed in the ancestors of a species; a vestigial organ or structure. M19.
2 A mark or trace left on the ground by the foot; a footprint, a track. *rare*. M17.

📖 **1a** H. ADAMS Vestiges of Saint Louis's palace remain at the Conciergerie. **b** T. PRINGLE Not a vestige of green pasturage was to be descried. A. KOESTLER If he still had a vestige of self-respect, he would clean his cell.

vestigial /vɛˈstɪdʒɪəl, -dʒ(ə)l/ *adjective*. L19.
[from prec. + -IAL.]
Of the nature of a vestige; remaining or surviving as a trace or remnant; rudimentary; BIOLOGY (of an organ or structure) degenerate or atrophied, having become functionless in the course of evolution.

📖 *Atlantic* He feels a vestigial flicker of anger from last night. **vestigial sideband** TELECOMMUNICATIONS a sideband which is partially attenuated (usu. at the higher frequencies) before transmission; *esp.* one transmitted along with a full sideband to improve the transmission of low-frequency components of the signal.

■ **vestigially** *adverb* E20.

vestigium /vɛˈstɪdʒɪəm/ *noun*. Pl. **-ia** /-ɪə/. M17.
[Latin: see VESTIGE.]
A vestige, a trace. Usu. foll. by *of*.

†vestiment *noun*. ME–M19.
[Old French, or Latin *vestimentum* clothing: see VESTMENT.]
A vestment, esp. an ecclesiastical one.

vestimentary /vɛstɪˈmɛnt(ə)ri/ *adjective*. Chiefly *formal* or *literary*. E19.
[formed as prec. + -ARY[1].]
Of or pertaining to clothing or dress; vestiary.
■ Also **vestimental** *adjective* (*rare*) M19.

vestimentiferan /ˌvɛstɪmɛnˈtɪf(ə)rən/ *noun & adjective*. L20.
[from mod. Latin *Vestimentifera* (see below), from Latin *vestimentum* (see VESTMENT) + -I- + -FER: see -AN.]
ZOOLOGY. ►**A** *noun*. A pogonophoran of the order Vestimentifera, members of which are found near hydrothermal vents. L20.
► **B** *adjective*. Of or pertaining to this order. L20.

Vestinian /vɛˈstɪnɪən/ *noun & adjective*. L16.
[from Latin *Vestini* + -AN.]
Hist. ►**A** *noun*. A member of an Oscan people inhabiting the Gran Sasso d'Italia area of ancient Italy; the language of this people. L16.
► **B** *adjective*. Of or pertaining to this people or their language. L16.

vestiture /ˈvɛstɪtjə, -tʃə/ *noun*. LME.
[from medieval Latin *vestitura*, from Latin *vestire* clothe: see VEST *verb*, -URE.]
1 Investiture of a person in office or *with* power etc. *rare*. LME.
2 †a = VESTURE 2. *rare*. Only in LME. ▸**b** Clothes, clothing, dress. *arch*. M19. ▸**c** ENTOMOLOGY. The characteristics of an insect's body-surface, as hairs, scales, etc. *rare*. E20.

vestment /ˈvɛs(t)m(ə)nt/ *noun*. ME.
[Old French *vestiment*, *vestement* (mod. *vêtement*) from Latin *vestimentum* clothing, from *vestire* clothe: see VEST *verb*, -MENT.]
1 A garment, *esp.* a ceremonial or official robe or gown (freq. in *pl.*); *collect.* (now *rare*) clothing, dress. ME.
2 Any of the official robes worn by members of the clergy, choristers, etc., during divine service, *esp.* a chasuble; a priestly robe. Freq. in *pl*. ME.
3 *transf. & fig.* A thing which covers as a garment; a covering. Now *arch. & poet.* L15.

📖 **3** W. HOGARTH Green. . . which colour nature hath chosen for the vestment of the earth.

■ **vestmental** *adjective* (*rare*) vestimentary M19. **vestmented** *adjective* (**a**) (of a person) dressed or robed in vestments; (**b**) (of a service) celebrated or conducted by clergy in vestments: M19.

vestock /ˈvɛstɒk/ *noun*. L20.
[Blend of VEST *noun* and STOCK *noun*[1].]
A clerical stock that extends to the waist.

vestry /ˈvɛstri/ *noun*. LME.
[from Anglo-Norman alt. of Old & mod. French *vestiaire*, †*vestiarie* (see VESTIARY) by assoc. with *-erie* -ERY: see -RY.]
1 A room or area within, or a building attached to, a church or chapel, used for keeping vestments, vessels, records, etc., and as a robing-room. Also ***vestry-room***. LME. ▸**b** A cloakroom, a changing-room. Formerly also, a treasure house. Now *rare*. L16.
2 An assembly or meeting of parishioners, orig. in the vestry of the parish church, to conduct parish business; a body of parishioners meeting in this way. Chiefly *Hist.* L16.

Comb.: **vestry book** a book for recording the proceedings of a parochial vestry or registering the births, marriages, and deaths of the parishioners; **vestryman** a member of a parochial vestry; **vestry-room** = sense 1 above.

■ **vestral** *adjective (rare)* of or pertaining to a vestry or vestries L19.

vestuary /ˈvɛstjʊəri/ *noun. arch.* L15.
[Old French *vestuaire* from medieval Latin *vestuarium* alt. (after *vestura*) of *vestiarium* VESTIARY, VESTRY.]
A vestiary, a vestry; a wardrobe.

vesture /ˈvɛstʃə/ *noun.* ME.
[Old French (mod. *vêture*) from medieval Latin *vestura* for late Latin *vestitura*, from Latin *vestire* clothe: see -URE.]
1 An article of clothing, a garment; *collect.* clothing, dress; *transf. & fig.* a covering. Now *arch.* or *poet.* ME.
2 LAW. All the vegetation growing on or covering land except trees; a product of land, as grass or corn. Now *rare.* LME.
■ **vestural** *adjective* (now *arch.* or *poet.*) of or pertaining to vesture or clothing, vestiary M19. **vestured** *adjective* (now *arch.* or *poet.*) clothed, dressed; covered: E16. **vesturer** *noun* (ECCLESIASTICAL, *rare*) a person responsible for care of clerical vestments and for other church duties L18.

Vesuvian /vɪˈsuːvɪən/ *adjective & noun.* Also (in sense B.2) **v-**. L17.
[from *Vesuvius* (see below) + -AN.]
▶ **A** *adjective.* Of, pertaining to, or resembling (that of) Vesuvius, an active volcano on the Bay of Naples in Italy. L17.
▶ **B** *noun.* **1** MINERALOGY. = VESUVIANITE. L18.
2 A kind of match used esp. for lighting cigars or pipes in the open air. Now chiefly *Hist.* M19.
■ **vesuvianite** *noun* (MINERALOGY) a silicate of calcium, magnesium, and aluminium, occurring as brown, yellow, or green crystals or masses in metamorphosed limestones L19.

vesuvin /vɪˈsuːvɪn/ *noun.* L19.
[German, from *Vesuvius* (see prec.), with allus. to the substance's explosive property: see -IN¹.]
= PHENYLENE **brown.**

Vesuvius /vɪˈsuːvɪəs/ *noun.* M19.
[See VESUVIAN.]
A great explosion of emotion; a thing or person liable to sudden outbursts.

vet /vɛt/ *noun*¹. M19.
[Abbreviation of VETERINARIAN or VETERINARY.]
1 A veterinary surgeon. *colloq.* M19.
2 A doctor of medicine. *slang.* E20.

vet /vɛt/ *noun*². *N. Amer. colloq.* M19.
[Abbreviation.]
A veteran.

🕮 D. DELILLO Officer Walker, a Vietnam vet.

vet /vɛt/ *verb trans.* Infl. **-tt-**. L19.
[from VET *noun*¹.]
1 Submit (an animal) to examination or treatment by a veterinary surgeon. *colloq.* L19.
2 Examine or treat (a person) medically. *slang.* L19.
3 Examine (work, a scheme, person, etc.) carefully and critically for deficiencies or errors; *spec.* investigate the suitability of (a candidate) for a post requiring particular loyalty and trustworthiness. E20.

🕮 **3** *Times* Vassall had been vetted as necessary for his special post. ***positive vetting***: see POSITIVE *adjective*.

■ **vetter** *noun* a person who vets people or things L20.

vetch /vɛtʃ/ *noun.* Also (earlier) †**fetch**. See also FITCH *noun*¹. ME.
[Anglo-Norman *veche* = Old French *vece* (mod. *vesce*), from Latin *vicia*.]
1 The seed of any plant of the genus *Vicia* (see sense 2 below), esp. in ref. to its small size or insignificance. ME.
2 Any of various leguminous plants of the genus *Vicia*, typically climbing plants with tendrils and numerous pairs of opposite leaflets; *spec.* (more fully ***common vetch***) *V. sativa*, which is sometimes grown for fodder (cf. TARE *noun*¹ 2b). Also, any of certain leguminous plants of other genera. LME.
2 ***bitter-vetch***, ***horseshoe-vetch***, ***kidney vetch***, ***milk-vetch***, etc.
■ **vetchy** *adjective (rare)* composed of vetches; having many vetches: L16.

vetchling /ˈvɛtʃlɪŋ/ *noun.* L16.
[from prec. + -LING¹.]
Any of various leguminous plants of the genus *Lathyrus*, allied to the vetches but often with fewer leaflets; *esp.* (in full ***meadow vetchling***, ***yellow vetchling***), *L. pratensis*, a common plant of grassland with yellow flowers.

veteran /ˈvɛt(ə)r(ə)n/ *noun & adjective.* E16.
[Old & mod. French *vétéran* or Latin *veteranus*, from *veter-*, *vetus* old: see -AN.]
▶ **A** *noun.* **1** A person who has grown old in or had long experience of military service; an old soldier. Freq. foll. by *of.* E16. ▸**b** Any ex-serviceman or servicewoman. Chiefly *N. Amer.* L18.
2 A person who has grown old in or had long experience of any office or position; an experienced or aged person. Freq. foll. by *of.* L16.
3 A veteran car. M20.

🕮 **1** W. H. PRESCOTT The Spanish infantry, who in a summer's campaign had acquired the .. weather-beaten aspect of veterans. R. SUTCLIFF He was a veteran of many campaigns, full of old wisdom. **Veterans' Day** 11 November, a public holiday in the US (replacing Armistice Day in 1954) held on the anniversary of the end of the First World War to honour US veterans and victims of all wars. **b** *Guardian* The story of a young Falklands veteran facing up to Aids. **2** D. LODGE Some long-haired, denim-clad veteran of the sixties.

▶ **B** *adjective.* **1** Of, pertaining to, or designating a veteran or veterans; experienced, long-serving. E17.
2 **a** Of a thing: old, long-continued. *rare.* M17. ▸**b** Designating a car made before a certain stipulated date, *spec.* before 1916 or (strictly) before 1905. Cf. VINTAGE *adjective* 2. M20.

🕮 **1** LD MACAULAY His professional skill commanded the respect of veteran officers. *Guardian* The veteran England midfielder is scheduled to play his last match .. on Saturday. **2b** *transf.*: *Guardian* His well-worn veteran Gretsch .. guitar.

veterinarian /vɛt(ə)rɪˈnɛːrɪən/ *noun & adjective.* M17.
[from Latin *veterinarius* (see next) + -AN.]
▶ **A** *noun.* A veterinary surgeon. Now chiefly *N. Amer.* M17.
▶ **B** *adjective.* = VETERINARY *adjective.* M17.

veterinary /ˈvɛt(ə)rɪn(ə)ri, ˈvɛt(ə)nri/ *adjective & noun.* L18.
[Latin *veterinarius*, from *veterinus* pertaining to cattle (*veterinae* (fem. pl.), *veterina* (neut. pl.) cattle) perh. from *veter-*, *vetus* old: see -INE¹, -ARY¹.]
▶ **A** *adjective.* Of, pertaining to, or intended for the diseases and injuries of esp. farm and domestic animals or their treatment. L18.
veterinary surgeon a person qualified to treat the diseases or injuries of esp. farm and domestic animals (freq. abbreviated *vet*).
▶ **B** *noun.* A veterinary surgeon. M19.

vetiver /ˈvɛtɪvə/ *noun.* Also **vetivert**. M19.
[French *vétiver*, *vétyver* from Tamil *veṭṭivēr*, from *vēr* root.]
(The fragrant root of) the cuscus grass, *Vetiveria zizanioides*.

vetkoek /ˈfɛtkʊk/ *noun. S. Afr.* Pl. same, **-s**, **-koeke** /-kʊkə/. E20.
[Afrikaans, from *vet* fat + *koek* cake.]
(A small, unsweetened cake of) deep-fried dough.

veto /ˈviːtəʊ/ *noun & verb.* E17.
[Latin = I forbid, used by Roman tribunes of the people to oppose measures of the Senate or actions of the magistrates.]
▶ **A** *noun.* Pl. **-oes**. A prohibition of a proposed or intended act, esp. a legislative enactment; the right or power of preventing an act in this way. Freq. in ***place a veto on***, ***put a veto on*** (also foll. by *to*). E17.

🕮 M. ARNOLD The bishop claimed .. the right of veto on the appointment of professors. P. H. GIBBS Patricia could not put a veto on Robin's wish to entertain .. friends. *Guardian* Give judges a veto over who could appear .. as advocates. *World Monitor* To .. offset the veto the Big Five powers wield in the Security Council. LIBERUM VETO. ***local veto***: see LOCAL *adjective*. ***pocket veto***: see POCKET *adjective*.

▶ **B** *verb trans.* Put a veto on (a measure etc.), refuse consent to, forbid authoritatively; refuse to admit or accept (a person). E18.

🕮 T. E. MAY Measures passed by the assembly were .. vetoed by the governor. L. M. MONTGOMERY Anne expanded socially, for Marilla .. no longer vetoed occasional outings.

■ **vetoer** *noun* L19. **vetoism** *noun (rare)* exercise or advocacy of the power of veto E19. **vetoist** *noun* a user or advocate of the right or power of veto E19. **vetoˈistic** *adjective* = VETOISTICAL M19. **vetoˈistical** *adjective* pertaining to or tending towards the use of a veto E19.

ve-tsin /veɪˈtsɪn/ *noun.* M20.
[Chinese *wèijīng*, from *wèi* taste, flavour, ingredient + *jīng* refined, essence, extract.]
Monosodium glutamate, as used in Chinese cookery.

vettura /veˈtʊərə, *foreign* vetˈtuːra/ *noun.* Pl. **-re** /-ri, *foreign* -re/. L18.
[Italian from Latin *vectura* transportation, from *vect-* pa. ppl stem of *vehere* convey.]
Chiefly *Hist.* A four-wheeled carriage used in Italy.

vetturino /vɛtʊˈriːnəʊ, *foreign* vettuˈriːno/ *noun.* Pl. **-ni** /-ni/. E17.
[Italian, formed as prec.]
Chiefly *Hist.* **1** In Italy: a person hiring out carriages or horses; a driver of a vettura. E17.
2 A vettura. L18.

vetust /vɛˈtʌst/ *adjective. rare.* E17.
[Latin *vetustus* rel. to *vetus* old.]
Old, ancient.
■ **vetustness** *noun* E18. **vetusty** *noun* ancientness, antiquity M19.

veuve /vəːv; *foreign* vœv (*pl. same*)/ *noun.* L18.
[French.]
1 In France, a widow. Freq. as a title prefixed to a name. L18.

vex /vɛks/ *verb, noun, & adjective.* LME.
[Old & mod. French *vexer* from Latin *vexare* shake, agitate, disturb.]
▶ **A** *verb.* **1** *verb trans.* **a** Trouble or harass by aggression, encroachment, or other interference. Now *rare.* LME. ▸**b** Of a disease etc.: afflict physically, affect with pain or suffering. Now *arch.* or *poet.* LME.
2 *verb trans.* **a** Distress mentally; make anxious or depressed, grieve, worry. LME. ▸**b** Puzzle, confound. E17.
3 *verb trans.* Anger by a slight or petty annoyance; irritate, annoy. LME.
4 *verb intrans.* Be distressed in mind; feel unhappy or dissatisfied, fret. Now *rare* or *obsolete.* L16.
5 *verb trans.* Disturb physically; toss about, agitate, stir up. Now *poet.* E17.
6 *verb trans.* Subject (a matter) to prolonged examination or discussion, debate at (excessive) length. E17.

🕮 **3** *Economist* He recently vexed rumour-mongers .. by declining to disclose Hongkong Bank's inner reserves. S. BUTLER Sorry for having done his lessons so badly and vexed his dear papa. **5** TENNYSON Thro' scudding drifts the rainy Hyades Vex the dim sea.

▶ **B** *noun.* **1** A cause or state of vexation or grief. *Scot.* E19.
2 Distressing or vexing commotion. *rare.* M19.
▶ **C** *adjective.* Vexed, annoyed, irritated. *Black English* (chiefly *W. Indies*). L19.
■ **vexable** *adjective (rare)* †(*a*) troublesome, oppressive; (*b*) able to be vexed: E16. **vexer** *noun* M16. **vexing** *adjective* that vexes someone or something, distressing, annoying, irritating L16. **vexingly** *adverb* M17.

vexata quaestio /vɛkˌsɑːtə ˈkwʌɪstɪəʊ, vɛkˌseɪtə ˈkwiːstɪəʊ/ *noun phr.* Pl. ***-tae -ones*** /-tiː -ˈəʊniːz/. E19.
[Latin.]
A vexed question.

vexation /vɛkˈseɪʃ(ə)n/ *noun.* LME.
[Old & mod. French from Latin *vexatio(n-)*, from *vexat-* pa. ppl stem of *vexare*: see VEX, -ATION.]
The action or an instance of vexing a person or thing; the state of being vexed; a thing or person causing someone to be vexed; (a) grief, (an) affliction; (an) annoyance, (an) irritation.

🕮 I. MURDOCH Ready to burst into tears of embarrassment and vexation. *Sunday Express* He will .. prosper despite credit squeezes, .. the rain, and other vexations.

vexatious /vɛkˈseɪʃəs/ *adjective.* M16.
[from prec. + -IOUS.]
1 Causing or tending to cause vexation, annoyance, or distress; annoying, troublesome. M16.
2 *spec.* in LAW. Of an action: instituted without sufficient grounds for winning purely to cause trouble or annoyance to the defendant. L17.
■ **vexatiously** *adverb* M17. **vexatiousness** *noun* M17. **vexatory** /ˈvɛksət(ə)ri/ *adjective* = VEXATIOUS 1 E20.

vexed /ˈvɛkst/ *adjective.* LME.
[from VEX *verb* + -ED¹.]
1 That has been vexed; troubled, distressed, grieved; annoyed, irritated. Freq. foll. by *at*, *by*, *with*. LME.
2 Of a question, issue, etc.: much debated or contested; difficult to solve, problematic. M17.

🕮 **1** H. JAMES Of course you're vexed at my interfering with you. W. H. AUDEN I must write home or mother will be vexed. **2** J. P. MAHAFFY The great vexed question of the .. composition of the Homeric poems.

■ **vexedly** /ˈvɛksɪdli/ *adverb* M18. **vexedness** *noun (rare)* M18.

vexilla *noun* pl. of VEXILLUM.

vexillary /ˈvɛksɪləri/ *noun.* L16.
[Latin *vexillarius* standard-bearer, formed as VEXILLUM: see -ARY¹.]
ROMAN HISTORY. A class of veterans in the Roman army, serving under a special standard. Also, a standard-bearer.

vexillation /vɛksɪˈleɪʃ(ə)n/ *noun.* M17.
[Latin *vexillatio(n-)*, formed as VEXILLUM: see -ATION.]
ROMAN HISTORY. A company of esp. veteran soldiers grouped under one standard.

vexillator /ˈvɛksɪleɪtə/ *noun.* E19.
[medieval Latin, formed as VEXILLUM: see -OR.]
A banner-bearer in a mystery or miracle play.

vexillology /vɛksɪˈlɒlədʒi/ *noun.* M20.
[formed as next + -OLOGY.]
The study of flags.
■ **vexilloˈlogical** *adjective* M20. **vexillologist** *noun* M20.

vexillum /vɛkˈsɪləm/ *noun.* Pl. **-lla** /-lə/. E18.
[Latin = flag, banner, from *vex-*, *vect-*, *vehere* carry, convey.]
1 **a** ROMAN HISTORY. A military standard or banner, esp. of a maniple; a body of soldiers grouped under this. E18. ▸**b** ECCLESIASTICAL. A small piece of linen or silk attached to the upper part of a crozier. L19.
2 BOTANY. The standard or large uppermost petal of a papilionaceous flower. E18.
3 ORNITHOLOGY. The vane of a feather. M19.

VFA *abbreviation. Austral.*
Victorian Football Association.

VFL *abbreviation. Austral.*
Victorian Football League.

VFR *abbreviation.*
Visual flight rules.

VFW *abbreviation. US.*
Veterans of Foreign Wars.

VG *abbreviation.*
1 Very good.
2 Vicar-General.

VGA *abbreviation.*
COMPUTING. Video graphics array.

VHD *abbreviation.*
Very high frequency.

VHS *abbreviation.*
Video home system, the video system and tape used by domestic video recorders and some camcorders.

VI *abbreviation.*
Virgin Islands.

via /ˈviːə, ˈvʌɪə/ *noun.* E17.
[Latin.]
A way, a road; a highway; *Hist.* any of the major Roman roads. Chiefly in phrs. below.
via affirmativa /əfəːməˈtʌɪvə/ THEOLOGY the approach to God through positive statements about his nature. ***Via Crucis*** /ˈkruːtʃɪs/ (*a*) = *the Way of the Cross* s.v. WAY *noun*; (*b*) *fig.* an extremely painful experience requiring strength or courage to bear. ***Via Dolorosa*** /dɒləˈrəʊzə/ (*a*) the route believed to have been taken by Christ through Jerusalem to Calvary; (*b*) *fig.* = *Via Crucis* (b) above. ***Via Lactea*** /ˈlaktɪə/ ASTRONOMY (now *rare*) the Milky Way. ***via media*** /ˈmiːdɪə/ a middle way; an intermediate course, a compromise. ***via negativa*** /nɛgəˈtʌɪvə/ THEOLOGY the approach to God believing no positive statements can be made about his nature; *transf.* a way of denial.

via /ˈvʌɪə, ˈviːə/ *preposition.* L18.
[Latin, abl. sing. of VIA *noun.*]
1 By way of; by a route passing through or over. L18.
2 By means of; with the aid of. M20.

> **1** *Great Hospitality* My flight . . to Paris took me via Los Angeles. **2** S. CISNEROS Flavio entered my life via a pink circular.

via /ˈvʌɪə/ *interjection.* Long *arch.* L16.
[Italian, formed as prec.]
1 Come on; come along. L16.
2 Go away; begone. L16. ▸**b** Expr. disbelief, derision, etc. L16.

> **1** SIR W. SCOTT Thy death-hour has struck—betake thee to thy sword—Via! **2b** SHAKES. *Merry W.* Ah, ha! Mistress Ford and Mistress Page, have I encompass'd you? Go to; via!

viable /ˈvʌɪəb(ə)l/ *adjective*[1]. E19.
[French, from *vie* from Latin *vita* life: see -ABLE.]
1 Able to live or exist, esp. in a particular place or climate. Esp. of a foetus: able to live at birth. E19. ▸**b** Of a seed or spore: able to germinate. L19.
2 *fig.* Workable, practicable; feasible, esp. economically or financially. M19.

> **2** *Bookseller* British publishers . . rely on coeditions with America to make their books viable.

■ **viaˈbility** *noun*[1] M19. **viably** *adverb* M20.

viable /ˈvʌɪəb(ə)l/ *adjective*[2]. *rare.* M19.
[from VIA *noun* + -ABLE.]
Traversable.
■ **viaˈbility** *noun*[2] L19.

viaduct /ˈvʌɪədʌkt/ *noun.* E19.
[from VIA *noun*, after AQUEDUCT.]
A long elevated structure, often consisting of a series of arches, designed to carry a railway or road over a valley, river, or low-lying ground.
■ **viaducted** *adjective* provided with a viaduct E20.

viaggiatory /vʌɪəˈdʒɛɪt(ə)ri/ *adjective. rare.* M19.
[from Italian *viaggiatore* travelling, from *viaggiare* to travel: see -ORY[2].]
Given to travelling about.

Viagra /vʌɪˈagrə/ *noun.* L20.
[Invented name: perh. influenced by *virile* or *virility*.]
PHARMACOLOGY. (Proprietary name for) the drug sildenafil citrate, taken to enhance erectile function, e.g. in the treatment of male impotence.

> *fig.*: S. KING The effect of judicious cutting is immediate and often amazing—literary Viagra.

vial /ˈvʌɪəl/ *noun.* ME.
[Alt. of PHIAL.]
Orig., a small vessel for holding liquids. Later *spec.*, a small glass bottle, a phial.
■ **vialled** *adjective* contained in a vial M17.

viale /ˈvjale/ *noun.* Pl. ***-li*** /-li/. E20.
[Italian.]
In Italy, a city street, *esp.* a broad one.

viand /ˈvʌɪənd/ *noun. formal.* LME.
[Old & mod. French *viande* †food, (now) meat from Proto-Romance alt. of Latin *vivenda* neut. pl. gerundive of *vivere* live.]
1 An item of food. Now usu. in *pl.*, provisions, victuals. LME.
2 Food. Now *rare.* LME.

> **1** DICKENS A decision . . in favour of veal-cutlet . . . R.W. himself went out to purchase the viand. U. SINCLAIR Two tables . . laden with dishes and cold viands. **2** TENNYSON Before us glow'd Fruit, blossom, viand, amber wine, and gold.

†viander *noun.* ME.
[Anglo-Norman *via(u)ndour*, *viandere* from Old French *viandier(e)*, formed as VIAND: see -ER[2].]
1 A person providing food, entertainment, etc., for a household or guests; a host, esp. of a specified kind. ME–L16.
2 A person fond of good living; a gourmand. M16–L18.
3 A supplier or seller of provisions. L16–E17.

†viatic *noun* see VIATICUM.

viatic /vʌɪˈatɪk/ *adjective. literary. rare.* M17.
[formed as VIATICAL: see -IC.]
Of or pertaining to travel or motion.

viatica *noun* pl. of VIATICUM.

viatical /vʌɪˈatɪk(ə)l/ *adjective.* M19.
[from Latin *viaticus* pertaining to a road or journey, formed as VIA *noun*: see -ATIC, -AL[1].]
Of or pertaining to a way or road; BOTANY growing by roadsides.
Special collocations: **viatical settlement** an arrangement whereby a person with a terminal illness sells his or her life insurance policy to a third party for less than its mature value, in order to benefit from the proceeds while alive.

viaticum /vʌɪˈatɪkəm/ *noun.* Pl. **-ca** /-kə/. Formerly also Anglicized as **†viatic**. M16.
[Latin, use as noun of neut. of *viaticus*: see prec.]
1 CHRISTIAN CHURCH. The Eucharist as administered to a person near or in danger of death. M16.
2 A supply or official allowance of money for a journey; travelling expenses. L16. ▸**b** A supply of food for a journey. M17.

viator /vʌɪˈeɪtə/ *noun.* E16.
[Latin, formed as VIA *noun*: see -OR.]
A traveller.

viatorial /vʌɪəˈtɔːrɪəl/ *adjective. rare.* M18.
[from Latin *viatorius*, formed as prec.: see -IAL.]
Of or pertaining to travel.

vibe /vʌɪb/ *noun & verb.* M20.
[Abbreviation.]
▸ **A** *noun. colloq.*
1 In *pl.* = VIBRAPHONE. M20.
2 = VIBRATION 4. Usu. in *pl.* M20.

> **2** *Time* Pat had bad vibes and knew what was coming.

▸ **B** *verb trans.* Transmit in the form of vibrations (VIBRATION 4); affect in a specified way by means of vibrations (VIBRATION 4). *slang.* L20.
■ **vibist** *noun* (*colloq.*) a player on the vibraphone M20.

vibex /ˈvʌɪbɛks/ *noun.* Pl. **vibices** /vʌɪˈbʌɪsiːz, vɪ-/. Now *rare.* L18.
[Latin = weal.]
MEDICINE. A narrow linear mark or patch on the skin caused by the subcutaneous effusion of blood. Usu. in *pl.*

vibraculum /vʌɪˈbrakjʊləm, vɪ-/ *noun.* Pl. **-la** /-lə/. M19.
[mod. Latin, from Latin *vibrare*: see VIBRATE, -CULE.]
ZOOLOGY. A defensive zooid with a long whiplike seta, found in some bryozoans.
■ **vibracular** *adjective* of, pertaining to, or having vibracula L19.

vibraharp /ˈvʌɪbrəhɑːp/ *noun.* M20.
[from HARP *noun*, after VIBRAPHONE.]
A vibraphone.
■ **vibraharpist** *noun* a player on the vibraharp M20.

Vibram /ˈvʌɪbrəm/ *noun.* M20.
[Origin unkn.]
(Proprietary name for) a kind of moulded rubber sole used on climbing boots; a boot having this sole.

vibrant /ˈvʌɪbr(ə)nt/ *adjective.* M16.
[Latin *vibrant-*, pres. ppl stem of *vibrare* VIBRATE: see -ANT[1].]
1 †**a** Stirred with anger. *rare.* Only in M16. ▸**b** Stirring or tense *with* a specified emotion etc.; full of vitality; flourishing, exuberant. M19. ▸**c** Of a colour: vivid, intense. L20.
2 Moving or acting rapidly; quivering, vibrating. E17.
3 Of a sound: characterized by vibration; resonant. M19.

> **1b** V. L. PARRINGTON Hungry for ideas, intellectually and emotionally vibrant. P. KAVANAGH The air was vibrant with revolutionary feeling. **c** *Country Life* Under the sea where the light plays on vibrant corals, tropical pinks and flamboyant ochres. **3** R. P. WARREN A distant hollow clamor, vibrant as in a cave.

■ **vibrance** *noun* = VIBRANCY M20. **vibrancy** *noun* the condition or quality of being vibrant L19. **vibrantly** *adverb* E20.

vibraphone /ˈvʌɪbrəfəʊn/ *noun.* Also **vibro-**. E20.
[from VIBRA(TO + -PHONE.]
MUSIC. A percussion instrument consisting of a series of tuned metal bars with tubular resonators suspended below, each tube having a motor-driven fan at the top to produce the vibrato effect.
■ **vibraphonist** *noun* a player on the vibraphone E20.

vibraslap /ˈvʌɪbrəslap/ *noun.* L20.
[formed as prec. + SLAP *noun*[2].]
MUSIC. A percussion instrument consisting of a V-shaped metal rod with a vibration box at one end which is vibrated by striking a ball fixed to the other end.

vibrate /vʌɪˈbreɪt/ *verb.* Pa. pple & ppl adjective **-ated**, (earlier) **†-ate**. LME.
[Latin *vibrat-* pa. ppl stem of *vibrare* move rapidly to and fro, brandish, shake, etc.: see -ATE[3].]
▸ **I** *verb trans.* **1** Emit (light, sound, etc.) (as) by vibration. LME.
2 Throw or hurl with vibratory motion. *arch.* M17.
3 Of a pendulum etc.: measure (seconds) by vibration. M17.
4 Cause to move back and forth or up and down rapidly and repeatedly; put in vibration; *spec.* compact (concrete, sand, etc.) with a vibrator. Formerly also (*rare*), brandish (a weapon). M17.

> **1** TENNYSON Star to star vibrates light.

▸ **II** *verb intrans.* **5** Esp. of a pendulum: move or swing to and fro; oscillate. E17. ▸**b** *fig.* Fluctuate *between* two extremes or *from* one extreme *to* another; vacillate. L18.
6 Move back and forth or up and down rapidly and repeatedly; quiver, shake, tremble. Also foll. by *with*. E18. ▸**b** *spec.* in PHYSICS, undergo vibration (VIBRATION 2a). L18.
7 (Of a sound) resonate, resound, continue to be heard; *fig.* move through or throughout, circulate. Also foll. by *in*, *on*, *through*, etc. M18.

> **6** N. CALDER An earthquake could set the planet vibrating. S. MIDDLETON Now his body shook, vibrated with anger. **7** BYRON He hears The clang of tumult vibrate on his ears. *Dance* Those supercharged roles . . still vibrate in the memories of many New Yorkers.

¶ Not recorded between LME and E17.
■ ˈ**vibrative** *adjective* (now *rare*) vibrating, vibratory M17.

vibratile /ˈvʌɪbrətʌɪl/ *adjective.* E19.
[Alt. of VIBRATORY by substitution of suffix -ATILE, after *pulsatile* etc.]
1 = VIBRATORY 1. E19.
2 ZOOLOGY. Of cilia etc.: having the capacity for vibration; characterized by rapid and constant oscillatory motion. M19.
■ **vibraˈtility** *noun* M18.

vibration /vʌɪˈbreɪʃ(ə)n/ *noun.* M17.
[Latin *vibratio(n-)*, formed as VIBRATE: see -ATION.]
1 *gen.* The action of vibrating or moving to and fro rapidly and repeatedly; an instance of this, a vibrating or tremulous movement. M17.
2 a PHYSICS. The rapid alternating or reciprocating motion about an equilibrium in the particles of an elastic body, as produced in air by the propagation of sound; the motion in the particles of a body by which sound is produced; a single cycle of this. M17. ▸**b** A supposed movement of this kind in the nerves, formerly believed to be the means by which sensory nerve impulses are transmitted to the brain. *obsolete* exc. *Hist.* E18.
3 The action of vacillating or fluctuating between extremes; an instance of this. L18.
4 A characteristic signal or impression about a person or thing, regarded as communicable to others; (an) atmosphere. Also, a mental (esp. occult) influence. Usu. in *pl.* L19.

> **1** T. C. WOLFE He felt a slight vibration in the massive walls around him. D. SHIELDS A whisper . . . Sibilant speech with little or no vibration of the vocal cords. **3** J. H. BURTON The same restlessness . . the same vibration between anarchy and abject submission. **4** T. K. WOLFE Something's getting up tight, there's bad vibrations. M. ROBERTS I must not attempt to approach too closely to the apparition lest I violate the vibrations surrounding her.

Comb.: **vibration damper** a device for damping vibration; *esp.* one for counteracting torsional vibration in a crankshaft; **vibration white finger** MEDICINE Raynaud's syndrome caused by prolonged use of vibrating hand tools or machinery.
■ **vibrationless** *adjective* L19.

vibrational /vʌɪˈbreɪʃ(ə)n(ə)l/ *adjective*. **L19.**
[from prec. + -AL[1].]
Of or pertaining to vibration; vibratory; *spec.* in PHYSICS, involving or resulting from particular modes of vibration or oscillation of the atoms in a molecule.
vibrational number MUSIC (now *rare*) = FREQUENCY 4b.
■ **vibrationally** *adverb* **M20.**

vibratiuncle /ˌvʌɪbreɪʃɪˈʌŋk(ə)l/ *noun*. **M18.**
[from VIBRATI(ON + -UNCLE.]
A minute or slight vibration.

vibrato /vɪˈbrɑːtəʊ/ *adverb & noun*. **M19.**
[Italian, pa. pple of *vibrare* vibrate.]
MUSIC. ▶**A** *adverb*. With a rapid slight variation in pitch. **M19.**
▶**B** *noun*. Pl. **-os**. A rapid slight variation in pitch in the singing or playing of a note. Cf. TREMOLO *noun* 1. **L19.**
■ **vibratoless** *adjective* without vibrato **L20.**

vibrator /vʌɪˈbreɪtə/ *noun*. **M19.**
[from VIBRATE + -OR.]
1 Any of the vibrating reeds of an organ etc. by which the sound is produced. **M19.**
2 Any of various instruments or parts which have or cause a vibratory motion; *spec.* (**a**) a machine for compacting concrete by vibration before it sets; (**b**) a small electrical device used in massage or for sexual stimulation. **L19.**

vibratory /ˈvʌɪbrət(ə)ri, vʌɪˈbreɪt(ə)ri/ *adjective*. **E18.**
[from VIBRATE + -ORY[2].]
1 Having the capacity or property of vibrating; exhibiting or characterized by vibration. **E18.**
2 Causing or producing vibration. **M18.**
3 Of or pertaining to vibration. **M19.**

vibrio /ˈvɪbrɪəʊ, ˈvʌɪbrɪəʊ/ *noun*. Also **V-**. Pl. **-os**, **-ones** /-ˈəʊniːz/. **M19.**
[mod. Latin *Vibrio* (see below), from Latin *vibrare* VIBRATE, after French *vibrion*.]
†**1** ZOOLOGY. A minute nematode worm of the former genus *Vibrio*. Only in **M19.**
2 MEDICINE & BACTERIOLOGY. A motile water-borne Gram-negative bacterium of the widespread genus *Vibrio* or a related genus, usu. occurring as curved flagellated rods, and including pathogens causing cholera, gastroenteritis, and septicaemia. Also more widely, any curved rod-shaped bacterium. **M19.**
■ **vibrioˈcidal** *adjective* (MEDICINE) destructive to vibrios **M20.** **vibrioid** *adjective* belonging or allied to the genus *Vibrio*; of a curved rod-shape with a slight helical twist: **M19.** **vibriˈonic** *adjective* (now *rare*) of, pertaining to, or caused by vibrios **M19.** **vibriˈosis** *noun*, pl. **-oses** /-ˈəʊsiːz/, VETERINARY MEDICINE infection with, or a disease caused by, vibrios **M20.**

vibrion /ˈvɪbrɪɒn/ *noun*. Now *rare*. **M19.**
[French: see prec.]
†**1** BIOLOGY. A vibratile filament or cilium. Only in **M19.**
2 BACTERIOLOGY. A vibrio or related bacterium. **L19.**

vibriones *noun pl.* see VIBRIO.

vibrissa /vʌɪˈbrɪsə/ *noun*. Pl. **-ssae** /-siː/. **L17.**
[Latin, from *vibrare* VIBRATE.]
1 Any of a number of long stiff hairs growing about the mouth or elsewhere on the face of many mammals, used as an organ of touch; a whisker; a nostril hair. Usu. in *pl.* **L17.**
2 ORNITHOLOGY. Each of the coarse bristle-like feathers growing about the gape of certain birds that catch insects in flight. Usu. in *pl.* **L19.**

vibro- /ˈvʌɪbrəʊ/ *combining form* of Latin *vibrare* VIBRATE: see -O-.
■ **vibrogram** *noun* a record produced by a vibrograph **M20.** **vibrograph** *noun* (**a**) *Hist.* a phonautograph; (**b**) an instrument for measuring or recording mechanical vibrations: **L19.** **vibˈrometer** *noun* a vibrograph that measures the amplitude of vibrations **L19.** **vibroscope** *noun* (*obsolete* exc. *Hist.*) an early type of vibrograph **L19.** **vibroˈtactile** *adjective* of, pertaining to, or involving the perception of vibration through touch **M20.**

vibronic /vʌɪˈbrɒnɪk/ *adjective*. **M20.**
[from VIBR(ATIONAL + ELECTR)ONIC.]
PHYSICS. Of or pertaining to electronic energy levels or transitions associated with the vibration of the constituent atoms of a molecule.
■ **vibronically** *adverb* **M20.**

vibrophone *noun* var. of VIBRAPHONE.

viburnum /vɪˈbəːnəm, vʌɪ-/ *noun*. **M18.**
[mod. Latin use as genus name of Latin = wayfaring-tree.]
Any of numerous Eurasian and N. American shrubs constituting the genus *Viburnum*, of the honeysuckle family, which have terminal clusters of small white or pink flowers; *esp.* one grown for ornament, as the wayfaring-tree, *V. lantana*, or the guelder rose, *V. opulus*.

vic /vɪk/ *noun*. **E20.**
[Arbitrary syllable.]
1 Used for *v* in telephone communications and in the oral spelling of code messages. **E20.**
2 MILITARY. A V-formation of aircraft. **M20.**

Vic. *abbreviation*.
Victoria.

vicar /ˈvɪkə/ *noun*. **ME.**
[Anglo-Norman *vicare*, *vikere* from Old & mod. French *vicaire* (now) assistant curate, deputy, from Latin *vicarius* substitute, deputy, from *vic-*: see VICE *noun*[4] & *preposition*, -AR[2].]
1 CHRISTIAN CHURCH. A person regarded as an earthly representative of God or Christ; *spec.* (**a**) the Pope; (**b**) St Peter. Also, Christ or the Holy Spirit regarded as representing God. **ME.**
2 Orig., a person ministering to a parish in place of the rector, or as the representative of a religious community to which the tithes had been passed. Later, in the Anglican Church, the incumbent of a parish of which the tithes were formerly passed to a chapter, religious house, or layman (cf. RECTOR 2); now also (in full ***team vicar***), a priest who is a member of a team ministry. **ME.**
3 In an Episcopal Church, a member of the clergy deputizing for another (esp. a bishop) in the performance of ecclesiastical functions; *spec.* (ROMAN CATHOLIC CHURCH) a bishop's deputy. Also with specifying adjective, as ***papal vicar***, ***vicar episcopal***, etc. **LME.**
4 More fully ***vicar choral***. A member of the clergy or choir appointed to sing certain parts of a cathedral service. **LME.**
5 *gen.* A person deputizing for another, esp. in administrative functions. Also (*rare*), a thing substituted for another. **LME.**
Phrases: **lay vicar** = sense 4 above. ***team vicar***: see sense 2 above. **vicar apostolic** ROMAN CATHOLIC CHURCH a missionary; a titular bishop. ***vicar choral***: see sense 4 above. **Vicar of Bray** [with allus. to a 16th-cent. vicar of Bray in Berkshire, popularly believed to have changed religion several times] a person who readily changes his or her principles according to circumstances. **Vicar of Christ** the Pope.
■ **vicarate** *noun* = VICARIATE *noun* 3b **L19.** **vicarish** *adjective* appropriate to or characteristic of a vicar **M20.** **vicarship** *noun* the office or position of a vicar **M16.**

vicarage /ˈvɪk(ə)rɪdʒ/ *noun*. **LME.**
[App. from prec. + -AGE: cf. Anglo-Latin *vicaragium*.]
1 The benefice or living of a vicar. **LME.**
2 The residence of a vicar; *transf.* those living in this. **M16.**
†**3** (A) payment due to a vicar; a tithe or tithes. *Scot.* **L16–E19.**
†**4** The office or position of a vicar. *rare*. **E17–M18.**
Comb.: **vicarage tea party** *transf.* a mild or innocuous event.

vicaress /ˈvɪk(ə)rɪs/ *noun*. **E17.**
[from VICAR + -ESS[1].]
1 A sister ranking immediately below the Abbess or Mother Superior in a convent. **E17.**
2 A female vicar or representative. *rare*. **M17.**
3 The wife of a parish vicar. **L18.**

vicar-general /vɪkəˈdʒen(ə)r(ə)l/ *noun*. **LME.**
[from VICAR + GENERAL, after medieval Latin *vicarius generalis*.]
†**1** (A title of) the Pope. **LME–M17.**
2 ROMAN CATHOLIC CHURCH. An ecclesiastical officer assisting or representing a bishop in matters of jurisdiction or administration. **LME.** ▸**b** In the Anglican Church, a lay official serving as a deputy or assistant to a bishop or Archbishop. **M16.**
3 *Hist.* (The title of) Thomas Cromwell (*c* 1485–1540) as the King's representative in ecclesiastical affairs. **L17.**
■ **vicar-generalship** *noun* the office or position of a vicar-general **L16.**

vicariad /vɪˈkɛːrɪad/ *noun*. **M20.**
[formed as VICARIANT + -AD[1].]
ECOLOGY. = VICARIANT *noun*.

vicarial /vɪˈkɛːrɪəl, vʌɪ-/ *adjective*. **E17.**
[from VICAR + -IAL, after *ministerial*.]
1 Delegated, deputed. **E17.**
2 Of or pertaining to a vicar or vicars. **M18.**
3 Holding the office of a vicar. **E19.**

vicarian /vɪˈkɛːrɪən, vʌɪ-/ *noun & adjective*. **L16.**
[Late Latin *vicarianus* of a deputy, formed as VICARIOUS: see -IAN.]
▶**A** *noun*. †**1** A substitute, a deputy. *rare*. Only in **L16.**
2 A person believing a person, esp. the Pope or a priest, to be an earthly representative of God. **M19.**
▶**B** *adjective*. Of, pertaining to, or governed by a deputy. **M17.**

vicariance /vɪˈkɛːrɪəns/ *noun*. **M20.**
[formed as next + -ANCE.]
BIOLOGY. The existence of vicariant forms; the subdivision of a population into distinct but related species etc. by the appearance of a geographical barrier.

vicariant /vɪˈkɛːrɪənt, vʌɪ-/ *noun & adjective*. **M20.**
[from Latin *vicarius* (see VICAR) + -ANT[1].]
BIOLOGY. ▶**A** *noun*. A species, variety, etc., of plant or animal forming the counterpart in one area or on one soil to a closely related form native to another area or a different soil, the two being considered to have evolved from a common ancestor. **M20.**
▶**B** *adjective*. That is a vicariant or exhibits vicariance. **M20.**

vicariate /vɪˈkɛːrɪət, vʌɪ-/ *noun*. **E17.**
[medieval Latin *vicariatus*, from Latin *vicarius*: see VICAR, -ATE[1].]
1 CHRISTIAN CHURCH. The office or authority of a vicar. **E17.**
2 The office or authority of a deputy or deputizing body. **E17.**
3 a A district governed by a deputy governor. **M18.** ▸**b** CHRISTIAN CHURCH. A church or parish ministered to by a vicar. **M18.** ▸**c** ROMAN CATHOLIC CHURCH. The see of a vicar apostolic. **E19.**

vicariate /vɪˈkɛːrɪət, vʌɪ-/ *adjective*. Long *rare* or *obsolete*. **E17.**
[from Latin *vicarius* (see VICAR) or from prec.: see -ATE[2].]
= VICARIOUS 2b.

vicariism /vɪˈkɛːrɪɪz(ə)m, vʌɪ-/ *noun*. Also **vicarism** /ˈvɪkərɪz(ə)m/. **M20.**
[formed as VICARIANT + -ISM.]
BIOLOGY. = VICARIANCE.

vicarious /vɪˈkɛːrɪəs, vʌɪ-/ *adjective*. **M17.**
[Latin *vicarius*: see VICAR, -ARIOUS.]
1 That acts in place of another thing or person; that is a substitute. **M17.**
2 Performed, accomplished, or undergone by or on behalf of another. **L17.** ▸**b** Of power, authority, etc.: held or exercised by a deputy; delegated, deputed. **E18.** ▸**c** Experienced in the imagination through another person or agency. **E20.**
3 PHYSIOLOGY. Designating or pertaining to the performance by or through one organ of functions normally discharged by another; substitutive. **L18.**
4 Of, pertaining to, or involving substitution. **M19.**
5 BIOLOGY. = VICARIANT *adjective*. **M20.**

> **2** J. L. ESPOSITO Unlike Christianity, there is no vicarious suffering or atonement for humankind. **c** R. K. NARAYAN The old lady . . seemed to get a vicarious thrill out of my romance. D. SIMPSON 'He was burnt to death.' Her fists clenched in vicarious pain.

■ **vicariously** *adverb* **L18.** **vicariousness** *noun* **E18.**

vicarism *noun* var. of VICARIISM.

†**vicary** *noun*. **LME–E18**
[Old French *vicarie* or medieval Latin *vicaria*, from Latin *vicarius*: see VICAR, -Y[3].]
The office or position of a vicar, a vicarship. Also, a benefice held by a vicar.

Vicat /ˈviːkɑː/ *noun*. **E20.**
[Louis Joseph *Vicat* (1786–1861), French engineer.]
ENGINEERING. Used *attrib.* with ref. to an apparatus for measuring the consistency and setting time of Portland cement and other materials.

vice /vʌɪs/ *noun*[1]. **ME.**
[Old & mod. French from Latin *vitium*.]
1 Extreme moral corruption; depravity; evil; grossly immoral or degrading habits or conduct. **ME.** ▸**b** An instance of this; an immoral or degrading habit or practice, *esp.* one involving prostitution, drugs, etc. **ME.** ▸**c** A character in a morality play representing (a) vice. *obsolete* exc. *Hist.* **M16.** ▸**d** *ellipt.* = ***vice squad*** below. *slang*. **M20.**
2 A defect in personal character or conduct, or in the action or constitution of a thing; a fault, a flaw. **ME.** ▸**b** A physical defect or weakness; a blemish, a deformity. **LME.** ▸**c** A bad habit or fault in a horse. **E18.**
3 Viciousness, harmfulness. Now *rare*. **M19.**

> **1** BYRON Vice cannot fix, and virtue cannot change . . For vice must have variety. C. CONNOLLY We pay for vice by the knowledge that we are wicked. **b** TENNYSON Doubling all his master's vice of pride. **2** D. H. LAWRENCE Not that James had any vices. He did not drink or smoke. *Times of India* In some cases, custodial interrogation was necessary, despite its many vices. **b vice of conformation** MEDICINE (now *rare*) a congenital deformity.

Comb.: **vice ring** a group of criminals involved in organized prostitution; **vice squad** a division of a police force appointed to enforce laws relating to prostitution, drug abuse, illegal gambling, etc.
■ **viceless** *adjective* **M16.**

vice /vʌɪs/ *noun*[2] & *verb*. Also ***vise**. **ME.**
[Old & mod. French *vis* from Latin *vitis* vine (stem), tendril, plant with tendrils.]
▶**A** *noun*. **1** A screw, a winch; a device operated with a screw. Formerly also *gen.*, any mechanical device. Now *rare* or *obsolete*. **ME.** ▸†**b** A tap or stopper for a vessel. **M16–M17.**
2 A spiral staircase. Long *arch.* **LME.**
3 A device consisting of two jaws moved by turning a screw, used to clamp an object being filed, sawn, etc., in position and freq. attached to a workbench. **E16.** ▸**b** A tool used to draw lead into calms, in making lattice windows. **E18.**

> **3** *Practical Woodworking* Support the wood end-up in the jaws of a vice.

▶**B** *verb*. †**1** *verb trans.* Fix *on* with a screw. *rare*. Only in **M16.**

2 *verb trans.* Secure in a vice; squeeze or press tightly (as) in a vice. Freq. as *viced ppl adjective.* **E17.**

> 📖 **2** M. S. POWER Sitting on the bottom step of the altar, the ciborium viced between his knees.

▪ **vicelike** *adjective* resembling (that of) a vice; holding or squeezing firmly: **M19.**

vice /vʌɪs/ *noun*^{3}. Long *obsolete* exc. *dial.* **LME.**
[Aphet.]
Advice.

vice /*as noun* vʌɪs, *as preposition* ˈvʌɪsiː/ *noun*^{4} *& preposition.* **M16.**
[Latin, abl. of *vix* (recorded in oblique forms in *vic-*) change, place, stead.]
▶ **A** *noun.* Chiefly *SCOTS LAW* (now *Hist.*).
1 A person's stead; the place *of* another. **M16.**
†**2** A turn in a sequence or succession. **M17–E19.**
▶ **B** *preposition.* In place of; in succession to. **L18.**

> 📖 THACKERAY He was gardener and out-door man, vice Upton, resigned.

vice /vʌɪs/ *noun*^{5}. **L16.**
[Absol. use of VICE-.]
A person acting as a substitute or deputy, as a vice-chairman, a vice-president, etc.

> 📖 DICKENS Thinking of the many Chancellors and Vices, and Masters of the Rolls, who are deceased.

vice- /vʌɪs/ *combining form.*
[Repr. Latin *vice* in place of.]
1 Forming nouns with the senses 'acting as a substitute or deputy for', 'next in rank to', as ***vice-abbot***, ***vice-captain***, ***vice-cardinal***, etc.
2 Forming nouns with the sense 'of, pertaining to, or administered by a substitute or deputy', as ***vice-chair***, ***vice-government***, etc.
▪ **vice-ˈchamberlain** *noun* a deputy chamberlain; *spec.* the deputy of the Lord Chamberlain: **M16.** **vice-ˈconsul** *noun* †(*a*) *ROMAN HISTORY* a proconsul; (*b*) the deputy of a consul: **M16.** **vice-ˈconsular** *adjective* of or pertaining to a vice-consul **M19.** **vice-ˈconsulate** *noun* = VICE-CONSULSHIP **E19.** **vice-ˈconsulship** *noun* the office or position of vice-consul; the term of office of a vice-consul: **L16.** **vice-god** *noun* a person regarded as an earthly representative or minister of God **E17.** **vice-ˈgovernor** *noun* an official who ranks below or deputizes for a governor **L16.** **vice-king** *noun* (now *rare*) a ruler exercising authority on behalf of a king; a viceroy: **L16.** **vice-ˈlegate** *noun* the representative or deputy of a legate, esp. a papal legate **M16.** **vice-ˈlegateship** *noun* the office or position of vice-legate **L17.** **vice-queen** *noun* (now *rare*) = VICEREINE **L16.** **vice-ˈrector** *noun* a deputy rector, esp. of a theological college **E17.** **vice-ˈregent** *noun* the deputy of a regent **M16.** **vice-ˈwarden** *noun* a deputy warden **M16.**

vice admiral /vʌɪs ˈadm(ə)r(ə)l/ *noun phr.* **E16.**
[Anglo-Norman *visadmirail*, Old French *visamiral* (mod. *viceamiral*), formed as VICE-, ADMIRAL.]
1 *Hist.* Any of various senior admiralty officers appointed, *spec.* one appointed to administer maritime law. **E16.**
2 A naval officer ranking below an admiral and above a rear admiral. **E16.**
†**3** A ship commanded by a vice admiral. **L16–E18.**
▪ **vice-admiralty** *noun* (*obsolete* exc. *Hist.*) the office, charge, or jurisdiction of a vice admiral **E17.**

vice anglais /vis ɑ̃glɛ/ *noun phr.* **M20.**
[French, lit. 'English vice'.]
A vice considered characteristic of the English; *esp.* the use of corporal punishment for sexual stimulation.

vice-chancellor /vʌɪsˈtʃɑːns(ə)lə/ *noun.* **LME.**
[from VICE- + CHANCELLOR.]
The deputy of a chancellor; *spec.* (*a*) the cardinal at the head of the papal Chancery; (*b*) orig. (now *Hist.*), each of a group of higher judges in the former Court of Chancery; now, the head of the Chancery division of the High Court of Justice; (*c*) the acting representative of the Chancellor of a university, discharging most of the administrative duties.
▪ **vice-chancellorship** *noun* the office or position of vice-chancellor; the period of office of a vice-chancellor: **L16.**

vice-comital /vʌɪsˈkɒmɪt(ə)l/ *adjective.* **M19.**
[from VICE-COUNTY after COMITAL.]
Of or pertaining to a vice-county (VICE-COUNTY 2) or vice-counties.

vice-county /vʌɪsˈkaʊnti/ *noun.* **M17.**
[from VICE- + COUNTY *noun*^{1}.]
†**1** = VISCOUNTY 1. **M17–E18.**
2 Any of a set of numbered divisions of Great Britain and Ireland, corresponding to counties or parts of counties, established as units for plant recording (now used also for animal recording). **M19.**

vicegerent /vʌɪsˈdʒɪər(ə)nt, -ˈdʒɛː-/ *noun & adjective.* **M16.**
[medieval Latin *vicegerent-*, *-gerens* deputy, formed as VICE-, GERENT.]
▶ **A** *noun.* **1** A person exercising delegated power on behalf of a sovereign or ruler. **M16.** ▸**b** *gen.* A person appointed to discharge the office of another. **M16.** ▸**c** A ruler *of* a country etc. through delegated power. **L16.**
2 A ruler, priest, etc., regarded as an earthly representative of God or a god; *spec.* the Pope. **M16.**
3 A thing acting as a substitute. **L16.**
▶ **B** *adjective.* That is a vicegerent; characterized by or exercising delegated power. **L16.**
▪ **vicegerence** *noun* (now *rare*) = VICEGERENCY **E16.** **vicegerency** *noun* (*a*) the (period of) office of a vicegerent; the fact of exercising delegated power; (*b*) a district or province ruled by a vicegerent: **L16.**

vicenary /ˈvɪs(ə)n(ə)ri, ˈvʌɪ-/ *noun & adjective. rare.* **E17.**
[Latin *vicenarius*, from *viceni* distrib. of *viginti* twenty: see -ARY^{1}.]
▶† **A** *noun.* A military commander of twenty men. Only in **E17.**
▶ **B** *adjective.* = VIGESIMAL. **E18.**

vicennial /vʌɪˈsɛnɪəl/ *adjective.* **M18.**
[from Latin *vicennium* period of twenty years, from *vic-* stem of *vicies* twenty times + *annus* year: see -AL^{1}.]
Lasting for twenty years (chiefly *SCOTS LAW*); occurring every twenty years.

Vicentine /vɪˈsɛntʌɪn/ *noun & adjective.* **E17.**
[Italian *vicentino*, from *Vicenza*: see below, -INE^{1}.]
▶ **A** *noun.* A native or inhabitant of Vicenza, a city in northern Italy. **E17.**
▶ **B** *adjective.* Of or pertaining to Vicenza or the Vicentines. **M17.**

vice-president /vʌɪsˈprɛzɪd(ə)nt/ *noun.* **E16.**
[from VICE- + PRESIDENT *noun.*]
A person representing or deputizing for a president; an official who ranks immediately below a president.
▪ **vice-presidency** *noun* the position or office of vice-president; the term of office of a vice-president: **E19.** **vice-presiˈdential** *adjective* **M19.** **vice-presidentship** *noun* = VICE-PRESIDENCY **L17.**

viceregal /vʌɪsˈriːg(ə)l/ *adjective.* **M19.**
[from VICE- + REGAL *adjective.*]
Of, pertaining to, or characteristic of a viceroy.

vicereine /ˈvʌɪsreɪn/ *noun.* **E19.**
[French, from *vice-* VICE- + *reine* queen.]
The wife of a viceroy. Also, a female viceroy.

viceroy /ˈvʌɪsrɔɪ/ *noun.* **E16.**
[Old French *viceroy*, *vis-* (mod. *viceroi*), from *vice-* VICE- + †*roy*, *roi* king.]
1 A ruler of a colony, province, etc., exercising authority on behalf of a sovereign. **E16.** ▸**b** *transf.* A person in a position of high authority; *esp.* one acting on behalf of another. **L16.**
2 A N. American nymphalid butterfly, *Limenitis archippus*, that closely mimics the monarch in appearance and behaviour. Also called ***mimic***. **L19.**
▪ **viceroyal** *adjective* /ˈvʌɪsrɔɪəl, vʌɪsˈrɔɪəl/ = VICEREGAL **E18.** **viceroyship** *noun* = VICEROYALTY **E17.**

viceroyalty /ˈvʌɪsrɔɪəlti, vʌɪsˈrɔɪəlti/ *noun.* **E18.**
[French *vice-royauté*, from *vice-* VICE- + *royauté* ROYALTY.]
1 The office, position, or authority of a viceroy; *transf.* the household of a viceroy. **E18.**
2 A territory governed by a viceroy. **E18.**
3 The period of office of a viceroy. **E18.**

vicesimal /vʌɪˈsɛsɪm(ə)l/ *adjective. rare.* **M17.**
[from Latin *vicesimus* twentieth, from *viceni*: see VICENARY, -AL^{1}.]
= VIGESIMAL.

vice-treasurer /vʌɪsˈtrɛʒ(ə)rə/ *noun.* **M16.**
[from VICE- + TREASURER.]
The deputy or representative of a treasurer; *Hist.* a British Government official acting in this capacity in Ireland.
▪ **vice-treasurership** *noun* the office or position of vice-treasurer **L17.**

vice versa /vʌɪsə ˈvəːsə, vʌɪs/ *adverbial phr.* **E17.**
[Latin, lit. 'the position being reversed', formed as VICE *noun*^{4} & *preposition* + *versa* abl. fem. sing. of *versus* pa. pple of *vertere*: see VERSATILE.]
With a reversal of the order of terms or conditions mentioned; contrariwise, conversely.

> 📖 S. BRETT The Live terminal had been attached where the Neutral should have been and vice versa.

vicey-versey /vʌɪsɪˈvəːsi/ *noun.* **M19.**
[Repr. a colloq. or joc. pronunc.]
= VICE VERSA.

Vichy /ˈviːʃi/ *noun & adjective.* **M19.**
[A town in central France.]
▶ **A** *noun.* **1** In full ***Vichy water***. A mineral water obtained from springs in the area around Vichy. **M19.**
2 *Hist.* The government of France administered from Vichy in collaboration with the Germans from 1940 to 1944. **M20.**
▶ **B** *attrib.* or as *adjective. Hist.* Of, pertaining to, or supporting the French government in Vichy. **M20.**
▪ **Vichyist** *noun* (*Hist.*) a supporter of the Vichy government **M20.** **Vichyite** *noun & adjective* (*Hist.*) (*a*) *noun* = VICHYIST; (*b*) *adjective* supporting the Vichy government: **M20.**

vichyssoise /viːʃiːˈswɑːz/ *noun.* **M20.**
[French *crème vichyssoise glacée* lit. 'iced cream soup of Vichy'.]
A soup made with potatoes, leeks, and cream, and usu. served cold.

Vici /ˈvʌɪsʌɪ, ˈviːki/ *noun.* **L19.**
[Perh. from Latin *vici* pa. t. of *vincere* conquer.]
More fully ***Vici kid***. A chrome-tanned kid leather used for shoes and boots.

vicinage /ˈvɪsɪnɪdʒ/ *noun.* **ME.**
[Old French *vis(e)nage*, *visné* (mod. VOISINAGE) from Proto-Gallo-Romance alt. of Latin *vicinus* neighbour.]
1 = VICINITY 3. **ME.** ▸**b** *transf.* The people living in a particular vicinity or neighbourhood. **M17.**
2 = VICINITY 1. **L16.**
1 in the vicinage of = *in the vicinity of* s.v. VICINITY 3.

vicinal /ˈvɪsɪn(ə)l, vɪˈsʌɪn(ə)l/ *adjective.* **E17.**
[French, or Latin *vicinalis*, from *vicinus* (as noun) neighbour, (as adjective) neighbouring: see -AL^{1}.]
1 Of or pertaining to a neighbour or neighbours; (esp. of a railway or road) serving a neighbourhood, local. **E17.**
2 Neighbouring, adjacent. **M18.** ▸**b** *MATH. & CRYSTALLOGRAPHY.* Nearly coincident with a given plane or face. *rare.* **L19.** ▸**c** *CHEMISTRY.* Of substituted groups or atoms: in neighbouring or adjacent positions on a carbon ring or chain. **L19.**

vicine /ˈvɪsiːn, ˈvʌɪ-/ *adjective.* Long *rare.* **E16.**
[Latin *vicinus*: see prec., -INE^{1}.]
Neighbouring, adjacent.

vicinism /ˈvɪsɪnɪz(ə)m/ *noun.* **E20.**
[from Latin *vicinus* (see VICINAL) + -ISM.]
BOTANY. A tendency to variation caused by natural crossing with related forms growing nearby.

vicinity /vɪˈsɪnɪti/ *noun.* **M16.**
[Latin *vicinitas*, from *vicinus*: see VICINAL, -ITY.]
1 The state, condition, or quality of being near in space; proximity. **M16.**
†**2** Similarity, resemblance; affinity. **M16–L17.**
3 The area within a limited distance from a place; a nearby or surrounding district; *the* neighbourhood. **M16.**

> 📖 **3** N. SHUTE A ship in the vicinity that could help. W. STYRON An ex-farmer from the vicinity of Miastoko, in the far north. **in the vicinity (of)** in the area or neighbourhood (of); near (to), approximately.

vicious /ˈvɪʃəs/ *adjective & noun.* Also (*arch.*) **vitious**. **ME.**
[Old French (mod. *vicieux*) from Latin *vitiosus*, from *vitium* VICE *noun*^{1}: see -IOUS.]
▶ **A** *adjective.* **1** Of, pertaining to, or characterized by vice or immorality; depraved, immoral; profligate. **ME.**
2 Morally or practically condemnable; reprehensible, blameworthy. **LME.**
3 *LAW.* Not satisfying legal requirements; legally flawed or invalid. Now *rare* or *obsolete.* **LME.**
4 *gen.* Impaired or weakened by a defect; faulty, unsound; (of language etc.) corrupt, debased. **LME.** ▸†**b** Of a person: wrong, mistaken. *rare* (Shakes.). Only in **E17.**
5 Noxious, harmful to health; foul. Long *rare* or *obsolete.* **L16.** ▸†**b** Of a part of the body: diseased. **E17–M18.**
6 **a** Of an animal: inclined to be savage or bad-tempered. **E18.** ▸**b** Malignantly bitter or severe; malicious, spiteful, violent; *transf.* (of weather) severe, inclement. **E19.**

> 📖 **1** BURKE His practical and speculative morals were vitious in the extreme. G. GREENE The most vicious men have sometimes narrowly evaded sanctity. **4** *Times Lit. Suppl.* It would make for vicious illation, proving Brown's 'detached perspective' a cloak for myopia. **b** SHAKES. *Oth.* Though I perchance am vicious in my guess. **6a** A. CARTER The rats grew fat as piglets and vicious as hyenas. **b** *Time* Described as the most vicious Mob boss of his generation. *Vanity Fair* The increasingly vicious threats Liman was receiving.

Special collocations: **vicious abstraction** *PHILOSOPHY* the abstraction of one quality or term from a thing at the expense of others. ***vicious circle***: see CIRCLE *noun* 12. **vicious cycle** = CIRCLE *noun* 12. ***vicious intromission***: see INTROMISSION 1. **vicious spiral** an undesirable progression of dependent causes and effects; *esp.* a cumulative rise in prices and wages.
▶ **B** *absol.* as *noun pl. The* people who are vicious, as a class. **LME.**
▪ **viciously** *adverb* **ME.** **viciousness** *noun* **LME.**

vicissitude /vɪˈsɪsɪtjuːd, vʌɪ-/ *noun.* **M16.**
[Old & mod. French, or Latin *vicissitudo*, from *vicissim* by turns, from *vic-*: see VICE *noun*^{4} *& preposition*, -TUDE.]
1 †**a** Reciprocation, return. *rare.* Only in **M16.** ▸**b** (An) alternation, (a) regular change; *esp.* a repeated succession of opposites. Now *arch. & poet.* **E17.**
2 The fact or liability of change occurring in a specified thing or area; an instance of this. **L16.**
3 Change or mutability regarded as a natural process or tendency in human affairs. **L16.**
4 In *pl.* Changes in circumstances; uncertainties or variations of fortune or outcome. **E17.**

📖 **1b** M. O. W. OLIPHANT Her girlish shyness . . made the colour come and go in rapid vicissitude upon her cheek. R. S. BALL Remarkable climatic vicissitudes during past ages. **2** S. JOHNSON There is likewise in composition . . a perpetual vicissitude of fashion. *New Yorker* Vicissitudes of taste can come into play. **3** J. H. NEWMAN A world of conflict, and of vicissitude amid the conflict. **4** R. DAVIES A fine discussion about the surprises and vicissitudes life brought to just about everybody.

■ **vicissi'tudinous** *adjective* characterized by vicissitude; subject to changes of fortune or circumstance: **M19.**

Vickers /ˈvɪkəz/ *noun.* Pl. same. **E20.**
[*Vickers* Ltd, the manufacturer.]
Any of a series of machine-guns manufactured by Vickers.

vicomte /vikɔ̃ːt (*pl. same*); ˈviːkɔːnt, -kɒmt/ *noun.* **M19.**
[French: see VISCOUNT.]
A French nobleman corresponding in rank to a British or Irish viscount.

vicomtesse /vikɔ̃tɛs (*pl. same*); viːkɔːnˈtɛs, -kɒm-/ *noun.* **L18.**
[French, formed as prec., -ESS¹.]
A French noblewoman corresponding in rank to an English viscountess.

Viconian /vɪˈkəʊnɪən/ *adjective.* **M20.**
[from *Vico* (see below) + -IAN.]
PHILOSOPHY. Of, pertaining to, or designating the theories of the Neapolitan philosopher, Giovanni Battista Vico (1668–1744), esp. those concerned with the cyclical nature of culture.

vicontiel /vɪˈkɒnʃ(ə)l/ *noun & adjective. obsolete* exc. *Hist.* **M16.**
[Anglo-Norman = Old French *vi(s)contal*, Anglo-Latin *visecomitalis*, formed as VISCOUNT: see -IAL.]
▶ **A** *noun.* In *pl.* Money for land rental regularly payable to the Crown by a sheriff. **M16.**
▶ **B** *adjective.* Of or pertaining to a sheriff; executable by or addressed to a sheriff. **E17.**

victim /ˈvɪktɪm/ *noun.* **L15.**
[Latin *victima.*]
1 A living creature killed and offered as a sacrifice to a god or in a religious rite. **L15.** ▸**b** THEOLOGY. Christ as a sacrifice of himself to expiate the sins of humankind. **M18.**
2 A person killed or tortured by another; a person subjected to cruelty, oppression, or other harsh or unfair treatment or suffering death, injury, ruin, etc., as a result of an event, circumstance, or oppressive or adverse impersonal agency. Also, a person killed, injured, ruined, etc., as a result of his or her own action in seeking to attain an object, gratify a passion, etc. **M17.**
3 A person who is taken advantage of; a dupe. **L18.**

📖 **2** J. WAINWRIGHT The victims were all children. Each child was manually strangled. I. HAMILTON Jean . . began falling victim to a series of minor illnesses. *Punch* Babel's characters . . victims of their own foolishness as well as of the march of events. *Times Educ. Suppl.* 45 per cent of youngsters claimed to be victims of racial harassment. *Journal of Refugee Studies* Proposed to recognize the victims of the . . civil wars as political persecutees. *transf.*: *New York Review of Books* The street lights were out in the alley . . victims of years of municipal neglect. **3** *Which?* He's the victim of a professional fraudster using a forged card.

Comb.: **victim support** the provision of advice and counselling to victims of crime.

■ **victimage** *noun* (*a*) the condition of being a victim; (*b*) the practice of seeking out a victim, esp. a symbolic one, in order to expiate the guilt of some social group: **M20. victimhood** *noun* the state or condition of being a victim **M19. victimless** *adjective* (orig. & chiefly *US*) (of a crime) in which there is no injured party **M20.**

†**victimary** *noun. rare.* **M17–L18.**
[Latin *victimarius*, formed as prec.]
A killer of sacrificial victims.

victimize /ˈvɪktɪmʌɪz/ *verb trans.* Also **-ise. M19.**
[from VICTIM + -IZE.]
1 Make a victim of; cause to suffer inconvenience, discomfort, harm, etc. Also, single out for punitive or unfair treatment; *spec.* impose penalties on (an employee taking industrial action). **M19.** ▸**b** Cheat, defraud. **M19.**
2 Kill as, or in the manner of, a sacrificial victim; slaughter. *rare.* **M19.**

📖 **1** *Scientific American* The extent to which people have been victimized by rape, robbery, assault, larceny, burglary. J. MASSON Women in particular are often victimized by being labeled or given a specific psychiatric diagnosis. G. GREER The poor old woman, whom he saw as victimized by a suspicious community. **2** *Tait's Edinburgh Magazine* Fifty thousand Gentoos were victimized by the scimitar.

■ **victimi'zation** *noun* the action of victimizing someone or something; the fact of being victimized: **M19. victimizer** *noun* **M19.**

victimology /vɪktɪˈmɒlədʒi/ *noun.* **M20.**
[French *victimologie*, from *victime* VICTIM + -OLOGY.]
The study of the victims of crime and esp. the psychological effects on them of their experience.

■ **victimologist** *noun* **L20.**

victor /ˈvɪktə/ *noun & adjective.* **ME.**
[Anglo-Norman *victo(u)r* or Latin *victor*, from *vict-* pa. ppl stem of *vincere* conquer: see -OR.]
▶ **A** *noun.* **1** A person who overcomes or conquers an adversary in battle etc.; the leader of a winning army. Also, a winning army or nation collectively. **ME.**
2 A winner in any contest or struggle. **LME.**

📖 **1** *Bulletin of Atomic Science* Another world war in the age of atomic . . weapons would be an unparalleled disaster for victor and vanquished alike. M. WARNER The outcome of the duel no longer proved the innocence of the victor or the wrongdoing of the loser. **2** *Golf Monthly* He . . finished joint fifth, 5-under par and only two behind play-off victor Christy O'Connor.

▶ **B** *attrib.* or as *adjective.* Of or pertaining to a victor or victory; victorious. Chiefly *poet.* **LME.**

📖 SHELLEY Why pause the victor swords to seal his overthrow?

■ †**victoress** *noun* a female victor **L16–M17.**

Victoria /vɪkˈtɔːrɪə/ *noun.* **M19.**
[Queen *Victoria* of Great Britain and Ireland who reigned from 1837 to 1901.]
▶ **I 1** Either of two water lilies of tropical S. America, *Victoria amazonica* and *V. cruziana*, having enormous leaves. **M19.**
2 A large red luscious variety of plum. **M19.**
3 A light low four-wheeled carriage with a collapsible hood, seats for (usu.) two passengers, and an elevated driver's seat in front. **L19.**
4 A sovereign minted in the reign of Queen Victoria. **L19.**
5 A rare variety of domestic pigeon resembling the hyacinth. **L19.**
▶ **II 6** Used *attrib.* to designate things associated with Queen Victoria or her reign. **M19.**
6 Victoria Cross a decoration awarded for conspicuous bravery in the armed services, instituted by Queen Victoria in 1856. **Victoria crowned pigeon** a large blue crowned pigeon, *Goura victoria*. **Victoria Day** (in Canada) the Monday preceding May 24, observed as a national holiday to commemorate the birthday of Queen Victoria. **Victoria plum** = sense 2 above. **Victoria sandwich**, **Victoria sponge** a sponge cake consisting of two layers of sponge with a jam filling. **Victoria water lily** = sense 1 above.

victoria /vɪkˈtɔːrɪə/ *interjection.* Now *rare.* **M17.**
[(Spanish, Portuguese from) Latin: see VICTORY.]
Expr. triumph. Cf. VICTORY 1.

📖 C. KINGSLEY 'There go the rest of them! Victoria!' shouted Cary.

Victorian /vɪkˈtɔːrɪən/ *adjective*¹. *rare.* **E18.**
[from *Victorius* (see below) + -AN.]
Of, pertaining to, or attributed to the 5th-cent. ecclesiastic Victorius.
Victorian cycle, **Victorian period** = LUNISOLAR *period*.

Victorian /vɪkˈtɔːrɪən/ *adjective*² & *noun*¹. **M19.**
[formed as VICTORIA *noun* + -AN.]
▶ **A** *adjective.* **I 1** Of, pertaining to, or characteristic of the reign of Queen Victoria (1837–1901). **M19.**
2 Resembling or typified by the attitudes attributed to the Victorian era; *esp.* prudish, morally strict; old-fashioned, out-dated. **M20.**

📖 **1** *Royal Victorian Chain*: see ROYAL *adjective*. *Royal Victorian Order*: see ROYAL *adjective*. **Victorian Gothic** (designating) the style of architecture typical of the Gothic revival. **2** *Time Out* An even worse example of what workers described as 'Victorian industrial relations.'

▶ **II 3** Of or pertaining to any of various places named after Queen Victoria, *spec.* the State of Victoria in SE Australia. **M19.**
▶ **B** *noun.* **I 1** A native or inhabitant of the State of Victoria or any of the cities called Victoria. **M19.**
▶ **II 2** A person, esp. a writer, who lived in the reign of Queen Victoria. Also, a person whose attitudes and values are characteristic of those attributed to the Victorian era. **L19.**
3 a An article of furniture from the time of Queen Victoria. *rare.* **E20.** ▸**b** A house built during the reign of Queen Victoria. *US.* **M20.**

■ **Victori'ana** *noun pl.* [-ANA] (*a*) attitudes characteristic of the Victorian period; (*b*) articles, esp. furniture and ornaments, or architecture of the Victorian period: **E20. Victorianism** *noun* the collective characteristics, esp. concerning attitudes or style, of the Victorian period; an example of something characteristic of this period: **E20. Victorianist** *noun* an expert in or student of the Victorian period **L20. Victorianize** *verb trans.* make Victorian; convert (a house etc.) to a Victorian style: **E20. Victorianly** *adverb* in a Victorian manner or style; prudishly, formally: **E20.**

victoriate /vɪkˈtɔːrɪeɪt/ *noun. obsolete* exc. *Hist.* **E17.**
[Latin *victoriatus*, from *victoria* VICTORY: see -ATE¹.]
An ancient Roman silver coin stamped with the image of the goddess of Victory, equal to half a denarius.

victorin /ˈvɪktərɪn/ *noun.* **M20.**
[from mod. Latin *victoriae* (see below), from *Victoria* variety of oats susceptible to the fungus: see -IN¹.]
BIOCHEMISTRY. A toxin produced by the fungus *Helminthosporium victoriae*, the causative agent of a blight affecting some varieties of oats.

victorine /ˈvɪktəriːn/ *noun*¹. **M19.**
[from VICTORIA *noun* + -INE⁴.]
A kind of fur tippet formerly worn by women, fastening in front of the neck and with two loose ends hanging down.

victorine /ˈvɪktəriːn/ *noun*² & *adjective.* **L19.**
[French *Victorin*, from St *Victor*: see below, -INE¹.]
▶ **A** *noun.* A founder or adherent of the type of mysticism developed at the monastery of St Victor near Paris in the 12th and 13th cents. **L19.**
▶ **B** *adjective.* Of or pertaining to the mysticism of St Victor. **L19.**

victorious /vɪkˈtɔːrɪəs/ *adjective.* **LME.**
[Anglo-Norman = Old & mod. French *victorieux* from Latin *victoriosus*, from *victoria* VICTORY: see -IOUS.]
1 Having won a victory; triumphant, conquering; successful in any contest or struggle. **LME.**
2 Of or characterized by victory; producing victory; emblematic of victory. **LME.**

📖 **1** O. SITWELL A libel action, in which we were victorious. *Golf Monthly* He was a member of the victorious Ryder Cup team. **2** POPE Honours shall be snatch'd away, And curs'd for ever this victorious day. *Guardian* A victorious campaign in the state elections.

■ **victoriously** *adverb* **LME. victoriousness** *noun* **E18.**

victor ludorum /vɪktə luːˈdɔːrəm/ *noun phr.* **E20.**
[Latin = victor of the games.]
The overall champion in a sports competition, esp. at a school or college; the sports competition itself.

victory /ˈvɪkt(ə)ri/ *noun.* **ME.**
[Anglo-Norman *victorie* = Old & mod. French *victoire* from Latin *victoria*, from *victor*: see VICTOR, -Y⁴.]
1 The state of having overcome or conquered an adversary in battle etc.; supremacy or superiority won as the result of armed conflict. Also as *interjection*, expr. triumph or encouragement (cf. VICTORIA *interjection*). **ME.** ▸**b** An instance or occasion of overcoming an adversary in battle etc. **ME.**
2 Supremacy or superiority, triumph or success, in any contest or struggle; an instance of this. **ME.**
3 (Also **V-**.) A representation of the Roman goddess of victory. **M16.**

📖 **1** J. BRAND The Grecians . . obtained the Victory over the Persians. H. KISSINGER The military situation was improving, but nothing like total victory seemed in sight. *attrib.*: *Daily Telegraph* The Falklands victory parade. **2** *Illustrated London News* Elections . . resulted in a landslide victory for the . . nationalist movement. *Independent* India retained the Asia cup with a seven-wicket victory over Sri Lanka. ***moral victory***: see MORAL *adjective*.

Comb.: **victory bond** a bond issued by the Canadian and British Governments during or immediately after the war of 1914–18; **victory point** BRIDGE a point scored in a championship representing a number of international match points in accordance with an agreed scale; **victory roll**: performed by an aircraft as a sign of triumph, esp. after a successful mission; **victory sign** a signal of triumph or celebration made by holding up the hand with the palm outwards and the first two fingers spread apart to represent the letter V (for *victory*) (cf. V-SIGN 2).

■ **victoryless** *adjective* (*rare*) **L19.**

victress /ˈvɪktrɪs/ *noun.* **E17.**
[from VICTOR + -ESS¹, after Latin VICTRIX.]
A female victor.

victrix /ˈvɪktrɪks/ *noun.* Pl. **-trices** /-trɪsiːz/. **M17.**
[Latin, fem. of VICTOR: see -TRIX.]
A female victor; a victress.

Victrola /vɪkˈtrəʊlə/ *noun.* Also **v-**. **E20.**
[from the *Victor* Talking Machine Co. + -OLA.]
Chiefly *Hist.* (Proprietary name for) a kind of gramophone.

victual /ˈvɪt(ə)l/ *noun.* **ME.**
[Old French *vitaille*, (later and mod.) *victuaille* from late Latin *victualia* neut. pl. of *victualis*, from Latin *victus* livelihood, food, from base of *vivere* live: see -AL¹. Spelling but not pronunc. assim. to Latin.]
1 Whatever is required or may be used for consumption to maintain life; food, sustenance. Now *rare.* **ME.** ▸†**b** Produce of the land able to be used as food. **LME–L18.** ▸**c** Grain, corn. *Scot.* **L15.**
2 In *pl.* Articles of food; supplies, provisions, now esp. as prepared for use. **ME.**
†**3** In *pl.* Animals used as food. *rare.* **M16–M17.**
4 An article of food. *rare.* **M16.**

📖 **1** BYRON Laura . . almost lost all appetite for victual. **2** JOHN ROGERS Slaving over a hot stove to provide you with nourishing victuals.

■ **victualage** *noun* (*rare*) victualling; victuals: **E17. victualless** /-l-l-/ *adjective* (*rare*) **M19.**

victual /ˈvɪt(ə)l/ *verb*. Infl. **-ll-**, ***-l-**. ME.
[Old French *vitailler, vi(c)tuaillier*, from *vitaille*: see prec.]
1 *verb trans.* Supply (a person, oneself) with victuals; *esp.* stock (a ship, an army, etc.) with sufficient stores to last for some time. ME.
2 *verb intrans.* **a** Eat. Also (of an animal), feed, graze. L16. ▸**b** Lay in stores; obtain a supply of victuals. E17.

📖 **1** P. WARNER Edward was . . forced to retire because the countryside afforded nothing to victual an army. **2a** R. D. BLACKMORE Peggy and Smiler [the horses] . . victualling where the grass was good. **b** DEFOE A voyage of such length, that no ship could victual for.

victualer, **victualing** *nouns* see VICTUALLER, VICTUALLING.

victualler /ˈvɪt(ə)lə/ *noun*. Also ***-ualer**. LME.
[Old French *vitaill(i)er, -our*, from *vitaille*: see VICTUAL *noun*, -ER².]
1 A supplier of victuals; *spec.* (*a*) a person whose business is the provision of food and drink; (*b*) = ***licensed victualler*** s.v. LICENSED *adjective* 2. LME.
2 *spec.* **a** A person who supplies, or undertakes to supply, an army with provisions; a sutler. LME. ▸**b** Orig., a person who undertook to victual a trading vessel in return for a share in the profits. Later, a person who supplies a ship or navy with stores. LME.
3 A ship employed to carry stores for a fleet or for troops overseas. LME.

victualling /ˈvɪt(ə)lɪŋ/ *noun*. Also ***-ualing**. LME.
[from VICTUAL *verb* + -ING¹.]
1 The action of VICTUAL *verb*; the business of a victualler. LME.
2 Victuals; supply of food for sale; a supply of food for one's own use. LME.
Comb.: **victualling-house** *arch.* a house where victuals are supplied or sold; an eating-house, an inn; **victualling-office** an office concerned with the victualling of ships, esp. those of the Royal Navy.

vicuña /vɪˈkjuːnjə, -ˈkuː-/ *noun*. Also **vicugna**; **vicuna** /-nə/. E17.
[Spanish from Quechua *wikuña*.]
1 A hoofed mammal of the high Andes, *Vicugna vicugna*, which is related to the llama and guanaco and has a fine silky coat used for textile fabrics. E17.
2 A fine fabric made from the wool of the vicuña (also more fully ***vicuña cloth***). Also, a garment made of this fabric. M19.
Comb.: ***vicuña cloth***: see sense 2 above; **vicuña wool** (*a*) the wool of the vicuña; (*b*) a fabric made from a mixture of fine wool and cotton.

vicus /ˈvʌɪkəs, ˈviːkəs/ *noun*. Pl. **-ci** /-kiː/. M19.
[Latin = village, group of dwellings.]
ARCHAEOLOGY. In the Roman Empire, a village, a settlement; *spec.* the smallest unit of ancient Roman municipal administration, consisting of a village, part of a town, etc. Also, a medieval European township.

Vicwardian /vɪkˈwɔːdɪən/ *adjective*. *colloq.* L20.
[Blend of VICTORIAN *adjective*² & *noun*¹ and EDWARDIAN.]
Esp. of architecture: pertaining to or characteristic of the reigns of Queen Victoria (1837–1901) and King Edward VII (1901–10).

vid /vɪd/ *noun*. *colloq.* (orig. *US*). M20.
[Abbreviation.]
= VIDEO *noun*.

vid. /vɪd/ *verb trans.* (*imper.*). E17.
[Abbreviation.]
= VIDE *verb*².

vidame /ˈviːdɑːm/ *noun*. E16.
[Old French *visdame* (mod. *vidame*) from late Latin *vicedominus*, formed as VICE- + *dominus* lord.]
FRENCH HISTORY. A person who held lands from a bishop as his representative and defender in temporal matters.

vidarabine /vʌɪˈdarəbiːn, vɪ-/ *noun*. L20.
[App. from VI(RUS + *d*(*extrorotatory*) + ARABIN(OS)E.]
PHARMACOLOGY. A nucleoside analogue used to treat some herpesvirus infections.

vide /vʌɪd/ *verb*¹. LME.
[Aphet.]
1 *verb trans.* = DIVIDE *verb* 1. Long *dial.* & *US Black English*. LME.
2 *verb intrans.* In *imper.* An instruction to the members of the House of Commons: divide for voting (see DIVIDE *verb* 14). L19.

vide /ˈvʌɪdi, ˈvɪdeɪ, ˈviːdeɪ/ *verb*² *trans.* (*imper.*). M16.
[Latin, imper. sing. of *videre* see.]
See, refer to, consult. Used as a direction in a text referring the reader to a specified passage, work, etc., for fuller or further information. Cf. VID.

videlicet /vɪˈdɛlɪsɛt, vʌɪ-, -kɛt/ *adverb* & *noun*. LME.
[Latin, from *vide* stem of *videre* see + *licet* it is permissible. Cf. SCILICET.]
▸ **A** *adverb*. = VIZ *adverb*. LME.

📖 SIR W. SCOTT One of Rob's original profession, *videlicet* a drover.

▸ **B** *noun*. The word 'videlicet' introducing an explanation or amplification, esp. in a legal document. Cf. VIZ *noun*. M17.

videnda /vɪˈdɛndə/ *noun pl.* *rare*. M18.
[Latin, pl. of *videndum*, from *videre* see.]
Things worth seeing or which ought to be seen.

video /ˈvɪdɪəʊ/ *adjective* & *noun*. M20.
[from Latin *videre* see + -O, after AUDIO.]
▸ **A** *adjective*. **1** Of or pertaining to the visual element of television broadcasts or the signals representing it. M20.
2 Of or pertaining to the recording, reproducing, or broadcasting of visual images on magnetic tape etc. M20.

📖 **1** T. MCGUANE People . . had huge video dishes next to their homes. **2** *Art* In the case of video art, there has not been a major exhibition since 1976. *Which?* A special . . connector . . to simplify connecting together video equipment.

▸ **B** *noun*. Pl. **-os**.
1 The image which is displayed or is to be displayed on a television screen or other cathode-ray tube; the signal corresponding to this. M20.
2 Television as a broadcasting medium. *US colloq.* M20.
3 = ***video recorder*** below. *colloq.* M20.
4 A film etc. recorded on videotape; *colloq.* = ***video cassette*** below. Also, videotape as a recording medium. M20.
5 The process of recording, reproducing, or broadcasting visual images on magnetic tape etc. L20.

📖 **1 *reverse video***: see REVERSE *adjective*. **3** *Which?* Teletext videos can record subtitles. **4** *New Scientist* Money to be made from selling archive programmes on video. *Life* The music industry's free promo videos of pop stars. **5** B. GELDOF I suspected that video would become very important to music.

Special collocations & comb. (of noun & adjective): **video amplifier**: designed to amplify the wide range of frequencies present in video signals and deliver the signal to the picture tube of a television set. **video arcade** (orig. & chiefly *US*) an amusement arcade having mainly video games. **video camera** a camera for recording images on videotape etc. or for transmitting them to a monitor screen. **video cassette** a cassette of videotape; ***video cassette recorder***, = ***video recorder*** below (abbreviation *VCR*). **videoconference** an arrangement in which television sets linked by telephone lines etc. are used to enable a group of people in different places to communicate with each other in both sound and vision. **videoconferencing** communication by means of a videoconference. **video diary** a record on videotape of a notable period of someone's life, or of a particular event, made using a camcorder. **videodisc** a metal-coated disc on which visual material is recorded for subsequent reproduction on a television screen. **video display terminal**, **video display unit** = ***visual display unit*** s.v. VISUAL *adjective*. **video film** †(*a*) a cinematographic film of a television broadcast; (*b*) a video recording. **video frequency** a frequency in the range employed for the video signal in television (i.e. a few hertz to several million hertz), *esp.* one in the higher part of this range. **video game** a game played by electronically manipulating computer-generated images displayed on a television screen. **video-grab** (*a*) *noun* a frame of video or television footage used as a still photo, in print or on a computer screen; the process of obtaining this; (*b*) *verb trans.* capture and digitize (an image, esp. a frame of video or television footage) for later display or printing. **videogram** a pre-recorded video recording, esp. of a commercial film. **video jock**, **video jockey** (orig. *US*) a person who introduces and plays music videos on TV, at a discotheque, etc. **video mail** electronic mail to which a short video recording or a still image may be attached, to be replayed by the recipient. **video map** a map produced electronically on a radar screen to assist in navigation. **video mapping** the production of video maps. ***video nasty***: see NASTY *noun*¹ 2. **videophone** a telephone incorporating a television screen allowing communication in both sound and vision. **video piracy** the production and sale of unauthorized copies of commercial video films. **video pirate** a person who produces and sells illegal copies of commercial video films. **video-player** a machine used in conjunction with a television for playing video recordings. **videorecord** *verb trans.* make a video recording of. **video recorder** a machine used in conjunction with a television for recording broadcast material and playing this video recording back. **video recording** the action or process of recording something on videotape etc.; a recording on videotape etc. **video signal** a signal that contains all the information required for producing the picture in television broadcasting. **video-telephone** = ***videophone*** above. **video terminal** = ***video display terminal*** above.
■ **videophile** *noun* a person devoted to watching television or video recordings L20.

video /ˈvɪdɪəʊ/ *verb trans.* L20.
[from prec.]
Make a recording of (something) on videotape.

📖 *Practical Computing* The pupils . . have also videoed school events.

videogenic /vɪdɪəʊˈdʒɛnɪk, -ˈdʒiːn-/ *adjective*. Orig. & chiefly *US*. M20.
[formed as prec. + -GENIC.]
= TELEGENIC.

videographic /vɪdɪəˈgrafɪk/ *adjective*. L20.
[formed as VIDEOGRAPHY + -IC.]
Of or pertaining to the making of video films. Also, pertaining to videographics.

videographics /vɪdɪəˈgrafɪks/ *noun*. L20.
[formed as prec. + -ICS.]
The manipulation of video images using a computer.

videography /vɪdɪˈɒgrəfi/ *noun*. L20.
[from VIDEO *adjective* & *noun* + -GRAPHY.]
The process or art of making video films; the use of a video camera.
■ **videographer** *noun* a person who makes video films L20.

videotape /ˈvɪdɪə(ʊ)teɪp/ *noun* & *verb*. M20.
[from VIDEO *adjective* & *noun* + TAPE *noun* & *verb*.]
▸ **A** *noun*. **1** Magnetic tape for use either with a video recorder for recording broadcast television material, or in a video camera. M20.
2 A recording made on such tape. M20.

📖 **1** *attrib.*: B. JACKSON A man hefting a videotape camera on his shoulder. **2** *Decision* The ministry would be extended to India via videotapes distributed through Mission World.

Comb.: **videotape recorder** a video recorder; **videotape recording** a recording on videotape; the making of such a recording.
▸ **B** *verb trans.* Make a recording of (something) on videotape. M20.

📖 *New York Times* Check your posture . . by having someone . . videotape you.

videotex /ˈvɪdɪə(ʊ)tɛks/ *noun*. Also **-text** /-tɛkst/. L20.
[from VIDEO *adjective* & *noun* + TEXT.]
An information system in which a television is used to display alphanumeric information selected by the user. Now *spec.*, such a system derived from a computer database and using a telephone line to provide two-way communication (also called ***viewdata***). Cf. PRESTEL, TELETEXT.

vidette *noun* see VEDETTE.

vidicon /ˈvɪdɪkɒn/ *noun*. M20.
[from VID(EO *adjective* & *noun* + ICON(OSCOPE.]
A small television camera tube in which the image is formed on a transparent electrode coated with photoconductive material, the current from which varies as it is scanned by a beam of (usu. low-speed) electrons.

vidimus /ˈvʌɪdɪməs/ *noun*. LME.
[Latin = we have seen, from *videre* see.]
1 a A copy of a document bearing an attestation of its authenticity or accuracy. LME. ▸**b** An inspection of accounts. M19.
†**2** ARCHITECTURE. A design for a painted or stained-glass window. *rare*. E16–M18.

vidiot /ˈvɪdɪət/ *noun*. *slang* (orig. & chiefly *US*). M20.
[Blend of VIDEO *adjective* & *noun* and IDIOT *noun*.]
A habitual, esp. undiscriminating, watcher of television or videotapes.

Vidonia /vɪˈdəʊnɪə/ *noun*. Now *rare*. E18.
[Origin unkn.]
A dry white wine made in the Canary Islands.

viduage /ˈvɪdjʊɪdʒ/ *noun*. *rare*. M19.
[from Latin *vidua* widow + -AGE.]
Widowhood; widows collectively.

vidual /ˈvɪdjʊəl/ *adjective*. *arch.* M16.
[Late Latin *vidualis*, formed as prec.: see -AL¹.]
Of, pertaining to, or befitting a widow or widowhood; widowed.

†**viduate** *verb trans.* L16–E18.
[Latin *viduat-* pa. ppl stem of *viduare*, from *viduus* destitute: see -ATE³.]
Leave widowed, desolate, or destitute. Chiefly as ***viduated*** *ppl adjective*.

viduity /vɪˈdjuːɪti/ *noun*. *arch.* LME.
[Old & mod. French *viduité* or Latin *viduitas*, from *vidua* widow: see -ITY.]
The state of being a widow; the time during which a woman is a widow; widowhood.

vie /vi/ *noun*. Pl. pronounced same. ME.
[Old & mod. French from Latin *vita* life.]
▸†**I 1** An account of the life of a saint. Only in ME.
2 Way of or lot in life. Only in ME.
▸ **II 3** Life. Only in French phrs. used in English L19.
3 *vie de Bohème* /də bɔɛm/ a Bohemian way of life. ***vie de château*** /də ʃɑto/ the way of life of a large country house; aristocratic social life. ***vie d'intérieur*** /dɛ̃terjœːr/ private or domestic life. ***vie en rose*** /ɑ̃ roz/ a life seen through rose-coloured spectacles. ***vie intérieure*** /ɛ̃terjœːr/ one's inner life, the life of the spirit. ***vie intime*** /ɛ̃tim/ the intimate private life of a person. ***vie romancée*** /rɔmɑ̃se/, pl. **-s -s** (pronounced same), a fictionalized biography.
¶ Formerly fully naturalized. See also TRANCHE ***de vie***.

vie /vʌɪ/ *verb*. Pa. t. & pple **vied** /vʌɪd/; pres. pple **vying** /ˈvʌɪɪŋ/. M16.
[Prob. aphet. from ENVY *verb*².]
†**1** CARDS. **a** *verb trans.* & *intrans.* Stake (a certain sum) on the strength of one's hand. M16–M17. ▸**b** *verb trans.* Back (a card) for a certain sum; declare oneself able to win (a game etc.). Freq. in ***vie it***. L16–L17.
†**2** *verb trans.* Set or present (something) against something else in competition or rivalry; contend or strive

with another in respect of (something). Usu. foll. by *with*. M16–E19.

3 *verb trans.* Match (something) *with* something else by way of return, rivalry, or comparison. *arch.* L16.

†**4** *verb trans.* Increase in number by addition or repetition. L16–M17.

5 *verb intrans.* Enter into or carry on rivalry; be rivals or competitors; compete for superiority (*with* a person etc., *for* or *in* a thing). E17.

†**6** *verb intrans.* Contend in debate. *rare.* E17–M18.

> 2 JONSON Thine eyes Vie teares with the Hyæna. 3 TENNYSON Vying a tear with our cold dews. 5 JOHN ROGERS Antique plates vied for attention with two corn dollies. H. DAVID Whistler . . soon created a public personality which vied with Swinburne's in its outrageousness. INA TAYLOR It . . boosted his ego to have three women vying with each other for his favours.

■ **vier** *noun* (*rare*) L17.

vielle /vɪˈɛl/ *noun.* M18.
[French: see VIOL *noun*[1].]
Any of various medieval stringed instruments played with a bow. Also, a hurdy-gurdy.

Vienna /vɪˈɛnə/ *noun.* L18.
[The capital of Austria.]
▶ **I 1** Used *attrib.* to designate things from or associated with Vienna; *spec.* designating (items made of) a hard-paste porcelain, often richly decorated, manufactured in Vienna from 1719 to 1864. L18.

2 Used *attrib.* to designate a grade of wheat-flour and types of bread and cake made from this. M19.

1 Vienna Circle a group of empiricist philosophers, scientists, and mathematicians based at Vienna University from the 1920s to 1938 who were chiefly concerned with methods of determining significance, the formalization of language, the unification of science, and the elimination of metaphysics. **Vienna coup** BRIDGE the playing of the highest ranking card of a suit as a preparation for eventually forcing an opponent to discard winning cards. **Vienna paste** a paste made up of equal parts of caustic potash and quicklime. **Vienna sausage** a small frankfurter made of pork, beef, or veal. **Vienna Secession** = SECESSION 3b. *Vienna* SCHNITZEL. **Vienna steak** a flat rissole made of minced meat. **Vienna white** = CREMNITZ WHITE.

▶ **II** *ellipt.* **3** Vienna porcelain. E20.

4 A Vienna sausage. M20.

Viennese /vɪəˈniːz/ *noun & adjective.* M19.
[from prec. + -ESE.]
▶ **A** *noun.* Pl. same.
1 A native or inhabitant of Vienna. M19.
2 The dialect of German spoken in Vienna. M19.
▶ **B** *adjective.* Of, pertaining to, or associated with Vienna. M19.

Viennese coffee a blend of coffee flavoured with fig extract. **Viennese Secession** = SECESSION 3b. **Viennese waltz** a waltz characterized by a slight anticipation of the second beat of the bar and having a romantic quality; a piece of music for this dance or in its rhythm.

Vierendeel /ˈviːrəndeɪl/ *noun.* M20.
[Arthur *Vierendeel*, Belgian engineer and architect.]
ENGINEERING. Used *attrib.* to designate a type of girder in which there are no diagonal members, overall rigidity of the structure being maintained by rigidity at the joints of the vertical and horizontal members.

viertel /ˈfɪrtəl/ *noun.* Also **V-**. Pl. same. M20.
[German = quarter.]
In Germany and Austria, a quarter of a litre (*of* wine etc.); a glass or jug holding this quantity.

Viet /ˈvɪɛt/ *noun & adjective.* M20.
[Abbreviation.]
▶ **A** *noun.* = VIETNAMESE *noun* 1. M20.
▶ **B** *adjective.* = VIETNAMESE *adjective.* M20.

vi et armis /viː ɛt ˈɑːmiːs/ *adverbial phr.* E17.
[Latin = with force and arms.]
Violently, forcibly, by compulsion; *spec.* in LAW (now *Hist.*), with unlawful violence. Cf. FORCE *noun*[1] 5b.

Viet Cong /vɪɛt ˈkɒŋ, vj-/ *noun & adjective.* Also **Vietcong**. M20.
[Vietnamese *Việt Cộng*, lit. 'Vietnamese Communist'.]
▶ **A** *noun.* Pl. same. A member of the Communist guerrilla forces active in Vietnam between 1954 and 1976. M20.
▶ **B** *adjective.* Of or pertaining to this movement or its members. M20.

Viet Minh /vɪɛt ˈmɪn, vj-/ *noun & adjective.* Also **Vietminh**. M20.
[Vietnamese *Việt Minh*, from *Việt-Nam Độc-Lập Đồng-Minh* Vietnamese Independence League.]
▶ **A** *noun.* Pl. same. A nationalist movement (1941–50) which fought for independence in French Indo-China; the movement succeeding this; a member of one of these movements. M20.
▶ **B** *adjective.* Of or pertaining to any of these movements or their members. M20.

Vietnamese /ˌvɪɛtnəˈmiːz, ˈvjɛt-/ *noun & adjective.* M20.
[from *Vietnam* (see below) + -ESE.]
▶ **A** *noun.* Pl. same.
1 A native or inhabitant of Vietnam, (formed in 1945 by the union of the former French colonial provinces of Annam, Tongking, and Cochin-China, and between 1954–76 divided into North and South Vietnam) in SE Asia. M20.
2 The language of this people, perhaps belonging to the Mon-Khmer family. M20.
▶ **B** *adjective.* Of or pertaining to Vietnam, its people, or their language. M20.

Vietnamize /ˈvɪɛtnəmʌɪz, ˈvjɛt-/ *verb trans.* Also **-ise**. M20.
[formed as prec. + -IZE.]
Give a Vietnamese character to; make Vietnamese.
■ **Vietnamiˈzation** *noun* M20.

Vietnik /ˈvɪɛtnɪk, ˈvj-/ *noun.* Orig. & chiefly *US.* M20.
[from *Viet(nam* + -NIK, after *beatnik*.]
An active opponent of American military involvement in the war between North and South Vietnam.

vieux /vjø/ *adjective.* L19.
[French.]
The French (masc.) for 'old', occurring in various phrases used in English
■ MON VIEUX. ***vieux jeu*** /ʒø/ *noun & adjective*, pl. of noun ***vieux jeux*** (pronounced same), [lit. 'old game'] (something or someone) old-fashioned, out-moded, passé L19. ***vieux marcheur*** /marʃœːr/, pl. ***vieux marcheurs*** (pronounced same), [lit. 'old campaigner'] an elderly womanizer E20. ***vieux rose*** /roz/ *noun & adjective* (of) a deep pink colour, old rose L19.

view /vjuː/ *noun.* ME.
[Anglo-Norman *vewe*, *vieue*, Old French *vëue* (mod. *vue*) use as noun of fem. pa. pple of *vëoir* (mod. *voir*) from Latin *videre* see.]
▶ **I 1** A formal inspection or survey of lands, property, etc., for a particular purpose; an official examination of something; the office or position of a person appointed to make such an inspection or examination. Now *rare* or *obsolete* exc. as passing into senses below. ME. ▸†**b** A review of troops etc. LME–E18. ▸**c** LAW. In court proceedings, a formal inspection, by a judge and jury or appointed viewers, of property mentioned in evidence or the scene of a crime. Cf. VIEWER 1. E16. ▸**d** An inspection of objects for sale, esp. by auction, by prospective purchasers; a viewing. L19.

2 *gen.* Any visual examination, inspection, or survey. M16.

> 1 H. HALLAM A view of this armour was to be taken twice in the year.

▶ **II 3 a** The exercise of visual perception; the faculty of sight. Freq. in ***to view***. ME. ▸**b** Range of sight or vision; extent of visibility. L16.

4 The action or an act of visually perceiving someone or something; the sight or prospect *of* a specified person or thing; an act of looking or seeing; a sight; a look, a glance. L15. ▸**b** *ellipt.* A view-halloo. E20.

5 Visual appearance or aspect; aspect from a given direction or position. M16.

6 That which may be seen or looked at from a particular point; *spec.* †(*a*) HUNTING the track of a deer; (*b*) an extent of land etc. covered by the field of vision from a particular point; a prospect, a scene. L16. ▸**b** A pictorial representation of a landscape or other scene. L17.

> 3a SHELLEY Like a glow-worm . . Among the flowers and grass, which screen it from the view. H. B. STOWE Tom was already lost to view among the distant swamps. J. MORLEY Between two or three thousand papers . . must have passed under my view. **b** L. GRANT-ADAMSON They were past the apple tree and out of view. 4 SHELLEY The thronging thousands, to a passing view, Seemed like an ant-hill's citizens. W. GODWIN The view of his figure immediately introduced a train of ideas into my mind. J. G. LOCKHART He proceeded to thread his way westwards . . until we lost view of him. R. WESTALL The parents loved it too; craning their necks . . for a view. 5 POPE Like furious, rush'd the Myrmidonian crew, Such their dread strength, and such their dreadful view. W. LEWIS There is a 'mountain' by Gaston Lachaise. Its back view is the best. 6 R. CAMPBELL This roof also commanded a magnificent view of the town. **b** *attrib.*: *Listener* Academic view painters . . used to set up their easels round the picturesque little harbour.

▶ **III 7** Mental contemplation or consideration; notice. ME. ▸**b** An act of contemplation or mental examination of a subject. L16.

8 A particular manner of considering or regarding something; a mental attitude; an opinion, idea, or belief concerning a particular subject or thing. Freq. in *pl.* L16. ▸**b** An aspect or light in which something is regarded or considered. E18.

9 An overview; a general or summary account *of* something. E17.

10 An aim, a purpose; a plan. M17.

11 A thing to anticipate; a prospect, an expectation. E18.

> 7 N. HAWTHORNE Rather a noteworthy personage in the view of our ancestors. 8 A. STORR Freud's final view . . came to be that there were simply two groups of instincts. JANET MORGAN The official view was that Agatha had crashed her car. *New York Review of Books* Her views were consistent only in the stubborn conviction with which she proclaimed them. 9 J. RAZ The two theses present a comprehensive view of the nature . . of legitimate authority. 10 *Society* I have told you my views for Jemima.

Phrases: ***in full view***: see FULL *adjective*. **in that view**, **in this view** (now *rare* or *obsolete*) on that account, for that reason. **in view** (*a*) in sight; (*b*) ***have in view***, ***keep in view***, have or bear in mind, keep under consideration; have or keep as a goal or ultimate aim. **in view of** (*a*) so as to be seen by; (*b*) near enough to see; (*c*) in anticipation or expectation of; (*d*) considering, in regard or on account of. ***long view***: see LONG *adjective*[1]. **on the view of** on visual inspection or perception of, *spec.* (LAW) by way of inquest. **on view** on exhibition; open to general observation or inspection. **on view of** = *on the view of* above. ***Pisgah view***. ***point of view***: see POINT *noun*[1]. ***press view***: see PRESS *noun*[1]. ***private view***: see PRIVATE *adjective*. ***take a dim view of***: see DIM *adjective* 4. ***take a poor view of***: see POOR *adjective*. **take a view of** take a look at, make an inspection, examination, or survey of. ***take the long view***: see *long view* s.v. LONG *adjective*[1]. **take the view that** hold or express the opinion that (esp. in contrast to the view of others). ***top view***: see TOP *adjective*. ***view of frank-pledge***: see FRANK-PLEDGE 2. **with a view of** = *with the view of* below. **with a view to** (*a*) with the aim of attaining or accomplishing; (*b*) with the hope or intention of. **with the view of** with the objective or plan of. **with this view** with this intention or aim, for this purpose. ***worm's-eye view***: see WORM *noun*.

Comb.: **view camera** a large format camera with a ground glass screen for viewing; **view card** a picture postcard showing a view; **viewfinder** a device on a camera showing the field of view of the lens, used in framing and focusing the picture; **viewgraph** a graph produced as a transparency for projection on to a screen, or for transmission during a teleconference; **view-halloo** HUNTING a shout given by a member of the hunt on seeing a fox break cover; **viewphone** = *videophone* s.v. VIDEO *adjective & noun*; **viewport** (*a*) a window in a spacecraft or in the conning tower of an oil rig; (*b*) COMPUTING = WINDOW *noun* 4e; **viewscreen** (in science fiction) a screen via which one may see and communicate remotely with another person; **viewsite** (chiefly *US*) a site (for a house or other building) with an attractive view.

view /vjuː/ *verb.* E16.
[from the noun.]
1 *verb trans.* Inspect or examine in a formal or official manner; survey carefully or professionally. Formerly also, review (troops). E16.

2 *spec.* †**a** *verb trans.* Inspect or examine (records, accounts, etc.) by way of check or control. M16–M17. ▸†**b** *verb trans.* Survey or explore (a country, coast, etc.). M16–L18. ▸**c** *verb intrans.* Look over a property to assess its suitability for purchase or rent. E20.

3 a *verb trans.* Look at; scrutinize; observe closely. M16. ▸**b** *verb trans.* See; catch sight of. L16. ▸**c** *verb trans.* HUNTING. See (a fox) break cover; give notice of (the fox as doing so) by hallooing. Usu. foll. by *away*. M19. ▸**d** *verb trans. & intrans.* Watch (television); watch (a programme etc.) on television. M20.

4 *verb trans.* Survey or examine mentally; pass under mental review; contemplate, consider. Also foll. by *with*. L16. ▸**b** Regard or approach in a particular manner or a certain light; form an opinion of. M18.

> 1 J. SMEATON We . . took the opportunity of viewing the progress of our moorstone works. *Harpers & Queen* Invite readers to a special evening to view the . . Ready-to-Wear collections. **2c** ***order to view***: see ORDER *noun*. **3a** *Choice* Another important diagnostic tool for viewing the colon is the barium X-ray. **b** *Skin Diver* Viewed from above, the archipelago is a vast tapestry of turquoise. 4 A. HELPS He . . has viewed the matter in hand more gravely. *Times Educ. Suppl.* Intellectuals are viewed with suspicion. **b** S. BELLOW He viewed himself as a person normally interested in girls. *Backpacker* Scientists pledged they would no longer view forests as a standing cash crop.

■ **viewaˈbility** *noun* ability to be viewed M20. **viewable** *adjective* able to be viewed; *spec.* (of a television programme) able to be watched with pleasure or interest, worth watching: E20.

viewdata /ˈvjuːdeɪtə/ *noun.* Also **V-**. L20.
[from VIEW *verb* + *data* pl. of DATUM.]
A videotex system employing a telephone connection to a computer database. Cf. PRESTEL.

viewer /ˈvjuːə/ *noun.* LME.
[from VIEW *verb* + -ER[1].]
1 A person appointed to examine or inspect something; *esp.* (*a*) an inspector or examiner of goods supplied by contract; (*b*) LAW a person appointed by a court to inspect the scene of a crime, property, etc. (cf. VIEW *noun* 1c). LME. ▸**b** An overseer, manager, or superintendent of a coalmine or colliery. E18.

2 *gen.* A person who views, watches, or looks at something; an observer, a spectator. M16. ▸**b** A person who watches television. M20.

3 An optical device for looking at film transparencies etc. M20.

■ **viewership** *noun* the audience for a particular television programme or channel; the number of such an audience: M20.

viewing /ˈvjuːɪŋ/ *noun*. **M16.**
[from VIEW *verb* + -ING[1].]
The action of VIEW *verb*; an instance of this; an opportunity or occasion to view; *spec.* (*a*) *N. Amer.* the action of seeing the deceased for a final time before a funeral; a time for mourners to view a body in this way; (*b*) the activity of watching television; an instance or period of this; (*c*) the inspection of a property by a prospective buyer, or of objects to be sold at auction; an instance of this (cf. VIEW *noun* 1d).

📖 *Video Maker* Video recorders . . now 'time-shift' programmes for future viewing. *Dancing Times* A new ballet may show its qualities best at a second viewing.

viewless /ˈvjuːlɪs/ *adjective*. **E17.**
[from VIEW *noun* + -LESS.]
1 That cannot be perceived by the eye; unable to be seen; invisible. Cf. SIGHTLESS *adjective* 2. *literary*. **E17.**
2 Lacking a view or prospect. **M19.**
3 Having no views or opinions. **L19.**

📖 **1** WORDSWORTH Gone are they, viewless as the buried dead.

■ **viewlessly** *adverb* (*literary*) invisibly **E19.**

viewly /ˈvjuːli/ *adjective*. Now *dial.* **M16.**
[from VIEW *noun* + -LY[1].]
Pleasant or attractive to the view, having a pleasing appearance.

viewpoint /ˈvjuːpɔɪnt/ *noun*. Also **view-point**. **M19.**
[from VIEW *noun* + POINT *noun*[1].]
1 A point of view; a mental standpoint from which a matter is considered. **M19.**
2 A point or position from which a view or prospect is seen; an observation point. **M19.**

📖 **1** R. HAYMAN The story was to be written from the viewpoint of a young man. **2** *Amateur Photographer* Using standard to wideangle focal length lenses allows the photographer to select a different viewpoint.

viewy /ˈvjuːi/ *adjective*. **M19.**
[from VIEW *noun* + -Y[1].]
1 Holding or characterized by speculative or fanciful views; lacking common sense. *colloq.* **M19.**
2 Eye-catching; showy. *slang*. Now *rare*. **M19.**

📖 **1** W. H. PATER Some knotty question or viewy doctrine.

■ **viewiness** *noun* (*rare*) the state or quality of being viewy; tendency to speculative or fanciful views: **M19.**

viff /vɪf/ *noun & verb*. *colloq.* **L20.**
[Acronym, from vectoring in forward flight.]
▶ **A** *noun*. A technique used by a vertical take-off aircraft to change direction abruptly by altering the direction of thrust of the aircraft's jet engines. **L20.**
▶ **B** *verb intrans.* Of a vertical take-off aircraft: change direction in this way. **L20.**

vig /vɪg/ *noun*. *US slang*. **M20.**
[Abbreviation.]
= VIGORISH.

viga /ˈviːgə/ *noun*. *US*. **M19.**
[Spanish.]
A rough-hewn roof timber or rafter, esp. in a Pueblo building.

Vigenere /vɪʒəˈnɛː/ *adjective & noun*. Also **-ère**. **E20.**
[Blaise de Vigenère (1523–96), French scholar and student of ciphers.]
(Designating or pertaining to) a polyalphabetic cipher first described by Vigenère in 1586.

vigent /ˈvʌɪdʒ(ə)nt/ *adjective*. Long *rare*. **L16.**
[Latin *vigent-*, pres. ppl stem of *vigere* thrive: see -ENT.]
Flourishing; vigorous; prosperous.

vigesimal /vɪˈdʒɛsɪm(ə)l, vʌɪ-/ *adjective*. **M17.**
[from Latin *vigesimus* var. of *vicesimus*, from *viceni* distrib. of *viginti* twenty + -AL[1]. Cf. VICENARY, VICESIMAL.]
Pertaining to twentieths or to the number twenty; reckoning or proceeding by twenties or twentieths.
■ **vigesimally** *adverb* **L20.**

vigia /ˈvɪdʒɪə/ *noun*. **M19.**
[Portuguese = lookout, from *vigiar*, from Latin *vigilia*: see next.]
A warning on a sea chart to denote a reported but as yet unverified danger.

vigil /ˈvɪdʒɪl/ *noun & verb*. **ME.**
[Old & mod. French *vigile* from Latin *vigilia* watch, wakefulness, from *vigil* awake, alert, rel. to *vigere* be vigorous or lively.]
▶ **A** *noun*. **1** ECCLESIASTICAL. The eve of a festival or holy day, as an occasion of religious observance. **ME.** ▸**b** A devotional watch, *esp.* the watch kept on the eve of a festival or holy day; a nocturnal service or devotional exercise. Usu. in *pl.* **LME.** ▸**c** In *pl.* Prayers said or sung at a nocturnal service, esp. for the dead. **L15.**
†**2** A wake. *rare*. **LME–E17.**
†**3** Each of the four watches into which the ancient Romans divided the night. **LME–M17.**
4 The action of keeping watch, orig. *spec.* devotional watch. Freq. in ***keep vigil***. **LME.**
5 *gen.* An occasion or period of keeping awake for any reason or purpose during a time usually given to sleep. **L17.** ▸**b** A stationary and peaceful demonstration in support of a particular cause, usu. characterized by the absence of speeches or other explicit advocacy of the cause. **M20.**
6 A period of wakefulness or insomnia. *rare*. **M18.**

📖 **1b** POPE Visits to ev'ry Church we daily paid . . The Stations duly, and the Vigils kept. **4** P. BAILEY My parents kept vigil in a room in the hospital. **5** J. BEERBOHM Some companion to enliven my weary vigil. **b** *Gay Times* Candlelit vigils . . against the murder . . are to take place at French embassies.

▶ **B** *verb intrans.* Keep a vigil or vigils. *rare*. **L19.**

📖 *Peace News* They vigiled and sang outside the cruise control base.

vigilance /ˈvɪdʒɪl(ə)ns/ *noun*. **L16.**
[French, or Latin *vigilantia*, formed as VIGILANT: see -ANCE.]
1 The quality or character of being vigilant; watchfulness, alertness to danger etc.; close monitoring of a situation; caution. **L16.** ▸†**b** A guard, a watch. *rare* (Milton). Only in **M17.**
2 The state of being awake; *spec.* in MEDICINE (now *rare*), insomnia. **M18.**

📖 **1** *Guardian* The Home Secretary . . urged greater public vigilance after the . . bombing.

Comb.: **vigilance committee** *US* a self-appointed body for the maintenance of justice and order in a community lacking well-established procedures for such matters.
■ Also †**vigilancy** *noun* **M16–M18.**

vigilant /ˈvɪdʒɪl(ə)nt/ *adjective & noun*. **L15.**
[Latin *vigilant-* pres. ppl stem of *vigilare* keep awake, from *vigil*: see VIGIL, -ANT[1].]
▶ **A** *adjective*. **1** Watchful against danger, difficulty, etc.; keeping steadily on the alert; closely monitoring a situation. **L15.** ▸**b** HERALDRY. Of an animal: positioned as if watching for prey. *rare*. **E19.**
2 Characterized by vigilance; assiduous. **M16.**
†**3** Wakeful; sleepless. *rare*. **E–M17.**

📖 **1** S. NAIPAUL He had been a vigilant and faithful watchdog of the state's interest. **2** H. H. WILSON It was impossible . . to exercise a vigilant personal supervision over the officers.

▶ **B** *noun*. *rare*.
1 A guardian, a keeper. **E19.**
2 A wakeful or watchful person. **E19.**
■ **vigilantly** *adverb* **M16.** †**vigilantness** *noun* (*rare*) vigilance **L16–E18.**

vigilante /vɪdʒɪˈlanti/ *noun*. Orig. *US*. **M19.**
[Spanish = VIGILANT.]
A member of a vigilance committee; any person executing summary justice in the absence or breakdown of legally constituted law enforcement bodies. Now also, a member of a self-appointed group undertaking law enforcement but without legal authority, operating in addition to an existing police force to protect property etc. within a localized area.

📖 *Guardian* Armed civilian vigilantes . . patrolled the streets of Lusaka. *attrib.*: *Sounds* A vigilante group to stamp out . . boorish male behaviour.

■ **vigilantism** *noun* the principles or practice of vigilantes **M20.**

vigintennial /vɪdʒɪnˈtɛnɪəl/ *adjective*. *rare*. **E20.**
[from Latin *viginti* twenty, after *biennial*, *triennial*, etc.: see -AL[1].]
Occurring every twenty years.

vigintillion /vɪdʒɪnˈtɪljən/ *noun*. **E20.**
[from Latin *viginti* twenty, after *million*, *billion*, etc.]
Orig. (esp. in the UK), the twentieth power of a million (10^{120}). Now usu. (orig. *US*), the twenty-first power of a thousand (10^{63}).

vigintivirate /vɪˈdʒɪntɪˌvɪrət/ *noun*. **L16.**
[Latin *viginti-viratus*, from *viginti-viri* (a committee of) twenty men: see -ATE[1].]
ROMAN HISTORY. The office or position of a member of an administrative committee of twenty men; this committee.

vigneron /ˈviːnjərɒn, *foreign* viɲərɔ̃ (*pl. same*)/ *noun*. **LME.**
[French, from *vigne* VINE.]
A person who cultivates grapevines; a vine-grower.
¶ Recorded earlier in **ME** as a surname.

vignette /viːˈnjɛt, vɪ-/ *noun & verb*. As noun also (earlier) †**vinet**. **LME.**
[Old & mod. French, dim. of *vigne* VINE: see -ET[1], -ETTE.]
▶ **A** *noun*. **1** A usu. small decorative design or illustration on a blank space in a book etc., esp. at the beginning or end of a chapter or on the title page; *spec.* one not enclosed in a border, or with the edges shading off into the surrounding paper. Formerly also, an ornamental title page etc. containing various symbolic designs or figures. **LME.**
2 ARCHITECTURE. A carved decoration representing the trailing tendrils, branches, or leaves of a vine. **LME.**
3 A photographic portrait showing only the head or the head and shoulders and with the edges gradually shading into the background. **M19.**
4 A brief descriptive account, anecdote, or essay; a character sketch; a short evocative episode in a play etc. **L19.**
▶ **B** *verb trans.* **1** Make a vignette of; *spec.* produce (a photograph) in the style of a vignette by softening away or shading off the edges of the subject. **M19.**
2 OPTICS. Cause vignetting of an image. **M20.**

📖 **1** *Graphics World* These include the softly vignetted sunsets . . of Japan.

■ **vignetter** *noun* a device for producing photographic vignettes, usu. consisting of a mask or screen with a central hole or of graduated opacity from the centre outwards **L19.** **vignetting** *noun* †(*a*) *rare* = VIGNETTE *noun* 2; (*b*) the action or process of producing vignettes, esp. in photography; (*c*) OPTICS a darkening or loss of the periphery of an image, as a result of the blocking of some off-axis rays during their passage through the optical system: **E17.** **vignettist** *noun* an artist or engraver who produces vignettes for books **L19.**

vignoble /ˈviːnjəʊb(ə)l/ *noun*. **L15.**
[Old & mod. French, from popular Latin, from Latin *vinea* vineyard.]
A vineyard.

vigogne /vɪˈgəʊn; *foreign* vigɔɲ (*pl. same*)/ *noun*. **M17.**
[French from Spanish VICUÑA.]
1 The vicuña. **M17.**
2 Vicuña cloth. Also, a cheap hosiery yarn. **L19.**
Comb.: **vigogne yarn** a mixture of the wool of the vicuña, or other fine wool, and cotton.

vigonia /vɪˈgəʊnɪə/ *noun*. **M18.**
[App. a Latinization of French VIGOGNE.]
The vicuña. Also, (in full ***vigonia wool***) vicuña wool; (in full ***vigonia cloth***) vicuña cloth.

vigor *noun* see VIGOUR.

†**vigorate** *verb trans.* **E17–L18.**
[Latin *vigorat-* pa. ppl stem of *vigorare* animate, invigorate, from *vigor* VIGOUR: see -ATE[3].]
Invigorate, strengthen.

vigorish /ˈvɪg(ə)rɪʃ/ *noun*. *US slang*. **E20.**
[Prob. from Yiddish from Russian *vyigrysh* gain, winnings.]
The percentage deducted from a gambler's winnings by the organizers of a game. Also, an excessive rate of interest on a loan.

vigorist /ˈvɪg(ə)rɪst/ *noun*. *rare*. **E19.**
[from Latin *vigor* VIGOUR + -IST.]
A person who acts with vigour or energy; a person who advocates vigorous action.

vigoro /ˈvɪg(ə)rəʊ/ *noun*. *Austral.* **E20.**
[from VIGOROUS *adjective*: see -O.]
A team game combining elements of cricket and baseball, played with a soft rubber ball.

vigorous /ˈvɪg(ə)rəs/ *adjective*. **ME.**
[Old French (mod. *vigoureux*) from medieval Latin *vigorosus*, from Latin *vigor* VIGOUR: see -OUS.]
1 (Of a person, animal, bodily part or function, etc.) physically strong and active, energetic, robust in health; (of a plant, vegetation, etc.) growing strongly and flourishingly. **ME.** ▸**b** Characterized by, requiring, or involving physical strength or activity. **L17.**
2 Full of or exhibiting operative force or vitality; having a powerful or invigorating effect. **LME.** ▸**b** Of language etc.: forceful, stirring, rousing. **E19.**
3 Acting, performed, or enforced with vigour or energy. **LME.**

📖 **1** J. R. GREEN He was so vigorous that he made his way to Scotland on foot. P. MANN Thorndyke was in vigorous health . . and kept himself fit by playing tennis. *Amateur Gardening* This vigorous climber is grown mainly for its fruits. **b** C. STORR Munching nut bars to replenish their strength after vigorous swimming races. **2** DRYDEN The too vig'rous Dose too fiercely wrought. J. MORLEY So vigorous and minutely penetrative was . . his understanding. A. REID Granted a more vigorous flow of water, the Northmuir need fear no local rival. **b** G. VIDAL The book opens with a vigorous description of Wanamaker's department store being torn down. **3** *New York Times* She waged a vigorous campaign but lost, receiving less than 25 percent of the vote.

■ **vigorously** *adverb* **LME.** **vigorousness** *noun* **LME.**

vigour /ˈvɪgə/ *noun*. Also ***-or**. **ME.**
[Old French (mod. *vigueur*) from Latin *vigor* liveliness, activity, from *vigere* be lively, flourish: see -OR, -OUR.]
1 Active physical strength; vitality; activity or energy of body or constitution. **ME.** ▸**b** Strong or flourishing growth in a plant or vegetation. **E17.**
2 Vital or powerful operative force or strength; powerfulness or intensity of effect or operation. **LME.**

▸**b** Forcefulness in the expression of ideas, artistic feeling, etc.; rousing or stirring quality. M16.
3 *LAW.* Legal or binding force; validity. Freq. in ***in vigour***, in force or operation. Now *rare*. LME.
4 A condition or state at which strength or activity are at a peak; the prime of life. Also formerly (*MEDICINE*), the height or peak of a disease. M16.
5 Mental or moral robustness, energy, or activity; animation or liveliness of thought or the faculties. L16.
6 Strong, firm, or energetic action, esp. in administration or government; the power or use of this. E17.

> 🕮 **1** G. CRABBE When Honour .. gave thee every charm, Fire to thy eye and vigour to thy arm. E. FIGES What .. gives him the vigour to go off .. as though time had not touched him? **2** W. LITHGOW The vigour of the day gone, and the cooling night come, we aduanced. *Independent* The downside of all this macho vigour is a tendency for the car to buck. **b** *Guardian* This .. recording fully captures the vigour .. which gave his piano playing such lasting quality. **4** A. N. WILSON Minto, still in the days of her vigour, feeding the fowls, exercising the dogs. **5** L. GRANT-ADAMSON An attractive man, whose physical energy was matched by intellectual vigour. **6** *Parliamentary Affairs* He .. chided those departments which had failed to pursue the new managerialism with sufficient vigour.

■ **vigourless** *adjective* M18.

viguier /vigje/ *noun.* Pl. pronounced same. M18.
[French, var. of *vicaire*: see VICAR.]
1 *Hist.* A magistrate in pre-Revolutionary southern France. M18.
2 Either of two government officials in Andorra acting as executive representatives of (ultimately) the French President and the Spanish Bishop of Urgel. L19.

vihara /vɪˈhɑːrə/ *noun.* L17.
[Sanskrit *vihāra*.]
A Buddhist monastery or nunnery.

vihuela /vɪˈ(h)weɪlə/ *noun.* M19.
[Spanish.]
An early Spanish stringed musical instrument, *spec.* (*a*) (more fully ***vihuela de mano*** /dɪ ˈmanəʊ/ [= of the hand]) a type of guitar; (*b*) (more fully ***vihuela de arco*** /dɪ ˈɑːkəʊ/ [= of the bow]) a type of viol.
■ **vihuelista** /vɪ(h)weɪˈliːstə/ *noun* a player of the vihuela E20.

Viking /ˈvʌɪkɪŋ/ *noun & adjective.* E19.
[Old Norse *víkingr*, Icelandic *víkingur*, either from *vík* creek, inlet or from Old English *wīc* WICK *noun*[2] (whence also Old English *wīcing* pirate): see -ING[3].]
Hist. ▸**A** *noun.* Any of the Scandinavian seafaring pirates and traders who raided and settled in parts of NW Europe in the 8th to the 11th cents.; *gen.* a warlike pirate or sea-rover. E19.

> 🕮 A. MACKAY Norse Vikings whose dragon boats preyed on the coasts.

▸**B** *attrib.* or as *adjective.* Of or pertaining to the Vikings. M19.
■ **Vikingism** *noun* the practices or customs of the Vikings L19.

vila /ˈviːlə/ *noun.* Pl. **vilas**; **vile** /ˈviːli/. E19.
[Serbo-Croat.]
In southern Slavonic mythology, a fairy, a nymph, a spirit. Cf. WILI.

vilayet /vɪˈlɑːjɛt/ *noun.* M19.
[Turkish *vilâyet* from Arab. *wilāya(t)* government, rule, administrative district.]
A province of Turkey (formerly of the Ottoman empire), ruled by a *vali* or governor.

vild /vʌɪld/ *adjective.* Long *arch. & dial.* M16.
[Alt. of VILE *adjective* with excrescent *d*.]
Vile.
■ **vildly** *adverb* L16. **vildness** *noun* L16.

vile *noun*[1] *pl.* see VILA.

vile /vʌɪl/ *adjective, adverb, & noun*[2]. ME.
[Old & mod. French *vil* masc., *vile* fem. from Latin *vilis* of low value or price, cheap, mean, base.]
▸**A** *adjective.* **1** Morally base; despicable, depraved, shameful; (of an insult etc.) implying depravity. ME.
2 Physically repulsive, esp. through filth or corruption; disgusting, sordid. ME.
3 Of a condition, situation, etc.: base, degrading, ignominious. *arch.* ME.
4 Of little worth or account; of low status; worthless. *arch.* ME. ▸†**b** Cheap, low in price. L15–E17.
5 Of poor quality, wretchedly inferior. Now chiefly *colloq.*, abominably bad, very unpleasant. ME.

> 🕮 **1** LD MACAULAY The vilest specimens of human nature are to be found among demagogues. T. C. WOLFE He used to .. call me vile names. B. HEAD An act of the most vile treachery. **2** W. PRYNNE My vile body I bequeath to the dust. **3** F. W. FARRAR A slave, in the vilest of all positions. **4** POPE A clamorous vile plebeian rose. ***in durance vile***: see DURANCE 2. **5** C. BRAYFIELD The vile climate of this .. land. L. GRANT-ADAMSON The coffee .. tasted vile without .. milk and sugar.

▸**B** *adverb.* Vilely. Now only in comb. ME.

> 🕮 W. OWEN Rough blankets and vile-tasting food.

▸†**C** *noun.* A base or despicable person. LME–M16.
■ **vilely** *adverb* ME. **vileness** *noun* †(*a*) foulness, filthiness, foul matter; (*b*) the quality or character of being vile; depravity, baseness; an instance of this: L15.

Vilene /ˈvʌɪliːn/ *noun.* M20.
[Invented word: see -ENE.]
(Proprietary name for) a backing or lining material for cloth.

†**viliaco** *noun.* Also **-iago**. Pl. **-oes**. L16–M17.
[Italian *vigliacco*, from Latin *vilis* VILE *adjective*.]
A vile or contemptible person; a villain.

vilify /ˈvɪlɪfʌɪ/ *verb trans.* LME.
[Late Latin *vilificare*, from Latin *vilis*: see VILE *adjective*, -FY.]
1 Lower in worth or value; make of little or less account. Now *rare* or *obsolete*. LME. ▸†**b** Make morally vile, degrade. Also, defile, dirty. E17–L18. ▸†**c** Disgrace, dishonour. M17–M18.
2 Depreciate or disparage with abusive or slanderous language; defame, revile, speak evil of. Formerly also, speak slightingly of. L16.
†**3** Regard as worthless or of little value; despise. L16–L17.

> 🕮 **2** J. P. STERN He extols Rome .. merely to vilify Judaeo-Christian subversiveness. W. SHEED Inclined to vilify the informers and canonize the resisters.

■ **vilifiˈcation** *noun* (*a*) *rare* the action of lowering a person etc. in worth or value; (*b*) the action of vilifying or reviling a person etc. with abusive language; an instance of this; (*c*) *rare* an abusive remark or speech: M17. **vilifier** *noun* E17. **vilifyingly** *adverb* L17.

vilipend /ˈvɪlɪpɛnd/ *verb trans. arch.* LME.
[Old & mod. French *vilipender* or Latin *vilipendere*, from *vilis* VILE *adjective* + *pendere* consider.]
1 Regard as worthless or of little value, despise; treat contemptuously or slightingly. LME.
2 Speak slightingly or abusively of; abuse, vilify. E16.
■ **vilipender** *noun* M19. **viliˈpensive** *adjective* abusive E19.

vility /ˈvʌɪlɪti/ *noun.* Long *arch.* LME.
[Latin *vilitas*, from *vilis* VILE *adjective*: see -ITY.]
1 Vileness of character or conduct; moral baseness or depravity. LME.
†**2a** Mean or low estimate. Only in LME. ▸**b** Lowliness of status or condition. M16–L17. ▸**c** Lowness of price, cheapness. Only in 17.

vill /vɪl/ *noun.* Also †**ville**. E17.
[Anglo-Norman = Old French *vil(l)e* farm, country house (mod. *ville* town) from Latin *villa*: see next.]
1 *Hist.* In medieval England, the smallest administrative unit under the feudal system, a subdivision of a hundred roughly corresponding to the Anglo-Saxon tithing and the modern parish; a feudal township. E17.
2 A village. *poet.* L17.
†**3** A villa. *rare.* L17–M18.

villa /ˈvɪlə/ *noun.* E17.
[Partly from Latin *villa* country house, farm, partly from Italian *villa* from Latin.]
1 In *ROMAN ANTIQUITIES*, a large country house with an estate. Now, a country residence; *spec.* a rented or privately owned holiday home, esp. abroad. E17.
2 A usu. detached or semi-detached house in a suburban or residential district. Freq. in proper names. M18.

> 🕮 **2** A. N. WILSON A substantial semi-detached house called Dundela Villas.

■ **villadom** *noun* suburban villas or their residents collectively L19. **villaed** *adjective* covered with villas L18. **villafy** *verb trans.* (*a*) turn into a villa; (*b*) cover with villas: M19. **villakin** *noun* (chiefly *joc.*) a small villa M18. **villaless** *adjective* M19. **villarette** *noun* a small villa L18.

Villafranchian /vɪləˈfraŋkɪən/ *adjective & noun.* L19.
[French *villafranchien*, from *Villafranca* d'Asti, a village in N. Italy near which exposures of this period occur: see -IAN.]
PALAEONTOLOGY. (Of, pertaining to, or designating) a stratigraphical stage in Europe crossing the boundary of the Upper Pliocene and the Lower Pleistocene, and *esp.* the mammalian fauna of this period.

village /ˈvɪlɪdʒ/ *noun.* LME.
[Old French, from Latin *villa*: see prec., -AGE.]
1 A self-contained group of houses and associated buildings, usu. in a country area; an inhabited place larger than a hamlet and smaller than a town. LME. ▸**b** A large town or city, *esp.* London. *joc.* E19. ▸**c** A small self-contained district or community within a city or town, regarded as having features characteristic of a village; *spec.* (***the Village***), Greenwich Village in New York. M19. ▸**d** A minor municipality with limited corporate powers. *US.* L19. ▸**e** A select suburban shopping centre. *Austral.* L20.
2 The inhabitants or residents of a village regarded as a community; the villagers. E16.
3 A small group or cluster of burrows of prairie dogs. Also ***village burrow***. Cf. TOWN *noun* 7. E19.

> 🕮 **1** J. PURSEGLOVE The Warwickshire village of Barton near Stratford. D. M. THOMAS It was scarcely a village—just three or four houses and a church spire. ***global village***, ***lake village***, ***post-village***, ***street village***, ***tent village***, etc. **c** *Harpers & Queen* Hampstead—the loveliest of London's historical 'villages'.

Comb.: **village burrow**: see sense 3 above; **village idiot** a person of very low intelligence resident and well known in a village; *transf.* a very foolish or apparently simple-minded person; **village pump** a village's communal water pump (freq. allusively: cf. ***PARISH pump***).
■ **villagedom** *noun* the condition or status of a village; the system of village communities: M19. **villageful** *noun* as many as a village contains, the whole population of a village L19. **villagehood** *noun* = VILLAGEDOM L19. **villageless** *adjective* L19. **village-like** *adjective* resembling (that of) a village M19. **villaget** *noun* (*rare*) a little village L18. **villageward(s)** *adverb* in the direction of a village L19. **villagey** *adjective* village-like L19.

villager /ˈvɪlɪdʒə/ *noun.* L16.
[from prec. + -ER[1].]
A person living in a village, now esp. a working-class native or resident of long standing.
■ **villageress** *noun* (*rare*) a female villager L19.

villagery /ˈvɪlɪdʒ(ə)ri/ *noun. arch.* L16.
[formed as prec. + -ERY.]
Villages collectively.

> 🕮 SHAKES. *Mids. N. D.* Are you not he That frights the maidens of the villagery.

villagization /vɪlɪdʒʌɪˈzeɪʃ(ə)n/ *noun.* Also **-isation**. M20.
[formed as prec. + -IZATION.]
In Africa and Asia, concentration of population in villages; the transfer of control of land to villagers communally; in Tanzania, *spec.* = UJAMAA.

villain /ˈvɪlən/ *noun & adjective.* ME.
[Old French *vilein*, *vilain* (mod. *vilain*) from Proto-Romance (medieval Latin *villanus* villager) from Latin *villa* VILLA.]
▸**A** *noun.* Also †**villein**. See also VILLEIN.
▸**I 1** Orig. (*arch.*), a simple or unsophisticated person; a rustic; a boor. Now, a person guilty or capable of great wickedness, an unprincipled or depraved person. ME. ▸**b** A rogue, a rascal. Chiefly *joc.* L16. ▸**c** (Usu. with *the*.) The character in a play, novel, etc., important to the plot because of his or her evil motives or actions; *transf.* a culprit. Freq. in ***the villain of the piece***. Cf. HERO 4. E19. ▸**d** A professional criminal. *colloq.* M20.
2 †**a** A bird, esp. a hawk, of a common or inferior species. L15–L16. ▸**b** A person or animal of a troublesome character. L19.

> 🕮 **1** *New Yorker* Innocents, lured into the clutches of charming villains. ***rogue and villain***: see ROGUE *noun*. **b** R. BAGOT If this .. post does not bring me a letter from Jim .. I shall telegraph to the young villain. **c** *Guardian* He played .. Nazi villains in British films. L. STARKE CFCs and halons, the villains in the eroding ozone-layer problem. **d** *Face* The .. British habit of turning petty villains into .. folk heroes.

▸**II** See VILLEIN.
▸**B** *adjective.* †**1** = VILLAINOUS 1. Only in ME.
2 = VILLAINOUS 2. Now *rare* or *obsolete*. ME.
†**3** Bringing opprobrium, shameful. Cf. VILLAINOUS 4. ME–M16.
4 = VILLAINOUS 6. Now *rare* or *obsolete*. LME.
5 = VILLAINOUS 5. *rare.* E17.
■ **villaindom** *noun* (*rare*) the world of villains, villains collectively L19. **villainess** *noun* a female villain L16. **villainize** *verb trans.* (*a*) make villainous; debase, degrade; (*b*) treat or revile as a villain: E17. **villainizer** *noun* L16.

†**villainage** *noun* var. of VILLEINAGE.

villainous /ˈvɪlənəs/ *adjective.* Also †**-anous**. LME.
[Sense 1 from Old French *vileneus*; later senses from VILLAIN + -OUS.]
†**1** Churlish, boorish, rude. *rare.* Only in LME.
2 Having the character of a villain; indicative or of the nature of villainy; depraved, wicked; criminal. LME.
3 Of words etc.: scurrilous, obscene, profane. L15.
†**4** Shameful, horrible. E16–E17.
5 Extremely bad or objectionable; atrocious, detestable. Now *colloq.* L16.
†**6** Low in status or social position; servile. Cf. VILLEIN. E17–M18.

> 🕮 **2** G. BORROW They were villainous-looking ruffians. *Guardian* A .. villainous landlord who goes to extreme lengths to evict his .. lodger. **3** R. L. STEVENSON He .. broke out with a villainous, low oath. **5** *Christian World* The weather was villainous It rained every day.

■ **villainously** *adverb* LME. **villainousness** *noun* (*rare*) E18.

villainy /ˈvɪləni/ *noun.* Also †**villany**. ME.
[Old & mod. French *vilenie* (medieval Latin *vilania*, *-enia*): see VILLAIN, -Y[3].]
1 Action or conduct characteristic or typical of a villain; villainous behaviour; depravity, wickedness; crime; an instance of this, a wicked act or deed. ME.
†**2** Injury, indignity, or insult suffered by a person; (a source of) disgrace, dishonour, or discredit. ME–L16.
†**3** Lack of politeness, rudeness, boorishness. ME–L17.
†**4** Lack of status or social position; servitude. LME–M16.

📖 **1** R. NORTH His Employments . . were forging, . . stealing and all Sorts of villainy. H. CONWAY Capable of any villainy that the heart of man could devise.

villan /ˈvɪlən/ *noun.* **M16.**
[medieval Latin *villanus* villager, from Latin VILLA.]
Hist. A villein.

†villanage *noun* var. of VILLEINAGE.

villancico /viʎanˈθiko/ *noun.* Pl. **-os** /-ɔs/. **E19.**
[Spanish, dim. of *villano* peasant, rustic from medieval Latin *villanus*: see prec.]
MUSIC. A form of Spanish and Portuguese song consisting of short stanzas separated by a refrain, orig. a kind of folk-song but later used in sacred music; now *esp.* a Christmas carol.

villanella /vɪləˈnɛlə/ *noun.* Pl. **-lle** /-leɪ/, **-llas.** **L16.**
[Italian: see next.]
MUSIC. A form of Italian part-song having a rustic character and a vigorous rhythm.

villanelle /vɪləˈnɛl/ *noun.* **L16.**
[French from Italian *villanella* fem. of *villanello* rural, rustic, from *villano* peasant, rustic from medieval Latin *villanus* villager from Latin *villa* VILLA.]
†**1** MUSIC. = VILLANELLA. **L16–L17.**
2 A usu. pastoral or lyric poem consisting normally of five three-line stanzas and a final quatrain, with only two rhymes throughout and some lines repeated. **L19.**

†villanous *adjective* var. of VILLAINOUS.

Villanova /vɪləˈnəʊvə/ *noun.* **E20.**
[A hamlet near Bologna in Italy, the scene of archaeological finds.]
ARCHAEOLOGY. Used *attrib.* to designate an Italian culture of the early Iron Age.

Villanovan /vɪləˈnəʊv(ə)n/ *noun & adjective.* **E20.**
[from prec. + -AN.]
ARCHAEOLOGY. ▶**A** *noun.* An inhabitant of Italy during the Villanova period. **E20.**
▶**B** *adjective.* Of, pertaining to, or designating the Villanova period. **E20.**

†villany *noun* var. of VILLAINY.

Villar y Villar /ˌvɪlɑːr iː ˈvɪlɑː/ *noun phr.* **L19.**
[Spanish = Villar (a surname) and Villar.]
(Proprietary name for) a kind of Havana cigar.

villatic /vɪˈlatɪk/ *adjective.* Chiefly *arch.* **L17.**
[Latin *villaticus*, from *villa* VILLA: see -ATIC.]
Of or pertaining to a villa or villas or the inhabitants; *esp.* rural, rustic.

📖 MILTON The . . roosts, And nests . . Of tame villatic Fowl.

ville /vɪl, vʌɪl/ *noun*[1]. *colloq.* (chiefly *US*). **M19.**
[French = town. Cf. -VILLE.]
A town, a village.

†ville *noun*[2] var. of VILL.

-ville /vɪl/ *suffix. colloq.* **M16.**
[from French *ville* town, as in many US town-names. Cf. VILLE *noun*[1].]
Forming the names of fictitious places with ref. to the particular quality suggested by the word to which it is added.

📖 F. H. BURNETT That girl is a winner from Winnersville. J. AITKEN Man, that's just dragsville.

villeggiatura /villeddʒaˈtuːra/ *noun.* Pl. **-re** /-re/. **M18.**
[Italian, from *villeggiare* live at a villa or in the country, from *villa* VILLA.]
Residence at a country villa or in the country, esp. in Italy; a holiday spent in this way.

villein /ˈvɪlən, -eɪn/ *noun.* Also **†villain**. See also VILLAIN *noun.* **ME.**
[Var. of VILLAIN *noun.*]
1 *Hist.* Under the feudal system: a peasant occupier or cultivator entirely subject to a lord or attached to a manor; a serf. Formerly also *gen.*, a peasant, a country labourer, a rustic. **ME.**
2 See VILLAIN *noun.*
Comb.: **villein service** service rendered by a villein to his lord as a condition of holding his land; **villein socage** socage or tenure by villein service.

villeinage /ˈvɪlənɪdʒ, -leɪn-/ *noun.* Also **†villa(i)nage.** **ME.**
[Anglo-Norman, Old French *vilenage*, medieval Latin *villenagium*: see prec., -AGE.]
Hist. **1** The state or condition of a feudal villein; serfdom. **ME.**
2 The tenure by which a feudal villein held or occupied his land. Also ***tenure in villeinage.*** **LME.**
3 The body of villeins, villeins collectively. **M19.**

ville lumière /vil lymjɛːr/ *noun.* **E20.**
[French = town or city of light(s).]
A brightly lit city or town; an exciting modern city or town; *spec.* (***la Ville Lumière***), Paris.

villi *noun* pl. of VILLUS.

villiform /ˈvɪlɪfɔːm/ *adjective.* **M19.**
[from VILLUS + -I- + -FORM.]
ZOOLOGY. Having the form of villi; resembling velvet.

villino /vilˈliːno, vɪˈliːnəʊ/ *noun.* Pl. **-ni** /-ni/. **M19.**
[Italian, dim. of *villa* VILLA.]
A small house in Italy.

Villonesque /viːjɒˈnɛsk, viːlɒˈnɛsk/ *adjective.* **M20.**
[from *Villon* (see below) + -ESQUE.]
Characteristic of the 15th-cent. French lyric poet François Villon or his work.

villose /ˈvɪləʊs/ *adjective.* **E18.**
[Latin *villosus* hairy, rough, from VILLUS: see -OSE[1].]
BOTANY & ENTOMOLOGY. = VILLOUS 3.

villosity /vɪˈlɒsɪti/ *noun.* **L18.**
[from prec. + -ITY: see -OSITY.]
1 BOTANY & ZOOLOGY. The condition or fact of being villous. **L18.**
2 A villous formation or surface; a villus. **E19.**

villotta /vilˈlɔtta/ *noun.* Pl. **-tte** /-tte/. **L19.**
[Italian.]
MUSIC. A type of villanella originating in northern Italy.

villous /ˈvɪləs/ *adjective.* **LME.**
[Latin *villosus*: see VILLOSE, -OUS.]
1 ANATOMY. Covered with villi. **LME.**
2 Of the nature of villi. **M17.**
3 BOTANY & ZOOLOGY. Thickly covered with long soft hairs; shaggy. **M18.**

villus /ˈvɪləs/ *noun.* Pl. **villi** /ˈvɪlʌɪ, ˈvɪliː/. **E18.**
[Latin = tuft of hair, shaggy hair.]
1 BOTANY. A long, slender, soft hair. Usu. in *pl.* **E18.**
2 ANATOMY. Any of numerous slender hairlike processes or minute projections closely set on a surface, esp. in the mucous membrane of the intestines. Usu. in *pl.* **E18.**

vim /vɪm/ *noun*[1]. Orig. *US.* **M19.**
[Prob. from Latin *vim* accus. sing. of *vis* strength, energy.]
Vigour, energy, spirit.

Vim /vɪm/ *noun*[2] *& verb.* Also **v-.** **L19.**
[App. from prec.]
▶**A** *noun.* (Proprietary name for) a scouring powder. **L19.**
▶**B** *verb trans.* Infl. **-mm-**. Clean with Vim. **E20.**

vimana /vɪˈmaːnə/ *noun.* **M19.**
[Sanskrit *vimāna.*]
In the Indian subcontinent: the central tower enclosing the shrine in a temple; MYTHOLOGY a heavenly chariot.

vimineous /vɪˈmɪnɪəs/ *adjective.* Now *rare.* **M17.**
[from Latin *vimineus*, from *vimin-*, *vimen* osier: see -EOUS.]
1 Made of pliable twigs or wickerwork. **M17.**
2 BOTANY. Producing slender flexible twigs. **M17.**

VIN *abbreviation.*
Vehicle identification number.

vin /vɛ̃/ *noun.* Pl. pronounced same. **L17.**
[French Cf. VINHO, VINO.]
(A) French wine: used in various phrases.
vin blanc /blɑ̃/, pl. **-s -s** (pronounced same), (a) white wine. ***vin compris*** /kɔ̃pri/ wine included in the price of a meal or other entertainment. ***vin cuit*** /kɥi/ [lit. 'cooked, boiled'] (*a*) grape juice boiled to a syrup and used to fortify or sweeten other wine (cf. VINO *cotto*); (*b*) a sweet aperitif wine. ***vin de paille*** /də pɑːj/, pl. ***vins de paille***, = ***straw wine*** s.v. STRAW *noun & adjective.* ***vin de table*** /də tabl/, pl. ***vins de table***, = ***table wine*** s.v. TABLE *noun* (cf. TAFELWEIN). ***vin d'honneur*** /dɔnœːr/, pl. ***vins d'honneur***, a wine formally offered in honour of a person or persons; a reception at which wine is so offered. ***vin doux (naturel)*** /du natyrɛl/, pl. ***vins doux (naturels)*** (pronounced same), [lit. 'sweet (natural)'] a sweet fortified wine. ***vin du pays*** /dy pe(j)i/, pl. ***vins du pays***, [lit. 'of the country'] a local wine. ***vin fou*** /fu/, pl. ***vins fous*** (pronounced same), [lit. 'mad'] a white or rosé sparkling wine from the Jura. ***vin gris*** /gri/, pl. ***vins gris***, [lit. 'grey'] a rosé wine of eastern France. ***vin jaune*** /ʒoːn/, pl. ***vins jaunes*** (pronounced same), [lit. 'yellow'] a yellowish wine from the Jura region of eastern France. ***vin mousseux***, pl. ***vins mousseux***, = MOUSSEUX *noun.* ***vin ordinaire*** /ɔrdinɛːr/, pl. **-s -s** (pronounced same), [lit. 'ordinary'] (a) simple (usu. red) table wine for everyday use. ***vin rosé*** /roze, ˈrəʊzeɪ/, pl. **-s -s** (pronounced same), (a) rosé wine. ***vin rouge*** /ruːʒ/, pl. **-s -s** (pronounced same), (a) red wine.

vina *noun* var. of VEENA.

vinaceous /vʌɪˈneɪʃəs/ *adjective & noun.* **L17.**
[from Latin *vinaceus*, from *vinum* wine.]
▶**A** *adjective.* Of the reddish colour of wine, wine-coloured. **L17.**
▶**B** *noun.* A vinaceous colour. *rare.* **E19.**

vinaigrette /vɪneɪˈgrɛt, vɪnɪ-/ *noun.* **LME.**
[French, from *vinaigre* VINEGAR *noun*: see -ETTE.]
†**1** **a** A stew, sauce, or other dish made with vinegar. Only in **LME.** ▸**b** A condiment prepared with vinegar. Only in **L17.**
2 *Hist.* A small two-wheeled carriage drawn or pushed by people, formerly used in France. **L17.**
3 A small ornamental bottle or box for holding a sponge saturated with smelling-salts etc. **E19.**
4 A salad dressing of oil and wine vinegar with seasoning. Also more fully ***vinaigrette dressing***, ***vinaigrette sauce.*** **L19.**

¶ In isolated use before **L17.**

vinal /ˈvʌɪn(ə)l/ *adjective.* **M17.**
[from Latin *vinum* wine + -AL[1].]
Produced by or originating in wine.

vinaya /ˈvɪnəjə/ *noun.* **M19.**
[Sanskrit = conduct.]
BUDDHISM. (The scripture containing) the code of conduct that regulates Buddhist monastic life.

vinblastine /vɪnˈblastiːn/ *noun.* **M20.**
[from mod. Latin *Vinca* former genus name (see next) + LEUCO)BLAST + -INE[5].]
PHARMACOLOGY. A cytotoxic alkaloid obtained from the Madagascar periwinkle, *Catharanthus roseus*, and used to treat lymphomas and other cancers. Cf. VINCRISTINE.

vinca /ˈvɪŋkə/ *noun*[1]. **M19.**
[mod. Latin (see below), from late Latin *pervinca*: see PERIWINKLE *noun*[1].]
Any plant belonging to (or formerly included in) the genus *Vinca* (family Apocynaceae); a periwinkle.
Comb.: **vinca alkaloid** any of several alkaloids (as vinblastine, vincristine) obtained from Madagascar periwinkle.

Vinča /ˈvɪntʃə/ *noun*[2]. **E20.**
[A village site near Belgrade in Serbia.]
ARCHAEOLOGY. Used *attrib.* to designate (artefacts of) a central Balkan culture of neolithic and chalcolithic age.

Vincennes /vanˈsɛn/ *noun & adjective.* **M18.**
[See below.]
▶**A** *noun.* A kind of fine porcelain produced at a château in the town of Vincennes (now a suburb of Paris) in the eighteenth cent., before the workshop was transferred to Sèvres. **M18.**
▶**B** *attrib.* or as *adjective.* Designating (an item made from) this porcelain. **L19.**

Vincent /ˈvɪns(ə)nt/ *noun.* **E20.**
[Jean Hyacinthe *Vincent* (1862–1950), French bacteriologist.]
MEDICINE. Used in *possess.* to designate a painful ulcerative condition of the inside of the mouth or of the gums, associated with infection with fusiform bacteria and spirochaetes.
Vincent's angina, ***Vincent's disease***, ***Vincent's gingivitis***, etc.

Vincentian /vɪnˈsɛnʃ(ə)n/ *noun*[1] *& adjective*[1]. **M19.**
[from *Vincent* (see below) + -IAN.]
▶**A** *noun.* A member of an order of Roman Catholic mission-priests founded by St Vincent de Paul (1576–1660). **M19.**
▶**B** *adjective.* Of or pertaining to St Vincent or his order. **L19.**

Vincentian /vɪnˈsɛnʃ(ə)n/ *noun*[2] *& adjective*[3]. **M20.**
[from St *Vincent* (see below) + -IAN.]
▶**A** *noun.* A native or inhabitant of St Vincent in the W. Indies. **M20.**
▶**B** *adjective.* Of or pertaining to St Vincent. **M20.**

Vincentian /vɪnˈsɛnʃ(ə)n/ *adjective*[2]. **L19.**
[from St *Vincent* of Lerins (see below) + -IAN.]
THEOLOGY. Designating a canon or rule originating or associated with St Vincent of Lerins (died *c* 450).

vinchuca /vɪnˈtʃuːkə/ *noun.* **M20.**
[Amer. Spanish, from Quechua *wihchuykuk* lit. 'fall violently'.]
Any of several bloodsucking triatomine bugs of Central and S. America, esp. *Triatoma infestans.*

vincible /ˈvɪnsɪb(ə)l/ *adjective.* Now *literary.* **M16.**
[Latin *vincibilis*, from *vincere* overcome: see -IBLE. Cf. earlier INVINCIBLE.]
Of an opponent, obstacle, etc.: able to be overcome or conquered; conquerable, surmountable.
■ **vinciˈbility** *noun* **M18.** **vincibleness** *noun* **E18.** **vincibly** *adverb* **M17.**

vincristine /vɪnˈkrɪstiːn/ *noun.* **M20.**
[formed as VINBLASTINE, the 2nd elem. perh. repr. CRISTA.]
PHARMACOLOGY. A cytotoxic alkaloid obtained from the Madagascar periwinkle, *Catharanthus roseus*, and used to treat acute leukaemia and other cancers. Cf. VINBLASTINE.

vinculum /ˈvɪŋkjʊləm/ *noun.* Pl. **-la** /-lə/. **M17.**
[Latin, from *vincire* bind: see -ULE.]
1 A bond, a tie. Chiefly *fig.* **M17.**
2 MATH. A horizontal line over two or more terms, denoting that they are to be treated as a unit in the following operation. **E18.**
3 ANATOMY. A connecting band or bandlike structure; *esp.* a narrow tendon. **M19.**

vindaloo /vɪndəˈluː/ *noun.* **L19.**
[Prob. from Portuguese *vin d'alho* wine and garlic sauce, from *vinho* wine + *alho* garlic.]
A highly spiced hot Indian curry dish made with meat, fish, or poultry. Also ***vindaloo curry***, etc.

vindemial /vɪnˈdiːmɪəl/ *adjective. rare.* **M17.**
[Latin *vindemialis*, from *vindemia* vintage: see -AL[1].]
Of, pertaining to, or associated with the gathering of grapes.

vindemiate /vɪnˈdiːmɪeɪt/ *verb intrans. rare.* **M17.**
[Latin *vindemiat-* pa. ppl stem of *vindemiare*, from *vindemia* vintage: see **-ATE**³.]
Gather ripe fruit, esp. grapes.

vindemiation /vɪnˌdiːmɪˈeɪʃ(ə)n/ *noun. rare.* **L16.**
[medieval Latin *vindemiatio(n-)*, formed as prec.: see **-ATION**.]
The gathering of grapes etc.

vindicate /ˈvɪndɪkeɪt/ *verb trans.* **M16.**
[Latin *vindicat-* pa. ppl stem of *vindicare* claim, set free, punish, avenge, from *vindic-*, *vindex* claimant, avenger: see **-ATE**³.]
†**1 a** Wreak (anger) in revenge. Only in **M16.** ▸**b** Avenge or revenge (a person, cause, wrong, etc.). **E17–E18.** ▸**c** Punish; take revenge *on* a person for (a wrong). **E17–L18.**
†**2** Make or set free; deliver, rescue. Usu. foll. by *from*. **M16–M18.**
3 Claim for oneself or as one's rightful property; assert or establish possession of. Freq. foll. by *for*, *to*. **L16.**
4 Clear of blame, criticism, or doubt by demonstration etc.; justify (a person, action, oneself, etc.) by evidence or argument; establish or maintain the existence or validity of (a quality, assertion, etc). **M17.**
5 Assert or maintain by means of action, esp. in one's own interest; defend against encroachment or interference. **M17.**

📖 **4** T. FERRIS Subsequent experiments have further vindicated Einstein's confidence. M. PATTISON To vindicate himself from the charge of treason. *Guardian* He has been vindicated, for the colliery is indeed earmarked for closure.

■ **vindicaˈbility** *noun* (*rare*) **E19.** **vindicable** *adjective* able to be vindicated **M17.** **vindicatingly** *adverb* **L19.**

vindication /vɪndɪˈkeɪʃ(ə)n/ *noun.* **L15.**
[Old French (now dial.) or Latin *vindicatio(n-)*, formed as prec.: see **-ATION**.]
†**1** The action of avenging or revenging a person, wrong, etc. **L15–L17.** ▸**b** Retribution, punishment. Only in **M17.**
†**2** Deliverance, emancipation. Only in **E17.**
3 The action or an act of vindicating a person etc. or of clearing of blame etc.; justification by evidence or argument; maintenance of the existence or validity of a quality etc. Freq. foll. by *of*. **M17.** ▸**b** A justifying fact or circumstance. **M19.**

vindicative /vɪnˈdɪkətɪv, ˈvɪndɪkeɪtɪv/ *adjective.* **LME.**
[Old & mod. French *vindicative*, *-tif* or medieval Latin *vindicativus*, formed as **VINDICATE**.]
†**1** = **VINDICTIVE** *adjective* 1. **LME–M18.**
2 = **VINDICTIVE** *adjective* 2. Now *rare*. **E17.**
3 Serving to vindicate a thing etc. by defence or assertion. **M17.**
■ **vindicativeness** *noun* vindictiveness **M17.**

vindicator /ˈvɪndɪkeɪtə/ *noun.* **M16.**
[Late (eccl.) Latin, formed as **VINDICATE**: see **-OR**.]
A person who vindicates a person or thing.
■ **vindicatress** *noun* (*rare*) a female vindicator **M19.**

vindicatory /ˈvɪndɪkeɪt(ə)ri/ *adjective.* **M17.**
[from **VINDICATE** + **-ORY**².]
1 Serving or tending to vindicate a thing etc.; justificatory, defensive. **M17.**
2 Of a law etc.: avenging; punitive, retributive. **M17.**
■ **vindicatorily** *adverb* **M19.**

vindictive /vɪnˈdɪktɪv/ *adjective.* **E17.**
[from Latin *vindicta* vengeance, revenge + **-IVE**.]
1 Tending to seek revenge; characterized by a desire for revenge; vengeful; spiteful. **E17.**
2 Involving retribution or punishment; punitive, avenging. Now *rare*. **E17.**

📖 **1** N. MONSARRAT The vindictive paying-off of old scores. N. BAWDEN You aren't vindictive, you haven't said even *one* bad thing about Pete! **vindictive damages** LAW damages exceeding simple compensation to the plaintiff and awarded also to punish the defendant.

■ **vindictively** *adverb* **E18.** **vindictiveness** *noun* **L17.**

vine /vʌɪn/ *noun & verb.* **ME.**
[Old French *vine*, (also mod.) *vigne* from Latin *vinea* vineyard, vine, use as noun of fem. of *vineus* pertaining to wine, from *vinum* **WINE** *noun*.]
▶ **A** *noun.* **1** Any of the climbing woody plants of the genus *Vitis* (family Vitaceae) grown for their grapes (esp. grapes used to make wine); *esp.* the Old World species *V. vinifera*, long grown in warm-temperate countries. Also *gen.*, any plant of the genus *Vitis*. **ME.** ▸**b** *fig.* Christ regarded as a vine, of which his followers are the branches. Chiefly in echoes of *John* 15:1 etc. **ME.**
2 With specifying word: any of numerous plants related to the cultivated vine or resembling it in their climbing habit. **LME.**
†**3** A vineyard. **LME–M16.**
†**4** A grape. *poet. rare.* **LME–L17.**
5 ROMAN ANTIQUITIES. = **VINEA**. *rare.* **LME.**
6 a The stem of any trailing or climbing plant. **M16.** ▸**b** A straw rope. *dial.* **L16.** ▸**c** A trailing or climbing plant; any plant whose stem needs support to stay erect. Chiefly *N. Amer.* **E18.**
7 A suit of clothes; *pl.* clothing. *US slang.* **M20.**

📖 **1** *Guardian* Glasses of strong ruby wine from the Baronessa's vines. **2** *balloon vine*, *caustic vine*, *kudzu vine*, *potato vine*, *Russian vine*, etc. **wild vine** (*a*) *N. Amer.* (now *rare*) the fox-grape, *Vitis labrusca*; (*b*) *dial.* any of several British climbing or trailing plants, esp. traveller's joy and white bryony. **6a** *New Yorker* She happened to have plenty of green tomatoes on the vine.

Comb.: **vine black** charcoal prepared from vine twigs or wood; **vine-dresser** a person engaged in the pruning, training, and cultivation of vines; **vine-fretter** (now *rare* or *obsolete*) a grub or insect, esp. an aphid, that feeds on vines; **vine-hook** an implement used in pruning vines; **vine leaf** a leaf of a vine (*STUFFED vine leaves*); **vine louse** = *grape* PHYLLOXERA; **vine moth** either of two small moths which infest vines, *Eupoecilia ambiguella* (family Cochylidae), and (more fully ***European vine moth***) *Lobesia botrana* (family Tortricidae); ***vine*** PHYLLOXERA; †**vine-press** a wine-press; **vine-rod** a staff of vine-wood, the badge of office of a Roman centurion; **vine-scroll** an ornamentation representing a vine; **vine snake** any of several very slender arboreal colubrid snakes, esp. of the genus *Oxybelis* (of tropical America) and *Thelotornis* (of Africa); **vine tree** = sense 1 above; **vine weevil** a weevil, *Otiorhynchus sulcatus*, which is destructive to many plants, esp. pot plants; **vine-wood** the wood of the vine.

▶ **B** *verb trans. & intrans.* †**1** *verb trans.* Graft into a vine. *rare.* Only in **L16.**
2 *verb intrans.* Develop tendrils like a vine; grow or twist like a vine. **L18.**
3 *verb trans.* Separate (peas) from their vines and pods, usu. by means of a mechanical viner. Chiefly as ***vining*** *verbal noun.* Chiefly *US.* **E20.**
■ **vineless** *adjective* **L19.** **viner** *noun* (orig. *US*) an implement for gathering the products of vines or trailing or climbing plants, *esp.* one used to harvest peas **E20.**

vinea /ˈvɪnɪə/ *noun.* Pl. **-eae** /-ɪiː/. **E17.**
[Latin: see prec.]
ROMAN ANTIQUITIES. A kind of protective shed or canopy used in siege operations.

vineal /ˈvɪnɪəl/ *adjective. rare.* **M17.**
[Latin *vinealis*, formed as prec.: see **-AL**¹.]
Of or pertaining to vines or wine; growing on vines.

vinegar /ˈvɪnɪɡə/ *noun & verb.* **ME.**
[Old French *vyn egre* (mod. *vinaigre*) ult. from Latin *vinum* wine + *acer*, *acre* sour.]
▶ **A** *noun.* **1** A sour-tasting liquid consisting chiefly of dilute acetic acid, produced by the oxidation of the alcohol in wine, other liquors, etc., and used (freq. with additives) as a condiment or food preservative. **ME.**
2 *fig.* Sour or acid speech, behaviour, or character; sourness, sharpness. **E17.**

📖 **1** ***malt vinegar***, ***raspberry vinegar***, ***strawberry vinegar***, ***tarragon vinegar***, ***wine vinegar***, etc. ***mother of vinegar***: see **MOTHER** *noun*² 2. ***oil and vinegar***: see **OIL** *noun*. ***piss and vinegar***: see **PISS** *noun*. ***thieves' vinegar***: see **THIEF**. **2** *She* My life isn't all sweetness. There's a little vinegar there. *attrib.*: E. MIALL A peevish and vinegar-hearted step-mother.

Comb.: **vinegar Bible** a 1717 Oxford edition of the Bible in which 'the parable of the vineyard' at *Luke* 20 read 'the parable of the vinegar'; **vinegar eel** a minute nematode worm, *Turbatrix aceti*, that breeds in vinegar; **vinegar-fly** a fruit fly of the genus *Drosophila*; **vinegar mother**, **vinegar plant** = ***mother of vinegar*** s.v. **MOTHER** *noun*² 2; **vinegar stick** *Hist.* a sword or walking-stick with a vinaigrette or holder for smelling-salts fitted into the handle; **vinegar worm** = ***vinegar eel*** above.

▶ **B** *verb trans.* Treat or flavour with vinegar; add or apply vinegar to; restore with vinegar. **E17.**

vinegarish /ˈvɪnɪɡ(ə)rɪʃ/ *adjective.* **M17.**
[from prec. + **-ISH**¹.]
Somewhat resembling vinegar; sour, sharp, (*lit. & fig.*).
■ **vinegarishly** *adverb* **L19.**

vinegarroon /ˌvɪnɪɡəˈruːn/ *noun. US.* Also **-aroon**. **M19.**
[Amer. Spanish *vinagrón*, from Spanish *vinagre* **VINEGAR** *noun*.]
A large harmless whip scorpion, *Mastigoproctus giganteus*, which is found in southern USA and Mexico, and when alarmed emits a secretion smelling like vinegar.

vinegary /ˈvɪnɪɡ(ə)ri/ *adjective.* **M18.**
[formed as prec. + **-Y**¹.]
Resembling vinegar, sour like vinegar; acid. Chiefly *fig.*

vinery /ˈvʌɪn(ə)ri/ *noun.* **LME.**
[In sense 1 from Old French *vignerie* (medieval Latin *vinarium*); in senses 2 & 3 from **VINE** + **-ERY**.]
1 A vineyard. **LME.**
2 A greenhouse or hothouse for grapevines. **L18.**
3 Vines collectively. **L19.**

†**vinet** *noun* see **VIGNETTE**.

vinew *adjective, verb, & noun* var. of **VINNY**.

vinewed *adjective* var. of **VINNIED**.

vineyard /ˈvɪnjɑːd, -jəd/ *noun.* **ME.**
[from **VINE** + **YARD** *noun*¹.]
1 A plantation of grapevines, *esp.* one cultivated for wine-making. **ME.**
2 *fig.* In biblical allusions, a sphere of action or labour, esp. of an elevated or spiritual character. **LME.**
■ **vineyarded** *adjective* enclosed as a vineyard; covered with vineyards: **E19.** **vineyarding** *noun* the cultivation of vineyards **L19.** **vineyardist** *noun* a person engaging in vine-growing **M19.**

vingerpol /ˈfɪŋərpɔl/ *noun.* **L19.**
[Afrikaans, from Dutch *vinger* **FINGER** *noun* + *pol* tuft.]
Any of several South African spurges producing succulent branches which resemble fingers, as *Euphorbia clavaroides* and *E. caput-medusae*.

vingt-et-un /vɛ̃t e œ̃/ *noun.* Also †**vingt-un**. **L18.**
[French = twenty-one. Cf. **PONTOON** *noun*².]
The card-game pontoon.

vingty /ˈvaŋti/ *noun. slang.* **M20.**
[Abbreviation.]
= **VINGT-ET-UN**.

vinho /ˈviɲu, ˈviːnəʊ/ *noun.* **M19.**
[Portuguese Cf. **VIN**, **VINO**.]
Portuguese wine: used in various phrases.
vinho branco /ˈbraŋku, ˈbraŋkəʊ/ white wine. ***vinho corrente*** /kəˈrrentə/ [lit. 'common, ordinary'] = ***VINO corriente***. ***vinho da casa*** /da ˈkaza/ [lit. 'of the house'] house wine. ***vinho de consumo*** /də kɔ̃ˈsumu/ [lit. 'for consumption'] = ***VINO corriente***. ***vinho tinto*** /ˈtintu, ˈtɪntəʊ/ red wine. ***vinho verde*** /ˈverdə, ˈvəːdi/ [lit. 'green wine'] young wine not allowed to mature.

vinic /ˈvʌɪnɪk/ *adjective.* Now *rare* or *obsolete*. **M19.**
[from Latin *vinum* wine + **-IC**.]
Chiefly CHEMISTRY. Obtained or derived from wine or alcohol.

viniculture /ˈvɪnɪkʌltʃə/ *noun.* **L19.**
[from Latin *vinum* wine + **-I-** + **-CULTURE**.]
The cultivation of grapes for the production of wine.
■ **viniˈcultural** *adjective* **L19.** **viniˈculturist** *noun* a person engaged in viniculture **L19.**

viniferous /vʌɪˈnɪf(ə)rəs/ *adjective. rare.* **M19.**
[formed as prec. + **-FEROUS**.]
Producing wine.

vinification /ˌvɪnɪfɪˈkeɪʃ(ə)n/ *noun.* **L19.**
[formed as prec. + **-FICATION**.]
The conversion of grape juice etc. into wine by fermentation.

vink /fɪŋk/ *noun. S. Afr.* Also **fink**. **M19.**
[Afrikaans = finch.]
A weaver-bird.

vinney *adjective, verb, & noun* var. of **VINNY**.

vinnied /ˈvɪnɪd/ *adjective.* Long *obsolete* exc. *dial.* Also **vinewed** /ˈvɪnjuːd/, **vinnowed** /ˈvɪnəʊd/; **f-** /f-/. **E16.**
[from **VINNY** *verb*, *noun*: see **-ED**¹, **-ED**².]
Mouldy, musty.

vinny /ˈvɪni/ *adjective, verb, & noun.* Long *obsolete* exc. *dial.* & in ***blue vinn(e)y (cheese)*** s.v. **BLUE** *adjective*. Also **vinew** /ˈvɪnjuː/, **vinney**, **vinnow** /ˈvɪnəʊ/, (earlier) **f-**; as adjective also **fenny** /ˈfɛni/.
[Old English *fynig*, formed as **FEN** *noun*²: see **-Y**¹.]
▶ **A** Mouldy, musty. **OE.**
▶ **B** *verb intrans. & trans.* (Cause to) become mouldy. **OE.**
▶ **C** *noun.* Mould, mouldiness. Also *ellipt.* (sc. cheese) in ***blue vinny***, ***blue vinney***. **M16.**

vino /ˈvino, *esp. in sense 3* ˈviːnəʊ/ *noun.* **L17.**
[Spanish, Italian = wine. Cf. **VIN**, **VINHO**.]
1 Spanish or Italian wine: used in various phrases. **L17.**
2 An alcoholic liquor distilled from nipa-palm sap, drunk in the Philippines. **E20.**
3 Wine, esp. of an inferior kind. *colloq.* (freq. *joc.*). **E20.**

📖 **1** ***vino blanco*** /ˈblaŋko/ [Spanish] white wine. ***vino corriente*** /koˈrrjente/ [Spanish, lit. 'common, ordinary'] cheap wine equivalent to *vin ordinaire*. ***vino cotto*** /ˈkɔtto/ [Italian, lit. 'cooked'] grape juice boiled to a syrup and used to fortify or sweeten other wine, esp. marsala (cf. ***VIN cuit***). ***vino crudo*** /ˈkruːdo/ [Italian, lit. 'raw'] wine in its natural state, not boiled (cf. ***vino cotto*** above). ***vino de color*** /de koˈlɔr/ [Spanish] a rich sweet wine, used in the blending of sherry and other fortified wines. ***vino de pasto*** /de ˈpasto/ [Spanish, lit. 'pasture wine'] (*a*) a pale and fairly dry sherry; (*b*) table wine for everyday consumption. ***vino dolce*** /ˈdoltʃe/ [Italian], ***vino dulce*** /ˈdulθe/ [Spanish] sweet wine. ***vino locale*** /loˈkaːle/ [Italian] local wine. ***vino maestro*** /maˈestro/ [Spanish, lit. 'master'] a sweet and strong wine used to fortify or sweeten other wines. ***vino nero*** /ˈneːro/ [Italian, lit. 'black'] dark red wine. ***vino rosso*** /ˈrosso/ [Italian] red wine. ***vino santo*** /ˈsanto/ = **VINSANTO**. ***vino secco*** /ˈsekko/ [Italian] dry wine. ***vino tierno*** /ˈtjerno/ [Spanish, lit. 'tender'] wine made from partially dried grapes, used esp. for fortifying malaga. ***vino tinto*** /ˈtinto/ [Spanish] red wine. **3** *Food & Wine* Any old vino . . will do.

vinolent /ˈvʌɪn(ə)l(ə)nt/ *adjective.* **LME.**
[Latin *vinolentus*, from *vinum* wine.]
Fond of drinking wine; tending to drunkenness.
■ **vinolence** *noun* (*rare*) drunkenness **LME.** **vinolency** *noun* (*rare*) drunkenness **E17.** **vinolentness** *noun* drunkenness **E18.**

vinologist /vʌɪˈnɒlədʒɪst/ *noun. rare.* **M19.**
[from Latin *vinum* wine + **-OLOGIST**.]
A connoisseur of wines.

vinometer /vʌɪˈnɒmɪtə/ *noun.* **M19.**
[formed as prec. + **-OMETER.**]
An instrument for measuring the strength or purity of wine.

vinose /vʌɪˈnəʊs/ *adjective.* **E18.**
[Latin *vinosus* full or fond of wine: see **-OSE**[1].]
Vinous.

vinosity /vʌɪˈnɒsɪti/ *noun.* **E17.**
[from next + **-ITY.**]
1 Fondness for wine. **E17.**
2 The state or quality of being vinous; vinous character or flavour. **M17.**

vinous /ˈvʌɪnəs/ *adjective.* **LME.**
[from Latin *vinum* + **-OUS.**]
1 Of the nature of or resembling wine; made of or prepared with wine. **LME.** ▸**b** Producing wine or similar liquor. *rare.* **L17.**
2 Of, pertaining to, or characteristic of wine. **E18.**
3 Fond of wine or of drinking; resulting from or affected by drinking wine etc.; drunken. **L18.**
4 Of the reddish colour of wine, wine-red, vinaceous. **M19.**
1 vinous liquor alcoholic drink made from grapes, wine. **2 vinous fermentation** (now *rare*) alcoholic fermentation.
■ **vinously** *adverb* **M19. vinousness** *noun* **E18.**

vinsanto /vinˈsanto, vɪnˈsantəʊ/ *noun.* **M20.**
[Italian, from *vino santo* holy wine.]
A sweet white Italian dessert wine. Cf. ***VINO santo.***

vint /vɪnt/ *noun*[1]. *rare.* **M17.**
[Back-form. from **VINTAGE** *noun.*]
(A) vintage.

vint /vɪnt/ *noun*[2]. **L19.**
[Russian.]
A Russian card-game resembling auction bridge.

vint /vɪnt/ *verb trans.* **E18.**
[Back-form. from **VINTAGE** *verb* or **VINTNER.**]
†**1** Sell (wine). Only in **E18.**
2 Make (wine or other liquor). **M19.**

vinta /ˈvɪntə/ *noun.* **E20.**
[Austronesian.]
A small sailing boat used by the Moros of the Philippines.

vintage /ˈvɪntɪdʒ/ *noun & adjective.* **LME.**
[Old & mod. French *vendange* from Latin *vindemia*, from *vinum* **WINE** *noun* + *demere* take away, alt. by assoc. with **VINTER, VINTNER** and assim. to **-AGE.**]
▶ **A** *noun.* **1 a** The produce of the vine, either as grapes or wine; the yield of a vineyard or district in a season; the wine made from this. **LME.** ▸**b** Wine, esp. of good quality. *poet.* **E17.** ▸**c** A wine of high quality made from the crop of a single identified district in a good year. **M18.**
2 The gathering of grapes for wine-making, the grape-harvest; the season or time of this. **LME.**
3 *transf. & fig.* The year or period when a person was born or flourished or a thing made or produced; a thing etc. made in a particular year or period. **L19.**

> 📖 **1a** SHELLEY The purple vintage . . Heaped upon the creaking wain. **c** *Washington Post* He rates a . . 1945 Mouton-Rothschild . . among the finest vintages. **2** BURKE The produce of the vintage in . . Languedoc. **3** J. HIGGINS A . . silk dress of pre-war vintage.

▶ **B** *adjective.* **1** Of or pertaining to the vintage; of high quality; characteristic of the best period of a person's or a producer's work, classic; of an old style, from the past, antique. **L19.**
2 *spec.* Designating a car made between 1917 or (strictly) 1905 and 1930. Cf. **VETERAN** *adjective* 2b. **E20.**

> 📖 **1** *Country Life* This [play] may be recommended as vintage Coward. JOHN MORRIS A bottle of the finest vintage claret. *Independent* It was not a vintage performance from the Wallabies. **vintage festival**: to celebrate the beginning of the vintage. **vintage port** port of special quality, all of one year, bottled early and aged in the bottle.

vintage /ˈvɪntɪdʒ/ *verb.* **L16.**
[from prec.]
1 *verb intrans.* Gather grapes to make wine. *rare.* **L16.**
2 *verb trans.* **a** Strip (vines or a vineyard) of grapes at the vintage. Now *rare* or *obsolete.* **E17.** ▸**b** Gather (grapes) to make wine; make (wine) from gathered grapes. **L19.**

vintager /ˈvɪntɪdʒə/ *noun.* **L16.**
[from **VINTAGE** *noun* + **-ER**[1].]
A person who gathers grapes or works at the vintage.

vintem /vɪnˈtɛm/ *noun.* **L16.**
[Portuguese, from *vinte* twenty.]
Hist. In Portugal, Brazil, etc., a small silver or copper coin of the value of 20 reis.

†**vinter** *noun.* **ME–L15.**
[Anglo-Norman *viniter, vineter*: see next.]
A vintner.
■ †**vinteress, -tress** *noun* = **VINTNERESS L17–E18.**

vintner /ˈvɪntnə/ *noun.* **LME.**
[Anglo-Latin *vintenarius* var. of *vinetarius* from Anglo-Norman *viniter, vineter*, Old French *vinetier* from medieval Latin *vinetarius, vinatarius* from Latin *vinetum* vineyard from *vinum* wine: see **-ER**[2].]
A person who deals in or sells wine, a wine-merchant. Formerly also, an innkeeper selling wine.
■ **vintneress** *noun* (*rare*) a female vintner **M17. vintnership** *noun* the occupation or position of a vintner **L17. vintnery** *noun* the trade of a vintner, wine-selling **M19.**

vintry /ˈvɪntri/ *noun.* Now *arch.* or *Hist.* **ME.**
[from **VINTER** + **-Y**[3]: see **-RY.**]
1 A place for the selling or storage of wine; a wine shop, a wine vault. **ME.**
2 Usu. ***the Vintry.*** A large wine store formerly existing in the City of London; the immediate neighbourhood of this as a part of the city. **LME.**

viny /ˈvʌɪni/ *adjective.* **L16.**
[from **VINE** + **-Y**[1].]
1 Of, pertaining to, or of the nature of vines; consisting of vines. **L16.**
2 Full of or covered with vines; bearing or producing vines. **E17.**

vinyl /ˈvʌɪnɪl, -(ə)l/ *noun & adjective.* **M19.**
[from Latin *vinum* wine + **-YL.**]
▶ **A** *noun.* **1** CHEMISTRY. The monovalent radical or group $CH_2{=}CH{-}$. **M19.**
2 A polyvinyl resin or plastic; a covering material or fabric made of or containing this. **M20.** ▸**b** This as the material of which gramophone records are made. Also, a gramophone record, esp. as opp. to a compact disc; records collectively. *colloq.* **L20.**

> 📖 **2b** Q With vinyl on its way out, the 45rpm single doesn't have much chance.

Comb.: **vinyl acetate** a colourless liquid ester, $CH_2CH{\cdot}O{\cdot}CO{\cdot}CH_3$, used in the production of polyvinyl acetate and other commercially important polymers; **vinyl chloride** a colourless toxic gas, CH_2CHCl, used in the production of polyvinyl chloride and other commercially important polymers; **vinyl resin** any resin that is composed of polyvinyl compounds.
▶ **B** *attrib.* or as *adjective.* Consisting or made of vinyl, covered with vinyl; *colloq.* of or pertaining to records, pressed as a record. **M20.**

vinylidene /vʌɪˈnʌɪlɪdiːn, vʌɪˈnɪlɪdiːn/ *noun.* **L19.**
[from prec. + **-IDENE.**]
CHEMISTRY. The divalent radical $CH_2{=}C{=}$. Usu. in *comb.* Cf. **POLYVINYLIDENE.**

Vinylite /ˈvʌɪnɪlʌɪt/ *noun.* **E20.**
[from **VINYL** + **-ITE**[1].]
(Proprietary name for) a vinyl resin used esp. in the manufacture of gramophone records.

vinylogue /ˈvʌɪnɪlɒɡ/ *noun.* Also ***-log.** **M20.**
[from **VINYL** + **-LOGUE.**]
CHEMISTRY. Each of two or more compounds that have the same molecular structure except for a $-CH{=}CH-$ group.
■ **viˈnylogous** *adjective* pertaining to or designating a vinylogue or a series of vinylogues **M20. vinylogy** /vʌɪˈnɪlədʒi/ *noun* the relationship between vinylogous compounds **M20.**

Vinylon /ˈvʌɪnɪlɒn/ *noun.* Also **V-. M20.**
[from **VINYL** + **-ON**, perh. after **NYLON.**]
Any of a class of synthetic fibres made from polyvinyl alcohol treated with formaldehyde, used esp. in the manufacture of water-resistant fabrics.

Vinyon /ˈvɪnjən/ *noun.* **M20.**
[from **VINY(L** + **-ON**, after **RAYON** *noun*[2].]
Any of several synthetic fibres which are copolymers of vinyl chloride with other vinyl compounds.

viol /ˈvʌɪəl/ *noun*[1]. **L15.**
[Old French *viel(l)e* (mod. **VIELLE**), alt. of *viole*, from Provençal *viola, viula*, prob. rel. to **FIDDLE** *noun.*]
1 †**a** A medieval musical instrument resembling a violin; a fiddle. Only in **L15.** ▸**b** A musical instrument of the Renaissance and afterwards, having five, six, or seven strings, often with frets, played with a bow and held vertically on the knees or between the legs. **M16.**
†**2** A player on this instrument. *rare.* **M16–M17.**
Phrases: *bass viol*: see **BASS** *adjective.* **viol d'amore** /daˈmɔːri/ = *viola d'amore* s.v. **VIOLA** *noun*[2].
■ **violer** *noun* (chiefly *Scot. arch.*) a player on the viol, formerly *esp.* one attached to a royal household **M16. violist** *noun* a player on the viol or viola **M17.**

†**viol** *noun*[2]. **E17–M19.**
[Origin unkn.]
NAUTICAL. A large rope attached to the capstan used to weigh an anchor.

viola /ˈvʌɪələ/ *noun*[1]. **LME.**
[Latin = violet, later used as a genus name.]
†**1** A violet. Also *fig. rare.* **LME–L15.**
2 Any plant of the genus *Viola* (family Violaceae), comprising the violets and pansies, which are characterized by irregular five-petalled flowers (the lowest petal being spurred). Also, a flower or flowering stem of such a plant. **M19.** ▸**b** HORTICULTURE. A type of pansy developed by hybridization of the garden pansy, *Viola wittrockiana*, with the Pyrenean *V. cornuta*, differing from the former in its tufted perennial growth and smaller, usu. uniformly coloured flowers. **L19.**

viola /vɪˈəʊlə/ *noun*[2]. **E18.**
[Spanish & Italian, prob. from Provençal: see **VIOL** *noun*[1].]
1 A four-stringed musical instrument of the violin family, larger and of lower pitch than a violin; an alto or tenor violin. **E18.** ▸**b** A player on this instrument. **L19.**
2 = **VIOLA DA GAMBA** 2. **L19.**
Phrases: **viola bastarda** = ***LYRA viol.*** **viola da braccio** any member of the violin family, as opp. to a viola da gamba; *spec.* a viol corresponding to the modern viola. **viola d'amore**, †**viola d'amour** a kind of tenor viol usu. having sympathetic strings and no frets. **viola pomposa** an 18th-cent. viola with an additional string.

violable /ˈvʌɪələb(ə)l/ *adjective.* **LME.**
[Latin *violabilis*, from *violare* **VIOLATE** *verb*: see **-ABLE.**]
†**1** Destructive. *rare.* Only in **LME.**
2 Able to be violated. **M16.**

violaceous /vʌɪəˈleɪʃəs/ *adjective.* **M17.**
[Latin *violaceus*, formed as **VIOLA** *noun*[1]: see **-ACEOUS.**]
Of a violet colour; purplish blue.

viola da gamba /vɪˌəʊlə də ˈɡambə/ *noun phr.* Also (earlier) **viol da gamba** /ˈvʌɪəl də ˈɡambə/. **L16.**
[Italian, lit. 'leg viol'.]
1 A viol held between the player's legs, *esp.* one corresponding to the modern cello. **L16.**
2 An organ-stop resembling this instrument in tone. **M19.**
■ **viola da gambist** *noun* a player on the viola da gamba **E20.**

violate /ˈvʌɪələt/ *adjective. arch.* **LME.**
[Latin *violatus*, formed as next.]
1 Violated. **LME.**
2 Impure, corrupt. **L15.**

violate /ˈvʌɪəleɪt/ *verb trans.* **LME.**
[Latin *violat-* pa. ppl stem of *violare* treat with violence etc.: see **-ATE**[3].]
1 Break, infringe, transgress; fail to keep or observe. **LME.** ▸**b** *transf.* Accuse or find (a prisoner) guilty of infringing the conditions of parole. *US slang.* **L20.**
2 Assault sexually; rape. **LME.**
3 Treat irreverently; desecrate, profane, defile. **LME.**
†**4 a** Cause (esp. physical) deterioration in; corrupt, spoil. **M16–M17.** ▸**b** Damage by violence. **L16–L17.**
†**5** Attack violently; assault, assail. **E–M17.**
6 Break in upon; interrupt or disturb rudely. **M17.**
7 Fail to respect; disregard. **L17.**

> 📖 **1** H. CARPENTER By undertaking paid work he was violating the terms of his entry visa. P. ABRAHAMS We do not violate their laws. **b** E. BRAWLEY My parole officer violated me . . and I wound up in the Joint again. **3** T. ARNOLD Some of the . . richest temples . . were violated and ransacked. **6** SHELLEY To violate the sacred doors of sleep. *New Yorker* 'Somebody's violated my space', she said. **7** J. GALSWORTHY He could not . . have violated his best instincts, letting other people into the secret.

■ **violater** *noun* (now *rare*) = **VIOLATOR E16. violative** *adjective* (chiefly *US*) involving or causing violation **M19. violator** *noun* a person who violates a person or thing; *arch.* a rapist: **LME. violatory** *adjective* (*rare*) = **VIOLATIVE** *adjective* **E19.**

violation /vʌɪəˈleɪʃ(ə)n/ *noun.* **LME.**
[Old & mod. French, or Latin *violatio(n-)*, formed as prec.: see **-ION.**]
1 The action or an act of violating a person or thing. **LME.**
2 *spec.* An infringement of the law; an infringement of the rules in a sports contest. Chiefly *N. Amer.* **M20.**

> 📖 **1** H. KUSHNER I was saddened by their violation of a sacred precinct. **2** *Philadelphia Inquirer* Leibowitz, 45, who had 630 outstanding tickets for moving violations, and . . Canning, 19, . . were led out of Traffic Court. *Sports Illustrated* This violation required a two-stroke penalty in the eyes of the . . officials.

■ **violational** *adjective* = **VIOLATIVE E19.**

violaxanthin /ˌvʌɪələˈzanθɪn/ *noun.* **M20.**
[from **VIOLA** *noun*[1] + **XANTHIN.**]
BIOCHEMISTRY. A xanthophyll occurring as a yellow pigment in daffodils and other plants.

viol da gamba *noun phr.* see **VIOLA DA GAMBA.**

violence /ˈvʌɪələns/ *noun.* **ME.**
[Old & mod. French from Latin *violentia*, from *violent-, -ens* or *violentus*: see **VIOLENT** *adjective & noun*, **-ENCE.**]
1 The exercise of physical force so as to cause injury or damage to a person, property, etc.; physically violent behaviour or treatment. **ME.** ▸**b** An instance of this; a violent or injurious act; a physical assault. **LME.** ▸**c** LAW. The unlawful exercise of physical force. **M19.**
2 The state or quality of being violent in action or effect; great force or strength in operation; vehemence, severity, intensity. Also, an instance of this. **LME.**
3 Strength or intensity of emotion; fervour, passion. **LME.**

4 The action or an act of constraining or forcing unnatural change upon something; *spec.* (a) misinterpretation or misapplication of a word etc. **L16.**

📖 **1** P. BARKER Men fought, . . but violence between women was unthinkable. G. SWIFT The land of violence, the land of the gun. W. F. DEEDES A near-criminal element, eager to organise violence on any pretext. **b** A. DESAI The heat of the sun was an assault, a violence. **2** ALDOUS HUXLEY Mrs. Viveash had been reduced, by the violence of her headache, to coming home. M. M. KAYE Shook her with a violence that forced the breath from her lungs. **3** SIR W. SCOTT Nothing to deserve such a horrid imputation as your violence infers. **4** J. YEOWELL Christian missionaries . . avoided all unnecessary violence to the ancient habits of the aborigines.

Phrases: **do violence to** (now chiefly *literary*) cause extreme harm or injury to; act contrary to, outrage.

■ Also **violency** *noun* (long *obsolete* exc. *Scot.*) **M16.**

violencia /vio'lenθja/ *noun.* **M20.**
[Spanish = violence.]
In Colombia: the period 1948–1958, during which there was violent political conflict.

violent /'vʌɪəl(ə)nt/ *adjective & noun.* **ME.**
[Old & mod. French from Latin *violentus* or *violens*, *-ent-*.]
▶ **A** *adjective.* **1** Having a marked or powerful (esp. physical) effect; (of pain, a reaction, etc.) very strong, severe, extreme. **ME.** ▸**b** Of colour: intense, vivid. **M18.**
2 Of an action: involving or using great physical force or strength, esp. in order to cause injury; not gentle or moderate. **LME.**
3 Of a storm or other natural force: operating with great force or strength, now esp. destructively. See also ***violent storm*** below. **LME.** ▸**b** Of a noise: extremely loud. **E17.**
4 Of a person: habitually using physical force or violence, esp. in order to injure or intimidate others. Formerly also, acting illegally. **LME.**
5 †**a** Due or subject to constraint; involuntary, forced. **L15–M17.** ▸**b** Of death: caused by external force or poison; unnatural. **L16.**
6 Characterized by or displaying passion or intense emotion; vehement, furious. **M17.**

📖 **1** G. ORWELL He was doubled up by a violent coughing fit. T. SHARPE Mirkin's reaction was so violent that he had to be sedated. **b** O. MANNING A lipstick of a violent mulberry colour. **2** A. LOOS Did I ever want to do a thing that was really violent, . . shoot someone, for instance. V. NABOKOV Found himself . . making violent love to Rose. **3** M. KINGSLEY It was highly dangerous . . because of the violent storms. **4** J. WELCH They don't parole repeat violent offenders.

Special collocations & phrases: **violent profits** *SCOTS LAW* damages payable by a tenant illegally remaining in a property. **violent storm** *METEOROLOGY* a wind of force 11 on the Beaufort scale (56–63 knots or 103–117 kph). **lay violent hands on** attack physically, assault.

▶ **B** *noun.* Orig., a violent thing, emotion, etc. Now, a violent person, *esp.* a violent criminal. **E17.**

📖 J. SCOTT The psychiatric wards are filled with violents.

¶ As noun not recorded between 17 and 20.

■ **violently** *adverb* **LME.** **violentness** *noun* (long *rare* or *obsolete*) violence **L17.**

†**violent** *verb.* **M16.**
[Old & mod. French *violenter*, or medieval Latin *violentare*.]
1 *verb trans.* Strain the meaning of (a text). *rare.* Only in **M16.**
2 *verb trans.* Constrain or force (*to do*) by physical force; coerce. Chiefly *Scot.* **L16–M18.**
3 *verb intrans.* Act violently; rage. *rare* (Shakes.). Only in **E17.**

violescent /vʌɪə'lɛs(ə)nt/ *adjective.* **M19.**
[formed as VIOLA *noun*[1] + -ESCENT.]
Tinged with violet.

violet /'vʌɪələt/ *noun.* **ME.**
[Old & mod. French *violet(te)*, †*-ete*, dims. of *viole* formed as VIOLA *noun*[1]: see -ET[1].]
1 Any of numerous low-growing plants of the genus *Viola* (see VIOLA *noun*[1] 2), characterized by horizontally directed lateral petals and freq. with cordate leaves and bluish-purple, lilac, or white flowers; *esp.* (more fully ***sweet violet***, ***common violet***) *V. odorata*, a spring-flowering plant of hedges and warm banks, much grown for its fragrant flowers. Also, a flower of such a plant. **ME.** ▸**b** With specifying word: any of various plants resembling the violet in the colour or fragrance of their flowers, their early flowering, etc. **L16.**
2 Material or clothes of a violet colour. **ME.** ▸**b** A purplish blue colour resembling that of the violet, occurring at the end of the spectrum opposite red; a pigment of this colour. **LME.**
3 The scent of violet, esp. as used in cosmetics. **M19.**
4 An onion; in *pl.*, spring onions. *slang.* **L19.**

📖 **1** ***dog violet***, ***marsh violet***, ***Parma violet***, etc. ***shrinking violet***: see SHRINK *verb.* **b** ***African violet***, ***dame's violet***, ***dog's tooth violet***, ***water violet***, etc. **2** W. H. PATER The mass said so solemnly, in violet, on Innocents' Day. **b** A. ALVAREZ Beyond . . , the blue merged into violet, became hazy.

Comb.: **violet-blue** (of) the colour violet; **violet cream** (*a*) a violet-scented cosmetic cream; (*b*) a chocolate with a violet-flavoured centre; **violet tea**: made from dried violet flowers; **violet wood** any of several purplish tropical timbers; *esp.* that of the S. American leguminous tree *Dalbergia cearensis*.

■ **violetish** *adjective* somewhat violet in colour **L19.**

violet /'vʌɪələt/ *adjective.* **LME.**
[Old & mod. French, attrib. use of prec.]
Of or resembling the colour of a violet; bluish-purple.

📖 A. SILLITOE Her opened . . coat showed a violet blouse underneath. **violet bee**, **violet carpenter bee** a large violet-coloured carpenter bee, *Xylocopa violacea*, which is found in southern Europe. **violet crab** a violet-coloured land crab, *Gecarcinus ruricola*, which is found on the Caribbean islands. **violet-ear** any of several Central and S. American hummingbirds of the genus *Colibri*, which have extended glittering purple ear coverts. **violet-eared waxbill** the common grenadier, *Uraeginthus granatina*, which has violet ear coverts and is found in southern Africa. **violet-green swallow** a dark-backed swallow with green and violet glosses, *Tachycineta thalassina*, found in western N. America. **violet ray** *noun & adjective* (*a*) *noun* a ray of violet (or ultraviolet) light; (*b*) *adjective* designating a device that produces or uses violet (or ultraviolet) light. **violet sea-snail** = ***violet snail*** below. **violet shift** = ***blue shift*** s.v. BLUE *adjective.* **violet snail** (the shell of) any of various small gastropod molluscs of the genus *Janthina*, which have thin violet-coloured shells and cling to floating rafts of bubbles in warm seas.

violet /'vʌɪələt/ *verb.* Infl. **-t(t)-**. **E17.**
[from VIOLET *noun*, *adjective*.]
1 *verb trans.* Colour or tinge with violet. **E17.**
2 *verb intrans.* Gather violets. **E19.**

violetta /vio'lɛtta/ *noun*[1]. Pl. **-tte** /-tte/. **M18.**
[Italian, dim. of *viola* VIOLA *noun*[2].]
MUSIC. A small viol.
violetta marina /ma'ri:na/ *Hist.* an obsolete stringed instrument, prob. resembling the viola d'amore.

violetta /vɪə'lɛtə/ *noun*[2]. **L19.**
[mod. Latin (see below), dim. of VIOLA *noun*[1].]
A miniature viola with small fragrant flowers that are usu. without dark markings.

violette *noun* pl. of VIOLETTA *noun*[1].

violette de Parme /vjɔlɛt də parm/ *noun phr.* Pl. ***violettes de Parme*** (pronounced same). **E20.**
[French.]
= ***Parma violet*** (a) s.v. PARMA *noun*[1] 1.

violin /vʌɪə'lɪn, 'vʌɪəlɪn/ *noun & verb.* **L16.**
[Italian *violino*, from *viola* VIOLA *noun*[2].]
▶ **A** *noun.* **1** A musical instrument with four strings of treble pitch, played with a bow; a fiddle. **L16.**
2 A player on this instrument; a violinist. **M17.**
Phrases: **play first violin** take a leading role. **play second violin** *rare* take a subordinate role.
Comb.: **violin spider** a small and deadly spider, *Loxosceles laeta*, which has a violin-shaped mark on the back and is native to S. America.
▶ **B** *verb. rare.*
†**1** *verb trans.* Entice by violin-playing. *rare.* Only in **E18.**
2 *verb intrans. & trans.* (with *it*). Play the violin. **L19.**
■ **violinist** *noun* a player on the violin **M17.** **violinistic** *adjective* of or pertaining to the violin **L18.**

violine /'vʌɪəli:n, -lʌɪn/ *noun.* Now *rare.* **M19.**
[from VIOLA *noun*[1] + -INE[5].]
1 *CHEMISTRY.* An emetic alkaloid found in the common violet. **M19.**
2 A particular violet-blue colouring matter or colour. **M19.**

violino piccolo /vi:ə,li:nəʊ 'pɪkələʊ/ *noun phr.* Pl. **-ni -li** /-ni -li/. **L18.**
[Italian, lit. 'small violin'.]
An early kind of small violin, tuned a third or (usu.) a fourth higher than the ordinary violin.

viologen /vʌɪ'əʊlədʒ(ə)n/ *noun.* **M20.**
[from VIOLET *noun* + -O- + -GEN.]
CHEMISTRY. Any of a series of salts of heteroaromatic cations of the formula $(C_5H_4NR)_2^{2+}$, which are used as redox indicators.

violon /'vʌɪələn/ *noun.* **M16.**
[Fr; in sense 2 formed as VIOLONE: see -OON.]
†**1** A violin. Also, a violinist. **M16–E17.**
2 A kind of organ-stop resembling a double bass in tone. **M19.**

violoncello /vʌɪələn'tʃɛləʊ, vi:ə-/ *noun.* Pl. **-os**. **E18.**
[Italian, dim. of VIOLONE.]
1 A cello. **E18.** ▸**b** A cellist. **M19.**
2 An organ-stop similar in tone to a cello. **L19.**
1 violoncello piccolo [= small] a small variety of cello.
■ **violoncellist** *noun* a cellist **M19.**

violon d'Ingres /vjɔlɔ̃ dɛ̃gr/ *noun phr.* Pl. ***violons d'Ingres*** (pronounced same). **M20.**
[French, lit. 'Ingres' violin', the painter Ingres having been a keen violinist.]
An interest or activity other than that for which a person is best known; an occasional pastime.

violone /vɪə'ləʊni/ *noun.* **E18.**
[Italian, from *viola* VIOLA *noun*[2].]
A double-bass viol.

violons d'Ingres *noun phr.* pl. of VIOLON D'INGRES.

viomycin /vʌɪə'mʌɪsɪn/ *noun.* **M20.**
[from *vio-* (of unkn. origin) + -MYCIN.]
PHARMACOLOGY. A bacteriostatic antibiotic produced by several bacteria, sometimes used to treat tuberculosis.

viosterol /vʌɪə(ʊ)'stɪərɒl/ *noun.* **E20.**
[from ULTRA)VIO(LET + -STEROL.]
BIOCHEMISTRY. = CALCIFEROL.

VIP *abbreviation.*
1 *BIOCHEMISTRY.* Vasoactive intestinal (poly)peptide.
2 Very important person.

VIP /vi:ʌɪ'pi:/ *noun.* **M20.**
[from initial letters of *very important person*.]
A very important person, *esp.* a high-ranking guest.

vipassana /vɪ'pasənə/ *noun.* **E20.**
[Pali = inward vision.]
In Theravada Buddhism, (the insight achieved by) meditation involving concentration on the body or its sensations.

viper /'vʌɪpə/ *noun.* **E16.**
[(Old & mod. French *vipère* from) Latin *vipera* snake, from *vivus* alive + *parere* bring forth.]
1 Any of various Old World viperid snakes of the genus *Vipera* or subfamily Viperinae, many of which are ovoviviparous; *spec.* the small Eurasian *Vipera berus* (also called ***adder***), which has a zigzag pattern on the back and is the only venomous snake found in Britain. Also, any venomous, dangerous, or repulsive snake. **E16.** ▸**b** More fully ***pit viper***. Any of various American and Asian viperid snakes of the subfamily Crotalinae, which have sensory pits on the head that can detect the heat of prey. **E16.**
2 *fig.* **a** A venomous or spiteful person. **L16.** ▸**b** A treacherous or deceitful person, *esp.* one who betrays those who have helped him or her. **L16.**
3 A smoker of marijuana or opium, *esp.* habitual one. Also, a heroin addict. Now *rare.* **M20.**

📖 **1** ***Gaboon viper***, ***horned viper***, ***Russell's viper***, etc. **b** ***palm viper***, ***red viper***, etc. **2a** SHAKES. *Coriol.* Where is this viper That would depopulate the city and Be every man himself?

Comb.: **viper-broth** a soup made by boiling vipers, formerly supposed to be highly nutritious; **viperfish** (*a*) any of several elongated deep-sea fishes of the family Chauliodontidae and genus *Chauliodus*, which have very long fangs and extensible jaws; (*b*) the lesser weever, *Trachinus vipera*; **viper's bugloss** a stiff bristly blue-flowered plant of the borage family, *Echium vulgare*, of open chalky, sandy, or shingly ground; also (with specifying word), any of several other plants of the genus *Echium*; **viper's grass** a plant of the genus *Scorzonera*, esp. *S. hispanica*; **viper-wine** wine with an added extract obtained from vipers, formerly taken as a restorative.

■ **viper-like** *adverb & adjective* (*a*) *adverb* in the manner of a viper; (*b*) *adjective* resembling a viper: **M17.** **viperling** *noun* a young viper **M19.**

viperid /vʌɪ'pɛrɪd/ *noun & adjective.* **E20.**
[mod. Latin *Viperidae* (see below), from *Vipera* genus name: see VIPER, -ID[3].]
ZOOLOGY. ▶**A** *noun.* Any snake of the family Viperidae, which comprises the true vipers and (in most classifications) the pit vipers, which are heavy-bodied venomous snakes with hollow fangs that are folded back in the mouth when not in use. **E20.**
▶ **B** *adjective.* Of, pertaining to, or designating this family. **E20.**

viperine /'vʌɪpərʌɪn, -ɪn/ *adjective & noun.* **M16.**
[Latin *viperinus*, from *vipera* VIPER: see -INE[1]. In senses 3b, B. from mod. Latin *Viperinae* (see below).]
▶ **A** *adjective.* **1** = VIPEROUS 2. **M16.**
2 Of, pertaining to, or obtained from a viper. **E17.**
3 *ZOOLOGY.* **a** Of a snake: resembling a viper. **E19.** ▸**b** Of, pertaining to, or designating the subfamily Viperinae, which comprises the true vipers, or the family Viperidae which contains it. Cf. CROTALINE *adjective.* **L19.**
3a viperine snake a harmless colubrid snake, *Natrix maura*, that resembles a viper and is found in SW Europe.
▶ **B** *noun. ZOOLOGY.* A snake of this subfamily. Cf. CROTALINE *noun.* **L19.**

viperish /'vʌɪp(ə)rɪʃ/ *adjective.* **M18.**
[from VIPER + -ISH[1].]
Resembling or characteristic of a viper; chiefly *fig.* venomous, spiteful.
■ **viperishly** *adverb* **L19.**

viperous /'vʌɪp(ə)rəs/ *adjective.* **M16.**
[from VIPER + -OUS.]
1 Of or pertaining to a viper or vipers; consisting of vipers. *arch.* **M16.**
2 Of the nature of or resembling (that of) a viper; characteristic of a viper; malignant, venomous. **M16.**

📖 2 COLERIDGE Those viperous journals, which deal out .. hate, fury and sedition. R. BRIDGES A savage beast, The viperous scourge of gods and humankind.

■ **viperously** *adverb* L16. **viperousness** *noun* M17.

vipoma /vʌɪˈpəʊmə/ *noun.* L20.
[from VIP (see below) + *-oma.*]
MEDICINE. A tumour which secretes vasoactive intestinal polypeptide (VIP).

†**vipseys** *noun pl.* var. of GIPSIES.

viraemia /vʌɪˈriːmɪə/ *noun.* Also ***-remia**. M20.
[from VIRUS + -AEMIA.]
MEDICINE. The presence of viruses in the blood.
■ **viraemic** *adjective* L20.

virage /viraʒ/ *noun.* Pl. pronounced same. M20.
[French.]
A hairpin bend; a sharp turn made in negotiating such a bend.

virago /vɪˈrɑːɡəʊ, -ˈreɪɡəʊ/ *noun & adjective.* OE.
[Latin, from *vir* man.]
▶ **A** *noun.* Pl. **-os**.
†**1** Woman. Only in biblical allusions with ref. to the name given by Adam to Eve. OE–L16.
2 A woman of masculine strength or spirit; a female warrior, an amazon. *arch.* LME. ▶†**b** A man of exceptional strength or spirit. *rare* (Shakes.). L16–E17.
3 A domineering woman; a fierce or abusive woman. LME.

📖 3 CLIVE JAMES A deranged virago who was famous for yelling angry obscenities.

▶ **B** *adjective.* That is a virago; of or pertaining to a virago or viragos. L16.
■ **viraˈginian** *adjective* = VIRAGINOUS *adjective* M17. **viraginous** *adjective* of the nature or characteristic of a virago M17. **viragoish** *adjective* resembling or characteristic of a virago L19.

viral /ˈvʌɪr(ə)l/ *adjective.* M20.
[from VIRUS + -AL¹.]
Of the nature of, caused by, or pertaining to a virus or viruses.
viral marketing a method of marketing that relies on customers to spread the word about a product or service, esp. by email.
■ **virally** *adverb* by a virus or viruses M20.

†**viranda**, †**virando** *nouns* see VERANDA.

Virchow-Robin space /vɪəkəʊˈrɒbã speɪs/ *noun phr.* L19.
[from R. L. K. *Virchow* (1821–1902), German pathologist + C. P. *Robin* (1821–85), French histologist.]
ANATOMY. An extension of the subarachnoid space surrounding a blood-vessel as it enters the brain or the spinal cord.

virelay /ˈvɪrəleɪ/ *noun.* LME.
[Old & mod. French *virelai* alt. of †*vireli* (perh. orig. a refrain) after *lai* LAY *noun*².]
A song or short lyric poem, originating in 14th-cent. France, usu. consisting of short-lined stanzas with two rhymes variously arranged.

virement /ˈvʌɪəm(ə)nt, virmɑ̃/ *noun.* E20.
[French, formed as VEER *verb*².]
The process of transferring items (esp. public funds) from one financial account to another.

viremia *noun* see VIRAEMIA.

virent /ˈvʌɪr(ə)nt/ *adjective.* L16.
[Latin *virent-*, pres. ppl stem of *virere* be green: see -ENT.]
†**1** Verdant; fresh. L16–M17.
2 Green in colour. *arch.* M19.

vireo /ˈvɪrɪəʊ/ *noun.* Pl. **-os**. M19.
[Latin, a bird, perh. the greenfinch; cf. *virere* be green.]
Any of various small American songbirds of the genus *Vireo* or the family Vireonidae, which have mainly green or brown upperparts and yellow or white underparts. Cf. GREENLET.
red-eyed vireo a vireo, *Vireo olivaceus*, that is the commonest bird in the woods of eastern N. America but is found throughout the Americas. ***shrike vireo***: see SHRIKE *noun*². ***solitary vireo***: see SOLITARY *adjective*. **WARBLING vireo**.

vires *noun* pl. of VIS *noun*¹.

virescent /vɪˈrɛs(ə)nt/ *adjective.* E19.
[Latin *virescent-*, pres. ppl stem of *virescere* turn green: see -ESCENT.]
Greenish, turning green; BOTANY exhibiting virescence.
■ **virescence** *noun* greenness; *esp.* (BOTANY) abnormal development of chlorophyll in petals or other parts normally coloured: M19.

virga /ˈvəːɡə/ *noun.* Pl. **virgae** /ˈvəːɡiː/. E20.
[Latin = rod.]
1 MUSIC. (A symbol designating) a note used in plainsong. E20.
2 METEOROLOGY, *sing.* & in *pl.* Streaks of precipitation that appear to hang from the undersurface of a cloud and usu. evaporate before reaching the ground. M20.

virgal /ˈvəːɡ(ə)l/ *adjective. rare.* M18.
[formed as prec. + -AL¹.]
Made of twigs or rods.

virgate /ˈvəːɡət/ *noun.* M17.
[medieval Latin *virgata*, from VIRGA: see -ATE¹.]
Hist. **1** In England, a former measure of land, varying in extent and averaging thirty acres. M17.
2 A rod or pole used as a measure. L18.
■ **virgater** *noun* a person holding or cultivating a virgate of land L19.

virgate /ˈvəːɡət/ *adjective.* E19.
[Latin *virgatus*, from *virga* rod: see -ATE².]
BOTANY. Of a stem or branch: wand-shaped; long, straight, and slender.
■ Also **virgated** *adjective* (*rare*) M18.

virgation /vəːˈɡeɪʃ(ə)n/ *noun.* L19.
[from Latin *virga* twig + -ATION.]
GEOLOGY. A system of branching and diverging faults.

†**virge** *noun.* M16.
[Var. of VERGE *noun*, after Latin *virga*.]
1 = VERGE *noun* 9. M16–L17.
2 = VERGE *noun* 3. E17–E18.
3 = VERGE *noun* 1a. E17–M18.

virger *noun* see VERGER.

virgie /ˈvəːdʒi/ *adjective & noun. colloq.* M20.
[Abbreviation.]
= VIRGIN *noun & adjective*.

Virgilian /vəˈdʒɪlɪən/ *adjective & noun.* Also **Ver-**. E16.
[Latin *Vergilianus*, from Publius *Vergilius* Maro (see below): see -IAN.]
▶ **A** *adjective.* **1** Of, pertaining to, or characteristic of the Roman poet Virgil (Publius Vergilius Maro, 70–19 BC) or his work. E16.
2 Of or following the agricultural methods described in Virgil's *Georgics*. E18.
1 Virgilian lots a method of divination by selecting a passage of Virgil at random.
▶ **B** *noun.* **1** A student of or expert in the works of Virgil. L16.
2 A person following Virgil's methods of agriculture. M18.
■ **Virgilianism** *noun* (an expression in) the characteristic style of Virgil M19.

virgin /ˈvəːdʒɪn/ *noun & adjective.* ME.
[Anglo-Norman & Old French *virgine*, *-ene* (mod. *vierge*), from Latin *virgo*, *virgin-*.]
▶ **A** *noun.* **1** ECCLESIASTICAL. An unmarried woman esteemed for her chastity and piety within the Christian Church; now *esp.* a member of any order of women under a vow of virginity. ME.
2 A person (esp. a young woman) who has never had sexual intercourse; *arch.* a young woman, a girl. ME. ▶**b** ENTOMOLOGY. A female insect that produces fertile eggs by parthenogenesis. L19. ▶**c** *fig.* A naive or innocent person; a person inexperienced in a specified sphere of activity. M20.
3 ASTRONOMY. (**V-**.) = VIRGO 1. LME.
4 *transf.* An uncaptured or unconquered place or thing; an uninhabited place. E17.
5 A cigarette made of Virginia tobacco. *slang.* Now *rare* or *obsolete*. E20.

📖 **2** *Publishers Weekly* Secretly a sexual virgin, Reich was one of Washington's .. eligible .. bachelors. HENRY MILLER Had an affair with a strange man because she was tired of being a virgin. **c** *Running* First-timers—or 'virgins'—like me will be .. aware of how important the .. Marathon has become.

Comb. & phrases: **the Virgin**, **the Blessed Holy Virgin** CHRISTIAN CHURCH the Virgin Mary; ***vestal virgin***: see VESTAL *adjective* 1; **Virgin Mary** (*a*) (CHRISTIAN CHURCH) *the* mother of Christ; (*b*) a drink of tomato juice (without vodka, cf. ***Bloody Mary*** s.v. BLOODY *adjective & adverb*); **virgin's bower** any of various kinds of clematis, esp. *Clematis vitalba* (traveller's joy), *C. flannula*, native to the Mediterranean region, and (*N. Amer.*) *C. virginiana*; **virgin's garland** a garland of flowers and coloured paper formerly carried at a virgin's funeral; †**virgin's milk** a milky cosmetic preparation containing benzoin, formerly used for cleansing the face or skin; †**Virgin's spike** the star Spica in Virgo.

▶ **B** *adjective.* **1** Resembling or characteristic of a virgin; pure, unstained, spotless. ME. ▶**b** Not yet used or taken; uncaptured, unconquered; (of land) uncharted, unexplored; (of a mountain) not yet climbed. LME.
2 Of, or pertaining to a virgin or virgins; that is a virgin; chaste; unmated. LME.

📖 **1** DE QUINCEY A glittering expanse of virgin snow. **b** G. ORWELL Coal .. in its virgin state is .. hard as rock. *Times* An expedition to a virgin Himalayan peak. **2** SHAKES. *Much Ado* Pardon, goddess of the night, Those that slew thy virgin knight. SIR W. SCOTT Ne'er again to braid her hair The virgin snood did Alice wear.

Special collocations: **virgin birth** (*a*) CHRISTIAN CHURCH (the doctrine of) the birth of Christ from a mother who was (and remained) a virgin; (*b*) ZOOLOGY parthenogenesis. **virgin clay** unfired clay; **virgin comb** a honeycomb that has been used only once for honey and never for brood; **virgin forest** a forest in its untouched natural state; **virgin metal**: freshly made from ore; **virgin olive oil**: obtained from the first pressing of the olives; **virgin queen** (*a*) ***the Virgin Queen***, Queen Elizabeth I of England, who died unmarried; (*b*) ZOOLOGY an unfertilized queen bee, ant, etc. **virgin reproduction** ZOOLOGY parthenogenesis; **virgin wax** †(*a*) fresh or unused beeswax; (*b*) a purified or fine quality of wax, esp. as used in candles; white wax; **virgin widow** a woman who has been widowed while still a virgin; **virgin wool**: that has never or only once been spun or woven.
■ **virginhood** *noun* (now *rare*) virginity M17. **virgin-like** *adjective* resembling (that of) a virgin; characteristic of or befitting a virgin: L16. **virginly** *adverb* as or like a virgin; in the manner of a virgin or virgins: L15.

†**virgin** *verb trans. rare* (Shakes.). Only in E17.
[from the noun.]
With *it*: remain a virgin.

virginal /ˈvəːdʒɪn(ə)l/ *noun & verb.* M16.
[formed as next, perh. from its use by young women.]
▶ **A** *noun sing.* & (usu.) in *pl.* An early keyboard instrument resembling a spinet and set in a box, used esp. in the 16th and 17th cents. Also ***pair of virginals***. M16.
▶ **B** *verb intrans.* Infl. **-l(l)-**. Tap with the fingers as on a virginal. *rare.* E17.
■ **virginalist** *noun* a player on or composer for the virginals E20.

virginal /ˈvəːdʒɪn(ə)l/ *adjective.* LME.
[Old & mod. French, or Latin *virginalis*, from *virgo*, *virgin-*: see VIRGIN *noun*, -AL¹.]
1 Of or pertaining to a virgin or virginity; characteristic of or befitting a virgin. LME.
2 That is a virgin; chaste; *fig.* pure, unsullied, untouched. L15.

📖 **1** C. G. WOLFF Maintaining .. this myth of virginal purity. R. WILBUR Wherever on the virginal frontier New men with rutting wagons came.

■ **virgiˈnality** *noun* (*rare*) virginity LME. **virginally** *adverb* L19.

Virginia /vəˈdʒɪnɪə/ *noun.* E17.
[See sense 1.]
1 Used *attrib.* to designate things found in, obtained from, or associated with Virginia, a State in the south-eastern US (orig. the first English settlement, 1607). E17.
2 *ellipt.* = ***Virginia tobacco*** below. Also, a cigarette made of this. E17.
1 Virginia Algonquian (of) the Algonquian language (now extinct) of the Powhatans. **Virginia bluebell** = ***Virginia cowslip*** below. **Virginia cowslip** a N. American woodland plant of the borage family, *Mertensia virginica*, bearing nodding blue trumpet-shaped flowers. **Virginia creeper** any of several woody climbing plants of the genus *Parthenocissus*, of the vine family; esp. *P. quinquefolia*, of the eastern US, and *P. tricuspidata*, of China and Japan, which both have tendrils ending in adhesive pads and are grown for covering walls and buildings. **Virginia deer** = ***Virginian deer*** s.v. VIRGINIAN *adjective*. **Virginia fence** *US* a rail fence made in a zigzag pattern; ***make a Virginia fence*** (*colloq.*), walk drunkenly. **Virginia nightingale** = ***Virginian nightingale*** s.v. VIRGINIAN *adjective*. **Virginia opossum** = ***Virginian opossum*** s.v. OPOSSUM 1. **Virginia poke** = POKE *noun*² 2a. **Virginia rail** a N. American rail, *Rallus limicola*, which resembles the water rail in appearance and habits. **Virginia reel** *N. Amer.* a country dance. ***Virginia snakeroot***: see ***snakeroot*** s.v. SNAKE *noun*. **Virginia stock** a low-growing cruciferous plant of the Mediterranean region, *Malcolmia maritima*, grown for its fragrant flowers, freq. lilac or white. **Virginia tobacco** a variety of tobacco grown and manufactured in Virginia. **Virginia water-leaf** a water-leaf, *Hydrophyllum virginianum*, with leaves edible when young (also called ***Shawnee salad***).

virginiamycin /vəˌdʒɪnɪəˈmʌɪsɪn/ *noun.* M20.
[from mod. Latin *virginiae* (see below) + -MYCIN.]
PHARMACOLOGY. Any of various antibacterial substances produced by the bacterium *Streptomyces virginiae*, used as antibiotics and as growth-promoting agents for food animals.

Virginian /vəˈdʒɪnɪən/ *noun & adjective*¹. L16.
[from VIRGINIA + -AN.]
▶ **A** *noun.* A native or inhabitant of Virginia. L16.
▶ **B** *adjective.* Of or pertaining to the State of Virginia. E17.
Virginian cowslip = ***Virginia cowslip*** s.v. VIRGINIA 1. **Virginian creeper** = ***Virginia creeper*** s.v. VIRGINIA 1. **Virginian deer** the white-tailed deer, *Odocoileus virginianus*. **Virginian eared owl** the great horned owl, *Bubo virginianus*. **Virginian nightingale** the common cardinal, *Cardinalis cardinalis*, which has a strong and clear song. ***Virginian opossum***: see OPOSSUM 1. **Virginian partridge** the northern bobwhite, *Colinus virginianus*. ***Virginian poke***: see POKE *noun*² 2a. **Virginian quail** = ***Virginian partridge*** above. **Virginian sea** the part of the Atlantic Ocean off the coast of Virginia.

†**virginian** *adjective*². E17–M18.
[from VIRGIN *noun & adjective* + -IAN.]
Virginal; virgin.

Virgin Islander /ˈvəːdʒɪn ˈʌɪləndə/ *noun.* M20.
[from *Virgin Islands* (see below) + -ER¹.]
A native or inhabitant of (any of) the Virgin Islands, the westernmost islands of the Lesser Antilles.

virginity /vəˈdʒɪnɪti/ *noun.* ME.
[Old & mod. French *virginité* from Latin *virginitas*, *-tat-*, from *virgo*, *virgin-*: see VIRGIN *noun & adjective*, -ITY.]
1 The state or condition of being a virgin; sexual chastity. Freq. in ***keep one's virginity***, ***lose one's virginity***. ME.
2 *fig.* **a** The state or condition of being fresh, pure, or untouched. E17. ▶**b** Innocence, inexperience. Also, virtue, integrity. L20.

virginium /və'dʒɪnɪəm/ *noun.* M20.
[from VIRGINIA + -IUM.]
HISTORY OF SCIENCE. The element of atomic no. 87 (later named ***francium***), mistakenly claimed to have been discovered spectroscopically.

Virgo /'vəːgəʊ/ *noun.* Pl. **-os.** OE.
[Latin *virgo* VIRGIN *noun*, Virgo.]
1 (The name of) a large constellation on the celestial equator between Leo and Libra; ASTROLOGY (the name of) the sixth zodiacal sign, usu. associated with the period 23 August to 22 September (see note s.v. ZODIAC); the Virgin. OE.
2 A person born under the sign Virgo. E20.
■ **Virgoan** *adjective & noun* (*a*) *adjective* of or pertaining to Virgo; designating or characteristic of a person born under the sign Virgo; (*b*) *noun* = VIRGO 2: M20.

virgo intacta /ˌvəːgəʊ ɪn'taktə/ *noun phr.* E18.
[Latin, lit. 'untouched virgin'.]
Chiefly LAW. A girl or woman who has never had sexual intercourse; a virgin with the hymen intact.

Virgoulee /'vəːgʊleɪ/ *noun.* Long *rare.* Also †**-goule.** L17.
[French from *Virgoulée* repr. pronunc. of *Villegoureux*, a village in central France.]
= VIRGOULEUSE.

Virgouleuse /vəːgʊ'ləːz, -'luːz/ *noun.* L17.
[French, from *Virgoulée*: see prec.]
A juicy variety of winter pear. Also ***Virgouleuse pear***.

virgula /'vəːgjʊlə/ *noun.* Pl. **-lae** /-liː/. M17.
[Latin, dim. of *virga* rod: see -ULE.]
1 ZOOLOGY & PALAEONTOLOGY. A small rodlike structure; *esp.* = NEMA 2. M17.
2 = VIRGULE 1. *rare.* E18.
3 MUSIC. = NEUME 2. E19.
Phrases: †**virgula divina** a divining-rod.

virgular /'vəːgjʊlə/ *adjective. rare.* E17.
[from prec. + -AR[1].]
Of an alphabet, system of notation, etc.: consisting of thin lines or strokes.

virgule /'vəːgjuːl/ *noun.* M19.
[French = comma from Latin VIRGULA.]
1 A slanting or upright line used esp. in medieval manuscripts to mark a caesura, or as a punctuation mark equivalent to a comma. Now also = SOLIDUS 2. M19.
2 WATCHMAKING. More fully ***virgule escapement***. A type of escapement in which the teeth of the wheel have the shape of a comma. Cf. VERGE *noun* 4a. L19.

†**virgult** *noun. rare.* E16.
[Latin *virgulta* neut. pl., from VIRGULA.]
1 A bush, a shrub; a set of young shoots. E16–M17.
2 A thicket; a copse. Only in M18.

virial /'vɪrɪəl/ *noun.* L19.
[from Latin *vir-* pl. stem of *vis* force, strength: see -IAL.]
PHYSICS. A simple function of the positions of, and the forces acting upon, the particles of a system, summed over that system.
Comb.: **virial coefficient** each of the (temperature-dependent) coefficients of inverse powers of *V* in a polynomial series used to approximate the quantity *pV/RT* in the virial equation; **virial equation, virial expansion** an equation that is used to determine the state of a real gas or similar collection of particles; **virial theorem** the theorem that for a steady-state system of particles obeying an inverse square law of force, the time average of the kinetic energy equals the time average of the virial.
■ **viriali'zation** *noun* the acquisition of internal kinetic energy by a contracting body of matter, as during formation of a galaxy etc. L20. **virialize** *verb intrans.* undergo virialization L20. **virialized** *adjective* that has undergone virialization L20.

viricidal /vʌɪrɪ'sʌɪd(ə)l/ *adjective.* E20.
[from VIRUS + -I- + -CIDE + -AL[1].]
Capable of killing viruses.
■ **'viricide** *noun* a viricidal substance M20.

virid /'vɪrɪd/ *adjective. poet. & literary.* E17.
[Latin *viridis*, from *virere* be green: see -ID[1].]
Green, verdant.

viridarium /vɪrɪ'dɛːrɪəm/ *noun.* Pl. **-ria** /-rɪə/. M17.
[Latin, from *viridis* VIRID: see -ARIUM.]
ROMAN ANTIQUITIES. A pleasure-garden or green court of a Roman villa or palace.

viridescence /vɪrɪ'dɛs(ə)ns/ *noun.* M19.
[formed as next: see -ESCENCE.]
The quality of being viridescent.

viridescent /vɪrɪ'dɛs(ə)nt/ *adjective.* M19.
[Late Latin *viridescent-* pres. ppl stem of *viridescere* become green, from Latin *viridis*: see VIRID, -ESCENT.]
Greenish, tending to become green.

viridian /vɪ'rɪdɪən/ *noun & adjective.* L19.
[from Latin *viridis* VIRID + -IAN.]
▶**A** *noun.* A bright bluish-green chromium oxide pigment; the colour of such a pigment. Also called ***Guignet's green***. L19.
▶**B** *adjective.* Bluish-green. E20.

viridin /'vɪrɪdɪn/ *noun.* M20.
[from mod. Latin *viride* (see below), from Latin *viridis* VIRID: see -IN[1].]
PHARMACOLOGY. An antibiotic with antifungal properties, derived from the mould *Trichoderma viride*.

viridine /'vɪrɪdʌɪn/ *noun.* Now *rare* or *obsolete.* M19.
[from Latin *viridis* VIRID + -INE[5]; in sense (c) from mod. Latin *viride* (see below).]
Any of various green substances; *esp.* †(*a*) chlorophyll; (*b*) a green aniline dye; (*c*) an alkaloid obtained from the American false hellebore, *Veratrum viride*.

viridity /vɪ'rɪdɪti/ *noun.* Now *rare.* LME.
[Old & mod. French *viridité* or Latin *viriditas* from *viridis* VIRID: see -ITY.]
1 The quality or state of being virid or green; greenness, verdancy. LME.
2 *fig.* Innocence; inexperience; naivety. E19.

virile /'vɪrʌɪl/ *adjective.* L15.
[Old & mod. French *viril* or Latin *virilis*, from *vir* man: see -ILE.]
1 Of, belonging to, or characteristic of a man; manly, masculine. Also, marked by strength, force or vitality. L15. ▶**b** Of dress: denoting the attainment of male adulthood; distinctively belonging to a man as opp. to a youth or woman. *arch.* E17.
2 (Of a person) potent, full of masculine energy or vigour; (of a man) having a strong sexual drive. E16.
3 Of or having procreative power. M16.

📖 **1** I. MURDOCH The bearded and ostentatiously virile appearance of his colleague. *Audubon* A virile new government agency . . made the . . bounty hunters obsolete. **2** *European* A virile . . Stalin imposed a divided Europe upon a dying . . Roosevelt. **3** ***virile member***: see MEMBER *noun*.

virilescence /vɪrɪ'lɛs(ə)ns/ *noun. rare.* M19.
[from VIRILE + -ESCENCE.]
The condition of becoming virile, *spec.* of assuming male physical characteristics.

virilisation *noun* var. of VIRILIZATION.

virilism /'vɪrɪlɪz(ə)m/ *noun.* L19.
[from VIRILE + -ISM.]
MEDICINE. The development of male physical and mental characteristics in a female; virilization.

virility /vɪ'rɪlɪti/ *noun.* L16.
[Old & mod. French *virilité* or Latin *virilitas*, from *virilis*: see VIRILE, -ITY.]
1 The period of life during which a person of the male sex is in his prime; mature or fully developed manhood or male vigour. Now *rare.* L16.
2 The power of procreation; male sexual potency. Formerly also, the male sexual organs. L16.
3 Strength and vigour of action or thought; energy or force of a virile character. E17.

📖 **1** J. M. GOOD At puberty it [the pulse] is only 80; about virility 75. **2** *Guardian* As the middle years encroach . . men . . fear a waning of virility. **3** T. W. WILSON Political vitality and vigour, civil virility.

virilization /vɪrɪlʌɪ'zeɪʃ(ə)n/ *noun.* Also **-isation.** M20.
[from VIRILE + -IZATION.]
MEDICINE. The development of male secondary sexual characteristics in a female or precociously in a male, as a result of excess androgen production.
■ **'virilized** *adjective* exhibiting virilization M20. **'virilizing** *adjective* causing virilization M20.

virilocal /vɪrɪ'ləʊk(ə)l/ *adjective.* M20.
[from Latin *virilis* VIRILE + LOCAL *adjective.*]
Designating or pertaining to a system of marriage in which a married couple settles in the husband's home or community. Cf. PATRILOCAL, UXORILOCAL.
■ **viriloˈcality** *noun* the custom of virilocal residence M20. **virilocally** *adverb* M20.

virino /vɪ'riːnəʊ/ *noun.* Pl. **-os.** L20.
[from VIRUS + *-ino* dim. suffix (cf. -INO).]
MICROBIOLOGY. A hypothetical infectious particle postulated as the cause of scrapie, consisting of a nucleic acid in a protective coat made from host cell proteins.

virion /'vʌɪrɪɒn/ *noun.* M20.
[from VIRUS + -I- + -ON.]
MICROBIOLOGY. The complete, infective form of a virus outside a host cell, with a core and a capsid.

viripotent /vɪ'rɪpə(ʊ)t(ə)nt/ *adjective.* Long *rare.* M17.
[Latin *viripotent-, -ens*, from *vires* strength: see -ENT.]
Full of strength or energy.

virl /vəːl/ *noun. obsolete* exc. *Scot.* LME.
[Old French *virol, virelle*: see VERREL. Cf. FERRULE, VIROLE.]
A ferrule.

viro- /'vʌɪrəʊ/ *combining form* of VIRUS 2b: see -O-.
■ **virogene** *noun* a gene sequence corresponding to the genome of a tumour virus but occurring, normally repressed, in a cell M20. **viroˈgenesis** *noun* the formation or production of viruses M20. **virogeˈnetic, viroˈgenic** *adjectives* giving rise to viruses M20. **viroˈpexis** *noun* [Greek *pēxis* fixing] the process by which a virus particle becomes attached to a cell wall and incorporated into the cell by phagocytosis M20. **virosome** *noun* [-SOME[3]] (*a*) a particle of ribonucleoprotein and virus DNA found in the cytoplasm of certain virus-infected cells; (*b*) a liposome into which viral proteins have been introduced: L20.

viroid /'vʌɪrɔɪd/ *noun.* M20.
[from VIRUS + -OID.]
BIOLOGY. Orig., a virus-like particle. Now, an infectious entity similar to a virus but smaller, consisting only of a strand of nucleic acid without the protein coat characteristic of a virus.

virola /vɪ'rəʊlə/ *noun.* L19.
[mod. Latin genus name, from a S. American word.]
(The wood of) any of various S.American trees of the genus *Virola* (family Myristicaceae), which are sources of timber, oils and fats, and resins.

virole /'vɪrəʊl/ *noun.* E18.
[French = ferrule, ring.]
HERALDRY. An encircling ring on a bugle-horn.
■ **viroled** *adjective* [cf. French *virolé*] provided with a virole E19.

virology /vʌɪ'rɒlədʒi/ *noun.* M20.
[from VIRUS + -OLOGY.]
The branch of science that deals with the study of viruses.
■ **viroˈlogic, viroˈlogical** *adjectives* M20. **viroˈlogically** *adverb* L20. **virologist** *noun* M20.

virose /vʌɪ'rəʊs/ *adjective.* Now *rare.* L17.
[Latin *virosus*, from VIRUS: see -OSE[1].]
(Esp. of a plant) poisonous; suggestive of poisonous qualities; (of a plant, its flavour, smell, etc.) unwholesome, nauseous.

virosis /vʌɪ'rəʊsɪs/ *noun.* Pl. **-roses** /-'rəʊsiːz/. E20.
[from VIRUS + -OSIS.]
A virus disease.

virous /'vʌɪrəs/ *adjective. rare.* L15.
[formed as VIROSE: see -OUS.]
†**1** Purulent. Only in L15.
2 = VIROSE *adjective.* M17.

virtu /vəː'tuː/ *noun.* Also **vertu, virtù.** E18.
[Italian *virtù* VIRTUE. The form *vertu* alt. as if from French.]
1 A love of or interest in works of art; a knowledge of or expertise in the fine arts; the fine arts as a subject of study or interest. E18.
2 *collect.* Objects of art; curios. M18.
3 The strength or worth inherent in a person or thing; *esp.* inherent moral worth or virtue. M20.

📖 **1 article of virtu, object of virtu** an article interesting because of its antiquity, quality of workmanship, etc.; an antique, a curio. **man of virtu, gentleman of virtu** a connoisseur, a virtuoso. **2** *Times* A sale of virtu which had only 8 per cent bought in. **3** N. ANNAN A society that seemed . . hypocritical, cowardly and without virtu.

virtual /'vəːtjʊəl/ *adjective.* LME.
[medieval Latin *virtualis*, from Latin *virtus* VIRTUE, after late Latin *virtuosus*: see VIRTUOUS, -AL[1].]
1 Possessed of certain physical virtues or powers; effective in respect of inherent qualities; capable of exerting influence by means of such qualities. Now *rare.* LME. ▶**b** Of a herb: possessing specific healing properties or virtues. *rare.* M17.
†**2** Morally virtuous. *rare.* LME–E17.
†**3** Capable of producing a certain effect or result; effective, potent, powerful; *spec.* in MECHANICS (of a dimension) effective. LME–E19.
4 That is so in essence or effect, although not recognized formally, actually, or by strict definition as such; almost absolute. LME. ▶**b** OPTICS. Designating the apparent focus or image resulting from the effect of reflection or refraction upon rays of light. E18. ▶**c** MECHANICS. Of velocity etc.: possible and infinitesimal. E19. ▶**d** NUCLEAR PHYSICS. Designating an excited state of an atomic nucleus which has energy in excess of that needed for the emission of a particle, but a lifetime sufficiently long for it to be regarded as a quasi-stationary state. M20. ▶**e** PARTICLE PHYSICS. Designating particles and processes that cannot be directly detected and occur over very short intervals of time and space with correspondingly indefinite energy and momenta. M20. ▶**f** COMPUTING. Not physically existing but made by software to appear to do so from the point of view of the program or the user; *esp.* in ***virtual memory*** below. M20.

📖 **1** BACON See if the Virtuall Heat of the Wine . . will not mature it. **3** J. MOXON Dr. Dee . . as a vertual Proof of his own Learned Plea, quotes two Authentique Authors. **4** R. HEILBRONER The virtual deification of Mao has made China . . a personal theocracy. *New York Review of Books* The courts have come to a virtual standstill.

Special collocations: **virtual cathode** ELECTRONICS a part of a space charge or electron beam where the potential is a minimum, so that electrons are repelled and positive ions attracted. **virtual displacement** a notional infinitesimal displacement in a mechanical system that is consistent with the constraints of the system. **virtual height** the height of an imaginary reflecting plane surface which in free space would give rise to the same travel time for reflected radio waves as an actual ionospheric layer. ***virtual image***: see sense 4b above. **virtual memory** COMPUTING memory that appears to exist as main storage although most of it is supported by data held in secondary storage, transfer between the two being made automatically as required. **virtual pet** a electronically-generated animal with which human interaction is possible, such as a Tamagotchi. **virtual reality** the generation by computer software of an image or environment that appears real to the senses. **virtual temperature** METEOROLOGY the temperature that dry air would have to have in order to have the same density as a given body of moist air when at the same pressure. **virtual work** the work done by a force making a virtual displacement.

■ **virtually** *adverb* in a virtual manner; *esp.* in effect; to all intents; as far as essential qualities or facts are concerned: LME.

virtualism /ˈvəːtjʊəlɪz(ə)m/ *noun*. L19.
[from prec. + -ISM.]
CHRISTIAN THEOLOGY. The Calvinistic doctrine of Christ's virtual presence in the Eucharist.
■ **virtualist** *noun* L19.

virtuality /vəːtjʊˈalɪti/ *noun*. L15.
[medieval Latin *virtualitas*, from *virtualis*: see prec., -ITY.]
†**1** The possession of force or power; something endowed with such power. *rare*. L15–E17.
2 Virtual or essential nature or being, as distinct from external form or embodiment. M17.
3 A virtual (as opp. to an actual) thing; a potentiality. M19.
4 Virtual reality. L20.

🕮 **2** H. BUSHNELL The government of the world is waiting on Christianity, and is . . in . . virtuality a supernatural kingdom. **4** D. BRIN Moments later, fully suited for virtuality, I held a flint knife in my hands.

virtue /ˈvəːtjuː, -tʃuː/ *noun*. ME.
[Old & mod. French *vertu* from Latin *virtus* valour, worth, merit, moral perfection, from *vir* man.]
▶ **I** As a personal attribute.
1 a The power or operative influence inherent in a supernatural or divine being. *arch*. ME. ▶**b** An embodiment of such power; *spec*. in Christian theology, a member of the fifth order of the ninefold celestial hierarchy, ranking directly below the dominations and above the powers (usu. in *pl*.). ME. ▶†**c** An act of superhuman or divine power; a miracle. ME–E16.
2 Conformity of life and conduct with moral principles; voluntary adherence to recognized laws or standards of right conduct; moral excellence; uprightness. ME. ▶**b** Industry, diligence. *Scot*. *rare*. M16. ▶**c** Chastity or sexual purity, esp. on the part of a woman. L16.
3 A particular form of moral excellence; a special manifestation of the influence of moral principles in life or conduct. Also, any of certain moral qualities regarded as of particular worth or importance, as each of the cardinal, natural, or theological virtues (see below). ME. ▶**b** A personification or representation of a moral quality. M19.
†**4** Physical strength, force, or energy. ME–E16. ▶**b** Flourishing state or condition. *rare*. LME–L15.
5 The possession or display of manly qualities; manly excellence, courage, valour. *arch*. ME.
6 †**a** An acquired skill or accomplishment. ME–E19. ▶**b** Superiority or excellence; outstanding ability, merit, or distinction. Now *rare*. LME. ▶†**c** = VIRTU 1. *rare*. E18–E19.

🕮 **2** EARL OF CHATHAM Honour, courage . . humanity, and in one word, virtue in its true signification. R. P. WARREN A . . mentor for virtue in the midst of the political hurly-burly. *personified*: J. TROLLOPE How tiresome virtue is . . blocking every path to pleasure. **3** *Guardian* The wifely virtues of patience, tolerance and self-sacrifice. **5** SHAFTESBURY His Arms or military Virtue.

▶ **II** As a quality of things.
7 †**a** Of a precious stone: magical or supernatural power, esp. in the prevention or cure of disease etc.; later, great worth or value. ME–E16. ▶**b** Esp. of a herb, drug, etc.: efficacy arising from inherent physical qualities; beneficial, restorative, or healing property. ME. ▶**c** Moral efficacy; influence working for good on human life or conduct. Now *rare*. ME. ▶**d** Inherent worth, merit, or efficacy of any kind. LME. ▶†**e** Of a law etc.: operation, force. LME–L17.
8 A particular power, property, beneficial quality or feature, inherent in or pertaining to something. ME.

🕮 **7b** E. RAFFALD It will draw all the virtue out of the . . herbs, and turn it to a good gravy. **c** F. MYERS If Divine virtue is to be ascribed to every letter of Scripture. **d** A. J. P. TAYLOR Halifax . . had learnt the virtue of appeasement during . . long negotiations. **8** W. DAMPIER The Sulphurousness or other Vertue of this Water. A. TOFFLER Singing the virtues of . . microcomputers. *Dissent* A special virtue of . . Walzer's essay . . is that it is written in a spirit of generosity.

Phrases: **by virtue of**, **in virtue of**, †**by the virtue of**, †**in the virtue of** by the power or efficacy of; now, on the strength of, in consequence of, because of. ***cardinal virtue***: see CARDINAL *adjective*. ***lady of easy virtue***: see LADY *noun & adjective*. **make a virtue of necessity**, **make virtue of necessity**, †**make a virtue of need**, †**make virtue of need** [after Old French *faire de necessité vertu*, Latin *facere de necessitate virtutem*] derive benefit or advantage from performing an unwelcome obligation with apparent willingness; submit to unavoidable circumstances with a good grace. ***natural virtue***: see NATURAL *adjective*. ***of easy virtue***: see EASY *adjective* 8. ***theological virtue***: see THEOLOGICAL *adjective* 1.

■ **virtued** *adjective* (*rare*) invested with virtue or efficacy E17. **virtueless** *adjective* (*a*) lacking efficacy or excellence; ineffective, worthless; (*b*) lacking moral excellence; immoral: LME.

virtuosa /vəːtjʊˈəʊsə, -zə/ *noun*. Now *rare*. M17.
[Italian, fem. of VIRTUOSO.]
A female virtuoso.

virtuosic /vəːtjʊˈɒsɪk/ *adjective*. L19.
[from VIRTUOSO + -IC.]
Having or displaying the skills of a virtuoso; of or pertaining to a virtuoso or virtuosi.

🕮 *Gramophone* His natural delight in his virtuosic prowess gets the better of his musical judgement.

virtuosity /vəːtjʊˈɒsɪti/ *noun*. LME.
[In sense 1 from medieval Latin *virtuositas*, from late Latin *virtuosus* VIRTUOUS *adjective* + -ITY. In other senses from VIRTUOSO + -ITY.]
†**1** Manly qualities or character. Only in LME. ▶**b** Virtuousness. Only in E18.
2 The pursuits or temperament characteristic of a virtuoso or connoisseur; interest or taste in the fine arts, esp. of a dilettante nature. L17.
3 Attention (orig., when considered excessive or contrived) to technique, or to the production of effects requiring a high degree of technical skill, in the fine arts, esp. in music. M19.

🕮 **3** *Guardian* Mr Heggie's remarkable linguistic virtuosity outstripped his flair for dramatic action. *Opera Now* Ferocious virtuosity . . reaches its peak . . in the aria '*Brilla nell'alma*'.

virtuoso /vəːtjʊˈəʊsəʊ, -zəʊ/ *noun & adjective*. E17.
[from Italian = learned, skilful from late Latin *virtuosus*: see next.]
▶ **A** *noun*. Pl. **-si** /-si/, **-sos**.
†**1** A person who has a general interest in arts and sciences, or who pursues special investigations in one or more of these; a learned person; a scientist or scholar. E17–L18.
2 A person who has a special knowledge of or interest in the fine arts; a student or collector of works of art or virtu; a connoisseur, *esp*. a person pursuing these interests in a dilettante manner. M17.
3 A person who has special knowledge or skill in the technique of a fine art, esp. music. Also, a person with outstanding technical skill in any sphere. M18.

🕮 **2** *Gentleman's Magazine* The Virtuoso will appreciate this . . instructive . . manual. **3** *Profession* Critical theory is the great virtuoso at this game of one-upmanship. *Time* He was famous during childhood as a keyboard virtuoso.

▶ **B** *attrib*. or as *adjective*. Of or pertaining to a virtuoso; displaying the skills of a virtuoso; characterized by virtuosity. M17.

🕮 *Art in America* A virtuoso display of 'voguing' . . which mimes the movements of fashion models.

■ **virtuosoship** *noun* the state or condition of being a virtuoso; the profession of a virtuoso: E18.

virtuous /ˈvəːtjʊəs, -tʃʊəs/ *adjective & noun*. ME.
[Old French *vertuous*, (also mod.) *vertueux* from late Latin *virtuosus*, from Latin *virtus* VIRTUE: see -OUS.]
▶ **A** *adjective*. **I** Of a person, a person's conduct, etc.
†**1** Distinguished by manly qualities; full of courage; valiant. ME–E17. ▶**b** Of an act: displaying a manly spirit; brave, heroic. *rare*. M16–M17.
2 Possessing or showing virtue in life and conduct; acting with moral rectitude or in conformity with moral standards and principles; free from vice, immorality, or wickedness; upright, good, righteous. ME. ▶**b** Esp. of a woman: chaste. LME. ▶†**c** Used as a title of courtesy, esp. in addressing a woman of rank or eminence. M16–L17. ▶**d** Diligent, industrious. *Scot*. E18.
3 Characterized by or of the nature of virtue; conforming to moral law or principles; morally good; estimable, worthy. LME.

🕮 **2** I. MURDOCH I've seen your love life . . tempting our virtuous leader to sodomy. P. THEROUX He woke feeling . . almost virtuous, as though . . purified. **virtuous circle** [after *vicious circle* s.v. CIRCLE *noun* 12] a recurring cycle of events, the result of each one being to increase the beneficial effect of the next. **3** D. LODGE He ought to be feeling a virtuous indignation at their adultery. M. FORSTER A life below stairs quite unlike her own virtuous existence.

▶ **II** Of a thing, its effect, etc.
4 Producing or capable of producing (great) effect; powerful, potent, strong. *arch*. ME.
5 Endowed with or possessing inherent virtue or power, esp. of a magical or supernatural kind; potent in effect or influence; *spec*. having potent medicinal properties; efficacious. *arch*. ME.

🕮 **4** MILTON With one vertuous touch Th'Arch-chimick Sun . . Produces . . precious things. **5** BROWNING Cutting the roots of many a virtuous herb To solace . . mortals!

▶ **B** *absol*. as *noun*. Virtuous people as a class. Usu. with *the*. LME.
■ **virtuously** *adverb* LME. **virtuousness** *noun* LME.

virtute officii /vəːˌtjuːti ɒˈfɪʃɪiː/ *adverbial phr*. E19.
[Latin.]
LAW. By virtue of (one's) office.

virucidal /vʌɪrʊˈsʌɪd(ə)l/ *adjective*. E20.
[from VIRUS + -CIDE + -AL[1].]
= VIRICIDAL.
■ **ˈvirucide** *noun* = VIRICIDE L20.

virulence /ˈvɪrʊl(ə)ns, ˈvɪrjʊ-/ *noun*. LME.
[from next: see -ENCE.]
†**1** Discharge from a wound; pus. Only in LME.
2 Extreme acrimony or bitterness of temper or expression; violent hostility or rancour. E17.
3 The property or quality of being physically virulent; extreme poisonousness or venomousness; exceptional severity (of disease). M18. ▶**b** MICROBIOLOGY. The relative capacity of (a strain of) a micro-organism to cause disease; degree of pathogenicity. M20.

🕮 **2** DICKENS The ill will of Miss Knag had lost nothing of its virulence. R. FULLER What . . drunken virulence from Sammy had sent me from the house.

■ **virulency** *noun* virulence E17.

virulent /ˈvɪrʊl(ə)nt, ˈvɪrjʊ-/ *adjective*. LME.
[Latin *virulentus* poisonous, from VIRUS: see -ULENT.]
1 MEDICINE. †**a** Of wounds or ulcers: containing or yielding toxic or purulent matter. LME–E18. ▶**b** Of diseases etc.: of exceptional severity. M16. ▶**c** Of micro-organisms: capable of producing disease. M20.
2 Possessing venomous or strongly poisonous qualities; extremely noxious. E16.
3 Violently bitter or rancorous; full of acrimony or hostility. E16.
4 MICROBIOLOGY. Of a phage: causing lysis of the host cell immediately after replicating within it, without a period as a prophage; lytic, not lysogenic. M20.

🕮 **3** H. BRODKEY He . . had a virulent curse-hurling harridan of a sister. *Guardian* Shocked by the virulent anti-Islam sentiments in so much of Chesterton.

■ **virulently** *adverb* E16. **virulentness** *noun* (long *rare* or *obsolete*) L17.

viruliferous /vɪrʊˈlɪf(ə)rəs/ *adjective*. M20.
[formed as VIRULENT + -I- + -FEROUS.]
MICROBIOLOGY. Of an insect vector: carrying a virus.

virus /ˈvʌɪrəs/ *noun*. LME.
[Latin = slimy liquid, poison, offensive odour or taste.]
1 The venom of a snake etc. L16.
2 a MEDICINE. A substance produced in the body as the result of disease; *esp*. one capable, after inoculation, of infecting other people or animals with the same disease. *obsolete* exc. *Hist*. E18. ▶**b** MEDICINE & MICROBIOLOGY. A submicroscopic organism that can multiply only inside living host cells, has a non-cellular structure lacking any intrinsic metabolism and usu. comprising a single DNA or RNA molecule inside a protein coat, and is freq. pathogenic. L19. ▶**c** An infection with such an organism. *colloq*. M20.
3 A moral or intellectual poison; a harmful, corrupting, or malignant influence. Also, an infectious fear, anxiety, etc. L18.
4 COMPUTING. More fully ***computer virus***. An unauthorized self-replicating program that can interfere with or destroy other programs, and can transfer itself to other systems via disks or networks. L20.

🕮 **2b** ***adenovirus***, ***Lassa virus***, ***orphan virus***, ***parainfluenza virus***, ***RNA virus***, etc. **3** *Daily Telegraph* The brutal plague of war is gone, but the virus remains as the peace matures.

■ **virus-like** *adjective* resembling a virus M20.

vis /vɪs/ *noun*[1]. Pl. ***vires*** /ˈvʌɪriːz/. E17.
[Latin.]
1 Strength, force, energy, vigour. Chiefly in various phrs. E17.
2 LAW. In *pl*. Legal validity; legal authority or power. (Earlier in INTRA VIRES, ULTRA VIRES.) L20.
1 ***vis a fronte*** /ɑː ˈfrɒnteɪ/ a force operating from in front, as in attraction or suction. ***vis a tergo*** /ɑː ˈtəːgəʊ/ a force operating from behind; a propulsive force. ***vis comica*** /ˈkɒmɪkə/ humorous energy; comic force or effect. ***vis inertiae*** /ɪˈnəːʃɪʌɪ/ (*a*) MECHANICS the resistance offered by matter to any force tending to alter its state of rest or motion; (*b*) *transf*. tendency to remain inactive or unprogressive. ***vis major*** /ˈmeɪdʒə/ LAW overpowering force, esp. of nature (used as a reason for damage done to, or loss of, property). ***vis medicatrix naturae*** /mɛdɪˌkeɪtrɪks naˈtʃʊərʌɪ/ the healing power of nature. ***vis viva*** /ˈviːvə/ MECHANICS the operative force of a moving or acting body, equal to the mass of the body multiplied by the square of its velocity.

vis /vɪz/ *noun*[2]. *colloq*. (orig. MILITARY). M20.
[Abbreviation.]
= VISIBILITY 1b.

Vis. *abbreviation*.
Also **Visc.** Viscount.

visa /ˈviːzə/ *noun & verb.* M19.
[French from Latin = things seen, neut. pl. of pa. pple of *videre* see. Cf. VISÉ.]
▶ **A** *noun.* An endorsement on a passport etc. indicating that it has been examined and found correct, esp. as permitting the holder to enter or leave a country. M19.
▶ **B** *verb trans.* Mark with a visa; put a visa on. M19.

visage /ˈvɪzɪdʒ/ *noun.* Now chiefly *literary.* ME.
[Old & mod. French from Old French *vis* (cf. VIS-À-VIS) from Latin *visus* sight, appearance, from pa. pple of *videre* see: see -AGE.]
1 The face, esp. of a person; the face with regard to the form or proportions of the features. ME.
2 The face or features as expressive of feeling or temperament; the expression on a person's face. ME.
3 External appearance or aspect. ME.
4 The face or visible side of the sun or moon. LME.
†**5** An image, a likeness; a portrait. LME–L16.
†**6** An assumed or misleading appearance; a show; a pretence. LME–L17.
📖 **1** *New Yorker* A large man, wide of jowl and dark of visage. **2** L. STRACHEY The forbidding visage became charged with smiles. **3** J. PINKERTON Noble serpentine . . is . . of an unctuous visage.
■ **visaged** *adjective* having a visage (usu. as 2nd elem. of comb., as ***grim-visaged***) ME.

visagiste /viːzɑːˈʒiːst/ *noun.* Also **visagist** /ˈvɪzədʒɪst/. M20.
[French, formed as prec. + *-iste* -IST.]
A make-up artist.

Visākha *noun* see VESAK.

visarga /vɪˈsɑːgə, vɪˈsəːgə/ *noun.* E19.
[Sanskrit, lit. 'emission'.]
A sign in the Sanskrit alphabet representing the aspiration of a vowel. Also, such aspiration.

vis-à-vis /viːzɑːˈviː/ *noun, preposition, & adverb.* M18.
[Old & mod. French, lit. 'face to face', from Old French *vis* VISAGE + *à* to + *vis*.]
▶ **A** *noun.* Pl. same.
1 A light horse-drawn carriage for two people sitting face to face. *obsolete* exc. *Hist.* M18.
2 A person or thing facing or situated opposite to another, esp. in certain dances. M18. ▶**b** A counterpart, an opposite number. Also (*US*), a social partner. E20.
3 A face-to-face meeting. M19.
📖 **2b** J. K. JEROME The Vosges peasant has not the . . air of contented prosperity that spoils his *vis-à-vis* across the Rhine. **3** S. W. BAKER My first *vis-à-vis* with a hippo.
▶ **B** *preposition.* Regarding, in relation to. Also, opposite to, face to face with. M18.
📖 *Dance Theatre Journal* Groups need to . . make their own policy decisions *vis-à-vis* experimentation. L. HUDSON He wants to sustain an impression *vis-à-vis* his audience.
▶ **C** *adverb.* Opposite; facing one another. E19.
📖 SIR W. SCOTT *Waverley* . . found himself in the desired vehicle, *vis-à-vis* to Mrs Nosebag. R. FIRBANK He would raise a cold, hypnotic eye . . towards the ladies *vis-à-vis*.

viscacha /vɪsˈkatʃə/ *noun.* Also **viz-** /vɪz-/, **bis-** /bɪs-/, †**biz-**. E17.
[Spanish *vizcacha* (†*bizcacha*) from Quechua (*h*)*uiscacha*.]
Any of several large S. American burrowing rodents of the chinchilla family: (*a*) (more fully ***mountain viscacha***) each of three long-eared and long-tailed rodents of the genus *Lagidium*, found in mountains from Peru to Patagonia; (*b*) (more fully ***plains viscacha***) a heavily built rodent, *Lagostomus maximus*, which has horizontal black and white bars across the face and is found in the grasslands of Argentina.

viscera /ˈvɪs(ə)rə/ *noun pl.* M17.
[Latin = internal organs, pl. of VISCUS.]
1 *ANATOMY.* The organs contained within the trunk, considered collectively; the digestive tract together with the heart, liver, lungs, etc. M17.
2 The bowels or innermost parts of anything. E18.
■ †**viscerous** *adjective* (*rare*) of the nature of the viscera M17–E18.

visceral /ˈvɪs(ə)r(ə)l/ *adjective.* L16.
[In sense 1 from Old French, or medieval Latin *visceralis* in same sense. In senses 2–5 from prec. + -AL[1].]
1 Affecting the viscera regarded as the seat of emotion; pertaining to or reaching deep-seated instinctive feelings. L16.
2 *MEDICINE.* Of disorders or diseases: affecting the viscera. L18.
3 *ANATOMY.* Of, pertaining to, or consisting of the viscera; situated in or among, or covering, the viscera. E19.
4 Pertaining to the viscera of animals used as a means of divination. *rare.* M19.
📖 **1** A. CROSS Whoever did it hated him for reasons far more visceral than the usual academic disagreements. J. C. OATES Feeling that stab of visceral horror.
Special collocations: **visceral arch** *ZOOLOGY* one of a set of parallel ridges in the region of the mouth in a fish's skull, or in the embryonic skull of a higher vertebrate. **visceral brain** (now *rare*) those parts of the brain which mediate bodily activity, esp. visceral activity, in response to emotion. **visceral cavity** that part of an animal body in which the viscera are contained. **visceral cleft** *ZOOLOGY* one of the intervals between the visceral arches. **visceral hump** *ZOOLOGY* a dorsal enlargement containing the viscera in snails and other shelled gastropods. **visceral layer** *ANATOMY* the innermost layer of a serous membrane covering an organ or lining a cavity. ***visceral pleura***: see PLEURA *noun*[1] 1.
¶ Sense 1 obsolete after 17: revived M20.
■ **viscerally** *adverb* M17.

visceralization /ˌvɪs(ə)r(ə)lʌɪˈzeɪʃ(ə)n/ *noun.* Also **-isation**. M20.
[from prec. + -IZATION.]
MEDICINE. The spreading of an infection to the viscera; the movement of a pathogen towards the viscera.
■ **ˈvisceralize** *verb intrans.* spread to or attack the viscera M20.

viscerate /ˈvɪsəreɪt/ *verb trans. rare.* E18.
[from VISCERA + -ATE[3], after *eviscerate*.]
Eviscerate, disembowel.

viscero- /ˈvɪs(ə)rəʊ/ *combining form* of Latin VISCERA: see -O-. *ANATOMY & MEDICINE.*
■ **visceroˈcranium** *noun* = SPLANCHNOCRANIUM E20. **viscerˈopˈtosis** *noun* abnormal mobility of an abdominal organ, causing it to take up an unusually low position due to gravity L19. **viscerotome** *noun* an instrument for obtaining post-mortem samples of liver tissue through a puncture in the abdominal wall, used esp. when yellow fever is suspected M20. **visceˈrotomy** *noun* the use of a viscerotome M20. **visceroˈtonia** *noun* viscerotonic personality or characteristics M20. **visceroˈtonic** *adjective & noun* (*a*) *adjective* temperamentally resembling or characteristic of an endomorph, with a comfort-loving, sociable, and easy-going personality; (*b*) *noun* a viscerotonic person: M20. **viscerotropic** /-ˈtrəʊpɪk, -ˈtrɒpɪk/ *adjective* tending to attack or affect the viscera M20. **viscerotropism** /-ˈtrəʊp-/ *noun* the tendency of micro-organisms or infection to attack or affect the viscera M20.

viscid /ˈvɪsɪd/ *adjective.* M17.
[Late Latin *viscidus*, from Latin *viscum* birdlime: see -ID[1].]
1 Glutinous, sticky; semifluid; ropy. M17.
2 Chiefly *BOTANY*, of a leaf, stem, etc.: having the surface covered with a sticky secretion or coating. M18.
📖 **1** A. LURIE The saucer of margerine was a viscid yellow pool.
■ **viˈscidity** *noun* (*a*) the quality of being viscid; (*b*) viscid matter, a viscid substance: E17.

viscidium /vɪˈsɪdɪəm/ *noun.* Pl. **-dia** /-dɪə/. M20.
[mod. Latin, formed as prec. + -IUM.]
In certain orchids, each of the one or two viscid bodies formed by the rostellum, which have the pollinia attached to them.

viscin /ˈvɪsɪn/ *noun.* M19.
[French from Latin *viscum* birdlime, mistletoe: see -IN[1].]
A sticky substance which occurs in the berries etc. of mistletoe and forms the main constituent of birdlime.

viscoelasticity /ˌvɪskəʊɛlaˈstɪsɪti, -iːl-, -ɪl-/ *noun.* M20.
[from VISCO(SITY + ELASTICITY.]
The property of a substance of exhibiting both elastic and viscous behaviour, the application of stress causing temporary deformation if the stress is quickly removed but permanent deformation if it is maintained.
■ **viscoeˈlastic** *adjective* exhibiting or pertaining to viscoelasticity M20.

viscoid /ˈvɪskɔɪd/ *adjective. rare.* L19.
[from VISCOUS + -OID.]
Of a viscid or viscous nature.

viscometer /vɪsˈkɒmɪtə/ *noun.* L19.
[from late Latin *viscosus* VISCOUS + -METER.]
An instrument for measuring the viscosity of liquids.
COUETTE viscometer. ***Redwood viscometer***: see REDWOOD *noun*[2].
■ **viscoˈmetric** *adjective* M20. **viscoˈmetrically** *adverb* M20. **viscometry** *noun* the measurement of viscosity; the use of a viscometer: L19.

viscose /ˈvɪskəʊz, -kəʊs/ *noun.* L19.
[from VISCOUS + -OSE[2].]
1 A viscous orange-brown solution obtained by treating cellulose with sodium hydroxide and carbon disulphide, later used to regenerate cellulose as either rayon fibre or flexible transparent film. L19.
2 Rayon fabric or fibre made by the viscose process. M20.
Comb.: **viscose process** the process for making rayon with viscose as an intermediate product; **viscose rayon** = sense 2 above.

†**viscose** *adjective*[1]. LME–L18.
[Late Latin *viscosus* VISCOUS: see -OSE[1].]
Viscid, viscous.

viscose /ˈvɪskəʊz, -kəʊs/ *adjective*[2]. E20.
[from the noun.]
Made of viscose.

viscosimeter /vɪskəˈsɪmɪtə/ *noun.* M19.
[formed as VISCOMETER.]
= VISCOMETER.
■ **ˌviscosiˈmetric** *adjective* L19. **ˌviscosiˈmetrically** *adverb* E20. **viscosimetry** *noun* = VISCOMETRY L19.

viscosity /vɪˈskɒsɪti/ *noun.* LME.
[Old & mod. French *viscosité* or medieval Latin *viscositas*, from late Latin *viscosus*: see VISCOUS, -ITY.]
1 a The quality or fact of being viscous; semifluidity; glutinousness. LME. ▶**b** A viscous substance; a quantity of viscous matter. M16.
2 *PHYSICS.* The tendency of a liquid or gas to resist by internal friction the relative motion of its molecules and hence any change of shape; the magnitude of this, as measured by the force per unit area resisting a flow in which parallel layers unit distance apart have unit speed relative to one another (also ***absolute viscosity***, ***dynamic viscosity***). M19.
📖 **1** A. T. ELLIS Lydia was . . faintly disgusted by tears . . and by the viscosity of their substance. **2 kinematic viscosity** the dynamic viscosity of a fluid divided by its density. ***specific viscosity***: see SPECIFIC *adjective*.
Comb.: **viscosity index** a number expressing the degree to which the viscosity of an oil is unaffected by temperature.

viscount /ˈvʌɪkaʊnt/ *noun.* Also (esp. in titles) **V-**. LME.
[Anglo-Norman *viscounte* (Old French *vi(s)conte*, mod. *vicomte*) from medieval Latin *vicecomes*, *-comit-*: see VICE-, COUNT *noun*[2].]
1 *Hist.* A person acting as the deputy or representative of a count or earl in the administration of a district; *spec.* (in England) a sheriff or high sheriff. LME. ▶**b** In the island of Jersey, a sheriff. L17.
2 A British or Irish nobleman ranking between an earl and a baron. LME.
3 The brother of a count. M19.
■ **viscountcy** *noun* the title, dignity, or rank, of a viscount M19. **viscountship** *noun* = VISCOUNTCY E17.

viscountess /ˈvʌɪkaʊntɪs/ *noun.* Also (esp. in titles) **V-**. L15.
[from prec. + -ESS[1].]
1 A viscount's wife or widow; a woman holding the rank of viscount in her own right. L15.
2 A medium (size of) roofing-slate. Cf. COUNTESS 2. L19.

viscounty /ˈvʌɪkaʊnti/ *noun.* LME.
[from VISCOUNT + -Y[5].]
1 *Hist.* The office or jurisdiction of a viscount; the district under a viscount's authority. LME.
2 = VISCOUNTCY. M19.

viscous /ˈvɪskəs/ *adjective.* LME.
[from Anglo-Norman, or late Latin *viscosus*, from Latin *viscum* birdlime: see -OUS.]
1 Glutinous, sticky; viscid. LME. ▶**b** *PHYSICS.* Semifluid; having a high viscosity; not flowing freely. M19.
2 *BOTANY.* = VISCID 2. E18.
📖 **1** V. SINGH A viscous red blob of chewed betel leaf slipped from the edge of her mouth. *fig.*: *Time* [They] . . specialize in producing viscous show tunes. The songs not only cloy, they choke. **b viscous flow** laminar flow.
■ **viscously** *adverb* L19. **viscousness** *noun* L16.

viscuous /ˈvɪskjʊəs/ *adjective.* Now *rare.* E17.
[Irreg. from Latin *viscum*: see prec., -OUS.]
Viscous.

viscus /ˈvɪskəs/ *noun.* Pl. VISCERA. E18.
[Latin.]
ANATOMY. Any of the well-defined internal organs of the body; *esp.* those contained within the trunk.

vise /viːz/ *noun*[1]. Chiefly *Scot.* L17.
[Origin unkn.]
MINING. A line of fracture of a fault in a coal seam, usu. marked by a deposit of clay, mineral, etc.

vise *noun*[2] & *verb* see VICE *noun*[2] & *verb.*

visé /ˈviːzeɪ/ *verb & noun. arch.* E19.
[French, pa. pple of *viser* scrutinize, look attentively at, from Proto-Romance, from Latin *vis-* pa. ppl stem of *videre* see. Cf. VISA.]
▶ **A** *verb trans.* = VISA *verb.* E19.
▶ **B** *noun.* = VISA *noun.* M19.

viseme /ˈvɪziːm/ *noun.* M20.
[from VIS(UAL + -EME.]
Orig., a recognizable visible contrastive movement of the lips. Now more generally, the movement of the lips made whilst speaking that corresponds to the phoneme prounounced.

†**visement** *noun.* ME–M16.
[Aphet. formed as ADVISEMENT, or directly from Old & mod. French *visement*, from *viser*: see prec., -MENT.]
= ADVISEMENT 2.

Vishnu /ˈvɪʃnuː/ *noun.* M17.
[Sanskrit *Viṣṇu*.]
One of the three major Hindu gods, regarded by his worshippers as the supreme being and saviour, but by others as the second member of the Trimurti.
■ **Vishnuism** *noun* the worship of Vishnu L19. **Vishnuite** *noun & adjective* (*a*) *noun* a worshipper of Vishnu; an adherent of Vishnuism; (*b*) *adjective* of or pertaining to Vishnuism: L19. **Vishnuvite** *noun & adjective* = VISHNUITE E19.

visibilia /vɪzɪˈbɪlɪə/ *noun pl.* M20.
[Latin, neut. pl. of *visibilis* VISIBLE: see -IA[2].]
Visible things; visual images.

visibility /vɪzɪˈbɪlɪti/ *noun.* LME.
[French *visibilité* or late Latin *visibilitas* from Latin *visibilis*: see next, -ITY.]
1 The condition, state, or fact of being visible; visible quality; ability to be seen. LME. ▸**b** The range or possibility of vision as determined by the conditions of light, atmosphere, etc., prevailing at a particular time; an instance of this. E20. ▸**c** The degree to which something impinges on public awareness or attracts general attention; prominence. M20.
2 A visible person, thing, or entity. Now *rare.* E17.
†**3** Sight; the exercise of visual perception. *rare.* E17–M18.

📖 **1** M. POOLE If Christ did indeed promise the perpetual visibility of his Church. R. A. PROCTOR The comet . . attracted more attention when it had passed from view than . . during the brief period of its visibility. **b** F. CHICHESTER Fog came, reducing visibility to half a mile. **c** *Software Magazine* He must be recognized for . . raising the visibility of the software industry.

visible /ˈvɪzɪb(ə)l/ *adjective & noun.* ME.
[Old & mod. French, or Latin *visibilis*, from *vis-* pa. ppl stem of *videre* see: see -IBLE.]
▶ **A** *adjective.* **1** Able to be seen; that by its nature is perceivable by the eye. ME.
2 That may be mentally perceived or noticed; clearly or readily evident; apparent, obvious. LME.
3 That can be seen or perceived under certain conditions, or with optical aid etc.; in sight; open to view. LME. ▸**b** Of exports, imports, etc.: consisting of tangible commodities, as opp. to invisible items such as tourism, insurance, etc. L19.
4 Of a person: able to be seen or visited; *esp.* disposed or prepared to receive visitors. *arch.* E18.
5 In a position of public prominence; attracting public attention; well known. L20.

📖 **1** N. CHOMSKY The planes attacked any visible target, even trails and cultivated fields. D. LODGE Vic returned the smile with a visible effort. *Guardian* The wealth visible all around . . is a result of sticking to Japan's formula for success. **2** T. MITCHELL A visible decrease in the offences which had been previously committed. *Guardian* How he managed to do this with little visible means of support . . was . . a mystery. **3** L. GRANT-ADAMSON He took a lane to East End, the hamlet visible from the windows of Butlers. **b** *Financial Times* The visible deficit fell sharply . . as imports responded to weak domestic demand. **5** *Times* The proposed flotation of fast growing Abbey Life . . would make it more visible. *Scientific American* He became highly visible in . . flood control and economic planning.

Special collocations & phrases: **outward visible sign**: see SIGN *noun.* ***the Church visible***: see CHURCH *noun* 3. ***visible horizon***: see HORIZON *noun* 1. **visible index** an index so arranged that each item is visible. **visible light**: within the visible spectrum. **visible spectrum** the range of wavelengths of electromagnetic radiation to which the human eye is normally sensitive. **visible speech** (*a*) a system of phonetic notation consisting of characters or symbols intended to represent the actual position of the vocal organs in the production of speech sounds; (*b*) speech rendered into a visible record by spectrography.
▶ **B** *noun.* **1** A visible person, thing, or entity. Usu. in *pl.* E17.
2 In *pl.* Visible exports or imports. M20.
3 = ***visible spectrum*** above. M20.

📖 **1** I. ZANGWILL The visibles of Art, the invisibles of Religion. **the visible** that which is visible, *esp.* the visible world.

■ **visibleness** *noun* L16. **visibly** *adverb* (*a*) so as to be visible to the eye; (*b*) evidently, manifestly, obviously: LME.

Visigoth /ˈvɪzɪɡɒθ/ *noun.* M16.
[Late Latin *Visigothus* (usu. in pl. *-gothi*; so Greek *Ouisigotthoi*), the 1st elem. of which may mean 'west', as opp. to OSTROGOTH.]
1 A member of the branch of the Goths which entered parts of France and Spain towards the end of the 4th century AD and subsequently ruled much of Spain until 711. M16.
2 *transf.* An uncivilized or barbarous person. M18.
■ **Visiˈgothic** *adjective* of or pertaining to the Visigoths L18.

visile /ˈvɪzʌɪl/ *adjective & noun.* E20.
[from Latin *vis-* pa. ppl stem of *videre* see + -ILE.]
▶ **A** *adjective.* Of, pertaining to, or predominantly involving the sense of sight; having a greater receptivity to visual images than to aural or tactile sensations. E20.
▶ **B** *noun.* A visile person. E20.

vision /ˈvɪʒ(ə)n/ *noun & verb.* ME.
[Old & mod. French from Latin *visio(n-)* sight, thing seen, formed as prec.: see -ION.]
▶ **A** *noun.* **1 a** A person who or thing which is apparently perceived otherwise than by ordinary sight; *esp.* an apparition of a prophetic, revelational, or supernatural nature presented to the mind in sleep or in a state of heightened spiritual or emotional awareness. ME. ▸**b** A distinct or vivid mental image or concept, *esp.* an attractive or fantastic one; an excursion into the imagination. Freq. in *pl.* L16. ▸**c** A person or thing seen in a dream or trance. E17. ▸**d** A person or thing of exceptional beauty. E19.
2 Perception or contemplation of an imaginative or spiritual nature; imaginative or mystical insight or foresight. LME. ▸**b** Ability to plan or form policy in a far-sighted way, esp. in politics; sound political foresight. E20.
3 The action or faculty of seeing with the eye; visual perception; sight. LME. ▸**b** An instance of seeing; a look. *rare.* M19.
†**4** A thing actually seen; an object of sight. *rare* (Shakes.). Only in E17.
5 The visual component of a television broadcast; television images collectively; the transmission or reproduction of such images. Also, the signal corresponding to these images. E20.

📖 **1** MILTON Prophetic Anna, warn'd By Vision, found thee in the Temple. *Opera Now* A . . shepherd, revealed there in a vision as the incarnation of . . Dionysus. ***BEATIFIC vision***. **b** G. BOYCOTT Antigua is . . every Englishman's vision of paradise. *National Trust Magazine* I had romantic visions of myself as a drystone waller, indomitable against the elements. **vision splendid** the dream of some glorious imagined time. **c** SIR W. SCOTT Thou, for so the Vision said, Must in thy Lord's repentance aid. **d** *Oxford Times* Among all those man mountains . . runs a vision of grace and loveliness. **2** F. W. FARRAR The divine vision of a Peter, and the inspired eloquence of a Paul. C. ISHERWOOD With a flash of vision, I saw myself ten years hence. **b** A. J. P. TAYLOR Truman . . had none of Roosevelt's vision as international leader. **3** E. FIGES Her eyes so . . dazzled by the sunlight that she saw spots swimming across her vision. *Practical Health* Throbbing pain in the eye with some disturbance of vision could be glaucoma. ***double vision***: see DOUBLE *adjective & adverb.* ***field of vision***: see FIELD *noun* 13. **line of vision** the straight line along which an observer looks. ***red vision***: see RED *adjective.* ***tubular vision***: see TUBULAR *adjective* 2b. **5** G. FREEMAN The sound came on a full minute before the vision.

Comb.: **vision-mixer** a person whose job is to switch from one camera, image, section of videotape, etc., to another in television broadcasting or recording; **vision quest** *N. Amer.* the attempt to achieve a vision traditionally undertaken by mature men of the Plains Indian peoples, usu. through fasting or self-torture.
▶ **B** *verb trans.* **1** Show (as) in a vision; present to the eye or mind; *rare* call *up* a vision of. L16.
2 See (as) in a vision; envisage, imagine. L18.

📖 **2** I. L. IDRIESS The boy stood staring . . , his mind visioning the story as told . . at the campfire.

■ **visioned** *adjective* (*a*) seen in a vision; (*b*) associated with or arising from a vision or visions; (*c*) gifted with the power of seeing visions: E16. **visioner** *noun* a person who has visions; a visionary: E18. **visioning** *noun* the action of seeing visions; an instance of this: M19. **visionist** *noun* (*a*) a visionary; (*b*) CHRISTIAN THEOLOGY a supporter of the view that the biblical account of creation was revealed to the writer in a vision or series of visions: M17. **visionless** *adjective* (*a*) sightless, blind; (*b*) lacking the ability to see visions; devoid of higher insight or imagination: E19.

visional /ˈvɪʒ(ə)n(ə)l/ *adjective.* L16.
[from VISION *noun* + -AL[1].]
1 Connected with, relating to, or based on, a vision or visions. L16.
2 Of the nature of, appearing in, or forming part of, a vision. M17.
■ **visionally** *adverb* as or in a vision M17.

visionary /ˈvɪʒ(ə)n(ə)ri/ *adjective & noun.* M17.
[from VISION *noun* + -ARY[1].]
▶ **A** *adjective.* **1** Given to seeing visions; capable of receiving impressions or obtaining knowledge by this means. Also *transf.*, far-sighted, percipient. M17. ▸**b** Given to fanciful and impractical ideas or theories; speculative, dreamy. E18.
2 Of the nature of a vision; presented in a vision; seen only in a vision; spectral. M17. ▸**b** Connected with or pertaining to a vision or visions. M18.
3 Existing in imagination only; having no base in reality; characterized by fantasy. Also, (of a scheme, plan, etc.) unable to be carried out or realized; purely speculative; unpracticable. E18.

📖 **1** A. B. JAMESON A strange . . visionary child, to whom an unseen world had revealed itself. *Omni* If visionary physicist Hal Puthoff is proved right, we may soon have a new . . energy source. **b** J. BONNYCASTLE We laugh at the absurdities of a visionary pretender. **2** DICKENS By what visionary hands she was led along. **b** J. ADAIR Having intimidated themselves . . with visionary notions. **3** POPE Vanish'd are all the visionary joys. D. LEAVITT He had been . . sidetracked by . . wrongheaded and visionary notions.

▶ **B** *noun.* **1** A person who receives knowledge of unknown or future things in visions. Also *transf.*, a person with vision or foresight. E18.
2 A person who indulges in speculative or fanciful ideas or schemes. E18.

📖 **1** *Methodist Recorder* Commitment to overseas students started with the work of visionaries like Hilda Porter. S. HILL That . . bliss which saints and visionaries . . attempted to describe. **2** H. MARTINEAU Being treated as a visionary, and . . laughed at as absurd.

■ **visionariness** *noun* E19.

visit /ˈvɪzɪt/ *noun.* E17.
[French *visite*, from *visiter*, or immed. from the verb.]
1 An act of visiting a person; a call on or temporary stay with a person for social, friendly, business, or other purposes. Also, an excursion to or temporary residence at a place. Freq. in ***make a visit***, ***pay a visit***. E17. ▸**b** A bitch's journey to and stay with a dog for mating purposes. M19. ▸**c** An occasion of going *to* a dentist, doctor, etc., for examination or treatment. L19. ▸**d** BILLIARDS & SNOOKER. A turn of play at the table. E20.
†**2** An occurrence of menstruation. Cf. VISITOR 5. M17–E18.
3 A professional, official, or pastoral call on a person made by a doctor, a member of the clergy, etc. E18.
4 A formal or official call for inspection or examination purposes. L18.
5 A chat. *US.* L20.

📖 **1** D. M. THOMAS He'd been put to bed early, exhausted after a visit from Konstantin. *Times Educ. Suppl.* She has been known to pay a flying visit to Paris just to see a movie. **3** *British Medical Journal* A district nurse may have a total of 1500 visits to patients a year. **4** M. PATTISON Sir Thomas More made . . a domiciliary visit in search of heretical books. **right of visit** = ***right of visitation*** s.v. VISITATION 1b.

visit /ˈvɪzɪt/ *verb.* ME.
[Old & mod. French *visiter* or Latin *visitare* go to see, frequentative of *visare* view, see to, visit, from *vis-* pa. ppl stem of *videre* see. Senses 1–7 are based on those of late Latin *visitare* in the Vulgate.]
▶ **I 1** *verb trans.* Of God: come to (a person) in order to bring comfort or salvation. *arch.* ME.
†**2** *verb trans.* Esp. of God: come to (a person) in order to observe or examine a person's behaviour; subject to scrutiny. ME–M17.
3 *verb trans.* Of a disease, a calamity, a fear, etc.: come upon, attack, afflict. Freq. in *pass.* and foll. by *with* or *by*. ME.
4 *verb trans.* Punish (wrongdoing) (foll. by *with*); inflict punishment for (wrongdoing) *on* a person. ME.
5 *verb trans.* & (*rare*) *intrans.* Inflict harm or punishment on (a person); deal severely with, afflict, (a person) *with* something as a punishment. ME.

📖 **1** W. COWPER For He . . Shall visit earth in Mercy. **2** J. CARYL The eye of God is alway upon us . . he visiteth us. **3** J. E. T. ROGERS Cornwall must have been . . lightly visited with the Plague. E. B. WHITE Publishers are often visited with vague forebodings. **4** J. A. FROUDE Mild offences were visited with the loss of eyes or ears. G. PRIESTLAND The sins of his father should in no way be visited on the son. **5** SMOLLETT Indignation . . directed to Cot Almighty, who visited his people with distempers. J. JORTIN Reasons why God doth not immediately visit the disobedient.

▶ **II 6** *verb trans.* Go to, or make a practice of going to, (the sick, the poor, etc.) in order to give comfort or assistance, esp. out of charity or in fulfilment of pastoral duty. ME.
7 *verb trans. & intrans.* Pay a sociable, polite, or friendly call on (a person); go to see (a person) for a particular purpose. Also, reside temporarily with (a person) as a guest. ME. ▸**b** *verb trans.* Orig., go to (a person for sexual intercourse). Now only *spec.*, (of a bitch) be put to mate with (a dog). LME. ▸**c** *verb trans.* Of a doctor etc.: attend (a patient) professionally; examine medically. LME. ▸**d** *verb trans.* Go to (a person etc.) with hostile intentions. Long *rare* or *obsolete.* M16. ▸**e** *verb intrans.* Foll. by *with*: go and see, esp. socially (now *N. Amer.*). Also (*US*), converse, chat (*with*). M19.
8 *verb trans.* Go to look at; inspect, examine; *esp.* examine (vessels, goods, baggage, etc.) officially. ME. ▸**b** *verb trans. & intrans. spec.* Go to (an institution) to ensure that everything is in order; make periodic official calls to (an institution) for supervisory purposes. ME.
9 *verb trans.* Go to or stay for a limited time at (a place) for interest or for a purpose; *spec.* (*a*) go to (a church etc.) for worship or as a religious duty; (*b*) (of a migratory bird or an animal) fly to or frequent (a certain locality etc.) at a particular time of the year. ME.
†**10** *verb trans.* Foll. by *with*: come to (a person) bringing something of benefit; enrich (a person) with some benefit. ME–M17.

📖 **6** SHAKES. *Meas. for M.* Bound by my charity . . I come to visit the afflicted spirits Here in the prison. ELIZABETH HAMILTON The minister . . had been sent for . . to visit a sick parishioner. **7** M. MOORCOCK Uncle Semya wanted me to . . visit him in Odessa. D. DELILLO Bee wants to visit at Christmas. **e** L. DUNCAN You two visit a minute while I get something I left in my room. **8** R. ORME A passport . . should exempt the goods . . from being visited or stopped by the officers. **b** LD MACAULAY A commission with power to visit . . the Church of England. **9** R. W. EMERSON In sweeping showers, the spring Visits the valley. *Which?* A full-time 'facilitator' (who visits GP practices to train the . . staff). *National Trust Magazine* Optional tour . . visits the . . museum of vernacular architecture.

■ **visited** *ppl adjective* †(*a*) afflicted with illness; attacked by plague or other epidemic; (*b*) (of a place, person, etc.) that has been visited, that is the object of a visit or visits: M16. **visiˈtee** noun a person to whom a visit is paid E18. **visiter** noun (now rare) a visitor LME.

visitable /ˈvɪzɪtəb(ə)l/ adjective. E17.
[from prec. + -ABLE.]
1 Of an institution etc.: liable to visitation; subject to official supervision or inspection. E17.
2 Esp. of a place: able to be visited; worth visiting. E18.
3 Of a person: able to be visited on more or less equal terms by those of some standing in society; socially acceptable. arch. M18.
4 Such as admits of receiving visitors. rare. M19.

2 *Maclean's Magazine* It has . . visitable old buildings.

visitador /ˌvɪzɪtəˈdɔː/ noun. rare. L17.
[Spanish & Portuguese, from *visitar* visit.]
An official visitor, inspector, or superintendent.

Visitandine /vɪzɪˈtandiːn/ noun & adjective. M18.
[French, irreg. from Latin *visitand-* gerundial stem of *visitare* visit + -INE[3].]
▶ **A** noun. A nun belonging to the Order of the Visitation, founded in 1610 by Mme. de Chantal (St Frances) under the direction of St Francis de Sales. M18.
▶ **B** adjective. Of or pertaining to the Visitandines or their Order. L19.

visitant /ˈvɪzɪt(ə)nt/ noun & adjective. L16.
[French, pres. pple of *visiter*, or Latin *visitant-* pres. ppl stem of *visitare*: see VISIT verb, -ANT[1].]
▶ **A** noun. **1** A person who visits a place, another person, etc.; a visitor, now esp. a supernatural one. L16.
2 A thing which affects or comes to a person, esp. for a temporary period. M18.
3 = VISITOR 4b. L18.

1 T. JEFFERSON Not written by a Virginian, but a visitant from another State. T. C. WOLFE Suddenly Cook appeared like a spectral visitant. 2 L. STRACHEY Her smile, so rare a visitant to those saddened features.

▶ **B** adjective. Of the nature of a visitant; visiting. arch. or poet. M17.

A. HECHT Vapor, like a visitant ghost, Hovers above a lake . . before the dawn.

visitation /vɪzɪˈteɪʃ(ə)n/ noun. ME.
[Old & mod. French, or late Latin *visitatio(n-)*, from Latin *visitare*: see VISIT verb, -ATION.]
▶ **I 1** The action, on the part of an appointed, qualified, or authorized person, of making an official visit of inspection for supervisory purposes; an instance of this; spec. (a) a visit of examination paid by a bishop or archdeacon to inquire into the state of a diocese, parish, etc.; (b) (now Hist.) a periodic visit made to a district by heralds in England and Wales between 1530 and 1689 to examine and enrol arms and pedigrees. ME. ▸**b** The boarding of a merchant vessel belonging to another State to ascertain its character and purpose. Formerly also, examination of goods by a customs officer. M18.
2 The action of visiting a place; an instance of this. LME. ▸†**b** The object of a visit. rare (Milton). Only in M17.
3 The action or practice of visiting the sick or poor as a charitable act; pastoral visiting; a pastoral or charitable visit. LME.
4 The action of paying a sociable or polite call or calls; an instance of this. Also (colloq.), an unduly prolonged visit, a visit which is disagreeable to the recipient. LME. ▸**b** A gathering at the home of a deceased person before the funeral; a wake. US. L20. ▸**c** US LAW. A divorced person's right to spend time with his or her children in the custody of a former spouse. L20.
5 (**V-**.) The visit paid by the Virgin Mary to Elizabeth (recorded in *Luke* 1:39–56); the festival commemorating this, 2 July; a picture representing the event. Also more fully ***the Visitation of our Lady***. L15.

1b right of visitation the right to conduct a visitation of a vessel, not including the right of search. **2** *Backpacker* Despite increases in visitation . . , the park service has kept the wilderness intact. **4** G. CRABBE To lose the . . day In dissipation wild, in visitation gay. D. DU MAURIER We had made do with the monthly visitations of . . the estate mason. **5 the order of the Visitation, the Visitation** the Visitandine order of nuns.

▶ **II 6** The action, on the part of God or some supernatural power, of visiting a person or people in order to comfort, help, judge, inflict punishment for wrongdoing, etc. ME. ▸**b** An appearance of a supernatural being. M19.
7 A grave affliction, blow, or trial, regarded as an instance of divine dispensation; retributive punishment operating by this means. LME.
8 Any catastrophe, disaster, or destructive agency afflicting a people, country, etc. M16.
9 An instance of an immaterial power or influence visiting or affecting the mind. L18.

6 J. ARCH A visitation of the Almighty . . upon a . . dissipated aristocracy. **b** *Guardian* Floods imprinted a black signature on the walls . . as if to mark a satanic visitation. **7** *Manchester Weekly Times* War is here regarded . . as a punitive visitation. **8** T. ARNOLD The period . . was marked by the visitations of pestilence. **9** GEO. ELIOT His voice was what his uncle's might have been . . modulated by . . a visitation of self-doubt.

visitator /ˈvɪzɪteɪtə/ noun. Now rare. M16.
[Late Latin, from *visitare* VISIT verb: see -OR.]
An official visitor.

visitatorial /ˌvɪzɪtəˈtɔːrɪəl/ adjective. L17.
[from prec. + -IAL, or from medieval Latin *visitatorius* visitatory + -AL[1].]
1 Of, pertaining to, or connected with, an official visitor or visitation. L17.
2 Having the power of official visitation; exercising authority of this kind. L19.

visite /vizit (pl. same), vɪˈziːt/ noun. M19.
[French = VISIT noun.]
1 A woman's light cape or short sleeveless cloak. M19.
2 ***visite de digestion*** /də diʒɛstjɔ̃/ [lit. 'visit of digestion'], a formal call paid in return for hospitality received, esp. after a dinner party. E20.
¶ See also CARTE-DE-VISITE.

visiting /ˈvɪzɪtɪŋ/ verbal noun. ME.
[from VISIT verb + -ING[1].]
The action of VISIT verb; an instance of this; a visitation, a visit.
Comb.: **visiting-book** a book containing the names of people calling or to be called on; **visiting-card** (a) a small card bearing a person's name, presented on, or left in lieu of, paying a visit; (b) ***leave one's visiting-card*** (slang, orig. Military) leave unpleasant evidence of having been at a place; **visiting hours** a time designated when visitors may call, esp. to see a person in a hospital or other institution; **visiting rights** the right to pay or receive visits to or from a child in the custody of another, esp. a divorced spouse; the right to receive visits while in an institution.

visiting /ˈvɪzɪtɪŋ/ ppl adjective. E17.
[from VISIT verb + -ING[2].]
That visits; that pays visits or is engaged in visiting.
visiting ant = DRIVER 6. **visiting fellow**, **visiting lecturer**, **visiting professor** an academic who accepts an invitation to work at another institution for a fixed term. **visiting fireman** US slang (a) a visitor to an organization given especially cordial treatment on account of his or her importance; (b) a tourist expected to spend freely.

visitor /ˈvɪzɪtə/ noun. LME.
[Anglo-Norman *visitour*, Old & mod. French *visiteur*, from *visiter* VISIT verb: see -OR.]
1 A person who makes an official visit of inspection or supervision, esp. to an institution; spec. (a) an ecclesiastic or a lay commissioner appointed to visit churches etc.; (b) a person with the right or duty of periodically inspecting and reporting on a college or other educational institution. LME.
2 A person who visits the sick, the poor, etc., in a professional capacity, from charitable motives, or with a view of doing good. LME.
3 A person who pays a visit to another person; a person staying as a guest. L16.
4 A person who visits a place, country, etc., esp. as a sightseer or tourist. E18. ▸**b** A migratory bird, or an animal, which frequents a certain locality only at particular times of the year. M19. ▸**c** SPORT. A member of a visiting team. Usu. in pl. E20.
5 An occurrence of menstruation. Cf. VISIT noun 2. colloq. L20.
2 *district visitor*: see DISTRICT noun. **HEALTH *visitor***.
Comb.: **visitor centre** (orig. US) a building in a tourist area in which exhibitions etc. are displayed as an introduction to the locality; **visitors' book** a book in which visitors to a hotel, church, etc., write their names and addresses and sometimes comments; **visitors' list** a public list of those making a visit to a place, esp. to a resort.
■ **visitorship** noun the office or position of an official visitor M19.

visitorial /vɪzɪˈtɔːrɪəl/ adjective. E19.
[from prec. or VISIT verb: see -IAL.]
= VISITATORIAL 1.

visitress /ˈvɪzɪtrɪs/ noun. Now rare. E19.
[from VISITOR: see -ESS[1].]
A female visitor.

†**visive** adjective. LME.
[French †*visif*, -*ive* or late Latin *visivus*, from Latin *visus* seeing, sight.]
1 Of or pertaining to sight or the power of seeing; visual. Freq. in ***visive faculty***, ***visive power***, etc. LME–M19. ▸**b** Serving as a means by which sight or vision is made possible. M17–E19. ▸**c** Having the power of vision; able to see. rare. L17–L18.
2 Forming the object of vision; visible; falling upon or appearing to the eye. L16–L17.
1 visive organ the eye.

Visking /ˈvɪskɪŋ/ noun. Also **v-**. M20.
[The *Visking* Corporation of Chicago, USA.]
(Proprietary name for) a type of seamless cellulose tubing used as a membrane in dialysis and as an edible casing for sausages.

visna /ˈvɪznə/ noun. M20.
[Old Norse = to wither.]
VETERINARY MEDICINE. A fatal disease of sheep in which there is progressive demyelination of neurones in the brain and spinal cord, caused by the maedi-visna virus. Cf. MAEDI.
Comb.: **visna-maedi** = MAEDI-visna.

visne /ˈviːni/ noun. LME.
[Anglo-Norman, Old French *visné* from Proto-Romance, from Latin *vicinus* neighbour: see VICINITY.]
LAW (now Hist.).
1 A neighbourhood, esp. as the area from which a jury is summoned. LME.
2 A jury summoned from the neighbourhood in which the cause of action lies. M17.
†3 = VENUE 2a. rare. M17–M18.

visnomy /ˈvɪznəmi/ noun. Now arch., Scot., & dial. E16.
[Var. of PHYSIOGNOMY.]
A person's face or expression, esp. viewed as indicative of the mind and character; a person's physiognomy.

vison /ˈvʌɪs(ə)n/ noun. Now rare or obsolete. L18.
[French, of unkn. origin.]
The American mink, *Mustela vison*.

visor /ˈvʌɪzə/ noun & verb. Also **vizor**. ME.
[Anglo-Norman *viser* = Old & mod. French *visière*, from Old French *vis* face: see VISAGE, -OR.]
▶ **A** noun. **1** The front part of a helmet, protecting the face but having apertures for air and light, and able to be raised and lowered; the upper portion of this. ME. ▸**b** The peak of a cap. N. Amer. M19. ▸**c** A shade for protecting the eyes from bright light, esp. a fixed or hinged shield at the top of the windscreen of a motor vehicle or aircraft. E20.
2 A mask (lit. & fig.). ME.
†3 A face; an outward aspect or appearance. L16–L17.
4 A variety of frilled pigeon. Now rare. L19.

1 C. THIRLWALL He was pierced with . . a javelin through the visor of his helmet. D. LODGE A blue plastic safety helmet with a transparent visor. 2 B. CAPES The eyelets in its woollen visor were like holes scorched through. C. MCWILLIAM The visor of chilliness I keep about my face.

Comb.: **visor-bearer** either of two Brazilian hummingbirds of the genus *Augastes*, which have glittering golden green foreheads and throats.
▶ **B** verb trans. Cover or disguise with a visor. rare. L15.
■ **visorless** adjective M19.

visored /ˈvʌɪzəd/ adjective. Also **vizored**. LME.
[from prec.: see -ED[2], -ED[1].]
1 Having the face covered or disguised with a visor or mask. LME.
2 (Of a helmet) having a visor; (of a cap) peaked. M19.

†**visorum** noun. M17–L18.
[mod. Latin *visorium* aphet. from medieval Latin *divisorium* a dividing thing or part.]
A device formerly used by compositors while setting type, to indicate the line on the copy.

Visqueen /ˈvɪskwiːn/ noun. US. Also **v-**. M20.
[from VISKING with humorous alt. of *king* to *queen*.]
(Proprietary name for) a durable polyethylene sheeting, used in various building applications and in the manufacture of waterproof household articles.

viss /vɪs/ noun. Now chiefly Hist. E17.
[Tamil *visai*.]
In southern India and Burma (Myanmar), a unit of weight equal to about 1½ kilograms (about 3½ lb).

vista /ˈvɪstə/ noun. Also †**visto**, pl. **-o(e)s**. M17.
[Italian = view.]
1 A view, a prospect, esp. one seen through an avenue of trees or other long narrow opening. M17.
2 a A long narrow opening, esp. one created deliberately in a wood etc., through which a view may be obtained, or in itself affording a pleasant prospect; an avenue, a glade. L17. ▸**b** An open corridor or long passage in or through a large building; an interior portion of a building affording a continuous view. E18.
3 fig. A broad prospect or vision presented to the imagination; a mental view, in prospect or retrospect, of an extensive period of time or series of events, experiences, etc. L17.

1 *Harper's Magazine* Sudden, swift vistas of peaks and . . valleys. **2a** S. RICHARDSON He employed hands to cut a vista through a coppice. **3** R. F. HOBSON Meetings . . opened up new vistas about language and life. *Jazz FM* The impact of that rich musical vista on a black plantation worker.

Comb.: **vista-dome** US a high glass-sided railway carriage enabling passengers to look at the view from above the normal level of the train.

vistaed /ˈvɪstəd/ *adjective*. M19.
[from prec. + -ED².]
1 Placed or arranged so as to make a vista or avenue. M19.
2 Provided with a vista or vistas. M19.
3 *fig.* Seen as if in a mental vista. M19.

Vistavision /ˈvɪstəvɪʒ(ə)n/ *noun*. Also **V-**. M20.
[from VISTA + VISION *noun*.]
A form of wide-screen cinematography employing standard 35 mm film in such a way as to give a larger projected image using ordinary methods of projection.
¶ Proprietary name in the US.

†visto *noun* var. of VISTA.

visual /ˈvɪʒjʊəl, -zj-/ *adjective & noun*. LME.
[Late Latin *visualis*, from Latin *visus* sight: see -AL¹.]
► **A** *adjective*. **1** Coming, proceeding, or directed from the eye or sight. *obsolete* exc. in ***visual line***, ***visual ray*** below (in which it is now understood in sense 2). LME.
2 Of, pertaining to, or connected with the faculty of sight or the process of vision. Cf. OPTIC *adjective* 1. L15.
3 That is by nature perceivable to the eye; able to be seen; visible. L15.
4 (Of knowledge) attained or obtained by sight; (of an action) performed by the eye; (of an impression etc.) received through the sense of sight; based on something seen. M17.
5 Of or pertaining to vision in relation to the object of sight; optical. E18.
6 Of the nature of a mental vision; produced or occurring as a mental image. E19.

> 🕮 **2** P. QUILLIN Poor visual adaptation to the dark. *Guardian* New technology can remove . . barriers for people with visual handicaps. **3** G. GORDON A photograph album which provides visual comment on these . . difficult times. *Omnibus* Characters performing a repertoire of visual slapstick. **4** *Skin Diver* The overwhelming visual impression was of color, of . . swarming life. *Guardian* There was no effective visual monitoring of crowd density. **6** I. MURDOCH He had a clear visual image of himself driving . . into a ditch.

Special collocations: **visual acuity** sharpness of vision, esp. as measured or expressed in terms of a definite scale. **visual agnosia** MEDICINE a loss of ability to recognize objects by sight. **visual aid** an item of illustrative matter, as a film, model, etc., designed to supplement or aid the assimilation of written or spoken information. **visual angle** the angle formed at the eye by the extremities of an object viewed. **visual axis** the straight line from the eye to the object or point of vision; the line of sight. **visual binary** ASTRONOMY a binary star of which the components are sufficiently far apart to be resolved by an optical telescope. **visual cortex** PHYSIOLOGY the part of the cerebral cortex that receives and processes sensory nerve impulses from the eyes. ***visual display***: see DISPLAY *noun* 2b. **visual display unit** a device for displaying on a screen data stored in a computer, usu. incorporating a keyboard for manipulating the data. **visual field** field of vision. **visual line** = ***visual axis*** above. **visual point** (now *rare*) the position from which an object is viewed. **visual purple** = RHODOPSIN. **visual range** (chiefly AERONAUTICS) the distance within which an object can be observed or identified visually. **visual ray** a light ray proceeding directly between the eye and an object viewed (orig. conceived as originating in the eye, now as passing from the object to the eye).
► **B** *noun*. **1** A visual ray. *rare*. E18.
2 A visile person. *rare*. L19.
3 A visual image or display, a picture; *spec.* the visual element of a film or television broadcast. Usu. in *pl.* M20.

> 🕮 **3** *Empire* Menzies . . gave the film its carefully stylized visuals. *Green Magazine* The best talks will be spectacular with experiments and visuals.

■ **visualist** *noun* a visile person; a visualizer: L19. **visually** *adverb* LME.

visualise *verb* var. of VISUALIZE.

visuality /vɪʒjʊˈalɪti, -zj-/ *noun*. M19.
[from VISUAL *adjective* + -ITY.]
1 Mental visibility; a mental image. M19.
2 Vision, sight. E20.
3 Visual aspect or quality; physical appearance. M20.

visualize /ˈvɪʒjʊəlʌɪz, -zj-/ *verb*. Also **-ise**. E19.
[from VISUAL *adjective* + -IZE.]
1 *verb trans. & (rare) intrans.* Make visible to the mind or imagination (something abstract or not visible or present to the eye); form a mental vision or image (of). E19.
2 *verb trans.* Make visible to the eye. E20.

> 🕮 **1** C. SHIELDS Visualize the pain, its substance and color. **2** *Artist* Polaroids prove very useful for instantly visualising houses from different angles.

■ **visualizaˈbility** *noun* M20. **visuaˈlizable** *adjective* M20. **visualiˈzation** *noun* (*a*) the action or process of visualizing; *spec.* a meditation technique in which a mental image (particularly of a hoped-for event) is formed and focused on as a psychological aid to confidence; (*b*) a mental image formed by visualizing: L19. **visualizer** *noun* a person who visualizes something; *spec.* (*a*) PSYCHOLOGY a person whose mental processes operate predominantly in terms of visual images rather than abstract ideas; (*b*) a commercial artist employed to design layouts for advertisements: L19.

visuo- /ˈvɪʒjʊəʊ, -zj-/ *combining form* of Latin *visus* sight, vision, forming terms in ANATOMY & PHYSIOLOGY: see -O-.
■ **visuoˈmotor** *adjective* pertaining to or involving motor activity as guided by or dependent on sight M20. **visuoˈpsychic** *adjective* designating either of two cortical areas adjacent to the striate cortex, orig. regarded as sites of mental processing of visual sense impressions E20. **visuoˈsensory** *adjective* pertaining to or involving the visual perception of sensory signals; *spec.* designating the striate cortex as the part of the brain that receives sensory nerve impulses from the eye: E20. **visuoˈspatial** *adjective* pertaining to the visual field as it involves perception of the spatial relationships of objects M20. **visuoˈtactual** *adjective* pertaining to or perceived by both visual and tactile senses M20.

Vita /ˈvʌɪtə/ *noun*¹. Also **v-**. E20.
[Latin *vita* life.]
In full ***Vita-glass***, ***Vitaglass***. (Proprietary name for) a glass which transmits most of the ultraviolet rays of sunlight.

vita /ˈviːtə/ *noun*². M20.
[Italian or Latin = life.]
1 ***vita nuova*** /ˈnwəʊvə/ [Italian = new life, a work by Dante describing his love for Beatrice], a fresh start or new direction in life, esp. after some powerful emotional experience. M20.
2 [Latin.] A biography, a life history; *spec.* a curriculum vitae. M20.

vital /ˈvʌɪt(ə)l/ *adjective & noun*. LME.
[As adjective from Old & mod. French, from Latin *vitalis*, from *vita* life + -AL¹; as noun from Latin *vitalia* use as noun of neut. pl. of *vitalis*.]
► **A** *adjective*. **1** Pertaining to or constituted by the animating force, power, or principle present in all living things and which is essential for continued existence. LME.
2 Full of life or energy; lively. Formerly also, animate, living. LME.
3 Maintaining, supporting, or sustaining life. Now chiefly *poet*. LME.
4 a Of parts, organs, etc.: essential or necessary to life; performing the functions indispensable to the maintenance of life. L15. ▸**b** *transf.* Of a part or component: essential to the functioning of the whole. Now passing into sense 8. M17.
5 Of, relating to, or characteristic of life; inherent in living things or organic bodies. M16. ▸**b** GEOLOGY. Produced or formed by living organisms; of organic origin. Now *rare*. M19. ▸**c** BIOLOGY. Of stains or their use: used or carried out on living tissue. E20.
6 Imparting life or vigour; invigorating; life-giving. Chiefly *poet*. L16.
7 Affecting life, esp. detrimentally; fatal to or destructive of life. *arch*. E17.
8 Essential to the existence of something; absolutely indispensable or necessary; extremely important, crucial. Freq. foll. by *for*, *to*. E17. ▸**b** Paramount, supreme, very great. E19.

> 🕮 **1** *She* Chinese medicine uses herbs to enhance . . the flow of vital energy. **2** SHELLEY That bright shape of vital stone which drew the heart out of Pygmalion. *Guardian* A stocky . . vital, robust . . and humorous man. **3** WORDSWORTH Every draught of vital breath. C. BERNHEIMER He associates their menstrual cycle with . . the circulation of vital fluids. **4b** *Guardian* One of the country's largest businesses . . a vital part of the economy. **5** G. BIRD To explain vital phenomena by the . . laws governing dead matter. *Quarterly* Death, the state in which the vital functions and powers have come to an end. **6** E. YOUNG O Joy . . ! twice three years I have not felt thy vital beam. **7** S. J. PRATT The surgeon . . assures me the wound is vital. **8** A. J. P. TAYLOR Surprise was supposed to be a vital ingredient of war. *Guardian* Rather than being optional, exercise is vital for health. W. PERRIAM It's vital to keep active. **b** H. MACMILLAN It was of vital importance to keep the railways going.

Special collocations: **vital air** CHEMISTRY (now *Hist.*) = OXYGEN. **vital capacity** PHYSIOLOGY the capacity of the lungs as determined by measuring the air expired between maximum inspiration and maximum expiration. **†vital flame** = ***vital spark*** below. **vital force** = ÉLAN ***vital***. **vital power** the power to sustain life. **vital signs** clinical measurements, *spec.* pulse rate, temperature, respiration rate, and blood pressure, that indicate the state of a patient's essential body functions. **vital spark** life-force. **†vital spirit(s)** = SPIRIT *noun* 11a. **vital statistics** (*a*) statistics concerned with or relating to human life, as births, deaths, etc.; (*b*) *colloq.* the measurements of a woman's bust, waist, and hips.
► **B** *noun*. **1** In *pl. & (rare) sing.* The parts or organs of the body essential to life or on which life depends, esp. the brain, heart, lungs, and liver. LME.
2 In *pl.* Parts or features essential or indispensable to something; essentials. M17.

> 🕮 **1** W. COWPER To transfix him where the vitals wrap The liver. B. PYM Hunger gnawed at his vitals. *fig.*: L. MANN Rents through which the vitals of the sofa oozed. STAP ***my vitals!*** **2** *Pall Mall Gazette* The Parnellite leaders approached the vitals of the issue.

■ **vitally** *adverb* in a vital manner; now *esp.* in a way or to an extent which is vital, absolutely essential, or paramount; essentially, indispensably: M17.

vitalise *verb* var. of VITALIZE.

vitalism /ˈvʌɪt(ə)lɪz(ə)m/ *noun*. E19.
[French *vitalisme*, or from VITAL *adjective* + -ISM.]
BIOLOGY. The doctrine or theory that the origin and phenomena of life are due to or produced by a vital principle, as distinct from a purely chemical or physical force.
■ **vitalist** *noun & adjective* (*a*) *noun* an advocate of or believer in vitalism; (*b*) *adjective* = VITALISTIC: M19.

vitalistic /vʌɪtəˈlɪstɪk/ *adjective*. M19.
[formed as prec. + -ISTIC.]
1 Of, pertaining to, involving, or denoting vitalism or a hypothetical vital principle. M19.
2 Pertaining to or denoting the germ theory, esp. in its relation to fermentation. *Hist*. L19.
3 ART. Pertaining to a style of modernist art characterized by vivid or kinetic representationalism. M20.

vitality /vʌɪˈtalɪti/ *noun*. L16.
[Latin *vitalitas*, from *vitalis* VITAL *adjective*: see -ITY.]
1 Vital force, power, or principle as present in all living things; the life principle or force. Also, the germinating power of a seed. L16.
2 The ability to endure or to continue to function. M19.
3 Mental or physical vigour; energy, animation, liveliness. M19.
4 A thing possessing vital force. *rare*. M19.

> 🕮 **1** S. SONTAG TB sufferers . . are . . deficient in vitality, in life force. A. S. BYATT A witch's wax dolls take on vitality when she warms them into shape. **2** R. HEILBRONER We . . hope . . that future man can rediscover the self-renewing vitality of primitive culture. **3** M. FORSTER She wanted to live in Florence . . and not be withdrawn from the vitality . . of city life. A. N. WILSON A person of a . . bubbly kindness and conversational vitality.

Vitalium *noun* var. of VITALLIUM.

vitalize /ˈvʌɪt(ə)lʌɪz/ *verb trans*. Also **-ise**. L17.
[from VITAL *adjective* + -IZE.]
1 Give life to; invest with vital force. L17.
2 Infuse with vitality or vigour; invigorate, animate. E19.

> 🕮 **2** *Rolling Stone* Urging his new pal . . to vitalize a boring yuppie life.

■ **vitaliˈzation** *noun* M19.

Vitallium /vʌɪˈtalɪəm/ *noun*. Also **v-**, **-talium** /-ˈteɪlɪəm/. M20.
[Origin unkn.]
METALLURGY. (Proprietary name for) an alloy of cobalt, chromium, and molybdenum that has a high resistance to abrasion, corrosion, and heat, used in surgery, dentistry, and engineering.

vitamin /ˈvɪtəmɪn, ˈvʌɪt-/ *noun*. Also **†-ine**. E20.
[from Latin *vita* life + AMINE, from a mistaken belief that vitamins contain amino acids.]
Any of various organic compounds of which small quantities are needed in the diet because they have a distinct biochemical role (often as coenzymes), and cannot be adequately synthesized by the body, so that a deficiency usu. produces characteristic symptoms or disease.
vitamin A retinol, a deficiency of which leads to night blindness and anaemia. **vitamin B** any of the vitamins in the B complex; ***vitamin B complex***, ***vitamin B group***, several chemically unrelated water-soluble vitamins mostly occurring together in liver, cereals, and yeast; ***vitamin*** B_1 = THIAMINE; ***vitamin*** B_2 = RIBOFLAVIN; ***vitamin*** B_6, pyridoxine and related compounds, deficiency of which can give rise to irritability, nervousness, or convulsions; ***vitamin*** B_{12}, cyanocobalamin and related compounds, synthesized by micro-organisms and present in meat, eggs, dairy products, etc., a deficiency of which leads to pernicious anaemia and neuropathy. **vitamin C** = ASCORBIC ***acid***. **vitamin D** any or all of several fat-soluble vitamins that cure or prevent rickets in children and osteomalacia in adults, being required for the correct metabolism of calcium; ***vitamin*** D_2 = CALCIFEROL; ***vitamin*** D_3 = CHOLECALCIFEROL. **vitamin E** = TOCOPHEROL. **vitamin H** (chiefly *US*) = BIOTIN. **vitamin K** either or both of two related fat-soluble derivatives of naphthoquinone, required for the proper clotting of blood; ***vitamin*** K_1 = PHYLLOQUINONE; ***vitamin*** K_2 = MENAQUINONE. **vitamin M** (chiefly *US*) = FOLIC ***acid***. **vitamin P** (chiefly *US*) = CITRIN.
■ **vitaˈminic** *adjective* pertaining to or containing a vitamin or vitamins E20. **viˈtaminous** *adjective* (*rare*) = VITAMINIC E20.

vitaminize /ˈvɪtəmɪnʌɪz/ *verb trans*. Also **-ise**. M20.
[from prec. + -IZE.]
Add a vitamin or vitamins to (food, esp. food lacking the vitamin concerned). Chiefly as ***vitaminized*** *ppl adjective*.

> 🕮 *fig.*: M. WOODHOUSE A home-grown, vitaminized, . . all-American boy.

■ **vitaminiˈzation** *noun* M20.

Vitaphone /ˈvʌɪtəfəʊn/ *noun*. E20.
[from Latin *vita* life + -PHONE.]
(Proprietary name for) an early process of sound film recording in which the soundtrack is recorded on discs.

vitativeness /vɪˈteɪtɪvnɪs/ *noun. rare.* **M19.**
[formed as prec. + -ATIVE + -NESS.]
PHRENOLOGY. The love of life, the desire to live.

vitellaria /vɪtəˈlɛːrɪə/ *noun.* Pl. **-iae** /-ɪiː/. **M20.**
[mod. Latin, formed as VITELLUS + *-aria* (see ARY[1] 3).]
ZOOLOGY. A nonfeeding larval stage of many holothuroid, crinoid, and some ophiuroid echinoderms, typically cylindrical and initially free-swimming.

vitellary /ˈvɪt(ə)ləri, vɪˈtɛləri, vʌɪ-/ *noun & adjective.* Now *rare.* **M17.**
[from Latin VITELLUS + -ARY[1]; cf. prec.]
ZOOLOGY. ▶ †**A** *noun.* **1** The place where the yolk of an egg is formed. **M–L17.**
2 The yolk of an egg. *rare.* Only in **M18.**
▶ **B** *adjective.* Of or belonging to the yolk; vitelline. **M19.**

vitelligenous /vɪtɛˈlɪdʒɪnəs/ *adjective.* **M19.**
[from Latin VITELLUS + -I- + -GENOUS.]
ZOOLOGY. Producing the vitellus or yolk.

vitellin /vɪˈtɛlɪn, vʌɪ-/ *noun.* **M19.**
[from VITELLUS + -IN[1].]
BIOCHEMISTRY. A phosphoprotein that is a major constituent of egg-yolk. Also, a similar protein found in plant seeds.

vitelline /vɪˈtɛlʌɪn, vʌɪ-, -lɪn/ *adjective.* **LME.**
[medieval Latin *vitellinus*, from VITELLUS: see -INE[1].]
1 Of a deep yellow colour like the yolk of an egg. Now *rare.* **LME.**
2 *ZOOLOGY & EMBRYOLOGY.* Of or belonging to the yolk of an egg or embryo; designating embryologically related structures in mammals in which the yolk-sac is rudimentary. **M19.**
2 vitelline duct a duct which conveys yolk from the yolk gland to the oviduct. **vitelline gland** a yolk-secreting gland present in many invertebrates. **vitelline layer**, **vitelline membrane** a transparent membrane surrounding and secreted by the ovum, and freq. surrounding the yolk.

vitello- /vɪˈtɛləʊ, ˈvɪt(ə)ləʊ/ *combining form.*
[from Latin VITELLUS: see -O-.]
BIOLOGY & BIOCHEMISTRY. Forming words with the sense 'of or pertaining to the yolk of an egg'.
▪ **vitelloˈgenesis** *noun* the formation of the yolk of an egg **M20.** **vitellogeˈnetic**, **vitelloˈgenic** *adjectives* producing the yolk **M20.** **vitelloˈgenin** *noun* a blood-borne protein from which the substance of the yolk is made **M20.** **vitellophage** *noun* (*ENTOMOLOGY*) any of the cells which metabolize the yolk of an insect egg during early embryonic development **L19.**

vitello tonnato /viˈtɛllo tonˈnaːto/ *noun phr.* **M20.**
[Italian, from *vitello* veal + *tonno* tuna.]
An Italian dish consisting of roast or poached veal served cold in a tuna and anchovy mayonnaise.

vitellus /vɪˈtɛləs, vʌɪ-/ *noun.* Now *rare.* **E18.**
[Latin = yolk of an egg.]
1 *EMBRYOLOGY.* The yolk of an egg or ovum. **E18.**
2 *BOTANY.* A fleshy sac situated between the albumen and the embryo in a seed. **E19.**

vitenge *noun* var. of KITENGE.

vitex /ˈvʌɪtɛks/ *noun.* **E17.**
[mod. Latin use as genus name of Latin = chaste-tree.]
Any of various shrubs and small trees, freq. aromatic and with palmately divided leaves, which constitute the chiefly tropical genus *Vitex*, of the verbena family; *esp.* the chaste-tree, *V. agnus-castus*.

vitiate /ˈvɪʃɪət/ *ppl adjective.* Now *arch. rare.* **LME.**
[Latin *vitiatus* pa. pple of *vitiare*: see next, -ATE[2].]
Vitiated.

vitiate /ˈvɪʃɪeɪt/ *verb trans.* **M16.**
[Latin *vitiat-* pa. ppl stem of *vitiare*, from *vitium* VICE *noun*[1]: see -ATE[3].]
1 Make incomplete, imperfect, or faulty; mar or spoil the quality of. Also, impair the purity of (a language) or the correctness of (a text). **M16.**
2 Corrupt morally; deprave; lower the moral standard of. **M16.** ▸**b** Pervert or debase (the eye, taste, etc.). **E19.**
†**3** Deprive (a woman) of her virginity; violate. **M16–L18.**
4 Contaminate the substance of; make bad, impure, or defective; *esp.* make (air) polluted and unfit for breathing. **L16.**
5 Invalidate; make ineffectual; *spec.* destroy or impair the legal validity or force of. **E17.** ▸**b** Make (an argument etc.) inconclusive or unsatisfactory. **M18.**

🕮 **1** S. BECKETT Lunch was a ritual vitiated by no base thoughts of nutrition. M. FRAYN The information that spies steal is . . vitiated by the possibility that its sources are corrupt. **2** GEO. ELIOT This vitiating effect of an offence against his own sentiment of right. J. S. MILL Moral beliefs . . have been vitiated . . by the absence of any distinct recognition of an ultimate standard. **4** S. COOPER Deleterious kinds of food, such as the ergot or vitiated rye. *Guardian* The poisoned waters and vitiated air. **5** G. WILL Giving government . . rights to involvement in business decisions, thereby vitiating the rights of the real owners. *Vanity Fair* The Soviet invasion of Czechoslovakia didn't immediately vitiate the resistance movement. **b** R. G. COLLINGWOOD Their theorizing . . is apt to be vitiated by weakness in its foundation of fact.

▪ **vitiˈation** *noun* **M17.** **vitiator** *noun* (*rare*) **M19.**

viticulture /ˈvɪtɪkʌltʃə/ *noun.* **L19.**
[from Latin *vitis* vine + -CULTURE.]
The cultivation of grapevines; the science or study of this.
▪ **vitiˈcultural** *adjective* of or pertaining to viticulture **M19.** **vitiˈculturist** *noun* a person who practises viticulture **L19.**

vitiligo /vɪtɪˈlʌɪgəʊ/ *noun.* **L16.**
[Latin = tetter.]
MEDICINE. A local depigmentation of the skin which results in well-defined whitish patches; *esp.* as a disorder of uncertain cause without any other symptom. Cf. LEUCODERMA.

vitilitigate /vɪtɪˈlɪtɪgeɪt/ *verb intrans. rare.* **L17.**
[Latin *vitilitigat-* pa. ppl stem of *vitilitigare*: see -ATE[3].]
Altercate or contend noisily; wrangle, argue.

vitiosity /vɪʃɪˈɒsɪti/ *noun.* Now *rare* or *obsolete.* **LME.**
[Latin *vitiositas*, from *vitiosus* VICIOUS: see -ITY.]
1 The state or character of being guilty of or devoted to vice or immorality. **LME.**
†**2** A defect, a fault; an imperfection. **M16–M17.**
3 *SCOTS LAW.* The quality of being faulty or improper in a legal aspect. **M18.**

vitious *adjective & noun* see VICIOUS.

vitraillist /ˈvɪtreɪlɪst/ *noun. rare.* **E17.**
[from French *vitrail* glass window + -IST.]
A maker of glass; a designer in stained glass.

vitrain /ˈvɪtreɪn/ *noun.* **E20.**
[from VITREOUS + *-ain*, after FUSAIN.]
GEOLOGY. A black, highly lustrous, and often brittle material which is one of the lithotypes of coal.

†**vitrean** *adjective. rare.* **M17–L18.**
[formed as VITREOUS + -AN.]
Of or resembling glass.

vitrectomy /vɪˈtrɛktəmi/ *noun.* **M20.**
[from VITREOUS + -ECTOMY.]
MEDICINE. (An instance of) the surgical operation of removing the vitreous fluid from the eyeball and replacing it with another fluid.

vitremanie /ˈviːtrəmani:/ *noun.* **L19.**
[from French *vitre* window-pane + *manie* fad.]
A form of decoration for window-panes using coloured designs to give a stained-glass effect, popular in the Victorian period.

Vitreosil /ˈvɪtrɪə(ʊ)sɪl/ *noun.* Also **v-**. **E20.**
[from VITREOUS + SILICA.]
(Proprietary name for) vitreous silica.

vitreosity /vɪtrɪˈɒsɪti/ *noun. rare.* **L19.**
[formed as next + -OSITY.]
The state or quality of being vitreous.

vitreous /ˈvɪtrɪəs/ *adjective.* **LME.**
[from Latin *vitreus*, from VITRUM: see -EOUS.]
1 Resembling glass in some way, esp. in colour, appearance, or texture, or *spec.* (*CHEMISTRY & MINERALOGY*) in physical properties and lack of crystalline structure; glassy. **LME.**
2 Of or pertaining to glass; consisting of, derived from, or containing glass. **M17.**

🕮 **1** P. THEROUX The silver vitreous rain crackling in the street.

Special collocations: **vitreous body** *ANATOMY* = ***vitreous humour*** below. **vitreous electricity** positive electricity obtained from glass by friction. **vitreous enamel** = ENAMEL *noun* 1. **vitreous humour** *ANATOMY* a transparent gel filling the eyeball behind the lens. **vitreous lustre** *MINERALOGY* a lustre resembling that of broken glass. **vitreous silica** an amorphous, translucent or transparent form of silica obtained by rapid quenching from the molten state. **vitreous sponge** *ZOOLOGY* = ***glass sponge*** s.v. GLASS *noun & adjective.*
▪ **vitreously** *adverb* **L18.**

vitrescence /vɪˈtrɛs(ə)ns/ *noun.* **L18.**
[from next: see -ENCE.]
The state of becoming vitreous or glassy; vitrified or vitreous condition.
▪ Also **vitrescency** *noun* (*rare*) **M18.**

vitrescent /vɪˈtrɛs(ə)nt/ *adjective.* **M18.**
[from Latin VITRUM + -ESCENT.]
Tending to become glass; able to be turned into glass; glassy.

vitrescible /vɪˈtrɛsɪb(ə)l/ *adjective.* **M18.**
[French, from *vitre* glass + -IBLE.]
Able to be vitrified; vitrifiable.

vitric /ˈvɪtrɪk/ *adjective.* **E20.**
[from Latin VITRUM + -IC.]
Vitreous; *spec.* in *GEOLOGY*, (of tuff) composed chiefly of glassy material.

vitrifaction /vɪtrɪˈfakʃ(ə)n/ *noun.* **E18.**
[Alt. of VITRIFICATION: see -FACTION.]
= VITRIFICATION.

†**vitrificate** *verb trans. rare.* **E17–E18.**
[from medieval Latin *vitrificatus* vitrified: see -ATE[3].]
Vitrify.

vitrification /ˌvɪtrɪfɪˈkeɪʃ(ə)n/ *noun.* **E17.**
[medieval Latin *vitrificatio(n-)*, from Latin VITRUM: see -FICATION.]
1 The action or process of vitrifying; an instance of this. **E17.**
2 A vitrified substance or body. **M17.**

vitriform /ˈvɪtrɪfɔːm/ *adjective.* **L18.**
[from Latin VITRUM + -I- + -FORM.]
Having the form or appearance of glass.

vitrify /ˈvɪtrɪfʌɪ/ *verb trans. & intrans.* **LME.**
[French *vitrifier* or directly from Latin VITRUM: see -FY.]
Convert or be converted into glass or a glassy substance, esp. by heat.
vitrified fort *ARCHAEOLOGY* a hill-fort of a type best known in Scotland and some parts of Continental Europe, the stones of which were vitrified by the intense heat generated when the timber lacings of the walls were burnt.
▪ **vitrifiaˈbility** *noun* (*rare*) ability to be vitrified **L19.** **vitriˈfiable** *adjective* able to be vitrified **M17.**

vitrine /ˈvɪtriːn/ *noun.* **L19.**
[French, from *vitre* glass: see -INE[4].]
A glass display case.

🕮 R. SCRUTON A vitrine full of silver-gilt.

vitrinite /ˈvɪtrɪnʌɪt/ *noun.* **M20.**
[from VITRAIN + -IN[1] + -ITE[1].]
GEOLOGY. One of the three major kinds of maceral that go to make up humic coal, rich in oxygen and characteristic of vitrain.

vitriol /ˈvɪtrɪəl/ *noun.* **LME.**
[Old & mod. French, or medieval Latin *vitriolum*, from Latin VITRUM.]
1 Any of various sulphates of metallic elements; *spec.* ferrous sulphate. Also, sulphuric acid. Usu. with specifying word. **LME.**
2 *fig.* Acrimonious, caustic, or scathing speech, criticism, or feeling. **M18.**

🕮 **1** ***vitriol of copper***, ***vitriol of iron***, ***vitriol of lead***, etc. **2** *Vanity Fair* The prime villain . . against whom all his vitriol would be directed.

Phrases: **blue vitriol**, **copper vitriol** copper sulphate. **green vitriol** ferrous sulphate. ***oil of vitriol***: see OIL *noun*. **white vitriol** zinc sulphate.

†**vitriolate** *adjective.* **M17.**
[from medieval Latin *vitriolum*: see prec., -ATE[2].]
1 Of, pertaining to, or resembling vitriol. **M–L17.**
2 Treated or impregnated with vitriol. **M17–L18.**

vitriolated /ˈvɪtrɪəleɪtɪd/ *adjective. arch.* **E17.**
[formed as prec. + -ED[1].]
1 Impregnated with vitriol; (of minerals etc.) affected by native sulphates. **E17.**
2 Treated with vitriol. **M17.**
2 vitriolated tartar potassium sulphate.

vitriolic /vɪtrɪˈɒlɪk/ *adjective.* **L17.**
[from VITRIOL + -IC.]
1 Of, belonging to, or resembling vitriol; impregnated with vitriol. **L17.**
2 *fig.* Of speech, criticism, etc.: acrimonious, caustic, scathing. **M19.**

🕮 **1 vitriolic acid** (concentrated) sulphuric acid. **2** *Guardian* A vitriolic letter, which hurled abuse at the Prime Minister.

▪ **vitriolically** *adverb* in an acrimonious or scathing manner **L20.**

vitriolize /ˈvɪtrɪəlʌɪz/ *verb.* Also **-ise**. **L17.**
[from VITRIOL + -IZE.]
†**1** *verb trans.* Convert into sulphate. **L17–L18.** ▸**b** *verb intrans.* Become converted into sulphate. **M–L18.**
2 *verb trans.* Throw sulphuric acid at (a person) with intent to injure. Now *rare.* **L19.**
▪ **vitrioliˈzation** *noun* the process of converting, or of being converted, into a sulphate **M18.**

Vitrolite /ˈvɪtrə(ʊ)lʌɪt/ *noun.* **M20.**
[from Latin VITRUM + -O- + -LITE.]
(Proprietary name for) opal glass.

vitrophyre /ˈvɪtrə(ʊ)fʌɪə/ *noun.* **L19.**
[from Latin VITRUM + -O- + *-phyre*, after *granophyre*.]
PETROGRAPHY. Any of a class of porphyritic rocks characterized by an igneous texture in which phenocrysts are embedded in a glassy groundmass.
▪ **vitroˈphyric** *adjective* **L19.**

vitrous /ˈvɪtrəs/ *adjective. rare.* **M17.**
[from next: see -OUS.]
Vitreous.

vitrum /ˈvɪtrəm/ *noun*. Pl. **vitrums**, **vitra** /ˈvɪtrə/. M17.
[Latin.]
Glass; a glassy substance; a glass vessel.
¶ Obsolete exc. in medical prescriptions.

Vitruvian /vɪˈtruːvɪən/ *adjective*. M18.
[from Marcus *Vitruvius* Pollio (see below) + -IAN.]
Of, relating to, or in the style of Vitruvius, a Roman architect and writer of the 1st cent. BC whose book *De Architectura* was later influential in the development of Renaissance architecture.
Vitruvian scroll a convoluted scroll pattern used as a decoration on friezes etc.
■ **Vitruvianism** *noun* (*rare*) the style or principles of architecture favoured by Vitruvius M19.

vitry /ˈvɪtri/ *noun*. Now *rare* or *obsolete*. LME.
[French *Vitré* a town in Brittany.]
In full ***vitry canvas***. A kind of light durable canvas.

vitta /ˈvɪtə/ *noun*. Pl. **vittae** /ˈvɪtiː/. L17.
[Latin = band, fillet, chaplet.]
†**1** ANATOMY. = AMNION. Only in L17.
2 ROMAN ANTIQUITIES. A leather strap on a soldier's suit of armour. Also, a sash. E18.
3 ZOOLOGY. A band or stripe of colour. E19.
4 BOTANY. Any of the resin canals in the fruit of most umbelliferous plants, four usu. occurring between the main ridges and two more on the inner faces. E19.
■ **vittate** *adjective* (*a*) ZOOLOGY marked or striped with vittae; (*b*) BOTANY having a given number of vittae (VITTA 4): E19.

Vittel /viːˈtɛl/ *noun*. L19.
[A town in the Vosges department of France.]
(Proprietary name for) a type of mineral water obtained from springs in the neighbourhood of Vittel. Also ***Vittel water***.

vituline /ˈvɪtjʊlʌɪn/ *adjective*. *rare*. LME.
[Latin *vitulinus*, from *vitulus* calf: see -INE[1].]
Of or belonging to a calf or calves; resembling that of a calf.

vituperable /vɪˈtjuːp(ə)rəb(ə)l, vʌɪ-/ *adjective*. Now *rare* or *obsolete*. LME.
[Latin *vituperabilis*, from *vituperare*: see VITUPERATE *verb*, -ABLE.]
That deserves or merits vituperation; blameworthy, reprehensible; disgraceful.

vituperant /vɪˈtjuːp(ə)r(ə)nt, vʌɪ-/ *adjective*. *rare*. M19.
[Latin *vituperant-* pres. ppl stem of *vituperare*: see VITUPERATE *verb*, -ANT[1].]
Abusive, vituperative.

vituperate /vɪˈtjuːpərɪt, vʌɪ-/ *adjective*. *rare*. M19.
[Latin *vituperatus* pa. pple of *vituperare*: see next, -ATE[2].]
Orig., worthy of vituperation. Now, vituperative.

vituperate /vɪˈtjuːpəreɪt, vʌɪ-/ *verb*. M16.
[Latin *vituperat-* pa. ppl stem of *vituperare*, from *vitu-* for *viti-* stem of *vitium* VICE *noun*[1] + *parare* prepare: see -ATE[3].]
1 *verb trans*. Blame, abuse, find fault with, in strong or violent language; vilify, revile. M16.
2 *verb intrans*. Employ abusive language. M19.

> 📖 **1** J. A. FROUDE He vituperated . . the vices of the court.

¶ Rare before E19.
■ **vituperator** *noun* M19. **vituperatory** *adjective* (now *rare* or *obsolete*) vituperative L16.

vituperation /vɪtjuːpəˈreɪʃ(ə)n, vʌɪ-/ *noun*. LME.
[Old French, or Latin *vituperatio(n-)* blaming, censuring formed as prec.: see -ATION.]
The action of vituperating; (an expression of) blame or censure; abuse, vilification. Also, vituperative or abusive language.

> 📖 *Locus* The book's received . . a nearly unanimous chorus of vituperation. *Vanity Fair* Barnes's vituperation spewed forth in geysers of mud.

¶ Rare before E19.

vituperative /vɪˈtjuːp(ə)rətɪv, vʌɪ-/ *adjective*. E18.
[Late Latin *vituperativus*, formed as prec.: see -IVE.]
1 Of words, language, etc.: containing or expressing strong depreciation; violently abusive or censorious. E18.
2 Characterized or accompanied by vituperation. M18.
3 Of a person: given to vituperation; employing or uttering abusive language. E19.

> 📖 **1** E. K. KANE His eloquence becoming more and more licentious and vituperative. *Art in America* Negative and . . vituperative criticism of young artists. **2** C. MCWILLIAM He . . saved me . . from the vituperative, obsessing voice of Margaret.

■ **vituperatively** *adverb* M19.

vituperous /vɪˈtjuːp(ə)rəs, vʌɪ-/ *adjective*. Now *rare*. L16.
[French †*vitupéreux* (= Provençal *vituperos*), or Spanish *vituperoso*, from late Latin *vituperosus*, from *vituperium* blame, dishonour, from *vituperare*: see VITUPERATE *verb*, -OUS.]
1 Vituperative. L16.
2 Worthy of blame or vituperation; shameful, ignominious. E17.
■ **vituperously** *adverb* L19.

viva /ˈviːvə/ *noun*[1] & *interjection*. M17.
[Italian = live!, 3rd person sing. pres. subjunct. of *vivere* live from Latin.]
(A cry or cheer) wishing long life and prosperity to or expressing approval of an admired person or thing: hurrah! long live! Cf. VIVAT, VIVE *interjection*.

viva /ˈvʌɪvə/ *noun*[2] & *verb*. *colloq*. L19.
[Abbreviation.]
► **A** *noun*. = VIVA VOCE *noun*. L19.
► **B** *verb trans*. Pa. t. **vivaed**, **viva'd** /ˈvʌɪvəd/. Subject to a viva voce examination, examine orally. Cf. VIVA-VOCE. L19.

vivace /vɪˈvɑːtʃi/ *adverb*, *noun*, & *adjective*. L17.
[Italian = brisk, lively from Latin *vivac-*, *vivax*: see next.]
MUSIC. ► **A** *adverb*. A direction: in a brisk lively manner. L17.
► **B** *noun*. A passage to be performed in this manner. L17.
► **C** *adjective*. Brisk, lively. E20.

vivacious /vɪˈveɪʃəs, vʌɪ-/ *adjective*. M17.
[from Latin *vivac-*, *vivax* conscious or tenacious of life, lively, vigorous from *vivus* alive, from *vivere* live: see -ACIOUS.]
1 Full of or characterized by animation or liveliness; animated, lively, spirited. M17.
2 Continuing to live; long-lived. Formerly also, (of a plant) perennial. Now *rare* or *obsolete*. M17.
3 Tenacious of life, difficult to kill or destroy. *rare*. M17.

> 📖 **1** DICKENS Mr. Snevelicci . . proposed 'The Ladies! Bless their hearts!' in a most vivacious manner. *Guardian* Edith, a writer, is the opposite of the vivacious, outgoing Sophie.

■ **vivaciously** *adverb* E18. **vivaciousness** *noun* M17.

vivacity /vɪˈvasɪti, vʌɪ-/ *noun*. LME.
[Old & mod. French *vivacité* from Latin *vivacitas* natural vigour, formed as prec.: see -ACITY.]
1 The state or condition of being vivacious or lively; animation, liveliness, spirit; intellectual or mental acuteness or vigour. LME. ►**b** A vivacious or lively act, expression, etc. Usu. in *pl*. L17.
2 The property or fact of living for a long time; longevity. Formerly also, vital force, vitality. Now *rare*. E17.
3 Activity, energy, vigour. Now *rare*. M17.

> 📖 **1** R. MACAULAY That quiet pale girl, so lacking in spirit and vivacity.

Vivaldian /vɪˈvaldɪən/ *adjective* & *noun*. M20.
[from *Vivaldi* (see below) + -AN.]
► **A** *adjective*. Of, pertaining to, or characteristic of the Italian composer Antonio Vivaldi (1678–1741) or his music. M20.
► **B** *noun*. An interpreter, student, or admirer of Vivaldi or his music. L20.

vivandier /vivɑ̃dje/ *noun*. Also (fem.) ***-ière*** /-jɛːr/. Pl. pronounced same. L16.
[French.]
Hist. In the French and other Continental European armies, a supplier of provisions to troops in the field.

vivarium /vʌɪˈvɛːrɪəm, vɪ-/ *noun*. Pl. **-ria** /-rɪə/, **-riums**. E17.
[Latin = warren, fish-pond, use as noun of *vivarius* from *vivus* alive, from *vivere* live: see -ARIUM.]
1 A place for keeping living animals, esp. fish, for food; a fish-pond. *obsolete* exc. *Hist*. E17.
2 An enclosure or structure adapted or prepared for keeping animals under conditions approximating to the natural conditions, for observation or study; *spec*. (*a*) an aquarium; (*b*) a terrarium. L17.

vivary /ˈvʌɪv(ə)ri/ *noun*. Now *rare* or *obsolete*. E17.
[formed as prec.: see -ARY[1].]
= VIVARIUM.

vivat /ˈvʌɪvat, ˈviː-/ *interjection* & *noun*. L16.
[Latin = may he or she live, 3rd person sing. pres. subjunct. of *vivere*.]
= VIVA *noun*[1] & *interjection*. Cf. VIVE *interjection*.

> 📖 THACKERAY The king was received with shouts and loyal vivats.

viva-voce /ˈvʌɪvəvəʊtʃi/ *verb trans*. Pres. pple & verbal noun **-voceing**. L19.
[from next.]
Subject to a viva voce examination, examine orally. Freq. abbreviated VIVA *verb*.

viva voce /vʌɪvə ˈvəʊtʃi/ *adverbial*, *adjectival*, & *noun phr*. M16.
[medieval Latin, lit. 'by or with the living voice'.]
► **A** *adverbial phr*. **1** Orally rather than in writing. M16.
2 Aloud rather than silently. Now *rare* or *obsolete*. M17.
► **B** *adjectival phr*. **1** Expressed in speech rather than writing, spoken, oral. E17.
2 Of an examination etc.: conducted orally; *spec*. designating a supplementary oral examination following the ordinary written examinations. E19.
► **C** *noun phr*. A viva voce examination. Freq. abbreviated to VIVA *noun*[2]. M19.

vivax /ˈvʌɪvaks/ *noun* & *adjective*. M20.
[mod. Latin specific name (see below), from Latin = long-lived.]
MEDICINE. ► **A** *noun*. A parasitic protozoan, *Plasmodium vivax*, which causes the commonest form of relapsing tertian malaria. M20.
► **B** *adjective*. Of, pertaining to, or designating this organism or disease. M20.

vive /viːv, vʌɪv/ *adjective*. Long *Scot*. or *arch*. L15.
[Old & mod. French, fem. of *vif* from Latin *viva*, *vivus* living, or directly from Latin.]
1 Brisk, vigorous. *rare*. L15. ►†**b** Of a mineral: having active properties. L16–L17.
2 Affecting or impressing the mind in a lively or vivid manner. E16.
3 a Of a picture etc.: lifelike, accurately representing that depicted. L16. ►**b** Of a colour: bright, vivid. L16. ►**c** Of an image seen: clear, distinct. *Scot*. E19.
†**4** Alive, living. L16–L17.
1b ***calx vive***: see CALX 2.
■ **vively** *adverb* L15.

vive /viv/ *interjection*. L16.
[French = may he, she, or it live, from *vivre* from Latin *vivere* live.]
Wishing long life and prosperity to or expressing approval of an admired person or thing; long live! Cf. VIVA *interjection*, VIVAT.

> 📖 *Guardian* Britons who believe in democracy will cry Vive La Revolution; Vive La France! ***vive la bagatelle*** /la bagatɛl/ [lit. 'success to frivolity or nonsense'] expr. a carefree attitude to life. ***vive la différence*** /la diferɑ̃s/ *joc*. expr. approval of the difference between the sexes. ***vive le roi*** /lə rwa/ acclaiming a sovereign: long live the king!

vivency /ˈvʌɪv(ə)nsi/ *noun*. *rare*. M17.
[from Latin *vivere* live + -ENCY.]
The quality or fact of being alive; vitality.

viver /ˈvʌɪvə/ *noun*[1]. Long *obsolete* exc. *dial*. ME.
[Anglo-Norman *viver*, Old & mod. French *vivier*, formed as VIVARIUM: see -ER[2]. Cf. VIVIER.]
A fish-pond.

†**viver** *noun*[2]. L16–L17.
[Old French *vivre* snake from Latin *vipera* VIPER.]
= DRAGONET 2.

viverra /vɪˈvɛrə/ *noun*. E18.
[Latin = ferret.]
ZOOLOGY. Orig., a ferret. Later, a civet of the genus *Viverra*. Now only as mod. Latin genus name.

viverrid /vɪˈvɛrɪd/ *noun* & *adjective*. E20.
[mod. Latin *Viverridae* (see below), from *Viverra*: see prec., -ID[3].]
ZOOLOGY. ► **A** *noun*. Any of various carnivorous mammals of the family Viverridae, which includes the civets and genets, and (usu.) the mongooses. Cf. next. E20.
► **B** *adjective*. Pertaining to or designating this family. E20.

viverrine /vɪˈvɛrʌɪn, vʌɪ-/ *adjective* & *noun*. E19.
[In sense A.1 from mod. Latin *viverrinus* specific name; in senses A.2, B. from mod. Latin *Viverrinae* (see below), formed as VIVERRA + -INE[1].]
ZOOLOGY. ► **A** *adjective*. **1** Resembling a civet. Now *rare*. E19.
2 Pertaining to or designating the viverrid subfamily Viverrinae, which comprises the true civets, genets, and linsangs. L19.
► **B** *noun*. A mammal of this subfamily. L19.

vivers /ˈvʌɪvəz/ *noun pl*. *Scot*. M16.
[Old & mod. French *vivres* use as noun of *vivre* live.]
Food, provisions, victuals.

vives /vʌɪvz/ *noun pl*. Now *rare* or *obsolete*. Also †**avives**, †**fives**. E16.
[French *avives*, also Old French *vives*, ult. from Arab. *aḍ-ḍība* glanders, lit. 'the she-wolf'.]
VETERINARY MEDICINE. Swelling and inflammation of the submaxillary glands of a horse.

viveur /vivœːr/ *noun*. Pl. pronounced same. M19.
[French = a living person.]
A person who lives a fashionable and social life. Cf. ***BON viveur***.

vivianite /ˈvɪvɪənʌɪt/ *noun*. E19.
[from John Henry *Vivian* (1785–1855), Brit. mineralogist + -ITE[1].]
MINERALOGY. A monoclinic phosphate of iron occurring as colourless prismatic crystals or masses which oxidize to blue or green, found as a secondary mineral in ore veins, phosphate pegmatites, and sedimentary clays.

vivid /ˈvɪvɪd/ *adjective*. M17.
[Latin *vividus*, from *vivere* live, *vivus* alive, lively: see -ID[1].]
1 Full of life; vigorous, animated, lively. M17.
2 a Of colour, light, etc.: intensely bright, brilliant, glaring. M17. ►**b** Brilliantly coloured or lit. L17.
3 Clearly or distinctly perceived; intensely or strongly felt or expressed. L17.
4 a Of an action or operation: proceeding or taking place with great vigour or activity. E18. ►**b** Of a mental

faculty: capable of strong and distinct impressions, producing clear images, active. E19. ▸**c** Of description etc.: making a sharp and clear impression on the senses, striking, graphic; lifelike. M19.

> 📖 **1** WILKIE COLLINS Her face expressed vivid interest and astonishment. S. BELLOW This pretty lady had been a vivid heroine of the Jazz Age. **2a** *Antique Collector* The most vivid hues or the gentler pastel shades. *Guardian* Their vivid blue, highlighted by sudden shafts of sunlight. **b** K. TYNAN He struts like a prize rooster, vivid in scarlet and gold. **3** H. READ The memory of that journey is still vivid in my mind. R. STRANGE Initial impressions, however powerful and vivid, fade. **4b** A. S. BYATT She had a vivid imagination. **c** *Oxford Today* A brilliantly vivid picture of prewar life in St Thomas's. D. M. THOMAS A vivid account of his first experience of a massacre.

■ **vi'vidity** *noun* (*a*) vitality; (*b*) the quality or state of being vivid; vividness: E17. **vividly** *adverb* M17. **vividness** *noun* M17.

vivier /vivje/ *noun*. Pl. pronounced same. LME.
[Old & mod. French: see VIVER *noun*[1].]
A fish-pond; a tank for storing live fish etc.
¶ Obsolete after LME until revived from mod. French in M20.

vivific /vʌɪˈvɪfɪk/ *adjective*. Now *literary* or *formal*. M16.
[Latin *vivificus* from *vivus* living: see -FIC.]
Life-giving, enlivening, vivifying.

vivificate /vɪˈvɪfɪkeɪt/ *verb trans.* Now *rare*. LME.
[Latin *vivificat-* pa. ppl stem of late Latin *vivificare* VIVIFY: see -ATE[3].]
= VIVIFY 1.
■ †**vivificative** *adjective* life-giving, vivifying E16–M18.

vivification /ˌvɪvɪfɪˈkeɪʃ(ə)n/ *noun*. LME.
[Late Latin *vivificatio(n-)*, formed as prec.: see -ATION.]
1 The action or fact of endowing a person with (physical or spiritual) life; the process or fact of being vivified. LME.
†**2** ALCHEMY. Restoration of a metal to its original state. E17–E18.

vivify /ˈvɪvɪfʌɪ/ *verb*. LME.
[Old & mod. French *vivifier* from late Latin *vivificare*, from Latin *vivus* alive, from *vivere* live: see -FY.]
1 *verb trans.* Give life to, endow with life; animate, enliven, make lively; brighten. LME.
2 *verb intrans.* **a** Impart life or animation. E17. ▸**b** Acquire life, become alive. M18.

> 📖 **1** S. PATERSON Are we not all originally . . sprung from the same vivified mass? H. MARTINEAU His ready wit seldom failed . . to illustrate and vivify what was said. **2a** J. TYNDALL The one may vivify, while the other kills.

■ **vivifier** *noun* M19. **vivifying** *adjective* (*a*) life-giving, enlivening; †(*b*) (of medicine) restorative: M17.

viviparous /vɪˈvɪp(ə)rəs, vʌɪ-/ *adjective*. M17.
[from Latin *viviparus*, from *vivus* alive: see -PAROUS.]
1 ZOOLOGY. Involving the production of living young; producing young which have developed inside the body of the parent. Cf. OVIPAROUS, OVOVIVIPAROUS. M17.
2 BOTANY. Reproducing from buds which form plantlets (instead of flowers) while still attached to the parent plant, or from seeds which germinate within the fruit; characterized by such methods of reproduction. L18.
1 viviparous blenny a common live-bearing blenny, *Zoarces viviparus*, which is found in northern European coastal waters; also called ***eelpout***. **viviparous lizard** a common Eurasian lizard, *Lacerta vivipara*, which is ovoviviparous and is the only lizard found throughout the British Isles and Scandinavia; also called ***common lizard***.
■ **viviparism** *noun* viviparous reproduction L19. **vivi'parity** *noun* the condition or character of being viviparous M19. **viviparously** *adverb* E19. **vivipary** *noun* viviparity E20.

vivisect /ˈvɪvɪsɛkt, vɪvɪˈsɛkt/ *verb*. M19.
[Back-form. from next.]
1 *verb trans.* Perform vivisection on. M19.
2 *verb intrans.* Practise vivisection. L19.

vivisection /vɪvɪˈsɛkʃ(ə)n/ *noun*. E18.
[from Latin *vivus* alive + SECTION *noun*, after *dissection*.]
1 The action of cutting or dissecting part of a living organism. Now usu. *spec.* (& usu. *depreciative*), dissection or other experimentation carried out on living animals for the purposes of scientific research. E18. ▸**b** An operation of this nature. M19.
2 *fig.* Excessively minute or ruthless investigation or criticism. L19.
■ **vivisectional** *adjective* (*a*) of, pertaining to, or of the nature of vivisection; (*b*) performing vivisection: M19. **vivisectionally** *adverb* L19. **vivisectionist** *noun* a practitioner or defender of vivisection L19. **vivisective** *adjective* = VIVISECTIONAL (b) L19. **vivisector** *noun* a practitioner of vivisection M19.

vivotoxin /ˈvʌɪvəʊtɒksɪn/ *noun*. M20.
[from Latin *vivus* alive + -O- + TOXIN.]
A substance which is produced in a diseased plant and is involved in the disease process.

vivres /ˈviːvəz, *foreign* viːvr/ *noun pl.* Now *rare* or *obsolete*. M17.
[French: see VIVERS.]
Food, provisions, victuals.

vixen /ˈvɪks(ə)n/ *noun*. Also †**fixen**.
[Old English *fyxe* fem. of FOX *noun*, *fyxen* adjective, = late Old High German *fuhsin*, Middle High German *vühsinne* (German *Füchsin*): see -EN[2]. For initial *v* cf. VAN *noun*[1], VANE.]
1 A female fox. OE.
2 An ill-tempered quarrelsome woman, a shrew. L16.
■ **vixenish** *adjective* characteristic of, appropriate to, or resembling a vixen; (of a woman) shrewish, ill-tempered: E19. **vixenishly** *adverb* in a vixenish or ill-tempered manner M19. **vixenishness** *noun* E19. **vixenly** *adjective & adverb* (*rare*) (*a*) *adjective* vixenish; (*b*) *adverb* vixenishly: L17.

Viyella /vʌɪˈɛlə/ *noun*. Also **v-**. L19.
[from *Via Gellia* a valley in Derbyshire where first made.]
(Proprietary name for) a fabric made from a twilled mixture of cotton and wool; a garment made of this material.

viz /vɪz/ *adverb & noun*. Also **viz.** (point). M16.
[Abbreviation of VIDELICET; the *z* repr. the usual medieval Latin symbol of contraction for *-et*.]
▸ **A** *adverb*. Usu. introducing an amplification or explanation of a previous statement or word: that is to say, namely, in other words. Cf. VIDELICET *adverb*. M16.

> 📖 W. COWPER The ingenious contriver of it, viz. myself.

▸ **B** *noun*. The word 'viz' used to introduce an amplification or explanation, esp. in a legal document. Also, a special clause in a deed introduced by 'viz'. Cf. VIDELICET *noun*. E18.

†**vizament** *noun*. *rare* (Shakes.). Only in E17.
[Alt.]
= ADVISEMENT 2, VISEMENT.

vizard /ˈvɪzəd/ *noun & verb*. *arch.* M16.
[Alt. of VISOR by confusion of ending: see -ARD. For a similar substitution cf. MAZARD *noun*[1].]
▸ **A** *noun*. **1** A mask worn to conceal or (formerly) protect the face; a disguise; *fig.* an outward show or appearance (freq. foll. by *of*). Also ***vizard-mask***. M16.
2 A masked person; *spec.* a woman wearing a mask in public, a prostitute. Now only in ***vizard-mask***. M17.
▸ **B** *verb trans.* †**1** Conceal or disguise under a false outward show or appearance; represent falsely. E–M17.
2 Cover or disguise (as) with a vizard; mask. E17.
■ **vizarded** *ppl adjective* wearing a vizard, masked, disguised; *fig.* assumed, pretended: L16.

vizcacha *noun* var. of VISCACHA.

†**Vizeeree** *noun & adjective* var. of WAZIR *noun*[2] & *adjective*.

vizier /vɪˈzɪə, ˈvɪzɪə/ *noun*. M16.
[French *visir*, *vizir* or Spanish *visir* from Turkish *vezir* from Arab. *wazīr* helper, assistant, (later) ruler's senior aide or minister: see -IER.]
Hist. In some Muslim countries, esp. Turkey under Ottoman rule: a high state official or minister; a governor or viceroy of a province; *esp.* (also ***grand vizier***) the chief minister of the sovereign.
■ **vi'zieral** *adjective* = VIZIERIAL L19. **vi'zierate** /-rət/ *noun* (*a*) the position or authority of a vizier; the period of a vizier's office; (*b*) a province or district governed by a vizier; (*c*) the department or residence of a vizier: L17. **vizierial** *adjective* of or pertaining to a vizier; (of a letter etc.) issued by or under the authority of a vizier: M19. **vi'ziership** *noun* the position or authority of a vizier, the period of a vizier's office; a province or district governed by a vizier; a vizierate: M17.

vizor *noun & verb* var. of VISOR.

vizored *adjective* var. of VISORED.

vizsla /ˈvɪʒlə/ *noun*. Also **V-**. M20.
[A town in Hungary.]
(A dog of) a breed of golden-brown pointer with large pendent ears.

vizy /ˈvɪzi/ *verb & noun*. *Scot.* Also **-zz-**. LME.
[from Old Northern French *viseer* from Latin *visitare* VISIT *verb*.]
▸ **A** *verb*. †**1** *verb trans.* Go to see, pay a visit to, visit. LME–E17.
2 *verb trans.* Look at closely or attentively; study, examine, view. LME. ▸†**b** Inspect or survey formally or officially. L15–L16.
†**3** *verb trans.* Afflict *with* illness or harm. LME–M16.
4 *verb intrans.* Look, gaze. E16.
5 *verb intrans.* Take aim with a gun etc.; aim *at*. L16.
▸ **B** *noun*. **1** The sight of a gun. M17.
2 An aim taken at an object etc. Esp. in ***take a vizy***. E18.
3 A look, a view; a sight *of* something; a glimpse. E18.
■ **vizyless** *adjective* E19.

VJ *abbreviation*.
1 Victory over Japan, in the war of 1939–45; chiefly in ***VJ Day***, the date when Japan ceased fighting (15 August 1945) or formally surrendered (2 September 1945).
2 Video Jockey.

VLA *abbreviation*.
ASTRONOMY. Very large array (a system of radio telescopes in the US).

Vlach /vlak/ *noun & adjective*. M19.
[Bulgarian, Serbo-Croat = Old Church Slavonic *Vlachŭ* Romanian or Italian, Czech *Vlach* Italian, Russian *Volokh*, ult. from Germanic word for 'foreigner'. Cf. WALACH, WALLACHIAN.]
▸ **A** *noun*. **1** A member of a Romanic people inhabiting esp. Romania and Moldova; a Romanian. M19.
2 The Romanian dialect of this people. E20.
▸ **B** *adjective*. Of or pertaining to this people or their language. L19.
■ **Vlachian** /ˈvleɪkɪən/ *adjective* = VLACH *adjective* L19.

vlakte /ˈflaktə/ *noun*. *S. Afr.* L18.
[Afrikaans from Dutch.]
An extent of flat open country; a plain. Freq. in *pl.*

vlast /vlast/ *noun*. Pl. **-i** /-i/. M20.
[Russian *vlast'*.]
In the countries of the former USSR: power, *esp.* political power. Also (usu. in *pl.*), those in authority, the Government, the establishment.

VLBI *abbreviation*. ASTRONOMY.
Very long baseline interferometry (a method of measuring signals from a radio source).

VLCC *abbreviation*.
Very large crude (oil) carrier.

VLDB *abbreviation*.
COMPUTING. Very large database.

VLDL *abbreviation*.
BIOCHEMISTRY. Very low-density lipoprotein.

vlei /fleɪ, vlʌɪ/ *noun*. L18.
[Afrikaans from Dutch *vallei* valley.]
1 In South Africa: a shallow pool of water; a piece of low-lying ground covered with water during the rainy season. L18.
2 A swamp. *US local*. L19.
Comb.: **vlei loerie**, **vlei lourie** *S. Afr.* any of several southern African coucals, *esp.* the white-browed coucal, *Centropus superciliosus*.

VLF *abbreviation*.
Very low frequency (designating radio waves with a frequency between 10 and 30 kHz).

VLSI *abbreviation*.
ELECTRONICS. Very large scale integration (*or* integrated).

VO *abbreviation*.
Royal Victorian Order.

vo. /vəʊ/ *adverb*. E19.
[Abbreviation.]
= VOCE *adverb*. Cf. VOC.

VOA *abbreviation*.
Voice of America (a radio station).

Vo-Ag /vəʊˈag/ *noun*. *US colloq.* M20.
[Abbreviation of Vocational Agriculture.]
Agriculture considered as a subject of study for those intending to make it their profession.

vobla /ˈvɒblə/ *noun*. Also **w-**. M20.
[Russian.]
Dried and smoked roach eaten in Russia as a delicacy.

voc. /vɒk/ *adverb*. E18.
[Abbreviation.]
= VOCE *adverb*.

vocab /ˈvəʊkab/ *noun*. *colloq.* E20.
[Abbreviation.]
(A) vocabulary.

vocable /ˈvəʊkəb(ə)l/ *noun*. LME.
[French, or Latin *vocabulum*, from *vocare* call: see -ABLE.]
†**1** A name, a designation. *rare*. LME–E17.
2 A word, a term, esp. with reference to form rather than meaning. M16.

vocable /ˈvəʊkəb(ə)l/ *adjective*. *rare*. E20.
[from Latin *vocare* call + -ABLE.]
Capable of utterance.
■ **vocably** *adverb* E20.

vocabular /və(ʊ)ˈkabjʊlə/ *adjective*. E17.
[from Latin *vocabulum* VOCABLE *noun* + -AR[1].]
Of or pertaining to words.

vocabulary /və(ʊ)ˈkabjʊləri/ *noun & adjective*. M16.
[medieval Latin *vocabularius*, *-um* from Latin *vocabulum* VOCABLE *noun*: see -ARY[1].]
▸ **A** *noun*. **1** A usu. alphabetical list of words with definitions or translations, as in a grammar or reader of a foreign language; a glossary. M16.
2 The range of language of a particular author, group, discipline, book, etc.; the sum of words known or habitually used by an individual. M18.
3 The sum or aggregate of words composing a language. L18.

4 A set of artistic or stylistic forms, techniques, movements, etc.; the range of such forms etc. available to a particular person etc. E20.

> 📖 **2** H. READ Realism is one of the vaguest terms in the vocabulary of criticism. A. PRICE The marvellous Old Testament vocabulary which had come naturally to seventeenth-century speakers. S. TOWNSEND 'Overview' is just one of the thousands of words in my vocabulary. **3** E. A. FREEMAN The largest infusion that the vocabulary of one European tongue ever received from another. **4** *New Yorker* Female fashion models, to demonstrate the vocabulary of the mannequin: poise, insouciance, charm . . hauteur.

▸ **B** *adjective.* Of, pertaining to, or composed of words. *rare.* E17.

■ **vocabu'larian** *noun* (*rare*) a person who gives much or undue attention to words L19. **vocabularize** *verb trans.* (*rare*) provide with a vocabulary M19. †**vocabuler** *noun* (*rare*) a vocabulary M16–E18. **vocabulist** *noun* †(*a*) a vocabulary; (*b*) a compiler of a vocabulary: M16.

vocal /'vəʊk(ə)l/ *adjective & noun.* LME.
[Latin *vocalis*, from *voc-*, *vox* voice: see -AL[1].]
▸ **A** *adjective.* **1** Uttered, communicated, or produced by the voice; spoken, oral; of or pertaining to the voice; of the nature of words or speech. LME.
2 ANATOMY. Operative or concerned in the production of voice or the articulation of speech sounds. LME.
3 a Of music: performed by or composed for the voice with or without instrumental accompaniment; that is sung or intended for singing. L16. ▸**b** Of or pertaining to singing. L18.
4 a Pertaining to or of the nature of a vowel; = VOCALIC. L16. ▸**b** PHONETICS. Uttered with voice as opp. to breath; voiced, sonant. M17.
5 Of a person, animal, or (*poet.*) inanimate object: possessing a voice, having the power of speech, able to produce sounds; uttering or producing sounds. E17.
6 *fig.* Conveying impressions or ideas as if by speech; expressive, eloquent. E17.
7 Full of sound, sounding, resounding. Freq. foll. by *with.* M17.
8 Readily or freely expressing one's views or opinions in speech; vociferous, outspoken. L19.

> 📖 **1** C. H. SPURGEON Silent worship is sweet, but vocal worship is sweeter. *Gamut* Performed against the vocal protests of the liberal factions. **2 vocal cord**, **vocal fold** either of two folds of mucous membrane in the larynx which vibrate when close together to produce voiced sounds. **vocal tract** the region of the body between the larynx and the lips which is responsible for the production of speech. **3b** *Guardian* Singing rhythm and blues inspired tunes in vocal harmony. **vocal line** the sung melody line of a song or vocal composition. **vocal score** a musical score showing the voice parts in full and a keyboard arrangement of the instrumental parts. **5** J. WESLEY Our Harps, no longer vocal now, We cast aside. GOLDSMITH These insects are generally vocal in the midst of summer. **7** F. W. FARRAR When all the air is vocal with whispering trees, and singing birds. **8** L. H. TRIBE An extremely vocal minority . . unalterably opposed to all forms of birth control.

▸ **B** *noun.* **1** A vowel. Long *rare* or *obsolete.* L16.
2 ECCLESIASTICAL. A member of a Roman Catholic body who has a right to vote in certain elections. M17.
3 Vocal faculty; power of speech. *rare.* M19.
4 a Vocal music; singing. E20. ▸**b** A musical composition or performance with singing; in *pl.* & *sing.*, the sung part of a song or vocal composition, a vocal part. M20.

> 📖 **4b** *Q* Jones was putting down the vocal for a song. *New Yorker* Chiming acoustic guitars, airy synthesizers, far-off backing vocals.

■ **vocally** *adverb* LME. **vocalness** *noun* (*rare*) E18.

vocalese /vəʊkə'liːz/ *noun.* M20.
[from prec. + -ESE, perh. partly after VOCALISE *noun*.]
A style of singing in which the singer puts words or meaningless syllables to a previously instrumental piece. Also = SCAT *noun*[4].

vocalic /və(ʊ)'kalɪk/ *adjective.* E19.
[from VOCAL *adjective* + -IC.]
Of, pertaining to, or consisting of a vowel or vowels; of the nature of a vowel; containing many vowels.

vocalion /və(ʊ)'keɪlɪən/ *noun.* L19.
[formed as prec. after *accordion*, *orchestrion*.]
A musical instrument similar to a harmonium with broad reeds, producing sounds somewhat resembling the human voice.

vocalise /vəʊkə'liːz, 'vəʊkəliːz/ *noun.* L19.
[French, from *vocaliser* vocalize.]
MUSIC. A singing exercise using individual syllables or vowel sounds; a vocal passage consisting of a melody without words. Also *derog.*, a technical vocal display.

vocalise *verb* var. of VOCALIZE.

vocalism /'vəʊk(ə)lɪz(ə)m/ *noun.* M19.
[from VOCAL *adjective* + -ISM.]
1 The use of the voice or vocal organs in speech or singing. M19.
2 a A system of vowels; the use of vowels. M19. ▸**b** A vocal sound or articulation. L19.

vocalist /'vəʊk(ə)lɪst/ *noun.* E17.
[formed as prec. + -IST.]
1 An utterer of words, a speaker. *rare.* E17.
2 A singer, esp. of popular or jazz songs. M19.
■ **voca'listic** *adjective* pertaining to vocal music or musicians L19.

vocality /və(ʊ)'kalɪti/ *noun.* L16.
[medieval Latin *vocalitas* utterance, formed as VOCAL *adjective*: see -ITY.]
1 The possession or exercise of vocal powers. L16.
2 The quality or fact of being uttered or utterable; vocal quality; in *pl.*, vocal properties or sounds, *spec.* as in singing. E17.
3 PHONETICS. The quality of being voiced or vocalic. M17.

vocalize /'vəʊk(ə)lʌɪz/ *verb.* Also **-ise**. M17.
[from VOCAL *adjective* + -IZE.]
1 *verb trans.* Form (a sound) or utter (a word etc.) with the voice; articulate; sing (a song etc.). M17.
2 *verb trans.* PHONETICS. ▸**a** Convert into a vowel. M19. ▸**b** Utter with voice rather than breath, make sonant. M19.
3 *verb trans.* Provide with a voice, make vocal or articulate. M19.
4 *verb trans.* Provide with vowels or vowel signs; *spec.* write (Hebrew etc.) with vowel points. M19.
5 *verb intrans.* **a** Perform vocal music, sing; *spec.* sing with several notes to one vowel. M19. ▸**b** Esp. of an animal: utter a vocal sound. M20.
■ **vocali'zation** *noun* the action or fact of vocalizing or being vocalized; an instance of this; (mode of) utterance, speech, or singing, (a) vocal expression: M19. **vocalized** *ppl adjective* that has been vocalized; *spec.* in JAZZ, (of the tone of an instrument) made to resemble that of the human voice: M19. **vocalizer** *noun* E20.

vocation /və(ʊ)'keɪʃ(ə)n/ *noun.* LME.
[Old & mod. French, or Latin *vocatio(n-)*, from *vocat-* pa. ppl stem of *vocare* call: see -ATION.]
1 The fact or feeling of being called by God to undertake a specific (esp. religious) career, function, or occupation; a divine call to do certain work; a strong feeling of fitness or suitability for a particular career etc. LME. ▸**b** CHRISTIAN THEOLOGY. The calling of humankind to salvation by God or Christ. E16.
2 The calling of a person to a public position, esp. to the ministry or another Church office. LME.
3 a The work or function to which a person is called; a mode of life or employment regarded as requiring dedication. L15. ▸**b** A career, an occupation; a trade, a profession. M16. ▸**c** *collect.* Those following a particular occupation or profession. L16.
†**4** The action of summoning an assembly or its members. *rare.* L15–L18.

> 📖 **1** W. S. MAUGHAM It's no good my being ordained if I haven't a real vocation. **3a** H. P. LIDDON In some quarters, the missionary's life . . is regarded as a profession rather than as a vocation. **b** W. IRVING In addition to his other vocations, he was the singing-master of the neighbourhood.

■ **vocationless** *adjective* E20.

vocational /və(ʊ)'keɪʃ(ə)n(ə)l/ *adjective.* M17.
[from prec. + -AL[1].]
Of or pertaining to a vocation or occupation; *spec.* (of education or training) directed at a particular occupation and its skills.

> 📖 *Independent* Vocational courses will benefit the economy.

■ **vocationalism** *noun* training for a vocation; educational emphasis on this: E20. **vocationalize** *verb trans.* direct towards vocational training M20. **vocationally** *adverb* L19.

vocative /'vɒkətɪv/ *adjective & noun.* LME.
[Old & mod. French *vocatif* or Latin *vocativus*, from *vocat-*: see VOCATION, -IVE.]
▸ **A** *adjective.* **1** GRAMMAR. Designating, being in, or pertaining to the case of nouns, adjectives, or pronouns used to address or invoke people or things. LME.
2 Characteristic of or pertaining to calling or addressing. M17.
▸ **B** *noun.* GRAMMAR. *The* vocative case; a word, form, etc., in the vocative case. LME.
■ **vocatively** *adverb* M17.

voce /'votʃe/ *noun.* M18.
[Italian = voice.]
MUSIC. The voice: occurring in various phrases with reference to quality or register.
voce di gola /di 'goːla/ a throaty or guttural voice. ***voce di petto*** /di 'petto/ the chest register. ***voce di testa*** /di 'testa/ (*a*) the head register; †(*b*) the falsetto voice.

voce /'vəʊtʃi/ *adverb.* M19.
[Latin, abl. sing. of *vox* voice, word.]
Under the word or heading (of). Cf. VO., VOC.

vociferant /və(ʊ)'sɪf(ə)r(ə)nt/ *adjective & noun.* E17.
[Latin *vociferant-* pres. ppl stem of *vociferari*: see next, -ANT[1].]
▸ **A** *adjective.* Vociferous. E17.
▸ **B** *noun.* A clamorous or noisy person. *rare.* L19.
■ **vociferance** *noun* (*a*) clamour or noise of shouting; (*b*) vociferousness: M19.

vociferate /və(ʊ)'sɪfəreɪt/ *verb.* L16.
[Latin *vociferat-* pa. ppl stem of *vociferari*, from *voc-*, *vox* voice + *fer-* stem of *ferre* carry: see -ATE[3].]
1 *verb trans.* Utter (words etc.) loudly, assert vehemently. L16. ▸**b** Drive by means of clamour. M19.
2 *verb intrans.* Cry out loudly; bawl, shout. E17.
■ **vociferative** *adjective* (*rare*) vociferous L16. **vociferator** *noun* E19.

vociferation /və(ʊ),sɪfə'reɪʃ(ə)n/ *noun.* LME.
[Old French *vociferation* (mod. *vociférations* pl.) or Latin *vociferatio(n-)*, formed as prec.: see -ATION.]
The action of vociferating; loud shouting; an act or instance of this, a clamour, an outcry.

vociferous /və(ʊ)'sɪf(ə)rəs/ *adjective.* E17.
[from Latin *vociferari* VOCIFERATE + -OUS.]
Uttering or characterized by loud cries or shouts; clamorous, noisy; insistently and forcibly expressing one's views, outspoken, vocal.

> 📖 T. C. WOLFE Shouting vociferous gayeties at Mr. Logan. *Insight* A vociferous opponent of deregulation in the 1970s.

■ **vocife'rosity** *noun* (*rare*) vociferousness M19. **vociferously** *adverb* E19. **vociferousness** *noun* M19.

vocoder /vəʊ'kəʊdə/ *noun.* M20.
[from VO(ICE *noun* + CODE *noun* + -ER[1].]
A synthesizer that produces or reproduces sounds from an analysis of speech or other vocal input.
■ **vocode** *verb trans.* transform or produce by means of a vocoder L20.

vocoid /'vəʊkɔɪd/ *adjective & noun.* M20.
[from VOC(AL + -OID.]
PHONETICS. (Designating or pertaining to) a speech sound of the vocalic type. Cf. CONTOID.

vocule /'vɒkjuːl/ *noun.* M19.
[from Latin *vocula* dim. of *vox* voice: see -ULE.]
The faint final sound produced in pronouncing certain consonants.

VOD *abbreviation.*
Video-on-demand.

Vodafone /'vəʊdəfəʊn/ *noun.* L20.
[from VO(ICE *noun* + DA(TA + *fone* alt. of PHONE *noun*[2].]
(Proprietary name for) a cellular telephone system operating in the UK; a telephone handset forming part of this system.

Vodian /'vəʊdɪən/ *noun & adjective.* Also **Votian** /'vəʊt-/. M20.
[from Russian *Vod'* + -IAN.]
▸ **A** *noun.* **1** A member of a minor Finnic people settled to the NW of Novgorod, mentioned in sources from the 11th cent. M20.
2 The almost extinct Finnic language of this people. M20.
▸ **B** *attrib.* or as *adjective.* Of or pertaining to the Vodians or their language. M20.

vodka /'vɒdkə/ *noun.* E19.
[Russian, dim. of *voda* water. Cf. Polish *wodka*.]
A colourless alcoholic spirit made esp. in Russia and Poland by distillation of grain etc.; a glass or drink of this.
vodka and tonic, ***vodka Collins***, etc.
Comb.: **vodka gimlet** a cocktail made of vodka and lime juice; **vodka martini** a Martini cocktail with vodka substituted for gin.

vodkatini /vɒdkə'tiːni/ *noun.* M20.
[Contr.]
A vodka martini.

vo-do-deo-do /,vəʊdəʊdɪəʊ'dəʊ/ *noun.* M20.
[A meaningless refrain.]
Used *attrib.* to designate a jazz song or style of singing characterized by speed, energy, and the repetition of *vo-do-deo-do* or a similar refrain.

vodun /'vəʊduːn/ *noun.* L19.
[Fon *vodũ* tutelary deity, fetish. Cf. VOODOO.]
A fetish, usu. one connected with the snake-worship and other rites practised first in Dahomey (now Benin) and later introduced by slaves esp. to Haiti and Louisiana.

voe /vəʊ/ *noun.* L17.
[Norwegian *våg*, Icelandic *vogur* bay, inlet from Old Norse *vágr* creek, bay.]
A creek, inlet, or small bay in Orkney or Shetland.

voetganger /'fʊtxaŋə/ *noun. S. Afr.* E19.
[Afrikaans from Dutch = pedestrian, from *voet* foot + *ganger* goer.]
1 A locust in its immature wingless stage. Cf. HOPPER *noun*[1] 2. E19.
2 A pedestrian. Also (*colloq.*), an infantryman. E20.

voetsek /ˈfʊtsɛk/ *interjection & verb. S. Afr.* Also **-sak** /-sak/. M19.
[Afrikaans *voe(r)tsek*, from Dutch *voort zeg ik* be off I say.]
▶ **A** *interjection.* Esp. to a dog: go away!, off you go! M19.
▶ **B** *verb.* **1** *verb trans.* Chase (a dog) away. L19.
2 *verb intrans.* Leave, go away. M20.

voetstoots /ˈfʊtstʊəts/ *adverb & adjective. S. Afr.* M20.
[Afrikaans, from Dutch *met de voet te stoten* to push with the foot.]
LAW. (Of a sale or purchase) without guarantee or warranty; at the buyer's risk. Also *fig.*, without reservation or conditions.

voeu /vø, vəː/ *noun.* Pl. **-x** (pronounced same). E20.
[French = vow, wish: see VOW *noun.*]
A non-mandatory recommendation made by an international conference.

vogesite /ˈvəʊdʒɪzʌɪt/ *noun.* L19.
[German *Vogesit* from *Vogesen* German name of the Vosges Mountains in NE France: see -ITE[1].]
GEOLOGY. A lamprophyre consisting essentially of phenocrysts of hornblende in a groundmass containing potash feldspar.

vogie /ˈvəʊgi/ *adjective. Scot.* E18.
[Origin unkn.]
1 Vain, proud, conceited. E18.
2 Merry, cheerful, delighted. E18.

vogt /fəʊkt, v-/ *noun.* Also **V-**. L17.
[German from medieval Latin use as noun of Latin *vocatus* pa. pple of *vocare* call.]
A steward, bailiff, or similar official in Germany or a German-speaking area.

vogue /vəʊg/ *noun, adjective, & verb.* L16.
[French from Italian *voga* rowing, fashion, from *vogare* row, be going well.]
▶ **A** *noun.* †**1 a** Natural bent or capacity. Only in L16. ▸**b** General course or tendency; usual character or condition. E17–E18.
†**2** *The* principal place in popular esteem, *the* greatest currency or popular success. L16–L18.
†**3 a** The approval or favour *of* a class or group. E17–E18. ▸**b** The current opinion or belief; the general report or rumour. E17–M18.
4 a Popularity (esp. short-lived), popular use or currency. Freq. in ***in vogue***, ***into vogue***, ***out of vogue***. E17. ▸**b** A prominent place in popular favour or fashion; a period of such favour, *esp.* a short-lived one. L17.
5 The prevailing fashion; a thing in (esp. short-lived) favour at a particular time. M17.

> 📖 **4a** R. FORD Travelling in a carriage with post-horses was brought into vogue by the Bourbons. C. BEATON Sagging tail coats, . . the remnants of a military fashion that was still in vogue. **b** J. BARZUN The medical use of hypnosis is enjoying a new vogue. **5** J. GALSWORTHY The days of her prime, when a drawl was all the vogue. C. LAMBERT Before the war he . . created a vogue for the Russian ballet.

▶ **B** *attrib.* or as *adjective.* Fashionable, currently in vogue. Freq. in ***vogue word***. M17.
▶ **C** *verb.* Pres. pple & verbal noun **vogueing**, **voguing**.
†**1** *verb trans.* Estimate or reckon as something; (foll. by *down* or *up*) extol or disparage (a thing). M17–E18.
2 *verb intrans.* [from the fashion magazine *Vogue*.] Perform a solo dance with movements reminiscent of a fashion model's posings and posturings. Freq. as ***vogueing***, ***voguing*** *verbal noun.* L20.
▪ **voguer** *noun* a person who vogues L20. **voguey** *adjective & noun* (*a*) *adjective* = VOGUISH; (*b*) *noun* (*slang*) a person aspiring to be fashionable, *esp.* one heavily influenced by the fashion magazine *Vogue*: E20. **voguish** *adjective* that is in vogue or temporarily fashionable E20.

vogue la galère /vɔg la galɛːr/ *interjection.* M18.
[French, lit. 'let the galley be rowed'.]
Let's get on with it! Let's give it a go!

Vogul /ˈvəʊg(ə)l/ *noun & adjective.* Also †**W-**. L18.
[Russian *Vogul*, German *Wogul*.]
▶ **A** *noun.* **1** A member of an Ugric people inhabiting Tobolsk and Perm in central Russia. L18.
2 The Ob-Ugrian language of this people. E20.
▶ **B** *adjective.* Of or pertaining to this people or their language. L18.
▪ Also **Voˈgulian** *noun & adjective* L18.

voice /vɔɪs/ *noun.* ME.
[Anglo-Norman *voiz*, *voice*, Old French *vois*, *voiz*, (also mod.) *voix* from Latin *vox*, *voc-* voice, sound.]
1 Sound produced by the vocal organs of man or animals and usu. uttered through the mouth or nose; *esp.* sound formed in the human larynx in speaking, singing, or other utterance; the faculty or power of producing this; this with a specified quality or tone. ME. ▸**b** PHONETICS. Expiration of air with vibration or resonance produced when the vocal cords are drawn loosely together and the air is forced through the resulting narrow passage. Cf. BREATH 3c. M19.
2 Sound produced by the vocal organs naturally made by and regarded as characteristic of an individual person; a specified manner of speaking, singing, etc.; a person perceived only through his or her voice. ME. ▸**b** (A supposed utterance of) an invisible guiding or directing spirit; a voice heard only by a mentally disturbed person. Usu. in *pl.* E20.
3 The sound *of* prayer, a crowd, etc.; a sound produced by something inanimate, as the wind, a musical instrument, etc. ME.
4 a The right to have a part or share in the control or deciding of something; an opportunity to express an opinion etc.; a say. ME. ▸**b** The expressed opinion or will of the people, a group, etc. (now freq. in the names of radio stations); an expression of a person's opinion or preference; a person expressing an opinion etc.; *spec.* in Parliament, a vote given with the voice. LME. ▸†**c** Support or approval in a suit or petition. *rare* (Shakes.). L16–E17. ▸**d** Utterance or expression of feeling, opinion, etc. M19.
†**5** A word, phrase, or sentence, uttered; a speech. LME–L18.
†**6** General or common talk; (a) rumour, (a) report. LME–M17.
7 GRAMMAR. A group of forms of a verb indicating the function of the subject in relation to the action implied; the quality of a verb as indicated by a particular voice. LME.
8 The agency or means by which something specified is expressed, represented, or revealed. L16.
9 MUSIC. **a** A person's capacity for singing, esp. with others; a person considered as the possessor of a voice, a singer. L16. ▸**b** A vocal part in music. Also, a constituent part of a fugue. M17. ▸**c** Each of the lines or notes able to be played simultaneously on a musical instrument, esp. an electronic one. M20. ▸**d** In an electronic musical instrument, each of a number of selectable pre-set or programmable tones. L20.

> 📖 **1** SHELLEY Muttering with hoarse, harsh voice. W. YOUATT The voice of animals is produced by the passage of air through this aperture. **2** A. MARSH-CALDWELL 'Come here, both of you', says the lady, in a deep, awful voice. W. K. KELLY 'I second that proposal', exclaimed a voice. *Guardian* A fabulous, rounded, bluesy voice and a terrific stage presence. J. HIGGINS He raised his voice 'Listen, everybody.' **3** SIR W. SCOTT The voice of thunder shook the wood. *Contact* Listening to the jerky voice of the engine. **4a** A. HELPS If we had more voice in the management of affairs. **b** J. MORSE A convention . . ratified the constitution without a dissenting voice. **d** *Whole Earth Review* Language gives voice to a nation's stories. **7** ***active voice***, ***middle voice***, ***passive voice***. **8** H. REED Poetry is the voice of imagination. J. BUCHANAN Rose was no longer there to act as the voice of reason. **9a** *Kaatskill Life* Medieval and Appalachian music for voices, recorder, . . banjo and mandolin.

Phrases: **at the top of one's voice** as loudly as possible. ***exclusive voice***: see EXCLUSIVE *adjective.* ***force one's voice***: see FORCE *verb*[1]. ***gravel voice***: see GRAVEL *noun.* ***head voice***: see HEAD *adjective.* **in good voice**, **in voice** in proper vocal condition for singing or speaking. ***lift up one's voice***: see LIFT *verb.* **lose one's voice** be (temporarily) deprived of the power of using the voice for singing or speaking, esp. through an infection or hoarseness. ***Pilate's voice***: see PILATE 2. **the voice of God** the expression of God's will, command, wrath, etc. ***voice in the wilderness***: see WILDERNESS 2. **with one voice** unanimously.

Comb.: **voice-box** (*a*) ANATOMY the larynx; (*b*) = ***speak-box*** s.v. SPEAK *verb*; **voice channel** TELECOMMUNICATIONS a channel with a bandwidth sufficiently great to accommodate speech; **voice coil** (*a*) = ***speech coil*** s.v. SPEECH *noun*; (*b*) a similar coil with the converse function in a moving-coil microphone; **voice-figure** a figure or graphic representation of a vocal sound; **voice frequency** a frequency within the range required for the transmission of speech (usu. 200 or 300 Hz to 3000 Hz or higher); **voice leading** *US* = ***part-writing*** s.v. PART *noun*; **voice level** the volume of a voice measured for recording purposes; **voice mail** a system for electronically storing, processing, and reproducing verbal messages left through the conventional telephone network; **voice message** a recording of a verbal message which is stored and reproduced using the telephone network; **voice-over** *noun & verb* (*a*) *noun* (a) narration spoken by an unseen narrator in a film or a television programme; the unseen person providing the voice; (*b*) *verb trans. & intrans.* do a voice-over (for); **voice part** MUSIC a part or melody written for the voice, a vocal part; **voice-print** a visual record of speech, analysed with respect to frequency, duration, and amplitude; **voice-printer** an apparatus for producing voice-prints; **voice-printing** the production or use of voice-prints; **voice radio** a two-way radio, a transceiver; **voice recognition** the technology or process of identifying, analyzing, and interpreting sounds produced by the human voice, *spec.* (*a*) computer recognition and interpretation of spoken words and phrases; (*b*) computer analysis and matching of the distinctive characteristics of an individual human voice. **voice synthesizer** a synthesizer for producing sounds in imitation of human speech; **voice-tube** a pipe or tube for conveying the voice, esp. as used on ships; **voice vote** a vote taken by noting the relative strength of the calls of *aye* and *no*.

voice /vɔɪs/ *verb trans.* LME.
[from prec.]
1 In *pass.* Be commonly said or stated, be spoken of generally or publicly; be reported or rumoured *abroad*. Formerly also *impers.* in ***it is voiced how***, ***it is voiced that***, etc. *arch.* LME.
†**2** Speak of, report, proclaim. L16–L17.
†**3** Speak of in a certain way, *esp.* speak highly of, praise. Also foll. by *up*. Usu. in *pass.* Only in 17.
†**4** Elect (a person) by voice or vote; nominate or appoint to an office. Also foll. by *out*. E–M17.
5 Give utterance or expression to (an emotion, opinion, etc.); express in words, proclaim openly or publicly; speak or utter (a word etc.). E17. ▸**b** Act as the mouthpiece or spokesman of, express the opinions of, (a group etc.). L19. ▸**c** = NARRATE *verb* 1b. M20.
6 a Provide with the faculty of speech or song. *poet. & rhet.* E18. ▸**b** MUSIC. Give the correct quality of tone to (an organ or organ-pipe). Also, write the voice parts for (a piece of music). E18.
7 PHONETICS. Utter with vibration or resonance produced when the vocal cords are drawn loosely together and air is expelled through the resulting narrow passage; cause to become voiced. L19.

> 📖 **5** U. HOLDEN An uncompromising child, voicing what other people only thought. *Guardian* The Kremlin . . voiced concern at Austria's application to join the European Community. **7** H. SWEET Dutch still voices final *s* in stressless words . . when a vowel follows.

▪ **voicer** *noun* †(*a*) *Scot.* a voter; (*b*) MUSIC a person who voices the pipes of an organ: M17.

voiced /vɔɪst/ *adjective.* LME.
[from VOICE *noun* or *verb*: see -ED[2], -ED[1].]
1 Possessing a voice, having a voice of a specified kind, quality, or tone. LME.
†**2** Much or highly spoken of; commended, famed. Only in M17.
3 PHONETICS. Uttered with voice or vibration or resonance of the vocal cords; sonant. Opp. VOICELESS 5. M19.
1 ***clear-voiced***, ***loud-voiced***, ***low-voiced***, ***soft-voiced***, ***sweet-voiced***, etc.
▪ **voicedness** *noun* M20.

voiceful /ˈvɔɪsfʊl, -f(ə)l/ *adjective.* Chiefly *poet. & rhet.* E17.
[from VOICE *noun* + -FUL.]
1 Possessing a voice, having power of utterance; sonorous, sounding; vocal *with* or expressive *of* something. E17.
2 Of or pertaining to the voice; uttered by the voice or voices. E19.
▪ **voicefulness** *noun* M19.

voiceless /ˈvɔɪslɪs/ *adjective.* M16.
[formed as prec. + -LESS.]
1 Having no voice, lacking the power of utterance; uttering no speech, dumb, mute; speechless. M16. ▸**b** *spec.* Having no voice in the control or management of affairs. M17.
2 Characterized by the absence of sound or voice, silent, still. Chiefly *poet. & rhet.* E19.
3 Not expressed or uttered by the voice or in speech; unspoken, unuttered. Chiefly *poet. & rhet.* E19.
4 Characterized by or causing loss of speech. Chiefly *poet. & rhet.* E19.
5 PHONETICS. Uttered without voice or vibration resonance of the vocal cords, uttered with the vocal cords held wide apart. Opp. VOICED 3. M19.
▪ **voicelessly** *adverb* M19. **voicelessness** *noun* M19.

voicespond /ˈvɔɪspɒnd/ *verb intrans.* M20.
[from VOICE *noun* + CORRE)SPOND.]
Correspond by means of recorded spoken messages.
▪ **voicespondence** *noun* correspondence in this way M20. **voicespondent** *noun* a person who voicesponds M20.

voicing /ˈvɔɪsɪŋ/ *noun.* E17.
[from VOICE *verb* + -ING[1].]
†**1** Voting, nomination, or decision by voice. E–M17.
2 The action or fact of uttering with the voice, the speaking or utterance *of* something; speech, vocal utterance; an instance of this. E17.
3 MUSIC. **a** The operation or process of giving the correct quality of tone to an organ or organ-pipe; the tone so obtained. M19. ▸**b** The tonal quality of a group of instruments in a jazz group etc.; a blend of instrumental sound, (a) harmonization. M20.
4 PHONETICS. The action or process of uttering a consonant etc. with voice; the change of a sound from unvoiced to voiced. L19.

void /vɔɪd/ *adjective & noun.* ME.
[Old French *voide* dial. var. of *vuide* (mod. *vide*) fem., superseding *vuit* masc., from Proto-Romance pa. ppl formation repr. also by Latin *vocivus*, *vacivus*, rel. to *vacare* (see VACANT).]
▶ **A** *adjective.* **1** Of an office, position, etc.: having no incumbent or holder; unoccupied, vacant. ME. ▸†**b** Marked by or pertaining to a vacancy or interregnum. L15–E17.
2 Having no occupants or inhabitants; not occupied or frequented by living creatures; deserted, empty; *spec.* (*a*) *arch.* (of a seat) in which no one is sitting; (*b*) *arch.* (of land) not occupied by buildings etc., vacant, waste; (*c*) (now chiefly *dial.*) (of a house or room) unoccupied, untenanted. ME.

3 Not occupied by visible contents; containing no matter; empty, unfilled. *arch.* ME. ▸**b** *spec.* Having the centre empty or not filled in. *rare.* L16.
†**4** Empty-handed; destitute. LME–M16.
5 Devoid of, free from, lacking; not tainted with; not possessing; not affected by. Usu. foll. by *of.* LME. ▸**b** Empty in respect *of*; cleared or rid *of.* L15.
6 a Of speech, action, etc.: ineffective, useless, leading to no result. Formerly also, (of a person) destitute of good qualities, worthless; (of a thing) superfluous. LME. ▸**b** ASTROLOGY. Of a planet etc. or its course: leaving a sign without making any further aspects etc. Formerly esp. in †*void of course.* *rare.* LME.
7 Having no legal force; not binding in law; (legally) invalid, ineffectual. Freq. in ***null and void***. LME.
8 Of time: free from work or occupation; idle, leisure. Now *rare.* LME.
9 CARDS (esp. BRIDGE). Of a hand etc.: having no cards in a given suit. M20.

> 📖 **1** I. WALTON The Provostship . . of Eaton became void by the death of Mr. Thomas Murray. **2** E. A. FREEMAN Most likely it stood in the void space between the mound . . and the later Castle. R. KIPLING 'We know the Shrine is void,' they said, 'The Goddess flown.' ***void and redd***: see REDD *ppl adjective.* **3** J. HUTTON It . . passes as freely through a transparent body as through the voidest space. A. C. SWINBURNE An eagle . . That . . with void mouth gapes after emptier prey. **5** W. GOLDING Their faces would be uncovered but void of . . make-up. *Christianity Today* All is presented with professional objectivity, void of scorn or ridicule. **b** *Church Times* World War II saw the College void of students. **6a** R. HOOKER Despaire I cannot, nor induce my minde to thinke his faith voide. **7** *Independent* The poll was declared null and void after less than . . 50 per cent . . bothered to turn out. W. GELDART A marriage between persons either of whom is under the age of 16 is void.

▸ **B** *noun.* **1** The absence or scarcity *of* something; a lack, a want. *rare.* LME.
2 Emptiness, vacancy, vacuity. LME.
3 An empty or vacant space; an unoccupied place or opening in something or between things; a vacancy caused by the absence or removal of something. LME. ▸**b** ARCHITECTURE. A space left in a wall for a window or door; the opening of an arch; an unfilled space in a building or structure. E17. ▸**c** Each of the small unoccupied spaces in a heap or mass which is not perfectly solid; *spec.* (***a***) a defect in a crystal lattice consisting of a space larger than a single vacancy; (***b***) an interatomic space in a crystal lattice. M19.
4 The empty expanse of space, air, or sky; *spec.* (an) absolutely empty space; (a) vacuum. Freq. with *the.* M17.
5 *fig.* An unsatisfied desire; a feeling of emptiness. L18.
6 A period during which a house or farm is unoccupied or unlet. L19.
7 CARDS. **a** In the game of skat, the seven, eight, or nine, which have no value in scoring. L19. ▸**b** The absence of any cards in a particular suit in a player's holding. M20.
8 MEDICINE. An act of emptying the bladder. L20.

> 📖 **4** P. DAVIES The majority of the universe is intergalactic void containing . . tenuous gas. **5** DICKENS With an aching void in his young heart.

void /vɔɪd/ *verb.* ME.
[Partly from Old French *voider, vuider* (mod. *vider*), from base also of the adjective and noun; partly aphet. from AVOID *verb.*]
▸ **I** *verb trans.* **1** Clear (a room, house, place) of occupants; empty or clear (a place, container, etc.) of something; *fig.* make free or clear of some quality or condition. Usu. foll. by *of.* *arch.* ME. ▸**b** Clear (a table). Long *arch.* LME. ▸**c** Empty (the stomach); clear or blow (the nose); clean out (a slaughtered animal). *rare.* LME. ▸†**d** Make (a benefice or office) vacant; vacate. M17–E18.
2 Deprive of legal validity; make legally void or invalid; avoid. Also *gen.* (now *rare*), deprive of effectiveness, meaning, force, or value; annul, cancel. ME. ▸†**b** Confute, refute. LME–L17.
†**3** Cause or compel (a person) to go away from or leave a place; send away, dismiss, expel. ME–M17.
†**4 a** Go away from, depart from, or leave (a place); give (ground); move out of (the way); get out of (a person's sight). ME–M18. ▸**b** Vacate (a seat). *rare.* M–L19.
5 †**a** Clear away by destruction or demolition; remove completely. ME–M17. ▸**b** Remove (something) so as to leave a vacant space; remove by emptying or taking out. LME.
†**6 a** = AVOID *verb* 7. ME–L17. ▸**b** = AVOID *verb* 8. LME–L17. ▸**c** = AVOID *verb* 9. LME–E18.
7 Of a person, an animal, a bodily organ, etc.: discharge (matter) through a natural vent or orifice, esp. through the excretory organs; eject by excretion or evacuation. LME.
8 Carry off, discharge, or drain away (water, etc.). Freq. foll. by *away.* LME.

> 📖 **2** J. DIDION Her hand trembled so hard that she had to void the first check. **7** *Nature* Pigeons . . feed on ripe berries and . . void viable seeds.

▸ **II** *verb intrans.* **9** Go away, depart, leave a place or position; retreat, make way; vanish, disappear; = AVOID *verb* 5. Also foll. by adverb or preposition. *arch.* ME.
10 Empty the bladder, urinate (now chiefly MEDICINE). Formerly also, vomit. LME.
†**11** Of a benefice, office, etc.: become or remain vacant. LME–M16.
†**12** Flow or pass out, esp. by evacuation or excretion; be discharged. M16–L18.
■ **voidless** *adjective* (*rare*) (***a***) LAW not voidable; (***b***) *poet.* unavoidable: M17.

voidable /ˈvɔɪdəb(ə)l/ *adjective.* L15.
[from prec. + -ABLE.]
Able to be voided; *spec.* (chiefly LAW) able to be annulled or made legally void, that may be either avoided or affirmed.
■ **voidaˈbility** *noun* E19. **voidableness** *noun* E18.

voidage /ˈvɔɪdɪdʒ/ *noun.* M20.
[from VOID *noun* + -AGE.]
Chiefly SCIENCE & ENGINEERING. Voids or empty spaces collectively; the proportion of a volume occupied by voids.

voidance /ˈvɔɪd(ə)ns/ *noun.* LME.
[Old French, from *voider, vuider*: see VOID *verb*, -ANCE.]
1 The action or process of emptying out the contents of something; discharge, evacuation, esp. by excretion from the body; the emptying out or carrying away of water etc., esp. by drainage. Now *rare.* LME.
†**2** The action of clearing away or removing something. LME–L17.
3 ECCLESIASTICAL. The fact of a benefice etc. becoming or being vacant. LME.
4 Chiefly LAW. Annulment; invalidation; = AVOIDANCE 4. L15.

voided /ˈvɔɪdɪd/ *ppl adjective.* LME.
[from VOID *verb* + -ED[1].]
1 *gen.* That has been voided. LME.
2 Having a part or portion cut out so as to leave a void or vacant space. Now only HERALDRY, (of a charge or ordinary) having the central area cut away following the outline of the charge so as to show the field. LME.
3 Emitted or discharged by regurgitation or excretion. L18.

voidee /ˈvɔɪdiː/ *noun. obsolete* exc. *Hist.* LME.
[Anglo-Norman, pa. pple of *voider* VOID *verb*, app with ref. to the withdrawal from a hall of those who were not to sleep there: see -EE[1].]
A collation or light meal of wine with spiced delicacies, comfits, etc., taken before retiring to rest, before the departure of guests, or after a feast or fuller meal; a parting dish.

voider /ˈvɔɪdə/ *noun.* ME.
[from VOID *verb* + -ER[1].]
†**1** A piece of armour covering a part left exposed by other pieces, esp at the elbow or knee. Only in ME.
†**2** A screen, a defence; a remover or driver away *of* something. LME–M16.
3 A receptacle into which or from which something is emptied; *esp.* (***a***) a tray, basket, etc., in which dirty utensils, waste food, etc., are placed during a meal or when clearing a table; †(***b***) a tray, basket, or large plate, usu. ornamental in design, for holding, carrying, or handing round sweets; (***c***) a wicker basket, esp. for laundry. Now *arch.* & *dial.* LME.
4 HERALDRY. A flanch; *esp.* one which encroaches only a small way on to the shield. Usu. in *pl.* M16.
5 a A person who or thing which voids, clears away, or empties something. *rare.* L16. ▸†**b** A servant or attendant who clears the table after a meal. Freq. *fig.* E–M17. ▸**c** MEDICINE. A person who passes urine. M20.

voidness /ˈvɔɪdnɪs/ *noun.* LME.
[from VOID *adjective* + -NESS.]
†**1** Freedom from work; leisure. Only in LME.
†**2** Vanity, futility. LME–E17.
3 The state or condition of being void, empty, or unoccupied; emptiness, vacancy, vacuity. LME. ▸**b** A void or vacant space. LME.
†**4** Freedom from or absence or lack of something. L15–L16.
5 The state or condition of being legally void; nullity. L19.

voilà /vwala, vwɑːˈlɑː/ *verb trans. & intrans. (imper. & impers.).* Also ***-la***. M18.
[French, from imper. of *voir* see + *là* there.]
There is, are, etc.; see there. As *interjection*, there it is!, there you are!
voilà tout /tu, tuː/ [French = all] that is all, there is nothing more to do or say.

voile /vɔɪl, vwal/ *noun & adjective.* L19.
[French = VEIL *noun.*]
▸ **A** *noun.* A lightweight open-texture material of cotton, wool, silk, or acetate, used esp. for blouses and dresses. L19.
▸ **B** *attrib.* or as *adjective.* Made of voile. L19.

voilette /ˈvɔɪlɛt, ˈvwalɛt/ *noun.* M19.
[French, dim. of *voile*: see prec., -ETTE.]
1 A little veil. M19.
2 A dress material resembling voile. E20.

voir dire /ˈvwɑː dɪə/ *noun.* Also **voire dire**. L17.
[Law French, from Old French *voir* true, truth + *dire* say.]
LAW. A preliminary examination by a judge or counsel of the competence of a witness or (occas.) a juror; an oath taken by such a witness. Also, an investigation into the truth or admissibility of evidence, held during a trial.

†**voisinage** *noun.* M17.
[French, from *voisin* neighbouring: cf. VICINAGE.]
1 The fact of being neighbouring or near; proximity. M–L17.
2 The neighbourhood; the adjoining district. Also foll. by *of* (a place). M17–E18.

voiture /ˈvwɑːtjʊə; *foreign* vwatyːr (*pl. same*)/ *noun.* L17.
[French from Latin *vectura.*]
Esp. in France and French-speaking countries: a carriage; a vehicle; a means of transport.

voiturette /vwɑːtjʊəˈrɛt; *foreign* vwatyrɛt (*pl. same*)/ *noun.* Now *rare.* L19.
[French, dim. of prec.: see -ETTE.]
Esp. in France and French-speaking countries: a small motor vehicle, *esp.* a motorized quadricycle.

voiturier /vwɑːˈtjʊərɪeɪ, -rɪə; *foreign* vwatyrje (*pl. same*)/ *noun.* M18.
[French, from VOITURE: see -IER.]
Chiefly *Hist.* Esp. in France and French-speaking countries: the driver of a carriage or coach.

voivode /ˈvɔɪvəʊd/ *noun.* Also **voivod**. L16.
[Bulgarian, Serbo-Croat *vojvoda*, Czech *vojvoda*, Polish *wojewoda* from Slavonic base also of VAIVODE. Cf. WAYWODE.]
A local governor or ruler in various parts of central and eastern Europe; *spec.* (***a***) *Hist.* any of the early semi-independent rulers of Transylvania; (***b***) an official in charge of an administrative district in modern Poland.
■ **voivodeship** *noun* the office of voivode; the district governed by a voivode: L18.

voix céleste /vwa selɛst, vwɑː sɪˈlɛst/ *noun phr.* Pl. ***voix célestes*** (pronounced same). L19.
[French = heavenly voice.]
An organ-stop having an 8-ft pitch, with 2 pipes to each note, tuned slightly apart, producing an undulating tone traditionally regarded as reminiscent of celestial voices. Also called ***vox angelica***.

vol /vɒl/ *noun*[1]. E18.
[French = flight, from *voler* from Latin *volare* to fly.]
HERALDRY. Two wings represented as joined at the base and displayed with the tips upward.

vol /vɒl/ *noun*[2]. Also **vol.** (point). L17.
[Abbreviation.]
1 = VOLUME *noun* 3. L17.
2 = VOLUME *noun* 7. M19.

vola /ˈvəʊlə/ *noun.* L17.
[Latin.]
ANATOMY. The hollow of the hand or foot.

volage /vɔˈlɑːʒ/ *adjective.* LME.
[Old & mod. French from Latin *volaticus*: see VOLATIC, -AGE.]
Giddy, foolish; fickle, inconstant.
¶ Formerly fully naturalized; now in literary use, reintroduced from mod. French.

Volans /ˈvəʊlənz/ *noun.* E20.
[Abbreviation of PISCIS VOLANS.]
(The name of) an inconspicuous constellation between Carina and the south celestial pole; the Flying Fish. Also called ***Piscis Volans***.

volant /ˈvəʊlənt/ *adjective & noun.* E16.
[French, pres. pple of *voler* fly, from Latin *volare*: see -ANT[1].]
▸ **A** *adjective.* **1** *Hist.* ***volant piece***, an addition to the front of a helmet as a protection for the face, used esp. in tournaments. E16.
†**2** MILITARY. Of a body of troops etc.: capable of rapid movement or action. M16–M17.
3 HERALDRY. Of a bird etc.: flying; having the wings expanded as if in flight. L16.
4 Passing rapidly through the air or space, as if by flight; floating lightly in the air. E17. ▸**b** Moving rapidly or lightly; active, nimble. M17.
5 Flying; able to fly, capable of flight. M17.
6 Of the nature of or characterized by flight. E19.
7 Flounced, frilled. E20.
▸ **B** *noun.* †**1** The state or position of remaining undecided or uncommitted between two parties, sides, or opinions. Chiefly in ***act the volant***, ***keep the volant***. Only in M18.
†**2** A volant piece. *rare.* M19.
3 A flounce on a dress, a frill. M19.
4 = VOLET. *rare.* L19.
■ **volantly** *adverb* L19.

volante /vəˈlanti/ *noun*[1]. L18.
[Spanish, from pres. pple of *volar* to fly, from Latin *volare*: cf. prec.]
A horse-drawn carriage or wagon, esp. of a two-wheeled covered type, used in Cuba and formerly in other Spanish-speaking countries.

volante /vəˈlanti/ *noun*[2]. L19.
[from Italian = flying.]
MUSIC. The rapid execution of a series of notes in singing or playing; *esp.* in violin-playing, a bowing technique in which the bow bounces from the string in a slurred staccato.

volapié /volaˈpje/ *noun*. M19.
[Spanish, lit. 'flying foot', from *volar* to fly + *pie* foot.]
BULLFIGHTING. A movement in which a bullfighter runs in to kill a stationary or slowly moving bull.

Volapük /ˈvɒləpʊk/ *noun*. Also **-puk**. L19.
[from *vol* repr. English *world* + connective *-a-* + *pük* repr. English *speak, speech*.]
An artificial language invented in 1879 for universal use by a German priest, J. M. Schleyer, and based on extremely modified forms of words from English and Romance languages, with a complex system of inflections. Also *transf.*, a universal language.
■ **Volapükist** *noun* an advocate or user of Volapük L19.

volar /ˈvəʊlə/ *adjective*. E19.
[from VOLA + -AR[1].]
ANATOMY. Of or pertaining to the palm of the hand or the sole of the foot; usu. *spec.*, designating the surface of the forearm continuous with the palm of the hand.

volary /ˈvəʊləri/ *noun*. Now *rare*. M17.
[French *volière*, from *voler* to fly, after words in -ARY[1].]
1 A large bird-cage; an aviary. M17.
†**2** *collect.* The birds kept in an aviary. L17–M18.

volatic /vəˈlatɪk/ *noun & adjective*. Now *rare* or *obsolete*. M17.
[Latin *volaticus* winged, inconstant, from *volat-*: see next, -IC.]
▶ **A** *noun*. A winged creature. *poet.* M17.
▶ **B** *adjective*. That flies or flits about. L17.

volatile /ˈvɒlətʌɪl/ *noun & adjective*. ME.
[Old French *volatil* (mod. *volatile*) or Latin *volatilis*, from *volat-* pa. ppl stem of *volare* to fly: see -ATILE.]
▶ **A** *noun*. †**1** *collect.* Birds; *esp.* wildfowl. ME–M17.
2 A winged creature; a bird, a butterfly, etc. Usu. in *pl.* Now *rare*. ME.
3 A volatile substance. L17.
▶ **B** *adjective*. †**1** Of meal: ground so fine as to fly about readily. Only in L16.
2 Of a substance: having the form of or readily converted to vapour; liable or susceptible to evaporation at ordinary temperatures. Formerly also, in a state liable to undergo or having undergone loss of weight on heating (due to evaporation, chemical combination, etc.). L16.
3 a Flying, capable of flying, volant. E17. ▶**b** Moving or flitting from one place to another, esp. with some speed. M17.
4 Of a person, the mind, etc.: readily changing from one interest or mood to another; flighty, fickle. Also more widely, characterized by unpredictable changes of emotion, fortune, etc. M17. ▶**b** Of a market, shares, etc.: showing sharp changes in price or value; unstable. M20.
5 Evanescent, transient; readily vanishing or disappearing; difficult to seize, retain, or fix permanently. M17. ▶**b** COMPUTING. Of a memory: retaining data only as long as there is a power supply connected. M20.
Special collocations: †**volatile alkali** ammonia. **volatile oil** an essential oil. **volatile salt** a solid substance which gives off a vapour; *spec.* = SAL VOLATILE.
¶ Cf. SAL VOLATILE.
■ **volatileness** *noun* (now *rare*) volatility L17.

volatilise *verb* var. of VOLATILIZE.

volatility /vɒləˈtɪlɪti/ *noun*. E17.
[from Latin *volatilis* VOLATILE *adjective*: see -ILITY.]
1 Readiness to vaporize or evaporate, especially at ordinary temperatures; the degree of this. E17.
2 Tendency to levity or flightiness; lack of steadiness or seriousness. Now *esp.*, unpredictability or changeableness of mood, behaviour, etc. M17.
3 Adaptability or capacity for flight. *rare*. E18.
4 Capacity for rapid movement. *rare*. L18.
5 COMPUTING. The property of a memory of not retaining data after the power supply is cut off. M20.

volatilize /vəˈlatɪlʌɪz, ˈvɒlətɪlʌɪz/ *verb*. Also **-ise**. M17.
[from VOLATILE *adjective* + -IZE.]
1 *verb trans.* Cause to evaporate, convert to vapour. Formerly, make volatile. M17. ▶**b** *fig.* Make light, airy, insubstantial, etc. M17.
2 *verb intrans.* Become volatile; evaporate. E18.
■ **volatilizable** *adjective* (*a*) readily evaporated, evaporable; †(*b*) able to be made volatile: E19. **volatiliˈzation** *noun* the action or process of making volatile; the state of being volatilized: M17. **volatilizer** *noun* an apparatus for volatilizing substances, a vaporizer L19.

volation /vəˈleɪʃ(ə)n/ *noun*. *rare*. M18.
[from Latin *volare* to fly + -ATION.]
The action of flying; = VOLITATION.

volatize /ˈvɒlətʌɪz/ *verb trans. & intrans*. Now *rare*. Also **-ise**. M17.
[from VOLAT(ILE *adjective* + -IZE.]
= VOLATILIZE.
■ †**volatization** *noun* (*rare*) = VOLATILIZATION M17–E19.

vol-au-vent /ˈvɒlə(ʊ)vɒ̃/ *noun*. E19.
[French, lit. 'flight in the wind'.]
A (usu. small) round flat-bottomed case of puff pastry filled with chopped meat, fish, egg, etc., in sauce.

volcan /ˈvɒlkən/ *noun*. Now *rare* or *obsolete*. L16.
[French, Spanish *volcán*, formed as VOLCANO.]
= VOLCANO *noun* 1.

volcanian /vɒlˈkeɪnɪən/ *adjective*. *rare*. E19.
[from VOLCANO + -IAN. Cf. VULCANIAN.]
= next.

volcanic /vɒlˈkanɪk/ *adjective & noun*. L18.
[French *volcanique*, from *volcan* VOLCANO + *-ique* -IC. Cf. VULCANIC.]
▶ **A** *adjective*. **1** Of or pertaining to a volcano or volcanoes; due to or formed by (the action of) a volcano or volcanoes; (of material) produced in or ejected by a volcano or volcanoes. L18.
2 a Characterized by the presence of volcanoes. L18. ▶**b** Of the nature of a volcano. M19.
3 *fig.* Resembling or characteristic of a volcano; violently explosive, capable of sudden and violent activity; (of the mind, emotions, etc.) intensely fervid or violent; full of latent or suppressed violence. E19.
1 volcanic ash loose fragmented solid material ejected from a volcano. ***volcanic bomb***: see BOMB *noun* 4. **volcanic glass** obsidian.
▶ **B** *noun*. A rock or mineral formed by volcanic action. Usu. in *pl.* L19.
■ **volcanically** *adverb* (*a*) with regard to volcanic nature or action; (*b*) in an explosive, eruptive, or fiery manner; with sudden violence: M19.

volcanicity /vɒlkəˈnɪsɪti/ *noun*. M19.
[French *volcanicité* or from (the same root as) prec.: see -ITY. Cf. VULCANICITY.]
Volcanic character; volcanic action or activity, volcanism.

volcaniclastic /vɒlˌkanɪˈklastɪk/ *adjective & noun*. M20.
[from VOLCANI(C + CLASTIC.]
GEOLOGY. ▶**A** *adjective*. Designating or pertaining to a clastic rock which contains volcanic material. M20.
▶ **B** *noun*. A volcaniclastic rock. M20.

volcanism /ˈvɒlkənɪz(ə)m/ *noun*. M19.
[French *volcanisme*, formed as VOLCANIC + -ISM. Cf. VULCANISM.]
The state or condition of being volcanic; volcanic action, volcanic phenomena collectively.

volcanist /ˈvɒlkənɪst/ *noun*. L18.
[French *volcaniste* or from VOLCANO + -IST. Cf. VULCANIST.]
1 = VULCANIST 2. L18.
2 A vulcanologist. E19.

volcanity /vɒlˈkanɪti/ *noun*. *rare*. L18.
[from VOLCAN(IC + -ITY.]
= VOLCANICITY.

volcano /vɒlˈkeɪnəʊ/ *noun & verb*. Also †**vul-**. E17.
[Italian from Latin *Volcanus*, *Vulcanus* VULCAN.]
▶ **A** *noun*. Pl. **-oes**.
1 A hill or mountain situated over an opening or openings in the earth's crust through which lava, cinders, steam, gases, etc. are or have been expelled continuously or at intervals. E17. ▶**b** A thing resembling a volcano, esp. in emitting smoke and flame. L18.
2 *fig.* **a** A violent feeling or passion, esp. in a suppressed state. L17. ▶**b** A state of things liable to burst out violently at some time. Freq. in ***sit on a volcano*** etc. M19.
1 ***active volcano***, ***extinct volcano***, ***shield volcano***, etc.
Comb.: **volcano rabbit** a small, dark brown rabbit, *Romerolagus diazi*, resembling a pika, having short ears and no tail, and found in the mountains of central Mexico.
▶ **B** *verb trans. & intrans.* Act or be like a volcano (towards). *rare*. M19.

volcanology /vɒlkəˈnɒlədʒi/ *noun*. L19.
[from prec. + -OLOGY.]
= VULCANOLOGY.
■ **volcanoˈlogic** *adjective* M20. **volcanoˈlogical** *adjective* L19. **volcanologist** *noun* L19.

vole /vəʊl/ *noun*[1]. L17.
[French, app. from *voler*, Latin *volare* to fly.]
CARDS. The winning of all the tricks in certain card-games, esp. écarté, quadrille, and ombre. Freq. in ***win the vole***.
go the vole run every risk in the hope of great gain; try every possibility.

vole /vəʊl/ *noun*[2]. E19.
[from Norwegian *voll* field (+ *mus* mouse).]
Orig. †***vole-mouse***. Any of various small thickset short-tailed herbivorous rodents of the genus *Microtus* and related genera of the family Muridae, widespread in cold and temperate parts of the northern hemisphere.
meadow vole, ***Orkney vole***, ***pine vole***, ***red-backed vole***, ***snow vole***, ***water-vole***, etc. **bank vole** a relatively long-tailed vole, *Clethrionomys glareolus*, of Eurasian woodland and scrub. **common vole** a light-coloured Eurasian vole, *Microtus arvalis*, found in the British Isles only in Guernsey and Orkney. **field vole** a vole of Eurasian grassland, *Microtus agrestis*.

volens /ˈvəʊlɛnz/ *adjective*. L19.
[Latin, pres. pple of *velle*: see next.]
LAW. Consenting to the risk of injury.

volent /ˈvəʊlənt/ *adjective*. M17.
[Latin *volent-* pres. ppl stem of *velle* will, wish, desire: see -ENT.]
Exercising or capable of exercising will or choice in one's conduct or course of action.

volet /ˈvɒleɪ; *foreign* vɔlɛ (*pl. same*)/ *noun*. M19.
[Old & mod. French, lit. 'shutter', from *voler* from Latin *volare* to fly: see -ET[1].]
Each of the wings or side-compartments of a triptych. Also called ***volant***.

volitant /ˈvɒlɪt(ə)nt/ *adjective*. Chiefly *literary*. M19.
[Latin *volitant-* pres. ppl stem of *volitare* frequentative of *volare* to fly: see -ANT[1].]
Flitting, flying, constantly moving about; capable of flying.

volitate /ˈvɒlɪteɪt/ *verb intrans*. Chiefly *literary*. E17.
[Latin *volitat-* pa. ppl stem of *volitare*: see prec., -ATE[3].]
†**1** Fly about; run to and fro. Only in Dicts. E–M17.
2 Fly with a fluttering motion. M19.

volitation /vɒlɪˈteɪʃ(ə)n/ *noun*. Chiefly *literary*. M17.
[Late Latin *volitatio(n-)*, formed as prec.: see -ATION.]
Flying, flight. Also, an act of flying or (*fig.*) gadding about.

volition /vəˈlɪʃ(ə)n/ *noun*. E17.
[French, or directly from Latin *volitio(n-)*, from *volo*, *velle* to wish, to will: see -ITION.]
1 An act of willing or resolving something; a decision or choice made after due consideration or deliberation. Now *rare*. E17.
2 The action of consciously willing or resolving something; the making of a definite choice or decision regarding a course of action; exercise of the will. M17.
3 The power or faculty of willing; will-power. M18.

> 📖 **2** I. MURDOCH I don't know when it would have occurred to us to leave of our own volition. **3** J. UGLOW She is totally deprived of volition, . . directed by agencies beyond her . . control.

■ **volitionless** *adjective* L19.

volitional /vəˈlɪʃ(ə)n(ə)l/ *adjective*. E19.
[from prec. + -AL[1].]
1 Of or pertaining to volition or the action of willing or resolving something. E19.
2 Possessing the faculty of volition; exercising or capable of exercising will. E19.
3 Of a force: leading or impelling to action. *rare*. M19.
4 Of an action, etc.: arising from or characterized by the exercise of volition or will; *esp.* (PHYSIOLOGY) = VOLUNTARY *adjective* 3. M19.
■ **volitioˈnality** *noun* the quality or state of being volitional L19. **volitionally** *adverb* with respect to volition; in a volitional manner: L19.

volitionary /vəˈlɪʃ(ə)n(ə)ri/ *adjective*. *rare*. L19.
[from VOLITION *noun* + -ARY[1].]
= VOLITIONAL.

volitive /ˈvɒlɪtɪv/ *adjective & noun*. L15.
[medieval Latin *volitivus*, from *volitio(n-)*: see VOLITION, -IVE.]
▶ **A** *adjective*. **1** Of or pertaining to the will; volitional. L15.
2 Performed deliberately or with express intention. M19.
3 GRAMMAR. Expressive of a wish or desire; = DESIDERATIVE *adjective* 1. M19.
▶ **B** *noun*. GRAMMAR. = DESIDERATIVE *noun*. E19.

volitorial /vɒlɪˈtɔːrɪəl/ *adjective*. Now *rare* or *obsolete*. L19.
[from mod. Latin *Volitores* noun pl., birds capable of flight + -IAL.]
Of or pertaining to flying; having the power of flight.

volk /fɒlk/ *noun*. Also **V-**. L19.
[Afrikaans (from Dutch), German = nation, people: see FOLK.]
1 The Afrikaner people. Also (freq. *derog.*), the non-white employees of a white (esp. Afrikaner) master collectively. *S. Afr.* L19.
2 The German people (esp. with ref. to Nazi ideology). M20.
Comb.: **volkspele** /ˈfɔlkspiːlə/ [Afrikaans *spele* games] *S. Afr.* Afrikaner folk-dances; **Volkspolizei** /ˈfɔlkspɒlɪˌtsʌɪ/ [German POLIZEI] *Hist.* a police force of the German Democratic Republic (cf. VOPO); **volkswil** /ˈfɔlksvɪl/ *S. Afr.* the will of the people (*spec.* of the Afrikaner people).

Völkerwanderung /ˈfœlkərˌvandərʊŋ, ˈfəːlkəˌvɑːndərʊŋ/ *noun*. Pl. **-en** /-ən/. M20.
[German, from *Völker* nations + *Wanderung* migration.]
A migration of peoples; *spec.* that of Germanic and Slavonic peoples into and across Europe from the second to the eleventh centuries.

völkisch /ˈfœlkɪʃ/ *adjective*. M20.
[German.]
Populist, nationalist, racialist.

Volksdeutscher /ˈfɔlksdɔytʃər, ˈfɒlksdɔɪtʃə/ *noun*. Pl. **-tsche** /-tʃə/. M20.
[German, from *Volks-* combining form of *Volk* (see VOLK) + *Deutscher* a German.]
A person of German origin living outside Germany and Austria; an ethnic German.
■ **Volksdeutsch** *adjective* of, pertaining to, or characteristic of the *Volksdeutsche* M20.

volkslied /ˈfɒlksliːd, -t/ *noun*. Pl. **-lieder** /-liːdə/. Also **V-**. M19.
[German, Afrikaans (from Dutch), formed as prec. + LIED.]
1 A German folk-song; a song or other piece of music in the style of German folk-songs. M19.
2 A national anthem; *spec*. (*Hist.*) that of the 19th-cent. Transvaal Republic. Also, a S. African folk-song. *S. Afr.* L19.

volley /ˈvɒli/ *noun*. L16.
[Old & mod. French *volée*, ult. from Latin *volare* to fly: see -Y⁵.]
1 A simultaneous discharge of a number of firearms or other weapons; a salvo; a shower of arrows, stones, etc. Freq. foll. by *of* (weapons, shots, etc.). L16. ▸**b** A storm or shower of hail, rain, etc. *poet.* M18.
2 a An uttering or outpouring *of* many words, shouts, laughs, etc., in rapid succession. Freq. foll. by *of*. L16. ▸**b** A rapid succession or (almost) simultaneously occurring group of sharp sounds, nervous impulses, etc. E17.
†**3** A crowd or large number *of* persons or things. L16–L17.
4 TENNIS (orig. REAL TENNIS), CRICKET & FOOTBALL etc. The flight of a ball in play before it has touched the ground; a stroke or shot in which a ball is hit or kicked before it has touched the ground. L16.

🕮 **1** G. P. R. JAMES Another volley shot rang out from behind the gateway. LD MACAULAY The royal troops . . fired such a volley of musketry as sent the rebel horse flying. J. G. FARRELL Another deadly volley . . and scarcely a man was left on his feet. **2a** W. CATHER Marie broke out with a volley of questions. **4** *Tennis* After my . . serve, I was going to hit a volley down the line. ***half-volley***: see HALF-. **on the volley** (*a*) (TENNIS, CRICKET, & FOOTBALL etc.) without waiting for the ball to bounce; †(*b*) *fig.* [after French *à la volée*] without consideration.

Comb.: **volley-firing** simultaneous firing at the word of command by successive parties of soldiers.

volley /ˈvɒli/ *verb*. L16.
[from the noun.]
▸ **I** *verb trans*. **1** Utter (words etc.) rapidly or impetuously. Usu. foll. by adverbs, as *off*, *out*. Chiefly *literary*. L16.
2 a Discharge (arrows, shot, etc.) in a volley. Orig. & chiefly as **volleyed** *ppl adjective*. M18. ▸**b** Fire a volley or volleys at. *rare*. E20.
3 Hit or strike (a ball) in a volley; *spec*. (*a*) (TENNIS etc.) return (a ball) in play before it touches the ground; (*b*) FOOTBALL kick (the ball) before it touches the ground; score (a goal) in this way; (*c*) CRICKET bowl or deliver (a ball) which reaches the batsman before bouncing. L19.
▸ **II** *verb intrans*. **4** Fire a volley or volleys. E17.
5 a Emit or produce short sounds simultaneously or in continuous succession. E19. ▸**b** Issue or be discharged in or like a volley; rush or stream with great rapidity; shoot rapidly. M19.
6 SPORT. Hit or return the ball before it bounces; make a volley. E19.
6 ***serve-and-volley***: see SERVE *verb*¹.
■ **volleyer** *noun* (SPORT) a person who volleys L19.

volleyball /ˈvɒlɪbɔːl/ *noun*. L19.
[from VOLLEY *noun*, *verb* + BALL *noun*¹.]
A game for two teams (now usu. of six players) in which a large ball is hit by the fingers, fist, or forearm over a high net without its touching the ground. Also, the ball used in this game.

volost /ˈvolost/ *noun*. L19.
[Russian *volost′*.]
Hist. In pre-revolutionary Russia and the USSR, an administrative subdivision, the smallest used in rural areas (abolished in 1930).

volplane /ˈvɒlpleɪn/ *noun* & *verb*. E20.
[French *vol plané*, from *vol* flight + *plané* pa. pple of *planer* PLANE *verb*².]
▸ **A** *noun*. A controlled dive or downward flight at a steep angle, esp. by an aeroplane with the engine stopped or shut off. E20.
▸ **B** *verb intrans*. Of an aeroplane, bird, etc.: make a volplane. E20.

Volscian /ˈvɒlʃ(ə)n/ *noun* & *adjective*. E16.
[from Latin *Volscus*, pl. *Volsci* + -IAN.]
▸ **A** *noun*. **1** *Hist.* A member of an ancient warlike people formerly inhabiting the east of Latium in central Italy, subdued by the Romans in the 4th cent. BC. E16.
2 The Italic language spoken by the Volscians. M19.
▸ **B** *adjective*. Of or pertaining to the Volscians or their language. E17.
■ Earlier †**Volsce** *noun* = VOLSCIAN *noun* 1 LME–E17.

volsella, **volsellum** *nouns* vars. of VULSELLA, VULSELLUM.

Volstead /ˈvɒlstɪd/ *noun*. E20.
[A. J. *Volstead* (1860–1947), American legislator and originator of the prohibition Act passed in 1919 by the US Congress.]
US HISTORY. Used *attrib*. to designate the legislation which enforced alcohol prohibition in the US or the period (1920–33) during which it was in force.
■ **Volsteadism** *noun* (US HISTORY) the policy of the Volstead Act; prohibition: E20.

volt /vəʊlt, vɒlt/ *noun*¹. L19.
[from A. *Volta*: see VOLTAIC *adjective*¹.]
PHYSICS etc. The SI unit of electromotive force; the difference of electric potential capable of sending a constant current of one ampere through a conductor whose resistance is one ohm (formerly, with a power dissipation of one watt). (Symbol V.)
kilovolt, ***millivolt***, etc. ***electronvolt***: see ELECTRON *noun*².
¶ Orig. suggested as the name for the unit of resistance (ohm).

volt *noun*² var. of VOLTE.

volt /vɒlt, vəʊlt/ *verb*¹. M17.
[French *volter*, formed as VOLTE.]
†**1** *verb intrans*. & *refl*. Turn (oneself) round or over; *fig.* perform a volte-face. *rare*. M–L17.
2 *verb intrans*. FENCING. Make a volte. Now *rare*. L17.
†**3** *verb intrans*. Leap; = VAULT *verb*² 2. *rare*. Only in M18.

volt /vəʊlt, vɒlt/ *verb*². *literary*. M20.
[from VOLT *noun*¹.]
1 *verb trans*. Charge (something) as with electricity; energize; shock. M20.
2 *verb intrans*. Travel like an electric current. M20.

volta /ˈvɒltə/ *noun*. L16.
[Italian = turn: see VOLTE.]
= LAVOLTA.

volta- /ˈvɒltə/ *combining form*. Now *rare* or *obsolete*.
[from VOLTAIC *adjective*¹.]
Voltaic, as ***volta-electric***, ***volta-electricity***, etc.

voltage /ˈvəʊltɪdʒ, ˈvɒltɪdʒ/ *noun*. L19.
[from VOLT *noun*¹ + -AGE.]
Electromotive force or potential difference, esp. expressed in volts.

🕮 ***high voltage***, ***low voltage***, ***overvoltage***, ***screen voltage***, ***surge voltage***, etc. *fig.*: *Times* Walton's first symphony is a work of extraordinarily high voltage.

Comb.: **voltage clamp** *noun* & *verb* (PHYSIOLOGY) (*a*) *noun* (the application of) a constant voltage artificially maintained across a cell membrane; (*b*) *verb trans*. apply a voltage clamp to (chiefly as ***voltage-clamped*** *ppl adjective*, ***voltage-clamping*** *verbal noun*); **voltage-controlled** *adjective* controllable by varying the applied voltage; **voltage divider** a linear resistor or series of resistors which can be tapped at any intermediate point to produce a specific fraction of the voltage applied between its ends.

voltaic /vɒlˈteɪɪk/ *adjective*¹. E19.
[from Alessandro *Volta* (1745–1827), Italian scientist + -IC.]
Of or pertaining to electricity produced by chemical action in a primary battery; *arch.* designating such electricity; = GALVANIC 1.
voltaic battery, **voltaic cell** = GALVANIC ***battery***. **voltaic pile** = GALVANIC ***pile***.
■ **voltaically** *adverb* (*arch.*) by means of or in respect of voltaic electricity; in the manner of a voltaic battery: M19.

Voltaic /vɒlˈteɪɪk/ *adjective*² & *noun*. M20.
[from the River *Volta* in W. Africa + -IC.]
▸ **A** *adjective*. Of or pertaining to a group of Niger-Congo languages of W. Africa; of or pertaining to Burkina Faso (formerly Upper Volta). Cf. UPPER VOLTAN *adjective* & *noun*. M20.
▸ **B** *noun*. **1** The group of Voltaic languages. M20.
2 A speaker of a Voltaic language; *esp.* a native or inhabitant of Burkina Faso. L20.

Voltairean /vɒlˈtɛːrɪən/ *adjective* & *noun*. Also (earlier) **-ian**. L18.
[from de *Voltaire*, name adopted by François Marie Arouet (1694–1778), French writer: see -EAN, -IAN.]
▸ **A** *adjective*. Of or pertaining to Voltaire; resembling Voltaire, esp. in a mocking and sceptical attitude characteristic of his opinions and views. L18.
▸ **B** *noun*. A follower or adherent of Voltaire in respect of opinions or the manner of expressing them; a person whose views on social and religious questions are characterized by a critical and mocking scepticism. M19.
■ **Voltaireanism** *noun* = VOLTAIRISM M19. **Voltairism** *noun* a thing characteristic of Voltaire; the body of opinions and views expressed by Voltaire; the mocking and sceptical attitude characteristic of these: L18.

voltaism /ˈvɒltəɪz(ə)m/ *noun*. Now *arch.* or *Hist.* E19.
[formed as VOLTAIC *adjective*¹ + -ISM.]
= GALVANISM 1.

voltameter /vɒlˈtamɪtə/ *noun*. M19.
[from VOLTA- + -METER.]
= COULOMETER.

voltammetry /vəʊlˈtamɪtri, vɒlt-/ *noun*. M20.
[from VOLT *noun*¹ + AM(PERE + -METRY.]
PHYSICAL CHEMISTRY. An electro-analytical technique for identifying and finding the concentrations of various ions in solution by plotting the relation of current and voltage in a micro-electrode.
■ **voltaˈmmetric** *adjective* M20. **voltaˈmmetrically** *adverb* by means of voltammetry M20.

volte /vɒlt, vəʊlt/ *noun*. Also (now *rare*) **volt**. L16.
[French from Italian *volta* turn, use as noun of fem. pa. pple of *volgere* to turn, from Latin *volvere* roll.]
†**1** = LAVOLTA. L16–E17.
2 FENCING (now *Hist.*). A sudden jump or other movement to avoid a thrust; *spec.* a swinging round of the rear leg to turn the body sideways. L17.
3 HORSEMANSHIP. A small circle of determined size (properly with a radius equal to the length of a horse); a movement by a horse sideways around the point of such a circle. E18.
4 (A) complete change. *rare*. E20.

volte-face /vɒltˈfɑːs, -ˈfas/ *noun*. E19.
[French from Italian *voltafaccia*, from *voltare* to turn (ult. from frequentative of Latin *volvere* roll) + *faccia* (ult. from Latin *facies*) face.]
The act or an instance of turning so as to face in the opposite direction. Chiefly *fig.*, a complete change of attitude, opinion, or position in an argument.

🕮 *Insight* Mitterrand's abrupt volte-face on the question of command and control.

Volterra /vɒlˈtɛrə/ *noun*. E20.
[A town in Tuscany, western Italy.]
Volterra alabaster, ***Volterra marble***, a form of alabaster quarried around Volterra.
■ **Volterran** *adjective* of or pertaining to Volterra M20.

voltinism /ˈvɒltɪnɪz(ə)m/ *noun*. E20.
[from *-voltine* in BIVOLTINE, UNIVOLTINE + -ISM.]
The number of broods typically produced per year by a population of a particular insect species.

voltmeter /ˈvəʊltmiːtə, ˈvɒlt-/ *noun*. L19.
[from VOLT *noun*¹ + -METER.]
An instrument for measuring electric potential in volts.
millivoltmeter: see MILLIVOLT. ***peak voltmeter***: see PEAK *noun*¹.

†**volubilis** *noun*. M16–E18.
[from Latin: see VOLUBLE.]
Bindweed, convolvulus.

volubility /vɒljʊˈbɪlɪti/ *noun*. L16.
[French *volubilité* or Latin *volubilitas*, from *volubilis*: see next, -ITY.]
†**1** Quickness in turning from one subject to another; versatility. *rare*. L16–E17.
2 The capacity of revolving, rolling, or turning round; ability to rotate about an axis or centre. Now *rare*. L16.
3 The character or state of being voluble in speech; great fluency of language; garrulousness. L16. ▸**b** Smooth or copious flow of verse or poetic utterance. Now *rare*. L16.
†**4** Capacity for rapid motion, *spec*. in an easy or gliding manner. E–M17.
†**5** Tendency to change or turn from one condition to another; changeableness, inconstancy. Only in 17.

🕮 **3** H. JAMES The charming visitor . . began to chatter with her usual volubility.

voluble /ˈvɒljʊb(ə)l/ *adjective*. LME.
[French, or directly from Latin *volubilis*, from *volu-*: see VOLUME *noun*, -UBLE.]
1 a Capable of or exhibiting ready rotation about a point or axis. Now *rare*. LME. ▸**b** BOTANY. Twisting round other plants; twining. M18.
2 Liable to change; inconstant, variable, mutable. Now *rare*. LME.
3 Moving rapidly and easily, esp. with a gliding or undulating movement. Now *rare*. L16.
4 Of a person, the tongue, etc.: characterized by fluent, vehement, or incessant speech. Of speech etc.: characterized by great fluency or readiness of utterance. L16.

🕮 **4** J. CARY She suddenly broke into voluble animated speech. W. PLOMER Mrs Bunstable was voluble, but I was hardly prepared for the flood of words.

■ **volubleness** *noun* E17. **volubly** *adverb* E17.

volume /ˈvɒljuːm/ *noun*. LME.
[Old French *volum*, (also mod.) *volume* from Latin *volumen* roll (of writing), book, etc., from *volu-* var. of base of *volvere* to roll. Cf. VOL *noun*².]
▸ **I 1** *Hist.* A roll of parchment, papyrus, etc., containing written matter; a literary work, or part of one, recorded or preserved in the form of a scroll. LME.
2 A collection of written or printed sheets bound together to form a book; a tome. LME.
3 Each of two or more usu. separately bound portions into which a work of some size is divided; each of a number of books forming a related set or series. E16.

4 *fig.* A thing which is comparable to a book, esp. in containing matter for study. **L16.**

> 1 *Times* The codex, or hinged book . . took the place of the volume or roll. **2** I. MURDOCH Several well-worn and learned-looking volumes from the London Library. ***omnibus volume, slim volume***, etc. **3** A. N. WILSON Lewis was writing the second volume of his space trilogy.

▶ **II** †**5** Size or extent (of a book). **M16–M18.**

6 The bulk, size, or magnitude of a mass of substance, an object, a number of things considered in bulk, etc., in terms of material content or esp. of space occupied or enclosed in three dimensions; the bulk or mass of a body of moving water etc. Freq. foll. by *of*. **E17.** ▸**b** The amount or quantity of something, esp. considered in relation to a continuing process; the number of things so considered in bulk; *COMMERCE* the number of transactions etc. in a given period. **L19.**

7 A quantity or mass (esp. a large one) regarded as matter occupying space; *CHEMISTRY* a determinate quantity or amount of a substance, in terms of bulk or space occupied. **M17.**

8 Without article: bulk, size, spacial extent in three dimensions. **L18.**

9 a *MUSIC.* Richness or fullness of tone. **E19.** ▸**b** Quantity, strength, or power of sound; loudness. **E19.**

> 6 D. ATTENBOROUGH Maintaining body temperature is easier . . the lower the ratio between . . volume and surface area. J. PURSEGLOVE The deepened channel . . designed to accommodate a given volume of water. ***atomic volume, critical volume, specific volume, swept volume***, etc. **b** C. WARWICK The volume of traffic . . was increased to bursting point. *Guardian* Retail sales volume grew by 0.8 per cent in the second quarter. *Fantasy* The volume of manuscripts has increased considerably over the last three years. **7** J. TYNDALL One volume of chlorine combines with one volume of hydrogen. **9b** M. DE LA ROCHE She began to sing, softly at first, but gaining in volume.

▶ **III 10** A coil, a wreath, a convolution; a coiled or rolling mass. Chiefly *poet.* **M17.**

Phrases: **speak volumes**, **express volumes**, **tell volumes** be highly expressive or significant.

Comb.: **volume control** (a knob etc. allowing) control of the volume of sound, esp. when reproduced or transmitted; **volume-density** the number *of* things per unit volume; **volume indicator** *ELECTRONICS* a device for measuring the power of a complex electrical signal corresponding to a sound pattern, to indicate the volume of the sound so represented; **volume table** *FORESTRY* a set of empirically derived figures relating the volume of timber in a given type of tree or log to measurable parameters such as height and girth, enabling estimation of timber yields; **volume unit** a unit equal in magnitude to the decibel, used for calibrating volume indicators, a sine wave of a power of one milliwatt being assigned a reference value of zero; usu. abbreviation *VU*.

▪ **volumeless** *adjective* (esp. in *PHYSICAL CHEMISTRY*, of an idealized polymer chain) occupying no volume **M20.**

volume /ˈvɒljuːm/ *verb.* **E19.**
[from the noun.]

1 a *verb trans.* Send up or pour out (smoke, sound, etc.) in volumes. **E19.** ▸**b** *verb intrans.* Rise or roll in or like a cloud or dense mass. **E19.**

2 *verb trans.* Collect or bind in a volume or book. Cf. earlier **VOLUMED** *adjective* 1. **M19.**

volumed /ˈvɒljuːmd/ *adjective.* **L16.**
[from **VOLUME** *noun* + **-ED**².]

1 Made into a volume or volumes (of a specified size, number, etc.); provided with books. **L16.**

2 Formed into a rolling, rounded, or dense mass. **E19.**

volumen /vəˈljuːmɛn/ *noun.* Pl. **-mina** /-mɪnə/. **M16.**
[Latin: see **VOLUME** *noun*.]

†**1** A volume, a book. Only in **M16.**

2 A roll (*of* parchment, etc.). **M19.**

volumenometer /vɒljuːməˈnɒmɪtə/ *noun.* **M19.**
[from Latin *volumen* **VOLUME** *noun* + **-OMETER.**]

An instrument for measuring the volume of a solid by the displacement of liquid or gas.

volumetric /vɒljʊˈmɛtrɪk/ *adjective.* **M19.**
[from **VOLU(ME** *noun* + **-METRIC.**]

Of, pertaining to, or involving measurement by volume.

volumetric analysis *CHEMISTRY* determination of the concentration, acidity, etc., of a liquid or solution by measuring the volume of a specific added reagent required for the completion of a particular reaction, esp. by titration. **volumetric efficiency** *MECHANICS* the ratio of the volume of fluid actually displaced by a piston or plunger to its swept volume.

volumetrical /vɒljʊˈmɛtrɪk(ə)l/ *adjective.* **M19.**
[formed as prec. + **-ICAL.**]
= **VOLUMETRIC** *adjective.*

volumetrically /vɒljʊˈmɛtrɪk(ə)li/ *adverb.* **M19.**
[from **VOLUMETRIC, VOLUMETRICAL**: see **-ICALLY.**]

By means of the measurement of volume; *esp.* by volumetric analysis. Also, as regards (the measurement of) volume.

volumetry /ˈvɒljʊmɪtri/ *noun. rare.* **M19.**
[formed as **VOLUMETRIC**: see **-METRY.**]

The scientific measurement of volume; *esp.* volumetric analysis.

volumina *noun* pl. of **VOLUMEN.**

voluminal /vəˈljuːmɪn(ə)l/ *adjective.* **L19.**
[from Latin *volumin-*, *volumen* **VOLUME** *noun*: see **-AL**¹.]

PHYSICS etc. Of, pertaining to, or possessing volume.

voluminous /vəˈljuːmɪnəs/ *adjective.* **E17.**
[Partly from late Latin *voluminosus* with many coils, sinuous; partly directly from Latin *volumin-*, *volumen* **VOLUME** *noun*: see **-OUS.**]

1 Full of turnings or windings; containing or consisting of many coils or convolutions. Now *rare.* **E17.**

2 Producing many books; writing or speaking at great length. **E17.**

3 Forming a large volume; consisting of many volumes. **E17.**

4 Extremely full or copious; forming a large mass or collection; *gen.* extensive, vast. **M17.**

5 Of great volume or size; massive, bulky, large; (of drapery etc.) loose and ample. **M17.**

> 2 *New Left Review* The most ardent and voluminous advocate of women's liberation. **3** D. PIPER His voluminous book on Milton's work. **4** R. K. NARAYAN My notes on this are voluminous. **5** N. BLAKE Petrov produced an envelope from the pocket of his voluminous overcoat. J. GATHORNE-HARDY Her nightdress spreading out round her voluminous as a tent.

▪ **voluminosity** /-ˈnɒsɪti/ *noun* the state of being voluminous; *rare* an instance of this: **L18.** **voluminously** *adverb* **M17.** **voluminousness** *noun* **M17.**

volumize /ˈvɒljuːmʌɪz/ *verb trans.* Also **-ise.** **L20.**
[from **VOLUME** *noun* + **-IZE.**]

Of a shampoo or other product: add body to or enhance the thickness of (hair). Freq. as ***volumizing ppl adjective.***

▪ **volumizer** *noun* **L20.**

voluntariate /vɒlənˈtɛːrɪət/ *noun.* **L19.**
[French *volontariat*, from *volontaire*, †*voluntaire* **VOLUNTARY** *adjective*: see **-ATE**¹.]

Voluntary service, esp. of a military character.

voluntarily /ˈvɒlənt(ə)rɪli, vɒlənˈtɛrɪli/ *adverb.* **LME.**
[from **VOLUNTARY** *adjective* + **-LY**².]

1 Of one's own free will or accord; without compulsion, constraint, or undue influence by others; freely, willingly. **LME.**

2 Without other determining force than natural character or tendency; naturally, spontaneously. Now *rare.* **M16.**

†**3** At will, at pleasure; extempore. Only in **L17.**

> 1 A. KENNY His lectures were so popular that we would turn up voluntarily to attend them.

voluntarism /ˈvɒləntərɪz(ə)m/ *noun.* **M19.**
[Irreg. from **VOLUNTARY** *adjective* + **-ISM.** Cf. **VOLUNTARYISM.**]

1 Chiefly *Hist.* The principle that the Church or schools should be independent of the State and supported by voluntary contributions. **M19.**

2 *PHILOSOPHY.* A theory or doctrine which regards will as the fundamental principle or dominant factor in the individual or in the universe. **L19.**

3 The principle of relying on voluntary action or participation rather than compulsion, esp. as regards the involvement of voluntary organizations in social welfare. **M20.**

voluntarist /ˈvɒlənt(ə)rɪst/ *noun & adjective.* **M19.**
[formed as prec. + **-IST.**]

▶ **A** *noun.* An advocate or adherent of voluntarism or voluntaryism; *esp.* an advocate of voluntary military service as opp. to conscription. **M19.**

▶ **B** *adjective.* Of, pertaining to, or characteristic of voluntarists. **E20.**

▪ **voluntaˈristic** *adjective* (*a*) of or pertaining to voluntarists or voluntarism; (*b*) of or pertaining to voluntary action: **E20.**

voluntary /ˈvɒlənt(ə)ri/ *adjective, adverb, & noun.* **LME.**
[Partly directly from Latin *voluntarius*, from *voluntas* will, partly after Old & mod. French *volontaire*, †*voluntaire* **VOLUNTEER** *noun*: see **-ARY**¹.]

▶ **A** *adjective.* **1** Of a feeling, sentiment, etc.: arising or developing in the mind without external constraint; purely spontaneous in origin or character. **LME.**

2 Of an action: performed or done of one's own free will, impulse, or choice; not constrained, prompted, or suggested by another. Also more widely, left to choice, not required or imposed, optional. **LME.** ▸**b** Of an oath, a confession, etc.: voluntarily made or given; not imposed or prompted by a promise or threat. **L16.** ▸**c** *LAW.* Of a conveyance, a disposition, etc.: made without money or other consideration being given or promised in return. **E17.** ▸†**d** Growing wild or naturally; of spontaneous growth. Cf. **VOLUNTEER** *noun* 3, *adjective* 4. *rare.* **E17–E18.**

3 *PHYSIOLOGY.* Of a bodily action: subject to or controlled by the will; under conscious control. **LME.** ▸**b** Of a muscle, etc.: acting or moving in response to the will; directing or controlling voluntary movements. **L18.**

4 a Assumed or adopted by free choice; freely chosen or undertaken; (of work) unpaid. **LME.** ▸**b** Brought about by one's own choice or deliberate action; self-inflicted, self-induced. **M16.** ▸**c** Of a society, association, etc.: entered into of free choice. Also, consisting of volunteers. **E17.**

5 Done by deliberate intent; designed, intentional. **L15.**

†**6** Of the will: free, unforced, unconstrained. **E–M16.**

7 Of a person: acting from personal choice or impulse, willingly, or spontaneously, in a specified capacity. Also, endowed with the faculty of willing. **L16.** ▸†**b** Serving as a volunteer soldier. Also, composed of such volunteers. **L16–M17.**

8 Freely or spontaneously bestowed or made; contributed from personal choice or impulse or from generous or charitable motives. **L16.**

†**9** Favourably inclined or disposed (*to* do something); willing, ready. **L16–M18.**

10 Of an institution, organization, etc.: maintained or supported solely or largely by voluntary contributions. Also more widely, existing through voluntary support, not established by statute; *spec.* in the UK, (of a school) built by a voluntary institution but maintained by a local education authority. **M18.** ▸**b** Of, pertaining to, or advocating voluntarism in respect of the Church, schools, etc. **M19.**

> 1 J. RUSKIN Were faith not voluntary, it could not be praised. **2** J. F. KENNEDY The essence of a democracy is voluntary action and co-operation. *Independent* Hand-written records are outside the law and subject only to a new voluntary code. **4a** F. HOYLE We could also choose . . activities that exposed us to voluntary dangers. *Guardian* Dockers made redundant . . after their company went into voluntary liquidation.

Special collocations: **Voluntary Aid Detachment** (in the UK) an organization of voluntary first-aid and nursing workers, founded in 1909. **voluntary patient** a person who enters a mental hospital without being committed to it. **Voluntary Service Overseas** a British organization promoting voluntary work in developing countries. **voluntary simplicity** a philosophy or way of life that rejects materialism in favour of human and spiritual values, and is characterized by minimal consumption, environmental responsibility, and community cooperation.

▶ **B** *adverb.* = **VOLUNTARILY** *adverb.* Now *rare.* **L15.**

▶ **C** *noun.* **1** †**a** Music added to a piece at the will of the performer. **M–L16.** ▸**b** An extempore musical performance, esp. as a prelude to more elaborate music. **L16.** ▸**c** An organ solo played before, during, or after a Church service or other religious or formal ceremony; the music for such a piece. **E18.**

†**2** Free will or choice. Chiefly in ***of a person's own voluntary, out of a person's own voluntary, at a person's own voluntary, at voluntary.*** **L16–M17.**

3 *ellipt.* A thing which is voluntary, as a voluntary oath, an extempore or voluntary piece of writing, etc.; in competitions, a special performance left to the performer's choice. Also, a voluntary organization. **L16.**

†**4** A person serving voluntarily, and usually without pay, as a soldier in a campaign, battle, etc.; = **VOLUNTEER** *noun* 1. **L16–L17.**

5 A person who undertakes or engages in some action, enterprise, etc., of his own choice or free will; = **VOLUNTEER** *noun* 2. Now *rare.* **L16.**

6 = **VOLUNTARYIST.** **M19.**

7 A rider's fall from a horse. Esp. in ***cut a voluntary.*** *colloq.* **M19.**

▪ **voluntariness** *noun* **E17.**

voluntaryism /ˈvɒlənt(ə)rɪɪz(ə)m/ *noun.* Now *rare.* **M19.**
[from **VOLUNTARY** *adjective* + **-ISM.**]
= **VOLUNTARISM** 1, 3.

▪ **voluntaryist** *noun* an advocate or adherent of voluntaryism **M19.**

voluntative /ˈvɒləntətɪv, -teɪtɪv/ *adjective & noun.* **M17.**
[from Latin *voluntat-*, *voluntas* + **-IVE** (see **-ATIVE**) after *cohortative*, *desiderative*, etc.]

▶ **A** *adjective.* †**1** Proceeding from the will; wilful. Only in Dicts. Only in **M17.**

2 *GRAMMAR.* = **VOLITIVE** *adjective* 3. **L19.**

3 Pertaining to voluntary action. *rare.* **L19.**

▶ **B** *noun. GRAMMAR.* = **VOLITIVE** *noun.* **L19.**

volunteer /vɒlənˈtɪə/ *noun & adjective.* Also †**-tier.** **L16.**
[Old & mod. French *volontaire*, †*voluntaire*, from Latin *voluntarius* (pl., sc. *milites* soldiers) **VOLUNTARY** *adjective*, assim. to **-IER, -EER.**]

▶ **A** *noun.* **1** *MILITARY.* **a** A person who voluntarily enrols for military service, a soldier who has not been conscripted. **L16.** ▸**b** *spec.* A member of an organized military or paramilitary company or force, formed by voluntary enrolment and distinct from a regular army; *Hist.* a member of any of the corps formerly organized and provided by the State with instructors, arms, etc. **M17.**

2 A person who voluntarily offers his or her services in any capacity; a person who voluntarily takes part in an enterprise. **M17.**

3 A plant which grows spontaneously without being planted; a self-sown plant. **M17.**
†**4** *ellipt.* A thing which is voluntary; a deliberate lie; a voluntary gift. *rare.* **L17–M18.**
5 *LAW.* A person to whom a voluntary conveyance is made; a person who benefits by a deed made without money or other consideration being given or promised in return. **M18.**

> 🕮 **2** C. ANGIER She worked for three days a week as a volunteer. A. FINE I need four strong volunteers to carry a table. *Vogue* Looking for volunteers willing to undergo simple skin and blood tests. **3** *Power Farming* A grass weed-killer is applied . . to take out volunteers and any grasses present.

▶**B** *attrib.* or as *adjective.* **1** That is a volunteer, of or pertaining to a volunteer or volunteers; consisting or composed of volunteers. **M17.**
2 Voluntarily performing an action or service; undertaking a service of one's own free will. **M17.**
3 Of a service, action, etc.: rendered or performed voluntarily. **E18.**
4 Of a plant, vegetation, etc.: growing spontaneously, self-sown. **L18.**
1 Volunteer State *US* the State of Tennessee (from which large numbers volunteered for the Mexican War of 1847).

volunteer /vɒlən'tɪə/ *verb.* **L17.**
[from the noun.]
1 *verb intrans.* Enrol voluntarily for military service; become a volunteer. (Foll. by *for, to do.*) **L17.**
2 *verb trans. & intrans.* Offer (oneself, one's services) for a particular purpose or enterprise; offer of one's own accord *to do.* **E19.** ▶**b** *verb trans.* Assign or commit (another person) to a particular undertaking, esp. without consultation; cause to volunteer. Usu. in *pass.* Freq. *iron.* **M20.**
3 *verb trans.* Offer to undertake or perform (a task) or to give or supply (a thing). Also, give (a thing) *away* of one's own accord. *rare.* **E19.**
4 *verb trans.* Communicate (information etc.), make (a suggestion), on one's own initiative; say without prompting (freq. with direct speech as obj.). **E19.**

> 🕮 **1** G. GREENE He had volunteered, though he was over military age. A. WALKER If they . . hadn't volunteered for the trenches in World War I. **2** P. H. GIBBS The villagers who had volunteered to do the digging. J. MASSON These people didn't volunteer for the study; they were coerced. *Drew Magazine* She has also volunteered her time in offering a computer keyboarding class. **b** R. HILL If Kedin had volunteered him, he really had no choice. *Times* Someone was volunteered to go and buy provisions. **4** L. M. MONTGOMERY Matthew . . had never been known to volunteer information about anything in his whole life.

volunteerism /vɒlən'tɪərɪz(ə)m/ *noun.* **M19.**
[from VOLUNTEER *noun* + -ISM.]
1 The system of having volunteer military forces. **M19.**
2 The use of volunteer labour, esp. in social services, voluntarism. *N. Amer.* **L20.**

†**voluntier** *noun* var. of VOLUNTEER *noun.*

volupté /vɔlypte/ *noun. literary.* **E18.**
[French: see VOLUPTY.]
Voluptuousness.

voluptuary /və'lʌptjʊəri/ *noun & adjective.* **E17.**
[Latin *voluptuarius* post-classical var. of *voluptarius*, from *voluptas* pleasure: see -ARY¹.]
▶**A** *noun.* A person devoted to luxury and sensual pleasure or the gratification of the senses. **E17.**

> 🕮 L. TRILLING We do not expect a voluptuary to seek his pleasure in domesticity.

▶**B** *adjective.* Of, pertaining to, or characterized by luxury and sensual pleasure. **E17.**

voluptuous /və'lʌptjʊəs/ *adjective.* **LME.**
[Old & mod. French *voluptueux, -euse* or Latin *voluptuosus*, from *voluptas* pleasure: see -UOUS.]
1 Pertaining to, derived from, characterized by, or addicted to sensuous or sensual pleasure, esp. of a refined or luxurious kind. **LME.**
2 Imparting a sense of delicious pleasure; suggestive of sensuous or sensual pleasure. **E19.** ▶**b** *spec.* Full of sexual promise, esp. through shapeliness or fullness of form. **M19.**

> 🕮 **1** BURKE That . . voluptuous satisfaction which the assured prospect of pleasure bestows. **2** BYRON When Music arose with its voluptuous swell. **b** A. THWAITE Men may misinterpret such voluptuous offerings—the upraised breasts, the yearning thighs.

■ **voluptuously** *adverb* **LME.** **voluptuousness** *noun* the quality of being voluptuous; an instance of this: **LME.**

volupty /və'lʌpti/ *noun. arch.* **LME.**
[Old French *volupte* (mod. *volupté*) or Latin *voluptas* pleasure.]
Pleasure, delight, esp. of a sensuous or sensual nature; an instance of this.

voluta *noun* see VOLUTE *noun.*

volutation /vɒljʊ'teɪʃ(ə)n/ *noun.* Now *rare* or *obsolete.* **E17.**
[Latin *volutatio(n-)*, from *volutat-* pa. ppl stem of *volutare* wallow: see -ATION.]
The action of rolling or wallowing; *fig.* the action of turning a thing over in the mind.

volute /və'l(j)uːt/ *noun.* Also (earlier) in Latin form †**-ta**, pl. **-tae**. **M16.**
[French, or Latin *voluta* use as noun of fem. of *volutus* pa. pple of *volvere* to roll, to wrap.]
1 *ARCHITECTURE.* A spiral scroll characteristic of Ionic capitals and also used in Corinthian and composite capitals. **M16.**
2 A spiral part or object; a convolution. **M18.**
3 (A shell of) any of numerous gastropod molluscs of the family Volutidae, which usu. have large apertures, short spires, and ornamental coloration. **M18.**

volute /və'l(j)uːt/ *adjective.* **M19.**
[Latin *volutus*, or directly from prec.]
Having the form of a volute; forming a spiral curve or curves; *BOTANY* rolled up.

voluted /və'l(j)uːtɪd/ *adjective.* **E19.**
[from VOLUTE *noun* + -ED².]
Spirally twisted or grooved; *ARCHITECTURE* provided with a volute or spiral scroll.

volutin /'vɒljʊtɪn/ *noun.* **E20.**
[from mod. Latin *volutans* specific epithet of the bacterium *Spirillum volutans*, from Latin *volutans* pres. pple of *volutare* to roll: see -IN¹.]
BIOCHEMISTRY. A basophilic compound containing polyphosphate found in metachromatic granules in the cytoplasm and vacuoles of various micro-organisms and fungi.

volution /və'luːʃ(ə)n/ *noun.* **L15.**
[Late Latin *volutio(n-)*, from Latin *volut-* pa. ppl stem of *volvere* to roll: see -ION.]
1 A rolling or revolving movement. **L15.**
2 A spiral twist; a coil, a convolution. **M18.**
3 A whorl of a spiral shell. **L19.**

volva /'vɒlvə/ *noun*¹. **M18.**
[mod. Latin, from Latin *volvere* to roll, to wrap.]
MYCOLOGY. In agarics and gasteromycetes, the veil which encloses the fruiting body, esp. as persisting after rupture as a sheath at the base of the stalk.

volva /'vɒlva/ *noun*². Also **völva**. **L19.**
[Old Norse *vǫlva* (Icelandic *völva*, Norwegian *volve*).]
In Scandinavian mythology, a prophetess, a female soothsayer.

volve /vɒlv/ *verb.* Long *rare* or *obsolete.* **LME.**
[Latin *volvere* to roll, to turn, or French †*volver*, from same source.]
Chiefly in ***volve and revolve***.
†**1** *verb intrans. & trans.* Consider, turn over in the mind. **LME–M18.**
2 *verb intrans. & trans.* Turn over, roll. **LME.**
†**3** *verb trans. & intrans.* Turn over the pages of (a book). **E16–L17.**

volvelle /'vɒlvɛl/ *noun. obsolete* exc. *Hist.* **LME.**
[medieval Latin *volvella, volvellum*, app. from Latin *volvere* to roll.]
A device consisting of one or more movable circles surrounded by other graduated or figured circles, for calculating the rising and setting of the sun and moon, the state of the tides, etc.

volvox /'vɒlvɒks/ *noun.* **L18.**
[mod. Latin (see below), from misreading in Pliny of *volvocem* for *volucrem* (accus.) a pest of vines, as if from Latin *volvere* to roll.]
BOTANY. Any of various photosynthetic flagellates constituting the genus *Volvox*, forming colonies which appear as minute greenish globules spinning round in the water.

volvulus /'vɒlvjʊləs/ *noun.* Pl. **-li** /-lʌɪ, -liː/. **L17.**
[medieval Latin (in mod. Latin sense), from Latin *volvere* to roll, to twist.]
MEDICINE. Intestinal obstruction caused by a twisting or knotting of the bowel; an instance of this.

vomer /'vəʊmə/ *noun.* **E18.**
[Latin = ploughshare.]
ANATOMY & ZOOLOGY. Any of various bones resembling a ploughshare in shape; *esp.* (*a*) a small thin bone forming the posterior part of the partition between the nostrils in man and most higher vertebrates; (*b*) a bone forming the front part of the roof of the mouth in fishes, often bearing teeth.
■ **vomerine** *adjective* of or belonging to a vomer; composing a vomer; (of teeth) situated on a vomer: **M19.**

†**vomic** *adjective. rare.* **M16–L18.**
[from medieval Latin (NUX) VOMICA.]
vomic nut, = NUX VOMICA.

vomica /'vɒmɪkə/ *noun.* Now *rare* or *obsolete.* Pl. **-cae** /-siː, -kiː/, **-cas**. **L16.**
[Latin = abscess, boil, app. from *vomere* vomit, eject.]
1 †**a** A vent, an opening. Only in **L16.** ▶**b** A source of a stream etc. **M19.**
2 *MEDICINE.* **a** A cavity or abscess in an internal organ, usu. a lung. **L17.** ▶**b** A sudden expectoration of a large quantity of purulent or putrid matter. **L19.**

vomit /'vɒmɪt/ *noun.* **LME.**
[Old French *vomite* or Latin *vomitus*, from *vomere* VOMIT *verb.*]
1 The action of vomiting or being sick; an instance of this. **LME.**
2 Matter ejected from the stomach by vomiting. **LME.** ▶**b** *transf.* Substance cast out by discharge or eruption. **E17.**
3 An emetic. *arch.* **LME.**
4 A person or thing of a loathsome or disgusting character. *contempt.* **E17.**
5 The hood or cover of a vomiting boiler. Now *rare.* **L19.**
2 *black vomit*: see BLACK *adjective.*
Phrases: **return to one's vomit** [in allus. to *Proverbs* 26:11] revert to one's bad old ways.
Comb.: **vomit bag** = ***sick-bag*** s.v. SICK *adjective.*

vomit /'vɒmɪt/ *verb.* **LME.**
[Latin *vomit-* pa. ppl stem of *vomere* or Latin frequentative *vomitare*.]
▶**I 1** *verb intrans.* Eject ingested matter from the stomach through the mouth; be sick. **LME.**
2 *verb trans.* Eject (ingested matter) from the stomach through the mouth. Also foll. by *out, up.* **LME.**
3 *verb intrans. & trans.* Cause (a person) to vomit. *arch.* **M17.**

> 🕮 **1** A. WALKER I vomited incessantly. **2** T. C. WOLFE He ate, and instantly vomited up again all he had eaten. **3** G. CATLIN He is vomiting and purging his patients with herbs.

▶**II 4** *verb trans.* Reject or cast *out, up,* or *forth,* esp. with abhorrence or loathing; utter or pour *forth* or *out* (abusive or objectionable language). *arch.* **M16.**
5 *verb trans.* Pour (matter) *out, forth,* or *up,* as if by vomiting, *esp.* eject violently (flames, molten lava, etc.). **M16.**
6 *verb intrans.* Issue or come out with force or violence; rush *out,* spout *up.* *rare.* **M17.**

> 🕮 **4** F. PARKMAN The Frenchman vomited against him every species of malignant abuse. **5** T. H. HUXLEY The fused rocks . . which are vomited forth by volcanoes. **b** A. LURIE A maroon over-stuffed chair . . lies on its side vomiting kapok.

■ **vomiter** *noun* (*a*) a person who vomits; †(*b*) an emetic: **M16.** **vomiting** *verbal noun* (*a*) the action of the verb; an instance of this; (*b*) vomited matter, vomit: **L15.** **vomiting** *ppl adjective* that vomits or causes to vomit; ***vomiting boiler*** (now *rare*), a boiler in which the water is forced up a pipe and then falls back on to the cloth etc. being boiled: **M19.**

vomition /və'mɪʃ(ə)n/ *noun.* **M17.**
[French †*vomition* or Latin *vomitio(n-)*, formed as prec.: see -ION.]
The action of vomiting.

†**vomitive** *adjective & noun.* **LME.**
[Old & mod. French *vomitif, -tive* or medieval Latin *vomitivus*, formed as prec.: see -IVE.]
▶**A** *adjective.* Of a medicine etc.: causing vomiting; emetic. **LME–M18.**
▶**B** *noun.* An emetic. **E17–M18.**

vomito /'vomito, 'vɒmɪtəʊ/ *noun.* Now *rare.* **M19.**
[Spanish (& Portuguese) *vómito* from Latin *vomitus* VOMIT *noun.*]
MEDICINE. Yellow fever in its virulent form, when it is usu. accompanied by black vomit.

vomitorium /vɒmɪ'tɔːrɪəm/ *noun.* Pl. **-ria** /-rɪə/. **M18.**
[Late Latin, use as noun of neut. of Latin *vomitorius* VOMITORY *adjective.*]
ROMAN ANTIQUITIES. **1** A passage or opening in an amphitheatre or theatre, leading to or from the seats. Usu. in *pl.* **M18.**
2 A room allegedly for vomiting deliberately during feasts, to make way for other food. **E20.**

vomitory /'vɒmɪt(ə)ri/ *noun.* **E17.**
[from next, partly through Anglicization of prec.]
†**1** An emetic. **E17–M18.**
2 A passage or opening in a theatre etc., esp. between banks of seats; *spec.* = VOMITORIUM 1. **M18.**
3 An opening through which smoke etc. is discharged. **E19.**

vomitory /'vɒmɪt(ə)ri/ *adjective.* **E17.**
[Latin *vomitorius*, from *vomit-*: see VOMIT *verb*, -ORY².]
1 Of or pertaining to vomiting. *arch.* **E17.**
2 Causing vomiting; emetic. Now *rare* or *obsolete.* **M17.**

vomitous /'vɒmɪtəs/ *adjective. US.* **M20.**
[from VOMIT *noun* + -OUS.]
Likely to make a person vomit; nauseating, disgusting.

vomitus /'vɒmɪtəs/ *noun.* **E20.**
[Latin: see VOMIT *noun.*]
Chiefly *MEDICINE.* Vomited matter.

vomity /'vɒmɪti/ *adjective. US.* **M20.**
[from VOMIT *noun* + -Y¹.]
Redolent of vomit; nauseating, disgusting.

von Gierke /fɒn ˈɡɪəkə/ *noun.* **M20.**
[Edgar O. K. *von Gierke* (1877–1945), German pathologist.]
MEDICINE. Used in *possess.* and *attrib.* to designate a type of glycogen storage disease, caused by an enzyme deficiency and characterized by an enlarged liver, obesity, and stunted growth.

von Hippel–Lindau /fɒn ˌhɪp(ə)l ˈlɪndaʊ/ *noun.* **M20.**
[from Eugen *von Hippel* (1867–1939), German pathologist + Arvid Vilhelm *Lindau* (1892–1958), Swedish pathologist.]
MEDICINE. Used *attrib.* and in *possess.* to designate a hereditary disease or syndrome characterized by the presence of angiomas in the cerebellum and retina, and abnormal growths in the kidney or pancreas.

von Recklinghausen's disease /fɒn ˈrɛklɪŋhaʊz(ə)nz dɪˌziːz/ *noun phr.* **E20.**
[Friedrich *von Recklinghausen* (1833–1910), German pathologist.]
MEDICINE. **1** A hereditary disease in which numerous neurofibromas develop on various parts of the body, esp. the skin, nerve trunks, and peripheral nerves. Also called ***Recklinghausen's disease***. **E20.**
2 A disease in which bones are weakened as a result of hyperparathyroidism, leading to bowing and fracture of long bones and sometimes deformities of the chest and spine. Also called ***osteitis fibrosa cystica***. **E20.**

von Willebrand /vɒn ˈwɪləbrand/ *noun.* **M20.**
[Erik Adolf *von Willebrand* (1870–1949), Finnish physician.]
MEDICINE. Used *attrib.* and in *possess.* to designate a hereditary condition characterized by prolonged bleeding, caused by deficiency or abnormality of a plasma coagulation factor.

voodoo /ˈvuːduː/ *noun & verb.* Also (earlier) †**vaudoo**, & other vars. **E19.**
[Louisiana French *voudou*, formed as VODUN. Cf. HOODOO.]
▶ **A** *noun.* **1** A black religious cult, practised in the W. Indies (esp. Haiti) and the southern US, characterized by sorcery and spirit possession, and combining elements of Roman Catholic ritual with traditional African religious and magical rites. Also (*ellipt.*), a voodoo deity, a voodoo spell. **E19.**
2 A person who practises voodoo. **L19.**

> 🕮 **1** *attrib.*: D. R. KOONTZ He's a voodoo priest who practices only white magic. *transf.*: F. EXLEY I haven't for years seen any validity whatever in the Freudian voodoo.

Comb.: **voodoo economics** (chiefly *US*, *derog.*) economic policies which involve maintaining or increasing levels of public spending whilst reducing levels of taxation, or are otherwise perceived as being fanciful or leading to debt.
▶ **B** *verb trans.* Cast a spell on (a person) by voodoo, practise voodoo on. **L19.**
▪ **voodooism** *noun* the belief in or practice of voodoo **M19.** **voodooist** *noun* a practitioner of voodooism **E20.**

voom /vuːm/ *interjection. colloq.* **M20.**
[Imit. Cf. VROOM.]
Repr. the sound of an explosion or of an engine being revved.

voorbok /ˈfʊəbɒk/ *noun. S. Afr.* Pl. **-bokke** /-bɒkə/. **E20.**
[Afrikaans, lit. 'front goat'.]
A goat which acts as bell-wether to a flock of sheep; *fig.* a leader, an instigator.

voorhuis /ˈfʊəhœys/ *noun. S. Afr.* **E19.**
[Afrikaans.]
The entrance hall of a house (esp. one in Cape Dutch style), often used as a living-room.

voorkamer /ˈfʊərkɑːmər/ *noun. S. Afr.* Also (earlier) †***fore-***. **L18.**
[Dutch = front room.]
= prec.

voorloper /ˈfʊəlʊəpə/ *noun. S. Afr.* (now *Hist.*). **M19.**
[Afrikaans, from *voor-* before + *loop* to run.]
The leader of a span of oxen, usu. a young African or Coloured boy.

voorslag /ˈfʊəslax/ *noun.* **M19.**
[Afrikaans.]
The lash forming the end of a wagon whip.

Voortrekker /ˈfʊətrɛkə/ *noun. S. Afr.* **L19.**
[Afrikaans, from *voor-* before + *trekken* TREK *verb*.]
Hist. A Boer pioneer, *esp.* one who took part in the Great Trek from Cape Colony *c* 1835.

Vopo /ˈfəʊpəʊ/ *noun.* Pl. **-os.** **M20.**
[German, from ***Vo(lks)po(lizei)*** s.v. VOLK.]
Hist. In the German Democratic Republic, a member of the Volkspolizei.

VOR *abbreviation.*
VHF omnirange.

voracious /vəˈreɪʃəs/ *adjective.* **M17.**
[Latin *vorac-*, *vorax*, from *vorare* devour: see -IOUS.]
1 Characterized by greed in eating, greedy; ravenous, insatiable. **M17.**
2 *fig.* Characterized by extreme eagerness in the pursuit of some desire or interest. **E18.**

> 🕮 **1** W. S. MAUGHAM His corpulence pointed to a voracious appetite. O. MANNING Voracious creatures who would devour him if they could. **2** *Times Lit. Suppl.* The fourth player's sexually voracious life. *Home & Freezer Digest* Robert's a voracious reader—everything from philosophy and politics to . . the latest popular novels.

▪ **voraciously** *adverb* **M18.** **voraciousness** *noun* **E18.**

voracity /vəˈrasɪti/ *noun.* **E16.**
[Old & mod. French *voracité* or Latin *voracitas*, formed as prec.: see -ACITY.]
The quality or character of being voracious; greediness in eating.

†**voraginous** *adjective.* **E17.**
[Latin *voraginosus*, from *voragin-*, VORAGO: see -OUS.]
1 Resembling an abyss or whirlpool. **E17–M18.**
2 Devouring, voracious. **M–L17.**

vorago /vəˈreɪɡəʊ/ *noun.* Long *rare.* Pl. **-oes.** **M17.**
[Latin, from *vorare* devour.]
An abyss, a gulf, a chasm.

vorant /ˈvɔːr(ə)nt/ *adjective.* **E17.**
[Latin *vorant-* pres. ppl stem of *vorare* devour: see -ANT[1].]
†**1** Devouring. *rare.* **E–M17.**
2 *HERALDRY.* Of an animal: swallowing its prey. **M18.**

-vore /vɔː/ *suffix.* Also (see below) **-ivore**.
[French *-vore* from Latin *-vorus* (see -VOROUS), or as back-form. from -VOROUS.]
Forming (usu. with intermediate -I-) nouns denoting 'an organism living on a given kind of food', as ***carnivore***, ***frugivore***.

vorlage /ˈfɔːlɑːɡə/ *noun.* Pl. **-ges**, **-gen** /-ɡən/. **M20.**
[German.]
1 a *SKIING.* A position in which the skier leans forward without lifting the heels from the skis. **M20.** ▸**b** In *pl.* Skiing trousers. **M20.**
2 An original version of a manuscript from which a copy is produced. **M20.**

vorlaufer /ˈfɔːlaʊfə/ *noun.* **M20.**
[German *Vorläufer*, from *vorlaufen* run on ahead.]
A skier who travels a course before a race to establish that it is within the capacity of the competitors.

-vorous /v(ə)rəs/ *suffix.* Also (see below) **-ivorous**.
[Repr. Latin *-vorus*, from *vorare* devour: see -OUS. Cf. -VORE.]
Forming (usu. with intermediate -I-) adjectives with the sense 'devouring, feeding on', as ***carnivorous***, ***insectivorous***, ***omnivorous***.

Vorspiel /ˈfoːrʃpiːl/ *noun.* Pl. ***-e*** /-ə/. **L19.**
[German, from *vor* before + *Spiel* play.]
MUSIC. A prelude.

Vorstellung /ˈfoːrʃtɛlʊŋ/ *noun.* Also ***v-***. Pl. ***-en*** /-ən/. **E19.**
[German.]
PHILOSOPHY & PSYCHOLOGY. An idea, a mental picture.

vortal /ˈvɔːt(ə)l/ *noun.* **L20.**
[from V(ERTICAL *adjective* + PORTAL *noun*[1].]
COMPUTING. An Internet site that provides a directory of links to information related to a particular industry.

vortex /ˈvɔːtɛks/ *noun.* Pl. **-exes**, **-ices** /-ɪsiːz/. **M17.**
[Latin (var. of VERTEX) an eddy of water, wind, or flame, from *vortere*, *vertere* to turn.]
1 a In Cartesian theory: any of the rapidly revolving collections of fine particles supposed to fill all space and by their rotation to account for the motions of the universe; the whirling movement of such a collection of particles. Usu. in *pl.* **M17.** ▸**b** *PHYSICS.* A rapid motion of particles round an axis; a whirl of atoms, fluid, or vapour. **M19.**
2 A violent eddy of the air; a cyclone; the central portion of this. Also, an eddying mass of fire. **M17.**
3 A swirling mass of water; a whirlpool. **E18.**
4 *fig.* **a** A whirl or constant round of frenetic activity, rapid change, etc. **M18.** ▸**b** A place or state into which people or things are irresistibly drawn. **L18.**
5 *The* group of vorticist artists. **E20.**

> 🕮 **2** *Monitor (Texas)* A tornado . . that sucked a man into its vortex. **4a** D. CECIL She plunged him into a vortex of social activity. M. IGNATIEFF Someone who . . kept his distance from the vortex of Petersburg intrigue. **b** J. WAIN Streatham, Tooting, Fulham—vanished places, swallowed up in the vortex of London.

Comb.: **vortex shedding** the periodic detachment of vortices from an object in a fluid flow, causing a varying force to be experienced by the object; **vortex sheet** a region of vortices that is created at the interface of two masses of fluid having different velocities along the interface; ***vortex street***: see STREET *noun* 3a; **vortex turbine**, **vortex wheel** a turbine in which the water enters tangentially at the circumference and is discharged at the centre.

vortical /ˈvɔːtɪk(ə)l/ *adjective.* **M17.**
[from Latin *vortic-*, VORTEX + -AL[1].]
Moving in a vortex; (of motion) resembling that of a vortex, rotatory.
▪ **vortically** *adverb* **L19.**

vorticella /vɔːtɪˈsɛlə/ *noun.* Pl. **-llae** /-liː/. **L18.**
[mod. Latin, dim. of Latin *vortic-*, VORTEX: see -ELLA.]
ZOOLOGY. A sessile protozoan of the genus *Vorticella*, which has a long contractile stalk and a ciliated body shaped like an inverted bell. Also called ***bell-animal***, ***bell-animalcule***.
▪ **vorticellid** *noun* a protozoan of the family Vorticellidae, which comprises *Vorticella* and related genera **M19.**

vortices *noun pl.* see VORTEX.

vorticism /ˈvɔːtɪsɪz(ə)m/ *noun.* **E20.**
[from Latin *vortic-*, VORTEX + -ISM.]
A British art-movement of *c* 1914–15, influenced by cubism and futurism and characterized by machine-like forms.

vorticist /ˈvɔːtɪsɪst/ *noun.* **M19.**
[formed as prec. + -IST.]
1 An advocate of the Cartesian theory of vortices. **M19.**
2 An exponent of vorticism in art. **E20.**

vorticity /vɔːˈtɪsɪti/ *noun.* **L19.**
[formed as VORTICAL + -ITY.]
PHYSICS. A measure of the degree of local rotation in a fluid, defined as the curl of the velocity at any point.

vorticose /vɔːtɪˈkəʊs/ *adjective.* **L18.**
[Latin *vorticosus*, from *vortic-* VORTEX: see -OSE[1].]
1 Of motion: = VORTICAL. **L18.**
2 Resembling a vortex. **L19.**
▪ **vorticosely** *adverb* **L19.**

vorticular /vɔːˈtɪkjʊlə/ *adjective.* **M19.**
[formed as prec. + -ULAR.]
Of motion: vortical, vorticose.

vortiginous /vɔːˈtɪdʒɪnəs/ *adjective.* Now *arch. rare.* **L17.**
[from Latin *vortigin-*, *vortigo* var. of VERTIGO: see -OUS. Cf. VERTIGINOUS.]
1 Of motion: vortical, vorticular. **L17.**
2 Moving in a vortex or vortices; rushing in whirls or eddies. **L18.**

vortograph /ˈvɔːtəɡrɑːf/ *noun.* **E20.**
[from VORT(EX + -O- + -GRAPH.]
An abstract photograph taken with a camera and a vortoscope.

vortoscope /ˈvɔːtəskəʊp/ *noun.* **E20.**
[formed as prec. + -SCOPE.]
A mirror device used for producing abstract photographs.

votable /ˈvəʊtəb(ə)l/ *adjective.* **M18.**
[from VOTE *verb* + -ABLE.]
1 Having the right to vote. *rare.* **M18.**
2 Able to be voted on or for; (of shares) carrying voting rights. **M20.**
▪ **votaˈbility** *noun* **M20.**

votal /ˈvəʊt(ə)l/ *adjective.* **E17.**
[from Latin *votum* a vow, a wish + -AL[1].]
†**1** Existing only in will or intention. Only in **E17.**
2 Of the nature of a vow; (of an offering) associated with a vow. **M17.**

votaress /ˈvəʊt(ə)rɪs/ *noun.* Also **-tress** /-trɪs/. **L16.**
[from VOTARY + -ESS[1].]
A female votary; *esp.* a woman devoted to a religious life or to a special saint.

votarist /ˈvəʊt(ə)rɪst/ *noun.* **E17.**
[from VOTARY + -IST.]
A person bound by a vow; a votary.

votary /ˈvəʊt(ə)ri/ *noun.* **M16.**
[from Latin *vot-* pa. ppl stem of *vovere* to vow: see -ARY[1].]
▶ **I 1** A person bound by a vow or vows, *spec.* to a religious life. **M16.**
2 A devoted follower of God, a deity, a cult, etc.; a worshipper. **L17.**

> 🕮 **2** E. A. FREEMAN Harold implored the help of the relic whose sworn votary he was.

▶ **II 3** *fig.* A person passionately addicted to a pursuit, occupation, etc; a devoted adherent or admirer of a person, cause, etc. **L16.**

votation /vəʊˈteɪʃ(ə)n/ *noun. rare.* **E19.**
[from VOTE *verb* + -ATION.]
The action of voting in an election or at a meeting.

vote /vəʊt/ *noun.* **LME.**
[Latin *votum* a vow, a wish, use as noun of neut. of pa. pple of *vovere*: see next.]
▶ **I 1** A formal expression of choice or opinion by means of a ballot, show of hands, etc., concerning esp. a choice of candidate or approval or rejection of a resolution; such an expression counted as a unit for or against. **LME.** ▸**b** A piece of paper or other token used to record this. **E19.**

2 An act or instance of voting, esp. by a legislative body on a proposed measure. L16.
3 A right to vote; spec. *the* right of voting in general elections, *the* franchise. L16. ▸**b** A person regarded merely as an embodiment of the right to vote. Also, a voter. M18.
4 An opinion expressed by a majority of votes; a resolution or decision passed or a sum of money granted by a legislative body etc. as the result of voting. M17.
5 The total number of votes that are or may be given by or for a particular group (freq. with specifying word); the total number of votes cast. M19.

> 🕮 **1** GOLDWIN SMITH Birney polled just enough votes to defeat Clay. *Outing (US)* You get my vote the next time you run for poundmaster. C. P. SNOW The motion was carried by seven votes to four. A. S. NEILL Each pupil and each staff member having one vote. ***block vote, casting vote, cumulative vote, postal vote, transferable vote,*** etc. **2** J. T. SMITH Put it to the Vote whether the meeting 'approve' and 'confirm' the minutes. *Church Times* The General Synod will take its crucial vote on the ordination of women . . next November. **3** G. B. SHAW Give women the vote. **4** DICKENS A vote of thanks was moved to the mayor for his able conduct. *Milton Keynes Express* A unanimous vote that a supporters' club be formed. *Times* The Government is not bound by the committee's vote. **5** A. J. P. TAYLOR The 'flapper vote' is supposed to have benefited . . Labour . . in the general election of 1929.

▸†**II 6** A vow; a solemn undertaking. M16–E18.
7 A prayer, an intercession. Also, an aspiration; an ardent desire. E–M17.

Phrases: ***free vote***: see FREE *adjective*. ***one man one vote***: see ONE *adjective* etc. ***put to a vote, put to the vote***: see PUT *verb*[1]. ***split the vote***: see SPLIT *verb*. **vote of censure** a motion tabled by the Opposition, showing that the majority do not support the party in office. **vote of confidence** a resolution showing majority support for a government, policy, etc. **vote of no confidence** = ***vote of censure*** above. **vote on account** a resolution at the close of the financial year to assign a sum of money to a government department as an advance payment before its full annual expenditure is authorized by law.

Comb.: **vote bank** in India, a group of people who can be relied upon to vote together in support of the same party; **vote-catcher** = *vote-winner* below; **vote-catching** *adjective* likely to attract the votes of the electorate; **Vote Office** the office from which Parliamentary bills and papers are issued to members of the House of Commons; **vote-winner** a measure etc. likely to appeal to the electorate.

¶ Before 1600 only in Scot. use.

■ **voteless** *adjective* having no vote L17.

vote /vəʊt/ *verb*. M16.
[Partly from Latin *vot-* pa. ppl stem of *vovere* to vow, desire; partly from the noun.]
1 *verb trans.* Dedicate by a vow, esp. to a deity. Now *rare*. M16.
2 *verb intrans.* Cast a vote; exercise one's right to do this; express a choice or preference by ballot, show of hands, etc. (Foll. by *against*, *for*, †*to*; also with adverbial compl.) M16.
3 *verb trans.* Of a legislative body, committee, etc.: enact, establish, or ratify by vote; grant or confer by vote. M16.
†**4** *verb trans.* Submit (a matter) to a vote; vote on. *rare*. L16–L17.
5 *verb trans.* Decide by vote *that*, *to do*. M17.
6 *verb trans.* Put in a specified position by a vote. Foll. by preposition or adverb. M17.
7 *verb trans.* **a** Declare or pronounce by common consent (*to be*). M17. ▸**b** Propose; suggest *that*. Chiefly in ***I vote***. *colloq.* E19.
8 *verb trans.* Present for voting; record the votes of (electors). *US*. M19.
9 *verb trans.* Exercise the voting rights of (shares). M20.

> 🕮 **2** C. P. SNOW He voted radical and she was a vehement tory. A. J. P. TAYLOR Some fifty Liberals voted against the bill. *Guardian* The pro-abortion lobby was looking hopefully . . at that 50 per cent of the adult population which does not vote. *Financial Times* At the June election, many Moslems voted for Dr Ahmet Sadik. **3** W. SELWYN Having in common council voted a petition to the king. E. FORSEY Monies are voted by Parliament to be disbursed for a stated purpose. **5** J. PURSEGLOVE Parliament voted that King George III award Elkington $1,000. *Financial Times* College lecturers have voted by a 0.5 majority to end their . . dispute. **6** *Longman's Magazine* My name has been voted off the list of your committee. *Guardian* Mr Gabor Roszik of the HDF was voted into Parliament. **7b** E. BOWEN I vote we take those two on again. **8** E. W. NYE I believe they vote people there who have been dead for centuries.

Phrases, & with adverbs in specialized senses: **vote down** defeat in a vote. **vote in** elect (a person) or approve (a measure) as a result of a vote. **vote with one's feet** indicate an opinion by one's presence or absence.

Vo-Tech /vəʊˈtɛk/ *adjective & noun*. *US colloq.* L20.
[Abbreviation.]
▸**A** *adjective*. Vocational and technical. L20.
▸**B** *noun*. A vocational and technical school. L20.

voteen /vəʊˈtiːn/ *noun*. *Anglo-Irish*. M19.
[Prob. from DE)VOTE *adjective* & *noun* + -EEN[2].]
A very religious person; a votary.

voter /ˈvəʊtə/ *noun*. L16.
[from VOTE *verb* + -ER[1].]
A person who has a right to vote, *esp.* an elector.

Votic /ˈvəʊtɪk/ *noun & adjective*. E20.
[from Russian *Voty* the Vodians + -IC.]
= VODIAN.

voting /ˈvəʊtɪŋ/ *verbal noun*. L16.
[from VOTE *verb* + -ING[1].]
The action of giving a vote.
Comb.: **voting machine** a vote-recorder; **voting-paper** a paper on which a vote is recorded.

voting /ˈvəʊtɪŋ/ *ppl adjective*. M17.
[from VOTE *verb* + -ING[2].]
†**1** Votive, dedicatory. Only in M17.
2 Possessing or exercising the right to vote. M19.

†**votist** *noun*. *rare*. E17–E18.
[from VOTE *noun* or *verb* + -IST.]
A person who makes a vow; a votary.

votive /ˈvəʊtɪv/ *adjective & noun*. L16.
[Latin *votivus*, from *votum* vow, VOTE *noun*.]
▸**A** *adjective*. **1** Consisting in or expressive of a vow, desire, or wish. L16.
2 Offered, undertaken, etc., in fulfilment of a vow, or as a thanksgiving. E17.

> 🕮 **1 votive mass** ROMAN CATHOLIC CHURCH a mass that does not correspond to the order of the day but is said for a special intention, at the choice of the celebrant. **2** W. IRVING A votive candle placed before the image of a saint. H. N. HUMPHREYS The altars for Apollo were besieged with votive offerings for the staying of the pestilence.

▸**B** *noun*. A votive offering. M17.

votress *noun* var. of VOTARESS.

Votyak /ˈvəʊtjak/ *noun & adjective*. M19.
[Russian.]
Hist. = UDMURT.

vouch /vaʊtʃ/ *noun*. Now *rare* or *obsolete*. E17.
[from the verb.]
An assertion; a formal attestation of fact.

vouch /vaʊtʃ/ *verb*. ME.
[Old French *vo(u)cher* summon, ult. from Latin *vocare* call.]
1 *verb trans.* LAW (now *Hist.*). Cite, call, or summon (a person) to court to give proof of a title to property; (foll. by *over*) (of a person so summoned) cite (another person) to court to provide the necessary proof. Freq. in ***vouch to warrant, vouch to warranty***. ME.
2 *verb trans.* **a** Call (a person) to witness. Now *rare* or *obsolete*. LME. ▸**b** Cite as an authority; adduce in corroboration. *arch.* M16.
3 *verb trans.* Affirm, declare. Formerly, assert to be. Now *rare* or *obsolete*. LME.
†**4** *verb trans.* **a** Assert a claim to (a thing). *rare*. L15–M16. ▸**b** Guarantee a person's title to (a thing). *rare*. E–M17.
5 *verb trans.* Condescend to give, vouchsafe (now *rare*). Formerly, deign *to do*. L16.
6 *verb trans.* Confirm or uphold (a statement etc.) by evidence or assertion; state authoritatively *that*; provide concrete evidence of. *arch.* L16.
7 *verb intrans.* Answer *for*, be surety *for*. L17.

> 🕮 **2b** R. SANDERSON It would be too long to vouch Texts for each particular. W. WOLLASTON For the truth of this I vouch the mathematicians. **3** SHAKES. *All's Well* Like a timorous thief . . steal What law does vouch mine own. SHELLEY What we have done None shall dare vouch, though it be truly known. **6** T. REID They will . . respect nothing but facts sufficiently vouched. *Law Times* All expenses so claimed must be strictly vouched. I. WATSON She was able to vouch that I was the person I said I was. **7** JOYCE Some things he could not vouch for . . but of others he had had personal experience. W. S. MAUGHAM He could vouch for its authenticity. D. JACOBSON Whether Amnon was telling the truth . . is something I can't vouch for.

vouchee /vaʊˈtʃiː/ *noun*. LME.
[from VOUCH *verb* + -EE[1].]
1 LAW (now *Hist.*). A person vouched or summoned to court to give proof of a title to property. LME.
2 A person cited or appealed to as an authority. *arch.* M17.

voucher /ˈvaʊtʃə/ *noun*. E16.
[In sense 1 Anglo-Norman use as noun of Old French inf. *voucher*, in later senses also directly from VOUCH *verb*: see -ER[4], -ER[1]. Cf. next.]
1 LAW (now *Hist.*). The summoning of a person to court to give proof of the title to a property. E16.
†**2** LAW. A vouchee; a vouchor. Only in 17.
3 A fact, circumstance, or thing serving to confirm or prove something; *esp.* a corroborative document, note, etc., attesting the correctness of accounts, proving the delivery of goods or valuables, etc. E17.
4 A person who vouches for a person, fact, statement, etc. M17.
†**5** A person who passes counterfeit coin. *Criminals' slang*. M17–E18.
6 A document which can be exchanged for goods or services as token of payment made or promised by the holder or another. M20.

> 🕮 **3** E. K. KANE The destruction of the vouchers of the cruise . . the log-books . . the surveys, and the journals. J. T. SMITH Produce accounts, with vouchers of all receipts and expenditure. **6** *She* Runners-up will each receive a £2 voucher to spend in Boots. ***gift voucher, luncheon voucher,*** etc.

Comb.: **voucher specimen** a specimen serving to substantiate a plant record.

vouchor /ˈvaʊtʃə/ *noun*. E17.
[Anglo-Norman, from *voucher*: see prec., -OR.]
LAW (now *Hist.*). A person who calls another to court to give proof of a title to property.

vouchsafe /vaʊtʃˈseɪf/ *verb trans.* Now chiefly *literary & formal*. ME.
[from VOUCH *verb* + SAFE *adjective*. Orig. as two words (sometimes separated or with inverted order).]
▸**I** †**1** Confer or bestow (a thing) *on* a person. ME–L17.
2 Give or grant in a gracious or condescending manner. (Foll. by indirect obj., *to*.) ME. ▸**b** Deign to utter (a word, answer etc.) in conversation or response. L16.
†**3 a** Be good enough to take part in (some pursuit). L16–M17. ▸**b** Receive (a thing) graciously, deign to accept. Also (*rare*), be prepared to bear or sustain. L16–E17.
†**4** Acknowledge (a person) in some favourable relationship or manner. L16–M17.

> 🕮 **2** J. LONDON The one rational moment that was vouchsafed her. *Times Lit. Suppl.* A reputation for erudition . . gained . . by claiming to know what was vouchsafed only to the adept. **b** W. BLACK All the reply that Tita vouchsafed was to wear a pleased smile of defiance.

▸**II 5** †**a** Permit or allow, as an act of grace or condescension. (Foll. by *that*.) ME–M17. ▸**b** Permit or allow (a person) *to do*. LME.
6 Show a gracious willingness *to do*, grant or permit readily, condescend or think fit *to do*. ME.

> 🕮 **5a** SHAKES. *Jul. Caes.* If Brutus will vouchsafe that Antony May safely come to him. **b** J. KEBLE Be it vouchsaf'd thee still to see Thy true, fond nurslings closer cling. **6** C. WORDSWORTH The Pope vouchsafed to give bulls of institution to the ecclesiastics named by the crown.

■ **vouchsafement** *noun* (*a*) an act of condescension or favour; a favour, blessing; (*b*) the action of conferring a boon or favour: E17.

voulu /vuly/ *adjective*. *literary*. L19.
[French, pa. pple of *vouloir* to wish.]
Lacking in spontaneity; contrived.

vour /ˈvaʊə/ *verb trans.* Long *obsolete* exc. *dial.* ME.
[Aphet. from DEVOUR, perh. after Latin *vorare*.]
Devour, eat.

voussoir /ˈvuːswɑː/ *noun*. ME.
[Old French *vausoir*, *vaussoir*, etc. (mod. *voussoir*) from popular Latin *volsorium* ult. from Latin *vols-* pa. ppl stem of *volvere* to roll, to turn.]
Each of the wedge-shaped or tapered stones, bricks, etc., forming an arch or vaulting.
¶ Not recorded between LME and E18.
■ **voussoired** *adjective* constructed with voussoirs L19.

Vouvray /ˈvuːvreɪ/ *noun*. L19.
[A village in the department of Indre-et-Loire, France.]
White wine (still or sparkling) produced in the Vouvray district.

vow /vaʊ/ *noun*. ME.
[Anglo-Norman *vou*, *vu(u)*, Old French *vo*, *vou* (mod. *vœu*), formed as VOTE *noun*.]
1 A solemn promise made to God, another deity, or a saint, to perform an action, make a sacrifice, etc.; *gen.* a solemn undertaking or resolve. Also (foll. by *of*), a solemn promise to observe a specified state or condition. ME.
†**2** A votive offering. *rare*. ME–L17.
3 a In *pl.* The promises by which a monk or nun is bound to poverty, chastity, and obedience. Freq. in ***take one's vows, take vows***. LME. ▸**b** A solemn promise of fidelity, *esp.* one made during a marriage ceremony. Usu. in *pl.* M16.
4 An earnest wish or desire; a prayer, a supplication. *arch.* LME.
5 A solemn affirmation of faith or allegiance. *rare*. L16.

> 🕮 **1** DRYDEN With Vows and suppliant Pray'rs appease. G. K. CHESTERTON I made a . . vow . . that I would not talk seriously. ***vow of poverty, vow of silence,*** etc. **3b** A. LAMBERT As a good Christian, she had never questioned her marriage vows. **4** BURKE You have my most ardent vows for an auspicious beginning.

Phrases: **baptismal vows** the promises given at baptism by the baptized person or by his or her sponsors. ***simple vow***: see SIMPLE *adjective*. **under a vow** bound by a vow.
Comb.: †**vow-breach** the breaking of a vow; **vow-breaker** a person who breaks a vow; †**vow-fellow** (*rare*, Shakes.) a person bound by the same vow as the speaker.

vow /vaʊ/ *verb.* ME.
[Old & mod. French *vouer*, from *vou* VOW *noun*. In branch II aphet. from AVOW *verb*[1].]
► **I 1** *verb trans.* Promise or undertake solemnly, esp. by making a vow; swear *that*, *to do*, etc. ME. ►**b** *verb trans.* Make a solemn resolve or threat to inflict (injury), exact (vengeance), etc. L16.
2 *verb intrans.* Make a vow or solemn undertaking. ME.
3 *verb trans.* Dedicate or consecrate *to* a deity etc.; devote *to* a person or cause. L15.

> **1** C. DEXTER He had reformed and vowed to turn from his sinful ways. **b** D. GARNETT Archer stood up . . vowing vengeance on the Chesapeakes. **2** TENNYSON The hall was . . in tumult—some Vowing and some protesting. **3** SIR W. SCOTT Connamore, who vowed his race, For ever to the fight and chase.

► **II** †**4** *verb trans.* Acknowledge, admit. ME–M16.
5 *verb trans.* Affirm, assert solemnly, proclaim; = AVOW *verb*[1] 3. *arch.* ME.

> **5** GOLDSMITH I vow, child, you are vastly handsome.

■ **vower** *noun* a person who makes or has taken a vow or vows M16. **vowess** *noun* (*arch.*) (*a*) a woman who has taken a vow of chastity, *esp.* a widow; (*b*) a woman who has taken religious vows: E16.

vow /vaʊ/ *interjection. Scot. arch.* M16.
[Prob. ellipt. from *I vow*. Cf. WOW *interjection*.]
= WOW *interjection*.

vowed /vaʊd/ *ppl adjective. literary.* M16.
[from VOW *verb* + -ED[1].]
†**1** Of a person: bound by or under a vow or vows. M16–E18.
2 Undertaken in accordance with a vow; confirmed or sworn in a vow or vows; solemnly promised. M16.
►†**b** Solemnly consecrated or dedicated. L16–L17.

> **1** SIR W. SCOTT The Crusader . . as a vowed champion of the Cross. **2** DRYDEN I sought with joy The vowed destruction of ungrateful Troy. SHELLEY That mother Whom to . . cheer . . Was my vowed task.

vowel /ˈvaʊəl/ *noun & verb.* ME.
[Old French *vouel* var. of *voiel* masc. (mod. *voyelle* fem.), from Latin *vocalis*, from *voc-*, VOX + *-alis* -AL[1].]
► **A** *noun.* **1** A speech sound produced by vibration of the vocal cords but without any closure or narrowing of the speech tract such as would cause audible friction, capable of forming a syllable; a letter of the alphabet representing such a sound. Cf. CONSONANT *noun* 1b. ME.
†**2** A word. L16–M17.
1 *cardinal vowel*, *indeterminate vowel*, *murmur vowel*, *neutral vowel*, etc. *long vowel*, *short vowel*, etc.
Comb.: **vowel colour** the precise timbre and quality of a vowel sound; **vowel diagram**: showing relative degrees of closeness, openness, or raising in the articulation of individual vowels; **vowel-glide**: produced in passing from one vowel to another; ***vowel gradation***: see GRADATION 9; **vowel harmony** a feature of a language, whereby successive syllables in a word are limited to a particular class of vowel, as in Finno-Ugric, Turkish, etc.; **vowel height** the degree to which the tongue is raised or lowered in the articulation of a particular vowel; **vowel-laxing** the articulation of a vowel with the speech organs relaxed; **vowel mutation** = UMLAUT *noun* 1; **vowel-point** *noun & verb* (*a*) *noun* any of a set of marks used to indicate a vowel in Hebrew, Syriac, and Arabic; (*b*) *verb trans.* supply with such marks; **vowel-quality** the identifying acoustic characteristic of a vowel; **vowel-quantity** the duration length of a vowel; **vowel shift** a phonetic change in a vowel or vowels; ***great vowel shift*** (*Hist.*), a series of changes between medieval and modern English affecting the long vowels of the standard language.
► **B** *verb.* Infl. **-ll-**, *__-l-__.
†**1** *verb intrans. & trans.* Articulate the vowels in singing. L15–M17.
2 *verb trans.* Convert into a vowel; vocalize. E17.
3 *verb trans.* Supply with vowels or vowel-points. E17.
†**4** Pay (a creditor) with an IOU. *slang.* Only in 18.
■ **vowelist** *noun* (*rare*) †(*a*) a student of vowels or vowel-points; (*b*) a poet etc. characterized by the use of vowels: M17. **vowelize** *verb trans.* (*a*) modify or produce with vowels; (*b*) = VOWEL *verb* 3: E19. **vowelled** *adjective* (*a*) provided with vowels, esp. to an unusual extent; (*b*) having vowels of a specified kind or quality: M17. **vowelless** /-l-l-/ *adjective* L19. **vowelly** *adjective* having many vowels; characterized by vowels: E18.

vox /vɒks/ *noun.* M16.
[Latin.]
Voice, sound. Only in phrs. below.
vox angelica /anˈdʒɛlɪkə/ [Latin = angelic] = VOIX CÉLESTE. **vox humana** /hjʊˈmɑːnə/ [Latin = human] an organ reed-stop, having an 8-ft pitch, producing a tone supposedly resembling the human voice. **vox nihili** /ˈnʌɪ(h)ɪlʌɪ, -liː/ [Latin = of nothing] a worthless or meaningless word, *esp.* one produced by a scribal or printer's error. **vox populi** /ˈpɒpjʊlʌɪ, -liː/ [Latin = of the people] expressed general opinion; common talk or rumour.

voxel /ˈvɒksɛl/ *noun.* L20.
[from VO(LUME *noun* after *pixel*.]
COMPUTING. (In modelling or graphic simulation) each of an array of elements of volume that constitute a notional three-dimensional space; *esp.* each of an array of discrete elements into which a representation of a three-dimensional object is divided.

vox pop /vɒks ˈpɒp/ *noun & adjectival phr. colloq.* M20.
[Abbreviation of *vox populi*.]
► **A** *noun.* Popular opinion as represented by informal comments from members of the general public; statements or interviews of this kind. M20.

> *Times Lit. Suppl.* Dreadful quotations in these chapters, including paragraphs of vox pop.

► **B** *attrib.* or as *adjective.* Of, pertaining to, or characteristic of vox pop. M20.

> *Times* ITN . . and TV-am combined for a down-to-earth, vox-pop view of the occasion.

voyage /ˈvɔɪɪdʒ/ *noun.* ME.
[Anglo-Norman, Old French *veiage*, *voiage*, etc. (mod. *voyage*), from Latin VIATICUM: see -AGE.]
1 Orig., an act of travelling, a journey from one (distant) place to another, freq. for a particular purpose, *spec.* (*a*) a pilgrimage; (*b*) a military expedition. Now, a long journey by sea, air, or in space, *esp.* one in which a return is made to the starting-point. ME.
†**2** An enterprise, an undertaking, *esp.* one involving a journey. ME–L17.
3 *fig.* The passage through life; the supposed journey to the afterlife. LME.
†**4** A navigational route. L16–M18.
5 A written account of a voyage. L16.
6 (The catch taken during) a single fishing, sealing, or whaling trip; the proceeds from this. Now *N. Amer. dial.* M19.

> **1** *American Heritage* To command *Apollo 14* on its voyage to the moon. *New York Review of Books* The voyages of Columbus launched a period of European exploration. ***run a voyage***: see RUN *verb*. †**voyage royal** an expedition undertaken by a sovereign. **3** TENNYSON Passing on thine happier voyage now Toward no earthly pole.

Comb.: **voyage policy** LAW a maritime insurance policy providing cover during a specified voyage.
¶ See also BON VOYAGE.

voyage /ˈvɔɪɪdʒ/ *verb.* L15.
[French *voyager* travel, or directly from prec.]
1 *verb intrans.* Make a voyage. L15.
2 *verb trans.* Make a voyage over or through; traverse, esp. by sea or air. M17.

> **1** E. M. FORSTER So the sailors of Ulysses voyaged past the Sirens. *fig.*: G. WILL His body was dying but his mind still voyaged. **2** POPE Him, thus voyaging the deeps below, . . The King of Ocean saw.

■ **voyageable** *adjective* able to be voyaged over or through; navigable: (cf. earlier UNVOYAGEABLE) E19. **voyager** *noun* a person who makes a voyage or voyages; a traveller: L15.

voyagé /vwajaʒe/ *noun & adjective.* Pl. of noun pronounced same. M20.
[French, pa. pple of *voyager* travel.]
BALLET. (Designating) a movement in which the pose is held during progression.

voyageur /vwɒjəˈʒəː; *foreign* vwajaʒœːr (*pl. same*)/ *noun.* L18.
[French: see prec.]
Hist. In Canada, a person formerly employed by a fur company to transport goods between trading posts.

voyant /vwajɑ̃/ *noun.* Pl. pronounced same. M20.
[French, formed as next.]
A visionary; a seer.

voyant /vwajɑ̃/ *adjective.* E20.
[French, pres. ppl adjective of *voir* see: see -ANT[1].]
Showy, gaudy, flashy.

voyeur /vwɑːˈjəː/ *noun & verb.* E20.
[French, from *voir* see + *-eur* -OR.]
► **A** *noun.* A person who obtains sexual stimulation from covert observation of the sexual organs or actions of others. Also (*transf.*), a person who observes a particular situation without participation; a powerless or passive spectator. E20.

> I. WATSON He spied at them . . through a glass like a voyeur. *Blitz* He is ultimately a world-weary voyeur, incapable of trust and riddled with suspicion.

► **B** *verb intrans.* Obtain stimulation or gratification by being a voyeur, indulge in voyeurism. Chiefly as ***voyeuring*** *verbal noun.* M20.
■ **voyeurism** *noun* the state or condition of being a voyeur E20. **voyeurist** *noun & adjective* (*a*) *noun* a voyeur, a person who indulges in voyeurism; (*b*) *adjective* voyeuristic: M20. **voyeuˈristic** *adjective* of or pertaining to voyeurism E20. **voyeuˈristically** *adverb* M20.

voyou /vwaju/ *noun.* Pl. pronounced same. E20.
[French.]
A street urchin; a lout, a hooligan.

vozhd /vəʊʒd/ *noun.* M20.
[Russian *vozhd'*.]
A leader, a person in supreme authority; *spec.* (*Hist.*) Stalin.

VP *abbreviation.*
1 Verb phrase.
2 Vice-President.

VPL *abbreviation.*
Visible panty line.

VR *abbreviation.*
1 Variant reading.
2 Latin *Victoria Regina*, Queen Victoria.
3 Virtual reality.

vraic /vreɪk/ *noun.* E17.
[French dial., var. of *vrec*, *vrac* from Middle Low German, Dutch *wrak* WRACK *noun*[2]. Cf. VAREC.]
In the Channel Islands: seaweed, esp. as used for fuel and fertilizer.

vrai réseau /vrɛ rezo/ *noun phr.* Pl. ***vrais réseaux*** (pronounced same). M19.
[French = true net.]
A fine net ground used in making handmade (esp. Brussels) lace. Cf. RÉSEAU 1.

vraisemblable /vrɛsɑ̃blabl/ *adjective.* M19.
[French, from *vrai* true + *semblable* like.]
Believable, plausible.

vraisemblance /vrɛsɑ̃blɑ̃ːs/ *noun.* Pl. pronounced same. E19.
[French, from *vrai* true + SEMBLANCE.]
1 Verisimilitude. E19.
2 A representation *of* a person or thing. M19.

vrais réseaux *noun* pl. of VRAI RÉSEAU.

vriddhi /ˈvrɪdhi/ *noun.* M19.
[Sanskrit *vṛddhi* increase.]
SANSKRIT GRAMMAR. The strongest grade of an ablaut series of vowels; the process of raising a vowel from the middle grade to this.

vriesia /ˈvriːzɪə/ *noun.* M19.
[mod. Latin (see below), from W. H. de *Vries* (1806–62), Dutch botanist + -IA[1].]
Any of various bromeliads constituting the tropical American genus *Vriesia*, having rosettes of freq. banded or variegated leaves and spikes of chiefly yellow or white tubular flowers.

vril /vrɪl/ *noun.* L19.
[Invented word. Cf. BOVRIL.]
An imaginary form of energy described in E. Bulwer-Lytton's *The Coming Race* (1871).

VRML *abbreviation.*
COMPUTING. Virtual reality modelling language.

vroom /vruːm/ *noun, interjection, & verb.* Also **varoom**; redupl. **v- v-**. M20.
[Imit. Cf. VOOM.]
► **A** *noun & interjection.* (Repr.) the roaring noise made by a motor vehicle accelerating or travelling at speed. M20.

> *Punch* Noisy as the pits . . whence the vrooms and fumes waft up before exploding into eardrum and nostrils.

► **B** *verb.* **1** *verb intrans.* (Of a motor vehicle or engine) make a roaring noise; travel or accelerate at speed. M20.
2 *verb trans.* Rev (an engine) to produce a roaring sound. L20.

> **1** *New Yorker* To go varooming all over the desert in a couple of jeeps.

vrouw /vraʊ/ *noun.* Chiefly *S. Afr.* Also **vrow**. E17.
[Dutch = German *Frau*. Cf. FROW *noun*[1].]
A woman, a wife, *esp.* one of Dutch origin.

VS *abbreviation.*
Veterinary Surgeon.

vs. *abbreviation.*
Versus.

V-sign /ˈviːsʌɪn/ *noun.* M20.
[from V, V + SIGN *noun*.]
1 a The letter V, esp. as used to symbolize victory during the war of 1939–45. M20. ►**b** The Morse Code representation of this letter. M20.
2 = ***VICTORY sign***. Also, a gesture resembling the victory sign but made with the back of the hand outwards, as a sign of abuse, contempt, etc. M20.

> **2** E. FAIRWEATHER He stands in the garden making V-signs and shouting 'Bastards! Bastards!'

VSO *abbreviation.*
Voluntary Service Overseas.

VSOP *abbreviation.*
Very Special Old Pale (brandy).

V/STOL /ˈviːstɒl/ *abbreviation.*
Vertical and short take-off and landing.

VT *abbreviation.* Also **Vt.**
Vermont.

VTEC *abbreviation.*
MEDICINE. Verocytotoxin-producing E. coli.

VTO *abbreviation.*
Vertical take-off.

VTOL /ˈviːtɒl/ *abbreviation.*
Vertical take-off and landing.

VTR *abbreviation.*
Video tape recorder.

VU *abbreviation.* Also **vu**.
ELECTRONICS. Volume unit; ***VU meter***, a volume indicator employing the VU scale.

vue d'ensemble /vy dɑ̃sɑ̃bl/ *noun phr.* Pl. ***vues d'ensemble*** (pronounced same). M19.
[French.]
A general view of matters; an overview.

vuelta /ˈvwɛltə/ *noun.* M20.
[Spanish = turn, round.]
BULLFIGHTING. The triumphal circuit of the ring awarded to a successful matador.
¶ See also MEDIA VUELTA.

vues d'ensemble *noun phr.* pl. of VUE D'ENSEMBLE.

vug /vʌg/ *noun.* Also †**vugh**. E19.
[from Cornish *vooga*, perh. ult. cogn. with Breton *mouger* cave.]
MINING & GEOLOGY. A cavity in a rock, which may contain a lining of crystalline minerals.
■ **vuggy** *adjective* full of cavities M19. **vugular** /ˈvʌgjʊlə/ *adjective* (GEOLOGY) containing vugs; of the nature of a vug: M20.

vuilgoed /ˈfœylxut/ *noun. S. Afr. slang.* Pl. same. E20.
[Afrikaans, from Dutch *vuil* filthy + *goed* things.]
Filth, rubbish. Freq. as a term of abuse, a despicable person.

Vulcan /ˈvʌlkən/ *noun.* LME.
[Latin *Vulcanus*.]
► **I** Chiefly *literary.*
†**1** A volcano. LME–E18.
2 *transf.* A blacksmith; an iron-worker. M17.
3 (A) fire. L17.
► **II 4** The Roman god of fire and metalworking, the lame son of Jupiter and Juno and the husband of Venus, identified by the Romans with the Greek god Hephaestus. Also, a representation of the god Vulcan. E16.
¶ Earliest with ref. to the Lipari Islands (cf. ***VULCANIAN Islands***).

Vulcanian /vʌlˈkeɪnɪən/ *noun & adjective.* L16.
[from Latin *Vulcanius*, formed as prec., in later senses perh. partly also from *vulcano* obsolete var. of VOLCANO: see -IAN.]
►†**A** *noun.* A person regarded as resembling Vulcan. *rare.* Only in L16.
► **B** *adjective.* **1** Of, pertaining to, or characteristic of the god Vulcan; produced or made by Vulcan. E17.
2 Of, belonging to, or having many volcanoes; volcanic. M17.
3 GEOLOGY. = PLUTONIC 1. Now *rare* or *obsolete.* M19.
4 GEOLOGY. Of, pertaining to, or designating (the stage of) a volcanic eruption characterized by periodic explosive events. E20.
Phrases: **Vulcanian Islands** the Lipari Islands, lying between Sicily and Italy.

vulcanic /vʌlˈkanɪk/ *adjective.* L18.
[In sense 1 from French *vulcanique* var. of *volcanique* VOLCANIC, in sense 2 from VULCAN: see -IC.]
1 = VOLCANIC 1. L18.
2 (**V-**.) Of, pertaining to, or characteristic of the Roman god Vulcan. E19. ▸**b** Of or pertaining to fire; fiery. M19.

vulcanicity /vʌlkəˈnɪsɪti/ *noun. rare.* L19.
[from prec. or French *vulcanicité* var. of *volcanicité* VOLCANICITY: see -ITY.]
= VOLCANICITY.

vulcanisation *noun,* **vulcanise** *verb,* vars. of VULCANIZATION, VULCANIZE.

vulcanism /ˈvʌlkənɪz(ə)m/ *noun. rare.* L19.
[French *vulcanisme* var. of *volcanisme* VOLCANISM.]
= VOLCANISM.

vulcanist /ˈvʌlkənɪst/ *noun.* L16.
[In sense 1 from VULCAN, in sense 2 from French *vulcaniste* var. of *volcaniste* VOLCANIST: see -IST.]
†**1** A person who works with fire; *esp.* a blacksmith. L16–E17.
2 An asserter of the igneous origin of certain geological and planetary formations. E19.

vulcanite /ˈvʌlkənʌɪt/ *noun.* M19.
[from VULCAN + -ITE¹.]
†**1** = PYROXENE. Only in M19.
2 A preparation of indiarubber and sulphur hardened by exposure to intense heat. Also called ***ebonite***. M19.

vulcanization /vʌlkənʌɪˈzeɪʃ(ə)n/ *noun.* Also **-isation**. M19.
[from next + -ATION.]
The method or process of treating crude indiarubber with sulphur and subjecting it to intense heat, thus rendering it more durable and adaptable.

vulcanize /ˈvʌlkənʌɪz/ *verb.* Also **-ise**. E19.
[from VULCAN + -IZE.]
1 *verb trans. gen.* Throw into a fire; burn. *rare.* E19.
2 *verb trans.* Subject (indiarubber etc.) to the process of vulcanization. Freq. as ***vulcanized*** *ppl adjective.* M19.
3 *verb intrans.* Undergo vulcanization. L19.
■ **vulcanizate** *noun* a material that has been vulcanized M20. **vulcanizer** *noun* a person who or thing which vulcanizes something; *esp.* the apparatus used in vulcanizing indiarubber: M19.

†**vulcano** *noun & verb* var. of VOLCANO.

vulcanology /vʌlkəˈnɒlədʒi/ *noun.* M19.
[formed as VULCANIC + -OLOGY. Cf. VOLCANOLOGY.]
The branch of science that deals with volcanoes and volcanic phenomena.
■ **vulcanoˈlogical** *adjective* L19. **vulcanologist** *noun* M19.

vulgar /ˈvʌlgə/ *noun. arch.* LME.
[from next.]
†**1** The common or usual language of a country; the vernacular. LME–M17.
2 †**a** A member of the common people, an ordinary person. Also, a person regarded as belonging to a low social class, an uneducated or unrefined person. Earliest in *pl.* E16–E19. ▸**b** *collect. pl. The* common people. L16.
†**3** In *pl.* English text for translation into Latin as a school exercise. E16–E17.
†**4** = VULGATE *noun* 1. E17–E18.

vulgar /ˈvʌlgə/ *adjective.* LME.
[Latin *vulgaris*, from *vulgus* the common people: see -AR¹.]
1 Employed in common or ordinary reckoning of time, distance, etc.; calculated according to common or standard practice. Now chiefly in ***vulgar fractu.*** LME. ▸†**b** = VULGATE *adjective* 1. M16–E19.
2 In common or general use; customary, standard; commonly current or prevalent; widely disseminated. LME.
3 (Of language etc.) commonly used by the people of a country; vernacular, esp. as opp. to Latin; (of a word) used in ordinary speech; common, familiar. Formerly also, written or spoken in the usual language of a country. *arch.* L15.
4 Of, pertaining to, or characteristic of the ordinary or common people; plebeian. M16. ▸†**b** Of a soldier etc.: of undistinguished rank. E17–L18.
5 Of the common or usual kind; ordinary, commonplace; not advanced or sophisticated. *arch.* M16.
6 Offensively coarse in manner or character; low. M17.

📖 **1** ***vulgar fraction***: see FRACTION 1. **2** BURKE The quality of labour which in the vulgar course we .. employ. R. G. COLLINGWOOD This current vulgar theory dominates the minds of classical scholars. **3** R. BARBER Songs of love's bitter-sweetness .. written in the vulgar tongue. T. BEWICK Foreign Birds, with their Vulgar and Scientific Names. **Vulgar Latin** informal Latin of classical times. **4** BYRON 'Tis easy to astonish .. The vulgar mass. **5** W. K. KELLY A very vulgar policy, and one within the scope of .. ordinary capacities. **7** H. JAMES A loud, vulgar, .. bullying man. D. ATHILL He loved having money and making a vulgar show with it.

■ **vulgarly** *adverb* LME. **vulgarness** *noun* (now *rare* or *obsolete*) vulgarity E17.

vulgarian /vʌlˈgɛːrɪən/ *adjective & noun.* M17.
[from prec. + -IAN.]
► **A** *adjective.* Vulgar. M17.
► **B** *noun.* A vulgar person. E19.

📖 G. WILL Johnson was a bullying vulgarian, often crudely unethical, sometimes corrupt.

■ **vulgarianism** *noun* vulgarity E20.

vulgarisateur /vylgarizatœːr/ *noun.* Pl. pronounced same. M20.
[French, from *vulgariser* popularize, vulgarize + *-ateur* -ATOR.]
A popularizer, a vulgarizer.

vulgarisation /vylgarizasjɔ̃/ *noun*¹. M20.
[French.]
= VULGARIZATION.
¶ See also HAUTE VULGARISATION, *OEUVRE* ***de vulgarisation***.

vulgarisation *noun*² var. of VULGARIZATION.

vulgarise *verb* var. of VULGARIZE.

vulgarism /ˈvʌlgərɪz(ə)m/ *noun.* M17.
[from VULGAR *adjective* + -ISM.]
†**1** A common or ordinary expression. *rare.* Only in M17.
2 A coarse or vulgar phrase or expression. M18.
3 Vulgarity; an instance of this. M18.

vulgarity /vʌlˈgarɪti/ *noun.* L16.
[Partly from late Latin *vulgaritas*, formed as VULGAR *adjective*, partly directly from VULGAR *adjective*: see -ITY.]
†**1** The common people. L16–M17. ▸**b** The ordinary sort or class *of* something. M–L17.
†**2** General use; prevalence. *rare.* E–M17.
†**3** The state or quality of being ordinary or commonplace; an instance of this. M17–E18.
4 The state or quality of being vulgar or coarse; an instance of this. Also, a vulgar person. L18.

📖 **4** R. MACAULAY A garish hugeness that smacked almost of vulgarity, and pained his fastidious taste. N. MONSARRAT To watch one's guests arriving was an unacceptable vulgarity.

vulgarization /vʌlgərʌɪˈzeɪʃ(ə)n/ *noun.* Also **-isation**. M17.
[from next + -ATION. Cf. VULGARISATION *noun*¹.]
The action or process of vulgarizing something; an instance of this.

vulgarize /ˈvʌlgərʌɪz/ *verb.* Also **-ise**. E17.
[from VULGAR *adjective* + -IZE.]
1 *verb intrans.* Act in a vulgar manner; be or become vulgar. E17.
2 *verb trans.* Make vulgar, *esp.* popularize, make commonplace. E18.

📖 **2** HAZLITT They vulgarise and degrade whatever is .. sacred to the mind. W. LEWIS It is just the popularization and vulgarizing of art that is responsible for the .. swarms of dilettante competitors.

■ **vulgarizer** *noun* L19.

vulgate /ˈvʌlgət/ *ppl adjective*¹. Long *arch. rare.* E16.
[Latin *vulgat-* pa. ppl stem of *vulgare*: see next, -ATE².]
In general or common use.

Vulgate /ˈvʌlgeɪt, -gət/ *adjective*² *& noun.* Also (in senses A.2, B.2, 3) **v-**. E17.
[Late Latin *vulgata* fem. (*editio* edition, *lectio* reading), *vulgatus* masc. (*textus* text), pa. pples of Latin *vulgare* make public or common, from *vulgus* common people: see -ATE².]
► **A** *adjective.* **1** Designating the standard accepted version of (a portion of) the Bible, *spec.* the Latin version prepared mainly by St Jerome (see sense B.1 below); (of a passage etc.) occurring in such a version. E17.
2 *gen.* Designating or occurring in the standard accepted version of any text. M19.
► **B** *noun.* **1** A Vulgate bible; *spec.* the Latin version of the Bible prepared mainly by St Jerome in the late 4th cent. E18.
2 *gen.* The standard accepted reading or version of any text. M19.
3 Common or colloquial speech. M19.

vulgate /ˈvʌlgət/ *verb trans. rare.* M19.
[Latin *vulgat-* pa. ppl stem of *vulgare*: see prec., -ATE³.]
Put into general circulation.

vulgo /ˈvʌlgəʊ/ *adverb.* Long *arch. rare.* E17.
[Latin, abl. of next.]
Commonly, popularly.

vulgus /ˈvʌlgəs/ *noun*¹. Long *arch. rare.* L17.
[Latin.]
The common people; the masses.

vulgus /ˈvʌlgəs/ *noun*². M19.
[Alt. of *vulgars* (see VULGAR *noun* 3) translating mod. Latin *vulgaria* use as noun of neut. pl. of Latin *vulgaris*, a title of Latin–English phrase books since L15: assim. to GRADUS.]
In some public schools, a short set of Latin verses on a given subject.

vuln /vʌln/ *verb trans.* Now only in HERALDRY. L16.
[Irreg. from Latin *vulnerare*: see VULNERATE.]
Wound; pierce with a weapon. Chiefly as ***vulned*** *ppl adjective.*

vulnerable /ˈvʌln(ə)rəb(ə)l/ *adjective.* E17.
[Late Latin *vulnerabilis* wounding, from *vulnerare* VULNERATE: see -ABLE. Cf. earlier INVULNERABLE.]
†**1** Wounding, injurious. *rare.* Only in E17.
2 Able to be wounded; (of a person) able to be physically or emotionally hurt; liable to damage or harm, esp. from aggression or attack, assailable. (Foll. by *to*.) E17.
3 BRIDGE. Of a side: liable to increased penalties or bonuses as a result of having won a game. E20.

📖 **2** W. PERRIAM I do understand you're feeling very vulnerable. D. HALBERSTAM Our troops .. were vulnerable to the night strikes of the Chinese. *Soldier of Fortune* The vulnerable vital points of the human anatomy.

■ **vulnerability** *noun* the state or quality of being vulnerable E19. **vulnerableness** *noun* E18. **vulnerably** *adverb* M19.

vulnerary /ˈvʌln(ə)rəri/ *adjective & noun.* L16.
[Latin *vulnerarius*, from *vulner-*, *vulnus* wound: see -ARY¹.]
► **A** *adjective.* **1** Useful in healing wounds; curative in respect of external injuries. Now *rare* or *obsolete.* L16.
2 Causing a wound or wounds; wounding. *arch. rare.* E17.
► **B** *noun.* A vulnerary preparation, plant, or drug. Now *rare* or *obsolete.* E17.

†**vulnerate** *verb trans.* L16–M18.
[Latin *vulnerat-* pa. ppl stem of *vulnerare*, from *vulner-*, *vulnus* wound: see -ATE³.]
= VULN.

vulpanser /vʌlˈpansə/ *noun.* E18.
[mod. Latin, from Latin *vulpes* fox + *anser* goose, after Greek *khēnalōpēx*.]
The shelduck, *Tadorna tadorna*.

Vulpecula /vʌlˈpɛkjʊlə/ *noun*. L18.
[Latin *vulpecula* dim. of *vulpes* fox: see -CULE.]
Orig. ***Vulpecula et Anser*** [Latin = fox and goose]. (The name of) a constellation of the northern hemisphere, lying in the Milky Way between Cygnus and Aquila; the Fox.

vulpic /ˈvʌlpɪk/ *adjective*. L19.
[from mod. Latin *vulpina* specific epithet of the lichen *Cetraria vulpina*, from Latin *vulpinus*: see VULPINE, -IC.]
CHEMISTRY. ***vulpic acid***, an acid, $C_{19}H_{14}O_5$, occurring in many lichens and also obtained artificially.
■ Also **vulˈpinic** *adjective* E20.

vulpicide /ˈvʌlpɪsʌɪd/ *noun*. E19.
[from Latin *vulpes* fox + -CIDE.]
1 A person who kills a fox, *spec*. otherwise than by hunting with hounds. E19.
2 The action of killing a fox, *spec*. otherwise than by hunting with hounds. E19.
■ **vulpiˈcidal** *adjective* of, pertaining to, or committing vulpicide E19. **vulpicidism** *noun* the practice of vulpicide M19.

†**vulpinary** *adjective*. *rare*. E18–E19.
[formed as next: see -ARY¹.]
= VULPINE 1.

vulpine /ˈvʌlpʌɪn/ *adjective*. E17.
[Latin *vulpinus*, from *vulpes* fox: see -INE¹.]
1 Characteristic of, or resembling (that of) a fox, foxlike; *fig*. cunning, crafty, sly. E17.
2 Of or pertaining to a fox or foxes; that is a fox. M19.

📖 **1** B. MOORE The boatman was young, vulpine, with a wild cub's grace. D. LODGE A mischievous, slightly vulpine smile, like a fox in a fable. **vulpine opossum**, **vulpine phalanger** the brushtail possum, *Trichosurus vulpecula*, of Australia. **2** *Field* Gorse . . seems to offer small inducement to the vulpine fraternity.

■ **vulpinism** *noun* vulpine nature or character; craft, guile: M19.

vulsella /vɒlˈsɛlə/ *noun*. Also **vol-**. L17.
[Latin = pair of tweezers, from *vuls-*, *vols-* pa. ppl stem of *vellere* pluck + -ELLA.]
= next.

vulsellum /vɒlˈsɛləm/ *noun*. Also **vol-**. L19.
[mod. Latin, app. from misunderstanding of prec. as neut. pl.]
MEDICINE. A kind of forceps with hooks or claws on each blade, used esp. in gynaecological operations.

vulture /ˈvʌltʃə/ *noun*. LME.
[Anglo-Norman *vultur*, Old French *voltour* (mod. *vautour*), from Latin *vulturius*, from *vultur*, *voltur*.]
1 a Any of various large Old World birds of prey of the family Accipitridae, most of which feed on carrion and have a mainly bald head and neck, traditionally reputed to gather with others in anticipation of a death. LME. ▸**b** Any of several similar New World birds of prey of the family Cathartidae. Cf. BUZZARD *noun*¹ 1b. L18.
2 *fig*. **a** A thing which preys on the mind; *esp*. a cause of mental anguish, a tormenting emotion or obsession. Chiefly *literary*. L16. ▸**b** A rapacious person. E17.
3 (Usu. **V-**.) Any of several northern constellations; *esp*. Lyra. Now *rare*. M17.
1a ***bearded vulture***, ***griffon vulture***, ***white-backed vulture***, etc. **b** ***king vulture***, ***turkey vulture***, etc.
Phrases: **king of the vultures** (now *rare*) the king vulture, *Sarcorhamphus papa*.
■ **vulturish** *adjective* somewhat like a vulture E19.

vulture /ˈvʌltʃə/ *verb*. E17.
[from prec.]
1 *verb trans*. Consume rapaciously. E17.
2 *verb intrans*. Move suddenly with rapacious intent; swoop *down*, *in*, etc. M20.

📖 **2** M. ALLINGHAM The tax harpies vultured down for death duties.

vulturine /ˈvʌltʃərʌɪn/ *adjective*. M17.
[Latin *vulturinus*, from *vultur*: see prec., -INE¹.]
Of, pertaining to, or resembling a vulture or vultures; vulturous; *fig*. rapacious.
vulturine guinea-fowl a large E. African guinea-fowl, *Acryllium vulturinum*, which has a bare head and upper neck, and a mantle of long, striped iridescent feathers. **vulturine parrot** either of two parrots which have bare foreheads and feed on soft fruit, *Gypopsitta vulturina* of Brazil and *Psittrichas fulgidus* of New Guinea.

vulturous /ˈvʌltʃərəs/ *adjective*. E17.
[formed as prec. + -OUS.]
Characteristic of or resembling (that of) a vulture; *esp*. rapacious.

📖 G. STEINEM She . . hadn't been subject to the criticism of this rather vulturous group.

vulva /ˈvʌlvə/ *noun*. Pl. **-vas**, **-vae** /-viː/. LME.
[Latin *vulva*, *volva* womb, matrix.]
ANATOMY. The female external genitals; ZOOLOGY the opening of the vagina in a female mammal; the external opening of the oviduct in some invertebrates.
■ **vulval**, **vulvar** *adjectives* of or belonging to the vulva M19. **vulˈvectomy** *noun* (an instance of) surgical removal of (part of) the vulva E20. **vulviform** *adjective* (BOTANY & ZOOLOGY) resembling a vulva M19. **vulˈvitis** *noun* (MEDICINE) inflammation of the vulva M19.

vulvovaginitis /ˌvʌlvəʊvadʒɪˈnʌɪtɪs/ *noun*. L19.
[from VULVA + -O- + VAGINITIS.]
MEDICINE. Inflammation of the vulva and vagina.

vum /vʌm/ *verb intrans*. & *trans*. *US colloq*. Infl. **-mm-**. L18.
[Alt. of vow *verb*.]
Vow, swear.

vurry /ˈvəːri/ *adjective*. *non-standard US*. L19.
[Repr. a pronunc.]
Very.

vv. *abbreviation*.
1 Verses.
2 Volumes.

VW *abbreviation*.
Volkswagen.

vygie /ˈfeɪxi/ *noun*. *S. Afr*. M20.
[Afrikaans, from Dutch *vyg* fig + *-ie* dim. suffix.]
Any of numerous succulent plants belonging to the genus *Mesembryanthemum* (family Aizoaceae) or related genera, esp. species of *Carpobrotus* with edible fruit.

vying *verb pres. pple* of VIE *verb*.

Vynide /ˈvʌɪnʌɪd/ *noun*. M20.
[Invented name.]
(Proprietary name for) a plastic material imitating leather.

Ww

W, w /ˈdʌb(ə)ljuː/.
The twenty-third letter of the modern English alphabet, originating from a ligature of the Roman letter represented by *U* and *V* of modern alphabets. The sound normally represented by the letter is the bilabial semivowel /w/, closely resembling the value of Roman consonantal *U* or *V*. The sound was at first represented by *uu*, but in Old English and early Middle English the runic character wynn was widely used, this in turn being replaced in Middle English by the ligature *w*. Consonantal *w* is now silent initially and medially before *r* and may be silent before *h* (see **WH**) and (in some words as ***answer***, ***sword***, ***two***) after *s* and *t*. It may also be elided in the unstressed 2nd elem. of a compound, as in place-names (***Norwich***) and in certain nautical terms (***forward***, ***gunwale***). Vocalic *w* results from the Middle English mutation of *g* and *y* (cf. **YOGH**) and medially and terminally forms a digraph with the preceding stressed vowel (as in ***bow***); also from Middle English *w* was freq. used instead of *u* as 2nd elem. of other digraphs (as in ***paw***, ***yew***). Pl. **W's**, **Ws**.
▶ **I 1** The letter and its sound.
2 The shape of the letter.
2 W-shaped *adjective* having a shape or a cross-section like the capital letter W.
▶ **II** Symbolical uses.
3 Used to denote serial order; applied e.g. to the twenty-third (or often the twenty-second, either I or J being omitted) group or section, sheet of a book, etc.
4 *GENETICS*. (Cap. W.) Denoting the female-determining sex chromosome in species in which the female rather than the male is the heterogametic sex (as in birds and some insects).
5 *PARTICLE PHYSICS*. [Initial letter of *weak*.] (Cap. W.) Denoting a heavy charged vector boson that is probably the quantum of the weak interaction.
▶ **III 6** Abbrevs.: **W** = west(ern); watt(s); Welsh; (*CHEMISTRY*) [mod. Latin] *wolframium* tungsten; women('s size). **w.** = wicket(s); wide(s); wife; with.

WA *abbreviation*.
1 Western Australia.
2 Washington (State). *US*.

Wa /wɑː/ *noun & adjective*. **M19**.
[Wa.]
▶ **A** *noun*. Pl. same, **-s**.
1 A member of a group of hill-dwelling peoples of E. Myanmar (Burma) and SW Yunnan. **M19**.
2 The Mon-Khmer language of this people. **M19**.
▶ **B** *attrib.* or as *adjective*. Of or pertaining to the Wa or their language. **E20**.

WAAC *abbreviation*.
Women's Army Auxiliary Corps (see next).

Waac /wak/ *noun*. Also **WAAC**. **E20**.
[Acronym.]
A member of the British Women's Army Auxiliary Corps (1917–19) or the American force of the same name (now the WAC) formed in 1942.

WAAF *abbreviation*.
Women's Auxiliary Air Force (see next).

Waaf /waf/ *noun*. Also **WAAF**. **M20**.
[Acronym.]
A member of the Women's Auxiliary Air Force (1939–48, subsequently reorganized as part of the Women's Royal Air Force).

waal /wal, wɑːl/ *interjection*. *US colloq*. **M19**.
[Repr. a pronunc.]
= **WELL** *interjection*.

wabbit /ˈwɒbɪt/ *adjective*. *Scot*. Also **wappit** /ˈwapɪt/, **wubbit** /ˈwʌbɪt/. **L19**.
[Origin uncertain: perh. rel. to **WOUBIT**.]
Tired out, exhausted; out of sorts, off colour.

📖 J. TORRINGTON The one-eyed moggy looked wabbit from trekking snowed-up pavements.

†**wabble** *noun*, *verb* vars. of **WOBBLE** *noun*, *verb*.

Wabenzi /wɑːˈbɛnzi/ *noun pl*. *joc*. Also **Wa-Benzi**. **M20**.
[Invented to resemble the name of an African people: from *wa-* human pl. prefix + Mercedes-*Benz* a make of luxury car.]
In Africa, black politicians, businessmen, businesswomen, etc., whose success is characterized by their ownership or use of a Mercedes-Benz car.

wabi /ˈwabi/ *noun*. **M20**.
[Japanese, lit. 'solitude'.]
In Japanese art, a quality of simple and serene beauty of a slightly austere or melancholy kind expressing a mood of spiritual solitude recognized in Zen Buddhist philosophy. Cf. **SABI**.

waboom /ˈvɑːbʊəm/ *noun*. Orig. (now *rare*) **wagenboom** /ˈvɑːx(ə)nbʊəm/. **L18**.
[Afrikaans, from *wa*, earlier *wagen* wagon + *boom* tree, from the use of the wood to build wagons.]
A South African protea, *Protea arborea*, forming a bushy tree with large pale yellow flowers.

WAC *abbreviation*. *US*.
Women's Army Corps.

Wac /wak/ *noun*. *US*. Also **WAC**. **M20**.
[Acronym.]
A member of the Women's Army Corps, formed in 1943.

Wachagga /wəˈtʃagə/ *noun pl*. Also **-chaga**. **L19**.
[Bantu *Wachaga*, from *wa-* human pl. prefix + **CHAGGA**.]
The Chagga people.

wack /wak/ *noun*[1]. *slang* (orig. *US*). **M20**.
[Prob. back-form. from **WACKY**.]
An eccentric, mad, or crazy person; a crackpot.

wack /wak/ *noun*[2]. *dial*. **M20**.
[Perh. from **WACKER**.]
A familiar term of address: pal, mate.

wack /wak/ *adjective*. *slang* (chiefly *US*). **L20**.
[Prob. from **WACKO**, **WACKY**.]
Bad, harmful; unfashionable.

wacke /ˈwakə/ *noun*. **E19**.
[German from Middle High German = large stone, from Old High German *wacko* pebble.]
PETROGRAPHY. Orig., any soft sandstone-like rock resulting from the decomposition of basaltic rocks. Now, any sandstone containing between 15 and 75 per cent mud matrix. Cf. **GREYWACKE**.

wacked *adjective* var. of **WHACKED**.

wacker /ˈwakə/ *noun*. *dial*. **M18**.
[Origin unkn.]
A Liverpudlian. Also = **WACK** *noun*[2].

Wacker process /ˈvakə ˈprəʊsɛs/ *noun phr*. **M20**.
[from *Wacker* Chemie G.m.b.H., German chemical company.]
CHEMISTRY. The catalytic oxidation of an alkene to an aldehyde, esp. of ethylene (ethene) to acetaldehyde (ethanal).

wacko /ˈwakəʊ/ *adjective & noun*. *slang* (orig. & chiefly *N. Amer.*). Also **wh-**. **L20**.
[from next + **-O**.]
▶ **A** *adjective*. Mad; eccentric. **L20**.
▶ **B** *noun*. Pl. **-o(e)s**. A mad or eccentric person. **L20**.

wacky /ˈwaki/ *noun & adjective*. Orig. *dial*. Also **wh-**. **M19**.
[from **WHACK** *noun* + **-Y**[1].]
▶ **A** *noun*. A crazy, mad, or peculiar person; an eccentric. **M19**.
▶ **B** *adjective*. **1** Left-handed. *dial*. **E20**.
2 Crazy, mad; eccentric, peculiar, weird. *slang* (orig. *US*). **M20**.

📖 **2** *She* The wackiest scheme of all . . a college for cats and dogs. *TV Times* A wacky . . chase movie about a truck driver who careers . . across the continent. **wacky baccy** *colloq*. cannabis.

■ **wackily** *adverb* **M20**. **wackiness** *noun* **M20**.

wad /wɒd/ *noun*[1] & *verb*[1]. **M16**.
[Obscurely rel. to Dutch *watten* (whence German *Watte*), French *ouate*, Italian *ovatta* padding, cotton wool, Spanish *bata* dressing-gown.]
▶ **A** *noun*. **1** A material composed of matted fibres used for padding; wadding. *obsolete* exc. *Scot*. **M16**.
2 A bundle of hay or straw; *esp*. a small bundle of hay, peas, beans, etc., made at the time of cutting or reaping; a portion of a sheaf. Now *dial*. **L16**. ▸**b** A heap. Also, a swath. *dial*. **M18**.
3 A small lump or compact bundle of soft, loose, or pliable material used esp. as a plug, as a pad, or to keep things apart. **L16**. ▸**b** A disc or plug of paper, cloth, etc., retaining the powder and shot in position in a gun or cartridge. **M17**. ▸**c** A thing rolled up tightly, as a roll of banknotes. **L18**.
4 A large quantity, esp. of money; a mass, a heap. Orig. *Scot. & north*. **E19**.
5 *CERAMICS*. A small piece of clay either placed on the rim of a saggar as a wedge, or to separate boxed pots etc. **E19**.
6 A bun, a cake; a sandwich. Also *gen*., something to eat. *slang*. **E20**.

📖 **3** P. LIVELY She went round . . stuffing wads of torn-up sheets against the worst leaks. *fig*.: T. C. BOYLE Something rose in her throat, a deep wad of . . regret. ***oily wad***: see **OILY** *adjective*. **b shoot one's wad** *colloq*. (chiefly *US*) do all that one can do. **c** N. DEMILLE A briefcase stuffed with wads of money. **4** A. COOKE Eggs and bacon and a wad of pancakes. **6** ALAN BENNETT Picking old men off bomb sites and feeding them tea and wads in some . . church hall.

Comb.: **wadcutter** (chiefly *US*) a bullet designed to cut a neat hole in a paper range target; **wad hook** a spiral tool for withdrawing a wad or charge from a gun.
▶ **B** *verb trans*. Infl. **-dd-**.
1 Put a wad in (a gun, a cartridge); plug (an aperture) with a wad. Also foll. by *up*. **L16**.
2 Press (loose, soft, or fibrous material) into a small space; form into a wad; *US* roll up tightly. Also foll. by *up*. **M17**.
3 Lay up (cut peas, beans, etc.) in bundles. Now *dial*. **L17**.
4 Line, stuff, or pad (as) with wadding; protect (a person, walls, etc.) with wadding. **M18**.

📖 **1** W. OWEN You had best wad up your ears if swearing upsets them. **2** G. VIDAL The T-shirt was wadded up. E. BOWEN She drew some shreds of Kleenex out . . and wadded them together. *New Yorker* He wads his damp clothes into the . . dryer. **4** M. MCCARTHY His royal-purple wadded dressing-gown.

■ **wadder** *noun* (*rare*) †(**a**) an implement for wadding a gun; (**b**) *dial*. a person who wads peas, beans, etc.: **L16**.

wad /wɒd/ *noun*[2] & *verb*[2]. **E17**.
[Perh. cogn. with Old Norse *vaðr* (masc.) measuring-line, Middle Swedish *vapi* (weak masc.) boundary line between properties, or Old English *wadan* go, **WADE** *verb*.]
▶ **A** *noun*. **1** *SURVEYING*. A straight line taken in measuring from one mark to another. Now *rare* or *obsolete*. **E17**.
2 A line, *esp*. one marked out between two tracts of land; a mark or guide in ploughing, shooting, etc. *dial*. **L18**. ▸**b** Way or course of travel, track (*lit. & fig.*). *dial*. **M19**.
▶ **B** *verb intrans*. Infl. **-dd-**. *SURVEYING*. Mark out a straight line. Now *rare* or *obsolete*. **E17**.

wad /wɒd/ *noun*[3]. Chiefly *north*. **E17**.
[Origin unkn.]
1 Graphite, black lead. **E17**.
2 An impure earthy ore of manganese. **L18**.

wadding /ˈwɒdɪŋ/ *noun*. **E17**.
[from **WAD** *noun*[1] & *verb*[1] + **-ING**[1].]
1 Any material from which wads for guns are made; a wad. **E17**.
2 Any soft, loose, or pliable material used as a padding, lining, stuffing, etc. Now *esp*., cotton wool formed into a fleecy layer. **M18**.
3 The action of **WAD** *verb*[1]. **L18**.

waddle /ˈwɒd(ə)l/ *verb & noun*. **LME**.
[Perh. frequentative of **WADE** *verb*: see **-LE**[3].]
▶ **A** *verb*. †**1** *verb intrans*. Fall heavily or as an inert mass. Only in **LME**.
2 *verb intrans*. Walk with short steps and a clumsy swaying motion, like a stout short-legged person or a bird (as a duck or goose) with short legs set far apart. **L16**. ▸**b** Become a lame duck or defaulter. Usu. foll. by *out*. *Stock Exchange slang*. Now *rare* or *obsolete*. **L18**.
3 *verb trans*. Of an animal: trample or tread down (grass). Now *dial*. **E17**.

📖 **2** H. E. BATES Ponderous and old and flabby, the Labradors waddled ten or twelve paces. A. CRAIG Old women . . waddling home with their shopping.

▶ **B** *noun*. The action of waddling; a waddling gait. **L17**.

📖 D. DELILLO I make believe I'm fat and walk with a waddle.

■ **waddler** *noun* **E19**. **waddlingly** *adverb* in a waddling manner **L19**. **waddly** *adjective* that waddles; moving with a waddling gait: **M20**.

waddy /ˈwɒdi/ *noun*[1] & *verb*. **L18**.
[Aboriginal, perh. alt. of **WOOD** *noun*[1].]
▶ **A** *noun*. **1** An Australian Aborigine's war-club. **L18**.
2 Any club or stick; *spec*. a walking-stick. *Austral. & NZ*. **E19**.

▶ **B** *verb trans.* Club or kill with a waddy. *Austral.* **M19.**

waddy /ˈwɒdi/ *noun*[2]. *US slang.* **L19.**
[Origin unkn.]
A cowboy, *esp.* a temporary cowhand.

wade /weɪd/ *verb & noun.*
[Old English *wadan* = Old Frisian *wada*, Middle Dutch, Middle Low German *waden*, Old High German *watan* (German *waten* weak), Old Norse *vaða*, from Germanic verb meaning 'go, go through', from Indo-European base repr. by Latin *vadere* go, *vadare* wade through, *vadum* ford.]
▶ **A** *verb.* †**1** *verb intrans.* **a** Go, advance, move onward. Usu. foll. by *over, through.* **OE–M17.** ▸**b** Esp. of a weapon: go *through* or penetrate *into* something. **OE–LME.**
2 *verb intrans.* Walk through water or any liquid or soft substance which acts as an impediment to motion. Formerly also, pass *over* a river etc. on foot. **ME.** ▸**b** *fig.* Go laboriously or doggedly *through* a tedious task, a long or uninteresting book, etc. Also, progress with difficulty or by force. **LME.**
3 *verb trans.* Walk through (water etc.). **ME.**
4 *verb intrans.* Go *into* or run *over* in one's mind; think *through* an argument etc. Now *obsolete* exc. as passing into sense 2b. **LME.**
5 *verb intrans.* Of the sun or moon: (appear to) move *through* clouds or mist; be clouded. Chiefly *Scot. & north.* **LME.**
†**6** Be *in* a certain condition, go about *in* certain clothing. Only in **L16.**

📖 **2** W. GOLDING I began to wade into the tall bracken. P. PEARCE He began wading ashore in hurried, splashing strides. *fig.*: S. RICHARDSON A man who is to wade into her favour . . through the blood of her brother. **wading pool** *N. Amer.* a paddling pool. **b** *Management Today* By the time the reader has waded through . . nine chapters, the book begins to lighten. **3** T. MCGUANE Skelton . . began to wade the tidal creek.

With adverbs & prepositions in specialized senses: **wade in** *colloq.* make a vigorous or concerted attack on an opponent; intervene, esp. vocally. **wade into** *colloq.* make a physical or verbal attack on; confront energetically.
▶ **B** *noun.* **1** A thing that can be waded through; a ford. *obsolete* exc. *Scot.* **ME.**
2 An act of wading. **M17.**
■ **wadable**, **wadeable** *adjective* **E17.**

Wade–Giles /weɪdˈdʒʌɪlz/ *noun & adjective.* **M20.**
[from Sir Thomas Francis *Wade* (1818–95), diplomat and first Professor of Chinese at Cambridge University + Herbert Allen *Giles* (1845–1935), Wade's successor at Cambridge.]
(Designating) a system of romanized spelling for transliterating the Chinese language devised by Wade and subsequently modified by Giles. (Now widely superseded by Pinyin.)

wader /ˈweɪdə/ *noun.* **L17.**
[from **WADE** *verb* + **-ER**[1].]
1 A person who or thing which wades. **L17.** ▸**b** A wading bird; *spec.* (*a*) a bird of the suborder Charadrii, which comprises plovers, sandpipers, snipes, and related birds; (*b*) *N. Amer.* any large long-legged, long-necked wading bird, as a heron, stork, or crane. **L18.**
2 In *pl.* High waterproof boots, or a waterproof garment for the legs and body, used esp. by anglers for wading. **M19.**

wadge *noun* var. of **WODGE.**

Wadhamite /ˈwɒdəmʌɪt/ *noun.* **M18.**
[from *Wadham* College (named from its founders, Nicholas and Dorothy Wadham) + **-ITE**[1].]
A member of Wadham College, Oxford.

wadi /ˈwɑːdi, ˈwɒdi/ *noun.* Also **wady**. Pl. **wadis**, **wadies**. **E17.**
[Arab. *wādī* valley, river-bed. Cf. **OUED.**]
In certain Arabic-speaking countries, a rocky watercourse which is dry except during the rainy season; the stream running through such a watercourse.

wadmal /ˈwɒdm(ə)l/ *noun & adjective.* Now *Hist.* **ME.**
[Old Norse *vaðmál*, from *váð* cloth, **WEED** *noun*[2] + *mál* measure (see **MEAL** *noun*[2]).]
▶ **A** *noun.* A coarse woollen cloth, in England used principally for covering horse-collars, and in Orkney, Shetland, and Scandinavia for warm garments, blankets, etc. **ME.**
▶ **B** *attrib.* or as *adjective.* Made of wadmal. **M16.**

wadset /ˈwɒdsɛt/ *noun.* Now *Hist.* **LME.**
[from the verb.]
1 SCOTS LAW. A mortgage of land or other heritable property as security for or in satisfaction of a debt etc., the debtor having the right to redeem the property on payment of the debt. **LME.**
2 *gen.* A pledge; something pledged. **L18.**

wadset /ˈwɒdsɛt/ *verb trans.* Chiefly *Scot.* Now *Hist.* Infl. **-tt-**. Pa. t. & pple **-set**, **-setted**. **ME.**
[from Scot. var. of **WED** *noun* + **SET** *verb*[1].]
Put in pledge; pawn, mortgage.
■ **wadsetter** *noun* (*Scot.*) (*a*) *rare* a mortgagor; (*b*) a mortgagee: **E17.**

wady *noun* var. of **WADI.**

waesucks /ˈwesʌks/ *interjection. Scot.* **L18.**
[from Scot. var. of **WOE** *noun*: the ending app. repr. *sakes* (see **SAKE** *noun*[1]).]
Expr. commiseration: alas!

WAF *abbreviation. US.*
Women in the Air Force.

w.a.f. *abbreviation.*
With all faults.

Wafdist /ˈwɒftɪst/ *adjective & noun.* **E20.**
[from the *Wafd* (see below) from Arab. *wafd* delegation (in full *al-wafd al-miṣrī* the Egyptian delegation), from *wafada* come, travel, esp. as an envoy + **-IST.**]
▶ **A** *adjective.* Of or pertaining to the Wafd, an Egyptian nationalist organization and later a political party, formed in 1918 and reconstituted as the New Wafd in 1978. **E20.**
▶ **B** *noun.* A member or supporter of the Wafd. **E20.**

wafer /ˈweɪfə/ *noun & verb.* **LME.**
[Anglo-Norman *wafre* (whence Anglo-Latin *wafra*) var. of Old Northern French *waufre*, Old & mod. French *gaufre* (see **GOFFER**) from Middle Low German *wāfel* **WAFFLE** *noun*[1].]
▶ **A** *noun.* **1** A very thin light crisp usu. sweet biscuit, formerly often eaten with wine, now esp. of a kind eaten with ice-cream. **LME.** ▸**b** A small bar of ice-cream sandwiched between wafers. **M20.**
2 CHRISTIAN CHURCH. A thin disc of unleavened bread used in the Eucharist in some Churches. **LME.**
3 A small disc of dried paste, which when moistened was formerly used for sealing letters, attaching papers, etc. (now *Hist.*). Also (LAW), a disc of red paper stuck on a document instead of a seal. **E18.**
4 MEDICINE. A thin leaf of paste, used to form a cachet for the administration of a powder. Now *rare.* **M19.**
5 Any round thin spot, mark, or object. **M19.**
6 ELECTRONICS. A very thin slice of a semiconductor crystal used as the substrate for solid-state circuitry. **M20.**
7 A very small gold ingot, weighing no more than a few ounces. **L20.**

📖 **5** J. BALDWIN The shirt was covered with round, paper-thin wafers, red and green. J. MCPHEE It was exquisite stone . . in blocks and wafers.

Comb.: †**wafer-cake** (*a*) (chiefly *derog.*) a communion wafer; (*b*) (*rare*, Shakes.) something fragile and easily broken; **wafer-iron** an implement for baking wafers, consisting of two iron plates between which the paste is held; **wafer-paper** paper for baking wafers on; paper used to administer medicaments; **wafer-scale** *adjective* (ELECTRONICS) on the scale of a wafer (sense 6); **wafer-thin** *adjective* very thin.
▶ **B** *verb trans.* Fasten or seal with a wafer. Also foll. by *up.* **M18.**

📖 G. A. SALA [He] had wafered the page of the book . . against the . . desk.

■ **waferer** *noun* (*obsolete* exc. *Hist.*) a maker or seller of wafers (known for being prepared to act as a go-between in love affairs); a confectioner in a royal or noble household: **LME.** **waferlike** *adjective* resembling a wafer; very thin: **L19.**

wafered /ˈweɪfəd/ *adjective.* **E19.**
[from prec.: see **-ED**[2], **-ED**[1].]
1 Fastened, sealed, or attached with a wafer or wafers. **E19.**
2 Of unleavened bread: made into communion wafers. *rare.* **M19.**

wafery /ˈweɪf(ə)ri/ *noun.* Now *Hist.* **LME.**
[Anglo-Norman *wafrie* (whence Anglo-Latin *wafria*) from *wafre* **WAFER** *noun*: see **-Y**[3].]
A room or building in which wafers are made; the department of the royal household occupied with the making of wafers and confectionery.

wafery /ˈweɪf(ə)ri/ *adjective.* **L19.**
[from **WAFER** *noun* + **-Y**[1].]
Resembling a wafer, extremely thin or fragile.

waff /waf/ *noun. Scot. & north.* **L16.**
[from **WAFF** *verb*[1]. Cf. **WAFT** *noun.*]
1 A puff or sudden gust of wind or air. **L16.** ▸**b** A whiff or waft of perfume. **E19.**
2 A waving movement; *esp.* a wave of the hand or of something held in the hand; a signal. **E17.**
3 An apparition, a wraith. **E18.**
4 A slight blow, *esp.* one given in passing. **M18.** ▸**b** A mild attack of illness, a touch of cold. **E19.**
5 A passing view, a glimpse. **E19.**

waff /waf/ *adjective. Scot.* **E18.**
[Var. of **WAIF** *adjective.*]
1 (Of an animal) wandering, stray; (of a person) solitary, lonely; homeless. **E18.**
2 Of no account, worthless; inferior in quality, shabby. **L18.**
■ **wafflike** *adjective* shabby-looking; having a disreputable appearance; of little account: **E19.**

waff /waf/ *verb*[1]. Chiefly *Scot. & north.* **LME.**
[Var. of **WAVE** *verb*[1].]
†**1** *verb trans.* Foll. by *away*: dismiss or put aside with a wave of the hand. Only in **LME.**
2 *verb intrans.* Of the wind: blow. **LME.**
3 *verb trans.* Of the wind: cause (something) to move to and fro. **E16.** ▸**b** *verb trans. & intrans.* Flap, flutter; (of a bird) move (the wings) in flight. **M19.**
4 *verb trans. & intrans.* Set (air) in motion; fan. **L17.**

waff /wɒf/ *verb*[2] *intrans.* Now *dial.* **L16.**
[Imit.]
Of a dog, esp. a puppy: bark, yap, yelp.

Waffen SS /ˈvaf(ə)n ɛsˈɛs/ *noun phr.* **M20.**
[German *Waffen-SS*, from *Waffen* armed + *SS* abbreviation of **SCHUTZSTAFFEL.**]
Hist. The combat units of the SS in Nazi Germany during the war of 1939–45.

waffie /ˈwafi/ *noun. Scot.* **E19.**
[from **WAFF** *adjective* + **-IE.**]
A worthless person, a vagabond.

waffle /ˈwɒf(ə)l/ *noun*[1] *& adjective.* Orig. *US.* **M18.**
[Dutch *wafel*, *waefel* = Middle Low German *wāfel* (see **WAFER**). Cf. **GOFFER.**]
▶ **A** *noun.* A small crisp batter-cake, baked in a waffle-iron, and eaten hot with syrup, butter, etc. **M18.**
Comb.: **waffle-iron** a utensil for baking waffles consisting of two hinged metal pans, with a grid or other pattern, which form indentations on the waffle during cooking; **waffle stomper** *US slang* a boot or shoe with a heavy ridged sole (usu. in *pl.*).
▶ **B** *attrib.* or as *adjective.* Designating a style of fine honeycomb weaving or a fabric woven to give a honeycomb effect. **M20.**

waffle /ˈwɒf(ə)l/ *noun*[2]. **M19.**
[from the verb.]
1 Orig. (*dial.*), chatter, gossip. Now (*colloq.*), verbose but empty or aimless talk or writing. **M19.**
2 The bark or yapping of a small dog. *dial.* **L19.**

📖 **1** *Boardroom* The statement . . is unusually blunt in comparison to the normal preference of . . Ministers for waffle and equivocation.

waffle /ˈwɒf(ə)l/ *verb.* **L17.**
[Frequentative of **WAFF** *verb*[2].]
1 *verb intrans.* Of a dog: yap, yelp. Now *dial.* **L17.**
2 **a** *verb intrans.* Waver; vacillate, equivocate. *colloq.* (orig. *Scot. & north.*). **E19.** ▸**b** *verb intrans.* Indulge in waffle; ramble *on. colloq.* **E20.** ▸**c** *verb trans.* Utter as waffle. *colloq.* **M20.** ▸**d** Of an aircraft or motor vehicle: travel *along* in an apparently purposeless, leisurely, or unsteady manner, usu. at low speed. *colloq.* **M20.**

📖 **2a** *Christianity Today* The denomination has waffled on such theological issues as the uniqueness of Christ. **b** *Golf Illustrated* Listening and watching the political pundits waffle on about marginal seats.

■ **waffler** *noun* (*a*) (chiefly *Scot. & north.*) an idler, a waverer; (*b*) *colloq.* a person given to waffling talk or writing: **E19.**

waffly /ˈwɒfli/ *adjective. colloq.* **L19.**
[from **WAFFLE** *noun*[2], *verb* + **-Y**[1].]
1 Wavering, vacillating, equivocal. **L19.**
2 Characterized by or given to waffling speech or writing. **L19.**

waft /wɒft, wɑːft/ *noun.* In sense 2 also **weft**, **wheft** /wɛft/. **M16.**
[App. from **WAFT** *verb*[1], *verb*[2]. Cf. **WAFF** *noun.*]
1 **a** A taste, a flavour, *esp.* an unpleasant one. Now *dial.* **M16.** ▸**b** A scent or odour passing through the air or carried on the breeze; a whiff. **E17.**
2 NAUTICAL. A flag, ensign, etc., knotted at the centre or with its fly stopped to the ensign staff, formerly used as a distress signal when hung on the mainstay, or for various other signals depending on the part of the ship from which it was flown; an act of displaying such a signal. Cf. **WHIFF** *noun*[1] 8. **M16.**
3 A current or rush of air, a breath of wind; *fig.* a transient sensation or quality. **E17.** ▸**b** A sound carried by the breeze. **M17.** ▸**c** A puff of smoke or vapour. **L19.**
†**4** An act of transporting something over water; a passage across the sea. **M17–L18.**
5 An act of waving; a waving movement. **M17.**
6 An apparition, a wraith. *dial.* **L19.**

📖 **1b** R. MACNEIL There was also a waft of stale body odour noticeable. **2 make a waft** hang out a flag etc. as a signal. **3** W. GOLDING The lamps flickered in the wafts of hot air. B. NEIL A waft of last night's bitter humour drifted through her. **b** B. TARKINGTON There came to his ears a waft of comment from a passing automobile. **5** I. DOIG His horse's tail giving a . . little waft as if wiping clean the field of vision.

†**waft** *verb*[1]. **L15.**
[App. alt. of **WAFF** *verb*[1].]
1 *verb trans.* Signal to (a person etc.) by waving the hand or something held in the hand. Also, wave (the hand or something held in the hand), esp. as a signal. **L15–E18.**

▸**b** Move (something) *aside* with a wave of the hand. Only in L18.
2 *verb intrans.* Move to and fro, wave. *rare.* L16–M17.
3 *verb trans.* Turn (the eyes) aside with a disdainful movement. *rare* (Shakes.). Only in E17.

waft /wɒft, wɑːft/ *verb*^{2}. E16.
[Back-form. from WAFTER.]
†**1** *verb trans.* Escort (a ship or fleet of ships) in a convoy. E16–L17.
2 †**a** *verb intrans.* Sail (freq. foll. by *about, along, off,* etc.); cross *over* by water. M16–E19. ▸**b** *verb trans.* Convey by water; carry *over* or *across* a stretch of water. Also, (of the sea or waves) carry, transport. Now *poet.* L16.
3 *verb trans.* Of the wind: propel (a sailing vessel) or convey (a person in a vessel) *to* or *from* a place. M17.
4 *verb intrans.* Travel easily or smoothly (as) through the air or through space; float or glide (as) on the wind. M17. ▸**b** Of the breeze: blow softly. E19.
5 *verb trans.* Convey or send (as) through the air or through space. E18. ▸**b** Carry (as) on wings. E18. ▸**c** *fig.* Transport instantaneously, as by magic or in the imagination. L18.
6 *verb trans.* Move, drive, or carry (a thing) *along, away,* etc., (as) by producing a current of air. M19.

📖 **2a** T. GAGE We that day wafted about for a good wind. **b** DRYDEN Nor wou'd th' Infernal Ferry-Man . . Be brib'd, to waft him to the farther shore. **3** *fig.*: R. BUCHANAN What wind of utter despair had wafted her to that place. **4** M. HUNTER The smell of hot, fresh bread wafting from the bakery door. E. TENNANT She wafted from the . . door in green raw silk. *Guardian* [They] . . wafted through the heats to . . the intermediate boys' 400 metres final. **5** V. WOOLF Big Ben . . whose stroke was wafted over the northern part of London. V. NABOKOV The flimsy paper was wafted toward a bench. J. SAYLES Old duffers . . wafting funnels of cigar smoke into the night sky. **b** A. N. WILSON The angels . . waft him heavenwards.

■ **wafting** *noun* (*a*) the action of the verb; (*b*) *rare* something wafted or carried by the wind: E16.

waftage /ˈwɒftɪdʒ, ˈwɑːf-/ *noun.* Now *arch. & literary.* M16.
[from prec. + -AGE.]
1 The action of wafting; the convoying of ships; conveyance across water. M16.
2 Passage (as) through the air or through space. M17.
3 The action or power of propulsion of the wind. M17.

📖 **1** *Fraser's Magazine* The crazy bark of old Charon, only fitted for the light waftage of ghosts. **3** L. WALLACE Let us give ourselves to waftage of the winds.

†**wafter** *noun.* L15.
[Low German, Dutch *wachter,* from *wachten* guard.]
1 An armed vessel employed as a convoy. L15–L17.
2 The commander of a convoying vessel. L15–E17.

wafture /ˈwɒftjʊə, ˈwɑːf-/ *noun.* Now *arch. & literary.* E17.
[from WAFT *verb*^{1}, *verb*^{2} + -URE.]
1 The action or an act of waving the hand or something held in the hand. E17. ▸**b** The waving of a wing or wings. L18.
2 The action of wafting or propelling by air or current. M18.
3 A thing wafted or carried by or on the breeze. E19.

📖 **1** G. MACDONALD A few mysterious waftures of the hand. **3** K. TENNANT The smell of manure . . , the human waftures of sweat.

wafty /ˈwɒfti, ˈwɑːf-/ *adjective. rare.* E17.
[from WAFT *noun, verb*^{2} + -Y^{1}.]
1 That wafts a perfume etc. E17.
2 That wafts or moves to and fro in the wind. E20.

wag /wag/ *noun*^{1}. M16.
[from WAG *verb.*]
1 An act of wagging; a single wagging movement. M16.
2 Power or inclination to wag. M19.

📖 **1** R. BUCHANAN Recognising her, he gave a faint wag of the tail.

wag /wag/ *noun*^{2}. M16.
[Prob. abbreviation of *waghalter* s.v. WAG *verb.*]
†**1** A mischievous boy (freq. used as a term of endearment to a baby boy). Also, a youth, a young man, a fellow. M16–L17.
2 A joker; a facetious or jocular person; a wit. L16.
3 [Cf. *play the wag* (a) below.] A child who plays truant. *Austral. slang.* L20.

📖 **1** R. GREENE Mothers wagge, pretie boy. **2** *Business Tokyo* The wag who . . defined a consultant as someone who borrows your watch to tell you the time. **play the wag** *slang* (*a*) = *hop the wag* s.v. HOP *verb*^{1}; (*b*) play jokes, play the fool.

wag /wag/ *verb.* Infl. **-gg-**. ME.
[Iterative from base of Old English *wagian*: see WAW *verb*^{1}. Cf. QUAG *verb.*]
▶**I** *verb intrans.* **1** Be in motion or activity; move. Now (*colloq.*), stir one's limbs (usu. in neg. contexts). ME.
†**2** Totter, stagger, threaten to fall. ME–L15.
†**3** Move about from place to place; wander. ME–M16.
4 Move, shake, or sway to and fro or from side to side, esp. in a rapid or energetic manner. LME. ▸**b** Of a plant, leaves, etc.: quiver, waver. *obsolete* exc. *Scot.* LME. ▸†**c** *fig.* Waver, vacillate. *rare.* LME–M16. ▸†**d** Swing on the gallows, be hanged. LME–M16. ▸**e** Of the tongue: move briskly in animated speech, esp. in gossip or idle talk. Esp. in ***tongues wag*** below. L16.
†**5** Shift or budge from a place. Usu. in neg. contexts. LME–M18.
6 **a** Of the world, times, etc.: go along with varied fortune or characteristics. *arch.* E16. ▸**b** Go, set off. Now *rare.* L16. ▸**c** Travel, proceed; go *along,* carry on. Also foll. by *on.* Now *Scot. & colloq.* L17.

📖 **1** G. J. WHYTE-MELVILLE Poor devil! . . could hardly wag coming up the hill. **4** A. DILLARD The floor wagged under my feet. *Guardian* Beards and earrings wagged in agreement. **5** T. HEARNE I cannot wag out of Oxford till the Term is ended. **6b** ALAN ROSS He . . never would wag any where without 60 Chariots. **c** A. MCNEILL He wagged along and helped to build up the commercial greatness . . of his country.

▶**II** *verb trans.* **7** Brandish (a weapon). Also, wave (something) to attract attention or as a signal etc. ME.
8 Move (esp. a limb or part of the body) to and fro or from side to side, esp. with rapid, repeated movements; shake (the head). ME. ▸**b** Of an animal: move (the tail) from side to side. LME. ▸†**c** Flap (the wings). L15–L16. ▸**d** Move (the tongue) in animated speech, esp. in gossip or idle talk. M16. ▸**e** Move, stir, (a limb, finger, etc.). Usu. in neg. contexts. Now *colloq.* L16.
†**9** Set in motion, cause to quiver or shake, stir. ME–L17.

📖 **7** G. MCCAUGHREAN He . . wagged his flag, but it only seemed to madden the horse. **8** T. C. WOLFE The little man . . wagged a finger roguishly. I. COLEGATE He twinkled . . at her, wagging his old head from side to side. **d** W. H. DIXON Every one who owed him grudge would eagerly . . wag his tongue.

▶**III** [from WAG *noun*^{2}.]
10 **a** *verb intrans. & trans.* (with *it*). Play truant. *slang.* L19. ▸**b** *verb trans.* Play truant from. *Austral. slang.* L20.

Phrases: **beards wag**, **chins wag**, **jaws wag**, **tongues wag** there is talk or gossip. **how the world wags** *arch.* how affairs are going or conducted. ***jaws wag***: see ***beards wag*** above. **let the world wag (as it will)** *arch.* regard the course of events with unconcern. ***the tail wags the dog***: see TAIL *noun*^{1}. ***tongues wag***: see ***beards wag*** above. ***wag one's finger at***: see FINGER *noun.*
Comb.: **wag-at-the-wall** *Scot. & north.* (*a*) a hanging wall clock with pendulum and weights exposed; (*b*) a household goblin; †**waghalter** a person likely to swing in the hangman's noose, a gallows-bird; †**wag-string** = ***waghalter*** above; WAGTAIL.
■ **waggable** *adjective* (*rare*) able to be wagged M19.

waganga *noun pl.* see MGANGA.

wage /weɪdʒ/ *noun.* ME.
[Anglo-Norman, Old Northern French (Anglo-Latin *vagium, wagium*) = Old French *guage,* (also mod.) *gage,* from Germanic, rel. to GAGE *noun*^{1}, WED *noun.*]
†**1** = GAGE *noun*^{1} 1, 2. ME–L16.
2 *sing.* & in *pl.* A payment made, usu. by an employer to an employee, in return for work or service rendered; formerly *esp.* a salary or fee paid to a person of official or professional status. Now *spec.* a fixed regular payment, usu. daily or weekly, by an employer to an unskilled or manual worker (cf. SALARY *noun* 1). ME. ▸†**b** *spec.* (Usu. in *pl.*) A soldier's pay. ME–M17. ▸**c** In *pl.* (ECONOMICS.) The part of total production that is the return to labour as earned income as distinct from the remuneration received by capital as unearned income. M20.
3 *sing.* & in *pl.* Reward, recompense, requital. ME.
†**4** A payment for the use or possession of property. *rare.* LME–E17.

📖 **2** B. BAINBRIDGE He had three weeks' wages saved. P. FITZGERALD She had been hired . . for an agreed weekly wage. *She* Women . . still earn only two-thirds of male wages. ***living wage***: see LIVING *noun*^{1}. ***social wage***: see SOCIAL *adjective.* **3** *Scientific American* Heart attacks . . thought of as . . the wages of overeating. *Guardian* That . . thriller about the wages of sin, Fatal Attraction.

Comb.: **wage-claim** a demand for an increase in wages, esp. by a trade union; **wage drift** the tendency for wages to rise above national rates through local overtime and other agreements; the extent of this increase; **wage-earner** a person who works for wages; **wage economy** a system of economic organization in which employees are paid wages in return for work (cf. ***share economy*** s.v. SHARE *noun*^{2}); **wage freeze** a temporary fixing of wages at a certain level; **wage scale** a graduated scale of wage rates for different levels of work; **wages council** any of various statutory bodies consisting of management and employee representatives responsible for determining minimum rates of pay in particular industries, esp. those in which collective bargaining is comparatively weak; **wage slave** a person dependent on income from employment of an extremely arduous or menial nature; **wage slavery** the condition of being a wage slave; **wage stop** the limitation of supplementary benefit to the level of the average wage.
■ **wagedom** *noun* (*rare*) the economic system under which wage-earners live L19. **wageless** *adjective* †(*a*) *rare* that does not pay a wage; (*b*) unpaid; not earning or receiving wages: E17. **wagelessness** *noun* E20.

wage /weɪdʒ/ *verb.* ME.
[Anglo-Norman *wager,* Old Northern French *wagier, waigier* = Old French *guagier* (mod. *gager*), from *guage*: see prec.]
▶**I** †**1** *verb trans.* Deposit or give as a pledge or security. ME–L18.
†**2** *verb trans. fig.* Offer (one's oath etc.) as security for the fulfilment of a promise etc. *rare.* LME–L16.
3 *verb trans.* LAW (now *Hist.*). ▸**a** ***wage one's law, wage the law,*** defend an action by wager of law; go to law. LME. ▸**b** ***wage battle***, pledge oneself to fight a lawsuit. M16.
4 *verb trans.* Venture, risk the loss of (*arch.*); (now *Scot.*) stake, wager, bet. LME.

📖 **4** HENRY FIELDING I would wage a shilling that the pedestrian outstripped the equestrian travellers.

▶**II** †**5** *verb trans.* **a** Engage or employ for wages; hire, esp. for military service. ME–M17. ▸**b** Bribe. LME–L18.
6 *verb trans.* Pay wages to. Now chiefly as **WAGED** *ppl adjective.* LME.
†**7** *verb trans.* Put out to hire. *rare* (Spenser). Only in L16.

📖 **6** I. D'ISRAELI The master dresses and wages highly his pampered train.

▶**III** **8** *verb trans.* Carry on (war, a conflict or contest). LME. ▸†**b** *verb intrans.* Struggle, contend *against*; struggle *through* difficulties; contend in rivalry. Only in 17.
9 *verb trans.* Wield (a weapon etc.). *rare* (now *Scot.*). M19.

📖 **8** I. MURDOCH I had . . waged a battle with Georgie's . . lack of taste. C. PHILLIPS ETA, . . of the Basque separatist movement, is waging a campaign against the Government.

waged /weɪdʒd/ *ppl adjective.* LME.
[from prec. + -ED^{1}.]
Of work: recompensed with wages, paid. Of a person: receiving a wage; in work; doing paid work.

📖 *Times Lit. Suppl.* Entitlement to 150 hours of free schooling . . was soon extended to waged and unwaged women.

wagel /ˈwag(ə)l/ *noun.* Chiefly *dial.* L17.
[Perh. from Cornish.]
An immature greater black-backed gull, *Larus marinus,* which has mottled grey and white plumage. Also ***wagel gull***.

wagenboom *noun* see WABOOM.

Wagener /ˈvɑːɡənə/ *noun.* M19.
[Abram *Wagener* (fl. 1796), US farmer, who first raised it.]
In full ***Wagener apple***. A late-ripening variety of apple, with a golden skin and pink flesh.

wager /ˈweɪdʒə/ *noun.* ME.
[Anglo-Norman *wageure,* from *wager* WAGE *verb.* In branch II perh. from WAGE *verb* + -ER^{4}.]
▶**I** †**1** A solemn pledge or undertaking. Only in ME.
2 A thing (esp. a sum of money) laid down as a stake. Now chiefly in ***lay a wager, win a wager, lose a wager.*** ME. ▸†**b** A prize in a contest. LME–M17.
3 A betting transaction. M16. ▸**b** A contest for a prize. Long *rare.* E17.
4 A thing on the outcome of which a bet is or may be laid; the subject of a bet. L16.

📖 **2** A. DILLARD Old-timers . . lay wagers on the exact day and hour it will occur. **3** *Greyhound Star* We used to have friendly wagers on whose dog would win. †**lie upon the wager** (*rare,* Spenser) be at stake.

▶**II** **5** LAW (now *Hist.*). ▸**a** ***wager of law***, a form of trial in which the defendant was required to produce witnesses who would swear to his or her innocence. E16. ▸**b** ***wager of battle***, a form of trial in which a defendant's guilt or innocence was decided by single combat between the parties or their champions. E17.
Comb.: **wager-boat** *Hist.* a light racing scull used in contests between single scullers; **wager-cup**: offered as a prize in a contest; **wager-policy** an insurance policy in which the insurer has no insurable interest in the thing insured.

wager /ˈweɪdʒə/ *verb.* LME.
[from the noun.]
1 *verb trans.* Stake (esp. a sum of money) on the outcome of an uncertain event or on an undecided or unresolved matter; bet (a person) a certain amount *that* something is or will be so. Earliest as ***wagering*** *verbal noun.* LME. ▸**b** *fig.* Offer as a pledge, guarantee, or forfeit; risk the loss of. M17.
†**2** *verb intrans.* Contend for a prize. *rare.* Only in L16.
3 *verb trans.* Foll. by obj. clause: offer or lay a wager, make a bet (*that*). Also (*colloq.*), confidently assert (*that*), be sure. E17.

📖 **1** WORDSWORTH I'd wager house and field That . . he has it yet. J. HERSEY Stirner wagered Dr. Bernhardt two loaves . . , a . . stake that might have meant life or death for some inmates. *Atlantic City* More that $1 billion is wagered annually at state tracks. **b** *Guardian* The Reagan Administration . . wagered the prestige of the US on the overthrow of the revolutionary government. **3** E. O'NEILL You didn't get much thanks from Mike, I'll wager, for your help. A. CROSS The elevators . . do not now work, and . . I am willing to wager that they never will.

■ **wagerer** *noun* M17.

Wagga /ˈwɒɡə/ *noun. Austral. slang.* E20.
[from *Wagga Wagga* a town in New South Wales, Australia.]
In full ***Wagga blanket***, ***Wagga rug***. A blanket or covering made from two sacks cut open and sewn together along one edge.

wagger /ˈwaɡə/ *noun*[1]. *rare.* LME.
[from WAG *verb* + -ER[1].]
†**1** A person who agitates or stirs something. Only in LME.
2 A person who wags his or her head etc.; an animal that wags its tail. M17.

wagger /ˈwaɡə/ *noun*[2]. *slang* (orig. *Oxford Univ. slang*). Also more fully **wagger-pagger-bagger** /ˌwaɡəpaɡəˈbaɡə/. E20.
[from *wa*(*ste*-*pa*(*per ba*(*sket* + *-agger*: see -ER[6].]
A waste-paper basket.

waggery /ˈwaɡ(ə)ri/ *noun.* L16.
[from WAG *noun*[2] + -ERY.]
1 Waggish behaviour; drollery, jocularity; (practical) joking. L16.
2 A waggish action or remark; a (practical) joke. E17.

📖 **1** S. SONTAG You might think they would mind . . but everyone here seems to enjoy the King's waggery.

waggish /ˈwaɡɪʃ/ *adjective.* L16.
[from WAG *noun*[2] + -ISH[1].]
1 Of a person: jocular, facetious; playfully mischievous. Formerly also, wanton, loose. L16.
2 Pertaining to or characteristic of a wag; (of an action, remark, etc.) done or made in a spirit of waggery. L16.

📖 **2** *Athenaeum* Mr Tarkington writes in . . a vein of waggish farce.

■ **waggishly** *adverb* E17. **waggishness** *noun* L16.

waggle /ˈwaɡ(ə)l/ *noun.* L19.
[from the verb.]
A waggling motion or movement; *spec.* (GOLF) an act of waggling the club-head over the ball before playing a shot.

📖 R. ANGELL Catchers had to flash him signals with hand gestures rather than with finger waggles.

Comb.: **waggle dance** ENTOMOLOGY a waggling movement performed by a honeybee at the hive or nest, to indicate to other bees the direction and distance of a source of food.

waggle /ˈwaɡ(ə)l/ *verb.* Also **woggle** /ˈwɒɡ(ə)l/. L16.
[Frequentative of WAG *verb*: see -LE[3]. Cf. WIGGLE *verb*.]
1 a *verb trans.* Move or shake (something held or fixed at one end) to and fro with short quick movements; *esp.* cause (part of the body) to shake, wobble, or move from side to side. Also (*joc.* & *colloq.*), wield or manipulate (a bat, oar, etc.). L16. ▸**b** *verb intrans.* GOLF. Swing the club-head to and fro over the ball before playing a shot. L19. ▸**c** *verb trans.* Get the better of, overcome. *US slang* (now *rare*). E20. ▸**d** *verb trans.* AERONAUTICS. Rock (the wings of an aircraft in flight) rapidly from side to side, usu. to convey a signal. E20.
2 *verb intrans.* **a** Shake or wobble while in motion; walk or move shakily; waddle. Usu. with adverbs. E17. ▸**b** Of a thing held or fixed at one end: move to and fro with short quick movements; wobble. E18.

📖 **1a** I. MURDOCH Waggling the oar vigorously . . to propel the boat. C. PHILLIPS The young girls waggling their hips crazily. **2a** R. BADEN-POWELL The men dance in a circle . . ; the women waggle round and round . . outside it. BEVERLEY CLEARY She had a loose tooth . . that waggled back and forth. **b** R. H. BARHAM His tail waggled more Even than before.

■ **waggler** *noun* (ANGLING) a type of float designed to be especially sensitive to movement of the bait, and chiefly used in semi-still water L20. **waggly** *adjective* waggling, unsteady; wiggly: L19.

waggon *noun* & *verb*, **-age** *noun*, etc., vars. of WAGON *noun*, *verb*, etc.

wag'n bietje /ˈvaxənbiki/ *noun phr. S. Afr.* L18.
[Afrikaans, lit. 'wait a bit': cf. WAIT-A-BIT.]
Any of various S. African acacias and other trees and shrubs with hooked and clinging thorns, such as *Ziziphus mucronata* of the buckthorn family.

Wagnerian /vɑːɡˈnɪərɪən/ *adjective* & *noun.* L19.
[from *Wagner* (see below) + -IAN.]
▶ **A** *adjective.* Of, pertaining to, or characteristic of the German operatic composer Richard Wagner (1813–83), his music and theories of musical and dramatic composition. Also *transf.*, grand, large-scale; grandiose; highly dramatic. L19.

📖 *Gramophone* Lushness . . can overlay the music when a hefty Wagnerian soprano tackles it. *Guardian* A strategic predicament of positively Wagnerian proportions.

▶ **B** *noun.* An interpreter, student, or admirer of Wagner or his music. L19.
■ **Wagnerianism** *noun* (adherence to) Wagnerian theories L19. **ˈWagnerism** *noun* Wagner's theory and practice in the composition of music dramas; the influence or cult of Wagner: M19.

Wagner tuba /ˈvɑːɡnə ˈtjuːbə/ *noun phr.* M20.
[from *Wagner* (see prec.) + TUBA *noun*[1].]
MUSIC. A brass instrument resembling a wide-bore horn invented by Wagner as a compromise between a horn and a tuba to give special tone-colour for *The Ring* cycle of operas.

Wagogo /wəˈɡəʊɡəʊ/ *noun pl.* & *adjective.* M19.
[Bantu, from *wa-* human pl. prefix + GOGO.]
▶ **A** *noun pl.* The Gogo people of central Tanzania. M19.
▶ **B** *attrib.* or as *adjective.* Of or pertaining to the Wagogo. L19.

wagon /ˈwaɡ(ə)n/ *noun.* Also **-gg-**. L15.
[Dutch *wagen*, †*waghen* = Old English *wæġn* WAIN *noun*[1].]
1 A sturdy four-wheeled vehicle for transporting heavy or bulky loads, often with a removable cover; *spec.* an open four-wheeled cart for carrying hay etc., with an elongated body and an extended framework attached to the sides. L15. ▸**b** (**W-**.) *The* Plough (PLOUGH *noun* 4). M19.
†**2** A carriage of any kind for the conveyance of passengers and luggage. Also (*poet.*), a triumphal or stately conveyance; a chariot. M16–M17.
3 A covered horse-drawn vehicle operating a regular service for the conveyance of goods and passengers by road. Now *Hist.* E17.
4 a A truck used to convey minerals, ore, etc., within the workings of a mine, or from a mine to a distribution point. M17. ▸**b** A railway goods vehicle, *esp.* an open truck. Formerly also, an open carriage for conveying passengers at the lowest fares; *gen.* any railway vehicle. M18.
5 A light wheeled vehicle, as a cart, trailer, cabin, etc., used as a mobile food-stall, shop, etc. Also, a dearborn. Chiefly *N. Amer.* M19.
6 A caravan used by gypsies, travelling showmen, etc. M19.
7 A child's pram. *US.* M19.
8 a A police patrol wagon. *slang* (orig. & chiefly *US*). L19. ▸**b** A trolley for carrying and serving meals, a dinner wagon. E20. ▸**c** A station-wagon, an estate car. Also *gen.*, any motor car. *colloq.* M20.

Phrases etc.: ***battle-wagon***: see BATTLE *noun*. ***chuck-wagon***: see CHUCK *noun*[5]. ***dinner wagon***: see DINNER *noun*. **fix a person's wagon** *US slang* bring about a person's downfall, spoil a person's chances of success. ***hitch one's wagon to a star***: see HITCH *verb*. ***Jersey wagon***: see JERSEY *noun*[1]. ***mammy wagon***: see MAMMY *noun*[2] 3. ***meat-wagon***: see MEAT *noun*. **on the wagon**, **on the water-wagon** *slang* (orig. *US*) abstaining from alcoholic drink, teetotal. ***pie-wagon***: see PIE *noun*[2]. ***sloven-wagon***: see SLOVEN *noun* 5. ***smoke-wagon***: see SMOKE *noun*.

Comb.: **wagon-bed** the body of a wagon; **wagon boss** *N. Amer.* the master of a wagon-train; **wagon box** *US* (*a*) a wagon-bed; (*b*) a large storage chest usu. kept under the front seat of a wagon; **wagon-ceiling** ARCHITECTURE a roof of either semicircular or polygonal section; **wagon-head** ARCHITECTURE a cylindrical or polygonal ceiling, roof, or vault; **wagon-load** as much or as many as can be carried in a wagon; ***a wagon-load of monkeys***: see MONKEY *noun*; **wagon-man** the driver of a wagon, a wagoner; **wagon-master** a person in charge of one or more wagons; *esp.* a person in overall charge of a wagon-train; **wagon-road** (*a*) a road for the passage of wagons; (*b*) a railway in a mine on which wagons are run; **wagon-roof** a barrel vault; **wagon-tent** *S. Afr.* the canopy of a covered wagon; **wagon-train** a train of wagons, *esp.* a train of covered wagons used by pioneers or settlers; **wagon-tree** *S. Afr.* = WABOOM; **wagon-vault** = ***wagon-roof*** above; **wagon-way** = ***wagon-road*** above; **wagon-wright** a maker or repairer of wagons; **wagon-yard** a depot for wagons, esp. those used on a railway.
■ **wagonful** *noun* as much or as many as a wagon will hold M19. **wagonry** *noun* (*rare*) †(*a*) *poet.* chariots collectively; (*b*) conveyance by wagon: L16.

wagon /ˈwaɡ(ə)n/ *verb.* Also **-gg-**. E17.
[from the noun.]
1 *verb intrans.* Travel in a wagon; transport goods by wagon. Chiefly *US.* E17.
2 *verb trans.* Load (goods etc.) into a wagon ready for transportation. M17.
3 *verb trans.* Transport (goods) in a wagon or by wagon-train. *US.* M18.

wagonage /ˈwaɡ(ə)nɪdʒ/ *noun.* Now *rare.* Also **-gg-**. E17.
[from WAGON *noun*, *verb* + -AGE.]
1 Conveyance or transport by wagon. E17.
2 The cost of conveying goods etc. by wagon; the charge so incurred. M18.
3 A wagon-train. M19.

wagoner /ˈwaɡ(ə)nə/ *noun*[1]. Also **-gg-**. M16.
[Dutch *wagenaar*, †*waghenaer*, formed as WAGON *noun*: see -ER[1].]
1 The driver of a wagon. Formerly also, a farmhand whose specific duties included driving a wagon. M16. ▸**b** The driver of any vehicle. *joc.* M19. ▸**c** A person in charge of the trucks in a mine. L19.
†**2** The driver of a chariot. *poet.* L16–M17.
3 (Usu. **W-**.) Orig., the constellation Boötes. Later, the constellation Auriga. Now *rare.* L16.

wagoner /ˈwaɡ(ə)nə/ *noun*[2]. *obsolete* exc. *Hist.* Also **-gg-**. L17.
[Anglicized from Dutch surname *Waghenaer* (see below).]
Orig., an atlas of nautical charts published by Lucas Janssen Waghenaer in 1584 under the title *Spieghel der Zeevaerdt* (English translation *The Mariners Mirror*, 1588). Later *gen.*, any book of charts for nautical use.

wagonette /waɡəˈnɛt/ *noun.* Also **-gg-**. M19.
[from WAGON *noun* + -ETTE.]
Chiefly *Hist.* A four-wheeled horse-drawn pleasure vehicle, open or with a removable cover, with facing side-seats and one or two seats arranged crosswise in front.

wagon-lit /vaɡɔ̃ˈliː/ *noun.* Pl. **wagon-lits** /vaɡɔ̃ˈliːz/, **wagons-lits** /vaɡɔ̃ˈliː/. L19.
[French, from *wagon* railway coach + *lit* bed.]
A sleeping-car on a train in Continental Europe.

wagon-restaurant /vaɡɔ̃ rɛstɔrɑ̃/ *noun.* Pl. ***wagons-restaurants*** (pronounced same). E20.
[French, from *wagon* railway coach + RESTAURANT.]
A dining-car on a train in Continental Europe.

wagons-lits, ***wagons-restaurants*** *nouns pl.* see WAGON-LIT, WAGON-RESTAURANT.

wagtail /ˈwaɡteɪl/ *noun.* E16.
[from WAG *verb* + TAIL *noun*[1].]
1 Any of various small Eurasian and African songbirds of the genera *Motacilla* and *Dendronanthus* (family Motacillidae), which have a long tail that is continually wagged up and down and which usu. frequent water-sides. E16. ▸**b** Any of various other tail-wagging songbirds; *esp.* (*a*) *Austral.* = ***willy wagtail***; (b) s.v. WILLY *noun*[2]; (*b*) *N. Amer.* = ***waterthrush*** s.v. WATER *noun*. M19.
†**2** Used as a familiar or contemptuous form of address to a man or young woman; *esp.* a licentious or unfaithful woman, a prostitute. L16–L18.
3 An artificial minnow used in trout-fishing. E20.
4 A vertical strip of wood placed in the side of the frame of a sash-window to keep the sashes separate when raised or lowered. M20.

1 ***pied wagtail***, ***white wagtail***, ***yellow wagtail***, etc.
Comb.: **wagtail dance** = ***waggle dance*** s.v. WAGGLE *noun*; **wagtail flycatcher** = sense 1b(a) above; **wagtail warbler** = sense 1b(b) above.

Wahabi /wəˈhɑːbi/ *noun* & *adjective.* Also **-hh-**. E19.
[Arab. *wahhābī* from Muḥammad ibn ʽAbd-al-*Wahhāb* (1703–92), founder of the sect.]
▶ **A** *noun.* A member of a conservative Islamic sect of strict Hanbalis. E19.
▶ **B** *attrib.* or as *adjective.* Of or pertaining to this sect. E19.
■ **Wahabism**, **Wahabiism** *noun* Wahabi culture or doctrines E19. **Wahabite** *noun* & *adjective* = WAHABI E19.

wahala /wəˈhala/ *noun.* L20.
[Hausa.]
In Nigeria: trouble, inconvenience; fuss, bother.

wahey /wəˈheɪ/ *interjection.* Also **-ay**. L19.
[Imit.]
Expr. delight, exhilaration, or pleasure.

Wahhabi *noun* & *adjective* var. of WAHABI.

wahine /wɑːˈhiːni, *foreign* waˈhine/ *noun.* L18.
[Maori. Cf. VAHINE.]
1 A Maori woman or wife. *NZ.* L18.
2 In Polynesia, = VAHINE. M19.
3 A girl surfer. *slang.* M20.

wahoo /wɑːˈhuː/ *noun*[1]. L18.
[Origin unkn.]
The winged elm, *Ulmus alata*, native to the US. Also ***wahoo elm***.

wahoo /wɑːˈhuː/ *noun*[2]. M19.
[Dakota *waⁿhu* lit. 'arrow-wood'.]
A N. American spindle tree, *Euonymus atropurpureus*. Also called ***burning bush***.

wahoo /wɑːˈhuː/ *noun*[3]. E20.
[Origin unkn.]
A large marine fish, *Acanthocybium solanderi* (family Scombridae), which is a streamlined and fast-swimming predator and is found in all tropical seas.

wahoo /wɑːˈhuː/ *interjection*, *verb*, & *noun*[4]. *US* (chiefly *dial.*). M20.
[Prob. natural exclam.]
▶ **A** *interjection.* Expr. exuberance or triumph. M20.
▶ **B** *verb intrans.* Cry 'wahoo!' M20.
▶ **C** *noun.* **1** A cry of 'wahoo!'; an exuberant shout. L20.
2 An uncouth person, a boor, a yahoo. L20.

wah-wah /ˈwɔːwɔː/ *noun*[1]. Also **wa-wa**. L19.
[Var.]
= WOW-WOW.

wah-wah /ˈwɑːwɑː/ *noun*[2] & *verb.* Also **wa-wa**. E20.
[Imit.]
▶ **A** *noun.* **1** A musical effect achieved on brass instruments by manipulation of a mute and on an electric guitar by means of a pedal controlling output from the amplifier; such a pedal. E20.
2 The sound of a baby's crying; a noise resembling this. M20.

1 *wah-wah effect, wah-wah guitar, wah-wah mute, wah-wah pedal*, etc.
▶ **B** *verb intrans.* Produce a wah-wah effect with an electric guitar etc. M20.

wai /wʌɪ/ *noun & verb.* M20.
[Thai.]
▶ **A** *noun.* A Thai gesture of greeting made by bringing the palms together in front of the face or chest and in some cases bowing. Cf. NAMASKAR. M20.
▶ **B** *verb intrans.* Make this gesture. L20.

waiata /ˈwʌɪətə/ *noun. NZ.* E19.
[Maori.]
A Maori song.

waif /weɪf/ *noun*[1] *& adjective.* LME.
[Anglo-Norman *waif, weif* (Anglo-Latin *waivium, weyvium*) var. of Old Northern French *gaif*, fem. *gaive*, prob. of Scandinavian origin (cf. Old Norse *veif* something wavering or flapping, rel. to *veifa* wave).]
▶ **A** *noun.* **1** LAW. **a** A piece of property which is found ownerless and which falls to the lord of the manor if unclaimed; the right of claiming such property. LME. ▸**b** A stolen item abandoned by the thief in flight. L16.
2 A homeless and helpless person, *esp.* a neglected or abandoned child. Freq. in ***waifs and strays***, neglected or abandoned children, *transf.* odds and ends. E17.

📖 **2** C. E. M. JOAD Those waifs and strays of the intelligentsia who had refused to participate in the war. B. DUFFY All the poor waifs . . without even shoes or a penny pie. *transf.*: *Sports Illustrated* A shy bony waif of 17 with the legs of an antelope.

▶ **B** *attrib.* or as *adjective.* **1** That is a waif; stray, wandering, homeless. Cf. WAFF *adjective* 1. Now chiefly *Scot.* E17.
2 a Of a rumour or saying: floating, current. *Scot. rare.* M18. ▸**b** Poor or inferior in quality. Cf. WAFF *adjective* 2. *Scot.* E19.
■ **waifish** *adjective* waiflike M20. **waifishly** *adverb* L20. **waiflike** *adjective* resembling (that of) a waif E20.

waif /weɪf/ *noun*[2]. E16.
[Perh. from Old Norse *veif*: see prec.]
†**1** A convolution, a coil. *Scot.* Only in E16.
2 A small flag used as a signal, *esp.* (WHALING) one used to mark the position of a whale. M16.

waif /weɪf/ *noun*[3]. M19.
[Origin uncertain: cf. WAFF *noun.*]
A thing carried or driven by the wind; a puff of smoke, a streak of cloud.

wail /weɪl/ *noun.* LME.
[from the verb.]
1 The expression of pain, grief, etc., by prolonged high-pitched crying; the action of wailing, esp. in lamentation for the dead. LME.
2 A high-pitched plaintive cry of pain, grief, etc., esp. loud and prolonged; a bitter lamentation or complaint; *transf.* a sound resembling this. E19.

📖 **2** C. SAGAN The wail of the night freight, as haunting . . as the cry of the loon. M. ROBERTS The funeral barge . . departs upstream to the wails of mourners.

wail /weɪl/ *verb.* ME.
[from Old Norse word from *vei* interjection = Old English *wā* WOE.]
1 *verb intrans.* Express pain, grief, etc., by prolonged high-pitched cries; utter a wail or wails. ME.
2 *verb intrans. & trans.* Lament or complain persistently and bitterly, say lamentingly, (*that*). ME.
3 *verb intrans.* Grieve bitterly. (Foll. by *at, for.*) LME.
4 *verb trans.* Feel deep sorrow for (a situation, event, etc.); mourn the loss of (a dead person etc.); bewail, lament. Now *poet. & rhet.* LME.
5 *verb intrans.* Of the wind, music, a bird, etc.: give out a mournful sound like a person wailing. L16.
6 *verb intrans.* Of a jazz or rock musician: play very well or with great feeling. Also foll. by *away. US slang.* M20.

📖 **1** *Guardian* She didn't just cry. She wailed. **2** A. TROLLOPE He went on wailing, complaining of his lot as a child complains. S. BARING-GOULD 'I wish I was dead,' wailed the poor creature. **4** W. MORRIS Well then might Psyche wail her wretched fate. **5** *Chambers's Journal* In the green reed-beds . . teal whistled and plover wailed. P. BOWLES A factory siren wailed.

■ **wailer** *noun* a person who wails; *spec.* a professional mourner: LME. **waily** *adjective* (*rare*) †(*a*) *dial.* full of woe; (*b*) (of a sound) resembling a wail: E19.

wailful /ˈweɪlfʊl, -f(ə)l/ *adjective.* Chiefly *poet.* M16.
[from WAIL *noun* + -FUL.]
1 Having the character of or resembling a wail; expressive of pain, grief, etc.; high-pitched and plaintive. M16.
†**2** That is to be bewailed, lamentable. M16–E17.
3 Full of lamentation, sorrowful; *transf.* producing a mournful sound like a person wailing. L16.
■ **wailfully** *adverb* E17.

wailing /ˈweɪlɪŋ/ *noun.* ME.
[from WAIL *verb* + -ING[1].]
The action of WAIL *verb*; an instance of this, a wail.
Comb.: **Wailing Wall** the remaining part of the wall of the Second Temple of Jerusalem destroyed in 70 BC, where Jews traditionally pray and lament on Fridays.

wailing /ˈweɪlɪŋ/ *ppl adjective.* LME.
[formed as prec. + -ING[2].]
That wails; (of a cry etc.) expressing lamentation; (of a sound) resembling a wail.
■ **wailingly** *adverb* M19.

wailsome /ˈweɪls(ə)m/ *adjective. rare.* M16.
[from WAIL *noun, verb* + -SOME[1].]
†**1** That is to be bewailed. Only in M16.
2 Having a wailing sound. L19.

wain /weɪn/ *noun*[1] *& verb.*
[Old English *wæg(e)n, wǣn* = Old Frisian *wein*, Old Low Frankish *reidi-wagan*, Middle & mod. Low German, Dutch *wagen*, Old High German *wagan* (German *Wagen*), Old Norse *vagn* cart, barrow, from Germanic from Indo-European base repr. also by WAY *noun*, WEIGH *verb.*]
▶ **A** *noun.* **1** = WAGON *noun* 1. Now *arch. & poet.* OE. ▸**b** A chariot. Chiefly *poet.* ME.
2 (**W-**.) *The* Plough (PLOUGH *noun* 4). OE.

📖 **1** W. COWPER From the sun-burnt hay-field, homeward creeps The loaded wain. **2 Lesser Wain** *the* group of seven principal stars in Ursa Minor which resembles that of the Plough.

Comb.: **wainman** (*obsolete* exc. *Hist.*) = WAINER; **wainwright** a wagon-builder.
▶†**B** *verb trans.* Carry or transport (as) in a wain. ME–E19.
■ **wainer** *noun* (*rare*) the driver of a wain, a wagoner ME. **wainful** *noun* (*rare*) as much as a wain will hold E18.

wain *noun*[2] var. of WEAN *noun.*

wainage /ˈweɪnɪdʒ/ *noun.* L15.
[Old Northern French *waaignage* (Anglo-Latin *wainnagium*), from *waaignier* till, earn, gain, from Germanic verb repr. also in *weidenen* pasture, forage, hunt: see GAIN *verb*[2].]
Hist. **1** *collect.* Feudal agricultural implements. L15.
2 Land under cultivation. E19.

wainscot /ˈweɪnskɒt/ *noun, adjective, & verb.* ME.
[Middle Low German *wagenschot*, app. from *wagen* wagon + *schot* perh. = boarding, planking (cf. *bokenschot* superior beechwood).]
▶ **A** *noun.* **1** Imported oak of high quality, chiefly used for fine panelling; logs, planks, or boarding of this oak. Now chiefly *Hist.* ME. ▸†**b** A piece or board of this oak. LME–M17.
2 Panelling of oak or other wood lining esp. the lower part of a room wall; an area of such panelling. M16.
†**3** *transf. & fig.* A thing or person resembling old wainscot in hardness or colour. L16–M17.
4 Any of numerous pale or drab-coloured noctuid moths, esp. of the genera *Mythimnia, Photedes*, and *Archanara.* E19.
▶ **B** *attrib.* or as *adjective.* **1** Made of or lined with wainscot; panelled. L16.
†**2** Resembling old wainscot in hardness or colour. L16–M18.
1 wainscot chair a panel-back chair.
▶ **C** *verb trans.* Infl. **-t-**, **-tt-**. Line (a wall, room, etc.) with wainscot; *transf.* line with marble, tiles, etc., panel with mirrors or pictures. Freq. as ***wainscoted, wainscotted*** *ppl adjective.* L16.
■ **wainscoting, wainscotting** *noun* (*a*) the action or process of lining a room, walls, etc., with wainscot; (*b*) a wainscot; the material for this; wooden panelling; wainscots collectively: L16.

waipiro /ˈwʌɪpɪrəʊ/ *noun. NZ.* M19.
[Maori, from *wai* water + *piro* putrid.]
Alcoholic liquor, spirits.

waist /weɪst/ *noun.* LME.
[App. repr. Old English word corresp. to Gothic *wahstus* growth, size, from Germanic base of WAX *verb*[1].]
1 The part of the human body below the ribs and above the hips, usu. of smaller circumference than these; the narrower middle part of the normal human figure; the circumference of this. LME.
2 a NAUTICAL. The middle part of the upper deck of a ship, between the quarterdeck and the forecastle. L15. ▸**b** NAUTICAL. In *pl.* Rails at a ship's waist (also ***waist-rails***); the sides of a ship at the waist. M17. ▸**c** The middle section of the fuselage of an aeroplane, esp. a bomber. Chiefly *US.* M20.
3 †**a** A belt worn around the waist, a girdle. M16–E17. ▸**b** The part of a garment encircling or covering the waist; the narrowed middle part of a woman's dress etc., usu. corresponding to the wearer's waist. Also, the part of a garment between the shoulders and the waist or narrowed part. L16. ▸**c** A bodice; a blouse. Chiefly *US.* E19.
4 The narrow middle part of a thing, as a bell, violin, hourglass, shoe, etc. E17. ▸**b** The constriction between the thorax and abdomen of a wasp, ant, etc. E18.

📖 **1** GOLDSMITH So tall, that the Spaniards only reached his waist. *Daily Telegraph* A . . woman, permanently paralysed from the waist down after a spinal injection. G. MURRAY Grasped around the waist by a lecherous man. M. ROBERTS Rosina laces me up tight to show off my neat pretty waist. **3b** C. COOKSON The bodice was plain and ribbed to the waist. D. HIGHSMITH The jacket had padded shoulders and a pinched waist. ***long waist, short waist***, etc.

Comb.: **waistband** a belt or girdle worn round the waist; *esp.* a band of cloth fitting about the waist and forming the upper part of a lower garment; **waist-cloth** (*a*) NAUTICAL (in *pl.*) decorative or protective coloured cloths hung about the upper parts of a ship; (*b*) NAUTICAL a protective cloth for a hammock, stowed in the waist of a vessel; (*c*) a loincloth; **waist-deep** *adjective & adverb* deep as the waist; (submerged) to the waist; **waist-gun** a gun set in the waist of an aircraft, esp. a bomber; **waist-gunner** an operator of such a gun; **waist-high** *adjective & adverb* = ***waist-deep*** above; **waist-length** *adjective* (of hair, a garment, etc.) reaching to the waist; **waistline** (*a*) a line outlining or following the contour of the waist; (*b*) a person's waist, esp. with reference to its size; (*c*) a notional line running round the body of a motor vehicle at the level of the bottom of the window frames; ***waist-rails***: see sense 2b above.
■ **waister** *noun* (NAUTICAL HISTORY) a (usu. inexperienced) seaman assigned to duties in the waist of a ship E19. **waistless** *adjective* (having the appearance of) having no waist E16.

waistcoat /ˈweɪs(t)kəʊt, ˈwɛskət/ *noun.* E16.
[from prec. + COAT *noun.*]
1 Orig., a man's garment usu. sleeveless and reaching to the knees or hips and worn under a coat. Now, a close-fitting waist-length garment, without sleeves or collar but usu. having buttons, worn by men usu. over a shirt and under a jacket; a similar garment worn for warmth or protection. E16.
2 †**a** A freq. elaborate short upper garment worn by women usu. beneath an outer gown. M16–E18. ▸**b** A woman's garment resembling a man's waistcoat. E18.
3 A short usu. sleeveless undergarment; a vest; a camisole. Now *rare* or *obsolete.* L16.
†**4** A short outer coat or jacket; a jersey. E17–M18.

📖 **1** A. S. BYATT He wore . . an elegant waistcoat . . under his town and country tweed jacket. ***strait waistcoat, strait-waistcoat***: see STRAIT *adjective*[1].

■ **waistcoated** *adjective* having a waistcoat (of a specified kind) L18. **waistcoaˈteer** *noun* (*obsolete* exc. *Hist.*) a low-class prostitute E17. **waistcoating** *noun* a fabric made esp. for men's waistcoats E19. **waistcoatless** *adjective* E19.

waisted /ˈweɪstɪd/ *adjective.* L16.
[from WAIST + -ED[2].]
Having a waist (of a specified size or form).
long-waisted, short-waisted, wasp-waisted, etc.

wait /weɪt/ *noun.* ME.
[Partly from Old Northern French noun from *waitier* WAIT *verb*, partly directly from the verb.]
▶ **I 1** A watchman, a sentinel, *esp.* one with a horn or trumpet to sound an alarm or make a signal; a scout, a spy. Long *obsolete* exc. *Hist.* ME.
2 a *Hist.* A member of a small body of wind instrumentalists maintained by a city or town. In *pl.*, such a body. ME. ▸†**b** A player on the flute, oboe, trumpet, etc.; a musician. E16–M17. ▸**c** A member of a band of musicians and singers singing carols in the streets. In *pl.*, such a body. *arch.* L18.
†**3** A wind instrument, as a shawm, oboe, flute, etc. Usu. in *pl.* M16–L17.
▶ **II 4** The action or process of watching out for an enemy etc. or of lurking in ambush; watchfulness, expectancy. Chiefly in ***lie in wait (for), lie wait (for)***. ME.
5 a The day's duty of a warder in the Tower of London. L17. ▸**b** A period of duty at court of a lord- or lady-in-waiting. L19.
6 A period of waiting. M19.

📖 **4** A. T. ELLIS She lay in wait for unsuspecting travellers. **6** *New Yorker* I settled at a table outside and prepared for a long wait.

Comb.: **wait-list** *noun & verb* (chiefly *N. Amer.*) (*a*) *noun* a waiting-list, esp. for a transport service; (*b*) *verb trans.* put (a person) on a wait-list; draw up a wait-list for places on (a transport service); **wait state** COMPUTING the condition of an operating system, central processing unit, etc., of being unable to process further instructions due to being occupied with some other task.

wait /weɪt/ *verb.* ME.
[Old Northern French *waitier* var. of Old French *guaitier* (mod. *guetter* watch for) from Germanic base repr. also by WAKE *verb.*]
†**1** *verb trans. & intrans.* Watch with hostile intent; lie in wait (for). ME–L16.
†**2** *verb trans.* Watch, observe closely; look out for; watch over, care for. Only in ME.
†**3 a** *verb intrans.* Keep watch; act as a watchman. ME–E17. ▸**b** *verb trans.* Observe carefully *how, what, when*, etc.; take precautions *that*, be careful *to do.* ME–L16.
4 a *verb trans.* Look forward with desire, apprehension, etc., to (an event etc.), continue in expectation of. Now *rare.* LME. ▸**b** *verb intrans.* Be expectant or on the watch; look forward in desire, apprehension, etc.; continue in expectation; remain for a time without something

expected or promised. Freq. foll. by *for* an event etc., *to do* a thing. M16.

5 a *verb trans.* Defer departure or action until the occurrence of (an event etc.); (of a thing) remain in readiness for, be in store for. Chiefly in ***wait one's turn***. LME. ▸**b** *verb intrans.* Defer departure or action until the occurrence of an expected event, the arrival of a person, etc.; (of a thing) remain in readiness, remain for a while neglected. Freq. foll. by *for* an event etc., *to do* a thing. LME. ▸**c** *verb trans.* Postpone (a meal) in expectation of someone's arrival. *colloq.* L18.

†**6** *verb trans.* Attend, escort, or accompany (a person etc.) to give assistance or show respect. LME–E19.

7 a *verb intrans.* Be in readiness to receive orders; act as an attendant or servant; *spec.* serve as a waiter at table. Foll. by *at* table, *on* a person or (*N. Amer.*) table. L15. ▸**b** *verb trans.* Serve as a waiter at (table). *Scot. & N. Amer.* E19.

> 🕮 **4b** H. CAINE The only condition on which he would agree to wait for his money. M. SARTON Things waited for with dread rarely turned out as expected. **5a** *Guardian* I am told to get to the back of the queue and wait my turn. **b** H. JAMES She would go and put on her hat; he must wait a little. G. VIDAL Men and women stood on the platform . . , waiting for the . . train. W. GOLDING For a time . . I waited to see what would happen. M. GORDON Her husband and her children, waiting for her in the car. A. T. ELLIS You'd better get going . . . You don't want to keep them waiting. **c** B. BRYSON I composed a letter to my parents telling them not to wait supper. **7a** J. MCGAHERN The two men ate in silence . . , waited on by the two girls. **b** *Publishers Weekly* He washed dishes and waited tables in Schrafft's.

Phrases: **cannot wait** (*a*) (of a situation etc.) needs to be dealt with immediately; (*b*) (of a person) is very impatient (*for* something). **can wait** (*a*) (of a situation etc.) need not be dealt with immediately; (*b*) (of a person) has sufficient patience to await a result etc. ***wait a minute***: see MINUTE *noun*. **wait and see** await the progress of events. ***wait ATTENDANCE (on)***. **wait for it!** (*a*) do not begin before the proper moment; (*b*) creating an interval of suspense before saying something unexpected or amusing. ***wait one's turn***: see sense 5a above. **wait the day**, **wait the hour**, **wait the opportunity** *arch.* defer action until an appropriate time. ***wait until the dust settles***: see DUST *noun*. **you wait!** (freq. *joc.*) implying a threat, promise, or warning.

With adverbs & prepositions in specialized senses: **wait about**, **wait around** linger expectantly, loiter, hang about. **wait on** (*a*) *Scot.* linger about a place or in expectation of death; (*b*) *Austral., NZ, Scot., & north.* wait for a while, be patient, (freq. as *imper.*). **wait on** — (*a*) (now *rare*) accompany or escort to give assistance or show respect; (*b*) serve as an attendant or waiter to, await the convenience of; ***wait on hand and foot***: see HAND *noun*; (*c*) pay a respectful visit to; (*d*) (of a thing) accompany, be associated with, attend as a consequence; (*e*) remain in expectation of, wait for; ***wait on God*** (in biblical contexts): place one's hopes in God; (see also sense 7a above). **wait out** (*a*) BASEBALL force (a pitcher) to throw a maximum number of pitches by refraining from striking at pitches; (*b*) (chiefly *N. Amer. colloq.*) wait during, wait for the end of; ***wait it out***, endure a period of waiting; (*c*) await the arrival or occurrence of, wait for. **wait up** defer going to bed, esp. in expectation of an arrival or occurrence.

wait-a-bit /ˈweɪtəbɪt/ *noun*. L18.

[from WAIT *verb* + A *adjective* + BIT *noun*², usu. translating Afrikaans WAG'N BIETJE.]

More fully ***wait-a-bit thorn***. Any of various plants which hinder progress by their thorny growth; *esp.* (*S. Afr.*) = WAG'N BIETJE.

wait-a-while /ˈweɪtəwʌɪl/ *noun*. M19.

[from WAIT *verb* + A *adjective* + WHILE *noun*: cf. prec.]

1 = WAIT-A-BIT. *S. Afr. rare.* M19.

2 Any of several shrubs or small trees forming dense thickets, esp. the leguminous plant *Acacia colletioides*. *Austral.* L19.

waiter /ˈweɪtə/ *noun*. LME.

[from WAIT *verb* + -ER¹.]

▸**I 1** †**a** A person watching or observing closely; *rare* a person lying in wait, a spy, a scout. LME–L17. ▸**b** A customs officer. Cf. ***tidewaiter*** s.v. TIDE *noun*. *obsolete* exc. *Hist.* L15. ▸**c** A warder at the Tower of London. More fully ***yeoman waiter***. M16. ▸**d** A watchman at the city gates. *Scot. obsolete* exc. *Hist.* L17.

2 †**a** A usu. high-ranking member of a royal or noble person's household. LME–L17. ▸**b** A bridesmaid. *obsolete* exc. *US dial.* or *Hist.* M16.

†**3** A (usu. male) household servant, as a groom or footman. L15–L18. ▸**b** MILITARY. A soldier employed as a domestic servant to an officer. *US.* E–M19.

4 A man employed to serve at table in a hotel, restaurant, large house, etc. E16.

5 †**a** A person visiting or paying court to another of superior rank; an attendant. M16–E17. ▸**b** A uniformed attendant at the Stock Exchange, Lloyd's of London, or other City of London institutions. L19.

▸**II 6** A person who waits for an event, opportunity, time, etc. M17. ▸**b** CHESS. = ***waiting problem*** s.v. WAITING *verbal noun*. E20.

7 a A salver, a small tray. M18. ▸†**b** = ***dumb waiter*** s.v. DUMB *adjective & noun*. L18–M19.

■ **waitering** *noun* the occupation of a waiter M19. **waiterlike** *adjective* resembling (that of) a waiter E19.

waiting /ˈweɪtɪŋ/ *verbal noun*. ME.

[from WAIT *verb* + -ING¹.]

The action of WAIT *verb*; *spec.* †(*a*) a lying in wait, ambush; †(*b*) watch, observation; (*c*) attendance *on* a social superior; (*d*) official attendance at court; one's period or term of this; (*e*) expectation, expectancy; remaining stationary or inactive in expectation of something; (*f*) the parking of a vehicle for a short time at the side of a road etc. (chiefly in ***no waiting***).

lady-in-waiting: see LADY *noun & adjective*. ***lord-in-waiting***: see LORD *noun*.

Comb.: **waiting game** a tactic in a contest etc. whereby one refrains from action in the earlier part so as to act more effectively at a later stage; **waiting-list** a list of people waiting for a thing, as selection, accommodation, treatment, etc., not immediately available; **waiting move** CHESS: intended to exploit a situation whereby the necessity to move is a disadvantage; **waiting problem** CHESS: for which the key is a waiting move; **waiting race**: in which the superiority of the winner is designedly not displayed until near the end of the course; **waiting-room**: provided for people obliged to wait for a service etc., as in a railway station or at a doctor's or dentist's; **waiting time** time spent waiting, as for a service, computer process, etc.

waiting /ˈweɪtɪŋ/ *ppl adjective*. M16.

[formed as prec. + -ING².]

1 That waits on or attends to another, that acts as an attendant or waiter. M16.

2 That waits for a person or thing; expectant. M17.

1 waiting-maid *arch.* a woman's personal servant or handmaid. **waiting-man** (now *US*) a man's personal male servant. **waiting-woman** *arch.* = ***waiting-maid*** above.

■ **waitingly** *adverb* L19.

waitperson /ˈweɪtpəːs(ə)n/ *noun*. Chiefly *US.* L20.

[from *wait-* in WAITER, WAITRESS + PERSON *noun*.]

A waiter or waitress. (Used to avoid sexual distinction.)

waitress /ˈweɪtrɪs/ *noun & verb*. L16.

[from WAITER + -ESS¹.]

▸**A** *noun*. †**1** A woman's handmaid. *rare*. Only in L16.

2 A woman employed to serve at table in a hotel, restaurant, large house, etc. M19.

Comb.: **waitress service** service by waitresses in a restaurant etc. (opp. ***self-service***).

▸**B** *verb intrans.* Work as a waitress. Chiefly as ***waitressing*** *verbal noun*. M20.

waitron /ˈweɪtrɒn/ *noun*. *US.* L20.

[Blend of WAITER, WAITRESS and PATRON *noun* or *-on* as in *automaton* (implying robotic activity).]

= WAITPERSON.

waive /weɪv/ *verb trans.* Also †**wave**. ME.

[Anglo-Norman *weyver* (whence Anglo-Latin *waiviare*, *weiviare*) var. of Old French *gaiver*, *guesver* allow to become a waif, abandon, from *gaif* WAIF *noun*¹.]

1 LAW. Deprive (*spec.* a woman) of the benefit and protection of the law, outlaw. *obsolete* exc. *Hist.* ME.

†**2** Abandon, give up, lay aside; resign (an office). ME–M17. ▸**b** Change one's mind about, give up, (an intention). LME–E19. ▸**c** Withdraw (legal proceedings, a motion) formally. Also, defeat (a proposal) on a vote. M17–M18.

3 Shun or avoid (now esp. a subject or discussion); elude, escape; evade *doing*. Now *rare*. ME. ▸**b** Avoid acceptance of (an offer, something offered); decline (an honour, combat, etc.). Now *rare* or *obsolete*. M17.

4 Refrain from insisting on or making use of (a right, claim, opportunity, etc.), relinquish; decline to press (an argument, objection, etc.). LME. ▸**b** Dispense with (formality etc.). L18.

†**5** Ignore, disregard, overlook; let pass (an opportunity). LME–E18.

6 LAW. Abandon (stolen goods). *obsolete* exc. *Hist.* M16.

7 Refrain from applying or enforcing (a rule etc.), make an exception to. M17. ▸**b** N. AMER. SPORT. Of a club: refrain from using the right to buy or sign (a player) from another club in the same league. Cf. WAIVER 2. E20.

8 Refrain from entering on (an action, discussion, etc.); put aside for the present, defer. M17. ▸†**b** Omit from a statement or narrative; leave out. M17–M18.

9 Dismiss or put aside (as) with a wave of the hand. Foll. by *aside*, *away*, *off*. *non-standard.* M19.

> 🕮 **4** A. MAUPIN 'What about the money involved?' 'Oh, I waived my fee.' **7** *Guardian* In these cases a school may waive some of the academic requirements.

■ **waivable** *adjective* LAW able to be waived E19.

waiver /ˈweɪvə/ *noun*. E17.

[Anglo-Norman *weyver* use as noun of *weyver* WAIVE: see -ER⁴.]

1 The action or an act of waiving a right, claim, etc.; a document attesting to such action. E17.

2 *spec.* (N. AMER. SPORT). A club's waiving of the right to sign a player from another club in the same league before he is offered to a club in another league. Freq. in ***on waivers***. L19.

Wai-Wai /ˈwʌɪwʌɪ/ *noun & adjective*. Also **Waiwai**. Pl. same, **-s**. M19.

[Origin unkn.]

▸**A** *noun*. A member of a people inhabiting parts of northern Brazil, southern Guyana, and Suriname; the language of this people. M19.

▸**B** *attrib.* or as *adjective*. Of or pertaining to this people or their language. L20.

waka /ˈwaka/ *noun*¹. *NZ.* E19.

[Maori.]

A Maori canoe.

waka /ˈwakə/ *noun*². Pl. same. M20.

[Japanese.]

1 A form of classic Japanese lyrical poetry developed from ancient traditional ballads. M20.

2 = TANKA *noun*². M20.

Wakamba /wəˈkambə/ *noun & adjective*. L19.

[Bantu, from *wa-* human pl. prefix + KAMBA.]

▸**A** *noun*. **1** The Kamba language. L19.

2 *pl.* The Kamba people. Also *sing.*, a member of the Wakamba. M20.

▸**B** *attrib.* or as *adjective*. Of or pertaining to the Wakamba or their language. M20.

wakame /ˈwakameɪ/ *noun*. M20.

[Japanese.]

An edible brown alga, *Undaria pinnatifida*, used in Chinese and Japanese cookery (esp. in dried form).

Wakash /wɑːˈkaʃ/ *adjective & noun*. Now *rare*. M19.

[Nootka *waukash* good, app. applied to the people by Captain Cook.]

= WAKASHAN.

Wakashan /wɑːˈkaʃ(ə)n/ *adjective & noun*. L19.

[from prec. + -AN.]

(Pertaining to or designating) a family of N. American Indian languages spoken in parts of British Columbia and Washington State, including Kwakiutl and Nootkan.

wake /weɪk/ *noun*¹.

[Old English *-wacu* (in *nihtwacu*) corresp. to Middle Low German, Middle Dutch *wake* (Dutch *waak*), Old High German *wahha* (German *Wache*) watch, watching, wakefulness, Old Norse *vaka* watch, vigil, eve, ult. rel. to WAKE *verb*. Partly a new formation in Middle English from WAKE *verb*. Sense 3 prob. from Old Norse *vaka*.]

1 Wakefulness, esp. during normal hours of sleep. Now only in ***sleep and wake***, ***sleep or wake***, ***wake and dream***. OE.

†**2** Avoidance of sleep as a religious observance on the eve of a festival etc.; an instance of this, a vigil. ME–M17.

3 a *sing.* & in *pl.* (freq. treated as *sing.*). The annual festival or fair of a (usu. rural) parish, orig. on the feast of the patron saint of the church. Later also, an annual holiday in (esp. industrial) northern England. Now chiefly *dial.* or *Hist.* ME. ▸**b** The vigil or eve of a religious festival, marked by celebrations; a religious festival. *obsolete* exc. *dial.* E16.

4 Now esp. among Irish people: a watch or vigil held by relatives and friends beside the body of a dead person before burial; this accompanied by merrymaking or lamentation. LME.

wake /weɪk/ *noun*². L15.

[Prob. from Middle Low German *wake* from Old Norse *vaka*, *vǫk* hole or opening in ice, perh. orig. as made by a vessel (whence also Dutch *wak*, German *Wake* hole or channel in ice).]

1 A track made by a person or thing; *spec.* (*a*) a trail of light behind a luminous object in motion; (*b*) a disturbance caused by a body swimming or moving in water; (*c*) turbulent air left behind a body in flight; (*d*) a track or trail on land. L15.

2 *esp.* The track left on the water's surface by a moving ship etc. (Earliest in ***in the wake of*** below.) M16. ▸**b** A ship's course. *rare*. L16.

3 A line of hay prepared for carting. *dial.* M19.

4 An open hole or unfrozen place in ice. *dial.* M19.

> 🕮 **2** A. GERAS The long white wake that the ship made in the dark water.

Phrases & comb.: **in the wake of** behind and in the track left by a ship etc.; behind, following; as a result or consequence of, in imitation of. **in wake of** NAUTICAL = ***in way of*** s.v. WAY *noun*. **wakeboard** a board used in wakeboarding. **wakeboarding** the sport of riding on a short, wide board resembling a surfboard and performing acrobatic manoeuvres while being towed behind a motor boat.

wake /weɪk/ *adjective* (chiefly *pred.*). Long *rare*. LME.

[Aphet. from AWAKE *adjective*.]

Not sleeping, awake.

wake /weɪk/ *verb*. Pa. t. **woke** /wəʊk/, **waked**; pa. pple **woken** /ˈwəʊk(ə)n/, **waked**.

[Old English strong verb repr. only in pa. t. *wōc* corresp. to Old Norse verb repr. by pa. pple *vakinn* awake; also partly from Old English weak verb *wacian* = Old Frisian *wakia*, Old Saxon *wakon*, Old High German *wahhēn*, *-ōn* (German *wachen*), from Germanic from Indo-European. Cf. WATCH *verb*.]

▸**I 1** *verb intrans.* Be or remain awake, be kept awake. Now *rare* exc. as WAKING *noun*, *ppl adjective*. OE. ▸**b** *verb trans.* Remain awake during (the night). *poet.* L15.

2 *verb intrans.* Stay awake to keep watch, provide care, or accomplish work; remain active or vigilant at night. Now only (*dial.*), sit up at night *with* a person, esp. a sick one. OE.

3 *verb intrans.* Avoid sleep as a religious observance; pass the night in prayer, keep a vigil in church, beside a dead body before burial, etc. *obsolete* exc. *dial.* OE.

4 *verb trans.* **a** Watch or guard at night, keep watch over. *obsolete* exc. *dial.* ME. ▸**b** Keep watch or vigil beside the body of (a dead person) before burial, hold a wake over. Now *dial.* (esp. *Anglo-Irish*). ME.

▶ **II 5** *verb intrans.* Come out of the state of sleep or unconsciousness, cease to sleep. Freq. foll. by *up*. ME. ▸**b** *transf.* & *fig.* Be roused to action or activity; become animated, alert, or lively, throw off lethargy. Usu. foll. by *up*. LME.

6 *verb trans.* Rouse from sleep or unconsciousness, cause to stop sleeping. Freq. foll. by *up*. ME. ▸**b** *transf.* & *fig.* Rouse to action or activity, make alert or lively. Also, disturb (silence, a place) with noise; cause to re-echo. Freq. foll. by *up*. LME.

7 *verb trans.* Bring (a feeling etc.) into being, arouse; stir up (strife etc.); evoke (an echo etc.). Also foll. by *up*. ME.

> 📖 **5** J. BARTH I must have waked at six o'clock, that morning. C. BRAYFIELD I feel like I'm dreaming and I never want to wake up. **6** P. USTINOV He was asleep . . . They went through the room quietly, without waking him up. **7** J. BUCHAN A surprising number of things which woke my curiosity.

Phrases: ***wake a sleeping wolf***: see WOLF *noun*. **wake to**, **wake up to** (cause to) become conscious, aware, or appreciative of.

■ **wakeless** *adjective* without awakening, unbroken, undisturbed E19. **waker** *noun* a person who wakes a person or thing; a person who wakes in a specified way; ***waker-upper*** (*colloq.*), a waker: ME. **waking** *noun* the action of the verb; an instance of this; being or remaining awake; *dial.* a vigil, a wake over a dead body: ME. **waking** *ppl adjective* that wakes; that remains awake; ***waking dream***: see DREAM *noun*[2]: ME.

wakeful /ˈweɪkfʊl, -f(ə)l/ *adjective.* LME.
[from WAKE *verb* + -FUL.]

1 Habitually keeping awake; alert, vigilant, watchful. LME.

2 Keeping awake, esp. while others sleep. M16.

3 Of a night etc.: passed with little or no sleep. E17.

†**4** That rouses a person from sleep, awakening. *rare* (Milton). Only in E17.

5 Of a dream etc.: waking. M17.

6 Unable to sleep, restless. L17.

■ **wakefully** *adverb* L16. **wakefulness** *noun* E17.

wakeman /ˈweɪkmən/ *noun. arch.* Pl. **-men**. ME.
[from WAKE *noun*[1] + MAN *noun*.]

1 A watchman. ME.

2 *Hist.* A member of a class of municipal officers in Ripon, Yorkshire; the chief magistrate or mayor of the borough of Ripon. L15.

waken /ˈweɪk(ə)n/ *verb.*
[Old English *wæcnan* = Old Norse *vakna* wake up, Gothic *gawaknan*, from Germanic base also of WAKE *verb*: see -EN[5].]

1 *verb intrans.* = WAKE *verb* 5, 5b. OE.

2 *verb trans.* = WAKE *verb* 6, 6b. ME.

3 *verb trans.* = WAKE *verb* 7. ME.

4 *verb trans.* SCOTS LAW. Revive (a court process allowed to remain inactive for a year and a day). Freq. as ***wakening*** *verbal noun.* M16.

5 *verb trans.* Watch over, keep an eye on. *Scot.* M16.

■ **wakener** *noun* E16.

wakerife /ˈweɪkrʌɪf, -rɪf/ *adjective. Scot.* & *north.* L15.
[from WAKE *verb* + RIFE *adjective*.]

Indisposed to sleep, wakeful, vigilant.

■ **wakerifely** *adverb* E19. **wakerifeness** *noun* E17.

wake-robin /ˈweɪkrɒbɪn/ *noun.* M16.
[App. from WAKE *verb* + ROBIN *noun*[1].]

1 The cuckoo-pint or wild arum, *Arum maculatum*. M16.

2 In N. America: (***a***) the arrow arum, *Peltandra virginica*; (***b***) any of various trilliums, esp. *Trillium erectum* and *T. sessile*. E18.

wake-up /ˈweɪkʌp/ *noun.* M19.
[from WAKE *verb* + UP *adverb*[1].]

1 †**a** ***wake-up kittle***, the kittiwake. Only in M19. ▸**b** = ***common flicker*** s.v. FLICKER *noun*[1]. M19.

2 An alert or resourceful person. *Austral.* & *NZ slang.* E20.

3 The action of waking a person or of being woken from sleep. L20.

2 be a wake-up be alert (*to*).

Comb.: **wake-up call** a telephone alarm call for awakening a sleeping person; **wake-up pill** *colloq.* = PEP ***pill***; **wake-up service** a telephone service specializing in wake-up calls.

wakey-wakey /weɪkɪˈweɪki/ *interjection* & *noun. colloq.* (orig. MILITARY). M20.
[Redupl. extension of WAKE *verb*.]

▶ **A** *interjection.* Exhorting a person or persons to wake up. M20.

> 📖 M. WOODHOUSE: 'Wakey-wakey,' he said. 'Stand by your beds.'

▶ **B** *noun.* = REVEILLE. Also, an utterance of 'wakey-wakey'. M20.

wakf /wakf/ *noun.* Also ***waqf***. M19.
[Arab. *waqf* stoppage, immobilization (*sc.* of ownership of property), from *waqafa* stop, come to a standstill.]

In Islamic countries, endowment or settlement of property under which the proceeds are to be devoted to a religious or charitable purpose; land or property endowed in this way.

wakizashi /wakɪˈzaʃi/ *noun.* Pl. same. L19.
[Japanese, from *waki* side + *-sashi*, from *sasu* put into position, wear at one's side.]

A Japanese sword shorter than a *katana*.

wakon /ˈwak(ə)n/ *noun.* L18.
[Dakota *wakʰáⁿ* spirit, being with supernatural power.]

= MANITOU.

Comb.: **wakon-bird** a mythical bird venerated by some N. American Indians.

Walach /ˈwɒlək/ *noun* & *adjective.* Also **-ll-**. L18.
[Var. of VLACH.]

▶ **A** *noun.* **1** = VLACH *noun.* L18.

2 The language of the Walachs or Vlachs. *rare.* L18.

▶ **B** *adjective.* Of or pertaining to the Walachs or their language. M19.

Walachian *noun* & *adjective* var. of WALLACHIAN.

Walapai /ˈwaləpʌɪ/ *noun* & *adjective.* M19.
[Walapai *Xawalapaiy* pine tree people.]

▶ **A** *noun.* Pl. **-s**, same.

1 A member of a Yuman people of NW Arizona. M19.

2 The language of this people. L19.

▶ **B** *attrib.* or as *adjective.* Of or pertaining to the Walapais or their language. L19.

Walcheren /ˈvalkərən, -x-/ *noun.* E19.
[An island at the mouth of the River Schelde in the Netherlands.]

MEDICINE. ***Walcheren ague***, ***Walcheren fever***, a severe form of malaria.

wald *noun*, *verb* see WIELD *noun*, *verb*.

Walden inversion /ˈwɒld(ə)n ɪnˌvəːʃ(ə)n; ˈvald(ə)n/ *noun phr.* E20.
[from P. von *Walden* (1863–1957), Latvian chemist.]

CHEMISTRY. = INVERSION *noun* 7b.

Waldenses /wɒlˈdɛnsiːz/ *noun pl.* M16.
[medieval Latin, app. from *Waldensis* var. of (Peter) *Valdes* (d. 1205), Lyonnese merchant, the founder.]

ECCLESIASTICAL. The adherents of a persecuted puritan sect originating in southern France *c* 1170, now existing chiefly in northern Italy and N. America. Cf. VAUDOIS *noun*[1].

■ **Waldense** *noun* (*rare*) = WALDENSIAN *noun* L19. **Waldensian** *noun* & *adjective* (***a***) *noun* a member of the Waldenses; (***b***) *adjective* of or pertaining to the Waldenses: E17.

Waldenström /ˈvaldənstrəːm/ *noun.* M20.
[Jan Gösta *Waldenström* (b. 1906), Swedish biochemist and physician.]

MEDICINE. Used in *possess.* to designate several diseases and syndromes, esp. a rare progressive form of macroglobulinaemia.

Waldeyer /ˈvaldʌɪə/ *noun.* E20.
[Heinrich W. G. von *Waldeyer*-Hartz (1836–1921), German anatomist.]

ANATOMY. Used in *possess.* to designate various anatomical structures described by von Waldeyer-Hartz.

Waldeyer's ring, **Waldeyer's tonsillar ring** a circular system of lymphoid tissue around the throat, formed by the tonsils and the pharyngeal and lingual adenoids.

waldflute /ˈwɔːldfluːt/ *noun.* M19.
[German *Waldflöte* lit. 'forest flute'.]

An organ-stop producing an open flutelike tone.

waldhorn /ˈvalthɔːn/ *noun.* M19.
[German.]

A French horn. Also, a natural valveless horn.

waldo /ˈwɔːldəʊ/ *noun.* Pl. **-os**, **-oes**. M20.
[*Waldo* F. Jones, fictional inventor described in a science-fiction story by Robert Heinlein.]

A remote-controlled device for handling or manipulating objects.

Waldorf salad /wɔːldɔːf ˈsaləd/ *noun.* E20.
[*Waldorf*-Astoria Hotel in New York, where first served.]

A salad made from apples, walnuts, and usu. celery, dressed with mayonnaise.

waldrapp /ˈwɔːldrap/ *noun.* E20.
[German, from *Wald* wood, forest + *Rapp* var. of *Rabe* raven.]

The hermit ibis, *Geronticus eremita*, which has mainly dark metallic green plumage and a bare head, and is now confined to Morocco and Turkey. Also called ***bald ibis***.

Waldsterben /ˈvaltʃtɛrbən/ *noun.* L20.
[German, from *Wald* wood, forest + *Sterben* dying, death.]

ECOLOGY. Disease and death in forest trees and vegetation as a result of atmospheric pollution.

wale /weɪl/ *noun*[1] & *verb*[1].
[Late Old English *walu* = Low German *wāle* weal, Old Norse *vala* knuckle. Cf. WEAL *noun*[2], *verb*.]

▶ **A** *noun.* †**1** A ridge of earth or stone. Only in LOE.

2 = WEAL *noun*[2] 1. LOE.

3 NAUTICAL. **a** = GUNWALE. ME. ▸**b** Any of the broad thick timbers forming the outer sides of a ship. Usu. in *pl.* ME.

4 A ridge or raised line of threads in a woven fabric; the texture of a fabric with such lines. L16.

5 Each of the horizontal timbers between the piles of a dam etc. Also ***wale-piece***. M17.

6 A ridge on a horse's collar. L18.

7 BASKET-MAKING. Any of the horizontal bands round the body of a basket of intertwined rods. E20.

Comb.: **wale-knot** = WALL-KNOT; ***wale-piece***: see sense 5 above.

▶ **B** *verb trans.* **1** = WEAL *verb* 2. LME.

2 a MILITARY. Weave (a gabion etc.). M19. ▸**b** BASKET-MAKING. Intertwine (rods) to make a wale; provide with a wale or wales. M19.

■ **waling** *noun* (***a***) the action of the verb; (***b***) (any of) the wales used to brace a dam etc.; (***c***) NAUTICAL the timbers forming the wale of a boat; (***d***) BASKET-MAKING the wales of a basket: M19.

wale /weɪl/ *noun*[2], *adjective*, & *verb*[2]. *Scot.* & *north.* ME.
[Old Norse *val* corresp. to Old High German *wala* (German *Wahl*), from Germanic base also of WILL *verb*[1].]

▶ **A** *noun.* **1** The action or an act of choosing; (a) choice. Also, scope for choice. ME.

2 A thing chosen as the best; a choice example. E16.

▶†**B** *adjective.* Chosen; choice, select. ME–L18.

▶ **C** *verb.* **1** *verb trans.* Choose, select; sort. ME.

2 *verb intrans.* Make a choice; choose. ME.

waler /ˈweɪlə/ *noun*[1]. *obsolete* exc. *Hist.* E19.
[from WALE *verb*[2] + -ER[1].]

MINING. A boy employed to pick out impurities from coal.

Waler /ˈweɪlə/ *noun*[2]. M19.
[from New South *Wales* + -ER[1].]

1 A horse imported into India from Australia, esp. from New South Wales; an Australian-bred horse. M19.

2 A native or inhabitant of New South Wales, Australia. Also *gen.*, an Australian. *slang.* L19.

waler *noun*[3] see WHALER.

wali /ˈwaːliː/ *noun.* E19.
[Arab. *al-wālī*.]

Hist. The governor of a province in an Arab country. Cf. VALI.

walia /ˈwaːlɪə/ *noun.* M20.
[Amharic.]

More fully ***walia ibex***. A smaller variety of the ibex, *Capra ibex*, found in Ethiopia.

Walian /ˈweɪlɪən/ *noun* & *adjective.* L19.
[from *Wales* + -IAN.]

▶ **A** *noun.* A native or inhabitant of either South Wales (***South Walian***) or North Wales (***North Walian***). L19.

▶ **B** *adjective.* Of or pertaining to either of these regions. Only in ***South Walian***, ***North Walian***. L20.

walk /wɔːk/ *noun.* ME.
[from WALK *verb*[1].]

▶ **I 1** The action or an act of walking; esp. a short journey on foot for exercise or pleasure; a stroll, a constitutional. ME. ▸†**b** Travel; wandering. LME–L17. ▸†**c** Line or path of movement. LME–L16.

2 *fig.* **a** Movement in time; progress, development. Formerly also (*rare*), expatiation, extended discourse. M16. ▸**b** Manner of behaviour; conduct. L16. ▸†**c** A course of action or conduct forming part of the plot of a drama. M17–M18.

3 *spec.* **a** A formal procession. M16. ▸**b** A walking race or sports contest. L19. ▸**c** BASEBALL. = ***base on balls*** s.v. BASE *noun*[1]. E20. ▸**d** A dance performed at a walking pace. Chiefly with specifying word, as ***Lambeth walk*** (see LAMBETH 3). M20. ▸**e** A sponsored event in which participants walk a certain distance for charity. L20.

4 An act of walking as distinguished from more rapid progress; the slowest gait or pace of a person or animal. E17.

5 A characteristic manner of walking; a person's gait. M17.

> 📖 **1** SARA MAITLAND Taking her for long weekend walks in the park. **2a** C. LAMB The . . infelicity which accompanies some people in their walk through life. **3e** *Guardian* Oxfam depended on walks for up to £175,000 of its year's £2½ millions budget. **4** DAY LEWIS At a brisk walk, which . . I prevent from degenerating into a trot. *Scientific American* In the walk at least two of the horse's legs touch the ground. **5** E. BIRNEY A small nimble fellow with . . a walk like a prowling tomcat.

▶ **II 6 a** A usual or favourite place for walking; a preferred route for walking. LME. ▸**b** A route chosen for walking. E17. ▸**c** A regular circuit of delivery etc.; a worker's usual round or run. E18.

7 a A poultry run (cf. RUN *noun* 11c). M16. ▸**b** The place in which a gamecock is kept. E17.

8 A place or route intended or suitable for walking; *spec.* (**a**) a cloister or aisle in a church or other public building; (**b**) (with specifying word) in the Royal Exchange, any of the areas of pathway in which a particular class of merchant was allowed to walk, as ***East India walk***, ***Virginia walk***, etc. **M16.** ▸**b** A broad path through or around a garden. Also, a pavement for pedestrians. **M16.** ▸**c** A tree-lined avenue. **L16.** ▸**d** A circular pavement walked on by a horse driving a mill. **M18.** ▸**e** = ***rope-walk*** s.v. ROPE *noun*[1]. **L18.**

9 A division of a forest in the charge of a particular forester, ranger, or keeper. **M16.** ▸**b** *Hist.* A plantation. **L18.**

10 (An area of) land used for pasturage; now *spec.* a sheepwalk. **M16.**

11 A distance to be walked; *esp.* such a distance defined by a specified length of time spent in walking. **M16.**

12 *fig.* **a** A branch or sphere *of* a specified activity or interest; a speciality. **E18.** ▸**b** = ***walk of life*** below. Now *rare.* **M19.**

13 A farm etc. where a hound-puppy is sent to accustom it to various surroundings. Freq. in ***at walk***, ***put to walk***. **M18.**

> 📖 **6b** J. MARTINEAU We can find walks that will vie with the Thiergarten. **c** *Times* A postwoman . . prevented from . . obtaining a particular postal 'walk'. **8** N. HAWTHORNE The great cloister . . has a walk of intersecting arches. **b** *New Yorker* A . . man is smoothing cement for his new walk. **c** ADDISON There is a long Walk of aged Elms. **11** J. RUSKIN A few hundred yards west . . , within ten minutes' walk, is the Baptistry. **12a** DICKENS He painted anything . . . 'He has no particular walk? . . No speciality?' said Mr. Dorrit. N. PEVSNER Dealing with the higher walks of administration.

Phrases etc.: ***cock-of-the-walk***: see COCK *noun*[1]. ***random walk***: see RANDOM *adjective*. **take a walk** (**a**) *N. Amer. slang* be dismissed; in *imper.*, go away, get out; (**b**) walk out as a form of industrial action. **walk in life** (now *rare* or *obsolete*) = ***walk of life*** below. **walk of life** (**a**) a person's social rank; (**b**) a person's profession, occupation, or calling. ***Whit walk***: see WHIT *adjective*. **win in a walk** *N. Amer. colloq.* win easily; walk over.

Comb.: (See also combs. of WALK *verb*[1].) **walk-clerk** (*obsolete* exc. *Hist.*) a bank clerk charged with collecting payment of cheques in a particular district; **walksman** (chiefly *Hist.*) an officer in charge of a particular stretch of the bank of a river or canal.

walk /wɔːk/ *verb*[1].

[Old English *wealcan* corresp. to Middle & mod. Low German, Middle & mod. Dutch *walken* WALK *verb*[2], Old Norse *valka* drag about, torment, (refl.) wallow, from Germanic base of unkn. origin.]

▸ **I** *verb intrans.* †**1** Roll, toss. **OE–LME.**

†**2** Go from place to place; journey, wander. **OE–E16.**

3 †**a** Circulate; pass or be passed around. **ME–L17.** ▸†**b** Of crime etc.: be rife; become widespread. **ME–E17.** ▸**c** Of a thing: move; progress. Now *obsolete* exc. *Scot.* **LME.** ▸†**d** *fig.* Be a substitute; pass *for*. **M16–E17.**

4 †**a** Go about in public; live or move *in* a particular place. **ME–E17.** ▸**b** (Of a ghost etc.) be seen about, appear; (of a dead person) return and be seen as a ghost. Orig. foll. by *out*. **ME.**

5 Travel or move about on foot; move in a specified direction on foot (foll. by *down*, *in*, *out*, etc.). **ME.** ▸**b** Move about or go from place to place on foot for exercise or pleasure. **ME.** ▸**c** *BASEBALL.* Of a batter: reach first base on balls. **M19.** ▸**d** In *imper.* Cross the road (indicated, together with the neg., on American road signs). *US.* **M20.**

6 *fig.* Behave or act in a specified manner. Freq. in ***walk with God***, lead a religious life. **ME.**

7 Go away, leave (formerly freq. in *imper.*); be turned out; *slang* die. **LME.** ▸**b** *transf.* Be stolen or got rid of; be carried off. Now *colloq.* **LME.** ▸**c** *CRICKET.* Leave the wicket without waiting to be given out. Also foll. by *out*. **M20.** ▸**d** Be released from suspicion or from a charge; avoid a sentence of imprisonment. *N. Amer. slang.* **M20.**

8 Go on foot in procession; follow a prescribed route on foot in the course of official duty; *Hist.* (of a proctor at Oxford University) march to and fro at a degree ceremony. **LME.**

9 **a** Of a quadruped: progress with the slowest gait, always having at least two feet on the ground at once. Also, (of a horse-rider) ride a horse at this pace. **LME.** ▸**b** Of a human or other biped: progress by lifting and setting down each foot in turn, so as to have one foot always on the ground; progress with similar movements *on* one's hands etc. **M18.** ▸**c** *JAZZ.* Of a bass player: play a walking bass (see WALKING *ppl adjective*). **M20.**

10 Leave one's place of work at short notice as a form of industrial action. Usu. foll. by *out*. Orig. *US.* **L19.**

> 📖 **4b** R. L. STEVENSON Would ye rob the man before his body? Nay, he would walk! **5** H. JAMES She walks in without knocking at the door. A. CARNEGIE Father and I walked over from Allegheny to Pittsburgh. **b** A. DAVIES The town . . is on the whole very pleasant to . . walk about in. **6** A. S. NEILL A difficult subject to tackle . . . but I tried to walk warily. **7** *Observer* Thompson and Co should not have accepted his offer to walk. **b** *Times* Cutlery, which, if interesting, tended to 'walk'. **c** J. FINGLETON Graveney should have walked but O'Neill dropped him at third slip. **9b** J. C. POWYS This . . baby . . could *just* walk. P. KAVANAGH One of the greatest scamps that ever walked on two feet. **10** *Daily Telegraph* The . . sound engineering crews . . walked out shortly before the programme was due . . on the air.

▸ **II** *verb trans.* **11** Travel through or traverse on foot; *fig.* pervade. **ME.** ▸†**b** Attend, frequent. **M17–M18.**

12 Go (a specified distance) on foot; undertake (a journey etc.) on foot. **LME.**

13 Lead or drive (a horse, dog, etc.) at a walk; exercise in this way. Also foll. by *out*. **L15.**

14 Walk on or along; walk round (a boundary). **M16.**

15 Walk about on. **M17.**

16 Bring into a specified state by walking; dispel the adverse effects of by walking (foll. by *off*). **M17.**

17 Cause or induce to walk with one; conduct or accompany on foot (esp. in a specified direction). **M17.** ▸**b** Force or help to walk by pushing from behind. **E19.** ▸**c** *BASEBALL.* Allow (a batter) to reach first base on balls. **E20.**

18 Go through (a dance etc.) at a walk. **E19.**

19 Cause to move or turn by walking; *spec.* (*NAUTICAL*) turn (a capstan) by walking round it. **M19.** ▸**b** Start (a game-bird) by beating the ground. Usu. foll. by *up*. **L19.**

20 **a** Take charge of (a puppy) at walk (see WALK *noun* 13). **M19.** ▸**b** Keep (a gamecock) in a walk. **M19.** ▸**c** *ANGLING.* Draw (a hooked fish) through the water with the rod, esp. to escape a current or obstruction. **L19.**

21 Move (a gun) so as to hit a target progressively in a straight line. **M20.**

> 📖 **11** BROWNING When man walks the garden of this world. **12** DICKENS They walked a few paces, and paused. **13** H. CARPENTER He met Gertrude walking her dog in the Jardin du Luxembourg. **14** SPENSER With a few to walke the narrow way. **15** *Independent* Pleasure from walking the beautiful heather moorlands. **16** *Philadelphia Inquirer* There is . . room for walking off all that food. **17** D. ABSE Shouldn't we walk him home? E. O'BRIEN He walked her through the . . passage and from room to room. **b** J. K. JEROME He took me by the two shoulders, walked me out into the street.

Phrases: †**let walk** dismiss from attention. ***someone walking on my grave***: see GRAVE *noun*[1]. **walk all over** *colloq.* (**a**) treat with contempt; (**b**) defeat decisively. **walk a person off his or her feet** = ***walk a person off his or her legs*** s.v. LEG *noun*. ***walk a person off his or her legs***: see LEG *noun*. ***walk on air***, ***walk as if on air***: see AIR *noun*[1] 1. **walk a turn** walk once up and once down. **walk before one can run** understand elementary points before proceeding to anything more difficult. **walk good!** *W. Indies* farewell! good luck! **walk home** *fig.* win a contest easily. ***walk hots***: see HOT *noun*[2] 1b. ***walk in a person's footsteps***: see FOOTSTEP 1. ***walk in a person's steps***: see STEP *noun*[1]. **walk in one's sleep** = SLEEPWALK. ***walk in the way with***: see WAY *noun*. **walk into a person's affections** win a person's love immediately and easily. ***walk Matilda***: see MATILDA 1. ***walk on air***: see AIR *noun*[1] 1. **walk on crutches** support oneself by crutches in walking. **walk one's rounds** *arch.* follow a usual or prescribed route on foot. ***walk Spanish***: see SPANISH *adverb*. ***walk tall***: see TALL *adverb*. **walk the chalk** *slang* walk along a chalked line as a proof of being sober. **walk the hospitals** *arch.* = ***walk the wards*** below. ***walk the plank***: see PLANK *noun*. **walk the streets** (**a**) traverse the streets in search of work etc.; be homeless; (**b**) be a prostitute. **walk the wards** receive clinical instruction as a medical student. **walk with a stick** etc. use a stick etc. as a partial support in walking. ***walk with God***: see sense 6 above. ***within walking distance***: see DISTANCE *noun*.

With adverbs & prepositions in specialized senses: (See also Phrases above.) **walk away (from)** (**a**) refuse to become involved (with); (**b**) leave the scene of (an accident) on foot without needing to be carried on a stretcher; (**c**) outdistance (an opponent) in a race. **walk away with** win or steal easily. **walk in** (**a**) *imper.* (*arch.*) come in; (**b**) arrive, enter, esp. unexpectedly or with surprising ease; (see also sense 5 above). **walk into** *colloq.* (**a**) attack vigorously, assail; (**b**) eat or drink a large quantity of; (**c**) arrive or find oneself in (an awkward situation) through unwariness. **walk off** depart suddenly or abruptly; (see also sense 16 above). **walk off with** *colloq.* (**a**) steal; (**b**) win easily. **walk on** (of an actor) go on stage with few or no lines to say; (see also sense 9b above). **walk out** (**a**) (of a soldier) go into town on a pass when off duty; (**b**) leave a gathering or place without warning, esp. in protest; (see also senses 4b, 5, 7c, 10, 13 above). **walk out on** (**a**) desert, abandon; (**b**) withdraw from (an agreement). **walk out with** *arch.* court, go out with. **walk over** (**a**) go over (a racecourse) at a walking pace to win a race with little or no opposition; (**b**) *transf.* win or defeat easily. **walk round** *N. Amer. colloq.* defeat easily. **walk through** perform (a dramatic role etc.) with little effort. **walk up** *imper.* a showman's invitation to see a show; (see also sense 19b above). **walk with** †(**a**) be in accord with, act harmoniously with; (**b**) *arch.* = ***walk out with*** above.

Comb.: **walk-around** (**a**) *Hist.* a kind of rotary mill; (**b**) *US* a dance in which participants move in a large circle; a piece of music accompanying this; **walk-away** *noun & adjective* (designating) a race in which the winner leaves the other competitors far behind; **walk-back** *US slang* a rear apartment; **walk-march** *noun & verb intrans. MILITARY* (a command to) march at a walking pace; (a command to cavalry to) proceed at the walk; **walk-off** an act of walking off from a stage, sports field, etc.; **walk-round** *noun & adjective* (**a**) *noun* (*US*) = ***walk-around*** (b) above; (**b**) *adjective* (of a shop) with goods arranged for a customer to walk around.

■ **walkable** *adjective* (**a**) suitable for walking on; (**b**) (of a distance) able to be walked: **M18.** **walkist** *noun* (now *rare* or *obsolete*) a race walker **L19.**

walk /wɔːk/ *verb*[2] *trans.* Now *dial.* & *Hist.* Also (*Scot.*) **waulk**. **ME.**

[Middle & mod. Low German, Middle & mod. Dutch *walken* (cf. prec.); perh. partly from WALKER *noun*[1].]

1 = FULL *verb*[1] 2. Also (*Scot.*), thicken, make hard or callous. **ME.**

†**2** *transf.* Beat (a person). **E16–E18.**

Comb.: **walk-mill** = ***fulling-mill*** s.v. FULL *verb*[1] 2; **waulking song** *Scot.* a rhythmic Gaelic song with many verses and a chorus, formerly sung while walking cloth.

walkabout /ˈwɔːkəbaʊt/ *noun*. **L19.**

[from WALK *verb*[1] + ABOUT *adverb*.]

▸ **I 1** Among Australian Aborigines: a person travelling on foot, a swagman. **L19.**

▸ **II 2** A period of wandering in the bush by an Australian Aborigine. *Austral.* **E20.**

3 *transf.* **a** A journey; a protracted walk, *esp.* one taking in a number of places. **E20.** ▸**b** An informal stroll through a crowd by a visiting dignitary. **L20.**

Phrases: **go walkabout** go on a walkabout.

walkathon /ˈwɔːkəθɒn/ *noun*. *colloq.* **M20.**

[from WALK *verb*[1] + -ATHON.]

A long-distance competitive walk, now *esp.* one organized as a fund-raising event for charity.

walker /ˈwɔːkə/ *noun*[1]. Now *Scot.*, *dial.*, & *Hist.* Also (*Scot.*) **waulker**.

[Late Old English *wealcere*, Middle & mod. Low German, Middle & mod. Dutch *walker*, Old High German *walkari* (German *Walker*), formed as WALK *verb*[2]: see -ER[1].]

= FULLER *noun*[1].

walker /ˈwɔːkə/ *noun*[2]. **LME.**

[from WALK *verb*[1] + -ER[1].]

1 *gen.* A person who walks. **LME.** ▸**b** An itinerant beggar; a vagrant. *dial.* **M19.**

†**2** A gamekeeper with charge of a particular area of forest. **L15–E18.**

3 A person who walks for exercise or recreation; a participant in an organized walk or walking race. **L16.**

†**4** *sing.* & in *pl.* The feet. *slang.* **E17–M19.**

5 †**a** A wandering insect, a palmer-worm. Only in **M17.** ▸**b** A bird, insect, etc., that uses walking as its usual gait, as opp. to hopping, running, etc. **E19.**

6 With qualifying adjective: a person who acts in the specified manner. Now *rare* or *obsolete.* **L17.**

7 *SPORT.* A person who walks up partridges (see WALK *verb*[1] 19b). **E20.**

8 A person employed to take dogs for walks. Also = ***puppy walker*** s.v. PUPPY *noun*. **M20.**

9 **a** = ***baby-walker*** s.v. BABY *noun*. **M20.** ▸**b** = ***walking frame*** s.v. WALKING *noun*. **M20.**

10 A man who accompanies women as an escort at fashionable social occasions. *US slang.* **L20.**

> 📖 **1** M. LEITCH He was the lone walker on this long white avenue. **3** J. HALPERIN His father, a great walker, often took the boy along on his rambles. **6** O. BLACKALL Cast out of the . . Communion of the Faithful as disorderly Walkers. **9b** G. PALEY A gathering of . . arguers were leaning . . on aluminum walkers.

Phrases & comb.: ***race walker***: see RACE *noun*[1]. ***TENNESSEE walker***. **walker-on** = WALK-ON *noun* 1b.

■ †**walkership** *noun* the position or office of forest walker **M17–E18.**

Walker /ˈwɔːkə/ *noun*[3]. **E20.**

[John W. *Walker*, 19th-cent. US sportsman.]

More fully ***Walker hound***. (An animal of) a breed of American foxhound, usu. black, white, and tan in colour.

Walker /ˈwɔːkə/ *interjection*. *arch.* **E19.**

[Origin unkn.]

Expr. incredulity. Cf. ***HOOKEY Walker***.

Walkerite /ˈwɔːkərʌɪt/ *noun*. **M19.**

[from *Walker* (see below) + -ITE[1].]

A member of an extreme Calvinistic sect founded in Ireland by John Walker (1768–1833).

walkies /ˈwɔːkɪz/ *noun pl. colloq.* **M20.**

[from WALK *noun* + -IE.]

A walk to exercise a dog; *joc.* a walk, a stroll. Freq. in ***go walkies***.

walkie-talkie /wɔːkɪˈtɔːki/ *noun*. **M20.**

[from WALK *verb*[1] + -IE + TALK *verb* + -IE.]

1 A small radio transmitter and receiver that can be carried to provide two-way communication while the user is walking. **M20.**

2 A doll that can be made to walk and talk. **M20.**

walk-in /ˈwɔːkɪn/ *adjective & noun*. **E20.**

[from WALK *verb*[1] + IN *adverb*.]

▸ **A** *adjective*. **1** Of, pertaining to, or designating a person able to walk into a place casually or without an appointment; of, pertaining to, or designating a service not requiring an appointment. **E20.**

2 **a** Of a storage area: large enough to walk into. **M20.** ▸**b** Of a cinema, bank, etc.: entered on foot, as opp. to a drive-in. *N. Amer.* M20. ▸**c** Of a room: entered directly rather than through an intervening passage. M20.

> 1 *Music & Letters* 50 per cent of the income was generated by walk-in customers. *Sunday Times* Family walk-in centres in . . inner-cities. **2a** ***walk-in closet***, ***walk-in larder***, ***walk-in refrigerator***, ***walk-in wardrobe***, etc.

▸ **B** *noun.* **1** A walk-in wardrobe or other storage area. M20.

2 A person who defects by walking into a foreign embassy or consulate unsolicited. L20.

walking /ˈwɔːkɪŋ/ *noun.* LME.
[from WALK *verb*¹ + -ING¹.]
1 The action of WALK *verb*¹; an instance of this. LME.
2 Orig., a civic procession on foot. Later more widely, a walk or journey on foot; the distance covered by this in a specified time. LME.
3 The condition of a surface for walking on. M17.

Comb. & phrases: ***race walking***: see RACE *noun*¹; **walking day** a day on which schoolchildren walk in procession; **walking frame** a free-standing metal frame held at the top as a support in walking; **walking leg** ZOOLOGY in certain arthropods, esp. crustaceans, a limb used for walking; **walking machine** a mechanical or robotic device attached to a person to enable performance beyond normal capacity or strength; **walking on two legs**, **walking with two legs** in the People's Republic of China, the complementary use of both small-scale or local methods and large-scale capital-intensive ones in production and education; **walking-orders**, **walking-papers** *N. Amer. colloq.* notice of dismissal; **walking party** a party undertaking an excursion on foot; **walking-rapier**, **walking-sword** *Hist.* a short sword formerly worn in civilian life; **walking-staff** (now *rare* or *obsolete*) = WALKING-STICK 1; ***walking-sword***: see ***walking-rapier*** above; **walking-ticket** *US colloq.* = ***walking-orders*** above; **walking-wheel** = PERAMBULATOR 2; ***walking with two legs***: see ***walking on two legs*** above.

walking /ˈwɔːkɪŋ/ *ppl adjective.* LME.
[from WALK *verb*¹ + -ING².]
That walks or is able to walk; moving or travelling on foot. Formerly also, vagrant, strolling.

Special collocations & phrases: TENNESSEE ***walking horse***. **walking bass** a bass part, freq. of broken octaves, going up and down the scale in 4/4 time in steps or small intervals. **walking catfish** a SE Asian freshwater catfish, *Clarias batrachus* (family Clariidae), which is able to crawl over land and has been introduced into Florida, USA. **walking corpse** a person hardly showing any signs of life or vitality. **walking delegate** a trade-union official who visits sick members, interviews employers, etc. **walking dictionary** *colloq.* a person possessing a great store of information. **walking doll** a mechanical doll with moving legs. **walking dragline** MINING a large dragline supported on movable feet. **walking encyclopedia** *colloq.* = ***walking dictionary*** above. **walking fern** an ornamental N. American fern, *Camptosorus rhizophyllus*, with fronds which root at the tip. **walking fish** any fish which is able to crawl over land; *esp.* (***a***) any of several Asian snake-heads of the genus *Ophicephalus*; (***b***) a S. American catfish of the genus *Callichthys*; (***c***) a mudskipper; (***d***) a climbing perch. **walking funeral** a funeral in which the coffin is wheeled by hand. **walking gentleman** an actor playing a non-speaking part requiring gentlemanlike appearance. **walking lady** an actress playing a non-speaking part requiring ladylike appearance. **walking leaf** (***a***) = ***walking fern*** above; (***b***) = ***leaf insect*** s.v. LEAF *noun*¹. **walking sickness** an illness which does not confine the sufferer to bed. **walking wounded** casualties able to walk despite their injuries.

walking-stick /ˈwɔːkɪŋstɪk/ *noun.* L16.
[from WALKING *noun* + STICK *noun*¹.]
1 A stick carried in the hand when walking. L16.
2 = ***stick insect*** s.v. STICK *noun*¹. *N. Amer.* M18.

Comb.: **walking-stick palm** an Australian palm, *Linospadix monostachya*, the stem of which is used for making walking-sticks.

Walkman /ˈwɔːkmən/ *noun.* Pl. **-mans**, **-men** /-mən/. L20.
[from WALK *verb*¹ + MAN *noun.*]
(Proprietary name for) a type of personal stereo.

walk-on /ˈwɔːkɒn/ *noun & adjective.* E20.
[from ***walk on*** s.v. WALK *verb*¹.]
▸ **A** *noun.* **1** A dramatic role with little or no speaking. E20. ▸**b** An actor playing such a role. M20.
2 SPORT. A member of a sports team who has no regular status. *US.* L20.

> 1 *Video for You* His parts were seldom more than walk-ons.

▸ **B** *adjective.* **1** Of, pertaining to, or designating an airline service not requiring prior booking. M20.
2 Of, pertaining to, or designating a dramatic role with little or no speaking; *transf.* unimportant, insignificant. M20.

> 1 D. LODGE Skytrain, the walk-on, no-reservation service. **2** J. SUTHERLAND Humphry Ward has a walk-on part in literary history.

walk-out /ˈwɔːkaʊt/ *noun & adjective.* L19.
[from ***walk out*** s.v. WALK *verb*¹.]
▸ **A** *noun.* **1** An act of walking out in protest; a sudden angry departure; *spec.* a strike called at short notice. L19.
2 A courtship; a love affair. M20.
3 A doorway or passage providing outdoor access; access provided by such a feature. *N. Amer.* M20.

▸ **B** *adjective.* Of a room etc.: having a door to the outside. *N. Amer.* M20.

walkover /ˈwɔːkəʊvə/ *noun.* M19.
[from ***walk over*** s.v. WALK *verb*¹.]
▸ **A** *noun.* **1** A race in which the winner is unchallenged, having merely to walk over the finish line; a contest easily won through lack of competition. M19.
2 *gen.* Any easy achievement. E20.

> 1 *Boxing* Stevenson won . . in a walkover, his opponent . . showing up with his hand in a cast. **2** *Business* A walkover in the PC market.

▸ **B** *adjective.* That is a walkover; easily won or achieved. M20.

walk-through /ˈwɔːkθruː/ *noun & adjective.* M20.
[from ***walk through*** s.v. WALK *verb*¹.]
▸ **A** *noun.* **1** An unchallenging part in a play or other performance; *transf.* an undemanding task. M20. ▸**b** A perfunctory or lacklustre performance. L20.
2 a A rough rehearsal of a play, film, etc., without cameras. M20. ▸**b** COMPUTING. A product review of software carried out before release. L20.
▸ **B** *adjective.* Of a building: permitting access from either end. M20.

walk-up /ˈwɔːkʌp/ *adjective & noun.* E20.
[from WALK *verb*¹ + UP *adverb*¹.]
▸ **A** *adjective.* **1** Of an apartment etc.: reached by stairs rather than by a lift; (of a building) allowing access to the upper floors only by stairs. Chiefly *N. Amer.* E20.
2 Of a shop, service counter, etc.: entered or approached directly from the street. M20.

> 1 P. AUSTER An old walk-up building with gloomy stairwells. **2** *Down East* Red's Eats, a one-window, walk-up, fast-food joint.

▸ **B** *noun.* **1** A walk-up apartment or building. Chiefly *N. Amer.* E20.
2 HORSE-RACING. The walk of a racehorse to a starting line or tape. *US.* M20.
3 SHOOTING. The action of walking up game-birds; a piece of land kept clear for this purpose during a shoot. L20.

> 1 D. LEAVITT He was living on the top floor of a walk-up.

walkway /ˈwɔːkweɪ/ *noun.* Orig. *US.* L18.
[from WALK *noun* or *verb*¹ + WAY *noun.*]
1 A path etc. for walking along. L18.
2 A pedestrian passageway linking different buildings or sections of a building, *esp.* one raised above ground level. Also, a specially built path through a garden or scenic area. E20.

> 2 *Courier-Mail (Brisbane)* The mangrove walkway . . will enhance this area of the Gardens. *Flight International* External walkways leading to and from the airbridges.

Walkyrie /wɒlˈkɪri/ *noun.*
[Old English *wælcyriġe*, from *wæl* (see VALHALLA) + root of *ċēosan* CHOOSE. Cf. VALKYRIE.]
MYTHOLOGY. In Anglo-Saxon England, any of a group of supernatural female warriors supposed to ride through the air over battlefields and decide who should die. Cf. VALKYRIE.

■ **Walkyric** *adjective* of or pertaining to a Walkyrie or Walkyries E20.

wall /wɔːl/ *noun*¹.
[Old English *wall*, (West Saxon) *weall* corresp. to Old Frisian, Old Saxon, Middle & mod. Low German, Middle & mod. Dutch *wal* from Latin *vallum* rampart from *vallus* stake.]
1 A rampart or bank of earth, stone, etc., used for defensive purposes; a defensive structure enclosing a city, castle, etc.; in *pl.* fortifications. OE. ▸**b** An embankment to hold back the water of a river or the sea. ME. ▸**c** *fig.* A person who or thing which serves as a defence. Also (*spec.*), a navy, an army. LME. ▸**d** HERALDRY. A charge representing an embattled wall. L17.
2 A structure of little width in proportion to its length and height, usu. erected with continuous courses of brick or stone, and serving to enclose, protect, or divide a space or property or to support a roof. OE. ▸**b** The side next to the wall. E17. ▸**c** In the Eton College wall game, each of the players who form the bully against the wall. M19.
3 The vertical surface of a wall, esp. within a building. OE.
4 *fig.* A barrier, impediment, or obstacle to communication, interaction, etc. ME. ▸**b** ATHLETICS. *The* point of onset of extreme fatigue in a long-distance race, esp. a marathon, after which an athlete needs considerable willpower to finish. L20.
5 A thing that resembles a wall in appearance; a tall or perpendicular barrier. ME. ▸**b** In mah-jong, the arrangement of tiles from which hands are drawn. E20. ▸**c** BASEBALL. The barrier marking the outer perimeter of the outfield. E20. ▸**d** FOOTBALL. A line of defenders forming a barrier against a free kick (to be) taken near the penalty area. M20. ▸**e** SURFING. The steep face of a wave before it breaks. M20.
6 ANATOMY & ZOOLOGY. The membranous investment or lining of an organ, cavity, etc. LME. ▸**b** The outer horny covering of the foot of a horse. M19. ▸**c** BOTANY & MICROBIOLOGY. A rigid layer of cellulose or other polysaccharides lying outside the plasma membrane of the cells of plants, fungi, and bacteria. M19.
7 Anything functioning like the wall of a house, prison, etc.; *spec.* (***a***) a side of a vessel or tent (usu. in *pl.*); (***b***) the pastry forming the sides of a pie. L16.
8 MINING. The (surface of) rock enclosing a lode or seam; the side of a mine next to this. E18.
9 In full ***wall brown***, also ***wall butterfly***. Any of several Eurasian satyrid butterflies of the genus *Lasiommata*, which have orange-brown wings with dark brown markings and small eyespots; *esp.* the common *L. megera* of Europe. M19.

> 1 R. BAKER The Emperor Adrian . . made a great wall of earth between England and Scotland. MILTON Others from the Wall defend With Dart and Jav'lin. **2** TENNYSON Four gray walls, and four gray towers. DICKENS Mr. Pickwick found himself . . within the walls of a debtor's prison. G. GREENE Faces separated by a safe wall of glass. ***blank wall***, ***breast wall***, ***cavity wall***, ***embankment wall***, ***fire wall***, ***honeycomb wall***, ***middle wall***, ***parapet wall***, ***parpen wall***, ***party wall***, ***retaining wall***, ***sleeper wall***, etc. **3** C. J. LEVER The walls were decorated with coloured prints. **4** R. ST BARBE He . . barricades himself behind an unassailable wall of self-sufficiency. T. S. ELIOT Is the wall of pride cast down that divided them? W. ABISH It is disconcerting to enter the bookstore and be met by a wall of silence. ***potential wall***, ***tariff wall***, etc. **b** J. F. FIXX In thirty-five marathons . . I've never hit the wall I get tired, but . . always keep going. **5** M. EDWARDES We were faced with a wall of reporters and photographers. **7** SHAKES. *John* Within this wall of flesh There is a soul counts thee her creditor.

Phrases: ***against the wall***: see ***up against the wall*** below. **bang one's head against a brick wall**, **knock one's head against a brick wall**, **run one's head against a brick wall** have one's efforts continually rebuffed, try repeatedly to no avail. CAVITY ***wall***. ***Chinese wall***: see CHINESE *adjective*. **drive to the wall** drive to the last extremity. **drive up the wall** infuriate. ***fly on the wall***: see FLY *noun*¹. ***four walls***: see FOUR *adjective*. ***fourth wall***: see FOURTH *adjective*. ***from wig to wall***: see WIG *noun*². **give a person the wall** allow a person to walk next to the wall as the cleaner and safer side of a pavement etc. **go over the wall** *slang* (***a***) go to prison; (***b***) escape from prison; (***c***) leave a religious order; (***d***) defect (to another country). **go to the wall** be defeated or pushed aside; *spec.* go out of business. ***hole in the wall***: see HOLE *noun*¹. ***knock one's head against a brick wall***: see ***bang one's head against a brick wall*** above. ***mani wall***: see MANI *noun*². MENDANG ***wall***. **off the wall** (*slang*, chiefly *N. Amer.*) (***a***) unconventional(ly); (***b***) = ***off the cuff*** s.v. CUFF *noun*¹. ***pellitory of the wall***: see PELLITORY 2. ***run one's head against a brick wall***: see ***bang one's head against a brick wall*** above. **see through a brick wall** be exceptionally perceptive or intelligent. **send to the wall**. †**thrust to the wall** thrust aside into a position of neglect. **talk to a brick wall** fail to elicit any understanding or response from one's audience. ***the writing on the wall***: see WRITING *noun*. ***thrust to the wall***: see ***send to the wall*** above. **turn one's face to the wall** (of a dying person) turn away one's face in awareness of impending death. **up against the wall**, **against the wall** (***a***) facing execution by a firing-squad; (***b***) in an inextricable situation, in great trouble or difficulty. **up the wall** angry, furious; distraught, crazy. **Wall of Death** a fairground sideshow in which a motorcyclist uses gravitational force to ride around the inside walls of a vertical cylinder. **within the walls** within the ancient boundaries (of a city) as opp. to the suburbs. ***with one's back to the wall***: see BACK *noun*¹. ***wooden walls***: see WOODEN *adjective*.

Attrib. & comb.: In the sense 'set or fixed on or against a wall, growing on or against a wall', as ***wall clock***, ***wall cupboard***, ***wall-hangings***, ***wall light***, ***wall phone***, ***wall safe***, ***wall socket***, etc. Special combs., as **wall-arcade** ARCHITECTURE: used as a decoration of a wall; **wall bar** any of a set of horizontal bars extending up the wall of a gymnasium and used for various exercises; **wall-bearing** a surface supporting a shaft as it enters or passes through a wall; **wall bed**: which can be folded up against a wall when not in use; **wall-board** (a piece of) board, made from wood pulp, fibre, etc., used for surfacing walls, ceilings, etc.; **wall-border** a garden border at the foot of a wall; **wall-box** (***a***) an aperture made in or through a wall to accommodate a wall-bearing; (***b***) a postbox fixed in or to a wall (as opp. to a pillar-box); **wall-bracket**: attached to a wall as a stand or support for a lamp, ornament, shelf, etc.; ***wall brown***, ***wall butterfly***: see sense 9 above; **wall chart** a chart or poster designed for display on a wall, esp. in a classroom; **wallcovering** a wallpaper or other material used to cover and decorate interior walls; **wallcreeper** a Eurasian songbird, *Tichodroma muraria*, allied to the nuthatches, which has broad bright red wings and lives among rocks in mountainous country; **wall-face** the surface of a wall; **wall fern** a polypody of the *Polypodium vulgare* aggregate species; **wallfish** *dial.* the edible snail; **wall-fruit** (***a***) a fruit growing on a tree or bush trained against a wall; (***b***) a tree or bush bearing such fruit; **wall game** *the* form of football peculiar to Eton College, played against a wall; **wall garden** (***a***) a garden surrounded by a wall; (***b***) a border planted beside a sheltering wall; ***wall*** GERMANDER; **wall-hook** †(***a***) *rare* a grappling-hook; (***b***) a hook-shaped holdfast for fastening wire, piping, etc., to a wall; **wall lizard** any of various small Eurasian lacertid lizards of the genus *Podarcis*, frequenting walls, rocks, etc.; *esp.* the common *P. muralis* of southern Europe; **wall-nail**: made for driving into walls; **wall newspaper** (***a***) a newspaper produced by a college, workplace, etc., and displayed on a wall; (***b***) (esp. in China) an official newspaper displayed on a public wall; **wall-painting** a mural, a fresco; **wall pass** FOOTBALL etc. = ***one-two*** (b) s.v. ONE *adjective, noun, & pronoun*; ***wall pennywort***: see ***pennywort*** (a) s.v. PENNY; **wall pepper** biting stonecrop, *Sedum acre*, whose leaves have a peppery taste; **wall-piece** (*a*) MILITARY HISTORY a large gun mounted on the wall of a fort etc.; (*b*) ARCHITECTURE = PENDANT *noun* 1b; **wall-plate** a timber placed horizontally on or in a wall as a support for joists or rafters; ***wall plug***: see PLUG *noun* 1c; **wall-pocket** (*a*) a receptacle for small household items, designed to hang on a wall; (*b*) = ***wall vase*** below; **wall-poster**: displayed on a public wall; *spec.* = DAZIBAO; **wall-rib** ARCHITECTURE: placed at the intersection of a vault or arch with the wall; **wall-rock** GEOLOGY the rock adjacent to or enclosing a vein, hydrothermal ore deposit, fault, etc.; **wall rocket** either of two European yellow-flowered cruciferous plants, *Diplotaxis muralis* and *D. tenuifolia*, naturalized in Britain on walls and waste ground; **wall rue** a small fern of old walls, *Asplenium ruta-muraria*, with leaves resembling those of rue; **wall-side** (*a*) the side of a wall; (*b*) the side of a pavement etc. next to or nearest the wall; **wall-sided** *adjective* (esp. of a ship) having perpendicular sides like a wall; **wall space** an expanse of unbroken wall surface, *esp.* one regarded as an area for displaying pictures etc.; **wall-stone** (*a*) a stone forming part of a wall; (*b*) masonry, (a) stone suitable for building; **wall-tent**: having perpendicular sides; **wall-tie** each of the pieces of iron, slate, etc., used to bind together the two parts of a hollow wall; **wall-to-wall** *adjective* (*a*) (esp. of a carpet) covering the whole floor of a room, extending from one wall to another; (*b*) *fig.* filling a space or area entirely, ubiquitous; **wall-tree** a fruit tree trained against a wall for protection and warmth; **wall unit** a piece of furniture having various sections, esp. shelves and cupboards, and designed to stand against a wall; **wall vase**: having one flat side, designed to be hung on a wall; **wall-walk** a footpath along the top of a wall (in a castle etc.); **wall-wash** liquid distemper applied to the surface of a wall; **wallwasher** a lighting fixture designed to illuminate a wall evenly without lighting the floor; **wall-work** †(*a*) work done in building a wall; (*b*) a defensive work consisting of walls. See also WALLFLOWER, WALLPAPER.

■ **waller** *noun*[1] (now *rare* or *obsolete*) †(*a*) *rare* a wall-tree; (*b*) LAW a person casually employed to copy or engross legal documents: L17. **wallful** *noun* as much as the surface of a wall will hold M20. **wall-less** /-l-l-/ *adjective* M19.

†wall *noun*[2]. E17–E18.

[Back-form. from WALL-EYE.]

A wall-eye; the quality of being wall-eyed. Freq. *attrib.*

wall /wɔːl/ *noun*[3]. M19.

[Ellipt.]

NAUTICAL. = WALL-KNOT.

wall /wɔːl/ *verb*[1]. Long *obsolete* exc. *dial.*

[Old English *weallan* (intrans.), corresp. to Old Frisian *walla*, Old Saxon, Old High German *wallan* boil, gush out, from Germanic: cf. WELL *verb*[1].]

†**1** *verb intrans.* Boil (*lit. & fig.*). OE–ME.

†**2** *verb intrans.* Of a liquid: bubble up; well up, flow abundantly. OE–LME. ▸**b** Swarm (with vermin). OE–LME.

3 a *verb trans.* Boil. ME. ▸**b** *verb intrans.* Boil brine in making salt. L16.

■ **waller** *noun*[2] a person in a salt-works who boils brine E17.

wall /wɔːl/ *verb*[2].

[Old English (in pa. pple) *geweallod*, from *weall* WALL *noun*[1].]

▸**I** *verb trans.* **1** Provide, surround, or fortify with or as with a wall or walls. Also foll. by *about, round (about)*. OE. ▸**b** Build (*up*) the wall or walls of. (*lit. & fig.*) LME.

2 Enclose with or as with a wall (foll. by *in*); shut *off* or *out*, divide, (as) with a wall. OE. ▸**b** Line the walls of (a room, gallery, etc.). M19.

3 Close or block up (a gate, window, etc.) with masonry. Usu. foll. by *up*. E16.

4 Shut up (a person or thing) within walls; entomb in a wall, immure. Usu. foll. by *up*. M16.

5 Build (stone) into a wall. *rare*. L18.

> 📖 **1** SHAKES. *Rich. II* This flesh which walls about our life. DICKENS The House of Correction . . is not walled, like other prisons. Z. GREY A shady . . glade, partly walled by . . masses of upreared rocks. **2** H. BROOKE A gravel-walk that was walled in on the left hand. J. TYNDALL A space for cooking walled off from the sleeping-room. *fig.*: C. NESS A weekly sabbath walls in our wild natures. **b** LYTTON The room was walled from . . floor to . . roof with books. **4** E. A. POE I had walled the monster up within the tomb!

▸**II** *verb intrans.* **6** Build a wall or walls. L16.

■ **waller** *noun*[3] a person who builds walls ME.

wall /wɔːl/ *verb*[3] *trans. & intrans.* Long *Scot. & US.* L15.

[Rel. to 1st elem. of WALL-EYED.]

Roll (the eyes).

¶ Not recorded between E16 and E19.

walla *noun* var. of WALLAH.

wallaba /ˈwɒləbə/ *noun.* E19.

[Arawak.]

A large S. American leguminous tree, *Eperua falcata*, noted for its durable timber; the wood of this tree.

Wallabee /ˈwɒləbi/ *noun.* Chiefly *N. Amer.* M20.

[Perh. rel. to next.]

(Proprietary name for) any of several types of shoe; *spec.* (*a*) a kind of loafer with contrasting stitching; (*b*) a kind of suede desert boot.

wallaby /ˈwɒləbi/ *noun.* L18.

[Aboriginal *wolabā*.]

1 Any of various smaller kangaroos, including the majority of the members of the family Macropodidae. L18.

2 (W-.) A member of the Australian international rugby union team. E20.

> 📖 **1** ***forest wallaby, red-necked wallaby, scrub wallaby, rock wallaby, whiptail wallaby***, etc. **on the wallaby (track)** *Austral. slang* tramping about as a vagrant; unemployed. **2** *Country Life* The Wallabies are about to play the first international of their tour against Scotland.

Comb.: **wallaby-bush** a small S. Australian tree with reddish wood, *Beyeria viscosa*; also called ***pinkwood***; **wallaby-grass** any of various tufted pasture grasses of Australia and New Zealand, mainly of the genus *Danthonia*.

Wallace /ˈwɒlɪs/ *noun.* M19.

[Alfred Russel *Wallace* (1823–1913), English naturalist.]

Used ***attrib.*** and in ***possess.*** to designate concepts originated by Wallace or related to his work on speciation and distribution.

Wallace effect the evolution of reproductive isolation between sympatric species. **Wallace line**, **Wallace's line** a suggested boundary between the oriental and Australasian biogeographical regions, now placed along the continental shelf of SE Asia east of the islands of Borneo, Bali, and the Philippines. ***Wallace's standardwing***: see STANDARDWING *noun*.

■ **Wallacea** /wɒˈleɪsɪə/ *noun* a zoogeographical area constituting a transition zone between the oriental and Australasian regions, usu. held to comprise Sulawesi and other islands situated between the respective continental shelves E20. **Wallacean** /wɒˈleɪsɪən/ *adjective* (*a*) of, pertaining to, or designating concepts originated by Wallace; (*b*) of or pertaining to Wallacea: M20.

Wallach *noun* var. of WALACH.

Wallachian /wɒˈleɪkɪən, vəˈlakɪən/ *noun & adjective.* Also -l-. E17.

[from *Wallachia* (see below) + -AN. Cf. VLACH.]

▸**A** *noun.* **1** A native of the former principality of Wallachia, now part of Romania. Also = VLACH *noun*. E17.

2 The language spoken by the Wallachians. E18.

▸**B** *adjective.* Of or pertaining to Wallachia, the Wallachians, or their language. L18.

wallah /ˈwɒlə/ *noun.* Orig. *Anglo-Indian.* Also **walla**. L18.

[Hindi *-vālā* suffix expr. relation (from Sanskrit *pālaka* keeper), commonly apprehended by Europeans as noun (with the sense 'man, fellow').]

1 A person, formerly esp. a servant or bearer, concerned with or in charge of a usu. specified thing, task, etc. Chiefly as 2nd elem. of comb. Now *colloq.* L18.

2 *ellipt.* = COMPETITION-***wallah***. *Anglo-Indian.* M19.

3 Any functionary doing a routine administrative job; a civil servant, a bureaucrat. *colloq.* M20.

> 📖 **1** B. TRAPIDO Roger . . being a music wallah, had always made a thing of St. Cecilia's Day. TIRESIAS I must pluck up courage to ask the medical wallahs whether malignant or benign. ***box-wallah, pani-wallah, punkah-wallah***, etc.

wallah-wallah /ˈwɒləwɒlə/ *noun.* Also **walla-walla**. M20.

[Origin unkn.]

In Hong Kong, a small boat used as a ferry for casual traffic.

wallaroo /ˈwɒləruː/ *noun.* E19.

[Aboriginal *wolarū*.]

Each of three large kangaroos of the genus *Macropus*; *esp.* (more fully ***common wallaroo***) the hill kangaroo, *M. robustus*.

Wallawalla /wɒləˈwɒlə/ *noun & adjective.* Pl. of noun -s, same. E19.

[App. from *Walla Walla*, a county of SE Washington.]

A member of, of or pertaining to, a N. American Indian people inhabiting parts of the States of Oregon and Washington; (of) the Sahaptin language of this people.

walla-walla *noun* var. of WALLAH-WALLAH.

wallbanger /ˈwɔːlbaŋə/ *noun.* Orig. *US.* L20.

[App. from WALL *noun*[1] + BANGER *noun*[1].]

= ***Harvey wallbanger*** s.v. HARVEY 3.

walled /wɔːld/ *adjective.* OE.

[from WALL *verb*[2] + -ED[1].]

1 Provided, surrounded, fortified, or enclosed with or as with a wall. OE. ▸**b** As 2nd elem. of comb.: having a wall or walls of a specified type, quality, construction, etc. LME.

2 ANATOMY & BIOLOGY. Furnished with a wall or investing structure; (as 2nd elem. of comb.) having walls of a specified kind or number. L19.

> 📖 **1** JOHN ROGERS They went through an archway and into a walled, paved garden. **b** ***double walled, mud-walled, thin-walled***, etc.

Comb.: **walled-in** *adjective* (*a*) (of a garden, courtyard, etc.) enclosed by walls; (*b*) = ***walled-up*** (b) below; **walled-off** *adjective* separated by a wall; **walled-up** *adjective* (*a*) (of a window, door, etc.) blocked or sealed up with masonry; (*b*) (of a person) entombed in a wall or behind walls.

Wallerian /wɒˈlɪərɪən/ *adjective.* Also w-. L19.

[from Augustus V. *Waller* (1816–70), English physiologist + -IAN.]

PHYSIOLOGY. Designating (a law describing) a type of degeneration affecting severed nerve fibres or spinal nerves.

wallet /ˈwɒlɪt/ *noun.* LME.

[Prob. from Anglo-Norman from Germanic base of WELL *noun*[1].]

1 A bag, pouch, or knapsack (usu. slung over the shoulder) for carrying food, clothing, books, etc., esp. on a journey; *spec.* (*a*) a pilgrim's scrip; (*b*) a beggar's bag; (*c*) a pedlar's pack. *arch.* LME.

2 A small flat bag or case, usually of leather and freq. closed by a flap fastened with a button or clasp; *esp.* one for carrying banknotes, tickets, etc. Orig. *US.* M19.

■ **walletful** *noun* as much as a wallet will hold E20.

wall-eye /ˈwɔːlʌɪ/ *noun.* In sense 2 usu. **walleye**. E16.

[Back-form. from next.]

1 An eye the iris of which is whitish, streaked, particoloured, or different in hue from the other eye, or which has a divergent squint. E16.

2 A large N. American pikeperch, *Stizostedion vitreum*, which has large prominent eyes and is valued as a food and sport fish. Also called ***wall-eyed pike***. L19.

wall-eyed /ˈwɔːlʌɪd/ *adjective.* LME.

[Old Norse *vagleygr*, from unkn. 1st elem. rel to Icelandic *vagl* film over the eye, Swedish *vagel* sty on the eye + *-eygr* -eyed (from *auga* EYE *noun*): see -ED[2]. Cf. WALL *verb*[3].]

1 Having one or both eyes with a whitish, streaked, or particoloured iris; having eyes of differing colour. Also, having a divergent squint. LME.

†**2** Of anger or jealousy: indicated by glaring eyes. L16–E17.

> 📖 **1 wall-eyed pike** = WALL-EYE 2. **2** SHAKES. *John* The vilest stroke, That ever wall-ey'd wrath . . Presented to the tears of soft remorse.

wallflower /ˈwɔːlflaʊə/ *noun.* L16.

[from WALL *noun*[1] + FLOWER *noun*.]

1 A Mediterranean cruciferous plant, *Erysimum cheiri*, much grown for its fragrant velvety golden-yellow, orange-red, bronze, etc., flowers and naturalized on old walls, rocks, etc. L16. ▸**b** A perfume derived from the flowers of this plant. E20.

2 A woman sitting out at a dance for lack of partners. Now also (*gen.*), a person at a social function who receives no attention; a shy or socially awkward person. *colloq.* E19.

1 ***Siberian wallflower***: see SIBERIAN *adjective*.

wallie *adjective, adverb, & noun* var. of WALLY *adjective*[1], *adverb, & noun*[1].

walling /ˈwɔːlɪŋ/ *noun.* LME.

[from WALL *verb*[2] + -ING[1].]

1 The action of WALL *verb*[2]. LME.

2 Walls collectively; (the materials for making) a stretch of wall. LME.

Comb.: **walling hammer**: used for dressing stones in a dry wall.

wallis /ˈwɒlɪs/ *noun. obsolete* exc. *dial.* L17.

[Origin unkn.]

The withers of a horse.

wall-knot /ˈwɔːlnɒt/ *noun.* E17.

[Rel. obscurely to Norwegian, Swedish *valknut*, Danish *valknude* double knot, secure knot.]

A secure knot made on the end of a rope by unlaying and intertwining the strands. Cf. ***wale-knot*** s.v. WALE *noun*[1].

Walloon /wɒˈluːn/ *noun & adjective.* M16.

[French *Wallon* from medieval Latin *Wallo(n-)*, from Germanic: see -OON. Cf. WELSH.]

▸**A** *noun.* **1** A member of a people of Gaulish origin inhabiting southern and eastern Belgium and neighbouring parts of France. M16.

2 The French dialect spoken by this people. M17.

▸**B** *adjective.* Of or pertaining to the Walloons. M16.

wallop /ˈwɒləp/ *noun.* ME.

[Old Northern French *walop* var. of Old & mod. French *galop*, from *galoper*: see next. Cf. GALLOP *noun*.]

1 A horse's gallop. Long *rare*. ME.

2 The noisy bubbling motion made by a liquid rapidly boiling or approaching boiling point; an instance of this. Chiefly in ***boil a wallop***, ***seethe a wallop***, boil with a rapid noisy bubbling. Now *dial.* M16. ▸**b** A flapping or fluttering rag. *Scot.* M18.

3 (The sound made by) a noisy violent, heavy, or clumsy movement of the body; a noisy lurch or plunge. Now *dial. & colloq.* M16.

4 A (violent) beat of the heart or pulse. *Scot.* L18.

5 A heavy resounding blow; a thump, a whack. Also, the ability to deliver such a blow. *colloq.* E19.

6 Alcoholic drink, *esp.* beer. *colloq.* M19.

3 go wallop fall noisily.

wallop /ˈwɒləp/ *verb.* LME.

[Old Northern French *waloper* var. of Old & mod. French *galoper*, perh. blend of Frankish *wala* well and *hlaupan* run, ult. from Germanic. Cf. GALLOP *verb*, LEAP *verb*.]

▶ **I** *verb intrans.* **1** Gallop. Now *dial. & colloq.* LME.
2 Boil hard with a noisy bubbling. Now *dial.* L16.
3 Make noisy violent or heavy movements; move clumsily or convulsively; flounder. Now *dial. & colloq.* E18.
4 Of the heart or blood: pulsate (violently). *Scot.* M18.
5 Dangle, flap about; wobble. *Scot. & dial.* E19.

1 R. GRAVES When I was a courser.. That like the wind would wallop along. **2** N. HAWTHORNE An immense pot over the fire, surging and walloping with some kind of.. stew. **5 wallop in a tether** *Scot.* (now *rare* or *obsolete*) be hanged.

▶ **II** *verb trans.* **6** Beat, thrash; strike violently, thump, whack. *colloq.* E19.
7 = GOLLOP *verb. dial. & colloq.* L19.
■ **walloper** *noun* (*colloq.*) (*a*) a person who or thing which wallops; (*b*) anything strikingly big of its kind; (*c*) *Austral.* a policeman: M19.

walloping /ˈwɒləpɪŋ/ *verbal noun.* LME.
[from prec. + -ING¹.]
The action of WALLOP *verb*; an instance of this, *esp.* a thrashing.

walloping /ˈwɒləpɪŋ/ *adjective.* LME.
[formed as prec. + -ING².]
1 That wallops. Now chiefly *spec.* (*dial. & colloq.*), that moves with a clumsy irregular gait. LME.
2 Strikingly large or powerful. Cf. THUMPING *adjective* 2. *colloq.* E19.

2 T. PARKS A walloping great nudge with his knee.

wallow /ˈwɒləʊ/ *noun.* L16.
[from WALLOW *verb*¹.]
1 a Orig., mire or filth in which a pig wallows. Now also, the action or an instance of wallowing (*lit. & fig.*). L16. ▸**b** A place used by a buffalo, rhinoceros, etc., for wallowing; a mud hole, dust hole, or depression formed by the wallowing of such an animal. Orig. *US.* L18. ▸**c** *fig.* A state of depression or stagnation. M20.
2 A rolling motion. *rare.* L17.

1a J. GROSS Nor was he.. averse.. as a reader, to a nice old-fashioned romantic wallow. **2** W. STYRON The boat is moving obediently to the river's sluggish seaward wallow.

wallow /ˈwɒləʊ/ *adjective.* Long *obsolete* exc. *dial.* See also WAUGH *adjective*.
[Old English *wealg* = Low German *walg* insipid, Norwegian *valg* tasteless, from Germanic.]
= WALLOWISH.

wallow /ˈwɒləʊ/ *verb*¹.
[Old English *w(e)alwian*, ult. from Germanic from Indo-European base repr. by Latin *volvere* to roll.]
▶ **I** *verb intrans.* **1** Esp. of a person or animal: roll about or toss from side to side while lying down. *rare* exc. as in sense 2. OE. ▸**b** Of a ship etc.: roll from side to side; sail with a rolling motion; be tossed about. ME. ▸**c** (Of the sea etc.) roll, heave, toss; (of a liquid, smoke, etc.) gush, surge (*up*). LME. ▸**d** Move (about) heavily, clumsily, or with a rolling gait. L16.
2 a Roll about, lie relaxed, in or *in* some liquid, viscous, or yielding substance (as mire, blood, water, etc.). OE. ▸**b** *fig.* Remain plunged, take delight, or indulge unrestrainedly in or *in* vice, sensuality, pleasure, misery, etc.; revel *in*. ME. ▸**c** Foll. by *in*: have plenty (of wealth or possessions). Chiefly *derog.* LME–M18.

1 DEFOE Some that were wounded and lame.. lay wallowing and screaming.. upon the ground.

▶ **II** *verb trans.* **3** Cause (a rounded object) to roll or turn over; trundle. Long *rare.* LME.
†**4** Cause (a person or animal) to wallow. Chiefly *refl.* or in *pass.* LME–L17.
■ **wallower** *noun* (*a*) MECHANICS a trundle, a lantern-wheel; (*b*) a person who or animal which wallows: M16. **wallowingly** *adverb* in a wallowing manner M16.

wallow /ˈwɒləʊ/ *verb*² *intrans.* Long *obsolete* exc. *dial.*
[Old English *wealwian*, from Germanic base of WALLOW *adjective*.]
Wither, fade, waste *away*, (*lit. & fig.*).

wallowish /ˈwɒləʊɪʃ/ *adjective.* Long *obsolete* exc. *dial.* M16.
[from WALLOW *adjective* + -ISH¹.]
Insipid, tasteless; sickly. Cf. WALLOW *adjective*.

wallpaper /ˈwɔːlpeɪpə/ *noun & verb.* E19.
[from WALL *noun*¹ + PAPER *noun*.]
▶ **A** *noun.* **1** Paper, usually printed or embossed with designs and sold in rolls, for pasting on to interior walls as decoration; paper-hangings. E19.
2 *fig.* An unobtrusive background, esp. of music or other sound. Chiefly *derog.* E20.
3 COMPUTING. A pattern or picture used as an optional background on a computer screen. L20.

2 C. DANE They faded into a mere wall-paper of sound.

▶ **B** *verb trans. & intrans.* Cover or decorate (a wall or walls) with wallpaper. M20.

Wallsend /ˈwɔːlzɛnd, wɔːlzˈɛnd/ *noun.* Now *rare* or *obsolete.* E19.
[A town in Northumberland.]
Orig., a coal of high quality obtained from a seam at Wallsend. Later, (a proprietary name for) a coal of a certain quality and size.

Wall Street /ˈwɔːl striːt/ *noun phr.* M19.
[A street in New York City where some of the most important US financial institutions are centred.]
The American financial world or money market. Freq. *attrib.*
Comb.: **Wall Street crash** *Hist.* the collapse of the American stock market in October 1929.
■ **Wall Streeter** *noun* a Wall Street financier, *esp.* one working in the New York stock market L19. **Wall Streetish** *adjective* of or characteristic of Wall Street or its financiers E20.

wallum /ˈwɒləm/ *noun. Austral.* M19.
[Aboriginal.]
A tall banksia of Queensland and New South Wales, Australia, *Banksia aemula*, with large cones; the heathy strip on the Queensland coast where this is common.

wallwort /ˈwɔːlwət/ *noun.*
[Old English *wealhwyrt*, from *wealh* foreigner (see WELSH *adjective*) + *wyrt* WORT *noun*¹, perh. because thought to spring where foreign blood had been spilt (cf. *danewort* s.v. DANE).]
The dwarf elder or danewort, *Sambucus ebulus*.

wally /ˈwɔːli, ˈwali/ *adjective*¹, *adverb*, & *noun*¹. *Scot.* Also **wallie.** L15.
[Origin unkn.]
▶ **A** *adjective.* Good, fine, handsome; large, ample; ornamental. L15.
▶ **B** *adverb.* Well, finely. M16.
▶ **C** *noun.* A toy, an ornament, a gewgaw. L17.

wally /ˈwɒli/ *adjective*² & *noun*². *slang.* M20.
[Origin uncertain: perh. shortened from male forename *Walter*. Cf. CHARLIE, WOLLY.]
▶ **A** *adjective.* Unfashionable, outmoded; characteristic of or pertaining to a wally. M20.
▶ **B** *noun.* A stupid, inept, or ineffectual person. Also used as a general term of abuse. L20.

walm /wɔː(l)m, wɒlm/ *noun & verb.* Long *obsolete* exc. *dial.*
[Old English *wælm* = mod. West Frisian *wâlm* smoke, vapour, Flemish dial. *walm* wave, bubble, a gushing, Dutch, Low German *walm* smoke, Old High German, Middle High German *walm* heat, passion, German dial. *Walm* boiling, whirlpool, from Germanic. Cf. WAMBLE *verb*.]
▶ **A** *noun.* †**1 a** Surging (of waves). Only in OE. ▸**b** A wave, a billow. Chiefly *poet.* ME–L16.
†**2** A gush of water; (the water of) a spring, fountain, etc. OE–LME.
3 The bubbling and heaving of boiling water etc.; an instance of this. Cf. WAMBLE *noun* 2. OE.
▶ **B** *verb intrans.* †**1 a** Of water: well up or *up*, gush forth or *forth*. ME–L17. ▸**b** Of smoke, vapour, etc.: swirl, billow. *rare.* E17–E20.
2 Seethe or bubble as in boiling; boil. Cf. WAMBLE *verb* 4. E17.

walnut /ˈwɔːlnʌt/ *noun & adjective.*
[Old English *walh-hnutu* corresp. to Middle Low German *wallnut* (whence Middle & mod. High German *walnuss*), Middle Dutch *walnote* (Dutch *walnoot*), Old Norse *walhnot*, from Germanic = foreign nut.]
▶ **A** *noun.* **1** The nut of trees of the genus *Juglans*, esp. *J. regia*, which consists of the stone of the green fleshy fruit, containing an edible kernel in separate halves; the kernel of this. Also ***Persian walnut***, (*US*) ***English walnut***. LOE.
2 The timber of any tree of the genus *Juglans*, esp. *J. regia*, used for furniture. L16. ▸**b** The reddish-brown colour of the wood of the walnut tree. L19.
3 Any tree of the genus *Juglans* (family Juglandaceae), members of which have drooping catkins and aromatic pinnate leaves; *esp.* the Eurasian *J. regia* and (more fully ***black walnut***) the N. American *J. nigra*. Also ***walnut tree***. E17.
Phrases: ***African walnut***: see AFRICAN *adjective*. ***English walnut***, ***Persian walnut***: see sense A.1 above. QUEENSLAND ***walnut***. ***shagbark walnut***: see SHAGBARK 2.
Comb.: **walnut-shell** (*a*) the hard shell of a walnut; either of the halves of this; (*b*) *transf.* a very light or fragile boat; ***walnut tree***: see sense 3 above.
▶ **B** *attrib.* or as *adjective.* **1** Made of or with walnuts; extracted from walnuts. E17.
2 Made of the wood walnut. M19.

Walpolian /wɔːlˈpəʊlɪən/ *adjective & noun.* M18.
[from the family name *Walpole* (sense 1 Horace, sense 2 his father Robert) + -IAN.]
▶ **A** *adjective.* **1** Of, pertaining to, or characteristic of (the writings of) the English author and letter-writer Horace Walpole (1717–97). Also, designating a neo-Gothic style of architecture popularized by him. M18.
2 Of, pertaining to, or characteristic of (the career of) the English statesman Sir Robert Walpole (1676–1745). E20.
▶ **B** *noun.* An admirer of Horace Walpole. M18.
■ **Walpoliˈana** *noun* publications or other items concerning or associated with Horace Walpole M20.

Walpurgis /valˈpɔːɡɪs, -ˈpʊəɡɪs/ *noun.* E19.
[German, genit. of *Walpurga* name of 8th-cent. Anglo-Saxon female saint. Cf. next.]
In full ***Walpurgis night***. The eve of May Day, marked (according to German folklore and esp. Goethe's *Faust*) by a witches' sabbath or a feast of the powers of darkness; *transf.* an orgiastic celebration or party.

Walpurgisnacht /valˈpʊrɡɪsnaxt/ *noun.* E19.
[German, formed as prec. + *Nacht* night.]
= prec.

Walras' law /ˈvalrɑːs lɔː/ *noun phr.* M20.
[M. E. L. *Walras* (1834–1910), French economist.]
ECONOMICS. The law that the total value of goods and money supplied equals that of goods and money demanded.
■ **Walrasian** /valˈreɪsɪən/ *adjective* of or pertaining to the economic theories of Walras M20.

walrus /ˈwɔːlrəs, ˈwɒl-/ *noun.* E18.
[Prob. from Dutch *walrus*, *-ros*, alt. (after *walvis(ch)* whale) by inversion of the elems. of such forms as Old English *horschwæl*, Old Norse *hrosshvalr* ('horse-whale').]
A large pinniped mammal, *Odobenus rosmarus*, allied to the eared seals, which is distinguished by two large downward-pointing tusks, and is found in the Arctic ocean.
Comb.: **walrus moustache** a long thick drooping moustache resembling the whiskers of a walrus.

Walschaerts /ˈwalʃɑːts, ˈval-, -ʃɑːts/ *noun.* L19.
[Egide *Walschaerts* (1820–1901), Belgian mechanic.]
MECHANICS. Used *attrib.* and in *possess.* to designate a kind of valve gear that was used on some steam railway locomotives.

Walsingham way /ˈwɔːlsɪŋəm ˈweɪ/ *noun phr.* L19.
[See below.]
The Milky Way, as fancifully supposed to have been used as a guide by pilgrims travelling to the shrine of Our Lady of Walsingham, a village in Norfolk.

†**walt** *adjective.* M16–M18.
[Rel. to next.]
NAUTICAL. = WALTY.

walt /wɔːlt/ *verb.* Long *obsolete* exc. *dial.* ME.
[Rel. to Old High German *walzan*, Middle High German, German *walzen* roll, revolve: cf. WALLOW *verb*¹, WELT *verb*².]
†**1** *verb trans.* Revolve in the mind, consider. *rare.* Only in ME.
2 *verb trans.* Throw, esp. to the ground; upset, overturn. LME.
3 *verb intrans.* Be thrown down, upset, or overturned; totter, fall over. LME.

Walt Disney /wɔːlt ˈdɪzni, wɒlt/ *noun phr.* M20.
[from *Walter* Elias *Disney*: see DISNEYESQUE.]
Used *attrib.* to designate the style of the (usu. animated) films or characters created by Walt Disney. Cf. DISNEYESQUE.

walter /ˈwɔːltə/ *verb. obsolete* exc. *dial.* LME.
[Frequentative of WALT *verb*: cf. WELTER *verb*¹.]
▶ **I** *verb intrans.* **1** Roll to and fro, tumble or toss about; lie sprawling; (foll. by *in*) wallow (*lit. & fig.*). LME. ▸†**b** Swing to and fro. LME–L19.
2 Of water etc.: flow, gush; surge. LME.
3 Move or go unsteadily; totter, stumble; waddle. LME.
▶ **II** *verb trans.* **4** Roll about, toss to and fro; *refl.* sprawl or wallow on the ground, in the mire, etc. Long *rare* or *obsolete.* LME.

Walter Scottish /wɔːltə ˈskɒtɪʃ/ *adjective.* E19.
[from Sir *Walter Scott* (see below) + -ISH¹.]
Of or characteristic of (the style or writings of) the novelist and poet Sir Walter Scott (1771–1832).

Walther /ˈwɔːltə, ˈvaltə/ *adjective & noun.* E20.
[See below.]
(Designating) a pistol or rifle made by Walther, a German firm of firearm manufacturers.

Waltonian /wɔːlˈtəʊnɪən/ *adjective & noun. arch.* E19.
[from *Walton* (see below) + -IAN.]
▶ **A** *adjective.* Of or pertaining to Izaak Walton (1593–1683), author of *The Compleat Angler* (1653); *esp.* of or pertaining to angling. E19.
▶ **B** *noun.* An angler. M19.
■ ˈ**Waltonizing** *noun* angling M19.

walty /ˈwɔːlti/ *adjective.* Now *rare.* M17.
[from WALT *adjective* + -Y¹.]
NAUTICAL. Of a ship: unsteady, liable to capsize.

waltz /wɔːl(t)s, wɒl-/ *noun.* L18.
[German *Walzer*, from *walzen* roll, revolve, waltz. Cf. VALSE *noun*.]
1 A dance in triple time performed by a couple who swing each other rhythmically round and round as they progress round the floor; (a piece of) music to accompany this dance. L18.
2 An easy task or achievement. *colloq.* M20.

📖 **1** *Spectator* A stately waltz at an even pace. HESITATION ***waltz***. ***old-fashioned waltz***: see OLD-FASHIONED *adjective*. ***Viennese waltz***: see VIENNESE *adjective*.

Comb.: **waltz king** *the* Viennese composer Johann Strauss the younger (1825–99); **waltz-length** *adjective* (of a garment) calf-length.

waltz /wɔːl(t)s, wɒl-/ *verb*. L18.
[from prec. or German *walzen*.]
▶ **I** *verb intrans*. **1** Dance a waltz; perform (the steps of) the waltz. L18.
2 *transf*. Move lightly, nimbly, or easily; move casually, unconcernedly, or boldly *around, into, off, up (to)*, etc. *colloq*. M19.

📖 **1** F. J. FURNIVALL Oh fair-haired Alice, how well you waltz! ***waltzing mouse*** = WALTZER 2. **2** *Cycle World* You just don't waltz over to England and start racing in British League. *World Soccer* Michailichenko waltzed through the defence to score from a difficult angle.

▶ **II** *verb trans*. **3** With adverb (phr.): move (a person) in or as in a waltz, casually, or easily. M19.
4 Carry or convey (a thing) easily. *joc*. L19.

📖 **3** R. P. JHABVALA I want to . . be waltzed all the way home in my evening gown. **4** ***waltz Matilda***: see MATILDA 1.

waltzer /ˈwɔːl(t)sə, ˈwɒl-/ *noun*. E19.
[from prec. + -ER¹.]
1 A person who dances the waltz. E19.
2 (An animal of) a mutant variety of house mouse which habitually spins round. Also called ***waltzing mouse***. E20.
3 A fairground ride in which cars spin round as they are carried round an undulating track. M20.
2 ***Japanese waltzer***: see JAPANESE *adjective*.

waly /ˈwɔːli, ˈweɪli/ *interjection*. *Scot. & north*. E18.
[Perh. rel. to WELLAWAY, WOE.]
Expr. sorrow.

wamara /wəˈmɑːrə/ *noun*. M19.
[Arawak.]
A leguminous tree of Guyana, *Swartzia tomentosa*, with wood resembling ebony; the wood of this tree.

wambais /ˈwambeɪs/ *noun*. M18.
[Old French: cf. GAMBESON, WAMUS.]
Hist. = GAMBESON.

wambenger /ˈwɒmbɛŋə/ *noun*. E20.
[Aboriginal.]
= PHASCOGALE.

wamble /ˈwɒmb(ə)l/ *noun*. *obsolete* exc. *dial*. Also **womble**. M16.
[from next.]
1 A churning of the stomach; queasiness, nausea. M16.
†**2** = WALM *noun* 3. E17–M18.
3 An unsteady motion; a roll of the body; a rolling or staggering gait. E19.
3 ***on the wamble*** staggering, wobbling.
Comb.: **wamble-cropped** *adjective* (now *US*) queasy, sick.

wamble /ˈwɒmb(ə)l/ *verb*. *obsolete* exc. *dial*. Also **womble**. LME.
[In branch I prob. corresp. to Danish *vamle* feel nausea; in branch II to Norwegian *vamla* stagger etc. In branch III perh. by metathesis from WALM *verb*.]
▶ **I 1** *verb intrans*. Be queasy, rumble queasily. LME.
▶ **II 2 a** *verb intrans*. Turn and twist about, wriggle; roll over and over. Also foll. by *about, over*. LME. ▸**b** *verb trans*. Turn (a thing) over or round; tangle, twist. M16.
3 *verb intrans*. Move unsteadily; stagger, totter, reel. L16.
▶ **III** †**4** *verb intrans*. = WALM *verb* 2. M17–E18.
■ **wambling** *verbal noun* the action of the verb; an instance of this: LME. **wamblingly** *adverb* in a wambling manner L17.

wambly /ˈwɒmbli/ *adjective*. Chiefly *dial*. M19.
[from WAMBLE *noun* or *verb*: see -Y¹.]
1 Shaky, tottering, unsteady. M19.
2 Affected with nausea, queasy. L19.
■ **wambliness** *noun* E20.

wame /weɪm/ *noun*. *Scot. & north*. LME.
[North. var. of WOMB *noun*.]
1 The belly, the abdomen. Long *obsolete* exc. *Scot*. LME.
2 The womb. LME.
3 *transf*. A hollow, a cavity. M18.

📖 **1** R. BURNS Food fills the wame, an' keeps us livin.

■ **wameful** *noun* (*Scot*.) a bellyful E18.

†**wampampeag** *noun* var. of WAMPUMPEAG.

Wampanoag /wɑːmpəˈnəʊəg/ *noun & adjective*. L17.
[Narragansett, lit. 'easterners'.]
▶ **A** *noun*. A member of a N. American Indian people of SE Massachusetts and the eastern shore of Narragansett Bay. L17.
▶ **B** *adjective*. Of, pertaining to, or designating this people. M20.

wampee /wɒmˈpiː/ *noun*¹. *N. Amer*. E19.
[Perh. from Algonquian.]
1 Jack-in-the-pulpit, *Arisaema triphyllum*. E19.
2 In the southern US, pickerel-weed, *Pontederia cordata*. L19.

wampee /wɒmˈpiː/ *noun*². Also **wampi**. M19.
[Chinese *huángpí* lit. 'yellow skin'.]
A Chinese tree of the rue family, *Clausena lansium*, grown in the tropics for its fruit; the fruit of this tree, resembling a small lime.

wampum /ˈwɒmpəm/ *noun*. Chiefly *N. Amer*. M17.
[Abbreviation of next (falsely analysed as *wampum* + *peag*): cf. PEAG.]
1 Chiefly *Hist*. Beads made from the ends of shells rubbed down, polished, and threaded on strings, worn by N. American Indians as decoration or (formerly) used as money or for mnemonic or symbolic purposes. M17.
2 *gen*. Money. *slang*. L19.
Comb.: **wampum snake** any of several N. American colubrid snakes with black and red bands or stripes; *esp*. the mud snake, *Farancia abacura*, and the rainbow snake, *Abastor erythrogrammus*.

wampumpeag /ˈwɒmpəmpiːg/ *noun*. *obsolete* exc. *Hist*. Also †**wampam-** & other vars. E17.
[Algonquian, from *wap* white + *umpe* string + *-ag* pl. suffix.]
= WAMPUM 1.

wampus /ˈwɒmpəs/ *noun*. *US slang*. E20.
[Origin unkn.]
A bad-tempered, objectionable, or loutish person.

wamus /ˈwaməs/ *noun*. *US*. E19.
[Prob. from Dutch *wammes* contr. of *wambuis* from Old French *wambois* GAMBESON: cf. WAMBAIS.]
In southern and western US, a warm knitted jacket resembling a cardigan.

WAN /wan/ *abbreviation*.
COMPUTING. Wide area network.

†**wan** *noun*¹. E17.
[Perh. from Dutch †*wanne* (now *wan*): see VAN *noun*¹.]
1 = VAN *noun*¹ 1. Only in E17.
2 = VAN *noun*¹ 3. M18–L19.

wan /wɒn/ *adjective*¹. OE.
[Origin unkn.]
1 Esp. of the sea or other water: lacking light or lustre; gloomy, dark. Chiefly *poet*. OE.
†**2** Of an unhealthy greyish colour; discoloured as by a bruise. OE–M17.
3 a Esp. of a person or a person's face: pallid, sickly; unusually or unhealthily pale. Freq. in ***pale and wan***. ME. ▸**b** Of the light of the moon, stars, etc.: faint, dull, partially obscured. E17.
4 Sad, dismal. Formerly also, fearful, deadly, cruel. *poet*. LME.

📖 **3a** D. H. LAWRENCE Lettie came home wan, sad-eyed, and self-reproachful. *absol*.: TENNYSON Melissa, tinged with wan from lack of sleep. **b** D. H. LAWRENCE The wan moon . . sank into insignificance.

Special collocations: **wan smile** a faint or forced smile (as of someone sick or unhappy).
■ **wanly** *adverb* with a wan look; pallidly; *fig*. dejectedly: ME. **wanness** /-n-n-/ *noun* the condition of being wan; pallidness: LME. **wannish** *adjective* somewhat wan LME.

wan /wan/ *adjective*², *noun*², & *pronoun*. *dial*. M17.
[Repr. a dial. pronunc.]
= ONE *adjective, noun, & pronoun*.

wan /wɒn/ *verb*. Now *poet*. Infl. **-nn-**.
[Old English *wannian*, from WAN *adjective*¹.]
†**1** *verb intrans*. Become dark, discoloured, or livid. OE–LME.
2 *verb trans*. Make pale. E16.
3 *verb intrans*. Grow pale. L16.

📖 **3** W. DE LA MARE The haze of noon wanned silver-grey.

wan- /wɒn/ *prefix*. Long *obsolete* exc. *Scot. & north*.
[Old English *wan-* corresp. to Old Frisian, Old Saxon, Middle Low German, Middle Dutch, Old High German, Middle High German *wan-* (German *wahn-*), Old Norse, Swedish, Danish *van-*.]
Prefixed to nouns & adjectives with the sense 'bad, wrong, mis-, un-', as ***wanfortune***, ***wanrest***.

wananchi /wəˈnantʃi/ *noun pl*. M20.
[Kiswahili, pl. of *mwananchi* inhabitant, citizen.]
In Kenya and Tanzania, the indigenous workers, the masses.

wanax /ˈwanaks/ *noun*. M20.
[Greek (*w*)*anax*.]
GREEK ANTIQUITIES. A Mycenaean or Minoan king or ruler.

wanchance /wɒnˈtʃɑːns/ *noun*. *Scot*. Now *arch. & literary*. L16.
[from WAN- + CHANCE *noun*.]
Ill luck, misfortune.

wanchancy /wɒnˈtʃɑːnsi/ *adjective*. *Scot*. Now *literary* or *arch*. M18.
[from prec. + -Y¹.]
Unlucky, dangerous. Also, eerie, uncanny.

wand /wɒnd/ *noun*. ME.
[Old Norse *vǫndr* = Gothic *wandus* (not in West Germanic), prob. from Germanic base meaning 'turn, wind' (cf. WEND *verb*¹).]
1 A straight slender stick. Now *Scot. & dial*. ME. ▸†**b** A light walking-stick, a cane. M16–M18. ▸**c** A stick used as a pointer. L16.
†**2** A sceptre. ME–L15.
3 a A rod, stick, or cane used for punishment. Long *rare*. ME. ▸**b** A stick or switch for urging on a horse. *obsolete* exc. *dial*. LME.
4 A young shoot, a sapling; a slender branch, a twig. *obsolete* exc. *poet. & dial*. LME. ▸**b** *spec*. A young shoot of willow cut to be used in basket-making, wattling, etc. Now *Scot. & dial*. LME.
5 A rod or staff carried as a sign of office; *esp*. a tall slender rod of wood, silver, etc., carried erect by a verger or official walking in front of a dignitary on ceremonial occasions. Also (*colloq*.), a conductor's baton. LME.
6 A staff or baton serving as a symbol in certain legal transactions. LME.
7 A magic rod used in casting spells by a fairy or a magician; a supposedly magic rod used by a conjuror for effect. Freq. in ***magic wand***. (Now the usual sense.) LME.
8 A fishing-rod. M16.
†**9** A measuring rod. M17–E19.
10 The straight rigid pipe linking the cleaning head to the hose of a vacuum cleaner. M20.
11 a More fully ***mascara wand***. A small applicator for mascara etc., usu. with a brush at one end. M20. ▸**b** In full ***curling wand***, ***styling wand***. A heated appliance used for curling or styling hair. L20.
12 A hand-held electronic device which can be passed over a bar code to read the data it represents. L20.

📖 **1** SHAKES. *Two Gent*. My sister . . is as white as a lily and as small as a wand. **5** V. WOOLF The conductor, . . bowing to the Queen, . . raised his wand. **6** ***wand of peace*** SCOTS LAW (now *Hist*.) a silver-topped baton carried by a king's messenger as a symbol of his office, and delivered to an outlaw as a sign of his restoration to the King's peace. **7** *fig*.: J. WAIN You can wave your magic wand and get me a pass.

Comb.: **wand flower** any of various ornamental plants of the South African genus *Dierama*, of the iris family, with flowers in nodding spikes, esp. *D. pendulum* and *D. pulcherrimum*.

wand /wɒnd/ *verb trans*. L15.
[from the noun.]
1 Wattle, interweave, plait. *Scot. & dial*. L15.
2 Beat with a wand or switch. *Scot. & dial*. L16.
3 Scan the bar code on (an article) using a wand (WAND *noun* 12). L20.

wanded /ˈwɒndɪd/ *adjective*. Now *rare*. M16.
[from WAND *noun* + -ED².]
Made of or (of a bottle) encased in wickerwork.

wander /ˈwɒndə/ *noun*. L18.
[from the verb.]
1 An act of wandering. L18.
2 A gradual change in the orientation of the axis of the earth, a gyroscope, or other spinning body. M20.

📖 **1** *Times* The mouth-watering wander through the food hall to the restaurant.

wander /ˈwɒndə/ *verb*.
[Old English *wandrian* = Old Frisian *wondria*, Middle Low German, Middle Dutch *wanderen*, from West Germanic verb rel. to WEND *verb*¹, WIND *verb*¹: see -ER⁵.]
▶ **I** *verb intrans*. **1 a** Go about from place to place without any fixed course, purpose, or destination; roam, ramble; have no fixed abode. Also foll. by *about, around*. OE. ▸**b** Make one's way in a leisurely manner or without a predetermined route; stroll, saunter. L16.
2 a Of an inanimate thing: move or be carried about on an uncertain course; stray. MEDICINE & PHYSIOLOGY. Of a disease, pain, cell, etc.: move randomly from one part of the body to another. OE. ▸**b** Of the mind, thoughts, etc.: pass in an uncontrolled manner from one subject to another. LME. ▸**c** Of a rumour, opinion, etc.: be in circulation. M16. ▸**d** Esp. of the eyes or a person's gaze: turn this way and that; rove. L16. ▸**e** Of a river, road, etc.: pursue a devious or circuitous course; wind, meander. M18. ▸**f** Of a gyroscope or other spinning body: undergo a gradual change in the orientation of its axis. M20.
3 a Of a person, his or her attention, etc.: digress from a purpose, course of action, or train of thought; go morally or intellectually astray. Also foll. by *away, from, off*. OE. ▸**b** Deviate from a fixed path or route; stray from one's home or company, or from protection or control. Also foll. by *from, off*. E16.
4 Of a person: be unsettled or incoherent in mind or purpose; be inattentive. Later also, be delirious from

illness or exhaustion; talk incoherently, ramble, rave. LME.

📖 **1a** B. PYM She wandered aimlessly about the room. G. VIDAL I wanted . . to wander unnoticed wherever I chose. *fig.*: B. JOWETT Wander at will from one subject to another. **b** J. HERRIOT I wandered as in a dream through the gate. J. LE CARRÉ He wandered off . . in search of soda for our whiskies. **2b** E. BOWEN Eva's attention did not wander once a lesson began. P. BAILEY Her mind was wandering, but she recognized my mother. **d** H. ROTH Her gaze wandered thoughtfully over the dishes. **3b** V. WOOLF Her mother would not like her to be wandering off alone like this. **4** P. MANSON The patient may wander or pass into a comatose state.

▶ **II** *verb trans.* **5** Roam about, in, or through (a place); traverse in wandering. L16.

6 Cause to wander, lead astray; *fig.* confuse in mind, bewilder. Chiefly *joc.* & *colloq.* L19.

📖 **5** *Today* Thousands of homeless war orphans wandered the roads of Europe. **6** J. BUCHAN It's weather that 'ud wander a good hunter.

Comb.: **wander-plug** a plug which can be fitted into any socket of an electrical device; **wander-witted** *adjective* = WANDERY.

■ **wanderable** *adjective* (*rare*) that one can wander in E20. **wandered** *ppl adjective* that has wandered from home, out of the way, etc.; stray; bewildered: LME. **wandery** *adjective* wandering in thought or speech; vague, distant: E20.

wanderer /ˈwɒnd(ə)rə/ *noun.* LME.
[from prec. + -ER¹.]
1 A person who or thing which wanders or has long wandered; a person of a roving nature. LME.
2 [translating Latin *planeta* or Greek *planētēs*.] A planet. Now *arch.* & *literary.* E17.
3 SCOTTISH HISTORY. Any of the Covenanters who left home to follow their dispossessed ministers in 1669. E18.

wandering /ˈwɒnd(ə)rɪŋ/ *verbal noun.* LME.
[formed as prec. + -ING¹.]
1 a Travelling from place to place without a fixed route or destination; aimless roaming. Also, an instance of this (freq. in *pl.*). LME. ▸**b** The process of a person's mind or thoughts passing from one subject to another. LME. ▸**c** Devious or erratic movement from place to place; irregular turning (esp. of the eyes) this way and that. E19.
2 Deviation from one's intended path; straying. E18.
3 Mental illness, delirium; (in *pl.*) incoherent ramblings. M19.
1c *polar wandering*: see POLAR *adjective.*

wandering /ˈwɒnd(ə)rɪŋ/ *ppl adjective.* OE.
[formed as prec. + -ING².]
1 Of a person or animal: travelling from place to place without a fixed route or destination, aimlessly roaming, vagrant. OE. ▸**b** Nomadic, migratory. LME.
2 a Of the mind, thoughts, etc.: passing randomly from one subject to another, vague, restless. LME. ▸**b** Of a celestial body, esp. a planet: not fixed, having a separate individual motion. E16. ▸**c** Of a road, river, etc.: lying in an irregularly bending line, winding, meandering. M16. ▸**d** Of a thing: travelling or carried along in an uncertain or frequently changing direction; moving to and fro. L16. ▸**e** Of the eyes: roving, turning this way and that. L16. ▸**f** Of a plant: sending out long tendrils, runners, or trailing shoots. Cf. ***wandering Jew*** (c), ***wandering sailor*** below. L16. ▸**g** MEDICINE & PHYSIOLOGY. Of a disease, pain, cell, etc.: moving randomly from one part of the body to another. L16. ▸**h** MEDICINE. Of an organ etc.: too loosely fixed in place; abnormally movable. L19.
3 Of a journey, life, etc.: characterized by wandering. L16.
4 Deviating or straying from the right path or a fixed course; *fig.* (of a person) erring, disloyal. E17.

Special collocations: **wandering cell** HISTORY OF SCIENCE an amoeboid cell. **wandering fire** will-o'-the-wisp. **wandering hands** *colloq.* (freq. *joc.*) a tendency on the part of a man to fondle female colleagues or acquaintances uninvited. **wandering Jew** (*a*) (with *the*) in medieval legend, a man who insulted Jesus on the day of the Crucifixion and was condemned to roam the world until the Day of Judgement; (*b*) *fig.* any person who indulges in restless and unprofitable travelling from place to place; (*c*) any of various creeping or trailing plants; *esp.* any of several spiderworts, *Tradescantia albiflora*, *T. fluminensis*, and *T. zonata*, grown as house-plants. **wandering nerve** = VAGUS. **wandering sailor** (*a*) ivy-leaved toadflax, *Cymbalaria muralis*; (*b*) creeping Jenny, *Lysimachia nummularia*. **wandering star** (now *arch.* & *literary*) a planet.

■ **wanderingly** *adverb* M16.

Wanderjahr /ˈvandərjaːr/ *noun.* Pl. **-e** /-ə/. L19.
[German: see WANDER-YEAR.]
= WANDER-YEAR.

wanderlust /ˈwɒndəlʌst/ *noun.* E20.
[German.]
An eagerness or fondness for wandering or travelling.

📖 A. CARTER But, pilgrim by name, pilgrim by nature, came the day the wanderlust seized him by the throat again.

■ **wanderluster** *noun* a person eager to travel E20. **wanderlusting** *adjective* eager to travel M20.

Wanderobo /wɒndəˈrəʊbəʊ/ *noun & adjective.* Pl. of noun same. E20.
[African name.]
Of or pertaining to, a member of, a nomadic hunting people of Kenya.

wanderoo /wɒndəˈruː/ *noun.* L17.
[Sinhalese *vandaru* monkey from Sanskrit *vānara*.]
In the Indian subcontinent, the hanuman langur, *Presbytis entellus*. Formerly also, the lion-tailed macaque, *Macaca silenus*.

Wandervogel /ˈvandərfoːɡəl/ *noun.* Pl. **-vögel** /-føːɡəl/. E20.
[German, lit. 'bird of passage'.]
A member of a German youth organization founded at the end of the 19th cent. for the promotion of outdoor activities (esp. hiking) and folk culture; *transf.* a rambler, a hiker.

wander-year /ˈwɒndəjɪə/ *noun.* L19.
[from WANDER *verb* + YEAR *noun*¹, after German WANDERJAHR.]
A year of wandering or travel. Formerly (*spec.*), a year of travel by an apprentice to improve in skill and knowledge.

Wandjina /wɒnˈdʒiːnə/ *noun. Austral.* Pl. same. M20.
[Aboriginal.]
A member of a spirit people depicted in Aboriginal rock paintings in western Australia.

wandle /ˈwɒnd(ə)l/ *adjective. Scot.* & *north.* Also **wanle** /ˈwɒn(ə)l/. E19.
[App. rel. to WAND *noun*.]
(Of a thing) flexible, supple; (of a person) lithe, agile, nimble.

📖 SIR W. SCOTT The bairn . . grew up to be a fine wanle fallow.

wandoo /wɒnˈduː/ *noun.* M19.
[Aboriginal.]
A white-barked eucalyptus, *Eucalyptus redunca*, of western Australia; the light to reddish-brown durable wood of this tree.

wandought /ˈwɒndɒxt/ *noun & adjective. Scot.* E18.
[from WAN- + DOUGHT.]
▶ **A** *noun.* A feeble or puny person. E18.
▶ **B** *adjective.* Feeble, ineffective, worthless. M18.

wandsman /ˈwɒn(d)smən/ *noun.* Pl. **-men.** M19.
[from WAND *noun* + -'S¹ + MAN *noun*.]
An official who carries a wand or rod; a verger of a cathedral.

wandy /ˈwɒndi/ *adjective. rare.* E17.
[formed as prec. + -Y¹.]
†**1** Full of wands. Only in E17.
2 Resembling a wand; long and flexible. E19.
3 Of a person: well-built and good-looking. *dial.* E19.

wane /weɪn/ *noun.*
[Old English *wana*, *wan* want, lack: cf. Dutch *wan* leakage etc., Gothic *wan* lack.]
▶ **I** †**1** Lack, shortage, absence *of*. OE–LME. ▸**b** Fault, defect. *rare.* OE–LME.
†**2** Need, poverty. OE–ME.
3 The amount by which a plank or roughly squared log falls short of a correctly squared shape; a bevelled edge left on a plank with one face narrower than the other; the imperfect angles of a rough-hewn log. M17.
▶ **II 4** Orig., decrease in size. Later, gradual decrease in power, importance, intensity, etc., esp. following the culmination of a gradual increase; a declining period; the latter part of a period of time. Now *rare* exc. in ***on the wane*** below. LME.
5 The gradual decrease of the visible illuminated area on the moon. Now *rare* exc. in ***in wane***, ***in the wane***, ***in her wane***, ***in its wane***, ***on the wane***, ***upon the wane***. M16. ▸**b** The period characterized by the waning of the moon, esp. regarded as a favourable or unfavourable time for various agricultural operations. Chiefly in ***at the wane of the moon***, ***in the wane of the moon***. M16.

📖 **4 on the wane** declining, decreasing. **5** KEATS She, like a moon in wane, Faded before him.

■ **waney** *adjective* (of unsquared timber) having wanes or natural bevels at the angles M17.

wane /weɪn/ *verb.*
[Old English *wanian* lessen = Old Frisian *wonia*, Old Saxon *wanon*, Old High German *wanōn*, *wanēn*, Old Norse *vana*, from Germanic base repr. also by Latin *vanus* vain.]
▶ **I** *verb intrans.* Opp. *wax*.
1 Decrease in size or extent; dwindle. Now *rare.* OE. ▸**b** Grow less in quantity or volume; (of the sea or other water) subside, ebb. Now *rare.* ME.
2 Of the moon: show a decrease in the extent of the portion illuminated, as occurs progressively from full moon to new moon. OE.
3 Of light, colour, etc.: decrease in brilliance; become faint or dim. OE.
4 Of a person, nation, etc.: decline in power, importance, or prosperity. OE. ▸**b** Decline in physical strength; age. *rare.* E19.
5 Of a condition, activity, feeling, etc.: become gradually less in degree, decline in intensity, abate. ME.
6 Of a period of time: draw to a close, conclude. M16.

📖 **1** B. JOWETT That which grows is said to wax, and that which decays to wane. **3** W. OWEN I walk till the stars of London wane And dawn creeps up. **4** H. WILSON The Cabinet Council . . waned in influence. **5** E. L. DOCTOROW Long after the girl's interest had waned. P. FULLER The waning of religious belief. A. HUTH The heat of her fury began to wane. **6** D. GARNETT The summer waned into autumn.

▶ **II** *verb trans.* **7** Lessen or diminish (a privilege, quality, etc.). Also foll. by *away*. Long *rare* or *obsolete*. OE.
8 Cause (the moon) to wane (*away*). *rare.* M19.
■ **waned** *ppl adjective* that has waned; diminished, decreased: L16.

wang /wɒŋ/ *noun*¹. *obsolete* exc. *dial.*
[Old English *wang*, corresp. to Old Saxon *wanga*, Middle Dutch, Middle Low German *wange*, Old High German *wanga* (Middle High German *wange*, German *Wange*), Old Norse *vange*, from Germanic.]
†**1** The cheek. OE–LME.
2 In full ***wang-tooth***. A molar tooth. OE.

wang *noun*², *verb*¹, *verb*² vars. of WHANG *noun*¹, *verb*¹, *verb*².

wanga /ˈwaŋɡə/ *noun.* M19.
[Haitian creole *ouanga*, from a W. African lang.]
Witchcraft, sorcery; a charm, a spell; a magical object.

wangan, **wangun** *nouns* vars. of WANIGAN.

wangle /ˈwaŋɡ(ə)l/ *verb*¹ *intrans. Scot.* & *dial.* E19.
[Perh. alt. of WAGGLE *verb* due to influence of WANKLE.]
Move shakily or unsteadily; dangle.

wangle /ˈwaŋɡ(ə)l/ *verb*² & *noun. colloq.* L19.
[Origin uncertain: perh. based on WAGGLE *verb* and WANKLE.]
▶ **A** *verb.* **1** *verb trans.* Obtain (something) in an irregular way by scheming etc.; accomplish by indirect or insidious means; alter or fake (an account, report, etc.). L19.
2 *verb intrans.* & *refl.* Obtain something or get somewhere by scheming, etc.; use irregular means to accomplish a purpose. E20.
3 *verb trans.* Influence or induce (a person) to do something. *rare.* E20.

📖 **1** C. CONNOLLY I hoped I could come . . to see you, but I couldn't wangle it. J. O'HARA He used his influence . . in wangling contributions for poorer parishes. S. WYNTER A friend in the colonial office wangled him a job. **2** P. LIVELY Gordon was trying to wangle himself into the Intelligence (everyone . . wangled and pulled strings).

▶ **B** *noun.* An act of wangling; an irregular method of working; something indirectly or insidiously contrived or manipulated. E20.
■ **wangler** *noun* E20.

wangrace /ˈwɒŋɡrɛs/ *noun. Scot.* & *Anglo-Irish.* M18.
[Origin unkn.]
A thin sweetened gruel given to invalids.

wanhap /ˈwɒnhap/ *noun. Scot.* E16.
[from WAN- + HAP *noun*.]
Misfortune.
■ **wanhappy** *adjective* unfortunate L16.

wanhope /ˈwɒnhəʊp/ *noun.* ME.
[from WAN- + HOPE *noun*¹.]
1 Hopelessness, despair. ME.
†**2** Orig., vain hope. Later (as two words), faint hope. LME–M17.

†**waniand** *noun.* LME–L16.
[from north. pres. pple of WANE *verb*.]
The waning (of the moon); *fig.* an unlucky time. Freq. in ***in the waniand*** = ***with a*** WANION.

wanigan /ˈwanɪɡ(ə)n/ *noun. N. Amer.* Also **wangan**, **wangun**, /ˈwaŋɡ(ə)n/. M19.
[Shortened from Montagnais *atawangan*, from *atawan* buy or sell.]
1 A receptacle for small supplies or a reserve stock; *esp.* a boat or chest containing outfit supplies for a lumber camp. M19. ▸**b** Stores, provisions. E20.
2 A mobile cabin, usu. wooden, mounted on runners. M20.

wanion /ˈwɒnjən/ *noun. arch.* Also **-nn-**. M16.
[Alt. of WANIAND.]
with a wanion, †***in a wanion***, with a curse, with a vengeance. Also as *interjection*, expr. asseveration or imprecation.

wank /waŋk/ *noun, verb, & adjective. coarse slang.* M20.
[Origin unkn.]
▶ **A** *noun.* **1** (An act of) masturbation, esp. by a boy or man. M20.
2 A contemptible or ineffectual person or thing; something worthless or inferior. L20.
▶ **B** *verb.* **1** *verb intrans.* Esp. of a boy or man: masturbate. Also foll. by *off*. M20.

2 *verb trans.* Masturbate (esp. a boy or man). Freq. foll. by *off*. **M20.**
1 wanking-pit *joc.* a bed.
▶ **C** *attrib.* or as *adjective*. Likely or intended to induce masturbation. **L20.**

📖 J. I. M. STEWART He has an enormous great wank picture in his room.

■ **wanked-out** *adjective* exhausted (by masturbation) **L20.** **wanky** *adjective* contemptible, ineffectual, worthless **L20.**

Wankel /ˈwaŋk(ə)l, ˈvaŋ-/ *noun.* **M20.**
[Felix *Wankel* (1902–88), German engineer and inventor.]
In full ***Wankel rotary engine***, ***Wankel engine***. A rotary internal-combustion engine in which a curved, triangular, eccentrically pivoted piston rotates in an elliptical chamber, forming three combustion spaces that vary in volume as it turns.

wanker /ˈwaŋkə/ *noun. coarse slang.* **M20.**
[from WANK *verb* + -ER[1].]
1 A person, esp. a boy or man, who masturbates. **M20.**
2 A contemptible or ineffectual person. **L20.**

📖 **1 wanker's doom** *joc.* disability supposedly caused by excessive masturbation. **2** *Melody Maker* Singer/frontman to take over lead vocals . . . No wankers!

wankle /ˈwaŋk(ə)l/ *adjective. obsolete* exc. *dial.*
[Old English *wancol* = Old Saxon *wankol*, Middle & mod. Dutch *wankel*, Old High German *wanchal*, Middle High German *wankel*: cf. Old High German *wankōn* (Middle High German, German *wanken*) waver, totter.]
Unsteady, insecure; changeable, unsettled.

†**wanlace** *noun.* **ME–L16.**
[Anglo-Norman *wanelace* (Anglo-Latin *wanlassum*), of unkn. origin.]
= WINDLASS *noun*[2].

wanle *adjective* var. of WANDLE.

Wan-Li /wanˈliː/ *noun & adjective.* **L19.**
[The royal name of Shen Zong, emperor of China 1573–1620.]
(Designating) pottery and porcelain made during the reign of Wan-Li.

wanluck /ˈwɒnlʌk/ *noun. Scot.* Now *rare*. **L16.**
[from WAN- + LUCK *noun*.]
Bad luck, misfortune.

wanna /ˈwɒnə/ *verb trans. non-standard.* **L19.**
[Repr. a pronunc. Cf. WANTA.]
Want to; want a.

📖 *Frendz* Right on, Paul! Wanna job? A. TAN I wanna see African elephants.

wannabe /ˈwɒnəbi/ *noun & adjective. slang* (orig. *US*). Also **-bee**. **L20.**
[Repr. a pronunc. of *want to be*. Cf. prec.]
▶ **A** *noun.* An admirer or fan who seeks to emulate a particular celebrity or type, esp. in dress or appearance. Cf. WOULD-BE *noun*. **L20.**
▶ **B** *attrib. adjective.* Aspiring, would-be. **L20.**

wannion *noun* var. of WANION.

wanrest /ˈwɒnrest/ *noun. Scot.* **M16.**
[from WAN- + REST *noun*[1].]
1 A state of anxiety or trouble; unrest. **M16.**
2 The pendulum of a clock. Now *rare*. **L18.**
■ **wanˈrestful** *adjective* restless **L18.**

wanruly /wɒnˈruːli/ *adjective. Scot.* **L18.**
[from WAN- + RULY.]
Unruly.

wanst /wɒnst/ *adverb & conjunction. dial.* (chiefly *Anglo-Irish*). **M19.**
[Var. of ONCE.]
Once.

want /wɒnt/ *noun*[1]. Now *dial.*
[Old English *wand*, *wond* = Swedish dial. *vand*, Norwegian *vand*, *vaand*, *vond*, *vønd* mole, shrew, from Germanic base meaning 'turn', prob. with ref. to the winding passages it makes.]
A mole (the animal).

want /wɒnt/ *noun*[2]. **ME.**
[Old Norse *vant* noun of *vanr* adjective (= Old English *wana*) lacking, missing; in later use often directly from the verb.]
†**1** A thing that is missing. *rare*. Only in **ME.**
2 Lack of something desirable or necessary, esp. a quality; deficiency, shortage. **ME.** ▶†**b** In *pl.* Instances of shortage. **M17–M18.**
3 The state of lacking the necessities of life; penury; poverty. Also, famine, starvation. **LME.** ▶†**b** In *pl.* Circumstances of hardship, suffering, etc. **L16–M18.**
4 Absence of a person or (rarely) a thing. Now *rare* or *obsolete*. **L15.**
5 a A condition marked by the lack of some necessity; need. **L16.** ▶**b** A thing that is needed or desired; a requirement, a request. Freq. in *pl.* **L16.**
†**6** A defect, a fault; a shortcoming. **L16–E18.**
7 A gap, a hole, a hollow. *rare. obsolete* exc. *dial.* **M17.**
8 MINING. An interruption in a seam of coal. **M19.**

📖 **2** *Country Walking* The Highlands . . are still more impracticable, from the want of road and bridges. **3** M. MEYER First year at university is often spent in circumstances of comparative want. **5b** *Stamps* We welcome wants from those of you who seek the rare or elusive.

Phrases: **for want of** for lack of; because of the absence or deficiency of. **have a want** *Scot.* be of very low intelligence. **in no want of** having abundantly. **in want of** in need of; not having (enough).
Comb.: **want list**, **wants list**: of desired stamps, books, etc., circulated among dealers by a collector etc.

want /wɒnt/ *verb.* **ME.**
[Old Norse *vanta* be lacking, lack: cf. prec. and WANE *verb*.]
1 *verb intrans.* **a** Be lacking or missing; be deficient in quantity or degree. *arch.* exc. *Scot.* and in ***be wanting*** (see WANTING 1a). **ME.** ▶†**b** Be lacking or insufficient to achieve a certain result. Usu. foll. by *of* or *impers.* in ***there wants***. **ME–M18.**
2 *verb trans.* **a** Be without, lack; have too little of (esp. a desirable quality); fail to get. **ME.** ▶**b** Come short by (a certain amount) of attaining a certain result. In later use chiefly *impers.* in expressions of time. *arch.* **LME.** ▶†**c** Be deprived of, lose. **L15–E18.** ▶**d** Go or do without. Usu. in neg. contexts. *obsolete* exc. *Scot. & dial.* **M16.** ▶†**e** Feel the loss of, miss. **E17–M18.** ▶†**f** Be free from (something undesirable). **M17–L18.**
3 *verb intrans.* Be in need; be in a state of poverty or destitution. Now *rare* exc. *Scot.* **ME.**
4 *verb trans.* Be in need of; have occasion for, require; need *doing*; *colloq.* need or ought *to do*, *to be done*. **L15.**
5 *verb trans.* Desire, wish for; wish to have possession of; wish *to do*. Now also *spec.*, desire sexually. **E18.** ▶**b** Wish to see or speak to (someone); desire the presence or assistance of (a person); *spec.* (of the police etc.) require (a person) in connection with some offence. Freq. in *pass.* **M18.** ▶**c** Desire (a person) *to do* or *be*. Also with adverbs and (esp. *US*) with clause as obj. **M18.**
6 *verb intrans.* Foll. by *in*, *out*, etc.: wish to go in the direction specified. *colloq.* (orig. *Scot. & US*). **M19.**

📖 **2a** L. NAMIER He . . does not want resolution, but it is mixed with too much obstinacy. **b** T. HARDY It . . wanted only ten days to the first of November. **4** T. HARDY He wants food and shelter, and you must see that he has it. V. WOOLF His manners certainly wanted improving. M. GEE You want to be careful. You're getting obsessed. **5** P. GALLICO My childhood was spent wanting things I couldn't have. G. SWIFT When I held her in my arms I never wanted to let go. **b** DICKENS You're wanted—some one at the door. V. S. PRITCHETT He is . . wanted internationally for theft. **c** SCOTT FITZGERALD I want you and Daisy to come over to my house. *Encounter* You want I should call a doctor, Missus? *Times* Feelings are running high and the students want him out. **6** E. AMBLER They can keep everything . . . We just want out.

With adverbs & prepositions in specialized senses, & phrases: **want for** suffer from the want of; be ill-provided with; be lacking in (chiefly in neg. context); ***want for nothing***, have no lack of any of the necessities or comforts of life. **want in (on)** wish to join (a group), take part in (a scheme), etc. (see also sense 6 above). †**want of** lack, be without, have in insufficient measure. **want out (of)** wish to leave (a group), opt out of (a scheme) etc. (see also sense 6 above). **what do you want with —?**, **what do they want of —?**, etc., what is your etc. object in dealing with or wishing to possess —?
■ **wantable** *adjective* desirable, likely to be sought after **L20.**

wa'n't *verb* see BE *verb*.

wanta /ˈwɒntə/ *verb trans. non-standard.* **L19.**
[Repr. a pronunc. Cf. WANNA.]
Want to.

wantage /ˈwɒntɪdʒ/ *noun. US.* **M19.**
[from WANT *verb* + -AGE.]
Deficiency, shortage.

wanted /ˈwɒntɪd/ *adjective & noun.* **L17.**
[from WANT *verb* + -ED[1].]
▶ **A** *adjective.* **1** Lacking, missing; desired, needed. **L17.**
2 Of a person: sought after by the police. **E19.**

📖 **2** R. TRAVERS The Newcastle detective recognised the seaman as the wanted man.

▶ **B** *noun.* A person who or thing which is wanted, esp. by the police. Usu. in *pl.* Chiefly *colloq.* **L18.**
■ **wantedness** *noun* **L20.**

wanter /ˈwɒntə/ *noun.* **E17.**
[formed as prec. + -ER[1].]
1 A person who is deficient in something. Now *rare* or *obsolete*. **E17.**
2 A person who desires or is in need of something. **E18.**
3 A person without a husband or wife. *Scot. & dial.* **E18.**

wanthrift /ˈwɒnθrɪft/ *noun. Scot.* **E16.**
[from WAN- + THRIFT *noun*[1].]
Lack of thrift or economy; extravagance.

wan-thriven /ˈwɒnθrɪv(ə)n/ *adjective. Scot.* **E16.**
[formed as prec. + THRIVEN.]
Poorly developed, stunted in growth.

wanting /ˈwɒntɪŋ/ *adjective.* **ME.**
[from WANT *verb* + -ING[2].]
1 a Absent, lacking, missing; not forthcoming, not supplied or provided. (Foll. by *to*.) **ME.** ▶**b** Foll. by *to*: failing to help or satisfy (a person or need); falling below (an expected standard). Now *rare*. **M17.**
2 Lacking in something; deficient; needy. (Foll. by *in*, †*of*.) **L16.**
†**3** Slow or backward *to do* something. **L17–M18.**
†**4** Requisite, necessary. **M18–E19.**
5 Of very low intelligence, weak-minded. *colloq.* **M19.**

📖 **1a** R. G. COLLINGWOOD Critics have not been wanting who were stupid enough to accuse them. **2** A. STORR Measuring himself against his father, he had always found himself to be wanting. **5** A. T. ELLIS The woman was probably the result of too much in-breeding, and wanting in the head.

■ **wantingness** *noun* (*rare*) **M17.**

wantless /ˈwɒntlɪs/ *adjective. rare.* **L16.**
[from WANT *noun*[2] + -LESS.]
Having no want or lack.
■ **wantlessness** *noun* **L19.**

wanton /ˈwɒntən/ *adjective, noun, & verb.* **ME.**
[from WAN- + Old English *togen* pa. pple of *tēon* discipline, train, from Germanic base rel. to that of TEAM *noun*.]
▶ **A** *adjective.* **1 a** Orig. (of a person), undisciplined, ungoverned; unmanageable, rebellious. Later *spec.* (of a boy), childishly cruel or unruly. **ME.** ▶†**b** Of an animal: skittish, refractory; unmanageable. **M16–M18.**
2 Of a person (orig. only of a woman), thought, action, etc.: lascivious, lewd, sexually promiscuous. Formerly also, flirtatious. **LME.**
3 †**a** Of a person: jovial, inclined to joking; carefree. **LME–M16.** ▶**b** Of a young animal: frisky, frolicsome. Chiefly *poet.* **M16.** ▶**c** Of colour or music: gay, lively. Now *poet.* **L16.** ▶**d** Of an object: moving freely as if alive; unrestrained. *poet.* **L16.**
4 Orig. of wealth, clothing, or diet, later of a way of life: luxurious, extravagant. Also (of a person or action), petulant, spoiled; self-indulgent. **LME.**
5 a Of a person: insolent in triumph or prosperity; reckless; merciless. **E16.** ▶**b** Of cruelty, violence, etc.: unprovoked and reckless; gratuitous. **M17.**
†**6** Fastidious or dainty in appetite. **M16–E18.**
7 Profuse in growth; luxuriant. *poet.* **L16.**
†**8** Of speech, imagination, etc.: extravagant, impetuous, unrestrained. **L17–M18.**

📖 **1a** SIR W. SCOTT The poor bird, around whose wing some wanton boy has fixed a line. **2** E. FERBER With a gesture utterly unpremeditated, wanton, overpowering, she threw her arms about his neck. *fig.*: SHAKES. *Mids. N. D.* To see the sails conceive, And grow big-bellied with the wanton wind. **4** P. ACKROYD He meditates on misery living side-by-side with wanton excess. **5b** J. BRYCE Tyranny consists in the wanton and improper use of strength by the stronger. *Independent* The wanton destruction of so much of this continent's . . fauna.

▶ **B** *noun.* †**1** A person treated with overindulgence and excessive leniency; *esp.* a spoilt or pampered child. **E16–M17.**
2 ***play the wanton***, †***play the wantons***, dally, trifle; formerly also, behave lewdly or lasciviously. *arch.* **E16.**
3 A lascivious or lewd person. **M16.**
†**4** A playful or skittish animal or bird (or, orig., child). **L16–E19.**

📖 **3** L. MANN She had been a wanton anxious to deck herself out in deceitful finery.

▶ **C** *verb.* Now *arch.* or *literary*.
1 a *verb intrans. & trans.* (with *it*). Play amorously, lasciviously, or lewdly (*with* a person). **L16.** ▶**b** *verb intrans.* Esp. of a child or young animal: play idly (*with* another); frolic unrestrainedly, gambol. **L16.** ▶**c** *verb intrans.* Go idly or move freely (*around*, *up and down*, etc.). Also, spend one's time carelessly. **L16.**
2 a *verb intrans. & trans.* (with *it*). Run into excesses or extravagances of conduct or living; revel (*in* a course of action). **M17.** ▶**b** *verb intrans.* Indulge in extravagances of language or thought. **M17.** ▶**c** *verb intrans.* Of nature, a garden, a plant, etc.: flourish profusely or extravagantly; grow or ramble at will. **M17.**
3 *verb intrans. & trans.* (with *away*). Deal carelessly or wastefully *with* (resources etc.); spend (time, resources, etc.) carelessly or wastefully. **M17.**

📖 **2c** W. E. GOSSE Untrimmed brambles wantoned into the likeness of trees. **3** J. PRATT A minister has no right to wanton away the support of his family.

■ **wantoner** *noun* (*rare*) a person given to wanton behaviour **E19.** **wantonize** *verb* (*a*) *verb intrans.* (*arch.*) dally, sport, frolic; indulge in lasciviousness; (*b*) *verb trans.* (*rare*) make wanton: **L16.**

wantonly /ˈwɒntənli/ *adverb.* **LME.**
[from WANTON *adjective* + -LY[2].]
1 Lewdly, lasciviously; voluptuously, luxuriously. **LME.**
2 Frolicsomely, playfully, light-heartedly. **LME.**

3 Without regard for right or consequences; recklessly, gratuitously; wilfully. LME.

📖 **1** C. DEXTER The front of her dressing-gown gaped wantonly open. **3** A. BURGESS A handsome coin called a half-crown (wantonly killed by the decimal reformists of the 1970s).

wantonness /ˈwɒntənnɪs/ *noun.* ME.
[formed as prec. + -NESS.]
1 a Lasciviousness, lewdness. ME. ▸†**b** Unbridled luxury, extravagance in expenditure. LME–E18. ▸**c** Arrogance, insolence in triumph or prosperity. Now *rare.* L15. ▸†**d** Caprice, whim. L16–M19. ▸**e** Lawless extravagance, unrestrained licence. E18. ▸**f** Reckless and unprovoked cruelty, violence, etc. L18.
2 An instance of wantonness; a whim; a reckless and unjustifiable act. Now *rare* or *obsolete.* M17.

want-wit /ˈwɒntwɪt/ *noun & adjective.* Now *arch.* or *dial.* LME.
[from WANT *verb* + WIT *noun.*]
(A person) lacking wit or sense.

wanty /ˈwɒnti/ *noun.* LME.
[Prob. from WAME + TOW *noun²* or TIE *noun¹.*]
†**1** A rope or band used to fasten a load on the back of a horse. LME–L19.
2 The bellyband of a shaft-horse. *Scot. & dial.* M19.

wanweird /ˈwɒnwɪəd/ *noun. Scot.* Now *rare.* E16.
[from WAN- + WEIRD *noun.*]
Bad luck, misfortune.

wanwordy /ˈwɒnwəːdi/ *adjective. Scot.* Now *rare* or *obsolete.* L18.
[from WAN- + WORTHY *adjective.*]
Worthless.

wanworth /ˈwɒnwəːθ/ *noun. Scot.* E18.
[from WAN- + WORTH *noun¹.*]
A very low price, a bargain.

Wanyamwezi /wanjamˈweɪzi/ *noun & adjective.* M19.
[African name, lit. 'people of the moon'.]
▶ **A** *noun.* Pl. same. A member of a Bantu-speaking people of Tanzania. M19.
▶ **B** *adjective.* Of or pertaining to the Wanyamwezi. M19.

wanze /wɒnz/ *verb.* Now *rare* or *obsolete.*
[Old English *wansian*, from *wane* wanting.]
†**1** *verb trans.* Orig., diminish, waste. Later, make lean. OE–M17.
†**2** *verb intrans.* Decrease, grow less; (of the moon) wane. Only in ME.
3 *verb intrans.* Wither, fade, waste away; become emaciated. LME.

WAP /wap/ *abbrev.*
Wireless Application Protocol, a set of protocols enabling mobile phones and other radio devices to be connected to the Internet.

wap /wɒp/ *noun¹.* LME.
[Rel. to WAP *verb¹.*]
1 A blow, a knock, a thump. *obsolete* exc. *Scot. & dial.* LME.
2 A shake, a flap; a sweeping or tossing movement. *Scot.* M17.
3 A gust of wind; a sudden storm. *Scot.* E19.
4 A fight; a quarrel. *Scot.* M19.

wap /wɒp/ *noun².* *Scot. & dial.* M16.
[Prob. from WAP *verb².*]
1 A turn of a string wrapped round something. *rare.* M16.
2 A bundle of straw or hay. E19.

wap /wɒp/ *verb¹.* Now *Scot. & dial.* Infl. **-pp-**. LME.
[Origin unkn.: cf. SWAP *verb*, WHOP *verb.*]
1 *verb intrans.* Strike or knock *on* or *through*; beat, hit. LME.
2 *verb intrans.* (Of the wind) blow in gusts; (of cloth, wings, etc.) flap, beat. Long *obsolete* exc. *Scot.* LME.
3 *verb trans.* Throw quickly or violently; pull roughly. (Foll. by *down, out*, etc.) LME.
4 *verb trans.* Shake, flap, wave. Long *obsolete* exc. *Scot.* L16.
5 *verb intrans.* Copulate. *slang.* Long *rare* or *obsolete.* E17.
6 *verb intrans.* Make the intermittent sound of shallow water over stones. E20.

wap /wɒp/ *verb² trans. obsolete* exc. *Scot. & dial.* Infl. **-pp-**. LME.
[Origin uncertain: perh. alt. of WARP *verb*. Cf. WRAP *verb.*]
Wrap, envelop; bind, tie.

wap /wɒp/ *verb³ intrans. obsolete* exc. *dial.* Infl. **-pp-**. LME.
[Imit.]
Of a dog: bark, yelp.

wapato /ˈwɒpətəʊ/ *noun.* Also **wapp-**, **-atoo** /-ətuː/. Pl. **-os**. E19.
[Chinook Jargon *wappatoo* from Cree *wapatowa* lit. 'white mushroom'.]
The tubers of either of two N. American kinds of arrowhead, *Sagittaria cuneata* and *S. latifolia*, formerly used as food by N. American Indians; either of the plants from which these are obtained.

wapentake /ˈwɒp(ə)nteɪk/ *noun.*
[Late Old English *wǣpen(ge)tæc* from Old Norse *vápnatak*, from *vápna* genit. pl. of *vápn* WEAPON + *tak* act of taking, from *taka* TAKE *verb.*]
Hist. A subdivision of certain northern and midland English counties, corresponding to the hundred of other counties. Also, the judicial court of such a subdivision. Cf. HUNDRED *noun* 3.

Wapishana /wapɪˈʃɑːnə/ *noun & adjective.* Also **-siana** /-ˈsjɑːnə/. M19.
[Arawak.]
▶ **A** *noun.* Pl. same, **-s**.
1 A member of an Arawak people of Guyana and Brazil. M19.
2 The language of this people. L19.
▶ **B** *adjective.* Of or pertaining to this people or their language. M19.

wapiti /ˈwɒpɪti/ *noun.* E19.
[Shawnee *wa:piti* lit. 'white rump'.]
A large deer, *Cervus canadensis*, which resembles a large red deer and is sometimes considered to be a race of it, and which is native to western N. America. Also (*N. Amer.*) called *elk*.

wappato, **wappatoo** *nouns* vars. of WAPATO.

†**wappened** *adjective. rare* (Shakes.). Only in E17.
[Origin unkn.]
Of a person: sexually exhausted through promiscuity.

wappenschaw /ˈwap(ə)nʃɑː/ *noun.* Also **-shaw**, **weapon-** /ˈwɛp(ə)n-/. E16.
[formed as WEAPON + SHOW *noun¹*; prob. orig. shortened from next.]
1 SCOTTISH HISTORY. = WAPPENSCHAWING. E16.
2 A volunteer rifle-meeting. *Scot.* M19. ▸**b** [translating Dutch *wapenschouwing*: see next.] A rifle-shooting competition. *S. Afr.* L19.

wappenschawing /ˈwap(ə)nˌʃɑːɪŋ/ *noun.* Also **-shawing**, **weapon-** /ˈwɛp(ə)n-/. LME.
[formed as WEAPON + SHOWING; = Dutch *wapenschouwing*.]
SCOTTISH HISTORY. A periodical muster or review of the men under arms in a particular lordship or district.

wapper /ˈwɒpə/ *verb intrans. obsolete* exc. *dial.* L16.
[Perh. cogn. with WAVE *verb¹*: cf. Dutch *wapperen* swing, oscillate, waver.]
Blink one's eyes. Also, tremble.
Comb.: **wapper-eyed** *adjective* blinking, bleary-eyed.

wappered /ˈwɒpəd/ *adjective. obsolete* exc. *dial.* E17.
[from prec. + -ED¹.]
Tired, fatigued.

wappie /ˈwɒpi/ *noun. W. Indies.* M20.
[Perh. from WAP *noun¹* + -IE.]
A gambling game played with cards.

†**Wappineer** *noun.* L17–L18.
[formed as WAPPINGER + -EER.]
= WAPPINGER.

wapping /ˈwɒpɪŋ/ *adjective.* Now *Scot. & dial.* E17.
[from WAP *verb¹* + -ING². Cf. WHOPPING.]
= WHOPPING.

Wappinger /ˈwɒpɪŋə/ *noun. rare.* M18.
[from *Wapping* (see below) + -ER¹.]
A native or inhabitant of Wapping, a part of London close to the docks.

wappit *adjective* var. of WABBIT.

waqf *noun* var. of WAKF.

war /wɔː/ *noun¹.* LOE.
[Anglo-Norman, Old Northern French *werre* var. of Old & mod. French *guerre*, from Frankish (or West Germanic) *werra* rel. to Old High German *werra* confusion, discord, strife, Old Saxon, Old High German *werran* bring into confusion (German *wirren* confuse, perplex), from Germanic base repr. by WORSE *adjective.*]
1 a The state of (usu. open and declared) armed conflict between nations or states; armed hostilities between nations or States, or between parties in the same nation or State; the employment of armed forces against a foreign power, or against an opposing party in the State. Also (now chiefly *arch.* or *joc.*) in *pl.* (treated as *pl.* or †*sing.*) in same sense. LOE. ▸**b** A specific conflict between armed forces carried on in a campaign or series of campaigns; the period of time during which such conflict exists. Freq. with specifying word. ME.
2 Any active hostility or struggle between living beings; (a) conflict between opposing forces or principles; a campaign against something pervasive and undesirable. ME.
3 a Fighting; a battle. Chiefly *poet.* Now *rare* or *obsolete.* ME. ▸†**b** A hostile attack, an invasion. LME–E17.
4 The operations by which armed hostilities are carried on; fighting as a department of activity, a profession, or an art. LME.
5 *collect. poet.* ▸†**a** Instruments of war, munitions. M17–E18. ▸**b** Soldiers in fighting array. Now *rare* or *obsolete.* M17.

📖 **1a** *Encounter* War was almost universally considered an acceptable . . way of settling international differences. **b** *Daily Telegraph* Any war in Europe would be a nuclear one. ***First World War, Great War, Gulf war, Hundred Years War, Opium War, Punic war, Second World War, Spanish Civil War, Wars of the Roses***, etc. **2** *Wall Street Journal* Gasoline price wars have been common in . . North Carolina. *Daily Mail* 27,000 official forms have been scrapped in a Whitehall war on red tape.

Phrases: **at war** engaged in war. ***cold war***: see COLD *adjective*. ***contraband of war***: see CONTRABAND *noun* 3. ***COUNCIL of war***. ***declaration of war***: see DECLARATION 4. ***gang war***: see GANG *noun*. **go to the war(s)** *arch.* go abroad as a soldier. **go to war** enter into hostilities. **have a good war** (freq. *iron.*) achieve success, satisfaction, or enjoyment during a war. **have been in the wars** *colloq.* show marks of injury; appear bruised, unkempt, etc. ***holy war***: see HOLY *adjective*. ***honours of war***: see HONOUR *noun*. ***limited war***: see LIMITED *adjective*. **make war** carry on hostilities (foll. by *against, on, with*). ***munitions of war***: see MUNITION *noun* 3. **open war** avowed active hostility. ***phoney war***: see PHONEY *adjective*. ***PRISONER of war***. ***private war***: see PRIVATE *adjective*. ***war of attrition***: see ATTRITION 5. ***war of detail***: see DETAIL *noun*. ***war of nerves***: see NERVE *noun*. **war of words** a sustained conflict conducted by means of the spoken or printed word; a propaganda war. **war to end war(s)**, **war to end all war(s)** a war which is intended to make subsequent wars impossible; *spec.* the war of 1914–18.

Attrib. & comb.: In the senses 'of or pertaining to war', 'used or occurring in war', 'suited for war', as ***war hospital***, ***war ration***, ***war relief***, ***war victim***, ***war wound***, etc. Special combs., as **war artist**: employed to produce paintings or drawings of a war; **war baby** (*a*) a baby born during a war, *esp.* a (freq. illegitimate) child of a man on active service; (*b*) *slang* a young or inexperienced officer; (*c*) *US slang* a bond etc. which is sold during a war or which increases in value because of a war; **war bag** *US*: containing money, clothing, or other supplies; **war-bird** *US* (*a*) = ***war-eagle*** below; (*b*) *fig.* a fighting aircraft or pilot; **war bonnet** a head-dress decorated with eagle feathers, worn by N. American Indians; **War Box** *slang* the War Office; **war bride** a woman who marries a serviceman (esp. a foreign one) met during a war; **War Cabinet**: having responsibility for the political decisions of a country during a war; **war chest** (a chest or strongbox for) funds used in waging war; *fig.* funds used by a political party to finance an election campaign; **war-cloud** (*a*) a cloud of dust and smoke rising from a battlefield; (*b*) *fig.* an international situation threatening war; **war college** (chiefly *US*): providing advanced instruction for senior officers of the armed services; **war communism** *Hist.* an economic policy, based on strict centralized control of the economy, adopted by the Bolsheviks during the Russian Civil War (1917–21); **war correspondent** a journalist reporting from a scene of war; **war crime** an offence committed in wartime which violates the accepted rules of war; **war criminal** a person who has committed a war crime; **war cry** (*a*) a phrase or name shouted by a body of fighters to encourage each other in battle; (*b*) a party slogan etc.; **war dance**: performed before a battle or in celebration of a victory; **war department** the State office in charge of the army etc.; **war diary**: recording the experiences of an individual during a war; **war-dog**: trained for use in war; *fig.* a fierce warrior; **war-drum**: beaten as a summons to war or an accompaniment to the battle; **war-eagle** the golden eagle, so called because of the use of its feathers for decoration by N. American Indians; **war economy** (*a*) a measure taken to save money or other resources during a war; (*b*) an economy in which a large part of the workforce is engaged in arms production etc. rather than in the production of goods for export or for civilian use; **war effort** the effort of a nation or an individual group to win a war; **war fever** an enthusiasm for war; **warfront** the foremost part of the field of operations of opposing armies; **war-game** (*a*) a game simulating war, *esp.* a battle conducted with model soldiers; (*b*) an exercise by which a military strategy is examined or tested; *spec.* = KRIEGSPIEL 1; **war-gamer** a person who plays a war-game; **war-gaming** the playing of war-games; the use of such games to examine or test strategies; **war gas** a gas or other chemical agent used in war to produce irritant or poisonous effects; **war generation**: which has experienced a war; **war-god**, **war-goddess** a god or goddess who presides over war; **war grave**: of a serviceman who died on active service, *esp.* one in a special cemetery; **war-guilt** the responsibility for having caused a war (freq. with ref. to the claim that Germany caused the war of 1914–18, which was embodied in an article of the Treaty of Versailles (1919)); †**war-hable** *adjective* (*rare*, Spenser) fit for war, of military age; **war-hatchet**: used by N. American Indians to symbolize the declaration or cessation of hostilities; **war-hawk** *US* a person eager for the fray, a brave; **warhead** the explosive head of a missile, torpedo, or similar weapon; **war hero**, **war heroine** a person who has acted heroically in a war; **War House** *slang* the War Office; **war hysteria** unhealthy emotion or excitement caused by war; an enthusiasm for war; **war-kettle** among N. American Indians, a kettle which was set on the fire as a part of the ceremony of inaugurating a war; **warload** the bombs or missiles carried on a military aircraft; **war machine** (*a*) an instrument or weapon of war; (*b*) the military resources of a country organized for waging war; **war-man** (orig. chiefly *Scot.*, now *rare*) a warrior, a soldier; **war medicine** *N. Amer.* magic formerly used by N. American Indians to ensure success in war; **war memorial** a monument etc. commemorating those (esp. from a particular locality) killed in a war; **war minister** a person who directs the war affairs of a State; the Secretary of State for War; **war-note** *poet.* a musical summons to war; **War Office** (*a*) *Hist.* the former department of the British Government in charge of the administration of the army (incorporated into the Ministry of Defence in 1964); the building in which the business of this department was conducted; (*b*) the US War Department; **war orphan** a child orphaned by war; **war-party** (*a*) a body of people, esp. N. American Indian braves, banded together for war; (*b*) a political party that favours war; **war pension**: paid to someone disabled or widowed by war; **war-plane** an aircraft equipped for fighting, bombing, etc., in wartime; **war poet**: writing on war themes, esp. of the two world wars; **war-post**: into which N. American Indians struck the war-hatchet; **war-proof** *noun & adjective* †(*a*) *noun* (*rare*, Shakes.) courage proved in war; (*b*) *adjective* capable of resisting a hostile attack; **war refugee** a person who seeks refuge in another country or region to escape from the effects of war; a displaced person in wartime; **war reporter** = ***war correspondent*** above; **war resistance** opposition to war, pacifism; **war resister** an opponent of war or of a particular war; **war risk** a risk of loss etc. during wartime (freq. in *pl.* & *attrib.*); **war road** *N. Amer.* = WARPATH; **war room**: from which a war is directed; **war-saddle** a saddle used by mounted warriors, usu. with a high pommel and cantle; **warship** an armoured ship used in war; **war-steed** *poet.* a warhorse; **war-substantive** *adjective* confirmed (in a rank) for the duration of a war; **wartime** (*a*) the period during which a war is waged; (*b*) *US HISTORY* daylight-saving time introduced during the war of 1939–45; **war trial** the trial of a person for a war crime or crimes; **war veteran** a veteran of a (freq. specified) war; **war-weary** *adjective* (*a*) exhausted and dispirited by war; (*b*) *US* (of aircraft) badly damaged in wartime and withdrawn from service; **war-whoop** a cry made esp. by N. American Indians on rushing into battle; **war-wolf** *Hist.* a siege engine; **war work** special work made necessary by war and intended to advance the war effort; **war-worker** a person undertaking war work.

■ **warful** *adjective* (*rare*) bellicose, warlike **M16**. **warless** *adjective* free or exempt from war; not engaging in war: **LME**. **warlessness** *noun* (*rare*) absence of war **E20**. **warspeak** *noun* jargon used during or in the description of a war, esp. by military personnel **M20**.

war /wɑː, wɔː/ *adjective, adverb, & noun*². *Scot. & north.* Also **waur**. **ME**.
[Old Norse *verre* adjective, *verr* adverb: cf. WORSE *adjective, noun, & adverb.*]
▶ **A** *adjective & adverb.* = WORSE *adjective, adverb.* **ME**.
▶ **B** *noun.* The worst of it; that which is inferior. **ME**.

war /wɔː/ *verb*¹. Infl. **-rr-**. **ME**.
[from WAR *noun*¹, partly after Old French *werreier* WARRAY.]
†**1** *verb trans.* Make war on. **ME–E17**. ▸**b** Ravage, harry; harass, persecute. **ME–E16**.
2 *verb intrans.* Make war; fight. (Foll. by *against, on, upon, with.*) Now *literary*. **ME**. ▸**b** Of peoples, rulers, etc.: be at war with each other. **ME**. ▸**c** Serve as a soldier. **M16**.
3 *verb intrans.* Fight verbally etc. as opp. to physically; (of forces, principles, etc.) be in strong opposition. **ME**.
4 *verb trans.* Carry on or wage (warfare etc.). Long *rare* or *obsolete*. **LME**.
■ **warring** *ppl adjective* (*a*) engaged in warfare; *fig.* feuding, contending; (*b*) ***Warring States***, designating the last period (475 BC onward) of Chinese history prior to the unification of China in 221 BC: **E17**.

war /wɑː, wɔː/ *verb*² *trans. Scot.* Infl. **-rr-**. Also **waur**. **LME**.
[from WAR *noun*².]
Defeat in a contest or competition; surpass, outdo.

War. *abbreviation.*
Warwickshire.

waragi /ˈwarəgi/ *noun.* **E20**.
[Kiswahili *wargi*.]
In Uganda, a strong alcoholic drink made from bananas or cassava.

Warao /wəˈraʊ/ *noun & adjective.* Also (earlier) **Waraw**. **E19**.
[Amer. Indian name.]
▶ **A** *noun.* Pl. **-s**, same. A member of an American Indian people inhabiting parts of Guyana, Suriname, and Venezuela; the language of this people. **E19**.
▶ **B** *adjective.* Of or pertaining to the Waraos or their language. **M19**.

waratah /ˈwɔːrətɑː/ *noun.* **L18**.
[Aboriginal.]
Any of several Australian shrubs constituting the genus *Telopea* (family Proteaceae), which bear crimson flowers in terminal clusters surrounded by large red bracts; esp. *T. speciosissima*, the emblem of New South Wales, Australia.

Waraw *noun & adjective* see WARAO.

warb /wɔːb/ *noun. Austral. slang.* **M20**.
[Perh. from WARBLE *noun*².]
A lazy, unkempt, or contemptible person.
■ **warby** *adjective* unprepossessing, unkempt; disreputable, contemptible: **E20**.

warble /ˈwɔːb(ə)l/ *noun*¹. **LME**.
[Old Northern French (esp. Picard) *werble*, from *werbler* WARBLE *verb*¹.]
1 Orig., a tune or melody played on an instrument or sung. Later (influenced by WARBLE *verb*¹), the action or an act of warbling; soft and sweet singing or sound, esp. of birds. **LME**.
2 A manner of warbling. **M16**.
Comb.: **warble tone** *PHYSICS* a constant amplitude tone whose frequency oscillates between certain limits, used in acoustic measurement.

warble /ˈwɔːb(ə)l/ *noun*². **LME**.
[Origin unkn. Cf. WORNIL.]
1 A small swelling or abscess on the back of cattle, deer, etc., produced by the larva of a warble fly developing under the skin; a hole in the hide left by the emerging larva. **LME**. ▸**b** The parasitic larva of any of several large flies of the genus *Hypoderma* (family Oestridae), which burrow through the tissues of hoofed mammals etc. Also (more fully ***warble fly***), an adult fly whose larvae are of this kind. **E19**.
2 A small hard tumour, caused by the pressure or friction of the saddle on a horse's back. Usu. in *pl.* **E17**.
■ **warbled** *adjective* (of a hide) injured by warbles **L19**.

warble /ˈwɔːb(ə)l/ *verb*¹. **LME**.
[Old Northern French (esp. Picard) *werbler*, *werbloier* trill, sing, from Frankish *hwirbilōn* whirl, trill: cf. Old High German *wirbil* whirlwind (German *Wirbel*).]
†**1** *verb trans.* Proclaim by a flourish of trumpets; sound (a trumpet etc.). *rare*. Only in **LME**.
2 *verb intrans.* Of a bird: sing softly and sweetly, trill. **L15**.
3 *verb intrans.* **a** Of a person: modulate the voice in singing; sing with trills and quavers. Later also, sing softly and sweetly, sing in a birdlike manner; *gen.* (freq. *joc.*) sing. **E16**. ▸**b** Of a stream: flow with a melodious sound. *poet.* **L16**. ▸**c** Of music: sound with a quavering melody; be produced with smooth and rapid modulations of pitch. Now *rare* or *obsolete*. **E18**.
4 *verb trans.* Sing with trills and runs; utter melodiously, express in song or verse; *gen.* (freq. *joc.*) sing. Also foll. by *forth, out*. **L16**.
†**5 a** *verb trans.* Manipulate (the strings of a musical instrument) in playing. **L16–M17**. ▸**b** *verb intrans.* Of a stringed instrument: emit melodious sounds. **E17–L18**.
6 *verb intrans.* Of a telephone (*spec.* a Trimphone): ring with a distinctive trilling sound. **M20**.

> 🕮 **2** MILTON Birds on the branches warbling. **4** T. H. WHITE Warbling the great medieval drinking-song.

warble /ˈwɔːb(ə)l/ *verb*² *trans. & intrans.* **L15**.
[Origin unkn.]
FALCONRY. Of a hawk: cross (the wings) together over the back after rousing and mantling.

warbler /ˈwɔːblə/ *noun.* **E17**.
[from WARBLE *verb*¹ + -ER¹.]
1 A person who or thing which warbles or sings sweetly; *gen.* (freq. *joc.*) a singer. **E17**. ▸**b** *spec.* A female singer. *slang*. **M20**.
2 a Any of numerous small plain-coloured Old World songbirds of the family Sylviidae, which are chiefly arboreal insectivores and are noted for their complex warbling songs. **L18**. ▸**b** Any of various small, usu. bright-coloured American songbirds of the family Parulidae. Also ***wood warbler***. **L18**. ▸**c** Any of various small mainly dull-coloured Australasian songbirds of the families Acanthizidae (more fully ***Australian warbler***, ***Australasian warbler***) and Maluridae. **L18**.
3 A group of grace-notes embellishing a tune on the bagpipe. *Scot.* **E19**.
4 A telephone which warbles. Cf. WARBLE *verb*¹ 6. *colloq.* **L20**.
2a *garden warbler*, *leaf warbler*, *reed warbler*, *sedge warbler*, *willow warbler*, etc. **b *Kentucky warbler*, *myrtle warbler*, *prairie warbler*, *Swainson's warbler***, etc. **c *rock warbler*, *wren warbler***, etc.
Comb.: **warbler finch** an emberizid finch, *Certhidea olivacea*, that occurs in the Galapagos Islands and has the appearance and feeding habits of an Old World warbler.

warbling /ˈwɔːblɪŋ/ *ppl adjective.* **M16**.
[formed as prec. + -ING².]
That warbles; *esp.* singing or sounding with sweet quavering notes.
warbling vireo a mainly grey-coloured vireo, *Vireo gilvus*, which is widespread from Canada to Peru and has a melodious warbling song.

Warburg /ˈwɔːbəːg/ *noun.* **M20**.
[Otto Heinrich *Warburg* (1883–1970), German biochemist and physiologist.]
BIOCHEMISTRY. Used *attrib.* and in *possess.* to designate apparatus for the study of the metabolism of tissue by the manometric measurement of oxygen consumption and carbon dioxide production.

Warburgian /wɔːˈbəːgɪən/ *adjective.* **M20**.
[from Aby *Warburg* (1866–1929), German-Jewish cultural historian, + -IAN.]
Of, pertaining to, or characteristic of Warburg or his work, or the Warburg Institute, founded in 1904 by him in Hamburg and transferred in 1933 to London.
■ **Warburgianism** *noun* **L20**.

warcraft /ˈwɔːkrɑːft/ *noun.* Pl. same. **M17**.
[from WAR *noun*¹ + CRAFT *noun.*]
1 Skill in warfare; the art of conducting a war. **M17**.
2 Warships or naval vessels collectively. Also, a warship. **L19**.

ward /wɔːd/ *noun.*
[Old English *weard* = Middle Low German *warde*, Old High German *warta* watch (German *Warte* watch-tower), Old Norse *varða*, *varði* cairn, from Germanic extension of stem of verb meaning 'be on guard' (cf. WARE *verb*¹); reinforced in Middle English by Old Northern French *warde* = Old & mod. French *garde* GUARD *noun.*]
▶ **I** Protection, defence, control.
1 The function of a watchman, sentinel, etc.; the action of keeping a lookout for danger; observation, surveillance. Freq. in ***hold ward***, ***keep ward***. Now *rare*. **OE**.
2 a *gen.* Guardianship, control. Now *rare*. **ME**. ▸**b** *spec.* Guardianship of a child, minor, etc.; the condition of being subject to a guardian. **ME**. ▸**c** *FEUDAL LAW.* The control and use of the lands of a deceased tenant by knight-service, and the guardianship of the infant heir during his or her minority. **ME**.
3 Care or charge of a prisoner; the condition of being a prisoner; custody, imprisonment. Now *rare*. **ME**.
4 *SCOTS LAW* (now *Hist.*). Land tenure by military service (freq. in ***hold ward***). Also, a payment in commutation of military service. **E16**.
5 A defensive posture or movement in fencing; *fig.* (*arch.*) a defensive position or attitude. **L16**. ▸†**b** Defence, protection, shelter. **L16–L17**.
▶ **II** A body of guards.
6 A company of watchmen or guards. Now *rare*. **OE**.
†**7** Any of the three main divisions of an army (the van, the rear, and the middle). Orig. as 2nd elem. of comb. **ME–M17**.
†**8** A garrison. **L15–M17**.
▶ **III** A place for guarding.
9 The inner or outer circuit of the walls of a castle; the ground between two encircling walls of a fortress. Formerly also, a portion of the defences of a fortress entrusted to a particular officer or division of the garrison; a guarded entrance. Now *arch.* or *Hist.* **ME**.
10 Orig., a prison. Later, each of the divisions or separate sections of a prison. **ME**.
11 a An administrative division of a borough or city, orig. under the jurisdiction of an alderman, now usu. electing its own councillors. Also, the people of such a district collectively. **ME**. ▸**b** Chiefly *Hist.* An administrative division of some Scottish and northern English counties. **LME**. ▸**c** An administrative division of the Mormon Church; a Mormon congregation. **M19**.
12 A division of a forest; an enclosed piece of land; a field. *Scot.* **LME**.
†**13** A store-cupboard, a storeroom. **E16–M18**.
14 A room in a hospital etc. containing a number of beds, or allocated to a particular class of patients; the smallest administrative division for in-patients in a hospital. Also more widely, a dormitory in any building providing temporary accommodation. **E17**. ▸**b** The patients in a hospital ward collectively. **M18**.

> 🕮 **10** E. WALLACE Lane . . was in the same ward at Dartmoor; we came out together. **14** *Look Now* A Nursing Officer responsible for three or more wards. ***casual ward***: see CASUAL *adjective*. ***Nightingale ward***: see NIGHTINGALE *noun*² 2. OBSERVATION ***ward***. ***open ward***: see OPEN *adjective*.

▶ **IV** A person under guardianship.
15 a A minor under the control of a guardian. Now also = ***ward of court*** below. **ME**. ▸**b** *gen.* A person who is under the protection or control of another. **LME**.
†**16** An orphan under age. **M–L16**.

> 🕮 **15a** ***ward in Chancery***: see CHANCERY. **ward of court** a minor for whom a guardian has been appointed by the Court of Chancery, or who has become directly subject to the authority of that court. **16** SHAKES. *Rom. & Jul.* His son was but a ward two years ago.

▶ **V** An appliance for guarding.
17 Usu. in *pl.* ▸**a** The ridges projecting from the inside plate of a lock, serving to prevent the passage of any key which does not have incisions of corresponding form and size. Also (*popularly*), the incisions in a lock. **LME**. ▸**b** The incisions in the bit of a key, corresponding to the projecting ridges of the lock. Also (*popularly*), the projections in a key. **LME**.
18 In *pl.* Any notches and projections in a mechanical device which resemble the wards of a lock and key. **L16**.

> 🕮 **17a** J. I. M. STEWART There was a harsh grating sound . . and the key turned in its wards.

Comb.: **ward aide** a person employed to do non-medical work in a hospital ward; **ward-book** a register of admissions to a hospital; **ward-heeler** *US* a local follower of the political head of a ward (sense 11a); a party worker in elections etc.; **ward-heeling** *adjective* (*US*) pertaining to, engaged in, or designating, the activities of a ward-heeler; **ward-holding** *SCOTS LAW* (now *Hist.*) a tenure of lands by military service (cf. sense 4 above); **ward maid** a female hospital orderly; **wardmote** (chiefly *Hist.*) a meeting of the citizens of a ward, orig. *esp.* (in the City of London) a meeting of the liverymen of a ward under the presidency of the alderman; **ward orderly** a person employed to assist nurses in a hospital ward; **ward-room** (*a*) the dining-room of naval commissioned officers above the rank of sub-lieutenant; commissioned officers as a body; (*b*) a military guardroom; **ward round** a visit paid by a doctor (sometimes accompanied by medical students) to each of the patients in his or her care or in a particular ward or wards; **wardsman**, **wardswoman** (*a*) an inmate appointed to supervise a ward in a prison or workhouse; (*b*) *Austral.* (**wardsman**) a hospital orderly; **ward-woman** *arch.* a lady's maid, a woman in charge of her mistress's wardrobe.

■ **wardatar** *noun* (SCOTS FEUDAL LAW) the person having wardship of lands while the heir is a minor **M16**. **warded** *adjective* (of a key or lock) constructed with wards **L16**.

ward /wɔːd/ *verb.*

[Old English *weardian* = Old Frisian *wardia*, Old Saxon *wardon*, Old High German *wartēn* (German *warten* nurse, look after), Old Norse *varða*, from Germanic base as prec.; reinforced in Middle English by Old Northern French *warder* var. of Old & mod. French *garder* GUARD *verb*. In sense 10 from the noun.]

1 a *verb trans.* Keep safe, take care of; guard, defend, protect. (Foll. by *from*.) *arch.* **OE**. ▸†**b** *verb intrans.* Keep guard. **LME–E18**.

†**2** *verb trans.* Rule or govern (a country); administer (an estate); act as guardian to (a child). **OE–LME**.

†**3** *verb trans.* Man *with* a garrison; protect or shield *with*; fortify (a castle). Orig. also, (of a castle) defend or protect (an area etc.). **OE–M17**.

†**4** *verb intrans.* Take up a position of defence, take precautions *against*. **ME–M18**.

5 *verb trans.* Keep in close custody; confine, imprison. Chiefly *Scot.* Now *rare*. **ME**.

6 *verb intrans.* Parry blows; stand on the defensive in a combat. *arch.* **LME**.

7 *verb trans.* **a** Repel, turn aside, (a blow, attack, etc.). Usu. foll. by *off*. **L16**. ▸**b** Avert, keep *off*, (harm, danger, etc.). **L16**.

8 *verb trans.* Enclose; hem *in*, shut *off*. *rare*. **L16**.

9 *verb trans.* Of a dog: line or cover (a bitch). **M18**.

10 *verb trans.* Place (a patient) in a particular hospital ward; lodge (a vagrant) in a casual ward. **L19**.

> 📖 **7a** G. GREENE Holding his palm over his eyes . . to ward off falling glass. **b** *Country Living* A healthy body needs a . . supply of minerals to ward off illness. A. STEVENS He insisted that Emilie sat behind him to ward off evil spirits. **10** P. D. JAMES She had a temperature of 103.8 when she was warded.

-ward /wəd/ *suffix.*

[Old English *-weard*, primarily forming adjectives with the sense 'having a specified direction', from Germanic base meaning 'turn' (cf. Latin *vertere*). See also -WARDS.]

1 Forming adverbs from nouns and adverbs with the sense 'towards the place or direction specified', or adjectives with the sense 'turned or tending towards', as in ***backward***, ***earthward***, ***homeward***, ***inward***, ***onward***, ***skyward***, etc.

2 Forming adverbial phrases from nouns, pronouns, and adverbs following *to* with the sense 'towards, the region towards or about', as ***to heavenward***, ***to herward***, ***to the eastward***, ***to theeward***, etc. Now *arch.* or *literary*.

†**3** Forming adverbial phrases from nouns, pronouns, and adverbs following *from* with the sense 'away from', as in ***from herward*** etc.

¶ Adverbs in sense 1 are now more usually formed from -WARDS.

warday /ˈwɔːdeɪ/ *noun. dial.* **L16**.

[Of Scandinavian origin: cf. Swedish *vardag*, Danish *hverdag*, lit. 'every day'.]

A weekday, a day other than Sunday. Cf. EVERYDAY *noun* 2.

warden /ˈwɔːd(ə)n/ *noun*^{1}. **ME**.

[Anglo-Norman, Old Northern French *wardein* var. of Old French *g(u)arden* GUARDIAN.]

†**1** A person who guards, protects, or defends something or someone; *spec.* a guardian angel. **ME–E16**.

2 a A person in charge of something specified; a keeper. *obsolete* exc. *poet.* **ME**. ▸**b** A gatekeeper, a porter, a sentinel. Now *rare*. **ME**.

†**3** A person having custody of the person and property of an orphan heir during his or her minority. Also more widely, a person in charge of young people. **ME–E18**.

4 a A regent or viceroy appointed to rule a country in the king or queen's absence or minority. *obsolete* exc. *Hist.* **ME**. ▸**b** The governor of a town, province, or district; the commander of a fortress. *obsolete* exc. *Hist.* in ***Warden of the Marches***. **ME**.

†**5 a** A custodian of a building, esp. of a temple or church. **ME–M17**. ▸**b** The dean of a cathedral or collegiate church, or of a royal chapel. **LME–M16**.

6 An officer to whose custody prisoners are committed; the governor of a prison. **ME**.

7 In certain guilds, esp. in the livery companies of the City of London: a member of the governing body under the authority of the Master or the Prime Warden. **ME**.

†**8 a** A person in charge of some work or enterprise. **LME–E17**. ▸**b** FREEMASONRY. Either of two officers (called ***Senior Warden*** and ***Junior Warden***) in a symbolic lodge who acted as assistants to the Worshipful Master. Only in **18**.

9 = CHURCHWARDEN *noun* 1. **LME**. ▸**b** An official with similar functions in a synagogue. **L19**.

10 †**a** The superior of a Franciscan convent. **LME–L16**. ▸**b** The head or presiding officer of certain colleges, schools, hospitals, youth hostels, etc. **M16**.

11 In titles of various officers holding positions of trust under the Crown, as ***Warden of the Cinque Ports***, ***Lord Warden of the Stannaries***, etc. **L15**.

12 A member of a committee appointed to be in charge of the repair and regulations for use of a bridge, highway, etc. **L15**.

13 a The superintendent of a harbour, market, etc. **M16**. ▸**b** As 2nd elem. of combs. designating certain officials or superintendents, as ***barrack-warden***, ***fire-warden***, ***game-warden***, etc. **M19**. ▸**c** An air-raid warden. **M20**.

14 a The officer who presides at ward-meetings or elections. **M18**. ▸**b** AUSTRAL. HISTORY A government official, with magisterial powers, in charge of a goldfield. **M19**. ▸**c** The head of a county council. *Canad.* **M19**.

■ **wardency** *noun* (*rare*) (*a*) the position of a warden; (*b*) the sphere or district in which a warden works: **M19**. **wardenry** *noun* (*a*) the office or position of a warden; (*b*) *Hist.* the jurisdiction of, or district under the care of, a Warden of the Marches: **LME**. **wardenship** *noun* (*a*) *rare* guardianship, safe-keeping; (*b*) the office or position of a warden: **ME**.

warden /ˈwɔːd(ə)n/ *noun*^{2}. **LME**.

[Origin unkn.]

An old variety of baking pear. Also ***pear warden***, ***warden pear***.

warden /ˈwɔːd(ə)n/ *verb.* **E20**.

[from WARDEN *noun*^{1}.]

1 *verb trans.* Watch over or guard as a warden; *spec.* patrol (a nature reserve etc.). **E20**.

2 *verb intrans.* Act as a (wildlife) warden. **M20**.

warder /ˈwɔːdə/ *noun*^{1} & *verb.* **LME**.

[Anglo-Norman *wardere*, *wardour*, from Old Northern French *warder*: see WARD *verb*, -ER^{1}.]

▸**A** *noun.* **1** A soldier or other person set to guard an entrance etc.; a watchman, a sentinel. **LME**.

†**2** A prisoner. *Scot. rare.* **L16–E17**.

3 An official in charge of prisoners in a jail. **M19**.

> 📖 **1** *fig.*: W. WATSON A fair-built seaport, warder of the land.

▸**B** *verb trans.* Provide with a warder or sentinel. **M19**.

■ **wardership** *noun* (*rare*) (*a*) the office or position of a warder; (*b*) the carrying out of the duties of a warder: **M19**.

warder /ˈwɔːdə/ *noun*^{2}. **LME**.

[Reduced form of WARDERER.]

In early use, a staff, a wand. Later, a baton or truncheon carried as a symbol of office, command, or authority, esp. as used to give the signal for the start or end of a battle or contest.

warder /ˈwɔːdə/ *noun*^{3}. *rare.* **L16**.

[from WARD *verb* + -ER^{1}.]

†**1** FENCING. A person who parries. Only in **L16**.

2 A person who wards something off. Also ***warder-off***. **L19**.

warderer /ˈwɔːd(ə)rə/ *noun. obsolete* exc. *Hist.* **LME**.

[Perh. from Anglo-Norman *ware* look out + *derere* (mod. French *derrière*) behind.]

A baton, a truncheon, a warder.

Wardian /ˈwɔːdɪən/ *adjective.* **M19**.

[from Nathaniel B. *Ward* (1791–1868), English botanist, the inventor + -IAN.]

Chiefly *Hist.* ***Wardian case***, a glass-sided airtight case used for growing ferns etc. indoors or for transporting living plants over long distances.

warding /ˈwɔːdɪŋ/ *noun.* **ME**.

[from WARD *verb* + -ING^{1}.]

1 The action of guarding a place etc.; an instance of this. Orig. also, a body of guards or watchmen. **ME**.

2 Imprisonment. *Scot.* **L15**.

3 Guardianship, keeping. *rare.* **M16**.

4 The creation of wards in locks and on keys. Esp. in ***warding-file***. **M19**.

wardite /ˈwɔːdʌɪt/ *noun.* **L19**.

[from H. A. *Ward* (1834–1906), US naturalist and dealer + -ITE^{1}.]

MINERALOGY. A hydrated basic tetragonal phosphate of sodium and aluminium, occurring as transparent light blue-green crystals.

Ward-Leonard /wɔːdˈlɛnəd/ *noun.* **E20**.

[Harry *Ward Leonard* (1861–1915), US electrical engineer and inventor.]

ELECTRICAL ENGINEERING. Used *attrib.* to designate a system for controlling a direct-current motor in which its armature current is supplied by an auxiliary generator, the field current of which is varied to vary the speed of the motor.

Wardour Street /ˈwɔːdə striːt/ *noun phr.* **L19**.

[A street in central London, formerly occupied mainly by dealers in antique furniture.]

1 Used *attrib.* to designate the pseudo-archaic diction affected by some modern writers, esp. of historical novels. **L19**.

2 Wardour Street as a centre of the British film industry. Freq. *attrib.* **E20**.

wardress /ˈwɔːdrɪs/ *noun.* **L19**.

[from WARDER *noun*^{1} + -ESS^{1}.]

A female warder in a prison.

wardrobe /ˈwɔːdrəʊb/ *noun.* **ME**.

[Old Northern French *warderobe* var. of Old & mod. French *garderobe*, from *garder* GUARD *verb* + *robe* ROBE *noun*^{1}. Cf. GARDEROBE.]

†**1** A private chamber; *esp.* a bedroom. **ME–L17**.

†**2** A room for storing clothes or armour, usu. adjoining a bedroom; a dressing-room. **LME–M19**.

3 A department of a royal or noble household in charge of clothing. Also, the building in which the officers of this department work. **LME**.

4 A person's entire stock of clothes; a collection of clothing for a particular season, activity, etc. **LME**.

5 A large movable or built-in cupboard, fitted with rails, shelves, hooks, etc., for storing clothes, esp. in a bedroom. **L16**.

6 A room in which theatrical costumes and props are kept; the costume department or costumes of a theatre, film studio, etc. **E18**.

> 📖 **4** J. CARLYLE The weather is grown horribly cold, and I am . . intent . . on getting my winter wardrobe into order. *Woman's Own* Add a dash of colour to your wardrobe with our . . cardi. **6** *Stage & Television Today* She was asked . . to help out in the wardrobe at the Flora Hall, Scarborough.

Comb.: **wardrobe mistress**, **wardrobe master** a person in charge of a theatrical or film wardrobe, or of the professional wardrobe of an actor or actress; **wardrobe-room**: in which the stage costumes are stored in a theatre; **wardrobe trunk**: fitted with rails, shelves, etc., for use as a travelling wardrobe.

■ **wardrober** *noun* (*obsolete* exc. *Hist.*) an officer of a royal household in charge of clothing **LME**.

-wards /wədz/ *suffix.*

[Old English *-weardes*, corresp. to Old Saxon, Middle Low German *-wardes*, Old High German, Middle High German *-wartes*, the ending of the neut. genit. sing. (used adverbially) of adjectives with Germanic base meaning 'turn': see -WARD.]

1 Forming adverbs from nouns and adverbs with the sense 'towards the place or direction specified', or adjectives with the sense 'turned or tending towards', as ***backwards***, ***eastwards***, ***heavenwards***, ***inwards***, etc.

2 Forming adverbial phrases from nouns, pronouns, and adverbs following *to* with the sense 'towards, the region towards or about', as in ***to you-wards***, etc. Now *arch.*, *literary*, or *dial.*

3 Forming adverbial phrases from nouns, pronouns, and adverbs following *from* with the sense 'away from', as in ***from herwards*** etc. *obsolete* exc. *dial.*

¶ Adjectives in sense 1 are now more usually formed from -WARD. In general, -WARDS is preferred to -WARD when a notion of manner as well as direction is implied (as in *she can write backwards*), or when a definite direction is being stated in contrast with other directions.

wardship /ˈwɔːdʃɪp/ *noun.* **LME**.

[from WARD *noun* + -SHIP.]

1 a The guardianship of a minor; *spec.* in FEUDAL LAW, the guardianship and custody of the person and property of an heir during his or her minority. **LME**. ▸**b** *gen.* Guardianship, protection, custody. **M17**.

2 The condition of being a ward; *spec.* in FEUDAL LAW, the condition of being under guardianship as a minor. **M16**.

> 📖 **1a** *attrib.*: *Daily Telegraph* In the wardship proceedings the applicant and his wife were refused access to the child.

ware /wɛː/ *noun*^{1}. *Scot. & dial.*

[Old English *wār* corresp. to Northern Frisian *wier* seaweed, pondweed (whence prob. Dutch *wier*) repr. Germanic base meaning 'bind': cf. OARWEED.]

Seaweed, *esp.* coarse seaweed washed up on the shore and used as manure.

SEA-ware.

ware /wɛː/ *noun*^{2}.

[Old English *waru* corresp. to Old Frisian *ware*, *were*, Middle Low German, Middle Dutch *ware* (Dutch *waar*), Old Norse *vara*, from Germanic. Perh. same word as next with the meaning 'object of care'. Cf. WARE *adjective*.]

1 a *sing.* & in *pl.* Articles of merchandise or manufacture; goods, commodities. Freq. as 2nd elem. of comb. **OE**. ▸**b** An article of merchandise, a saleable commodity. *rare*. **L19**.

2 *collect.* A person's skills, talents, products, etc. **ME**.

3 a *sing.* & in *pl.* Textile fabrics. *obsolete* exc. in ***MANCHESTER wares***. **ME**. ▸†**b** *sing.* & in *pl.* Livestock. **ME–M18**. ▸**c** *collect.* Field-produce, crops, vegetables (now *dial.*); *spec.* large potatoes intended for sale (also ***ware potatoes***). **LME**. ▸**d** A young oyster in its third year. **L19**.

4 *collect.* †**a** The genitals. Also in ***lady ware***. LME–E18. ▸**b** Women. Freq. in ***piece of ware***. *joc. arch.* M16.
5 *collect.* Articles made of pottery; ceramics. Chiefly with specifying word, as ***chinaware***, ***glassware***, ***Jasper-ware***, ***Parian ware***, ***Staffordshire ware***, etc. M18.

📖 **1a** M. IGNATIEFF The booksellers setting out their wares on the quais. ***iron ware***, ***paper ware***, ***stationery ware***, etc. **2** J. G. HOLLAND There is nothing immodest . . in the advertisement of a man's literary wares. **5** *Artist* A selection of art pottery and functional ware is also for sale.

Phrases: **the hale ware** *Scot.* the whole number or amount; the sum total.

ware /wɛː/ *noun*³. Long only *Scot.*
[Old English *waru* fem. corresp. to Old Frisian *ware*, Old Saxon, Old High German *wara* (Middle High German *ware*, war), from Germanic base also of WARE *adjective*. Cf. WARE *noun*².]
Watchful care, heed, cautiousness; safe-keeping, defence, protection.

ware /wɛː/ *noun*⁴. *Scot. & north.* ME.
[Old Norse *vár* (Icelandic *vor*, Swedish, Norwegian, Danish *vår*).]
The season of spring.

ware /wɛː/ *adjective*.
[Old English *wær*, *ġewær* corresp. to Old Saxon *war*, Old High German *giwar* (German *gewahr*), from Germanic base meaning 'observe, take care'. Cf. WARE *noun*², *noun*³, WARE *verb*¹, WARN *verb*¹.]
▸ **I** *pred.* **1** Aware, conscious, having knowledge (*of*, *that*, etc.). Now *arch.* or *Scot.* OE.
2 Prepared, on one's guard, vigilant, cautious. *arch.* OE.
3 Careful or cautious in avoiding a person or thing. *arch.* Foll. by *of*, †*that*, †*to do*, †*with*. OE.
4 Prudent, sagacious, cunning. Freq. in ***ware and wise***. *arch.* OE.
†**5** Careful or guarded in action. Foll. by *in*, *of*, *to do*, *with*. ME–L16.
▸† **II** *attrib.* **6** Prudent, cautious, cunning. LME–E17.

ware /wɛː/ *verb*¹.
[Old English *warian* corresp. to Old Frisian *waria*, Old Saxon *waron*, Old High German *biwarōn* beware, Old Norse *vara*, from Germanic base also of prec.; in Middle English coalescing with Old Northern French *warer* (mod. *garer*), from Germanic.]
1 *verb intrans.* & †*refl.* Take care, be on one's guard. Foll. by †*of*, *that*, †*to*, †*with*. *arch.* OE. ▸**b** In *imper.* As a warning cry, a call to animals, and in hunting: beware. *obsolete* exc. *dial.* OE.
2 *verb trans.* Beware of, guard against; avoid, shun. Usu. in *imper.* *arch.* OE. ▸**b** In *imper.* As a warning cry and in hunting: watch out for, beware. Freq. in ***ware horse***. E16.
▪ **wareful** *adjective* (now only *poet.*) watchful, cautious M16.

ware /wɛː/ *verb*² *trans.* *obsolete* exc. *Scot.* & *dial.* ME.
[Old Norse *verja* invest (money), lay out.]
1 Spend (money); consume or use up (resources or goods). Also foll. by *out*. ME.
2 *fig.* Expend, use up (one's time, energy, etc.). LME.

waree *noun* var. of WAREE.

warehou /ˈwɑːrəhaʊ/ *noun*. *NZ.* M19.
[Maori.]
A large marine food fish, *Seriolella brama* (family Centrolophidae), found in the shallow inshore waters of New Zealand and Australia.

warehouse /ˈwɛːhaʊs/ *noun*. ME.
[from WARE *noun*² + HOUSE *noun*¹.]
1 A building or part of a building used for the storage of retail goods, furniture, etc.; *spec.* = ***bonded warehouse*** s.v. BOND *verb* 4. ME.
2 A shop; now *esp.* a large wholesale or retail store. E18.
3 A large impersonal institution providing accommodation for psychiatric patients, the old, or the poor. *US colloq.* L20.

📖 **1** G. STEIN Pulling great loads from the ships to the warehouses.

Phrases: ***bonded warehouse***: see BOND *verb* 4. ***Italian warehouse***: see ITALIAN *adjective*. **warehouse to warehouse** *adjectival phr.* designating (a clause in) a cargo insurance policy which provides that the policy applies throughout all of the normal course of transit.
Comb.: **warehouse club** an organization operating from a large store which sells goods in bulk at discounted prices to business and private customers who must first become club members; **warehouseman** (*a*) a man employed in or in charge of a warehouse; (*b*) a wholesale merchant (esp. a trader in textile materials) who has a warehouse for storing merchandise; **warehouse party** a large, usu. illegal, party with dancing, held in a warehouse or other spacious building.

warehouse /ˈwɛːhaʊs, -haʊz/ *verb trans.* L18.
[from the noun.]
1 Deposit or store (goods, furniture, etc.) in a warehouse; place (imported goods) in a bonded warehouse pending payment of the import duty. L18.
2 Place (a person, esp. a psychiatric patient) in a large impersonal institution. *US colloq.* L20.
3 Buy (shares) as a nominee of another trader, with a view to a takeover. Freq. as ***warehousing*** *verbal noun*. *Stock Exchange slang.* L20.

wareless /ˈwɛːlɪs/ *adjective*. Now *rare* or *obsolete* exc. *dial.* M16.
[from WARE *noun*³ + -LESS.]
1 Unwary, incautious, imprudent. M16.
2 Unguarded; unconscious (*of* danger). M16.

warely /ˈwɛːli/ *adverb*. *obsolete* exc. *Scot.*
[Old English *wærlīce*, from *wær*: see WARE *adjective*, -LY².]
Watchfully, cautiously; prudently.

wareness /ˈwɛːnɪs/ *noun*. *obsolete* exc. *poet.*
[Old English *wærnes*, from *wær*: see WARE *adjective*, -NESS.]
Cautiousness, vigilance.

Warerite /ˈwɛːrʌɪt/ *noun*. M20.
[Respelling of WEAR *verb*¹ + RIGHT *adverb*.]
(Proprietary name for) a hard durable plastic laminate used as a surfacing material.

wareshi /waˈrɛʃi/ *noun*. E20.
[Origin unkn.]
In Guyana, a basket worn on the back and held by a headband round the forehead.

warfare /ˈwɔːfɛː/ *noun & verb*. LME.
[from WAR *noun*¹ + FARE *noun*¹.]
▸ **A** *noun*. **1** The action of going to war or engaging in war; military life or operations. LME.
2 *transf.* & *fig.* Fighting, conflict, hostilities; campaigning. M16.

📖 **1** *Newsweek* Up to 12,000 troops . . trained in desert warfare. ***bacteriological warfare***, ***biological warfare***, ***nuclear warfare***: see NUCLEAR *adjective*. ***psychological warfare***: see PSYCHOLOGICAL *adjective*. ***push-button warfare***: see PUSH-BUTTON 2. **2** H. BRODKEY He was in a very trance of warfare, fighting with his mother, with his analyst. ***economic warfare***. ***gang warfare***: see GANG *noun*.

▸ **B** *verb intrans.* Wage war; take part in war. Now *rare* exc. as WARFARING *ppl adjective*. LME.
▪ **warfaring** *ppl adjective* that wages war; militant, warlike: M16.

warfarin /ˈwɔːfərɪn/ *noun*. Also **W-**. M20.
[from Wisconsin Alumni Research Foundation + *-arin*, after COUMARIN: see -IN¹.]
PHARMACOLOGY. A water-soluble tricyclic anticoagulant used as a selective rodenticide and in the treatment of thrombosis as a prophylactic against embolism; 3-(α-acetonylbenzyl)-4-hydroxycoumarin, $C_{19}H_{16}O_4$.

Warholian /wɔːˈhəʊlɪən/ *adjective*. L20.
[from Andy *Warhol* (see below) + -IAN.]
Of or characteristic of the work or ideas of the US artist, film-maker, and proponent of pop art Andy Warhol (1927–87).

warhorse /ˈwɔːhɔːs/ *noun*. M17.
[from WAR *noun*¹ + HORSE *noun*.]
1 A powerful horse ridden in war by a knight or trooper; a charger. Now *Hist.* M17.
2 A veteran soldier or politician. Also more widely, a veteran of any activity; a dependable or stalwart person. M19.
3 A tough or determined woman. E20.
4 A thing which is frequently used or very familiar; *spec.* a work of art, esp. music, which is frequently performed. M20.

wari /wɒˈriː, ˈwɒri/ *noun*. E20.
[Prob. from a Ghanaian language.]
An originally W. African board game, a variation of mancala.

†**wariangle** *noun*. LME–L19.
[Origin unkn.]
A shrike, *esp.* the red-backed shrike, *Lanius collurio*.

†**wariment** *noun*. *rare* (Spenser). Only in L16.
[from WARY *adjective* + -MENT.]
Precaution.

Waring /ˈwɛːrɪŋ/ *noun*¹. E20.
[Edward *Waring* (1734–98), English mathematician.]
MATH. Used in *possess.* to designate a conjecture (proved by Hilbert in 1909) that every integer is equal to the sum of not more than g sth powers, g depending on s but not on the integer.

Waring /ˈwɛːrɪŋ/ *noun*². M20.
[*Waring* Products Corporation, New York.]
Waring blender, (proprietary name for) a food processor (chiefly *US*); SCIENCE a homogenizer.

waringin /wəˈrɪŋɡɪn/ *noun*. L19.
[Indonesian.]
A large tree of SE Asia, *Ficus benjamina*, resembling the banyan.

wark /wɑːk/ *noun & verb*. *obsolete* exc. *dial.*
[Old English *wærc* corresp. to Old Norse *verkr* (Swedish *värk* pain, Danish *værk* gout, rheumatism), from Germanic base also of WORK *noun*.]
▸ **A** *noun*. A pain, an ache. OE.
▸ **B** *verb intrans.* Ache, throb; suffer pain. Cf. WORK *verb* 17. OE.

warlike /ˈwɔːlʌɪk/ *adjective*. LME.
[from WAR *noun*¹ + -LIKE.]
1 Of a person, nation, etc.: naturally disposed to warfare or fighting; skilled or courageous in war; bellicose. LME. ▸**b** Of a sound, action, etc.: martial in character. LME. ▸**c** Favouring or threatening war; hostile. E20.
†**2** Equipped for fighting or for war. LME–E18.
3 Of or pertaining to war; for use in war; military. M16.
4 Of or belonging to a warrior or soldier. M16.

warling /ˈwɔːlɪŋ/ *noun*. Now *rare*. M16.
[App. arbitrary formation to rhyme with *darling*.]
A person who is despised or disliked. Chiefly in ***it is better to be an old man's darling than a young man's warling*** (proverbial).

warlock /ˈwɔːlɒk/ *noun*¹ & *adjective*.
[Old English *wǣrloga* corresp. to Old Saxon *wārlogo*, from Old English *wǣr* covenant + weak base of *lēogan* LIE *verb*². The mod. form with final *-ck* is Scot. in origin.]
▸ **A** *noun*. **1** †**a** An oath-breaker, a traitor. OE–LME. ▸**b** A wicked person, a scoundrel. Freq. used as a term of abuse. Long *obsolete* exc. *Scot.* OE.
†**2** The Devil; Satan. OE–M16. ▸**b** A devil, a demon. *rare.* OE–LME.
†**3** A savage hostile creature; a monster, a giant. OE–L16.
4 A man in league with the Devil and so possessing occult and evil powers; a sorcerer, a wizard; a man who practises witchcraft. Orig. *Scot. & north.* ME. ▸**b** A magician, a conjuror. *Scot.* E18.
▸ **B** *attrib.* or as *adjective*. Orig. (now only *Scot.*), malignant, wicked. Later, designating or pertaining to a warlock or wizard; magical. LME.
¶ The modern currency of the word is due chiefly to Sir Walter Scott.
▪ **warlockry** *noun* (*arch.*) the practice of magic; wizardry: E19.

warlock /ˈwɔːlɒk/ *noun*². *obsolete* exc. *dial. rare.* LME.
[Origin uncertain: prob. assim. to CHARLOCK.]
Any of several cruciferous weeds, *esp.* wild radish, *Raphanus raphanistrum*, and black mustard, *Brassica nigra*.

warlord /ˈwɔːlɔːd/ *noun*. M19.
[from WAR *noun*¹ + LORD *noun*.]
1 A military commander or commander-in-chief. M19.
2 [translating Chinese *jūnfá*.] In China: a military commander having a regional power base and ruling independently of the central government, orig. and esp. in China in the period 1916–28. Now also, any regional military commander with more or less independent control of an area or military group. E20.
▪ **warlordism** *noun* the policies or practices of a warlord; government by warlords: M20.

warm /wɔːm/ *adjective & noun*.
[Old English *wearm* corresp. to Old Frisian, Old Saxon *warm*, Old High German *war(a)m* (Dutch, German *warm*), Old Norse *varmr*, from Germanic, prob. from Indo-European base repr. by Latin *formus* warm, Greek *thermos* hot, Sanskrit *gharma* heat.]
▸ **A** *adjective*. **1** Having a fairly high temperature; giving out a considerable degree of heat. OE.
2 Of a person or animal, or a part of the body: at the normal temperature of the living body; feeling a comfortable sensation of heat. OE. ▸**b** *spec.* Of a person: glowing with a sensation of heat from physical exertion, eating and drinking, etc. E17.
3 Of clothing, or an animal's coat: made of a material or substance which retains heat in the body; suitable for cold weather. ME. ▸**b** Of soil: quick to absorb heat; retaining warmth. L16.
†**4** Comfortably settled in a seat, official position, etc.; securely established in possession of something. Usu. foll. by *in*. LME–E19.
5 Ardent, zealous, impulsive; eager *for* something; (of a debate etc.); excited, heated. Now *rare*. LME.
6 (Of a person, the heart, feelings, etc.) full of love, affection, gratitude, etc.; cordial, tender; (of a kiss, embrace, etc.) expressive of such feelings; (of an utterance, praise, etc.) enthusiastic, hearty. L15.
7 Hot-tempered, angry. M16.
8 Comfortably off, well-to-do; rich, affluent. Now chiefly *colloq.* L16.
9 Characterized by or prone to sexual desire; amorous. L16.
10 (Of fighting or conflict) vigorous, hard, aggressive; (of a place or situation) dangerous or difficult to be in. E17.
11 **a** Of a report, representation, a person's imagination, etc.: lively, glowing, vivid. M17. ▸**b** Of a composition or description: indelicate; sexually explicit or titillating. E19.
12 HUNTING. Of a scent or trail: fresh, strong. E18.
13 Of a drug or item of food: producing a sensation of heat in the body. M18.
14 Of a colour or light: suggestive of warmth, as a rich red or yellow. M18.

15 Of a participant in esp. a children's seeking or guessing game: near to the object sought. Also more widely, on the verge of finding out or guessing something. M19.

📖 **1** D. H. LAWRENCE A warm hollow in the sandhills where the wind did not come. M. HOCKING The day, although early, was already warm. **keep a place warm**, **keep a seat warm**, etc., *fig.* occupy a place temporarily for another who is not yet qualified to hold it. **2** J. STEINBECK She could feel his warm breath against her skin. M. PYKE A coarse grey shirt keeps one . . warmer than, a delicate bleached white one. **warm and fuzzy** *colloq.* comfortable, cosy; evoking emotional or sentimental feelings (cf. *warm fuzzy* below). **3** I. MURDOCH He put on warm clothes, a woollen sweater. **5** G. GROTE A warm and even angry debate arose upon his . . speech. **6** L. URIS The greetings were warm, with affectionate hugs. *Times* Emperor Haile Selassie . . was given a warm welcome when he landed at Khartoum. I. MURDOCH My parents . . send their very warmest wishes. A. N. WILSON Mum's a very *warm* person. She *means* well. **7** CONAN DOYLE I don't know why you should be so warm over such a trifle. **10** G. WASHINGTON If he be detected in any . . pranks I will make the country too warm to remain in. **11** E. W. ROBERTSON Bridforth has drawn a very warm picture of the scene. **15** R. A. KNOX In what spirit? Penitence? No . . . Adoration? No; but you're getting warmer.

Special collocations & comb.: **warm-air** *adjective* that produces warm air for heating. **warm bath**: in warm water. **warmblood** a horse of mixed genetic background refined by the use of Arab or Thoroughbred blood. **warm-blooded** *adjective* (*a*) = ENDOTHERMIC; (*b*) *fig.* ardent, fervent, passionate. **warm-bloodedness** the character or condition of being warm-blooded. **warm boot** COMPUTING a reloading or restart of an operating system etc. without switching off the computer, esp. when changing programs. **warm front**: see FRONT *noun* 11b. **warm fuzzy** *colloq.* (orig. & chiefly *US*) a comfortable or cosy feeling; a person or thing inducing such a feeling, *esp.* a compliment (cf. *warm and fuzzy* above). **warm-headed** *adjective* (now *rare*) having an excitable temperament or vivid imagination. **warm-hearted** *adjective* of a generous and affectionate disposition; hearty, cordial. **warm-heartedly** *adverb* in a warm-hearted manner. **warm-heartedness** the quality of being warm-hearted. **warm reception** *iron.* a demonstration of hostile feeling. **warm sector** METEOROLOGY a region of warm air bounded by the cold and warm fronts of an active depression. **warm-temperature** *adjective* designating or characterized by a climate with warm summers and cool winters, typical of middle latitudes, nearer the pole than or overlapping with subtropical regions. **warm-water** *adjective* living in or characteristic of the seas of warm or tropical regions; (of a port etc.) not freezing in winter. **warm work** (*a*) hard work or strenuous activity, esp. fighting; (*b*) dangerous conflict.

▶ **B** *noun.* **1** A state or sensation of being warm; warmth. Now chiefly in ***in the warm***, ***into the warm***, indoors, out of the cold. ME.

2 An act of warming; the process of becoming warm. Freq. in ***give a warm***, ***have a warm***. Now chiefly *colloq.* M18.

3 In full ***British Service warm***, ***British warm***. A warm short overcoat worn especially by officers of the army. E20.

📖 **2** *Scots Magazine* Coming into his house to . . have a warm at the fire.

▪ **warmish** *adjective* L16. **warmly** *adverb* E16. **warmness** *noun* OE.

warm /wɔːm/ *verb.*

[Old English *werman*, *wirman* (branch I) = Old Saxon *wermian* (Dutch *warmen*), Old High German *wermen* (German *wärmen*), Old Norse *verma*, Gothic *warmjan*, from Germanic; also Old English *wearmian* (branch II) = Old High German *war(a)mēn* (early mod. German *warmen*); both from Germanic base of WARM *adjective*.]

▶ **I** *verb trans.* **1** Make (a person's body, limbs, etc.) warm by exposure to heat; impart warmth to; cause to feel warm. OE.

2 a Heat (an object, substance, building, etc.) to a fairly or comfortably high temperature. OE. ▸**b** Impart warmth of colour to. M19.

3 a Inspire with affection, love, or gratitude; cause to feel pleasure. E16. ▸**b** Make enthusiastic or interested, rouse; *spec.* put (an audience) into a receptive mood prior to a show or broadcast by entertaining, chatting, etc. Now usu. foll. by *up*. L16. ▸**c** Of drink: excite, stimulate. *rare.* E17. ▸†**d** Exhort (troops etc.) to valour. L17–E18.

†**4** Celebrate a move to or the completion of (a new house) by a party or other entertainment. E17–E19.

5 Beat, flog. *dial.* E19.

📖 **1** G. VIDAL She sat close to the window so that the morning sunlight would warm her. M. KEANE Warming her bottom in front of the fire. **2a** E. WAUGH One thing about a party, it does warm the room. **3a** W. GOLDING I was warmed by Summer's belief in my ability. B. HEAD Just seeing him . . every day warmed their hearts because there were so few good men left.

▶ **II** *verb intrans.* **6 a** Become warm; be raised to a fairly or comfortably high temperature. OE. ▸**b** Of colour: become warmer or more ruddy. M19. ▸**c** Foll. by *up*: (of an athlete etc.) prepare oneself by light exercise or practice immediately before the start of a contest or other form of physical exertion. L19. ▸**d** Foll. by *up*: (of an engine, electrical appliance, etc.) reach a temperature high enough for efficient working. M20.

7 Of a person, the heart, feelings, etc.: become affectionate, kindly, or friendly (*to* or *towards* a person). LME.

8 Become eager, animated, or enthusiastic; liven *up*; (foll. by *to*) become more interested in or keen on (one's work, a plan, etc.). M18.

📖 **6c** L. M. ALCOTT Beth put a pair of slippers down to warm. M. ANGELOU He ran out . . to warm up before a . . basketball game. **d** W. SOYINKA The plane . . had begun to warm up on the airstrip. **7** G. LORD For the first time since their meeting, Beth warmed a little to her. **8** A. JOHN Shy and reserved, he would warm up after a few tankards of beer. A. WILSON He soon warmed to the subject and told Robin about the new history. A. WEST My mother had not warmed to the idea of taking her on.

Phrases, & with adverbs in specialized senses: ***like*** DEATH ***warmed up***. **warm down** recover from strenuous physical exercise by doing gentle exercise. **warm over** *N. Amer.* = *warm up* below. **warm the bell** *Nautical slang* (strike a bell and) prepare for something earlier than the correct time (from the practice of warming a ship's hourglass to make the sand run more freely). **warm up** make warm again; *esp.* reheat (cooked food that has become cold): see also senses 3b, 6c, d, 8 above.

Comb.: **warm-down** recovery from strenuous physical exercise with gentle exercise.

▪ **warmable** *adjective* (*rare*) M19. **warming** *noun* (*a*) the action of the verb (also foll. by *up*); an instance of this; (*b*) *rare* a house-warming; (*c*) *rare* a thrashing, a trouncing: LME.

warm /wɔːm/ *adverb.*

[Old English *wearme*, from the adjective.]

Warmly; so as to be warm.

warmer /ˈwɔːmə/ *noun.* L16.

[from WARM *verb* + -ER¹.]

1 A person who warms. *poet.* L16.

2 Any of various things for warming something. Freq. with specifying word, as ***foot-warmer***, ***leg warmer***, ***plate-warmer***, etc. E19.

Comb.: **warmer-up**, **warmer-upper** something that warms a person up; *spec.* (*a*) a preliminary act or person provided to put an audience in a receptive mood; (*b*) a stimulating drink.

warming-pan /ˈwɔːmɪŋpan/ *noun.* L16.

[from WARMING *verbal noun* + PAN *noun*¹.]

1 *Hist.* A long-handled, usu. brass, covered pan with a flat body, filled with live coals etc. and used for warming beds. L16.

2 a A woman for a man to have in bed with him. *slang* (long *rare* or *obsolete*). M17. ▸**b** A person who temporarily holds a place or employment until the intended occupant is ready to take it. *arch. slang.* M19.

warmonger /ˈwɔːmʌŋɡə/ *noun.* L16.

[from WAR *noun*¹ + MONGER *noun*.]

†**1** A mercenary soldier. *rare* (Spenser). Only in L16.

2 A person who seeks to bring about or promote war. E19.

▪ **warmongering** *noun & adjective* (the action of) seeking to bring about war M20.

warmouth /ˈwɔːmaʊθ/ *noun.* L19.

[Origin unkn.]

A freshwater fish, *Lepomis gulosus*, of the sunfish family Centrarchidae, found in the eastern US.

warmth /wɔːmθ/ *noun.* ME.

[Corresp. to Middle Low German *wermede* (Dutch *warmte*), Middle High German *wermede* (early mod. German *Wärmte*), from West Germanic: see WARM *adjective*, -TH¹.]

1 A fairly hot or comfortably heated state of the atmosphere, esp. as an essential of physical comfort and well-being; a temperate heat radiating from the sun, a fire, etc. ME. ▸**b** A moderate degree of heat produced in or retained by a substance. M18.

2 The natural heat of a living body; vital heat. L16.

3 a An excited or heated emotional state; ardour, enthusiasm; cordiality, heartiness. L16. ▸**b** A heated state of temper approaching anger; heated language or argument. E18.

4 A glowing hue; *spec.* a glowing effect in painting produced by the use of warm colours. E18.

📖 **1** J. HERRIOT A pleasant warmth met me as I went into the pub. J. FRAME Those with no homes depending for warmth . . on the doorways of . . places like banks. **2** G. ORWELL Her cheek was almost near enough for him to feel its warmth. **3a** T. C. WOLFE McHarg, too, began to show wholehearted warmth for the plan.

▪ **warmthless** *adjective* (*rare*) M19.

warm-up /ˈwɔːmʌp/ *noun.* L19.

[from *warm up* s.v. WARM *verb*.]

1 = WARM *noun* 2. L19.

2 a The action or process of warming up for a contest etc. by light exercise or practice. E20. ▸**b** A preliminary action in preparation for something. M20.

3 The action or process of raising the temperature of an engine, electrical appliance, etc., to a level high enough for efficient working. M20.

4 The warming up of an audience into a receptive mood, esp. before a show or broadcast. M20.

5 a A garment designed for warmth. M20. ▸**b** A garment worn during light exercise or practice; a track suit. Also ***warm-up suit***. *N. Amer.* M20.

📖 **2a** *Dance Theatre Journal* An extensive warm-up involving . . stretches and strengthening exercises. *attrib.*: T. O'BRIEN Down to the beach for warm-up exercises. **b** ANNE STEVENSON Sylvia's plan was to write stories . . as a warm-up for marketable fiction. **4** *attrib.*: *New Musical Express* The new bands . . are alright, but I consider them all just warm up acts.

warn /wɔːn/ *noun. rare.* ME.

[from WARN *verb*¹.]

†**1** An intimation or notice of something as about to happen. Only in ME.

2 Warning. *poet.* M19.

warn /wɔːn/ *verb*¹.

[Old English *war(e)nian*, *wearnian*, corresp. to Middle Low German *warnen*, Old High German *warnōn*, *warnēn* (German *warnen*), from West Germanic base meaning 'be cautious': cf. WARE *adjective*.]

▶ **I** †**1** *verb intrans. & refl.* Take heed, be on one's guard, beware. Only in OE.

▶ **II 2** *verb trans.* Give notice to (a person) of impending or possible danger or misfortune. Freq. foll. by *against*, *of*, *that*. OE.

3 *verb trans.* Give (a person) cautionary advice with regard to actions or conduct; counsel *against* neglect of duty or *against* wrong action or belief. Also foll. by †*of*, *that*, *to do*. OE.

4 *verb trans.* Put (a person) on his or her guard; caution *against* someone or something as dangerous. Also foll. by †*from*, *of*. ME.

5 a *verb trans.* Inform or notify of something requiring attention; give advance notice to. Usu. foll. by *of*, *that*, *to do*. ME. ▸†**b** *verb trans.* Tell (a person) when it is time *to do* something. ME–L17. ▸**c** *verb intrans.* Of a clock: make a clicking or whirring noise prior to striking. *Scot. & dial.* M19.

6 *verb trans.* **a** Summon (a person) *to* a duty, place, etc. Later *esp.*, summon officially; command the attendance of. ME. ▸†**b** Call, give notice of (a meeting). LME–L18.

7 *verb trans.* **a** Notify of something commanded; order under penalties. LME. ▸**b** Forcefully notify (a person) to go *away*, *from*, *out of* (a place), etc. L16. ▸**c** Foll. by *off*: give notice to (a person) to keep at a distance or to keep off an area; *fig.* advise forcefully against or prohibit from a particular action or involvement. E19.

†**8** *verb trans.* Give (a person) notice to leave his or her employment or tenancy. Usu. foll. by *out*. L15–M19.

📖 **2** A. LAMBERT The doctor . . warned me he might not last the month. *absol.*: *Times* He has warned . . of the dangers of securitizing debts. **3** B. WEBB I warned Susan to be careful what she said. A. N. WILSON Gutch had been right to warn him against coming. **4** P. LIVELY His father had warned him against strange men. **5a** E. M. FORSTER Then came your telegram warning me that Aunt Juley was coming by that train. **7b** L. M. ALCOTT She never saw Laurie mount guard in the hall to warn the servants away. **c** A. BRIGGS A husbandman, warned off the field because battle was about to begin. S. MIDDLETON You don't think he was trying to warn you off marriage to me? **warn off the course** RACING (*Hist.*) prohibit (a defaulter against the laws of the Jockey Club) from riding or running horses at meetings under the Jockey Club's jurisdiction.

†**warn** *verb*² *trans.*

[Old English *wiernan* corresp. to Old Frisian *werna*, Old Saxon *wernian*, Old High German *wernen*, Old Norse *verna*; partly also Old English *wearnian* (by confusion with prec.) = Old Frisian *warna*, Old Norse *varna*: both from Germanic base meaning 'obstruct, defend'.]

1 Refuse or deny *to* a person; refuse to grant (a request etc.); refuse *to do*. OE–L15.

2 Refuse to allow (some action) *to* a person; forbid *to do*. OE–L16.

3 Prevent, hinder, or restrain from action. OE–E16.

4 a Stop the way of. Only in ME. ▸**b** Refuse or deny (entry, the door, right of way, etc.). LME–E17. ▸**c** Forbid, exclude *from* a place or position; keep *from* a person. LME–L16.

📖 **4c** SPENSER Carelesse heauens . . can . . not warne death from wretched wight.

†**warnel** *noun* var. of WORNIL.

warner /ˈwɔːnə/ *noun.* E16.

[from WARN *verb*¹ + -ER¹.]

1 COOKERY. An elaborate table decoration, usu. made of sugar. Cf. SUBTLETY 3. *obsolete* exc. *Hist.* E16.

2 A person who or thing which gives warning; *spec.* a mechanical device for giving warning. M16.

3 A person who summons people to attend a gathering. Now *rare* or *obsolete*. L16.

warning /ˈwɔːnɪŋ/ *noun.*

[Old English *war(e)nung*, *wearning*, from *war(e)nian*, *wearnian* WARN *verb*¹: see -ING¹.]

†**1** Heed, precaution. OE–L16.

2 Indication, intimation, or threatening of impending misfortune or danger; a sign or message of this. OE.
3 a Deterrent counsel; cautionary advice against neglect of duty or imprudent or wrongful action. OE. ▸**b** An experience, sight, etc., that serves as a caution; a deterrent example. E17. ▸**c** The action or an instance of warning someone *off* (see WARN *verb*[1] 7c). L20.
4 Advice to beware of a person or thing as being dangerous; an instance of this. ME.
5 a Advance notice of an event; length of time allowed for preparation for an event. ME. ▸**b** In some clocks, the clicking or whirring noise which precedes the striking. L18. ▸**c** A signal given by means of a siren etc. to indicate that an aerial attack is imminent; an air-raid warning. E20.
6 Notice of termination of a business connection, esp. by a landlord to a tenant, an employer to an employee, or vice versa. Now *rare*. LME.
†**7** Advance notice of being called on to perform some duty. LME–M18.
†**8 a** Notification of a fact or occurrence. LME–E17. ▸**b** A notice or signal that a certain time has come, or that it is time to do something. LME–E19.
9 A summons, a command for attendance. Now *formal*. LME.

> **2** *New Scientist* Finches and sandgrouse gave warning of the approach of predators. D. ACHESON Without warning a hurricane struck. J. LE CARRÉ A man whose warnings go unheeded until it's too late. **3b** O. NASH My head is on a pole as a warning to all young men . . planning to be too bright. **5a** LD MACAULAY At a moment's warning the Sheriff adjourned the poll.

Phrases: ***Gypsy's warning***: see GYPSY *noun*. ***red warning***: see RED *adjective*. ***Scarborough warning***: see SCARBOROUGH 1. ***sound a note of warning***: see NOTE *noun*[2]. **take warning** alter one's course of action when warned of its danger. **the usual warning** the customary caution given by a police officer when making an arrest, viz. that anything the suspect says may be taken down and used in evidence. ***yellow warning***: see YELLOW *adjective*.
Comb.: **warning bell** (*a*) a bell for giving alarm of fire or attack; (*b*) a bell announcing the imminent departure of a vessel; (*c*) a bell alerting people to prepare for a meal etc.; **warning-piece** (*a*) a signal-gun discharged to give notification of arrival, danger, etc.; (*b*) HOROLOGY a piece in a clock which produces the warning just before striking (see sense 5b above); **warning-pipe** an overflow pipe serving to show when a cistern is too full; **warning track** BASEBALL a strip around the outside of the outfield which warns approaching fielders of the proximity of a wall; **warning triangle** a triangular red frame carried by motorists, and set up on the road as a danger signal to warn approaching drivers of the proximity of a broken-down vehicle or other hazard; **warning-wheel** HOROLOGY: that produces the warning (see sense 5b above).
■ **warningfully** *adverb* (*rare*) warningly E20.

warning /ˈwɔːnɪŋ/ *ppl adjective*. M16.
[from WARN *verb*[1] + -ING[2].]
That warns.

> G. M. FRASER Susie glanced at me, lifting a warning finger. **warning coloration** ZOOLOGY a conspicuous pattern or colour which indicates that an animal is unpalatable or poisonous.

■ **warningly** *adverb* in a warning manner, by way of warning M19.

warnish /ˈwɔːnɪʃ/ *verb trans. obsolete* exc. *Scot*. ME.
[Anglo-Norman *warniss-* lengthened stem of *warnir* from Germanic; rel. to WARN *verb*[1]: see -ISH[2].]
Warn or inform beforehand.

warp /wɔːp/ *noun*.
[Old English *wearp* from base of the verb; in later senses directly from the verb.]
1 WEAVING. The threads stretched lengthwise in a loom, usu. twisted harder than the weft or woof, with which these threads are crossed. OE.
2 NAUTICAL. A rope or light hawser attached at one end to a fixed object, used esp. in hauling or for towing a ship in a harbour etc.; a warping hawser. ME. ▸**b** A rope attached to a net used in trawl-fishing. M19.
3 A group of four fish or oysters. LME.
4 Alluvial sediment deposited by water; silt. Also, a bed or layer of this. L17.
5 The state of being warped or twisted, esp. of shrunken or expanded timber; (a) distortion. L17.
6 Bias, perverse inclination; bitterness of the mind or character; a mental twist. M18.
7 SCIENCE FICTION. *ellipt*. = ***space warp*** s.v. SPACE *noun*, ***time warp*** s.v. TIME *noun*. M20.

> **1** *fig.*: *Listener* Enoch Powell has . . changed the warp and woof of British politics. **3** A. H. PATTERSON 'Tellers' . . count the herring warp by warp.

Comb.: **warp-beam** WEAVING the roller on which the warp is wound and from which it is drawn as the weaving proceeds; **warp drive** a fictional or hypothetical propulsion mechanism for a spaceship which is capable of manipulating space–time so as to travel faster than light; **warp factor** (in science fiction) the degree to which the velocity of a spaceship etc. exceeds that of light; usu. with numeral, as ***warp factor 8*** etc.; **warp knitting** machine knitting in which the yarns chiefly run lengthwise; **warp-lace**: having threads resembling the warp of a fabric; **warp print** a material design in which the warp yarns are printed with a pattern before weaving, giving a shadowy effect; **warp speed** a speed faster than light attained by means of a warp drive; *colloq.* very high speed.

warp /wɔːp/ *verb*.
[Old English *weorpan* corresp. to Old Saxon *werpan*, Old High German *werfan* (Dutch *werpen*, German *werfen*), Old Norse *verpa*, Gothic *wairpan*, from Germanic. Cf. WAP *verb*[2].]
▸**I 1** *verb trans*. **a** Project through space; throw, fling. Long *obsolete* exc. *dial*. OE. ▸†**b** Cast (lots). OE–ME.
†**2** *verb trans*. Sprinkle, scatter *on* a surface; spurt or shoot *out*. OE–ME.
3 a *verb trans*. Open (a gate) violently or suddenly; fling *open*, throw *up*. Long *obsolete* exc. *dial*. OE. ▸†**b** *verb intrans*. Of a door: open. LME–E16.
†**4** *verb trans*. **a** Drive *away* or *out*, expel, reject, renounce. OE–ME. ▸**b** Throw (a person) suddenly or roughly *into* prison, distress, etc. ME–L16.
†**5** *verb trans*. Strike, hit (*with* a missile). OE–ME.
†**6** *verb trans*. Throw *down*; overthrow. Only in ME.
†**7** *verb trans*. Utter, pronounce (a word, speech); utter (a cry), heave (a sigh). Also with *out*. ME–E16.
8 *verb trans*. & *intrans*. **a** Lay (eggs). *dial*. ME. ▸**b** Of a ewe, cow, etc.: give birth to (young) prematurely. *dial*. E18.
▸**II 9** *verb trans*. **a** Orig., weave (a fabric). Later, arrange (yarn) so as to form a warp; wind on a warp-beam. ME. ▸†**b** *fig*. Weave, contrive, devise. Also foll. by *up*. LME–L18.
10 *verb trans*. ANGLING. Fasten (an artificial fly) to the hook. Foll. by *on*, *up*, etc. L17.
11 *verb trans*. In rope-making, stretch (yarn) into lengths to be tarred. E19.
12 *verb trans*. Twist, insert (one thing *into* another); intertwine. *obsolete* exc. *Scot*. E19.
▸**III 13** *verb trans*. Bend or twist (an object) out of shape, distort; *spec*. curve (timber) by the application of steam. LME. ▸**b** AERONAUTICS (now *Hist*.). Bend or twist (a wing or aerofoil) by an attached wire to stabilize or turn an aeroplane. E20.
14 *verb intrans*. Of timber, metal, etc.: become bent or twisted out of shape, esp. by the action of heat or damp. LME.
15 *verb intrans*. & *trans*. Shrink, shrivel, contract. *rare*. L16.
16 *verb trans*. Distort (the mind, judgement, etc.); bias; make perverted or strange. Also foll. by *from*, *out of*, *to*. L16.
†**17** *verb intrans*. **a** Be biased, be perversely drawn or attracted (*to*, *towards*). Also, bend, yield (*to*); submit *to do* something. L16–L18. ▸**b** Be influenced in one's judgement or sentiments, become biased; deviate, go astray. (Foll. by *from*.) E17–E19.
18 a *verb intrans*. Turn or incline in a specified direction. *rare* exc. *Scot*. L17. ▸**b** *verb trans*. Turn aside or divert (a moving object) from its path or orbit; deflect. Now *rare*. E18.
19 *verb trans*. Distort (a word or statement), misinterpret, falsify (a fact, account, etc.). E18.
20 *verb intrans*. SCIENCE FICTION. Travel through space by way of a space or time warp. M20.

> **13** E. BOWEN Warped by sea damp, the doors were all stuck ajar. L. ALTHER She accused him of warping the Beatles album she'd given him. **14** A. AYCKBOURN We have to climb out of the . . window . . because the front door warps when it rains. **16** E. WAUGH The poor old girl had plainly had her tastes warped by Roger Fry. J. CHEEVER O'Brien warped my whole outlook on sex.

▸**IV 21** NAUTICAL. **a** *verb trans*. Move or tow (a ship) by hauling on a rope or warp. Freq. foll. by *away*, *in*, *out*, *round*. E16. ▸**b** *verb intrans*. Of a ship: move by warping. M16.
22 *verb intrans*. Float or whirl through the air. Chiefly *poet*. M16.
23 *verb trans*. **a** Heap up (alluvial sediment) by gradual deposit from a current. Also foll. by *up*. Now *rare* or *obsolete*. L17. ▸**b** Choke or silt *up* (a channel) with alluvial deposit. M18.
24 *verb trans*. Silt over (land) by flooding. L18.
25 *verb intrans*. & *refl*. Progress slowly or with effort using one's hands and feet; haul oneself along. Now *rare*. L18.

> **21a** T. PYNCHON Men stand on shore waiting to take lines and warp the barges in.

■ **warpage** *noun* (*a*) *rare* a charge for warping or hauling ships into a harbour; (*b*) the extent or result of (esp. timber) warping or bending: M19. **warped** *ppl adjective* (*a*) bent, twisted out of shape; (*b*) distorted, perverted; (*c*) (of land) enriched with alluvial warp: LME.

warpaint /ˈwɔːpeɪnt/ *noun*. E19.
[from WAR *noun*[1] + PAINT *noun*.]
1 Paint used, esp. by N. American Indians, to decorate the face and body before going into battle. E19.
2 a A person's best clothes and finery; *esp*. ceremonial or official costume. *colloq*. M19. ▸**b** Cosmetics, make-up. *colloq*. M19.

> **2b** *Daily Express* Jane Russell wouldn't even go out to buy a newspaper without full warpaint.

warpath /ˈwɔːpɑːθ/ *noun*. M18.
[from WAR *noun*[1] + PATH *noun*[1].]
The path or route taken by a warlike expedition of N. American Indians.
on the warpath (*a*) going to war, seeking the enemy; (*b*) *colloq*. taking a hostile course or attitude, displaying one's anger.

warper /ˈwɔːpə/ *noun*. OE.
[from WARP *verb* + -ER[1].]
†**1** A person who throws something, a thrower. Only in OE.
2 A person who winds yarn in preparation for weaving; a person who lays the warp for the weaver. E17.
3 A warping-machine. M19.

warping /ˈwɔːpɪŋ/ *noun*. ME.
[formed as prec. + -ING[1].]
†**1** The action of throwing something. ME–L15.
2 a The preparation of a warp for weaving. LME. ▸**b** = WARP *noun* 1. L17.
3 a Silt or alluvial sediment deposited by water. *rare*. LME. ▸**b** The process of silting over low-lying land by flooding. L18.
4 a The action of twisting, bending, or distorting something; the fact of becoming twisted or bent out of shape; an instance of this. LME. ▸**b** *fig*. The action or an act of distorting or perverting a person's behaviour, thoughts, etc., from the right course or direction; the fact of deviating or going astray. E17.
5 The action of towing a ship by means of warps. E16.
†**6** The action of scheming or plotting; a fabrication. L16–E19.
7 ANGLING. The wound thread attaching an artificial fly to a hook. L17.
8 CARPENTRY. A strengthening brace, a strut. M19.
Comb.: **warping-buoy**: used in warping a ship; **warping-frame**, **warping-mill**: on to which the threads are run in weaving; **warping-post** a strong post used in warping ropeyarn.

warple /ˈwɔːp(ə)l/ *noun*. *dial*. M16.
[Origin unkn.]
A country lane, a bridle-road. More fully ***warple way***.

warple /ˈwɔːp(ə)l/ *verb*. *Scot*. M18.
[Origin unkn.]
1 *verb trans*. Entangle, intertwine. M18.
2 *verb intrans*. Move with difficulty; walk unsteadily, stagger. M18.
3 *verb intrans*. Twist or wind *round*. M19.

warragal *noun* var. of WARRIGAL.

warrandice /ˈwɒr(ə)ndɪs/ *noun*. Chiefly *Scot*. LME.
[Anglo-Norman *warandise* var. of *warantise*: see WARRANTISE, -ICE[1].]
1 A guarantee, an undertaking to secure another against risk; *spec*. in SCOTS LAW, an obligation to indemnify the grantee or purchaser of land if an evictive or paramount claim should be established against the lands through defect of title. LME.
†**2** Security from danger; safety. E16–E19.

warrant /ˈwɒr(ə)nt/ *noun*[1]. ME.
[Old Northern French *warant* var. of Old French *guarant*, *-and* (mod. *garant*) from Frankish *werēnd* (= Old High German *werēnt*), from *giwerēn*, German *gewähren* corresp. to Old Frisian *wera* be surety for, guarantee. Cf. GUARANTEE.]
▸**I** *gen*. A person or thing.
†**1** A protector, a defender. ME–E19.
†**2** A safeguard, a protection; security or safety from one's enemies. Also, a place of refuge, a shelter. ME–L16.
3 a A person answerable for a fact or statement; an authoritative witness. ME. ▸**b** A conclusive proof. LME. ▸**c** With qualifying adjective, esp. *good* or *great*: a person who may be relied on *to do* a thing to the extent specified. *Anglo-Irish*. M19.
4 A command from a superior freeing a person from blame or legal responsibility for an action; authorization, sanction; evidence of this. ME.
5 A person granting authorization or sanction for another's action. ME.
†**6 a** Assurance given, guarantee. LME–E19. ▸**b** A guarantor, a surety; bail. *Scot*. & *dial*. L15–M19.
7 Justifiable grounds for an action, belief, or feeling. L16.

> **4** HOBBES That Assembly, which is without warrant from the Civil Soveraign, is unlawful. **5** SIR W. SCOTT Use axe and lever, Master Foster—I will be your warrant! **7** R. C. TRENCH There is no warrant for ascribing to them such treachery here.

▸**II** *spec*. A document.
8 A document issued by a monarch, an officer of State, or an administrative body, authorizing a particular action. Earliest as †***warrant dormant***. LME.

9 A writ or order issued by some authority, empowering a police or other officer to make an arrest, search premises, or carry out some other action relating to the administration of justice. LME.

10 A document authorizing payment of a sum of money; *spec.* a certificate entitling the holder to subscribe for shares of a company. LME.

†**11** A voucher, a certificate. LME–L16.

12 a = *warrant officer* below. E18. ▸**b** An official certificate of service rank issued to a warrant officer. L18.

13 A receipt given to a person who has deposited goods in a warehouse, by assignment of which the title to the goods is transferred. E19.

📖 **9** V. BRITTAIN Feeling as though I were signing the warrant for my own execution. R. HAYMAN The court where the warrant for his arrest had been issued.

Phrases: DIVIDEND **warrant**. **general warrant** a warrant for the arrest of the person or people suspected of an offence, no individual being named or described. †**of warrant** held in esteem, important. †**out of warrant** (*rare*, Shakes.) unlawful. ***royal warrant***: see ROYAL *adjective*. ***search warrant***: see SEARCH *noun*[1]. **warrant of attorney** (now *rare*) a legal document conferring authority to a person to act as one's representative in certain legal or business matters. **warrant of fitness** *NZ* a certificate of roadworthiness legally required for most motor vehicles in New Zealand and valid for six months. ***vouch to warrant***: see VOUCH *verb* 1.

Comb.: **warrant card** a document of authorization and identification carried by a police officer; **warrant chief** an African local official in Nigeria, formerly *esp.* one appointed by the colonial power; **warrant-officer** (*a*) an officer in certain armed services (formerly also in the Navy) who holds office by a warrant, ranking between a commissioned officer and an NCO; (*b*) an officer whose duty it is to serve warrants.

■ **warrantless** *adjective* (*a*) *rare* without justification, unwarrantable; (*b*) without judicial authorization; without a search warrant: M19.

warrant /ˈwɒr(ə)nt/ *noun*[2]. L19.
[Origin unkn.]
MINING. Underclay.

warrant /ˈwɒr(ə)nt/ *verb trans.* ME.
[Old French *warantir, warandir* vars. of *g(u)arantir, -andir* from Proto-Romance, from base of WARRANT *noun*[1].]

†**1** Keep safe from danger; protect (*from*). ME–L16.

2 a Guarantee as true; make oneself answerable for (a statement). Now chiefly in ***I warrant***, ***I'll warrant***, I am certain, I'll be bound. ME. ▸†**b** Promise or predict as certain. L16–E19.

3 LAW. **a** Guarantee the security of (land, possessions, etc.) *to* a person. Also (*gen.*), guarantee the safety or security of (a person or thing) *from*, †*for*, or *against* danger, harm, etc. LME. ▸**b** Give warranty of (title); give warranty of title to (a person). L15.

4 Guarantee (goods etc.) to be of the specified quality, quantity, etc. LME. ▸**b** Promise under guarantees. M19.

5 a Assure (a person) of a fact. Chiefly in ***I warrant you***, ***I'll warrant you***. E16. ▸**b** Provide (a person) with a formal guarantee, promise or assurance. Also with double obj. Now *rare*. M16.

6 Attest the truth of; authenticate. M16.

7 Grant (a person) authorization *to do* something; authorize, sanction, (a course of action). L16.

8 †**a** Justify by appeal to authority or evidence, find warrant for. E–M17. ▸**b** Of a thing: provide sufficient grounds for (a course of action); justify. M17. ▸**c** Justify (a person) in a course of action. L17.

9 Appoint (an officer) by a warrant. *rare*. M18.

📖 **2a** TENNYSON I warrant, man, that we shall bring you round. **3a** T. FULLER He had so cunningly contrived all his plots, as to warrant himself against all events. **4** L. M. MONTGOMERY It was warranted to dye any hair . . black and wouldn't wash off. **5a** SOUTHEY I'll warrant thee thou'lt drain His life-blood dry. **7** G. MACKENZIE Nor can the Council . . warrand any to do what would otherwise be a crime. **8b** A. J. AYER He thought that the evils of Nazism warranted armed resistance. D. MURPHY He judged our numerous discomforts too trivial to warrant . . expert attention.

warrantable /ˈwɒr(ə)ntəb(ə)l/ *adjective.* L16.
[from prec. + -ABLE.]

1 Of an action, thing, sentiment, etc.: that may be authorized, sanctioned, or permitted; justifiable. L16.

†**2** That may be guaranteed as good, true, etc.; praiseworthy, acceptable. L16–E19.

3 HUNTING. Of a stag: old enough to be hunted (5 or 6 years). L17.

4 That can be legally guaranteed. L19.

■ **warrantaˈbility** *noun* (earlier in UNWARRANTABILITY) L20. **warrantableness** *noun* L16. **warrantably** *adverb* E17.

warranted /ˈwɒr(ə)ntɪd/ *ppl adjective.* E17.
[formed as prec. + -ED[1].]

1 Permitted by law or authority; authorized, justified, sanctioned. E17.

2 Provided with a legal or official warrant; guaranteed; *spec.* (of an officer) holding a rank by warrant. M18.

¶ Earlier in UNWARRANTED.

warrantee /wɒr(ə)nˈtiː/ *noun.* M17.
[formed as prec. + -EE[1].]

1 A person who gives a guarantee; a warranty. M17.

2 LAW. A person to whom a warranty is given. E18.

warranter /ˈwɒr(ə)ntə/ *noun.* LME.
[formed as prec. + -ER[1].]

†**1** A person who assures another of safety; a protector. *rare*. LME–E19.

2 A person who assures, authorizes, or guarantees something. L16.

3 LAW. = WARRANTOR. E18.

warrantise /ˈwɒr(ə)ntʌɪz/ *noun.* Long *arch.* ME.
[Old French *warantise*, from *warantir* WARRANT *verb*: see -ISE[1]. Cf. WARRANDICE.]

1 LAW. = WARRANTY 1a. Chiefly in ***clause of warrantise***. ME.

2 a A person or thing serving as a guarantee or surety. ME. ▸**b** The action of warranting, guaranteeing, or giving assurance; the state or fact of being guaranteed. LME.

†**3** Defence, protection. *rare*. LME–L15.

4 Authorization, permission, sanction. L16.

†**5** Confidence, assurance. *rare*. L16–E17.

2b †**of warrantise**, †**on warrantise** for certain, without fail.

warrantor /ˈwɒr(ə)ntə/ *noun.* L17.
[from WARRANT *verb* + -OR.]
LAW. A person who gives a warranty.

warranty /ˈwɒr(ə)nti/ *noun.* ME.
[Anglo-Norman *warantie* var. of *garantie*: see GUARANTY.]

1 LAW. **a** A covenant annexed to a conveyance of real estate, by which the vendor warrants the security of the title conveyed. ME. ▸**b** An undertaking by one of the parties to a contract, breach of which entitles the innocent party to damages but not to terminate the contract; *esp.* a manufacturer's written promise as to the extent to which defective goods will be repaired, replaced, etc. LME. ▸**c** In an insurance contract, an engagement by the insured party that certain statements are true or that certain conditions shall be fulfilled, the breach of this engagement involving the invalidation of the policy. E19.

2 *gen.* A guarantee, an assurance. Now only *Scot. & dial.* M16.

3 Substantiating evidence. M16.

4 Formal or official sanction for a course of action etc.; authorization. Now *rare*. L16.

5 Justification; grounds *for* an action or belief. M19.

1a ***vouch to warranty***: see VOUCH *verb* 1.

Comb.: **warranty deed** LAW: containing a covenant of warranty.

†**warray** *verb trans. & intrans.* ME–M19.
[Old French *werreier* var. of *guerreier* (mod. *guerroyer*), from *guerre* WAR *noun*[1].]
Make war (on); carry out persecution (of).

warree /ˈwɒriː/ *noun.* Also **waree**. L17.
[App. from Spanish *jabalí* through Miskito.]
The white-lipped peccary, *Tayassu pecari*, of Central and S. America.

warren /ˈwɒr(ə)n/ *noun*[1]. LME.
[Anglo-Norman, Old Northern French *warenne* var. of Old & mod. French *garenne* game-park, now esp. rabbit warren, from a Gaulish base meaning 'post' (cf. Irish *farr* pillar, post) evidenced in Gaulish place-names.]

1 *Hist.* **a** A piece of land enclosed and preserved for breeding game. LME. ▸**b** The right to keep or hunt game. More fully ***free warren***. L15.

2 Orig., a piece of land set aside for the breeding of rabbits (formerly also of hares). Now usu., a piece of ground on which rabbits breed wild in burrows; a network of interconnecting rabbit burrows. More fully ***rabbit warren***. LME.

3 A number of a rabbits (formerly also hares) occupying a warren; *transf.* any collection of small animals. E17.

4 Orig. (*spec.*), a brothel. Later (*gen.*), any building or settlement compared to a rabbit warren, as a densely populated cluster of houses; any building or area characterized as a labyrinthine mass of passages and rooms. M17.

📖 **2** A. HIGGINS The rabbits were out of their warrens, feeding. **4** J. LE CARRÉ The warren of Dickensian corridors and crooked staircases.

Warren /ˈwɒr(ə)n/ *noun*[2]. M19.
[James *Warren* (fl. 1848), Brit. engineer.]
ENGINEERING. Used *attrib.* and (formerly) in *possess.* to designate a girder or truss composed of alternately inclined diagonal members joining two horizontal ones, forming a series of non-overlapping triangles pointing alternately up and down.

warrener /ˈwɒr(ə)nə/ *noun.* LME.
[Anglo-Norman *warener* (= Old Northern French *warennier*, Old & mod. French *garennier*), from *warenne* WARREN *noun*[1]: see -ER[2].]

1 *Hist.* **a** An officer employed to watch over the game in a park or preserve. LME. ▸**b** An officer or employee in charge of a rabbit warren. LME.

2 A person who owns or rents a rabbit warren. Now chiefly *Hist.* M19.

3 A rabbit occupying a warren. *rare*. M19.

warrer /ˈwɔːrə/ *noun.* ME.
[Anglo-Norman *werrour*, from *werrer* to war, from *werre* WAR *noun*[1], in later use from WAR *verb*[1] + -ER[1].]

†**1** A person who engages in warfare, a soldier, a warrior. Also, an antagonist, a persecutor. ME–L15.

2 A person who wars or contends against something. *rare*. M19.

warrigal /ˈwɒrɪg(ə)l/ *noun & adjective.* *Austral.* Also **warragal**. L18.
[Aboriginal *warregal, wor-re-gal, worrikul*, etc.]

▸ **A** *noun.* **1** = DINGO *noun* 1. L18.

2 = MYALL *noun*[1] 2. M19.

3 A wild or untamed horse. L19.

▸ **B** *adjective.* Wild, savage. M19.

Warrington /ˈwɒrɪŋtən/ *noun.* M20.
[A town in Cheshire.]
Used *attrib.* to designate a type of cross-peen joiner's hammer.

warrior /ˈwɒrɪə/ *noun & adjective.* ME.
[Old Northern French *werreior, werreieur* var. of Old French *guerreieor* (mod. *guerroyeur*), from *werreier, guerreier*: see WARRAY, -ER[2], -OR.]

▸ **A** *noun.* **1** A person whose occupation is warfare; a soldier, a member of an armed force. Now usu., a person experienced or distinguished in fighting, esp. of the ages celebrated in epic and romance or among primitive peoples; *fig.* a hardy, courageous, or aggressive person. ME. ▸**b** *transf.* An animal regarded as a brave fighter. L17.

2 In full ***bloody warrior***. The wallflower, *Erysimum cheiri*, *esp.* the dark red variety. *dial.* E19.

Phrases: ***bloody warrior***: see sense 2 above. ***cold warrior***: see COLD *adjective*. ***happy warrior***: see HAPPY *adjective*. ***Unknown Warrior***: see UNKNOWN *adjective*.

▸ **B** *attrib.* or as *adjective*. Of, pertaining to, or characteristic of a warrior; martial. M16.

■ **warriorism** *noun* L19. **warriorship** *noun* M19.

warrioress /ˈwɒrɪərɪs/ *noun.* L16.
[from prec. + -ESS[1].]
A female warrior.

warsle /ˈwɑːs(ə)l/ *verb & noun.* *Scot. & north.* LME.
[Metath. alt. of WRESTLE *verb, noun*.]

▸ **A** *verb.* **1 a** *verb intrans.* Wrestle (*with*), struggle. LME. ▸**b** *verb trans.* Wrestle with (an adversary). L18.

2 *verb intrans.* Move with difficulty; struggle *through*, *over*, etc. (*lit. & fig.*). L15. ▸**b** *verb trans.* Get (a thing) *on*, *out*, *up* with a struggle. L18.

▸ **B** *noun.* A struggle, a tussle (*lit. & fig.*); a wrestling bout. L18.

wart /wɔːt/ *noun.*
[Old English *wearte* corresp. to Old Frisian *warte, worte*, Old Saxon *warta*, Old High German *warza* (Dutch *wrat*, German *Warze*), Old Norse *varta*, from Germanic.]

1 MEDICINE. A small, benign, usu. hard excrescence on the skin; *esp.* infectious squamous papilloma, which is caused by a virus and is common in children; condyloma. Also called **verruca**. OE.

2 An unsightly protuberance; a disfiguring feature. E17.

3 ZOOLOGY & BOTANY. Any rounded excrescence on the skin of an animal or the surface of a plant. L18.

4 a A very young subaltern. *Military slang*. L19. ▸**b** An obnoxious or objectionable person. *colloq.* L19. ▸**c** A junior midshipman or naval cadet. *Nautical slang*. E20.

📖 **1a** ***soft wart***: see SOFT *adjective*. **2** C. GRAVES Betting shops, those terrible warts on the soul of Ireland. **warts and all** *colloq.* with no attempt to conceal blemishes, inadequacies, or unattractive features or qualities. **4b** A. MACRAE People . . think Karl's a little wart because he says what he thinks.

Comb.: **wart-biter** a large European bush-cricket, *Decticus verrucivorus*; **wart-cress** a small cruciferous plant with warty fruit, *Coronopus squamatus*, found in trampled ground; also called ***swine-cress***; **wart disease** a disease of potatoes caused by the fungus *Synchytrium endobioticum*, which produces warty outgrowths on the tubers; **warthog** a wild pig, *Phacochoerus aethiopicus*, which has pronounced warts on the face and bristly grey skin, and is common on the African savannah; **wart snake** any of various stout-bodied aquatic non-venomous snakes of the family Acrochordidae, which have coarse three-spined scales and are found in SE Asia and northern Australia; also called ***file snake***; **wartweed** any of several plants having an acrid milky juice reputed to cure warts; *esp.* sun spurge, *Euphorbia helioscopia*; **wartwort** = *wartweed* above.

■ **warted** *adjective* (*a*) covered with warts; (*b*) BOTANY & ZOOLOGY studded with wartlike knobs or excrescences; verrucose: E17. **wartless** *adjective* M19. **wartlike** *adjective* resembling (that of) a wart. L17.

warth /wɔːθ/ *noun. obsolete exc. dial.*
[Old English *waroþ* etc. corresp. to Middle Low German *werde, -er,* Old High German *werid* (German *Wert, Werder* island).]
A shore, a stretch of coast. Also, a flat meadow, *esp.* one close to a stream.

†**wartle** *noun.* L16–E18.
[Dim. of WART: see -LE[1].]
A swollen gland or ganglion in the neck or groin; *gen.* a lump.

warty /ˈwɔːti/ *adjective.* L15.
[from WART *noun* + -Y[1].]
1 Afflicted with warts on the skin. L15.
2 Rocky, rough. *rare.* M17.
3 ZOOLOGY & BOTANY. Having wartlike knobs or excrescences. L17.
4 Of the nature of, or resembling, a wart. M18.
3 warty newt = *crested newt* s.v. CRESTED 1.

wary /ˈwɛːri/ *adjective.* L15.
[from WARE *adjective* + -Y[1].]
1 Habitually on one's guard; cautious, careful, circumspect. (Foll. by †*in, of.*) L15.
2 Of action, behaviour, etc.: proceeding from or characterized by caution. L15.
†**3** Careful in expenditure, thrifty. E17–E19.

📖 **1** G. VIDAL He was a wary man, accustomed to disappointment. INA TAYLOR He . . was wary of enmeshing himself in another relationship. **2** T. HARDY With a wary grimness . . he evaded an answer.

■ **warily** *adverb* M16. **wariness** *noun* M16.

†**wary** *verb.*
[Old English *wierġan, wærġan* curse, corresp. to Old Saxon *waragean*, Old High German *gawergen*, Gothic *gawargjan* condemn, from Germanic, whence also Old English *wearg* felon.]
1 *verb trans.* Invoke a curse on. OE–M18. ▸**b** Of God, the Church, etc.: pronounce a formal curse against. LME–M16.
2 *verb trans.* Speak impiously or profanely against; blaspheme. OE–L15.
3 *verb trans.* Afflict with an evil regarded as the result of divine wrath or malignant fate. ME–L16.
4 *verb intrans.* Utter a curse or curses. ME–M18.

was /wɒz/ *noun.* ME.
[from *was* pa. t. sing. of BE *verb.*]
What was; something past.

was *verb* see BE *verb.*

wasabi /wəˈsɑːbi/ *noun.* E20.
[Japanese.]
A cruciferous plant, *Eutrema wasabi*, whose thick green root is used in Japanese cookery, usu. ground as an accompaniment to raw fish.

wase /weɪz/ *noun. obsolete* exc. *Scot. & dial.* ME.
[Perh. of Scandinavian origin (cf. Swedish, Danish, Norwegian *vase* bundle of straw, fascine).]
1 A bundle of straw or reeds, *esp.* one used as a torch. ME.
2 A pad of straw, cloth, etc., worn to relieve pressure when carrying a load on the head. M16.
3 A pad or washer used for sealing the joints of a pipe. M19.

wash /wɒʃ/ *noun.*
[Late Old English *(ġe)wæsc* corresp. to Old High German *wasga, wesga* (Middle High German *wasch(e), wesche,* German *Wäsch(e), Wasch*); later uses directly from the verb.]
▸**I 1** The action or an act of washing; the process of being washed. LOE. ▸**b** The action or an act of washing clothes etc.; *the* process of being washed or set aside or sent away for washing. Freq. in ***in the wash, at the wash***. E18. ▸**c** A quantity of clothes etc. set aside for washing or recently washed. L18.
2 A thin coat of paint, whitewash, etc., on a wall; a preparation used for this; a broad thin layer of watercolour laid on freely with the brush; *transf.* a broad area *of* a particular colour, light, shade, etc. L16.
3 (An application of) a liquid preparation used for cleansing, colouring, etc.; *spec.*: (**a**) a medicinal solution (freq. as 2nd elem. of comb.); (**b**) (now *Hist.*) a liquid cosmetic or hair preparation; (**c**) a liquid preparation used to protect plants against pests or disease; (**d**) a solution applied to metals to give the appearance of gold or silver; (**e**) PHOTOGRAPHY the liquid in which a newly developed photographic plate or print is washed. E17.

📖 **1** E. BLAIR She never failed to enjoy her wash at the baths. **wash and brush-up** a brief wash of one's face and hands and tidying of one's hair. **b** DICKENS The pocket-handkerchiefs . . . We've just looked 'em out, ready for the wash. S. CISNEROS The stream where the women do the wash. **come out in the wash** become known, be clarified; (of a situation, difficulty, etc.) be resolved or put right in due course. ***shrunk in the wash***: see SHRINK *verb.* **c** J. CHEEVER A laundry basket full of wash. **2** H. MOORE I used some of the cheap wax crayons . . in combination with a wash of watercolour. P. BARKER Rain had blurred the landscape, dissolving sky and hills together in a wash of grey. **black wash** (**a**) (now *rare*) a skin lotion; (**b**) a wash for colouring a surface black; (**c**) the blackening of someone's character, defamation; (**d**) *colloq.* a heavy defeat in a sporting contest etc., esp. one in which one fails to score. **3** ***eyewash, mouthwash***, etc.

▸**II 4** The washing or breaking of the waves on the seashore; a rush or surging movement of the sea or other water; the sound of this. LOE. ▸**b** Erosion due to wave action; the removal or displacement of soil by rain and running water. Freq. as 2nd elem. of comb. LOE. ▸**c** A swell caused by the passage of a vessel through water. Also, a current of air caused by the passage of an aircraft. L19.
5 a A sandbank, mud-flat, etc., alternately covered and exposed by the sea; part of an estuary able to be forded at low tide. LME. ▸**b** A low-lying tract of land, periodically flooded, and interspersed with shallow pools and marshes; an area of pasture etc. enclosed between banks and deliberately flooded in winter to contain the overflow of a river (cf. ***washland*** s.v. WASH-). L15. ▸**c** The dry bed of an intermittent stream. Also more fully ***dry-wash***. *US.* L19.
6 An expanse of shallow water, a lagoon. Also, a shallow pool or runnel formed by the overflow of a river; a flooded stretch of road. Now *local.* M16.

📖 **4** *Blackwood's Magazine* The wash of the swell on rocks met my ear. J. M. COETZEE In a wash of water driven through the windows by high winds lay broken furniture. *fig.*: A. SCHLEE The intimate wash of small sounds that are indecipherable in a strange place. **b** ***rain-wash, sheet-wash***, etc. **c** G. HUNTINGTON He had to manage the boat when the wash of the steamer caught it.

▸**III 7** A unit of measure used for weighing oysters and whelks. ME.
8 The blade of an oar. *rare.* M18.
9 The underground den of a beaver or a bear. E19.
10 = ***wash-sale*** s.v. WASH-. *Stock Exchange slang.* L19. ▸**b** A balanced outcome; a situation or result which is of no net benefit to either of two opposing sides, values, etc. *US colloq.* (orig. COMMERCE). L20.
▸**IV 11** Waste water discharged after use in washing; liquid refuse. Now *rare.* LME.
12 Kitchen slops and scraps or brewery refuse as food for pigs. Earliest as ***hogwash*** s.v. HOG *noun.* LME. ▸**b** *gen.* Liquid food for animals. M19.
13 Stale urine, as used as a detergent and a mordant. *Scot. & north.* L15.
14 Orig. (*rare*), vapid discourse. Later, insipid or weak liquor. M16.
15 Orig., the partially fermented wort remaining after beer has been brewed from it; this wort as subjected to further fermentation and used in the distillation of spirits. Later, malt etc. steeped in water to undergo fermentation preparatory to distillation. L17.
16 Nonsense, rubbish. *slang.* E20.
▸**V 17** Silt or gravel carried away by a stream and deposited as sediment; alluvial deposit. E18.
18 Soil from which gold or diamonds can be extracted by washing. L19.

wash /wɒʃ/ *adjective.* Now *rare* or *obsolete.* M16.
[Perh. from WASH *verb.*]
Washy, weak, insipid; tender.

wash /wɒʃ/ *verb.* Pa. pple **washed**, (now *arch. & dial.*) **washen** /ˈwɒʃ(ə)n/.
[Old English *wæsċan, wasċan, waxan* corresp. to Old Saxon *wascan* (Dutch *wassen*), Old High German *wascan* (German *waschen*), Old Norse *vaska* (weak), from Germanic, from base also of WATER *noun.*]
▸**I 1** *verb trans.* Remove the dirt from (something, as dirty clothes, dishes, etc.) by application of or immersion in liquid, esp. water, and usu. soap or detergent; clean with liquid. Also with adverbial obj. OE. ▸**b** *verb intrans.* Wash clothes etc., esp. as an occupation or as part of one's household duties. L16. ▸**c** *verb trans.* with adverbial obj. & *intrans.* Of fabric, dye, or a garment: withstand cleaning with soap and water without detrimental effects on colour or texture. M18. ▸**d** *verb trans.* Do the washing for (a person, esp. a lodger). *dial.* L18. ▸**e** *verb intrans.* Bear investigation, stand the test; prove to be convincing or genuine, be believed. Chiefly in ***(it) won't wash***. *colloq.* M19. ▸**f** *verb intrans.* Wash crockery, cutlery, etc., after use. See also ***wash up*** below. Also foll. by *up.* M20.
2 *verb trans.* Clean (oneself, a part of the body, etc.) with water and usu. soap; bathe (a cut or wound). Also, (of an animal, esp. a cat) clean (itself) by licking and rubbing with the paws. ME. ▸**b** *verb intrans.* Clean oneself, esp. one's face and hands; (of an animal, esp. a cat) clean itself by licking etc. ME. ▸**c** *verb trans. fig.* Purify (a person) from sin. Formerly also, bathe (a person) for symbolic purposes; baptize. ME. ▸**d** *verb trans.* Rinse (the mouth etc.) with water, a medicinal solution, etc. Freq. foll. by *out.* M16.
3 *verb trans.* Wet or moisten thoroughly; saturate or drench with water, dew, tears, etc. Chiefly *poet.* ME. ▸†**b** Moisten (the throat) with wine. LME–E17.
4 *verb trans.* Of the sea or a river: flow over or lap against (a shore or coast); beat or break on (walls, cliffs, etc.); touch (a town, country, etc.). Also, (of a river) flow through (a country). ME. ▸**b** *verb intrans.* Of waves: sweep *over* a surface; rush *in*; break or surge *against* (the shore etc.); make a rushing or splashing sound when breaking. L18.
5 *verb trans. & intrans.* Immerse (oneself, a person) in a river, pool, etc.; bathe. Long *rare.* LME.
†**6** *verb trans.* Sweat (gold or silver coin) by the application of acids. LME–E18.
7 *verb trans.* Brush a thin coat of watery paint over (a wall etc.); whitewash, colour-wash. Also, smear (a surface) with a thin coating of a liquid substance. E17. ▸**b** Coat (inferior metal) *with* a film of gold etc. deposited from a solution. L18.
8 *verb trans.* Cover (paper) with a broad thin layer of watercolour laid on freely with the brush; lay (colour) in washes; paint *in* (part of a picture) with a wash of colour. Also (*transf.*), appear to cover (any object or surface) with a broad area of a particular colour, light, shade, etc. E17.
9 *verb trans.* In the game of mah-jong, shuffle (the tiles). E20.

📖 **1** N. STREATFEILD I'll just wash your jersey through. *Cook's Magazine* Wash the spinach with the red roots attached. B. OKRI When the water drained away, the street was washed . . clean. E. O'BRIEN She . . goes to the sink to wash the glasses. **b** S. CISNEROS When you wash, it ain't enough to separate the clothes by temperature. **c** A. LURIE They chose sturdy, practical clothes that . . washed and wore well. **e** S. BELLOW I was tempted to believe that she didn't hear . . . But that didn't wash. **f** *Listener* Let's pack away the tea. I'll wash, you dry. **2** *Guardian* I washed my hands . . with soap and water. *transf.*: *Sunday Express* The fresh face of a Welsh schoolgirl washed clean by the rain. **b** A. BROOKNER I shall have to unpack and wash. **c** I. WATTS We are wash'd in Jesus' blood, We're pardon'd thro' his name. **d** J. T. STORY She . . tasted it, spat and washed her mouth out. **3** SHAKES. *Tam. Shr.* She looks as clear As morning roses newly wash'd with dew. **4** G. BORROW A small village, washed by the brook. J. L. WATEN The alcove . . was safe from the waves that occasionally washed the deck. **b** K. LINES Gigantic waves would wash over the earth. *transf.*: *Tennis* The applause washed over him as he left. **5** SHAKES. *A.Y.L.* He went but forth to wash him in the Hellespont. **7** W. COBBETT The windmills . . are all painted or washed white. **b** C. MCCULLOUGH A silver tea service and . . china cups washed with a delicate coating of gold leaf. **8** *Draw It! Paint It!* Wash in the shadows broadly. D. SIMPSON The trees . . washed with an . . eerie crimson glow from the setting sun.

▸**II 10** *verb trans.* Remove by washing. Also (*fig.*), remove (something regarded as a stain or taint, as sin, etc.). Usu. foll. by *away, out, off.* ME. ▸**b** *verb trans.* Blot out, obliterate, cancel. Usu. foll. by *away.* LME. ▸**c** *verb intrans.* Be removed by washing; (of dye or colouring matter) disappear when washed. Usu. foll. by *away, out, off.* M18.
11 *verb trans.* Of waves, running water, rain, etc.: remove, carry away; carry along in a specified direction. Freq. foll. by *away, down, off, out of,* etc. LME. ▸**b** *verb trans.* Separate (metallic particles) by treating metalliferous earth with water. Freq. foll. by *out.* M16. ▸**c** *verb trans. & intrans.* Agitate in water or pass flowing water through (metalliferous earth) so as to sift out the metallic particles. M16. ▸**d** *verb intrans.* Be removed or swept away by moving water; *esp.* (of soil etc.) be eroded, wear away by inundation. Usu. foll. by *away, down.* L16.
12 *verb trans.* **a** Of running water, rain, etc.: pass over (a surface) so as to carry off adherent or loose matter; erode. Also foll. by *out.* E16. ▸**b** Flush or drench (a substance) with water or other liquid in order to remove impurities or dissolve out a component. M17. ▸**c** Scoop out (a channel, depression, etc.) by water erosion. M18.
13 *verb trans.* Foll. by *down*: accompany or follow (food) with a drink, esp. to aid swallowing or digestion. E17.
14 *verb intrans.* Be tossed about, be carried or driven along, by waves or running water. Freq. foll. by *up, ashore,* etc. E17.
15 ROWING. **a** *verb trans.* Steer so as to impede (a competitor) by the wash of one's own boat. M19. ▸**b** *verb intrans.* Foll. by *out*: fail to lift out the blade of an oar squarely at the finish of a stroke. L19.

📖 **10** LD MACAULAY This merit was thought sufficient to wash out even the stain of his Saxon extraction. **c** *New Age Journal* Henna . . gives hair a semipermanent protein coating . . and it washes out gradually. **11** C. FRANCIS Sir Cloudesly's flagship . . was sunk and his body washed ashore. R. INGALLS Not even the rain could wash away the soot and . . grime. **d** W. COBBETT [The soil] . . does not wash away like sand or light loam. **12a** BYRON A pathway, which the torrent Hath wash'd since winter. **b** W. A. MILLER By washing the distilled liquid with water, the acetone . . may be removed. **13** B. TRAPIDO We ate kebabs . . and washed them down with beer. **14** *Sea Frontiers* World War II shells . . occasionally wash up on the beaches. *transf.*: *Times* There was a lot of confidence washing around in the computer business.

▸**III** *slang.* **16** *verb trans.* **a** PRINTING. Punish or tease (a fellow-worker) by hammering on his desk. Also, congratulate (an apprentice) on the end of his apprenticeship in a similar way. Now *rare* or *obsolete*. E19. ▸**b** Subject (stock) to a wash-sale. *Stock Exchange slang*. L19. ▸**c** Murder. Also foll. by *away*. M20. ▸**d** Launder (money). L20.

Phrases: **wash a person's head (without soap)** *slang* scold a person. **wash its face** *slang* (of an investment, enterprise, etc.) justify its cost, pay its way. †**wash one's brain**, **wash one's head** *joc.* drink alcohol. ***wash one's dirty linen in public***: see LINEN *noun* 1. **wash one's eyes** *arch. joc.* drink alcohol (as if to clear or sharpen the sight). **wash one's hands** *euphem.* go to the lavatory. **wash one's hands of** (orig. with allus. to *Matthew* 27:24) renounce responsibility for; refuse to have any further dealings with. ***wash one's head***: see ***wash one's brain*** above. **wash one's mouth out (with soap)** (now chiefly *fig.*) wash out the mouth as a punishment, esp. for swearing (usu. in *imper.*).

With adverbs & prepositions in specialized senses: **wash down** wash (esp. a large surface) completely; (see also sense 11, 11d, 13 above). **wash out** (*a*) clean the inside of (a thing) by washing; (*b*) rinse out (soap etc.) from clothes; (*c*) obliterate, cancel; (*d*) *colloq.* call off (an event) esp. due to rain; (*e*) *Air Force slang* kill (an airman) in a crash; crash (an aircraft); (*f*) fade in the wash; *fig.* become pale, lose all vitality; (*g*) *US* eliminate (esp. a student) as unsatisfactory or as failing to meet required standards; (*h*) *US* (esp. of a student) be eliminated as unsatisfactory, fail to meet required standards; (see also senses 2d, 10, 10c, 11, 12a, 15 b above). **wash up** (*a*) *verb phr. trans. & intrans.* wash (crockery, cutlery, etc.) after a meal; (*b*) *US slang* bring to a conclusion; end or finish (something); (*c*) *N. Amer.* have a wash, wash one's face and hands; (*d*) *verb phr. trans. & intrans.* retrieve (particles of gold) from the sluices etc. in which the particles have collected during washing.

wash- /wɒʃ/ *combining form*. OE.
[from WASH *noun*, *verb*.]
Forming nouns and adjectives with the senses 'of or pertaining to washing or a wash', 'used for washing'.

wash-and-wear *adjective* (of a garment or fabric) easily washed, drying readily, and not requiring to be ironed. **washbag** a small waterproof bag for holding toilet articles; a sponge bag. **wash-ball** (*a*) (now chiefly *Hist.*) a ball of soap used for washing the hands and face, and for shaving; (*b*) a hollow plastic ball which is filled with liquid detergent and placed in the drum of a washing machine together with the washing. **wash-basin** a basin for washing one's hands, face, etc. **wash-basket** (*a*) *US* a basket for holding a wash of oysters (see WASH *noun* 7); (*b*) a basket for holding washing. **wash-bottle** CHEMISTRY (*a*) a bottle containing liquid through which gases are passed for purification; (*b*) a bottle with a nozzle and either a mouthpiece or compressible sides, for directing a stream of liquid on to a substance or utensil to be washed. **wash-bowl** †(*a*) a washtub; (*b*) a wash-basin; (*c*) a pan for washing gold. **washbrew** *dial.* a dish made of boiled oatmeal; flummery. **wash-brush** a large paint-brush for laying on broad washes of colour. **washcloth** *N. Amer.* a face-cloth. **wash-coat** an undercoat of paint, *esp.* one for improving or preparing the surface rather than giving a colour. **washday** the day when the household washing is done. **wash-deck** *adjective* (NAUTICAL) used in or pertaining to the washing of a ship's deck. **wash-dirt** auriferous soil or gravel to be subjected to washing. **wash-dish** (*a*) *dial.* the pied wagtail; (*b*) *US* a wash-basin. **wash-fast** *adjective* able to be washed without fading or the dye running. **wash-kettle** *US* a kettle in which water is heated for washing. **washland** = WASH *noun* 5b. **wash-leather** *noun & adjective* (*a*) *noun* a soft kind of leather, usually of split sheepskin, dressed to imitate chamois leather and used for washing windows etc.; (*b*) *adjective* made of or resembling wash-leather. **wash-line** (chiefly *US*) a washing-line. **washman** (*a*) a washerman; (*b*) a workman employed in applying the wash or coating of tin in the manufacture of tinplate. **wash-off** *noun & adjective* (*a*) *noun* loose material that is washed off by running water; (*b*) *adjective* able to be washed off. **wash-pan** *US* a metal washing-bowl; a pan for washing ore. **wash-pen** *Austral.* & *NZ* a pen for holding sheep waiting to be washed. **washplain** a flat tract of land covered with alluvial deposits, washed by seasonally flooded streams. **wash-pool** (chiefly *Austral.*) a pool for washing sheep. **wash-pot** (*a*) (now *arch.* or *fig.* with allus. to *Psalms* 60:8) a vessel for washing one's hands; †(*b*) a servant employed to wash pots; (*c*) *US* a vessel in which to wash clothes etc. over a fire. **wash-primer** a wash coat for use on metallic surfaces. **washrag** *US* a face-cloth. **washroom** (chiefly *N. Amer.*) (*a*) a room with facilities for washing oneself; (*b*) a lavatory. **wash-sale** *Stock Exchange slang* a fictitious sale of securities by a broker who has corresponding commissions from an intending seller, and who instead of making separate transactions, makes a direct transfer from one account to the other, the difference going to his or her own profit (cf. WASH *noun* 10). **washstand** a piece of furniture designed to hold a basin, jug, soap, etc. **wash-table** (now *Hist.*) a table for holding a wash-basin and jug. **wash-trough** (*a*) a trough in which ore is washed; (*b*) a trough for washing the hands and face. **washtub** (*a*) a tub for washing clothes; (*b*) (in full ***washtub bass***) a washtub converted into a musical instrument like a double-bass by stretching a string across it. **wash-water** water for washing or that has been used for washing. **wash-way** (chiefly *dial.*) (*a*) a portion of a road crossed by a shallow stream; (*b*) a road with a concave surface. **wash-wipe** a vehicle's built-in window-cleaning system, comprising windscreen wipers and water bottle. **washwoman** (now *US*) a washerwoman.

Wash. *abbreviation*.
Washington.

washable /ˈwɒʃəb(ə)l/ *adjective & noun*. E17.
[from prec. + -ABLE.]
▸ **A** *adjective*. †**1** Able to be used for washing, with which one can wash. *rare*. Only in E17.
2 Able to be washed, esp. without damage. E19.

> 📖 **2** *Independent* The cushion has two washable covers.

▸ **B** *noun* in *pl.* Garments that may be washed without being damaged. M20.
■ **washaˈbility** *noun* L19.

washaway /ˈwɒʃəweɪ/ *noun*. Chiefly *Austral.* L19.
[from WASH *verb* + AWAY *adverb*.]
The removal by flood of a portion of a hillside; the destruction of part of a railway line or road by flood; a hole or breach produced by the washing away of soil. Cf. WASHOUT 3.

washboard /ˈwɒʃbɔːd/ *noun & adjective*. M18.
[from WASH- + BOARD *noun*.]
▸ **A** *noun*. **1** NAUTICAL. A board on the side of a boat, or the sill of a lower-deck port, to prevent the sea breaking over. M18.
2 Orig., a flat piece of wood fixed on an axis within the barrel of an early washing machine, and made to revolve so as to agitate the clothes in the water. Now (orig. *US*), a hardwood board, with a ribbed surface or covered with corrugated zinc, on which clothes are scrubbed in washing. L18. ▸**b** A washboard used mainly by skiffle bands as a percussion instrument and played with the fingers; the kind of music produced by bands using this instrument. E20.
3 A skirting-board. *dial.* E19.
4 A corrugated surface, esp. of a road. M20.

> 📖 **1** *Motor Boat & Yachting* The foredeck, including the washboard, has been restyled. **2b** *New Yorker* They . . played a washboard, a washtub bass, a banjo . . and a jawbone. **4** *California Bicyclist* After 16 miles of washboard to jumble our brains, the lead riders peeled off.

▸ **B** *attrib.* or as *adjective*. **1** Of a surface, esp. a road: corrugated, esp. as a result of weather and usage. E20.
2 Of or pertaining to the use of a washboard as a musical instrument. M20.

washdown /ˈwɒʃdaʊn/ *noun*. M20.
[from *wash down* s.v. WASH *verb*.]
The action or an act of washing something down; *spec.* an act of washing oneself completely at a wash-basin as distinct from in a bath or under a shower.

wash-drawing /ˈwɒʃdrɔː(r)ɪŋ/ *noun*. L19.
[from WASH *verb*, *noun* + DRAWING *noun*.]
The technique of producing a picture or sketch in which washes of watercolour are laid on over a pen or pencil drawing; a picture or sketch produced by this technique.

washed /wɒʃt/ *ppl adjective*. M16.
[from WASH *verb* + -ED[1].]
1 That has been washed; that has been swept *away* or scooped *out* by washing. M16. ▸**b** Of material etc.: faded, bleached; *spec.* (of a carpet) specially treated so as to soften the colours and impart a sheen. E20.
2 ***washed out***: ▸**a** Of a fabric, dye, etc.: that has faded in the wash. L18. ▸**b** *fig.* Pale; lacking in vitality. M19.
3 ***washed up***, ***all washed up***, finished; without prospects; having failed. (Foll. by *with*.) *slang* (chiefly *N. Amer.*). E20.

> 📖 **1** J. IMISON Adding . . one part of washed whiting to three parts of carmine. *Here's Health* Any vegetable offcuts may be used including washed peelings. **2a** E. JOLLEY Her washed-out dress looked mauve and silky. **b** N. MAILER She was looking tired, even washed out. **3** *Literary Review* His . . decline accelerated and he fell in with the . . view that he was a washed-up has-been.

¶ Earlier in UNWASHED.

washen /ˈwɒʃ(ə)n/ *ppl adjective*. *arch.* & *dial.* LME.
[Strong pa. pple of WASH *verb*: see -EN[6].]
Washed.

washen *verb* see WASH *verb*.

washer /ˈwɒʃə/ *noun*[1]. ME.
[from WASH *verb* + -ER[1].]
1 a The pied wagtail, *Motacilla alba*. ME. ▸**b** *N. Amer.* The racoon (which habitually washes its food). L19.
†**2** A person who sweats coin. LME–L18.
3 A person who washes something, esp. as an occupation. E16.
4 A cock or outlet valve of a water pipe. Also, the outlet valve of a basin, cistern, etc., to which the waste pipe is attached. L16.
5 An apparatus for washing as used in various industries or for various applications; a domestic washing machine; a dishwasher; a windscreen washer. Also as 2nd elem. of comb., as ***dishwasher***, ***windscreen-washer***, etc. E19.
6 A face-cloth. *Austral.* M20.
Comb.: **washer bottle** in a vehicle, a container holding the reservoir of water for the windscreen washer; **washer-drier** a machine that both washes clothes and dries them; **washerman** a man whose occupation is the washing of clothes; **washer-up** a person who washes up dishes etc., esp. as a job; **washer-upper** *colloq.* a washer-up; **washer-wife** *Scot.* a washerwoman.

washer /ˈwɒʃə/ *noun*[2] *& verb*. ME.
[Origin unkn.]
▸ **A** *noun*. **1** A perforated annular disc or flattened ring of metal, leather, etc., placed between two rotating surfaces to relieve friction and prevent lateral movement. ME.
2 A perforated metal disc or plate placed under a nut, head of a bolt, etc., to spread the load when tightened. E19.
3 An annular disc of leather, rubber, plastic or other compressible material placed between pipes, beneath the plunger of a tap, etc., to provide a seal. M19.
▸ **B** *verb trans.* Provide with a washer. M19.

washerette /wɒʃəˈrɛt/ *noun*. M20.
[from WASHER *noun*[1] + -ETTE.]
A launderette.

washerwoman /ˈwɒʃəwʊmən/ *noun*. Pl. **-women** /-wɪmɪn/. M17.
[from WASHER *noun*[1] + WOMAN *noun*.]
1 A woman whose occupation is washing clothes etc.; a person who takes in washing. *arch.* M17.
2 = WASHER *noun*[1] 1a. *dial.* E19.
Comb.: **washerwoman's fingers**, **washerwoman's hand** (now *rare*) a condition of the hands characteristic of cholera, resembling the wrinkling of the skin of the hands of washerwomen; **washerwoman's itch**, **washerwoman's scall** (now *rare*) a form of eczema or psoriasis affecting the hands of washerwomen; **washerwoman's skin** skin that is much wrinkled as a result of immersion in water.

washery /ˈwɒʃ(ə)ri/ *noun*. L19.
[from WASH- + -ERY.]
A place where coal, ore, wool, etc., is washed. Also (*rare*), a laundry.

washeteria /wɒʃəˈtɪərɪə/ *noun*. Orig. & chiefly *US*. M20.
[from WASH- after *cafeteria*.]
A launderette.
car washeteria a self-service car-wash.

wash-hand /ˈwɒʃhand/ *adjective*. M18.
[from WASH- + HAND *noun*.]
Intended for use in washing the hands and face. Only in comb. as below.
Comb.: **wash-hand basin** a wash-basin; **wash-hand stand** a washstand.

wash-house /ˈwɒʃhaʊs/ *noun*. OE.
[from WASH- + HOUSE *noun*[1].]
†**1** A bath-house. *rare*. OE–E18.
2 A building where clothes etc. are washed; *spec.* (*a*) an outhouse or room where domestic washing is done; (*b*) *US* a commercial laundry; (*c*) a public building provided with washing facilities. L16.

washi /ˈwaʃi/ *noun*. L20.
[Japanese.]
Japanese paper; *spec.* a thin handmade variety used to make lantern shades, kites, etc.

washin /ˈwɒʃɪn/ *noun*. Also **wash-in**. E20.
[from WASH *verb* + IN *adverb*, after WASHOUT.]
AERONAUTICS. An increase in the angle of incidence of an aeroplane wing towards the tip. Cf. WASHOUT 5.

washing /ˈwɒʃɪŋ/ *noun*. ME.
[from WASH *verb* + -ING[1].]
1 The action of WASH *verb*; an instance of this. Also foll. by *away*, *off*, *out*, *up*, etc. ME. ▸**b** *spec.* A ceremonial or religious ablution. LME.
2 a In *pl.* & †*sing.* The liquid that has been used to wash something; matter removed when something is washed. ME. ▸**b** In *pl.* Metal obtained by washing ore or metalliferous earth. E17. ▸**c** In *pl.* Matter carried away by rain or running water; alluvial deposit. E18. ▸**d** In *pl.* Places containing soil from which gold or diamonds are obtained by washing. M19.
3 Clothes etc. just washed or set aside for washing. ME.
†**4** A medical lotion. ME–M16.

> 📖 **1** W. MORRIS The wind . . Howled round about, with washing of the rain. **3** L. GRANT-ADAMSON He extricated his dirty washing and tossed it into the washing machine. **take in one another's washing** provide mutual help, esp. by buying one another's goods or services in transactions where no new wealth accrues overall.

Comb.: **washing bat** *Hist.* a wooden implement used to beat dirty washing after it had been soaked; **washing-bowl** †(*a*) a wash-basin; (*b*) (*obsolete* exc. *local*) a pan or tub for washing clothes etc.; **washing-day** = ***washday*** s.v. WASH-; **washing-house** a wash-house; **washing-line** a clothes-line; **washing machine** a machine for washing clothes and linen etc.; **washing-pan** a pan for washing ore, a wash-pan; **washing-place** (*a*) a place where washing is done; a laundry; (*b*) a place where gold is washed out from sand or earth; **washing-powder** powder of detergent or soap for washing clothes etc.; ***washing soda***: see SODA 1; **washing-stand** a washstand; **washing-stock** *Hist.* a wooden bench on which washing was beaten with a washing bat; **washing-stuff** *Austral. slang* auriferous earth; **washing-up** the process of washing crockery etc. after use; used dishes awaiting washing; ***washing-up liquid***, liquid detergent for washing up with.

washing /ˈwɒʃɪŋ/ *adjective.* M16.
[from WASH *verb* + -ING[2].]
1 That washes; *esp.* surging, overflowing, streaming with water. M16. ▸**b** Of a garment or fabric: washable. M16.
†**2** Of a blow: slashing, powerful. Cf. SWASHING 2. M16–E17.

Washington /ˈwɒʃɪŋtən/ *noun. US.* M19.
[George *Washington* (1732–99), first president of the United States, the US federal capital and seat of government (Washington DC), and a State in the north-western US.]
▸ **I** *attrib.* **1** Used to designate things named after or associated with Washington or the state of Washington. M19.
1 Washington clam a large edible clam, *Saxidomus nuttalli*, found off the coasts of south-western N. America. **Washington lily** a tall lily, *Lilium washingtonianum*, with fragrant pure white flowers, found in the mountains of California and Oregon. **Washington pie** a light cake made of sponge layers with a jam or filling.
▸ **II 2** *fig.* The US government or any of its departments. E20.
■ **Washingtoˈnologist** *noun* a person who studies or is an expert in the workings of the US government etc. M20.

Washingtonia /wɒʃɪŋˈtəʊnɪə/ *noun.* M20.
[mod. Latin (see below), from George *Washington*: see prec., -IA[1].]
Either of two fan palms constituting the genus *Washingtonia*, *W. filifera* and *W. robusta*, natives of California, Arizona, and Mexico and planted as street trees.

Washingtonian /wɒʃɪŋˈtəʊnɪən/ *noun & adjective.* L18.
[from WASHINGTON + -IAN.]
▸ **A** *noun.* **1** *Hist.* A supporter or admirer of George Washington and his political standpoint. L18.
2 *Hist.* A member of an American temperance society founded in 1840. M19.
3 A native or inhabitant of Washington DC or of the State of Washington. M19.
▸ **B** *adjective.* **1** Of, pertaining to, or characteristic of George Washington or his politics. E19.
2 Of or pertaining to the Washingtonian Temperance Society or the practice of temperance that it advocated. M19.
3 Of, pertaining to, or characteristic of an inhabitant of Washington DC or the State of Washington. M20.

Washita /ˈwɒʃɪtɔː/ *noun.* M19.
[Ouachita or *Washita* Mountains in Arkansas, USA.]
Washita stone, ***Washita oilstone***, a porous variety of novaculite used for sharpening cutting tools.

Washo /ˈwɒʃəʊ, -ʃuː/ *noun & adjective.* Also **-oe**. M19.
[Washo *ˈwášiw*.]
▸ **A** *noun.* Pl. same, **-s**.
1 A member of a N. American Indian people inhabiting the area around Lake Tahoe on the border of California and Nevada. M19.
2 The Hokan language of this people. L19.
▸ **B** *attrib.* or as *adjective.* Of or pertaining to the Washo or their language. M19.
Washo canary *US colloq.* a burro. **Washo zephyr** a strong west wind that blows in Nevada.

washout /ˈwɒʃaʊt/ *noun.* Also **wash-out**. L19.
[from *wash out* s.v. WASH *verb.*]
1 An act of washing out something; *spec.* (**a**) the washing out of a cistern etc.; a pipe or other appliance for doing this; (**b**) BIOLOGY & MEDICINE the removal of material, esp. from a physiological system, by means of a fluid; the fluid used for, or matter removed by, this; (**c**) METEOROLOGY the removal of particles from the air by falling water droplets. L19.
2 GEOLOGY. A narrow channel cut into a sedimentary deposit by swiftly flowing water; *esp.* one that is later filled by younger sediments; *spec.* in MINING, a channel cut into a coal deposit during its formation and replaced with sandstone etc. L19.
3 The removal by flood of a portion of a hillside; a hole or breach in a railway or road caused by flood or erosion. Cf. WASHAWAY. Orig. *US.* L19.
4 a A complete failure, something disappointingly bad. *colloq.* E20. ▸**b** A useless or unsuccessful person (*colloq.*); *spec.* (*Air Force slang*) a person who is eliminated from a course of training. E20. ▸**c** A wrecked aircraft. *Air Force slang.* E20.
5 AERONAUTICS. A decrease in the angle of incidence of an aeroplane wing towards the tip. Cf. WASHIN. E20.

📖 **3** S. BURNFORD The road was pure sand and treacherous with spring washouts. **4a** *Atlantic* Illogical, unmotivated, the new happy ending is, as narrative, a total washout. **b** K. AMIS I'm such a washout I couldn't be trusted to boil an egg.

wash-up /ˈwɒʃʌp/ *noun.* M19.
[from *wash up* s.v. WASH *verb.*]
1 An act of washing crockery etc. after use; *rare* a place where this is done, a scullery. M19. ▸**b** A person employed to wash dishes in a restaurant, hotel, etc. *colloq.* L20.
2 An act of washing oneself, a wash. *N. Amer.* L19.
3 MINING. The washing of a collected quantity of ore; the quantity of gold obtained by washing. L19.
4 A dead body washed up by the sea. *rare.* E20.
5 A follow-up discussion or debriefing. Also, an outcome. *colloq.* (orig. NAUTICAL). M20.

washy /ˈwɒʃi/ *adjective.* M16.
[from WASH *noun*, *verb* + -Y[1]. Cf. WISHY-WASHY.]
†**1** Having too much moisture, waterlogged. Also, (of wind or weather) moisture-laden, bringing rain. M16–M18.
2 a Of food, drink, etc.: too diluted; weak, sloppy, watery. E17. ▸**b** Of literary style, a person's opinions or remarks, etc.: lacking force or vigour, feeble, insipid. E19.
3 Of the stomach: having an accumulation of liquid and undigested food. *rare.* E17.
4 Of colour, painting, etc.: thinly or loosely applied; lacking strength or intensity; pale. M17.
5 Of a horse or cow: poor in quality or condition, *esp.* liable to sweat or have diarrhoea after slight exertion. M17.
6 Of a person: lacking strength or stamina; weak, ineffectual, feeble; exhausted, washed-out. Now *rare* exc. in WISHY-WASHY. M17.

📖 **2b** M. O. W. OLIPHANT The publication . . was a weak and washy production. **4** G. ALLEN Blue eyes . . look so mild and gentle and washy. P. BENSON The canvas was covered with thin lines of . . brown paint beneath a big washy block of blue. **6** S. GIBBONS Nice-looking boy but a bit washy, thought Reenie.

■ **washiness** *noun* M17.

wasm /ˈwɒz(ə)m/ *noun. joc.* M20.
[Blend of WAS *verb* and ISM *noun.*]
An 'ism' that has gone out of fashion; an obsolete or obsolescent belief, doctrine, or theory.

wasn't *verb* see BE *verb.*

wasp /wɒsp/ *noun*[1]. Also (now *dial.* & *joc.*) **wops** /wɒps/.
[Old English *wæsp*, *wæps*, *wæfs*, corresp. to Old Saxon *wepsia*, *wespa*, *wasp*, Old High German *wafsa*, *wefsa* (German *Wespe*), Middle Low German *wepse*, *wespe*, from West Germanic, from Indo-European base meaning WEAVE *verb*[1], with ref. to the construction of the paper nest.]
1 A stinging hymenopterous social insect of the genus *Vespula* and related genera of the family Vespidae, which usu. have yellow black-banded bodies, feed on other insects and sweet materials, and construct a nest made of paper; a colony consists of several perfect females (queens) and males, and numerous sterile females (workers). Also in ENTOMOLOGY, any of numerous solitary and parasitic hymenopterous insects mainly of the suborder Apocrita, other than the bees and ants (usu. with specifying word). OE.
2 *fig.* **a** A person characterized by irascibility and persistent petty malignity; *esp.* (in *pl.*) a multitude of irritating critics or attackers. E16. ▸**b** A thing that irritates or offends. L16.
3 In full ***wasp-fly***. A kind of artificial fly for salmon-fishing made to imitate the appearance of a wasp. L17.

📖 **1** ***cuckoo wasp***, ***gall wasp***, ***mason wasp***, ***potter wasp***, ***wood-wasp***, etc. ***SEA wasp***. **2a** N. AMHURST I had no sooner undertaken this task, but I raised a nest of holy wasps . . about my ears.

Comb.: **wasp beetle** a European longhorn beetle, *Clytus arietis*, which resembles a wasp in appearance and behaviour; **wasp-fly** (**a**) any hoverfly which resembles a wasp; (**b**) see sense 3 above; **wasp-paper** the thin dry material of which wasps' nests are made, produced by the mastication of wood; **wasp's nest** (**a**) the nest of a wasp; (**b**) *fig.* a difficult, unpleasant, or troublesome situation, place, etc.; †**wasp-stung** *adjective* (*rare*, Shakes.) irritable (as if stung by a wasp); **wasp-waist** a very slender waist, esp. one accentuated from wearing a tight corset; **wasp-waisted** *adjective* having a very slender waist, esp. as the result of wearing a tight corset.
■ **wasplike** *adjective* resembling (that of) a wasp M17.

Wasp /wɒsp/ *noun*[2]. Chiefly *N. Amer.* Freq. *derog.* Also **WASP**. M20.
[from White Anglo-Saxon Protestant.]
A member of the American white Protestant middle or upper class descended from early northern European settlers.

📖 *attrib.*: R. JAFFE The leading prestigious Wasp law firm in New York.

■ **Waspdom** *noun* the sphere or beliefs of Wasps; Wasps collectively: M20.

wasp /wɒsp/ *verb.* M19.
[from WASP *noun*[1].]
1 *verb trans.* Sting as a wasp does. *rare.* M19.
2 *verb intrans.* Foll. by *around*, *about*: dart about in the manner of a wasp, in an irritating, noisy, or persistent fashion. M20.

waspie /ˈwɒspi/ *noun.* M20.
[from WASP *noun*[1] + -IE.]
A woman's corset designed to accentuate the slenderness of the waist; a belt of similar design.

waspish /ˈwɒspɪʃ/ *adjective*[1]. M16.
[from WASP *noun*[1] + -ISH[1].]
1 Quick to resent any petty affront; irritable, touchy, petulantly spiteful; given to making pointed or spiteful remarks. M16.
2 Of, pertaining to, or resembling a wasp or some characteristic of one. L16.

📖 **1** SOUTHEY So bad a judgement and so waspish a temper. B. LEIGH The dancers . . brought . . whispers of waspish dressing-room tiffs and wretchedness.

■ **waspishly** *adverb* L17. **waspishness** *noun* L16.

Waspish /ˈwɒspɪʃ/ *adjective*[2]. Chiefly *N. Amer.* Freq. *derog.* Also **WASPish**. M20.
[from WASP *noun*[2] + -ISH[1].]
Of, pertaining to, or characteristic of an American Wasp.

📖 L. ELLMANN She held tentative WASPish prejudices . . . such as her deep ignorance of the working class.

waspy /ˈwɒspi/ *noun.* Long *obsolete* exc. *dial.* E16.
[from WASP *noun*[1] + -Y[6].]
A wasp.

waspy /ˈwɒspi/ *adjective*[1]. M17.
[from WASP *noun*[1] + -Y[1].]
1 Resembling a wasp in shape, wasplike. M17.
2 Full of wasps. L17.
■ **waspily** *adverb*[1] (*rare*) waspishly M19.

Waspy /ˈwɒspi/ *adjective*[2]. Chiefly *N. Amer.* Freq. *derog.* Also **WASPy**. M20.
[from WASP *noun*[2] + -Y[1].]
= WASPISH *adjective*[2].
■ **Waspily** *adverb*[2] L20. **Waspiness** *noun* L20.

wassail /ˈwɒseɪl, ˈwɒs(ə)l, ˈwas(ə)l/ *noun & verb.* Now *arch.* or *Hist.* ME.
[Old Norse *ves heill* be in good health, corresp. to Old English *wes hāl*: see HALE *adjective.*]
▸ **A** *noun.* **1** A salutation used when presenting a cup of wine to a guest, or a toast used to drink a person's health, a customary pledge in early English times (cf. ***drink hail*** s.v. DRINK *verb*). ME.
2 The liquor in which healths were drunk; *esp.* the spiced ale or mulled wine drunk during celebrations for Twelfth Night and Christmas Eve. ME.
†**3** A custom observed on Twelfth Night and New Year's Eve of drinking healths from the wassail-bowl. L16–M17.
4 A drinking-bout; riotous festivity, revelling. E17.
5 The custom of going from house to house at Christmas time singing carols or songs; a carol or song sung by wassailers. *rare.* E17.
Comb.: **wassail-bowl**, **wassail-cup** a large bowl or cup in which wassail was made and from which healths were drunk; the liquor contained in the bowl.
▸ **B** *verb.* **1** *verb intrans.* Make merry; sit carousing and drinking toasts. ME.
2 *verb trans.* Drink to (fruit trees or cattle) in a custom intended to ensure vigorous growth. *local.* M17.
3 *verb intrans.* Go from house to house at Christmas time singing carols and songs. Chiefly as ***wassailing*** *verbal noun.* M18.
■ **wassailer** *noun* (**a**) a person who takes part in riotous festivities; a reveller; (**b**) a person who goes from house to house singing carols etc.: M17.

wassell *noun* var. of WASTEL.

wasser /ˈwɒzə/ *noun. colloq.* E20.
[from WAS *verb* + -ER[1].]
= HAS-BEEN.

†**wasserman** *noun. rare* (Spenser). Only in L16.
[German *Wassermann* lit. 'water man'.]
A mythical sea-monster partly in the form of a man, supposed to destroy ships.

Wassermann /ˈwɒsəmən, *foreign* ˈvasərman/ *noun.* E20.
[August Paul *Wassermann* (1866–1925), German bacteriologist.]
MEDICINE. Used *attrib.* and *absol.* with ref. to a test for syphilis in which antibodies to the pathogen are detected by a complement-fixation test.

wast *verb* see BE *verb.*

wastable /ˈweɪstəb(ə)l/ *adjective.* LME.
[from WASTE *verb* + -ABLE.]
That may be wasted; subject to wastage. Also *spec.* (LAW), (of a thing) in respect of which a tenant may be chargeable with waste.

wastage /ˈweɪstɪdʒ/ *noun.* M17.
[from WASTE *verb* + -AGE.]
1 A ruined or deserted place; (a piece of) waste ground. *Scot.* M17.
2 a Loss incurred by wastefulness; the action of using something wastefully. L17. ▸**b** Loss or diminution by

For other words beginning with *wash-* see the entry for **wash-**

use, decay, erosion, leakage, damage or theft of stock, etc. M18. ▸**c** The action of laying land waste. E20. ▸**d** More fully ***natural wastage***. The loss of students through failure to complete a course; the loss of employees other than by redundancy (esp. by retirement or resignation). E20.

3 Waste material. L19.

waste /weɪst/ *noun & adjective*. ME.
[Old Northern French *wast(e)* var. of Old French *guast(e)*, *gast(e)*, partly repr. Latin (*vastum* neut. of) *vastus* waste, desert, partly from the verb.]

▸ **A** *noun*. **I** Waste land.

1 (An) uninhabited or sparsely inhabited and uncultivated country; (a) desert, (a) wilderness. Now chiefly *rhet.* ME. ▸**b** A vast expanse of water, snow-covered land, etc. Chiefly *literary*. M16.

2 A piece of land not cultivated or used for any purpose, and supporting few or no plants useful for pasture or wood; *spec.* in LAW, a piece of common land of this nature. Now *rare* exc. *dial.* & in LAW. LME.

3 A devastated region; a place that has been laid waste. E17.

4 MINING. A disused working; a part of a mine from which the coal etc. has been extracted. L17.

> 📖 **1** A. MOOREHEAD We ascended Mount Hopeless, . . nothing but an endless waste of barren rock. **b** SIR W. SCOTT Broad black raindrops mingle with the waste of waters. *fig.*: DICKENS Miss Brass . . brought . . a dreary waste of cold potatoes, looking as eatable as Stonehenge.

▸ **II** The action or process of wasting.

5 Useless expenditure or consumption; extravagant or ineffectual use (*of* money, goods, time, effort, etc.). Also, an instance of this. ME. ▸**b** A profusion, a lavish abundance *of* something. E18.

6 LAW. Damage (or occas. simply alteration) to an estate caused by neglect or unauthorized action, esp. by a life tenant. LME.

7 Gradual loss or diminution from use, wear and tear, decay or natural process. Now *rare*. LME. ▸**b** A wasting of the body by disease; a decline in health. Now *dial.* L16.

8 The consumption or using up of material, resources, time, etc. (orig. *spec.* of candles etc. at a funeral or memorial). Long *obsolete* exc. as passing into sense 5. L15.

9 Destruction or devastation caused by war, floods, fire, etc. Now *rare*. L15. ▸†**b** In *pl.* Ravages. E17–M18.

> 📖 **5** A. LURIE It's a waste of time talking to someone who does nothing but lie. J. G. FLEMING Separate litigation . . entails enormous waste of resources.

▸ **III 10** Waste matter, refuse; unusable material left over from a process of manufacture, the use of consumer goods, etc.; the useless by-products of a process; material or manufactured articles so damaged as to be useless or unsaleable. Also *spec.*, surplus or spoiled sheets produced in printing; *ellipt.* cotton waste, rock waste, etc. LME.

11 Orig., an overflow of surplus water. Now usu. *spec.*, waste water, effluent, esp. when free of excrement (cf. SOIL *noun*[2] 5a). L16. ▸**b** A pipe, drain, etc., for carrying off waste matter or surplus water, steam, etc. Cf. ***waste pipe*** below. M17.

> 📖 **10** *Independent* An alternative to the . . practice of dumping waste in old mineral workings. ***cotton waste***, ***industrial waste***, ***nuclear waste***, ***radioactive waste***, ***rock waste***, ***silk waste***, ***trade waste***, etc. **11b** *Do-It-Yourself* Draw a scale plan of your bathroom and mark all supplies and wastes on it.

▸ **B** *adjective*. **1** Of land: uncultivated and uninhabited or sparsely inhabited; not applied to any purpose, not used for cultivation or building. Also, unfit for cultivation, uninhabitable, barren, desert. ME.

†**2** That has been laid waste; devastated, ruinous. ME–E19.

†**3** Of speech, thought, or action: profitless, serving no purpose, idle, vain. ME–L16.

†**4** Void, destitute *of*. *Scot.* LME–L16.

†**5** Superfluous, needless. LME–E17.

†**6** Of time, leaves in a book: spare, unoccupied, unused. Of a building or room: unoccupied, empty. L16–M18.

7 Of a material, a by-product, etc.: eliminated or thrown aside as worthless after the completion of a process; refuse. Also PHYSIOLOGY, eliminated from the body as excreta. M19. ▸**b** Of a manufactured article: rejected as defective. Also, (e.g. of sheets of a printed book) produced in excess of what can be used. M19.

> 📖 **1** M. SINCLAIR The waste ground covered with old boots and rusted . . tins. **7** ***waste material***, ***waste product***, etc.

Phrases: **go to waste** be wasted. ***impeachment of waste***: see IMPEACHMENT 3b. **lay waste** devastate, ravage (occas. foll. by *to*). **lie waste** remain in an uncultivated or desert condition. **run to waste** (of liquid) flow away so as to be wasted; *fig.* (of wealth, powers, etc.) be expended uselessly.

Comb. & special collocations: **waste-basket** *noun & verb* (now chiefly *N. Amer.*) (*a*) *noun* = ***waste-paper basket*** below; (*b*) *verb trans.* put in a waste-paper basket; **waste-bin** a dustbin; a rubbish bin; a bin for waste-paper, food scraps, or other waste; **waste-book** COMMERCE a rough account-book in which entries are made of all transactions as they occur, to be copied formally afterwards; **waste-cock** a cock or tap to regulate the discharge of waste water; **waste disposal unit** a mechanical device (usu. electrically powered) set at the top of a waste pipe for grinding kitchen waste into small fragments; **waste-disposer** = ***waste disposal unit*** above; **waste-gate** (*a*) a gate for regulating the outflow of waste water; (*b*) ENGINEERING a device in a turbocharger which regulates the pressure at which exhaust gases pass to the turbine by opening or closing a vent to the exterior; **waste-heap** (*a*) a pile of refuse; (*b*) CARDS a pile of cards formed during a game from those which are not wanted or cannot be played; **waste heat** heat produced as the by-product of some process; ***waste-heat boiler***, a boiler employing this; **waste mould** SCULPTURE a simple negative mould which has to be broken or chipped away to free the cast inside; **waste moulding** a moulding made using a waste mould; **waste paper** (*a*) paper put aside as spoiled, superfluous, or useless for its original purpose; †(*b*) blank or unused paper; **waste-paper basket** a basket into which waste paper is thrown; **waste-pile** = ***waste-heap*** above; **waste pipe** a pipe to carry off waste water or steam; *spec.* a pipe for the drainage of dirty water from a sink, bath, etc. (in contrast to a soil-pipe); **waste plug** (*a*) a plug used to stop up a waste pipe temporarily; †(*b*) = PLUG *noun* 1b; **waste products** useless by-products of a manufacturing process or of an organism's metabolic processes; **waste silk** silk waste, inferior silk from the outer part of the cocoons; **waste water**, **wastewater** (*a*) superfluous water, or water that has served its purpose, allowed to run away; (*b*) water that has been used in some industrial process; (*c*) sewage; **waste-way** *US* a channel for the passage of waste or surplus water; **waste-weir** a weir allowing the overflow of surplus water from a canal or reservoir.

■ **wasteless** *adjective* without diminution, unwasting L16. **wasteness** *noun* (*a*) the state of lying waste; barrenness; *arch.* destruction; (*b*) (*obsolete* exc. *dial.*) an uninhabited or unfrequented region or place: LME.

waste /weɪst/ *verb*. ME.
[Old Northern French *waster* var. of *g(u)aster* from Proto-Romance from Latin *vastare*, from *vastus*: see prec.]

▸ **I** *verb trans.* **1** Lay waste, devastate, ravage, ruin, (a place, its inhabitants, property, etc.). Now *literary*. ME.

2 Consume, use up, wear away, diminish or reduce (a thing) by gradual loss. Also foll. by *away*. *obsolete* exc. as passing into sense 5. ME.

3 Consume or destroy (a person or living creature, the body, the strength, etc.) by decay, disease, or atrophy; emaciate, enfeeble. Also foll. by *away*, †*up*. Freq. as ***wasted*** *ppl adjective*. ME.

†**4** Destroy, annihilate, put an end to (something immaterial, e.g. sin, sorrow). Also foll. by *away*. ME–L17.

5 a Consume or expend (money, property) uselessly, extravagantly, or to no profit; squander. Freq. foll. by *in*, *on*, †*away*. ME. ▸**b** Spend, pass, occupy (time, one's life, etc.) idly or unprofitably; employ or expend (energy, effort, qualities, one's self, etc.) uselessly or without adequate return. Freq. foll. by *in* (an activity), *on* or *over* (an activity, a person), and formerly with inf. ME. ▸**c** Bestow or expend (something) *on* an unappreciative recipient. Also in *pass.*, fail to be appreciated; make no impression *on* a person; (of a person, a person's qualities or abilities) have no opportunity for distinction or usefulness. M18. ▸**d** Cause or allow (a substance, energy, etc.) to be used unprofitably or lost. E19. ▸**e** Fail to take advantage of, throw away, (an opportunity). M19.

6 LAW. Destroy, injure, damage, (property); cause to deteriorate in value; allow to fall into decay. Now *rare*. LME.

†**7** Spend, part with, diminish one's store of, (money, property); spend, pass, occupy, (time); get over (a distance in travelling). LME–M18.

8 Spoil, cause to deteriorate. Long *obsolete* exc. *dial.* L16.

†**9** Diminish or consume the livelihood of, impoverish, (a person); *refl.* impoverish oneself. L16–E18.

10 Treat (material, esp. paper or books) as waste. L19.

11 Beat up, kill, murder, (someone); devastate (a place). *slang* (chiefly *N. Amer.*). M20.

> 📖 **3** M. PUZO He was wasted away to no more than a skeleton. **5a** AV *Luke* 15:13 The younger sonne . . wasted his substance with riotous liuing. F. KING What is the point of wasting money at expensive restaurants? **b** E. M. FORSTER Pray don't waste time mourning over me. E. WAUGH The . . day was wasted on a visit to a house . . which was entirely unsuitable. ***waste words***: see WORD *noun*. ***waste BREATH***. **c** U. HOLDEN Further school education would be wasted on her. **d** J. TYNDALL A considerable portion of the heat . . is wasted by radiation. **7** SHAKES. *Merch. V.* Companions That do converse and waste the time together. **11** C. WESTON They wasted Barrett because he blew their deal.

▸ **II** *verb intrans.* **12** Lose strength, health, or vitality; lose flesh or substance, pine, decay; become gradually weak or enfeebled. Freq. foll. by *away*. ME. ▸**b** SPORT. Esp. of a jockey: lose weight by dieting and training. M18.

13 Be used up or worn away; be diminished or decreased by gradual loss, wear, or decay. Now *literary*. LME.

14 Of time: pass away, be spent. Also foll. by *away*. Now chiefly *literary*. LME.

> 📖 **12** A. KENNY Watching an invalid waste away at home. **13** J. PALSGRAVE All thyng wasteth but the grace of God. **wasting asset** COMMERCE an asset which gradually diminishes while producing income. **14** M. TWAIN The afternoon wasted away.

■ **wastingly** *adverb* (*rare*) in a wasting manner, wastefully, so as to waste something M16.

wasted /ˈweɪstɪd/ *adjective*. LME.
[from prec. + -ED[1].]

1 That has been wasted; expended or consumed uselessly or unprofitably; emaciated, enfeebled. LME.

2 Under the influence or suffering the after-effects of drink or drugs; drunk, stoned. *slang* (chiefly *N. Amer.* & *Austral.*). M20.

> 📖 **2** N. BLINCOE He knew Sunday was the last chance to get really wasted before work started again.

wasteful /ˈweɪstfʊl, -f(ə)l/ *adjective*. ME.
[from WASTE *noun* + -FUL.]

1 That causes devastation, desolation, or ruin; that destroys or lays waste something. Now *rare* or *obsolete* exc. as passing into sense 5. ME.

†**2** Useless, worthless; unused; (of desires, words, etc.) empty, profitless; (of time) unoccupied, spare. LME–L16.

3 Of a person, a style of living, etc.: given to or characterized by waste or useless or excessive expenditure; uneconomical, extravagant. Cf. WASTY 1. LME.

4 Of a place: desolate, unfrequented, uninhabited. Now *arch. poet.* LME.

5 Of a person, an action, a process, etc.: that wastes, consumes, or expends unprofitably something specified or implied; not economical. (Foll. by *of*.) LME.

6 That causes bodily wasting or emaciation. Now *rare*. E17.

■ **wastefully** *adverb* LME. **wastefulness** *noun* L15.

wastel /ˈwɒst(ə)l/ *noun*. *obsolete* exc. *Hist.* Also **wassell** /ˈwɒs(ə)l/. ME.
[Old Northern French var. of Old French *guastel* (mod. *gâteau* cake), prob. of Germanic origin.]

1 Bread made of the finest flour; a cake or loaf of this. Also ***wastel-bread***, ***wastel cake***. ME.

2 HERALDRY. = TORTEAU. *rare*. L15.

wasteland /ˈweɪs(t)land, -lənd/ *noun*. M19.
[from WASTE *adjective* + LAND *noun*[1].]

1 a (A piece of) land in its natural uncultivated state. Also, (a) waterless or treeless desert. M19. ▸**b** (A piece of) land, esp. surrounded by developed land, unused or unfit for cultivation or building. E20.

2 *fig.* A place, time, situation, etc., regarded as spiritually or intellectually barren. M19.

3 (A piece of) land in public ownership. *NZ*. M19.

> 📖 **1b** L. NKOSI Traversing a wasteland of sand, rock, and heaps of industrial rubble. **2** *Opera Now* Demolish the image abroad of Australia as a cultural wasteland.

waster /ˈweɪstə/ *noun*. LME.
[Anglo-Norman *wastere*, *wastour*, from *waster* WASTE *verb* (see -ER[2]), coalesced with later formation on WASTE *verb* + -ER[1].]

1 A person who lives in idleness and extravagance; a person who wastes resources, an extravagant spender, a squanderer, a spendthrift. Now also (*colloq.*), a worthless person, an idler (cf. WASTREL *noun* 3). LME. ▸**b** A person who wastefully expends or consumes something specified. Foll. by *of*. LME.

2 A person who lays waste, despoils, or plunders a place etc.; a ravager, a plunderer. LME.

3 An animal that is wasting away or that will not fatten. Now chiefly *dial.* LME.

4 A thing rejected as waste or useless; an article of faulty or inferior manufacture; an animal, bird, etc. not considered good enough to be kept for breeding. Cf. WASTREL *noun* 2. E18.

5 A thing which causes or allows waste or loss of material; *esp.* (*dial.*) a piece of matter in the wick which causes a candle to gutter and burn too fast. L18.

wastery *noun* var. of WASTRY.

wastethrift /ˈweɪs(t)θrɪft/ *noun*. Now *rare*. E17.
[from WASTE *verb* + THRIFT *noun*[1].]
A spendthrift.

wastrel /ˈweɪstr(ə)l/ *noun & adjective*. L16.
[from WASTE *verb* + -REL.]

▸ **A** *noun*. **1** In Cornwall: a tract of waste land. Now only *spec.*, a strip of waste ground alongside a road. L16.

2 An article of imperfect workmanship; an unhealthy or wasted-looking animal. Cf. WASTER *noun* 4. L18.

3 An idle, worthless, or disreputable person; a wasteful person, a spendthrift; *arch.* a neglected child, a waif. M19.

> 📖 **3** V. WOOLF A set of gifted but good for nothing wastrels.

▸ **B** *adjective*. **1** Of inferior quality, rejected as imperfect. Now *rare*. L16.

2 Of an animal: feeble, lacking strength or vigour. Now chiefly *dial.* L16.

3 Wasteful. *poet.* L19.

■ **wastreldom**, **wastrelism** *nouns* extravagance (esp. with ref. to government spending) E20.

wastrife /ˈweɪstrɪf/ *adjective & noun*. *Scot.* E19.
[from WASTE *adjective* + RIFE. Cf. CAULDRIFE.]
▶ **A** *adjective*. Wasteful, extravagant. E19.
▶ **B** *noun*. Wastefulness, extravagance. E19.

wastry /ˈweɪstri/ *noun*. *Scot. & north.* Also **wastery**. M17.
[from WASTE *verb* + -RY.]
Reckless extravagance; waste, wastefulness; an instance of this.

wasty /ˈweɪsti/ *adjective*. E19.
[from WASTE *noun* + -Y[1].]
1 = WASTEFUL 3. *US. rare*. E19.
2 Resembling cotton-waste. *US. rare*. L19.
3 Liable to waste from deterioration. E20.

Wasukuma /wasʊˈkuːmə, -ˈkjuː-/ *noun pl.* M19.
[Bantu, from *wa-* human pl. prefix + *sukuma* north.]
The Sukuma people.

Waswahili *noun pl.* see SWAHILI.

WAT *abbreviation*.
AERONAUTICS. Weight and Temperature.

wat /wɒt/ *noun*[1]. Long *obsolete* exc. *dial.* L15.
[Prob. from *Wat* dim. of male forename *Walter*.]
A hare.

📖 SHAKES. *Ven. & Ad.* Poor Wat, far off upon a hill, Stands on his hinder legs with list'ning ear.

wat /wat/ *noun*[2]. M19.
[Thai from Sanskrit *vāṭa* enclosure.]
In Thailand or Cambodia, a Buddhist monastery or temple.

wat *verb pres. t.*: see WIT *verb*.

watap /ˈwɒtap/ *noun*. Also **wattap**, **watape**. M18.
[N. Amer. French from Ojibwa.]
A fibre or thread made by some N. American Indian peoples from the split roots of conifers, esp. white spruce.

watch /wɒtʃ/ *noun*.
[Old English *wæċċe*, from stem repr. also by the verb. In some later senses directly from the verb.]
▶ **I** Wakefulness, act of watching.
†**1** The state of being awake; voluntary or involuntary going without sleep; wakefulness. OE–M17.
2 Watching as a devotional exercise or religious observance; an act or instance of this, a vigil, a wake. Now *rare* exc. in ***watch-night*** below. OE. ▸**b** A flock of nightingales. *rare*. LME.
3 The action or a continued act of keeping awake and vigilant for the purpose of attending, guarding, observing, etc. OE.
4 = ***night-watch*** (c) s.v. NIGHT *noun*. Now chiefly *poet.*, esp. in ***the watches of the night***, the night-time. Cf. sense 12 below. OE.
5 The action or an act of watching or observing with continuous attention; a continued lookout, as of a sentinel or guard; surveillance. Also, the duty or office of watchman or sentinel. Chiefly in ***keep a watch***, ***keep watch***, ***set a watch***. LME. ▸†**b** Watchfulness, vigilance. Only in LME.
6 A sentinel. Also, the body of soldiers constituting the guard of a camp, town, gate, etc. *obsolete* exc. *Hist.* LME.
7 The action of keeping guard and maintaining order in the streets, esp. during the night, by a group chosen from the community. Long *rare* exc. *Hist.* LME. ▸†**b** A payment or tax for the upkeep of town watchmen. LME–E16.
8 A person who watches; a lookout. Formerly also, a spy. LME. ▸**b** CRICKET. A fielder. Also, a fielding position. Now *rare* or *obsolete*. M19.
†**9** A lying in wait, an ambush; an insidious plot. LME–M17.
10 A person who watches, or people who watch, to guard and protect life and property; *esp.* (*Hist.*) a watchman or body of watchmen who patrolled and guarded the streets of a town, proclaimed the hour, etc., before the introduction of the police force. M16.
11 A hill serving as a lookout station. Also more fully ***watch hill***. *Scot. & north. obsolete* exc. in place-names. M16.
12 a NAUTICAL. Each of the periods into which a 24-hour period is divided; *esp.* each of the alternating periods of time for which a part of a ship's company remains on duty (usu. four hours, except the dogwatches). Cf. sense 4 above. L16. ▸**b** A part, often one half or one third, of the officers and crew, who together attend to the working of a vessel during a watch. E17. ▸**c** A sailor's turn or period of duty. E18.
13 Any of various companies of irregular Highland troops in the 18th cent. Now *Hist.* exc. in ***Black Watch*** s.v. BLACK *adjective*. M18.

📖 **1** SHAKES. *Haml.* Fell into a sadness, then into a fast, Thence to a watch. **2** *Church Times* A watch was kept all night. **4** D. J. ENRIGHT In the long watches, When the leaves litter the misty streets. **5** E. WELTY Kept a watch on the front walk through the parlor curtains. **10** D. W. JERROLD The woman, with a piercing shriek, called the watch, but the watch . . answered not. **12** ***dogwatch***, ***graveyard watch***, ***middle watch***, ***morning watch***, etc.

▶ **II** A timepiece.
†**14** An alarm clock; an alarm attached to a clock. LME–M16.
†**15 a** A dial, a clock-face; the circle of figures on a dial. L16–L17. ▸**b** The moving parts of a clock. L17–E19.
16 A small portable timepiece for carrying on one's person, either in a pocket, attached to the clothing, or (now usu.) worn on a band around the wrist. L16. ▸**b** A chronometer as used on board ship. L18.
17 [app. mistranslation of French *montre* show-piece, wrist-watch, from *montrer* show.] A trial-piece of glass, pottery, copper, etc., put in a furnace and taken out again, to assess the degree of heating and the condition of the material. E17.

📖 **16** G. VIDAL He glanced at his watch: fifteen minutes to eight. ***fob watch***, ***hunting-watch***, ***lever watch***, ***verge watch***, ***wrist-watch***, etc.

Phrases: ***Black Watch***: see BLACK *adjective*. **crazy as a two-bob watch** *Austral. slang* extremely stupid, mad. ***DEATH-watch***. ***hack watch***: see HACK *noun*[2] 6. †**her watch** *slang* herself. †**his watch** *slang* himself. †**my watch** *slang* myself. ***NEIGHBOURHOOD watch***. ***night watch***: see NIGHT *noun*. **off the watch** NAUTICAL off duty. **on the watch**, **on watch** on the lookout, exercising vigilance (foll. by *for* or with inf.). ***the watches of the night***: see sense 4 above. **watch and ward** *noun phr.* the performance of the duty of a watchman or sentinel, esp. as a feudal obligation; now only *rhet.*, a careful guard. **watch and watch** (according to) the arrangement by which divisions of a ship's crew take duty alternately every four hours. **watch below**, **watch off** NAUTICAL the time during which a sailor is off duty.

Comb.: **watchband** *N. Amer.* = ***watch-strap*** below; **watch-bell** (*a*) *arch.* a bell rung every half-hour on board ship; a bell marking the beginning of a period of watch duty; †(*b*) an alarm bell; **watch-bill** †(*a*) a bill or halberd (as) carried by a watchman; (*b*) NAUTICAL a document setting out the duties of the members of a ship's crew; **watch-boat** a boat on patrol duty; **watch-box** a small shelter for a person on watch; **watch cap** a close-fitting knitted cap, as used in bad weather in the US Navy; **watch-care** *US* watchful care; **watch-case** orig., a hinged metal case or cover for a pocket watch; now also, the metal case enclosing the works of a watch; **watch-chain** a metal chain to which a pocket watch is attached; **watch-charm** *US* a small ornament that may hang from a watch-chain; **watch-cloak**, **watch-coat** a thick heavy cloak or coat worn by seamen, soldiers, watchmen, etc., when on duty in bad weather; **Watch Committee** *Hist.* the committee of a county borough council dealing with the policing and public lighting of the borough; **watch-fire** a fire maintained during the night as a signal, or for the use of a person or group of people on watch; **watch-glass** †(*a*) an hourglass; (*b*) a concave glass disc, covering the dial of a watch; a similar concave glass disc used in a laboratory etc. to hold material for observation or experiment; **watch-guard** a chain, cord, ribbon, etc., used to fasten a watch to the clothing; ***watch hill***: see sense 11 above; **watch-house** a house in which a watch or guard is stationed; *spec.* a building used as a station for town watchmen, and for the detention until morning of any disorderly people brought in by the watchmen; **watch-keeper** a person who keeps watch or acts as a lookout, esp. as a member of a watch on board ship; an officer in charge of a watch; **watch-keeping** *noun & adjective* (of or pertaining to) the action of keeping watch, esp. on board ship; **watch-light** (*a*) a night-light, esp. in the form of a slow-burning candle with a rush wick; (*b*) *rare* a light carried by a watchman; **watch-list** a list of items or names which require close surveillance, esp. for legal or political reasons; **watch-mate** a fellow-member of a ship's watch; **watch-night** (*a*) *Hist.* a religious service extending over midnight held monthly by Wesleyan Methodists; (*b*) the last night of the year, New Year's Eve; a religious service held on this night (or now also on Christmas Eve), usu. extending over midnight; (*c*) *W. Afr.* a night-watchman; **watch-officer** an officer who takes his or her turn as the officer in charge of the watch; **watch-paper** a disc of inscribed or ornamented paper, silk, or other material, inserted as a lining in the outer case of an old-fashioned watch; **watch room** a room from or within which a watch is kept; **watch-setting** MILITARY the posting of the watch; **watch-spring** the mainspring of a watch; **watch-stand** †(*a*) a lookout position for a sentinel or watchman; (*b*) a small stand on which a watch may be placed with its face visible; **watch-strap** a strap for fastening a watch on the wrist; **watch-tower** (*a*) a tower from which a watch can be kept, esp. for the approach of danger; †(*b*) a lighthouse; **watch-wheel** (now *rare*) the balance-wheel of a clock; **watchwork** the part of the movement of a clock which measures the time and drives the hands, as distinguished from the part which strikes the hour; also, the works or the movement of a watch.

■ **watchless** *adjective* (*a*) unwatched; (*b*) unwatchful: E17. **watchlessness** *noun* lack of watchfulness L17.

watch /wɒtʃ/ *verb*.
[Old English (in pres. pple) *wæċċende*, from same source as *wacian*: see WAKE *verb*.]
▶ **I** *verb intrans.* **1** †**a** Be or remain awake. OE–M17. ▸†**b** Keep awake intentionally. OE–M17. ▸**c** Remain awake with a sick person or at a person's bedside, esp. to give help or comfort. L17.
2 Remain awake for purposes of devotion; keep vigil. OE.
3 Be on the alert, be vigilant; be on one's guard against danger or surprise. Freq. foll. by *for*. ME.
4 Look at or observe something over a period of time, esp. so as to be aware of any movement or change; be on the lookout. LME. ▸**b** Be on the watch *for* (something expected). E17.
5 Fulfil the duty of a watchman, sentinel, or guard; keep watch; (of a sailor) be on duty during a watch. LME.
6 NAUTICAL. Of a buoy: be in operation on the surface of the water. M17.

📖 **1c** H. JAMES Ladies of the parish had . . offered . . piously to watch with her. **4** C. P. SNOW My father was watching with mild interest. J. FOWLES I . . watched out of the corner of my eye. **b** C. RAYNER Staring abstractedly . . but quite clearly watching . . for new arrivals. **5** A. RADCLIFFE Peter was ordered to watch at the door.

▶ **II** *verb trans.* **7** Orig., keep under guard to prevent escape or rescue. Now more widely, keep under observation or surveillance; keep an eye on; set a watch on. ME.
†**8** Guard against attack; provide with guards or watchmen; serve as a guard to. LME–E19.
9 Observe, use one's sight to ascertain (now *spec.* over a period of time) *whether, what, who, how, which*, etc.; see *that* something occurs, is the case, or is (not) done. LME.
10 Keep the eyes fixed on; look attentively at; observe by looking at, over a period of time. Also with adverb or phr. implying motion or change, as *watch* a person who is passing *down, in, out, to* a place, etc. E16. ▸**b** Follow observantly; keep oneself informed about (a course of events, etc.). L17. ▸**c** Exercise care, caution, or restraint about (something); pay attention to. M19. ▸**d** LAW. Attend to (a case) in accordance with a watching brief. L19.
11 Exercise protecting vigilance over; guard, look after; tend (a flock). E16. ▸**b** Sit up beside (a sick person) to give help or comfort; keep watch beside (a dead body). E16.
12 Be on the alert for (an opportunity, an advantage); be vigilant to choose (one's time for action). Formerly also, look out for, wait expectantly for (a coming event). M16.
13 FALCONRY. Prevent (a hawk) from sleeping, as a means of taming. L16.

📖 **7** D. STEEL She could watch the children playing outside. *Independent* Groups which the Israelis would have liked to watch. *Proverb*: A watched pot never boils. **10** J. TYNDALL I watched the clouds forming. M. FRAYN She watched me very closely . . to see . . what my reaction was. *Venue* A great place to rest and watch the world go by. A. MOTION To find his father watching the news on television. **b** LD MACAULAY The war . . raging in Hungary . . was watched by all Europe. **c** *Flex* Like all bodybuilders, they watch their diets carefully. **11** ARNOLD BENNETT Watch the iron for me, love, will you? **12** DICKENS Winkle eagerly watched his opportunity: it was not long wanting.

Phrases & comb.: ***bird-watch***: see BIRD *noun*. ***clock-watch***: see CLOCK *noun*[1]. †**watch and ward** *verb phr.* keep watch and ward. ***watch a person's back***: see ***watch one's back*** below. **watching brief** (*a*) LAW an instruction to a barrister to follow a case on behalf of a client not directly involved; (*b*) *gen.* a state of interest maintained in a proceeding in which one is not directly or immediately concerned. **watching-chamber** *Hist.* a room or chamber in which a watch or vigil is kept, esp. by a shrine. **watch it** *colloq.* be careful (freq. imper., as a threat or warning). ***watch one's step***: see STEP *noun*[1]. **watch one's back**, **watch a person's back** be alert for or guard oneself or another against danger from behind or from some unexpected quarter. ***watch someone's smoke***: see SMOKE *noun*. ***watch the clock***: see CLOCK *noun*[1]. ***watch this space!***: see SPACE *noun* 14.

With adverbs & prepositions in specialized senses: **watch after** — follow (a person) with one's eyes, watch the movements of. ***watch for***: see senses 3, 4b above. **watch out** (*a*) *colloq.* be alert, look out (freq. as imper.); (*b*) (CRICKET, now *rare*) field; (*c*) ***watch out for*** —, be on the watch for, be alert for. **watch over** = sense 11 above. **watch up** *rare* sit up at night.

watchable /ˈwɒtʃəb(ə)l/ *adjective*. E17.
[from WATCH *verb* + -ABLE.]
That may be watched; *spec.* that may be watched with pleasure or profit at the theatre or cinema, or on television.

■ **watchaˈbility** *noun* M20.

watchdog /ˈwɒtʃdɒg/ *noun, adjective, & verb*. E17.
[from WATCH *noun* + DOG *noun*.]
▶ **A** *noun*. **1** A dog kept to guard a house, property, etc., and warn of intruders. E17.
2 *fig.* A person or body of people appointed to monitor others' rights, behaviour, etc., esp. as a safeguard against abuses by the authorities, business interests, etc. M19.
▶ **B** *attrib.* or as *adjective*. Characteristic of or acting as a watchdog. M19.
▶ **C** *verb trans.* Infl. **-gg-**. Attend, follow, or guard (a person); maintain surveillance over (an activity, situation, etc.). E20.

watcher /ˈwɒtʃə/ *noun*. LME.
[from WATCH *verb* + -ER[1].]
1 A person who is occupied in watching; a watchman, a guard, a sentry; a spy who keeps someone under surveillance. LME.

2 A person who keeps awake at night, esp. in vigil. Now *rare*. E16.

3 A person who watches by a sickbed, or by a dead body. M16.

4 [translating Aramaic *ʿîr*.] An angel (of a kind) characterized as ever wakeful. *arch.* M16.

5 *gen.* A person who watches (something), or who keeps watch. Freq. foll. by *of*, occas. *over*. L16. ▸**b** An eye so personified. *poet.* L16.

6 With preceding noun, freq. hyphenated: a person who closely follows the affairs of (a particular person, country, or institution). *colloq.* (orig. *US*). M20.

5 ***bird-watcher***: see BIRD *noun*. ***clock-watcher***: see CLOCK *noun*[1]. **6** ***China-watcher***, ***Kremlin-watcher***, etc.

watchet /ˈwɒtʃɪt/ *noun & adjective*. Now *arch. & dial.* LME.

[App. from Old Northern French *watchet*, earlier *waschet*, Anglo-Latin *waschetum*, of unkn. origin.]

▸ **A** *noun*. **1** A light blue colour (also ***watchet-blue***); cloth or garments of this colour. LME.

2 ANGLING. (An artificial fly imitating) a small bluish mayfly. Also ***watchet fly***. L18.

▸ **B** *adjective*. Light blue, sky-blue. L15.

¶ Formerly occas. used of greenish colours.

watchful /ˈwɒtʃfʊl, -f(ə)l/ *adjective*. L15.

[from WATCH *noun* + -FUL.]

1 Characterized by vigilance or careful observation; engaged in or accustomed to watching or close observation; vigilant. Also foll. by *of*. L15.

2 Wakeful, sleepless. *arch.* M16.

†**3** Of a place, a duty, etc.: in which one must be on the watch. L16–M19.

📖 **1** *She* Ever anxious and watchful of her mother. **2** SHAKES. *Two Gent.* Twenty watchful, weary, tedious nights.

■ **watchfully** *adverb* M16. **watchfulness** *noun* L16.

watchmaker /ˈwɒtʃmeɪkə/ *noun*. M17.

[from WATCH *noun* + MAKER.]

A person whose trade is to make and repair watches and clocks.

■ **watchmaking** *noun* the making of watches E18.

watchman /ˈwɒtʃmən/ *noun*. Pl. **-men**. LME.

[from WATCH *noun* + MAN *noun*.]

1 A member of a military guard; a sentinel, a sentry, a lookout. Now *rare* exc. in biblical allusions. LME.

†**2** A person who keeps vigil, a watcher; a person who watches over or guards a person or thing, a guardian (*of* something). LME–E17.

3 Each of a body of people appointed to keep watch in a town from sunset to sunrise; *spec.* a constable of the watch who, before the Police Act of 1839, patrolled the streets by night to safeguard life and property. Cf. WATCH *noun* 10. Now chiefly *Hist.* LME.

†**4** A scout, a spy. Only in M16.

5 A person employed to guard private property, a building, etc., while the owner, tenant, or workpeople are away, esp. during the night. E17.

6 A dor-beetle. Also ***watchman beetle***. M19.

📖 **1** AV *Ps.* 127:1 Except the Lord keepe the citie, the watchman waketh but in vain. **2** JAMES MELVILLE The Watchmen and fathfull Pastours of the Kirk. **3** J. MARQUAND The clatter of a watchman's rattle . . warning thieves. **5** *Independent* Terrorists were disturbed by a watchman while planting semtex bombs. ***night-watchman***: see NIGHT *noun*.

watchword /ˈwɒtʃwəːd/ *noun*. LME.

[from WATCH *noun* + WORD *noun*.]

†**1** MILITARY. A word or short phrase used as a password. LME–M17. ▸**b** The call of a sentinel on his rounds. E17–L18.

†**2** A cautionary word or speech. Also, a premonitory sign, a warning event. L15–M18.

†**3** A preconcerted signal to begin an attack etc. M16–M19.

4 a A password used among the members of a sect, society, etc. *arch.* M16. ▸**b** A word or phrase used as embodying the guiding principle or rule of action of a party or individual. M18.

water /ˈwɔːtə/ *noun*.

[Old English *wæter* = Old Frisian *weter*, Old Saxon *watar*, Old High German *wazzar* (Dutch *water*, German *Wasser*), from West Germanic (Old Norse *vatn*, Gothic *wato*, gen. *watins*, show a var. with *-n-* formative), from Indo-European base repr. also by Old Church Slavonic, Russian *voda* (cf. VODKA).]

▸ **I 1** The liquid (in its pure form transparent, colourless, tasteless, and odourless) which forms the main constituent of seas, lakes, rivers, and rain, and is put to many domestic and industrial uses: it is a compound of hydrogen and oxygen (formula H_2O), and was formerly regarded as one of the four elements. OE. ▸**b** Water as a drink or as basic to animal and plant life. OE. ▸**c** Water as used for washing, cleansing, etc.; (as a count noun) any of the successive quantities of this used in a gradual process of washing. OE. ▸**d** Water as used to dilute drinks etc. LME. ▸**e** Water viewed as a chemical substance, which may exist also as ice or steam. E19. ▸**f** COMMERCE. Fictitious capital consisting of unsold stock of a trading company: see WATER *verb* 5b. L19.

2 Water as collected in seas, lakes, rivers, etc. Freq. in *pl.*, with ref. to flowing water or water moving in waves. OE. ▸**b** Quantity or depth of water, as sufficient or insufficient for navigation. M16. ▸**c** In *pl.* The seas and oceans of a particular part of the world; the part of the sea regarded as under the jurisdiction of a particular State (cf. ***territorial waters*** s.v. TERRITORIAL *adjective*). M17. ▸**d** *The* sea (esp. the Atlantic Ocean) or *the* strait (esp. the Irish Sea) separating Great Britain from some other country; *the* river separating one half of a city (esp. London) from the other. Chiefly in ***across the water***, ***over the water***, ***cross the water***. M17.

3 A particular expanse or body of water; a pool, a lake, a sea. ME. ▸**b** A stream, a river; *esp.* a small river. Freq. in place-names. Now chiefly *Scot. & north.* ME.

4 In *pl.* Floods (esp. in ***the waters are out***). Formerly *sing.*, a flood. ME.

5 The water of a mineral spring, used, esp. medicinally, for bathing or for drinking. Freq. in *pl.*, esp. in ***drink the waters***, ***take the waters***. M16.

📖 **1** P. FRANCIS Surface water percolating downwards . . comes into contact with hot magma. *Guardian* Cardiff was flooded, and firemen were called to pump water away. ***ice-water***, ***salt water***, ***spring water***, ***tap water***, etc. **b** D. CUSACK Mrs Mac brings Sheila a powder and a drink of water. **c** *Town & Country* A bathroom with hot and cold water, soap and *real* towels. E. K. KANE Butter . . my own invention, melted from salt beef and washed in many waters. **d** G. K. CHESTERTON I don't care where the water goes if it doesn't get into the wine. *fig.*: *Times Lit. Suppl.* The epigrams . . were Wilde and water with . . more water than Wilde. **2** LD MACAULAY The water in the bay was as even as glass. F. W. FARRAR They . . had been baptised in the waters of their native river. DAY LEWIS Poems . . emerge . . with the compulsive force of waters that have stealthily massed behind a dam. **c** P. V. WHITE Two ships . . cruising in Southern waters. *Undercurrents* The Italians claimed . . that the ship was in Jugoslav waters. R. HUNTFORD *Discovery* was bound for some of the roughest waters in the world. **d** D. MURPHY Their two sons are . . in Enniskillen and soon . . will be off to study 'across the water'. **3** A. E. HOUSMAN Like a skylit water stood The bluebells in the azured wood. *Coarse Fishing* He knew of six waters which held 30 lb carp. **b** ***Allan Water***, ***Water of Leith***, etc. **4** E. MONTAGU I . . agreed to . . send a messenger to see if the waters had fallen. **5** *New Scientist* Victims of rheumatic complaints . . are particularly attracted to the waters. *Country Living* You can take the waters at the Pump Room. ***Malvern water***, ***Perrier water***, ***seltzer water***, ***Vichy water***, etc.

▸ **II** A liquid resembling (and usually containing) water.

6 A solution or infusion of a substance, esp. one used medicinally or as a cosmetic or perfume. ME.

7 a Tears. LME. ▸**b** Saliva. Now only, flow of saliva provoked by appetite. L16. ▸**c** Usu. in *pl.* The amniotic fluid discharged from the womb before childbirth. Freq. in ***the waters have broken***. L17.

8 Urine. Chiefly in ***make water***, ***pass water***, void urine. LME. ▸**b** A patient's urine examined as a means of diagnosing disease. Cf. ***cast water*** s.v. CAST *verb*. LME.

9 Any of certain vegetable juices. L16.

📖 **6** ***barley water***, ***lavender water***, ***potash-water***, ***rose-water***, etc. **7a** DICKENS A . . rap on the nose . . which brought the water into his eyes. **b** W. S. GILBERT The thought of Peter's oysters brought the water to his mouth. **9** C. PHILLIPS A glass of coconut water.

▸ **III** Transf. and miscellaneous uses.

10 Degree of transparency and brilliancy in a diamond or a pearl (formerly graded ***first water***, ***second water***, ***third water***). E17. ▸**b** ***of the first water***, ***of the purest water***, ***of the rarest water***, etc. (*fig.*), unsurpassed in one's (or its) class. Freq. *derog.* E19.

11 = WATERCOLOUR 2, 3. L18.

📖 **10** J. FOWLES It's only small stones . . but all very fine water. **b** D. L. SAYERS The shock was a staggerer of the first water. B. W. ALDISS Hitler . . a 'villain of the first water'.

Phrases: **above water** above the surface of the water (cf. ***keep one's head above water*** below). ***a fish out of water***: see FISH *noun*[1]. ***back water***: see BACK *verb* 10. ***between wind and water***: see WIND *noun*[1]. ***blue water***: see BLUE *adjective*. ***bread and water***: see BREAD *noun*[1]. ***break water***: see BREAK *verb*. **by water** by ship or boat (as a means of travel or transport). **cast one's bread upon the waters** [cf. *Ecclesiastes* 11:1] give generously in the belief that one's kindness will ultimately be repaid. ***cold water***: see COLD *adjective*. ***dead water***: see DEAD *adjective*. ***deep water(s)***: see DEEP *adjective*. ***dip one's toe in (the water)***, ***dip one's toes in (the water)***: see TOE *noun*. ***drink the waters***: see sense 5 above. ***heavy water***: see HEAVY *adjective*. ***hell and high water***, ***hell or high water***: see HELL *noun*. ***high water***: see HIGH *adjective*. ***hold water***: see HOLD *verb*. HOLY WATER. ***hot water***: see HOT *adjective*. **keep one's head above water** avoid ruin by a continued struggle. ***light water***: see LIGHT *adjective*[1]. ***like water off a duck's back***: see DUCK *noun*[1]. ***low water***: see LOW *adjective*. ***make a hole in the water***: see HOLE *noun*[1]. **make water** (*a*) (of a boat) take in water through a leak; (*b*) see sense 8 above. ***oil on water***, ***oil on the water(s)***: see OIL *noun*. ***pass water***: see sense 8 above. ***pour oil on the waters***, ***pour oil on troubled waters***: see POUR *verb* 1. ***slack water***: see SLACK *adjective*. **spend money like water** spend lavishly. ***strong water***: see STRONG *adjective*. **take the water** (*a*) (of an animal etc.) enter a lake, river, etc., and begin to swim; (*b*) embark, take ship. ***take the waters***: see sense 5 above. ***take to something like a duck to water***: see DUCK *noun*[1]. **take water** = ***take the water*** above. ***test the water***: see TEST *verb*[2] 2. **the king over the water** *Hist.* Jacobite designation for the son and grandson of James II, James Stuart (1688–1766) and Charles Stuart (1720–80), who in exile successively asserted the Stuart claim to the British throne against the house of Hanover (cf. ***the Old Pretender***, ***the Young Pretender*** s.v. PRETENDER). ***tread water***: see TREAD *verb*. **under water** below the surface of water; (of land) flooded, submerged. ***waste water***: see WASTE *noun & adjective*. **water bewitched** *joc.* an excessively diluted drink, *esp.* very weak tea. **Water of Ayr stone** a kind of stone found on the banks of the River Ayr in Scotland, used for whetstones and polishing. ***water of crystallization***: see CRYSTALLIZATION *noun* 1. **water of life** (*a*) a drink imparting life or immortality to the drinker; (*b*) *rare* brandy; whisky (cf. AQUA VITAE); (*c*) THEOLOGY spiritual enlightenment. **water on the brain** hydrocephalus. **water on the knee** fluid in the knee-joint. **water over the dam** = ***water under the bridge*** below. **water under the bridge** past events which it is unprofitable to bring up or discuss. ***white water***: see WHITE *adjective*.

Comb.: **water-ash** an ash tree, *Fraxinus caroliniana*, of swamps in the southern US; **water authority** a body administering a system of water supply; ***water*** AVENS; **water-bag** a bag of skin, leather, or canvas for carrying water, esp. one used in Eastern countries for transporting and distributing water, or in Australia by travellers in dry areas; ***a hundred in the water-bag*** (*Austral. slang*), very hot; **water-bailie** *Scot.* = ***water bailiff*** below; **water bailiff** (*a*) *Hist.* a custom-house officer at a port; (*b*) an official responsible for the enforcement of fishing laws; *esp.* a river-policeman employed to prevent poaching; **water balance** (*a*) any of various counterbalancing devices which use the weight of water to raise loads; (*b*) PHYSIOLOGY equilibrium between water intake and water loss; (*c*) HYDROLOGY etc. an assessment of the water resources or turnover of a lake, catchment area, etc. after all input and output has been taken into account; **water-ballast** NAUTICAL (tanks etc. filled with) water placed in a vessel to serve as ballast, esp. after the cargo is unloaded; **water barometer** an early form of barometer in which the pressure of the atmosphere is measured by the height of a column of water; **water-based** *adjective* having water as the main ingredient; **water bat** any of various bats that habitually fly over water; *esp.* Daubenton's bat; **water-bath** CHEMISTRY a vessel containing water heated to a given temperature, used for heating preparations placed in smaller vessels; **water bear** (*a*) = TARDIGRADE *noun* 2; (*b*) *Canad.* a polar bear; **water-bearer** (*a*) a person employed to carry water from a spring etc. for domestic use, esp. in an Eastern country; (*b*) (**W-**) the constellation and zodiacal sign Aquarius; **water-bed** a bed with a flexible water-filled mattress in a rigid frame, designed to adapt itself to the posture of the sleeper; **water beech** a N. American hornbeam, *Carpinus caroliniana*; **water beetle** any of numerous beetles that live in water, esp. carnivorous beetles of the family Dytiscidae, and scavenging beetles of the family Hydrophilidae; **water betony** = ***water figwort*** below; **waterbird** any bird which frequents water; *esp.* one which wades or swims; **water birth** a birth in which the mother spends the final stages of labour in a birthing pool, with delivery taking place either in or out of the water; **water biscuit** a thin crisp biscuit made from flour and water; ***water-blinks***: see BLINK *noun* 4; **water blister** a blister containing a colourless serous fluid rather than blood or pus; ***water-bloom***: see BLOOM *noun*[1] 3c; **water-boa** the anaconda *Eunectes murinus*; **Water Board** an administrative body controlling the supply of water to a town or district; **water-boatman** a water bug that has hind legs shaped like oars for swimming, *esp.* a carnivorous bug of the family Notonectidae (also called ***backswimmer***), and a phytophagous bug of the family Corixidae (also ***lesser water-boatman***); **waterbody** a body of water forming a physiographical feature, as a sea, reservoir, etc.; **waterbok** /-bɒk/ = ***water-buck*** below; **water-bomber** *Canad.* an aircraft used for extinguishing forest fires by dropping water; **water-borne** *adjective* (*a*) floating on the water; (*b*) (of goods etc.) conveyed by ship or boat; (*c*) (of disease) communicated or propagated by contaminated drinking-water; **water bottle** (*a*) a vessel of skin, glass, metal, etc., for holding or carrying drinking-water; (*b*) = ***hot-water bottle*** s.v. HOT *adjective*; **water bouget** HERALDRY = BOUGET; **water-bough** (*obsolete* exc. *dial.*) a small bough on a tree trunk overshadowed by a larger bough; **water-bound** *adjective* (*a*) cut off by floods; (*b*) (of macadam roads) solidified by rolling and watering; **water-boy** (chiefly *N. Amer.*) a boy or man who brings drinking water to people engaged in strenuous exercise; **waterbrash** MEDICINE a sudden filling of the mouth with dilute saliva or regurgitated fluid, accompanying dyspepsia or nausea; **water break** (a piece of) broken water; **water-breather** any animal capable of breathing in water by means of gills etc.; **water-breathing** *adjective* designating an animal which is a water-breather; **water-buck** a large antelope, *Kobus ellipsiprymnus*, which has a coat of various shades of brown or grey and is found in watered districts of the African savannah (cf. SING-SING); **water budget** (*a*) HERALDRY = BOUGET; (*b*) HYDROLOGY etc. = ***water balance*** (c) above; **water-buffalo** a large Asiatic buffalo, *Bubalus arnee*, which occurs widely as a domesticated beast of burden, but whose ancestral wild form in the Indian subcontinent and SE Asia is now endangered; **water bug** (*a*) any of numerous heteropteran bugs that live in water; (*b*) *US* the common cockroach, *Blatta orientalis*; **water-bull** a legendary semi-aquatic animal resembling a bull; **water-bus** a motor-boat or steamer carrying paying passengers as part of a scheduled service; **water-butt** a large open barrel for catching rainwater; ***water caltrop(s)***: see CALTROP 1; **water cannon** a device for discharging water at high pressure, esp. to disperse crowds; **Water-carrier** = ***water-bearer*** (b) above; **water-cart** a cart carrying water; *esp.* (now *Hist.*) a vehicle of this kind used for watering the streets; **water-caster** (*obsolete* exc. *Hist.*) a person who professes to diagnose disease by examining a patient's urine; **water chestnut** (*a*) any of several aquatic plants constituting the genus *Trapa* (family Trapaceae), esp. *T. natans*, which have horned edible nuts; (*b*) (in full ***Chinese water chestnut***) the edible starchy tuber of a spike-rush, *Eleocharis dulcis*, used in Chinese cookery; **water chickweed** a straggling succulent white-flowered plant of riversides etc., *Myosoton aquaticum*, of the pink family, resembling a large chickweed; **water-chute** an artificial cascade of water to be descended as an amusement; **water clerk** a clerk from a shipowner's or agent's office, who boards an arriving ship; **water-clock** a water-driven instrument for measuring time; *esp.* = CLEPSYDRA; **water-closet** (a small room containing) a large bowl for urinating and defecating, the excreta being flushed away by a stream of water (cf. ***earth closet*** s.v. EARTH *noun*[1]); **water company** a commercial association for supplying water to the inhabitants of a town or district; **water-cool** *verb trans.* cool (an engine etc.) by circulating water (chiefly as ***water-cooled*** *ppl adjective*); **water-cooler** a vessel in which water is kept cool; *spec.* (*N. Amer.*) a tank of cooled drinking water in a place of work; **water-cow** (*a*) = ***water-buffalo*** above; (*b*) a legendary semi-aquatic animal resembling a cow; **water cracker** *US* = ***water biscuit*** above; **watercraft** (*a*) skill in matters pertaining to activities on water; (*b*) a vessel that plies on the water, such vessels collectively; ***personal watercraft*** (chiefly *US*), a jet-ski; ***water crane***: see CRANE *noun*[1] 3; **water-cricket** †(*a*) the larva of a stonefly; (*b*) any of several water bugs of the genus *Velia* that run on the surface film; **water-crow** any of various dark-coloured waterbirds; *esp.* the dipper *Cinclus cinclus*; **water-crowfoot** any of a group of buttercups (genus *Ranunculus*) with white flowers and finely dissected submerged leaves, occurring in ponds and streams; **water cure** (*a*) a course of medical treatment by hydrotherapy; (*b*) a form of torture in which a person is forced to drink large quantities of water; **water cushion** a depth of water that acts to lessen the impact or force of something; **water cycle** the cycle of processes by which water circulates between the earth's oceans, atmosphere, and land, involving precipitation as rain and snow, drainage in streams and rivers, and return to the atmosphere by evaporation and transpiration; **water deer** a small Chinese deer, *Hydropotes inermis*, that has been introduced into England; **water diviner** = ***water-finder*** below; **water-drinker** a person who drinks water; *esp.* a total abstainer; **water-drinking** *adjective* drinking water (and abstaining from alcohol); **water drive** OIL INDUSTRY the use of water to force oil out of a reservoir rock; ***water-dropwort***: see DROPWORT 2; **water drum** a drum containing water, or placed in water, which is played as a musical instrument; **water-dust** water in the form of fine spray; **water elder** the guelder rose, *Viburnum opulus*; **water elm** the planer-tree, *Planera aquatica*; **water engine** †(*a*) a fire engine; (*b*) an engine for pumping water; **water fern** any of several small floating ferns; esp. *Azolla filiculoides*, a mosslike freq. reddish plant of tropical and subtropical America (naturalized in Great Britain); **water figwort** a European figwort, *Scrophularia auriculata*, with obtuse bluntly toothed leaves, found by streams and ponds; **water finder** a person who dowses for water; **water-finding** dowsing for water; ***water flag***: see FLAG *noun*[1] 1; **water-flea** any of various minute freshwater cladoceran crustaceans, which swim by flicking their branched antennae; **water-flood** (*a*) a body or mass of water in flood; (*b*) OIL INDUSTRY water-flooding; an instance of this; **water-flooding** OIL INDUSTRY the injection of water into a reservoir rock in order to force oil into neighbouring production wells; **water-fly** any fly or similar insect that frequents water or waterside habitats; **waterfront** (orig. *US*) the part of a town adjoining a harbour, river, lake, etc.; **watergall** †(*a*) a boggy part of a field; (*b*) (now *dial.*) a secondary or imperfectly formed rainbow; †**watergang** a watercourse, *esp.* an artificial one; **water garden** a garden with pools or a stream, for growing aquatic plants; **water gas** (*a*) a gas made by blowing steam over incandescent coke and consisting mainly of carbon monoxide and hydrogen; (*b*) water in the form of vapour; **water gauge** (*a*) a transparent tube etc. indicating the level of water in a reservoir, steam boiler, etc.; (*b*) pressure expressed in terms of a head of water; ***water* GERMANDER**; **water-gilder** a person who practises water-gilding; **water-gilding** the former process of gilding metal surfaces by immersion in liquid gold amalgam; **water-gilt**, **water-gold** liquid gold amalgam used in water-gilding; gold that has been applied by this means; **water-gruel** *noun & adjective* (*a*) *noun* thin gruel made with water rather than milk; formerly *fig.*, as a type of something insipid; †(*b*) *adjective* insipid, namby-pamby, characterless; **water-guard** a body of customs officers employed to watch ships in order to prevent smuggling; **water gum** any of several Australian trees of the myrtle family, esp. *Tristaniopsis laurina*, which grows near streams; **water gun** (chiefly *N. Amer.*) a water pistol; **water-head** (*a*) (the land adjoining) the head or source of a stream; (*b*) = HEAD *noun* 19; **water hemlock** (*a*) the European cowbane, *Cicuta virosa*; (*b*) = ***water-dropwort*** s.v. DROPWORT 2; **waterhen** any of various aquatic rails, such as the moorhen and other birds of the genus *Gallinula*; **water-house** *Hist.* a building in which water was raised from a river or well into a reservoir to be conveyed by pipes for domestic use; ***water* HYACINTH**; **water-ice** (*a*) a confection of water and sugar, flavoured and frozen; a sorbet; (*b*) ice formed by the direct freezing of water; (*c*) ASTRONOMY frozen water or water vapour; **water injection** (*a*) OIL INDUSTRY the forcing of water into a reservoir formation, esp. as a technique of secondary recovery; (*b*) AERONAUTICS the injection of water into the cylinders of a piston engine or the air intake of a jet engine, to provide cooling and increase engine efficiency; **water-insoluble** *adjective* insoluble in water; **water-intoxicated** *adjective* (MEDICINE) suffering from water intoxication; **water intoxication** MEDICINE a condition resulting from the intake of too much water, leading progressively to drowsiness, confusion, convulsions, coma, and death; **water-jacket** a casing containing water surrounding a thing, to prevent undue heating or chilling; **water-jacketed** *adjective* surrounded by a water-jacket; **water jump** a water-filled ditch or hollow to be jumped by horses and riders, or by runners in an obstacle race; ***water-kelpie***: see KELPIE *noun*[1]; **water-knot** a kind of knot used in joining together the sections of a fishing-line; **water-laid**, **water-lain** *adjectives* (GEOLOGY) designating strata deposited by water; **water-lane** (*a*) *dial.* a green lane with a stream running along it; (*b*) a narrow passage of open water, as between masses of reeds or lines of shipping; **water-leaf** (*a*) any of several N. American woodland plants constituting the genus *Hydrophyllum* (family Hydrophyllaceae), with bell-shaped flowers and lobed or pinnate leaves looking as if stained with water; (*b*) ARCHITECTURE a stylized representation of the leaf of an aquatic plant, used as an ornament in sculptured capitals; (*c*) paper at an early stage of manufacture; **water leech** = LEECH *noun*[2] 1; **water lemon** the edible fruit of a species of passion-flower, *Passiflora laurifolia*; ***water lentils***: see LENTIL 1b; **water lettuce** a tropical aquatic plant of the arum family, *Pistia stratiotes*, which forms a floating rosette of leaves; **water lily** any aquatic plant of the family Nymphaeaceae, with broad flat floating leaves and large solitary cup-shaped flowers; *esp.* the white-flowered *Nymphaea alba* (more fully ***white water lily***), of Europe, and the yellow-flowered *Nuphar lutea* (more fully ***yellow water lily***), of Eurasia; **water lizard** a newt or other lizard-like animal inhabiting water; **water-lungs** ZOOLOGY = ***respiratory tree*** s.v. TREE *noun* 7(c); **water main** the main pipe in the water-supply system of a house etc.; **water mass** OCEANOGRAPHY a large body of seawater that is distinguishable by its characteristic temperature and salinity range; **water-meadow** a meadow periodically flooded by a stream; **water-measure** *Hist.* a unit or system of measurement for coal, salt, fruit, etc., sold from vessels in port or on a river; **water measurer** any of several long thin water bugs of the genus *Hydrometra* and family Hydrometridae, which walk slowly on the surface film; **water meter** a device for measuring and recording the amount of water supplied to or used by a household; ***water milfoil***: see MILFOIL 2; **water-mill** (*a*) a mill with machinery driven by a water-wheel; (*b*) a water-wheel; **water-miller** the owner or manager of a water-mill; **water-mite** any of numerous aquatic mites of the suborder Protostigmata, most of which are parasitic as larvae and predatory as adults; ***water moccasin***: see MOCCASIN 2; **water-mole** *Austral.* a platypus; **water mongoose** a dark brown African mongoose, *Atilax paludinosus*, found in marshes and near rivers; **water monitor** any semi-aquatic monitor lizard; *esp.* the Nile monitor, *Varanus niloticus*; **water-mouse** orig., the water-vole, *Arvicola terrestris*; now, any of several mice that frequent water, esp. Central American mice of the genus *Rheomys*; **water-mouth** *Scot.* the mouth of a river; **water-net** = HYDRODICTYON; **water-nymph** MYTHOLOGY a nymph living in or under water; a naiad; **water oak** any of several N. American oaks which grow near water, esp. *Quercus nigra* of the southern US; **water opossum** = YAPOK; **water-organ** = HYDRAULUS; **water ouzel** the dipper *Cinclus cinclus*; **water-ox** = ***water-buffalo*** above; **water-parsnip** any of several aquatic umbelliferous plants with pinnate leaves, esp. *Sium latifolium* (more fully ***greater water-parsnip***) and *Berula erecta* (more fully ***lesser water-parsnip***); **water-parting** = WATERSHED 1; **water-pepper** a Eurasian knotweed of damp ground, *Persicaria hydropiper*, the leaves of which have a peppery taste; **water-pheasant** any of various long-tailed waterbirds; *esp.* the pheasant-tailed jacana, *Hydrophasianus chirurgus*, of India and SE Asia; ***water pimpernel***: see PIMPERNEL 2b; **water pipe** (*a*) a pipe for conveying water; (*b*) a hookah; **water pipit** a dark-coloured European pipit, *Anthus spinoletta*, that frequents waterside habitats; **water-pistol** a toy pistol shooting a jet of water; **water plane** (*a*) a canal constructed on a level, without locks; (*b*) a plane passing through a floating body, as a ship etc., on a level with the water-line; †(*c*) a seaplane; **water plantain** a Eurasian aquatic plant, *Alisma plantago-aquatica* (family Alismataceae), with ovate leaves resembling those of a plantain (genus *Plantago*) and with panicles of lilac flowers; also (with specifying word), any of several other plants of the genus *Alisma* or formerly included in it; **water polo** a game played by teams of swimmers, using a ball like a football; **water-pore** ZOOLOGY a minute ciliated opening through the oral wall of the disc of a crinoid; **water-pot** (*a*) a vessel for holding water; (*b*) ASTRONOMY the part of the constellation Aquarius represented as a vase or urn; (*c*) a watering-can; **water-power** (*a*) mechanical force derived from the weight or motion of water; (*b*) a fall or flow of water which can be so utilized; **water pressure** hydraulic pressure; **water-pressure** *adjective* designating an engine etc. operating by means of hydraulic pressure; **water-privilege** *US* the right to use water, esp. in order to turn machinery; a stream or body of water able to be used for this purpose; **water pump** a pump for raising water; **water pumper** a person using a water pump; ***water* PURPIE**; **water purslane** (*a*) a low-growing plant of damp and wet habitats, *Lythrum portula*, of the purple loosestrife family; (*b*) *US* an aquatic plant, *Ludwigia palustris*, of the willow-herb family; **waterquake** a seismic disturbance in the sea; **water rail** a Eurasian rail, *Rallus aquaticus*, which frequents dense vegetation near water; **water-rate**, **water-rent** a charge levied on a householder for the supply of water; **water-repellent** *adjective* not easily penetrated by water; **water-resistant** *adjective* (of a fabric etc.) able to resist but not entirely prevent the penetration of water (cf. WATERPROOF *adjective*); **water-ret** *verb trans.* ret (flax or hemp) by steeping in water (opp. ***dew-ret***); **water ring** ZOOLOGY = ***ring-canal*** s.v. RING *noun*[1]; **water-rot** *verb trans.* (*US*) = ***water-ret*** above; †**water-rug** *rare* (Shakes.) a kind of shaggy water-dog; **water-sail** (now *Hist.*) in square-rigged ships, a small sail beneath a lower studding-sail, spread in calm weather; **water sapphire** (*a*) a colourless or pale variety of sapphire; (*b*) an intense blue variety of cordierite occurring chiefly in Ceylon (also called ***saphir d'eau***); **waterscape** (a picture of) a view or piece of scenery consisting of water; **water-scorpion** any of several flattened water bugs of the family Nepidae, which have raptorial front legs and breathe through a bristle-like tubular tail; esp. *Nepa cinerea* of Europe; **water-screw** = ***ARCHIMEDEAN screw***; **water-serpent** (*a*) = ***water snake*** below; (*b*) = ***sea-serpent*** (*a*) s.v. SEA; **water-shield** a purple-flowered N. American aquatic plant, *Brasenia schreberi* (family Cabombaceae), having leaves like those of a water lily; **water shrew** any of various semi-aquatic or waterside shrews, esp. Eurasian shrews of the genus *Neomys* and N. American shrews of the genus *Sorex*; **water silk** (a garment of) watered silk (see WATERED *ppl adjective* 4a); **water skater** = ***pond-skater*** s.v. POND *noun*; **watersmeet** a meeting-point of two streams; **water snake** (*a*) any of various snakes that frequent fresh water, esp. harmless colubrid snakes of the genus *Natrix* and other genera; (*b*) = ***sea-snake*** (a) s.v. SEA; (*c*) (**W- S-**) *the* constellation Hydrus; (*d*) = WART ***snake***; **water-softener** an apparatus or chemical for making hard water soft; ***water soldier***: see SOLDIER *noun* 4; **water-soluble** *adjective* soluble in water; **water spaniel** (an animal of) any variety of spaniel used for retrieving waterfowl; **water spider** any of several, usu. large, semi-aquatic spiders; *esp.* (*a*) the spider *Argyroneta aquatica*, which dives under water, where it constructs a web containing air to act as a diving-bell; (*b*) a raft spider; **water-spirit** a supernatural being believed to inhabit water; **water-splash** a shallow stream or ford crossing a road; **water sports** (*a*) sports that are carried out on water, such as waterskiing and windsurfing; (*b*) *slang* sexual activity involving urination; **water-spot** *verb intrans.* (of fabric) show permanently any mark made on it by a drop of water; ***water starwort***: see STARWORT 1(c); **water stick insect** any of several very long and narrow water bugs of the genus *Ranatra*, allied to the water-scorpions; **water stoma** BOTANY a hydathode; **water-stop** (*a*) a place where a traveller or train stops for water; (*b*) a sealant to prevent water from leaking through joints; **water-stream** (now *rare*) a stream or current of water; a river, a brook; **water strider** = ***pond-skater*** s.v. POND *noun*; **water-swallow** †(*a*) a wagtail; (*b*) a sand martin; (*c*) a swallow-hole; **water taxi** a small boat picking up casual passengers on a river, canal, etc.; **water-thief** *poet.* a pirate; **waterthrush** either of two N. American birds of the genus *Seiurus* (family Parulidae), resembling small thrushes and found near woodland streams and swamps; **water thyme** Canadian waterweed (see ***waterweed*** below); **water tortoise** any of various African or S. American side-necked turtles of the family Pelomedusidae; **water-torture** any of several forms of torture involving water, esp. one in which the victim is placed under an incessant drip of water; **water-tower** a tower with an elevated tank to give pressure for distributing water; **water tree** any of several trees and shrubs yielding abundant drinkable sap, esp. *Tetracera potatoria* (family Dilleniaceae) of tropical Africa; **water tube** each of the tubes carrying water through a water-tube boiler; **water-tube** *adjective* designating a form of boiler in which the water circulates through tubes exposed to the source of heat; **water tunnel** a device resembling a wind tunnel, but using a flow of water instead of air to test models; **water vapour** water as a gas evaporated below the boiling point; **water-vascular** *adjective* (ZOOLOGY) pertaining to or consisting of water vessels; ***water-vascular system***, a network of water vessels in the body of an echinoderm, the tube-feet being operated by the pressure within the vessels; **water vessel** ZOOLOGY any of a system of vessels in some invertebrates in which water circulates; **water vine** any of several plants which yield an abundant watery sap, *esp.* the W. Indian *Doliocarpus calinea* (family Dilleniaceae); **water violet** an aquatic plant of the primrose family, *Hottonia palustris*, with lilac flowers and finely pinnate submerged leaves; **water-vole** (*a*) either of two large semi-aquatic Eurasian voles of the genus *Arvicola*, which burrow into the banks of rivers and streams; *esp.* the common *A. terrestris*; (*b*) *N. Amer.* a similar but smaller vole, *Microtus richardsoni*; **water-wagon** (orig. *US*) = ***water-cart*** above; chiefly in ***on the water-wagon*** (*slang*), abstaining from alcoholic drink, teetotal; **water-wagtail** (*a*) = WAGTAIL 1; (*b*) *US* = ***waterthrush*** above; **water-wave** *noun & verb* (*a*) *noun* a wave of water; a seismic wave in the sea; a scalloped wave in the hair set on the forehead with water; (*b*) *verb trans.* set (hair) in water-waves; **water-waved** *adjective* having a wavelike pattern; (of hair) set in water-waves; **water-waving** (*a*) a wavy or watered appearance given to silk etc. by pressing two pieces together; (*b*) the setting of hair in water-waves; **waterweed** (*a*) any aquatic plant with inconspicuous flowers; (*b*) *spec.* any of several freq. invasive N. American or S. American plants of the genus *Elodea*, of the frogbit family; *esp.* (more fully ***Canadian waterweed***) *E. canadensis*, widely naturalized in Europe; **water-wheel** (*a*) a wheel driven by water and used to power machinery, esp. that of a mill or pump; (*b*) a wheel for raising water, esp. for irrigation, by means of buckets fitted on its circumference; ***water whorl-grass***: see WHORL *noun*; **water-willow** any of various plants with narrow leaves resembling those of a willow, e.g. the N. American *Justicia americana*, of the acanthus family; **water-wings** inflatable floats fixed to the upper arms of a person learning to swim to give increased buoyancy; **water-witch** (*a*) a witch inhabiting water; (*b*) *US* any of various waterbirds noted for their diving, *esp.* a grebe; (*c*) *US* a water-finder; **water-witching** *US* dowsing; **water-wolf** *colloq.* the otter; **water-worm** any aquatic annelid; **waterwort** any of several aquatic plants of the genus *Elatine* (family Elatinaceae), with inconspicuous pinkish flowers in the axils of the leaves; **water yarrow** *arch.* any of several aquatic plants with finely divided leaves, *esp.* water violet.

■ **waterless** *adjective* unsupplied with water, containing no water; (of a process, apparatus, etc.) using or needing no water: OE. **waterlessness** *noun* L19. **waterward(s)** *adverb* [orig. *to the waterward(s)*] towards the water ME.

water /ˈwɔːtə/ *verb*.

[Old English *wæterian*, from *wæter* WATER *noun*.]

▶ **I** *verb trans.* **1 a** Give a drink of water to (an animal, esp. a horse on a journey); take (cattle) to water to drink. OE. ▸**b** Supply water to (troops on the march etc.); furnish (a boat, a fleet) with a supply of fresh water. OE. ▸**c** Supply (an engine) with water. L19.

2 Drench or sprinkle (a plant, crop, etc.) with water to encourage growth; pour or sprinkle water on (soil) to promote plant growth. OE.

3 Irrigate (land, crops). Of a river etc.: (*a*) supply water to (vegetation, land); †(*b*) surround (a site) (usu. in *pass.*). LME.

4 a Soak in water. Now *Canad.* LME. ▸**b** Sprinkle or drench (a material) for moistening or (a road etc.) to settle the dust. L15.

5 Dilute or adulterate (a drink) with water; *fig.* make less vivid, forceful, or shocking (now usu. ***water down***). LME. ▸**b** COMMERCE. Increase in nominal amount (the stock or capital of a trading company) by the creation of extra stock that is not sold. M19.

6 Produce a wavy lustrous finish on (a fabric) by sprinkling it with water and passing it through a calender. LME.

📖 **3** I. COLEGATE Flat meadowland, watered by slow winding rivers. **5** G. ORWELL The . . danger of watering the . . Socialist movement down to . . pale-pink humbug. *Journal (Newcastle-upon-Tyne)* Brewery man denies watering beer.

▶ **II** *verb intrans.* **7** Of the eyes: fill and run with moisture; shed water, flow with tears. Also (*rare*) (of tears) gather in the eyes. ME.
8 Secrete saliva in anticipation of food. Chiefly in ***make a person's mouth water*** & vars. below. M16.
9 Of a ship etc.: take fresh water on board. M16.
10 Drink water; obtain water to drink. E17.
11 Urinate. *rare.* E17.

📖 **7** A. BURGESS Closing his eyes in the full sunlight that made them water. **8** A. SILLITOE Delicious sniffs of salt and vinegar . . made our mouths water.

Phrases, & with adverbs in specialized senses: **make a person's mouth water**, (now *Scot.*) **make a person's teeth water** (of food) make a person salivate with a desire to eat; *fig.* fill a person with pleasurable anticipation or desire. **one's mouth waters**, (now *Scot.*) **one's teeth water** one salivates at the sight of food; *fig.* one is filled with pleasurable anticipation or desire. **water in** give water to (a seedling) on planting. **water with one's tears** *arch.* make wet with one's tears (chiefly *hyperbol.* or *fig.*).

waterage /ˈwɔːt(ə)rɪdʒ/ *noun.* L17.
[from WATER *noun* + -AGE.]
Conveyance by water; the charge made or the money paid for this.

Waterbury /ˈwɔːtəb(ə)ri/ *noun.* L19.
[A town in Connecticut, USA.]
1 Used *attrib.* to designate a low-priced watch or clock of a type manufactured at Waterbury. L19.
2 *ellipt.* A Waterbury watch. L19.

watercolour /ˈwɔːtəkʌlə/ *noun.* Also *-**color**. LME.
[from WATER *noun* + COLOUR *noun.*]
†**1** The colour of water; blue, greyish-blue. LME–L16.
2 A pigment for which water, not oil, is used as a solvent. Usu. in *pl.* L16.
3 A picture painted with watercolours; the art of painting with watercolours. L17.
▪ **watercoloured** *adjective* (*a*) *rare* of the colour of water; (*b*) painted in watercolours: E18. **watercolourist** *noun* a person who paints in watercolours M19.

watercourse /ˈwɔːtəkɔːs/ *noun.* E16.
[from WATER *noun* + COURSE *noun*[1].]
1 A stream of water; a river, a brook. Also, an artificial channel for conveying water. E16.
2 The bed or channel of a river or stream. M16.

watercress /ˈwɔːtəkrɛs/ *noun.* ME.
[from WATER *noun* + CRESS.]
Any of several pungent-tasting cruciferous plants, *Rorippa nasturtium-aquaticum*, *R. microphylla*, and their hybrid, found near springs and in running water; (*sing.* & (now *rare* or *obsolete*) in *pl.*) the leaves of such a plant, eaten as a salad.
fool's watercress: see FOOL *noun*[1].

water-dog /ˈwɔːtədɒg/ *noun.* LME.
[from WATER *noun* + DOG *noun.*]
1 A dog trained to enter water, esp. for retrieving waterfowl; any kind of dog that swims well. LME.
2 a Any of various aquatic mammals; *esp.* the otter. Now *rare.* L16. ▸**b** An aquatic N. American salamander of the genus *Necturus*; a mud puppy. M19.
3 A person at home on or in the water, as a sailor or swimmer. M17.
4 A small dark floating cloud supposed to indicate rain. Cf. DOG *noun* 10. E19.

watered /ˈwɔːtəd/ *ppl adjective.* LME.
[from WATER *verb* + -ED[1].]
†**1** Of the eyes etc.: filled with or wet with tears. LME–L16.
2 Soaked, sprinkled, or kept moist with water. LME. ▸**b** Of meadowland: subject to flooding. M18. ▸**c** Of a country etc.: supplied with streams (freq. with adverb). Of a road: within easy distance of water. L18.
3 Diluted with water (*lit.* & *fig.*). Now usu. ***watered-down***. M16.
4 a Of silk or other textile: having a wavy lustrous damask-like pattern. L16. ▸**b** Of steel: damascened. M19.
5 Of trading stock or capital: artificially increased by watering: see WATER *verb* 5b. L19.

📖 **3** *Times* A compromise plan . . would have involved a watered-down selection procedure.

waterer /ˈwɔːtərə/ *noun.* L15.
[from WATER *verb* + -ER[1].]
1 A person who supplies animals with drinking water. L15.
2 A person who waters plants, crops, etc. M16.
3 A container used for supplying water to animals or plants. L19.

waterfall /ˈwɔːtəfɔːl/ *noun* & *verb.* LME.
[from WATER *noun* + FALL *noun*[2]. Cf. Old English *wætergefeall*.]
▶ **A** *noun.* **1** A vertically descending part of a stream where it falls from a height over a rock, precipice, etc.; a cascade. LME.
2 An inclination of the ground sufficient to facilitate the fall or drainage of water. E16.
†**3** A swift stream tumbling in a rocky bed, a rapid. L17–M18.
4 *MINING.* A special head of water to be turned down a pit-shaft when needed. L18.
5 A neckcloth with long drooping ends worn in the early 19th cent. M19.
6 A chignon. Also, a wave of hair falling down the neck below the chignon or net. Orig. *US.* M19.
7 In a woman's garment, a cascading arrangement of material or attached decoration (orig., a series of flounces worn over a bustle). L19.
8 *CERAMICS.* A continuously flowing stream of glaze material applied to the upper surfaces of tiles. M20.
▶ **B** *verb.* **1** *verb intrans.* Tumble like a waterfall; cascade. M20.
2 *verb trans.* Cover with a stream of running water. M20.

Waterford /ˈwɔːtəfəd/ *noun.* L18.
[A city in SE Ireland.]
Used *attrib.* to designate glassware first manufactured at Waterford in the 18th and 19th cents., esp. drinking-glasses and chandeliers.

waterfowl /ˈwɔːtəfaʊl/ *noun.* Pl. same, (now *rare*) -**s**. ME.
[from WATER *noun* + FOWL *noun.*]
A bird that frequents the margin of lakes, rivers, seas, etc. Now usu., any of the larger swimming birds, esp. a duck or goose, regarded as game. Usu. in *pl.*
▪ **waterfowler** *noun* (*US*) a hunter of waterfowl L20. **waterfowling** *noun* (*US*) the hunting of waterfowl L20.

watergate /ˈwɔːtəgeɪt/ *noun*[1]. ME.
[from WATER *noun* + GATE *noun*[1].]
1 A gate of a town, castle, etc., giving access to the waterside. ME. ▸**b** A gate through which to bring supplies of water. M16.
†**2** A sluice, a floodgate. LME–M18.
3 A place through which water traffic passes. L19.

watergate /ˈwɔːtəgeɪt/ *noun*[2]. *Scot.* & *north.* LME.
[from WATER *noun* + GATE *noun*[2].]
A channel for water, a watercourse.

Watergate /ˈwɔːtəgeɪt/ *noun*[3] & *verb.* L20.
[A building in Washington DC, USA, containing the national headquarters of the Democratic Party, the bugging and burglary of which in 1972 by people connected with the Republican administration led to a national scandal and the resignation of President R. M. Nixon.]
▶ **A** *noun.* A political or commercial scandal on a large scale. Cf. -GATE. L20.
▶ **B** *verb intrans.* Engage in activities reminiscent of the Watergate scandal, esp. those involving the use of hidden bugging devices or the suppression of evidence. Chiefly as ***Watergating*** *verbal noun.* L20.
▪ **Watergater** *noun* L20.

water-glass /ˈwɔːtəglɑːs/ *noun.* E17.
[from WATER *noun* + GLASS *noun.*]
1 A glass vessel for holding water, *esp.* a vase for flowers or plants. E17.
2 A water-clock. M17.
†**3** A glass finger-bowl. M–L18.
4 An instrument for making observations beneath the surface of water, consisting of a bucket with a glass bottom. E19.
5 An aqueous solution of sodium or potassium silicate which solidifies when exposed to the air, used as a vehicle for fresco painting, as a fire-resistant paint, for pickling eggs, etc. M19.

water-hammer /ˈwɔːtəhamə/ *noun.* E19.
[from WATER *noun* + HAMMER *noun.*]
1 An evacuated tube partly filled with water which falls on the end with a noise like that of a hammer when the tube is reversed, used to illustrate the fact that in a vacuum liquids and solids fall at the same rate. E19.
2 The (sound of) concussion or reverberation in a water pipe when the flow is suddenly stopped, when there is an airlock, or when steam is admitted. L19.
3 *MEDICINE.* Used *attrib.* to designate a jerky pulse with a full expansion followed by a sudden collapse. L19.

water-hole /ˈwɔːtəhəʊl/ *noun.* L17.
[from WATER *noun* + HOLE *noun*[1].]
1 A hole or depression in which water collects; a pond, a pool; a cavity in the bed of a river, *esp.* one that retains water when the river itself is dry; this as regularly drunk from by animals. L17.
2 *ASTRONOMY.* The part of the radio spectrum between the frequencies of hydrogen atoms and hydroxyl radicals. L20.

water-horse /ˈwɔːtəhɔːs/ *noun.* LME.
[formed as prec. + HORSE *noun.*]
†**1** The hippopotamus. LME–M17.
2 A stack of split cod piled up to dry after being salted or washed. *Canad. dial.* L18.
3 A water-spirit appearing in the form of a horse. Cf. KELPIE *noun*[1]. E19.

Waterhouse–Friderichsen syndrome /wɔːtəhaʊsˈfriːd(ə)rɪks(ə)n ˌsɪndrəʊm/ *noun phr.* M20.
[from Rupert *Waterhouse* (1873–1958), English physician + Carl *Friderichsen* (1886–1979), Danish physician.]
MEDICINE. A fulminating meningococcal septicaemia with haemorrhagic destruction of the adrenal cortex, which occurs chiefly in children and can be fatal within hours.

watering /ˈwɔːt(ə)rɪŋ/ *noun.* OE.
[from WATER *verb* + -ING[1].]
1 The action of WATER *verb.* OE.
†**2** A place where horses and cattle were taken to drink. LME–E17.
†**3** A place where ships obtained a supply of fresh water. L16–L17.
4 †**a** Water for irrigation. E17–E18. ▸**b** A ditch draining a marsh; the tract drained by such a ditch. *dial.* L18.
5 A wavy variegated appearance given to silk, metal, etc.; a moiré pattern. L17.
Comb.: **watering-can** a portable container for watering plants, having a long spout usu. ending in a perforated sprinkler; **watering-hole** (*a*) a water-hole where animals regularly drink; (*b*) *joc.* a place supplying alcoholic refreshment; †**watering-house** an inn where coachmen obtained water for their horses and refreshment for themselves; **watering-place** (*a*) a place in a river or lake regularly drunk from by animals; a pool or trough for cattle and horses; (*b*) a place where a supply of water can be obtained; (*c*) a place for bathing in or drinking the waters of a mineral spring, a spa; a seaside resort; **watering-pot** (*a*) a watering-can; (*b*) *ZOOLOGY* (the shell of) any of several burrowing bivalve molluscs of the genus *Penicillus* (family Clavagellidae), which secrete a long perforated shelly tube to which the small valves are fused.

waterish /ˈwɔːt(ə)rɪʃ/ *adjective.* LME.
[from WATER *noun* + -ISH[1].]
1 Resembling water in appearance or colour. Cf. WATERY 4. LME. ▸†**b** Of colour: light grey, pale blue. M16–L17.
†**2** = WATERY 7. M–L16.
3 = WATERY 2. M16.
†**4** = WATERY 6. M16–E18.
5 = WATERY 1. M16.
†**6** Native to or inhabiting the water, aquatic. Cf. WATERY 5. L16–E18.
▪ **waterishly** *adverb* L16. **waterishness** *noun* M16.

Waterlander /ˈwɔːtəlandə/ *noun.* M19.
[from *Waterland* a district in the northern Netherlands + -ER[1].]
ECCLESIASTICAL. A member of a moderate or liberal grouping of Mennonites.
▪ Also **Waterlandian** *noun* M18.

water-level /ˈwɔːtəlɛv(ə)l/ *noun.* M16.
[from WATER *noun* + LEVEL *noun.*]
1 An instrument using water to determine the horizontal. Cf. ***spirit-level*** s.v. SPIRIT *noun.* M16.
2 *MINING.* A road driven on the strike of a seam to carry off water. L17.
3 = WATER-TABLE 4. M19.
4 (The position of) the horizontal surface of still water. M19.

water-line /ˈwɔːtəlʌɪn/ *noun.* E17.
[formed as prec. + LINE *noun*[2].]
1 *NAUTICAL.* The line along which the surface of the water touches the side of a floating ship etc. (marked on a ship's hull for use in loading); a ship's line of flotation. Also ***load-water-line*** s.v. LOAD *noun.* E17.
2 *SHIPBUILDING.* Any of various structural lines of a ship, parallel with the surface of the water, representing the contour of the hull at various heights above the keel. M18.
3 The outline of a coast. L18.
4 = WATER-TABLE 4. M19.
5 A linear watermark in paper. M19.
6 A stain on a wall showing where a roof formerly terminated. L19.
▪ **waterlined** *adjective* (of paper) marked with water-lines E20. **waterliner** *noun* a shot that hits a vessel on the water-line L19.

waterlog /ˈwɔːtəlɒg/ *verb trans.* Infl. -**gg**-. L18.
[App. from WATER *noun* + LOG *verb*[1].]
1 Make (a ship etc.) unmanageable by flooding or filling with water. See also WATERLOGGED. L18.
2 Impair or make unserviceable by saturating with water; *gen.* soak. L19.
▪ **waterlogger** *noun* E20.

waterlogged /ˈwɔːtəlɒgd/ *adjective.* M18.
[from prec. + -ED[1].]
1 Of a ship etc.: unmanageable or deprived of buoyancy through being flooded or filled with water. M18.

2 Impaired or made unserviceable by saturation with water; *gen.* soaked. **E19.**
■ **waterloggedness** *noun* **M19.**

Waterloo /wɔːtəˈluː/ *noun.* **E19.**
[A village in Belgium near Brussels, where Napoleon was finally defeated in 1815.]
1 A decisive and final defeat or contest; a cause of such a defeat. Freq. in ***meet one's Waterloo***. **E19.**
2 A bright blue tint. Also ***Waterloo blue***. **E19.**
Comb.: **Waterloo ball** a frivolous entertainment etc. preceding a serious occurrence (with ref. to a ball given in Brussels on the eve of the Battle of Waterloo); ***Waterloo blue***: see sense 2 above; **Waterloo Cup** an annual race in hare-coursing.

waterman /ˈwɔːtəmən/ *noun.* Pl. **-men. ME.**
[from WATER *noun* + MAN *noun*.]
1 A person working on a boat or among boats, *esp.* a boatman plying for hire on a river etc. Formerly also, a seaman, a mariner. **ME.** ▸**b** An oarsman or sailor of a specified level of knowledge or skill. **E20.**
2 A person employed in the supply or distribution of water. **E18.** ▸**b** *Hist.* An attendant at a cab- or coach-stand, occupied primarily in watering the horses. **M18.**
3 An imaginary being living in or under water; a merman. **M19.**
■ **watermanship** *noun* the art of a waterman, skill in rowing or managing boats etc. **L19.**

watermark /ˈwɔːtəmɑːk/ *noun & verb.* **M17.**
[formed as prec. + MARK *noun*[1].]
▸ **A** *noun.* †**1** A boundary-mark indicating the line of separation between the waters of different rivers. *Scot.* Only in **M17.**
2 a The level to which the tide, a river, etc., has risen or usually rises; a line marking this. **L17.** ▸**b** A mark left by a flood. **E19.**
3 A mark or device impressed in paper during manufacture, usu. barely noticeable except when held against the light, identifying the maker etc.; a metal design used to make such a mark. **E18.**
4 A line showing the draught of a ship. **M18.**
▸ **B** *verb trans.* **1** Mark or stamp with a watermark. **M19.**
2 Embody (a design etc.) as a watermark. **L19.**

watermelon /ˈwɔːtəmɛlən/ *noun.* **L16.**
[from WATER *noun* + MELON *noun*[1].]
The fruit of the gourd *Citrullus lanatus*, which has a green rind and sweet, very juicy flesh; the plant bearing this fruit, native to Africa and widely grown in warmer parts of the world.

Water Pik /ˈwɔːtə pɪk/ *noun phr.* **M20.**
[from WATER *noun* + PICK *noun*[1].]
(Proprietary name for) a device for cleaning the teeth by directing a jet of water at them.

waterproof /ˈwɔːtəpruːf/ *adjective, noun, & verb.* **M18.**
[formed as prec. + PROOF *adjective*.]
▸ **A** *adjective.* Impervious to water, completely resistant to the action of water. **M18.**
▸ **B** *noun.* A waterproof fabric or garment. **L18.**
▸ **C** *verb trans.* Make waterproof or impervious to water. **M19.**
■ **waterproofed** *adjective* made waterproof; provided with or wearing a waterproof garment or garments: **L19.** **waterproofer** *noun* (*a*) a person who waterproofs something; (*b*) material with which to waterproof something: **M19.** **waterproofing** *noun* (*a*) the action of the verb; (*b*) the quality of being waterproof; (*c*) material with which to waterproof something: **M19.** **waterproofness** *noun* **M20.**

water-rat /ˈwɔːtərat/ *noun.* **M16.**
[from WATER *noun* + RAT *noun*[1].]
1 Any of various larger semi-aquatic rodents of the family Muridae; *esp.* (*a*) the water-vole, *Arvicola terrestris*; (*b*) *US* the muskrat; (*c*) *Austral.* any rat of the genus *Hydromys*. **M16.**
2 *fig.* A water-borne thief, a pirate; *derog.* a sailor, a boatman. **L16.**
3 In *pl.* (**Water Rats**). A philanthropic show-business society. Also more fully ***Grand Order of Water Rats***. **E20.**

watershed /ˈwɔːtəʃɛd/ *noun.* **E19.**
[formed as prec. + SHED *noun*[1], after German *Wasserscheide*.]
1 The line separating waters flowing into different rivers, basins, or seas; a narrow ridge between two drainage areas. **E19.** ▸**b** *fig.* A turning-point in affairs, a crucial time or occurrence. **L19.**
2 a The slope down which the water flows from a watershed. **M19.** ▸**b** The whole gathering ground of a river system. **L19.**
3 A structure for throwing off water. **L19.**

📖 **1** A. J. TOYNBEE A ridge that is the watershed between the Atlantic and the basin of the River Paraná. **b** M. MEYER The publication of this book marked a watershed in their relationship.

watershoot /ˈwɔːtəʃuːt/ *noun.* **L16.**
[from WATER *noun* + SHOOT *noun*[1].]
1 A vigorous but unproductive shoot from the trunk, main branch, or root of a tree. **L16.**
2 †**a** Outflow of drainage water from land; water carried off by drainage. **E17–M19.** ▸**b** A gutter or channel for the overflow of water. **E17.**
†**3** A waterfall, a cascade. Only in **M18.**
4 = ***water-chute*** s.v. WATER *noun.* **E20.**

waterside /ˈwɔːtəsʌɪd/ *noun & adjective.* **ME.**
[formed as prec. + SIDE *noun*.]
▸ **A** *noun.* **1** The bank or margin of a sea, river, or lake. **ME.**
2 The side towards the water. **M19.**
▸ **B** *attrib.* or as *adjective.* Situated or found at the waterside; characteristic of or pertaining to the waterside. **M17.**
■ **watersider** *noun* (*Austral. & NZ*) a dockside worker **E20.**

water-ski /ˈwɔːtəskiː/ *noun, adjective, & verb.* **M20.**
[from WATER *noun* + SKI *noun*.]
▸ **A** *noun.* Either of a pair of skis, or a single ski, enabling the wearer to skim the surface of water when towed by a motor boat. **M20.**
▸ **B** *attrib.* or as *adjective.* Of, pertaining to, or suitable for water-skiing. **M20.**
▸ **C** *verb intrans.* Skim the surface of water on water-skis. **M20.**
■ **water-skier** *noun* a person who water-skis **M20.**

water-souchy /wɔːtəˈsuːtʃi, -ˈsuːʃi/ *noun.* Now chiefly *Hist.* **M18.**
[Dutch *waterzootje*, from *water* WATER *noun* + *zootje*, *zoodje* boiling (of fish).]
Fish, esp. perch, boiled and served in its own liquor.

waterspout /ˈwɔːtəspaʊt/ *noun.* **LME.**
[from WATER *noun* + SPOUT *noun*.]
1 A spout, pipe, or nozzle for discharging water. **LME.** ▸†**b** A jet of water from a fountain etc. **E17–E19.**
2 A gyrating column of spray and water between sea and cloud, produced by the action of a whirlwind. **M18.**
3 A sudden and violent fall of rain; a cloudburst. **L18.**

water-stone /ˈwɔːtəstəʊn/ *noun.* **LME.**
[formed as prec. + STONE *noun*.]
†**1** A stone basin for holy water. Only in **LME.**
†**2** ALCHEMY. A kind of philosophers' stone. *rare.* Only in **M17.**
3 A variety of Scottish building stone. **E19.**
4 Any of various stones which are pale-coloured, or which have a cavity containing water. **M19.**
5 A stratum of sandstone, shale, or limestone which contains water. **L19.**
6 A whetstone used with water rather than oil. **L19.**

water-table /ˈwɔːteɪb(ə)l/ *noun.* In sense 4 usu. as two words. **LME.**
[from WATER *noun* + TABLE *noun*.]
1 ARCHITECTURE. The sloping top of a plinth. Also, a horizontal projecting ledge or moulding with a sloping top, set along the side of a wall to throw off rain. **LME.**
2 A channel or gutter at the side of a road. **E18.**
3 A window-ledge or -sill in a ship or railway carriage. **L19.**
4 (The position of) the plane below which the soil or substrate is saturated with water. **L19.**
■ **water-tabling** *noun* (*a*) ARCHITECTURE water-tables collectively; a line of water-tables; (*b*) *dial.* the action or process of renovating with sods the side of a ditch worn away below the roots of a hedge: **L16.**

watertight /ˈwɔːtətʌɪt/ *adjective & noun.* **LME.**
[formed as prec. + TIGHT *adjective*.]
▸ **A** *adjective.* Constructed, fastened, or fitted so as to prevent the passage or leaking of water; *fig.* (of a scheme, argument, etc.) unassailable, invulnerable, without flaws. **LME.**

📖 A. T. ELLIS Only the most watertight of excuses could save her from the party. **watertight compartment** each of the compartments, with watertight partitions, into which the interior of a large ship is now usually divided for safety.

▸ **B** *noun.* A watertight boot. Usu. in *pl.* **M19.**
■ **watertightness** *noun* **M19.**

waterway /ˈwɔːtəweɪ/ *noun.* **OE.**
[from WATER *noun* + WAY *noun*.]
†**1** A channel connecting two pieces of water; a path with a stream running along it. Only in **OE.**
2 A channel for the escape or passage of water. **LME.**
3 NAUTICAL. A thick plank at the side of a deck hollowed into a channel to carry off water through the scuppers. **M17.**
4 a The breadth of a navigable watercourse, *esp.* that allowed under a bridge or tunnel. **M18.** ▸**b** A route for travel or transport by water; a river, canal, area of sea, etc., viewed as a medium of transit. **L18.** ▸**c** An opening for the passage of vessels; a navigable course or passage, *esp.* one to and from a harbour. **L19.**
5 The full-open passage area in a cock or valve. **M18.**

waterwork /ˈwɔːtəwəːk/ *noun.* **LME.**
[formed as prec. + WORK *noun*.]
†**1** A structure built in, to contain, or as a defence against water, as a tank, pier, sea wall, etc. **LME–L18.**
†**2** A kind of imitation tapestry, painted with size or distemper. **M–L16.**
3 In *pl.* & *sing.* Work concerned with hydraulic engineering, irrigation, drainage, etc. Now *rare.* **M16.** ▸**b** A thing done in, on, or by means of water. *rare.* **E17.**
4 In *pl.* (treated as *sing.* or *pl.*) & †*sing.* An establishment for storing, purifying, and to supply an area or town. **L16.**
5 †**a** An ornamental fountain or cascade. Usu. in *pl.* **L16–M19.** ▸**b** In *pl.* (The shedding of) tears; *rare* the falling of rain. *colloq.* **M17.** ▸**c** In *pl. euphem.* The urinary system. *colloq.* **E20.**

📖 **5c** L. LOCHHEAD Nowt up with the ticker, any trouble with the waterworks?

■ **water-worker** *noun* a person engaged in working with water; *spec.* an employee at a waterworks: **L16.**

watery /ˈwɔːt(ə)ri/ *adjective.* Also †**watry**.
[Old English *wæterig*, from WATER *noun* + -Y[1].]
1 Of land etc.: full of water, damp, well-watered. Of clouds, weather, etc.: rainy, wet. **OE.** ▸**b** Covered with water; positioned or built in or near water. Chiefly *poet.* **L16.**
2 Resembling water in consistency; thin, (excessively) fluid; (of food etc.) containing too much water, flavourless. **OE.**
3 Of speech, style, a person, etc.: vapid, uninteresting, insipid. **ME.**
4 Resembling water in appearance or colour; (of colour, sunshine, etc.) pale; (of the sky etc.) rainy-looking, overcast. **LME.**
5 Of, pertaining to, or inhabiting water; aquatic; (of a portent, season, etc.) heralding or bringing rain. Now *rare.* **LME.**
6 Of the eyes etc.: suffused with tears, tearful; running with or exuding moisture. **LME.**
7 Of the nature or consisting of water. Now chiefly *arch.* & *literary.* **LME.** ▸**b** Of a chemical extract or solution: made with water, aqueous. **E19.**
8 HERALDRY. = UNDEE. **L15.**

📖 **2** I. MURDOCH A bottomless morass of watery mud and weed. C. BRAYFIELD Rows of watery English lettuces. **3** *Times Lit. Suppl.* A watery but harmless story of London society. D. LODGE Marjorie . . gave a watery smile in acknowledgement. **4** K. WATERHOUSE The sun was still out, in a watery sort of way. **5** T. GRAY She mew'd to ev'ry watry God. **6** R. J. GRAVES His eyes became very red, watery, and intolerant of light. **7** J. PURSEGLOVE The river Blackwater . . forms the watery gulf between northern and southern Ireland.
watery grave, †**watery tomb** the bottom of the sea etc. as a place where a person lies drowned.

■ **waterily** *adverb* **L19.** **wateriness** *noun* †(*a*) watery constituent or element, aqueous matter in a liquid or solid; (*b*) the state of being watery, watery quality or nature: **LME.**

wath /wɑːθ/ *noun. obsolete* exc. *dial.* **LME.**
[Old Norse *vað* (Swedish, Danish *vad*) = Old English *wæd* sea, waves, Middle Low German, Old High German *wat* (Dutch *wad*), from Germanic word repr. by Latin *vadum* ford rel. to WADE *verb*.]
A ford; a fordable stream.
■ **wathstead** *noun* (*dial.*) a ford **E17.**

†**watry** *adjective* var. of WATERY.

WATS *abbreviation. N. Amer.*
Wide Area Telephone Service.

Watson /ˈwɒts(ə)n/ *noun*[1]. **E20.**
[Dr. *Watson*, the stolid faithful foil and assistant to the detective Sherlock Holmes in the stories of A. Conan Doyle.]
A person acting as a foil or assistant, esp. to a detective.

Watson /ˈwɒts(ə)n/ *noun*[2]. *Austral. colloq.* **M20.**
[App. the name of two brothers known at the beginning of the 20th cent. for betting large sums.]
bet like the Watsons, wager large sums.

watsonia /wɒtˈsəʊnɪə/ *noun.* **E19.**
[mod. Latin (see below), from Sir William *Watson* (1715–87), Scot. naturalist + -IA[1].]
Any of various chiefly South African bulbous plants constituting the genus *Watsonia*, of the iris family, which bear spikes of white, pink, or red flowers similar to gladioli and are sometimes grown for ornament.

Watsonian /wɒtˈsəʊnɪən/ *adjective.* **E20.**
[from *Watson* (see below) + -IAN.]
1 Of or pertaining to the US behavioural psychologist J. B. Watson (1878–1958). **E20.**
2 Of or pertaining to Henry Cottrell Watson (1804–81), British botanist, founder of the vice-county system of recording. **M20.**
3 Of, pertaining to, or characteristic of Dr Watson, friend and assistant of Sherlock Holmes (see WATSON *noun*[1]) or a person resembling him. **M20.**

Watsu /ˈwɒtsuː/ *noun.* **L20.**
[Blend of WATER *noun* and SHIATSU.]
A form of shiatsu massage that takes place in water.
¶ Proprietary name in the US.

watt /wɒt/ *noun*. L19.
[James Watt (1736–1819), Scot. engineer and inventor of the steam engine.]
PHYSICS. Orig., a unit of electrical power (or rate of heat generation) represented by a current of one ampere flowing through a potential difference of one volt. Now (equivalently), the derived SI unit of power, equal to the expenditure or production of one joule of energy per second. (Symbol W.)
Comb.: **watt-hour** the work done by one watt in one hour; **wattmeter** an instrument for measuring electric power; **watt-second** = JOULE 1.
■ **wattage** *noun* an amount of electrical power, esp. the operating power of a lamp, appliance, etc. expressed in watts; *colloq.* electricity, electrical illumination: E20. **wattless** *adjective* (of a current, electromotive force, etc.) consuming no power E20.

wattap *noun* var. of WATAP.

Watteau /ˈwɒtəʊ/ *noun*. M19.
[See below.]
Used *attrib.* to designate things, esp. women's clothing, associated with or reminiscent of those found in the paintings of the French artist Antoine Watteau (1684–1721).
Watteau back an arrangement of the back of a dress, coat, etc. with a double pleat falling from the neck to the extremity of the skirt without being gathered in at the waist. **Watteau bodice** a bodice with a square opening at the neck and short ruffled sleeves. **Watteau mantle** a kind of cloak having a Watteau back. **Watteau pleat** the pleat of a Watteau back.
■ **Watteauˈesque** *adjective* reminiscent of or in the style of Watteau E20. **Watteauish** *adjective* resembling the style of Watteau M19. **Watteaulike** *adjective* = WATTEAUESQUE M19.

wattle /ˈwɒt(ə)l/ *noun*[1] & *verb*.
[Old English *watul*, of uncertain origin but app. cogn. with *wætla* bandage.]
▶**A** *noun*. **1** Rods or stakes interlaced with twigs or branches as a material for making fences, walls, roofs, etc.; *sing.* & in *pl.*, rods and branches collected for this purpose. OE.
2 A rod, a stick. *dial.* L16.
3 A wicker hurdle. *dial.* M17.
4 More fully ***wattle-tree*** [from the early settlers' use of the boughs to build huts]. In Australia: any of numerous indigenous acacias, chiefly with long pliant boughs and freq. with fragrant golden flowers. L18.
1 wattle and daub wattle twigs plastered with clay or mud and used as a building material. **4 *Cootamundra wattle*, *golden wattle*, *silver wattle***, etc.
▶**B** *verb trans.* **1** Construct (a building, wall, fence, etc.) of wattle. LME. ▸**b** Construct (a sheepfold) with hurdles. L18.
2 Interlace (rods, twigs, etc.) to form wattle. L15.
3 Cover, enclose, or fill up with wattle. Also foll. by *about*. M16.
4 Bind together (rods or stakes) with interlaced twigs or branches. Also foll. by *across*. E17.
5 Enclose (sheep) in a sheepfold. *dial.* L19.
■ **wattling** *noun* (*a*) = WATTLE *noun*[1] 1; (*b*) the action of the verb: ME.

wattle /ˈwɒt(ə)l/ *noun*[2]. E16.
[Origin unkn.]
1 A coloured fleshy lobe hanging from the head or neck of certain birds, as the domestic fowl, turkey, etc. E16.
2 A flap of skin hanging from the throat or neck of some pigs, sheep, and goats. L16.
3 = BARBEL 2. M17.
Comb.: **wattlebird** (*a*) any of several Australian honeyeaters of the genera *Anthochaera* and *Melidectes*, which have a wattle hanging from each cheek; (*b*) (in *pl.*) the songbirds comprising the New Zealand family Callaeidae, which have wattles hanging from the base of the bill, and include the saddleback, the kokako, and the extinct huia; **wattle-eye** any of various African songbirds of the genus *Platysteira* (family Platysteiridae), which have a small coloured wattle above the eye.

wattled /ˈwɒt(ə)ld/ *adjective*. M16.
[from WATTLE *noun*[2] + -ED[2].]
†**1** Having folds of flesh. *rare*. Only in M16.
2 Of a bird etc.: having a wattle or wattles; HERALDRY having the wattles of a specified tincture. L17.
2 †**wattled bee-eater** = *wattlebird* (a) s.v. WATTLE *noun*[2]. **wattled crane** an African crane, *Bugeranus carunculatus*, which has partially feathered wattles hanging from the chin. †**wattled crow** = *wattlebird* (b) s.v. WATTLE *noun*[2]. **wattled jacana** a Central and S. American jacana, *Jacana jacana*, which has small red wattles at the base of the bill. **wattled lapwing**, **wattled plover** any of several African and Asian lapwings which have a wattle above or in front of the eye.

Watusi /waˈtuːsi/ *noun, adjective, & verb*. Also **-tutsi** /-ˈtʊtsi/. L19.
[Bantu, from *wa-* human pl. prefix + TUTSI.]
▶**A** *noun*. Pl. same.
1 A member of a people forming a minority of the population of Rwanda and Burundi but who formerly dominated the Hutu majority. Also called ***Tutsi***. L19.
2 (Also **w-**.) A popular dance of the 1960s. M20.
▶**B** *attrib.* or as *adjective*. Of or pertaining to the Watusi. M20.
▶**C** *verb intrans.* Dance the Watusi. M20.

wau *noun* var. of WAW *noun*[3].

waugh /wɑf/ *adjective*. *Scot. & north.* E18.
[Var. of WALLOW *adjective*.]
Tasteless, insipid; unpleasant to the smell or taste, sickly; faint, weak.

waugh /wɔː/ *interjection*. M18.
[Natural exclam.]
Expr. grief, indignation, disgust, etc.

Waughian /ˈwɔːɪən/ *adjective*. M20.
[from *Waugh* (see below) + -IAN.]
Of, pertaining to, or characteristic of the English novelist Evelyn Waugh (1903–66) or his writing.
■ **Waughism** *noun* (*a*) ideas or style characteristic of Waugh or his novels; (*b*) a word or expression characteristic of Waugh: M20.

waught /waxt/ *verb & noun*. *Scot. & north.* E16.
[Origin uncertain: perh. rel. to QUAFF.]
▶**A** *verb trans. & intrans.* Drink in large draughts; drain (a glass). Also foll. by *over*, *out*. E16.
▶**B** *noun*. A copious draught, a large drink. L16.

waul /wɔːl/ *verb & noun*. Also **wawl**. E16.
[Imit.]
▶**A** *verb intrans.* Give a loud plaintive cry like a cat or newborn baby. E16.
▶**B** *noun*. An act of wauling, a loud plaintive cry. M19.

waulk *verb* see WALK *verb*[2].

waur *adjective, adverb, & noun, verb* vars. of WAR *adjective, adverb, & noun*[2], *verb*[2].

wave /weɪv/ *noun*. L15.
[Alt., by assoc. with the verb, of WAW *noun*[1]; in branch II a new formation on WAVE *verb*[1].]
▶**I 1 a** Any of a succession of undulations which travel over the surface of the sea or other body of liquid, which are caused by each part of the surface successively rising and falling, and which may rise to a crest and break in strong wind etc.; a moving ridge or swell of water between two depressions; any of a series of long coastal rollers which follow each other at regular intervals, arch over, and break on the shore. L15. ▸**b** *sing.* & in *pl.* Water; the sea. *poet.* L16.
2 a A rough, stormy, or fluctuating condition (of life, passion, etc.). Usu. in *pl.* M16. ▸**b** A swelling and subsidence of feeling, excitement, etc.; a movement of common sentiment, activity, etc. sweeping over a community. Also, a sharp increase in the extent or degree of some phenomenon. M19.
3 a A formation with undulating shape; each of the rises and falls of such a formation, *spec.* in hair. Also, a set that leaves the hair in waves. M16. ▸**b** An undulating line or streak of colour. M17. ▸**c** ARCHITECTURE. An undulated moulding; a cyma or ogee moulding. M17. ▸**d** A wavy or zigzag pattern; something made in this pattern. M19.
4 PHYSICS. Any of a succession of oscillations or periodic disturbances in a fluid or solid which is propagated in a particular direction without progressive movement of the particles affected, as in sound, seismic shock, etc. Also, an analogous oscillation or disturbance in a field (as in light or gravitation) or in a time-varying quantity (as a voltage). M18. ▸**b** METEOROLOGY. A temporary rise or fall in atmospheric pressure or temperature which takes place at successive points in a particular direction on the earth's surface; *colloq.* a spell of abnormal heat or cold. M19. ▸**c** PHYSICS. A de Broglie wave. E20.
5 a A long convex strip of land between two long broad hollows; any of a series of such strips. Also, a rounded ridge of sand or snow formed by the action of the wind. L18. ▸**b** An undulatory movement, or each of an intermittent series of movements, of something passing over a surface or through the air. E19. ▸**c** MEDICINE. = ***pulse-wave*** s.v. PULSE *noun*[1]. M19. ▸**d** A forward movement of a large body of people (esp. advancing invaders or soldiers), or of military vehicles or aircraft, which either recedes and returns after an interval, or is followed after a time by another body repeating the same movement. M19. ▸**e** A rising-and-falling effect produced by successive sections of a crowd standing up, raising and lowering their arms, and sitting down again. Usu. more fully ***human wave***, ***Mexican wave***, ***Mexico wave***. L20.
6 Any of numerous geometrid moths that have wavy markings on the wings. E19.

🕮 **1a** V. BRITTAIN White crests of . . waves which swung rather than broke against the shore. N. CALDER Great waves that raced in from the Atlantic. ***bow wave***, ***seventh wave***, ***standing wave***, ***tidal wave***, etc. **b** TENNYSON We came to warmer waves, and deep Across the boundless east we drove. **2b** J. C. RANSOM The university is . . not too old to experience waves of reformational zeal. *International Business Week* Each new wave of technology unleashed vast demand. B. BETTELHEIM Goethe's *Werther* was blamed for causing a wave of suicides. A. LAMBERT Alistair had been killed . . . I remember the grief, how it came in waves. ***crime wave***, ***new wave***, etc. **3a** *Hairdo Ideas* This sensational look . . with its tight waves through the crown and full, buoyant curls. ***marcel wave***, ***permanent wave***, etc. **4 *alpha wave***, ***carrier wave***, ***electromagnetic wave***, ***gravitational wave***, ***lee wave***, ***matter wave***, ***medium wave***, ***radio wave***, ***seismic wave***, ***shock wave***, ***stationary wave***, ***travelling wave***, etc. **b *cold wave***, ***heat wave***, etc. **5d** *Armed Forces* Co-ordinated waves attacking . . as many targets as possible. *EuroBusiness* Turkey's geographical position . . has always made it host to waves of . . migrants.

▶**II** An act of waving.
7 A swaying to and fro. M17.
8 A motion to and fro of the hand or of something held in the hand, used as a signal. L17.

🕮 **8** R. BROUGHTON With a would-be-valedictory wave of the hand.

Phrases: ***human wave***: see sense 5e above. **make waves** stir up trouble, make things worse, make a fuss. ***Mexican wave***, ***Mexico wave***: see sense 5e above. ***on the crest of the wave***: see CREST *noun* 6. **the wave of the future** the inevitable future fashion or trend. **wave of contraction** PHYSIOLOGY the onward contraction of a muscle from the point where the stimulus is applied. ***Welsh wave***: see WELSH *adjective*.
Comb.: **wave-action** GEOLOGY the action of water flowing in waves; **wave analyser** an instrument for Fourier analysis of a wave motion; **waveband** a range of electromagnetic wavelengths or frequencies between specified limits; **wave base** PHYSICAL GEOGRAPHY the greatest depth of water at which sediment can be disturbed by surface waves; **wave-bread**: presented as a wave-offering; **wave-change** *adjective* (RADIO) designating a switch or rotary control for changing the wavelength (range) to which a transmitter or receiver can be tuned; **wave changer** RADIO a wave-change switch or control; a tuner; **wave cloud** METEOROLOGY any of a series of parallel elongated clouds that form at the crests of atmospheric waves in the lee of high ground and remain stationary in relation to the ground; **wave drag** AERODYNAMICS the drag experienced by a body at supersonic speeds as a result of the formation of a shock wave; **wave energy**: obtained by harnessing wave power; **wave equation** PHYSICS an equation that represents wave motion; *esp.* (*a*) the differential equation $\partial^2U/\partial t^2 = c^2\nabla^2U$; (*b*) Schrödinger's equation; **wave filter** ELECTRONICS = FILTER *noun* 4(e); **waveform** the shape of a wave at any moment, or that of the graphical representation of a (usu. periodically) varying physical quantity; a wave regarded as characterized by a particular shape or manner of variation, esp. a varying voltage; **wavefront** PHYSICS a continuous line or surface that is a locus of points where the phase is the same at a given instant; **wave function** PHYSICS a function that satisfies a wave equation, esp. Schrödinger's equation; **wave group** PHYSICS a short group of waves, not necessarily of uniform wavelength or amplitude; **waveguide** a device which constrains or guides electromagnetic waves along a defined path with minimum energy loss; *spec.* a metal tube, usu. of rectangular cross-section, doing this in the hollow space along its length; **wave-hop** *verb intrans.* (*colloq.*) fly low over the sea; **wave-line** (*a*) *rare* an outline recommended by some naval architects for the hull of a vessel as facilitating movement through the waves; (*b*) PHYSICS the path of a wave of light, sound, etc.; the graphic representation of this; **wave machine**: for producing waves in water; **wave-mark** (*a*) GEOLOGY a ripple mark on the surface of sedimentary rock, produced by waves at the time of deposition; (*b*) a wavy mark or stain; **wave-mechanical** *adjective* concerned with or involving wave mechanics; **wave mechanics** PHYSICS a form of non-relativistic quantum mechanics in which particles are regarded as having some of the properties of waves, the waves being described by Schrödinger functions; **wavemeter** (*a*) ELECTRICITY an instrument for measuring the wavelength or frequency of radio waves; (*b*) an instrument for measuring and recording the heights of water waves; **wave-motion** (*a*) motion in curves alternately concave and convex; (*b*) the movement of water waves; **wave-motor** a machine designed to utilize wave energy for motive power; **wave number** PHYSICS & CHEMISTRY the number of waves per unit length, used esp. to represent the frequency of electromagnetic radiation; the reciprocal of wavelength, or this multiplied by 2π; **wave-off** AERONAUTICS a signal or instruction to an approaching aircraft that it is not to land; **wave-offering**: presented by a priest before the altar (see WAVE *verb*[1] 2); **wave packet** PHYSICS a group of superposed waves which together form a travelling localized disturbance; *esp.* one described by Schrödinger's equation and regarded as representing a particle; **wave–particle** *adjective* (PHYSICS) designating the twofold description of matter and energy in terms of the two seemingly incompatible concepts of waves and particles; **wave-path** SEISMOLOGY the line along which a shock wave is propagated; **wave pattern** ARCHITECTURE = *VITRUVIAN scroll*; **wave period** PHYSICS the period between the arrivals at a given point of successive peaks or troughs of a travelling wave; **wave picture** PHYSICS the conception of subatomic particles as waves, in accordance with wave theory; **wave-power**: derived from the motion of waves, esp. on the coast or in an estuary; **waverider** AERONAUTICS a wing that derives lift from a shock wave close to its undersurface; an aeroplane having such wings; **waveshape** = *waveform* above; **wave-siren**: in which a current of air is driven through a narrow slit against an undulatory curve on the periphery of a cylinder or disc; **wave-surface** PHYSICS a geometrical surface which is the locus of all points reached at one instant by an undulatory agitation propagated from any centre; **wave-system** a series of waves; **wave theory** (*a*) (*obsolete* exc. *Hist.*) the undulatory theory; (*b*) PHYSICS a theory which treats subatomic particles as waves; (*c*) PHILOLOGY = WELLENTHEORIE; **wave train** PHYSICS a limited succession of waves travelling in the same direction, with equal or only slightly differing wavelengths; **wave trap** RADIO = TRAP *noun*[1] 6d; **wave vector** PHYSICS a vector whose direction is the direction of propagation of a wave and whose magnitude is the wave number; **wave velocity** PHYSICS = ***phase velocity*** s.v. PHASE *noun*; **wave winding** a kind of armature winding in which the coils are wound between commutator

bars just over 180 degrees apart so that there are two routes in parallel between the positive and the negative brush.

¶ See also WAVES.

■ **waveless** *adjective* having no waves or undulation; not agitated or disturbed by waves: L16. **wavelessly** *adverb* in a waveless manner E19. **wavelet** *noun* a small wave, a ripple E19. **wavelike** *adjective & adverb* (*a*) *adjective* resembling a wave; (*b*) *adverb* in the manner of a wave or waves: L17.

wave /weɪv/ *verb*[1].

[Old English *wafian* (corresp. to Middle High German *waben*), reinforced in Middle English by Old Norse *veifa* (see WEAVE *verb*[2]), from Germanic, partly from Germanic base also of WAVER *verb*; in branch III directly from the noun. See also WAFF *verb*[1].]

▸ **I** Of voluntary movement.

†**1** *verb intrans.* Make a movement to and fro with the hands. Only in OE.

2 *verb trans.* Move (a thing) to and fro or from side to side; *spec.* (*a*) move (one's hand, arm, etc., or something held in the hand) through the air with a sweeping gesture, often up or down or from side to side as a sign of greeting or farewell; (*b*) brandish (a weapon); (*c*) (in the Levitical ritual) raise and move from side to side (an offering) before the altar. ME. OE. ▸**b** *verb intrans.* (Of the hand, arm, etc., or something held in the hand) be moved to and fro; (of a weapon) be brandished. E17.

†**3** Chiefly NAUTICAL. ▸**a** *verb intrans.* Make a signalling motion with one's uplifted hands or with something held in one's hands. E16–M17. ▸**b** *verb trans.* Signal to (a person). M16–E17.

†**4** **a** *verb trans.* & (*rare*) *intrans.* Move (the wings) up and down in or as in flight. M16–E19. ▸**b** *verb intrans.* Move the body from side to side. Only in 17. ▸**c** *verb trans.* Move (one's head) up and down; incline (one's head). E17–M18.

5 **a** *verb trans.* Signify (something) by a wave of the hand or arm. (Foll. by *at* or *to* a person.) E19. ▸**b** *verb intrans.* Give a wave of the hand or arm (*at* or *to* a person or thing). E19. ▸**c** *verb trans.* Motion (a person etc.) *away, in, over, to do* something, etc., by a movement of the hand. M19.

> **2** G. VIDAL She waved her hands in the air to dry the lacquer. R. FULLER She waved her stick in greeting. *fig.*: J. G. WOOD Where the corn waves its yellow ears. **b** DAY LEWIS His arms waved like signals of distress. **5a** A. SETON Katherine . . waved goodbye until the . . horses faded from sight. **waving base** an observation terrace at an airport from which the public may watch the aircraft and wave to the travellers. **b** K. AMIS Nash politely waved me out of the room. *fig.*: *Economist* Other much more dubious . . takeovers were waved through.

▸ **II** Of involuntary movement.

6 **a** *verb intrans.* Of a thing: move to and fro; shake or sway by the action of the wind. ME. ▸**b** *verb intrans.* Of long hair: hang down loose. *poet.* L17.

†**7** *verb intrans.* **a** Move to and fro restlessly or unsteadily; waver, totter. LME–M17. ▸**b** Of a floating body: move restlessly by the impulse of the air or water. E17–E18.

†**8** *verb intrans.* Wander, stray, (of a person, the mind, etc.) alternate between different opinions or courses of action; vacillate, waver. LME–L18.

9 *verb intrans.* **a** (Of water, the sea) move in waves; (of a field of corn etc.) undulate like the waves of the sea. M16. ▸**b** Of a crowd: move to and fro restlessly in a body. L16.

10 *verb trans.* Of the wind etc.: cause (a thing) to sway or move to and fro. E17.

▸ **III** **11** *verb trans.* Ornament with an undulating design; make wavy in form or outline. M16.

12 *verb intrans.* Undulate in form or outline. L18.

> **11** *Hair* The hair has been softly waved.

With adverbs in specialized senses: **wave aside** dismiss as intrusive or irrelevant. **wave down** wave to (a vehicle or its driver) as a signal to stop.

■ **wavingly** *adverb* in the manner of a wave or waves M18.

†**wave** *verb*[2] var. of WAIVE.

waved /weɪvd/ *adjective.* M16.

[from WAVE *noun*, *verb*[1]: see -ED[2], -ED[1].]

1 Having undulated markings. M16.

2 Presenting a wavy outline or appearance, undulating. L16. ▸**b** HERALDRY = UNDEE. Now *rare.* E17. ▸**c** Of a sword, dagger, etc.: having the edge undulated. L17.

3 BOTANY & ZOOLOGY. Having a wavy surface or edge, undulate; having wavy markings. M17.

4 Held high and moved to and fro. L19.

wavel /ˈweɪv(ə)l/ *verb. Scot.* Infl. **-ll-**. M17.

[Frequentative of WAVE *verb*[1]: see -EL[1], -LE[3].]

1 †**a** *verb trans.* Twist (the mouth). Only in M17. ▸**b** *verb intrans.* Move backwards and forwards, wave; flutter, waver. *rare.* L17.

2 *verb trans.* Embroider with a wavy pattern. *rare.* M19.

3 *verb intrans.* Move unsteadily, stagger. L19.

wavelength /ˈweɪvlɛŋθ, -lɛŋkθ/ *noun.* M19.

[from WAVE *noun* + LENGTH.]

1 The distance between successive peaks or maxima of a wave or wavelike curve; *esp.* this as the distinguishing feature of the radio waves used to carry a particular broadcast service. M19. ▸**b** PHYSICS. Electromagnetic radiation having a specified wavelength. E20.

2 A particular mode or range of thinking and communicating. Esp. in ***be on the same wavelength***, understand each other. E20.

> **2** R. HARRIES She really isn't one of us, she isn't on our wavelength. *Blitz* He had a remarkable wavelength of communication with Indira Gandhi.

Comb.: **wavelength constant** = *PROPAGATION constant.*

wavellite /ˈweɪv(ə)lʌɪt/ *noun.* E19.

[from William *Wavell* (d. 1829), English physician + -ITE[1].]

MINERALOGY. An orthorhombic hydrated basic phosphate of aluminium, occurring in globular aggregates with a fibrous radiating structure.

waver /ˈweɪvə/ *noun*[1]. E16.

[from the verb.]

1 A condition of vacillation or faltering. Freq. in ***on the waver***, uncertain, unsteady. E16.

2 A condition of trembling; a flutter. E19.

waver /ˈweɪvə/ *noun*[2]. M16.

[Origin uncertain: perh. from WAIVE in the sense 'leave untouched'.]

A young tree left standing when the surrounding wood is felled.

waver /ˈweɪvə/ *noun*[3]. M16.

[from WAVE *verb*[1] + -ER[1].]

†**1** (**W-**.) The star Fomalhaut in the constellation Piscis Austrinus. Only in M16.

†**2** A person who vacillates. *rare.* Only in M17.

3 A person who waves, or causes something to undulate, swing, or flutter. M19.

4 PRINTING. A roller which distributes ink diagonally. Also ***waver roller***. L19.

5 An implement for making hair wavy. L19.

waver /ˈweɪvə/ *verb.* ME.

[Old Norse *vafra* move unsteadily, flicker (Norwegian *vavra* go to and fro, stagger) = Middle High German *waberen* (German *wabern*) move about, frequent, from Germanic: see -ER[5]. Cf. WAVE *verb*[1].]

▸ **I** *verb intrans.* **1** **a** Of a person, sentiment, etc.: show doubt or indecision; falter in resolution or allegiance; vacillate. ME. ▸**b** Of a soldier, body of troops, etc.: become unsteady, flinch, give way. M19.

2 **a** Travel without a fixed destination; wander, rove *about*. LME. ▸†**b** Stray *from*. LME–E17.

3 Sway to and fro unsteadily; reel, stagger, totter. LME.

4 Swing or wave in the air; float, flutter. LME.

5 Change, vary, fluctuate. L15.

6 Of the voice, eyes, etc.: become unsteady; shake, tremble, falter. E17.

7 Of light, an object, etc.: flicker, quiver. M17.

> **1a** L. P. HARTLEY In war . . his hostility never wavered, just as . . loyalty to his own side never wavered. L. BLUE I began to waver in my vegetarianism. **5** DICKENS Mr Benjamin Allen had been wavering between intoxication partial and intoxication complete. **6** V. WOOLF Her voice in its indignation wavered as if tears were near. **7** P. S. BUCK There wavered upon the child's face a flickering smile. E. MANNIN Figures moved with lanterns, the light wavering against mud walls.

▸ **II** *verb trans.* **8** Cause to waver; set in a waving or fluttering motion. Now *rare.* LME.

■ **wavery** *adjective* characterized by wavering or fluttering; tremulous, unsteady: E19.

waverer /ˈweɪv(ə)rə/ *noun.* L16.

[from prec. + -ER[1].]

1 A person who vacillates in opinion, hesitates, or falters in allegiance. L16.

2 (**W-**.) *Hist.* Any of a group of peers who were willing to make terms with the Reform government of 1832 rather than wreck the Upper House. M19.

wavering /ˈweɪv(ə)rɪŋ/ *adjective.* ME.

[formed as prec. + -ING[2].]

1 Vacillating, undecided; faltering in allegiance. ME.

†**2** Wandering, vagrant. LME–E17.

3 Tottering, shaking, reeling. LME.

4 Fluttering, floating, waving. LME.

5 Orig. (of a person), having a doubtful right to something. Later (of fortune, affairs, etc.) variable, mutable. LME.

6 Changing in intensity; flickering, intermittent; tremulous, unsteady. LME.

■ **waveringly** *adverb* LME. **waveringness** *noun* (*rare*) E17.

Waves /weɪvz/ *noun pl. US.* M20.

[Acronym, from Women Appointed (later Accepted) for Volunteer Emergency Service.]

The women's section of the US Naval Reserve, established in 1942, or, since 1948, of the US Navy.

waveson /ˈweɪvs(ə)n/ *noun.* E16.

[from WAIVE (later assim. to WAVE *noun*) + *-son* after Anglo-Norman *floteson* FLOTSAM.]

MARITIME LAW. = JETSAM 1.

wavey /ˈweɪvi/ *noun. N. Amer.* Pl. **-veys**, **-vies**. L18.

[Cree *we:hwe:w*, Ojibwa *we:ˀwe:*.]

The snow goose, *Anser caerulescens.*

wavicle /ˈweɪvɪk(ə)l/ *noun.* E20.

[Blend of WAVE *noun* and PARTICLE.]

PHYSICS. An entity having characteristic properties of both waves and particles.

wavies *noun pl.* see WAVEY.

wavy /ˈweɪvi/ *adjective & noun.* M16.

[from WAVE *noun* or *verb*[1] + -Y[1].]

▸ **A** *adjective.* **1** **a** HERALDRY. = UNDEE. M16. ▸**b** Forming an undulating line or a series of wavelike curves. E18. ▸**c** BOTANY & ZOOLOGY. (Of marks, margins, etc.) undulating in outline; sinuate. M19. ▸**d** Of a dog: having a coat that is undulating, not curly. Also more fully ***wavy-coated***. M19.

2 (Of the sea etc.) full of waves; *transf.* (of the air, clouds, etc.) billowy. L16.

3 Moving to and fro or up and down with a wavelike motion; sinuous. E18.

4 Fluctuating, wavering, changing. L18.

5 Of land: rising and falling gently. L18.

6 MEDICINE. Designating respiration in which the inspiratory, and sometimes the expiratory, sounds are broken into two or more separate parts. L19.

> **1a barry wavy** (of a field) divided into waving bands of generally horizontal direction. **b** D. H. LAWRENCE Her hair . . lies low upon her neck in wavy coils.

Special collocations: **Wavy Navy** *colloq.* the Royal Naval Volunteer Reserve, so nicknamed from the wavy braid worn by officers on their sleeves prior to 1956.

▸ **B** *noun.* A wavy-coated retriever. L19.

■ **wavily** *adverb* M19. **waviness** *noun* L18.

waw /wɔː/ *noun*[1]. *obsolete* exc. *Scot.* ME.

[Rel. to Old English *wagian* wave, shake, totter.]

A wave of the sea.

waw /wɔː/ *noun*[2]. *Scot. & north.* M18.

[from WAW *verb*[2].]

The cry of a cat.

waw /wɔː/ *noun*[3]. Also **wau**. M19.

[Var. of VAV.]

The sixth letter of the Hebrew alphabet; the corresponding letter in the Arabic and other Semitic alphabets.

waw consecutive, **waw conversive** HEBREW GRAMMAR the conjunction *wa* 'and' used with the imperfect to express the perfect, or used with the perfect to express the imperfect.

†**waw** *verb*[1].

[Old English *wagian*, corresp. to Middle Low German, Middle Dutch *wagen*, Old High German *wagōn*, Old Norse *vaga*, ult. from Germanic. Cf. WAG *verb*.]

1 *verb intrans.* Shake, totter. Only in OE.

2 *verb intrans.* Sway on a base; wave in the wind. OE–ME.

3 *verb intrans.* Of water or wind: move restlessly. ME–M16.

4 *verb trans. & intrans.* (Cause to) move or go *away*. Only in ME.

waw /wɔː/ *verb*[2] *intrans. Scot. & north.* L16.

[Imit.]

Utter a sound similar to the cry of a cat.

wa-wa *noun*[1], *noun*[2] & *verb* vars. of WAH-WAH *noun*[1], *noun*[2] & *verb*.

wawl *verb & noun* var. of WAUL.

wax /waks/ *noun*[1].

[Old English *wæx*, *weax* = Old Frisian *wax*, Old Saxon, Old High German *wahs* (Dutch *was*, German *Wachs*), Old Norse *vax*, from Germanic.]

1 = BEESWAX *noun.* OE. ▸**b** Beeswax melted down, bleached, or otherwise prepared for a special purpose, as for candles, modelling material, protective coatings, etc. Also with qualifying adjective. OE. ▸**c** An object made of beeswax, as a candle, modelled figure, etc. M19.

2 **a** = ***SEALING-wax***. OE. ▸**b** = ***COBBLER'S wax***. E17. ▸**c** = ***earwax*** s.v. EAR *noun*[1]. E18.

3 *fig.* A person or thing likened to wax, with ref. to its softness and readiness to receive impressions, mouldability, fusibility, etc. OE.

4 Any of a class of thermoplastic water-repellent lipid substances with low softening temperatures, esters of long-chain fatty acids and alcohols, which are secreted by animals or form a protective outer layer on the stem, leaves, etc., of plants. L18. ▸**b** Any of various mineral and synthetic hydrocarbons with similar properties, as paraffin wax and some polyethers. M19.

5 A thick syrup produced by boiling down the sap of the sugar maple and cooling. *US.* M19.

6 Paraffin wax rubbed on a ski or surfboard to prevent slipping. E20.

7 A gramophone record (so called from the wax discs in which the recording stylus cuts its groove). Freq. in ***on wax***, in record form. *colloq.* E20.

Phrases: **close as wax** extremely close (with ref. to the adhesive nature of wax). ***JAPANESE wax***. **man of wax**, **lad of wax** (now *arch.* & *dial.*) a good, clever, or faultless man. ***mineral wax***: see MINERAL *adjective*. ***nose of wax***: see NOSE *noun*. ***paraffin wax***: see PARAFFIN noun. ***vegetable wax***: see VEGETABLE *adjective*. ***virgin wax***: see VIRGIN *adjective*.

Attrib. & comb.: In the sense 'made of wax', as ***wax candle***, ***wax taper***, etc. Special combs., as **wax bath** an application of warm liquid wax, which is allowed to solidify, to a part of the body, for cosmetic or medical purposes; **wax bean** *N. Amer.* = ***wax-pod bean*** below; **wax berry** any of certain plants having berries with a waxy coating, *esp.* the bayberry, *Myrica cerifera*, of the US, and the allied *M. cordifolia*, of South Africa; the berry of such a plant; **wax-billed** *adjective* (of a bird) having a bill resembling sealing-wax; **wax borer** *Austral. slang* a person who talks too much; **wax-chandler** a person whose trade is to make or sell wax candles; **wax-cloth** (*a*) cloth coated with wax as a protection from wet; (*b*) oil cloth for covering floors or tables; **wax-cluster** a Tasmanian shrub, *Gaultheria hispida*, of the heath family, with white flowers and berries; **wax-colour** (*a*) a pigment ground with wax for encaustic painting; (*b*) the yellow colour of wax; **wax doll** (*a*) a doll with a head and bust (often also limbs) of wax; (*b*) (in *pl.*) fumitory, *Fumaria officinalis*, so called from its waxy pink flowers; **wax-end** thread coated with cobbler's wax, used by shoemakers; **wax-eye** *Austral. & NZ* = ***silver-eye*** s.v. SILVER *noun & adjective*; **wax flower** (*a*) an imitation flower made of wax; (*b*) any of certain plants having flowers with a waxen appearance; *esp.* = HOYA; **wax gland** ENTOMOLOGY a gland which secretes wax; **wax-insect** an insect that produces wax; *esp.* a scale insect; **wax jack** a device for holding a coiled taper with its end ready for lighting, to provide a flame for melting sealing-wax; **wax-kernel** (*obsolete* exc. *dial.*) a hard glandular swelling in the neck or armpit or under the jaw; **wax-light** a candle, taper, or night-light made of wax; **wax moth** any of several pyralid moths which have larvae that feed on beeswax; esp. *Galleria mellonella*, which is a pest of honeycomb in beehives; **wax museum** a waxworks; **wax myrtle** the bayberry, *Myrica cerifera*; **wax-painting** encaustic painting; **wax palm** either of two S. American wax-yielding palms, *Ceroxylon alpinum*, of Colombia, and the carnauba, *Copernicia prunifera*, of Brazil; **wax paper** paper waterproofed with a layer of wax; *N. Amer.* greaseproof paper; **wax plant** any of various plants yielding a vegetable wax or having flowers with a waxen appearance; *esp.* (*a*) the bayberry, *Myrica cerifera*; (*b*) = ***wax flower*** (b) above; **wax pocket** ENTOMOLOGY each of the sacs on the abdomen of a honeybee, for receiving the wax secreted by the wax glands; **wax-pod (bean)** a dwarf French bean belonging to any of several varieties having yellow, stringless pods; = ***butter-bean*** (a) s.v. BUTTER *noun*[1]; **wax print** cloth patterned by a batik process; **wax resist** a process similar to batik used in pottery and printing; **wax shot** (*obsolete* exc. *Hist.*) a customary payment made for the maintenance of lights in churches; **wax tablet** a board coated with wax, written on with a stylus; **wax-tree** any of various trees yielding wax; *esp.* (more fully ***Japanese wax-tree***) an eastern Asian sumac, *Rhus succedanea*, having white berries which are used as a substitute for beeswax.

■ **waxlike** *adjective* resembling wax in appearance or consistency M18.

wax /waks/ *noun*[2]. Now *rare* exc. *dial.* ME.
[from WAX *verb*[1].]
1 The process of waxing; growth. ME.
2 Stature; size (of something growing). LME.

wax /waks/ *noun*[3]. *slang*. M19.
[Perh. evolved from usage such as *wax angry* (see WAX *verb*[1]).]
Angry feeling; a bad temper. Chiefly in ***be in a wax***.

wax /waks/ *verb*[1] *intrans.* Pa. pple **-ed**, (*arch.*) **-en** /-(ə)n/.
[Old English *weaxan* = Old Frisian *waxa*, Old Saxon, Old High German *wahsan* (Dutch *wassen*, German *wachsen*), Old Norse *vaxa*, Gothic *wahsjan*, from Germanic strong verb from Indo-European, repr. by Greek *auxanein* increase, Latin *augere*, Sanskrit *ukṣ* grow.]
▶**I** Increase. (Opp. ***wane***.)
1 Of a plant or its parts: increase gradually in size and vigour; develop, sprout. *obsolete* exc. *dial.* OE.
2 Of a person or animal (orig. also of part of the body): increase gradually in size and strength. *arch. & dial.* OE. ▸†**b** MEDICINE. Of a growth or disease: arise and develop on or in the body. OE–LME.
†**3** Of a company of people: increase in numbers. OE–M17.
4 Of a person, nation, etc.: advance in power, importance, prosperity, etc. (Foll. by *in*.) *arch. & literary*. OE.
5 Of an inanimate thing: increase in size, quantity, volume, intensity, etc.; *spec.* (*a*) (of the sea) rise, swell; (*b*) (of day or night) grow longer. *literary*. OE.
6 Of the moon: show an increase in the extent of the portion illuminated, as occurs progressively from new moon to full moon. OE.
7 Of a quality, state, activity, etc.: become gradually greater or more striking; increase in potency or intensity. *literary*. OE.
†**8** Of a quality, activity, event, etc.: come into being, begin, occur. OE–LME.

> 📖 **6** W. DE LA MARE That shadowed moon now waxing in the west. **7** W. GOLDING The slow thoughts waxed and waned.

▶**II** Become.
9 With compl. (esp. adjective): pass into a specified state or mood, begin to use a specified tone; become gradually, grow, turn. ME.
†**10** Of fire: burn *out*. LME–L16.

> 📖 **9** *Guardian Weekly* Merchants are waxing fat on imports. *Face* He waxed enthusiastic about Australia.

Phrases: **wax in age** advance in years.

wax /waks/ *verb*[2] *trans.* LME.
[from WAX *noun*[1].]
1 Cover with a layer of wax; polish or stiffen with a dressing of wax; saturate or impregnate with wax. LME.
†**2** Stop (an aperture) with or as with wax. Also foll. by *up*. LME–E18.
3 In leather manufacture, dress (a skin) with a mixture of lampblack, oil, etc. L19.
4 Make a gramophone record of (music etc.); record. Cf. WAX *noun*[1] 7. *colloq.* M20.
5 Remove unwanted hair from (legs etc.) by applying wax and peeling off the wax and hairs together. M20.
■ **waxer** *noun* L19. **waxing** *noun* (*a*) the process of covering or dressing with wax; (*b*) depilation by means of wax; (*c*) *colloq.* a gramophone record or phonograph cylinder: LME.

wax /waks/ *verb*[3] *trans.* M19.
[Perh. rel. to prec.]
1 Beat (a person) thoroughly; gain victory over, get the better of. *US colloq.* M19.
2 Kill, murder. *slang*. M20.

waxbill /ˈwaksbɪl/ *noun*. M18.
[from WAX *noun*[1] + BILL *noun*[2].]
Any of numerous small finchlike birds of the African genus *Estrilda* (family Estrildidae), whose bills have a waxy appearance; *spec.* (more fully ***common waxbill***) the red-billed *E. astrild*. Also, a bird of any of several other genera of this family.
swee waxbill, ***violet-eared waxbill***, ***yellow-bellied waxbill***, etc.

waxed /wakst/ *ppl adjective*. LME.
[from WAX *verb*[2] + -ED[1].]
1 Coated with a layer of wax; polished or stiffened with wax; dressed, saturated, or impregnated with wax, as for waterproofing. LME.
2 Of a skin: dressed on the flesh side with a mixture of lampblack, oil, etc. M19.
1 waxed jacket an outdoor jacket made of waterproof waxed cotton. **waxed paper** paper that has been impregnated with wax to make it waterproof or greaseproof, or to use for insulation etc.

waxen /ˈwaks(ə)n/ *adjective*.
[Old English *wexen*, superseded by a new formation from WAX *noun*[1] + -EN[4].]
1 Made of wax. *arch.* OE.
2 a Able to receive impressions like wax; soft. L16. ▸**b** Having a smooth pale translucent surface as of wax. L17.
3 Covered, coated, or loaded with wax. L16.

> 📖 **2b** M. IGNATIEFF She . . watched the life slip away from their waxen faces.

Special collocations: **waxen chatterer** the Bohemian waxwing, *Bombycilla garrulus*. **waxen image** an effigy in wax representing a person whom it is desired to injure by witchcraft.

†**waxen** *verb*[1]. M16–M17.
[Unexpl. alt. of WAX *verb*[1].]
= WAX *verb*[1].

> 📖 SHAKES. *Mids. N. D.* And then the whole quire hold their hips and laugh, And waxen in their mirth.

waxen *verb*[2] *pa. pple*: see WAX *verb*[1].

waxwing /ˈwakswɪŋ/ *noun*. E19.
[from WAX *noun*[1] + WING *noun*.]
Each of three crested perching birds of the genus *Bombycilla*, which have red waxlike tips to the inner wing feathers; *esp.* (more fully ***Bohemian waxwing***) *B. garrulus*, which breeds in northern Eurasia and N. America and wanders widely in winter.

waxwork /ˈwakswəːk/ *noun*. L17.
[from WAX *noun*[1] + WORK *noun*.]
1 Modelling in wax; an object, esp. a lifelike dummy, or objects modelled in wax. L17.
2 An exhibition of wax figures representing famous characters; the place of such an exhibition. Now only in *pl.* M18.
3 The climbing bittersweet, *Celastrus scandens*, so called from the waxy scarlet aril of the fruit. *US*. E19.

waxy /ˈwaksi/ *adjective*[1]. LME.
[from WAX *noun*[1] + -Y[1].]
†**1** Made of wax. LME–E17.
2 a Of a person, the mind, etc.: soft, impressionable like wax. L16. ▸**b** Having the nature or distinctive properties of wax. L18.
3 a Resembling wax in colour or consistency; *spec.* (of boiled potatoes) not dry or powdery. M19. ▸**b** MEDICINE. Affected with amyloid degeneration. M19.
4 Soiled or covered with wax. M19.
■ **waxily** *adverb* L19. **waxiness** *noun* M19.

waxy /ˈwaksi/ *adjective*[2]. *slang*. M19.
[from WAX *noun*[3] + -Y[1].]
Angry, in a temper.

way /weɪ/ *noun*.
[Old English *weg* = Old Frisian *wei*, *wī*, Old Saxon, Old High German *weg* (Dutch *weg*, German *Weg*), Old Norse *vegr*, Gothic *wigs*, from Germanic base meaning 'move, journey, carry' (cf. WAIN *noun*[1] & *verb*, WEIGH *verb*), repr. also by Latin *vehere* carry.]
▶**I** A path.
1 a A track for travelling along; a road, a lane, a path; *spec.* (*a*) a main road (now *rare* exc. in names of Roman roads) or path connecting different parts of a country; (*b*) a path in a wood or through fields. OE. ▸**b** A place or means of passage, as a door, a gate, an opening made through a crowd, etc. Freq. in ***way in***, ***way out***. ME.
†**2** ANATOMY. Any duct or channel in the body. LME–E17.
3 In *pl.* ▸**a** NAUTICAL. Baulks laid down for rolling or sliding heavy objects along. M17. ▸**b** Parallel wooden rails or planks, forming an inclined plane for heavy loads to slide down on. M19. ▸**c** MECHANICS. Parallel sills forming a track for the carriage of a lathe or other tool. M19.

> 📖 **1a** LD MACAULAY In winter, when the ways were bad and the nights long. J. BETJEMAN In among the silver birches winding ways of tarmac wander. *Daily Mail* The Pennine Way . . goes from Edale in Derbyshire . . to Teesdale. *fig.*: SHAKES. *Haml.* But, in the beaten way of friendship, what make you at Elsinore? **b** *fig.*: *Argosy* Now that he had that damned cheque in his pocket, there was no way out.

▶**II** Course of travel.
4 a A line or course of travel or progression by which a place may be reached, or along which a person or thing may pass. (Foll. by *into*, *out of*, *to*, etc.) OE. ▸**b** Mode of transport. E18.
5 a Travel or motion along a particular route or in a particular direction. Freq. with possess. OE. ▸†**b** A journey, a voyage; a pilgrimage. ME–L15. ▸**c** NAUTICAL. Movement of a vessel through the water; velocity. M17.
6 Distance (to be) travelled along a particular route; the distance from one place to another. Usu. with qualifying adjective. Also (now *N. Amer. & dial.*) in *pl.* (treated as *sing.*). OE.
7 a Direction of motion, relative position, or aspect. Freq. preceded by demonstrative, possessive, or pronominal adjective, as *my*, *this*, *that*, *which*, etc., or (*colloq.*) by place-name indicating the or its neighbourhood. Also (now *dial.*) in *pl.* (treated as *sing.*). ME. ▸**b** Direction of thought, situation, opinion, etc. Freq. preceded by *this* or *that*. L16.
8 a Course or line of actual movement. LME. ▸†**b** The wake of a vessel. M16–E18. ▸**c** ENGRAVING. The series of parallel paths made by a cradle rocked on a mezzotint. L19.
9 a Opportunity for passage or advance; absence of obstruction to forward movement; *fig.* freedom of action, scope, opportunity. Chiefly in phrs. below. LME. ▸**b** LAW. = ***right of way*** s.v. RIGHT *noun*[1]. M18.
†**10** NAUTICAL. The course of a ship. Only in 17.

> 📖 **4a** D. EDEN Nurse Ellen knows the way home. R. K. NARAYAN Gaffur always chose this way to the river. *fig.*: J. H. NEWMAN Two alternatives, the way to Rome, and the way to Atheism. **5a** W. IRVING The river forces its way between perpendicular precipices. R. S. THOMAS Pedestrian man holds grimly on his way. M. WHEELER I . . thanked him . . for his lunch, and went my way. **6** J. AGEE He . . walked again, by now a good way behind the others. T. O'BRIEN Across the street and down a ways, he saw the shoddy frame building. **7a** SIR W. SCOTT To ask her lady, which way she proposed to direct her flight. WILKIE COLLINS Will you step this way, and see her at once? P. MARSHALL Uncle Sam will toss a few millions our way. A. THWAITE She comes Of a very good family, up Inverness way. **b** J. WHITTAKER The War . . did the ordinary social movements no good—at least, I feel that way. D. EDEN If it had not happened that way she would have contrived something else.

▶**III** Means, manner.
11 a A path or course of life; a person's activities and fortunes. *biblical & arch.* OE. ▸**b** In *pl.* Habits of life, esp. with regard to moral conduct. OE. ▸**c** *sing.* & in *pl.* A prescribed course of life or conduct; the law or commandments (of God). OE.
12 a The course of actions chosen for the doing of something; the course of events in the occurrence of something; a method of performing an action. Formerly freq. in ***any manner of way(s)***, ***all manner of way(s)***. OE. ▸†**b** Literary style or method. M–L17.
13 a A course of action. Freq. in ***go the right way***, ***go the wrong way***. Now *rare*. ME. ▸†**b** A person's best or most advisable course. L16–E17.
14 a A method, means, or course of action by which some end may be attained or a danger escaped. Foll. by *of*, *to*, *to do*. ME. ▸**b** An aspect, a feature, a respect; a point of comparison. Chiefly in adverbial phrs. ***in any way***, ***in some way***, etc. L16.
15 a The customary or usual manner of acting or behaving. E17. ▸**b** In *pl.* Customary modes of behaviour; usages, customs. M18.
†**16** A particular form of church government or polity. M17–M18.
17 Kind of occupation, work, or business. Now only *Scot.* & in ***way of business***, or preceded by specifying word. L17.
18 a *sing.* & in *pl.* A habitual or characteristic manner of action, behaviour, expression, etc. Freq. with possess.

E18. ▸**b** *transf.* A tendency or liability of a thing to act in a particular manner. L19.

> 📖 **11b** M. CREIGHTON Your letter . . may in time lead to an amendment of my ways. **12a** I. FLEMING If I . . wanted a market for his stones, this was no way to go on. D. EDEN He talked in a light amusing way. L. DEIGHTON He smiled and held the smile in a way that only actors can. **14a** ALDOUS HUXLEY There is no way of telling. G. VIDAL She tried to think of some way she could get to know him. D. BOGARDE She had found a way to help these poor soldiers. *Proverb:* Where there's a will there's a way. **b** M. R. RINEHART It's a dead end, in more ways than one. **15b** B. PYM He . . was steeped in English ways and conventions. **18a** G. STEIN It was always Melanctha's way to be good to anyone in trouble. L. P. HARTLEY We are getting rather set in our ways. **b** *Times Lit. Suppl.* Each of our nerves has a nature of its own and ways of its own.

Phrases: †**a foul way out** (*rare*, Shakes.) miserably unsuccessful. ***a good way(s)***: see GOOD *adjective*. †**a great way** to a great extent. **all the way** completely. **all the way (from — to —)** (*a*) throughout the specified interval, at every point in it; (*b*) *US* (estimated etc.) at any amount between the specified quantities. **be in a way** *dial.* be in a state of mental distress or anxiety. **be in the way of** be likely to do or obtain, have a good chance of. **be on one's way** set off immediately. **be on your way, on your way** *imper.* (*colloq.*) go away, get going. ***both ways***: see BOTH *adjective*. **by a long way** (usu. with a compar.) by a great amount, by far. **by the way** (*a*) during a journey, on the way; (*b*) incidentally, in passing, as a side-topic or casual remark; †(*c*) (*rare*, Shakes.) indirectly, by a side channel of information; (*d*) as a subordinate piece of work. **by way of** (*a*) via; (*b*) as an instance or a form of; in the capacity or with the function of; (*c*) by means of, through the medium of; (*d*) *arch.* in the habit of; making a profession of, having a reputation for. **clear the way** (*a*) remove obstacles; (*b*) stand aside. ***come one's way***: see COME *verb*. **come a long way, go a long way** achieve much, make much progress. **come one's ways, go one's ways** (usu. in *imper.*, now only *dial.*) come on, move forward. **come in one's way, lie in one's way** be met with in one's experience. ***cut both ways***: see CUT *verb*. **dry way** a chemical process or assay carried out in the absence of water or other liquid. ***each way***: see EACH *adjective*. **either way** = ***one way or other*** below. **everything coming one's way, everything going one's way** everything happening in one's favour. ***every way, every which way***: see EVERY *adjective* 1. ***feel one's way***: see FEEL *verb*. ***find its way, find one's way to***: see FIND *verb*. †**from the way** (*rare*, Shakes.) out of the way, in a secluded place. ***gather way***: see GATHER *verb* 12. **get one's own way, get one's way, have one's own way, have one's way** get what one wants; ensure one's wishes are met. **give way** (*a*) retreat in the face of attack; †(*b*) make way, leave the way clear; (*c*) (foll. by *to*) make room for, be superseded by, allow precedence to (***give-way sign***: instructing some road users to allow priority to some others); †(*d*) allow free scope or opportunity (*to*); (*e*) (of a structure etc.) be dislodged or broken under a load, collapse; (*f*) make concessions (*to*), yield, fail to resist; (*g*) (foll. by *to*) be overcome by an emotion, break down; (*h*) (of a rowing crew) row hard. **go all the way, go the whole way** (*a*) continue a course of action to its conclusion; *spec.* (*slang*) engage in sexual intercourse (*with* someone) as opp. to just petting; (*b*) agree completely *with* someone. **go a long way**: (*a*) last for a considerable time; (*b*) see ***come a long way*** above. ***go down the wrong way***: see WRONG *adjective*. **go one's own way** behave as one pleases. ***go one's ways***: see ***come one's ways*** above. **go out of one's way to do something** do something which the circumstances do not call for or invite. **go separate ways** cease to work or operate together, take up different paths. ***go the way of all the earth, go the way of all flesh***: see GO *verb*. ***go the whole way***: see ***go all the way*** above. ***go the wrong way***: see WRONG *adjective*. ***Great White Way***: see GREAT *adjective*. HALFWAY. **have a way with** have skill in dealing with. **have a way with one** have a persuasive manner. **have everything one's own way, have it all one's own way** have one's wishes carried out exactly. ***have it both ways***: see HAVE *verb*. ***have one's own way, have one's way***: see ***get one's own way*** above. **have one's way with** have sexual intercourse with. **have way** †(*a*) (*rare*, Shakes.) be allowed liberty of action; (*b*) (of a feeling) find vent. †**here lies our way**, †**here lies your way** it is time to go. **hold one's way, keep one's way** travel without interruption; *fig.* continue one's course of action. ***how way!***: see HOW *noun*[1] & *interjection*[1] 1. ***in a bad way***: see BAD *adjective*. ***in a big way***: see BIG *adjective*. ***in a fair way to***: see FAIR *adjective*. ***in a family way***: see FAMILY *noun*. **in a great way** (living) on a large scale of income and expenditure. ***in a small way***: see SMALL *adjective*. **in a way** (*a*) in a certain respect but not altogether or completely; (*b*) *dial.* distressed, anxious. **in a — way** in the condition specified. **in his way, in its way**, etc., if regarded from a particular standpoint appropriate to that person or thing; *spec.* (*a*) suited to one's capacity, tastes, or requirements (usu. in neg. contexts); (*b*) (now *rare*) on the path by which one is travelling; †(*c*) in the course of one's journey; (*d*) = ***in the way*** (a) below. **in that way** *euphem.* pregnant. ***in the family way***: see FAMILY *noun*. **in the way** (*a*) forming an obstacle or hindrance; (*b*) (now *rare* or *obsolete*) within reach, at hand; (*c*) *euphem.* pregnant. **in the — way** of the nature of or belonging to the class of —. **in the way of** †(*a*) as an instance or manifestation of; †(*b*) with a view to, as a means of attaining; when one is concerned with; (*c*) of the nature of, belonging to the class of; (*d*) (now *rare*) by means of; (*e*) in the course or routine of. †**in the way of honesty** under honourable conditions; so far as honour allows. †**in the way of marriage** with a view to matrimony. **in way of** NAUTICAL in a direct line aft from. **it is always the way with someone** someone always acts so. **it's this way** *colloq.* it's like this (introducing an explanation). ***keep one's way***: see ***hold one's way*** above. **keep out of a person's way** avoid a person. **know one's way around, know one's way about** know how to get from place to place in a neighbourhood. ***lead the way***: see LEAD *verb*[1]. ***lie in one's way***: see ***come in one's way*** above. ***look the other way***: see LOOK *verb*. ***lose one's way, lose the way***: see LOSE *verb*. ***lose way***: see LOSE *verb*. ***make in one's way***: see MAKE *verb*. **make its way** (of a thing) travel, make progress; (of an opinion, custom, etc.) gain acceptance. **make one's way** (*a*) travel or proceed in an intended direction or to a certain place; (*b*) make progress in one's career; advance in wealth, status, etc., by one's own efforts. ***make the best of one's way***: see BEST *adjective, noun, & adverb*. **make way** (*a*) remove obstacles to progress; allow room *for* others to proceed; (*b*) achieve progress; †(*c*) make a hole in something; (*d*) leave a place vacant *for* a successor or substitute. †**means and ways** = ***ways and means*** below. ***middle way***: see MIDDLE *adjective*. MILKY WAY. ***narrow way***: see NARROW *adjective*. ***not know which way to turn***: see TURN *verb*. **no two ways about it** there can be no doubt of the fact. **no way** not at all, definitely not. ***ONCE in a way***. **one way and another** taking various considerations into account. **one way or another** by some means, for any of various reasons. **one way or other, one way or the other** in either direction; regarding either of two possibilities. **on one's way** on, or in the course of, a journey. **on one's way in, on one's way up** *colloq.* going up in status, popularity, etc. **on one's way out, on one's way down** *colloq.* going down in status, popularity, etc. **on the way** (*a*) *colloq.* pregnant; (*b*) *colloq.* (of a child) conceived but not yet born; (*c*) = ***on one's way*** above. **on the way in, on the way up** = ***on one's way in*** above. **on the way out, on the way down** = ***on one's way out*** above. ***on your way***: see ***be on your way*** above. **out of a person's way** (*a*) not on a person's intended route, away from a person's path of travel; (*b*) (now *rare* or *obsolete*) not in accordance with a person's purpose or taste, outside a person's scope. ***out of harm's way***: see HARM *noun* 1. †**out of one's way** entailing a loss of (a specified sum). **out of the way** (*a*) remote from a centre of population, secluded; (*b*) not or no longer an obstacle or hindrance; disposed of, settled; clear *of*; (*c*) out of place, inappropriate; unusual, remarkable (usu. with neg.); †(*d*) (of a thing) lost, missing; (*e*) (of a person) imprisoned; killed; (see also OUT-OF-THE-WAY). ***over the way***: see OVER *preposition*. ***pave the way***: see PAVE *verb*. ***pay its way, pay one's way***: see PAY *verb*[1]. ***permanent way***: see PERMANENT *adjective*. ***plane the way***: see PLANE *verb*[1] 1. ***prepare the way***: see PREPARE *verb*. ***push one's way***: see PUSH *verb*. **put out of the way** (*a*) *arch.* do away with, kill; (*b*) disturb, inconvenience, trouble (freq. *refl.*). ***right of way***: see RIGHT *noun*[1]. ***sacred way***: see SACRED *adjective*. **see one's way** (*a*) have a view of the path immediately ahead along which one is travelling; (*b*) (also ***see one's way clear***) know that some object is attainable (foll. by *to*); feel justified in deciding *to do* something (usu. in neg. contexts). ***show the way***: see SHOW *verb*. ***stop a person's way***: see STOP *verb*. ***swing both ways***: see SWING *noun*. **take one's way** *arch.* set out on a journey; travel. **take the way** *arch.* enter on and follow the route leading *to* a place. **that way** (*a*) homosexual; (*b*) (foll. by *about*) in love, infatuated; (see also senses 7a, b above). ***the hard way***: see HARD *adjective, adverb, & noun*. **the other way about, the other way around, the other way round** conversely, vice versa. ***the parting of the ways***: see PARTING 2. **there are no two ways about it** = ***no two ways about it*** above. †**there is but one way** death or ruin is certain. **there is no way** — *colloq.* there is no possibility that —. †**there lies your way** please go away. **the Way** in the Acts of the Apostles, the Christian religion. **the Way of the Cross** a series of images representing the Stations of the Cross, ranged round the interior of a church, or on the road to a church or shrine; the series of devotions prescribed to be used at these stations in succession. **the ways of God** *arch.* the course of God's providence. ***the wrong way***: see WRONG *adjective*. ***under way***: see UNDERWAY. †**walk in the way with** in biblical use, accompany, *fig.* associate with. **way in** a means of entry or introduction; an entrance (see sense 1b above). **way of life** the principles or habits governing all one's actions etc. **way of looking at it, way of looking at things** the personal perspective from which one views a situation or event; a point of view. **way of thinking** a set of opinions or principles characteristic of an individual or group. **way out** a means of exit or escape; an exit (see sense 1b above). **ways and means** (*a*) the methods and resources at a person's disposal for achieving some end; (*b*) methods of raising government revenue (freq. in ***Committee of Ways and Means***, a committee of the House of Commons or of the US House of Representatives); *gen.* financial resources. **way to go!** *N. Amer. colloq.* expr. encouragement, approval, or pleasure. **well on one's way** having made considerable progress. **wet way** a chemical process or assay carried out in the presence of water or other liquid. ***WHAT way?*** ***which way the wind blows, which way the wind lies***: see WIND *noun*[1].

Comb.: **wayboard** MINING a thin layer or band that divides or separates thicker strata; **way-chain** a brake for the wheel of a vehicle; **way fare** *US*: charged for travelling between intermediate stations on a railway; **way-freight** *N. Amer.* goods that are picked up or set down at intermediate stopping places on a railway or shipping route; a train carrying such freight; **waygate** *Scot. & north.* (*a*) a passageway; (*b*) speed, progress, headway; **wayleave** (payment for) right of way granted by the owner of land to a particular body for a particular purpose, as for carrying telephone wires over or along buildings, or laying paths or pipes across land; a document conferring the right; **way letter** *US*: given to a mail carrier to take to a post office; **wayman** †(*a*) a waywarden; †(*b*) a traveller, a wayfarer; (*c*) a workman employed in fixing the rails of a railway, a platelayer; **waymark** *noun & verb* (*a*) *noun* a conspicuous object which serves as a guide to travellers; (*b*) *verb trans.* provide or identify (a path) with waymarks; **way passenger** *US*: getting on or off at a stage or station intermediate between the main stops on a route; **way-point** (orig. *US*) a stopping-place on a journey; (on an air journey) the computer-checked coordinates of each stage of a long flight; **way-port**: which normally serves as a port of call rather than as an ultimate destination; **way-post** a signpost; **way station** *N. Amer.* (*a*) an intermediate station on a railway route; (*b*) a point marking progress in a certain course of action etc.; **way-stop** (chiefly *US*) an intermediate stop on a journey; **way-ticket** *Hist.* = WAYBILL 4; **way train** *US*: which stops at intermediate stations on a railway; **way-up** GEOLOGY orientation as regards which part is uppermost or was deposited last; **way-wise** *adjective* (*US*) (of a horse) familiar with the roads it is required to travel; *dial.* (of a person) experienced, trained; **way-worn** *adjective* worn or wearied by travel.

■ **wayless** *adjective* having no way or road; *esp.* (of a country or region) trackless, pathless: OE.

†**way** *verb*[1]. L16.
[from the noun.]
1 *verb intrans.* Go, travel. L16–E18.
2 *verb trans.* Train (a horse) to be familiar with travelling on paths. M17–E18.
3 *verb trans.* Set (a wagon) on the running path or track. Only in M18.

†**way** *verb*[2] var. of WEIGH *verb*.

way /weɪ/ *adverb*. ME.
[Aphet. from AWAY.]
1 Away (to or at another place). Now chiefly *Scot., north., & US dial.* ME.
2 At or to a great distance; long, far. With adverbs & prepositions of direction or time. M19.
3 Much, to a considerable degree. (Usu. with a compar. or superl.) Orig. *US*. M20. ▸**b** Extremely, very. *slang*. L20.

> 📖 **2** BARONESS ORCZY The three men had become mere specks, 'way down the road. H. KURNITZ They live way up top. K. HULME It's late, Holmes, way after eleven. N. GORDIMER The country's always been way ahead in industrial . . development. **3** A. TYLER He was way overdressed, for August. T. MCGUANE You're way prettier than she is.

Comb. & phrases: **way-in** *adjective* (*colloq.*) conventional; fashionable, sophisticated; **way off** *fig.* far away from an intention or aim; greatly mistaken; **way-out** *adjective* unconventional, eccentric; progressive, avant-garde; **way-outness** *colloq.* unconventionality.

way /weɪ/ *interjection*. M19.
[Cf. WO.]
A call to a horse to stop.

-way /weɪ/ *suffix*.
[from WAY *noun*.]
= -WAYS.

wayang /ˈwɑːjaŋ/ *noun*. E19.
[Javanese *wajang*, *wayang*.]
In Indonesia and Malaysia: a theatrical performance employing puppets or human dancers; *spec.* a Javanese and Balinese shadow puppet play (also ***wayang kulit*** /ˈkuːlɪt/ [Javanese = skin, leather]).

way-back /ˈweɪbak/ *adverb, adjective, & noun*. *colloq.* (chiefly *N. Amer., Austral., & NZ*). As adverb usu. **way back**; as adjective & noun also **wayback**. M19.
[from WAY *adverb* + BACK *adverb*.]
▸ **A** *adverb*. **1** Far away; in a remote rural area. M19.
2 A long time ago; for a long period in time before; *transf.* through and through. L19.
2 from way back for a long period in time before. **way back when** *colloq.* (orig. *US*) a long time ago.
▸ **B** *adjective*. **1** Of long ago. L19.
2 Hailing from, or located in, a remote rural area. L19.
▸ **C** *noun*. **1** A person inhabiting or coming from a remote district. L19.
2 A remote rural area; *spec.* the Australian outback. L19.

waybill /ˈweɪbɪl/ *noun & verb*. L18.
[from WAY *noun* + BILL *noun*[3].]
▸ **A** *noun*. **1** A list of passengers booked for seats in a stagecoach or other public vehicle. Also, a statement of goods entrusted to a public carrier for delivery at stated destinations. L18.
2 A list of places to be visited on a journey. E19.
3 A label attached to a shipment or an article in transit to indicate its destination, mode of transport, etc. *N. Amer.* E19.
4 *Hist.* A pass produced by a traveller to obtain financial assistance at certain stages of his or her journey. L19.
▸ **B** *verb trans.* List (goods) on a waybill. *US*. M19.

waybread /ˈweɪbrɛd/ *noun*. Also **waybred**.
[Old English *weġbræde*, *-brāde*, corresp. to Old Saxon *wegabrēda*, Old High German *wegabreita* (German *Wegbreit* masc., *Wegebreite* fem.), West Germanic compound of WAY *noun* + adjective corresp. to BROAD *adjective* = 'the broad-leaved plant of the roadside'.]
The greater plantain, *Plantago major*.

wayfare /ˈweɪfɛː/ *noun*. *arch.* LME.
[from WAY *noun* + FARE *noun*[1], after WAYFARING *adjective*.]
Wayfaring, travelling.

wayfare /ˈweɪfɛː/ *verb intrans.* *arch.* M16.
[Back-form. from WAYFARING *noun*.]
Travel, esp. on foot.

wayfarer /ˈweɪfɛːrə/ *noun*. LME.
[formed as next + FARER.]
A traveller by road, *esp.* one on foot.

wayfaring /ˈweɪfɛːrɪŋ/ *noun*. M16.
[from WAY *noun* + FARE *verb* + -ING[1], after next.]
Travelling; an instance of this.

Comb.: **wayfaring-tree** a Eurasian viburnum, *Viburnum lantana*, characteristic of chalk and limestone scrub, with broad leaves downy underneath, white flowers in dense cymes, and berries turning from green through red to black; ***American wayfaring-tree***, an allied N. American shrub, the hobblebush, *V. alnifolium*.

wayfaring /ˈweɪfɛːrɪŋ/ *ppl adjective. arch.* OE.
[from WAY *noun* + pres. pple of FARE *verb*.]
Travelling by road. Esp. in ***wayfaring man***.

way-gang /ˈweɪgaŋ/ *noun. Scot.* M18.
[from WAY *adverb* + GANG *noun*.]
= WAY-GOING *noun*.

way-going /ˈweɪgəʊɪŋ/ *noun & adjective. Scot. & north.* LME.
[from WAY *adverb* + GOING *noun, adjective*.]
▶ **A** *noun*. The action or fact of going away; departure. LME.
Comb.: **way-going crop** *Hist.*: allowed to a tenant on quitting land rented.
▶ **B** *adjective*. Departing, outgoing. M17.

waygoose /ˈweɪguːs/ *noun. obsolete* exc. *dial.* L17.
[Earlier form of WAYZGOOSE.]
= WAYZGOOSE.

waylay /weɪˈleɪ/ *verb trans.* Pa. t. & pple **waylaid** /weɪˈleɪd/. E16.
[from WAY *noun* + LAY *verb*¹, after Middle Low German, Middle Dutch *wegelāgen*, from *wegelage* from Old Saxon, Old High German form meaning 'besetting of ways'.]
1 Lie in wait for in order to surprise and attack; ambush. E16. ▸**b** Intercept and seize (a thing in transit); *fig.* seize (an opportunity). L16.
2 Wait for and accost (a person); stop (a person) in order to converse. E17.
†**3** Block the path of (a person); obstruct (an activity); impede, intercept. Only in 17.
4 Blockade (a road, an area) with an armed force etc. Now *rare* or *obsolete*. E17.

> 🕮 **1** L. GARFIELD The two men . . would waylay the magistrate and murder him. *fig.*: P. ACKROYD Problems of his family to waylay and beset him. **2** I. WALLACE He must make haste . . without letting himself be waylaid by press or colleagues.

■ **waylayer** *noun* E17.

†**wayment** *verb & noun.* ME.
[Old French *waimenter*, *guaimenter*, from *wai*, *guai* alas, prob. after *lamenter* lament.]
▶ **A** *verb intrans.* Lament, wail; sorrow bitterly. ME–L19.

> 🕮 SPENSER For what bootes it to weepe and to wayment, When ill is chaunst?

▶ **B** *noun*. Lamentation. LME–M17.

-ways /weɪz/ *suffix.*
[from WAY *noun* + -'s¹.]
Forming adverbs & adjectives with the sense 'relating to direction, position, or manner', from nouns, as ***edgeways***, ***endways***, ***lengthways***, ***sideways***, etc., or (occas.) from adjectives, as ***flatways***, ***longways***, etc. Cf. -WISE.

wayside /ˈweɪsʌɪd/ *noun & adjective.* LME.
[from WAY *noun* + SIDE *noun*.]
▶ **A** *noun*. The side of a road; the land bordering either side of a road or path. LME.
fall by the wayside fail to stay the course, drop out of an undertaking.
▶ **B** *attrib.* or as *adjective*. Of or pertaining to the wayside; situated on or near, occurring or living by, the wayside. LME.

> 🕮 R. K. NARAYAN They stopped under a wayside tree. **wayside pulpit** a board, usu. placed outside a place of worship, displaying a religious text or maxim.

wayward /ˈweɪwəd/ *adjective.* LME.
[Aphet. from AWAYWARD.]
1 Childishly self-willed or perverse; disobedient, refractory. LME. ▸†**b** (Of judgement) perverse, wrong, unjust. LME–M17. ▸†**c** Of an action etc.: indicating obstinate self-will. LME–E19. ▸†**d** Of a thing, condition, etc.: untoward. M16–E19.
2 Conforming to no fixed rule or principle of conduct; erratic; unaccountable, freakish. M16.

> 🕮 **1** N. BAWDEN She . . was still a child to her mother; awkward and wayward, always in the wrong. **2** G. GREENE The dim and wayward light of the kerosene lamp. B. BAINBRIDGE The Greek gods were essentially cruel and wayward.

■ **waywardly** *adverb* LME. **waywardness** *noun* LME.

waywarden /ˈweɪwɔːd(ə)n/ *noun.* M17.
[from WAY *noun* + WARDEN *noun*¹.]
Hist. A person elected to supervise the highways of a parish or district.

way-wiser /ˈweɪwʌɪzə/ *noun.* Now *Hist.* M17.
[Anglicized from German *Wegweiser*, from *Weg* WAY *noun* + *Weiser* agent-noun from *weisen* show.]
An instrument for measuring and indicating a distance travelled by road.

waywode /ˈweɪwəʊd/ *noun.* M17.
[Var. of VOIVODE, repr. an early Hungarian form of a common Slavonic title.]
Hist. = VOIVODE.
■ **waywodeship** *noun* the province or district ruled by a waywode L17.

wayzgoose /ˈweɪzguːs/ *noun.* M18.
[Alt. of earlier WAYGOOSE, of unkn. origin.]
Orig., an entertainment given by a master printer to his workers around St Bartholomew's Day (24 August), marking the beginning of the season of working by candlelight. Later, an annual festivity held in summer by the members of a printing establishment, consisting of a dinner and (usu.) an excursion into the country.

wazir /wəˈzɪə/ *noun*¹. E18.
[Arab. *wazīr*: see VIZIER.]
Hist. = VIZIER.
■ **wazirate** *noun* = VIZIERATE L19.

Wazir /wəˈzɪə/ *noun*² *& adjective.* Also **Waziri** /wəˈzɪəri/, †**Vizeeree**, & other vars. E19.
[Local name, perh. with ref. to descent from a vizier: see prec.]
▶ **A** *noun*. Pl. **-s**, same. A member of a Pathan people of NW Pakistan. E19.
▶ **B** *adjective*. Of or pertaining to this people. M19.

wazoo /wəˈzuː/ *noun. US coarse slang.* M20.
[Origin unkn.]
The buttocks, the anus.

> 🕮 G. KEILLOR Your public-radio audience is a pain in the wazoo. **up, out the wazoo** in great quantities, in abundance, to excess.

wazzock /ˈwazək/ *noun. slang.* L20.
[Origin unkn.]
A stupid or annoying person.

Wb *abbreviation.*
PHYSICS. Weber(s).

WBA *abbreviation.*
World Boxing Association.

WBC *abbreviation.*
World Boxing Council.

WC *abbreviation.*
1 Water-closet.
2 West Central (a postal district of London).

WCC *abbreviation.*
World Council of Churches.

W/Cdr. *abbreviation.*
Wing Commander.

WCT *abbreviation.*
World Championship Tennis.

WCTU *abbreviation. N. Amer.*
Women's Christian Temperance Union.

WD *abbreviation.*
1 War Department.
2 Works Department.

WDC *abbreviation.*
Woman Detective Constable.

WDS *abbreviation.*
Woman Detective Sergeant.

we /wiː, *unstressed* wɪ/ *pers. pronoun, 1 pl. subjective (nom.), & noun.*
[Old English *wē*, *we*, corresp. to Old Frisian *wī*, *wi*, Old Saxon *wī*, *wē*, Old High German *wir* (Dutch *wij*, German *wir*), Old Norse *vér*, *vær*, Gothic *weis*, from Germanic.]
▶ **A** *pronoun*. **1** Used by the speaker or writer referring to himself or herself and one or more other people considered together as the subject of predication or in attributive or predicative agreement with that subject. OE. ▸**b** With a preceding verb in imper., in exhortations. Now only *poet. & rhet.* OE. ▸**c** Used by the speaker or writer referring to people or society in general. OE. ▸**d** Used confidentially or playfully (often implying condescension) to mean the person addressed, with whose interests the speaker thus identifies himself or herself, as by a doctor to a patient. E18.
2 a Used by and with reference to a monarch or ruler, esp. in formal pronouncements and declarations. Cf. OUR *adjective* 2. OE. ▸**b** Used by the speaker or writer to establish an impersonal or inclusive tone, or *spec.* by a newspaper editor expressing views understood to be supported by the editorial staff collectively. Cf. OUR *adjective* 3. OE.
3 Objective: us. Now *colloq. & dial.* L15.
4 Possessive: our. *dial. & W. Indies.* M19.

> 🕮 **1** H. JAMES I dare say we seem to you a vulgar lot of people. *Woman's Illustrated* We Naval men never smile when on duty. I. MURDOCH We two have our separate histories. C. RAYNER We are Mr and Mrs Lucas from Boston in Massachusetts. **b** SHAKES. *Rich. II* Put we our quarrel to the will of heaven. **c** L. STEFFENS We have to . . establish a steady demand for good government. M. ROBERTS Solitude is a necessity which we enjoy too rarely. **d** J. B. PRIESTLEY Good-morning . . Are we all very well this morning? **2a** M. THATCHER We are in the fortunate position . . of being . . the senior person in power. ***royal we***: see ROYAL *adjective*. **3** SHAKES. *Coriol.* And to poor we Thine enmity's most capital.

▶ **B** *noun*. The speaker or writer together with one or more people, referred to as a group. M19.

> 🕮 E. HARDWICK I am alone here in New York, no longer a *we*.

■ **we-ness** *noun* = US-NESS E20.

WEA *abbreviation.*
Workers' Educational Association.

weak /wiːk/ *adjective & noun.*
[Old English *wāc* corresp. to Old Norse *veikr*, Old Saxon *wēk*, Old High German *weih* (Dutch *week*, German *weich* soft), from Germanic, from base meaning 'yield, give way'. Reinforced in Middle English by forms from Old Norse.]
▶ **A** *adjective*. †**1** Pliant, flexible, not rigid. OE–E16.
†**2** Insignificant, mean; of little account or worth; inconsiderable. OE–E19.
3 Lacking courage or strength of purpose or will; not steadfast, wavering. OE. ▸**b** Indicative of weakness of character. M17. ▸**c** Unable to control one's emotions, unduly swayed by grief, compassion, or affection. M18.
4 a Lacking in strength and skill as an opponent or enemy; having little or inferior fighting power. Also (occas.) more widely, poorly supplied with people or things of a specified kind. ME. ▸**b** Lacking in skill as a competitor, athlete, etc.; (of an action) exhibiting lack of skill. E19.
5 a Physically lacking in power; unable to exert great muscular force; deficient in physical vigour or robustness; lacking in energy; feeble, infirm. ME. ▸**b** Exhausted; faint. Now chiefly *dial.* E18. ▸**c** Performed with or exhibiting a lack of muscular strength. L18.
6 Lacking in power or vigour, not intense; lacking in force, not strong; feeble, soft; (of a person) lacking conviction, unsure; (of the pulse or respiration) having little force; (now *rare*) (of a disease etc.) not severe or acute. ME.
7 a (Of the mind or mental faculties) deficient in power; not retentive; without force of intellect or strength of mind; easily deceived, credulous. LME. ▸**b** Lacking mental power (*in* one's intellect, the brain, etc.). M17.
8 Lacking in ability, ill-qualified, unskilled or inefficient *in*, *of* or *to do* something. Also, (of a quality, attribute, etc.) held to a low degree. LME. ▸**b** Of a literary work or composition: showing little evidence of ability. *rare.* E18.
9 Having little control or authority over others. Formerly also, (of power) little, diminished. LME.
10 Lacking in material strength; unsound, insecure; *spec.* (of a fortress, town, military position, etc.) not having powerful defences; easy to take or invade. LME. ▸**b** CHESS. Of a pawn: insufficiently protected against capture. Of a square: difficult to defend. M19.
11 Of a bodily organ or its function: deficient in functional strength. L15.
12 a (Of an argument, evidence, proof, etc.) not convincing; (of a case) ill-supported by evidence or precedent. M16. ▸**b** Of an action etc.: ineffectual. L16.
13 a Of a solution, a drink, etc.: containing a low proportion of an essential (esp. dissolved) substance; diluted; *spec.* in CHEMISTRY (of an acid or alkali) only partially dissociated in aqueous solution into anions and cations. L16. ▸**b** Of flour: made with less glutinous wheat so as to rise less, be less absorbent, etc. L19.
14 Lacking in solidity or firmness; slight; easily broken, fragile, frail. L16.
15 Not vivid, not strongly marked, faint; PHOTOGRAPHY (of a negative) not having marked contrast of light and shade. L16.
16 (Of a syllable or musical beat) unstressed, unaccented; (of stress) having relatively little force. M17.
17 CARDS. Not composed of commanding cards; not having commanding cards (*in* a specified suit). L17.
18 a Of language, an expression, a word: lacking in force or emphasis. L18. ▸**b** MATH. Of an entity or concept: implying less than others of its kind; defined by fewer conditions. M20.
19 COMMERCE. **a** Of prices, a market, etc.: having a downward tendency, not firm; fluctuating, depressed. M19. ▸**b** Of money or stock: insufficient to meet a demand or to carry on operations. L19.
20 GRAMMAR. **a** Of a Germanic noun or adjective: belonging to a declension in which the original Germanic stem ended in *n*. M19. ▸**b** Of a Germanic verb: forming the past tense and past participle by the addition of a suffix. Also (occas.), used to designate a particular verb-type in a non-Germanic language. M19.
21 a (Of a drug, chemical reagent, etc.) not powerful in operative effect; (of a lens) having little magnifying power. L19. ▸**b** PHYSICS. Of a field: having a low strength, exerting only a small force on particles, charges, etc. E20. ▸**c** PHYSICS. Designating the weakest of the known kinds of force between particles, which acts only at distances less than about 10^{-15} cm, is very much weaker than the electromagnetic and the strong interactions, and conserves neither strangeness, parity, nor isospin. M20.

📖 **5a** V. Woolf He despises me for being too weak to play. M. Holroyd He felt so weak . . that he found it impossible to lift a match. **6a** C. Ryan The signals they received . . were so weak as to be barely audible. C. Thubron There must be a power shortage . . the light is so weak. **8** *Business Franchise* Board members who . . have expertise in areas where you feel weak. **10** Tennyson The gate, Half-parted from a weak and scolding hinge, Stuck. **11** D. H. Lawrence I've got a weak chest. **12a** B. Neil I listened to his excuses . . getting weaker and weaker. **13a** A. Lambert The Head and her Deputy sat . . over a pot of weak coffee.

Special collocations, comb., & phrases: ***the weaker sex***: see SEX *noun*. **the weaker vessel** (long *joc.*) a wife, a female partner. **weak ending** PROSODY an unstressed syllable in a normally stressed place at the end of an iambic line. **weakest link** = *weak link* below. **weak grade** PHILOLOGY the reduced ablaut-form. **weak-handed** *adjective* (*a*) having weak hands; *fig.* not capable of effective exertion; (*b*) = SHORT-HANDED 2. **weak-headed** *adjective* lacking strength of mind or purpose. **weak-hearted** *adjective* (*rare*) faint-hearted; soft-hearted. **weak interaction** PHYSICS interaction at short distances between subatomic particles mediated by the weak force (see sense 21c above). **weak mixture** = *lean mixture* s.v. LEAN *adjective*. **weak moment** a time when one is unusually careless, compliant, or temptable. **weak link** the weakest or least dependable of a number of interdependent items. **weak point** (*a*) a point or feature where a thing is defective or unsound; a place where defences are assailable; (*b*) a flaw or weakness in a person's argument, character, or ability, or in a person's resistance to temptation. **weak side** the defective, unsound, or vulnerable aspect of a person or thing. **weak-sighted** *adjective* having poor sight. **weak sister** *colloq.* an ineffectual or unreliable person; a person of weak character. **weak spot** = *weak point* above.

▶ **B** *absol.* as *noun*. A weak person. Usu. *collect. pl.*, *the* class of weak people. OE.

■ **weakish** *adjective* L16.

†**weak** *verb trans.* LME–M19.
[from the adjective.]
Make weak or weaker; weaken, enfeeble.

weaken /ˈwiːk(ə)n/ *verb*. LME.
[from WEAK *adjective* + -EN[5]: in earliest use perh. of Scandinavian origin (cf. Norwegian dial. *veikna*, Swedish *vekna* become weak).]
▶ **I** *verb trans.* **1** Enfeeble, decrease the vigour of, (the mind etc.). LME.
2 Lessen (authority, influence, etc.). M16.
3 Lessen the physical strength or vigour of (an animal, plant, etc.); lessen the functional vigour of (an organ etc.). M16.
4 Reduce the strength of (a body of people) in numbers or fighting power; make (a position) less secure. M16.
5 Make weaker in resources, authority, power, etc. M16.
6 a Lessen or destroy the strength of (an argument, conviction, etc.); reduce the likelihood of. E17. ▸**b** Make less efficacious. M17.
7 Reduce the intensity of (a colour, sound, etc.). L17. ▸**b** PHONETICS. Reduce in force of utterance. M19.
8 CARDS. Lessen the strength of (one's hand etc.). M18.
9 Make (a material thing) less strong or more liable to fracture. E19.
10 Make (market prices, a market) less firm. L19.

📖 **1** Day Lewis I must have weakened my capacity for attention and observation. **2** B. Neil Don't keep apologising to the boys . . . It weakens your standing. **3** P. P. Read Weakened by her sickness and a sleepless night, she wept. **weaken the hands of** (in biblical use) reduce the effectiveness of (a person or group), hinder, discourage. **6a** J. le Carré Had Bella softened his head and weakened his will?

▶ **II** *verb intrans.* **11** Grow or become weak or weaker. M16. ▸**b** Take a less firm attitude, recede from a standpoint; give way. Orig. *US*. L19.

📖 **11b** E. Bowen Dread of chaos filled the room, so that Karen's heart weakened.

■ **weakener** *noun* L16. **weakening** *noun* (*a*) the action of the verb; an instance of this; (*b*) (now *rare* or *obsolete*) a cause or source of weakness: M16.

weakfish /ˈwiːkfɪʃ/ *noun*. Pl. **-es** /-ɪz/, (usu.) same. L18.
[Dutch †*weekvisch*, from *week* soft + *visch* fish.]
Any of several sciaenid sea-trout of the genus *Cynoscion*, of the coastal waters of eastern N. America; esp. *C. regalis*, which is a popular food fish. Also called ***squeteague***.

weakie /ˈwiːki/ *noun*. *slang*. Also **weaky**. M20.
[from WEAK *adjective* + -IE, -Y[6].]
A weak person (chiefly *Austral.*); *spec.* a weak player at chess.

weak-kneed /wiːkˈniːd, ˈwiːkniːd/ *adjective*. M19.
[from WEAK *adjective* + KNEE *noun* + -ED[2].]
Lacking resolution or determination. Also occas. (*lit.*), physically weak and unsteady.
■ **weak-ˈkneedness** *noun* L19.

weakling /ˈwiːklɪŋ/ *noun & adjective*. E16.
[from WEAK *adjective* + -LING[1].]
▶ **A** *noun*. †**1** An effeminate or unmanly person. E16–E17.
2 A person who is spiritually weak or lacks religious faith. Now *rare*. M16.
3 A person or animal lacking physical strength or weak in health or constitution. L16.
4 A person who is weak in character or intellect. L16.

📖 **3** *Sport* I myself was once a 7 stone weakling. **4** *Times* We are not a nation of weaklings.

▶ **B** *attrib.* or as *adjective*. Weak, feeble. M16.

weakly /ˈwiːkli/ *adjective*. L16.
[formed as prec. + -LY[1].]
1 Weak in constitution, not strong or robust; delicate, fragile. L16.
2 Characterized by moral weakness. L19.
■ **weakliness** *noun* E19.

weakly /ˈwiːkli/ *adverb*. ME.
[formed as prec. + -LY[2].]
1 a With little energy, force, or strength. ME. ▸**b** In an infirm or enfeebled manner. LME.
†**2 a** Insecurely, unsubstantially. E16–L18. ▸**b** With weakness of constitution. *rare* (Shakes.). Only in E17.
3 With slight defensive strength. L16.
4 a With deficiency of numbers; sparsely, meagrely. Now *rare* or *obsolete*. E17. ▸**b** In a slight degree; to a small extent. L18.
5 With weakness of mind or character; with lack of mental grasp or firmness of will. E17.
6 With little vigour of action; inefficiently. M17.
7 With little force of argument; unconvincingly. M17.
8 PHYSICS. By means of the weak interaction. M20.

weak-minded /wiːkˈmʌɪndɪd/ *adjective*. L16.
[from WEAK *adjective* + MINDED.]
1 Lacking strength of purpose. L16.
2 Mentally handicapped; of very low intelligence. L19.
■ **weak-mindedness** *noun* M19.

weakness /ˈwiːknɪs/ *noun*. ME.
[formed as prec. + -NESS.]
1 The quality or condition of being weak; (a) deficiency of strength, power, or force. ME.
2 a A weak point, a defect; an infirmity of character, a failing. L16. ▸†**b** A weakened physical condition; an attack of faintness. E17–M18.
3 a A self-indulgent liking or inclination (*for* a person or thing); an inability to resist a certain temptation. E18. ▸**b** A person whom or thing which one greatly likes or is unable to resist. E19.

📖 **1** E. Longford Wellington's deafness was a family weakness. **2a** Day Lewis His power to sustain the singer, . . cover up weaknesses of tone. M. Drabble She feels sorry for almost everybody. It is one of her weaknesses. **3a** H. James If she had a weakness it was for prawns.

weaky *noun* var. of WEAKIE.

weaky /ˈwiːki/ *adjective*. *north*. M17.
[from WEAK *adjective* + -Y[1].]
Moist, damp; juicy.

weal /wiːl/ *noun*[1]. *arch.*
[Old English *wela* = Old Saxon *welo* (cf. Old High German *wela*, *wola* adverb), from West Germanic base also of WELL *adverb*.]
†**1** *sing.* & in *pl.* Wealth, riches. Freq. in ***worldly weal***. OE–M19.
2 *sing.* & †in *pl.* Welfare, well-being; good fortune, prosperity. OE. ▸†**b** *transf.* A source of well-being or good fortune. ME–M16.
3 = COMMONWEAL. LME.

📖 **2** O. Nash What I'll have, come woe, come weal, Is coffee . . *with* the meal. **3** *Economist* Distortions against the national weal . . rightly blamed on special-interest groups. ***public weal***.

Comb.: †**weal-public** (*a*) = *public weal*; (*b*) = COMMONWEALTH 2; †**wealsman** (*rare*, Shakes.) a person devoted to the public weal.
■ †**wealsome** *adjective* happy, prosperous LME–L18.

weal /wiːl/ *noun*[2]. Also (esp. in sense 2) **wh-**. E19.
[Var. of WALE *noun*[1] after WHEAL *noun*[1].]
1 A ridge raised on the flesh by the blow of a rod, whip, etc. E19.
2 MEDICINE. A raised area of the skin, usu. red and rounded, and freq. accompanied by itching, as in urticaria. E19.
3 *gen.* A ridge. M19.

📖 **1** P. Lively A plum-coloured weal across her cheek-bone.

weal *noun*[3] var. of WEEL *noun*[1].

weal /wiːl/ *verb*. Also (earlier) **wh-**. L16.
[Var. of WALE *verb*[1] after WHEAL *verb*[1].]
1 *verb intrans.* Be marked with weals. *rare*. L16.
2 *verb trans.* Mark with weals. L17.

📖 **2** V. S. Reid He talked o' getting Romsey's whip and showed me . . where he was wealed.

weald /wiːld/ *noun*.
[Old English (West Saxon) var. of *wald* WOLD.]
1 (Now usu. **W-**.) *sing.* & in *pl.* *The* formerly wooded district including the parts of East Sussex, Kent, and Surrey lying between the North and South Downs. OE.
2 *gen.* A wooded district; a wold. *obsolete* exc. *poet.* M16.
Comb.: **wealdsman** a native or inhabitant of the Weald.

Wealden /ˈwiːld(ə)n/ *noun & adjective*. E19.
[from prec. + -EN[4].]
▶ **A** *noun*. GEOLOGY. A formation or series of Lower Cretaceous estuarine and freshwater deposits, extensively developed in the Weald. E19.
▶ **B** *adjective*. **1** GEOLOGY. Of or pertaining to the Wealden formation. E19.
2 Of or pertaining to the Weald; *spec.* designating a style of timber house built in the Weald in the late medieval and Tudor periods. L19.

we-all /ˈwiːɔːl/ *pronoun*. *US dial.* L19.
[from WE + ALL *adjective*.]
= WE.

wealth /wɛlθ/ *noun*. ME.
[from WELL *adverb* or WEAL *noun*[1] + -TH[1], after *health*.]
1 *arch.* **a** = WEAL *noun*[1] 2. ME. ▸**b** An instance or kind of prosperity; a blessing. Usu. in *pl.* ME. ▸**c** = COMMONWEAL 2. LME.
2 Abundance of valuable possessions or money; the state or condition of possessing this; material prosperity, opulence, affluence. ME. ▸†**b** In *pl.* Valuable or expensive goods; luxuries. LME–M16. ▸†**c** Degree of material prosperity. E–M17. ▸**d** The valuable possessions or products characteristic of a people or country; the collective riches *of* a people or country. M17. ▸**e** A particular product considered as the chief source of a country's riches. M17.
†**3** Spiritual well-being. Freq. in ***for the wealth of one's soul***. LME–M16.
4 Plenty; abundance or profusion *of* a specified thing. L16.
5 ECONOMICS. A possession or possessions considered useful and having an exchangeable value. E19.

📖 **2** E. Heath There was no display of wealth; that came later . . when I saw the crown jewels. J. Aiken I summoned Parkson . . . How easily . . we acquire the habits of wealth. **d** A. Trollope Not for all the wealth of India would he have given up his lamb to that . . wolf. **4** Clive James Immediately you are impressed by the wealth of detail.

Comb.: **wealth tax**: levied on the basis of a person's capital or financial assets.
■ **wealthful** *adjective* (now *rare* or *obsolete*) rich, wealthy, prosperous ME. **wealthless** *adjective* (*rare*) E17.

wealthy /ˈwɛlθi/ *adjective & noun*. LME.
[from WEALTH + -Y[1].]
▶ **A** *adjective*. †**1** Possessing well-being; happy; comfortable. LME–M16.
2 Of a person, country, etc.: possessing (esp. financial) wealth; rich, affluent, prosperous. LME.
†**3** Valuable. M16–M18.
4 *fig.* Rich *in* some possession or advantage; abundant, copious. E17.

📖 **2** R. Macdonald 'Does Elizabeth have much money?' 'Of course—she's wealthy'. **4** Tennyson Revealings deep . . are thine Of wealthy smiles.

▶ **B** *noun*. (**W-**.) A N. American red-skinned variety of cooking or eating apple. M19.
■ **wealthily** *adverb* M16. **wealthiness** *noun* (now *rare*) wealth E16.

wean /wiːn, weɪn/ *noun*. *Scot. & dial.* Also **wain** /weɪn/. L17.
[Contr. of *wee ane*: see WEE *adjective*, ANE.]
A young child.

wean /wiːn/ *verb*.
[Old English *wenian* = Old Frisian *wenna*, Old Saxon *wennian* (Dutch *wennen*), Old High German (*gi*)*wennen* (German *entwöhnen*), Old Norse *venja*, from Germanic.]
1 *verb trans.* Accustom (an infant or other young mammal) to food other than (esp. the mother's) milk. OE.
2 *verb trans.* & (*rare*) *intrans.* *fig.* Detach or disengage (oneself or another) from a habit etc. by enforced discontinuance; reconcile to the loss of something by degrees. Freq. foll. by (*away*) *from*, *off*. E16.
3 *verb trans.* Remove or abate gradually. *rare*. E18.

📖 **1** C. Freeman Esther . . weaned baby Shlomo away from her breast. **2** R. Fuller Dr Stembridge was right in trying to wean me from my sleeping pills.

■ **weanable** *adjective* L16. **weanedness** *noun* (*literary*) spiritual detachment E17.

weanel /ˈwiːn(ə)l/ *noun*. *obsolete* exc. *dial.* L15.
[from prec. + -EL[2].]
A newly weaned animal.

weaner /ˈwiːnə/ *noun*. L16.
[formed as prec. + -ER[1].]
†**1** A person who weans a child. *rare*. Only in L16.
2 A calf, lamb, or pig weaned during the current year. Freq. *attrib.* Orig. *Austral. & NZ*. M19.

weanie /ˈwiːni/ *noun*. *Scot. & dial.* Also **-ny**. L18.
[from WEAN *noun* + -IE, -Y[6].]
A very young child.

weanling /ˈwiːnlɪŋ/ *noun & adjective*. M16.
[from WEAN *verb* + -LING[1].]
▶ **A** *noun*. A newly weaned infant or young animal. M16.
▶ **B** *adjective*. That is a weanling; newly weaned. M17.

weany *noun* var. of WEANIE.

weapon /ˈwɛp(ə)n/ *noun*.
[Old English *wǣp(e)n* = Old Frisian *wēpen*, Old Saxon *wāpan* (Dutch *wapen*), Old High German *waf(f)an* (German *Waffe*), Old Norse *vápn*, from Germanic verb of unkn. origin.]
1 An instrument used or intended to inflict bodily harm, *esp.* one so used in warfare to overcome an enemy or repel a hostile attack. OE. ▸†**b** Such instruments collectively; weaponry, arms. OE–L16. ▸**c** *transf.* A part of the body of a bird or animal used as a means of attack or defence, as a claw, tusk, etc.; *spec.* (in *pl.*), the spurs of a gamefowl. M17.
2 *fig.* Any means of gaining an advantage in a conflict; a means of attack. OE.
3 The penis. *coarse slang*. OE.

📖 **1** J. WYNDHAM I had no kind of weapon but my knife. G. GREENE Something so big that the H-bomb will become a conventional weapon.

Phrases: **at all weapons, at any weapons** *arch.* with weapons of any kind. ***binary weapon***: see BINARY *adjective*. **fight a person with his or her own weapons, beat a person with his or her own weapons**, etc., *fig.* fight, beat, etc., a person using his or her own typical manner or procedure. ***secret weapon***: see SECRET *adjective & noun*.
Comb.: **weapon-carrier** = ***weapons-carrier*** below; **weapon-salve** (*obsolete* exc. *Hist.*) an ointment believed to heal a wound when applied to the weapon producing the wound; **weapons-carrier** a vehicle or aircraft designed to carry weapons; **weapons-grade** *adjective* designating fissile material of a suitable quality for making nuclear weapons; **weaponsman** a military expert in the use of weapons; **weapon-smith** *Hist.* a maker of weapons; **weapons system, weapon system** (orig. *US*) a military weapon together with all the equipment required to make use of it, such as detection and control apparatus, a launcher, and a delivery vehicle; **weapon-training** military training in the use of weapons.
▪ **weaponed** *adjective* provided with a weapon or weapons; armed: OE. **weapoˈneer** *noun* (*US*) (*a*) a person in charge of a military weapon before its deployment; (*b*) an expert or specialist in the development of military weapons: M20. **weapoˈneering** *noun* the development and production of military weapons M20. **weaponiˈzation** *noun* (*a*) the process of equipping a country etc. with military weapons; (*b*) the process of adapting a thing for use as a weapon: M20. **weaponized** *adjective* (*a*) equipped with military weapons; (*b*) adapted for use as a weapon: L20. **weaponless** *adjective* OE. **weaponry** *noun* weapons collectively, *esp.* military weapons M19.

weaponschaw, weaponschawing *nouns* see WAPPENSCHAW, WAPPENSCHAWING.

wear /wɛː/ *noun*. LME.
[from WEAR *verb*[1].]
1 The action of wearing an article of clothing etc.; the condition or fact of being worn. LME.
2 A thing or things worn; *esp.* fashionable or suitable clothing for a specified activity or occasion. L16. ▸**b** *fig.* Custom, habit. E17.
3 Ability to be worn further or over a (specified) period of time; degree of resistance to the effects of being worn. L17.
4 The process or condition of being worn or impaired by continued use, friction, attrition, etc.; deterioration of quality due to this. E18.

📖 **1** *Daily Express* I want to discourage the . . wear to school of tracksuits. **2** ***formal wear, menswear, sportswear, summer wear***, etc. **b** *Saturday Review* That mood of . . knowingness which is all the wear among some . . short-story writers. **3** J. O'FAOLAIN A pair of old boots with wear in them yet. **4** A. LURIE We often discard garments that show little or no wear. R. BRAUTIGAN A tin roof coloured reddish by years of wear.

Phrases: **in wear** being regularly worn; in vogue, in fashion. **tear and wear** = ***wear and tear*** (a) below. **the worse for wear** damaged or deteriorated through being worn; *joc.* drunk. **wear and tear** (*a*) damage or deterioration from continuous ordinary use; (*b*) ***wear and tear pigment*** (BIOCHEMISTRY) = LIPOFUSCIN.
Comb.: **wear-dated** *adjective* (of a garment) guaranteed to last for a specified amount of time.

wear /wɛː/ *verb*[1]. Pa. t. **wore** /wɔː/; pa. pple **worn** /wɔːn/.
[Old English *werian* = Old Saxon *werian*, Old High German *werien*, Old Norse *verja*, Gothic *wasjan* clothe, from Germanic and Indo-European base repr. also by Old Norse *vest* cloak, Latin *vestis* clothing.]
▶ **I** Bear, carry.
1 a *verb trans.* Carry or bear on (a part of) the body for protection, warmth, decoration, etc.; be dressed in; have on. Formerly also foll. by *on, upon*. OE. ▸**b** *verb trans.* Be dressed habitually in; in *pass.*, be generally or habitually worn. ME. ▸†**c** *verb intrans.* Dress; be dressed. *rare*. ME–L16.
2 *verb trans.* Bear or carry about; *fig.* carry *in* one's mind, memory, etc. Also, display or fly (a flag etc.). OE.
3 *verb trans. transf.* Bear (one's own hair, beard, etc.); allow (one's hair or beard) to grow to a specified length; arrange (one's hair) in a specified style. OE. ▸**b** *gen.* Bear or possess as a part of the body. E16.
4 *verb trans.* Exhibit, present, (a facial expression, appearance, etc.). E17.
5 *verb trans.* Tolerate, accept; agree to. Usu. in neg. contexts. *colloq.* E20.

📖 **1** G. VIDAL He wore the frock coat and striped trousers of an earlier time. *New Yorker* I never wear scent. **b** V. WOOLF We wore . . a great many petticoats then. E. BOWEN Waistcoats of plush were worn. **2** SHAKES. *Macb.* I shame To wear a heart so white. **3** T. HARDY The equestrian wore a grizzled beard. A. TYLER You're wearing your hair a little fuller. **b** THACKERAY Steyne wore the scar to his dying day. **4** H. ROTH His face wore an expression of grim aloofness. **5** J. WEBSTER Don't impose your ideas about marriage . . on her. She won't wear it.

▶ **II** Waste (away), decay.
6 *verb trans. & intrans.* (Cause to) diminish in strength, effectiveness, or intensity; (cause to) fade or disappear gradually over time. Usu. foll. by *away, off, out*, etc. ME.
7 *verb trans.* Impair the surface of or obliterate gradually by friction, use, attrition, etc. (also foll. by *away, down, out*); rub *off* gradually. Also, bring into a specified state by this action. See also ***wear out*** below. LME.
8 *verb intrans.* Become impaired or decay gradually from friction, use, attrition, etc. (also foll. by *away, down, out*); (foll. by *off*) rub off gradually, *fig.* lose effectiveness or intensity. Also, be brought into a specified state by this action. See also ***wear out*** below. LME.
9 *verb trans.* Sap the strength of, tire, fatigue, exhaust (also foll. by *away, out*) (freq. as ***wearing ppl adjective***); (foll. by *down*) overcome by persistence. E16. ▸**b** *verb intrans.* Foll. by *on* or *upon*: affect adversely, weigh on. M19.
10 *verb trans.* Form or produce by friction, use, or attrition. L16.

📖 **6** G. GREENE He fixed pictures in our minds that thirty years have been unable to wear away. P. P. READ The effects of the wine had worn off. **7** J. STEINBECK The limb is worn smooth by men who have sat on it. W. TREVOR We're deprived of grass . . due to footsteps wearing it down. **8** W. READE The gilt beginning to wear off. **9** A. LURIE Being both delicate and conscientious, she would wear herself out. W. RAEPER The wintry chills . . began to wear down his health. **b** M. PIERCY The New England winter had begun to wear on her. **10** F. WARNER Soft napkins For the wounds your chains have worn.

▶ **III** Move, pass.
11 a *verb intrans.* Proceed, advance, esp. slowly or gradually. Chiefly *Scot.* LME. ▸**b** *verb trans.* Travel over. *rare. poet.* L16. ▸**c** *verb trans.* Lead (sheep or cattle) gradually into an enclosure. Also foll. by *in, up*. *Scot.* E18.
12 a *verb intrans.* Of (a period of) time: pass, esp. tediously; pass *on* or *away* (see also ***wear on*** below). Freq. (*poet.*) as ***worn ppl adjective***. LME. ▸**b** *verb trans.* Spend or pass (time). Also foll. by *away, out*. Chiefly *poet.* M16.
13 *verb trans. & intrans.* (Cause to) pass gradually *into* (a state or condition). M16.
14 *verb intrans.* Remain in a specified condition over time; retain pristine condition, popularity, youthful appearance, etc., to a specified degree. M16.

📖 **12a** R. CAMPBELL As the grim night wore, The fury of the tempest grew more blind. C. CHAPLIN As the afternoon wore on, I began to miss them. **13** D. MADDEN Autumn wore into winter. **14** G. CHARLES He had been so handsome . . . But how many men about this age . . had worn infinitely better. *Nature* Re-reading the books, I find they don't wear at all well.

Phrases: **wear a crown, wear the purple** hold the office of sovereign, emperor, etc. ***wear motley***: see MOTLEY *noun* 3. **wear on** be prolonged or continued. **wear one's arm in a sling** support one's arm in a sling when injured. ***wear one's heart on one's sleeve***: see HEART *noun*. ***wear one's — hat***: see HAT *noun*. **wear one's years well, wear well** remain young-looking. **wear out** (*a*) use or be used until no longer usable; (*b*) tire or be tired out. **wear the breeches** = ***wear the trousers*** below. †**wear the horn(s)** be a cuckold. **wear the pants** *N. Amer.* = ***wear the trousers*** below. ***wear the* PETTICOAT**. ***wear the purple***: see ***wear a crown*** above. **wear the trousers** be the dominant member of a couple, household, etc. ***wear the willow***: see WILLOW *noun* 1c. **wear thin** *fig.* (of patience etc.) begin to fail. ***wear two hats***: see HAT *noun*. ***wear well***: see ***wear one's years well*** above. ***wear willow***: see WILLOW *noun* 1c. †**wear yellow hose** be jealous. **win and wear** *arch.* win and enjoy as a possession.
Comb.: **wear-out** (*rare*) destruction or damage from use.
▪ **wearer** *noun* (*a*) a person who wears a specified garment etc.; (*b*) *rare* a thing which wears away a surface etc.: LME.

wear /wɛː/ *verb*[2]. Pa. t. & pple **wore** /wɔː/. E17.
[Origin unkn.]
NAUTICAL. **1** *verb intrans.* Of a ship: change from one tack to another by turning the head away from the wind. Freq. foll. by *round*. Opp. TACK *verb*[1] 9. Cf. VEER *verb*[2] 2. E17.
2 *verb trans.* Bring (a ship) about by turning its head away from the wind. E18.

wearable /ˈwɛːrəb(ə)l/ *adjective & noun*. L16.
[from WEAR *verb*[1] + -ABLE.]
▶ **A** *adjective*. Able to be worn; fit or suitable to wear. L16.
▶ **B** *noun*. A wearable item; a garment. Usu. in *pl.* E18.
▪ **wearaˈbility** *noun* E20.

weariful /ˈwɪərɪfʊl, -f(ə)l/ *adjective*. *arch.* LME.
[from WEARY *verb* + -FUL.]
1 Causing weariness; wearisome. LME.
2 Suffering or expressing weariness; fatigued, exhausted. M19.

📖 **2** G. MEREDITH Colney cast a weariful look backward.

▪ **wearifully** *adverb* L19. **wearifulness** *noun* M19.

wearing /ˈwɛːrɪŋ/ *noun*. ME.
[from WEAR *verb*[1] + -ING[1].]
1 *gen.* The action of WEAR *verb*[1]. ME.
†**2** *sing.* & (*rare*) in *pl.* = WEAR *noun* 2. ME–M19.
†**3** = WEAR *noun* 3. *rare*. M16–M18.
4 A wasting disease; *spec.* tuberculosis. *dial.* E19.
5 In *pl.* Worn areas on a surface; marks of wear. *rare*. L19.
1 the worse for wearing = ***the worse for wear*** s.v. WEAR *noun*.
Comb.: **wearing apparel** *arch.* clothing; **wearing course** the top layer of a road surface which is worn down by traffic; **wearing gear** *arch.* = ***wearing apparel*** above.

wearish /ˈwɪərɪʃ/ *adjective*. LME.
[Origin unkn. Cf. WERSH *adjective*.]
1 Dull in flavour; tasteless. Cf. WERSH 2. Long *obsolete* exc. *dial.* LME.
2 Sickly in health or appearance; feeble, delicate. Cf. WERSH 1. Now chiefly *dial.* E16.

wearisome /ˈwɪərɪs(ə)m/ *adjective*. LME.
[from WEARY *verb, adjective* + -SOME[1].]
†**1** = WEARIFUL 2. LME–M17.
2 Causing weariness through monotony or length; tedious. LME.
3 Causing weariness from exertion or pain; fatiguing, exhausting. Now *rare*. L16.

📖 **2** D. MADDEN Could there be anything more wearisome . . than to stand alone . . before a mirror?

▪ **wearisomely** *adverb* M18. **wearisomeness** *noun* M16.

weary /ˈwɪəri/ *adjective & adverb*.
[Old English *wērig, wǣrig*, corresp. to Old Saxon *sīpwōrig* weary from a journey, Old High German *wuarag* drunk, from West Germanic.]
▶ **A** *adjective*. **I 1** Suffering from loss of strength and need for rest as a result of continued exertion or endurance; tired, fatigued, now esp. intensely so; expressing extreme tiredness or fatigue. OE.
2 Depressed, dispirited. (Foll. by *of, with*.) OE.
3 Dismayed at the continued presence or recurrence *of* a thing; exhausted in patience *with*. Formerly also foll. by *in, to do*. ME.
4 Of a person: frail, sickly. *Scot. & dial.* LME.

📖 **1** O. MANNING The weary faces of other passengers. I. MURDOCH We are both weary, we have not the energy for real communication. **weary Willie** [see ***TIRED Tim***] a tramp, a work-shy person. **2** SHAKES. *Macb.* So weary with disasters, tugg'd with fortune. **3** J. B. PRIESTLEY She was weary of stopping to ask the way. A. P. HERBERT Weary we are of blood and noise and pain.

▶ **II 5** Fatiguing, exhausting. Now passing into sense 6. ME.
6 Irksome, wearisome, tedious. LME.
7 a Sad, sorrowful. *Scot. & north.* E18. ▸**b** Vexatious, irritating. *Scot. & north.* L18.

📖 **5** R. KIPLING Now we have walked a weary way. **6** A. UTTLEY So the weary time dragged on.

▶ **B** *adverb*. Extremely, very. *Scot. & dial.* OE.
▪ **wearily** *adverb* LME. **weariness** *noun* (*a*) the state or condition of being weary; (*b*) a thing that produces this, a cause of tiredness or fatigue: OE. †**wearyish** *adjective* (*rare*) wearisome E17–E18.

weary /ˈwɪəri/ *verb*.
[Old English *wēr(i)gian, gewērigian*, formed as prec.]
1 *verb intrans.* Grow weary (*of*); tire (*of*). Also (*arch.*) foll. by *to do*. OE. ▸**b** *verb trans.* Foll. by *out*: endure wearily to the end of. *rare*. L16. ▸**c** *verb intrans.* Wait wearily *for* or *to do*; languish *for*. Chiefly *Scot.* E19.
2 *verb trans.* Make weary. Freq. as ***wearying ppl adjective***. OE. ▸**b** Foll. by *out*: fatigue completely; tire out. M17.

📖 **1** R. L. STEVENSON He had wearied . . of Woolwich, and . . slipped up to London for a spree. **c** R. CAMPBELL I wearied for a flash of . . sunlight. **2** *Times Lit. Suppl.* Spending a wearying amount of time working for not very much. D. MADDEN The whole Northern Irish political issue wearied and bored him.

▪ **weariable** *adjective* L18. **weariless** *adjective* that does not become weary, tireless LME. **wearilessly** *adverb* L18. **wearyingly** *adverb* in a wearying way, so as to weary someone E19.

weasand /ˈwiːz(ə)nd/ *noun*. Now *arch.* or *dial.* Also †**wyson**.
[Old English *wāsend*, corresp. to Old Frisian *wāsanda, -enda*, Old Saxon *wāsend(i)*, Old High German *weisant*; app. a West Germanic pres. ppl formation.]
1 The oesophagus, the gullet. OE.
†**2** The trachea, the windpipe. LME–L18.
3 The throat generally. LME.

weasel /ˈwiːz(ə)l/ *noun & adjective.*
[Old English *wesule, wesle, weosule* = Middle Low German *wesel, wezel*, Old High German *wisula* (German *Wiesel*), from West Germanic noun of unkn. origin.]
▶ **A** *noun.* **1** A small carnivorous mustelid mammal, *Mustela nivalis*, which has a slender brown and white body with a short tail, is noted for its ferocity, and is found in Eurasia and N. America; *fig.* a treacherous or deceitful person. Also *colloq.*, a stoat. OE. ▸**b** With specifying word: any of several other carnivorous mammals (now chiefly those of the genus *Mustela* and related genera) that resemble *M. nivalis.* L18.
2 A native or inhabitant of S. Carolina. *US colloq.* M19.
3 A tracked vehicle capable of travelling over difficult terrain; *spec.* (*a*) US MILITARY a light cargo and personnel carrier; (*b*) a snow tractor. M20.
4 An equivocal or ambiguous statement or claim, *esp.* one intended to mislead. M20.
1 *pop goes the weasel*: see POP *adverb*.
Comb.: **weasel-faced** *adjective* having thin sharp features; **weasel-lemur** a small short-tailed lemur, *Lepilemur mustelinus*; **weasel's snout** a cornfield weed with two-lipped pink flowers, *Misopates orontium*, allied to the snapdragon; **weasel word** an equivocal or ambiguous word used intentionally to mislead; **weasel-worded** *adjective* equivocating, ambiguous.
▶ **B** *attrib.* or as *adjective.* Of a word, statement etc.: equivocating; intentionally ambiguous or misleading. E20.

> 🕮 R. M. PIRSIG The whole business seemed . . merely a new and pretentious jargon of weasel concepts.

■ **weaselly** *adjective* resembling or characteristic of a weasel; weasel-faced, thin, angular; equivocating, deceitful: M19. **weaselship** *noun* (*rare*) †(*a*) (with possess. adjective, as *his weaselship* etc.) a mock title of respect given to a weasel; (*b*) the characteristic nature of a weasel: E18.

weasel /ˈwiːz(ə)l/ *verb. colloq.* Infl. **-ll-**, ***-l-**. E20.
[from the noun.]
1 a *verb trans.* Make ambiguous or intentionally misleading. E20. ▸**b** *verb intrans.* Equivocate, prevaricate; quibble. M20.
2 *verb intrans.* Extricate oneself from an awkward position, situation, obligation, etc. (foll. by *out of*). Also, default *on* an obligation or promise. E20.
3 *verb trans.* Obtain or extract (a thing), esp. by cunning. Usu. foll. by *out of.* L20.

> 🕮 **1b** C. WESTON He listened to the younger detective weaseling at the other end. **2** P. DICKINSON Pibble weaseled out of the car. *Spectator* Cooper was too kind-hearted to name those who weaseled out of the exercise. **3** L. DEIGHTON He . . 'weaseled' luggage for the boat-train passengers.

weather /ˈwɛðə/ *noun.*
[Old English *weder* = Old Frisian, Old Saxon *wedar*, Old High German *wetar* (Dutch *weer*, German *Wetter*), Old Norse *veðr*, from Germanic, prob. from base of WIND *noun*[1].]
1 The condition of the atmosphere at a given place and time with respect to heat, cold, sunshine, rain, cloud, wind, etc. OE. ▸**b** (A spell of) a particular kind of weather. Now *rare* exc. in *in all weathers*. OE. ▸**c** Bad weather; destructive rain, frost, wind, etc.; *spec.* (now *dial.* & NAUTICAL) violent wind accompanied by heavy rain or rough sea. OE. ▸**d** Weather suitable for some purpose; *spec.* fine weather. Long *obsolete* exc. *Scot.* LME. ▸†**e** Rain, snow, etc., falling from the clouds. LME–E19. ▸†**f** Air, sky. LME–E17.
2 NAUTICAL. The direction in or side towards which the wind is blowing; windward. Freq. *attrib.* LME.
3 More fully *angle of weather*. The angle made by a windmill's sails with the perpendicular to the axis. M18.

> 🕮 **1** O. WILDE The weather . . is . . awful—real snow and other horrors. A. S. BYATT They talked about the weather in an English way. *Guardian* Perfect weather for Mr Bush's garden party. *bad weather, cold weather, fine weather, good weather, hot weather, rainy weather*, etc. *fig.*: *Times* High Commissioners may come and go according to the political weather. **b** C. BRAYFIELD She obediently played sports in all weathers without complaint. **c** SIR W. SCOTT Weather and war their rougher trace Have left on that majestic face.

Phrases etc.: *angle of weather*: see sense 3 above. *fine-weather*: see FINE *adjective*. *fine weather for ducks*: see DUCK *noun*[1]. *have the weather gauge of*: see GAUGE *noun* 2. **in the weather** exposed to the elements, in the open air, outdoors. **keep a weather eye (on)**, **keep one's weather eye (on)**, **keep a weather eye open (for)**, **keep one's weather eye open (for)** be watchful and alert (for), keep one's wits about one (for). *keep the weather gauge of*: see GAUGE *noun* 2. **make good weather of it**, **make bad weather of it**, etc., NAUTICAL (of a ship) behave well, badly, etc., in a storm. **make heavy weather of** perform (an apparently simple task) clumsily or ineptly, exaggerate the difficulty or burden presented by (a problem etc.). **under the weather** indisposed, slightly unwell. **weather permitting** (as an announcement referring to a ship's sailing, a sports fixture, etc.) conditional on the weather being favourable. *wind and weather*: see WIND *noun*[1].
Comb.: **weather balloon** a balloon sent up to provide meteorological information; **weather-beaten** *adjective* (*a*) buffeted by wind, rain, etc., exposed to the weather; (*b*) worn, damaged, or discoloured by such exposure; †**weather-bit** *adjective* (*rare*) weather-beaten; **weatherbitt** *noun & verb* (NAUTICAL) (*a*) *noun* an extra turn of a cable about the bitts in bad weather; (*b*) *verb trans.* give such an extra turn to (a cable); **weather-blate**, **weather-bleat** *Anglo-Irish* [formed as HEATHER-*bleat* after *weather*] the snipe; **weather-bound** *adjective* prevented by bad weather from travelling or proceeding; **weather bow** NAUTICAL the bow turned towards the wind; **weather-box** = *weather-house* below; **weather-breeder** (chiefly *dial.*) a day of exceptionally sunny and calm weather, thought of as heralding a storm; **weather bureau** *US* an agency established esp. by the government to observe and report on weather conditions; **weather centre** an office providing weather information and analysis; **weather chart** a diagram showing the current or future state of the weather over a large area; **weathercoat** a weatherproof coat, a raincoat; **weather-cottage** = *weather-house* below; **weather cycle** a recurring pattern of weather or of a tendency in the weather; **weather deck** NAUTICAL a deck exposed to the weather, the uppermost unprotected deck; **weather-fend** *verb trans.* (*arch.*) protect from the weather, shelter; **weather forecast** a usu. broadcast or printed analysis of the state of the weather with an assessment of likely developments over a certain time; **weather forecaster** a presenter of a weather forecast on radio, television, etc.; **weather-gall** (now *dial.*) = *watergall* (b) s.v. WATER *noun*; **weather-glass** †(*a*) a kind of thermometer used to gauge air temperature and predict changes in the weather; (*b*) a barometer; (*c*) *poor man's weather-glass*: see POOR MAN; †**weather-headed** *adjective* [prob. from WETHER after *weather*] empty-headed, foolish; *weather helm*: see HELM *noun*[2]; **weather-house** a toy hygroscope in the form of a small house with figures of a man and woman standing in two porches, the man coming out of his porch in wet weather and the woman out of hers in dry; **weatherman** (*a*) an observer of the weather, a meteorologist; *spec.* a male weather forecaster; (*b*) (with cap. initial) (a member of) a violent revolutionary group in the US; **weather map** = *weather chart* above; **weather prophet** a person who foretells the weather; **weather resistance** the quality of being weather-resistant; **weather-resistant** *adjective* resistant to the effects of bad weather, esp. rain; **weather side** (*a*) NAUTICAL the windward side of a vessel etc.; (*b*) the side of a building, tree, etc., most exposed to the weather; **weather station** a meteorological observation post; **weather-strip** *noun & verb* (*a*) *noun* a strip of wood, rubber, etc., applied to a door or window to exclude rain and wind; (*b*) *verb trans.* apply a weather-strip to; **weather-stripping** material used to weather-strip a door or window; the process of applying this; **weather-tile** a kind of overlapping tile used to cover a wall; **weather-tiled** *adjective* covered with weather-tiles; **weather-tiling** the process of covering a wall with weather-tiles; the tiling used for this; **Weather Underground** the revolutionary organization formed by the Weathermen; *weather-vane*: see VANE 1; *weather window*: see WINDOW *noun* 3c; **weather woman** (*a*) (with cap. initial) a female member of the revolutionary Weatherman organization; (*b*) a female weather forecaster.
■ **weatheri'zation** *noun* (*US*) the act or process of weatherizing something L20. **weatherize** *verb trans.* (*US*) make weatherproof; *spec.* make (a building) impervious to the weather by insulation, double-glazing, etc.: M20. **weathermost** *adjective* (NAUTICAL) furthest to windward M16. **weather'ology** *noun* the branch of science that deals with the weather and its phenomena E19. **weatherward** *noun & adverb* (NAUTICAL) windward M16. **weatherwise** *adverb* as regards the weather M20. **weathery** *adjective* (*rare*) fitful, changing like the weather M16.

weather /ˈwɛðə/ *verb.*
[Old English *wed(e)rian* = Old Norse *viðra*. In branch II directly from the noun.]
▶†**I** **1** *verb intrans.* Be (good or bad) weather. Cf. WEATHERING I. Only in OE.
▶ **II** **2** *verb trans.* Subject to the beneficial action of the wind and sun, air; dry or season in the open air; FALCONRY allow (a hawk) to perch in the open air. LME
3 *verb trans.* NAUTICAL. Sail to the windward of (a headland, another ship, etc.); (foll. by *on* or *upon*) gain on in a windward direction, *fig.* gain an advantage over, take liberties with. L16.
4 *verb trans.* Withstand and come safely through (a storm); *fig.* survive (a period of trouble etc.), sustain without disaster. Also foll. by *out.* M17.
5 a *verb trans.* Wear away, disintegrate, or discolour (rock, stone, etc.) by exposure to the elements. Freq. as *weathered ppl adjective.* M18. ▸**b** *verb intrans.* Become worn, disintegrated, or discoloured by exposure to the elements; weather in a specified way; (foll. by *out*) become prominent by the decay or disintegration of the surrounding rock. L18.
6 *verb trans.* Set (the sails of a windmill) at the proper angle to obtain the maximum effect from the wind. M18.
7 *verb trans.* ARCHITECTURE. Slope or bevel (a surface) to throw off rain etc.; make (boards, tiles, etc.) overlap downwards for this purpose. M19.

> 🕮 **4** B. MONTGOMERY We had weathered these storms successfully and the end of the war was in sight. **5a** C. BRAYFIELD A permanent tan and a lean, weathered look. **b** I. MURDOCH Old brick . . weathered to a rich blackish red.

■ **weathera'bility** *noun* the quality of being weatherable M20. **weatherable** *adjective* able to withstand the effects of the weather M20.

weatherboard /ˈwɛðəbɔːd/ *noun & verb.* M16.
[from WEATHER *noun* + BOARD *noun, verb.*]
▶ **A** *noun.* **1** Each of a series of boards nailed to outside walls horizontally, with edges overlapping downwards, to keep out rain etc.; *collect.* such boards as a covering material. M16. ▸**b** A board laid over builders' work or material as a protection. M19. ▸**c** A building covered with weatherboards. *Austral.* E20.
2 A sloping board fixed over a window, to the bottom of an outside door, etc., to keep out rain etc. M16.
3 NAUTICAL. The windward side of a ship. E17.
▶ **B** *verb trans.* Nail or fix weatherboards on. M16.
■ **weatherboarding** *noun* the work of covering a building etc. with weatherboards; weatherboards collectively: E16.

weathercock /ˈwɛðəkɒk/ *noun & verb.* ME.
[formed as prec. + COCK *noun*[1].]
▶ **A** *noun.* **1** A weather-vane in the form of a cock; *gen.* a weather-vane of any form; *fig.* a changeable or inconstant person or thing. ME.
2 AERONAUTICS. The tendency of an aircraft to turn away from the set compass direction into the relative wind. Usu. *attrib.* L19.

> 🕮 **1** M. E. BRADDON In affairs of the heart, Mr. Turchill belonged to the weathercock species.

▶ **B** *verb.* †**1** *verb trans.* with *it.* Veer or vary like a weathercock. M17–E19.
2 *verb trans.* Provide with a weathercock; serve as a weathercock for. M17.
3 a *verb intrans.* NAUTICAL. (Tend to) head into the wind. M20. ▸**b** *verb intrans. & trans.* AERONAUTICS. Turn away from the set compass direction into the relative wind. M20.
■ **weathercockism** *noun* changeableness M19. **weathercock-like** *adjective* resembling a weathercock; fickle, changeable: E18.

weathering /ˈwɛð(ə)rɪŋ/ *noun.* OE.
[from WEATHER *verb* + -ING[1].]
▶†**I** **1** Weather conditions; (good or bad) weather. OE–M16.
2 Propitious or suitable weather. ME–M16.
3 Stormy weather; a storm. LME–E17.
▶ **II** **4** The action of WEATHER *verb*; exposure to the beneficial or adverse effects of the elements; the result of such exposure; damage, discoloration, etc., caused by the weather. M16.
5 ARCHITECTURE. A projecting course on the face of a wall to throw off rain etc.; a slope or bevel given to a surface for this purpose. M18.

weatherly /ˈwɛðəli/ *adjective.* M17.
[from WEATHER *noun* + -LY[1].]
†**1** Of or pertaining to the weather. *rare.* Only in M17.
2 NAUTICAL. Able to sail close to the wind without drifting to leeward; making little leeway. E18.
■ **weatherliness** *noun* L19.

Weatherometer /wɛðəˈrɒmɪtə/ *noun.* Also **w-**. E20.
[from WEATHER *noun* or *verb* + -OMETER.]
(Proprietary name for) a device for subjecting substances to simulated weather conditions to determine their weather-resistance.

weatherproof /ˈwɛðəpruːf/ *adjective, noun, & verb.* E17.
[formed as prec. + PROOF *adjective.*]
▶ **A** *adjective.* Impervious to the weather, completely resistant to the effects of bad weather, esp. rain. E17.
▶ **B** *noun.* Weatherproof material. Also, a weatherproof coat; a raincoat. L19.
▶ **C** *verb trans.* Make weatherproof. Freq. as *weatherproofed ppl adjective.* E20.
■ **weatherproofness** *noun* M20.

Weatings /ˈwiːtɪŋz/ *noun pl.* Also **w-**. M20.
[Respelling of WHEAT + *-ings* as in *middlings*.]
(Proprietary name for) the residue of the milling of wheat, as food for farm animals.

weave /wiːv/ *verb*[1] *& noun.*
[Old English *wefan*, corresp. to Old Frisian *weva*, Middle & mod. Low German, Middle & mod. Dutch *weven*, Old High German *weban* (German *weben*), Old Norse *vefa*, from Germanic, from Indo-European base repr. also by Greek *huphē, huphos* web, *huphainein* weave, Sanskrit *ūrṇavābhi* spider, lit. 'wool-weaver'. Cf. WASP *noun*[1], WEB *noun*, WEEVIL, WEFT *noun*[1].]
▶ **A** *verb.* Pa. t. **wove** /wəʊv/; pa. pple **woven** /ˈwəʊv(ə)n/, (*rare*) **weaved**.
1 *verb trans.* Form (fabric) by interlacing alternate threads stretched lengthwise (the warp) with transverse threads (the weft), esp. on a loom. Also, make (a garment etc.) in this way. OE. ▸**b** Depict in tapestry. *arch.* LME. ▸**c** *fig.* Contrive, devise, or construct (a poem, spell, narrative, etc.), esp. skilfully. LME. ▸**d** Form (a basket, wreath, etc.) by interlacing rods, twigs, flowers, etc. LME. ▸**e** Knit (stockings etc.) (*Scot.*). Also (*dial.*), plait (hair). L17.
2 *verb intrans.* Make fabric by weaving; work at a loom. OE.
3 *verb trans. & intrans.* Of a spider or insect: spin (a web or cocoon). ME.
4 *verb trans.* Form (threads etc.) into fabric, a finished item, etc., by interlacing; blend *in* thus. M16. ▸**b** *verb trans. fig.* Intermingle or blend *in* closely as if by weaving; work up (separate elements) *into* an intricate and connected whole. M16. ▸**c** *verb trans.* Entwine or wreathe (branches, flowers, etc.) together. L16. ▸**d** *verb intrans.* Become entwined or interwoven. Also, be weavable. *rare.* E17.

5 *verb trans.* Cause to move in a devious or intricate course; make (one's way) or direct (one's steps) in such a course, as in dancing. Also (*literary*), go through the intricate movements of (a dance). *rare.* M17.

> 📖 **1** *Yankee* A Navajo woman knows how to weave a rug. **c** D. DELILLO Men . . gathered to weave their tales of gunfire and . . mobs. *Guardian* The magic of the market . . can weave its spell on the water business. **d** W. KENNEDY Francis's mother wove crosses from the dead dandelions. **2** W. COWPER Yon cottager who weaves at her own door. **4** C. BIGG The art of weaving flax had been introduced from Babylon. **b** B. BRYSON Otherwise serious religious poems into . . which he artfully wove acrostics of his own name. **5** DE QUINCEY Sarah was going about the crowd, and weaving her person in and out.

▶ **B** *noun.* **1** A thing that has been woven, a woven thread or fabric. Now *rare.* L16.

2 A particular method or pattern of weaving. L19.

> 📖 **1** *fig.*: T. C. BOYLE A weave of silver in his hair. **2** *Highlife* The trench coat—despite its . . tight weave . . —is still only what they call 'showerproof'.

■ **weavable** *adjective* able to be woven L15. **weavingly** *adverb* (*rare*) in a weaving manner M20.

weave /wiːv/ *verb*[2]. L16.

[Prob. from Old Norse *veifa* move from place to place, wave, brandish, corresp. to Middle & mod. Dutch *weiven*, Old High German *weiben*, from Germanic, ult. rel. to Latin *vibrare* VIBRATE.]

1 *verb intrans.* Move repeatedly from side to side; sway the body alternately to one side and the other; take a devious course, (as if) to avoid obstructions. L16. ▸**b** *spec.* Of a horse or a captive wild animal: move the head, neck, and body restlessly from side to side of the stall or cage. M19. ▸**c** Of an aircraft or its pilot: fly a devious course; take evasive action. Orig. *RAF slang.* M20.

†**2** *verb trans.* Make a signal to (a ship or its occupants) by waving a flag etc. L16–E17.

3 *verb trans.* Move or wave (the hand or something held by it) *to and fro, about,* etc. Long *rare.* E17.

4 *verb trans. & intrans.* BOXING. Step in feinting and try to approach (one's opponent) closely before delivering one's blow. E19.

> 📖 **1** W. PERRIAM A cyclist . . weaves in and out of cars. **c** **get weaving** *colloq.* begin action briskly; start at once; hurry. **4** ***bob and weave***: see BOB *verb*[3] 1.

weaver /ˈwiːvə/ *noun*[1]. ME.

[from WEAVE *verb*[1] + -ER[1].]

1 A person engaged or occupied in weaving fabric. ME. ▸**b** A person who plaits hair (*dial.*). Also (*Scot.*), a person who knits stockings etc. L18.

2 *fig.* A person who contrives or devises a narrative etc. Usu. foll. by *of.* LME.

3 A spider. *Scot.* E19.

4 Any of numerous sparrow-like, chiefly African birds of the family Ploceidae, many of which build elaborately interwoven nests. Also = ***weaver finch*** below. Also more fully ***weaver-bird***. E19.

5 BASKET-MAKING. A cane woven between the stakes of a basket. L19.

> 📖 **2** W. COWPER Sedentary weavers of long tales Give me the fidgets. **4** ***cutthroat weaver, sociable weaver, social weaver,*** etc.

Comb.: **weaver ant** any of several tropical ants of the genera *Oecophylla* and *Camponotus*, which build nests of leaves fastened together by the silk of their larvae; ***weaver-bird***: see sense 4 above; **weaver finch** a finch of the family Estrildidae; *spec.* either of two small birds of the genus *Parmoptila*; **weaver's knot** a sheet-bend or single bend, used for joining threads in weaving.

■ **weaveress** *noun* (*rare*) a female weaver E18.

weaver /ˈwiːvə/ *noun*[2]. E19.

[from WEAVE *verb*[2] + -ER[1].]

A person, animal, or thing which weaves from side to side; *esp.* (*a*) a horse etc. that weaves the head, neck, and body from side to side; (*b*) *RAF slang* a pilot or aircraft taking evasive action; (*c*) *colloq.* a motorist who changes lanes continuously, esp. to overtake other vehicles.

weazen /ˈwiːz(ə)n/ *adjective.* Now *rare.* M18.

[Alt. of WIZEN *adjective.*]

Wizened.

■ **weazeny** *adjective* somewhat wizened M19.

weazen /ˈwiːz(ə)n/ *verb intrans. & trans.* Now *rare.* E19.

[Alt. of WIZEN *verb.*]

Shrink, shrivel, wizen. Chiefly as ***weazened*** *ppl adjective.*

web /wɛb/ *noun.*

[Old English *web(b)*, corresp. to Old Frisian *webb*, Old Saxon *webbi* (Middle Dutch *webbe*, Dutch *web*), Old High German *wappi, weppi*, Old Norse *vefr*, from Germanic base also of WEAVE *verb*[1].]

▶ **I 1** (A) woven fabric; *spec.* a whole piece of cloth in the process of being woven or after it comes from the loom. OE. ▸**b** Warp thread or threads. M16. ▸**c** *transf. & fig.* Something resembling a woven fabric; an intricate or interconnecting structure or series of elements; a network. L16. ▸**d** A radio or television broadcasting network. *US.* M20. ▸**e** (Usu. **W-**.) *The* World Wide Web (see WORLDWIDE). L20.

2 An article, as a garment, tapestry, etc., made of woven fabric. Also, woven fabric of a particular material or pattern. Now *arch.* or *literary.* OE. ▸**b** A bandana, a large handkerchief. Now *rare* or *obsolete.* M19.

3 A strong band of material woven without pile. Also, webbing. Cf. ***girth-web*** s.v. GIRTH *noun*[1]. ME.

4 A network of fine threads of scleroprotein constructed by a spider to catch its prey and secreted from its spinnerets; a cobweb; the material of this. Also, a similar filmy network produced by certain insect larvae etc. ME. ▸**b** *fig.* A subtly woven snare or entanglement. Also, anything flimsy and insubstantial. L16. ▸**c** A single thread spun by a spider. L19.

5 A continuous wire mesh on rollers carrying paper pulp; a large roll of paper for use in continuous printing processes. E19. ▸**b** A continuously moving plastic sheet or film. M20.

> 📖 **1** R. S. SURTEES Peter was dressed like his master—coat, waistcoat, and breeches of the same web. **b** ***loom the web***: see LOOM *verb*[1] 2. **c** C. STOLL Technicians had woven a web of cables . . interconnecting most of the computers. *Guardian* An accusation . . that 'ministers entered into a detailed web of deception.' **e** C. FREELAND The Web's potent combination of words and images . . muddles up McLuhan's basic distinctions between the verbal and the visual, the left and the right brain. **2** W. MORRIS With richest webs the marble walls were hung. **4b** DICKENS Accident and artifice had spun a web about him. *Guardian* Hungary is caught in a web of conflicting legislation.

▶ **II 6 a** ANATOMY & MEDICINE. A membrane or thin sheetlike structure in the body. ME. ▸**b** ZOOLOGY. The omentum. Now *rare* or *obsolete.* E19.

†**7** MEDICINE. A thin white film or opacity growing over the eye, as a cataract, leucoma, pterygium, etc. LME–E19.

8 a The membrane or fold of skin between the digits of a hand or foot; *esp.* that which connects the toes of an aquatic bird, mammal, or frog, forming a palmate foot. L16. ▸**b** MEDICINE. An extension of the normal interdigital fold which occurs as a congenital malformation of the human hand or foot. M19.

9 The vane of a bird's feather. E18.

▶ **III 10** A sheet of lead, as used for roofing and for coffins. Long *rare* or *obsolete.* L15. ▸†**b** A quantity of glass. *rare.* M16–M17.

11 The piece of bent iron forming a horseshoe. L16.

12 †**a** The blade of a sword or of a carpenter's plane; the iron head of an axe or hatchet. E17–E19. ▸**b** The thin sharp part of the coulter of a plough. L18. ▸**c** The detachable long narrow blade of a frame-saw or fretsaw. M19.

13 MINING. The extent of a face of a wall of coal, esp. with regard to its depth or thickness. Chiefly *Scot.* M18.

14 The bit of a key; each of the steps or incisions in this. L18.

15 a The thin partition on the inside of the rim of a sheave. *rare.* L18. ▸**b** The vertical plate connecting the upper and lower laterally extending flanges in a beam or girder. Also, a longitudinal vertical member joining the upper and lower components of a wooden rib or spar in an early aircraft. M19. ▸**c** The upright portion between the tread and the bottom flange of a rail. M19. ▸**d** The arm of a crank, connecting the shaft and the wrist. L19. ▸**e** A solid disc connecting the centre and the rim of a wheel, instead of spokes. L19. ▸**f** The part of an oar between the blade and the loom. E20. ▸**g** In *pl.* Snowshoes. *N. Amer.* E20.

Comb.: **web-beam** the roller in a loom on which the web is wound as it is woven; **webcast** a live video broadcast of an event transmitted across the Internet; **web-fed** *adjective* = *reel-fed* s.v. REEL *noun*; **web-fingered** *adjective* (MEDICINE) having the fingers united for all or part of their length by a web (sense 8b above); **web-foot** (*a*) a foot with webbed toes; (*b*) a bird or other animal with webbed feet; (*c*) a person who lives in a wet environment or climate; *spec.* (*US*) a native of Oregon; **web-footed** *adjective* having web-feet; **weblog** COMPUTING a personal website, on which an individual or group of users record opinions, links to other sites, etc., on a regular basis; **weblogger** COMPUTING a person who creates and maintains a weblog; **web-machine** a printing machine which is automatically fed with paper from a large roll; **webmaster** COMPUTING a person who is responsible for a particular server on the World Wide Web; **web-nest** a filmy network of threads enclosing a group of insects, insect larvae, or young spiders; **web offset** offset lithographic printing on a web of paper; **website** COMPUTING a set of linked documents associated with a particular person, organization, or topic that is held on a computer system and can be accessed as part of the World Wide Web; **web-spinner** (*a*) a web-spinning spider; (*b*) a brownish gregarious insect of the small order Embioptera, whose members live in silken tunnels and have wingless females; **web-toed** *adjective* (MEDICINE) having the toes united for all or part of their length by a web (sense 8b above); **web-wheel** a wheel with a plate or web instead of spokes, or with rim, spokes, and centre in one piece, as in watch-wheels; **web-work** a material like that of a woven fabric; **web-worm** *US* any of various moth larvae which are more or less gregarious and spin large webs in which they feed or rest.

■ **weblike** *adjective* resembling (that of) a web M18.

web /wɛb/ *verb.* Infl. **-bb-**. OE.

[from the noun.]

1 *verb trans.* Weave (a fabric) on a loom. Now *rare* or *obsolete.* OE.

2 *verb intrans.* Weave or spin a web. E17.

3 *verb trans.* Connect (fingers, toes, etc.) with a web or membrane. L18.

4 *verb trans.* Cover with a web, esp. a cobweb; weave a web on or over (*lit. & fig.*). M19.

5 *verb trans.* Entangle or enfold (as) in a cobweb. *rare.* M19.

> 📖 **1** J. BARLOW She seeks the wool to web the fleece. **4** J. CAREW Premature age and drink webbed her face with wrinkles. J. FRAME Spiders weave their webs (. . your letterbox is webbed shut).

webbed /wɛbd/ *adjective.* M17.

[from WEB *noun* + -ED[2].]

1 Esp. of a bird's foot: having the digits connected by a membrane or fold of skin. M17. ▸**b** MEDICINE. Of the fingers or toes: united for all or part of their length by a fold of skin (cf. WEB *noun* 8b). M19.

2 Covered (as) with a cobweb or cobwebs. E19.

Webbian /ˈwɛbɪən/ *adjective.* M20.

[from Sidney J. and M. Beatrice *Webb* (see below) + -IAN.]

Of, pertaining to, or characteristic of the English social reformers Sidney and Beatrice Webb (1859–1947 and 1858–1943), or their theories.

webbing /ˈwɛbɪŋ/ *noun.* LME.

[from WEB *verb* + -ING[1].]

1 The action or process of weaving. Long *rare* or *obsolete.* LME.

2 A woven fabric; a web; a network. M18. ▸**b** *spec.* Strong closely woven material, usu. in the form of a wide band, used to support upholstery, for belts, etc. L18.

3 Palmation; MEDICINE a webbed state of the fingers or toes. L19.

> 📖 **2** T. C. WOLFE An old building, with a . . harsh webbing of fire escapes. **b** *attrib.*: *Blackwood's Magazine* Trench coat, rifle, bayonet, webbing belts.

webby /ˈwɛbi/ *adjective.* LME.

[from WEB *noun* + -Y[1].]

1 Consisting of web; resembling a web, esp. a cobweb. LME.

2 Of the fingers or toes: having a web or membrane. E19.

> 📖 **1** E. NESBIT The big darn in the . . carpet was all open and webby like a fishing-net.

webcam /ˈwɛbkam/ *noun.* L20.

[from WEB *noun* + CAM(ERA).]

COMPUTING. A video camera connected to a computer, producing images that can be transmitted across the Internet.

¶ Proprietary name in the US.

weber /ˈveɪbə, ˈwɛbə/ *noun*[1]. L19.

[Wilhelm Eduard *Weber* (1804–91), German physicist.]

ELECTRICITY. †**1 a** A coulomb. Only in L19. ▸**b** An ampere. Only in L19.

†**2** A unit of magnetic pole strength in the cgs system, equal to the pole strength that produces a field of 1 oersted at 1 centimetre. Only in L19.

3 The SI unit of magnetic flux, equal to 100 million maxwells; one volt-second. (Symbol Wb.) L19.

Weber /ˈveɪbə/ *noun*[2]. L19.

[Ernst Heinrich *Weber* (1795–1878), German physiologist and anatomist.]

PHYSIOLOGY. **1** ***Weber's law***, the observation that the increase in a stimulus that is just noticeable is a constant proportion of the initial stimulus. L19.

2 ***Weber fraction, Weber ratio***, this constant proportion. M20.

Comb.: **Weber–Fechner law** (*a*) = ***Weber's law*** above; (*b*) = FECHNER'S LAW.

Weberian /veɪˈbɪərɪən, wɪ-/ *adjective*[1]. M19.

[from WEBER *noun*[2] + -IAN.]

ANATOMY & ZOOLOGY. Designating anatomical structures descibed by Weber.

Weberian apparatus the set of structures which connect the air bladder with the ear in certain fishes. **Weberian ossicles** a chain of small bones forming part of the Weberian apparatus.

Weberian /veɪˈbɪərɪən/ *adjective*[2]. M20.

[from *Weber* (see below) + -IAN.]

Of, pertaining to, or characteristic of the German composer Carl Maria von Weber (1786–1826) or his music.

Weberian /veɪˈbɪərɪən/ *adjective*[3]. M20.

[from *Weber* (see below) + -IAN.]

Of, pertaining to, or characteristic of the German sociologist and political economist Max Weber (1864–1920) or his philosophy or writings.

Webernesque /veɪbəˈnɛsk/ *adjective*. M20.
[from *Webern* (see below) + -ESQUE.]
Of, pertaining to, or characteristic of the music of the Austrian composer Anton von Webern (1883–1945).

Weber number /ˈveɪbə nʌmbə; ˈwɛbə/ *noun phr*. M20.
[from Moritz *Weber* (1871–1951), German naval engineer.]
PHYSICS. A dimensionless quantity used in the study of surface tension, bubbles, and waves, usu. expressed as $\rho l v^2/\gamma$ or the reciprocal of this, where γ is the surface tension of the fluid, ρ its density, l the characteristic length, and v the velocity of the fluid or of waves in the fluid; the square root of either of these quantities.

Webley /ˈwɛbli/ *noun*. L19.
[from P. *Webley* & Son (see below).]
(Proprietary name for) any of various types of revolver and other small arms originally made by the English firm of P. Webley & Son of Birmingham.

webster /ˈwɛbstə/ *noun*. *obsolete* exc. *Hist. & Scot*.
[Old English *webbestre* fem. of *webba* weaver: see -STER.]
A weaver, orig. *esp*. a female one.

Websterian /wɛbˈstɪərɪən/ *adjective*[1]. L19.
[from Noah *Webster* (1758–1843), American lexicographer + -IAN.]
Of, pertaining to, or characteristic of the dictionary compiled by Noah Webster (first published in 1828) or any of its later revisions and abridgements.

Websterian /wɛbˈstɪərɪən/ *adjective*[2]. E20.
[from *Webster* (see below) + -IAN.]
Of, pertaining to, or characteristic of the English dramatist John Webster (1580–1625) or his plays.

websterite /ˈwɛbstəraɪt/ *noun*. L19.
[from *Webster*, a village in N. Carolina, USA + -ITE[1].]
PETROGRAPHY. An ultramafic intrusive igneous rock composed essentially of orthorhombic and monoclinic pyroxenes.

webzine /ˈwɛbziːn/ *noun*. L20.
[from WEB *noun* + MAGA)ZINE.]
COMPUTING. A magazine published electronically on the World Wide Web.

Wechsler /ˈwɛkslə/ *noun*. M20.
[David *Wechsler* (1896–1981), US psychologist.]
PSYCHOLOGY. Any of various intelligence tests and scales devised by Wechsler. Freq. *attrib*.

wed /wɛd/ *noun*. *obsolete* exc. *Scot*.
[Old English *wedd*, corresp. to Old Frisian *wedd*, Old Saxon *weddi* (Dutch *wedde*), Old High German *wetti* (German *Wette*), Old Norse *veð*, Gothic *wadi*, from Germanic base rel. to Latin *vad-*, *vas* surety: see GAGE *noun*[1], WAGE *noun*.]
1 A pledge, something deposited as security for a payment or the fulfilment of an obligation. Also (*rare*), a hostage. OE.
2 The condition of being given or held as a wed or pledge; the state of being pawned or mortgaged. Chiefly in phrs. below. OE.
3 A stake in a game or wager. ME.
2 in wed as a pledge or hostage. †**in wed of** as security for (a payment etc.). **to wed** = *in wed* above.

wed /wɛd/ *verb*. Now chiefly *literary*, *dial*., or *formal*. Infl. **-dd-**. Pa. t. & pple **wedded**, **wed**.
[Old English *weddian*, corresp. to Old Frisian *weddia*, Middle Low German *wedden*, Old High German *wettōn* (German *wetten*) pledge, wager, Old Norse *veðja* pledge, Gothic *gawadjōn* espouse, from Germanic base also of prec.]
†**1** *verb intrans*. Enter into a covenant (*to do*). *rare*. Only in OE.
2 *verb trans*. Orig., make (a woman) one's wife by the giving of a pledge. Later, (of a person of either sex) marry; become the husband or wife of (a person) by participating in a recognized ceremony or formal act. OE.
3 *verb trans*. & *intrans*. Join (a couple) in marriage; conduct the wedding ceremony for. OE. ▸**b** *verb trans*. Give (a woman) in marriage; cause to be married. *rare*. LME.
4 *verb trans*. In *pass*. Be joined in marriage *to* (a husband or wife); be joined together as husband and wife. Formerly also foll. by *with*. ME.
5 *verb intrans*. Enter into matrimony, get married. Freq. foll. by †*to*, *with*. ME.
6 *verb trans*. Wager or stake (money, one's life, etc.). *obsolete* exc. *Scot. & north*. LME.
7 *verb trans*. **a** Attach (a person etc.) indissolubly by affection or inclination to something; *esp*. in *pass*., be obstinately attached or devoted *to* (an opinion, habit, etc.). LME. ▸**b** Unite (a thing) closely or intimately *with* or *to* something else; join in close association. E19.
8 *verb trans*. Espouse or adopt (a cause, course of conduct, custom, etc.). Now *rare* or *obsolete*. E17.

> **2** J. WILSON The husband, now no longer tied May wed a new and blushing bride. **3** R. BROUGHTON The *Helmsley Courier* devotes three columns to . . describing . . how they were clad, who wed them. **4** SIR W. SCOTT I found her wedded to a Gascon squire. **7a** *Economist* He . . seems wedded to a view of China common in the late Maoist period. **b** J. BARZUN The high middle class . . wedded knowledge and elegance.

■ **wedded** *ppl adjective* (*a*) that has been wed, married; (*b*) of or pertaining to marriage or married persons; (*c*) obstinately attached (*to* an opinion, habit, etc.); (*d*) (of things) united or joined closely together: OE.

Wed. *abbreviation*. Also **Weds.**
Wednesday.

Weddell seal /ˈwɛd(ə)l siːl/ *noun*. E20.
[James *Weddell* (1787–1834), Scot. navigator.]
A large mottled grey seal, *Leptonychotes weddellii*, that breeds on fast ice in the Antarctic.

†**wedder** *noun* var. of WETHER.

wedding /ˈwɛdɪŋ/ *noun*. OE.
[from WED *verb* + -ING[1].]
1 The action of WED *verb*; marriage. Formerly also, the married state, matrimony. OE.
2 A marriage ceremony; the performance of the ceremony itself; this with its accompanying celebrations. ME. ▸**b** With specifying adjective, as *diamond*, *golden*, *silver*, *ruby*, etc. A wedding anniversary. M19.

> **2** J. MCGAHERN She set her heart on a . . wedding . . at the little village church. L. GRANT-ADAMSON The family things . . weddings, funerals and whatnot. S. HILL After the wedding, there was luncheon in a hotel. *double wedding*, *shotgun wedding*, *white wedding*, etc.

Comb.: **wedding anniversary** the anniversary of a wedding; **wedding band** *N. Amer*. a wedding ring; **wedding breakfast** a meal etc. usu. served between the marriage ceremony and the departure for the honeymoon; **wedding-bush** any of various Australian shrubs constituting the genus *Ricinocarpos*, of the spurge family, bearing clusters of fragrant starry white or pink flowers; esp. *R. pinifolius* and *R. bowmanni*; **wedding cake** a rich iced and decorated fruit cake, often with two or more tiers, served to guests at a wedding reception; *fig*. (freq. *derog*.) a building resembling a wedding cake in the ornateness of its architecture; **wedding-cake** *adjective* (*fig*., freq. *derog*.) designating or pertaining to a style of architecture characterized by its sumptuous ornateness; **wedding canopy** = CHUPPAH; **wedding-card**: bearing the names of the bride and groom and sent out as an announcement of the wedding (usu. in *pl*.); **wedding-chest**, **wedding coffer** *Hist*. an ornamental chest made to contain a bride's trousseau, a cassone; **wedding day** the day on which a marriage takes place or is due to take place; an anniversary of this day; **wedding-favour** *arch*. a white rosette or knot of ribbons worn by guests at a wedding; **wedding-finger** = *ring finger* s.v. RING *noun*[1]; **wedding-garment** (*a*) a garment appropriate to or worn at a wedding; (*b*) *fig*. (with allus. to *Matthew* 22:11) a qualification for participating in a feast of some kind; **wedding group** (a photograph of) a wedding party; **wedding knives** *Hist*. a pair of knives given to a bride as a symbol of marital status; **wedding-knot** (*a*) *fig*. the bond of matrimony; (*b*) NAUTICAL a tie for uniting the looped ends of two ropes; **wedding list** a list of items which a couple about to be married would find acceptable as wedding presents; **wedding-march** a march (esp. that by Mendelssohn) composed for performance at a wedding, usu. played to signal the entrance of the bride or the exit of the couple; **wedding night** the night after a wedding, esp. as the night of a marriage's consummation; **wedding-party** the whole group of people gathered for a wedding; **wedding reception** a party at which the wedding guests are formally greeted and entertained after the marriage ceremony; **wedding ring** a ring worn to indicate married status; **wedding-sheet** *Hist*. a sheet laid on the bridal bed and sometimes kept to form a shroud for the bride at her death; **wedding tackle** *slang* a man's genitals.

■ **weddinger** *noun* (*Scot. & dial*.) a wedding guest; in *pl*., the whole wedding-party, including the bride and groom: E19.

wedeln /ˈveɪd(ə)ln/ *noun*. Also **wedel** /ˈveɪd(ə)l/. M20.
[German: see next.]
SKIING. A technique using a swaying movement of the hips to make a series of short parallel turns.

wedeln /ˈveɪd(ə)ln/ *verb intrans*. Also **wedel** /ˈveɪd(ə)l/, infl. **-ll-**, *-**l-**. M20.
[German, lit. 'wag (the tail)'.]
SKIING. Use the wedeln technique. Also, perform a similar movement on a skateboard.

†**wedenonfa'** *noun*. *Scot*. L15–E19.
[from Old English *wēden-* mad (in combs.) + ONFALL.]
= WEED *noun*[3] 1.

wedge /wɛdʒ/ *noun*. See also WODGE.
[Old English *wecg*, corresp. to Old Saxon *weggi*, Old High German *weggi*, *wecki* (Dutch *wegge*, German *Weck(e)* wedge-shaped piece of cake etc.), Middle Low German, Middle Dutch *wigge* (Dutch *wigge* wedge, piece of cake), Old Norse *veggr*, from Germanic.]
1 A piece of wood, metal, etc., which has a narrow triangular cross-section and is driven between two objects or parts of an object to split, tighten, or secure them, or to widen an opening etc.; MECHANICS this considered as a simple machine, now regarded as a variety of the inclined plane. OE. ▸**b** ARCHITECTURE. A voussoir. E18.
2 †**a** An ingot of gold, silver, etc. (perh. orig. in the form of a wedge). OE–E18. ▸**b** Silver money or plate. *slang* (now *rare*). E18.
3 *fig*. A thing acting as a wedge; *esp*. something creating a split or divide. L16.
4 A lump or cake of any solid substance. Now *rare* or *dial*. L16. ▸**b** A wad of banknotes; (a significant amount of) money. *slang* (orig. *Criminals'*). L20.
5 A thing resembling a wedge in shape or form; a wedge-shaped part or piece of anything; *spec*. (*a*) a formation of people (formerly esp. of troops) tapering towards the front, in order to drive a way through opposition; a similar formation adopted by birds, esp. geese, in flight; (*b*) the wedge-shaped stroke in cuneiform characters; (*c*) METEOROLOGY = RIDGE *noun*[1] 3b; (*d*) a V-shaped sign or symbol used in various musical and other notations; (*e*) GOLF a golf club with a wedge-shaped head, used for lofting the ball at approach shots or out of a bunker etc.; a shot made with such a club; (*f*) a wedge-shaped heel (also ***wedge-heel***); a shoe with such a heel (also ***wedge-shoe***); (*g*) a hairstyle in which the ends of the hair are slightly graduated to form a series of wedges. E17.
6 GEOMETRY. A triangular prism; a simple solid formed by cutting a triangular prism by any two planes. Also (in full ***spherical wedge***), a solid formed by two planes meeting along the axis of a sphere. E18.
7 HERALDRY. A charge consisting of an isosceles triangle with a very acute angle at its vertex. E18.

> **1** *Traditional Woodworking* Assemble the joint, tapping the wedge into position. **3** *Economist* To make a bid for . . power by driving a wedge between the parties of the . . coalition. **the thin end of the wedge** a relatively insignificant change, action, measure, etc., which promises or threatens to open the way to further more serious changes or consequences. **5** V. GLENDINNING The monumental wedge of chocolate cake. *attrib*.: *Time Out* The police . . adopting their familiar flying wedge formation to break up the picket.

Comb.: **wedgebill** a bird with a wedge-shaped bill, as (*a*) an Australian logrunner, *Sphenostoma cristatum*, which has an upright crest; (*b*) a hummingbird, *Schistes geoffroyi*, of Central and S. America; **wedge-form**, **wedge-formed** *adjectives* wedge-shaped; ***wedge-heel***: see sense 5(f) above; **wedge issue** *US* a divisive political issue, esp. one that is raised by a candidate for public office in the hope of attracting or alienating an opponent's supporters; **wedge photometer**: in which the illumination reaching two sides of a wedge of glass from different sources is compared; **wedge-shaped** *adjective* (*a*) shaped like a solid wedge, cuneiform; (*b*) BOTANY = CUNEATE; **wedge shell** (a shell of) any of various marine bivalves of the genus *Donax* and family Donacidae, which have generally triangular shells; ***wedge-shoe***: see sense 5(f) above; **wedgetail** *Austral*. = ***wedge-tailed eagle*** below; **wedge-tailed** *adjective* having a wedge-shaped tail; ***wedge-tailed eagle***, a large eagle, *Aquila audax*, which is found throughout Australia; **wedge tent** an A tent.

■ **wedgelike** *adjective* wedge-shaped; resembling a wedge: L16. **wedgewise** *adverb* after the manner or in the form of a wedge M16. **wedgy** *adjective* (*rare*) resembling a wedge; wedge-shaped: L18.

wedge /wɛdʒ/ *verb*[1]. LME.
[from prec.]
1 *verb trans*. Tighten, secure, or fasten by driving in a wedge or wedges. Also foll. by *in*, *up*. LME.
2 *verb trans*. Drive or force (a thing, oneself) tightly in or into something; secure by driving in or pressing tight. Freq. foll. by *between*, *in*, *into*, *under*, etc. E16.
3 *verb trans*. Split by driving in a wedge; force apart or open (as) by driving in a wedge. Now chiefly with adverbs. M16.
4 *verb intrans*. **a** Force one's way *in*. *rare*. E17. ▸**b** Become fixed or jammed tight (as) by the operation of a wedge. *rare*. E18.
5 *verb trans*. Pack, crowd, or mass (a number of people or animals) in close formation, or in a limited space. Usu. in *pass*. Freq. foll. by *in*, *into*, *together*. E18.
6 *verb intrans*. GEOLOGY. Of a body of rock: thin out, lens out. Usu. foll. by *out*. E19.

> **1** V. WOOLF The window shook, and Rebecca . . wedged it. D. HIGHSMITH The main lights were on, . . the exit doors wedged open. **2** D. LODGE A cigar wedged between manicured fingers. L. GRANT-ADAMSON A drunken gossip columnist . . was wedged in the revolving doors. **3** SHAKES. *Tr. & Cr*. My heart, As wedged with a sigh, would rive in twain. P. FRANCIS Magma forces its way up into the crack, widening it . . by hydraulically wedging the walls apart. **5** CARLYLE The 2,000 human figures, wedged . . into one dark mass.

Phrases: †**wedge their way** (*rare*, Milton) fly in a wedge-shaped formation.

wedge /wɛdʒ/ *verb*[2] *trans*. L17.
[Origin unkn.]
POTTERY. Prepare (wet clay) for use by cutting, kneading, and throwing down, in order to expel air-bubbles.
■ **wedger** *noun* L19.

wedged /wɛdʒd/ *adjective*. M16.
[from WEDGE *noun*, *verb*[1]: see -ED[2], -ED[1].]
Shaped like a wedge.

wedgie /ˈwɛdʒi/ *noun*. *colloq*. M20.
[from WEDGE *noun* + -IE.]
1 A wedge-heeled shoe. Now also, a shoe with a platform sole. Usu. in *pl*. M20.

2 The action of pulling up the material of someone's underwear tightly between the buttocks, esp. as a practical joke. Orig. *US.* L20.

> 2 S. KING The bullies were still giving Gerald wedgies in study-hall.

wedging /ˈwɛdʒɪŋ/ *noun.* L17.
[from WEDGE *verb*[1] + -ING[1].]
1 The action of WEDGE *verb*[1]; the condition of being wedged. L17. ▸**b** A wedge-shaped piece or pieces of some hard material driven in for tightening or securing. E19.
2 GEOLOGY. The lensing or thinning out of a body of rock. Usu. foll. by *out.* E19.

Wedgwood /ˈwɛdʒwʊd/ *adjective & noun.* L18.
[See below.]
▸ **A** *adjective.* 1 Designating or pertaining to the ceramic ware made by the English potter Josiah Wedgwood (1730–95) and his successors, esp. a kind of fine stoneware with classical white cameo designs on a blue, green, or black ground. L18.
2 Of the characteristic pale or greyish blue colour of some Wedgwood ware. E20.
▸ **B** *noun.* 1 (A piece of) Wedgwood ware. M19.
2 Wedgwood blue. E20.
¶ Proprietary name in relation to ceramics.

wedlock /ˈwɛdlɒk/ *noun & verb.* LOE.
[from WED *noun* + -LOCK.]
▸ **A** *noun.* †1 The marriage vow or obligation. Chiefly in phrs. below. LOE–E17.
2 The condition of being married; marriage as a state of life or as an institution; (a) matrimonial relationship. Now chiefly *literary & formal* exc. in ***born in wedlock, born out of wedlock*** below. ME.
†3 A wife. M16–L17.

> 1 †**break one's wedlock**, †**break wedlock** commit adultery. †**hold wedlock**, †**keep wedlock** be faithful in marriage. 2 J. FLETCHER 'Tis sacriledge to violate a wedlock. *Guardian* Wedlock is . . accepted as socially tidier. **born in wedlock** born of parents married to each other, legitimate. **born out of wedlock** born of parents not married to each other, illegitimate.

Comb.: †**wedlock-bound** *adjective* (*rare*, Milton) bound in marriage.
▸†**B** *verb trans.* Unite in marriage. Usu. in *pass. rare.* M17–M18.

Wednesday /ˈwɛnzdeɪ, -di, ˈwɛdn-/ *noun, adjective, & adverb.*
[Old English *wōdnesdæg*, corresp. to Old Frisian *wōnsdei*, Middle Low German *wōdensdach* (Dutch *woensdag*), Old Norse *óðinsdagr* 'day of Odin', translating late Latin *Mercurii dies* 'day of the planet Mercury'.]
▸ **A** *noun.* The fourth day of the week, following Tuesday. OE.
Ash Wednesday: see ASH *noun*[2].
▸ **B** *attrib.* or as *adjective.* Of Wednesday; characteristic of Wednesday; taking place on Wednesday(s). LME.
▸ **C** *adverb.* On Wednesday. Now *colloq.* E17.
■ **Wednesdays** *adverb* (*colloq.*) on Wednesdays, each Wednesday L20.

wee /wiː/ *noun*[1] *& adjective.* Orig. *Scot.* ME.
[Ult. from Old English (Anglian) *wēg(e*, corresp. to West Saxon *wǣge*: see WEY. Cf. PEEWEE, WEESHY.]
▸ **A** *noun.* 1 †**a** A little or young thing; a child. Only in ME. ▸**b** A small quantity, measure, or degree. Now only *Scot.* LME.
2 A short time. Formerly also (*rare*), a short distance. Now chiefly *Scot.* ME.
▸ **B** *adjective.* Extremely small, tiny (*colloq.*). Also (chiefly *Scot.*), small, little. LME.

> R. PARK A wee house that crouched between . . two factories.

Phrases: **a wee**, †**a little wee** (now chiefly *Scot.*) (*a*) to a small extent, in a small degree; (*b*) somewhat, rather; (*c*) for a short time. **a wee bit** a little; somewhat, rather. **a wee bit of a —** *colloq.* a small or unimportant example of, a mild case of. **the wee folk** fairies. **Wee Free** *colloq.* (usu. *derog.*) a member of the Free Kirk (after 1900). **Wee Free Kirk** *colloq.* (usu. *derog.*) the Free Kirk (after 1900). **wee hours**, **wee small hours** *colloq.* = ***small hours*** s.v. SMALL *adjective, adverb, & noun.*

wee /wiː/ *noun*[2] *& verb. colloq.* M20.
[Imit. Cf. WEE-WEE.]
▸ **A** *noun.* Urine; the action or an act of urinating. M20.
▸ **B** *verb.* Pa. t. & pple **weed**.
1 *verb intrans.* Urinate. M20.
2 *verb refl.* Urinate involuntarily; wet oneself. L20.

wee /wiː/ *interjection.* Usu. redupl. **wee wee.** M19.
[Imit.]
Repr. the squeal of a pig.

weed /wiːd/ *noun*[1].
[Old English *wēod*, corresp. to Old Saxon *wiod* rel. to Old High German *wiota* fern, of unkn. origin.]
1 A plant that grows, esp. profusely, where it is not wanted; *spec.* a plant of no utility growing wild among crops, garden plants, etc., and competing with them for light, nutrients, etc. Freq. as 2nd elem. in plant-names. OE. ▸**b** Weeds collectively; dense or luxuriant plant growth. ME. ▸**c** A plant growing wild in fresh or salt water. Chiefly as 2nd elem. in combs. M16.
2 **a** *gen.* A plant. Chiefly *poet.* OE. ▸**b** A shrub or tree, *esp.* one abundant in a particular area. Now chiefly *rhet.* L17.
3 *fig.* A troublesome, harmful, or unprofitable thing or person. LME.
4 **a** Tobacco. Now usu. with *the. colloq.* E17. ▸**b** A cigar, a cheroot. *colloq.* M19. ▸**c** Marijuana; a marijuana cigarette. Freq. with *the. slang* (orig. *US*). E20.
5 **a** A poor leggy loosely built horse. *slang.* M19. ▸**b** A tall thin weak-looking person lacking a sturdy physique; a feeble or contemptible person. *colloq.* M19.

> 1 R. QUIRK Grass is a weed in a flower bed but not in a lawn. *Garden Answers* Kill off all perennial weeds, such as . . nettles. ***bindweed***, ***cudweed***, ***hogweed***, ***knapweed***, ***milkweed***, etc. **b** D. HIGHSMITH Lower slopes choked with thornbushes and tangled weed. **c** ***duckweed***, ***pondweed***, ***river-weed***, ***seaweed***, etc. **2b** J. B. MOZLEY The ash is the weed of the county. **3** *Guardian* No one who is now . . pulling out . . the weeds of Marxism can claim any originality. **4a** *Company* The weed is responsible for one third of all cancer deaths in the UK. **5b** *Smash Hits* She's *such* a weed that she enjoys . . sitting at home . . making little toy pigs.

Comb.: **weed-grown** *adjective* overgrown with weeds; **weedhead** *slang* (chiefly *US*) a (habitual) marijuana smoker (cf. ***hophead*** (a) s.v. HOP *noun*[1]); **weed-hook** a hook for cutting down weeds; **weed inspector** an official in charge of controlling the growth of harmful weeds; **weedkiller** something that kills weeds; *esp.* any of various chemical preparations in liquid or powder form used for killing weeds; **weed whacker** *N. Amer.* an electrically-powered grass trimmer with a nylon cutting cord that rotates on a spindle.
■ **weedery** *noun* (*rare*) (*a*) weeds collectively; (*b*) a place filled with weeds: M17. **weedful** *adjective* (*rare*) full of weeds E17. **weedicide** *noun* (*a*) chemical weedkiller M20. **weedless** *adjective* free from weeds (*lit.* & *fig.*) E17. **weedling** *noun* (*rare*) (*a*) a small weed; (*b*) a slight feeble person: E19.

weed /wiːd/ *noun*[2]. *arch.*
[Old English *wǣd*, corresp. to Old Frisian *wēd*, Old Saxon *wād* (in Dutch *lijnwaad*), Old High German *wāt*, Old Norse *váð*, *vōð*, from Germanic; or Old English *wǣde*, *gewǣde*, corresp. to Old Frisian *wēde*, Old Saxon *wādi*, *giwādi* (Dutch *gewaad*), Old High German *giwāti*, from Germanic, of disputed origin.]
1 An article of clothing; a garment. OE.
2 Clothes collectively, clothing, dress. OE.
3 *transf. & fig.* Something resembling or compared to clothing, a covering. Now *rare.* ME.
4 *sing.* & †in *pl.* Defensive covering, armour, mail. Now *rare.* ME.
5 *sing.* & in *pl.* (An article of) clothing distinctive of a person's sex, profession, condition in life, etc. Freq. with specifying word. ME.
†6 A cloth, a hanging; cloths or hangings collectively. ME–L16.
7 With specifying word, as *funeral*, *mourning*, etc.: a black garment worn to signify bereavement. Also, a scarf or band of crape worn by a mourner. M16.
8 In *pl.* & †*sing.* More fully ***widow's weeds***. The deep mourning worn by a widow. L16.

> 1 POPE An aged mendicant in tatter'd weeds. **2** SPENSER Each mans worth is measured by his weed. **3** R. BURNS Autumn, in her weeds o'yellow. **5** TENNYSON This poor gown . . this beggar-woman's weed. **8** E. BOWEN The day of the funeral they turned out . . draped in widow's weeds.

weed /wiːd/ *noun*[3]. *Scot. & Anglo-Irish.* Also **weid.** L18.
[Abbreviation of WEDENONFA'.]
1 A sudden febrile attack; *esp.* puerperal fever. L18.
2 VETERINARY MEDICINE. A feverish disease of farm animals; *esp.* (*a*) mastitis in cows and ewes; (*b*) recurrent fever and lameness in horses. E19.

weed /wiːd/ *verb*[1].
[Old English *wēodian*, corresp. to Old Saxon *wiodon*, Middle & mod. Low German *weden*, Middle & mod. Dutch *wieden*, from WEED *noun*[1].]
1 *verb intrans.* Clear an area of weeds; uproot or cut down weeds. OE.
2 *verb trans.* Free (an area, a crop, etc.) from weeds. ME. ▸**b** *fig.* Remove unwanted or harmful elements from. LME.
3 *verb trans.* Remove (weeds) from land, esp. from cultivated land or from a crop. Also foll. by *out.* LME. ▸**b** *fig.* Eradicate (errors, faults, sins, etc.); remove (a thing or person) as harmful or useless. Usu. foll. by *out*, *away.* E16. ▸†**c** *transf.* Remove (vermin, destructive animals). *rare* (Shakes.). Only in L16.
4 **a** *verb trans.* Clear *away* (plants, not necessarily harmful or useless ones); thin *out* (plants or trees). *rare.* M16. ▸**b** *verb trans. & intrans.* Foll. by *away*: carry off by death or die. *Scot.* (chiefly *literary*). M18. ▸**c** *verb trans.* Remove (inferior or unwanted individuals) from a company, herd, etc. Freq. foll. by *out.* M19. ▸**d** *verb intrans. & trans.* Foll. by *down*: reduce (a group of people) by selection. L19. ▸**e** *verb trans.* Perform a process of selection on (documents, a file, etc.), so as to reject unimportant or superfluous items; select (papers etc.) in this manner. Also, sort (papers, esp. official documents) so as to withhold sensitive material from the public. Also foll. by *out.* L19.
5 *verb trans.* Steal (part of a larger quantity of something). *Criminals' slang* (now *rare*). E19.
6 *verb intrans. & refl.* ANGLING. Of a trout: bury itself in weeds when hooked. L19.

> 1 JULIA HAMILTON He had seen Macindoe in the border weeding. **2** R. L. STEVENSON The alleys . . were smoothed and weeded like a boulevard. **b** J. A. FROUDE The Senate was . . weeded of . . its disreputable members. **3b** *Atlantic* The FDA's testing hurdles . . weed out most unsafe or ineffective drugs. **4c** *Racing Pigeon Pictorial* It is important to weed out the poor birds that will . . crop up with inbreeding. **e** *Listener* 90 per cent of departmental paperwork is 'weeded out' and destroyed.

■ **weeder** *noun* (*a*) an implement for weeding; (*b*) a person who removes weeds from a crop, esp. as an occupation etc.; (*c*) an official in a government department employed to weed documents, letters, etc., so as to withhold sensitive material from the public: LME.

weed *verb*[2] *pa. t. & pple* of WEE *verb.*

weeded /ˈwiːdɪd/ *adjective*[1]. M18.
[from WEED *noun*[1], *verb*[1]: see -ED[2], -ED[1].]
1 Freed from weeds. M18.
2 Covered with weeds; full of or choked with weeds (also foll. by *up*). E19.
3 Thinned out; sparse. *Scot.* M19.

weeded /ˈwiːdɪd/ *adjective*[2]. *arch. rare.* L19.
[from WEED *noun*[2] + -ED[2].]
Dressed in widow's weeds.

weeding /ˈwiːdɪŋ/ *noun.* OE.
[from WEED *verb*[1] + -ING[1].]
1 The action of WEED *verb*[1] (*lit.* & *fig.*). OE.
2 A plant removed by weeding or thinning out. Usu. in *pl.* L16.
Comb.: **weeding-hook** a weed-hook.

weedy /ˈwiːdi/ *adjective*[1]. LME.
[from WEED *noun*[1] + -Y[1].]
1 Full of or overgrown with weeds. LME.
2 Of the nature of or resembling a weed; made or consisting of weeds; having a taste or smell of weeds. E17.
3 **a** Of an animal, esp. a horse or hound: lean, leggy, and lacking in strength and stamina. *slang.* E19. ▸**b** Esp. of a person: tall and thin; lanky and weak-looking; of poor physique. Also, feeble; lacking strength of character. *colloq.* M19.

> 1 A. PILLING He could see right down the weedy drive to the front gate. **2** I. MURDOCH The cool weedy smell of the water. *fig.*: F. C. BURNAND A long-legged gentleman with weedy whiskers. **3b** *Guardian* A . . weedy collage of lights and sound effects. J. C. OATES Tall, rangy, weedy, with long lank . . hair.

■ **weediness** *noun* E20.

weedy /ˈwiːdi/ *adjective*[2]. *rare.* M19.
[from WEED *noun*[2] + -Y[1].]
Of a woman: wearing widow's weeds, clad in mourning.

Weejuns /ˈwiːdʒənz/ *noun pl.* Chiefly *US.* M20.
[Fanciful.]
(Proprietary name for) moccasin-style shoes for casual wear.

week /wiːk/ *noun.*
[Old English *wice*, *wicu*, corresp. to Old Frisian *wike*, Old Saxon *-wika* in *crūcewika* Holy Week (Dutch *week*), Old High German *wehha*, *wohha* (German *Woche*), Old Norse *vika*, Gothic *wikō* (translating Greek *taxis* order), from Germanic noun prob. meaning 'series, succession' and rel. to Latin *vic-*: see VICE *preposition*, VICE-.]
1 The cycle of seven successive days recognized in the Jewish calendar and from there adopted in the calendars of Christian, Muslim, and various other peoples; a single period of this cycle, beginning with the day traditionally fixed as the first day of the week (now usu. reckoned from and to midnight on Saturday–Sunday). OE. ▸**b** With specifying word: a particular week of the year, the whole or part of which is assigned to a specific event, purpose, cause, action, or observance; the date of a specific festival etc. OE.
2 **a** A period of seven days, reckoned from any point. Freq. in ***a week today***, ***a week yesterday***, ***a week Saturday***, etc. OE. ▸**b** Seven days as a term for periodical payments of wages, rent, etc., or as a unit of reckoning for time of work or service. LME. ▸**c** An indefinite time; in *pl.*, a long indefinite period of time. LME.
3 The period of time spent at work, formerly the six days between Sundays and now usu. the five days from Monday to Friday, excluding the weekend. Also, an amount of work done during this period. OE.
4 With specifying word, as *Monday*, *tomorrow*, *yesterday*, etc.: seven days before or after the day mentioned. LME.

🕮 **1** M. DORRIS She . . listens to the radio every week instead of going to . . church. *Independent* Heads of foreign missions plan to meet next week. **b** *Police Chief* The ceremony . . took place during National Police Week. ***Easter Week, Ember Week, Holy Week***, etc. **2a** BEVERLEY CLEARY A week's collection of dirty socks . . under her bed. P. BARKER I believe he volunteered . . . The first week of the war. **b** J. HERSEY Fired him. After thirty-four years, they gave him two weeks' notice. **c** C. BRAYFIELD Why not . . think about it for a week or two? *Reader's Digest* None of our children came over to see us for weeks. **3** *Architects' Journal* Generous benefits including . . a 35-hour week with flexitime. **4** E. O'BRIEN He would be drawing the dole by the following Monday week.

Phrases: **a week** every week, weekly, per week. †**be in by the week** be ensnared or caught; *fig.* be deeply in love. **day of the week** each of the seven days constituting a week, as Sunday, Monday, Tuesday, etc. **feast of weeks** = PENTECOST 1. ***knock into the middle of next week***: see KNOCK *verb*. ***the other week***: see OTHER *adjective*. ***three day week***: see THREE *noun*. ***TODAY week***. **too late a week** *joc.* far too late (now chiefly with allus. to Shakes. *A.Y.L.*). **week and week about** in alternate weeks. ***week in, week out***: see IN *adverb*. **week of Sundays** an indefinitely long period (cf. ***MONTH of Sundays***).

Comb.: **weeklong** *adjective & adverb* (lasting) for a whole week; **weeknight** a night in the week other than at the weekend or (formerly) other than Sunday night; **weeknightly** *adverb* (*US*) occurring every weeknight; **week-to-week** *adjective* continuing or recurring in successive weeks; continual; **week-work** *LAW* (now *Hist.*) work done for a lord by a tenant for a certain number of days a week.

week /wiːk/ *interjection*. **L16.**
[Imit.]
Repr. the squeak of a pig, mouse, guinea pig, etc.

weekday /ˈwiːkdeɪ/ *noun*. **OE.**
[from WEEK *noun* + DAY *noun*.]
†**1** A day of the week. **OE–LME.**
†**2** A day of the week other than market-day or Sunday. **L15–L16.**
3 A day of the week other than at a weekend or (formerly) other than Sunday; a working day. **M16.**

🕮 **3** D. LODGE The weekdays were not so bad, when he could distract himself with work. *attrib.*: T. HARDY She . . came down in her ordinary weekday clothes.

weekend /wiːkˈɛnd, ˈwiː-/ *noun, adjective, & verb*. Also **week-end**. **M17.**
[from WEEK *noun* + END *noun*.]
▶ **A** *noun*. The end of a week; a period at the end of a week's work, usu. Sunday and Saturday or part of Saturday, often a time during which business is suspended and most shops are closed; this period extended slightly, esp. for a holiday or a visit. **M17.**

🕮 *Guardian* Delays experienced by . . British air travellers two week-ends ago. *Golf for Women* Whether you stay for a weekend or a month you'll . . remember the warm atmosphere. ***long weekend***: see LONG *adjective*¹. ***lost weekend***: see LOST *adjective*.

▶ **B** *attrib.* or as *adjective*. **1** For use at weekends; occurring at or for the duration of a weekend. **L19.**
2 Carrying out a specific activity or hobby, or fulfilling a particular role, only at weekends or for pleasure; amateur, casual. **M20.**

🕮 **1** L. ELLMANN Holding her weekend bag with its pyjamas. *Here's Health* Weekend introductory courses learning basic massage skills in a relaxed . . setting. **2** D. HALLIDAY The boat was . . full of tanned, husky weekend sailors.

▶ **C** *verb intrans.* Spend a weekend. **E20.**

🕮 M. FITZHERBERT He . . dined often at Downing Street, weekended at The Wharf.

weekender /wiːkˈɛndə/ *noun*. **L19.**
[from prec. + -ER¹.]
1 A person who spends weekends away from home. **L19.**
2 A weekend or holiday cottage. *Austral. colloq.* **E20.**
3 A bag large enough to carry everything needed for a weekend away; a weekend bag. *N. Amer.* **M20.**
4 A person who indulges in occasional drug-taking, esp. at weekends. *slang* (orig. *US*). **M20.**
5 A small pleasure-boat, *esp.* one designed for private use at weekends. Chiefly *US*. **M20.**

weekly /ˈwiːkli/ *adjective & noun*. **L15.**
[from WEEK *noun* + -LY¹.]
▶ **A** *adjective*. **1** Occurring, done, produced, etc., once a week. **L15.** ▶**b** Performing an action, or employed in a particular capacity, once a week; having a contract by the week. **E18.**
2 Of or pertaining to a week (either as a seven-day period or as opp. to the weekend or Sunday). **M16.**

🕮 **1** E. SEGAL The only . . bright spot . . had been Laura's weekly letters. *Holiday Which?* Charter flights are usually sold on a weekly basis. **b weekly boarder** a pupil boarding at school during the week and returning home at weekends.

▶ **B** *noun*. A newspaper, magazine, etc., published once each week. **M19.**

weekly /ˈwiːkli/ *adverb*. **LME.**
[from WEEK *noun* + -LY².]
Once a week, from week to week, in each or every week.

🕮 *Guardian* Meetings are held weekly. *Plants & Gardens* Plants are fed weekly between March and October.

weel /wiːl/ *noun*¹. *Scot. & north.* Also **weal**, **weil**.
[Old English *wǣl*, corresp. to Middle Dutch *wael*, Middle Low German *wēl*.]
A deep pool; a deep place in a river or the sea; a whirlpool, an eddy.

weel /wiːl/ *noun*². **ME.**
[Reduced form of WILLY *noun*¹.]
1 A wicker trap for catching fish, esp. eels. **ME.** ▶**b** *HERALDRY.* A charge representing this. **L17.**
2 A basket, *esp.* one in which fish are kept. **LME.**

ween /wiːn/ *verb. arch.*
[Old English *wēnan* = Old Frisian *wēna*, Old Saxon *wānian* (Dutch *wanen* fancy, imagine), Old High German *wan(n)ēn* (German *wähnen* suppose wrongly), Old Norse *vǽna*, Gothic *wēnjan* hope, from Germanic base also of WISH *verb*, WONT *adjective*.]
▶ **I** *verb trans.* **1** Think, surmise, or suppose *that*. Freq. in parenthetical use. Formerly also foll. by direct obj. and inf. or compl. **OE.** ▶†**b** Believe, credit, (something). **OE–L16.**
2 Expect, think possible or likely, anticipate. Now foll. by subord. clause or adverbial compl. **OE.** ▶**b** Intend, hope, wish, or be minded *to do*. **OE.**

🕮 **1** J. DEE The eye weeneth a round Globe . . to be a flat and plaine Circle. W. FULKE Let him looke in his lexicon, where I weene al his Greeke is. R. H. BARHAM A stalwart knight, I ween, was he.

▶†**II** *verb intrans.* **3** Dream of, look for. Foll. by *of*. *rare* (Shakes.). Only in **E17.**

weeny /ˈwiːni/ *noun*¹. **M19.**
[from WEENY *adjective*.]
1 A very young child. *colloq.* **M19.**
2 An objectionable, insignificant, or feeble person. *N. Amer. slang.* **E20.**

🕮 **2** T. CLANCY The CIA weenies who sat at desks and judged people in the field for a living.

weeny /ˈwiːni/ *noun*². *N. Amer. colloq.* **E20.**
[Alt. of WEINER. Cf. WIENIE.]
A Vienna sausage.

weeny /ˈwiːni/ *adjective. colloq.* **L18.**
[from WEE *adjective* after TINY *adjective*. Cf. TEENY *adjective*².]
Very small, tiny.
Comb.: **weeny-bopper** a very young usu. female pop fan (cf. TEENY-BOPPER).

weep /wiːp/ *noun*. **ME.**
[from next.]
†**1** Weeping, lamentation. **ME–M16.**
2 a A tear. Usu. in *pl.* **L18.** ▶**b** A fit or bout of weeping. **M19.**
3 An exudation, percolation, or sweating of moisture. **M19.**

🕮 **2b** J. GARDNER She sometimes had a quiet weep about his death. **the weeps** *colloq.* a fit of weeping or melancholy. **3** F. CHICHESTER There was no sign of a leak—only a slight weep at one place.

Comb.: **weep-hole** an opening through which water percolates or drips.

weep /wiːp/ *verb*. Pa. t. & pple **wept** /wɛpt/.
[Old English *wēpan*, corresp. to Old Frisian *wēpa* cry aloud, Old Saxon *wōpian* bewail, Old High German *wuofan*, Old Norse *œpa* scream, shout, Gothic *wōpjan*, from Germanic, prob. of imit. origin.]
▶ **I** *verb intrans.* **1** Manifest pain, misery, grief, etc., by tears, usu. accompanied by sobs and inarticulate moans; shed tears. Freq. foll. by *for*. **OE.** ▶**b** Cry or pray *to* with weeping. *rare*. **LME.**
2 Shed or exude liquid, drops of water, or moisture; *spec.* (***a***) (of a boiler, pipe, etc.) allow usu. small drops of water to percolate or leak through; (***b***) (of a sore) exude a serous fluid. **LME.**
3 Issue in drops; trickle or fall like tears. **L16.**
4 Hang limply, droop; *esp.* (of a tree) droop its branches. **M18.**

🕮 **1** MILTON She embrac'd him, and for joy Tenderly wept. DICKENS I knew . . how you had mourned for me, and wept for me. G. GREENE He began to weep—the tears ran . . out of the one good eye. W. GOLDING My mother wept to see me go. ***weep on a person's shoulder***: see SHOULDER *noun*.

▶ **II** *verb trans.* **5** Shed tears over; lament with tears; bewail. *arch.* **OE.**
6 Let fall from the eyes, shed, (tears etc.). **ME.** ▶**b** Declare, express, or utter with tears or lamentation. Also foll. by *out*, *forth*. **L16.**
7 Bring into a specified state or condition by weeping. Foll. by *into*, *to*, or with adjectival or (now *rare*) adverbial compl. **L16.**
8 Foll. by *away*: spend or consume in tears and lamentation; remove or wash away with tears. **L16.**
9 Shed (moisture or water) in drops; exude (a liquid etc.). **M17.**

🕮 **5** SIR W. SCOTT Edith, for whom he dies, will know how to weep his memory. **6** KEATS She . . wept a rain Of sorrows at his words. J. BALDWIN No child had ever wept such tears as he wept that morning. **b** SHAKES. *Wint. T.* Leontes opening his free arms and weeping His welcomes forth. W. COWPER I . . wept a last adieu! M. FORSTER 'I cannot,' she wept, 'I cannot.' **7** SHAKES. *Macb.* Let us . . Weep our sad bosoms empty. *Temple Bar* Phil wept herself to sleep in her sister's arms. **8** W. M. PRAED The mild Charity which . . Weeps every wound . . away. TENNYSON Nothing left But . . to . . weep my life away. **9** SIR W. SCOTT Its branches grew Where weep the heavens their holiest dew.

weeper /ˈwiːpə/ *noun*. **ME.**
[from prec. + -ER¹.]
1 A person who weeps, esp. habitually; *spec.* (***a***) (now chiefly *Hist.*) a hired mourner at a funeral etc.; (***b***) *ECCLESIASTICAL HISTORY* a member of the lowest class of penitents in the early Eastern Church. **ME.** ▶**b** A small image of a mourner in a niche on a funeral monument. **M17.**
2 Chiefly *Hist.* Anything worn as a conventional badge of mourning; *spec.* (***a***) a strip of white material worn on a man's cuff; (***b***) a man's black crape hat-band; (***c***) a widow's black crape veil or white cuff. Usu. in *pl.* **E18.**
3 In full ***weeper capuchin***. A capuchin monkey of northern S. America, *Cebus olivaceus*, which has a pale face and dark V-shaped cap. **L18.**
4 A hole or pipe in a wall for the escape of dripping water. **L19.**
5 In *pl.* Long side-whiskers worn without a beard. Also ***DUNDREARY weepers***, ***PICCADILLY weepers***. **L19.**
6 = WEEPIE. *colloq.* **M20.**
7 A wine bottle that leaks gradually through the cork. **M20.**

weepie /ˈwiːpi/ *noun. colloq.* Also **-py**. **E20.**
[from WEEP *verb* + -IE: cf. MOVIE, TALKIE.]
A sentimental film, story, play, etc.

weeping /ˈwiːpɪŋ/ *noun*. **ME.**
[from WEEP *verb* + -ING¹.]
1 The action of WEEP *verb*; an instance of this. **ME.**
2 In *pl.* & *sing.* Liquid or fluid that has wept or exuded from the body, a tree, etc. **M17.**
Comb.: **weeping-hole** an opening through which moisture percolates; †**weeping-ripe** *adjective* ready to weep.

weeping /ˈwiːpɪŋ/ *adjective*. **OE.**
[from WEEP *verb* + -ING².]
1 That weeps, characterized by weeping; (of the voice, face, etc.) tearful, lachrymose; (of emotion, an utterance, etc.) accompanied or expressed by weeping. **OE.**
2 Exuding moisture, oozing; (of soil) swampy; (of the eyes) running, watering; (of weather, skies, etc.) dripping, rainy. **OE.** ▶**b** Of water, a spring, etc.: falling or issuing in drops like tears. Now *rare* or *obsolete*. **L17.**
3 Of a tree, esp. a variety (usu. cultivated) of one that normally has spreading branches: having long drooping branches. **E17.**

🕮 **3** LADY BIRD JOHNSON The weeping juniper, whose branches droop as though they are about to draw their last breath.

Special collocations: **weeping capuchin** = WEEPER 3. **Weeping Cross** *fig.* severe disappointment, failure, (esp. in ***come home by Weeping Cross***, suffer failure or severe disappointment). ***weeping myall***: see MYALL *noun*². †**weeping tear(s)** abundant weeping. **weeping willow** (***a***) any of several willows with drooping branches grown for ornament, orig. *Salix babylonica*, reputedly native to China, now usu. either of its hybrids with the white willow and crack-willow; (***b***) *rhyming slang* a pillow.
■ **weepingly** *adverb* in a weeping manner; with tears: **ME.**

weepy *noun* var. of WEEPIE.

weepy /ˈwiːpi/ *adjective*. **LME.**
[from WEEP *verb* + -Y¹.]
†**1** Weeping, mournful. **LME–E17.**
2 Exuding moisture, damp, oozy. Chiefly *dial.* **E19.**
3 Inclined to shed tears, tearful. *colloq.* **M19.**
4 Of a story, film, etc.: intended to evoke a tearful reaction; sentimental, tear-jerking. Cf. WEEPIE. *colloq.* **M20.**
■ **weepily** *adverb* **L20.** **weepiness** *noun* **M20.**

weequashing /ˈwiːkwɒʃɪŋ/ *noun*. *US*. **L18.**
[from Algonquian *wigwas* birch-bark (canoe) + -ING¹.]
The spearing of eels or fish from a canoe by torchlight.

weer *noun* var. of WERE *noun*².

weese /wiːz/ *verb intrans.* Long *obsolete* exc. *dial.* Also **weeze**.
[Old English *wēsan*, from OOZE *noun*¹.]
Ooze, drip, or distil gently.

weeshy /ˈwiːʃi/ *adjective*. *Anglo-Irish*. **E19.**
[Origin unkn. Cf. WEE *adjective*.]
Very small, tiny.

weet /wiːt/ *verb*¹. Long *arch.* ME.
[Var. of WIT *verb*.]
1 *verb trans.* Know (a fact, an answer, etc.). Freq. foll. by obj. clause. ME.
2 *verb intrans.* Know of or *of* something. LME.

1 SPENSER That aged Sire . . looked forth, to weet, if true indeede Those tydings were. 2 G. OWEN When Percellye weareth a hatte, All Pembrokeshire shall weete of that.

■ †**weetingly** *adverb* = WITTINGLY (a) LME–M16.

weet /wiːt/ *verb*² *intrans.* M19.
[Imit.]
Of a bird: make a call resembling 'weet'.

weetless /ˈwiːtlɪs/ *adjective. pseudo-arch.* L16.
[from WEET *verb*¹ + -LESS.]
†**1** Meaningless. *rare* (Spenser). Only in L16.
2 Unknowing, unconscious. L16.

weet-weet /ˈwiːtwiːt/ *noun*¹. *obsolete* exc. *dial.* M19.
[Imit. of the bird's call.]
The common sandpiper, *Actitis hypoleucos*.

weet-weet /ˈwiːtwiːt/ *noun*². L19.
[Aboriginal *wij wij*.]
An Australian toy or (*Hist.*) Aboriginal weapon, consisting of a flexible handle with a knob on the head, that can be thrown to a great distance.

weever /ˈwiːvə/ *noun*. E17.
[Perh. transf. use of Old French *wivre* serpent, dragon, var. of *guivre* from Latin *vipera* VIPER.]
More fully ***weever-fish***. Any of various elongated NE Atlantic fishes of the genus *Trachinus* and family Trachinidae, which lie half buried in sand and have venomous dorsal and opercular spines with which they can inflict painful wounds; *esp.* (more fully ***lesser weever***) *T. vipera*, which is common along European and Mediterranean coasts (also called ***viperfish***). Also (*Austral.*), any of various sand perches of the family Mugiloididae.

weevil /ˈwiːv(ə)l, ˈwiːvɪl/ *noun*.
[Old English *wifel* beetle, corresp. to Old Saxon *wivil* (in *goldwivil* glow-worm), Old High German *wibil*, *wipil* beetle, chafer, from Germanic base meaning 'move briskly', repr. also by WAVE *verb*¹, WEAVE *verb*¹.]
1 Orig., a beetle of any kind. Now, any of numerous beetles of the family Curculionidae and certain related families, which are characterized by an elongated snout or rostrum and whose larvae (and adults) often bore into grain, fruit, nuts, bark, and stored plant products. OE.
2 *fig.* A despicable person. *rare.* L16.
1 ***boll-weevil***, ***nut-weevil***, ***palm weevil***, ***pea-weevil***, ***vine weevil***, etc.
■ **weevily** *adjective* infested with weevils M18.

wee-wee /ˈwiːwiː/ *verb & noun*. M20.
[Imit. Cf. WEE *noun*² & *verb*.]
▶ **A** *verb intrans.* Pa. t. & pple **-weed**. Urinate. *nursery & colloq.* M20.
▶ **B** *noun*. **1** Urine; the action or an act of urinating. *nursery & colloq.* M20.
2 The penis. *slang.* M20.
1 **do a wee-wee**, **have a wee-wee**, **make a wee-wee** urinate.

weeze *verb* var. of WEESE.

w.e.f. *abbreviation*.
With effect from.

weft /weft/ *noun*¹.
[Old English *weft(a)*, corresp. to Old Norse *veptr*, *vipta* weft, Middle High German *wift* fine thread, from Germanic base also of WEAVE *verb*¹.]
1 WEAVING. The threads woven at right angles across a warp in making fabric. Cf. WOOF *noun*¹ 1. OE. ▸**b** Yarn (to be) used for this. L18. ▸**c** The strips of cane, palm leaf, straw, etc., used as filling in weaving baskets, mats, etc. M19.
2 A thing that is spun or woven (*lit.* & *fig.*). LME.
3 A streak or thin layer of smoke, mist, etc. E19.
4 BOTANY. A form of growth resembling a weft; (***a***) a layer of closely interwoven hyphae produced in certain fungi; (***b***) a mass of loosely interwoven shoots formed by certain mosses. L19.

1 E. TUNIS Two strands of weft were carried across the warp together.

Comb.: **weft fork**: for stopping a loom automatically when a weft-thread breaks or fails.
■ **weftage** *noun* the arrangement of the threads of a woven fabric etc. L17. **wefty** *adjective* (*rare*) of the nature of a weft M19.

†**weft** *noun*². L16–M19.
[Alt.]
= WAIF *noun*¹.

weft *noun*³ see WAFT *noun*.

Wegener's granulomatosis /ˈveɪg(ə)nəz ˌgranjʊləʊməˈtəʊsɪs/ *noun phr.* M20.
[from F. *Wegener* (1907–1990), German pathologist.]
MEDICINE. An often fatal disease characterized by granulomatosis of the respiratory tract and necrotizing blood-vessels.

Wegener's theory /ˈveɪg(ə)nəz ˌθɪəri/ *noun phr.* E20.
[from Alfred *Wegener* (1880–1930), German geophysicist.]
GEOLOGY. The theory of continental drift developed by Wegener.
■ **Wegeˈnerian** *adjective* M20.

wegotism /ˈwiːgətɪz(ə)m/ *noun. joc.* Now *rare.* L18.
[Blend of WE and EGOTISM.]
Obtrusive or excessive use of the first person plural by a speaker or writer. Cf. WEISM.

†**wehee** *interjection, noun, & verb.* Also **wihy** & other vars. LME.
[Imit.]
▶ **A** *interjection & noun.* (Repr. the sound of) a horse's whinny or neigh. LME–L17.
▶ **B** *verb intrans.* Whinny, neigh. E17–M19.

Wehmut /ˈveːmuːt/ *noun*. E20.
[German.]
Sadness, melancholy, wistfulness, nostalgia.

wehrlite /ˈveːlʌɪt, ˈwəː-/ *noun*. M19.
[from Adolf *Wehrle* (1795–1835), Austrian mining official + -ITE¹.]
1 GEOLOGY. A peridotite mainly consisting of olivine and monoclinic pyroxene with common accessory opaque oxides. M19.
2 MINERALOGY. A native rhombohedral alloy of bismuth and tellurium occurring as silvery to steel-grey foliated masses. L19.

Wehrmacht /ˈveːrmaxt/ *noun*. M20.
[German, lit. 'defence force'.]
Hist. The German armed forces, esp. the army, between 1921 and 1945.

Wehrwirtschaft /ˈveːrvɪrtʃaft/ *noun*. M20.
[German, from *Wehr* defence + *Wirtschaft* economy.]
The principle or policy of directing a nation's economic activity towards preparation for or support of a war effort, esp. (*Hist.*) as applied in Germany in the 1930s.

wei ch'i /weɪ ˈtʃiː/ *noun*. L19.
[Chinese *wéiqí* (Wade–Giles *wei-ch'i*), from *wei* to surround + *qí* (*ch'i*) chess.]
A traditional Chinese board game of territorial possession and capture. Cf. GO *noun*².

Weichsel /ˈvʌɪks(ə)l/ *adjective & noun*. M20.
[German = the River Vistula in Poland.]
GEOLOGY. (Designating or pertaining to) the final Pleistocene glaciation in northern Europe, possibly corresponding to the Würm in the Alps.
■ Also **Weichselian** /-ˈsiːl-/ *adjective & noun* M20.

weid *noun* var. of WEED *noun*³.

Weierstrass /ˈvʌɪəstrɑːs/ *noun*. L19.
[Karl T. W. *Weierstrass* (1815–97), German mathematician.]
MATH. Used *attrib.* and in *possess.* with ref. to equations, theorems, functions, etc., developed or investigated by Weierstrass.
■ **Weierˈstrassian** *adjective* L19.

weigela /wʌɪˈdʒiːlə/ *noun*. Also **weigelia** /-ˈdʒiːlɪə/. M19.
[mod. Latin (see below), from C. E. *Weigel* (1748–1831), German physician + -A¹, -IA¹.]
Any of various Chinese and Japanese shrubs constituting the genus *Weigela*, of the honeysuckle family, which bear nearly regular pink, white, or red flowers on the previous season's wood; esp. *W. florida*, grown for ornament.

weigh /weɪ/ *noun*¹. L18.
[from WAY *noun* by erron. assoc. with *weigh anchor*.]
under weigh, (of a vessel etc.) in motion through the water, under way.

weigh *noun*² var. of WEY *noun*.

weigh /weɪ/ *verb*. Also †**way** & other vars.
[Old English *weġan* = Old Frisian *wega*, *weia* move, weigh, Old Saxon *wegan* (Dutch *wegen*) weigh, Old High German *wegan* move, shake, weigh (German *bewegen* move), Old Norse *vega* lift, weigh, from Germanic, from Indo-European base repr. also by Latin *vehere* convey: cf. WAIN *noun*¹ & *verb*, WEY.]
▶ **I** Carry, lift.
†**1** *verb trans.* Carry round or from one place to another, transport. OE–LME.
†**2** *verb trans.* Bear (arms); wear (a robe etc.). OE–ME.
3 a *verb trans.* NAUTICAL. Draw up (the anchor) before sailing. ME. ▸**b** *verb trans.* Raise up or *up* (a sunk ship, gun, etc.) from the bottom of the water. L15. ▸**c** *verb intrans.* = ***weigh anchor*** s.v. ANCHOR *noun*¹. Also *gen.*, set sail. E16.
†**4** *verb trans.* Hoist or lift *up*. LME–M17.

3a SIR W. SCOTT Hoisted his sail, his anchor weigh'd. **b** W. COWPER Weigh the vessel up . . she may float again.

▶ **II** Determine or measure (a) weight.
5 *verb trans.* Determine the heaviness of (a body or substance), esp. by balancing it in a pair of scales or against a counterpoise of known heaviness. OE. ▸**b** Hold (an object) in the hand or hands (as if) to estimate its weight; heft. M16.
6 *verb trans. fig.* ▸**a** Measure the value of (a person, condition, quality, etc.) as if on scales. ME. ▸**b** Compare (something) *with* or *against* another object, consideration, etc. E16.
7 *verb trans.* **a** Ponder the force of (words or expressions). ME. ▸**b** Consider, estimate, or take into account the relative value or importance of (a fact, circumstance, statement, etc.); ponder with a view to choice or preference. LME.
†**8** *verb trans.* **a** Esteem, value, think highly of; count dear or precious. Freq. in neg. contexts. ME–L17. ▸**b** With adjectival compl.: consider to be, count as. L16–E17.
9 *verb trans.* Use scales to measure a definite quantity of (a substance); take out or *out* (a specified weight) from a larger quantity; (foll. by *out*) apportion by weight (a specified quantity) *to* a person or persons; (foll. by *in*, *into*) introduce a specified weight of (a substance), add as an ingredient. LME. ▸†**b** *spec.* Measure out or *out* (a sum of money) by weight. Chiefly in biblical use. LME–E17. ▸**c** *fig.* Impartially dispense or administer (justice). *rare.* LME.
†**10** *verb intrans.* Think or judge *of*. Only in L16.
†**11** *verb trans.* Keep (the wings) evenly spread in flight. *poet. rare.* Only in M17.
12 *verb intrans.* RACING. Of a jockey: (stand on scales to) have his or her declared weight checked. E19.

6a G. BERKELEY Were all men to be weighed in the exact scale of merit. J. S. BLACKIE God . . weighs the hearts Of them that worship. B. MONTGOMERY But when weighed in the balance they are not found wanting. **b** SHAKES. *Temp.* Then wisely . . weigh Our sorrow with our comfort. J. RULE Whenever there were generalizations about women, Evelyn weighed herself against them. U. LE GUIN He weighed the moral discomfort against the practical advantage. **7a** DICKENS Mr. Carker read this slowly; weighing the words as he went. **b** HENRY FIELDING I weighed the consequences on both sides as fairly as I could. S. SMILES Action becomes suspended in nicely weighing the pros and cons. J. BUCHAN I have collected all my evidence and carefully weighed it. **8b** SHAKES. *Hen. V* 'Tis best to weigh The enemy more mighty than he seems.

▶ **III 13 a** *verb trans.* Be equal to, balance in heaviness, (a usu. specified weight). OE. ▸**b** *verb intrans.* Have a specified degree of heaviness. With adjectival or adverbial compl. ME. ▸†**c** *verb intrans. fig.* Amount or be equivalent *to*. Only in 16. ▸**d** *verb trans.* Have the same weight or value as; counterbalance. L16. ▸†**e** *verb intrans.* Be of equal value or importance *with*. L16–M17. ▸**f** *verb intrans.* Foll. by *against*: counterbalance; count or be counted against. L16.
14 *verb intrans.* Be (regarded as) valuable or important; have influence *with* a person forming a judgement. LME.

13a SHAKES. *Much Ado* I know them, yea, And what they weigh, even to the utmost scruple. G. GREENE Folios of landscape gardening weighed a lot. W. TREVOR She weighed seven stone and eight pounds. *fig.*: J. R. LOWELL All the beautiful sentiments in the world weigh less than a single lovely action. **b** T. GAINSFORD Knavery makes . . the country-man to water his corne, to make it weigh heavy. W. COWPER Like barrels with their bellies full, They only weigh the heavier. *fig.*: SHAKES. *John* One must prove greatest. While they weigh so even, We hold our town for neither. **f** H. MARTINEAU Such evils . . can neither be helped nor be allowed to weigh against the advantages of union. J. GILMOUR He believes that every sin will weigh against him. **14** MILTON Pleasing to God, or not pleasing, with them weighed alike. CONAN DOYLE His opinion would weigh with any judge.

▶ **IV** Affect or be affected by weight.
15 *verb trans.* Foll. by *down*: draw, force, or bend down by pressure of weight; *fig.* depress, oppress, lie heavy on. ME.
16 *verb intrans.* Of the scale of a balance: go *up* or *down* through holding the lesser or greater weight. Also *gen.*, sink or go *down* through excessive heaviness or load. Long *rare.* LME.
17 *verb trans.* Of an object on scales: cause (the scale) to go *down* or *up*; turn the scale when weighed against (something else); (foll. by *down*, †*out*) outweigh. Chiefly *fig.* LME.
18 *verb intrans.* Foll. by *on*, *upon*: lie heavy on, depress, (a person, mood, etc.). L18.

15 AV *Wisd.* 9:15 The earthy tabernacle weigheth downe the minde. W. COWPER The plentiful moisture incumber'd the flower, And weigh'd down its beautiful head. H. T. BUCKLE The people were weighed down by an insufferable taxation. **17** SHAKES. *Hen. VIII* My friends, they that must weigh out my afflictions. SWIFT One Whig shall weigh down ten Tories. DICKENS The . . carelessness of his disposition . . weighed down the scale on the same side. *Westminster Gazette* Whose mistakes . . are a thousand times weighed up by his . . deeds of true friendship. **18** KEATS Care weighs on your brow. M. BARING A load that . . had been weighing on him for years.

Phrases, & with adverbs & prepositions in specialized senses: ***weigh anchor***: see ANCHOR *noun*¹. **weigh a person against gold** weigh an Indian raja etc. and distribute the same weight of gold as charity. ***weigh a ton***: see TON *noun*¹. **weigh in** (***a***) check the weight of (a jockey) after a race; (***b***) (of a jockey) have his or her weight checked after a race (cf. sense 12 above); (***c***) (of a boxer etc.) be weighed before a fight; ***weigh in at***: turn the scales at (a particular weight), *transf.* (*colloq.*) cost (a particular price); (*d*) *colloq.* bring one's weight or influence to bear, contribute (esp. forcefully) to a discussion, enterprise, etc.; ***weigh in with***: introduce, contribute, produce, (esp. something forceful, significant, or additional); (*e*) weigh (an air passenger's luggage) before a flight; subject (a passenger) to this procedure; (*f*) (of an angler) have (one's catch) officially weighed at the end of a competition; (see also sense 9 above). **weigh into** *colloq.* attack, belabour, launch into, (a person). **weigh off** *slang* punish, convict, sentence, (a criminal or delinquent). **weigh one's words** choose one's words carefully and speak deliberately. **weigh up** appraise, form an estimate of, (a person, situation, etc.).

Comb.: **weigh-bar** = *weigh-shaft* below; **weigh-beam** a balance, *esp.* a steelyard; **weighboard** = ***wayboard*** s.v. WAY *noun*; **weighbridge** a weighing-machine, usu. flush with the road, for weighing vehicles or animals; **weigh-house** a public building to which commodities are brought to be weighed; **weigh-in** (*a*) the weighing of a boxer before a fight; (*b*) the weighing of an angler's catch at the end of a competition; **weighman** a man employed to weigh goods, *esp.* a collier who weighs tubs of coal as they leave the pit-head; **weighmaster** an official in charge of a weigh-house or public scales; **weigh-out** the verification of a jockey's declared weight before a race; **weigh-scale** (orig. *north.*) the pan of a balance; **weigh-shaft** MECHANICS a shaft which rocks or oscillates about its axis rather than making complete revolutions.

■ **weighable** *adjective* able to be weighed, esp. on scales LME. †**weighage** *noun* a duty or toll paid for the weighing of goods M16–M19. **weighed** *adjective* that has been weighed; *spec.* (of a judgement, opinion, etc.) considered, balanced: LME. **weighment** *noun* (*Anglo-Indian*) the action or an act of weighing a commodity L19.

weigher /ˈweɪə/ *noun.* ME.
[from prec. + -ER¹.]

1 A person employed to weigh commodities; an official appointed to test weights, supervise weighing, etc. ME.

2 A person who weighs anchor. L16.

📖 **1** *fig.*: B. JOWETT Do you, like a skilful weigher, put into the balance the pleasures and pains.

Comb.: **weigher-in** an official who weighs in a boxer, an angler's catch, etc.

weighing /ˈweɪɪŋ/ *verbal noun.* LME.
[from WEIGH *verb* + -ING¹.]

The action or process of ascertaining the weight of something (*lit.* & *fig.*); an instance of this.

Attrib. & *comb.*: In the sense 'in or on which weighing takes place', as *weighing-house*, *weighing-room*, *weighing-scales*, etc.; **weighing-engine**, **weighing-machine** a machine or apparatus for weighing people or large weights.

weight /weɪt/ *noun.*
[Old English (*ge*)*wiht*, corresp. to Old Frisian *wicht*, Middle Dutch *wicht*, *ghewichte* (Dutch *wicht*, *gewicht*, German *Gewicht*), Old Norse *vétt*, *vætt*, from Germanic, the mod. form being infl. by WEIGH *verb*.]

▸ **I 1** Orig., the quantitative dimension or measure determined by weighing. Later also, relative heaviness. OE. ▸**b** *transf.* A pair of scales, a balance. Usu. in *pl.* ME. ▸**c** Weighable matter. M17.

2 a A standard of weight. Long *obsolete* exc. as in senses b, c. OE. ▸**b** A unit or system of units used for expressing how much an object or a quantity of matter weighs. ME. ▸**c** A measure of an illegal drug. *slang.* L20.

3 A piece of metal etc., weighing a known amount equal to (a multiple or an aliquot part of) a unit in some recognized scale. ME. ▸**b** ATHLETICS. *The* heavy lump of stone or ball of metal used in shot-putting; the shot. Chiefly *Scot.* M19. ▸**c** In *pl.* Heavy objects (usually weighing a known amount) used in lifting to demonstrate or improve strength, fitness, etc. M19.

4 A heavy object, block of metal, etc., used to pull, press, or hold something down, to give an impulse to machinery (as in a clock), to act as a counterpoise, etc. LME.

📖 **1** A. T. THOMSON The proportions of acid and water were equal by weight. A. KOESTLER The most conspicuous quality in which all bodies on earth shared was weight. **2b** *Times* The Weights and Measures Bill was considered in committee. ***avoirdupois weight***: see AVOIRDUPOIS 2. ***apothecaries' weight***: see APOTHECARY 1. ***stone-weight***: see STONE *noun* 12. ***TROY weight***. **3b** *Field* Throwing the hammer, putting the weight. **4** JOHN HOLLAND A weight being attached to the hook *b*, the spring . . is drawn downwards. N. HAWTHORNE There was a clock without a case, the weights being visible. ***letter-weight***, ***paperweight***, ***sash weight***, etc.

▸ **II** A weighable amount or quantity.

5 A portion or quantity weighing a definite amount. Abbreviation *wt.* OE. ▸**b** *ellipt.* A pennyweight of gold. *Austral.* L19.

6 The amount that a thing weighs; the quantitative expression of this in terms of conventional units, esp. as measured using scales, a balance, etc.; the quantity of substance as measured by the downward force exerted on its mass by a gravitational field. LME. ▸**b** MECHANICS. The resistance to be overcome by a machine. Now *rare* or *obsolete.* E19.

7 The amount which an article (sold by weight) of given price or value ought to weigh. LME.

8 A heavy mass, *esp.* one that is lifted or carried; (a) load. LME. ▸**b** *spec.* RACING. The amount which a jockey is required or expected to weigh, or which a mount can easily carry. M17. ▸**c** *ellipt.* (A competition for boxers of) a particular boxing weight. E20.

9 Impetus, motive force. LME.

📖 **5** SHAKES. *Merch. V.* I rather choose to have a weight of carrion flesh. G. DODD About 112 lbs. weight of biscuits are put into the oven. *British Medical Journal* A powder consisting of equal weights of . . bleaching powder and powdered boric acid. **6** D. BREWSTER The weight of all bodies is diminished by the centrifugal force . . at the equator. ***combining weight***, ***dead weight***, ***equivalent weight***, ***live weight***, etc. **7** DEFOE It was near two ounces more than weight in a pound. **8** SIR W. SCOTT Mine arms . . little care A weight so slight as thine to bear. J. TYNDALL The simplest form of work is the raising of a weight. D. JACOBSON Shifting his weight from one strong leg to another. **c** ***catch-weight***, ***fighting-weight***, ***flyweight***, ***heavyweight***, ***middleweight***, etc.

▸ **III** *fig.* **10** A burden (of responsibility, suffering, etc.). LME.

11 Importance, moment. LME. ▸**b** A relative value assigned to an observation, factor, etc.; *spec.* (STATISTICS) a multiplier associated with any of a set of numerical quantities that are added together. E19.

12 a The force of a blow or attack; pressure. L15. ▸**b** The weightiest or heaviest part; preponderance, esp. of evidence. M16.

13 Power to persuade, convince, or impress a person; influence, authority. M16.

📖 **10** DICKENS Overpowered by the weight of her sorrows. S. C. HALL An aged man . . enfeebled by the weight of years. G. W. TARGET Such a weight off my mind. **11** W. LAW All such bodily actions as affect the soul, are of great weight in Religion. A. HELPS Care and trouble cease to weigh as if they were the only things of weight. S. HAZZARD Fashion was indiscriminate, giving the same weight to whim as to conviction. **12a** SIR W. SCOTT Forced asunder, by the weight and press of numbers. C. ACHEBE I finally felt the full weight of the previous night's humiliation. **b** DEFOE The Parish of St. Giles's, where still the Weight of the Infection lay. J. E. T. ROGERS The weight of evidence is in favour of the latter hypothesis. **13** SOUTHEY This detracts not from the weight of your reasoning. LD MACAULAY No man spoke with more weight and dignity in council. G. ORWELL The Communist Party . . had thrown its whole weight against revolution. C. KEAREY He carries a lot of weight . . he'll do his best to obtain the concessions.

▸ **IV 14** The degree of blackness or boldness of a typeface or font of type. E19.

15 The heaviness of a fabric as a measure of its quality or suitability. L19.

15 ***dress weight***, ***suit-weight***, ***summer-weight***, etc.

Phrases: **by weight** as determined by weighing. ***carry weight***: see CARRY *verb*. **feel the weight of** receive a heavy blow from, (*fig.*) undergo severe pressure from. **give weight to**, **give due weight to**, **give full weight to** recognize or carefully consider the validity, force, or importance of a plea, argument, circumstance, etc. ***lay weight on***: see LAY *verb*¹. **lose weight** (of a person) decrease one's weight, become thin or thinner. ***pull one's weight***: see PULL *verb*. **put on weight** increase one's weight, become fat or fatter. ***put one's weight behind***, ***swing one's weight behind***: see ***throw one's weight behind*** below. **take the weight off (one's feet)** *colloq.* sit down and rest. **throw one's weight about**, **throw one's weight around** *colloq.* unpleasantly assert oneself or one's authority, act officiously. **throw one's weight behind**, **put one's weight behind**, **swing one's weight behind** use one's influence to promote (a campaign, candidate, plan, etc.). ***tropical weight***: see TROPICAL *adjective* 3b. **weight for weight** taking an equal weight of each. **worth one's weight in gold**, **worth one's weight in silver**, **worth its weight in gold**, **worth its weight in silver** extremely valuable, helpful, or useful.

Comb.: **weight belt** a belt to which weights are attached, designed to help divers and underwater swimmers stay submerged; **weight-clock**: operated by weights; **weight cloth** RACING: carried by a jockey to make up his weight; **weight function** PHYSICS a function that specifies the weight (sense 11b above) of some quantity; **weightlifter** a person who takes part in weightlifting; **weightlifting** the sport or exercise of lifting heavy weights; **weight-train** *verb intrans.* practise weight-training; **weight-training** physical training involving the use of weights.

weight /weɪt/ *verb trans.* Orig. *Scot.* M17.
[from prec.]

1 Oppress with or as with weight, weigh down or *down*. Usu. in *pass.* M17.

2 Ascertain the weight of (goods etc.); weigh (*lit.* & *fig.*). E18.

3 Load (*down*) with a weight; supply with an additional weight; make weighty. M18. ▸**b** Treat (a fabric) to make it seem stouter. Also, add weight to (an inferior product) by using an adulterant. M19. ▸**c** STATISTICS. Multiply (components of an average etc.) by factors reflecting their relative importance. E20.

4 Assign to (a horse) the weight that must be carried in a handicap race. M19.

📖 **1** T. BOSTON Their weighted and sorrowful life . . succeeded with . . joy. GEO. ELIOT A House of Commons . . not weighted with . . the landed class. M. SINCLAIR You walked slowly, weighted . . by your immense fatigue. **3** A. POWELL Those toys . . cannot be pushed over because heavily weighted at the base. J. MCGAHERN He covered the . . heap . . with clear plastic, weighted down with stones. **c** ***weighted average***: resulting from the multiplication of each component by a factor reflecting its importance. **4** *Horse & Hound* Trying to find a free horse weighted at . . my minimum of 10 st. 4 lb.

■ **weightage** *noun* (the assignment of) a weighting factor compensating for some usu. numerical disadvantage E20. **weightedness** *noun* (*rare*) the quality or condition of being weighted M17.

weighting /ˈweɪtɪŋ/ *noun.* M19.
[from prec. + -ING¹.]

1 The action of WEIGHT *verb.* M19.

2 A thing used as a weight to press down or balance something. L19.

3 An amount added to a salary for a special reason, esp. to compensate for the higher cost of living in a given locality. M20.

📖 **3** *attrib.*: *Daily Telegraph* The London weighting index . . used . . for calculating extra payments for employees in London.

weightless /ˈweɪtlɪs/ *adjective.* M16.
[from WEIGHT *noun* + -LESS.]

Lacking weight, having comparatively little weight (*lit.* & *fig.*); *spec.* (of a body having mass) not apparently acted on by gravity, either because the gravitational field is locally weak, or because both the body and its surroundings are freely and equally accelerating under the influence of the field (as in an orbiting satellite).

■ **weightlessly** *adverb* M20. **weightlessness** *noun* L19.

Weight Watcher /ˈweɪt wɒtʃə/ *noun.* Orig. *US.* M20.
[from WEIGHT *noun* + WATCHER *noun*.]

1 In *pl.* (Proprietary name for) an organization promoting dietary control as a means of slimming, and any club associated with this organization; *sing.* a member of this organization or an associated club. M20.

2 (**weight-watcher**.) A person who tries to lose weight, esp. by dieting; a person who is habitually aware of or concerned about his or her weight. M20.

■ **weight-watching** *adjective* & *noun* (*a*) *adjective* concerned about one's (excessive) weight, *esp.* keeping to a diet; (*b*) *noun* concern about one's weight, dieting: L20.

weighty /ˈweɪti/ *adjective.* LME.
[from WEIGHT *noun* + -Y¹.]

▸ **I** In literal use.

1 Of considerable or appreciable weight; heavy. LME. ▸**b** Of a person or animal: unusually large or bulky of body, corpulent. L16. ▸**c** Heavy in proportion to bulk, of high density. L16. ▸†**d** Of a coin: of full weight, of the standard or legal weight. E17–M18.

2 Falling heavily, or with force or violence. L16.

📖 **2** POPE Up-bore my load, and prest the sinking sands With weighty steps.

▸ **II** *fig.* **3** Hard to bear; oppressive, burdensome, grievous. L15. ▸†**b** Rigorous, severe. *rare* (Shakes.). Only in E17.

4 Of great gravity or significance, momentous; requiring or deserving careful thought or consideration; important, serious. L15. ▸**b** Substantial, solid; of high value. M16.

5 a Of an argument, utterance, etc.: producing a powerful effect; convincing, persuasive; forcible, telling. M16. ▸**b** Of a person: having great authority or stature; influential, authoritative. M17.

†**6** Of a face etc.: expressing earnestness or gravity; solemn. Only in 17.

📖 **3** STEELE The weighty Cares . . to undergo for the publick Good. **b** SHAKES. *Timon* We banish thee for ever . . . If after two days' shine Athens contain thee, Attend our weightier judgment. **4** BURKE War and peace, the most weighty of all questions. DICKENS Four secrets. Mind! Serious, grave, weighty secrets. **b** S. W. SINGER Dibdin whose authority on the subject is the weightiest. **5a** W. ROBERTSON Several weighty objections had to be urged. E. A. FREEMAN Few and weighty were the words the . . Earl spoke that day.

■ **weightily** *adverb* (chiefly *fig.*) in a weighty manner, with or as with weight M16. **weightiness** *noun* M16.

weil *noun* var. of WEEL *noun*¹.

Weil–Felix reaction /vʌɪlˈfiːlɪks rɪˌakʃ(ə)n/ *noun.* E20.
[from Edmund *Weil* (1880–1922), Austrian bacteriologist + Arthur *Felix* (1887–1956), Polish-born bacteriologist.]

MEDICINE. An agglutination reaction which takes place when serum from a patient infected with typhus is added to certain strains of bacteria of the genus *Proteus*, used as a diagnostic test for the disease.

Weil's disease /ˈvʌɪlz dɪˌziːz/ *noun phr.* L19.
[H. Adolf *Weil* (1848–1916), German physician.]

MEDICINE. A severe, sometimes fatal, form of leptospirosis that is characterized by fever, jaundice, and muscle pains, and is acquired by infection from rats via contaminated water.

Weimar /ˈvʌɪmɑː/ *attrib. adjective.* M20.
[A city in Thuringia, Germany, where the constitution of 1919–33 was adopted.]
Designating or pertaining to political, social, or cultural aspects of Germany during the period from 1919 to 1933.
Weimar Republic Germany under the democratic republican constitution that it had from 1919 to the beginning of the Third Reich in 1933.
■ **Weimaraner** /vʌɪməˈrɑːnə, wʌɪ-/ *noun* (an animal of) a breed of grey short-coated drop-eared pointer, originally bred as a hunting dog in the Weimar region M20.

Weinberg–Salam /ˌwʌɪnbəːgsəˈlɑːm/ *noun.* L20.
[from Steven *Weinberg* (b. 1933), US physicist + Abdus *Salam* (1926–96), Pakistani physicist.]
PARTICLE PHYSICS. Used **attrib.** with ref. to the unified field theory (or electroweak theory) postulated by Weinberg and Salam.

weiner *noun* var. of **WIENER**.

weinkraut /ˈvʌɪnkraʊt/ *noun.* M20.
[German, from *Wein* wine + *Kraut* cabbage.]
Pickled cabbage cooked with white wine and apples.

Weinstube /ˈvaɪnʃtuːbə, -st-/ *noun.* Pl. **-ben** /-bən/, **-bes**. L19.
[German, from *Wein* wine + *Stube* room.]
A small German wine bar or tavern. Cf. **BIERSTUBE**.

Wein, Weib, und Gesang /ˈvaɪn ˈvaɪp ʊnt gəˈzaŋ/ *noun phr.* L19.
[German.]
Wine, woman, and song (see **WINE** *noun*).

weir /wɪə/ *noun & verb.*
[Old English *wer*, corresp. to Old Saxon *werr*, Middle Low German, Middle High German *wër(e)* (Low German *wër(e)*, German *Wehr*), from *werian* dam up: see **WERE** *verb*[1] & *noun*[3].]
▶ **A** *noun.* **1** A barrier or dam to restrain water, *esp.* (**a**) a mill-dam; (**b**) a dam across a canal or navigable river, to retain the water or regulate its flow. OE.
2 A fence or enclosure of stakes in a stream, river, harbour, etc., for trapping fish. OE.
3 A pond or pool; *spec.* a deep pool or whirlpool for fishing. *obsolete exc. dial.* ME.
4 A fence or embankment to prevent the encroachment of a river or sea-sand, or to divert a stream. *local.* L16.
5 A hedge. *Scot.* L18.
▶ **B** *verb trans.* Provide with a weir. Chiefly as ***weired*** pa. pple. E17.
■ **weiring** *noun* (materials for) the construction of a weir or weirs L18.

weird /wɪəd/ *noun. arch.* (now chiefly *Scot.*).
[Old English *wyrd* = Old Saxon *wurd*, Old High German *wurt*, Old Norse *urðr*, from Germanic.]
1 (Inexorable) fate, destiny. Long *rare.* OE.
2 MYTHOLOGY. In *pl.* The Fates. Cf. **FATE** *noun* 1b. OE. ▸**b** A person claiming or thought to have the power to foresee and control future events; a witch, a wizard, a soothsayer. E17.
3 A person's future fate; a person's appointed lot or destiny. *sing.* & in *pl.* OE. ▸**b** *spec.* An evil fate inflicted by supernatural power, esp. by way of retribution. ME.
4 a A happening, event, occurrence. OE. ▸**b** That which is destined or fated to happen; predetermined events collectively. LME.
5 †**a** A decree (of a god). LME–E16. ▸**b** A prediction of a person's fate; a prophecy. L18.
3 ***dree one's weird***: see **DREE** *verb.*
■ **weird-like** *adjective* suggestive of the supernatural, eerie, uncanny M19. **weirdsome** *adjective* (*rare*) uncanny, mysterious L19.

weird /wɪəd/ *adjective.* LME.
[Orig. attrib. use of prec. in *weird sisters* (see sense 1 below).]
1 Having or claiming preternatural power to control the fate or destiny of human beings etc. LME.
2 Partaking or suggestive of fate or the supernatural, unearthly, eerie; unaccountably or uncomfortably strange; queer, uncanny. E19.
3 Orig., out of the ordinary, strange, unusual, esp. in appearance. Now also freq. *gen.*, odd, bizarre, incomprehensible. E19.

> 🕮 **1** SHELLEY Like some weird Archimage sit I, Plotting dark spells. **weird sisters** (**a**) *the* Fates; (**b**) witches, *esp.* those in Shakespeare's *Macbeth*. **2** S. SMILES Awakened by a weird and unearthly moaning. **3** *English Historical Review* 'Guacciadim' . . is a weird misprint for Guicciardini. C. BLACKWOOD My grandmother's behaviour became increasingly weird and unbalanced. G. SWIFT I don't understand . . . I mean that's really *weird*, isn't it? **weird and wonderful** (freq. *iron.* or *derog.*) marvellous in a strange or eccentric way; both remarkable and peculiar or unfathomable; exotic, outlandish.

■ **weirdish** *adjective* M19. **weirdity** *noun* a weird thing, *esp.* a weird characteristic (usu. in *pl.*) M20. **weirdly** *adverb* M19. **weirdness** *noun* M19.

weird /wɪəd/ *verb trans.* ME.
[from the noun.]
▶ **I** *obsolete* exc. *Scot.* **1** Preordain or predestine by the decree of fate. Usu. in *pass.* ME.
2 Assign to (a person) as his or her fate; apportion as a person's destiny or lot. M16.
3 Warn ominously, prophesy. M18.
▶ **II 4** Foll. by *out*: annoy; make depressed or bored. Freq. as ***weirded out*** *ppl adjective. slang* (chiefly *US*). L20.

weirdie /ˈwɪədi/ *noun. colloq.* Also **-dy**. L19.
[from **WEIRD** *adjective* + **-IE**.]
1 = **WEIRDO**. L19.
2 Anything, esp. a film or story, that is bizarre, incomprehensible, or grotesque. M20.

weirdo /ˈwɪədəʊ/ *noun & adjective. colloq.* M20.
[from **WEIRD** *adjective* + **-O**.]
▶ **A** *noun.* Pl. **-os**. An odd, eccentric, or unconventional person; *spec.* any long-haired bearded young man. M20.
▶ **B** *adjective.* Bizarre, eccentric, odd. M20.

weirdy *noun* var. of **WEIRDIE**.

weism /ˈwiːɪz(ə)m/ *noun.* E19.
[from **WE** + **-ISM**.]
Too frequent use of first person plural pronouns. Cf. **WEGOTISM**.

Weismannism /ˈvʌɪsmənɪz(ə)m/ *noun. obsolete* exc. *Hist.* Also **W-**. L19.
[from August F. L. *Weismann* (1834–1914), German biologist + **-ISM**.]
A theory of evolution and heredity propounded by Weismann, esp. in regard to the continuity of the germplasm and the non-transmission of acquired characteristics.
■ **Weismannian** /-ˈman-/ *adjective* of or pertaining to Weismann or his theory E20.

Weissenberg /ˈvʌɪs(ə)nbəːg/ *noun.* M20.
[Karl *Weissenberg* (b. 1893), Austrian-born physical chemist.]
1 CRYSTALLOGRAPHY. Used **attrib.** with ref. to a technique of single-crystal X-ray diffraction in which a metal shield allows the diffracted X-rays to produce only one set of parallel lines of spots which are recorded over the whole of the photographic film by rotating it synchronously with the crystal. M20.
2 PHYSICS. ***Weissenberg effect***, an effect observed when a viscoelastic liquid is stirred, in which the liquid rises in the centre and climbs the stirring rod rather than forming a concave surface like normal fluids. M20.

Weisswurst /ˈvʌɪsvəːst, *foreign* ˈvaɪsvʊrst/ *noun.* M20.
[German, from *weiss* white + *Wurst* sausage.]
(A) whitish German sausage made chiefly of veal.

weka /ˈwɛkə/ *noun.* M19.
[Maori, imit. of the bird's call.]
More fully ***weka rail***. A large flightless rail, *Gallirallus australis*, which has brown and black plumage and is confined to New Zealand. Also ***weka rail***. Also called ***woodhen***.

†**Welch** *adjective & noun* var. of **WELSH** *adjective & noun.*

welch *verb* var. of **WELSH** *verb.*

welcome /ˈwɛlkəm/ *noun*[1], *interjection, & adjective.*
[Old English *wilcuma* (from *wil-* desire, pleasure + *cuma* comer), with later alt. of 1st elem. to *wel-* **WELL** *adverb* infl. by Old French *bien venu* or Old Norse *velkominn*.]
▶†**A** *noun.* A person whose arrival is pleasing or desirable; an acceptable person or thing. Only in OE.
▶ **B** *interjection.* Used to greet a visitor or guest; expr. pleasure at the arrival of a person. OE.

> 🕮 J. BURCHILL Welcome back to the land of the living.

▶ **C** *adjective.* **1** Of a person: acceptable as a visitor, companion, etc. OE.
2 Of a thing: acceptable, agreeable, pleasing. ME.
3 Freely allowed or cordially invited to do or have something. Foll. by *to*, *to do*. ME.

> 🕮 **1** E. F. BENSON Maud would be a welcome guest. **2** *American Speech* Contributions to the Atlas Fund . . to defray . . costs are welcome. E. HEALEY They reached the welcome shade of the great trees. **3** J. AUSTEN You would be . . welcome to any other in my trinket-box. E. H. ERIKSON She is quite welcome to keep the pencils. *iron.*: G. MITCHELL If nudists excite you, you're welcome to them.

Phrases etc.: **and welcome**: added to a statement to imply that its subject or addressee is freely allowed or cordially invited to do or have something specified. **bid welcome** express gladness on receiving (a person) home, as a guest, etc. **make welcome** receive (a person) hospitably. **welcome aboard** *joc.* (with allus. to nautical usage) greeting a person joining a particular group, enterprise, etc. **welcome-home-husband** *dial.* cypress spurge, *Euphorbia cyparissias*. **wish welcome** = *bid welcome* above. **you are welcome, you're welcome**: a polite response to an expression of thanks.

■ **welcomely** *adverb* (**a**) with an expression or feeling of welcome; gladly, hospitably; (**b**) in a manner that is welcomed: L16. **welcomeness** *noun* E17.

welcome /ˈwɛlkəm/ *noun*[2]. E16.
[from prec. or next.]
1 An assurance to a visitor or stranger that he or she is welcome; a glad, kind, hearty, or hospitable reception given to a person arriving, a new idea, etc. E16. ▸**b** A greeting or reception of a specified (friendly or unfriendly) kind. M16. ▸†**c** A special award for the person or persons first drawing lots or blanks on the opening or each subsequent day of a lottery. M16–E17.
2 Glad or hospitable reception of a visitor or stranger. L16.
3 A welcoming salute with guns etc. E17.

> 🕮 **1** A. MARSH-CALDWELL That he was . . beloved by Everard, was sufficient to insure him a welcome. J. R. GREEN The welcome of the townsmen made up . . for the ill-will. **outstay one's welcome, overstay one's welcome** stay too long as a visitor etc. **b** SHAKES. *Temp.* And to thee and thy company I bid A hearty welcome. T. STAFFORD The Invaders finding so ill a welcome, returned. **2** TENNYSON And welcome turns a cottage to a palace. R. P. JHABVALA She got up . . holding out both hands to him in welcome. **3** SIR W. SCOTT The cannon from the ramparts glanced, And thundering welcome gave.

Comb.: **welcome home** (**a**) a party or reception to celebrate a person's homecoming (freq. *attrib.*); (**b**) *dial.* a bell tolled to mark a person's death; **welcome mat** (orig. *N. Amer.*) a mat put out to greet welcome visitors (*lit.* & *fig.*); **welcome wagon** *N. Amer.* a car bringing gifts and samples from local merchants to newcomers in a community.

welcome /ˈwɛlkəm/ *verb trans.*
[Old English *wilcumian*, formed as **WELCOME** *noun*[1] with similar later alt. of 1st elem.]
1 Greet or receive with pleasure, gladness, or a welcome; give a friendly reception to; make welcome. Freq. with adverb (phr.). OE.
2 Greet or receive *with* or *by* something of a specified (usu. unpleasant) kind. L16.
3 Be pleased at the prospect or occurrence of (an event etc.). M19.

> 🕮 **1** J. AUSTEN Their landlord, who called to welcome them to Barton. LD MACAULAY The . . loyalty with which Charles had been welcomed back to Dover. CONAN DOYLE Not too proud to admit that he . . would welcome any help. M. FORSTER Lizzie, baby in her arms, beaming and welcoming her in. **2** A. RADCLIFFE If you return . . you will be welcomed by a brace of bullets. **3** W. S. MAUGHAM She did not know that Madame Berger had welcomed the marriage.

■ **welcomer** *noun* ME. **welcoming** *noun* the action of the verb; a welcome: ME. **welcoming** *adjective* that gives a welcome, friendly M17. **welcomingly** *adverb* L19.

weld /wɛld/ *noun*[1]. LME.
[= Middle Low German *waude* (for *walde*), Middle Dutch *woude* (Dutch *wouw*), perh. rel. to **WEALD**, **WOLD**. Perh. already in Old English.]
A Eurasian mignonette, *Reseda luteola*, of bare or disturbed, freq. chalky places, formerly grown as the source of a yellow dye (also called ***dyer's rocket***). Also, the dye obtained from this plant.

weld /wɛld/ *noun*[2]. M19.
[from next.]
1 A joining or joint made by welding. M19.
2 The action, process, or result of welding; the state or fact of being welded. M19.
1 ***butt weld***, ***fusion weld***, ***lap weld***, ***seam weld***, ***spot weld***, etc.
Comb.: **weld decay** (increased susceptibility to) corrosion in chromium-nickel stainless steel adjacent to a weld, owing to the precipitation of chromium carbide and the consequent lowering of the chromium content; **weld pool** the pool of molten metal formed about a joint in welding.
■ **weldless** *adjective* made without a weld M19.

weld /wɛld/ *verb.* L16.
[Alt. of **WELL** *verb*[1] (under infl. of pa. t. & pple), prob. after Swedish *välla*.]
▶ **I** *verb intrans.* **1** Orig., become joined or united together. Later, become or admit of being welded. Now *rare*. L16.
▶ **II** *verb trans.* **2 a** Join together (pieces of metal, esp. iron or steel) by heating and hammering or pressure. L17. ▸**b** Join together (pieces of metal, plastic, etc.) by melting, using local heat provided (for metals) by an electric arc, oxyacetylene torch, or laser, usu. with the addition of extra metal. L19.
3 *fig.* Unite, esp. closely or inseparably; join closely together. E19.

> 🕮 **2** ***lap-weld***, ***microweld***, ***spot-weld***, ***stitch weld***, ***tack weld***, etc. **3** T. S. ELIOT While the late Archbishop was Chancellor, no one . . did more to weld the country together. *Your Business* My job is to weld individual departments into a team. *Sunday Times* Critics . . show signs . . of welding themselves into an organized opposition.

■ **welda'bility** *noun* the quality or property of being weldable M19. **weldable** *adjective* able to be welded (together) M19. **welder** *noun* a person or machine employed in welding E19. **weldment** *noun* a unit consisting of pieces welded together M20.

welded /ˈwɛldɪd/ *adjective.* M19.
[from prec. + -ED[1].]
1 Joined or united by or as by welding. M19.
2 *GEOLOGY.* **a** Designating pyroclastic rock formed by the union of small heat-softened particles. E20. ▸**b** Designating an intimate close-fitting contact between two bodies of rock that have not been heat-softened or tectonically disrupted. M20.

welding /ˈwɛldɪŋ/ *noun.* E17.
[from WELD *verb* + -ING[1].]
1 The action or process of welding (*lit.* & *fig.*). E17.
2 The property of uniting under the combined operation of heat and pressure. E19.
1 ***arc welding, friction welding, percussion welding, spot welding, submerged-arc welding,*** etc.
Comb.: **welding heat** the degree of heat to which iron or steel is brought for pressure welding; **welding rod** a thin metal rod, usu. coated with flux, which is progressively melted to supply the additional metal needed in a welded joint; **welding steel** a steel alloy suitable for welding, esp. electric arc welding; **welding torch** a blowpipe used in oxyacetylene welding.

weldmesh /ˈwɛldmɛʃ/ *noun.* M20.
[from WELD *noun*[2] or *verb* + MESH *noun.*]
(Proprietary name for) wire mesh formed by welding together two series of parallel wires crossing at right angles.

welfare /ˈwɛlfɛː/ *noun.* ME.
[Contr. of *well fare*, from WELL *adverb* + FARE *verb.*]
1 Happiness, well-being, good health or fortune, (of a person, community, etc.); successful progress, prosperity. ME.
†**2** A source of well-being or happiness. Only in LME. ▸**b** Good cheer; extravagant living or entertainment. LME–L16.
3 a Organized provision for the basic (esp. physical and economic) well-being of needy members of a community; financial support for this. E20. ▸**b** *ellipt.* (Usu. **W-**.) (The officials of) a welfare department or office. E20. ▸**c** Benefit paid by the State to people in need. Orig. *US.* M20.

> **1** D. JACOBSON He enquires . . after Amnon's welfare . . He is fine, he assures David. R. DAWKINS Admire those who put the welfare of others first. **3b** D. LESSING She asked Welfare if Aurora could go to a council nursery. **c on welfare, on the welfare** receiving financial assistance from the State for basic living needs.

Attrib. & comb.: In the senses 'pertaining to or concerned with the welfare of (workers, the poor, etc.)', 'provided by the State for the needy', as ***welfare benefit, welfare centre, welfare cheque, welfare clinic, welfare department, welfare office, welfare policy, welfare service, welfare worker,*** etc. Special combs., as **welfare capitalism** a capitalist system combining a desire for profits with concern for the welfare of employees; **welfare hotel** *US*: providing temporary accommodation for people on welfare; **welfare roll** *N. Amer.* a list of people entitled to State welfare benefits; **welfare state** (a country practising) a system whereby the State provides services, grants, allowances, pensions, etc., to protect the health and well-being of citizens, esp. those in need; **welfare statism** (orig. *US*) the social conditions or organization associated with a welfare state; **welfare work** organized effort for the welfare of the poor, disabled, or disadvantaged.
■ **welfarism** *noun* (orig. *US*) the principles or policies associated with a welfare state, welfare-statism M20. **welfarist** *noun* (*a*) a person concerned with welfare, esp. that of animals; (*b*) (orig. *US*) a person who supports the principles or policies associated with a welfare state (freq. *attrib.*): M20.

†**welfare** *verb* (*imper.*) & *interjection.* M16–L17.
[formed as prec.: see FAREWELL.]
Chiefly in optative phrases expr. (genuine or ironic) good wishes.

> SPENSER But thine my Deare (welfare thy heart my deare).

welk /wɛlk/ *verb*[1]. Long *obsolete* exc. *dial.* ME.
[Prob. of Low Dutch origin: cf. Middle & mod. Low German, Middle & mod. Dutch *welken.*]
1 *verb intrans.* Of a flower, plant, etc.: lose freshness or greenness; droop; wilt, wither, fade. ME.
†**2** *verb intrans.* Become less, shrink. Of the sun or moon: wane, lose brightness. LME–M17.
3 *verb trans.* Cause to fade or wither. L16.

†**welk** *verb*[2] *trans. rare.* LME–E19.
[Rel. to WALK *verb*[1], *verb*[2].]
Roll or knead together.

welked *adjective* var. of WHELKED.

welkin /ˈwɛlkɪn/ *noun.* Long only *poet.*
[Old English *weolcen, wolc(e)n*, corresp. to Old Frisian *wolken, wulken*, Old Saxon, Old High German *wolkan* (Dutch *wolk*, German *Wolke*).]
†**1** A cloud. OE–ME.
2 a The vault formed by the sky, the firmament. OE. ▸**b** *spec.* The abode of God or the gods; the celestial regions, heaven. M16.
†**3** In Ptolemaic astronomy: a celestial sphere. Only in ME.
4 The upper atmosphere; the region of the air in which the clouds float, birds fly, etc. LME.

> **2** SIR W. SCOTT If a sail but gleam'd white 'gainst the welkin blue.

Phrases & comb.: **make the welkin ring, rend the welkin** make a very loud sound. †**welkin-eye** (*rare*, Shakes.) a heavenly or blue eye.

well /wɛl/ *noun*[1].
[Old English (Anglian) *wella* corresp. to Old High German *wella* (German *Welle*) wave, Old Norse *vella* boiling heat, bubbling, turbulence, from Germanic base also of WALL *verb*[1], WELL *verb*[1].]
1 a A spring of water rising to the earth's surface to form a pool or stream. Now *arch.* & *poet.* OE. ▸**b** A spring of water supposed to be of miraculous origin or to have healing powers. Now *spec.* a medicinal or mineral spring; in *pl.*, a place or resort with this, a spa. OE. ▸**c** A fountain fed by a spring; a pump, pipe, or similar device erected above a spring; a drinking-fountain. Chiefly *Scot.* L16.
2 *transf.* & *fig.* A source *of* something, *esp.* an abundant one. OE. ▸†**b** A copious flow of tears or blood; a weeping person. ME–E17. ▸**c** A whirlpool. Now chiefly *dial.* M17.
3 A shaft sunk into the ground to reach and tap a supply of water; *spec.* a circular one lined with masonry, with a stone border and a structure built above it for lowering and raising a bucket. OE. ▸**b** *HERALDRY.* A charge representing this structure. L18.
4 *NAUTICAL.* **a** An enclosed space in the bottom of a ship containing the pump or its suction pipes, into which bilge-water runs. E17. ▸**b** A tank in a fishing boat, in which the catch is preserved alive. E17.
5 Any shaft or pit sunk or dug into the ground; *spec.* (*a*) a pit dug for the storage of ice; (*b*) a shaft sunk in the ground to reach and tap a supply of oil, brine, gas, etc. Freq. with specifying word. L17.
6 a The open space or shaft enclosing a staircase in a tall building, or in which a lift operates; a similar deep narrow space in the middle of a building or group of buildings, to provide light and ventilation. Esp. ***stairwell*** s.v. STAIR. L17. ▸**b** A space left in a stack of hay for ventilation. *dial.* E18. ▸**c** A railed open area in a lawcourt, where the solicitors sit. M19. ▸**d** = ***orchestra pit*** s.v. ORCHESTRA 3. M20. ▸**e** An area in the centre of a legislative chamber, lecture theatre, etc. around which the seating is arranged in tiers. *US.* M20.
7 a *Hist.* A boxlike receptacle in the body of a carriage, for luggage. L18. ▸**b** A comparatively deep receptacle at the bottom of a desk, cabinet, etc. M19. ▸**c** A sunken receptacle or depression containing or designed to contain a liquid, esp. one in a dish for gravy etc. or in a desk for ink; *spec.* (*CERAMICS*) the depressed central portion of a plate, saucer, or dish. M19.
8 *PHYSICS.* = ***potential well*** s.v. POTENTIAL *noun.* M20.

> **1** E. MUIR A fountain in a waste, A well of water in a country dry. **2** E. FITZGERALD The secret Well of Life. **3** V. WOOLF She has to draw her water from a well in the garden. **5** ***gas well, oil well, test well,*** etc. **6** G. F. NEWMAN He looked down at the compound in the well of the building. W. GOLDING He looked . . down the well of the stairs. *HomeFlair* A safe working platform is essential when . . decorating a stairwell. **7c** E. DAVID Rub it into the flour . . make a well in the centre, put in the egg.

Comb.: **well-boat** a fishing boat with a well or tank for the storage and transport of live fish; **well-brick** a curved brick for lining a well; **well-bucket** a bucket used to draw water from a well, *esp.* one attached to a rope and pulley; **well-cistern**: fed by a spring; **well-cress** (now *dial.*) = WATERCRESS; **well-curb** the stone border round the mouth of a well; **well-deck** an open space on the main deck of a ship, lying at a lower level between the forecastle and poop; **well-decked** *adjective* having a well-deck; **well-decker** a ship with a well-deck; **well-dish** a meat-dish with a depression at one end to collect fat and gravy; **well-dresser** a person who takes part in well-dressing; **well-dressing** the decoration of wells with flowers etc., an ancient custom at Whitsuntide esp. in Derbyshire; **well-grate**: level with the hearth with an air-chamber below; **well-hole** an opening through a floor or series of floors for a staircase, lift, the admission of light, etc.; a stairwell; the empty space round which the stairs of a winding staircase turn; **well-house** a small building or room enclosing a well and its apparatus; **well-kerb** = ***well-curb*** above; **well-kick** an exertion of pressure by an oil-well in excess of that of the drilling fluid pumped into it, leading to loss of circulation; **well-point** *noun* & *verb* (*CIVIL ENGINEERING*) (*a*) *noun* each of a system of pipes sunk into the ground around an excavated area in order to lower the water table; (*b*) *verb trans.* supply with well-points; **well-room** = ***well-house*** above; **well shrimp** any of various freshwater crustaceans found in wells and underground water, which are freq. blind and white; **well-staircase, well-stairs, well-stairway**: with a well or open centre; **wellstead** (now *obsolete* exc. *dial.*) a site for a well; **well-sweep** a long pole mounted as a lever for raising buckets of water from a well; **well-tomb** a prehistoric tomb with a vertical shaft as the entrance; **well-trap** a depression in a drain, in which water lies to prevent the escape of foul air; **well water**: issuing or drawn from a well or spring; **well-way** the shaft of a well; **well-wheel** the wheel turning the axle of a windlass at a well.
■ **welled** *adjective* (*a*) having a well or hollow on the surface, pitted; (*b*) (of a fishing boat) having a tank in which to preserve the catch alive: M19. **well-like** /-l-l-/ resembling (that of) a well *adjective* E19.

well /wɛl/ *adjective.* Compar. BETTER *adjective*, superl. BEST *adjective.* OE.
[from WELL *adverb* in pred. use.]
1 *pred.* Happy; favoured by good fortune. *arch.* OE.
2 *pred.* In favour, on good terms, *with* a person. Chiefly in ***keep well with, stand well with.*** *arch.* (*rare* before 18.) LME. ▸**b** *spec.* On terms of intimate friendship or familiarity *with* a woman. *arch.* E18. ▸†**c** Pleased *with* (oneself). L18–M19.
3 *pred.* Prosperous, affluent, rich. Now *rare* exc. in ***be well left, well-to-do*** below. LME. ▸**b** Favourably circumstanced. Now *rare.* LME.
4 *pred.* Esp. of a ship: in a sound or undamaged state. LME.
5 *pred.* In a satisfactory state; of such a nature as to meet with approval. LME. ▸**b** Ready; *esp.* ready to eat, cooked. *Scot.* E19.
6 *pred.* **a** Advisable, desirable. Also foll. by *as.* L15. ▸**b** Fortunate, lucky; being a cause for thankfulness. Now usu. with *as.* M17.
7 In good health; free or recovered from illness. Formerly foll. by *of* an illness or wound. Usu. *pred.* M16. ▸**b** Of a person's health: good. Of an illness: cured. *arch.* E18.
8 a In conformity with approved standards of action or conduct; right, proper. Usu. & now only *pred. arch.* exc. in ***all very well*** below. M16. ▸**b** Of unexceptionable quality; good. *arch.* exc. in ***all very well*** below. M17.
9 *pred.* Of good or satisfactory appearance. Now *rare* or *obsolete.* E17.

> **5** W. IRVING She saw . . that all was not well with him. P. S. BUCK Fifty eggs, not new laid, but still well enough. *Proverb*: All's well that ends well. **6a** DICKENS I never thought to look at him again . . but it's well I should, perhaps. **b** TENNYSON Well is it that no child is born of thee. *News of the World* It was just as well that Brighton's promotion rivals faltered. *Today* It is as well I had no idea that ahead of me lay . . frightening years. **7** M. MITCHELL Ellen looked after sick people and made them well again. R. CHANDLER If a well man prays, that's faith. A sick man prays and he is just scared. R. P. JHABVALA I'm worried about her . . she hasn't been keeping too well. *absol.*: *City Limits* Calls for help coming from AIDS patients and the concerned well.

Phrases, comb., & special collocations: **all very well** (*a*) right and proper in itself or only under certain circumstances; (*b*) of unexceptionable quality according to some standards. ***be well left***: see LEAVE *verb*[1]. ***get well***: see GET *verb.* **leave well alone, let well alone** refrain from trying to improve that which is already satisfactory, avoid needless change or disturbance. **well and good**: expr. dispassionate acceptance of a decision etc. **well-baby** *adjective* designating or pertaining to a clinic providing routine health check-ups and immunizations and general health care advice for young children. **well day**: on which one is free from (an attack of an intermittent) illness. ***well-man***: see ***well-woman*** below. **well-to-do** *adjective* [well sometimes interpreted as the adverb] prosperous, affluent, rich; *transf.* thriving; ***the well-to-do***, those who are well-to-do. **well to live** (now *rare*) well-to-do. **well to pass** (now *Scot.*) well-to-do. **well-wish** (now *rare*) an act of wishing another well, a good wish. **well-woman, well-man** *adjectives* designating or pertaining to a clinic providing advice and information on, and routine check-ups for, health problems specific to or particularly common amongst women or men.
■ **wellness** *noun* the state of being well or in good health M17.

well /wɛl/ *verb*[1].
[Old English *wællan, wellan* (West Saxon *wiellan, wyllan*) causative from WALL *verb*[1]. Cf. Middle & mod. Low German, Middle & mod. Dutch *wellen*, Old Norse *vella*, from Germanic.]
†**1** *verb trans.* Boil (a liquid, ingredients, etc.). OE–L17.
2 *verb trans.* †**a** Liquefy (metal) by heat; cast, found. ME–L16. ▸**b** = WELD *verb* 2. *obsolete* exc. *dial.* LME.
3 *verb intrans.* Of a liquid, the containing vessel, etc.: boil. Also foll. by *up*. Long *obsolete* exc. *dial.* ME.
4 *verb intrans.* Rise up to the surface (of the earth, a wound, etc.) and (usu.) flow in a copious or steady stream; (of tears) appear in the eyes in copious amounts; *fig.* (of sound, an idea, etc.) issue, emanate, be perceived, as if from beneath a surface. Freq. foll. by *up.* ME. ▸**b** Foll. by *over*. Overflow (*lit.* & *fig.*). M19.
5 *verb trans.* (Of a spring) pour forth (water); *fig.* pour out (something) as in a stream. Also foll. by *forth, out, up.* LME.
6 *verb intrans.* Of the eyes: fill *with* tears. L20.

> **4** J. REED Through his clothes fresh blood came welling up with every heart-beat. J. DIDION Maria watched the tears welling in Helene's eyes. S. CHITTY New peace and happiness welled up inside her. M. LEITCH A thick brown liquid welled up and quickly filled the hollow. **6** S. WEINTRAUB His eyes often welled with tears when he became sentimental.

well /wɛl/ *verb*[2]. *arch. slang.* E19.
[from WELL *noun*[1].]
Defraud (one's accomplices) by embezzling part of the booty; conceal (booty) from one's accomplices.

well /wɛl/ *adverb, interjection, & noun*[2].
[Old English *wel(l)* = Old Frisian, Old Saxon (Dutch) *wel*, Old Norse *vel*; also with adverbial suffix (and vowel variation) Old Saxon *wela, wala, wola*, Old High German *wela, wola* (German *wohl*), Gothic *waila*; prob. from Indo-European base also of WILL *verb*[1]. Cf. WEAL *noun*[1].]

▸ **A** *adverb*. Compar. BETTER *adverb*, superl. BEST *adverb*.
▸ **I 1** In accordance with a good or high standard of conduct or morality. OE.
2 In such a manner as to constitute good treatment or confer a benefit; kindly, considerately; in a friendly manner; with approval; favourably. OE. ▸**b** With equanimity or good nature. Chiefly with *take*. OE.
3 With courage and spirit; bravely. *arch.* ME.

> 📖 **1** WORDSWORTH By acting well, And understanding, I should . . love The end of life. **2** T. HARDY Shaking hands heartily . . and wishing each other well. W. S. MAUGHAM Everyone likes him and thinks well of him. M. LASKI Perhaps they mean well, perhaps they'll come back. **b** N. BAWDEN My mother . . thanked me for 'taking it well'. **3** SIR W. SCOTT Well . . did De Bracy . . maintain the fame he had acquired.

▸ **II 4** Carefully, attentively. OE.
5 In a way appropriate to the facts or circumstances; fittingly, properly, suitably. OE.
6 Happily, successfully, with fortunate outcome; without disaster. Also, luckily, opportunely. OE. ▸**b** Profitably; advantageously. Esp. in ***marry well*** s.v. MARRY *verb*. Formerly also *spec.*, profitably for the seller or buyer. LME.
7 In a state of plenty or comfort; prosperously. OE.
8 With good reason. Chiefly with *may*. OE. ▸†**b** Certainly. L15–M17.
9 a Without difficulty; readily, easily. Chiefly with *can*. OE. ▸**b** In all likelihood, probably. Chiefly with *may*. LME.
†**10 a** To all appearance. ME–M16. ▸**b** With shrewd reasoning. LME–L17.

> 📖 **4** LD MACAULAY Feversham . . had looked at himself well in the glass. **5** SHAKES. *A.Y.L.* It would do well to set the deer's horns upon his head. S. FOOTE Well said, my young limb of the law. G. WILL It has been well said that rock turns revolt into a style. **6** S. BEDFORD It hasn't turned out well at all. M. DICKENS She was well out of it, because of what he had done to her. S. WYNTER Sue felt herself well rid of them and their resentments. I. MURDOCH I hope the campaign is going well. **7** J. MITCHELL He had a small private income . . not enough to live well. **8** G. GREENE Our imaginary observer might well wonder at this great harvest of tablets. *Dimensions* You may well ask if any food can be worth . . £400 . . a pound. **9** T. HARDY Fifty pounds, which Barnett could well afford to lose. **b** H. JAMES A great experience, which they might very well find . . useful. *Practical Health* Being short of breath . . may well be the first sign of asthma.

▸ **III 11** In a thorough manner; to an extent approaching completeness. Passing into sense 13 below. OE.
12 To a high point or degree; extensively, soundly, deeply, etc. OE.
13 Skilfully, expertly; with some talent or distinction. OE. ▸**b** With good appearance or effect. ME.
14 Satisfactorily; successfully. OE.
15 a Clearly, definitely; without any doubt. ME. ▸**b** Intimately; closely, in detail. ME.

> 📖 **11** J. C. LOUDON Pots . . well cleaned in the inside. W. GASS He hid them so well he couldn't find them himself. **12** H. JAMES There are worse fates . . than being loved too well. E. WAUGH Papa never left me anything. He thought I was well provided for. G. GREENE A good bourbon won't hurt you. You'll sleep well. **13** N. MOSLEY He and his eldest son rowed quite well. J. BERGER Those . . who are able to speak well speak on public platforms. **b** M. KEANE Her expensive clothes became her very well. **14** H. GREVILLE A fine child, and the Queen doing well. M. BRAGG Doing the job well. *Which?* Easispray 4190 . . performed fairly well. *Forestry* Non-native species . . have been shown to grow well in Britain. **15a** D. HAMMETT Did you remember it well enough that you could've described it? M. ROBERTS She knows perfectly well she is spoiling them. **b** S. BEDFORD A friend of mine knew him very well.

▸ **IV 16** To the full degree or extent; to a considerable extent, certainly, thoroughly. Now *rare* exc. in ***well able***, ***well aware***, ***well worth***, ***well worthy***. OE.
†**17** Qualifying a numeral or term of measurement: at least. OE–L16.
18 †**a** Qualifying adverbs: very. ME–M16. ▸**b** Qualifying adverbs & prepositions of place or direction: to a considerable extent, more than slightly. ME. ▸†**c** Qualifying compars.: much, rather. ME–E17. ▸**d** Qualifying adjectives, esp. adjectives of quality or emotion: very, extremely. *non-standard & slang*. L20.
19 Used with preceding adverb as *bloody, damn, jolly*, etc., to form intensive phrs. L19.

> 📖 **16** DRYDEN Nor well alive nor wholly dead they were. *Which?* It's well worth fitting a smoke-detector . . since many people die from the smoke of a house-fire. **18b** E. TEMPLETON The party had continued until well after midnight. *Observer* They should be located well away from existing conurbations. A. POWELL She was well into her thirties when they became engaged. **d** T. BARLING Eyetie . . had kept Archie well busy ducking and diving. *Blitz* I was well chuffed to see him as November's 'cover star'.

Phrases: **as well** (*a*) in addition, also; (*b*) to the same extent; (*c*) (chiefly with *may*) with equal reason or result; with no loss of advantage or cause for regret. **as well as** (*a*) in as good, satisfactory, etc., a way as; (*b*) to the same extent as, in the same degree as; (*c*) in addition to. ***be well served***: see SERVE *verb*[1]. **deserve well of** be entitled to gratitude or good treatment from. **do well to do** act prudently or sensibly in doing. **just as well** = *as well* (c) above. ***like well***: see LIKE *verb*[1] 5a. ***live well***: see LIVE *verb*. ***marry well***: see MARRY *verb*. ***pretty well***: see PRETTY *adverb* 1. ***set well with***: see SET *verb*[1]. ***speak well of***: see SPEAK *verb*. ***strip well***: see STRIP *verb*[1] 1b. ***very well***: see VERY *adjective*[1] & *adverb*. ***well and truly***: see TRULY 5b. **well away** (*a*) having made *esp.* considerable progress; (*b*) *colloq.* fast asleep; (*c*) *colloq.* very drunk. **well enough** sufficiently well, adequately. **well met!** *arch.*: used in greeting a person one has been wanting to meet; (***hail-fellow-well-met***: see HAIL *interjection*). **well off** favourably or comfortably situated as regards money or other personal circumstances; ***the well off***, those so situated. ***well on one's way***: see WAY *noun*. See also ***well-to-do*** s.v. WELL *adjective*.

Comb.: †**well-accomplished** *adjective* accomplished; **well-acquainted** *adjective* having a good acquaintance with or knowledge of; familiar *with*; **well-adjusted** *adjective* (*a*) in a good state of adjustment; (*b*) mentally and emotionally stable; **well-advised** *adjective* (*a*) (of a person) prudent, wise, (*to do*); (*b*) (of an action etc.) carefully considered; **well-affected** *adjective* favourably disposed, friendly, (*to* or *towards*); **well-aged** *adjective* (now *rare*) advanced in years, old; **well-appointed** *adjective* having all the necessary equipment; **well-attended** *adjective* (of a meeting etc.) attended by a large number of people; **well-balanced** *adjective* (*a*) having an orderly disposition of parts; (*b*) having no constituent lacking or in excess; (*c*) sane, sensible; **well-becoming** *adjective* (*arch.*) highly befitting or suiting; **well-behaved** *adjective* (*a*) showing or having good conduct or manners; (*b*) MATH. designating entities which are susceptible to various manipulations, as continuity or differentiability (of a function), convergence (of a series); (*c*) (of a computer program) communicating with hardware via standard operating system calls rather than directly, and therefore able to be used on different machines; **well-being** healthy, contented, or prosperous condition; moral or physical welfare (of a person or community); *transf.* satisfactory condition (of a thing); **well-beloved** *adjective* & *noun* (*a*) *adjective* dearly loved; (*b*) *noun* a dearly loved person; dearly loved people collectively; †**well-beseeming** *adjective* (*rare*) highly becoming; †**well beseen** *adjective* of good appearance, well appointed, well dressed; **well-blooded** *adjective* (*obsolete* exc. *dial.*) (of the face etc.) flushed, rosy; **well-bodied** *adjective* (now *rare* or *obsolete*) (of a person) having an attractive or impressive body or figure; **well-born** of noble birth; **well-breathed** /-briːðd, -brɛθt/ *adjective* having a good capacity for breathing, sound of wind; not out of breath; **well-bred** (*a*) of good family and upbringing; *esp.* showing good breeding, courteous or refined in speech and behaviour; (*b*) (of an animal) of good or pure stock; **well-breeched** *adjective* prosperous, well-to-do; **well-built** *adjective* (*a*) of good construction; (*b*) (of a person) big, strong, and well-proportioned; **well-chosen** *adjective* carefully or aptly selected; (esp. of words) carefully chosen for effect, *spec.* sharp, abusive, denunciatory (freq. in ***a few well-chosen words***); **well-conditioned** *adjective* (*a*) of good morals or behaviour, right-minded; (*b*) in good physical condition, sound, healthy; (*c*) established on good terms or conditions; (*d*) MATH. such that a small error in measurement or change in data gives rise to only a small change in the calculated result; **well-conducted** *adjective* (*a*) properly organized, managed, or carried out; (*b*) well-behaved; (*c*) well conducted musically; ***well-connected***: see CONNECTED 2; **well content**, **well contented** *adjectives* highly pleased or satisfied; **well-covered** *adjective* (*a*) comprehensively or thickly covered; (*b*) *colloq.* (of a person) plump, corpulent; **well-defined** *adjective* clearly indicated, marked, or determined; **well-deserved** *adjective* (*a*) rightfully merited or earned; †(*b*) *rare* (Shakes.) having well deserved something; **well-developed** *adjective* substantially or fully developed; fully grown, mature; of generous size; **well-disposed** *adjective* †(*a*) in good physical condition, healthy; (*b*) suitably or skilfully placed or arranged; (*c*) of a favourable disposition, friendly, (*towards*); **well-documented** *adjective* supported or attested by much documentary evidence; **well-done** *adjective* & *interjection* †(*a*) wise, prudent, virtuous; (*b*) performed or executed skilfully or well; also as *interjection*, expr. approval of a person's actions etc.; (*c*) (of meat) thoroughly cooked; **well-dressed** *adjective* (*a*) wearing smart and usu. stylish clothing; (*b*) properly prepared or trimmed; **well-earned** *adjective* fully deserved; **well-educated** *adjective* educated to a high level or standard; **well-endowed** *adjective* (*a*) well provided with talent or resources, having a substantial endowment; (*b*) *colloq.* (of a man) having large genitals; (of a woman) large-breasted; **well-established** *adjective* firmly placed; well-authenticated; long-standing; **well-faring** *adjective* (*arch.*) †(*a*) handsome, good-looking; robust, healthy; (*b*) doing well, prosperous; **well-favoured** *adjective* handsome, attractive, good-looking; †**well-favouredly** *adverb* in a well-favoured manner; **well-favouredness** (now *rare* or *obsolete*) the quality or condition of being well-favoured; **well-fed** *adjective* having or having had plenty of (esp. good-quality) food to eat; **well-formed** *adjective* properly or attractively proportioned, correctly or becomingly constructed or shaped; *spec.* (LINGUISTICS) formed according to stated grammatical rules, (LOGIC) designating any sequence of symbols conforming to the formation rules of a logical system (esp. as ***well-formed formula***); **well-formedness** (chiefly LINGUISTICS) the quality of being well-formed; **well-found** *adjective* †(*a*) as *interjection*: used as a greeting; †(*b*) of established merit or value, commendable; (*c*) = ***well-appointed*** above; **well-founded** *adjective* (*a*) built on a firm and solid base; (*b*) *esp.* (of a belief, suspicion, statement, etc.) having a foundation in fact or reason, based on good grounds or evidence; **well-foundedly** *adverb* in a well-founded manner; **well-foundedness** the quality of being well-founded; **well-gotten** *adjective* (long *arch.*) obtained by good means, honourably gained, (opp. ***ill-gotten***); **well-groomed** *adjective* (*a*) (of a horse) well-brushed; (*b*) (of a person) smartly turned out, with carefully tended hair, skin, clothes, etc.; **well-grounded** *adjective* (*a*) = ***well-founded*** (b) above; (*b*) having a good training in or knowledge of the groundwork of a subject; **well-grown** *adjective* showing a substantial or satisfactory growth or development; **well-heeled** *adjective* (*colloq.*) wealthy; **well-hung** *adjective* (*a*) having large pendent organs; now (*colloq.*, of a man), having large genitals; (*b*) decorated with rich hangings or tapestry; (*c*) (now *rare*, of the tongue) glib, fluent; (*d*) (of a gate, skirt, etc.) suspended or attached so as to hang well; (*e*) (of meat or game) hung up for a sufficient time; **well-in** *adjective* (*Austral. slang*) = ***well off*** above; **well-informed** *adjective* well equipped with information; having much knowledge in general or of a special subject; **well-intended** *adjective* well-meant; **well-intentioned** *adjective* (of a person) having good intentions, well-meaning; (of an action etc.) due to or based on good intentions, well-meant; **well-judged** *adjective* opportunely, skilfully, or discreetly done, judicious; **well-kempt** *adjective* = KEMPT *adjective*; **well-kept** *adjective* maintained in good order or condition; carefully preserved or stored; (of a secret etc.) well concealed; **well-knit** *adjective* (*a*) firmly compacted, closely linked or connected; (*b*) (of a person) strongly and compactly built, not loose-jointed; **well-known** *adjective* (*a*) known to many, widely or generally known, famous; (*b*) intimately or thoroughly known; **well-knownness** the quality of being well known, fame, celebrity; ***well languaged***: see LANGUAGED *adjective* 1; **well-liked** *adjective* regarded with much affection or approval; **well-lined** *adjective* having a good lining; *spec.* (of a purse) full of money; **well-looking** *adjective* (*arch.*) good-looking, attractive; **well-lost** *adjective* (long *arch.*) lost in a good cause or for a good consideration; **well-loved** *adjective* dearly loved, well-beloved; regarded with great affection or approval; **well-made** *adjective* (*a*) (of a person or animal) well-proportioned, of good build; (*b*) (of a thing) strongly or skilfully constructed; **well-mannered** *adjective* †(*a*) having good morals, virtuous; (*b*) having or showing good manners, courteous, polite; **well-marked** *adjective* clearly defined, distinct, easy to distinguish or recognize; **well-matched** *adjective* suited, compatible; fit to be a pair, be adversaries, etc.; **well-meaner** a well-meaning person; **well-meaning** *adjective* (of a person or thing) having or based on good intentions but freq. ineffective or ill-advised; **well-meaningly** *adverb* in a well-meaning manner; **well-meant** *adjective* (of a thing) well-meaning; ***well-meated***: see MEAT *verb* 2; **well-nourished** *adjective* having been amply provided with nourishment, well-fed; **well-oiled** *adjective* (*a*) sufficiently or generously lubricated; *transf.* operating smoothly; (*b*) (of a compliment etc.) easily expressed through habitual use; (*c*) *colloq.* drunk, intoxicated; **well-order** *verb trans.* (MATH.) arrange the elements of (a set) in such an order as to produce a well-ordered set; **well-ordered** *adjective* (*a*) orderly, properly regulated, carefully arranged; (*b*) MATH. (of an ordered set) having the property that every non-empty subset of it has a first or least element; **well-ordering** MATH. the property of being well-ordered; a well-ordered set; **well-padded** *adjective* provided with sufficient padding; *transf.* fleshy, plump; **well-paid** *adjective* (*a*) (of a person) amply rewarded for a job; (*b*) (of a job) that pays well; **well-placed** *adjective* (*a*) set in a good place or position; properly, conveniently, or judiciously placed; (*b*) holding a good social position; **well-pleased** *adjective* highly gratified or satisfied; **well-pleasing** *adjective* giving great pleasure or satisfaction; **well-plucked** *adjective* (*arch. colloq.*) plucky, fearless; **well-preserved** *adjective* carefully stored, remaining in good condition; *spec.* (of a mature or old person) youthful-looking, showing comparatively few signs of ageing; **well-proportioned** *adjective* having good, graceful, or correct proportions; **well-read** *adjective* knowledgeable through much reading, having read a wide variety of literature etc. (foll. by *in* a subject); **well-received** *adjective* favourably received or reviewed, welcomed; **well-rested** *adjective* having had sufficient rest or sleep, relaxed, restored; **well-rounded** *adjective* (*a*) *lit.* fleshy, plump; buxom; (*b*) *fig.* (of a person, character, life, etc.) complete and symmetrical, well-balanced, full and varied; (of a phrase etc.) complete and well expressed; ***well-saved***: see SAVE *verb*; **well-set** *adjective* (*a*) (of a person etc.) strongly built, sturdy, of good figure, (also ***well set up***); (*b*) skilfully, fittingly, or happily placed, settled, or arranged; (*c*) CRICKET (of a batsman) playing the bowling with ease and apparently unlikely to get out; **well-shaped** *adjective* having a good form or figure, gracefully shaped; ***well-shapen***: see SHAPEN *ppl adjective* 1; **well-spaced** *adjective* (of items) placed neither too close nor too far apart from each other; **well-spent** *adjective* (of time, money, etc.) expended or spent profitably or judiciously; **well-spoken** *adjective* (of a person or voice) articulate, fluent; of educated or refined speech; ***well-stacked***: see STACKED 2; **well-stocked** *adjective* (of a shop, garden, etc.) plentifully filled with goods, plants, etc.; **well-studied** *adjective* †(*a*) (of a person) well-read, learned, proficient, (*in*); (*b*) produced or learned by careful study, carefully studied; **well-suited** *adjective* (*a*) well-matched, suitable; adapted *to*, fit *for*; (*b*) wearing a smart suit of clothes; **well-tasted** *adjective* (now *rare*) (*a*) having a good taste or flavour; (*b*) (of a person) having good taste; **well-tempered** *adjective* †(*a*) having a good bodily constitution; (*b*) even-tempered; good-tempered; (*c*) (of steel) brought to the right degree of hardness and elasticity; (*d*) (of clay or mortar) well mixed or compounded; (*e*) [German *wohltemperirt*] MUSIC tuned in equal temperament; **well-thought-of** *adjective* having a good reputation, esteemed, respected; **well-thought-out** *adjective* properly planned in advance, carefully devised; **well-thumbed** *adjective* (of a book etc.) bearing marks of frequent handling, well-used; **well-timbered** *adjective* (*a*) strongly constructed of wood; (*b*) (now *rare*, of a person etc.) well-built; (*c*) well-wooded; **well-timed** *adjective* (*a*) timely, opportune; judicious; (*b*) actuated or wielded in regular time; **well-travelled** *adjective* that has travelled far, experienced in travel; **well-tried** *adjective* often used or tested with good results, thoroughly tried, reliable; **well-trodden** *adjective* frequently trodden, much walked on; *fig.* much frequented, visited, or dealt with; **well-turned** *adjective* (*a*) (of the body or limbs, esp. a leg or ankle) elegantly shaped or displayed; (*b*) (of a compliment, phrase, verse, etc.) elegantly expressed; (*c*) skilfully turned or rounded; **well-turned-out** *adjective* smartly dressed, well-groomed; ***well-*UPHOLSTERED**; **well-used** *adjective* †(*a*) well practised or exercised; (*b*) rightly or effectively used; (*c*) much or often used; **well-willed** *adjective* (*obsolete* exc. *Scot. & north.*) kindly or favourably disposed (*to, to do, that*); **well-willer** (now *rare*) a well-wisher; **well-willing** *noun* & *adjective* †(*a*) *noun* good will, favour, kindly regard; good intention;

(*b*) *adjective* (now *rare* exc. *dial.*) well-disposed, benevolent (*to*, *towards*); ready *to do*; **well-willy** *adjective* (long *obsolete* exc. *dial.*) well-disposed, benevolent; †**well-wished** *adjective* (*rare*, Shakes.) attended by good wishes; **well-wisher** a person who wishes another well, a well-disposed person; **well-wishing** *noun* & *adjective* (*a*) *noun* the action of wishing another well; (*b*) *adjective* that wishes another well, benevolent; (see also ***well-wish*** s.v. WELL *adjective*); **well-won** *adjective* gained by hard or honourable effort, creditably won; **well-wooded** *adjective* thickly covered with woods; **well-worked** *adjective* (*a*) thoroughly or cleverly operated or treated; (*b*) skilfully wrought; **well-worn** *adjective* (*a*) much worn by use; *fig.* (of a phrase etc.) trite, hackneyed; (*b*) becomingly carried or displayed; **well-wrought** *adjective* well-made, skilfully constructed or put together.

▶**B** *interjection.* Expr. surprise, resignation, insistence, etc., or resumption or continuation of talk, used esp. after a pause in speaking. Also redupl. (*well, well!*). OE.

oh well: see OH *interjection*. ***well, I never!*** **well then**: introducing a conclusion or further statement, or implying that one can be drawn or made.

▶**C** *noun.* An utterance of 'well!'. M19.

¶ A hyphen is normally used in combinations of *well* when used attributively, but not when used predicatively, e.g. *a well-made coat* but *the coat is well made*.

■ **wellish** *adverb* (*dial.* & *colloq.*) pretty well, fairly well M18.

welladay /wɛlə'deɪ/ *interjection* & *noun.* Now *arch.* & *dial.* M16.
[Alt. of WELLAWAY by substitution of DAY *noun*, as in *lackaday*.]
▶**A** *interjection.* Expr. grief or lamentation: alas! M16.
▶**B** *noun.* An utterance of 'welladay!'; (a) lamentation. L16.

wellanear /wɛlə'nɪə/ *interjection. obsolete* exc. *dial.* E17.
[App. alt. of WELLAWAY by substitution of ANEAR *adverb* & *preposition*.]
Expr. grief or lamentation: alas!

wellaway /wɛlə'weɪ/ *interjection* & *noun. arch.*
[Old English *weg lā weg*, *wei lā wei*, alt. of *wā lā wā* after Scandinavian: see WOE, LO *interjection*[1]. Cf. WELLADAY, WELLANEAR.]
▶**A** *interjection.* Expr. grief or lamentation: alas! OE.
▶**B** *noun.* **1** An utterance of 'wellaway'; (a) lamentation. ME.
†**2** Grief, misery, woe. ME–M17.

wellawins /wɛlə'wɪnz/ *interjection. Scot.* L18.
[Alt.]
= WELLAWAY *interjection*.

Wellentheorie /'vɛlənteo,riː/ *noun.* M20.
[German, from *Welle* wave + *Theorie* theory.]
PHILOLOGY. The theory that linguistic changes spread like waves over a speech-area and the dialects of adjacent districts resemble each other most.

Wellerism /'wɛlərɪzm/ *noun.* Also **w-**. M19.
[from Samuel *Weller* or his father, two characters in Dickens's *Pickwick Papers* + -ISM.]
A form of humorous comparison in which a familiar saying or proverb is identified with something said by a person in a specified but inapposite situation.

📖 *New Society* The Wellerism: 'Meet you at the corner as one wall said to another.'

well-head /'wɛlhɛd/ *noun.* ME.
[from WELL *noun*[1] + HEAD *noun*.]
1 The place at which a spring breaks out of the ground; the source of a stream or river, a fountain-head. Freq. *fig.*, a source of anything. ME. ▸**b** A spring in a marsh. *Scot.* E19.
2 The top of a draw-well; a structure erected over this. E17. ▸**b** A structure erected over an oil- or gas-well. Freq. *attrib.* M20.

📖 **1** E. PAGITT Oxford, and Cambridge, two Well-heads of Divinity.

wellie *noun* & *verb* var. of WELLY *noun* & *verb*.

Wellington /'wɛlɪŋtən/ *noun.* Also **w-**. E19.
[Arthur Wellesley, first duke of *Wellington* (1769–1852), Brit. general and statesman.]
1 In full ***Wellington boot***. Orig., a high boot covering the knee in front and cut away behind; a somewhat shorter boot worn under the trousers. Now usu., a waterproof rubber or plastic boot usu. reaching the knee, worn in wet or muddy conditions. Usu. in *pl.* Freq. abbreviated WELLY *noun*. E19.
2 Used *attrib.* to designate clothing introduced by or named after the Duke of Wellington. E19.
3 A variety of cooking apple with yellowish white flesh. Also ***Wellington apple***. E19.
4 ***beef Wellington***, a dish consisting of fillet of beef coated in pâté and wrapped in puff pastry. M20.
2 ***Wellington coat***, ***Wellington hat***, ***Wellington trousers***, etc.

wellingtonia /wɛlɪŋ'təʊnɪə/ *noun.* M19.
[mod. Latin (see below), formed as prec. + -IA[1].]
A Californian conifer, *Sequoiadendron giganteum* (formerly *Wellingtonia gigantea*), which is related to the redwood and is the largest known tree. Also called ***big tree***, ***giant sequoia***, ***mammoth tree***.

Wellingtonian /wɛlɪŋ'təʊnɪən/ *adjective* & *noun.* M19.
[formed as WELLINGTON + -IAN.]
▶**A** *adjective.* Of, pertaining to, or characteristic of the first duke of Wellington. M19.
▶**B** *noun.* **1** A follower or adherent of the first duke of Wellington. M19.
2 A (former) pupil of Wellington college in Berkshire. M19.

well-near /wɛl'nɪə/ *adverb. obsolete* exc. *dial.* ME.
[from WELL *adverb* + NEAR *adverb*[2].]
= WELL-NIGH.

well-nigh /wɛl'nʌɪ/ *adverb.* Now *arch.* & *literary.*
[Old English *wel nēah*, formed as WELL *adverb* + NIGH *adverb*.]
Very nearly, almost wholly or entirely.

📖 F. HOYLE They had been exposed to well-nigh unbearable heat.

Wellsian /'wɛlzɪən/ *adjective.* E20.
[from *Wells* (see below) + -IAN.]
Of, pertaining to, or resembling the ideas and writings of the English science fiction writer H. G. Wells (1866–1946).

well-spring /'wɛlsprɪŋ/ *noun.*
[Old English *welspryng*, *wylspring*, formed as WELL *noun*[1] + as SPRING *noun*[1].]
= WELL-HEAD 1.

welly /'wɛli/ *noun* & *verb.* Also **-ie**. M20.
[Abbreviation of WELLINGTON.]
▶**A** *noun.* **1** A wellington boot. Also ***welly boot***. *colloq.* M20.
2 A powerful kick; acceleration, force, thrust. *slang.* L20.

📖 **2** *Daily Mirror* 'Daredevil Divi' gave the car a bit more welly. *Guardian* The tactic most likely to succeed . . was the long welly upfield.

▶**B** *verb trans.* Kick powerfully; trip up. *slang.* M20.

welly /'wɛli/ *adverb. dial.* E17.
[Var. of WELL-NIGH.]
Almost, nearly.

wels /wɛls, v-/ *noun.* Pl. same. L19.
[German.]
A very large elongated catfish, *Silurus glanis*, which is found in fresh water from central Europe to central Asia. Also called ***sheat-fish***, ***silurus***.

Welsbach /'vɛlzbax/ *noun.* L19.
[C. A. F. von *Welsbach* (1858–1929), Austrian chemist and engineer.]
Used *attrib.* to designate the gas-mantle, which was invented by von Welsbach, and lamps employing it.
¶ Proprietary name in the US.

Welsh /wɛlʃ/ *adjective* & *noun.* Also †**Welch**.
[Old English (Anglian, Kentish) *Węlisc*, *Wǣlisc*, (West Saxon) *Wālisc*, *Wȳlisc* corresp. to Old High German *wal(a)hisc*, *walesc* (German *welsch*) Roman, Italian, French, Dutch *waalsch* WALLOON, Old Norse *Valskr* Gaulish, French; from Old English *W(e)alh* corresp. to Old High German *Wal(a)h*, Old Norse *Valir* pl., from Germanic word meaning 'foreign (Celtic or Roman)' from Latin *Volcae* a Celtic people, of unkn. origin: see -ISH[1]. Cf. VLACH, WALACH.]
▶**A** *adjective.* Orig. (*Hist.*), of or pertaining to the native Celtic population of England as distinguished from the Anglo-Saxons. Now, designating a native or inhabitant of Wales, a western part of Great Britain and before union with England an independent country; of, pertaining to, or characteristic of Wales, its inhabitants, or its language. OE.

Special collocations & comb.: **Welsh aunt** a parent's first (female) cousin. **Welsh Black** (an animal of) a black-coated breed of cattle developed in N. Wales, now usu. kept for both meat and milk production. **Welsh clearwing** a dark-bodied clearwing moth, *Synanthedon scoliaeformis*, now confined in the British Isles to parts of Scotland and Ireland. †**Welsh comb** the thumb and forefingers. **Welshcomb** *verb trans.* comb (one's hair) using one's thumb and fingers instead of a comb. ***Welsh*** CORGI. ***Welsh cotton***: see COTTON *noun*[2]. **Welsh dragon** a red heraldic dragon as the emblem of Wales. **Welsh dresser** a kind of sideboard with cupboards and drawers below and open shelves above. **Welsh harp** a harp with three rows of strings. **Welsh hound** (an animal of) a breed of dog similar to the English foxhound but wire-haired. ***Welsh main***: see MAIN *noun*[1] 3. **Welsh mountain** (*a*) (in full ***Welsh mountain pony***) a small, strong, slender, hardy breed of pony, used as a riding pony or in harness; (*b*) (in full ***Welsh mountain sheep***) a small hardy breed of sheep developed in the uplands of Wales. **Welsh Nationalist** a person wanting home rule for Wales; *spec.* a member of the Welsh Nationalist Party; ***Welsh Nationalist Party*** = PLAID *noun*[2]. **Welsh niece** a first (female) cousin. **Welsh Office** the government department responsible for Welsh affairs; the building where this is housed. **Welsh onion** a tufted plant, *Allium fistulosum*, related to the onion, grown for its slender elongated bulbs which are used like spring onions; also called ***ciboule***. **Welsh poppy** a yellow-flowered poppy of shady rocky places, *Meconopsis cambrica*, native to western Europe (including Wales and SW England) and freq. grown for ornament. **Welsh rabbit** = ***Welsh*** RAREBIT. ***Welsh springer (spaniel)***: see SPRINGER 6. **Welsh terrier** (an animal of) a stocky, rough-coated, usu. black and tan breed of terrier with a square muzzle and drop ears. **Welsh uncle** a parent's male first cousin. **Welsh Wales** *colloq.* the parts of Wales where Welsh culture is especially strong or which are most distinctively Welsh. **Welsh wave** a small European geometrid moth, *Venusia cambrica*, which has pale wings with dark wavy markings.

▶**B** *noun.* Pl. same, (in sense 1c) **Welshes**.
1 a *collect. pl.* *The* Celtic ancient Britons as distinguished from the Anglo-Saxons. *obsolete* exc. *Hist.* OE. ▸**b** *collect. pl.* *The* natives or inhabitants of Wales. ME. ▸**c** A Welshman. Long *rare* or *obsolete*. LME.
2 The Celtic language of Wales. OE. ▸**b** *transf.* A strange language; speech not readily understood. Now *rare*. M17.
2 ***Old Welsh***: see OLD *adjective*.

■ **Welsher** *noun*[1] (*slang*) a Welsh person M19. **Welshness** *noun* Welsh character L16. **Welshy** *noun* (*slang*) a Welsh person M20.

welsh /wɛlʃ/ *verb.* Also **welch** /wɛltʃ/. M19.
[Origin unkn.]
1 a *verb intrans.* Of the loser of a bet, esp. a bookmaker: evade paying a debt; *transf.* evade an obligation. M19. ▸**b** *verb trans.* Swindle (a person) out of money won in a bet. M19.
2 *verb intrans.* Foll. by *on*: fail to carry out a promise to (a person); fail to honour (an obligation). M20.

📖 **2** S. BELLOW He had betrayed me, welshed on an agreement.

■ **welsher** *noun*[2] a person, esp. a bookmaker, who welshes M19.

Welshman /'wɛlʃmən/ *noun.* Pl. **-men**. OE.
[from WELSH *adjective* + MAN *noun*.]
1 a A Celtic ancient Briton. *obsolete* exc. *Hist.* OE. ▸**b** A man of Welsh birth or descent. OE.
2 The large-mouth bass, *Micropterus salmoides*. *US.* E18.

Welshry /'wɛlʃri/ *noun.* ME.
[formed as prec. + -RY. Cf. Anglo-Latin *Wallescheria*.]
†**1** Welsh people collectively. Only in ME.
2 *Hist.* The part of a town or area inhabited by Welsh or Celtic as opp. to English people. E17.
3 Welsh origin or nationality. L19.

Welshwoman /'wɛlʃwʊmən/ *noun.* Pl. **-women** /-wɪmɪn/. LME.
[formed as prec. + WOMAN *noun*.]
A woman of Welsh birth or descent.

welt /wɛlt/ *noun*[1] & *verb*[1]. LME.
[Origin uncertain: perh. from Old English.]
▶**A** *noun.* **1** A strip of leather etc. sewn around the edge of a shoe upper and attached to the sole. LME.
2 A strip of ribbed or reinforced material put on the edge of a garment etc. as a border or binding; an edging, a trimming. E16. ▸**b** HERALDRY. A fringe or edging on the sides of a charge. L17.
3 a A ridge on flesh, *esp.* one raised by a blow from a whip etc.; a weal. M16. ▸**b** *gen.* A narrow ridge, a raised stripe; a decorative or reinforcing strip. L16.
†**4** A binding strip or band. Only in 17.
5 A stroke with a whip etc.; a heavy blow with the fist etc. M19.

Comb.: **welt pocket** a slit pocket having a welt on the lower edge that extends upward to cover the slit.

▶**B** *verb trans.* **1** Provide or mark with a welt or welts; repair or renew the welts of. L15.
2 Beat, thrash, flog. E19.

■ **welting** *noun* (*a*) the action of the verb; (*b*) a welt, an edging, a border; (*c*) a beating, a thrashing: E16.

welt /wɛlt/ *noun*[2]. *dial.* M20.
[Origin unkn.]
The practice by which members of a gang of dockers take turns to have an unauthorized break while the rest work.

welt /wɛlt/ *verb*[2]. *obsolete* exc. *dial.* LME.
[from Old Norse verb corresp. to Old English *-wæltan*, *wyltan*, Old High German *walzen*, *welzen*, Gothic *waltjan*: see WALT *adjective*, *verb*.]
1 *verb intrans.* Roll or turn over, fall over; sway, be unsteady. LME.
2 *verb trans.* Throw to the ground, overturn; beat down. Also, roll, trundle. LME.

welt /wɛlt/ *verb*[3]. Chiefly *dial.* M18.
[Prob. alt. of WELK *verb*[1]. Cf. earlier WELTER *verb*[2], WILT *verb*[1].]
1 *verb trans.* Wither (cut grass etc.). Usu. in *pass.* M18.
2 *verb intrans.* Become withered, wilt. M19.

welt /wɛlt/ *verb*[4] *intrans. dial.* M20.
[from WELT *noun*[2].]
Of a docker: take an unauthorized break under the welt system.

Weltanschauung /'vɛltan,ʃaʊʊŋ/ *noun.* Pl. **-en** /-ən/, **-s**. M19.
[German, from *Welt* world + *Anschauung* perception.]
A particular philosophy or view of life; the world-view of an individual or group.

Weltbild /'vɛltbɪlt/ *noun.* M20.
[German, from *Welt* world + *Bild* picture.]
= WELTANSCHAUUNG.

welted /ˈwɛltɪd/ *adjective*. E16.
[from WELT *noun*[1], *verb*[1]: see -ED[2], -ED[1].]
1 Furnished with a welt or raised border or edging. Now chiefly of a boot or shoe. E16.
2 BOTANY. Furnished with a raised welt or projecting edge. Now only in ***welted thistle***, a European thistle, *Carduus crispus*, the stem of which is continuously winged for most of its length. L16.
3 Marked with a welt or raised mark of a lash. M19.

welter /ˈwɛltə/ *noun*[1]. L16.
[from WELTER *verb*[1].]
1 A state of confusion, upheaval, or turmoil. L16.
2 The rolling or tossing of the sea. M19.
3 A surging or confused mass (*of* material things or people); a disorderly or contrasting mixture *of* immaterial things. M19.

> 📖 **1** *Saturday Review* The present welter of English politics. **3** E. BIRNEY To organize the welter of notes . . pencilled down from Turvey's bewildering conversation. *Guardian* Lost in the welter of new and shocking experience.

welter /ˈwɛltə/ *noun*[2]. L16.
[from WELT *noun*[1] & *verb*[1] + -ER[1].]
A person who makes or inserts a welt in a shoe etc.

welter /ˈwɛltə/ *noun*[3]. E19.
[Origin uncertain: perh. from WELT *verb*[1] + -ER[1].]
1 A heavy rider or boxer. Cf. WELTERWEIGHT. E19. ▸**b** HORSE-RACING. In full ***welter handicap***, ***welter race***, etc. A race for heavy riders. E19.
2 A thing exceptionally big or heavy of its kind; a heavy blow. *colloq.* & *dial.* M19.

welter /ˈwɛltə/ *verb*[1]. ME.
[Middle Low German, Middle Dutch *welteren*.]
1 *verb intrans.* **a** Roll, tumble, or wriggle about; writhe, wallow. ME. ▸**b** Roll or lie prostrate *in* one's blood; be soaked or steeped *in* blood or gore. Now *arch.* & *poet.* L16.
2 *verb intrans.* †**a** Revel, live at ease. *rare.* ME–L16. ▸**b** Indulge *in* unrestrained licentiousness, pleasure, etc. Now *rare.* M16. ▸**c** Be sunk or deeply involved *in*. E17.
3 *verb intrans.* Of a ship etc.: roll or be tumbled to and fro, be washed about. LME.
4 *verb intrans.* Roll down in a stream; flow. Now *rare.* LME.
5 *verb intrans.* **a** Of waves, the sea, etc.: toss and tumble, surge. Now *poet.* LME. ▸**b** *transf.* Of a mass of things or people: be in a state of confusion, upheaval, or turmoil. M19.
†**6** *verb trans.* Move, turn, or force by rolling; cause to roll, toss up and down. LME–L16.
7 †**a** *verb intrans.* Of a vehicle: sway or rock unsteadily; be overturned. *rare.* LME–M16. ▸**b** *verb trans.* Overthrow, overturn, upset. Chiefly *Scot.* LME. ▸**c** *verb intrans.* Move with a heavy rolling gait; flounder; *dial.* reel, stagger. Now *rare.* L16.

> 📖 **1b** D. G. MITCHELL They lie—the fifty corpses—weltering in their blood. **2b** TENNYSON Happier are those that welter in their sin.

welter /ˈwɛltə/ *verb*[2] *intrans. obsolete* exc. *dial.* M17.
[Origin uncertain: cf. WELT *verb*[3], -ER[5].]
Wither.

welterweight /ˈwɛltəweɪt/ *noun & adjective*. E19.
[from WELTER *noun*[3] + WEIGHT *noun*.]
▶ **A** *noun*. **1** HORSE-RACING. †**a** Heavy weight of a rider. *rare.* Only in E19. ▸**b** A heavy rider. M19. ▸**c** An extra weight sometimes imposed in addition to that based on age. L19.
2 A weight at which boxing etc. matches are made, intermediate between lightweight and middleweight, in the amateur boxing now being between scale 63.5 and 67 kg, though differing for professionals, wrestlers, and weightlifters and according to time and place; a boxer etc. of this weight. L19.
Phrases: **junior welterweight** (of) a weight in professional boxing of between 61.2 and 63.5 kg; (designating) a boxer of this weight. **light welterweight** (of) a weight in amateur boxing of between 60 and 63.5 kg; (designating) a boxer of this weight.
▶ **B** *adjective*. (Of a boxer etc.) that is a welterweight; of or pertaining to welterweight. L19.

Weltliteratur /ˈvɛltlɪtera,tuːr/ *noun*. Also **-litt-**. E20.
[German, from *Welt* world + *Literatur* literature.]
A literature of all nations and peoples; universal literature.

Weltpolitik /ˈvɛltpoli,tiːk/ *noun*. E20.
[German, from *Welt* world + *Politik* politics.]
International politics; a particular country's policy towards the world at large.

Weltschmerz /ˈvɛltʃmɛrts/ *noun*. L19.
[German, from *Welt* world + *Schmerz* pain.]
A weary or pessimistic feeling about life; an apathetic or vaguely yearning attitude.

Weltstadt /ˈvɛltʃtat/ *noun*. Pl. ***-städte*** /-ʃtɛːtə/. L19.
[German, from *Welt* world + *Stadt* town.]
A city of international importance or cosmopolitan character; a cosmopolis.

welwitschia /wɛlˈwɪtʃɪə/ *noun*. M19.
[mod. Latin (see below), from Friedrich *Welwitsch* (1806–72), Austrian botanist + -IA[1].]
A gymnospermous plant, *Welwitschia mirabilis*, of desert regions in SW Africa, which has a dwarf, massive trunk, two very long strap-shaped leaves, and male and female flowers in the scales of scarlet cones.

wely /ˈwɛli/ *noun*. E19.
[Arab. *walī* friend (of God), saint.]
1 A Muslim saint. E19.
2 The tomb or shrine of a Muslim saint. M19.

wem /wɛm/ *noun*. *arch.* ME.
[Alt. of Old English *wam* under the infl. of WEM *verb*.]
1 Moral blemish, taint of sin, stigma. Chiefly in ***without wem***. ME.
2 Material blemish, defect, or stain. *obsolete* exc. *dial.* ME.
3 Bodily blemish, disfigurement, or defect; the mark of a bodily injury, a scar. ME.
■ **wemless** *adjective* (*obsolete* exc. *dial.*) ME.

†**wem** *verb trans.* Infl. **-mm-**.
[Old English *wemman*, from *wam(m)*, *wom(m)* scar. Cf. Old High German *biwemman*, *gi-*, Gothic *anawammjan* to blame.]
1 Disfigure, mutilate; impair, injure, harm. OE–LME.
2 Taint with sin, defile. ME–L15.
3 Stain, mark with spots. LME–M16.
¶ Survived in UNWEMMED.

Wemyss /wiːmz/ *noun*. E20.
[A town and parish in Fife, Scotland.]
In full ***Wemyss ware*** etc. A type of pottery produced at the Fife Pottery in Kirkcaldy and characteristically decorated with colourful underglaze illustrations of flowers, fruit, birds, etc.

wen /wɛn/ *noun*[1].
[Old English *wen(n)*, *wæn(n)* = Dutch *wen*, prob. rel. to Middle Low German *wene*, Low German *wehne* tumour, wart, of unkn. origin.]
1 A lump or protuberance on the body; *spec.* †(***a***) a wart; (***b***) MEDICINE a sebaceous cyst under the skin, esp. on the head; †(***c***) a swelling on the throat characteristic of goitre; †(***d***) an excrescence or tumour on the body of a horse; †(***e***) an excrescence on a tree. OE.
†**2** A spot, a blemish, a stain, (*lit.* & *fig.*). ME–L16.
3 *transf.* & *fig.* An unsightly or disfiguring addition etc.; *esp.* a large and congested city. L16.
3 the great wen London.
■ **wenny** *adjective* (now *rare* or *obsolete*) (***a***) of the nature of or similar to a wen; (***b***) afflicted with wens: L16.

wen *noun*[2] var. of WYNN.

wench /wɛn(t)ʃ/ *noun & verb*. ME.
[Abbreviation of WENCHEL.]
▶ **A** *noun*. **1** A girl, a young woman; a female child. Now *arch.* & *dial.* exc. *joc.* ME. ▸**b** A rustic or working-class girl. *arch.* L16.
2 A licentious woman; a prostitute; a mistress. *arch.* LME.
3 A female servant, a maidservant, a serving-maid. *arch.* LME. ▸**b** A black woman, esp. a servant. *US slang* (now *Hist.*). M18.

> 📖 **1** C. SEDLEY Yonder goes an odd Fellow with a very pretty Wench. T. C. WOLFE She was well built . . and was not a bad-looking wench.

▶ **B** *verb intrans.* Of a man: consort with licentious women or prostitutes; womanize. *arch.* L16.
■ **wencher** *noun* (*arch.*) L16. **wenchless** *adjective* (*rare*) E17. **wenchlike** *adjective* (*arch.*) girlish M16.

†**wenchel** *noun*. OE–ME.
[Perh. rel. to WANKLE.]
A child; a servant, a slave; a prostitute.
¶ The form from which *wench* is abbreviated.

Wend /wɛnd/ *noun*.
[Old English *Winedas*, *Weonod(land* = Old High German *Winida*, Old Norse *Vindr*, of unkn. origin. Readopted in 18 from German *Wende*, pl. *Wenden*.]
A member of a Slavonic people inhabiting Lusatia in eastern Germany. Also called ***Sorb***.

wend /wɛnd/ *verb*[1]. Now *arch.* & *literary.* Pa. t. & pple **wended**, †**went**.
[Old English *wendan* = Old Frisian *wenda*, Old Saxon *wendian*, Old High German *wentan* (Dutch, German *wenden*), Old Norse *venda*, Gothic *wandjan*, from Germanic base rel. to WIND *verb*[1].]
1 †**a** *verb trans.* Alter the position or direction of; turn (a thing) round or over. OE–L15. ▸†**b** *verb intrans.* ***wend again***, turn back, return. OE–LME. ▸†**c** *verb intrans.* NAUTICAL. Of a ship etc.: turn in the opposite direction. ME–E18. ▸**d** *verb trans.* NAUTICAL. Turn (a ship, a ship's bow) to the opposite direction. Now *dial.* M16.
†**2** **a** *verb trans.* Turn (one's thoughts etc.) in a new direction; change (one's mind); turn (a person) *to* or *from* a course of life or action. OE–LME. ▸**b** *verb intrans.* Of a person: turn in thought or purpose *to* or *from* a person, course of action, etc.; change one's mind or purpose. OE–M16.
†**3** *verb intrans.* & *trans.* Turn from one condition or form to another; change *to* or *into*, alter, transform. OE–L16.
†**4** *verb intrans.* Of an event etc. or with impers. subj.; take place, happen, come about. OE–LME.
5 *verb refl.* Turn, direct, or betake oneself. Freq. with adverbs & prepositions. Long *arch.* OE.
6 *verb intrans.* Go off, away, or out; depart. Freq. with adverbs & prepositions. OE. ▸†**b** Depart by death. Freq. in ***wend forth from life***, ***wend hence***, ***wend to heaven***, etc. OE–M16. ▸†**c** *transf.* & *fig.* Of a thing: pass away; disappear, decay. Also foll. by *away*. OE–M16.
7 *verb intrans.* & *trans.* (with adverbial obj.). Go forward, proceed; journey, travel; make *one's way*. OE. ▸**b** *transf.* & *fig.* Of a thing: move, flow, or run in a specified course or direction. Of a road: extend, stretch. ME.
†**8** *verb intrans.* Turn round, over, or from side to side; turn or twist the body. ME–M16.

> 📖 **6** SIR W. SCOTT Wend on your way, in the name of God and St. Dunstan. **7** M. TWAIN Certain witnesses did see them wending thither. *Los Angeles* We suggest . . slowly wending your way south by bus. **b** S. BARING-GOULD A river wending towards a portal of black rock.

Phrases: †**be went** be gone, departed, or past. ***wend again***: see sense 1b above.

†**wend** *verb*[2] *pa. t.* & *pple*: see WEEN.

Wendic /ˈwɛndɪk/ *adjective & noun*. Now *rare*. M19.
[from WEND *noun* + -IC.]
= WENDISH.

wendigo *noun* var. of WINDIGO.

Wendish /ˈwɛndɪʃ/ *adjective & noun*. E17.
[from WEND *noun* + -ISH[1].]
▶ **A** *adjective*. Of or pertaining to the Wends or their language. E17.
▶ **B** *noun*. The W. Slavonic language of the Wends, Sorbian. E17.

Wendy house /ˈwɛndi haʊs/ *noun phr*. Also **W-**. M20.
[from the small house built around *Wendy* in J. M. Barrie's play *Peter Pan*.]
A small structure or tent resembling a house, for children to play in.

wenge /ˈwɛŋgeɪ/ *noun*. M20.
[Name in the Democratic Republic of Congo (Zaire).]
The dark brown timber of *Millettia laurentii*, a leguminous tree of central Africa.

wen jen /ˈwɛn ʒɛn/ *noun phr. pl.* M20.
[Chinese *wénrén* man of letters, from *wén* writing + *rén* (Wade-Giles *jên*) man.]
Chinese men of letters.

wen li /ˈwɛn liː/ *noun phr*. L19.
[Chinese *wén lǐ* grammar, literary style, from *wén* writing + *lǐ* texture, reason.]
= WEN-YEN.

Wensleydale /ˈwɛnzlɪdeɪl/ *noun*. L19.
[A district of North Yorkshire, England.]
1 In full ***Wensleydale sheep***. A breed of long-woolled sheep originally raised in Wensleydale; a sheep of this breed. L19.
2 In full ***Wensleydale cheese***. A variety of blue or white cheese made chiefly in Wensleydale. L19.

went /wɛnt/ *noun*. *obsolete* exc. *dial.* ME.
[Rel. to WEND *verb*[1].]
1 A path, a way, a passage. ME. ▸†**b** A journey, a course of movement. LME–L16.
†**2** A plan; a trick. Only in ME.
†**3** A turn or course of affairs; an occasion, a chance. ME–L16.
†**4** A turn or change of direction; a turning about. LME–L15.

went *verb*[1] *pa. t.* & *pple*: see GO *verb*.

†**went** *verb*[2] *pa. t.* & *pple* of WEND *verb*[1].

wentletrap /ˈwɛnt(ə)ltrap/ *noun*. M18.
[Dutch *wenteltrap* winding staircase, spiral shell from earlier *wendeltrap*, from *wenden* wind, turn + *trap* stair.]
(A shell of) any of various marine gastropod molluscs of the family Epitoniidae, which have spiral conical shells and (usu.) ridged whorls. Cf. STAIRCASE *noun* 2.

wen-yen /ˈwɛnjɛn/ *noun*. Also **wenyen**, **-yan**. M20.
[Chinese *wényán*, from *wén* writing + *yán* speech, words.]
The traditional literary language or style of China, now superseded by pai-hua.

Wepsian *noun & adjective* see VEPSIAN.

wept *verb pa. t.* & *pple of* WEEP *verb*.

wer- *combining form* var. of WERE-.

Werdnig–Hoffmann /ˌvəːdnɪɡˈhɒfmən/ *noun*. **E20.**
[from Guido *Werdnig* (1844–1919), Austrian neurologist + Johann *Hoffmann* (1857–1919), German neurologist.]
MEDICINE. Used *attrib.* and in *possess.* to designate a fatal familial disease that is present at birth or develops soon afterwards and is characterized by muscular hypotonia, progressive atrophy, paralysis, and loss of sucking ability.

were /wɪə/ *noun*¹. **OE.**
[Abbreviation of WERGELD.]
Hist. = WERGELD.

were /ˈwɪə/ *noun*². Long *obsolete* exc. *Scot.* Also **weer**. **ME.**
[Origin uncertain: perh. var. of WAR *noun*¹.]
1 Danger, peril, jeopardy. Freq. in ***in were of***, ***in weers of***, in danger of. **ME.**
†**2** A condition of trouble or distress. **ME–E16.**
3 Apprehension, fear, dread. **ME.**
4 Perplexity; doubt, uncertainty; something giving cause for uncertainty, a matter of doubt. **ME.**

were /wɪə/ *verb*¹ & *noun*³. Long *obsolete* exc. *Scot.*
[Old English *werian*, *wergan* = Old Saxon *werian*, *werean*, Old Frisian *wera*, Middle & mod. Dutch *weren*, Old High German *warian*, *werian*, Old Norse *verja* (Icelandic *verja*, Norwegian *verge*, Swedish *värja*, Danish *værge*, *verge*), Gothic *warjan*, from Germanic.]
▶ **A** *verb trans.* **1** Check, restrain; ward off, repel. Also foll. by *away*, *off*. **OE.**
2 (Foll. by *against*, *from*, *of*, *with*.) Protect from assault or injury; defend, guard. **OE.** ▸**b** Keep or hold (esp. an entrance or exit). **ME.**
▶ **B** *noun*. †**1** A defender, a protector. *rare*. Only in **ME.**
2 Defence. *Scot. rare*. **M19.**

were *verb*² see BE.

were- /wɛː, wɪə, wəː/ *combining form*. Also **wer-** /wəː/. **L19.**
[from next.]
Used with names of animals to denote a human being imagined to be able to change at times into a specified animal, as ***were-bear***, ***were-leopard***, etc.
■ **were-jaguar** *noun* in Olmec mythology, a creature partly human and partly feline **M20.**

werewolf /ˈwɛːwʊlf, ˈwɪə-, ˈwəː-/ *noun*. Also **werwolf** /ˈwəːwʊlf/. Pl. **-wolves** /-wʊlvz/.
[Late Old English *werewulf* = Low German *werwulf*, Middle & mod. Dutch *weerwolf*, Middle High German *werwolf* (German *Werwolf*, *Wehr-*): 1st elem. perh. from Old English *wer* man (= Latin *vir*).]
1 A mythical being able to change at times from a person to a wolf. **LOE.**
2 A member of a right-wing paramilitary German underground resistance movement. **M20.**
¶ Rare between **E17** and **E19.**
■ **werewolfery** *noun* = LYCANTHROPY 2 **M19.** **werewolfish** *adjective* resembling or of the nature of a werewolf **L19.** **werewolfism** *noun* = LYCANTHROPY 2 **M19.**

werf /wɛrf/ *noun*. *S. Afr.* Also **werft**. **E19.**
[Dutch (now dial.) = Northern Frisian *werw*, *werrew*, Middle Low German *warf*: see WHARF *noun*.]
A homestead; the space surrounding a farm.

wergeld /ˈwəːɡɛld/ *noun*. Also **-gild** /-ɡɪld/.
[Old English *wergeld*, (West Saxon) *-gild*, Anglo-Latin *weregildum*, from *wer* man + *gield* YIELD *noun*.]
Hist. In Germanic and Anglo-Saxon law, the price put on a man according to his rank, payable as a fine or compensation by a person guilty of homicide or certain other crimes.

†**werkeday** *noun* & *adjective* see WORKADAY.

Wernerian /wəˈnɪərɪən/ *adjective* & *noun*. Also **w-**. **E19.**
[from Abraham Gottlob *Werner* (1750–1817), German mineralogist and geologist + -IAN.]
GEOLOGY. ▶**A** *adjective*. = NEPTUNIAN *adjective* 2b. **E19.**
▶ **B** *noun*. = NEPTUNIST 2. **E19.**
■ **Wernerianism** *noun* = NEPTUNISM **L19.**

wernerite /ˈwəːnərʌɪt/ *noun*. **E19.**
[formed as prec. + -ITE¹.]
MINERALOGY. = SCAPOLITE.

Werner's syndrome /ˈwəːnəz ˌsɪndrəʊm, ˈvɛː-/ *noun phr.* **M20.**
[Carl Otto *Werner* (1879–1936), German physician + SYNDROME.]
MEDICINE. A rare hereditary syndrome whose symptoms include short stature, endocrine and vascular disorders, and premature ageing and death.

Wernicke /ˈwəːnɪkə, ˈvɛː-/ *noun*. **L19.**
[Karl *Wernicke* (1848–1905), German neuropsychiatrist.]
MEDICINE. Used in *possess.* to designate things studied by Wernicke.
Wernicke's aphasia a neurological disorder in which there is an inability to understand speech and (usu.) to speak intelligibly, caused by a lesion of Wernicke's area. **Wernicke's area** an area of the cerebral cortex comprising part of the dominant temporal lobes. **Wernicke's disease**, **Wernicke's encephalopathy**, **Wernicke's syndrome** an encephalopathy caused by vitamin B_1 deficiency and characterized by severe amnesia, confabulation, and disordered eye movements.
Comb.: **Wernicke–Korsakoff disease**, **Wernicke–Korsakoff syndrome** the presence of both Wernicke's disease and Korsakoff's syndrome in an individual.

werowance /ˈwɛrəʊwɑːns, -ans/ *noun*. **L16.**
[Delaware *wirowántësu* he is rich from *wiro* be rich.]
Hist. A N. American Indian chief in Virginia and Maryland.

wersh /wəːʃ/ *adjective*. *Scot. & north.* **L15.**
[Prob. contr. of WEARISH.]
1 = WEARISH 2. **L15.**
2 = WEARISH 1. Freq. *fig.* **L16.**
3 Of weather or wind: unrefreshing; raw. **M19.**
■ **wershly** *adverb* **M17.**

Werterean, **Werterian** *adjectives* vars. of WERTHERIAN.

Werterism *noun* var. of WERTHERISM.

wertfrei /ˈveːrtfraɪ/ *adjective*. **E20.**
[German, from *Wert* WORTH *noun*¹ + *frei* FREE *adjective*.]
Free of value judgements; morally neutral.
■ ***Wertfreiheit*** /ˈveːrtfraɪhaɪt/ *noun* [-*heit* -HOOD] the quality of being *wertfrei* **M20.**

Wertherian /vəːˈtɪərɪən/ *adjective*. Also **-terian**, **-ean**. **M19.**
[from German *Werther* the hero of Goethe's romance *Die Leiden des jungen Werther* + -IAN, -EAN.]
Morbidly sentimental.

Wertherism /ˈvəːtərɪz(ə)m/ *noun*. Also **-terism**. **M19.**
[formed as prec. + -ISM.]
Morbid sentimentality.

werwolf *noun* var. of WEREWOLF.

Wesak *noun* var. of VESAK.

Wesen /ˈveːzən/ *noun*. *rare*. **M19.**
[German.]
A person's nature as shown in characteristic behaviour; the distinctive nature or essence of a thing.

Wesleyan /ˈwɛslɪən, ˈwɛzlɪən, wɛzˈliːən/ *adjective* & *noun*. **L18.**
[from *Wesley* (see below) + -AN.]
▶ **A** *adjective*. Of or pertaining to the English evangelist John Wesley (1703–91) or his teaching; of or pertaining to the Protestant denomination founded by Wesley; Methodist. Also ***Wesleyan Methodist***. **L18.**
▶ **B** *noun*. A follower of John Wesley; a member of the Wesleyan denomination; a Methodist. Also ***Wesleyan Methodist***. **L18.**
■ **Wesleyanism** *noun* the system of theology introduced and taught by John Wesley; the doctrine and practice of the Wesleyans: **L18.** **Wesleyanized** *adjective* affected by Wesleyanism **M19.** **Wesleyism** *noun* (*rare*) = WESLEYANISM **M19.**

wessel /ˈwɛs(ə)l/ *adverb*. *Scot.* **E19.**
[Obscurely from WEST *adverb*.]
Westward, westerly.

Wessex /ˈwɛsɪks/ *noun*. **L19.**
[An Anglo-Saxon kingdom (see WEST SAXON), the name being revived by Thomas Hardy to designate the counties of SW England (esp. Dorset) in which his novels are set.]
Used *attrib.* to designate things originating in or associated with Wessex.
Wessex culture ARCHAEOLOGY an early Bronze Age culture in southern England represented by a characteristic range of grave-goods. **Wessex saddleback** (an animal of) a former breed of saddleback pig.

Wessi /ˈwɛsɪ, v-/ *noun*. *colloq.* (freq. *derog.*). Pl. **-is**, **-ies**. **L20.**
[German, prob. abbreviation of *Westdeutsche* West German.]
A term used in Germany to denote someone who was a citizen of the Federal Republic of Germany before reunification; a West German. Cf. OSSI.

west /wɛst/ *noun*¹. *obsolete* exc. *dial.* **M16.**
[Origin unkn.]
A sty or inflammatory swelling on the eyelid.

west /wɛst/ *adverb*, *noun*², *adjective*, & *verb*.
[Old English *west* corresp. to Old Frisian, Old Saxon, Old High German, (Dutch, German) *west*, Old Norse *vestr*, from Germanic, from Indo-European base repr. also by Greek *hesperos*, Latin *vesper* evening.]
▶ **A** *adverb*. **1** In the direction of that part of the horizon where the sun sets; towards the cardinal point which is 90 degrees clockwise from the south point. **OE.** ▸**b** Foll. by *of*: further in this direction than. Also (*Scot.*) without *of*. **L16.** ▸**c** In or to the States of the western US. *US.* **L19.**

> 🕮 **1** *Guardian* The wealth . . flows west to the richest regions of the Soviet Union. SARA MAITLAND Further west she saw her own street from above. **b** *Bon Appetit* Grand Teton National Park . . lies just west of the Continental Divide.

▶ **B** *noun*. In senses 1–4 usu. with *the*.
1 (The direction of) that part of the horizon or the sky where the sun sets; *spec.* the cardinal point which is 90 degrees clockwise from the south point. **ME.**
2 (Freq. **W-**.) The western part of the world, relative to another part, or of a (specified) country, region, town, etc.; *spec.* (*a*) Europe and N. America as distinguished from Asia, China, etc.; the culture and civilization of these regions as opp. to that of the Orient; (*b*) the non-Communist States of Europe and N. America (now *Hist.*); non-Communist States or regions in general; (*c*) *Hist.* = ***Western Empire*** s.v. WESTERN; (*d*) the western part of England, Great Britain, Scotland, or Ireland; (*e*) the States of the western US, now usu. those west of the River Mississippi; (*f*) Western Australia. Also (*transf.*), the inhabitants of such a part of the world, such a region, country, etc. **ME.**
3 ECCLESIASTICAL HISTORY. The Catholic Church in the Western Roman Empire and countries adjacent to it; the Latin Church. **L16.**
4 The west wind. Chiefly *poet.* **E17.**
5 (**W-**.) In bridge, (formerly) whist, or other four-handed partnership game: the player who occupies the position so designated, and who sits opposite 'East'. In mah-jong, = ***west wind*** (a) below. **E20.**

> 🕮 **1** G. LIDDY The wind was reported to be from the west. W. BRONK Venus, tonight, was beautiful in the west. **2** J. L. ESPOSITO Neotraditionalism . . seeks to emphasize those areas that distinguish Islam from the West. **4** A. C. SWINBURNE As roses, when the warm West blows, Break to full flower.

▶ **C** *adjective*. **1** Situated in or lying towards the west or western part of something; on the westerly side. **ME.** ▸**b** *spec.* Designating or situated in the end of a Christian church which is furthest from the (high) altar, traditionally but not necessarily the geographical west. **LME.** ▸**c** Facing west. **L16.**
2 (Also **W-**.) Designating (a person or the people of) the western part of a country, region, city, etc. **L15.** ▸**b** Of western as opp. to eastern Europe; *esp.* belonging to the Latin Church. Now *rare* or *obsolete*. **M16.**
3 Of or pertaining to the west; (of a wind) coming from the west. **L16.**

> 🕮 **1** J. COX The road that hugs the west bank of the Delaware River. **b** J. BARNES The medieval frieze on the west end of the church. **c** D. ROBERTS The hopvines on the west window. **2** ***West Africa***, ***West London***, ***West Midlands***, ***West Sussex***, etc.; ***West African***, ***West European***, etc.

▶ **D** *verb intrans.* Move towards the west; *esp.* (of the sun) draw near to or set in the west. *rare* (chiefly *literary*). **LME.**

> 🕮 C. M. DOUGHTY The sun at length westing to the valley brow.

Phrases: ***Far West***: see FAR *adjective*. **go west** (*a*) (of the sun) set; (*b*) *fig.* die, disappear; (*c*) *colloq.* be killed, destroyed, or lost. ***Middle West***: see MIDDLE *adjective*. **to the west (of)** in a westerly direction from. WILD WEST.
Special collocations & comb.: **westabout** *adverb* (NAUTICAL) by a westerly route; westwards. **West African** *noun* & *adjective* (a native or inhabitant of) western Africa. ***West African nutmeg***: see NUTMEG *noun* 1. ***West African teak***: see TEAK *noun* 2. **West Bank** *the* region west of the River Jordan and north-west of the Dead Sea assigned to Jordan in 1948 and occupied by Israel since 1967. **West Banker** an inhabitant of the West Bank. **westbound** *adjective* & *noun* (*a*) *adjective* travelling or heading westward; (*b*) *noun* (chiefly *N. Amer.*) a westbound train. **West Briton** †(*a*) a native or inhabitant of Wales; (*b*) a native or inhabitant of Ireland, now (chiefly *derog.*) one who favours a close political connection with Great Britain. **west-by-north**, **west-by-south** (in the direction of) the compass point 11¼ degrees or one point north, south, of the west point. **west country** the western part of any country; *spec.* the south-western counties of England (Somerset, Devon, Cornwall, etc.). **west end** the western end of something; *spec.* (*a*) (**W-E-**) the district of London lying between Charing Cross Road and Park Lane, a fashionable shopping and entertainment area; the inhabitants of this area; the theatres of this area or their personnel; (*b*) *transf.* the fashionable or aristocratic quarter of any other town or place. **West-ender** a person who lives at the west end of a town etc. esp. London. ***West* GERMANIC**. **West Indies** †(*a*) the parts of America first discovered by Columbus and other early navigators, and believed by them to be the coast of Asia; (*b*) the chain of islands extending from the coast of Florida in N. America to that of Venezuela in S. America. **west-north-west** (in the direction) midway between west and north-west. **West-of-England** *adjective* designating a type of high-quality woollen broadcloth from the west of England. **west side** (*a*) the side situated in or lying towards the west; (*b*) *spec.* (**W- S-**) *US* the western part of Manhattan. **West Sider** *US* a native or inhabitant of Manhattan's West Side. **west-south-west** (in the direction) midway between west and south-west. **west wind** (*a*) (usu. with cap. initials) one of the four players in mah-jong; (*b*) each of the four tiles so designated in mah-jong; (see also sense C.3 above).
■ **westmost** *adjective* (now *rare* exc. *Scot.*) most westerly; westernmost: **OE.**

west coast /wɛst ˈkəʊst/ *noun* & *adjectival phr.* **LME.**
[from WEST *adjective* + COAST *noun*.]
▶ **A** *noun phr.* The western coast of a country or region. **LME.**
▶ **B** *adjectival phr.* **1** Designating or pertaining to the western coast of a country. **M19.**
2 *spec.* (Usu. with cap. initials.) ▸**a** Designating or pertaining to the western coast of the US, esp. California (freq. with allus. to the relaxed and informal lifestyle and attitudes of its inhabitants). Orig. *US.* **M20.** ▸**b** Of or pertaining to a style of modern jazz centred on Los Angeles in the 1950s, typified by small ensembles, technical sophistication, and elaborate writing. **M20.**
3 Designating a kind of large rear-view mirror for lorries etc. Orig. *US.* **M20.**

■ **West Coaster** *noun* (*a*) a native or inhabitant of the west coast of a country; (*b*) a player or devotee of West Coast jazz: L19.

wester /ˈwɛstə/ *noun. colloq.* E20.
[from WEST *noun*² + -ER¹.]
A (strong) wind blowing from the west.

wester /ˈwɛstə/ *adjective. obsolete* exc. *Scot. & dial.*
[Old English *westra* (from *west* WEST *adverb*), corresp. to Old Norse *vestari*, Icelandic *vestri* (Norwegian, Danish *vestre*, Swedish *väster*).]
Lying towards or nearest the west; western.

wester /ˈwɛstə/ *verb intrans.* LME.
[from WEST *adverb* + -ER⁵.]
1 Of the sun, moon, etc.: travel westward; draw near the west. Chiefly *poet.* or *literary.* LME.
2 Of the wind: shift or veer westward. L16.
■ **westering** *adjective* (chiefly *poet.*) (*a*) (esp. of the sun) nearing the western horizon; (*b*) moving in a westward direction; (of the wind) shifting or veering to the west: M17.

westerling /ˈwɛstəlɪŋ/ *noun.* Now *rare.* M17.
[from WESTER *adjective* + -LING¹.]
A native or inhabitant of a western country or district.

westerly /ˈwɛstəli/ *adverb, adjective, & noun.* L15.
[from WESTER *adjective* + -LY², -LY¹.]
▸ **A** *adverb.* **1** In a westward position or direction; towards the west. L15.
2 Esp. of a wind: (nearly) from the west. E18.

> **1** W. IRVING Our plan was . . to keep westerly, until we should pass through . . the Cross Timber.

▸ **B** *adjective.* **1** Esp. of a wind: coming (nearly) from the west. L16.
2 Situated towards or facing the west; directed towards the west. L16.

> **2** *Guardian* My rides have circled the whole westerly arc of the Alps.

▸ **C** *noun.* A westerly wind. Usu. in *pl.* L19.
■ **westerliness** *noun* (*rare*) M18.

†**westermost** *adjective.* LME–E19.
[from WESTER *adjective* + -MOST.]
= WESTERNMOST.

western /ˈwɛst(ə)n/ *adjective, noun, verb, & adverb.*
[Old English *westerne*, from WEST *adverb*, corresp. to Old Saxon, Old High German *westrōni*, from Germanic base of WEST *adverb, noun*², *adjective, & verb.*]
▸ **A** *adjective.* **1** Coming from the west; *esp.* (of a wind) blowing from the west. OE.
2 Living in or originating from the west, esp. of England or Europe; *spec.* living or originating in the English West Country. OE. ▸**b** Belonging to the English West Country. M16.
3 Situated in the west; directed, facing, or lying towards the west; having a position relatively west. LME.
4 Of, pertaining to, or characteristic of the west or its inhabitants; found or occurring in the west. L16.
5 *spec.* Of, pertaining to, or in the West (WEST *noun*² 2, 3); now *esp.* (*a*) *Hist.* of or pertaining to the alliance of states which fought against Germany and her allies in the wars of 1914–18 and 1939–45; (*b*) *Hist.* of or pertaining to the non-Communist States of Europe and N. America; (*c*) of or pertaining to (any of) the States of the western US. E17. ▸**b** Of or pertaining to a film or novel belonging to the genre of the western. Orig. *US.* E20.
6 *fig.* Of a person's life or days: declining. *rare.* E17.

> **3** J. CONRAD He . . fixed his clear eyes . . on the western sky. J. STEINBECK The sun was setting toward the western mountains. **4** E. K. KANE He himself would take the western search. **5** J. SILK Not until the thirteenth century did . . Aristotle . . become read in the Western world. *World Monitor* Exposed for selling Western top-secret technology to the Russians. ***Far Western***: see FAR *adjective.* ***Middle Western***: see MIDDLE *adjective.*

Special collocations: **Western** ABNAKI. **Western American** = ***General American*** s.v. AMERICAN *noun* 4. **Western Approaches** the area of sea immediately to the west of Great Britain. †**Western barge**, †**Western boat**, etc., a barge or other boat used on the River Thames westward of London. **Western blot**, **Western blotting** [after SOUTHERN BLOT] *BIOCHEMISTRY* an adaptation of the Southern blot procedure, used to identify specific peptide and amino-acid sequences. ***Western boat***: see ***Western barge*** above. **Western Church** the Latin Church as distinguished from the Orthodox or Eastern Church. **Western Empire** the more westerly of the two parts into which the Roman Empire was divided in AD 395. **western equine encephalitis**, **western equine encephalomyelitis** a mosquito-borne viral encephalitis that affects chiefly horses but also humans and is sometimes fatal, esp. to children. **Western European Union** an association formed in 1955 from the former Western Union (see below), with the addition of Italy and West Germany, chiefly in order to coordinate defence and promote economic cooperation. **Western Front** the front in Belgium and northern France in the wars of 1914–18 and 1939–45. ***Western hemisphere***: see HEMISPHERE *noun* 1b. ***western hemlock***: see HEMLOCK *noun* 2. **Western Isles** (*a*) the Hebrides; (*b*) the Azores. **western man** humankind as shaped by the culture and civilization of western Europe and N. America. **Western Ocean** the Atlantic. ***Western pug***: see PUG *noun*² 2a. ***western red cedar***: see ***red cedar*** (b) s.v. RED *adjective.* **western roll** a method of highjumping in which the athlete jumps from the inside foot, swings up the other leg, and rolls over the bar on his or her side. **Western saddle**: with a deep seat, high pommel and cantle, and long broad stirrups. **western sandwich** *N. Amer.*: in which the filling is an omelette containing onion and ham. **western swing** a style of country music influenced by jazz, popular in the 1930s. **Western Union** *Hist.* an association of West European nations (Belgium, France, Luxembourg, the Netherlands, and the UK) formed in 1948 with similar aims to, and later superseded by, the Western European Union. **western white pine** (the whitish timber of) a pine of western N. America, *Pinus monticola*. **western yellow pine** the ponderosa pine, *Pinus ponderosa*.
▸ **B** *noun.* **1** A native or inhabitant of the west; a westerner. E17. ▸**b** *spec.* A native or inhabitant of the States of the western US. *US.* M19.
2 A member of the Western Church. M19.
3 A film or novel belonging to a genre depicting life in the American West in the 19th and early 20th cents., usu. featuring cowboys in heroic rules, gunfights, etc. Orig. *US.* E20.

> **3** R. BANKS Cast as the decent . . leader of the sheepherders in . . westerns of the '50s.

▸ **C** *verb intrans.* Of the sun: begin to set. *rare* (chiefly *literary*). M19.
▸ **D** *adverb.* *HORSEMANSHIP.* In the manner of a cowboy; in a relaxed style with a deep-seated saddle and almost straight legs (cf. ***Western saddle*** above). L20.
■ **westerner** *noun* (freq. **W-**) (*a*) a native or inhabitant of the western part of any country, esp. the US; a person belonging to the West as opp. to the East or a Communist State (*Hist.*); (*b*) *Hist.* an advocate of or believer in the concentration of forces on the Western Front during the war of 1914–18 (cf. EASTERNER (b)): L16. **westernism** *noun* (*a*) an idiom or expression peculiar to the States of the western US; (*b*) western quality; western characteristics etc., as distinguished from those of the East: M19. **westernly** *adjective & adverb* (*a*) *adjective* (now *rare*) = WESTERLY *adjective*; (*b*) *adverb* in a Western manner; (*rare*) westerly: L16. **westernmost** *adjective* situated further to the west; most westerly: E18. **westernness** /-n-n-/ *noun* M20.

westernize /ˈwɛstənʌɪz/ *verb.* Also **-ise**. M19.
[from prec. + -IZE.]
1 *verb trans.* Make western in character, quality, etc.; *esp.* influence with or convert to the ideas and customs of the West. M19.
2 *verb intrans.* Become western in character. *rare.* E20.

> **1** *Newsweek* Washington's efforts to bring China . . to a more Westernized view of the world.

■ **westerniˈzation** *noun* E20. **westernizer** *noun* M20.

West Highland /wɛst ˈhʌɪlənd/ *adjectival & noun phr.* M18.
[from WEST *adjective* + HIGHLAND.]
▸ **A** *adjective.* Of or pertaining to the western part of the Highlands of Scotland. M18.
West Highland cattle = ***Highland cattle*** s.v. HIGHLAND. **West Highland terrier** (an animal of) a small short-legged breed of terrier with a white coat and erect ears and tail, developed in the West Highlands (also called ***Poltalloch terrier, westie***).
▸ **B** *noun.* **1** In *pl.* The western part of the Highlands of Scotland. M19.
2 = ***West Highland terrier*** above. M20.
■ **West Highlander** *noun* (an animal of) the breed of Highland cattle M19.

westie /ˈwɛsti/ *noun.* Also **-ty**. M20.
[from WEST *adjective* + -IE.]
A West Highland terrier.

West India /wɛst ˈɪndɪə/ *noun & adjectival phr.* Now *rare.* M16.
[from WEST *adjective* + INDIA.]
▸†**A** *noun phr.* = ***West Indies*** s.v. WEST *adjective.* M16–M17.
▸ **B** *adjectival phr.* Of or pertaining to the West Indies. M17.
Comb.: **West-Indiaman** a vessel engaged in the West India trade.

West Indian /wɛst ˈɪndɪən/ *noun & adjectival phr.* L16.
[formed as prec. + -AN.]
▸ **A** *noun phr.* †**1** An original inhabitant of the West Indies. Usu. in *pl.* L16–M17.
2 A native or inhabitant of any island of the West Indies, of European or African origin or descent. M17.
3 A person of West Indian descent. E20.
▸ **B** *adjectival phr.* Of or pertaining to the West Indies. E17.

West Indy /wɛst ˈɪndi/ *noun & adjectival phr.* Long *obsolete* exc. *colloq. & dial.* Also **West Indie**. E17.
[from WEST INDIA: cf. INDIES.]
(Of or pertaining to) the West Indies.

westing /ˈwɛstɪŋ/ *noun.* E17.
[from WEST *adverb* or *verb* + -ING¹.]
1 Chiefly *NAUTICAL.* Distance travelled or measured westward. E17. ▸**b** *CARTOGRAPHY.* Distance westward from a point of origin; a unit of measurement used to calculate this (usu. in *pl.*). Also, a line of longitude west of a given meridian. M18.
2 The fact of a wind's blowing from or shifting to the west. M19.

Westinghouse /ˈwɛstɪŋhaʊs/ *noun.* L19.
[George *Westinghouse* (1846–1914), US inventor and manufacturer.]
In full ***Westinghouse brake***. A brake of a kind used on railway trains, operated by compressed air on a fail-safe principle.

westland /ˈwɛs(t)lənd/ *adjective & noun.* Chiefly *Scot.* LME.
[from WEST *adjective* + LAND *noun*¹.]
▸ **A** *adjective.* **1** Of, pertaining to, or inhabiting the western part of a country, esp. the west of Scotland. LME.
2 Of a place: situated in the west, western. E16. ▸**b** Westerly. *rare.* M17.
▸ **B** *noun.* The western part of a country, esp. Scotland. L15.
■ **westlander** *noun* L17.

westlin /ˈwɛs(t)lɪn/ *adjective. Scot.* E18.
[Alt. of prec.]
Western; westerly.

West Lothian /wɛst ˈləʊðɪən/ *noun.* L20.
[The name of a former parliamentary constituency in Central Scotland, whose MP, Tam Dalyell, persistently raised the issue in debates on Scottish and Welsh devolution during 1977–78.]
West Lothian question, the UK constitutional anomaly that, following devolution, Westminster MPs for Scottish and Welsh constituencies are unable to vote on Scottish or Welsh matters that have been devolved to the assemblies of those countries, but are able to vote on equivalent matters concerning England, whilst MPs for English constituencies have no reciprocal influence on Scottish or Welsh matters.

Westmark /ˈwɛs(t)mɑːk/ *noun.* M20.
[German, from *West* west + *Mark* MARK *noun*².]
Hist. The basic monetary unit of the Federal Republic of Germany, as distinguished from the Ostmark of the German Democratic Republic. Cf. DEUTSCHMARK.

Westminster /ˈwɛs(t)mɪnstə/ *noun.* M16.
[*Westminster* Abbey (see below) or the City of *Westminster*, an inner London borough: from WEST *adjective* + MINSTER.]
1 Used *attrib.* to designate people or things associated with Westminster Abbey, the collegiate church of St Peter in inner London, esp. with ref. to the Hall used as a court of justice, to the assembly of divines held in 1643, or to St Peter's College. M16. ▸**b** *ellipt.* A present or former pupil of St Peter's College. L17.
2 The Palace of Westminster, a former royal residence where Parliament sat until the destruction of the buildings by fire in 1834, the present Houses of Parliament later built on the same site; *allus.* parliamentary life; parliament; politics. E19.
2 Westminster chimes, **Westminster quarters** the pattern of chimes struck at successive quarters by Big Ben in the Houses of Parliament, used for other clocks and door chimes; the chime uses four bells struck in five different four-note sequences, each of which occurs twice in the course of an hour.

West Nile /wɛs(t) ˈnʌɪl/ *noun phr.* M20.
[from WEST *adjective* + NILE.]
MEDICINE. Used *attrib.* to designate a mosquito-borne virus and the disease it causes, usu. a mild fever but sometimes a fatal encephalitis.

Weston /ˈwɛst(ə)n/ *noun.* E20.
[Edward *Weston* (1850–1936), English-born electrical engineer.]
1 ***Weston cell***, a primary cell with electrodes of mercury and of cadmium amalgam and electrolyte of cadmium sulphate, used as a standard voltage source for calibrating electrical instruments. E20.
2 ***Weston number***, ***Weston speed***, a photographic film speed using a former system based on exposure meters made by Weston's company. M20.

Westphalia /wɛs(t)ˈfeɪlɪə/ *noun.* M17.
[medieval Latin, from Old High German *Westfalo* an inhabitant of the district of *Westfalen* in Germany (see below).]
Used *attrib.* to designate various products associated with Westphalia (*Westfalen*), a former Prussian province of NW Germany, now part of the State of North Rhine-Westphalia.
Westphalia bacon, ***Westphalia ham***, etc.
■ **Westphalian** *adjective* of or pertaining to Westphalia E17.

West-Pointer /wɛs(t)ˈpɔɪntə/ *noun. US.* M19.
[from *West Point* a village on the west bank of the Hudson River in New York State + -ER¹.]
An officer trained at the US military academy at West Point.

Westpolitik /ˈvɛstpɒlɪˌtiːk/ *noun.* L20.
[German, from *West* west + *Politik* policy: cf. OSTPOLITIK.]
Hist. In European politics, a policy of establishing or developing diplomatic and trading relations with Western nations, esp. formerly on the part of Communist States.

Westralian /wɛˈstreɪlɪən/ *adjective & noun.* L19.
[from *Westralia* contr. of *Western Australia* + -AN.]
▸ **A** *adjective.* Of or pertaining to the State of Western Australia. L19.

▶**B** *noun.* A native or inhabitant of Western Australia; in *pl.* Western Australian mining shares. L19.

West Saxon /wɛs(t) 'saks(ə)n/ *noun & adjectival phr.* OE.
[from WEST *adjective* + SAXON. Cf. WESSEX.]
Hist. ▶**A** *noun.* **1** A native or inhabitant of the powerful Anglo-Saxon kingdom of Wessex, established in the 6th cent. and ultimately including much of southern England. OE.
2 The dialect of Old English used by the West Saxons. M19.
▶**B** *adjective.* Of, pertaining to, or characteristic of the West Saxons or their dialect. L16.

westward /'wɛstwəd/ *adverb, noun, & adjective.* OE.
[from WEST *adverb* + -WARD.]
▶**A** *adverb.* Towards the west (*of*); in a westerly direction. OE.

Nation He was consumed by the idea of sailing westward across the ocean.

▶**B** *noun.* The direction or area lying to the west, or the west *of* a place etc. L16.

J. FORREST The tracks of horses coming from the westward.

▶**C** *adjective.* Situated or directed towards the west; moving or facing towards the west. L18.
westward position a west-facing position of the celebrant standing behind the altar facing the congregation at the Eucharist.
■ **westwardly** *adverb & adjective* (*a*) *adverb* in or from a westerly direction; (*b*) *adjective* (of a wind) blowing (nearly) from the west; moving, lying, or facing towards the west: E16. **westwardmost** *adjective* (*rare*) westernmost L17. **westwards** *adverb* & (now *rare*) *noun* = WESTWARD *adverb & noun* M16.

westy *noun* var. of WESTIE.

westy /'wɛsti/ *adjective. obsolete* exc. *dial.* L16.
[Origin unkn.]
Confused; giddy.

wet /wɛt/ *noun.*
[Old English *wǣt*, *wǣta*, formed as WET *adjective*. In branch II from WET *verb*.]
▶**I 1** Moisture; liquid or moist substance. OE.
2 Alcohol, drink. Now chiefly in ***heavy wet*** (slang), malt liquor. OE.
3 a Rainy or damp weather. ME. ▸**b** Atmospheric moisture deposited as precipitation. ME. ▸**c** Dampness; moisture or rain regarded as detrimental. LME. ▸**d** A downpour, shower, or spell of rain. Now *rare.* LME. ▸**e** *The* wet season. *colloq.* (chiefly *Austral.*). L19.
4 A person who supports the unrestricted sale and consumption of alcohol; an anti-prohibitionist. *colloq.* L19.
5 A feeble or inept person. Also (*derog.*), a politician with liberal tendencies, esp. as regarded by the right-wing members of his or her party. *colloq.* M20.
6 = ***wetback*** s.v. WET *adjective. US slang.* L20.
7 A wet-weather tyre. *slang.* L20.

1 M. PEMBERTON The floor . . was covered with wet and slime. **3a** Z. N. HURSTON A . . rattlesnake had come in out of the wet. **b** W. BLACK The . . thin wet that seemed to hang in the atmosphere like a vapour. **c** T. HARDY The gable-end of the cottage was stained with wet. †**take wet** be harmed by damp. **5** W. PERRIAM He didn't *want* a party . . party-games were just for . . wets.

▶**II 8** An alcoholic drink; a glass of liquor. *colloq.* E18.
9 An act of urinating; urine. *slang.* E20.

8 J. LE CARRÉ Enjoying what he and Meg called a small wet.

wet /wɛt/ *adjective.* Compar. & superl. **-tt-**.
[Old English *wǣt*, *wēt* corresp. to Old Frisian *wēt*, Old Norse *vátr*, ult. rel. to WATER *noun*; superseded in Middle English by *wet* pa. pple of WET *verb*.]
1 Dampened or moistened with water or other liquid; sprinkled, covered, dipped in, or soaked with water or other liquid (freq. foll. by *with*). Also (of a young child etc.), incontinent of urine. OE. ▸**b** Suffused with tears; moist from weeping. Freq. foll. by *with*. ME. ▸**c** Designating a removable liner or sleeve for the cylinder of an internal-combustion engine that has cooling water flowing between the liner and the cylinder wall. M20. ▸**d** Of the activities of an intelligence organization, esp. the KGB: involving bloodshed, esp. assassination. *slang.* L20.
2 Of the weather, a place, etc.: rainy. OE. ▸**b** Of the air, wind, etc.: moisture-laden. *rare.* LME.
3 Consisting of moisture, watery, liquid. Chiefly *literary.* OE.
4 Of land or soil: holding water, waterlogged, heavy. OE.
5 Of timber: full of sap, unseasoned. LME.
6 Of paint, varnish, or ink: tacky, sticky, liable to smudge. E16.
7 MEDICINE. **a** Designating certain diseases which are characterized by moist secretions. *rare.* M16. ▸**b** Designating various items used in hydropathic treatment. M19.
8 Of a defensive ditch: containing water. L16.
9 Of fish: cured with salt or brine. Also, fresh, not dried. L16.
10 Of measure: used for liquids. Long *rare.* L16.
11 Of or pertaining to alcohol, esp. as drunk in substantial quantities; addicted to drink; tipsy, drunk. *colloq.* L16. ▸**b** Consisting of alcoholic drink, or concerned with its sale and consumption; *spec.* (of a country, legislation, etc.) permitting the unrestricted sale of alcohol; (of a person) favouring the unrestricted sale of alcohol, anti-prohibitionist. L18.
12 a Of a confection: preserved in syrup; of a syrupy nature. Now *rare* or *obsolete.* E17. ▸**b** Of surgical or natural history specimens: kept in alcohol or other liquid preservative. M19.
13 a Of a Quaker: not rigidly adhering to the observances of his or her sect. *colloq.* E18. ▸**b** Inept, ineffectual, feeble. Also, *derog.* (of a politician), having liberal tendencies, esp. Conservative with anti-monetarist or liberal tendencies. *colloq.* E20.
14 Designating technical processes, chemical tests, etc., involving the use of water, solvents, or other liquids. E19.
15 NAUTICAL. Of a vessel: liable to ship water over the bows or gunwale. M19.
16 Of natural gas: containing significant amounts of the vapour of higher hydrocarbons. E20.

1 J. CALDER She messed about on the river . . and wasn't afraid to get wet. V. GLENDINNING She sprawled on . . the wet pavement. C. BRAYFIELD His . . shirt, wet with spray, flapped damply in the wind. **b** C. COOKSON Agnes' face too was wet with her laughter. She dried her eyes. **2** *Guardian* We were 2,000 feet up in one of the wettest corners of France. **3** R. KIPLING The little cargo-boats, that sail the wet seas roun'. **13b** M. GEE Hugo, don't be so *wet* I'm not the marrying kind. *Marxism Today* There is nothing wet about Heseltine. What he represents is not caring capitalism.

Phrases: **all wet** (orig. & chiefly *N. Amer.*) mistaken, completely wrong. **come with a wet sail** make swift progress to victory, like a ship with sails wetted in order to keep close to the wind. ***dripping wet***: see DRIP *verb* 2. **get a person wet** *NZ slang* gain the upper hand over a person; have a person at one's mercy. **get wet** *Austral. slang* lose one's temper, become angry. ***soaking wet***: see SOAKING *adverb*. ***sopping wet***: see SOPPING *adverb*. ***wet behind the ears***: see EAR *noun*[1]. **wet from the press** *arch.* (of a newspaper etc.) just printed or published. **wet through**, **wet to the skin** with one's clothes soaked. **with a wet finger** *arch.* easily, with little effort.

Special collocations & comb.: **wet-and-dry bulb** *adjective* designating an instrument comprising two thermometers, used as a psychrometer. **wetback** *colloq.* (orig. & chiefly *US*) an illegal immigrant, orig. one who entered the US by swimming the Rio Grande from Mexico. **wet bar** *N. Amer.* a bar or counter in the home for serving alcoholic drinks. **wet bargain** *arch.*: closed with a drink. **wet blanket** a person who throws a damper over anything; a gloomy person who stifles others' enjoyment. **wet-blanket** *verb trans.* throw a damper over; discourage, depress. ***wet-bob***: see BOB *noun*[5] 1. **wet bulb** one of the two thermometers of a psychrometer, the bulb of which is enclosed in wetted material. ***wet canteen***: see CANTEEN 1. **wet cell** a voltaic cell in which the electrolyte is a liquid. ***wet cupping***: see CUPPING *noun* 1. **wet diggings** (orig. *US*) gold diggings in or near a river or stream. **wet dock** a watertight dock in which the water is maintained at the level of high tide, so that vessels can remain constantly afloat in it. **wet dream** an erotic dream with an involuntary ejaculation of semen. **wet-eared** *adjective* = ***wet behind the ears*** s.v. EAR *noun*[1]. **wet fish** (*a*) *colloq.* a feeble or inept person; (*b*) fresh fish, as opp. to fish which has been frozen, cooked, or dried. **wet fly** ANGLING an artificial fly allowed to sink below the surface of the water. **wetland** a marsh, swamp, or other stretch of land that is usually saturated with water (usu. in *pl.*). **wet lease** *noun & verb* (*a*) *noun* a lease of an aircraft in which the lessor provides a flight crew and sometimes also fuel; (*b*) *verb trans.* lease (an aircraft) together with a flight crew etc. **wet look** an appearance of a wet or glossy surface, esp. one given to clothing fabrics. **wet meter** a gas meter in which the gas passes through a body of water. **wet-nurse** *noun & verb* (*a*) *noun* a woman employed to breast-feed and nurse another's baby (opp. ***dry-nurse***); (*b*) *verb trans.* act as a wet-nurse to; *colloq.* treat tenderly or care for as if helpless. **wet plate** PHOTOGRAPHY a sensitized collodion plate exposed in the camera while the collodion is moist. **wet process** a manufacturing process involving the use of water or other liquid. **wet rent** a levy paid to a brewery by a publican in a tied public house in proportion to the amount of beer sold. **wet rot** a brown rot affecting timber with a high moisture content; the fungus causing this, which is commonly *Coniophora puteana*. **wet season** a time of year in which there is the most rainfall. **wet shave** a shave carried out with soap and water or other lubricant as opp. to a (usu. electric) razor alone. **wet-shod** *adverb & adjective* (*obsolete* exc. *Scot. & dial.*) (*a*) *adverb* with wet feet; (*b*) *adjective* wet-footed. **wet smack** *slang* (chiefly *US*), a spoilsport. ***wet steam***: see STEAM *noun*. **wet strength** the strength of paper and textiles when wet. **wetsuit** a close-fitting garment, usu. of rubber, worn by skin-divers, surfers, etc., to protect them from the cold. **wet time** in the building trade, time during which work cannot be carried out owing to bad weather. **wet trade** an occupation involving the use of cement, water, lime, etc., as bricklaying or plastering. **wetware** [after *hardware*, *software*] brain cells regarded as chemical materials organized so as to perform arithmetic or logical operations. ***wet way***: see WAY *noun*. **wet-weather** *adjective* (*a*) associated with or occurring in rainy weather; (*b*) intended for use in rainy weather. **wet-white** liquid white theatrical make-up. **wet wing** (of an aircraft) having fuel pumped directly into the wings as opp. to being pumped into rubber bags contained in the wings.
■ **wetly** *adverb* M16. **wettish** *adjective* somewhat wet LME.

wet /wɛt/ *verb.* Infl. **-tt-**. Pa. t. & pple **wet**, **wetted**. OE.
[from WET *adjective*.]
1 *verb trans.* Make wet by the application of water or other liquid; cover, sprinkle, moisten, or drench (freq. foll. by *with*); dip or soak *in*. OE. ▸**b** Of water, rain, etc.: make wet or damp; drench. ME. ▸**c** SCIENCE. Of a liquid: cover or penetrate (a substance or object) readily, so that a small quantity spreads uniformly over it rather than lying as droplets upon it. M19.
2 *verb trans.* Of a person or animal: get (oneself, one's body or clothes, a thing, etc.) wet by contact with or immersion in water or other liquid. ME. ▸**b** Urinate in or on (one's bed, clothes); *refl.* urinate involuntarily. M18.
3 *verb intrans.* Become wet. ME.
4 *verb trans.* Of a river, sea, etc.: water or irrigate (land). Also (*rare*), wash against, border with water (a coast or country). LME.
5 *verb intrans.* & †*refl.* Drink alcohol; take drink. LME. ▸**b** *verb trans.* Accompany (solid or dry food) with (alcoholic) drink. L19.
6 *verb trans.* Celebrate by drinking; have a (usu. alcoholic) drink over. L17.
7 *verb trans.* **a** Steep or soak (grain) in water in order to convert it into malt. L17. ▸**b** Infuse (tea) by pouring boiling water on. *dial. & colloq.* E20.
8 *verb intrans.* Rain, drizzle. *Scot. & dial.* E18.
9 *verb trans.* Foll. by *down*: dampen (ash, paper, etc.) with water. M19.
10 *verb intrans.* NAUTICAL. Of a vessel: ship water. L19.
11 *verb intrans.* Urinate. E20.

1 BUNYAN They . . kissed his feet, and wetted them with tears. N. HAWTHORNE We were caught in . . showers . . without being very much wetted. E. J. HOWARD I got some water out of a . . bottle . . and wet the towel. A. TAN She wetted her palm and smoothed the hair above my ear. **2** A. MARSH-CALDWELL In traversing the ford . . they have wetted the bag of powder. **b** *fig.*: G. F. NEWMAN The Sunday editors would wet themselves; they liked nothing better than a sordid purge in an institution. **6** F. MARRYAT I should give them a dinner to wet my commission. **9** *Ships Monthly* The red hot clinker . . was wetted down by the trimmer. **11** J. STEINBECK House-broken dogs wet on the parlor rug.

Phrases: ***wet one's clay***: see CLAY *noun* 3. **wet one's line** *colloq.* start fishing, fish. **wet one's pants** *fig.* become excited or upset (as if to the extent of involuntarily urinating). ***wet one's whistle***: see WHISTLE *noun*. **wet the baby's head** *colloq.* celebrate the birth of a child with a (usu. alcoholic) drink. **wet the other eye** *colloq.* (now *rare*) have a second (esp. alcoholic) drink. **wet through**, **to the skin** soak the clothes of, drench completely.
■ **wetted** *adjective* (*a*) *gen.* made wet; moistened, damped; (*b*) *spec.* (of an aircraft surface) in contact with the moving airflow: E17. **wetter** *noun* (*a*) a person who wets or damps something; (*b*) *Scot. & colloq.* a wetting, a soaking: M18.

weta /'wɛtə/ *noun. NZ.* M19.
[Maori.]
Any of various large wingless orthopterous insects of the families Stenopelmatidae and Rhaphidophoridae, which are confined to New Zealand.

wether /'wɛðə/ *noun.* Also †**wedder**.
[Old English *weþer*, corresp. to Old Frisian *withar*, Old Saxon *wiþar* (Dutch *weer*), Old High German *widar* (German *Widder*), Old Norse *veðr* ram, Gothic *wiþrus* lamb, from Germanic, of disputed origin.]
1 A male sheep, a ram; *esp.* a castrated ram. Also ***wether sheep***. OE. ▸**b** *transf.* A man; *esp.* a eunuch. M16.
2 The fleece obtained from the second or any subsequent shearing of a sheep. L19.
Phrases: **grey wethers** any large boulders which resemble sheep in the distance; *esp.* the sarsen stones of Wiltshire.
Comb.: **wether head** a sheep's head; *fig.* a stupid person; **wether hog** (chiefly *Scot. & north.*) a male sheep (castrated or not) before its first shearing; **wether lamb** a male lamb; ***wether sheep***: see sense 1 above.

Wetmore order /'wɛtmɔːr ˌɔːdə/ *noun phr.* M20.
[Alexander *Wetmore* (1886–1978), US ornithologist + ORDER *noun*.]
ORNITHOLOGY. A system and sequence of bird classification developed by Wetmore, used as the basis of most modern systems.

wetness /'wɛtnɪs/ *noun.* OE.
[from WET *adjective* + -NESS.]
1 The state or condition of being wet (*lit. & fig.*); moisture, wet. OE.
2 A wet spot or patch of ground. *rare.* E19.

1 R. D. EDWARDS A profession which regards loyalty as weakness and decency as wetness. C. FREMLIN Each blade of . . grass glittering with wetness.

wettable /'wɛtəb(ə)l/ *adjective.* L19.
[from WET *verb* + -ABLE.]
Able to be wetted.
■ **wetta'bility** *noun* the property of being wettable; the degree to which something may be wetted: E20.

wetting /ˈwɛtɪŋ/ *noun*. ME.
[from WET *verb* + -ING[1].]
1 The action of WET *verb*; an instance of this, a soaking. ME.
2 A liquid used to wet or moisten something; *esp.* a small quantity of water or alcohol used to moisten the throat. Chiefly *colloq.* ME.

📖 **1** SOUTHEY A thorough wetting under a succession of heavy showers. P. FRANCIS The ash swelled slightly as a result of the wetting.

Comb.: **wetting agent** a chemical that can be added to a liquid to reduce its surface tension and make it more effective in wetting things.

WEU *abbreviation*.
Western European Union.

wevet /ˈwɛvət/ *noun*. *dial.* L15.
[from WEAVE *verb*[1] + -ET[2].]
A cobweb.

wey /weɪ/ *noun*. *obsolete* exc. *Hist.* & *dial.* Also **weigh**.
[Old English *wǣg*, *wǣge*, corresp. to Old Saxon, Old High German *wāga* (Dutch *waag*, German *Wage*), Old Norse *vág*, from Germanic, rel to WEIGH *verb*.]
1 †*sing.* & in *pl.* (also treated as *sing.*). A balance, a pair of scales. OE. ▸**b** In *pl.* A weighbridge, a (public) weighing-machine. *Scot.* L19.
2 A former unit of weight or volume, used for cheese, wool, salt, coal, etc., varying greatly with different commodities. OE.

Weyl /vʌɪl/ *noun*. M20.
[Hermann *Weyl* (1885–1955), German mathematician.]
MATH. Used *attrib.* to designate concepts introduced by Weyl.
Weyl group a factor group constructed from two subgroups that satisfy certain conditions. **Weyl tensor** a tensor in general relativity that gives the space–time curvature component not determined locally by matter.

Weymouth /ˈweɪməθ/ *noun*. M18.
[In sense 1, from Sir Thomas Thynne, first Lord *Weymouth* (1640–1714). In sense 2, of uncertain origin.]
1 ***Weymouth pine***, the N. American white pine, *Pinus strobus*, extensively planted by the first Lord Weymouth on his estate at Longleat, Wiltshire. M18.
2 ***Weymouth bit***, ***Weymouth bridle***, a type of simple curb bit, or a double bridle comprising this bit and a snaffle with two sets of reins. L18.

w.f. *abbreviation*.
PRINTING. Wrong font.

wff *abbreviation*.
LOGIC. Well-formed formula.

WFTU *abbreviation*.
World Federation of Trade Unions.

Wg. Cdr. *abbreviation*.
Wing Commander.

wh.
A consonantal digraph occurring initially in words of Old English (Germanic) origin, representing *hw*, as in *hwæt* what, or, in words of other origin, probably ult. imit., as in ***whip***, ***whisk***. Old English pronunciation of a voiced bilabial consonant preceded by a breath developed in two ways: (***a***) it was reduced to a simple voiced consonant /w/; (***b***) influenced by the accompanying breath, the voiced /w/ became unvoiced to give /hw/ (now esp. in Scottish and Irish pronunciation). In a few words with *who-*, the /w/ was lost, resulting in simple /h/, as in ***who***, ***whoop***; by analogy with these, some *ho-* words became spelt *who-*, as ***whole***, ***whore***. Used in LINGUISTICS to represent an interrogative or relative pronoun or adverb (as ***which***, ***where***, ***how***, etc.); pronounced as the names of the individual letters. Usu. in comb., as ***wh-clause***, ***wh-movement***, etc.

whack /wak/ *verb*, *noun*, *interjection*, & *adverb*. E18.
[Imit., or perh. alt. of THWACK. Cf. prec.]
▸**A** *verb*. **1** *verb trans.* Beat vigorously, thrash; strike with a sharp or resounding blow. *colloq.* E18. ▸**b** Defeat in a contest. *colloq.* L19.
2 *verb trans.* Put, bring, or take, with vigorous action. Foll. by adverb. *colloq.* E18.
3 *verb trans.* Share, divide. Also foll. by *up*. *slang.* E19.
4 *verb intrans.* Foll. by *off*: masturbate. *US slang.* M20.

📖 **1** K. AMIS The new batsman . . whacked the ball towards Jenny. K. A. PORTER She . . whacked them . . on the skull with a folded paper fan. M. ATWOOD Her father . . whacks her with his belt. **2** *Fortune* The . . agency had to whack $30 million off pretax earnings. *Sea Angling Quarterly* Lash a new bait to the hook . . and whack it back out there. *Mountain Biker* Whack on the front brake and watch for flex.

▸**B** *noun*. **1** A sharp or resounding blow; the sound of this. *colloq.* M18. ▸**b** A chance, a turn; an attempt, an attack. *slang.* L19.
2 A portion, a share, an amount. *slang.* L18. ▸**b** A bargain, an agreement. *US slang.* M19.

📖 **1** K. ROBERTS He caught you an awful whack . . How do you feel? **b** P. G. WODEHOUSE I was . . merry . . as always when about to get another whack at Anatole's cooking. **2** M. INNES There were lawyers . . settling the affair, and they got their whack. D. ADAMS He probably apportioned a fair whack of his time to . . breaking down doors.

Phrases & comb.: **have a whack at** *slang* (***a***) strike a blow at; (***b***) attempt. **out of whack** *slang* (chiefly *N. Amer.*) out of order, malfunctioning; out of line, maladjusted. **take a whack at** = *have a whack at* above. **whack-up** *slang* a sharing out, a dividing up.
▸**C** *interjection* & *adverb*. With a whack. *colloq.* E19.

📖 F. MARRYAT Whack came the cane on Johnny's shoulders.

■ **whacked** *adjective* (also **wacked**) (*colloq.*) (***a***) tired out, exhausted; (***b***) ***whacked out*** (*US slang*), mad, crazy; *spec.* intoxicated with drugs: E20. **whacker** *noun* (*colloq.*) (***a***) *dial.* a sharp blow; (***b***) *US* a drover; (***c***) a thing very large of its kind; *esp.* a big lie: E19. **whacking** *noun* (*colloq.*) the action of the verb; an instance of this, a beating, a thrashing: M19. **whacking** *adjective* & *adverb* (*colloq.*) (***a***) *adjective* very large; (***b***) *adverb* very, exceedingly (*big*, *great*, etc.): L18.

whacko *adjective* & *noun* var. of WACKO.

whacko /ˈwakəʊ/ *interjection*. *slang* (chiefly *Austral.*). M20.
[from WHACK *noun* + -O.]
Expr. delight or excitement.

whacky *noun* & *adjective* var. of WACKY.

whakapapa /fakəˈpapə/ *noun*. M20. *NZ.*
[Maori.]
Maori genealogy; a Maori genealogical table.

whale /weɪl/ *noun* & *verb*[1].
[Old English *hwæl* = Old High German *wal* (German *Walfisch*), Old Norse *hvalr*.]
▸**A** *noun*. Pl. **-s**, (occas.) same.
1 Any of various large fishlike marine mammals of the order Cetacea, which have forelimbs modified as fins, a tail with horizontal flukes, and nasal openings on top of the head, and which comprise the suborder Mysticeti and (usu. esp. the larger members of) the suborder Odontoceti (freq. with specifying word). OE.
2 (Usu. **W-**.) (The name of) *the* constellation Cetus. M16.
3 In *pl.* Anchovies on toast. *School & Univ. slang* (now *Hist.*). L19.
1 ***blue whale***, ***humpback whale***, ***killer whale***, ***sperm whale***, etc. ***a sprat to catch a whale***: see SPRAT *noun*[1]. ***a tub for a whale***: see TUB *noun*[1]. **a whale of a** — *colloq.* an exceedingly good or fine etc. —. BALEEN ***whale***. ***throw a tub to a whale***: see TUB *noun*[1]. ***toothed whale***: see TOOTHED 1.
Comb.: **whale acorn-shell**, **whale barnacle** an acorn barnacle, esp. one of the family Coronulidae, that lives attached to whales etc.; **whale-bird** a bird which follows a whaling vessel to feed on offal etc., or which is found in the same locality as whales; *esp.* a prion; **whaleboat** (***a***) *Hist.* a long narrow double-bowed boat formerly used in whaling; (***b***) a boat of this kind carried for use as a lifeboat etc.; **whale-feed**, **whale-food** any small animal upon which whales feed; *spec.* krill; **whale-fin** (now *rare* or *obsolete*) whalebone (formerly supposed to be the fin of a whale); **whale-fisher**, **whale-fisherman** a person engaged in the business of whaling; **whale-fishery** the business, occupation, or industry of whaling; **whale-fishing** whaling; ***whale-food***: see *whale-feed* above; **whalehead** = *whale-headed stork* below; **whale-headed stork** an African stork, *Balaeniceps rex* (family Balaenicipitidae), which has a very large clog-shaped bill and grey plumage; also called ***shoebill***; **whale louse** any of various small amphipod crustaceans of the genus *Cyamus* and family Cyamidae, which live commensally on whales, esp. on the heads of right whales; **whaleman** = WHALER 1, 2; **whale-oil** oil obtained from the blubber of a whale; **whale shark** a very large spotted shark, *Rhincodon typus* (family Rhincodontidae), which feeds on plankton etc. in tropical seas, and is the largest living fish; **whalesucker** a remora (fish), *Remora australis*, which attaches itself to whales and porpoises.
▸**B** *verb intrans.* Engage in whaling; hunt and kill whales. OE.
■ **whalery** *noun* (***a***) the industry of whaling; (***b***) a whaling-station: L17.

whale /weɪl/ *verb*[2]. Now *US colloq.* L18.
[Prob. var. of WALE *verb*[2].]
1 *verb trans.* Beat, flog. L18.
2 *verb intrans.* Foll. by adverb: do something implied by the context continuously or vehemently. M19.

📖 **1** K. TENNANT I'll have to whale the hide off them one of these days. **2** H. DAY You don't think I've whaled up here . . to . . talk about women, do you?

whaleback /ˈweɪlbak/ *noun* & *adjective*. L19.
[from WHALE *noun* + BACK *noun*[1].]
▸**A** *noun*. A thing shaped like a whale's back; *spec.* (***a***) an arched structure over the bow or stern part of the deck of a steamer, a turtle-back; (***b***) (chiefly *Hist.*) a steamship with a spoon bow and a very convex main deck; (***c***) PHYSICAL GEOGRAPHY a large elongated mound, hill, or sand-dune; a *roche moutonnée*. L19.
▸**B** *attrib.* or as *adjective*. Having a whaleback; shaped like a whale's back, very convex. L19.
■ **whalebacked** *adjective* shaped like a whale's back, very convex M19.

whalebone /ˈweɪlbəʊn/ *noun* & *adjective*. Also (in sense A.1) †**whale's bone**. ME.
[from WHALE *noun* + BONE *noun*.]
▸**A** *noun*. †**1** Ivory from the walrus or some similar animal confused with the whale. ME–M19.
2 An elastic horny substance which grows in a series of thin parallel plates in the upper jaw of baleen whales, and is used by them to strain plankton from the seawater. Also called ***baleen***. E17.
3 A strip of whalebone, esp. used as stiffening in stays, dresses, etc. E17. ▸**b** A riding-crop made of whalebone. M19.
Comb.: **whalebone whale** = BALEEN ***whale***.
▸**B** *attrib.* or as *adjective*. Made of whalebone; stiffened with strips of whalebone. E17.
■ **whaleboned** *adjective* provided with whalebone, *esp.* stiffened with strips of whalebone M17.

†**whalefish** *noun*. E16–E18.
[from WHALE *noun* + FISH *noun*[1]. Cf. Middle Low German, Middle & mod. Dutch *walvisch*.]
A whale.

whaler /ˈweɪlə/ *noun*. In sense 5 also **waler**. L17.
[from WHALE *noun* or *verb*[1] + -ER[1].]
1 A person engaged in the business of whaling. L17.
2 A ship used in whaling. Also, a long narrow double-bowed boat carried by a ship for use as a lifeboat etc., a whaleboat. E19.
3 A thing unusually large of its kind. *US slang.* M19.
4 Any of several sharks of the family Carcharinidae, formerly encountered in the vicinity of whales; spec. *Carcharinus brachyurus* (also ***whaler shark***), a large and dangerous shark common in Australian waters. Freq. with specifying word. Chiefly *Austral.* L19.
5 A tramp. *arch. Austral. slang.* L19.
Comb.: **whalerman** = sense 1 above; ***whaler shark***: see sense 4 above.

†**whale's bone** *noun* see WHALEBONE.

whaling /ˈweɪlɪŋ/ *noun*[1]. L17.
[from WHALE *noun* or *verb*[1] + -ING[1].]
The practice, business, occupation, or industry of hunting and killing whales, esp. for their oil, meat, or whalebone.
Comb.: **whaling-master** the captain of a whaler; **whaling station** a land base where whales which have been caught are flensed and rendered.

whaling /ˈweɪlɪŋ/ *verbal noun*[2]. Now *dial.* & *US*. M19.
[from WHALE *verb*[2] + -ING[1].]
The action of WHALE *verb*[2]; an instance of this.

whally /ˈwɔːli/ *adjective*. *rare.* L16.
[Perh. from WALL *noun*[2] + -Y[1].]
Of an eye: showing much white, glaring.

wham /wam/ *noun*, *interjection*, *adverb*, & *verb*. *colloq.* E20.
[Imit.]
▸**A** *noun*. A heavy blow, a forcible impact; the sound of this. Also, a resounding success; an attempt *at* something. E20.

📖 C. BONINGTON The peg held, another half-dozen whams of the hammer, and it was in.

▸**B** *interjection* & *adverb*. With a wham. E20.

📖 J. M. CAIN And then, wham, I pleaded her guilty. R. DAHL Down comes a . . nut . . on to the top of his bald-head. Wham!

Comb.: **wham-bam**, **wham-bang** *adverbs*, *interjections*, & *adjectives* (***a***) *adverb* & *interjection* with quick forceful or violent action (*spec.* with ref. to sexual intercourse); (***b***) *adjective* characterized by such action, forceful, violent.
▸**C** *verb trans.* & *intrans.* Infl. **-mm-**. Strike with force; (cause to) move with speed, violence, or noise. E20.

📖 J. THURBER She . . picked up a shoe, and whammed it through a pane of glass. K. KESEY The black boy whammed flat against the wall.

whame /weɪm/ *noun*. *obsolete* exc. *dial.* M17.
[Origin unkn.]
A gadfly, a horsefly.

whammo /ˈwaməʊ/ *interjection* & *adverb*. *colloq.* M20.
[from WHAM + -O-.]
= WHAM *interjection* & *adverb*.

whammy /ˈwami/ *noun*. *N. Amer. colloq.* M20.
[from WHAM *noun* + -Y[6].]
An evil or unlucky influence; an unpleasant or problematic effect or situation.

📖 S. BELLOW Girls . . had the power to put the sexual whammy . . on him. *International Business Week* California . . is suffering a double whammy of cold and drought.

whang /waŋ/ *noun*[1]. Also **wang**. E16.
[Alt. of THONG *noun*. Cf. WHANG *verb*[1].]
1 A narrow strip of hide or leather, a thong. *Scot.* & *dial.* E16.
2 A thick slice of bread, cheese, etc. *Scot.* & *dial.* L17.
3 The penis. *coarse slang* (chiefly *US*). M20.

whang /waŋ/ *noun*^{2}. E19.
[Imit. Cf. next.]
A resounding blow; the noise of this.

whang /waŋ/ *verb*^{1}. Also **wang**. L17.
[Alt. of THONG *verb*. Cf. WHANG *noun*^{1}, *noun*^{2}.]
1 a *verb trans.* Beat (as) with a thong; lash. *Scot. & dial.* L17. ▸**b** *verb trans. & intrans.* Strike, drive, throw or be thrown, etc., with force or violent impact. (Not always distinguishable from WHANG *verb*^{2}.) *colloq.* E19.
2 *verb trans.* Cut in large slices. *Scot. & dial.* M18.

> **1b** E. BIRNEY The corporal . . whanged his pipe spitefully against the table leg. D. BOGARDE A stone . . whanged . . against the bonnet of the car. P. THEROUX They had flown the . . gunship into the darkness, their rotor blades whanging the low branches.

■ **whanger** *noun* †(*a*) *rare* a violent thief; (*b*) *US coarse slang* the penis: E18.

whang /waŋ/ *verb*^{2} *intrans. colloq.* Also **wang**. M19.
[Imit.]
Make a loud resounding noise; move or strike with such a noise. (Not always distinguishable from WHANG *verb*^{1} 1b.)

> J. LEASOR The bullets whanged off a door. *Motor* You rush from the pits just as the leading Porsches whang past.

whang /waŋ/ *interjection & adverb. colloq.* M19.
[from WHANG *noun*^{2}, *verb*^{2}.]
Repr., with, a loud resounding noise, with a whang.

whangdoodle /waŋˈduːd(ə)l/ *noun. N. Amer. colloq.* Also **whang-doodle**. M19.
[Arbitrary.]
An imaginary creature. Also, something unspecified, a thingummy.

whangee /waŋˈgiː/ *noun.* L18.
[Chinese *huáng* old bamboo shoots, a hard white-skinned bamboo.]
Any of several Chinese bamboos of the genus *Phyllostachys*, esp. *P. nigra*; (more fully ***whangee cane***) a yellow knobbed cane made from the stem of such a bamboo.

> *attrib.*: *Times* A blue, red, and white umbrella with a whangee . . handle.

whare /ˈwɒri/ *noun.* E19.
[Maori.]
A (Maori) house or hut; *gen.* a hut, a shed, *spec.* one on a sheep station, where the hands sleep or eat.

wharf /wɔːf/ *noun.* Pl. **wharves** /wɔːvz/, **wharfs**.
[Late Old English *hwearf*, *w(e)arf* corresp. to Middle Low German *warf*, *werf* mole, dam, wharf (whence Dutch *werf* shipyard, German *Werft* wharf, shipyard).]
1 A level structure of timber, stone, etc., built alongside water to allow ships to moor for loading and unloading. LOE.
†**2** An embankment, a mole, a dam. LOE–E17. ▸**b** The bank of a river. Only in E17.
Comb.: **wharf-boat** (*a*) *US* a boat supporting a platform and moored at a bank, used as a wharf; (*b*) a boat used at a wharf; **wharf crane**: fixed in position on a wharf; **wharf-lumper** *Austral.* a wharf-labourer; **wharf-rat** (*a*) any rat, esp. a brown rat, that infests wharfs; (*b*) *arch. slang* a person who loiters about wharfs, esp. with the intention of stealing.
■ **wharfie** *noun* (*Austral. & NZ colloq.*) a stevedore, a docker E20. **wharfing** *noun* †(*a*) *rare* = WHARFAGE 1; (*b*) a structure in the form of a wharf; material used for the construction of wharves: LME. **wharfless** *adjective* E19.

wharf /wɔːf/ *verb.* M16.
[from the noun.]
†**1** *verb trans.* Strengthen (a river-bank etc.) with planks of timber or stone. M16–L19.
2 *verb trans.* Unload or store (goods) at a wharf. L16.
3 *verb intrans.* Of a ship: moor at a wharf. L19.
4 *verb trans.* Moor (a ship) at a wharf. E20.

wharfage /ˈwɔːfɪdʒ/ *noun.* LME.
[from WHARF *noun* + -AGE.]
1 (The provision of) storage at a wharf; the loading or unloading of goods at a wharf. LME.
2 The charge for this. LME.
3 Wharfs collectively. E18.

wharfinger /ˈwɔːfɪn(d)ʒə/ *noun.* Orig. †**wharfager**. ME.
[from WHARFAGE + -ER^{1}.]
An owner or keeper of a wharf.

wharl /wɑːl/ *verb intrans.* LME.
[Imit.]
Use a uvular trill; burr.

Wharncliffe /ˈwɔːnklɪf/ *noun.* M19.
[James Archibald Stuart-Wortley-Mackenzie, 1st Baron *Wharncliffe* (1776–1845).]
Used *attrib.* to designate a standing order in Parliament requiring the directors of a company wishing to promote a private Bill for the extension of the company's powers to secure the consent of its shareholders, or a meeting at which this consent is sought.

wharrow /ˈwarəʊ/ *noun. obsolete* exc. *dial.* E16.
[Alt.]
= WHARVE *noun*.

Wharton /ˈwɔːt(ə)n/ *noun.* M19.
[Thomas *Wharton*, English anatomist (1610–73).]
ANATOMY. Used in *possess.* to designate anatomical structures discovered or described by Wharton.
Wharton's duct the duct conveying saliva from either of the two submandibular salivary glands into the mouth. **Wharton's jelly** the jelly-like mucoid connective tissue which surrounds the blood-vessels in the umbilical cord.

wharve /wɔːv/ *noun.*
[Old English *hweorfa* (corresp. to Old Saxon *hwervo*, Old High German *hwerbo*), from *hweorfan* to turn, from Germanic base also of WHIRL *noun*. Cf. WHARROW.]
The whorl of a spindle.

wharves *noun pl.* see WHARF *noun*.

what /wɒt/ *pronoun, noun, adverb, interjection, conjunction, & adjective* (in mod. usage also classed as a *determiner*). Also (*non-standard*) **wot** /wɒt/.
[Old English *hwæt* = Old Frisian *hwet*, Old Saxon *hwat* (Dutch *wat*), Old High German *(h)waz* (German *was*), Old Norse *hvat*, Gothic *hwa*, from Germanic from Indo-European neut. form of base of WHO (repr. also in Latin *quod*). Cf. WHEN, WHERE, WHY.]
► **A** *pronoun & noun.* **I** *interrog. pronoun.* **1** Used in asking the identity or name of a thing or (later) things specified, indicated, or understood. OE.
2 Used in asking (orig.) the identity or name, (now) the character, function, etc., of a person or persons specified, indicated, or understood. OE. ▸**b** A thing or person of what consequence, value, or force? With noun phr. as answer: cf. sense E.2b below. OE.
3 How much? how many? OE.
4 *ellipt.* Used as or in a direct question asking for repetition, clarification, or confirmation of something just said. Cf. WHO *pronoun & noun* 1b. LME.
5 Preceded by *or*: representing the unknown final alternative in a set of proposed options. *colloq.* M18.

> **1** T. HARDY She ventured to enquire . . in what quarter Mr Henchard could be found. E. BOWEN 'I don't want him, if that's what you mean,' said Veronica. J. BUCHAN What was the cause? J. RHYS What could I . . say against all this? J. WAIN What the hell has it got to do with you where I work? I. MURDOCH What's that funny noise that keeps coming? P. ACKROYD The doctor will soon find out what's wrong. M. AMIS I don't know what it's like to write a poem. **2** SHAKES. *Oth.* What are you? *Rod.* My name is Rodrigo. DISRAELI I was to be something great, . . but what, we could not determine. SCOTT FITZGERALD What are you going to be when you grow up? E. WAUGH What's she? Some kind of inspector, I suppose. **b** POPE What's Fame? a fancy'd life in others' breath. **3** H. HAWKINS Lloyd must have made £20,000 . . what I made is of no consequence. **4** DICKENS 'Cold punch,' murmured Mr Pickwick, as he sunk to sleep again. 'What?' demanded Captain Boldwig. No reply. J. MORTIMER 'Well, I gave it to her.' 'You what?' **5** M. MITCHELL Not knowing whether you . . were amused, interested or what. J. MCGAHERN Not that, sweetie, not this, sweetie, are you stupid or what?

► **II** *rel. pronoun.* **6** Referring to a preceding pronoun (esp. *all*) or noun: which, who; that. Formerly also with preceding preposition. Now *non-standard.* OE.
7 That or those which, the thing(s) which; as much or as many as; the kind or sort that; *gen.* something which. Also used in parenthetic clauses qualifying a following word or phr., or in parenthetic or introductory clauses (esp. ***what is more*** below) qualifying a following clause. ME. ▸**b** Referring to a preceding noun: the one which; *esp.* the ones which, those which. Usu. after conjunction. ME.
8 Anything that, whatever. Formerly also, whoever. Now only in phrs. ME.
9 Used redundantly after *than* or *as* introducing a clause. *non-standard.* E19.

> **6** DICKENS Them's her lights, Miss Abbey, wot you see a-blinking yonder. J. B. MORTON If I sat down to write a book, I'd want to shove in all what I saw. K. TENNANT A man what don't profit from all a woman's telling . . ain't worth the trouble. **7** SIR W. SCOTT She wore, what was then . . unusual, a coat . . and hat resembling those of a man. LD MACAULAY The country was not what it had been. T. HARDY On opening it he found it to be what she called her will. D. BARNES What she steals she keeps. O. MANNING Harriet returned to hear what he had to say. R. P. JHABVALA The office . . is right in what used to be the British residential area. M. ROBERTS Why don't you say what you mean? *Amateur Gardening* Many seeds . . need a period of what is called vernalisation. **b** L. MURRAY All fevers, except what are called nervous. M. ARNOLD The Revolution made a clean sweep of . . endowments; what exist date from a time since the Revolution. **8** S. PEPYS Their service was six biscuits a-piece, and what they pleased of burnt claret. **9** M. SPARK 'He's the same as what we are,' Dixie said.

► **III** Indefinite (non-rel.) pronoun.
†**10** Something; anything. ME–L16.

> **10** SPENSER Come downe, and learne the little what, that Thomalin can sayne.

► **IV 11** In exclams.: what thing(s)! LME.

> **11** AV *Num.* 23:23 It shalbe said of Iacob, and of Israel, What hath God wrought!

► **V** *noun.* (With *pl.*)
12 A question as to what something is, what is or was to be done, etc.; a reply to such a question. Also, the essence or substance of the thing in question. M17.
13 A thing. *rare.* M17.

> **12** J. L. MOTLEY I . . wrote my name and my whences and whats . . in a great book. **13** O. NASH Why, that's the what, the special what, That you're allergic to.

► **B** *adverb.* **1** Introducing a question, simply as a sign of interrogation. *obsolete* exc. *dial.* OE.
2 In exclams.: to what an extent! in what a way! *obsolete* exc. *dial.* OE.
3 *interrog.* †**a** For what reason or purpose? why? OE–M17. ▸**b** In what respect or way? how? *arch.* ME. ▸**c** To what degree or extent? how much? LME.
†**4** In correlative phrs. ***what . . . what***, ***what . . . and***: some . . . others; both . . . and; partly . . . partly. ME–L17.
5 In phrs. formed with prepositions, now only in ***what with***: on account of, in view of, considering, (usu. more than one thing). ME.

> **1** E. RAVENSCROFT What's he a Spy too? **3a** MILTON What sit we then projecting Peace and Warr? **b** SIR W. SCOTT It just cam open . . in my hand—what could I help it? **c** J. RUSKIN What do we, as a nation, care about books? **4** C. COTTON A hundred and fifty Horse (what Gentlemen and what of his own Guards). **5** M. SPARK We are a little upset, what with one thing and another. J. MORTIMER I might find that . . painful, what with the situation at home. W. BOYD The heat was intense, what with the lights and the press of people.

► **C** *interjection.* †**1** Used to introduce or call attention to a statement: lo! now! OE–LME.
2 Expr. surprise or astonishment. Usu. preceding a question. ME.
3 Used to hail, summon, or command the attention of a person. Earlier in WHAT HO. *arch.* M16.
4 Used interrogatively to invite assent or convey emphasis. *colloq.* L18.

> **2** A. DILLARD What! No further? Yike! **4** T. SHARPE Damn fine shooting, what!

► **D** *conjunction.* †**1** Till, until. Only in ME.
2 To the extent that; as far as. Long *obsolete* exc. *dial.* LME.

> **2** N. WARD I speak . . to excuse what I may, my Country-men.

► **E** *adjective.* **I** *interrog. adjective.* **1** Used in asking the identity of a choice made from an indefinite or (*colloq.*) definite set of alternatives. Cf. WHICH *adjective* 2. ME.
2 Used in asking about the nature of the person(s) or thing(s) designated: what kind of —? ME. ▸**b** *pred.* Of what kind or character? With adjectival phr. as answer: cf. sense A.2b above. ME.
3 How much —? how many —? LME.

> **1** SHELLEY What hope of refuge, or retreat? C. BRONTË A story! What story? J. M. MURRY By what means . . he is perpetuated . . I cannot pause to inquire. SCOTT FITZGERALD You ought to have understood . . what kind of a picture I wanted. I. MURDOCH What number is that psalm, Pinkie, can you remember? W. HORWOOD What we wish to know . . is who you are and what news you have. **2** F. D. MAURICE He wants a God . . what God he cares very little. *Interview* Food snobbism about what wine to drink with what meal. **b** SHAKES. *Twel. N.* I see you what you are: you are too proud. R. BAGOT You know what he is about anything disagreeable—how he simply ignores its existence. **3** H. JAMES She never knew afterwards what time had elapsed.

► **II** *rel. adjective.* **4** The . . . that, as much . . . as, as many . . . as. ME.
5 *gen.* Any . . . that; whatever. Formerly also foll. by *ever*, *so*, *soever*, *somever*: see also WHATEVER, WHATSO, WHATSOEVER, WHATSOMEVER. *arch.* ME.

> **4** B. T. WASHINGTON What little clothing and household goods we had were placed in a cart. W. GOLDING I exerted what strength I had left. **5** POPE Spirits . . Assume what sexes and what shapes they please.

► **III 6** In exclams. or after verbs of thinking or perceiving: that is such to a great, strange, or remarkable degree. As *sing.* chiefly & now only (exc. with collective or abstract nouns) followed by indef. article. Also (*arch.*) with inverted construction. ME.

> **6** DICKENS You may judge with what devotion he clung to this girl. RIDER HAGGARD What rubbish you talk. E. WAUGH Vicountess Metroland . . What a name! J. C. POWYS What things they do tell us! M. KEANE We do realise what a ghastly time she went through.

► **IV** Indefinite (non-relative) adjective.
7 Any . . . at all, any . . . whatever. Usu. with *soever*. *arch.* L16.

📖 **7** SIR W. SCOTT She wore not . . any female ornament of what kind soever.

Phrases etc.: **but what**: see BUT *conjunction & pronoun* 2c. ***for what it is worth***: see WORTH *adjective*. ***have what it takes***: see TAKE *verb*. ***I know what***: see KNOW *verb*. ***I'll tell you what, I tell you what***: see TELL *verb*. ***know what's what***: see KNOW *verb*. **THAT'S** ***what***. ***what about***: see ABOUT *preposition* 6. ***what and if***: see ***what if*** below. ***what a vengeance***: see VENGEANCE *noun*. **what countryman?** *arch.* a man of what country? ***what do you say to?***: see SAY *verb*[1]. **what else?** what else should be the case? of course! **what for** (*a*) (long *dial.*) (introducing a clause) why; (*b*) *colloq.* (as an independent question) why? (*c*) ***give what for*** (*slang*), inflict severe pain or chastisement on. **what have you** (preceded by *and, or*) other similar things. **what if,** (*arch.*) **what and if** (*a*) what would be the case if? what would happen if? (*b*) what does it matter if? **what is more** and as an additional point; moreover. ***what matter?***: see MATTER *noun*. ***what NEXT?*** ***what price***: see PRICE *noun*. **what of?** what is the news concerning? **what of it?** why should that be considered significant? ***what's trumph?*** s.v. TRUMPH. **what's with?** *colloq.* what's the matter with? what has happened to? ***what's your will?***: see WILL *noun*[1]. **what then?** what would happen in that case? ***what the vengeance***: see VENGEANCE *noun*. ***what time***: see TIME *noun*. **what way?** *Scot. & north.* how? why? ***what with***: see sense B.5 above. ***what would you say to?***: see SAY *verb*[1]. ***what you will***: see WILL *verb*[1].

Comb.: **whatchamacallit** *colloq.* [repr. a pronunc. of *what you may call it*] = **whatsit** below; **what-d'you-call-'em** *colloq.* persons or things of a category or type whose name one cannot recall, does not know, or does not wish to specify; **what-d'you-call-it** *colloq.* = **whatsit** below; **what-if** *adjective & noun* (that involves) speculation as to what might have been, had antecedent conditions been different; **what's-her-face, what's-his-face** *colloq.* = ***what's-her-name, what's-his-name*** below; **what's-her-name, what's-his-name, what's-its-name** *colloq.* a person or thing whose name one cannot recall, does not know, or does not wish to specify; **whatsit** *colloq.* a thing whose name one cannot recall, does not know, or does not wish to specify; **what-the-hell** *verb & adjective* (*slang*) (*a*) *verb intrans.* exclaim 'what the hell . . ?'; (*b*) *adjective* insouciant, devil-may-care.

■ **whatness** *noun* [translating Latin *quidditas*] PHILOSOPHY = QUIDDITY 1 E17.

whata /ˈfʌtə/ *noun. NZ.* Also **futtah**. M19.
[Maori.]
A Maori food-store raised on posts.

whatabouts /ˈwɒtəbaʊts/ *noun pl. rare.* M19.
[from WHAT *pronoun* after WHEREABOUTS.]
One's activities, what one is about.

whatever /wɒtˈɛvə/ *pronoun, noun, adjective, & adverb.* Also (*poet.*) **-e'er** /-ˈɛː/. ME.
[from WHAT *pronoun, adjective* + EVER.]
► **A** *pronoun.* **I** Interrog. use.
1 (Also as two words.) Used with emphatic force in place of *what* in a question. Now *colloq.* ME.

📖 **1** T. HARDY Whatever has made you come now, sir? E. DAVID Cupids in the kitchen? Whatever next? C. P. SNOW Whatever do you mean?

► **II 2** Anything that; (chiefly *poet.*) everything that. LME.
3 No matter what; the unknown thing that. Also with ellipsis of verb: being what — may be. LME.
4 With loss of relative force: anything at all (*rare*); *colloq.* (usu. preceded by *or*) something similar. M17.

📖 **2** T. HARDY He was always ready to do . . whatever lay in his power. I. MCEWAN I'll do whatever you want . . but please get a doctor for Mary. **3** J. H. NEWMAN Men of one idea and nothing more, whatever their merit, must be . . narrow-minded. H. JAMES Whatever it is, I hereby offer to accept it. J. RHYS This business of looking cheerful whatever happens. W. GOLDING Speaking nothing but whatever it is they speak in the island. **4** M. INNES There isn't a handy second title around. Viscount Tom Noddy or whatever. J. BARNES Bourgeois monarchy, or . . totalitarianism, or anarchy, or whatever.

► **III** *noun.* **5** An unnamed or unspecified person, thing, quality, etc. E20.

📖 **5** TOLKIEN The whatever-it-was was . . getting close behind Gimli. *New Yorker* He cooked his beans and bacon, his mutton . . , his whatever.

► **B** *adjective.* **I 1** Any . . . that; *poet.* all or every . . . that. LME.
2 Any . . . all. *obsolete* exc. as in sense B.3 below. LME.
3 No matter what. Also (after preposition) with ellipsis of verb: any . . . all. (Cf. sense B.2 above.) M16.
4 *postpositive.* At all; of any kind. Chiefly & now only in neg. contexts with *any, no, none*, etc. Cf. earlier WHATSOEVER *adjective* 2. E17.

📖 **1** J. M. MURRY We must be content with whatever hints we may glean. DAY LEWIS Whatever meaning there is in my life . . should unfold itself. **2** INIGO JONES Their chiefest Glory to be wholly ignorant in whatever Arts. **3** A. THWAITE The writer knows whatever nonsense he writes will be well received. *City Limits* We can . . take it in whatever direction. **4** R. C. HUTCHINSON There was nothing whatever wrong with the motor-car. O. NASH I'd rather have my facts all wrong Than have no facts whatever.

► **II** Interrog. use.
5 (Also as two words.) Used with emphatic force in place of *what* in a question. E20.

📖 **5** OED Whatever contrivance is that?

► **C** *adverb.* Whatever may be the case, at any rate. *colloq.* L19.

📖 *New Musical Express* Whatever, the myth looks momentous in its . . new American threads.

Phrases: **or whatever** *colloq.* or something similar (used esp. to suggest substitution of a more accurate or appropriate term).

what ho /wɒtˈhəʊ/ *interjection & adjectival phr.* LME.
[from WHAT *interjection* + HO *interjection*[1].]
► **A** *interjection.* Used to hail, summon, or call the attention of a person. Cf. WHAT *interjection* 3. *arch.* LME.

📖 SHAKES. *Temp.* What ho! slave! Caliban! R. M. BALLANTYNE 'What ho! Coleman,' cried Bax.

► **B** *adjective.* With hyphen. Having the characteristics supposedly typical of a person who says 'what ho!'; hearty, upper-class. *colloq.* M20.

📖 *Time* A what ho English blueblood.

†**whatkin** *adjective. Scot. & dial.* ME.
[from WHAT *adjective* + KIN *noun*. Cf. WHATTEN.]
1 *interrog.* What kind or sort of —? ME–M16.
2 *rel.* That kind of . . . which; whatever. Only in ME.

what-like /ˈwɒtlʌɪk/ *interrog. adjective.* Orig. *Scot.* Now *arch.* & *dial.* Also as two words. E18.
[from WHAT *pronoun* + LIKE *adjective*, as in '*what* is it *like*?', after SUCHLIKE.]
Of what appearance? of what kind or character? Usu. *pred.*

Whatman /ˈwɒtmən/ *noun.* L19.
[Name of manufacturer.]
In full ***Whatman paper***. (Proprietary name for) a kind of paper used for drawing, engraving, etc.

what'n *interrog. adjective* var. of WHATTEN.

whatnot /ˈwɒtnɒt/ *noun.* Also **what-not**, (in sense 1) **what not**. L16.
[from WHAT *pronoun* + NOT *adverb*.]
1 Orig., anything; everything. Now only *collect.* (as final item of a list, usu. after *and*), other similar things or (*occas.*) people. L16.
2 An unspecified thing (freq. *euphem.*); a trivial thing. E17.
3 A stand with shelves, used for keeping or displaying small objects. E19.

📖 **1** W. C. WILLIAMS Investigating . . the ground for birds' nests or whatnot. J. WAIN Lines, sidings, embankments, tunnels and what-not. P. LIVELY I do office stuff. Orders and whatnot. **2** *Blitz* I was a raving lunatic. Hair down to my whatnot.

whatso /ˈwɒtsəʊ/ *pronoun & adjective.* Now *arch. & poet.* ME.
[from WHAT *pronoun, adjective* + SO *adverb*, reduced form of Old English *swā hwæt swā* so what so.]
► **A** *pronoun.* **1** = WHATEVER *pronoun* 2, 3. ME.
†**2** = WHOEVER 2. ME–M16.
► **B** *adjective.* **1** = WHATEVER *adjective* 1. L16.
2 = WHATEVER *adjective* 3. M19.

whatsoever /wɒtsəʊˈɛvə/ *pronoun & adjective.* Also (*poet.*) **-soe'er** /-səʊˈɛː/. ME.
[from prec. + EVER.]
► **A** *pronoun.* **1** = WHATEVER *pronoun* 2, 3. Now *poet.* ME.
†**2** = WHOEVER 2. LME–E17.
†**3** = WHATEVER *pronoun* 4. L16–M17.
► **B** *adjective.* **1** = WHATEVER *adjective* 1, 3. Now *poet.* L15.
2 *postpositive.* At all; of any kind; = WHATEVER *adjective* 4. Now only in neg. contexts with *any, no, none*, etc. L15.
†**3** = WHATEVER *adjective* 2. L16–L17.

📖 **2** K. CROSSLEY-HOLLAND There was nothing whatsoever he could do about it. JULIA HAMILTON He has no sense of humour whatsoever.

whatsomever /wɒts(ə)mˈɛvə/ *pronoun & adjective. obsolete* exc. *dial.* ME.
[from WHAT *pronoun* + SOMEVER.]
► **A** *pronoun.* **1** = WHATEVER *pronoun* 2, 3. ME.
†**2** = WHOEVER 2. LME–E17.
► **B** *adjective.* = WHATEVER *adjective* 1, 3, 4. LME.

whatten /ˈwɒt(ə)n/ *interrog. adjective. Scot. & north.* Also **what'n**. M16.
[Reduced form of WHATKIN.]
What kind of —? what?

whau /waʊ/ *noun.* M19.
[Maori.]
A New Zealand shrub or small tree, *Entelea arborescens*, of the linden family, with cordate leaves, white flowers, and bristly fruits; the very light porous wood of this tree. Also called ***corkwood***.

whaup /wɔːp, wɑːp/ *noun. Scot. & north.* M16.
[Imit.]
The curlew, *Numenius arquata*.

whb *abbreviation.*
Wash-hand basin.

wheak *verb & noun* var. of WHEEK.

†**wheal** *noun*[1]. LME–E18.
[Rel. to WHEAL *verb*[1]. Cf. WHELK *noun*[2], WEAL *noun*[2].]
A pimple, a pustule.

wheal /wiːl/ *noun*[2]. *local.* M19.
[Cornish *huel*, from †*wheyl* work.]
A mine.

wheal *noun*[3] see WEAL *noun*[2].

†**wheal** *verb*[1]. LOE.
[Origin unkn. Cf. WHEAL *noun*[1], WEAL *verb*.]
1 *verb intrans.* Suppurate; become affected with pustules. LOE–E19.
2 *verb trans.* Cause to suppurate; affect with pustules. Only as ***whealed*** *ppl adjective.* LOE–L17.

wheal *verb*[2] see WEAL *verb*.

wheat /wiːt/ *noun & adjective.*
[Old English *hwǣte* = Old Saxon *hwēti* (Dutch *weit*), Old High German *weizi* (also *weiʒʒi*, whence German *Weizen*), Old Norse *hveiti*, Gothic *hwaiteis*, from Germanic base also of WHITE *adjective & adverb*.]
► **A** *noun.* **1** Any of various cereal grasses of the genus *Triticum*, with spikelets in dense distichous spikes; *esp.* (more fully ***bread wheat***) *Triticum aestivum*, widely grown in temperate climates, the source of the best bread flours, and *T. durum* (more fully ***durum wheat***), the flour from which is used to make pasta. OE.
2 The grain of this, ground to make flour etc. OE.
3 A pale gold colour like that of ripe wheat. M20.
1 hard wheat, red wheat, rivet-wheat, soft wheat, white wheat, etc. **2** ***separate the wheat from the chaff***: see CHAFF *noun*[1]. ***shredded wheat***: see SHRED *verb*.

Comb.: **wheat-belt** a region where wheat is the chief agricultural product; **wheat-bird** a bird that feeds on wheat, *esp.* (*a*) the chaffinch; (*b*) *N. Amer.* the horned lark, *Eremophila alpestris*, or the white-throated sparrow, *Zonotrichia albicollis*; **wheat bulb fly** (the larva of) a small fly, *Delia coarctata* (family Anthomyiidae), which attacks the base of wheat stems; **wheat-corn** (now *rare*) a grain of wheat; **wheat-duck** the American wigeon, *Anas americana*, which sometimes frequents wheat-fields; **wheatflakes** flavoured flakes of wheat as a breakfast cereal; **wheat-fly** any of various insects, esp. midges of the family Cecidomyiidae whose larvae infest the wheat plant; **wheat germ** the embryo of the wheat grain, extracted during milling as a source of vitamins; **wheat-grass** any of several N. American grasses of the genus *Agropyron* grown as fodder, including *A. spicatum* (in full ***bluebunch wheat-grass***) and *A. smithir* (in full ***western wheat-grass***); **wheat-land** land suitable for growing wheat on or on which wheat is grown; **wheatsheaf** a bundle of wheat tied in a sheaf after reaping; **Wheat State** *US* either of the States of Kansas and Minnesota.

► **B** *adjective.* Of a pale gold colour like that of ripe wheat. E20.

■ **wheatish** *adjective* in the Indian subcontinent, designating or having a light-brown complexion M20. **wheatless** *adjective* M19. **wheaty** *adjective* †(*a*) containing grains of wheat; (*b*) of or pertaining to wheat: L16.

wheatear /ˈwiːtɪə/ *noun*[1]. LME.
[from WHEAT + EAR *noun*[2].]
An ear of wheat.

wheatear /ˈwiːtɪə/ *noun*[2]. Also (earlier) **-ears**. L16.
[App. from WHITE *adjective* + ARSE *noun* (with ref. to the bird's white rump), with assim. to WHEAT, EAR *noun*[2].]
Any of several birds of the mainly Old World genus *Oenanthe* (family Turdidae), which have black tails and conspicuous white rumps; esp. *O. oenanthe* of Europe and neighbouring areas, which has a bluish-grey back, buff breast, and black eyestripe and wings.

wheaten /ˈwiːt(ə)n/ *adjective & noun.* OE.
[from WHEAT *noun* + -EN[4].]
► **A** *adjective.* **1** Made of the grain or flour of wheat; *spec.* (of bread) made of the whole grain, wholemeal. OE.
2 Of or pertaining to wheat as a plant; made of the stalks or straw of wheat. OE.
3 Of a pale gold colour like that of ripe wheat. M20.

📖 **3** D. LEAVITT He had straight brown hair that turned wheaten in summer. **wheaten terrier** (a dog of) a breed of terrier with a pale golden soft wavy coat.

► **B** *noun.* A pale gold colour like that of ripe wheat. Also, a wheaten terrier. M20.

wheatmeal /ˈwiːtmiːl/ *noun.* OE.
[from WHEAT *noun* + MEAL *noun*[1].]
Flour made from wheat with some of the bran and germ removed.

†**wheat-plum** *noun.* M16–M19.
[from WHEAT + PLUM *noun*, orig. from misinterpretation of Latin *cerea pruna* waxen or wax-coloured plums as 'wheaten plums' (from *ceres* wheat, corn); later prob. assoc. with *white* (cf. WHEATEAR *noun*[2], Dutch *witte pruim* white plum).]
A large variety of plum.

Wheatstone /ˈwiːtstən, -stəʊn/ *noun.* M19.
[Sir Charles *Wheatstone* (1802–75), English physicist.]
Used in *possess.* and *attrib.* to designate things invented by or associated with Wheatstone.
Wheatstone bridge, Wheatstone's bridge a simple circuit for measuring an unknown resistance by connecting it so as to

form a quadrilateral with three known resistances and applying a voltage between a pair of opposite corners.

whee /wiː/ *interjection, noun, & verb.* E20.
[Natural exclam.]
▶**A** *interjection.* Expr. delight or exhilaration. E20.
▶**B** *noun.* A high-pitched sound or cry; an utterance of 'whee!'. M20.
▶**C** *verb.* Pa. t. & pple **wheed**.
1 *verb intrans.* Utter a high-pitched sound; utter 'whee!'. M20.
2 *verb trans.* Foll. by *up*: excite. *US colloq.* M20.

wheech /hwiːx, hwiːk/ *verb. Scot.* E19.
[Imit.]
1 *verb intrans.* Move quickly, esp. through the air; rush, dash. E19.
2 *verb trans.* Snatch, take away quickly. M19.

wheedle /'wiːd(ə)l/ *verb & noun.* M17.
[Perh. from German *wedeln* fawn (on), cringe (to), from *Wedel* tail, fan.]
▶**A** *verb.* **1** *verb trans.* Coax or persuade by flattery or endearments. Freq. foll. by *into*, or with direct speech as obj. M17.
2 *verb intrans.* Use flattery or endearments. M17.
3 *verb trans.* Get (a thing) *from* or *out of* a person by wheedling; *arch.* cheat (a person) *out of* a thing by wheedling. L17.

> 🕮 **1** N. SAHGAL Kiran and I had gone to wheedle him into taking us to the cinema. A. WEST He had to pacify her and wheedle her into a better humour. A. BROOKNER 'Mama, Mama,' wheedles Betty on the telephone. 'Don't be cross with me'. **2** V. GLENDINNING He continued to wheedle and plead, but she had no intention of giving in. **3** SIR W. SCOTT I wheedled an old woman out of these ballads. V. ACKLAND I . . wheedled permission from my inattentive mother.

▶**B** *noun.* **1** An act or instance of wheedling; a piece of insinuating flattery or cajolery. Now *rare.* M17.
2 A wheedler. *slang.* Now *rare* or *obsolete.* L17.

> 🕮 **1** THACKERAY So were the Sirens ogres—pretty blue-eyed things . . singing their melodious wheedles.

■ **wheedlingly** *adverb* in a wheedling manner M19. **wheedler** *noun* a person who wheedles L18.

wheek /wiːk/ *verb & noun.* Chiefly *dial.* Also **wheak**. E16.
[Imit.]
▶**A** *verb intrans.* Squeak. E16.
▶**B** *noun.* A squeak. E19.

wheel /wiːl/ *noun.*
[Old English *hwēol*, *hwēogol*, *hweowol* = Middle & mod. Low German *wēl*, Middle & mod. Dutch *wiel*, Old Norse *hjól*, *hvél*, from Germanic word from Indo-European base repr. by Sanskrit *cakra-* wheel, circle, Greek *kuklos* CYCLE *noun*, redupl. of verb meaning 'move around', repr. by Greek *polos* axis, Latin *colus* distaff.]
▶**I 1** A solid disc or a circular ring with spokes radiating from the centre, attached or able to be attached at its centre to an axle around which it revolves and used to facilitate the motion of a vehicle or for various mechanical purposes. OE.
2 A wheel-like structure or a device having a wheel as its essential part, used for a specific purpose; *spec.* (*a*) a large wheel used in various ways as an instrument of punishment or torture; (*b*) the revolving part of a lathe; *esp.* a potter's wheel; (*c*) a steering-wheel; (*d*) a revolving disc or drum used in various games of chance (also ***wheel of fortune***); †(*e*) a turnstile at the entrance of a convent. OE.
3 a A bicycle; a tricycle; ***the wheel***, cycling. Chiefly *US.* L19. ▸**b** In *pl.* A car. *slang.* M20.
▶**II** A thing resembling a wheel in form or movement.
4 An object having the form of a wheel, a circle, a disc; *spec.* (*a*) an ornament, design, or decoration resembling a spoked wheel; (*b*) *US slang* a dollar coin; (*c*) an item of food, esp. a cheese, made in the form of a shallow round which may be cut into sections. OE.
5 The celestial sphere, or any of the spheres of the planets etc. in ancient astronomy, regarded as revolving like a wheel. Now only *fig.* ME.
6 A firework which rotates when let off. Now *rare* exc. in ***CATHERINE wheel***, PIN-WHEEL. E17.
7 Each of the wards of a lock, which are rotated by the key. L18.
▶**III 8** The wheel which Fortune is fabled to turn, as an emblem of mutability (cf. ***Fortune's wheel***, ***wheel of Fortune*** below). OE.
9 A constituent part or element of something regarded as a machine or as moving forwards as if on wheels. ME. ▸**b** An important person; = ***big wheel*** (b) s.v. BIG *adjective*. *slang* (chiefly *US*). M20.
10 A recurring course of actions or events; an endless cycle. ME.
11 [Partly from WHEEL *verb*.] A movement about an axis or centre or in a circular or curved course; a rotation; a turn (usually, not completely around); *spec.* the movement of a line of people (esp. troops) with one end as a pivot. E17.
12 *PROSODY.* A set of short lines concluding a stanza. M19.
13 A leg. Usu. in *pl. US slang.* E20.

> 🕮 **8** S. MIDDLETON Now, in old age, when he expected little, looked forward to less, the wheel had come full circle. **9** C. LAMB Night's wheels are rattling fast over me. N. BLAKE A certain amount of hypocrisy is necessary to oil the wheels of society. **10** R. KIPLING I go to free myself from the Wheel of Things. **11** R. BOLDREWOOD The reckless speed and practised wheel of the trained . . horses.

Phrases: ***a spoke in one's wheel***: see SPOKE *noun*. **at the wheel** (*a*) driving a vehicle; (*b*) directing a ship; (*c*) in control of affairs. **be on a person's wheel** *slang* (chiefly *Austral.*) be close behind him or her; put pressure on him or her. ***big wheel***: see BIG *adjective*. ***break a butterfly on a wheel***: see BUTTERFLY 1. ***break on the wheel***: see BREAK *verb*. ***Egyptian wheel***: see EGYPTIAN *adjective*. ***fifth wheel***: see FIFTH *adjective*. ***fly on the wheel***: see FLY *noun*[1]. **Fortune's wheel** = sense 8 above. ***free wheel***, ***free-wheel***: see FREE *adjective*. ***grease the wheels***: see GREASE *verb*. ***hell on wheels***: see HELL *noun*. ***idle wheel***: see IDLE *adjective*. ***Ixionian wheel***. ***leading wheels***: see LEADING *adjective*. ***meals-on-wheels***: see MEAL *noun*[2]. **on oiled wheels**, **on wheels** (*a*) smoothly; quickly; (*b*) (as an intensive) in the extreme. ***pair of wheels***: see PAIR *noun*[1] 1. ***Persian wheel***: see PERSIAN *adjective*. ***phonic wheel***: see PHONIC *adjective*. ***potter's wheel***: see POTTER *noun*[1]. ***put a spoke in a person's wheel***: see SPOKE *noun*. ***put one's shoulder to the wheel***, ***set one's shoulder to the wheel***: see SHOULDER *noun*. ***reinvent the wheel***. **silly as a wheel** *Austral. slang* extremely silly. ***slow wheel***: see SLOW *adjective*. ***split wheel***: see SPLIT *ppl adjective*. ***square wheels***: see SQUARE *adjective*. ***trailing wheel***: see TRAILING *ppl adjective*. **wheel and axle** *MECHANICS* one of the simple machines which transmit force or direct its application. **wheel of Fortune** (*a*) = sense 8 above; (*b*) see sense 2(d) above. **wheels within wheels** (*a*) intricate machinery; (*b*) *colloq.* indirect or secret agencies.

Comb.: **wheel animalcule** = ROTIFER; **wheel arrangement** the relative positioning of driving-wheels and idle wheels on a locomotive; **wheel-back** *noun & adjective* (a chair) with a back shaped like or containing the design of a wheel; **wheel balance** *MECHANICS* an even distribution of mass about the axis of a wheel so that it rotates without wobbling or vibrating; **wheel balancing** *MECHANICS* the process of achieving wheel balance for the wheels of a motor vehicle; **wheel barometer** a mercurial barometer having a float attached to a string passing over a pulley-wheel on which the index turns; **wheelbase** the distance between the front and rear axles of a vehicle; **wheel brace** (*a*) a tool for screwing and unscrewing nuts on the wheel of a vehicle; (*b*) a hand drill worked by turning a wheel; **wheel bug** a large reduviid bug, *Arilus cristatus*, which is found in the southern US and the W. Indies and has a semicircular serrated crest resembling a cog-wheel; **wheel car** a simple farm cart; **wheel-carriage** *arch.* a wheeled vehicle; **wheelchair** a chair on wheels for an invalid or a disabled person; **wheelchaired** *adjective* in or confined to a wheelchair; **wheel clamp** a clamp designed to be locked to one of the wheels of an illegally parked motor vehicle to immobilize it; **wheel-clamp** *verb trans.* immobilize (a motor vehicle) with a wheel clamp; **wheel-cross** a ring-cross with arms radiating from a small circle in the centre of the ring; **wheel-dog** *Canad.* the dog harnessed nearest to the sleigh in a dog team; **wheel-dwelling** *ARCHAEOLOGY* (now *rare*) = ***wheel-house*** (b) below; **wheel-engraved** *adjective* (of glassware) engraved by means of wheel-engraving; **wheel-engraving** the art or process of engraving patterns on glass using a rotating copper wheel and an abrasive mixture of emery and oil, sand and water, etc.; **wheel-horse** (*a*) a horse next to the wheels of a vehicle; (*b*) *fig.* a person who bears the main burden of a business etc.; *spec.* (*US*) an experienced and conscientious member of a political party; **wheel-house** (*a*) a structure enclosing a large wheel; *spec.* the structure on a vessel containing the steering wheel, a steersman's shelter; (*b*) *ARCHAEOLOGY* an Iron Age circular stone dwelling having partition walls, which act as roof supports, radiating from the centre; (*c*) = ROUNDHOUSE 3; **wheel landing** *AERONAUTICS* a landing in which the main wheels touch down first, followed by the tail; **wheel-lock** *Hist.* (*a*) a type of gunlock having a steel wheel to rub against the flint etc.; (*b*) a gun with such a gunlock; **wheel-made** *adjective* (of pottery) made on a potter's wheel; **wheelman** (chiefly *US*) (*a*) a person in charge of a wheel in a machine piece; *esp.* a steersman; (*b*) *colloq.* a male cyclist; (*c*) the driver of a wheeled vehicle; *spec.* (*Criminals' slang*) the driver of a getaway car; **wheel-map** a medieval map of the world having Jerusalem depicted as the centre with lines radiating from it to other major cities etc.; **wheel-organ** *ZOOLOGY* the trochal disc of a rotifer; **wheel-ore** = BOURNONITE; **wheel-pit** (*a*) a space enclosed by masonry for a large wheel, as a turbine, to turn in; (*b*) *dial.* a whirlpool; **wheel-plate** the part of a solid wheel between the rim and the hub; **wheel-plough**: having wheels running on the ground to reduce friction or regulate the depth of the furrow; **wheel-press** a hydraulic press for moulding a solid wheel, or for fixing it on to an axle; **wheel-seat** the part of an axle that fits into the centre of a wheel; **wheel-set** a pair of wheels attached to an axle; **wheel slip** slipping of the wheels of a vehicle caused by lack of traction; **wheelsman** *US* a steersman; **wheel-spin** rotation of a vehicle's wheels without traction; **wheel-tax** *Hist.*: on wheeled carriages; **wheel well** (*a*) the recess under the wing of a vehicle into which a wheel fits; (*b*) the recess on an aircraft into which the landing gear is retracted; **wheel-window** a circular window with mullions radiating from the centre like spokes; **wheel wobble** vibration of the wheels of a moving vehicle, esp. when travelling at speed; **wheelwork** (the set of) connected wheels forming part of a mechanism, esp. in a watch or clock.

■ **wheelage** *noun* (*Hist.*) a toll paid for the passage of a wheeled vehicle; cost of carriage in a wheeled vehicle: E17. **wheelless** /-l-l-/ *adjective* E19. **wheel-like** *adjective* resembling (that of) a wheel M19. **wheelwise** *adverb* in the manner or form of a wheel L16. **wheely** *adjective* (*rare*) of or pertaining to a wheel E17.

wheel /wiːl/ *verb.* ME.
[from the noun.]
▶**I** Move like a wheel or by means of wheels.
1 *verb intrans.* Turn or revolve on an axis or pivot; rotate. ME. ▸**b** Reel; be giddy. L16.
2 *verb trans.* Cause to turn or revolve on an axis or pivot; rotate. LME. ▸**b** *verb trans. & intrans. spec.* Flourish (a stick) menacingly. Chiefly *Anglo-Irish.* E17.
3 *verb intrans. & trans.* (Cause to) change direction or face another way, esp. quickly or suddenly. Freq. foll. by *about*, *round*. E16. ▸**b** *verb trans. fig.* Change one's mind or a course of action. M17.
4 *MILITARY.* **a** *verb intrans.* Of a rank or body of troops: swing round in line with one end as a pivot, so as to change front. L16. ▸**b** *verb trans.* Cause (a rank or body of troops) to do this. M17.
5 *verb intrans.* Move in a circle or curve; circle; go round in circles. E17. ▸**b** *verb trans.* Cause to move in this way; trace (a circular or curved course). E18.
6 *verb trans.* Convey in or on a wheeled thing, (as a chair, vehicle, etc.). E17. ▸**b** *verb trans. & intrans. fig.* Convey or move easily or smoothly, as if on wheels; roll. *rare.* M17. ▸**c** *gen.* Bring *in*, *on*, or *out*. *colloq.* L20.
7 *verb intrans.* Travel in or on a wheeled vehicle; go along on wheels. *arch.* E18.
8 *verb trans.* Push or pull (a wheeled thing). L18. ▸**b** Drive or (esp.) manoeuvre (a car) slowly. *colloq.* M20.

> 🕮 **1** F. HARRISON The gates . . to the Elysian fields may . . wheel back on their adamantine hinges. *fig.*: J. M. COETZEE Summer is wheeling slowly towards its end. **3** K. A. PORTER She turned her head aside, wheeled about and walked away. A. PRICE Mitchell had wheeled his horse at the foot of the ridge. R. INGALLS She wheeled around and ran across the lawn. **5** F. KING The dead leaves whirled and wheeled in . . concentric circles. K. LETTE Julian wheeled drunkenly to the left. **b** DAY LEWIS Over the hill three buzzards are wheeling On the glass sky their skaters' curves. **6** A. BROOKNER A little girl . . whom Vadim wheeled about in her pram. J. MCPHEE A lackey with a handcart . . wheeled her luggage to the . . Hotel. E. SEGAL A nurse swiftly wheeled the young man into the . . Trauma room. **c** J. L. CARR I suppose they wanted to wheel me out like a museum piece. *Times* Worthy statistics will be wheeled out . . in time for the election. **8** G. SWIFT I . . wheeled my bike across the footbridge. **b** J. POYER It was quite late when Bethwig wheeled his Lancia into the . . car park.

▶**II** Have the form of a wheel.
†**9** *verb intrans.* Of a peacock: spread out its tail. E16–M18.
†**10** *verb trans.* Encircle, surround. *rare.* L16–M17.
†**11** *verb intrans.* Extend in a circle or curve. M17–L18.
12 *verb trans.* Give a circular or curved form to. *rare.* M17.
13 *verb intrans.* *NEEDLEWORK.* Embroider an ornamental design resembling a spoked wheel. Only as ***wheeling*** *verbal noun*. L19.
▶**III 14** *verb trans.* Provide with a wheel or wheels. M17.
Phrases: **wheel and deal** *colloq.* engage in political or commercial scheming.
■ **wheeling** *verbal noun* the action of the verb; an instance of this: L15. **wheeling** *adjective* (*a*) that wheels; (*b*) (of a chair etc.) that has wheels, that may be wheeled: L16.

wheelbarrow /'wiːlbarəʊ/ *noun & verb.* ME.
[from WHEEL *noun* + BARROW *noun*[3].]
▶**A** *noun.* **1** A shallow open box mounted on a single wheel at the front and legs at the back and having two shafts, used for the transportation of esp. garden loads. ME. ▸**b** A children's game in which one partner walks or runs on his or her hands with the legs supported off the ground by the other partner. Cf. ***wheelbarrow race*** (b) below. Usu. in *pl.* M18.
†**2** *transf.* A light carriage. L16–E19.
Comb.: **wheelbarrow race** (*a*) a race in which each contestant pushes a wheelbarrow (usu. occupied by a team-mate); (*b*) a race between two or more pairs, in which one of each pair runs on his or her hands with the legs supported off the ground by the other partner.
▶**B** *verb trans.* Convey in a wheelbarrow. E18.

wheeled /wiːld, *poet.* 'wiːlɪd/ *adjective.* E16.
[from WHEEL *noun* + -ED[2].]
1 Having a wheel or wheels; (as 2nd elem. of comb.) having wheels of a specified number or kind. E16.
2 *transf.* Effected on wheels or by wheeled vehicles. M19.

> 🕮 **1** G. GREENE He was on a wheeled bed passing down long corridors. ***four-wheeled***, ***large-wheeled***, ***two-wheeled***, etc.

wheeler /'wiːlə/ *noun.* ME.
[from WHEEL *noun*, *verb* + -ER[1].]
▶**I** Senses from the noun.
1 A wheelwright. ME.
2 A draught animal positioned next to the wheels or nearest the driver, and behind another. E19.
3 A vehicle or boat having a wheel or wheels esp. of a specified number or kind. Chiefly as 2nd elem. of comb. M19.
▶**II** Senses from the verb.

4 A person who wheels a vehicle, or conveys something in a wheeled vehicle (esp. a wheelbarrow). **L17.**
5 A cyclist. *colloq.* **L19.**
Comb.: **wheeler-dealer** *colloq.* [from ***wheel and deal*** s.v. WHEEL *verb*] a political or commercial schemer; **wheeler-dealing** *colloq.* political or commercial scheming.

wheelie /ˈwiːli/ *noun. slang.* **M20.**
[from WHEEL *noun* + -IE.]
1 The stunt of riding a bicycle or motorcycle for a short distance with the front wheel off the ground, or of riding a skateboard with either pair of wheels off the ground. **M20.**
2 A sharp U-turn made by a motor vehicle, causing skidding of the wheels. **L20.**
3 A person in or confined to a wheelchair. *Austral.* **L20.**
4 ***wheelie bin***, a large refuse bin on wheels. Orig. *Austral.* **L20.**

wheelwright /ˈwiːlrʌɪt/ *noun.* **ME.**
[from WHEEL *noun* + WRIGHT.]
A person who makes or repairs (esp. wooden) wheels and wheeled vehicles.
■ **wheelwrighting** *noun* the making of (esp. wooden) wheels and wheeled vehicles **L19.**

wheen /wiːn/ *adjective* (in mod. usage also classed as a *determiner*) & *noun. Scot., N. Ir., & north.* **LME.**
[Repr. Old English *hwēne* in some degree, instr. case of *hwōn* a few.]
▶ **A** *adjective.* Few, not many. Usu. preceded by *a*: a few, a fair amount or number of. **LME.**

📖 SIR W. SCOTT A wheen idle gowks coming to glower at the hole. I. RANKIN Those are two questions; I've got a wheen more.

▶ **B** *noun.* **1** ***a wheen of***, a few, a fair amount or number of. **LME.**
2 *adverbial.* ***a wheen***, somewhat. **M19.**

📖 **2** C. GIBBON The auld wife's a wheen better.

wheep /wiːp/ *noun*[1]. *rare.* **L19.**
[Imit.]
The sound of a sword etc. being drawn from a sheath.

wheep /wiːp/ *verb & noun*[2]. **E19.**
[Imit.]
▶ **A** *verb intrans.* = WHEEPLE *verb* 1. *Scot. & north.* **E19.**
▶ **B** *noun.* **1** = WHEEPLE *noun. Scot. & north.* **M19.**
2 A short high-pitched noise, a bleep. *colloq.* **L19.**

wheeple /ˈwiːp(ə)l/ *noun & verb. Scot., N. Ir., & north.* **L18.**
[Imit.]
▶ **A** *noun.* A shrill protracted cry made by a bird; a feeble or tuneless whistle. **L18.**
▶ **B** *verb.* **1** *verb intrans.* Of a bird: utter a shrill protracted cry. **L18.**
2 *verb trans. & intrans.* Whistle (a tune), esp. feebly or tunelessly. **L18.**

wheetle /ˈwiːt(ə)l/ *verb intrans.* Chiefly *Scot.* **E19.**
[Imit.]
Whistle shrilly.

wheeze /wiːz/ *verb & noun.* **LME.**
[Prob. from Old Norse *hvæsa* to hiss.]
▶ **A** *verb.* **1** *verb intrans.* Breathe with an audible whistling or rasping sound, due to dryness or obstruction in the air passages. **LME.** ▸**b** *transf.* Make a whistling or rasping sound. **M19.**
2 *verb trans.* Utter with such a sound. Also foll. by *out.* **M19.**

📖 **1** A. CRAIG Joggers pounded past, wheezing slightly in the autumnal air. **2** C. J. LEVER 'You'll soon see!' wheezed out the old man.

▶ **B** *noun.* **1** An act of wheezing; a whistling or rasping sound. **LME.**
2 A joke or comic phrase introduced (esp. repeatedly) into a performance by a clown or comedian; a catchphrase; a clever scheme. *colloq.* (orig. *Theatrical slang*). **M19.**

📖 **1** V. NABOKOV The poor girl developed a dry cough and a wheeze in the bronchia. A. TYLER A bus . . stopped with a wheeze and let them climb on. B. UNSWORTH The thin wheeze of his breathing was audible in the quiet room. **2** H. ROBBINS 'May all your troubles be little ones.' Johnny winced at the old wheeze. *Times* Thought it would be a jolly wheeze to buy one.

■ **wheezer** *noun* **M19.** **wheezing** *verbal noun* the action of the verb; an instance of this: **M16.** **wheezingly** *adverb* in a wheezing manner, with a wheeze **L19.** **wheezle** *noun & verb* (chiefly *Scot. & north.*) (*a*) *noun* a wheeze; (*b*) *verb intrans.* wheeze: **M18.**

wheezy /ˈwiːzi/ *adjective.* **E19.**
[from WHEEZE *noun, verb* + -Y[1].]
Characterized by or affected by wheezing; resembling a wheeze. Also, making a wheezing sound.

📖 J. K. JEROME The strains of 'He's got 'em on,' jerked . . out of a wheezy accordion. B. MUKHERJEE The younger man managed a wheezy laugh. *Parents* The wheezy attacks most commonly start with ordinary coughs.

■ **wheezily** *adverb* **L19.** **wheeziness** *noun* **L19.**

wheft *noun* see WAFT *noun.*

whelk /wɛlk/ *noun*[1].
[Old English *weoloc*, *wioloc*: cf. Western Flemish *willok*, *wullok*. The spelling with *wh-* (15) is perh. due to assoc. with next.]
(The shell of) any of various marine gastropod molluscs of the family Buccinidae and related families, most of which are predators of bivalve molluscs and have turbinate shells; esp. *Buccinum undatum*, which is common on N. Atlantic coasts and is used as food.
dog-whelk: see DOG *noun & adjective.*
Comb.: **whelk-stall** a stall at which whelks are sold; ***unable to run a whelk stall***, incompetent, esp. in business; **whelk-tingle** = TINGLE *noun*[2].

whelk /wɛlk/ *noun*[2]. Now chiefly *dial.*
[Late Old English *hwylca* rel. to WHEAL *noun*[1].]
1 A pimple, pustule. **LOE.**
2 [By confusion.] = WEAL *noun*[2]. **M18.**
■ **whelky** *adjective* (*rare*) pimply **E19.**

whelked /wɛlkt/ *adjective.* Also **welked** /wɛlkt/. **M16.**
[from WHELK *noun*[1] + -ED[2]. In later use, sense 2 prob. from WHELK *noun*[2].]
1 Twisted, convoluted, or ridged like a whelk's shell. **M16.**
2 Marked with weals or ridges on the flesh. Cf. WHELK *noun*[2] 2. **L16.**

whelm /wɛlm/ *verb & noun.* **ME.**
[Repr. unrecorded Old English verb parallel to WHELVE. Cf. WHEMMEL.]
▶ **A** *verb.* †**1** *verb intrans.* Overturn, capsize. **ME–E16.**
2 *verb trans.* Turn (a hollow vessel) upside down; *esp.* place (a hollow vessel) upside down *over* something as a cover. Now *dial.* **ME.** ▸†**b** Cover (a thing) with an upside-down vessel. **LME–M17.** ▸**c** Throw or heap (a thing) over something else, esp. so as to cover or crush it. Foll. by *over, upon.* **E17.** ▸†**d** *verb trans. & intrans.* Turn *over* (soil). **M17–L18.**
3 *verb intrans.* Pass *over* and cover (a thing) *literary.* Long *rare.* **LME.**
4 *verb trans.* Cover with a great mass of water, earth, etc.; submerge, drown, bury; *transf. & fig.* engulf or destroy like a flood, avalanche, etc.; overpower emotionally. **M16.**

📖 **4** TENNYSON Some were whelmed with missiles of the wall. A. JESSOPP Flocks, and herds, and corn and hay being whelmed in the deluge.

▶ **B** *noun.* **1** A wooden drainpipe, originally made from a hollowed tree-trunk. Long *obsolete* exc. *dial.* **L16.**
2 A surge (*of* activity, water, etc.). Chiefly *poet.* **E19.**

whelp /wɛlp/ *noun*[1] *& verb.*
[Old English *hwelp* = Old Saxon *hwelp* (Dutch *welp*), Old High German *hwelf*, (also mod.) *welf*, Old Norse *hvelpr*, from a Germanic word of which no cognates are known.]
▶ **A** *noun.* **1** A young dog; a puppy. **OE.**
2 A young wolf, lion, tiger, bear, etc.; a cub. *arch.* **OE.** ▸**b** *transf.* A young child. Now *joc.* **L15.**
3 a An offspring of a monstrous or evil being. *arch.* **ME.** ▸**b** Orig., a contemptible person. Later, an ill-mannered child or youth. **ME.**
4 NAUTICAL. Any of the longitudinal projections on the barrel of a capstan or the drum of a windlass. Usu. in *pl.* **LME.**
5 NAUTICAL. [After use as support for HMS *Lion*.] An auxiliary war vessel established in Charles I's reign. Long *obsolete* exc. *Hist.* **E17.**

📖 **3b** G. B. SHAW This unmannerly young whelp Chubbs-Jenkinson.

Phrases: **in whelp** (of a female animal) pregnant.
▶ **B** *verb.* **1** *verb trans. & intrans.* Of a female animal or (*derog.*) a woman: give birth (to). **ME.**
2 *transf. & fig.* Bring forth; originate (an evil scheme etc.). **L16.**

📖 **1** *Time* A child-woman of the '60s who whelps children out of wedlock. *Daily Telegraph* Bitches that whelp in quarantine over here. *Greyhound Star* Candy Floss has whelped a litter of . . three dogs and two bitches. **2** W. COWPER Having whelped a prologue with great pains.

■ **whelphood** *noun* the condition of being a whelp; the time during which an animal is a whelp: **M19.** **whelpish** *adjective* **L16.** **whelpless** *adjective* **L16.** **whelpling** *noun* a whelp, *esp.* a little or young whelp **E17.**

whelp /wɛlp/ *noun*[2]. *colloq.* **E20.**
[Alt.]
= WELT *noun*[1].

whelve /wɛlv/ *verb trans. obsolete* exc. *dial.*
[Late Old English *hwylfan* = Old Saxon *bihwelbian* cover over, Middle & mod. Dutch, Middle & mod. Low German *welven*, Old High German *welben* (German *wölben* to vault, arch), Old Norse *hvelfa* to arch, turn upside down, from Germanic verb from base (meaning 'rounded, arched') of Old English *hwealf* arch, vault & other Germanic cognates, Greek *kolpos* bosom. Cf. WHELM.]
1 Turn (a vessel etc.) upside down so as to cover something; *gen.* turn over, overturn. **LOE.**
†**2** Hide; bury. **LME–E18.**

whemmel /ˈwɛm(ə)l/ *verb & noun. Scot. & dial.* Also **whomm-** /ˈwɒm-/, **whumm-** /ˈwʌm-/. **M16.**
[Metathetic var. of WHELM.]
▶ **A** *verb.* Infl. **-l(l)-.**
1 *verb trans.* Turn (a vessel etc.) upside down; *transf. & fig.* upset, throw into confusion. **M16.** ▸**b** Cover (a thing) with an upside-down vessel etc.; hide. **L18.**
2 *verb trans.* Submerge; drown. **M16.**
3 *verb intrans.* Tumble over. **L18.**
▶ **B** *noun.* An overthrow; an upset; a state of confusion. **E19.**

when /wɛn/ *adverb, conjunction, & noun.*
[Old English *hwenne*, *hwænne*, *hwanne*, *hwonne* corresp. to Old Frisian *hwanne*, *hwenne* until, if, Old Saxon *hwan(na)* when, Old High German *wenne*, *wanne* (German *wenn* if, *wann* when), Gothic *hwan* when, how, from Germanic adverb from Indo-European base also of WHO, WHAT.]
▶ **A** *adverb.* **1** *interrog.* At what time? on what occasion? in what circumstances? **OE.**
2 *rel.* Referring to an antecedent denoting a period of time: at or on which. **ME.**
3 In the past. *N. Amer. colloq.* **M20.**

📖 **1** SWIFT I wonder when this letter will be finished. D. H. LAWRENCE When will the car come? *Sunday Correspondent* When would it be possible to meet him? *New York Review of Books* Some wondered when it would happen again. **2** P. MARSHALL He remembered . . the time when he had worked . . for a white family. **3** H. WAUGH She needn't try those airs with me. I knew her when.

▶ **B** *conjunction.* **1** At the time that, on the occasion that; in the circumstances which; *gen.* at any time that, on any or every occasion that. Also *ellipt.* with only predicate expressed. **OE.**
2 Introducing a clause as obj. of verb, or qualified by a preposition: the or a time at which. **OE.**
3 At which time; after or upon which; and then; (with implication of suddenness) but just then. **OE.**
4 Seeing that, considering that. **ME.**
5 While on the contrary, whereas. **ME.**

📖 **1** M. KEANE You will come out . . when hounds meet at nine o'clock. Not earlier. E. BOWEN My uncle, a . . versatile and when necessary inventive talker. P. S. BUCK This woman came into our house when she was a child. DAY LEWIS Wasps and bees only sting . . when they are annoyed. V. S. PRITCHETT We wondered which room you had when you lived there. **2** G. VIDAL Remember when we used to talk about seeing more of Italy? *New Yorker* I came across . . the tights . . from when I waited table. **3** S. BARING-GOULD Scarcely had she touched the spindle when she pierced her hand on it. D. H. LAWRENCE They were eating . . when the boy jumped off his chair. V. S. PRITCHETT It was disturbing when you thought about it. **4** D. GILL How can we love the plainsmen when they burn / our houses . . and rape our wives. **5** F. MARRYAT I . . received fifty shillings, when I ought to have received . . ten pounds.

Phrases & comb.: ***as and when***: see AS *adverb* etc. ***if and when***: see IF *conjunction.* **say when** *colloq.*: used by a person performing an action (esp. pouring out drink) for another, to ask when the action should stop. **when-issued** *adjective* (chiefly *US*) designating or pertaining to an agreement to buy securities in which payment is not required until delivery.
▶ **C** *pronoun & noun.* **1** *pronoun.* After a preposition: what time? which time. **ME.**
2 *noun.* The or a time at which something happens (or did or will happen). **M16.**

📖 **1** *Daily Telegraph* A hearing is due on July 15, by when the court may have disappeared.

■ **whenabouts** *noun & adverb* (*rare*) (*a*) *noun* the approximate time at which something happened; (*b*) *adverb* about what time?: **L19.**

whenas /wɛnˈaz/ *conjunction. arch.* Also as two words. **LME.**
[from WHEN *conjunction* + AS *adverb.*]
1 = WHEN *conjunction* 1. **LME.**
†**2** = WHEN *conjunction* 3. **M16–L17.**
3 = WHEN *conjunction* 4, 5. **M16.**

whence /wɛns/ *adverb, conjunction, pronoun, & noun.* Now *formal.* **ME.**
[from WHENNE + -S[3]. The spelling *-ce* is phonetic, to retain the unvoiced sound denoted in the earlier spelling by *-s*. Cf. HENCE, THENCE.]
▶ **A** *adverb & conjunction.* **I** *interrog. adverb.* **1** From what place? **ME.**
2 From what source, origin, or cause? **ME.**

📖 **1** TENNYSON O babbling brook . . Whence come you? E. MUIR I did not know whence came my breath. **2** L. STERNE But whence . . have you concluded . . that the writer is of our church?

▶ **II** *rel. adverb & conjunction.* **3** From which place; from or out of which. **LME.** ▸†**b** From the place in which. *rare* (Shakes.). Only in **E17.**
4 From which source, cause, or circumstance. **M16.**

📖 **3** *Times* He was educated at Sywell House School . . whence he went up to Oxford. D. PIPER Void lobster shells whence the meat has . . been abstracted. **4** G. L. GOODALE A tip bows or nods . . to all points of the compass; whence the name nutation.

▶**B** *pronoun & noun.* **1** ***from whence***, from which place, from which source, from which circumstance. **LME.**
2 The place of origin of a thing; a source. **M19.**
■ **whenceforward** *adverb* (*rare*) from which time or place onward **M17.**

whencesoever /wɛnssəʊˈɛvə/ *pronoun, adverb, & conjunction.* Also (*poet.*) **-soe'er** /-səʊˈɛː/. **E16.**
[from WHENCE + SOEVER.]
▶**A** *pronoun.* ***from whencesoever***, from whatever place or source. **E16.**
▶**B** *rel. adverb & conjunction.* From whatever place or source. **L16.**
■ Also **whencever** *pronoun, adverb, & conjunction* **E18.**

whenever /wɛnˈɛvə/ *adverb & conjunction.* Also (*poet.*) **-e'er** /-ˈɛː/. **ME.**
[from WHEN *adverb, conjunction* + EVER.]
▶**I** *rel. adverb & conjunction.* **1** At whatever time that, no matter when; every time that. **ME.**
2 As soon as. Now only *Scot. & Anglo-Irish.* **M17.**
📖 **1** *Oxford Magazine* When the official story . . is published, whenever that may be. D. CUSACK Whenever I dream of vegetables something terrible happens! A. CARTER She gave Victoria a banana whenever she saw her.
▶**II** *interrog. adverb.* **3** (Also as two words.) Used with emphatic force in place of *when* in a question. Now *colloq.* **LME.**
📖 **3** OED When ever did I say that?
▶**III 4** With loss of relative force: at some similar time. Usu. preceded by *or. colloq.* **E20.**
📖 **4** H. JAMES I said to myself . . three weeks ago, or whenever, that . . I was going to come over.

†**whenne** *adverb & conjunction.* **OE–L15.**
[Old English *hwanon(e)*, *hwonan* = Old Saxon *hwanon*, Old High German *wanan(a)*, *wannen* (Middle High German *swannen*), from Germanic from Indo-European base also of WHEN. Cf. WHENCE.]
= WHENCE *adverb & conjunction.*

whenso /ˈwɛnsəʊ/ *rel. adverb & conjunction. arch.* **ME.**
[from WHEN *adverb, conjunction* + SO *adverb.*]
†**1** = WHEN *conjunction* 1. **ME–M16.**
2 = WHENEVER 1. **ME.**

whensoever /wɛnsəʊˈɛvə/ *rel. adverb & conjunction.* Also (*poet.*) **-soe'er** /-səʊˈɛː/. **ME.**
[from WHEN *adverb, conjunction* + SOEVER.]
= WHENEVER 1.

whensomever /wɛns(ə)mˈɛvə/ *rel. adverb & conjunction.* Now *dial.* **LME.**
[from WHEN *adverb, conjunction* + SOMEVER.]
= WHENEVER 1.

where /wɛː/ *adverb, conjunction, pronoun, & noun.*
[Old English *hwǣr*, *hwar(a)* corresp. to Old Frisian *hwēr*, Old Saxon *hwār* (Du *waar*), Old High German *(h)wār*, *wā* (German *wo*), Old Norse *hvar*, Gothic *hwar*, from Germanic derivs. from Indo-European base also of WHO, WHAT.]
▶**A** *adverb.* **I** *interrog.* **1** In or at what place. **OE.** ▸**b** After an interjection or verb of looking, as *lo*, *see*, etc.: here, there. *arch.* **ME.**
2 To what place. **OE.**
3 *gen.* In what situation or circumstances; at what point or stage; in what passage or part (of a writing); in what respect or particular; from what source. **ME.**
📖 **1** G. GREENE Where are your bags? W. PERRIAM He's always refused to tell me where he lives. **2** SHAKES. *Mids. N. D.* Where shall we go? C. SANDBURG I don't know where I'm going but I'm on my way. **3** C. BRONTË 'But where is the use of going on,' I asked.
▶**II** *rel.* **4** Referring to an antecedent denoting a place or receptacle, or *gen.* a situation, circumstance, etc.: in, at, or to which. **ME.**
📖 **4** A. CARTER A . . country station where cow parsley foamed along the line. H. R. HALDEMAN We are now at a point where fact and fiction are becoming badly confused. I. MCEWAN We're looking for a place where we can get something to eat. P. O. DUDGEON My niece and I set out from Oxford, where she works.
▶**B** *conjunction.* **1** In, at, or to the (or a) place in or at which. **ME.**
2 Introducing a clause as obj. of a verb or preposition, or as predicate: the (or a) place in or to which. **ME.**
3 In or to any (or every) place in or to which; wherever. **ME.**
4 Introducing a clause as obj. of the verb or preposition, or as predicate: orig., a case in which, a person to whom (now only *spec.* as the object of love or marriage); now, the respect or particular in which. **ME.**
5 In the passage or part (of a writing) in which; at or to the point or stage at which; in the situation or circumstances in which; in the respect or particular in which. **LME.** ▸**b** To or at a point such that. Usu. preceded by *to. US dial.* **M20.**
†**6** Chiefly LAW. Seeing that, considering that. **LME–M17.**
7 While on the contrary, whereas. **LME.**
8 That. *N. Amer. colloq.* **E20.**
📖 **1** E. BOWEN The low ceiling was kept where it was by two heavy cross-beams. **2** R. P. JHABVALA He . . propelled her back to where the others were. J. JOHNSTON Brushing yesterday's dust . . into the garden, from where it had come. M. ROBERTS Tell me a story . . . Go on from where you left off. **4** T. HARDY It would be better she should marry where she wished. OED That was where he failed. **5** E. BOWEN My conversation with Miss Banderry did not end where I leave off recording it. **7** R. A. CRAM Where Roman and Byzantine art had striven to achieve space in its simplest form, the North worked for interior space. **8** *New Yorker* I see where the St. Regis has changed hands again.
Phrases: ***get where***: see GET *verb.* ***where it's at***: see AT *preposition.*
▶**C** *pronoun & noun.* **I** *pronoun.* **1** What, which. Only in comb. with adverbs & prepositions. No longer productive exc. *poet.* **ME.**
2 What place? **M18.**
📖 **2** L. STEFFENS No matter who you are or where you come from, Chicago will give you a . . boost. G. GREENE I went to beg for money . . for expatriation—to where?
▶**II** *noun.* **3** A place; *esp.* the or a place at which something happens (or did or will happen). **LME.**
Comb.: **whereafter** *rel. adverb & conjunction* (*arch.*) after which; **whereanent** *rel. adverb & conjunction* (chiefly *Scot.*) concerning which; **whereat** *adverb & conjunction* (*arch.*) (*a*) *interrog. adverb* (*rare*) at what?; (*b*) *rel. adverb & conjunction* at which; **whereaway** *adverb* (*arch.*) in what direction; **wherefrom** *rel. adverb & conjunction* (now *arch. & formal*) from which, whence; **whereinto** *rel. adverb & conjunction* (*arch.*) into which; **whereout** *rel. adverb & conjunction* (*arch.*) out of which, out from which; **wherethrough** *rel. adverb & conjunction* (*arch.*) (*a*) through which; (*b*) on account of which; in consequence of which; **whereto** *adverb & conjunction* (now *arch. & formal*) (*a*) *interrog. adverb* to what; to what end; for what; (*b*) *rel. adverb & conjunction* to which; **whereunder** *rel. adverb & conjunction* (now *arch. & formal*) under which; **whereunto** *adverb & conjunction* (now *arch. & formal*) (*a*) *interrog. adverb* unto what; for what purpose; (*b*) *rel. adverb & conjunction* unto which.
■ **whereness** *noun* the fact or condition of a thing being where it is; situation, location: **L17.**

whereabout /wɛːrəˈbaʊt/; *as noun* ˈwɛːrəbaʊt/ *adverb & noun.* Now *rare.* **ME.**
[from WHERE *adverb, conjunction* + ABOUT *preposition.*]
▶**A** *adverb.* **1** *interrog.* **a** = WHEREABOUTS *adverb* 1a. **ME.** ▸†**b** Concerning what; on what business. **ME–L16.**
†**2 a** *rel.* Concerning or in regard to which. **M16–M17.** ▸**b** Near or in the neighbourhood of which. **M17–E18.**
▶**B** *noun.* = WHEREABOUTS *noun.* **E17.**

whereabouts /wɛːrəˈbaʊts/; *as noun* ˈwɛːrəbaʊts/ *adverb & noun.* **LME.**
[from prec. + -S³. Cf. WHATABOUTS.]
▶**A** *adverb.* **1** *interrog.* **a** Where; about or approximately where. **LME.** ▸†**b** = WHEREABOUT *adverb* 1b. Only in **M16.**
†**2** *rel.* = WHEREABOUT *adverb* 2a. **L16–M17.**
▶**B** *noun.* With possess. or *of*: the place in or near which a person or thing is; (approximate) location. Cf. earlier WHEREABOUT *noun.* **L18.**

whereas /wɛːrˈaz/ *rel. adverb, conjunction, & noun.* **ME.**
[Comb. WHERE *adverb, conjunction* + AS *adverb.*]
▶**A** *rel. adverb.* = WHERE *adverb* 4. Long *arch.* **ME.**
▶**B** *conjunction.* †**1** = WHERE *conjunction.* **LME–L16.**
2 Taking into consideration the fact that; seeing that, considering that. Chiefly & now only introducing a preamble in a legal or other formal document. **LME.**
3 Introducing a statement of fact in contrast or opposition to that in the main clause: while on the contrary; the fact on the other hand being that. **L15.**
📖 **3** *Times Educ. Suppl.* Individual responsibility is mentioned . . four times whereas legislation is mentioned only once.
▶**C** *noun.* A statement introduced by 'whereas'; the preamble of a formal document. **L18.**

whereby /wɛːˈbʌɪ/ *adverb & conjunction.* **ME.**
[from WHERE *pronoun* + BY *preposition.*]
▶**I** *interrog. adverb.* **1** By or near what; in what direction; by what means. Now *rare* or *obsolete.* **ME.**
📖 **1** S. JOHNSON Whereby wilt thou accomplish thy design?
▶**II** *rel. adverb & conjunction.* **2** Beside or near which; along, through, or over which. Now *rare.* **ME.**
3 By means of which; according to which, in which. **ME.**
4 As a result of or owing to which; so that, in order that. Now *rare.* **LME.**
5 Whereupon. *dial.* **L16.**
📖 **3** D. SIMPSON That strange osmosis whereby news . . is transmitted without apparent means of communication. J. EPSTEIN An arrangement whereby I would . . pay 10 percent.

wherefore /ˈwɛːfɔː/, *in sense A.2* wɛːˈfɔː/ *adverb, conjunction, & noun.* Also (now only in sense A.2) **-for.** **ME.**
[from WHERE *pronoun* + FOR *preposition.*]
▶**A** *adverb.* Now *arch. & formal.*
▶**I** *interrog.* **1** For what; for what purpose or end; for what cause or reason; why. **ME.**
📖 **1** W. OWEN Why sit they here in twilight? Wherefore rock they, purgatorial shadows.
▶**II** *rel.* **2** For which. **ME.**
3 On account of which; as a result of which. **ME.**
📖 **2** R. BRIDGES The secret purpose wherefor Nature plann'd their industry. **3** R. HOOKER The true reason wherfore Christ doth loue belieuers is because their belief is the gift of God.
▶**B** *conjunction.* Introducing a clause expr. a consequence or inference from what has just been stated: for which reason; which being the case. Now *arch. & formal.* **ME.**
📖 M. TWAIN A . . touch upon his arm . . saved him this indiscretion; wherefore he gave the royal assent.
▶**C** *noun.* A question beginning with 'wherefore' (*rare*); the answer to such a question, a reason. **M16.**
📖 *Gramophone* I was desperate to know all the whys and wherefores of a really advanced technique.

wherein /wɛːrˈɪn/ *adverb & conjunction.* Now *arch. & formal.* **ME.**
[from WHERE *pronoun* + IN *preposition.*]
▶**I** *interrog. adverb.* **1** In what (thing, matter, respect, etc.). **ME.**
📖 **1** F. W. FARRAR Oh, Britannicus! wherein have we offended?
▶**II** *rel. adverb & conjunction.* **2** In which (place, receptacle, writing, etc.). **ME.** ▸†**b** Into which. **LME–L16.** ▸**c** During or in the course of which (time). **M16.**
3 In which (matter, fact, etc.); in respect of which. **ME.**
4 In that respect in which; that in which. **L16.**
📖 **2** M. KEANE The garden wherein was walled their . . chief sport in life. **3** T. HARDY The only case wherein the gain could be considered . . worth the hazard. **4** SHAKES. *Mids. N. D.* Wherein it doth impair the seeing sense, It pays the hearing double recompense.
Comb.: **whereinsoever** *rel. adverb & conjunction* in whatever matter, respect, etc.

whereof /wɛːrˈɒv/ *adverb & conjunction.* Now *arch. & formal.* **ME.**
[from WHERE *pronoun* + OF *preposition.*]
▶**I** *interrog. adverb.* †**1** From what source; to what purpose; for what reason. **ME–L16.**
2 Of what. **LME.**
▶**II** *rel. adverb & conjunction.* **3** Of which. **ME.**
†**4** From or out of which. **ME–L17.**
†**5** On account of which. **ME–E17.**
†**6** By means of which. **ME–E17.**
3 know whereof one speaks know what one is talking about.

whereon /wɛːrˈɒn/ *adverb & conjunction.* Now *arch. & formal.* **ME.**
[from WHERE *pronoun* + ON *preposition.*]
▶**I** *interrog. adverb.* **1** On what. **ME.**
▶**II** *rel. adverb & conjunction.* **2** On which. **ME.**
3 On to which. **ME.**
4 = WHEREUPON 4. **L16.**

whereso /ˈwɛːsəʊ/ *rel. adverb & conjunction. arch.* **ME.**
[from WHERE *adverb, conjunction* + SO *adverb.*]
= WHEREVER 2, 3, 4.

wheresoever /wɛːsəʊˈɛvə/ *rel. adverb & conjunction.* Now *arch. & formal.* **ME.**
[from WHERE *adverb, conjunction* + SOEVER.]
1 = WHEREVER 2, 3, 4. **ME.**
2 *ellipt.* = WHEREVER 5. **M16.**

wheresomever /wɛːs(ə)mˈɛvə/ *rel. adverb & conjunction.* *obsolete* exc. *dial.* **ME.**
[from WHERE *adverb* + SOMEVER.]
= WHEREVER 2, 3.

whereupon /wɛːrəˈpɒn/ *adverb & conjunction.* **ME.**
[from WHERE *pronoun* + UPON *preposition.*]
▶**I** *interrog. adverb.* †**1** Upon what; concerning what; for what reason. **ME–M17.**
▶**II** *rel. adverb & conjunction.* **2** Of position: upon which. Now *arch. & formal.* **ME.** ▸†**b** On to which. **M16–M17.**
3 †**a** With clause as antecedent: on which account, for which reason; of derivation from which (by inference). **LME–L17.** ▸**b** Upon which as a basis of action, argument, etc. Now *rare* or *obsolete.* **E16.**
4 Upon the occurrence of which; immediately after and in consequence of which. **LME.**
5 Concerning which. Now *rare* or *obsolete.* **M16.**
📖 **4** T. HARDY The room began to darken, whereupon Christopher arose to leave.

wherever /wɛːrˈɛvə/ *adverb & conjunction.* Also (*poet.*) **-e'er** /-ˈɛː/. **ME.**
[from WHERE *adverb, conjunction* + EVER *adverb.*]
▶**I** *interrog. adverb* (Also as two words.)
1 Used with emphatic force in place of *where* in a question. Now *colloq.* **ME.**
📖 **1** R. BOLDREWOOD Wherever did the cayenne come from?

▶ **II** *rel. adverb & conjunction.* **2** At, in, or to any or every place in or to which. ME.

📖 **2** G. GREENE He would have liked to leave visible footprints wherever he walked. J. MITCHELL They . . could hunt wherever they liked.

▶ **III 3** Introducing a qualifying dependent clause: in or to whatever place; no matter where. LME.

4 In any case or circumstances in which. E17.

5 With loss of relative force: at, in, or to some similar place. Now usu. preceded by *or. colloq.* M17.

📖 **3** A. M. FAIRBAIRN Wherever the laws of mechanics rule, necessity rules. **4** O. WILDE Wherever you are . . you will make a mark. A. PRICE Wherever Audley was, that would be the centre of things. **5** *Bookseller* A jet flies off to London, New York, Paris, or wherever.

wherewith /wɛːˈwɪð/ *adverb, conjunction, & noun.* Now *arch. & formal.* ME.

[from WHERE *pronoun* + WITH *preposition.*]

▶ **A** *adverb & conjunction.* **I** *interrog. adverb.* †**1** With what. ME–L16.

▶ **II** *rel. adverb & conjunction.* **2** With which; by means of which, whereby. ME.

3 In consequence of which; on account of which. LME.

†**4** Together with which; in addition to or besides which. LME–M17.

5 Whereupon. M16.

📖 **2** J. BUCHAN There was nothing on the globe wherewith to bribe him.

▶ **B** *noun.* = WHEREWITHAL *noun.* Usu. without article. ME.

wherewithal /wɛːwɪˈðɔːl/ *adverb, conjunction, & noun.* M16.

[from WHERE *adverb, conjunction* + WITHAL *adverb.*]

▶ **A** *adverb & conjunction.* **I** *interrog. adverb.* **1** With what. *arch.* M16.

▶ **II** *rel. adverb & conjunction.* †**2** Whereupon. M16–M17.

3 With which; whereby. *arch.* M16.

▶ **B** *noun.* That with which to do something, the means by which to do something; *esp.* the money needed for a purpose. (Foll. by *to do.*) Also without article. Cf. earlier WHEREWITH *noun.* L16.

📖 R. P. JHABVALA When he did not have the wherewithal to pay his soldiers, they mutinied. F. FORSYTH Somewhere in London there has to exist the wherewithal to discover any . . knowledge known to man. G. KEILLOR He doubted they had the wherewithal to hold up a gas station. T. O'BRIEN Sarah had resources. There was no shortage of wherewithal.

wherret /ˈwɛrɪt/ *noun & verb.* Now *dial.* L16.

[Perh. imit.]

▶ **A** *noun.* A sharp blow; *esp.* a slap. L16.

▶ **B** *verb trans.* Strike sharply; *esp.* slap. L16.

wherry /ˈwɛri/ *noun & verb.* LME.

[Origin unkn.]

▶ **A** *noun.* **1** A light rowing boat used chiefly on rivers and in harbours for carrying passengers. LME.

2 A large light barge. L16.

3 A large four-wheeled dray. *local.* L19.

Comb.: **wherryman** a man employed on a wherry.

▶ **B** *verb trans.* Carry in a wherry. *rare.* E17.

¶ Recorded earlier in ME as a surname.

whet /wɛt/ *verb & noun.*

[Old English *hwettan* = Middle & mod. Low German, Middle & mod. Dutch *wetten*, Old High German *wezzan* (German *wetzen*), Old Norse *hvetja*, Gothic *gahwatjan*, from Germanic verb from adjective meaning 'sharp' (whence also Old English *hwæt* quick, active, brave).]

▶ **A** *verb.* Infl. **-tt-**.

1 *verb trans.* Sharpen (a tool or weapon) esp. on a stone; (of an animal) sharpen (the teeth, tusks, or beak) in preparation for an attack. OE. ▸**b** *verb intrans.* Prepare for an attack. Long *rare* or *obsolete.* LME.

†**2** *verb trans. fig.* Incite or urge on (*to, to do*). OE–M18.

3 *verb trans.* Stimulate (the appetite or a desire, interest, etc.). Also foll. by *up.* LME.

†**4** *verb trans.* [translating Hebrew *šānan.*] In biblical translations and allusions: inculcate. E16–M17.

5 *verb trans. & intrans.* Of a bird: preen (the feathers). Long *rare* or *obsolete.* E17.

📖 **3** R. TRAVERS A vengeful . . public, its temper whetted by . . sensational journalism. J. LONDON The many books he read but served to whet his appetite.

Phrases: ***whet one's whistle***: see WHISTLE *noun* 2.

▶ **B** *noun.* **1** An act of sharpening something, esp. on a stone. Also (now *dial.*), the interval between two sharpenings; *fig.* an occasion. E17.

2 (A small quantity of) something that stimulates one's appetite (*lit. & fig.*); *esp.* a dram. L17.

📖 **2** M. A. LOWER Should any facts I may state, serve as a whet for the visitor's curiosity. W. JERDAN He . . swallowed . . oysters as a whet, and proceeded to dine.

■ **whetten** *verb trans.* (long *obsolete* exc. *dial.*) whet L16. **whetter** *noun* a person who or thing which whets something (*lit. & fig.*) LME.

whether /ˈwɛðə/ *pronoun, noun, adjective* (in mod. usage also classed as a *determiner*), *& conjunction.*

[Old English *hweþer, hwæþer* corresp. to Old Frisian *hwed(d)er*, Old Saxon *hweþar*, Old High German *(h)wedar* (German *weder* neither), Old Norse *hvaðarr*, Gothic *hwaþar*, from Germanic word from base of WHO + compar. suffix repr. also in OTHER *adjective.*]

▶ **A** *pronoun & noun.* **1** *pronoun.* Which of the two; *gen.* whichever of the two, no matter which of the two. Also (*occas.*) of more than two. Now *arch. & dial.* OE.

2 *noun.* A question expr. a doubt or choice between two alternatives; a reply to such a question. E19.

📖 **1** TENNYSON Whether would ye? gold or field?

▶ **B** *adjective.* Which — of the two; *gen.* whichever — of the two, no matter which — of the two. Also (*occas.*) of the more than two —, of the three or more —. Long *rare.* OE.

▶ **C** *conjunction.* **1** Introducing a direct question (now *rare* or *obsolete*), or indirect question, expr. a doubt or choice between alternatives, or a clause following a verb expr. doubt etc. referring to alternatives. Usu. with correl. *or* or ***or whether*** before the second or last alternative. OE.

†**2** Introducing a direct question as a mere sign of interrogation. Freq. with verb in subjunctive; usu. without inversion of subject and verb. OE–L16.

3 Introducing an indirect question with the second alternative implied only, expr. simple inquiry, or a conditional clause expr. an opinion: if. OE.

4 Introducing a qualifying or conditional clause expressing two alternatives, usu. with correlative *or* before the second alternative: whichever of the alternative possibilities or suppositions is the case. ME.

5 With ellipsis in both alternatives: either. ME.

📖 **1** SHAKES. *John* Whether hadst thou rather be a Faulconbridge . . Or the reputed son of Coeur-de-Lion? M. KEANE He . . cared not at all whether George entangled himself for good or ill. B. PYM She had not been sure whether to come . . or not. **3** LD MACAULAY The Londoners flocked . . to hear whether there was any news. V. WOOLF One doesn't mind . . whether she disappears for ever. **4** R. MACAULAY Whether Jane had ever been in love with Herbert or not, she was not so now. **5** E. A. FREEMAN William, whether by accident or by design, was not admitted. R. COBB He was a tireless walker, whether exercising . . dalmatians or alone.

Phrases: **whether or no**, (*occas.*) **whether or not** (*a*) introducing an indirect question or a qualifying or conditional clause expressing one alternative and implying the other (its negative); (*b*) in any case, at all events.

whetstone /ˈwɛtstəʊn/ *noun.* OE.

[from WHET *verb* + STONE *noun.*]

1 A fine-grained stone used for giving a smooth edge to cutting tools after grinding. OE. ▸**b** Any hard fine-grained rock, as novaculite, of which whetstones are made; hone stone. L16.

2 [After former custom of hanging a whetstone round the neck of a liar.] A liar. *obsolete* exc. *dial.* LME.

3 *fig.* Something that sharpens the wits, appetite, interest, etc. M16.

whew /fjuː, hwjuː/ *interjection, noun, & verb.* LME.

[Imit.]

▶ **A** *interjection.* Expr. surprise, consternation, or relief. LME.

▶ **B** *noun.* †**1** A simple wind instrument, a pipe. LME–L15.

2 A whistling or rushing sound, *spec.* made by a bird. E16. ▸**b** A factory hooter. *dial.* M19. ▸**c** A hurry. *dial.* E20.

3 An utterance of 'whew!' M18.

▶ **C** *verb intrans.* **1** Whistle; make a whistling or rushing sound; *esp.* say 'whew!' L15.

2 Move quickly; hurry; bustle. *dial.* L17.

■ †**whewer** *noun* the European wigeon, *Anas penelope*, which has a whistling call, *esp.* a female one M17–E19.

whewl /wjuːl/ *verb intrans.* Now *dial.* L15.

[Imit.]

Cry plaintively; whine, howl.

whey /weɪ/ *noun & verb.*

[Old English *hwæg, hweg* = Middle Dutch *wey* (Dutch *wei*), from Germanic whence also (by ablaut) Middle Low German *huy, hoie*, Dutch *hui* whey. Cf. WHIG *noun*[1].]

▶ **A** *noun.* **1** The watery part of milk which remains after the formation of curds. OE.

†**2** MEDICINE. = SERUM 1. L16–E18.

Comb.: **whey-butter**: made from whey or from whey-cream; **whey-cream**: which remains in the whey after the curd has been removed; **whey-face** (a person with) a pale face; **whey-faced** *adjective* pale, esp. with fear.

▶†**B** *verb trans.* Separate the whey from (milk); *transf.* make (the blood) thin. M17–M18.

■ **wheyey** *adjective* consisting of, containing, or resembling whey LME. **wheyish** *adjective* resembling whey in consistency or colour LME. **wheyishness** *noun* M17.

which /wɪtʃ/ *adjective* (in mod. usage also classed as a *determiner*), *pronoun, & conjunction.* Also in (written) abbreviated form **wh', wh.** (point).

[Old English *hwilc* = Old Saxon *(h)wilik*, Middle Low German, Middle Dutch *wilk*, Old Norse *hvílíkr*, Gothic *hwileiks*, ult. from Germanic bases of WHO, ALIKE *adjective.* Cf. EACH, SUCH *demonstr. adjective & pronoun.*]

▶ **A** *adjective.* **I** *interrog. adjective.* †**1** Of what kind, quality, or character; what kind of. Corresp. to SUCH *demonstr. adjective.* OE–LME.

2 Used in asking the identity of a choice made from an indefinite set of alternatives. Cf. WHAT *adjective* 1. *obsolete* exc. as in sense A.3 below. OE.

3 Used in asking the identity of a choice made from a definite (stated or implied) set of alternatives. Cf. WHAT *adjective* 1. OE.

📖 **2** J. LEONI Nor ought any one to wonder, which way such vast Quantities of earthen Ware came here. **3** T. HARDY Which gin had broken a man's leg, which gun had killed a man. V. WOOLF Which will it be? . . Wet or fine? E. BAKER He knew which office it was. G. VIDAL One of the columnists. You can guess which one. I. MCEWAN Can you remember which way we went?

▶†**II 4** = WHAT *adjective* 6. OE–LME.

▶ **III 5** Any — that; whichever. Also foll. by *ever, soever. arch.* OE.

📖 **5** MILTON Which way I flie is Hell; my self am Hell.

▶ **IV** *rel. adjective.* **6** Introducing a clause and qualifying a noun referring to and esp. summing up the details of the antecedent in the preceding clause or sentence. Also (*arch.*) preceded by *the.* ME.

📖 **6** DEFOE It rain'd all Night and all Day . . during which time the Ship broke in pieces.

▶ **B** *pronoun.* **I** *interrog. pronoun.* **1** = WHAT *pronoun* 1. Also (*occas.*), who. *obsolete* exc. *dial. & joc.* OE.

2 Which person(s); which thing(s). OE.

📖 **1** W. FAULKNER Yankee say, 'Sartoris, John Sartoris,' and Marse John say, 'Which? Say which?' **2** T. HARDY Hard to say in which of the two . . any particular obliteration had its origin. D. H. LAWRENCE Which of these two men was to win? ***tell tother from which***: see TOTHER *pronoun* 1. **which is which**: used in asking about two or more persons who or things which are difficult to distinguish from each other.

▶ **II** *rel. pronoun.* **3** Introducing a clause describing or stating something additional about the antecedent, the sense of the main clause being complete without the relative clause. Also, introducing a parenthetic clause with the referent following. Used to refer to things and people (now (exc. *arch. & dial.*) only people when regarded as a collective body or with respect to their function or character): cf. WHO *pronoun* 5. Also (*arch.*) preceded by *the.* Cf. THAT *rel. pronoun* 7. ME.

4 Introducing a clause defining or restricting the antecedent, esp. a clause essential to the identification of the antecedent; that; *rare* (as correlative to *same, such*, etc.) as. Used as in sense 3 above: cf. WHO *pronoun* 4. Also (*arch.*) preceded by *the.* Cf. THAT *rel. pronoun* 6. ME.

†**5** That or those which; something that; one or those who. ME–E18.

📖 **3** A. URE Yellow rosin contains some water, which black rosin does not. W. BESANT When, which happened every day, they forgot their disguises. I. HAY They conformed to the rules . . . Which was just as well. E. J. HOWARD His chair which was covered with a greasy car rug. I. MURDOCH The bar, against which leaned a number of . . men. **but which** which nevertheless, which however. **4** AV *Matt.* 6:9 Our father which art in heauen, hallowed be thy name. J. H. NEWMAN He was not quite the craven . . which she thought him. G. GREENE A shop which would pack and post your Christmas parcels. W. S. MAUGHAM The life into which she had led him had made him spend more money than he could afford. E. WAUGH Nothing which she wore . . had been chosen by or for a man.

▶ **III 6** Any that; whichever. Also foll. by *ever, soever. arch.* OE.

▶ **C** *conjunction.* †**1** Used to link clauses, with a pers. pronoun or equivalent (as *thereof*) in the relative clause functioning as a rel. pronoun to refer to the antecedent. Cf. WHO *conjunction.* LME–M18.

2 Used to link clauses or to introduce a clause, without referring to an antecedent; and. Long *dial.* L16.

📖 **1** J. LOCKE Provisions . . which how much they exceed the other in value, . . he will then see. **2** THACKERAY 'That noble young fellow,' says my general . . . Which noble his conduct I own it has been.

Comb.: **whichaway** *pronoun* (*US colloq. & dial.*) [after THATAWAY] which way? in what direction?; **which-so** *pronoun* (*arch.*) whichever; **whichsoever** *pronoun & adjective* (*arch.*) whichever; **whichway(s)** *adverb* (*colloq.*, chiefly *N. Amer.*) in all directions, in every direction, (freq. preceded by *all, every*).

whichever /wɪtʃˈɛvə/ *adjective & pronoun.* ME.

[from WHICH *adjective, pronoun* + EVER *adverb.*]

1 Any or either of a definite (stated or implied) set of people or things that. Formerly also of an indefinite set. ME.

2 No matter which. L17.

📖 **1** M. ROBERTS They shout for her from whichever room they happen to be in. *Today* 75 per cent on a small packet or £1 . . a gross, whichever is the greater. **2** SWIFT Both Sides hang out their Trophies too, which ever comes by the worst. W. BESANT In politics you are used . . . You get nothing, whichever side is in.

whicker /ˈ(h)wɪkə/ *verb & noun.* M17.
[Imit. Cf. NICKER *verb*, SNICKER.]
▶ **A** *verb intrans.* **1** Utter a half-suppressed laugh; snigger, titter. M17.
2 Of a horse: give a soft breathy whinny. M18.
3 Move with a sound as of something hurtling through or beating the air. E20.

📖 **3** A. S. BYATT The horses whickered with pleasure when she came into the yard. G. MAXWELL My aunt's . . pigeons whickered past my window.

▶ **B** *noun.* A snigger; a soft breathy whinny. Also, the sound of something beating the air. L19.
■ **whickering** *noun* the action of the verb; an instance of this: L19.

whid /wɪd/ *noun*¹ & *verb*¹. M16.
[Perh. dial. devel. of Old English *cwide* speech.]
▶ **A** *noun.* **1** A word. Usu. in *pl. Criminals' slang.* M16.
2 A lie, a fib; an exaggerated story. *Scot.* L18.
1 *stubble your whids!*: see STUBBLE *verb.*
▶ **B** *verb intrans.* Infl. **-dd-**. Lie, fib. *Scot.* E17.

whid /wɪd/ *noun*² & *verb*². *Scot.* L16.
[Perh. ult. from Old Norse *hviða* squall.]
▶ **A** *noun.* †**1** A squall. Only in L16.
2 A quick noiseless movement. E18.
▶ **B** *verb intrans.* Infl. **-dd-**. Move quickly and noiselessly. E18.

whidah *noun* var. of WHYDAH.

whiddle /ˈwɪd(ə)l/ *verb intrans. arch. slang.* M17.
[Perh. from WHID *noun*¹: see -LE³.]
Divulge a secret, turn informer.

Whieldon /ˈwiːldən/ *noun.* M19.
[Thomas *Whieldon* (1719–95), Staffordshire potter.]
Used *attrib.* to designate a kind of coloured earthenware.

whiff /wɪf/ *noun*¹. See also QUIFF *noun*¹. L16.
[Imit. Cf. WHIFT.]
▶ **I 1** A puff or slight gust of wind. L16.
2 An inhalation of tobacco smoke; smoke so inhaled; an act or (*rare*) the action of smoking. L16. ▶†**b** A sip or draught of liquor. E–M17.
3 A smell, *esp.* a faint unpleasant one. Also foll. by *of.* M17.
4 *transf. & fig.* A trace or hint *of* something; (now *Scot.*) a slight attack *of* an illness. M17.
5 A puff of smoke or vapour. Also foll. by *of.* E18. ▶**b** *transf.* A cigarette or small cigar. L19.
6 A puffing or whistling sound; a short or gentle whistle. E18.
7 A small discharge *of* shot or explosive. M19.

📖 **1** DICKENS Give her a whiff of fresh air with the bellows. **2** R. L. STEVENSON Silver took a whiff or two of his pipe. **3** H. KELLER I . . had never had so much as a whiff of salt air. J. RABAN In the doorways, you catch a whiff of bacon fat. R. CARVER A faint whiff of formaldehyde on his clothes. **4** R. OWEN Nothing has emerged about Mr. Chernenko's relatives—certainly no whiff of scandal. *Observer* British nostrils are always aquiver for any whiff of pretension. **5** A. LEE Up the laundry chute . . floated whiffs of steamy air. **6** LYTTON Sir Willoughby . . made . . no other reply than a long whiff.

▶ **II 8** NAUTICAL. A flag hoisted as a signal. Cf. WAFT *noun* 2, WHIFT 2. L17.
▶ **III 9** A light narrow outrigged sculling-boat. M19.
Phrases: **in a whiff** *dial.* in a short time.
■ **whiffy** *adjective* (*colloq.*) having an unpleasant smell M19.

whiff /wɪf/ *noun*². E18.
[Perh. same as prec.]
Any of various N. Atlantic flatfishes; *spec.* (*a*) the megrim or sail-fluke, *Lepidorhombus whiffiagonis*; (*b*) *N. Amer.* any of the genus *Citharichthys* (family Bothidae).

whiff /wɪf/ *verb*¹. L16.
[from WHIFF *noun*¹.]
1 *verb intrans.* Of the wind: blow with a slight gust; move with or make the sound of this. L16. ▶**b** *verb trans.* Utter with a puff of air. M18.
2 *verb trans.* Drive or carry (as) by a puff of air; blow *away, out,* etc. E17. ▶**b** *verb intrans.* Move lightly as if blown by a puff of air. E17.
3 *verb trans. & intrans.* Puff out (smoke) from a pipe etc.; smoke (a pipe etc.). E17.
†**4** *verb trans.* Drink (liquor). Only in 17.
5 *colloq.* **a** *verb trans.* Get a (slight) smell of, smell. M17. ▶**b** *verb intrans.* Sniff, smell. M19. ▶**c** *verb intrans.* Emit an unpleasant odour. L19.
6 *US slang.* **a** *noun intrans.* Of a baseball batter or a golfer: miss the ball. E20. ▶**b** *verb trans.* Cause (a baseball batter) to strike out. E20.
■ **whiffer** *noun* E17.

whiff /wɪf/ *verb*² *intrans.* M19.
[Perh. same word as prec.]
ANGLING. Fish from a swiftly moving boat with a hand-line towing the bait near the surface.

whiffet /ˈwɪfɪt/ *noun. US.* E19.
[Prob. from WHIFF *noun*¹ + -ET¹.]
1 A small dog. Also ***whiffet dog***. E19.
2 *transf.* An unimportant person. *colloq.* M19.

whiffle /ˈwɪf(ə)l/ *noun.* L17.
[from WHIFF *noun*¹ + -LE². In senses 2, 3 prob. from WHIFFLE *verb.* Cf. WIFFLE.]
1 An unimportant thing; a trifle. Long *rare.* L17.
2 An act of whiffling; a puff or slight movement of air etc. M19.
3 A sound as of gently moving air. L20.
Comb.: **whiffle-ball** *US* a light hollow ball used in a variety of baseball (cf. *WIFFLE-ball*); a game played with such a ball.

whiffle /ˈwɪf(ə)l/ *verb.* M16.
[from WHIFF *verb*¹ + -LE³.]
1 *verb intrans.* (Of the wind) blow in puffs or slight gusts, shift about; *fig.* vacillate, be evasive. M16.
2 *verb trans.* Blow or drive (as) with a puff of air. M17.
3 *verb intrans.* Move lightly as if blown by a puff of air; flicker, flutter. M17.
†**4** *verb intrans.* Drink. Cf. WHIFF *verb*¹ 4, WHIFFLED. *rare.* Only in L17.
5 *verb intrans.* Talk idly. Cf. WHIFFLING *adjective* 2. *dial.* E18.
6 *verb intrans.* Make a soft sound as of a gentle wind, in breathing etc. M19.

whiffled /ˈwɪf(ə)ld/ *adjective. slang.* E20.
[Origin unkn. Cf. WHIFFLE *verb* 4.]
Drunk.

whiffler /ˈwɪflə/ *noun*¹. *obsolete* exc. *Hist.* M16.
[Perh. from WIFLE + -ER¹, with spelling assim. to WHIFF *noun*¹, *verb*¹, WHIFFLE *verb.*]
An attendant armed with a javelin, battleaxe, sword, or staff and employed to keep the way clear for a procession or other public spectacle.

whiffler /ˈwɪflə/ *noun*². E17.
[from WHIFFLE *verb* + -ER¹.]
†**1** A smoker. E17–M19.
2 An insignificant or contemptible person; an evasive person. M17.

whiffletree *noun* see WHIPPLETREE.

whiffling /ˈwɪflɪŋ/ *noun.* L17.
[from WHIFFLE *verb* + -ING¹.]
The action of WHIFFLE *verb*; an instance of this.

whiffling /ˈwɪflɪŋ/ *adjective.* M16.
[from WHIFFLE *verb* + -ING².]
1 That whiffles. M16.
2 Pettifogging, fussy; paltry, insignificant. E17.

whift /wɪft/ *noun. obsolete* exc. *dial.* E17.
[Alt. of WHIFF *noun*¹.]
1 A puff of wind, air, etc. E17.
2 A small flag hoisted as a signal. Cf. WHIFF *noun*¹ 8. M17.

whig /wɪg/ *noun*¹. Now *Scot. & dial.* E16.
[Prob. rel. to WHEY.]
Whey; a drink made from this. Also, buttermilk.

Whig /wɪg/ *noun*² & *adjective.* Orig. *derog.* M17.
[Prob. abbreviation of WHIGGAMORE.]
Hist. ▶**A** *noun.* **1** An adherent of the Presbyterian cause in Scotland in the 17th cent. M17.
2 A person who opposed the succession of James II to the crown; an exclusioner. Opp. TORY *noun* 2. L17.
3 A member or supporter of the English, later British, reforming and constitutional party that after 1688 sought the supremacy of Parliament and was eventually succeeded in the 19th cent. by the Liberal Party. Opp. TORY *noun* 3. E18.
4 *US.* **a** An American colonist who supported the American Revolution. E18. ▶**b** A member of an American political party, favouring a protective tariff and strong central government, succeeded by the Republican Party. M19.
▶ **B** *adjective.* Of, pertaining to, or supporting the Whigs; characteristic of a Whig or Whigs. L17.
Whig historian: who interprets history as the continuing and inevitable victory of progress over reaction. **Whig history**: written by or from the point of view of a Whig historian.
■ **Whiggery** *noun* (chiefly *derog.*) Whiggism L17. **Whiggess** *noun* (*rare*) a female Whig L18. **Whiggify** *verb trans.* make Whiggish L17. **Whiggism** *noun* the principles or practices of the Whigs M17. **Whiglet** *noun* a petty Whig L17. **Whigling** *noun* = WHIGLET E19. **Whigship** *noun* (*joc.*) (with possess. adjective, as *your Whigship* etc.) a mock title of respect given to a Whig L18.

whig *noun*³ var. of WIG *noun*¹.

whig /wɪg/ *verb*¹. *Scot.* Infl. **-gg-**. M17.
[Origin unkn.]
1 *verb trans.* Urge forward, drive briskly. M17.
2 *verb intrans.* Jog along; move or work briskly. L17.

Whig /wɪg/ *verb*² *trans. arch.* Infl. **-gg-**. L17.
[from WHIG *noun*².]
Behave like a Whig towards.

whig /wɪg/ *verb*³ *trans. & intrans. dial.* Infl. **-gg-**. M18.
[from WHIG *noun*¹.]
Turn sour; curdle.

whiggamore /ˈwɪgəmɔː/ *noun.* Orig. *Scot.* M17.
[Prob. from WHIG *verb*¹ + MARE *noun*¹. Cf. WHIG *noun*² & *adjective.*]
Hist. Orig., a member of a body of rebels from the western part of Scotland who in 1648 marched on Edinburgh in opposition to Charles I. Later (*derog.*), = WHIG *noun*² 1.

Whiggish /ˈwɪgɪʃ/ *adjective.* L17.
[from WHIG *noun*² + -ISH¹.]
1 Of, supporting, or characteristic of a Whig or Whigs (usu. *derog.*, now *Hist.*); pertaining to or characteristic of a Whig historian. L17.
2 *transf.* Liberal, unprejudiced, open to new ideas. *rare.* E18.
■ **Whiggishly** *adverb* L17. **Whiggishness** *noun* M19.

whigmaleery /ˈwɪgməlɪəri/ *noun.* Chiefly *Scot.* M18.
[Origin unkn.]
Something fanciful or whimsical; a whim; a trifling frivolous ornament, a trinket.

while /wʌɪl/ *noun.*
[Old English *hwīl* = Old Frisian *hwīle*, Old Saxon *hwīl(a)* time, Old High German *(h)wīla* point or period of time (Dutch *wijl*, German *Weile*), Old Norse *hvíla* bed, Gothic *hweila* time, from Germanic, from Indo-European base repr. also by Latin *quies* QUIET *noun*, *tranquillus* TRANQUIL.]
▶ **I 1** A period of time, considered with respect to its duration; *esp.* a (relatively) short period of time. OE. ▶**b** The duration of or time needed for a specified activity. Long *arch.* LME.
2 Used adverbially. ▶**a** With indef. article & freq. adjective of quantity: for a (*long, short*, etc.) time. See also AWHILE. OE. ▶**b** With def. article: in the meantime, meanwhile. OE. ▶**c** With *that, this*: during that or this time. Now only preceded by *all.* L15.
3 With def. article, used as conjunction: during the time that, while. *arch.* OE.
†**4** Sufficient or available time, leisure. ME–M17.
5 *spec.* The time spent (connoting trouble, effort, or work) in doing something. *obsolete* exc. in phrs. below. LME.

📖 **1** S. BELLOW The refrigerator . . would take a while to get cold. J. HIGGINS This rain's with us for a while yet. G. SWIFT I was home for a brief while in the summer. **b** SHAKES. *Ven. & Ad.* It shall . . Bud and be blasted in a breathing while. **2a** M. SINCLAIR She stood a little while, looking out. **b** E. BLYTON Joanna . . listened to their adventures . . getting the lunch ready all the while. M. M. KAYE He had pressed refreshments on them, talking volubly the while. **3** KEATS Beseeching him, the while his hand she wrung. **4** P. HOLLAND If they might have had while and time as well to follow it.

▶ **II 6** A time when something happens or is done, an occasion. Formerly also, a proper or suitable time. Also used adverbially. Now *arch. & dial.* OE.

📖 **6** R. L. STEVENSON There are whiles . . when ye are altogether too canny.

Phrases: **all the while** during the whole time (that). **at whiles** at times, sometimes. ***between-whiles***: see BETWEEN *adverb.* ***once in a while***: see ONCE *adverb* etc. **one while** †(*a*) at one time, on one occasion; (*b*) *US* a long time. **worth one's while**, (*arch.*) **worth the while** worth the time or effort spent; worth doing, profitable, advantageous.
■ **whilie** *noun* (*Scot.*) a short time E19.

while /wʌɪl/ *verb.* E17.
[from the noun.]
†**1** *verb trans.* Engage or occupy (a person) for a time; occupy the time of. E–M17.
2 *verb trans.* Pass (a period of time) in a leisurely and esp. pleasant manner. Usu. foll. by *away.* M17.
3 *verb intrans.* Of time: pass tediously. Now *dial.* E18.

📖 **2** G. SWIFT To while away the heavy hours, they told each other stories. G. DALY He was happily whiling away the evenings by reading aloud.

while /wʌɪl/ *adverb, conjunction, & preposition.*
[Old English *hwīle* (adverb) accus. of *hwīl* WHILE *noun*; as conjunction, abbreviation of Old English *þā hwīle þa* during the time that.]
▶ **A** *adverb.* †**1** At times, sometimes; *esp.* (introducing parallel phrs. or clauses) now . . . then; = WHILES *adverb* 2. OE–M17.
†**2** At one time, formerly; = WHILOM 2. OE–LME.
†**3** For a time, temporarily; at the same time, meanwhile. *rare.* L15–M17.
4 *rel.* Referring to a noun denoting a period of time: during which, when. M19.

📖 **4** *Guardian* The Bulgarians have stopped people coming over for the period while I am here.

▶ **B** *conjunction.* **1** During the time that; *spec.* (*a*) for as long as; (*b*) before the end of the time that. Also with ellipsis of pronominal subject and *be*. Formerly also foll. by *that.* ME. ▶†**b** At the time that; when. ME–L15. ▶**c** During which time; and meanwhile. LME.

2 Up to the time that; until. Formerly also foll. by *at*, *that*. Now *north*. ME.
3 So long as, provided that. *arch*. LME.
4 When on the contrary, whereas; granted that, although. L16.
5 In addition to the fact that; and at the same time. M19.

📖 **1** DICKENS The confidence of this house . . is not to be abused . . while I have eyes and ears. G. VIDAL I listened . . while he explained the state of the world. R. WEST He enjoyed drawing while he was being read to. *Amateur Gardening* This natural covering prevents the corms drying out while in store. **c** M. KEANE She . . proceeded to soothe Jane while he proceeded to soothe Jessica. **2** BUNYAN Run . . while thou art weary, and then I will . . carry thee. **4** D. MACDONALD While his works are sometimes absurd, they are rarely dull. D. MELTZER While Mathilde was an active, thriving baby, Matthieu was a cause of . . concern to the nurses. **5** *Times* The walls . . are decorated with . . panelling, while the frieze and ceiling are in modelled plaster.

► **C** *preposition*. Up to (a time); until. Now *north*. LME.

📖 W. G. COLLINGWOOD Father will be happy while dinner time.

Comb.: **while as**, **whileas** *arch*. = sense B.1 above; **while-you-wait** *attrib. adjective* (of a service) performed immediately.

whilere /wʌɪlˈɛː/ *adverb*. *arch*.
[Orig. two words, from WHILE *adverb* + ERE *adverb*.]
A while before, some time ago; = EREWHILE.

whiles /wʌɪlz/ *noun*, *conjunction*, *preposition*, & *adverb*. *arch*. ME.
[from WHILE *noun* + -S³.]
► **A** *noun*. †**1** With indef. article, def. article, demonstr. adjective, or adjective of quantity, used adverbially: = WHILE *noun* 2. ME–M17.
2 With def. article, used as conjunction: = WHILE *noun* 3. Now *rare* or *obsolete*. ME.

📖 **2** SIR W. SCOTT They feasted . . The whiles a Northern harper . . Chanted a rhime.

► **B** *conjunction*. **1** = WHILE *conjunction* 1. ME.
†**2** = WHILE *conjunction* 2. LME–E17.
†**3** = WHILE *conjunction* 3. M16–M17.
►†**C** *preposition*. = WHILE *preposition*. LME–M16.
► **D** *adverb*. †**1** = WHILE *adverb* 2. *Scot*. LME–L16.
2 At times, sometimes; *esp*. (introducing parallel phrs. or clauses) now . . . then. Cf. WHILE *adverb* 1. Chiefly & now only *Scot*. L15.

📖 **2** R. L. STEVENSON So we lay . . whiles whispering, whiles lying still.

whillaloo /ˈwɪləluː/ *noun & interjection*. *dial*. M17.
[Imit. Cf. Irish *liúgh* shout, cry, and ULULU.]
(A wailing cry) expr. lamentation.

Whillans /ˈwɪlənz/ *noun*. L20.
[Don *Whillans* (1933–85), Brit. mountaineer.]
Used *attrib*. to designate various pieces of climbing equipment designed by Whillans.

whilly /ˈwɪli/ *verb trans*. *Scot*. E18.
[Abbreviation.]
= WHILLYWHA *verb*.

whillywha /ˈwɪlɪwɑː/ *noun & verb*. *Scot*. M17.
[Origin unkn.]
► **A** *noun*. **1** A wheedling or insinuating person; a flattering deceiver. M17.
2 Flattery, cajolery. E19.
► **B** *verb trans*. Trick or persuade by flattery; wheedle, cajole. Cf. WHILLY. E19.

whilom /ˈwʌɪləm/ *adverb*, *adjective*, & *conjunction*.
[Old English *hwīlom* dat. pl. of WHILE *noun*.]
► **A** *adverb*. †**1** = WHILE *adverb* 1. OE–L16.
2 At one time, formerly. Cf. WHILE *adverb* 2. Now *literary*. ME.
†**3** At a future time, in future. ME–E16.

📖 **2** A. R. AMMONS The spider, whilom serene, / attacks to feed.

► **B** *adjective*. That existed or was such at a former time. Formerly also, (of a person) late, deceased. Now *literary*. LME.

📖 *Nature* There . . speaks the whilom managing editor of the *Journal of Bacteriology*.

► **C** *conjunction*. = WHILE *conjunction* 1, 2. *dial*. E17.

whilst /wʌɪlst/ *noun*, *conjunction*, & *adverb*. LME.
[from WHILES + *t* as in *amidst*, *amongst*, etc.]
► **A** *noun*. **1** With def. article (formerly also indef. article), used adverbially: = WHILE *noun* 2b. Long *arch*. LME.
2 With def. article., used as conjunction: during the time that, = WHILE *noun* 3. Now *rare* or *obsolete*. LME.
► **B** *conjunction*. **1** = WHILE *conjunction* 1. LME.
2 = WHILE *conjunction* 2. *obsolete* exc. *dial*. E16.
3 = WHILE *conjunction* 3, 4, 5. M16.

📖 **1** *Ships Monthly* The huge mound of ashes . . which had accumulated . . whilst the ship had been in port. *Gardener* If you move it whilst in bud many of the buds may drop. **3** *Hair* It cares for your hair whilst encouraging it to curl. *Photo Answers* Whilst most fisheye lenses provide a circular image, the Sigma . . produces a 180° diagonal image.

► **C** *adverb*. **1** In the meantime, meanwhile. Cf. sense A.1 above. *obsolete* exc. *dial*. E17.
2 *rel*. = WHILE *adverb* 4. L20.

whim /wɪm/ *noun & verb*. M17.
[Origin unkn.]
► **A** *noun*. **I** †**1** A pun, a play on words. Only in M17.
†**2** A fanciful or fantastic (esp. artistic) creation; something odd or quaint. L17–E19.
3 A sudden fancy; a freakish idea; a caprice. L17.
4 Capriciousness. E18.

📖 **3** P. G. WODEHOUSE A woman's whims have to be respected, however apparently absurd. L. DURRELL The whim seized him to drive me to Montaza. **4** POPE Sneering Goode, half malice and half whim.

► **II 5** A kind of windlass turned by a horse and used esp. for raising ore or water from a mine. *arch*. M18.
► **B** *verb*. Infl. **-mm-**.
1 *verb trans*. Orig., spurn or put *off* on a whim. Now, have a sudden fancy or desire for. Also foll. by *to do*. E18.
2 *verb intrans*. Of the head: swim. *dial*. E18.
■ **whimmery** *noun* a piece of whimsicality M19. **whimmy** *adjective* whimsical, capricious L18.

whimberry *noun* var. of WHINBERRY.

whimbrel /ˈwɪmbr(ə)l/ *noun*. M16.
[from dial. *whimp* or WHIMPER (with ref. to the bird's cry) + -REL.]
A small curlew, *Numenius phaeopus*, which has a striped head, a trilling call, and breeds in northern parts of Europe, Asia, and Canada.

whimp *noun*, *adjective*, & *verb*¹ var. of WIMP *noun*², *adjective*, & *verb*.

whimp /wɪmp/ *verb*² *intrans*. *local*. M16.
[Imit. Cf. WHIMPER.]
Whimper.

whimper /ˈwɪmpə/ *verb & noun*. E16.
[from WHIMP *verb*² + -ER⁵. Cf. WIMP *noun*², *adjective*, & *verb*.]
► **A** *verb*. **1** *verb intrans*. Utter a feeble intermittent cry expressive of fear, pain, or distress; make a low complaining sound. E16. ►**b** *fig*. Complain; cry *after*, *for*. M16.
2 *verb trans*. Utter or express in a whimper. L18.
3 *verb intrans*. Of running water etc.: make an intermittent murmuring sound. L18.

📖 **1** P. SAYER I heard him whimper, . . and I realised he was still alive. W. PERRIAM The baby . . is whimpering pathetically. **b** G. ORWELL You have whimpered for mercy. **2** T. SHARPE 'I thought you were a gentleman,' she whimpered. **3** W. IRVING The little brook that whimpered by his school-house.

► **B** *noun*. **1** A feeble intermittent cry expressive of fear, pain, or distress, a low complaining sound. L17.
2 *fig*. A dull or disappointing note or tone. E20.

📖 **1** P. FARMER The crying had stopped . . I couldn't hear so much as a whimper. D. R. KOONTZ Ineffectual whimpers and breathless protests. **2** *Times* Here the world ends neither with a bang nor a whimper.

■ **whimperer** *noun* M18. **whimpering** *noun* the action of the verb; an instance of this: E16. **whimperingly** *adverb* in a whimpering manner M19.

whimpish *adjective* var. of WIMPISH.

whimsey *noun & adjective* var. of WHIMSY.

whimsical /ˈwɪmzɪk(ə)l/ *adjective & noun*. M17.
[from WHIMSY + -ICAL.]
► **A** *adjective*. **1** Subject to or characterized by a whim or whims; capricious. M17.
†**2** Uncertain, liable to change. M17–M18.
3 Fantastic, fanciful; odd, quaint. L17.

📖 **1** Y. MENUHIN I don't think my parents found my request far-fetched . . but they may have found it more whimsical than urgent. M. WESLEY My uncle was . . whimsical, a fanciful old man. **2** S. RICHARDSON Poor man! he stands a whimsical chance between us. **3** C. THUBRON The heraldic . . dragons . . appeared more whimsical than frightening. G. BODDY A . . manor house furnished in a . . somewhat whimsical style.

► **B** *noun*. A member of a section of the Tories in the reign of Queen Anne. *slang* (now *Hist*.). E18.
■ **whimsiˈcality** *noun* the quality or state of being whimsical; an instance or example of this: M18. **whimsically** *adverb* E18. **whimsicalness** *noun* E18.

whimsy /ˈwɪmzi/ *noun & adjective*. Also **-sey**. E17.
[Prob. based on WHIM-WHAM: see -SY.]
► **A** *noun*. **I 1** A sudden fancy; a caprice; a whim. E17.
2 Capriciousness. L17.
3 A fanciful or fantastic (esp. artistic) creation; something odd or quaint; *spec*. a small fanciful object or trinket made by a glass-maker or potter. E18.

📖 **1** M. BRADBURY The train had . . stopped at some chance spot . . someone's whimsy. **2** *Design* Until more excitement and whimsy is injected into the work, success . . could prove a problem. **3** G. KEILLOR Not so much a City as a . . whimsy built on a swamp.

► **II 4** = WHIM *noun* 5. *local*. L18.
Comb.: **whimsy-whamsy** [after next] = WHIM *noun* 3.
► **B** *adjective*. Whimsical. M17.

📖 TIRESIAS Pasold's factory with its unashamedly whimsy picture of ladybirds spinning.

■ †**whimsied** *adjective* (*rare*) filled with whims E17–M19. **whimsily** *adverb* M17. **whimsiness** *noun* E20.

whim-wham /ˈwɪmwam/ *noun*. E16.
[Fanciful redupl. with vowel variation: cf. FLIMFLAM, JIMJAM.]
1 A fanciful or fantastic object; *fig*. a trifle; a trifling ornament, a trinket. E16.
2 = WHIM *noun* 3. L16.

whin /wɪn/ *noun*¹. *Scot. & north*. ME.
[Origin unkn.]
= WHINSTONE.

whin /wɪn/ *noun*². Chiefly *Scot. & north*. LME.
[Prob. of Scandinavian origin: cf. Swedish *hven*, Old Danish *hvine*, *hvinegræs*, Norwegian *hvine*, applied to certain grasses.]
Gorse, *Ulex europaeus*; a gorse-bush. Also (with specifying word), any of several other prickly shrubs.
petty whin: see PETTY *adjective*.

whinberry /ˈwɪnb(ə)ri/ *noun*. Also **whim-** /ˈwɪmb-/. LOE.
[Alt. of *wineberry* s.v. WINE *noun*, by assoc. with WHIN *noun*².]
(The fruit of) the bilberry, *Vaccinium myrtillus*.

whinchat /ˈwɪntʃat/ *noun*. L17.
[from WHIN *noun*² + CHAT *noun*³.]
A small migratory chat, *Saxicola rubetra*, which resembles the stonechat and is found in similar habitats.

whindle /ˈwɪnd(ə)l/ *verb & noun*. *obsolete* exc. *dial*. E17.
[App. from WHINE *verb* + -LE³.]
► **A** *verb intrans*. Whine, whimper. E17.
► **B** *noun*. A whining person; a whine. M17.

whine /wʌɪn/ *verb & noun*.
[Old English *hwīnan* = Old Norse *hvína* whizz, whistle in the air. Cf. WHINGE.]
► **A** *verb*. †**1** *verb intrans*. Of an arrow: whistle through the air. *rare*. Only in OE.
2 *verb intrans*. Utter a subdued high-pitched prolonged cry, expressive esp. of pain, distress, or complaint; emit a high-pitched prolonged sound resembling this; cry in a subdued plaintive tone. ME.
3 *verb intrans*. Complain in a querulous tone or in a feeble or undignified way. M16.
†**4** *verb trans*. Drive *away* by whining; waste *away* in whining. E–M17.
5 *verb trans*. Utter in a querulous or nasal tone. L17.

📖 **2** BYRON My dog will whine in vain, Till fed by stranger hands. THACKERAY The . . beggars . . whining for alms. E. HARDWICK A gate whined on its rusty hook. **3** L. M. ALCOTT You can't go, Amy; so don't be a baby and whine about it. J. EPSTEIN They whined . . and cursed the gods when they lost. **4** SHAKES. *Coriol*. At his nurse's tears He whin'd and roar'd away your victory. **5** J. HELLER 'You never trust me with information,' he whined truculently.

► **B** *noun*. A subdued high-pitched prolonged cry, expressive esp. of pain, distress, or complaint; a high-pitched prolonged sound resembling this; a querulous or nasal tone; a feeble or undignified complaint. M17.

📖 HAZLITT A peevish whine in his voice like a beaten schoolboy. R. BANKS Muffled sounds of . . a radio, the whine of an electric shaver.

■ **whiner** *noun* E17. **whining** *noun* the action of the verb; an instance of this: LME. **whiningly** *adverb* in a whining manner M17.

whing /wɪŋ/ *verb*, *interjection*, & *noun*. L19.
[Imit.]
► **A** *verb trans. & intrans*. Move with great force and a high-piched ringing sound. L19.
► **B** *interjection* & *noun*. (Repr.) a high-pitched ringing sound. E20.

whinge /wɪn(d)ʒ/ *verb & noun*. Now *colloq*. (earlier *Scot. & north*.).
[Late Old English *hwinsian* = Old High German *win(i)sōn* (German *winseln*), from Germanic. Cf. WHINE.]
► **A** *verb intrans*. Pres. pple & verbal noun **-g(e)ing**. Whine; *esp*. complain peevishly, grumble. LOE.

📖 B. PEARSON The door whinged and Heath came in. A. TAYLOR Gamblers shouldn't whinge when they lose. *Times Educ. Suppl*. To stop whingeing about low morale.

► **B** *noun*. A whine, *esp*. a peevish complaint, a grumble. E16.

📖 D. HEWETT The landlady . . with some whinge about the other tenants.

¶ Not recorded between OE and E16.

whinger /ˈwɪŋ(g)ə, ˈwɪn(d)ʒə/ *noun*[1]. Chiefly *Scot.* Now *Hist.* **L15.**
[Alt.]
= WHINYARD.

whinger /ˈwɪn(d)ʒə/ *noun*[2]. Now *colloq.* (orig. *Scot. & north.*). **L18.**
[from WHINGE *verb* + -ER[1].]
A person who whines or grumbles.

whinner /ˈwɪnə/ *verb & noun. local.* **L17.**
[Frequentative of WHINE *verb*: see -ER[5].]
▶ **A** *verb intrans.* Whine. **L17.**
▶ **B** *noun.* A whine. **M19.**

whinny /ˈwɪni/ *noun.* **E19.**
[from the verb.]
An act of whinnying; a gentle high-pitched neigh; a sound resembling this.

📖 K. A. PORTER She gave a . . whinny between hysteria and indignation.

whinny /ˈwɪni/ *adjective*[1]. **L15.**
[from WHIN *noun*[2] + -Y[1].]
Covered with or having many whins or furze-bushes.

whinny /ˈwɪni/ *adjective*[2]. *obsolete* exc. *Scot. dial.* **L18.**
[from WHIN *noun*[1] + -Y[1].]
Of the nature of or containing whinstone.

whinny /ˈwɪni/ *verb.* Also (earlier) †**whrinny**. **LME.**
[Imit.]
1 *verb intrans.* (Of a horse) give a gentle high-pitched neigh, esp. to express pleasure; *transf.* emit a sound or sounds resembling this. **LME.**
2 *verb trans.* Utter with a whinnying sound; express by whinnying. **E19.**

📖 **1** S. HEANEY The refrigerator whinnied into silence. W. KOTZWINKLE The pony whinnied and tossed his head. **2** A. C. GUNTER The donkeys . . whinny their pleasure as they drink.

whinstone /ˈwɪnstəʊn/ *noun.* **E16.**
[from WHIN *noun*[1] + STONE *noun.*]
1 Any of various hard dark-coloured rocks or stones, *esp.* compact igneous rocks, as basalt, dolerite, etc.; greensand, chert, etc. **E16.**
2 A boulder or slab of this. **L16.**

whiny /ˈwʌɪni/ *adjective.* **M19.**
[from WHINE *noun, verb* + -Y[1].]
Resembling a whine; disposed to whine, fretful.

📖 P. LIVELY I want to go, I say, in a whiny voice. *Chicago Sun-Times* The Yankees . . hysterically paranoid, whiny . . and obnoxious.

■ **whininess** *noun* **M20.**

whinyard /ˈwɪnjəd/ *noun. obsolete* exc. *Hist.* See also WHINGER *noun*[1]. **L15.**
[Origin. unkn.: for the ending cf. PONIARD.]
A type of short sword, orig. hung from the belt.

whio /ˈwiːəʊ, *foreign* ˈfiɔ/ *noun. NZ.* Pl. same, **-os. M19.**
[Maori.]
The blue or mountain duck, *Hymenolaimus malacorhynchos*, of New Zealand.

whip /wɪp/ *noun.* **ME.**
[Partly from the verb; partly from Middle & mod. Low German *wip(pe)* quick movement, leap, etc.]
▶ **I 1** An instrument for flogging or beating, consisting either of a rigid rod or stick with a leather etc. lash attached, or of a flexible switch, used for urging on animals, punishing, etc. **ME.** ▸**b** *fig.* A thing causing (mental or physical) pain or acting as a stimulus to action. Chiefly *poet.* **LME.** ▸**c** *transf.* The occupation or art of driving horses. **L18.**
2 A blow or stroke (as) with a whip; a lash; in *pl.*, a flogging. *obsolete* exc. *Scot.* **LME.** ▸**b** In *pl.* Large quantities, plenty, abundance, (*of*). Cf. LASHING *noun*[1] 2. *dial., Austral., & NZ.* **L19.**
3 A slender unbranched shoot, *esp.* (chiefly *US*) the first year's growth of a bud or graft. Also (FORESTRY), a tree tall and thin for its height. **L16.** ▸**b** = ***whip aerial*** below. **M20.**
4 A light fluffy dessert made with whipped cream or beaten eggs etc. Usu. with specifying word. **M18.**
5 a A person who drives a horse-drawn carriage, esp. skilfully. Usu. with specifying adjective. **L18.** ▸**b** PRINTING. A compositor who sets type speedily. **L19.**
6 POLITICS. **a** The action of summoning the attendance of the members of a party for a parliamentary division. **E19.** ▸**b** A member of a party in Parliament appointed to control its parliamentary discipline and tactics and esp. to ensure attendance and voting in debates. Cf. earlier ***whipper-in*** s.v. WHIPPER 3b. **M19.** ▸**c** The parliamentary whips' written notice requesting or requiring attendance for voting at a division etc., variously underlined according to the degree of urgency; the discipline of such a notice. **L19.** ▸**d** *The* discipline and instructions associated with being a member of a party in Parliament. **M20.**
7 More fully ***whip-round***. An informal appeal for and collection of money from a group of people. **M19.**
8 HUNTING. A whipper-in (see WHIPPER 3a). **M19.**

📖 **1b** DISRAELI Fanatics, who had . . smarted under the satirical whips of the Dramatists. **3c** ***three-line whip, two-line whip.*** **d** *Times* Mr. Walker was asked if he would accept the Conservative whip. **5** J. K. JEROME The German driver is not . . a first-class whip.

▶ **II 9** A sudden movement; a start; the brief time taken by this, an instant. *obsolete* exc. *Scot.* **LME.**
10 An abrupt sweeping movement as of a whip; FENCING an act or instance of whipping the blade in parrying; MECHANICS a slight vibration or bending movement in a mechanical part, caused by sudden strain; CRICKET a springy action of the wrist in playing or delivering a ball; WRESTLING a technique by which one's opponent is hurled into a somersault by a sharp wrench of the forearm. **L18.**

📖 **10** Z. GREY The long swing and whip of his arm that produced the jump ball.

▶ **III 11** NEEDLEWORK. An overcast stitch. **L16.**
12 WEAVING. An extra yarn not forming part of the warp or the weft. **E19.**
▶ **IV 13** NAUTICAL. In full ***whipstaff***. A handle attached to the tiller, formerly used in small ships. *obsolete* exc. *Hist.* **E17.**
14 Each of the arms carrying the sails in a windmill. **M18.**
15 A simple rope-and-pulley apparatus for hoisting (esp. light) objects. **M18.**
16 A fairground ride in which freely pivoting cars revolve jerkily round a track. **E20.**

Phrases: ***a crack of the whip, a fair crack of the whip***: see CRACK *noun* 1. ***ride whip and spur***: see SPUR *noun*[1]. **whip and tongue grafting** a method of grafting in which both stock and scion are cut diagonally and their surfaces are provided with matching tongues which interlock when the graft is tied.

Comb.: **whip aerial, whip antenna** an aerial in the form of a long flexible wire or rod with a connection at one end; **whipbird** any of various Australian birds which have a call resembling the crack of a whip; *esp.* (*a*) a logrunner of the genus *Psophodes*; †(*b*) any of several whistlers of the genus *Pachycephala*; **whip-club** a carriage-driving club; **whip-craft** the art of driving carriages; **whip-crane** a light derrick with tackle for hoisting; **whip-crop** *dial.* any of several shrubs or trees whose shoots are used for whip-handles, *esp.* the wayfaring-tree, *Viburnum lantana*; **whip graft** HORTICULTURE a simple graft in which both stock and scion are cut diagonally; **whip hand** (*a*) the hand which holds the whip in riding or driving a carriage etc.; (*b*) *fig.* the advantage or control in a situation (freq. in ***have the whip hand***); **whip-hem** NEEDLEWORK a hem formed by whipping; **whip line** (*a*) = WHIPCORD 1; (*b*) the rope forming part of a whip (WHIP *noun* 15); **whipman** (now *rare*) a carriage-driver; *dial.* a carter; **whip-ray** an eagle ray, a stingray; *spec.* (*N. Amer.*) the spotted eagle ray, *Aetobatus narinari*; **whip-roll** WEAVING a roller carrying the yarn from the yarn-beam to the reed; **whip scorpion** an arachnid of the order Uropygi, resembling a scorpion with a long narrow caudal flagellum, raptorial pedipalps, and slender tactile front legs; **whip-snake** any of various snakes having a long slender form; esp. colubrids of the genera *Coluber* (in Eurasia), *Masticophis* (in N. America: cf. COACHWHIP 2), and *Psammophis* (in Africa), various tree and vine snakes, and Australian elapids of the genus *Demansia*; **whip-socket** a socket fixed to the dashboard of a carriage to hold the end of a whip; ***whipstaff***: see sense 13 above; **whipstall** AERONAUTICS a stall in which an aircraft changes suddenly from a nose-up attitude to a nose-down one; **whip-stick** (*a*) a pliant stick used as a whip; (*b*) *Austral.* = MALLEE; **whipstock** (*a*) the handle of a whip; (*b*) OIL INDUSTRY a long tapered steel wedge placed at the bottom of a hole to cause the drilling bit to deviate sideways; **whip tail** an animal's tail resembling a whip; **whipworm** any of various parasitic nematode worms of the family Trichuridae, which have a stout posterior and slender anterior part, esp. worms of the genus *Trichuris* which infest the intestines of domestic animals.

■ **whipless** *adjective* (of a Member of Parliament) having resigned, or having been deprived of, the whip of a party: **M20.** **whiplike** *adjective* resembling (that of) a whip **E19.** **whipship** *noun* (*rare*) (*a*) *joc.* (with possess. adjective, as ***his whipship***: etc.) a mock title of respect given to a coachman; (*b*) the rank or office of parliamentary whip: **E19.**

whip /wɪp/ *verb.* Infl. **-pp-. ME.**
[Prob. from Middle & mod. Low German, Middle & mod. Dutch *wippen* swing, vacillate, leap, from Germanic base meaning 'move quickly' repr. also in Dutch *wipplank* see-saw, *wipstaart* wagtail. Cf. WIPE *verb.*]
▶ **I** Move swiftly or abruptly.
†**1** *verb intrans.* Of a bird: flap the wings violently. Only in **ME.**
2 *verb intrans.* & †*trans.* with *it.* Make an abrupt movement; move hastily or swiftly; dart, dash; thrash about. Usu. foll. by adverb or adverbial phr. **LME.**
3 *verb trans.* Move, take, put, pull, etc., with an abrupt, hasty, or swift movement or action. Usu. foll. by adverb or adverbial phr. **LME.** ▸**b** Drink quickly. Usu. foll. by *off, up. slang.* **L16.** ▸**c** Make *up* or prepare quickly or hastily. **E17.** ▸**d** Orig., swindle. Now, steal. *slang* (orig. *Criminals'*). **M19.**
4 †**a** *verb trans.* Pierce *through* the body etc. with a sword-thrust. *slang.* **L17–M19.** ▸**b** *verb trans.* & *intrans.* FENCING. Cause (one's blade) to move round the point of contact with the opponent's parrying blade. **L18.**
5 *verb trans.* Hoist or lower with a whip (WHIP *noun* 15). **M18.**

📖 **2** R. L. STEVENSON He whipped out of sight in a moment. R. INGALLS He made himself promise not to . . whip through the pages. M. ROBERTS I whipped round and pressed the light switch beside the door. **3** V. WOOLF He had whipped a tape measure from his pocket. R. INGALLS Agnes . . whipped the screen door open. **c** *Boston Sunday Globe* Mrs Kelly had a local dressmaker whip up a coat and dress. *What Food?* Have these to hand and you will be able to whip up a good meal anytime.

▶ **II** Use (as) a whip, strike (as) with a whip.
6 *verb trans.* Strike with a whip as a punishment; punish with repeated blows of a whip, flog; *loosely* beat, spank; drive *away, out*, etc. **LME.** ▸**b** Urge (a horse etc.) on with a whip. Also foll. by *up.* **L16.** ▸**c** Spin (a top) by striking it with a whip. **L16.**
7 *verb trans.* Chastise, reprove severely; afflict, torment. Formerly also used in *imper.* as an oath. *arch.* **M16.**
8 *verb trans.* Strike like a whip, lash; ANGLING cast a fly-line over (a stretch of water) repeatedly; drive *forward, out*, etc., produce, as by striking like a whip. **L16.**
9 *verb trans.* Defeat; excel. Now *colloq.* (chiefly *N. Amer.*). **L16.**
10 *verb trans.* Beat (cream, an egg-white, etc.) vigorously until thick or stiff. **L17.** ▸**b** *verb intrans.* Of cream: thicken as a result of vigorous beating. **M20.**
†**11** *verb trans.* [After French *fouetté*.] As *pa. pple.* Streaked, striped. **L17–E18.**
12 *verb trans.* & *intrans.* **a** Foll. by *in*: (of a huntsman) have the special duty of bringing (straying hounds) back into the pack. **M18.** ▸**b** Foll. by *in, up*: summon the attendance of (the members of a party) for a division in Parliament. **M18.**
13 *verb trans.* Rouse, excite, or stir up (feeling etc.). Usu. foll. by *up.* **E19.**

📖 **6** STEELE The . . boys . . were whipped away by a beadle. THACKERAY She deserves to be whipped, and sent to bed. **b** J. RATHBONE The coachman whipped up the mules. **8** *Cornhill Magazine* The cold has whipped red roses on her cheeks. S. HILL A burst of rain and spray whipped his face. **9** J. IRVING The Steering wrestling team whipped Bath Academy . . 9–2. **13** A. MASON Whipping the credulous into a frenzy of faith. S. MIDDLETON They'd . . whipped up considerable support.

▶ **III** Bind round or over.
14 *verb trans.* **a** Overlay (a rope etc.) with cord wound closely and regularly round and round; bind (twine) in this way round something. Cf. earlier WHIPCORD. **LME.** ▸**b** Fasten by binding in this way. **M18.**
†**15** *verb trans.* Wreathe, entwine. *Scot.* **L15–E16.**
16 *verb trans.* NEEDLEWORK. Sew with overcast stitches; gather by sewing with overcast and running stitches. **M16.**

📖 **14** *Motorboats Monthly* Having bought the rope . . divide it up into lengths and whip the ends. **16** D. PARKER She began whipping narrow lace along the top of the half-made garment.

Phrases: **whip creation**: see CREATION 4. **whip into shape** make presentable or efficient. **whip the cat** *Austral. & NZ colloq.* complain, moan; be sorry, show remorse.
Comb.: **whip-pan** *noun & verb* (CINEMATOGRAPHY) (*a*) *noun* a panning movement fast enough to give a blurred picture; (*b*) *verb intrans.* pan quickly to give a blurred picture.
■ **whippable** *adjective* (*a*) able or liable to be whipped; (*b*) (of cream) capable of thickening when whipped: **M19.** **whipped** *ppl adjective* (*a*) that has been whipped; *N. Amer. slang* exhausted, tired out (foll. by *up*); (*b*) (of a vote etc.) subject to a parliamentary whip: **M16.**

†**whip** *interjection & adverb.* **LME–E19.**
[from the verb.]
Suddenly, in a trice; presto!

whipcord /ˈwɪpkɔːd/ *noun, verb, & adjective.* **ME.**
[Prob. from WHIP *verb* + CORD *noun*[1], with later assoc. with WHIP *noun.*]
▶ **A** *noun.* **1** Thin tough tightly twisted cord such as is used for making whiplashes; a length of this. **ME.**
2 A close-woven ribbed worsted material used for riding breeches etc. **L19.**
▶ **B** *verb trans.* Provide (a whip) with a whipcord. *rare.* **L18.**
▶ **C** *adjective.* Tough as whipcord; made of whipcord. **M19.**

📖 T. C. WOLFE Their arms were . . lean with the play of whipcord muscles.

whip-jack /ˈwɪpdʒak/ *noun. arch.* **M16.**
[App. from WHIP *verb* + JACK *noun*[1].]
A beggar who pretends to be an impoverished sailor.

whiplash /ˈwɪplaʃ/ *noun & verb.* **L16.**
[from WHIP *noun* + LASH *noun*[1].]
▶ **A** *noun.* **1** The flexible end of a whip; (chiefly *fig.*) a blow with a whip, the sound of this. **L16.**
2 BOTANY & ZOOLOGY. A whiplike organism or structure, as a vibraculum. Also *spec.*, the seaweed *Chorda filum* (sea lace). **M19.**

3 Damage to the neck or spine caused by a severe jerk of the head, esp. as in a car accident. Chiefly in ***whiplash injury***. **M20.**

> 📖 **1** *attrib.*: J. WAINWRIGHT I . . put whiplash scorn into my voice.

▶**B** *verb*. **1** *verb trans.* Propel, strike, etc., suddenly and forcefully, like the lash of a whip; jerk in a contrary direction, *spec.* cause a whiplash injury to; inflict sudden or severe harm on. **M20.** **2** *verb intrans.* Move suddenly and forcefully, like the lash of a whip. **M20.**

> 📖 **1** M. IGNATIEFF He shifted gears, popped the clutch, and they were whiplashed forward. *fig.*: C. DEXTER *'Thought?'* Morse's . . repetition . . sounded like a whiplashed retaliation for such impertinence. **2** *Washington Post* The cable . . snapped. It . . whiplashed around the deck and caught the Chief in the spine.

whipper /ˈwɪpə/ *noun*. **E16.**
[from WHIP *verb* + -ER[1].]
1 A person who or thing which excels others. *obsolete* exc. *dial.* **E16.** **2** A person, esp. an official, who inflicts a whipping as a punishment. **M16.** ▸**b** = FLAGELLANT *noun* 1. *rare*. **M17.** **3** *whipper-in*: ▸**a** A huntsman's assistant who brings straying hounds into the pack. **M18.** ▸**b** = WHIP *noun* 6b. *obsolete* exc. *Hist.* **L18.** **4** *Hist.* A person or apparatus raising coal from a ship's hold by means of a pulley; = ***coal-whipper*** s.v. COAL *noun*. **M19.** **5** A person who stitches the edge of a blanket. Chiefly *dial.* **L19.**

whipperginny /ˈwɪpədʒɪni/ *noun*. Long *arch.* **L16.**
[Origin unkn.]
†**1** A promiscuous woman. *slang*. Only in **L16.** **2** A particular old card-game. **E17.**

whippersnapper /ˈwɪpəsnapə/ *noun*. **L17.**
[Perh. from WHIP *noun* + SNAPPER *noun*[1], after earlier SNIPPER-SNAPPER.]
A small or insignificant person; *esp.* an insignificant but impertinent or intrusive (usu. young) person.

> 📖 J. GALSWORTHY A whipper-snapper of a young fellow.

■ **whippersnap** *verb intrans.* [back-form.] behave like a whippersnapper, be impertinent or intrusive **E20.**

whippet /ˈwɪpɪt/ *noun*. **L15.**
[Partly from WHIP *noun*, *verb* + -ET[1]; partly from next.]
†**1** A type of light wine. *rare*. Only in **L15.** **2** Orig., a lively young woman. Now (*dial.*), a nimble, diminutive, or puny person. **M16.** **3** Orig., a small breed of dog. Now *spec.* (a dog of) a breed which is a cross between a greyhound and a terrier or spaniel, used for racing. **E17.** ▸**b** *transf. Hist.* A light kind of tank used in the war of 1914–18. Also ***whippet tank***. **E20.**
■ **whippeˈteer** *noun* a person who keeps a whippet or whippets **L19.**

†**whippet** *verb intrans.* **M–L16.**
[App. from *whip it*: see WHIP *verb* 2. Cf. prec.]
Move briskly.

whippin /ˈwɪpɪn/ *noun*. *dial.* **L17.**
[Origin. unkn. Cf. WHIPPLETREE.]
= WHIPPLETREE. Also more fully ***whippintree***.

whipping /ˈwɪpɪŋ/ *noun*. **M16.**
[from WHIP *verb* + -ING[1].]
1 The action of WHIP *verb*; an instance of this; *spec.* (a) beating, esp. with a whip. **M16.** **2** Cord used to overlay a rope etc.; each turn of a length of this. **L17.**
Comb.: **whipping-bench**, **whipping-block** *Hist.*: on which offenders were laid for public whippings; **whipping-boy** (*a*) *Hist.* a boy educated with a young prince or other royal person and punished instead of him; (*b*) a scapegoat; **whipping-cream**: suitable for whipping; **whipping-girl** *rare* a scapegoat; **whipping-post** *Hist.*: to which offenders were tied for public whippings; **whipping-stock** *rare* a person frequently whipped; *transf.* an object of blame; **whipping-top**: kept spinning by being whipped.

Whipple's disease /ˈwɪp(ə)lz dɪˌziːz/ *noun phr.* **M20.**
[from George Hoyt *Whipple* (1878–1976), US pathologist.]
MEDICINE. Intestinal lipodystrophy.

whippletree /ˈwɪp(ə)ltriː/ *noun*. Also ***whiffle-** /ˈwɪf(ə)l-/. **M18.**
[1st elem. app. from WHIP *verb*. Cf. WHIPPIN.]
A swingletree.

whippoorwill /ˈwɪpəwɪl/ *noun*. **E18.**
[Imit. of the bird's call.]
A nightjar, *Caprimulgus vociferus*, found in North and Central America.

whippy /ˈwɪpi/ *adjective*. **M19.**
[from WHIP *noun* + -Y[1].]
Flexible, springy.

> 📖 R. DAHL The branches above him were very thin and whippy.

■ **whippiness** *noun* **L19.**

whipsaw /ˈwɪpsɔː/ *noun & verb*. **M16.**
[from WHIP *noun* or *verb* + SAW *noun*[1].]
▶**A** *noun*. **1** A saw with a narrow blade held at each end by a frame, used esp. for curved work. **M16.** **2** *fig.* Something that is disadvantageous in two ways. Chiefly *US*. **L19.**
▶**B** *verb*. **1** *verb trans.* **a** Cut with a whipsaw. **M19.** ▸**b** Cheat by joint action on two others; STOCK EXCHANGE cause to lose in two ways. *US slang*. **L19.** **2** *verb intrans.* **a** Use a whipsaw. **E20.** ▸**b** Suffer the loss incurred by buying a security before the price falls and selling before the price rises. Orig. & chiefly as ***whipsawing*** *verbal noun*. *US Stock Exchange slang*. **E20.**

whipster /ˈwɪpstə/ *noun*. **L16.**
[App. from WHIP *verb* + -STER.]
1 a A lively, reckless, or mischievous person. *obsolete* exc. *dial.* **L16.** ▸**b** A promiscuous or licentious person. Long *obsolete* exc. *dial.* **L16.** ▸**c** A whippersnapper. *arch.* **E17.** **2** A person who uses a whip. Now *rare* or *obsolete*. **M17.**

whip-stitch /ˈwɪpstɪtʃ/ *verb & noun*. **L16.**
[from WHIP *verb*, *noun* + STITCH *verb*[1].]
▶**A** *verb trans.* Sew with overcast stitches. **L16.**
▶**B** *noun*. An overcast stitch; overcast sewing. **M17.**
at every whip-stitch, **every whip-stitch** *dial.* & *US* at frequent intervals, at every opportunity.

whipsy-derry /ˈwɪpsɪˌdɛri/ *noun*. Now *rare*. **M19.**
[Prob. connected with WHIP *noun* and DERRICK.]
A hoisting apparatus consisting of a derrick with a whip or simple pulley attached, worked by a horse or horses.

whiptail /ˈwɪpteɪl/ *adjective & noun*. **L18.**
[from WHIP *noun* + TAIL *noun*[1].]
▶**A** *adjective*. Designating any of various animals having a long slender tail. **L18.**
whiptail lizard any of various American lizards of the genus *Cnemidophorus* (family Teiidae). **whiptail ray** *Austral.* = ***whip-ray*** s.v. WHIP *noun*. **whiptail wallaby** a pale slender-shouldered wallaby, *Macropus parryi*, found in woodland in NE Australia; also called ***pretty-face (wallaby)***.
▶**B** *noun*. A whiptail lizard, ray, wallaby, etc. Also (*Austral.*) a rattail. **L19.**

whip-tom-kelly /wɪptɒmˈkɛli/ *noun*. **M18.**
[Imit. of the birds' call.]
Either of two vireos, *Vireo olivaceus* of N. and S. America, and *V. altiloquus* of the W. Indies and Florida.

whir *noun*, *verb*, *interjection*, & *adverb* vars. of WHIRR *noun*, *verb*, *interjection*, & *adverb*.

whirl /wəːl/ *noun*. **LME.**
[Partly from Middle & mod. Low German, Middle & mod. Dutch *wervel* †spindle etc. corresp. to Old High German *wirbil* (German *Wirbel*), or Old Norse *hvirfill* circle etc., ult. from Germanic base meaning 'to turn'; partly from the verb. Cf. WHARVE, WHORL.]
▶**I 1** = WHORL *noun* 1. **LME.** ▸**b** ROPE-MAKING. A cylinder of wood with a hook on which the ends of the fibre are hung in spinning. **L18.** **2** = WHORL *noun* 2. **L17.** **3** BOTANY. = WHORL *noun* 3. **E18.** **4** ZOOLOGY. = WHORL *noun* 3b. **L19.**
▶**II 5 a** The action or an act of whirling; (a) swift circling movement, (a) rapid rotation about an axis or centre. **L15.** ▸**b** (A part of) a body of water, air, etc., which is rotating rapidly; an eddy, a vortex. **M16.** **6** *transf.* & *fig.* **a** Confused and hurried activity; a busy or frantic series of activities etc.; tumult, bustle, rush. **M16.** ▸**b** A state of confusion. **E18.** **7** An attempt, *esp.* an initial or tentative attempt. Freq. in ***give it a whirl***. *colloq.* (orig. *US*). **L19.**

> 📖 **5a** E. K. KANE The whirl of the snow-drift. **b** J. CONRAD The dry dust rose in whirls. TOLKIEN A whirl of bats . . flurried over them. **6a** *Rolling Stone* At the center of the social whirl: . . hosting banquets . . , organizing charity bashes. E. F. BENSON In these weeks of whirl and rush, one's duties had to come first. A. HIGONNET Fashionable resorts generated a whirl of events. **b** R. S. SURTEES His head was in a complete whirl. **7** SNOO WILSON Give it a whirl, try it for a month. *New Yorker* First, he gave the family business a whirl.

whirl /wəːl/ *verb*. **ME.**
[Old Norse *hvirfla* turn about, whirl, rel. to *hvirfill*: see prec.]
1 *verb intrans.* Move in a circle or curve, esp. rapidly or with force; rush about in various directions. **ME.** **2** *verb trans.* Cause to move in a circle or curve, esp. rapidly or with force; *spec.* throw or fling a missile etc. in a curve. Formerly also *gen.* [by confusion], hurl. **LME.** ▸†**b** *verb trans.* & *intrans.* Throw (a die, dice) in gaming. **L16–L18.** **3** *verb intrans.* & *trans.* Turn swiftly about an axis or centre; revolve rapidly; spin round and round. **LME.** ▸**b** Turn quickly to face in another direction. **M19.** **4 a** *verb intrans.* Travel fast (as if) in a wheeled vehicle; move along swiftly, rush or sweep along. **LME.** ▸**b** *verb trans.* Drive (a wheeled vehicle), convey in a wheeled vehicle, swiftly; *gen.* carry *along*, *away*, *down*, etc., swiftly (now only with implication of circular movement). **LME.** **5** *verb intrans.* (Of the brain, senses, etc.) seem to spin round, be confused, follow each other in bewildering succession. **M16.** ▸**b** *verb trans.* Cause (the brain etc.) to reel; affect with giddiness. Now *rare* or *obsolete*. **L16.**

> 📖 **1** N. COWARD The Palace Hotel Skating Rink . . everybody whirling round in vivid colours. G. GREENE Dust which . . whirled around us in the wind. D. LESSING Suddenly alive with energy, she whirled about opening doors. **2** J. M. COETZEE The wind rises . . , my cap is whirled from my head. P. THEROUX Dust that had been whirled against . . walls. **3** T. H. WHITE He saw the stars . . whirling on their silent . . axes. A. CARTER The snow came whirling down in huge . . flakes. B. MOORE Little boys, whirling their school satchels in the air. **b** F. HERBERT She whirled and strode from the room. G. PALEY He whirled me around and took my hands. **4a** C. KINGSLEY Travellers . . whirling through miles of desert. S. LEWIS The ambulance whirled under the . . carriage-entrance of the hospital. **b** TENNYSON The winds begin to rise . . ; The last red leaf is whirl'd away. N. MITFORD I found myself being whirled through the suburbs . . in a large . . Daimler. **5** S. WYNTER Your head whirling with words spoken by 'unknown tongues'. J. HIGGINS So much had happened and it was all whirling around in her head.

Comb.: **whirl-about** *noun & adjective* (a thing) that whirls about; **whirl-blast** (orig. *dial.*) a whirlwind; **whirl-bone** (*obsolete* exc. *dial.*) (*a*) the round head of a bone (*spec.* the thigh-bone) turning in the socket of another bone; (*b*) the round bone of the knee, the patella; **whirl-puff** (long *obsolete* exc. *dial.*) a puff of wind that raises dust in a whirl.
■ **whirler** *noun* **LME.**

†**whirlbat** *noun*. Also (earlier) **hurl-**, **whorl-**. **ME.**
[App. from WHIRL *verb*, HURL *verb* + BAT *noun*[1].]
CLASSICAL ANTIQUITIES. **1** Orig., a type of club used as a weapon. Later [glossing Latin *aclys*], a small javelin. **ME–L18.** **2** [Glossing Latin *caestus*.] = CESTUS *noun*[2]. **M16–L18.**

whirled /wəːld/ *adjective*. **E18.**
[from WHIRL *noun*, *verb*: see -ED[2], -ED[1].]
1 Whorled. **E18.** **2** That has been whirled. **L19.**

whirlicote /ˈwəːlɪkəʊt/ *noun*. *arch.* **LME.**
[from WHIRL *verb*, with unkn. 2nd elem.]
A coach, a carriage.

whirligig /ˈwəːlɪgɪg/ *noun*, *adjective*, *adverb*, & *verb*. **LME.**
[from WHIRL(NG *adjective* or WHIRLY + GIG *noun*[1]. Cf. TWIRLIGIG.]
▶**A** *noun*. **1** Any of various toys that are whirled or spun round; *spec.*, a toy with four arms like miniature windmill-sails, which whirl round when it is moved through the air. **LME.** **2** Any of various mechanical devices having a whirling or rotatory movement; *spec.* †(*a*) a former instrument of punishment consisting of a large cage suspended on a pivot; (*b*) a merry-go-round. **L15.** **3** (A) rapid circling movement; something characterized by constant frantic activity or change; a whirl. **L16.** ▸**b** A fickle, flighty, or lively person. Cf. GIG *noun*[1] 1. *arch.* **E17.** **4** More fully ***whirligig beetle***. Any of various small water beetles of the family Gyrinidae, which have paddle-like legs and are freq. found in large numbers circling rapidly over the surface of still water. **E18.**

> 📖 **3** R. MACAULAY Life is a whirligig, and who knows what next? H. JACOBSON The whirligig of reason came to rest at truth.

▶**B** *attrib.* or as *adjective*. Resembling a whirligig; characterized by a whirling movement. **L16.**

> 📖 SIR W. SCOTT The changes of this trumpery whirligig world.

▶**C** *adverb*. With a whirling movement. *rare*. **L16.**
▶**D** *verb intrans.* & *trans.* with *it*. Infl. **-gg-**. Whirl, spin round. **L16.**

whirling /ˈwəːlɪŋ/ *noun*. **LME.**
[from WHIRL *verb* + -ING[1].]
The action of WHIRL *verb*; an instance of this.
whirling disease a disease of trout caused by the parasitic sporozoan *Myxosoma cerebralis*, which affects the balance of the fish.

whirling /ˈwəːlɪŋ/ *adjective*. **LME.**
[from WHIRL *verb* + -ING[2].]
That whirls.
whirling DERVISH. **whirling plant** = ***telegraph plant*** s.v. TELEGRAPH *noun*. **whirling-table** a machine with a rapidly revolving table, used for experiments in centrifugal force etc.
■ **whirlingly** *adverb* **E19.**

whirlpool /ˈwəːlpuːl/ *noun*. **E16.**
[from WHIRL *verb* + POOL *noun*[1].]
1 A constant powerful circular motion in a river, the sea, etc., caused by the meeting of adverse currents, an obstruction, etc., and often causing suction to its centre. Also *fig.*, a destructive or absorbing agency; a scene of confused and turbulent activity. **E16.**

2 In full ***whirlpool bath***. A bath or pool with underwater jets of hot, usu. aerated, water, used for physiotherapy or relaxation. Also, a pumping unit for producing such jets. M20.

whirlwind /ˈwəːlwɪnd/ *noun & adjective*. ME.
[Old Norse *hvirfilwindr*, from *hvirfill* WHIRL *noun* + *vindr* WIND *noun*[1].]
▶ **A** *noun*. **1** A small rotating storm of wind in which a vertical column of air whirls rapidly around a core of low pressure and moves progressively over land or sea. ME.
2 *transf. & fig.* A violent or destructive agency; a confused tumultuous process or state. LME.

> **1** J. HERSEY A whirlwind ripped through the park. Huge trees crashed down. **2** C. KINGSLEY The whirlwind of town pleasure. *Company* The case prompted a . . media whirlwind that threw up many similar cases of . . neglect.

▶ **B** *attrib.* or as *adjective*. Violent, impetuous; very rapid or hasty. E17.

> J. SUTHERLAND There followed a whirlwind romance and the couple were married three months later.

whirly /ˈwəːli/ *adjective*. M16.
[from WHIRL *noun* or *verb* + -Y[1].]
Characterized by whirling; confused, frantic, rapid.
Comb.: **whirlybird** *colloq.* a helicopter; **whirly-whirly** *Austral.* a whirling air current or dust cloud.

whirr /wəː/ *noun*. Also **whir**. LME.
[Rel. to next.]
1 Orig. (now only *Scot.*), rapid or forceful movement, rush, hurry. Now, a continuous rapid buzzing or softly clicking sound as of the fluttering of a bird's or insect's wings or of cog-wheels in constant motion. LME.
†**2** *fig.* Mental confusion; a mental shock. E17–E18.

> **1** R. L. STEVENSON The . . marsh-birds rose again . . with a simultaneous whirr. J. CHEEVER The only sound is the whirr of moving-picture cameras.

whirr /wəː/ *verb, interjection, & adverb*. Also **whir**, infl. **-rr-**. LME.
[Prob. of Scandinavian origin (cf. Danish *hvirre*, Norwegian *kvirra*, Swedish dial. *hvirra*) from unrecorded Old Norse verb rel. to *hvirfill*, *hvirfla*: see WHIRL *noun, verb*. Later prob. also imit. Cf. prec., HURRY *verb*.]
▶ **A** *verb*. †**1** *verb trans.* Throw with violence and noise; fling, hurl. LME–E17.
2 *verb intrans.* & (*rare*) *trans.* Move swiftly with a whirr. LME.
3 *verb intrans.* Emit a whirr; *dial.* growl, purr. E18.

> **2** R. K. NARAYAN Bats were whirring about. **3** A. BURGESS The clock whirred and got ready to strike.

▶ **B** *interjection & adverb*. Repr. a whirr or whirring sound; with a whirr. E17.

> DISRAELI Whirr! the exploded cork whizzed through the air. R. FRAME Taking photographs with a long lens . . . Click-whirr-click, click.

■ **whirring** *noun* the action of the verb; an instance of this; a whirr: L16.

whirry /ˈwəːri/ *adjective*. M20.
[from WHIRR *noun* + -Y[1].]
Characterized by or of the nature of a whirr.

whirry /ˈwɪri/ *verb*. Now *Scot.* L16.
[Perh. blend of WHIRR *verb* and HURRY *verb*.]
1 *verb trans.* Carry or drive swiftly; hurry along. L16.
2 *verb intrans.* Move rapidly, hurry. E17.

whish /wɪʃ/ *verb*[1], *interjection*[1], *& noun*. E16.
[Imit.]
▶ **A** *verb*. **1** *verb trans.* Drive or chase off by uttering a soft sibilant sound. *rare*. E16.
2 *verb intrans.* Emit a soft sibilant sound as of something moving rapidly through air or water. M16.
▶ **B** *interjection*. Repr. the sound of something moving rapidly through air or water. M16.
▶ **C** *noun*. Such a sound. E19.

whish /wɪʃ/ *verb*[2] *& interjection*[2]. Now *dial.* M16.
[Natural exclam. Cf. WHISHT *interjection* etc.]
▶ **A** *verb*. **1** *verb trans.* Silence, cause to be quiet, hush. M16.
2 *verb intrans.* Become or keep quiet. E17.
▶ **B** *interjection*. Demanding silence or quiet: hush! M16.

whisht /wɪʃt/ *interjection, noun, adjective, & verb*. M16.
[Natural exclam. Cf. prec., HUSH *interjection*, HUSHT *interjection*, ST *interjection*, WHIST *interjection*.]
▶ **A** *interjection*. Demanding silence or quiet: hush! (Cf. sense D.1 below.) Now chiefly *Scot., Anglo-Irish, & dial.* M16.
▶ **B** *noun*. **1** An utterance of 'whisht!' to demand silence. *rare*. M16.
2 Silence. Chiefly in ***hold one's whisht***, be quiet. *Scot.* L18.
3 A slight sound, a whisper. Only in neg. contexts. *Scot.* L18.
▶ **C** *adjective*. Silent, quiet, hushed. Now *dial.* L16.
▶ **D** *verb*. Now chiefly *Scot., Anglo-Irish, & dial.*
1 *verb intrans.* Become or keep silent, hush. (In imper. not distinguishable from sense A. above.) M18.
2 *verb trans.* Make silent, hush. E19.

whisk /wɪsk/ *noun*[1]. Orig. *Scot.* Also (earlier) †**wisk**. LME.
[Partly from Old Norse *visk* wisp, from Germanic base also of WISP *noun*; partly from the verb.]
▶ **I 1** A light rapid sweeping movement or action. LME.

> **1** LYTTON Giving a petulant whisk of her tail. **in a whisk**, **with a whisk** suddenly, in a flash.

▶ **II 2 a** ANGLING. Any of the slender hairlike tail cerci of a mayfly, stonefly, etc. E17. ▸**b** A bundle of grass, twigs, bristles, etc., fixed on a handle and used for removing dust or flies. Also ***whisk broom***. E18. ▸**c** Any of several grasses of warm countries having inflorescences that can be made into brushes or brooms, esp. *Chrysopogon gryllus* (more fully ***French whisk***) and broom-corn (more fully ***Venetian whisk***); the inflorescence of such a grass. M18.
3 A utensil for beating eggs, whipping cream, etc., *esp.* one with wire loops fixed to a handle. M17.
4 A woman's collar worn in the late 17th cent. *obsolete* exc. *Hist.* M17.

> **3** J. CLAVELL Buntaro . . beat the powder and water with the bamboo whisk to blend it.

▶†**III 5** A whippersnapper. *slang*. Only in 17.

whisk /wɪsk/ *noun*[2]. *obsolete* exc. *dial.* E17.
[Perh. from WHISK *verb*.]
= WHIST *noun*[2].

whisk /wɪsk/ *verb, adverb, & interjection*. Also (earlier) †**wisk**. LME.
[Prob. of Scandinavian origin: cf. Swedish *viska* whisk (off), Danish *viske* and WHISK *noun*[1].]
▶ **A** *verb*. †**1** *verb trans.* In *pass.* Become entangled. Only in LME.
2 *verb intrans.* Move with a light rapid sweeping motion; go (esp. out of sight) lightly or quickly, rush, dart. Usu. foll. by preposition. L15.
3 *verb trans.* Move (something) with a light sweeping movement; take or put with a sudden movement; convey lightly or quickly. Usu. foll. by preposition or adverb. E16.
4 *verb trans.* Beat with a bundle of twigs etc. Now only *spec.*, stir or beat up (eggs, cream, etc.) with a light rapid movement, esp. by means of a whisk (WHISK *noun*[1] 3). M16.
5 *verb trans.* Brush lightly and rapidly from a surface. Usu. foll. by *away*, *off*. E17.

> **2** L. M. ALCOTT Scrabble [the pet rat] whisked into his hole. E. BOWEN The van whisked over the bridge. **3** R. PARK Carrie quickly whisked the papers under a cushion. R. JAFFE She . . whisked people's plates away. C. J. CHERRYH The lift whisked them up with a knee-buckling force. J. WINTERSON She . . whisked me off to hospital. **4** E. DAVID Whisk the mixture until it will hold a soft peak. *Food & Wine* Whisk together the shallots, orange juice . . and olive oil.
> **5** W. IRVING His . . horse stood, stamping and whisking off the flies. DICKENS The beadle . . whisked the crumbs off his knees.

Comb.: **whisk tail** a tail that may be whisked; **whisk-tailed** *adjective* having a whisk tail.
▶ **B** *interjection & adverb*. With a sudden light movement. M18.
■ **whisking** *verbal noun* the action of the verb; an instance of this: M16. **whisking** *adjective* (*a*) that whisks; (*b*) *arch. colloq.* active, lively; (*c*) (*obsolete* exc. *dial.*) great, huge, excessive: E16.

whisker /ˈwɪskə/ *noun & verb*. LME.
[from WHISK *verb* + -ER[1].]
▶ **A** *noun*. **1** A thing used for whisking, as a switch, a bundle of feathers, twigs, etc. *obsolete* exc. *dial.* LME.
2 a In *pl.* & (*arch.*) *collect. sing.* The hair growing on a man's chin, upper lip, and cheeks; orig. (now *colloq.*), a moustache; now *esp.*, the hair growing on the cheeks or sides of the face alone. LME. ▸**b** Orig., a moustache. Now, a patch of hair growing on one cheek or side of a man's face (chiefly in ***pair of whiskers***); any of the hairs growing on a man's chin, upper lip, and cheeks or sides of the face, or on a woman's face. E18.
†**3** A large or excessive thing; *esp.* a big lie. *slang*. M–L17.
4 Any of a number of long projecting hairs or bristles growing on the face (esp. on the snout) of many mammals; each of a similar set of feathers around the bill of certain insectivorous birds. Also, moustachial markings on a bird. L17. ▸**b** *fig.* A very small distance or amount. *colloq.* E20. ▸**c** ELECTRICITY. A wire used to form a rectifying contact with the surface of a semiconductor. E20.
5 NAUTICAL. **a** More fully ***whisker pole***. Either of two spars extending laterally on each side of the bowsprit, for spreading the guys of the jib-boom. M19. ▸**b** A lever for detonating a torpedo. L19.
6 A single crystal that has grown in a filamentous form a few microns thick, characterized by a lack of dislocations and a tensile strength much greater than the bulk material. M20.

> **2a** DICKENS A shaggy fellow . . with a good deal of hair and whisker. S. LEACOCK This photograph is of a man with whiskers. **b** A. CRAIG Tim (whose face . . was bracketed by a pair of long whiskers). **4b** *Dressage Review* His trot music . . appeared to be just a whisker too slow. *Mail on Sunday* John Emburey came within a whisker of capturing his . . first wicket. *Autosport* Perkins swept around the outside . . to claim victory by a whisker.

Phrases: ***cat's whisker***: see CAT *noun*[1]. **grow whiskers** (of food) become mouldy. **have whiskers**, **have grown whiskers** (of news, a story, etc.) be very old.
▶ **B** *verb trans.* Provide with whiskers. *rare*. E19.
■ **whiskerage** *noun* whiskers collectively M19. **whiskerless** *adjective* M19. **whiskery** *adjective* (*a*) having whiskers; (*b*) suggestive of or resembling whiskers or a whisker: M19.

whiskerando /wɪskəˈrandəʊ/ *noun*. *joc.* Pl. **-os**. E19.
[Don Ferolo *Whiskerandos*, a character in Sheridan's play 'The Critic' (1779).]
A heavily whiskered man.

whiskered /ˈwɪskəd/ *adjective*. M18.
[from WHISKER *noun* + -ED[2].]
1 Of a man: having whiskers. M18.
2 Of a mammal or bird: (*a*) having whiskers; (*b*) having moustachial markings. M18.
2 whiskered auklet a dark auklet, *Aethia pygmaea*, that has three white plumes on each side of the face and breeds on islands in the N. Pacific. **whiskered bat** any of several small Eurasian bats of the genus *Myotis*; *esp.* the widespread *M. mystacinus*. **whiskered tern** an Old World tern, *Chlidonias hybrida*, which has a black cap and white cheeks.

whiskey *noun*[1] *& verb*, *noun*[2] see WHISKY *noun*[1] *& verb*, *noun*[2].

whiskey jack *noun phr.* var. of WHISKY JACK.

whisky /ˈwɪski/ *noun*[1] *& verb*. Also (see note below) **whiskey**. E18.
[Var. of USQUE.]
▶ **A** *noun*. A spirit distilled chiefly in Scotland and Ireland from malted barley, or from barley with maize or rye; a similar spirit distilled chiefly in the US from either rye or maize; a drink of this. E18.

> V. GLENDINNING On top of the whiskies the wine made her truculent. ANNE STEVENSON She stood drinking whisky and ginger . . in Miller's bar. ***blended whisky***: see BLEND *verb*[2] 1b. ***corn-whiskey***: see CORN *noun*[1] 3c. ***grain whisky***: see GRAIN *noun*[1]. ***Irish whiskey***: see IRISH *adjective*. ***malt whisky***: see MALT *noun*[1] *& adjective*. ***rye whiskey***: see RYE *noun*[1]. ***Scotch whisky***: see SCOTCH. ***single malt whisky***: see SINGLE *adjective & adverb*.

Comb.: **whiskey-straight** *US colloq.* a drink of whiskey without water; **whiskey-water** *N. Amer.* a drink of whiskey and water; **whisky mac** (also with cap. initials) (a drink of) whisky and ginger wine mixed in equal amounts; **whisky money** *Hist.* the proportion of the beer and spirit duty which was allocated by law to technical education; **whisky priest** *slang* a habitually drunken priest; **whisky-soda** *N. Amer., Austral., & NZ* (a drink of) whisky and soda; **whisky sour** a drink of whisky and lemon or lime juice; **whisky voice** *colloq.* a hoarse or rough voice.
▶ **B** *verb trans.* Supply with whisky, give a drink of whisky to. *rare*. M19.
¶ The Irish and US product is now usu. spelt *whiskey*.
■ **whiskied** *adjective* saturated with or smelling of whisky M19. **whiskified** *adjective* affected by excessive drinking of whisky E19. **whiskyish** *adjective* affected by whisky, smelling of whisky E20.

whisky /ˈwɪski/ *noun*[2]. Also **whiskey**. M18.
[from WHISK *verb* + -Y[1], from its light swift movement. Cf. TIMWHISKY.]
Chiefly *Hist.* A kind of light two-wheeled one-horse carriage, a type of gig.

whisky jack /ˈwɪski dʒak/ *noun phr.* *Canad.* Also **whiskey jack**. L18.
[Alt. of next after *Jack*.]
The grey jay, *Perisoreus canadensis*.

whisky john /ˈwɪski dʒɒn/ *noun phr.* *Canad.* (now *rare* or *obsolete*). L18.
[Alt. of Cree *wiskatjan*, Montagnais *wi:skača:n* after *whisky*, *John*. Cf. prec.]
= prec.

whisp /wɪsp/ *noun*. *rare*. LME.
[Imit.]
A slight gust *of* wind; a light shower *of* rain.

whisper /ˈwɪspə/ *noun*. E16.
[from the verb.]
1 A soft rustling sound. E16.
2 An act of whispering or speaking softly; a soft non-resonant quality of voice characterizing such speech; a whispered word or phrase. L16.
3 A brief mention, a suggestion, a hint, (chiefly in neg. contexts); a rumour, a piece of gossip. L16.

📖 1 *Shooting Life* The rifle slides from its cover with a whisper of canvas on metal. 2 G. GISSING Her voice had sunk to a whisper. M. MITCHELL The talk would die to whispers. W. MARCH A whisper that hardly carried to Christine's ears. ***pig's whisper, stage whisper. Chinese whispers***: see CHINESE *adjective*. 3 *Essentials* A slight tint to give your skin just a whisper of colour. J. GALSWORTHY The old scandal had been . . kept from her. . . He wouldn't have a whisper of it reach her. *Times* Reed International . . advanced 13p . . on whispers that a stakebuilding operation was again under way.

▪ **whisperless** *adjective* absolutely silent M19. **whispery** *adjective* characterized by whispers; resembling a whisper: M19.

whisper /ˈwɪspə/ *verb.*
[Old English *hwisprian* = early Flemish *wisperen*, German *wispern* (of Low German origin), rel. to synon. Middle Low German, Middle Dutch *wispelen*, Old High German *(h)wispalōn* (German *wispeln*), Old Norse *hvískra*, *hvísla*, from Germanic imit. base also of WHISTLE *verb*.]
▸ **I 1** *verb intrans.* Speak very softly without vibration of the vocal cords; talk or converse in this way, esp. for the sake of secrecy. OE. ▸**b** *verb trans.* Foll. by *adverb*: bring by soft speech. Chiefly *poet.* L17.
2 *verb trans.* Say or report privately or confidentially; in *pass.*, be rumoured; (in neg. contexts) say the least word of. LME. ▸**b** *verb intrans.* Speak or converse privately or conspiratorially about a person or thing; *esp.* (in neg. contexts) say the least word *against* etc. E16. ▸**c** *verb trans.* Foll. by *adverb*, *adverbial phr.*: bring by private (esp. malicious) speech. M17.
3 *verb trans.* Say, utter, or express very softly, esp. for the sake of secrecy; *arch.* address, tell, or ask very softly. M16.

📖 1 ALDOUS HUXLEY He took the trouble to whisper. **b** DRYDEN Rising Fears are whisper'd thro' the Crowd. **2a** L. STRACHEY It was whispered that Lady Flora was with child. **b** S. PEPYS Ne'er a prince in France dare whisper against it. **c** H. BUSHNELL The great majority . . are . . beckoned, whispered into their calling. **3** DICKENS Miss Jane . . whispered her sister to observe how jealous Mr. Cheggs was. W. SHEED Catholic recusants . . who . . held whispered Masses in makeshift chapels. W. CATHER Amédée . . whispered . . that they were going to play a joke on the girls. A. MAUPIN 'Sorry,' whispered Brian, backing away.

▸ **II 4** *verb intrans.* Make a soft rustling sound. E16. ▸**b** *verb trans.* Express or communicate by a soft rustling sound. M17.
5 *verb trans.* Suggest (something) secretly or mysteriously to the mind; *arch.* suggest secretly or mysteriously to the mind of (a person). E17.

📖 4 J. STEINBECK The trees whispered softly in the breeze. **5** DISRAELI Nature seemed to whisper me the folly of learning words instead of ideas. P. BOWLES Her intuition whispered to her to lie absolutely still.

▪ **whisperer** *noun* M16. **whisperingly** *adverb* in a whispering manner, in a whisper L16.

whispering /ˈwɪsp(ə)rɪŋ/ *noun.* OE.
[from WHISPER *verb* + -ING¹.]
The action of WHISPER *verb*; an instance of this.
Comb.: **whispering campaign** a systematic circulation of a rumour, esp. in order to denigrate a person or thing; **whispering-gallery** a usu. circular or elliptical gallery situated under a dome, whose acoustic properties are such that a whisper may be heard round its entire circumference.

whiss /wɪs/ *verb intrans.* Now *Scot. dial.* LME.
[Imit.: cf. Icelandic *hvissa* whizz, run with a hissing sound.]
Orig., make a sibilant sound, whistle, hiss, whizz. Later, whisper.

whist /wɪst/ *noun*¹. E17.
[from WHIST *interjection*, *verb*¹.]
†**1** = WHISHT *noun* 1. *rare.* Only in E17.
2 = WHISHT *noun* 2. *Anglo-Irish.* L19.

whist /wɪst/ *noun*². M17.
[Alt. of WHISK *noun*².]
A card-game with the players (usu. four) grouped into pairs of partners and in which points are scored according to the number of tricks won and (in some forms) by the highest trumps or honours held by each pair.
duplicate whist: see DUPLICATE *adjective*. **long whist**: in which the score is ten points with honours counting. **short whist**: in which the score is five points with honours counting. ***solo whist***: see SOLO *adjective*.
Comb.: **whist-drive** a social occasion at which progressive whist is played.

whist /wɪst/ *adjective.* Now *arch.* & *dial.* LME.
[from WHIST *interjection*.]
Silent, quiet. Chiefly *pred.*

whist /wɪst/ *verb*¹. Now *arch.* & *dial.* M16.
[from WHIST *interjection*.]
1 *verb intrans.* = WHISHT *verb* 1. In *imper.* not distinguishable from WHIST *interjection*. M16.
†**2** *verb trans.* = WHISHT *verb* 2. M16–E17.

whist /wɪst/ *verb*² *intrans. rare.* E19.
[from WHIST *noun*².]
Play whist.
▪ **whister** *noun* a person who plays whist E19.

whist /wɪst/ *interjection.* Now *arch.* & *dial.* LME.
[Natural exclam. Cf. WHISHT.]
= WHISHT *interjection*. Cf. WHIST *verb*¹ 1.

whister /ˈwɪstə/ *verb trans.* & *intrans. obsolete* exc. *dial.* LME.
[Repr. Old English *hwæstrian* whisper, rustle, with partial assim. to WHISPER *verb*.]
Whisper.

whistle /ˈwɪs(ə)l/ *noun.* OE.
[Rel. to next.]
1 A short tubular instrument producing a shrill tone by means of breath, air, or steam forced through a narrow slit, used esp. for signalling. Also, a simple musical instrument resembling a recorder; formerly, a pipe, a flute. OE. ▸†**b** *fig.* A person speaking on behalf of another; a person giving a secret signal. LME–M17. ▸**c** A suit. Also more fully ***whistle and flute***. *rhyming slang.* M20.
2 The mouth or throat as used in speaking or singing. Chiefly in ***wet one's whistle***, ***whet one's whistle*** below. *colloq.* LME.
3 An act of whistling; a clear shrill sound produced by forcing the breath through the narrow opening made by contracting the lips, (and sometimes further narrowed by inserting two fingers), used esp. as a call or signal or to express surprise, approval, or derision; such a sound made by blowing through a whistle; *rare* an act of whistling a tune. LME.
4 *transf.* A similar sound made by a bird, the wind, a moving missile, etc. M17.

📖 1 J. CHEEVER The train blows its whistle. J. KOSINSKI Police whistles shrilled in the silence. *Smithsonian* A toy company that makes wooden tops, whistles, and kazoos. ***Swanee whistle, tin whistle***, etc. **3** SIR W. SCOTT Klepper knows my whistle, and follows me. CONAN DOYLE The shrill whistle of the fifes. *Glasgow Herald* Succumbing to their . . opponents only on the final whistle.

Phrases: **(as) clean as a whistle, (as) clear as a whistle, (as) dry as a whistle** very clean or clear or dry. ***bells and whistles***: see BELL *noun*¹. ***blow the whistle on***: see BLOW *verb*¹. ***hunt the whistle***: see HUNT *verb*. ***kist o' whistles***: see KIST *noun*¹ 1. **pay for one's whistle, pay too dear for one's whistle** pay much more for something than it is worth. ***penny whistle***: see PENNY *adjective*. ***silent dog whistle, silent whistle***: see SILENT *adjective*. **wet one's whistle, whet one's whistle** (chiefly *joc.* & *colloq.*) have a drink, esp. an alcoholic one. ***whistle and flute***: see sense 1c above.
Comb.: **whistle-blower** a person who blows the whistle on a person or activity (see BLOW *verb*¹); **whistle-language** = ***whistle-speech*** below; **whistle punk** *N. Amer.* a logger who signals by means of a whistle to those operating a donkey-engine; **whistle-speech** a system of communication by whistling, based on spoken language and used to communicate over long distances; **whistle-wood** *Scot.* & *north.* peeled wood used by children to make whistles; any of the trees providing such wood, *esp.* alder and sycamore.

whistle /ˈwɪs(ə)l/ *verb.*
[Old English *(h)wistlian* corresp. to Old Norse *hvísla* whisper, Middle Swedish *hvisla*, Swedish *vissla* whistle, Danish *hvistle* hiss, from Germanic imit. base also of WHISPER *verb*.]
▸ **I 1** *verb intrans.* Orig., play on a pipe. Now, blow or sound a whistle. OE.
2 *verb intrans.* Produce a whistle or clear shrill sound by forcing the breath through contracted lips, esp. as a signal or to express surprise, approval, or derision; produce a series of such sounds; *spec.* produce a tune consisting of a series of such sounds. OE.
3 *verb intrans.* (Of a bird, the wind, etc.) emit a whistle; (foll. by adverb) (of the wind, a missile, etc.) move or go with a whistle. OE. ▸**b** Of a fabric or garment: rustle shrilly. *obsolete* exc. *dial.* M17.
4 *verb trans.* Produce (a tune), express, by whistling. Also with cognate obj., emit (a whistle). M16.
5 *verb trans.* **a** Shoot or drive with a whistling sound. L17. ▸**b** Foll. by *down*, *off*: apply, take off, (the brakes of a train). M19. ▸**c** Make (one's way) with whistling. M19.

📖 1 SIR W. SCOTT She whistled on a small silver call . . used to summon domestics. **2** G. VIDAL Whistling tonelessly (he had no ear for music). J. DICKEY I put my thumb and forefinger in my mouth and whistled. L. HELLMAN He whistled when he saw the prices on the menu. **3** J. M. COETZEE Jet fighters whistled high overhead. A. TYLER Wind whistled in under the canvas flaps. **4** C. RAYNER A song that was . . popular, being whistled . . by every errand boy. *Peace News* Arrested . . for whistling the Irish National Anthem.

▸ **II** *transf.* & *fig.* **6** *verb trans.* Give a signal to by whistling; call, summon, get (as) by whistling. Freq. foll. by *up*. L15. ▸**b** Send (a hawk) *away*, *off*, etc., by whistling; *fig.* dismiss or abandon lightly. M16.
7 *verb intrans.* Issue a call or summons (*for*), summon. Now *rare* or *obsolete* exc. as in senses 1, 3 above. M16.
8 *verb intrans.* & *trans.* Speak of (something) secretly, give secret information (about). Now *rare* or *obsolete.* L16.
9 *verb intrans.* Foll. by adverb or adverbial phr.: go, come, etc., rapidly. *colloq.* L17.

📖 6 G. GREENE Shall I whistle a taxi, sir? G. NORTH Cluff whistled Cline from the hearth-rug. *fig.*: I. MURDOCH One can't whistle up happiness. It's a gift of nature. **9** I. ASIMOV The blow whistled past, with little room to spare.

Phrases: **go whistle**: expr. unceremonious or contemptuous dismissal or refusal. **whistle down the wind** (*a*) turn (a hawk) loose; (*b*) *fig.* let go, abandon. **whistle for** *colloq.* await or expect in vain, fail to get. ***whistle in the dark***: see DARK *noun*¹ 1.
▪ **whistleable** *adjective* (of a tune) able to be whistled M20. **whistled** *adjective* (*a*) that has been whistled (***whistled language*** = ***whistle-language*** s.v. WHISTLE *noun*); (*b*) *slang* drunk: M18.

whistler /ˈwɪs(ə)lə/ *noun.* OE.
[from WHISTLE *verb* + -ER¹.]
1 a A person who plays on a whistle. Now *rare.* OE. ▸**b** A person who whistles with the lips. LME.
2 A bird, mammal, etc., that whistles; *esp.* (*a*) any of various thickheads with loud melodious calls, esp. of the genus *Pachycephala*; (*b*) *Canad.* the goldeneye *Bucephala clangula*, whose wings make a whistling sound in flight; (*c*) the hoary marmot, *Marmota caligata*, which has a whistling call; (*d*) a broken-winded horse that breathes hard with a shrill sound. L16.
3 A thing that makes a whistling sound. E19. ▸**b** *spec.* An atmospheric radio disturbance heard as a whistle that falls in pitch, caused by lightning and guided by the lines of force of the earth's magnetic field. E20.

Whistlerian /wɪˈslɪərɪən/ *adjective.* L19.
[from *Whistler* (see below) + -IAN.]
Of, pertaining to, or characteristic of the American-born painter and wit James McNeill Whistler (1834–1903) or his work.
▪ **ˈWhistlerism** *noun* the style of Whistler; a statement or expression characteristic of Whistler: E20.

whistle-stop /ˈwɪs(ə)lstɒp/ *noun*, *adjective*, & *verb.* M20.
[from WHISTLE *noun* + STOP *noun*².]
▸ **A** *noun.* **1** A small station at which trains only stop when given a signal; *transf.* a small unimportant town. *US.* M20.
2 A politician's brief halt for a speech while on an electioneering tour. M20.
▸ **B** *attrib.* or as *adjective.* Designating a journey or tour with many brief halts. M20.
▸ **C** *verb intrans.* Infl. **-pp-**. Make a whistle-stop tour. M20.

whistling /ˈwɪs(ə)lɪŋ/ *verbal noun.* OE.
[from WHISTLE *verb* + -ING¹.]
The action of WHISTLE *verb*; an instance of this.
Comb.: **whistling-shop** *arch. slang* a room in a prison where spirits were secretly sold without a licence (a whistle being given to escape detection).

whistling /ˈwɪst(ə)lɪŋ/ *ppl adjective.* LME.
[from WHISTLE *verb* + -ING².]
1 That whistles. LME. ▸**b** *transf.* Of a place: full of whistling. E17.
2 Of a sound: of the nature of a whistle. M17.
Special collocations: **whistling atmospheric** = WHISTLER 3 b. **whistling duck** any of various ducks which make whistling calls or flight sounds; *esp.* (*a*) the goldeneye; (*b*) the wigeon; (*c*) a duck of the genus *Dendrocygna*, of tropical and subtropical regions (also called ***tree duck***). **whistling eagle**, **whistling eagle-hawk** = ***whistling kite*** below. **whistling kettle**: fitted with a device that emits a whistle as the water boils. **whistling kite** an Australasian kite, *Haliastur sphenurus*, which makes a series of shrill whistling calls. **whistling marmot** = WHISTLER 2(c). **whistling moth** the death's head hawkmoth, *Acherontia atropos*, which is capable of producing a high-pitched whistle. **whistling swan** the N. American race of the tundra swan, *Cygnus columbianus*, which breeds in the Arctic and winters in the US. **whistling thorn** a small prickly acacia of E. Africa, *Acacia drepanolobium*. **whistling thrush** a thrush of the genus *Myiophoneus*, of southern and eastern Asia.
▪ **whistlingly** *adverb* M19.

whistly /ˈwɪs(ə)li/ *adjective. rare.* E20.
[from WHISTLE *noun* + -Y¹.]
Of a sound: of the nature of a whistle.

whistly /ˈwɪstli/ *adverb. arch.* LME.
[from WHIST *adjective* + -LY². Cf. WISTLY.]
Silently, quietly.

whit /wɪt/ *noun*¹. LME.
[App. alt. of WIGHT *noun*.]
The very least or a very little part or amount, a jot. Usu. in neg. contexts.

📖 S. T. FELSTEAD Other things which matter not a whit. R. GODDEN Mam did not care one whit about family pedigrees. **every whit** the whole; wholly. **no whit** not at all, not in the least.

Whit /wɪt/ *adjective* & *noun*². M16.
[Extracted from WHITSUN, WHIT SUNDAY.]
▸ **A** *attrib. adjective.* Pertaining to, connected with, or occurring on or at Whit Sunday or Whitsuntide; *spec.* designating the week or any of the days of the week (now only the Monday and Tuesday) following Whit Sunday or the Saturday before Whit Sunday. M16.
Whit walk a Whitsuntide event in which church congregations walk in procession through the streets.
▸ **B** *noun.* The weekend or week including Whit Sunday; Whitsuntide. L20.

whit /wɪt/ *interjection*, *adverb*, & *noun*³. Also redupl. **whit-whit**. M19.
[Imit.]
(Repr.) a shrill abrupt sound; with such a sound.

whitbed /ˈwɪtbɛd/ *noun*. E19.
[from WHITE *adjective* + BED *noun*.]
A high quality variety of Portland stone, valued for building.

white /wʌɪt/ *noun*. LOE.
[The adjective used ellipt. or absol.]
1 The translucent viscous fluid surrounding the yolk of an egg, which turns white when cooked; albumen. Chiefly in ***white of an egg***, ***egg-white***. LOE.
2 White colour; a shade of this; whiteness; *poet*. fairness of complexion. LOE. ▸**b** A white pigment or dye. Freq. with specifying word. M16.
3 A white textile. Usu. with specifying word and in *pl*. *arch*. ME.
4 White clothing. ME. ▸**b** In *pl*. White clothes; *spec*. (*a*) (chiefly *Hist*.) ecclesiastical vestments; (*b*) white clothes (*spec*. trousers) worn for cricket, tennis, etc. E17.
5 The visible white part of the eyeball surrounding the iris. Freq. in ***the whites of the eyes***. LME.
6 The white or light-coloured part of anything. Formerly also, a white mark or spot. LME.
7 ARCHERY. Orig. (now *Hist*.), the white target placed on a butt. Now, a circular band of white on the target, or either of two such bands; a shot that hits this. LME.
8 Orig., silver money, silver. Later (*slang*), a silver coin; *gen*. money. LME.
9 White wine. LME.
10 A thing distinguished by white colour, as a white butterfly, a white pigeon, a white diamond, a loaf of white bread, the white ball in snooker etc., a white piece in a game etc.; the player of the white pieces in chess or draughts. LME. ▸**b** Heroin; an amphetamine tablet. *slang*. E20.
11 PRINTING. Any part of a sheet of paper not printed on; *esp*. a blank space between words or lines or at the foot of a short page. Cf. ***river of white*** s.v. RIVER *noun*[1] 4. L16.
12 In *pl*. with *the*. MEDICINE. = LEUCORRHOEA. Now *rare*. L16.
13 (Usu. **W-**.) A member of a light-skinned people, a white person. L17.
14 A member of a political party, faction, etc., adopting white as its colour (cf. BLACK *noun* 7); *spec*. (*Hist*.) = WHITE RUSSIAN *noun phr*. 2. L17.

📖 **1** *Poultry World* Eggs . . with pale yolks, watery whites and . . meat spots. *Guardian* Beat the egg-whites stiff and gently fold into potato mixture. **2** W. ROBERTSON Their skin is covered with a fine hairy down of a chalky white. W. B. MARRIOTT White was regarded as the colour . . appropriate to things divine. *Antique Collector* A Chinese porcelain ewer . . all glazed in white. **b** ***Chinese white***, ***indigo-white***, etc. **4** A. S. BYATT The village girls . . dressed in white, to celebrate May Day. **b** M. GALLANT He was dressed in clean, not too new summer whites. *New Yorker* She saw him . . in his doctor's whites. *Thames Valley Now* All weekend fixtures, played in whites. **5** A. CARTER Her eyes rolled until they were all whites. **9** *Elle* The choice of dry whites now available includes . . Chardonnay and Sauvignon Blanc. **10** ***Bath white***, ***cabbage white***, ***marbled white***, etc. **13** M. L. KING A plant that hired both Negroes and whites. K. MILLETT South African whites training in guerilla warfare.

Phrases & comb.: **Admiral of the White** *Hist*.: of the White squadron (one of the three divisions of the Royal Navy made in the 17th cent.). ***in black and white***: see BLACK *noun* 2. **in the white** (of cloth) in an undyed state; (of a manufactured article) unfinished. ***pearly whites***: see PEARLY *adjective*. ***river of white***: see RIVER *noun*[1] 4. **white balance** (a control or system for adjusting) the colour balance on a video camera. **white-on-white** *adjective* designating a garment etc. made of white cloth with a white woven-in design.

white /wʌɪt/ *adjective & adverb*.
[Old English *hwīt* = Old Frisian, Old Saxon *hwīt*, Old High German (*h*)*wīz* (German *weiss*), Old Norse *hvítr*, Gothic *hweits*, from Germanic from Indo-European. Cf. WHEAT.]
▸ **A** *adjective*. **I 1** Of the colour of fresh milk or snow; having that colour produced by reflection, transmission, or emission of all wavelengths of visible light without absorption, being fully luminous and devoid of any hue. OE. ▸**b** (Of hair) having lost its colour esp. in old age; (of a person) having white hair. Also, albino. ME. ▸**c** PHYSICS. Designating (non-optical) radiation, esp. sound, having approximately equal intensities at all the frequencies of its range. E20.
2 Approaching the colour white; of a light colour; *spec*. (*a*) (of a crop) light-coloured when ripening, i.e. consisting of cereals (as opp. to roots, legumes, etc.); (of land) suitable for cereals; (*b*) (of a metal or metal object) silvery grey and lustrous. OE. ▸**b** Of glass: colourless; transparent. OE. ▸**c** Of wine: made from white grapes or dark grapes with the skins removed, and of an amber, golden, or pale yellow colour. ME. ▸**d** Of paper: blank, not written or printed on. Formerly also, (of a document) unendorsed. LME. ▸**e** [translating Italian *voce bianca* white voice.] Of a singing voice or its sound: lacking emotional coloration and resonance. L19. ▸**f** Of coffee or (occas.) tea: served with milk, cream, etc. E20.
3 a (Of the skin or complexion) light in colour, fair; having fair skin. Chiefly *poet*. exc. as in sense 3b below. OE. ▸**b** Of or belonging to a light-skinned people, chiefly inhabiting or descended from those having inhabited Europe; of or pertaining to white people. E17.
4 Wearing white clothing; *spec*. belonging to an ecclesiastical order distinguished by a white habit. ME. ▸**b** [Orig. with ref. to the white flag of the Bourbons.] Pertaining to or supporting a royalist or legitimist cause; *esp*. counter-revolutionary, reactionary. Cf. RED *adjective* 8b. M18.
5 Orig., of or pertaining to an illness marked by pallor. Now, pale (of face) from illness, fear, anger, etc. LME.

📖 **1** D. H. LAWRENCE All the ground was white with snowdrops. G. GREENE The kitchen was like a snowdrift with its white casement and white dresser and white table. I. MURDOCH His very white teeth flashing under his moustache. ***blue-white***, ***grey-white***, ***snow-white***, etc. **2** W. A. MILLER Tin is a white metal with a tinge of yellow. *Times* The familiar wrapped and sliced white loaf. **c** E. DAVID A few bottles of glorious white Burgundy. **3a** J. CHEEVER Careful never to expose her white skin to the sun for long. **b** L. NKOSI The Government is going to stop them . . going to the white universities. H. BASCOM A White woman with yellowish hair. *Harper's Magazine* The . . general squalor that poor people, white or black, endured in the land of dreams. *Listener* This cocktail of dance and dialectic defines the best of white British soul. **4** A. SETON White nuns, Cistercians, shrouded in snowy wimples and habits. **5** D. CUSACK She went white as a sheet and . . slid off her chair. R. RENDELL He wondered if his face was as white as it felt.

▸ **II** *fig*. **6 a** Morally or spiritually pure; innocent. OE. ▸**b** Free from malignity or evil intent; beneficent, harmless. Chiefly in special collocations below. Cf. BLACK *adjective* 7, 8a. M17. ▸**c** Of propaganda: truthful. *colloq*. M20.
7 Highly prized, precious; dear, favourite. Long *obsolete* exc. in WHITE BOY 1. LME.
†**8** Specious, plausible. LME–E19.
9 Of a period of time, season, etc.: auspicious, happy. Now *rare*. E17.
10 Honourable, decent, fair. *colloq*. (orig. *Austral*.). M19.

📖 **6** A. TROLLOPE Duty to see that your name be made white again. A. GARVE They expect standards of personal behaviour whiter than white. **10** *Times* He didn't want to see them put in a difficult spot . . which . . was rather white of him.

Phrases: ***black and white***: see BLACK *adjective*. ***bleed white***: see BLEED *verb* 12. ***Dashing White Sergeant***: see DASHING *ppl adjective*. ***dead white***: see DEAD *adjective* etc. ***free, white, and over twenty-one***: see FREE *adjective*. ***Great White Way***: see GREAT *adjective*. ***Red and White Friesian***: see RED *adjective*. ***red, white, and blue***: see RED *adjective*. ***the white feather***: see FEATHER *noun*. ***the Great White Throne***: see THRONE *noun*. ***white about the gills***: see GILL *noun*[1] 2b.

Special collocations & comb.: **white admiral** any of several nymphalid butterflies of the genus *Limenitis*, which have blackish wings with white markings; esp. *L. camilla* of Europe, and *L. arthemis* of N. America. **White Africa** the white inhabitants of Africa; the parts of Africa ruled by white people. ***white alder***: see ALDER 1b. **white ant** (*a*) = TERMITE 1; (*b*) in *pl*. (*Austral. slang*) loss of sanity; lack of intelligence. **white-ant** *verb trans*. (*Austral. slang*) destroy in the manner of termites; undermine; sabotage. ***white* ANTIMONY**. **White Army** *Hist*. any of the armies which opposed the Bolsheviks during the Russian Civil War (1918–21). ***white arsenic***: see ARSENIC *noun* 2. **white ash** (*a*) *N. Amer*. a kind of ash, *Fraxinus americana*, with leaflets paler or silvery-white below; the wood of this tree, highly valued for making oars; *colloq*. an oar; (*b*) *S. Afr*. = ***white alder*** (b) s.v. ALDER 1b; (*c*) refined sodium carbonate, as distinct from the crude black ash. **White Australia policy** AUSTRAL. HISTORY a policy restricting immigration into Australia to white people only. **white-backed** *adjective* having a white back or rump; ***white-backed vulture***, either of two large Old World vultures of the genus *Gyps*, which have a white rump visible in flight; esp. *G. africanus* of Africa. **white backlash** reaction on the part of white people against demands by or concessions to black people. **whitebait** (*a*) a small silvery-white fish caught in large numbers and eaten whole, comprising the fry of the herring and sprat; (*b*) any similar young or small fishes caught for food, esp. of the genera *Galaxias*, *Lovettia*, *Retropinna*, and *Engraulis* (*Austral. & NZ*), and silversides of the genus *Atherina* or family Atherinidae (*N. Amer. & S. Afr*.). **white-bark pine** a pine with pale flaky bark, *Pinus albicaulis*, native to western N. America. **white bass** a N. American freshwater bass, *Morone chrysops* (family Percichthyidae). **white bear** *N. Amer*. (*a*) a polar bear; (*b*) a light-coloured form of the grizzly bear. **whitebeard** a man with a white beard; (freq. *derog*.) an old man. **white-bellied** *adjective* having a white belly or underparts; ***white-bellied sea-eagle***, an Asian and Australasian sea-eagle, *Haliaeetus leucogaster*, which is mainly white with grey-brown wings. **white belt** (the holder of) a belt marking the rank of beginner in judo or karate. **white birch** the paper birch, *Betula papyrifera*. **white bird** (*a*) any of various birds with white or pale plumage; (*b*) in Irish folklore, a bird of fairyland. **white blood cell** = LEUCOCYTE. **whiteboard** a board with a white surface, like a blackboard, for writing or drawing on with felt-tipped pens. **white book** [translating medieval Latin *liber albus*: cf. ALBUM] a book of official records or reports bound in white; *spec*. (LAW) (with cap. initials) (a copy of) the official book entitled *Supreme Court Practice*. **white box** any of several Australian box-gums with pale foliage or wood, esp. *Eucalyptus albens*. **white brass** a brass alloy containing a large proportion of zinc, used in ornamental work etc. **white bread** bread of a light colour made from sifted or bleached flour, as distinguished from brown bread; **white-bread** *adjective* (*N. Amer. colloq*.) of, belonging to, or representative of the white middle classes; not progressive, radical, or innovative; **white-breasted** *adjective* having a white breast; ***white-breasted nuthatch***, a common N. American nuthatch, *Sitta carolinensis*, with a black cap and white face. **whitebrick** a hard, durable variety of brick made from gault. **white bronze** any light-coloured bronze, *esp*. a hard white alloy which is high in zinc. ***white bryony***: see BRYONY 1. **white-burning** *adjective* (of clay) giving a white product when fired. **white butterfly** any of various mainly white butterflies, esp. of the family Pieridae. **white campion** a campion of cultivated ground, roadsides, etc., *Silene latifolia*, with white evening-scented flowers. **white cane** = ***white stick*** (b) below. **white cast iron** = ***white iron*** (b) below. **white cedar** (*a*) any of several N. American conifers, esp. *Thuja occidentalis* and *Chamaecyparis thyoides*; (*b*) an Australian variety of the azedarac, *Melia azedarach*. **white cell** = LEUCOCYTE. ***white chameleon***: see CHAMELEON *noun* 2. **white chauvinism** prejudice against non-white people. **white chauvinist** a person prejudiced against non-white people. **white Christmas** Christmas with snow on the ground. **white clay** kaolin. **White Cliffs opal** a variety of opal mined near White Cliffs, a town in New South Wales, Australia. ***white clover***: see CLOVER *noun*. **white coal** water as a source of power, *spec*. electricity. **whitecoat** (*a*) (*obsolete* exc. *Hist*.) a soldier wearing a white or light-coloured coat; (*b*) a young seal, having a coat of white fur; the skin or fur of this; (*c*) a doctor or hospital attendant who wears a white coat. **white coat** *spec*.: worn as a protective overall by doctors, laboratory workers, etc. ***white coffee***: see COFFEE *noun*. ***white* COHOSH**. **white comb** VETERINARY MEDICINE a form of favus attacking the combs of fowls, caused by the fungus *Trichophyton gallinae*. ***white* COPPERAS**. **white corpuscle** = LEUCOCYTE. ***white crow***: see CROW *noun*[1] 1. **white-crowned** *adjective* having a white crown; ***white-crowned sparrow***, a N. American sparrow-like emberizid, *Zonotrichia leucophrys*, with a black and white striped crown. ***white* CURRANT**. **white-damp** carbon monoxide as occurring in coalmines. ***white dead-nettle***: see DEAD *adjective*. ***white deal***: see DEAL *noun*[2] 2. **white death** (*a*) tuberculosis; (*b*) = ***white shark*** below. **white dwarf** ASTRONOMY a small, faint, very dense star lying below the main sequence, representing the stable phase assumed by stars having less than 1.4 solar masses when their nuclear reactions cease. **white-eared** *adjective* having white ears; (of a bird) having a white patch at the side of the head; ***white-eared monarch (flycatcher)***, a black and white monarch flycatcher, *Monarcha leucotis*, found near the eastern coast of Queensland, Australia, and on neighbouring islands. **white earth** earthy material that is light-coloured, as chalk, kaolin; pigment made from this. **white egret** = ***great white egret*** s.v. GREAT *adjective*. **white elephant** a useless or troublesome possession or thing. ***white elm***: see ELM 1. **white embroidery** = ***white work*** below. ***white ensign***: see ENSIGN *noun* 4. **white-eye** any of various birds with a white iris, or with white plumage around the eyes; *spec*. any of numerous small Old World perching birds of the family Zosteropidae, esp. of the genus *Zosterops*, which have greenish plumage and a ring of white feathers around the eye. **white-eyed** *adjective* having the iris of the eye white; (of a bird) having white plumage around the eyes (***white-eyed* POCHARD**). **whiteface** (*a*) an animal with a white face (chiefly *attrib*.); *spec*. (chiefly *N. Amer*.) a Hereford; (*b*) white stage make-up. **White Father** (*a*) a white man regarded as controlling people of another race; (*b*) [translating French *Père Blanc*] a member of the Society of Missionaries of Africa, a Roman Catholic order founded in Algiers in 1868. **white finger(s)** = ***RAYNAUD's disease***. **white fir** any of several N. American firs, esp. *Abies concolor*, of the south-western US. ***white flag***: see FLAG *noun*[4]. **white flight** *US* the migration of white people from inner-city areas (esp. those with a large black population) to the suburbs. **white flour** fine wheat flour, usu. bleached, from which most of the bran and germ have been removed. **white flux** = LEUCORRHOEA. **whitefly** any of various small bugs of the family Aleyrodidae, with waxy white wings, many of which are pests of garden and greenhouse plants. **white-footed** *adjective* having white feet; ***white-footed mouse***, a N. American mouse, *Peromyscus leucopus*, which is related to the deer mouse and is found mainly in the US. **white fox** = ***Arctic fox*** s.v. ARCTIC *adjective*. **white friar** [from the colour of the order's habit] a Carmelite friar. **whitefront** = ***white-fronted goose*** below. **white-fronted** *adjective* having a white breast or forehead; ***white-fronted goose***, a grey goose, *Anser albifrons*, that has a white forehead and breeds in northern Eurasia and N. America. ***white frost***: see FROST *noun*. **white fuel** = ***white coal*** above. **white goat** = ***ROCKY MOUNTAIN goat***. **white gold** any of various silver-coloured alloys of gold with palladium, platinum, or silver, or with nickel and other base metals, used as substitutes for platinum in jewellery. **white goods** (*a*) household linen; (*b*) large domestic electrical equipment that is conventionally white, as washing machines and refrigerators. **white grape**: that is green or amber when ripe. **white grub** the larva of a chafer, esp. the cockchafer, which is a pest of grass and cereal roots. **White Guard**, **White Guardist** *Hist*. (*a*) a member of a force fighting for the government in the Finnish civil war of 1918; (*b*) a member of a counter-revolutionary force fighting in the Russian civil war of 1918–21. **white-gum** any of numerous Australian eucalypts, with white or light-coloured bark. **white-haired** *adjective* having white hair (***white-haired boy*** (*colloq*.), a favourite, a pet). ***white hake***: see HAKE *noun*[1] 2a. **white-hat** *slang* a good man; a hero. **whitehead** (*a*) *colloq*. a white or white-topped skin-pustule; (*b*) *NZ* a bird of a race of the yellowhead, *Mohoua ochrocephala*, with a white head and underparts, found on North Island and neighbouring islands. **white-headed** *adjective* (*a*) (of an animal) having white hair or plumage on the head; ***white-headed eagle***, ***white-headed sea-eagle***, the N. American bald eagle, *Haliaeetus leucocephalus*; (*b*) (of a person) having white or very fair hair, flaxen-haired; ***white-headed boy*** (*colloq*.), a favourite, a pet. **white-heart** (*a*) (more fully ***white-heart cherry***) a pale yellow, red-tinged, variety of sweet cherry; (*b*) malleable cast iron made by keeping white iron at a high temperature for several days in an oxidizing environment, so as to remove the carbon from the surface layers. **white heat** (*a*) (the degree of heat corresponding to) the condition of being white-hot; (*b*) *fig*. a state of intense passion or activity. ***white* HELLEBORE**. **white heron** = ***great white egret*** s.v. GREAT *adjective*. **White Highlands** *Hist*. an area in western Kenya formerly (1909–59) reserved for Europeans. **white hole** ASTRONOMY a hypothetical celestial object which expands outwards from a space–time singularity emitting energy, in the manner of a time-reversed black hole. **white** hope (*a*) *Hist.* a white boxer thought capable of beating Jack Johnson, the first black boxer to be world heavyweight champion (1908–15); (*b*) *transf.* a person or thing expected to achieve much for a group, organization, etc. ***white horehound***: see HOREHOUND 1. **white horse** (*a*) a representation of a white horse; *spec.* any of several cut on chalk-downs in England; (*b*) (usu. in *pl.*) a white-crested wave; (*c*) a tough sinewy substance lying between the upper jaw and junk of a sperm-whale. **white-hot** (*a*) sufficiently hot to radiate white light; (*b*) *fig.* (of emotion) intense, violent; (of a person) very talented; (of news etc.) sensational, completely new; (cf. RED-HOT). **white house** (*a*) (with cap. initials) [the official residence of the US President in Washington] the US President; the US Presidency; the US Government; (*b*) *Scot.* (*obsolete* exc. *Hist.*) a house built of mortared stone in NW Scotland and the Hebrides. **White Hun** *Hist.* a member of a nomadic people who lived in Bactria in the 5th and 6th cents. **white hunter** a white man who hunts big game professionally. **white information** positive information about a person's creditworthiness held by a bank etc. ***white ipecacuanha***: see IPECACUANHA 2. **white iron** (*a*) (now *rare* or *obsolete*) tin-plate; (*b*) cast iron of a silvery colour containing most or all of its carbon in combination; (*c*) ***white iron pyrites***, marcasite. ***White Kaffir***: see KAFFIR *noun* 2c. ***white KARANTEEN***. ***white kerria***: see KERRIA 2. **white knight** (*a*) a person who or thing which comes to the aid of someone; *spec.* (*Stock Exchange slang*) a welcome company bidding for a company facing an unwelcome takeover bid; (*b*) [with allus. to a character in Lewis Carroll's *Through the Looking-Glass*] an enthusiastic but ineffectual person. **white-knuckle** *adjective* (*colloq.*) (esp. of a fairground ride) causing fear or terror; showing fear or terror. **white-knuckled** *adjective* having white knuckles, *esp.* tense from fear or terror. **white label** a musical recording for which the fully printed commercial label is not yet available, and which has been supplied with a plain label before general release for promotional purposes. **White Lady** (*a*) a cocktail made with gin, orange liqueur, and lemon juice; (*b*) *Austral. slang* a drink of or containing methylated spirits; (*c*) an apparition of a woman, a ghost. **white land** (*a*) *slang* [after its being uncoloured on planning maps] open land not designated for development or change of use, or on which development is not allowed; (*b*) see sense 2 above. **white lead** (*a*) basic lead carbonate, used as a white pigment in paint, mixed with linseed oil to make putty, and in ointments (also called ***ceruse***); (*b*) basic lead sulphate or basic lead silicate used as a similar white pigment; (*c*) ***white lead ore*** = CERUSSITE. **white leg** MEDICINE = ***PHLEGMASIA alba dolens***. **white letter** (*a*) *arch.* (printing in) roman type; (*b*) ***white-letter hairstreak***, a small European lycaenid butterfly, *Strymonidia w-album*, which is mainly dark brown with a white W-shaped streak on the underside of the hindwing. **white level** TELEVISION the signal level corresponding to the maximum brightness in transmitted pictures. **white lie** a harmless or trivial untruth. **white lightning** *slang* (*a*) *US* inferior or illicitly distilled whiskey; (*b*) a type of LSD. **white lime** lime mixed with water as a coating for walls; whitewash. **white-lime** *verb trans.* (now *rare* or *obsolete*) whitewash. **white line** (*a*) PRINTING a space equivalent to one line left blank between two lines of type; (*b*) ENGRAVING an engraved line which prints white; the art or technique of using such lines; (*c*) *US slang* alcohol as a drink; (*d*) a narrow white strip painted on the road surface to guide or direct motorists. **white-lipped** *adjective* having white lips, *esp.* tense from fear, terror, or rage; ***white-lipped peccary***, a Central and S. American peccary, *Tayassu pecari*, with white bristles on the lips and chin. **white list** *colloq.* [after ***blacklist*** s.v. BLACK *adjective*] a list of the names of people or things considered acceptable. **white liver** *arch.* [from the belief that a deficiency of bile or 'choler' resulted in a light-coloured liver and lack of spirit] the supposedly pale liver of a coward (cf. ***LILY liver***). **white-livered** *adjective* (*arch.*) feeble-spirited, cowardly. ***white loaf***: see LOAF *noun*[1]. ***white magic***: see MAGIC *noun*. ***white magnesia***: see MAGNESIA 3. **white mahogany** (*a*) a W. Indian tree, *Antirhea jamaicensis*, of the madder family; (*b*) an Australian eucalypt, *Eucalyptus robusta*. ***white maidenhair***: see MAIDENHAIR 2. **white man** a man belonging to a light-skinned people, a white (***the white man's burden***, the supposed task of white people to civilize black people; ***the white man's grave***, equatorial W. Africa considered as being particularly unhealthy for white people). ***white mangrove***: see MANGROVE 2. **white matter** the whitish tissue in the vertebrate central nervous system consisting mainly of myelinated nerve fibres, situated below the grey matter of the cortex and next to the core of the spinal cord. **white meat** (*a*) *collect. sing. & pl.* (*obsolete* exc. *dial.*) dairy produce (also occas. eggs); foods prepared from milk; (*b*) pale meat, as poultry, veal, pork, and rabbit; (*c*) *coarse slang* (chiefly *US*) white women regarded collectively as a means of sexual gratification. ***white MERGANSER***. **white metal** any of various alloys of a light silvery-grey colour. **white meter** a meter for measuring the off-peak consumption of electricity. **white mica** a light-coloured mica; *spec.* muscovite. **white money** silver coins. **white monk** a Cistercian monk. **white mouse** (*a*) an albino form of the house mouse, widely bred as a pet and laboratory animal; (*b*) the collared lemming, *Dicrostonyx torquatus*. ***white mulberry***: see MULBERRY *noun* 1. **white mule** *US slang* illicitly distilled whiskey. **white muscle disease** a nutritional disease of calves and lambs due to vitamin E deficiency, causing weakness, dysphoea, collapse, and heart failure. ***white mustard***: see MUSTARD *noun* 2. **white-necked** *adjective* having a white neck; ***white-necked raven***, either of two ravens with some white neck feathers, *Corvus albicollis* of Africa, and *C. Cryptoleucus* of southern N. America. **white negro** (*a*) a black person, or a person with black ancestry, who has a pale or albino complexion; (*b*) a white person who defends the rights or interests of black people. **white nickel (ore)** = CHLOANTHITE. **white nigger** *US slang* (*derog.* & considered *racially offensive*) (*a*) a white person who does menial labour; (*b*) a black person who is regarded as deferring to white people or accepting a role prescribed by them. **white night** (*a*) [translating French *nuit blanche*] a sleepless night; (*b*) a night when it is never properly dark, as in high latitudes in summer. **white noise**: having approximately equal intensities at all the frequencies of its range. **white note** MUSIC (*a*) a note with an open head; (*b*) a note corresponding to a white key on a keyboard. **white nutmeg** an old variety of peach with white aromatic flesh. **white oak** any of several N. American oaks, esp. *Quercus alba*, which has a pale bark and resembles the English oak, *Q. robur*; the wood of such a tree; ***swamp white oak***: see SWAMP *noun*. **white oil** (*a*) crude oil that is pale in colour; (*b*) a colourless petroleum distillate; *spec.* liquid paraffin used medicinally and in the food and plastic industries. **white owl** an owl with white plumage; *esp.* (*a*) the barn owl; (*b*) the snowy owl. **whitepainter** *Canad. colloq.* a renovator of houses. **whitepainting** *Canad. colloq.* renovation of houses. **White Paper** (*a*) *Hist.* a corrected and revised version of an Order Paper of the House of Commons issued earlier the same day; (*b*) a British Government report giving information or proposals on an issue. ***white park cattle***: see ***park cattle*** s.v. PARK *noun*. **white pelican** a pelican with white plumage; esp. *Pelecanus onocrotalus* of the Old World, and *P. erythrorhynchos* of North and Central America. ***white pepper***: see PEPPER *noun* 1. **white perch** *N. Amer.* any of several pale-coloured percoid fishes; esp. *Morone americana* (family Percichthyidae), found in the fresh and coastal waters of eastern N. America. ***white PEROBA***. **white phosphorus** the ordinary allotrope of phosphorus, a translucent waxy whitish or yellowish solid which is poisonous and very reactive; also called ***yellow phosphorus***. **white pine** (*a*) *N. Amer.* (the pale timber of) any of several pines, esp. the Weymouth pine, *Pinus strobus* (***western white pine***: see WESTERN *adjective*); ***white pine weevil***, a brown weevil, *Pissodes strobi*, the larvae of which tunnel into the shoots of the Weymouth pine and other conifers; (*b*) any of several Australasian conifers, *esp.* (*Austral.*) a cypress pine, *Callitris glaucophylla*, and (*NZ*) the kahikatea, *Podocarpus dacrydioides*. ***white pipe tree***: see PIPE *noun*[1]. **white plague** *arch.* tuberculosis. **white-point** a European noctuid moth, *Mythimna albipuncta*, which has a white dot on each forewing. **white pointer** = ***white shark*** below. ***white pomfret***: see POMFRET 1. **white poplar** a freq. planted Eurasian poplar, *Populus alba*, with palmately lobed leaves covered with dense white down beneath. **white port**: made from white grapes. ***white potato***: see POTATO *noun* 2. **whitepox** a poxvirus isolated from monkeys, causing variola minor infection. ***white precipitate***: see PRECIPITATE *noun* 1. **white-print** a document printed in white on a dark ground. **white pudding** a kind of sausage made of oatmeal and suet. **white racism** belief in the superiority of white people over non-white people, esp. black people. **white racist** *adjective & noun* (*a*) *adjective* of, pertaining to, or characterized by white racism; (*b*) *noun* a believer or practitioner of white racism. **White Raja** *Hist.* any of the three Rajas belonging to the English family of Brooke who ruled Sarawak from 1841 to 1941. ***white rat***: see RAT *noun*[1]. **white rent** (*obsolete* exc. *Hist.*) rent payable in silver money. ***white rhinoceros***: see RHINOCEROS 1. **white ribboner** a person who wears a white ribbon as a badge of temperance, a teetotaller. **white rod** *Hist.* = ***white staff*** below. **white room** a clean dust-free room for the assembly, repair, or storage of spacecraft. ***white rose***: see ROSE *noun* 6. **white rot** (*a*) any of several fungal diseases of wood or living plants indicated by white patches of decay; (*b*) (with hyphen) any of several plants of damp ground believed to cause liver rot in sheep, *esp.* marsh pennywort, *Hydrocotyle vulgaris*, and butterwort, *Pinguicula vulgaris*. **white rum** (a drink of) a colourless variety of rum. **white rust** (*a*) any of various fungal diseases of plants characterized by white blisters on leaves or stems, *esp.* one caused by *Albugo candida* (affecting cruciferous plants) or *Puccinia horiana* (affecting chrysanthemums); (*b*) a white coating that forms on zinc in moist air, consisting of zinc oxide and (usu.) some basic carbonate. ***white sage***: see SAGE *noun*[1] 1b. **white sale** a shop sale of household linen. ***white sandalwood***: see SANDALWOOD 1. ***white sanicle***: see SANICLE 2. **white sapphire** a colourless variety of corundum. ***white satin***: see SATIN *noun* 2, 3, 4. **white sauce**: made with flour, melted butter, and milk or cream. **white scour** a bacterial disease of young calves due to enteric infection with *Escherichia coli*, causing severe diarrhoea, dehydration, and often death. **white scourge** *arch.* tuberculosis. **white scours** = ***white scour*** above. ***white SEA-bass***. ***white SERAYA***. **white shark** a large and dangerous shark, *Carcharadon carcharias*, which is found in the temperate and tropical regions of all oceans. **white-shoe** *adjective* (*colloq.*) (*a*) (chiefly *US*) effeminate; immature; (*b*) *US* denoting a company (esp. a law firm) owned and run by white upper-class Americans and typically regarded as cautious and conservative; (*c*) AUSTRALIAN POLITICS of, belonging to, or supporting the conservative Queensland National Party. **White Sister** a nun belonging to an order or congregation distinguished by a white habit. **white-skin** a white person (cf. ***redskin*** s.v. RED *adjective*). **white slave** *spec.* a (white) woman who is trapped or forced into prostitution, usu. abroad. **white slavery** *spec.* traffic in white slaves. ***white sock***: see SOCK *noun*[1]. **white soup** soup made with white stock. **white spirit** (*a*) a volatile colourless liquid distillate of petroleum that boils between about 150°C and 200°C and is widely used as a paint thinner and solvent; (*b*) in *pl.*, colourless spirits as gin, vodka, etc. **white spot** a Eurasian noctuid moth, *Hadena albimacula*, which has a large white spot on each forewing. **white spruce** a N. American spruce, *Picea glauca*, with blue-green foliage. ***white squall***: see SQUALL *noun*[1] 1. ***white squill***: see SQUILL 2a. **white staff** *Hist.* any of various royal or governmental offices symbolized by a white staff; an official holding such an office. **white stick** *spec.* (*a*) *Hist.* = ***white staff*** above; (*b*) a white walking-stick carried by a blind person both as a distinguishing feature and to locate obstacles. **white stock** stock made with chicken, veal, or pork. ***white STOMPNEUS***. **white stone** (*a*) a colourless gemstone; (*b*) (freq. ***whitestone***) a form of rendering; (*c*) ***mark with a white stone***, regard as specially fortunate or happy (with allus. to the ancient practice of using a white stone as a memorial of a happy event). ***white stopper***: see STOPPER *noun* 5. ***white stork***: see STORK *noun* 1. **white stuff** *slang* (chiefly *US*) heroin; cocaine. **white sugar** purified sugar. **white supremacism** the doctrine or practice of white supremacists. **white supremacist** *noun & adjective* (*a*) *noun* a believer or practitioner of white supremacy; (*b*) *adjective* of, pertaining to, or characterized by white supremacy. **white supremacy** domination by white people over non-white people, esp. black people. ***white swallowwort***: see SWALLOWWORT 1. **whitetail (deer)** = ***white-tailed deer*** below. **white-tailed** *adjective* having a white tail; ***white-tailed deer***, a deer, *Odocoileus virginianus*, which has a white underside to the tail and is found from Canada to northern S. America (also called ***Virginian deer***); ***white-tailed GNU***; ***white-tailed sea-eagle***, a large sea-eagle, *Haliaeetus albicilla*, found from Europe and Greenland to Japan; ***white-tailed spider***, an Australian spider, *Lampona cylindrata*, which has a venomous bite that can cause extensive tissue damage. **White Terror** *Hist.* any of various periods of persecution by counter-revolutionaries, *spec.* that in Hungary in 1919–20 and in China in the years following 1927. **whitethorn** the hawthorn, *Crataegus monogyna*, which has a light-coloured bark compared to the blackthorn. **whitethroat** (*a*) any of several white-throated Eurasian warblers of the genus *Sylvia*, esp. *S. communis*, and (more fully ***lesser whitethroat***), *S. curraca*; (*b*) *N. Amer.* = ***white-throated sparrow*** below. **white-throated** *adjective* having a white throat; ***white-throated sparrow***, a N. American sparrow-like emberizid, *Zonotrichia albicollis*. **white tie** *spec.* a man's white bow-tie worn as part of full evening dress; *ellipt.* full evening dress. **white tin** (*a*) refined metallic tin, in contrast to black tin; (*b*) the ordinary (beta) allotrope of tin, which predominates between 13.6 and 161 degrees Celsius. **whitetip (shark)** either of two large sharks of the genus *Carcharinus*, with white-tipped fins, *C. albimarginatus* (more fully ***reef whitetip***), and *C. longimanus* (more fully ***ocean whitetip***). ***white titi***: see TITI *noun*[2]. ***white TOMBAC***. **white-toothed** *adjective* having white teeth; ***white-toothed shrew***, any of numerous Old World shrews of the genus *Crocidura*, with unpigmented teeth, esp. *C. russula* and *C. suaveolens* which reach western Europe. ***white trash***: see TRASH *noun*[1] 4. **white trout** (*a*) a pale form of the brown trout, *Salmo trutta*; (*b*) *N. Amer.* = WEAKFISH. ***white truffle***: see TRUFFLE *noun* 1. **white van man** *colloq.* an aggressive male driver of a delivery or workman's van (typically white in colour). ***white VITRIOL***. **white wagtail** a grey, black, and white Eurasian wagtail, *Motacilla alba*; *spec.* one of the widespread grey-backed race (cf. ***PIED wagtail***). **whitewall** *noun & adjective* (a tyre) having white side walls. **white-walled** *adjective* (of a tyre) having white side walls. **white walnut** the butter-nut, *Juglans cinerea*, whose wood is lighter than that of other walnuts; the wood of this tree. **white ware** (*a*) white goods; (*b*) white earthenware. **white water** shallow water; *esp.* turbulent foamy water in rapids or in shallows at sea. **whitewear** = ***white goods*** (a) above. **white wedding** a wedding at which the bride wears a formal white dress. **whiteweed** *N. Amer.* any of several white-flowered plants, *esp.* the ox-eye daisy, *Leucanthemum vulgare*. **white whale** = BELUGA 2. **white wheat** a variety of wheat with light-coloured grains. **white whiskey** *US* (a drink of) colourless (esp. illicit) whiskey. **white willow** a Eurasian streamside willow, *Salix alba*, with narrow leaves having silky white hairs on both sides. **white window** a stained-glass window in grisaille. **whitewing** (*a*) a chaffinch; (*b*) *N. Amer.* a white-winged dove, a white-winged scoter. **white-winged** *adjective* having white or partly white wings; ***white-winged dove***, an American dove, *Zenaida asiatica*, which is grey with white wing patches; ***white-winged scoter*** (*N. Amer.*), the velvet scoter, *Melanitta fusca*. **white witch** a person who practises white magic. **white work** embroidery worked in white thread on a white ground. **white worm** an errant (free-living) polychaete, *Nephtys hombergi*, which is bluish-white with iridescent pink shading.

▶ **B** *adverb.* Honourably, decently. *colloq.* (orig. *Austral.*). L19.

■ **whitelike** *adjective* (*rare*) pale E17. **whiteness** *noun* the quality or condition of being white; *poet.* a white substance or part: OE.

white /wʌɪt/ *verb.* OE.

[from the adjective.]

†**1** *verb intrans.* Become white, whiten. OE–L15.

2 *verb trans.* Make white, whiten; *spec.* (*a*) whitewash; (*b*) bleach. *arch.* ME.

3 Foll. by *out.* ▸**a** *verb intrans.* Of vision: become impaired by exposure to a sudden bright light. L20. ▸**b** *verb trans.* Impair the vision of (a theatre audience) by such means. L20. ▸**c** *verb trans.* Obliterate (a typing or writing mistake) with white correction fluid. L20.

Comb.: **white-out** (*a*) a dense blizzard; (*b*) a weather condition caused by uniform lighting in snow-covered country, in which shadows, horizon, and physical features are indistinguishable; (*c*) a white correction fluid for obliterating typing or writing mistakes.

whitebeam /ˈwʌɪtbiːm/ *noun.* E18.

[App. from WHITE *adjective* + BEAM *noun*.]

A small tree of the rose family, *Sorbus aria*, chiefly of chalk and limestone woodland, having white flowers, red berries, and ovate serrate leaves with white downy undersides (also ***whitebeam tree***). Also, chiefly with specifying word, any of various similar and closely related trees.

white boy /ˈwʌɪt bɔɪ/ *noun phr.* In sense 2 **Whiteboy**. L16.

[from WHITE *adjective* + BOY *noun*.]

1 A boy or (esp.) man who is a favourite. L16.

2 (**Whiteboy**.) ▸†**a** A member of an illegal rebellious association. M–L17. ▸**b** IRISH HISTORY. A member of an illegal agrarian organization wearing white shirts at meetings etc., active in the 18th and 19th cents. M18.

■ **Whiteboyism** *noun* (*Hist.*) the principles and practices of the Irish Whiteboys L18.

whitecap /ˈwʌɪtkap/ *noun & verb.* Also **white-cap**. M17.

[from WHITE *adjective* + CAP *noun*[1].]

▶ **A** *noun.* **1** Any of several birds with a white or light-coloured patch on the head. *obsolete* exc. *dial.* M17.

2 A crested wave, a breaker. L18.

3 A member of a self-constituted vigilante group using violence against people or groups regarded as objectionable. Usu. in *pl.* *US.* L19.

▶ **B** *verb trans.* Infl. **-pp-**. Use violence against (a person) in the style of the whitecaps. *US.* L19.

■ **whitecapper** *noun* = WHITECAP *noun* 3 L19.

Whitechapel /ˈwʌɪttʃap(ə)l/ *noun.* M18.
[A district in the East End of London.]
1 In CARDS, a lead of a singleton with a view to subsequent trumping. In BILLIARDS, an act of pocketing an opponent's ball. Also more fully ***Whitechapel play.*** M18.
2 ***Whitechapel needle***, a make of sewing-needle. *arch.* Chiefly *US.* L18.
3 Chiefly *Hist.* A light two-wheeled sprung cart used by shopkeepers etc. Also ***Whitechapel cart.*** M19.

white-collar /wʌɪtˈkɒlə/ *adjective & noun.* E20.
[from WHITE *adjective* + COLLAR *noun.*]
▶ **A** *adjective.* **1** (Of a person) engaged in non-manual, esp. clerical or administrative, work; (of work or an occupation) not manual or industrial, *esp.* clerical, administrative. E20.
2 *transf.* (Of crime) non-violent, esp. financial; (of a person) guilty of such crime. M20.
▶ **B** *noun.* A white-collar worker. M20.
■ **white-collared** *adjective* (*a*) wearing a white collar; (*b*) (of a worker) white-collar: L19.

whited /ˈwʌɪtɪd/ *ppl adjective. arch.* ME.
[from WHITE *verb* + -ED[1].]
1 Covered or coated with white; whitewashed. Now chiefly *fig.* in ***whited sepulchre*** s.v. SEPULCHRE *noun* 1. ME.
2 Lightened in colour; bleached. E16.
3 Of a horse: having white socks on the hind legs. M18.

Whitefieldian /ˈwʌɪtfiːldɪən/ *noun.* Also **Whitfield-** /ˈwɪtfiːld-/. M18.
[from *Whitefield* (see below) + -IAN.]
Hist. A follower of the English Methodist preacher George Whitefield (1714–70); a Calvinistic Methodist.
■ **Whitefieldism** *noun* the doctrines of the Whitefieldians L19. **Whitefieldite** *noun* = WHITEFIELDIAN M18.

whitefish /ˈwʌɪtfɪʃ/ *noun.* Also **white fish**. Pl. **-es** /-ɪz/, (usu.) same. LME.
[from WHITE *adjective* + FISH *noun*[1].]
1 Fish with pale flesh, as cod, haddock, whiting, etc. LME.
†**2** = BELUGA. M17–L18.
3 Any of various salmonid fishes of the genera *Coregonus* and *Prosopium*, found in the lakes of northern Eurasia and N. America and valued as food. M18.
3 ***Menominee whitefish***: see MENOMINEE *adjective.*
■ **whitefisher** *noun* a person who catches white fish E16. **whitefishing** *noun* the business, occupation, or industry of catching white fish E17.

Whitehall /ˈwʌɪthɔːl/ *noun.* E19.
[A street in London in which Government offices are situated.]
The British Government; its offices or policy; the civil service.

> 🕮 C. S. FORESTER Heaven only knew what Whitehall and Downing Street would say.

Comb.: **Whitehall Warrior** *slang* (*a*) a civil servant; (*b*) an armed forces officer employed in administration rather than on active service.
■ **Whitehallese** *noun* jargon regarded as typical of the civil service M20. **Whitehallism** *noun* attitudes or personnel regarded as typical of the civil service E20.

Whiteheadian /wʌɪtˈhɛdɪən/ *adjective.* M20.
[from *Whitehead* (see below) + -IAN.]
Of, pertaining to, or characteristic of the English mathematician and philosopher A. N. Whitehead (1861–1947) or his ideas.

whitely /ˈwʌɪtli/ *adjective.* Long *obsolete* exc. *Scot.* LME.
[from WHITE *adjective* + -LY[1].]
Pale, esp. of complexion.

whitely /ˈwʌɪtli/ *adverb.* Now *poet.* LME.
[from WHITE *adjective* + -LY[2].]
So as to be or appear white.

> 🕮 T. HARDY A whitely shining oval of still water.

whiten /ˈwʌɪt(ə)n/ *verb.* ME.
[from WHITE *adjective* + -EN[5].]
1 *verb trans.* Make white or whiter; make pale or paler; *spec.* (*a*) whitewash; (*b*) bleach. ME. ▸**b** *fig.* Free or clear from evil, guilt, etc.; cause to seem right or good; give a specious appearance to. LME.
2 *verb intrans.* Become or grow white or whiter; turn pale, esp. from fear. M17.

> 🕮 **1** M. CHABON A hard heel of brown bread whitened with margarine. *absol.*: P. BENSON He was in the stripping shed, whitening. **b** H. SPENCER By selecting the evidence any society may be relatively . . whitened. **2** T. MCGUANE Around the bases of the piers the green water was racing and whitening. S. RUSHDIE The whitened knuckles of the hand which gripped the sack revealed his determined frame of mind.

■ **whitener** *noun* a person who or thing which whitens; *spec.* a bleaching agent: E17. **whitening** *noun* (*a*) the action of the verb; an instance of this; (*b*) = WHITING *noun*[2] 2: E17.

White Russian /wʌɪt ˈrʌʃ(ə)n/ *noun & adjectival phr.* M19.
[from WHITE *adjective* + RUSSIAN.]
▶ **A** *noun phr.* **1** = BELORUSSIAN *noun.* M19.
2 *Hist.* An opponent of the Bolsheviks during the Russian Civil War (1918–21). E20.
▶ **B** *adjectival phr.* **1** = BELORUSSIAN *adjective.* L19.
2 *Hist.* Of or pertaining to the White Russians. E20.

whitesmith /ˈwʌɪtsmɪθ/ *noun*[1]. ME.
[from WHITE *adjective* + SMITH *noun.*]
A metalworker; *spec.* (*a*) a tinsmith; (*b*) a person who polishes or finishes as opp. to forging, metal goods.
■ **whitesmithery** *noun* = WHITESMITHING E19. **whitesmithing** *noun* performing whitesmith's work M19.

whitesmith /ˈwʌɪtsmɪθ/ *noun*[2]. M19.
[from WHITE *adjective* + surname of Sir William Sidney *Smith* (1764–1840), English admiral.]
A variety of gooseberry with white fruit.

White's thrush /ˈwʌɪts ˈθrʌʃ/ *noun phr.* M19.
[Gilbert *White* (1720–93), English naturalist.]
A large Asian thrush, *Zoothera dauma*, which has the plumage boldly patterned with black crescent-shaped markings.

whitewash /ˈwʌɪtwɒʃ/ *verb & noun.* L16.
[from WHITE *adjective* + WASH *verb.*]
▶ **A** *verb trans.* **1** Plaster over (a wall etc.) with a white substance; cover or coat with whitewash. L16.
2 *fig.* (Attempt to) clear or uphold the reputation of (a person, institution, etc.) by concealment of faults or mistakes. M18. ▸**b** In *pass.* Of an insolvent: be cleared from liability for his or her debts by passage through a bankruptcy court. M18.
3 Beat (an opponent) in a sporting match without allowing any opposing score; defeat by a large margin. *colloq.* M19.

> 🕮 **1** G. M. WOODWARD The floor is reddled; the walls whitewashed. *absol.*: SIR W. SCOTT Workmen . . repairing, painting, and white-washing. **2** J. COLVILLE Those who blamed the Nazis and whitewashed the Germans. B. BETTELHEIM Trying to whitewash his own behaviour toward her. **3** *Pot Black* Karen . . got off to a flying start . . looking as though she would whitewash Lynette.

▶ **B** *noun.* †**1** A cosmetic imparting a light colour to the skin. L17–M18.
2 A solution of lime and water, or of whiting, size, and water, for whitening walls etc. L17.
3 *fig.* Something that conceals faults or mistakes in order to clear or uphold the reputation of a person or institution; a cover-up. M19.
4 The action or an act of whitewashing; *colloq.* a victory in a sporting match in which an opponent fails to score or is defeated by a large margin. M19.

> 🕮 **3** *Satellite Times* Biographical whitewash of the controversial FBI director. *Independent* Frank Dobson, Labour's energy spokesman, called the report 'a whitewash'. **4** *Pot Black* Fisher avenged last year's defeat . . with a punishing 5–0 whitewash. *Listener* No national policy is more important than showing . . there has been no whitewash at the White House.

Comb.: **whitewash gum** either of two Australian eucalypts with powdery white bark, *Eucalyptus apodophylla* and *E. terminalis*.
■ **whitewasher** *noun* M18.

whitewood /ˈhwʌɪtwʊd/ *noun.* L17.
[from WHITE *adjective* + WOOD *noun*[1].]
1 Any of various trees with white or light-coloured wood; *esp.* (*a*) *N. Amer.* the tulip tree, *Liriodendron tulipifera*; the basswood, *Tilia americana*; (*b*) *Austral.* a small tree of arid regions, *Atalaya hemiglauca* (family Sapindaceae), with grey-green foliage valuable as fodder. Also ***whitewood tree***. L17.
2 Any light-coloured wood, esp. as not (yet) stained or varnished; *spec.* wood of the Norway spruce, *Picea abies*, imported from Continental Europe, or (more fully ***American whitewood***) that of the tulip tree, *Liriodendron tulipifera*. E18.

Whitey /ˈwʌɪti/ *noun. Black slang* (freq. *derog.* & *racially offensive*). E19.
[from WHITE *adjective* + -Y[6].]
A white person; white people collectively.

whitey *adjective* var. of WHITY.

Whitfieldian *noun* var. of WHITEFIELDIAN.

†**whitflaw**, **whitflow** *nouns* vars. of WHITLOW.

Whitgiftian /wɪtˈgɪftɪən/ *noun & adjective.* L19.
[from *Whitgift* (see below) + -IAN.]
▶ **A** *noun.* A past or present member of Whitgift School in Croydon, SE England, founded by John Whitgift (*c* 1530–1604), Archbishop of Canterbury. L19.
▶ **B** *adjective.* Of, pertaining to, or characteristic of John Whitgift; of or pertaining to Whitgiftians. M20.

whither *verb & noun*[1] see WUTHER.

whither /ˈwɪðə/ *adverb, conjunction, pronoun, & noun*[2]. *arch.*
[Old English *hwider* from Germanic base also of WHICH. Cf. HITHER, THITHER.]
▶ **A** *adverb & conjunction.* **I** *interrog. adverb.* **1** To what place. OE.
2 To what result, state, action, etc. OE.

> 🕮 **1** DICKENS 'Whither are we going?' inquired the lady. T. HARDY He was gone for good, nobody knew whither. **2** G. GREENE The great question of whither her genius was tending.

▶ **II** *rel. adverb & conjunction.* **3** To the place to or in which. OE.
4 To or in any place to which; to whatever place. ME.
5 To which place; to which. LME.

> 🕮 **3** A. TATE It must be plain from this train of ideas whither I am leading this discussion. **4** DEFOE They were at Liberty to travel whither they pleased. **5** M. PEMBERTON At Cowes, whither I had taken my yacht.

▶ **B** *pronoun & noun.* **1** ***to whither***, to which place. *rare.* L17.
2 The place or state to which a person or thing moves; direction. *rare.* E19.

whitherso /ˈwɪðəsəʊ/ *rel. adverb & conjunction. arch.*
[from WHITHER *adverb* + SO *adverb.*]
= next.

whithersoever /wɪðəsəʊˈɛvə/ *rel. adverb & conjunction. arch.* ME.
[from WHITHER *adverb* + SOEVER.]
1 To or in any place to which. ME.
2 No matter to what place. L16.

whitherward /ˈwɪðəwəd/ *adverb. arch.* ME.
[from WHITHER *adverb* + -WARD.]
1 *interrog.* Towards or to what place, in what direction, whither. Also *fig.* or *gen.*, towards what. ME.
2 *rel.* Towards the or any place which; towards which. ME.
■ Also **whitherwards** *adverb* (*rare*) ME.

whiting /ˈwʌɪtɪŋ/ *noun*[1]. LOE.
[from WHITE *verb* + -ING[1]. Cf. WHITTEN.]
1 In full ***whiting tree***. = WHITTEN. Long *obsolete* exc. *dial.* LOE.
2 The action of WHITE *verb.* LME.
3 Ground chalk used for whitewashing, cleaning plate, etc. LME.

whiting /ˈwʌɪtɪŋ/ *noun*[2]. ME.
[Middle & mod. Dutch *wijting*, from *wijt* white: see -ING[3].]
1 A gadid food fish, *Merlangius merlangus*, which is common off European coasts; the flesh of this as food. ME.
2 Any of various other fishes; *esp.* (*a*) *N. Amer.* a hake of the genus *Merluccius*; (*b*) *N. Amer.* a barb, *Menticirrhus saxatilis*; (*c*) *Austral.* any of several food and game-fishes of the percoid family Sillaginidae. L19.
2 ***blue whiting***: see BLUE *adjective.* ***rock whiting***: see ROCK *noun*[1].
Comb.: ***whiting-mop***: see MOP *noun*[4]; **whiting pollack** the pollack, *Pollachius pollachius*; **whiting pout** = BIB *noun* 2.

whitish /ˈwʌɪtɪʃ/ *adjective.* LME.
[from WHITE *adjective* + -ISH[1].]
Somewhat white; (of a colour) approaching white.
■ **whitishness** *noun* M16.

whitleather /ˈwɪtlɛðə/ *noun.* LME.
[from WHITE *adjective* + LEATHER *noun.*]
Soft white or pale leather, prepared by tawing.

Whitley /ˈwɪtli/ *adjective.* E20.
[J. H. *Whitley* (1866–1935), chairman of a committee set up in 1916 which recommended the setting up of such bodies.]
Designating a negotiating body for discussing and settling matters of industrial relations, pay and conditions, etc. Freq. in ***Whitley Council***.
■ **Whitleyism** *noun* the use of Whitley Councils for dealing with industrial relations E20.

whitling /ˈwɪtlɪŋ/ *noun. Scot. & north.* L16.
[from WHITE *adjective* + -LING[1].]
A salmonid fish, app. a young sea-trout.

whitlockite /ˈwɪtlɒkʌɪt/ *noun.* M20.
[from Herbert P. *Whitlock* (1868–1948), US mineralogist + -ITE[1].]
MINERALOGY. A rhombohedral calcium hydrogen phosphate containing iron and magnesium, found as transparent or translucent crystals in meteorites etc., and often occurring in dental calculi.

whitlow /ˈwɪtləʊ/ *noun.* Also †**-flaw**, †**-flow**. LME.
[Prob. from WHITE *adjective* + FLAW *noun*[1]; but perh. rel. to Dutch *fijt*, †*vijt*, Low German *fit*. The alt. to *whitlow* is unexpl.]
MEDICINE. (An infection causing) an abscess or swelling in the pulp around a fingernail or toenail. Cf. PARONYCHIA 1.
Comb.: **whitlow-grass** (*a*) a dwarf early-flowering white-flowered cruciferous plant of wall-tops etc., *Erophila verna*, formerly reputed to cure whitlows; (*b*) (with specifying word) any of several plants of the related genus *Draba*, found esp. on mountain rocks.

Whitmanesque /wɪtmə'nɛsk/ *adjective.* L19.
[from *Whitman* (see below) + -ESQUE.]
Characteristic or suggestive of the US poet Walt Whitman (1819–92), or his work.
■ **Whitmanish** *adjective* = WHITMANESQUE *adjective* E20. **Whitmanism** *noun* Whitman's metrical or poetical style; a feature of this: L19. **Whitmanite** *noun* an admirer or imitator of Whitman L19.

whitret /'wɪtrɪt/ *noun. Scot. & dial.* LME.
[Prob. from WHITE *adjective* + RAT *noun*¹.]
A weasel. Also, a stoat.

Whitstable /'wɪtstəb(ə)l/ *noun.* L19.
[See below.]
In full *Whitstable oyster*. An oyster of a type farmed at Whitstable, a coastal town in SE England.

whitster /'wɪtstə/ *noun.* Now *local.* LME.
[from WHITE *verb* + -STER.]
A person who bleaches (esp. textiles), a bleacher.

Whitsun /'wɪts(ə)n/ *adjective & noun.* ME.
[from WHIT SUNDAY, analysed as *Whitsun Day*. See also WHIT *adjective & noun*².]
▸ **A** *attrib. adjective.* = WHIT *adjective.* ME.
Special collocations & comb.: **Whitsun ale** *Hist.* a parish festival formerly held at Whitsuntide, involving feasting, dancing, games, etc. **Whitsun Day**, **Whitsunday** (*a*) Whit Sunday; (*b*) (usu. *Whitsunday*) one of the Scottish quarter days, now 28 May, formerly 15 or 26 May. †**Whitsun eve** the day before Whit Sunday. **Whitsuntide** the weekend or week including Whit Sunday.
▸ **B** *noun.* The weekend or week including Whit Sunday; Whitsuntide. M19.

Whit Sunday /wɪt 'sʌndi/ *noun phr.*
[Late Old English *Hwīta (Sunnandæg)* lit. 'white (Sunday)', prob. from the white robes of the newly baptized at Pentecost. See also WHIT *adjective & noun*², WHITSUN.]
CHRISTIAN CHURCH. **1** The seventh Sunday after Easter, commemorating the descent of the Holy Spirit on the disciples. Cf. PENTECOST 2. LOE.
†**2** The particular day of the descent of the Holy Spirit. Only in ME.

whittawer /'wɪtɔːə/ *noun. obsolete* exc. *dial.* ME.
[from WHITE *adjective* + TAWER *noun.*]
Orig., a person who tawed hide into whitleather, a tawer. Later, a currier, a tanner.

whitten /'wɪt(ə)n/ *noun.* Long *obsolete* exc. *dial.* M16.
[Var. of WHITING *noun*¹.]
In full *whitten tree*. Any of several small trees having leaves with white downy undersides, *esp.* whitebeam.

whitter /'wɪtə/ *noun. Scot.* L18.
[Prob. from WHITTLE *verb.*]
A drink of liquor.

whittie-whattie /'wɪtɪˌwɒti/ *noun & verb. Scot. & north.* L17.
[Perh. redupl. of WHAT *pronoun.*]
▸ **A** *noun.* Vague talk; indecision; a frivolous excuse. L17.
▸ **B** *verb intrans.* Be undecided. Also, mutter, whisper. L17.

Whittington /'wɪtɪŋt(ə)n/ *noun.* E20.
[Sir Richard *Whittington* (d. 1423), merchant and Mayor of London.]
Used *attrib.* to designate a pattern of eight chimes (traditionally supposed to have been heard by Whittington in London), used in some chiming clocks.

whittle /'wɪt(ə)l/ *noun*¹. Now *dial.*
[Old English *hwītel* (corresp. to Old Norse *hvítill* white bed-cover), formed as WHITE *adjective* + -LE¹.]
Orig., a blanket. Later, a cloak; a shawl.

whittle /'wɪt(ə)l/ *noun*². Now *dial.* LME.
[Var. of THWITTLE *noun.*]
A knife; *spec.* (*a*) a long knife used in butchery etc.; (*b*) a clasp-knife.

whittle /'wɪt(ə)l/ *verb.* M16.
[from WHITTLE *noun*².]
▸ **I 1** *verb trans. & intrans.* (with *at*, or *absol.*). Cut thin slices or shavings from the surface of (a wooden stick etc.); pare with a knife; (freq. foll. by *away*, *down*) reduce or sharpen by doing this. M16.
2 *verb trans. & intrans. transf. & fig.* Wear (a thing) away by some process; reduce or make (a thing) smaller by successive subtractions; diminish gradually the amount, force, or importance of (a thing). Freq. foll. by *away, down.* M18.
3 *verb trans.* Make or shape by whittling. M19.

> 🕮 **1** M. FITZGIBBON He whittled away at a stick. *Scottish World* Mr McKillips.. began whittling as a lad in Washington State. J. HARVEY Ted.. started.. whittling a pencil down to the stub. **2** P. THEROUX A succession of hills, whittled and fissured by the wind. *Times* The FT index.. having opened 8.5 up, saw its lead slowly whittled away. B. DUFFY Can there be no middle.. ground while we whittle away at the problem? M. FORSTER The list of fourteen is whittled down to four. **3** A. SETON Amusing himself by whittling a set of chessmen from an alder slab.

▸†**II 4** *verb trans.* Ply with drink; make drunk. M16–L17.
▸ **III 5** *verb intrans.* Worry, fret. *dial.* L19.
■ **whittler** *noun* M19. **whittling** *noun* (*a*) the action of the verb; (*b*) in *pl.*, fragments cut off in whittling, shavings: E17.

Whitworth /'wɪtwəθ/ *noun.* M19.
[Sir Joseph *Whitworth* (d. 1887), English engineer and inventor.]
1 A type of rifle having a hexagonal bore with a rapid twist, and firing an elongated shot. Also *Whitworth rifle*. M19.
2 Used *attrib.* (and formerly also in *possess.*) to designate a series of standard screw-thread for metal, and fasteners having such a thread. L19.

whity /'wʌɪti/ *adjective.* Also **whitey**. L16.
[from WHITE *adjective* + -Y¹. See also WHITEY *noun.*]
Whitish; rather white. Freq. in *comb.*
whity-brown *adjective & noun* (paper) of a pale brown colour.

whiz *noun, verb, interjection, & adverb* vars. of WHIZZ *noun, verb, interjection, & adverb.*

whiz-bang *interjection, noun, & adjective* var. of WHIZZ-BANG.

whizgig /'wɪzgɪg/ *noun. arch.* E19.
[from WHIZZ *verb* + GIG *noun*¹.]
An object, esp. a toy, that whizzes round.

whizz /wɪz/ *noun.* Also **whiz**, (in sense 4) **wiz** /wɪz/. E17.
[from the verb. Branch-II perh. a different word: cf. WIZARD *noun.*]
▸ **I 1** The action or an act of whizzing; a sibilant sound as made by the friction of a body moving through the air at great speed; a swift movement producing such a sound. E17. ▸**b** The practice of picking pockets (chiefly in *on the whizz*); a pickpocket. *slang* (chiefly *US*). E20.
2 An agreement, a bargain. *US slang.* M19.
3 Amphetamines. *slang.* L20.

> 🕮 **1** G. MEREDITH Amid a whizz of scythe-blades. M. STOTT A quick whizz round with the carpet sweeper.

▸ **II 4** A very remarkable thing. E20.
5 A person who is wonderfully skilful or talented in some specified respect. E20.

> 🕮 **4** *Times* A massive iron key that.. makes a whizz of a paper-weight. *New Scientist* The latest technological whizz is the so-called 'expert system'. **5** T. MALLON He was not.. a whizz at shorthand. *Pilots International* A 15 year old computer whizz who designed the program.

Comb.: **whizz-kid** *colloq.* an exceptionally successful or brilliant young person.

whizz /wɪz/ *verb, interjection, & adverb.* Also **whiz**. M16.
[Imit.]
▸ **A** *verb.* **1** *verb intrans.* Make a sibilant sound as of a body moving through the air at great speed. Now *dial.* exc. as in sense 2 below. M16. ▸†**b** Wheeze. L16–M18.
2 *verb intrans.* Move swiftly (as) with such a sound. L16. ▸**b** *fig.* Have a sensation of such a sound. L18.
3 *verb trans.* Cause to whizz; hurl, shoot or convey swiftly with a whizz; *spec.* rotate rapidly in a machine, esp. a food processor. M19.
4 Pickpocket. Chiefly as *whizzing verbal noun.* E20.
5 *verb intrans.* Urinate. *slang.* E20.

> 🕮 **2** F. KING Rockets were whizzing up into the leaden sky. I. BANKS I can't go whizzing off to conferences. A. BEATTIE The little girl whizzes by again on the skateboard. **3** S. SPENDER I was whizzed off to the radio station and did a broadcast. M. SPARK He put a stone in the sling and whizzed it beautifully, far into the air. *TV Times* Chop chicken breasts and place in a food processor... Whizz until smooth.

▸ **B** *interjection & adverb.* Repr. a whizzing sound; with a whizz. E19.
■ **whizzer** *noun* (*a*) a person who or thing which whizzes; (*b*) *slang* an extraordinary or wonderful person or thing: L19. **whizzing** *verbal noun* the action of the verb; an instance of this: E17. **whizzing** *adjective* (*a*) that whizzes; (*b*) *slang* excellent, remarkable: L16. **whizzingly** *adverb* M19.

whizz-bang /'wɪzbaŋ/ *interjection, noun, & adjective. colloq.* Also **whiz-bang**. M19.
[from WHIZZ *verb, interjection* + BANG *noun*¹.]
▸ **A** *interjection.* Repr. a whizzing sound that ends with a bang. M19.
▸ **B** *noun.* **1** A high-velocity shell from a small-calibre gun, whose passage is heard before the gun's report. E20.
2 A resounding success. E20.
3 A firework that jumps around making a whizzing noise and periodic bangs. M20.
▸ **C** *adjective.* Fast-paced, very lively. M20.

whizzo /wɪ'zəʊ/ *interjection, adjective, & noun. slang.* Also **wizzo** /wɪ'zəʊ/. E20.
[from WHIZZ *noun* + -O.]
▸ **A** *interjection.* Expr. delight. E20.
▸ **B** *adjective.* Excellent, wonderful. M20.
▸ **C** *noun.* Pl. **-os**. = WHIZZ *noun* 4. L20.

whizzy /'wɪzi/ *adjective.* M19.
[from WHIZZ *noun, verb* + -Y¹.]
1 Characterized by whizzing; *dial.* dizzy, giddy. *rare.* M19.
2 Technologically innovative or advanced; up-to-date, modern. *colloq.* L20.

WHO *abbreviation.*
World Health Organization.

who /huː, *unstressed* hʊ/ *pronoun, noun, & conjunction.*
[Old English *hwā* corresp. to Old Frisian *hwa*, Old Saxon *hwē, hwie*, Old High German *(h)wer* (Dutch *wie*, German *wer*), Old Swedish *ho*, Old Danish *hwa* (Danish *hvo*), Gothic *hwas*, from Germanic from Indo-European base parallel to that repr. in Latin *quis* who, what.]
▸ **A** *pronoun & noun.* (As pronoun functioning as subject or (exc. *formal*) object: cf. WHOM.)
▸ **I** *interrog. pronoun.* **1** Used in asking the identity of a person or persons specified, indicated, or understood; what or which person(s). OE. ▸**b** *ellipt.* Used as or in a direct question asking for repetition, clarification, or confirmation of something just said involving a reference to a person's name. Cf. WHAT *pronoun & noun* 4. M18.
2 Used in asking the character, function, etc., of a person or persons; what sort of person(s). LME.

> 🕮 **1** W. S. MAUGHAM Who the hell d'you suppose he is, Evie? I. MURDOCH Who had said that, about perfection and reality? O. MANNING He was waiting for her to ask who it was. G. VIDAL Peter looked about the room to see who was missing. M. ROBERTS You might go far,.. who knows? **b** DICKENS 'I heerd 'em.. saying how they'd done old Fireworks.' 'Old who?' said Mr Pickwick. **2** T. HARDY: 'Who is Mr Boldwood?' said Bathsheba. J. WYNDHAM Who am I to say what's best for her?

▸ **II** *rel. pronoun.* **3** Any person, whoever. Now *literary* & usu. without pronominal in correl. clause. ME. ▸†**b** No matter what person; whoever. ME–M16.
4 Introducing a clause defining or restricting the antecedent, esp. a clause essential to the identification of the antecedent; that. Formerly also, (as correl. to *such*) as. Used to refer to people and to things denoting or connoting a group of people or having an implication of personality: cf. WHICH *pronoun* 4, THAT *pronoun* 6. ME.
5 Introducing a clause stating something additional about the antecedent, the sense of the main clause being complete without the relative clause; *occas.* and he (she, they). Used as in sense 4 above: cf. WHICH *pronoun* 3. LME.
6 The person or (esp. persons) that. *arch.* L16.

> 🕮 **3** R. KIPLING Who rides at the tail of a Border thief, he sits not long at his meat. A. AUSTIN Who holds the sea, perforce doth hold the land. **4** S. T. WARNER Every one who could squeeze.. into Oris' house did so. M. KEANE A.. nervous man who.. preferred the company of his inferiors. *Amateur Stage* Theatres and companies who offer interpretative performance of their productions. I. MURDOCH The Meeting should be.. attended by any guests who happened to be present. *Times* Over half.. our sample who we assessed as working class concurred. **5** DEFOE Our Surgeons, who we all call Doctors at Sea. E. J. HOWARD Pamela, who had been married for nearly a year. A. CARTER Miss Brown, who lisped and wore glasses. I. MURDOCH A 'minute', which I sent to Duncan, who sent it to Mrs Fredericksson. S. DELANEY This.. dog, who'd been sleeping under the porch. **6** WORDSWORTH There are who ask not if thine eye Be on them.

▸ **III** *noun.* **7** A person. *rare.* M17.
8 (A question as to) the identity of a person. L18.
Phrases: *as who*: see AS *adverb* etc. †**but who** who.. not; but what. *who goes there?*: see GO *verb.* **who's who** (*a*) used in asking about two or more people who are difficult to distinguish from each other; *know who's who*: see KNOW *verb*; (*b*) a list or directory with facts about notable people. **you and who else?** expr. incredulity about a person's ability to carry out a threat.
Comb.: **who-all** *pronoun* (*US dial.*) who. **who-does-what** *adjective* (of a dispute etc.) concerning which group of workers should do a particular job. **whosis**, **whosit** *colloq.* a person whose name one cannot recall, does not know, or does not wish to specify (freq. in titles).
▸†**B** *conjunction.* Used to link clauses with a pers. pronoun in the relative clause functioning as a rel. pronoun to refer to the antecedent. Cf. WHICH *conjunction* 1. E16–E17.
■ **whoness** *noun* (*rare*) the inherent nature of a person; the state of being an individual: E20.

whoa /wəʊ/ *interjection.* Orig. **who**. LME.
[Var. of HO *interjection*². Cf. WOA.]
Commanding a horse or other draught animal or (now *joc.*) a person to stop or slow down.
¶ The spelling *whoa* is not recorded before M19.

whodunit /huː'dʌnɪt/ *noun. colloq.* Also **-dunnit**. M20.
[from *who done it?* non-standard form of *who did it?*]
A story, play, etc., about the detection of a crime etc., esp. a murder.
■ **whodunitry**, **-dunnitry** *noun* writing or subject matter characteristic of a detective story M20.

whoever /huː'ɛvə/ *pronoun.* Also (*poet.*) **-e'er** /-'ɛː/. ME.
[from WHO *pronoun* + EVER.]
▸ **I 1** Any person or persons who. ME. ▸**b** Any person or persons whom. L16.
2 No matter who; the unknown person or persons who; *colloq.* some similar person (usu. preceded by *or*). E16.

> 🕮 **1** B. BETTELHEIM Whoever saves a life.. remains beholden to the person he saved. **b** SHAKES. *Rom. & Jul.* Whoe'er you find attach. **2** V. WOOLF Listening to Miss La Trobe or whoever it was, practising her scales. *She*: Whoever wields the hardware, family photography can be a battleground.

▶ **II** *interrog.* **3** (Also as two words.) Used with emphatic force in place of *who* in a question. *colloq.* L19.

📖 **3** E. BOWEN Whoever is she talking to on the stairs?

whole /həʊl/ *adjective, noun, adverb, & interjection.* Also (earlier) †**hole**. See also HALE *adjective.*
[Old English *hāl*, *gehāl* = Old Frisian, Old Saxon *hēl* (Dutch *heel*, *geheel*), Old & mod. High German *heil*, Old Norse *heill*, Gothic *hails*, *gahails*, from Germanic. The spelling with *wh-* (from 15) reflects a widespread dial. pronunc. with /w/ (see WH).]
▶ **A** *adjective.* **I** In good condition, sound.
1 Of a person, animal, or part of the body: uninjured, unhurt; recovered from injury. *arch.* OE.
2 Of a material object: free from damage or defect; not broken; intact. Passing into senses A.5, 6 below. OE.
3 Free from disease; healthy; restored to health, recovered from disease. *arch.* OE. ▸†**b** Of the mind: sound. OE–L16.
†**4** Good, wholesome. ME–E16.

📖 **1** BROWNING The evil thing . . Left the man whole and sound of body. **2** N. HAWTHORNE She is . . as whole as when she left the hands of the sculptor.

▶ **II** Complete, total.
5 Not divided into parts; not broken up or cut into pieces; entire. Passing into sense A.2 above. OE. ▸†**b** Undivided in allegiance or devotion; loyal, steadfast. Cf. ***whole-hearted***, ***whole-souled*** below. ME–M16. ▸†**c** Not divided in opinion; united, unanimous. LME–M16.
6 Having all its parts or elements; not lacking any part; full, perfect. Passing into sense A.2 above. ME. ▸**b** Containing all its proper or essential constituents. Chiefly in special collocations: see below. L18.
7 *attrib.* **a** With *noun sing.* The total amount or extent of; every part of; (with collect. noun) each or every one of. Following article, possess. or demonstr. adjective, etc., or other determiner; formerly also without article. ME. ▸**b** With *noun pl.* The total number of; all of, each or every one of. Following determiner (def. article, indef. article, possess. adjective, etc.) and preceding numeral and noun; (now chiefly *Scot.*) following determiner and preceding noun (without numeral). In emphatic use: with article omitted and following (formerly, preceding) any numeral. LME.
8 Designating or pertaining to a family relationship in which both the parents are the same; full; pure. Opp. ***half***. LME. ▸†**b** Not sharing the specified charge or function with any one else, sole. LME–E17. ▸**c** BOOKBINDING. Forming the whole of the cover. M19.

📖 **5** *Nature* Synaptosomes were prepared from whole rat brain. B. FUSSELL Sand dabs are so small they can be sautéed whole and eaten in two bites. *Health Guardian* The holistic approach . . treats patients as whole people. *Country Homes* Basmati rice, cooked with . . whole cardamom pods. **6** TENNYSON That so my pleasure may be whole. **7a** E. NESBIT She would scream 'Fire!' and 'Murder!' and she didn't mind if the whole street heard. J. BUCHAN His whole body was one huge ache. J. OSBORNE He was upset by the whole idea. G. GORDON Children know they have not been told the whole truth by grown-ups. M. ROBERTS The whole weekend, right through to Monday morning. **b** J. JACKSON The Church had no breathing for whole twenty yeares together. *Time* Bagwell taught himself to speed-read, gulping whole paragraphs at a glance. D. F. GALOUYE I feel . . I've stood still for two whole years.

▶ **B** *adverb.* Wholly, entirely, fully, perfectly. Now *rare* & chiefly in comb. Formerly also with pleonastic *all*. ME.

📖 W. COWPER War and the chase engross the savage whole.

▶ **C** *noun.* **1** *The* full, complete, or total amount or extent (*of*); all the parts, members, inhabitants, etc. *of*. LME.
2 A thing made up of combined or connected parts; a complex system; a thing complete in itself. Usu. with indef. article. L16.
3 MINING. A seam of coal not yet worked, or in an early stage of working. M18.

📖 **1** *Rail* A park and ride facility for the whole of the Vale. B. LEIGH Alice in Wonderland was his favourite book and he could recite the whole of it. **2** I. ASIMOV Lines and curves . . entwined into a coalescing whole.

Phrases: **as a whole** as a unity; in its entirety; not as separate parts. **a whole lot** (*colloq.*, orig. *US*) very much (usu. preceding a compar.). ***give the whole show away***: see SHOW *noun*[1]. ***go the whole hog***: see HOG *noun*. ***go the whole way***: see WAY *noun*. **in the whole** (now *rare*) all together, in all. **in whole** in full, entirely, wholly (opp. ***in part***). ***lick whole***: see LICK *verb*. **on the whole** (*a*) taking everything relevant into account, all things considered; (*b*) in general, for the most part. ***the whole kit and boodle***, ***the whole kit and caboodle***: see KIT *noun*[1]. ***the whole shoot***: see SHOOT *noun*[1]. ***with a whole skin***: see SKIN *noun*.
Special collocations & comb.: **whole cloth** cloth of the full size as manufactured, as distinguished from a piece cut off for a garment etc.; (***cut out of the whole cloth***, ***cut out of whole cloth***, ***made out of the whole cloth***, ***made out of whole cloth*** (*US slang*), wholly fabricated, totally false). **whole-colour**, **whole-coloured** *adjectives* (of an animal) of a uniform colour. **whole-earther** *colloq.* a person concerned about the protection and conservation of natural resources and wildlife. **wholefood** food which has not been unnecessarily processed or refined. **whole gale** NAUTICAL (now chiefly *US*) a storm wind of 48–55 knots (force 10 on the Beaufort scale). **wholehearted** *adjective* (of a person) completely devoted or committed; (of an action etc.) done with all possible effort, attention, or sincerity; thorough. **wholeheartedly** *adverb* in a wholehearted manner. **wholeheartedness** the quality or condition of being wholehearted. **whole holiday** a whole day taken as a holiday (opp. ***half-holiday***). **whole-hoofed** *adjective* = SOLIDUNGULATE *adjective*. **whole-length** *noun & adjective* (*a*) *noun* a portrait showing the whole height of the human figure, a full-length portrait; (*b*) *adjective* (of a portrait etc.) full-length. **whole-life** *adjective* pertaining to or designating an insurance policy for which premiums are payable until the death of the person insured. **wholemeal** *adjective & noun* (designating or made from) meal or flour made from the whole grain of wheat or other cereals with none of the bran or germ removed. **whole milk** milk with none of its fats or other constituents removed; *spec.* unskimmed milk. **whole note** MUSIC †(*a*) a whole tone; (*b*) (now *N. Amer.*) a semibreve. **whole number** (*a*) MATH. any of the numbers exactly divisible by one (usu. taken to include zero); an integer; *spec.* such a number representing a positive quantity, as used in counting (as 2, 6, 42, etc.); (*b*) ***whole-number rule*** PHYSICS, the empirical law that the atomic weights of the elements are mostly close to being whole numbers. **whole-rock** *adjective* (GEOLOGY) designating a complete rock sample as used in an analytical procedure, as distinct from the individual minerals composing it. **whole-souled** *adjective* (chiefly *US*) wholehearted. **whole step** MUSIC an interval of a (whole) tone. **whole-stitch** LACE-MAKING a stitch in which the threads are woven together as in cloth. ***whole sum***: see SUM *noun*. **whole-time** full-time. **whole-timer** a full-timer. **whole-tone scale** MUSIC: consisting entirely of tones, with no semitones. **wholewheat** *noun & adjective* (*a*) *noun* wheat with none of the bran or germ removed; (*b*) *adjective* designating or made from flour made from wholewheat.
■ **wholeness** *noun* LOE. **wholewise** *adverb* (*rare*) as a whole, with respect to the whole L17.

wholely *adverb* see WHOLLY.

wholesale /ˈhəʊlseɪl/ *noun, adjective, verb, & adverb.* LME.
[from WHOLE *adjective* + SALE *noun*.]
▶ **A** *noun.* The selling of goods in large quantities, usu. for retail by others. Orig. in ***by wholesale*** below. Cf. RETAIL *noun* 1. LME.
by wholesale *fig.* (*a*) (of selling) in large quantities; (*b*) in abundance; extensively; indiscriminately.
▶ **B** *attrib.* or as *adjective.* **1** Of, pertaining to, or involved in wholesale. M17.
2 *fig.* Done on a large scale; extensive; indiscriminate. M17.

📖 **1** L. L. PRICE Greater friction . . in the retail than in the wholesale market. DAY LEWIS My grandfather, being a wholesale chemist, not a retailer, could never be suspected of handing articles across a counter. **2** *Tree News* The wholesale removal of all trees.

▶ **C** *verb trans. & intrans.* **1** Sell (goods) wholesale. E18.
2 *verb intrans.* Of goods: be sold wholesale, esp. for a specified price. Freq. foll. by *at*, *for*. L19.

📖 **1** *New Yorker* I make . . ornaments . . and wholesale them to gift shops. **2** *New Yorker* A cassette that wholesaled for forty dollars.

▶ **D** *adverb.* By wholesale; at a wholesale price; *fig.* on a large scale. M19.

📖 G. M. TREVELYAN Factories, producing goods wholesale, ruining craftsmanship. R. WESTALL The price of bacon wholesale was now beyond belief.

■ **wholesaler** *noun* a person who sells goods wholesale M19.

wholescale /ˈhəʊlskeɪl/ *adjective.* M20.
[from WHOLE *adjective* + SCALE *noun*[4], after WHOLESALE *adjective*.]
= WHOLESALE *adjective* 2.

wholesome /ˈhəʊls(ə)m/ *adjective & noun.* ME.
[from WHOLE *adjective* + -SOME[1]; prob. already in Old English (cf. Old High German *heilsam*, Old Norse *heilsamr*). Cf. HALESOME.]
▶ **A** *adjective.* **1** Conducive to general well-being; promoting mental or moral health; beneficial; prudent, safe. ME.
2 Promoting physical health; salubrious. Formerly also, curative, medicinal. LME.
3 Having a sound (physical or moral) constitution; healthy. E16.
4 NAUTICAL. (Of a ship) not liable to roll; (of a sea) not causing ships to roll. Now *rare*. E17.

📖 **1** STEELE Bestow a little of your wholesome Advice upon our Coachmen. *Blitz* The kind of provincial trad jazz that wholesome hobbies are built upon. **2** TOLKIEN The air is wholesome there because of the outlets through fissures in the rock. **3** T. BERGER The most vicious types . . would today qualify as the most wholesome of citizens.

▶ **B** *noun.* In *pl.* Wholesome things. *rare.* M18.
■ **wholesomely** *adverb* ME. **wholesomeness** *noun* ME.

wholism /ˈhəʊlɪz(ə)m/ *noun.* M20.
[Alt. after WHOLE *noun*.]
= HOLISM.
■ **wholist**, **who'listic** *adjectives* = HOLISTIC M20. **who'listically** *adverb* = HOLISTICALLY M20.

wholly /ˈhəʊlli, ˈhəʊli/ *adverb.* Also (earlier, now *dial.*) **holly** /ˈhɒli/, (now *rare*) **wholely**. ME.
[from WHOLE *adjective* + -LY[2]; prob. already in Old English. Current form and pronunc. results from the influence of WHOLE *adjective* on the normal development (now dial.) *holly*; for spelling with *wh-* see WHOLE.]
1 As a whole, in its entirety, in full. Formerly also, all together, in a body. Now *rare*. ME.
2 Completely, entirely; without limitation or diminution. ME.
3 Exclusively, solely, only. LME.

📖 **1** J. RUSKIN A man who can see truth at all, sees it wholly. **2** J. BUCHAN I found a large room wholly without frippery. H. NICOLSON Release me either wholly or partially from my contract. J. BARNES Though . . frank by nature, he is never wholly sincere. **3** TENNYSON A creature wholly given to brawls and wine.

Comb.: **wholly-owned** *adjective* designating a company all of whose shares are owned by another company.

whom /huːm/ *pronoun.* Now chiefly *formal*.
[Old English *hwām*, *hwǣm* dat. of *hwā* WHO *pronoun*, *hwæt* WHAT *pronoun* (corresp. to Old Frisian *hwam*, Old Saxon *hwem*, Old High German *(h)wemu* (German *wem*), Old Norse *hveim* (Danish †*hvam*), Gothic *hwamma*), superseding in function Old English *hwone*, *hwane*, *hwæne* accus. masc. of *hwā*.]
1 Objective of WHO *pronoun*. OE.
2 Objective of WHICH *pronoun*. Now only (passing into sense 1) used to refer to things denoting or connoting a group of people or having the implication of personality. ME.
3 Subjective: who. E16.

📖 **1** BYRON: 'Whom the gods love die young' was said of yore. M. KEANE Younger ladies to whom Cynthia sold her horses. W. S. MAUGHAM His wife and daughter whom he had come . . to spend Easter with. J. RHYS My brother whom I scarcely knew. O. MANNING To whom would you award Bessarabia? B. BAINBRIDGE The servant, whom I believe to be a good girl. **2** P. LUCKOMBE The vowels . . are seventeen in number; five of whom are pronounced long. J. STEINBECK A dog of whom passers-by said, 'He is an American dog.' **3** *Nature* The initiated—whom are not synonymous with the intelligent. *Daily Telegraph* Whom am I to defend Daphne du Maurier?

¶ Sense 3 is often regarded as incorrect.

whomever /huːmˈɛvə/ *pronoun.* Chiefly *literary*. Also (*poet.*) **-e'er** /-ˈɛː/. ME.
[from WHOM + EVER.]
Objective of WHOEVER.

📖 L. MICHAELS Twisting his head as though whomever he addressed lived on his hip.

whommel *verb & noun* var. of WHEMMEL.

whomp /wɒmp/ *noun & verb. colloq.* (chiefly *N. Amer.*). E20.
[Imit.]
▶ **A** *noun.* A dull heavy sound; a heavy blow. E20.
▶ **B** *verb.* **1** *verb trans.* Strike heavily, thump; *transf.* defeat decisively. E20.
2 *verb trans.* Foll. by *up*. ▸**a** Produce quickly, with little preparation or planning. E20. ▸**b** Stir up (an emotion, disturbance, etc.). E20.
3 *verb intrans.* Fall with a dull heavy sound. E20.

📖 **1** *New England Monthly* A man who died . . after being whomped with a baseball bat. **3** *New Scientist* The Sunday edition of the New York Times . . whomped to the floor.

whomso /ˈhuːmsəʊ/ *pronoun. arch.* ME.
[from WHOM + SO *adverb*.]
Objective of WHOSO.

whomsoever /huːmsəʊˈɛvə/ *pronoun.* Chiefly *literary*. Also (*poet.*) **-e'er** /-ˈɛː/. LME.
[from WHOM + SOEVER.]
1 Objective of WHOSOEVER. LME.
2 Subjective: whosoever. (Often regarded as incorrect.) L16.

📖 **1** R. BARBER The knights . . jousting . . with whomsoever they chanced to meet. **2** J. RUSKIN They shall not be impeded by whomsoever it may be.

whoo /wuː/ *verb.* L16.
[Rel. to next.]
†**1** *verb trans. & intrans.* Of an owl: hoot. L16–E17.
2 *verb intrans.* Give a cry of 'whoo!'. L19.

whoo /wuː/ *interjection & noun.* Also redupl. **whoo-whoo**. E17.
[Var. of HOO *interjection* etc.]
▶ **A** *interjection.* **1** Expr. surprise, delight, etc. E17.
2 Repr. the hoot of an owl. M17.
▶ **B** *noun.* A call or cry of 'whoo!'. M19.

whoof /wuːf, wʊf/ *interjection, noun, & verb.* In sense 2 also **woof**. M18.
[Imit.]
▶ **A** *interjection & noun.* **1** (Repr.) an abrupt gruff cry. Now *rare*. M18.
2 (Repr.) a sound (as) of a sudden expulsion of air. E20.
▶ **B** *verb intrans.* Utter an abrupt gruff cry (*rare*); make a sound as of air being expelled. M19.

whoofle /ˈwuːf(ə)l, ˈwʊf-/ *verb intrans.* & (*rare*) *trans.* E20.
[Imit.: cf. prec., WHUFFLE *verb.*]
Make a snorting, gurgling, or snuffling sound; *rare* drink *up* with such a sound.

whoom /wʊm/ *noun & verb.* M20.
[Imit.]
▶ **A** *noun.* A resonant booming or rushing sound. M20.
▶ **B** *verb intrans.* Make such a sound. M20.

whoompf /wʊm(p)f/ *interjection & noun.* M20.
[Imit.]
(Repr.) a sudden violent rushing sound (as) of an object bursting into flame.

whoop /huːp, wuːp/ *noun.* Also (earlier) **hoop** /huːp/. ME.
[Rel. to next. In branch II shortened from ***whoop-de-do*** s.v. WHOOP *verb.*]
▶ **I 1** A cry of 'whoop!'; a loud cry (as) of excitement, triumph, etc. ME. ▶**b** A long rasping indrawn breath following a fit of coughing in whooping-cough. E19.
2 A form of the game of hide-and-seek. L18.

🕮 **1** A. MAUPIN Mary Ann let out a whoop 'You're an angel, DeDe!' D. ADAMS They let out whoops of delight. **a whoop and a holler** *slang* (chiefly *N. Amer.*) a short distance. **not care a whoop**, **not give a whoop**, etc., be indifferent.

▶ **II 3** A bump or (occas.) dip on an off-road motorcycle or cycle racetrack or rally course. L20.

whoop /huːp, wuːp/ *verb.* Also **hoop** /huːp/. LME.
[Prob. imit.: cf. Old & mod. French *houper* (from *houp* interjection), prec.]
1 *verb intrans.* Utter a whoop or series of whoops; shout out in excitement, exultation, defiance, etc. LME. ▶**b** *verb trans.* Utter with a whoop; express by whooping; (foll. by adverb or adverbial phr.) bring or urge by or with whooping. LME. ▶**c** *verb trans.* Shout at. *rare.* L17. ▶**d** Foll. by *up*: arouse enthusiasm for; encourage; praise. *colloq.* (chiefly *US*). L19.
2 *verb intrans.* Of an owl: hoot. M17. ▶**b** Express by hooting; hoot at. L17.
3 *verb intrans.* Make the sound characteristic of whooping-cough. E19.

🕮 **1** A. HALEY Whooping out loud with the pleasure of feeling so wildly free. **b** T. MCGUANE The cows had mouths of long grass . . . Lucien whooped them out onto hard ground. **d whoop it up** *colloq.* (*a*) engage in revelry; (*b*) *US* create a stir.

Comb.: **whoop-de-do** *N. Amer. colloq.* (*a*) a fuss, a commotion; (*b*) a very bumpy stretch of road to ride a motorcycle along; **whoop-up** (*colloq.*, chiefly *N. Amer.*) a noisy celebration or party; revelry.

whoop /huːp, wuːp/ *interjection.* Also (*rare*) **hoop** /huːp/. LME.
[Natural exclam. Cf. Old & mod. French *houp*, prec.]
Expr. excitement, exultation, defiance, etc. Also, repr. the sound of a siren.

whoopee /*as interjection* wʊˈpiː, *as noun* ˈwʊpi/ *interjection & noun. colloq.* M19.
[from WHOOP *interjection* + -EE².]
▶ **A** *interjection.* Expr. exuberant joy. M19.
▶ **B** *noun.* Exuberant or boisterous merrymaking; revelry. E20.
make whoopee (*a*) indulge in exuberant merrymaking, revel; (*b*) *euphem.* have sexual intercourse.
Comb.: **whoopee cushion** a rubber cushion that when sat on makes a sound like the breaking of wind.

whooper /ˈhuːpə, w-/ *noun.* Also (earlier) **hoop-** /ˈhuːp-/. M16.
[from WHOOP *verb* + -ER¹.]
A person who or animal that whoops; *spec.* (*a*) = ***whooper swan*** below; (*b*) *N. Amer.* = ***whooping crane*** s.v. WHOOPING *ppl adjective.*
Comb.: **whooper swan** a large swan, *Cygnus cygnus*, which has a yellow and black bill and breeds in northern Eurasia and Greenland.

whooping /ˈhuːpɪŋ, w-/ *verbal noun.* Also (earlier) **hoop-** /ˈhuːp-/. M16.
[from WHOOP *verb* + -ING¹.]
The action of WHOOP *verb*; an instance of this.

whooping /ˈhuːpɪŋ, w-/ *ppl adjective.* Also (earlier) **hoop-** /ˈhuːp-/. M17.
[from WHOOP *verb* + -ING².]
1 That whoops; (of a sound or cry) of the nature of a whoop. M17.
2 Unusually large. Also, very noisy, uproarious. *slang* (chiefly *US*). M19.
Special collocations: **whooping cough** a contagious disease chiefly affecting children, caused by the bacterium *Bordetella pertussis*, and characterized by convulsive coughs followed by a long sonorous inspiration. **whooping crane** a large endangered N. American crane, *Grus americana*, with mainly white plumage.

whoops /wʊps/ *interjection.* Also **whoops-a-daisy** /ˈwʊpsəˌdeɪzi/. M20.
[Prob. from WHOOPSIE *interjection.* Cf. OOPS.]
Expr. surprise, dismay, or apology, esp. after stumbling or making an obvious mistake.

🕮 *New Yorker* Whoops! You're not supposed to tell where he is.

whoopsie /ˈwʊpsi/ *noun. nursery & slang.* L20.
[from next.]
A lump or piece of excrement. Usu. in *pl.*
do whoopsies, **do a whoopsie** defecate.

whoopsie /ˈwʊpsi/ *interjection. colloq.* Also **whoopsie-daisy** /ˈwʊpsɪˌdeɪzi/. E20.
[Prob. alt. of UPSY-DAISY.]
= WHOOPS *interjection.*

whoosh /wʊʃ, wuːʃ/ *verb, noun, & interjection.* M19.
[Imit.]
▶ **A** *verb.* **1** *verb intrans.* Emit a dull soft sibilant sound as of something rushing through the air; move with a rushing sound. M19.
2 *verb trans.* Cause to move with a rushing sound. E20.

🕮 **1** D. HEWETT A Council truck whooshed past, sending . . water into the gutters. T. O'BRIEN His skis whooshed on the powdered snow. **2** B. HINES He whooshed the curtains open. R. CRITCHFIELD The Channel Tunnel . . will . . whoosh you from London to Paris.

▶ **B** *noun.* A rushing sound; a movement accompanied by a rushing sound. Also, an utterance of 'whoosh!' L19.

🕮 T. C. BOYLE She listened to the whoosh of traffic from the distant freeway.

▶ **C** *interjection.* Repr. a rushing sound; expr. a rushing movement. L19.

whoo-whoop /huːˈhuːp/ *interjection & noun.* E17.
[Origin unkn.]
HUNTING. (A shout) signalling the death of the quarry.

whop /wɒp/ *noun. colloq.* LME.
[from the verb.]
An act of whopping; a heavy blow or impact.

whop /wɒp/ *verb & adverb.* LME.
[Var. of WAP *verb*¹.]
▶ **A** *verb.* Infl. **-pp-**.
1 *verb trans.* Take, put, etc., suddenly or violently. *dial.* LME.
2 *verb trans.* Strike with heavy blows; beat soundly, thrash. *slang.* L16. ▶**b** *fig.* Defeat utterly; surpass or excel greatly. *slang.* M19.
▶ **B** *adverb.* With a sudden movement or impact. E19.

whopper /ˈwɒpə/ *noun. slang.* L18.
[from prec. + -ER¹.]
Something unusually large of its kind; *spec.* a blatant or gross lie.

🕮 *Sunday Express* It's a whopper of around 1,500 pages. *Independent* The case . . comes down to the reliability of Nonna and Mr Redmond and they have told some whoppers.

whopping /ˈwɒpɪŋ/ *adjective. slang.* E18.
[from WHOP *verb* + -ING². Cf. earlier WAPPING *adjective.*]
Unusually large; huge; (of a lie) blatant, gross.

🕮 L. OLIVIER A whopping great thrombosis in my right leg. R. OWEN Some outrageous assertion or whopping untruth. *Natural History* A whopping two-thirds of the world's oil lies under the sands.

whore /hɔː/ *noun & verb.*
[Late Old English *hōre* corresp. to Middle & mod. Low German *hore*, Middle Dutch *hoere* (Dutch *hoer*), Old High German *huora* (German *Hure*), Old Norse *hóra*, from Germanic base repr. also by Old Norse *hórr*, Gothic *hōrs* adulterer, from Indo-European base repr. by Latin *carus* dear. For change to spelling with *wh-* see WH (cf. WHOLE).]
▶ **A** *noun.* **1** A prostitute. LOE.
2 A promiscuous woman; a man's mistress; an adulteress. *derog.* ME. ▶**b** *fig.* A corrupt or idolatrous community. LME.
3 *transf.* A male prostitute; a promiscuous or unprincipled person. Esp. as a term of abuse. M17.
Phrases: **play the whore** *arch.* (of a woman) engage in immoral or promiscuous sexual relations; commit adultery. ***scarlet whore***: see SCARLET *adjective.* **the whore of Babylon** *arch. derog.* the Roman Catholic Church.
Comb.: **whore-hunt** *verb intrans.* (*arch.*) (of a man) engage in promiscuous sexual relations; **whoremaster** (*a*) *arch.* a sexually promiscuous man, a lecher; (*b*) a pimp; †**whoremasterly** *adjective* lecherous; **whoremistress** a brothel-keeper; **whoremonger** *arch.* a sexually promiscuous man, a lecher; **whore's bird** *arch.* an illegitimate child, a bastard (chiefly as a term of abuse); **whore's egg** *N. Amer.* a sea urchin; **whore-shop** *slang* a brothel.
▶ **B** *verb.* **1** *verb intrans.* (Of a man) engage in promiscuous sexual relations with prostitutes; (of a woman) engage in immoral or promiscuous sexual relations. LOE. ▶**b** *fig.* Pursue or seek *after* (something false, unworthy, or idolatrous). M16.
2 *verb trans.* Debauch (a woman); corrupt, deprave. Now *rare.* E17.
3 *verb trans.* Spend in whoring; get or bring by whoring. *rare.* L17.
■ **whorage** *noun* (*rare*) a group of whores L19. **whoredom** *noun* immoral or promiscuous sexual activity; in *pl.*, instances of such activity: ME. †**whorer** *noun* a sexually promiscuous man, a lecher M17–E18. **whoreship** *noun* (*joc.*, now *rare* or *obsolete*) (with possess. adjective, as ***her whoreship*** etc.) a mock title of respect given to a whore E17. **whorism** *noun* (*rare*) whoredom L16. **whory** *adjective* whorish L17.

whore-house /ˈhɔːhaʊs/ *noun.* Now chiefly *N. Amer.* ME.
[from WHORE *noun* + HOUSE *noun*¹.]
A brothel.
¶ Obsolete after L17; revived in 20.

whoreson /ˈhɔːs(ə)n/ *noun & adjective. arch.* ME.
[from WHORE *noun* + SON *noun*¹, after Anglo-Norman *fiz a putain.*]
▶ **A** *noun.* A bastard son; *gen.* a despicable man, a scoundrel. ME.
▶ **B** *attrib.* or as *adjective.* Vile, abominable, detestable. LME.

Whorfian /ˈwɔːfɪən/ *adjective.* M20.
[from *Whorf* (see below) + -IAN.]
Designating the views and theories of the American linguist Benjamin Lee Whorf (1897–1941); esp. in ***Whorfian hypothesis***, the theory that one's perception of the world is determined by the structure of one's native language. Cf. SAPIR–WHORF HYPOTHESIS.

whorish /ˈhɔːrɪʃ/ *adjective.* M16.
[from WHORE *noun* + -ISH¹.]
1 Having the character of a whore, sexually promiscuous; characteristic of a whore; lewd. M16.
2 *fig.* Corrupt; idolatrous. M16.

🕮 **1** D. WELCH The hideous picture of a . . whorish wife and an idiot baby. *Washington Post* Whorish come-ons in a riverside hamlet.

■ **whorishly** *adverb* M16. **whorishness** *noun* M16.

whorl /wɔːl, wəːl/ *noun & verb.* LME.
[App. var. of WHIRL *noun*, infl. by WHARVE *noun* and Dutch †*worvel, wervel.*]
▶ **A** *noun.* **1** A small fly-wheel fixed on the spindle of a spinning-wheel to maintain or regulate the speed; a small pulley by which the spindle is driven in a spinning-machine. LME.
2 A convolution, a coil; *spec.* each of the turns or convolutions of a spiral structure, esp. (ZOOLOGY) of the shell of a gastropod mollusc. L16.
3 BOTANY. A set of leaves, flowers, branches, etc., springing from the axis at the same level and encircling it; a verticil. Also (more fully ***floral whorl***), each of the sets of floral organs (*esp.* the petals and sepals) arranged concentrically round the receptacle. L17. ▶**b** ZOOLOGY. A set of radial or encircling parts or structures. *rare.* M19.
4 A complete circle in a fingerprint. L19.

🕮 **2** J. M. COETZEE The hairy whorl of his ear. W. STEGNER Currents stirred the pool into whorls.

Comb.: **whorl-flower** a Nepalese plant, sometimes cultivated, *Morina longifolia*, of the teasel family, having flowers in axillary whorls; **whorl-grass** (more fully ***water whorl-grass***) the grass *Catabrosa aquatica*, of north temperate regions, which has the branches of its panicle in whorls.
▶ **B 1** *verb intrans.* Form or imitate a whorl; spiral or move in a twisted convoluted fashion, whirl, swirl. Freq. *poet.* E19.
2 *verb trans.* Draw up by means of a whorl or pulley. *rare.* L19.
3 *verb trans.* Arrange in whorls or convolutions. *poet.* E20.
■ **whorled** *adjective* having or arranged in a whorl or whorls; (of leaves, flowers, etc.) verticillate; (of a shell etc.) convoluted, turbinate; ***whorled knotgrass***: see KNOTGRASS 2: L18.

whorlbat *noun* see WHIRLBAT.

whort /wəːt/ *noun. dial.* L16.
[Dial. var. of HURT *noun*³.]
= WHORTLEBERRY.

whortle /ˈwəːt(ə)l/ *noun.* L16.
[Abbreviation.]
= WHORTLEBERRY.

whortleberry /ˈwəːt(ə)lbəri/ *noun.* L16.
[Dial. var. of HURTLEBERRY.]
(The fruit of) the bilberry, *Vaccinium myrtillus*; (chiefly with specifying word) any of several other dwarf moorland shrubs of the genus *Vaccinium*.
red whortleberry: see RED *adjective.*

whose /huːz/ *possess. adjective* (in mod. usage also classed as a *determiner*) *& pronoun.*
[Old English *hwæs* genit. of *hwa* (masc.), *hwæt* (neut.) WHAT *pronoun*, with vowel lengthening and mutation in Middle English through influence of WHO, WHOM.]
▶ **A** *attrib. adjective.* **I** *interrog. adjective.* **1** Of what person or persons? OE.

🕮 **1** J. CONRAD 'What's his name?' 'Whose name?' V. WOOLF A voice asserted itself. Whose voice it was no one knew.

▶ **II** *rel. adjective.* **2** Subjective genitive. ▶**a** Of whom; belonging or pertaining to whom. ME. ▶**b** Of which; belonging or pertaining to which. Usu. replaced by *the—of which*, except where an unacceptably clumsy construction would result. LME.
3 Objective genitive: of whom, of which. Now *rare.* LME.

4 With ellipsis of antecedent: the or any person whose. Now *rare* or *obsolete*. LME.

> 📖 **2a** I. MURDOCH The blond youngster, whose name is Leo. DAY LEWIS A curate . . whose income was about £150 a year. **b** M. MCLUHAN 'Credit' whose natural tendency is towards debt. *New Yorker* It was clearly a good idea whose time had come. **4** G. HERBERT Whose house is of glasse, must not throw stones at another.

▶ **B** *pronoun.* [Absol. use of the adjective.]

1 *interrog.* The one or ones belonging to what person or persons? ME.

2 *rel.* The one or ones belonging to whom. E17.

> 📖 **1** S. CISNEROS 'Whose is this?' Mrs Price says. **2** AV *Gen.* 38:25 The man whose these are.

Comb.: **whosesoever**, **whosever** *possess. adjectives & pronouns* (*a*) *adjective* of whomever; (*b*) *pronoun* the one or ones of whomever.

whoso /ˈhuːsəʊ/ *pronoun. arch.* ME.
[from WHO *pronoun* + SO *adverb*, reduced from Old English *swā hwā swā* so who so.]
1 = WHOEVER 1. ME.
2 = WHOEVER 2. ME.

whosoever /huːsəʊˈɛvə/ *pronoun & postpositive adjective.* Also (*poet.*) **-e'er** /-ˈɛː/. ME.
[from prec. + EVER.]
▶ **A** *pronoun.* **1** = WHOEVER 1. ME.
2 = WHOEVER 2. LME.
3 Any one at all. Cf. WHATEVER *pronoun* 4. Now *rare* or *obsolete*. L16.
▶ **B** *postpositive adjective.* Qualifying a preceding personal noun or *any*: = WHATEVER *adjective* 4. Long *rare* or *obsolete*. L16.

†**whosomever** *pronoun.* LME–M17.
[from WHO *pronoun* + SOMEVER.]
= WHOEVER.

> 📖 SHAKES. *Tr. & Cr.* Who some ever you take him to be, he is Ajax.

†**whrinny** *verb* see WHINNY *verb*.

whuff /wʌf/ *verb intrans. & trans. rare.* L19.
[Imit.]
Make or utter with a sound as of a forcible blast of breath or wind.
■ **whuffle** *verb intrans.* whuff E20

whummel *verb & noun* var. of WHEMMEL.

whump /wʌmp/ *verb, noun, & interjection. colloq.* L19.
[Imit.]
▶ **A** *verb.* **1** *verb intrans.* Make or move or knock with a dull thudding sound. L19.
2 *verb trans.* Strike heavily or with a dull thudding sound. L20.
▶ **B** *noun & interjection.* (Repr.) a dull thudding sound, as of a body landing heavily. E20.

whup /wʌp/ *verb trans. colloq.* Chiefly *N. Amer.* Infl. **-pp-**. L19.
[Var. of WHIP *verb*.]
Beat; thrash. Also, defeat convincingly.

> 📖 M. FRUTKIN The natives of this land don't know a rifle from a dowsing stick . . . Sometimes I'm ashamed to be whupping them. R. KENAN Paw and Hugh went out and I figured they was going to the woodpile so Paw could whup Hugh good.

†**whurl** *verb intrans.* L15–L18.
[Imit.]
Make a roaring or rumbling noise; purr.

whush /wʌʃ/ *verb intrans.* Now *dial.* L16.
[Imit.]
Of the wind, water, etc.: make or move with a soft rushing sound.

why /wʌɪ/ *adverb, conjunction, noun, interjection, & verb.*
[Old English *hwī*, *hwȳ* instr. of *hwæt* WHAT corresp. to Old Saxon *hwī*, Old Norse *hví*, from Germanic from Indo-European locative form of base of WHO, WHAT (cf. Greek (Doric) *pei* where).]
▶ **A** *adverb.* **I** *interrog.* **1** For what reason; from what cause or motive; for what purpose. OE.
2 Used with the negative form of the simple present tense in a direct question, to express a positive suggestion. M20.

> 📖 **1** R. LEHMANN It turned into a . . celebration, I don't know why. DAY LEWIS Why didn't you stop him? I. MURDOCH Why did you leave Russia? J. KOSINSKI Chance did not understand why she laughed. *ellipt.*: F. HOYLE Why the air of great solemnity? **2** DODIE SMITH Why don't I drive you over to hear it?

▶ **II** *rel. adverb & conjunction.* **3** On account of which, because of which, for which. Chiefly after *reason*. ME.
4 The reason for which. E17.

> 📖 **3** R. MACAULAY Both saw every reason why they should make a success of life. **4** N. COWARD *Victor* Do you love me? *Amanda* Of course, that's why I'm here. E. BOWEN She had never cared . . for London, which was why she'd put pressure on him to retire.

▶ **B** *noun.* Pl. **whys**.
1 A reason, a cause; an explanation. Now only with ref. to something specified, and with conscious allusion to the interrog. use. ME.
2 A question as to the reason for something; a problem, an enigma. M16.

> 📖 **1** W. C. WILLIAMS She . . had come up to find out the why of the festivities. **2** H. JACOBSON Who can explain the whys and wherefores of attraction between the sexes?

▶ **C** *interjection.* **1** Expr. of surprise, esp. surprised discovery or recognition. E16.
2 Emphasizing a following statement, expr. impatience, objection, or reflection. M16.
†**3** As an emphasized call or summons, expr. impatience. *rare* (Shakes.). Only in L16.

> 📖 **1** G. VIDAL 'Do you play bridge?' 'Why yes,' said Philip. L. GARFIELD 'Why, it's charming, charming,' twittered Laughing Lady. **2** W. GOLDING If he had more savage wishes why they had been common enough in the world. B. DUFFY Why, it would have been enough to unhinge anyone.

Phrases: ***know the reason why***: see KNOW *verb*. **why, so!** *arch.* expr. content, acquiescence, or relief. **why so?** on what grounds? for what reason or purpose? See also FORWHY.
Comb.: **whydunit** *colloq.* [after WHODUNIT] a story, play, etc., about the detection of the motive for a crime etc.; **whyever** *adverb* (*colloq.*) (*a*) *rel.* for whatever reason; (*b*) *interrog.* (also as two words) used with emphatic force in place of *why* in a question implying perplexity or surprise; **why-not** (now *rare* or *obsolete*) (*a*) an argument which attempts to leave the opponent without a reply; (*b*) ***at a why-not***, at an advantage.

▶ **D** *verb intrans.* Ask the question 'why?'; ask for an explanation. Chiefly as ***whying*** *verbal noun*. E20.

> 📖 D. H. LAWRENCE Once you start whying, there's no end to it.

■ **whyness** *noun* that which causes a thing to be as it is; the essential reason for something: L19.

whydah /ˈwɪdə/ *noun.* Also **whidah**. L18.
[*Ouidah*, a town in Benin, W. Africa. Cf. WIDOW-BIRD.]
Any of various African weaver-birds having males with predominantly black plumage and very long tail feathers; *spec.* (*a*) a parasitic weaver of the genus *Vidua* and subfamily Viduinae (also called ***widow-bird***); (*b*) a true weaver of the genus *Euplectes* (now usu. ***widow-bird***). Also ***whydah bird***.

WI *abbreviation.*
1 West Indies.
2 Wisconsin. *US*.
3 Women's Institute.

wibbly-wobbly /wɪblɪˈwɒblɪ/ *adjective. colloq.* (orig. *dial.*). E20.
[Redupl. of WOBBLY *adjective* with vowel variation.]
Wobbling badly, showing great unsteadiness.

Wicca /ˈwɪkə/ *noun.* M20.
[Repr. Old English *wicca*: see WITCH *noun*[1].]
The practices and religious cult of modern witchcraft.
■ **Wiccan** *noun & adjective* (a follower or practitioner) of Wicca L20.

wich /wɪtʃ/ *noun. local* (now *Hist.*). Also **wych**. OE.
[App. a differentiated var. of WICK *noun*[2]. Cf. the place-names of (former) salt-making towns *Droitwich* (formerly *Wich*), *Nantwich*, *Northwich*.]
A salt-works, salt-pit, or brine-spring in the salt-manufacturing district of Cheshire and neighbouring parts; in *pl.*, the salt-making towns of these parts.

wichert /ˈwɪtʃət/ *noun. local.* E20.
[Origin uncertain: perh. repr. a local pronunc. of 'white earth'.]
A variety of chalk marl subsoil found near the Chilterns in Buckinghamshire, which is mixed with chopped straw and used for making walls.

Wichita /ˈwɪtʃɪtɔː/ *noun & adjective.* M19.
[Osage *wicita* or from a related name.]
▶ **A** *noun.* Pl. **-s**, same. A member of an Indian people of southern central N. America (now Oklahoma, formerly also Kansas and Texas); the language of this people. M19.
▶ **B** *attrib.* or as *adjective*. Of or pertaining to the Wichitas or their language. L19.

wichuraiana /wɪˌtʃʊrʌɪˈɑːnə/ *noun.* E20.
[mod. Latin (see below), from Max Ernst *Wichura* (1817–66), German botanist.]
Any of several rambling roses, usu. with small glossy leaves and clustered flowers, derived from *Rosa wichuraiana*, a prostrate evergreen rose of eastern Asia. Also more fully ***wichuraiana rose***.

wick /wɪk/ *noun*[1].
[Old English *wēoc* (in *candelwēoc*), *wēoce*, corresp. to Middle Dutch *wiecke* (Dutch *wiek*), Middle Low German *wēke*, Old High German *wiohha* (German *Wieche*), of unkn. origin.]
1 A strip or thread of fibrous or spongy material in a lamp, candle, cigarette-lighter, etc., which supplies fuel to the flame. OE. ▸**b** The material from which wicks are made; wicking. LME.
2 MEDICINE. A gauze strip inserted in a wound to drain it. M17.

> 📖 **1** P. ABRAHAMS Mrs Bruce turned up the wick of the lamp.

Phrases: ***dip one's wick***: see DIP *verb*. **get on a person's wick** *colloq.* get on a person's nerves, irritate a person.

wick /wɪk/ *noun*[2].
[Old English *wīc* = Old Frisian *wīk*, Old Saxon *wīc* (Dutch *wijk* district, ward), Old High German *wīh* (German in *Weichbild* municipal area), Gothic *weihs* village, prob. from Germanic from Latin *vicus* row of houses, street, village, cogn. with Greek *oikos* house.]
†**1** A residence, a dwelling-place. OE–ME.
†**2** A town, a village, a hamlet. OE–E17.
3 A farm, *esp.* an outlying farm of a village or manor; *spec.* a dairy farm. Now only in place-names. OE.
†**4** An enclosed piece of ground, a close. *local*. ME–E19.
3 ***Ardington Wick, Eton Wick, Hackney Wick***, etc.

wick /wɪk/ *noun*[3]. Now *dial.* ME.
[Old Norse *vik* as in *munnvik* (Danish *mundvig*) corner of the mouth, from Germanic base also of next.]
The corner of the mouth or eye.

wick /wɪk/ *noun*[4]. *Scot. & north.* M17.
[Old Norse *vik* fem. (in place-names), whence app. also Middle Low German *wīk* (Low German *wiek*, *wicke*), Middle Dutch *wijck*, Frisian *wik*, from Germanic base meaning 'bend'.]
An inlet, a small bay.

wick /wɪk/ *adjective*[1]. *obsolete* exc. *Scot. & dial.* ME.
[Prob. formed as WICKED *adjective*[1].]
= WICKED *adjective*[1] 1, 2.

wick /wɪk/ *adjective*[2]. *north.* M18.
[Alt.]
= QUICK *adjective*.

wick /wɪk/ *verb*[1] *& noun*[5]. L18.
[Origin unkn. Cf. INWICK, OUTWICK.]
CURLING. ▶**A** *verb intrans.* Make a shot so as to strike the inside or outside of another stone and move it. L18.
▶ **B** *noun.* Such a shot. E19.

wick /wɪk/ *verb*[2]. M20.
[from WICK *noun*[1].]
1 *verb intrans.* Of a liquid: migrate by capillary action, esp. through absorbent cloth. M20.
2 *verb trans. & intrans.* Absorb or draw off (liquid) by capillary action. (Foll. by *away*.) M20.

> 📖 **2** *Footloose* The pile on the inside wicks moisture . . off the skin so keeping the wearer warm and dry.

-wick /-wɪk/ *suffix.*
[Old English *wīce*.]
Forming nouns from names of officials etc. meaning 'the post or jurisdiction of such an official', as in ***bailiwick, Herdwick, sheriffwick***.

wicked /ˈwɪkɪd/ *adjective*[1], *noun, & adverb.* ME.
[Prob. from Old English *wicca* (see WITCH *noun*[1]) + -ED[2]. Cf. WICK *adjective*[1].]
▶ **A** *adjective.* **1** Marked by, or having a character disposed to, serious and wilful wrongdoing (freq. cruel and injurious acts); morally depraved. Also *hyperbol.*, shamefully extravagant or sensuous. ME. ▸**b** Spiteful, malicious, ill-tempered; (of an animal) vicious. LME.
2 a Harmful, trying, unpleasant; (of a road) difficult, impassable (now *US*). Formerly also, (of a wound) malignant. Now chiefly *dial.* or *colloq.* ME. ▸**b** Of bad quality; poor. *arch.* LME.
3 Playfully mischievous; roguish. E17.
4 a Dauntingly skilful; mean, formidable. *slang* (orig. *US*). E20. ▸**b** Excellent, great, wonderful. *slang*. L20.

> 📖 **1** DENNIS POTTER The boy might have wicked thoughts, like wanting his father to die. R. MAYER Children were . . terrified by Snow White's wicked stepmother. *Heritage Outlook* Buildings towards which the wicked developer is driving his bulldozer. A. LAMBERT She thought lesbianism was unnatural and wicked. **Wicked Bible** an edition of 1631, in which the seventh commandment was misprinted 'Thou shalt commit adultery'. **b** JAS. HOGG It's hard to gar a wicked cout leave off flinging. G. W. TARGET I've got a wicked tongue and I've probably been unfair. **2a** G. A. SMITH Tents may be carried away by wicked gusts. *Newmarket Journal* I didn't sleep a wink. The pain was wicked. *Times* To work with he was wicked He was such a perfectionist. *Amateur Gardening* Pyracanthas . . possess rather wicked prickles. **b** HOR. WALPOLE They talk wicked French. **3** *She* Wicked impersonations of Margaret Thatcher. **4a** SCOTT FITZGERALD Tell 'em to play 'Admiration'! . . Phoebe and I are going to shake a wicked calf. **b** *Time Out* I've been to . . Acid House parties. We have a wicked time but never . . take any drugs.

▶ **B** *absol.* as *noun.* **1** *The* class of wicked people. LME.
†**2** A wicked person. L15–M19.
1 no peace for the wicked, no rest for the wicked [*Isaiah* 48:22, 57:21] (freq. *joc.*) no rest or tranquillity for the speaker; incessant activity, responsibility, or work.
▶ **C** *adverb.* Wickedly; fiercely, savagely, furiously; very badly, terribly. Now *colloq.* LME.

> 📖 R. BANKS My father laid into me something wicked.

■ **wickedly** *adverb* ME. **wickedness** *noun* wicked character, conduct, or speech; a wicked act: ME.

wicked /wɪkt/ *adjective*[2]. E16.
[from WICK *noun*[1] + -ED[2].]
Of a candle etc.: having a wick. Usu. in comb., as ***long-wicked***.

wicker /ˈwɪkə/ *noun, adjective, & verb*. ME.
[Of E. Scandinavian origin (cf. Swedish *viker*, Danish *viger* willow), from base of Swedish *vika* to bend (cf. Old English *wīcan* give way, collapse, and WEAK *adjective & noun*).]
▶ **A** *noun*. **1** Pliant twigs, usu. of willow, plaited together in basketry; wickerwork. ME.
2 A pliant twig esp. as used for making baskets etc. Usu. in *pl.* (= sense 1). LME. ▸**b** Such a twig forming part of the living plant. Now *rare*. E16.
3 A wickerwork basket, cradle, chair, etc. L16.
Comb.: **wickerwork** = sense 1 above.
▶ **B** *adjective*. Made, consisting of, or covered with wicker. E16.
▶ **C** *verb trans*. Furnish, cover, or enclose with wicker. Chiefly as **WICKERED** *adjective*. E16.
▪ **wickered** *adjective* encased in or made of wickerwork L16.

wicket /ˈwɪkɪt/ *noun*. ME.
[Anglo-Norman, Old Northern French *wiket* = Old & mod. French *guichet*, usu. referred to the Germanic base appearing in Old Norse *víkja* to move, to turn (Swedish *vika*, Danish *vige*).]
1 A small door or gate made in, or placed beside, a large one, for entrance and exit when the large one is closed. Also, any small gate for pedestrians, as at the entrance of a field. ME.
2 A small opening or grille in a door, wall, etc. Now chiefly (*US*), an opening in the window of a ticket office or cashier's desk, closed by a grille or sliding panel. ME.
3 CRICKET. A framework of three stumps, fixed upright in the ground and surmounted by (formerly) a bail or (now) two bails (**BAIL** *noun*[2] 2b), forming the structure at which the bowler aims the ball and which the batsman defends. L17. ▸**b** A wicket as representing an individual batsman's turn at batting. With ordinal numeral: the player who goes in to bat at the fall of the designated wicket. M18. ▸**c** The ground between the wickets, esp. in respect of its condition; the pitch. M19.
4 A croquet hoop. *US* (now *Hist.*). M19.

> 🕮 **3** ***break the wicket***: see **BREAK** *verb*. ***hit wicket***: see **HIT** *verb*. ***keep wicket***: see **KEEP** *verb*. **b** G. BOYCOTT We lost those early wickets .. to shrewd, professional bowling. *Cricketer* An extraordinary day's cricket continued with five more wickets going down in 30 overs. **first-wicket partnership** (& with other numerals) the pair of batsmen batting before the first etc. wicket falls. **take a wicket** (of a bowler) dismiss a batsman, get a batsman out. **win by three wickets** (& with other numerals) win with three etc. batsmen not yet out or still available to play. **c** ***soft wicket***: see **SOFT** *adjective*. ***sticky wicket***: see **STICKY** *adjective*[2] 2.

Comb.: **wicket-gate** = sense 1 above.

wicket-keeper /ˈwɪkɪtkiːpə/ *noun*. E18.
[from prec. + **KEEPER** *noun*.]
CRICKET. The player on the fielding side positioned just behind the batsman's wicket to stop any balls that pass it, to stump the batsman, etc.
▪ **wicket-keep** *noun & verb* (*a*) *noun* (*colloq.*) = **WICKET-KEEPER**; (*b*) *verb intrans*. act as wicket-keeper: M19. **wicket-keeping** *noun* the occupation of a wicket-keeper E19.

Wickham /ˈwɪkəm/ *noun*. L19.
[Prob. from Dr T. C. *Wickham*, Hampshire angler.]
ANGLING. In full ***Wickham's fancy***. A kind of artificial fly.

wicking /ˈwɪkɪŋ/ *noun*. M19.
[from **WICK** *noun*[1] + -ING[1].]
Material for making wicks; cord or tape of cotton or other fibre, to be cut into lengths for wicks.

wickiup /ˈwɪkɪʌp/ *noun*. *US*. Also **wickyup**. M19.
[Algonquian (Menominee *wikiop*), perh. a var. of *wikiwam* **WIGWAM**.]
A rough hut consisting of a frame covered with brushwood, used by nomadic peoples in the west and south-west; *colloq.* any small hut or shanty.

wickless /ˈwɪklɪs/ *adjective*. L19.
[from **WICK** *noun*[1] + -LESS.]
That burns without a wick; not fitted with a wick.

wickner /ˈwɪknə/ *noun*. *obsolete* exc. *local*.
[Old English *wīcnere*, from *wīcnian*, from *wīce* office, function (see -WICK).]
A steward, a bailiff; *spec.* an official who collects rents and fines due to the lord of a manor.

wickyup *noun* var. of **WICKIUP**.

Wicliffian /wɪˈklɪfɪən/ *noun & adjective*. Also **-ifian**. Orig. †**Wicleuian**. L16.
[medieval Latin *Wyclyvianus*, with later assim. to forms of the name *Wycliffe*: see **WYCLIFFITE**, -IAN.]
ECCLESIASTICAL HISTORY. ▶†**A** *noun*. = **WYCLIFFITE** *noun*. L16–E18.
▶ **B** *adjective*. Of or pertaining to (the teaching of) John Wycliffe or his followers. E18.

Wicliffist, **Wicliffite** *nouns & adjectives* vars. of **WYCLIFFIST**, **WYCLIFFITE**.

wicopy /ˈwɪkəpi/ *noun*. *US*. L18.
[Algonquian: cf. Cree *wi:kopiy* inner bark of the linden.]
The leatherwood, *Dirca palustris*. Also, the basswood, *Tilia americana*.

Widal /vɪˈdɑːl, w-/ *noun*. L19.
[G. F. *Widal* (1862–1929), French physician.]
MEDICINE. Used ***attrib.*** and in ***possess.*** to designate an agglutination test for typhoid and other Salmonella infections.

widdendream /ˈwɪd(ə)ndriːm/ *noun*. Long *obsolete* exc. *Scot.* Also (now *literary*) **widdrim** /ˈwɪdrɪm/.
[Old English *wōdendrēam*, formed as **WOOD** *adjective*[2] + **DREAM** *noun*[1].]
A state of great mental confusion; a wild fit. Chiefly in ***in a widdendream***, in a daze; all of a sudden.
¶ Not recorded after **LME** until (*Scot.*) M18.

widdershins /ˈwɪdəʃɪnz/ *adverb & adjective*. Orig. & chiefly *Scot.* Also **wither-** /ˈwɪðə-/, (as adjective) **-shin**. E16.
[Middle Low German *weddersin(ne)s* from Middle High German *widersinnes*, from *wider-* counter- (cf. **WITHER** *adjective & adverb*) + genit. of *sin* direction, way. In sense A.2 assoc. (through Scot. pronunc.) with **SUN** *noun*[1].]
▶ **A** *adverb*. **1** In a direction opposite to the usual one; the wrong way round. Freq. in ***stand widdershins***, ***start widdershins***, (of hair) stand on end. E16.
2 In a direction contrary to the apparent course of the sun (considered unlucky or associated with occult rites); anticlockwise. M16.
▶ **B** *adjective*. Moving etc. in a direction contrary to the apparent course of the sun; unlucky, relating to the occult. M18.

widdiful /ˈwɪdɪfʊl, -f(ə)l/ *noun & adjective*. *Scot.* E16.
[from **WIDDY** *noun*[1] + -**FUL**, lit. 'person who would fill the hangman's noose'.]
▶ **A** *noun*. A person who deserves hanging; a scamp, a rascal. E16.
▶ **B** *adjective*. Fit for the hangman's noose; rascally. M16.

widdle /ˈwɪd(ə)l/ *noun*[1]. *Scot. & north.* L18.
[Origin unkn.]
(A) commotion, (a) bustle; (a) struggle, contention.

widdle /ˈwɪd(ə)l/ *noun*[2]. *colloq.* M20.
[formed as **WIDDLE** *verb*[2].]
An act of urinating.

widdle /ˈwɪd(ə)l/ *verb*[1] *intrans*. *Scot. & north.* Also redupl. **widdle-waddle** /wɪd(ə)lˈwɒd(ə)l/. M17.
[Alt. of **WADDLE** *verb*.]
Move with slow, waddling, or irregular movement; *fig.* progress with difficulty.

widdle /ˈwɪd(ə)l/ *verb*[2] *intrans*. *colloq.* M20.
[Alt. of **PIDDLE** *verb*. Cf. **TIDDLE** *verb*[2].]
Urinate.

widdrim *noun* see **WIDDENDREAM**.

widdy /ˈwɪdi/ *noun*[1]. Chiefly *Scot.* Also **widdie**, **woodie** /ˈwʊdi/, & other vars. LME.
[Scot. & north. var. of **WITHY** *noun*.]
1 A band or rope, *spec.* one made of intertwined osiers. LME.
2 The hangman's rope. Also [perh. by erron. association with **WOOD** *noun*[1]], the gallows. LME.
†**3** A certain quantity of iron (perh. orig. a bundle bound with a 'widdy'). L15–E17.
2 cheat the widdy escape hanging.

widdy /ˈwɪdi/ *noun*[2]. *dial.* M19.
[Abbreviation.]
= next.

widdy-widdy-way /ˌwɪdɪwɪdɪˈweɪ/ *noun*. *dial.* M19.
[A rhyme used during the game.]
A children's chasing game, a form of tag.

wide /wʌɪd/ *noun*. ME.
[Absol. use of next.]
†**1** Width, breadth. Only in ME.
2 †**a** The open sea. Only in ME. ▸**b** *gen.* A wide expanse. Chiefly *poet.* M19.
3 CRICKET. A ball bowled wide of the wicket, counting one against the bowler's side. M19.
Phrases: **to the wide** [alt. of *to the world*] *slang* (after an adjective) utterly and completely, esp. in ***broke to the wide*** s.v. **BROKE** *adjective* 2, ***dead to the wide*** s.v. **DEAD** *adjective*.

wide /wʌɪd/ *adjective*.
[Old English *wīd* = Old Frisian, Old Saxon *wīd*, Old High German *wīt* (Dutch *wijd*, German *weit*), Old Norse *víðr*, from Germanic, of unkn. origin.]
▶ **I 1** Spacious, extensive. Now usu., having great horizontal extent; *esp.* as a conventional epithet (chiefly *literary*) of words denoting a large area, as *earth, sea, world*, etc. OE. ▸**b** Of a garment etc.: capacious; large and loose. *obsolete* exc. *dial.* in ***wide coat***, an overcoat. ME. ▸†**c** Large, substantial. ME–M16.
2 Extending over or affecting a large area; far-reaching. Chiefly *poet.* OE.
3 *fig.* Having a large range or scope; embracing a great number or variety of people or things; extensive, comprehensive. M16. ▸**b** Of opinions or the person holding them: liberal, broad, unprejudiced. E19.

> 🕮 **1** COVERDALE *Prov.* 21:9 It is better to dwell in a corner .. then with a braulinge woman in a wyde house. M. MOORCOCK The train moved into wide, horizonless steppe-land. *Commercials* The dolphins hadn't been brought up in the big wide underwater world. **3** J. RUSKIN I want a definition of art wide enough to include all its varieties of aim. J. AGATE F. Y.'s interests are very wide, and he can write equally well about church organs and flying. *Economist* The managers have a wide discretion in their investment policy. S. BELLOW He was a wide reader. **b** A. F. DOUGLAS-HOME He was credited with a wide and liberal outlook on human affairs.

▶ **II 4** Measuring a considerable distance from side to side; broad (opp. ***narrow***). Also, extending throughout a specified area (only as 2nd elem. of comb., as ***country-wide***, ***nationwide***, ***worldwide***, etc.). OE.
5 Having a specified transverse measurement; (a specified extent) in breadth. OE.
6 Now chiefly of the eyes: opened widely. E16. ▸**b** PHONETICS. Of a vowel sound: pronounced with the vocal muscles relaxed. Opp. **NARROW** *adjective* 7a. M19.

> 🕮 **4** E. O'NEILL They make wide detours to avoid the spot. *Listener* A coffee-table book, with .. wide margins. R. TRAVERS He sent them further afield, covering a wider area. G. VIDAL The .. palace .. is approached by a wide straight avenue. **5** *Skin Diver* The ship was 120 feet long and 30 feet wide. **6** KEATS Many a door was wide. J. STEINBECK Juana stared at him with wide unfrightened eyes.

▶ **III 7** †**a** Situated at a great or specified distance from something. Usu. foll. by *of*. LME–M19. ▸**b** *fig.* Far (apart) in nature, character, opinion, etc.; not in accordance, divergent. Foll. by *from, of*. Now *rare*. M16.
8 Deviating from the point aimed at or the direct course; CRICKET (of a ball) bowled too far to one side of the wicket for the batsman to strike it (cf. **WIDE** *noun* 3). Freq. *fig.*, foll. by *of* or (now *rare*) *from*, esp. in ***wide of the mark*** below. M16.
9 Of an interval, distinction, etc.: extending far between limits; existing between two things which are far apart. L16.
10 Going beyond bounds of restraint, moderation, etc.; excessive; *spec.* (now *slang*) loose, immoral. L16.
11 [Short for *wide awake*.] Shrewd, wary, alert; *esp.* skilled in sharp practice, engaging in shady dealings. (Cf. ***wide boy*** below.) *slang*. L19.

> 🕮 **7a** O. HEYWOOD A place .. 4 miles wide of St. Albans. **b** J. BENTHAM My own notions .. were too wide of the notions prevalent among lawyers. **8** G. BERKELEY Your Comment must be wide of the Author's meaning. **9** J. RUSKIN There is a wide difference between elementary .. and superficial knowledge. *Independent* The gap is surely too wide to bridge. **10** *Daily News* Prices asked are very wide, and are beyond the values that merchants are disposed to give. **11** *Church Times* Local councillors .. are .. thought of as wide, power-seeking or pompous.

Phrases: ***all wool and a yard wide***: see **WOOL** *noun* 2. ***give a wide berth to***: see **BERTH** *noun* 1a. **wide of the mark** not to the point, irrelevant; mistaken. ***wide open spaces***: see ***open space*** (b) s.v. **OPEN** *adjective*.
Special collocations & comb.: **wide-angle** *adjective* having a wider field of view than the standard. **wide area network** a network similar to a local area network but joining computers that are further apart (e.g. in different towns); abbreviation ***WAN***. **wide-band** *adjective* having a wide band of frequencies or wave-lengths. **wide-bodied** *adjective* (of a large jet aeroplane) having a wide fuselage. **wide-body** *adjective* = ***wide-bodied*** above. **wide boy** *slang* a man who lives by his wits, esp. dishonestly; a petty criminal, a spiv. **wide brown land** (*Austral.*) the country of Australia. **wide-cut** *adjective* (OIL INDUSTRY) involving or produced by fractional distillation over a wide temperature range. **wide-eyed** *adjective* having the eyes wide open with amazement; *fig.* naive, innocent. **wideout** = ***wide receiver*** below. **wide receiver** AMER. FOOTBALL a pass receiver positioned several yards to the side of an offensive formation. **wide-scale** *adjective* that occurs on a wide scale; extensive, widespread. **wide screen** a cinema screen which presents a wide field of vision in proportion to its height. **wide world** all *the* world great as it is.

wide /wʌɪd/ *adverb*.
[Old English *wīde*, from *wīd* **WIDE** *adjective*.]
1 Over a large area; widely, extensively. Chiefly *poet.* exc. in ***far and wide*** s.v. **FAR** *adverb* & in comb. OE.
2 With a large space or spaces between; far apart. OE. ▸**b** Loosely apart; so as not to remain close or in contact. L18.
3 To the full extent. Chiefly with *open*. See also ***wide open*** below. OE.
4 At, to, or from a great or specified distance; far off. Now *dial.* OE.
5 At a distance to one side; away from the target or the proper course. (Foll. by *of*.) M16.

📖 **1** G. W. Knight He welcomes disorder and confusion, would let them range wide over the earth. ***wide-reaching***, ***wide-stretched***, ***wide-sweeping***, etc. **2** J. Steinbeck Lifted it with the tips of thumb and forefinger and spread the other three fingers wide. E. O'Neill Light-brown eyes, set wide apart. **b** Shelley Shaking wide thy yellow hair. **3** A. Carter He opened his eyes wide as if surprised. H. Secombe Sid spread his arms wide. **4** N. Hawthorne Not only in this district, but wide away. **5** Rider Haggard [He] fired . . but the ball went wide. C. N. Parkinson Water from the broken skylight drips wide of the bucket placed to catch it.

Phrases & comb.: **wide awake**: see WIDE-AWAKE. **wide open** (*a*) fully open, open to the full extent; (*b*) exposed to attack, unprotected (foll. by *to*); freq. *fig.*, esp. in ***leave oneself wide open***, ***lay oneself wide open***; (*c*) (of an issue or case) not resolved or decided. **wide-ranging** *adjective* covering an extensive range.

wide-awake /ˈwʌɪdəweɪk/ *adjective & noun*. Also (as pred. adjective) **wide awake** /wʌɪd əˈweɪk/. E19.
[from WIDE *adverb* + AWAKE *adjective*.]
▶ **A** *adjectival phr.* **1** Awake with the eyes wide open; fully awake. Usu. *pred.* E19.
2 *fig.* Thoroughly vigilant or alert; sharp-witted, knowing. *colloq.* (orig. *slang*). M19.
3 ***wide-awake hat***, a soft felt hat with broad brim and low crown [punningly so named as not having a nap]. M19.
▶ **B** *noun*. **1** A wide-awake hat (see sense A.3 above). M19.
2 The sooty tern, *Sterna fuscata*, so called from its cry. L19.
■ **wide-aˈwakeness** *noun* M19.

widely /ˈwʌɪdli/ *adverb*. L16.
[from WIDE *adjective* + -LY².]
1 Over or through a wide area; in or to various places. L16.
2 With, at, or by a wide interval or intervals (of space or time); far apart. L16.
3 Over a wide range; in relation to many or various things, subjects, cases, etc.; extensively. L17.
4 To a large extent, considerably; *esp.* so as to be far apart in nature, character, etc. Formerly also, so as to be wide of the mark. L17.

📖 **1** E. Waugh A man of many interests . . well read, widely travelled. **2** Dickens Widely staring eyes. **3** C. P. Snow I began to read widely outside science. O. Manning Nowadays we do not use the word so widely. **4** M. Edgeworth Negligence and inhumanity are widely different.

widen /ˈwʌɪd(ə)n/ *verb*. E17.
[from WIDE *adjective* + -EN⁵.]
†**1** *verb trans.* Open wide. *rare*. Only in E17.
2 *verb trans.* Make wide or wider, broaden; *fig.* extend, make more comprehensive. M17.
3 *verb intrans.* Become wide or wider (*lit.* & *fig.*). M17.

📖 **1** M. Drayton The gates thus widen'd . . Their ample entrance to the English gaue. **2** C. Milne It was man . . who tramped out the tracks he needed and later widened them into roads. P. Ackroyd Dickens decided to widen his attack from educational matters alone. **3** I. Murdoch The river widened into a pool. E. Fromm The gap between rich and poor nations has ever widened.

■ **widener** *noun* a person who or thing which widens; an apparatus for widening something, *spec.* a drill constructed to bore a hole of greater diameter than its own: L17.

wideness /ˈwʌɪdnɪs/ *noun*. Now *rare*. OE.
[from WIDE *adjective* + -NESS.]
1 Transverse measurement; diameter, breadth. Also, extent of opening, distance apart. *obsolete* exc. *dial.* OE.
2 Large extension, spaciousness; a vast expanse. ME.
3 Great extent from side to side. M16.
4 *fig.* Width of range; extensiveness, comprehensiveness. M16.
¶ Replaced in general use by WIDTH.

widespread /ˈwʌɪdsprɛd, -ˈsprɛd/ *adjective*. E18.
[from WIDE *adverb* + SPREAD *ppl adjective*.]
1 Distributed over a wide area; extensively diffused or disseminated. E18.
2 Extended over a wide space; broad. M18.

wide-where /ˈwʌɪdwɛː/ *adverb*. Long *arch.*
[from WIDE *adverb* + WHERE *adverb*.]
Over a wide area; far and wide.

widgeon *noun* var. of WIGEON.

widger /ˈwɪdʒə/ *noun*. M20.
[A word from a nonsense definition in a series of memory tests.]
A small spatular gardening tool used to transplant seedlings.

widget /ˈwɪdʒɪt/ *noun*. Orig. *US*. E20.
[Prob. alt. of GADGET.]
1 A gadget, a mechanical contrivance; *esp.* a small manufactured item. *colloq.* E20.
2 COMPUTING. A component of a user interface which operates in a particular way. L20.
3 A plastic device, used in some beer cans and bottles, which introduces nitrogen into the beer giving it a creamy head in imitation of draught beer. L20.

widgie /ˈwɪdʒi/ *noun*. *Austral. & NZ*. Now *Hist.* M20.
[Origin unkn.]
An Australasian Teddy girl. Cf. BODGIE.

widish /ˈwʌɪdɪʃ/ *adverb & adjective*. L18.
[from WIDE *adverb, adjective* + -ISH¹.]
▶ **A** *adverb*. Somewhat widely. L18.
▶ **B** *adjective*. Somewhat wide. M19.

Widmanstätten /ˈwɪdmənʃtɛtən, ˈvɪt-/ *noun*. M19.
[Alois Josep *Widmanstätten* (1754–1849), Austrian mineralogist.]
Used *attrib.* with ref. to an orderly pattern of intersecting bands seen in some meteorites and steels when a polished section is etched, attributed to the crystallization or precipitation of a new solid phase along the crystal planes of a parent solid phase.

widow /ˈwɪdəʊ/ *noun*¹.
[Old English *widewe*, *wuduwe* = Old Frisian *widwe*, Old Saxon *widowa*, Old High German *wituwa* (Dutch *weduwe*, *weef*, German *Witwe*), Gothic *widuwō*, adjective formation of Indo-European base repr. by Sanskrit *vidhavā* widow, Greek *ēitheos* unmarried man, Latin *viduus* bereft, void, widowed.]
1 A woman who has lost her husband by death and has not married again. Formerly (now *arch.* & *dial.*) prefixed as a title before the surname of such a woman. OE. ▸**b** A female animal, esp. a hen bird, that has lost its mate. ME. ▸**c** (More fully ***widow bewitched***) a wife separated from or deserted by her husband (now *dial.*). Now chiefly (*colloq.*) as 2nd elem. of comb., a wife whose husband devotes most of his time to a specified activity and is seldom at home. LME. ▸**d** ECCLESIASTICAL. Any of a class of devout widows in the early Christian Church. L16.
2 = WIDOW-BIRD. M18.
3 An extra hand dealt to the table in certain card-games. L19.
4 TYPOGRAPHY. A short (esp. single-word) last line of a paragraph left at the top of a page or column and considered undesirable. M20.

📖 **1** A. S. Byatt This stone is dedicated to Randolph Henry Ash . . by his sorrowing widow and wife of more than 45 years. **c** *Guardian* One . . unit, aware of the dangers of creating 'TA widows' opens its bar . . to wives. ***business widow***, ***golf widow***, etc.

Phrases: ***black widow***: see BLACK *adjective*. **grass widow**. ***Merry Widow***: see MERRY *adjective*. MOURNFUL **widow**. ***mourning widow***: see MOURNING *ppl adjective*. **the widow** [translation of French *la Veuve* Clicquot, a firm of wine merchants] *colloq.* champagne. **the Widow of Windsor**, **the Widow at Windsor** *slang* (orig. *Services*) Queen Victoria, whose husband predeceased her by forty years. ***virgin widow***: see VIRGIN *adjective*. ***widow bewitched***: see sense 1c above.

Comb.: **widow-finch** a widow-bird, an indigo-bird; **widow-maker** a killer or potential killer of men; *spec.* (*N. Amer. slang*) a dead branch caught high in a tree which may fall on a person below; **widow-man** *dial.* a widower; ***widow's cruse***; **widow's men** *Hist.* fictitious crewmen whose names were entered on a ship's books, their pay being credited to a widows' pension fund; ***widow's mite***: see MITE *noun*² 1b. ***widow's peak***: see PEAK *noun*¹ 1e; **widow's walk** *N. Amer.* a railed or balustraded platform built on the roof, orig. in early New England houses, esp. for providing an unimpeded view of the sea; ***widow's weeds***: see WEED *noun*² 8; **widow-wail** the shrub mezereon, *Daphne mezereum*; also, a dwarf evergreen shrub of the western Mediterranean region, *Cneorum tricoccon* (family Cneoraceae), with pink sweet-scented flowers; **widow woman** (chiefly *arch.* & *dial.*) = sense 1 above.
■ **widowhood** *noun* (*a*) the state or condition of a widow (or widower); the time during which one is a widow (or widower); †(*b*) (*rare*, Shakes.) an estate settled on a widow: OE. **widowly** *adjective & adverb* (*a*) *adjective* pertaining to, characteristic of, or befitting a widow; (*b*) *adverb* in a way befitting a widow, like a widow: M16.

widow /ˈwɪdəʊ/ *noun*². *obsolete* exc. *dial.*
[Old English *widewa* masc. corresp. to *widewe* WIDOW *noun*¹.]
= WIDOWER 1.

widow /ˈwɪdəʊ/ *verb trans.* ME.
[from WIDOW *noun*¹ or *noun*².]
1 Make a widow (or, rarely, widower) of; bereave of one's husband (or wife). Chiefly as ***widowed ppl adjective***. ME. ▸**b** *fig.* Deprive *of* a highly prized possession (person, thing, or quality); bereave. *literary*. L16.
†**2** Survive as a widow, become the widow of. *rare* (Shakes.). Only in E17.
†**3** Endow with a widow's right. *rare* (Shakes.). Only in E17.

📖 **1b** E. Young Wit, widow'd of good-sense, is worse than nought.

widow-bird /ˈwɪdəʊbəːd/ *noun*. L18.
[from WIDOW *noun*¹ (with ref. to the black plumage of the males) + BIRD *noun*.]
A whydah, *esp.* one of the genus *Euplectes*.

widower /ˈwɪdəʊə/ *noun*. LME.
[from WIDOW *noun*¹ + -ER¹.]
1 A husband who has lost his wife by death and has not married again. LME. ▸**b** As 2nd elem. of comb.: a husband whose wife devotes most of her time to a specified activity (cf. WIDOW *noun*¹ 1c). *colloq.* M20.
†**2** Any of an ecclesiastical class of men corresponding to that of widows (WIDOW *noun*¹ 1d). L16–E17.

📖 **1** M. Cox William was a widower, but . . he married again. **b** *Listener* He's a football widower because I'm the one . . trooping away to . . matches.

■ **widowered** *adjective* (*rare*) having become a widower M19. **widowerhood** *noun* the state or condition of a widower; the time during which a man is a widower: L18. **widowership** *noun* = WIDOWERHOOD M17.

width /wɪtθ, wɪdθ/ *noun*. E17.
[from WIDE *adjective* + -TH¹, formed on the analogy of *breadth* to replace WIDENESS.]
1 The linear extent of a thing as measured across or from side to side; breadth. E17. ▸**b** A distance equal to the width of a thing; *esp.* the transverse extent of a swimming pool, taken as a measure of the distance swum (cf. LENGTH 3d). M19. ▸**c** A strip of material of full width as woven. L19.
2 Largeness of transverse or horizontal extent; *fig.* breadth or liberality of thoughts, views, etc. L17. ▸**b** A wide expanse. M19.
3 *transf.* The magnitude or range of magnitudes of a non-spatial quantity represented graphically as extent along an axis. Cf. ***bandwidth*** s.v. BAND *noun*². L19.

📖 **1** Dickens Large round eyes, opened to their utmost width. S. E. White Strips of certain arbitrary lengths and widths. **b** L. Grant-Adamson His [room] was spacious, the width of the house. **2** *Guardian* The pocket cartoons are formidable social history, limited in width. **b** M. Franklin Weeks and weeks spent . . crossing widths of saltbush country.

■ **widthways** *adverb* in the direction of the width, transversely L18. **widthwise** *adverb* = WIDTHWAYS L19.

Wiedemann–Franz /viːdəmanˈfraːnts/ *noun*. E20.
[from Gustav H. *Wiedemann* (1826–99) + Rudolf *Franz* (1827–1902), German physicists.]
PHYSICS. **1** ***Wiedemann–Franz law***, the law (valid at sufficiently low or high temperatures) that at any given temperature the ratio of the thermal to the electrical conductivity has approximately the same value for all metallic elements. E20.
2 ***Wiedemann–Franz ratio***, this ratio, equivalent to the Lorenz constant. M20.

wiederkom /ˈviːdəkɒm/ *noun*. Also **-komm**, **W-**. L19.
[French *vidrecome* goblet, ult. from German *wiederkommen* return, come again.]
A tall cylindrical German drinking-vessel made of (usu. coloured or painted) glass.

wield /wiːld/ *noun*. Long *obsolete* exc. *Scot.* Also (*Scot.*) **wald** /wɔːld/.
[Old English *weald* (rare), usu. *ġeweald*, Anglian *ġewald* = Old Saxon *giwald*, Old High German *gawalt* (German *Gewalt*), partly from Old English *ġewild*: see Y-, next.]
1 Command, control. OE.
†**2** Power, strength. ME–E16.

wield /wiːld/ *verb*. Also (*Scot.*) **wald** /wɔːld/.
[Old English *wealdan* (strong) verb = Old Saxon *waldan*, Old High German *waltan* (German *walten*), Old Norse *valda*, Gothic *waldan*, partly Old English *wieldan* (weak) verb, from a mutated form of this.]
1 †**a** *verb trans.* Rule, govern. OE. ▸†**b** *verb trans.* Overcome, subdue. OE–ME. ▸**c** *verb intrans.* Rule, have the command; *fig.* prevail. *obsolete* exc. *Scot.* LME.
†**2** *verb trans.* **a** Have at one's command or disposal; hold, possess, enjoy. Also, get possession of, obtain. OE–L18. ▸**b** Experience, suffer; suffer patiently, endure, tolerate. ME–L16.
†**3** **a** *verb trans.* Decide, ordain; bring about; carry out, perform. OE–E16. ▸**b** *verb intrans.* Occupy oneself; act, do, fare (well etc.). LME–E17.
4 *verb trans.* Direct the movement or action of, control, (a bodily member, a faculty, etc.); guide, direct; deal with successfully, manage. *obsolete* exc. *Scot.* & *dial.* OE. ▸†**b** Carry (something heavy or requiring effort). ME–L16. ▸†**c** Express, utter. *rare*. L16–M17.
5 *verb trans.* Use or handle with skill and effectiveness; ply (a weapon or tool, now always one held in the hand). OE. ▸**b** Exercise (power, influence). Freq. *fig.* in ***wield a sceptre***, ***wield the sceptre***, exercise supreme authority, rule. L16.

📖 **4** P. Fletcher Her daughters . . Much pain'd themselves her stumbling feet to weeld. E. Young Whose mind was . . strong to weild all science. **5** F. Forsyth A group of soldiers, . . wielding rifles by the barrels, had burst into the hotel. M. Warner Wielding her dressmaker's shears she began slicing into the cloth. *fig.*: A. Menzies Who could wield such scathing invective? **b** H. T. Buckle Over the inferior order of minds, they still wield great influence. J. Fane A time in which women wielded their power behind the scenes.

■ **wieldable** *adjective* (*rare*) M18. **wielder** *noun* †(*a*) a ruler, a governor; (*b*) a person who wields a weapon, implement, etc.: LME. †**wieldless** *adjective* unmanageable, unwieldy M–L16.

wieldy /ˈwiːldi/ *adjective*. LME.
[from prec. + -Y¹. In later use back-form. from UNWIELDY.]
†**1** Skilful in directing the movement of one's limbs etc.; vigorous, lithe, active. LME–L17.

2 Easy to wield or handle; manageable, handy. L16.

2 *Times* The pretence that university senates are wieldy management bodies.

Wien /viːn/ *noun*. E20.
[Max Carl *Wien* (1866–1938), German physicist.]
1 *ELECTRICITY*. ***Wien bridge***, an alternating-current bridge circuit used to measure capacitance (or frequency) in terms of resistance and frequency (or capacitance). E20.
2 *PHYSICAL CHEMISTRY*. ***Wien effect***, the increase in the electrical conductivity of an electrolytic solution as the field strength is increased. M20.

wiener /ˈviːnə, *in N. Amer. senses also* w-/ *noun*. In sense 2 also **weiner**. L19.
[German, adjective from *Wien* Vienna.]
▶ **I** *attrib*. **1** Used *attrib*. to designate things from or associated with Vienna. L19.
1 Wiener dog *N. Amer. colloq.* a dachshund. **Wiener Kreis** [= circle] = ***Vienna Circle*** s.v. VIENNA 1. **Wiener** SCHNITZEL. **wienerwurst** [= sausage] *N. Amer.* = ***Vienna sausage*** s.v. VIENNA 1.
▶ **II** *ellipt*. **2** = ***wienerwurst*** above. *N. Amer.* E20.
Comb.: **wiener roast** *N. Amer.* a barbecue at which Vienna sausages are cooked and served.

wienie /ˈwiːni/ *noun*. *N. Amer. slang*. Also **winny** /ˈwɪni/. M19.
[Alt. of prec.: see -IE.]
= WIENER 2. Cf. WEENY *noun*[2].

Wien's law /ˈviːnz lɔː/ *noun phr*. L19.
[from Wilhelm *Wien* (1864–1928), German physicist.]
PHYSICS. Either of two laws promulgated by Wien: (*a*) an approximation to Planck's law that holds at short wavelengths, according to which the flux of radiant energy of wavelength λ emitted by a black body at temperature T is proportional to $1/\lambda^5 \exp(hc/\lambda kT)$; (*b*) the law that the wavelength of the radiation of maximum intensity from a black body is proportional to the absolute temperature.

wife /wʌɪf/ *noun*. Pl. **wives** /wʌɪvz/.
[Old English *wīf* = Old Frisian, Old Saxon *wīf* (Dutch *wijf*), Old High German *wīp* (German *Weib* woman), Old Norse *víf*, of unkn. origin.]
1 A woman; in later use *esp.* one engaged in the sale of some commodity. Now (chiefly *Scot.*, freq. *derog.*), a middle-aged or elderly woman. Also as 2nd elem. of comb., as ***alewife***, ***fishwife***. OE.
2 A married woman esp. in relation to her husband. OE. ▸**b** The female mate of a male animal. LME.
3 The female head of a household; the landlady of an inn. *obsolete* exc. as GOODWIFE 1, HOUSEWIFE *noun* 1. LME.

1 A. GRAY The village school . . had . . a kitchen where a wife from the village made flavourless meals. **2** DICKENS He had never been married; but he was still on the look-out for a wife. P. ACKROYD He . . blamed his wife for all the woes of their marriage.

Phrases: ***all the world and his wife***: see WORLD *noun*. ***battered wife***: see BATTER *verb*[1] 1. ***Dutch wife***: see DUTCH *adjective*. **have to wife** *arch.* be the husband of (a woman). ***man and wife***: see MAN *noun* 7a. OLD WIFE. **take a wife** *formal* (of a man) get married. **take to wife** *arch.* become the husband of (a woman). **wife and mother** (freq. *joc.*) a woman who shows a zealous devotion to her family. **Wife of Bath** *noun & adjectival phr.* (a woman) resembling the Wife of Bath in Chaucer's *Canterbury Tales* in sexual appetite, sexual frankness, etc.
Comb.: **wife-swapper** a person who engages in wife-swapping; **wife-swapping** the interchange of marital partners for sexual purposes within a group of friends or acquaintances.
■ **wifedom** *noun* (*a*) = WIFEHOOD; (*b*) wives collectively: M19. **wifehood** *noun* (*a*) the state or position of a wife; (*b*) the character of a wife; wifely qualities: LME. **wifeless** *adjective* having no wife; unmarried: OE. **wifelessness** *noun* L19. **wifelike** *adjective & adverb* (*a*) *adjective* resembling (that of) a wife; (*b*) *adverb* after the manner of a wife: L16.

wife /wʌɪf/ *verb intrans*. *rare*. LME.
[from the noun. Cf. WIVE.]
†**1** Take a wife; marry. LME–E18.
2 Be a wife; act as a wife. Chiefly as ***wifing*** *verbal noun*. E20.

wifely /ˈwʌɪfli/ *adjective*.
[Old English *wīflīc*: see -LY[1].]
†**1** Of or pertaining to a woman or women; womanly. OE–M16.
2 Pertaining to, characteristic of, or befitting a wife; having a character befitting a wife. OE.

2 E. SIMPSON The typing chore Jean seemed to accept as a wifely duty.

■ **wifeliness** *noun* wifely character or quality M19.

wifey *noun* var. of WIFIE.

Wiffle /ˈwɪf(ə)l/ *noun*. *US*. Also **w-**. M20.
[Var. of WHIFFLE *noun*.]
Used *attrib.* in the proprietary names of certain items of sporting equipment (see below).
Wiffle ball a light perforated ball used in a variety of baseball (cf. ***whiffle-ball*** s.v. WHIFFLE *noun*); a game played with such a ball. **Wiffle bat** a bat designed for use with a Wiffle ball.

wifie /ˈwʌɪfi/ *noun*. Also **wifey**. L18.
[from WIFE *noun* + -IE, -Y[6].]
A little wife; *Scot.* a little or young woman. Chiefly as a term of endearment or familiarity.

wifish /ˈwʌɪfɪʃ/ *adjective*. Orig. †**wivish**. M16.
[from WIFE *noun* + -ISH[1].]
†**1** Belonging to or characteristic of a woman; *derog.* womanish. Only in M16.
2 Characteristic of or resembling a wife. Formerly also, excessively devoted to one's wife. Chiefly *derog.* E17.

†**wifle** *noun*. OE–LME.
[Old English *wifel* from Germanic, from Indo-European base meaning 'wave, swing, shake'.]
A javelin, a battleaxe, a spear.
¶ Perh. the 1st elem. of WHIFFLER *noun*[1].

wift /wɪft/ *verb intrans*. *obsolete* exc. *dial*. M16.
[Imit.]
Orig., go astray. Later, drift to and fro, drift along.

wig /wɪɡ/ *noun*[1]. Now *Scot. & dial*. Also **whig**. LME.
[Middle Low German, Middle Dutch *wigge* wedge, wedge-shaped cake: see WEDGE *noun*.]
A kind of small bun made with currants and butter.

wig /wɪɡ/ *noun*[2]. *Scot. & north*. Now *rare*. E17.
[Old Norse *veggr* wall.]
from wig to wall, from wall to wall; backwards and forwards.

wig /wɪɡ/ *noun*[3]. L17.
[Shortened from PERIWIG *noun*, as WINKLE *noun* from PERIWINKLE *noun*[2].]
1 An artificial covering of hair for the head, worn to conceal baldness, as a disguise, to enhance one's appearance, or as part of professional or ceremonial costume (now only by judges and barristers). L17. ▸**b** A natural head of hair, esp. of a child (*joc.*). Also (*US slang*), the head, the brain. E20. ▸**c** The wool growing above and around the eyes of a sheep, removed during shearing. *Austral.* M20.
2 A severe reprimand. Cf. WIG *verb* 2, WIGGING. *colloq.* L18.
3 A person who wears a wig (professionally); a dignitary. Cf. ***bigwig*** s.v. BIG *adjective*. *colloq.* E19.
4 The coarse hair on the shoulders of a full-grown male fur-seal; a seal bearing this. M19.

1 P. ROTH Over her real . . hair she wears a wig . . , an oversized aureole of black corkscrew curls. ***bag-wig***, ***full-bottomed wig***, ***ramillie wig***, etc. **wigs on the green** *colloq.* (orig. *Anglo-Irish*) violent or unpleasant developments, ructions. ***b flip one's wig***: see FLIP *verb* 5. **2** *Daily Chronicle* As often as not a 'wig' ended by the offer of a cheroot.

Comb.: **wig-picker** *US slang* a psychiatrist; **wig-stand** a support for placing a wig on when not in use; **wig-tree** the Venetian sumac, *Cotinus coggygria*.
■ **wigless** *adjective* L18. **wiglet** *noun* a small wig or hairpiece M19.

wig /wɪɡ/ *verb*. Infl. **-gg-**. E19.
[from WIG *noun*[3].]
1 *verb trans.* Put a wig on; *spec.* provide (actors etc.) with wigs for a theatrical performance. E19. ▸**b** Clip the wig (WIG *noun*[3] 1c) of a sheep. Chiefly as ***wigging*** *verbal noun*. *Austral.* E20.
2 *verb trans.* Reprimand severely. *colloq.* E19.
3 *verb intrans.* Lose control of one's emotions (cf. ***flip one's wig*** s.v. FLIP *verb* 5). Chiefly foll. by *out*. *US slang*. M20.

2 *Times* A subordinate . . who presumably has been severely 'wigged' by his chief. **3** *American Speech* He wigged out at the prof's gag. G. LEES I just wigged. I banged the table . . and I grabbed this guy.

Wigan /ˈwɪɡ(ə)n/ *noun*. M19.
[A town in Lancashire.]
A stout make of calico, orig. manufactured at Wigan.

wigeon /ˈwɪdʒ(ə)n/ *noun*. Also **widgeon**. Pl. **-s**, same. E16.
[Perh. from imit. base, after PIGEON *noun*[1].]
1 Each of three ducks of the genus *Anas*, the males of which have a whitish forehead and crown and a whistling call; *esp.* (more fully ***European wigeon***) *A. penelope* of northern Eurasia, and (more fully ***American wigeon***) *A. americana* of N. America. E16. ▸**b** Any of various other wild ducks. *obsolete* exc. *dial.* M17.
2 [With allus. to the supposed stupidity of the bird.] A fool, a simpleton. *arch.* E17.
1b red-headed wigeon the pochard, *Aythya ferina*.
Comb.: **wigeon-grass**, **wigeon-weed** eel-grass, *Zostera marina*.

wigged /wɪɡd/ *adjective*. L18.
[from WIG *noun*[3] + -ED[2].]
Provided with or wearing a wig.

wigger /ˈwɪɡ(ə)r/ *noun*. *US slang*. L20.
[Abbreviation of *white nigger* (see WHITE *adjective*).]
A white person who tries to emulate or acquire cultural behaviour and tastes attributed to black people.

wiggery /ˈwɪɡ(ə)ri/ *noun*. L18.
[from WIG *noun*[3] + -ERY.]
1 Wigs or false hair collectively; the practice of wearing a wig. L18.
2 Dignity or formality associated with the wearing of a wig, freq. regarded as empty. M19.

2 A. TROLLOPE Their outward appearance of the august wiggery of statecraft.

wigging /ˈwɪɡɪŋ/ *noun*. *colloq*. E19.
[from WIG *noun*[3] or WIG *verb* + -ING[1].]
A severe reprimand; a scolding.

D. ACHESON Woodward and I were prepared for a good wigging for sloppy work.

wiggle /ˈwɪɡ(ə)l/ *verb & noun*. Now *colloq. & dial.* ME.
[Middle & mod. Low German, Middle & mod. Dutch *wiggelen*, frequentative of Low German *wiggen*: see -LE[3]. Cf. WAG *verb*, WAGGLE *verb*, WRIGGLE *verb*.]
▶ **A** *verb*. **1** *verb intrans.* Move irregularly to and fro or from side to side, waggle; *esp.* go or move sinuously, wriggle. Freq. *fig.* ME.
2 *verb trans.* Cause (a thing, esp. a part of the body) to move in this way. L17.

1 J. MALCOLM They wiggled and squirmed but couldn't free themselves. *Sailplane & Gliding* A large town with a river wiggling through it. *Ring* Tyson is . . looking for . . a way to wiggle out of his contract. **2** J. CAREY An exponent of the fleshly style, all hip-wiggling and provocativeness.

▶ **B** *noun*. **1** An act of wiggling; a wriggling movement. E19.
2 A wavy line drawn by a pen, pencil, etc. M20.

1 L. M. ALCOTT Rob's footstool had a wiggle in its uneven legs. C. BRAYFIELD Jo tottered forward on her high heels and curtseyed to the audience with a wiggle. **get a wiggle on** (*slang*, chiefly *US*) get a move on, hurry. **2** ***SUESS wiggle***.

Comb.: **wiggletail** the aquatic larva of a gnat or a mosquito.
■ **wiggler** *noun* a thing that wiggles; *esp.* (*a*) the aquatic larva of a gnat or a mosquito; (*b*) *PHYSICS* a magnet designed to make a beam of particles in an accelerator describe a sinusoidal path, in order to increase the amount of radiation they produce (cf. UNDULATOR 2): M19.

wiggle-waggle /ˈwɪɡ(ə)lwaɡ(ə)l/ *adjective, noun, & verb*. *dial. & colloq.* As noun & verb also **wiggle-woggle** /-wɒɡ(ə)l/. L18.
[Redupl. formation combining WIGGLE and WAGGLE *noun, verb*, emphasizing the alternation of movement. Cf. WIG-WAG.]
▶ **A** *adjective*. That wiggles and waggles; *fig.* vacillating. L18.
▶ **B** *noun*. **1** A tremulous undulating movement. E19.
2 = CAKEWALK *noun* 2. E20.
▶ **C** *verb trans. & intrans.* (Cause to) move with a tremulous undulating movement. M19.

wiggly /ˈwɪɡli/ *adjective*. *colloq*. E19.
[from WIGGLE *verb* or *noun* + -Y[1].]
Characterized by or suggestive of wiggling movement; (of a line, pattern, etc.) having small irregular undulations.

Blackwood's Magazine Black . . tie with a white wiggly bacterial pattern. *TV Times* Spawn . . become wiggly tadpoles.

wiggly-waggly /ˈwɪɡlɪwaɡli/ *adjective*. *dial. & colloq.* Also **wiggly-woggly** /-wɒɡli/. L19.
[Redupl. formation combining WIGGLY and WAGGLY. Cf. WIGGLE-WAGGLE.]
That wiggles and waggles.

wiggy /ˈwɪɡi/ *adjective*. E19.
[In sense 1 from WIG *noun*[3], in sense 2 from WIG *verb* 3: see -Y[1].]
1 Wearing or distinguished by a wig; *transf.* extremely grave, formal, or ceremonious. E19.
2 Not in control of one's emotions; freaky. *US slang*. M20.

wight /wʌɪt/ *noun*.
[Old English *wiht* corresp. (with variation of gender and meaning) to Old Saxon *wiht*, Middle & mod. Low German, Middle & mod. Dutch *wicht*, Old High German *wiht* (German *Wicht*), Old Norse *vættr* fem., Gothic *waihts* fem.: ult. connections uncertain.]
1 †**a** A living being; a creature. OE–L16. ▸**b** A supernatural being. Now chiefly *arch. & Scot.* OE. ▸**c** A human being; a person. Now *arch., dial., & literary*. ME.
†**2** A certain (esp. small) amount. Usu. in neg. contexts. Cf. WHIT *noun*[1]. OE–LME.

1b W. MORRIS Our protection against uncouth wights. **c** *Motor* The poor wight in Paris . . struggling to bend his limited English to . . complex technical terminology. **2 no wight** not at all, not in the least.

wight /wʌɪt/ *adjective & adverb*. Now *arch., Scot., & dial.* ME.
[Old Norse *vígt* neut. of *vígr* of fighting age, skilled in arms, cogn. with Old English *wīg* battle, conflict, *wiga* warrior, from Indo-European base repr. also by Latin *vincere*, *vic-* conquer.]
▶ **A** *adjective*. **1** Strong and courageous, esp. in warfare; valiant, brave. ME.
2 Strong, robust, mighty; exercising strength, energetic. ME. ▸†**b** Forcible, violent; powerful in effect,

strong. ME–L16. ▸†c Strongly built or constructed; stout. ME–L16.

3 Moving briskly or rapidly; agile, swift. LME.

1 W. MORRIS They ought to sing of him who was as wight As Launcelot or Wade. 3 SIR W. SCOTT Mount thee on the wightest steed.

▸ B *adverb*. 1 Actively, energetically. *obsolete* exc. *Scot*. ME.
†2 Quickly, without delay. ME–E17.

■ **wightly** *adverb* ME. **wightness** *noun* LME.

wighty /ˈwʌɪti/ *adjective*. *obsolete* exc. *dial*. LME.
[from WIGHT *adjective* + -Y[1].]
= WIGHT *adjective*.

wigsby /ˈwɪgzbi/ *noun*. *joc*. *arch*. L18.
[from WIG *noun*[3]: see -BY.]
(A designation for) a person wearing a wig.

wig-wag /ˈwɪgwag/ *adjective*, *verb*, & *noun*. L16.
[Redupl. of WAG *verb*, *noun*[1] with vowel variation. Cf. WIGGLE-WAGGLE.]
▸ A *adjective*. Moving repeatedly to and fro; following a tortuous or zigzag course. *rare*. L16.
▸ B *verb trans*. & *intrans*. Infl. **-gg-**. (Cause to) move lightly to and fro, wag; *esp*. wave (a flag etc.) to and fro in signalling. L19.

Sun (Baltimore) The order: 'Splice the mainbrace' was wig-wagged to all ships. G. TALBOT Wipers wig-wagging to keep windscreens clear. R. SILVERBERG Alleluia was standing in the middle of the road, wigwagging her arms.

▸ C *noun*. 1 An act of waving a flag to and fro in signalling; a message sent by such means. L19.
2 WATCHMAKING. A machine operating a reciprocating polisher. L19.

wigwam /ˈwɪgwam/ *noun*. E17.
[Ojibwa *wigwaum*, *wigiwam* var. of Algonquian *weekuwom*, *wikiwam* lit. 'their house'.]
1 A chiefly dome-shaped or oval hut characteristic of the N. American Indians about the Great Lakes and eastward, consisting of bark, matting, or hides stretched over a framework of poles (cf. TEPEE); a similar structure among other peoples. E17.
2 Any house or dwelling (*joc*.); *US slang* a large building (formerly often a temporary structure) for political gatherings. E19.
3 A pyramidal framework of poles etc., *spec*. one used to support beans, sweet peas, etc. L20.

3 J. HEGLEY Seeing a wigwam of planks / being burned.

†**wihy** *interjection*, *noun*, & *verb* var. of WEHEE.

Wilburite /ˈwɪlbərʌɪt/ *adjective* & *noun*. *US*. M19.
[from John *Wilbur* (1774–1856), New England Quaker + -ITE[1]. Cf. GURNEYITE.]
▸ A *adjective*. Of, pertaining to, or characteristic of a conservative American Quaker movement founded in 1845 by John Wilbur. M19.
▸ B *noun*. A member of this movement. M19.

wilco /ˈwɪlkəʊ/ *interjection*. *colloq*. (orig. MILITARY). M20.
[Abbreviation of *will comply*.]
Expr. compliance or agreement, esp. acceptance of instructions received by radio or telephone.

Wilcoxon /ˈwɪlkɒks(ə)n/ *noun*. M20.
[Frank *Wilcoxon* (1892–1965), Irish statistician.]
STATISTICS. Used *attrib*. with ref. to a non-parametric test for assessing whether two populations have identical distributions.

wild /wʌɪld/ *adjective*, *noun*, & *adverb*.
[Old English *wilde* = Old Frisian *wilde*, Old Saxon, Old High German *wildi* (Dutch, German *wild*), Old Norse *villr*, Gothic *wilþeis*, from Germanic.]
▸ A *adjective*. I 1 Of an animal: living in, or having reverted to, a natural state; not living with or under the control of humans, not tame or domesticated. OE.
2 Of a plant: growing in a natural state; growing freely without human intervention; not cultivated. Freq. in the names of uncultivated plants related to or resembling cultivated plants. OE.
3 Of a place or region: left uncultivated; free of human intervention or habitation; desolate. OE. ▸b Belonging to or characteristic of a desolate region; of or in a wilderness. L17.
4 a Produced or deriving from wild animals or plants; produced without domestication or cultivation. ME. ▸b MINING. Of a mineral or ore: impure, inferior. L18.
5 Of a person etc.: uncivilized; barbarous. Also, rebellious. ME.

1 R. MACAULAY Wild creatures . . scuttered out among the bushes. 2 I. MURDOCH She picked . . wild flowers in the grass near the lake. *wild carrot*, *wild grape*, *wild olive*, *wild plum*, *wild sage*, etc. 3 *Country Living* Wild moorlands, blue with lochs. 4a *Scotsman* I had my first experience of 'wild' meat . . in Tanzania. Zebra steak was the main dish. 5 SIR W. SCOTT It's ill taking the breeks aff a wild Highlandman.

▸ II 6 Uncontrolled, unrestrained; taking or disposed to take one's own way; acting or moving unrestrictedly. OE. ▸b Resisting control or restraint, wilful, unruly, wayward; disorderly; reckless, careless. Also, irregular, erratic. ME. ▸c Yielding to sexual desire; licentious; dissolute. ME. ▸d Of game, a horse, etc.: shy; fearful of humans; easily startled. L16.
7 Not having control of one's mental faculties; distracted, distraught; (of the eyes) indicating distraction. ME.
8 Fierce, savage, ferocious; violent; cruel. ME. ▸b Of the sea, the weather, etc.: violently agitated, rough, stormy; *fig*. tumultuous, turbulent. ME. ▸c Of a vocal or instrumental sound: loud and unrestrained. M16.
9 Of an action, notion, statement, etc.: going beyond the bounds of what is prudent or reasonable; rash; fantastically or absurdly unreasonable. Freq. in ***in one's wildest dreams***, ***beyond one's wildest dreams***, in or beyond one's most fantastic or unrestrained imaginings or expectations. E16. ▸†b Of or designating the extreme Evangelical party in the Church of Scotland. L18–E19.
10 Of an emotion or its expression: highly excited or agitated; frantic; passionately vehement. L16.
11 a Strange or fantastic in appearance. E17. ▸b Artless, free, fanciful, or romantic in style; pleasingly unconventional or primitive. M17. ▸c A general term of approval: amazing, wonderful, exciting. *US slang*. M20.
12 *colloq*. a Extremely irritated; angry, infuriated. M17. ▸b Passionately desirous or anxious *to do* something; extremely attracted to or infatuated with a person (foll. by *about*, *for*). L18. ▸c Overwhelmed or carried away by enthusiasm. Freq. foll. by *about*, *for*. E19.
13 a Aimed wide of the mark or at random; haphazard. E19. ▸b Of a playing-card: having any rank chosen by the player holding it. E20.

6 DICKENS The children wild in the streets. A. SILLITOE He woke himself . . by a wild clawing at his clothes. **b** F. MARRYAT An only son, very wild, who would go to sea in spite of his remonstrances. *Sounds* With pierced nose, wild red hair and . . tattoos. **c** *Guardian* We started to crack up . . having a real wild time, taking drugs, drinking. **d** P. HAWKER The birds were so . . wild that it was almost impossible to get near them. 7 M. ROBINSON I am really almost wild with affliction! L. THOMAS Tremulous, hallucinating, wild-eyed, unhinged men. 8 SHAKES. *John* This is the bloodiest shame, The wildest savagery. **b** DICKENS A bad winter's night in the wild Atlantic. **c** J. MCGAHERN They exploded into wild laughter. 9 A. C. CLARKE The envious rumour . . was wild hyperbole. *Harpers & Queen* Cosmetics companies making wild claims for their products. 10 SARA MAITLAND She heard . . wild terrified screaming. **11b** MILTON If . . sweetest Shakespear fancies childe, Warble his native Wood-notes wilde. *Flowers* If you want the decorated pot to appear wild, choose weeping willow. **c** G. PALEY This dress is wild It must've cost a dime. **12a** J. K. JEROME It made me awfully wild, especially as George burst out laughing. **b** J. MCGAHERN After a week in the house . . you're . . wild to get out. **c** *New York Woman* Beware the black catsuit . . . Designers are . . wild for these body-hugging numbers. **13a** *Guardian* A wild tee shot . . missed the green by 20 yards.

▸ B *noun*. †1 A wild animal; wild animals collectively; *spec*. an animal or animals of the chase; game. ME–L16.
2 A wild or desolate place; an uncultivated or uninhabited region; a wilderness; in *pl*., *the* wild parts *of* a particular region. L16.

2 *Daily Telegraph* Summer adventure camps in the wilds of Wester Ross.

▸ C *adverb*. In a wild manner; wildly; randomly. M16.

G. P. R. JAMES The soldier who fronted him, struck wild, reeled, staggered.

Phrases: ***beyond one's wildest dreams***, ***in one's wildest dreams***: see sense A.9 above. **in the wild** in an untamed, undomesticated, or uncultivated state. **in the wilds**, **out in the wilds** *colloq*. far from normal habitation; remote from urban life and culture; on the furthest limits or boundaries. **like wild** *colloq*. with passionate enthusiasm or great excitement. **play the wild** *US colloq*. behave in a careless or reckless manner; play havoc with. ***run wild***: see RUN *verb*. ***sow one's wild oats***: see OAT *noun*. **the wild** the state of being untamed, undomesticated, or uncultivated.

Special collocations & comb.: ***wild angelica***: see ANGELICA *noun*[1] 1. ***wild ARUM***. ***wild basil***: see BASIL *noun*[1] 2. **wild beast** an undomesticated or ferocious animal (*lit*. & *fig*.). ***wild bergamot***: see BERGAMOT *noun*[2] 3. ***wild boar***: see BOAR 1b. **wild card** (*a*) see sense 13b above; (*b*) SPORT a player or team chosen to enter a competition at the organizers' discretion after the regular places have been taken up; (*c*) COMPUTING a character that will match any character or combination of characters in a search etc. **wild cattle** (*a*) undomesticated or feral cattle; (*b*) (animals of) any of various species of wild bovid. ***wild CELERY***. **wild cherry** a tall Eurasian woodland tree, *Prunus avium*, bearing white flowers in spring, the ancestor of cultivated sweet cherries; also called *gean*. **wild chestnut** the Cape chestnut, *Calodendrum capense*. ***wild cinnamon***: see CINNAMON *noun*. **wildcraft** *verb* & *noun* (*US*) (*a*) *verb trans*. gather (herbs, fungi, etc.) from the wild; (*b*) *noun* the action or practice of wildcrafting natural produce. **wild dog** any of various wild members of the dog family; *esp*. (*a*) the hunting dog of Africa; (*b*) the dhole of India; (*c*) the dingo of Australia. **wild duck** any of numerous undomesticated ducks; *spec*. the mallard. ***wild endive***: see ENDIVE 2. **wild garden** a group of hardy plants planted in an informal setting and intended to appear to be growing without human intervention. **wild gardening** the practice or activity of growing a wild garden. ***wild GARLIC***. **wild ginger** *N. Amer*. a kind of birthwort, *Asarum canadense*, with a rootstock tasting of ginger. **wild goat** any wild species of goat, as the ibex; any goat-antelope, as the chamois. **wild horse** (*a*) a horse not domesticated or broken in, a feral horse; (*b*) = ***PRZEWALSKI'S horse***; (*c*) in *pl*. (*colloq*.) even the strongest inducement or most powerful influence (chiefly in neg. contexts). ***wild HYACINTH***. ***wild Irish***: see IRISH *noun* 1. ***wild IRISHMAN***. **wild leek** (*a*) a southern European plant, *Allium ampeloprasum*, from which the leek is thought to be derived; (*b*) ramsons, *Allium ursinum*; (*c*) *N. Amer*. ramp, *Allium tricoccum*. ***wild liquorice***: see LIQUORICE 3. ***wild mare***: see MARE *noun*[1] 3. ***wild MARJORAM***. ***wild mignonette***: see MIGNONETTE 2. **wild mustard** charlock, *Sinapis arvensis*. ***wild NAVEW***. ***wild oat***: see OAT *noun* 2. ***wild oats***: see OAT *noun*. **wild orange** (*a*) the wild form of the cultivated orange, *Citrus sinensis*, or a closely related plant; (*b*) any of various trees resembling this in fruit, flowers, or foliage, *esp*. the Kaffir orange, *Strychnos pungens*, and a N. American cherry-laurel, *Prunus caroliniana*. ***wild pansy***: see PANSY *noun* 1. **wild parsley** *colloq*. any of several fine-leaved umbelliferous plants. **wild parsnip** (*a*) a Eurasian plant of calcareous grassland, *Pastinaca sativa*, from which the cultivated parsnip is derived; (*b*) *N. Amer*. a kind of cowbane, *Cicuta maculata*. **wild pig** a wild boar. ***wild pine***: see PINE *noun*[2] 5. **wild pitch** *noun* & *verb* (BASEBALL) (*a*) *noun* a pitch which is not hit by the batter and cannot be stopped by the catcher, enabling a base-runner to advance; (*b*) *verb trans*. enable (a base-runner) to advance in this way. **wild radish** a cornfield weed, *Raphanus raphanistrum* subsp. *raphanistrum*, allied to the cultivated radish. ***wild rape***: see RAPE *noun*[3] 3. ***wild rice***: see RICE *noun*[2] 2. **wild rye** (*a*) any of several European kinds of wild barley, esp. *Hordeum secalinum* and *H. murinum*; (*b*) *N. Amer*. any of several grasses of the genus *Elymus*. ***wild sarsaparilla***: see SARSAPARILLA 2. **wildscape** a wild, uncultivated, or desolate landscape; an area of land free from human intervention. ***wild service (tree)***: see SERVICE *noun*[2] 1b. **wild silk** silk produced by wild silkworms; an imitation of this made from short silk fibres. ***wild snapdragon***: see SNAPDRAGON 1. ***wild strawberry***: see STRAWBERRY 2. **wild talent** any of various psychic powers such as extrasensory perception, telepathy, telekinesis, etc. ***wild tansy***: see TANSY 1b. ***wild teasel***: see TEASEL *noun* 1. ***wild THYME***. ***wild tobacco***: see TOBACCO 2. **wild turkey** the wild bird from which the domesticated turkey is derived. **wild type** GENETICS the type of strain, gene, or characteristic that prevails among individuals in natural conditions, as opp. to an atypical mutant type. **wild-type** *adjective* (GENETICS) of, pertaining to, or of the nature of a wild type. ***wild valerian***: see VALERIAN 1. ***wild vine***: see VINE *noun* 2. **wild well** an oil well which is out of control and blowing oil or gas from the borehole. ***wild woad***: see WOAD *noun* 2.

■ **wildish** *adjective* somewhat wild; inclining to wildness: E18. **wildling** *noun* a wilding; a wild plant, flower, or animal: M19. **wildness** *noun* (*a*) the quality or condition of being wild; (*b*) (now *rare* or *obsolete*) a wild place, a wilderness: LME.

wild /wʌɪld/ *verb*. ME.
[from prec.]
1 *verb intrans*. Of an animal or plant: grow or become wild; run wild. *rare*. ME.
†2 *verb trans*. Make wild; *esp*. make demented or distraught, madden. LME–M17.

wildbore /ˈwʌɪl(d)bɔː/ *noun*. *local*. L18.
[Origin unkn.]
A stout and closely woven unglazed tammy or fine worsted.

wildcat /ˈwʌɪl(d)kat/ *noun* & *adjective*. Also **wild cat**. LME.
[from WILD *adjective* + CAT *noun*[1].]
▸ A *noun*. 1 A small native Eurasian and African cat, *Felis silvestris*, that is usu. grey with black markings and a bushy black-tipped tail, is noted for its ferocity, and is the supposed ancestor of the domestic cat. Also, any of various other smaller members of the cat family, as the bobcat. LME.
2 A hot-tempered, violent, or spiteful person (esp. a woman). L16.
3 a A person who plans a rash project or engages in a risky enterprise. Also, a financially unsound commercial enterprise. *colloq*. (chiefly *US*). E19. ▸b An exploratory oil well, drilled where there is only a possibility of success. Orig. *US*. L19. ▸c *ellipt*. Illicitly distilled whiskey. Chiefly *US*. L19. ▸d *ellipt*. A wildcat strike (see sense B.2d below). M20.
▸ B *attrib*. or as *adjective*. 1 Of or pertaining to a wildcat. E17.
2 a (Of an enterprise etc.) risky, financially unsound; (of a business or its products) illicit; *gen*. reckless, rash. Orig. & chiefly *US*. M19. ▸b Of or pertaining to an exploratory oil well (see sense A.3b above). Orig. *US*. L19. ▸c Of a train: running in addition to the timetable or without official permission. *US*. L19. ▸d Of industrial action, esp. a strike: called at short notice, usu. without union backing. Orig. *US*. M20.

■ **wildcatter** *noun* (*a*) a prospector who sinks wildcat oil wells; (*b*) a wildcat striker: L19. **wildcatting** *noun* (*a*) the drilling of a wildcat oil well; (*b*) participation in a wildcat strike: L19.

wild deer /ˈwʌɪld dɪə/ *noun phr*. Pl. same.
[Old English *wil(d)dēor*, *wildedēor*, alt. of deriv. of base of WILD *adjective*; in sense 2 from WILD *adjective* + DEER.]
†1 A wild animal; *pl*. wild animals collectively. OE–ME.
2 A deer in an untamed or wild state. Usu. *pl*., deer in such a state collectively. M18.

Wildean /ˈwʌɪldɪən/ *adjective.* E20.
[from Oscar *Wilde* (see below) + -AN.]
Of, pertaining to, or characteristic of the Irish writer and wit Oscar Fingal O'Flahertie Wills Wilde (1854–1900) or his works.

wildebeest /ˈwɪldəbiːst, ˈvɪ-/ *noun.* Pl. **-s**, same, **-e** /-ə/. E19.
[Afrikaans, from *wild* wild + *beest* beast.]
Either of two large African grazing antelopes of the genus *Connochaetes*, having a long shaggy head, hooked horns, and a long tail. Also called ***gnu***.
black wildebeest a dark brown wildebeest with a white tail, *Connochaetes gnou*; also called ***white-tailed gnu***. **blue wildebeest** a light-coloured wildebeest, *C. taurinus*; also called ***brindled gnu***.

wilder /ˈwɪldə/ *verb. arch.* (now chiefly *poet.*). E17.
[Origin uncertain: perh. from next, but cf. Middle Dutch *verwildern*, and BEWILDER, which is, however, later.]
1 *verb trans.* Cause to lose one's way, as in a wilderness; lead or drive astray; *refl.* lose one's way, go astray. E17. ▸**b** *fig.* Make at a loss as to how to act or what to think; bewilder. M17.
2 *verb intrans.* Lose one's way, go astray, wander; be bewildered. M17.
†**3** *verb trans. & intrans.* Make or become wild or uncivilized. *rare.* L18–E19.
📖 **1** SOUTHEY Ye whom Youth has wilder'd on your way. **2** J. KEBLE Ye too, who tend Christ's wildering flock.
■ **wildered** *adjective* (*a*) straying, lost; bewildered; confused, mingled confusedly; (*b*) (of a place or region) in which one may lose one's way; pathless, wild: M17.

wilderness /ˈwɪldənɪs/ *noun.*
[Old English *wil(d)dēornes*, from *wil(d)dēor* WILD DEER + -NESS.]
1 Land which is wild, uncultivated, and inhabited only by wild animals; a wild, uncultivated, or uninhabited region. OE. ▸**b** Part of a large garden or park, planted so as to give an uncultivated or bewilderingly wild appearance, often laid out as a maze. M17.
2 *fig.* Anything compared to a wild or desolate region, or in which one wanders or becomes lost or lonely; *arch.* (THEOLOGY) the present world or life as contrasted with the afterlife. ME.
†**3** Wildness, uncultivated condition. Also *fig.* (*rare*, Shakes.), wildness of character, licentiousness. LME–M17.
4 *transf.* Any wild or desolate area or expanse. L16.
5 A mingled or confused collection *of* things or (*rare*) people. L16.
📖 **1** J. PURSEGLOVE Wildernesses of scattered birch, where adders sun themselves among the fern. *Backpacker* Despite . . pressures from developers, the park service has kept the wilderness intact. **2** BUNYAN As I walk'd through the wilderness of this world. M. FOOT Would he not be left to roam the political wilderness. **in the wilderness** [with allus. to *Numbers* 14:33] (*a*) (of a politician, political party, etc.) out of office; (*b*) *gen.* unregarded, out of favour. **voice in the wilderness** [with allus. to *Matthew* 3:3 etc.] an unheeded advocate of reform. **4** BYRON This blue wilderness of interminable Air. **5** DICKENS The wilderness of masts on the river, and . . steeples on the shore. D. LODGE That wilderness of factories and warehouses.

wildfire /ˈwʌɪl(d)fʌɪə/ *noun.* OE.
[from WILD *adjective* + FIRE *noun.*]
1 Destructive or uncontrollable fire; a conflagration. OE.
2 a MEDICINE. Any of various inflammatory eruptive skin diseases, *esp.* those in which the infection spreads from one part to another; *spec.* erysipelas. Now *rare.* OE. ▸**b** A leaf-spot disease of tobacco, caused by a variety of the bacterium *Pseudomonas syringae*. E20.
3 *Hist.* A composition of highly flammable substances, readily ignited and difficult to extinguish, esp. as used in warfare. ME.
4 *fig.* Anything compared to a destructive or uncontrollable agency; an excited, violent, or heated emotion etc. ME.
5 a Lightning; *esp.* sheet lightning without audible thunder. *rare* (chiefly *Scot.*). E16. ▸**b** (A) will-o'-the-wisp (*lit.* & *fig.*). M17. ▸**c** Firedamp in a coalmine. Formerly also, volcanic fire. L17.
📖 **1** J. MCPHEE Wildfires have raced through the forest. **4** C. M. DOUGHTY There is a wild-fire in my heart which cannot be appeased till I be avenged. **like wildfire** very swiftly and forcibly; freq. in ***spread like wildfire***.

wildflysch /ˈwʌɪl(d)flɪʃ, *foreign* ˈvɪltflɪʃ/ *noun.* Also **W-**. E20.
[German, from *wild* wild, rugged + Swiss German FLYSCH.]
GEOLOGY. Flysch containing large, irregularly distributed blocks and occupying beds that are distorted.

wildfowl /ˈwʌɪl(d)faʊl/ *noun.* Pl. same. OE.
[from WILD *adjective* + FOWL *noun.*]
Orig., a wild bird. Now, a game-bird, *esp.* a duck, a goose. Usu. in *pl.*
■ **wildfowler** *noun* a person who shoots or catches wildfowl M19. **wildfowling** *noun* the pursuit or capture of wildfowl L19.

wild goose /wʌɪl(d) ˈguːs/ *noun & adjectival phr.* Pl. **wild geese** /giːs/. OE.
[from WILD *adjective* + GOOSE *noun.*]
▶ **A** *noun phr.* **1** Any of various undomesticated or feral geese; *esp.* (*a*) the greylag, *Anser anser*; (*b*) *N. Amer.* the Canada goose, *Branta canadensis*. OE.
2 *fig.* **a** A flighty or foolish person. L16. ▸**b** *Hist.* In *pl.* (A nickname for) the Irish Jacobites who served as professional soldiers in Europe on the abdication of James II and later. M19.
▶ **B** *attrib.* or as *adjectival phr.* Wild, fantastic; foolish; fruitless. L18.
Comb.: **wild-goose chase** †(*a*) *rare* a horse-race in which the second or any succeeding horse had to follow accurately the course of the leader, like a flight of wild geese; (*b*) orig., an erratic course taken by one person (or thing) and followed (or that may be followed) by another; now, a foolish, fruitless, or hopeless quest, a pursuit of something unattainable.

wildie /ˈwʌɪldi/ *noun. slang.* Also **-dy**. M20.
[from WILD *adjective* + -IE.]
A fish, esp. a carp, which is truly wild, as opp. to one bred artificially as stock for anglers. Usu. in *pl.*

wilding /ˈwʌɪldɪŋ/ *noun*[1] & *adjective.* E16.
[from WILD *adjective* + -ING[3].]
▶ **A** *noun.* **1** A crab-apple; a crab-apple tree. E16.
2 *gen.* Any wild or uncultivated plant; the fruit or flower of such a plant. L16.
3 A wild person, thing, or (*rare*) animal. E17.
📖 **3** E. WHARTON You are not a heathen wilding, but a child of Christ.
▶ **B** *attrib.* or as *adjective.* **1** ***wilding apple***, a crab-apple. ***wilding tree***, a crab-apple tree. M16.
2 Of a plant: growing wild. Of a fruit or flower: obtained from such a plant. Chiefly *poet.* L17.

wilding /ˈwʌɪldɪŋ/ *noun*[2]. *US slang.* L20.
[from WILD *adjective* + -ING[1].]
The activity by a gang of youths of going on a protracted and violent rampage in a public place, attacking or mugging passers-by; an instance of this.

wildlife /ˈwʌɪl(d)lʌɪf/ *noun.* L19.
[from WILD *adjective* + LIFE *noun.*]
The native fauna and flora of a region, freq. *spec.* the fauna only.
📖 *attrib.*: *BBC Wildlife* We will protect wildlife habitat, open spaces and wilderness.
Comb.: **wildlife park** a park in which the public may view wild animals in conditions as close as possible to those of their natural environment; **wildlife sanctuary** a designated conservation area in which the wildlife is protected from hunting, collecting, etc.

wildly /ˈwʌɪl(d)li/ *adverb.* LME.
[from WILD *adjective* + -LY[2].]
1 In a wild, confused, or random manner; in disorder, erratically. LME.
2 Without restraint; uncontrollably; excitedly, frantically; as if demented or distraught; *colloq.* exceedingly, extremely. LME.
3 Without the moderating influence of culture or training; roughly, savagely. Also, in a free or pleasingly unconventional style; with the romantic aspect of uncultivated country. L16. ▸†**b** Without cultivation, naturally, like a wild plant. *rare* (Shakes.). E–M17.
📖 **1** D. MORAES The ship rolled wildly, so that at meals the stewards had to cleat the plates down. **2** J. HERSEY Most animals . . thrash about wildly when they . . find themselves with a foot trapped. R. GODDEN My eyes were green—not for nothing; I was wildly jealous. B. W. ALDISS She had thrown a wildly expensive party in her hotel suite. **3** JAS. ROBERTSON The wildly wooded banks of the Ardoch.

wild man /ˈwʌɪld man/ *noun phr.* Pl. **wild men** /mɛn/. Also **wildman**. ME.
[from WILD *adjective* + MAN *noun.*]
1 A man who is wild; a man of a rough, savage, or fierce nature; a man noted for dissolute or unruly behaviour. ME. ▸**b** An uncivilized or primitive man; a man reverted to a primitive state. ME. ▸**c** An extremist in a political party, a profession, etc. Usu. in *pl.* E20.
2 The orang-utan. Also ***wild man of the woods***. *arch.* L18.
Phrases: **wild man of the woods** (*a*) a man or supposed semi-human creature living in a wild state in woodland; (*b*) see sense 2 above.

Wild West /wʌɪld ˈwɛst/ *noun phr.* M19.
[from WILD *adjective* + WEST *noun*[2].]
1 The western part of the US during its lawless frontier period. M19.
2 *transf.* & *fig.* Any place or area compared to the N. American Wild West, esp. with regard to its lawlessness. L19.
📖 **1** *attrib.*: A. NICOL She removed the Wild West novels and romance magazines.
Comb.: **Wild West show** a circus or fairground entertainment depicting cowboys and N. American Indians with displays of riding, shooting, etc.
■ **wild western** *adjective & noun* (*a*) *adjective* characteristic of or resembling the Wild West; (*b*) *noun* a film about the Wild West; a western: M19. **Wild Westerner** *noun* M20.

wildwood /ˈwʌɪldwʊd/ *noun.* Now chiefly *poet.* & ECOLOGY. OE.
[Orig. two words, from WILD *adjective* + WOOD *noun*[1].]
A forest of natural growth, or one allowed to grow naturally; uncultivated or unfrequented woodland; *the* primeval forest prior to its modification by humans.

wildy *noun* var. of WILDIE.

wile /wʌɪl/ *noun.* Now usu. in *pl.* ME.
[Perh. from unrecorded Old Norse noun whence *vél* craft, artifice rel. to *véla* defraud.]
1 A crafty, cunning, or deceitful trick; a stratagem, a ruse. Formerly also, a piece of deception, a delusion. ME. ▸**b** A subtle or skilful device or scheme; a clever or resourceful procedure. *obsolete* exc. as passing into prec. ME. ▸**c** An amorous or playful trick; an enticing or charming ploy. L16. ▸**d** *spec.* A cunning trick of a hare to escape its hunters. L17.
2 Deceit, deceitfulness; cunning, trickery, guile. Now *rare.* LME.
3 Any of various mechanical devices; *spec.* (*Scot.*) a device for twisting straw ropes. L17.
📖 **1** *Guardian* Now . . people are wise to the wiles of the credit card companies. **c** B. TRAPIDO They used their considerable girlish wiles to draw him out. **2** LYTTON This Godwin is a man of treachery and wile.
■ †**wilely** *adjective* wily M16–L18.

wile /wʌɪl/ *verb.* ME.
[from the noun.]
1 *verb trans.* Bring, entice, or get by a wile or wiles; lead, induce, or obtain by deception, cunning, or enticement. Freq. foll. by *away, into, over.* ME.
2 Divert attention pleasantly from (something unpleasant or tedious); *esp.* while away (time) pleasantly or divertingly. Freq. foll. by *away.* L18.
📖 **1** R. L. STEVENSON She could neither be driven nor wiled into the parish kirk. **2** *Cook's Magazine* While waiting for responses . . , he began baking bread to wile away the time.

Wilfridian /wɪlˈfrɪdɪən/ *noun.* M19.
[from St *Wilfrid* (634–709) + -IAN.]
ECCLESIASTICAL HISTORY. A member of a religious fraternity founded by Father F. W. Faber (1814–63) for his fellow converts to Roman Catholicism.

wilful /ˈwɪlfʊl, -f(ə)l/ *adjective, adverb, & noun.* Also ***will-**. ME.
[from WILL *noun*[1] + -FUL. Earlier in WILFULLY *adverb.*]
▶ **A** *adjective.* **1** Asserting or disposed to assert one's own will contrary to persuasion, instruction, or command; headstrong; obstinate; determined to have one's own way. ME. ▸†**b** Resolute; firm in resolve. *rare.* ME–M17.
†**2** Having the will *to do* something; wishful, desirous. ME–L16.
3 Of an action etc.: done on purpose; deliberate, intentional. ME.
†**4** Willing; ready to comply with a request, desire, or requirement. LME–L16.
†**5** Done or undergone of one's own free will; voluntary. LME–L17.
📖 **1** H. CHAPONE The smallest disappointment . . will put wilful young people out of temper. E. O'BRIEN Allowing the car, like a wilful animal, to pursue its own course. **3** S. TOWNSEND He has been suspended . . pending an enquiry into his wilful neglect and cruelty to a rubber plant. W. GELDART A marriage is . . voidable . . because of one party's wilful refusal to consummate it. **5** S. PURCHAS He there died . . through his wilfull want of bread and water.
▶†**B** *adverb.* Wilfully. ME–E17.
▶ **C** *noun.* A wilful person; *rare* a wilful act. E19.
■ **wilfulness** *noun* (*a*) the quality or character of being wilful; (*b*) *rare* an instance of this, a wilful act: ME.

wilfully /ˈwɪlfʊli, -f(ə)li/ *adverb.* Also ***will-**.
[Late Old English *wilfullīċe*: see prec., -LY[2].]
†**1** Willingly, readily; patiently, submissively. LOE–E16.
†**2** Of one's own free will, voluntarily. LOE–E18. ▸**b** At will, freely. ME–E17.
†**3** With desire, longingly. *rare.* ME–E17.
4 On purpose; intentionally, deliberately. LME.
5 In an obstinately self-willed or stubborn manner. L16.
📖 **4** *Which?* An offence for anyone to fell . . or wilfully damage the tree without consent. **5** *SLR Camera* Olympus are still wilfully employing pointless gimmicks in the design.

wilga /ˈwɪlgə/ *noun. Austral.* L19.
[Aboriginal *wilgar*.]
Any of several white-flowered drought-resistant trees of the genus *Geijera*, of the rue family; esp. *G parviflora*, valuable as fodder.

wilgie /ˈwɪlgi/ *noun. Austral.* M19.
[from Aboriginal *wilgi*.]
A kind of red ochre used by Aborigines as a body paint.

Wilhelmine /ˈvɪlhelmʌɪn/ *adjective.* M20.
[from German male forename *Wilhelm* William (see below) + -INE[1].]
Of or pertaining to (the reign of) William II, emperor of Germany 1888–1918.
■ Also **Wilhelˈminian** *adjective* M20.

Wilhelmstrasse /ˈvɪlhɛlm,ʃtrɑːsə/ *noun.* E20.
[German, from *Wilhelm* William + *Strasse* street.]
A street in Berlin, the site of the German foreign office until 1945; *allus.* the pre-war German foreign office and its policies.

wili /ˈvɪli/ *noun.* Also **willi**. M20.
[German or French, from Serbo-Croat *vila* nymph, fairy.]
MYTHOLOGY. In Slavonic and eastern German legends, a spirit of a betrothed girl who has died from grief at being jilted by her lover (used esp. with ref. to the ballet *Giselle*). Cf. VILA.

wiliwili /ˈwiːlɪwiːliː/ *noun.* L19.
[Hawaiian.]
A coral tree, *Erythrina tahitensis*, of Hawaii and Tahiti, which bears clusters of orange flowers; the wood of this tree, used to make surfboards.

Wilkism /ˈwɪlkɪz(ə)m/ *noun.* M18.
[Irreg. from John *Wilkes* (see below) + -ISM.]
Hist. The principles or policies associated with John Wilkes (1727–97), English radical politician and proponent of parliamentary reform.
■ **Wilkite** *noun* a follower or adherent of Wilkism L18.

will /wɪl/ *noun*[1].
[Old English *willa* corresp. to Old Frisian *willa*, Old Saxon *willio*, Old High German *willo*, *willio* (Dutch *wil*, German *Wille*), Old Norse *vili*, Gothic *wilja*, from Germanic, from base also of WELL *adverb*.]
▸ **I 1** Desire, wish, longing; (a) liking or disposition (*to do*); (an) inclination *to do*. Long *obsolete* exc. as passing into senses 5, 6, and 6b. OE.
†**2** Sexual desire or appetite. OE–E17.
3 That which one desires. Chiefly in ***have one's will (of)*** below. Now *arch. & poet.* OE. ▸**b** A desire or wish as expressed in a request; the expression of a wish, a request, a petition. Freq. in ***what's your will*** below. Now *arch. & Scot.* ME.
4 Pleasure, delight, joy. Long *obsolete* exc. in ***have no will of*** below. OE.

> 🕮 **1** SHAKES. *Jul. Caes.* I have no will to wander forth of doors. SIR W. SCOTT The faculty of the present proprietor to entertain his friends is greatly abridged, . . the will . . remains the same. **3** A. C. SWINBURNE Have all thy will of words; talk out thine heart.

▸ **II 5** The action of willing or deciding to do something; the exercising of the mind with conscious intention towards initiating a chosen action; volition. OE. ▸**b** Intention, intent, purpose, determination; an instance of this. Now *rare* or *obsolete.* ME. ▸**c** A (psychological) drive; *gen.* a deliberate or fixed desire or intention (*to do*). Freq. in ***will to*** below. E19.
6 The faculty by which a person exercises his or her capacity for initiating conscious and intentional action; power of choice in regard to action. Cf. FREE WILL. OE. ▸**b** Control over one's own will; self-control; degree of deliberate imposition of this over instinct or impulse; an instance of this. Freq. with specifying word. Also ***will-power***. LME.
7 Intention or determination that what one wishes or ordains be done by another or others; force or energy of intention; an expression or embodiment of this, an order, an injunction; *arch.* (with possess. adjective) what one wills should be done. Also (with specifying word), disposition towards another or others. OE. ▸†**b** Consent, acquiescence; favourable disposition. ME–M16. ▸**c** Purport or substance of a legal document. Chiefly in ***the will of the letters***, ***the will of the summons*** below. *obsolete* exc. *Hist.* LME.
8 Undue assertion of one's own will; wilfulness. Long *obsolete* exc. *Scot.* ME.

> 🕮 **5** E. YOUNG The naked will obtains thy smile, Beneath this monument of praise unpaid. *Henry James Review* His will bent on the improvement of his art. **b** J. ARBUTHNOT My Will at present is to have Dinner. **c** U. LE GUIN Shevek's . . incredulity turned to rage . . , a blind will to violence, which he had never felt before. **6** W. MAXWELL He hated himself for being weak, for having no will. B. HEAD They had a hang-dog air as though the society and its oppressive ways had broken their will. **b** *Sports Illustrated* The . . blond with the . . iron will has taken command of her game and her emotions. **7** SHAKES. *Coriol.* Direct me, if it be your will, Where great Aufidius lies. D. ACHESON To acknowledge frankly that the will of the people had been constitutionally and clearly expressed. G. PRIESTLAND Nervous of . . confusing the theology of any one church with the Will of God. ***goodwill***, ***ill will***, etc.

▸ **III 9** A person's formal declaration as to the disposal of his or her property after death, having or intended to have legal force and usu. made in writing, to be signed and witnessed; the document in which this declaration of intention is expressed. Cf. TESTAMENT 3. OE.

> 🕮 **9** A. CARTER His will left instructions he should be cremated.

Phrases: **against one's will** in opposition to one's inclination or liking, unwillingly; contrary to one's choice, intention, or desire. **at the will of** at the mercy of, subject to the desires or intentions of. **at will** (*a*) according to one's volition or choice; as and when one pleases; (*b*) *arch.* at one's command or disposal; (*c*) LAW (of an estate) held during the owner's or lessor's pleasure by a tenant able to be evicted without notice; (of a tenant) able to be evicted without notice. **a will of one's own** a strong or self-assertive will; *euphem.* obstinacy, wilfulness. **by one's will**, **by will** (*obsolete* exc. *Scot.*) with one's consent or approval, willingly; as one would wish. **come in a person's will** *Scot.* submit oneself to a person's will; put oneself at a person's disposal. ***evil will***: see EVIL *adjective*. GOODWILL. **have no will of** *Scot.* take no pleasure in, have no liking for. **have one's will (of)** (now *arch. & poet.*) obtain what one wants (of something); have one's way (with a person). ***ill will***: see ILL *adjective & adverb*. ***latter-will***: see LATTER *adjective*. ***living will***: see LIVING *adjective*. **of one's will**, **of will** of one's own accord, spontaneously, voluntarily (now only with possess. and *own*). **o' will** *Scot.* spontaneously, of one's own accord. ***publish a will***: see PUBLISH 1. SELF-WILL. **take one's will** (chiefly *Scot.*) do as one pleases (in respect *of*). **take the will for the deed** *arch.* accept an expressed intention to do something as evidence of a commitment to perform it (whether or not this occurs). **the will of the summons**, †**the will of the letters** SCOTS LAW (now *Hist.*) the part of a writ of citation requiring the officer of law to cite the defendant to answer the summons in court. **to one's will**, **to will** (*obsolete* exc. *Scot.*) as one pleases or chooses; to one's liking. **what's your will?** (now *arch. & Scot.*) what do you want? what do you wish me to do? **will to** [after German *Wille zu*] chiefly with noun or *to do*, used esp. in PSYCHOANALYSIS & PHILOSOPHY to describe instincts or drives; *spec.* (*a*) ***will to power***, [translating German *Wille zur Macht*] esp. in Nietzschean philosophy and analytic psychology, the driving force behind all human behaviour; (*b*) ***will to be***, ***will to live***, an overriding, usu. innate drive or instinct to survive; (*c*) ***will to art***, an innate human drive towards artistic creation. **with a will** with determination; vigorously, energetically. **with one's will**, **with will** (*obsolete* exc. *Scot.*) = ***by one's will*** above. **with the best will (in the world)** however good or well-meaning one's intentions. ***work one's will***: see WORK *verb*.

Comb.: **will-form** a form on which a will is or may be made out; ***will-power***: see sense 6b above.

■ **will-less** /-l-l-/ *adjective* (*a*) not having a will of one's own; not exercising the will; (*b*) lacking the faculty of volition: M18.

will /wɪl/ *noun*[2]. L17.
[from WILL *verb*[1].]
An utterance or use of the auxiliary verb 'will'; a determination expressed by this.

will /wɪl/ *adjective & adverb.* Now only *Scot. & dial.* ME.
[Old Norse *villr* WILD *adjective*.]
▸ **A** *adjective.* **1** Going or gone astray; straying, wandering. ME.
2 *fig.* Not knowing what to do or how to proceed; at a loss, perplexed. ME.
3 Of a place: out-of-the-way; strange; desolate. LME.
▸ **B** *adverb.* Astray (*lit. & fig.*). Chiefly in **go will**, lose one's way, wander, err. ME.

will /wɪl, *unstressed* w(ə)l/ *verb*[1]. Pres.: 1, 2, 3 sing. & pl. **will**, (*informal*, esp. after pronouns) **'ll**; 2 sing. (*arch.*) **wilt** /wɪlt/. Pa.: 1, 2, 3 sing. & pl. **would** /wʊd, *unstressed* wəd/, (*informal*, esp. after pronouns) **'d**; 2 sing. (*arch.*) **wouldst** /wʊdst/ or **wouldest** /ˈwʊdɪst/. Neg.: **will not**, (*informal*) **won't** /wəʊnt/; **would not**, (*informal*) **wouldn't** /ˈwʊd(ə)nt/. No other parts used.
[Old English *wyllan* = Old Frisian *willa*, Old Saxon *willian* (Dutch *willen*), Old Norse *vilja*, Gothic *wiljan*, from Germanic, parallel with Germanic verb repr. by Old Frisian *wella*, Old High German *wellen* (German *wollen*), Old Norse *velja*, Gothic *waljan* choose, from Indo-European base also of Latin *velle*, *volo*. In branch I not always clearly distinguishable from WILL *verb*[2].]
▸ **I** As full verb (not always clearly distinguishable from WILL *verb*[2]).
1 *verb trans.* Desire, want, wish for, have a mind to, (something); wish or intend (*that* or that something be done or happen). Chiefly *arch.* OE.
2 *verb trans.* Give authoritative expression of a wish or intention *that*; decree, order. Long *obsolete* exc. as passing into WILL *verb*[2] 2. OE.

> 🕮 **1** J. GRANGE Who wil the curnell of the nut must breake the shell. SHAKES. *Tr. & Cr.* Hector! where's Hector? I will none but Hector. TENNYSON I would not one of thine own doves, Not ev'n a rose, were offer'd to thee. *Essentials* Moles, beauty spots, call them what you will . . , might be the warning sign of skin cancer.

▸ **II** The present tense ***will*** as auxiliary verb. Foll. by inf. without *to* or *ellipt.*
3 Desire to, wish to. *arch.* OE.
4 In response to another's desire or requirement: be disposed or willing to; consent to. OE. ▸**b** In the 2nd person: expr. a request, esp. a polite one. ME.
5 Choose to; intend consciously or voluntarily to. OE.
6 Be accustomed to; have the habitual or inevitable tendency to; do habitually. OE.
7 In the 1st person (also the 2nd and 3rd in interrog. use or indirect statements): expr. the speaker's determination, wish, or intention to bring about (or with neg., prevent) some action, event, or state of things in the future. OE.
8 Forming (with present infinitive) the future, and (with perfect infinitive) the future perfect tense; in more or less definite contexts. Latterly esp. in the 2nd and 3rd persons, ***shall*** being more usual (exc. *colloq.*) in the 1st person (in informal and unemphatic contexts ***'ll*** is now more usual than either); in hypothetical, relative, temporal, and final clauses used for all persons. Also used in the 2nd and 3rd persons for commands, esp. those of an abrupt or impersonal nature. OE. ▸**b** *ellipt.* Will go. *arch.* OE.
9 Expr. probability or expectation: must as a logical or necessary consequence. OE.
10 Be able to, be capable of (doing); have a (specified) ability, potential, or capacity. LME.
11 †**a** Resolve to. L15–M16. ▸**b** *emphatic* (in positive contexts). Be determined to; insist on or persist in (doing). E17.

> 🕮 **3** THACKERAY He . . points . . to the dishes which he will have served. **4** WORDSWORTH There's neither dog nor heifer . . Will wet his lips within that cup of stone. *Fast Forward* My problem is girls—they won't go out with me. **b** SIR W. SCOTT I desire you will found nothing on an expression hastily used. **5** R. BAXTER When God will tell us we shall know. J. BUCHAN They won't believe it. They'll think it's a dodge. **6** SIR T. BROWNE Crabs move sideling, Lobsters will swim swiftly backward. J. RUSKIN Men, by their nature, are prone to fight; they will fight for any cause, or for none. **7** SHAKES. *Temp.* Her waspish-headed son . . Swears he will shoot no more. I. MURDOCH I will, if I may, telephone you . . tomorrow evening. V. SINGH I'll beat him to a pulp. *Village Voice* Then I learn I am pregnant. I won't abort it. **8** J. RUSKIN I hope it may do you some good, as it won't me. J. CONRAD This calm will last . . many hours. A. MAUPIN 'You'll shrivel up.' 'No I won't.' E. SEGAL I think you'll make a wonderful doctor. J. ASHBERY The truth will out. **b** SIR W. SCOTT 'Thither will I then,' said the Constable. **9** BOLINGBROKE He who abandons . . his country, will abandon . . his friend. *Gamut* If a nuclear physicist makes a statement about nuclear physics, it will be presumed to be . . accurate. **10** *Practical Motorist* A full-size hacksaw won't fit into the average tool box. *Modern Railways* Each binder will hold . . 12 issues of the magazine. **11b** T. L. PEACOCK There is a girl concealed in this tower, and find her I will. W. GOLDING I *must* and *will* recover my composure.

▸ **III** The past form ***would*** as auxiliary verb with temporal function. Foll. by inf. without *to* or (now *rare*) *ellipt.*
12 Desired to, wished to. Now *arch. & literary.* OE.
13 Was willing or disposed to; consented to. OE.
14 Was accustomed to; had the habitual or inevitable tendency to; did habitually. OE.
15 As past tense corresp. to ***will*** in senses 7, 8. OE.
16 In indirect reported speech: in statements in the 2nd and 3rd persons reporting an original statement (esp. of intention) in the 1st person. OE.
17 Could; was capable of (doing). LME.
18 Was determined to; insisted on or persisted in (doing). Also (*colloq.*), could typically or inevitably be expected to, esp. in the light of a person's known character or tendencies. E18.

> 🕮 **12** SHAKES. *Temp.* This damn'd witch . . was banish'd; for one thing she did They would not take her life. DEFOE Mrs. Bargrave asked her whether she would drink some tea. DICKENS Look where you would, some exquisite form glided . . through the throng. **13** JOSEPH HALL In the Creation hee could haue made all at once, but hee would take dayes for it. D. MADDEN She . . wanted to marry you, but . . you would have none of it. **14** THACKERAY The girls would ask her . . for a little music, and she would sing her three songs. **15** E. WAUGH It was the wet season . . . At the end of August the rain would stop. V. WOOLF Lucy's way of coming in—as if she did not know what she would find. J. CASEY Working his way up to master wouldn't have been a piece of cake. **16** *Holiday Which?* Passengers were told that they would be taken to a hotel overnight. **17** *Which?* Keys which would fit only a limited number of locks. **18** C. MACKENZIE 'He always pushes me out.' 'He would.' T. HINDE 'He would, wouldn't he,' she says. 'It's what you'd expect of a born capitalist.'

▸ **IV** The past form ***would*** as auxiliary verb with modal function. Foll. by inf. without *to* or *ellipt.*
19 In statements of desire, intention, choice, preference, etc.: should like, wish, or desire (to). Now *esp.*, should wish earnestly (*that*) (now *arch. & poet.*); (foll. by *rather*, *sooner*) should prefer; ***would have*** (foll. by obj. and inf. or compl.), should like (a person or thing) to be or do something. OE. ▸**b** Esp. in tentative, polite, or deferential contexts: might be disposed to, should venture to (mean, say, or do, if permitted). LME.
20 In the apodosis of a hypothetical proposition (expressed or implied), indicating that the supposition is a possibility or contingent or conditional upon something, or to express hesitation or uncertainty. Latterly esp. in the 2nd and 3rd persons, *should* being more usual in the 1st, exc. where *should* could be interpreted as having the meaning 'ought to'. OE.
21 In a conditional clause with implication of intention or volition: chose to; was willing to. OE.

22 In the apodosis of hypothetical proposition (expressed or implied), with implication of intention or volition: should choose or be willing to. Also (*colloq.*), in 1st person statements of advice or recommendation. ME.

23 In a noun-clause (freq. introduced by *that*) dependent on expressions of desire, advice, or request. L16.

> **19** BYRON Come hither, child, I would a word with you. J. G. WHITTIER Would I might die now. A. E. HOUSMAN I hear the bugle blow To call me where I would not go. A. BROOKNER If there were illness he would rather not witness it. **b** *Rhythm* We would hope that age has not withered him . . but we cannot be sure. **20** SHAKES. *Rom. & Jul.* A rose By any other name would smell as sweet. T. HARDY A hat that seemed as if it would open and shut like an accordion. E. WAUGH Would the signor . . like a buttonhole? G. GREENE That information could have been conveyed, I would have thought, more easily in writing. A. TYLER Would you believe he was once the size of this little tyke? *Nation* The less one was willing to think of kids, it would seem, the more one thought of Ellis. **21** H. JAMES Something she wished him to understand if he only would. H. JOHNSON Vouvray tends to be . . rounder than champagne, a reason why . . many people prefer it, if they would but admit it. **22** V. NABOKOV She'd send me packing if I were to grow enterprising; my career would be ruined. D. MADDEN She'd have married him too, if she could have managed it. *New York Woman* You could dine out . . but I wouldn't. **23** TENNYSON I wish the snow would melt. P. THEROUX He hoped that he would be struck down by a thunderbolt.

Phrases: **nill I, will I, nill he, will he**, etc., *arch.* = ***will I, nill I*** etc. below. ***reason will, reason would***: see REASON *noun*[1]. **what you will** whatever you like or want. **will and nill** *arch.* = ***will or nill*** below. **will do** *colloq.* expr. willingness to carry out a request. **will I, nill I, will he, nill he**, etc., *arch.* (*a*) willingly or unwillingly; (*b*) one way or another; in any case; anyhow (cf. WILLY-NILLY). **will or nill** *arch.* (*a*) choose or refuse (something); intend or prevent (something); (*b*) ***whether a person will or nill***, whether a person will or not; willingly or unwillingly. **would God, would to God** *arch. & literary* O that it were God's will. **wouldn't it?** (chiefly *Austral. & NZ slang*) expr. annoyance, disgust, etc.

¶ Cf. SHALL *verb*.

will /wɪl/ *verb*[2]. Pres.: 3 sing. **wills**, (*arch.*) **willeth** /ˈwɪlɪθ/; pa. t. & pple **willed** /wɪld/.

[Old English *willian* = Old High German *willōn*, from Germanic base of WILL *noun*[1]. In early uses not always clearly distinguishable from WILL *verb*[1].]

1 *verb trans.* = WILL *verb*[1] 1. OE.

2 *verb trans.* Leave instructions in one's will or testament (*that* something be done, or for something *to be* done after death). OE. ▸**b** Bequeath by the terms of a will. Freq. in *pass.* LME.

3 *verb trans.* Have as the object of one's will; intend consciously or unconditionally. Usu. foll. by *that, to do*. OE. ▸**b** *verb intrans.* Exercise will-power; use volition to make a choice or decision. L16. ▸**c** *verb trans.* Bring, instigate, or compel *into* or *out of* a given state or position by exercise of one's will. Also, control or influence (another person) or induce (a person or thing) *to do* by the exercise of one's will. M19.

4 *verb trans.* **a** Enjoin, order; decree, ordain. Freq. foll. by *to do*. *arch.* ME. ▸†**b** Request, entreat. LME–L17. ▸†**c** *fig.* Of a thing: require, demand; persuade (a person) *to do*. LME–M17.

> **1** I. BARROW Two things he willeth, that we should be good, and that we should be happy. **2** H. PEACHAM Willing his body to be buried in the Cathedrall Church of Rochester. **b** T. DREISER He was . . on this farm because it had been willed to him. **3** A. E. HOUSMAN Others . . Have willed more mischief than they durst. F. FERGUSSON Oedipus suffers forces he can neither control nor understand . . ; yet at the same time he wills . . his every move. *absol.*: CARLYLE All shall be as God wills. **b** F. QUARLES My Sin-bemangled body lies, Not having pow'r, to will; nor will, to rise! **c** C. FREEMAN Rachel willed herself to forget the moment of . . her deliverance. M. DORRIS I willed the car to start. **4** DRYDEN 'Tis yours . . to will The Work, which Duty binds me to fulfil. **c** SHAKES. *Coriol.* What custom wills, in all things should we do't?

will /wɪl/ *verb*[3] *intrans.* Now only *Scot.* Pa. t. & pple **willed**, **wilt** /wɪlt/. ME.

[Old Norse *villask* refl. of *villa* lead astray, from *villr* WILL *adjective*.]

Go astray, lose one's way; stray.

willable /ˈwɪləb(ə)l/ *adjective. rare.* LME.

[from WILL *verb*[1], *verb*[2] + -ABLE.]

†**1** That is to be willed or desired. Only in LME.

2 Able to be willed. L19.

willed /wɪld/ *adjective*[1]. LME.

[from WILL *noun*[1] + -ED[2].]

1 Having a will of a specified kind. Chiefly as 2nd elem. of comb., as ***self-willed, strong-willed, weak-willed***, etc. LME.

2 Having one's will directed to some (specified) action; minded or disposed (*to do*). *arch.* LME.

willed /wɪld/ *adjective*[2]. M19.

[from WILL *verb*[2] + -ED[1].]

1 Bequeathed by the terms of a person's will or testament. *rare.* M19.

2 Consciously intended or effected by one's will; voluntary. L19. ▸**b** Controlled by another's will. L19.

> **2** *Guardian* His friends are wondering how long his willed seclusion will last.

willemite /ˈwɪləmʌɪt/ *noun.* M19.

[from *Willem* I (1772–1843), king of the Netherlands + -ITE[1].]

MINERALOGY. A trigonal silicate of zinc occurring in masses or crystals of greenish yellow and other colours, and often strongly fluorescent.

willer /ˈwɪlə/ *noun.* LME.

[from WILL *verb*[2] + -ER[1].]

1 A person who desires something; a wisher. Chiefly, & now only, as 2nd elem. of comb., as ***ill-willer, well-willer***, etc. LME.

2 A person who exercises his or her will; a voluntary agent. LME.

Willesden /ˈwɪlzd(ə)n/ *adjective.* L19.

[A suburb in NW London, where the product was originally made.]

Designating any of various forms of paper or canvas that have been toughened and waterproofed by being treated with cuprammonium solution.

willet /ˈwɪlɪt/ *noun.* M19.

[Imit. of the bird's call.]

A large N. American sandpiper, *Catoptophorus semipalmatus*, that has greyish-brown plumage with a striking black and white wing pattern visible in flight.

willey *noun & verb* var. of WILLY *noun*[1] & *verb*.

willful *adjective, adverb, & noun*, **willfully** *adverb* see WILFUL, WILFULLY.

willi *noun* var. of WILI.

William /ˈwɪljəm/ *noun.* Also **w-**. L16.

[Male forename. In sense 3, with pun on BILL *noun*[3].]

▸ **I 1** Any of several pinks or related plants. Now chiefly in ***sweet William*** s.v. SWEET *adjective*. L16.

2 *Hist.* A former Dutch coin equal to 10 guilders. M19.

3 a An account for payment, a bill. *slang.* M19. ▸**b** A banknote. *US slang.* M19.

1 wild Williams *arch.* ragged robin, *Lychnis flos-cuculi*.

▸ **II 4** Used *attrib.* to designate styles of architecture, furniture, etc., characteristic of the reign of monarchs of Great Britain and Ireland named William, esp. William III and Mary (reigned jointly 1689–94), and William IV (reigned 1830–7). E20.

Williamite /ˈwɪljəmʌɪt/ *noun & adjective.* M17.

[In sense 1 from mod. Latin *Wilhelmita, Guilhelmita*, French *Guillemite*, from Old French *Guillemin* (mod. *Guillaume*) William (see below) + -ITE[1]. In sense 2 from *William* of Orange (see below) + -ITE[1].]

▸ **A** *noun.* **1** A member of an order of Augustinian hermits founded in the 12th cent. by followers of St William. M17.

2 *Hist.* A supporter of William of Orange, later King William III (see WILLIAM 4). Cf. JACOBITE *noun*[2]. L17.

▸ **B** *adjective.* Of glass: bearing portraits or emblems of William III, as an indication of anti-Jacobite feelings. E20.

William Morris /wɪljəm ˈmɒrɪs/ *adjective.* M20.

[See MORRIS *adjective*[2].]

= MORRIS *adjective*[2].

■ **William Morrisy** *adjective* resembling the life of William Morris; characteristic of his work: M20.

william-nilliam /wɪljəmˈnɪljəm/ *adverb. joc. & colloq.* E20.

[Extended form of WILLY-NILLY *adverb*.]

Willy-nilly.

Williams /ˈwɪljəmz/ *noun*[1]. E19.

[from *Williams*'s Nursery, Turnham Green, Middlesex, where the fruit was first raised.]

A juicy early-ripening variety of *bon chrétien* pear. Also more fully ***Williams Bon Chrétien, Williams pear, Williams's Bon Chrétien, Williams's pear***. Cf. BARTLETT.

Williams /ˈwɪljəmz/ *noun*[2]. M20.

[Frederick Callard *Williams* (1911–77), English electrical engineer.]

COMPUTING. Used *attrib.* with ref. to a cathode-ray tube used in some early computers to store and display an array of spots representing bits.

Williamsburg /ˈwɪljəmzbəːɡ/ *noun.* Chiefly *US.* M20.

[The former capital of the State of Virginia.]

Used *attrib.* to designate architectural and decorative styles and colours (esp. a shade of blue) considered characteristic of Williamsburg in colonial times or of its modern reconstruction, and objects made in such styles.

williamsite /ˈwɪljəmzʌɪt/ *noun.* M19.

[from L. White *Williams*, 19th-cent. US mineralogist + -ITE[1].]

MINERALOGY. A massive variety of antigorite resembling jade.

willie *noun* var. of WILLY *noun*[2].

willies /ˈwɪlɪz/ *noun pl. colloq.* (orig. *US*). L19.

[Origin unkn.]

the willies, nerves, jitters; a fit of nervous apprehension. Chiefly in ***give a person the willies, get the willies***.

willing /ˈwɪlɪŋ/ *noun.* OE.

[from WILL *verb*[2] + -ING[1].]

1 Wishing, desire. *arch.* & now only in conjunction with ***nilling***. OE.

2 The action of exercising one's will, volition; (now *rare*) an instance of this. Also, cheerful intention, readiness of will, obliging disposition. ME. ▸**b** The action of controlling or influencing another by the exercise of one's will. L19.

3 The action of bequeathing something by will. M19.

> **2** *Daily News* The two first are of human willing; the last is purely . . necessary. ***show willing***: see SHOW *verb*.

willing /ˈwɪlɪŋ/ *adjective & adverb.* OE.

[from WILL *verb*[1] + -ING[2]. In Old English recorded only with prefix.]

▸ **A** *adjective.* **1** Having a ready will; disposed to undertake or consent to a thing without reluctance; ready to be of use or service; obliging. Freq. foll. by *to do*. OE. ▸**b** *fig.* (Of a thing) compliant, yielding; (of the wind) favourable. E16. ▸**c** Given, offered, performed, or undergone willingly or readily; done or offered by a willing person. M16.

†**2** Wishing, wishful, desirous. LME–E19.

†**3** Done or undergone of one's own will; voluntary, intentional, deliberate. M16–E17.

> **1** S. BELLOW I was a more than willing listener. *Guardian* Charities . . were willing to help. *She* Shoppers who are willing to pay more for meat . . less intensively farmed. **c** LD MACAULAY The . . willing obedience of his subjects. J. HIGGINS Willing hands reached down to help them up the ladder.

▸ **B** *adverb.* Willingly, without reluctance. Chiefly & now only in ***willing or nilling, willing nilling***, whether one likes it or not, willy-nilly. *arch.* L16.

■ **willingly** *adverb* in a willing manner; *spec.* (*a*) readily, without reluctance, gladly; †(*b*) intentionally, deliberately; †(*c*) without compulsion, voluntarily: OE. **willingness** *noun* M16.

williwaw /ˈwɪlɪwɔː/ *noun.* M19.

[Origin unkn. Cf. WILLY *noun*[3].]

A sudden violent squall, orig. in the Straits of Magellan.

willock /ˈwɪlək/ *noun. obsolete* exc. *dial.* M17.

[formed as next + -OCK.]

An auk; *esp.* the guillemot.

will-o'-the-wisp /wɪləðəˈwɪsp/ *noun & verb.* Orig. †**will with the wisp**. E17.

[from *Will* abbreviation of male forename *William* + O' *preposition*[2] + THE *adjective* + WISP *noun*.]

▸ **A** *noun.* = IGNIS FATUUS (*lit. & fig.*). Also, an elusive person. E17.

> *Times Lit. Suppl.* A separate peace with Austria-Hungary was the great will o' the wisp of the First World War. *attrib.*: J. KRANTZ To run off to London in pursuit of a hauntingly perverse will-o'-the-wisp girl.

▸ **B** *verb trans.* Lead astray like a will-o'-the-wisp. *rare.* M17.

■ **will-o'-the-wispish** *adjective* of the nature of or resembling a will-o'-the-wisp M19.

willow /ˈwɪləʊ/ *noun, adjective, & verb.*

[Old English *welig* = Old Saxon *wilgia*, Middle & mod. Low German *wilge*, Dutch *wilg*, from Germanic base also of WILLY *noun*[1].]

▸ **A** *noun.* **1** Any of various shrubs and small trees of the genus *Salix*, chiefly of north temperate regions, which bear inconspicuous flowers in catkins and are typically plants of streamsides with pliant branches and long narrow leaves. OE. ▸**b** The timber or flexible shoots of the willow, often used for cricket-bats, baskets, etc.; *fig.* a flexible or compliant person. L15. ▸**c** A branch or the leaves of the willow as a symbol of grief for unrequited love or the loss of a loved one. Freq. in ***wear the willow, wear willow, wear the willow garland, wear the green willow***, grieve for the loss of a loved one, be in mourning. *arch.* L16. ▸**d** A pale green shade or tint of the colour of willow leaves. Also more fully ***willow-green***. L19.

†**2** = WILLY *noun*[1] 2. LME–M16.

3 Any of various plants resembling a willow in some way, esp. in having flexible branches or long narrow leaves; *esp.* (more fully ***native willow***) the couba, *Acacia salicina*. Usu. with specifying word. M16.

4 = WILLY *noun*[1] 3. M19.

5 A cricket-bat. Cf. ***King Willow*** s.v. KING *noun*. M19.

1 *crack-willow, goat-willow, grey willow, weeping willow, white willow*, etc. **3 flowering willow** a desert shrub of south-western N. America, *Chilopsis linearis* (family Bignoniaceae), with willow-like leaves and white flowers.

▸ **B** *attrib.* or as *adjective.* **1** Made of, decorated with, or resembling the wood or leaves of the willow; resembling the willow, willowy. L15.

2 Made of willow-pattern porcelain etc. E20.

Comb. & special collocations: **willow beauty** a European geometrid moth, *Peribatodes rhomboidaria*, that is greyish with dark speckling; **willow beetle** (*a*) the osier weevil, *Cryptorhynchus* *lapathi*; (**b**) = ***willow leaf beetle*** below; **willow borer** (*a*) the larva of the osier weevil, *Cryptorhynchus lapathi*, which is a pest of willows; (**b**) a large longhorn beetle, *Saperda carcharias*, whose larvae bore into the wood of willows and poplars; **willow gentian** a European gentian, *Gentiana asclepiadea*, with deep blue flowers, curving stems, and willow-like leaves; **willow-green**: see sense A.1d above; **willow grouse** (*a*) a grouse of northern Eurasia and Canada, *Lagopus lagopus*, which turns white in winter and is conspecific with the British red grouse; (**b**) *Canad.* the ruffed grouse, *Bonasa umbellus*; **willowherb** †(*a*) (more fully ***yellow willowherb***) yellow loosestrife, *Lysimachia vulgaris*; (**b**) any of numerous plants constituting the genus *Epilobium* (family Onagraceae), with pink flowers of various shades and opposite freq. lanceolate or narrow leaves; *esp.* (more fully ***great hairy willowherb***) *E. hirsutum*, a plant of streamsides with cherry-coloured flowers and usu. softly hairy leaves; (***rosebay willowherb***: see **rosebay** (b) s.v. ROSE *noun*); **willow leaf** (*a*) a leaf of the willow; (**b**) a design or shape resembling this; **willow leaf beetle** any of various chrysomelid beetles that feed on willow leaves, esp. of the genera *Phyllodecta* and *Galerucella*, and (*N. Amer.*) of the genus *Chrysomela*; **willow-leaved** *adjective* having long narrow leaves; **willow myrtle** any of several western Australian trees constituting the genus *Agonis*, of the myrtle family, with willow-like leaves; **willow oak** an oak of the eastern US, *Quercus phellos*, having narrow entire leaves like those of a willow; **willow-pattern** *noun & adjective* (designating porcelain etc. having) a conventional design representing a Chinese scene, often with a willow tree, of blue on white porcelain, stoneware, or earthenware; **willow ptarmigan** (chiefly *N. Amer.*) = ***willow grouse*** (a) above; **willow tit** a Eurasian tit, *Parus montanus*, which has a sooty black cap; **willow tree** = sense A.1 above; **willow warbler** (*a*) a small Eurasian leaf warbler, *Phylloscopus trochilus*; (**b**) any of various related warblers found mainly in Asia; **willow-ware** (*a*) porcelain, earthenware, or stoneware with a willow-pattern design; (**b**) articles woven from osiers; **willow weed** (*a*) = ***willowherb*** (a) above; (**b**) any of several persicarias with willow-like leaves, *esp.* redshank, *Persicaria maculosa*; **willow-wren** = ***willow warbler*** (a) above.

▶ **C** *verb trans.* Treat (cotton etc.) with a willow or willy (WILLY *noun*[1] 3). *rare*. **M19.**

■ **willowed** *adjective* (*rare*) bordered or grown with willows **M18.** **willow-like** *adjective* resembling (that of) a willow **E18.** **willowish** *adjective* (*a*) resembling that of a willow, esp. with regard to the colour of willow-leaves; (**b**) *rare* like a willow; *fig.* pliant: **M17.**

willowy /ˈwɪləʊi/ *adjective.* **M18.**
[from WILLOW *noun* + -Y[1].]
1 Bordered, shaded, or covered with willows. **M18.**
2 Slender, lithe; graceful. **L18.**

> 🕮 **1** SHELLEY The willowy plain of the Rhone. **2** C. BRAYFIELD Tall but so delicate, willowy, thin.

■ **willowily** *adverb* (*rare*) **M20.** **willowiness** *noun* (*rare*) **L20.**

willsome *adjective* var. of WILSOME *adjective*[2].

†will with the wisp *noun & verb phr.* see WILL-O'-THE-WISP.

will-worship /ˈwɪlwəːʃɪp/ *noun. arch.* **M16.**
[from WILL *noun*[1] + WORSHIP *noun*, translating Greek *ethelothrēskeia* (Colossians 2:23).]
Worship according to one's own will or inclination; worship seen as imposed by human will without divine authority.

willy /ˈwɪli/ *noun*[1] *& verb.* Also **willey**.
[Old English *wilige*, *wiliga*.: see WILLOW. Cf. TWILLY *noun*[2] & *verb*, WEEL *noun*[2].]
▶ **A** *noun.* **1** A basket. *dial.* **OE.**
2 A weel, a fish-trap. *local.* **E17.**
3 A revolving conical or cylindrical machine fitted with internal spikes for opening and cleaning wool, cotton, or flax. **M19.**
▶ **B** *verb trans.* Treat (cotton etc.) with a willy. **M19.**

willy /ˈwɪli/ *noun*[2]. Also **willie**. **M19.**
[Pet-form of male forename *William*: see -Y[6].]
1 Any of various birds; *esp.* a guillemot. Cf. WILLOCK. *dial.* **M19.**
2 The penis. *slang.* **E20.**
Comb.: **willy wagtail** (*a*) *dial.* the pied wagtail; (**b**) a common Australian fantail flycatcher, *Rhipidura leucophrys*, which has striking black and white plumage.

willy /ˈwɪli/ *noun*[3]. **M19.**
[Prob. rel. to WILLIWAW.]
A sudden squall in the South Atlantic; a whirlwind of spray above the sea's surface.

†willy *adjective.* **ME.**
[from WILL *noun*[1] + -Y[1].]
1 Willing, eager. **ME–L15.**
2 Well-disposed, benevolent. **LME–L15.**
¶ Survived in ***well-willy*** s.v. WELL *adverb*.

willya /ˈwɪljə/ *verb* (*2 sing. pres.*). *non-standard.* **M20.**
[Repr. an informal pronunc.]
Will you?

willyart /ˈwɪljɑːt/ *adjective. Scot.* **L16.**
[Rel. to WILL *adjective*; later assoc. with WILL *noun*[1].]
1 Wild; shy. **L16.**
2 Self-willed, obstinate. **L18.**

willy-nilly /wɪlɪˈnɪli/ *adverb & adjective.* **E17.**
[= *will I, nill I*: see WILL *verb*[1]. Cf. HITTY-MISSY.]
▶ **A** *adverb.* Whether one likes it or not; willingly or unwillingly. Also, haphazardly, anyhow, at random. **E17.**

> 🕮 Q. BELL A mission, which had to be imposed, willy-nilly, upon the Colonial Office. *Yankee* Ancient cars and trucks . . were parked willy-nilly.

▶ **B** *adjective.* Existing or occurring whether one likes it or not. **L19.**

willy-willy /ˈwɪlɪˌwɪli/ *noun.* **L19.**
[Aboriginal.]
In NW Australia, a cyclone or dust-storm.

Wilms /wɪlmz, vɪlmz/ *noun.* **E20.**
[Max *Wilms* (1867–1918), German surgeon.]
MEDICINE. Used *attrib.* and in *possess.* to designate a malignant tumour of the kidney (nephroblastoma) that occurs in young children.

wilsome /ˈwɪls(ə)m/ *adjective*[1]. *obsolete* exc. *Scot.* **ME.**
[Old Norse *villusamr*, from *villr* WILL *adjective* + *-samr* -SOME[1].]
1 Of a region or path: lonely and wild; dreary. **ME.**
2 Erring, wandering, straying; bewildered, perplexed; doubtful, uncertain (*of*). **ME.**
■ **wilsomely** *adverb*[1] **LME.** **wilsomeness** *noun*[1] **ME.**

wilsome /ˈwɪls(ə)m/ *adjective*[2]. *obsolete* exc. *dial.* Also **-ll-**. **LME.**
[Perh. orig. a use of prec., later assoc. with WILL *noun*[1].]
Wilful, obstinate, stubborn.
■ **wilsomely** *adverb*[2] **M19.** **wilsomeness** *noun*[2] **LME.**

Wilson /ˈwɪls(ə)n/ *noun*[1]. **E19.**
[Alexander *Wilson* (1766–1813), Scottish-born Amer. ornithologist.]
Used in *possess.* in the names of birds described by Wilson.
Wilson's petrel = ***Wilson's storm petrel*** below. **Wilson's phalarope** a long-billed phalarope, *Phalaropus tricolor*, found chiefly in inland parts of N. America. **Wilson's snipe** a snipe, *Gallinago gallinago*, of a race found in N. America. **Wilson's storm petrel**, a storm petrel, *Oceanites oceanicus*, which breeds around the Southern Ocean and migrates to northern oceans.

Wilson /ˈwɪlsən/ *noun*[2]. **E20.**
[S. A. Kinnier *Wilson* (1878–1937), English neurologist.]
MEDICINE. ***Wilson's disease***, ***Wilson's syndrome***, a degenerative disease affecting the liver and the lentiform nucleus. Also called ***hepatolenticular degeneration***.

Wilsonian /wɪlˈsəʊnɪən/ *adjective*[1] *& noun*[1]. **E20.**
[from *Wilson* (see below) + -IAN.]
▶ **A** *adjective.* Of, pertaining to, or characteristic of Woodrow Wilson (1856–1924), US president 1913–21, or his policies. **E20.**
▶ **B** *noun.* A supporter of Woodrow Wilson or his policies. **E20.**
■ ˈ**Wilsonism** *noun* the policies of Woodrow Wilson **E20.**

Wilsonian /wɪlˈsəʊnɪən/ *adjective*[2] *& noun*[2]. **M20.**
[from *Wilson* (see below) + -IAN.]
▶ **A** *adjective.* Of, pertaining to, or characteristic of Harold Wilson (1916–95), British prime minister 1964–70 and 1974–6, or his policies. **M20.**
▶ **B** *noun.* A supporter of Harold Wilson or his policies. **M20.**
■ ˈ**Wilsonite** *noun* = WILSONIAN *noun*[2] **M20.**

wilt /wɪlt/ *verb*[1] *& noun.* Orig. *dial.* **L17.**
[Perh. alt. of WELK *verb*[1].]
▶ **A** *verb.* **1** *verb intrans.* **a** Of a plant, leaf, or flower: become limp through heat, drought, etc.; wither, droop. **L17.** ▸**b** *transf.* Lose one's energy or vigour; become dispirited or despondent, flag, tire. **L18.**
2 *verb trans.* Cause to wilt. **E19.** ▸**b** *AGRICULTURE.* Leave (mown grass etc.) in the open to dry partially before being put in a silo. **L20.**

> 🕮 **1a** A. SILLITOE Leaves of aspidistras wilted in the fumes of beer and smoke. **b** P. G. WODEHOUSE She eyed the speaker sternly. He wilted. 'Yes, ma'am,' he mumbled sheepishly.

▶ **B** *noun.* The action or an act of wilting; *spec.* any of various plant diseases characterized by wilting of the foliage, chiefly caused by verticilliums and other hyphomycetous fungi. **M19.**
oak wilt, ***spotted wilt***, ***vascular wilt***, etc.

wilt *verb*[2] see WILL *verb*[1].

wilt *verb*[3] *pa. t. & pple*: see WILL *verb*[3].

Wilton /ˈwɪlt(ə)n/ *noun*[1]. **L18.**
[A town in Wiltshire noted for the manufacture of carpets.]
In full ***Wilton carpet***. A kind of woven carpet resembling a Brussels carpet but having a thick velvet pile.

Wilton /ˈwɪlt(ə)n/ *noun*[2]. **E20.**
[A farm near Grahamstown in South Africa.]
ARCHAEOLOGY. Used *attrib.* to designate a later Stone Age culture of southern Africa.

Wilts. *abbreviation.*
Wiltshire.

Wiltshire /ˈwɪltʃə/ *noun.* **L18.**
[A county in SW England.]
1 In full ***Wiltshire Horned sheep***, ***Wiltshire Horn***. (An animal of) a recently revived breed of large horned sheep kept for its meat rather than its short wool. **L18.**
2 In full ***Wiltshire bacon***. A kind of smoked bacon. **E19.**
3 In full ***Wiltshire cheese***. A kind of hard-pressed mild cheese made from whole milk. **E19.**

wily /ˈwʌɪli/ *adjective & adverb.* **ME.**
[from WILE *noun* + -Y[1].]
▶ **A** *adjective.* Full of or characterized by wiles; crafty, cunning; sly, artful. **ME.**

> 🕮 POPE The Knave of Diamonds tries his wily arts, And wins . . the Queen of Hearts. *Guardian* The wily old fox of South Asian politics. **wily beguile**, **wily beguily** *arch. slang* a wily person or action, *esp.* one excessively or counter-productively so.

▶†**B** *adverb.* In a wily manner, wilily. **LME–E17.**
■ **wilily** *adverb* **LME.** **wiliness** *noun* **LME.**

wimble /ˈwɪmb(ə)l/ *noun & verb.* Now *dial.* & *techn.* In sense A.4 also **-bel**, **-brel** /-br(ə)l/. **ME.**
[from Anglo-Norman from Germanic base also of GIMLET.]
▶ **A** *noun.* **1** A gimlet. **ME.**
2 An auger. Also, a brace. **LME.**
3 An instrument for boring in soft ground or for extracting rubbish from a bore-hole in mining. **L17.**
4 An implement for twisting together strands of straw etc. to make rope. **M19.**
▶ **B** *verb.* **1** *verb trans.* **a** Pierce (as) with a wimble; make (a hole) with a wimble. *obsolete* exc. *dial.* **LME.** ▸**b** Make (a rope) using a wimble. *dial.* **L19.**
2 *verb intrans.* Bore *into*. Chiefly *fig.*, penetrate or insinuate oneself *into*. *obsolete* exc. *dial.* **E17.**
■ **wimbler** *noun* **M20.**

Wimbledon /ˈwɪmb(ə)ld(ə)n/ *noun.* **E20.**
[A district of SW London.]
The annual tennis championship played at the All-England Lawn Tennis and Croquet Club in Wimbledon.

wimble-wamble /wɪmb(ə)lˈwɒmb(ə)l/ *adverb & noun. dial.* **L19.**
[Redupl. of WAMBLE *noun*, *verb*.]
▶ **A** *adverb.* ***go wimble-wamble***, roll about in walking. **L19.**
▶ **B** *noun.* The mass of people, the ordinary crowd. **M20.**

wimbly-wambly /wɪmblɪˈwɒmbli/ *adjective. dial.* **L19.**
[Redupl. of WAMBLY.]
Shaky, unsteady; feeble, effeminate.

wimbrel *noun* see WIMBLE.

Wimmera ryegrass /ˈwɪmərə ˈrʌɪgrɑːs/ *noun phr.* **E20.**
[A river and the region surrounding it in Victoria, Australia.]
A drought-resistant variety of a Mediterranean rye-grass, *Lolium rigidum*, grown as a pasture grass in Australia.

wimmin /ˈwɪmɪn/ *noun pl. non-standard.* **M19.**
[Repr. pronunc. of *women*, orig. *joc.*, later adopted by some feminists to avoid the ending *-men*. Cf. WOMYN.]
Women.

wimp /wɪmp/ *noun*[1]. *slang.* Now *rare.* **E20.**
[Origin uncertain: perh. alt. of *women*.]
A woman or girl.

wimp /wɪmp/ *noun*[2], *adjective, & verb. colloq.* Also **wh-**. **E20.**
[Origin uncertain: perh. from WHIMPER.]
▶ **A** *noun.* A feeble, timid, or ineffectual person. **E20.**

> 🕮 *Ice Hockey News Review* Goalies were wimps if they wore facemasks. *Quarterly* She's such a wimp If only she had some guts.

▶ **B** *attrib.* or as *adjective.* = WIMPISH. **L20.**
▶ **C** *verb intrans.* Foll. by *out*: feebly fail to act, timidly withdraw from or avoid an undertaking. **L20.**

WIMP /wɪmp/ *noun*[3]. Also **wimp**, **W-**. **L20.**
[Acronym, from windows, icons, mouse, and program (or pointer, product, pull-down menu, etc.).]
COMPUTING. A set of software features and hardware devices (as windows, icons, mice, pull-down menus, etc.) designed to simplify or demystify computing operations for the user. Freq. *attrib.*

WIMP /wɪmp/ *noun*[4]. **L20.**
[Acronym, from weakly interacting massive particle.]
Any of several hypothetical subatomic particles of large mass which interact only weakly with ordinary matter, postulated as constituents of the dark matter of the universe. Usu. in *pl.*

wimpish /ˈwɪmpɪʃ/ *adjective. colloq.* Also **wh-**. **E20.**
[from WIMP *noun*[2] + -ISH[1].]
Characteristic of a wimp; feeble, ineffectual, timid.

> 🕮 J. ASHBERY The puny efforts at repeal that I and my wimpish cohorts advocated. M. BLONSKY Americans who love excess . . demand the bold and crude and consider anything less, wimpish.

■ **wimpishly** *adverb* **L20.** **wimpishness** *noun* **L20.**

wimple /ˈwɪmp(ə)l/ *noun & verb.*
[Late Old English *wimpel* = Old Frisian, Middle & mod. Low German *wimpel*, Old Saxon *wimpal*, Old High German *winfila* (German *Wimpel* streamer, pennon), Old Norse *vimpill*: see -LE[1].]

▶ **A** *noun.* **1** A usu. linen or silk head-dress folded to cover the hair, sides of the face, and neck, formerly worn by women and still worn by some nuns. **LOE.**
2 A fold, a wrinkle; a turn, a twist; a ripple in a stream etc.; a crafty turn or twist, a wile. Chiefly *Scot.* **E16.**
▶ **B** *verb.* **1** *verb trans.* Envelop in a wimple; arrange in folds; *gen.* veil, cover. **ME.** ▸†**b** Enfold, enwrap, wrap *up.* **E16–M17.**
2 *verb intrans.* Orig. (*rare*), wear a wimple. Later, (of a veil etc.) fall in folds. *arch.* **ME.**
3 *verb intrans.* Meander, twist and turn; ripple; move shiftily or unsteadily. Chiefly *Scot.* **E18.**
■ **wimpled** *adjective* enveloped in or wearing a wimple, veiled; arranged or falling in folds; wrinkled, rippled; *Scot.* involved, intricate: **L16.** **wimpler** *noun* (*obsolete* exc. *Hist.*) a maker of wimples **ME.**

wimpy /ˈwɪmpi/ *adjective. colloq.* Also **wh-**. **M20.**
[from **WIMP** *noun*² + **-Y**¹.]
= **WIMPISH.**

📖 B. BRYSON [He] doesn't want to appear wimpy because his girlfriend is watching.

■ **wimpily** *adverb* **L20.** **wimpiness** *noun* **L20.**

Wimshurst machine /ˈwɪmzhəːst məˌʃiːn/ *noun phr.* **L19.**
[James *Wimshurst* (1832–1903), English engineer.]
PHYSICS. A hand-operated electrostatic generator consisting of two or more counterrotating insulating discs, each with a peripheral ring of metal sectors which connect successively with a stationary pair of brushes, become inductively charged, and transfer a high voltage to a pair of electrodes.

win /wɪn/ *noun*¹.
[Old English *win(n)*: mod. senses are from the verb.]
†**1** Strife, contention, conflict; tumult, disturbance, agitation. **OE–ME.**
2 Gain, acquisition, profit; advantage, benefit; possessions, riches, wealth. Long *obsolete* exc. *Scot.* **ME.**
3 A victory in a race, contest, bet, etc. **M19.**
4 A gain. In *pl.*, gains, winnings. *colloq.* **L19.**

📖 **3** *Times* The new champions . . well deserved their win.

win /wɪn/ *noun*². Long *obsolete* exc. *Scot.* See also **WYNN.**
[Old English *wynn* corresp. to Old Saxon *wunnia*, Old High German *wunja* (German *Wonne*), from Germanic base also of **WISH** *verb.* Cf. **WINSOME.**]
(A source of) pleasure or joy; a delight.

win /wɪn/ *noun*³. *slang.* Now *rare.* **M16.**
[Origin unkn.]
A penny.

win /wɪn/ *verb*¹. Infl. **-nn-**. Pa. t. & pple **won** /wʌn/.
[Old English *winnan* = Old Frisian *winna*, Old Saxon *winnan* suffer, win, Old High German *winnan* contend, *gewinnan* gain by labour (German *gewinnen* earn, gain, produce), Old Norse *vinna*, Gothic *(ga)winnan* suffer, of unkn. origin.]
†**1** *verb intrans.* Work, labour; strive, contend, fight. **OE–ME.**
2 *verb trans.* Subdue and take possession of; seize, capture, catch. *arch.* **OE.** ▸**b** *euphem.* Steal. **L17.** ▸**c** *CARDS.* Be of higher value than (another card, hand, or suit); gain possession of, take, (a trick). **L17.**
3 a *verb trans.* Get, obtain, acquire, (now usu. something immaterial); *esp.* gain as something profitable or desired. **OE.** ▸†**b** *verb intrans.* Make profit, gain. **ME–L17.**
4 *verb trans. spec.* ▸**a** Of a man: secure the affections of (a woman), esp. with a view to marriage. (Passing into sense 9 below.) **ME.** ▸**b** Gain or acquire as a result of a race, contest, bet, etc., or as a reward. **ME.** ▸**c** Gain by labour or as profit, earn. Now *Scot.* & *dial.* **ME.** ▸**d** Gather in or harvest (crops etc.). Now *Scot.* & *dial.* **LME.** ▸**e** Extract (coal, stone, ore, etc.) from a mine or quarry. Also, sink a shaft or make an excavation to reach (a seam or vein). **LME.** ▸†**f** Gain (ground) *upon*; gain (time). **LME–E18.**
5 *verb trans.* Conquer, overcome, defeat. Long *obsolete* exc. *Scot.* & *US dial.* **ME.**
6 *verb trans.* Be victorious in (a race, contest, bet, etc.). **ME.**
7 *verb intrans.* Be victorious in a race, contest, bet, etc., overcome one's opponent or competitor; *fig.* prevail, succeed. **ME.**
†**8** *verb trans.* Regain or recover (something lost); make up for (loss or waste); rescue, deliver; redeem. Also **win again.** **ME–M17.**
9 *verb trans.* Overcome the unwillingness or indifference of; gain (esp. gradually) the support or affection of; convert, sway; attract, allure; persuade, induce. Foll. by adverb or preposition, (*arch.*) *to do.* **ME.**
10 a *verb intrans.* Make or find one's way with an effort. Foll. by adverb or preposition. **ME.** ▸**b** *verb intrans.* Prevail over opposition etc., prevail despite difficulties; overcome obstacles, attain a desired end eventually. Foll. by adverb or preposition, esp. *out, through.* **ME.** ▸**c** *verb trans.* Succeed in bringing or putting (a person etc.) into a place, state, etc. Foll. by preposition or adverb. Long *rare* or *obsolete.* **ME.** ▸**d** *verb intrans.* Reach the place implied, get there. *Scot.* & *dial.* **LME.**
11 *verb intrans.* Manage or contrive *to do* something. Now *Scot.* & *dial.* **ME.**
12 *verb intrans.* Foll. by *on, upon,* †*of*: get the better of; gain or encroach on; gain influence over, impress, become appealing to. Formerly also, prevail *(up)on* a person *to do.* Now *rare* or *obsolete.* **LME.**
13 *verb trans.* †**a** Get across, cross; get through, accomplish. *rare.* **LME–L16.** ▸**b** Reach (a place etc.) with an effort. *arch.* **L15.**

📖 **3a** R. NIEBUHR The victory for equality of rights was won. D. CARNEGIE People sometimes become invalids in order to win sympathy. *Independent* His strategic aim is to win the credit for solving the deficit problem. **4a** JOHN CLARKE Faint heart never won faire lady. **b** V. S. PRITCHETT Failure to win a scholarship was a blow to vanity. G. GREENE She was a head warden in the blitz and won the George Medal. E. TENNANT Mrs Hyde, apparently, had won some money on a horse. **c** SIR W. SCOTT Every one wins his bread in this country. **6** DISRAELI I never heard that moral force won the battle of Waterloo. *Daily Telegraph* Road hauliers win test case. *Guardian* A side which believes totally in its ability to win matches. **7** F. W. FARRAR Yet, unaided by any, . . Christianity won. *Manchester Examiner* The M.C.C. winning by an innings and four runs. *Guardian* They played Charlton's youngsters . . the next day and won 12-0. **9** F. SHERIDAN She has won me to her party. H. ROTH He had been won over and . . growled his consent. **10a** BYRON Had Selim won . . To where the strand and billows met. R. L. STEVENSON When we won in by the pier. **b** R. F. BURTON He labours to win free from every form. *Listener* Finally won through opposition to become one of the most controversial commanders of the last war. E. CRISPIN I won through, though . . . I survived. *Times Educ. Suppl.* All good ordinary people who win out in the end. **13b** J. BUCHAN I . . crawled down the side of a tributary burn, and won the highroad.

Phrases & comb.: ***heads I win, tails you lose***: see **HEAD** *noun.* ***win again***: see sense 8 above. ***win and wear***: see **WEAR** *verb*¹. ***win by a head***: see **HEAD** *noun.* ***win one's spurs***: see **SPUR** *noun*¹. ***win over***: see sense 9 above. **win some, lose some** = ***you can't win them all*** below. **win the day** be victorious in a battle, argument, etc. ***win the exchange***: see **EXCHANGE** *noun.* ***win the kirn***: see **KIRN** *noun*². **win the peace** (of a country defeated in war) undergo successful reconstruction and become stronger economically than the victors. ***win the saddle or lose the horse***: see **SADDLE** *noun.* **win-win** *adjective* (*colloq.*) denoting a situation in which all parties benefit and no-one loses, or in which all possible outcomes are advantageous. **you can't win**: expr. a (usu. exasperated or frustrated) view that one's actions in a particular situation will always be unsuccessful or judged as wrong. **you can't win them all**: expr. resignation at or consolation for failure or disappointment.

win /wɪn/ *verb*² *intrans. Scot.* & *north.* Infl. **-nn-**. **LME.**
[Var. of **WON** *verb*¹.]
Dwell, reside, live.

win /wɪn/ *verb*³ *trans. Scot.* & *north.* Infl. **-nn-**. Pa. t. & pple **won** /wʌn/. **M16.**
[Perh. from **WIN** *verb*¹, but assoc. also with **WIND** *verb*².]
Dry (hay, turf, wood, etc.) by exposure to the air or a fire.

wince /wɪns/ *noun*¹. **E17.**
[from **WINCE** *verb*¹.]
1 A kick. Now *dial.* **E17.**
2 An involuntary grimace or shrinking movement. **M19.**

wince /wɪns/ *noun*². **L17.**
[Var. of **WINCH** *noun.*]
1 = **WINCH** *noun* 1, 3. **L17.**
2 *DYEING.* **a** A reel or roller placed over the division between two vats to allow fabric spread on it to be let down into one or the other. **M19.** ▸**b** A machine in which one or more endless lengths of fabric are drawn through the vat by a roller. **L20.**

wince /wɪns/ *verb*¹ *intrans.* **ME.**
[from Anglo-Norman var. of Old French *guencir, guenchier* turn aside, avoid: see **WINCH** *verb*¹.]
1 Kick restlessly from impatience or pain; *fig.* be recalcitrant or impatient. Now *dial.* **ME.**
2 Make an involuntary grimace or shrinking movement in response to pain, alarm, distress, etc., or to avoid pain; start, recoil, flinch. Freq. *fig.* **M18.**

📖 **2** A. CRAIG They always made me wince with shame at their arrogance. *Guardian* Blistered toes that caused him to limp and wince throughout the day.

■ **wincer** *noun*¹ **LME.** **wincingly** *adverb* in a wincing manner **L19.**

wince /wɪns/ *verb*² *trans.* **M19.**
[from **WINCE** *noun*².]
DYEING. Immerse in or pass through a vat by means of a wince.
■ **wincer** *noun*² a person who tends a wince **L19.**

wincey /ˈwɪnsi/ *noun & adjective.* Also **-sey.** **E19.**
[App. alt. of *woolsey* in **LINSEY-WOOLSEY.**]
▶ **A** *noun.* A strong lightweight fabric of wool and cotton or linen; a garment made of this. **E19.**
▶ **B** *attrib.* or as *adjective.* Made of wincey. **E19.**

winceyette /wɪnsɪˈɛt/ *noun & adjective.* **E20.**
[from prec. + **-ETTE.**]
(Made of) a lightweight napped cotton fabric used esp. for nightclothes.

winch /wɪn(t)ʃ/ *noun.* See also **WINCE** *noun*².
[Late Old English *wince* from Germanic base also of **WINK** *verb*¹.]
1 A reel; a roller; a pulley. **LOE.** ▸**b** *spec.* An angler's reel. **M17.** ▸†**c** *NAUTICAL.* A small machine used for making ropes and spunyarn. Also, a quantity of yarn so made. **M17–E20.**
†**2** A well-wheel. Also, a well. **ME–M17.**
3 A hoisting or hauling apparatus consisting of a horizontal drum or axle round which a rope, cable, or chain passes, turned by a crank or motor. **L16.** ▸**b** *Hist.* On the River Thames: a riverside winch used to haul craft through difficult places; a toll levied for the use of this. **E17.**
4 The crank of a wheel, shaft, axle, etc. **M17.**
5 *DYEING.* = **WINCE** *noun*² 2. **L18.**
Comb.: **winchman** (*a*) a person who operates a winch; (*b*) a person lowered by a winch from a helicopter, esp. to rescue people from shipwrecks etc.

winch /wɪn(t)ʃ/ *verb*¹. *obsolete* exc. *dial.* **ME.**
[from Anglo-Norman var. of Old French *guenchier* turn aside, avoid, from Germanic: see **WINK** *verb*¹. Cf. **WINCE** *verb*¹.]
1 *verb intrans.* = **WINCE** *verb*¹ 2. **ME.**
2 *verb intrans.* = **WINCE** *verb*¹ 1. **L15.**

winch /wɪn(t)ʃ/ *verb*² *trans.* **E16.**
[from **WINCH** *noun.*]
1 Hoist or haul (as) with a winch; lift *up* thus. **E16.**
2 *DYEING.* = **WINCE** *verb*². **M19.**

📖 **1** *Sunday Express* Ten crewmen . . were winched to safety by helicopter.

Winchester /ˈwɪntʃɪstə/ *noun.* **M16.**
[Branch I from the city (see sense 1). Branch II from Oliver F. *Winchester* (1810–80), US gun manufacturer.]
▶ **I** **1** Used *attrib.* to designate things originating in or associated with Winchester, a city in Hampshire, southern England. **M16.**
2 Chiefly *Hist.* A bottle or container holding a bushel, gallon, or quart in Winchester measure. **E18.**
1 Winchester bushel *Hist.*: in Winchester measure. **Winchester fives** [from the public school at Winchester] a form of fives with four players in a four-walled court, in which a buttress on a side wall makes one end of the court a little narrower than the other. **Winchester gallon** *Hist.*: in Winchester measure. ***Winchester goose***: see **GOOSE** *noun* 4. **Winchester measure** *Hist.* a system of dry and liquid measure the standards of which were originally deposited at Winchester. **Winchester quart** (*a*) *Hist.* a quart in Winchester measure; (*b*) *PHARMACOLOGY* 4 imperial pints (2.27 litres); a bottle holding this amount. **Winchester school**, **Winchester style** a style of manuscript illumination of the 10th and 11th cents. originating at Winchester.
▶ **II** **3** In full ***Winchester rifle***. (Proprietary name for) a kind of breech-loading repeating rifle. **L19.**
4 [So called because its original numerical designation, 3030, corresponded to that of a famous Winchester rifle.] *COMPUTING.* Used *attrib.* & *absol.* to designate a hermetically sealed data-storage device incorporating one or more high-capacity hard disks with heads and sometimes a drive unit. **L20.**

wind /wɪnd, *poet. also* waɪnd/ *noun*¹.
[Old English *wind* = Old Frisian, Old Saxon *wind*, Old High German *wint* (Dutch, German *wind*), Old Norse *vindr*, Gothic *winds*, from Germanic from Indo-European base repr. also by Latin *ventus*.]
▶ **I** *lit.* **1** Air in motion; a state of movement in the air; a perceptible current of air, usu. parallel to the surface of the ground etc. **OE.** ▸**b** A symbolical representation of the wind. **M19.**
2 A natural current of air blowing from a specified direction or defined in a particular way; *transf.* (in *pl.*) points of the compass, directions. Freq. in ***the four winds***. **OE.** ▸**b** In mah-jong: each of the four compass points taken up by the players; the player occupying such a place; also, any of sixteen tiles (four of each sort) used to represent one of the four winds. **E20.**
3 A scent carried by the wind, *esp.* one conveying the presence or proximity of a person or animal in hunting etc. **ME.**

📖 **1** SWIFT I set up my sail, the wind being fair. J. BRAINE I wanted . . to have the wind and the rain in my face. B. OKRI The wind from the ocean blew hard, sending sprays of salt water to the shore. **2** ***east wind, north wind, south wind, west wind, north-east wind***, etc.; ***Chinook wind, sirocco wind***, etc. **3** *Field* Four rhebok, which had . . got our wind shortly before.

▶ **II** *transf.* **4** (Excessive) gas in the stomach or intestines. **OE.**
5 a Air inhaled and exhaled by the lungs, breath; breathing as a vital process, *transf.* life. Now *rare* exc. as passing into sense 5c. **OE.** ▸**b** Breath as used in speaking; *transf.* speech, talk. Now *rare* exc. as in ***long-winded***. **ME.** ▸**c** Breath as needed for physical exertion; easy or regular breathing; capacity for regular breathing during

physical exertion. ME. ▸**d** A place on the body in front of the stomach where a blow temporarily takes away the breath. *slang.* E19.

†**6** Air in general as a substance. ME–E18.

7 Compressed or confined air; air contained within or filling a body. Now *rare* or *obsolete* exc. as in senses 4, 8. ME.

8 a Naturally or artificially produced air as used for sounding a trumpet, organ, or other wind instrument. LME. ▸**b** *collect. sing.* & in *pl.* The wind instruments of an orchestra; the players of these. L19.

9 The rush of air caused by a rapidly moving body. Foll. by *of.* L16.

10 *ASTRONOMY.* A stream of particles emanating from the sun or other star. M20.

> 📖 **4** *Guardian* Gripe water, which is used . . to relieve babies suffering from . . wind. **5a** P. V. WHITE The fall had only knocked the wind out of me. **c** A. UTTLEY The pony rested for a few minutes to get her wind. **7** G. MARKHAM A great ball of double leather fild with winde.

▶ **III** *fig.* **11** The wind as a type of something unaffected by any action, or as something unrestrained, swift, or mutable. ME.

12 A vain or insubstantial thing; mere empty talk, meaningless rhetoric; vanity, conceit. ME.

13 A force or influence acting on or carrying along a thing or person; a tendency or trend of affairs. LME.

> 📖 **11** SHAKES. *Temp.* Thou shalt be as free As mountain winds. C. M. YONGE 'Have you spoken to her?' 'As well speak to the wind'. **12** SWIFT The nation then too late will find . . Directors' promises but wind. **13** *Economist* The mining complex . . is adapting itself to the winds of change in Africa.

Phrases: ***beat the wind***: see BEAT *verb*[1] 1. ***before the wind***: see BEFORE *preposition.* **between wind and water** (*a*) *NAUTICAL* on the part of a ship's side lying sometimes above water and sometimes below; (*b*) *fig.* at a vulnerable point. ***break one's wind***, ***break wind***: see BREAK *verb.* BROKEN **wind**. ***close to the wind***: see CLOSE *adjective & adverb.* ***eat the wind out of***: see EAT *verb.* ***gain the wind of***: see GAIN *verb*[2]. **get the wind up** *colloq.* become alarmed or frightened. **get wind** (now *rare*) be revealed or divulged, become known. **get wind of** (*a*) smell out, detect by scent; (*b*) begin to suspect, hear a rumour of, become aware of. **have the wind up** *colloq.* be alarmed or frightened. **how the wind blows**, **how the wind lies** = *which way the wind blows* below. **in the wind** (*a*) to windward (*of*); (*b*) so as to perceive or to be perceived (as) by scent; (*c*) happening; about to happen; rumoured. ***in the wind's eye***: see EYE *noun.* **into the wind** towards the direction from which the wind is blowing, so as to face the wind. ***leading wind***: see LEADING *adjective.* **like the wind** very swiftly. **near the wind** = *close to the wind* s.v. CLOSE *adjective & adverb.* **off the wind** *NAUTICAL* with the wind on the quarter. **on a wind** *NAUTICAL* against a wind on either bow. **on the wind** (of a sound or scent) carried by the wind. ***on the wings of the wind***: see WING *noun.* ***piss and wind***: see PISS *noun.* ***piss in the wind***: see PISS *verb.* **put the wind up** *colloq.* alarm, frighten. ***raise the wind***: see RAISE *verb.* **recover the wind of** = *gain the wind of* s.v. GAIN *verb*[2]. ***red wind***: see RED *adjective.* ***row against the wind and tide***: see ROW *verb*[1]. **save one's wind** (now *rare*) abstain from useless talk, save one's breath. ***second wind***: see SECOND *adjective.* ***sink the wind***: see SINK *verb.* ***slip one's wind***: see SLIP *verb*[1]. ***sniff the wind***: see SNIFF *verb* 3. ***solar wind***: see SOLAR *adjective*[1]. ***soldier's wind***: see SOLDIER *noun.* ***straw in the wind***: see STRAW *noun.* **take the wind out of a person's sails** frustrate or deflate a person, esp. by making an unexpected remark or anticipating an action, remark, etc. **take wind** = *get wind* above. ***three sheets to the wind***: see SHEET *noun*[2]. **to the winds**, **to the four winds** in all directions; *fig.* into a state of abandonment or neglect; ***cast to the (four) winds***, ***fling to the (four) winds***, ***throw to the (four) winds***, cast away, reject utterly. ***twist in the wind***: see TWIST *verb.* **under the wind** (chiefly *NAUTICAL*) on the side away from the wind, to leeward; *spec.* in a position of shelter from the wind. **which way the wind blows**, **which way the wind lies** what is the state of opinion; which are the current trends; what developments are likely. ***whistle down the wind***: see WHISTLE *verb.* **wind and weather** exposure to the effects of the elements. **with the wind** in the direction in which the wind is blowing; ***gone with the wind***, gone completely, disappeared without trace.

Comb.: **wind axis** *AERONAUTICS* each of a set of rectangular coordinate axes having their origin in the aircraft and the *x*-axis in the opposite direction to the relative wind (usu. *pl.*); **wind band** a group of wind instruments as a band or a section of an orchestra; **wind-bells** = *wind chimes* below; **wind-blow** (*a*) a stretch of land eroded by wind; (*b*) a destructive gale; (*c*) = *windthrow* below; **wind-blown** *adjective* †(*a*) blown up, inflated; (*b*) blown on, along, or about by the wind (***wind-blown bob***, a bobbed hairstyle popular among women in the 1930s); **wind-bound** *adjective* unable to sail or proceed because of contrary or stormy winds; **wind-brace** a diagonal brace connecting the rafters of a roof; **wind-bracing** (the provision of) connecting members designed to stiffen a building etc. against the wind; **wind-break** a thing, as a row of trees, a fence, a wall, a screen, etc., used to break the force of the wind; **windbreaker** †(*a*) a carminative; (*b*) *US* = *wind-break* above; (*c*) (**W-**) (US proprietary name for) any of various items of clothing; **wind-broken** *adjective* brokenwinded; **windburn** (usu. superficial) inflammation or discoloration of the skin caused by exposure to wind; **wind-burned**, **-burnt** *adjective* affected by windburn; **windcharger** a small windmill which generates electricity for a farm, house, etc.; **windcheater** (*a*) *GOLF* a ball driven low into the wind, *spec.* one played with strong back-spin; (*b*) a kind of thick wind-resistant short jacket with close-fitting cuffs, neck, and lower edge; **wind-chest** *MUSIC* a chest or box in an organ which receives wind from the bellows and admits it to the pipes or reeds; **wind chill** (*a*) the cooling effect of wind blowing on a person or surface; (*b*) (in full ***wind-chill factor***, ***wind-chill index***) a measure or scale of the combined effect of low temperature and wind-speed on body temperature; **wind chimes** small pieces of glass etc. suspended from a frame so as to tinkle against one another in the wind; **wind-cone** = ***wind-sock*** below; **wind-crust** *MOUNTAINEERING* a crust formed on the surface of soft snow by the wind; **wind-drift** (*a*) (*rare*) a drift or current of wind; (*b*) the action of wind currents on water, vessels, etc.; **wind-egg** an imperfect or unproductive egg, *esp.* one with a soft shell; **wind energy**: obtained from harnessing the wind with windmills, wind turbines, etc.; ***wind-fanner***: see FANNER 4; **wind farm** a group of energy-producing windmills or wind turbines; **windflower** [translating the Greek name] any plant of the genus *Anemone*, of the buttercup family; *esp.* the wood anemone, *Anemone nemorosa*; **wind-force** the force of the wind, esp. as measured on the Beaufort scale or a similar system; **wind-furnace**: in which the draught is obtained by means of a (high or narrow) chimney rather than by mechanical means as in a blast-furnace; **wind gall** a swelling on a horse's leg just above and on either side of the fetlock, caused by distension of the synovial bursa; **wind-gap** a gap between ridges or hills, *spec.* one formed by a dried-up former river valley; **wind-gauge** (*a*) = ANEMOMETER 1; (*b*) a graduated apparatus attached to the sights of a gun to enable allowance to be made for the effect of wind on the projectile; (*c*) = ANEMOMETER 2; **wind-harp** an Aeolian harp; **wind-hole** †(*a*) the opening at the top of the windpipe, the glottis; (*b*) an opening in brickwork for the passage of air; (*c*) the hole in the lower board of a pair of bellows; (*d*) a ventilating shaft in a mine; (*e*) each of the openings in the soundboard of an organ for admitting wind to the pipes; **windhover** the kestrel; **wind instrument** a musical instrument played by means of a current of air, esp. the breath (now freq. *esp.* a woodwind instrument); **windjammer** (*a*) *US slang* a bugler, a bandsman; (*b*) *Hist.* a merchant sailing ship; (*c*) *US slang* a rumour-monger, a loquacious person; (*d*) = ***windcheater*** (b) above; **windjamming** *slang* (*a*) sailing a windjammer; (*b*) *US slang* talking, gossiping; (*c*) *US slang* playing a wind instrument; **wind load**, **wind loading** *ENGINEERING* the force on a structure arising from the impact of wind on it; **wind machine** (*a*) a machine driven by the wind; (*b*) a device for producing a blast of air, *spec.* of relatively warm air for protecting crops against frost; (*c*) in theatrical productions etc., a machine for simulating the sound of wind; **windpipe** = TRACHEA 1; (*a* ***sleeve across the windpipe***: see SLEEVE *noun*); **wind player** a player of a wind instrument; **windproof** *adjective & noun* (*a*) *adjective* (esp. of an outer garment) impervious to wind; (*b*) *noun* a windproof garment; **windrock** damage to the roots of young plants, caused by the movement of the stem in the wind; **wind-rose** *METEOROLOGY* a rose diagram indicating the relative frequency and strength of winds from the various points of the compass at a given place; **windsail** (*a*) a sail of a windmill; (*b*) *NAUTICAL HISTORY* a long wide tube or funnel of sailcloth used for ventilating a ship; **wind-scorpion** = SOLPUGID; **windscreen** a screen for protection from the wind; now *esp.* the glass screen ahead of the front seat or seats of a motor vehicle etc.; (***windscreen washer***, a device which washes the exterior of a windscreen by directing a jet or jets of water on to it; ***windscreen wiper***, a device for automatic wiping of the exterior of a windscreen during rain, snow, etc., usu. consisting of a mechanically or electrically operated rubber blade on an arm, moving in an arc); **wind-shake** a flaw or crack in timber (supposedly) caused by the force of the wind; †**wind-shaked** *adjective* (*rare*) = ***wind-shaken*** (a) below; **wind-shaken** *adjective* (*a*) shaken or agitated by the wind; (*b*) (of timber) affected with wind-shake; **wind shear** a (usu. vertical) gradient in wind velocity at right angles to the wind's direction, caused by friction with the ground surface etc.; **windshield** (chiefly *N. Amer.*) = ***windscreen*** above; **wind-slab** *MOUNTAINEERING* a thick wind-crust of a kind liable to slip and create an avalanche (cf. ***slab avalanche*** s.v. SLAB *noun*[1]); **wind-sleeve**, **wind-sock** a usu. canvas cylinder or cone flown from a mast, esp. at an airfield, to indicate the direction of the wind; **wind-spider** = SOLPUGID; **wind-splitter** *colloq.* (chiefly *US*) something very sharply formed or very swift; **wind sprint** *ATHLETICS* a form of exercise involving moving from a walk or slow run to a faster run and repeatedly reversing the process; **wind-stocking** = ***wind-sock*** above; **wind-stream** an air-stream, *esp.* the disturbed air in the wake of an aircraft; **wind-suck** (of a horse) have the vice of noisily drawing in and swallowing air (cf. ***crib-biting*** s.v. CRIB *noun*); **wind-sucker** a horse given to wind-sucking; **windsurf** *verb intrans.* engage in windsurfing; **windsurfer** (*a*) (**W-**, proprietary name in US for) a kind of sailboard; (*b*) a person who engages in windsurfing; **windsurfing** the sport of riding on water standing on a sailboard; **windswept** *adjective* exposed to or blown by the wind; *spec.* (of a hairstyle) designed to give the appearance of having been blown by the wind, tousled; **windthrow** the uprooting and blowing down of trees by the wind; timber so uprooted; **wind-tie** = ***wind-brace*** above; **wind-tight** *adjective* impervious to wind; **wind-trunk** *MUSIC* a tube in an organ through which wind passes from the bellows to the wind-chest; **wind tunnel** a tunnel-like apparatus for producing an air-stream of known velocity past models of aircraft, buildings, etc., in the study of wind flow or wind effects on the full-size object; **wind turbine**, a turbine driven by wind, *esp.* one having a large vaned wheel rotated by the wind to generate electricity; ***wind-vanner***: see VANNER *noun*[1] 2; **wind-way** (*a*) a ventilating passage in a mine; (*b*) the narrow slit in an organ-pipe or woodwind instrument through which the wind strikes the lip of the instrument to produce sound; (*c*) access of the wind to a sailing vessel so as to give freedom of passage.

■ **windlike** *adjective* resembling (that of) the wind M17. †**windermost** *adjective* furthest to windward E17–E18.

wind /wʌɪnd/ *noun*[2]. LME.

[Partly from Middle Dutch, Middle Low German *winde* windlass; partly from WIND *verb*[1].]

1 An apparatus for winding something; a winch, a windlass. *obsolete* exc. *dial.* LME.

2 An act or instance of winding; curved or twisted form; a coil, a twist; a bend or turn in a course; a single turn when winding. E19.

1 ***motor wind***: see MOTOR *noun & adjective.* **2** **out of wind** no longer twisted.

wind /wʌɪnd/ *verb*[1]. Pa. t. & pple **wound** /waʊnd/, (now *dial.* & *non-standard*) **winded**.

[Old English *windan* = Old Frisian *winda*, Old Saxon *windan* (Dutch, German *winden*), Old Norse *vinda*, Gothic -*windan*, from Germanic base rel. to WANDER *verb*, WEND *verb*[1].]

1 †**a** *verb intrans.* Of a thing: move quickly or forcefully, run, fly; *gen.* pass. Freq. with adverbs. OE–LME. ▸**b** *verb intrans. & refl.* Of a person or animal: proceed, go. Long *obsolete* exc. *Scot.* OE.

2 *verb trans.* Wield (a weapon or implement). Long *obsolete* exc. *dial.* OE. ▸†**b** Haul, hoist, lift. LME–L17.

3 *verb intrans.* Turn this way and that; writhe, wriggle. *obsolete* exc. *dial.* OE.

4 *verb trans.* Form or construct by twining or plaiting, plait; twine or weave *together*, intertwine. Formerly *spec.*, make or repair (a wall) with windings or rods. Long *obsolete* exc. *Scot.* OE.

5 †**a** *verb trans.* Put into a curved or twisted form, bend, twist; wring. OE–E17. ▸**b** *verb intrans.* Take or have a bent form; be twisted. Now *dial. & techn.* LME.

6 a *verb intrans.* & (*arch.*) *refl.* Move along in a sinuous, curving, or meandering course; go or travel on a road etc. which turns this way and that. Freq. with adverbs. ME. ▸**b** *verb trans.* & †*intrans.* (Cause to) move in a curve; turn. *arch.* LME. ▸**c** *verb intrans.* Of a road, course, etc.: have a sinuous, curving, or meandering course; turn this way and that. Formerly also (of an object), have a curved or sinuous form. Freq. with adverbs. M16. ▸**d** *verb trans.* Make (one's way) in a sinuous, curving, or meandering course; *arch.* traverse in a sinuous etc. course. M17.

7 a *verb trans.* Turn or pass (a thing) around a thing or person so as to encircle or enfold; wrap (closely) *about* or *around*; put (wool, thread, etc.) in coils around a thing or itself so as to form a compact mass or ball; arrange in coils. ME. ▸**b** *verb intrans.* Turn so as to encircle or enfold a thing or person; be or become twisted or coiled; (of a plant or animal) twist or coil itself. Freq. foll. by *about*, *around.* L16.

8 *verb trans.* Encircle or enfold (as) *with* coils; bind round *with* tape, wire, etc. ME. ▸**b** *spec.* Wrap (a corpse) in a shroud or winding-sheet, shroud. *obsolete* exc. *dial.* ME.

9 *verb trans.* Haul, hoist, or draw with a winch, windlass, etc. ME.

†**10** *verb trans. & intrans.* Draw or pull *out* with a twisting movement. LME–E17.

11 a *verb trans.* Turn or deflect in a certain direction; *esp.* direct or lead (a person) according to one's will. Now *rare.* LME. ▸**b** *verb trans.* & †*intrans.* Draw *out*, extricate or disentangle (a thing or person, oneself). Long *rare* or *obsolete.* LME. ▸**c** *verb trans.* & †*intrans.* Draw *in* or *into* by alluring or enticing; insinuate (a thing, oneself) *in* or *into.* M16. ▸†**d** *verb trans.* Circulate, put in circulation, (money or merchandise). Chiefly in ***turn and wind***. L16–L17.

12 *verb intrans.* & †*trans.* (*refl.* & with *it*). Pursue a devious or circuitous course in behaviour, argument, or thought. (Foll. by *about*, *through*.) *arch.* LME.

13 *NAUTICAL.* **a** *verb intrans.* Of a ship: turn or lie in a particular direction; swing round when at anchor. E17. ▸**b** *verb trans.* Turn (a ship) about or in a particular direction. E17.

14 *verb trans.* †**a** Tighten (a string of a musical instrument) so as to tune; turn (a tuning-peg) in tuning. Also foll. by *up.* Only in 17. ▸**b** Make (a watch, clock, etc.) operate by turning a key etc. to tighten a coiled or coiling spring. Usu. foll. by *up.* E17. ▸**c** *fig.* Work up or intensify *to* a certain pitch. Now usu. foll. by *up.* E17.

15 *verb trans. & intrans.* Direct or turn (a horse) to the left. *Scot.* M18.

> 📖 **6a** T. GRAY The lowing herd wind slowly o'er the lea. J. CLARE Glad I wind me down the lane. L. GRANT-ADAMSON He wound through the . . pedestrians, kept his eyes on his route. **b** J. DYER Or where the Lune or Coker wind their streams. **c** J. BUCHAN A white ribbon of road . . wound up the narrow vale. O. MANNING There were queues winding out from the platform barriers. **d** E. BLAIR The procession slowly wound its way to the cemetery. **7a** C. MORGAN Barbet wound the scarf round his neck. C. BRAYFIELD He wound an arm around her waist. A. S. BYATT The pale, pale hair in fine braids was wound round her head. **b** *Birder's World* Large vines that wound round every tree. **8** D. JOHNSON Wound round with a few turns of fine silk. **14b** R. SHAW He glanced at his watch—he had forgotten to wind it: it had stopped.

With adverbs in specialized senses, & phrases: **wind down** (*a*) draw gradually to a close; (*b*) become relaxed, unwind, (*lit.* & *fig.*); (*c*) let down with a winch etc., *spec.* lower (a window of a motor vehicle) by rotating a handle. **wind off** unwind (string, wool, etc.). **wind on** *PHOTOGRAPHY* turn (the film in a camera) to the next position in readiness for taking another photograph (cf. ***wind-on*** below). ***wind round one's finger***, ***wind round one's little finger***: see FINGER *noun.* **wind up** (*a*) draw up or hoist with a winch etc., *spec.* raise (a window of a motor vehicle) by rotating a handle; †(*b*) bind or wrap up; *fig.* involve, implicate; †(*c*) roll or fold up, furl; (*d*) coil (the whole of a piece of string etc.) into a compact mass or ball; (*e*) bring to a close, form the conclusion of, end; COMMERCE arrange the affairs of and dissolve (a company or business); (*f*) come to a close; COMMERCE (of a company etc.) cease business and go into liquidation; (*g*) *colloq.* end up in a specified state, place, or circumstance, find oneself eventually; (*h*) *colloq.* deliberately provoke, esp. by misleading or hoaxing; tease, annoy, trick; (see also senses 14a, b, c above, & cf. WIND-UP *noun*1 & *adjective*).

Comb.: **wind-down** *colloq.* a gradual lessening of excitement or reduction of activity (cf. WIND-UP *noun*1 & *adjective*); **wind-on** *adjective & noun* (PHOTOGRAPHY) (*a*) *adjective* designating or pertaining to the mechanism for advancing a film to the next position; (*b*) *noun* the function performed by this mechanism;

■ **windster** *noun* (now *rare* or *obsolete*) a person (orig. a woman) engaged in winding silk etc. LME.

wind /wɪnd, *in sense 3 also* wʌɪnd/ *verb*2. Pa. pple **winded**, (in sense 3, by assoc. with prec., freq.) **wound** /waʊnd/. LME.
[from WIND *noun*1.]
1 a *verb trans.* Perceive (an animal, person, etc.) by the scent conveyed by the wind; *fig.* detect as by scenting, get wind of. LME. ▸**b** *verb intrans.* Of an animal: sniff in order to scent or on scenting something. LME.
2 a *verb trans.* Expose to the wind or air; air; dry or taint by such exposure. Now *dial.* LME. ▸**b** *verb intrans.* Become tainted by exposure to air. *dial.* M19.
3 *verb trans. & intrans.* Sound or blow (a wind instrument, esp. a horn); blow (a blast or note) on a wind instrument, esp. a horn. L16.
4 *verb trans.* Deprive of wind or breath by exertion or a blow, put out of breath. Also, renew the wind of by rest. E19.
5 *verb trans.* Cause (a baby) to bring up wind after feeding. M20.

📖 **4** B. ENGLAND Ansell had crashed down with such force that he was winded. J. CHEEVER The climb up the stairs winded him.

windage /ˈwɪndɪdʒ/ *noun*. E18.
[from WIND *noun*1 + -AGE.]
1 The difference between the diameters of a gun's bore and the projectile, as measuring the space necessary for the escape of gas in firing. E18.
2 Allowance made, esp. in shooting, for the effect of the wind in deflecting a missile; such deflection. M19.
3 = WIND *noun*1 9. L19.
4 The air resistance of a moving object, esp. a vessel or a rotating machine part. Also, the force of the wind on a stationary object. L19.

windas /ˈwɪndəs/ *noun*. Pl. **-as(s)es**. ME.
[Anglo-Norman = Old French *guindas* from Old Norse *vindáss*, from *vinda* WIND *verb*1 + *áss* pole.]
1 = WINDLASS *noun*1 1. Long *obsolete* exc. *Scot.* ME.
2 A contrivance like a winch used for bending a cross-bow. Cf. WINDLASS *noun*1 2. Long *obsolete* exc. *Hist.* LME.

windbag /ˈwɪn(d)bag/ *noun*. L15.
[formed as prec. + BAG *noun*.]
1 a The bag of a bagpipe. Formerly also, the bellows of an organ. L15. ▸**b** *sing.* & in *pl.* The lungs; the chest. Now *joc.* M16.
2 A person who talks pompously and at length but says little of value, a foolishly long-winded person. *colloq.* E19.
3 A sailing ship. *Nautical slang.* E20.
■ **windbaggery** *noun* inflated talk M19. **windbagging** *noun & adjective* (*a*) *noun* verbosity, long-windedness; (*b*) *adjective* verbose, long-winded: L20.

winded /ˈwɪndɪd/ *adjective*1. LME.
[from WIND *noun*1 + -ED2.]
Having wind or breath of a specified kind or in a specified condition. Chiefly in comb., as ***broken-winded***, ***long-winded***, ***short-winded***, etc.

winded /ˈwɪndɪd, *in sense 2 also* ˈwʌɪndɪd/ *adjective*2. L16.
[from WIND *verb*2 + -ED1.]
1 Exposed to the wind or air; dried or tainted by such exposure. Now *dial.* L16.
2 Of a musical instrument: sounded with the breath, blown. E17.
3 Put out of breath, made breathless. L19.
■ **windedness** *noun* L16.

winder /ˈwʌɪndə/ *noun*1. M16.
[from WIND *verb*1 + -ER1.]
1 a A person employed in winding wool etc. M16. ▸**b** A person who turns or manages a winch or windlass, esp. at a mine. E18. ▸**c** A person who winds a clock or other mechanism. E19.
†**2 a** A tendril of a climbing plant. L16–L17. ▸**b** A twining plant. L16–L17.
3 a An apparatus for winding or on which to wind something, as a winch, spool, shaft, etc.; the handle of a winch etc. L16. ▸**b** A key for winding a clock, watch, etc.; the winding mechanism of a clock etc. E17.
4 Each of a series of steps wider at one end than the other, forming a winding (part of a) staircase. M17.
Comb.: **winder-up** a person who or thing which winds up something, esp. a business.

winder /ˈwɪndə/ *noun*2. *obsolete* exc. *dial.* M16.
[Early Flemish *winder*, *wender*.]
A wigeon.

winder /ˈwɪndə/ *noun*3. E17.
[from WIND *verb*2 + -ER1.]
1 A person who blows a wind instrument. E17.
2 A blow, run, climb, etc., that winds one or puts one out of breath (*colloq.*). Formerly *spec.* (*slang*), a sentence of transportation for life. E19.

winder /ˈwɪndə/ *noun*4. *non-standard*. L17.
[Repr. a pronunc.]
A window.

windfall /ˈwɪn(d)fɔːl/ *noun*. LME.
[from WIND *noun*1 + FALL *noun*2, perh. infl. by Middle High German *wintval* (German *Windfall*).]
1 a A tree or branch blown down by the wind; timber thus blown down; *spec.* (chiefly *US*) a heap of fallen trees blown down by a tornado. LME. ▸**b** An apple or other fruit blown down by the wind from a tree or bush. L16.
2 A thing unexpectedly acquired, a piece of unexpected good fortune, *esp.* a legacy. M16.

📖 **1b** *attrib.*: W. BESANT August apples, and windfall pears. **2** J. B. PRIESTLEY The windfall of the morning, six hundred pounds out of the blue.

Comb.: **windfall profit** ECONOMICS unexpectedly large or unforeseen profit; **windfall profits tax**, **windfall tax** ECONOMICS: levied on an unforeseen or unexpectedly large profit, esp. one judged to be excessive or unfairly obtained.
■ **windfallen** *adjective* blown down by the wind M16.

Windies /ˈwɪndɪz/ *noun pl. colloq.* M20.
[Contr. of *W(est Indies.)*]
West Indians, *spec.* the West Indian cricket team.

windigo /ˈwɪndɪgəʊ/ *noun*. Also **wen-** /ˈwɛn-/. Pl. **-o(e)s**. E18.
[Ojibwa *wintiko*.]
In the folklore of the northern Algonquian Indians: a cannibalistic giant, the transformation of a person who has eaten human flesh.

winding /ˈwʌɪndɪŋ/ *noun*1. OE.
[from WIND *verb*1 + -ING1.]
▸ **I 1** A thing that winds or is wound round something; a coil, a coiled object. Formerly also, a curved, circular, or twining pattern, ornament, piece of material, etc. OE. ▸**b** ELECTRICITY. An electrical conductor that is wound round a magnetic material, *esp.* (*a*) a coil encircling part of the stator or rotor of an electric motor or generator, or an assembly of such coils connected to form one circuit; (*b*) one forming part of a transformer. L19.
2 A curving, sinuous, or meandering path, course, etc.; in *pl.*, meanderings, twists and turns. LME.
3 A flexible rod or withy, esp. as used in making or repairing walls; (the use of) such rods as a material. *obsolete* exc. *dial.* LME.

📖 **2** WORDSWORTH The stream-like windings of that glorious street.

▸ **II 4** The action of WIND *verb*1; the condition of being wound; an act or instance of winding; *spec.* (*a*) sinuous, curving, or meandering course or motion; (*b*) the coiling, twining, or enfolding of something; (*obsolete* exc. *dial.*) wrapping in a shroud. LME. ▸**b** *fig.* In *sing.* & (usu.) *pl.* Devious or circuitous behaviour, argument, or thought. *arch.* E17. ▸†**c** MUSIC. A melodic alternation or variation. M17–E20.
4 out of winding = *out of wind* s.v. WIND *noun*2.
Comb.: **winding engine** a machine for hoisting something, a powered winch; **winding-hole** /ˈwɪnd-/ a place in a canal or river for turning a long boat; **winding-sheet** (*a*) a sheet in which to wrap a corpse for burial, a shroud; (*b*) a mass of solidified wax clinging to the side of a candle, likened to a sheet folded in creases and regarded as a bad omen; **winding up** conclusion, finish; now usu., arrangement of affairs and dissolution of a company etc.

winding /ˈwɪndɪŋ, ˈwʌɪnd-/ *verbal noun*2. L15.
[from WIND *verb*2 + -ING1.]
The action of sounding a wind instrument, esp. a horn. Foll. by *of*.

winding /ˈwʌɪndɪŋ/ *ppl adjective*1. LME.
[from WIND *verb*1 + -ING2.]
1 That winds; following a curving, sinuous, or meandering course or path; (of a staircase) spiral. LME.
2 *fig.* †**a** Devious, crooked, wily. L16–L17. ▸**b** Of a narrative: circuitous, rambling. L19.

📖 **1** S. TOWNSEND Happy exploration of the winding alleys and steep narrow streets.

■ **windingly** *adverb* L16. **windingness** *noun* M18.

winding /ˈwɪndɪŋ, *in sense 1 also* ˈwʌɪnd-/ *ppl adjective*2. M18.
[from WIND *verb*2 + -ING2.]
1 Of a wind instrument, esp. a horn: that is sounded. M18.
2 That winds one or takes one's breath away. M19.

windlass /ˈwɪndləs/ *noun*1 & *verb*. LME.
[App. alt. of WINDAS.]
▸ **A** *noun*. **1** = WINCH *noun* 3. LME.
†**2** Any of various similar smaller contrivances, *esp.* one used in discharging a crossbow or pistol. Cf. WINDAS 2. L15–E19.
1 Spanish windlass: see SPANISH *adjective*.
▸ **B** *verb trans.* Hoist or haul (as) with a windlass. M19.

†**windlass** *noun*2. M16.
[Alt. of WANLACE.]
1 A circuit made to intercept game in hunting; *gen.* a circuit, a circuitous movement. M16–E17.
2 *fig.* A crafty or devious course of action, a plot. M16–M18.

windle /ˈwɪnd(ə)l/ *noun*1. Now *dial.*
[Old English *windel*, from *windan* WIND *verb*1 + -LE3.]
1 A basket. OE.
2 A measure of corn etc., usu. equal to about 3 bushels. *local.* ME.
3 A bundle of straw etc. *Scot.* E19.

windle /ˈwɪnd(ə)l/ *noun*2. *obsolete* exc. *Scot. & dial.* L17.
[2nd elem. of GARNWINDLE, YARNWINDLE.]
= GARNWINDLE.

windle /ˈwɪnd(ə)l/ *verb*1. *obsolete* exc. *dial.* LME.
[from WIND *verb*1 + -LE3.]
1 *verb intrans.* = WIND *verb*1 6a. LME.
2 *verb trans.* = WIND *verb*1 7a. L16.

windle /ˈwɪnd(ə)l/ *verb*2 *intrans. obsolete* exc. *dial.* ME.
[Perh. back-form. from WINDLESTRAW.]
Lose strength or vigour; wither, waste away, dwindle.

windless /ˈwɪndlɪs/ *adjective*. LME.
[from WIND *noun*1 + -LESS.]
1 Breathless, out of breath. Now *rare*. LME.
2 Free from wind; not exposed to or stirred by the wind, in or on which no wind blows. L16.
■ **windlessly** *adverb* L19. **windlessness** *noun* E20.

windlestraw /ˈwɪnd(ə)lstrɔː/ *noun*. Now *arch.*, *Scot.*, & *dial.* OE.
[from WINDLE *noun*1 + STRAW *noun*.]
1 An old dry withered stalk of grass. OE.
2 Any of various long-stalked grasses, e.g. crested dog's tail, *Cynosurus cristatus*, and tufted hair-grass, *Deschampsia cespitosa*. Also ***windlestraw grass***. OE.
3 *fig.* Something light, trifling, or flimsy; a thin lanky person; a person of feeble health or character. M17.

windling /ˈwɪndlɪŋ/ *noun*. ME.
[Perh. from WIND *verb*1 + -LING1, or perh. two words. Cf. WINDLE *noun*1.]
†**1** *sing.* & in *pl.* Small ropes or cords. Only in ME.
2 A bundle of straw or hay. *Scot.* M17.

windmill /ˈwɪn(d)mɪl/ *noun & verb*. ME.
[from WIND *noun*1 + MILL *noun*1.]
▸ **A** *noun*. **1** A mill for grinding corn etc. having machinery driven by the action of the wind on its sails; a similar structure used for drawing water or generating electricity. ME.
2 A figure of a windmill; a sign or character resembling this, as a cross or asterisk. Now *rare* or *obsolete*. LME.
3 A model of a windmill; a toy consisting of curved vanes attached to a stick so as to revolve in the wind like the sails of a windmill. M16. ▸**b** CRICKET. A style of bowling with a high overarm delivery. Now *rare* or *obsolete*. M19.
†**4** *fig.* A fanciful notion; a visionary scheme or project. E17–M18.
5 An airscrew or propeller, *esp.* one for an autogiro. Now *Hist.* M20.
1 fight windmills = *tilt at windmills* below. **throw one's cap over the windmill** act recklessly or unconventionally. **tilt at windmills** [from a story in *Don Quixote*] attack an imaginary enemy or wrong.
Comb.: **windmill aeroplane** = AUTOGIRO; **windmill grass** an Australian grass, *Chloris truncata*, with horizontal or reflexed digitately arranged spikes; **windmill plane** = ***windmill aeroplane*** above; **windmill plant** = TELEGRAPH *plant*.
▸ **B** *verb*. †**1** *verb intrans.* Turn or change like a windmill. Only in L17.
2 *verb trans. & intrans.* Whirl or fling (one's limbs) around in a manner suggestive of a windmill. E20.
3 *verb intrans.* AERONAUTICS. Of a propeller or rotor: spin unpowered. Also (foll. by *down*), descend with the rotor etc. spinning. M20.

📖 **2** D. R. KOONTZ He windmilled his arms in a brief attempt to keep his balance.

■ **windmiller** *noun* the keeper of a windmill E16. **windmill-like** /-l-l-/ *adjective* resembling (that of) a windmill M19.

Windmill Hill /wɪn(d)mɪl ˈhɪl/ *noun phr.* M20.
[The site of a causewayed camp near Avebury in Wiltshire.]
Used *attrib.* to designate the culture, and esp. the pottery, characteristic of the earliest neolithic period in Britain.

windolite /ˈwɪndəʊlʌɪt/ *noun*. Also **W-**. E20.
[from WINDOW *noun* + *-lite* alt. of LIGHT *noun*. Cf. LITE *noun*[2].]
(Proprietary name for) a transparent material used as a substitute for glass.

windore /ˈwɪndɔː/ *noun*. *obsolete* exc. *dial*. M16.
[Alt. of next by assoc. with *door*.]
A window.

window /ˈwɪndəʊ/ *noun & verb*. ME.
[Old Norse *vindauga*, from *vindr* WIND *noun*[1] + *auga* EYE *noun*.]
▶ **A** *noun*. **1** An opening in a wall or roof of a building, vehicle, etc., now usu. fitted with glass in a fixed, hinged, or sliding frame, to admit light or air and provide a view of what is outside or inside; the glass filling this opening; this glass with its frame. ME.
2 The space or area beside or behind a window, *spec.* as used for displaying goods etc. at the front of a shop. Freq. in ***in the window***. ME.
3 *fig.* **a** An organ of sense, *esp.* an eye (usu. in *pl.* in ***windows of the mind***, ***windows of the soul***); an opportunity for study or insight (freq. foll. by *into*, *on*). ME. ▸**b** A continuous range of electromagnetic wavelengths for which the atmosphere (or some other medium) is relatively transparent. M20. ▸**c** An interval during which astronomical and atmospheric conditions are suitable for the launch of a spacecraft (also ***launch window***) or the weather allows oil-rig maintenance and construction at sea (also ***weather window***); *gen.* a free or suitable interval or period of time, an opportunity for action, (freq. in ***window of opportunity***, ***window of vulnerability***). Chiefly *US*. M20.
4 An opening resembling or likened to a window; now *spec.* (*a*) a transparent panel in an envelope to show the contents or address; (*b*) an aperture in a wall or screen through which to serve customers in a bank, ticket office, etc.; (*c*) a facet cut on a gemstone, esp. a rough one. LME. ▸**b** ANATOMY. = FENESTRA 2. E17. ▸**c** GEOLOGY. = FENSTER. E20. ▸**d** (Freq. **W-**.) = CHAFF *noun*[1] 5. M20. ▸**e** COMPUTING. The screen of a VDU regarded as a means of displaying an image stored in a computer; the part of a drawing, program, etc., chosen for display. Also, a defined part of a VDU display allocated to a particular category of information etc. M20. ▸**f** In pl. **Windows**. COMPUTING. (Proprietary name for) any of a series of widely-used graphical user interface systems for PCs and desktop computers. L20.

📖 **1** W. COWPER Trees are to be seen From ev'ry window. *Spectator* One of them wanting the window open and the other wanting it shut. *Daily News* The thieves . . smashed the window. E. M. BRENT-DYER 'No walk this day!' said that young person, looking sadly out of the window. ***French window***, ***oriel window***, ***rose window***, ***stained-glass window***, ***Venetian window***, etc. **2** DICKENS A . . draper's shop, with goods of all kinds . . in the window. THACKERAY The ticket in the window which announced 'Apartments to Let'. **3a** *Notes & Queries* A book which opens a window on one of the great-est periods of English history.

Phrases: **be thrown out of the window**, **go out of the window** be abandoned or made worthless, be no longer taken into account. ***Judas window***. ***open window unit***: see OPEN *adjective*. ***Piccadilly window***. ***shop window***: see SHOP *noun*. **throw the house out of the window** (now *rare*) make a great commotion, turn everything topsy-turvy. ***white window***: see WHITE *adjective*.
Comb.: **window-box** a box placed on an outside window-sill in which to grow flowers; **window-cleaner** a person employed to clean windows; **window display** a display of goods in a shop window; **window-dress** *verb trans. & intrans.* engage in window-dressing (of); **window-dresser** a person, organization, etc., engaged or employed in window-dressing; **window-dressing** †(*a*) the fittings and ornaments of a window; (*b*) the arrangement and display to the best advantage of goods in a shop window; (*c*) *fig.* the adroit presentation of facts etc. to give a deceptively favourable impression, *esp.* the arrangement of a balance-sheet so as to show a business etc. as more prosperous than it is; **window-envelope**: having a transparent panel to show the contents or address; **window-ledge** = ***window-sill*** s.v. SILL *noun*[1] 2a; **window-pane** (*a*) see PANE *noun*[1] 6; (*b*) *arch. slang* a monocle; (*c*) (in full ***window-pane check***) a kind of large check pattern on clothes; a single square of this; (*d*) a flatfish, *Scophthalmus aquosus*, of the W. Atlantic; **window plant** (*a*) a plant grown indoors on a window-sill; (*b*) any of several South African and Namibian desert plants of the mesembryanthemum family, e.g. *Lithops optica* and *Fenestraria rhopalophylla*, which grow buried in sand with only a transparent section of the leaf-tip visible above ground; **window-screen** (*a*) an ornamental device for filling a window-opening, as lattice-work or stained glass; (*b*) *US* a mesh screen put across a window-opening to admit air but exclude insects etc.; **window scrim** = SCRIM *noun* 2; **window-seat** (*a*) a seat below a window, esp. in an alcove or bay; (*b*) a seat next to a window in a train, bus, aircraft, etc.; **window-shop** *verb intrans.* go from shop to shop to look at the goods displayed in shop windows without buying anything (chiefly as ***window-shopping*** *verbal noun & ppl adjective*); **window-shopper** a person engaged in window-shopping; ***window-sill***: see SILL *noun*[1] 2a; **window table** a table by a window in a restaurant etc.; **window-tax** *Hist.* a duty levied on windows or similar openings; **window-trimmer** *US* = ***window-dresser*** above; **window-trimming** *US* = ***window-dressing*** above; **window-washer** (chiefly *US*) (*a*) = ***windscreen washer*** s.v. WIND *noun*[1]; (*b*) a window-cleaner.

▶ **B** *verb trans.* **1** Place in a window. *rare*. E17.
2 Provide with windows or similar openings. *rare*. M17.
■ **windowed** *adjective* (*a*) provided with or having windows (of a specified kind); having (esp. decorative) openings; *spec.* (of the thread mark of a banknote) having only some sections exposed to view; (*b*) *poet. & joc.* full of holes: LME. **windowful** *noun* as much as will fill a window L19. **windowing** *noun* †(*a*) the fittings or furniture of a window; (*b*) COMPUTING the process of selecting part of a stored image for display or enlargement: E17. **windowless** *adjective* LME. **windowlessness** *noun* E20. **window-like** *adjective* resembling a window M19. **windowy** *adjective* having many or large windows or similar openings M17.

windrow /ˈwɪndrəʊ/ *noun & verb*. Also **winrow** /ˈwɪnrəʊ/. E16.
[from WIND *noun*[1] + ROW *noun*[1].]
▶ **A** *noun*. A row of mown grass or hay, sheaves of corn, peats, etc., laid out to be dried by exposure to the wind. E16.
▶ **B** *verb trans.* Lay or set in windrows. E18.
■ **windrower** *noun* a machine for cutting and raking crops into windrows M20.

Windsor /ˈwɪnzə/ *adjective & noun*. L15.
[A town in Berkshire in southern England, site of the royal residence Windsor Castle.]
▶ **A** *adjective*. **1** Designating things originating in or associated with Windsor. L15.
2 Of, pertaining to, or characteristic of the British royal family since 1917 (formerly called *Saxe-Coburg-Gotha*). E20.
1 Windsor bean a variety of broad bean with short pods. **Windsor blue** = ***phthalocyanine blue*** s.v. PHTHALOCYANINE 2. **Windsor brick** a kind of red fire-resistant brick. **Windsor chair** a kind of wooden chair with the back formed of or supported by upright rods. **Windsor knot** a large loose knot in a necktie. **Windsor Red** a type of English cheese containing red wine. **Windsor soap** a kind of scented (usu. brown) soap. **Windsor tie** *US* a broad bias-cut necktie or scarf. **Windsor uniform** a uniform consisting of a blue coat with red collar and cuffs and a blue or white waistcoat, worn on certain ceremonial occasions at Windsor Castle.
▶ **B** *noun*. **1** *ellipt.* A Windsor brick, chair, tie, etc. L18.
2 A member of the Windsor royal family; (more fully ***House of Windsor***) the British royal family since 1917. E20.

wind-up /ˈwʌɪndʌp/ *noun*[1] *& adjective*. L16.
[from *wind up* s.v. WIND *verb*[1].]
▶ **A** *noun*. **1** The action or an act of winding up or concluding something; the close, conclusion, or finish *of* something. L16.
2 BASEBALL. The motions of a pitcher preparing to pitch the ball. M20.
3 Material that has become wound round something; the action of winding or coiling something round something else; the action of becoming twisted or stressed by the application of torque. M20.
4 A deliberate attempt to provoke someone by misleading or hoaxing; a trick, a tease, a practical joke. *colloq.* L20.
5 *ellipt.* A device operated by being wound up, as a wind-up gramophone or a clockwork toy. L20.
▶ **B** *adjective*. **1** Operated by being wound up; *spec.* clockwork; (of a window of a motor vehicle) raised and lowered by the rotation of a handle. L18.
2 Forming the conclusion of something; concluding, closing. M19.

wind-up /ˈwɪndʌp/ *noun*[2]. *colloq.* E20.
[from ***get the wind up*** s.v. WIND *noun*[1].]
A state of nervous anxiety or fear; an occurrence of this.

windward /ˈwɪndwəd/ *noun, adjective, & adverb*. As adverb also **-wards** /-wədz/. M16.
[from WIND *noun*[1] + -WARD. Cf. LEEWARD.]
Chiefly NAUTICAL. ▶**A** *noun*. The side or region towards which the wind blows; the direction from which the wind blows. Chiefly in ***to the windward***, ***to windward***. M16.
cast an anchor to windward adopt measures for security. **get to windward of** (*a*) gain an advantage over; (*b*) move to windward to avoid the smell of. **keep to windward of** keep out of the reach of.
▶ **B** *adjective*. Situated on the side facing the wind; having a direction towards the wind; (of a vessel) having a specified ability to sail close to the wind, weatherly. E17.
▶ **C** *adverb*. Towards the wind, to windward. L17.
■ **windwardly** *adjective* windward, weatherly M17. **windwardmost** *adjective* furthest to windward E17. **windwardness** *noun* windward or weatherly quality E17.

windy /ˈwɪndi/ *noun*[1]. *Scot., Anglo-Irish, & non-standard*. M19.
[Repr. a pronunc.]
A window. Cf. WINDER *noun*[4].

windy /ˈwɪndi/ *noun*[2]. *N. Amer. slang*. M20.
[from WINDY *adjective*[1].]
A tall story; a piece of boasting or exaggeration.

windy /ˈwɪndi/ *adjective*[1].
[Old English *windig*: see WIND *noun*[1], -Y[1].]
1 Consisting of wind; of or pertaining to the wind; resembling the wind. OE. ▸**b** Of music or a musical instrument: produced or sounded by wind or air. Chiefly *poet*. M19.
2 Of a place: exposed to the wind, blown on or through by the wind, windswept. Of weather etc.: characterized by or stormy with wind. OE. ▸**b** Stirred by the wind; moving so as to produce a current of air. *poet*. LME.
3 a = FLATULENT 2. OE. ▸**b** = FLATULENT 1. LME.
4 Of speech, a speaker, etc.: verbose, long-winded, wordy; empty, inflated, bombastic; boastful; *gen.* insubstantial, trivial, worthless. LME.
5 a Inducing pride or vanity. *obsolete* exc. as passing into sense 4. L16. ▸**b** Puffed up, inflated with pride, vain. Now *Scot.* E17.
6 a Nervous, frightened, anxious. *colloq.* E20. ▸**b** Of a place or situation: frightening, nerve-racking. *Military slang*. E20.

📖 **1** W. BASSE March, departed with his windy rage. **2** T. H. HUXLEY A windy day soon dries a wet pavement. *Guardian* The wide and windy streets of Ulan Bator. **4** *Illustrated London News* The windy speeches made at public political meetings. *Listener* Milton may be grandiloquent but he is not windy. **6a** *Daily Mirror* The Liberal MPs were too windy to give him his marching orders.

Phrases: **on the windy side of** *fig.* so as not to be detected by, out of reach of; away from, clear of. **the Windy City** Chicago.
■ **windily** *adverb* M19. **windiness** *noun* LME.

windy /ˈwʌɪndi/ *adjective*[2]. L20.
[from WIND *verb*[1] + -Y[1].]
Of a road, course, etc.: that winds about, twisting and turning.

wine /wʌɪn/ *noun*.
[Old English *wīn* = Old Frisian, Old Saxon, Old High German *wīn* (Dutch *wijn*, German *Wein*), Old Norse *vín*, Gothic *wein*, from Germanic, from Latin *vinum* prob. borrowed with Greek *oinos* etc. from a common Mediterranean source.]
1 Alcoholic liquor produced from fermented grape juice; (with specifying word) a type of this; a drink of this. OE.
2 Alcoholic liquor resembling wine made from the fermented juice of other fruits, or from grain, flowers, the sap of various trees, etc. Usu. with specifying word. LME.
3 PHARMACOLOGY. A solution of a medicinal substance in wine; a medicated wine. Usu. foll. by *of*. M17.
4 In full ***wine-party***. A party, esp. of undergraduates, the main purpose of which is wine-drinking. *arch.* E19.
5 A wineglass. M19.
6 A dark red colour; the colour of red wine. L19.

📖 **1** F. FYFIELD Wine and cheese parties . . to show off the wonders of your house. ***claret wine***, ***Loire wine***, ***Madeira wine***, ***pink wine***, ***red wine***, ***Rhone wine***, ***white wine***, etc. *fig.*: D. C. PEATTIE The sparkling wine of her daily adventure. *Guardian* If employers 'intoxicated with the wine of Thatcherism' had been less arrogant. **2** ***barley wine***, ***birch wine***, ***gooseberry wine***, ***rhubarb wine***, etc.

Phrases: ***bread and wine***: see BREAD *noun*[1]. ***flower of wine***: see FLOWER *noun* 11. ***high wine***: see HIGH *adjective*. **in wine** intoxicated with wine. ***made wine***: see MADE *ppl adjective*. **new wine in old bottles** [*Matthew* 9:17] something new or innovatory added to an existing or established system, order, etc. ***sops-in-wine***: see SOP *noun*[1]. ***spirit of wine***, ***spirits of wine***: see SPIRIT *noun*. ***sweet wine***: see SWEET *adjective & adverb*. **take wine** *arch.* drink wine with another person in a ceremonial manner, esp. as a token of friendship or regard. **wine of the country** = VIN *du pays*. **wine, women, and song**, **wine, woman, and song** [German WEIN, WEIB, UND GESANG]: proverbially required by men for carefree entertainment and pleasure.
Attrib. & comb.: In the sense 'of the colour of wine', as ***wine-red***, ***wine-yellow***, etc. Special combs., as **wine bar** (*a*) a counter in a club, shop, etc., where wine is kept or sold; (*b*) a bar or small licensed restaurant where wine is the main drink available; **wineberry** any of various shrubs or small trees bearing berries resembling wine in colour or taste, *esp.* (more fully ***Japanese wineberry***) a bramble of China and Japan, *Rubus phoenicolasius*, with edible orange fruit, and (*NZ*) the tutu, *Coriaria arborea*, or the mako, *Aristotelia racemosa*; the fruit of such a plant; **wine book** (*a*) a book for keeping records of wines bought and consumed; (*b*) a book about wines; **wine bottle** a glass bottle for wine, the standard size holding 75 cl or 26⅔ fluid ounces; **wine box** a square carton of wine fitted with a dispensing tap; **wine buff** a wine enthusiast; **wine butler**: in charge of the wine cellar and responsible for serving wine at meals etc.; ***wine cellar***: see CELLAR 3; **wine-dark** *adjective* of the colour of deep-red wine (used esp. to render Greek *oinops* as an epithet of the sea); **wine-dot** *Austral. slang* [joc. from WYANDOT] an addict of cheap wine; **wine farm** *S. Afr.*: on which grapes are grown for wine-making and usually wine is made; **wine-farmer** a wine-grower; **winefat** *arch.* = ***wine-vat*** below; **wine fly** any of various flies that are attracted to wine etc., or that have larvae that live in wine; *esp.* a vinegar fly; **wine fountain** a large vessel for holding and dispensing wine; **wine-gallon** a former measure of liquid capacity equal to 231 cubic inches; **wine-god** a god associated with wine, *esp.* Bacchus or Dionysus; **wine-grape** (orig. *US*) a grape suitable for making into wine; **wine-grower** a cultivator of vines for wine production; **wine-growing** the cultivation of vines for wine production; **wine gum** a small fruit-flavoured sweet made with gelatin; **wine-house** (*a*) (now chiefly *Hist.*) a public house where wine is drunk; (*b*) a firm of wine-merchants; **wine label** (*a*) a

label hung round the neck of a decanter to indicate what wine it holds; (*b*) a paper label on a wine bottle, stating the wine's name and provenance; **wine lake** a stockpile or surplus of wine; **wine-lees** the sediment of wine; **wine list** a list of the wines available at a restaurant etc.; **wine lodge** (*a*) a storage room for wine; (*b*) a licensed establishment selling wine, beer, and soft drinks; **wine-palm** any palm from which palm wine is obtained, esp. *Caryota urens*; ***wine-party***: see sense 4 above; **wine-porter** (now *rare*): employed to carry wine, esp. to deposit it in cellars; **wine-pot** a pot or flagon for wine; **wine rack** a frame with compartments for holding bottles of wine in a horizontal position; **winesap** a large red American winter apple; **wineskin** (*a*) a container for wine made from the whole skin of an animal; (*b*) *fig.* a person who fills his or her skin with wine, a tippler; **wine snob** a person who pretentiously uses an often flawed knowledge of wine in order to impress others; **winesour** a small acid variety of plum; **wine steward**: responsible for serving wine in a restaurant etc.; **wine-taster** (*a*) a person who judges the quality of wine by tasting; (*b*) an instrument for drawing a small sample of wine from a cask; **wine-tasting** judging the quality of wine by tasting; an occasion when this is done; **wine-vat** a winepress; **wine-vault(s)** (*a*) a vault in which wine is stored; (*b*) a public-house; **wine-vinegar** vinegar made from wine (as opp. to ***malt vinegar*** etc.); **wine waiter**, **wine waitress**: responsible for advising on and serving wine in a restaurant etc.

■ **wineless** *adjective* LME. †**winish** *adjective* (*rare*) having the quality or nature of wine; resembling wine: M16–M18.

wine /wʌɪn/ *verb*. E17.
[from prec.]

†**1** *verb trans.* **a** Foll. by *out*: spend (time) in drinking wine. *rare*. Only in E17. ▸**b** Provide (a cellar) with wine. *rare*. Only in M17.

2 *verb intrans.* Drink wine. Chiefly in ***wine and dine*** below. E19.

3 *verb trans.* Entertain with wine. Chiefly in ***wine and dine*** below. M19.

📖 **2** *Cook's Magazine* Weekend of cooking, wining, dining and fun on the California coast. **3** *TV Times* We are wined, dined and serenaded in a most gallant manner.

Phrases: **wine and dine** entertain or have a meal with wine.

winebibber /ˈwʌɪnbɪbə/ *noun*. Now *arch. & literary*. M16.
[from WINE *noun* + BIBBER.]

A tippler, a drunkard.

■ **winebibbing** *noun* tippling; frequent or convivial drinking: M16.

Winebrennarian /wʌɪnbrəˈnɛːrɪən/ *noun & adjective*. *US*. M19.
[from *Winebrenner* (see below) + -ARIAN.]

▸ **A** *noun*. A member of the Church of God, an evangelical sect founded by John Winebrenner (1797–1860) and others in 1830 in Pennsylvania. M19.

▸ **B** *attrib.* or as *adjective*. Of or pertaining to the Winebrennarians or their beliefs. L19.

wined /wʌɪnd/ *adjective*. E17.
[from WINE *noun, verb*: see -ED[2], -ED[1].]

1 Mixed with wine; coloured or flavoured with wine. *rare*. E17.

2 That has drunk wine, esp. in abundance. Also foll. by *up*. M17.

wineglass /ˈwʌɪnglɑːs/ *noun*. L16.
[from WINE *noun* + GLASS *noun*.]

▸ **A** *noun*. A glass for wine, usu. having a stem and a foot. Also, the contents of this, a wineglassful. L16.

▸ **B** *attrib.* or as *adjective*. Of or pertaining to a wineglass; resembling the typical shape of a wineglass. M19.

■ **wineglassful** *noun* the capacity or contents of a wineglass; as much as a wineglass will hold, a measure of liquid usu. reckoned as 2 fluid ounces: E19.

winepress /ˈwʌɪnprɛs/ *noun*. LME.
[from WINE *noun* + PRESS *noun*[1].]

A press in which the juice is extracted from grapes in making wine.

📖 *fig.*: SHELLEY Drunk from the winepress of the Almighty's wrath.

winer /ˈwʌɪnə/ *noun*. M16.
[from WINE *noun, verb* + -ER[1].]

1 A vintner. Now *rare*. M16.

2 A person who drinks wine. *colloq.* E20.

winery /ˈwʌɪn(ə)ri/ *noun*. Orig. *US*. L19.
[from WINE *noun* + -ERY.]

An establishment where wine is made.

winey *adjective* var. of WINY.

wing /wɪŋ/ *noun*. ME.
[Old Norse *vængir* accus., *vengi* pl. of *vængr* wing of a bird, aisle, repl. Old English *feþra* wings pl. of *feþer* FEATHER *noun*.]

▸ **I 1** Either of the modified forelimbs of a bird, which are usu. specialized for flight and bear large feathers for this purpose. ME. ▸**b** Any of various appendages of other animals which are specialized for flight; *esp.* (*a*) either of the modified forelimbs of a bat or pterodactyl, formed by skin stretched between the digits or behind the fifth digit respectively; (*b*) each of two or four flat extensions of the thoracic cuticle in most insects, usu. either transparent or covered in scales. LME. ▸**c** The wing of a bird used as food. Also, the shoulder of a hare or rabbit. LME. ▸**d** A representation, image, or imitation of a wing. M16.

2 a A wing as the means of flight of a supernatural being or mythical creature, as an angel, demon, dragon, etc. ME. ▸**b** The means by which something inanimate or abstract is regarded or represented as having the ability to fly, or to carry one swiftly along. Usu. in *pl.* LME.

3 Power or means of flight, or of movement or action represented as flight; action or manner of flying (*lit. & fig.*). ME. ▸**b** Shelter; protecting care (esp. with ref. to *Matthew* 23:37). Chiefly in ***under the wing of*** etc. below. ME.

4 *transf.* A bird; birds collectively, *esp.* game-birds. L16. ▸**b** A flock of plover. *rare*. E19.

📖 **2a** BYRON The Angel of Death spread his wings on the blast. **b** SHAKES. *Rich. III* When I should mount with wings of victory. **3** SHAKES. *2 Hen. VI* Knowledge the wing wherewith we fly to heaven.

▸ **II 5** A thing resembling or analogous to a wing in form or function, as (*a*) an apparatus intended to enable human flight when attached to the arms or shoulders; (*b*) in *pl.* = ***water-wings*** s.v. WATER *noun*; (*c*) a sail of a windmill; (*d*) *poet.* a ship's sail; the sails of a ship collectively; (*e*) *slang* an arm. ME. ▸**b** *spec.* A rigid horizontal winglike structure forming a supporting part of an aircraft; *transf.* (in *pl.*), a pilot's certificate of ability to fly an aeroplane (often indicated by a badge representing a pair of wings). E20.

6 A lateral part, appendage, boundary, or extension of a structure, as (*a*) a lateral or outlying part of an area or space; (*b*) either of the retaining walls at the ends of a bridge; (*c*) a lateral projection or member of a tool, implement, mechanism, etc.; (*d*) in a horse-drawn carriage, either of a pair of curved pieces extending over the wheels to protect passengers from mud splashes; in a motor vehicle, each of the parts of the bodywork incorporating the mudguards and covering the wheels; (*e*) either of a pair of side-pieces projecting forwards at the top of the high back of some armchairs; (*f*) a platform or deck extending out from the side of a boat. LME.

7 a Either of the divisions on the right or left side of the main body of an army or fleet in battle array. Also, either of the two divisions of a regiment; an operational unit of an air force consisting of two or more squadrons. LME. ▸**b** In FOOTBALL and other games, (the position of) a forward player on the far right or left of the centre; the part of the playing area in which a wing normally plays. L19. ▸**c** A section of a group or a political party, holding more progressive or reactionary views than those of the more moderate centre. L19.

8 Either of a pair of lateral projecting pieces of a garment on or near the shoulder; in military uniform, a kind of epaulette (now worn by bandsmen) which stands out from the seam at the top of the shoulder. Also, a side-flap of a cap etc. Now chiefly *Hist.* LME.

9 A subordinate part of a building which projects or is extended in a certain direction from the side of the main or central part. Also, any more or less separate section of a building, esp. of an institution such as a hospital or prison. E16. ▸**b** NAUTICAL. The part of a ship's hold nearest the side of the vessel. Also, the sponson of a steamer. M18. ▸**c** THEATRICAL. Either of the side scenes of a stage; *sing.* & (usu.) in *pl.*, the space at either side of the stage where these pieces of scenery stand. L18.

10 ANATOMY. = ALA 1. M17.

11 BOTANY. †**a** Each of the lateral divisions or leaflets of a pinnate leaf. L17–M18. ▸**b** Either of the two lateral petals on either side of the keel in a papilionaceous flower or the flower of a fumitory. L18. ▸**c** A thin membranous appendage of a seed (e.g. of the elm or sycamore) assisting its dispersal; a membranous flange extending along a stem or stalk. L18.

12 PHYSICS. A part of a spectral line where the intensity tails off to zero. M20.

📖 **5** BYRON While flew the vessel on her snowy wing. **b** *Publishers Weekly* Mike Hagen earns his wings as a crop duster in rural Florida. **6** J. S. BLACKIE The Hill of Howth, forming the north wing of the bay of Dublin. *Sports Illustrated* Rick . . slouched against the rear wing of his Penske–Chevy. **7a** *Guardian* Reduction . . involving . . elimination of five fighter wings and the closure of 15 bases. **b** *Rugby News* Modern wings must be able to kick accurately to touch and to . . sidestep and swerve. **c** *New York Review of Books* Wright . . wanted to use the speakership to restore to life the old liberal wing of the Democratic party. **9** A. S. BYATT Christabel's room was in the east wing . . closed since 1918.

Phrases: **a wing and a prayer** [a song (1943) by H. Adamson] (*a*) an emergency landing by an aircraft; (*b*) *fig.* reliance on hope or the slightest chance in a desperate situation. ***bastard wing***: see BASTARD *adjective*. **be on wings** be going with light steps as in a joyously ebullient mood. ***clip the wings of***: see CLIP *verb*[2] 1. ***feel one's wings***: see FEEL *verb*. **give wings to**, **lend wings to** (*a*) give the power of flight to; (*b*) *fig.* give full rein to; speed up. LEFT WING. ***lend wings to***: see ***give wings to*** above. **make wing** *arch.* make one's way by flying, fly. **on the wing** (*a*) flying, in flight; (*b*) *fig.* moving or travelling swiftly; astir, on the move; departing; ready to start or depart. **on the wings of the wind** swiftly. RIGHT WING. **spread one's wings**, **stretch one's wings**, **try one's wings** test or develop one's powers; expand one's horizons; lead a life of wider scope than hitherto. **take under one's wing** protect; treat as a protégé. **take wing** (*a*) (of a bird etc.) take flight, fly away; (*b*) *fig.* depart swiftly, make off, flee. ***try one's wings***: see ***spread one's wings*** above. ***under a person's wing***: see ***under the wing of*** below. **under the wing of**, **under a person's wing** under the protection, care, or patronage of (a person). **waiting in the wings** holding oneself in readiness to act; (for the moment) taking no part in the action. **wing-and-wing** NAUTICAL (of a ship) sailing directly before the wind, with the foresail hauled over on one side and the mainsail on the other.

Attrib. & comb.: In the senses 'of or pertaining to the wing of a bird, insect, etc.', as ***wing-feather***, ***wing-power***, etc., 'of or pertaining to the wing of an aircraft', as ***wing flutter***, ***wing-tank***, etc., 'of or pertaining to the wing of an army (now *rare*) or an air force', as ***wing-adjutant***, ***wing-headquarters***, etc., 'of or pertaining to the position of wing in sport', as ***wing-forward***, ***wing-half***, etc., 'having wings or side appendages', as ***wing-bonnet***, etc. Special combs., as **wing-back chair** = ***wing chair*** below; **wing-band** = ***wing-bar*** (a) below; **wing-bar** (*a*) a line of contrasting colour on the feathers of a bird's wing, esp. on the greater or median coverts; (*b*) AERONAUTICS a line of runway lights extending sideways at right angles to the runway; **wing-beat** one complete cycle of movements made by a wing in flying; **wing-bow** a band of contrasting colour on the shoulder or bend of the wing of a domestic fowl, esp. on the lesser coverts; **wing-bud** ENTOMOLOGY in an insect larva, a rudiment from which a wing develops; **wing-case** ENTOMOLOGY either of a pair of modified toughened forewings which cover the functional wings in certain insects; *esp.* an elytron of a beetle; **wing chair** a high-backed armchair with wings or projecting side-pieces; **wing-clap** *noun & verb* (*a*) *noun* a loud crack made by a bird striking its wings together; (*b*) *verb intrans.* produce a wing-clap or series of wing-claps; **wing-clapping** the production of a wing-clap or series of wing-claps; **wing collar** a high stiff shirt collar with the upper corners bent down; **wing commander** a rank in the Royal Air Force next below a group captain and above a squadron leader; **wing-cover** = ***wing-case*** above; **wing covert** any of the small coverts overlying the flight-feathers of a bird's wing; **wing-dam** *noun & verb* (*a*) *noun* a dam or barrier built into a stream to deflect the current; (*b*) *verb trans.* provide with a wing-dam; **wing-fish** any of various fishes with enlarged winglike pectoral fins; *esp.* a flying fish; **wing-footed** *adjective* (chiefly *fig.*) having winged feet; swiftly-moving; **wing formula** ORNITHOLOGY a record of the shape of a bird's wing, usu. comprising an indication of the length of each primary feather in relation to the wing tip or the longest primary covert; **wing-game** game-birds collectively (as opp. to ***ground game*** s.v. GROUND *noun*); ***wing loading***: see LOADING 6; **wingman** (*a*) the pilot of an aircraft which is positioned behind and to one side of the leading aircraft, as in combat formation; the aircraft itself; (*b*) a player in the wing position; **wing mirror** (*a*) a side mirror (freq. adjustable) on a dressing-table; (*b*) a rear-view mirror projecting from the side of a motor vehicle; **wing-nut** a screwed nut with winglike projections for turning with the fingers; also called ***butterfly nut***; **wingover** AERONAUTICS a manoeuvre in which an aircraft turns at the top of a steep climb and flies back along its original path; **wing oyster** (the shell of) any of various marine bivalve molluscs of the genus *Pteria* and family Pteriidae, with a winglike extension to each valve projecting from an elongated straight hinge; **wing rib** the end rib of a loin of beef; **wing root** the part of an aircraft wing where it is attached to the fuselage; **wing-sail** a rigid or semi-rigid structure similar to an aircraft wing fixed vertically on a boat to provide thrust from the action of the wind; **wing-sheath** = ***wing-case*** above; **wing-shell** †(*a*) = ***wing-case*** above; (*b*) (the shell of) any of various bivalve molluscs with a winglike shell or extension to it; *esp.* a wing oyster, *US* a piddock; (*c*) = PTEROPOD; **wing-shooting** the practice of shooting birds that are in flight; **wing-shot** *noun & adjective* (*a*) *noun* a shot aimed at a flying bird; a person skilled in wing-shooting; (*b*) *adjective* shot while flying; shot in the wing; **wing-snail** = PTEROPOD; ***wingspan***: see SPAN *noun*[1] 3c; **wing-tag** *verb trans.* attach a distinguishing marker to the wing of a bird; **wing-tip** (*a*) the tip of the wing of a bird, bat, insect, or aircraft; (*b*) (chiefly *N. Amer.*) a shoe with a toecap having a backward extending point and curving sides, resembling the shape of a wing; **wing-walking** acrobatic stunts performed on the wings of an airborne aircraft as a public entertainment; **wing-wall** a lateral wall forming a support to an abutment and to the adjacent earth.

■ **wingless** *adjective* having no wings; (of a kiwi, moa, etc.) having rudimentary wings: L16. **winglessness** *noun* (*rare*) L19. **winglike** *adjective* resembling a wing L18.

wing /wɪŋ/ *verb*. LME.
[from the noun.]

▸ **I 1** *verb intrans.* Use the wings, take flight, fly; *fig.* pass swiftly, speed. Also (of an aircraft), fly; (of a passenger) travel by aircraft. LME.

†**2** *verb trans.* Carve (a quail or partridge). L15–E19.

3 *verb trans.* Put wings on, provide with wings for flying; *fig.* enable to fly or soar; give swiftness to; hasten. L16.

4 *verb trans.* Fly through, on, or across; traverse (as) on wings; make (one's way) thus. E17.

5 *verb trans.* Convey (as) by means of wings; carry through the air as if flying, waft. E17.

6 *verb trans.* Send (as) in flight, let fly (a missile etc.); send off swiftly. E18. ▸**b** Cause to sail through the air; throw, fling; lob. *N. Amer. colloq.* L20.

7 *verb trans.* Shoot (a bird) in the wing, so as to prevent flight without causing death; *transf.* wound (a person) superficially, esp. in the arm or shoulder; disable by a shot. Also, pull off the wings of (an insect). E19.

📖 1 C. SAGAN A single bit of radio information, sent winging across space to earth. *Time* As Air Force One winged toward Washington. *Times* The Prince . . flies back from Monaco . . to wing off within hours for Papua New Guinea. M. WESLEY A flight of herring gulls winging out to sea. **3** LYTTON The Convent was at some distance, but . . fear would wing her steps. **4** *Fast Forward* Another chance to wing your way overseas to . . Hollywood! **5** C. EGLETON The VC 10 winged him back to Heathrow. **6** G. MEREDITH The desire to wing a telegram to her. **7** L. ARMSTRONG Slippers was a fast man on the draw. He winged the guy in the leg.

▶**II 8** *verb trans.* †**a** Reinforce (an army etc.) *with* additional troops on the wings; (of reinforcements) form the wings of. L16–L17. ▸**b** Provide (a building) with wings; fit with lateral parts or projections. L17.

9 *NAUTICAL.* **a** *verb trans.* Carry *up* (ballast) in the wings of a ship. L18. ▸**b** *verb intrans.* Foll. by *out*: set a sail on a boom projecting sideways when a ship is sailing before the wind. Cf. ***wing-and-wing*** s.v. WING *noun.* M19.

10 *verb intrans. & trans.* (with *it*). Study (a part) in or near the wings of a stage, having undertaken the role at short notice. Now *esp.* (orig. & chiefly *N. Amer.*), improvise; speak or act without preparation. *slang* (orig. *THEATRICAL*). L19.

📖 **10** *Globe & Mail (Toronto)* Mr. Trudeau came without notes, choosing to wing it.

Wing Chun /wɪŋ ˈtʃʊn/ *noun.* L20.
[Chinese, app. from Yim *Wing Chun* (fl. mid 18th cent.), by whom the system was developed.]
A simplified form of kung fu used principally as a system of self-defence.

Wingco /ˈwɪŋkəʊ/ *noun. RAF slang.* Pl. **-os**. M20.
[Abbreviation of ***wing commander*** s.v. WING *noun.*]
A wing commander.

wingding /ˈwɪŋdɪŋ/ *noun.* E20.
[Origin unkn.]
1 A fit or spasm, esp. as experienced or simulated by a drug addict; a furious outburst. Freq. in ***throw a wingding***. *US slang.* E20.
2 A wild party; a celebration, a social gathering. *slang* (orig. & chiefly *N. Amer.*). M20.

winged /wɪŋd, *poet.* ˈwɪŋɪd/ *adjective*[1]. LME.
[from WING *noun* + -ED[2].]
1 Having wings for flight, esp. of a specified kind or number; represented with wings; *spec.* (*HERALDRY*) having wings of a specified tincture. Freq. as 2nd elem. of comb. LME. ▸**b** Of a ship: with sails set. *poet.* L16.
2 *fig.* Capable of or performing some movement or action represented as flight; flying or passing swiftly, swift, rapid. E16.
3 Provided with or having one or more lateral parts, appendages, or projections. L16. ▸**b** *spec.* Of a stem, seed, etc.: having membranous appendages or flanges. L18.
†**4** = PINNATE 1. M17–L18.

📖 **1** *BBC Wildlife* Mayflies . . the only insect group to have a winged larval stage. *Allure* The winged monkeys in *The Wizard of Oz*. ***four-winged, long-winged, swift-winged***, etc. **2** SHAKES. *A.Y.L.* A woman's thought runs before her actions . . . So do all thoughts; they are wing'd. J. CLARE With double speed the wing'd hour gallops by. **3** G. MCCAUGHREAN She dragged the winged armchair . . behind the telephone engineer.

Special collocations: **winged bean** the Goa bean, *Psophocarpus tetragonolobus*. **winged elm** a small N. American elm, *Ulmus alata*, having branchlets with corky wings. **winged oyster** = ***wing oyster*** s.v. WING *noun.* **winged thistle** *NZ* either of two European thistles with winged stems, *Carduus tenuiflorus* and *C. pycnocephalus*, occurring as introduced weeds. **winged words** highly significant or apposite words (travelling swiftly as arrows to the mark).
■ **wingedly** /-ɪdli/ *adverb* M17. **wingedness** /-ɪdnɪs/ *noun* L18.

winged /wɪŋd/ *adjective*[2]. L18.
[from WING *verb* + -ED[1].]
Shot or wounded in the wing, arm, etc.; disabled by a superficial wound.

winger /ˈwɪŋə/ *noun.* L18.
[from WING *noun* + -ER[1].]
1 *NAUTICAL.* A small cask or tank stowed in the wing of a ship's hold. *rare.* L18.
2 In *FOOTBALL* and other games, a player on the right or left wing. L19.
3 *Nautical slang.* **a** A ship's steward. E20. ▸**b** A comrade or friend. Also, a young seaman taken under the wing of a more experienced rating etc. M20.

winglet /ˈwɪŋlɪt/ *noun.* E17.
[from WING *noun* + -LET.]
1 *gen.* A little wing; a thing resembling this; *rare* a small winglike appendage on an article of clothing. Chiefly *poet.* E17.
2 = ALULA. E19.
3 **a** A small winglike projection on a mechanism etc. *rare.* M19. ▸**b** A specially shaped vertical projection on the tip of an aircraft wing for reducing drag; a similar structure on a boat's keel. L20.

wingmanship /ˈwɪŋmənʃɪp/ *noun. rare.* M19.
[from WING *noun* + -MANSHIP, after *oarsmanship, penmanship*, etc.]
Skill in the use of wings for flight; flying regarded as an art or accomplishment.

wingy /ˈwɪŋi/ *noun. colloq.* L19.
[from WING *noun* + -Y[6].]
(A nickname for) a one-armed man.

wingy /ˈwɪŋi/ *adjective.* L16.
[from WING *noun* + -Y[1].]
1 Having wings, winged (*poet.*); having large or conspicuous wings. L16.
†**2** Of, pertaining to, or resembling a wing or wings; winglike. *rare.* M–L17.
3 *fig.* Capable of swift or soaring movement, soaring, aspiring; eluding grasp or comprehension. M17.

wink /wɪŋk/ *noun*[1]. ME.
[from WINK *verb*[1].]
1 A closing of the eyes for sleep; a (brief) spell of sleep, a nap. Usu. in ***forty winks, a wink of sleep***, etc. below. ME.
2 The action or an act of winking; a glance or significant movement (now a closing and opening) of one eye, esp. as a signal expressing command, assent, invitation, collusion, friendliness, etc. E16.
3 **a** A brief moment, as being the time it takes to wink. L16. ▸**b** The slightest amount. Chiefly in neg. contexts. L16. ▸**c** In time-and-motion study, a unit of time equivalent to one two-thousandth of a minute. Orig. *US.* M20.
4 A temporary closure or flicker of the eyelid. E17.

📖 **1** J. K. JEROME Every night I woke up at seven o'clock and never got a wink afterwards. **2** M. GEE Bill emphasized his one foreign phrase with a long rolling wink. E. BLAIR Oh aye! smirked Moira . . giving them a coy wink. *Guardian* Contrary to all the nods and winks of senior . . policy-makers. **4** SIR W. SCOTT The smallest twitch of the features, or wink of the eyelid.

Phrases: **a wink of sleep** *emphatic* a very brief spell of sleep (chiefly in neg. contexts). ***forty winks***: see FORTY *adjective*. **in a wink** any moment now, in a trice. ***nudge, nudge, wink, wink***: see NUDGE *noun.* ***sleep a wink***: see SLEEP *verb.* ***tip the wink to***: see TIP *verb*[4] 1.
■ **winkless** *adjective* (*rare*) without a wink, unwinking M19.

wink /wɪŋk/ *noun*[2]. Orig. *US.* L19.
[Abbreviation.]
A counter in the game of tiddlywinks.

wink /wɪŋk/ *verb*[1].
[Old English *wincian* = Old Saxon *wincon* (Middle Low German, Middle Dutch *winken*) rel. to Old High German *winchan* (German *winken*) move sideways, stagger, nod, from Germanic, from Indo-European base also of WINCE *verb*[1], WINCH *verb*[1].]
1 *verb intrans.* †**a** Close the eyes. OE–E19. ▸**b** Of the eyes: close. Now *arch. rare.* ME.
2 *verb intrans.* Give a significant glance, as of command, assent, invitation, collusion, etc. Usu. foll. by *on, to, at*. Now *rare* exc. as passing into sense 7 below. OE. ▸†**b** *verb trans.* Bring into a specified state by a glance or nod. *rare.* M17–E18.
3 *verb intrans.* Close and open the eyes momentarily and involuntarily. ME. ▸**b** Of a light, a glowing object, etc.: emit quick intermittent flashes; twinkle. Also (of a thing), disappear or go *out* suddenly; come *on* suddenly. L16. ▸**c** Of the eyes: flicker; close and open quickly. Now *rare.* M17.
†**4** *verb intrans.* Close one eye, as in aiming at a target; aim. ME–L17.
†**5** *verb intrans.* Have the eyes closed in sleep; sleep; doze. LME–M17.
6 *verb intrans.* Avoid acknowledging or noticing something faulty, wrong, or improper. Now *rare* exc. as in ***wink at*** below. L15.
7 *verb intrans.* Close and open one eye, esp. in a deliberate, intimate, or collusive manner, to convey a message to a person or as a signal of friendliness or good-humoured interest. M19.
8 *verb trans.* **a** Close (an eye, the eyes) for a moment, either deliberately as a signal etc. or involuntarily. M19. ▸**b** Move swiftly, cause to flicker like an eyelid. *rare.* L19. ▸**c** Give (a signal), send (a message), etc. by means of a flashing light. E20. ▸**d** Convey (a message) by a wink of the eye. L20.

📖 **1b** *fig.*: W. DAVENANT Shadows vanish when the world's eye wincks Behind a cloud. **2** ADDISON I winked upon my Friend to take his Leave. **3** *Quarterly Review* When there is a loud report close at hand we instinctively wink. **b** D. WELCH He spread his wares . . and . . moonstones and rubies and sapphires winked at us. R. SILVERBERG Still the vision went on, and on . . . Then it was gone, winking out with a snap. **6** W. COWPER Too just to wink, or speak the guilty clear. **7** *Quarterly* 'Does wonders for an old guy's libido,' he says, winking at Paula. **8** H. T. LANE He just . . mischievously winked one eye as I left the room. **c** J. BARTH The channel buoys winked their various rhythms.

Phrases: **wink at** (*a*) deliberately avoid acknowledging or noticing (an offence, fault, impropriety, etc.); connive at; (*b*) (now *rare* or *obsolete*) disregard or overlook (a fact or occurrence); †(*c*) be complaisant with (a wrongdoer); connive at the doings of. **wink away** remove (tears) by blinking the eyes. **wink hard** (now *rare*) deliberately avoid noticing something. †**wink on**, †**wink upon** wink at.

wink /wɪŋk/ *verb*[2]. Orig. *US.* M20.
[from WINK *noun*[2].]
1 *verb trans.* Flick (a counter) in tiddlywinks. M20.
2 *verb intrans.* Play tiddlywinks. M20.

wink-a-peep /ˈwɪŋkəpiːp/ *noun.* E17.
[from WINK *verb*[1] + euphonic *-a-* + PEEP *noun*[4].]
†**1** In *pl.* The eyes. *rare.* Only in E17.
2 The scarlet pimpernel, *Anagallis arvensis*. *dial. & US.* E17.

winkel /ˈvɪŋk(ə)l/ *noun.* E19.
[Dutch.]
In South Africa: a general store.

winker /ˈwɪŋkə/ *noun*[1]. M16.
[from WINK *verb*[1] + -ER[1].]
1 A person who winks. Now *rare.* M16.
2 A horse's blinker. Usu. in *pl.* L16.
3 An eye; an eyelash. Usu. in *pl.* Now *dial. & slang.* M18.
4 A flashing indicator light on a motor vehicle. M20.

winker /ˈwɪŋkə/ *noun*[2]. Orig. *US.* M20.
[from WINK *verb*[2] + -ER[1].]
A tiddlywinks player.

winking /ˈwɪŋkɪŋ/ *verbal noun.* ME.
[from WINK *verb*[1] + -ING[1].]
The action of WINK *verb*[1]; an act or instance of this.
as easy as winking *colloq.* very easy. **like winking** *colloq.* (now *rare*) (*a*) in an instant, very rapidly; (*b*) with vigour or persistency.

winkle /ˈwɪŋk(ə)l/ *noun.* L16.
[Abbreviation of PERIWINKLE *noun*[2].]
1 An edible marine gastropod mollusc of the genus *Littorina*. L16.
2 The penis, esp. of a baby or young boy. *nursery & slang.* M20.
Comb.: **winkle-picker** *slang* a shoe with a long pointed toe; **winkle-pin** *Military slang* a bayonet.

winkle /ˈwɪŋk(ə)l/ *verb*[1] *intrans. dial. rare.* L18.
[from WINK *verb*[1] + -LE[3].]
Emit light intermittently; twinkle.

winkle /ˈwɪŋk(ə)l/ *verb*[2]. Chiefly *colloq.* (orig. *Military slang*). M20.
[from WINKLE *noun.*]
1 *verb trans.* Foll. by *out*: extract, eject; find out, elicit. Also (*slang*), evict (a tenant) from rented property by underhand or dubious means to enable the property to be sold (chiefly as ***winkling*** *verbal noun*). M20.
2 *verb trans. & intrans.* Make (one's way) by picking one's steps cautiously; insinuate (oneself). L20.

📖 **1** D. ATHILL Never used the common rooms except . . when I was winkled out of my own. P. BARKER I swore I wasn't gunna tell her . . but she winkled it . . out of me.

■ **winkler** *noun* (*a*) *rare* a person who gathers winkles; a boat used for this; (*b*) *slang* a person who assists in the eviction of tenants: L19.

winky /ˈwɪŋki/ *noun. colloq.* (now *rare*). M19.
[from WINK *verb*[1] + -Y[6].]
like winky, like winking, very rapidly or vigorously.

winless /ˈwɪnlɪs/ *adjective. N. Amer.* M20.
[from WIN *noun*[1] + -LESS.]
Characterized by an absence of victories in a series of sporting contests.

winnable /ˈwɪnəb(ə)l/ *adjective.* M16.
[from WIN *verb*[1] + -ABLE.]
Able to be won.

📖 *Daily Telegraph* Party managers believe there are at least 50 winnable seats at a General Election.

■ **winnaˈbility** *noun* the quality of being winnable; *colloq.* capacity for winning: L20.

Winnebago /wɪnəˈbeɪgəʊ/ *noun & adjective.* M18.
[Algonquian *wi:nepye:ko:ha* lit. 'person of dirty water', with allus. to the muddy Fox River.]
▶**A** *noun.* Pl. same, (in sense 3 always) **-os**.
1 A member of a Siouan people originating in eastern Wisconsin and now living mainly in southern Wisconsin and Nebraska. M18.
2 The language of this people. M19.
3 In full ***Winnebago camper***. (US proprietary name for) a motor vehicle with insulated panels used as living accommodation by campers. M20.
▶**B** *attrib.* or as *adjective.* Of or pertaining to the Winnebago or their language. M18.

winner /ˈwɪnə/ *noun.* LME.
[from WIN *verb*[1] + -ER[1].]
1 A person who gains something, esp. by effort or merit; *spec.* a person who gets (a living) by labour, an earner (*obsolete* or *dial.* exc. in ***breadwinner***). LME.
2 A person who is victorious in a contest; a person, horse, etc., who wins a game, race, competition, etc.; in games of skill, a winning shot, piece, card, move, etc.;

colloq. a person who or thing which scores or is likely to score a success; a potentially successful person, project, etc. LME.

> 1 G. A. BIRMINGHAM A woman, a careless winner of the hearts of men. 2 *Grimsby Evening Telegraph* The winner of the game . . will represent Humberside. *New Yorker* I always knew she was a winner, and that she'd be a success. *Sports Illustrated* Sabatini jabbed volleys, slugged winners from the baseline.

Comb.: **winner-take-all**, **winner-takes-all** *adjectives* designating a contest or conflict in which victory is outright or the successful competitor alone is rewarded.

winning /ˈwɪnɪŋ/ *noun.* ME.
[from WIN *verb*[1] + -ING[1].]
1 Conquest, capture (of a place). Formerly also, conquered territory. Long *arch.* ME.
2 The action or an act of gaining, getting, or obtaining; acquisition; *esp.* victory in a game or contest. Formerly, gain (in general, as opp. to *loss*). ME. ▸†**b** *spec.* Getting of money or wealth; financial gain, profit; moneymaking. ME–M18. ▸†**c** Profit (in general), advantage. LME–L16. ▸**d** The action of getting, gathering, or taking (produce, fish, coal, stone, etc.); MINING the process of excavation and other preparation for working a bed of coal or other mineral. L15.
3 That which is won; a thing or amount obtained or gained; gain, profit. Now *rare* or *obsolete* exc. as in sense 4 below. ME.
4 In *pl.* Things or sums gained, profits; (now only *dial.*) earnings; now usu. *spec.*, money won by gaming or betting. LME.
5 Gaining of a person's affection or allegiance; gaining of an adherent or convert. Freq. foll. by *over*. LME.
6 The action of making one's way or getting somewhere. Chiefly *Scot.* & *dial.* M17.
7 MINING. A shaft or pit together with the associated apparatus for extracting the coal etc.; a portion of a coal field or mine laid out for working. Cf. sense 2d above. E18.

> 2a *a winning streak*: see STREAK *noun.* **d** *New Scientist* The mining of coal . . and the winning of oil from the ocean are not risk-free. 4 D. R. KOONTZ He always took his winnings in cash to avoid the taxman.

Comb.: **winning-chair** an umpire's seat set at the end of a racecourse; **winning-gallery** REAL TENNIS the last gallery on the hazard side of the court; **winning opening** REAL TENNIS each of the three openings around the court into which the ball may be struck from the far side of the net to gain a point (the dedans, grille, and winning-gallery); **winning-post** a post set up at the end of a racecourse, the racer who first passes it being the winner.

winning /ˈwɪnɪŋ/ *ppl adjective.* LME.
[from WIN *verb*[1] + -ING[2].]
†**1** Gaining or producing money or wealth; profitable, lucrative. LME–M16.
2 Gaining or resulting in victory or superiority in a contest or competition; victorious. (In *US colloq.* use also in superl.) L16.
3 Persuasive; alluring, endearing, attractive. L16.

> 2 *Sports Illustrated* Prost is the winningest driver ever, with 44 victories. ***winning hazard***: see HAZARD *noun.* **winning stroke**: that gains a point in a game, or by which a game is won. 3 J. WAINWRIGHT A touch of sweet-talk and a winning smile.

■ **winningly** *adverb* M17. **winningness** *noun* E18.

Winnipeg couch /ˈwɪnɪpɛɡ ˌkaʊtʃ/ *noun phr.* *N. Amer.* M20.
[formed as next.]
A couch convertible into a double bed.

Winnipegger /ˈwɪnɪpɛɡə/ *noun.* L19.
[from *Winnipeg* (see below) + -ER[1].]
A native or inhabitant of Winnipeg, the capital of Manitoba, Canada.

winnock /ˈwɪnək/ *noun.* *Scot.* L15.
[Alt. of WINDOW *noun*: see -OCK.]
A window.

winnow /ˈwɪnəʊ/ *noun.* L16.
[from the verb.]
1 A winnowing-fan or other device for winnowing grain etc. L16.
2 An act of winnowing; a motion resembling this, as the swing of a hanging object, the sweep of wings. Chiefly *poet.* E19.

winnow /ˈwɪnəʊ/ *verb.*
[Old English *windwian*, from *wind* WIND *noun*[1].]
1 *verb trans.* & *intrans.* Expose (grain etc.) to the wind or to a current of air so that unwanted lighter particles of chaff etc. are separated or blown away; clear of waste material in this way. OE. ▸**b** *fig.* Subject to a process which separates the various parts or components, esp. the good from the bad; clear of worthless or inferior elements. LME.
2 *verb trans.* **a** Separate or drive off (lighter or unwanted particles) by exposing to the wind or a current of air; *fig.* separate (the worthless part *from* the valuable); get rid of, clear away, eliminate (something undesirable). OE. ▸**b** Separate (the valuable part *from* the worthless); extract, select, or obtain (something desirable) by such separation (now usu. foll. by *out*). E17.
3 *verb trans.* & *intrans.* Move (something) as if in the process of winnowing; beat, fan, (the air), flap (the wings), wave (the fins). L16.
4 *poet.* **a** *verb trans.* Waft, diffuse; fan with a breeze. M18. ▸**b** *verb intrans.* Of the air etc.: blow fitfully or in gusts. L18.

> 1 E. FORBES The tea is . . winnowed and sifted, so as to free it from impurities. **b** G. MACDONALD Sorrow is not a part of life . . but a wind blowing throughout it, to winnow and cleanse it. **2b** SIR W. SCOTT Winnowing out the few grains of truth . . contained in this mass of empty fiction. 3 R. BURNS Winnowing blythe her dewy wings In morning's rosy eye.

Comb.: **winnow-cloth**, **winnow-sheet** (long *obsolete* exc. *dial.*) a large sheet of cloth used in winnowing grain.
■ **winnower** *noun* LME.

winny /ˈwɪni/ *noun.* *US colloq.* M19.
[from WIENER + -Y[6].]
A Vienna sausage.

wino /ˈwʌɪnəʊ/ *noun*[1]. *slang* (orig. *US*). Pl. **-os**. E20.
[from WINE *noun* + -O.]
A habitual drinker of cheap wine; an alcoholic, a drunkard, esp. one who is destitute.

wino /ˈwiːnəʊ/ *noun*[2]. Pl. **-os**. L20.
[from *W* (see below) + -INO.]
PARTICLE PHYSICS. Either of two hypothetical subatomic particles that are supersymmetric counterparts of W particles, with spin ½ instead of 1.

winrow *noun* & *verb* var. of WINDROW.

winsey *noun* & *adjective* var. of WINCEY.

winsome /ˈwɪns(ə)m/ *adjective.*
[Old English, from WIN *noun*[2] + -SOME[1].]
†**1** Pleasant, delightful, agreeable. OE–ME.
†**2** Kindly, gracious; merciful. *rare.* OE–ME.
3 Pleasing or attractive in appearance; winning or innocently appealing in appearance, character, or manners; charming, engaging. L17.
4 Cheerful, joyous. *dial.* L18.
¶ Not recorded between 14th and 17th cents., though prob. in Scot. and dial. use.
■ **winsomely** *adverb* L18. **winsomeness** *noun* M19.

Winstonian /wɪnˈstəʊnɪən/ *adjective.* E20.
[from *Winston* (see below) + -IAN.]
Of, pertaining to, or characteristic of the British statesman Sir Winston Spencer Churchill (1874–1965). Cf. CHURCHILLIAN *adjective.*

winter /ˈwɪntə/ *noun.*
[Old English *winter* = Old Frisian *winter*, Old Saxon, Old High German *wintar* (Dutch, German *winter*), Old Norse *vetr*, earlier *vettr*, *vittr*, Gothic *wintrus*, from Germanic, prob. from nasalized var. of Indo-European base also of WATER *noun*, WET *adjective*.]
1 The fourth and coldest season of the year, between autumn and spring: in the northern hemisphere freq. regarded as comprising December, January, and February, or (ASTRONOMY) reckoned from the winter solstice to the vernal equinox; in the southern hemisphere corresponding to the northern summer (June to August). OE. ▸**b** *transf.* Winter weather; a season resembling winter; wintry or cold weather. OE.
2 In *pl.* A specified number of years, esp. of a person's age. Now chiefly *poet.* & *rhet.* OE.
3 *fig.* A time or state of old age, decay, affliction, hostility, emotional coldness, etc. L16.

> 1 DAY LEWIS It smelt now of the apples which had been stored there through the winter. ***OLD-FASHIONED winter***. ***summer and winter***, ***winter and summer***: see SUMMER *noun*[1]. **b** ***BLACKTHORN winter***. ***NUCLEAR winter***. 2 R. S. THOMAS Davies, eighty-five Winters old, and still alive. 3 M. L. KING Men whose hearts had been hardened by the long winter of traditionalism. J. BARTH Intellectual discussion . . is the real joy of the winter of life.

Attrib. & *comb.*: In the senses 'characteristic of, suitable for, or used or occurring in winter', (of plants and animals) 'active or flourishing in winter', (of fruits) 'ripening in winter', (of crops) 'sown in autumn for an early harvest', as ***winter barley***, ***winter clothes***, ***winter-fly***, ***winter gull***, ***winter months***, ***winter plumage***, ***winter resort***, ***winter salad***, ***winter snow***, ***winter wheat***, ***winter wind***, etc. Special combs., as ***winter aconite***: see ACONITE 1b; **winter annual** a plant which germinates in the autumn, bears fruit, and (usu.) dies in late winter or spring; **winterberry** any of several deciduous N. American hollies with toothed, non-prickly leaves and with berries which persist through the winter; esp. *Ilex verticillata* (also called ***black alder***) and *I. laevigata* (smooth winterberry); also, the fruit of any of these shrubs; **winterbourne** an intermittent stream, as in chalk and limestone districts, which flows only in winter or at long intervals; **winter bud** ZOOLOGY a statoblast (formed at the approach of, or quiescent during, winter); **winter bunting** = ***snow bunting*** s.v. SNOW *noun*[1]; **winter cherry** any of several plants of the nightshade family with cherry-like fruit ripe in winter; esp. (*a*) the alkekengi, *Physalis alkekengi*, (*b*) a S. American nightshade, *Solanum capsicastrum*, grown as a pot plant for its orange berries; **winter coat** (*a*) the coat of an animal in winter, where this differs from that in summer; (*b*) a (woman's) coat suitable for winter weather; **winter count** a pictorial record or chronicle of the events of each year, kept by various N. American Indian peoples; **winter country** *NZ* land where livestock can be wintered; **winter-crack** *dial.* a yellowish plum which ripens in November (and cracks in frosty weather); **winter cress** any of several yellow-flowered cruciferous plants constituting the genus *Barbarea*, the leaves of which are, or were formerly, used as a winter salad; esp. *B. vulgaris*, a plant of streamsides etc.; **winter daffodil** an ornamental autumn-flowering Mediterranean amaryllid, *Sternbergia lutea*, resembling a yellow crocus; **winter day** = ***winter's day*** below; **winter duck** the pintail duck; also (*US*), the long-tailed duck; **winter egg** = ***winter ovum*** below; **winter-fallow** *verb* & *noun* (*a*) *verb trans.* lay (land) fallow during the winter; (*b*) *noun* a lying or laying fallow during the winter; land that lies fallow in winter; **winter-feed** *verb* & *noun* (*a*) *verb trans.* feed or maintain (animals etc.) during winter; (*b*) *noun* food supplied to animals during winter; **winter flounder** a cryptically coloured edible flatfish, *Pseudopleuronectes americanus*, of the Atlantic coast of N. America; also called ***mud dab***; **winter-flying** *adjective* (of an insect) active in winter; **winter garden** (*a*) a garden of plants that flourish in winter, as evergreens; (*b*) a greenhouse or conservatory in which plants are kept flourishing in winter; (*c*) a building used for concerts, plays, dances, etc., at a seaside resort; **winter gnat** any of various gnats of the family Trichoceridae, common in dancing swarms esp. in winter; **winter grape** a N. American vine, *Vitis vulpina*, with acid fruit which becomes sweet after frost; **winter heliotrope** a winter-flowering plant of the composite family (related to butterbur), *Petasites fragrans*, grown for its fragrant lilac flowers; **winter-house** a house for winter occupation (now esp. by a migratory people); ***winter jasmine***: see JASMINE 1; **winter kill** loss of crops etc. during winter; **winter-kill** *verb trans.* (chiefly in *pass.*) & *intrans.* become killed or blasted by the cold of winter; **winter-long** *adjective* & *adverb* (*a*) *adjective* as (tediously) long as winter; (*b*) *adverb* through a whole winter; **winter midge** = ***winter gnat*** above; **winter-moth** any of various geometrid moths which emerge in winter, esp. *Operophtera brumata* and (more fully ***northern winter-moth***) *O. fagata*, the females of which have vestigial or much reduced wings; **Winter Olympic Games**, **Winter Olympics** international competitive winter sports held under the auspices of the International Olympic Committee, usu. every four years; **winter ovum** ZOOLOGY a dormant, resistant resting egg produced by various invertebrates at the approach of winter (usu. in *pl.*); **winter packet** CANAD. HISTORY a boat or land party carrying mail in winter-time between trading posts; the mail itself; **winterpick** *dial.* a sloe, esp. one picked when mellowed by frost; **winter-proof** *adjective* resistant to the effects of winter weather; **winter-proud** *adjective* (of wheat or other crops) too luxuriant in winter; **winter quarters** accommodation for the winter, esp. for soldiers, or during an expedition etc.; (now *arch.* or *joc.*) a place in which an animal hibernates; **winter road** *Canad.* a road or route used in winter when the ground is frozen or there is snow; **winter rose** (*a*) a rose blooming in winter; (*b*) the Christmas rose, *Helleborus niger*; ***winter savory***: see SAVORY *noun*[1]; **winter's day** a day in winter; **winter sleep** hibernation; **winter sleeper** an animal that hibernates; **winter snipe** the purple sandpiper, *Calidris maritima*; **winter solstice** the occasion of the shortest day in the year, when the sun is at its lowest altitude north of the equator, on approx. 21 December (or in the southern hemisphere, south of the equator, on approx. 21 June); **winter-sport** *verb intrans.* engage in winter sports; **winter sports**: performed on snow or ice esp. in winter (e.g. skiing, ice-skating); ***winter squash***: see SQUASH *noun*[2]; †**winter's tale** an idle tale; **wintersweet** a Chinese shrub, *Chimonanthus praecox*, (family Calycanthaceae), grown for its pale yellow fragrant flowers which appear in winter before the leaves; **winter teal** the green-winged teal, *Anas crecca*; **Winter War** *the* war between the USSR and Finland in 1939–40; **winter-weed** any one of various small weeds, esp. speedwells, which survive and flourish in winter; **winter-weight** *adjective* (of clothes) warm and thick, suitable for wear in winter; ***winter woollies***: see WOOLLY *noun* 1; ***winter wren***: see WREN *noun*[1] 1.
■ **winterish** *adjective* of winter; somewhat wintry: M16. **winterless** *adjective* having no winter, free from or not experiencing winter M19. **winters** *adverb* (*N. Amer.*) during the winter; each winter: E20. **winterward(s)** *adverb* towards winter L19.

winter /ˈwɪntə/ *verb.* LME.
[from the noun, orig. translating Latin *hiemare*, *hibernare*.]
1 *verb intrans.* Spend the winter; stay or reside (at a specified place) during the winter; (of animals) find or be provided with food and shelter in the winter. Also foll. by *over*, (*Canad.*) *out*. LME.
2 *verb trans.* **a** Keep or maintain during the winter; *esp.* provide (animals) with food and shelter in the winter. Also foll. by *over*. LME. ▸†**b** *fig.* Maintain (an opinion) through a period of trial. *rare.* Only in E17.
3 *verb trans.* Affect like winter, subject to wintry conditions; make wintry; chill, freeze. Chiefly *fig.* E17.

> 1 J. J. AUDUBON Enormous numbers of waterfowl wintered in its vast marshes. **2a** *Yachting World* Yachts can be taken out of the water . . and wintered . . in the shed.

winterage /ˈwɪnt(ə)rɪdʒ/ *noun.* Chiefly *dial.* E19.
[from WINTER *noun*, *verb* + -AGE.]
Food or pasture for livestock in winter.

winterer /ˈwɪnt(ə)rə/ *noun.* L18.
[from WINTER *verb* + -ER[1].]
1 An animal kept over the winter, esp. for fattening. Chiefly *Scot.* L18.
2 A person, migratory bird, etc., that spends the winter in a specified place; a winter visitor or resident; *spec.* (*Hist.*) an employee of the Hudson's Bay Company in the far interior of N. America. E19.

3 A person who tends animals during winter. *rare.* M19.

wintergreen /ˈwɪntəgriːn/ *noun.* In sense 2 usu. **winter green**. M16.
[from WINTER *noun* + GREEN *noun*, after Dutch *wintergroen*, German *Wintergrün*.]
1 Any of certain plants whose leaves remain green in winter; *esp.* (*a*) any of various low-growing woodland plants of the genus *Pyrola* (family Pyrolaceae), typically with drooping racemes of bell-shaped white flowers (cf. PYROLA); also, any of several plants of related genera; (*b*) *N. Amer.* the checkerberry, *Gaultheria procumbens.* M16. ▸**b** In full ***oil of wintergreen***. An oil containing methyl salicylate, orig. distilled from the leaves of *Gaultheria procumbens* but now usu. made synthetically, which is used medicinally in liniments etc., and as a flavouring. M19.
2 Any evergreen plant. Usu. in *pl.* L17.
1 CHICKWEED *wintergreen*. **one-flowered wintergreen** a wintergreen, *Moneses uniflora*, with a single drooping flower. **spotted wintergreen** a wintergreen of the US, *Chimaphila maculata*, resembling the pyrolas but with leaves in whorls on the stem.

Winterhalter /ˈvɪntəhaltə/ *noun.* E20.
[F. X. *Winterhalter* (1806–73), German painter, esp. of royal portraits.]
Used **attrib.** to designate things characteristic of Winterhalter's pictures, esp. a style of women's formal dress with low necklines and crinolines.

winterim /ˈwɪntərɪm/ *adjective & noun.* *US.* L20.
[Blend of WINTER *noun* and INTERIM.]
(Of or pertaining to) a short winter term in some private schools in the US, part of which is spent by some pupils on projects away from the school.

wintering /ˈwɪnt(ə)rɪŋ/ *verbal noun.* L15.
[from WINTER *verb* + -ING[1].]
▸ **I** The action of WINTER *verb*.
1 The keeping or tending of animals during the winter. L15.
2 The action of passing the winter in a particular place; a stay or residence during the winter. L16.
▸ **II 3** Chiefly *Scot. & north.* ▸**a** A yearling. E18. ▸**b** = WINTERER 1. M18. ▸**c** = WINTERAGE. L18.

winterize /ˈwɪntərʌɪz/ *verb trans.* Orig. & chiefly *N. Amer.* Also **-ise**. M20.
[from WINTER *noun* + -IZE.]
Adapt or prepare (something) for operation or use in cold weather.
■ **winteri'zation** *noun* M20.

winterly /ˈwɪntəli/ *adjective.* LOE.
[from WINTER *noun* + -LY[1].]
1 Of, pertaining to, or occurring in winter. Now *rare* exc. as passing into sense 2. LOE.
2 Having the character of, or characteristic of, winter; resembling winter or that of winter; wintry; cold (*lit. & fig.*). M17.
¶ Not recorded between OE and M16.
■ **winterliness** *noun* L19.

Winter's bark /ˈwɪntəz bɑːk/ *noun phr.* E17.
[= mod. Latin *cortex Winteranus*, named after its discoverer, William *Winter* (or *Wynter*), English naval officer (d. 1589), who accompanied Francis Drake to the Straits of Magellan.]
The pungent bark of a S. American tree, *Drimys winteri*, (family Winteraceae), formerly valued as an antiscorbutic and stimulant; the tree yielding this bark, which has aromatic leaves and jasmine-scented white flowers.

wintertide /ˈwɪntətʌɪd/ *noun. arch.* OE.
[from WINTER *noun* + TIDE *noun*.]
= next.
¶ Not recorded E17–E19 (when re-formed).

wintertime /ˈwɪntətʌɪm/ *noun.* Also **winter time**. LME.
[from WINTER *noun* + TIME *noun*.]
The season or period of winter.

wintery *adjective* var. of WINTRY.

wintle /ˈwɪnt(ə)l/ *verb & noun. Scot.* L18.
[Early Flemish *windtelen*, *wend(t)elen*, from *winden* WIND *verb*[1].]
▸ **A** *verb intrans.* **1** Roll or swing from side to side. L18.
2 Tumble, capsize, be upset. M19.
▸ **B** *noun.* A rolling or staggering movement. L18.

wintry /ˈwɪntri/ *adjective.* Also **wintery** /ˈwɪnt(ə)ri/.
[Old English *wintriġ*, from WINTER *noun* + -Y[1].]
1 Of or pertaining to winter; occurring, existing, or found in winter; adapted or suitable for winter. Now *rare* exc. as passing into sense 2. OE.
2 Having the quality of winter; characteristic of winter. L16. ▸**b** *fig.* Aged, infirm or withered from age; (of hair) white with age. Also, devoid of fervour or affection; dismal, dreary, cheerless. M17.
3 Exposed to the effect of winter; chilled by winter. L17.
¶ Not recorded between OE and L16 (when re-formed).
■ **wintrify** *verb trans.* (*rare*) make wintry M19. **wintrily** *adverb* E19. **wintriness** *noun* E19.

Wintun /ˈwɪntuːn, wɪnˈtuːn/ *noun & adjective.* Also **Wintu**. Pl. of noun same, **-s**. L19.
[Wintun, lit. 'people'.]
A member of, of or pertaining to, a N. American Indian people inhabiting western areas of Sacramento Valley, California; (of) the Penutian language of this people.

winy /ˈwʌɪni/ *adjective.* Also **winey**. LME.
[from WINE *noun* + -Y[1].]
1 Of, pertaining to, or characteristic of wine; of the nature of wine; resembling wine in taste, appearance, etc.; containing wine. LME.
2 Affected by or due to (excessive) consumption of wine. L16.

winze /wɪnz/ *noun*[1]. M18.
[Perh. from WIND *noun*[2].]
MINING. A shaft or an inclined passage leading from one level to another, but not rising to the surface.

†**winze** *noun*[2]. *Scot.* L18–E19.
[Early Flemish *wensch* rel. to base of WISH *verb*.]
An imprecation, a curse.

WIP *abbreviation.*
Work in progress (chiefly in business and financial contexts).

wipe /wʌɪp/ *noun.* M16.
[from the verb.]
1 A slashing blow, a sweeping cut, a swipe; *fig.* a stroke of misfortune. Also (*rare*, Shakes.), a mark as of a blow or lash; a scar, a brand. M16.
2 *fig.* A cutting remark; a sarcastic reproof or rebuff; a gibe, a jeer. L16.
3 An act of wiping. M17. ▸**b** *CINEMATOGRAPHY & TELEVISION.* An effect in which an existing picture seems to be wiped out by a new one as the boundary between them moves across the screen (the pictures themselves remaining stationary). Orig. more fully ***wipe-dissolve***. M20.
4 a A handkerchief. *slang.* E18. ▸**b** A disposable piece of soft absorbent cloth or tissue, sometimes impregnated with a cleansing agent, for wiping clean one's hands or anything small. L20.
5 *MECHANICS.* = WIPER 3a. L19.

📖 **1** G. B. SHAW Take the poker, and fetch it a wipe across the nose. **3** S. MIDDLETON Give your feet a good wipe . . On that doormat. **4b** *Mother & Baby* Wrestling with a wet baby in one hand and a wipe in the other.

Phrases: **a wipe in the eye** = ***a smack in the eye*** s.v. SMACK *noun*[2]. ***nose-wipe***: see NOSE *noun*. SIDE-WIPE. ***sky the wipe***: see SKY *verb* 1.

wipe /wʌɪp/ *verb.*
[Old English *wīpian*, corresp. formally to Old High German *wīfan* wind round, Gothic *weipan* crown (cf. *waips* wreath), rel. to base of WHIP *verb*.]
1 *verb trans.* Rub (something) gently with a soft cloth, a hand, etc., or *on* something else, so as to clear the surface of dust, dirt, moisture, etc.; clean or dry in this way. OE.
2 *verb trans.* Remove or clear away (moisture, dirt, dust, etc.) from something by gentle rubbing. Freq. foll. by *away, off, up.* OE.
3 *verb intrans.* Be removed by wiping. Foll. by *off, away.* ME.
†**4** *verb trans.* Take *away* completely, as by theft or fraud; make off with. ME–M17.
5 *verb trans.* †**a** Remove or clear *away* or *off* (something deleterious, unwanted, or offensive). LME–M17. ▸**b** Take or put away (a stain, a defilement); remove the guilt, blame, or dishonour of; clear a person, or oneself, of (a charge or imputation). Usu. foll. by *away, off, out.* LME. ▸**c** Foll. by *away, out*: efface, erase (something written or painted). Now *rare* or *obsolete.* M16. ▸**d** Foll. by *off*: cancel (an account or score); discharge, pay off (a debt). Also, subtract (a certain portion) from a value, debt, etc. M17.
6 *verb trans.* Clear or cleanse *from* or *of* something. Chiefly *fig.* LME.
7 *verb trans.* Strike, beat, or attack (with a blow, or verbally). Long *dial. & slang.* E16.
†**8** *verb trans.* Deprive, rob, cheat of some possession or advantage. Foll. by *of, from.* M16–M18.
9 *verb trans.* Usu. foll. by *out*, occas. *away, off,* etc. ▸**a** Obliterate, efface; destroy or greatly reduce the effect or value of, eliminate; (foll. by *out*) do away with, put an end to, abolish, annihilate. M16. ▸**b** *spec.* Destroy completely, exterminate (a body of people). Also *slang*, kill (a person). Foll. by *out.* L16.
10 *verb trans.* Apply or spread (a soft or liquid substance) over a surface by rubbing with a cloth, pad, etc.; apply a substance to (an object) in this way; *spec.* in *PLUMBING*, apply solder by this method to finish off a joint (cf. WIPED *ppl adjective* 1). L18.
11 *verb trans.* **a** Erase (a magnetic recording, data stored on a magnetic medium). Freq. foll. by *off, out.* E20. ▸**b** Remove a recording or stored data from (a magnetic tape, memory, etc.). M20.
12 *verb trans.* Demagnetize (a ship) by passing a horizontal current-carrying cable up and down the hull; degauss. *colloq.* M20.
13 *verb intrans.* = DRY *verb* 5. Also foll. by *up.* M20.
14 *verb trans.* Dismiss, reject, repudiate (esp. a person). *Austral. & NZ slang.* M20.
15 *verb intrans.* *CINEMATOGRAPHY & TELEVISION.* Pass from or *from* one scene to another by means of a wipe. M20.
16 *verb intrans. & trans.* (in *pass.*). Foll. by *out*: orig. *spec.* in *SURFING*, fall or be knocked from one's surfboard, or from a wave; now also more widely, fall or crash while manoeuvring a skateboard, bicycle, skis, etc. Cf. WIPE-OUT 2. *slang.* M20.
17 *verb trans.* Foll. by *out*: overwhelm, overcome; *spec.* (of drink etc.) render intoxicated or senseless. *slang* (orig. *US*). L20.
18 *verb trans.* Pass (a plastic card) by hand through a device that reads data encoded on it; pass (a light-pen) over a bar code for the same purpose. L20.

📖 **1** P. FITZGERALD Daisy . . wiped her face with the back of her hand. A. HUTH Rosie looked down at her earth-stained fingers . . . She wiped them on . . her dress. N. WILLIAMS It was Henry who . . scrubbed the kitchen floor, wiped down the surfaces. **2** M. WARNER He . . stopped to wipe the chalky dust from his shined shoes. *Which?* Wipe up spills to stop children . . slipping. J. C. OATES Her eyes began to sting with tears she wiped impatiently away. **3** OED The spots will easily wipe off. **5b** DEFOE By his fidelity to wipe out all that was past. **d** *Guardian* Share dealers reacted by wiping 12 per cent off the company's stock market value. **6** *Independent* Amendments which could wipe the US cupboard bare of foreign investment capital. **9a** P. CARTER I just wanted to forget, to wipe out the past. *Independent* A counter-offensive . . could wipe away all the gains the resistance has made. *Nature* Drift nets could wipe out the South Pacific's albacore tuna fishery. **b** *Century Magazine* A tragedy which wiped out an entire crew. **11a** *Independent* Several viruses . . which can wipe information from computer hard discs. **b** E. SALTER The tape was sometimes wiped so's it could be used again. **13** R. V. BESTE He wiped while Huskion . . scrubbed away in the sink. **18** *Which?* When you hand over your card to pay, the shop assistant wipes it through the terminal.

Phrases & comb.: **wipe-clean** *adjective* designating fabrics or furnishings that may be cleaned simply by wiping. **wipe one's eye**, **wipe a person's eye** *slang* (*a*) orig., shoot a game-bird missed by a companion; now *gen.*, get the better of, score off; (*b*) punch in the eye. **wipe the — off a person's face**, **wipe the — off one's face**, etc., *colloq.* (cause a person to) cease showing the facial expression indicated by the noun (smile etc.). ***wipe the floor with***: see FLOOR *noun*. ***wipe the slate clean***: see SLATE *noun*. **wiping head** a head for removing a recording from magnetic tape or wire; an erase head.
■ **wipeable** *adjective* able to be wiped; esp. easily wiped clean: E20.

wiped /wʌɪpt/ *ppl adjective.* L19.
[from WIPE *verb* + -ED[1].]
1 That has been wiped; *spec.* in *PLUMBING*, (of a joint) finished with solder applied with a cloth or pad (cf. WIPE *verb* 10). L19.
2 *slang* (orig. *US*), usu. with *out*. ▸**a** Reduced to physical incapacity, tired out, exhausted. M20. ▸**b** Intoxicated or incapacitated by drugs or alcohol. M20. ▸**c** Financially ruined, penniless. L20.

wipe-out /ˈwʌɪpaʊt/ *noun.* E20.
[from *wipe out*: see WIPE *verb*.]
1 *RADIO.* The condition in which a strong received signal renders impossible the reception of other signals (either wanted ones or interference). E20.
2 Orig. *spec.* in *SURFING*, a fall from one's surfboard, or from a wave. Now also more widely, a fall from a skateboard, bicycle, etc., esp. while manoeuvring at speed. Cf. WIPE *verb* 16. *slang.* M20.
3 Destruction, annihilation; a crushing defeat. Also, an overwhelming experience. *slang* (orig. *US*). M20.

wiper /ˈwʌɪpə/ *noun.* M16.
[from WIPE *verb* + -ER[1].]
1 A person who wipes something; *spec.* a worker, sailor, etc., employed chiefly in wiping something clean or dry. Also with adverb, *away, out,* etc. M16. ▸**b** A weapon. Also, a gunman. *slang.* E17.
2 A cloth, pad, appliance, etc., used for wiping; *slang* (now *rare*) a handkerchief. L16. ▸**b** *spec.* A windscreen wiper. Freq. in *pl.* (exc. when **attrib.**). E20.
3 a *MECHANICS.* A cam, a tappet. L18. ▸**b** *ELECTRICITY.* A moving component that rotates or slides to make electrical contact with one or more terminals; a moving contact. Also ***wiper arm***. E20.
2 ***penwiper***: see PEN *noun*[2]. **b** attrib.: ***wiper blade***, ***wiper motor***, ***wiper switch***, etc.

WIPO *abbreviation.*
World Intellectual Property Organization.

Wiradjuri /wəˈradʒəri/ *noun & adjective.* Also **-djeri** & other vars. L19.
[Aboriginal, app. from Wiradjuri word for 'no', *wirai* (contrasted with related languages).]
▸ **A** *noun.* Pl. same.

1 A member of an Australian Aboriginal people of western and central New South Wales, Australia. L19.

2 The language of this people; (any of) a group of related languages spoken in parts of New South Wales, Australia and southern Queensland. L19.

▶ **B** *attrib.* or as *adjective*. Of or pertaining to this people or their language. L19.

wirble /ˈwəːb(ə)l/ *verb & noun. rare.* M19.
[German *wirbeln* verb, *Wirbel* noun.]
▶ **A** *verb intrans.* Turn round and round; whirl; eddy. M19.
▶ **B** *noun.* A whirl, a vortex. M19.

wire /wʌɪə/ *noun.*
[Old English *wīr*, corresp. to Middle Low German *wīre* (Low German *wīr*), rel. to Old Norse *víra virki* filigree work, Old High German *wiara* (ornament of) finest gold, prob. from base of Latin *viere* plait, weave.]

1 Metal wrought into the form of a slender rod or thread, formerly by hammering, now by rolling or usu. by the operation of wire-drawing, and used in fastenings, ornamentation, electric circuitry, delicate mechanisms, etc. Freq. with specifying word. OE. ▸**b** *spec.* = ***barbed wire*** s.v. BARBED *adjective*[1]. Also, a barricade made of this; *the* wire fencing of a prison or frontier (chiefly in phrs.). E20.

2 A piece or length of wire used for some purpose. (See also sense 7.) OE. ▸**b** A snare for hares or rabbits. M18. ▸**c** A wire stretched across and above the track at the start and finish of a racecourse. Chiefly in phrs. below. *N. Amer.* L19.

3 Usu. in *pl.* or *collect. sing.* ▸**a** Metallic strings (of a musical instrument). LME. ▸**b** The metallic lines or rods by which puppets are worked. Chiefly *fig.* in ***pull wire(s)***, ***pull the wires*** below. E17. ▸**c** Metallic bars (of a cage). M17. ▸**d** Knitting needles. *Scot.* L18. ▸**e** CROQUET. (The sides of) the metal hoops or arches through which the balls are driven. *rare.* M19.

4 A network or framework of wire; wirework. Now usu., wire netting. M16.

5 In *pl.* Things resembling shining wires, as hairs, rays, etc. *poet. & rhet.* (now *rare*). L16.

6 A thing resembling wire or a wire, as a long thin plant stem, a strawberry runner, a cylindrical piece of native silver. E17.

7 A line of wire used as a conductor of electric current. M18. ▸**b** *spec.* A line of wire connecting the transmitting and receiving instruments of a telegraph or telephone system. M19. ▸**c** The telegraphic system; a telegraphic message, a telegram. M19. ▸**d** A private warning or message. Chiefly in ***give the wire***. *slang.* L19. ▸**e** The telephone system; an individual telephone connection. Now chiefly *arch.* E20. ▸**f** [perh. abbreviation of WIRE-TAP *noun.*] An electronic listening device, a bug; *esp.* one which can be concealed on the person. Freq. in ***wear a wire***. L20.

8 A pickpocket (orig. so called from the practice of extracting handkerchiefs from pockets with a piece of wire). *slang.* M19.

9 In full ***wire rope***, ***wire cable***. Rope or cable made from wires twisted together as strands. L19.

10 A wire-haired dog, esp. a fox terrier or a dachshund. L19.

> 🕮 **1** A. KOESTLER Opens a complicated lock with a crude piece of bent wire. ***copper wire***, ***piano wire***, ***picture-wire***, ***plated wire***, ***steel wire***, etc. **b** S. HOOD A German machine gun opened up enfilading the wire. **2** *Garden Answers* Espalier . . trees need a system of horizontal training wires. ***bell-wire***, ***cross-wire***, ***fuse-wire***, ***saddle wire***, ***stub wire***, etc. **3a** MILTON Apollo sings To th' touch of golden wires. **4** ***chicken-wire***: see CHICKEN *noun*[1]. ***fly-wire***: see FLY *noun*[1]. **7** *Which?* Any strain on the mains flex could pull the wires out of the plug. **c** I. SHAW I'd send him a wire telling him where he could call me in Paris. **e** L. GRANT-ADAMSON A voice said down the wire: 'Good morning'.

Phrases etc.: **behind the wire** in prison. **by wire** by telegraph. ***cross wires***: see CROSS *verb*. **down to the wire** all the way (to the finishing-line). ***fly-by-wire***: see FLY *verb*. **from wire to wire** from start to finish (of a race). ***get one's wires crossed***: see CROSS *verb*. **go over the wire**, **go through the wire**, **go under the wire** defect from a former Eastern bloc country. ***high wire***: see HIGH *adjective, adverb, & noun*. ***live wire***: see LIVE *adjective*. ***mulga wire***: see MULGA 3. ***pull one's wire***: see PULL *verb*. **pull the wires** = ***pull the strings*** s.v. STRING *noun*. **pull wire(s)** = ***pull strings*** s.v. STRING *noun*. **straight wire** *Austral. slang* (now *rare*) (*the*) honest truth. **under the wire** at the finishing-line; *fig.* (falling) within the limits or scope of something.

Attrib. & comb.: In the senses 'made of wire or wirework', as ***wire basket***, ***wire cage***, ***wire cloth***, ***wire clothes-hanger***, ***wire fence***, ***wire mesh***, etc.; 'pertaining to wire' as ***wire-gauge***, ***wire-manufacture***, etc. Special combs., as **wire act** an acrobatic act performed on a tightrope; **wire bar** a bar of copper cast into a suitable form for drawing or rolling into wire; **wire bed** (*a*) a bed fitted with a wire spring base or mattress; (*b*) PAPER-MAKING a moving bed of wire over which the pulp is passed at the stage of beginning to form a web; **wire birch** *Canad.* = ***grey birch*** s.v. GREY *adjective*; **wire brush** (*a*) = BRUSH *noun*[2] 8; (*b*) a brush with stiff wire bristles used in cleaning, esp. for removing rust; **wire-brush** *verb trans.* clean with a wire brush; ***wire cable***: see sense 9 above; **wire-cut** *adjective* designating or pertaining to materials, esp. machine-made bricks, cut by using wire; **wire-cutter** (*a*) (freq. in *pl.*) nippers or pliers for cutting wire; (*b*) a person employed to cut a wire or wires; (*c*) a machine for cutting bricks with wire; **wire edge** the turned-over strip of metal produced on the edge of a cutting tool by faulty grinding or honing; **wire entanglement** MILITARY a barricade of (barbed) wire stretched over the ground to impede the advance of an enemy; **wire-frame** *adjective & noun* (*a*) *adjective* wire-framed; (of a picture or computer-generated image) depicting an object by representing all its edges as lines (including those out of sight when viewing the object itself); (*b*) *noun* (COMPUTING) a skeletal three-dimensional image of an object in which only lines and vertices are represented; **wire-framed** *adjective* (esp. of spectacles) having a frame made of wire; **wire gauge** (*a*) an instrument for measuring the diameter of wire; (*b*) a standard series of sizes in which wire etc. is made (***standard wire gauge***: see STANDARD *noun & adjective*); ***wire gauze***: see GAUZE *noun* 2; **wire-glass** sheet glass in which wire netting is embedded; **wire-grass** any of various grasses or grasslike plants having tough wiry stems; *esp.* (*a*) *N. Amer.* flattened meadow-grass, *Poa compressa*, a naturalized European grass; (*b*) *Austral.* any grass of the genus *Aristida*; **wire ground** LACE-MAKING = KAT STITCH; **wire-guided** *adjective* (esp. of a missile) directed by means of electric signals transmitted along a connecting wire; **wire-hair** a wire-haired terrier; **wire-haired** *adjective* having a rough coat of a stiff and wiry texture; *esp.* designating a kind of fox-terrier; **wire house** *US* a brokerage firm having branch offices connected to its main office by private telephone and telegraph wires; **wire-mark** PAPER-MAKING (*a*) (in *pl.*) the faint lines in laid paper made by the impression of the wires of the mould; (*b*) a watermark; **wire mattress** a mattress supported by wires stretched in a frame; **wire nail** a nail made from cut and shaped wire, elliptical or (usu.) circular in section, and pointed but not tapering; **wire netting**: made of wire twisted into meshes; **wirephoto** a facsimile process for transmitting pictures over telephone lines; *colloq.* a photograph transmitted by this means; **wirepull** *verb trans.* control or influence esp. from behind the scenes; **wirepuller** a person who exerts control or influence esp. from behind the scenes, a string-puller; **wire recorder** an apparatus for recording sounds, etc., magnetically on wire and afterwards reproducing them; **wire recording** a recording made with a wire recorder; the process of making one; **wire-rim** *adjective* = ***wire-frame*** (b) above; ***wire rope***: see sense 9 above; **wirescape** [SCAPE *noun*[3]] scenery, or a scene, dominated by overhead wires and their supports; **wire service** *N. Amer.* a news agency that supplies syndicated news by wire to its subscribers; **wire-stitched** *adjective* fastened using a wire-stitcher; **wire-stitcher** an automatic stapling machine which takes continuous wire and forms the staples as an integral part of the stapling operation; **wire-stitching** the operation of using a wire-stitcher; **wire story** JOURNALISM a story distributed by a wire service; **wire-strainer** *Austral. & NZ* = ***wire-stretcher*** below; **wire-stretcher** (chiefly *N. Amer.*) a tool or device for making taut the wire of a fence etc.; **wire-walker** an acrobat who performs feats on a wire rope; **wire-walking** tightrope walking; **wireway** a channel or duct, esp. of sheet metal, for enclosing lengths of wiring; ducting of this nature; **wire wheel** a wheel on a vehicle having narrow metal spokes (used esp. on sports cars); **wire wool** matted thin wire, used esp. for scouring kitchen utensils; **wire-wound** *adjective* wound or encircled with wire; **wire-wove** *adjective* (*a*) designating a very fine kind of paper; (*b*) made of woven wire.

wire /wʌɪə/ *verb.* ME.
[from the noun.]

†**1** *verb trans.* Adorn or entwine with or as with (gold) wire. *rare.* ME–M17.

2 *verb trans.* **a** Fasten, join, or fit with wire or wires; *spec.* secure (the cork of a bottle, the bottle itself) with wire. LME. ▸**b** Fence *in* with wire; cover *over* with wire. L17. ▸**c** Provide with a wire support; stiffen with wire. M19. ▸**d** Strengthen or protect with (barbed) wire. L19. ▸**e** Provide with electric wires; make electrical connections to; connect electrically *to*; provide *with* by means of connecting wires; *spec.* fit with a concealed listening device. Also foll. by *up*. L19. ▸**f** Incorporate (a facility etc.) *into* a device by electric wiring. Also more widely (*colloq.*), provide with a permanent or built-in facility or faculty, equip *for*, *with*, or *to do* something. M20.

3 *verb trans.* Catch or trap in a (wire) snare. M18.

4 *verb trans.* CROQUET. Place one's own or an opponent's ball so that a hoop or peg intervenes between it and its object (with ball or player as obj.). Usu. in *pass.* M19.

5 *verb trans. & intrans.* Send (a message) by telegraph. Also, send a telegraph message to (a person, place, etc.). *colloq.* M19.

6 *verb intrans. & trans.* = PICKPOCKET *verb. slang.* M19.

7 *verb trans. & refl.* Cause (someone) to become tense or excited. Also, prepare psychologically, psych up. Foll. by *up*. *colloq.* L20.

> 🕮 **2c** C. SPRY A temptation to wire . . the stem of a recalcitrant tulip. **e** P. THEROUX Fisher wired his computer terminal to the video screen. **5** E. BOWEN Stuart wired his apologies to Ireland. P. MORTIMER Their ship . . wired to say that the weather had broken.

With adverbs & prepositions in specialized senses: **wire in** *colloq.* get to work with a will, apply oneself energetically to something. **wire into** *colloq.* set about with gusto.

wired /wʌɪəd/ *ppl adjective.* LME.
[from WIRE *noun* or *verb*: see -ED[1], -ED[2].]

1 Supported, strengthened, or stiffened with wire; *spec.* (of glass) containing embedded wire mesh. LME.

2 Provided with or consisting of a wire fence or netting for confinement or protection. M18.

3 Fastened or secured with wire. Also foll. by *on*, *up*. L18.

4 CROQUET. Prevented from taking a particular course by an intervening hoop or peg. M19.

5 a Employing wires or similar physical connections to convey electrical signals, *esp.* for television or radio; involving or fitted with electrical connections. Also foll. by *up*. E20. ▸**b** Fitted with or wearing a piece of electrical sound equipment, as radio headphones or *spec.* an electronic listening device. Also more fully ***wired for sound***, ***wired up***. *colloq.* M20. ▸**c** Making use of computers and information technology to transfer or receive information, esp. by means of the Internet. *colloq.* L20.

6 a Foll. by *up*: annoyed, incensed, provoked. *US slang. rare.* E20. ▸**b** In a state of nervous excitement; tense, edgy, psyched up. Also foll. by *up*. *slang* (orig. & chiefly *US*). L20. ▸**c** Under the influence of drugs or alcohol; intoxicated, high. Also foll. by *up*. *slang* (chiefly *US*). L20.

7 Furnished or equipped with a facility or faculty; *esp.* having an inbuilt ability *for* or *to do* something. L20.

Phrases & comb.: **get wired** *colloq.* get (something) finished, sorted out, under control, etc. **have got it wired**, **have it wired** *colloq.* = ***have got it made*** s.v. MAKE *verb*. **have wired** *colloq.* have (something) finished, sorted out, under control, etc. **wired-in** *adjective* (*a*) bounded by wire, in the form of netting or fencing; (*b*) incorporated in or connected to a device or system by means of (electrical) wiring.

wire-draw /ˈwʌɪədrɔː/ *verb trans.* Now *rare*. Pa. t. **-drew** /-druː/; pa. pple **-drawn** /-drɔːn/. L16.
[Back-form. from next.]

1 Draw out (metal) into wire; practise wire-drawing. Also more widely, draw out (any material thing) to an elongated form; stretch. L16. ▸**b** Cause (steam or water) to pass through a small aperture. M18.

2 *fig.* **a** Prolong to an inordinate length; protract unduly, spin out. Also, reduce to great slenderness, attenuate. L16. ▸**b** Refine, apply, or press (an argument etc.) with idle or excessive subtlety. Formerly also, induce, extract, introduce, etc., by subtle persuasion or cunning persistence. E17.

> 🕮 **2a** F. BURNEY To fill up the middle and end of an evening by wire-drawing the comments afforded by the beginning. **b** R. SOUTH Nor am I for forcing, or wiredrawing the Sense of the Text. S. RICHARDSON She sought only to gain time, in order to wire-draw me into a consent.

wire-drawer /ˈwʌɪədrɔːə/ *noun.* ME.
[from WIRE *noun* + DRAWER.]

1 A person who draws metal into wire; a person who practises or is skilled in wire-drawing. ME.

†**2** *fig.* A person who spins out a matter to extreme length or tenuousness. M16–E19.

wire-drawing /ˈwʌɪədrɔːɪŋ/ *noun.* M17.
[from prec. + -ING[1].]
The action of WIRE-DRAW *verb* (*lit.* & *fig.*); the action or operation of making wire by drawing a piece of ductile metal through a series of holes of successively smaller diameter in a draw-plate.

wire-drawn, **wire-drew** *verbs* see WIRE-DRAW.

wireless /ˈwʌɪəlɪs/ *adjective, noun, & verb.* L19.
[from WIRE *noun* + -LESS.]

▶ **A** *adjective* (partly the noun used *attrib.*). Lacking or not requiring a wire or wires; *spec.* of, pertaining to, or employing radio transmission (rather than conducting wires); of or pertaining to a wireless. L19.
wireless cabinet, ***wireless licence***, ***wireless set***, ***wireless shack***, ***wireless silence***, ***wireless transmission***, etc. **wireless telegraphy** = RADIO-TELEGRAPHY. **wireless telephony** = RADIO-TELEPHONY.

▶ **B** *noun.* **1** Wireless telegraphy or telephony; sound broadcasting. Also, a particular radio station. E20.

†**2** A radio-telegram. E–M20.

3 A radio receiving set; = RADIO *noun* 4. E20.

▶ **C** *verb trans. & intrans.* = RADIO *verb*. Now *rare*. L19.

¶ With ref. to sound transmission now increasingly old-fashioned, being replaced by *radio* exc. in *Hist.* contexts.

■ **wirelessly** *adverb* without wires; by wireless: L19.

wireline /ˈwʌɪəlʌɪn/ *noun.* M19.
[from WIRE *noun* + LINE *noun*[2].]

1 In *pl.* Wire-marks (see ***wire-mark*** (a) s.v. WIRE *noun*). *rare.* M19.

2 OIL INDUSTRY. **a** A cable for lowering and raising tools and equipment in a well shaft. E20. ▸**b** An electric cable used to connect measuring devices in a well with indicating or recording instruments at the surface. L20.

3 A telegraph or telephone line of wire. M20.

4 A fishing-line of metal wire. L20.

wireman /ˈwʌɪəmən/ *noun.* Pl. **-men.** M16.
[from WIRE *noun* + MAN *noun*.]

†**1** A person who makes or works in wire. M16–M17.

2 A workman who fixes and attends to the conducting wires of an electrical system. L19.

3 A wire-tapper. *colloq.* L20.

4 A journalist working for a telegraphic news agency. L20.

wirer /ˈwʌɪərə/ *noun.* M19.
[from WIRE *verb* + -ER[1].]
A person who wires (in various senses of the verb); *slang* a pickpocket; a snarer of game; a worker who deals with wire; a telegraphist.

wire-tapper /ˈwʌɪətapə/ *noun.* L19.
[from WIRE *noun* + TAPPER *noun*[1].]
A person who makes a (usu. secret) connection to a telephone or telegraph circuit in order to intercept messages or eavesdrop.
■ **wire-tap** *noun & verb* (*a*) *noun* an act of tapping a telephone line, esp. as a form of surveillance; the device by which this is done; (*b*) *verb trans.* tap the telephone line of; monitor (a call) by means of a wire-tap: M20. **wire-tapping** *verbal noun* the practice or activity of a wire-tapper E20.

wirework /ˈwʌɪəwəːk/ *noun.* L16.
[from WIRE *noun* + WORK *noun*.]
1 The making of wire; work done in or with wire; fabrics or objects made of wire. L16.
2 Wire-walking. E20.
■ **wire-worker** *noun* (*a*) a person who makes wire or wire objects; (*b*) a wire-walker; (*c*) *fig.* a wire-puller: L17.

wireworm /ˈwʌɪəwəːm/ *noun.* L18.
[from WIRE *noun* + WORM *noun*.]
The slender hard-skinned larva of a click-beetle (family Elateridae), destructive to the roots of plants; any of various similar larvae, *esp.* the leather-jacket grub of a crane-fly. Also, a myriapod, esp. of the millipede genus *Iulus*, which damages plant roots.

wirey *adjective* see WIRY.

wirily /ˈwʌɪərɪli/ *adverb.* M19.
[from WIRY + -LY[2].]
In a wiry manner, like wire.

wiriness /ˈwʌɪərɪnɪs/ *noun.* E19.
[from WIRY + -NESS.]
The quality or condition of being wiry.

wiring /ˈwʌɪərɪŋ/ *noun.* E19.
[from WIRE *verb* + -ING[1].]
1 The action of WIRE *verb.* E19.
2 Wires collectively; wirework; *esp.* the electric wires in an apparatus or building. E19.
Comb.: **wiring diagram** a diagram of the wiring of an electrical installation or device, showing the electrical relationship of connections and components and usu. also their physical disposition.

wirra /ˈwɪrə/ *noun.* *Austral.* L19.
[Aboriginal: prob. repr. different words.]
1 A shallow wooden scoop used by Aborigines. L19.
2 = COUBA. E20.

wirra /ˈwɪrə/ *interjection.* *Anglo-Irish.* See also WURRA. E19.
[Preceded by *oh*, = Irish *a Mhuire* oh Mary!]
In full ***oh wirra***! Expr. sorrow or anxiety.
■ **wirrasthru** /wɪrəsˈθruː/ *noun* [Irish *a Mhuire is truagh* oh Mary it is a pity] a lament; also as *interjection*: L19.

wirrah /ˈwɪrə/ *noun.* *Austral.* L19.
[Aboriginal.]
A serranid fish, *Acanthistius serratus*, of Australian coasts, greenish brown with blue spots.

wirrwarr /ˈwəːwɑː, *foreign* ˈvɪrvar/ *noun.* M19.
[German.]
Turmoil, mess; a welter.

Wirt /vɪrt/ *noun.* Pl. **-e** /-ə/. M19.
[German.]
In German-speaking countries, a landlord of an inn.

Wirtschaft /ˈvɪrtʃaft/ *noun.* M19.
[German: in sense 2 abbreviation of *Gastwirtschaft*.]
1 (Domestic) economy, housekeeping. M19.
2 = WIRTSHAUS. E20.
Comb.: ***Wirtschaftswunder*** /ˈvɪrtʃaftsˌvʊndər/ an economic miracle; *spec.* the economic recovery of the Federal Republic of (West) Germany after the war of 1939–45.

Wirtshaus /ˈvɪrtshaʊs/ *noun.* Pl. **-häuser** /-hɔyzər/. E19.
[German, from genit. of *Wirt* innkeeper, landlord + *Haus* HOUSE *noun*[1].]
A hostelry or inn in a German-speaking country.

wiry /ˈwʌɪəri/ *adjective.* Also occas. **wirey**. L16.
[from WIRE *noun* + -Y[1].]
1 Made or consisting of wire; in the form of wire. L16.
2 Resembling wire in form and texture; tough and flexible. L16. ▸**b** *MEDICINE.* Of the pulse: small and tense. E19.
3 Of sound: produced by or as by the plucking or vibration of a wire. Also occas., (of music) played on stringed instruments; (of a voice) thin and metallic. E19.
4 Of a person or animal: lean, tough, and sinewy; *fig.* resilient, untiring. E19.

> 📖 **2** R. C. HUTCHINSON A man in early middle age, his wiry hair thinning prematurely. **3** *Gramophone* String tone is wiry, even a bit sour. **4** I. WATSON She was wiry, and carried no spare flesh.

wis /wɪs/ *verb*[1] *trans.* Long *obsolete* exc. *Scot.* Infl. **-ss-**.
[Old English *wissian* alt. of *wīsian* WISE *verb*[1] after (*ge*)*wis* IWIS.]
†**1** Make known, give information of; indicate, *esp.* point out (the way). OE–M16.
2 Show the way to, direct, guide, (a person). OE. ▸†**b** Manage, govern, control. OE–LME.
†**3** Instruct, teach, (a person). Freq. foll. by *to do*. OE–L15.

wis /wɪs/ *verb*[2] *intrans.* (*pres.*). Long *arch.* 3 sing. **wisses**. E16.
[Orig. in *I wis* alt. of IWIS *adverb* understood as 'I know' & assoc. with *wist* pa. t. of WIT *verb*. Cf. WIST *verb*[1].]
Know well.

Wis. *abbreviation.*
Wisconsin.

Wisconsin /wɪˈskɒnsɪn/ *adjective & noun.* L19.
[A north central state of the US.]
GEOLOGY. (Designating or pertaining to) the last (or last two) of the Pleistocene glaciations of N. America, approximating to the Weichselian of northern Europe.
■ Also **Wisconsinan** *adjective & noun* M20.

Wisconsinite /wɪˈskɒnsɪnʌɪt/ *noun.* M20.
[from WISCONSIN + -ITE[1].]
A native or inhabitant of the State of Wisconsin in the US.

Wisd. *abbreviation.*
Wisdom of Solomon (Apocrypha).

wisdom /ˈwɪzdəm/ *noun.* Also †**wise-**.
[Old English *wīsdōm* = Old Frisian, Old Saxon *wīsdōm*, Old High German *wīstuom* (German *Weistum* legal sentence, precedent), Old Norse *vísdómr*: see WISE *adjective*, -DOM.]
1 The quality of being wise, esp. in relation to conduct and the choice of means and ends; the combination of experience and knowledge with the ability to apply them judiciously; sound judgement, prudence, practical sense. OE. ▸**b** This quality personified (usu. as feminine) or regarded as expressing the essence or nature of God. OE. ▸**c** A wise thing *to do*; a wise act, policy, or proceeding. *sing.* & (occas.) in *pl. arch.* LME. ▸**d** With possess. pronoun: (a respectful or mock complimentary title given to) a person of wisdom or high status, esp. a member of a deliberative assembly. Usu. in *pl.* Now *rare* or *obsolete.* LME.
2 Knowledge, esp. of an abstruse kind; enlightenment, learning, erudition. Now chiefly *Hist.* OE. ▸†**b** In *pl.* Kinds of learning, branches of knowledge. *rare.* OE–M19.
3 Wise discourse or teaching; *spec.* (*ECCLESIASTICAL*) (*a*) the apocryphal book of *The Wisdom of Solomon*; †(*b*) *rare* the apocryphal book of *Ecclesiasticus*. Also (*collect. sing.* & †in *pl.*), wise sayings, precepts, etc. Formerly also, a wise statement or maxim. ME.
†**4** Sanity, reason. (Cf. WISE *adjective* 4.) *rare* (Shakes.). Only in E17.

> 📖 **1** P. USTINOV Wisdom is far slower to mature than scientific knowledge. **b** COLERIDGE Wisdom forbids her children . . to act and feel further than they know. **c** SHAKES. *3 Hen. VI* Till then 'tis wisdom to conceal our meaning.

Comb. & phrases: **in her wisdom**, **in his wisdom**, **in its wisdom**, etc., (now chiefly *iron.*) in the belief that it would be the best thing to do; **Wisdom literature** (*a*) the biblical books of Job, Proverbs, Ecclesiastes, Song of Songs, Wisdom of Solomon, and Ecclesiasticus collectively; (*b*) similar works (esp. from the ancient Near East) containing proverbial sayings, practical maxims, etc.; **wisdom tooth** each of the hindmost molar teeth in the upper and lower jaws in man, which usu. erupt about the age of twenty; ***cut one's wisdom teeth***, achieve wisdom or discretion.
■ †**wisdomness** *noun* (*rare*) (*a*) sound reasoning; (*b*) affected or spurious wisdom: L16–M17.

wise /wʌɪz/ *noun*[1]. *arch.*
[Old English *wīse*, corresp. to Old Frisian *wīs*, Old Saxon *wīsa* (Dutch *wijze*), Old High German *wīs*(*a*) manner, custom, tune (German *Weise*), Old Norse *vísa* stanza, from Germanic base also of WIT *verb*: cf. -WISE.]
1 A manner, way, mode, fashion, or degree. Formerly also *spec.*, a habitual manner of action, a habit, a custom. OE.
†**2** Song, melody. *rare.* OE–ME.

> 📖 **1** W. WATSON Some in scoffing manner; others in malicious wise. F. ROUS One who was in no wise averse to that common Learning. L. OLIPHANT He did it this wise. ***in such a wise***, ***in such wise***: see SUCH *demonstr. adjective & pronoun.*

wise /wʌɪz/ *adjective & noun*[2].
[Old English *wīs* = Old Frisian, Old Saxon, Old High German *wīs*(*i* (Dutch *wijs*, German *weise*) Old Norse *víss*, Gothic *-weis*, from Germanic, from Indo-European base also of WIT *verb*.]
▶ **A** *adjective.* **1** Of a person etc.: having or exercising (the power of) sound judgement or discernment, esp. in relation to conduct and the choice of means and ends; having and judiciously applying experience and knowledge; characterized by good sense and prudence. OE. ▸**b** Of behaviour, an action, a quality, etc.: proceeding from, indicating, or suggesting wisdom or discernment; sagacious, prudent, sensible, discreet. OE.
2 a Of a person: clever, skilled. Formerly also foll. by *of*. Long *obsolete* exc. as in b. OE. ▸**b** *spec.* Skilled in magic or occult arts. Now *dial.* or *Hist.* M17.
3 Having knowledge, well-informed; instructed, learned, (*in* a subject). Later also, informed, aware, (*of* something specified or implied). Now chiefly in phrs. OE.
4 In one's right mind, sane. Now *Scot.* & *dial.* ME.

> 📖 **1** AV *Rom.* 16:19 I would haue you wise vnto that which is good, and simple concerning euill. COLERIDGE The first duty of a wise advocate is to convince his opponents, that he understands their arguments. H. JAMES An ambitious diplomatist would probably be wise to marry. *Scotsman* A wise man . . knows his own limitations. **b** LD MACAULAY By a wise dispensation of Providence. G. SWIFT You say such wise, such clever things. **3** HOBBES Wiser and better learned in cases of Law . . than themselves. T. GRAY Where ignorance is bliss, 'Tis folly to be wise. *Century Magazine* Not one whit the wiser of the world than when he left home. *Times* A man wise in the ways of the world, shrewd in affairs.

▶ **B** *absol.* as *noun.* Formerly, a wise person, a sage. Now, *the* wise people as a class. OE.
Special collocations, comb., & phrases: **a word to the wise** = VERB. SAP. ***be wise after the event***: see EVENT *noun.* **make wise to do** (*obsolete* exc. *dial.*) pretend to do. **no wiser**, **none the wiser**, **not much wiser** knowing no more than before. ***one of the wisest***: see ONE *adjective, noun, & pronoun.* PENNY ***wise and pound foolish***. **put wise to** (*colloq.*, orig. *US*) inform of, enlighten about, enable to be wise to. ***three wise men***: see THREE *adjective.* ***three wise monkeys***: see MONKEY *noun.* **wise-ass** *slang* (orig. *US*) = ***wise guy*** below. **wisecrack** *noun & verb* (*colloq.*, orig. *US*) (*a*) *noun* a clever, pithy, or snide remark; (*b*) *verb intrans.* make a wisecrack. **wisecracker** a person given to making wisecracks. **wise guy** (*colloq.*, orig. *US*) a know-all; a person who makes sarcastic or annoying remarks. **wisehead** a wiseacre, a know-all. **wise man** a wise, discerning, or prudent man; *spec.* (*a*) (now *arch. rare*) a learned man, a scholar; (*b*) (now *colloq.*) a man chosen as an adviser in matters of state, a councillor; (*c*) a man versed in magic, astrology, etc., *esp.* each of the three Magi (see also ***three wise men*** s.v. THREE *adjective*); (*d*) ***wise man of Gotham***. **wise to** (*colloq.*, orig. *US*) aware of, esp. so as to know what to do or how to act. **wise woman** a woman who is wise; *spec.* (now *dial.* or *Hist.*) a female magician or witch, *esp.* a harmless or beneficent one who deals in charms against disease, ill luck, etc. **without anyone's being the wiser** undetected.
■ **wiseling** *noun* (now *rare*) a pretender to wisdom, a wiseacre M17. **wiseness** *noun* ME.

wise /wʌɪz/ *verb*[1]. Now chiefly *Scot.*
[Old English *wīsian* = Old Frisian *wīsa*, Old Saxon *wīsian* (Dutch *wijzen*), Old High German *wīsen* (German *weisen*), Old Norse *vísa*, from Germanic base also of WISE *adjective*. Cf. WIS *verb*[1].]
▶ **I** *verb trans.* **1** Show the way to (a person); guide, lead, direct; instruct, inform. OE.
2 Move in some direction or into some position; convey, conduct; turn. ME. ▸**b** Direct, aim, (a missile etc.). *Scot. rare.* ME.
3 *verb trans.* Show, point out, (the way). LME.
▶ **II 4** *verb intrans.* Direct one's course, go. ME.

wise /wʌɪz/ *verb*[2]. E20.
[from WISE *adjective*.]
1 *verb intrans.* & *trans.* Foll. by *up*: become or make aware, informed, or enlightened (about a person or thing). Freq. foll. by *on* or *to*. *colloq.* (chiefly *US*). E20.
2 *verb intrans.* Foll. by *off*, make wisecracks *at* (a person). *US slang.* M20.

> 📖 **1** *Wall Street Journal* Antique dealers are wising up to the growing demand for old radios.

■ **wised-up** *adjective* (*colloq.*, chiefly *US*) (made) aware or informed; knowing: E20.

-wise /wʌɪz/ *suffix.*
[from WISE *noun*[1]: cf. -WAYS.]
Forming (*a*) adverbs & adjectives chiefly from nouns, with the sense '(that is) in the manner, form, or direction of', as ***crosswise***, ***latticewise***, ***lengthwise***, ***otherwise***; (*b*) adverbs from nouns with the sense 'as regards, in terms of', as ***pairwise***, ***plotwise*** (now freely productive in the formation of nonce-words, as ***employment-wise***, ***moneywise***, ***publicity-wise***, etc.).

wiseacre /ˈwʌɪzeɪkə/ *noun.* *colloq.* L16.
[Middle Dutch *wijsseggher* soothsayer, prob. (with assim. to *segghen* say) from Old High German *wīssago*, alt. (by assoc. with *wīs* WISE *adjective* + *sagēn* say) of *wīzago* = Old English *witega* prophet, from Germanic base also of WIT *verb*. Assim. to ACRE is unexplained.]
1 A pretender to wisdom; a foolish person with an air or affectation of wisdom; a know-all. L16.
2 A wise or learned person, a sage. Chiefly *derog.* M18.

> 📖 **1** *Cincinnati Enquirer* The wiseacres said from the start it couldn't be done, but they were wrong.

†**wisedom** *noun* var. of WISDOM.

wiselike /ˈwʌɪzlʌɪk/ *adjective & adverb.* *Scot.* & *dial.* E19.
[from WISE *adjective* + -LIKE.]
▶ **A** *adjective.* **1** Reasonable, rational. E19.
2 Becoming, seemly, respectable, or proper, esp. in appearance. E19.
▶ **B** *adverb.* Fittingly, becomingly, respectably. E19.

wisely /ˈwʌɪzli/ *adverb*.
[Old English *wīslīce*, from WISE *adjective* + -LY^{2}.]
1 In a wise manner. OE. ▸**b** With an air or assumption of wisdom; knowingly. L16.
†**2** Attentively, carefully. OE–L16.
†**3** Skilfully, cleverly, ingeniously; cunningly. OE–E17.

wisenheimer /ˈwʌɪz(ə)nhʌɪmə/ *noun*. *US colloq.* E20.
[from WISE *adjective* + -(*n*)*heimer* as in such surnames as *Oppenheimer*.]
A wiseacre, a know-all; = SMART ALEC.

wisent /ˈwiːz(ə)nt/ *noun*. M19.
[German: see BISON.]
The European bison.

wiser /ˈwʌɪzə/ *noun & adverb*. ME.
[Compar. of WISE *adjective*: see -ER^{3}.]
▸ **A** *noun*. A person who is (one's) superior in wisdom. Usu. in *pl.* Now *rare*. ME.

📖 SIR W. SCOTT These Delilahs seduce my wisers and my betters.

▸ **B** *adverb*. More wisely. *rare*. E17.

📖 SHAKES. *A.Y.L.* Thou speak'st wiser than thou art ware of.

wish *adjective* var. of WISHT.

wish /wɪʃ/ *verb & noun*.
[Old English *wȳscan* = Middle Low German *wünschen*, Middle Dutch *wonscen*, *wunscen*, Old High German *wunsken* (German *wünschen*), from Germanic base also of WEEN *verb*, WONT *adjective*.]
▸ **A** *verb*. **I** *verb trans.* **1** Have or feel a wish, desire, or aspiration for; be so disposed that (if possible or practicable) one would like. Foll. by simple obj., obj. clause, (obj. &) inf., obj. & compl. or adverb (phr.). OE.
2 Express a wish or (usu. benevolent) hope for, say that one has a desire for, (usu. foll. by double obj., or obj. & compl.); *spec.* (now *rare*) invoke, call down, (an evil or curse). OE.
3 W. cognate obj.: make, have, (a wish). LME.
4 Request, ask; require. M16.
5 Recommend (a person) *to* another, a place, etc. Cf. WIS *verb*^{1} 2. *obsolete* exc. *Scot. & north.* L16.
6 Foist or impose (something or someone) *on (to)* a person. E20.

📖 **1** SHAKES. *Temp.* I would not wish Any companion in the world but you. J. AUSTEN She hears that Miss Biggs is to be married . . . I wish it may be so. C. LAMB I wished both magazine and review at the bottom of the sea. DICKENS Let us remember James by name and wish him happy. L. M. ALCOTT You should do just what your grandfather wishes. T. HARDY 'I wish we could marry now,' murmured Stephen, as an impossible fancy. J. B. MOZLEY If men really wish to be good, they will become good. I. MURDOCH These words were a barrier between us which she wished me . . to remove. **2** O. NASH I wish him moths, I wish him mice, I wish him cocktails lacking ice. ***wish a person good luck***, ***wish a person happy birthday***, ***wish a person many happy returns of the day***, ***wish a person merry Christmas***, etc. ***wish a person joy (of)***, ***wish a person the joy (of)***: see JOY *noun*. **4** SHAKES. *Meas. for M.* You were not bid to speak . . . No . . Nor wish'd to hold my peace. DICKENS Whatever we wished done was done with great civility. T. S. ELIOT Certainly, Sir Claude, if that is what you wish. **6** A. BROOKNER This troublesome nephew . . has been wished on him.

▸ **II** *verb intrans.* **7** Have or feel a wish, desire, or yearning *for*. Formerly also foll. by *after*. ME.
8 Make or have a wish. M16.
9 Feel or express a (good) wish for someone. Only in ***wish a person well***. L16.

📖 **7** ROBERT BURTON Vtopian parity is a thing to be wished for rather than effected. COLERIDGE I should not have wished for a more vanquishable opponent. **8** SHAKES. *All's Well* If yourself . . Did ever . . Wish chastely and love dearly. **9** A. T. ELLIS She stopped by his door, wished him well.

▸ **B** *noun*. **1** A thing one wishes or wishes for; = DESIRE *noun* 4. ME.
2 An act or instance of wishing; a (feeling of) desire for or *for* something one believes would give satisfaction, pleasure, etc., esp. something one thinks cannot be attained, possessed, or realized. LME. ▸†**b** The fact or condition of desiring. *rare*. LME–E18.
3 a A desire expressed in words; a verbal expression of a desire, a request. E16. ▸**b** *spec.* An expression of desire for another's welfare, happiness, etc., esp. as a farewell greeting. In *pl.* & †*sing.* L16. ▸**c** An imprecation, a malediction. Now *rare* or *obsolete*. L16.

📖 **1** MILTON Thy wish, exactly to thy hearts desire. **2** S. JOHNSON The whole world is put in motion by the wish for riches. SIR W. SCOTT Form but a wish for her advantage, and it shall be fulfilled. *Proverb*: If wishes were horses, beggars would ride. **3a** R. BAGOT At Anthony's wish she wore the Cuthbert diamonds.

Phrases: †**at high wish** at the height of the fulfilment of one's wishes. **best wishes**, **good wishes** (expr.) hopes for a person's happiness etc. **to a wish**, **to one's wish** (now *rare* or *obsolete*) as one wishes, *esp.* as much as one wishes or could wish. †**upon a wish**, †**upon one's wish** according to one's wish, just as one wishes.

Comb.: **wish book** *N. Amer. slang* a mail-order catalogue; **wish-dream** *noun & attrib. adjective* (having or indulging) a dream or fantasy that reflects some hidden wish; **wish list** a list of desired objects or occurrences; **wish-thinking** = ***wishful thinking*** s.v. WISHFUL *adjective* 2a.

■ **wishable** *adjective* (*rare*) that may be wished for, desirable M16. **wished** *ppl adjective* (**a**) (now *rare*) that is the object of a wish; (**b**) that is wished or longed *for*: L16. **wisher** *noun* a person who makes a wish or wishes (for) something (now *rare* exc. in comb., as ***ill-wisher***, ***well-wisher***, etc.) LME. **wishingly** *adverb* (*rare*) desirously, longingly L16. **wishless** *adjective* (*rare*) E19.

wisha /ˈwɪʃə/ *interjection*. *Anglo-Irish*. E19.
[Irish *mhuise* indeed or alt. of (*a*) *Mhuire* (O) Mary: cf. MUSHA.]
Expr. disbelief, dismay, emphasis, or surprise.

wishbone /ˈwɪʃbəʊn/ *noun*. M19.
[from WISH *noun* + BONE *noun*, with ref. to the custom of two people pulling the furcula of a cooked fowl until it breaks, the person left holding the longer part being entitled to make a wish.]
1 A forked bone between the neck and breastbone of a bird, the furcula. M19.
2 An object, part, etc., shaped like the wishbone of a bird; *spec.* (**a**) NAUTICAL a boom composed of two halves that curve outward from the mast on either side of the sail and in again, the clew of the sail between them being attached to the point where they meet aft; (**b**) a wishbone-shaped element in the independent suspension of a motor vehicle, having two arms which are hinged to the chassis at their ends and to the wheel at their join. Freq. *attrib.* M20.

wishful /ˈwɪʃfʊl, -f(ə)l/ *adjective*. E16.
[from WISH *noun* + -FUL.]
†**1** Such as is (to be) wished; desirable; desired. E16–M17.
2 a Of the eye, a look, a feeling, etc.: full of desire; longing, yearning, wistful. Later also, expressing or indicative of a wish. L16. ▸**b** Of a person: possessed by a wish for something specified or implied; wishing, desiring *to do*. M18.

📖 **2a** SHAKES. *3 Hen. VI* To greet mine own land with my wishful sight. C. BRIDGES The forlorn wandering child casting a wishful, penitent look towards his Father's house. **wishful thinker** a person who indulges in wishful thinking. **wishful thinking** belief or expectation founded on wishes rather than on what one has reason to suppose to be true.

■ **wishfully** *adverb* L16. **wishfulness** *noun* E19.

wish-fulfilment /ˈwɪʃfʊlˌfɪlm(ə)nt/ *noun*. Also *-**fill-**. E20.
[translating German *Wunscherfüllung*.]
PSYCHOANALYSIS. (A tendency towards) the fulfilment of acknowledged or unconscious wishes in dreams and fantasies; a dream or other event or object in which the fulfilment of a wish is given (usu. imaginary or symbolic) expression.
■ **wish-fulfilling** *adjective* that tends towards or expresses wish-fulfilment E20.

wishing /ˈwɪʃɪŋ/ *noun*. ME.
[from WISH *verb*: see -ING^{1}.]
The action of WISH *verb*; desire; an instance of this, a wish. Formerly occas. coupled with *woulding*.
Attrib. & comb.: In the sense 'that is supposed to be capable of magically conferring the fulfilment of a wish', as ***wishing-cap***, ***wishing-stone***, etc. Special combs., as **wishing-well** a well into which a coin is dropped as a wish is made.

wishly /ˈwɪʃli/ *adverb*. Long *obsolete* exc. *dial.* M16.
[Perh. alt. of WISTLY *adverb*, infl. by WISH *verb & noun*.]
Steadfastly, fixedly, intently; longingly. Usu. with ref. to a look, gaze, etc.

wishmay /ˈwɪʃmeɪ/ *noun*. *rare*. M19.
[translating Old Norse *óskmær*, from *ósk* wish + *mær*: see MAY *noun*^{1}.]
A Valkyrie.

Wishram /ˈwɪʃram/ *noun & adjective*. M19.
[Sahaptin *Wišxam*.]
▸ **A** *noun*. Pl. same.
1 A member of a N. American Indian people living in the southern part of the State of Washington. M19.
2 The Chinook dialect of this people. E20.
▸ **B** *attrib.* or as *adjective*. Of or pertaining to the Wishram or their dialect. M20.

wisht /wɪʃt/ *adjective*. Chiefly *dial.* Also **wish**. L18.
[Origin unkn.]
1 Uncanny, eerie, weird. L18.
2 Dreary, dismal; miserable. E19.
3 Sickly, wan. M19.
■ **wishtness** *noun* eeriness L18.

wishtonwish /ˈwɪʃtənwɪʃ/ *noun*. *US*. Now *rare*. E19.
[N. Amer. Indian, of imit. origin.]
1 The prairie dog. E19.
†**2** The nighthawk, *Chordeiles minor*. E–M19.

wish-wash /ˈwɪʃwɒʃ/ *noun*. L18.
[Redupl. of WASH *noun*: cf. SWISH-SWASH.]
1 Weak, insipid, or watery drink (or liquid food). L18.
2 *fig.* Insipid or excessively sentimental talk or writing. M19.

wishy-washy /ˈwɪʃɪwɒʃi/ *adjective*. E18.
[Redupl. of WASHY: cf. -Y^{1}.]
1 Feeble or insipid in quality or character; indecisive; trivial, trashy. Also (now *rare* or *obsolete*) weakly, sickly. E18.
2 Of drink or liquid food: weak and insipid; watery, sloppy. L18.

📖 **1** R. LOWELL A wishy-washy desire to be everything to everybody. *Toronto Sun* Our politicians are too wishy-washy to take a firm stand on this issue.

■ **wishy-washiness** *noun* L19.

†**wisk** *noun, verb, adverb, & interjection* see WHISK *noun*^{1}, *verb*, *adverb*, *& interjection*.

†**wismuth** *noun* see BISMUTH.

wisp /wɪsp/ *noun & verb*. ME.
[Origin uncertain: cf. West Frisian *wisp* wisp, twig, handful of straw, from Germanic base also of WHISK *noun*^{1}.]
▸ **A** *noun*. **1** A handful, bunch, twisted band, or small bundle of hay, straw, grass, etc.; *esp.* one used to wipe something dry or clean, as to rub down a horse. Also (now *rare*), a ring or wreath of other twisted material, used as a pad. ME.
2 *spec.* A bunch or twisted bundle of hay or straw, used for burning as a torch etc. ME. ▸**b** A will-o'-the-wisp, an ignis fatuus. Chiefly *poet.* Now *rare* or *obsolete*. E17.
3 a A bundle or parcel containing a definite quantity of certain commodities, esp. steel or fish. *Scot. & north.* L15. ▸**b** *transf.* A flock *of* birds, esp. snipe. E19.
4 a Any of various things that are twisted or form a bundle so as to be reminiscent or suggestive of a wisp of straw etc., as (**a**) a twist of paper; (**b**) a bundle of clothes. L16. ▸**b** *spec.* A thin, filmy, or curling small piece, fragment, or quantity (*of* hair, smoke, etc.). Now also = SLIP *noun*^{2} 8. M19.

📖 **2b** TENNYSON We did not know the real light, but chased The wisp that flickers where no foot can tread. **4b** A. RANSOME Thin wisps of smoke . . rose from the embers of the charcoal mound. P. MORTIMER A small woman . . must have been known as a wisp of a girl. I. COLEGATE Her fine white hair . . escaped in stray wisps on both sides of her face. *fig.*: A. T. ELLIS A faint wisp of memory floated into her mind and away again.

▸ **B** *verb*. **I** *verb trans.* **1** Rub (an animal, esp. a horse) *down* or *over* with a wisp. L16.
2 Put a twisted band of hay on (the legs of a horse). Long *obsolete* exc. *Scot.* E17.
3 Twist into or as a wisp; *dial.* rumple. M18.
▸ **II** *verb intrans.* **4** Vanish *away* like a wisp of vapour. L19.
5 Of hair etc.: hang or twine in wisps. E20.
■ **wispish** *adjective* of the nature of or resembling a wisp L19.

wispy /ˈwɪspi/ *adjective*. E18.
[from prec.: see -Y^{1}.]
Consisting of or resembling a wisp or wisps.

📖 A. TAN She would brush back her wispy bangs.

■ **wispily** *adverb* E20. **wispiness** *noun* M20.

wissel /ˈwɪs(ə)l/ *noun*. Chiefly *Scot.* L15.
[Middle Low German *wissele* or Middle & mod. Dutch *wissel*, corresp. to Old Frisian *wix(e)le*, Old High German *wehsal* (Middle High German *wehsel*, German *Wechsel*), Old Norse *víxl*, from Germanic.]
†**1** = EXCHANGE *noun* 3a. Only in L15.
2 Change for an amount of money. Chiefly *fig.*, esp. in ***get the wissel of one's groat***, get one's just deserts. E18.

Wissenschaft /ˈvɪsənʃaft/ *noun*. M19.
[German.]
(The systematic pursuit of) knowledge, science; learning, scholarship.
Comb.: ***Wissenschaftslehre*** /-ʃafts,leːrə/ a theory or philosophy of knowledge or science, esp. with ref. to German idealistic philosophy.

wist /wɪst/ *verb*^{1}. Long *arch.* E16.
[Partly from *I wist* alt. of IWIS *adverb* (cf. WIS *verb*^{2}), partly use of *wist* pa. t. of WIT *verb*.]
Know.

wist *verb*^{2} *pa. t. & pple* of WIT *verb*.

Wistar /ˈwɪstə, -ɑː/ *noun*. M20.
[The *Wistar* Institute of Anatomy and Biology, Philadelphia, USA, founded by I. J. Wistar (1827–1905).]
MEDICINE & BIOLOGY. Used *attrib.* to designate rats bred from a strain developed for laboratory purposes.

wisteria /wɪˈstɪərɪə/ *noun*. Also **wistaria** /-ˈstɛːrɪə/. M19.
[mod. Latin (see below), from Caspar *Wistar* (or *Wister*) (1761–1818), US anatomist + -IA^{1}.]
1 Any of various climbing leguminous shrubs constituting the genus *Wisteria*, native to N. America, Japan, and China, and bearing pinnate leaves and pendent racemes of showy blue-lilac papilionaceous flowers; esp. *Wisteria sinensis* (more fully ***Chinese wisteria***) and *W. floribunda* (more fully ***Japanese wisteria***), both much grown to cover walls. M19.

2 A light blue-purple shade, the colour of wisteria blossom. E20.

wistful /ˈwɪstfʊl, -f(ə)l/ *adjective*. E17.
[App. from WISTLY, infl. by WISHFUL: see -FUL.]
†**1** Closely attentive, intent. E17–M19.
2 Of a person, look, etc.: expectantly eager or watchful (now *rare*); mournfully or yearningly expectant or wishful. M17.
■ **wistfully** *adverb* M17. **wistfulness** *noun* L18.

wistiti *noun* var. of OUISTITI.

†**wistless** *adjective*. *poet.* M18–E19.
[Irreg. from next, or from WIST(FUL + -LESS.]
Inattentive, unobservant.

†**wistly** *adverb*. L15–M18.
[Perh. var. of WHISTLY *adverb*.]
With close attention; intently.

wit /wɪt/ *noun*.
[Old English *wit(t)*, *gewit(t)* corresp. to Old Frisian, Old Saxon *wit*, Old High German *wizzi* (Dutch *weet*, German *Witz*), Old Norse *vit*, from Germanic base of the verb.]
▶ **I** †**1** The mind as the seat of consciousness, thought, etc. OE–M17. ▶**b** Consciousness. Only in ME.
2 In *sing.* & (now usu.) *pl.* The mind or understanding considered in respect of its condition; *esp.* right mind, sanity. OE.
3 a The faculty of thinking and reasoning; understanding, intellect, reason. *arch.* ME. ▶**b** A person considered in respect of his or her intellect. *arch.* M16.
4 a Any of the faculties of perception or sensation. Esp. in ***the five wits*** below. Long *arch.* exc. as in b. ME. ▶**b** In *pl.* The mental or intellectual powers of a person collectively. LME.
5 Mental quickness, inventiveness, or sharpness; intellectual ability; genius, talent, cleverness. Now chiefly *spec.*, talent for speaking or writing wittily or amusingly. ME. ▶†**b** Practical ability, ingenuity, or skill. ME–E18. ▶†**c** Sagacity in an animal. LME–E17.
6 Wisdom, good sense or judgement, discretion, prudence. *obsolete* exc. in ***have the wit to***. ME. ▶†**b** A wise or prudent deed, practice, policy, or plan. ME–E17.
7 a A talented, clever, or intellectually gifted person; a genius. *obsolete* exc. as in sense b. LME. ▶**b** A person with a talent for speaking or writing wittily or amusingly; a witty person. L17.
8 (The quality which consists in) the apt, clever, unexpected, or (now esp.) humorous expression of thought or juxtaposition of ideas, expressions, etc., calculated to delight an audience. M16.

> 📖 **2** SHAKES. *Twel. N.* I am as well in my wits, fool, as thou art. M. FOTHERBY It is a thing so euident . . that whosoeuer denieth it, is (surely) out of his wit. **3a** SHAKES. *Mids. N. D.* I have had a dream, past the wit of man to say what dream it was. POPE In Wit a Man; Simplicity, a Child. **4a** J. MORLEY Morality depends not merely on the five wits, but on the mental constitution within. **b** S. RICHARDSON That my wits may not be sent a wooll-gathering. J. BUCHAN My wits were coming back to me, and I could think again. **5** W. DAVENANT Wit is not only the luck and labour, but also the dexterity of thought. T. YALDEN His flowing wit, with solid judgment join'd. W. COWPER Gilpin had a pleasant wit And lov'd a timely joke. **6** DRYDEN Lavish Grants suppose a Monarch tame, And more his Goodness than his Wit proclaim. J. RUSKIN One piece of good fortune, of which I had the wit to take advantage. I. WATSON Jambi had had the wit to pull up the gangplank. **7b** S. TOWNSEND My father is quite a wit after a couple of glasses of vodka. **8** J. DENNIS Scarron's Burlesque has . . little of good Sense, and consequently little of true Wit. POPE True Wit is Nature to advantage dress'd, What oft was thought, but ne'er so well express'd. J. A. HAMMERTON There is more 'heart' in humour, and more 'head' in wit. P. ACKROYD There are flashes of acid if high-spirited wit in all these sketches.

▶ **II 9** †**a** Knowledge acquired by study, learning; awareness. ME–M17. ▶**b** Information, intelligence. Esp. in ***get wit of***. *Scot. & north.* LME.
†**10** An opinion, a view, a judgement. LME–L16.

> 📖 **10** J. BELL The old Proverbe . . so many heades, so many wittes.

Phrases: ***a sport of wit***: see SPORT *noun*. ***at one's wits' end***: see ***one's wits' end*** below. **have one's wits about one**, **keep one's wits about one** be vigilant, mentally alert, or of lively intelligence. **live by one's wits** make a living by ingenious or crafty expedients, without a settled occupation. **one's wits' end**, **one's wit's end** the limit of one's ability to reason or cope; freq. in ***at one's wits' end***, in a state of utter perplexity. **out of one's wits** insane, mad, distracted. **set one's wits to** argue with. **the five wits** (long *arch.*) five (bodily) senses; *gen.* the perceptual or mental faculties.
Comb.: †**wit-cracker** (*rare*, Shakes.) a wisecracker; **wit-craft** †(*a*) the art of reasoning, logic; (*b*) exercise of one's wits; †**wit-snapper** = ***wit-cracker*** above; †**wit-wanton** *verb trans.* (with *it*) & *intrans.* (long *rare*) indulge wantonly in wit; **wit-worm** (long *rare*) a person who has developed into a wit (with allus. to the caterpillar emerging from the egg); **wit-writing** *rare* self-consciously witty or clever poetic composition.

wit /wɪt/ *verb*. Now *arch.* & *dial.* exc. in ***to wit*** below. Pres. t. **wot** /wɒt/, (*Scot.* & *north.*) **wat** /wat/, †**wote**. Pres. pple **witting**. Pa. t. & pple **wist** /wɪst/.
[Old English *witan* = Old Frisian *wita*, Old Saxon *witan*, Old High German *wizzan* (Dutch *weten*, German *wissen*), Old Norse *vita*, Gothic *witan*, from Germanic base also of WISE *adjective*, ult. from Indo-European base also of Sanskrit *veda* (see VEDA), Latin *videre* see: see also WOT *verb*[1]. Cf. GUIDE *verb*, WEET *verb*[1].]
▶ **I** *verb trans.* **1 a** Be acquainted with; be aware of; know (a fact or thing). OE. ▶†**b** Become aware of, gain knowledge of; find out, ascertain, learn; be informed of. OE–L17. ▶**c** Recognize; distinguish, discern. Long *rare* or *obsolete*. ME.
2 †**a** Be conversant with or versed in (a subject etc.). OE–ME. ▶**b** Know how or be able *to do*. Long *rare*. ME.
†**3** Expect (with certainty or confidence) *to do*. Only in ME.

> 📖 **1a** SPENSER The perill of this place I better wot then you. A. MONTGOMERIE All day I wot not what to do. *Century Magazine* They . . witting little that the tide has long since turned.

▶ **II** *verb intrans.* **4** Be aware *of*, know *of*. ME. ▶†**b** Have experience *of*. Only in LME.

> 📖 **4** A. D. T. WHITNEY We wit well of many things that we would never prove.

Phrases: ***God wot***: see GOD *noun*. **let wit** (*a*) let (a person) know (something); (*b*) inform (a person), disclose (something). **to wit** (*a*) that is to say, *scilicet*, namely; †(*b*) to be sure, truly, indeed; †(*c*) LAW indicating (and placed after the name of) the venue of a trial.

witan /ˈwɪtən/ *noun*. E19.
[Repr. Old English pl. of *wita* (see WITE *noun*[1]), from base of prec.]
Hist. (The members of) the national council in Anglo-Saxon times; = WITENAGEMOT.

witblits /ˈvɪtblɪts/ *noun*. *S. Afr.* Also **-blitz**. M20.
[Afrikaans, from *wit* white + *blits* lightning.]
Home-brewed brandy, a strong and colourless raw spirit.

witch /wɪtʃ/ *noun*[1].
[Old English *wiċċa*, fem. *wiċċe* (see also WICCA), formed as WITCH *verb*[1]. Cf. WICK *adjective*[1], WICKED *adjective*[1].]
1 A person, esp. a woman, who practises magic or sorcery. Later also *spec.*, (*a*) a person supposed or professing to have dealings with evil spirits and to be able to perform supernatural acts with their help; (*b*) a follower or practitioner of the religious cult of modern witchcraft, a Wiccan. OE. ▶**b** An ugly, repulsive, or malevolent (usu. old) woman; a hag. LME. ▶**c** A fascinating, bewitching girl or young woman. M18.
†**2** *transf.* The nightmare. *rare*. LME–L16.
3 Any of various animals or objects associated with or reminiscent of a witch, as (*a*) the stormy petrel; (*b*) = DOBBY 4. L18.

> 📖 **1** J. RHYS I have heard of one old witch changing herself into a pigeon. K. THOMAS A witch was a person . . (more often female) who could mysteriously injure other people.

Phrases: **as cold as a witch's tit** *slang* extremely cold. **as nervous as a witch** *US colloq.* very restless. **the witch is in it** it is bewitched. **witch of Agnesi** [translating Italian *versiera* witch + Maria Gaetana *Agnesi* (1718–99), Italian mathematician] MATH. a simple plane curve, symmetric about the *y*-axis and asymptotic to the *x*-axis, with an equation of the type $x^2y = 4a^2(2a - y)$.
Comb.: **witch-ball** a ball of decorated usu. coloured or silvered blown glass, (orig. as a charm against witchcraft); **witch bottle** *Hist.* a stone or glass bottle, filled with urine, nails, hair, etc., burned or heated to repel or break a witch's power over a bewitched person; **witch-bowl** a decorative circular glass bowl; **witch broom** = ***witches' broom*** below; **witch dance** a ritual dance performed by witches; **witch-doctor** (*a*) a person who professes to cure disease and counteract witchcraft by magic arts, *esp.* a tribal magician among primitive people; (*b*) *slang* a psychiatrist; **witch-doctoring**, **witch-doctory** the characteristic practice or practices of a witch-doctor; **witches' brew** (*a*) a magic brew prepared by witches; (*b*) *joc.* any harmful, suspicious, or disgusting concoction; **witches' broom** a dense twiggy outgrowth in a tree, resulting from infection by any of various fungi (esp. rusts), mites, or viruses; **witches' butter** any of certain gelatinous fungi of the Tremellales, esp. *Exidia glandulosa*; ***witches' sabbath***: see SABBATH 3; ***witches' thimble(s)***: see THIMBLE *noun* 8; **witch-finder** *Hist.* a person employed to search for and obtain evidence against witches; **witch-hat** a hat with a conical crown and flat brim, represented as worn by witches; **witch-hopple** *US* the hobblebush, *Viburnum alnifolium*; **witch-knot** (*a*) an elf-lock; (*b*) a knot tied to make or avert a spell; (*c*) = ***witches' broom*** above; **witch-lock** = ***witch-knot*** (a) above; **witch-mark** a mark on the body, supposed by witch-finders to denote that its possessor was a witch; **witch-post** in Yorkshire, a wooden post (usually of mountain ash) marked with a cross and built into a house as a protection against witches; **witch-smelling** the smelling out of witches; *fig.* witch-hunting; **witch-stone** a flat stone with a natural perforation, used as a charm against witchcraft; **witchweed** *S. Afr.* any of several parasitic plants of the genus *Striga*, of the figwort family; esp. *S. asiatica*, with bright red flowers; **witchwork** witchcraft.
■ **witchiness** *noun* the quality of being witchy M20. **witchlike** *adjective* characteristic of or resembling a witch E18. **witch-mania** *noun* a mania regarding witches and witchcraft M19. **witchmonger** *noun* a person who has dealings with witches or believes in witchcraft L16. **witchy** *adjective* of the nature of or resembling a witch, characteristic or suggestive of a witch M17.

witch /wɪtʃ/ *noun*[2]. Also **wych**.
[Old English *wiće*, *wić*, app. from Germanic base of WEAK *adjective*.]
(A vague or general name for) any of various trees having pliant branches: *esp.* (*a*) (now *dial.*) the mountain ash, *Pyrus aucuparia*; †(*b*) = WYCH ELM.
Comb.: **witch alder** a small shrub of the southern US, *Fothergilla gardenii*, with leaves like the alder, related to the witch hazel; ***witch elm***: see WYCH ELM; WITCH HAZEL.

witch /wɪtʃ/ *noun*[3]. *local*. L19.
[Origin unkn.]
A flatfish, *Glyptocephalus cynoglossus*, which resembles the lemon sole and is found in deeper water on both sides of the N. Atlantic. Also (chiefly *N. Amer.*) ***witch flounder***.

witch /wɪtʃ/ *verb*[1].
[Old English *wiċċian*, corresp. to Middle & mod. Low German *wikken*, *wicken*, of unkn. origin. In later senses prob. aphet. from BEWITCH.]
†**1** *verb intrans.* Practise magic arts or witchcraft; use sorcery. OE–E17.
2 *verb trans.* Affect or change (a person etc.) by witchcraft or sorcery; put a spell on. Also with adverb (phr.). ME.
3 *fig.* **a** *verb trans.* Enchant, charm, fascinate. L16. ▶**b** *verb intrans.* Use enchanting wiles. *rare*. L16.
■ **witched** *adjective* (*a*) bewitched, under a magic spell; (*b*) possessed of magic power: L16.

witch /wɪtʃ/ *verb*[2] *intrans.* & *trans.* *US*. M20.
[from WITCH *noun*[2].]
Dowse for (water) with a divining rod.
■ **witcher** *noun* a dowser M20.

witchcraft /ˈwɪtʃkrɑːft/ *noun*. OE.
[from WITCH *noun*[1] + CRAFT *noun*.]
1 The practices of a witch or witches, *esp.* the use of magic or sorcery; the exercise of supernatural power supposed to be possessed by a person in league with the Devil or evil spirits. OE. ▶**b** In *pl.* Acts or instances of this; magic arts. Long *rare* or *obsolete*. OE.
2 *fig.* Power or influence like that of a magician, as exercised by beauty or eloquence; *spec.* bewitching or fascinating attraction or charm. L16.

witchen /ˈwɪtʃən/ *noun*. Now *dial.* L16.
[from WITCH *noun*[2] + -EN[4].]
1 In full ***witchen elm***. = WYCH ELM. L16.
2 The mountain ash, *Pyrus aucuparia*. M17.

witchery /ˈwɪtʃ(ə)ri/ *noun*. M16.
[from WITCH *noun*[1]: see -ERY.]
1 The use or practice of witchcraft. M16. ▶**b** In *pl.* Deeds of witchcraft. L16.
2 *fig.* Bewitching or fascinating power or influence. L16.

witchetty /ˈwɪtʃɪti/ *noun*. *Austral.* M19.
[Aboriginal, from *wityu* hooked stick + *varti* grub.]
†**1** A hooked stick used to obtain witchetty grubs. M19–E20.
2 In full ***witchetty grub***. A large white grub, the larva of any of several moths and longhorn beetles which infest the roots and stem of the witchetty bush (see below), used as food by Aborigines and as bait by fishermen. L19.
Comb.: **witchetty bush** any of several small acacias, *esp.* the broad-leaved mulga, *Acacia kempeana*.

witch-grass /ˈwɪtʃgrɑːs/ *noun*. *US*. L18.
[Alt. of QUITCH-*grass*.]
A grass with creeping roots that occurs as a weed; *esp.* couch grass, *Elytrigia repens*.
old witch-grass: see OLD *adjective*.

witch hazel /ˈwɪtʃheɪz(ə)l/ *noun phr.* Also **wych hazel**. M16.
[from WITCH *noun*[2] + HAZEL *noun*[1].]
1 The wych elm, *Ulmus glabra*. M16.
2 A N. American shrub, *Hamamelis virginica* (family Hamamelidaceae), with yellow flowers; an extract of the leaves and bark of this shrub used to treat bruises, sprains, etc. Also, any other shrub of the genus *Hamamelis*, *esp.* the winter-flowering *H. mollis*, of China, and *H. japonica*, of Japan, both grown in gardens. Cf. HAMAMELIS. L17.

witch-hunt /ˈwɪtʃhʌnt/ *noun*. L19.
[from WITCH *noun*[1] + HUNT *noun*[2].]
1 A search for witches; a persecution of a person or persons suspected or accused of witchcraft. L19.
2 *fig.* A usu. malicious campaign against a group of people with unpopular or unorthodox views or behaviour, esp. Communists; a campaign *against* an individual. M20.
■ **witch-hunter** *noun* (*a*) *Hist.* a witch-finder; (*b*) *fig.* a person who takes part in or advocates a witch-hunt: M19. **witch-hunting** *noun* (*a*) *Hist.* the action or process of seeking out and obtaining evidence against people suspected of witchcraft; (*b*) participation in or advocacy of a witch-hunt: M17.

witch-hunt /ˈwɪtʃhʌnt/ *verb*. L19.
[Back-form. from WITCH-HUNTING.]
1 *verb intrans*. Take part in or advocate a witch-hunt. L19.
2 *verb trans. fig*. Subject to a witch-hunt. M20.

witching /ˈwɪtʃɪŋ/ *adjective*. LME.
[from WITCH *verb*[1] + -ING[2].]
1 That casts a spell; enchanting, bewitching. *lit. & fig*. LME.
2 Of or pertaining to witchcraft or sorcery. L16.

📖 **2** SHAKES. *Haml*. 'Tis now the very witching time of night. **the witching hour** midnight, the time when witches are proverbially active.

■ **witchingly** *adverb* bewitchingly M18.

witdoek /ˈvɪtdʊk/ *noun*. *S. Afr*. Pl. **-e** /-ə/, **-s**. L20.
[Afrikaans, from *wit* white + DOEK.]
A member of a largely black conservative vigilante movement operating in the townships around Cape Town, identifiable by the wearing of a white cloth or scarf about the head. Usu. in *pl*.

wite /wʌɪt/ *noun*[1]. Long *obsolete* exc. *Hist*.
[Old English *wita* weak masc. (also *gewita* in sense 2) = Old Frisian *wita*, Old Saxon *giwito* (Middle Low German *wete*) witness, Old High German *wizo* (*giwizo* witness), from Germanic stem rel. to WIT *verb*.]
1 A wise man, a councillor; *spec*. a member of the witan. OE.
2 A witness. OE–ME.

wite /wʌɪt/ *noun*[2]. *obsolete* exc. *dial*. & *Hist*. Also **wyte**.
[Old English *wīte* = Old Frisian *wīte*, Old Saxon *wīti*, Old High German *wīzzi*, Old Norse *víti* punishment, based on var. of Germanic verb meaning 'know': see WIT *verb*.]
1 Punishment; penalty; pain inflicted in punishment or torture, *esp*. the torments of hell. Long *arch*. OE. ▸**b** *Hist*. In Anglo-Saxon law, a fine imposed for certain offences or privileges. Freq. as second elem. in compounds, esp. ***bloodwite*** (see BLOOD *noun*). OE.
2 Blame, reproach; blameworthiness, fault. Now *Scot*. & *north*. ME. ▸†**b** The person who or thing which is to blame. *Scot*. E16–E18.
†**3** Offence, wrongdoing; a wrong. Only in ME.

📖 **2** R. L. STEVENSON But now it's done, Alan; and who's to bear the wyte of it?

■ **witeless** *adjective* (*Scot*., now *rare*) blameless M16.

wite /wʌɪt/ *verb trans*. *obsolete* exc. *Scot*. & *north*. Also **wyte**.
[Old English *wītan*, corresp. to Old Frisian *wīta*, Old Saxon *wītan*, Old High German *wīzan*, Old Norse *víta*, Gothic *-weitan* (*fraweitan* avenge), rel. to prec. Cf. TWIT *verb*.]
1 Lay the blame for (a thing) on a person etc. (Foll. by *on*, *to*, *upon*.) OE. ▸†**b** Impute as guilt. Also, in neutral sense, impute. LME–M16.
2 Impute the guilt to, blame, (a person). (Foll. by *for*, †*of*, *with* the thing imputed.) ME.

witenagemot /ˈwɪt(ə)nəɡɪˌməʊt/ *noun*.
[Old English *witena gemōt* assembly of wise men: see WITAN, WITE *noun*[1] and GEMOT, MOOT *noun*[1].]
Hist. The assembly of the witan, the national council of Anglo-Saxon times; *transf*. a modern parliament or other deliberative assembly.

📖 M. FOSTER The first select Witenagemote of the science of the world.

witereden /ˈwɪtərɛd(ə)n/ *noun*.
[Old English *wīterǣden*, from *wīte* WITE *noun*[2] + *rǣden* -RED.]
Hist. A fine (formerly erron. explained as a royal imposition or aid).

witful /ˈwɪtfʊl, -f(ə)l/ *adjective*. ME.
[from WIT *noun* + -FUL.]
†**1** Wise, sagacious. ME–E17.
2 Full of wit (in modern senses). M18.

witgat /ˈvɪtxat/ *noun*. *S. Afr*. E19.
[Afrikaans, from *wit* white + *gat* hole.]
Any of several trees of the genus *Boscia*, of the caper family, which have pale pitted bark and are found in dry areas of southern Africa; *esp*. the evergreen *B. albitrunca*. Also ***witgatboom*** [Afrikaans *boom* tree].

with /wɪθ/ *noun*[1]. E18.
[Perh. alt. of WIDTH.]
A partition between flues in a chimney stack.

with *noun*[2] var. of WITHE *noun*.

with /wɪð/ *preposition & adverb*.
[Old English *wiþ* = Old Frisian *with*, Old Saxon *wiþ*, prob. shortening of Germanic preposition repr. by WITHER *adjective & adverb*.]
▸**A** *preposition*. **I** Denoting opposition and derived notions.
1 †**a** In a position opposite; over against. OE–ME. ▸**b** Close to, alongside. Chiefly in ***close in with***. *obsolete* exc. NAUTICAL. OE.
2 In exchange or payment for. *obsolete* exc. *dial*. OE.
3 After words expr. conflict, dispute, competition, etc.: in opposition to; against. (Passing into sense 5 below.) OE. ▸†**b** As a defence or protection against. OE–LME.
4 After words expr. separation or release: from. Long *obsolete* exc. as in sense 14 below. OE.

📖 **1b** T. NORTH By force of weather driven with the coast of Sicile. **3** C. KINGSLEY He challenges all comers to wrestle with him. H. SPENCER A belief utterly at variance with probability. H. JAMES The notion of a battle with her only son. B. MALAMUD The Knights returned to their home grounds for a three-game set with the . . Reds. ***at war with***, ***compete with***, ***fight with***, ***go to law with***, ***quarrel with***, ***struggle with***, ***vie with***, etc.

▸**II** Denoting personal relation etc.
5 After words denoting speech or other communication or transactions between persons (with the person as obj.). OE. ▸**b** After words expressing conduct or feeling: towards (a person etc.). OE. ▸**c** Foll. by refl. pronoun, after words denoting reflection, soliloquy, etc. *arch*. M16.
6 Expr. a general relation to a person or thing, usu. as affected in some way by the action etc. spoken of: in the matter of, in regard to; in the performance, functioning, use, etc., of. OE. ▸**b** Used in emphatic commands, esp. after adverbs used with ellipsis of verb. LME.
7 In the estimation of; in the eyes of. OE.
8 In the case of; *esp*. so far as the practice or experience of (a person) is concerned. ME.

📖 **5** C. THIRLWALL To give audience to all who had business to transact with him. M. PATTISON During Edward's wars our commerce with France was wholly broken off. A. GARVE I'm . . anxious to square my account with him. J. HIGGINS If you're thinking of raising my case again with the Home Secretary. F. FORSYTH He had exchanged no words with the barman. ***deal with***, ***interfere with***, ***speak with***, ***trifle with***, etc. **b** C. E. RIDDELL You may as well be frank with me. J. K. JEROME I . . lost my temper with him. R. WEST A woman . . hopelessly in love with a man. A. HUNTER Since when were you on first-name terms with His Nibs? ***cross with***, ***gentle with***, ***patient with***, etc. **6** M. EDGEWORTH What do you want with me? E. A. FLOYER I . . soon got pretty handy with my sextant. F. W. ROBINSON If you will help me on with my coat. E. HEMINGWAY What's the matter with you, son? G. VIDAL I tried to continue with my writing. E. TAYLOR She may have made a mistake with her dates. R. WILKES Florence was becoming irritated by Charles's meanness with money. **b** B. H. MALKIN Get along with you, and go to bed. L. CARROLL Off with his head! J. THURBER He said to hell with the flag. **7** A. L. ROWSE He was very unpopular with the big boys. M. MILLAR What you want doesn't carry much weight with us. **8** F. COWLES I fell into the habit . . common with lonely people, of . . watching the passers-by. O. NASH With women's watches you need a microscope to read them. L. SANDERS You want her to suffer. It's . . become an obsession with you.

▸**III** Denoting agreement (or disagreement) in some respect.
9 Indicating relation to a standard or stated term, after words expr. comparison, resemblance, equality, identity, correspondence, agreement, disagreement, etc. OE.
10 Expr. unanimity: (as a member) of the same party or cause as; of the same opinion as. Chiefly in ***be with***. ME.
11 In the same way as (another person); as — does or did, is or was, etc. ME. ▸**b** As well or as thoroughly as (a person). Chiefly foll. by *the* and superl. adjective used *absol*. Now only in ***with the best (of them)*** s.v. BEST *adjective*. ME.
12 a Expr. coincidence in time: at the very moment of or immediately consequent upon (an event); at the same moment as (another doing or experiencing the same thing). ME. ▸**b** In the course of; as a consequence of the lapse of. Freq. in ***with time***. LME. ▸**c** Expr. correspondence of variation: at the same rate as; in proportion to. L17.
13 In the same direction as; *esp*. in the direction of the movement of (the tide, wind, sun, etc.). L15.

📖 **9** W. IRVING Her slender form contrasted finely with his . . person. T. HARDY She turned . . and faced in the same direction with himself. R. KIPLING The snow lay level with the window-sill. I. MURDOCH Godlike beings in comparison with whom my own parents seemed insignificant. *BBC Wildlife* As with other primates, male chimpanzees have a clear hierarchy. ***compare with***, ***correspond with***, ***identical with***, ***parallel with***, ***on equal terms with***, etc. **10** NEB *Matt*. 12:30 He who is not with me is against me. *Manchester Examiner* Only one Liberal voted with the Conservatives. W. S. BLUNT Morris is with me about Ireland. **11** T. ARNOLD I believe with you that savages could never civilize themselves. I. MURDOCH He ought to have remained, with Pinn, bland . . and aloof. **b** R. GREENE A young stripling . . that can sleep with the soundest, eate with the hungriest. **12a** T. L. PEACOCK John . . was determining to take possession with the first light of morning. R. S. SURTEES Mrs. Jorrocks, and Benjamin, were up with the lark. E. FITZGERALD Alas, that Spring should vanish with the Rose! *New Scientist* With the discovery of the sabkha dolomite, the picture changed. **b** J. R. ACKERLEY With the passage of time . . my father's habits altered. **c** B. WOLFE With each passing day the sportscaster's voice lost a few more decibels. *Nature* The abundance of condensible vapour will always decrease with height in a cloud. **13** J. MOXON Joyners work as well upon the Traverse . . as with the Grain of the wood.

▸**IV** Denoting association or accompaniment.
14 After words expr. combination, association, mixture, juxtaposition, etc., indicating that to which a person or thing is joined, connected, etc. Also, by analogy, after words, esp. verbs, expr. separation, as ***break***, ***part***. Cf. sense 4 above. OE.
15 Joining in the same activity, experience, etc., as; *spec*. acting on the same side as (another lawyer) in a case. ME.
16 a Foll. by pers. pronoun after *bring*, *carry*, *take* and similar verbs: as part of one's accompanying baggage, entourage, etc. ME. ▸**b** In the possession, keeping, or charge of. ME. ▸**c** In the character of; as a quality of. Chiefly with ***way***. LME.
17 In the company, society, or presence of; as a partner or companion to; *spec*. (***a***) at the house or staying as a guest of; in the household or service of; (***b***) in the employment of, working for, (a company etc.). Also, in the company of (a person etc.) as guide or protector. ME.
18 Having in one's possession or keeping; bringing, carrying, wearing, containing, riding, driving, etc. ME. ▸**b** Having (developing offspring) in the womb. Now *literary* exc. of animals. ME.
19 Having, possessing, (a feature, distinctive part, adjunct, or characteristic). Also (with explanatory or causal force) having as one does, did, etc.; considering, in view of. ME. ▸**b** Though having or possessing. Usu. foll. by noun qualified by *all*. LME.
20 a Accompanied by; having (a person or thing) as an addition or accompaniment. Freq. used to connect two nouns, in sense 'and — as well'. ME. ▸**b** Including, counting. ME. ▸**c** As part of the same combination, arrangement, outfit, etc., as; in the same category as. LME. ▸**d** *ellipt*. (passing into *adverb*). Having (an ingredient implied by the context) added, e.g. ***hot brandy with*** (= with sugar), ***coffee with*** (= with cream). *slang*. M19.
†**21** In addition to, besides; (with neg.) except. ME–L16.
22 Expr. the manner, emotional or mental state, etc., in which an action is carried out: in a manner characterized by (a quality etc.); under the influence of (an emotion etc.). ME.
23 Indicating a circumstance accompanying the action expressed by the verb. ME. ▸**b** In an imprecation etc., invoking misfortune at the same time on the person concerned. Long *rare* exc. in ***with a vengeance*** s.v. VENGEANCE *noun*. ME. ▸**c** When or if one has or is granted (a thing). Freq. in polite formulas, as ***with your leave***, ***with permission***, etc. LME. ▸**d** Introducing a refrain in a song or ballad. LME.
24 (Contextually.) Under the circumstance of; given the fact or circumstance of; in view of the fact of. Also, introducing an amplifying or explanatory feature, circumstance, etc. Freq. with noun qualified by pple. ME.

📖 **14** LD MACAULAY He allied himself closely with Castlemaine. *Christian World* He had never lost touch with his brethren. W. S. MAUGHAM Three girls . . wanted to come and share my squalor with me. G. ORWELL Dreams . . which have no connection with the physical world. G. GREENE I had chosen to combine my visit with the Christmas holiday. *Observer* Close to the frontier with Zaire. ***collaborate with***, ***combine with***, ***join with***, ***mingle with***, ***participate with***, ***unite with***, etc.; ***alliance with***, ***marriage with***, etc.; ***along with***, ***together with***. **15** M. KEANE She asked him to lunch with her on Thursday. R. WILKES I was playing cards with my husband. *Proverb*: Laugh and the world laughs with you; weep and you weep alone. **16a** J. R. ACKERLEY He would return . . bringing with him a present for my mother. L. SANDERS Eddie, can I take this copy with me? **b** R. WHATELY The 'burden of proof' lies with the accusers. *Times* This duty rests with the retailer. *Spectator* Investments are deposited with a bank. **c** J. H. NEWMAN What a way those fellows have with them! **17** T. HARDY Could not you go with me to show me the way . . ? P. G. WODEHOUSE He's got a job with the British Broadcasting Company. E. WAUGH You can come and buy carpets with me. M. MILLAR Peace be with you, Brothers. E. TAYLOR Miss Allot was to spend Christmas with the Townsends. V. S. PRITCHETT She is the only accompanist he can work with. G. HOUSEHOLD Both her parents had died young and she lived with her grandmother. J. HIGGINS Second-lieutenant with the Ulster Rifles. *Oxford Mail* The woman was returning . . after a night out with friends. **18** J. CONRAD Six months of knocking about at sea with valuable merchandise. F. FORSYTH If you were caught with a false driving license. J. HIGGINS The head waiter returned with their drinks himself. **b** ***with calf***, ***with foal***, ***with young***, etc. **19** T. HARDY Uniform of the period, with its immense epaulettes, . . would look strange . . now. *Harper's Magazine* She liked people with snap. CONAN DOYLE He was young . . with a strong masculine face. D. DU MAURIER Anyone with a gift for telepathy could read your . . mind. D. WELCH I must say you don't look very ill, with that colour. *Headlight* Convicted . . for using a lorry . . with inefficient brakes. B. MALAMUD How come with all your sex appeal that you never got hitched? J. HIGGINS Her English was excellent, but with a German accent. **b** W. COWPER England, with all thy faults, I love thee still. I. MURDOCH An incident . . which even the British Foreign Service, with its wide tolerance of eccentricity, could not overlook. **20a** A. RANSOME Sentenced to two years' imprisonment with hard labour. E. HEMINGWAY The doctor left three different medicines . . with instructions for giving them. D. WELCH We ordered . . green figs with cream. **b** D. E. WESTLAKE It costs around eighteen bucks, with the tax. **c** *Contemporary Review* All the neuroses should be classified with neurasthenia. C. F. BURKE A new chain to wear with his turtle neck sweater. L. SANDERS They had ale with their roast beef. **21** T. NORTH Very wise . . and with his wisdome . . very valiant. **22** S. BARING-GOULD The king escaped with difficulty. W. S. MAUGHAM They ate their simple meal with appetite. C. BAX A poet . . remembered with glowing affection. R. MAUGHAM He spoke English with a foreign accent. R. P. JHABVALA The Nawab treated him with . . exaggerated courtesy. ***with abandon***, ***with bated breath***, ***with gusto***, ***with impunity***, ***with one accord***, etc. **23** C. BAX He married again—with seemingly better results. B. MALAMUD She greeted him . . with a fresh kiss. A. GARVE He . . went off . . with scarcely a word. E. TAYLOR He . . got up with a jerk. *Oxford Mail* People went hopping mad . . with all sorts of crazy capers for charity. **b** SHAKES. *Meas. for M.* Show your knave's visage, with a pox to you! **c** E. WATERTON With these general data, I now proceed to examine some of the details. I. MURDOCH With so much rain it was hard to tell who was weeping. L. SANDERS It was an audacious scheme, but with foresight and a bit of luck, they could pull it off. ***with the exception that***, ***with the proviso that***, ***with the qualification that***, etc. **d** SHAKES. *Wint. T.* When daffodils begin to peer, With heigh! the doxy over the dale. **24** E. BOWEN He stood with his weight on one leg. G. GREENE It was odd how close we had become with Sarah gone. A. GARVE The road became very picturesque, with giant oaks . . lining the route. F. FORSYTH With the door safely shut behind him . . he went to work. D. DU MAURIER An old woman found with her throat slit. J. ROSSNER The room was very quiet with the radio off.

▸ **V** Denoting instrumentality or cause.

25 †**a** Through the medium or instrumentality of (a person). **OE–L16.** ▸**b** By the use of (a thing) as an instrument or means. Formerly also *gen.*, by means of. **ME.** ▸**c** After verbs of making etc.: out of (given materials or (now esp.) ingredients). Formerly also after verbs of subsisting: on (a food). **ME.** ▸†**d** In ref. to procreation: by (a male or female parent). **LME–E18.** ▸**e** After *begin*, *end*, and similar verbs, used to indicate the initial or final part of a proceeding, the person or thing dealt with first or last, etc. **LME.**

26 After words, esp. verbs, expr. giving, providing, filling, covering, etc.: by the addition, supply, acquisition, or possession of (a thing) as a material, content, provision, etc. **ME.**

27 As a consequence of; by reason of, on account of; in consequence of having or being full of; *esp.* from the effects of (an emotion). **ME.**

28 Expr. direct agent after pass. verb: by. Now chiefly *arch. & dial.* exc. in certain verbs used *fig.* **ME.**

📖 **25a** SHAKES. *Com. Err.* He did arrest me with an officer. **b** M. M. SHERWOOD She will be killing two birds with one stone. R. M. BALLANTYNE He walked with a crutch. P. KERLEY To map out an outline with a pencil. W. S. MAUGHAM Sibert Mason . . bought with his savings and hers a few acres. J. JOHNSTON Father made an angry gesture with his hand. J. ROSSNER Why do the Jesuits answer every question with another question? **c** SHAKES. *L.L.L.* You shall fast a week with bran and water. E. DAVID Make a fish stock with the heads and tails. **d** J. LISTER I had but two children with my wife. **e** J. RUSKIN We may close her national history with the seventeenth century. J. C. POWYS The morning . . opened . . with a sunrise out of a clear sky. D. WELCH We began the meal with insipid lettuce soup. **26** F. W. ROBERTSON Christianity . . permeates all evil with good. W. S. JEVONS China supplies us with vast quantities of tea. R. MACAULAY Both parties credited them with too much idealism. V. WOOLF A dispatch box stamped with the Royal Arms. D. WELCH Crumpets spread with anchovy paste. G. GREENE Drinking . . in some bierhaus decorated with holly. D. DU MAURIER Plates piled high with spaghetti. J. HIGGINS Everything you need you'll be provided with. **27** F. MARRYAT Jacob . . returned home well satisfied with the profit he had made. J. LONDON Genevieve sighed with relief. *Blackwood's Magazine* The ground sheet was crawling with scorpions. W. S. MAUGHAM Charley . . went white with anxiety. E. HEMINGWAY The road was dusty with cars passing. D. ABSE Uncle stood up . . shaking with rage. J. STEINBECK His forehead streamed with perspiration. *Times* Three electricians were taken to hospital with burns. N. E. HICKIN The little fields were . . yellow with cowslips. E. TAYLOR It poured with rain nearly all the time. L. SANDERS He chattered along . . making her laugh with his descriptions. M. FORSTER She . . surprised him with an open show of her affection. **28** SHAKES. *Wint. T.* He was torn to pieces with a bear. T. HERBERT Hyrcania . . is limited on the North with the Caspian Sea. J. RICE They're eaten up with envy. D. DU MAURIER John was seized with the . . thought that this was no coincidence.

Phrases & comb.: **be with** *spec.* †(*a*) be avenged on; (*b*) *colloq.* follow the reasoning etc. of. **with costs**, **with damages** (of a judgement in a lawsuit) accompanied by an order to the losing party to pay all legal expenses. **with it** (*a*) besides; in addition; (*b*) (also *attrib.*) with hyphen) aware of what is going on; alert and comprehending; *spec.* up to date, conversant with modern or fashionable ideas etc. **with-profit(s)** *adjective* (of a life assurance policy) allowing the insured to receive a share of the profits of the insurance company, usu. in the form of a bonus. **with that** *spec.* thereupon; saying, or having just said, that. **with us** *spec.* alive.

▸†**B** *adverb.* **1** With it (me, them, etc.); in company or association, together. **OE–LME.**

2 With that, with which; therewith, wherewith: = WITHAL *adverb* 2. **ME–M16.**

with- /wɪð/ *prefix* (no longer productive).
[Old English *wiþ-*.]
Prefixed to verbs and verbal derivs. (few of which survive) with the senses (*a*) 'away, back', as ***withdraw***, ***withhold***; (*b*) 'against, in opposition', as ***withstand***.

withal /wɪˈðɔːl/ *adverb & preposition. arch.* **ME.**
[Orig. two words, from WITH *preposition* + ALL *pronoun*.]

▸ **A** *adverb.* **1** Along with the rest; besides, moreover. Often in ***and withal***. **ME.** ▸**b** W. concessive force: at the same time; in spite of that. **L16.**

2 With that, with it. **ME.**

📖 **1** D. C. MURRAY She . . was so sweet and kind, and withal seemed . . so dependent on him. **b** A. MILLER He was a crank and a nuisance, but withal a . . brave man. **2** E. B. BROWNING Having spoiled the gods Of honours, crown withal thy mortal men.

▸ **B** *postpositive preposition* (placed after a verb, esp. one following a rel. pronoun, expressed or implied, governed by the preposition). = WITH *preposition*. Cf. ***therewithal***, ***wherewithal***. **ME.**

📖 J. PRESTON Whatsoever you part withall, you shall have a hundred fold in this life. W. ALLEN If such were indulgently dealt withal and tolerated. GOLDSMITH Though we took the best telescope to observe him withal.

withdraught /wɪðˈdrɑːft/ *noun. arch.* **ME.**
[from WITH- + DRAUGHT *noun*, after *withdraw* verb.]

†**1** Withdrawal. **ME–E17.** ▸**b** *spec.* Withdrawal from an action in court; a fine imposed for this. **E–M17.**

†**2** A private chamber; a closet, a recess. **L15–M16.**

3 A privy; a lavatory; a sewer. Now *local.* **L15.**

withdraw /wɪðˈdrɔː/ *noun.* Now *rare* or *obsolete.* **LME.**
[from the verb.]
Withdrawal, removal; *spec.* = WITHDRAUGHT 1b.

withdraw /wɪðˈdrɔː, wɪθ-/ *verb.* Pa. t. **-drew** /-ˈdruː/; pa. pple **-drawn** /-ˈdrɔːn/. **ME.**
[from WITH- + DRAW *verb*.]

▸ **I** *verb trans.* **1** Draw back or remove (a thing) from its place or position; take (one's eyes etc.) off something. (Foll. by *from*.) **ME.** ▸**b** Draw (a veil, curtain, etc.) back or aside; draw back (a bolt). Now *rare.* **L18.**

2 Take back or away (something bestowed or enjoyed). **ME.** ▸†**b** Cause to decrease or disappear. **LME–M16.** ▸**c** Remove (money) from a place of deposit. **L18.**

3 *fig.* **a** Take back, retract, (one's words, a statement or expression). Formerly, rescind (a judgement). **ME.** ▸**b** Remove from circulation, from the scope of an enquiry, etc. (Foll. by *from*.) **E18.** ▸**c** Refrain from proceeding with (a course of action, a proposal, etc.); cease to support (a candidate etc.). **L18.**

†**4 a** Keep back, stay (one's hand). Also, withhold (a blow). Only in **ME.** ▸**b** Keep back, withhold, (something due, customary, or necessary). **ME–L16.** ▸**c** Keep back, restrain (a person, his or her desires, etc.). **ME–M16.**

5 Draw away, deflect, divert (a person, his or her mind, etc.) from an object, pursuit, line of conduct, etc. Usu. foll. by *from*. Now *rare.* **ME.**

6 *refl.* Remove oneself *from* a place or position; *fig.* remove oneself *from* a condition, sphere, society, etc. Now *rare.* **ME.** ▸†**b** Cease *to do*, refrain *from* doing. Only in **ME.** ▸**c** Cause (a person) to undergo withdrawal from an addictive drug. **M20.**

7 Cause (a person) to retire from a position; *spec.* cause (troops) to retire from a position or engagement. (Foll. by *from*.) **LME.** ▸**b** LAW. Remove (a juror) from the panel in order to put an end to the proceedings. **L17.**

📖 **1** W. CATHER Alexandra tried to withdraw her hand, but Frank held on to it. **2** D. ATHILL An Egyptian whose passport had been withdrawn because he was a Communist. E. FORSEY The Quebec government, having given a tentative consent, withdrew it. **c** *Guardian* Savers withdrew £206.9 million more than they invested. **3a** *Guardian* He challenged the Opposition to withdraw its allegation. **b** H. R. FORSTER The next two lots were withdrawn. *She* Saab agreed to withdraw an advert . . after a complaint from Friends of the Earth. **c** J. PURSEGLOVE In 1984 the Thames Water Authority withdrew its drainage proposals for Otmoor. *Guardian* She withdrew her claim for unfair dismissal. **5** J. WAIN They've withdrawn their energy from everything else and put it into one thing. **6** DICKENS I am withdrawing myself from engagements of all kinds. **7** THACKERAY Walter . . was withdrawn from Eton, and put into a merchant's house. G. GREENE The Americans had withdrawn their ambassador. D. FRASER The British Army had been withdrawn from the Aisne front . . and moved northward.

▸ **II** *verb intrans.* **8** Depart or retire from a place or position, from a person's presence, to another room or a private place. (Foll. by *from*.) **ME.** ▸**b** Of combatants: retire from a field of battle, a contest, an advanced position, etc. **ME.** ▸†**c** Of water: subside, ebb. **ME–E17.** ▸†**d** Of an immaterial thing, a condition, etc.: depart, disappear. Only in **ME.**

9 Remove oneself or retire from a society or community, from public life, etc.; abandon participation (in an enterprise etc.). **ME.**

†**10** Foll. by *of*, *to do*: cease or refrain from doing something. Only in **ME.**

11 In parliamentary procedure: retract an unparliamentary remark etc. at the insistence of other MPs. Usu. in *imper.* **L18.**

12 Practise coitus interruptus. **M20.**

13 Cease to use an addictive drug, undergo withdrawal from an addiction. **L20.**

📖 **8** G. A. BIRMINGHAM The servant, after leaving coffee on the table, finally withdrew. E. BOWEN They withdrew early to their own rooms. C. S. FORESTER Hunter and Wingatt heard what she said and withdrew out of earshot. **b** H. MACMILLAN As the Israeli troops withdrew those of the United Nations occupied the territory behind them. **9** G. STEINER The holy man . . withdraws . . from the temptations of worldly action. A. GRAY I want you to withdraw from this case and start on someone more important. A. F. LOEWENSTEIN When . . told . . she wanted to go to the party alone, he'd withdrawn into wounded silence. **withdraw into oneself** become reserved or uncommunicative. ***withdraw into one's shell***: see SHELL *noun*.

■ **withdrawable** *adjective* **M19.**

withdrawal /wɪðˈdrɔː(ə)l/ *noun.* **E19.**
[from WITHDRAW *verb* + -AL[1], repl. the earlier WITHDRAWMENT.]

1 The act of retiring or retreating from a place or position. **E19.** ▸**b** PSYCHIATRY & PSYCHOLOGY. The state or process of psychic retreat from objective reality or social involvement. **E20.**

2 The act of taking back or away what has been granted, possessed, etc. **M19.** ▸**b** The removal of money etc. from a place of deposit. **M19.**

3 The act of withdrawing a person or thing from a place or position; *esp.* the removal of troops by way of retreat. **M19.** ▸**b** EDUCATION. The (usu. temporary) withdrawal of a child from class for remedial teaching. **M20.**

4 The retraction of a statement, proposal, etc. **M19.**

5 Cessation of use or provision of a drug; *spec.* the interruption of doses of an addictive drug, with resulting craving and physical reactions. **L19.**

6 = COITUS *interruptus*. **L19.**

📖 **5** D. W. GOODWIN The better the taste of the food, the harder the withdrawal.

Comb.: **withdrawal slip** a form which must be filled in when withdrawing money from a bank etc.; **withdrawal symptoms** unpleasant pathophysiological reactions resulting from the process of ceasing to take an addictive drug.

withdrawer /wɪðˈdrɔːə/ *noun.* **LME.**
[from WITHDRAW *verb* + -ER[1].]
A person who withdraws; *spec.* in SCOTTISH HISTORY, a person who did not conform to the Established Church in the 17th century.

withdrawing /wɪðˈdrɔːɪŋ/ *verbal noun.* **ME.**
[from WITHDRAW *verb* + -ING[1].]
The action of WITHDRAW *verb*.
Comb.: **withdrawing-chamber** (*Hist.*), **withdrawing-room** *arch.* a room to withdraw to; = DRAWING-ROOM 1.

withdrawment /wɪðˈdrɔːm(ə)nt/ *noun.* Now *rare.* **M17.**
[from WITHDRAW *verb* + -MENT.]
= WITHDRAWAL.

withdrawn /wɪðˈdrɔːn/ *adjective.* **E17.**
[pa. pple of WITHDRAW *verb*.]
That is or has been withdrawn; *esp.* (*a*) (of a place) private, secluded; (*b*) (of mental state) detached; PSYCHOLOGY characterized by isolation and loss of contact with objective reality (cf. WITHDRAWAL 1b).
■ **withdrawnness** /-n-n-/ *noun* **E20.**

withdrew *verb pa. t.* of WITHDRAW *verb*.

withe /wɪθ, wɪð, wʌɪð/ *noun.* Also **with.**
[Old English *wiþþe* = Old Frisian *withthe*, Middle Dutch *wisse* (Dutch *wis*), Old High German *wit*, *withi*, *wid*, *widi*, Old Norse *við*, *viðja* (cf. Gothic *kunawida* bonds), from Germanic, ult. from base repr. by WIRE *noun*. Cf. WITHY *noun*.]

1 A band consisting of a tough flexible shoot of a willow etc., or of several such shoots twisted together; such a shoot used for binding, tying, or plaiting. **OE.** ▸†**b** A willow wand or garland carried into the monarch's or a nobleman's house at Easter; the ceremony or festivity itself. **LME–L16.** ▸**c** *gen.* A pliant shoot or bough. **E19.**

†**2** A halter, properly one made with withes. **ME–L17.**

3 Any of several plants with flexible shoots; *esp.* (*a*) (now *dial.*) a willow; (*b*) *W. Indies* (more fully ***black withe***) a shrub, *Trichostigma fruticosum* (family Phytolaccaceae), whose stems are used for making baskets. **ME.**

4 In technical uses: (*a*) NAUTICAL an iron ring through which a spar is secured to a mast or boom; (*b*) a handle of elastic material for a tool, used to absorb shock. **M19.**

📖 **1c** R. C. PRAED A trailing withe of orange begonia. **3** ***prickly withe***.

Comb.: **withe-rod** either of two N. American viburnums, *Viburnum nudum* and *V. cassinoides*; a thin flexible twig from such a shrub.

withe /wɪð, wʌɪð/ *verb trans.* Now *dial. & US.* LME.
[from the noun.]
1 Twist like a withe. Now *rare.* LME.
2 Bind with a withe or withes; *US* take (deer) with a noose made of withes. E17.

withen /ˈwɪð(ə)n, ˈwʌɪð(ə)n/ *noun. obsolete* exc. *dial.* ME.
[from WITHE *noun* or WITHY *noun* after *aspen* etc.]
A withy, a willow.

wither /ˈwɪðə/ *noun*¹. E16.
[App. from WITHER *adverb* + -S¹.]
sing. & (usu.) in *pl.* **1** In a horse, ox, sheep, etc., the highest part of the back, lying between the shoulder-blades. E16. ▸**b** *fig.* [After Shakes. *Haml.*] The emotions, the sensibilities. Chiefly in ***wring the withers*** (see also UNWRUNG). E17.
†**2** In *pl.* The part of a saddle which comes over a horse's withers. E–M18.

📖 **1b** M. WESLEY Emily's pathetic accents would wring the best of withers.

Comb.: **witherwrung** *adjective* injured in the withers.

wither /ˈwɪðə/ *noun*². M17.
[from WITHER *verb.*]
†**1** A disease of cows. M17–E18.
2 In tea manufacture, the process of drying tea leaves before roasting. L19.

wither /ˈwɪðə/ *adjective & adverb. obsolete* exc. *dial.*
[Old English *wiþer* adverb & adjective, related to *wiþer* preposition = Old Saxon *wiþar*, Old High German *widar*, Old Norse *viðr*, Gothic *wiþra*, from Indo-European root denoting separation or division.]
▶ **A** *adjective.* **1** Orig., hostile, adverse. Now (*dial.*), fierce. OE.
†**2** Contrary, opposite; (of a side) wrong. Only in ME.
▶†**B** *adverb.* Hostilely; perversely; fiercely. Only in ME.

wither /ˈwɪðə/ *verb.* LME.
[App. var. of WEATHER *verb*, ult. differentiated for certain senses.]
▶ **I** *verb intrans.* **1** Of a plant: become dry and shrivel up. Freq. in fig. context. LME. ▸**b** Of a crop: become dry. Now only in tea manufacture, (of tea leaves) become dry before roasting (cf. sense 4b below). E16.
2 Of the body or its parts, a person, etc.: become shrunken from age, disease, etc.; lose vigour or robustness. (Foll. by *away.*) LME.
3 *fig.* Cease to flourish; languish, decline, fall into decay. (Foll. by *away.*) E16. ▸**b** *spec.* In Marxist theory: ***wither away***, (of the State) disappear as no longer being necessary after the dictatorship of the proletariat has effected the necessary changes in society. E20.

📖 **1** K. LINES No rain fell, and the grain withered in the parched ground. **wither on the vine** *fig.* perish for lack of attention. **2** B. MASON His physique fell away to a shrunken body and a leg withered from poliomyelitis. R. FULLER We're all growing old and withering away. **3** D. C. PEATTIE The desert days open, blaze, and wither one after another. S. MIDDLETON None of these women had gone out of her way, and thus temptation withered.

▶ **II** *verb trans.* **4** †**a** Air (clothes). M16–E17. ▸**b** Dry (tea leaves) before roasting. M18.
5 Cause (a plant, flower, etc.) to dry up and shrivel. M16.
6 Cause (the body or its powers) to shrink, become wasted or decayed, or lose freshness. L16.
7 *fig.* Cause to decline; blight, affect injuriously. Now chiefly *hyperbol.*, mortify (a person) with a look of extreme contempt. L16.

📖 **5** E. CLODD The fierce heat that withered the approaching harvest. **6** J. DYER Enfeebling vice Withers each nerve. **7** B. BAINBRIDGE Whenever the poor man asks her opinion . . she withers him with her eyes. D. W. WINNICOTT Sarcasm in a teacher has withered the growing point of many a child's learning.

▪ **withered** *ppl adjective* that has withered or lost its vitality; *arch.* (of a limb) paralysed: L15. **witheredness** *noun* M16. **witherer** *noun* (*rare*) a person who or thing which withers E19.

withering /ˈwɪð(ə)rɪŋ/ *noun.* E16.
[from WITHER *verb* + -ING¹.]
1 The action of WITHER *verb.* E16.
2 In *pl.* Withered branches or brushwood, used in making fences etc. M19.

withering /ˈwɪð(ə)rɪŋ/ *ppl adjective.* L16.
[from WITHER *verb* + -ING².]
1 Fading, decaying (*lit. & fig.*). L16.
2 Causing to fade or decay (*lit. & fig.*). Chiefly *hyperbol.*, of scornful looks, severe criticism, etc.: having a paralysing effect. L16.

📖 **2** E. BLISHEN He'd been visited by Mr Jepp, who'd subjected his lesson to a withering analysis. I. BANKS Obviously my withering look needed more work in front of the mirror.

▪ **witheringly** *adverb* E19.

witherite /ˈwɪðərʌɪt/ *noun.* L18.
[from William *Withering* (1741–99), English physician and scientist who first described it: see -ITE¹.]
MINERALOGY. A scarce orthorhombic mineral of the aragonite group, native barium carbonate, occurring as white, grey, or yellowish crystals, masses, etc., especially in veins of galena.

witherling /ˈwɪðəlɪŋ/ *noun.* Long *arch.* E16.
[from WITHER *verb* + -LING¹.]
A withered branch. Also, a stunted person.

withernam /ˈwɪðənɑːm/ *noun.* ME.
[Law French (whence Anglo-Latin *withernamium*), app. from Old Norse *viðrnám*, from *viðr* WITHER *adverb* + *nám* NAAM.]
LAW (now *Hist.*).
1 (In an action of replevin, where the goods distrained have been eloigned) the taking by the sheriff of the distrainor's own goods to an equivalent amount and delivering them to the plaintiff. Also, the writ, more fully ***capias in withernam***, commanding the sheriff to do this. ME.
2 A process of distress (or arrest) for debt, formerly current in the Cinque Ports. ME.

withershin *adjective*, **-shins** *adverb & adjective* vars. of WIDDERSHINS.

withery /ˈwɪð(ə)ri/ *adjective. rare.* E17.
[from WITHER *verb* + -Y¹.]
Inclined to wither; wilting.

withhold /wɪðˈhəʊld/ *verb.* Pa. t. **-held** /-ˈhɛld/; pa. pple **-held**, (*arch.*) **-holden** /-ˈhəʊld(ə)n/. ME.
[from WITH- + HOLD *verb.*]
1 *verb trans.* Restrain or hold back from action; keep under restraint. (Foll. by *from*, †*to do.*) ME. ▸†**b** *verb trans.* Keep off, ward off. LME–M16. ▸†**c** Prevent (a thing) from being done. Foll. by *that, to be done.* LME–M18. ▸**d** Keep separate *from. rare.* E16. ▸†**e** *verb intrans.* Refrain from doing something. Foll. by *from, to do.* M17–E19.
2 *verb trans.* Keep back (what belongs to, is due to, or is desired by another); refrain from giving, granting, or allowing. ME.
†**3** *verb trans.* Detain; keep in custody or under control. ME–E18.
†**4** *verb trans.* Keep in use or possession; *esp.* retain in the memory. ME–L15. ▸**b** Keep attached to one's person or engaged in one's service. ME–E16.
†**5** *verb trans.* Keep, maintain, preserve. Only in ME.

📖 **1** DEFOE So I withheld my Passion, though I was indeed enrag'd to the highest Degree. HENRY FIELDING Had not some awe of the company . . withheld his rage. P. WARUNG Blake . . though tempted, yet withheld himself from yielding. **2** *Times* The identity of the adopting parents should be withheld from the natural mother. M. RENAULT To offer or withhold her love in a system of rewards and punishments.

▪ **withholdable** *adjective* E19. **withholder** *noun* LME. **withholdment** *noun* (*rare*) = WITHHOLDING *verbal noun* M17.

withholding /wɪðˈhəʊldɪŋ/ *verbal noun.* LME.
[from WITHHOLD *verb* + -ING¹.]
The action of WITHHOLD *verb*; an instance of this.
Comb.: **withholding rate** *US* the rate for a withholding tax; **withholding table** *US* a table showing amounts of tax to be deducted from a dividend payment, salary, etc.; **withholding tax** (orig. *US*) a tax deducted at source, *spec.* one levied by some countries on interest or dividends paid to a person resident outside that country.

within /wɪðˈɪn/ *adverb, preposition, adjective, & noun.*
[Late Old English *wiþinnan*, from WITH *preposition & adverb* + *innan* (adverb & preposition) 'within', assim. to IN *adverb.*]
▶ **A** *adverb.* (In most senses opp. WITHOUT *adverb.*) *arch. & literary.*
1 In the interior, on the inner side; inside, internally. LOE. ▸**b** In the limits of a region; inside a State, organization, etc. LOE. ▸**c** In this document; herein. Now only LAW. LME.
2 *fig.* In the inward being; in the soul or heart, inwardly. LOE.
3 *spec.* In or into the house; indoors. Also, in the inner part of the house; (in stage-directions) behind the scenes. ME.

📖 **1** I. ASIMOV A small . . flower, yellow without and white-streaked within. **b** *Marxism Today* Capitalism . . faces an enemy within. **c** *Observer* To complete the purchase . . subject to the stipulations within mentioned. **2** J. DAVIDSON Be your own star, for strength is from within. **3** J. WESLEY The rain obliged me to preach within.

▶ **B** *preposition.* **1** Inside or not beyond the limits or boundaries of (a place); inside (specified boundaries). LOE. ▸**b** = IN *preposition* 1. *arch. & Scot.* ME. ▸**c** To the interior of; into. Now *rare* or *obsolete.* ME. ▸**d** *ellipt.* (passing into *adverb*). In place-names: lying within an area implied from the context, e.g. ***Bishopsgate Within*** (i.e. within the walls of London), ***Hensington Within*** (i.e. within the borough of Woodstock). LME. ▸**e** Among (or to) the membership of (a class, society, etc.); included in, forming part of, etc. Also, forming part of (a larger unit) but able to be treated independently; esp. in ***a play within a play*** s.v. PLAY *noun.* L17. ▸**f** On the inner (esp. landward) side of; further in than. Now *rare* or *obsolete.* M18.
2 *fig.* In the inner being, soul, or mind of. Chiefly in ***within oneself*** (see below). LOE.
†**3** Among (people); in the house or possession of. ME–E17.
4 Expr. temporal limits: (**a**) before the end of (a period); also, not more than — ago; (**b**) between the beginning and end of (a period). ME. ▸†**b** At some time during. L15–M17.
5 Not beyond or in excess of; by a degree or amount, at a distance, etc., of no more than. Freq. expr. a small margin of error, or the difference by which a measurement etc. falls short of a figure. LME.
6 *fig.* In the scope or sphere of action of (authority, knowledge, a law, etc.). L15.
7 a Expr. range of action or perception: inside, not beyond; close enough to be reached by. M16. ▸**b** Inside the guard or defences of. Chiefly FENCING, on the inside of (one's sword, arm, etc.). Now *rare.* M16.

📖 **1** I. WATTS To leave Obscurities in the Sentence, by confining it within too narrow Limits. LD MACAULAY Privileged districts, within which the Papal government had no . . power. J. CONRAD Her whole body swayed within the loose wrapper. **b** KEATS It shall comfort me within the tomb. **c** SHAKES. *Temp.* I would Have sunk the sea within the earth. **e** A. WHITE The importance of being in an organised body and having true friends within that body. *Listener* Fitzgerald was featured creating . . short stories . . . This device allowed for a film within a film. **2** D. H. LAWRENCE Her clear face scarcely showed the elation which rose within her. **4** R. DAHL If a black mamba bit you, you died within the hour. **5** D. EDEN Two women had baby girls within an hour of one another. J. THURBER I stood within a few feet of where the . . girl and I had sat for lunch. R. WILKES She had always lived within her income. **6** J. CONRAD No sailing within the meaning of our charter-party would ever take place. G. GREENE The examinations . . have to be rather simple—within the capacity of the tutors. **7a** T. HARDY She could feel her antagonist's arm within her grasp. X. HERBERT This island lay within rifle-shot of the mainland. J. WAIN Milk-bars within striking distance of American airfields. P. KAVANAGH There was wealth within his view. ***within earshot***, ***within sight***, ***within striking distance***, etc.

Phrases: †**within land** inland. **within oneself** (**a**) in one's inner thoughts or feelings; (**b**) so as to be self-contained or independent, without external connection (now *dial.*); †(**c**) in control of oneself; (**d**) living within the limits of one's own resources, without external aid (now *dial.*); (**e**) not beyond one's normal capacity of exertion.
▶ **C** *adjective.* That is within. Formerly, (of a letter or document) enclosed. *rare.* M18.
▶ **D** *noun.* That which is within or inside. Chiefly *fig.* E20.

within-door /wɪðˈɪndɔː/ *adverb & adjective.* Now *rare.* L16.
[from WITHIN *preposition* + DOOR. Cf. INDOOR.]
▶ **A** *adverb.* = INDOORS. L16.
▶ **B** *adjective.* = INDOOR. E17.

within doors /wɪðˈɪn dɔːz/ *adverbial phr. arch.* Also **within-doors.** L16.
[formed as prec. + -S¹. Cf. INDOORS.]
= INDOORS.

withinside /wɪðˈɪnsʌɪd/ *adverb & preposition.* Now *arch. & dial.* Also **within side.** L16.
[from WITHIN + SIDE *noun*, after INSIDE.]
▶ **A** *adverb.* **1** On the inner side. L16.
2 In (or to) the inner part; *spec.* indoors. L16.
Phrases: **withinside of** inside, within.
▶ **B** *preposition.* In the inner part or on the inner side of; inside, within. L17.
▪ **withinsides** *adverb* L19.

withness /ˈwɪðnɪs/ *noun. rare.* E20.
[from WITH *preposition* + -NESS.]
The fact of being with someone or something; collocation, association.

without /wɪðˈaʊt/ *adverb, preposition, conjunction, & noun.*
[Late Old English *wiþūtan*, from WITH *preposition & adverb* + *ūtan* from the outside.]
▶ **A** *adverb.* Now *literary & formal.* (For other apparent examples of the adverb see senses B.1b, 12 below.)
1 On the outside or outer surface; externally. LOE.
2 Outside the place mentioned or implied; *esp.* outside the house or room. LOE. ▸**b** Outside a body or community; not among the membership. Now only with allus. to *1 Corinthians* 5:12. ME.
3 *fig.* Outside the inward being or soul; in relation to others than the self. LOE.

📖 **2** J. BUCHAN He would leave the House . . and join the young men without. **b** A. MARSH-CALDWELL The secrets of my trade . . not to be lightly communicated to those who are without. **3** H. MARTINEAU You will be at ease without and at peace within.

▶ **B** *preposition.* Also (*arch.*) **withouten** /-ˈaʊt(ə)n/.
▶ **I** Outside, beyond (in various senses). Opp. WITHIN *preposition.* Now *literary.*
1 On, at, or (*arch.*) to the outside of (an area, receptacle, etc.); outside. LOE. ▸**b** *ellipt.* (passing into *adverb*). Outside something implied from the context. Chiefly in place-names, as ***Bishopsgate Without*** (= without the City walls). ME. ▸**c** On the outer side of; (in or to the space) beyond. E17.

2 *fig.* Not within the limits of; external(ly) to. **OE.**
3 Outside the range of (some action or perception); beyond the scope or sphere of action of. Now *rare.* **M16.**

📖 **1** *Christadelphian* Jesus was crucified without the gate of the city. **2** W. SPARROW One whose sources of happiness are without him. **3** E. A. KENDALL The happy consequences . . are without description.

▸**II** Senses intermediate between I and III.
†**4** Exclusive of; except. **LOE–ME.**
†**5** In addition to; besides. **ME–M16.**
▸**III** Expressing absence or privation. Opp. **WITH** *preposition.*
6 Not using or being acted on by (an instrument, means, etc.); not having the help, cooperation, etc., of (a person). **LOE.**
7 Not having with it or with one; not accompanied by, bringing, etc. **ME.** ▸**b** Not counting. *colloq.* **ME.**
8 (In a state of) not having (a thing etc.) as a possession, advantage, characteristic, etc.; destitute of. Freq. following a noun, forming a descriptive phr. equivalent to a rel. clause (= that does, did, etc., not have —) (cf. **WITH** *preposition* 19). **ME.** ▸**b** Not with (something that might be granted or obtained); not having got or received. **ME.**
9 In phrs. expr. manner, circumstance, etc.: with absence of or freedom from (a condition, effect, etc.); so as to experience or show a lack of (a feeling etc.). **ME.** ▸**b** Followed by a verbal noun: with omission or avoidance of (an action). **ME.**
10 So, or such, as not to admit the possibility of. **ME.**
11 With conditional implication: in default of, supposing the negation or omission of. Chiefly in neg. context. **ME.**
12 *ellipt.* (passing into *adverb*). In the absence of something implied from the context; *spec.* served without the omission of some ingredient (e.g. sugar). Also (usu. in neg. contexts), lacking some resource or quality, esp. money. **LME.**

📖 **6** T. HARDY He felt his way upstairs without a light. *Oxford Mail* Miss Warman would not be able to cope with the children without him. *Proverb:* You cannot make bricks without straw. **7** R. HARDY He walked free, without rifle, pack or bottle. J. HIGGINS Up on the fellside with you and don't come back without those sheep. A. CARTER She did bread pudding plain and fancy, with or without currants. M. KEANE He said he wanted to talk to her without Nurse. **8** N. HAWTHORNE It resembled an unspeakably bad dough nut, without any sweetening. D. ABSE A man without a woman in his life is driven to drink. G. GREENE He was desperate; he was without a job. Y. MENUHIN Bread was . . not to be played with in a world where some were without it. **b** LD MACAULAY He would as soon die without their absolution as with it. *Scotsman* The power which the Government have to exile Africans . . without trial. **9** V. WOOLF He is testy without much occasion. J. CONRAD He looked at it without any animosity. W. COOPER She could break social conventions without a qualm. ***without end, without fail, without a murmur, without prejudice, without warning,*** etc. **b** W. S. MAUGHAM They sat for a while without speaking. C. BAX Crabbe wrote about village life without sentimentalising it. G. GREENE You don't think I'll tell her—without you knowing? A. MCCOWEN I decided to leave RADA without completing the course. **10** S. JOHNSON These wounds . . are without cure. D. HUME The great lords . . could punish without appeal any thieves . . they caught. ***without price, without redress,*** etc. **11** F. MARRYAT Without a sense of your fault, how can repentance . . be expected? **12** E. A. FREEMAN I don't get any worship here; but I am better without.

Phrases: **not without** with a slight but appreciable amount or degree of (a feeling, quality, etc.). †**without that that**, †**without this that** *LAW:* expr. a defendant's assertion of special matter of exception or justification against the plaintiff's claim, while reserving his or her denial of the whole cause of action.
Comb.: **without-profit(s)** *adjective* (of a life assurance policy) providing normal cover but not allowing the insured to receive a share of the profits of the insurance company.

▸**C** *conjunction.* **1** ***without that***, †(*a*) except that; (*b*) (now *rare* or *obsolete*) = sense 2 below. **LOE.**
2 If . . not, unless. Also, without its being the case that. Now chiefly *dial.* & *non-standard* exc. *US.* **LME.**

📖 **2** *Listener:* Without you have a bit of class already, your town gets no new theatre. J. HIGGINS He won't be able to go to the bathroom without we know it.

▸**D** *noun.* That which is external; the outside. *rare.* **L19.**

without door /wɪð'aʊt dɔː/ *adverbial & adjectival phr. arch.* As adjective **without-door**. **ME.**
[from **WITHOUT** *preposition* + **DOOR**. Cf. **OUTDOOR**.]
▸**A** *adverbial phr.* = **OUTDOORS**. **ME.**
▸**B** *adjectival phr.* = **OUTDOOR** *adjective*; *fig.* relating to the outer world, external. **E17.**

without doors /wɪð'aʊt dɔːz/ *adverbial phr. arch.* **E17.**
[formed as prec. + **-S**[1].]
1 Out of doors, in the open air. **E17.**
2 *fig.* Outside the community. Formerly *spec.*, outside Parliament. **L17.**

withouten *preposition* see **WITHOUT** *preposition.*

withoutside /wɪð'aʊtsʌɪd/ *adverb & preposition. arch.* **L16.**
[from **WITHOUT** + **SIDE** *noun*, after **OUTSIDE**.]
▸**A** *adverb.* On the outer side; in (or to) the space outside. Opp. ***withinside.*** **L16.**

📖 C. ROSSETTI We build our houses . . Comely withoutside and within.

Phrases: **withoutside of** outside.
▸**B** *preposition.* Outside. **L17.**

withstand /wɪð'stand/ *verb.* Pa. t. & pa. pple **-stood** /-'stʊd/. **OE.**
[from **WITH-** + **STAND** *verb.*]
1 *verb trans.* Maintain one's (or its) position against; resist, oppose, esp. successfully. **OE.** ▸†**b** Contradict, gainsay. Only in **16.** ▸**c** Resist the influence or cogency of. **E18.**
2 *verb intrans.* Offer resistance or opposition. **OE.**
3 *verb trans.* †**a** Prevent (a person or thing) from doing something. Foll. by *to do, that.* **ME–L16.** ▸†**b** Keep off or away; withdraw. **LME–E16.** ▸**c** Stand in the way of; impede the performance or progress of. Now *rare* or *obsolete.* **LME.**

📖 **1** J. TYNDALL Ground to mud by an agency which the hardest rocks cannot withstand. J. K. JEROME I never could withstand an appeal for help. N. FARAH The stone houses had withstood the weather. **c** E. A. FREEMAN It seems impossible to withstand this evidence. **2** J. R. GREEN Langton prepared to withstand and rescue his country from the tyranny of John. **3c** SIR W. SCOTT The entrance of Queen Berengaria . . was withstood . . by the chamberlains.

■ **withstander** *noun* **ME.**

withwind /'wɪθwʌɪnd/ *noun.* Now *dial.*
[Old English *wiþowinde*, *wiþe-*, from *wiþo-*, *wiþe-* (rel. to **WITHE** *noun*) + *winde* (rel. to **WIND** *noun*[2]).]
Either of two bindweeds, *Convolvulus arvensis* (field bindweed) and *Calystegia sepium* (hedge bindweed).

withy /'wɪði/ *noun.*
[Old English *wīþig* rel. to Old High German *wīda* (German *Weide*), Old Norse *víðir* willow. Cf. **WITHE** *noun.* See also **WIDDY** *noun*[1].]
1 Any of the willows (genus *Salix*); *spec.* one grown for its flexible branches, *esp.* the crack-willow, *S. fragilis.* **OE.**
2 A flexible branch of a willow, esp. as used for tying or binding, as a noose, etc.; a leash, hoop, etc., made of a withy. **LME.** ▸**b** *collect.* Withies as a material. **M19.**
Comb.: **withy-bed** a thicket of withies.

withy /'wɪθi/ *adjective. rare.* **L16.**
[from **WITHE** *noun* + **-Y**[1].]
Resembling a withe in flexibility.

withywind /'wɪðɪwʌɪnd/ *noun.* Now *dial.* **L16.**
[Alt. of **WITHWIND**, after **WITHY** *noun.*]
= **WITHWIND**. Also, traveller's joy, *Clematis vitalba.*

witless /'wɪtlɪs/ *adjective.*
[Old English *witlēas*: see **WIT** *noun* + **-LESS**.]
1 Mentally handicapped; mentally ill; out of one's wits, crazy. Formerly also, stupefied, dazed. Now esp. in ***drive witless, send witless.*** **OE.** ▸**b** Out of one's wits due to extreme fear. Chiefly in ***be scared witless.*** **L20.**
2 Lacking wisdom or sense; foolish. **ME.**
†**3** Having no intellectual faculty; lacking the ability to reason. **LME–L16.**
4 Deficient in understanding; having undeveloped or imperfect intellectual power; unintelligent, stupid. Also, uncomprehending (*of* or of something specified). **M16.**
5 Not knowing; unaware or ignorant *of. arch.* **L16.**
6 Not witty; lacking the ability to make witticisms. *rare.* **M18.**

📖 **1** J. TROLLOPE It drives me witless to have to agree with Mrs Betts, but I do. **2** J. L. MOTLEY It was witless to believe that Parma contemplated any such measure. J. WILSON I want to impress her . . but I just keep up a witless chant of 'How beautiful.' **4** BROWNING The man is witless of . . The value in proportion of all things. D. R. KOONTZ She couldn't get interested in the conversations that . . Carson conducted with a witless actress. **5** J. S. BLACKIE He lay all witless of his doom.

■ **witlessly** *adverb* **L16.** **witlessness** *noun* **OE.**

witling /'wɪtlɪŋ/ *noun. arch.* & chiefly *derog.* **L17.**
[from **WIT** *noun* + **-LING**[1].]
A person who fancies himself or herself as a wit; a person who utters light or feeble witticisms.

witloof /'wɪtluːf/ *noun.* **L19.**
[Dutch, lit. 'white leaf'.]
A variety of chicory grown for blanching, with broad leaves and midribs.

witness /'wɪtnɪs/ *noun.*
[Old English *witnes*, from *wit* **WIT** *noun* + *-nes* **-NESS**.]
†**1** Knowledge, understanding, wisdom. **OE–L15.**
2 Attestation of a fact, event, or statement; testimony, evidence. Also *spec.*, open profession or testimony (to the power) of one's religious faith through one's actions or words. **OE.** ▸**b** The inward testimony of the conscience (after *2 Corinthians* 1:12). **ME.**
3 A person who gives evidence concerning matters of fact under investigation; *spec.* a person who gives evidence on oath or affirmation in a court of justice or judicial inquiry. **OE.**
4 A person who is called on, selected, or appointed to be present at a transaction, so as to be able to testify to its having taken place; *spec.* (more fully, ***attesting witness, subscribing witness***) a person who is present at the execution of a document and subscribes it in attestation thereof. **OE.** ▸†**b** A sponsor or godparent at baptism. **L16–M19.**
5 Attestation by signature, oath, etc. Chiefly in legal contexts, as ***in witness of, in witness hereof, in witness whereof,*** etc. **ME.**
6 A person present at an event etc. and able to provide information about it from personal observation. Usu. foll. by *of, to.* **ME.** ▸**b** God, heaven, or a person invoked for confirmation, to attest to one's actions, etc. Freq. in ***(as) God is my witness, be my witness that, call to witness*** below. **ME.**
7 A person or thing whose existence, condition, etc. attests or proves something; a token. Freq. foll. by *to, of.* **ME.** ▸**b** Introducing a name, designation, phrase, or clause denoting a person who or thing which provides evidence of the fact or exemplifies the statement. Also ***as witness.*** **ME.** ▸**c** *spec.* In textual criticism, a manuscript or an early version which is regarded as evidence of authority for the text. Usu. in *pl.* **M19.**
8 A person who testifies for Christ or the Christian faith by his or her actions or words; formerly *esp.* a martyr. **LME.** ▸**b** = ***Jehovah's Witness*** s.v. **JEHOVAH** *noun.* Orig. *US.* **M20.**

📖 **2** B. JOWETT Agamemnon . . if the witness of Homer be accepted, brought the greatest number of ships. M. L. KING The early Christians . . made a triumphant witness for Christ. A. S. BYATT To . . recount the true pre-history of the race through the witness of folk-tale and legend. **3** *Guardian* A key witness for the prosecution . . told the court he was hired to attack the bouncer. **6** J. S. C. ABBOTT I have been . . witness to the singular effect which the sound of a bell had upon Napoleon. *Guardian* Witnesses said the aircraft . . ploughed into several cars before breaking in two. ***ear-witness, eyewitness,*** etc. **b** DRYDEN That still I love, I call to Witness al the Pow'rs above. **7** E. A. FREEMAN Gifts yet more costly were now the witness of his personal presence. I. COLEGATE The . . gallery which he was letting without rent . . was there as witness to his concern with things other than profit. **b** V. WOOLF He was of course a gentleman; witness socks and trousers.

Phrases: ***as witness:*** see sense 7b above. ***auricular witness:*** see **AURICULAR** *adjective* 4. ***bear witness:*** see **BEAR** *verb*[1]. **call to witness** appeal to for confirmation etc. ***hearsay witness:*** see **HEARSAY** *noun.* ***hostile witness:*** see **HOSTILE** *adjective* 2. **in witness** (*obsolete* exc. as in sense 5 above) as proof (of). ***Jehovah's Witness, Jehovah Witness:*** see **JEHOVAH**. **with a witness** *arch.* with clear evidence, without a doubt; with a vengeance.
Comb.: **witness-box** an enclosure in a lawcourt from which witnesses give evidence; ***witness-stand:*** see **STAND** *noun*[1] 12b.

witness /'wɪtnɪs/ *verb.* **ME.**
[from prec.]
1 *verb trans.* Bear witness to (a fact or statement), esp. orally or in writing; testify to, attest; provide evidence of. **ME.** ▸**b** *fig.* Serve as proof of; be a token or indication of. **LME.** ▸**c** *transf.* Of a document: provide formally attested evidence of. Usu. with obj. clause. **L15.** ▸**d** Show evidence of or as to (an object of allegiance) by faithful speech or conduct; be a witness for. Now *rare.* **E16.** ▸†**e** Give evidence of by one's behaviour; evince. **L16–E18.**
2 *verb intrans.* Bear witness; testify. Now freq. foll. by *to, against.* **ME.**
3 *verb trans.* **a** Give formal or sworn evidence of (a fact etc.); depose in evidence. Now *rare* or *obsolete.* **ME.** ▸**b** Attest formally by signature; sign (a document) as a witness of its execution. **ME.** ▸**c** Be formally present as a witness of (a transaction). **LME.**
4 *verb trans.* Be a witness of (an event etc.); experience by personal observation. **L16.** ▸**b** *fig.* Of a place, time, etc.: be associated with (a fact or event); be the scene or setting of. **L18.**

📖 **1** T. INNES The antiquity of the settlement of the Scots in Britain witnessed by our own country writers. DICKENS Witness you three—I'm not afraid of him. **b** J. PURSEGLOVE The price of land continued to soar, as witnessed by the increasing investment in farmland by financial institutions. **2** *Decision* To meet the spiritual needs of sports people and . . encourage them to witness to their faith. *fig.:* R. GREENE Lette their owne works serue to witnesse against their owne wickednesse. **4** *Guardian* I witnessed three young Englishmen . . smash a bottle over the head of a Finnish woman. **b** *International Affairs* The events of that period . . witnessed . . all the elements of the thorny process of decolonization.

■ **witnessable** *adjective* (*rare*) able to be witnessed **L19.** **witnesser** *noun* a witness **LME.** **witnessing** *noun* (*a*) the action of the verb; an instance of this; †(*b*) oral or written testimony: **ME.**

Witney /'wɪtni/ *noun & adjective.* **E18.**
[A town in Oxfordshire (see below).]
▸**A** *noun.* A heavy loose woollen material with a nap, manufactured and made up into blankets at Witney in Oxfordshire; a blanket made from this material. For-

merly also, a kind of cloth or coating made at Witney. E18.
▶ **B** *attrib.* or as *adjective.* Made of Witney. M18.

witogie /vɪˈtʊəxi/ *noun. S. Afr.* Also ***witoo-***. M19.
[Afrikaans, from Dutch *wit* white + *oog* eye + *-ie* dim. suffix.]
Either of two South African white-eyes of the genus *Zosterops*; *esp.* the Cape white-eye, *Z. pallida*.

witteboom /ˈvɪtəbʊəm/ *noun. S. Afr.* L18.
[Afrikaans, lit. 'white tree'.]
The silver-tree, *Leucadendron argenteum*.

witted /ˈwɪtɪd/ *adjective.* LME.
[from WIT *noun* + -ED².]
1 Having wit or wits; (as 2nd elem. of comb.) having wits of a specified quality or amount. LME.
†**2** Possessed of understanding or intelligence. LME–E17.
1 ***dull-witted, half-witted, keen-witted, quick-witted,*** etc.

witter /ˈwɪtə/ *noun*¹. *Scot. & north.* E16.
[Prob. of Scandinavian origin: cf. Norwegian *vitr, vitring* warning, sign.]
1 A thing serving as a mark, sign, or token. E16.
2 The tee towards which stones are aimed in curling. L18.

witter /ˈwɪtə/ *noun*². *Scot. & north.* L18.
[Origin unkn.]
The barb of an arrow, fishing-spear, fish-hook, etc. Usu. in *pl.*

witter /ˈwɪtə/ *verb*¹ *trans.* Long *obsolete* exc. *Scot.* ME.
[Ult. origin unkn. Cf. WITTER *noun*¹.]
Inform, instruct; make clear (to a person).

witter /ˈwɪtə/ *verb*² *intrans. colloq.* (orig. *Scot. & dial.*). E19.
[Prob. imit.]
Chatter or mutter; grumble; speak tediously and at length on trivial matters. Freq. foll. by *on*.

🕮 M. SYAL Women . . who . . snivelled if he didn't smile patiently while they wittered on about their problems.

wittering /ˈwɪt(ə)rɪŋ/ *noun. Scot. & north.* ME.
[from WITTER *verb*¹ + -ING¹.]
Information, cognizance. Now *esp.*, a sign, a token, a hint.

Wittgensteinian /ˌvɪtgənˈʃtʌɪnɪən, -ˈstʌɪn-/ *adjective & noun.* M20.
[from *Wittgenstein* (see below) + -IAN.]
▶ **A** *adjective.* Of or pertaining to the Austrian-born philosopher Ludwig Wittgenstein (1889–1951), or his theories or methods. M20.
▶ **B** *noun.* An follower or adherent of Wittgenstein. M20.

witticism /ˈwɪtɪsɪz(ə)m/ *noun.* L17.
[Irreg. from WITTY + -ISM, coined by Dryden after *criticism*.]
A wittily amusing remark; a sparklingly clever joke. Formerly also, a feeble attempt at wit; a jeer.

🕮 *Premiere* Webb . . caricatures Lydecker expertly, delivering empty witticisms with arrogantly perfect timing.

■ **witticize** *verb intrans.* (*rare*) utter witticisms E18.

Wittig /ˈvɪtɪg/ *noun.* M20.
[Georg Friedrich Karl Wittig (1897–1987), German chemist.]
CHEMISTRY. Used *attrib.* to designate synthetic techniques introduced by Wittig.
Wittig reaction a method for the preparation of substituted alkenes utilizing the action of an alkyl phosphorus ylid on a carbonyl compound (aldehyde or ketone). **Wittig rearrangement** the conversion of benzyl or allyl ethers in the presence of a strong base to the corresponding secondary or tertiary alcohol.

wittily /ˈwɪtɪli/ *adverb.* ME.
[from WITTY *adjective* + -LY².]
†**1** Intelligently, cleverly, ingeniously. Passing into sense 2. ME–L17.
2 Wisely, discreetly, sensibly. *arch.* ME.
3 In a sparklingly clever and amusing way. M16.

🕮 **2** EVELYN Dr. Pritchard . . preached . . very gravely and wittily. **3** G. MURRAY He . . wittily intensified the quality of caricature.

witting /ˈwɪtɪŋ/ *noun. obsolete* exc. *Scot. & dial.* ME.
[Partly from Old Norse *vitand* (in *at minni, várri*, etc., *vitand* to my, our, etc. knowledge); partly from WIT *verb* + -ING¹.]
1 The fact of knowing or being aware of something; knowledge, cognizance. Freq. in ***at one's witting, by one's witting, of one's witting, to one's witting***, to or with one's knowledge; as (far as) one knows. ME.
2 *sing.* & (usu.) in *pl.* Knowledge obtained or (esp.) communicated; information, intelligence, news; notice, warning. Chiefly in ***get witting(s), have witting(s)***. LME.

witting /ˈwɪtɪŋ/ *adverb & adjective.* LME.
[from WIT *verb* + -ING².]
▶†**A** *adverb.* Wittingly; with awareness of what one is doing. Chiefly in conjunction with *wilfully* or *willing*. LME–E17.
▶ **B** *adjective.* **1** Aware, cognizant. Chiefly *pred.* E16.
2 Of an action: done consciously (and so with responsibility), intentional, deliberate. M16. ▸**b** Conscious as an agent; that is consciously (what is denoted by the noun). L17.

🕮 **1** N. MAILER The victim was not witting of the experiment. **2** *Times Lit. Suppl.* Spiritualists . . would emphasize the scientific . . nature of their calling, despite the many exposures of witting and unwitting fraud. **b** *Newsweek* There is no proof that the Chinese are witting accomplices in a bomb-building program.

■ **wittingly** *adverb* (*a*) with knowledge or awareness of what one is doing; consciously; deliberately; †(*b*) (*rare*) skilfully; wisely: ME.

wittol /ˈwɪt(ə)l/ *noun & adjective. arch.* LME.
[App. from WIT *verb* + ending of CUCKOLD with later loss of *d*.]
▶ **A** *noun.* **1** A man who is aware and tolerant of his wife's infidelity; an acquiescent cuckold. LME.
2 A person who has little sense; a fool. L16.
▶ **B** *attrib.* or as *adjective.* Of or pertaining to a wittol. E17.
■ **wittolly** *adjective* L16.

witty /ˈwɪti/ *adjective.*
[Old English *wit(t)ig*, from WIT *noun* + -Y¹.]
†**1** Having wisdom; wise, having good judgement; prudent, sensible. OE–E17.
2 Intelligent, clever; skilful, expert, capable. Now *arch. & dial.* OE. ▸†**b** Crafty, cunning, artful. Also, foolishly ingenious in devising something harmful to oneself. LME–E18.
†**3** Orig., endowed with reason, rational. Later, in full possession of one's wits, of sound mind. *rare.* OE–L17.
†**4** Showing or demanding intellectual ability. Later (esp. of discourse), ingenious or subtle in conception or expression. LME–E18. ▸**b** Skilfully devised for an evil purpose. Only in 17.
†**5** Showing or originating from good judgement or discernment. LME–E18.
6 Capable of or given to saying or writing sparklingly clever and amusing things; fond of making witticisms. L16. ▸†**b** Sharply critical, censorious, sarcastic. E17–M18.
7 Esp. of speech or writing: characterized by or full of clever and sparkling humour; cleverly amusing. L16.

🕮 **2** R. EDEN In workemanship and artes they are marueylous wyttie. **b** T. HERBERT As simple as they seeme, they are witty enough in craft, revenge, and villany. **4** J. LOCKE The Fallacies that are often concealed in florid, witty or involved Discourses. **6** R. S. WOOLHOUSE Bacon was obviously an entertaining, civil, and witty personal companion. **7** S. TOWNSEND There was no witty repartee . . not a single hilarious anecdote was told. *Guardian* Courting the buyers with ever more witty, young and charming variations on the Chanel look.

■ **wittiness** *noun* LME.

†**witwall** *noun.* M16.
[Early mod. German †*wittewal(e)* (dial. *Wiedewal*), from Middle Low German *wedewale* (early Flemish *widewael*), from *wede* WOOD *noun*¹ + *-wale* of unkn. origin. Cf. HICKWALL, WOODWALL.]
1 The golden oriole *Oriolus oriolus*. M16–L17.
2 A woodpecker. M17–M19.

wiv /wɪv/ *preposition. dial. & non-standard.* L19.
[Repr. a cockney pronunc.]
With.

wive /wʌɪv/ *verb. arch.*
[Old English *(ge)wīfian* = Middle Low German, Middle Dutch *wīven*, from *wīf* WIFE *verb*.]
1 *verb intrans.* Take a wife, marry. Freq. foll. by *with*. OE.
2 *verb trans.* Provide with a wife, obtain a wife for. E16.
3 *verb intrans. & trans.* (with *it*). Be a wife, act as a wife. *rare.* L16.
4 *verb trans.* Marry, become the wife or husband of. L16.

wivern *noun* var. of WYVERN.

wives *noun* pl. of WIFE *noun*.

†**wivish** *adjective* see WIFISH.

wiwi /ˈwiːwi/ *noun. NZ.* M19.
[Maori.]
Rushes or rushlike plants collectively.

wi-wi /ˈwiːwiː/ *noun*². *Austral. & NZ slang* (now *rare* or *obsolete*). M19.
[Repr. pronunc. of French *oui, oui* yes, yes, taken as typical of the French language.]
A French person; in *pl.*, the French.

Wiyot /ˈwiːjɒt/ *noun & adjective.* M19.
[Wiyot *wiyat* (people of) the Eel River delta.]
▶ **A** *noun.* Pl. same.
1 A member of an Algonquian people formerly living on the coast of northern California. M19.
2 The language of this people. M19.
▶ **B** *attrib.* or as *adjective.* Of or pertaining to the Wiyot or their language. E20.

wiz *noun* see WHIZZ *noun*.

wizard /ˈwɪzəd/ *noun, adjective, & verb.* LME.
[formed as WISE *adjective* + -ARD.]
▶ **A** *noun.* **1** A philosopher, a sage. *arch.* (freq. *derog.*). LME.
2a A man (formerly also, a woman) skilled in the practice of magic or the occult arts; a sorcerer. Now also, a man who practises witchcraft, a warlock. M16. ▸**b** A person noted for his or her remarkable powers or exceptional ability within a certain sphere; an expert in a particular field of activity. Freq. in ***financial wizard***, a person skilled in making money, or in organizing financial affairs. E17. ▸**c** A professional conjuror. *US* (now *rare* or *obsolete*). M19. ▸**d** A traditional healer, a medicine man. Chiefly *N. Amer.* M19.
3 COMPUTING. A software tool that operates automatically to guide a user through a particular process. L20.

🕮 **2a** J. HALIFAX A shaman, an entranced wizard whose spirit is in mystical flight. **b** *Home Office Computing* You don't need to become a technical wizard to take advantage of these . . error-eliminating tips.

▶ **B** *adjective.* **1** Having the powers or properties of a wizard; having magical power or influence. L16.
2 Of, pertaining to, or associated with wizards or wizardry; magic, enchanted, bewitched. M17.
3 Excellent, marvellous, wonderful. *slang.* E20.

🕮 **1** SHELLEY The wizard lady sate aloof, Spelling out scrolls of dread antiquity. **2** N. MUNRO Like as they were in some wizard fortress cut from rock. **3** H. E. BATES Above all . . being young and alive and loved was the wizardest thing of all.

▶ **C** *verb trans.* †**1** Call (a person) 'wizard'. *rare.* Only in E17.
2 Practise wizardry on, bewitch; drive *away* as by magic. M17.
■ **wizardly** *adjective* of, pertaining to, or characteristic of a wizard or wizardry L16.

wizardry /ˈwɪzədri/ *noun.* L16.
[from WIZARD *noun* + -RY.]
1 The art or practice of a wizard or wizards; wizardly or magic skill; witchcraft. L16.
2 Inexplicable and remarkable power, ability, or influence. Now *esp.*, remarkable skill or expertise in a particular field of activity; the result of this. L19.

🕮 **2** C. AIKEN What wizardry this slow waltz works upon us! *Stage* New technical wizardry includes a full flying system for scenery changes with flying over the forestage.

wizen /ˈwɪz(ə)n/ *adjective.* L18.
[Abbreviation from WIZENED.]
= WIZENED 2.

wizen /ˈwɪz(ə)n/ *verb.*
[Old English *wisnian* = Old High German *wesanēn*, Old Norse *visna*, from Germanic base rel. to Latin *viescere* wither.]
1 *verb intrans.* Of a plant: dry up, wither. Also (of a person, a person's features, etc.), shrivel; wrinkle, esp. with age. Now chiefly as WIZENED *adjective*. OE.
2 *verb trans.* Cause to wither or shrivel. *Scot.* E16.

wizened /ˈwɪz(ə)nd/ *adjective.* E16.
[from prec. + -ED¹.]
1 Of a plant, fruit, etc.: dried up, withered. E16.
2 Of a person, a person's features, etc: wrinkled and dried up, thin and shrivelled, esp. with age. E16.

WIZO *abbreviation.*
Women's International Zionist Organization.

wizzo *interjection, adjective, & noun* var. of WHIZZO.

wk. *abbreviation.*
1 Weak.
2 Week.
3 Work.

WKB *abbreviation.*
PHYSICS. Wentzel–Kramers–Brillouin (used *attrib.* with ref. to a method for obtaining an approximate solution of the Schrödinger equation based on the expansion of the wave function in powers of Planck's constant).

wks. *abbreviation.*
Weeks.

WLA *abbreviation.*
Hist. Women's Land Army.

WLTM *abbreviation.*
Would like to meet (used in lonely hearts advertisements).

Wm. *abbreviation.*
William.

WMO *abbreviation.*
World Meteorological Organization.

WNW *abbreviation.*
West-north-west.

WO *abbreviation.*
1 War Office.
2 Warrant Officer.

wo /wəʊ/ *interjection.* L16.
[Var. of WHOA. Cf. WAY *interjection*.]
1 ***wo ho (ho), wo ha (ho)***, a falconer's call to a hawk. L16.
2 A call ordering a horse to stop; whoa. L18.

w/o *abbreviation.*
1 Also **witho.** Walkover.

2 Without.

woa /wəʊ/ *interjection.* M19.
[Var. of WHOA.]
Whoa.

woad /wəʊd/ *noun & verb.*
[Old English *wād* = Old Frisian *wēd*, Middle Low German, Middle Dutch *wēt*, *weede*, Old High German *weit* (Dutch *weede*, German *Waid*), from West Germanic source (whence medieval Latin *waida*, *waisdo*, *waisda*, French *guède*).]
▶ **A** *noun.* **1** A blue dye (now superseded by indigo and synthetic dyes) prepared from the leaves of *Isatis tinctoria* (see sense 2) dried, powdered, and exposed to air. OE.
2 A glaucous yellow-flowered cruciferous plant, *Isatis tinctoria*, formerly much grown for the blue colouring matter yielded by it. OE.

> 📖 **1** H. WILSON To believe .. that when you pass Basingstoke the natives paint themselves with woad. **2 wild woad** the plant weld, *Reseda luteola*.

Comb.: †**woad-ashes** (*a*) the ashes of burnt wine-lees, used by dyers; (*b*) the ashes of burnt wood used to make a lye.
▶ **B** *verb trans.* **1** Dye, colour, or stain (cloth, the skin, etc.) with woad. LME.
2 Treat (a dye) with woad. L16.

> 📖 **1** *fig.*: W. GURNALL The hypocrite is not thus woaded with impudency, to sinne at noonday.

■ **woader** *noun* (*rare*) (*a*) a dyer with woad; (*b*) a grower of woad: LME.

woadwaxen *noun*: see WOODWAXEN.

wobbegong /ˈwɒbɪɡɒŋ/ *noun.* Also **wobby-**. M19.
[Aboriginal.]
A brown carpet shark, *Orectolobus maculatus*, which is patterned with light-edged spots and bars, and is found off the coasts of Australia.

wobble /ˈwɒb(ə)l/ *noun.* Also †**wabble**. L17.
[from next.]
1 The action or an act of wobbling; an unsteady rocking motion or movement; an instance of hesitation, vacillation, or uncertainty. L17.
2 BIOCHEMISTRY. The variable pairing that is possible between a base in a transfer RNA anticodon and the corresponding base in a messenger RNA codon. Freq. *attrib.* M20.

> 📖 **1** R. HOGGART Twopence a pound on meat .. can cause a bad wobble in the week's planning. *Hippocrates* The spiked heel adds a wobble to the ankle.

wobble /ˈwɒb(ə)l/ *verb.* Also †**wabble**. M17.
[Corresp. to Low German *wabbeln*, Old Norse *vafla* (synon. with *vafra* WAVER *verb*), from Germanic base also of WAVE *verb*[1], WAVER *verb*: see -LE[3].]
1 *verb intrans.* Proceed unsteadily; sway erratically from side to side whilst in onward motion. M17. ▸**b** Bubble; boil. Now *dial.* E18. ▸**c** Move or shake from side to side or to and fro whilst remaining stationary; quiver; vibrate. Also (of the voice), tremble, quaver. M18.
2 *verb trans.* Cause to shake, vibrate, or tremble. M19.
3 *verb trans.* Crumple *up*. US. M19.
4 *verb intrans.* Hesitate or waver between different opinions or courses of action; act uncertainly; vacillate. L19.

> 📖 **1** W. STEGNER Jordan, drunk on his own eloquence .. wobbled out of the lobby. L. NIVEN The harpoon wobbled in flight, until the trailing line dragged it straight again. **c** M. DORRIS The table wobbles where the one leg is too short. J. DISKI The excess pounds wobbled as the slap .. of his soles on the stone juddered his flesh. **2** W. STEGNER Weakness wobbled her knees. J. SAYLES The noon sun makes the blacktop gooey and wobbles the air above it. **4** *Guardian* After an encouraging performance in the morning .. GB and Ireland wobbled but .. recovered to win. *Atlantic* Pressured from both political flanks, the Administration wobbled into making an open-ended commitment.

Comb.: **wobble plate** = *swashplate* s.v. SWASH *noun*[1].
■ **wobbling** *verbal noun* the action of the verb; an instance of this: M19.

wobbler /ˈwɒblə/ *noun.* L18.
[from prec. + -ER[1].]
1 A person who or thing which wobbles. L18.
2 ENGINEERING. A projection on a roll in a rolling-mill, by which it may be turned. E20. ▸**b** = ***wobble plate*** s.v. WOBBLE *verb.* M20.
3 ANGLING. A lure that wobbles and does not spin. E20.
4 = WOBBLY *noun*[2]. *colloq.* M20.

wobbly /ˈwɒbli/ *noun*[1]. Orig. *US.* E20.
[Origin unkn.]
Hist. A member of the Industrial Workers of the World, a labour organization advocating syndicalism which enjoyed its greatest support in the western US during the early 20th cent.

wobbly /ˈwɒbli/ *noun*[2]. *colloq.* L20.
[from WOBBLY *adjective.*]
A fit of panic, temper, etc. Chiefly in ***throw a wobbly***, lose one's composure in a fit of panic, temper, etc.; act unpredictably. Cf. WOBBLER *noun* 4.

wobbly /ˈwɒbli/ *adjective.* M19.
[from WOBBLE *verb* + -Y[1].]
Wobbling or tending to wobble; unsteady or weak due to shock, an illness, etc.; (of a line, handwriting) shaky, not straight or regular; wavering, vacillating, uncertain; unsound.

> 📖 P. THEROUX There was a wobbly quality to his fifteen-year-old's voice. *Women's Review* He regarded women as inferior, and .. used wobbly and sometimes bemusing theories to prove female subordination. W. PERRIAM A rabbit jelly, a wobbly gleaming scarlet one.

■ **wobbliness** *noun* L19.

wobbulator /ˈwɒbjʊleɪtə/ *noun.* Also **wobul-**. M20.
[from WOBB(LE *noun* or *verb* + MOD)ULATOR.]
ELECTRONICS. A device for producing a signal whose frequency varies rapidly and repeatedly between two limits.
■ **wobbulated** *adjective* varied or produced by means of a wobbulator M20. **wobbu'lation** *noun* repeated variation of a frequency by a wobbulator M20.

wobbygong *noun* var. of WOBBEGONG.

wobla *noun* var. of VOBLA.

WOC *abbreviation.* Also **WOCS**.
Waiting on cement (to set).

Wodehousian /wʊdˈhaʊsɪən/ *noun & adjective.* M20.
[from *Wodehouse* (see below) + -IAN.]
▶ **A** *noun.* **1** A typical character in one of the comic novels of the English author Sir Pelham Grenville Wodehouse (1881–1975). M20.
2 An admirer or reader of Wodehouse's novels. *rare.* L20.
▶ **B** *adjective.* Pertaining to or characteristic of Wodehouse or his works. M20.

wodge /wɒdʒ/ *noun. colloq.* (orig. *dial.*). Also **wadge**. M19.
[Alt. of WEDGE *noun.*]
A bulky mass; a chunk or lump; a wad; a substantial amount.

> 📖 GODFREY SMITH Coal .. made from immense wodges of compressed peat. *Economist* An active secondary market for trading the wodges of third-world debt gathering dust in .. Japanese banks.

■ **wodgy** *adjective* solid, bulky E20.

woe /wəʊ/ *interjection, noun, & adjective.*
[Old English *wā* (also *wǣ*) corresp. to Old Frisian, Old Saxon, Middle Low German *wē*, Middle & mod. Dutch *wee*, Old High German *wē* (German *weh*), Old Norse *vei*, *væ*, Gothic *vai*, Greek *ouai*, *oua*, *oa*, Latin *vae*, Latvian *wai*, Welsh *gwae*: a natural exclam. Cf. WALY, WELLAWAY.]
▶ **A** *interjection.* **I 1** Expr. grief or lamentation: alas! *arch.* OE.

> 📖 **1** C. PATMORE And if, ah woe, she loves alone.

▶ **II** W. dat. (or, later, its equivalent).
2 In exclams. or statements of grief, distress, affliction, etc., with or without verb. Now *arch.*, *dial.*, & *literary.* OE.
2 woe betide: see BETIDE 1. **woe be to us** may affliction or distress overtake us. **woe is him** cursed is he. **woe is me** I am distressed, unhappy, unfortunate, etc. **woe to** there will be unfortunate consequences for. **woe worth the day**, **woe worth the time**, etc., (now chiefly *Scot.* cursed be, may evil befall the day, time, etc.
▶ **B** *noun.* **1** Misery, affliction, distress; misfortune, trouble. Chiefly *arch.* & *literary* exc. in ***tale of woe*** below. ME. ▸**b** In *pl.* Misfortunes, troubles, griefs (*arch.* & *literary*); *colloq.* problems. LME.
2 Physical pain; disease or infirmity. Also (*spec.*), pain due to torment in hell. *obsolete* exc. as passing into sense 1. ME.
3 The emotion of sorrow or anguish. *obsolete* exc. as passing into sense 1. ME.
†**4** Lamentation, mourning. Chiefly in ***make woe***. ME–E16.
5 An utterance of 'woe' in warning or denunciation; a curse. *arch.* LME.

> 📖 **1** MILTON The Fruit Of that Forbidden Tree, whose mortal tast Brought Death .. and all our woe. *New Age* The usual tangle of human woe: early pregnancy, dropping out of school. **tale of woe** (chiefly *joc.*) a catalogue or narrative of problems or misfortunes. **b** W. SEWEL The Lord sent me .. to warn you of the woes that are coming upon you. *Vanity Fair* On one issue all .. agreed, that the Barnes's financial woes are not over.

▶ **C** *adjective* (orig. & chiefly *pred.*).
1 Grieved, wretched, miserable, sorrowful. *obsolete* exc. *Scot.* & *north.* ME.
†**2** Of an event, situation, etc.: woeful, miserable. L16–L18.

> 📖 **1** J. CARLYLE Poor Queen! .. I was wae to look at her, wae to think of her.

■ **woesome** *adjective* (*rare*, chiefly *Scot.*) woeful E19.

woebegone /ˈwəʊbɪɡɒn/ *adjective.* ME.
[from prec. + *begone* pa. pple of BEGO, as in *me is woe begone* woe has beset me.]
1 Overwhelmed or afflicted with misfortune, distress, sorrow, or grief. *arch.* ME.
2 Exhibiting a state of distress, misery, or grief; sad, miserable, or dismal in appearance. E19.

> 📖 **1** H. F. CARY That lofty shade, who .. seems too woe-begone to drop a tear. **2** I. DOIG In that woebegone log house .. my father was born. N. BAWDEN She glowered at me like a reproachful woebegone child.

¶ The rise of sense 2 in the modern period was due to an archaistic revival of the word in E19.

woeful /ˈwəʊfʊl, -f(ə)l/ *adjective.* ME.
[from WOE *noun* + -FUL.]
1 Afflicted with sorrow, distress, or misfortune; sorrowful, mournful. ME.
2 Of a time, a place, etc.: fraught with woe, affliction, or misery. ME.
3 Causing commiseration or dissatisfaction; very bad or poor, deplorable, pitiful. E17.

> 📖 **1** E. ARNOLD Be sure that woeful father wept. A. BROOKNER Lizzie .. was .. a distraction, with her woeful face and her grubby tracksuit. **2** B. LOPEZ The early history of Hudson Bay .. is a woeful chronicle of fatal disasters. **3** *Guardian* Steps were being taken to offer women equal opportunities ... But the .. efforts made in medicine were woeful.

¶ Revived or newly formed in M18.
■ **woefully** *adverb* in a woeful manner; now *esp.* deplorably, pitifully; terribly, exceedingly: LME. **woefulness** *noun* (*arch.*) woeful condition E16.

wog /wɒɡ/ *noun*[1]. *slang* (*derog.* & *racially offensive*). E20.
[Origin uncertain: perh. acronym from westernized oriental gentleman, or abbreviation of GOLLIWOG.]
A foreigner, *esp.* a non-white person or one of Arab extraction.

wog /wɒɡ/ *noun*[2]. *Austral. slang.* M20.
[Origin unkn.]
A small insect; a germ or organism causing infection; an illness or disease, *esp.* influenza, dysentery, or a gastric complaint.

wog /wɒɡ/ *verb trans. slang.* Infl. **-gg-**. L20.
[Origin unkn.]
Steal.

Wogdon /ˈwɒɡdən/ *noun.* E19.
[Robert *Wogdon* (fl. 1776–1800), a noted gunsmith.]
A type of duelling pistol made by Wogdon.

woggle /ˈwɒɡ(ə)l/ *noun.* M20.
[Origin unkn. Cf. TOGGLE *noun.*]
A loop or ring of leather, cord, etc., through which the ends of a Scout's neckerchief are threaded.

woggle *verb* var. of WAGGLE *verb.*

†**Wogul** *noun & adjective* var. of VOGUL.

Wöhler test /ˈvəːlə tɛst/ *noun phr.* E20.
[August *Wöhler* (1819–1914), German railway engineer.]
MECHANICS. A fatigue test in which a horizontal bar is rotated axially while supported at one end and loaded at the other.

wok /wɒk/ *noun.* M20.
[Chinese (Cantonese).]
A large bowl-shaped frying-pan used in esp. Chinese cookery.

woke *verb pa. t.*: see WAKE *verb.*

woken *verb pa. pple*: see WAKE *verb.*

wold /wəʊld/ *noun.* In sense 3b also **W-**.
[Old English (Anglian) *wald*, (West Saxon) *weald* (see WEALD) = Old Frisian, Old Saxon, Old High German *wald* (Dutch *woud*, German *Wald*) forest, Old Norse *vǫllr* untilled field, plain, from Germanic, perh. rel. to WELD *noun*[1] and cogn. with WILD *adjective* & *noun.*]
1 Forest, forest land; wooded upland. Long *obsolete* exc. *dial.* OE.
†**2** A hill, a down. ME–E16.
3 A piece of open country; a plain. Now *esp.* a tract of high open uncultivated country or moorland; in *pl.* & *collect. sing.* rolling uplands. Chiefly *literary.* ME. ▸**b** *spec.* In *pl.* & *collect. sing.* *The* hill country of N. Yorkshire and Humberside; *the* Cotswold district; *the* hilly districts of Leicestershire and Lincolnshire. L15.

> 📖 **3** TENNYSON The wind, that beats the mountain, blows More softly round the open wold. *attrib.*: A. S. BYATT The Mercedes was having difficulty with a hay-wain in the twisting little wold roads.

¶ After E16 fell out of general use and was restricted to names of particular areas (e.g. the Yorkshire Wolds) which were probably once wooded, whence it was generalized in literary use (sense 3) after *c* E17.

wolf /wʊlf/ *noun.* Pl. **wolves** /wʊlvz/.
[Old English *wulf* corresp. to Old Frisian *wolf*, Old Saxon *wulf* (Dutch *wolf*), Old High German *wolf* (German *Wolf*), Old Norse *ulfr*, Gothic *wulfs*, from Germanic, from Indo-European base repr. also by Latin *lupus*, Greek *lukos*, Sanskrit *vrka*.]
1 A large doglike mammal, *Canis lupus*, which is native to Europe, Asia, and N. America, esp. the tundra and taiga, lives in packs, and is noted for its supposed ferocity and rapacity (also ***grey wolf***, ***timber wolf***). Also, any of several other American canids. **OE.** ▸**b** *fig.* Anything compared to a wolf in respect of the animal's ferocity or rapacity. **OE.** ▸**c** (Usu. with specifying word.) Any of various other carnivorous mammals that resemble the wolf, as a hyena, a thylacine. **E19.** ▸**d** The skin, hide, or fur of the wolf. **E19.**
2 A person or being (orig. esp. the Devil) of a cruel, ferocious, or rapacious disposition; an enemy or persecutor of the Christian flock (with ref. to *Matthew* 7:15, *Acts* 20:29, etc.). **OE.** ▸†**b** A person who deserves to be hunted down like a wolf. Cf. ***wolf's-head*** below. **M16–M17.** ▸**c** A man with a voracious sexual appetite; a man who habitually pursues and seduces women. *slang.* **M19.** ▸**d** A male homosexual seducer; a male homosexual who adopts an active role with a partner. *slang* (orig. *US*). **E20.**
3 *fig.* A wolf as a type of a destructive or devouring agency, esp. hunger or famine. Chiefly in ***keep the wolf from the door*** below. **LME.** ▸**b** A ravenous appetite; an insatiable craving for food. **L16.**
4 Any of various kinds of apparatus; *spec.* †(***a***) a military engine with sharp teeth for grasping battering rams used by besiegers; (***b***) a kind of fishing net (also ***wolf-net***). **L15.**
5 a An image or representation of a wolf. **M16.** ▸**b** (**W-.**) *ASTRONOMY.* *The* constellation Lupus. **M16.**
6 Any of various other animals likened to a wolf in some way; *esp.* a voracious fish, as a wolf-fish, a pike. **M16.**
†**7** *MEDICINE.* Any of various malignant and erosive diseases; *esp.* lupus. **M16–E19.**
8 *MUSIC.* **a** An out-of-tune effect giving a harsh sound when chords in certain extreme keys are played on old keyboard instruments, esp. the organ, before the introduction of tuning by equal temperament; a chord or interval characterized by such a sound. **L18.** ▸**b** A jarring sound which sometimes occurs from a bowed stringed instrument when the instrument's body resonates to a certain note. Also ***wolf-note***. **L19.**
9 In full ***wolf tree***. A tree occupying more space than has been allowed for it, so restricting the growth of its neighbours. **E20.**

📖 **1b** BYRON The Assyrian came down like the wolf on the fold. *Guardian* The media finger the suspects like wolves watching the stragglers in the herd of deer. **2** P. SIDNEY Such a slye wolfe was entred among them, that could make justice the cloake of tirannye. **c** S. J. PERELMAN This guy . . is a . . wolf who is constantly slavering after secretaries.

Phrases etc.: **AARDWOLF**. **cry wolf (too often)** (with ref. to the fable of the shepherd boy who tricked people with false cries of 'Wolf!') raise repeated false alarms (so that a genuine cry for help goes unheeded). **have a wolf by the ears**, **hold a wolf by the ears** be in a precarious situation; be in a predicament where any course of action presents problems. **keep the wolf from the door** avert or stave off hunger, starvation, or poverty. ***loafer wolf***: see **LOAFER** 2. ***lone wolf***: see **LONE** *adjective & adverb*. **MANED** ***wolf***. ***PRAIRIE-wolf***. ***red wolf***: see **RED** *adjective*. **see a wolf** *arch.* be lost for words (from the old belief that on seeing a wolf a person lost his or her voice). ***Tasmanian wolf***: see **TASMANIAN** *adjective*. **throw to the wolves** sacrifice (a subordinate, friend, etc.) in order to avert danger or difficulties for oneself. ***tiger-wolf***: see **TIGER** *noun*. †**wake a sleeping wolf** (*rare*, Shakes.) invite trouble or disturbance. ***water-wolf***: see **WATER** *noun*. **wolf in sheep's clothing** (with ref. to *Matthew* 7:15) a person whose hostile or malicious intentions are concealed by a pretence of gentleness or friendliness.

Attrib. & comb.: In the senses 'made of the hide or fur of a wolf', as ***wolf coat***, ***wolf hat***, ***wolf jacket***, etc., 'of or pertaining to the (esp. spiritual) association of human beings with wolves', as ***wolf clan***, ***wolf people***, ***wolf totem***, etc. Special combs., as **wolfberry** a N. American shrub, *Symphoricarpos occidentalis*, allied to the snowberry; **wolf call** *colloq.* (orig. *US*) a wolf-whistle; **wolf-cry** a false alarm; **wolf cub** (***a***) a young wolf; (***b***) (former name for) a Cub Scout; **wolf-dog** (***a***) = ***wolfhound*** below; (***b***) a hybrid between a domestic dog and a wolf; **wolf-fish** any of various large deep-water marine fishes of the family Anarhichadidae, which have long bodies and large doglike teeth (also called ***sea-cat***, ***sea-catfish***, ***sea-wolf***); esp. *Anarhichas lupus*, of the N. Atlantic; †**wolf fly** = ***ROBBER-fly***; **wolf-head** (***a***) the head of a wolf; an image or representation of this; (***b***) *LAW* (now *Hist.*) in Anglo-Saxon England, a cry for the pursuit of an outlaw as one to be hunted down like a wolf; *transf.* (orig. in ***cry wolf's head***) an outlaw; **wolfhound** (an animal of) any of several large breeds of dog formerly kept for hunting wolves; **wolf-madness** = **LYCANTHROPY** 1; **wolf-moth** the corn moth, *Nemapogon granella*, whose larvae infest stored grain; **wolf-net** = sense 4(b) above; **wolf-note** = sense 8b above; **wolf-pack** (***a***) a number of wolves naturally associating as a group, esp. for hunting; (***b***) any group of people or things which operate as a hunting and attacking pack, as a group of submarines, aircraft, etc.; *spec.* (*US*) an urban gang of criminal youths; **wolfsbane** an aconite, *esp.* (***a***) monkshood, *Aconitum napellus*; (***b***) *Aconitum vulparia*, which has dull yellow flowers and occurs in mountainous regions of Europe; **wolf's claw** the common club-moss, *Lycopodium clavatum*; **wolf's head** = ***wolf-head*** above; **wolfskin** the skin or pelt of a wolf; a garment etc. made of this; **wolf's milk** [with ref. to the acrid milky juice] any of several spurges, *esp.* sun spurge, *Euphorbia helioscopia*, and leafy spurge, *E. esula*; **wolf-snake** any of various harmless Asian colubrid snakes of the genus *Lycodon*; esp. *L. aulicus*, which has variable markings and is common in the Indian subcontinent; **wolf-spider** any of various spiders of the family Lycosidae, which run after and spring on their prey; **wolf's tooth** a rudimentary tooth in a horse, which grows out sideways from the jaw and can cut the cheek; ***wolf tree***: see sense 9 above; **wolf-whistle** *noun & verb* (***a***) *noun* a whistle, esp. one by a man, expressing sexual admiration or attraction; (***b***) *verb intrans.* make a wolf-whistle; **wolf willow** *Canad.* the silverberry, *Elaeagnus commutata*.

■ **wolfess** *noun* (*rare*) (***a***) a female wolf; (***b***) a woman who habitually pursues and seduces men: **LME**. **wolfkin** *noun* (*rare*) a young wolf **E18**. **wolflike** *adjective* like (that of) a wolf; ferocious, ravening, rapacious: **L16**. **wolfling** *noun* a young or little wolf **ME**.

wolf /wʊlf/ *verb.* **M19.**
[from prec.]
1 *verb trans.* Eat like a wolf; devour ravenously. Freq. foll. by *down*. Cf. **WOOF** *verb*² 3. **M19.**
2 *verb intrans. & trans.* (with *it*). Behave like a wolf; habitually pursue and seduce women. **M19.**
3 *verb trans.* Delude with false alarms. Cf. ***cry wolf*** s.v. **WOLF** *noun*. *rare.* **E20.**
4 *verb trans. & intrans.* Make fun (of); criticize (a person). *Black slang.* **M20.**

📖 **1** *Ladies Home Journal (US)* Everybody around you . . is wolfing down hot dogs, peanuts and ice cream.

wolfer /ˈwʊlfə/ *noun.* **L19.**
[from **WOLF** *noun, verb* + **-ER**¹.]
1 A wolf-hunter. **L19.**
2 A person who wolfs food or drink. *rare.* **L19.**

Wolff /vɒlf/ *noun.* **M20.**
[Ludwig *Wolff* (1857–1919), German chemist.]
CHEMISTRY. ***Wolff rearrangement***, a molecular rearrangement, important in the conversion of an organic acid to its next higher homologue, in which a diazoketone loses a molecule of nitrogen and forms a ketene.
Comb.: **Wolff–Kishner reduction** [Nikolai M. *Kishner* (1867–1935), Russian chemist] the reduction of an aldehyde or ketone to an alkane by heating the hydrazone or semicarbazone derivative in a strongly basic solution.

Wolffian /ˈwʊlfɪən/ *adjective.* **M19.**
[from Kaspar Friedrich *Wolff* (1733–94), German embryologist + **-IAN**.]
ANATOMY & ZOOLOGY. Designating various embryological structures described by Wolff.
Wolffian body = **MESONEPHROS**. **Wolffian duct** the duct of the mesonephros, which is the urinogenital duct in male anamniotes and the vas deferens etc. in male amniotes. **Wolffian ridge** either of two longitudinal ridges on either side of the embryo on which the limb buds arise.

Wolfian /ˈvɒlfɪən, ˈwʊlfɪən/ *adjective*¹ & *noun*¹. **L18.**
[from *Wolf(f)* (see below) + **-IAN**.]
▸ **A** *noun.* A follower or adherent of the German philosopher Christian Freiherr von Wolf(f) (1679–1754), or of his philosophical system, an eclectic adaptation of Leibnitzian philosophy and scholasticism. **L18.**
▸ **B** *adjective.* Of or pertaining to Wolf(f) or his philosophy. **M19.**

Wolfian /ˈvɒlfɪən, ˈwʊlfɪən/ *adjective*² & *noun*². **E19.**
[from *Wolf* (see below) + **-IAN**.]
▸ **A** *adjective.* Of or pertaining to the German classical scholar and philologist Friedrich August Wolf (1759–1824), or his theory that the Homeric poems are texts deriving from an oral tradition rather than being the unified work of a single author. **E19.**
▸ **B** *noun.* A follower or adherent of Wolf. **L19.**

wolfing /ˈwʊlfɪŋ/ *verbal noun.* Chiefly *N. Amer.* **L19.**
[from **WOLF** *noun* + **-ING**¹.]
Hunting for wolves.

wolfish /ˈwʊlfɪʃ/ *adjective.* **L16.**
[from **WOLF** *noun* + **-ISH**¹.]
1 Of or pertaining to a wolf or wolves. **L16.**
2 Characteristic of or resembling that of a wolf. **L17.**
3 Resembling a wolf in appearance or disposition; ferocious; *US colloq.* ravenously hungry. **L18.**

📖 **3** P. THEROUX The sense of being trapped and victimized by someone who was wolfish and unpredictable.

■ **wolfishly** *adverb* **M19**. **wolfishness** *noun* **L17**.

wolfram /ˈwʊlfrəm/ *noun.* **M18.**
[German, perh. an old miners' word, from *Wolf* **WOLF** *noun* + *Rahm* cream or Middle High German *rām* soot. Presumably orig. a pejorative term, with ref. to the ore's inferiority compared to the tin with which it occurred. Cf. **COBALT**, **NICKEL** *noun & adjective*.]
1 *MINERALOGY.* = **WOLFRAMITE**. **M18.**
2 The metal tungsten. **M19.**
■ **wolframate** *noun* = **TUNGSTATE** **M19**. **wolˈframic** *adjective* = **TUNGSTIC** **M19**. **wolframite** *noun* (*MINERALOGY*) a monoclinic tungstate of iron and manganese, which occurs as black to brown crystals, blades, granules and masses, and is the chief ore of tungsten **M19**.

Wolf–Rayet star /wʊlfˈrʌɪeɪ stɑː/ *noun phr.* **L19.**
[from C. J. E. *Wolf* (1827–1918) + G. A. P. *Rayet* (1839–1906), French astronomers.]
ASTRONOMY. Any of a class of hot white to blue stars characterized by bright broad spectral lines due to hydrogen, helium, carbon, or nitrogen, believed to be short-lived and unstable.

wolfy /ˈwʊlfi/ *adjective. US.* **E19.**
[from **WOLF** *noun* + **-Y**¹.]
Wolflike; characterized by or suggestive of the presence of wolves; ferocious, uncivilized.

†**wol(l)** *verb* see **WOOLD** *verb*.

Wollaston /ˈwʊləstən/ *noun.* **L19.**
[William Hyde *Wollaston* (1766–1828), English physicist and chemist.]
PHYSICS. Used *attrib.* and in *possess.* with ref. to things designed by Wollaston.
Wollaston prism, **Wollaston's prism** a prism made from two prisms of calcite or quartz with their optic axes perpendicular to each other and to the incident light, which is split into two diverging beams of polarized light.
■ **wollastonite** *noun* (*MINERALOGY*) a triclinic metasilicate of calcium, usu. occurring in white to grey fibrous tabular masses and used as a source of rock wool (also called ***tabular spar***) **E19**.

wolly /ˈwɒli/ *noun. slang.* **L20.**
[Origin unkn. Cf. **WALLY** *noun*¹.]
A uniformed policeman, *esp.* a constable. Cf. **WOOLLY** *noun* 3.

Wolof /ˈwəʊlɒf/ *noun & adjective.* **E19.**
[Wolof. Cf. earlier **JOLLOF**.]
▸ **A** *noun.* Pl. same, **-s**. A member of an African people of Senegal and (The) Gambia; the Niger-Congo language of this people. **E19.**
▸ **B** *adjective.* Of or pertaining to the Wolof or their language. **M19.**

Wolstonian /wʊlˈstəʊnɪən/ *adjective & noun.* **M20.**
[from *Wolston*, a village in Warwickshire, England + **-IAN**.]
GEOLOGY. (Designating or pertaining to) the penultimate Pleistocene glaciation in Britain, identified with the Saale of northern Europe (and perhaps the Riss of the Alps).

wolve /wʊlv/ *verb. rare.* **E18.**
[from *wolv-* stem of **WOLF** *noun*.]
1 *verb intrans. & trans.* (with *it*). Behave like a wolf. *lit. & fig.* **E18.**
2 *MUSIC.* Of an organ: emit a hollow wailing sound due to deficient wind supply. **M19.**

wolver /ˈwʊlvə/ *noun. rare.* **L16.**
[from (the same root as) prec. + **-ER**¹.]
1 A person who behaves like a wolf; a ravenous or savage creature. **L16.**
2 = **WOLFER** 1. **E20.**

wolverine /ˈwʊlvəriːn/ *noun.* Also **-ene**, (earlier) †**-ing**. **L16.**
[Obscurely from *wolv-* stem of **WOLF** *noun*.]
1 A heavily built thick-furred mustelid mammal, *Gulo gulo*, found in the coniferous forests and tundra of northern Eurasia and N. America. Also called ***glutton***. **L16.** ▸**b** The fur of the wolverine. **L16.**
2 (A nickname for) a native or inhabitant of the State of Michigan in the US. **M19.**
Comb.: **Wolverine State** *US* the State of Michigan.

wolves *noun* pl. of **WOLF** *noun*.

wolvish /ˈwʊlvɪʃ/ *adjective.* **LME.**
[from *wolv-* stem of **WOLF** *noun*: see **-ISH**¹. Cf. **WOLFISH**.]
1 Characteristic of a wolf; wolflike. **LME.**
2 Of or pertaining to a wolf or wolves. **M16.**
■ **wolvishness** *noun* (*rare*) **M16**.

woman /ˈwʊmən/ *noun.* Pl. **women** /ˈwɪmɪn/.
[Old English *wīfman(n)*, *-mon(n)*, pl. *wīfmen(n)*, from *wīf* woman, **WIFE** *noun* + *man(n)*, *mon(n)* **MAN** *noun*. Cf. **WIMMIN**.]
▸ **I 1** An adult female person, as opp. to a man or girl or both; an individual female person. **OE.** ▸**b** Used as a form of address to a female person (cf. **LADY** *noun* 4). Now freq. *joc. & derog.* **LME.** ▸**c** As 2nd elem. of comb.: an adult female person having a specified nationality, status, character, profession, occupation, or interest; an adult female person using or skilled in the use of a specified implement; an adult female person associated with or described as something specified. **LME.**
2 Chiefly *Hist.* A female servant, *esp.* a lady's maid; *spec.* a queen's female attendant ranking below lady. **OE.** ▸**b** A female domestic help, a charwoman. **L19.**
3 (Also **W-.**) (Without article.) The female human person, esp. viewed as a type; the female sex. **OE.**
4 A (kept) mistress; a female lover or sexual partner; (now chiefly *dial. & US*) a wife. **LME.**

📖 **1** *Athenaeum* Defendant pleaded . . that the person described as a woman was in fact a lady. M. AMIS My mother, a lean, nervous and intelligent woman. D. LESSING A bulky girl, no, a woman, with short black curls. **b** NEB *Matt.* 15:28 Jesus replied, 'Woman, what faith you have!' D. SHANNON Let me relax in peace, woman. **c** ***bondwoman, businesswoman, chairwoman, charwoman, clergywoman, countrywoman, Englishwoman, fancy woman, Frenchwoman, gentlewoman, horsewoman, laywoman, man's woman, needlewoman, penwoman, saleswoman, serving-woman, townswoman, trencherwoman***, etc. **3** DRYDEN Woman's a various and a changeful Thing! S. RICHARDSON Woman is the glory of all created existence:—But you, madam, are *more* than woman! **4** J. W. SCHULTZ I must get home. I want to see my woman . . before I die.

▶ **II** *transf. & fig.* **5** *The* character or qualities (traditionally regarded as) typical of a woman, womanliness; *the* feminine side or aspect (of a person). Now also, a man with characteristics traditionally associated with women. **M17.**

6 The reverse of a coin used in tossing (as the side of a penny having Britannia as opp. to the king's head). Cf. MAN *noun* 12. *arch.* **L18.**

📖 **5** LYTTON I believe . . I have a great deal of the woman in me.

Phrases: ***a woman's reason***: see REASON *noun*[1]. ***be one's own woman***: see OWN *adjective & pronoun*. ***fallen woman***: see FALLEN *ppl adjective* 1. ***fancy woman***: see FANCY *adjective*. ***inner woman***: see INNER *adjective*. ***make an honest woman of***: see HONEST *adjective*. ***man's woman***: see MAN *noun*. ***new woman***: see NEW *adjective*. ***old woman's tooth***. ***outer woman***: see OUTER *adjective*. ***own woman***: see OWN *adjective & pronoun*. ***public woman***: see PUBLIC *adjective*. ***scarlet woman***: see SCARLET *adjective*. ***sporting woman***: see SPORTING *adjective*. ***strange woman***: see STRANGE *adjective*. ***strong woman***: see STRONG *adjective*. ***the little woman***: see LITTLE *adjective*. ***the other woman***: see OTHER *adjective*. ***wine, women, and song, wine, woman, and song***: see WINE *noun*. ***wise woman***: see WISE *adjective & noun*[2]. ***woman about town***: see TOWN *noun*. ***woman of ideas***: see IDEA. ***woman of letters*** a female scholar or writer. ***woman of means***: see MEAN *noun*[1]. ***woman of pleasure***: see PLEASURE *noun*. ***woman of the streets*** a prostitute. ***woman of the town***: see TOWN *noun*. ***write oneself woman***: see WRITE *verb*. ***young woman***: see YOUNG *adjective*.

Comb.: Appositional with the sense 'female', esp. in names of professions etc. (formerly) more usually pursued by men, as ***woman doctor, woman driver, woman police officer, woman-servant, woman teacher***, etc. (pl. ***women doctors*** etc.). **woman-body** *dial.* a woman; **woman-born** *adjective* (*poet.*) born of woman; **woman-child**, pl. **women-children**, *arch.* a female child; **woman-grown** *adjective* (*poet.*, now *rare* or *obsolete*) that has become a woman; **woman-hour** *joc. & colloq.* an hour's work done by a woman; **woman-man** (chiefly *derog.*) an effeminate man; **woman-movement** (*a*) (*Hist.*) *the* movement for the emancipation of women; (*b*) = ***women's movement*** below; †**woman-post** a female messenger or courier; **woman-power** (*a*) the exercise of authority or political influence by women; (*b*) (the number of) women available for work; **woman question** *Hist.* the issue of the rights of women as a matter of political controversy in the 19th cent.; ***woman's estate***: see ESTATE *noun* 1b; **woman-slaughter** *rare* manslaughter of a woman; **woman's man** a ladies' man; **woman's movement** = ***women's movement*** below; **woman's magazine, women's magazine** a magazine designed primarily for women (freq. *attrib.* with allus. to superficiality or stereotypical attitudes regarded as characteristic of such magazines); **woman's page, women's page** a page of a newspaper devoted to topics intended to be of special interest to women; **woman's work, women's work** work traditionally undertaken by women; **woman's righter** (now *rare*) an advocate of women's rights; **woman's rights** = ***women's rights*** below; **woman's woman** a woman whose qualities etc. are particularly appreciated by other women, a woman who is popular with other women; †**woman-tired** *adjective* (*rare*, Shakes.) henpecked; **woman trouble** *colloq.* (*a*) gynaecological problems; (*b*) difficulties caused to a man by a relationship with a woman or women; **womenpower** = ***woman-power*** above; **women's college** a university college that admits only women as students; **women's group**: formed for the discussion or furtherance of the interests of women; **Women's Institute** an organization of women in rural areas who meet regularly and engage in various social and cultural activities; **women's lib** *colloq.* = ***women's liberation*** below; **women's libber** *colloq.* a supporter of women's liberation; **women's liberation** (*a*) the liberation of women from inequalities and subservient status in relation to men, and from all forms of sexism; (*b*) (usu. with cap. initials) a movement campaigning for these aims; **women's liberationist** a supporter of women's liberation; ***women's magazine***: see ***woman's magazine*** above; **women's movement** (*a*) *the* movement for the recognition and extension of women's rights; (*b*) (usu. with cap. initials) = ***women's liberation*** (b) above; ***women's page***: see ***woman's page*** above; **women's rights** the human rights of women, *esp.* those that promote or secure legal and social equality with men; **women's room** *US* a women's lavatory in a hotel, office, etc.; ***Women's Rural Institute***: see RURAL *adjective*; **women's studies** academic studies concerning women, their role in society, etc.; **women's suffrage** the political enfranchisement of women; **women's wear** clothes for women; ***women's work***: see ***woman's work*** above.

■ **womandom** *noun* (*rare*) women collectively **M19.** **womanhead** *noun* (long *arch.* *rare*) = WOMANHOOD **LME.** **womanity** /-ˈmanɪti/ *noun* (*joc.*, now *rare*) the normal disposition or character of womankind **M19.** **womanless** *adjective* lacking a woman or women, wifeless **ME.** **womanness** /-n-n-/ *noun* womanliness, the fact or quality of being a woman **M19.**

woman /ˈwʊmən/ *verb. colloq.* Infl. **-nn-** (esp. in sense 2), **-n-**. **L16.**
[from the noun.]
†**1 a** *verb intrans.* Become like a woman; behave like a woman. **L16–E17.** ▸**b** *verb trans.* Make like a woman, esp. in weakness or subservience. *rare* (Shakes.). Only in **E17.**
2 *verb trans.* Provide with (esp. a crew or staff of) women. Cf. MAN *verb.* **E18.**
3 *verb trans.* Address as 'woman'. **M18.**

womanfully /ˈwʊmənfʊli, -f(ə)li/ *adverb.* **E19.**
[from WOMAN *noun* after *manfully*: see -LY[2].]
With womanly courage or perseverance.

📖 *Bucks Examiner* The two sopranos . . rose womanfully to Mozart's demands.

womanhood /ˈwʊmənhʊd/ *noun.* **LME.**
[from WOMAN *noun* + -HOOD.]
1 The state or condition of being a woman (as opp. to a man). **LME.** ▸**b** The state of being a grown woman; female maturity. **E17.**
2 The disposition, character, or qualities natural to a woman; womanliness. **LME.**
3 Women collectively, womankind. **E16.**

📖 **1b** J. DUNN Sisters groping their way towards womanhood, with no sympathetic older woman as . . guide. **2** DICKENS Miss Brass's maiden modesty and gentle womanhood.

womanise *verb* var. of WOMANIZE.

womanish /ˈwʊmənɪʃ/ *adjective.* **LME.**
[from WOMAN *noun* + -ISH[1].]
1 Of, pertaining to, or used by a woman or women. Now *rare.* **LME.**
2 Now chiefly *derog.* ▸**a** Characteristic of or suitable for a woman or women. **LME.** ▸**b** Resembling a woman, womanlike; *spec.* (*a*) (of a man) effeminate; (*b*) (of a girl) behaving like a woman. **LME.**
†**3** Excessively fond of women. *rare.* Only in **16.**
■ **womanishly** *adverb* **L16.** **womanishness** *noun* **M16.**

womanism /ˈwʊmənɪz(ə)m/ *noun.* **M19.**
[from WOMAN *noun* + -ISM.]
Advocacy of or enthusiasm for the rights, achievements, etc., of women; *spec.* (chiefly *Black English*) a form of feminism emphasizing the celebration of the contribution of women to society as a whole.

womanist /ˈwʊmənɪst/ *noun.* **E17.**
[from WOMAN *noun* + -IST; in sense 2 after *feminist*.]
†**1** A womanizer. *rare.* Only in **E17.**
2 An advocate of womanism. **L20.**

womanize /ˈwʊmənʌɪz/ *verb.* Also **-ise**. **L16.**
[from WOMAN *noun* + -IZE.]
1 *verb trans.* Make a woman of; make effeminate, emasculate, (a man). **L16.**
2 *verb intrans.* Of a man: pursue or engage in casual sexual encounters with women; philander. **L19.**
■ **womanizer** *noun* a philanderer **E20.**

womankind /ˈwʊmənkʌɪnd/ *noun.* **LME.**
[from WOMAN *noun* + KIND *noun*. Cf. WOMENKIND.]
†**1** A female person; a woman. **LME–E19.**
2 The female sex; women collectively or in general. **LME.**
3 The women of a family, household, country, etc., collectively; (one's) female relatives, friends, etc. **L16.**

womanlike /ˈwʊmənlʌɪk/ *adjective & adverb.* **LME.**
[from WOMAN *noun* + -LIKE.]
▶ **A** *adjective.* Resembling or characteristic of a woman or women; *derog.* womanish. **LME.**
▶ **B** *adverb.* In a womanly or womanlike manner. **LME.**

womanly /ˈwʊmənli/ *adjective.* **ME.**
[from WOMAN *noun* + -LY[1].]
1 (Of a person, an act, etc.) having or showing the qualities or attributes (as gentleness, devotion, fearfulness, etc.) regarded as characteristic of or appropriate for women; (of a quality) characteristic of or appropriate for a woman, feminine. Formerly also, (of a man) effeminate. **ME.**
2 Having the character of, befitting, or characteristic of a woman as opp. to a girl. **E18.**

📖 **1** SOUTHEY Womanly sobs were heard, and manly cheeks Were wet with silent tears. M. KENNEDY Telemachus . . upbraids his mother for not behaving like a womanly woman. A. BROOKNER Harmless womanly things, like spending money on clothes. **2** STEELE The Girl was very proud of the Womanly Employment of a Nurse. DICKENS A short, brown, womanly girl of fourteen.

■ **womanliness** *noun* **M16.**

womanly /ˈwʊmənli/ *adverb. arch.* **ME.**
[from WOMAN *noun* + -LY[2].]
In a womanly manner; like a woman.

📖 W. M. SPACKMAN She was as womanly sweet as she was sexually delicious.

womanthrope /ˈwʊmənθrəʊp/ *noun. rare.* **L19.**
[Joc. formation on WOMAN *noun* after *misanthrope*.]
A hater of women.

womb /wuːm/ *noun.*
[Old English *wamb, womb* = Old Frisian, Middle Low German, Middle Dutch *wamme* (Dutch *wam*), Old Frankish *wamba*, Old High German *wamba, wampa* (German *Wamme*), Old Norse *vǫmb*, Gothic *wamba*, from Germanic, of unkn. origin. See also WAME.]
1 The organ in the body of a woman or female mammal in which offspring are carried, protected, and nourished before birth; the uterus. **OE.** ▸**b** *fig.* A place of origin, development, or growth. **LME.**
†**2** The abdomen, the belly; the stomach. **OE–E19.**
3 (A thing resembling) a hollow space or cavity. Formerly also, a round hollow object or part. **OE.**
1 ***suffocation of the womb***: see SUFFOCATION 2.
Comb.: **womb-to-tomb** *adjective* (of a procedure etc.) spanning an entire lifetime.
■ **wombed** *adjective* (*rare*) having a womb of a specified kind **ME.** **womblike** *adjective* resembling a womb; providing protection, containment, or isolation: **M20.** **womby** *adjective* (having a cavity) that resembles a womb, hollow **L16.**

womb /wuːm/ *verb trans.* **M16.**
[from the noun.]
Enclose as in a womb.

wombat /ˈwɒmbat/ *noun.* **L18.**
[Aboriginal.]
Each of three Australian burrowing marsupials constituting the genera *Vombatus* and *Lasiorhinus* (family Vombatidae), which have a thick heavy bearlike body and short legs; *esp.* (more fully ***common wombat***) *V. ursinus*, of SE Australia and Tasmania.

womble *noun* var. of WAMBLE *noun*.

women *noun* pl. of WOMAN *noun*.

womenfolk /ˈwɪmɪnfəʊk/ *noun pl.* Also (chiefly *US colloq.*) **-folks**. **M19.**
[from *women* pl. of WOMAN *noun* + FOLK.]
1 Women collectively, womankind. **M19.**
2 The women of a particular family, household, or other group. **M19.**

womenish /ˈwɪmɪnɪʃ/ *adjective. rare.* **L19.**
[formed as prec. + -ISH[1].]
Of, pertaining to, or characteristic of women.

womenkind /ˈwɪmɪnkʌɪnd/ *noun.* **LME.**
[formed as prec. + KIND *noun*.]
1 = WOMANKIND 2. **LME.**
2 = WOMANKIND 3. **M17.**

wommera *noun* var. of WOOMERA.

wompoo /ˈwɒmpuː/ *noun.* **L19.**
[Imit. of the bird's call.]
More fully ***wompoo fruit-dove, wompoo pigeon***. A large colourful Australian fruit-dove, *Ptilinopus magnificus*, with green upperparts, pale grey head, purple breast, and yellow abdomen. Also called ***magnificent fruit-dove***.

womyn /ˈwɪmɪn/ *noun pl. non-standard.* **L20.**
[Alt. of *women*, adopted by some feminists to avoid the ending *-men*. Cf. WIMMIN.]
Women.

won /wɒn, wɔːn/ *noun.* Pl. same. **M20.**
[Korean *wŏn*.]
The basic monetary unit of North and South Korea, equal to 100 jun in North Korea and 100 jeon in South Korea.

won /wɒn/ *verb*[1]. Now *arch., Scot., & north.* Infl. **-nn-**; pa. t. & pple **wonned**, **wont** /wɒnt/; see also WONT *adjective*. Also **wone** /wəʊn/.
[Old English *wunian, gewunian*, = Old Frisian *wunia, wonia*, Old Saxon *wunon, wonon*, Old High German *wonēn* (Dutch *wonen*, German *wohnen*), Old Norse *una*, from Germanic base also of WONE *noun*: cf. WONT *adjective*, WONTED *adjective*. See also WIN *verb*[2].]
▶ **I 1** *verb intrans.* Stay habitually, reside, have one's home. **OE.**
†**2** *verb intrans.* Continue to be, remain; exist, live. **OE–M17.**
†**3** *verb trans.* Inhabit, live in. **OE–E17.**
▶ **II 4** *verb intrans.* Be accustomed *to do* something. Cf. WONT *adjective*. Long *obsolete* exc. *Scot.* **OE.**
†**5** *verb trans.* Accustom (a person, oneself) *to* something. **ME–L15.**
¶ See note s.v. WONT *verb*[1].

won *verb*[2], *verb*[3] *pa. t. & pple*: see WIN *verb*[1], *verb*[3].

wonder /ˈwʌndə/ *noun.*
[Old English *wundor* = Old Frisian *wunder*, Old Saxon *wundar*, Old High German *wuntar* (Dutch *wonder*, German *Wunder*), Old Norse *undr*, of unkn. origin.]
1 An amazing, remarkable, or astonishing person or thing, a prodigy, a remarkable specimen or example *of*. Also, *the* object of profound admiration for a particular people, age, etc. **OE.** ▸**b** Amazing, remarkable, or astonishing character or quality; wonderfulness; *rare* wonders collectively. **ME.**

2 a A miraculous or supernatural act or event, a miracle. *arch.* OE. ▸**b** A remarkable or astonishing act or achievement. Freq. in ***do wonders***, ***perform wonders***, etc. ME.
3 An astonishing or surprising occurrence or event, a surprising thing. Formerly *spec.*, an extraordinary natural occurrence regarded as an omen or portent (usu. in *pl.*). ME.
†**4** An evil act, evil; destruction, disaster; great distress or grief. ME–L16.
5 The emotion or attitude excited by the perception of something unexpected, unfamiliar, or inexplicable; *esp.* surprise or astonishment mingled with admiration, perplexity, or curiosity. Formerly also, an instance of this. ME. ▸†**b** Profound admiration. L16–E17.
6 A state of wondering (*whether*, *if*, etc.). *rare.* M19.
7 = CRULLER. *US.* M19.

> 📖 **1** GOLDSMITH The wonders of the Mediterranean sea. A. ALVAREZ He looked at her with awe, as though she were unique, a wonder. **b** T. GRAY Great things and full of wonder . . I shall unfold. **2b** SHAKES. *1 Hen. VI* Where valiant Talbot . . Enacted wonders with his sword and lance. M. WHEELER With limited time and means he wrought wonders. **3** W. COWPER The chilling tale of midnight murder was a wonder . . told to frighten babes. T. MCGUANE It's a wonder we found anything. **5** AV *Acts* 3:10 They were filled with wonder and amazement at that which had happened vnto him. GOLDSMITH Still the wonder grew, That one small head could carry all he knew. P. FITZGERALD Mach's principle that the element of wonder never lies in the phenomenon, but always in the person observing.

Phrases: **boneless wonder** (*a*) a gymnast; (*b*) *fig.* a person lacking backbone. **eighth wonder of the world** *hyperbol.* a particularly impressive object etc. **for a wonder** surprisingly, remarkably; strange to say. **in the name of wonder** *colloq.* as an intensive, adding emphasis to a question. ***nine days' wonder***: see NINE *adjective*. **no wonder**, **small wonder**, etc., one cannot be surprised, it is natural, (*that, if*); one might have guessed (*that*). **seven wonders of the world** the seven buildings and monuments traditionally regarded as the most spectacular of the ancient world. ***small wonder***: see ***no wonder*** above. **the wonder is** what is surprising is (*that*). **to a wonder** *arch.* wonderfully, marvellously well. **work wonders** (*a*) do miracles; (*b*) succeed remarkably, produce remarkable or marvellous results.
Attrib. & comb.: In the sense 'of the nature of a wonder, having marvellous or amazing properties' as ***wonder boy***, ***wonder drug***, ***wonder woman***, etc. Special combs., as **wonder-horn** (*a*) *rare* a cornucopia of marvels; (*b*) a magical horn; **wonderland** (*a*) a fairyland; (*b*) a land or realm full of surprises or marvels; **wonder-monger** (*arch.*, chiefly *derog.*) a person who deals in or relates wonders, a wonder-worker; **wonder rabbi** in Hasidic Judaism, a tsaddik; **wonderstone** GEOLOGY (*a*) (now *rare*) a red and transparent yellow breccia found in the Mendips area of Somerset, England; (*b*) a soft bluish-grey South African rock of volcanic origin that takes a high polish; **wonder-stricken**, **wonder-struck** *adjectives* reduced to silence by wonder; **wonder-work** (*a*) a marvellous achievement, *esp.* a miracle; (*b*) a wonderful structure or artefact; (*c*) *rare* marvellous work or workmanship; **wonder-worker** a person who performs wonders, *esp.* a thaumaturge; **wonder-working** *adjective* that performs wonders, esp. miracles.
■ **wonderly** *adjective* (long *obsolete* exc. *US dial.*) of the nature of a wonder, wonderful OE.

wonder /ˈwʌndə/ *verb.* OE.
[from the noun.]
1 *verb intrans.* Be filled with wonder, great surprise, or astonishment (*at, over*). OE. ▸**b** *verb trans.* Be surprised to find (*that, to do*). OE.
2 *verb trans.* Desire or be curious to know, (*how, whether, why*, etc.). Now also introducing a tentative inquiry or polite request (*if, whether*, etc.). ME.
†**3** *verb trans.* Regard with (admiring) wonder; marvel at. M16–L19.
†**4** *verb trans.* Cause to wonder, astonish. M16–L18.

> 📖 **1** SHAKES. *Cymb.* Whilst I am bound to wonder, I am bound to pity too. SIR W. SCOTT It cannot be wondered at if he took such opportunities as offered. B. CAPES His benevolent truthfulness was a thing to wonder over. **b** SHAKES. *Much Ado* I wonder that you will still be tacking. **2** J. M. BARRIE I wonder if you would give me a mug of tea. J. WAIN People . . wondered . . how you were getting on. I. MURDOCH Bruno wondered if he could tell Nigel. E. WELTY Where am I? he wondered. **3** GOLDSMITH It is not . . to be wondered, that there were many complaints.

Phrases: **I shouldn't wonder** *colloq.* it would not surprise me; I think it quite likely. **I wonder** I rather doubt it.
■ **wonderer** *noun* a person who wonders at a person or thing L16. **wondering** *noun* (*a*) the action of the verb; †(*b*) *rare* an object of wonder, a marvel: OE. **wondering** *adjective* that wonders, marvelling; filled with wonder: L16. **wonderingly** *adverb* in a wondering manner, in or with wonder M16.

wonder /ˈwʌndə/ *adverb.* Long *obsolete* exc. *Scot.* ME.
[from the noun.]
Wondrously, surprisingly; exceedingly, very.

wonderful /ˈwʌndəfʊl, -f(ə)l/ *adjective & adverb.* LOE.
[from WONDER *noun* + -FUL. Cf. WUNNERFUL.]
▸**A** *adjective.* **1** That arouses wonder or astonishment, marvellous; very remarkable or admirable; extremely good, excellent. LOE.
†**2** Filled with wonder or admiration. *rare.* LME–L16.

> 📖 **1** DICKENS Mr. Tomkins . . had a wonderful eye for the picturesque. *Punch* A wonderful performer for such a small horse-powered car. ***weird and wonderful***: see WEIRD *adjective*.

▸**B** *adverb.* In a wonderful manner; to a wonderful degree or extent. Now *dial.* LME.
■ **wonderfully** *adverb* (*a*) in a wonderful manner, to a wonderful degree or extent; (as an intensive) remarkably well or much, extraordinarily, exceedingly; †(*b*) *rare* with wonder or admiration: ME. **wonderfulness** *noun* LME.

wonderment /ˈwʌndəm(ə)nt/ *noun.* Chiefly *literary.* LME.
[from WONDER *verb* + -MENT.]
1 An expression of wonder (*arch.*, esp. in ***make a wonderment***); a state of wonder, surprise, or awe. LME.
2 An object of or matter for wonder; a wonderful thing. LME. ▸**b** A wonderful example or instance *of* something. E17.
3 Wonderful quality, marvellousness. L16.

> 📖 **1** COLERIDGE *'Nor cold, nor stern, my soul!'* They gape for wonderment. F. TROLLOPE What wonderments you do make about nothing. G. H. LEWES The mind passes from wonderment at the miraculous. **3** R. COBB The sheer wonderment of his first fortnight of liberty.

†**wonders** *adjective & adverb.* ME–E17.
[from WONDER *noun* + -'S[1]. Cf. next.]
= WONDROUS.

wondrous /ˈwʌndrəs/ *adjective & adverb.* Now *arch. & poet.* L15.
[Alt. of WONDERS by substitution of -OUS after *marvellous.*]
Wonderful(ly).
■ **wondrously** *adverb* in a wondrous manner; to a wonderful degree: E16.

†**wone** *noun.* Also **wonne**. ME.
[Aphet. from Old English *gewuna*, corresp. to Old Saxon *giwono*, Old High German *giwona* from Germanic base also of WON *verb*[1]. Cf. WONT *noun.*]
1 Established usage or custom, an instance of this, a habit; habitual action or conduct, habits collectively. ME–M16.
2 A dwelling-place, an abode, a home. Orig. *spec.*, a world. ME–M18.

†**wone** *verb* var. of WON *verb*[1].

wong /wɒŋ/ *noun.* Long *obsolete* exc. in place-names.
[Old English *wang*, *wong* = Old Saxon, Old High German *wang* (German dial. *Wang* mountain slope), Old Norse *vangr* (Swedish dial. *vång*, Danish *vang*), from Germanic.]
A plain, a field; a piece of meadowland; *spec.* a piece of unenclosed land, a common.

wonga /ˈwɒŋɡə, ˈv-/ *noun. slang.* L20.
[Perh. from Romany *wongar* coal, money.]
Money.

> 📖 A. ENRIGHT But do they go home empty handed? Or do they wander off with a wad of wonga?

wongai /ˈwɒŋɡʌɪ/ *noun. Austral.* M20.
[Aboriginal.]
The jujube tree, *Ziziphus jujuba* (also ***wongai tree***); the fruit of this tree.

wonga-wonga /ˈwɒŋɡəˈwɒŋɡə/ *noun. Austral.* Also **wonga** /ˈwɒŋɡə/. E19.
[Aboriginal.]
1 A large Australian pigeon, *Leucosarcia melanoleuca*, which has mainly grey plumage, and a white belly with black markings. Also ***wonga-wonga pigeon***. E19.
2 In full ***wonga-wonga vine***. A woody twining Australian plant, *Pandorea pandorana* (family Bignoniaceae), with pinnate leaves and tubular creamy white flowers which are suffused with red or purple at the throat. L19.

wongi /ˈwɒŋɡi/ *noun. Austral. slang.* E20.
[Aboriginal.]
A talk, a chat; a speech.

wonk /wɒŋk/ *noun*[1]. E20.
[Perh. repr. Chinese (Cantonese) *wōng kaú* yellow dog.]
In China, a dog. Also ***wonk dog***.

wonk /wɒŋk/ *noun*[2]. *slang* (chiefly *derog.*). E20.
[Origin unkn.]
1 NAUTICAL An incompetent or inexperienced sailor; *spec.* a naval cadet. E20.
2 *Austral.* **a** A white person. M20. ▸**b** An effeminate or homosexual man. M20.
3 A studious or hard-working person. Esp. in ***policy wonk***, a person obsessively interested in the details of political policy, legislation, etc. *US.* M20.

wonky /ˈwɒŋki/ *adjective. slang.* E20.
[Fanciful.]
Shaky, loose, unstable, unsteady; faulty, unreliable; crooked.
■ **wonkily** *adverb* L20. **wonkiness** *noun* L20.

wonner /ˈwɒnə/ *noun.* Long *arch.* Also †**woner**. ME.
[from WON *verb*[1] + -ER[1].]
A dweller, an inhabitant.
¶ Not recorded between E16 and M19.

wonning /ˈwʌnɪŋ/ *noun.* Long *rare* or *obsolete* exc. *dial.* OE.
[from WON *verb*[1] + -ING[1].]
†**1** The action of WON *verb*[1]; the state of dwelling or abiding (in a place). OE–LME.
2 A dwelling-place; a dwelling, a habitation. OE.
†**3** (A) custom, (a) habit. *rare.* LME–E17.

wont /wəʊnt/ *noun.* Now *formal* or *joc.* ME.
[Perh. from a conflation of *it is my wone* and *I am wont*: see WONE *noun*, WONT *adjective*.]
What is habitual or customary; a custom, a habit.

> 📖 W. TREVOR He would, as was his wont . . , walk for a mile. *Nature* It was the wont to rank science . . among the highest . . pursuits. **of wont** *arch.* customary, usual. ***use and wont***: see USE *noun*.

wont /wəʊnt/ *adjective. arch.* OE.
[pa. pple of *gewunian*: see WON *verb*[1]. Cf. WONTED, -ED[1].]
1 Familiar *with* or (formerly also) used *to* a thing, practice, or condition. Long *obsolete* exc. *Scot.* OE.
2 Accustomed, apt, liable. Usu. foll. by *to do*. OE.
3 = WONTED 2. Long *obsolete* exc. *Scot.* LME.

> 📖 **2** SIR W. SCOTT The lark was wont my matins ring. DICKENS All is going on as it was wont. W. D. WHITNEY Such a distinction is wont to be termed 'inorganic'. A. STORR Someone . . toward whom she was wont to turn for . . support.

wont /wəʊnt/ *verb*[1]. *arch.* 3 sing. pres. **wonts**, **wont**. Pa. t. & pple **wont**, **wonted**. LME.
[from WONT *adjective* or back-form. from WONTED.]
1 *verb trans.* Make (a person) accustomed or used *to*; *refl.* become accustomed or used *to*. LME.
2 *verb intrans.* Be or become accustomed (*to, to do*). M16.

> 📖 **2** W. BURKITT Had he not wonted to converse formerly with them, he had not now been sought. J. BRUCE He who had wont to come to the patriarchs . . had actually come to him.

¶ Pa. t. & pple *wont* not always distinguishable from pa. t. & pple of WON *verb*[1].

wont *verb*[2] *pa. t. & pple*: see WON *verb*[1], WONT *verb*[1].

won't /wəʊnt/ *noun. colloq.* E20.
[from *won't*: see WILL *verb*[1].]
An utterance of 'won't'; a refusal to do something.

won't *verb*: see WILL *verb*[1].

wonted /ˈwəʊntɪd/ *adjective.* LME.
[from WONT *noun* or as extension of *wont* pa. pple of WON *verb*[1]: see -ED[2], -ED[1]. Cf. WONT *adjective*.]
1 †**a** = WONT *adjective* 2. LME–E17. ▸**b** Used *to* a thing, practice, or condition. Also, (made) familiar with one's environment. Cf. WONT *adjective* 1. Now *N. Amer.* E17.
2 Habitual, customary, usual. LME.

> 📖 **2** F. NORRIS McTeague had relapsed to his wonted stolidity.

■ **wontedly** *adverb* customarily, habitually, usually M16. **wontedness** *noun* (*rare*) accustomedness, habituation M17.

†**wontless** *adjective. poet.* L16—M19.
[from WONT *noun* + -LESS.]
Unaccustomed, unwonted, unusual.

wonton /wɒnˈtɒn/ *noun.* Also **won ton**. M20.
[Chinese (Cantonese) *wān t'ān*.]
In Chinese cookery: (a dish consisting of) a small round dumpling or roll with a savoury filling (esp. of minced pork), usually eaten boiled in soup.
Comb.: **wonton soup** soup containing wontons.

woo /wuː/ *noun. colloq.* M20.
[from next.]
(A spell of) caressing or lovemaking; *spec.* sexual intercourse, love.

> 📖 *Guardian* Couples making woo in motor-cars should be careful not to rock them too much. ***pitch the woo***, ***pitch woo***: see PITCH *verb*[2].

woo /wuː/ *verb*[1]. Now *literary.*
[Late Old English *wōgian* (intrans.), *āwōgian* (trans.), of unkn. origin.]
▸**I** *verb intrans.* **1** Court a woman; behave amorously. LOE.
2 Make an appeal, solicit, plead. *arch.* E17.
▸**II** *verb trans.* **3** Pay court to, court, seek the hand or love of, (esp. a woman); seek the favour or support of (a person, group, etc.); try to gain, win, or achieve (fame, fortune, etc.). LOE.
4 Entreat, importune; coax. LME.

> 📖 **3** W. COWPER They that woo preferment. W. BALLANTINE A theatre which . . had wooed in vain the patronage of the public. C. STEAD A woman that Sam had loved, wooed and given his name to. *Economist* Advertisers—those keen to woo the teenage and yuppie markets. **4** ROBERT BURTON To little purpose he wooed the King and Queen for Reparation. W. COWPER Begone!—I woo thee not to stay. T. G. BOWLES A splendid summer day, wooing the very coat off your back.

■ **wooable** *adjective* suitable for wooing E20.

woo /wuː/ *verb*[2] *trans.* E20.
[Origin unkn.]
= MAH-JONG *verb*.

wood /wʊd/ *noun*[1] *& adjective*[1].

[Old English *wudu* later form of *widu*, *wiodu* = Old High German *witu*, Old Norse *viðr*, from Germanic word rel. to Old Irish *fid* tree, wood, Irish *fiodh*, Welsh *gwŷdd* trees.]

▶ **A** *noun*. **I 1** †**a** A tree. OE–ME. ▶**b** *transf.* An object made from trees or their branches, as a ship, a spear, the Cross. Long *arch.* exc. as passing into sense 7. OE.

2 *sing.* & in *pl.* A collection of trees growing more or less thickly together (esp. naturally, rather than as a plantation) over a considerable area; a piece of ground covered with trees, with or without undergrowth. OE. ▶**b** *transf. & fig.* [After Latin *silva*.] A collection or crowd of spears etc. suggesting the trees of a wood; *gen.* a collection, a crowd. Now *rare* or *obsolete*. L16.

3 Wooded country, woodland; trees collectively (growing together). OE.

📖 **1b** J. M. NEALE His precious Body . . broken on The Wood. **2** E. O'BRIEN It is a young wood, and the pine trees have not grown to any reasonable height. DENNIS POTTER He remembered the cottage, nearly three miles along a track into the woods. **3** ***brushwood, copsewood, hedge-wood, shelter wood, underwood***, etc.

▶ **II 4 a** The substance of which the roots, trunks, and branches of trees and shrubs consist; trunks or other parts of trees collectively. Also *spec.*, the hard compact fibrous part of this, consisting largely of secondary xylem, which forms the strengthening and water-transporting tissue of the plant. OE. ▶**b** This material as cut for use in building, as fuel, in crafts and manufacturing, etc. Freq. with specifying word. OE. ▶**c** In biblical use, wood as the material of an idol or image. M16. ▶**d** *fig.* [After Greek and Latin use.] The stuff of which a person is made. L16.

5 *spec.* in HORTICULTURE. The substance of the branches of a tree or shrub; branches collectively, esp. (in a fruit tree) those primarily leaf-bearing not fruit-bearing. E16.

6 A particular kind of wood. L16.

7 A thing made of wood: *spec.* (**a**) the wooden part of something, as the shaft of a spear, the frame or handle of a tennis racket; (**b**) a cask or barrel as a container for wine, beer, etc. (as distinct from a bottle); (**c**) *arch. slang* the pulpit; (**d**) (now *rare*) the woodwind section of an orchestra. L17. ▶**b** Each of the large bowls used in the game of bowls. L19. ▶**c** GOLF. Orig., a golf club with a wooden head. Now more widely, a club with a head which is relatively broad from front to back, of wood, plastic, or light metal. Also (more fully ***wood shot***), a shot made with such a club. E20.

📖 **4a** A. D. IMMS Lucanid larvae inhabit the rotting wood of trees. J. COX The cambium, a thin film of tissue . . that sheathes the wood. ***reaction wood, tension wood***, etc. **b** SIR W. SCOTT Heap on more wood!—the wind is chill. *She* Construct a four-poster bedframe from 2 × 2 inch wood. ***balsa wood, elm wood, olive-wood, rosewood, sandalwood, yellow-wood***, etc. ***brushwood, firewood, kindling-wood, lop-wood, pit-wood, round wood***, etc. **6** *Country Living* He uses six native woods: yew, cherry, ash, lime, sycamore and walnut. **7** I. MURDOCH Michael knocked briskly with his fist on the wood of the door. *Wine & Spirits* A gran reserva must be aged for . . two years in wood.

Phrases: ***babes in the wood***: see BABE noun 2. ***cock-of-the-wood***: see COCK noun[1]. ***dead wood***: see DEAD adjective. ***early wood***: see EARLY adjective. ***greenwood***: see GREEN adjective. **have the wood on** *Austral. & NZ colloq.* have the upper hand over, have a hold on. ***hewers of wood and drawers of water***: see HEWER. **in a wood** (now *rare* or *obsolete*) in difficulty, trouble, or perplexity; at a loss. ***knock on wood, knock wood***: see KNOCK verb. ***late wood***: see LATE adjective. ***neck of the woods***: see NECK noun[1]. **not see the wood for the trees, see the wood for the trees** (fail to) grasp the main issue or gain a general view among a mass of details (usu. in neg. contexts). ***open woods***: see OPEN adjective. **out of the wood(s)** out of danger or difficulty. ***plastic wood***: see PLASTIC adjective & noun[3]. ***saw wood***: see SAW verb[1]. ***see the wood for the trees***: see ***not see the wood for the trees*** above. TOUCHWOOD. ***touch wood***: see TOUCH verb.

Comb.: **wood-acid** = ***wood-vinegar*** below; **wood alcohol** = ***wood spirit*** (b) below; **wood-and-water joey** *Austral. slang* an odd job man; ***wood anemone***: see ANEMONE 1; **wood ant** (*a*) a large reddish European ant, *Formica rufa*, which builds domed nests especially noticeable in woodland; (*b*) *W. Indies* a kind of termite; **wood apple** a gum-yielding tree of tropical Asia, *Limonia acidissima*, allied to the citruses; the edible fruit of this tree; ***wood AVENS***; **wood-axe** an axe for hewing wood or felling trees; **wood barley** a European grass of calcareous woodland, *Hordelymus europaeus*, resembling barley but with hermaphrodite lateral spikelets; **wood betony** (*a*) the plant betony, *Stachys officinalis*; (*b*) *N. Amer.* a kind of lousewort, *Pedicularis canadensis*; **wood-bill** = BILL noun[1] 2; **wood bison, wood buffalo** a variety of American bison found in wooded parts of western Canada; **woodblock** a block of wood, as used for making floors etc.; *spec.* (*a*) one from which a woodcut is made; (*b*) MUSIC = ***temple block*** s.v. TEMPLE noun[1]; **wood-borer** a thing that bores wood; *esp.* any of various insects and other invertebrates which make holes in wood; **wood-boring** *adjective* that makes holes in wood; ***wood buffalo***: see ***wood bison*** above; **wood-burner** (*a*) an engine, ship, etc., that is fuelled with wood; (*b*) a wood-burning stove or fire; **wood-burning** *adjective* using wood as fuel, heated or driven by the burning of wood; **wood-butcher** *US slang* a carpenter, *esp.* an inexperienced one; **wood-carpet** (*a*) a floor-covering made of thin pieces of wood, often arranged in patterns; (*b*) a brown and white geometrid moth, *Epirrhoe rivata*; **woodchat (shrike)** a shrike, *Lanius senator*, of southern Europe, northern Africa, and the Middle East, having black and white plumage with a chestnut head; **woodchip** (*a*) a chip of wood; (*b*) (in full ***woodchip paper***) wallpaper with woodchips etc. embedded in it to give an uneven surface texture; **wood-chop** *Austral. & NZ* a wood-chopping contest; **wood-chopper** (chiefly *N. Amer.*) = WOODCUTTER 1; **wood-coal** (*a*) *arch.* charcoal made from wood; (*b*) = LIGNITE; **wood-copper** MINERALOGY a banded brown fibrous variety of olivenite; **woodcreeper** any of the birds of the Neotropical family Dendrocolaptidae, which have the tail feathers stiffened to aid in climbing tree-trunks; **wood-dove** (*a*) = WOODPIGEON; (*b*) any of several African doves of the genus *Turtur* (usu. with specifying word); **wood-drake** a male wood-duck; **wood-duck** any of various ducks which inhabit woodland, *esp.* the N. American *Aix sponsa* and the Australian *Chenonetta jubata*; **wood-engraver** (*a*) a person who makes wood-engravings; (*b*) any of various N. American wood-boring beetles, esp. *Xyleborus caelatus*; **wood-engraving** (*a*) a design cut in relief on a block of wood, *spec.* across the grain (cf. WOODCUT); (*b*) a print made from the impression of such a relief; (*c*) the technique of making such reliefs and prints; **wood-fibre**: obtained from wood, esp. as a material for making paper; **wood-fire** a fire made (primarily) of wood; **wood-fired** *adjective* = ***wood-burning*** above; **wood-flour** powdered wood or fine sawdust, as used in the manufacture of explosives, plastics, linoleum, etc.; **wood-free** *adjective* †(*a*) entitled to take wood without payment; (*b*) PAPER-MAKING not made from mechanically-produced wood pulp (though usu. made from chemical wood pulp); **wood-frog** a frog found in woods, *esp.* the N. American *Rana sylvatica*; **wood germander** = ***wood sage*** below; **wood-god** = ***wood-spirit*** (a) below; **wood-grain** (a surface or finish imitating) the grain of wood; **woodgrouse** any of several game-birds, as the capercaillie, the spruce grouse, and the willow grouse; **wood grub** the larva of any of several wood-boring insects; **woodhack** (long *obsolete* exc. *dial.*) [cf. NUTHATCH] a woodpecker; **wood-heap** *Austral.* = WOODPILE 1; **wood-hen** (*a*) (now *rare*) a woodcock, *esp.* a female one; (*b*) = WEKA; **wood-hole** a hole or recess in which wood is stored for fuel (cf. ***coal-hole*** s.v. COAL noun); **wood hoopoe** any of several African birds of the genus *Phoeniculus* or family Phoeniculidae, which have dark glossy plumage and a long bill and tail; ***wood HYACINTH***; **wood-ibis** (*a*) a stork, *Mycteria americana*, of wooded swamps from the southern US to central S. America (also called ***wood-stork***); (*b*) (more fully ***crested wood ibis***) an ibis, *Lophotibis cristata*, of Madagascar; **wood-knife** (*a*) (now *arch.* or *Hist.*) a dagger or short sword used by huntsmen for cutting up game, or generally as a weapon; (*b*) a large knife for cutting off branches or twigs; **wood laurel** the spurge laurel, *Daphne laureola*; **wood-leopard** = ***leopard moth*** s.v. LEOPARD noun; **wood lily** any of various chiefly white-flowered shade-loving plants; *spec.* a trillium, esp. *Trillium grandiflorum*; **wood-lot** (orig. *US*) a plot of land containing or consisting of woodland; **wood-meal** (*a*) a kind of flour resembling sawdust in appearance, prepared from the root of the manioc or cassava; (*b*) *rare* powdered wood, as used in explosives, or produced by wood-worms; **wood millet** a woodland grass, *Milium effusum*, with one-flowered spikelets on fine spreading branches; **woodmote** *Hist.* a court for determining cases in forest law; **wood mouse** a mouse which lives in woodland; spec. *Apodemus sylvaticus* of western and central Eurasia and N. Africa, which is brown with white underparts (also called ***long-tailed field mouse***); **woodnote** a natural untrained musical note or song like that of a wild bird (freq. in *pl.*, in later use often with allus. to Milton's description of Shakespeare in *L'Allegro*); **wood nymph** (*a*) a nymph associated with woods or trees, a dryad, a hamadryad; (*b*) (usu. ***woodnymph***) any of several hummingbirds of the genus *Thalurania*; (*c*) any of several N. American satyrid butterflies of the genus *Cercyonis*; **wood-oil** any of several oils or oily substances obtained from various trees; *esp.* (*a*) = ***GURJUN oil***; (*b*) = ***tung oil*** s.v. TUNG 2; **wood-opal** opal with markings like the grain of wood, formed by the replacement of woody tissue with silica; **wood-owl** an owl which lives in woods, *esp.* the tawny owl; **wood-paper**: made (primarily) from wood-pulp; **wood-partridge** (now *rare*) = ***woodgrouse*** above; **wood-pheasant** (now *rare*) = ***woodgrouse*** above; ***wood pimpernel***: see PIMPERNEL 2b; **wood-print** a print from an engraved woodblock, a woodcut; **wood pulp** a wood-fibre reduced mechanically or chemically to pulp as raw material for making paper; **wood-pussy** *N. Amer. colloq.* = ***woods-pussy*** below; **woodquest** (now *dial.*) [QUEEST] the woodpigeon; **wood-rabbit** a rabbit which lives in woods; *US* a cottontail; **wood-ranger** a person who ranges through the woods or countryside (cf. RANGER noun 1b, 2, 3a); **wood rat** any rat of the N. American genus *Neotoma*; **wood-reeve** the steward or overseer of a wood or forest; **wood-rock** a compact variety of asbestos resembling dry wood; **wood rot** a fungal growth that causes wood to rot; **woodrush** any of various grasslike plants (orig. those growing in woods) constituting the genus *Luzula*, of the rush family, which have flat leaves fringed with long hairs; **wood sage** a European labiate plant, *Teucrium scorodonia*, of woods and heaths, having greenish-yellow flowers and a heavy aromatic smell; ***wood sanicle***: see SANICLE 1; **wood-saw** a saw for cutting wood; **woods boss** *N. Amer.* a foreman in charge of lumberjacks; **woods colt** *US colloq.* (*a*) a horse of unknown paternity; (*b*) a foundling, an illegitimate child; **wood-screw** a metal male screw with a slotted head and a sharp point; **wood-sear** *noun & adjective* (now *dial.*) (*a*) *noun* (the insect which produces) cuckoo-spit; also, the season in which a tree or shrub will decay or die if its wood is cut; (*b*) *adjective* = ***wood-seary*** below; **wood-seary** *adjective* (now *dial.*) (of land or soil) sandy, loose and dry; **wood-sere** *noun & adjective* = ***wood-sear*** above; **woodskin (canoe)** in Guyana, a light canoe made of bark; **wood-snail** a snail that inhabits woods, esp. *Cepaea nemoralis*; **wood sorrel** (*a*) a small delicate spring-flowering woodland plant, *Oxalis acetosella* (family Oxalidaceae), having sharp-tasting trifoliate leaves and solitary white flowers veined with purple; (*b*) (with specifying word) a similar plant of the genus *Oxalis*; **wood-spell** *US colloq.* a turn of work at piling or storing wood for fuel; **wood-spirit** (*a*) MYTHOLOGY a spirit associated with or said to dwell in woods; (*b*) crude methanol obtained by destructive distillation of wood; **woods-pussy** *N. Amer. colloq.* a skunk; **woodstar** any of several small hummingbirds (usu. with specifying word); **wood-stork** = ***wood-ibis*** (a) above; **wood-stove** a wood-burning stove; **wood strawberry** the wild strawberry, *Fragaria vesca*; **wood sugar** = XYLOSE; **wood-swallow** any of several Asian and Australasian songbirds of the genus *Artamus* and family Artamidae, which have long wings and short tails, and feed on airborne insects; **wood-tar** a bituminous liquid obtained by distillation of wood; **wood-thrush** (*a*) a thrush of eastern N. America, *Hylocichla mustelina*, with a brown back and dark-spotted white breast, and a loud liquid song; (*b*) *local* the mistle thrush, *Turdus viscivorus*; **wood-tick** an ixodid tick which infests wild and domestic animals and is often found clinging to plants, *esp.* the American *Dermacentor andersoni*; **wood-tin** MINERALOGY a brownish fibrous variety of cassiterite, resembling dry wood; **wood-turner** a person who shapes wood with a lathe; **wood-turning** shaping wood with a lathe; **wood vinegar** crude acetic acid obtained by destructive distillation of wood; also called ***pyroligneous acid***; **wood warbler** (*a*) a small greenish-yellow Eurasian warbler, *Phylloscopus sibilatrix*; (*b*) = WARBLER 2b; **woodware** articles made of wood, woodenware; **woodwasp** (*a*) any of various wasps or similar insects that live in woodland or burrow in rotten wood; (*b*) *spec.*, a member of the family Siricidae of large insects related to sawflies, characterized by long ovipositors and wood-boring larvae (also called ***horntail***); *esp.* (more fully ***giant woodwasp***) the very large *Urocerus gigas*, which superficially resembles a hornet; **wood-wing** THEATRICAL a wing shaped and decorated to represent a tree or trees; **wood-wool** †(*a*) cotton; (*b*) fine shavings of wood, used esp. as a packing material; **wood-wren** (*a*) = ***wood warbler*** (a) above; (*b*) = ***WILLOW warbler***; **woodwright** (chiefly *poet.*) a worker in wood, a carpenter.

▶ **B** *attrib.* or as *adjective*. Made of wood, wooden. M16.

📖 *Daily Telegraph* Decor . . somewhat dated, with flock wallpaper, dark wood tables.

▪ **woodless** *adjective* devoid of woods, not wooded, treeless M16. **woodlet** *noun* (*rare*) a little wood E19.

Wood /wʊd/ *noun*[2]. M19.

[B. *Wood*, 19th-cent. US chemist.]

Wood's alloy, Wood's metal, an easily melted alloy consisting of bismuth, lead, tin, and cadmium in decreasing proportions and used esp. for soldering.

Wood /wʊd/ *noun*[3]. E20.

[Robert W. *Wood* (1868–1955), US physicist.]

MEDICINE. **1** ***Wood's glass***, a form of glass containing cobalt which is opaque to visible light but transmits ultraviolet. E20.

2 ***Wood's light***, ultraviolet light obtained by using a filter of Wood's glass. E20.

wood /wʊd/ *adjective*[2], *noun*[4], *& adverb*. *arch.* exc. *Scot. & dial.*

[Old English *wōd* = Old High German *wuot*, Old Norse *óðr*, Gothic *wōþs* possessed by a devil, from Germanic from Indo-European base repr. also by Latin *vates* seer, poet, Old Irish *fáith* poet.]

▶ **A** *adjective*. **1** Mad, insane, lunatic; (of an animal) rabid. OE.

2 Going beyond all reasonable bounds; senseless; extremely rash or reckless, wild; vehemently excited. OE.

3 a *fig.* Of the sea, wind, fire, etc.: violently agitated, raging. OE. ▶**b** Extremely fierce or violent; irascible; violently angry, enraged, furious. ME.

▶†**B** *noun*. Madness. Only in ME.

▶ **C** *adverb*. Madly, frantically, furiously. Long *rare*. ME.

▶†**D** *verb intrans.* Go mad; rave, rage. Only in LME.

▪ **woodly** *adverb* OE. **woodness** *noun* OE.

wood /wʊd/ *verb*. OE.

[from WOOD noun[1] or (in sense 4) back-form. from WOODED adjective.]

†**1** *verb intrans.* Fell wood. Only in OE.

†**2** *verb intrans.* Hide or take refuge in a wood. LME–M17.

†**3** *verb trans.* Surround with or enclose in a wood; *refl.* hide oneself in a wood. M–L16.

4 a *verb trans.* Supply with wood for fuel; load (a vessel) with wood. Also foll. by *up*. E17. ▶**b** *verb intrans.* Procure or take in a supply of wood for fuel. Also foll. by *up*. M17.

5 *verb trans.* Cover (land) with trees; plant with trees, convert into woodland. E19.

6 *verb trans.* Provide with a wooden support; prop with wood. *rare*. E20.

¶ Not recorded between OE and M16.

woodbine /ˈwʊdbʌɪn/ *noun*. Orig. (now *rare*) **-bind** /-bʌɪnd/. OE.

[from WOOD noun[1] + (alt. of) BIND verb.]

1 Any of various climbing plants, *esp.* (now *dial.*), hedge bindweed, *Calystegia sepium*, and (*US*) Virginia creeper, *Parthenocissus quinquefolia*. OE. ▶**b** *spec.* The common honeysuckle of Europe, *Lonicera periclymenum*. ME.

2 (Usu. **W-**.) ▶**a** (Proprietary name for) a brand of cheap cigarettes; a cigarette of this brand. E20. ▶**b** An Englishman, esp. a soldier (considered as a habitual smoker of Woodbine cigarettes). *Austral. slang*. E20.

▪ **woodbined** *adjective* overgrown or adorned with woodbine L18.

Woodbury /ˈwʊdb(ə)ri/ *noun*. M19.

[See below.]

PHOTOGRAPHY (now *Hist.*). Used *attrib.* & in *comb.* to designate processes invented by the English photographer W. B. Woodbury (1834–85).

Woodbury gravure, *Woodbury process*, etc. **Woodburytype** a photomechanical process by which continuous tone gelatin images are produced from a lead mould; a print so produced.

woodchuck /ˈwʊdtʃʌk/ *noun*. **L17.**
[Alt. of N. Amer. Indian name (prob. Algonquian), by assoc. with WOOD *noun*¹ (cf. Narragansett *ockqutchaun*).]
A common large N. American marmot, *Marmota monax*, with reddish-brown and grey fur. Also called ***groundhog***.

woodcock /ˈwʊdkɒk/ *noun*. Pl. **-s**, (in sense 1 freq.) same. **LOE.**
[from WOOD *noun*¹ + COCK *noun*¹.]
1 A migratory Eurasian bird, *Scolopax rusticola*, related to the snipe, which has a long straight bill and variegated plumage, and is esteemed as a game-bird; occas. *spec.*, the male of this. Also (freq. with specifying word), any of various similar or related birds, esp. (more fully ***American woodcock***) the smaller *Scolopax minor* of eastern N. America. **LOE.**
2 *fig.* A fool, a simpleton, a dupe (with ref. to the bird's ease of capture). *arch.* **LME.**
3 a A variety of large cider apple. **E18.** ▸**b** In full ***woodcock clay***, ***woodcock soil***. A loose soil of clay and gravel. **M18.** ▸**c** Any of various murexes (shells) with a long spine like a woodcock's bill; *esp.* (more fully ***thorny woodcock***) *Murex pecten*. **E19.**
1 Scotch woodcock [fanciful, after *Welsh rabbit*] a savoury dish usu. of scrambled or chopped boiled eggs or an egg and cream sauce served on toast with an anchovy paste.

woodcraft /ˈwʊdkrɑːft/ *noun*. **ME.**
[from WOOD *noun*¹ + CRAFT *noun*.]
1 Skill in matters pertaining to woods or forests, esp. with regard to hunting or stalking deer, or now (chiefly *N. Amer. & Austral.*) to survival and journeying in forested country. **ME.**
2 Skill in woodwork. **M19.**

Wood Cree /wʊd ˈkriː/ *noun & adjectival phr.* **L19.**
[from WOOD *noun*¹ + CREE *noun & adjective*.]
▶**A** *noun*. Pl. **-s**, same.
1 A member of a Cree people originally inhabiting woodland areas of Saskatchewan and Manitoba in Canada. **L19.**
2 The language of this people. **M20.**
▶**B** *attrib.* or as *adjective*. Of or pertaining to this people or their language. **L20.**

woodcut /ˈwʊdkʌt/ *noun*. **M17.**
[from WOOD *noun*¹ + CUT *noun*².]
A design cut in relief on a block of wood, *spec.* with or along the grain (cf. ***wood-engraving*** s.v. WOOD *noun*¹ & *adjective*¹); a print from the impression of such a relief.

woodcutter /ˈwʊdkʌtə/ *noun*. **M18.**
[from WOOD *noun*¹ + CUTTER.]
1 A person who cuts wood; *spec.* a person who cuts down or fells trees, or cuts off their branches, for the wood. **M18.**
2 A maker of woodcuts. **E19.**
■ **woodcutting** *noun* (*a*) the making of woodcuts; (*b*) the action or employment of cutting timber: **L17.**

wooded /ˈwʊdɪd/ *adjective*. **E17.**
[from WOOD *noun*¹, though also taken as pa. pple of WOOD *verb*: see -ED¹, -ED².]
Covered with growing trees; having many woods or forests; provided with wood.
📖 A. MAUPIN A densely wooded ridge lined with eucalyptus trees.

wooden /ˈwʊd(ə)n/ *adjective & verb*. **M16.**
[from WOOD *noun*¹ + -EN⁴, -EN⁵.]
▶**A** *adjective*. **1** Made of wood. Also (*arch. rare*) produced by means of wood; (of employment) concerned with wood. **M16.**
2 Having the quality of wood; resembling (that of) wood; *fig.* stiff, clumsy, or stilted; without animation or flexibility. Formerly also, of inferior character, poor, worthless. **M16.**
3 †**a** Of the woods, sylvan. *rare.* Only in **E17.** ▸**b** = WOODED. *US* (now *rare* or *obsolete*). **E19.**
📖 **2** D. HALBERSTAM Vital in personal contact, he became wooden and stilted in front of the camera.
Special collocations, phrases, & comb.: **accept a wooden nickel**, **accept wooden money**, **take a wooden nickel**, **take wooden money**, etc., *US slang* be fooled or swindled. **up the wooden hill** *colloq.* upstairs to bed (usu. said to children). **wooden cross** a wooden cross on a serviceman's grave; *fig.* death in action regarded ironically as an award of merit. **wooden cut** = WOODCUT. †**wooden dagger** a dagger of laths worn by the personification of Vice in medieval morality plays. **wooden-head** *colloq.* a stupid person, a blockhead. **wooden-headed** *adjective* (*colloq.*) stupid, insensitive. **wooden-headedness** *colloq.* stupidity. **wooden horse** (*a*) *arch.* a ship; (*b*) *Hist.* = HORSE *noun* 5(a); (*c*) = ***Trojan horse*** s.v. TROJAN *adjective* 1. ***wooden leg***: see LEG *noun* 6. ***wooden nutmeg***: see NUTMEG 1. ***wooden overcoat***: see OVERCOAT 2. **wooden pear** = ***woody pear*** s.v. WOODY *adjective* 5. **wooden spoon** a booby prize (orig. a wooden spoon presented to the candidate coming last in the Cambridge mathematical tripos); last place in a competition. **wooden spoonist** a person (in a team) coming last in a competition etc. **wooden suit** *slang* a coffin. **wooden tongue** an infectious disease chiefly of cattle in which the tongue becomes enlarged and hardened, caused by various bacteria, esp. *Actinobacillus lignieresi*. **woodentop** *slang* (*a*) a uniformed policeman; (*b*) a soldier belonging to the Guards; (*c*) = ***wooden-head*** above. **wooden walls** (*a*) *poet. & rhet.* [after Greek (Herodotus) *xulinon teikhos*wooden wall] ships or shipping as a defensive force; (*b*) *CANAD. HISTORY* the large wooden ships formerly used in the Newfoundland seal fishery. **woodenware** articles, esp. household utensils, made of wood. **wooden wedding** (orig. *US*) a fifth wedding anniversary, on which presents made of wood are often given.
▶**B** *verb trans.* **1** Make wooden. *rare.* **M17.**
2 Knock *out*; render unconscious. *Austral. & NZ slang.* **E20.**
■ **woodener** *noun* (*Austral. slang*) a knock-out blow **L19.** **woodenly** *adverb* **M17.** **woodenness** /-n-n-/ *noun* **M19.** **woodeny** *adjective* of a wooden quality **M19.**

wooder /ˈwʊdə/ *noun*. Long *rare* or *obsolete*. **LOE.**
[from WOOD *verb* + -ER¹. Cf. WOODYER.]
A cutter or collector of wood, esp. for fuel.
¶ Not recorded between **LME** and **M18.**

woodhenge /wʊdˈhɛn(d)ʒ/ *noun*. **E20.**
[from WOOD *noun*¹ + HENGE *noun*¹, after *Stonehenge*.]
ARCHAEOLOGY. A prehistoric henge in the form of a circular bank and ditch believed to have contained a circular timber structure; orig. and *spec.* (**W-**) the first such to be discovered, near Stonehenge.

woodhouse *noun* var. of WOODWOSE.

wood-house /ˈwʊdhaʊs/ *noun*. **ME.**
[from WOOD *noun*¹ + HOUSE *noun*¹.]
A house, shed, or room for the storage of wood.

woodie /ˈwʊdi/ *noun*¹. *colloq.* **M20.**
[Abbreviation: see -IE.]
A woodpigeon.

woodie *noun*² var. of WIDDY *noun*¹.

woodiness /ˈwʊdɪnɪs/ *noun*. **E17.**
[from WOODY *adjective* + -NESS.]
1 Woody texture or appearance. **E17.**
2 The condition of being wooded; prevalence or abundance of woodland; woody growth. **L18.**

wooding /ˈwʊdɪŋ/ *noun*. **E17.**
[from WOOD *verb* + -ING¹. Cf. late Old English *wudung* (from *wudian*).]
1 The action of WOOD *verb*; *esp.* the collection of wood for fuel. **E17.**
2 A plantation or collection of trees. *Scot.* **L18.**

woodish /ˈwʊdɪʃ/ *adjective*. Now *rare*. **M16.**
[from WOOD *noun*¹ + -ISH¹.]
1 Having the nature, quality, or consistency of wood; (somewhat) woody. **M16.**
†**2** Pertaining to woods or wooded country; sylvan. **L16–M17.**

woodland /ˈwʊdlənd/ *noun*. **OE.**
[from WOOD *noun*¹ + LAND *noun*¹.]
1 Land covered with trees; a wooded region or piece of ground. **OE.**
2 *ARCHAEOLOGY.* (**W-.**) A hunting and farming culture which flourished in the wooded country of eastern N. America from about 1000 BC to the European settlement, characterized by burial mounds and a distinctive style of pottery. **E20.**
📖 **1** *Natural World* Ancient woodlands are . . often destroyed through misuse or wilful damage. *attrib.*: ***woodland garden***, ***woodland scenery***, etc.
Comb.: **woodland caribou** a caribou of a population found in forested areas of Canada.
■ **woodlanded** *adjective* covered with woodland, wooded *rare* **M20.** **woodlander** *noun* an inhabitant of woodland; *occas.* an animal or plant whose natural habitat is in woodland: **L18.**

woodlark /ˈwʊdlɑːk/ *noun*. **ME.**
[from WOOD *noun*¹ + LARK *noun*¹.]
A lark, *Lullula arborea*, of Europe, NW Africa, and the Middle East, smaller than the skylark and having a shorter tail.

woodlouse /ˈwʊdlaʊs/ *noun*. Pl. **-lice** /-lʌɪs/. **E17.**
[from WOOD *noun*¹ + LOUSE *noun*.]
1 Any small isopod crustacean of the suborder Oniscoidea, typically having a rounded segmented carapace (some forms being able to roll into a ball) and found mainly in damp shady terrestrial habitats. Also called ***sowbug*** & other names. **E17.**
2 Any of various other small invertebrates found in woodwork or in woods, as a mite, a termite, a booklouse, a pill-millipede. **M17.**

woodman /ˈwʊdmən/ *noun*. Pl. **-men**. **LME.**
[from WOOD *noun*¹ + MAN *noun*. Cf. WOODSMAN.]
1 A person who hunts game in a wood or forest; a huntsman. Long *arch.* **LME.**
2 A person who looks after the trees in a wood or forest, a forester or forester's assistant; a person who fells or lops trees for timber or fuel. Also, a person who provides or sells wood. **LME.**
†**3** An inhabitant of the woods, (a figure representing) a wild man; = WOODWOSE. **LME–L18.**
4 A workman who makes something of wood, esp. the woodwork of a carriage. *rare.* **L19.**
Comb.: **woodmancraft**, **woodmanscraft** = WOODMANSHIP.
■ **woodmanship** *noun* the business or skill of a woodman **L16.**

woodmonger /ˈwʊdmʌŋgə/ *noun*. Now chiefly *Hist.* **ME.**
[from WOOD *noun*¹ + MONGER *noun*.]
A dealer in wood; a timber-merchant; *esp.* a seller of wood for fuel.

woodpecker /ˈwʊdpɛkə/ *noun*. Also †**-peck**. **M16.**
[from WOOD *noun*¹ + PECKER.]
1 Any of numerous perching and climbing birds of the subfamily Picinae (family Picidae), which are characterized by the habit of tapping or pecking holes in the trunks and branches of trees in search of invertebrate prey, typically have variegated or strongly marked plumage, and are found in most continents. Freq. with specifying word. **M16.**
2 A machine-gun. *US & Austral. Military slang.* **L19.**
1 ***green woodpecker***, ***hairy woodpecker***, ***ladder-back woodpecker***, ***pied woodpecker***, ***spotted woodpecker***, ***three-toed woodpecker***, etc.

woodpigeon /ˈwʊdpɪdʒɪn, -dʒ(ə)n/ *noun*. **E17.**
[from WOOD *noun*¹ + PIGEON *noun*¹.]
Orig., any of various kinds of pigeon that may live in woods, as the stock dove, *Columba oenas*. Now usu. *spec.* the large *Columba palumbus* of western Eurasia and NW Africa, which has blue-grey plumage with white crescent markings on the wings (also called ***ring-dove***).

woodpile /ˈwʊdpʌɪl/ *noun*. **M16.**
[from WOOD *noun*¹ + PILE *noun*⁴.]
1 A pile of wood stored esp. for fuel. **M16.**
2 A xylophone. *slang.* **M20.**
1 ***nigger in the woodpile***: see NIGGER *noun* 1.

woodruff /ˈwʊdrʌf/ *noun*. Also **-roof** /-ruːf/.
[Old English *wudurofe*, from *wudu* WOOD *noun*¹ + unexpl. 2nd elem.]
A low-growing Eurasian woodland plant of the madder family, *Galium odoratum*, with whorled leaves and clusters of small white flowers which smell of hay when dry. Also (with specifying word), any of several related plants.

Woodruff key /ˈwʊdrʌf kiː/ *noun phr.* **L19.**
[from *Woodruff* Manufacturing Co., Hartford, Connecticut, US.]
A key whose cross-section is part circular (to fit into a curved keyway in a shaft) and part rectangular, used chiefly in machinery.

woodshed /ˈwʊdʃɛd/ *noun*. **M19.**
[from WOOD *noun*¹ + SHED *noun*².]
1 A shed for storing wood, esp. for fuel. Also *euphem.*, a lavatory. **M19.**
2 A private place, out of the sight or hearing of others; *slang* a place where a musician may (or should) practise in private. **M20.**
Phrases: ***something nasty in the woodshed***: see NASTY *adjective*. **take into the woodshed** *N. Amer. colloq.* (discreetly) reprimand or punish (i.e., orig., by giving a child a spanking out of sight in the woodshed).

woodshed /ˈwʊdʃɛd/ *verb trans. & intrans. slang.* Infl. **-dd-**. **M20.**
[from the noun.]
MUSIC. Practise or rehearse, esp. privately. Also, harmonize spontaneously. Freq. as ***woodshedding*** *verbal noun*.

woodsia /ˈwʊdzɪə/ *noun*. **M19.**
[mod. Latin (see below), from Joseph Woods (1776–1864), English architect and botanist + -IA¹.]
Any of various small tufted rock-loving ferns constituting the genus *Woodsia*, widespread in mountains in temperate and cool regions of the world, two species of which, *W. ilvensis* (more full ***oblong woodsia***) and *W. alpina* (more fully ***Alpine woodsia***) are rare natives of Britain.

woodside /ˈwʊdsʌɪd/ *noun*. **ME.**
[from WOOD *noun*¹ + SIDE *noun*.]
The side or edge of a wood.
📖 *Atlantic Monthly* The snow may be gone . . except . . along fences and woodsides.

woodsman /ˈwʊdzmən/ *noun*. Pl. **-men**. **L17.**
[from WOOD *noun*¹ + -S¹ + MAN *noun*. Cf. ***backwoodsman*** s.v. BACK-, WOODMAN.]
A person who inhabits, frequents, or ranges the woods, for hunting, sport, woodcutting, etc.; a person who is acquainted with or accustomed to the woods.
¶ Recorded in **ME** as a surname.

woodspite /ˈwʊdspʌɪt/ *noun.* Now *dial.* Also (earlier) **†-sp(e)ight.** M16.
[from WOOD *noun*¹ + SPEIGHT.]
A woodpecker, *esp.* the green woodpecker, *Picus viridis.*

woodsy /ˈwʊdzi/ *adjective.* Orig. and chiefly *N. Amer.* M19.
[from WOOD *noun*¹ + -S¹ + -Y¹ (irreg. formed to distinguish from *woody*).]
Of or pertaining to woods; characteristic or suggestive of the woods.

woodwall /ˈwʊd(w)ɔːl/ *noun.* Now *dial.* ME.
[from or cogn. with Middle Low German *wedewale*: see WITWALL. Perh. partly imit. in origin (cf. HICKWALL).]
†**1** The golden oriole, *Oriolus oriolus.* ME–M17.
2 A woodpecker, *esp.* the green woodpecker, *Picus viridis.* L15.

woodward /ˈwʊdwəd/ *noun*¹. LOE.
[from WOOD *noun*¹ + WARD *noun.*]
1 *Hist.* The keeper of a wood; an officer of a wood or forest, having charge of the growing timber. LOE.
2 An officer of one of the Orders of Foresters. L19.

woodward /ˈwʊdwəd/ *noun*² & *adverb. rare.* E17.
[from WOOD *noun*¹ + -WARD.]
▶†**A** *noun.* ***from the woodward***, from a wood. Only in E17.
▶**B** *adverb.* In the direction of a wood. M19.
■ Also **woodwards** *adverb* M19.

woodwax /ˈwʊdwaks/ *noun.* Now *rare* or *obsolete.* OE.
[from WOOD *noun*¹ + base of WAX *verb*¹, the name prob. meaning 'woody growth'.]
= WOODWAXEN.

woodwaxen /ˈwʊdwaks(ə)n/ *noun.* Also **woad-** /ˈwəʊd-/. LME.
[App. from oblique case of prec. in Old English understood as nom.; later also assoc. with WOAD *noun.*]
The plant dyer's greenweed, *Genista tinctoria.*

woodwind /ˈwʊdwɪnd/ *noun.* L19.
[from WOOD *noun*¹ + WIND *noun*¹.]
MUSIC. **1** Wind instruments (mostly) originally made of wood (flute, clarinet, oboe, bassoon, etc.); *the* section of an orchestra playing such instruments. L19.
2 An instrument of this kind. Usu. in *pl.* E20.

woodwork /ˈwʊdwəːk/ *noun.* M17.
[from WOOD *noun*¹ + WORK *noun.*]
1 †**a** *sing.* & in *pl.* Articles made of wood; woodware. M17–L18. ▶**b** Wood that has been worked, carved, shaped, etc.; *esp.* those parts of a manufactured object, structure, building, etc., which are made of wood; the wooden part *of* something. L17. ▶**c** *The* frame of a football goalpost. *colloq.* M20.
2 a Work done in woods, forestry. M18. ▶**b** Work done in or with wood, carpentry. E20.
1b crawl back into the woodwork, **vanish into the woodwork**, etc., disappear into obscurity. **crawl out of the woodwork** come out of hiding, emerge from obscurity; (of something unwelcome) appear, become known.
■ **woodworker** *noun* (*a*) a worker in wood, a person who makes things of wood; (*b*) a machine for working in wood: L19. **woodworking** *noun* = WOODWORK 2a, b L19.

woodworm /ˈwʊdwəːm/ *noun.* Pl. same, **-s**. M16.
[from WOOD *noun*¹ + WORM *noun.*]
Any of various invertebrates which burrow in wood, *spec.* †(*a*) a shipworm; (*b*) the larva of a furniture beetle, which bores tunnels in the wood of buildings, furniture, etc. Also, the damaged condition of wood affected by this.

woodwose /ˈwʊdwəʊz, -s/ *noun. obsolete* exc. *Hist.* Also **-house** /-haʊs/ & other vars. LOE.
[from WOOD *noun*¹ + unexpl. 2nd elem.]
1 A wild man of the woods; a savage; a satyr, a faun; a person dressed to represent such a being in a pageant. LOE.
2 The representation of such a being, esp. as a decoration, a heraldic bearing or supporter. LME.

woody /ˈwʊdi/ *noun. colloq.* Chiefly *US.* M20.
[from WOOD *noun*¹ + -Y⁶.]
An estate car with timber-framed sides.

woody /ˈwʊdi/ *adjective.* LME.
[from WOOD *noun*¹ + -Y¹.]
▶**I 1** Covered or overgrown with trees or shrubs; full of woods or forests; wooded. LME.
†**2** Belonging to, inhabiting, or growing in woods or woodland; sylvan. L16–M17.
3 Of, pertaining to, or situated in a wood. E18.

> 📖 **1** W. HOWITT The hills . . became wilder and woodier.

▶**II** †**4** Made of wood, wooden. *rare.* Only in M16.
5 Chiefly of plants, their stems, tissues, etc.: of the nature of or consisting of wood; ligneous, lignified. L16.
6 Resembling (that of) wood; having the texture or consistency of wood; redolent of wood. L18.

> 📖 **5** *Gardening from Which?* Prune just as the base of the shoot becomes woody. ***woody*** NIGHTSHADE. **woody pear** any of several small Australian trees constituting the genus *Xylomelum* (family Proteaceae), which bear hard pear-shaped fruits. **woody plant** a tree or shrub, as distinct from a herbaceous plant. **woody tongue** = ***wooden tongue*** s.v. WOODEN.

woodyard /ˈwʊdjɑːd/ *noun.* ME.
[from WOOD *noun*¹ + YARD *noun*¹.]
A yard or enclosure in which wood is chopped, sawn, or stored, esp. for fuel.

†**woodyer** *noun.* LOE–E19.
[from WOOD *verb* + -IER. Cf. WOODER.]
= WOODMAN 2.

wooer /ˈwuːə/ *noun.* OE.
[from WOO *verb*¹ + -ER¹.]
A person who woos another, *esp.* a man who woos a woman with a view to marriage, a suitor; *gen.* & *fig.*, a person who seeks to win over or gently persuade another person.

> 📖 *Notes & Queries* Another of this difficult lady's unchancy wooers was a Scottish laird. C. TOMALIN Virginia was always the wooer, Katherine . . unresponsive.

woof /wuːf/ *noun*¹ & *verb*¹. OE.
[Alt. of ABB after WEAVE *verb*¹; later also infl. by *warp.*]
▶**A** *noun.* **1** WEAVING. The threads that cross from side to side of a loom, crossing the warp; = WEFT *noun*¹ 1. OE. ▶**b** Thread used to make the woof. M16.
2 A woven fabric, esp. as being of a particular texture. Also, the texture of a fabric. Chiefly *poet.* L17.
▶**B** *verb trans.* Arrange (threads) so as to form a woof; weave. *rare.* L19.

woof /wʊf/ *verb*² & *noun*². E19.
[Imit. In sense A.3 alt. of WOLF *verb*, in sense B.2 back-form. from WOOFER. Cf. WUFF *noun*, WOUGH *noun*².]
▶**A** *verb.* **1** *verb intrans.* Of a dog: utter a gruff abrupt bark. E19.
2 *verb intrans.* & *trans.* Say (something) in an ostentatious or aggressive manner; speak to (a person) in such a way. Freq. as **woofing** *verbal noun. Black slang* (chiefly *US*). M20.
3 *verb trans.* Consume ravenously. Also foll. by *down. colloq.* M20.
▶**B** *noun.* **I 1** The gruff abrupt bark of a dog; a sound or utterance resembling this. Also as *interjection.* M19.
2 Low-frequency sound of poor quality from a loudspeaker. M20.
▶**II** See WHOOF.

woofer /ˈwʊfə, *in sense 2* ˈwuːfə/ *noun.* M20.
[from (the same root as) WOOF *verb*² + -ER¹.]
1 A person who talks loudly or constantly, esp. in an ostentatious or aggressive manner. *Black slang* (chiefly *US*). M20.
2 A large loudspeaker designed to reproduce low frequencies. Cf. TWEETER. M20.

woofits /ˈwuːfɪts/ *noun. slang.* E20.
[Origin unkn.]
A feeling of being unwell, esp. in the head; moody depression. Usu. with *the.*

woofter /ˈwʊftə, ˈwuːftə/ *noun. slang. derog.* Also **-tah**. L20.
[Alt. of POOFTER.]
A homosexual; an effeminate man.

> 📖 J. ARNOTT Tosses me a poncey silk dressing gown . . . Probably look a right woofter in this thing.

woofy /ˈwʊfi, ˈwuːfi/ *adjective*¹. *rare.* E19.
[from WOOF *noun*¹ + -Y¹.]
Resembling a woven fabric.

woofy /ˈwʊfi/ *adjective*². M20.
[from WOOF *noun*² + -Y¹.]
Of reproduced sound: having too much bass, or bass that is indistinct.

wooingly /ˈwuːɪŋli/ *adverb.* LME.
[from *wooing* pres. pple of WOO *verb*¹: see -ING², -LY².]
In the manner of a wooer; *esp.* enticingly, alluringly; formerly, wantonly, impudently.

wool /wʊl/ *noun* & *adjective.*
[Old English *wull* = Old Frisian *wolle*, *ulle*, Middle Low German, Middle Dutch *wulle*, *wolle*, Old High German *wolla* (Dutch *wol*, German *Wolle*), Old Norse *ull*, Gothic *wulla*, from Germanic, from Indo-European base also of Latin *lana* wool, *vellus* fleece.]
▶**A** *noun.* **1** The fine soft curly or wavy hair forming the coat of a sheep, goat, or similar animal; *spec.* this hair shorn and prepared for use in making cloth, yarn, etc. Now also, twisted woollen yarn for the knitting, mending, etc., of garments. OE. ▶**b** A quantity, supply, or particular class of wool. Usu. in *pl.* LME. ▶**c** The complete fleece of a sheep etc. LME. ▶**d** The underhair or down of some other mammals. E17.
2 (An article of) woollen clothing, cloth, or fabric. ME. ▶**b** The nap of a woollen fabric. M16.
3 A thing regarded as resembling sheep's wool, *spec.* (*a*) a dense covering of long, curled, and matted hairs found on certain plants; the thick furry hair of some insects or larvae; (*b*) *colloq.* the hair of a person's head; (chiefly *derog.*) short curly hair. LME. ▶**b** Any fine fibrous mineral substance. M18.

> 📖 **1** TENNYSON I hear Dead sounds at night . . Like footsteps upon wool. *Illustrated London News* The wool is shorn, combed and when necessary dyed. ***Berlin wool***, ***botany wool***, ***combing wool***, ***goat's wool***, ***lambswool***, ***Lincoln wool***, ***sheep's wool***, ***teg wool***, etc. **2** H. ALLEN I *am* a little cold . . till I change into my wool. **3** ***bull's wool***, ***cotton wool***, etc. **b** ***glass wool***, ***mineral wool***, ***rock wool***, ***slag wool***, ***steel wool***, etc.

Phrases: **all wool and a yard wide** *fig.* of excellent quality, thoroughly sound. ***dyed-in-the-wool***, ***dyed-in-wool***: see DYE *verb* 1. ***great cry and little wool***: see CRY *noun.* **keep one's wool on**, **lose one's wool** *slang* keep or lose one's temper. ***much cry and little wool***: see CRY *noun.* **out of the wool** recently shorn. **philosopher's wool**, **philosophic wool** zinc oxide as a white flocculent powder. ***plucked wool***: see PLUCKED *adjective*¹. ***pulled wool***: see PULL *verb.* **pull the wool over a person's eyes** deceive or hoodwink a person. ***slipe wool***: see SLIPE *noun*³. ***slut's wool***: see SLUT *noun.* ***virgin wool***: see VIRGIN *adjective.*
▶**B** *attrib.* or as *adjective.* Made of wool. E16.
Comb. & special collocations: **wool alien** a plant introduced into a country by means of imported wool waste containing its seed; **wool-bearer** an animal that bears or produces wool, *esp.* a sheep; **wool-bearing** *adjective* (*rare*) (of an animal) that bears or produces wool; **wool-blind** *Austral.* & *NZ* (of a sheep) having its sight obscured by its growth of wool; **wool-blindness** *Austral.* & *NZ* the condition of being wool-blind; **wool-broker** *Austral.* & *NZ* a company which prepares a wool-grower's wool-clip for sale; **wool-card** an instrument used in carding wool; **wool-carder** a person who cards wool; **wool cheque** *Austral. colloq.* (a) payment for wool-clip; **wool church** *Hist.* any of the English churches built or modified out of the wealth produced by the Tudor wool trade; **woolclasser** *Austral.* & *NZ* a person who grades wool shorn from sheep etc.; **wool-classing** *Austral.* & *NZ* the task or occupation of a woolclasser; **wool-clip** the total quantity of wool shorn in any place or season; **wool-clipper** NAUTICAL a clipper for carrying wool; **wool-comb** a toothed instrument or (later also) a machine for carding wool; **wool-comber** a person who combs or cards wool; **wool-combing** the action or process of carding wool; **wool-dyed** *adjective* = ***dyed-in-the-wool*** s.v. DYE *verb* 1; **wool-fat** = LANOLIN; **wool-fell** the skin of a sheep etc. with the fleece attached; **wool-flock** coarse inferior wool; **wool-gather** *verb intrans.* [back-form.] indulge in aimless or inattentive thought or imagining; **wool-gathering** *noun* & *adjective* (*a*) *noun* the action of gathering wool, esp. fragments torn from sheep by bushes etc.; *fig.* indulgence in aimless thought or imagining; (*b*) *adjective* that wool-gathers, given to wool-gathering; **wool-grass** name for various grasses or grasslike plants having woolly spikelets, as the N. American club-rush *Scirpus cyperinus*; **wool-grower** a breeder of sheep etc. for wool; **wool-hat** *US slang* a Southern small farmer or ignorant countryman; **wool-hawk** *Austral.* a sheep-shearer, *esp.* an expert one; **wool-house** (now *Hist.*) a building for storing or manufacturing wool; **woolman** (now chiefly *Austral.*) a wool-grower, a dealer in wool; **Woolmark** an international quality symbol for wool instituted by the International Wool Secretariat; **woolmaster** (now *Hist.*) a wool-grower; **wool moth** a moth, *Endrosis sarcitrella*, whose larvae feed on sheep's wool and woollen articles; **wool-needle** a blunt needle used for wool-work; **wool-oil** †(*a*) oil used to salve the wool of sheep; (*b*) = LANOLIN; **wool-pated** *adjective* woolly-headed; **wool-press**: used in packing wool; **wool-pulling** (*a*) the removal of wool from a sheepskin; (*b*) *fig.* the action of pulling the wool over a person's eyes; **wool-roller** *Austral.* a person who pulls off coarse edges before the woolclasser receives the wool; **wool-scour** *Austral.* a large shed where wool is washed; **wool-shears**: for shearing sheep; **woolshed** (chiefly *Austral.* & *NZ*) the large building at a sheep-station in which the shearing and wool-packing are done; **wool-skin** = ***wool-fell*** above; **wool-sorter** a sorter of wool; ***wool-sorters' disease***, anthrax; **wool-staple** a market for the sale of wool; ***wool-stapler***: see STAPLER *noun*¹ 2; **wool table** *Austral.* & *NZ* a slatted table in a woolshed where fleeces are skirted and the wool graded; **wool team** *Austral.* & *NZ* a team of draught animals for transporting wool; **wool-track** *Austral.* a route along which consignments of wool are conveyed to a port; **wool-wax** = LANOLIN; **wool-wheel**: for spinning wool; **wool-winder** (*a*) a person who packs up fleeces for transport or sale; (*b*) a frame on which wool is wound; **wool-work** †(*a*) working in wool, manufacture of woollen goods; (*b*) needlework executed in wool, esp. on a canvas foundation; knitted wool fabric; **wool-worker** a person who works in wool.
■ **wool-like** /-l-l-/ *adjective* resembling (that of) wool M17. †**woolling** *noun* (*a*) *rare* the combing of wool; (*b*) the smuggling of wool, owling: L16–M18. **woolsey** /ˈwʊlzi/ *adjective* (*rare*) [cf. LINSEY-WOOLSEY] woolly, woollen M19.

wool /wʊl/ *verb trans. rare.* M17.
[from the noun.]
1 †**a** Coat or line with wool. Only in M17. ▶**b** Stuff *up* with wool. L19.
2 Pull the hair of (a person), esp. in anger. M19.

woold /wuːld/ *noun.* E17.
[Rel. to the verb.]
NAUTICAL. In full ***woold rope***. A woolding for a mast, spar, etc.

woold /wuːld/ *verb trans.* E17.
[Back-form. or formed as next.]
1 NAUTICAL. Wind rope or chain round (a broken or weakened mast, spar, etc.). E17.
2 *gen.* Wrap or bind round. L18.

■ **woolder** *noun* †(*a*) *NAUTICAL* a woold rope; (*b*) a stick or lever used in woolding or rope-making: **M16.**

woolding /ˈwuːldɪŋ/ *noun.* **LME.**
[from Middle Low German *wōlen*, Middle Dutch *woelen* bind (Dutch = *woold* a mast). Cf. prec.]
Chiefly *NAUTICAL.* The action of **WOOLD** *verb.* Also, a wrapping; *esp.* the rope or chain used in woolding a mast, spar, etc. (usu. in *pl.*).

wooled *adjective* see **WOOLLED.**

woolen *adjective & noun* see **WOOLLEN.**

Woolfian /ˈwʊlfɪən/ *adjective.* **M20.**
[from *Woolf* (see below) + **-IAN.**]
Of, pertaining to, or characteristic of (the work of) the English writer Virginia Woolf (1882–1941).

woolled /wʊld/ *adjective.* Also ***wooled.** **LME.**
[from **WOOL** *noun* + **-ED**².]
1 Bearing wool, covered with wool; unshorn. **LME.**
2 Having wool of a specified kind. Chiefly as 2nd elem. of comb. **L16.**

woollen /ˈwʊlən/ *adjective & noun.* Also ***woolen.** **LOE.**
[from **WOOL** *noun* + **-EN**⁴.]
▶ **A** *adjective.* **1** Made (wholly or partly) of or manufactured from (esp. short fibres of) wool. **LOE.**
†**2** Wearing woollen clothing. *rare.* **L15–E17.**
▶ **B** *noun.* **1** Fabric made (chiefly) of or from wool. **ME.**
2 In *pl.* Woollen cloths or garments. **L16.**
1 be buried in woollen (*obsolete* exc. *Hist.*) have a woollen shroud.
Comb.: **woollen-draper** (*obsolete* exc. *Hist.*) a dealer in woollen goods; **woollen-drapery** (*obsolete* exc. *Hist.*) woollen goods; **woollen-witted** *adjective* dull-witted.
■ **woollenize** *verb trans.* (*rare*) impart to (vegetable fibres) the appearance and texture of wool **L19.** **woolleny** *adjective* (*rare*) made of or having the texture of woollen cloth **L18.**

woolly /ˈwʊli/ *adjective & noun.* Also ***wooly.** **LME.**
[from **WOOL** *noun* + **-Y**¹.]
▶ **A** *adjective.* **1** Of the nature, texture, or appearance of wool; resembling or suggesting wool, wool-like; *spec.* (of a food) having a (usu. unpleasant) soft clinging texture. **LME.**
2 Consisting of or pertaining to wool; containing wool. **L16.**
3 Bearing or naturally covered with wool. **L16.** ▸**b** Of an animal or (*derog.*) a person: having hair resembling wool. **M18.** ▸**c** Rough, uncouth; barbarous, unrefined. Freq. in ***wild and woolly.*** **L19.**
4 Of a plant or its parts: covered with a pubescence resembling wool; having dense, curled, and matted hairs. **L16.**
5 Lacking definiteness, definition, or incisiveness, vague; confused, hazy; (of a sound) indistinct. **E19.**

> 🕮 **1** GEO. ELIOT The sky had the white woolly look that portends snow. **2** J. DAVIES He had upon his upper Garment, some black Sheep-skin, the woolly side out. KEATS Silent was the flock in woolly fold. **5** B. BROWN The . . auditorium acts as a speaking tube, and reproduction is woolly and blurred. *Photography* The woolly guidelines . . forbid 'any unwarrantable intrusion of privacy'.

Special collocations & comb.: **woolly aphid** an aphid, *Eriosoma lanigerum*, which is coated with waxy fluff and is found on the bark of apple trees. **woolly bear** (*a*) a hairy caterpillar, esp. of a tiger moth; (*b*) the small hairy larva of a carpet beetle, which is destructive to carpets, insect collections, etc.; (*c*) *Military slang* a type of high-explosive shell. **woollybutt** any of several Australian eucalypts with thick fibrous bark, esp. *Eucalyptus longifolia.* **woolly foot** a yellowish-brown toadstool, *Collybia peronata*, with a slender stem, the base of which bears long woolly hairs, found commonly in woodland in both Eurasia and North America. **woolly-head** (orig. *US*) (*a*) a person with hair resembling or suggestive of wool; *esp.* (*derog. & racially offensive*) a black person; (*b*) *US HISTORY* an advocate of the abolition of slavery. **woolly-headed** *adjective* (*a*) having woolly hair or a woolly head; ***woolly-headed thistle***, a thistle of calcareous grassland and scrub, *Cirsium eriophorum*, having large heads with densely cottony involucres; (*b*) dull-witted, confused. **woolly lemur** a lemur, *Avahi laniger*, which has a thick dark coat. **woolly mammoth** a mammoth with a coat of long woolly hair; *spec.* one of the Eurasian species *Mammuthus primigenius*, sometimes found preserved in the Siberian permafrost. **woolly monkey** either of two Central and S. American monkeys of the genus *Lagothrix*, which have a thick woolly coat and a prehensile tail; *esp.* (more fully ***common woolly monkey, Humboldt's woolly monkey***) *L. lagothricha.* **woolly rhinoceros** an extinct two-horned Eurasian rhinoceros of the genus *Coelodonta*, that had a long woolly coat and was adapted to the cold periods of the Pleistocene. **woolly spider monkey** a large spider monkey, *Brachyteles arachnoides*, with dense woolly fur and a large protruding belly, native to the rainforests of SE Brazil. **woolly worm** *US* = ***woolly bear*** (a) above.
▶ **B** *noun.* **1** A woollen garment or covering; *spec.* a knitted pullover. **M19.**
2 A sheep, *esp.* one before shearing. *US, Austral., & NZ colloq.* **L19.**
3 A uniformed policeman. Cf. **WOLLY.** *slang.* **M20.**

> 🕮 **1** *Royal Air Force Journal* Warm clothing, roll-necked woollies . . and odd knitted headgear. **winter woollies** (freq. *joc.*) warm underwear.

■ **woollily** *adverb* in a vague, confused, or indecisive manner **M20.** **woolliness** *noun* **L16.** **woollyish** *adjective* (*rare*) somewhat woolly **L18.**

wool-pack /ˈwʊlpak/ *noun.* **ME.**
[from **WOOL** *noun* + **PACK** *noun.*]
1 A large bag, made of jute etc., for packing a quantity of wool or shorn fleeces (now chiefly *NZ*); (*obsolete* exc. *Hist.*) a bale of wool. **ME.** ▸†**b** = **WOOLSACK** 2. **M17–E18.**
2 *transf.* Something resembling a wool-pack; *esp.* a fleecy cumulus cloud. **L16.**
■ **wool-packer** *noun* a person who or (later) machine which packs wool for transport or sale **LME.** **wool-packing** *noun* the occupation of a wool-packer **M19.**

Woolpit /ˈwʊlpɪt/ *attrib. adjective.* **L19.**
[See below.]
Designating a pale-coloured brick made from earth in or around Woolpit, a village in Suffolk.

woolsack /ˈwʊlsak/ *noun.* In sense 2 now **W-.** **ME.**
[from **WOOL** *noun* + **SACK** *noun*¹.]
1 A large package or bale of wool. **ME.** ▸†**b** A fat person. *rare* (Shakes.). Only in **L16.**
2 Orig., a seat made of a bag of wool for the use of judges attending the House of Lords (now only at the opening of Parliament). Later, *the* wool-stuffed seat of the Lord Chancellor in the House of Lords; *the* position of Lord Chancellor. **L16.**

Woolton pie /ˈwʊlt(ə)n pʌɪ/ *noun phr.* **M20.**
[from F. J. Marquis (1883–1964), 1st Earl of *Woolton*, who was Minister of Food during the war of 1939–45 when the pie was publicized.]
Hist. More fully ***Lord Woolton pie.*** A type of vegetable pie.

†**woolver** *noun* see **WOLVER.**

†**woolward** *adjective.* **ME–E19.**
[formed as **WOOL** *noun* + base of **WEAR** *verb*¹.]
Wearing wool next the skin, esp. as a penance.

Woolwich /ˈwʊlɪdʒ/ *noun.* **L18.**
[See below.]
Used ***attrib.*** to designate (products of) the old dockyard and the Royal Arsenal in Woolwich, an area of Greater London (formerly in Kent).

Woolworth /ˈwʊlwəːθ/ *noun.* **M20.**
[Frank Winfield *Woolworth* (1852–1919), American businessman.]
Used ***attrib.*** to designate low-priced goods regarded as typical of the merchandise of the stores of the retailing company F. W. Woolworth.
■ **Woolˈworthian** *adjective* **M20.**

wooly *adjective & noun* see **WOOLLY.**

woomera /ˈwuːm(ə)rə/ *noun. Austral.* Also **wommera** /ˈwɒm(ə)rə/ & other vars. **L18.**
[Aboriginal.]
= ***THROWING-stick.*** Cf. next.

woomerang /ˈwuːmərаŋ/ *noun. Austral.* **M19.**
[Aboriginal, perh. alt. after *boomerang.*]
= ***throwing-stick*** (b) s.v. **THROWING.** Cf. prec.

woomph /wuːmf, wʊmf/ *interjection.* **M20.**
[Imit.]
Expr. a sound like that of a sudden blow or impact accompanied by an expulsion of air.

woon /wuːn/ *noun.* **E19.**
[Burmese *wun.*]
Chiefly *Hist.* An administrative officer in Myanmar (Burma).

woonerf /ˈvuːnəːf/ *noun.* Pl. **-nerfs, -nerven** /-nəːv(ə)n/. **L20.**
[Dutch, from *woon-* residential (from *wonen* live, reside) + *erf* ground, premises. Cf. **ERF.**]
A road in a residential area, in which a number of devices are employed to create a safer environment by reducing and slowing the flow of traffic.

woopie /ˈwuːpi, ˈwʊpi/ *noun. colloq.* (orig. *N. Amer.*). Also **-py.** **L20.**
[from well-off older person: see **-IE, -Y**⁶. Cf. **YUMPIE, YUPPIE.**]
An affluent retired person able to pursue an active lifestyle.

woop woop /ˈwʊp wʊp/ *noun. Austral. & NZ. joc.* Also **woop woops** /wʊps/. **E20.**
[Pseudo-Aborig.]
1 A remote rural town or district; *the* outback; (with cap. initials) the name of an imaginary place in a remote area. **E20.**
2 A country bumpkin. *rare.* **M20.**

woopy *noun* var. of **WOOPIE.**

woorara *noun* see **WOURALI.**

Wooster /ˈwʊstə/ *adjective & verb.* **M20.**
[See below.]
▶ **A** *adjective.* Characteristic of or resembling Bertie Wooster, an amiable but vacuous young man about town in the novels of P. G. Wodehouse. **M20.**
▶ **B** *verb intrans.* Behave like Bertie Wooster. *rare.* **M20.**
■ **Woosterish** *adjective* characteristic of or resembling Bertie Wooster **M20.** **Woosterism** *noun* a remark or action characteristic of Bertie Wooster **M20.**

wootz /wuːts/ *noun.* **L18.**
[Prob. from Marathi *ūc* high(-quality steel), from Sanskrit *ucca* high.]
METALLURGY. A hard crucible steel made in India by fusing magnetic iron ore with carbonaceous plant material.

woozy /ˈwuːzi/ *adjective. colloq.* (orig. *US*). **L19.**
[Origin unkn. Cf. **WUZZY.**]
1 Dizzy, unsteady; dazed, fuddled; slightly intoxicated. **L19.**
2 Representing or marked by sloppy, muddled, or vague thinking or expression; undisciplined. **M20.**

> 🕮 **1** R. PILCHER Dolly, woozy with champagne . . took Penelope's hands in her own. B. A. MASON She feels woozy from this morning's medicine. **2** *New Yorker* There are gaps in the plot and woozy lapses in time.

■ **woozily** *adverb* **E20.** **wooziness** *noun* **E20.**

wop /wɒp/ *noun*¹ *& adjective. slang* (*derog. & racially offensive*). Orig. *US.* **E20.**
[Perh. from Italian *guappo* bold, showy, from Spanish *guapo* dandy.]
▶ **A** *noun.* **1** An Italian or other southern European, esp. as an immigrant or foreign visitor. **E20.**
2 The Italian language. **M20.**
▶ **B** *adjective.* Italian. **M20.**

wop /wɒp/ *noun*². *RAF slang.* **M20.**
[Acronym, from wireless operator: cf. **OP** *noun*⁴.]
A radio operator.

wops *noun* see **WASP** *noun*¹.

Worcester /ˈwʊstə/ *noun & adjective.* **M16.**
[A city, the county town of Worcestershire, in the West (Midlands) of England.]
1 (Designating) a product originating in or associated with Worcester. **M16.**
2 More fully ***Royal Worcester.*** A type of fine porcelain orig. manufactured in Worcester. **E19.**
3 More fully ***Worcester pearmain.*** An early, slightly conical, red-skinned variety of eating apple, introduced to cultivation about 1875 by Richard Smith, a Worcester nurseryman. **L19.**
1 Worcester sauce = ***WORCESTERSHIRE sauce.***

Worcesterberry /ˈwʊstəbɛri/ *noun.* **E20.**
[from prec. + **BERRY** *noun*¹.]
A small black gooseberry of the N. American species *Ribes divaricatum*, once believed to be a hybrid of the blackcurrant and the gooseberry and sold as such by a Worcester nurseryman.

Worcestershire /ˈwʊstəʃə/ *attrib. adjective.* **L17.**
[A county in the West (Midlands) of England, from **WORCESTER** + **SHIRE** *noun.*]
Designating things originating or made in Worcester or Worcestershire.
Worcestershire sauce a pungent sauce containing soy, vinegar, and condiments, first made in Worcester; also called ***Worcester sauce.***

Worcs. *abbreviation.*
Worcestershire.

word /wəːd/ *noun.*
[Old English *word* = Old Frisian, Old Saxon *word* (Dutch *woord*), Old & mod. High German *wort*, Old Norse *orð*, Gothic *waurd*, from Germanic base rel. also to Latin *verbum* word.]
▶ **I** Speech, utterance.
1 *sing.* & in *pl.* A thing or things said, a remark or remarks, (a) speech, (an) utterance, (freq. as contrasted with thought, action, or, formerly, writing). Also, a conversation; a person's language or form of expression; verbal expression; *arch.* a phrase used. **OE.**
2 *spec.* **a** (In expressed or implied neg. contexts.) Any utterance, statement, comment, etc., however brief or insignificant. **OE.** ▸**b** A pithy saying, a maxim, a proverb, (*arch.*); = **MOTTO** 1. **LME.** ▸**c** A watchword, a password. **M16.**
3 News, information, intelligence. **OE.** ▸**b** (*The*) rumour. **OE.** ▸†**c** Fame, renown, high repute. **OE–L15.** ▸**d** Reputation *of* being or having something. *Scot.* **E18.**
4 A command, an order; a request. **OE.**
5 A promise, an undertaking. Later also, any assertion or affirmation involving the good faith of its maker; an assurance. **LME**
6 In *pl.* The lyrics of a song etc.; an actor's lines. **LME.**
7 *sing.* & in *pl.* Contentious, angry, or violent talk between people; an argument, a quarrel. Now chiefly in ***have words, have a word.*** **LME.**

1 W. COWPER Rome shall perish—write that word In the blood that she has spilt. G. P. R. JAMES We have striven . . to draw some word from her; but she . . answers nothing. H. CONWAY To use his own words, he was in a cleft stick. *Proverb*: Actions speak louder than words. **2a** L. P. HARTLEY You talk too much, Janice . . you don't let Jeremy get a word in. K. AMIS What was the matter with you this morning? I couldn't get a word out of you. **b** SPENSER Round about the wreath this word was writ. DE QUINCEY Shakspere's deep word would be realized and 'darkness be the burier of the dead'. **c** F. MARRYAT He gave the word, and the gate was opened. **3** SHAKES. *Ant. & Cl.* Bring me word how tall she is. DICKENS Ask her to leave word with the man at the door. M. L. KING The arrest . . was becoming public knowledge. Word of it spread around the community. E. FEINSTEIN I have sent Frederick our new address, but so far there has been no word. **b** P. O'DONNELL I know of him. The word is that he's good. **4** TENNYSON In my time a father's word was law. DICKENS I gave Rames the word to lower the Longboat. **5** SHAKES. *Mids. N. D.* I would I had your bond . . I'll not trust your word. H. KINGSLEY What surety had he? . . none but his word—the word of a villain. J. FOWLES If I gave you my word, I wouldn't break it. F. WELDON In the country . . the word of a gentleman still means something. People trust one another. **7** Z. N. HURSTON Celestine is not mad any more about the word we had last week. B. BAINBRIDGE Freda's had words with him. He's crying.

▶**II** *ECCLESIASTICAL.* **8** A divine communication, message, revelation, or proclamation; *spec.* (*CHRISTIAN CHURCH*) (***a***) *the* message of the gospel; (***b***) (**W-**) *the* Son of God, *the* second person of the Trinity; (***c***) (usu. **W-**) *the* Bible. **OE.**

8 GEO. ELIOT Carrying the word of life to the sinful and desolate. H. KINGSLEY Read us a chapter out of the Bible . . I like to hear the Word. *Church Times* Reverend Brothers in the Sacred Ministry of Word and Sacrament. *Islamic Studies* The . . simple form of Islam which consists of obeying the word of God as embodied in the Qur'ān.

▶**III** A linguistic element.

9 Any of the sequences of one or more sounds or morphemes (intuitively recognized by native speakers as) constituting the basic units of meaningful speech used in forming a sentence or sentences in a language; a lexical unit other than a phrase or affix, a term, an item of vocabulary; *spec.* (***a***) the standardly cited form of an item of vocabulary (e.g. the infinitive of a verb), as opp. to a grammatical inflection; (***b***) this form considered together with its grammatical inflections as expressing a common lexical meaning or range of meanings. Also, a sequence of (written, typed, engraved, etc.) letters representing this, *esp.* one flanked by spaces. **OE.**

†**10** A name or title designating a thing or person. **OE–L16.**

11 *The* right term; *the* most apt or appropriate expression. Also (*colloq.*), *the* relevant notion, consideration, or action (identified contextually). **L16.**

12 *TELEGRAPHY.* Any of the sequences of a fixed number of characters (including a space) in a telegraphic message that has been coded or redivided for transmission. **L19.** ▶**b** *MATH.* An ordered sequence of generators of a group. **M20.** ▶**c** *COMPUTING.* A consecutive string of bits that is treated as a unit by computer hardware, now usu. consisting of (a multiple of) 16 bits. Also more fully ***machine word***. **M20.**

9 J. LOCKE Words are sensible Signs necessary for Communication. G. D. CAMPBELL Words, which should be the servants of Thought, are too often its masters. *New York Times* 'Makuta' is the plural form of the word 'likuta'. R. HEILBRONER Radical analysts . . assume that the word 'capitalism' is synonymous with the words 'United States'. **11** SHAKES. *Cymb.* Are you ready for death? . . Hanging is the word, sir. W. S. GILBERT When I think of man, Contempt is not the word.

Phrases: **a person of his or her word** a reliable person. ***a sport of words***: see SPORT *noun*. **at a word** (***a***) as soon as a word is given or a request made, without more ado, at once; (***b***) in short, briefly. **a word and a blow** a brief angry or defiant utterance followed immediately by the delivery of a blow, as the beginning of a fight; *gen.* (chiefly with allus. to Shakes. *Romeo & Juliet*) any sudden or unpremeditated act. **a word in a person's ear** *colloq.* a brief oral message privately to a person. ***a word to the wise***: see WISE *noun*[2]. ***be as good as one's word***: see GOOD *adjective*. ***be at a loss for words***: see ***at a loss*** (b) s.v. LOSS. **be better than one's word** exceed or do more than one has promised. ***be worse than one's word***: see WORSE *adjective, noun, & adverb*. ***beyond words***: see BEYOND *preposition*. ***book of words***: see BOOK *noun*. **break one's word** fail to do what one has promised. ***by word of mouth***: see MOUTH *noun*. ***chaffer words***: see CHAFFER *verb* 2. ***dirty word***: see DIRTY *adjective*. ***eat one's words***: see EAT *verb*. ***empty word***: see EMPTY *adjective*. ***from the word go***: see GO *verb*. ***full word***: see FULL *adjective*. **get a word in edgeways** seize the opportunity to say something at a brief pause in a monologue or conversation. **give one's word** make a solemn promise. **good word** a friendly, favourable, or appreciative utterance; something (that can be) said on behalf of or in commendation of a person or thing (freq. in ***put in a good word for***, ***say a good word for***). ***hang on a person's words***: see ***hang on*** (d) s.v. HANG *verb*. **have a word (with)** speak briefly (to). **have no words for** be unable to express. ***have the last word***: see ***last word*** (a) s.v. LAST *adjective*. ***high words***: see HIGH *adjective*. *IMITATIVE* ***word***. **in a word**, **in one word** briefly, in short, in sum. **in other words** expressing the same thing differently. **in so many words** in those very words; explicitly, bluntly. ***in words of one syllable***: see SYLLABLE *noun* 1a. ***last word***, ***last words***: see LAST *adjective*. **latest word** *the* most recent news, fashion, achievement, etc. ***leave word (with)***: see LEAVE *verb*[1]. ***logical word***: see LOGICAL *adjective*. ***long word***: see LONG *adjective*[1]. **my word!** *colloq.* expr. surprise or (*Austral.*) agreement. ***not BREATHE a word of***. **of few words** not given to much or lengthy speaking, taciturn. **of many words** given to much or lengthy speaking, loquacious; verbose. **on my word** = ***upon my word*** below. ***play of words***: see PLAY *noun*. ***play on a word***, ***play on words***: see ***play on*** (b) s.v. PLAY *verb*. ***play on words***, ***play upon words***: see PLAY *noun*. *PRECATORY* ***words***. **put into words** express in speech or writing. ***put the hard word on (a person)***: see HARD *adjective* etc. ***put words into a person's mouth***: see MOUTH *noun*. ***radical word***: see RADICAL *adjective* 4. ***send word (to)***: see SEND *verb*[1]. **Seven Last Words**, **Seven Words** *the* seven utterances of the crucified Christ recorded in the Gospels. ***suit the action to the word***: see SUIT *verb*. **take a person at his or her word** (***a***) assent to a person's statement or proposal (and act accordingly); (***b***) interpret a person's words literally or exactly. **take a person's word** believe a person's statement or assurance (***take a person's word for it***, believe a person's claim or assertion without (further) investigation etc.). ***take the word***: see ***take up the word*** below. ***take the words out of a person's mouth***: see MOUTH *noun*. **take the word**, **take up the word** begin speaking, esp. immediately after or instead of someone else. **Ten Words** *arch. the* Decalogue. ***the Comfortable words***: see COMFORTABLE *adjective* 2. ***the spoken word***: see SPOKEN *ppl adjective*. **too — for words** too — to be adequately described. **upon my word** expr. asseveration or surprise. ***war of words***: see WAR *noun*[1]. **waste words** talk in vain. ***weigh one's words***: see WEIGH *verb*. ***winged words***: see WINGED *adjective*[1]. †**with a word** (*rare*, Shakes.) = ***in a word*** above. **word by word** taking each word in its turn; *spec.* (in alphabetization) treating a space as prior to any letter (so that e.g. *New York* precedes *Newark*). **word for word** in or using exactly the same or (in a translation) precisely corresponding words; verbatim, literal(ly). ***word of command***: see COMMAND *noun* 1. **word of honour** an assurance given on one's honour, a pledge of good faith. **word of mouth** (***a***) oral communication or publicity; (***b***) done, given, etc., by speaking; oral. **words fail me** an exclamation of astonished disbelief, extreme emotion, etc. ***world of words***: see WORLD *noun*.

Comb.: **word association** the bringing to mind of one word in response to another; *spec.* in *PSYCHOANALYSIS*, a psychodiagnostic technique based on (the analysis of) a person's immediate prereflective verbal response to the presentation of stimulus words, esp. as revealing the contents and character of his or her subconscious; **word-base** *PHILOLOGY*, *rare* the simple word from which its derivatives and inflected forms arise; **word-blind** *adjective* (*MEDICINE*) affected with word-blindness; **word-blindness** *MEDICINE* inability to understand written or printed words when seen, owing to disorder of the visual word-centre; **word-book** (***a***) a book containing a list or lists of systematically (esp. alphabetically) arranged words, vocabulary, a glossary, a dictionary; (***b***) *rare* a libretto; **word-bound** *adjective* restrained or impeded in speech etc., esp. by extreme self-consciousness regarding the use of words; **word-break** the point at which a printed etc. word which would overrun the margin is hyphenated to indicate that it continues on the next line; **word-catcher** *arch. derog.* (***a***) a person who cavils at words, a carping critic; (***b***) a collector of words, a lexicographer; **word-category** *LINGUISTICS* = ***word-class*** below; **word-centre** *ANATOMY* each of certain centres in the brain which govern the perception and use of spoken and written words; **word-class** *LINGUISTICS* a category of words of similar form or function, *esp.* a part of speech; **word-deaf** *adjective* (*MEDICINE*) affected with word-deafness; **word-deafness** *MEDICINE* inability to understand words when heard, owing to disorder of the auditory word-centre; **word-field** *LINGUISTICS* a group of lexical items seen as associated in meaning because occurring in similar contexts; **word-final** *adjective* (of a letter or sound) occurring at the end of a word; **word-finally** *adverb* in word-final position; **word frequency** the relative frequency of occurrence of a word in a given text or corpus; **word-game**: requiring the discovery, making, selection, etc., of words; **word geography** the or a study of the regional distribution of words and phrases; **word-hoard** *arch.* a store of words, *esp.* the vocabulary of a person, group, or language; **word-index** an alphabetical list of words used in a given work or corpus, with references to the passages in which they occur but without quotations; **word-initial** *adjective* (of a letter or sound) occurring at the beginning of a word; **word-initially** *adverb* in word-initial position; **word-internally** *adverb* = ***word-medially*** below; **word-ladder** a puzzle in which a given word is to be converted into another by way of a series of words each formed by changing just one letter of its predecessor; **word length** *COMPUTING* the number of bits in a word; **wordlore** (***a***) (the study of) the words of a language and their history; (***b***) *arch.* morphology; **word-magic** *ANTHROPOLOGY* magical power supposed to reside in or be exercised by the use of the name of a person or thing; **wordman** *rare* a master of words or language; **wordmanship** skill in the use of words; **word mark** (***a***) a (real or invented) word used as a trade mark; (***b***) *COMPUTING* a bit that takes a different value according to whether the character containing it does or does not begin (or end) a word; a character containing such a bit; **word-medial** *adjective* (of a letter or sound) occurring in the middle of a word; **word-medially** *adverb* in word-medial position; **word method** *EDUCATION* the look-and-say method of teaching reading; **wordmonger** (usu. *derog.*) a person who deals in (esp. strange, pedantic, or vacuous) words; **wordmongering** (usu. *derog.*) the practice of a wordmonger, verbal trickery; **word order** the order of succession of the words in a sentence etc., esp. as affecting meaning; **word-paint** *verb trans.* describe vividly in words; **word-painter** a writer with a talent for vivid description; **word-painting** a vivid written description; **word-pair**: of words of similar sound or form; **word-perfect** *adjective* knowing perfectly every word of one's lesson, part, etc.; **word-picture** a vivid description in words; **wordplay** (a) witty use of words (esp. of verbal ambiguities), a pun; (an instance of) playing with words; **word problem** *MATH.* the problem of determining whether two different products are equal, or two sequences of operations are equivalent; **word-process** *verb trans.* [back-form.] keyboard, edit, or produce (a letter, text, etc.) using a word processor; **word processing** the electronic production, storage, and manipulation of text, *esp.* the action of using a word processor; **word processor** a computer system designed or used for electronically storing, manipulating, editing, and (usually) displaying and printing text entered from a keyboard; a software package controlling such functions; **word recognition** *EDUCATION & PSYCHOLOGY* the process or faculty whereby a reader perceives and correctly understands words; **word-salad** *PSYCHIATRY* a type of speech indicative of advanced schizophrenia in which random words and phrases are mixed together unintelligibly; **word-sign** a thing, esp. a graphic character, representing a complete word; **word size** *COMPUTING* = ***word length*** above; **wordsman** a person who deals with words, *spec.* a lexicographer; **wordsmanship** = ***wordmanship*** above; *spec.* verbal one-upmanship; **wordsmith** a skilled user or maker of words; **word-square** (a puzzle requiring the discovery of) a set of words of equal length arranged one under another so as to read the same down as across; **word-stock** the vocabulary or sum of words available to a language, dialect, etc.; **word-symbol** = ***word-sign*** above; **word time** *COMPUTING* the time between the reading of the first bits of successive words; **word-type** a particular word or item of vocabulary considered in abstraction from the number of times it is used or occurs; **word-watch** *verb intrans.* observe linguistic usage, esp. with ref. to changes and innovations; **word-watcher** an observer of (esp. changes and innovations in) linguistic usage; **word-wrap**, **word-wrapping** in word processing, the automatic shifting of a word too long to fit at the end of one line to the beginning of the next line; **word-writing** *LINGUISTICS* ideographic writing.

▪ **wordage** *noun* (***a***) words collectively, *esp.* the quantity or number of words in a text etc.; (***b***) = VERBIAGE 1: **E19.** **wordly** *adjective* (*rare*) verbal **M17.** **wordster** *noun* a person who deals in words; a student of words and their meanings: **E20.**

word /wəːd/ *verb*. **ME.**
[from prec.]

▶**I** *verb intrans.* **1** Utter words; speak, talk. Now *rare* or *obsolete*. **ME.**

▶**II** *verb trans.* **2** Utter in words, say, speak; recite. Formerly also, speak of, mention. *obsolete* exc. *dial.* **ME.**

†**3a** Urge verbally. *rare* (Shakes.). Only in **E17.** ▶**b** Bring (a person etc.) to or into a specified condition by means of words. **M17–E18.**

4 Put into words, select words to express; compose, draft, (esp. in a specified manner or style). Freq. as ***worded*** *ppl adjective*. **E17.** ▶†**b** Verbally represent or cause to be represented as. *rare* (Shakes.). Only in **E17.**

5 Speak to, accost; tell. Also, rebuke. *Austral. slang*. **E20.**

3a SHAKES. *Ant. & Cl.* He words me, girls, he words me, that I should not Be noble to myself. **b** R. SOUTH Men are not to be Worded into new Tempers, or Constitutions. **4** *Times* Many psychiatrists word . . reports and personal opinions in ways . . unintelligible to other people. R. C. HUTCHINSON My letter . . had to be worded carefully. H. CARPENTER Her journal is full of strongly worded pieces of art criticism. **b** SHAKES. *Cymb.* This matter of marrying his king's daughter . . words him . . a great deal from the matter. **5 word a person up** advise or give advance warning to a person.

▪ **worder** *noun* (*rare*) †(***a***) a chatterer; (***b***) a person who puts something into words: **E17.**

wording /ˈwəːdɪŋ/ *noun*. **M16.**
[from WORD *noun* or *verb*: see -ING[1].]

†**1** Angry or abusive speech. Cf. WORD *noun* 7. **M16–E17.**

2 Speaking, talking, utterance. Cf. WORD *verb* 1. Now *rare* or *obsolete*. **E17.**

3 The action of putting something into words; the way in which something is verbally expressed or composed; the form of words used, phrasing. **M17.**

4 An inscription. *rare*. **E20.**

2 KEATS Fine wording, Duke! but words could never yet Forestall the fates. **3** W. BLACKSTONE Some forms necessary in the wording of last wills and testaments. DICKENS I entreat . . attention . . to the wording of this document. *Spectator* The meaning . . is plain, though the wording is, to say the least, . . involved.

wordless /ˈwəːdlɪs/ *adjective*. **ME.**
[from WORD *noun* + -LESS.]

1 Inexpressible in words; unutterable. *obsolete* exc. as passing into sense 2. **ME.**

2 Not expressed in words; unspoken. **L15.**

3 Not uttering a word; silent, speechless. **L15.** ▶**b** Incapable of speech or verbal self-expression. **M17.**

4 Unaccompanied by words. **L16.**

3b W. D. HOWELLS The innocence of wordless infancy. **4** G. K. CHESTERTON The man . . cast it down with a wordless sound more shocking than a curse.

▪ **wordlessly** *adverb* **M19.** **wordlessness** *noun* **L19.**

Wordsworthian /wəːdzˈwəːθɪən/ *noun & adjective*. **E19.**
[from *Wordsworth* (see below) + -IAN.]

▶**A** *noun*. An admirer or imitator of the English poet William Wordsworth (1770–1850); a student or admirer of his works. **E19.**

▶**B** *adjective*. Of, pertaining to, or characteristic of Wordsworth; (of a poem) composed by, or in the style of, Wordsworth. **E19.**

▪ **Wordsworthiˈana** *noun pl.* publications or other items concerning or associated with Wordsworth **L19.** **Wordsworthianism** *noun* interest in Wordsworth; Wordsworthian quality: **L19.**

wordy /ˈwəːdi/ *adjective*. LOE.
[from WORD *noun* + -Y[1].]
1 Containing, expressed in, or using many or (esp.) too many words; prolix, verbose. LOE. ▸**b** Consisting of or expressed in words; of words; verbal. E17.
†**2** Skilled in the use of words. *rare*. Only in 17.

1 R. DAVIES His sardonic smile as we haggled was worth pages of wordy argument.

■ **wordily** *adverb* in a wordy manner, verbosely E16. **wordiness** *noun* the quality of being wordy, verbosity E18.

wore *verb*[1] *pa. t. & pple* of WEAR *verb*[1].

wore *verb*[2] *pa. t. & pple* of WEAR *verb*[2].

work /wəːk/ *noun*.
[Old English *weorc*, *werc*, *worc*, *wurc*, = Old Frisian, Old Saxon *werk*, Old High German *werah*, *werc* (Dutch *werk*, German *Werk*), Old Norse *verk*, from Germanic, from Indo-European base also of Greek *ergon*.]
▶ **I** Act, action, process.
1 A thing done; an act, a deed, a proceeding; *spec.* one involving toil or strenuous effort. *arch. & literary* in *gen.* sense. OE. ▸**b** THEOLOGY, in *pl.* Good or moral acts or deeds considered in relation to justification (usu. as opp. to ***faith*** or ***grace***). LME. ▸**c** A criminal act or activity. Cf. JOB *noun*[1] 1b. *Criminals' slang*. E19.
†**2** Doings, deeds *collect. sing.*; conduct. OE–E17.
3 Purposive action involving effort or exertion, esp. as a means of making one's living; (one's) regular occupation or employment. Also, labour, toil; *spec.* (***a***) the operation of making or repairing something, (in *pl.*) architectural or engineering operations; (***b***) (the cost of) the labour involved in making something, as contrasted with the material used; (***c***) investigation, study. OE. ▸**b** Chiefly SPORT. Practice, training; exertion or movement proper to a particular sport etc. M19.
4 Orig., trouble, affliction. Later (*arch.*), (a) disturbance, (a) fuss. OE.
5 A thing to be done or to do; what a person (or thing) has to do; a task, a function. OE.
6 Action of a particular (freq. specified) kind, production of a characteristic effect; functioning, operation. LME. ▸**b** CRICKET. = BREAK *noun*[1] 9. M19.
†**7** MATH. The process of or an operation in calculation; a process of calculation written out in full. Cf. WORKING *noun* 7. M16–M19.
8 PHYSICS & MECHANICS. The operation of a force in producing movement or other physical change, esp. as a definitely measurable quantity. M19.

1 R. BOYLE Another Work of Charity upon my hands . . to reform an extravagant Husband. R. WHATELY The works performed by Jesus . . were beyond the unassisted powers of man. **b** Q. BELL Concerned with works rather than with faith. **3** J. BUCHAN It was hard work rowing, for the wind was against him. D. BLOODWORTH A paleo-zoologist . . doing some work on prehistoric monkeys. C. WARWICK Her work as a freelance political journalist. *Reader's Digest* People know I'm a writer, but they don't really regard what I do as work. ***needlework***, ***woodwork***, etc. ***building works***, ***clerk of works***, ***roadworks***, etc. **b** A. C. H. SMITH He's never been tried on a racecourse before, but I've ridden him out in work. **4** C. M. YONGE There's no harm done yet, so don't make such a work. **5** SHAKES. *1 Hen. IV* Fie upon this quiet life! I want work. A. TROLLOPE To fight the devil was her work—was the appointed work of every living soul. J. C. SWANNELL Mrs Jessie Coulson took over the work. **6** R. SIBBES The work of God's spirit in his children, is like fire. BYRON Famine, despair, cold, thirst, and heat, had done Their work on them by turns.

▶ **II** Product, result.
9 *gen.* A thing, structure, or result produced by the operation, action, or labour of or *of* a person or other agent; things made collectively, creation, handiwork. Also, something achieved or accomplished, the doing *of* an agent. OE.
10 An architectural or engineering structure, as a house, bridge, pier, etc.; an edifice. Now *Hist. & dial.* exc. as in senses b, c below. OE. ▸**b** *sing.* & in *pl.* MILITARY. A fortified building or other defensive structure, a fortification; any of the sides, walls, etc., of such a structure. Freq. as 2nd elem. of comb. OE. ▸**c** An excavated space or structure; *spec.* (***a***) a mine; (***b***) *local* a kind of trench in draining. Now *rare* or *obsolete*. L15.
11 A literary or musical composition. Later also, a painting, sculpture, or other piece of fine art; *collect. (sing. & in pl.)* the literary, musical, or artistic output of a person etc. ME.
12 a (A style of) workmanship, esp. ornamental workmanship. Now chiefly *collect. sing.*, things or structures, esp. of an ornamental nature, (being) made from particular materials or with specified tools. LME. ▸**b** A thing consisting of or (being) made from a textile fabric; the fabric itself, esp. while being worked on; a piece of knitting, needlework, embroidery, etc. LME. ▸†**c** An ornamental pattern or figure. LME–L17.
13 Orig., a set of parts forming a machine or mechanism. Now *spec.* (in *pl.*), the internal working parts of a machine; *esp.* the mechanism of a clock or watch. E17. ▸**b** In *pl.* A drug addict's equipment for taking drugs. *US slang*. M20.

9 DRYDEN The waxen Work of lab'ring Bees. LD MONBODDO Man in his natural state is the work of God. K. P. OAKLEY Stones . . faceted by sandstorms . . are occasionally mistaken for the work of man. **10** MILTON The work some praise And some the Architect. **b** ***earthwork***, ***fieldwork***, ***hornwork***, ***outwork***, etc. **11** V. WOOLF The works of Byron in one volume. R. G. COLLINGWOOD The artist may take his audience's limitations into account when composing his work. K. CLARK Haydn's earlier works, particularly those for small orchestras and strings. *American Speech* It . . cannot be recommended as a reference work. **12a** EVELYN A rare clock of German worke. ***bead-work***, ***chain-work***, ***glass work***, ***ironwork***, ***lacquer-work***, ***poker-work***, ***shell-work***, ***silver-work***, etc. **b** DICKENS The work she had knitted, lay beside her. W. BESANT A girl, with work on her lap, sewing. ***Berlin work***, ***drawn-work***, ***laid-work***, ***shadow work***, etc.

▶ **III 14** †*sing.* & in *pl.* (now usu. treated as *sing.*). A place or premises where industrial activity, esp. manufacture, is carried on. L16.

14 ***works bus***, ***works canteen***, ***works manager***, ***works outing***, ***works supervisor***, etc.

Phrases: ***a demon for work***: see DEMON *noun*[1] 6. **a good day's work** a large or satisfying amount of work done in a day; a day spent conscientiously or productively working. ***all in a day's work***, ***all in the day's work***: see DAY *noun*. ***a nasty bit of work***, ***a nasty piece of work***: see NASTY *adjective*. **at work** in action; engaged in work, esp. one's regular employment. **a work of time** a proceeding which takes a long time. ***clerk of the works***, ***clerk of works***: see CLERK *noun*. ***Covenant of Works***: see COVENANT *noun*. **cut out work for a person** prepare work to be done by a person, give a person something to do. ***dead work***: see DEAD *adjective* etc. ***dirty work***, ***dirty work at the crossroads***: see DIRTY *adjective*. **give a person the works** (***a***) *colloq.* give or tell a person everything; (***b***) *colloq.* treat a person harshly; (***c***) *slang* kill a person. ***good works***: see GOOD *adjective*. **go to work** (***a***) proceed to some action (expressed or implied), commence operations; (***b***) set off for or travel to one's place of employment. **have one's work cut out** have as much to do as one can manage, esp. in the time available; be faced with a hard task. ***in-and-out work***: see IN AND OUT *adjectival phr.* **in the works** being planned, worked on, or produced. ***maid of all work***: see MAID *noun*. **make a work** create or cause confusion, (a) fuss, or (a) disturbance. ***make light work of***: see LIGHT *adjective*[1]. ***make short work of***: see SHORT *adjective*. ***nice work***: see NICE *adjective*. **out of work** (so as to be) without work or employment. **out-of-work** *attrib. adjective & noun* (a person who is) unemployed. ***piece of work***: see PIECE *noun*. ***public works***: see PUBLIC *adjective & noun*. ***rid-work***: see RID *noun* 2. ***ride work***: see RIDE *verb*. ***rough work***: see ROUGH *adjective*. ***rustic work***: see RUSTIC *adjective* 2. ***sale of work***: see SALE *noun*. ***servile work***: see SERVILE *adjective* 1. **set to work** (cause to) begin to work. ***shoot the works***: see SHOOT *verb*. ***social work***: see SOCIAL *adjective*. ***spanner in the works***: see SPANNER *noun*[1] 2. **the work of** — a proceeding occupying (a stated length of time). ***to work***: see TO *preposition*. ***upper works***: see UPPER *adjective*. VIRTUAL ***work***. ***warm work***: see WARM *adjective*. ***white work***: see WHITE *adjective*. **work in progress** work undertaken but not yet completed; *spec.* in COMMERCE (usu. with hyphens), the total cost of materials, labour, etc. incurred up to a given point in a process of production, manufacture, etc. ***work of art***: see ART *noun*[1].

Comb.: **work-bag**, **work-basket**: for storing implements and materials for needlework; **workbench** a bench at which mechanical or practical work, esp. carpentry, is done; **workbook** (***a***) in a business etc., a book containing a record of daily duties, work (to be) done, etc.; (***b***) (chiefly *N. Amer.*) a book of practical instruction, *esp.* one which sets out exercises, problems, etc., to be worked through; (***c***) COMPUTING a single file containing several different types of related information as separate worksheets; **workbox** a box containing tools, materials for sewing, etc.; **work camp** (orig. *US*) (***a***) a camp at which community work is done, esp. by young volunteers; (***b***) = ***labour camp*** s.v. LABOUR *noun*; **work card** (***a***) a card issued by an employer and serving as a kind of identity document; (***b***) a card setting out questions, problems, etc., for a pupil to work through; **workday** *noun & adjective* (***a***) *noun* a day on which work is ordinarily done, a weekday; (***b***) *adjective* = WORKADAY *adjective*. **work ethic** the principle that hard work is intrinsically virtuous or worthy of reward; see also ***Protestant work ethic*** s.v. PROTESTANT *adjective*; **work experience** (the provision of) experience of employment, esp. for school-leavers; **workfellow** = ***workmate*** below; **work-flow** (the organization of) the sequence of industrial, administrative, etc., processes through which a piece of work passes from initiation to completion; **workfolk** workpeople, *esp.* farm labourers; **workforce** the (number of) people engaged in or available for work, esp. in a particular firm or industry; **work function** PHYSICS (***a***) the minimum quantity of energy which is required to remove an electron to infinity from the surface of a given solid (usu. a metal) (symbol ϕ); (***b***) a thermodynamic property of a system, being its internal energy minus the product of its temperature and entropy (symbol *A*); **work furlough** *US* = ***work release*** below; **work group** SOCIOLOGY: of people in a workplace who normally work together; **work-hand** an assistant employed by another person, *esp.* = HAND *noun* 12b; **work-harden** *verb* (METALLURGY) (***a***) *verb trans.* toughen (a metal) by cold-working; (***b***) *verb intrans.* (of a metal) become tough as a result of cold-working; **workhead** (***a***) the part of a lathe which carries the mandrel; (***b***) an interchangeable working attachment for a powered implement or tool; **workhorse** (***a***) a horse used for work on a farm; (***b***) *fig.* a machine, person, etc., that dependably performs arduous work; †**work-jail** a penal workhouse; **workload** the amount of work to be done by a person or persons; **work-master** (now *rare* or *obsolete*) (***a***) a master workman, an overseer or employer of workmen; (***b***) *fig.* a producer or creator of a thing, *esp.* God as creator and ruler; **workmate** a person engaged in the same work as another, *esp.* a fellow labourer; **work measurement** the application of ergonomic techniques in establishing the time required for performing a particular task; **work-minded** *adjective* eager to work, esp. hard; **work-mistress** (now *rare*) a woman who controls or superintends work, *fig.* nature personified; **workmonger** THEOLOGY (*derog.*, now *rare* or *obsolete*) a person who expects to be justified by works; **workpeople** people in paid employment, esp. in manual or industrial labour; **work permit** an official document giving a foreigner permission to take a job in a country; **workpiece** a thing (being) worked on with a machine or tool; **workplace** a or the place at which a person works, as an office, factory, etc.; **work point** in Communist China, a unit used in calculating wages due, based on the quality and quantity of work done; **work rate** a rate at which work is done, the amount of work done in a period of time; *spec.* the amount of fatiguing running and chasing a football player does in a game; **work release** *US* leave of absence from prison by day enabling a person to continue in normal employment; **workroom** a room for working in, *esp.* one equipped for a particular kind of work; **works committee**, **works council**: of workers or their representatives, formed for joint discussions with employers; **workshadow** *verb trans. & intrans.* accompany (a person at work) for a short period in order to gain understanding of or receive training in a job; (chiefly as ***workshadowing*** *verbal noun*); **work-sharing** short-time working by all employees in an overmanned industry, as an alternative to redundancies; **worksheet** (***a***) = ***workbook*** (a) above; (***b***) a paper on which are recorded notes, calculations, etc., relating to work in progress; (***c***) a paper listing exercises, problems, etc., for a student to work through; **work-shy** *adjective* disinclined to work; **work-space** (***a***) COMPUTING = ***working storage*** s.v. WORKING *noun*; (***b***) space for people to work in; **workstation** (***a***) a location on an assembly line at which an operation in a manufacturing process is carried out; (***b***) (a desk with) a computer or computer terminal and keyboard; a powerful desktop computer; **work study** the assessment of methods of working with a view to maximizing output and efficiency; **work surface** = ***worktop*** below; **work table**: for supporting working materials, tools, etc., *esp.* one used for sewing or needlework; **work-team** a team of animals (esp. horses or oxen) or people who work together; **worktop** a flat surface for working on, esp. in a kitchen; **workweek** *N. Amer.* the total number of hours or days worked in a week.
■ **workwise** *adverb* as far as work is concerned M20.

work /wəːk/ *verb*. Pa. t. & pple **worked**, (earlier, now *arch.*, *literary*, & *techn.*) **wrought** /rɔːt/. See also WORKED, WROUGHT *ppl adjectives*.
[Old English *wyrċan* (pa. t. *worhte*, pa. pple *ġeworht*), (Mercian) *wircan*, late Old English *wercan*, *weorc(e)an*, (with later substitution of final *k* due mainly to the noun), from Germanic, from Indo-European base also of ORGAN *noun*[1], ORGY. Cf. WRIGHT *noun*.]
▶ **I** *verb trans.* Perform, produce.
1 Do, perform, practise (a task, deed, process, etc.). Freq. with cogn. obj. (in ***work miracles***, ***work wonders*** now passing into sense 5 below). *arch.* OE. ▸**b** Commit (a sin or crime), do (evil, wrong, etc.). *arch.* OE. ▸**c** Observe (a rite or ceremony). Long *obsolete* exc. FREEMASONRY. OE.
2 Carry out or execute (a person's will, advice, etc.). Now only as passing into sense 5 below. OE.
3 Produce (as) by labour or exertion, make, construct; now usu. *spec.*, make or form (an ornamental object, design, etc.) artistically or skilfully. Now freq. foll. by *in* a material or medium. OE. ▸**b** Of God: create. Long *rare*. OE. ▸†**c** Compose (a written work). OE–M18.
4 Weave (a fabric); make (a garment etc.) by means of needlework or knitting; ornament with or *with* an embroidered design, embroider. ME.
5 Produce as a result, bring about, cause; accomplish, achieve. ME.
6 †**a** Act in order to effect (something); plan, contrive; manage (a matter or proceeding). ME–M17. ▸**b** Arrange, engineer, successfully contrive. Usu. foll. by *it*. *colloq.* L19.
7 Put in, insert, incorporate, esp. in the process of construction or composition. M17. ▸**b** HORTICULTURE. Graft *on* a stock. M17.

1 *English Historical Review* The special work . . and the rich ability with which he wrought it. **b** AV *Matt.* 7:23 Depart from me, ye that worke iniquity. T. HOOD Methought, last night, I wrought A murder, in a dream! **3** W. COWPER A goblet exquisitely wrought. U. LE GUIN Patterns of vines worked in painted wire. **4** SHAKES. *Ven. & Ad.* Now she unweaves the web that she hath wrought. TENNYSON A damask napkin wrought with horse and hound. L. M. ALCOTT I'm going to work Mr. Laurence a pair of slippers. **5** DICKENS The beer had wrought no bad effect upon his appetite. P. BARKER The changes that sickness and pain had wrought in her appearance. *National Law Journal (US)* Power failures can often work havoc. **6a** MILTON To work in close design, by fraud or guile What force effected not. **b** J. RULE Have you got time off? . . Ask Bill . . . He can work it for you. **7** STEELE Those occasional Dissertations, which he has wrought into the Body of his History.

▶ **II** *verb trans.* Do something to, influence, affect.
8 a Cause to be in, bring into, a specified state (now esp. as a result of exertion or artificial agitation); make, render; change, convert. With obj. & adjective compl. or adverbial phr. Now freq. *refl.* OE. ▸**b** Make (up), compound, or shape (materials, ingredients, etc.) into or *into* something. M16.

9 Expend effort or energy on, operate in or on, or apply force to; *spec.* (*a*) till or cultivate, (land, soil, etc.); (*b*) obtain (ore, coal, stone, etc.) by mining or quarrying; extract materials from (a mine, quarry, etc.); (*c*) knead or stir (a mixture); (*d*) shape (stone, metal, etc.) by cutting or hammering; (*e*) = ***work out*** (g) below; (*f*) practise one's occupation, perform, or operate in or at (a place, site, etc.) or for (a specified period) or according to (an agreed system of hours); (*g*) (of a train, bus, etc.) operate along (a specified line or route). OE.

10 a Set to work, exact labour from; employ in work; *spec.* use (a dog) for herding sheep or cattle. LME. ▸**b** Exercise (a faculty etc.); cause (a thing) to act; actuate, operate, use, direct the action of, (a machine, plan, institution, etc.). LME.

11 Act on the mind, will, or feelings of; influence, persuade; affect, stir the emotions of. Later also, try to persuade, urge. L16. ▸**b** Hoax, cheat, take advantage of. *US.* L19.

12 Make (one's or its way), esp. gradually or laboriously. Also *refl.* L16.

13 a Cause to progress or penetrate into or move out of some position, esp. against resistance. E17. ▸**b** Direct the movement of, guide or drive in a particular course; *spec.* (*a*) steer, manoeuvre, (a ship, boat, etc.); (*b*) (chiefly *Austral.* & *NZ*) herd (sheep, cattle, etc.). M17.

> **8a** SHAKES. *Hen. VIII* This imperious man will work us all From princes into pages. *Manchester Examiner* It would take some time for the trade to work itself right. J. RHYS I'd worked myself into a frenzy. **9** *Jazz Journal International* I came back . . and worked a few clubs and so forth. *Finescale Modeler* Work the paint into the brush by stroking on the palette. *Countryside Campaigner* Minerals can only be worked where they naturally occur. *New Civil Engineer* Main contractor Jones Bros . . has been working 11 hour shifts, six and a half days a week. **10a** M. DICKENS Jane is working you too hard. *Sporting Dog* Terry Harris . . worked a brace of dogs towards the sheep. **b** C. RYAN A lone signaller . . began to work his radio set. P. FITZGERALD There were lifts, worked by electricity. **11** SHAKES. *Macb.* My dull brain was wrought With things forgotten. *Times* The born politician's art of working a crowd. **12** B. EMECHETA A big bead of perspiration working its way . . down the bridge of Nina's nose. **13a** B. TAYLOR In vain I . . worked my benumbed hands. *Times Lit. Suppl.* A neighbouring battery of guns . . were being worked into position. *refl.*: *Skin Diver* The hull has worked itself about three feet into the hard clay bottom. **b** DEFOE Having no Sails to work the Ship with. F. D. DAVISON Sheep dogs . . working lost flocks in the mountain gullies.

▸**III** *verb intrans.* Act, function, labour.

14 Of a person: do something, act, proceed, behave. Long *rare* or *obsolete* in *gen.* sense. OE. ▸**b** Proceed (in a particular way) in performing a calculation or solving a problem. LME.

15 Exert oneself physically or mentally, esp. in order to achieve a purpose or result; do work, labour, toil, (*at* or *on* a subject, occupation, project, etc.); perform a task or tasks; conduct a campaign; strive (*for, to do*). Also (long *arch. rare*), plan, contrive, (*that, to do*). OE.

16 Do one's daily or ordinary business or work; pursue a regular occupation, have a job, be employed, (*in* some trade, profession, field of study or activity, etc.). Also (*slang*), operate as a thief or swindler. ME.

17 a (Of a thing) perform a function; (of a machine, device, etc.) run, operate, or function, esp. properly or effectively; *spec.* revolve, go through regular motions; (of an action, plan, etc.) be practicable, succeed. ME. ▸**b** Have or produce an effect, take effect, have or exert an influence; *spec.* use one's persuasive power, (strive to) prevail. Foll. by *on, upon,* (*arch.*) *with.* LME.

18 Of a part of the body: ache, hurt. Cf. WARK *verb. obsolete* exc. *dial.* LME.

19 Of a substance, material, etc.: behave in a specified way while being worked (sense 9 above). L15.

20 Of wine etc.: ferment. Cf. earlier WORKING *noun* 9. M16.

> **14** R. CROWLEY If he haue wrought against the lawes. **b** D. BAGLEY This gadget is working in octal instead of decimal. **15** SHAKES. *Hen. VIII* Without the King's assent or knowledge You wrought to be a legate. G. GODWIN How hard some folks do work at what they call pleasure. J. LUBBOCK Ants work not only all day, but . . often all night too. *Sea Spray* These lads have worked like dogs all winter. **16** R. HOGGART The employed inhabitants of these areas work for a wage. P. A. ADAMS Leaving the Society to work as a secular priest in the Clifton diocese. **17a** A. C. GUNTER Maurice . . closes the door . . trying it to be sure the spring lock has worked. W. LIPPMANN Trying out all sorts of schemes to find out whether they work. *Entertainment Weekly* If this is author Anthony Browne's image for emotional withdrawal, it doesn't work for this reader. **b** SHAKES. *Twel. N.* I know my physic will work with him. S. PEPYS The King may yet be wrought upon . . to bring changes in our Office. LD MACAULAY She . . worked on his feelings by pretending to be ill. H. JAMES She worked . . upon the sympathy . . of her associates.

▸**IV** *verb intrans.* Move.

21 Move or travel on a particular course or route, proceed in a particular direction; make one's or its way, progress, penetrate, esp. gradually, laboriously, or in a specified way. LME. ▸**b** *spec. NAUTICAL.* Sail in a particular course or direction; *esp.* sail against the wind, tack. M17.

22 Move restlessly, violently, or convulsively; be in or cause a state of agitation; *spec.* (*a*) (of the sea etc.) toss, seethe; (*b*) *NAUTICAL* (of a ship) strain or labour so that the fastenings become slack; (*c*) (of the face or features) twitch, move convulsively. L16.

23 Arrive gradually at a specified state or position as a result of constant or continual movement. L18.

> **21** A. BRASSEY After midnight . . the wind worked gradually round. *fig.*: E. GASKELL Their religion did not work down into their lives. **22** JOHN TAYLOR The well . . doth continually work and bubble with extreame violence. E. WELTY Her face worked and broke into strained, hardening lines. *fig.*: C. STANFORD Tempests of feeling often work beneath an unchanged face. **23** R. H. DANA The anchor on the lee bow had worked loose, and was thumping the side.

Phrases: ***be subdued to what one works in***: see SUBDUE *verb* 2. ***music while you work***: see MUSIC *noun.* **work a point** *Austral. slang* take unfair advantage. ***work like a beaver***: see BEAVER *noun*[1]. ***work like a charm***: see CHARM *noun*[1]. ***work like a nigger***: see NIGGER *noun* 1. ***work one's arse off***: see ARSE *noun* 1. ***work one's fingers to the bone***: see BONE *noun.* ***work one's guts out***: see GUT *noun.* **work one's passage** pay for one's journey on a ship with work instead of money. ***work one's tail off***: see TAIL *noun*[1]. ***work one's ticket***: see TICKET *noun.* **work one's way through college** etc. obtain the money for educational fees, one's maintenance as a student, etc., by working. **work one's will** *arch.* accomplish one's purpose *on* or *upon* a person or thing. ***work on tribute***: see TRIBUTE *noun* 3. ***work out one's own salvation.*** ***work scathe***: see SCATHE *noun* 2. ***work the oracle***: see ORACLE *noun.* ***work the rabbit's foot on***: see *rabbit's foot* (a) s.v. RABBIT *noun.* ***work to rule***: see RULE *noun.* ***work wonders***: see WONDER *noun.*

With adverbs & prepositions in specialized senses: **work away** work continuously or unremittingly. **work back** *Austral. colloq.* do overtime. **work in** (*a*) insert, introduce, incorporate, find a place for; (*b*) cooperate or get along *with.* **work off** (*a*) print off (as from a plate), *esp.* print in final form ready for publication or distribution; (*b*) dispose of, palm off, pass off; (*c*) take off or away by degrees; get rid of, free oneself from, esp. by continuous action, effort, or work. **work on** continue working. **work out** (*a*) bring, fetch, or get out by some process or course of action; get rid of, expel; (*b*) (of something enclosed or embedded) make its way out, esp. gradually; work loose and come out; (*c*) work (a mine etc.) until it is exhausted; (*d*) discharge (a debt etc.) by labour instead of with money; (*e*) bring about or produce (a result) by labour or effort; attain, accomplish, esp. with difficulty; †(*f*) (*rare,* Shakes.) preserve to the end; (*g*) solve (a problem or question) by reasoning or calculation; find out by calculating, calculate (an answer, sum, amount, etc.); (*h*) give or produce a definite result, have or issue in a particular or specified result; (*i*) be calculated *at* a quantity or total; (*j*) bring to a fuller or finished state, produce or express completely or in detail, develop, elaborate; (*k*) engage in physical exercise or training; *spec.* (*BOXING*) fight a practice bout. **work out of** use (a place, office, etc.) as a base for one's work or business. **work over** (*a*) *colloq.* beat up or violently attack (a person); (*b*) examine thoroughly. **work to** be responsible to (a person) as one's immediate superior, supervisor, etc. **work up** †(*a*) build up or construct (a wall etc.); (*b*) stir up, mix, mingle, (ingredients etc.); make up (material) *into* something by labour, bring (material) into some condition, esp. into efficient working order or readiness for use; (*c*) elaborate, enlarge, develop, (*to* or *into* something); (*d*) bring by work or an influence *to* or *into* a specified state or condition; (*e*) painstakingly make, construct, form, or fashion (cf. sense 3 above); (*f*) *NAUTICAL* (now *rare* or *obsolete*) set to or keep at needless and disagreeable hard work as a punishment; (*g*) learn, study, or master (a subject); (*h*) arouse, excite, agitate (a person, the emotions, etc.), esp. gradually; induce or persuade (a person) *to do* something; (*i*) be gradually stirred up or excited; proceed or advance to a climax or state of agitation.

Comb.: **workaway** *US* a person who works his passage on a ship; **work-in** a protest, usu. against threatened closure of a factory etc., in which workers occupy the workplace and continue working; **workout** (*a*) *BOXING* a practice bout; (*b*) *gen.* a session of exercise or training; a test, a trial; **workover** the repair or maintenance of an oil well; **work-to-rule** the action or an instance of working to rule; **work-up** (*a*) *PRINTING* (a smudge made by) a piece of spacing material that works loose and rises in the forme; (*b*) *MEDICINE* (orig. *US*) a diagnostic examination of a patient; (*c*) *CHEMISTRY* the experimental procedures carried out to separate and purify substances for analysis or the products of a chemical reaction; (*d*) (an instance of) the process of bringing a ship into seaworthy condition.

workable /ˈwəːkəb(ə)l/ *adjective.* M16.
[from prec. + -ABLE.]

1 (Of a substance or material) able to be worked, manipulated, or moulded for use; (of a condition, property, etc.) that enables a substance or material to be worked. M16.

2 That can be managed, conducted, or (made to) function or operate, esp. satisfactorily; practicable, feasible. M18.

> **1** E. WAUGH There is tin in the Ngumo mountains in workable quantities. **2** *New Yorker* Every problem carries with it the chance of a workable solution. G. PRIESTLAND To think in terms of workable law . . not just moral indignation.

■ **workaˈbility** *noun* the condition, quality, or fact of being workable; *spec.* the degree to which or ease with which a substance or material can be worked, manipulated, or moulded: L19. **workableness** *noun* L18. **workably** *adverb* M20.

workaday /ˈwəːkədeɪ/ *noun & adjective.* Also (earlier) †**werke-**, (now *rare* or *obsolete*) **worky-** /ˈwəːkɪ-/, & other vars. ME.
[Origin uncertain: perh. from WORK *noun* + DAY *noun* after trisyllabic vars. of *Sunday, mass-day.*]

▸**A** *noun.* A day on which work is ordinarily done (as opp. to a holiday); a workday. *obsolete* exc. *dial.* ME.

▸**B** *attrib.* or as *adjective.* Pertaining to or characteristic of a workday or its occupations; characterized by a regular succession or round of tasks, humdrum, routine; ordinary, everyday, practical. M16.

> L. WHISTLER The work-a-day interior struck him as 'something between a school and a sanatorium'. *Atlantic* Acquaintances for whom weekend activities seem more important than workaday existence.

¶ The forms with medial *-a-* are not recorded before E19.

workaholic /wəːkəˈhɒlɪk/ *noun. colloq.* (orig. *US*). M20.
[from WORK *noun, verb* + -AHOLIC.]
A person addicted to work; a person who voluntarily works excessively hard, esp. for too long.

> M. SEYMOUR Too much of a workaholic to allow illness to interrupt his work plans. *attrib.*: *Sunday Express* Try to take time off from your workaholic life.

■ ˈ**workaholism** *noun* the condition of being a workaholic M20.

workalike /ˈwəːkəlʌɪk/ *noun & adjective.* L20.
[from WORK *verb* + ALIKE *adverb.*]
(A computer) able to use the software of another specified machine without special modification; (a piece of software) identical in function to another software package.

worked /wəːkt/ *ppl adjective.* L16.
[pa. pple of WORK *verb*: see -ED[1].]

▸**I** *gen.* **1** That has been worked. Later also foll. by *-out, -up,* etc. L16.

> **1** *Daily Telegraph* Miners . . voted not to go on strike, not even over closure of worked-out pits. J. WILSON He got all worked up and started shouting and swearing. ***worked to*** DEATH.

▸**II** *spec.* **2** Executed or ornamented with needlework, engraving, etc. M18.

3 *ARCHAEOLOGY.* Of a flint etc.: artificially shaped or fashioned. M19.

worker /ˈwəːkə/ *noun.* ME.
[from WORK *verb* + -ER[1].]

1 A creator or producer of or *of* a thing or effect; *spec.* †(*a*) God as creator; (*b*) a doer *of* evil, a deed, etc.; a performer *of* a specified kind of action. *arch.* ME.

2 A person who works or does work of any kind, nature, or quality; *spec.* (*a*) one who works *in* a specified medium; (*b*) one employed in a specified trade, industry, or position (freq. as 2nd elem. of comb.); (*c*) a waged industrial employee or manual labourer; (*d*) in *pl.*, working-class people collectively. LME. ▸**b** A person who works hard. E17.

3 a A bullock, horse, etc., used as draught animal. Now *Austral.* E17. ▸**b** A dog or other animal that works (well). M19.

4 (An individual of) a caste in social insects, as ants and bees, which consists of sterile females that supply food and perform other services for the colony. M18.

> **1** W. MORRIS She grew to be the sorceress, Worker of fearful things. R. ELLISON As a numbers runner he is . . a worker of miracles. **2** *Black Panther* Karl Marx's famous credo: 'Workers of the World, Unite'. *New Society* Some increase . . in the proportion of . . salaried workers. A. STORR Freud was . . an extremely hard worker. ***cloth-worker, factory-worker, metalworker,*** etc. ***fast worker***: see FAST *adjective.* PSYCHIATRIC ***social worker. slave worker***: see SLAVE *noun*[1] & *adjective*[1]. ***social worker***: see SOCIAL *adjective.* **b** H. B. STOWE A dreamy, neutral spectator . . when he should have been a worker.

Comb.: **worker-director** a worker who is also on the board of directors of a firm; **worker participation** participation of workers in the management of their firm or industry; **worker priest** (*a*) a Roman Catholic priest in postwar France who earned his living as a factory-worker or the like; (*b*) *gen.* a priest engaged (usually part-time) in secular work; **workers' cooperative** a business or industry owned and managed by those who work for it.

■ **workerist** *adjective* of, pertaining to, or characteristic of a proletarian or worker-oriented view of society; (too) sympathetic to the role of labour in the class struggle: M20. **workerless** *adjective* without workers; *spec.* (*ENTOMOLOGY*) designating a (usu. parasitic) ant species that lacks a caste system: E20.

workfare /ˈwəːkfɛː/ *noun.* Orig. *US.* M20.
[from WORK *noun* + WEL)FARE *noun.*]
A policy of requiring recipients of certain State benefits to do some work in exchange for them.

workful /ˈwəːkfʊl, -f(ə)l/ *adjective.* ME.
[from WORK *noun* + -FUL.]

†**1** Active, operative. ME–L17.

2 Full of (hard) work; hard-working. M19.

■ **workfulness** *noun* †(*a*) *rare* activity; (*b*) laborious activity: L16.

workhouse /ˈwəːkhaʊs/ *noun.* LOE.
[from WORK *noun* + HOUSE *noun*[1].]
1 *Hist.* A house, shop, or room in which work is regularly done; a workshop, a factory. LOE.
2 *Hist.* Orig., a house established to provide work for the unemployed poor of a parish. Later, an institution in which the destitute of a parish received board and lodging, usually in return for work done. M17.
3 A prison or house of correction for petty offenders. *US.* M17.
2 *Union Workhouse*: see UNION *noun*[2] 5b.
Comb.: **workhouse sheeting** strong twilled unbleached cotton material used for sheeting, curtains, etc.; **workhouse test** *Hist.* the test of good faith put to an applicant for poor relief by which he or she was obliged to consent to go to the workhouse if required.
■ **workhoused** /-haʊzd/ *adjective* (*rare*) lodged in or habituated to a workhouse M19.

working /ˈwəːkɪŋ/ *noun.* ME.
[from WORK *verb* + -ING[1].]
▶ **I** *gen.* **1** The action of WORK *verb*; an instance or the result of this; the activity or performance of work; the way a thing works. (Foll. by *-off, -out, -over, -up*, etc.) ME.
🕮 **1** *Westminster Gazette* Working is agreeable to my nature and to my health. *Guardian* The government said it would improve the working of the economy.
▶ **II 2 a** *collect. sing.* & in *pl.* A person's actions or deeds. *arch.* LME. ▸**b** *collect. sing.* & (now usu.) in *pl.* The processes or functioning of the mind, conscience, etc. L16.
3 †**a** Performance or execution *of* a particular work or act. LME–L17. ▸**b** FREEMASONRY. (The observance of) a rite, a system of ritual. L19.
†**4** Making, manufacture, construction; the manner or style in which something is made, handiwork, workmanship. LME–E18.
5 The action of operating or performing work on something, manipulation, management; *spec.* (*a*) exploitation of the resources of (a mine, quarry, etc.); (*b*) the putting into operation *of* a scheme, system, legislation, etc. LME.
6 Influential operation; influence, effectiveness. *arch.* LME.
7 Mathematical calculation or calculations. Now chiefly *spec.*, the record of the successive steps taken or calculations made in solving a mathematical problem. Cf. WORK *noun* 7. LME.
†**8** Aching; pain (*rare*). Also, stomachic or intestinal disturbance. LME–E18.
9 Fermentation of liquor. M16.
10 Restless movement of water, esp. the sea; straining of a ship etc. so as to slacken the fastenings. L16. ▸**b** Agitated twitching or convulsive movement of the face or features. E19.
11 The proper action or movement of (a part of) a machine etc. M17.
🕮 **2a** W. P. MACKAY In the twelfth chapter of Revelation we have depicted a remarkable series of Satan's workings. **b** N. ROWE The secret workings of my Brain Stand all reveal'd to thee. **5** W. RALEIGH The working of a Myne There. J. MOXON A piece of Ivory . . strong enough to bear working till they bring it to as small a Cilinder as they can.
▶ **III** †**12** Decorative work. *rare.* M16–E18.
13 A mine, a quarry; a part of this which is being worked or has been worked. M18.
🕮 **13** *Mineral Magazine* While examining and surveying the disused workings of the . . mine.
Comb. (not all clearly separable from collocations of the adjective): ***working breakfast***: see *working lunch* below; **working copy**: of a book or other document used or annotated by someone working on its contents; **working day** (*a*) a workday; (*b*) the part of a day or amount of time per day devoted or allotted to work; ***working dinner***: see *working lunch* below; **working drawing** a scale drawing of a building, machine, part, etc., serving as a guide in construction or manufacture; **working hours**: normally devoted to work; †**working-house** = WORKHOUSE 1, 2; **working hypothesis**: used as a basis for action; **working knowledge**: adequate to work with; **working load** the maximum load that (a part of) a machine or other structure is designed to bear; the amount of work a person is assigned to do; **working lunch** etc. a lunch etc. at which those present discuss business; **working memory** PSYCHOLOGY the part of short-term memory which is concerned with immediate conscious perceptual and linguistic processing; ***working model***: see MODEL *noun* 2b; **working order** the condition in which a machine, system, etc., works satisfactorily or in a specified way; **working-out** (*a*) the calculation of results; (*b*) the elaboration of details; **working outline**: forming the basis of a finished drawing; **working party** (*a*) MILITARY a party detailed for a special piece of work outside ordinary duties; (*b*) (now *Hist.*) a group of women, meeting to do work (esp. sewing) for a good cause; (*c*) a committee or group appointed to study and report on a particular question, and to make recommendations based on its findings; (*d*) a group of prisoners engaged on outdoor work, esp. outside the perimeter of the prison; **working plan**: serving as the basis for the construction of a building, management of a project, etc.; working drawings; **working space** (*a*) COMPUTING = ***working storage*** below; (*b*) = ***work-space*** (b) s.v. WORK *noun*; **working storage** COMPUTING part of a computer's memory that is used by a program for the storage of intermediate results or other temporary items; **working surface**, **working top** = ***worktop*** s.v. WORK *noun*.

working /ˈwəːkɪŋ/ *adjective.* LME.
[from WORK *verb* + -ING[2].]
▶ **I** *gen.* **1** That works. LME.
▶ **II 2** Active, energetic. *arch.* LME. ▸†**b** That produces an effect, effective; *spec.* (of words or events) stirring. L16–E18.
†**3** Aching, throbbing with pain. LME–M16.
4 Of the sea etc.: agitated, tossing. *poet.* L16.
5 Of a mechanism etc.: that functions (esp. in a specified manner); *spec.* that moves (as opp. to being fixed or stationary). E17.
6 Of an animal: used for work, esp. in farming, hunting, or for guard duties; not kept as a pet or for show. E17. ▸†**b** Designating a social insect of the worker caste. M18–E19.
7 Engaged in work, working for one's living; *esp.* employed in a manual or industrial occupation. M17. ▸**b** Of a partner in a firm: taking an active part in the business (opp. ***sleeping***). E19.
8 Of the face or features: twitching, moving convulsively, esp. with agitated emotion. M18.
🕮 **4** POPE Oars they seize . . and brush the working seas. **7** I. MURDOCH Us working hacks who have to earn our living. N. PAINTING Not an ordinary working chap like you and me.
Special collocations (not all clearly separable from combs. of the noun): ***working capital***: see CAPITAL *noun*[2] 2. **working class** *adjective* of, pertaining to, or characteristic of the working class or classes. **working class(es)** the class or classes consisting of the people who are (normally) employed for wages, esp. in manual or industrial work; the proletariat. **working girl** (*a*) *colloq.* a girl or woman who goes out to earn her living rather than remaining at home; (*b*) *US slang* a prostitute. **working man** a man employed for wages (esp. in a manual or industrial job), a working-class man. **working title** a provisional title given to a book, film, or other work before the final title is settled. **working woman** a woman employed for wages (esp. in a manual or industrial job), a working-class woman.
■ **workingly** *adverb* (*rare*) †(*a*) effectively; (*b*) industriously: M17.

workless /ˈwəːklɪs/ *adjective.* L15.
[from WORK *noun* + -LESS.]
1 Doing no work; idle. Long *rare* exc. as in sense 3 below. L15.
†**2** THEOLOGY. Of faith: without works. M16–M17.
3 Having no work to do; unemployed, redundant. M19.
■ **worklessness** *noun* unemployment L19.

workman /ˈwəːkmən/ *noun.* Pl. **-men**. OE.
[from WORK *noun* + MAN *noun*.]
1 A man employed to do (usually) manual or industrial work; an operative. OE.
2 A skilled or expert craftsman. Now *rare* or *obsolete.* L15. ▸**b** HUNTING. A skilful or experienced rider. M19.
3 A person considered with regard to skill or expertise in a job, craft, or art. L15.
†**4** *The* Creator. M16–E17.
🕮 **3** J. H. PARKER One of the characteristics of a good workman not to waste his material. *Proverb*: A bad workman blames his tools.

workmanlike /ˈwəːkmənlʌɪk/ *adverb & adjective.* LME.
[from prec. + -LIKE.]
▶ **A** *adverb.* In a manner or style characteristic of a good workman; competently. LME.
▶ **B** *adjective.* **1** Of, pertaining to, or characteristic of a workman. *rare.* M17.
2 Characteristic of a good or diligent workman; showing practised skill; well executed, competent, efficient. M18.
🕮 **2** *Daily Telegraph* The orchestra gave . . a workmanlike performance.
■ Also **workmanly** *adverb & adjective* (*rare*) LME.

workmanship /ˈwəːkmənʃɪp/ *noun.* LME.
[from WORKMAN + -SHIP.]
†**1 a** The performance or execution of (a) work; labour, esp. the (amount of) labour spent on a particular task or job. LME–E19. ▸**b** Action, agency, operation. M16–M17. ▸**c** Creation, manufacture, production. L16–L17.
2 A thing produced or made by a workman, craftsman, etc.; *spec.* the work of a particular person, faculty, etc. E16.
3 (The degree of) skill, art, or craftsmanship exhibited in a piece of work. E16.
🕮 **2** J. BUTLER Human nature, considered as the divine workmanship. G. BERKELEY Inconsistent ideas which are often the workmanship of their own brains. **3** R. BOYLE Idiots admire in things the Beauty of their Materials, but Artists that of the Workmanship.

workshop /ˈwəːkʃɒp/ *noun & verb.* M16.
[from WORK *noun* + SHOP *noun*.]
▶ **A** *noun.* **1** A room, building, etc., in which work (esp. manufacture) is carried on. M16.
2 A meeting or session (orig. in education or the arts, but now in any field) for discussion, study, experiment, etc.; the people attending or organizing such a meeting. M20.
🕮 **1** *fig.*: SIR W. SCOTT Fergus's brain was a perpetual workshop of scheme and intrigue.
▶ **B** *verb trans.* Infl. **-pp-**. Stage an experimental or preliminary performance of (a play, musical, etc.). Cf. sense A.2 above. L20.

worksome /ˈwəːks(ə)m/ *adjective. rare.* M19.
[from WORK *noun*, *verb* + -SOME[1].]
Industrious, diligent.

workwoman /ˈwəːkwʊmən/ *noun.* Pl. **-women** /-wɪmɪn/. M16.
[from WORK *noun* + WOMAN *noun*.]
A female worker or operative. Also (*arch.*), a woman who does needlework.

worky /ˈwəːki/ *noun. colloq.* (orig. *US*). M19.
[from WORK *noun* + -Y[6].]
A worker, an operative.

workyday *noun & adjective* see WORKADAY.

world /wəːld/ *noun & verb.*
[Old English *world*, *weorold* = Old Frisian *wrald*, *warld*, Old Saxon *werold* (Dutch *wereld*), Old High German *weralt* (German *Welt*), Old Norse *verǫld*, from Germanic base cogn. with Latin *vir* man + Germanic base of OLD *noun*[1], hence meaning 'age or life of man'.]
▶ **A** *noun.* **I** (A period of) human existence.
1 (Earthly) human existence; *this* present life. OE. ▸**b** *gen.* A state of (present or future) existence. ME.
2 a Earthly human pursuits and interests; secular or lay (as opp. to religious or clerical) life, pursuits, and interests, temporal or mundane affairs. OE. ▸**b** *gen.* The events, affairs, and conditions of human life. OE. ▸†**c** A state of human affairs; a state of things, a situation. LME–E17.
3 †**a** An age or period in human existence or history. OE–L17. ▸**b** *spec.* An age or period of human history identified by or associated with particular cultural, intellectual, or economic characteristics or conditions. Now *rare* or *obsolete* exc. as passing into sense 9. M16.
🕮 **1** W. PALEY A Christian's chief care being to pass quietly through this world to a better. DICKENS She was too good for this world and for me, and she died. **b** WORDSWORTH Blank misgivings of a Creature Moving about in worlds not realised. **2a** W. COWPER Renounce the world—the preacher cries. R. BARNARD Father Anselm furrowed his brow. 'I believe his name in the world was Denis Crowther.' **b** SHAKES. *Haml.* To be honest, as this world goes, is to be one man pick'd out of ten thousand. S. BARING-GOULD What was the world coming to, when police poked their noses into his shop? **3b** LD MACAULAY Men whose minds had been trained in a world which had passed away.
▶ **II** The earth; a natural environment or system.
4 *The* earth and everything on it; *the* globe; *the* human environment; *collect.* the countries on earth. OE. ▸**b** A section or part of the earth, esp. as a place of inhabitation or settlement. M16. ▸**c** *sing.* & in *pl.* A great quantity or number (*of*), a vast amount (*of*). Also in *pl.* (adverbial), by a great deal, vastly. L16.
5 The (material) universe, the cosmos; creation as a whole; everything that exists. Also (with specifying word), any part of the universe considered as an entity. ME. ▸**b** A planet or other celestial body, *esp.* one viewed as inhabited. E18.
6 A person's normal or habitual sphere of interest, action, or thought; a realm of activity or endeavour; *fig.* a characteristic atmosphere or environment. L16.
7 a A particular realm of natural or created things; *esp.* the animal, vegetable, and mineral kingdoms. L17. ▸**b** Any group or system of (usu. similar) things or beings considered as constituting a unity. L17.
🕮 **4** SHAKES. *A.Y.L.* All the world's a stage, And all the men and women merely players. N. SHUTE I had travelled the world. *Economist* Siporex is a . . concrete product . . now used all over the world. *Sunday Times* Board a luxury liner to cruise the most colourful waters in the world. **b** I. WATTS Alexander the Great . . wept for want of more worlds to conquer. **c** F. LOCKER I'd give worlds to borrow Her yellow rose with russet leaves. *Autocar* There's not a world of difference between the carb 1.6 fitted to this estate and the injected version. **5b** W. COWPER The sun, a world whence other worlds drink light. *fig.*: K. MANSFIELD The oranges were little worlds of burning light. **6** H. MARTINEAU The taint of contempt which infects all the intercourses of his world. V. BRITTAIN The sceptical, indifferent world of London journalism. M. ESSLIN Ionesco's own peculiar world of nightmare, Chaplinesque humour, and wistful tenderness. **7b** W. COWPER Then, all the world of waters sleeps again. WORDSWORTH Dreams, books, are each a world.
▶ **III** People, society.
8 a The human race; humankind as a whole; human society. OE. ▸**b** Human society considered with ref. to its activities, occupations, problems, etc. Later also, the practices, customs, or social hierarchy of one's society;

the concerns of society at large. LME. ▸c Society at large, the public; public opinion. M16.

9 Usu. with specifying word: a particular part or section of the earth's inhabitants or of (a) human society, esp. with ref. to the place or time of their existence, or to their status, interests, or pursuits. LME. ▸b *The* people with exclusively secular, mundane, or worldly interests and pursuits; *the* worldly and irreligious. Cf. sense 2a above. LME. ▸c Fashionable society or circles. L17.

> 8a TENNYSON These two parties still divide the world—Of those that want, and those that have. **b** SHAKES. *Merry W.* Old folks, you know, have discretion . . and know the world. W. COWPER Low in the world, because he scorns its arts. **c** *Bookman* From the world's point of view, his unpopularity was richly deserved. **9** G. M. TREVELYAN To prevent the domination . . of the European world by France. ***business world, fashion world, pop world***, etc.

Phrases: **against the world** in opposition to or in the face of everyone; against all opposition. ***all the time in the world***: see TIME *noun*. **all the world and his wife** (*a*) any large mixed gathering of people; (*b*) everyone with pretensions to fashion. **all the world over** = ***the world over*** below. ***before the secular worlds***: see SECULAR *adjective* 5. ***begin the world***. ***brave new world***: see BRAVE *adjective*. ***bring into the world***: see BRING *verb* 5. **carry the world before one** have rapid and complete success. ***citizen of the world***. **come into the world** be born. ***dead to the world***: see DEAD *adjective*. ***dispatch out of the world***: see DISPATCH *verb*. ***done to the world***: see DONE *ppl adjective*. ***eighth wonder of the world***: see WONDER *noun*. ***external world***: see EXTERNAL *adjective*. ***First World***: see FIRST *adjective*. **First World War** the war of 1914–18. **for all the world** taking account of everything in the world; in every respect, exactly, precisely (*like, as if*). ***Fourth World***: see FOURTH *adjective*. ***free world***: see FREE *adjective*. ***go to a better world***: see GO *verb*. †**go to the world** be married. ***how the world wags***: see WAG *verb*. **in the world** (used as an intensifier) on earth, in existence; of all, at all. ***let the world wag (as it will)***: see WAG *verb*. ***looking-glass world***. ***lower world***: see LOWER *adjective*. ***man of the world***: see MAN *noun*. ***middle world***: see MIDDLE *adjective*. ***New World***: see NEW *adjective*. ***next world***. ***not be long for this world***: see LONG *adverb*. ***Old World***: see OLD *adjective*. ***on top of the world***: see TOP *noun*[1]. ***other world***: see OTHER *adjective*. **out of this world** extremely good, delightful, wonderful; beyond description; amazing. ***pride of the world***: see PRIDE *noun*[1]. ***prince of this world***: see PRINCE *noun*. ***renounce the world***: see RENOUNCE *verb* 1b. ***rise in the world***: see RISE *verb*. ***roof of the world***: see ROOF *noun*. ***Second World***: see SECOND *adjective*. **Second World War** the war of 1939–45. **see the world** travel widely; gain wide experience. ***set the world on fire***: see FIRE *noun*. ***seven wonders of the world***: see WONDER *noun*. ***small world***: see SMALL *adjective*. ***tell the world***: see TELL *verb*. **the best of both worlds** get the benefits of two different desirable outcomes, possibilities, etc., without having to choose between them. ***the end of the world***: see END *noun*. ***the outer world***: see OUTER *adjective*. ***the soul of the world***: see SOUL *noun*. **the world over** throughout the world. **the world's end** the farthest limit of the earth, the farthest attainable point of travel. **the world, the flesh, and the Devil** the temptations of earthly life. **the world to come** the afterlife, a supposed life after death. **the worst of both worlds** the least desirable results of two different outcomes, possibilities, etc. **think the world of** have a very high opinion of or regard for. THIRD WORLD. **Third World War** a hypothetical future war involving most of the nations of the world. ***twilight world***: see TWILIGHT *adjective*. ***with the best will in the world***: see WILL *noun*[1]. †**world of words** a dictionary. **worlds apart** vastly different, quite incompatible. **world without end** (*a*) for ever, eternally; (*b*) *rare* eternal existence, endlessness. ***would give the world***: see GIVE *verb*.

Comb.: **world-all** *rare* [translating German *Weltall*] the universe; **World Bank** *colloq.* an international banking organization established to control the distribution of economic aid between member nations (officially called the International Bank for Reconstruction and Development); **world-beater** a person or thing (capable of) surpassing all others of the kind in some respect; **world-class** *adjective* of a quality or standard regarded as high or outstanding throughout the world; **World Cup** SPORT an international tournament open to (qualifying) national teams from all parts of the world, in which the winning team is awarded a cup; *esp.* (SOCCER) the world championship tournament held every four years in a different country; **World English** a variety of, or the fundamental features of, English regarded as standard or acceptable wherever English is spoken; **world fair** = ***world's fair*** below; **world-famous** *adjective* known throughout the world; **world-ground** PHILOSOPHY a (transcendent or immanent) reality or principle underlying or sustaining the cosmos; **World Heritage Site** a natural or man-made site, area, or structure recognized by UNESCO as being of outstanding international importance and therefore as deserving special protection; **world-historical** *adjective* of or pertaining to world history, of global historic importance; **world history** history embracing the events of the whole world, global history; **world language** (*a*) a language universally known by educated people, a language spoken in many countries; (*b*) an artificial language for international use; **world-life** (long *rare*) life in the world, earthly life; **world-line** PHYSICS & PHILOSOPHY (a curve joining) the set of points in space–time successively occupied by a particle etc.; **world literature** (*a*) a body of work drawn from many nations and recognized as literature throughout the world; (*b*) (the sum of) the literature of the world; **world music** traditional local or ethnic music, esp. from the developing world; commercial pop music influenced by or incorporating elements of this; **world-old** *adjective* (that is) as old as the world; **world order** a system of laws or regularities governing events in this or another world; *spec.* an international set of arrangements for preserving global political stability; **world-point** PHYSICS & PHILOSOPHY a point in space–time, a particular point in space at a particular instant of time; **world power** a nation, State, etc., having great power or influence in world affairs; **world-ranking** *adjective* that ranks among the best in the world; **World Series** (US proprietary name for) a series of games contested annually as a playoff between the champions of the two major N. American baseball leagues; **world's fair** (orig. *US*) an international exhibition of arts, science, industry, and agriculture; **world-shaking** *adjective* of supreme importance, of enormous significance; **world-soul** PHILOSOPHY the immanent cause or principle of order, life, etc., in the physical world; **world-spirit** (*a*) the spirit of the secular world; (*b*) = ***world-soul*** above; (*c*) = ***world-ground*** above; **world-view** a set of fundamental beliefs, attitudes, values, etc., determining or constituting a comprehensive outlook on life, the universe, etc.; **world war**: involving several world powers (freq. in ***First World War, Second World War, Third World War*** above); **world-weariness** the condition of being world-weary; **world-weary** *adjective* weary of the world, tired of life; **world-wise** *adjective* (*rare*) = ***worldly-wise*** s.v. WORLDLY *adverb*.

▸ **B** *verb trans.* Populate, inhabit. *rare*. L16.

■ **worlded** *adjective* (*rare, poet.*) containing worlds L19. **worldful** *noun* (*hyperbol.*) as much as would fill a world M19. **worldish** *adjective* (*rare*) worldly; (as 2nd elem. of comb.) of or belonging to a specified world: ME. **worldless** *adjective* E19. **worldlet** *noun* (chiefly SCIENCE FICTION) a little world, a planetoid E20. **worldling** *noun* (*a*) a worldly person; †(*b*) a citizen of the world, an inhabitant of the world: M16.

worldhood /ˈwəːldhʊd/ *noun*. *rare*. M16.
[from WORLD *noun* + -HOOD.]

†**1** Worldly possessions. Only in M16.
2 The quality or condition of being a world. L17.

worldly /ˈwəːldli/ *adjective*. OE.
[from WORLD *noun* + -LY[1].]

1 Of or pertaining to this world or this life; earthly, temporal, mundane. Formerly also, mortal. OE.
2 Of or belonging to the secular (as opp. to religious) realm or world; secular. OE.
3 Engrossed in or devoted to temporal affairs, esp. the pursuit of wealth and pleasure. ME.

> **1** MILTON Thou . . seem'st otherwise inclin'd Then to a worldly Crown. *Sunday Express* All my worldly goods . . in a battered suitcase. **2** L. M. MONTGOMERY She thought puffed sleeves were too worldly for a minister's wife. **3** N. HAWTHORNE Genuine love . . brings back our early simplicity to the worldliest of us.

Special collocations & comb.: **worldly-minded** *adjective* having a worldly mind, intent on the things of this world. **worldly wisdom** knowledge or good sense in worldly affairs, *spec.* prudence as regards one's own interests.

■ **worldlily** *adverb* in a worldly manner E19. **worldliness** *noun* LME.

worldly /ˈwəːldli/ *adverb*. ME.
[from WORLD *noun* after prec.: see -LY[2].]

In a worldly manner; with a worldly intent or disposition.

Comb.: **worldly-wise** *adjective* having worldly wisdom.

worldward /ˈwəːldwəd/ *noun, adverb, & adjective*. LME.
[from WORLD *noun* + -WARD.]

▸†**A** *noun*. ***to the worldward***, in regard to the world, in worldly respects. LME–M17.
▸ **B** *adverb*. Towards the world. M17.
▸ **C** *adjective*. Directed towards or facing the world. M19.

worldwide /ˈwəːldwʌɪd, wəːldˈwʌɪd/ *adjective & adverb*. M19.
[from WORLD *noun* + WIDE *adjective, adverb*.]

▸ **A** *adjective*. Extending over, known or occurring in, or affecting, all parts of the world. M19.

World Wide Web a system for accessing and retrieving multimedia information over the Internet, whereby documents stored at numerous locations worldwide are cross-referenced using hypertext links, which allow the user to move from one document to another; the network of information accessible via this system.

▸ **B** *adverb*. Throughout the world. L19.

WORM /wəːm/ *abbreviation*.

COMPUTING. Write once read mostly (or many times), designating optical memory or an optical storage device on to which data may be written once only by laser, and which is thereafter used as ROM.

worm /wəːm/ *noun*.
[Old English *wyrm*, (later) *wurm*, corresp. to Old Frisian *wirm*, Old Saxon, Old & mod. High German *wurm* (Dutch *worm*), Old Norse *ormr* serpent, Gothic *waurms*, from Germanic base rel. to Latin *vermis* worm, Greek *rhomos*, *rhomox* woodworm. Cf. WORSUM.]

▸ **I 1** A serpent, a snake, a dragon. *arch.* OE.
2 An animal that creeps or crawls; a reptile; an insect. *obsolete* exc. in comb., as ***slow-worm, galleyworm, glow-worm***, etc. OE.
3 Any of numerous slender elongated invertebrate animals, usu. with soft moist bodies and inhabiting marine or fresh water, or burrowing in the soil; *esp.* any of the segmented worms or annelids, the roundworms or nematodes, and the flatworms; *spec.* an earthworm. OE. ▸**b** Any of these animals which are internal parasites of humans and animals. Also, the disease or disorder constituted by the presence of these. Usu. in *pl.* OE.
4 Any insect larva with an elongated body; a maggot, a grub, a caterpillar, *esp.* one that feeds on and destroys flesh, fruit, leaves, timber, textiles, stored products, etc. Also ***the worm***, infestation with such larvae. OE. ▸**b** A silkworm. OE.
5 A maggot or earthworm as a consumer of dead bodies in the grave. Freq. *fig.* OE.
†**6** A parasitic tick or mite which infests the skin and causes itching. Cf. RINGWORM. OE–E17.
7 Any of various long slender marine crustaceans and molluscs which destroy submerged timber by boring; *esp.* the shipworm. Also ***the worm***, infestation with these. E17.

> **3** ***eelworm, lug worm, palolo worm, rag worm, tube worm***, etc. **b** ***Guinea worm, hair-worm, round worm, tapeworm, thread worm***, etc. **4** ***bookworm, hornworm, measuring worm, nose-worm, slug-worm, wireworm***, etc.

▸ **II** *fig.* **8** A human being likened to a worm or reptile, esp. as an object of contempt, scorn, or pity; an insignificant person; an abject miserable creature. OE. ▸**b** A policeman. *slang*. M19.
9 a A grief or passion that torments the heart or conscience, *esp.* remorse. OE. ▸†**b** A perverse fancy, a whim; a streak of insanity. L15–E18.
10 ***the worm***, (a popular name for) any of various ailments supposed to be caused by a worm or worms; *spec.* †(*a*) colic; (*b*) toothache. *Scot.* L15.

▸ **III 11** The lytta in a dog's tongue, formerly cut out as a supposed safeguard against rabies. Now *rare* or *obsolete*. M16.
12 *techn.* Any of various implements of spiral form, as (*a*) a screw fixed on the end of a rod, for withdrawing the charge or wad from a muzzle-loading gun; (*b*) *local* (the screw of) an auger or gimlet; (*c*) the spiral tube or pipe of a still, in which the vapour is cooled and condensed; (*d*) the spiral part of a screw; (*e*) a short screw working in a worm-gear. M16.
13 a An (artificial or natural) object resembling an earthworm. E18. ▸**b** In *pl.* (The coiled pods of) a leguminous plant of southern Europe, *Astragalus hamosus*, sometimes grown as a curiosity. M19.

Phrases: **a worm will turn** = ***even a worm will turn*** below. ***be food for worms***. **can of worms** a complex and largely uninvestigated matter (esp. one likely to prove problematic or scandalous). **even a worm will turn** even the meekest person will resist or retaliate if pushed too far. **worm's-eye view** a view as seen from below or from a humble position.

Comb.: **worm-burrow** the hole made by a worm in soil, mud, or sand; a fossil perforation of this sort; **worm-cast** a convoluted mass of soil, mud, or sand thrown up by a worm on the surface after passing through the worm's body; **worm-conveyor** a conveyor working on the principle of the Archimedean screw; **worm-eel** any of various long slim-bodied eels of the families Moringuidae and Ophichthidae, found in tropical and warm-temperate seas; **worm-fence** *US* = ***snake-fence*** s.v. SNAKE *noun*; **worm-fishing** fishing with worms for bait; **worm-gear** an arrangement consisting of a toothed wheel worked by a revolving spiral; **worm grass** either of two pinkroots, *Spigelia marilandica*, of the southern US, and *S. anthelmia*, of the W. Indies, which are used as anthelmintics; **worm-hole** (*a*) a hole made by a burrowing worm or insect in wood, fruit, books, etc.; (*b*) PHYSICS a hypothetical interconnection between widely separated regions of space–time; **worm-holed** *adjective* perforated with worm-holes; **worm-killer** a preparation for destroying garden worms; **worm-lizard** = AMPHISBAENIAN *noun*; **worm pipefish** a thin wormlike pipefish, *Nerophis lumbriciformis*, found on the rocky coasts of the NE Atlantic; **worm red** (of) a dull brownish-red colour; **wormseed** (the dried heads of) any of various plants considered to have anthelmintic properties, esp. Mexican tea, *Chenopodium ambrosioides* (***Levant wormseed***: see LEVANT *adjective*[2]); **worm-shell** (*a*) (the shell of) a marine gastropod mollusc, esp. of the genus *Vermetus*, which has a shell that becomes loosely and irregularly twisted towards the mouth; (*b*) = ***worm-tube*** below; **worm-snake** any of various small harmless snakes that resemble worms; *esp.* (*a*) a blind snake; (*b*) the colubrid *Carphophis amoena* of N. America; **worm-spring** a spiral spring; **worm-tube** the twisted calcareous tube of some sedentary polychaetes, as *Serpula*.

■ **wormery** *noun* a place or container in which worms are kept M20. **wormish** *adjective* (*rare*) wormlike, *fig.* weak, despicable LME. **wormless** *adjective* (*rare*) M19. **wormlike** *adjective & adverb* (*a*) *adjective* resembling (that of) a worm (*lit.* & *fig.*); (*b*) *adverb* (*rare*) after the manner of a worm: E18.

worm /wəːm/ *verb*. M16.
[from the noun.]

▸ **I 1** *verb trans.* Extract the worm or lytta from the tongue of (a dog) as a supposed safeguard against rabies. *obsolete* exc. *Hist.* M16.
2 *verb trans.* **a** Rid (plants, esp. tobacco) of insect larvae. E17. ▸**b** Treat (a person or an animal) with a preparation designed to expel parasitic worms. M20.

▸ **II 3** *verb intrans.* Hunt or catch worms. L16.
4 *verb trans.* Cause to be eaten by worms; in *pass.*, be damaged or destroyed by worms, become wormeaten. E17.

> **3** RIDER HAGGARD The old thrush goes on worming. **4** J. GALT The Manse had fallen into a sore state of decay—the doors were wormed on the hinges.

▸ **III 5** *verb trans.* **a** Get rid of or expel by persistent or subtle pressure or underhand means (foll. by *out*); (foll. by *out of*) deprive or dispossess of (property etc.) by underhand dealing. Now *rare* or *obsolete*. L16. ▸**b** Extract

(esp. confidential information) by insidious questioning, persistence, or cunning. E18.
†**6** *verb trans.* Pry into the secrets of (a person); spy on. E17–E19.

7 **a** *verb intrans.* Move or progress with a crawling or twisting motion. E17. ▸**b** *verb trans.* Move (*oneself*) or make (one's way) with a crawling or twisting motion. (Foll. by *in*, *into*.) E19. ▸**c** *verb trans.* Cause to move or progress *off*, *down*, *through*, etc., gradually or tortuously. M19.

8 *fig.* **a** *verb intrans.* Foll. by *in*, *into*: make one's way insidiously into a person's confidence, a desirable position, etc., esp. with damaging or destructive effect. E17. ▸**b** *verb trans.* Foll. by *in*, *into*: insinuate (*oneself*) or make (one's way) into a person's favour or confidence, a desirable position, etc., esp. with damaging or destructive effect. E18.

> 🕮 **5b** A. CRAIG He would be so sympathetic, he'd worm all their secrets out of them. R. DAVIES The Notable British Trials series, which he wormed out of the Reserved Shelves in the library. **7b** *Reader's Digest* Worming her way into places no one else could reach. **8a** *Cornhill Magazine* Imposters . . wormed into his confidence. **b** *New Republic* He isn't the only former Soviet official to have wormed his way into the new order.

▸ **IV** *techn.* **9** *verb trans.* Make a screw-thread on. L16.

10 *verb trans.* **a** NAUTICAL. Wind spunyarn or small rope spirally round (a rope or cable) to fill the grooves between the strands and render the surface smooth for parcelling and serving. M17. ▸**b** Wind packing strips between (the cores of a multicore electric cable) so as to give a more nearly circular cross-section; wind (conductors) together to form such a cable. E20.

11 *verb trans.* Remove the charge or wad from (a muzzle-loading gun) by means of a screw fixed on the end of a rod. E19.

■ **worming** *ppl adjective* winding, twisting; *fig.* working or advancing insidiously or tortuously: E17.

†**worm-eat** *verb trans.* Infl. as EAT *verb*; pa. t. usu. **-ate**, pa. pple usu. **-eaten**. L16–M18.
[Back-form. from next.]
Eat into in the manner of a worm.

wormeaten /ˈwəːmiːt(ə)n/ *adjective.* LME.
[from WORM *noun* + *eaten* pa. pple of EAT *verb*. Cf. prec.]
1 Eaten into by a worm or worms. LME.
2 (Of organic tissue) indented with small holes; eroded as by worms. L16.
3 *fig.* Decayed, rotten; decrepit, old and dilapidated; antiquated, outworn. L16.
■ †**worm-eatenness** *noun* E17–M18.

†**worm-eaten** *verb pa. pple*: see WORM-EAT.

worm-eater /ˈwəːmiːtə/ *noun.* E18.
[from WORM *noun* + EATER.]
1 A bird or other creature that feeds on worms; *spec.* (*US*) the worm-eating warbler. E18.
2 A person who drills holes in fake antique furniture to simulate worm-holes. *slang.* L19.

worm-eating /ˈwəːmiːtɪŋ/ *adjective.* E19.
[from WORM *noun* + *eating* pres. pple of EAT *verb*.]
That eats worms.
worm-eating warbler a small New World warbler of the eastern US, *Helmitheros vermivorus*, which has a yellowish head boldly striped with black.

wormed /wəːmd/ *adjective.* L17.
[from WORM *noun*, *verb*: see -ED², -ED¹.]
1 Formed with a screw-thread. Also (as 2nd elem. of comb.), having a specified number of screw-threads. L17.
2 Eaten into or infested with worms. M19.

wormer /ˈwəːmə/ *noun.* E17.
[from WORM *verb* + -ER¹.]
1 A person who tries to find something out or extract secrets from someone. E17.
2 ANGLING. A person who collects worms for, or uses worms as, bait. L19.
3 A screw fixed on the end of a rod, for withdrawing the charge or wad from a muzzle-loading gun. *N. Amer.* L19.
4 A preparation used to rid animals of worm infestations. M20.

wormian /ˈwəːmɪən/ *adjective.* M19.
[from mod. Latin (*ossa*) *Wormiana*, from Olaus *Worm* (1588–1654), Danish physician: see -IAN.]
ANATOMY. Designating small irregular bones frequently found in the sutures of the skull.

wormling /ˈwəːmlɪŋ/ *noun.* L16.
[from WORM *noun* + -LING¹.]
A small worm; *fig.* a poor despicable creature.

wormstall /ˈwəːmstɔːl/ *noun.* Long *obsolete* exc. *dial.* E17.
[App. alt. of †*oumer* UMBER *noun*¹ + STALL *noun*¹.]
An outdoor shelter for cattle in warm weather.

wormwood /ˈwəːmwʊd/ *noun* & *adjective.*
[Old English *wermōd* = Old Saxon *wer(i)moda*, Old High German *wer(i)muota* (German *Wermut*), alt. in late Middle English as if from WORM *noun* + WOOD *noun*¹: cf. VERMOUTH.]
▸ **A** *noun.* **1** A hoary aromatic plant of the composite family, *Artemisia absinthium*, a traditional ingredient of vermouth and absinthe with a proverbially bitter taste, and formerly used as a tonic, anthelmintic, etc. Also, with specifying word, any of various other artemisias or similar plants. OE.
2 *fig.* A type of what causes bitterness and grief; (a source of) bitter mortification or vexation. Freq. in ***gall and wormwood***. M16.
3 Either of two European noctuid moths, *Cucullia absinthii* and *C. artemisiae*, the larvae of which feed on wormwood and mugwort. M19.
1 ***Roman wormwood***, ***sea wormwood***, etc. †**salt of wormwood** impure potassium carbonate obtained from the ashes of wormwood.
▸ **B** *attrib.* or as *adjective.* Made or flavoured with wormwood; *fig.* causing bitterness and grief. L16.
Comb. & *special collocations*: **wormwood-beer**: in which wormwood is infused; †**wormwood lecture** a scolding; **wormwood water**, **wormwood wine** a cordial or liqueur flavoured (like absinth or vermouth) from wormwood.

wormy /ˈwəːmi/ *adjective.* LME.
[from WORM *noun* + -Y¹.]
1 Eaten into by worms or grubs. LME. ▸**b** *fig.* = WORMEATEN 3. *rare.* E17.
2 Wormlike. M16.
3 Infested or affected with worms, itch-mites, etc.; full of worms. L16.
4 Of or pertaining to worms. *poet.* E19.

worn /wɔːn/ *adjective.* LME.
[pa. pple of WEAR *verb*¹.]
1 Impaired or damaged by wear, use, or exposure (also ***worn-down***); *fig.* hackneyed, stale; often heard. LME.
2 Of a person etc.: (looking) wasted, enfeebled, or exhausted, as by toil, age, anxiety, etc. Also ***worn-down***. LME. ▸**b** Of land: no longer fertile. *rare.* L17.
†**3** Of time, a period: past, departed. *rare* (Shakes.). Only in E17.
Comb.: ***worn-down***: see senses 1, 2 above; **worn-out** *adjective* (**a**) that has worn out or been worn out; (**b**) outworn; †(**c**) (*rare*, Shakes.) = sense 3 above.
■ **wornness** /-n-n-/ *noun* L19.

worn *verb* pa. pple of WEAR *verb*¹.

wornil /ˈwɔːnɪl/ *noun.* *obsolete* exc. *dial.* Also †**warnel**. OE.
[Perh. from stem meaning 'pus' + NAIL *noun*.]
= WARBLE *noun*².

worricow /ˈwʌrɪkaʊ/ *noun.* *Scot.* E18.
[from WORRY *verb* + COW *noun*³.]
A scarecrow, a hobgoblin; a person of frightening or repulsive appearance. Formerly also, *the* Devil.

worried /ˈwʌrɪd/ *adjective.* LME.
[from WORRY *verb* + -ED¹.]
†**1** Killed, struck dead. Only in LME.
2 That has been worried; *esp.* harassed; troubled, perturbed, uneasy, or distressed in mind; suggesting or exhibiting worry. M16.

> 🕮 DICKENS 'I don't mean that,' said Mrs. Boffin, with a worried look. *Times* I'm frankly very worried about it. ***worried sick***: see SICK *adjective*.

■ **worriedly** *adverb* in a worried or distressed manner, concernedly E20.

worriment /ˈwʌrɪm(ə)nt/ *noun.* Chiefly *US.* M19.
[from WORRY *verb* + -MENT.]
The action or state of worrying; worry, distress, anxiety. Also, a cause of worry.

worrisome /ˈwʌrɪs(ə)m/ *adjective.* M19.
[from WORRY *noun* or *verb* + -SOME¹.]
Causing or apt to cause worry or distress.
■ **worrisomely** *adverb* L17.

worrit /ˈwʌrɪt/ *verb* & *noun.* *colloq.* L18.
[App. alt. of WORRY *verb*.]
▸ **A** *verb.* **1** *verb trans.* Worry, distress, vex. L18.
2 *verb intrans.* Give way to or experience worry, distress, impatience, etc. M19.
▸ **B** *noun.* A state or cause of worry or mental distress; an anxiety, a fret. M19.

worry /ˈwʌri/ *noun.* LME.
[from the verb.]
1 A dog's action of biting and shaking an animal so as to injure or kill it, *spec.* a hound's worrying of its quarry; an instance of this. LME.
2 A state or feeling of mental unease or anxiety regarding or arising from one's cares or responsibilities, uncertainty about the future, fear of failure, etc.; anxious concern, anxiety. Also, an instance or cause of this. E19.

> 🕮 **2** *Times* His chief worry was that he was unable to be of any further use. E. WELTY Enough . . to retire on free of financial worry. C. DEXTER She would have found it . . difficult to swallow anything that lunchtime, for she was sick with worry.

Comb.: **worry beads** a string of beads manipulated by the fingers to occupy one's hands and calm the nerves; **worry lines** lines or wrinkles on the forehead supposedly formed by a habitual expression of worry.
¶ Rare before E19.

worry /ˈwʌri/ *verb.*
[Old English *wyrgan* = Old Frisian *wergia* kill, Middle Low German, Middle Dutch *worgen*, Old High German *wurgan* (Dutch *wurgen*, German *würgen*), from West Germanic. Cf. WORRIT.]
1 *verb trans.* Strangle. Formerly also, kill, strike dead. Long *obsolete* exc. *Scot.* OE.
2 Long *obsolete* exc. *Scot.* ▸**a** *verb trans.* Choke (a person or animal) *on* or with a mouthful of food; (of food) cause to choke. ME. ▸**b** *verb intrans.* Be choked (*on*), choke *on*. LME.
3 *verb trans.* Devour, gobble *up*. Now *Scot.* & *north.* ME.
4 *verb trans.* Esp. of a dog or wolf: seize by the throat with the teeth and pull about or tear; kill or injure by biting and shaking. Later also *gen.*, bite at or use the teeth on (an object), esp. repeatedly or vigorously. ME. ▸**b** *verb intrans.* Pull or tear *at* (an object) with the teeth. L19.
5 *verb trans.* Harass, harry, attack repeatedly or persistently; handle roughly; get or bring into a specified state, place, etc., by harassment or persistent effort. M16.
6 *verb trans.* Irritate or distress by inconsiderate or demanding behaviour; pester. L17.
7 *verb intrans.* W. adverb (phr.): advance or progress by persistent effort; force or make one's way. L17.
8 *verb trans.* Cause mental distress or agitation to (a person, oneself); make anxious and ill at ease; *refl.* (usu. in neg. contexts) take needless trouble. E19.
9 *verb intrans.* Give way to anxiety, unease, or disquietude; allow one's mind to dwell on difficulties or troubles. M19.

> 🕮 **4** T. MEDWIN A dog who once takes to worry sheep never leaves off the habit. *transf.*: DRYDEN He grew familiar with her hand, Squeez'd it, and worry'd it with ravenous kisses. **b** G. MCINNES A huge airedale was worrying at my leg. **5** E. A. FREEMAN Edward the Third was worried into war by the aggression of Philip. ANTHONY HOPE If he got hold of a problem, he would worry it to a solution. **worry out** obtain (the solution of a problem etc.) by dogged effort. **6** DICKENS You worry me to death with your chattering. J. B. PRIESTLEY They won't really do anything but worry you with questions. **7** W. IRVING He worried from top to bottom of the castle with an air of infinite anxiety. R. KIPLING When the wind worries through the 'ills. **worry along**, **worry through** manage to advance by persistence in spite of obstacles, persevere, keep going. **8** DICKENS I quite fret and worry myself about her. A. TROLLOPE Men when they are worried by fears . . become suspicious. E. BOWEN He did not allow his handicap to worry him. ***worry oneself sick***: see SICK *adjective*. **9** *Time* Leave everything to me and don't worry. B. SPOCK They worry about the baby's crying . . suspecting that something is seriously wrong. **I should worry** *Austral. colloq.* it doesn't worry me at all. ***not to worry***: see NOT *adverb*.

Comb.: **worry-guts**, **worry-wart** *colloq.* an inveterate worrier, a person who habitually worries unduly.
■ **worrier** *noun* (**a**) an animal that kills or injures others by biting and rough treatment; (**b**) a habitually anxious person, a person inclined to worry: M16. **worryingly** *adverb* in a worrying manner; to a worrying degree: M19.

worse /wəːs/ *adjective*, *noun*, & *adverb.*
[Old English *wiersa*, *wyrsa* = Old Frisian *werra*, *wirra*, Old Saxon *wirsa*, Old High German *wirsiro*, Old Norse *verri*, Gothic *wairsiza*, from Germanic base repr. also by WAR *noun*¹: cf. WAR *adjective*, *adverb*, & *noun*². As adverb from Old English *wiers* = Old Saxon, Old High German *wirs*, Old Norse *verr*, Gothic *wairs*, from Germanic: cf. BETTER *adjective*, *noun*², & *adverb*. See also WUSS *adjective* & *noun*.]
▸ **A** *adjective.* Compar. of the adjectives ***bad***, ***evil***, ***ill***. (In pred. & ellipt. uses merging with the adverb.)
1 More reprehensible, wicked, or cruel. OE.
2 Less advantageous or desirable, as (**a**) more harmful, painful, damaging, or unpleasant; (**b**) more unfavourable or unlucky. OE. ▸**b** Less appropriate or suitable; more faulty or ill-conceived. M17. ▸**c** Less effective, competent, or skilful; that does a task etc. less well. E18.
3 Of lower quality or value; less good, inferior. OE.
4 *pred.* Less fortunate, less well off; in poorer health or condition. Freq. with *the*. OE.

> 🕮 **1** B. HINES I'm not that bad, I'm no worse than stacks o' kids. **2** I. MURDOCH I will . . recover, I have had worse blows than this. *Sunday Times* Everything's getting worse and not better. **b** R. BOYLE The argument was bad, the plot worse, the contempt of authority worst of all. **3** ADAM SMITH The commodity of the distant country is of a worse quality than that of the near one. **4** W. BEVERIDGE Thou art never the worse, for others being better. R. H. BARHAM Nobody seem'd one penny the worse! G. GORDON Hospitals were to make people better, not worse.

▸ **B** *absol.* as *noun.* **1** A thing that is worse; that which is less good; (with *the*) a worse condition. OE.
2 A person inferior in virtue, goodness, attainments, etc.; *the* worse people. ME.

> 🕮 **1** SPENSER For feare of worse, that may betide. SIR W. SCOTT With fair warning not to come back on such an errand, lest worse come of it. J. AGATE A . . teacher suspected of flirting, and worse, with his pupils.

▸ **C** *adverb.* Compar. of the adverbs ***badly***, ***ill***, ***evil***, ***evilly***. (In pred. & ellipt. uses merging with the adjective.)

1 In a worse manner; more wickedly, harshly, carelessly, unfortunately, etc.; to a lesser or lower degree. OE.

2 With intensive force after verbs of hurting, fearing, etc.: more intensely; to a greater degree. L16.

> **1** SHAKES. *Ven. & Ad.* Your treatise makes me like you worse and worse. MILTON With ruin upon ruin, rout on rout, Confusion worse confounded. WORDSWORTH Some thought far worse of him, and judged him wrong. **2** SHAKES. *Coriol.* I do hate thee Worse than a promise-breaker. SHELLEY That stern yet piteous look, those solemn tones, Wound worse than torture.

Phrases & special collocations: ***a fate worse than*** DEATH. **be worse than one's word** fail to fulfil what one has promised. ***for better, for worse, for better or for worse***: see BETTER *adjective, noun*[2], & *adverb*. **for the worse** in such a way as to deteriorate; into a worse condition, state, etc. **from bad to worse** to or into an even worse state, decline, etc. ***go by the worse***: see GO *verb*. **have the worse (of)** be worsted or defeated in a contest. **none the worse (for)** not adversely affected (by). **one's worse half** *joc.* one's spouse, *esp.* one's husband. **or worse** or as an even worse alternative. †**put to the worse** defeat or worst in a contest etc. **the worse for drink** (rather) intoxicated, (fairly) drunk. ***the worse for wear***: see WEAR *noun*. ***worse luck***: see LUCK *noun*. **worse off** in a worse position as regards money or other personal circumstances. ***worse than*** DEATH.

■ **worseness** *noun* LME.

worse /wəːs/ *verb*. Long *non-standard*.
[Old English *wyrsian*, from *wyrsa*: see prec.]
†**1** *verb intrans.* = WORSEN 2. OE–M19.
2 *verb trans. & refl.* = WORSEN 1, 3. ME.

> **2** A. TROLLOPE Them as goes away to better themselves, often worses themselves.

worsement /ˈwəːsm(ə)nt/ *noun*. L19.
[from prec. + -MENT, after *betterment*. Cf. WORSENMENT.]
Chiefly LAW. Deterioration and depreciation of real property caused by the action of people outside without the owner's consent.

worsen /ˈwəːs(ə)n/ *verb*. ME.
[from WORSE *adjective* + -EN[5].]
1 *verb trans.* Make worse; impair, cause to deteriorate. ME. ▸**b** *spec.* Depreciate, disparage. L19.
2 *verb intrans.* Become worse, deteriorate. L18.
3 *verb refl.* Make oneself worse or (*dial.*) worse off. E19.

> **1** D. MADDEN This weariness is not eased by lying down but worsened. **2** N. BAWDEN The situation had worsened. P. BAILEY My condition worsened. Death now seemed inevitable.

■ **worsenment** *noun* deterioration, *esp.* worsement L19.

worser /ˈwəːsə/ *adjective, adverb, & noun*. Now *arch.* & *non-standard*. L15.
[from WORSE *adjective, noun, & adverb* + -ER[3] (a double compar.): cf. LESSER.]
▸**A** *adjective*. = WORSE *adjective*. Chiefly, & now only, *attrib.* L15.
▸**B** *adverb*. = WORSE *adverb*. M16.
▸**C** *absol.* as *noun*. = WORSE *noun*. L16.

worser /ˈwəːsə/ *verb trans. rare*. Chiefly *dial.* & *non-standard*. M19.
[from WORSER *adjective* after BETTER *verb*.]
Make worse.

worserer /ˈwəːs(ə)rə/ *adjective. rare. dial. & joc.* M18.
[from WORSER *adjective*, with joc. redupl. of -ER[3].]
= WORSE *adjective*.

worserment /ˈwəːsəm(ə)nt/ *noun. rare.* L19.
[from WORSER *adjective* or *verb* + -MENT, after *betterment*.]
= WORSEMENT.

worsest /ˈwəːsɪst/ *adjective. joc., dial., & non-standard.* M19.
[from WORSE *adjective* + -EST[1], or joc. refash. of WORST *adjective*.]
= WORST *adjective*.

worship /ˈwəːʃɪp/ *noun*.
[Old English *weorþscipe*, from *weorþ* WORTH *adjective* + *-scipe* -SHIP.]
▸**I** Worth, dignity.
1 The condition of being held in or of deserving esteem, honour, or repute; renown, good reputation; worthiness, merit, credit. Long *arch.* OE. ▸†**b** A source or ground of honour or esteem. ME–L16.
2 The possession of high rank or position; prominence, importance, high standing. *arch.* OE. ▸†**b** A distinction, a dignity; a position of honour. ME–E17.
3 (Also **W-**.) With possess. adjective (as ***your worship*** etc.): an honorific title for an important or high-ranking person, esp. a magistrate or mayor. M16.

> **1** TENNYSON It will be to your worship, as my knight . . To see that she be buried worshipfully. **2** SIR W. SCOTT Worship and birth to me are known By look, by bearing, and by tone. **b** SHAKES. *Lear* Men . . That . . in the most exact regard support The worships of their name. **3** DICKENS A pick-pocketing case, your worship.

▸**II** Acknowledgement of worth, homage.
4 Respectful recognition or honour shown to a person or thing. *arch.* OE.
5 Religious reverence, adoration, or homage paid to a being or power regarded or treated as supernatural or divine; the expression of this in acts, ritual, ceremony, or prayer, esp. of a public or formal nature. Now also *transf.*, veneration or devotion similar to religious homage shown to a person or principle. ME.
6 A particular form or type, or (formerly) an instance, of religious homage. Usu. in *pl.* E17.

> **5** J. B. MOZLEY Mystical thought quickens worship. D. POWELL Her . . face glowed with worship when she looked at Rosenbaum. *Christianity Today* These people, when they gather for worship, pray, preach, and sing in a particular way. *Independent* The Hindu religion . . left its mark, particularly in the worship of the . . divine phallus. *Times Educ. Suppl.* The deeply-ingrained worship of tidy-looking dichotomies. ***devil-worship, fire worship, hero worship, image worship, moon worship***, etc. ***place of worship***: see PLACE *noun*[1]. **6** T. MITCHELL A faith, which . . stood far . . above the baser worships.

■ **worshipless** *adjective* †(*a*) *rare* not worshipping; (*b*) not worshipped; lacking worship: M18.

worship /ˈwəːʃɪp/ *verb*. Infl. **-pp-**, ***-p-**. ME.
[from prec.]
▸**I** *verb trans.* **1** Honour or adore as divine or sacred, esp. with religious rites or ceremonies; offer prayer or prayers to (a god). ME. ▸**b** *transf.* Regard with extreme respect, devotion, or love; idolize. E18.
†**2** Regard or treat (a person) with honour or respect; *spec.* salute, bow down to. ME–M18.
†**3** Invest with honour or repute; confer honour or dignity on. ME–E17.

> **1** J. L. ESPOSITO God reminds his people that He . . is to be worshipped. **b** A. BRONTË He worships the very ground I tread on. D. M. FRAME He likes learned men but . . does not worship them. J. HALPERIN James . . was respected by Hardy, and worshipped by Conrad.

▸**II** *verb intrans.* **4** Engage in worship; attend a religious service. Now also, feel or be full of adoration. E18.

> **4** *Atlantic* No longer do we join . . a church because it was where our family worshipped.

■ **worshipper** *noun* LME. **worshippingly** *adverb* in a worshipping manner, adoringly LME.

worshipable /ˈwəːʃɪpəb(ə)l/ *adjective*. Also **-pp-**. LME.
[from prec. + -ABLE.]
†**1** Entitled to honour or respect; honourable. Only in LME.
2 Able to be worshipped. M19.

worshipful /ˈwəːʃɪpfʊl, -f(ə)l/ *adjective & noun*. ME.
[from WORSHIP *noun* + -FUL.]
▸**A** *adjective*. **1** Distinguished or outstanding in respect of character, rank, or a (good) quality; reputable, honourable; entitled to honour or respect. *arch.* ME.
2 (Usu. **W-**.) Designating honorifically a person or body of importance or distinguished rank, as a mayor, justice of the peace, livery company, (the master of) a masonic lodge. Formerly also in gen. use in respectful forms of address. LME.
†**3** Showing or bringing honour or distinction *to* a person; honourable. LME–L15.
4 Full of worship, adoring. E19.
5 Deserving to be worshipped. L19.

> **1** CARLYLE If not the noblest and worshipfulest of all Englishmen, at least the strongest and terriblest. E. A. FREEMAN His look was worshipful and kingly. **4** T. HARDY Her large, worshipful eyes . . looking at him from their depths.

▸**B** *noun*. An honourable, reputable, or distinguished person; *spec.* a magistrate. Long *arch.* (*joc.*). LME.

■ **worshipfully** *adverb* †(*a*) with due honour; †(*b*) in such a way as to express or confer honour; †(*c*) so as to obtain or deserve honour or praise; (*d*) in a spirit of worship, adoringly: ME. **worshipfulness** *noun* LME.

worsification /ˌwəːsɪfɪˈkeɪʃ(ə)n/ *noun. rare. joc.* M19.
[Alt. of VERSIFICATION, as if from WORSE *adjective* + -FICATION.]
The composition of bad verses; poor versification.

worst /wəːst/ *adjective, adverb, & noun*.
[Old English *wierresta*, *wyrresta* = Old Frisian *wersta*, Old Saxon *wirsista*, Old High German *wirsisto*, Old Norse *verstr*, from Germanic: see WORSE *adjective*, -EST[1].]
▸**A** *adjective*. Superl. of the adjectives ***bad, evil, ill***.
1 Most reprehensible, wicked, or cruel. OE.
2 Least advantageous or desirable, as (*a*) most harmful, painful, damaging, or unpleasant; (*b*) most unfavourable or unlucky. OE. ▸**b** Hardest, most difficult to deal with. LME.
3 Least good; of the lowest quality, value, or importance; most lacking in the required or expected good qualities. ME.
†**4** *pred.* Most unfortunate or badly off. *rare* (Shakes.). Only in E17.

> **1** LYTTON The worst passions are softened by triumph. *Cornhill Magazine* Editors . . often quoted what was worst and most Prussian in Carlyle. W. J. BURLEY Nicky is a born worrier . . he's his own worst enemy. **2** DEFOE We thought they ought to be . . put to the worst of Deaths. G. GREENE Wormold's worst fears about the new model had been justified. **3** HENRY FIELDING To charge the same for the very worst provisions, as if they were the best. LYTTON That class . . , with the best intentions, have made the worst citizens.

▸**B** *adverb*. **1** In the worst manner; to the worst degree; least well or usefully. (With (ppl) adjectives & in comb. freq. with hyphen.) OE.
2 With a verb of liking, allowing, pleasing, etc.: least well, least. *arch.* OE.

> **1** R. BURNS A miller us'd him worst of all, For he crush'd him between two stones. J. S. LE FANU We are the worst-governed and the worst-managed people on earth. **2** SHAKES. *Per.* Of all the faults beneath the heavens the gods Do like this worst.

▸**C** *absol.* as *noun*. **1** *The* person or (usu.) persons most objectionable or least estimable in character, behaviour, etc. ME.
2 *The* worst or most objectionable thing, circumstance, event, behaviour, etc. LME. ▸**b** *spec.* *The* worst aspect or part *of* a thing, a person's character, etc. E17.
3 ***the worst, one's worst***, the utmost evil or harm possible. LME.
4 (Usu. with *the*.) Defeat in a contest. LME.
5 *The* harshest view or judgement (*of* a person or thing). LME.

> **1** YEATS The best lack all conviction, while the worst Are full of passionate intensity. **2** H. MACMILLAN I went through all the emergency plans so as to be prepared for the worst. **b** L. P. HARTLEY That's the worst of being a novelist—we never answer letters. **3** SHAKES. *Hen. V* To our best mercy give yourselves Or, like to men proud of destruction, Defy us to our worst. W. MORRIS I did the worst to him I loved the most. J. WAIN I decided to have her up here . . and let the gossips do their worst. **4** W. GODWIN In these wars, the Peris generally came off with the worst. **5** J. RUSKIN The worst he can venture to say is, that it is ridiculous.

Phrases, special collocations, & comb.: **at its worst**, **at one's worst** (when) in its or one's worst state or mode. **at the worst**, **at worst** (*a*) even on the least favourable view, estimate, etc.; (*b*) in the worst possible state or case. **do your worst**: expr. defiance (cf. sense C.3 above). **get the worst of it**, **have the worst of it** be defeated. ***go by the worst***: see GO *verb*. ***have the worst of it***: see ***get the worst of it*** above. **if it comes to the worst**, **if the worst comes to the worst** if things turn out as badly as possible or conceivable. **make the worst of** regard or represent in the most unfavourable light. **the worst kind** *US colloq.* most thoroughly or severely. **worst-case** *adjective* designating or pertaining to the worst of the possible foreseeable outcomes, scenarios, etc. **worst-seller** (the author of) a book having a very small sale. ***the worst of both worlds***: see WORLD *noun*.

worst /wəːst/ *verb*. E17.
[from the adjective.]
†**1** *verb trans.* Make worse, damage, inflict loss on. E17–L18. ▸**b** *verb intrans.* Grow worse, deteriorate. *rare.* L18–E19.
2 *verb trans.* Defeat, overcome, get the better of (an adversary etc.); outdo, prove better than. Freq. in *pass.* M17.

> **2** J. F. RUSLING Blücher now took pleasure in getting even with Napoleon for worsting him at Ligny. P. GOODMAN Carlos has stolen twenty-six cars, Pedro twenty-three, and each is driven by necessity not to be worsted. B. UNSWORTH You can't bear to be worsted in argument.

worsted /ˈwʊstɪd/ *noun & adjective*. ME.
[from *Worste(a)d* a parish in Norfolk, England.]
▸**A** *noun*. **1** A woollen fabric made from closely twisted yarn spun of combed long-staple wool. ME. ▸**b** *ellipt.* A garment, esp. a jacket or suit, made of this. M20.
2 A closely twisted yarn made of long-staple wool in which the fibres lie parallel. Later also, a fine soft woollen yarn used for knitting and embroidery. LME.
▸**B** *attrib.* or as *adjective*. Made of worsted. LME.
worsted work (an) embroidery in worsted yarn on canvas.

†**worsum** *noun*. Also **wursum**. OE–M19.
[Old English *worsm*, *wursm*, app. rel. (by metathesis) to WORM *noun*.]
Purulent matter, pus.

wort /wəːt/ *noun*[1].
[Old English *wyrt* = Old Saxon *wurt*, Old & mod. High German *wurz*, Old Norse *urt*, Gothic *waurts*, from Germanic base rel. to that of ROOT *noun*[1]. Cf. next.]
1 A plant, *esp.* one used as food or medicinally; a potherb. *arch.* exc. as 2nd elem. in plant-names. OE.
†**2** A cabbage or other kind of brassica. ME–M17.
†**3** In *pl.* Broth, pottage. LME–M16.

> **1** T. O. COCKAYNE We find the healing power of worts spoken of as a thing of course. ***butterwort, liverwort, lungwort, marshwort, St John's wort, soapwort, woundwort***, etc.

wort /wɔːt/ *noun*².
[Old English *wyrt* = Old Saxon *wurtja* spicery, Middle & mod. High German *würze* spice, brewer's wort, from base also of prec.]
1 BREWING. A sweet infusion of ground malt or other grain before fermentation, used to produce beer, distilled malt liquors, etc.; unfermented beer. OE.
†**2** An infusion or decoction of malt formerly used to treat ulcers, scurvy, etc. L17–L18.
1 *sweet wort*: see SWEET *adjective & adverb*.

Wörter und Sachen /ˈvœrtər ʊnt ˈzaxən/ *noun & adjectival phr.* M20.
[German, lit. 'words and things'.]
LINGUISTICS. (Designating) a method of research in semantics in which the history and meanings of words are studied through correlation with the things they represent.

worth /wɔːθ/ *noun*¹.
[Old English *w(e)orþ, wurþ* = Old Frisian *werth*, Old Saxon *werþ*, Old High German *werd* (German *Wert*), Old Norse *verð*, Gothic *wairþ*: use as noun of WORTH *adjective*.]
1 Pecuniary value. Formerly also, money, price. OE. ▸**b** The equivalent *of* a specified sum or amount; *spec.* the equivalent *of* a specified sum of money in a commodity. E16.
2 The proper or relative value of a thing in respect of its qualities, reputation, etc. ME. ▸**b** High merit or value, excellence. E17.
3 The (intrinsic or moral) character, dignity, or quality of a person; *spec.* (high) personal merit or attainments. L16.
4 The material position or standing of a person, esp. in respect of property. Also, possessions, property, means. *arch.* L16.

📖 **1** DICKENS Some poverty-stricken legatee . . selling his chance . . for a twelfth part of its worth. ***present worth***: see PRESENT *adjective*. **b** A. TAN Two thousand dollars' worth of TVs and refrigerators. **2** T. DRAXE A man knoweth not the worth of a thing before that he wanteth it. C. GEIKIE The worth of man's homage to God does not depend on the place where it is paid. **b** I. BARROW Nothing of worth . . can be atchieved . . with a faint heart. **3** M. PUZO He was held down . . , his worth was not recognized. J. DUNN She needed a mother's approval, as a reconfirmation of her . . worth. **4** SHAKES. *Rom. & Jul.* They are but beggars that can count their worth.

worth /wɔːθ/ *noun*². *obsolete* exc. *Hist.*
[Old English *worþ* = Old Saxon *wurþ* soil, Middle Low German *wurt, wort* homestead, of unkn. origin.]
An enclosed place, a homestead.
¶ Until L16 recorded chiefly in place-names.

worth /wɔːθ/ *pred. adjective* (now usu. with prepositional force).
[Old English *w(e)orþ, wurþ* = Old Frisian *werth*, Old Saxon *werþ*, Middle Dutch *w(a)ert*, Old High German *werd* (Dutch *waard*, German *wert*), Old Norse *verðr*, Gothic *wairþs*, from Germanic.]
1 Of the value of (a usu. specified amount or sum); of the same or as much value as (something specified). Freq. used contemptuously in neg. contexts. OE. ▸**b** W. preceding adverb: able to be estimated valuable as a possession or property. Long *arch.* ME. ▸**c** Of a person: having a certain (usu. specified) value or status in respect of possessions, property, or income; possessed of, owning. LME.
2 a Deserving or worthy of (something). Now *rare* exc. as passing into sense 5 below. OE. ▸†**b** Of sufficient merit, deserving, *to be* or *do* something. OE–LME.
†**3** Esp. of a person: important; respectable; worthy. OE–M16.
4 Valuable, worthwhile (*rare*); (long *obsolete* exc. *Scot.*) of use or service. ME.
5 Sufficiently important or valuable to be an equivalent or good return for (something); such as to justify or repay; bringing compensation for. LME.

📖 **1** WORDSWORTH Tell me what this land is worth by the acre. K. AMIS Originals, I shouldn't be surprised. Must be worth quite a packet. ***not worth a fig, not worth a halfpenny, not worth a hill of beans, not worth a tinker's curse, not worth two pins***, etc. **2a** T. MUDGE It flatters me . . that you should think any thing of mine . . worth your trouble. **5** W. KING The crown of France was well worth the trouble of hearing one mass. R. BROOKE A blasphemy scarce worth me saying, A sorry jest. *Forbes* An engaging . . spy thriller well worth anyone's time. *Investors Chronicle* The extra return . . is ultimately not worth the risk.

Phrases: ***a trick worth two of that***: see TRICK *noun*. ***for all it is worth, for all one is worth*** *colloq.* to the fullest extent; without reserve, with the utmost effort. ***for what it is worth***: expr. (usu. parenthetically) a refusal or disinclination to guarantee or vouch for the truth or value of a statement etc. ***not worth an hour's purchase, not worth a day's purchase***: see PURCHASE *noun*. ***not worth the candle***: see CANDLE *noun*. ***nought worth***: see NOUGHT *pronoun & noun* 1. ***worth one's weight in gold, worth one's weight in silver, worth its weight in gold, worth its weight in silver***: see WEIGHT *noun*. ***worth it*** *colloq.* worth the time, effort, etc., spent. ***worth's one's salt***: see SALT *noun*¹. ***worth one's while, worth the while***: see WHILE *noun* 5.

worth /wɔːθ/ *verb. obsolete* exc. in phr.
[Old English *weorþan, wurþan* = Old Frisian *wertha*, Old Saxon *werþan*, Old High German *werdan* (Dutch *worden*, German *werden*), Old Norse *verða*, Gothic *wairþan*, from Germanic from Indo-European base also of Latin *vertere* (earlier *vortere*) turn, Sanskrit *vartate* turns, proceeds, takes place.]
1 †**a** *verb intrans.* Come to pass, happen, take place. OE–LME. ▸**b** *verb intrans.* (with dat.) & *trans.* Used in subjunct. to expr. a wish: happen to, be upon, befall (a person etc.). Long *obsolete* exc. in ***woe worth the day, woe worth the time***, etc., s.v. WOE *interjection* 2. ME.
†**2** *verb intrans.* **a** Become, come to be; turn or be changed *to*. OE–E16. ▸**b** Get *on* or *upon* a horse etc.; mount *up*. ME–L15. ▸**c** Foll. by *of*: happen to, become of. LME–E19.

worthful /ˈwɔːθfʊl, -f(ə)l/ *adjective*. Now *arch. & formal*.
[Old English *weorþful, wurþful*, from WORTH *noun*¹ + -FUL. App. re-formed in 16–17 (partly after WORTHLESS) and in 19 (perh. after German *wertvoll*).]
1 Of a person: honourable; deserving of honour, respect, or reverence; having worth or merit. OE.
2 Having worth or value; valuable. ME.
▪ **worthfulness** *noun* (*rare*) ME.

worthily /ˈwɔːðɪli/ *adverb*. ME.
[from WORTHY *adjective* + -LY².]
1 In a worthy manner; *spec.* (***a***) according to desert or merit; (***b***) deservedly, justly, rightly. ME. ▸†**b** *spec.* With due dignity, pomp, or splendour. ME–E16.
2 With due reverence, devoutly; in a fitting spirit, appropriately, properly. ME.
3 In a manner befitting a person of high standing or character; in accordance with one's dignity or personal worth; honourably, nobly. LME.

📖 **1** T. STANLEY Ingratitude is worthily hateful to all men. R. G. PRESTON That which cannot be taken away is worthily esteemed the most excellent. **3** SHAKES. *Ant. & Cl.* Worthily spoken, Maecenas. G. CHALMERS He worthily fell, in fighting for his people.

†**worthing** *noun*. ME–L19.
[App. from WORTH *adjective* + -ING¹. Cf. GOODING.]
Dung; manure.

worthless /ˈwɔːθlɪs/ *adjective*. L16.
[from WORTH *noun*¹ + -LESS.]
1 (Of a thing) having no worth or intrinsic value; (of a person) lacking merit or moral character, contemptible, despicable. L16.
†**2** Unworthy *of* something. L16–M17.

📖 **2** SHAKES. *Jul. Caes.* A peevish schoolboy, worthless of such honour.

▪ **worthlessly** *adverb* M19. **worthlessness** *noun* E17.

worthwhile /wɔːθˈwʌɪl, *attrib. also* ˈwɔːθ-/ *adjective*. Also **worth-while** & (earlier, usu. *pred.*) as two words. M17.
[from ***worth the while*** s.v. WHILE *noun*.]
That is worth the time or effort spent; of (sufficient) value or importance.

📖 *Good Housekeeping* For some people a collection is only worthwhile if the pieces are rare. *Veterinary Record* The campaign against the disease is achieving worthwhile results.

▪ **worthwhileness** *noun* L19.

worthy /ˈwɔːði/ *adjective, adverb, & noun*. ME.
[from WORTH *noun*¹ + -Y¹.]
▶ **A** *adjective*. **1** Of a thing: having worth, value, or importance; good; excellent. Long *arch.* ME. ▸†**b** Having a specified value or worth. ME–E19.
2 (Of a person) distinguished by good qualities, deserving honour or respect, estimable; (of an action, project, etc.) meritorious, morally upright. Now freq. *iron.*, estimable yet somewhat unimaginative, ineffectual, or sanctimonious. ME. ▸†**b** Of a person: socially prominent; of (high) rank or standing. LME–L15. ▸†**c** Of a thing: honourable; held in honour or esteem. LME–E18. ▸**d** Of mind, character, etc.: having a high moral standard. L16.
3 a Deserving (*of*) or meriting (something). ME. ▸**b** Of sufficient value; sufficiently good; suitable. ME. ▸**c** Appropriate, becoming, of such a kind as to be expected; *esp.* good enough for (a person). Now usu. foll. by *of*. ME. ▸†**d** *spec.* Of blame, a punishment, etc.: sufficiently heavy or severe; deserved. M16–E17.

📖 **1** J. PLAYFORD All the . . Graces . . in this most worthy manner of singing. **2a** LYTTON Alred, Bishop of Winchester, the worthiest prelate in . . the land. W. SHEED Real writers, not just worthy people with something to say. *Oxford Today* All this . . fund-raising for new posts . . . Worthy enough in its way, but quite wrong-headed. *Times* Worthy committees deciding what consumers want hardly ever get it right. **3a** R. GRAVES He would try to be worthy of Augustus's loving generosity. *Christian* Qualities which will colour . . all Christian education . . worthy the name. J. WAINWRIGHT A simple fact not worthy of either mention or discussion. **b** BYRON Thou Shalt one day, if found worthy, . . See thy God. F. R. WILSON It was improved by the insertion of worthy windows. *Manchester Evening News* Bent on proving that he is a worthy successor to Mr. Russell Lowell. **c** POPE The host to succour, and thy friends to save Is worthy thee. J. BRYCE Pontiffs whose fearlessness and justice were worthy of their exalted office. *New York Review of Books* A mud-slinging logic . . worthy of a gutter moralist. **d** SHAKES. *All's Well* He has much worthy blame laid upon him.

▶ **B** *adverb*. Worthily; in a manner worthy *of* (something). Now *non-standard*. LME.
▶ **C** *noun*. **1** A worthy, distinguished, eminent, or famous person. LME. ▸**b** A person, *esp.* one who has a marked personality or is well known in a particular area. *joc.* M18.
†**2** A thing of worth or value. *rare* (Shakes.). Only in L16.

📖 **1** *Times* The boards are full of local businessmen, worthies and professionals. **the nine worthies** nine famous personages of ancient Jewish and classical and medieval Christian history and legend (Joshua, David, and Judas Maccabaeus; Hector, Alexander, and Julius Caesar; and King Arthur, Charlemagne, and Godfrey of Bouillon).

▪ **worthiness** *noun* (***a***) the state, character, or quality of being worthy; an instance of this; †(***b***) (with possess. adjective, as *your* etc.) an honorific title for a dignitary, patron, etc.: ME.

†**worthy** *verb trans.* ME–E17.
[from the adjective.]
Render or hold worthy (*of* something); raise to honour or distinction.

-worthy /ˈwɔːði/ *suffix*.
[from WORTHY *adjective*.]
Forming adjectives from nouns, with the senses 'deserving of', 'suitable or fit for', as ***blameworthy, newsworthy, roadworthy, trustworthy***.

wortle /ˈwɔːt(ə)l/ *noun*. LME.
[Origin unkn.]
A small steel plate containing tapered holes, used in the drawing of wire.
Comb.: **wortle plate** (***a***) = WORTLE; (***b***) a high carbon steel used to make wortles.

wot *pronoun, noun, adverb, interjection, conjunction, & adjective* see WHAT.

wot /wɒt/ *verb*¹ *trans. & intrans. arch.* Infl. **-tt-**. ME.
[Extension of the present stem *wot* of WIT *verb* to other parts of the verb.]
Know.
▪ †**wottingly** *adverb* (*rare*) wittingly, knowingly M16–M19.

wot *verb*² *pres. t.*: see WIT *verb*.

wotcher /ˈwɒtʃə/ *interjection. slang.* Also **watcha**, **watcher**. L19.
[Corrupt. from ***what cheer?*** s.v. CHEER *noun*¹.]
Expr. casual greeting.

†**wote** *verb pres. t.*: see WIT *verb*.

woubit /ˈwuːbɪt/ *noun. obsolete* exc. *dial.* Also **oubit** /ˈuːbɪt/. LME.
[App. from WOOL *noun* + unexpl. 2nd elem.]
More fully ***hairy woubit***. A hairy caterpillar; *esp.* a woolly bear.

wough /waʊ, wɔː/ *noun*¹. *obsolete* exc. *dial.*
[Old English *wāg, wǣg, wāh* = Old Frisian *wach*, Old Saxon *wēg* rel. to Gothic *waddjus*, Old Norse *veggr*.]
1 A wall of a house; a partition. OE.
2 MINING. The side of a vein. M17.

wough /wɒf/ *noun*². E19.
[Imit.: cf. WOOF *noun*², WUFF *noun*.]
The bark of a dog or other animal.

would /wʊd/ *noun*. LME.
[from *would* pa. t. of WILL *verb*¹.]
An instance of what is expressed by the auxiliary verb ***would***; a (mere) wish, a conditional desire or intention.

would *verb* see WILL *verb*¹.

would-be /ˈwʊdbiː/ *adjective & noun*. ME.
[from *would* pa. t. of WILL *verb*¹ + BE.]
▶ **A** *attrib. adjective*. **1** Of a person: that would (like to) be, potential; wishing to be, aspiring; posing as. Freq. *derog.* ME.
2 Of a thing: intended as or to be. M19.

📖 **1** *Howard Journal* Education . . might well be crucial in providing . . social objectives to the would-be or actual recidivist. R. JAFFE Hollywood was full of would-be starlets.

▶ **B** *noun*. A person aspirng or wishing to be something specified or implied. E17.

woulder /ˈwʊdə/ *noun*. Now *rare* or *obsolete*. E16.
[Irreg. from *would* pa. t. of WILL *verb*¹ + -ER¹.]
A person given to indulging idle wishes instead of making active efforts. Esp. in ***wishers and woulders***.

wouldest *verb* see WILL *verb*¹.

would-have-been /ˈwʊd(h)əvbiːn/ *adjective*. M18.
[from *would* pa. t. of WILL *verb*¹ + HAVE *verb* + *been* pa. pple of BE.]
That would have liked to be, that aimed at being (something specified).

woulding /ˈwʊdɪŋ/ *noun*. Long *rare*. M16.
[from *would* pa. t. of WILL *verb*¹ + -ING¹.]
1 The action or fact of desiring something, esp. idly or ineffectually. M16.
2 In *pl.* Desires, inclinations. M17.

📖 **1** M. HENRY Wishing and woulding is but trifling.

wouldst *verb* see **WILL** *verb*[1].

Woulfe bottle /ˈwʊlf bɒt(ə)l/ *noun.* E19.
[Peter *Woulfe* (c 1727–1803), English chemist.]
CHEMISTRY. A glass bottle with two or more necks, used for passing gases through liquids, and (formerly) in distillation.

wound /wuːnd/ *noun.*
[Old English *wund* = Old Frisian *wund(e)*, Old Saxon *wunda*, Old High German *wunta* (Dutch *wond*, German *Wunde*), Old Norse *und*, of unkn. origin.]
1 An injury to body tissue caused by a cut, blow, hard or sharp impact, etc., *esp.* one in which the skin is cut or broken; an external injury. OE. ▸**b** *transf.* An injury to a plant, caused by pruning, lopping, or mechanical causes, in which the tissue is exposed. L16. ▸**c** MEDICINE. An incision or opening made by a surgeon. M17.
2 *fig.* An injury to a person's reputation; a hurt to a person's feelings, an instance of emotional pain or grief; *poet.* the pangs of love. OE.
3 In *pl.* as *interjection.* Used, esp. in phrs. with possessive combinations, to express asseveration or adjuration, as in ***by Christ's wounds***, ***God's wounds***, etc. Cf. **OONS**, **WOUNDS**, **ZOUNDS**. *arch.* ME.
4 A thing which causes a wound (*lit. & fig.*). *rare.* E18.

📖 **1** V. BRITTAIN A gangrenous leg wound . . with the bone laid bare. JONATHAN MILLER Gaping wounds and flowing blood. J. RATHBONE Scalp wounds always bleed alarmingly. **2** H. BROOKE The wounds of honour never close. R. JACKSON What a wound that was to me, to think he would make so light a gift of God. S. MIDDLETON There's some gap, some wound in him. He's a misfit.

Phrases: ***lick one's wounds***: see **LICK** *verb.* ***rub salt in a person's wound(s)***: see **SALT** *noun*[1]. **the Five Wounds** the wounds in the hands, feet, and side of the crucified Jesus.
Comb.: **wound cork** a protective layer of phellem formed over a damaged part of a plant; **wound hormone** a substance which is produced in a plant in response to a wound and stimulates healing; **wound parasite** a parasitic fungus which invades the host plant only through wounds and exposed tissue; **wound-stripe** (chiefly *Hist.*) a strip of gold braid worn by a wounded soldier on the sleeve; **wound tumour virus** a plant virus of the genus *Phytoreovirus*, transmitted by leafhoppers, which gives rise to tumours on leaf veins, stems, and roots, the effects being increased by artificial wounding; **wound wood** protective wood formed round a wound in a damaged tree by the cambium.

wound /waʊnd/ *ppl adjective.* LME.
[pa. pple of **WIND** *verb*[1].]
That has been wound, subjected to winding. Freq. foll. by adverb.

📖 DICKENS That . . old gentleman is still murmuring like some wound-up instrument running down. M. PIERCY I'm too wound up to study.

wound /wuːnd/ *verb*[1].
[Old English *wundian*, formed as the noun.]
▸ **I** *verb trans.* **1** Of a person, weapon, etc.: inflict a wound or physical injury on (a person, the body, etc.). OE.
2 *fig.* Inflict hurt or pain on; upset, offend, grieve; damage the reputation of. ME. ▸**b** Make an unpleasant impression on, grate on, (the ear). M17.
3 *transf.* Pierce, cut; damage in this way. ME. ▸†**b** Damage (a mast), esp. in a naval action. M–L18.
†**4** Of wine: overpower. *rare.* E17–E19.

📖 **1** E. WAUGH He had been wounded in the foot by Mr Prendergast's bullet. **2** J. AUSTEN She dared not . . speak lest, she might wound Marianne still deeper. C. KINGSLEY You have . . wounded my credit with the King, past recovery.

▸ **II** *verb intrans.* **5** Inflict a wound or wounds (*lit. & fig.*); do harm, hurt, or injury. OE.

📖 **5** THACKERAY We wound where we never intended to strike.

■ **woundable** *adjective* able to be wounded, vulnerable E17. **wounder** *noun* LME.

wound *verb*[2], *verb*[3] *pa. t. & pple*: see **WIND** *verb*[1], *verb*[2].

wounded /ˈwuːndɪd/ *adjective.*
[Old English *gewundod*, pa. pple of **WOUND** *verb*[1].]
That has been wounded (*lit. & fig.*); suffering from or damaged by a wound or wounds.
■ **woundedly** *adverb* †(*a*) *rare* = **WOUNDILY**; (*b*) in the manner of a wounded person; as though wounded: L18. **woundedness** *noun* (*rare*) M17.

woundily /ˈwaʊndɪli/ *adverb. arch.* E18.
[from **WOUNDY** *adjective*[2] + **-LY**[2].]
Excessively, extremely, dreadfully.

wounding /ˈwuːndɪŋ/ *noun.* LME.
[from **WOUND** *verb*[1] + **-ING**[1].]
1 The action of **WOUND** *verb*[1]; an instance of this; the fact of being wounded. LME.
2 A wound or injury to a person. L16.

wounding /ˈwuːndɪŋ/ *adjective.* ME.
[from **WOUND** *verb*[1] + **-ING**[2].]
That wounds or injures; capable of causing hurt or pain.
■ **woundingly** *adverb* LME.

woundless /ˈwuːndlɪs/ *adjective.* L16.
[from **WOUND** *noun* + **-LESS**.]
1 Free from a wound or wounds; unwounded. L16.
†**2** That cannot be wounded; invulnerable. Only in E17.

woundly /ˈwaʊndli/ *adverb. arch.* M17.
[from next + **-LY**[2].]
= **WOUNDILY** *adverb.*

wounds /waʊndz/ *interjection. arch.* E17.
[Ellipt. for *God's wounds*. Cf. **WOUND** *noun* 3.]
= **ZOUNDS**.

woundwort /ˈwuːndwəːt/ *noun.* M16.
[from **WOUND** *noun* + **WORT** *noun*[1].]
Any of various plants which have been used to heal wounds; *esp.* a labiate plant of the genus *Stachys*, the members of which bear whorls of freq. purple, pink, or red flowers in spikelike inflorescences.
Saracen's woundwort: see **SARACEN** *noun.*

woundy /ˈwuːndi/ *adjective*[1]. *rare.* LME.
[from **WOUND** *noun* + **-Y**[1].]
1 Full of wounds; characterized by wounds. LME.
2 Causing wounds. E19.

woundy /ˈwaʊndi/ *adverb & adjective*[2]. *arch.* E17.
[from **WOUNDS** + **-Y**[1]. Cf. **BLOODY** *adjective & adverb.*]
▸ **A** *adverb.* Very; extremely; excessively. E17.
▸ **B** *adjective.* Very great; extreme. M17.

wourali /wʊˈrɑːli/ *noun.* Now *rare.* Also (earliest) **woorara** /wʊˈrɑːrə/, & other vars. M18.
[from a Carib word repr. also by **CURARE**, **URARI**.]
= **CURARE**.

wove /wəʊv/ *adjective & noun.* E18.
[Var. of next.]
▸ **A** *adjective.* **1** = **WOVEN** *adjective.* E18.
2 Of paper: made on a wire-gauze mesh so as to have a uniform unlined surface. E19.
2 wove mould the particular kind of mould used in making wove paper.
▸ **B** *noun.* Paper made on a wire-gauze mesh so as to have a uniform unlined surface. M19.

wove *verb pa. t.* of **WEAVE** *verb*[1].

woven /ˈwəʊv(ə)n/ *adjective.* See also prec. LME.
[pa. pple of **WEAVE** *verb*[1].]
1 That has been woven; formed or made by weaving. LME.
2 Formed by interlacing or intertwining after the manner of weaving. LME.
3 Interlaced, intertwined. E19.

woven *verb pa. pple*: see **WEAVE** *verb*[1].

WOW *abbreviation.*
Waiting on weather.

wow /waʊ/ *noun*[1]. L18.
[Imit.]
1 A bark or similar sound. L18. ▸**b** = **WAUL** *noun.* E19.
2 Fluctuations in pitch in reproduced sound that are sufficiently slow to be heard as such in long notes; a property in a reproducer that gives rise to this, *esp.* uneven speed. Cf. **FLUTTER** *noun* 1d. M20.

wow /waʊ/ *noun*[2] *& adjective. slang* (orig. *US*). E20.
[from the interjection.]
▸ **A** *noun.* A sensational success. E20.

📖 P. G. WODEHOUSE 'A friend . . tipped me off that this company was a wow' 'A what?' 'A winner.'

▸ **B** *adjective.* Exciting or expressing admiration and delight. E20.

wow /waʊ/ *verb*[1] *intrans.* E19.
[Imit.: cf. **WOW** *noun*[1], **WOWSER**.]
= **WAUL** *verb.*

wow /waʊ/ *verb*[2] *trans. slang* (orig. *US*). E20.
[from **WOW** *noun*[2], *interjection.*]
Impress or excite (esp. an audience) greatly; make enthusiastic.

📖 *Sunday Express* Yet another new look . . wowed London last week.

wow /waʊ/ *interjection.* E16.
[Natural exclam. Cf. **VOW** *interjection*, **ZOWIE**.]
Expr. astonishment, admiration, or (*Scot.*) aversion, sorrow, or mere asseveration. Cf. **YOW** *interjection* 3.
■ **wowee**, **-ie** *interjection* expr. astonishment or admiration E20.

wowser /ˈwaʊzə/ *noun. slang* (chiefly *Austral.*). L19.
[Perh. from **WOW** *verb*[1]: see **-ER**[1].]
A puritanical enthusiast or fanatic; a killjoy, a spoilsport; *spec.* a (fanatical) teetotaller.
■ **wowserish** *adjective* of the nature of a wowser, puritanical E20. **wowserism** *noun* the characteristic behaviour or beliefs of a wowser or wowsers, puritanism E20.

wow-wow /ˈwaʊwaʊ/ *noun.* See also **WAH-WAH** *noun*[1]. E19.
[Malay *wauwau*, Javanese *wâwâ*, imit. of the animal's call.]
A gibbon; *esp.* the silvery gibbon or the agile gibbon.

woy /wɔɪ/ *interjection.* L18.
[Natural exclam.]
Commanding a horse to stop.

WP *abbreviation.*
Word processing; word processor.

w.p. *abbreviation.*
Weather permitting.

WPA *abbreviation. US.*
Works Progress Administration.

w.p.b. *abbreviation.*
Waste-paper basket.

WPC *abbreviation.*
Woman Police Constable.

w.p.m. *abbreviation.*
Words per minute.

WRAC *abbreviation.*
Hist. Women's Royal Army Corps.

wrack /rak/ *noun*[1].
[Old English *wræc*, from var. of base of *wrecan* **WREAK** *verb.* See also **WREAK** *noun.*]
1 Vengeance, revenge. Also, hostile action, active enmity, persecution. Now *arch. & poet.* OE.
2 Destruction, havoc; an instance of this. Freq. in ***go to wrack***. Cf. **RACK** *noun*[5] 1. Now *arch. & dial.* LME. ▸**b** The ruin or overthrow of a person; adversity, misfortune. *obsolete* exc. *Scot.* LME.
†**3** A means of destruction or downfall. L16–L17.
4 A vestige or trace left by a destructive agency. Cf. **WRECK** *noun*[1] 6. E17.

📖 **1** SPENSER There gan he . . with bitter wracke To wreake on me the guilt of his owne wrong. **2** M. ARNOLD The wind . . Has made in Himalayan forests wrack. L. HODSON Fences be going to wrack, and drainin' isn't what it should be.

wrack /rak/ *noun*[2]. LME.
[Middle & mod. Dutch *wrak* (= Middle Low German *wrak*, *wracke*, whence German *Wrack*), corresp. to Old English *wræc* **WRACK** *noun*[1]. In sense 3 cf. **VAREC**, **VRAIC**.]
▸ **I 1** A wrecked ship or other vessel. Now chiefly *Scot. & dial.* LME. ▸**b** *transf.* A broken-down person or thing. L16.
2 Remnants of, or goods from, a wrecked vessel, esp. as driven or cast ashore. Formerly also, the right to have these. *arch.* LME.
3 Seaweed and other marine vegetation cast ashore by the waves; any of certain seaweeds, esp. of the genus *Fucus*, growing in the intertidal zone. Also, weeds, rubbish, etc., floating on or washed down a river, pond, etc. Cf. **WRECK** *noun*[1] 2a. E16. ▸**b** Roots of couch grass and other weeds, esp. as loosened from the soil to be collected for burning. Cf. **WRECK** *noun*[1] 2b. Chiefly *Scot.* L16.
4 Disablement or destruction of a vessel; shipwreck. Now *rare.* L16.
3 ***bladderwrack***, ***grass-wrack***, ***sea wrack***, etc.
▸ **II 5** That which is of poor or worthless quality; waste material. Now *rare.* L15.

wrack *noun*[3] see **RACK** *noun*[1].

wrack /rak/ *verb*[1] *trans.* Long *obsolete* exc. *Scot.* ME.
[Irreg. var. of **WREAK** *verb.* Cf. **WRAKE**.]
1 Avenge; punish. ME.
2 Give vent to (spite, malice, etc.). M17.

wrack /rak/ *verb*[2]. Now *arch. & dial.* L15.
[from **WRACK** *noun*[2].]
†**1** *verb intrans.* Suffer shipwreck. L15–M17.
2 *verb trans.* Wreck (a vessel or those on board); cast ashore by shipwreck. Usu. in *pass.* M16.
3 *verb trans.* **a** Cause the downfall of (a person etc.); ruin, overthrow. M16. ▸**b** Injure or spoil severely; destroy. L16.

wrack *verb*[3] var. of **RACK** *verb*[1].

wrackful /ˈrakfʊl, -f(ə)l/ *adjective.* Long *arch.* M16.
[from **WRACK** *noun*[2], *noun*[1] + **-FUL**.]
1 Causing shipwreck. M16.
2 Causing destruction or devastation; destructive. L16.
3 Subject to or attended by injury, harm, etc. L16.

WRAF *abbreviation.*
Women's Royal Air Force.

wrain-bolt *noun* see **WRING-BOLT**.

wraith /reɪθ/ *noun.* Orig. *Scot.* E16.
[Origin unkn.]
1 a An apparition of a dead person; a ghost. E16. ▸**b** A spectral appearance of a living person, freq. regarded as portending that person's death. E16.
2 A spirit or sprite inhabiting pools etc. M18.
3 A person or thing suggestive of a phantom or wraith in paleness or insubstantial quality; *esp.* a wisp of cloud, smoke, etc. E19.

📖 **3** W. C. WILLIAMS A tall wraith of a woman looking as though any wind might blow her away. B. ENGLAND The mist was maddeningly slow to lift . . . Then, quite suddenly the drifting wraiths were gone.

■ **wraithlike** *adjective* resembling a wraith; pale and insubstantial: **M19.**

†**wrake** *verb trans.* **ME.**
[Irreg. var. of **WREAK** *verb.* Cf. Middle Low German *wraken* to torture.]
1 = **WRACK** *verb*¹ 1. Only in **ME.**
2 = **WRACK** *verb*¹ 2. **L16–M18.**

wramp /ramp/ *noun & verb. Scot. & north.* **M17.**
[Origin uncertain: cf. Middle Low German *wrampachtich*, Danish *vrampet* warped, twisted.]
▶ **A** *noun.* A twist, a sprain. Chiefly *fig.* **M17.**
▶ **B** *verb trans.* Twist, sprain, (the ankle etc.). **E19.**

wrang *verb* see **WRING** *verb.*

wrangle /ˈraŋɡ(ə)l/ *noun.* **LME.**
[from the verb.]
A (freq. angry or noisy) dispute, argument, or altercation, *esp.* a convoluted or public one. Also, the action of wrangling.

📖 T. DE W. TALMAGE The Book of Job has been the subject of unbounded theological wrangle. J. REED There was a fearful wrangle over who should be commander-in-chief.

■ **wranglesome** *adjective* (chiefly *dial.*) given to wrangling; quarrelsome: **E19.**

wrangle /ˈraŋɡ(ə)l/ *verb.* **LME.**
[Prob. of Low Dutch origin: cf. Low German, German dial. *wrangeln* wrestle, frequentative of Middle & mod. Low German *wrangen* rel. to *wringen* (see **WRING** *verb*).]
1 *verb intrans.* Quarrel or dispute angrily or noisily; engage in convoluted or public debate or in controversy. Formerly also, take part in a public disputation at a university (cf. **WRANGLER** 1b). (Foll. by *about*, *over*, etc., a subject; *with*, *against*, an opponent.) **LME.** ▸**b** *transf.* Make a harsh discordant noise; jangle. **E19.**
2 *verb trans.* †**a** Foll. by *out*: argue (a case, dispute, etc.) to the end. **E17–E18.** ▸**b** Argue (a person) *out of* a possession etc. or *into* a state. **M17.** ▸**c** Foll. by *away*, *out*: waste (time etc.) in wrangling. *rare.* **L18.**
3 *verb trans.* Get (a thing) *out of* or *from* a person by argument or persuasion. Now *US.* **E17.**
4 *verb trans.* [Cf. **WRANGLER** 2.] Round up, herd, and care for (horses etc.). *US.* **L19.**

📖 **1** A. J. CRONIN Andrew . . wrangled long and stubbornly with the short man over prices. A. BURGESS The two men amiably wrangle about their respective faiths. **2b** T. BROOKS All the devils in hell shall never wrangle a believer out of his heavenly inheritance. **3** *Atlanta* They were bent on wrangling from state officials whatever was needed.

■ **wrangling** *noun* the action of the verb; an instance of this, a wrangle: **LME.** **wrangling** *adjective* (*a*) given to, marked by, or of the nature of noisy dispute; contentious; (*b*) clamorous, jangling: **L15.**

wrangler /ˈraŋɡlə/ *noun.* **E16.**
[from prec. + -**ER**¹.]
1 A person who wrangles or quarrels noisily; a person who engages in debate or controversy. **E16.** ▸**b** At Cambridge University, a student placed in the first class of the mathematical tripos. **M18.**
2 [Prob. in part alt. of Spanish *caverango*, *caballerango* stable-boy.] A person appointed to herd horses on a ranch etc.; *gen.* a cowboy. *US.* **L19.**
3 (Also **W-**.) In *pl.* exc. *attrib.* (Proprietary name for) a kind of jeans. Orig. *US.* **M20.**
1b *senior wrangler*: see **SENIOR** *adjective.*
■ **wranglership** *noun* the position or rank of a wrangler at Cambridge University **L18.**

WRANS *abbreviation. Austral.*
Women's Royal Australian Naval Service.

wrap /rap/ *noun.* **LME.**
[from the verb.]
1 A wrapper, a covering; *spec.* a blanket or rug used to wrap about oneself when travelling, sleeping, etc. **LME.** ▸**b** Material used for wrapping, *esp.* very thin plastic film. **M20.**
2 A loose garment wrapped about the person; *spec.* (*a*) a woman's shawl, scarf, etc.; a loose robe, a wrapper; (*b*) (usu. in *pl.*) a loose outer garment worn when travelling. **E19.**
3 An act of wrapping something; a single twist or winding of cord in fastening an object. **L19.**
4 *fig.* In *pl.* A veil of secrecy maintained about something, esp. a new project. Chiefly in ***keep under wraps***, ***take the wraps off***. **M20.**
5 CINEMATOGRAPHY & TELEVISION. The end of a session of filming or recording. **L20.**

📖 **1** M. ARNOLD To penetrate through wraps and appearances to the essence of things. **2** A. MANNING I was taking off my wraps, and making ready to go up stairs. H. JAMES The haste I made to get into slippers and into a wrap. H. ROBBINS She let her evening wrap fall from her shoulders. **4** *Times* Only now was the truth about battered wives being revealed 'because the wraps have just been pulled off a taboo subject'. C. MCCULLOUGH The book stays under wraps until I say it can be displayed. **5** *Listener* The director says: 'Cut! Thank you, . . that's a wrap'.

Attrib. & comb.: In the sense 'that wraps around the body, wrap-around', as ***wrap coat***, ***wrap dress***. Special combs., as **wrap party** CINEMATOGRAPHY: held to celebrate the completion of filming; **wrap reel**, **wrap wheel** a large revolving framework on which yarn can be wound and measured.
¶ Rare before **19.**

wrap /rap/ *verb.* Infl. **-pp-**. Pa. pple **wrapped**, (esp. in sense 4b, by assoc. with **RAPT** *adjective*) **wrapt**. **ME.**
[Origin unkn.: cf. Northern Frisian *wrappe* stop up, Danish dial. *vrappe* to stuff. Cf. also **WAP** *verb*².]
▶ **I** **1** *verb trans.* Cover (a person or part of the body) by enfolding in a cloth etc.; clothe in an enfolding garment. (Foll. by *in*, *with*, etc.) **ME.** ▸**b** *verb trans.* (usu. in *pass.*) & *intrans.* Foll. by *up*: dress (oneself) in warm clothes. **M19.**
2 *verb trans.* Cover (an object) by winding or folding something round it, esp. so as to protect from injury, loss, etc., or as concealment for a gift etc. Freq. foll. by *up*. **LME.**
3 *verb trans.* **a** Envelop in or *in* a surrounding medium (as flames, mist, etc.). Freq. in *pass.* **LME.** ▸†**b** Entangle. Usu. in *pass.* **LME–L16.** ▸**c** Enfold in the arms; clasp. **L16.**
4 *verb trans.* **a** Involve, immerse, or absorb in or *in* a state or condition. Freq. in *pass.* **LME.** ▸**b** In *pass.* Be engrossed *in*, have one's whole attention or interest taken up *with*, a person or thing (now usu. foll. by *up*). Also, be absorbed *in* thought, contemplation, etc. Cf. **RAPT** *adjective.* **M16.** ▸**c** In *pass.* Foll. by *in*: be entirely bound up with or dependent on. Also foll. by *up*. **M17.**
5 *verb trans.* Involve (a matter) in obscurity or perplexing language so as to disguise its true nature. Freq. foll. by *up*. **LME.** ▸**b** Veil or conceal *from* a person etc. **E19.**
6 Foll. by *up*: ▸**a** *verb trans.* Conclude, finalize. Also, defeat. *colloq.* **E20.** ▸**b** *verb intrans.* Stop talking. Freq. in *imper. slang.* **M20.**
7 *verb intrans.* CINEMATOGRAPHY & TELEVISION. Finish filming or recording. **L20.**

📖 **1** QUILLER-COUCH The clothes that wrapped his diminutive body were threadbare. M. IGNATIEFF She soon had him up in a bath chair, wrapped in blankets. **b** A. T. ELLIS 'You need to wrap up', said Eric . . . It was December. **2** S. KINGSLEY Patsy is wrapping . . the more fragile articles in several layers of cloth. M. ROBERTS Christmas presents bought for the family and not yet wrapped up. **3a** J. TYNDALL A thick fog . . wrapped the mountain quite closely. **c** J. POYER He wrapped his friend in a bear hug. **4a** DICKENS The house is wrapped in slumbers. *Westminster Gazette* We were living from day to day wrapped in anxiety. **b** L. M. MONTGOMERY Little mistakes, such as . . walking . . into the brook while wrapped in imaginative reverie. J. CAREW You're . . selfish and wrapped up in yourself. *Look Now* I love getting completely wrapped up in a book. *Christian Aid News* She lived a life wrapped up with her . . family, friends and church. **c** H. BROOKE He was the only child . . and . . the lives of his parents were wrapt up in him. **5** *Times* He wrapped it up for you. Maybe the blunt truth would have been better. **6a** *Motoring News* We should wrap up the deal this week. **wrap it up** stop doing something.

▶ **II** **8** *verb trans.* Wind or fold up or together; roll or gather up (a pliant or flexible object) in successive layers. Freq. foll. by *up*, *together*. Now *rare* or *obsolete*. **ME.**
9 *verb trans.* Fold, wind, or roll (something) *round* or *about* a person or thing as a garment or wrapping; entwine (something flexible) *round* or *about* a thing. **LME.**
10 *verb intrans.* Of a thing: twine or extend itself round or about a thing like a wrapper or covering. **E17.** ▸**b** Of a garment: extend over the figure etc. so as to cover it or form a lap. **L18.**
11 *verb refl.* Foll. by *round*: eat or drink (an item of food or drink). *colloq.* **L19.**
12 *verb trans.* Crash (a vehicle) into a stationary object. Foll. by *around*, *round*. *colloq.* **M20.**
13 COMPUTING. **a** *verb trans.* Cause (a word, a unit of text) to be carried over *to* or *onto* a new line automatically as the right margin is reached. **L20.** ▸**b** *verb intrans.* Of a word: be so carried over. **L20.**

📖 **8** W. RAMESEY Thunder is . . an exhalation . . thickened and wraped into a cloud. **9** V. BRITTAIN I shivered so much . . that G. took off the scarf . . and wrapped it round me. B. ENGLAND The boy . . wrapped his small brown arms round MacConnachie's neck. ***wrap round one's finger***, ***wrap round one's little finger***: see **FINGER** *noun.* **10** P. BARKER He tried to put Ian down, but the child's arms and legs wrapped tightly round him. *Blueprint* A . . series of . . courts that wrap around the office towers.

wraparound /ˈrapəraʊnd/ *noun & adjective.* Also **wrapround** /ˈrapraʊnd/. **L19.**
[from **WRAP** *verb* + **AROUND**.]
▶ **A** *noun.* **1** A garment wrapped round the body; *esp.* a wraparound skirt or top (see sense B.1a below). **L19.**
2 A fastening or label that wraps round a bottle. **M20.**
3 COMPUTING. A procedure or facility by which a linear sequence of memory locations or positions on a screen is treated cyclically, so that when the last has been counted or occupied the first is returned to automatically. **M20.**
▶ **B** *adjective.* **1** **a** Of a garment, esp. a woman's skirt or top: that wraps around the body. **M20.** ▸**b** Of sunglasses, goggles, etc.: having lenses or lens frames extending around the side of the head. **M20.**
2 That surrounds or curves round another thing; *spec.* (*a*) (of a part of a building or of a motor vehicle) that extends round a corner; (*b*) (of a cinema screen) having a greater sideways extent than normal. **M20.**
3 PRINTING. Of a flexible relief printing plate: wrapped round the cylinder of a rotary press. Of a machine: employing such a plate. **M20.**
4 PUBLISHING. Of a book cover: made from a single sheet of material. Of a jacket: in which the design extends from front to back without being divided by the spine. **M20.**
5 (Of a mortgage) financed by a new lender who pays the monthly instalments of the mortgage to the original lender at the original rate of interest, and at the same time provides the borrower with additional funds for the purchase; pertaining to such a mortgage. Also, designating a tax-deferral scheme in which the interest on certain investments goes into paying the premiums for an annuity. *US.* **M20.**

wrap-over /ˈrapəʊvə/ *noun & adjective.* **M20.**
[from **WRAP** *verb* + **OVER** *adverb.*]
▶ **A** *noun.* Part of a thing, usu. a garment, that overlaps another part of itself. **M20.**
▶ **B** *adjective.* That overlaps another part of itself; *esp.* (of a garment) having a wrap-over. **M20.**

wrappage /ˈrapɪdʒ/ *noun.* **E19.**
[from **WRAP** *verb* + -**AGE**.]
1 That which wraps or covers; a wrapper of a parcel or packet. **E19.** ▸**b** Wrapping material. **L19.**
2 A loose outer garment; a wrapper. **M19.**

wrapper /ˈrapə/ *noun & verb.* **LME.**
[from **WRAP** *verb* + -**ER**¹.]
▶ **A** *noun.* **1** A thing in which something is wrapped. Now chiefly *spec.*, a flexible piece of paper, foil, etc., forming a protective covering for a product. **LME.** ▸**b** More fully ***wrapper leaf***. Tobacco-leaf of a superior quality prepared to form the outer casing of a cigar. Chiefly *US.* **L17.** ▸**c** The outer paper cover or jacket of a book or magazine. Usu. in *pl.* **E19.** ▸**d** A cover wrapped round a newspaper or magazine, for posting. **M19.** ▸**e** A sheet put over furniture, shop goods, etc., as protection from dust or fading. **M19.**
2 **a** A shawl, cloak, etc., for wrapping round the shoulders or head. **M16.** ▸**b** A loose outer garment, esp. for informal indoor wear or for use in household work; *esp.* a woman's loose gown or negligée. **M18.**
3 A person who wraps or packs up anything; *spec.* a person whose occupation consists in wrapping parcels. Also ***wrapper-up***. **L16.**

📖 **1** S. RADLEY Quantrill tore the wrapper from a packet of cigarettes. C. DEXTER A diminutive bar of soap (unopened) in a pink-paper wrapper. **c** P. ACKROYD The first number of *Bleak House* appeared . . in bluish-green wrappers. **2b** M. FRENCH She put on a wrapper and . . padded out in . . slippers.

▶ **B** *verb trans.* Enclose in a wrapper; cover with a dust-jacket. **L19.**
■ **wrapperer** *noun* a person who covers (esp. magazines or books) with wrappers **E20.** **wrappering** *noun* (*a*) coarse material for wrapping; (*b*) a loose outer garment: **M19.**

wrapping /ˈrapɪŋ/ *noun.* **LME.**
[from **WRAP** *verb* + -**ING**¹.]
1 The action of **WRAP** *verb.* **LME.**
2 **a** A thing used for wrapping up an object; a wrap, a covering. Freq. in *pl.* **LME.** ▸**b** A loose outer garment; a wrapper. **M17.**

📖 **2a** *Independent* What counts is . . the quality of the wrapping, and only lastly the present itself.

Comb.: †**wrapping-gown** a nightgown; **wrapping-paper** strong or decorative paper for wrapping up parcels.

wrap-rascal /ˈraprɑːsk(ə)l/ *noun.* Now *Hist.* & *dial.* **E18.**
[from **WRAP** *verb* + **RASCAL** *noun.*]
A loose overcoat worn esp. in the 18th cent.

wrapround *noun & adjective* var. of **WRAPAROUND**.

wrapt *verb pa. pple*: see **WRAP** *verb.*

wrap-up /ˈrapʌp/ *noun & adjective.* **M20.**
[from **WRAP** *verb* + **UP** *adverb*¹.]
▶ **A** *noun.* **1** An easily satisfied customer; an easy sale or task. *US slang.* **M20.**
2 A summary or résumé, esp. of news; a conclusion. **M20.**
▶ **B** *adjective.* That concludes or sums up a programme, book, etc. **M20.**

wrasse /ras/ *noun.* Pl. **-s**, same. **L17.**
[Cornish *wrah* from Middle Cornish *gwrah* = Welsh *gwrach* lit. 'old woman, hag'. Cf. **OLD WIFE** 2(a).]
Any of numerous perciform marine fishes of the family Labridae, esp. the genus *Labrus*, which have a single long dorsal fin of which the anterior part is spiny, are frequently brightly coloured, and are common inshore

fishes in all temperate and tropical seas. Usu. with specifying word.
Ballan wrasse, cuckoo wrasse, Maori wrasse, rainbow wrasse, red wrasse, etc.

wrassle *noun, verb*, **wrassler** *noun*, **wrassling** *noun* see WRESTLE *noun* etc.

†**wrast** *verb* var. of WREST *verb*.

wrastle *noun, verb*, **wrastler** *noun*, **wrastling** *noun* var. of WRESTLE *noun* etc.

wrath /rɒθ, rɔːθ/ *noun*. Now *literary*.
[Old English *wrǣþþu*, from *wrāþ* WROTH *adjective*.]
1 Intense anger or indignation; a fit or manifestation of such feeling. OE. ▸**b** *spec.* Divine displeasure or retribution; an instance of this. OE.
†**2** Impetuous ardour or fury. L15–E17.

📖 **1** J. A. SARGEANT The referee . . brings down on his head the wrath of the fans. A. S. NEILL He isn't afraid of arousing wrath or moral indignation. *fig.*: SIR W. SCOTT A wasted female form, Blighted by wrath of sun and storm. **b** AV *Matt.* 3:7 O generation of vipers, who hath warned you to flee from the wrath to come? E. ERSKINE No Man can read his Bible . . but he must hear of a wrath to come from God upon Impenitent Sinners. **like the wrath of God** dreadful, terrible; dreadfully. **2** SHAKES. *A.Y.L.* They are in the very wrath of love, and they will together.

■ **wrathless** *adjective* (now *rare*) ME.

wrath /rɒθ, rɔːθ/ *adjective*. *rare*. M16.
[Var. of WROTH *adjective*, infl. by assoc. with prec.]
Intensely angry; deeply resentful.

†**wrath** *verb*. ME.
[from the noun.]
1 *verb intrans. & refl.* Be or become intensely angry or indignant. (Foll. by *against, with*, etc.) ME–E19.
2 *verb trans.* **a** Make (a person etc.) angry; provoke to deep resentment. ME–L15. ▸**b** Be or become angry with (a person); treat with extreme anger or deep resentment. LME–M16.
¶ In isolated use after L15.

wrathful /ˈrɒθfʊl, -f(ə)l, ˈrɔːθ-/ *adjective*. Now *literary*. ME.
[from WRATH *noun* + -FUL. Cf. WROTHFUL.]
Full of or characterized by wrath or intense anger.

📖 P. ACKROYD He discarded the concept of a wrathful and avenging God.

■ **wrathfully** *adverb* ME. **wrathfulness** *noun* LME.

wrathy /ˈrɒθi, ˈrɔːθi/ *adjective*. Chiefly *N. Amer.* E19.
[from WRATH *noun* + -Y[1]. Cf. WROTHY.]
= WRATHFUL.
■ **wrathily** *adverb* M19.

wraw /rɔː/ *adjective*. Long *obsolete* exc. *dial.* ME.
[Origin unkn.]
Angry, wrathful.

wrawl /rɔːl/ *verb intrans. obsolete* exc. *north.* LME.
[Imit. Cf. Norwegian *vraula, raula*.]
1 Utter an inarticulate noise; bawl, squall. Also, quarrel, brawl. LME.
†**2** Of a cat: miaow. Only in L16.

wraxle /ˈraks(ə)l/ *verb intrans.* Long *obsolete* exc. *dial.*
[Old English *wraxlian* = Old Frisian *wraxlia* (West Frisian *wrakselje, wrokselje*): cf. WRESTLE *verb*.]
Wrestle; contend, strive.

wray /reɪ/ *verb*. Long *obsolete* exc. *north.* Also (*north.*) **wree** /riː/.
[Old English *wrēgan* = Old Frisian *wrēia*, Old Saxon *wrōgian*, Old High German *ruogen* (German *rügen*), Old Norse *rœgja*, from Germanic. Cf. BEWRAY *verb*[1].]
†**1** *verb trans.* **a** Denounce, inform on, (a person). OE–L15. ▸**b** Assert by way of accusation. OE–LME.
†**2** *verb trans.* Reveal (a secret) treacherously or prejudicially; *gen.* disclose, make known. ME–L16.
†**3** *verb trans.* Betray or expose (a person). ME–M18.
4 *verb trans. & intrans.* Insinuate or make an insinuation *against* a person. *north.* L18.

wreak /riːk/ *noun*. *arch.* ME.
[Var. of WRACK *noun*[1], later assim. to WREAK *verb*. Cf. WRECK *noun*[2].]
1 Vengeance, revenge (freq. in ***take wreak***). Formerly also, an instance of taking revenge. ME.
†**2** Harm, injury; damage. M–L16.

📖 **1** S. BATMAN No creature is more . . feruent to take wreak than is the Bee when he is wrath.

■ **wreakful** *adjective* marked by desire for revenge, vengeful M16. **wreakless** *adjective* (*poet.*, *rare*) (**a**) unpunished; (**b**) unavenged: E17.

wreak /riːk/ *verb*. Pa. t. **wreaked**, (*arch.*) **wroke** /rəʊk/. Pa. pple **wreaked**, (*arch.*) **wroke** /rəʊk/, (*arch.*) **wroken** /ˈrəʊk(ə)n/.
[Old English *wrecan* = Old Frisian *wreka*, Old Saxon *wrekan*, Old High German *rehhan* (Dutch *wreken*, German *rächen*), Old Norse *reka*, Gothic *wrikan* persecute, from Germanic, from Indo-European base prob. repr. also in Latin *urgere* URGE *verb*, Greek *eirgein* shut up. See also WRAKE, WRACK *noun*[1], *verb*[1], WRECK *noun*[1], *verb*[2], WRETCH.]
†**1** *verb trans.* Drive, press, force to move. Only in OE.
†**2** *verb trans.* Banish, expel; drive out or away. OE–LME.
3 *verb trans.* Give vent or expression to (a feeling, esp. anger). Freq. foll. by *on, upon*. OE. ▸**b** Bestow or spend (care etc.) *on*. Now *rare*. L16.
†**4** *verb trans.* **a** Punish (a person, a misdeed, etc.). OE–M17. ▸**b** Injure, harm. LME–L17.
5 *verb trans.* **a** Avenge (a person); (*refl. & in pass.*) take revenge. (Foll. by *on, upon*, or *of* the person who has done the injury, †*of* a wrong etc.) *arch.* OE. ▸**b** Exact retribution for, avenge, (a wrong or injury). (Foll. by *on* or *upon* a person.) *arch.* OE. ▸†**c** Vindicate (a cause etc.) by an act of retribution. LME–L16.
†**6** *verb intrans.* Take vengeance. (Foll. by *on*.) OE–E17.
7 *verb trans.* **a** Inflict (vengeance etc.) on or upon a person. L15. ▸**b** Cause (harm, damage, etc.). Freq. in ***wreak havoc***. (Foll. by *on, upon*.) E19. ▸**c** Deliver (a blow etc.). E19.

📖 **3** DICKENS The dwarf . . wanting somebody to wreak his ill-humour upon. N. HAWTHORNE In the education of her child, the mother's enthusiasm of thought had something to wreak itself upon. P. LIVELY Bulldozers . . monsters unleashed to wreak their mechanical will upon the London clay. **b** J. H. WIFFEN To wreak Such love upon the task. **5a** T. BOSTON They usually wreaking themselves on the ministers as the cause of all public evils. **b** SIR W. SCOTT Vanoc's death must now be wroken. **7a** W. S. CHURCHILL The French wreaked their vengeance on the burghers of the Netherlands. R. TRAVERS An opportunity to wreak private justice on the returning murderer. J. N. ISBISTER Freud wreaked his pyschoanalytic revenge on Wilson. **b** P. L. FERMOR The transformation that beer . . can wreak on the human frame. D. HALL One mosquito can wreak havoc on a picnic or a night's sleep. *Daily Telegraph* The damage wreaked overnight by drunken trippers.

■ **wreaker** *noun* (long *arch.*) an avenger ME.

wreath /riːθ/ *noun*. Pl. **wreaths** /riːðz, riːθs/.
[Old English *wriþa*, from weak grade of *wrīþan* WRITHE *verb*.]
1 An object wound or coiled into a circular shape; a circular band of (usu. precious) metal etc., *esp.* one worn as an ornament. OE. ▸**b** HERALDRY. A representation of the twisted band by which a crest is joined to a helmet. L15.
2 *spec.* A circular band of interwoven flowers, leaves, etc., worn on the head as an ornament, as a mark of honour (esp., in classical times, by victorious contestants), or placed on a grave, at a monument, etc., as a token of respect. Also, a representation of this in metal, stone, etc. LME. ▸**b** A trailing cluster of flowers, tendrils, etc. E17.
3 A crease, a wrinkle. Now *rare* or *obsolete*. LME.
4 A pad supporting a load carried on the head. Now *dial.* M16.
5 A single turn or coil of a coiled thing; a curving or spiral mass of cloud, vapour, etc. Also, a winding motion. L16. ▸**b** A single convolution of a spiral structure or shell; a whorl. M17. ▸**c** A snowdrift. Freq. in ***wreath of snow***. Chiefly *Scot.* E18. ▸†**d** ZOOLOGY. In full ***wreath shell***. A turbinate shell. L18–E19.
6 A curve in the handrail of a circular staircase; the part of the handrail which bends round such a curve. E19.

📖 **2** A. DUGGAN He was bareheaded save for the laurel wreath. B. MALAMUD A young girl . . laid . . in a casket covered with wreaths of hothouse flowers. **5** SHELLEY Then does the dragon . . twine his vast wreaths round the forms of the daemons. TED HUGHES Cows . . looping the hedges with their/warm wreaths of breath.

■ **wreathless** *adjective* E19. **wreathlet** *noun* M19.

wreathe /riːð/ *verb*. M16.
[Prob. partly back-form. from WRETHEN, partly from WREATH. Cf. WRITHE *verb*.]
▸ **I** *verb trans.* **1** Twist in or into a coil or coils; twine (something flexible) round or over a thing (freq. foll. by *round, about*). M16. ▸**b** *fig.* Fasten or secure (a yoke of oppression) *about* or *(up)on* the neck of a person etc. *Scot.* M17.
2 Twist together, entwine; intertwine to form a single structure. M16. ▸**b** *spec.* Form (a wreath) from intertwined flowers or leaves; intertwine (flowers etc.) to form a garland or wreath. L16.
3 Surround with something twisted; *esp.* encircle or adorn (as) with a wreath. Usu. foll. by *with, in*. M16.
4 **a** Strain or turn forcibly round or to one side; wrench, wrest. Formerly also, force the meaning of (a passage). Now *Scot.* L16. ▸**b** Contort, writhe, (the limbs etc.). Now *rare*. M17. ▸**c** Arrange (the face or features) *in* or (now *rare*) *into* a smile. Freq. as ***wreathed*** *ppl adjective*. E19.

📖 **1** J. MARSTON Shall I once more . . wreathe my arms about Antonio's neck? SIR W. SCOTT Fitz-James . . wreath'd his left hand in the mane. **b** W. ROBERTSON Troops . . employed . . for subduing the Scots, and wreathing the yoke about their neck. **2** SHELLEY I behold . . An Eagle and a Serpent wreathed in fight. **b** MILTON The Garland wreath'd for Eve. **3** R. BROOKE Pale flowers wreathed her . . brows. B. CHATWIN The pulpit had been wreathed with old man's beard. *Great Outdoors* The hallowed views were wreathed in mist. **4a** *fig.*: J. LYLY To wrest the will of man, or to wreathe his heart to our humours. **b** J. GAY Impatient of the wound, He rolls and wreaths his shining body round. **c** C. KINGSLEY Gilbert . . walked up to the pair, his weather-beaten countenance wreathed into . . paternal smiles.

▸ **II** *verb intrans.* **5** Twist, coil; (of vapour) move in spirals. L16.
6 Assume or move in the shape of a wreath or wreaths. L18. ▸**b** Of snow: form into drifts. *Scot.* M19.

📖 **5** H. ROTH He could feel its ghastly emanation wreathing about him in ragged tentacles. **6** *Lancashire Life* I could see wreathing smoke . . lifting slowly.

■ **wreathed** *ppl adjective* that has been wreathed; *esp.* formed into or arranged in coils, twisted; (of a column etc.) having a twisted or spiral form or ornamentation; (of a bird) having a line encircling the head: M16. **wreather** *noun* a person who or thing which wreathes or twists something M16. **wreathing** *verbal noun* the action of the verb; an instance of this: M16. **wreathingly** *adverb* in a wreathing or spiral manner M19.

wreathen /ˈriːð(ə)n/ *ppl adjective*. *arch.* Orig. †**wrethen**. LME.
[App. var. of *writhen* pa. pple of WRITHE *verb*, later assim. to WREATH, WREATHE: see -EN[6].]
1 Formed or arranged in coils or curves; twisted. LME.
2 Formed (as) by interweaving; entwined, intertwined. E17.

📖 **1** AV *Exod.* 28:14 Thou shalt make . . two chaines of pure gold . . ; of wreathen worke shalt thou make them.

wreathy /ˈriːθi/ *adjective*. M17.
[from WREATH + -Y[1].]
1 Having the form of a wreath or coil; marked by spiral motion or arrangement. M17.
2 Of the nature of a wreath or garland. E18.

📖 **1** D. M. MOIR The wreathy smoke ascends.

wreck /rɛk/ *noun*[1]. ME.
[Anglo-Norman *wrec* from Old Norse (Norwegian, Icelandic *rek*), from verb meaning 'drive' repr. also in WREAK *verb*.]
▸ **I** Concrete senses.
1 **a** LAW. Cargo, or a piece of wreckage, washed ashore from a wrecked or stranded vessel. Also ***wreck of the sea***. ME. ▸**b** *gen.* = WRECKAGE 2. M18.
2 **a** = WRACK *noun*[2] 3. Now chiefly *Scot. & north.* LME. ▸**b** = WRACK *noun*[2] 3b. *Scot. & dial.* M18.
3 A ship that has been wrecked; the remains of such a vessel. L15.
4 A tossed-up or confused mass; a large quantity. Now *north.* E17.
5 **a** The battered residue or wretched remains *of* a thing which or person who has suffered ruin, destruction, debilitating disease, etc. E18. ▸**b** A ruined or dilapidated building, vehicle, etc.; a person whose health, strength, etc., has totally broken down. L18.
6 = WRACK *noun*[1] 4. L18.

📖 **1a** W. BLACKSTONE If any persons . . take any goods so cast on shore, which are not legal wreck. **3** C. FRANCIS Even large natural harbours . . are littered with wrecks of ships which . . ran on the rocks. **5a** M. ARNOLD There he was joined by the wreck of the consul's army. F. C. SELOUS All the Portuguese here were mere wrecks of men—frail, yellow, and fever-stricken. **b** B. A. MASON Steve is a wreck, still half drunk. *Best* The front of my car was completely gone, it was a wreck. ***NERVOUS wreck***.

▸ **II** Abstract senses.
7 The destruction or complete disablement of a ship at sea; an instance of this. LME. ▸**b** *gen.* Physical destruction or demolition. E18. ▸**c** A road or rail crash. *N. Amer.* E20. ▸**d** The death of a large number of pelagic or migrating birds, usu. as the result of a storm at sea. M20.
8 *fig.* The downfall or overthrow of an established order of things, a system, etc.; an instance of this. Freq. in ***go to wreck (and ruin)***. M16.

📖 **7** C. WILKES In leaving the harbour we had a narrow escape from wreck. **8** CONAN DOYLE What brought all his wicked scheme to wreck was your discovery of . . Heidegger's dead body. I. MURDOCH I had not . . enjoyed observing the wreck of my brother's marriage.

Comb.: **wreckfish** a fish that frequents wrecks; *spec.* the stone-bass, *Polyprion americanus*; **wreck-fishing** fishing in the vicinity of a wreck; **wreck master** an officer appointed to take charge of goods etc. cast up from a wrecked ship; **wreck-wood** wood washed ashore from a wreck.
■ **wreckfree** *adjective* (LAW, now *Hist.*) exempt from forfeiture of shipwrecked cargo or vessels ME.

†**wreck** *noun*[2]. *rare*. Only in L16.
[Alt. of WREAK *noun*.]
Vengeance; revenge.

wreck /rɛk/ *verb*[1]. LME.
[from WRECK *noun*[1].]
▸ **I** *verb trans.* †**1** Wash ashore. LME–E19.
2 Reduce (a structure, vehicle, etc.) to a ruined or shattered condition by force or violence; destroy. E16. ▸**b** *spec.*

Cause the wreck of (a vessel); involve (a person) in a shipwreck; lose or damage (cargo) thus. Usu. in *pass.* L16.
3 *fig.* **a** Bring (a person) to disaster; ruin. L16. ▸**b** Cause the ruin or destruction of (a condition, system, etc.); severely upset or impair (a person's health, nerves, etc.). M18. ▸**c** Frustrate, thwart; prevent the passing of (a measure). M19.

> 📖 **2** G. GREENE A stampede of elephants wrecks the village. E. LONGFORD Machines were wrecked by Luddites. **b** C. SMITH A young Gentleman . . wrecked himself, and wandering along the unhospitable shore. D. A. THOMAS The submarine *Santa Fe* was abandoned and wrecked. **3b** T. C. WOLFE His . . bouts of drinking had wrecked his health. W. S. CHURCHILL Many felt that a formal defiance would wreck their cause. *Daily Telegraph* Injuries which put an end to his sporting life and wrecked his marriage.

▸ **II** *verb intrans.* **4** Suffer shipwreck. L17.
5 Salvage wreckage; *US* engage in breaking up wrecked or damaged vehicles for spares or scrap. E20.

> 📖 **4** G. BERKELEY My letters were in one of the vessels that wreck'd.

■ **wrecked** *ppl adjective* (*a*) that has suffered shipwreck, destruction, or (*fig.*) ruin or disaster; (*b*) *N. Amer. slang* intoxicated by drink or drugs: E18. **wrecking** *ppl adjective* that wrecks or destroys a thing; ***wrecking amendment*** (POLITICS), an amendment designed to defeat the purpose of the bill concerned: L17.

wreck /rɛk/ *verb*[2] *trans.* L16.
[Alt. of WREAK *verb*.]
= WREAK *verb.* Now *obsolete* exc. (*US*) in ***wreck havoc***.

wreckage /ˈrɛkɪdʒ/ *noun.* M19.
[from WRECK *verb*[1] + -AGE.]
1 The action or process of wrecking something; the fact of being wrecked. M19.
2 Fragments of a wrecked vessel, a shattered structure, etc. Cf. WRECK *noun*[1] 1b. L19. ▸**b** *fig.* People who have suffered ruin or extreme misfortune. L19.

> 📖 **2** H. E. BATES After storms the woods were filled with a wreckage of broken branches.

wrecker /ˈrɛkə/ *noun*[1]. Orig. & chiefly *N. Amer.* L18.
[from WRECK *noun*[1] + -ER[1].]
1 A ship or person employed in salvaging wrecked or endangered vessels. L18.
2 A railway vehicle with a crane or hoist for removing crashed trains or similar obstructions. Also, a breakdown truck. E20.
3 A person who breaks up damaged vehicles for spares or scrap. *US.* M20.

wrecker /ˈrɛkə/ *noun*[2]. E19.
[from WRECK *verb*[1] + -ER[1].]
1 A person who causes shipwreck; *esp.* (*Hist.*) a person who lured vessels ashore by false signals in order to plunder them. Also, a person who unlawfully appropriates wreck washed ashore. E19.
2 **a** A person who wrecks or ruins a structure, institution, etc. L19. ▸**b** *fig.* A person who successfully obstructs the passing of a measure etc. L19.
3 A demolition worker. Chiefly *N. Amer.* M20.

wreckful /ˈrɛkfʊl, -f(ə)l/ *adjective. arch.* L16.
[from WRECK *noun*[1] + -FUL.]
Causing shipwreck, ruin, or disaster; dangerous, destructive.

wrecking /ˈrɛkɪŋ/ *verbal noun*[1]. L18.
[from WRECK *verb*[1] + -ING[1].]
The action of WRECK *verb*[1]; *spec.* the action or business of demolishing a building etc.
Comb.: **wrecking ball** a heavy metal ball which may be swung from a crane into a building to demolish it; **wrecking bar** an iron bar with one end chisel-shaped for prising and the other bent and split to form a claw.

wrecking /ˈrɛkɪŋ/ *noun*[2]. *N. Amer.* E19.
[from WRECK *noun*[1] + -ING[2].]
The action or business of salvaging or clearing away a wreck or wrecks. Freq. *attrib.*
attrib.: ***wrecking car, wrecking crane, wrecking truck***, etc.

wreckling *noun* var. of RECKLING.

wree *verb* see WRAY.

wren /rɛn/ *noun*[1].
[Old English *wrenna*, obscurely rel. to Old High German *wrendo, wrendilo*, Old Norse (Icelandic) *rindill*.]
1 A very small Eurasian and N. American songbird, *Troglodytes troglodytes*, which has brown barred plumage and a short cocked tail. Also more fully ***northern wren***, ***common wren***, (*N. Amer.*) ***winter wren***. OE. ▸**b** Any of various other birds of the genus *Troglodytes* or family Troglodytidae, resembling the northern wren. Usu. with specifying word. M19.
2 **a** Any of various small European warblers and kinglets. Usu. with specifying word. Now *colloq.* L17. ▸**b** Any of various small Australasian and Central and S. American birds that resemble wrens in some way. Usu. with specifying word. M19.
3 A woman, *esp.* a young woman. *US slang.* E20.
1 ***bobby wren, jenny-wren, St Kilda wren.*** **b** ***marsh wren, rock wren, tule wren***, etc. **2a** ***golden-crested wren, reed-wren, willow-wren***, etc. **b** ***emu-wren, fairy-wren, rock wren, scrub-wren***, etc.
Comb.: **wren-babbler** any of various Asian babblers that resemble wrens; **wren-boy** (chiefly *Anglo-Irish*) any of a party of boys or young men going from house to house on Boxing Day carrying a holly-bush decorated with a figure of a wren (orig. with a dead wren) and asking for presents; **wren-tail** an artificial fly for trout-fishing, made from the tail feather of a wren; **wren-tit** a small N. American songbird of the babbler family, *Chamaea fasciata*, with dark plumage and a long tail; **wren-warbler** (*a*) any of several warblers of the genera *Camaroptera* and *Prinia*, found in tropical Africa or Asia; (*b*) a fairy-wren.
■ **wrenlet** *noun* a young wren M19.

Wren /rɛn/ *noun*[2]. E20.
[Orig. in pl., from abbreviation ***WRNS***.]
A member of the Women's Royal Naval Service, formed in 1917; (in *pl.*) the Service itself.
■ **Wrennery** *noun* (*joc.*) a building used to accommodate Wrens M20.

Wrenaissance /rɛˈneɪs(ə)ns/ *noun. joc.* M20.
[from *Wren* (see WRENIAN) after RENAISSANCE.]
An architectural style modelled on that of Sir Christopher Wren, esp. as represented by some of the work of Sir Edwin Lutyens.

wrench /rɛn(t)ʃ/ *noun.* LME.
[from the verb.]
1 An act of wrenching or pulling aside; a violent twist or turn. Also, the fact of being wrenched. LME. ▸**b** A sudden twist or jerk causing pain or injury to a limb or muscle; a sprain, a strain. M16. ▸**c** *fig.* A painful parting or uprooting; the distress resulting from such an event. M19. ▸**d** PHYSICS. A force together with a couple which is in a plane perpendicular to the force. L19.
2 †**a** A sharp or abrupt turning movement. *rare.* M16–M17. ▸**b** COURSING. An act of turning round a hare or rabbit at less than a right angle. E17.
3 **a** A mechanical screw. M16. ▸**b** A tool, e.g. a spanner, consisting of a metal bar with (freq. adjustable) jaws for gripping and turning a bolt-head, nut, etc. L18. ▸**c** MEDICINE. A surgical instrument with adjustable jaws for gripping a part, esp. a deformed foot to be rectified by torsion. Now *rare.* L19.
4 A strained or wrested meaning; a forced interpretation. E17.

> 📖 **1** W. GOLDING He gave a convulsive wrench of his whole body. †**on wrench** *rare* crosswise. **c** C. CHAPLIN It was a wrench leaving Keystone, for I had grown fond of . . every-one there. **3b** ***monkey wrench, spud wrench, Stillson wrench, torque wrench***, etc.

Comb.: **wrench fault** GEOLOGY = ***strike-slip fault*** s.v. STRIKE *noun*[1].

wrench /rɛn(t)ʃ/ *verb.*
[Late Old English *wrencan* corresp. to Old High German *renchen* (German *renken*), of unkn. origin.]
1 *verb intrans.* Make a sudden or violent turning or twisting motion. Now *rare.* LOE.
2 *verb trans.* Twist or pull violently round or sideways. ME. ▸**b** Tighten (as) with a wrench. L16.
3 *verb trans.* Injure (a limb etc.) by undue twisting or stretching; sprain, strain. M16. ▸**b** *fig.* Cause pain to; distress greatly. L18.
4 *verb trans.* Misinterpret (a passage) or distort (facts) to suit a theory etc. M16.
5 *verb trans.* Pull, draw, or detach with a wrench or twist; *transf.* take forcibly. Freq. foll. by *from, away, off*, etc. L16.
6 COURSING. **a** *verb intrans.* Of a hare etc.: veer or come round at less than a right angle. L16. ▸**b** *verb trans.* Divert or bring round (a hare etc.) at less than a right angle. E17.
7 *verb intrans.* Pull at a thing with a wrench or twist. Usu. foll. by *at.* L17.

> 📖 **1** J. REED We hurtled furiously on, wrenched right and left to avoid collisions. **2** R. C. HUTCHINSON Without braking he wrenched his car round the corner. P. LIVELY Time, like the city, is blown apart, wrenched into a shattered parody of itself. **b** *fig.*: SHAKES. *Coriol.* For thy revenge Wrench up thy power to th'highest. **3** J. AIKEN Each step . . wrenched my injured joints. **b** J. M. COETZEE His confusion and distress . . wrenched my heartstrings. **4** A. WINCHELL It is . . better to learn how God really did proceed, than to . . wrench our Bible to make it fit a misconception. **5** H. MARTINEAU Those from whose hands he had wrenched the means of subsistence. J. OSBORNE He makes a great effort to wrench himself free, but Cliff hangs on. S. MIDDLETON He . . began to unlace his shoes, then wrench his tie loose. **7** G. GREENE M. Morin drove with clumsy violence, wrenching at his gears.

■ **wrencher** *noun* (*a*) *rare* an instrument for wringing or tightening; (*b*) a person who or thing which wrenches or twists something: L15. **wrenching** *verbal noun* the action of the verb; an instance of this: LME.

Wrenean /rɛˈniːən/ *adjective.* E19.
[from Sir Christopher *Wren* (see next) + -EAN.]
= WRENIAN.

Wrenian /ˈrɛnɪən/ *adjective.* M19.
[from *Wren* (see below) + -IAN.]
Of, pertaining to, or in the style of the English architect Sir Christopher Wren (1632–1723).

wrest /rɛst/ *noun*[1]. ME.
[from the verb.]
1 A twist, a wrench; a tug, a violent pull. ME. ▸**b** A wrenching of a muscle; a sprain. *Scot.* E17.
2 *Hist.* An implement for tuning certain wire-stringed instruments, as the harp or spinet; a tuning-key. LME.
†**3** An instance of wresting or straining the meaning of words etc. L16–E17.
Comb.: **wrest block** MUSIC = ***wrest-plank*** below; **wrest-pin** MUSIC = ***tuning-pin*** s.v. TUNING *noun*; **wrest-plank** MUSIC the board in which the wrest-pins are fixed.

wrest /rɛst/ *noun*[2]. Now *dial.* M17.
[Alt. of REEST *noun*, by assoc. with prec.]
A piece of iron (or formerly wood) fastened beneath the mould-board in certain ploughs; the mould-board itself.

wrest /rɛst/ *verb.* Also †**wrast**.
[Old English *wrǣstan* rel. to Old Norwegian, Icelandic *reista*, Middle Danish *vreste* (Danish *vriste*).]
▸ **I** *verb trans.* **1** Turn, twist. Also foll. by *away, round*, etc. OE. ▸†**b** Tighten (the strings of a musical instrument) or tune (a stringed instrument) by means of a wrest. Also foll. by *up.* OE–E17. ▸†**c** Put *in* with a twisting movement. Chiefly *fig.* L16–L17.
2 Pull, pluck, or detach with a wrench or twist; *fig.* seize or obtain (esp. power or control) with effort or difficulty; take forcible control of. Freq. foll. by *from.* ME. ▸†**b** Force *out* (a sound or word); utter, esp. with difficulty. LME–L16.
†**3** **a** Dispose or influence (a person, a person's feelings) in a given direction. Freq. foll. by *to do.* ME–E17. ▸**b** Divert, draw (the attention, gaze, etc.) away from one thing to another. LME–M18.
4 Deflect or divert to a different purpose, esp. an improper one. E16.
5 **a** Affect with griping pain; rack. Now *rare* or *obsolete.* E16. ▸**b** Strain the muscles of (a joint etc.); sprain (the foot etc.). Chiefly *Scot.* M16.
6 Strain or distort the meaning or interpretation of (words, a writer, a law, etc.), esp. to suit one's own interest or views. (Earlier as ***wresting*** *verbal noun.*) M16. ▸†**b** Derive (a pedigree) improperly *from* a person; corrupt the form of (a word). L16–E18.

> 📖 **1** MARVELL The heliotrope flower . . wrests its neck in turning after the warm sun. **2** R. L. STEVENSON These . . tried in vain to catch the stick and wrest it from his grasp. H. A. L. FISHER In two brief campaigns he wrested from the Lombards all the country which they had won. R. NIEBUHR A minority . . may attempt to wrest control of the state apparatus from the majority. S. KINGSLEY You've got to wrest the leadership of the Federalist Party away from him! R. MACNEIL It built character to go to sea, to wrest your living from it. **3a** R. GREENE A yong man is like a tender plant, apt to be wrested by nurture either to good or euill. **4** G. BERKELEY Cunning men, who bend and wrest the public interest to their own private ends. **6** SIR W. SCOTT You appear convinced of my guilt, and wrest every reply I have made. C. KINGSLEY When you try to wrest Scripture and history to your own use. H. P. BROUGHAM A Pemberton wresting the rules of evidence, to the sacrifice of innocent persons.

▸† **II** *verb intrans.* **7** Struggle, contend. ME–E17.
8 Force a way. LME–L16.
■ **wrester** *noun* a person who wrests something; *esp.* †(*a*) a person who tunes a musical instrument with a wrest; (*b*) a person who strains or distorts the meaning of words etc.: E16. **wresting** *verbal noun* the action of the verb; an instance of this: LME.

wrestle /ˈrɛs(ə)l/ *noun.* Also (now *dial.*, chiefly *N. Amer.*) **(w)rassle**, **(w)rastle**, /ˈras(ə)l/. ME.
[from the verb. See also WARSLE *noun*.]
1 The action of wrestling or struggling. ME.
2 A wrestling bout or contest, esp. as an athletic sport under a code of rules. L17. ▸**b** *fig.* A hard struggle. M19.

wrestle /ˈrɛs(ə)l/ *verb.* Also (now *dial.*, chiefly *N. Amer.*) **(w)rassle**, **(w)rastle**, /ˈras(ə)l/.
[Old English (implied in WRESTLING), corresp. to Low Dutch word repr. by Northern Frisian *wrassele*, Middle Low German *wrostelen*, *wrostelen*, Middle & mod. Dutch *worstelen*. See also WARSLE *verb*. Cf. WRAXLE.]
▸ **I** *verb intrans.* **1** Engage in the practice or sport of wrestling. (Foll. by *with.*) OE.
2 Contend resolutely *with* or *against* circumstances, natural forces, feelings, etc. ME. ▸**b** Strive earnestly *with* God in prayer. E17.
3 **a** Strive with difficulty to cope *with* a problem, task, etc.; struggle *to do.* LME. ▸**b** Make one's way with effort. Freq. foll. by *through.* L16.
4 Twist or writhe about; wriggle, move sinuously. Now *rare.* LME.

📖 **1** S. WYNTER He wrestled with her savagely, trying to . . bend her body to his will. **2** P. KURTH They will try to persuade me [to become Catholic]. And I cannot. I must still wrestle. *Time* The . . types who wrestled with their consciences over whether to serve their country in time of war. **3** F. TUOHY She was wrestling ineffectively with the key, which fitted badly into the lock. W. BOYD I spend befuddled hours wrestling with these arcane epistemological riddles. JOHN ROGERS She watched her mother . . close the heavy . . book and wrestle to get it into her bag.

▸ **II** *verb trans.* **5** Engage in (a wrestling bout or contest). LME.

6 Contend with (a person) in wrestling; overcome by, throw in, wrestling. E19. ▸**b** Throw (a calf) for branding. *US dial.* L19.

7 Drive or push (as) by wrestling; force *from* or *out* of (as) by wrestling; move (an object etc.) with laborious application of force, manhandle. E19.

📖 **6** *Listener* He rides horses, climbs mountains and wrassles Indian chiefs. **7** T. C. WOLFE Maggie . . had gone to court and wrestled the motherless boy from the sinful keeping of his father. A. GRAY He picked up his mother and wrestled her out of the room. A. LURIE She hauls the bag off the conveyor and wrestles it into her cart.

With adverbs in specialized senses: **wrestle down** bring (an opponent) to the ground in wrestling; *fig.* suppress with a struggle. **wrestle out** go through or perform with struggle or effort.

wrestler /ˈrɛslə/ *noun.* Also (now *dial.*, chiefly *N. Amer.*) **(w)rassler**, **(w)rastler**, /ˈras-/. LOE.
[from WRESTLE *verb* + -ER¹.]
1 A person who wrestles; *esp.* a person who practises wrestling as a sport. LOE.
2 *fig.* A person who contends with difficulties, against adverse circumstances, etc. ME.
3 A person who throws cattle for branding. *US dial.* L19.

wrestling /ˈrɛslɪŋ/ *noun.* Also (now *dial.*, chiefly *N. Amer.*) **(w)rassling**, **(w)rastling**, /ˈras-/.
[Old English *wræstlung*, formed as WRESTLE *verb* + -ING¹.]
1 A form of hand-to-hand fighting in which two opponents grapple and try to pin or throw each other to the ground; *esp.* such fighting as an athletic contest under a code of rules. OE. ▸**b** A wrestling bout or contest. ME.
2 *fig.* The action of striving, struggling, or contending. OE.

1 *all-in wrestling*, *Cumberland wrestling*, *mud-wrestling*, *sumo wrestling*, etc. attrib.: *wrestling bout*, *wrestling match*, *wrestling ring*, etc.

wretch /rɛtʃ/ *noun & adjective.*
[Old English *wreċċa* corresp. to Old Saxon *wrekkio*, Old High German *(w)recch(e)o* exile, adventurer, knight errant (German *Recke* warrior, hero, (dial.) giant), from West Germanic base repr. also by WREAK *verb*.]
▸ **A** *noun.* †**1** A banished person; an exile. OE–LME.
2 A deeply unfortunate or pitiable person or creature. Freq. as a term of commiseration. OE.
3 A vile, despicable, or reprehensible person. Freq. as a term of playful depreciation. OE.
4 A niggardly person; a miser. Now *Scot.* ME.

📖 **2** T. GRAY The Wretch, that long has tost On the thorny bed of Pain. S. MOSTYN I see my wife wants me. The poor wretch is terribly jealous. P. CARTER A lonely, miserable wretch living a furtive life in a shabby room. **3** DEFOE Wretch! . . look back upon a mis-spent Life. A. HELPS A wretch of a pedant who knows all about tetrameters. M. FORSTER I am an ungrateful wretch to venture to criticise her.

▸† **B** *adjective.* **1** = WRETCHED *adjective* 1. OE–L16.
2 = WRETCHED *adjective* 2, 3. Only in ME.

wretched /ˈrɛtʃɪd/ *adjective & noun.* ME.
[Irreg. from WRETCH *noun* + -ED². Cf. WICKED *adjective*¹, *noun*, & *adverb*.]
▸ **A** *adjective.* **1** **a** Of a person or creature: in a pitiful state of misery, poverty, or dejection; deeply unhappy or unfortunate. ME. ▸**b** (Of conditions etc.) fraught with misery, distress, or unhappiness; (of weather) uncomfortable. ME.
2 Having unworthy qualities or character; (of a person) reprehensible, hateful. Also as intensifier. ME.
3 Of poor or inferior character; worthless, inadequate; deplorably bad. LME.

📖 **1a** R. HODGSON Angry prayers For . . wretched, blind pit ponies. E. SEGAL Both heaven and earth had turned their backs on those wretched victims. **feel wretched** feel miserable with illness or embarrassment. **b** D. H. LAWRENCE We had had a wretched week, with everybody mute and unhappy. **2** COLERIDGE The wretched tyrant . . had exhausted the whole magazine of animal terror. D. DU MAURIER The wretched fellow must have stayed somewhere drinking . . to be so late. Y. MENUHIN It was wretched of me to repay him and his friend by subjecting them to an embarrassing . . confrontation. M. FORSTER How can Ba recover if this wretched abscess is clogging up her lung? **3** DENNIS POTTER At work . . with one thin sandwich and one wretched cup of coffee to sustain me. D. LODGE Rows of wretched hovels.

▸ **B** *noun.* *The* class of wretched people. Formerly, a wretched person. LME.

📖 K. WHITE I heard the wretched's groan, and mourn'd the wretched's doom. P. ACKROYD To alleviate the plight of the poor and wretched.

■ **wretchedly** *adverb* ME. **wretchedness** *noun* the state or quality of being wretched; a cause or instance of misery: ME.

wretchock /ˈrɛtʃək/ *noun.* Now *dial.* E16.
[from WRETCH *noun* + -OCK.]
The smallest or weakest of a brood or litter; a diminutive person, a little wretch.

†**wrethen** *ppl adjective* see WREATHEN.

wrick /rɪk/ *noun & verb.* Chiefly *dial.* M19.
[Perh. rel. to Low German *wrikken* move here and there, sprain. Cf. earlier RICK *verb*².]
▸ **A** *noun.* A sprain, a strain. M19.
▸ **B** *verb trans.* Sprain, strain. L19.

wride /rʌɪd/ *noun & verb.* Now *dial.*
[Old English *wrīd*, from *wrīdan*, *wrīdian* put out shoots, grow.]
▸ **A** *noun.* A shoot, a stem; a group of shoots or stems growing from one root. OE.
▸ **B** *verb intrans.* Put out shoots, spread out. ME.

wrier *compar. adjective* see WRY *adjective.*

wriest *superl. adjective* see WRY *adjective.*

wrig /rɪg/ *verb.* Now *dial.* Infl. **-gg-**. L15.
[Prob. from Low German *wriggen* twist or turn.]
1 *verb intrans.* Move sinuously; wriggle, writhe. L15.
†**2** *verb trans.* Twist or bend (a flexible object) about; cause to wriggle. E16–M17.

wriggle /ˈrɪg(ə)l/ *noun.* L17.
[from the verb.]
1 A quick wriggling or writhing movement of the body etc.; *fig.* (*rare*) a piece of equivocation. L17. ▸**b** A sinuous formation, marking, or shape; a wriggling or meandering course. E19.
2 A sand eel. *dial.* E19.

Comb.: **wriggle-work** zigzag decoration on antique pewter etc., formed by rocking the gouge from side to side when tracing the design.

wriggle /ˈrɪg(ə)l/ *verb.* L15.
[Middle & mod. Low German (= Dutch) *wriggelen* frequentative of *wriggen*: see WRIG *verb*, -LE³. Cf. WIGGLE *verb*, WRY *verb*¹.]
1 *verb intrans.* Twist the body about; writhe, squirm. L15. ▸**b** Move or proceed with writhing or twisting movements; flow or run sinuously. E17.
2 *verb trans.* **a** Cause (esp. a part of the body) to make short writhing or twisting movements; bring into a specified state or form by wriggling. L16. ▸**b** Foll. by *in*, *into*: insert or introduce by wriggling. L16. ▸**c** Make (one's way) by wriggling. M19.
3 **a** *verb intrans. & refl.* Manoeuvre oneself into or *into* favour, office, etc., by ingratiating or shifty means. L16. ▸**b** *verb intrans.* Practise evasion or equivocation; *esp.* get *out of*, escape *from*, one's responsibilities by means of a contrived pretext. M17.
4 *verb trans.* Form in, or (formerly) cut with, a wriggly or sinuous pattern. *rare.* E17.

📖 **1a** A. HARDY The little fish hatches out and wriggles free. M. FORSTER Our precious baby wriggles like an eel in my arms. **b** HOR. WALPOLE The Trent wriggles through a lovely meadow. D. WELCH I undressed and wriggled into my bathing suit. E. BLYTON They wriggled over the cliff on their tummies. **2a** B. BAINBRIDGE He slid backwards . . and wriggling his body from side to side slowed the swing. **b** M. GEE He . . wriggled a red glass stud into his earlobe. **c** *fig.*: D. HOGAN Joly seemed . . able to wriggle her way around any problem. **3a** ALBERT SMITH He wriggled himself into the good opinion of the coachman. C. KINGSLEY A scheme by which to wriggle into Court favour. **b** A. FRASER He . . tried to wriggle out of the situation.

■ **wriggled** *ppl adjective* that has been wriggled; *wriggled work* = *wriggle-work* s.v. WRIGGLE *noun*: L16. **wriggler** *noun* (**a**) *fig.* a person who advances by ingratiating or shifty means; (**b**) a person who or thing which wriggles; *esp.* a wriggling fish or animalcule: M17. **wriggling** *verbal noun* the action of the verb; an instance of this: L16. **wrigglingly** *adverb* in a wriggling manner E17.

wriggly /ˈrɪgli/ *adjective.* L19.
[from WRIGGLE *noun*, *verb* + -Y¹.]
Given to wriggling; full of wriggles, winding, sinuous.

wright /rʌɪt/ *noun.* Now *arch. & dial.*
[Old English *wryhta* metath. form of *wyrhta* = Old Frisian *wrichta*, Old Saxon *wurhtio*, Old High German *wurhto*, from West Germanic base repr. by WORK *verb*.]
1 A craftsman, a maker, a builder; *spec.* (chiefly *Scot. & north.*) a carpenter. Freq. as 2nd elem. of comb. OE.
†**2** A person who does or performs something; a doer. OE–ME.

1 *cartwright*, *playwright*, *plough-wright*, *shipwright*, *wheelwright*, etc.

■ **wrighting** *noun* (now chiefly *Scot.*) the occupation or activity of a carpenter L15.

wrily *adverb* var. of WRYLY.

wring /rɪŋ/ *noun*¹.
[Old English *wringe*, from *wringan* WRING *verb*.]
1 A cider-press; a wine-press. OE.
2 A cheese-press. L19.

wring /rɪŋ/ *noun*². LME.
[from WRING *verb*.]
1 The action or an act of wringing; *esp.* a squeeze or clasp of the hand. LME.
2 A griping pain, esp. in the intestines. Now *rare* or *obsolete.* E16.

📖 **1** *Century Magazine* She gave the shirt . . a vicious wring.

wring /rɪŋ/ *verb.* Pa. t. **wrung** /rʌŋ/, (*arch. & dial.*) **wrang** /raŋ/; pa. pple **wrung** /rʌŋ/.
[Old English *wringan* = Old Saxon *-wringan* (Middle Low German, Dutch *wringen*), from West Germanic strong verb from base rel. to WRONG *adjective*.]
▸ **I** *verb trans.* **1** Squeeze or twist (something wet or juicy), so as to force out the liquid; *spec.* squeeze and twist (a wet garment etc.) in the hands or with a wringer so as to force out water. Freq. foll. by *out*. OE.
2 **a** Extract (the moisture) from something wet (esp. wet clothes) by squeezing or by twisting; *transf.* force (tears) *out of* the eye or *from* a person. Usu. foll. by *from*, *out (of)*. OE. ▸**b** *fig.* Obtain (a thing) with effort or difficulty from a person; elicit or extract, esp. by pressure. Usu. foll. by *from*, *out (of)*. ME.
3 Twist forcibly, wrench; *esp.* break (a person's or animal's neck) by twisting. Also, twist (esp. the mast of a ship) out of position. OE. ▸**b** Contort, screw up, (the features etc.). ME. ▸**c** Twist spirally, coil. L16.
4 **a** Twist (the clasped hands or fingers) together, as a sign of distress. ME. ▸**b** Clasp vigorously (a person's hand); press (a person) *by* the hand. M16.
5 Bring into a specified position or condition by twisting or wringing (foll. by *down*, *up*, etc.); put *in* or *into* a thing with a twisting movement. LME.
6 Rack with pain or anguish. Of a shoe: pinch. LME. ▸**b** Subject to harassment or oppression. M16.
7 Strain or distort the meaning of; wrest. Now *rare* or *obsolete.* M16.

📖 **1** G. HUNTINGTON They were . . scrubbing the clothes with soap . . and then wringing them out. B. CHATWIN He would wring out the sponge. **2a** EVELYN A laundress wringing water out of a piece of linen. GOLDSMITH It is not a small distress that can wring tears from these old eyes. *fig.*: S. BRETT The last drop of sentiment had been wrung from the occasion. **b** G. SANTAYANA A miser, grown rich on . . miserable payments wrung from the poor. J. DAVIS Their leaders were able to wring concessions from . . the rulers of Saudi Arabia. J. DUNN Female relations intent on cornering them and wringing from them a suitably doleful response. **3** M. DICKENS If he ever makes a pass at you, I'll wring his neck. W. GOLDING We have no topmasts . . and a ship that has been badly wrung. **4a** *fig.*: *Business* The City will . . wring its hands when it sees what it's missed. **b** EVELYN He wrung me by the hand. **6** K. MANSFIELD His heart was wrung with such a spasm that he could have cried out. A. FRASER It was a scene which wrung all who witnessed it. *Listener* It will wring the withers and bring tears to the eyes of all their colleagues.

▸ **II** *verb intrans.* †**8** Flow *out* under pressure; force a way *out*. ME–L16.
9 Writhe, twist; *esp.* (of the hands) clasp and twist together as a sign of distress. LME.
10 **a** Twist the body in convulsive struggling. (Foll. by *with*, *against*.) L15. ▸**b** Writhe in or be racked by pain or anguish. L15.

📖 **10a** *fig.*: V. WOOLF I have strained and wrung at journalism and proof correction.

■ **wringing** *noun* (**a**) the action of the verb, *esp.* the squeezing of water from a wet cloth; an instance of this; in *pl.*, the water etc. which is wrung out; †(**b**) a griping pain, esp. in the intestines; *fig.* a pang of remorse: ME. **wringing** *ppl adjective* (**a**) (of hands) twisting together or wrung in distress; *wringing wet*, so wet that water may be wrung out; (**b**) causing anguish: ME.

wring-bolt /ˈrɪŋbəʊlt/ *noun.* Also (earlier) **wrain-** /ˈreɪn-/. M18.
[App. var. of *ringbolt* s.v. RING *noun*¹.]
In shipbuilding, a large ringbolt used to hold planks in place until they are permanently fastened.

wringer /ˈrɪŋə/ *noun.* ME.
[from WRING *verb* + -ER¹.]
1 An extortioner; an oppressor. ME.
2 A person who wrings clothes after washing, esp. as an occupation. L16. ▸**b** A machine for wringing water from washed clothes; a mangle. L18.
2b **put through the wringer** *slang* (orig. *US*) subject (a person) to a taxing experience, esp. by severe interrogation.

†**wringle** *verb.* L16.
[Corresp. in sense 1 to Danish *vringle*, Swedish & Norwegian *vringla*, in sense 2 to Flemish *wringelen*.]
1 *verb trans.* Entwine; twist together. Only in L16.
2 *verb intrans.* Move sinuously; writhe. L16–E19.

wrinkle /ˈrɪŋk(ə)l/ *noun*[1]. LME.
[Origin uncertain: in sense 1 repr. the rare Old English pa. ppl form *gewrinclod* winding (as a ditch), of which no inf. is recorded. Cf. WRINKLED.]
▶ **I** †**1** A sinuous movement or formation; a winding, a sinuosity. LME–E16.
2 a A crease or ridge in a fabric etc. caused by folding, puckering, etc. LME. ▸**b** *fig.* A minor difficulty; a snag. Chiefly in ***iron out the wrinkles***. M20.
3 A small fold or crease of the skin caused by old age, care, displeasure, etc. LME.
4 *fig.* A moral stain or blemish. Chiefly in ***without spot or wrinkle***, ***without any spot or wrinkle***. LME.
5 *gen.* A slight narrow ridge or depression breaking the smoothness of a surface; a corrugation. Also (chiefly *poet.*), a ripple on the surface of water. E16.

> 📖 **2a** S. JOHNSON His stockings [were] without a wrinkle. A. TYLER Rivulets of . . water were running down the wrinkles in her skirt. **b** *Guardian* The BBC wanted to make . . advances in technical practices . . . Wrinkles still remained. **3** W. BLACK The calm . . forehead that had as yet no wrinkle of age or care. P. LIVELY The fretwork of wrinkles on an old man's neck. **4** J. CARYL Believers have now a righteousness in Christ without spot or wrinkle. **5** T. HERBERT The Sea . . was as smooth as Glass, not the least curl or wrinkle discernable. A. COMBE The numerous folds or wrinkles which line the inner surface of the duodenum.

▶ **II** †**6** A crooked or tortuous action; a trick, a wile. LME–L16.
7 a A clever expedient or device. Now chiefly (orig. *US*, more fully ***new wrinkle***) a clever innovation in technique, style, etc.; a new development or complication. *colloq.* E19. ▸**b** A piece of useful information or advice; a helpful tip. *colloq.* E19.

> 📖 **7a** W. C. HANDY In addition to twirling their batons, they added the new wrinkle of tossing them. *Billings (Montana) Gazette* Electronics Funds Transfer Systems . . are the latest wrinkle in computerized banking. **b** *Daily Telegraph* Hitler is . . studying Napoleon's Continental System in the hope of getting a few wrinkles for present use.

Comb.: **wrinkle ridge** ASTRONOMY a long, irregular ridge on the surface of the moon, Mars, etc.
■ **wrinkleless** /-l-l-/ *adjective* L18.

wrinkle /ˈrɪŋk(ə)l/ *noun*[2]. Now *dial.* & *N. Amer.* L16.
[Alt. of WINKLE *noun* after prec.]
A periwinkle. Formerly also, a whelk.

wrinkle /ˈrɪŋk(ə)l/ *verb*. LME.
[from WRINKLE *noun*[1].]
1 *verb trans.* Form wrinkles or folds in (a surface, esp. the face). Freq. foll. by *up*. LME.
2 *verb intrans.* Of a surface, esp. the face: become puckered into or marked by wrinkles or small folds. Also foll. by *up*. E16.

> 📖 **1** J. L. WATEN The doctor came out, a large smile wrinkling his red face. J. DAWSON She would . . wrinkle up her forehead, smile apologetically and sigh. *Scientific American* A whirligig . . can wrinkle the water into as many as 14 consecutive ripples. **2** T. HOOK The neckcloth, after four vain attempts, wrinkled round his neck in folds. A. PRICE The Minister's nose wrinkled with instinctive distaste.

wrinkled /ˈrɪŋk(ə)ld/ *adjective*. LME.
[from WRINKLE *noun*[1] + -ED[2], but in sense 1 repr. Old English pple *gewrinclod*: see WRINKLE *noun*[1].]
†**1** Full of windings, tortuous; twisted, coiled. LME–L16.
2 Having the surface puckered into or broken by small furrows and ridges; corrugated. E16. ▸**b** Of a person, the face, etc.: marked with wrinkles, lined with age or care. E16.

> 📖 **2** G. ORWELL The hills . . were grey and wrinkled like the skins of elephants. C. DEXTER She . . smoothed the wrinkled coverlet on which she had . . been lying. **b** E. M. FORSTER Her brow was wrinkled, and she still looked furiously cross.

■ **wrinkledness** *noun* M16.

wrinklie *noun* var. of WRINKLY *noun*.

wrinkling /ˈrɪŋklɪŋ/ *noun*. LME.
[from stem of Old English *gewrinclod* (see WRINKLE *noun*[1]) + -ING[1].]
†**1** A twisting, a sinuosity. LME–M16.
2 A series of wrinkles; a puckered surface, formation, etc. L15.
3 The action of creasing or puckering into wrinkles; the fact of becoming wrinkled; an instance of this. E16.

wrinkly /ˈrɪŋkli/ *adjective* & *noun*. As noun also **wrinklie**. L16.
[from WRINKLE *noun*[1] + -Y[1].]
▶ **A** *adjective*. Full of wrinkles; creased, puckered. L16.
▶ **B** *noun*. A person regarded as old by teenagers; a middle-aged or elderly person. Cf. CRUMBLY *noun*. *slang*. *derog.* M20.

wrist /rɪst/ *noun*.
[Old English *wrist*, corresp. to Old Frisian *wrist*, *wirst*, Middle & mod. Low German *wrist*, Middle & mod. High German *rist* wrist, instep, withers, Old Norse *rist* instep, from Germanic, prob. ult. from base also of WRITHE *verb*.]
1 The joint connecting the hand to the forearm; the region around this joint. OE. ▸**b** The part of a sleeve or glove which covers the wrist. E19.
2 The ankle; the instep. Usu. ***wrist of the foot***. Now *dial.* E16.
3 ZOOLOGY. The carpus or carpal joint in the foreleg of a quadruped or the wing of a bird; the analogous part in certain fishes. M19.
4 MECHANICS. More fully ***wrist-pin***. A stud projecting from a crank etc. as an attachment for a connecting-rod. M19.

> 📖 **1** A. LAMBERT She took his wrist: it was cold and the pulse was faint. ***limp wrist***: see LIMP *adjective*. ***slap a person's wrist***: see SLAP *verb*[1]. ***a tap on the wrist***: see TAP *noun*[2] 1.

Attrib. & comb.: In the senses 'worn or carried on the wrist', as ***wrist-bag***, ***wrist-radio***, or (CRICKET etc.) 'effected or directed by wrist-play', as ***wrist hit***, ***wrist-stroke***, etc. Special combs., as **wristband** (*a*) the part of a sleeve (esp. a shirt-sleeve) which covers the wrist; a cuff; (*b*) = WRISTLET; (*c*) in sport, a strip of material worn round the wrist to absorb perspiration; **wrist-bone** any of the small bones of the wrist; **wrist clonus** PHYSIOLOGY spasmodic contraction of the muscles of the hand, produced by forcible extension of the hand at the wrist; **wrist-drop** MEDICINE an affection marked by inability to extend the hand and fingers, resulting from paralysis of the forearm extensor muscles; **wrist jerk** = *wrist clonus* above; **wrist-length** *adjective* reaching to the wrist; ***wrist-pin***: see sense 4 above; **wrist-plate** MECHANICS an oscillating plate bearing one or more wrist-pins on its face; **wrist-play** CRICKET batting in which runs are scored by using the muscles of the wrist rather than by full striking; **wrist-slap** *colloq.* a mild rebuke; **wrist-slapping** *colloq.* mild scolding; **wrist-watch** a small watch worn on a strap or wristlet round the wrist; **wrist-work** = ***wrist-play*** above; **wrist-wrestling** a form of arm-wrestling in which the contestants lock thumbs instead of gripping hands.

wristed /ˈrɪstɪd/ *adjective*. E17.
[from WRIST + -ED[2].]
Having a wrist; (as 2nd elem. of comb.) having a wrist of a specified kind.
strong-wristed, ***thin-wristed***, etc.

wrister /ˈrɪstə/ *noun*. *US*. L19.
[from WRIST + -ER[1].]
A knitted covering for the wrist.

wristlet /ˈrɪstlɪt/ *noun*. M19.
[from WRIST + -LET, after *bracelet*.]
A band, ring, or small strap worn on the wrist for decoration, protection, etc.; a bracelet; a handcuff.

wristy /ˈrɪsti/ *adjective*. M19.
[from WRIST + -Y[1].]
Chiefly CRICKET. Performed by flexing of the wrist; marked by clever wrist-play.
■ **wristily** *adverb* M20.

writ /rɪt/ *noun*.
[Old English *writ* corresp. to Old High German *riz* stroke, written character (German *Riss* as in *Umriss* outline), Old Norse *rit* writing, writ, letter, Gothic *writs* stroke of a pen, from Germanic base also of WRITE *verb*. See also next.]
1 Written matter; a writing; *spec.* †(*a*) a written work, a book; (*b*) (*obsolete* exc. in ***Holy Writ***, ***Sacred Writ*** below) Holy Scripture; †(*c*) a written communication; a letter. Now *rare* in *gen.* sense. OE.
2 A formal document; a legal instrument; *spec.* (LAW) (*a*) a written command or order issued in the name of a sovereign, court, State, or other competent authority, directing a specified person or persons to act or refrain from acting in a specified way; (*b*) a document issued by the Crown to summon a peer to Parliament or to order an election of a member or members of Parliament. Now also (*transf.* & *fig.*), authority, power to enforce compliance or submission, effective influence. ME.
3 Written record. ME. ▸**b** Written words or characters. Long *obsolete* exc. in phr. below. ME. ▸†**c** Written form; = WRITING *noun* 4. Esp. in ***in writ***. ME–L17.

> 📖 **1 Holy Writ**, **Sacred Writ** sacred writings collectively; *esp.* the Bible. **2** *Insight* He hires an attorney to file a writ of habeas corpus requesting a new trial. T. DUPUY The Porte's writ was law as far east as the Persian Gulf. **one's writ runs** one has authority (of a specified kind or extent). **serve a writ on** deliver a writ to. **writ of execution** a judicial order that a judgement be enforced. **writ of inquiry**: by which a sheriff is directed to summon a jury to hold an inquiry, *spec.* for the assessment of damages in a case where a defendant has failed to appear. **writ of summons**: by which an action is started in the High Court. ***original writ***: see ORIGINAL *adjective*. ***purchase a writ***: see PURCHASE *verb* 4b. **3** POPE He . . Of ancient writ unlocks the learned store. **b** ***hand of writ***: see HAND *noun*.

writ *verb pa. t.* & *pple*: see WRITE *verb*.

write /rʌɪt/ *noun*. ME.
[Var. of prec. after next, or directly from next.]
†**1** The Scriptures. Chiefly in ***Holy Write***. ME–M16.
†**2** Written matter; a writing. LME–M18.
3 Chiefly LAW. = WRIT *noun* 2. *obsolete* exc. *Scot.* LME.
4 Written record or form; writing (as opp. to oral communication). *obsolete* exc. *Scot.* L15. ▸**b** *spec.* Handwriting; style of calligraphy. *Scot.* E17.

write /rʌɪt/ *verb*. Pa. t. **wrote** /rəʊt/, (now *dial.*) **writ** /rɪt/. Pa. pple **written** /ˈrɪt(ə)n/, (*arch.*) **writ** /rɪt/, (now *dial.*) **wrote** /rəʊt/.
[Old English *wrītan* corresp. to Old Frisian *wrīta* score, write, Old Saxon *wrītan* cut, write, Old High German *rīzan* tear, draw (German *reissen* sketch, tear, pull, drag), Old Norse *rīta* score, write, from Germanic base of unkn. origin.]
▶ **I** *verb trans.* **1** †**a** Score, outline, or draw the shape of (a thing). OE–L16. ▸**b** Form (letters, symbols, or words) by carving, engraving, etc.; trace in or on a hard or plastic surface, esp. with a sharp instrument; record in this way. Now chiefly as passing into sense 2a. OE. ▸**c** Carve, engrave, or trace letters or words on (a hard or plastic surface). Now *rare* or *obsolete*. ME. ▸**d** *fig.* Indicate clearly or unmistakably (some personal condition or quality). Usu. in *pass.* E17.
2 a Form or mark (a letter, characters, words, etc.) on paper etc. with a pen, pencil, typewriter, etc. Later also, produce (a specified kind or style of handwriting). OE. ▸**b** Cover, fill, or mark (a paper, sheet, etc.) with writing. ME. ▸**c** Enter or record (a name) with a pen etc.; *arch.* mention (a person) in this way. ME.
3 Set down in writing; express or present (words, thoughts, feelings, etc.) in written form. OE. ▸**b** Paint (a message or sign). LME. ▸**c** COMPUTING. Enter (an item of data) *in*, *into*, *on*, or *to* a storage medium (esp. a disk or tape) or a location in store; enter data in or on (a storage medium). M20. ▸**d** Of a recording device: produce (a graphical record). M20.
4 a State, relate, describe, depict, or treat in writing; compose or produce a written statement, chronicle, or record of (circumstances, events, etc.). OE. ▸**b** Convey (news etc.) by letter; communicate (information etc.) in writing. LME. ▸**c** Decree, ordain, or enjoin in writing. Usu. in *pass.* M16.
5 Compose and set down on paper (a literary composition, narrative, verse, etc.); *spec.* compose and set down (a text, report, article, novel, etc.) for written or printed reproduction or publication. OE. ▸**b** Compose and set down (music, a melody, etc.) in notes. L17.
6 a Draw up, draft (a document, writing, etc.); put into proper written form. Also, insert (a provision etc.) *into* a law, agreement, etc. OE. ▸**b** Compose and commit to paper (a letter, note, etc.); communicate with a person by (letter etc.). Later also (now *US* or *colloq.*), write and send a letter to (a person). OE. ▸**c** Fill in, complete, (a cheque etc.) with writing. M19.
7 Spell (a word, name, etc.) in a specified or particular manner in writing. ME.
8 a (Be able to) use (a particular language) in writing. ME. ▸**b** Use (a name, word, etc.) in designating oneself. Now *rare* or *obsolete* exc. as in sense 9. L16.
9 Designate (a person, oneself) as something in writing, set down as; style, call, or term in writing. *arch.* LME. ▸**b** Bring or reduce (a person, esp. oneself) to a specified state by writing. M18.
10 a = UNDERWRITE *verb* 2b. L19. ▸**b** STOCK EXCHANGE. Make (an option) available for purchase by creating a contract; enter into (an option contract) with a buyer. M20.
11 Sit, take, (a written examination). Chiefly *S. Afr.* M20.

> 📖 **1b** *British Museum Magazine* The cuneiform inscription is written in the Babylonian language. *fig.*: BYRON Roll on, thou . . dark blue Ocean! . . Time writes no wrinkle on thy azure brow. **d** I. HAY It must be written all over me . . . You are right . . I'm in love. E. WELTY The young man saw him examine it . . with wonder written all over his face. **3** S. RICHARDSON My heart is full, and I can't help writing my mind. C. REEVE I will get these instructions wrote in a proper form. **4a** SHAKES. *Sonn.* If I could write the beauty of your eyes. T. S. ELIOT The great poet, in writing himself, writes his time. **b** SHAKES. *Coriol.* Have you . . perused What I have written to you? E. BOWEN Anna wrote thanks to Rodney. **c** G. BORROW 'It was not so written,' said Antonio, who . . was a fatalist. **5** O. W. HOLMES The style of . . 'Prelude' shows that it was written under cerebral excitement. DAY LEWIS Short stories and sketches she had written for parish magazines. D. HEALEY Wordsworth wrote a sonnet to Milton. **6a** *Time* The coffee-break has been written into union contracts. *Chicago Tribune* The energy bill will be written by a Senate-House conference. **b** M. MOORE The young man . . writ her a polite note. M. MITCHELL An old gentleman . . wrote me in sorrow because Belle did not have a parrot. **7** R. DUPPA In this MS . . Virgil is uniformly written Vergil. **9** AV *Jer.* 22:30 Thus saith the Lord, Write ye this man childlesse. A. TROLLOPE He took his degree, and wrote himself B.A. **b** THACKERAY You have . . written yourself out of five hundred a-year.

▶ **II** *verb intrans.* **12** Carve, trace, or engrave letters *in*, *on*, or *upon* a hard or plastic surface. OE.
13 Form or mark words, characters, etc. with a pen, pencil, etc.; produce writing, esp. of a specified kind or style. OE. ▸**b** Print by means of a typewriter etc.; typewrite. L19. ▸**c** COMPUTING. Enter data into a storage medium (esp. a disk or tape) or a location in store. M20.
14 Compose or produce a literary composition, report, book, or other text (*of*, *on*, or *about* a subject, person, etc.); practise literary composition; engage in authorship.

Later also, work as a clerk, amanuensis, or (now usu.) a journalist, professional writer, etc. OE. ▸**b** Compose and set down music, a melody, etc. L17.

15 Compose and commit to paper a letter, note, etc.; compose and send a letter *to* a person, organization, etc.; communicate information in writing (freq. foll. by *to do*); conduct correspondence. L16.

> 🕮 **13** T. GRAY My having at last found a Pen that writes. J. BUCHAN He sat down . . and wrote to my dictation. **14** H. BRODKEY Her third husband, a . . novelist from Montana, wrote for the movies between novels. A. BELL Lord Glenbervie, who wrote disapprovingly of Sydney Smith in his *Diaries*. P. BAILEY 'What I Did In My Holidays' was the subject my classmates and I were asked to write about. **15** R. C. LEHMANN Tell Mary she hasn't written for an age. *Lancet* We write to draw attention to Von Foerster's paper. G. DALY Gabriel wrote to his little sister praising Lizzie.

Phrases: ***nothing to write home about, not much to write home about***: see HOME *adverb*. **write oneself man, write oneself woman** *arch*. reach one's majority, attain maturity or a specified age. ***write one's own ticket***: see TICKET *noun*. **writ large** in magnified, emphasized, or elaborated form.

With adverbs in specialized senses: **write down** (*a*) commit to or record in writing, note down; (*b*) designate or reveal (a person, oneself) as; (*c*) disparage, depreciate, or decry in writing; (*d*) reduce the nominal value of (an account, stock, assets, etc.); (*e*) write as though for readers of inferior intelligence or taste, adapt one's literary style *to* such readers. **write in** (*a*) insert (a fact, statement, etc.) in writing; (*b*) send (a suggestion, query, etc.) in written form to an organization; (*c*) (orig. & chiefly *US*) insert (the name of an unlisted person) on a ballot-paper as the candidate of one's choice. **write off** (*a*) note the deduction of (money) in a financial statement, *esp*. cancel the record of (a bad debt etc.), acknowledge the loss of or failure to recover (an asset); (*b*) *fig*. dismiss from consideration as insignificant, irrelevant, a hopeless failure, etc.; (*c*) compose (a letter etc.) with facility; (*d*) damage (a vehicle etc.) beyond repair. **write out** (*a*) make a transcription or fair copy of, copy out; transcribe in full or detail, as from brief notes or shorthand; (*b*) exhaust oneself by excessive writing; (*c*) eliminate, or contrive the temporary absence of, (a character, etc., in a long-running radio or television serial) by writing an appropriate story-line. **write up** (*a*) write a full account, statement, description, or record of (something); elaborate in writing; (*b*) commend or praise in writing; (*c*) make entries to bring (a diary, report, etc.) up to date, complete (a record) in writing.

Comb.: **write-back** the process of restoring to profit a provision for bad or doubtful debts previously made against profits and no longer required; **write-down** a reduction in the estimated or nominal value of stock, assets, etc.; **write-in** (*a*) (orig. & chiefly *US*) (a vote for) an unlisted candidate written in by a voter on a ballot-paper; (*b*) a demonstration of public opinion in the form of mass letters of protest; **write-off** (*a*) the cancellation from an account of a bad debt, worthless asset, etc.; a debt or asset so treated; (*b*) an object, esp. a vehicle, so badly damaged as to not be worth repair; (*c*) a worthless or ineffectual person or thing, a failure; **write-once** *adjective* (COMPUTING) designating a memory or storage device (esp. an optical one) on which data, once written, cannot be modified; **write-permit ring** COMPUTING a ring which has to be inserted in the hub of a tape reel before the tape can be written to or erased; **write-protect** *verb & adjective* (COMPUTING) (*a*) *verb trans*. protect (a disk) from accidental writing or erasure, as by removing the cover from a notch in its envelope; (*b*) *adjective* designating such a notch etc.; **write-up** orig., a written account in commendation of a person or thing; now *esp*. a (favourable or unfavourable) journalistic account or review.

■ **writable** *adjective* (*a*) able to be written or set down in writing; (*b*) suitable for writing with: L18. **writative** *adjective* (now *rare*) disposed to write, given to writing M18. **writee** *noun* (*rare*) a person for whom something is written, a reader E17.

writer /ˈrʌɪtə/ *noun*.

[Old English *wrītere*, formed as prec. + -ER¹.]

1 A person who can write or has written something; a person who writes in a specified manner or style. OE. ▸**b** A person who paints words etc. on a sign; a sign-writer. M19. ▸**c** A pen etc. that writes in a specified manner. E20.

2 A functionary whose business or occupation consists in writing; *spec*. (*a*) a clerk, esp. in the Navy or in government offices; (*b*) (chiefly *Hist*.) a scribe; (*c*) (chiefly *Scot*.) a solicitor. OE. ▸**b** STOCK EXCHANGE. A broker who makes an option available for purchase; a seller of options. M20.

3 A person who writes books or produces literary compositions, articles, reports, or other texts; an author; the composer *of* a book etc. OE. ▸**b** *The* person who is writing. Esp. (as a circumlocution) in ***the present writer***, I. L16. ▸**c** A composer of music, songs, etc. L17.

4 *ellipt*. The writings or work of an author. E17.

> 🕮 **1c** M. RUSSELL The pen you've chosen. It's a bad writer. **3** *Modern Painters* Many writers on cubism . . write as though Cubism were a system of painting waiting to be discovered. **4** HAZLITT Able writers . . are suffered to moulder in obscurity on the shelves of our libraries. A. HELPS I saw . . in an American writer a humorous account.

Comb. & phrases: ***the present writer***: see sense 3b above; **writer-in-residence** a writer holding a residential post in a university etc., in order to share his or her professional insights; **writer's block** a periodic lack of inspiration afflicting creative writers etc.; **writer's cramp** a form of muscular cramp or spasm in the hand resulting from excessive writing; **writer's writer**: whose appeal is primarily to his or her fellow writers; **Writer to the Signet** SCOTS LAW †(*a*) a clerk employed to prepare writs for the royal signet; (*b*) a solicitor belonging to the society of solicitors formerly having the exclusive privilege of preparing writs in the Court of Session.

■ **writeress** *noun* (*rare*) a female writer or author E19. **writerly** *adjective* appropriate to or characteristic of a professional author; consciously literary: M20. **writership** *noun* (chiefly *Hist*.) the office or position of writer, a clerkship, esp. in the East India Company M18.

writhe /rʌɪð/ *noun*. In sense 1a also **writh**. ME.

[from next.]

1 a An object twisted or formed into a circular shape; a twisted band; a wreath. Long *obsolete* exc. *dial*. ME. ▸**b** A curled or twisted formation; a twist. M19.

2 An act of writhing; a twisting movement of the body, face, etc.; a contortion. E17.

writhe /rʌɪð/ *verb*. Pa. pple **writhen** /ˈrɪð(ə)n/, **writhed**.

[Old English *wrīþan* corresp. to Old High German *rīdan*, Old Norse *ríða*, rel. to WREATHE *verb*, WROTH, from Germanic.]

▸ **I** *verb trans*. †**1 a** Envelop or swathe (a thing) by winding or folding. OE–LME. ▸**b** Confine or fasten with a cord etc.; bind, fetter. OE–LME. ▸**c** Surround or wreathe *with* something. *rare*. E16–E18.

2 Twist, coil, (a thing); fashion into or *into* coils, folds, or a certain shape; arrange in a coiled or twisted form; distort by twisting. Freq. foll. by *about*. Now chiefly *literary*. OE.

3 Unite, combine, or make by twisting, entwining, or plaiting; plait, intertwine. Freq. foll. by *together*. Long *rare* or *obsolete* exc. *dial*. OE.

4 Turn or wrench round or to one side; twist forcibly about. Now chiefly *spec*., twist about or *about*, contort, (the body, limbs, face, oneself, etc.). ME. ▸†**b** *fig*. Divert, deflect, cause to turn away or incline, (*from* or *to* a person, course, etc.). Also foll. by *to do*. ME–M17.

5 Twist or wrench out of place, position, or relation. Freq. foll. by *off*, *from*. LME.

†**6** *fig*. Twist, strain, or pervert the meaning of (a word, passage, etc.); perversely misinterpret or misapply. M16–M17.

7 Utter, speak *out*, with a writhe. *rare*. L19.

> 🕮 **2** C. ROSSETTI Who twisted her hair . . And writhed it shining in serpent-coils. J. A. SYMONDS Snow lies . . writhed into loveliest wreaths. **4** MILTON Then Satan first knew pain, And writh'd him to and fro convolv'd. STEELE A Way of appearing Wise by writhing the Head. W. GOLDING He moaned and writhed his body as if the grief were a physical pain. **6** S. R. GARDINER The pelagians . . searched out places of scripture, and writhed them violently . . to their purpose.

▸ **II** *verb intrans*. **8** Move in a turning or sinuous manner; change posture by twisting, twist about; *spec*. twist or contort the body, limbs, etc., (as if) in acute pain, distress, etc. Now also, suffer severe embarrassment or mental discomfort. ME.

9 Change position or proceed with a writhing or twisting motion. Usu. with adverb (phr.). ME.

> 🕮 **8** M. CHOLMONDELEY [He] lit the paper, and . . watched it writhe under the . . flame. G. GISSING When she awoke, it was to toss and writhe for hours in uttermost misery. R. CHURCH I writhed under the lash of his tongue. SARA MAITLAND Phoebe had writhed in shame at the thought. **9** F. TENNYSON Snakes writhed to their holes.

■ **writhed** *adjective* (now chiefly *literary*) that has undergone writhing, twisted; *spec*. (*a*) fashioned (as) by twisting or convolution; (*b*) (of the features etc.) contorted, wry: M16. **writher** *noun* a person who writhes or twists LME. **writhing** *verbal noun* the action of the verb; an instance of this: LME. **writhingly** *adverb* in a writhing manner M16.

writhen /ˈrɪð(ə)n/ *adjective*. OE.

[pa. pple of prec.]

1 Combined, made by, or subjected to, twining or plaiting; intertwined, entwined, plaited. Now *dial*. OE.

2 Subjected to twisting, wrenching, or turning; twisted or contorted out of normal shape or form. Now *arch*. or *literary*. ME. ▸**b** *spec*. Of antique glass or silver: having spirally twisted ornamentation. E20.

3 Arranged in coils, folds, or windings; formed or fashioned (as) by coiling or convolution. *arch*. M16.

writhled /ˈrɪð(ə)ld/ *adjective*. *arch*. M16.

[App. from stem of WRITHE *verb* (see -LE³), but perh. alt. of RIVELLED. See also WRIZZLED.]

Of a person, the skin, etc.: wrinkled; shrivelled, withered.

writing /ˈrʌɪtɪŋ/ *noun*. ME.

[from WRITE *verb* + -ING¹.]

▸ **I 1** The action, process, or practice of writing; the occupation of a person who writes; the use of written characters for purposes of record, communication, etc. ME.

2 The art or practice of penmanship or handwriting; *spec*. the characteristic handwriting of a person. LME.

3 Style, form, manner, or method of literary or musical composition. LME.

4 The state or condition of having been written; written form. LME.

†**5** Manner of setting down a word etc.; orthography. E16–E18.

> 🕮 **1** A. H. GARDINER Writing is a genuine, though secondary, form of speech. *Scientific American* The invention of writing took place in Mesopotamia around 3500 B.C. **2** T. S. ELIOT You did send me postcards from Zurich; But . . I can't decipher your writing. **3** R. W. CHURCH Easy and unstudied as his writing seems.

▸ **II 6** That which is (recorded) in a written or printed state or form; written information; literary output. ME.

7 a A written composition, a piece of literary work done, as a book, article, etc.; (usu. in *pl*.) the work or works of an author or group of authors. ME. ▸**b** A written document; *spec*. (*a*) a letter; (*b*) a legal instrument, a deed, (a document relating to) an agreement or contract. LME.

8 Written or printed letters, characters, or symbols; lettering; *arch*. an inscription. ME.

> 🕮 **6** *New York Review of Books* Much of the writing consists of wild generalization. **7a** B. BETTELHEIM From Trilling's writings one can gain a better comprehension of . . psychoanalysis. *New Yorker* The most recent compilation of scholarly writings on the subject.

Phrases etc.: **at this present writing, at this writing** at the time of writing this. ***automatic writing***: see AUTOMATIC *adjective* 3. **in writing** in written form. ***mirror writing***: see MIRROR *noun*. ***sacred writing***: see SACRED *adjective*. ***script-writing***: see SCRIPT *noun*¹ 2c. **the writing on the wall** evidence or a sign of approaching disaster; an ominously significant event, situation, etc. (with allus. to *Daniel* 5:5, 25–8). **the Writings** = HAGIOGRAPHA.

Comb.: **writing bed** a board or level surface for writing on; **writing block** (*a*) a pad of writing-paper; (*b*) = ***writer's block*** s.v. WRITER; **writing-board**: on which to rest the paper while writing; **writing-book** a blank book for keeping records, practising handwriting, etc.; a book containing or consisting of writing-paper; **writing-box** (chiefly *Hist*.) (*a*) a small box for keeping paper and other writing requisites; (*b*) a small portable writing-desk; **writing cabinet** an article of furniture combining a writing-desk with drawers, shelves, and other facilities for writing; **writing-case** a portable case for holding writing requisites, and providing a surface to write on; **writing-desk** (*a*) a desk for writing at, esp. one equipped for holding writing materials, papers, etc.; (*b*) *rare* a type of writing-case; **writing ink**: prepared or suitable for writing with a pen; **writing-lark** [with ref. to the markings on the egg-shells] *dial*. the yellowhammer, *Emberiza citrinella*; **writing-master** (*a*) a teacher of or instructor in writing, penmanship, or calligraphy; (*b*) *dial*. the yellowhammer (see ***writing-lark*** above); **writing-pad** a pad or blotter for writing on, *esp*. a pad of notepaper; **writing-paper**: designed for writing on; now *esp*. notepaper; **writing-pen**: suitable or adapted for writing; **writing slider** a sliding shelf which draws out at the top of a chest of drawers; **writing speed** (*a*) ELECTRONICS the maximum speed at which an electron beam can scan the screen of a cathode-ray tube and its path still be able to be recorded; (*b*) the effective speed of videotape past a head when the rotation of the head is taken into account; **writing-table** †(*a*) a writing-tablet; (*b*) a table used for writing at, *esp*. one having drawers and other accessories for writing materials etc.; **writing-tablet** a thin tablet, sheet, or plate of wood etc., for writing on.

writing /ˈrʌɪtɪŋ/ *adjective*. L16.

[from WRITE *verb* + -ING².]

That writes; engaged in or excessively devoted to writing.

written /ˈrɪt(ə)n/ *adjective*. ME.

[pa. pple of WRITE *verb*.]

1 That has been written; composed, recorded, or mentioned in writing; committed to writing; that is in writing (as opp. to oral or printed). Later also, that is or has been written *about*, *down*, *off*, *out*, *up*, etc. ME. ▸**b** Of a law: reduced to or established by writing; formulated in a document, code, or printed work. ME. ▸**c** Expressed in due literary form. E20.

2 Bearing a carved or written inscription etc.; covered with writing. Also foll. by *on*. LME.

written *verb pa. pple*: see WRITE *verb*.

writter /ˈrɪtə/ *noun*. Now *rare*. L19.

[from WRIT *noun* + -ER¹.]

A person who serves a writ or process.

wrizzled /ˈrɪz(ə)ld/ *adjective*. *obsolete* exc. *dial*. L16.

[Perh. var. of WRITHLED.]

Marked with creases, wrinkles, or corrugations; wrinkled, shrivelled.

WRNS *abbreviation*.

Women's Royal Naval Service (cf. WREN *noun*²).

wro /rəʊ/ *noun*. *obsolete* exc. *north*. Pl. **wros**. ME.

[Rel. to Old Norse *rá* nook, cabin, whence also Middle Swedish *vra*(*a*, Swedish *vrå*, Danish *vrå*, Norwegian *raa*, *ro*.]

A nook, a corner; a secluded or sheltered spot.

†**wroath** *noun*. *rare* (Shakes.). Only in L16.

[Var. of RUTH *noun*¹.]

Calamity, misfortune. Cf. RUTH *noun*¹ 4b.

wroke *verb pa. t. & pple*: see WREAK *verb*.

wroken *verb pa. pple*: see WREAK *verb*.

wrong /rɒŋ/ *noun*¹. *obsolete* exc. *dial.*
[Old English, from Old Norse *rǫng* rel. to *rangr*: see WRONG *adjective & adverb*.]
†**1** A rib of a ship or other vessel; a floor-timber of a ship. Cf. RUNG *noun* 4. OE–E16.
2 A large crooked bough or branch, *esp.* one cut off and lopped for timber. M18.

wrong /rɒŋ/ *noun*². LOE.
[Prob. use as noun of next (though recorded earlier).]
1 (An instance of) that which is morally unjust, unfair, or improper, (an) injustice; unjust or inequitable treatment; (a) wrong action; (an) evil, harm, or injury inflicted or received. LOE. ▸**b** *LAW*. (A) violation or infringement of law; (an) invasion of right to the damage or prejudice of another or others. Orig. *Scot.* ME. ▸**c** Physical hurt or harm caused to a thing or person; treatment causing material injury or damage. Now *rare*. LME.
2 Claim, possession, or seizure that is (legally or morally) unjustifiable or unwarranted. Now *rare* or *obsolete*. ME.
3 The fact or position of acting unjustly or indefensibly; the state of being or appearing wrong in respect of attitude, fact, procedure, or belief. Esp. in ***in the wrong***. ME.

🕮 **1** T. SECKER The Abilities of the Man, that uses them to his Neighbour's Wrong. COLERIDGE The innumerable multitude of wrongs By man on man inflicted. A. MARSH-CALDWELL One who never sees wrong, without the noble resolution to revenge it. F. A. PALEY If the wrong has been wholly on one side. J. WYNDHAM So young, Terry. So sure of right and wrong. **b** ***civil wrong***: see CIVIL *adjective*. ***private wrong***: see PRIVATE *adjective*. ***public wrong***: see PUBLIC *adjective & noun*. **c** POPE Lest time or worms had done the weapon wrong. **3** H. KINGSLEY I quarrelled with her last night. I was quite in the wrong.

Phrases: **by wrong** (now *rare* or *obsolete*) by virtue or reason of an illegal or unjustifiable claim or seizure. **do (a person) wrong** act unjustly or unfairly to a person; *spec.* be unfaithful to a spouse or lover. **do wrong to** malign, mistreat. ***in the wrong***: see sense 3 above. **put in the wrong** make a person (appear to be) responsible for a quarrel, mistake, offence, etc. ***under a sense of wrong***: see SENSE *noun*.
■ **wronglessly** *adverb* (*rare*) without doing wrong or injury, harmlessly L16.

wrong /rɒŋ/ *adjective & adverb*. ME.
[Corresp. to Old Norse *rangr* awry, unjust (Middle Swedish *vranger*, Swedish *vrång*, (M)Da. *vrang*) = Middle Low German *wrangh* sour, tart, Middle Dutch *wrangh* bitter, hostile, Dutch *wrang* acid, rel. to WRING *verb*. Prob. already in Old English.]
▶**A** *adjective*. **I** †**1** Having a crooked or curved course, form, or direction; twisted, bent; wry. ME–E17.
2 Of a person: misshapen; deformed. Long *obsolete* exc. *dial.* LME.
▶**II 3** Of an action etc.: deviating from equity, justice, or goodness; not morally correct or equitable; unjust. ME.
4 Of a person: deviating from integrity, rectitude, or probity; of bad character; doing or disposed to do wrong. Now *rare* or *obsolete* exc. in ***wrong'un*** below. ME. ▸**b** Unreliable or untrustworthy (from the criminal's point of view); not friendly or sympathetic to criminals. *Criminals' slang*. M19.
5 a Not conforming to some standard, rule, convention, or principle; contrary to what is approved or proper. ME. ▸**b** Incorrect, false, mistaken; (of a belief etc.) involved in or based on error. LME. ▸**c** Of a work of art: misattributed. *colloq.* M20.
6 Amiss; not in satisfactory or proper state or order; in (a) bad, abnormal, or unsatisfactory condition. LME.
7 Not answering to what is required or intended; unsuitable; inappropriate; less or least desirable. LME. ▸**b** *spec.* (*TYPOGRAPHY*). Of a font etc.: not of the proper size, character, or face. L18. ▸**c** *MUSIC*. Of a note etc.: discordant. M20.
8 Leading in a direction not intended, desired, or expected (*lit.* & *fig.*). LME.
9 Not sound or healthy *in* mind; not sane. Now chiefly in colloq. phrs., esp. ***wrong in the head***. M18.

🕮 **3** J. S. MILL Actions are wrong . . [in proportion] as they tend to produce the reverse of happiness. W. S. JEVONS Nothing . . morally wrong in a strike . . when properly conducted. J. MCCARTHY It was very wrong of him to make such a request. **5a** POPE Most by Numbers judge a Poet's song; And smooth or rough, with them is right or wrong. G. BERKELEY Revenues that in ignorant times were applied to a wrong use. **b** J. S. LE FANU Her watch . . being seldom more than twenty minutes wrong, either way. T. HARDY Giles did not contradict him, though he felt sure that the gentleman was wrong. L. GRANT-ADAMSON I was wrong about the date of it . . . I told you he wrote five weeks ago but really it was six. **6** S. DELANEY Doctors say there's something wrong with the brain. W. STEGNER Please . . not another tirade about what's wrong with the world. A. PRICE There's nothing wrong with funerals . . I met my wife at a funeral. **7** GEO. ELIOT The fatal step of choosing the wrong profession. E. H. YATES Never did a man so persistently . . do the wrong thing in the wrong place. I. MURDOCH In an unlucky inauspicious time when any move would be a wrong one. **8** F. L. OLMSTED Inquirers into Nature . . upon a wrong road, groping their way through the labyrinth of error. *Sail* We have gotten ourselves into trouble . . by telling the helmsman the wrong course to steer.

▶**III 10** †**a** Of a person: that has no legal right, title, or claim; not legitimate; = WRONGFUL 3b. ME–L16. ▸**b** Illegal; not legally valid. L15.
†**11** Situated on the left side. *rare*. LME–M16.

Phrases & special collocations: ***bark up the wrong tree***: see BARK *verb*¹. ***born on the wrong side of the blanket***: see BLANKET *noun*. ***come to the wrong shop***: see SHOP *noun*. ***get hold of the wrong end of the stick***: see STICK *noun*¹. ***get in wrong***: see GET *verb*. ***get off on the wrong foot***: see ***on the wrong foot*** s.v. FOOT *noun*. **get on the wrong side of** incur the dislike or disfavour of. ***get out of bed on the wrong side***: see BED *noun*. ***get the wrong end of the stick***: see STICK *noun*¹. **go down the wrong way** (of food) enter the windpipe instead of the gullet. ***have the wrong end of the stick***: see STICK *noun*¹. ***laugh on the wrong side of one's face***, ***laugh on the wrong side of one's mouth***: see LAUGH *verb*. ***not put a foot wrong***: see FOOT *noun*. ***on the wrong side (of)***: see ***wrong side*** below. ***on the wrong track***: see TRACK *noun*. ***rub the wrong way***: see RUB *verb* 6a. ***stroke a person the wrong way***, ***stroke a person's hair the wrong way***: see STROKE *verb*¹. ***the wrong side of the tracks***: see TRACK *noun*. **the wrong way** (in) a mistaken, incorrect, unsuitable, or ineffective manner; ***the wrong way round***, in the opposite or reverse of the normal or desirable orientation or sequence. ***wrong scent***: see SCENT *noun*. **wrong side** (*a*) the reverse; the side intended to be turned inward, downward, or away; ***wrong side out***, inside out; (*b*) ***on the wrong side***, on the less favoured or losing side; (*c*) ***on the wrong side of***, on the unsafe, disadvantageous, inappropriate, undesirable, etc., side of (something), of an age greater than (the age specified), out of favour with (a person); ***on the wrong side of the post(s)***: see POST *noun*¹. **wrong'un** *colloq.* (*a*) *RACING* a horse dishonestly held back so as to lose a race; (*b*) a bad, dishonest, or untrustworthy person, a rogue, a crook; (*c*) *CRICKET* a deceptive delivery requiring a defensive stroke; a googly.

▶**B** *adverb*. **1** Not in accordance with equity, justice, or goodness; in an unjust or morally wrong manner. ME.
2 Not in the right, proper, or correct manner; improperly, unfittingly, unsatisfactorily. ME.
3 Falsely; erroneously, incorrectly. ME.
4 In a wrong direction, by or on a wrong course, (*lit.* & *fig.*). LME. ▸†**b** In an oblique line or position; askew. LME–L15.

🕮 **2** T. JEFFERSON They will amend it whenever they find it works wrong. O. WISTER Every guest's uneasiness lest he drink his coffee wrong. **3** THACKERAY In spite of her care . . she guessed wrong. **4** W. S. GILBERT He loved to send old ladies wrong, And teach their feet to stray. G. GREENE Your pronunciation of the name . . set me wrong.

Phrases: **get wrong** (*a*) *colloq.* misunderstand (a person, statement, etc.); (*b*) reach or give an incorrect answer to (a question etc.). **go wrong** (*a*) take a wrong path, road, turn, etc.; go astray; (*b*) make a mistake, fall into error; (*c*) deviate from moral or suitable behaviour, fall into evil ways; (*d*) happen amiss, result in failure; (*e*) stop functioning properly.

Comb.: **wrong-foot** *verb trans.* (*a*) *SPORT* cause (an opponent) to be awkwardly balanced by a deceptive move, shot, etc.; (*b*) *fig.* disconcert by an unexpected move, catch unprepared; **wronghead** *noun & adjective* (*a*) *noun* a perversely erroneous or wrong-headed person; (*b*) *adjective* = ***wrong-headed*** below; **wrong-headed** *adjective* having a perverse judgement or intellect; perversely or obstinately wrong or erroneous; **wrong-headedly** *adverb* in a wrong-headed manner; **wrong-headedness** the quality or character of being wrong-headed; **wrong-slot** *verb intrans.* in rally driving, take the wrong road.
■ **wrong-wise** *adverb* (*rare*) in a wrong direction or manner M19.

wrong /rɒŋ/ *verb*. ME.
[from prec.]
▶**I** *verb trans.* **1** Do wrong to (a person); treat unjustly, unfairly, or harshly. ME. ▸**b** Violate, do damage to (something immaterial); bring discredit on, take unfair advantage of (something). LME.
2 Defraud or wrongfully dispossess (a person) *of* something, esp. money. *arch.* L15.
3 Malign unwarrantedly or mistakenly; unjustly attribute evil motives to; try to discredit. L16.
4 Cause undeserved physical harm or injury to (a person etc.); hurt, damage. *obsolete* exc. *Scot.* L16. ▸†**b** Affect detrimentally or harmfully; mar, spoil. L16–L18.
5 *NAUTICAL*. Outsail (a vessel etc.); *esp.* = BLANKET *verb* 4. Now *rare* or *obsolete*. L17.

🕮 **1** TENNYSON He that wrongs his friend Wrongs himself more. *L.A. Style* She saw that she'd been grievously wronged by the Welfare Department. **b** SHAKES. *Haml.* I do receive your offer'd love like love, And will not wrong it. DICKENS Rely on my not wronging your forbearance and consideration. **3** N. HAWTHORNE I should wrong her if I left the impression of her being . . obtrusive. TENNYSON I wrong the grave with fears untrue.

▶†**II** *verb intrans.* **6** Act wrongly, harmfully, or injuriously; do wrong (*to* a person etc.). LME–L17.
■ **wronger** *noun* (*a*) a person who does wrong to another, a wrongdoer; †(*b*) (foll. by *of*) a person who abuses or misuses something: LME.

wrongdoer /ˈrɒŋduːə/ *noun*. LME.
[from WRONG *noun*² + DOER.]
1 A person who commits wrongful or immoral acts; a person whose behaviour deviates from integrity or rectitude. LME.
2 *LAW*. A person who is guilty of a wrong; a law-breaker. E16.

wrongdoing /ˈrɒŋduːɪŋ/ *noun*. LME.
[formed as prec. + DOING *noun*.]
Action or behaviour contrary to morality or law, misconduct; moral or legal transgression; an instance of this; a wrongful action.

wrongful /ˈrɒŋfʊl, -f(ə)l/ *adjective*. ME.
[from WRONG *noun*² + -FUL.]
1 Full of wrong or injury (now *rare* or *obsolete*); characterized by wrong, unfairness, or injustice. ME.
†**2** Of a person: behaving evilly or immorally, doing or disposed to do wrong. LME–E17.
3 Contrary to law; unlawful, illegal. LME. ▸**b** Of a person: not entitled to his or her position or claimed standing; holding office etc. unlawfully or illegally. M16. ▸†**c** Unjustly detained. *rare* (Spenser). Only in L16.
4 Mistaken, erroneous. Long *rare*. LME.
■ **wrongfully** *adverb* ME. **wrongfulness** *noun* LME.

wrongly /ˈrɒŋli/ *adverb*. ME.
[from WRONG *adjective* + -LY².]
1 In a wrong, unjust, or inequitable manner; unjustly; unfairly. ME.
2 In an inappropriate or unsuitable manner; improperly. ME.
3 Incorrectly, erroneously, mistakenly. M17.

wrongness /ˈrɒŋnɪs/ *noun*. LME.
[from WRONG *adjective* + -NESS.]
†**1** The state or condition of being curved or crooked; wryness. *rare*. LME–L15.
2 The state or condition of being wrong, incorrect, or inappropriate; faultiness, error; unsuitability, inappropriateness. Now also, something wrong or amiss. E18.
3 A wrong tendency or inclination; a wrongful act. *rare*. M18.
4 The character or quality of being morally wrong; injustice, wrongfulness. M19.

🕮 **2** M. ANGELOU I sensed a wrongness around me, like an alarm clock that had gone off without being set. **4** R. ALTER In the . . 1980s the wrongness of racism . . is taken to be self-evident in most intellectual circles.

wrongo /ˈrɒŋ(g)əʊ/ *noun*. *slang* (chiefly *US*). Pl. **-os**. M20.
[from WRONG *adjective* + -O.]
A bad, dishonest, or untrustworthy person. Also, a counterfeit coin.

wrongous /ˈrɒŋəs/ *adjective*. Long only *Scot.* & *north*. ME.
[from WRONG *adjective* after RIGHTEOUS.]
†**1** Of a person: acting wrongfully, inequitably, or unjustly; rascally, iniquitous, unjust. ME–E17.
2 = WRONGFUL *adjective* 1. ME.
3 Improper in nature or application; inappropriate, unsuitable. ME. ▸**b** Wrongly directed or constituted. *rare*. M18.
4 †**a** Obtained by illegal or wrongful means; ill-gotten. LME–M18. ▸**b** *SCOTS LAW*. Contrary to law; unlawful, illegal. L17.
■ **wrongously** *adverb* (*a*) in a wrongous manner, *esp.* wrongfully, unfairly; †(*b*) incorrectly: ME.

†**wroot** *verb* see ROOT *verb*².

wrot /rɒt/ *noun*. M20.
[Alt. of WROUGHT *adjective*.]
BUILDING. Timber with one or more surfaces planed smooth; wrought or dressed timber.

wrote *verb pa. t. & pple*: see WRITE *verb*.

wroth /rəʊθ, rɒθ/ *adjective & noun*. *arch.*
[Old English *wrāþ* = Old Frisian *wrēth*, Old Saxon *wrēþ* (Dutch *wreed* cruel), Old High German *reid*, Old Norse *reiðr*, from Germanic base also of WRITHE *verb*. Cf. WRATH *noun*, *adjective*.]
▶**A** *adjective*. **1** Of a person: stirred to intense anger or indignation; wrathful, incensed, irate. Also foll. by *against*, *at*, †*to*, *with*. OE. ▸**b** *transf.* Of the wind, sea, etc.: stirred up, stormy. ME.
†**2** Of words, action, etc.: characterized by or indicative of wrath or indignation. OE–M17.
†**3** Fierce, savage, violent. OE–E16.
†**4** Bad, evil; grievous, perverse. OE–LME.

🕮 **1** WORDSWORTH Some . . Waxed wroth and with foul claws . . On Bard and Hero clamorously fell.

▶†**B** *noun*. Wrath, fury; anger. LME–M17.

Wrotham /'ru:təm/ *adjective & noun*. L19.
[See below.]
(Designating) pottery made at Wrotham in Kent in the 17th and 18th cents., esp. red clay slip-ware with a yellowish lead glaze.

†**wrothful** *adjective*. L15–E19.
[Alt. of WRATHFUL after WROTH *noun* or *adjective*.]
Esp. of a person: wrathful, angry.
■ †**wrothfully** *adverb* L15–M19.

wrothy /'rəʊθi, 'rɒθi/ *adjective*. LME.
[from WROTH *adjective* + -Y¹, infl. in later use by WRATHY.]
Wrathful, angry.

wrought /rɔ:t/ *adjective*. Now *arch., literary, & techn.* ME.
[Early pa. pple of WORK *verb*. Cf. WROT.]
1 That has been worked; *esp.* worked into shape or condition, fashioned, formed. Freq. as 2nd elem. of comb. ME. ▸**b** *spec.* Shaped, dressed, or prepared for use from the raw or rough material. M16.
2 (Of a textile, esp. silk) manufactured, spun; (of a garment, tapestry, etc.) decorated as with needlework, embellished, embroidered. LME.
3 a Of a metal: beaten out or shaped with a hammer or other tools. M16. ▸**b** Of metalwork: made by hammering or handwork. Opp. ***cast***. E19.
4 Of coal: mined. *rare*. E18.

📖 **1** C. D. E. FORTNUM Most elegantly wrought earthen vases. **b** W. SPALDING The country exports . . the marble of Carrara, both wrought and unwrought. **3b wrought iron** a tough malleable form of iron which has a low carbon content (largely superseded by steel).

Comb.: **wrought-up** stirred up, excited, stimulated.

wrought *verb pa. t. & pple*: see WORK *verb*.

w.r.t. *abbreviation*.
With respect to.

wrung *verb pa. t. & pple* of WRING *verb*.

WRVS *abbreviation*.
Women's Royal Voluntary Service.

wry /rʌɪ/ *noun*. Now *rare* or *obsolete* exc. *Scot*. LME.
[from WRY *verb*¹.]
†**1 on wry, upon wry**, = AWRY *adverb*. *Scot*. LME–M16.
2 A twisting or tortuous movement. LME.

wry /rʌɪ/ *adjective & adverb*. Compar. **wryer**, **wrier**. Superl. **wryest**, **wriest**. E16.
[from next.]
▶ **A** *adjective*. **1** Of the features, neck, etc.: turned to one side, contorted, distorted; *spec.* (of the face, a look, etc.) twisted or contorted as a manifestation of dislike, disgust, disappointment, or (now freq.) quiet or sardonic amusement. E16. ▸**b** *transf.* Drily or obliquely humorous; sardonic, ironic. E20.
2 a That has been twisted; wrung out of shape; crooked, bent. M16. ▸**b** Deflected from a straight course; inclined or turned to one side. Now *rare* exc. as passing into sense 1. L16.
3 Perverted; unfair, unjust. Now *rare*. M16.
4 Of words, thoughts, etc.: aberrant, wrong; cross. *arch.* L16.

📖 **1** J. AGEE A hen, with a wry neck which could never be straightened. A. S. NEILL Over the beer she made a wry face, and said, 'Nasty!' *Times* The laudatory article . . must have brought a wry smile to the face of many a jet-lagged businessman. ***make a wry mouth***: see MOUTH *noun*. **b** E. O'NEILL He smiles with a wry amusement. *Times Lit. Suppl.* Sharp, often wry, accounts of human relationships about to go wrong. **2b** F. ATTERBURY Every wry Step . . from the Path of Duty. **4** SIR W. SCOTT Art thou not a hasty coxcomb, to pick up a wry word so wrathfully?

▶ **B** *adverb*. Obliquely; awry. L16.
Comb.: **wrybill**, **wry-billed plover** a small New Zealand plover, *Anarhynchus frontalis*, which has a bill that bends to the right; **wry-faced** *adjective* (*a*) having the face out of line with the neck and chest; (*b*) that makes a wry face; **wry-tail** a congenital deformity of dogs, poultry, etc., characterized by a tail that is crooked or deflected to one side.
■ **wryness** *noun* L16.

wry /rʌɪ/ *verb*¹.
[Old English *wrīgian* strive, go forward, tend = Old Frisian *wrīgia* bend, stoop. Cf. AWRY, WRIGGLE *verb*.]
▶ **I** *verb intrans.* †**1 a** Move, proceed. Only in OE. ▸**b** Have a specified tendency; incline. OE–L16.
2 †**a** Of a person: go, swerve, or turn (*aside* or *away*). ME–E17. ▸**b** *fig.* Deviate from the right or proper course; go wrong, err. Long *rare*. LME. ▸†**c** Of a thing: turn obliquely or from side to side; undergo twisting or bending; bend, wind. LME–M17.
3 Contort the limbs, features, etc., (as) in pain or agony; wriggle, writhe. Now *rare*. ME.
▶ **II** *verb trans.* †**4 a** Deflect or divert (a person or thing) from some course or in some direction; cause to turn aside, away, or back. LME–M17. ▸**b** Avert (the head, face, etc.); turn aside or *away*. LME–M17.
5 Twist or turn (the body, neck, etc.) round or about; contort, wrench. LME. ▸†**b** *fig.* Twist the meaning of, misinterpret (a text etc.). E16–M17. ▸†**c** Pervert. M16–E17. ▸**d** Twist out of shape or form; give a twist to; pull, make wry. L16.
6 Twist or distort (the face or mouth), esp. as a manifestation of dislike, disgust, or quiet amusement. E16.

wry /rʌɪ/ *verb*² *trans*. Long *obsolete* exc. *dial.*
[Old English *wrēon*, *wrion* = Northern Frisian *wreye*, from Germanic.]
1 †**a** Lay, place, or spread a cover over (something); cover up or over. OE–E19. ▸**b** *spec.* Cover or rake up (a fire) so as to keep it alive. LME.
†**2** Clothe with a garment or armour. OE–LME. ▸**b** Put trappings or armour on, harness, (a horse). Only in ME.
†**3** Conceal, hide, keep secret. OE–L15.
†**4** Serve as a covering to (a person or thing); be spread over. OE–M17.
†**5** Cover or stretch over (an expanse of ground). Only in ME.

wryer *compar. adjective* see WRY *adjective*.

wryest *superl. adjective* see WRY *adjective*.

wryly /'rʌɪli/ *adverb*. Also **wrily**. LME.
[from WRY *adjective* + -LY².]
In a wry manner.

wry-mouth /'rʌɪmaʊθ/ *noun & adjective*. E17.
[from WRY *adjective* + MOUTH *noun*.]
▶ **A** *noun*. †**1** A condition in which the mouth is persistently twisted. *rare*. E17–M19.
2 Any of several marine fishes of the family Cryptacanthodidae, allied to the prickle-backs, having a very oblique mouth, and found in the NW Atlantic and N. Pacific. M19.
▶ **B** *attrib.* or as *adjective*. = WRY-MOUTHED. E17.
■ **wry-mouthed** *adjective* (*a*) having a wry mouth; (*b*) characterized by contortion of the mouth: M16.

wryneck /'rʌɪnɛk/ *noun*. L16.
[from WRY *adjective* + NECK *noun*¹.]
1 Either of two Old World birds with cryptic plumage of the genus *Jynx* (family Picidae), characterized by their habit of twisting and writhing the neck when disturbed; *esp.* (more fully ***northern wryneck***) *Jynx torquilla*, of Eurasia and N. Africa. L16.
2 A person with torticollis. E17.
3 MEDICINE. = TORTICOLLIS. M18.

wry-necked /'rʌɪnɛkt, -'nɛkt/ *adjective*. L16.
[from prec. + -ED².]
Having a crooked neck; affected with torticollis.

WSPU *abbreviation*.
Hist. Women's Social and Political Union.

WSW *abbreviation*.
West-south-west.

WT *abbreviation*. Also **W/T**.
Wireless telegraphy.

wt. *abbreviation*.
Weight.

WTO *abbreviation*.
World Trade Organization.

Wu /wu:/ *adjective & noun*. E20.
[Chinese *wú*.]
▶ **A** *adjective*. Of or pertaining to the form of Chinese, comprising a group of dialects, spoken in Shanghai, the south of Jiangsu province and most parts of Zhejiang province, China. E20.
▶ **B** *noun*. Chinese of the Wu group. L20.

wubbit *adjective* var. of WABBIT.

wuff /wʌf/ *noun*. E19.
[Imit.: cf. WOOF *noun*², WOUGH *noun*².]
A low suppressed canine bark.

wuff /wʌf/ *verb intrans*. M19.
[Imit.]
Give a low suppressed bark.

wulfenite /'wʊlfənʌɪt/ *noun*. M19.
[from F. X. von *Wulfen* (1728–1805), Austrian scientist + -ITE¹.]
MINERALOGY. A tetragonal molybdate of lead, usu. occurring as orange-yellow tabular crystals, and (sometimes) in massive and granular forms.

Wulfilian /wʊl'fɪlɪən/ *adjective*. E20.
[from Gothic *Wulfila* Ulfilas (see below) + -IAN.]
Of or pertaining to Ulfilas, 4th-cent. Christian missionary, translator of the Bible into Gothic, and inventor of the Gothic alphabet.

Wulfrunian /wʊl'fruːnɪən/ *noun*. M20.
[from *Wulfrun* a 10th-cent. lady of the manor from whose name *Wolverhampton* (see below) is derived + -IAN.]
A native or inhabitant of Wolverhampton, a city in the English W. Midlands.

wump /wʌmp/ *noun*. *slang*. *rare*. E20.
[Origin unkn.]
A foolish or feeble person.

wumph /wʌmf, wʊmf/ *noun*. E20.
[Imit.]
A sudden deep sound, as of the impact of a soft heavy object.

Wunderkammer /'vʊndərkamər/ *noun*. Pl. ***-ern*** /-ərn/. L20.
[German, from *Wunder* wonder + *Kammer* chamber.]
A chamber or cabinet of wonders; *spec.* a place exhibiting the collection of a connoisseur of curiosities.

wunderkind /'vʊndəkɪnt/ *noun*. *colloq.* Also **W-**. Pl. **-s**, **-er** /-də/. L19.
[German, from *Wunder* wonder + *Kind* child.]
1 A highly talented child; a child prodigy, esp. in music. L19.
2 A person who achieves remarkable success at an early age. M20.

Wundtian /'vʊntɪən/ *adjective*. L19.
[from *Wundt* (see below) + -IAN.]
PSYCHOLOGY. Of or pertaining to the school of experimental and physiological psychology founded in Leipzig by the German psychologist Wilhelm Wundt (1832–1920) or his ideas or methods.

wunnerful /'wʌnəfʊl, -f(ə)l/ *adjective*. *joc. & colloq.* E20.
[Repr. dial. or US pronunc.]
Wonderful, marvellous, very good.

wurley /'wə:li/ *noun*. *Austral.* Also **-ie**. M19.
[Aboriginal *wa(d)li*.]
1 An Aboriginal's hut or shelter. M19.
2 Any temporary shelter. M19.

Wurlitzer /'wə:lɪtsə/ *noun*. E20.
[Rudolf *Wurlitzer* (1831–1914), German-born US instrument-maker.]
(Proprietary name for) a large pipe organ or electric organ, esp. one of a kind used widely in cinemas in the 1930s.

Würm /vʊəm/ *adjective & noun*. E20.
[Former name of a lake (the Starnberger See) in Bavaria, Germany.]
GEOLOGY. (Designating or pertaining to) the final Pleistocene glaciation in the Alps, possibly corresponding to the Weichselian of northern Europe.
■ Also **Würmian** *adjective & noun* E20.

wurra /'wʌrə/ *interjection*. *Anglo-Irish*. L19.
[Var. of WIRRA *interjection*.]
Expr. grief or despair.

wurst /və:st, w-; *foreign* vʊrst/ *noun*. M19.
[German.]
Sausage, esp. of the German or Austrian type; a German or Austrian sausage.

†**wursum** *noun* var. of WORSUM.

Württemberger /'və:təmbə:gə/ *noun*. L19.
[German, from *Württemberg*: see below, -ER¹.]
A native or inhabitant of Württemberg, a former State in SW Germany, now part of Baden-Württemberg.

Wurtz /vʊəts, və:ts/ *noun*. E20.
[C. A. *Wurtz* (1817–84), French chemist.]
CHEMISTRY. Used ***attrib.*** and in ***possess.*** to designate the condensation of an alkyl halide, usu. in the presence of metallic sodium, to form a larger symmetrical alkane.
Comb.: **Wurtz–Fittig** /-'fɪtɪg/ [Rudolph *Fittig* (1835–1910), German chemist] used ***attrib.*** to designate an analogous condensation of an alkyl halide and an aryl halide to give a molecule containing the hydrocarbon residues of both (e.g. $C_6H_5CH_3$ from C_6H_5Cl and CH_3Cl).

wurtzite /'wʊətsʌɪt, 'wə:t-/ *noun*. M19.
[formed as prec. + -ITE¹.]
MINERALOGY. Native zinc sulphide, a hexagonal mineral occurring as brownish-black pyramidal crystals and in radiating, fibrous, and massive forms.

wurzel /'wə:z(ə)l/ *noun*. *rare*. L19.
[Abbreviation.]
= MANGEL-WURZEL.

wushu /wu:'ʃu:/ *noun*. L20.
[Chinese *wǔshù*, from *wǔ* military + *shù* technique, art.]
The Chinese martial arts.

wuss /wʌs/ *noun*¹ *& adjective*. *colloq.* M19.
[Repr. colloq. or dial. pronunc.]
= WORSE *adjective & noun*.

wuss /wʊs/ *noun*². *colloq. derog.* L20.
[Back-form. from next.]
A weak or ineffectual person; a wimp.

📖 J. KEENAN You're such a wuss! . . What are you afraid of? That we'll get *caught*?

wussy /'wʊsi/ *noun & adjective*. *colloq. derog.* L20.
[Prob. short for *pussy-wussy*, redupl. of PUSSY *noun* 1.]
▶ **A** *noun*. A weak or ineffectual person; a wimp; an effeminate man. L20.
▶ **B** *adjective*. Weak or ineffectual; wimpish; effeminate. L20.

📖 M. SAWYER The men [were] burly and blokish, even in their wussy pink tank tops.

wüstite /ˈvʊstʌɪt/ *noun.* Also **wus-**. E20.
[from Ewald *Wüst* (1875–1934), German metallurgist.]
CHEMISTRY. A metastable cubic mineral consisting of a solid solution of magnetite in ferrous oxide, formed in iron/iron oxide systems at high temperatures.

wuther /ˈwʌðə/ *verb & noun. Scot. & dial.* Also (earlier) **whither** /ˈwɪðə/. LME.
[Prob. of Scandinavian origin: cf. Norwegian *kvidra* go to and fro with abrupt movements, rel. to Old Norse *hviða*: see WHID *noun*².]
▶ **A** *verb.* **1** *verb intrans.* Move with force or impetus, rush; make a rushing sound. LME.
2 *verb intrans.* Tremble, shake. LME.
3 *verb trans.* Strike or throw forcefully. E19.
▶ **B** *noun.* A violent or impetuous movement, a rush; a forceful blow; a gust of wind; a tremble; a rushing sound. L15.
■ **wuthering** *verbal noun* the action of the verb; an instance of this: L18.

wu ts'ai /wuːˈtsʌɪ/ *noun.* E20.
[Chinese *wǔcǎi* (Wade–Giles *wu ts'ai*), from *wǔ* five + *cǎi* colour.]
Polychrome; polychrome decoration in enamels applied to porcelain; porcelain with polychrome decoration, esp. of the Ming and Qing dynasties.

wu-wei /wuːˈweɪ/ *noun.* M19.
[Chinese *wúwéi*, from *wú* no, without + *wéi* doing, action.]
1 The Taoist doctrine of letting things follow their own course. M19.
2 *Hist.* In China, a minor sect characterized by this doctrine. M19.

wuz /wʌz/ *verb (pa.). non-standard & joc.* L19.
[Repr. colloq. or dial. pronunc.]
Was.

wuzzy /ˈwʌzi/ *adjective. colloq.* L19.
[Origin unkn.: cf. WOOZY, MUZZY.]
Confused, fuddled, vague.

WV *abbreviation. US.*
West Virginia.

w/v *abbreviation.*
Weight in volume.

W.Va. *abbreviation.*
West Virginia.

WW *abbreviation.*
Often as ***WW I***, ***WW II***. World War (One, Two).

WWF *abbreviation.*
1 Orig., World Wildlife Fund; now, World Wide Fund for Nature.
2 World Wrestling Federation.

WWW *abbreviation.*
1 World Weather Watch.
2 World Wide Web. Freq. **www** (the form used in addresses of sites on the Web).

WX *abbreviation.*
Women's extra-large (size).

WY *abbreviation. US.*
Wyoming.

Wyandot /ˈwʌɪəndɒt/ *noun & adjective.* Also (earlier & now usu. in sense A.2) **-otte**. M18.
[French *Ouendat* from Huron *Wendat*.]
▶ **A** *noun.* Pl. **-s**, same.
1 A member of a N. American Indian people belonging to the Huron nation and originally living in Ontario; the language of this people. M18.
2 (A bird of) a medium-sized American breed of domestic fowl. L19.
▶ **B** *attrib.* or as *adjective.* Of or pertaining to the Wyandots or their language. L18.

Wyatt /ˈwʌɪət/ *adjective.* E19.
[See below.]
Designating a building or architectural feature, esp. a type of tripartite window, designed by, or in the characteristic style of the English architect James Wyatt (1746–1813).
■ **Wyaˈttesque** *adjective* characteristic of the architecture of James Wyatt M20.

wych *noun*¹ var. of WICH.

wych *noun*² var. of WITCH *noun*².

wych elm /ˈwɪtʃ ɛlm/ *noun phr.* Also **witch elm**. E17.
[from *wych* var. of WITCH *noun*² + ELM.]
A Eurasian elm, *Ulmus glabra*, with large rough obovate leaves, found in woods and by streams.

wych hazel *noun phr.* var. of WITCH HAZEL.

Wycliffism /ˈwɪklɪfɪz(ə)m/ *noun.* M17.
[formed as WYCLIFFITE + -ISM.]
ECCLESIASTICAL HISTORY. The religious doctrines or tenets advocated or propagated by Wycliffe or his followers.

Wycliffist /ˈwɪklɪfɪst/ *noun.* Now *rare* or *obsolete.* Also (earlier) **-ifist**, **Wic-**. LME.
[formed as next + -IST.]
ECCLESIASTICAL HISTORY. = WYCLIFFITE *noun.*

Wycliffite /ˈwɪklɪfʌɪt/ *noun & adjective.* Also **-ifite**. Orig. **Wic-**. L16.
[medieval Latin *Wiclefita*, from *Wycliffe* (also spelt *Wyclif*, *Wiclif*): see below, -ITE¹.]
ECCLESIASTICAL HISTORY. ▶**A** *noun.* A person who held or propagated the religious tenets or doctrines of the English theologian and reformer John Wycliffe (*c* 1320–84); a follower of Wycliffe. L16.
▶ **B** *adjective.* **1** Of or pertaining to Wycliffe or his followers. M19.
2 Of a person: advocating, following, or adhering to Wycliffism. L19.
■ **Wycliffian** *noun & adjective* (now *rare*) †(*a*) *noun* = WYCLIFFITE *noun*; (*b*) *adjective* = WYCLIFFITE *adjective*: L16.

Wyclifist *noun* see WYCLIFFIST.

Wyclifite *noun & adjective* var. of WYCLIFFITE.

wye /wʌɪ/ *noun. techn.* M19.
[Repr. pronunc. of the letter Y.]
A support or other structure in a form resembling a Y; *spec.* (*a*) PLUMBING a short pipe with a branch joining it at an acute angle; (*b*) ELECTRICAL ENGINEERING = STAR *noun*¹ 9d; (*c*) an arrangement of three sections of railway track, used for turning locomotives.

wyerone /ˈwʌɪərəʊn/ *noun.* M20.
[from *wyer-* (of unkn. origin) + -ONE.]
BIOCHEMISTRY. A fungitoxic phytoalexin, $C_{15}H_{14}O_4$, produced by the broad bean plant.
Comb.: **wyerone acid** the organic acid of which wyerone is the methyl ester, and which has similar properties.

Wykehamical /wɪˈkamɪk(ə)l/ *adjective.* M18.
[from *Wykeham* (see next) + -ICAL.]
1 Of or pertaining to Winchester College or its pupils or staff. M18.
2 That is a (former) pupil of, or connected with, Winchester College. M19.

Wykehamist /ˈwɪkəmɪst/ *noun & adjective.* M18.
[mod. Latin *Wykehamista*, from William of *Wykeham* (1324–1404), Bishop of Winchester and founder of Winchester College: see -IST.]
▶ **A** *noun.* A past or present member of Winchester College, the oldest English public school. M18.
▶ **B** *adjective.* = WYKEHAMICAL *adjective* 1. M19.
■ **Wykehamite** *noun* = WYKEHAMIST *noun* E19.

wyn *noun* var. of WYNN.

wynd /wʌɪnd/ *noun.* Chiefly *Scot. & north.* ME.
[App. from stem of WIND *verb*¹.]
A narrow side-street or passage; a lane, an alley.

wynn /wɪn/ *noun.* Also **wen** /wɛn/, **wyn** /wɪn/.
[Old English *wyn*(*n*, lit. 'joy': see WIN *noun*².]
The Old English runic letter ᚹ (= w) and the manuscript form of this (ƿ, ƿ) in Old and early Middle English.
¶ In this dictionary w is substituted for wynn.

Wyo. *abbreviation.*
Wyoming.

wyomingite /wʌɪˈəʊmɪŋʌɪt/ *noun.* In sense 2 **W-**. L19.
[from *Wyoming*, a State in the western US + -ITE¹.]
1 GEOLOGY. A volcanic rock, usu. of a dull red colour, which consists of leucite and ferromagnetic minerals, and contains conspicuous crystals of phlogopite. L19.
2 (**W-**.) A native or inhabitant of Wyoming. M20.

wype /wʌɪp/ *noun.* Now *dial.* ME.
[Prob. imit. of the bird's call. Cf. Middle & mod. Swedish & Norwegian *vipa*, Swedish *tofsvipa*, Danish *vibe*; cf. also PEESWEEP.]
The lapwing, *Vanellus vanellus*.

WYSIWYG /ˈwɪzɪwɪɡ/ *adjective.* L20.
[Acronym, from *what you see is what you get*.]
COMPUTING. Denoting the representation of text, graphics, etc., onscreen in a form exactly corresponding to its appearance on a page.

†**wyson** *noun* var. of WEASAND.

wyte *noun, verb* vars. of WITE *noun*², *verb.*

wyvern /ˈwʌɪv(ə)n/ *noun.* Also **wivern**, (earlier) †**wyver**. LME.
[Old French *wivre* (mod. *guivre*) from Latin *vipera* snake, with excrescent *-n*: see VIPER.]
†**1** A viper. Only in LME.
2 Chiefly HERALDRY. (An image or figure of) a winged dragon with two feet like those of an eagle, and a serpent-like barbed tail. L16.

Xx

X, x /ɛks/.
The twenty-fourth letter of the modern English alphabet and the twenty-first of the ancient Roman one, in the latter an adoption of Greek *khi*. The sound most commonly denoted by the letter in English, as in Latin, is the double sound /ks/. However, this is often modified to /gz/ before a vowel or silent *h* (esp. in the prefix *ex-* when unstressed), as in ***exact***, ***exhaust***, ***Alexandrian***, and to /kʃ/ or /gʒ/ by reduction of /ksj/ or /gzj/ (in the manner of *ci* and *si*), as in ***noxious***, ***luxurious***, and words ending in *-xion*. Initial X occurs chiefly in words derived from Greek words beginning with the letter xi, and is generally pronounced /z/ (and occas. erroneously replaced by *z*); in adoptions from other languages it may retain (or approximate) the foreign pronunciation, as in ***Xavante***, ***Xhosa***, ***xu***, etc. (see also senses 13, 14 below). In the transliteration of oriental names X has been used to represent foreign sounds usually rendered as /sj/ or /ʃj/. Pl. **X's**, **Xs**.
▶ **I 1** The letter and its sound.
2 The shape of the letter; a diagonal cross, esp. as used to mark a location on a map, indicate incorrectness, register a vote, denote a kiss, etc., or as the signature of a person who cannot write.
1 x-height TYPOGRAPHY & CALLIGRAPHY the height of a lower-case x, esp. as representative of the size of the font or script to which it belongs. **2 X chair** a chair in which the underframe resembles the letter X in shape. **X-frame** the frame of an X chair. **X's and O's** noughts and crosses. **X-shaped** *adjective* having a shape or a cross-section like the capital letter X.
▶ **II** Symbolical uses.
3 Used to denote serial order; applied e.g. to the twenty-fourth (or often the twenty-third, either I or J being omitted) group or section, sheet of a book, etc.
4 The roman numeral for ten.
5 a MATH. (Usu. italic *x*.) The first unknown or variable quantity. ▸**b** Used to denote an unknown or unspecified person, thing, number (cf. X *adjective*), etc. Also (denoting a person) *X.Y.*, *XYZ*. ▸**c** BRIDGE. (Lower-case *x*.) A card between 2 and 9 inclusive. ▸**d** *X disease*, either of two diseases of originally unknown cause: (**a**) MEDICINE (chiefly *Austral.*) Murray Valley encephalitis; (**b**) VETERINARY MEDICINE a disease of poultry now known to be caused by a mycotoxin. ▸**e** LINGUISTICS. ***x-question***, a question requiring more than a 'yes' or 'no' answer, and usu. introduced by a specifically interrogative word.
6 GEOMETRY etc. (Italic *x*.) Used to denote a quantity measured along the principal or horizontal axis (abscissa); the first coordinate.
7 GENETICS. **a** (Cap. X.) Used to denote a sex chromosome of which the number in normal female somatic cells is twice that in male cells; ***X-linked***, (determined by a gene) that is carried on the X chromosome. ▸**b** (Lower-case *x*.) Used to denote the basic ancestral number of chromosomes which make up a genome, esp. with preceding number indicating degree of polyploidy. Cf. N, N 6d.
8 ***X factor***, the aspects of military life that have no civilian equivalent; pay made in recognition of these. *Military slang*.
9 (Cap. X.) Used to indicate the strength of brands of ale, stout, or porter, XX or double X denoting a medium quality, XXX or treble X the strongest quality. Also, indicating qualities of tin-plate.
10 ***X-band***, the range of microwave frequencies around 10,000 megahertz, used in radar transmission.
11 (Cap. X.) Used to denote films classified as suitable for adults only, or to which only those older than a certain age (usu. 18) are to be admitted; ***X-rated***, so classified; ***X-certificate***, (having) such a rating. (Superseded by 18.)
12 ZOOLOGY. ***X organ***, a group of cells in the eye-stalk of some crustaceans which secrete a substance that inhibits the production of hormone by the Y organ.
6 X-axis (**a**) (written *x-axis*) the principal or horizontal axis of a system of coordinates, points along which have a value of zero for all other coordinates; (**b**) ELECTRONICS the principal axis of a quartz crystal, joining two vertices of the hexagonal cross-section. **X-cut** *adjective* (ELECTRONICS) of, pertaining to, or designating a quartz crystal cut in a plane normal to the X-axis. **X-plate** ELECTRONICS either of a pair of electrodes in an oscilloscope that control the horizontal movement of the spot on the screen.
▶ **III 13** Representing Greek *khi* as the first letter of *Khristos* Christ, in written abbreviations, as ***Xt***, Christ, ***Xtian***, Christian, ***Xtianity***, Christianity, etc. Cf. ***chi-rho*** s.v. CHI; XMAS.
14 Representing various syllables, esp. *ex-*, *cross-*, in respelt abbreviations and contractions (usu. informal), either pronounced /ɛks/ or retaining the pronunciation of the uncontracted syllable, as ***ped-xing***, ***Xtal***, etc.

x /ɛks/ *adjective*. M19.
[from the letter: see X, X 5b.]
Designating or indicating an unknown or unspecified number etc. Freq. in ***x number of*** —.

📖 S. BELLOW An engagement ring from a man who loved me . . not just an object worth X dollars.

x /ɛks/ *verb trans.* 3 sing. pres. **x's**; pa. t. & pple **x-ed**, **x'd**; pres. pple & verbal noun **x-ing**. M19.
[from the letter.]
1 PRINTING. Supply with x's in place of types that are wanting. *rare*. M19.
2 Obliterate (a written or esp. typed character) with a superimposed 'x'; cross *out* in this way; = EX *verb*. M20.

X-acto /ɪg'zaktəʊ/ *noun*. Orig. & chiefly *US*. Also **Xacto**. Pl. **-os**. M20.
[Respelling of EXACT *adjective* + -O.]
(Proprietary name for) any of various hand-tools for craftwork, esp. a kind of knife.

Xanadu /'zanədu:/ *noun*. M20.
[Alt. of *Shang-tu*, an ancient city in SE Mongolia, residence of Kublai Khan (1216–94), as portrayed in S. T. Coleridge's poem *Kubla Khan* (1816).]
A place of dreamlike magnificence and luxury.

xanthan /'zanθan/ *noun*. M20.
[from mod. Latin *Xanthomonas* (see below), formed as XANTHO- + Greek *monas* MONAD: see -AN.]
CHEMISTRY. More fully ***xanthan gum***. A polysaccharide composed of glucose, mannose, and glucuronic acid, produced by fermentation (either by the bacterium *Xanthomonas campestris* or synthetically) and used in foods as a gelling agent, thickener, etc., and in oil-well drilling fluids.

xanthate /'zanθeɪt/ *noun*. M19.
[from XANTHIC, XANTHINE + -ATE[1].]
CHEMISTRY. **1** A salt or ester of a xanthic acid. M19.
2 A compound of xanthine with an alkali. *rare*. L19.

xanthate /'zanθeɪt/ *verb trans.* M20.
[Back-form. from next: see -ATE[3].]
CHEMISTRY. Cause to undergo xanthation.

xanthation /zan'θeɪʃ(ə)n/ *noun*. E20.
[from XANTHATE *noun* + -ATION.]
A stage in the viscose process for making rayon, in which alkaline cellulose is treated with carbon disulphide to form cellulose xanthate.

xanthelasma /zanθɪ'lazmə/ *noun*. M19.
[mod. Latin, formed as XANTH(O- + Greek *elasma* beaten metal.]
MEDICINE. Xanthoma, esp. as occurring around the eyes in elderly people.
■ **xanthelasmic** *adjective* E20.

xanthene /'zanθi:n/ *noun*. L19.
[from XANTH(O- + -ENE.]
CHEMISTRY. A yellowish tricyclic crystalline compound, $C_{13}H_{10}O$, whose molecule contains two benzene rings joined by a methylene group and an oxygen atom, and whose derivatives include brilliant, often fluorescent dyes such as fluoresceins and rhodamines.
attrib.: ***xanthene colour***, ***xanthene dye***, etc.

Xanthian /'zanθɪən/ *adjective & noun*. L17.
[from *Xanthus* (see below) + -IAN.]
▶ **A** *adjective*. Of or pertaining to Xanthus, an ancient town in Lycia in Asia Minor. L17.
▶ **B** *noun*. A native or inhabitant of Xanthus. L17.

xanthic /'zanθɪk/ *adjective*. E19.
[from XANTH(O- + -IC.]
1 CHEMISTRY. Orig., designating, pertaining to, or producing any of various yellow compounds, including xanthine. Now only *spec.*, designating or derived from a xanthic acid (see below). E19.
2 Yellow, yellowish. *rare*. M19.
1 xanthic acid an organic acid containing sulphur, $C_2H_5OCS{\cdot}SH$, many of whose salts are yellow; any of the colourless reactive acids of the general formula RO·CS·SH or RO·CS·SR′ (where R and R′ are alkyl or similar groups). **xanthic oxide** (now *rare* or *obsolete*) [from its yellow compound with nitric acid] = XANTHINE.

xanthin /'zanθɪn/ *noun*. See also next. M19.
[from XANTH(O- + -IN[1].]
CHEMISTRY. **1** Any of various yellow or orange carotenoid pigments present in plants. M19.
2 See next.

xanthine /'zanθʌɪn/ *noun*. Also **-in** /-ɪn/. See also prec. M19.
[from XANTHIC + -INE[5].]
BIOCHEMISTRY. A crystalline purine, $C_5H_4N_4O_2$, found in blood and urine and in some plants, which is an intermediate in the breakdown of nucleic acids to uric acid and is the parent compound of caffeine and related alkaloids. Also, any of several substituted derivatives of this.
Comb.: **xanthine oxidase** an enzyme containing molybdenum which catalyses the oxidation of hypoxanthine to xanthine and of xanthine to uric acid.
■ **xanthi'nuria** *noun* (MEDICINE) the presence of abnormally large amounts of xanthine in the urine L19.

Xanthippe /zan'tɪpi/ *noun*. Also **Xantippe**. L16.
[The wife of Socrates: see SOCRATIC *adjective*.]
A shrewish, scolding, or ill-tempered woman or wife.

xanthism /'zanθɪz(ə)m/ *noun*. *rare*. M20.
[from XANTH(O- + -ISM, after *erythrism*, *melanism*.]
ZOOLOGY. Abnormal or excessive yellowness, as in the plumage or fur of a bird or animal.
■ **xan'thistic** *adjective* exhibiting xanthism L20.

xantho- /'zanθəʊ/ *combining form*.
[from Greek *xanthos* yellow: see -O-.]
1 Yellow.
2 CHEMISTRY. Of, derived from, or related to xanthic acid.
■ **xanthochroism** /zan'θɒkrəʊɪz(ə)m/ *noun* [cf. XANTHOCHROIC] ZOOLOGY = XANTHISM; *spec.* loss of pigments other than yellow or orange ones, esp. in goldfish: L19. **xanthochro'matic** *adjective* = XANTHOCHROMIC E20. **xantho'chromia** *noun* (MEDICINE) a yellowish discoloration of the skin, or of the cerebrospinal fluid as a result of haemorrhage in or near the spinal cord or brain L19. **xantho'chromic** *adjective* (MEDICINE) of, pertaining to, or exhibiting xanthochromia M20. **xanthoderm** *noun* a person who is yellow-skinned, *spec.* a person of a Mongoloid physical type E20. **xanthophore** *noun* (ZOOLOGY) a cell (as in the skin of an animal) containing a yellow pigment E20. **xan'thopsia** *noun* (MEDICINE) a condition of the eyes in which objects appear yellowish; yellow vision: M19. **xanthopterin** /zan'θɒpt(ə)rɪn/ *noun* (CHEMISTRY) a yellow pterin pigment found esp. in certain butterflies and moths and in mammalian urine E20.

xanthochroic /zanθə(ʊ)'krəʊɪk/ *adjective*. Now *rare*. M19.
[from mod. Latin *Xanthochroi*, app. intended to be formed as XANTHO- + Greek *ōkhros* pale: see -IC.]
ANTHROPOLOGY. Designating, of, or pertaining to peoples typically having yellow or light-coloured hair and pale complexion.
■ **xanthochroid** /zan'θəʊkrɔɪd/, **xanthochrous** /zan'θəʊkrəs/ *adjectives* = XANTHOCHROIC M19.

xanthoma /zan'θəʊmə/ *noun*. Pl. **-mas**, **-mata** /-mətə/. M19.
[from XANTHO- + -OMA.]
MEDICINE. A condition characterized by the formation of yellowish patches or nodules on the skin due to deposition of lipids. Now usu., such a patch or nodule.
■ **xanthoma'tosis** *noun*, pl. **-toses** /-'təʊsi:z/, a metabolic disorder marked by the accumulation of lipids in the blood and the presence of multiple and widespread xanthomas E20. **xanthomatous** *adjective* pertaining to or of the nature of xanthoma E20.

xanthone /'zanθəʊn/ *noun*. L19.
[formed as XANTHENE + -ONE.]
CHEMISTRY. A tricyclic compound, $C_{13}H_8O_2$, which is a ketone analogue of xanthene and forms the basis of various natural pigments.

xanthophyll /'zanθə(ʊ)fɪl/ *noun*. M19.
[from XANTHO- + Greek *phullon* leaf.]
BIOCHEMISTRY. Any of a group of yellow or brown oxygen-containing carotenoids which act as accessory pigments in photosynthesis; *spec.* lutein. Also ***xanthophyll-pigment***.
■ **xantho'phyllic** *adjective* of or containing xanthophyll M20.

xanthorrhoea /zanθə(ʊ)'ri:ə/ *noun*. Also ***-rrhea**. E19.
[from mod. Latin (see below), formed as XANTHO- + -RRHOEA, from the yellow gum exuded at the base of the old leaves.]
Any of various palmlike Australian woody plants constituting the genus *Xanthorrhoea* (family Xanthorrhoeaceae), popularly called ***blackboy***, ***grass-tree***.

xanthous /'zanθəs/ *adjective*. E19.
[from Greek *xanthos* yellow + -OUS.]
ANTHROPOLOGY. Having or designating yellow or yellowish hair and a light complexion.

Xantippe *noun* var. of XANTHIPPE.

Xavante /ʃəˈvanti/ *noun & adjective.* E20.
[Portuguese, of unkn. origin.]
► **A** *noun.* Pl. same, **-s**.
1 A member of any of several semi-nomadic S. American Indian peoples of the interior savannah of central Brazil. E20.
2 The Tupi-Guarani language of any of these peoples. E20.
► **B** *attrib.* or as *adjective.* Of or pertaining to the Xavante or their languages. L20.

Xaverian /zeɪˈvɪərɪən/ *adjective & noun.* L19.
[from St Francis *Xavier* (1506–52), Spanish Jesuit missionary to southern and eastern Asia + -IAN.]
► **A** *adjective.* **1** Of, pertaining to, or designating a teaching order of Roman Catholic monks founded in 1839 and named in honour of St Francis Xavier. L19.
2 Of, pertaining to, or characteristic of St Francis Xavier. M20.
► **B** *noun.* A member of the Xaverian order. E20.

XC *abbreviation.* Also **x-c**.
Cross-country (skiing).

xd *abbreviation.*
Ex dividend.

Xe *symbol.*
CHEMISTRY. Xenon.

xebec /ˈziːbɛk/ *noun.* Also **zebec(k)**, **†chebec**. M18.
[French *chebec*, Spanish †*xabeque* (mod. *jabeque*) or Catalan *xabec*, ult. from Arab. *šabbāk* small warship or fishing vessel.]
A small three-masted (orig. two-masted) vessel with lateen and usu. some square sails, formerly much used in the Mediterranean.

xen- *combining form* see XENO-.

xenia /ˈziːnɪə/ *noun*[1]. L19.
[Greek: see XENIAL.]
BOTANY. The influence of a pollen genotype on the maternal tissue or endosperm of the fruit, shown in the form, colour, etc., of the seed.

xenia *noun*[2] pl. of XENIUM.

xenial /ˈziːnɪəl/ *adjective.* M19.
[from Greek *xenia* the state of being a guest + -AL[1].]
Of or pertaining to the friendly relation between host and guest, or between a person and a foreign country (esp. with ref. to the ancient Greek world).

Xenical /ˈzɛnɪk(ə)l/ *noun.* L20.
[Invented name.]
(Proprietary name for) a synthetic drug which blocks pancreatic enzymes involved in the absorption of fats and is given orally in the treatment of obesity.

xenium /ˈziːnɪəm/ *noun.* Pl. **-ia** /-ɪə/. E18.
[Latin from Greek *xenion* a present (esp. of table delicacies) given to a guest or stranger, use as noun of neut. of *xenios* pertaining to a stranger or guest, from *xenos*: see XENO-.]
1 *Hist.* An offering or gift, *esp.* one made (sometimes compulsorily) by medieval subjects to their lord as he passed through their estates. Usu. in *pl.* E18.
2 ROMAN ANTIQUITIES. A picture representing (the giving of) gifts. Usu. in *pl.* L18.

xeno- /ˈzɛnəʊ/ *combining form* of Greek *xenos* stranger, guest, foreigner: see **-O-**. Before a vowel also **xen-**. Foreign, strange, alien; occas., pertaining to or of the nature of a guest or guests.
■ **xeˈnarthral** *adjective* [Greek *arthron* joint] ZOOLOGY of or having peculiar accessory articulations in the vertebrae, characteristic of the order Edentata L19. **xenoˈantibody** *noun* (IMMUNOLOGY) an antibody produced in response to a xenoantigen L20. **xenoˈantigen** *noun* (IMMUNOLOGY) an antigen which originates from an individual of a different species L20. **xenoantiˈgenic** *adjective* (IMMUNOLOGY) of or pertaining to a xenoantigen L20. **xenobiˈologist** *noun* an expert in or student of xenobiology M20. **xenobiˈology** *noun* the branch of science that deals with (hypothetical or fictional) extraterrestrial life-forms; exobiology: M20. **xenobiosis** /-bʌɪˈəʊsɪs/ *noun* (ZOOLOGY) a form of symbiosis among ants in which two colonies of different species live in the same nest, without rearing their broods in common E20. **xenobiˈotic** *adjective & noun* (BIOLOGY) (designating) a substance, esp. a synthetic chemical, foreign to the body or to an ecological system M20. **xenoblast** *noun* (PETROGRAPHY) a mineral crystal which has grown in metamorphic rock without forming its characteristic crystal faces (opp. ***idioblast***) E20. **xenoˈblastic** *adjective* (PETROGRAPHY) of, pertaining to, composed of, or of the nature of a xenoblast or xenoblasts M20. **xeˈnocracy** *noun* a ruling body of foreigners M20. **xenocryst** *noun* (GEOLOGY) a crystal in an igneous rock which is not derived from the original magma L19. **xenoˈcrystal** *adjective* (GEOLOGY) pertaining to or of the nature of a xenocryst or xenocrysts M20. **xenoˈcrystic** *adjective* = XENOCRYSTAL L20. **xenodiagˈnosis** *noun* (MEDICINE) a diagnostic procedure in which clean, laboratory-bred vectors of a disease are allowed to feed on the individual or material that may be infected and are then examined for the pathogen M20. **xenodiagˈnostic** *adjective* (MEDICINE) of or pertaining to xenodiagnosis M20. **xeˈnogamous** *adjective* (BOTANY) of or pertaining to cross-fertilization E20. **xeˈnogamy** *noun* (BOTANY) cross-fertilization L19. **xenogeˈneic** *adjective* (IMMUNOLOGY) (involving material) derived from an individual of a different species M20. **xenoˈgenesis** *noun* (BIOLOGY, *rare*) (supposed) production of offspring permanently unlike the parent L19. **xeˈnogenous** *adjective* (chiefly MEDICINE) produced by external agency E19. **xenoˈglossia** *noun* = XENOGLOSSY L20. **xenoglossy** *noun* the (alleged) faculty of speaking a language one has not learned E20. **xenograft** *noun* (MEDICINE) a graft of tissue between individuals of different species; a heterotransplant, a heterograft: M20. **xenoˈlalia** *noun* = XENOGLOSSY L20. **xenolith** *noun* (GEOLOGY) a piece of rock within an igneous mass which differs from the surrounding rock and is thought to have been picked up by the mass when the latter was in the form of magma L19. **xenoˈlithic** *adjective* (GEOLOGY) pertaining to or containing xenoliths; occurring as a xenolith: E20. **xeˈnologist** *noun* an expert in or student of xenology M20. **xeˈnology** *noun* the branch of science that deals with extraterrestrial phenomena; *spec.* xenobiology: M20. **xenoˈmania** *noun* a mania for or inordinate attraction towards foreigners or things foreign, xenophilia L19. **xenoˈmaniac** *noun* a person affected with xenomania L19. **xenoˈmorphic** *adjective* (GEOLOGY) (of a mineral in a rock) having a form different from the characteristic one, owing to the pressure of other constituents L19. **xenotransplant** *noun* an organ or tissue transplanted from one species to another, esp. a transplant of animal tissue or organs into a human M20. **xenotransplanˈtation** *noun* the process of transplanting organs or tissues between members of different species M20. **xenotropic** *adjective* (MICROBIOLOGY) (of a virus) present in a host species in an inactive form and able to infect and replicate only in organisms of other species L20. **xenotropism** /-ˈtrəʊp-/ *noun* (MICROBIOLOGY) the phenomenon of inactivity of a virus in the usual host species; lack of susceptibility to a virus in the usual host species: L20.

xenodochium /zɛnəˈdɒkɪəm/ *noun.* Pl. **-chia** /-kɪə/. Also **-chion** /-kɪɒn/, (earlier)†**-chy**. M16.
[Late Latin from late Greek *xenodokheion*, formed as XENO- + *dekhesthai* receive.]
Hist. A house of reception for strangers and pilgrims; a hostel or guest-house, esp. in a monastery.

xenon /ˈzɛnɒn, ˈziː-/ *noun.* L19.
[Greek, neut. of *xenos* foreign, strange.]
CHEMISTRY. A colourless odourless gaseous chemical element, atomic no. 54, one of the noble gases, which is a trace constituent of the earth's atmosphere and is used in fluorescent lamps, lasers, anaesthetics, etc. (Symbol Xe.)
■ **xenic** *adjective*: ***xenic acid***, an aqueous solution of xenon trioxide M20.

xenophile /ˈzɛnəfʌɪl/ *noun & adjective.* Also **-phil** /-fɪl/. M20.
[from XENO- + -PHILE.]
► **A** *noun.* A person who is fond of or attracted to foreign things or people; a lover of the foreign. M20.
► **B** *adjective.* That is a xenophile; attracted to foreign things or people. M20.
■ **xenoˈphilia** *noun* the state of being (a) xenophile M20. **xenoˈphiliac**, **xenoˈphilic** *adjectives* = XENOPHILE *adjective* L20.

xenophobia /zɛnəˈfəʊbɪə/ *noun.* E20.
[from XENO- + -PHOBIA.]
A deep antipathy to foreigners or to foreign things.
> F. FITZGERALD A haven for . . a fierce traditionalism, and a concomitant xenophobia.

■ **ˈxenophobe** *noun & adjective* (***a***) *noun* a xenophobic person; (***b***) *adjective* = XENOPHOBIC: E20. **xenophobic** *adjective* pertaining to or affected with xenophobia E20. **xenophobically** *adverb* L20.

Xenophontean /zɛnəˈfɒntɪən/ *adjective.* Also **-ian**. L16.
[from Greek *Xenophônt-*, *Xenophôn* Xenophon (see below) + -EAN, -IAN.]
Pertaining to, characteristic of, described by, or resembling (that of) the Greek historian and biographer Xenophon (*c* 444–354 BC).
■ **Xenophontic** *adjective* E19.

Xenopus /ˈzɛnəpəs/ *noun.* L19.
[mod. Latin (see below), formed as XENO- + Greek *pous* foot.]
A clawed frog of the African genus *Xenopus*, esp. *X. laevis*, much used in embryological research and formerly in pregnancy testing, as it produces eggs in response to substances in the urine of a pregnant woman. Chiefly as mod. Latin genus name.

xenotime /ˈzɛnətʌɪm/ *noun.* M19.
[formed as XENO- (app. in error for Greek *kenos* vain, empty) + *timē* honour (with ref. to the false supposition that the mineral contained a new metal).]
MINERALOGY. Native yttrium phosphate, occurring in igneous rocks as yellowish brown crystals of the tetragonal system, and often containing other rare-earth elements.

xer- *combining form* see XERO-.

xeranthemum /zɪəˈranθɪməm/ *noun.* M18.
[mod. Latin (see below), formed as XERO- + Greek *anthemon* flower.]
Any of several Mediterranean composite plants constituting the genus *Xeranthemum*, having flower-heads with chaffy pink, purplish, or whitish petal-like bracts; *esp.* the immortelle, *X. annuum*, grown as an everlasting.

xerarch /ˈzɛrɑːk, ˈzɪər-/ *adjective.* E20.
[from XER(O- + Greek *arkhē* beginning, origin.]
ECOLOGY. Of a succession of plant communities: originating in a dry habitat.

Xeres /ˈzɛrɪs, ˈzɪərɪz/ *noun.* Now *rare* or *obsolete.* M17.
[A town in Andalusia, Spain (now Jerez de la Frontera).]
In full ***Xeres sack***, ***Xeres wine***. = SHERRY *noun* 1.

xeric /ˈzɪərɪk, ˈzɛ-/ *adjective.* E20.
[formed as XER(O- + -IC.]
ECOLOGY. Characterized by dry conditions.

xeriscape /ˈzɪərɪskeɪp/ *noun & verb.* Orig. and chiefly *US.* L20.
[from XERI(C + SCAPE *noun*[3].]
► **A** *noun.* A style of landscape design suitable for arid regions, which aims to minimize the need for irrigation and other maintenance by the appropriate choice of plants and other features; a garden or landscape designed in this way.
► **B** *verb trans.* Landscape (an area) in this style.

xero- /ˈzɪərəʊ, ˈzɛrəʊ/ *combining form.* Before a vowel **xer-**.
[Greek *xērо-* combining form of *xēros* dry: see **-O-**.]
Dry, dryness.
■ **xeroˈderma** *noun* (MEDICINE) any of several diseases characterized by excessive dryness of the skin, esp. a mild form of ichthyosis; ***xeroderma pigmentosum*** /pɪgmɛnˈtəʊzəm/, a rare hereditary condition in which skin and eyes are extremely sensitive to the ultraviolet light of the sun because of a fault in the DNA repair mechanism, often leading to cancer: M19. **xeroˈdermatous** *adjective* pertaining to or characteristic of xeroderma L19. **xeromorph** *noun* (BOTANY) a xeromorphic plant M20. **xeromorphic** *adjective* (BOTANY) pertaining to or exhibiting xeromorphy E20. **xeromorphy** *noun* (BOTANY) the possession by a plant in a relatively moist habitat of features characteristic of a xerophilous plant E20. **xerophile** *noun & adjective* (***a***) *noun* (BOTANY) a xerophilous plant; (***b***) *adjective* = XEROPHILOUS: L19. **xeroˈphilic** *adjective* = XEROPHILOUS M20. **xerophilous** /-ˈrɒfɪləs/ *adjective* (BOTANY & ZOOLOGY) adapted to a very dry climate or habitat, or to conditions where moisture is scarce M19. **xeˈrophily** *noun* (BOTANY & ZOOLOGY) the condition or character of being xerophilous E20. **xerophyte** *noun* (BOTANY) a xerophilous plant L19. **xerophytic** /-ˈfɪtɪk/ *adjective* (BOTANY) pertaining to or having the character of a xerophyte, xerophilous L19. **xerophytism** /-ˈrɒfɪtɪz(ə)m/ *noun* (BOTANY) = XEROPHILY E20. **xerosere** *noun* (ECOLOGY) a plant succession originating in a dry habitat E20. **xerostomia** /-ˈstəʊmɪə/ *noun* [Greek *stoma* mouth] MEDICINE excessive dryness of the mouth L19. **xeroˈthermic** *adjective* (BIOLOGY & GEOLOGY etc.) of, pertaining to, or characteristic of a hot, dry climate E20.

xerocopy /ˈzɪərəʊkɒpi, ˈzɛrəʊ-/ *noun.* M20.
[from next + COPY *noun*[1].]
A xerographic copy; a photocopy.
■ **xerocopying** *noun* the action of photocopying by xerography M20.

xerography /zɪəˈrɒgrəfi, zɛ-/ *noun.* M20.
[from XERO- + -GRAPHY, after *photography*.]
A dry copying process in which black or coloured powder adheres to those parts of a surface which remain electrically charged after exposure to light, corresponding to dark regions of an image, a permanent copy being obtained by fusing the powder by heat to a sheet of paper; photocopying.
■ **xeroˈgraphic** *adjective* M20. **xeroˈgraphically** *adverb* M20.

xeroma /zɪəˈrəʊmə, zɛ-/ *noun. rare.* M19.
[from XER(O- + -OMA.]
MEDICINE. = XEROSIS.

xerophagy /zɪəˈrɒfədʒi/ *noun.* M17.
[from XERO- + -PHAGY.]
The eating of dry food only, esp. of food cooked without oil as a form of fasting practised in the early Christian Church.

xerophthalmia /zɪərɒfˈθalmɪə, zɛ-/ *noun.* M17.
[from XER(O- + OPHTHALMIA.]
MEDICINE. Inflammation of the conjunctiva of the eye with abnormal dryness and corrugation, associated esp. with vitamin A deficiency.
■ **xerophthalmic** *adjective* M20.

xeroradiography /ˌzɪərəʊreɪdɪˈɒgrəfi, ˌzɛrəʊ-/ *noun.* M20.
[from XERO- + RADIOGRAPHY.]
A process for obtaining an X-ray picture, in which the X-rays impinge on an electrically charged surface like light in conventional xerography.
■ **xeroˈradiograph** *noun* a radiograph obtained by xeroradiography M20. **xeroradioˈgraphic** *adjective* M20.

xerosis /zɪəˈrəʊsɪs, zɛ-/ *noun.* L19.
[from XERO- + -OSIS.]
MEDICINE. Abnormal dryness, esp. of the skin, conjunctiva, or mucous membranes.

Xerox /ˈzɪərɒks, ˈzɛrɒks/ *noun & verb.* As verb also **x-**. M20.
[from XERO(GRAPHY with arbitrary ending.]
► **A** *noun.* (Proprietary name for) a machine for making copies by xerography; *loosely* a photocopy. M20.
► **B** *verb trans.* Reproduce or copy by xerography; photocopy. M20.

Xhosa /ˈkəʊsə, ˈkɔːsə/ *noun & adjective.* E19.
[Nguni.]
► **A** *noun.* Pl. same, **-s**.
1 A member of a Bantu-speaking people living mainly in Cape Province, South Africa. E19.

2 The language of this people, forming part of the Nguni language group (which also includes Zulu). **L19.**
▶**B** *adjective.* Of or pertaining to this people or their language. **E19.**

xi /ksʌɪ, gzʌɪ, sʌɪ, zʌɪ/ *noun.* **LME.**
[Greek.]
1 The fourteenth letter (Ξ, ξ) of the Greek alphabet. **LME.**
2 PARTICLE PHYSICS. Either of a pair of hyperons (and their antiparticles) having a mass of approximately 1320 MeV, spin of ½, hypercharge −1, isospin ½, and even parity, which on decaying usually produce a lambda particle and a pion. Freq. written Ξ. Also ***xi hyperon, xi particle.*** **M20.**

Xiang /ʃiːˈaŋ/ *noun.* Also **Hsiang. L20.**
[Chinese.]
A dialect of Chinese spoken mainly in Hunan province.

xiphi- /ˈzɪfi/ *combining form.*
[from Greek *xiphos* sword: see -I-.]
ANATOMY & ZOOLOGY. Forming terms relating to sword-shaped objects.
■ **xiphiˈplastral** *adjective & noun* (*a*) *adjective* pertaining to or constituting a xiphiplastron; (*b*) *noun* a xiphiplastron: **L19. xiphiˈplastron** *noun*, pl. **-tra**, each of the hindmost pair of bony plates in the plastron of a turtle **L19. xiphiˈsternal** *adjective* belonging to or constituting a xiphisternum **M19. xiphiˈsternum** *noun*, pl. **-na, -nums**, the posterior or lowest part of the sternum, which is cartilaginous in humans and many animals **M19.**

Xiphias /ˈzɪfɪas/ *noun.* Also †**x-. M17.**
[mod. Latin from Greek, from *xiphos* sword.]
1 ZOOLOGY. The swordfish, *Xiphias gladius*. Now only as mod. Latin genus name. **M17.**
†**2** ASTRONOMY. The constellation Dorado. Only in **18.**
■ **xiphioid** *adjective & noun* (*a*) *adjective* resembling or allied to the swordfish; belonging to the perciform superfamily Xiphioidea, which comprises the swordfish, sailfishes, spearfishes, and marlins; (*b*) *noun* a xiphioid fish: **M19.**

xiphoid /ˈzɪfɔɪd/ *adjective.* **M18.**
[Greek *xiphoeidēs*, from *xiphos* sword: see -OID.]
ANATOMY & ZOOLOGY. Sword-shaped; *esp.* designating an ensiform cartilage or bone.
xiphoid cartilage the xiphisternum in those animals where it is cartilaginous. **xiphoid process** (*a*) the xiphisternum; (*b*) the telson of a horseshoe crab.
■ **xiˈphoidal** *adjective* pertaining to or constituting the xiphoid cartilage or bone **E20.**

xiphopagus /zɪˈfɒpəgəs/ *noun.* Pl. **-gi** /-dʒʌɪ/. **M19.**
[formed as XIPHI- + -O- + Greek *pagos* thing firmly fixed.]
(The condition of) a pair of Siamese twins united by a band extending downwards from the xiphoid cartilage.
■ **xiphopagous** *adjective* **L19.**

xiphosuran /zɪfəʊˈsjʊərən/ *noun & adjective.* **L19.**
[from mod. Latin *Xiphosura* (see below), irreg. from Greek *xiphos* sword + *oura* tail: see -AN.]
ZOOLOGY. ▶**A** *noun.* A chelicerate arthropod of the subclass Xiphosura, which comprises the horseshoe crabs. **L19.**
▶**B** *adjective.* Of, pertaining to, or designating this subclass. **L19.**
■ **xiphosurid** *noun & adjective* (of or pertaining to) a xiphosuran of the family Xiphosuridae, the only family in the subclass Xiphosura **M20.**

X-irradiation /ˈɛksɪreɪdɪˌeɪʃ(ə)n/ *noun.* **M20.**
[Blend of X-RAY and IRRADIATION.]
Irradiation with X-rays. Also, X-radiation.
■ **X-irradiate** *verb trans.* irradiate with X-rays (chiefly as *X-irradiated ppl adjective*) **M20.**

XL *abbreviation.*
Extra large (esp. as a size of clothing).

Xmas /ˈkrɪsməs, ˈɛksməs/ *noun & verb. colloq.* **M16.**
[Abbreviation with *X* for Greek *khi*: see X, X 13.]
▶**A** *noun.* = CHRISTMAS *noun.* **M16.**
▶**B** *verb intrans.* Infl. **-ss-, -s-.** = CHRISTMAS *verb* 2. *rare.* **L19.**
¶ Orig. only a written form.

XML *abbreviation.*
COMPUTING. Extensible Markup Language, a metalanguage which allows users to define their own customized markup languages (esp. in order to display documents on the World Wide Web).

xoanon /ˈzəʊənɒn/ *noun.* Pl. **-ana** /-ənə/. **E18.**
[Greek, rel. to *xein* carve.]
Chiefly GREEK ANTIQUITIES. A primitive simply carved image or statue of a deity, orig. of wood, and often said to have fallen from heaven.

xography /ˈzɒgrəfi/ *noun.* **M20.**
[from *x* (of uncertain meaning, perh. from *parallax*) + -OGRAPHY.]
A photographic process producing stereo pairs of images which are divided into narrow strips, interleaved, and mounted under a plastic sheet embossed with a lens grid to give a three-dimensional effect.
■ **xograph** *noun* an image produced by this process **L20.**

XOR *abbreviation.*
COMPUTING. Exclusive OR (see OR *noun*[2]).

X-radiograph /ˈɛksreɪdɪə(ʊ)grɑːf/ *noun.* **L19.**
[from next + RADIOGRAPH *noun.*]
A radiograph made using X-rays.
■ **X-radiˈography** *noun* **M20.**

X-ray /ˈɛksreɪ/ *noun & verb.* **L19.**
[translating German *x-Strahlen* (pl.), from *Strahl* ray, so called because at the time of discovery in 1895 the nature of the rays was unknown.]
▶**A** *noun.* **1** In *pl.* Electromagnetic radiation of high energy and very short wavelength (between ultraviolet light and gamma rays, *c* 10^{-8}–10^{-11} m), capable of passing through many substances opaque to light, and used in medical diagnosis and treatment and in many methods of analysis. Formerly also called ***Roentgen rays. L19.***
2 (An) examination in which X-rays are passed through a person or object to fall on a photographic plate, showing internal structure (e.g. the position of bones in the body) by the differential absorption of the rays. **M20.**
3 = X-RADIOGRAPH. **M20.**
4 (Without article.) An X-ray department in a hospital. **M20.**

📖 **1** *Cancer Research* Exposure to leukemogenic doses of X-rays. **2** *Daily Telegraph* After a great deal of pain and misery I had an X-ray. **3** *New York Times* Pictures of bones or organs that are far more detailed than X-rays. **4** R. GORDON The cheerful girls in X-ray.

Attrib. & comb.: Esp. in the senses 'using X-rays', as ***X-ray analysis, X-ray microscope, X-ray spectrometer, X-ray spectroscopy, X-ray telescope***, etc.; 'emitting X-rays', as ***X-ray source, X-ray star***, etc.; 'of or pertaining to the (esp. medical) use of X-rays', as ***X-ray department, X-ray room, X-ray table***, etc. Special combs., as **X-ray astronomer** a person engaged in X-ray astronomy; **X-ray astronomy** the branch of astronomy that deals with the X-ray emissions of celestial objects; **X-ray burster** ASTRONOMY a cosmic source of intermittent short-lived powerful bursts of X-rays, which typically last about a second; **X-ray crystallographer** a person engaged in X-ray crystallography; **X-ray crystallography** the study of crystals and their structure by means of the diffraction of X-rays by the regularly spaced atoms of a crystalline material; **X-ray eyes** *fig.* the apparent or supposed ability to see beyond an outward form or through opaque material; very acute discernment; **X-ray spectrum** a graph of intensity against wavelength or frequency for the X-rays absorbed or emitted by a material; **X-ray tube** an electron tube for generating X-rays by accelerating electrons to high energies and causing them to strike a target anode from which X-rays are emitted; **X-ray vision** = *X-ray eyes* above.
▶**B** *verb trans.* Examine, photograph, or treat with X-rays. Also *fig.*, look penetratingly at, examine in great detail. Usu. in *pass.* **L19.**

📖 *Daily Telegraph* Suitcases, parcels and handbags go through the conveyor and their contents are X-rayed. Z. TOMIN She was being X-rayed because of a suspected weak chest.

■ **X-radiation** *noun* X-rays **L19.**

Xtal /ˈkrɪst(ə)l/ *noun.* Also **xtal. M20.**
[Abbreviation: see X, X 14.]
ELECTRONICS & ELECTRICITY. = CRYSTAL *noun.*

xu /suː/ *noun.* Pl. same. **M20.**
[Vietnamese from French *sou*: see SOU.]
A former monetary unit of Vietnam, equal to one-hundredth of a dong.

xyl- *combining form* see XYLO-.

xylan /ˈzʌɪlan/ *noun.* **L19.**
[from XYL(O- + -AN.]
CHEMISTRY. A hemicellulose contained in wood and other plant tissues and formed of long chains of pentose monomers.

xylary /ˈzʌɪləri/ *adjective.* **M20.**
[from XYL(EM + -ARY[1].]
BOTANY. Of, pertaining to, or constituting xylem.

xylem /ˈzʌɪləm/ *noun.* **L19.**
[from Greek *xulon* wood + *-ēma* pass. suffix.]
BOTANY. One of the two chief components of a vascular bundle, which conducts water and dissolved nutrients upwards from the root and also serves as a strengthening tissue, helping to form the woody element in the stem. Cf. PHLOEM.

xylene /ˈzʌɪliːn/ *noun.* **M19.**
[from XYL(O- + -ENE.]
CHEMISTRY. Each of three isomeric volatile liquid hydrocarbons with the formula $C_6H_4(CH_3)_2$, obtainable by distillation of wood, coal tar, and petroleum, and used in fuels, in solvents, and in chemical synthesis; dimethylbenzene. Also, a mixture of these. Also called ***xylol.***
■ **xylenol** /ˈzʌɪlɪnɒl/ *noun* each of five solid toxic isomeric compounds having the formula $C_6H_3(CH_3)_2OH$ (dimethylphenol); a mixture of these: **L19.**

xylidine /ˈzʌɪlɪdiːn/ *noun.* **M19.**
[from XYL(ENE + -IDINE.]
CHEMISTRY. Each of five isomeric amine derivatives of xylene having the formula $C_6H_3(CH_3)_2NH_2$, used in the making and pharmaceuticals.

xylitol /ˈzʌɪlɪtɒl/ *noun.* **L19.**
[from XYL(OSE + -ITOL.]
CHEMISTRY. A sweet-tasting crystalline alcohol, $CH_2OH(CHOH)_3CH_2OH$, derived from xylose, present in some plant tissues and used as an artificial sweetener in foods.

xylo /ˈzʌɪləʊ/ *noun. colloq.* **E20.**
[Abbreviation.]
= XYLONITE.

xylo- /ˈzʌɪləʊ/ *combining form.* Before a vowel **xyl-**.
[Greek *xulo-*, from *xulon* wood: see -O-.]
1 Of, pertaining to, involving, or resembling wood.
2 CHEMISTRY. Derived from or related to xylene or xylose.
■ **xylocaine** *noun* (PHARMACOLOGY, now *rare*) = LIGNOCAINE **M20. xylocopid** /-ˈkəʊpɪd/ *adjective & noun* [Greek *-kopos* -cutting] ENTOMOLOGY (of, pertaining to, or designating) a carpenter bee of the genus *Xylocopa* or family Xylocopidae **E20. xyloˈglucan** *noun* (BIOCHEMISTRY) a hemicellulose composed of chains of glucose residues to which are attached side-chains of xylose residues **M20. xylophage** *noun* (ZOOLOGY) a wood-eating animal, esp. an insect **L19. xylophagous** /zʌɪˈlɒfəgəs/ *adjective* (ZOOLOGY) feeding on wood; boring into and destroying wood: **M19. xylotomist** /-ˈlɒt-/ *noun* an expert in or practitioner of xylotomy **M20. xylotomous** /-ˈlɒt-/ *adjective* (of an insect etc.) that bores or cuts into wood **L19. xylotomy** /-ˈlɒt-/ *noun* the practice or technique of preparing sections of wood for microscopic examination **M20.**

xylobalsamum /zʌɪləʊˈbalsəməm/ *noun.* **M16.**
[Latin from Greek *xulobalsamon*, formed as XYLO-, BALSAM *noun.*]
The fragrant wood of the Arabian tree *Commiphora opobalsamum* (family Burseraceae), which yields the resin called balm of Gilead.

xylography /zʌɪˈlɒgrəfi/ *noun.* **E19.**
[from XYLO- + -GRAPHY.]
The art of making woodcuts or wood-engravings, esp. of an early or primitive kind. Also, printing from wood blocks as distinct from type.
■ **ˈxylograph** *noun & verb* (*a*) *noun* an image cut or engraved on wood; an impression from one, esp. of an early kind; (*b*) *verb trans.* make or reproduce by xylography: **M19. xylographer** *noun* a maker of woodcuts, esp. of the early period **E19. xyloˈgraphic** *adjective* of, pertaining to, or executed by xylography **E19. xylographica** /-ˈgrafɪkə/ *noun pl.* examples of xylography, as woodcuts, block-books, etc. **M20. xyloˈgraphical** *adjective* = XYLOGRAPHIC **E19. xyloˈgraphically** *adverb* by means of xylography **L19. xylographist** *noun* = XYLOGRAPHER **M19.**

xylol /ˈzʌɪlɒl/ *noun.* **M19.**
[from XYL(O- + -OL.]
CHEMISTRY. = XYLENE.

Xylonite /ˈzʌɪlənʌɪt/ *noun.* Also **Z-. M19.**
[from XYLO- + *-n-* + -ITE[1].]
(Proprietary name for) a type of celluloid.

xylophone /ˈzʌɪləfəʊn/ *noun.* **M19.**
[from XYLO- + -PHONE.]
A musical percussion instrument consisting of a graduated series of wooden bars, usu. played by striking with two small round-ended hammers. Now also occas., a similar instrument with metal bars.
■ **xylophonic** /-ˈfɒnɪk/ *adjective* of, pertaining to, or resembling a xylophone **L19. xylophonist** /zʌɪˈlɒfənɪst/ *noun* a person who plays a xylophone **E20.**

xylorimba /ˈzʌɪlərɪmbə/ *noun.* **M20.**
[Blend of prec. and MARIMBA.]
A large xylophone with a range extended to include that of the marimba.

xylose /ˈzʌɪləʊz, -s/ *noun.* **L19.**
[from XYLO- + -OSE[2].]
CHEMISTRY. A pentose (aldose) which occurs widely in plants, esp. as a constituent of xylan. Also called ***wood sugar.***

xylulose /ˈzʌɪljʊləʊz, -s/ *noun.* **M20.**
[from XYLO- + -ULOSE[2].]
CHEMISTRY. A ketase corresponding to the aldose xylose.

xylyl /ˈzʌɪlʌɪl, -ɪl/ *noun.* **M19.**
[from XYLENE + -YL.]
CHEMISTRY. Any of the radicals with the formula C_8H_9·, derived from xylenes.

xysma /ˈzɪzmə/ *noun. rare.* **M19.**
[Greek *xusma* shavings, filings, from *xuein* scrape.]
MEDICINE. Membranous particles in the faeces.

xystus /ˈzɪstəs/ *noun.* Pl. **xysti** /ˈzɪstʌɪ/. Also Anglicized as **xyst. M17.**
[Latin from Greek *xustos* smooth, from *xuein* scrape.]
CLASSICAL ANTIQUITIES. A long covered portico or court used by ancient Greek athletes for exercises. Also, an open colonnade or terrace walk planted with trees and used by the Romans for recreation and conversation.

Yy

Y, y /wʌɪ/.
The twenty-fifth letter of the modern English alphabet and the twenty-second of the ancient Roman one, repr. Greek upsilon, a differentiated form of the early Greek vowel-symbol, now also represented by U and V. Y was originally used in Old English to represent a fronted *u*, which in Middle English merged with short *i*. After the Norman Conquest the fronted *u* was increasingly represented by U, following French orthography, resulting in Y being used as an alternative to I, esp. where legibility might be improved by its use. After the introduction of printing Y gradually became used according to the following conventions: (i) in final position (***fly***, ***family***, ***destroy***); (ii) before *i* in inflectional forms of verbs (***lying***, ***tying***); (iii) in the plural of nouns in -*y* preceded by a vowel as (***boys***, ***rays***, ***alleys***); (iv) in words from Greek, transliterating upsilon (***hymn***). Y was occasionally used as an alternative to *th*-, as in *ye* for *the*, deriving from its similarity when handwritten to þ (thorn) (cf. TH). In Middle English it was also used to represent the letter yogh (ʒ), finally taking its place in all but a few words which dropped it entirely. Pl. **Y's**, **Ys**.

▶**I 1** The letter and its sound.
2 The shape of the letter. ▸**b** A forked clamp or support. ▸**c** In full ***Y moth***. Any of several Eurasian noctuid moths of the genera *Autographa* and *Syngrapha*, which have a pale marking on the forewing resembling the letter Y.

2 Y cross (*a*) a cross in the form of the letter Y, esp. (ECCLESIASTICAL) as an ornamental device on a vestment; (*b*) a piece of piping consisting of three branches diverging at acute angles. **Y-fronts** (proprietary name for) men's or boys' briefs with a Y-shaped seam at the front. **Y junction** a junction at which a road forks into two branches; a junction at which a road joins another at an acute angle. **Y-shaped** *adjective* having a shape or a cross-section like the capital letter Y. **Y track** a short track on a railway at right angles to the main track and connected with it by two switches in opposite directions, used for reversing a locomotive etc. *c silver Y*: see SILVER *noun & adjective*.

▶**II** Symbolical uses.
3 Used to denote serial order; applied e.g. to the twenty-fifth (or often the twenty-fourth, either I or J being omitted) group or section, sheet of a book, etc.
4 a MATH. (Usu. italic *y*.) The second unknown or variable quantity. ▸**b** An unknown or unspecified person or example; (*esp.* in connection with X) the second hypothetical person or example.
5 GEOMETRY etc. (Italic *y*.) A quantity measured along the secondary or vertical axis (ordinate); the second coordinate.
6 GENETICS. (Cap. Y.) Used to denote a sex chromosome which occurs in only one of the sexes (in mammals, the male) or is absent altogether, its presence or absence in the zygote determining in many species the sex of the organism; ***Y-linked***, (determined by a gene) that is carried on the Y chromosome.
7 ZOOLOGY. ***Y organ***, an endocrine gland in decapod crustaceans which secretes the moulting hormone ecdysone.
8 PARTICLE PHYSICS. (Cap. Y.) The hypercharge quantum number of subatomic particles.

5 Y-axis (*a*) (written *y-axis*) the secondary or vertical axis of a system of coordinates, points along which have a value of zero for all other coordinates; (*b*) ELECTRONICS the principal axis of a quartz crystal, joining the midpoints of two of the opposite sides of the hexagonal cross-section. **Y-cut** *adjective* (ELECTRONICS) of, pertaining to, or designating a quartz crystal cut in a plane normal to the Y-axis. **Y-plate** ELECTRONICS either of a pair of electrodes in an oscilloscope that control the vertical movement of the spot on the screen.

▶**III 9** Abbrevs.: **Y** = yen; Yeomanry; (*colloq.*, chiefly *N. Amer.*) a YMCA or YWCA hostel; (CHEMISTRY) yttrium; yuan (monetary unit). **y.** = year(s).

y' *pers. pronoun* see YOU *pronoun & noun*.

y- /ɪ/ *prefix*. *arch.*
[Repr. Old English *ge-*, from Germanic (German, Dutch *ge-*), perh. identical with Latin *co-*: see CO-. Cf. A-⁴, I-¹.]
†**1 a** Forming nouns and adjectives with the senses 'association', 'similarity', 'appropriateness'; forming nouns denoting mutual or collective relation. ▸**b** Forming nouns and verbs with the senses '(attainment of) result, stage in a process'; forming adjectives denoting a state.
2 Forming pa. pples and ppl adjectives, and verbs from verbs.

¶ Y- was largely lost in sense 1 by LME but survived in sense 2 (chiefly in pa. pples and ppl adjectives) as a deliberate archaism, as in *yclad*, *yclept*, *yravish*.

-y /i/ *suffix*¹. Also (after *y*) **-ey**.
[Repr. Old English *-ig*, from Germanic.]
Forming adjectives: (*a*) from nouns, with the senses 'of or pertaining to', 'having the nature, qualities, or appearance of', 'full of', as ***angry***, ***clayey***, ***happy***, ***icy***, ***horsy***, ***messy***, ***milky***, ***tidy***; 'addicted to', as ***booky***, ***boozy***; (chiefly *derog.*) 'having the bad or objectionable qualities of or associated with', as ***beery***, ***churchy***, ***tinny***; (*b*) from (chiefly monsyllabic) adjectives, with the sense 'approaching the quality of, somewhat, rather', as ***bluey***, ***chilly***, ***dusky***, ***haughty***, ***lanky***, ***slippery***; (*c*) from verbs, with the senses 'inclined or apt to', 'giving cause or occasion to', as ***clingy***, ***drowsy***, ***runny***, ***sticky***.

-y /i/ *suffix*² (not productive).
[Repr. Old English *-ian*, corresp. to Old Frisian *-ia*, Old Saxon *ōian*, *ōn*, Old High German, Gothic *ōn* (German *-en*), from Germanic.]
Forming verbs, esp. intransitive verbs derived from adjectives, as ***vinny***.
¶ After Late Middle English only productive in SW dial. as the infinitive ending of a verb used intransitively.

-y /i/ *suffix*³.
[Repr. (partly through Old & mod. French *-ie*) Latin *-ia*, Greek *-eia*, *-ia*: cf. -CY, -ERY, -GRAPHY, -IA¹, -LOGY, -PATHY, -PHILY, -TOMY, etc.]
1 Forming nouns of quality, state, or condition, as ***beggary***, ***courtesy***, ***folly***, ***glory***, ***jealousy***, ***orthodoxy***. ▸**b** *spec.* Forming learned and scientific nouns (after Greek) from adjectives in *-ic* and *-ous*, as ***brachycephaly***, ***metaboly***, ***syntony***.
2 Forming nouns denoting an action or its result, as ***blasphemy***, ***felony***, ***liturgy***, ***victory***; forming nouns with senses 'a collectivity', 'a place where — stay', as ***ewery***, ***family***, ***friary***.

-y /i/ *suffix*⁴.
[Repr. (partly through Anglo-Norman *-ie*) Latin *-ium* as appended to verbal roots.]
Forming nouns denoting an action or its result, as ***colloquy***, ***remedy***, ***subsidy***.

-y /i/ *suffix*⁵.
[Repr. Anglo-Norman, Old French *-e(e)*, (French *-é(e)*), from Latin *-atus*, *-ata*, *-atum*: see -ATE¹, -ATE².]
1 Forming nouns, as ***army***, ***county***, ***deputy***, ***embassy***, ***entry***, ***parley***, ***treaty***.
2 Forming adjectives, as ***easy***, esp. descriptive adjectives in HERALDRY, as ***bendy***, ***fleury***, ***gobony***, ***pily***, ***undy***.

-y /i/ *suffix*⁶. Orig. *Scot.* Also **-ey**.
[Origin unkn. See also -IE.]
Forming nicknames, pet names, and familiar diminutive nouns (occas. adjectives and verbs), as ***Charley***, ***doggy***, ***goody***, ***Johnny***, ***Limey***, ***loony***, ***Mummy***, ***shinny***, ***shorty***, ***Willy***.

-y /i/ *suffix*⁷ (not productive).
[Repr. Old & mod. French *-if*, *-ive* -IVE.]
Forming adjectives, often with (current or obsolete) synonyms in *-ive*, as ***hasty***, ***jolly***, ***tardy***.

Y2K *abbreviation*. *colloq.*
The year 2000.

ya /ja, jə/ *pers. pronoun & possess. adjective*. *colloq.* (chiefly *US*). M20.
[Repr. a pronunc.]
▶**A** *pers. pronoun*. You. M20.
▶**B** *possess. adjective*. Your. M20.

yaas /jas, jɑːs/ *adverb & interjection*. *colloq.* (chiefly *US*). L19.
[Repr. a pronunc. Cf. YAS, YERSE.]
= YES *adverb & interjection*.

yabba /ˈjabə/ *noun*. L19.
[Twi *ayawâ* earthen vessel, dish.]
In Jamaica, a large wooden or earthenware vessel used for cookery or storage.

yabber /ˈjabə/ *verb & noun*. *Austral. & NZ colloq.* M19.
[Aboriginal.]
▶**A** *verb intrans. & trans.* Talk, speak, esp. in an Aboriginal language. M19.
▶**B** *noun*. Talk, chatter; (esp. Aboriginal) speech or language. M19.

yabby /ˈjabi/ *noun & verb*. *Austral.* Also **-ie**. L19.
[Aboriginal.]
▶**A** *noun*. **1** A small edible freshwater crayfish, esp. of the genus *Charax*, found in the eastern part of Australia. L19.
2 = NIPPER *noun* 1d. M20.
▶**B** *verb intrans.* Fish for yabbies. M20.

yaboo /jɑːˈbuː/ *noun*. M18.
[Persian & Urdu *yābū*.]
(An animal of) a breed of large pony found in Afghanistan, Iran, and neighbouring countries.

ya boo *interjection & noun phr.* var. of YAH BOO.

yacca /ˈjakə/ *noun*¹. *W. Indies*. M19.
[Amer. Spanish *yaca* from Taino.]
Either of two podocarps, *Podocarpus coriacea* and *P. purdieana* (also ***yacca tree***); the wood of either of these trees, used esp. in cabinet-work.

yacca /ˈjakə/ *noun*². *Austral.* Also **yakka**. L19.
[Aboriginal.]
Any of various grass-trees (genus *Xanthorrhoea*).

yacca *noun*³ var. of YAKKA *noun*¹.

†**Yache** *noun* var. of YAKÖ.

yacht /jɒt/ *noun & verb*. M16.
[Early mod.Dutch *jaghte* (now *jacht*), from *jaghtschip* fast pirate-ship, from *jag(h)t* hunting (from *jagen* to hunt) + *schip* ship.]
▶**A** *noun*. Orig., a light fast sailing ship, esp. for conveying royal or other important people. Later, any of various (usu. light and comparatively small) vessels propelled by sail or engine; *spec.* (*a*) a small light sailing vessel, *esp.* one equipped for racing; (*b*) an engine-driven vessel of moderate size equipped for cruising. Also (*ellipt.*), a sand-yacht; an ice-yacht. M16.
Comb.: **yacht basin** a dock for mooring yachts, a marina; **yacht broker** a dealer in yachts; **yacht-club**: for owners or sailors of (esp. racing) yachts; **yachtsman** a person, esp. a man, who sails in a yacht, esp. regularly; **yachtsmanship** (skill in) the art or practice of yachting; **yachtswoman** a woman who sails in a yacht, esp. regularly; **yacht-yard**: where yachts are built or repaired.
▶**B** *verb intrans.* Race or cruise in a yacht. Chiefly as ***yachting*** *verbal noun*. M19.
■ **yachter** *noun* a person who sails in a yacht E19. **yachtie** *noun* (*colloq.*, chiefly *Austral. & NZ*) a yachtsman, a yachtswoman M20. **yachty** *adjective* (*colloq.*) of or pertaining to yachts M20.

yack /jak/ *noun*¹. *slang* (chiefly *Criminals'*). Now *rare*. L18.
[Prob. from Romany *ya(c)k* eye.]
A watch.

yack /jak/ *noun*². In sense 2 also **yak**. M19.
[Imit.]
1 Repr. a snapping sound. *rare*. M19.
2 *colloq.* **a** Trivial or unduly persistent talk. Also redupl. **yack yack**. M20. ▸**b** An accent, a tone of voice. M20.

yack /jak/ *verb intrans.* In sense 2 also **yak** (infl. **-kk-**). L19.
[Imit., or from prec.]
1 Make a snapping sound. *rare*. L19.
2 Engage in trivial or unduly persistent talk or conversation; chatter. *colloq.* M20.

yacker /ˈjakə/ *noun*¹. *slang*. Also **yakker**. L19.
[In sense 1 imit.; in sense 2 from prec. + -ER¹.]
1 Talk, conversation, chatter. *Austral.* L19.
2 A chatterbox, a gossip. M20.

yacker *noun*² var. of YAKKA *noun*¹.

yacker /ˈjakə/ *verb intrans.* *slang*. M20.
[from YACK *verb* + -ER⁵.]
= YACK *verb* 2.

yackety-yack /jakɪtɪˈjak/ *noun & verb*. *colloq.* Also **yaketty-yak** (infl. **-kk-**). M20.
[Imit.]
▶**A** *noun*. (The sound of) incessant chatter. M20.
▶**B** *verb intrans.* Chatter incessantly. M20.

yad /jɑːd/ *noun*. E20.
[Hebrew *yād* lit. 'hand'.]
JUDAISM. A pointer used by a reader of the Torah in a synagogue to follow the text, usu. in the form of a rod terminating in a hand with an outstretched index finger.

yada /ˈjɑːdə, ˈjadə/ *noun*. *N. Amer. colloq.* Also **-dd-**. Also redupl. **yada-yada**. M20.
[Imit.]
Trivial, tedious, or meaningless talk or writing; chatter.

> 🕮 J. MCINERNEY The doctor . . gives me this big lecture on AIDS—yada yada yada.

yaffingale /ˈjafɪŋgeɪl/ *noun*. *dial.* E17.
[Imit. (cf. next), with ending after *nightingale*.]
= YAFFLE *noun*.

yaffle /ˈjaf(ə)l/ *noun & verb*. L18.
[Imit. of the bird's call. Cf. YUCKLE.]
▶ **A** *noun*. The green woodpecker, *Picus viridis*. *dial*. L18.
▶ **B** *verb intrans*. Of a green woodpecker: utter its characteristic call. L19.

yag /jag/ *noun*. Also **YAG**. M20.
[Acronym, from yttrium aluminium garnet.]
A synthetic crystal of yttrium aluminium garnet, used in certain lasers and as an imitation diamond in jewellery.

yagé /ˈjɑːʒeɪ, *foreign* jaˈxɛ/ *noun*. E20.
[Amer. Spanish.]
An Amazonian liana, *Banisteriopsis caapi* (family Malpighiaceae), used by the Indians to make a hallucinogenic drink; this drink.

yager /ˈjeɪɡə/ *noun*¹. *US*. E19.
[App. Anglicized from German JÄGER. Cf. JAEGER *noun*².]
A type of short-barrelled large-bore rifle formerly used in the southern states of the US. Also *yager rifle*.

yager *noun*², **yagger** *noun* vars. of JAGGER *noun*².

†**Yaghan** *noun* see YAHGAN.

Yaghnobi /jɑːɡˈnəʊbi/ *noun & adjective*. Pl. of noun same, -S. M20.
[Yaghnobi.]
(Of) the modern Iranian language of a people inhabiting parts of Tajikistan, descended from a dialect of Sogdian; (a member) of this people.

Yagi /ˈjɑːɡi/ *noun*. M20.
[Hidetsugu *Yagi* (1886–1976), Japanese electrical engineer.]
BROADCASTING. In full *Yagi aerial*. A highly directional aerial that receives or transmits within a narrow frequency band, consisting of a number of short rods mounted transversely on an insulating support.

yagna *noun* var. of YAJNA.

yah /jɑː/ *noun*. *colloq. derog*. L20.
[from next.]
An upper-class person.

yah /jɑː/ *adverb & interjection*¹. *non-standard*. M19.
[Repr. an affected pronunc. Cf. YEAH, YEH.]
= YES *adverb & interjection*.

yah /jɑː/ *interjection*². E17.
[Natural exclam.]
Expr. disgust, aversion, derision, or defiance.

yah boo /jɑː ˈbuː/ *interjection & noun*. *slang*. Also **ya boo**. E20.
[from YAH *interjection*² + BOO *interjection*.]
▶ **A** *interjection*. Orig. among children: expr. scorn or derision. E20.
▶ **B** *noun*. An utterance of 'yah boo!'. E20.

Yahgan /ˈjɑːɡ(ə)n/ *noun & adjective*. Also (earlier) †**Yaghan**. Pl. of noun same, -S. L19.
[Local name.]
A member of, of or pertaining to, an indigenous people of Tierra del Fuego, found in the southernmost part of the islands; (of) the language of this people.

yahoo /ˈjɑːhuː, jəˈhuː/ *noun & verb*. M18.
[An imaginary race of brutish creatures resembling human beings in Swift's *Gulliver's Travels*. In sense A.2 perh. a different word.]
▶ **A** *noun*. **1** A coarse bestial person; a lout, a hooligan. M18.
2 A large hairy manlike monster supposedly inhabiting eastern Australia. Cf. YOWIE *noun*. *Austral*. M19.
▶ **B** *verb intrans*. Behave like a yahoo. M19.
■ **yahooism** *noun* style or behaviour characteristic of a yahoo M19.

yahoo /jɑːˈhuː, jaˈhuː/ *interjection*. L20.
[Natural exclam.]
Expr. exuberance or excitement.

yahrzeit /ˈjɑːtsʌɪt/ *noun*. M19.
[Yiddish from Middle High German *jarzît* anniversary, from Old High German *jar* (German *Jahr*) year + *zît* (German *Zeit*) time.]
JUDAISM. The anniversary of the death of a person, esp. a parent.

Yahudi /jəˈhuːdi/ *noun & adjective*. Now chiefly *US slang*. Also **Ye-**. E19.
[Hebrew *yĕhūḏī*, Arab. *yahūdī*.]
▶ **A** *noun*. Pl. **-dim** /-dɪm/, **-dis**. A Jew. E19.
▶ **B** *attrib*. or as *adjective*. Jewish. E19.

Yahweh /ˈjɑːweɪ/ *noun*. Also (now *rare*) **-veh** /-veɪ/; **Jahveh** /ˈjɑːveɪ/. M19.
[Hebrew *YHWH*, with added vowels generally thought by scholars to represent the most likely vocalization of the Tetragrammaton.]
(The personal name of) God in the Old Testament and Hebrew Scriptures. Cf. JEHOVAH, ELOHIM.

Yahwism /ˈjɑːwɪz(ə)m/ *noun*. Also **Jahvism** /ˈjɑːvɪz(ə)m/ L19.
[from prec. + -ISM.]
The religion associated with the worship of Yahweh; the use of 'Yahweh' as a name for God.
■ **Yahwist** *noun* the postulated author or authors of the parts of the Pentateuch in which God is regularly called 'Yahweh' (cf. ELOHIST, JEHOVIST 2) L19. **Yahˈwistic** *adjective* of, pertaining to, or characteristic of Yahwism or the Yahwist L19.

yair /jɛː/ *adverb*. *Austral. colloq*. M20.
[Repr. a pronunc.]
= YEAH *adverb*.

yajna /ˈjʌdʒnjə/ *noun*. Also **yagna**. E19.
[Sanskrit *yajña* worship, sacrifice.]
In Hinduism, a sacrificial rite with a specific objective, often involving the burning of substantial offerings.

yak /jak/ *noun*¹. L18.
[Tibetan *gyag*.]
A heavily built domesticated ox, *Bos grunniens*, with long shaggy hair and a humped back, kept in the uplands of central Asia for its milk and soft dense underfur, and as a pack animal. Also, a rare wild animal ancestral to this, *B. mutus*, found high on the Tibetan plateau.

yak *noun*², *verb* see YACK *noun*², *verb*.

yakdan /ˈjakdan/ *noun*. E19.
[Persian *yakdān* ice-house, portmanteau, from *yak* ice + *-dān* denoting a holder or container.]
In Iran (or Persia): a trunk, a portmanteau.

yakety-yak *noun & verb* var. of YACKETY-YACK.

Yakima /ˈjakɪmə/ *noun & adjective*. M19.
[Sahaptin.]
▶ **A** *noun*. Pl. same, -S.
1 A member of a N. American Indian people of south central Washington State. M19.
2 The Sahaptin language of the Yakima. M20.
▶ **B** *attrib*. or as *adjective*. Of or pertaining to the Yakima or their language. M19.

yakitori /jakɪˈtɔːri/ *noun*. M20.
[Japanese, from *yaki* toasting, grilling + *tori* bird.]
A Japanese dish consisting of pieces of chicken grilled on a skewer.

yakka /ˈjakə/ *noun*¹. *Austral. slang*. Also **yacca**, **yacker**. L19.
[Aboriginal.]
Work, toil. Esp. in *hard yakka*.

yakka *noun*² var. of YACCA *noun*².

yakka *noun*³ var. of YAKKHA.

yakker *noun* var. of YACKER *noun*¹.

yakkha /ˈjʌkə/ *noun*. Also **yakka**, (esp. in sense 2) **Y-**. M19.
[Pali.]
1 INDIAN MYTHOLOGY. = YAKSHA. M19.
2 = VEDDA. M19.

Yakö /ˈjɑːkəʊ, -ɔː/ *noun & adjective*. Also †**Yache**. Pl. of noun same. E20.
[Niger-Congo.]
Of or pertaining to, a member of, a Nigerian people centred on the town of Umor in the Cross River region.

yaksha /ˈjʌkʃə/ *noun*. L18.
[Sanskrit *yakṣa*.]
INDIAN MYTHOLOGY. (A statue or carving of) any of a class of demigods or nature spirits often serving as tutelary guardians, *esp*. one ministering to Kubera, the Hindu god of wealth.

Yakut /jaˈkʊt/ *noun & adjective*. M18.
[Russian from Yakut.]
▶ **A** *noun*. Pl. **-s**, same.
1 A member of a Mongolian people of NE Siberia. M18.
2 The Turkic language of this people. E20.
▶ **B** *attrib*. or as *adjective*. Of or pertaining to the Yakuts or their language. M19.

yakuza /jəˈkuːzə/ *noun*. Pl. same. M20.
[Japanese, from *ya* eight + *ku* nine + *za* three, with ref. to the worst kind of hand in a gambling game.]
A Japanese gangster or racketeer. Usu. *pl*., such gangsters etc. collectively.

Yale /jeɪl/ *adjective & noun*. M19.
[Linus Yale, Jr. (1821–68), US locksmith, the inventor.]
▶ **A** *attrib. adjective*. (Proprietary name designating) (a component of) a type of cylinder lock operated by means of a flat key with a specially serrated edge inserted so as to displace a number of pins by the correct distances. M19.
▶ **B** *noun ellipt*. A Yale lock or key. E20.

yali /jəˈliː/ *noun*. L19.
[Turkish *yali* shore from mod.Greek *gialo* shoreline from Greek *gialos* seashore.]
A large wooden house of a type once common on the shores of the Bosphorus.

Yalie /ˈjeɪli/ *noun*. *US colloq*. M20.
[from *Yale* (see below) + -IE.]
A student or graduate of Yale University.

y'all /jɔːl/ *noun*. *US dial*. Also **yall**. E20.
[Contr.]
You all; you (sing. & pl.).

> P. BAKER You guys smell and look like y'all been dipped in a cess pit. R. OLVER Well brother, how y'all doin'?

yaller *noun, adjective* see YELLOW *noun, adjective*.

yam /jam/ *noun*¹. L16.
[Portuguese *inhame* or Spanish †*iñame* (mod. *ñame*), prob. of W. African origin (cf. Fulani *nyami* eat).]
1 Any of various chiefly tropical vines constituting the genus *Dioscorea* (family Dioscoreaceae), which are grown for their edible starchy tubers, esp. (in SE Asia) *D. alata* and (in W. Africa) *D. × cayenensis* (more fully ***yellow yam***); the root of such a plant used as food. L16.
2 A variety of the sweet potato, *Ipomoea batatas*. *N. Amer*. L18.
3 A large coarse variety of potato. *Scot. obsolete* exc. *dial*. E19.
Comb.: **yam-bean** any of several leguminous plants which have edible tubers as well as edible pods, *esp*. the Central American *Pachyrhizus erosus*; **yam house** a building for storing yams; **yam potato** = sense 2 above; **yam-stick** *Austral*. a long sharpened stick used by Australian Aborigines for digging and as a weapon.

†**yam** *noun*². *rare*. M16–E19.
[Russian, ult. from Persian *yām* post-horse, post-house.]
A (Russian) post-house.

Yamasee /ˈjaməsiː/ *noun & adjective*. Also **-assee**. L17.
[Creek *yamasi* tame, gentle.]
Hist. ▶ **A** *noun*. Pl. same, -S. A member of a N. American Indian people of S. Carolina and Georgia. L17.
▶ **B** *attrib*. or as *adjective*. Of or pertaining to the Yamasee. M18.

Yamato-e /jaˈmatəʊeɪ/ *noun*. L19.
[Japanese, from *Yamato* Japan + *e* picture.]
The style or school of art in Japan which culminated in the 12th and 13th centuries and dealt with Japanese subjects in a distinctively Japanese (rather than Chinese) way.

Yami /ˈjɑːmi/ *noun & adjective*. E20.
[Yami.]
▶ **A** *noun*. Pl. same, -S.
1 A member of a people inhabiting the island of Botel-Tobago, north of the Batan Islands in the Philippines. E20.
2 The Austronesian language of this people. M20.
▶ **B** *attrib*. or as *adjective*. Of or pertaining to the Yami or their language. M20.

yammer /ˈjamə/ *noun*. Orig. *Scot*. E16.
[from the noun.]
Yammering, an instance of this, (*Scot. & dial.*); *colloq*. a loud noise, a din, *esp*. voluble talk.

yammer /ˈjamə/ *verb*. *colloq*. LME.
[Alt. of YOMER *verb* after Middle Dutch, Middle Low German *jammeren*.]
1 a *verb intrans*. Lament, mourn; cry out or howl in distress, wail; whine, whimper. *obsolete* exc. *Scot. & dial*. LME. ▶**b** *verb trans*. Utter complainingly, grumble. L18. ▶**c** *verb intrans*. Complain, grumble. E19.
2 *verb intrans*. Make a loud noise or din; yell, shout; talk volubly. E16.
3 *verb intrans*. Long, yearn, crave. *obsolete* exc. *Scot. & dial*. E18.

> **2** C. SANDBURG They banged their spoons . . on the table And went on yammering for more to eat.

■ **yammerer** *noun* L19.

†**Yampai** *noun* see YAVAPAI.

yamstchik /ˈjamstʃɪk/ *noun*. M18.
[Russian *yamshchik*, formed as YAM *noun*².]
Hist. The driver of a post-horse in Russia etc.

Yana /ˈjɑːnə/ *noun & adjective*. L19.
[Yana *ya·na* person, people.]
▶ **A** *noun*. Pl. same, -S. A member of a N. American Indian people of northern California; the Hokan language of this people. L19.
▶ **B** *attrib*. or as *adjective*. Of or pertaining to the Yana or their language. M20.

yandy /ˈjandi/ *noun & verb*. *Austral*. E20.
[Aboriginal.]
▶ **A** *noun*. A long shallow oval dish used for separating seeds etc. or particles of ore from refuse. E20.
▶ **B** *verb trans. & intrans*. Separate (grass seed) *from* refuse by shaking in a yandy; separate (ore) similarly or by winnowing. E20.

yang /jaŋ/ *noun & adjective*. L17.
[Chinese *yáng* sun, positive, male genitals.]
▶ **A** *noun*. In Chinese philosophy, the male or active principle of the two opposing forces of the universe. Cf. YIN *noun*¹. L17.
▶ **B** *attrib*. or as *adjective*. That represents yang; masculine. L17.
Comb.: **yang-yin** = *yin-yang* s.v. YIN *noun*¹ & *adjective*¹.

yangban /ˈjaŋban/ *noun.* Pl. **-s**, same. L19.
[Korean, *ˈyangpan*, from *ˈyang* both, a pair + *pan* social class.]
A member of the former ruling class in Korea.

yang ch'in /jaŋ ˈtʃɪn/ *noun phr.* L19.
[Chinese *yángqín*, from *yáng* high-sounding, foreign + *qín* (Wade–Giles *ch'in*) musical instrument, zither.]
A Chinese dulcimer.

yanggona /jaŋˈgəʊnə/ *noun.* Also **yaqona**. M19.
[Fijian *yaqona*.]
= KAVA.

Yang–Mills /jaŋˈmɪlz/ *noun.* M20.
[from C. N. *Yang* (b. 1922), Chinese-born US physicist + R. L. *Mills* (b. 1927), US physicist.]
PHYSICS. Used *attrib.* with ref. to a class of gauge theories with non-abelian gauge invariance.

Yang Shao /jaŋ ˈʃaʊ/ *noun & adjective.* E20.
[See below.]
ARCHAEOLOGY. (Designating or pertaining to) a neolithic Chinese culture (*c* 5000–3000 BC), evidence of which was first discovered at Yang Shao, a village in the Henan province of China.

Yank /jaŋk/ *noun[1] & adjective. colloq.* (freq. *derog.*). L18.
[Abbreviation of YANKEE.]
▶ **A** *noun.* **1** = YANKEE *noun* 1a. *US.* L18.
2 A native or inhabitant of the United States, an American; = YANKEE *noun* 1b. L19.
▶ **B** *attrib.* or as *adjective.* = AMERICAN *adjective* 2. M19.
Yank tank *Austral. slang* a large American car.

yank /jaŋk/ *noun[2]. colloq.* L18.
[Rel. to next.]
1 A sudden sharp blow, esp. with the hand. *Scot.* L18.
2 A sudden vigorous pull, a jerk. Orig. *US.* L19.

📖 **2** *Sport* Finley . . opens the clubhouse door with an angry yank.

yank /jaŋk/ *verb. colloq.* (orig. *dial.* & *US*). E19.
[Origin unkn. Cf. prec.]
1 *verb intrans.* Pull or jerk vigorously (*at* something). E19.
2 *verb trans.* Pull with a jerk. E19. ▸**b** Withdraw (a theatrical show, an advertisement, etc.); cancel. *US.* M20.

📖 **1** W. KOTZWINKLE Twiller jumped after him, yanking at the . . door of the car and opening it. **2** C. MCCULLOUGH Fee's . . arm yanked the brush ruthlessly through knots and tangles. *fig.*: J. I. M. STEWART I had to yank him out of Oxford—a shocking place.

Yankee /ˈjaŋki/ *noun & adjective. colloq.* (orig. *US*). M18.
[Perh. from Dutch *Janke* dim. of *Jan* John. Recorded in L17 as nickname.]
▶ **A** *noun.* **1 a** A native or inhabitant of New England or of any of the Northern States (*US*); US HISTORY a Federal soldier in the Civil War. M18. ▸**b** A native or inhabitant of the United States, an American. Freq. *derog.* L18.
2 The dialect of New England; *loosely*. American English generally. E19.
3 Whisky sweetened with molasses. *US local.* E19.
4 In *pl.* American stocks or securities. L19.
5 *ellipt.* = ***Yankee jib*** below. E20.
6 A composite bet on four or more horses to win or be placed in different races. M20.
▶ **B** *adjective.* That is a Yankee; of, pertaining to, or characteristic of a Yankee or Yankees; *loosely* pertaining to the United States, American. L18.
Special collocations & comb.: **Yankee bet** = sense A.6 above. **Yankee bond** a dollar bond issued in the US by an overseas borrower. **Yankee Doodle** (*a*) a popular American tune and song regarded as characteristically national; (*b*) = sense A.1 above. **Yankee jib (topsail)** a large jib topsail used in light winds, set on the topmast stay. **Yankee-land** (*a*) *US* New England; (*b*) the United States. **Yankee notions** small wares or useful articles made in New England or the Northern States. **Yankee State** *US* Ohio.
▪ **Yankeedom** *noun* (*rare*) (*a*) the United States; (*b*) Yankees collectively: M19. **Yankeeish** *adjective* characteristic of or resembling a Yankee M19. **Yankeeism** *noun* (*a*) Yankee character or style; (*b*) a Yankee characteristic or idiom: E19. **Yankeeize** *verb trans.* give a Yankee character to M19.

Yankton /ˈjaŋkt(ə)n/ *noun & adjective.* Also (earlier) †**H-**. L17.
[Dakota *ihanketonwan* lit. 'end village'.]
▶ **A** *noun.* Pl. **-s**, same.
1 A member of a Siouan people of the Great Plains of North and South Dakota, related to the Yanktonais. L17.
2 The language of this people. L19.
▶ **B** *attrib.* or as *adjective.* Of or pertaining to the Yanktons or their language. M19.

Yanktonai /ˈjaŋktənʌɪ/ *noun & adjective.* L18.
[Dakota *ihanketonwanna* lit. 'little end village'.]
▶ **A** *noun.* Pl. **-s**, same.
1 A member of a Siouan people of the Great Plains of North and South Dakota, related to the Yanktons. L18.
2 The language of this people. L20.
▶ **B** *attrib.* or as *adjective.* Of or pertaining to the Yanktonais or their language. E20.

Yanomami /ˈjanəmaːmi/ *noun & adjective.* Also **-mamö** /-maːməʊ/ & other vars. M20.
[Yanomami, from *yanoman* pl. of *yanan* person.]
▶ **A** *noun.* Pl. same. A member of a S. American Indian people inhabiting parts of southern Venezuela and northern Brazil; the Chibchan language of this people. M20.
▶ **B** *attrib.* or as *adjective.* Of or pertaining to the Yanomami or their language. M20.

Yanqui /ˈjaŋki/ *adjective & noun.* E20.
[Spanish.]
Esp. in Latin American contexts: = YANKEE *noun* 1b, *adjective.*

yantra /ˈjantrə/ *noun.* L19.
[Sanskrit = device or mechanism for holding or fastening, from *yam* hold, support.]
A geometrical diagram used as an aid to meditation in tantric worship; any object used similarly.

Yao /jaʊ/ *noun[1] & adjective[1].* Pl. of noun same. M19.
[Chinese *Yáo* lit. 'precious jade'.]
Of or pertaining to, a member of, a mountain-dwelling people of the Guangxi, Hunan, Yunnan, Guangdong, and Guizhou provinces of China and northern parts of Vietnam; (of) the language of this people.

Yao /jaʊ/ *noun[2] & adjective[2].* Pl. of noun same, **-s**. L19.
[Bantu.]
Of or pertaining to, a member of, a Bantu-speaking people found east and south of Lake Nyasa in E. Africa; (of) the language of this people.

yaourt /ˈjaʊət/ *noun.* Now *rare* or *obsolete.* E19.
[Repr. pronunc. of Turkish *yoğurt* YOGHURT.]
Yoghurt.

yap /jap/ *noun.* E17.
[Imit. Cf. YAP *verb.*]
1 a A dog that barks sharply, shrilly, or fussily. *obsolete* exc. *dial.* E17. ▸**b** A short sharp bark or cry. Also as *interjection.* E19.
2 A fool, *esp.* a dupe; an uncultured or unsophisticated person. *dial.* & *US slang.* L19.
3 a The mouth. *slang* (orig. *US*). E20. ▸**b** Idle or loquacious talk; tiresome or insistent chatter. *colloq.* E20. ▸**c** A chat. *slang.* M20.

📖 **1b** C. FREMLIN Snatches of loud music . . a strident yap of laughter. **3a** J. WAIN The money's paid . . the kidnapped person gets back home . . and nobody opens their yap.

yap /jap/ *adjective.* Chiefly *Scot.* & *north.* LME.
[Alt. of YEPE.]
1 Clever, cunning; shrewd, astute; nimble, active. LME.
2 Eager, ready, (*to do*). LME.
3 Hungry. E18.
▪ **yaply** *adverb* (*obsolete* exc. *Scot.*) LME. **yapness** *noun* (*rare*) E19.

yap /jap/ *verb intrans.* Infl. **-pp-**. M17.
[Imit. Cf. YAP *noun*, YAWP.]
1 Bark sharply, shrilly, or fussily; yelp. M17.
2 *transf.* Speak snappishly or complainingly; talk loudly, foolishly, or loquaciously; chatter. Orig. *Scot.* E19.
▪ **yapper** *noun* a dog or person that yaps E19.

yapok /ˈjapɒk/ *noun.* Also **-ock**. E19.
[from the River *Oyapock*, which runs from Brazil into French Guiana.]
A semi-aquatic central and S. American opossum, *Chironectes minimus*, which has grey fur with dark bands. Also called ***water opossum***.

yapon *noun* var. of YAUPON.

yapp /jap/ *noun.* L19.
[William *Yapp* (1854–75), owner of London bible warehouse, for whom it was first produced.]
A style of bookbinding with a limp leather cover projecting to overlap the edges of the leaves.
▪ **yapped** *adjective* (of a binding) made in this style L19.

yappet /ˈjapɪt/ *verb intrans. rare.* L17.
[Frequentative of YAP *verb.*]
= YAP *verb* 1. Chiefly as ***yappeting*** *ppl adjective.*

yappy /ˈjapi/ *adjective.* E20.
[from YAP *noun* or *verb.*]
Inclined to yap; of the nature of a yap or sharp bark.

yaqona *noun* var. of YANGGONA.

Yaqui /ˈjaki/ *noun & adjective.* E19.
[Spanish from earlier *Hiaquis* (pl.) from Yaqui *Hiaki*.]
▶ **A** *noun.* Pl. same, **-s**.
1 A member of an American Indian people of NW Mexico. E19.
2 The Uto-Aztecan language of this people. E20.
▶ **B** *attrib.* or as *adjective.* Of or pertaining to the Yaqui or their language. M19.

yar /jɑː/ *verb intrans.* Long *obsolete* exc. *dial.* Infl. **-rr-**. ME.
[Imit.]
Esp. of a dog: snarl, growl.

yarak /ˈjarak/ *noun.* M19.
[Perh. from Persian *yārakī* power, strength, ability, or from Turkish *yarağ* readiness, right heat for tempering metal.]
FALCONRY. Fit and proper condition (of a hawk) for hunting. Only in ***in yarak***.

yarborough /ˈjɑːb(ə)rə/ *noun.* E20.
[App. from an Earl of *Yarborough* said to have bet 1000 to 1 against the occurrence of such a hand.]
CARDS. In whist and bridge, a hand with no card above a nine.

yard /jɑːd/ *noun[1].*
[Old English *ġeard*, corresp. to Old Frisian *garda*, Old Saxon *gardo*, Old High German *gart* (Dutch *gaard*, German *Garten* garden), Old Norse *garðr*, Gothic *gards*, house *gards* enclosure, stall, from Germanic base rel. to Old Church Slavonic *gradŭ* city, garden, Russian *gorod* town. Cf. GARDEN *noun*, GARTH *noun[1]*, ORCHARD.]
†**1** A building, a house, a home. Only in OE.
†**2** A region, a land. Only in OE.
3 A usu. small uncultivated area adjoining or enclosed by a house or other building; *esp.* one surrounded by walls or buildings within the precincts of a house, castle, inn, etc. Later also *spec.* (*a*) a school playground; (*b*) (esp. in proper names) = COURT *noun[1]* 4; (*c*) *US* the area enclosed by the main buildings of a college campus. OE.
4 The garden of a private house. Now *dial., N. Amer., & Austral.* ME.
5 A piece of enclosed ground set apart for a particular purpose (freq. with specifying word); *spec.* (*a*) an enclosure on a farm, forming a pen for cattle or poultry, a storing place for hay etc., or containing a barn or similar building; (*b*) *ellipt.* = ***railway-yard*** s.v. RAILWAY *noun*; (*c*) an enclosed area in the precincts of a prison where prisoners may take exercise; (*d*) *Austral.* an enclosure for the sale of cars. ME.
6 An area in which moose and deer congregate, esp. during the winter months. *N. Amer.* E19.
3 ***backyard***, ***castle yard***, ***courtyard***, ***palace yard***, ***stable-yard***, etc. **5** ***brickyard***, ***dockyard***, ***exercise yard***, ***shipyard***, ***timber-yard***, ***vineyard***, etc.
Phrases: **the Yard** (*a*) = SCOTLAND YARD; (*b*) *US* the quadrangle formed by the original college buildings at Harvard University. **the Yards** *US* the stockyards where cattle are collected for slaughter, esp. in Chicago.
Comb.: **yard-dog** a watchdog kept in the yard of a house; **yard-grass** a low tropical grass, *Eleusine indica*, with digitate spikes, a common weed in parts of the US; **yard-man** *noun[1]* (*a*) a person in charge of or working in a yard, esp. a railway-yard or a timber-yard; (*b*) *US* a gardener; a person employed to do various outdoor jobs; **yard sale** *N. Amer.* a sale of miscellaneous second-hand items held in the garden of a private house; **yardsman** = ***yard-man*** above; **yardswoman** a woman in charge of or employed in a yard.
▪ **yardage** *noun[1]* (a charge for) the use of a yard for storage etc. M19. **yardful** *noun* as much or as many as a yard will hold M19.

yard /jɑːd/ *noun[2].*
[Old English *ġerd* = Old Frisian *jerde*, Old Saxon *gerdia* switch, *segalgerd* sailyard (Dutch *gard* twig, rod), Old High German *gart(e)a*, *gerta* (German *Gerte*), from West Germanic.]
▶ **I 1** NAUTICAL. A long spar (usually cylindrical and tapering to each end) slung at its centre from and forward of a mast for a square sail to hang from. OE.
†**2** A straight slender shoot or branch of a tree; a twig. OE–LME.
3 A staff, a stick, a rod; *spec.* (*a*) a shepherd's walking-stick; (*b*) a rod used for administering punishment; *fig.* punishment, chastisement; (*c*) a rod, wand, or staff carried as a symbol of authority or office; (*d*) a rod or stick three feet long, used for measuring. Long *rare* or *obsolete* OE.
1 ***jackyard***, ***main-yard***, ***mizzen yard***, ***spritsail yard***, etc.
▶ **II** Measure.
4 †**a** In full ***yard of land***. = YARDLAND 1. OE–E17. ▸**b** A former measure of area for land, equal to a quarter of an acre. Cf. ROOD *noun* 5a. Now *rare* or *obsolete.* LME.
5 A unit of linear measure equal to 16½ feet (5.0292 m) but varying locally. Also ***land-yard***. Now *rare.* OE.
6 The traditional English unit of length and distance, divided into three feet and 36 inches, and formerly defined legally by means of a metal bar or rod and now as 0.9144 metre exactly; a quantity of fabric etc. of this length. OE. ▸**b** A great length or amount. Usu. in *pl.* LME. ▸**c** A square or cubic yard of something; *spec.* (BUILDING) a cubic yard of sand. M19.

📖 **6** *Law Times* The railway line . . was perfectly straight for a distance of over 700 yards. *Yankee* She bought a few yards of quilted fabric. **b** H. JAMES He had a face a yard long; I wondered what ailed him. *Listener* We have heard anti-Wagnerian criticism before—academic traditionalists wrote yards of it.

▶ **III 7** The penis. Now *coarse slang.* LME.
8 One hundred dollars; a bill for this amount. *US slang.* E20.
Phrases: ***all wool and a yard wide***: see WOOL *noun* 2. **by the yard** *fig.* at great length; in vast quantities. **cubic yard** the volume

equal to that of a cube with edges three feet in length. **square yard** the area equal to that of a square with sides three feet in length. **yard of ale** (the contents of) a deep slender beer glass about a yard long and holding two to three pints.

Comb.: **yard-man** *noun*² (NAUTICAL) a sailor occupied on specified yards; **yard-measure** a three-foot rod, bar, or tape for measuring; **yard-rope** NAUTICAL †(*a*) in *pl.*, the permanent rigging of a yard; (*b*) a rope attached to a ship's yard; **yardstick** (*a*) a three-foot rod for measuring; (*b*) *fig.* a standard used for comparison; **yard-wand** (now *rare* or *obsolete*) = ***yardstick*** (a) above.

■ **yardage** *noun*² (*a*) (now *rare* or *obsolete*) the cutting of coal at a fixed rate per yard; (*b*) an amount or distance measured in yards: L19.

yard /jɑːd/ *verb*¹ *trans.* M17.

[from YARD *noun*². In sense 1 translating Manx *slattys*, from *slat* rod, wand of authority.]

1 *Hist.* In the Isle of Man, summon for hiring. M17.

2 Provide with sailyards. L17.

yard /jɑːd/ *verb*². M18.

[from YARD *noun*¹.]

1 *verb trans.* **a** Pen (*up*) or enclose (cattle etc.) in a yard. M18. ▸**b** Store (corn, wood, etc.) in a yard. Chiefly *N. Amer.* M18.

2 *verb intrans.* Of moose etc.: resort to winter quarters. *N. Amer.* M19.

■ **yarder** *noun* (*a*) *Austral.* a person who yards animals; (*b*) *N. Amer.* a kind of donkey engine used in logging: L19. **yarding** *noun* (*a*) the action of the verb; (*b*) (the cost of) storage in a yard: M19.

yardang /ˈjɑːdaŋ/ *noun.* E20.

[Turkish, abl. of *yar* cleft, precipice.]

PHYSICAL GEOGRAPHY. A sharp irregular ridge of sand etc., lying in the direction of the prevailing wind in exposed desert regions and formed by the wind erosion of adjacent less resistant material.

yard-arm /ˈjɑːdɑːm/ *noun.* L15.

[from YARD *noun*² + ARM *noun*¹.]

NAUTICAL. Either end of a ship's yard; the part of either end of a yard which is outside the sheave-hole.

when the sun is over the yard-arm *slang* at the time of day when it is permissible to begin drinking. **yard-arm and yard-arm**, **yard-arm to yard-arm** (of two ships) so close to one another that their yard-arms touch or cross.

Comb.: **yard-arm iron** a metal ring attached to each yard-arm to house the studding-sail boom.

yardbird /ˈjɑːdbəːd/ *noun. US slang.* M20.

[from YARD *noun*¹ + BIRD *noun*, perh. after *jailbird*.]

1 MILITARY. A new recruit. Also, a soldier under discipline for a misdemeanour, *esp.* one assigned to menial tasks. M20.

2 A convict. M20.

yardland /ˈjɑːdland/ *noun. obsolete* exc. *Hist.* LME.

[Contr. of *yard of land*, from YARD *noun*² + LAND *noun*¹.]

1 A measure of land usually equal to 30 acres but varying locally; a quarter of a hide. LME.

†**2** = YARD *noun*² 4b. M16–L17.

■ **yardlander** *noun* a holder of a yardland L19.

yare /jɛː/ *adjective & adverb.* Now *arch.* & *dial.*

[Old English *gearu* = Old Saxon *garu* (Dutch *gaar* done, dressed, clever), Old High German *garo* (German *gar* ready, prepared), Old Norse *gǫrr*, *gorv* ready-made, prompt, skilled from Germanic. Cf. GAR *verb*.]

▶**A** *adjective.* **1** Ready, prepared. OE.

2 Alert, nimble, active, brisk, quick. ME. ▸**b** Of a ship: moving lightly and easily; answering readily to the helm; easily manageable. LME.

▶**B** *adverb.* †**1** Without delay, promptly, immediately; soon. OE–E16.

†**2** Well, thoroughly; certainly, plainly. OE–E16.

3 Chiefly NAUTICAL. Used as imper.: be quick! *arch.* E17.

■ **yarely** *adverb* = YARE *adverb* OE.

yark *verb & noun* var. of YERK.

Yarkand /ˈjɑːkand, jɑːˈkand/ *noun.* L19.

[A city and district in the autonomous region of Sinkiang Uigur in western China.]

1 Used *attrib.* to designate things from or associated with Yarkand. L19.

2 = ***Yarkand carpet*** below. E20.

1 Yarkand carpet a type of Turkoman carpet. **Yarkand deer** a heavily built red deer, with short antlers, belonging to an endangered race occurring in Sinkiang Uigur. **Yarkand rug** = ***Yarkand carpet*** above.

Yarkandi /jɑːˈkandi/ *noun & adjective.* M19.

[formed as prec. + -I².]

▶**A** *noun.* A native or inhabitant of the city or district of Yarkand. M19.

▶**B** *adjective.* Of or pertaining to Yarkand or its people. M19.

yarm /jɑːm/ *verb & noun.*

[Old English *ġyrman*, of unkn. origin.]

▶**A** *verb intrans.* Utter a discordant or mournful cry; scream, yowl; wail. *obsolete* exc. *dial.* OE.

▶**B** *noun.* A discordant cry; a scream, a yowl. Long *obsolete* exc. *Scot. dial.* LME.

Yarmouth /ˈjɑːməθ/ *noun.* E17.

[See below.]

Used *attrib.* to designate things originating in or associated with Yarmouth, a fishing town on the coast of Norfolk.

Yarmouth bloater (*a*) a slightly salted smoked herring; (*b*) *colloq.* a native of Yarmouth.

yarmulke /ˈjɑːmʊlkə/ *noun.* Also **-ka**. E20.

[Yiddish *yarmolke* from Polish *jarmułka* cap, prob. from Turkish *yağmurluk* raincoat, cape, from *yağmur* rain.]

A skullcap worn by male Jews.

yarn /jɑːn/ *noun & verb.*

[Old English *ġearn* = Middle Dutch *gaern* (Dutch *garen*), (Old High German), Old Norse *garn*, prob. from Germanic base repr. also in Old Norse *gǫrn*, pl. *garnar* guts.]

▶**A** *noun.* **1** Orig., spun fibre of cotton, silk, wool, or flax. Now chiefly *spec.*, fibre prepared for use in weaving, knitting, the manufacture of sewing-thread, etc. OE. ▸**b** A fisherman's net. *dial.* M16. ▸**c** In ROPE-MAKING, any of the strands of which a rope is composed; these strands collectively. E17.

2 A (usu. long or rambling) story or tale, *esp.* an implausible, fanciful, or incredible one. Freq. in ***spin a yarn***. E19. ▸**b** A chat, a talk. *colloq.* (chiefly *Austral.* & *NZ*). M19.

1 knickerbocker yarn, **linen yarn**, **loop yarn**, **stocking yarn**, **textured yarn**, **woollen yarn**, etc. **metallic yarn**: see METALLIC *adjective.* **twist yarn**: see TWIST *noun*¹ 4. **2 GALLEY-yarn**.

Comb.: **yarn-beam** WEAVING the roller on which the yarn is wound; **yarn count**: see COUNT *noun*¹ 4b; **yarn-dyed** *adjective* (of fabric) dyed as yarn, before being woven; **yarn-spinner** (*a*) a person who spins yarn; (*b*) *colloq.* a person who tells yarns.

▶**B** *verb intrans.* Tell a yarn or yarns. Also, chat. *colloq.* E19.

yarnwindle /ˈjɑːnwɪnd(ə)l/ *noun.* Long *obsolete* exc. *dial.* ME.

[from YARN *noun* + as WINDLE *noun*¹.]

= GARNWINDLE.

yarooh /jaˈruː/ *interjection.* Also **yaroo**. E20.

[Natural exclam.]

Expr. pain.

Yarra-banker /ˈjarəbaŋkə/ *noun. Austral. colloq.* L19.

[from *Yarra* the river on which Melbourne stands + BANK *noun*¹ + -ER¹.]

A vagrant. Also, a soapbox orator.

yarraman /ˈjarəmən/ *noun. Austral.* Pl. **-mans**, **-men**. M19.

[Aboriginal.]

A horse.

yarran /ˈjarən/ *noun.* L19.

[Aboriginal.]

Any of several Australian acacias; esp. *Acacia omalophylla*, a small tree with scented wood used for fencing, fuel, etc.

†**yarringle** *noun.* E17–L19.

[Alt.]

= YARNWINDLE.

yarrow /ˈjarəʊ/ *noun.*

[Old English *ġearwe*, corresp. to Middle Dutch *garwe*, *gherwe* (Dutch *gerwe*), Old High German *gar(a)wa* (German *Schafgarbe*), from West Germanic: ult. origin unkn.]

A Eurasian plant of dry grassland, *Achillea millefolium*, of the composite family, with finely-divided bipinnate leaves and close flat clusters of white- or pink-rayed flower-heads (also called ***milfoil***). Also, with specifying word, any of several other plants mainly of the genus *Achillea*.

sweet yarrow: see SWEET *adjective.* ***water yarrow***: see WATER *noun.*

yas /jas/ *adverb & interjection.* Chiefly *US dial.* & *Black English.* L19.

[Repr. a pronunc. Cf. YAAS, YERSE.]

= YES *adverb & interjection.*

Yasa /ˈjɑːsɑː/ *noun.* Also **-ss-**, ***y-***. E18.

[Turkish, from Mongolian *jasaǧ*, from *jasa-* construct, arrange.]

Hist. A codification of Mongolian customary laws ascribed to Genghis Khan (1162–1227), used as the basis of law in much of Asia under Mongol rule.

yashiki /ˈjaʃɪki/ *noun.* Pl. same. E18.

[Japanese, from *ya* house + *shiki* laying out, space, site.]

Hist. The residence of a Japanese feudal nobleman, including the grounds and the quarters for his retainers.

yashmak /ˈjaʃmak/ *noun.* Also (earlier, *rare*) †**asmak**. M19.

[(Arab. *yašmak* from) Turkish *yaşmak* use as noun of *yaşmak* hide oneself.]

A veil concealing the face below the eyes, worn by Muslim women in public.

■ **yashmaked** *adjective* (*rare*) wearing a yashmak E20.

Yassa *noun* var. of YASA.

yataghan /ˈjatəgan/ *noun.* Also **at-** /ˈat-/. E19.

[Turkish *yatağan*.]

Chiefly *Hist.* In Muslim countries, a sword or long dagger having a handle without a guard and often a double-curved blade.

yate /jeɪt/ *noun.* M19.

[Aboriginal.]

Any of several eucalypts of SW Australia yielding a very tough wood, esp. *Eucalyptus cornuta*; the wood of these trees.

Yates' correction /ˈjeɪts kəˈrɛkʃ(ə)n/ *noun phr.* Also **Yates correction**, **Yates's correction**. M20.

[from Frank *Yates* (1902–94), English statistician.]

STATISTICS. A correction for the discreteness of the data that is made in the chi-square test when the number of cases in any class is small and there is one degree of freedom, consisting of the subtraction of ½ from each difference when evaluating chi squared.

yatra /ˈjɑːtrɑː/ *noun.* E19.

[Sanskrit *yātrā* journey, from *yā* go.]

A Bengali theatrical entertainment or song recital staged during a religious festival. Also, a pilgrimage, a procession; a festival.

yatter /ˈjatə/ *verb & noun. colloq.* (orig. *Scot.*). E19.

[Imit., perh. after YAMMER *verb* and CHATTER *verb*.]

▶**A** *verb intrans.* Talk idly, complainingly, or incessantly; chatter; gossip; gabble. Freq. foll. by *at*, *(on) about*. E19.

▶**B** *noun.* Idle, complaining, or incessant talk; chatter; gossip. E19.

yauld /jɔːld/ *adjective. Scot.* & *north.* L18.

[Origin unkn.]

Active, nimble; strong, vigorous.

yaup *verb & noun* var. of YAWP.

yaupon /ˈjɔːpɒn/ *noun.* Also **yapon**. E18.

[N. American Indian.]

A holly of the southern US, *Ilex vomitoria*.

yautia /jaʊˈtiːə/ *noun.* L19.

[Amer. Spanish, from Maya *yaaj* wound, poison + *té* mouth, from its caustic properties.]

Any of several Central American plants of the genus *Xanthosoma*, of the arum family, which are grown for their edible tubers; *esp.* the tannia, *X. sagittifolium*.

Yavapai /ˈjavəpʌɪ/ *noun & adjective.* As noun also (earlier) †**Yampai**. M19.

[Spanish, prob. from Mohave *yavapay*.]

▶**A** *noun.* Pl. **-s**, same. A member of a Yuman people of NW Arizona; the language of this people. M19.

▶**B** *attrib.* or as *adjective.* Of or pertaining to the Yavapais or their language. E20.

yaw /jɔː/ *noun*¹. M16.

[Rel. to YAW *verb*¹.]

The action or an act of yawing; (a) deviation of a ship from its course; (an) angular motion or displacement of an aircraft etc. about a yawing axis.

> 🕮 H. ALLEN The captain gave the ship a sudden wide yaw to port. *fig.*: *Listener* The first six years of ITV saw the yaw from suicidal pessimism to inglorious financial success.

Comb.: **yaw axis** = ***yawing axis*** s.v. YAW *verb*¹.

yaw /jɔː/ *noun*². L17.

[Back-form. from YAWS.]

1 = YAWS. Only *attrib.* and in comb. L17.

2 Any of the lesions characteristic of the disease yaws. M18.

yaw /jɔː/ *verb*¹. L16.

[Origin unkn.]

1 *verb intrans.* **a** Of a ship: deviate temporarily from its course, esp. through faulty steering or adverse weather conditions; turn from side to side. L16. ▸**b** *fig.* Deviate; move unsteadily. L16. ▸**c** Of an aircraft, missile, etc.: rotate about a vertical axis; turn from side to side. Cf. PITCH *verb*² 14e. Chiefly as ***yawing*** *verbal noun.* E20.

2 *verb trans.* Cause to yaw. M18.

> 🕮 **1a** J. DICKEY The canoe yawed and I braced back to equalize the weights. **c** CLIVE JAMES The aircraft was pitching and yawing over the bumpy grass. **2** P. H. GOSSE The man at the wheel . . neglecting his helm, 'yaws' the ship about sadly. L. J. CLANCY The aircraft is yawed to starboard.

Phrases: **yawing axis** a vertical axis of a ship, aircraft, or spacecraft about which yawing takes place, perpendicular to its longitudinal axis or direction of travel.

yaw /jɔː/ *verb*² & *interjection. rare.* Also redupl. **yaw-yaw**. L18.

[Imit. Cf. YAW-HAW.]

▶**A** *verb trans.* & *intrans.* Say or speak affectedly. L18.

▶**B** *interjection.* Expr. affected speech. L18.

Yawelmani /jɑːwɛlˈmɑːni/ *noun & adjective.* E20.
[Yawelmani *yaw'elmani* pl.]
▶**A** *noun.* Pl. same. A member of a N. American Indian people of California; the Yokuts language spoken by this people. E20.
▶**B** *attrib.* or as *adjective.* Of or pertaining to the Yawelmani or their language. E20.

yaw-haw /ˈjɔːhɔː/ *verb & noun.* M19.
[Imit. Cf. HAW-HAW, YAW *verb*² & *interjection.*]
▶**A** *verb intrans.* Laugh noisily; guffaw. Also, speak in an affected manner. M19.
▶**B** *noun.* A loud laugh; a guffaw. E20.

yawl /jɔːl/ *noun*¹. Also (*Scot.*) **yole** /jəʊl/. L16.
[Middle & mod. Low German *jolle* or Dutch *jol*, ult. origin unkn. Cf. JOLLY-BOAT.]
NAUTICAL. **1** A two-masted fore-and-aft rigged sailing boat with a short mizzen stepped far abaft of the rudder post; a small undecked two-masted fishing boat. L16.
2 *Hist.* A ship's jollyboat with usu. four or six oars. L16.
Comb.: **yawl-rigged** *adjective* rigged like a yawl.
▪ **yawler** *noun* a person who rows or sails in a yawl M19.

yawl /jɔːl/ *verb & noun*². Now *Scot. & dial.* ME.
[Parallel to YOWL *verb* & *noun*: cf. Low German *jaulen* (of a cat) howl.]
▶**A** *verb.* **1** *verb intrans.* Give a loud cry, esp. of pain or grief; howl, scream; shout, yell. ME.
2 *verb trans.* Shout out. M16.
▶**B** *noun.* A loud cry; a howl, a scream; a yell. E18.

yawmeter /ˈjɔːmiːtə/ *noun.* E20.
[from YAW *noun*¹ + -METER.]
An instrument for detecting changes in the direction of flow round an aircraft or other body.

yawn /jɔːn/ *noun.* E17.
[from the verb.]
1 A gaping aperture; *esp.* a chasm, an abyss. E17.
2 An act of yawning, from sleepiness or boredom. E18.
3 A boring or tedious thing. *colloq.* L19.

🕮 **1** J. MARSTON Now gapes the graves, and through their yawnes let loose Imprison'd spirits. **2** J. LE CARRÉ I could almost hear the yawns of the . . analysts as they waded through such turgid stuff. **3** *Times* Books about the European Economic Community are usually a yawn.

▪ **yawnful** *adjective* full of yawns L19.

yawn /jɔːn/ *verb.*
[Old English *ġeonian*, *ġinian* = Old High German *ginōn*, *ginēn*, Middle Dutch *ghēnen*.]
†**1** *verb intrans.* Open the mouth wide voluntarily, esp. to swallow something. OE–L17.
2 *verb intrans.* (Of a chasm, abyss, aperture, etc.) lie or be wide open, present a wide gap; (of the ground etc.) form a chasm, gape. OE.
3 *verb intrans.* Open the mouth wide and inhale (silently or audibly), as an involuntary reflex when sleepy or bored. LME. ▸**b** Open the mouth wide from surprise; gape. *obsolete* exc. *dial.* E17.
4 *verb trans.* Cause to open wide; make or produce by opening wide. LME.
5 *verb trans.* **a** Say or utter with a yawn or with the mouth wide open. E18. ▸**b** Bring into a position or condition by yawning; spend (a period) in a lethargic manner. M18.

🕮 **2** DICKENS When the silent tomb shall yawn . . I shall be ready for burial; not before. J. KEROUAC Great fogs yawned beyond stone walls along the precipices. E. BOWEN The . . writing desk . . yawned open, too overflowing to close. **3** G. A. BIRMINGHAM The Major yawned without an attempt to hide the fact he was bored. S. O'FAOLÁIN I yawned, dry-eyed for lack of sleep. **b** SHAKES. *Oth.* Methinks it should be now a huge eclipse Of sun and moon, and that th'affrighted globe Did yawn at alteration. **4** SOUTHEY She stood beside the murderer's bed, and yawn'd Her ghastly wound. **5a** N. ROWE Scorning the wound he [the lion] yawns a dreadful roar. **b** S. MORGAN The . . *haut ton*, who yawn away their existence in the assemblies of London.

▪ **yawner** *noun* (**a**) a person who yawns, esp. from sleepiness; (**b**) *colloq.* a boring or tedious thing; (**c**) *colloq.* a wide ditch: L17.

yawning /ˈjɔːnɪŋ/ *adjective.* OE.
[from YAWN *verb* + -ING².]
1 That yawns. OE.
2 Characterized by or producing yawning; sleepy; bored. E17.
▪ **yawningly** *adverb* E17.

yawny /ˈjɔːni/ *adjective.* E19.
[from YAWN *noun*, *verb* + -Y¹.]
Characterized by or producing yawning; inclined to yawn; sleepy.
▪ **yawniness** *noun* E19.

yawp /jɔːp/ *verb & noun.* Also **yaup**. ME.
[Imit. Cf. YAP *verb*, YELP *verb*.]
▶**A** *verb intrans.* **1** Shout or exclaim hoarsely; (of a dog) yelp; (of a bird) give a raucous or querulous cry. Chiefly *dial.* ME.
2 Gape, gawp. *dial.* M19.
3 Speak foolishly or noisily. *US.* L19.

🕮 **1** K. S. PRICHARD Frogs . . yawped through the long hours. **2** P. G. WODEHOUSE He just yawped at me like a half-wit. **3** *Brooklyn Eagle* The Eagle is opposed to free trade nonsense and anti-Imperialist yawping.

▶**B** *noun.* **1** A hoarse, raucous, or querulous cry. Chiefly *dial.* E19.
2 Foolish or noisy talk. Chiefly *US.* M19.

🕮 **2** J. H. INGRAHAM 'Hold your yaup' . . roared the old man. W. WHITMAN I sound my barbaric yawp over the roofs of the world.

▪ **yawper** *noun* L17.

yaws /jɔːz/ *noun.* L17.
[Prob. from Carib *yaya*, prob. ult. from a S. Amer. Indian lang.; *-s* prob. orig. the pl. suffix.]
A contagious disease of tropical countries, caused by the spirochaete *Treponema pertenue*, which enters skin abrasions and gives rise to small crusted lesions which may develop into deep ulcers. Also called ***framboesia***, ***pian***.

yawy /ˈjɔːi/ *adjective.* L17.
[from YAW *noun*² + -Y¹.]
Affected with or characteristic of yaws (the disease).

yay /jeɪ/ *adverb. N. Amer. slang.* Also **yea**. M20.
[Prob. var. of YEA *adverb*¹.]
With adjectives of size, height, etc.: so, this, (*big*, *high*, etc.).

🕮 P. THEROUX A daughter . . whom I've loved . . ever since she was yay high.

yay /jeɪ/ *interjection. slang.* M20.
[Perh. from prec. or alt. of YEAH.]
Expr. triumph, approval, or encouragement.

🕮 *New Wave* The Slits won the argument (Yay!) but we didn't get the interview (Boo!).

yayla /ˈjeɪlə/ *noun.* Also (earlier) **-lak** /-lak/. E19.
[Turkish.]
In central Asia, a high summer pasture used by nomads; an encampment pitched there.

Yayoi /ˈjɑːjɔɪ/ *adjective.* E20.
[A quarter in Tokyo.]
Designating a type of early pottery found in Japan and characterized by simple shapes and scored patterns. Also, designating the mainly neolithic culture characterized by this ware.

Yazidi *noun* var. of YEZIDI.

Yb *symbol.*
CHEMISTRY. Ytterbium.

†**yblent** *pa. pple & ppl adjective*¹. ME–L16.
[from Y- + pa. pple of BLEND *verb*¹.]
Blinded (*lit.* & *fig.*); dazed.

†**yblent** *pa. pple & ppl adjective*². LME–M18.
[from Y- + pa. pple of BLEND *verb*².]
Blended; confused, blurred.

†**yborn** *pa. pple & ppl adjective.* OE.
[from Y- + BORN *ppl adjective*, *borne* pa. pple of BEAR *verb*¹.]
1 Born. OE–M18.
2 Borne. OE–M17.

†**ybound** *pa. pple & ppl adjective.* OE–E18.
[from Y- + *bound* pa. pple of BIND *verb.*]
Bound.

†**ybrent** *pa. pple & ppl adjective.* ME–M18.
[from Y- + *brent* pa. pple of BURN *verb.*]
Burnt. Also, burnished.

yclad /ɪˈklad/ *pa. pple & ppl adjective. arch.* ME.
[from Y- + *clad* pa. pple of CLOTHE.]
Clothed (*lit.* & *fig.*).

🕮 BYRON Spring yclad in grassy dye.

yclept /ɪˈklɛpt/ *pa. pple & ppl adjective.* Now *arch.* & *joc.* Also **ycleped** /ɪˈkliːpt/, *poet.* ɪˈkliːpɪd/. OE.
[from Y- + *clept* obsolete pa. pple of CLEPE *verb.*]
Called, named, styled.

🕮 MILTON But com thou Goddes fair and free, In Heav'n ycleap'd Euphrosyne. K. VONNEGUT They were painted the palest rose-orange, not unlike the . . shade yclept 'Mani Eventide'.

yd. *abbreviation.*
Yard(s).

†**ydred** *pa. pple & ppl adjective.* ME–M17.
[from Y- + *dred* obsolete pa. pple of DREAD *verb.*]
Dreaded.

yds. *abbreviation.*
Yards.

YE *abbreviation.*
Your Excellency.

ye /jiː, *unstressed* jɪ/ *pers. pronoun, 2 pl. & sing. subjective (nom.) & objective (accus. & dat.).* Now *arch. & dial.* (repl. in general use by YOU *pronoun*). Also (now *dial.*) **'ee** /iː/.
[Old English *ġe ġē* = Old Frisian *jī*, Old Saxon *gi*, *ge* (Dutch *gij*), Old High German *ir* (German *ihr*), Old Norse *ér*, modified form (on the analogy of WE) of Germanic root repr. by Gothic *jūs*, from *ju-* (with pl. ending): see YOU *pronoun*, YOUR.]
Subjective & (later) objective (direct & indirect): used by the speaker or writer to refer to the persons or (later, orig. as a mark of respect) single person he or she is addressing, as the subject of predication or in attributive or predicative agreement with that subject.

🕮 SHAKES. *Rich. II* Look not to the ground, Ye favourites of a king. AV *Matt.* 5:46 If yee loue them which loue you, what reward haue yee? R. HERRICK Gather ye rosebuds, while ye may. LYTTON The morrow's sun shall light ye homeward both. T. HARDY Have ye heard about the King coming, Miss Maidy Anne? U. SINCLAIR Mebbe he was playing a joke on ye. ***ye gods (and little fishes)***: see GOD *noun.*

¶ See notes s.v. THOU *pers. pronoun & noun*², YOU *pers. pronoun & noun.*

ye *adjective* see THE.

yea /jeɪ/ *adverb*¹, *interjection, & noun.*
[Old English *ġē*, (West Saxon) *ġēa*, corresp. to Old Frisian *gē*, *jē*, Old Saxon, Old High German *jā* (Dutch, German *ja*), Old Norse *já*, Gothic *ja*, *jai*, from Germanic. Cf. YES *adverb & interjection.*]
▶**A** *adverb & interjection.* Now *arch. & dial.*
1 = YES *adverb & interjection.* OE.
†**2** Even; truly. OE–L16.
3 Indeed, and more. ME.
4 Introducing a reply to a statement, freq. expressing an objection: indeed?; well then. ME.

🕮 **1 say yea** answer in the affirmative; give assent. **2** A. HALL Helene . . did him earnestly behold, and swelling yea with wrath. **3** J. WESLEY Some . . use improper, yea, indecent, expressions in prayer. **4** TENNYSON 'Yonder comes a knight.' . . 'Yea, but one? Wait here, and when he passes fall upon him.'

▶**B** *noun.* **1** An utterance of 'yea'; an affirmative reply or statement; an assent. Also, (an) absolute truth, (a) certainty. Now *arch. & dial.* ME.
2 An affirmative vote; a person who votes in the affirmative. Now *N. Amer.* M17.
Phrases & comb.: **yea and nay** (**a**) affirmation and denial, *esp.* alternate affirmation and denial, shilly-shallying; ***by yea and nay***, a formula of asseveration substituted for an oath; (**b**) *attrib.* (with hyphens) disposed to assent or deny indifferently; vacillating, ambivalent. **yea-say** *verb trans. & intrans.* assent (to). **yea-sayer** a person who assents or is inclined to assent.
¶ Opp. NAY *adverb, interjection, & noun.*

yea *adverb*² var. of YAY *adverb.*

yeah /jɛː/ *adverb & interjection. colloq.* (orig. *US*). E20.
[Repr. an informal pronunc. Cf. YAH *adverb & interjection*¹, YEH.]
= YES *adverb & interjection.*

yealm *noun & verb* var. of YELM.

yean /jiːn/ *verb trans. & intrans.* Now *arch. & dial.* LME.
[Repr. Old English verb rel. to *ġeēan* pregnant, from Y- + EAN.]
Of an animal, esp. a ewe: give birth (to).
▪ **yeanling** *noun & adjective* (**a**) a young or newborn lamb or kid; (**b**) *attrib. adjective* young, newborn: M17.

year /jɪə/ *noun*¹. Pl. **-s**, (now *dial.*) same.
[Old English (Anglian) *ġēr*, (West Saxon) *ġēar* = Old Frisian *jār*, *jēr*, Old Saxon *jār*, *gēr* (Dutch *jaar*), Old High German *jār* (German *Jahr*), Old Norse *ár*, Gothic *jēr*, from Germanic, from Indo-European base repr. also by Avestan *yārə* year, Greek *hōra* season (whence Latin *hora* hour).]
1 More fully ***natural year***, ***solar year***, ***astronomical year***. The time taken by the earth to travel once round the sun, equal to 365 days, 5 hours, 48 minutes, and 46 seconds. OE. ▸**b** More fully ***planetary year***. The period of revolution of any planet round the sun. E18.
2 A period of roughly this length in a calendar, *esp.* (in the Gregorian calendar) a period of 365 or 366 days divided into twelve months beginning on 1 January and ending on 31 December, denoted by a number in a particular era. Also ***calendar year***, ***civil year***. OE.
3 A period of twelve months starting at any point; *spec.* a twelve-month (or shorter or longer) period reckoned for a special purpose (usu. with specifying word); a twelve-month period (identified contextually) as a unit in a person's age, forming part of a term of imprisonment or service. etc. OE. ▸**b** More fully ***Christian year***, ***Church year***. A twelve-month period arranged for religious observance in the Christian Church, usu. beginning with Advent. LME. ▸**c** Following a date: a year before or after the time specified. Cf. WEEK *noun* 4. *arch.* M16. ▸**d** A group of students entering college in the same academic year. L19.
4 In *pl.* ▸**a** A person's age. OE. ▸**b** Old age; maturity. *arch.* L16.
5 **a** In *pl.* Period, times; (with *possess. pronoun*) time of life. ME. ▸**b** A very long time. Usu. in *pl.* L17.

6 A year as the period of the seasons, and of the growth of crops and vegetation in general; a year regarded in terms of the quality of produce, *spec.* wine. LME.

📖 **1b** *Scientific American* The Martian year is 687 earth days long. **2** *Canoeist* In July their bookings were . . doubled on the same month last year. *Esquire* In the year 1815 a battle would be fought near Waterloo. ***Jewish year, Muslim year***, etc. ***year of the hare, year of the pig***, etc., (in the Chinese calendar). ***Christian Heritage Year, Tree Planting Year***, etc. **3** TENNYSON A nurse of ninety years. F. O'CONNOR I reckon she was forty year old. G. MAXWELL Streets . . paved with cobbles in the Spanish style of 300 years ago. E. TAYLOR She was fifteen years older than Polly. *Venue* With my form, I'd get three to five years for housebreaking. B. VINE He must apply to return to college. 'They'll make me do my whole second year again.' ***academic year, fiscal year, school year, tax year***, etc. **c** DISRAELI I should not be surprised . . if he were to change his name again before this time year. **d** S. SMILES At the following Christmas examination he was the first of his year. **4a** E. A. FREEMAN William, still a boy in years but a man in conduct and counsel. M. L. KING With . . his thoughtful expression, he looked older than his years. **b** SHAKES. *Rich. II* Till my infant fortune comes to years. L. BINYON Age shall not weary them, nor the years condemn. **5a** E. O'NEILL How hard these last years have been for you. SCOTT FITZGERALD He had changed since his New Haven years. **b** *Contemporary Review* For years the supply of teachers exceeded the demand. E. O'NEILL First time he's done that in years. W. F. HARVEY It's years since I've been there. **6** *Decanter* The unmistakable nose on Château de Beaucastel in a good year.

Phrases: ***astronomical year***: see sense 1 above. **a year and a day** LAW a period constituting a term for certain purposes, in order to ensure the completion of a full year. ***calendar year***: see sense 2 above. ***Christian year***: see sense 3b above. ***Church year***: see sense 3b above. ***civil year***: see sense 2 above. ***common year***: see COMMON *adjective*. ***dominical year***: see DOMINICAL *adjective* 1. **ecclesiastical year** = sense 3b above. **from year to year** continuous or without interruption from one year to the next. ***great year***: see GREAT *adjective*. ***Julian year***. ***leap year***: see LEAP *noun*[1]. ***lunar year***: see LUNAR *adjective*. ***lunisolar year***. ***Metonic year***. ***natural year***: see sense 1 above. ***planetary year***: see sense 1b above. ***Platonic year***: see PLATONIC *adjective* 1. ***regnal year***. ***sabbatical year***: see SABBATICAL *adjective*. ***sidereal year***: see SIDEREAL *adjective* 3. ***solar year***: see sense 1 above. ***Sothic year***: see SOTHIC 2. ***stepped in years***: see STEPPED *adjective*. ***stricken in years***: see STRIKE *verb*. ***the tother year***: see TOTHER *adjective*. **the year dot, the year one** *colloq.* a time in the remote past. ***tother year***: see TOTHER *adjective*. ***tropical year***: see TROPICAL *adjective* 1. ***well stepped in years***: see STEPPED *adjective*. **year after year** each year as a sequel to the preceding one, esp. in an unvarying sequence. **year by year** in each successive year, annually without ceasing. ***year in, year out***: see IN *adverb*. ***year of grace***: see GRACE *noun*. **year of Our Lord** in a year as reckoned from the birth of Jesus. **year-on-year** *adjective* ECONOMICS (of figures) as compared with the corresponding ones for a date twelve months earlier. ***years of discretion***. See also NEW YEAR.

Comb.: **year-bird** a hornbill, *Aceros plicatus*, found from Myanmar (Burma) to New Guinea, which has corrugations on its casque formerly thought to represent annual growth; **year class** the individuals of a particular animal (esp. a fish) that were born in any one year; **year-long** *adjective* lasting for a year; **year-old** *adjective & noun* (an animal) one year old; **year-ring** each of the rings formed by successive years' growth in the wood of a tree; **year-round** *adjective & adverb* (existing, occurring, used, etc.) all the year round; **year's mind** CHRISTIAN CHURCH (*a*) the anniversary of a person's death or burial, as an occasion for special prayers; †(*b*) a Requiem Mass held on such an anniversary.

year /jɪə, jəː/ *noun*[2]. *dial.* (chiefly *US*). M19.
[Repr. a pronunc.]
= EAR *noun*[1].

yearbook /ˈjɪəbʊk/ *noun*. L16.
[from YEAR *noun*[1] + BOOK *noun*.]
1 *Hist.* In *pl.* The books of reports of cases in the English law-courts between *c* 1283 and 1535. L16.
2 An annual publication by a society etc., dealing with events or aspects of the (usu. preceding) year; *spec.* (*N. Amer.*) one published by the graduating class of a high school or college. E18.

yeared /jɪəd/ *adjective*. Long *arch.* or *poet.* LME.
[from YEAR *noun*[1] + -ED[2].]
That has lived or lasted a (specified) number of years.

yearling /ˈjɪəlɪŋ/ *noun & adjective*. LME.
[from YEAR *noun*[1] + -LING[1].]
▶ **A** *noun*. **1** An animal (esp. a sheep, calf, or foal) a year old, or in its second year. Also, a racehorse in the calendar year after the year of foaling. LME.
2 A plant a year old. M19.
3 A student in his or her first year or beginning his or her second year at college. *US colloq.* E20.
4 ECONOMICS. A yearling bond (see sense B.2 below). M20.
▶ **B** *adjective*. **1** Of an animal or (*rare*) a child: a year old; in its second year. E16. ▸**b** Of a plant or seed: of the previous year's growth. M19.
2 ECONOMICS. Of a bond: issued by a local authority usu. for one year. M20.

yearly /ˈjɪəli/ *adjective*.
[Old English *ġēarlīc* = Old Frisian *ier(a)lik*, Old High German *jārlich* (Middle High German *jaerlich*, German *jährlich*), Old Norse *árligr*, from Germanic base of YEAR *noun*[1], -LY[1].]
1 Of or pertaining to a year (*rare*). Now *spec.*, payable every year. OE.
2 Done, recurring, produced, etc., once a year or every year. OE.
2 Yearly Meeting a national assembly held annually by the Society of Friends to deal with legislation and questions of policy.

yearly /ˈjɪəli/ *adverb*.
[Old English *ġēarlīce* = Middle Low German *jārlik*, Old High German *jārlich* (Middle High German *jaerlich*, German *jārlich*), Old Norse *árliga*, from Germanic base of YEAR *noun*[1], -LY[2].]
Once a year; in each or every year; annually. Also, year by year.

📖 E. NORTH Christmas cards were exchanged yearly.

yearn /jəːn/ *noun*. L18.
[from YEARN *verb*[1].]
A yearning.

📖 N. MAILER Phil Mansen was reputed to have a yearn for attractive ladies.

yearn /jəːn/ *verb*[1].
[Old English *ġiernan* = Old Saxon *gernean, girnean*, Old Norse *girna*, Gothic *gairnjan*, from Germanic base also of YERN *adjective*.]
▶ **I 1 a** *verb intrans.* Have a deep or passionate longing. Usu. foll. by *for, after, to do*. OE. ▸†**b** *verb trans.* Have a deep longing for. OE–M16.
†**2** *verb trans.* Ask for, request. OE–ME.
†**3** *verb intrans.* Of a hound: give tongue. E16–L17.
4 a *verb intrans.* Of sound: express or suggest strong desire or emotion. E19. ▸**b** *verb trans.* Utter in an emotional voice. M19. ▸**c** *verb trans.* Have an appearance as of longing; esp. strain forward. L19.

📖 **1a** D. DU MAURIER An agony of loneliness made me . . yearn for company. B. SPOCK The boy yearns to be like his idealized father. J. A. MICHENER Urbaal lay . . dreaming of the slave girl whom he yearned for with such passion. A. T. ELLIS Betty was beginning to pine and to yearn after Beuno. **4a** KEATS The music, yearning like a God in pain. **b** W. C. RUSSELL The jibs yearning from their sheets taut as fiddle-strings.

▶ **II 5** †**a** *verb trans.* Have compassion on, pity. *rare*. Only in E16. ▸**b** *verb intrans.* Be filled with compassion or tender feelings; be deeply moved. Usu. foll. by *at, to, towards*. M16.
†**6** *verb trans.* Cause to mourn; move to compassion. L16–M17.

📖 **5** O. W. HOLMES Just as my heart yearns over the unloved, just so it sorrows for the ungifted. **6** SHAKES. *Merry W.* She laments, sir, for it, that it would yearn your heart to see it.

■ **yearner** *noun* E20.

yearn *verb*[2] see EARN *verb*[2].

yearnful /ˈjəːnfʊl, -f(ə)l/ *adjective*. OE.
[In sense 1 from YERN *adjective*. In sense 2 from YEARN *verb*[1]: see -FUL.]
†**1** Eagerly desirous, anxious, solicitous. OE–LME.
2 Mournful, sorrowful. M16.
■ **yearnfully** *adverb* L19. †**yearnfulness** *noun* eagerness, diligence OE–ME.

yearning /ˈjəːnɪŋ/ *noun*[1]. OE.
[from YEARN *verb*[1] + -ING[1].]
1 The action of YEARN *verb*[1]; an instance of this. OE.
2 An object of intense desire. *rare*. LME.

yearning *noun*[2] see EARNING *noun*[2].

yearning /ˈjəːnɪŋ/ *ppl adjective*. E17.
[from YEARN *verb*[1] + -ING[2].]
That yearns; characterized by longing, desire, or compassion.
■ **yearningly** *adverb* M19.

yeast /jiːst/ *noun*. Also (now *arch. & dial.*) **yest** /jɛst/.
[Old English (late West Saxon *ġist*), corresp. to Middle Low German *gest* dregs, dirt, Middle Dutch *ghist, ghest* (Dutch *gist, gest* yeast), Middle High German *jist, gest, gist* yeast, froth (German *Gischt* sea-foam), Old Norse *jǫstr*, rel. to Old High German *jesan, gesan* to ferment, Greek *zein* to boil, *zestos* boiled.]
1 Any of several unicellular ascomycetous fungi of the genus *Saccharomyces*, esp. *S. cervisiae* and *S. ellipsoideus*, capable of converting sugar into alcohol and carbon dioxide; a yellowish-grey preparation of such a fungus used esp. as a fermenting agent or to raise bread dough etc. OE. ▸**b** *gen.* A unicellular fungus in which vegetative reproduction takes place by budding or fission. L19.
2 Froth or foam, esp. on new or fermenting beer or on agitated water. LME.
Comb.: **yeast cake** (*a*) (chiefly *US*) a small cake of compressed yeast and starch, used as a raising or fermenting agent; (*b*) a light cake raised with yeast; **yeast powder** *US* baking-powder used as a substitute for yeast in bread-making.
■ **yeasted** *adjective* containing added yeast, esp. as a raising agent E20. **yeastless** *adjective* M20. **yeastlike** *adjective* resembling (that of) yeast M19.

yeast /jiːst/ *verb intrans. & refl. rare*. E19.
[from the noun.]
Ferment; be covered or cover with froth.

yeasty /ˈjiːsti/ *adjective*. Also (now *arch. & dial.*) **yesty** /ˈjɛsti/. L16.
[from YEAST *noun* + -Y[1].]
1 Of or pertaining to yeast; full of yeast; resembling (that of) yeast, esp. in taste or smell. L16.
2 *fig.* Swelling, exuberant; (of talk) light and superficial. L16.
3 *transf.* Foamy, frothy. E17.

📖 **2** *Publishers Weekly* This is yeasty, up-to-the-minute reading. **3** W. DE LA MARE The yeasty surf curdled over the sands.

■ **yeastily** *adverb* L18. **yeastiness** *noun* M19.

Yeatsian /ˈjeɪtsɪən/ *adjective & noun*. E20.
[from *Yeats* (see below) + -IAN.]
▶ **A** *adjective*. Of, pertaining to, or characteristic of the Irish poet and playwright William Butler Yeats (1865–1939) or his work. E20.
▶ **B** *noun*. An admirer or student of Yeats or his work. M20.

yech /jɛk, jɛx/ *interjection, noun, & adjective*. *slang* (chiefly *N. Amer.*). Also **yecch**. M20.
[Imit. Cf. YUCK *interjection*.]
= YUCK *interjection, noun*[3], *& adjective*.

📖 *Rolling Stone* I went to . . folk festivals which were just yecch, awful. *Sunday Express* Shaving, yech it's the bane of my existence.

■ **yechy** *adjective* = YUCKY *adjective* M20.

yed /jɛd/ *noun & verb*. Chiefly *Scot.* Now *rare* or *obsolete*.
[Old English *ġiedd*, perh. ult. from same root as GATHER *verb*.]
▶ **A** *noun*. **1 a** A poem; a speech; a tale; a riddle. OE–ME. ▸**b** A fib; an exaggerated tale. *rare*. E19.
2 Contention, wrangling; strife. E18.
▶ **B** *verb intrans.* Infl. **-dd-**.
1 †**a** Sing; recite; talk. OE–LME. ▸**b** Fib; exaggerate a tale. *rare*. E19.
2 Contend, wrangle. L16.

yedda /ˈjɛdə/ *noun*. Also **yeddo** /ˈjɛdəʊ/, pl. **-os**. E20.
[Origin unkn.]
A type of straw used for making hats. Freq. *attrib*.
yedda braid, yedda plait, yedda straw, etc.

yedder /ˈjɛdə/ *noun*. *Scot. & north.* Also **yether** /ˈjɛðə/. LME.
[Var. of EDDER.]
1 A mark made by a blow, or by tight binding; a weal. Also, a sharp blow. LME.
2 An osier or a rod of pliant wood, used for binding a hedge. E16.

Yeddo /ˈjɛdəʊ/ *noun*[1]. M19.
[Var. of *Edo*, former name of Tokyo.]
Used *attrib.* to designate a few things found or originating in Tokyo in Japan.
Yeddo spruce the Japanese spruce, *Picea jezoensis*. **Yeddo hawthorn** a Japanese evergreen shrub, *Rhaphiolepis umbellata*, related to the hawthorn.

yeddo *noun*[2] var. of YEDDA.

†**yede** *verb*[1] *intrans.* M16–M18.
[from *yede* obsolete pa. t. of GO *verb*.]
Go, proceed.

†**yede** *verb*[2] *pa. t.*: see GO *verb*.

yeehaw /ˈjiːhɔː/ *interjection*. Chiefly *US*. Also **-ha(h)**. L20.
[Natural exclam. Cf. YAHOO *interjection*.]
Expr. enthusiasm or exuberance.

yeeow, yee-ow *interjections* vars. of YEOW.

yeep /jiːp/ *verb intrans. rare*. M19.
[Imit.]
Of a young bird: cheep.

yeeuch *interjection* var. of YEUCH.

yegg /jɛg/ *noun*. Chiefly *US*. E20.
[Origin unkn.]
A burglar, a safe-breaker, *esp.* one who travels from place to place.

yeh /jɛː/ *adverb & interjection*. *colloq.* E20.
[Repr. an informal pronunc. Cf. YAH *adverb & interjection*[1], YEAH.]
= YES *adverb & interjection*.

Yehudi *noun & adjective* var. of YAHUDI.

Yeibichai /ˈjeɪbɪtʃʌɪ/ *noun*. Also **Y-**. M20.
[Navajo *Ye'ii Bichaii* lit. 'Grandfather of the Giants', from *yé'ii* fearful one, giant + *bicheii*, *-aii* his maternal grandfather.]
A Navajo curative or initiation ceremony performed by masked dancers representing deities. Also, any of the dancers performing this ceremony; the deity represented by such a dancer.

Yekke /ˈjɛkə/ *noun*. *slang*. *derog.* Also **y-**, **-kkie** /-ki/. M20.
[Yiddish, of unkn. origin.]
In Israel, a member of a Jewish community of German origin.

yeld /jɛld/ *adjective & noun. Scot. & dial.* (chiefly *north.*).
[Late Old English *gelde*, corresp. to Middle Low German, Old High German *galt* (German *gelt*), Old Norse *geldr*. Cf. EILD, GELD *adjective*.]
▶ **A** *adjective.* **1** Of a female animal: barren; that has aborted or is not old enough to bear young. LOE.
2 Of a cow: not yielding milk. L17.
3 Of an inanimate object: sterile, unproductive. E18.
▶ **B** *noun.* A barren cow or ewe; a hind that is not pregnant. M19.

yelek *noun* var. of JELICK.

yelk *noun* see YOLK *noun*¹.

yell /jɛl/ *noun.* LME.
[from the verb.]
1 A loud sharp cry expressing pain, fear, anger, delight, triumph, etc.; *gen.* a loud cry, a shout. LME.
2 An organized rhythmical cry, used esp. to cheer on a sports team. *US.* L19.
3 A hilariously funny person or situation. Cf. SCREAM *noun* 3. *slang.* E20.

📖 **1** W. H. PRESCOTT The victorious enemy . . celebrated their success with songs or rather yells of triumph. A. GRAY Ozenfant began speaking in a quiet voice which grew steadily to a deafening yell.

yell /jɛl/ *verb.*
[Old English (Anglian) *ġellan*, (West Saxon) *ġiellan* = Middle Low German, Middle Dutch *ghellen*, Old High German *gellan* (Dutch *gillen*, German *gellen*), Old Norse *gjalla*, from Germanic base repr. also by Old English, Old High German *galan*, Old Norse *gala* sing, cry out. Cf. YELLOW *verb*².]
1 *verb intrans.* Utter a yell or yells; shout. Also, (of a bird or animal) utter its characteristic strident cry. OE. ▸**b** Of an inanimate thing: make a strident or crashing noise. Now *rare*. OE.
2 *verb trans.* Utter with a yell. ME.

📖 **1** SIR W. SCOTT She yelled out on seeing him as if an adder had stung her. R. GRAVES Thousands slowly sank out of sight, yelling with rage and despair. D. JACOBSON Yelling at him at the top of my voice. **2** C. M. YONGE Otho . . fled . . hunted by the students, all yelling abuse. C. S. FORESTER 'Sir!' yelled Hornblower back through the Captain's megaphone.

■ **yeller** *noun* E19.

yellow /ˈjɛləʊ/ *noun.* Also (*slang & dial.*, chiefly *US*) **yaller** /ˈjalə/. OE.
[The adjective used ellipt. or absol.]
▶ **I 1** A thing distinguished by yellow colour, as the yolk of an egg, a yellow variety of fruit or vegetable, a yellow bird, a yellow butterfly or moth, the yellow ball in snooker and similar games; *spec.* (*US*) gold. OE. ▸**b** = *yellow alert* s.v. YELLOW *adjective*. OE.
2 Yellow colour; a shade of this; yellowness; a yellow pigment or dye (freq. with specifying word). Also, yellow fabric, yellow clothes. ME.
3 A person with a naturally yellowish or olive skin; *esp.* (*derog. & racially offensive*) (**a**) a Chinese or Japanese person; (**b**) a person of mixed race. Usu. in *pl.* E19.

📖 **1** *clouded yellow*: see CLOUD *verb* 3. **double yellow** = *double yellow line* s.v. YELLOW *adjective*. **2** H. BELLOC His skin is of a dirty yellow. *gamboge yellow*, *Indian yellow*, *Naples yellow*, etc. **3** *high yellow*: see HIGH *adjective*.

▶ **II** In *pl.* (treated as *sing.*).
4 Jaundice, esp. in horses, cattle, and sheep. M16.
5 Any of various viral, fungal, and deficiency diseases of plants, marked by yellowing of the leaves and stunting. L18.
5 *peach yellows*: see PEACH *noun*¹. SPECKLED *yellows*. *tea yellows*: see TEA *noun*.
Comb.: **yellow spot** *noun*¹ the spot on which the yellow ball is placed in snooker.

yellow /ˈjɛləʊ/ *adjective.* Also (*slang & dial.*, chiefly *US*) **yaller** /ˈjalə/.
[Old English *ġeolu*, *-lo* = Old Saxon *gelo*, Middle & mod. Low German *geel*, Middle Dutch *gel(e)u*, *geel*, Old High German *gelo* (Dutch *geel*, German *gelb*), from West Germanic, rel. to Latin *helvus*, Greek *khloos*. Cf. GOLD *noun*¹.]
1 Of the colour of butter, egg-yolk, gold, or a lemon, between green and orange in the spectrum; of the colour of ripe wheat, faded leaves, or discoloured paper. OE. ▸**b** Having a naturally yellowish or olive skin; *esp.* (*derog. & racially offensive*) (**a**) Asian; *esp.* Chinese or Japanese; (**b**) of mixed white and (*US colloq.*) black or (*Austral. colloq.*) Aboriginal parentage or descent. L18. ▸**c** Dressed in yellow. *rare*. M19.
2 *fig.* **a** Affected with or expressive of jealousy, envy, or suspicion; jaundiced. Cf. *wear yellow hose* s.v. WEAR *verb*¹. *arch.* E17. ▸**b** Cowardly. *colloq.* (orig. *US*). M19. ▸**c** Of a trade union, its policies, etc.: favouring the interests of the employers; opposed to militant action or strikes. E20.
3 Of a novel, newspaper, etc.: luridly or unscrupulously sensational. M19.

📖 **1** M. ARNOLD The field strewn with its dank yellow drifts Of withered leaves. D. WELCH A huge yellow moon began to rise. S. GATES Chemical plants spewing bilious yellow smoke. *Best* The bright primary colours of the sunny yellow tiger lilies. *brownish-yellow*, *canary yellow*, *lemon yellow*, *mustard yellow*, etc. **2b** *Guardian* It frightens me when moderate voices are taken to be from weak and yellow men.

Special collocations & comb.: **yellow admiral** *Hist.* a post captain promoted to the rank of rear admiral on retirement without having actually served at that rank. **yellow alert** the preliminary stage of an alert, when danger is thought to be near but not actually imminent; a warning of such a situation. **yellow ant** any of various ants of a yellowish colour; *esp.* the small *Lasius flavus*, which is abundant in Eurasia and constructs anthills in grassland. *yellow archangel*: see ARCHANGEL 2. *yellow arsenic*: see ARSENIC *noun* 1. **yellow atrophy** MEDICINE (more fully *acute yellow atrophy*) a shrunken yellow condition of the liver after massive necrosis, as resulting from severe hepatitis. **yellow baboon** the common yellowish-brown baboon, *Papio cynocephalus*, of lowland E. and central Africa. **yellow-back** *colloq.* a cheap, orig. yellow-backed, novel. **yellow badge** *Hist.* a badge of identification that Jews have sometimes been required to wear, esp. in Nazi Germany (cf. *yellow star* below). **yellow bean** any of the yellow seeds of one of several varieties of soya bean. **yellow belle** a Eurasian geometrid moth, *Aspitates ochrearia*, with yellowish forewings. **yellow belt** (in judo or karate) (the holder of) a belt marking the attainment of the next grade above that of white belt. **yellowbill** any of various birds with a yellow bill; *esp.* (**a**) an African duck, *Anas undulata*; (**b**) *N. Amer.* = *black scoter* s.v. BLACK *adjective*; (**c**) an African coucal, *Ceuthomacheres aeneus*. **yellow-billed** *adjective* having a yellow bill; *yellow-billed cuckoo*, a N. American cuckoo, *Coccyzus americanus*; *yellow-billed duck* = *yellowbill* (a) above. **yellow birch** a N. American birch, *Betula lutea*, with yellow or grey bark. **yellowbird** any of several birds with yellow plumage; *esp.* (*N. Amer.*) (**a**) the American goldfinch, *Carduelis tristis*; (**b**) (more fully *summer yellowbird*) = *yellow warbler* (b) below. **yellow boa** a large boa, *Epicrates subflavus*, with yellowish coloration found in the W. Indies. **yellow bob** the yellow robin of eastern Australia, *Eopsaltria australis*. **yellow box** an Australian eucalyptus, *Eucalyptus melliodora*, with yellowish inner bark. **yellow-boy** *slang* (now *Hist.*) a gold coin, *esp.* a guinea or sovereign. **yellow-breasted** *adjective* having a yellow breast; *yellow-breasted chat*, a large New World warbler, *Icteria virens*, which has brown upperparts and a bright yellow throat and breast. **yellow bunting** = YELLOWHAMMER 1. **yellowcake** an oxide of uranium (and other elements) obtained as a yellow precipitate in the processing of uranium ores. **yellow card** *noun & verb* (**a**) *noun* (esp. in SOCCER) a card shown by the referee to a player being cautioned; (**b**) *verb trans.* (*yellow-card*) caution (a player) by the showing of a yellow card. **yellow cartilage** ANATOMY cartilage containing yellow or elastic fibres. **yellow cat**, **yellow catfish** the flathead catfish, *Pylodictis olivaris*. **yellow cedar** = *Nootka cypress* s.v. NOOTKA *adjective* 1. **yellow cell** BIOLOGY (**a**) a symbiotic yellow-green alga found in the bodies of certain aquatic invertebrates; (**b**) a storage cell in the intestinal wall of annelid worms. **yellow centaury** (**a**) (now *dial.*) = *yellow-wort* below; (**b**) a small annual plant of damp sandy heaths, *Cicendia filiformis*, related to the centauries. **yellow-cress** any of several yellow-flowered plants of the cruciferous genus *Rorippa* found by rivers, ponds, etc., allied to watercress. *yellow deal*: see DEAL *noun*² 2. **yellow dog** *US* (**a**) a (mongrel) dog with yellowish fur; (**b**) *fig.* a contemptible person or thing; (**c**) *yellow-dog Democrat*, a diehard Democrat who will vote for a Democratic candidate regardless of their personal qualities. **yellow earth** (**a**) a yellowish variety of bole; impure yellow ochre; (**b**) a yellowish loess occurring in northern China. **yellow elder** the yellow trumpet-tree, *Tecoma stans*. **yellow-eyed** *adjective* having yellow or yellowish eyes; *yellow-eyed grass*, (**a**) a plant of the monocotyledonous genus *Xyris* (family Xyridaceae), of warm and tropical countries, with grasslike leaves and yellow flowers; (**b**) a yellow-flowered plant of the genus *Sisyrinchium* (cf. *blue-eyed grass* s.v. BLUE *adjective*). **yellow fever** a tropical disease caused by an arbovirus and transmitted by mosquitoes, characterized by fever and jaundice and leading to degeneration of the liver and kidneys. **yellow fibre** = ELASTIC *fibre*. **yellow-fish** any of several fishes with yellow coloration; *esp.* (**a**) *N. Amer.* an Alaskan mackerel, *Pleurogrammus monopterygius*; (**b**) *S. Afr.* any of several freshwater cyprinid fishes of the genus *Barbus*. **yellow flag** (**a**) see FLAG *noun*¹ 1; (**b**) a flag flown by a vessel in quarantine. *yellow Geordie*: see GEORDIE 1. *yellow George*: see GEORGE 3. **yellow ground** kimberlite that is exposed at the surface and has become yellow as a result of atmospheric oxidation. **Yellow Hat** a member of the dominant Tibetan Buddhist order. **yellowhead** (**a**) a New Zealand warbler, *Mohoua ochrocephala*, with bright yellow head and underparts; (**b**) *N. Amer.* = *yellow-headed blackbird* below. **yellow-headed** *adjective* having a yellow head; *yellow-headed blackbird*, a N. American blackbird, *Xanthocephalus xanthocephalus*, the male of which has a black body with a yellow head and breast. **yellow horned** a Eurasian moth, *Achlaya flavicornis* (family Thyatiridae), which has mottled greyish forewings and yellow antennae. **yellow jack** (**a**) = *yellow flag* (b) above; (**b**) = *yellow jacket* (b) below; (**c**) *US slang* yellow fever; (**d**) a carangid fish, *Caranx bartholomaei*, of the western Atlantic. **yellow jacket** (**a**) *N. Amer. colloq.* a social wasp of the genus *Vespula*; (**b**) *Austral. colloq.* any of several eucalypts with yellowish bark. **yellow jersey** [orig. translating French *maillot jaune*] a cycling jersey worn by the overall leader in a cycle race, esp. the Tour de France, at the end of any one day, and ultimately presented to the winner. **yellow leaf** (*literary*) the process of ageing. **yellow-leg** *N. Amer. colloq.* [with ref. to the yellow stripe on the trousers of the uniform] a member of the US cavalry or of the Royal Canadian Mounted Police. **yellowlegs** a bird with yellow legs; *spec.* either of two migratory sandpipers, *Tringa flavipes* and *T. melanoleuca*. **yellow light** *N. Amer.* an amber traffic light. **yellow line** a line painted in yellow along the edge of a road, indicating that parking is restricted; *double yellow line*, (either of) a pair of such lines, indicating that parking is forbidden (usu. in *pl.*). **yellow metal** *spec.* a type of malleable brass that consists of about 60 per cent copper, 40 per cent zinc, and a little lead. **yellow Monday** [*Yellowmundee*, an Aborigine (fl. 1791)] *Austral. colloq.* the yellow form of a cicada, *Cyclochila australasiae*, common in the Sydney area. *yellow oat*: see OAT *noun*. **yellow ochre** a yellow variety of ochre containing limonite, used as a pigment. *yellow* OLEANDER. **yellow ore** *spec.* chalcopyrite. *yellow ox-eye*: see OX-EYE 1. **Yellow Pages** (proprietary name for) the classified section of or supplement to a telephone directory, printed on yellow paper and listing firms, products, and services. *yellow perch*: see PERCH *noun*¹ 1. **yellow peril** (*derog. & racially offensive*) the political or military threat regarded as being posed by Asian peoples, esp. the Chinese. **yellow phosphorus** = *white phosphorus* s.v. WHITE *adjective*. *yellow pimpernel*: see PIMPERNEL 2b. **yellow pine** the ponderosa pine, *Pinus ponderosa*. **yellow-poll (warbler)** a race of the yellow warbler found in southern Canada and the central US. **yellow poplar** the tulip-tree, *Liriodendron tulipifera*. *yellow* PUCCOON. **yellow rain** a yellow substance reported as falling in SE Asia, alleged to be a chemical warfare agent but now believed to consist of bee droppings. *yellow rattle*: see RATTLE *noun* 2. **yellow robin** either of two Australian robins of the genus *Eopsaltria* (family Eopsaltridae), which have mainly grey upperparts and mainly or partly yellow underparts; *esp.* (also *yellow bob*, *yellowhammer*) *E. australis* of eastern Australia. **yellow rocket** a kind of winter cress, *Barbarea vulgaris*. **yellow-root** either of two N. American plants of the buttercup family, the golden seal, *Hydrastis canadensis*, and (more fully *shrub yellow-root*) *Xanthorhiza simplicissima*, a low shrub with pinnate leaves; the yellow root of either of these plants, used medicinally or as the source of a yellow dye. **yellow-rumped** *adjective* having a yellow rump; *yellow-rumped warbler*, a N. American warbler, *Dendroica coronata*, with mainly blackish-grey plumage and a yellow rump. **yellow rust** a disease of wheat caused by the fungus *Puccinia striiformis*. **yellow sally** [*Sally*, female forename] ANGLING a lemon-yellow stonefly, esp. *Isoperla grammatica*, used as bait. **yellow-shafted flicker** a form of the common or northern flicker, *Colaptes auratus*, with yellowish-brown underwings. **yellowshank** = *yellowlegs* above. **yellow shell** a Eurasian geometrid moth, *Camptogramma bilineata*, the typical form of which has yellowish wings marked with dark wavy lines. **yellow snake** any of several yellowish snakes; *esp.* (*W. Indies*) = *yellow boa* above. *yellow snapdragon*: see SNAPDRAGON 1. **yellow soap** a soap containing rosin and tallow. **yellow spot** *noun*² = *macula lutea* s.v. MACULA 2. **yellow-staining mushroom** an inedible mushroom, *Agaricus xanthoderma*, which turns bright yellow where it is bruised. **yellow star** *Hist.* a piece of yellow cloth bearing the Star of David, which the Nazis required Jews to wear. *yellow star-thistle*: see *star-thistle* s.v. STAR *noun*¹ & *adjective*. **yellow streak** *colloq.* a trait of cowardice. *yellow suckling*: see SUCKLING *noun*² 1. **yellowthroat** any of several New World warblers of the genus *Geothlypis*; *esp.* (more fully *common yellowthroat*, *Maryland yellowthroat*) *G. trichas* of N. America, the male of which has a black mask and yellow underparts. **yellow tissue** = ELASTIC *tissue*. *yellow toadflax*: see TOADFLAX 1. *yellow topaz*: see TOPAZ *noun* 1. **yellow trout** = *brown trout* s.v. BROWN *adjective*. **yellow underwing** any of various Eurasian noctuid moths, esp. of the genus *Noctua*, which have yellow hindwings with a dark band near the margin. *yellow* VETCHLING. **yellow wagtail** a migratory Eurasian wagtail, *Motacilla flava*, with yellow underparts and a greenish back. **yellow warbler** (**a**) each of three small African warblers of the genus *Chloropeta*, with greenish upperparts and a yellow breast; spec. *C. natalensis* of central and southern Africa; (**b**) a small New World warbler, *Dendroica petechia*, with predominantly yellow plumage. **yellow ware** earthenware or stoneware made from yellow clay and covered with a yellow glaze. **yellow warning** = *yellow alert* above. **yellow-wood** (the timber of) any of several trees with wood which is yellow or yields a yellow dye, *esp.* (**a**) *Cladrastis lutea*, a leguminous tree of the southern US (also called **gopher-wood**); (**b**) = IROKO. **yellow-wort** a plant of calcareous grassland, *Blackstonia perfoliata*, of the gentian family, with bright yellow flowers and connate leaves. *yellow yam*: see YAM *noun*¹ 1. *yellow* YITE.

yellow /ˈjɛləʊ/ *verb*¹. OE.
[from the adjective.]
1 *verb intrans.* Become yellow; *esp.* fade to a yellow colour. OE.
2 *verb trans.* Make yellow. L16. ▸**b** Make a yellow admiral of. *Nautical slang* (now *Hist.*). M18.

📖 **1** S. E. WHITE The old piano with the yellowing keys. *fig.*: *Guardian Weekly* All that is left is a batch of yellowing declarations of good intentions.

†**yellow** *verb*² *intrans. rare.* E–M17.
[App. extension of YELL *verb*.]
Yelp; bellow.

yellow-bellied /ˈjɛlə(ʊ)bɛlɪd/ *adjective.* E18.
[from YELLOW *adjective* + BELLIED *adjective*.]
1 Of an animal: having yellow underparts. E18.
2 Cowardly. *colloq.* (orig. *US*). E20.
Special collocations: *yellow-bellied sapsucker*: see SAP *noun*¹. **yellow-bellied toad** a small European toad, *Bombina variegata*, which has a mainly bright yellow or orange underside. **yellow-bellied turtle** a turtle of a race of the N. American pond slider, *Pseudemys scripta*, having a yellow plastron. **yellow-bellied waxbill** = SWEE *waxbill*.

yellow-belly /ˈjɛlə(ʊ)bɛli/ *noun.* Also **yellowbelly**. L18.
[from YELLOW *adjective* + BELLY *noun*.]
1 A native of Lincolnshire. *colloq.* L18.
2 a A frog. E19. ▸**b** The yellow-bellied turtle; the tortoiseshell obtained from this. M19. ▸**c** Any of various fishes with yellow underparts; *esp.* (**a**) *Austral.* the golden perch, *Plectroplites ambiguus*; (**b**) *Austral. & NZ* any of several flatfishes, as certain flounders of the genera *Ammotretis* and *Rhombosolea*. L19.

3 A person having a yellowish skin; *esp.* (**a**) *US* a Mexican; (**b**) a person of mixed descent. *offensive.* **M20.**
4 A coward. *colloq.* (orig. *US*). **M20.**

yellowfin /ˈjɛlə(ʊ)fɪn/ *noun & adjective.* **E19.**
[from YELLOW *adjective* + FIN *noun*¹.]
▶ **A** *noun.* Any of various fishes with fins that are yellow or have yellow colouring on them. **E19.**
▶ **B** *attrib.* or as *adjective.* Having fins that are yellow or have yellow colouring on them. **E20.**
yellowfin croaker a shallow-water grey-green game-fish, *Umbrina roncador*, of the southern Californian coast. **yellowfin sole** a flatfish of the N. Pacific, *Limanda aspera*, caught for food esp. in the Bering Sea. **yellowfin tuna** a tuna, *Thunnus albacares*, which is found in all warm and tropical seas and is fished extensively for food.

yellowhammer /ˈjɛlə(ʊ)hamə/ *noun.* **M16.**
[from YELLOW *adjective*; 2nd elem. perh. from Old English *amore* a kind of bird, possibly conflated with *hama* covering, feathers.]
1 A common Eurasian bunting, *Emberiza citrinella*, the male of which has a bright yellow head and underparts. **M16.**
2 Any of several other birds with yellow plumage; *esp.* (**a**) *N. Amer.* the common or northern flicker, *Colaptes auratus*; (**b**) *Austral.* the yellow robin, *Eopsaltria australis*. **M19.**

yellowish /ˈjɛləʊɪʃ/ *adjective.* **LME.**
[from YELLOW *adjective* + -ISH¹.]
Somewhat yellow; having a yellow tinge.
■ **yellowishness** *noun* **M16.**

yellowly /ˈjɛləʊli/ *adverb.* **E17.**
[from YELLOW *adjective* + -LY².]
With a yellow colour or light.

yellowness /ˈjɛlə(ʊ)nɪs/ *noun.* **LME.**
[from YELLOW *adjective* + -NESS.]
1 The quality or state of being yellow; yellow colour. **LME.**
†**2** *fig.* Jealousy. **L16–E17.**

📖 **2** SHAKES. *Merry W.* I will incense Page to deal with poison; I will possess him with yellowness.

yellowtail /ˈjɛlə(ʊ)teɪl/ *noun & adjective.* **E17.**
[from YELLOW *adjective* + TAIL *noun*¹.]
▶ **A** *noun.* †**1** An earthworm with a yellow tail. Only in **17.**
2 Any of various marine fishes with a tail that is yellow or has yellow colouring on it; *esp.* (**a**) a large carangid game-fish of the genus *Seriola* (cf. ***amberjack*** s.v. AMBER *adjective*); (**b**) a trevally or kingfish of the genus *Caranx*; (**c**) a small estuarine carangid, *Trachurus novaezelandiae*, found in Australasian waters; (**d**) = MADEMOISELLE 4. **E18.**
3 A white European moth, *Euproctis similis* (family Lymantriidae), which has a yellow tip to the abdomen. **M18.**
4 A female or an immature male of the American redstart, *Setophaga ruticilla*, marked by yellow patches on the tail. *N. Amer.* Now *rare.* **L18.**
▶ **B** *attrib.* or as *adjective.* Having a yellow tail. **L18.**
Special collocations & comb.: **yellowtail damselfish**, **yellowtail demoiselle** a tropical Atlantic damselfish, *Microspathodon chrysurus*, which has a dark body and a contrasting bright yellow tail. **yellowtail flounder** a right-eye flounder of the NW Atlantic, *Limanda ferruginea*, which is yellowish with reddish-brown spots and was formerly an important food fish; also called ***rusty dab***. **yellowtail kingfish** a large carangid game-fish, *Seriola grandis*, of Australasian waters. **yellowtail rockfish** a scorpaenid food fish, *Sebastes flavidus*, found off the Pacific coast of N. America. **yellowtail scad** = sense A.2(c) above. **yellowtail snapper** a large snapper fish of the tropical Atlantic, *Ocyurus chrysurus*, which has a yellow lateral stripe merging with a yellow tail, and is a popular food and game-fish. **yellowtail warbler** (now *rare*) = sense A.4 above.

yellowy /ˈjɛləʊi/ *adjective.* **M17.**
[from YELLOW *adjective* + -Y¹.]
Yellowish.

yelm /jɛlm/ *noun & verb.* Long *dial.* Also **yealm**.
[Old English *gielm*, *gelm*, *gilm*, *gylm*, of unkn. origin.]
▶ **A** *noun.* Orig., a handful, a bundle, a sheaf. Now *spec.*, a bundle of straw laid straight for thatching. **OE.**
▶ **B** *verb trans. & intrans.* Separate, select, and arrange (straw) for thatching. **L16.**

yelp /jɛlp/ *noun.*
[Old English *gielp*, *gelp*, *gilp* = Old Saxon *gelp* defiant speech, Old High German, Middle High German *gelph*, *gelf* outcry, Old Norse *gjálp* noise of the sea: cf. next.]
▶†**I 1** Glory; ostentation. Only in **OE.**
2 Pride, arrogance. Only in **OE.**
3 Boasting, vainglorious speaking. **OE–LME.**
▶ **II 4** A short shrill cry of pain, excitement, etc., esp. as uttered by a dog. **E16.**

yelp /jɛlp/ *verb.*
[Old English *gielpan*, *gelpan*, *gilpan* = Middle High German *gelfen*, *gelpfen*, from Germanic imit. base repr. also in Old Saxon *galpon* (Low German *galpen*).]
▶ **I** †**1** *verb intrans.* Boast, speak vaingloriously. (Foll. by *of*, *that*.) **OE–LME.**
▶ **II** †**2** *verb intrans.* Cry or sing with a loud voice. **LME–M16.**
3 *verb intrans.* Esp. of a dog: utter a yelp or yelps. **M16.**
▶**b** *fig.* Complain, whine. **E18.**
4 *verb trans.* Utter with a yelp or in a yelping tone. **M17.**

📖 **3b** *Publishers Weekly* Writers yelp vainly when directors muscle in on their screen credits.

■ **yelper** *noun* **ME.**

†**yeman** *noun* var. of YEOMAN.

Yemeni /ˈjɛməni/ *noun & adjective.* **E20.**
[Arab. *yamanī*: see -I².]
▶ **A** *noun.* A native or inhabitant of Yemen, a country in southern Arabia. **E20.**
▶ **B** *adjective.* Of or pertaining to Yemen or its inhabitants. **M20.**

Yemenite /ˈjɛmənʌɪt/ *noun & adjective.* **M19.**
[from prec. + -ITE¹.]
▶ **A** *noun.* **1** = YEMENI *noun.* **M19.**
2 A Jew who was, or whose ancestors were, formerly resident in the Yemen. **E20.**
▶ **B** *adjective.* Of, pertaining to, or designating a Yemeni Arab or a Yemeni Jew. **L19.**

yen /jɛn/ *noun*¹. Pl. same. **L19.**
[Japanese *en* round. Cf. YUAN *noun*².]
The basic monetary unit of Japan, equal to 100 sen.

yen /jɛn/ *noun*² *& verb.* **L19.**
[Chinese (Cantonese) *yăn*, (Mandarin) *yǐn* addiction, craving for drugs, strong interest.]
▶ **A** *noun.* **1** The craving of a drug addict for a drug (orig. *spec.* for opium). Also, (a restless sleep characteristic of) the withdrawal symptoms of drug addiction. *slang* (orig. *US*). **L19.**
2 *gen.* A craving, a yearning, a longing (*for*). *colloq.* **E20.**

📖 **2** S. GIBBONS Ezra . . had a secret yen for horticulture.

▶ **B** *verb intrans.* Infl. **-nn-**. Crave for a drug; yearn, have a strong desire (*for*, *to do*). *slang.* **E20.**

yen /jɛn/ *noun*³. *US slang & techn.* **L19.**
[Prob. from Chinese *yān*, (Cantonese) *yin*.]
Opium.
Comb.: **yen hock**, **yen hok** a needle used in the preparation of opium in the form of pills or pellets for smoking; **yen hop** an opium pipe; **yen pock**, (*collect. sing. & pl.*) **yen pox** an opium pill; opium prepared as pills; **yen shee**, **yen shi** /ʃiː/ (**a**) the ash formed in the bowl of an opium pipe; (**b**) *loosely* opium; **yen siang**, **yen tsiang** /sɪˈaŋ/ an opium pipe.

Yenan /jɛˈnan/ *noun.* **M20.**
[A town in northern Shaanxi province, NE China.]
Hist. Used **attrib.** to designate the period 1936–49 in the history of the Chinese Communist Party, during which Yenan was its headquarters, or principles and policies evolved by the Party at that time.

Yenisei /ˈjɛnɪseɪ, jɛnɪˈseɪ/ *noun & adjective.* **L19.**
[A river in central Siberia.]
In full ***Yenisei Samoyed***. (Of) the Enets language.
Comb.: **Yenisei-Ostyak** *noun & adjective* (of) a central Siberian language of uncertain affinities.

yenta /ˈjɛntə/ *noun. N. Amer.* Also **yente**. **E20.**
[Yiddish, orig. a personal name.]
A gossip, a busybody; a noisy, vulgar person; a scolding woman, a shrew.

yentz /jɛnts/ *verb trans. US slang.* **M20.**
[Yiddish *yentzen* lit. 'copulate'.]
Cheat, swindle.

yen-yen /ˈjɛnjɛn/ *noun. US slang.* **L19.**
[Prob. from Chinese, formed as YEN *noun*² + YEN *noun*³.]
A craving for opium, addiction to opium.

yeo /jəʊ/ *noun. colloq.* Pl. **yeos**. **M19.**
[Abbreviation.]
= YEOMAN.

yeoman /ˈjəʊmən/ *noun.* Pl. **-men**. Also †**yoman**, †**yeman**. **ME.**
[Prob. reduced form of ***young man*** s.v. YOUNG *adjective*.]
▶ **I 1** *Hist.* A servant or attendant in a royal or noble household, typically ranking between a sergeant and a groom or between a squire and a page; an officer of a specified department or function esp. in a royal or noble household (usu. with following designation of office). Also *gen.*, an assistant to an official, an attendant. **ME.**
2 A junior naval officer or naval rating who has charge of or assists in a particular department; *esp.* (**a**) (in full ***yeoman of signals***) a petty officer concerned with visual signalling; (**b**) *US* a petty officer performing clerical duties on board ship. **M17.**
1 ***yeoman bedel***, ***yeoman of the wardrobe***, ***yeoman porter***, etc. **2** ***engineer's yeoman***, ***navigator's yeoman***, etc.
▶ **II 3** *Hist.* A man holding a small landed estate; a freeholder below the rank of a gentleman; *spec.* a person qualified by possessing free land of an annual value of 40 shillings to serve on juries, vote for the knight of the shire, etc. Also more widely, a commoner or countryman of respectable standing, *esp.* a person who cultivates his own land; *spec.* a freeman of a livery company. **LME.**
4 A man of this standing or rank serving as a (foot-)soldier. Now *Hist.* exc. as in sense 5 below. **LME.**
5 *spec.* A member of the Yeomanry force (see YEOMANRY 3). **L18.**
Comb. & phrases: ***yeoman of signals***: see sense 2 above; **Yeoman of the Guard** a member of the bodyguard of the sovereign of England (orig. archers appointed at the accession of Henry VII, now ceremonial); ***yeoman pricker***: see PRICKER 1(b); **yeoman service**, **yeoman's service** good, efficient, or useful service esp. at a time of need; **Yeoman Usher** the deputy to Black Rod; ***yeoman waiter***: see WAITER 1c; **Yeoman Warder** a member of the guard of the Tower of London; **yeoman work** = ***yeoman service*** above.
■ **yeomaness** *noun* (*rare*) = YEOWOMAN **E17.** **yeomaˈnette** *noun* (*US colloq.*, now *Hist.*) a woman yeoman of the US navy (esp. during and just after the war of 1914–18) **E20.** **yeomanhood** *noun* the position or station of a yeoman **L19.** **yeomanly** *adjective & adverb* (**a**) *adjective* having the character or status of a yeoman; pertaining to, characteristic of, or befitting a yeoman, sturdy, homely; (**b**) *adverb* in the manner befitting a yeoman, like a yeoman, doughtily, handsomely: **LME.**

yeomanry /ˈjəʊmənri/ *noun.* **LME.**
[from prec. + -RY.]
▶ **I 1** The body of yeomen or small landed proprietors, yeomen collectively. Now *Hist.* **LME.** ▶**b** The general body of freemen of a livery company. Long *obsolete* exc. *Hist.* **L15.**
†**2** A company of yeomen or attendants. Only in **17.**
3 A volunteer cavalry force in the British army, originally formed in 1794 chiefly of men of the yeomanry class and now incorporated in the Territorial Army. Also (*Hist.*) ***The Yeomanry Cavalry***, ***The Imperial Yeomanry***. **L18.**
▶†**II 4** The condition of a yeoman; yeomanhood. **LME–E17.**
5 A thing pertaining to or characteristic of a yeoman; honest or homely speech (befitting a good yeoman); yeoman's dress. **L15–L16.**

yeow /jiːˈaʊ/ *interjection. colloq.* (orig. *US*). Also **yee(-)ow**. **E20.**
[Natural exclam.]
1 Repr. the cry of a wolf, cat, etc. *rare.* **E20.**
2 Expr. pain or shock. **E20.**

yeowoman /ˈjəʊwʊmən/ *noun. rare.* Pl. **-women** /-wɪmɪn/. **M19.**
[from WOMAN *noun* after YEOMAN.]
A woman having the rank or position of a yeoman.

yep /jɛp/ *adverb & interjection*¹. *colloq.* (orig. *US*). Also **yip** /jɪp/, **yup** /jʌp/. **L19.**
[Alt. of YES *adverb & interjection*. Cf. NOPE *adverb & interjection*, YUP.]
= YES *adverb & interjection.*

yep /jɛp/ *interjection*². **L17.**
[Natural exclam.]
Urging on a horse.

†**yepe** *adjective.*
[Old English *gēap*, prob. rel. to Old Norse *gaupn* (see GOWPEN), from Germanic.]
1 Cunning, crafty, sly. **OE–ME.**
2 Prudent, wise, sagacious, astute. **OE–L15.**
3 Active, nimble, brisk; bold, daring. **ME–E16.**
¶ Earlier form of YAP *adjective.*

yepsen /ˈjɛps(ə)n/ *noun. dial.* Now *rare* or *obsolete.* **ME.**
[Prob. from unrecorded Old English word corresp. to Middle Low German *gespe*, *gepse*, Low German *geps(e)*, *göps(e)* (German *Gäspe*). Cf. GOWPEN.]
= GOWPEN 1.

yer /jə/ *pers. pronoun. slang & dial.* **M19.**
[Repr. a pronunc.]
= YOU *pronoun.*

yer /jə/ *possess. adjective. slang & dial.* **E19.**
[Repr. a pronunc.]
= YOUR *adjective.*

-yer /jə/ *suffix.*
Var. of -IER, now used chiefly after *w* as in ***bowyer***, ***lawyer***, ***sawyer***.

yerba /ˈjəːbə/ *noun.* Pl. same, **-s**. **E19.**
[Spanish = herb.]
More fully ***yerba maté***. = MATÉ 2.
yerba plant, ***yerba tea***, ***yerba tree***, etc.
■ **yerbal** /jəːˈbɑːl/ *noun* a grove or plantation of yerba **M19.**

yerba buena /ˈjəːbə bʊˈeɪnə/ *noun phr.* **M19.**
[Spanish, lit. 'good herb'.]
A trailing aromatic labiate plant of the western US, *Satureja douglasii*, with lilac or whitish flowers, which was used medicinally by the Californian Indians.

yerba santa /ˈjəːbə ˈsantə/ *noun phr.* **L19.**
[Spanish, lit. 'holy herb'.]
Any of several shrubs of the genus *Eriodictyon* (family Hydrophyllaceae), of south-western N. America; esp. *E. californicum*, whose aromatic leaves are used medicinally.

†**yerd-hunger** *noun*. *Scot*. E18–L19.
[from *yerd* dial. var. of EARTH *noun*[1] + HUNGER *noun*.]
Voracious desire to possess land.

yere /jɪə/ *adverb, noun, & pronoun*. *Scot. dial.* M19.
[Repr. a pronunc.]
= HERE *adverb, noun*[2], *& pronoun*.

yerk /jəːk/ *verb & noun*. Now chiefly *Scot. & dial.* Also **yark** /jɑːk/. LME.
[Origin uncertain: perh. partly imit. Cf. JERK *verb*[1], *noun*[1].]
▶ **A** *verb*. **1** *verb trans. & intrans.* Orig., sew (shoes or leather) tightly. Now also, bind (something) tightly with cords; tie firmly together. LME.
2 *verb trans.* Strike smartly, esp. with a rod or whip; slap, flog, lash. Now *rare*. E16.
3 *verb trans.* Pull, push, or throw with a sudden movement; wrench, tug; toss, jerk. M16.
4 a *verb intrans.* Lash or strike *out* with the heels, kick. M16. ▶**b** *verb trans.* Move (some part of the body) with a jerk or twitch; *esp.* (of a horse) lash out with (the heels). L16.
5 *verb trans.* Rouse, stir up, excite. L16. ▶**b** *verb intrans.* Nag, carp *at*. E17.
6 *verb intrans.* Esp. of an animal: spring or rise suddenly. E17.
7 *verb trans.* Utter abruptly; rattle off, strike up, (a song etc.). E17.
8 *verb intrans.* Engage eagerly in something. M18.
▶ **B** *noun*. **1** A smart blow or stroke; the sound of such a blow; the crack of a whip; a thud. E16.
2 An act (of a horse) of lashing out with the heels; an abrupt movement, a jerk, a twitch. L16.
3 A throbbing feeling, a twitching sensation. E19.

Yerkish /ˈjəːkɪʃ/ *noun & adjective*. L20.
[from R. M. *Yerkes* (1876–1956), US primatologist + -ISH[1].]
▶ **A** *noun*. A sign language devised for chimpanzees, based on geometric symbols. L20.
▶ **B** *attrib.* or as *adjective*. Of, pertaining to, or designating this sign language. L20.

yern /jəːn/ *adjective*. Long *obsolete* exc. *dial.*
[Old English *georn* = Old Saxon *gern*, Old High German *gern*, *kern* (Middle High German *gern*, German *gern*), Old Norse *gjarn*, from Germanic: cf. YEARN *verb*[1].]
1 Eager, keen; greedy, covetous. OE.
†**2** Swift; brisk; nimble. LME–E16.

yerra /ˈjɛrə/ *interjection*. *Anglo-Irish*. L19.
[Irish.]
Expr. asseveration or deprecation.

yerse /jəːs/ *adverb & interjection*. *non-standard*. Also **yers**. M20.
[Repr. a pronunc. Cf. YAAS, YAS.]
= YES *adverb & interjection*.

yersinia /jəːˈsɪnɪə/ *noun*. Pl. **-iae** /-ɪiː/, **-ias**. M20.
[mod. Latin (see below), from A. E. J. *Yersin* (1863–1943), Swiss-born French bacteriologist + -IA[1].]
BACTERIOLOGY. A bacterium of the genus *Yersinia* (formerly included in *Pasteurella*), which includes Gram-negative bacilli that are facultative anaerobes present in many animals, causing plague and yersiniosis in humans.
▪ **yersiniˈosis** *noun*, pl. **-oses** /-ˈəʊsiːz/, (a disease caused by) infection with yersiniae other than *Y. pestis* (the cause of plague), which in humans is self-limiting and usu. marked by lymphadenitis of the mesentery and ileitis or by enteritis L20.

yes /jɛs/ *noun*. Pl. **yeses**, **yes's**. E18.
[from YES *adverb & interjection*.]
An utterance of the word 'yes'; an instance of the use of 'yes'; an affirmative reply, an expression of assent.
say yes agree to a request; assent, comply.
Comb.: **yes-girl** *colloq.* = *yes-woman* below; **yes-man** *colloq.* a man who habitually says 'yes'; a person who habitually expresses agreement with a superior; an obsequious or weakly acquiescent subordinate; **yes-woman** *colloq.* an obsequiously subordinate or weakly acquiescent woman.

yes /jɛs/ *verb*. Infl. **-ss-**. E19.
[from next.]
1 *verb intrans.* Say 'yes'; assent. E19.
2 *verb trans.* Say 'yes' to or agree with (someone); flatter by habitual assent. *US*. E20.

yes /jɛs/ *adverb & interjection*.
[Old English *gēse*, *ġise*, *ġyse*, prob. from an unrecorded form equivalent to YEA *adverb*[1] + *sīe* may it be (so). Cf. YAAS, YAH *adverb & interjection*[1], YAS, YEAH, YEH, YEP *adverb & interjection*[1], YERSE.]
Equivalent to an affirmative sentence: *esp.* (**a**) giving an affirmative reply to a question, request, etc.; (**b**) agreeing with, affirming, or emphasizing a positive statement; (**c**) introducing a contradiction of a negative statement, usu. followed by an assertive phrase; (**d**) introducing a more emphatic or comprehensive statement, followed by *and*; (**e**) acknowledging one's presence when summoned, addressed, or approached (freq. *interrog.*); (**f**) *interrog.* inviting assent or approval; (**g**) *interrog.* expr. interest or mild disbelief and inviting further information. Also repeated for the sake of emphasis or as a sign of impatience.

📖 SHAKES. *A.Y.L.* Didst thou hear these verses? . . O, yes, I heard them all. O. W. HOLMES Tender-eyed blonde. Long ringlets . . . Says 'Yes?' when you tell her anything. DICKENS 'It's not in the way, Charley.' 'Yes, it is,' said the boy, petulantly. DAY LEWIS Yes, I accept all this. *Daily Telegraph* They found the process exciting, yes, and invigorating. R. LUDLUM His intercom buzzed; he flipped the switch on his console. 'Yes?' **Yes and No** (*a*) = ***twenty questions*** s.v. TWENTY *adjective*; (**b**) a game in which questions must be answered without using 'yes' or 'no'. **yes and no** (in answer to a question) partly, perhaps, to a certain degree. **yes-no**, **yes-or-no** *attrib. adjective* answerable by or definable in terms of a simple affirmation or negation. **yes sir** *colloq.* (chiefly *US*) certainly, indeed (cf. YESSIR). ***yes siree***.

¶ Peculiar to English, and formerly used spec. in response to a neg. question (in distinction from *yea*).

yeshiva /jəˈʃiːvə/ *noun*. Pl. **-vas**, **-vot(h)** /-vɒt/. M19.
[Hebrew *yĕšīḇāh*, from *yāšaḇ* sit.]
An Orthodox Jewish college or seminary; a Talmudic academy.

yesk *verb & noun* var. of YEX.

yeso /ˈjɛsəʊ/ *noun*. Also †**yesso**. M16.
[Spanish from Latin GYPSUM. Cf. GESSO.]
Gypsum, plaster of Paris; *esp.* gypsum-rich dust used to control acidity during the making of sherry.
¶ Obsolete after E17; reintroduced M19.

yessir /ˈjɛsə, jɛsˈsəː/ *interjection, noun, & verb*. *colloq.* E20.
[Alt. of ***yes sir*** s.v. YES *adverb & interjection*. Cf. NOSSIR.]
▶ **A** *interjection*. Expr. assent, esp. to a superior, or (chiefly *N. Amer.*) emphatic affirmation. E20.
▶ **B** *noun*. An utterance of 'yessir'. M20.
▶ **C** *verb trans. & intrans.* Infl. **-rr-**. Defer to (someone) as a superior; say 'yes, sir' to (someone). M20.

†**yesso** *noun* var. of YESO.

yessum /ˈjɛsəm/ *interjection*. *US dial.* E20.
[Alt. of *yes, ma'am*. Cf. YESSIR.]
A polite form of assent addressed to a woman.

yest *noun* see YEAST *noun*.

yester /ˈjɛstə/ *adjective, adverb, & noun*.
[Old English *geostra*, *giestra* = Old High German *gestaron*, *gesterēn* (German *gestern*), Middle Low German *ghist(e)ren*, Dutch *gisteren*, from Germanic base + compar. suffix *-t(e)r-*, from Indo-European base repr. also in Greek *khthes*, Sanskrit *hyas*, Latin *heri* yesterday (cf. also Latin *hesternus* of yesterday). In later use extracted from YESTERDAY.]
▶ **A** *adjective*. Of, pertaining to, or designating the day before today, yesterday. Now *poet.* exc. in comb. OE.

📖 DAY LEWIS Betwixt My yester and my morrow self.
YESTERDAY. **yestereve**, **yester-evening** *adverbs & nouns* (now *arch. & poet.*) (on) the evening of yesterday, YESTER-EVEN. **yestermorn**, **yester-morning** *adverbs & nouns* (now *arch.*, *poet.*, *& dial.*) (on) the morning of yesterday, yesterday morning.

▶†**B** *adverb*. On the day before today, yesterday. OE–L18.
▶†**C** *noun*. The day before today, yesterday. E18–M19.

yesterday /ˈjɛstədeɪ, -di/ *adverb, noun, & adjective*.
[Old English *ġeostran dæġ*, *ġiestran dæġ*, from Germanic base of YESTER, DAY *noun*: cf. Gothic *gistradagis* tomorrow.]
▶ **A** *adverb*. On the day before today; *fig.* in the (recent) past. Also *hyperbol.*, extremely urgently, immediately. OE.

📖 M. KEANE I flew in yesterday from Brazil. *Independent* Everybody wants something, and they want it yesterday. **not born yesterday** not wholly naive, not a fool (esp. in ***wasn't born yesterday***).

▶ **B** *noun*. The day before today; the previous day; *fig.* the (recent) past. OE.

📖 A. M. FAIRBAIRN To enrich the church of to-day with the wealth of all her yesterdays. *Guardian* Yesterday's talks . . do not herald any dramatic shift or achievement.

▶ **C** *adjective*. Belonging to yesterday or the immediate past; bygone. Now *rare* or *obsolete*. M16.
Comb.: **yesterday afternoon**, **yesterday evening**, **yesterday morning**, **yesterday night**, etc. (during) the afternoon, evening, morning, night, etc., of yesterday; **yesterday's man** a man, esp. a politician, whose career is finished or past its peak; **yesterday's news** *fig.* a thing which (or person who) is no longer of interest.

yester-even /ˈjɛstəriːv(ə)n/ *adverb & noun*. Now *arch. & dial.* Also **yestere'en** /-ˈiːn/. LME.
[from YESTER + EVEN *noun*[1]. Cf. YESTREEN.]
(On) the evening of yesterday, yesterday evening.

yestern /ˈjɛst(ə)n/ *adjective & adverb*. *arch. & dial.* M19.
[App. from YESTER after adjectives in *-ern*, as *eastern*.]
Yesterday.

yesternight /ˈjɛstənʌɪt/ *adverb & noun*. Now *arch. & dial.* OE.
[from YESTER + NIGHT *noun*.]
▶ **A** *adverb*. On the night of yesterday, last night. Also, yesterday evening. OE.
▶ **B** *noun*. Last night, the night just past. Also, yesterday evening. E16.

yester-year /ˈjɛstəjɪə/ *noun*. *literary*. L19.
[from YESTER + YEAR *noun*[1], orig. coined by D. G. Rossetti to render Villon's French *antan*.]
Last year. Also, time not long past (esp. nostalgically recalled).

📖 D. G. ROSSETTI Where are the snows of yester-year? G. CLARE Our wars of yester-year seem so heroic.

yestreen /ˈjɛstriːn/ *adverb & noun*. *Scot. & poet.* LME.
[Contr. from YESTER-EVEN.]
▶ **A** *adverb*. On the evening of yesterday; yesterday evening. LME.
▶ **B** *noun*. The evening of yesterday. E19.
¶ Taken up by English writers in 18th cent.

yesty *adjective* see YEASTY.

yet /jɛt/ *verb*. Long *obsolete* exc. *dial.* Infl. **-tt-**.
[Old English *ġēotan* = Old High German *giozan* (German *giessen*), Old Norse *gjóta*, Gothic *giutan*, from Germanic base rel. to Latin *fundere* pour. Cf. YOTE.]
1 *verb trans.* Pour; shed. OE.
2 *verb intrans.* Pour out, gush out. OE.
3 *verb trans.* **a** Cast (metal, a metal object). OE. ▶**b** Set in lead; *gen.* fix firmly. LME.

yet /jɛt/ *adverb, conjunction, & adjective*.
[Old English *ġiet*, *ġieta* = Old Frisian *iēta*, *ēta*, *ita*, of unkn. origin, like the synon. Old English *ġēn*, *ġēna*.]
▶ **A** *adverb*. **1 a** In addition, in continuation; besides, also, moreover; (with a numeral etc.) more. *arch.* exc. with *again*, *another*. OE. ▶**b** Emphasizing a compar.: even more, even, still. OE. ▶**c** [After Yiddish *noch*.] As an ironic intensive at the end of a sentence etc.: too, what's more. *colloq.* (orig. *US*). M20.
2 a Even now or at a particular time, as formerly; = STILL *adverb* 4 (freq. implying contrast to a future or subsequent state). OE. ▶**b** With following inf.: in future as not up till now (implying incompleteness and usu. preceded by *have* or *has*). M17.
3 Up to this (or that) time, until now (or then) (usu. implying expectation of possible change). Also (with superl. or *only*), so far, up to the present; (in interrog. & neg. contexts) so soon as this (or that), by now (or then). OE.
4 a At some time in the future, in the remaining time available, before all is over. OE. ▶**b** Even now (or then); as late as now (or then). OE. ▶**c** From this (or some stated or implied) time onwards; henceforth (or thenceforth). Now only contextually with words denoting time, as *awhile*, passing into sense 1a. OE.
5 Nevertheless, and in spite of that, but for all that. ME.

📖 **1a** *Guardian* The authorities are . . planning to make yet another startling concession. **b** T. HARDY This pine-clad protuberance was yet further marked out . . by . . a tower. **c** J. WAIN She wrote me a letter. On the typewriter, yet. **2a** K. LINES That song I heard is yet ringing in my ears. **b** *Independent* The deal has yet to be approved by the regulatory authorities. **3** I. MURDOCH She had not yet been down to the sea. O. MANNING The only encouraging sight I've seen here yet. J. AIKEN I had not become used to being Lady Fortuneswell yet. **4a** A. BROOKNER Elinor might yet learn those lessons. **b** *Guardian* Changes . . which could yet be reversed. **c** AV *John* 7:33 Then said Iesus vnto them, Yet a litle while am I with you, and then I goe vnto him that sent me. **5** M. PATTISON The style of Bede, if not elegant Latin, is yet correct.

Phrases: ***as yet***: see AS *adverb, conjunction, & rel. pronoun*. ***ere yet***: see ERE *conjunction* 1.
▶ **B** *conjunction*. In spite of that, but nevertheless, even then. Freq. correl. to *though* etc., and more emphatic than *but*. ME.

📖 V. WOOLF Writing is an agony . . . Yet we live by it. DAY LEWIS The whole picture, clear yet elusive, is bathed in a brooding, sub-aqueous light. R. F. HOBSON He has asked for an urgent appointment and yet arrives late.

▶ **C** *adjective*. That is still or as yet such; still continuing or subsisting. Now *rare*. E17.

yether *noun* var. of YEDDER.

yeti /ˈjɛti/ *noun*. M20.
[Tibetan *yeh-teh* little manlike animal.]
A creature said to resemble a large ape, whose tracks have supposedly been found in snow on the Himalayan mountains. Also called ***Abominable Snowman***.

yetling /ˈjɛtlɪŋ/ *noun & adjective*. *Scot. & north.* Also **yet(t)lin** /-lɪn/. LME.
[from YET *verb* + -LING[1].]
▶ **A** *noun*. **1** A pot or kettle, usu. of cast iron; *esp.* one with a bow-handle and three feet. LME.
2 Any of various articles made of cast iron; *esp.* a girdle on which cakes are baked. M16.
3 Cast iron. L18.
▶ **B** *adjective*. Made of cast iron; (of iron) cast. Now *rare* or *obsolete*. L15.

yett *noun* see GATE *noun*[1].

yettlin *noun* var. of YETLING.

yeuch /jəːx, jiːˈʌx/ *interjection*. *slang*. Also **yeeuch**, **yeugh**. L20.
[Imit.]
= YUCK *interjection*.

yeuk *verb & noun* var. of YUKE.

yew /juː/ *noun.*
[Old English *īw*, *ēow*, corresp. (with consonant-alt. and variation of gender) to Old English *ī(o)h*, *ēoh*, Old Saxon *īh*, Middle Low German, Middle Dutch *īwe*, *īewe*, *uw*, Old High German *īwu*, *īwa*, etc. (German *Eibe*), Old Norse *ýr* (chiefly 'bow') from Germanic, with parallel forms in Celtic and Balto-Slavonic.]
1 Any of various coniferous trees of the genus *Taxus* (family Taxaceae), with dark green narrow distichous leaves and seeds surrounded by a scarlet aril; esp. *T. baccata*, of Europe and western Asia, formerly much planted in churchyards. Also ***yew tree***. OE.
2 The dense springy wood of any of these trees; *esp.* that of *Taxus baccata*, formerly popular for making bows. Also ***yew-wood***. LME.
3 Branches of yew, as an emblem of mourning. LME.
4 A bow made of yew-wood. *poet.* L16.
1 ***Irish yew***: see IRISH *adjective*. ***stinking yew***: see STINKING *adjective*.
■ **yewen** *adjective* (*arch. rare*) made of the wood of the yew; consisting of yew trees: E16.

yew /jʊu:/ *pers. pronoun. colloq.* L19.
[Repr. a pronunc.]
= YOU *pronoun*.

yex /jɛks/ *verb & noun*. Long *obsolete* exc. *Scot. & dial.* Also **yesk** /jɛsk/.
[Old English *ġeocsian*, *ġiscian* corresp. to Old High German *gescōn*: of imit. origin.]
▶ **A** *verb*. †**1** *verb intrans.* Sob. OE–E17.
2 *verb intrans.* Hiccup. LME.
3 a *verb intrans.* Belch; hawk; expectorate. LME. ▸**b** *verb trans.* Belch forth. E16.
▶ **B** *noun*. A hiccup; the hiccups. Formerly also, a sob. OE.

yé-yé /jeje/ *adjective & noun.* M20.
[French, repr. *yeah-yeah* redupl. of YEAH, common in popular songs of the 1960s.]
▶ **A** *adjective*. Designating or pertaining to a style of popular music, dress, etc., typical of the 1960s, esp. in France; associated with or enthusiastic about this or subsequent forms of popular optimistic youth culture. M20.
▶ **B** *noun*. A person associated with the yé-yé style. Also, rock or pop music. M20.

yez /jɛz, jɪz/ *pers. pronoun. dial.* (esp. *Anglo-Irish*). Also **yiz**. E19.
[from YE *pers. pronoun* + *-z* repr. -S[1].]
You (said to more than one person).

Yezidi /ˈjɛzɪdi:/ *noun.* Also **Yaz-** /ˈjaz-/. E19.
[Origin unkn.]
A member of an exclusive community found chiefly in Kurdistan, Armenia, and the Caucasus, which, while believing in a supreme God, worships seven angels including the Devil, who is held to have repented.

YFC *abbreviation.*
Young Farmers Club.

†**yfere** *noun* var. of FERE *noun*.

†**yfere** *adverb.* ME–M18.
[Prob. pred. use of the noun.]
In company; together.
¶ Much used as a rhyming tag in Middle English poetry; *arch.* from 16.

†**ygo** *adverb. pseudo-arch.* L16–M18.
[Alt. of AGO *adverb*.]
Ago; formerly; ***late ygo***, recently.

📖 SPENSER And great Augustus long ygoe is dead.

YHA *abbreviation.*
Youth Hostels Association.

Yi /iː/ *noun & adjective.* Pl. of noun same. M20.
[Chinese.]
= LOLO.

yichus /ˈjɪkəs, -x-/ *noun.* Chiefly *US colloq.* E20.
[Yiddish from Hebrew *yiḥūs* pedigree.]
Social status, prestige.

Yid /*derog.* jɪd; *neutral (among Yiddish-speakers)* ji:d/ *noun. slang* (chiefly *derog.* & *offensive*). L19.
[Yiddish from Middle High German *Jude*, *Jüde* ult. from Latin *Judaeus* JEW *noun*.]
A Jew.

Yiddish /ˈjɪdɪʃ/ *noun & adjective.* L19.
[Yiddish *yidish*, short for *yidish daytsh* from Middle High German *jüdisch diutsch* Jewish German. Cf. German *jiddisch* Yiddish.]
(Of or pertaining to) a vernacular used by Jews in or from central and eastern Europe, based chiefly on High German with Hebrew and Slavonic borrowings, and written in Hebrew characters.

Yiddisher /ˈjɪdɪʃə/ *noun & adjective.* M19.
[German *Jüdischer*.]
▶ **A** *noun*. A Jew. M19.
▶ **B** *adjective*. Also **Yiddische**. Jewish. L19.

Yiddishism /ˈjɪdɪʃɪz(ə)m/ *noun.* E20.
[from YIDDISH + -ISM.]
1 A Yiddish word, idiom, or grammatical feature, *esp.* one adopted in another language. E20.
2 Advocacy of Yiddish culture and language. M20.
■ **Yiddishist** *noun & adjective* (*a*) *noun* a supporter of Yiddishism; *spec.* an advocate of the use of Yiddish as the worldwide language of Jews; also, a student of Yiddish language or literature; (*b*) *adjective* pertaining to Yiddishism or Yiddishists: E20.

Yiddishkeit /ˈjɪdɪʃkʌɪt/ *noun.* L19.
[Yiddish *yidishkeyt*.]
Jewish or Yiddish quality.

yield /ji:ld/ *noun.*
[Old English *ġield* payment (see GUILD *noun*[1]) from Germanic base of next. In senses 3, 4 from the verb.]
†**1** Payment; a sum of money paid or exacted, *spec.* = GELD *noun*. OE–L16. ▸**b** Payment for loss or injury, compensation. OE–E16.
†**2** The offering of sacrifice to a deity; worship. OE–ME.
3 The action of yielding crops or other products, production; that which is produced, produce; *esp.* amount of produce. LME. ▸**b** The amount of money brought in (e.g. interest from an investment, revenue from a tax); return. L19. ▸**c** CHEMISTRY etc. The amount obtained from a process or reaction relative to the theoretical maximum amount obtainable. E20.
4 The action of yielding or giving way, as a metal or other elastic material under pressure or tension, esp. under a stress greater than the yield stress. Also, the stage in the progressive stressing and deformation of a body when the yield point is reached. L19.

📖 **3** A. PATON They would get rid of the cows that gave the smallest yield. P. MARSHALL He had planted the dwarf coconut trees because of their quick yield. ***sustained yield***. **b** M. BRETT Investors . . accept much lower initial yields on shares than on fixed-interest stocks. ***redemption yield***. **c** QUANTUM ***yield***.

Comb.: **yield gap** the difference between the return of Government stocks and that of ordinary shares; **yield point** (*a*) (the stress corresponding to) a point on a stress–strain diagram at which strain or elongation begins to increase substantially without a corresponding increase in stress or loading; (*b*) (*esp.* in GEOLOGY) the elastic limit or the yield strength; **yield strength** in materials that do not exhibit a well-defined yield point, the stress at which a specific amount of plastic deformation is produced (usu. taken as 0.2 per cent of the unstressed length); **yield stress** the value of stress at a yield point or at the yield strength; **yield table** FORESTRY: giving the average growth-rate or timber yield of a given kind of tree that can be expected from unit area of woodland each successive year.

yield /ji:ld/ *verb.* Pa. t. & pple **yielded**, †**yold**.
[Old English *ġeldan*, (West Saxon) *ġieldan* = Old Frisian *gelda*, *ielda*, Old Saxon *geldan*, Old High German *geltan* (Dutch *gelden*, German *gelten*), Old Norse *gjalda*, from Germanic base meaning 'pay, requite'. Cf. GUILD *noun*[1].]
▶ **I** Pay, repay.
1 *verb trans.* †**a** Give in payment, render as due, (a debt, tax, etc.). OE–M17. ▸**b** Give as due or required (service, thanks, etc.). Formerly also, perform (a promise, a vow). *arch.* OE.
†**2** *verb trans.* Pay compensation for, make good, (loss or injury). OE–ME.
†**3** *verb trans.* Pay back; give back, restore. Also ***yield again***. OE–M16.
4 *verb trans.* †**a** Give in return for something received; return (a benefit, injury, etc.). OE–L16. ▸**b** Return (an answer, greeting, etc.). Now only, vouchsafe (an assent). ME.
5 *verb trans.* †**a** Requite or make return for (an action etc.). Freq. in ***God yield it you***. OE–M16. ▸**b** Reward or repay (a person). In later use only in ***God yield you*** etc. (a common expression of gratitude or goodwill). Long *arch.* OE.

📖 **1b** G. P. R. JAMES Yield him obedience in lawful things. **4b** SHAKES. *Meas. for M.* Leave me your snatches and yield me a direct answer. **5b** SHAKES. *Ant. & Cl.* Tend me to-night two hours, I ask no more, And the gods yield you for't!

▶ **II** Produce, exhibit.
6 a *verb trans.* Produce, bear, generate, (fruit, crops, etc.). Now chiefly, provide (a given amount of produce); bring in (so much revenue). ME. ▸**b** *verb intrans.* Bear produce; be productive or fertile. ME. ▸**c** *verb trans.* Give as a mathematical result. Now *rare*. M16.
7 *verb trans.* **a** Present, offer. *obsolete* exc. as passing into other senses. ME. ▸**b** Grant as a favour; bestow. ME. ▸†**c** Exercise (a function, force, etc.); deal (blows), give (battle); execute (a sentence, vengeance). ME–L16.
†**8** *verb trans.* Communicate in speech; *esp.* declare (a reason etc.). ME–M17.
†**9** *verb trans.* With compl.: render, make, cause to be. LME–L17.
10 *verb trans.* Emit, discharge; utter. *obsolete* exc. as passing into senses 11a, c. LME.
11 *verb trans.* **a** Provide so as to supply a need or serve a purpose. M16. ▸**b** Give rise to (a state or feeling). Now *rare*. L16. ▸†**c** Present to view, exhibit. E17–E18.

📖 **6a** *National Trust Magazine* The orchard yielded plums, pears, and apples. A. N. WILSON Father's investments only yielded an income of some £190 per annum. *Angler* A small E. Anglian stillwater yielded 172 lb of pike. *Farmers Weekly* The barley yielded more than 4t / acre last year. **b** J. C. MORTON Spalding's Prolific Red Wheat . . yields remarkably well, and weighs well in the bushel. **7a** S. PURCHAS Where the holy Trinitie did first yeeld it selfe in sensible apparition to the world. **b** J. R. GREEN The King yielded the citizens the right of justice. **8** J. USSHER What reason can you yeeld for this? **9** A. HALL This threat . . doth yeelde the Gods amazde and dum. **10** BACON Violets . . yeeld a pleasing Sent. M. ESSLIN These difficult plays could be forced to yield their secret. **11a** H. DRUMMOND Two flints struck together yielded fire. R. A. FREEMAN This soft loam . . yields beautifully clear impressions. **b** A. BAIN Curved forms . . yield . . a certain satisfaction through the muscular sensibility of the eye.

▶ **III** Surrender, give way, submit.
12 *verb trans.* Relinquish possession of, surrender (esp. a military position or forces to an enemy); *fig.* relinquish (a position of advantage etc.); give *up*. ME.
13 *verb trans.* †**a** Acknowledge (a person or thing) to be or *to be*; admit *that*. ME–M18. ▸**b** Concede the fact, validity, or cogency of. Now *rare*. L16.
†**14** *refl.* Betake oneself, go (*to*). ME–L16.
15 *verb intrans.* & (*arch.*) *refl.* Acknowledge defeat in a battle, contest, etc.; submit, surrender, (*to*). ME.
16 *verb intrans. fig.* ▸**a** Give way (*to* persuasion, entreaty, etc.); submit (*to* a proposal etc.). Formerly also, consent *to do*. L15. ▸**b** Give way or succumb *to* an overpowering feeling, condition, influence, etc. L16.
17 a *verb intrans.* Give way to or *to* pressure so as to collapse, bend, crack, etc.; *spec.* deform inelastically; undergo a large increase in strain without a corresponding increase in stress. (Foll. by *to*.) M16. ▸**b** Submit *to* and be affected by some physical action or agent (e.g. pressure, friction, heat, etc.). L18.
18 *verb intrans.* Be inferior or confess inferiority *to*. Now chiefly in ***yield to no one***. M16.
†**19** *verb intrans.* Be deflected *from* a path or course. L16–E19.
20 *verb intrans.* Give precedence (*to*); *spec.* (*a*) *US* relinquish the floor *to* another speaker in a debate; (*b*) (chiefly *N. Amer.*) give right of way to or *to* other traffic. E17.

📖 **12** A. DAVIS The overseers of the jail . . were not going to yield an inch without a fierce struggle. W. GELDART At the end of the lease the tenant must yield up the premises. ***yield the ghost***, ***yield up the ghost***: see GHOST *noun*. **yield one's breath**, **yield up one's breath** *arch.* die. **13a** MILTON I yeild it just, said Adam, and submit. **b** STEELE All which wise Men mean was yielded on both sides by our Lawyers. **15** E. HERBERT Genoua also was constrained to yield it self, and shake off the French yoke. E. A. POE You have conquered and I yield. LD MACAULAY The Whigs . . though defeated, . . did not yield without an effort. **16a** C. STEAD The worst thing about temptation is . . that you want to yield to it. W. S. CHURCHILL He was too ready . . to yield to the popular clamour which demanded the recall of an unsuccessful general. J. MCGAHERN Maggie yielded to Moran and stayed. **b** DICKENS The child . . soon yielded to the drowsiness that came upon her. **17a** J. LE CARRÉ He tugged at the string to break it, but it refused to yield. J. S. FOSTER Ductile materials which allow them to yield rather than break. **b** *Physiological Review* Many of the photo-autotrophic organisms have yielded to this treatment. **18** SWIFT Their mutton yields to ours, but their beef is excellent. L. AUCHINCLOSS I yield to nobody in admiration of my . . wife.

Comb.: **yield sign** *N. Amer.* a road sign instructing vehicles to give way;
■ **yieldable** *adjective* L16.

†**yieldance** *noun.* E17–E18.
[from YIELD *verb* + -ANCE.]
The action of yielding; submission, compliance.

yielder /ˈji:ldə/ *noun.* ME.
[from YIELD *verb* + -ER[1].]
†**1** A person who owes something; a debtor. Only in ME.
2 A person who gives up or concedes something, a person who gives in. L16.
3 An animal, crop, etc., that yields produce (of a given quantity). M18.

yielding /ˈji:ldɪŋ/ *ppl adjective.* ME.
[from YIELD *verb* + -ING[2].]
†**1** Owing, indebted. *rare*. Only in ME.
2 Bearing produce; fertile. Now *rare* or *obsolete*. M16.
3 Giving in, submitting; submissive, compliant. L16.
4 Giving way to pressure or other physical force; not stiff or rigid. L16.
■ **yieldingly** *adverb* M16. **yieldingness** *noun* E17.

yieldless /ˈji:dlɪs/ *adjective.* Chiefly *poet. rare*. M17.
[from YIELD *noun* or *verb* + -LESS.]
Not yielding or surrendering. Also, not productive.

yieldy /ˈji:ldi/ *adjective. rare.* L16.
[from YIELD *noun* or *verb* + -Y[1].]
1 Productive, fertile. L16.
2 Having the quality of yielding or giving way physically. M19.

YIG *abbreviation.*
Yttrium iron garnet.

Yi-hsing /iːˈʃɪŋ/ *adjective & noun.* E20.
[See below.]
(Designating) a type of unglazed red stoneware produced at Yi-hsing, a town in Jiangsu province, China, esp. in the later part of the Ming dynasty.

yike /jʌɪk/ *noun. Austral. slang.* M20.
[Origin unkn.]
A squabble, a fight.

yikes /jʌɪks/ *interjection. colloq.* L20.
[Origin unkn. Cf. YOICKS.]
Expr. great astonishment.
New York Woman I tried the Turkish steam room, then a dip in the 40-degree pool (yikes!).

yikker /ˈjɪkə/ *verb intrans.* M20.
[Imit.]
Of a bird or animal: make repeated short sharp cries.

yill /jɪl/ *noun. Scot.* L18.
[Alt. of ALE.]
= ALE 1.

yin /jɪn/ *noun*[1] *& adjective*[1]. L17.
[Chinese *yin* shade, feminine, the moon.]
► **A** *noun.* In Chinese philosophy, the female or negative principle of the two opposing forces of the universe. Cf. YANG. L17.
Kuan Yin: see KUAN 2.
► **B** *attrib.* or as *adjective.* That represents yin; feminine. M20.
Comb.: **yin-yang** the harmonious interaction of the female and male forces of the universe; ***yin-yang symbol***, a circle divided by an S-shaped line into a dark and a light segment, representing respectively yin and yang.

Yin /jɪn/ *noun*[2] *& adjective*[2]. Also (earlier) †**Ing**. L18.
[The dynasty's final capital in Honan Province.]
(Designating or pertaining to) the Shang dynasty of China, esp. in the period between the 15th and the 12th cents. BC.

ying ch'ing /jɪŋ tʃɪŋ/ *adjectival & noun phr.* E20.
[Chinese *yingqing* (Wade–Giles *ying ch'ing*) lit. 'shadowy blue'.]
(Designating) a type of Chinese porcelain with a bluish-white glaze produced in Jiangxi and other provinces, chiefly during the Song dynasty.

Yinglish /ˈjɪŋglɪʃ/ *noun & adjective. joc.* (orig. *US*). M20.
[Blend of YIDDISH and ENGLISH *adjective & noun.*]
(Of or pertaining to) a form of English containing many Yiddishisms.

yip /jɪp/ *noun.* Orig. *US.* E20.
[from the verb.]
A short high-pitched cry, as of a dog; a shout, an exclamation; a complaint.
P. G. WODEHOUSE If I'd been a life-insurance company I'd have paid up on him without a yip.

yip /jɪp/ *verb intrans.* Infl. **-pp-**. LME.
[Imit.]
1 Cheep, as a young bird. *obsolete* exc. *dial.* LME.
2 Utter a sharp cry or yelp; *transf.* complain. Orig. *US.* E20.

yip *adverb* var. of YEP *adverb.*

yipes /jʌɪps/ *interjection. colloq.* Also **yipe** /jʌɪp/. M20.
[Cf. CRIPES, YIKES.]
Expr. fear, dismay, or excitement.

yippee /ˈjɪpiː, jɪˈpiː/ *noun, interjection, & verb. colloq.* (orig. *US*). E20.
[Natural exclam.]
► **A** *noun.* A cry of 'yippee!' E20.
► **B** *interjection.* Expr. excited delight. M20.
A. CORNELISEN It's a boy! *A boy!* Yippee!
► **C** *verb intrans.* Cry 'yippee!' M20.

yippie /ˈjɪpi/ *noun.* Orig. *US.* Also **Y-**. M20.
[from Youth International Party + -IE, after HIPPY *noun.*]
A member of a group of politically active hippies, orig. in the US.

yips /jɪps/ *noun pl. colloq.* M20.
[Origin unkn.]
A state of nervousness which causes a golfer to miss an easy putt in a competition. Chiefly in ***the yips***.

Yishuv /jɪˈʃuːv, ˈjɪʃʊv/ *noun.* E20.
[Hebrew *yiššūḇ* settlement.]
The Jewish community or settlement in Palestine during the 19th cent. and until the formation of the State of Israel in 1948.

yite /jʌɪt/ *noun.* Chiefly *Scot.* E19.
[Origin unkn.]
More fully ***yellow yite***. The yellowhammer, *Emberiza citrinella.*

yiz *pers. pronoun* var. of YEZ.

Yizkor /ˈjɪzkə/ *noun.* Pl. same, **-s**. M20.
[Hebrew *yizkōr* lit. 'may he (sc. God) remember'.]
A memorial service held by Jews on certain holy days for deceased relatives, martyrs, etc.

-yl /ʌɪl, ɪl/ *suffix.* Also †**-ule**.
[Greek *hulē* wood, material.]
1 CHEMISTRY. Forming names of various groups and radicals, *esp.* those containing (***a***) any element combined with either oxygen or hydrogen, as ***carbonyl***, ***chromyl***, ***hydroxyl***, ***sulphydryl***; (***b***) carbon and hydrogen alone, as ***amyl***, ***butyl***, ***ethyl***; (***c***) carbon and hydrogen with oxygen, as ***acetyl***, ***carboxyl***, ***lactyl***. ►**b** Forming names of compounds containing such a group or radical, as ***alkyl***, ***biphenyl***.
2 Forming trade and proprietary names of various drugs, man-made fibres, etc., as ***Drinamyl***, ***Rhovyl***, ***Thermolactyl***.

ylang-ylang /iːlaŋˈiːlaŋ/ *noun.* Also **ilang-ilang**. L19.
[Tagalog *ilang-ilang.*]
A tree of tropical Asia, *Cananga odorata*, of the custard-apple family, with fragrant greenish-yellow flowers from which a perfume is distilled; the perfume obtained from this tree.

ylem /ˈʌɪlɛm/ *noun.* M20.
[Late Latin *hylem* accus. of HYLE.]
ASTRONOMY. In the big bang theory, the primordial matter of the universe, orig. conceived as composed of neutrons at high temperature and density.

ylid /ˈɪlɪd/ *noun.* Also **-ide** /-ʌɪd/. M20.
[from -YL + -ID[5], -IDE.]
ORGANIC CHEMISTRY. Any neutral compound containing a negatively charged carbon atom directly bonded to a positively charged atom of another element (esp. sulphur, phosphorus, or nitrogen).
■ **yˈlidic** *adjective* L20.

YMCA *abbreviation.*
Young Men's Christian Association; a hostel run by this.

-yne /-ʌɪn/ *suffix.*
[Alt. of -INE[5].]
CHEMISTRY. Forming the names of unsaturated hydrocarbons having a triple bond between two carbon atoms, as ***butyne***, ***propyne***, etc. Cf. ALKYNE.

yo /jəʊ/ *noun. dial.* (chiefly *US*). Pl. **yoes**. L19.
[Repr. a pronunc.]
= EWE *noun*[1].

yo /jəʊ/ *pers. pronoun & possess. adjective. dial.* (chiefly *Black English*). Also **yo'**. M19.
[Repr. a pronunc.]
► **A** *pers. pronoun.* You. M19.
► **B** *possess. adjective.* Your. M20.

yo /jəʊ/ *interjection.* Also redupl. **yo-yo(-yo)**. LME.
[Natural exclam.]
Attracting someone's attention, expr. encouragement or excitement, or (chiefly *US slang* (orig. *Black English*)) used as a greeting; NAUTICAL = YO-HO *interjection.*

yoaks /jəʊks/ *interjection. obsolete* exc. *dial.* Also **yoax**. L18.
[Cf. YOICKS.]
= YOICKS.

yob /jɒb/ *noun. colloq.* M19.
[Back slang for BOY *noun.*]
Orig., a boy. Now, an uncouth, loutish, ignorant youth or man; *esp.* one given to violent or aggressive behaviour, a hooligan.
B. ASHLEY A crowd of yelling yobs passed them a street away. *Times* I would not want anybody looking at me to think this man is a thick, stupid, illiterate yob.
■ **yobbery** *noun* yobbish behaviour L20. **yobby** *adjective* = YOBBISH M20.

yobbish /ˈjɒbɪʃ/ *adjective. colloq.* M20.
[from YOB + -ISH[1].]
Behaving like a yob, characteristic of a yob.
■ **yobbishly** *adverb* L20. **yobbishness** *noun* L20.

yobbo /ˈjɒbəʊ/ *noun. colloq.* Also **yobo**. Pl. **-o(e)s**. E20.
[Extended form of YOB.]
= YOB.
Railnews Beer swilling, transistor blaring yobbos heading for football troubles.

yock /jɒk/ *noun & verb. Theatrical slang* (chiefly *US*). Also **yok** (infl. **-kk-**). M20.
[Prob. imit. Cf. YUCK *verb & noun*[2].]
► **A** *noun.* A laugh, esp. a loud hearty one. M20.
► **B** *verb intrans.* Laugh, esp. loudly and heartily. M20.

yod /jɒd, jəʊd/ *noun.* In sense 1 also **yodh**. M18.
[Hebrew *yōḏ*. Cf. earlier JOD.]
1 The tenth and smallest letter of the Hebrew alphabet. M18.
2 PHONETICS. The semi-vowel /j/, which has the sound of the Hebrew *yod.* M18.

†**yode** *verb pa. t.*: see GO *verb.*

yodel /ˈjəʊd(ə)l/ *verb & noun.* Also (earlier) **j-**. E19.
[German *jodeln.*]
► **A** *verb.* Infl. **-ll-**, ***-l-**.
1 *verb intrans.* Practise a form of singing or calling marked by rapid alternation between the normal voice and falsetto, which is used esp. by people living in the Swiss and Tyrolean mountains. E19.
2 *verb trans.* Utter (a melody etc.) with yodelling. M19.
► **B** *noun.* A yodelled song, melody, or call. M19.
■ **yodeller** *noun* a person who yodels L19.

yodh *noun* see YOD.

yodization /jɒdʌɪˈzeɪʃ(ə)n/ *noun.* Also **-isation**. M20.
[from YOD + -IZATION.]
PHONETICS. = YOTIZATION.

yoga /ˈjəʊgə/ *noun.* L18.
[Sanskrit, lit. 'union': see YOKE *noun*[1].]
In Hindu philosophy, union of the self with the supreme being; a system of ascetic practice, meditation, etc., designed to achieve this. Freq. *spec.* = HATHA YOGA.
HATHA YOGA. *KARMA-yoga. Kundalini yoga*: see KUNDALINI 2. RAJA YOGA.

Yogacara /jəʊgɑːˈtʃɑːrə/ *noun.* L19.
[Sanskrit *yogācāra*, formed as YOGA + *ā-cāra* conduct, practice.]
1 A school of Mahayana Buddhism which teaches that only consciousness is real. L19.
2 An adherent of the Yogacara school. E20.
■ **Yogacarin** *noun* = YOGACARA 2 M20.

yogh /jɒg/ *noun.* ME.
[Origin unkn.]
The letter ȝ, originally a loose writing of *g* in Old English but developing in Middle English as a distinct letter to represent a palatal semivowel (/j/) initially and medially, a voiced velar or palatal fricative medially, and a voiceless velar or palatal fricative medially and finally. In later Middle English it was replaced by silent *gh*, *y*, and medial and final *w*. The letter *z* in some Scottish words (now chiefly place-names and surnames), such as *Menzies* /-ŋ-/, *Kirkgunzeon* /-nj-/, is an adaptation of yogh.

yoghurt /ˈjɒgət/ *noun.* Also **yogurt**. E17.
[Turkish *yoğurt*. Cf. YAOURT.]
A semi-solid, somewhat sour foodstuff, now often fruit-flavoured, made from milk curdled by the addition of certain bacteria; a carton of this substance.
■ **yoghurty** *adjective* full of, smeared with, or resembling yoghurt L20.

yogi /ˈjəʊgi/ *noun.* In sense 1 also **yogin** /-ɪn/. E17.
[Sanskrit *yogī* nom. sing. of *yogin*, from YOGA.]
1 A person practising, or proficient in, yoga. E17.
2 = YOGA. E20.
1 R. K. NARAYAN These Yogis can travel to the Himalayas just by a thought. B. W. ALDISS A yogi . . had once told him that, through correct breathing, modern man could regenerate himself.

yogic /ˈjəʊgɪk/ *adjective.* E20.
[from YOG(A + -IC.]
Of or pertaining to yoga.
yogic flying a technique used chiefly by Transcendental Meditation practitioners which involves thrusting oneself off the ground while in the lotus position.

yogin *noun* see YOGI.

yogini /ˈjəʊgɪniː/ *noun.* L18.
[Sanskrit *yoginī* fem. of *yogin*: see YOGI.]
1 HINDU MYTHOLOGY. A female demon, *esp.* one of a group attendant on Durga or Siva. L18.
2 A female yogi. M20.

yogism /ˈjəʊgɪz(ə)m/ *noun.* L17.
[from YOGA or YOGI + -ISM.]
The system of yoga or the yogis.

yogurt *noun* var. of YOGHURT.

yo-heave-ho /jəʊhiːvˈhəʊ/ *interjection & noun.* E19.
[from YO *interjection* + HEAVE-HO.]
NAUTICAL (now *Hist.*). (An exclamation) expr. effort in hauling together on a rope etc.
■ **yo-heave-hoing** *noun* the uttering of cries of 'yo-heave-ho!' M19.

yohimbe /jəʊˈhɪmbeɪ, -biː/ *noun.* Also **yohimbehe** /jəʊˈhɪmbəheɪ, -hiː/. L19.
[Prob. from a W. African lang.]
A W. African tree of the madder family, *Pausinystalia johimbe*, the bark of which yields yohimbine.
■ **yohimbine** /-biːn/ *noun* (CHEMISTRY) a crystalline toxic alkaloid, $C_{21}H_{26}O_3N_2$, obtained from the bark of the yohimbe, used as an adrenergic blocking agent and also as an aphrodisiac L19.

yo-ho /jəʊˈhəʊ/ *interjection, verb, & noun.* Also **yo-ho-ho** /jəʊhəʊˈhəʊ/. M18.
[from YO *interjection* + HO *interjection*[1].]
Chiefly NAUTICAL. ►**A** *interjection.* Attracting attention. Also = YO-HEAVE-HO. M18.
R. L. STEVENSON Fifteen men on the dead man's chest—Yo-ho-ho, and a bottle of rum!

▶ **B** *verb intrans.* Shout 'yo-ho!'. L18.
▶ **C** *noun.* A cry of 'yo-ho!'. E19.

yoi /jɔɪ/ *interjection.* Now *rare*. Also redupl. **yoi-yoi**. E19.
[Cf. next.]
= YOICKS.

yoicks /jɔɪks/ *interjection.* M18.
[Cf. YOI and HOICKS.]
Urging on hounds. Also, expr. excitement or exultation.

yoi-yoi *interjection* see YOI.

yojan /ˈjəʊdʒ(ə)n/ *noun.* Also **-na** /-nə/. L18.
[Sanskrit *yojana* yoking, distance travelled at one time without unyoking, formed as YOGA.]
In the Indian subcontinent: a measure of distance, varying locally from about 4 to 10 miles (6 to 15 km).

yok /jɒk/ *noun*¹. *slang* (*derog.*). E20.
[from Yiddish, GOY reversed with unvoicing of final consonant.]
Among Jews: a Gentile.

yok *noun*² & *verb* var. of YOCK.

yoke /jəʊk/ *noun*¹.
[Old English *ġeoc* = Old Saxon *juc* (Dutch *juk*), Old High German *joh* (German *Joch*), Old Norse *ok*, Gothic *juk*, from Germanic from Indo-European base corresp. to Latin *jugum*, Greek *zugon*, Sanskrit *yuga*, from base repr. also by Latin *jungere* join, Greek *zeugnunai*, Sanskrit YOGA.]
▶ **I 1** A wooden framework joining two oxen, horses, etc., at the neck and enabling them to pull a plough or wagon together. OE. ▸**b** ROMAN HISTORY. An uplifted yoke, or arrangement of three spears symbolizing it, under which a conquered army was made to pass. OE. ▸**c** A wooden frame fitted on the neck of a pig or other animal, to prevent it from breaking through a hedge etc. L16.
2 *fig.* **a** A burden of servitude or oppressive rule. OE. ▸**b** A bond of partnership or cooperation; *esp.* that of marriage. LME.
3 Any of various objects, esp. transverse bars, resembling a yoke; *esp.* (*a*) a crossbar on which a bell swings; (*b*) NAUTICAL a crosspiece fixed to the head of a rudder, which has ropes attached to its ends for steering; (*c*) ELECTRICAL ENGINEERING the part of a magnet or electromagnet that joins the poles or pole-pieces; (*d*) AERONAUTICS a control lever. LME.
4 a A frame fitted to the shoulders for carrying a pair of pails, baskets, etc. E17. ▸**b** A fitted part of a garment, usu. placed across the shoulders (or around the hips), from which the rest hangs. L19.

> 🕮 **2a** L. STRACHEY He had shaken the parental yoke from his shoulders; he was . . beginning to do as he liked. **b** SHAKES. *Merch. V.* Companions . . Whose souls do bear an equal yoke of love.

▶ **II 5** A pair of animals, esp. oxen, coupled by a yoke. (Pl. after numeral usu. same.) OE. ▸†**b** *gen.* A couple. LME–L16.
6 *Hist.* A measure of land in Kent, about 50 or 60 acres (20 or 25 hectares); vaguely, a small manor. OE.
7 = YOKING 2. *Scot. & dial.* M18.
8 A horse and cart or carriage; *gen.* a vehicle; a contraption, outfit, etc. *Scot. & Anglo-Irish.* L19.

> 🕮 **5** J. C. OATES Forty yoke of oxen were required to haul the enormous limestone slab.

Comb.: **yoke-elm** the hornbeam, *Carpinus betulus*, whose wood is used for yokes and whose leaves resemble those of the elm; **yoke-mate** an animal yoked with another; *fig.* = YOKE-FELLOW; **yoke-skey** *S. Afr.* = SKEY; **yoke-toed** *adjective* = ZYGODACTYL *adjective*; **yoke-tree** the main part of a yoke.

yoke *noun*² var. of YOLK *noun*².

yoke /jəʊk/ *verb.*
[Old English *ġeocian*, from YOKE *noun*¹.]
1 *verb trans.* **a** Put a yoke on (a pair of draught animals etc.); couple with a yoke. Also (*Austral.*) foll. by *up*. OE. ▸**b** Attach (an animal) *to* a plough or vehicle (orig. with a yoke); provide (a plough or vehicle) with yoked animals. LME.
2 *verb trans.* Bring into or hold in subjection; subjugate, oppress. Now *rare* or *obsolete*. ME.
3 *fig.* **a** *verb trans.* & (now *rare*) *intrans.* Bring or enter into association. ME. ▸**b** *verb intrans.* & (*in pass.*) *trans.* Become or be married. L16. ▸**c** *verb trans. gen.* Attach, put on or in (as a yoke). M19.
4 *verb trans.* Restrain (a pig or other animal) with a neck-yoke. M16.

> 🕮 **1b** *fig.*: W. R. NICOLL He yoked his great imagination to constant labour. **2** MILTON But foul effeminacy held me yok't. **3a** TENNYSON The care That yokes with empire. *Review of English Studies* Instances which illustrate different phenomena are yoked together.

■ **yokable**, **yokeable** *adjective* (*rare*) L15. **yoker** *noun* (*rare*) L15.

yoked /jəʊkt/ *adjective.* L15.
[from YOKE *noun*¹, *verb*: see -ED², -ED¹.]
1 Of draught animals: coupled by a yoke; attached by a yoke to a plough, vehicle, etc. L15.
2 a Of pails, baskets, etc.: carried on a shoulder-yoke. M19. ▸**b** Of a garment: fitted with a yoke. E20.

yoke-fellow /ˈjəʊkfɛləʊ/ *noun. arch.* E16.
[from YOKE *noun*¹ + FELLOW *noun*, translating Greek *suzugos*.]
1 A person yoked or associated with another, esp. in some work or activity. E16.
2 *spec.* A marriage partner, a spouse. M16.
■ **yoke-fellowship** *noun* E19.

yokel /ˈjəʊk(ə)l/ *noun. derog.* E19.
[Origin unkn.]
A (stupid or ignorant) rustic; a country bumpkin.

> 🕮 THACKERAY Black legs . . inveigle silly yokels with greasy packs of cards in railroad cars.

■ **yokelish** *adjective* characteristic of a yokel L19.

yoking /ˈjəʊkɪŋ/ *noun.* LME.
[from YOKE *verb* + -ING¹.]
1 The action of YOKE *verb*; an instance of this; *esp.* the coupling or attaching of animals by a yoke. LME. ▸**b** Harness. *Scot. & US.* L19.
2 A spell of work at the plough etc., done by a team of horses at a stretch, between being yoked and unyoked. E16. ▸**b** *transf.* An unbroken spell of any activity. E18.
3 A measure of land, prob. representing the amount ploughed at one yoking. *obsolete* exc. *Hist.* L16.
4 MINING. In *pl.* Pieces of wood joined together within a pit to prevent falls of earth or used in conjunction with stowces to mark out a claim. M17.

> 🕮 **2** G. S. KEITH A pair of horses can plough an English acre in three journies, or yokings, of four hours each. **b** A. J. CUPPLES 'A double yoking' . . a service when two successive sermons were preached without any mid-day interval.

Yokohama /jəʊkəˈhɑːmə/ *noun.* L19.
[A city in Japan.]
Used *attrib.* to designate things native to or associated with Yokohama.
Yokohama fowl (a bird of) a Japanese breed of fowl with a long tail.

yoko-shiho-gatame /ˈjəʊkəʊʃiːhəʊgaˌtameɪ/ *noun.* M20.
[Japanese, lit. 'lateral four-quarters hold', from *yoko* side, transverse direction + *shihō* (from *shi* four + *hō* direction, quarter) + *katame* to lock, hold.]
JUDO. A hold from the side in which the opponent's shoulders and hips are pinned to the ground.

yokozuna /jəʊkəˈzuːnə/ *noun.* Pl. same. M20.
[Japanese, from *yoko* crosswise + *tsuna* rope (orig. a kind of belt presented to the champion).]
A grand champion sumo wrestler.

Yokuts /ˈjəʊkʌts/ *noun & adjective.* L19.
[Yawelmani *yokʰoc'* an Indian.]
▶ **A** *noun.* Pl. same.
1 A member of any of about 40 closely related N. American Indian peoples of central California. L19.
2 The language family of the Yokuts; the language of any Yokuts group. E20.
▶ **B** *attrib.* or as *adjective.* Of or pertaining to the Yokuts or their languages. L19.

†**yold** *verb pa. t. & pple*: see YIELD *verb*.

yole *noun* see YAWL *noun*¹.

yolk /jəʊk/ *noun*¹. Also (now *rare* or *obsolete*) **yelk** /jɛlk/.
[Old English *ġeoloca*, *ġeolca*, from YELLOW *adjective*.]
1 The yellow internal part of a bird's egg, which is surrounded by the white, is rich in protein and fat, and nourishes the developing embryo. Also more fully ***egg-yolk***, ***yolk of egg***. OE. ▸**b** ZOOLOGY. The corresponding part in the ovum or larva of all egg-laying vertebrates and many invertebrates. M19.
2 *fig.* The best or innermost part of anything; the core. Now *Scot.* LME.
3 a A hard nodule in softer stone, rock, etc. Also, a soft type of coal. Chiefly *dial.* E18. ▸**b** A rounded opaque thickened part in window-glass; a pane of such glass. *Scot.* E19.
Comb.: **yolk duct** = ***vitelline duct*** s.v. VITELLINE 2; **yolk gland** a yolk-secreting gland present in most animals; a vitelline gland; **yolk sac** (*a*) a sac containing yolk attached to the embryos of reptiles and birds and the larvae of some fishes; (*b*) a sac lacking yolk in the early embryo of a mammal.
■ **yolkless** *adjective* L19.

yolk /jəʊk/ *noun*². Also **yoke**. E17.
[Backform. from YOLKY *adjective*¹. Cf. Middle Dutch *ieke*.]
A mixture of fat and suint found naturally in the wool of sheep. Cf. SUINT.
in the yolk (of wool) in its natural unwashed state.

yolked /jəʊkt/ *adjective.* L16.
[from YOLK *noun*¹ + -ED².]
Having or containing a yolk or yolks. Chiefly as 2nd elem. of comb.
double-yolked, ***small-yolked***, ***two-yolked***, etc.

yolky /ˈjəʊki/ *adjective*¹.
[Old English *eowocig*, ult. formed as EWE *noun*¹: see -Y¹. See also YOLK *noun*².]
Of wool: full of yolk or natural grease.

yolky /ˈjəʊki/ *adjective*². E16.
[from YOLK *noun*¹ + -Y¹.]
Resembling or consisting of egg-yolk; full of or containing yolk.

†**yoman** *noun* var. of YEOMAN.

†**yomer** *adjective & verb.*
[Old English *ġeōmor* = Old Saxon, Old High German *jāmar*.]
▶ **A** *adjective.* Sorrowful, wretched; doleful. OE–ME.
▶ **B** *verb intrans.* Murmur, complain; lament, mourn. OE–LME.
¶ Survives in altered form as YAMMER *verb*.

Yom Kippur /jɒm ˈkɪpə, kɪˈpʊə/ *noun phr.* M19.
[Hebrew *Yōm Kippūr*, from *yōm* day + *kippūr* atonement.]
= ***Day of Atonement*** s.v. ATONEMENT 4.
Comb.: **Yom Kippur War** an Arab–Israeli war that began on Yom Kippur on 6 October 1973.

yomp /jɒmp/ *verb intrans. & trans. slang* (orig. *Military*). L20.
[Origin unkn.]
March or trudge over (difficult terrain) with heavy equipment.

> 🕮 *Guardian* Our boys . . who yomped all those miles in the Falklands.

■ **yomper** *noun* L20.

yom tov /ˈjɒm tɒv/ *noun phr.* M19.
[Yiddish, from Hebrew *yōm* day + *ṭōb* good.]
A Jewish holiday or holy day.

Yomud /ˈjəʊmʌd, jɒˈmuːd/ *noun & adjective.* M19.
[Local name.]
▶ **A** *noun.* Pl. **-s**, same. A member of a Turkoman people of Turkmenistan. M19.
▶ **B** *adjective.* Of or pertaining to the Yomuds; *esp.* designating a type of rug made by this people, freq. having a characteristic diamond-shaped motif. E20.

yon /jɒn/ *adjective, pronoun, & adverb.* Now *Scot., dial., & literary.*
[Old English *ġeon*, corresp., with variation of vowels, to Old Frisian *jen*(*a*, *-e*, Middle Low German *gene*, Middle Dutch *ghens*, Old High German *jenēr* (German *jener* that one), Gothic *jains* that; cf. the parallel series of forms without initial consonant, viz. Old High German *enēr*, Old Norse *enn*, *inn* (def. article), cogn. with Greek *enē* day after tomorrow, *enioi* some, Sanskrit *ana-* this one.]
▶ **A** *demonstr. adjective.* **1** Designating some thing(s) or person(s) pointed out, esp. an object or objects at a distance but within view; yonder. Also *gen.* (now chiefly *Scot.*), that, those. OE.
2 = YONDER *adjective* 1. *local.* OE.

> 🕮 **1** W. H. DAVIES My eyes go far beyond, Across that field to yon far hill. ARNOLD BENNETT Let us hie hence in yon Aston Martin. L. GILLEN You'll be woman enough to stand up to yon Bruce.

▶ **B** *demonstr. pronoun.* Yonder person(s) or thing(s); that; those. Now chiefly *Scot. & dial.* ME.
▶ **C** *adverb.* = YONDER *adverb.* Now *Scot. & dial.* exc. in ***hither and yon*** s.v. HITHER *adverb* 1. LME.

yond /jɒnd/ *adjective*¹ & *pronoun. obsolete* exc. *dial.* ME.
[Use as adjective of YOND *adverb* after YON *adjective*.]
▶ **A** *adjective.* †**1** = YONDER *adjective* 1. Esp. in ***the yond side***. ME–E17.
2 = YON *adjective* 1. ME.
▶ **B** *demonstr. pronoun.* = YON *pronoun.* ME.

†**yond** *adjective*². *pseudo-arch.* (Spenser). L16–E17.
[App. due to misunderstanding of a passage in Chaucer using YOND *adverb* with ref. to a tiger.]
Furious, savage.

yond /jɒnd/ *preposition & adverb.* Also (*Scot.*) **yont** /jɒnt/.
[Old English *ġeond*(*an*) preposition, corresp. to Middle Low German *gent*(*en*), *jint*, Low German *gunt*(*en*), early Flemish *ghins* (Dutch *ginds*), Gothic *jaind*: cf. BEYOND.]
▶ **A** *preposition.* †**1** Through, throughout, over, across. OE–ME.
2 On or to the further side of, beyond. Chiefly *poet. & Scot.* LME.
▶ **B** *adverb.* **1 a** = YONDER *adverb* 2. *obsolete* exc. *dial.* OE. ▸**b** = YONDER *adverb* 1. *obsolete* exc. *dial.* ME.
2 At or to a distance; (far or further) away. Long *obsolete* exc. *Scot.* ME.

yonder /ˈjɒndə/ *adverb, adjective, pronoun, & noun.* ME.
[Corresp. to Old Saxon *gendra* (adjective), West Frisian *gindra* (adjective) on this side, Middle Dutch *ghinder*, *gunder* (Dutch *ginder*), Gothic *jaindrē*.]
▶ **A** *adverb.* **1** At or in the indicated place, there (esp. at a distance but within view); at some distance in the indicated direction; over there. ME.
2 To that place. ME.

> 🕮 **1** R. SUTCLIFF Yonder where the valley opens. F. O'CONNOR Look down yonder . . See that blind man down there? R. MACDONALD I found it in the clump of trees yonder. L. K. JOHNSON There's a glow on the hill, way over yonder.

▶ **B** *demonstr. adjective.* **1** Further, more distant. LME.
2 Situated yonder. Cf. YON *adjective* 1. LME.

1 H. FRASER His dead name . . by which his shadowy companions call him in the yonder world. G. MEREDITH A beech in May With the sun on the yonder side. *Dublin Review* Something on the yonder side of imagery. 2 SHAKES. *Mids. N. D.* You, the murderer, look as bright . . as yonder Venus in her glimmering sphere.

▶**C** *demonstr. pronoun*. = YON *pronoun*. *obsolete* exc. *dial*. LME.
▶**D** *noun*. †**1** A yonder aspect. *rare* Only in L19.
2 The far distance; a remote place. Usu. with qualifying adjective *colloq*. M20.

2 C. COCKBURN The ex-editor . . suddenly appeared out of the deep green yonder of Ireland.

■ **yonderly** *adjective* (*fig*., *dial*.) (*a*) distant, reserved; (*b*) depressed, gloomy: E19. **yonderway** *adverb* by that way, in that manner L16.

†**yong** *adjective & noun* see YOUNG *adjective & noun*.

†**yonger** *adjective & noun* see YOUNGER.

yoni /ˈjəʊni/ *noun*. L18.
[Sanskrit.]
Chiefly HINDUISM. A figure or representation of the female genitals as a sacred symbol or object.

yonker *noun* var. of YOUNKER.

yonks /jɒŋks/ *noun*. *slang*. M20.
[Perh. rel. to *donkey's years* S.V. DONKEY.]
A long time, ages. Chiefly in ***for yonks***.

J. GASH It was something I should have done yonks ago. *Big Issue* Rage . . isn't a new phenomenon. It's been around for yonks.

yonnie /ˈjɒni/ *noun*. *Austral*. *slang*. M20.
[Aboriginal.]
A small stone; a pebble.

yonside /ˈjɒnsʌɪd/ *noun & adverb*. M16.
[from YON *adjective* + SIDE *noun*.]
▶**A** *noun*. The further side; the other side. M16.
▶**B** *adverb*. On the further side (*of*). L17.

yont *preposition & adverb* see YOND *preposition & adverb*.

yoof /juːf/ *noun*. *colloq*. L20.
[Repr. a non-standard pronunc. of YOUTH.]
A young person; young people, esp. as a group to be catered for as regards entertainment, marketing, etc. Freq. *attrib*.

M. SYAL The voice of Brit-Asian Yoof. M. BURGESS Scabby-looking yoofs with boots two sizes too big. R. TOPPING Waving the camera around in an attempt to copy funky yoof TV angles.

yoo-hoo /ˈjuːhuː, juːˈhuː/ *interjection*, *noun*, *& verb*. As verb usu. **yoohoo**. E20.
[Natural exclam.]
▶**A** *interjection & noun*. (A call) used to attract a person's attention, esp. to one's arrival or presence. E20.
▶**B** *verb intrans. & trans*. Call 'yoo-hoo!' (to). M20.

yoop /juːp/ *noun & interjection*. M19.
[Imit.]
(Repr.) a convulsive sob or sudden cry.

yopo *noun* var. of NIOPO.

yordim /jɔːˈdɪm/ *noun pl*. L20.
[Hebrew, pl. of *yōrēd* person who descends.]
Emigrants from the State of Israel.

yore /jɔː/ *adverb & noun*. *arch*.
[Old English *ġeāra*, *ġeāre*, *ġeāro*, of unkn. origin.]
▶†**A** *adverb*. **1** Long ago or *ago*; of old. Freq. in ***full yore***. OE–E17.
2 In time past; formerly. ME–L16.
3 For a long time, esp. in the past. ME–E16.
▶**B** *noun*. The distant past; an earlier period. Long *obsolete* exc. in ***of yore***. LME.

TENNYSON A little lonely church in days of yore. W. C. WILLIAMS I inscribe this missive . . in the style of . . courteous sages of yore.

yorgan /jɔːˈɡʌn/ *noun*. E20.
[Turkish.]
A Turkish quilt.

York /jɔːk/ *noun*. L16.
[See below.]
▶**I** [A city in NE England, formerly the county town of Yorkshire.]
1 *Hist*. Used *attrib*. to designate (things pertaining to) the royal house descended from Edmund of Langley (1341–1402), fifth son of Edward III, first Duke of York, which ruled England from 1461 to 1485. L16.
2 Used *attrib*. to designate things originating from or peculiar to York or Yorkshire. L18.
2 York–Antwerp rules MARITIME LAW an international set of rules governing the application of general average in marine insurance.
▶**II** [from New York, a city and State in the US.]
3 Used *attrib*. to designate things found, used, or originating in New York. *N. Amer*. L17.
3 York shilling *Hist*. a coin formerly used in New York, worth about 12½ cents.

■ **Yorkish** *adjective* (*rare*) = YORKIST *adjective* M16.

york /jɔːk/ *verb trans*. L19.
[Back-form. from YORKER *noun*².]
CRICKET. Bowl (a batsman) with a yorker.

York boat /jɔːk ˈbəʊt/ *noun phr*. *obsolete* exc. *Hist*. M19.
[from *York* Factory, a trading settlement on the shore of Hudson Bay in north-eastern Manitoba, Canada.]
A type of inland cargo boat formerly used in Canada.

Yorker /ˈjɔːkə/ *noun*¹. L16.
[from YORK *noun* + -ER¹.]
1 A native or inhabitant of York or Yorkshire. L16.
2 A New Yorker. Formerly also (*spec*.), a soldier from New York. M18.

yorker /ˈjɔːkə/ *noun*². M19.
[Prob. formed as YORK *noun*, as having been introduced by Yorkshire players: see -ER¹.]
CRICKET. A fast ball pitching just under the bat.

York gum /jɔːk ˈɡʌm/ *noun phr*. M19.
[from *York*, a town in Western Australia + GUM *noun*².]
A eucalyptus, *Eucalyptus loxophleba*, of western Australia; the timber of this tree.

Yorkie /ˈjɔːki/ *noun*. *colloq*. E19.
[from YORK(SHIRE + -IE.]
1 A person who is a native of Yorkshire, N. England. E19.
2 A Yorkshire terrier. M20.

Yorkist /ˈjɔːkɪst/ *noun & adjective*. E17.
[from YORK *noun* + -IST.]
Hist. ▶**A** *noun*. An adherent or supporter of the house of York, esp. in the Wars of the Roses. E17.
▶**B** *adjective*. Of or pertaining to the house of York or the Yorkists. E19.

Yorks. *abbreviation*.
Yorkshire.

Yorkshire /ˈjɔːkʃə/ *noun*. E17.
[A former county in N. England, now divided into the three counties of North, South, and West Yorkshire.]
▶**I** **1** Used *attrib*. to designate things found or originating in, or associated with, Yorkshire. E17.
1 Yorkshire chair a type of 17th-cent. upright chair, usu. distinguished by an open backrest and arched cross-rails. **Yorkshire fog** a softly hairy pasture grass, *Holcus lanatus*, with greyish often pink-tinged panicles (also called ***meadow soft-grass***). **Yorkshireman** a man who is a native of Yorkshire. **Yorkshire pud** *colloq*. (a) Yorkshire pudding. **Yorkshire pudding** (a) baked batter pudding, orig. baked under meat, now usu. cooked separately and eaten with roast beef. **Yorkshire teacake** a kind of baked yeast teacake. **Yorkshire terrier** (an animal of) a small, long-coated, tan and blue-grey breed of terrier developed in the West Riding of Yorkshire. ***Yorkshire tyke***: see TYKE 3. **Yorkshirewoman** a woman who is a native of Yorkshire.
▶**II** *ellipt*. **2** Yorkshire dialect. E18.
3 (A) Yorkshire pudding. L19.
4 A Yorkshire terrier. E20.
■ **Yorkshireism** *noun* an action or expression characteristic of a native of Yorkshire M17.

Yoruba /ˈjɒrʊbə/ *noun & adjective*. M19.
[Yoruba.]
▶**A** *noun*. Pl. **-s**, same. A member of a people of western Nigeria and neighbouring coastal parts; the Kwa language of this people. M19.
▶**B** *attrib*. or as *adjective*. Of or pertaining to the Yorubas or their language. M19.
■ Also **Yoruban** *noun & adjective* M19.

Yoshiwara /jɒʃɪˈwɑːrə/ *noun & adjective*. L19.
[Japanese.]
Hist. In Japan: (of, designating, or pertaining to) an area, esp. in Tokyo, where brothels were officially recognized.

yote /jəʊt/ *verb trans*. *dial*. LME.
[Var. of YET *verb*.]
1 Pour. LME.
2 = YET *verb* 3a. LME. ▸**b** = YET *verb* 3b. M16.
3 Pour liquid on, soak. E17.

yotization /jəʊtʌɪˈzeɪʃ(ə)n/ *noun*. Also **-isation**. M20.
[Alt. of IOTA + -IZATION.]
PHONETICS. The prefixing of the semivowel /j/ to another sound or syllable; the change of a sound into /j/.

you /juː, *unstressed* jə/ *pers. pronoun*, *2 pl. & sing. subjective (nom.) & objective (accus. & dat.)*, *& noun*. Also (*informal*) **y'** /jə/.
[Old English *īow*, *ēow* (Northumbrian *iuih*) = Old Frisian *ju*, Old Saxon *ju* (Dutch *u*), Old High German (dat.) *iu*, *eu*, (accus.) *iuw*, *iuwih* (German *euch*), from West Germanic: cf. THEE *pers. pronoun & noun*, THOU *pers. pronoun & noun*², YE *pers. pronoun*.]
▶**A** *pronoun*. **1** Used by the speaker or writer to refer to the person or persons he or she is addressing (and also, sometimes, to one or more persons he or she regards as associated, esp. as belonging to the same category or class), as the subject of predication or in attributive or predicative agreement with that subject. Also as *interjection* in apposition to and preceding a noun, freq. in expressions of reproach or contempt. OE. ▸**b** Orig., yourselves. Later also, yourself. *arch*. OE.
2 Used to refer indefinitely to any possible hearer, reader, witness, interested party, etc.: one, anyone. L16.

1 SHAKES. *Mids. N. D.* Fie, fie! you counterfeit, you puppet you! DEFOE You English gentlemen . . are too forward in the wars. HENRY FIELDING Your religion . . serves you only for an excuse for your faults. SIR W. SCOTT The dog will not do you harm. GEO. ELIOT Sinners! . . Ah! dear friends, does that mean you and me? A. HELPS I declare you are all very unkind to me. F. WHISHAW How should poor little you deal with a maiden who dares to call the Tsar a bear? *transf*.: TENNYSON Old year, you shall not go. **b** SHAKES. *Jul. Caes.* Hence! home, you idle creatures, get you home! W. S. GILBERT Coward! get you hence. **2** D. H. LAWRENCE You don't elbow your neighbour if he's got a pistol on his hip. I. MURDOCH You can't see anything from here, except in winter. R. P. JHABVALA His clothes were in tatters and you could see his . . skin through them.

Phrases & comb.: ***same to you***, ***the same to you***: see SAME *pronoun & noun*. ***true for you***: see TRUE *adjective*, *noun*, *& adverb*. **you-all** (*US colloq. & dial*.) you (sing. & pl.); cf. Y'ALL. ***you and who else?***: see WHO *pronoun & noun*. **you and whose army?** = ***you and who else?*** **you and your —!** *colloq*. expr. (contemptuous, impatient, or good-natured) dismissal of the thing or person mentioned. **you and yours** you together with your family, property, etc. **you-know-what**, **you-know-who** a deliberately unnamed thing or person whose identity is (assumed to be) understood by the hearer. ***you lot***: see LOT *noun*.
▶**B** *noun*. The personality or essential nature of the person(s) being addressed. E18.

J. GRENFELL Let the music through, find the inner you.

¶ Orig. restricted to objective (direct & indirect) use, later extending to subjective use, finally replacing *ye* completely, and now the ordinary 2nd person pronoun for any number and case. See also note S.V. THOU *pers. pronoun & noun*².

you /juː/ *adjective*. M17.
[from prec.]
1 *possess*. Your. *rare*. Long *obsolete* exc. *dial*. M17.
2 *pred*. Expressive of or suited to the taste, personality, etc., of the person being addressed. E20.

you /juː/ *verb trans*. M16.
[formed as prec.]
Address (a person, esp. God) with 'you' instead of 'thou'.

A. N. WILSON No one called their friends *thou* . . . But it didn't mean we were all clamouring to *You* the Almighty.

young /jʌŋ/ *adjective & noun*. Also (earlier) †**yong**. See also YOUNGER.
[Old English *ġ(e)ong*, *gung*, later *iung* = Old Frisian, Old Saxon *jung*, Old High German *junc* (Dutch *jong*, German *jung*), Old Norse *ungr*, Gothic *juggs*, from Germanic, ult. from Indo-European base repr. also in YOUTH and in Sanskrit *yuvaśa* youthful, Latin *juvencus* young bull.]
▶**A** *adjective*. **1** That has lived a (relatively) short time; that is at an early stage of life or growth; not yet old, not far advanced in life. OE. ▸**b** *spec*. Designating the younger of two people of the same name or title (esp. the son as opp. to the father). Cf. JUNIOR *adjective* 1. ME. ▸**c** *pred*. & in *comb*. [After OLD *adjective* 3.] Of a specified age. Chiefly *joc*. L20.
2 **a** Of, pertaining to, or characteristic of youth or a young person; *spec*. (*a*) immature; (*b*) (freq. **Y-**) (of a group, party, or movement) representing or claiming to represent the interests or aspirations of young people, members, etc. OE. ▸**b** Having the characteristics of young people or of youth, youthful; *esp*. having or showing the freshness or vigour of youth. E16.
3 Newly or recently initiated, recruited, or (*Austral*.) arrived; inexperienced, having little experience; unpractised. OE.
4 Recently or newly begun, formed, introduced, or brought into use; not far advanced; recent, new; *spec*. (*a*) designating the moon in the early part of the lunar month, soon after new moon, when it appears as a crescent; (*b*) NAUTICAL designating thin salt-water ice newly formed in a bay or harbour, esp. before winter sets in. LME.
5 *fig*. Small, miniature. Now *joc*. & *colloq*. M16.

1 J. C. LOUDON The heart wood is . . darker . . than the soft or young wood. A. TROLLOPE He was still a young man, only just turned forty. *New Scientist*: *Dealing with Dirt* is . . aimed at a fairly young audience. **c** SARA MAITLAND She had come there when she was two years young, thirteen years ago. **2a** SHAKES. *Two Gent.* By love the young and tender wit Is turn'd to folly. D. M. MULOCK A remnant of my young days. ***Young Conservatives***, ***Young Farmers***, ***Young Liberals***, ***Young Socialists***, etc. **b** M. W. MONTAGU 'Tis a maxim with me to be young as long as one can. G. SWIFT You're the youngest sixty-four-year-old I know. **4** H. KINGSLEY It's a young country. *Times* A severe tax on a young concern not earning profits. D. HOGAN The night was young . . there were many bars in this city to travel through. **5** G. MITCHELL George . . has . . a torch in the car like a young searchlight.

Special collocations, comb., & phrases: ***an old head on young shoulders***: see SHOULDER *noun*. ***love's young dream***: see LOVE *noun*. **not so young as one used to be**, **not so young as one was** (*colloq*., freq. *joc*.) getting old or elderly. ***the Young Chevalier***: see CHEVALIER. **the young idea** the child's mind. ***the Young Pretender***: see PRETENDER 2. **Young America** (*a*) US HISTORY an expansionist movement within the Democratic Party in the mid 19th cent.; (*b*) American youth collectively. ***young blood***: see BLOOD *noun*. **Young England** *Hist.* a group of Tory politicians in the early years of Queen Victoria's reign. ***young entry***: see ENTRY 10. **young-eyed** *adjective* having the bright or lively eyes of a young person. **young flood** the beginning of the flood tide. ***young fogy***: see FOGY *noun* 1. ***young FUSTIC***. **young-gentlemanly** *adjective* pertaining to or characteristic of a young gentleman. **young-girlish** *adjective* pertaining to or characteristic of a young girl. **young grammarians** LINGUISTICS = JUNGGRAMMATIKER. ***young hopeful***: see HOPEFUL *noun*. **young lady** (*a*) a lady who is young, a young (esp. unmarried) woman, a girl; (*b*) *colloq.* a girlfriend, a female sweetheart. **young-ladydom** *rare* young ladies collectively. **young-ladyish**, **young-ladylike** *adjectives* resembling or characteristic of a young lady. **young lion** a young vigorous man. **young man** a man who is young; *spec.* †(*a*) = YEOMAN 1; (*b*) a boyfriend, a male sweetheart. **young manhood** †(*a*) *rare* courage befitting a young man; (*b*) the condition of being a young man, early manhood. **young-mannish** *adjective* (chiefly *derog.*) resembling, pertaining to, or characteristic of a young man. ***young master***: see MASTER *noun*[1] 19. **young offender** LAW a criminal between 14 and 17 years of age or (*Canad.*) between 12 and 17 years of age; ***young offender institution*** (in the UK): for the detention of criminals between the ages of 14 and 20, replacing the former detention centres and youth custody centres. **young person** LAW a person between 14 and 17 years of age. **youngstock** young farm animals. **young thing** *arch. & colloq.* a young person (esp. as a familiar form of address). ***Young Turk***: see TURK *noun*[1]. **young 'un**, **youngun** *colloq.* a youngster, *esp.* a child. **young woman** a woman who is young; *spec.* a girlfriend, a female sweetheart.

▶**B** *noun*. **1** Orig., a young person, *spec.* a young woman or girl. Now (usu. with *the*), young people collectively. OE.

2 The offspring of an animal, esp. before or soon after birth. Formerly also, a young animal. ME.

†**3** The time of youth. *rare*. LME–M17.

> 🕮 **1** SHAKES. *Merry W.* He woos . . both rich and poor, Both young and old. STEELE That Vigour which the Young possess. **2** D. ATTENBOROUGH The eggs . . hatch; . . the young crawl out. D. MORRIS Carnivores with young go to considerable trouble to provide food for their growing offspring. *transf.*: M. WESLEY In . . 1926 middle-class English families took their young to Brittany. **with young** (of a female animal) pregnant.

■ **youngish** *adjective* somewhat young M17. **younglet** *noun* (*rare*) a young animal M19. **younglike** *adjective* (now *rare*) of the nature of or resembling a young person, youthful M16. **youngly** *adverb* (now *rare*) (*a*) in the manner of a young person; youthfully, immaturely; (*b*) in youth, early in life: E16.

young /jʌŋ/ *verb intrans.* M20.
[from prec.]
GEOLOGY. Of a structure or formation: present the apparently younger side (in a specified direction).

youngberry /ˈjʌŋb(ə)ri/ *noun*. E20.
[from B. M. *Young* (fl. 1905), US horticulturist, who first raised it + BERRY *noun*[1].]
A hybrid bramble thought to be a cross between the loganberry and a N. American dewberry, *Rubus flagellaris*; the large reddish-black fruit of this shrub.

younger /ˈjʌŋgə/ *adjective & noun*. Also (earlier) †**yonger**. OE.
[from YOUNG *adjective* + -ER[3].]
▶**A** *adjective*. **1** Compar. of YOUNG *adjective* (opp. *elder*, *older*). OE.

2 *spec.* **a** After a person's name: that is the younger of two people of the same name in a family (chiefly *Scot.*); *esp.* (*Scot.*) designating the heir of a landed commoner. Cf. JUNIOR *adjective* 1. LME. ▸**b** Belonging to the earlier part of life; earlier. Now only in ***younger days***. L16.

Special collocations: ***Younger EDDA***. **younger generation** *the* next or rising generation (as opp. to the current one or one's own). **younger hand** the one who plays second in a card-game for two.

▶**B** *noun*. Pl. **-s**, (now *rare*) same. A person who has lived a shorter time; a person's junior. OE.

> 🕮 J. WOODALL It is fit that the yonger obey the elder. TENNYSON Answer'd Sir Gareth graciously to one Not many a moon his younger.

■ **youngerly** *adjective* (*colloq.*, chiefly *US*) somewhat young (opp. *elderly*) E19. **youngership** *noun* (*rare*) the condition of one who is younger, juniority E17.

Young–Helmholtz /jʌŋˈhɛlmhɒlts/ *noun*. L19.
[from Thomas *Young* (see YOUNG'S MODULUS) + H. L. F. von HELMHOLTZ.]
Used ***attrib.*** to designate the theory that in the eye there are receptors sensitive to one of three colours (red, green, and violet), and that colour perception is due to the stimulation of these in different proportions.

youngling /ˈjʌŋlɪŋ/ *noun*. OE.
[from YOUNG *adjective* + -LING[1].]
1 A young person or animal. OE. ▸†**b** *spec.* A young scholar, a disciple; a beginner, a novice, a tiro; an inexperienced person, *esp.* a young one. ME–L17.

2 A young shoot or blossom of a plant. M16.

> 🕮 **1** R. BLY The mother hawk pushes the younglings out of the nest one day.

youngness /ˈjʌŋnɪs/ *noun*. ME.
[from YOUNG *adjective* + -NESS.]
1 The state or quality of being young; youthfulness; the character or appearance of a person who is young. ME.

†**2** The time of (a person's) youth. *rare*. Only in L16.

Young's modulus /jʌŋz ˈmɒdjʊləs/ *noun phr*. Pl. **-li** /-lʌɪ, -liː/, **-luses**. M19.
[from Thomas *Young* (1773–1829), English physician and physicist.]
PHYSICS & MECHANICS. = ***modulus of elasticity*** s.v. MODULUS 3.

youngster /ˈjʌŋstə/ *noun*. Now chiefly *colloq.* L16.
[from YOUNG *adjective* + -STER, suggested by YOUNKER.]
1 A young person, a youth; *spec.* a boy or junior seaman on board ship. L16.

2 A child. M18.

3 A young animal. M19.

younker /ˈjʌŋkə/ *noun*. *arch.* Also **yonker** /ˈjɒŋkə/. E16.
[Middle Dutch *jonckher*, from *jonc* young + *hēre* lord: cf. JUNKER *noun*[1], YOUNGSTER.]
1 A young nobleman or gentleman, a youth of high rank. Long *obsolete* exc. *Hist.* E16.

2 *gen.* A youth. Formerly also *spec.*, (*a*) a fashionable young man; (*b*) a boy or junior seaman on board ship. E16.

3 A child. E17.

your /jɔː, jʊə/ *possess. pronoun & adjective* (in mod. usage also classed as a *determiner*), *2 sing. & pl.*
[Old English *ēower* genit. of YE *pronoun*, corresp. to Old Frisian *iuwer*, Old Saxon *iuwar*, Old High German *iuwēr* (German *euer*): cf. YOU *pers. pronoun & noun*.]
▶†**A** *pronoun*. **1** Genit. of YOU *pronoun*; of you. OE–M16.

2 = YOURS. OE–E17.

▶**B** *attrib. adjective*. **1** Of you; of yourself or yourselves; which belongs or pertains to you, yourself, or yourselves. OE. ▸**b** In respectful forms of address (as ***your Majesty***): that you are. LME.

2 Designating the speaker or writer himself or herself, esp. in the subscription of a letter. LME.

3 Used to designate a (type of) person or thing known or familiar to the person being addressed. Also (freq. *derog.*), designating any (esp. a typical) example of a class or kind. *colloq.* M16.

4 One's, anyone's. L16.

> 🕮 **1** T. FULLER Abler Men are undertaking your Confutation. J. RHYS I was . . pleased to have your letter. J. STEINBECK Let me help you to take off your coat. I. MURDOCH Are you going to tell me about your childhood? **b** ***your university***: see UNIVERSITY 3a. **2** ALLAN RAMSAY Yet may I please you, while I'm your devoted Allan. ***your servant***: see SERVANT *noun*. **3** A. HALL Your Anglo-Saxon doesn't panic easily. J. IRVING A serious place . . not your ordinary hospital. *Times* Quiet-spoken, not one of your brash oil types. *Stage* He does not strike you as your typical 'arts' man. **4** W. S. MAUGHAM The way . . firms . . keep their accounts is enough to turn your hair grey.

yourn /jɔːn, jʊən/ *possess. pronoun*. *dial.* LME.
[from prec. after *my, mine, thy, thine*, etc.: cf. OURN.]
= YOURS *pronoun*.

> 🕮 G. F. NEWMAN A talent like yourn, you could get a job in the library or administration where there's some fiddle.

yours /jɔːz, jʊəz/ *possess. pronoun & adjective*. ME.
[from YOUR *pronoun* + -'S[1].]
▶**A** *pronoun*. **1** Your one(s); that or those belonging or pertaining to you; *spec.* your family, friends, etc. ME. ▸**b** *ellipt.* W. ref. to (now esp. commercial) correspondence: your letter, the letter from you. M16.

2 ***of yours***, belonging or pertaining to you. ME.

3 Used as or in a formula ending a letter. LME.

4 *ellipt.* Your business, your affair. M19.

> 🕮 **1** BOSWELL I was . . doubly uneasy;—on my own account and yours. M. EDGEWORTH You should not meddle with them; they are not yours. J. CONRAD Speaking to a superior mind like yours. I. MURDOCH It is our duty, yours and mine. ***up yours***: see UP *preposition*[2]. **what's yours?** *colloq.* what would you like to drink? ***you and yours***: see YOU *pronoun*. **b** D. O'CONNELL I got yours of the 28th . . and am . . delighted to find your spirits better. **2** W. S. MAUGHAM I don't know that it's any business of yours. SCOTT FITZGERALD Saw an old friend of yours last night. **3** ***yours faithfully***, ***yours sincerely***, etc. ***EVER yours***. ***yours EVER***. ***yours TRULY***. **4** *Chile Pepper* Chiles add a robust flavor, and the texture is yours.

▶**B** *adjective*. Followed by another possessive qualifying the same noun: your. Now *rare* or *obsolete*. M16.

> 🕮 T. CRANMER By yours and their agreement I may obtain the next lease.

yourself /jɔːˈsɛlf, jʊə-, jə-/ *pronoun*. Also (now *rare* exc. in sense 2b) **your self**. See also YOURSELVES. ME.
[from YOUR *pronoun* + SELF *adjective* (but long interpreted as from YOUR *adjective* + SELF *noun*).]
▶**I** Orig. *emphatic*.
1 In apposition to *you*: you personally (sing.). Formerly also, in apposition to *ye*: yourselves. ME.

2 (Not appositional.) ▸**a** *sing. & †pl.* Subjective, predicative, & objective: you. ME. ▸**b** Your true or natural self or personality. L16. ▸**c** Added as a retort after repeating something just said to one. *colloq.* L19.

> 🕮 **1** SHAKES. *Two Gent.* Henceforth carry your letters yourself. F. C. BURNAND You . . gave me to understand you had been there yourself. E. GLYN You English are naturally asleep, and you yourself are the Sleeping Beauty. **2a** SWIFT Conversation is but carving; Carve for all, yourself is starving. A. SEWARD Not one of them equals yourself or Southey. R. S. SURTEES 'What a mess you're in . . !' . . 'I can't be much worse than yourself'. D. M. MULOCK A strong friendship used to exist between Uncle Brian, yourself, and Anne Valery. N. MARSH Spoke with a superb brogue . . 'Ah, it's yourself again.' **by yourself** on your own. **b** SHAKES. *Sonn.* O that you were yourself!

▶**II** *refl.* **3** Refl. form (direct, indirect, & after prepositions) corresp. to the subjective pronoun *you*: you personally, you (sing.). Formerly also, yourselves. ME.

> 🕮 **3** L. STEFFENS You have to think for yourself. J. FRASER Just give yourself, baby. I want you. *Sunday Mail (Brisbane)* Buy yourself a strawberry job with frozen yoghurt.

▶**III** *indef.* **4** = ONESELF. Cf. YOU *pronoun* 2, YOUR *adjective* 4. M17.

> 🕮 **4** *Times Lit. Suppl.* Everything that cannot be eaten must be used to scratch yourself with. DO-IT-YOURSELF. ***teach yourself***: see TEACH *verb*.

yourselves /jɔːˈsɛlvz, jʊə-, jə-/ *pronoun pl.* Also (now *rare*) as two words. E16.
[from prec. with pl. inflection.]
1 *emphatic & refl.* Freq. in apposition to *you* or (formerly) *ye*: your particular group of people personally, you individually. E16.

2 Your true or natural selves or personalities. E18.

> 🕮 **1** M. MANLEY Where your selves shall be Judges of his Conversation. DICKENS You ought to be ashamed of yourselves. M. TWAIN I honor . . you Pilgrim stock as much as you do yourselves. J. WELCH Help yourselves, boys. Don't be shy. **by yourselves** on your own.

yourt *noun* var. of YURT.

youth /juːθ/ *noun*. Pl. **youths** /juːðz/.
[Old English *ġeoguþ*, (late) *iuguþ* = Old Frisian *jogethe*, Old Saxon *jugup* (Dutch *jeugd*), Old High German *jugund* (German *Jugend*), from West Germanic, from base repr. by YOUNG *adjective*: see -TH[1].]
1 The fact or state of being young; youngness. Also, youthful freshness, vigour, appearance, etc. OE. ▸**b** *fig.* Novelty, recentness. *rare*. L16.

2 The time when one is young; *spec.* the period between childhood and full adulthood. OE. ▸**b** *fig.* An early stage in the existence of a thing. E17.

3 Young people collectively; the young. OE.

4 A young person; *esp.* a young man between boyhood and mature age. ME. ▸**b** A member of certain societies of bellringers. Usu. in *pl.* *obsolete* exc. *Hist.* M17.

> 🕮 **1** CONAN DOYLE His antagonist was tiring . . . His own youth and condition were beginning to tell. E. WAUGH Having for many years . . feigned youth, he now aspired to the honours of age. *personified*: A. WILSON He was . . always on youth's side against the absurdities of middle age. **b** SHAKES. *Merch. V.* If that the youth of my new int'rest here Have power to bid you welcome. **2** D. L. COHN Many American men dislike women because they were dominated by them throughout childhood and early youth. **b** *Church Times* Lutheranism . . covers a smaller area to-day than it did in its early youth. **3** T. R. FYVEL Russian youth has . . not remained untouched by the unrest of our age. *Guardian Weekly* Youth who need apprenticeship opportunities. **4** I. COMPTON-BURNETT Grant Edgeworth was a spare, dark youth of twenty-five. M. M. KAYE Had her . . bridegroom been a boy of her own age, or even a youth in his teens.

Comb.: **Youth Aliyah** [Hebrew *ʿălīyyāh* ascent] a movement begun in 1933 for the emigration of young Jews to Palestine; **youth and old age** = ZINNIA; **youth camp** any of the various camps established for young people in Germany under the Nazis; **youth centre** a building providing social and recreational facilities for young people; **youth club** a social club providing leisure activities for young people; **youth hostel** [translating German *Jugendherberge*]: providing cheap accommodation for (orig. young) people, esp. on hiking or cycling holidays; **youth-hostel** *verb intrans.* stay at youth hostels (chiefly as ***youth-hostelling*** *verbal noun*); **youth hosteller** a person who stays at youth hostels; **youth leader** a person having charge of young people in any youth organization; **Youth Opportunities Programme** a Government-sponsored service introduced in Britain in 1978 to provide temporary work experience for unemployed young people; **Youth Training Scheme** a Government-sponsored scheme introduced in Britain in 1983 to replace the Youth Opportunities Programme and offering job experience and training for unemployed school-leavers.

■ **youthless** *adjective* lacking youth or youthful characteristics E20.

youthen /ˈjuːθ(ə)n/ *verb trans. & intrans.* *rare*. L19.
[from YOUTH + -EN[5].]
Make or become youthful.

youthful /ˈjuːθfʊl, -f(ə)l/ *adjective.* M16.
[from YOUTH + -FUL.]
1 Pertaining to or characteristic of the young; juvenile. M16.
2 That is still young. L16. ▸**b** *fig.* That is in its early stage or has the freshness or vigour of youth. L16.

> **1** A. HUTH Youthful skittishness would look pretty silly in middle age. **2b** *Pall Mall Gazette* A youthful and astringent Tinta, an aromatic Malmsey of fabulous value.

■ **youthfully** *adverb* L16. **youthfulness** *noun* L16.

youthhead /ˈjuːθhɛd/ *noun.* Chiefly *Scot.* ME.
[from YOUTH + -HEAD.]
= YOUTH 1, 2, 3.

youthhood /ˈjuːθhʊd/ *noun. arch.* OE.
[from YOUTH + -HOOD.]
= YOUTH 1, 2, 3.

youthify /ˈjuːθɪfʌɪ/ *verb trans.* M20.
[from YOUTH + -I- + -FY.]
Make (a person) appear more youthful.

youthly /ˈjuːθli/ *adjective.* Now *rare.* OE.
[from YOUTH + -LY^{1}.]
= YOUTHFUL.

youthy /ˈjuːθi/ *adjective.* Now *Scot.* E18.
[from YOUTH + -Y^{1}.]
Having or pretending to have the character of youth.
■ **youthily** *adverb* M19. **youthiness** *noun* E19.

yow /jaʊ/ *interjection & verb.* LME.
[Natural exclam. & imit.]
▸**A** *interjection.* †**1** Expr. disgust or reproach. *rare.* Only in LME.
2 Repr. the natural cry of a dog or cat. M19.
3 = **WOW** *interjection. Austral. & NZ.* M20.
▸**B** *verb intrans.* Usu. redupl. **yow-yow**. Of a dog or cat: utter its natural cry; yelp, miaow. E19.

yowe /jaʊ/ *noun.* Now *dial.* LME.
[Repr. a pronunc.]
= EWE *noun*^{1}.

yowie /ˈjaʊi/ *noun. Austral.* L20.
[Aboriginal *yuwi* dream spirit.]
A large hairy manlike creature supposedly inhabiting SE Australia.

yowl /jaʊl/ *verb & noun.* ME.
[Imit.: cf. YAWL *verb* and Old Norse *gaula*, German *johlen*.]
▸**A** *verb.* **1** *verb intrans.* Esp. of a cat or dog: utter a yowl. ME.
2 *verb trans.* Express by yowling; utter with a yowl. M19.
▸**B** *noun.* A prolonged loud wailing cry, now esp. of a dog or cat. LME.
■ **yowler** *noun* M20.

yow-yow *verb* see YOW.

yowza /ˈjaʊzə/ *interjection.* Chiefly *US.* Also **-zer** & other vars. M20.
[Perh. rel. to German *Jauchzer* cry of delight.]
Expr. approval, excitement, or enthusiasm.

yo-yo /ˈjəʊjəʊ/ *noun, adjective, & verb.* E20.
[Prob. from a Philippine lang.]
▸**A** *noun.* Pl. **yo-yos**.
1 (Also **Yo-Yo**.) (Proprietary name for) a toy in the form of two joined discs with a deep groove between them in which a string is attached and wound, its free end being held so that the toy can be made to fall under its own weight and rise again by its momentum. E20. ▸**b** The pastime of playing with a Yo-Yo. M20.
2 *fig.* A thing which or person who is continually going up and down or to and fro; such motion or fluctuation. M20. ▸**b** A stupid or crazy person; a person of unpredictable moods. *slang.* L20.

> **2** *Times* Alarming yo-yos in the quality of food and service. **b** F. FORSYTH What's the point in handing over Saudi Arabia to these yo-yos?

▸**B** *adjective.* Marked by continual up-and-down or to-and-fro movement; continually passing into and out of a condition. M20.

> *Lancet* Severe on-off disabilities with freezing and rapid oscillations ('yo-yo' effect).

▸**C** *verb.* **1** *verb intrans.* Play with a Yo-Yo. M20.
2 *fig.* **a** *verb intrans.* Move up and down, or between one point and another; fluctuate. M20. ▸**b** *verb trans.* Manipulate or manoeuvre like a Yo-Yo. L20.

> **2** *Time* He has yo-yoed between 210 and 296 lbs., now carries a bulky 263. **b** W. BAYER I don't want the job if it means he gets to Yo-Yo me around.

■ **yo-yoer**, **yo-yoist** *nouns* a person who plays or performs with a Yo-Yo M20.

yo-yo *interjection* see YO *interjection.*

ypent /ɪˈpɛnt/ *pa. pple & ppl adjective. arch.* LME.
[from Y- + *pent* obsolete pa. pple of PEN *verb*^{1}.]
Penned, confined.

yperite /ˈiːpərʌɪt/ *noun.* E20.
[French *ypérite*, from *Ypres*, a town in Belgium where this gas was first used: see -ITE^{1}.]
= ***mustard gas*** s.v. MUSTARD *noun.*

†**ypight** *pa. pple & ppl adjective.* LME–M18.
[from Y- + *pight* pa. pple of PITCH *verb*^{2}.]
Pitched, fixed.

yr. *abbreviation.*
1 Year(s).
2 Younger.
3 Your.

yrast /ˈɪrast/ *adjective.* M20.
[Swedish, lit. 'dizziest', 'most bewildered', from *yr* dizzy, bewildered + *-ast* -EST^{1}.]
NUCLEAR PHYSICS. Pertaining to or designating a nuclear energy level that is the lowest for a specified value of spin.
yrast line a line on a graph of spin against nuclear rotational energy (or a function of these), connecting points representing the various yrast states of a nuclide.

†**yravish** *verb trans. pseudo-arch.* Only in E17.
[from Y- + RAVISH.]
= RAVISH.

yrs. *abbreviation.*
1 Years.
2 Yours.

†**ysame** *adverb.* ME–L16.
[App. from *i-* IN-^{1} + SAME *adverb.*]
Together.

†**ysprung** *pa. pple & ppl adjective.* Also **ysprong**. ME–M18.
[from Y- + *sprung* pa. pple of SPRING *verb*^{1}.]
Sprung, arisen.

YTS *abbreviation.*
Youth Training Scheme.

ytter /ˈɪtə/ *adjective.* Now *rare.* E19.
[from *Ytterby*: see next.]
MINERALOGY. Combined with, containing, or yielding yttria or yttrium.
ytter earth = YTTRIA.

ytterbium /ɪˈtəːbɪəm/ *noun.* L19.
[from *Ytterby*, a Swedish quarry where ytterbite was first found: see -IUM.]
A soft malleable silvery metallic chemical element of the lanthanide series, atomic no. 70, used in lasers, x-ray sources, etc. (Symbol Yb.)
¶ The name was originally applied to a mixture later separated into ytterbium proper and lutetium.
■ **ytterbia** *noun* ytterbium oxide, Yb_2O_3, a colourless, hygroscopic, weakly basic powder obtained from gadolinite etc. and used in special alloys, catalysts, etc. L19. **ytterbite** /ˈɪtəbʌɪt/ *noun* (now *rare*) = GADOLINITE M19.

yttrium /ˈɪtrɪəm/ *noun.* E19.
[from *Ytter(by*: see prec., -IUM.]
A dark grey metallic chemical element, atomic no. 39, belonging to the group of transition metals and used in special alloys, microwave ferrites, etc. (Symbol Y.)
Comb.: **yttrium metal**, **yttrium subgroup** any of a group of metals occurring together in certain ores, including yttrium and five rare earths of the lanthanide series.
■ **yttria** *noun* yttrium oxide, Y_2O_3, a yellowish-white powder obtained from gadolinite etc. and used in phosphors for colour television tubes, in incandescent mantles, etc. E19. **yˈttriferous** *adjective* containing or yielding yttrium L19.

yttro- /ˌɪtrəʊ/ *combining form.* E19.
[from prec.: see -O-.]
MINERALOGY. Forming the names of minerals containing yttrium, the second element usu. indicating the other metallic constituent, as ***yttrotungstite*** etc.

yu /juː/ *noun.* Pl. same. E20.
[Chinese *yǒu*.]
An ancient Chinese wine vessel in the form of a small metal pail with a swing handle and a decorative cover.

Yuan /ˈjuːɑːn, jʊˈɑːn/ *noun^{1} & adjective.* L17.
[Chinese *yuán* first.]
(Designating or pertaining to) the Mongol dynasty ruling China in the 13th and 14th cents.

yuan /jʊˈɑːn/ *noun^{2}.* Also **yüan**. Pl. same. E20.
[Chinese *yuán* lit. 'round'. Cf. YEN *noun*^{1}.]
The basic monetary unit of China, equal to 10 jiao or (formerly) 100 cents.

yuan /jʊˈɑːn/ *noun^{3}.* Also **Y-**. Pl. same. E20.
[Chinese *yuàn* courtyard.]
In China: any of several government departments.

yuca *noun* see YUCCA.

Yucatec /ˈjuːkətɛk/ *noun & adjective.* Also **Yucateco** /-ˈtɛkəʊ/, pl. **-os**. M19.
[Spanish *yucateco*, from *Yucatán*, earlier *Yocotán*, adapted from a Maya name for the language of the Mayan Indians of Oaxaca, Mexico.]
▸**A** *noun.* Pl. **-s**, same.
1 A member of an American Indian people of the Yucatán peninsula in eastern Mexico; *colloq.* a native or inhabitant of the peninsula or the State of Yucatán in its northern part. M19.
2 The Mayan language of the Yucatecs. M20.
▸**B** *attrib.* or as *adjective.* Of or pertaining to the Yucatecs or their language. L19.
■ Also **Yucatecan** /-ˈtɛkən/ *adjective & noun* M19.

yucca /ˈjʌkə/ *noun.* In sense 1 usu. **yuca** /ˈjuːkə/. M16.
[Carib.]
1 In western S. America and Central America: = CASSAVA. M16.
2 Any of various plants constituting the genus *Yucca*, of the agave family, which have a woody stem with a crown of rigid sword-shaped leaves and a panicle of bell-shaped flowers and are native to desert regions of N. America, though grown for ornament elsewhere. Also called ***Adam's needle***. M17.
Comb.: **yucca-borer** (*a*) a N. American moth, *Megathymus yuccae*, whose larva bores into the roots of yucca plants; (*b*) a Californian weevil, *Yuccaborus frontalis*; **yucca moth** any of several small American moths of the genus *Tegeticula* (family Prodoxidae) which lay their eggs in the ovary of a yucca plant and deposit a ball of pollen on the stigma, so fertilizing the seeds on which the larvae feed; **yucca-palm**, **yucca-tree** an arborescent species of *Yucca*.

Yuchi /ˈjuːtʃi/ *noun.* Also **Uchee**. Pl. **-s**, same. M18.
[Creek.]
1 A member of a N. American Indian people now incorporated into the Creek Confederacy in Oklahoma. M18.
2 The language of the Yuchis. M19.

yuck /jʌk/ *noun^{1}. slang* (orig. *US*). Also **yuk**. M20.
[Origin uncertain: perh. identical with next.]
A fool; a boor; anyone disliked or despised.

> M. SHULMAN The yucks who look at television don't know the difference between Ernest Hemingway and Huntz Hall.

yuck /jʌk/ *verb & noun^{2}. slang* (chiefly *N. Amer.*). Also **yuk** (verb infl. **-kk-**). M20.
[Origin uncertain. Cf. YOCK.]
▸**A** *verb intrans. & trans.* (with *it*). Fool around; laugh heartily. M20.
▸**B** *noun.* A (hearty) laugh. L20.

yuck /jʌk/ *interjection, noun^{3}, & adjective. slang.* Also **yuk**. M20.
[Imit. of the sound of vomiting. Cf. YECH *interjection.*]
▸**A** *interjection.* Expr. strong distaste or aversion. M20.

> BEVERLEY CLEARY Leftovers—yuck! thought Ramona. *Catch* I got asked to dance . . but always by the older, ugly men. Yuck!

▸**B** *noun.* Messy or distasteful material (*lit. & fig.*). M20.

> *New Statesman* Rotting wodges of chilly yuck which once were apples and pears. M. E. ATKINS Syndicated advice columns . . . All noble sentiments and romantic yuck.

▸**C** *adjective.* = YUCKY. L20.

> P. DICKINSON She's got a really yuck family, even worse than mine.

yuckle /ˈjʌk(ə)l/ *noun. dial.* M19.
[Var. of HICKWALL, infl. by YAFFLE.]
The green woodpecker, *Picus viridis*.

yucky /ˈjʌki/ *adjective. slang.* Also **yukky**. L20.
[from YUCK *noun*^{3} + -Y^{1}.]
1 Messy, gooey. L20.
2 Nasty, unpleasant; sickly sentimental. L20.

> **1** J. J. HENNESSY Chris, too, has had to go through the 'yukky' ordeal of make-up. **2** *TV Times* I got . . a yukky card from my mother.

■ **yuckiness** *noun* L20.

Yüeh /ˈjyə/ *noun^{1} & adjective.* Also **Yueh**. E20.
[from *Yuè Zhōu* (Wade–Giles *Yüeh Chou*): see below.]
(Designating) a type of stoneware with a celadon glaze made at Yuè Zhōu (now Shaoxing), a town in Zhejiang Province, China, esp. during the Tang dynasty.

Yüeh /ˈjyə/ *noun^{2} & adjective.* M20.
[Chinese *Yuè* a former name of Guangdong Province.]
▸**A** *noun.* The form of Chinese spoken in parts of the provinces of Guangdong and Guangxi, Cantonese. M20.
▸**B** *attrib.* or as *adjective.* Of or pertaining to Yüeh, Cantonese. L20.

yüeh ch'in /ˈjʊə tʃɪn, kɪn/ *noun.* M19.
[Chinese *yuèqín* (Wade–Giles *yüeh-ch'in*) lit. 'moon guitar'.]
A Chinese lute with four strings and a flat circular body.

yuffrouw /ˈjʊfraʊ/ *noun*. L15.
[Early mod.Dutch *jongvrouw*, later *juffrouw*, *juffer*, from *jong* YOUNG *adjective* + *vrouw* woman. Cf. JUFFER, UFER, UPHROE.]
1 NAUTICAL. Orig., a deadeye. Now *spec*., one used to extend the lines of a crowfoot. L15.
2 A young (Dutch) woman. Now *rare*. L16.

yuft /jʌft/ *noun*. L18.
[Russian *yuft'*, prob. ult. from Persian.]
= ***Russia leather*** s.v. RUSSIA 1.

yuga /ˈjʊgə/ *noun*. Also **yug** /jʊg/. L18.
[Sanskrit *yuga* YOKE *noun*[1], an age of the world.]
In Hindu cosmology, each of four periods, each shorter than and inferior to its predecessor, together totalling 4,320,000 years. Cf. KALPA.

yugen /ˈjuːg(ə)n/ *noun*. E20.
[Japanese, from *yū* faint, distant + *gen* dark, unfathomable.]
In traditional Japanese court culture and Noh plays, a hidden quality of graceful beauty or mystery; profound aestheticism.

Yugo /ˈjuːgəʊ/ *noun*. *colloq*. (now *Hist*.). Pl. **-os**. M20.
[Abbreviation.]
= YUGOSLAVIAN *noun*.

Yugoslav /ˈjuːgə(ʊ)slɑːv, juːgəʊˈslɑːv/ *noun & adjective*. Also **J-**. M19.
[Austrian German *Jugoslav*, from Serbo-Croat *jugo-* combining form of *jug* south + SLAV.]
▶ **A** *noun*. Orig., a member of any of various groups of southern Slavs (Serbs, Croats, and Slovenes). Later (*Hist*.), a Yugoslavian. M19.
▶ **B** *adjective*. Of or pertaining to the southern Slavs or the Yugoslavians. M19.

Yugoslavian /juːgə(ʊ)ˈslɑːvɪən/ *adjective & noun*. Also **J-**. E20.
[formed as prec. + -IAN.]
▶ **A** *adjective*. Of or pertaining to Yugoslavia, a State of SE Europe on the Adriatic coast, formed in 1918 from the union of Serbia, Montenegro, and the Slavonic provinces of the Austro-Hungarian Empire. E20.
▶ **B** *noun*. A native or inhabitant of Yugoslavia. E20.

yuh /jə/ *pers. pronoun*. *colloq*. (esp. *Black English*). E20.
[Repr. a pronunc.]
= YOU *pronoun*.

Yuit /ˈjuːɪt/ *noun & adjective*. E20.
[Siberian Yupik, lit. 'people', pl. of YUK *noun*[1].]
▶ **A** *noun*. Pl. same, **-s**.
1 An Eskimo of Siberia, the Aleutian Islands, and Alaska. E20.
2 The Yupik language, spoken by the Yuit. M20.
▶ **B** *adjective*. Of or pertaining to the Yuit or their language. M20.

Yuk /jʊk/ *noun*[1] *& adjective*. M20.
[Siberian Yupik, lit. 'person': see YUIT.]
(Of) a dialect of Yupik, spoken in parts of Alaska.

yuk *noun*[2] var. of YUCK *noun*[1].

yuk *verb & noun*[3] var. of YUCK *verb & noun*[2].

yuk *interjection*, *noun*[4], *& adjective* var. of YUCK *interjection*, *noun*[3], *& adjective*.

Yukaghir /ˈjuːkəgɪə, juːkəˈgɪə/ *noun & adjective*. M19.
[Yakut.]
▶ **A** *noun*. Pl. same, **-s**.
1 A member of a people of Arctic Siberia. M19.
2 The Palaeo-Siberian language of this people. M19.
▶ **B** *attrib*. or as *adjective*. Of or pertaining to the Yukaghir. M19.

yukata /jʊˈkata/ *noun*. E19.
[Japanese, from *yu* hot water, bath + *kata(bira)* light kimono.]
A light cotton kimono, freq. with stencil designs, worn indoors (orig. after a bath) or informally in hot weather.

Yukawa /jʊˈkɑːwə/ *noun*. M20.
[Hideki *Yukawa* (1907–1981), Japanese physicist.]
NUCLEAR PHYSICS. Used *attrib*. with ref. to a theory put forward by Yukawa, according to which the strong interaction between nucleons is mediated by the exchange of particles subsequently identified with pions.
Yukawa potential a potential function of the form $V = V_0(r/r_0)^{-1}\exp(-r/r_0)$, occurring in Yukawa's theory of the nuclear force.

yuke /juːk/ *verb & noun*. *Scot. & north*. Also **yeuk**. LME.
[Alt. of Old English *ġiċċan*, *gyccan* ITCH *verb*, after Middle Dutch *jeuken*.]
▶ **A** *verb intrans*. Itch. LME.
▶ **B** *noun*. Itching, an itch. M16.

Yuki /ˈjuːki/ *noun & adjective*. M19.
[Wintun *yu-keh* lit. 'stranger, enemy'.]
▶ **A** *noun*. Pl. same, **-s**.
1 A member of a group of N. American Indian peoples of the north-west Californian coast. M19.
2 The language spoken by the Yuki. L19.
▶ **B** *attrib*. or as *adjective*. Of or pertaining to the Yuki or their language. L19.

yukky *adjective* var. of YUCKY.

Yukon /ˈjuːkɒn/ *noun*. L19.
[*Yukon* Territory, NW Canada.]
Used *attrib*. to designate things native to or found in Yukon.
Yukon stove a lightweight portable stove consisting of a small metal box divided into firebox and oven.
■ **Yukoner** *noun* a native or inhabitant of the Yukon Territory L19.

yuky /ˈjuːki/ *adjective*. *Scot. & north*. E18.
[from YUKE + -Y[1].]
Itchy; itching with curiosity.
■ **yukiness** *noun* M19.

yulan /ˈjuːlən/ *noun*. E19.
[Chinese *yùlán*, from *yù* gem + *lán* plant.]
A Chinese magnolia, *Magnolia heptapeta*.

yule /juːl/ *noun & interjection*. Now *Scot., north., & literary* exc. in comb. Also **Y-**.
[Old English *ġēol*, *geo(h)ol*, *ġeh(h)ol*, *ġēola* Christmas Day, corresp. to Old Norse *jól* (pl.) heathen feast lasting twelve days, (later) Christmas, rel. to Old English (Anglian) *giuli* December and January = Old Norse *ýlir* month beginning on the second day of the week falling within 10–17 November, Gothic *jiuleis* in *fruma jiuleis* November: ult. origin unkn.]
▶ **A** *noun*. †**1** December; January. OE–ME.
2 Christmas and the festivities connected with it. OE.
▶†**B** *interjection*. Expr. joy or revelry at the Christmas festivities. M16–M19.
Comb.: **yule-clog** = *yule-log* (a) below; **yule-day** (chiefly *Scot*.) Christmas Day; **yule even** *Scot*. Christmas Eve; **yule-log** (*a*) a large log of wood burnt on the hearth at Christmas; (*b*) a log-shaped chocolate cake eaten at Christmas; **yule-tide** the Christmas season.

yuloh /ˈjuːləʊ/ *noun & verb*. Also **yulo**, pl. **-os**. L19.
[Prob. from Chinese (Cantonese) *iū-lō* scull a boat, from *iū* shake + *lō* oar.]
▶ **A** *noun*. A long flexible oar with a fixed fulcrum, operated from the stern to propel a sampan or similar small boat. L19.
▶ **B** *verb intrans*. Propel a boat by such an oar. L19.

yum /jʌm/ *interjection*. Also redupl. **yum-yum**. L19.
[Imit. Cf. NUM *noun & interjection*.]
Expr. the sound of smacking the lips in anticipation of food etc.; *gen*. expr. pleasurable enjoyment.

> 🕮 *Beano* Yum! Fish and chips! S. PARETSKY Homemade enchiladas, yum-yum.

Yuma /ˈjuːmə/ *noun*[1] *& adjective*. E19.
[Pima *yumĭ*.]
▶ **A** *noun*. Pl. same, **-s**. A member of a Yuman people of SW Arizona and adjoining areas of Mexico and California. Also, the language of this people. E19.
▶ **B** *attrib*. or as *adjective*. Of or pertaining to the Yuma or their language. L19.

Yuma /ˈjuːmə/ *noun*[2]. M20.
[*Yuma* County, Colorado, USA.]
Used *attrib*. to designate the remains of a prehistoric culture discovered at Yuma, esp. a type of projectile point.

Yuman /ˈjuːmən/ *adjective & noun*. L19.
[from YUMA *noun*[1] + -AN.]
▶ **A** *adjective*. Of or pertaining to various related N. American Indian peoples of Arizona, Mexico, and California, or the languages spoken by them. L19.
▶ **B** *noun*. A member of this group of peoples. Also, a language family of the Hokan group to which the languages of these peoples belong. E20.

yummy /ˈjʌmi/ *interjection & adjective*. L19.
[from YUM + -Y[1].]
▶ **A** *interjection*. = YUM. L19.

> 🕮 H. KURNITZ I adore movie stars. Gregory Peck! Yummy! *Beano* Choc drops—yummy!

▶ **B** *adjective*. (Of food etc.) highly appetizing; *fig*. highly attractive, desirable, etc. M20.

> 🕮 *Woman* The yummy smell of freshly-baked bread. I. MURDOCH Akiba Lebowitz was yummy of course but just married.

yump /jʌmp/ *verb & noun*. *slang*. M20.
[Prob. repr. a supposed pronunc. of JUMP *verb* by Swedish speakers.]
▶ **A** *verb intrans*. Of a rally car or its driver: leave the ground while taking a crest at speed. M20.
▶ **B** *noun*. An instance of yumping; a sharp crest in a road which causes a car to take off at speed. L20.

yumpie /ˈjʌmpi/ *noun*. *colloq*. (chiefly *US*). L20.
[from young upwardly mobile people: see -IE. Cf. YUPPIE.]
= YUPPIE.

yum-yum /jʌmˈjʌm/ *adjective & noun*. *slang*. L19.
[from *yum-yum* var. of YUM.]
▶ **A** *adjective*. Mouth-wateringly delicious; *fig*. excellent, first-rate. L19.

> 🕮 A. BUCHWALD All her girls are really yum-yum girls from the dance halls.

▶ **B** *noun*. **1** An action providing a pleasurable sensation; *esp*. love-making. L19.
2 An item of delicious food. L19.

yum-yum *interjection* see YUM.

Yunca /ˈjʊŋkə/ *noun & adjective*. M19.
[Amer. Spanish, from Quechua *yunca* plain, valley.]
▶ **A** *noun*. Pl. same, **-s**. = MOCHICA *noun*. M19.
▶ **B** *adjective*. = MOCHICA *adjective*. M20.

Yung Chêng /jʊŋ ˈtʃɛŋ/ *noun*. E20.
[Chinese *Yōngzhèng* (Wade–Giles *Yung-cheng*), third emperor of the Ching dynasty.]
(Designating) porcelain produced during the reign (1723–35) of Yung Chêng, characterized by its delicate colouring.

Yunnanese /jʊnəˈniːz/ *noun & adjective*. M19.
[from *Yunnan* (see below) + -ESE.]
▶ **A** *noun*. Pl. same. A native or inhabitant of Yunnan, a province of SW China; the Chinese dialect of Yunnan. M19.
▶ **B** *adjective*. Of or pertaining to Yunnan, its people, or their dialect. M20.

yup *adverb & interjection* var. of YEP *adverb & interjection*[1].

Yupik /ˈjuːpɪk/ *noun & adjective*. M20.
[Alaskan Yupik *Yup'ik* real person.]
▶ **A** *noun*. The language of the Yuit, a major division of the Eskimo-Aleut family, with dialects spoken in Siberia and parts of Alaska. Cf. INUPIAQ. M20.
▶ **B** *adjective*. Of or pertaining to this language. M20.

yuppie /ˈjʌpi/ *noun & adjective*. *colloq*. (usu. *derog*.). Also **yuppy**. L20.
[Acronym, from young urban (or upwardly mobile) professional (person): see -IE. Cf. YUMPIE.]
▶ **A** *noun*. A member of a socio-economic group comprising young professional people working in cities and noted for their careerism and affluent lifestyle. L20.

> 🕮 D. M. THOMAS I regarded with distaste a group of sleek young yuppies in city suits.

▶ **B** *attrib*. or as *adjective*. That is a yuppie; typical of, suitable for, or favoured by yuppies. L20.

> 🕮 *Daily Telegraph* It is . . likely to find favour at the yuppier end of the market. *Sunday Mail (Brisbane)*: *Food Glorious Food* is the complete yuppie cookbook. This is . . strictly posh nosh.

Comb.: **yuppie flu** *colloq*. myalgic encephalomyelitis, once thought to be a psychosomatic condition peculiar to yuppies.
■ **yuppiedom** *noun* the condition or fact of being a yuppie; yuppies as a class: L20. **yuppieism** *noun* yuppyish behaviour; a yuppyish expression etc.: L20. **yuppifiˈcation** *noun* the action of yuppifying a thing L20. **yuppify** *verb trans*. make (a neighbourhood, organization, etc.) typical of or suitable for yuppies L20. **yuppyish** *adjective* = YUPPIE *adjective* above L20.

Yurak /ˈjʊərak/ *noun*. L19.
[Yurak name.]
More fully ***Yurak Samoyed***. = NENETS.

yuro *noun* var. of EURO *noun*[1].

Yurok /ˈjʊərɒk/ *noun & adjective*. M19.
[Karok *yúruk* downstream. Cf. KAROK.]
▶ **A** *noun*. Pl. **-s**, same. A member of a N. American Indian people of northern California; the language of this people, distantly related to Algonquian. M19.
▶ **B** *attrib*. or as *adjective*. Of or pertaining to the Yuroks or their language. L19.

yurt /jʊət/ *noun*. Also **yourt**. L18.
[Russian *yurta* (through French *yourte* or German *Jurte*) from Turkic *jurt*.]
A circular tent of felt, skins, etc., on a collapsible framework, used by nomads in Mongolia and Siberia. Also, a semi-subterranean hut, usu. of timber covered with earth or turf.

Yuruk /ˈjʊərʊk/ *noun & adjective*. M17.
[Turkish *yürük* lit. 'nomad'.]
▶ **A** *noun*. Pl. **-s**, same. A member of a nomadic people inhabiting Anatolia. M17.
▶ **B** *attrib*. or as *adjective*. Of or pertaining to this people; *esp*. designating a type of rug made by the Yuruks. L20.

yus /jʌs/ *adverb. dial. & non-standard.* **E19.**
[Repr. pronunc.]
= **YES** *adverb.*

yusho /ˈjuːʃəʊ/ *noun.* **M20.**
[Japanese, from *yu* oil + *shō* disease.]
MEDICINE. A disease characterized by the development of brown staining of the skin and severe acne, caused by the ingestion of polychlorinated biphenyls.

Yusufzai /ˈjuːsʊfzʌɪ/ *noun & adjective.* **E19.**
[Persian, from *yūsuf* Joseph + *-zāy* bringing forth.]
▶ **A** *noun.* Pl. **-s**, same. A member of a Pathan people of the Pakistan–Afghanistan borders. **E19.**
▶ **B** *adjective.* Of or pertaining to this people. **M19.**

Yuvaraja /jʊvəˈrɑːdʒə/ *noun.* **L19.**
[Sanskrit *yuvarāja*, from *yuvan* young + *rājan* **RAJA** *noun*[1].]
Hist. The male heir to an Indian principality.

yuzbashi /juːzˈbɑːʃi/ *noun.* **E19.**
[Turkish *yüzbaşı*, from *yüz* hundred + *baş* head. Cf. **BIMBASHI.**]
A captain in the Turkish or (formerly) the Persian army.

yūzen /ˈjuːzɛn/ *noun.* **E20.**
[from Miyazaki *Yūzen-sai* (fl. mid 18th cent.), Japanese inventor of the process.]
Used *attrib.* to designate (designs produced by) a technique of dyeing silk in which rice-paste is applied to areas which are not to be dyed.

YWCA *abbreviation.*
Young Women's Christian Association; a hostel run by this.

†**ywhere** *adverb.* **OE–ME.**
[from **Y-** + **WHERE** *adverb.*]
Everywhere.
¶ The 2nd elem. of early uses of **EVERYWHERE.**

ywroken /ɪˈrəʊk(ə)n/ *ppl adjective. arch.* **OE.**
[from **Y-** + *wroken* arch. pa. pple of **WREAK** *verb.*]
Avenged; taken vengeance on, punished.

Zz

Z, z /zɛd/.
The last letter of the modern English alphabet and of the ancient Roman one, corresp. to Greek ζ and Hebrew *zayin*. Originally used in alien words and certain loan-words in Old English and Middle English with the phonetic value /ts/; the sound normally represented by the letter in modern English is the voiced sibilant /z/. Initially and medially *z* occurs largely in words of Greek or oriental origin (***zeal***, ***azimuth***, ***Amazon***, ***zenith***) and in the suffix ***-ize*** and its derivatives. In other classes of words the choice between *z* and *s* has been determined or influenced by various circumstances, e.g. the immediate source of the word (***bronze***), the desirability of a distinctive spelling (***ooze***), and the difficulty of writing the character rapidly and intelligibly. In some Scottish words *z* is an adaptation of ȝ: see **YOGH**. Pl. **Z's**, **Zs**. See also **IZZARD**, **ZED**, **ZEE**.
► **I 1** The letter and its sound. ▸**b** Used (usu. repeated) to represent the sound of buzzing or snoring.
2 The shape of the letter. ▸**b** One of the two directions of twist in spinning yarn. Usu. *attrib.* Cf. **S**, **S** 2b.
1 *A to Z*, *from A to Z*: see **A**, **A** 1. **b catch a few z's**, **catch some z's**, **get a few z's**, **get some z's** (chiefly *US*) get some sleep. **2 Z-bar** a metal bar having a Z-shaped cross-section. **Z-bed** a folding bed, *esp.* one that folds up like a Z or N. **Z-bend** a pair of opposite bends in a road. **Z-DNA** (*BIOCHEMISTRY*) DNA in which the double helix has a left-handed rather than the usual right-handed twist and the sugar phosphate backbone follows a zigzag course. **Z-plan** *ARCHITECTURE* the ground-plan of a type of Scottish castle having a central block with two towers at diagonally opposite corners. **Z-plastic** *adjective* (*MEDICINE*) (of surgery) involving the use of Z-shaped incisions. **Z-plasty** *MEDICINE* (an instance of) a surgical operation or technique in which one or more Z-shaped skin incisions are made (the diagonals forming one straight line), and the two triangular flaps so formed are drawn across the diagonal before being stitched. **Z-shaped** *adjective* having a shape or a cross-section like the capital letter Z.
► **II** Symbolical uses.
3 Used to denote serial order; applied e.g. to the twenty-sixth (or often the twenty-fifth, either I or J being omitted) group or section, sheet of a book, etc.
4 *MATH.* (Usu. italic *z*.) The third unknown or variable quantity. ▸**b** Used to denote an unknown or unspecified person, thing, number, etc. Cf. **X**, **X** 5b.
5 *GEOMETRY* etc. (Italic *z*.) Used to denote a quantity measured along the third axis in a three-dimensional system of coordinates.
6 *ANATOMY & ZOOLOGY.* [Initial letter of German *Zwischenscheibe* 'intermediate disc'.] ***Z disc***, ***Z line***, (also ***Z band***), a narrow transverse line between sarcomeres in a myofibril of striated muscle.
7 *GENETICS.* (Cap. Z.) Used to denote the male-determining sex chromosome in species in which the female rather than the male is the heterogametic sex.
8 *PHYSICS.* (Italic Z.) Used to denote the atomic number of an element.
9 *PARTICLE PHYSICS.* (Cap. Z.) Used to denote a heavy uncharged vector boson that forms a triplet with the two Ws.
5 Z-axis (written *z-axis*) (*a*) the third axis in a three-dimensional system of coordinates; (*b*) *ELECTRONICS* the optic axis of a quartz crystal.

za /zɑː/ *noun. US slang.* **M20.**
[Abbreviation.]
= **PIZZA**.

zabaglione /zabɑːˈljəʊni/ *noun.* **L19.**
[Italian, perh. ult. from late Latin *sabaia* an Illyrian drink.]
A dessert consisting of egg-yolks, sugar, and (usu. Marsala) wine, whipped to a frothy texture over a gentle heat and served either hot or cold. Cf. **SABAYON**.

zabra /ˈzɑːbrə/ *noun.* Also (earlier) †**zabre**. **E16.**
[Spanish.]
A small boat used off the coasts of Spain and Portugal.

zabuton /zaˈbuːtɒn/ *noun.* **L19.**
[Japanese, from *za* sitting, seat + *buton* var. of **FUTON**.]
A flat floor cushion for sitting or kneeling on.

zac /zak/ *noun. Austral. slang.* Now *rare.* Also **zack**. **L19.**
[Perh. from dial. form of **SIX**.]
A sixpence.

zacate *noun* var. of **SACATE**.

zacaton *noun* var. of **SACATON**.

zack *noun* var. of **ZAC**.

'zackly /ˈzakli/ *adverb. colloq.* Also **'zactly** /ˈzak(t)li/. **L19.**
[Repr. a dial. or colloq. pronunc.]
= **EXACTLY**.

zad *noun* see **ZED**.

Zadokite /ˈzeɪdəkʌɪt/ *noun & adjective.* **E20.**
[from *Zadok* (see below) + **-ITE**[1].]
► **A** *noun.* A member of a Jewish sect established in the 2nd cent. BC and tracing its leaders' authority back to Zadok, a high priest of Israel in the time of King David. **E20.**
► **B** *adjective.* Of or pertaining to the Zadokites. **E20.**

zadruga /zaˈdruːgə/ *noun.* Pl. ***-ge*** /-geɪ/. **L19.**
[Serbo-Croat.]
(The customs and rules of) a type of patriarchal social unit traditional to (agricultural) Serbians and other southern Slavonic peoples, orig. comprising an extended family group working the land and living communally round the main house.

zaffre /ˈzafə/ *noun.* Also †**-er**, †**saffer**. **M17.**
[Italian *zaffera* or its source Old & mod. French *safre*, perh. rel. to **SAPPHIRE**.]
Impure cobalt oxide, used in the preparation of smalt and as a blue colouring matter for pottery, glass, etc.

zaftig /ˈzaftɪg/ *adjective. N. Amer. colloq.* Also **zoftig** /ˈzɒftɪg/. **M20.**
[Yiddish from German *saftig* juicy.]
Of a woman: plump, having a full rounded figure.

zag /zag/ *verb & noun. colloq.* **L18.**
[from **ZIG)ZAG** *verb* or *noun.* Cf. **ZIG**.]
► **A** *verb intrans.* Infl. **-gg-**. Turn sharply away from a direction taken in a preceding zig. **L18.**

> 🕮 *New Yorker* The front wheel wobbled, the cycle zigged and zagged.

► **B** *noun.* A sharp turn away from a direction taken in a preceding zig. **M19.**

> 🕮 *Time* You don't go . . in a straight line. You go through zigs and zags.

Zaghlulist /zaˈgluːlɪst/ *noun & adjective.* **E20.**
[from *Zaghlūl Sa'd* (see below) + **-IST**.]
Hist. ► **A** *noun.* An adherent or supporter of the nationalist and separatist principles and policies of the Egyptian politician Zaghlūl Sa'd (1857–1927). **E20.**
► **B** *adjective.* Of or pertaining to the Zaghlulists. **E20.**

zaguan /zaˈgwan, s-/ *noun.* **M19.**
[Spanish *zaguán* vestibule, hall, from Arab. *'ustuwān*, perh. ult. from Greek *stoa* porch.]
A passage running from the front door to the central patio in houses in South and Central America and in the south-western US.

Zahal /zɑːˈhɑːl, tsaˈhal/ *noun.* **M20.**
[Hebrew, acronym from *Ṣĕbā' Hăgannāh Lĕ-Yiśrā'ēl* Israel Defence Force.]
The Israeli defence forces, formed originally in 1948 by the fusion of existing military organizations.

zaibatsu /zʌɪˈbatsuː/ *noun.* Pl. same. **M20.**
[Japanese, from *zai* wealth + *batsu* clique.]
COMMERCE. Orig., a Japanese capitalist organization usu. based on a single family having controlling interests in a variety of companies. Now, (the members of) a Japanese business cartel or conglomerate.

zaikai /ˈzʌɪkʌɪ/ *noun.* **M20.**
[Japanese, from *zai* wealth + *kai* world.]
In Japan: (the élite who control) the world of business and high finance.

zaim /zaˈiːm/ *noun.* **E19.**
[(Turkish from) Arab. *za'īm* chieftain.]
1 *Hist.* A Turkish feudal chief supporting a mounted militia bearing his name. **E19.**
2 In Lebanon: a powerful sectarian popular leader. **L20.**

zaire /zʌɪˈɪə/ *noun.* **M20.**
[from *Zaire* local name of the Congo River in central Africa.]
Hist. The basic monetary unit of Zaire (now the Democratic Republic of Congo), equal to 100 makuta.

Zairean /zʌɪˈɪərɪən/ *noun & adjective.* **L20.**
[from *Zaire* (see below, prec.) + **-EAN**.]
► **A** *noun.* A native or inhabitant of Zaire (now the Democratic Republic of Congo) in central Africa. **L20.**
► **B** *adjective.* Of or pertaining to Zaire. **L20.**
■ Also **Zairian** *noun & adjective* **L20.**

Zairese /zʌɪˌɪəˈriːz/ *noun & adjective.* Pl. of noun same. **L20.**
[formed as prec. + **-ESE**.]
= prec. Cf. next.

Zairois /zʌɪˌɪəˈrwɑː/ *noun & adjective.* Pl. of noun same. **L20.**
[French.]
= **ZAIREAN**.

zakat /zəˈkɑːt/ *noun.* **E19.**
[Persian & Urdu *zakā(t)*, Turkish *zekât* from Arab. *zakā(t)* almsgiving.]
An obligatory payment made annually under Islamic law on certain kinds of property and used for charitable and religious objects.

zakuska /zaˈkuskə/ *noun.* Also ***-kou-***. Pl. ***-kas***, ***-ki*** /-ki/. **L19.**
[Russian (usu. as pl. *zakuski*).]
An hors d'oeuvre.

zamacueca /zaməˈkwɛkə, s-/ *noun.* **M19.**
[Amer. Spanish: cf. **CUECA**.]
A S. American, esp. Chilean, dance in which a couple move around one another to the accompaniment of guitar chords and rhythmic handclapping.

zaman /ˈzaman/ *noun.* Also **-ng** /-ŋ/. **E19.**
[Spanish *samán* from Carib *zamang*.]
The rain-tree of tropical S. America, *Albizia saman*.

zamarra /θaˈmarra/ *noun.* **M19.**
[Spanish.]
In Spain: a kind of sheepskin jacket.

Zambian /ˈzambɪən/ *noun & adjective.* **M20.**
[from *Zambia* (see below) + **-AN**.]
► **A** *noun.* A native, citizen, or inhabitant of Zambia, a country in south central Africa. **M20.**
► **B** *adjective.* Of, pertaining to, or characteristic of Zambia or its people. **M20.**
■ **Zambianize** *verb trans.* make Zambian in character by replacing foreign personnel by black Zambians **M20.** **Zambiani'zation** *noun* the process of Zambianizing a firm, an industry, etc. **M20.**

zambo *noun* see **SAMBO** *noun*[1].

zambra /ˈzambrə, *foreign* ˈθambra/ *noun.* **L17.**
[Spanish.]
A kind of flamenco dance.

zambuk /ˈzambʌk/ *noun. Austral. & NZ colloq.* Also **-uck**. **E20.**
[Proprietary name for a type of antiseptic ointment.]
A first-aider, esp. a member of the St John's Ambulance Brigade, in attendance at a sporting fixture or other public gathering.

zamia /ˈzeɪmɪə/ *noun.* **E19.**
[mod. Latin (see below), from *zamiae*, misreading of *azaniae* pine cones, in a passage of Pliny.]
Any of various cycads constituting the tropical American genus *Zamia* (family Zamiaceae) or the allied Australian genus *Macrozamia* formerly included in it. Also (*Austral.*) ***zamia palm***.

zamindar /zəˈmiːndɑː, zəmiːnˈdɑː/ *noun.* Also **ze-**. **L17.**
[Urdu from Persian *zamīndār*, from *zamīn* land + *-dār* holding, holder.]
In the Indian subcontinent: a landed proprietor; *spec.* (*Hist.*) one who held land on which tax was paid direct to the British Government (cf. **RYOT**); formerly, an official who collected revenue held by a number of cultivators.
■ **zamindarship** *noun* = **ZAMINDARI** **L17.**

zamindari /zəˈmiːndəri, zəmiːnˈdɑːri/ *noun.* Also **ze-**, **-ary**. **M18.**
[Urdu from Persian *zamīndārī*, from *zamīndār*: see prec.]
Chiefly *Hist.* The system of holding land or farming tax by zamindars; the office or territory of a zamindar.

Zamorin *noun* var. of **SAMORIN**.

zampogna /zamˈpɒnjə, *foreign* tsamˈpoɲa/ *noun.* **M18.**
[Italian from (late) Latin *symphonia*: see **SYMPHONY**.]
MUSIC. A traditional mouth-blown bagpipe of southern Italy having two chanters and two drones. Also, any of various other woodwind instruments.

Zande /ˈzandi/ *noun & adjective.* Orig. †**Zandey**. As adjective also **Azande** /aˈzandi/. **L19.**
[Zande.]
► **A** *noun.* Pl. **Azande**.
1 A member of a central African people of mixed ethnic origin. **L19.**

2 The language of this people. **M20.**
▶ **B** *attrib.* or as *adjective.* Designating, of, or pertaining to this people or their language. **L19.**

zander /ˈzandə/ *noun.* **M19.**
[German.]
A large European pikeperch, *Stizostedion lucioperca*, which is native to central and northern Europe and has been introduced widely in western Europe.

†**Zandey** *noun & adjective* see ZANDE.

zanella /zəˈnɛlə/ *noun & adjective.* **L19.**
[Perh. from Antonio *Zanelli*, author of *Le lane italiane* (1878).]
(Designating) a satiny cotton fabric used for linings and esp. for covering umbrellas.

Zantac /ˈzantak/ *noun.* **L20.**
[Prob. from *Z* + ANTAC(ID.]
PHARMACOLOGY. (Proprietary name for) the drug ranitidine.

ZANU *abbreviation.*
Zimbabwe African National Union.

zany /ˈzeɪni/ *noun & adjective.* **L16.**
[French *zani*, or its source Italian *zan(n)i*, orig. Venetian and Lombardic form of *Gianni* = *Giovanni* John, stock name of the servants acting as clowns in the *commedia dell'arte*.]
▶ **A** *noun.* **1** A comic performer attending on a clown, acrobat, or mountebank, and imitating his master's acts in a ludicrously awkward way, a merry Andrew (*Hist.*); a professional jester or buffoon. Now *arch.* or *Hist.* **L16.**
2 a An attendant, a follower, a companion; *esp.* a hanger-on. *arch.* (usu. *derog.*). Now *rare.* **E17.** ▸†**b** An imitator, a mimic, *esp.* a poor or feeble one. **E17–M18.** ▸**c** A person who acts like a buffoon or plays the fool. Now *rare.* **E17.** ▸**d** An idiot, a simpleton. *obsolete* exc. *dial.* **L18.**

> 🕮 **1** SHAKES. *L.L.L.* Some carry-tale, some please-man, some slight zany. **2d** TENNYSON The printers are awful zanies, they print erasures and corrections too.

▶ **B** *attrib.* or as *adjective.* Comically idiotic; crazily or bizarrely ridiculous or comic. Now also, bizarre, crazy. **L16.**

> 🕮 *Washington Flyer* Complete with a zany plot and downright peculiar characters.

▪ **zanily** *adverb* **M20.** **zaniness** *noun* **M20.**

zany /ˈzeɪni/ *verb trans.* Now *arch. rare.* **E17.**
[from prec.]
Play the zany to; imitate awkwardly like a zany; mimic.

Zanzibari /zanzɪˈbɑːri/ *noun & adjective.* **L19.**
[from *Zanzibar* (see below) + -I[2].]
▶ **A** *noun.* A native or inhabitant of Zanzibar, an island on the east coast of Africa, now part of Tanzania. **L19.**
▶ **B** *attrib.* or as *adjective.* Of, pertaining to, or characteristic of Zanzibar or its people. **L19.**

zap /zap/ *interjection, verb, & noun. slang* (orig. *US*). **E20.**
[Imit.]
▶ **A** *interjection.* Repr. the sound or impact of a ray gun, laser, bullet, etc. Also (*fig.*), expr. the sudden or dramatic nature of an event. **E20.**

> 🕮 R. BANKS Put me onto something like this school bus case . . and zap! all those feelings disappear.

Comb.: **zap gun** a ray gun.
▶ **B** *verb.* Infl. **-pp-**.
▶ **I** *verb trans.* **1 a** Kill, esp. with a gun; deal a sudden blow to (a person). **M20.** ▸**b** Put an end to, do away with, destroy (a thing) abruptly. **L20.** ▸**c** *COMPUTING.* Erase or alter (an item in a program or memory) by direct intervention. **L20.**
2 Take action against (a person etc.); *spec.* (**a**) punish; (**b**) demonstrate against. **M20.**
3 Move, send, put, or strike quickly or forcefully. **M20.** ▸**b** Make more powerful or exciting; enliven, revitalize. Also foll. by *up.* **L20.**
4 Overwhelm, esp. emotionally. **M20.**

> 🕮 **1a** *New York Review of Books* A young man . . was zapped in the face . . with an aerosol spray can. **b** *Psychology Today* If this were just a tool for zapping stress . . it would be awesome enough. *Sky Warriors* Their . . tracking radars had been successfully zapped by Navy-launched anti-radar missiles. **3** *National Observer (US)* When Ms Klutz limberly zaps the ball over the net. *Japan Times* Fax machines . . are used for . . zapping news releases to the media. *Science News* They have induced silicon . . to emit light when zapped with electrical current. **b** P. HOWARD A first sentence so compelling that it will zap the . . sub-editor into . . animation. *New York Times* A silky textured duck liver pâté was zapped with . . brandy. **4** C. MCCULLOUGH Punctured. Pricked. Deflated. Zapped.

▶ **II** *verb intrans.* **5** Move quickly and vigorously. **M20.**
6 Wind a videotape rapidly forwards *through* a section, esp. of commercials, in a recorded programme; operate a remote control to switch rapidly *through* or between television channels etc., esp. during commercials. **L20.**

> 🕮 **5** J. WAIN Ill-health . . put a stop to his zapping back and forth across the Atlantic. **6** N. HORNBY He found the remote control . . and zapped through the channels.

▶ **C** *noun.* **1** Energy, power, vigour, drive; a strong emotional effect. **M20.**
2 A demonstration (against something). **L20.**
3 A charge or bolt of electricity etc.; a beam or burst of radiation etc. **L20.**
▪ **zapper** *noun* (**a**) a person, device, or technique that kills or does away with something, esp. insects; *spec.* (**Z-**, US proprietary name for) an agricultural machine which destroys pests that attack crops; (**b**) *slang* a remote control for operating a television, video recorder, etc.: **M20.** **zapping** *verbal noun* the action of the verb; *spec.* the practice of avoiding commercials when watching television programmes: **L20.** **zappy** *adjective* lively, amusing, energetic; striking: **M20.**

Zapata /zəˈpɑːtə/ *noun.* **M20.**
[Emilio *Zapata* (1879–1919), Mexican revolutionary, portrayed with a moustache of this kind by Marlon Brando in the film *Viva Zapata!* in 1952.]
Used *attrib.* to designate a type of moustache in which the two ends extend downwards to the chin.

zapateado /zaˌpatɪˈɑːdəʊ, *foreign* θapateˈaðo/ *noun.* Pl. **-os** /-əʊz, *foreign* -os/. **M19.**
[Spanish, from *zapato* shoe.]
1 A flamenco dance involving complex syncopated stamping of the heels and toes in imitation of castanets. **M19.**
2 Dancing or footwork of this kind. **M20.**

zapote /zəˈpəʊteɪ/ *noun.* **M19.**
[Spanish: see SAPOTA.]
= MAMMEE 2.

Zapotec /ˈzapətɛk/ *noun & adjective.* **L18.**
[Spanish *zapoteco*, *-ca* from Nahuatl *tzapoteca* pl. of *tzapotecatl* lit. 'person of the place of the sapotilla'.]
▶ **A** *noun.* **1** A member of an American Indian people of southern Mexico. **L18.**
2 The language of this people, comprising several distinct dialects. **L19.**
▶ **B** *adjective.* Of or pertaining to the Zapotecs or their language. **M19.**
▪ Also **Zapoˈtecan** *noun & adjective* **E20.**

†**zappe** *noun* see SAP *noun*[2].

zaptieh /ˈzaptɪeɪ/ *noun.* **M19.**
[Turkish *zabtiye* gendarmerie, gendarme, from colloq. Arab. *ḍābitiyya* police, from Arab. *ḍābit* officer.]
A Turkish policeman.

ZAPU *abbreviation.*
Zimbabwe African People's Union.

Zar /zɑː/ *noun.* **M19.**
[Arab. *zār*, from Amharic, prob. ult. from Cushitic *Jār* (name of) a sky deity.]
In several N. African countries: a malignant spirit, possession by which is traditionally held to explain attacks of (esp. religious) mania, esp. in women.

zarape *noun* var. of SERAPE.

Zarathustrian /zarəˈθʊstrɪən/ *adjective & noun.* **L19.**
[Avestan *Zarat̰uš* Zoroaster: see ZOROASTRIAN.]
= ZOROASTRIAN.

zarda /ˈzɑːdə/ *noun.* **L19.**
[Persian & Urdu *zardah*, from Persian *zard* yellow.]
A Persian and Indian sweet dish consisting of rice cooked with saffron and often almonds and raisins or sultanas.

zareba /zəˈriːbə/ *noun.* Also **zer-**, **-riba**. **M19.**
[Arab. *zarība* pen or enclosure for cattle.]
1 In Sudan and neighbouring countries: (a camp fortified by) a fence, usu. made of thorn trees, for defence against enemies or wild animals. **M19.**
2 *transf.* & *fig.* A defensive force or barrier. **L19.**

> 🕮 **1** D. REITZ We had taken every precaution, building zarebas at night. **2** G. GREENE Shadows of the palms pointed at him like a zareba of sabres.

zarf /zɑːf/ *noun.* **M19.**
[Arab. *ẓarf* vessel.]
A cup-shaped holder for a hot coffee-cup, used in the eastern Mediterranean region, usually of metal and of ornamental design.

zari /ˈzari/ *noun.* **M20.**
[Persian & Urdu *zarī*, from Persian *zar* gold.]
Indian gold and silver brocade; *colloq.* a sari decorated with this.

zariba *noun* var. of ZAREBA.

zarnich /ˈzɑːnɪk/ *noun. rare.* **E17.**
[Hispano-Arab. *zarnīk*, perh. from Persian *zarnī(k)* orpiment, from *zar* gold.]
A sulphide of arsenic; orpiment, realgar.

Zarp /zɑːp/ *noun. S. Afr. obsolete* exc. *Hist.* **L19.**
[Dutch acronym, from Dutch *Zuid Afrikaansch Republikeinsch Politie* South African Republican Police.]
A member of the Boer police force, esp. in the pre-1902 South African Republic.

zarzuela /θarˈθwela, zɑːˈzweɪlə/ *noun.* **L19.**
[Spanish.]
1 A traditional form of operetta in Spain, with spoken dialogue, songs, and dances. **L19.**
2 A Spanish dish consisting of various kinds of seafood cooked in a rich sauce. **M20.**

zastruga *noun* var. of SASTRUGA.

zat /zat/ *interjection. slang.* **M20.**
[Repr. a pronunc.]
CRICKET. = OWZAT.

zawiya /ˈzɑːwɪə/ *noun.* Also †**-yeh**. **M19.**
[Arab. *zāwiya* corner, prayer room.]
In N. Africa, a Sufi religious community's mosque, esp. when containing the shrine of a holy person.

zax *noun* see SAX *noun*[1].

zayat /ˈzɑːjət/ *noun.* **E19.**
[Burmese.]
In Myanmar (Burma): a public building for rest or shelter.

zazen /zɑːˈzɛn/ *noun.* **E18.**
[Japanese, from *za* sitting, a seat + *zen* ZEN.]
Zen meditation.

zazzy /ˈzazi/ *adjective. slang* (chiefly *US*). **M20.**
[Perh. blend of ZIPPY and JAZZY: cf. SASSY *adjective*, SNAZZY.]
Colourful, vivid; stylish, striking.

zea /ˈziːə/ *noun.* **L16.**
[Late & mod. Latin from Greek *zeia*.]
†**1** Spelt, *Triticum spelta*. **L16–E17.**
2 A cereal grass of the genus *Zea*; *spec.* maize, Indian corn, *Z. mays*. Also ***zea maize***. **L18.**

zeal /ziːl/ *noun.* **LME.**
[Latin (esp. ecclesiastical Latin) *zelus* from Greek *zēlos*.]
1 In biblical translations or allusions: ardent feeling manifested in love, jealousy, or righteous indignation. **LME.**
2 Fervent love or devotion. *obsolete* or merged in sense 3. **LME.**
3 Intense or passionate desire. Now usu., such desire displayed in pursuit of an objective, or in advancing a cause; hearty and persistent endeavour. (Foll. by *for*, †*of*, *to do*.) **LME.**
†**4** Disposition, intent. Chiefly in ***good zeal***. Chiefly *Scot.* **LME–L16.**

> 🕮 **1** AV *Ezek.* 5:13 I the Lord haue spoken it in my zeale, when I haue accomplished my fury. **3** SLOAN WILSON He had pursued her with all the zeal he always devoted to anything he wanted. A. S. BYATT Her collector's zeal for catalogued information. *Times* There was an almost missionary zeal in the Schoenberg circle to spread the . . gospel of the master.

▪ **zealless** /-l-l-/ *adjective* **E17.**

Zealander /ˈziːləndə/ *noun.* **L16.**
[from *Zealand* (see below) + -ER[1].]
1 A native or inhabitant of Zealand, a province of the Netherlands. **L16.**
2 A native or inhabitant of New Zealand; *esp.* a Maori. See also NEW ZEALANDER. **L18.**

zealot /ˈzɛlət/ *noun & adjective.* **M16.**
[ecclesiastical Latin *zelotes* from Greek *zēlōtēs*, from *zēloun* be jealous, from *zēlos* zeal.]
▶ **A** *noun.* **1** *Hist.* A member of a Jewish sect in Palestine, whose passionate opposition to foreign rule led to the Jewish uprising of AD 66–70 against Rome. **M16.**
2 A person who is zealous (*for* a cause). Usu., a person who is carried away by excess of zeal; a fanatical enthusiast. **M17.**

> 🕮 **2** W. W. NEWCOMB Dedicated, and single-minded, he became a zealot in his determination to record . . the rock art of Texas. W. STYRON The Professor was also a practicing Catholic, though hardly a zealot.

▶ **B** *attrib.* or as *adjective.* That is a zealot; characteristic of a zealot. **M16.**
▪ **zealotism** *noun* zealotry **E18.**

zealotic /ziːˈlɒtɪk/ *adjective.* Also **zel-**. **M17.**
[from ZEALOT + -IC: in form *zel-* assim. to Greek *zēlōtikos*, from *zēlōtēs* ZEALOT.]
Of the nature of or characteristic of a zealot.

zealotry /ˈzɛlətri/ *noun.* **M17.**
[from ZEALOT + -RY: cf. *bigotry*.]
(An) action or feeling characteristic of a zealot.

zealous /ˈzɛləs/ *adjective.* **E16.**
[from medieval Latin deriv. of Latin *zelus* (cf. medieval Latin *gelositas*): see ZEAL, -OUS.]
1 Full of zeal; active in the promotion of a person or cause. (Foll. by *for*, *to do*.) **E16.** ▸**b** Of an action etc.: marked by zeal. **M16**
†**2** Jealous (*of*). *rare.* **M16–M17.**

📖 **1** LD MACAULAY The House of Commons . . more zealous for royalty than the king. D. L. SAYERS The money . . might, by zealous enquirers, have been traced to Lord Peter Wimsey's banking account. **b** W. S. CHURCHILL The zealous campaign of the Whig Opposition in favour of the French revolutionaries.

■ **zealously** *adverb* L16. **zealousness** *noun* (now *rare*) M16.

zearalenone /ziːəˈralənəʊn/ *noun*. M20.
[from ZEA + *-ral-* (from resorcylic *acid lactone*) + -EN(E + -ONE.]
BIOCHEMISTRY. A bicyclic lactone which is a toxic metabolite of certain cereal fungi and causes disorders of the reproductive system in pigs.
■ **zearalanol** *noun* = ZERANOL M20.

zearat *noun* var. of ZIARAT.

zeatin /ˈziːətɪn/ *noun*. M20.
[from ZEA + euphonic *-t-* + -IN¹.]
BIOCHEMISTRY. A purine derivative occurring as a cytokinin in maize kernels and other plant materials.

zebec(k) *nouns* vars. of XEBEC.

zebra /ˈzɛbrə, ˈziːbrə/ *noun*. Pl. same, **-s**. E17.
[Italian, Spanish, Portuguese (earlier †*zevra*), orig. = wild ass, perh. ult. from Latin *equiferus*, from *equus* horse + *ferus* wild.]
1 Each of three wild African horses which have erect manes and whitish hides that are distinctively striped with black; esp. *Equus burchelli*, which is abundant on the E. African savannah. Also, the extinct quagga. E17.
2 *transf.* Any of various things striped like a zebra. E19. ▸**b** A striped prison uniform; a convict wearing such a uniform. *arch. slang*. L19. ▸**c** = ***zebra finch*** below. L19. ▸**d** = ***zebra crossing*** below. *colloq.* M20.
1 BURCHELL'S ZEBRA. GREVY'S ZEBRA. ***MOUNTAIN zebra***.
Comb.: **zebra angelfish** a tropical marine angelfish, *Pomacanthus semicirculatus* (family Pomacanthidae), of which the juvenile is very dark blue with pale vertical stripes, and the adult is yellowish with blue spots, head, and fins; **zebra crossing** a pedestrian crossing marked by broad black and white stripes on the road and Belisha beacons on the kerb; **zebra danio** a small Indian freshwater cyprinid fish, *Brachydanio rerio*, which has horizontal dark and light stripes and is popular as an aquarium fish; **zebra eel** an Indo-Pacific eel, *Echidna zebra* (family Muraenidae), which has a black body with numerous white transverse bands; **zebra finch** a gregarious Australasian waxbill, *Poephila guttata*, which has black and white stripes on the face and orange-brown cheeks, and is popular as a cage-bird; **zebra firefish** an Indo-Pacific scorpion fish, *Dendrochirus zebra*, which has black and white stripes and dangerously venomous spines; **zebra fish** any of various striped tropical fishes; *esp.* the zebra danio, the zebra firefish; **zebra mussel** a small freshwater bivalve, *Dreissena polymorpha*, with zigzag markings, native to NE Europe and introduced in western Europe and N. America, sometimes blocking drainpipes; **zebra-plant** any of several plants with ornamentally striped leaves, e.g. the Brazilian *Calathea zebrina* (family Marantaceae); **zebra scorpion fish** = ***zebra firefish*** above; **zebra spider** any of several small striped jumping spiders of the family Salticidae; *esp.* the common *Salticus scenicus*; **zebra-wolf** = THYLACINE; **zebrawood** any of several kinds of ornamentally striped wood used by cabinet-makers, e.g. that of the tropical tree *Connarus guianensis* (family Connaraceae); any of the trees or shrubs supplying such wood.
■ **zebraed** *adjective* striped like a zebra M19. **zebrine** *adjective* related to or characteristic of the zebra M19.

zebrano /zɪˈbrɑːnəʊ/ *noun*. E20.
[Irreg. from ZEBRA.]
Striped wood furnished by various African trees, esp. those of the genus *Microberlinia* (family Leguminosae).

zebrina /zɪˈbrʌɪnə/ *noun*. M20.
[mod. Latin (see below), formed as ZEBRA + -INA².]
Any of several Central American tradescantias grown for their ornamentally striped leaves and formerly distinguished as the genus *Zebrina*.

zebroid /ˈzɛbrɔɪd, ˈziː-/ *adjective & noun*. L19.
[from ZEBRA + -OID.]
▸ **A** *adjective*. Resembling or characteristic of a zebra. L19.
▸ **B** *noun*. An offspring of a horse and a zebra. L19.

zebrule /ˈzɛbruːl, ˈziː-/ *noun*. E20.
[Blend of ZEBRA and MULE *noun*¹.]
= ZEDONK.

zebu /ˈziːbuː/ *noun*. L18.
[French *zébu*, of unkn. origin.]
A humped ox, *Bos indicus*, orig. domesticated in India, which is tolerant of heat and drought and is now kept widely in tropical and warm-temperate countries.

zecchin /ˈzɛkɪn/ *noun*. L16.
[Italian *zecchino*: see SEQUIN.]
= SEQUIN *noun* 1.

Zech. *abbreviation*.
Zechariah (in the Bible).

Zechstein /ˈzɛkstʌɪn/ *noun & adjective*. E19.
[German, lit. 'mine-stone'.]
GEOLOGY. ▸**A** *noun*. An Upper Permian limestone developed in northern Germany and the North Sea basin, corresponding to magnesian limestone; the series of strata containing this. E19.
▸ **B** *attrib.* or as *adjective*. Pertaining to or designating the stratigraphic sequence of these rocks, or the shallow sea under which they were laid down. E20.

zed /zɛd/ *noun*. Also (*obsolete* exc. *dial.*) **zad** /zad/. LME.
[Old & mod. French *zède* (= Spanish, Italian *zeta*) from late Latin *zeta* from Greek *zēta*.]
1 The letter Z, z. Cf. ZEE. LME.
2 In full ***zed-bar***. = ***Z-bar*** s.v. Z, Z. L19.

📖 **1** G. CRABBE With study sad, I labour'd on to reach the final Zad.

zedoary /ˈzɛdəʊəri/ *noun*. LME.
[medieval Latin *zedoarium* from Persian *zadwār*.]
An Indian plant, *Curcuma zedoaria*, which is allied to turmeric and cultivated for its aromatic gingery rhizome; the root of this plant, used in parts of Asia as a condiment and tonic.

zedonk /ˈziːdɒŋk, ˈzɛ-/ *noun*. L20.
[Blend of ZEBRA and DONKEY.]
The offspring of a male zebra and a female donkey. Cf. ZONKEY.

zee /ziː/ *noun*. Now *US*. L17.
[Var. of ZED.]
The letter Z, z. Cf. ZED.

Zeeman /ˈzeɪmən/ *noun*. L19.
[Pieter *Zeeman* (1865–1943), Dutch physicist.]
PHYSICS. Used ***attrib.*** with ref. to the splitting of a spectral line into three or more closely spaced components when the light source is in a magnetic field not strong enough to produce the Paschen–Back effect.

zeera *noun* var. of JEERA.

zein /ˈziːɪn/ *noun*. Also †**zeine**. E19.
[from ZEA + -IN¹.]
BIOCHEMISTRY. A protein of the prolamine class found in maize, used in coatings, varnishes, inks, etc.

zeitgeber /ˈtsaɪtɡeːbər, ˈzʌɪtɡeɪbə/ *noun*. Pl. same, **-s**. M20.
[German, from *Zeit* time + *Geber* giver.]
PHYSIOLOGY. A rhythmically occurring event, esp. in the environment, which acts as a cue in the regulation of certain biological rhythms in an organism.

Zeitgeist /ˈtsaɪtɡaɪst, ˈzʌɪtɡʌɪst/ *noun*. M19.
[German, from *Zeit* time + *Geist* spirit.]
The spirit of the age; the trend of thought or feeling in a period, esp. as reflected in its literature, art, etc.

📖 S. REYNOLDS The dawn of a nineties zeitgeist that emphasized caring and sharing.

zek /zɛk/ *noun*. M20.
[Russian, repr. pronunc. of *z/k*, abbreviation of *zaklyuchënnyĭ* prisoner.]
In countries of the former USSR, a person held in a prison or forced labour camp.

zelator /ˈzɛlətə/ *noun*. *rare*. LME.
[(Old & mod. French *zélateur* from) ecclesiastical Latin *zelator*, from *zelare* be zealous: see -ATOR.]
A zealot, a fanatic; a zealous defender or supporter (*of*).

Zeldovich /ˈzɛldəvɪtʃ/ *noun*. L20.
[Ya. B. *Zel'dovich* (1914–87), Russian physicist.]
CHEMISTRY. Used ***attrib.*** to designate a mechanism for the oxidation of nitrogen to nitric oxide in flames via a two-stage free-radical reaction.

Zelig /ˈzɛlɪɡ/ *noun*. Chiefly *US*. L20.
[Leonard *Zelig*, central character in the US film *Zelig* (Woody Allen, 1983).]
(The name of) a person resembling Leonard Zelig in being able to change his or her appearance, behaviour, attitudes, etc., so as to be comfortable or appropriate in any circumstance.

📖 *New York Times* Mr. Gates . . has become a veritable Zelig of high technology, burrowing into every information industry nook.

■ **Zelig-like** *adjective* L20.

zelkova /zɛlˈkəʊvə/ *noun*. L19.
[mod. Latin (see below), from *zelkoua*, *tselkwa*, cited as local names of *Zelkova carpinifolia* in the Caucasus: cf. Russian *dzel'kva grabolistnaya*.]
Any of several deciduous trees constituting the genus *Zelkova*, of the elm family, which are chiefly native to China, Japan, and the Caucasus, and bear toothed leaves and small green flowers. Also ***zelkova tree***.

zelotic *adjective* var. of ZEALOTIC.

zeme /ˈziːmi/ *noun*. Also **zemi**. M16.
[Carib *cemi*.]
An idol or tutelary spirit, worshipped by the Caribs.
■ **zemeism** *noun* the worship of zemes E20.

zemindar, **zemindari**, **zemindary** *nouns* vars. of ZAMINDAR, ZAMINDARI.

zemirah /zəˈmɪərə/ *noun*. Pl. ***-rot(h)*** /-rəʊt/. M19.
[Hebrew *zĕmīrāh*, from *zimmēr* sing.]
JUDAISM. A religious song sung in Hebrew at Sabbath meals.

zemstvo /ˈzɛmstvəʊ, *foreign* ˈzemstvo/ *noun*. Pl. **-vos**, ***-va*** /-və/. M19.
[Russian, from †*zem'* (now *zemlya*) land.]
Hist. Any of the elected district or provincial councils set up in Russia by Alexander II in 1864 as part of his reforms.
■ **zemstvoist** *noun* a member of a zemstvo E20.

Zen /zɛn/ *noun*. E18.
[Japanese *zen* from Chinese *chán* quietude from Sanskrit *dhyāna* meditation.]
A school of Mahayana Buddhism emphasizing meditation and personal awareness, which became influential in Japanese life from the 13th cent. after being introduced from China. Also more fully ***Zen Buddhism***.

zenana /zəˈnɑːnə/ *noun*. M18.
[Persian & Urdu *zanānah*, from *zan* woman.]
1 In the Indian subcontinent: the part of a house in which high-caste women are or were secluded. M18.
2 A light quilted thin fabric used for women's dresses and negligées. E20.
Comb.: **zenana mission**: conducted among Hindu women by female Christian missionaries.

Zend /zɛnd/ *noun*. E18.
[French, abstracted from Persian *Awastā wa Zand* (see next), and orig. erron. taken for an attrib. elem. denoting the language of the Scriptures.]
†**1** The Zend-Avesta. Only in 18.
2 Avestan. Now *rare*. E18.
3 The Pahlavi translation and commentary forming part of the Zend-Avesta. L19.
■ **Zendic** *adjective* (*arch.*) of or pertaining to the Zend-Avesta or Avestan M19.

Zend-Avesta /zɛndəˈvɛstə/ *noun*. M17.
[Alt. of Persian *zand-(a)wastā*, *zandastā* = *Awastā wa Zand* lit. 'Avesta plus interpretation'.]
The Zoroastrian sacred writings of the Avesta, consisting of an Avestan text with a translation and commentary in Pahlavi.
■ **Zend-Aveˈstaic** *adjective* E19. **Zend-Aˈvestan** *noun & adjective* (of) the Avestan language L20.

Zendik /ˈzɛndɪk, zɛnˈdiːk/ *noun*. Also **Zindiq** /zɪnˈdiːk/. M19.
[Arab. *zindīk* from Persian *zandīk* fire-worshipper, heretic.]
Among Muslims, any of several kinds of heretic; *esp.* one who does not believe in revealed religion.
■ **Zendicism** /ˈzɛndɪsɪz(ə)m/ *noun* the belief of Zendiks L17.

zendo /ˈzɛndəʊ/ *noun*. Pl. **-os**. M20.
[Japanese *zendō*, formed as ZEN + *dō* hall.]
A place for Zen Buddhist meditation and study.

Zener /ˈziːnə/ *noun*¹. M20.
[Karl Edward *Zener* (1903–61), US psychologist.]
PSYCHOLOGY. Used ***attrib.*** with ref. to a type of card, used in packs of 25 in card-guessing tests in ESP experiments.

Zener /ˈziːnə/ *noun*². M20.
[Clarence Melvin *Zener* (1905–93), US physicist.]
ELECTRONICS. **1** Used ***attrib.*** to designate various concepts, devices, etc., connected with or arising from Zener's research. M20.
2 A Zener diode. M20.
1 Zener breakdown = ***Zener effect*** below. **Zener diode** a junction diode in which the forward characteristic is like that of an ordinary diode but there is a sudden large increase in reverse current at a certain constant reverse voltage owing to the Zener effect or the avalanche effect. **Zener effect** the increase in reverse current of a Zener diode when attributed to the tunnelling of current-carriers through the transition region rather than to the avalanche effect. **Zener voltage** the voltage at which the Zener effect occurs; the reverse breakdown voltage of a Zener diode.

Zengakuren /zɛŋɡəˈkuːrən/ *noun*. M20.
[Japanese, acronym from *Zen Nihon Gakusei Jichikai Sōrengō* = All-Japan Federation of Student Self-Government Associations (formed 1948).]
An extreme left-wing student movement in Japan.

zenick /ˈziːnɪk/ *noun*. Now *rare*. E19.
[French *zénik*, of unkn. origin.]
= ***grey meerkat*** (a) s.v. MEERKAT 2.

zenith /ˈzɛnɪθ/ *noun*. LME.
[Old French *cenit* (mod. *zénith*) or medieval Latin *cenit* (also *zenith*), ult. from Arab. *samt* in *samt-ar-ra's* 'path over the head': cf. AZIMUTH.]
1 The point of the heavens directly overhead (opp. ***nadir***). Formerly (*poet.*), course towards the zenith. LME. ▸**b** *loosely*. The expanse of sky overhead; the highest point reached by a celestial object. M17.
2 *fig.* The highest or culminating point in power, prosperity, etc. E17.

📖 **1** H. W. HERBERT There was not a speck of cloud from east to west, from zenith to horizon. **b** WORDSWORTH The clear bright Moon her zenith gains. **2** M. DRABBLE A pop singer whose fame was currently at its dizzy histrionic zenith. D. HALBERSTAM The idea of America's attaining the full zenith of its power was . . idealistic.

Comb.: **zenith distance** *ASTRONOMY* angular distance from the zenith; cf. ALTITUDE 1; **zenith sector** *ASTRONOMY* (now *Hist.*) an

instrument for determining the zenith distance of a celestial body; **zenith sweep** *ASTRONOMY* a series of observations of a region of the sky containing the zenith; **zenith telescope**, **zenith tube** *ASTRONOMY* (now *Hist.*) an optical instrument for determining the zenith distance of a celestial object.
■ **zenithward(s)** *adverb* towards the zenith **M19.**

zenithal /ˈzɛnɪθ(ə)l/ *adjective.* **M19.**
[from prec. + -AL¹.]
Pertaining to, situated or occurring at, the zenith; *fig.* supreme, culminating.
zenithal projection a map projection in which a portion of the globe is projected on to a plane tangential to a point on that portion, usu. made the centre of the map.

Zenker /ˈzɛŋkə/ *noun*¹. **L19.**
[Friedrich Albert von *Zenker* (1825–98), German pathologist.]
MEDICINE. Used in *possess.* (and *attrib.*) to designate pathological conditions etc. described by von Zenker.
Zenker degeneration, **Zenker hyaline degeneration** = *Zenker's degeneration* below. **Zenker diverticulum**, **Zenker pulsion diverticulum** = *Zenker's diverticulum* below. **Zenker's degeneration**, **Zenker's hyaline degeneration** a degeneration of striated muscle occurring chiefly in cases of acute infectious disease, esp. typhoid and cholera. **Zenker's diverticulum**, **Zenker's pulsion diverticulum** an abnormal diverticulum at the junction of the pharynx and oesophagus.

Zenker /ˈzɛŋkə/ *noun*². **E20.**
[Konrad *Zenker* (d. 1894), German histologist.]
Used in *possess.* to designate a fluid mixture developed by Zenker for use as a histological tissue fixative.

zeno- /ˈziːnəʊ/ *combining form.*
[Greek *Zēno-* combining form of *Zeus* Jupiter: see -O-.]
ASTRONOMY. Used to form adjectives with the sense 'pertaining to the planet Jupiter'.
■ **zeno'centric** *adjective* measured or expressed with Jupiter as centre **M20.** **zeno'graphic** *adjective* measured or expressed in relation to the surface of Jupiter **L20.** **zeno'graphical** *adjective* (*rare*) pertaining to the description or study of Jupiter **L19.**

Zenonian /ziːˈnəʊnɪən/ *adjective & noun.* **M19.**
[from Latin *Zeno(n-)*, Greek *Zēnōn* Zeno (see below) + -IAN.]
▶ **A** *adjective.* Of or pertaining to Zeno of Elea, a dialectician of the 5th cent. BC, or Zeno of Citium (fl. *c* 300 BC), the founder of the Stoic school of philosophy. **M19.**
▶ **B** *noun.* A follower of Zeno, esp. of Zeno of Citium. **M19.**
■ **Zenonic** /ziːˈnɒnɪk/ *adjective* = ZENONIAN *adjective* **L19.**

zeolite /ˈziːəlʌɪt/ *noun.* **L18.**
[from Greek *zein* to boil + -O- + -LITE.]
MINERALOGY. Any of a large group of minerals consisting of hydrated aluminium silicates of sodium, potassium, calcium, and barium, characterized by the ease with which they may be dehydrated and rehydrated, and utilized for their ion-exchange properties.
■ **zeolitic** /-ˈlɪtɪk/ *adjective* pertaining to, consisting of, or of the nature of zeolite **M19.** **zeo'litically** *adverb* as in a zeolite **M20.** **zeoliti'zation** *noun* transformation into a zeolite **L19.** **zeolitize** *verb trans.* transform into a zeolite; chiefly as **zeolitized** *ppl adjective*: **E20.**

Zep /zɛp/ *noun & verb. colloq.* **E20.**
[Abbreviation.]
▶ **A** *noun.* = ZEPPELIN *noun.* **E20.**
▶ **B** *verb trans.* Infl. **-pp-**. = ZEPPELIN *verb.* **E20.**

Zeph. *abbreviation.*
Zephaniah (in the Bible).

Zephiran /ˈzɛfɪran/ *noun.* **M20.**
[Origin unkn.]
PHARMACOLOGY. (Proprietary name for) an antiseptic preparation of a toxic aromatic quaternary ammonium salt.

Zéphirine Drouhin /ˌzeɪfɪriːn ˈdruːã/ *noun.* **M20.**
[A woman's name.]
A thornless climbing Bourbon rose with fragrant carmine-pink flowers, first introduced in France in 1868.

zephyr /ˈzɛfə/ *noun & adjective.* In sense A.1a freq. **Z-**. Earliest in Latin form **-rus** /-rəs/.
[Late Old English *zefferus* from Latin *zephyrus* from Greek *zephuros.*]
▶ **A** *noun.* **1 a** The west wind, esp. as personified, or regarded as a god. **LOE.** ▶**b** *gen.* A soft gentle breeze. **E17.**
2 a Any of various very light articles of clothing; *esp.* a sportsman's lightweight jersey. **L18.** ▶**b** A fine light soft gingham. **M19.**
3 A N. American nymphalid butterfly, *Polygonia zephyrus*, allied to and resembling the comma. Also ***zephyr angle-wing***. **L19.**

📖 **1a** S. JOHNSON Regions in which no wind is heard but the gentle Zephyr. **b** F. CHICHESTER During the day the wind dropped to a zephyr. H. BASCOM A zephyr ripples . . the branches of a coconut palm. **2a** A. DOUGLAS I was clad only in a 'zephyr' and running shorts.

▶ **B** *adjective.* Of certain fabrics: very light, soft, and fine. Of a garment: made of zephyr or soft gingham. **M19.**
zephyr gingham, ***zephyr merino yarn***, ***zephyr silk barège***, ***zephyr worsted***, etc.
Comb.: **zephyr lily** any of various bulbous plants constituting the genus *Zephyranthes*, of the lily family, with solitary lily-like plants, native to warm or tropical parts of America.
■ **zephy'rean** *adjective* of the nature of a zephyr **M19.** **zephyrous** *adjective* = ZEPHYREAN **M19.** **zephyry** *adjective* (*a*) full of zephyrs; (*b*) = ZEPHYREAN: **L18.**

zephyr /ˈzɛfə/ *verb intrans. rare.* **E20.**
[from the noun.]
Blow like a zephyr.

zephyrus *noun* see ZEPHYR *noun.*

Zeppelin /ˈzɛpəlɪn/ *noun & verb.* **E20.**
[Count Ferdinand von *Zeppelin* (1838–1917), its first constructor. Cf. ZEP.]
Hist. ▶**A** *noun.* In full ***Zeppelin airship***. A large dirigible airship (orig. one designed by von Zeppelin) of the early 20th cent., orig. for military use. **E20.**
▶ **B** *verb trans.* Drop bombs on (a place) from a Zeppelin. **E20.**

zeppole /ˈzɛpɒleɪ/ *noun. US.* Pl. **-li** /-li/. **M20.**
[Italian.]
A kind of doughnut.

zeranol /ˈzɛrənɒl/ *noun.* **L20.**
[from ZE(A)RA(LA)NOL.]
VETERINARY MEDICINE. A synthetic derivative of zearalenone used to promote growth in animals reared for food.

zereba, **zeriba** *nouns* vars. of ZAREBA.

zerk /zəːk/ *noun. US.* **L20.**
[Oscar U. *Zerk*, 20th-cent. US inventor.]
A fitting on a bearing, axle, etc., by which lubricant can be introduced under pressure. Also ***zerk fitting***.

zero /ˈzɪərəʊ/ *noun & adjective.* **E17.**
[French *zéro* or its source Italian *zero* from Old Spanish *zero* (mod. *cero*) from Arab. *ṣifr*: cf. CIPHER *noun.*]
▶ **A** *noun.* Pl. **-os**, **-oes**.
1 The arithmetical figure 0, representing absence of quantity or magnitude; nought. **E17.** ▶**b** The compartment numbered 0 on a roulette table. **M19.**
2 The point marked 0 on a graduated scale, from which a positive or negative quantity is reckoned, esp. in a thermometer or other measuring instrument. **L18.** ▶**b** The temperature corresponding to 0° on the Celsius and Réaumur scales (= 32° Fahrenheit), marking the freezing point of water. **E19.** ▶**c** A gunsight setting made to take allowance of wind deflection and elevation under normal conditions. **E20.**
3 The mathematical value denoted by 0, representing the transition between positive and negative values. Also, in expressing the amount of something, none at all. **E19.** ▶**b** *fig.* The lowest point or degree; nothingness. Also, an absence or lack of anything; nothing, nil. **E19.** ▶**c** *MATH.* In the theory of functions, a value of a variable for which a function has the mathematical value zero. **L19.** ▶**d** *LINGUISTICS.* The absence of a feature (e.g. an inflection, a phonetic or syntactic element) that is present in other instances. **L19.**
4 A worthless person or thing; a cipher. **E19.**
5 The initial point of a process or reckoning; *spec.* (in full ***zero hour***, ***zero day***) the hour or day when an attack or (chiefly military) operation is timed to begin. **M19.**
6 A zero-coupon bond. **L20.**

📖 **1** T. E. LAWRENCE At zero 8 hours to be exact, the united mass would attack. **2** *Farmers Weekly* A delay timer, variable between zero and 180 seconds, holds the elevator at the end of the slew. ***mechanical zero***: see MECHANICAL *adjective.* **b** M. SARTON A little warmer this morning, zero instead of twenty below. M. DEWAR Despite the blizzard . . the temperature was just above zero. **absolute zero** the lowest temperature theoretically possible, being zero on the Kelvin scale (equivalent to −273.15° Celsius). **3** C. DARWIN Their fertility ranges from zero to perfect fertility. J. R. LOWELL Dante's direct acquaintance with Plato may be reckoned at zero. A. FRANCIS The GDP growth rate would fall from 3 per cent to nearly zero. K. BARRATT All our numerical concepts are based upon the interaction of three numbers, zero, one, and two. **b** T. HOOD Merely to look at such a sight my courage sinks to zero. *Washington Post* My oath is not to disclose anything . . I can say nothing, absolutely zero. *Golf Monthly* Their sales resistance . . is zero. **d** *Language* In *sheep: sheep* the plural-suffix is replaced by zero. **4** P. BOOTH Don't you realise . . you're just a nobody, a great big zero with no past, no present, and no future? **5** *Business* Troops learned that they were participating only 36 hours before zero. ***ground zero***: see GROUND *noun.*

▶ **B** *attrib.* or as *adjective.* **1** Marked by temperatures of zero or below. **M19.**
2 That amounts to zero; *colloq.* no, not any. **L19.**
3 *LINGUISTICS.* Marked by the absence of a feature (e.g. an inflection) which is sometimes present. **E20.**

📖 **1** W. STEVENS Even in zero weather this [one snowdrop] has now increased to three. **2** *Guardian* I just had two weeks on a zero-calory diet. C. RYAN In zero visibility, unable to see their tow planes, many gliders cut loose. *Weekend Australian Financial News Network* . . zoomed from zero subscribers . . to 17.5 million.

Comb. & special collocations: **zero-balance** *adjective* (of a bank account) operated with no continuing balance, funds being transferred to it to just the extent required to meet drawings made on it; **zero-base**, **zero-based** *adjectives* (of a budget or budgeting) in which each item is costed anew, rather than in relation to its size or status in the previous budget; **zero beat** a condition in which two equal frequencies fully cancel one another, so that no beats are produced; **zero-beat** *adjective* (*RADIO*) designating a method of reception in which the incoming signal is mixed with a receiver-generated oscillation of the same frequency as the carrier wave; **zero-coupon** *adjective* (of a bond) carrying no interest but issued below its redemption price; **zero-crossing** *noun & adjective* (*a*) *noun* the crossing of the horizontal axis by a function as it passes through zero and changes sign; a point where this occurs; (*b*) *adjective* pertaining to the analysis of complex waveforms through the study of such points; ***zero day***: see sense A.5 above; **zero-derivation** *LINGUISTICS* derivation in which the form of the word is not altered; the use of a word with a different grammatical function or in a different (though related) sense; **zero-dimensional** *adjective* having no dimensions in space; **zero-energy** *adjective* (*NUCLEAR PHYSICS*) designating a small reactor, usu. built for research purposes, that develops so little power that no cooling and little shielding are required; **zero G** = *zero gravity* below; **zero grade** *PHILOLOGY* the absence or extreme reduction of an ablaut vowel from a syllable; **zero gravity** the state or condition in which there is no apparent force of gravity acting on a body, either because the force is locally weak, or because both the body and its surroundings are freely and equally accelerating under the force; weightlessness; **zero-graze** *verb trans.* (*AGRICULTURE*) feed (cattle) with cut grass brought to them instead of putting them out to pasture; **zero growth** an absence of increase (in population, production, etc.); ***zero hour***: see sense A.5 above; **zero option** *Hist.* a disarmament proposal that if the Soviet Union would withdraw its SS-20 missiles from Europe the US would abandon its plan to deploy Pershing and cruise missiles there; **zero-point** *adjective* (*PHYSICS*) designating or pertaining to properties and phenomena in quantized systems at absolute zero; **zero-power** *adjective* (*NUCLEAR PHYSICS*) = ***zero-energy*** above; **zero-rate** *verb trans.* assess (an item) at a VAT rate of zero; **zero rating** a rating of zero for VAT on a particular item; **zero sound** *PHYSICS* a form of longitudinal wave which has a slightly higher velocity than ordinary sound and is observed in superfluid helium under high frequency excitation; **zero-sum** *adjective* (of a game, political situation, etc.) in which whatever is gained by one side is lost by the other so that the net change is always zero; **zero tillage** *AGRICULTURE* = ***sod planting*** s.v. SOD *noun*¹; **zero tolerance** non-acceptance by the police or other authority of anti-social behaviour, esp. by strict and uncompromising enforcement of the law; **zero-zero** *adjective* (of flying conditions) in which both horizontal visibility and cloud ceiling are zero.

zero /ˈzɪərəʊ/ *verb.* **E20.**
[from the noun.]
1 *verb trans.* Set the sights of (a rifle) using targets at known distances. **E20.**
2 *verb trans.* Foll. by *in*: (*a*) train (a weapon) *on* a target; (*b*) concentrate guns or missiles on (a target). **M20.**
3 *verb intrans.* Foll. by *in*: (*a*) focus one's attention etc. *on*; (*b*) close in *on* an object of pursuit etc. **M20.**
4 *verb trans.* = ZEROIZE. **M20.**
5 *verb trans.* Foll. by *out*: eliminate, suppress. **M20.**

📖 **2** *Time* The Russians now have . . ICBMs . . zeroed in on U.S. targets. H. KAHN American bases overseas . . are at all times zeroed in by Soviet missiles. **3** *Daily News* Undercover cops . . have been assigned to zero in on the sellers of the . . cocaine derivative. G. ADAIR Like a camera, the eye consumes vistas whole then zeroes in on individual details. D. FRANCIS Creditors were zeroing in on the . . proceeds. **4** *Homes & Gardens* One button . . can zero the read-out at any point, allowing you to add ingredients. **5** *Word* We 'zero out' the voicing of /b/, which is not . . to deny that /b/ is voiced.

■ **zeroable** *adjective* (*a*) *LINGUISTICS* that may be omitted from a sentence without loss of meaning; (*b*) (of an instrument) able to be set to zero: **M20.** **zeroing** *verbal noun* the action of the verb; *spec.* (*LINGUISTICS*) the deletion or omission of part of a linguistic form or structure: **M20.**

zeroize /ˈzɪərəʊʌɪz/ *verb trans.* Also **-ise**. **E20.**
[from ZERO *noun* + -IZE.]
Adjust (an instrument or device) to give a zero reading, esp. in order to calibrate it; assign a value of zero to.

zeroth /ˈzɪərəʊθ/ *adjective.* **L19.**
[from ZERO *noun* + -TH².]
Coming next in a series before the one conventionally regarded as the first.

zerovalent /zɪərəʊˈveɪl(ə)nt/ *adjective.* **M20.**
[from ZERO *noun* + -VALENT.]
CHEMISTRY. Having a valency of zero, as is assigned for example to some metals in coordination compounds.
■ **zerovalency** *noun* **M20.**

zerumbet /zɪˈrʌmbɛt/ *noun.* **L16.**
[Portuguese from Persian *zarunbād.*]
An aromatic root of a plant of the genus *Curcuma*, prob. a form of zedoary, which is used medicinally in India and neighbouring countries.

zest /zɛst/ *noun.* Also **zeste**. **L15.**
[French *zeste*, †*zest*, *zec* thick skin dividing a walnut kernel, orange or lemon peel, of unkn. origin.]
1 Citrus-fruit (esp. orange or lemon) peel used as a flavouring or for preserving. Also, the oil squeezed from such peel to flavour liquor etc. **L15.**
2 *fig.* A piquant quality which adds to the enjoyment or agreeableness of something. **E18.**
3 Keen relish or enjoyment displayed in speech or action; gusto. (Foll. by *for.*) **L18.**

4 A thing which provides a savoury addition to a meal; an appetizer. Also, a piquant flavour. M19.

> 2 THACKERAY The sense that, perhaps, it was imprudent to take a cab or drink a bottle of wine, added a zest to those enjoyments. 3 J. BUCHAN They played with tremendous zest. K. TYNAN At fifty-three he retains all the heady zest of adolescence. D. CECIL That he should . . still enjoy life was due to . . his sheer, unquenchable zest for living. 4 DICKENS Mr. Wilkins had brought a pint of shrimps . . to give a zest to the meal.

■ **zestful** *adjective* full of piquancy, keen relish, or enjoyment M19. **zestfully** *adverb* L19. **zestfulness** *noun* L19.

zest /zɛst/ *verb trans.* E18.
[from the noun.]
Flavour with zest; *fig.* give a piquant quality to.

> M. MANLEY Heaven is sometimes pleased with Bitterness to Zest the Bowl of Bliss!

■ **zester** *noun* a device for shredding off the peel of an orange, lemon, etc. M20.

zeste *noun* var. of ZEST *noun*.

zesty /ˈzɛsti/ *adjective.* M20.
[from ZEST *noun* + -Y¹.]
1 Of a taste or food: piquant, agreeably sharp. M20.
2 *fig.* Energetic, stimulating. M20.

> 1 *Essentials* Zesty, tangy-flavoured . . Sandwich Pickle. 2 *Oxford Magazine* The little farrago ends with a bound of zesty life-assertion and merriment.

Zeta /ˈziːtə/ *abbreviation.*
Zero Energy Thermonuclear Assembly, an experimental thermonuclear fusion apparatus.

zeta /ˈziːtə/ *noun.* LME.
[Greek *zēta*, the letter Z, ζ: see Z, Z.]
The sixth letter (Z, ζ) of the Greek alphabet; ASTRONOMY (preceding the genitive of the Latin name of the constellation) the sixth brightest star in a constellation.
Comb.: **zeta function** MATH. an analytic function of a complex variable *s*, equal almost everywhere to $\{1^{-s} + 2^{-s} + 3^{-s} + \ldots\}$; also ***Riemann zeta function***; **zeta hypothesis** MATH. = RIEMANN ***hypothesis***; **zeta potential** PHYSICAL CHEMISTRY the potential difference that exists across the electrical double layer at the interface of a solid and a liquid.
■ **zetacism** /-sɪz(ə)m/ *noun* excessive or faulty use of the letter zeta or Z L19.

zetetic /zɪˈtɛtɪk/ *adjective & noun. rare.* M17.
[Greek *zētētikos*, from *zētein* seek, enquire: see -IC.]
▶ **A** *adjective.* Investigating; proceeding by inquiry. M17.
▶ **B** *noun.* **1** An inquirer; *spec.* an adherent of the ancient Greek sceptic school of philosophy. M17.
2 *sing.* & in *pl.* Investigation, inquiry (as in mathematics, etc.). L17.
■ **zetetically** *adverb* M17.

Zetlandic /zɛtˈlandɪk/ *adjective.* E18.
[from *Zetland* former official name of *Shetland*: see SHETLAND, -IC.]
= SHETLAND *adjective* 1.
■ **Zetlander** *noun* = SHETLANDER E18.

zeuglodon /ˈzjuːglədɒn/ *noun.* Also **Z-**. M19.
[mod. Latin (see below), from Greek *zeuglē* strap or loop of a yoke: see -ODON.]
Any of several primitive extinct whales of the genus *Basilosaurus* (formerly *Zeuglodon*) or family Zeuglodontidae, which had long narrow bodies and occurred in the Eocene.
■ **zeuglodont** *noun & adjective* (**a**) *noun* = ZEUGLODON; (**b**) *adjective* of or pertaining to this genus or family: M19.

zeugma /ˈzjuːgmə/ *noun.* LME.
[Latin from Greek, lit. 'yoking', from *zeugnunai* to yoke, rel. to *zugon* a yoke.]
A rhetorical figure by which a single word is made to refer to two or more words in a sentence, esp. when applying to them in different senses. Formerly also = SYLLEPSIS.
■ **zeugmatic** /-ˈmatɪk/ *adjective* pertaining to or involving zeugma M19. **zeugmatically** *adverb* so as to involve zeugma M19.

zeugmatography /zjuːgməˈtɒgrəfi/ *noun.* L20.
[from Greek *zeugmat-*, *zeugma* (see prec.) (with ref. to the coupling of the electromagnetic and magnetic fields) + -O- + -GRAPHY.]
MEDICINE. An imaging technique using nuclear magnetic resonance to obtain and display the structural details of soft tissue.
■ **zeugˈmatogram** *noun* a visual record produced by zeugmatography L20. ˌ**zeugmatoˈgraphic** *adjective* involving or produced by zeugmatography L20.

zeunerite /ˈzɔɪnərʌɪt, ˈzjuː-/ *noun.* L19.
[from Gustav A. *Zeuner* (1828–1907), German physicist and engineer + -ITE¹.]
MINERALOGY. A hydrated copper uranium arsenate, occurring as green tetragonal crystals similar to those of the related torbernite.

Zeus /zjuːs/ *noun.* E17.
[Greek, rel. to Latin *Jovis*: see JOVE.]
1 The chief god of the ancient Greeks, corresponding to the Roman Jupiter. E17.
2 The John Dory, *Zeus faber*, a fish anciently sacred to Zeus or Jupiter. Now only as mod. Latin genus name. E18.

zeze /ˈzeɪzeɪ/ *noun.* M19.
[Bantu.]
A stringed instrument of eastern and central Africa, resembling a zither.

Zhdanovism /ˈʒdɑːnɒvɪz(ə)m, -əvɪz(ə)m/ *noun.* M20.
[from *Zhdanov* (see below) + -ISM.]
Hist. The policy of rigorous ideological control of literature and cultural life, developed in postwar Russia by the politician A. A. Zhdanov (1896–1948).
■ **Zhdanovist**, **Zhdanovite** *adjectives* of, pertaining to, or advocating Zhdanovism M20.

zho *noun* var. of DZO.

Zhou /dʒəʊ/ *noun & adjective.* Also **Chou** /tʃəʊ/. L18.
[Chinese *Zhōu*.]
(Designating or pertaining to) a dynasty ruling in China from the 12th to the 3rd cent. BC.

ziamet /ˈziːəmɛt/ *noun.* E19.
[Turkish *zeamet*, from ZAIM.]
Hist. In feudal Turkey: the estate or fiefdom of a *zaim*.

ziarat /ziːˈɑːrət/ *noun.* Also **zea-**. L18.
[Urdu from Persian *ziyārat* from Arab. *ziyāra(t)* visit, pilgrimage.]
A Muslim pilgrimage to a shrine.

zibeline /ˈzɪbəlɪn, -iːn, -ʌɪn/ *noun.* L16.
[French, of Slavonic origin: see SABLE *noun*², -INE⁴.]
1 The sable. Now *rare* or *obsolete.* L16. ▸**b** The fur of this animal. M19.
2 A soft smooth woollen material with a long nap pressed flat, used esp. for women's coats. Also ***zibeline cloth***. L19.

zibet /ˈzɪbɪt/ *noun.* Now *rare* or *obsolete.* L16.
[medieval Latin *zibethum*: see CIVET *noun*¹.]
A civet; *esp.* the large Indian civet *Viverra zibetha*.

zibib /ˈzɪbɪb, zəˈbiːb/ *noun.* M19.
[Arab. *zabīb* (Egyptian Arab. *zibīb*) dried grapes, raisins.]
A strong colourless spirit made in Egypt from raisins.

ziczac /ˈzɪkzak/ *noun.* Also **ziczic** /ˈzɪkzɪk/, **sicsac** /ˈsɪksak/. M19.
[Arab. *zakzāk*, *saksak* plover; prob. imit.]
More fully ***ziczac bird***, ***ziczac plover***. The crocodile bird, *Pluvianus aegyptius*.

zidovudine /zɪˈdɒvjʊdiːn, -ˈdəʊv-/ *noun.* Also **Z-**. L20.
[App. by arbitrary alt. of AZIDOTHYMIDINE.]
PHARMACOLOGY. = AZIDOTHYMIDINE.

Ziebart /ˈziːbɑːt, ˈtsiː-/ *noun & verb.* M20.
[Kurt *Ziebart*, 20th-cent. German-born US mechanic.]
▶ **A** *noun.* (Proprietary name for) a process invented by Ziebart for rustproofing vehicles. M20.
▶ **B** *verb intrans.* Treat by this process. L20.

Ziegfeld /ˈziːgfɛld/ *noun.* E20.
[Florenz *Ziegfeld* (1869–1932), US theatre manager and producer.]
Used *attrib.* with ref. to the revues staged by Ziegfeld annually from 1907 to 1931.
Ziegfeld girl an actress taking part in a revue produced by Ziegfeld.

Ziegler /ˈziːglə/ *noun.* M20.
[Karl *Ziegler* (1898–1973), German chemist.]
CHEMISTRY. Used *attrib.* to designate a trialkyl aluminium–titanium tetrachloride catalyst used in the synthesis of polyethylenes and polypropylenes of high density and crystallinity. Also (more fully ***Ziegler–Natta*** [Giulio *Natta* (1903–79), Italian chemist]) used *attrib.* to designate any catalyst of a class including the Ziegler catalyst, consisting in general of a transition metal halide and a non-transition metal organic derivative, and used with any alkene monomer.

Ziehl /ziːl/ *noun.* L19.
[Franz *Ziehl* (1857–1926), German bacteriologist.]
BACTERIOLOGY. Used *attrib.* and in *possess.* to designate a red stain consisting of an alcoholic solution of fuchsine in an aqueous solution of phenol.
Comb.: **Ziehl–Neelsen** [F. K. A. *Neelsen* (1854–94), German pathologist] used *attrib.* to designate a method for identifying acid-fast organisms such as tuberculosis bacilli by staining with Ziehl's stain, decolourizing, and counterstaining with methylene blue.

ziff /zɪf/ *noun. Austral. & NZ slang.* E20.
[Origin unkn.]
A beard.

ZIFT /zɪft/ *abbreviation.*
Zygote intrafallopian transfer (the transfer of zygotes into the Fallopian tubes of a woman to facilitate conception).

zig /zɪg/ *verb & noun.* M20.
[from ZIG(ZAG *verb* or *noun*. Cf. ZAG.]
▶ **A** *verb intrans.* Infl. **-gg-**. Move at an angle, esp. abruptly as part of a zigzag movement, and in a direction contrary to that indicated by 'zag'. M20.
▶ **B** *noun.* An abrupt angled movement, esp. followed by another in a different direction. L20.

Zigeuner /tsɪˈgɔɪnə/ *noun.* Pl. same. Fem. **-rin** /-rɪn/, pl. **-rinnen** /-rɪnən/. M19.
[German.]
A Gypsy.

ziggurat /ˈzɪgʊrat/ *noun.* Also **zikk-** /ˈzɪk-/. L19.
[Akkadian *ziqqurratu* height, pinnacle.]
A rectangular stepped tower or pyramid of ancient Mesopotamia in which each storey is smaller than that below it, so having a terrace all round, and which is surmounted by a temple. Also, a building or structure resembling this.

zigzag /ˈzɪgzag/ *noun, adjective, & adverb.* E18.
[French *zigzag*, †*ziczac* from German *Zickzack*, of symbolic formation suggesting alternation of direction, applied first to fortifications.]
▶ **A** *noun.* **1** A line or course having a series of abrupt alternate right and left turns; a series of short lines inclined at angles in alternate directions. Orig. in ***in zigzag*** [= French *en zigzag*]. E18. ▸**b** Each of the turns or sections of such a line or course; *fig.* an abrupt change in direction. Usu. in *pl.* E18.
2 A thing having a zigzag shape; *esp.* (**a**) a road or path turning sharply at angles in alternate directions, esp. to reduce the gradient on a steep slope; each of the sharp turns forming such a road; (**b**) FORTIFICATION a trench leading towards a besieged place, constructed in a series of angles so as not to be enfiladed by the defenders; (**c**) ARCHITECTURE a chevron moulding. E18.
3 (**Z-**.) (Proprietary name for) a kind of cigarette-paper. E20.

> 1 E. BLAIR Lightning flashed, an enormous zigzag of it ripping across the sky. **b** K. ISHIGURO The path . . rose up the mountain in zig-zags. *fig.*: *Times* Current developments might merely be the zigzags of Communist policy.

Comb.: **zigzag machine** a sewing machine with a swing needle that may be used to produce a zigzag stitch and decorative stitches derived from it.
▶ **B** *adjective.* **1** Having the form of a zigzag; turning sharply at angles in alternate directions; characterized by turns of this kind. M18. ▸**b** ARCHITECTURE. Of a moulding or other ornament: having a zigzag pattern. M18.
2 Of a bird, shell, etc.: having zigzag markings. L18.
3 Drunk. *Military slang* (chiefly *US*). E20.

> 1 TOLKIEN They slithered . . in the dusk down the steep zig-zag path. **b** C. WORDSWORTH Columns of green basalt, with fantastic zigzag ornaments. **zigzag connection** ELECTRICAL ENGINEERING a form of star connection of three-phase circuits, each branch of which is interconnected and contains portions of two consecutive phases. **zigzag fence** (*N. Amer.*, now *rare*) = ***snake-fence*** s.v. SNAKE *noun*.

▶ **C** *adverb.* In a zigzag manner or direction. M18.

> D. DELILLO Scott found her walking zigzag in a nearly empty street.

zigzag /ˈzɪgzag/ *verb.* Infl. **-gg-**. L18.
[from the noun.]
1 *verb intrans.* Go or move in a zigzag course; have a zigzag course or direction; undergo a series of abrupt alternations in direction, gradient, degree, success, etc. L18. ▸**b** Of a sewing-machine: make zigzag stitches. M20.
2 *verb trans.* **a** Give a zigzag form to; mark a zigzag line on. Chiefly as ZIGZAGGED *adjective.* L18. ▸**b** Make *one's way* in a series of abrupt turns in alternate directions. L19. ▸**c** Cross in a zigzag manner. M20.
3 *verb trans.* Cause to move in a zigzag direction. E19.

> 1 J. WYNDHAM We made our way northward, zigzagging to avoid derelicts . . in the middle of the road. J. FANE A Chinese screen zigzagged between the door and one of the armchairs.

zigzagged /ˈzɪgzagd/ *adjective.* L18.
[from ZIGZAG *noun* or *verb*: see -ED², -ED¹.]
Having a zigzag form or marking.
■ **zigzaggedly** /-gɪdli/ *adverb* in a zigzag manner or course E20.

zigzaggery /ˈzɪgzag(ə)ri/ *noun.* M18.
[formed as prec. + -ERY.]
Zigzag course or proceeding (*lit.* & *fig.*).

zigzaggy /ˈzɪgzagi/ *adjective.* M19.
[from ZIGZAG *noun* + -Y¹.]
Characterized by zigzags or short sharp turns at alternate angles.

zikkurat *noun* var. of ZIGGURAT.

zikr /zɪkr/ *noun.* Also **dhikr** /ðɪkr/ M19.
[Arab. *ḏikr*.]
A Muslim invocatory prayer in which an expression of praise is continually repeated.

zilch /zɪltʃ/ *noun, adjective, & verb. slang* (orig. & chiefly *N. Amer.*). M20.
[Origin unkn.]
▶ **A** *noun.* Nothing, nil. M20.
▶ **B** *adjective.* No; non-existent. M20.

▶ **C** *verb trans.* SPORT. Defeat by preventing from scoring. Cf. ZIP *verb* 3. M20.

zillah /ˈzɪlə/ *noun.* Also **-a.** E19.
[Persian & Urdu *zila'* from Arab. *ḍila'* division.]
Hist. An administrative district in India.
Comb.: ***zillah parishad*** a district council in the Indian subcontinent.

zillion /ˈzɪljən/ *noun. colloq.* (orig. *US*). M20.
[Arbitrarily after *million, billion,* etc. (perh. from *z* repr. an unknown quantity).]
A very large but indefinite number.
📖 J. GRISHAM Most of the ten zillion condos were empty.
■ **zillio'naire** *noun* a very rich person M20. **zillionth** *adjective & noun* (*a*) *adjective* following very many others; umpteenth; (*b*) *noun* a tiny fraction of something: L20.

Zimba /ˈzɪmbə/ *noun.* Pl. same, **-s.** E20.
[African name.]
Hist. A member of an African people that lived in the vicinity of the Zambezi in the 16th cent.

Zimbabwe /zɪmˈbɑːbwi, -ˈbab-/ *noun.* E20.
[Shona *dzimbabwe* walled grave.]
▶ **A** *noun.* Any of the ruined stone-walled settlements scattered across Zimbabwe and neighbouring countries and dating from medieval times. E20.
▶ **B** *attrib.* or as *adjective.* Pertaining to or designating these settlements or the culture which produced them. M20.

Zimbabwean /zɪmˈbɑːbwɪən, -ˈbab-/ *noun & adjective.* M20.
[from *Zimbabwe* (see below) + -AN. Cf. prec.]
▶ **A** *noun.* Orig. (among African nationalists until independence in 1980), a black Rhodesian. Now, a native or inhabitant of Zimbabwe, a country in southern Africa. M20.
▶ **B** *adjective.* Of or pertaining to Zimbabweans or Zimbabwe. M20.

zimbalom *noun* var. of CIMBALOM.

zimbel /ˈtsɪmb(ə)l/ *noun.* E20.
[German from Latin *cymbalum*: see CYMBAL.]
MUSIC. A kind of high-pitched mixture-stop in an organ.

Zimmer /ˈzɪmə/ *noun.* Also **z-.** L20.
[from *Zimmer* Orthopaedic Limited, manufacturer.]
In full ***Zimmer frame***. (Proprietary name for) a kind of walking frame.

zinc /zɪŋk/ *noun & verb.* M17.
[German *Zink*, †*Zinken*, of unkn. origin. In sense A.3 from French.]
▶ **A** *noun.* **1** A hard lustrous bluish-white metallic chemical element, atomic no. 30, which is obtained from sphalerite and other ores, and is used for roofing, galvanizing iron, and making alloys with copper etc. (Symbol Zn.) M17.
2 Galvanized iron. L19.
3 The zinc-covered bar of a café or public house; *transf.* a café. E20.
Phrases: **flowers of zinc** crude zinc oxide. ***ruby zinc***: see RUBY *noun & adjective.*
Comb.: **zinc-air** *adjective* designating a type of primary cell employing a zinc anode, a porous carbon cathode using atmospheric oxygen, and an alkaline electrolyte; **zinc blende** = SPHALERITE; **zinc chloride** a white, crystalline, deliquescent solid, $ZnCl_2$, with numerous uses as a catalyst, polish, antiseptic, etc.; **zinc chromate** a toxic, yellow, water-insoluble powder, $ZnCrO_4$, used as a pigment; **zinc chrome** = *zinc yellow* below; **zinc-coated** *adjective* (of iron etc.) coated with a layer of zinc to prevent rust; **zinc finger** BIOCHEMISTRY a finger-like loop of peptides enclosing a bound zinc ion at one end, usu. part of a larger protein molecule (esp. one regulating transcription); **zinc green** a mixture of zinc and cobalt oxides used as a pigment; **zinc grey** a grey colour resembling that of zinc; **zinc ointment**: containing zinc oxide; **zinc ore** any ore used as a source of zinc, *esp.* sphalerite; **zinc oxide** a water-insoluble white powder, ZnO, used as a pigment, and in ointments, ceramics, etc. (also called ***Chinese white, zinc white***); **zinc roof** a corrugated roof of galvanized iron; **zinc sulphide** a yellow, water-insoluble powder, ZnS, used as a pigment and as a phosphor; **zinc white** zinc oxide used as a white paint; **zinc yellow** a greenish-yellow pigment consisting principally of zinc chromate.
▶ **B** *verb trans.* Cover or coat (iron etc.) with zinc or a compound of zinc to prevent rust; treat with zinc. Freq. as ***zinced*** *ppl adjective.* M17.
■ **zincate** *noun* a salt containing oxyanions of zinc L19. **zincian** *adjective* (of a mineral) having a proportion of a constituent element replaced by zinc M20. **zincic** *adjective* (now *rare*) of, pertaining to, or containing zinc M19. **zincifi'cation** *noun* (now *rare*) the process of zincing L19.

zincite /ˈzɪŋkʌɪt/ *noun.* M19.
[from ZINC *noun* + -ITE[1].]
MINERALOGY. A native form of zinc oxide, ZnO, which usu. occurs as granular or foliated masses of a deep red or orange-yellow colour, esp. in New Jersey, USA, where it is mined as an ore of zinc. Also called ***red zinc ore***.

†**zinckenite** *noun* var. of ZINKENITE.

zinco /ˈzɪŋkəʊ/ *noun.* Pl. **-os.** L19.
[Abbreviation.]
A zincograph; a zincographic plate or block.

zinco- /ˈzɪŋkəʊ/ *combining form.*
[from mod. Latin *zincum* ZINC: see -O-.]
Forming terms with senses (*a*) 'containing zinc and —'; (*b*) 'involving or using zinc'.
■ **zincotype** *noun* = ZINCOGRAPH L19.

zincode /ˈzɪŋkəʊd/ *noun. obsolete* exc. *Hist.* M19.
[from ZINC *noun* + -ODE[2].]
ELECTRICITY. The positive plate or anode of a voltaic cell (orig. made of zinc). Opp. PLATINODE.

zincography /zɪŋˈkɒɡrəfi/ *noun.* M19.
[from ZINCO- + -GRAPHY.]
The art or process of lithography using zinc plates.
■ **zincograph** /ˈzɪŋkəɡrɑːf/ *noun & verb* (*a*) *noun* a design or impression produced by zincography; (*b*) *verb trans.* engrave or print by zincography: L19. **zincographer** *noun* a person who practises zincography, an engraver on zinc M19. **zincographic** /zɪŋkəˈɡrafɪk/ *adjective* pertaining to or produced by zincography M19.

zindabad /ˈzɪndəbad/ *interjection & noun.* M20.
[Urdu, lit. 'may — live'.]
▶ **A** *interjection.* In the Indian subcontinent: expr. loud approval or encouragement for a specified person or thing. M20.
▶ **B** *noun.* A shout of this kind. M20.

zindan /zɪnˈdɑːn/ *noun.* L19.
[Turkish from Persian *zindān*.]
In Iran (Persia) and parts of central Asia: a prison.

Zindiq *noun* var. of ZENDIK.

zine /ziːn/ *noun. US colloq.* Also **'zine.** M20.
[Abbreviation.]
A magazine, *esp.* a fanzine.

zineb /ˈzɪnɛb/ *noun.* M20.
[from ZIN(C + E(THYLENE + B(IS- in the systematic name (see below).]
A white compound used as a fungicidal powder on vegetables and fruit; $C_4H_6N_2S_4Zn$, zinc ethylene bisdithiocarbamate.

Zinfandel /ˈzɪnfand(ə)l/ *noun.* M19.
[Origin unkn.]
A red or white dry wine of California. Also (more fully ***Zinfandel grape***), the red grape from which this is made.

zing /zɪŋ/ *noun. colloq.* (orig. *US*). E20.
[Imit.]
1 A sharp, high-pitched ringing sound; a twang. E20.
2 Energy, vigour, liveliness; zest; a quality that induces alertness or vitality. E20.

zing /zɪŋ/ *verb. colloq.* (orig. *US*). E20.
[from the noun or interjection.]
1 *verb intrans.* **a** Make a sharp, high-pitched ringing or whining sound; travel rapidly producing such a sound. E20. ▸**b** *fig.* Move energetically and with ease; abound *with* energy. M20.
2 *verb trans.* Foll. by *up*: enliven, invigorate. *US.* L20.
3 *verb trans.* Abuse; criticize. *US.* L20.
4 *verb trans.* Deliver (a witticism, question, etc.) with speed and force. *US.* L20.

zing /zɪŋ/ *interjection.* Chiefly *US.* E20.
[Imit. Cf. BING *interjection.*]
Indicating a sudden action or event.

zingana /ˈzɪŋɡənə, zɪŋˈɡɑːnə, ts-/ *noun.* In sense 1 **Z-.** E18.
[Italian, fem. of next.]
1 A Gypsy girl or woman. *rare.* E18.
2 = ZEBRANO. M20.

Zingano /ˈzɪŋɡənəʊ, ts-/ *noun.* Now *rare.* Pl. **-ni** /-ni/. L16.
[Italian = Greek *Athigganoi* an oriental people. Cf. next.]
A Gypsy.

Zingaro /ˈzɪŋɡərəʊ, ts-/ *noun & adjective.* Also **z-.** E17.
[Italian Cf. prec.]
▶ **A** *noun.* Pl. **-ri** /-ri/. Fem. **-ra** /-rə/, pl. **-re** /-reɪ/. A Gypsy. E17.
▶ **B** *attrib.* or as *adjective.* Of or pertaining to Gypsies. L18.

zingel /ˈzɪŋ(ə)l/ *noun.* E19.
[German.]
A freshwater percid fish, *Aspro zingel*, which has a somewhat elongated body with dark mottling on the back, and is found in central European rivers such as the Danube.

zinger /ˈzɪŋə/ *noun. US slang.* E20.
[from ZING *verb* + -ER[1].]
1 A thing outstandingly good of its kind. E20.
2 a A wisecrack; a punch-line. L20. ▸**b** A surprise question; an unexpected turn of events, e.g. in a plot. L20.

Zingg /zɪŋ, *foreign* tsɪŋ/ *noun.* M20.
[Theodor Zingg (b. 1905), Swiss meteorologist and engineer.]
PETROGRAPHY. Used *attrib.* with ref. to a system of classification of pebble shapes, in which two ratios formed from three mutually perpendicular diameters are used to assign a pebble to one of a series of basic shape classes.

zingiber /ˈzɪndʒɪbə/ *noun.* E20.
[mod. Latin (see below): see GINGER *noun & adjective*[1].]
A plant of the genus *Zingiber* (family Zingiberaceae), which includes the ginger, *Z. officinale*; the root of such a plant.

zingiberaceous /ˌzɪndʒɪbəˈreɪʃəs/ *adjective.* M19.
[from mod. Latin *Zingiberaceae*, formed as prec.: see -ACEOUS.]
BOTANY. Of the Zingiberaceae or ginger family.

zingo /ˈzɪŋɡəʊ/ *interjection.* Chiefly *US.* E20.
[from ZING *interjection* + -O.]
= ZING *interjection.*

zingy /ˈzɪŋi/ *adjective.* M20.
[from ZING *noun* + -Y[1].]
Energetic, exciting, lively.
■ **zingily** *adverb* L20.

Zinjanthropus /zɪnˈdʒanθrəpəs/ *noun.* M20.
[Former mod. Latin genus name, from *Zinj* early medieval (Arabic) name for E. Africa + Greek *anthrōpos* man.]
= ***Nutcracker Man*** s.v. NUTCRACKER *adjective* 2.

zinke /ˈtsɪŋkə/ *noun.* Also **zink.** L18.
[German.]
MUSIC (now *Hist.*). A musical instrument of wood or horn, similar to or identical with a cornett and common in 17th- and 18th-cent. Europe. Also, a loud reed-stop in an organ.

zinkenite /ˈzɪŋkənʌɪt/ *noun.* Also †**zinck-.** M19.
[from J. K. L. *Zincken* (d. 1862), German mine-director + -ITE[1].]
MINERALOGY. A sulphide of antimony and lead, occurring in steel-grey fibrous or feathering masses.

†**zinky** *adjective.* M–L18.
[from ZINC *noun* + -Y[1].]
Pertaining to or containing zinc.

zinnia /ˈzɪnɪə/ *noun.* M18.
[mod. Latin (see below), from J. G. *Zinn* (1727–59), German physician + -IA[1].]
Any of the plants constituting the chiefly Mexican genus *Zinnia*, of the composite family, several of which are grown for their showy daisy-like flowers.

zinnober green /ˈzɪnəbə ˈɡriːn/ *noun phr.* L19.
[from German *Zinnober* cinnabar + GREEN *noun.*]
= ***chrome green*** (b) s.v. CHROME *noun.*

zino /ˈziːnəʊ/ *noun.* Pl. **-os.** L20.
[from *Z* (see below) + -INO.]
PARTICLE PHYSICS. A hypothetical subatomic particle that is the supersymmetric counterpart of the Z particle, with spin ½ instead of 1.

Zion /ˈzʌɪən/ *noun.* Also **Sion** /ˈsʌɪən/. OE.
[ecclesiastical Latin *Sion*, Greek *Seōn, Seiōn* from Hebrew *ṣīyôn*, one of the hills of Jerusalem, on which the city of David was built, and which became the centre of ancient Jewish life and worship.]
The house or household of the God of Israel; the Jewish people and religion. Also in Christian use, the Christian Church; the Kingdom of God; heaven; a place of worship.
Stake of Zion: see STAKE *noun*[1] 5.
■ **Zionward** *adverb* towards Zion; *esp.* (*fig.*) heavenward: E18. **Zionwards** *adverb* = ZIONWARD M19.

Zionism /ˈzʌɪənɪz(ə)m/ *noun.* L19.
[from prec. + -ISM.]
A movement for (orig.) the reestablishment of a Jewish nation in Palestine, and (since 1948) the development of the State of Israel.

Zionist /ˈzʌɪənɪst/ *noun & adjective.* L19.
[formed as prec. + -IST.]
▶ **A** *noun.* **1** An advocate of Zionism. L19.
2 A member of any of a group of independent Christian churches in southern Africa similar to Pentecostal churches but having distinctive African elements of worship and belief. M20.
▶ **B** *attrib.* or as *adjective.* **1** Of or pertaining to Zionism. L19.
2 Of or pertaining to (Christian) Zionists. L20.
■ **Zio'nistic** *adjective* = ZIONIST *adjective* E20.

zip /zɪp/ *noun*[1]. In senses 1, 4 also (now *rare*) **zipp.** L19.
[Imit.]
1 A light sharp sound as of a bullet or other small or slender object passing rapidly through the air or through some obstacle, or of the tearing of cloth, etc.; a sound of this kind, a movement accompanied by such sound. L19.
2 *fig.* Energy, force, vigour. *colloq.* E20.
3 Nothing, nought, zero. Cf. ZILCH *noun. colloq.* (chiefly *N. Amer.*). E20. ▸**b** A Vietnamese person; any oriental person; (*derog.* & *racially offensive*). Also, any person regarded as worthless. *US slang.* M20.
4 A form of fastener for clothes, luggage, etc., consisting of two flexible strips with interlocking projections closed or opened by a sliding clip pulled along them. Also more fully ***zip-fastener, zip-fastening***. E20.

📖 **2** P. G. WODEHOUSE An orchestra was playing something with a good deal of zip. **4** J. BRAINE Too much messing about with buttons and zips and straps.

Attrib. & comb.: In the sense 'having a zip-fastener', as **zip bag**, **zip jacket**, **zip pocket**, etc. Special combs., as **zip gun** *US colloq.* a cheap home-made or makeshift gun; **zip-fastener**, **zip-fastening**: see sense 4 above; **zip-lock** *adjective* (*US*) designating a plastic bag with a special strip along two edges so that it can be sealed shut by pressing them together and readily reopened; **zip-top** *adjective* (*a*) = **ring-pull** *adjective* s.v. RING *noun*[1]; (*b*) having a top with a zip-fastener.

■ **zipless** *adjective* (*a*) *rare* lacking a zip-fastener; (*b*) *slang* (of a sexual encounter) brief and passionate: L20.

zip /zɪp/ *noun*[2]. *US*. M20.
[Acronym, from *Zoning Improvement Plan*.]
In full *zip code*. A series of (usu. five) digits representing a particular area in a city etc., used in addressing mail.

zip /zɪp/ *verb*. Infl. **-pp-**. M19.
[Imit.; in sense 2 from ZIP *noun*[1].]
1 *verb intrans.* Make the sound expressed by 'zip'. Also, move briskly or rapidly. M19.
2 *verb trans.* Close with a zip-fastener; fasten the zip of a garment on (a person). Freq. foll. by *up*. M20.
3 *verb trans.* Cause to move, arrive, or be produced rapidly. *colloq.* M20.
4 *verb trans.* SPORT. Defeat by preventing from scoring; = ZILCH *verb*. Cf. ZIP *noun*[1] 3. *slang* (chiefly *N. Amer.*). L20.
5 *verb trans.* COMPUTING. Compress a file or files (*spec.* by means of the program PKZIP) so as to take less space in storage. L20.

📖 **1** P. BARKER A rocket zipped into the sky. *Q* The . . director . . keeps the movie zipping along. **2** JAYNE PHILLIPS His father's leather toilet case was zipped shut. M. IGNATIEFF Reaching behind to zip up the skirt she was going to wear to church.

Comb.: **zip-out** *adjective* able to be removed by unfastening one or more zip-fasteners; **zip-up** *adjective* able to be fastened with zip-fasteners.

Zipf's law /ˈzɪpfs lɔː/ *noun phr.* M20.
[George Kingsley *Zipf* (1902–50), Amer. linguist + LAW *noun*[1].]
LINGUISTICS. Any of several principles investigated by Zipf, *esp.* the principle that frequently-used words tend to decrease in length.

zipp *noun* see ZIP *noun*[1].

zipped /zɪpt/ *adjective*. M20.
[from ZIP *noun*[1]: see -ED[2].]
Provided or fastened with a zip.

zipper /ˈzɪpə/ *noun & verb*. Chiefly *US*. E20.
[from ZIP *noun*[1] + -ER[1].]
▶**A** *noun*. = ZIP *noun*[1] 4. E20.
▶**B** *verb trans.* Fasten with a zipper. Freq. foll. by *up*. M20.
Comb.: **zipperhead** *slang* (*derog. & racially offensive*) = ZIP *noun*[1] 3b.
■ **zippered** *adjective* fastened with a zipper; having a zipper: M20.

Zippo /ˈzɪpəʊ/ *noun*. M20.
[Origin unkn.]
(Proprietary name for) a make of cigarette-lighter.

zippy /ˈzɪpi/ *adjective*. *colloq.* E20.
[from ZIP *noun*[1] + -Y[1].]
Bright, lively, energetic; fresh, invigorating; fast, speedy. Cf. ZIP *noun*[1] 2.

📖 V. SETH The first movement . . ends with . . a tremendously zippy set of ascending and descending scales.

■ **zippily** *adverb* L20. **zippiness** *noun* E20.

ziram /ˈzʌɪram/ *noun*. M20.
[from ZI(NC + CA)R(B)AM(ATE in the systematic name (see below).]
A white compound used as a fungicidal powder on vegetables and some fruit crops; $C_6H_{12}N_2S_4Zn$, zinc dimethyl dithiocarbamate.

zircaloy /ˈzəːkəlɔɪ/ *noun*. Also **-ll-**. M20.
[from ZIRC(ONIUM + ALLOY *noun*.]
METALLURGY. Any of several alloys of zirconium, tin, and other metals that are used chiefly as cladding for nuclear reactor fuel.

zircon /ˈzəːk(ə)n/ *noun*. L18.
[German *Zirkon*. Cf. JARGON *noun*[2].]
A tetragonal silicate of zirconium, occurring in variously coloured prismatic crystals, and mined as the main ore of zirconium. Also, a stone of a translucent variety of this, cut as a gem.
Comb.: **zircon blue** a light blue colour.
■ **zirconate** *noun* a salt containing oxyanions of zirconium M19. **zirconian** /zəːˈkəʊnɪən/ *adjective* zirconic; *spec.* in MINERALOGY, designating a mineral in which zirconium replaces a (small) proportion of some constituent element: M19. **zirconic** /zəːˈkɒnɪk/ *adjective* of, pertaining to, or resembling zircon; containing zirconia or zirconium: E19.

zirconia /zəːˈkəʊnɪə/ *noun*. L18.
[from prec. + -IA[1].]
1 Zirconium dioxide, ZrO_2, a white powder usu. obtained by heating zirconium salts and used in refractory coatings, ceramic glazes, etc. L18.
2 In full ***cubic zirconia***. The fused form of this used as a hard transparent synthetic substitute for diamonds in jewellery. L20.

zirconium /zəːˈkəʊnɪəm/ *noun*. E19.
[from ZIRCON + -IUM.]
A hard lustrous grey metallic chemical element, atomic no. 40, which belongs to the transition-metal group and is used as a coating for nuclear fuel rods, in corrosion-resistant alloys, etc. (Symbol Zr.)

zirconyl /ˈzəːkənʌɪl, -nɪl/ *noun*. L19.
[from ZIRCON(IUM + -YL.]
CHEMISTRY. The radical :ZrO, present in certain compounds of zirconium. Usu. in *comb.*

zit /zɪt/ *noun*. *colloq.* M20.
[Origin unkn.]
A pimple.

zita /ˈziːtə/ *noun*. Pl. **-te** /-teɪ/, **-ti** /-ti/. M19.
[Italian.]
Pasta in the form of tubes resembling large macaroni; an Italian dish consisting largely of this and usu. a sauce.

zither /ˈzɪðə/ *noun & verb*. M19.
[German formed as CITHARA. In transf. verbal use partly imit.]
MUSIC. ▶**A** *noun*. A musical instrument of central European origin, having four or five melody strings over a fretboard and thirty to forty accompanying strings, all running the length of a flat shallow resonator box, and played by striking or plucking. Also more widely, any instrument in which strings run the full length of the body, which is usu. also a resonator. M19.
▶**B** *verb intrans.* Play the zither. Also *transf.*, make a humming or buzzing sound. E20.
■ **zitherist** *noun* (*rare*) a performer on the zither L19.

ziti *noun pl.* see ZITA.

Ziv /zɪv/ *noun*. LME.
[Hebrew *zīw* lit. 'brightness, radiance'.]
Hist. In the Jewish calendar, = IYYAR.

ziz *noun* see ZIZZ *noun*.

zizania /zɪˈzeɪnɪə/ *noun*. Orig. (in sense 2 rarely) Anglicized as †**zizany**. ME.
[In sense 1 late Latin, noun pl. from Greek *zizania* darnel pl. of *zizanion*. In sense 2 adopted (as fem. sing.) as genus name.]
†**1** Tares: see TARE *noun*[1] 3. ME–E18.
2 Any of various aquatic grasses constituting the genus *Zizania*; *esp.* Indian rice, *Z. aquatica*. ME.

zizel /ˈzɪz(ə)l/ *noun*. Now *rare*. Also **sisel** /ˈsɪz(ə)l/. L18.
[German *Ziesel*.]
A souslik; *esp.* the European souslik, *Spermophilus citellus*.

zizyphus /ˈzɪzɪfəs/ *noun*. LME.
[(mod. Latin from) late Latin from Greek *zizuphos*, *-on*. Cf. JUJUBE.]
Any of various thorny shrubs and trees of the genus *Ziziphus*, of the buckthorn family, some of which have an edible fruit, the jujube.

zizz /zɪz/ *noun & verb*. In sense A.3 also **ziz**. E19.
[Imit.]
▶**A** *noun*. **1** A whizzing or buzzing noise; *esp.* the noise made by the rapid motion of a wheel. E19.
2 Gaiety, liveliness, sparkle. *colloq.* M20.
3 A short sleep, a nap. Cf. Z, Z 1b. *slang*. M20.
▶**B** *verb intrans. & trans.* **1** (Cause to) make a whizzing or buzzing sound. Also *fig.* (*colloq.*), liven *up*. M20.
2 Doze, sleep; (foll. by *away*) pass (time) in sleep. *slang*. M20.

📖 **1** I. WATSON When I woke . . insects were zizzing about me.

zizzy /ˈzɪzi/ *adjective*. *colloq.* M20.
[from ZIZZ *noun* + -Y[1].]
Showy, spectacular; lively, uninhibited.

zloty /ˈzlɒti/, *foreign* /ˈzwɔti/ *noun*. Pl. same, **-s**. E20.
[Polish *złoty*, from *złoto* gold.]
The basic monetary unit of Poland.

Zn *symbol*.
CHEMISTRY. Zinc.

zo *noun* var. of DZO.

zoa *noun pl.* see ZOON *noun*.

-zoa *suffix* pl. of -ZOON.

†**zoaea** *noun* var. of ZOEA.

-zoan /ˈzəʊən/ *suffix*.
[from Greek *zōion* animal + -AN; in sense 1 through mod. Latin taxonomic names in *-zoa*.]
ZOOLOGY. **1** Forming nouns and adjectives from names of zoological classes etc. ending in *-zoa*, as ***anthozoan***, ***hydrozoan***, ***protozoan***, ***sporozoan***, etc.
2 = -ZOON 1.

zoantharian /zəʊanˈθɛːrɪən/ *noun & adjective*. L19.
[from mod. Latin *Zoantharia* (see below), from Greek *zōion* animal + *anthos* flower: see -ARIAN.]
ZOOLOGY. ▶**A** *noun*. An anthozoan of the subclass Zoantharia, which includes sea anemones and stony corals with polyps that bear more than eight, rarely pinnate, tentacles. L19.
▶**B** *adjective*. Of or pertaining to this subclass. L19.
■ **zoˈanthid**, **zoanˈthidean** *nouns & adjectives* (*a*) *noun* a zoantharian of the small order Zoanthidea, which includes small animals like sea anemones with a single siphonoglyph; (*b*) *adjective* of or pertaining to this order: L20.

zoanthropy /zəʊˈanθrəpi/ *noun*. *rare*. M19.
[from ZO(O- + *-anthropy*, after CYNANTHROPY, LYCANTHROPY.]
A form of madness in which a person believes himself or herself to be an animal and behaves accordingly.
■ **zoanˈthropic** *adjective* of or pertaining to zoanthropy; affected with zoanthropy: L19.

zocalo /ˈzɒkələʊ/ *noun*. Pl. **-os**. L19.
[Spanish *zócalo*.]
In Mexico: a public square, a plaza.

†**zocco** *noun*. Pl. **-os**. M17–E18.
[Italian: cf. next.]
= SOCLE.

zocle /ˈzəʊk(ə)l, ˈzɒk-/ *noun*. Now *rare*. E18.
[Italian *zoccolo*: see SOCLE.]
= SOCLE.

zoco /ˈzɒkəʊ/ *noun*. Pl. **-os**. L19.
[Spanish from Arab. *sūk* SOUK *noun*[1].]
In Spain and N. Africa: a souk; a market-place.

zodiac /ˈzəʊdɪak/ *noun*. LME.
[Old & mod. French *zodiaque* from Latin *zodiacus* from Greek *zōidiakos* (sc. *kuklos* circle) of figures or signs, from *zōidion* sculptured figure (of an animal), sign of the zodiac, dim. of *zōion* animal: see -AC.]
1 ASTRONOMY & ASTROLOGY. A belt of the celestial sphere extending about 8 or 9 degrees on each side of the ecliptic, within which the apparent motions of the sun, moon, and principal planets take place, and which is usu. divided into twelve signs (see below). LME. ▸**b** In full ***zodiac of the moon*** etc. A belt of the celestial sphere within which the apparent motion of the moon or other specified celestial object takes place. E18.
2 A representation of the zodiac or of a similar astrological system (e.g. that used by the Chinese). LME.
†**3** A year; the calendar. M16–E17.
4 *fig. & allus.* A recurrent series, a complete course; *esp.* a set of twelve. Also, *the* compass or range of something. M16.
5 (**Z-**.) (Proprietary name for) a kind of inflatable dinghy, *esp.* one powered by an outboard motor. M20.

📖 **4** P. SIDNEY Freely ranging . . within the Zodiack of his owne wit.

Phrases: **sign of the zodiac** (now chiefly ASTROLOGY) each of the twelve equal parts into which the zodiac is divided, through one of which the sun passes in a month, and which are named after the twelve constellations Aries, Taurus, Gemini, Cancer, Leo, Virgo, Libra, Scorpio, Sagittarius, Capricorn, Aquarius, and Pisces (see note below).
Comb.: **zodiac ring** a ring bearing figures of one or more signs of the zodiac.

¶ Owing to the earth's precession the dates on which the sun is held by astrologers to enter the various signs of the zodiac no longer correspond to the sun's actual position in the constellations. These dates were established by Greeks of the Ptolemaic period (the 3rd–1st cents. BC); the discrepancy is now about a month, and a further constellation (Ophiuchus) is involved.

zodiacal /zəʊˈdʌɪək(ə)l/ *adjective*. L16.
[French, from *zodiaque*: see prec., -AL[1].]
Of, pertaining to, or situated in the zodiac.
zodiacal light a faint elongated ellipse of light extending along the zodiac on each side of the sun, visible (in the north temperate zone) chiefly after sunset in late winter and early spring, and before sunrise in autumn.

zoea /zəʊˈiːə/ *noun*. Pl. **-eae** /-ˈiːiː/, **-eas**. Also †**zoaea**, †**zooea**. E19.
[mod. Latin *zoe*, *zoea* (orig. the name of a supposed genus), from Greek *zōē* life: see -A[1].]
ZOOLOGY. A larval stage in certain crustaceans, esp. decapods, usu. characterized by one or more spines on the carapace and rudimentary thoracic and abdominal limbs; a crustacean in this stage.
■ **zoeal** *adjective* of or pertaining to a zoea L19.

Zoellner *noun* var. of ZÖLLNER.

zoetrope /ˈzəʊɪtrəʊp/ *noun*. M19.
[Irreg. from Greek *zōē* life + *-tropos* turning.]
A mechanical toy consisting of a cylinder with a series of slits in the circumference, and a series of figures on the inside representing successive positions of a moving object, which when viewed through the slits while the cylinder is rapidly rotating produce an impression of movement of the object.

zoftig *adjective* var. of ZAFTIG.

Zogist /ˈzɒgɪst/ *noun & adjective*. M20.
[from *Zog* (see below) + -IST.]
Hist. ▶**A** *noun*. A supporter of Zog (1895–1961), king of Albania from 1928 until deposed in 1939. M20.
▶**B** *adjective*. Of or pertaining to the Zogists. M20.

zograscope /ˈzɒgrəskəʊp/ *noun. obsolete* exc. *Hist.* M18.
[Perh. from ZOOGRAPHY + -SCOPE.]
An optical instrument consisting of a vertically suspended convex lens in front of an adjustable mirror, for the viewing of prints in magnified form and with stereoscopic effect.

Zohar /ˈzəʊhɑː/ *noun*. L17.
[Hebrew *zōhar* lit. 'light, splendour'.]
The chief text of the Jewish cabbala, presented as an allegorical or mystical interpretation of the Pentateuch.

zoic /ˈzəʊɪk/ *adjective*. M19.
[Greek *zōikos*, from *zōion* animal; or (in sense 1) extracted from AZOIC *adjective*[1]: see -IC.]
1 *GEOLOGY*. Showing traces of life; containing organic remains. Now *rare*. M19.
2 = ZOOMORPHIC 1, 2b. L19.

-zoic /ˈzəʊɪk/ *suffix*.
[from Greek *zōē* life + -IC; in sense 3 from mod. Latin taxonomic names in *-zoa*.]
1 *GEOLOGY*. Forming nouns and adjectives denoting or designating (organisms etc. of) a geological era characterized by a specific form of life, as ***Palaeozoic***, ***Mesozoic***, ***Cenozoic***, etc.
2 *ECOLOGY*. Forming adjectives designating animals having a specific mode of life or metabolism, as ***cryptozoic***, ***epizoic***, ***holozoic***, ***phanerozoic***, etc.
3 *ZOOLOGY*. Forming adjectives designating or pertaining to (animals belonging to) specific higher taxa, as ***hydrozoic***, ***metazoic***, ***polyzoic***, etc. Now *rare*.

zoid /ˈzəʊɪd/ *noun*. M19.
[from Greek *zōion* animal + -ID[2], or (in sense 1) abbreviation of ZOOID.]
1 *ZOOLOGY*. = ZOOID. Now *rare*. M19.
2 *BIOLOGY*. A zoospore; a zoogamete, a planogamete. M20.
▪ **zoiˈdogamous** *adjective* = PLANOGAMETIC L19.

Zoilus /ˈzəʊɪləs/ *noun*. Pl. **-li** /-lʌɪ/, **-luses**. M16.
[A Greek critic and grammarian (4th cent. BC) famous for his severe criticism of Homer.]
A censorious, malignant, or envious critic.
▪ **Zoilean** *adjective* characteristic of Zoilus or of a Zoilist E17. **Zoilism** *noun* carping criticism E17. **Zoilist** *noun* a carping critic M16.

zoisite /ˈzɔɪsʌɪt/ *noun*. E19.
[from Baron S. von Edelstein *Zois* (1747–1819), Austrian scholar + -ITE[1].]
MINERALOGY. An orthorhombic basic silicate of calcium and aluminium, usu. occurring in greyish-white or greenish prismatic crystals.

zoite /ˈzəʊʌɪt/ *noun*. M20.
[from next.]
ZOOLOGY. An infective stage, esp. a spore or cyst, of a protozoan parasite.

-zoite /ˈzəʊʌɪt/ *suffix*.
[from Greek *zōion* animal + -ITE[1].]
ZOOLOGY. Forming nouns denoting (esp. infective) stages in the life cycles of protozoan parasites, as ***merozoite***, ***sporozoite***, ***tachyzoite***, ***trophozoite***, etc.

Zolaism /ˈzəʊlə-ɪz(ə)m/ *noun*. L19.
[from Émile *Zola* (1840–1902), French novelist + -ISM.]
Extremely or excessively realistic treatment of the coarser sides of human life, as in the novels of Zola.
▪ **Zolaˈesque** *adjective* characteristic of or resembling the style of Zola L19. **Zolaist** *noun* a student of the writings of Zola; an admirer or imitator of Zola: L19. **Zolaˈistic** *adjective* characteristic of a Zolaist L19.

Zollinger–Ellison syndrome /ˌzɒlɪndʒəˈɛlɪs(ə)n ˌsɪndrəʊm/ *noun phr*. M20.
[from M. *Zollinger* (1903–92) + E. H. *Ellison* (1918–70), US physicians.]
MEDICINE. A syndrome characterized by excessive gastric acid secretion, producing recurrent peptic ulcers, and associated with a gastrin-secreting tumour or hyperplasia of the islet cells in the pancreas.

Zöllner /ˈzɒlnə, *foreign* ˈtsœlnər/ *noun*. Also **Zoe-**. L19.
[Johann Karl Friedrich *Zöllner* (1834–82), German astronomer and physicist.]
PSYCHOLOGY. Used *attrib.* and in *possess.* to designate the optical illusion of parallel lines which, when marked with short diagonal lines, appear to converge.

zollverein /ˈtsɔlfəraɪn/ *noun*. M19.
[German, from *Zoll* TOLL *noun*[1] + *Verein* union.]
Hist. A union of States with a uniform rate of customs duties from other countries and free trade within the union; *spec.* that between States of the German Empire in the 19th cent.

zombie /ˈzɒmbi/ *noun & verb*. E19.
[Of Bantu origin: cf. JUMBY.]
▶**A** *noun*. **1** Orig., a snake-deity in voodoo cults of or deriving from W. Africa and Haiti. Now (esp. in the W. Indies and southern US), a soulless corpse said to have been revived by witchcraft. E19.
2 A dull, apathetic, unresponsive, or unthinkingly acquiescent person. *colloq.* M20.
3 In the war of 1939–45, a man conscripted for home defence. *Canad. Military slang (derog.)*. M20.
4 A long mixed drink consisting of several kinds of rum, liqueur, and fruit juice. M20.
▶**B** *verb trans*. Foll. by *out*: exhaust; disorientate. M20.
▪ **zombie-like** *adjective* characteristic of or resembling a zombie; lifeless, unfeeling: M20. **zombiˈesque** *adjective* = ZOMBOID L20. **zombifiˈcation** *noun* (*colloq.*) the process of turning somebody into a zombie L20. **zombified** *adjective* (*colloq.*) made into a zombie; dull, apathetic: L20. **zombiism** *noun* M20. **zomboid** *adjective* (*colloq.*) zombie-like L20.

zomotherapy /zəʊməʊˈθɛrəpi/ *noun*. *rare*. E20.
[from Greek *zōmos* soup + THERAPY.]
MEDICINE. The use of raw meat or juice from it in the treatment of disease, esp. tuberculosis.

zona /ˈzəʊnə/ *noun*. E18.
[Latin: see ZONE *noun*.]
1 *MEDICINE*. Shingles. Also more fully ***zona ignea*** /ˈɪgnɪə/ [Latin, fem. of *igneus* of fire]. E18.
2 *ANATOMY & ZOOLOGY*. Usu. with mod. Latin specifying word. Any of several structures or parts of structures; *spec.* the zona pellucida (see below). M19.
2 zona fasciculata /faˌsɪkjʊˈlɑːtə/ [= fasciculate] the middle layer of the adrenal cortex. **zona glomerulosa** /ˌglɒmɛrjʊˈləʊsə/ [= glomerulose] the outer layer of the adrenal cortex. **zona pellucida** /pɪˈluːsɪdə/ [= pellucid] the transparent membrane surrounding the mammalian ovum. **zona radiata** /reɪdɪˈɑːtə/ [= RADIATE *adjective*] a radially striated form of the zona pellucida surrounding the ova of fishes etc.; **zona reticularis** /rɪˌtɪkjʊˈlɑːrɪs/ [= reticular] the inner layer of the adrenal cortex.

zonal /ˈzəʊn(ə)l/ *adjective & noun*. M19.
[from ZONE *noun* + -AL[1].]
▶**A** *adjective*. **1 a** Marked with zones or circular bands of colour. M19. ▸**b** Characterized by or arranged in zones, circles, or rings; forming a zone or ring. L19.
2 Of, pertaining to, involving, or constituting a zone or zones; regional. M19.
3 Of a soil, fossil, etc.: characteristic of a particular climatic, geographic, latitudinal, stratigraphic, etc., zone. E20.
4 *METEOROLOGY*. Aligned with lines of latitude. M20.
Special collocations: **zonal defence** *SPORT* = *zone defence* s.v. ZONE *noun*. **zonal fossil**, **zonal guide fossil** = *zone fossil* s.v. ZONE *noun*. **zonal index** *METEOROLOGY* a conventional measurement indicating the strength of the west-to-east airflow over middle latitudes. **zonal pelargonium** any of various hybrids of *Pelargonium zonale*, often with dark horseshoe-shaped markings on the leaves.
▶**B** *noun*. A zonal pelargonium. M19.
▪ **zoˈnality** *noun* zonal character or distribution E20. **zonally** *adverb* in or according to zones L19.

zonate /ˈzəʊneɪt/ *adjective*. M19.
[mod. Latin *zonatus*, from ZONA: see -ATE[2].]
ZOOLOGY & BOTANY. = ZONED *adjective*[1] 3b.
▪ Also **zonated** *adjective* E19.

zonation /zəʊˈneɪʃ(ə)n/ *noun*. L19.
[from next + -ATION.]
Distribution in zones or regions of definite character; *spec.* (*a*) *ECOLOGY* the distribution of plants or animals into specific zones according to altitude, depth, etc., each characterized by its dominant species; (*b*) *CYTOLOGY* formation of zones in the cytoplasm during mitotic division of some oocytes.

zone /zəʊn/ *noun*. LME.
[Old & mod. French, or Latin *zona* girdle, from Greek *zōnē*.]
1 *GEOGRAPHY*. Each of the five latitudinal belts broadly distinguished by temperature, into which the surface of the earth is divided by the two tropics and the two polar circles. Formerly also, each of the corresponding belts of the celestial sphere. LME. ▸**b** Any region extending around the earth between definite limits, esp. between two parallels of latitude. Also in *ASTRONOMY*, a similar region of the sky or on the surface of a planet or the sun. M16.
2 A region or tract of the world, *esp.* one distinguished by its climate. Chiefly *literary*. L16.
3 a A girdle or belt, as a part of dress. Also, a money-belt. *arch.* L16. ▸**b** A thing that encircles something like a girdle; a circumscribing or enclosing line, a band, a ring. L16.
4 A band or stripe of colour, or of light or shade, extending over or esp. around something; each of a number of concentric or alternate markings of this kind. M18.
5 a *MATH*. A part of the surface of a sphere contained between two parallel planes, or of the surface of a cone, cylinder, etc., contained between two planes perpendicular to the axis. L18. ▸**b** *CRYSTALLOGRAPHY*. A series of faces of a crystal extending around it and having their lines of intersection parallel. L18.
6 A definite (physical or conceptual) region or area, distinguished from adjacent regions by some particular feature, property, purpose, or condition. Usu. with specifying word or phrase. E19. ▸**b** A district or an area of land subject to particular restrictions concerning use and development. E20. ▸**c** *ICE HOCKEY, AMER. FOOTBALL, & BASKETBALL*. A specific area of the rink, field, or court; *spec.*, one to be defended by a particular player; a mode of defensive play employing this system (cf. ***zone defence*** below). E20. ▸**d** Each of the areas of Germany and Austria occupied by British, American, French, or Russian forces after the war of 1939–45 until 1955; ***the Soviet Zone***, ***the Zone*** (*Hist.*) East Germany. M20.
7 *ANATOMY & ZOOLOGY*. A growth or structure surrounding another in the form of a ring or cylinder. Also more widely, a distinct region, area, or layer extending around, through, or over a part. Cf. ZONA. E19.
8 *GEOLOGY & ECOLOGY*. A region, or each of a series of regions, situated between definite limits of altitude, depth, or time, and distinguished by characteristic fossils, forms of animal and plant life, etc. E19.
9 *COMPUTING*. A hole in certain punched cards that is punched above the column of holes representing non-zero digits, used in conjunction with the latter to represent non-numerical characters. Usu. *attrib.* M20.

> 📖 **1** ***frigid zone***, ***temperate zone***, ***torrid zone***, etc. **2** MILTON We may . . in some milde Zone Dwell. **6** P. LIVELY That shadowy zone between sleeping and waking. D. CAUTE We are entering an officially designated war zone. ***buffer zone***, ***crumple zone***, ***exclusion zone***, ***Roche zone***, ***smokeless zone***, ***subduction zone***, ***time zone***, ***twilight zone***, etc. **zone of fire** *MILITARY* the area into which an armed unit is ready to fire. **c** ***end zone***: see END *noun*. **8** ***littoral zone***, ***neritic zone***, ***oceanic zone***, etc.

Comb.: **zone centre** *TELEPHONY* an exchange which acts as a main switching centre in an area containing a number of exchange groups; **zone defence** *SPORT* a system of defensive play whereby each player guards an allotted portion of the field of play, rather than marking an allotted opponent; **zone electrophoresis** *BIOCHEMISTRY* electrophoresis in which an appropriate medium is used to ensure that the components remain separated in zones or bands according to their differing electrophoretic mobilities; **zone fossil** a guide fossil diagnostic of a particular zone or belt of strata; **zone-level** *verb trans.* subject to zone levelling; **zone leveller** an apparatus used for zone levelling; **zone levelling** a process similar to zone refining in which the molten zone is passed repeatedly to and fro to produce a more homogeneous material; **zone-melt** *verb trans.* = *zone-refine* below; **zone plate** a plate of glass marked out into concentric zones or rings alternately transparent and opaque, used like a lens to bring light to a focus; **zone-refine** *verb trans.* subject to zone refining; **zone refiner** an apparatus used for zone refining; **zone refining** a method of refining used to produce semiconductors and metals of very high purity by causing narrow molten zones to travel slowly along an otherwise solid rod or bar, so that impurities become concentrated at one end; **zone therapy** a technique in which different parts of the feet (or palms) are massaged or pressed to relieve conditions in different parts of the body with which they are held to be associated, as in reflexology; **zone time** mean solar time at the standard meridian on which a local time zone is based, taken as the standard time throughout the zone.
▪ **zoneless** *adjective* M18.

zone /zəʊn/ *verb*. L18.
[from prec.]
▶**I** *verb trans*. **1** Provide with or surround like a zone or girdle; encircle. L18.
2 *BOTANY & ZOOLOGY*. Mark with zones, rings, or bands of colour. Only as ***zoned*** pa. pple. L18.
3 Divide, distribute, or arrange into zones. E20.
4 Divide (a city, land, etc.) into areas subject to particular planning restrictions; designate (a specific area) for use or development in this manner. Also *US* (foll. by *out*), forbid (the siting of an enterprise) in a given area. Freq. as ***zoning*** *verbal noun*. E20.
5 Restrict the distribution of (a commodity) to a designated area. Now *rare* exc. *Hist.* (with ref. to British food allocation 1939–45). M20.

> 📖 **4** *Construction News* The site has been zoned for office, commercial and hotel development.

▶**II** *verb intrans*. **6** Foll. by *out*: lose concentration, cease paying attention; go to sleep. *US slang*. L20.
▪ **zoner** *noun* a person employed in the application of planning restrictions to particular areas M20.

zoned /zəʊnd/ *adjective*[1]. M17.
[from ZONE *noun, verb*: see -ED[2], -ED[1].]
†**1** Located in a zone or region of the celestial sphere. Only in M17.
2 Wearing a zone or girdle. Hence, virgin, chaste. E18.
3 a Characterized by or arranged in zones, rings, or bands. L18. ▸**b** Marked with zones, circles, or bands of colour. L18.

4 Arranged or distributed according to zones or definite regions. **L18.**

5 Designated for a particular type of use or development. **E20.**

zoned /zəʊnd/ *adjective*². *slang*. **L20.**
[Blend of **ZONKED** and **STONED**, infl. by **SPACED**.]
= **ZONKED**.

Zonian /ˈzəʊnɪən/ *noun & adjective*. **E20.**
[from Panama Canal *Zone* + **-IAN**.]
▶ **A** *noun*. An American inhabitant of the Panama Canal Zone, a strip of land on either side of the Panama Canal, controlled by the US between 1904 and 1979. **E20.**
▶ **B** *attrib*. or as *adjective*. Of or pertaining to Zonians. **M20.**

zonite /ˈzəʊnʌɪt/ *noun*. *rare*. **L19.**
[from **ZONE** *noun* + **-ITE**¹.]
ZOOLOGY. Any of the body rings of a segmented or apparently segmented animal, esp. a millipede or worm.

zonk /zɒŋk/ *verb*. *slang*. **M20.**
[from next.]
1 *verb trans.* Hit, strike, knock; *fig.* (also foll. by *out*) amaze, astound, overcome. **M20.**
2 *verb intrans.* Fail; lose consciousness; die. **M20.**
3 *verb intrans.* Foll. by *out*: fall heavily asleep. **L20.**

📖 **1** *Daily Telegraph* We fly to Los Angeles, where we are zonked with another three-hour time change.

■ **zonking** *adjective* great, remarkable **M20.**

zonk /zɒŋk/ *interjection & noun*. *slang*. **E20.**
[Imit.]
(Repr.) the sound of a blow or heavy impact, used esp. to indicate finality.

zonked /zɒŋkt/ *adjective*. *slang*. **M20.**
[from **ZONK** *verb* + **-ED**¹.]
1 Intoxicated by drugs or alcohol. Freq. foll. by *out*. **M20.**
2 Exhausted, tired *out*. **L20.**

zonkey /ˈzɒŋki/ *noun*. **M20.**
[Blend of **ZEBRA** and **DONKEY**.]
The offspring of a zebra and a donkey. Cf. **ZEDONK**.

zonky /ˈzɒŋki/ *adjective & noun*. *slang*. **L20.**
[from **ZONKED** + **-Y**¹, **-Y**⁶.]
▶ **A** *adjective*. Odd, weird. **L20.**
▶ **B** *noun*. A person in a zonked state. **L20.**

zonula /ˈzəʊnjʊlə/ *noun*. Pl. **-lae** /-liː/, **-las**. **M19.**
[mod. Latin, dim. of Latin *zona* **ZONE** *noun*.]
ANATOMY. A little zone; *spec.* (in full ***zonula ciliaris*** /sɪlɪˈɑːrɪs/ [mod. Latin = **CILIARY**]) a ring-shaped fibrous structure which forms the suspensory ligament of the eye lens.
■ **zonular** *adjective* pertaining to or forming a zonula or zonule; *spec.* belonging to or affecting the zonula ciliaris: **M19.**

zonule /ˈzəʊnjuːl/ *noun*. **M19.**
[from prec.: see **-ULE**.]
1 ANATOMY. = **ZONULA**. **M19.**
2 GEOLOGY. A limited biostratigraphic unit that is defined by the vertical and horizontal extent of a faunule. **E20.**
1 zonule of Zinn /zɪn/ [formed as **ZINNIA**] the zonula ciliaris.

zonure /ˈzəʊnjʊə/ *noun*. **L19.**
[mod. Latin *Zonurus* (former genus name), from Greek *zōnē* girdle + *oura* tail.]
ZOOLOGY. = ***girdle-tailed lizard*** s.v. **GIRDLE** *noun*¹.

zoo /zuː/ *noun*. **M19.**
[Short for ***ZOOLOGICAL gardens***.]
1 A place where wild animals are kept for breeding, study, or exhibition to the public (orig. *spec.* the Zoological Gardens in Regent's Park, London). **M19.**
2 A (diverse or motley) collection of people or things. Also, a place where such a collection is assembled. **E20.** ▸**b** A situation characterized by confusion and disorder. *colloq.* **L20.**

📖 **2** *Science News* The discovery of a new zoo of elementary particles: kaons, pions and muons. **b** S. PHILLIPS It's a zoo in the lobby.

Comb.: **zoo-keeper** an animal attendant employed in a zoo; a zoo owner or director; **zooman** *US colloq.* a male zoo-keeper.

zoo- /ˈzəʊəʊ/ *combining form*.
[from Greek *zōion* animal: see **-O-**.]
Forming nouns and adjectives with senses 'of or pertaining to animals', 'having (supposed) animal characteristics'.
■ **zooarchaeˈologist** *noun* an expert in or student of zooarchaeology **L20.** **zooarchaeˈology** *noun* the branch of science that deals with the animal remains at archaeological sites **L20.** **zooˈcentric** *adjective* centred upon the animal world, esp. to the exclusion of plants or humans **L19.** **zooˈchemistry** *noun* (now *rare*) animal biochemistry **M19.** **zoochore** *noun* [Greek *khōrein* to advance, to spread] a zoochorous plant **E20.** **zoˈochorous** *adjective* (of a plant) having its seeds dispersed by animals **E20.** **zoˈochory** *noun* the dispersal of plant seeds by animals **M20.** **zooˈcultural** *adjective* = **ZOOTECHNIC** **L19.** **zooculture** *noun* = **ZOOTECHNY** **E20.** **zoodyˈnamics** *noun* the mechanics of animal bodies **L19.** **zoˈoecial** *adjective* pertaining to or forming a zooecium **L19.** **zoˈoecium** *noun*, pl. **-cia**, [Greek *oikos* house] a thickened and hardened part of the cuticle forming a sheath enclosing each zooid in a colony of bryozoans **L19.** **zooˈflagellate** *noun & adjective* (pertaining to or designating) a flagellate with animal characteristics, esp. the lack of photosynthetic ability **M20.** **zooˈgamete** *noun* = **PLANOGAMETE** **L19.** **zooˈgenic** *adjective* produced from or caused by animals; (GEOLOGY) designating formations of animal origin: **M19.** **zoogeˈology** *noun* = **PALAEOZOOLOGY** **M19.** **zoogloea**, **-glea** /-ˈgliːə/ *noun* [Greek *gloios* glutinous substance] a mass of bacteria etc. forming a gelatinous mass, esp. in polluted fresh water **L19.** **zooˈgloeal**, **-ˈgleal** *adjective* pertaining to or consisting of a zoogloea **M20.** **zoˈolatrous** *adjective* pertaining to, of the nature of, or practising zoolatry **L19.** **zoˈolatry** *noun* the worship of animals **E19.** **zooˈmagnetism** *noun* (*Hist.*) animal magnetism **M19.** **zoomeˈchanics** *noun* = **ZOODYNAMICS** **L19.** **zooˈmelanin** *noun* melanin, esp. in feathers **M19.** **zoˈometry** *noun* (**a**) measurement of the dimensions and proportions of the bodies of animals; (**b**) the use of statistical methods in the study of animals: **L19.** **zooˈnosis** *noun*, pl. **-noses**, [Greek *nosos* disease] a disease naturally transmitted from one species of animal to another, esp. to humans **L19.** **zooˈnotic** *adjective* designating, causing, or involving a zoonosis; transmitted from animals to humans: **E20.** **zoopaˈthology** *noun* the pathology of animals **L19.** **zoˈophagous** *adjective* (of an animal) feeding on other animals; carnivorous: **M19.** **zooˈphobia** *noun* irrational fear of animals **E20.** **zooˈplankter** *noun* an individual organism of the zooplankton **M20.** **zooˈplankton** *noun* plankton consisting of small animals and the immature stages of larger animals **E20.** **zooplankˈtonic** *adjective* of, pertaining to, or consisting of zooplankton **E20.** **zoopraˈxography** *noun* the branch of zoology that deals with animal locomotion **L19.** **zoˈoscopy** *noun* hallucination in which imaginary animal forms are seen **L19.** **zoosemiˈotics** *noun* the branch of ethology that deals with communication within and between animal species **M20.** **zoˈosophy** *noun* (now *rare*) the knowledge or study of animals **M17.** **zoosperm** *noun* a motile spermatozoon **M19.** **zootaxy** *noun* (now *rare*) zoological classification, systematic zoology **M19.** **zooˈtechnic** *adjective* pertaining to zootechny **L19.** **zooˈtechnics** *noun* = **ZOOTECHNY** **L19.** **zootechny** /-tɛkni/ *noun* the art of rearing and using animals **L19.** **zooˈthecium** *noun*, pl. **-ia**, a gelatinous sheath produced and inhabited by certain ciliates **L19.** **zooˈtheism** *noun* the attribution of divine status to animals (cf. **ZOOLATRY**) **L19.** **zootheˈistic** *adjective* pertaining to or characterized by zootheism **L19.** **zoˈotic** *adjective* (**a**) GEOLOGY (of a rock etc.) containing fossil remains; (**b**) ECOLOGY (of a climax community) determined by the effects of animals, esp. grazing (cf. **BIOTIC** 2): **M19.** **zooˈtoxic** *adjective* of the nature of, or caused by, a zootoxin **E20.** **zooˈtoxin** *noun* a toxin derived from an animal **E20.** **zootype** *noun* (**a**) (a figure of) an animal as the type of a deity, as in Egyptian hieroglyphics; (**b**) a representative type of animal: **E20.** **zootypic** /-ˈtɪpɪk/ *adjective* (*rare*) pertaining to the animal type or types **L19.**

zoochlorella /ˌzəʊə(ʊ)kləˈrɛlə/ *noun*. Pl. **-llae** /-liː/. **L19.**
[mod. Latin, from **ZOO-** + **CHLOR-**² + Latin **-ELLA**.]
Any of numerous unicellular green algae present as symbionts in the cytoplasm of many (esp. freshwater) invertebrates. Cf. **ZOOXANTHELLA**.

†**zooea** *noun* var. of **ZOEA**.

zoogeography /ˌzəʊə(ʊ)dʒɪˈɒgrəfi/ *noun*. **L19.**
[from **ZOO-** + **GEOGRAPHY**.]
The science of the geographical distribution of animals.
■ **zoogeographer** *noun* **L19.** ˌ**zoogeoˈgraphic** *adjective* **L19.** ˌ**zoogeoˈgraphical** *adjective* **M19.** ˌ**zoogeoˈgraphically** *adverb* **L19.**

zoography /zəʊˈɒgrəfi/ *noun*. Now *rare*. **L16.**
[from **ZOO-** + **-GRAPHY**.]
1 Description of animals; descriptive zoology. Latterly *esp.* a survey of animal populations (cf. **DEMOGRAPHY**). **L16.**
2 The art of depicting animals; pictorial art in general. **M17.**
■ **zoˈographer** *noun* **M17.** **zooˈgraphic** *adjective* (**a**) describing or representing animals; relating to zoography; (**b**) = **ZOOGEOGRAPHIC**: **M18.** **zooˈgraphical** *adjective* = **ZOOGRAPHIC** **M17.** **zooˈgraphically** *adverb* in relation to zoography **L19.**

zooid /ˈzəʊɔɪd/ *noun*. **M19.**
[from **ZOO-** + **-OID**.]
Chiefly ZOOLOGY. An animal arising from another by budding or division; *esp.* each of the individuals which make up a colonial organism and often have different forms and functions. Formerly also, a motile cell. Cf. **ZOON** *noun*.
■ **zoˈoidal** *adjective* **L19.** **zooidiˈogamous** *adjective* = **PLANOGAMETIC** **L19.**

zookers /ˈzʊkəz/ *interjection*. Now *arch. & dial.* **E17.**
[Origin unkn.: cf. next.]
= next.

zooks /zʊks, zuːks/ *interjection*. Now *arch. & dial.* **M17.**
[Abbreviation of **GADZOOKS**.]
Expr. vexation, surprise, etc.

zoological /zəʊəˈlɒdʒɪk(ə)l, zuːə-/ *adjective*. **E19.**
[from **ZOOLOGY** + **-ICAL**.]
1 Pertaining to or concerned with zoology. **E19.**
2 Animal; of or pertaining to animals or figures of animals. Freq. *joc.* **M19.**

📖 **2** DICKENS One of the apartments has a zoological papering on the walls.

Special collocations: **zoological gardens** = **ZOO** 1. **zoological park** a zoo situated in parkland; a zoo in which animals are kept in open enclosures rather than cages.
■ **zoologic** *adjective* (chiefly *N. Amer.*) = **ZOOLOGICAL** **E19.** **zoologically** *adverb* in a zoological way; as regards zoology: **E19.**

zoologise *verb* var. of **ZOOLOGIZE**.

zoologist /zəʊˈɒlədʒɪst, zuː-/ *noun*. **M17.**
[formed as **ZOOLOGY** + **-IST**.]
An expert in or student of zoology.

zoologize /zəʊˈɒlədʒʌɪz, zuː-/ *verb*. Also **-ise**. **M19.**
[formed as **ZOOLOGY** + **-IZE**. Cf. **BOTANIZE**.]
1 *verb intrans.* Seek animals for zoological purposes; study animals, esp. in the field. **M19.**
2 *verb trans.* Explore or examine zoologically. *rare*. **M19.**

zoology /zəʊˈɒlədʒi, zuːˈɒl-/ *noun*. **M17.**
[mod. Latin *zoologia*, mod Greek *zōologia*, from Greek *zōion* animal: see **ZOO-**, **-LOGY**.]
The science of the structure, physiology, behaviour, classification, and distribution of animals. Formerly also, a treatise on or system of this.
■ **zoologer** *noun* (*rare*) = **ZOOLOGIST** **M17.**

zoom /zuːm/ *verb, noun, & interjection*. **L19.**
[Imit.]
▶ **A** *verb*. **1** *verb intrans.* Make a continuous low-pitched humming or buzzing sound; travel or move (as if) with such a sound; move at speed, hurry. *colloq.* **L19.**
2 AERONAUTICS. **a** *verb intrans.* Climb rapidly at a steep angle (passing into sense 1). **E20.** ▸**b** *verb trans.* Cause (an aircraft) to zoom; fly over (an obstacle) in this manner. **E20.** ▸**c** *verb intrans. fig.* Of prices, costs, etc.: rise sharply; soar, rocket. *colloq.* **L20.**
3 PHOTOGRAPHY & TELEVISION. **a** *verb intrans.* Of a camera or lens: close up on a subject without losing focus; alter range by changing focal length. Freq. foll. by *in* (*on*). **M20.** ▸**b** *verb trans.* Cause (a lens or camera) to alter range in this manner. **M20.**

📖 **1** C. DEXTER Two youngsters . . zoomed nearer on their L-plated motor bikes. **3a** *transf.*: *Nature* The interactive graphics section provides facilities for zooming in on smaller regions.

▶ **B** *noun*. **1** AERONAUTICS. An act of zooming. **E20.**
2 PHOTOGRAPHY & TELEVISION. **a** A camera shot in which the range is shortened to that of a close-up without loss of focus (also ***zoom shot***); this process. **M20.** ▸**b** = ***zoom lens*** below. **L20.**
3 *fig.* Zest, energy; sparkle. *colloq.* **M20.**
Comb.: **zoom lens** a camera lens for which the focal length, and hence the magnification and the field of view, can be smoothly varied while the image remains in focus; ***zoom shot***: see sense 2a above.
▶ **C** *interjection*. Repr. a zooming sound, such as that made by something travelling at speed; *fig.* denoting a sudden rise or fall. **M20.**
■ **zoomy** *adjective* (**a**) that makes a zooming sound; (**b**) impressively powerful, flashy: **M20.**

zoomorph /ˈzəʊə(ʊ)mɔːf/ *noun*. **L19.**
[from **ZOO-** + **-MORPH**.]
A representation of an animal form in decorative art or symbolism.

zoomorphic /zəʊə(ʊ)ˈmɔːfɪk/ *adjective*. **L19.**
[from prec. + **-IC**.]
1 Representing or imitating animal forms, as in decorative art or symbolism. **L19.**
2 Attributing the form or nature of an animal to something, esp. to a deity or superhuman being. **L19.** ▸**b** Of a god, spirit, etc.: (conceived or represented as) having the form of an animal. **L19.**

zoomorphism /zəʊə(ʊ)ˈmɔːfɪz(ə)m/ *noun*. **E19.**
[formed as prec. + **-ISM**.]
1 Attribution of animal form or nature to a god etc. **E19.**
2 Imitation or representation of animal forms in decorative art or symbolism. **L19.**
■ **zoomorphize** *verb trans.* make zoomorphic; attribute an animal form or nature to: **L19.**

zoomorphosed /zəʊə(ʊ)ˈmɔːfəʊzd/ *adjective*. *rare*. **M20.**
[from **ZOOMORPH** after *metamorphosed*.]
Of a decorative or symbolic design: given a zoomorphic form.

zoon /ˈzəʊɒn/ *noun*. *rare*. Pl. **zoons**, **zoa** /ˈzəʊə/. **M19.**
[mod. Latin from Greek *zōion* animal.]
An individual animal which is the total product of an impregnated ovum, not being either asexually produced or part of a colonial organism; opp. **ZOOID**. Formerly also, a zooid.

zoon /zuːn/ *verb*. *US colloq.* **L19.**
[Imit.: cf. **ZOOM**.]
1 *verb intrans.* Make a humming or buzzing sound; move quickly. **L19.**
2 *verb trans.* Cause to travel with such a sound; propel. **L19.**
■ **zooning** *noun* (**a**) the action of the verb; (**b**) *Black English* a style of preaching and response characterized by the repetition of words and phrases with tonal variation: **M20.**

-zoon /ˈzəʊən/ *suffix*. Pl. **-zoa** /ˈzəʊə/.
[from Greek *zōion* animal; in sense 2 from mod. Latin taxonomic names in *-zoa*: see **-ON**.]
ZOOLOGY. **1** Forming nouns denoting individual animals etc. (esp. small invertebrates or single-celled organisms) having a specific mode of life or function, as ***cryptozoon***, ***epizoon***, ***spermatozoon***, etc.
2 Forming nouns from names of zoological classes etc. ending in *-zoa*, as ***hydrozoon***, ***protozoon***. Cf. **-ZOAN 1**.

zoonomy /zəʊˈɒnəmi/ *noun*. *obsolete* exc. *Hist*. **E19**.
[mod. Latin *zoonomia*, from Greek *zōion* animal (or *zōē* life) + *nomos* law: see **-Y**[3].]
Animal physiology; the biology of animals.
■ **zooˈnomical** *adjective* pertaining or relating to zoonomy **E19**.

zoon politikon /ˌzəʊɒn pəˈlɪtɪkɒn/ *noun phr*. **M20**.
[Greek (after Aristotle's *politikon zōion*): cf. **ZOON** *noun*, **POLITIC** *adjective*.]
= ***political animal*** s.v. **POLITICAL** *adjective*.

zoophile /ˈzəʊəfʌɪl/ *noun*. **L19**.
[from **ZOO-** + **-PHILE**.]
1 *BOTANY*. (The seed of) a zoophilous plant. *rare*. **L19**.
2 A lover of animals; an opponent of cruelty to animals, *esp*. an anti-vivisectionist. **E20**.
■ **zoophilia** /zəʊəˈfɪlɪə/ *noun* (*PSYCHOLOGY*) attraction to animals that acts as an outlet for some form of sexual energy, now usu. implying copulation or bestiality **E20**. **zoophilic** /zəʊəˈfɪlɪk/ *adjective* (**a**) animal-loving; characterized by zoophilism or zoophilia; (**b**) (of a pathogenic organism) infecting animals and sometimes spread from them to humans: **M20**. **zoophilism** /zəʊˈɒfɪlɪz(ə)m/ *noun* an emotional attachment to, or love of, animals; passionate opposition to cruelty to animals: **L19**. **zoophilist** /zəʊˈɒfɪlɪst/ *noun* = **ZOOPHILE 2 E19**. **zoophilous** /zəʊˈɒfɪləs/ *adjective* (**a**) *BOTANY* (of a plant) pollinated by, or (*rare*) having its seeds dispersed by, animals; (**b**) = **ZOOPHILIC**: **L19**. **zoophily** /zəʊˈɒfɪli/ *noun* (**a**) = **ZOOPHILISM**; (**b**) = **ZOOPHILIA**: **L19**.

zoophorus *noun* var. of **ZOPHORUS**.

zoophyte /ˈzəʊəfʌɪt/ *noun*. **E17**.
[mod. Latin *zoophyton* from Greek *zōiophuton*, from *zōion* animal: see **ZOO-**, **-PHYTE**.]
†**1** Any of certain plants formerly reputed to have some animal qualities, e.g. the sensitive plant. Only in **17**.
2 *ZOOLOGY*. Any of various sessile invertebrate animals that resemble plants or flowers, such as crinoids, hydrozoans, sponges, and bryozoans. Formerly *spec*., an animal of the former group Zoophyta, which included some or most of these. **E17**.
■ **zoophytic** /zəʊəˈfɪtɪk/ *adjective* of, pertaining to, or produced by zoophytes; of the nature of a zoophyte: **E19**. **zoophyˈtology** *noun* (now *rare* or *obsolete*) the branch of zoology that deals with zoophytes **E19**.

zoospore /ˈzəʊəspɔː/ *noun*. **M19**.
[from **ZOO-** + **SPORE**.]
BOTANY & ZOOLOGY. A motile flagellated spore, occurring in certain algae, fungi, and protozoans. Also called ***planospore***, ***swarm-spore***.
■ **zoospoˈrangium** *noun*, pl. **-gia**, a sporangium producing zoospores **L19**. **zooˈsporic** *adjective* = **ZOOSPOROUS L19**. **zoˈosporous** *adjective* producing, of the nature of, or involving zoospores **M19**.

zoot /zuːt/ *noun*. *US slang*. **M20**.
[Abbreviation.]
= **ZOOT SUIT**.
Comb.: **zoot-shirt** a (brightly coloured) shirt designed to be worn with a zoot suit.
■ **zooty** *adjective* in the style of a zoot suit; (strikingly) fashionable: **M20**.

zootomy /zəʊˈɒtəmi/ *noun*. Now *rare*. **M17**.
[mod. Latin *zootomia*, prob. after late Latin *anatomia* **ANATOMY**: see **ZOO-**, **-TOMY**.]
The anatomy of animals; the dissection of animals. Latterly *esp*., comparative anatomy.
■ **zooˈtomic** *adjective* = **ZOOTOMICAL L19**. **zooˈtomical** *adjective* belonging or relating to zootomy **M19**. **zooˈtomically** *adverb* in relation to or by means of zootomy **M19**. **zootomist** *noun* an expert in or student of zootomy; *esp*. a comparative anatomist: **L17**.

zoot suit /ˈzuːt suːt, sjuːt/ *noun phr*. **M20**.
[Rhyming formation on **SUIT** *noun*.]
1 A man's suit of an exaggerated style popular in the 1940s (orig. worn by black Americans), characterized by a long, draped jacket with padded shoulders, and high-waisted tapering trousers. **M20**.
2 Any of various kinds of clothing for the whole body, *esp*. a windproof suit issued to some US and British troops during the war of 1939–45. *slang* (chiefly *Military*). **M20**.
■ **zoot-suited** *adjective* (*colloq*.) dressed in a zoot suit **M20**. **zoot-suiter** *noun* (*colloq*.) a zoot-suited person; *spec*. any of a group or gang of young men wearing zoot suits: **M20**.

zooxanthella /ˌzəʊəzanˈθɛlə/ *noun*. Pl. **-llae** /-liː/. **L19**.
[mod. Latin, from **ZOO-** + **XANTH(O-** + Latin **-ELLA**.]
Any of numerous yellow-brown dinoflagellates present as symbionts in the cytoplasm of many marine invertebrates. Cf. **ZOOCHLORELLA**.

zophorus /ˈzəʊf(ə)rəs/ *noun*. Also **zoophorus** /zəʊˈɒf(ə)rəs/. Pl. **-ri** /-rʌɪ/. **M16**.
[Latin from Greek *zōi(o)phoros*, from *zōion* animal + *-phoros* bearing.]
ARCHITECTURE. A continuous frieze bearing human and animal figures carved in relief.

zopilote /ˈzəʊpɪləʊt/ *noun*. **L18**.
[Spanish from Nahuatl *azopilotl*.]
An American vulture, *esp*. the turkey-buzzard, *Cathartes aura*.

zopissa /zəʊˈpɪsə/ *noun*. *rare*. **E17**.
[Latin from Greek *zōpissa*, from *pissa* pitch.]
†**1** A medicinal application made from pitch scraped from the sides of ships. **E17–M19**.
2 A patent waterproof coating for metal, wood, etc. **M19**.

zoppa /ˈtsɒppa/ *adjective & adverb*. **M18**.
[Italian, fem. of *zoppo* limping.]
MUSIC. In a syncopated rhythm, esp. one in which the second quaver of a two-four bar is accented.

zorb /zɔːb/ *verb & noun*. **L20**.
[Invented word.]
▶ **A** *noun*. (Usu. **Z-**.) A large transparent ball containing an inner capsule in which a person can be secured and then rolled along the ground, down hills, etc. **L20**.
▶ **B** *verb intrans*. Be rolled along in such a ball. Chiefly as ***zorbing verbal noun***, the sport of travelling in a zorb. **L20**.
¶ *Zorb* is a proprietary name in New Zealand (where the sport originated) and Australia.

zori /ˈzɔːri/ *noun*. Pl. **-s**, same. **E19**.
[Japanese *zōri*, from *sō* grass, (rice) straw + *ri* footwear, sole.]
A Japanese sandal, having a simple thong between the toes and a flat sole originally of straw but now often of rubber, felt, etc.

zorilla /zɒˈrɪlə/ *noun*. Also **zoril**, (earlier) **zorille** /ˈzɒrɪl/. **L18**.
[mod. Latin *Zorilla* former genus name, or directly from French *zorille*, Spanish *zorilla*, *-illo* dim. of *zorra*, *zorro* fox.]
1 A striped carnivorous mammal of the weasel family, *Ictonyx striatus*, of sub-Saharan Africa. **L18**.
2 = **ZORINO**. **M19**.

zorino /zɒˈriːnəʊ/ *noun*. Also **-rr-**. Pl. **-os**. **L19**.
[Spanish *zorrino* dim. of *zorro* fox.]
(The fur of) any of several Central and S. American skunks of the genus *Conepatus*.

Zoroastrian /zɒrəʊˈastrɪən/ *adjective & noun*. **M18**.
[from Latin *Zoroastres* from Greek *Zōroastrēs* from Avestan *Zaraθuštra* Zoroaster: see **-IAN**.]
▶ **A** *adjective*. Of or pertaining to Zoroaster, the Persian founder of Zoroastrianism (10th cent. BC or earlier), or Zoroastrianism. **M18**.
▶ **B** *noun*. A follower of Zoroaster. Cf. **PARSEE**. **E19**.
■ **Zoroastrianize** *verb trans*. & *intrans*. make or become Zoroastrian in character **L19**. **Zoroastric** *adjective* (*rare*) = **ZOROASTRIAN** *adjective* **M19**.

Zoroastrianism /zɒrəʊˈastrɪənɪz(ə)m/ *noun*. **M19**.
[from prec. + **-ISM**.]
The religious system taught by Zoroaster and his followers in the Zend-Avesta, which, while recognizing a single creator, is dualistic in seeing two opposing powers in the world, one of light and good and one of darkness and evil.

zorrino *noun* see **ZORINO**.

zorro /ˈzɒrəʊ/ *noun*. Pl. **-os**. **M19**.
[Spanish = fox.]
Either of two S. American foxes, *Dusicyon thous* and *D. microtis*.

zos-grass /ˈzɒsgrɑːs/ *noun*. **M20**.
[from **ZOS(TERA** + **GRASS** *noun*.]
= **ZOSTERA**.

zoster /ˈzɒstə/ *noun*. **E17**.
[Latin from Greek *zōstēr* girdle.]
†**1** A kind of seaweed. *rare*. Only in **E17**.
2 The disease shingles; = ***HERPES zoster***. **E18**.
3 *GREEK ANTIQUITIES*. A belt or girdle, esp. as worn by men. **E19**.

zostera /ˈzɒst(ə)rə, zɒˈstɪərə/ *noun*. **L18**.
[mod. Latin (see below), from Greek **ZOSTER**: see **-A**[1].]
Any of several submerged marine flowering plants with ribbon-like leaves, constituting the genus *Zostera* (family Zosteraceae), esp. *Z. marina*. Also called ***eel-grass***, ***grass-wrack***.

zosterops /ˈzɒstərɒps/ *noun*. Pl. same. **M19**.
[mod. Latin genus name (see below), from Greek **ZOSTER** + *ōps* eye, face.]
ORNITHOLOGY. A small bird of the genus *Zosterops* (see ***white-eye*** s.v. **WHITE** *adjective*).

Zouave /zuːˈɑːv, zwɑːv/ *noun*. **M19**.
[French from Berber (Kabyle) *Zouaoua* name of a people.]
1 A member of a body of light infantry in the French army, originally formed of Algerian Kabyles, and long retaining the original oriental uniform. **M19**. ▸**b** *Hist*. More fully ***Papal Zouave***, ***Pontifical Zouave***. A member of a corps of French soldiers formed in Rome for the defence of the Pope between 1860 and 1871. **M19**. ▸**c** *Hist*. A member of any of several volunteer regiments of Union troops in the American Civil War which adopted the name and in part the uniform of the French Zouaves. **M19**.
2 A garment resembling part of the Zouave uniform; *spec*. (**a**) *Hist*. (in full ***Zouave jacket***, ***Zouave bodice***) a woman's short embroidered jacket or bodice, with or without sleeves; (**b**) in *pl*., pegtop trousers, as worn by men in the late 19th cent. and women in the late 20th cent. (also ***Zouave trousers***, ***Zouave pants***); (**c**) a wide loose skirt with a looped or tucked up hemline (also ***Zouave skirt***). **M19**.

zouk /zuːk/ *noun*. **L20**.
[French, app. from Antillean creole.]
An exuberant style of popular music originating in Guadeloupe in the Lesser Antilles.
■ **zoukish** *adjective* **L20**.

zounds /zaʊndz/ *interjection*. *arch*. **L16**.
[Abbreviation from (*God*)'*s wounds*.]
Expr. surprise, indignation, or asseveration.

Zou-Zou /ˈzuːzuː/ *noun*. *colloq*. *obsolete* exc. *Hist*. **M19**.
[French, dim. of **ZOUAVE**.]
= **ZOUAVE 1**.

zowie /ˈzaʊi, zaʊˈiː/ *interjection*. *US colloq*. **E20**.
[Natural exclam. Cf. **WOW** *interjection*.]
Expr. astonishment, admiration, etc.

zoysia /ˈzɔɪzɪə/ *noun*. **M20**.
[mod. Latin (see below), from Carl von *Zoys* zu Laubach (1756–c 1800), Austrian botanist + **-IA**[1].]
A perennial grass of the genus *Zoysia*, of eastern Asia, used for lawns in subtropical regions. Also ***zoysia grass***.

ZPG *abbreviation*.
Zero population growth.

Zr *symbol*.
CHEMISTRY. Zirconium.

zubr /ˈzuːbrə, ˈzuːbə/ *noun*. **M18**.
[Russian.]
The European bison or wisent, *Bison bonasus*.

zubrowka /zʊˈbrɒvkə/ *noun*. Also **-ovka**. **M20**.
[Polish *żubrówka*, Russian *zubrovka*, also the name of plants said to be favoured by the bison (zubr).]
Vodka flavoured with the stalks of a Polish sweet-grass, *Hierochloe odorata*.

zucchetto /tsʊˈkɛtəʊ/ *noun*. Pl. **-ttos**, **-tti** /-ti/. Also **-tta** /-tə/. **M19**.
[Italian *zucchetta* dim. of *zucca* gourd, head.]
The skullcap worn by Roman Catholic ecclesiastics, black for priests, purple for bishops, red for cardinals, and white for the Pope.

zucchini /zʊˈkiːni/ *noun pl*. Chiefly *N. Amer*. & *Austral*. Also **-nis**. **E20**.
[Italian, pl. of *zucchino* small marrow, courgette, dim. of *zucca* gourd.]
Courgettes.

Zuckerkandl /ˈzʊkəkand(ə)l/ *noun*. **E20**.
[E. *Zuckerkandl* (1849–1910), Austrian anatomist.]
ANATOMY. Used *attrib*., in *possess*., and with *of* to designate the para-aortic bodies.

zufolo /ˈtsuːfələʊ, z-/ *noun*. Also **-ff-**. Pl. **-li** /-li/. **E18**.
[Italian.]
MUSIC. A flageolet, a small flute or whistle.
¶ Only in Dicts. before **20**.

zug /tsuːɡ/ *noun*. **L19**.
[Invented word, perh. with allus. to German *Zug*.]
A variety of waterproofed leather used esp. for the uppers of climbing boots. Also ***zug leather***.
¶ Formerly a proprietary name.

Zugunruhe /ˈtsuːkˌʊnruːə/ *noun*. **M20**.
[German.]
ORNITHOLOGY. Migratory restlessness; the migratory drive in birds.

zugzwang /ˈzʌɡzwaŋ/ *noun*. **E20**.
[German, from *Zug* move + *Zwang* compulsion, obligation.]
CHESS. A position in which a player must move but cannot do so without disadvantage; the obligation to make a move even when disadvantageous. Freq. in ***in zugzwang***.

Zulu /ˈzuːluː/ *noun & adjective*. **E19**.
[Zulu *umzulu*, pl. *amazulu*.]
▶ **A** *noun*. Pl. same, **-s**.
1 a A member of a black South African people orig. inhabiting Zululand and Natal. **E19**. ▸**b** The Bantu language of this people. **M19**. ▸**c** A black person. *US slang* (*derog*. & considered *racially offensive*). **M20**.
2 *ANGLING*. A kind of mainly black artificial fly. **L19**.
3 *Hist*. A kind of Scottish fishing boat first built at the time of the Zulu War, 1879–97. **L19**.

4 [from use as radio code word for the letter *z*.] More fully ***Zulu time***. ▸**a** = ***zone time*** s.v. ZONE *noun*. *Aeronautics slang*. **M20.** ▸**b** [repr. zero] = ***Greenwich Mean Time*** s.v. GREENWICH 1. *Astronautics slang*. **L20.**

▸**B** *attrib.* or as *adjective*. Of or pertaining to the Zulus or their language. **E19.**

Zulu hat *Hist.* a kind of straw hat with a wide brim.

zumbooruk /ˈzʌmbʊrʌk/ *noun*. Also **-uck**, **-ak**. **E19.**
[Urdu from Persian *zambūrak*, from *zambūr* bee.]
A small swivel-gun, *esp.* one mounted on the back of a camel.

†**zumo-** *combining form* var. of ZYMO-.

Zuñi /ˈzuːnji/ *noun & adjective*. Also **Zuni**. **M19.**
[A river in New Mexico, USA.]
▸**A** *noun*. Pl. same, **-s**.
1 A member of a Pueblo Indian people inhabiting the valley of the River Zuñi. **M19.**
2 The language of this people. **L19.**
▸**B** *attrib.* or as *adjective*. Of or pertaining to the Zuñi or their language. **L19.**
■ **Zuñian** *adjective* (*rare*) **L19.**

zuppa /ˈtsuppa/ *noun*. **M20.**
[Italian.]
Soup (in Italian cookery). Chiefly with specifying words.
zuppa di pesce / di ˈpeʃe/ fish soup. ***zuppa inglese*** /iŋˈglese/ [= English] a rich Italian dessert resembling trifle.

Zurich /ˈz(j)ʊərɪk, *foreign* ˈtsyːrɪç/ *noun*. **L19.**
[A city in Switzerland.]
Used *attrib.* to designate things associated with Zurich, esp. porcelain manufactured there in the 18th cent.
Zurich gnome: see GNOME *noun*² 3.
■ **Zuricher** *noun* a native or inhabitant of Zurich **L17.**

zurla /ˈzʊələ/ *noun*. Pl. ***-le*** /-leɪ/. **M20.**
[Serbo-Croat *sûrla*, from (the same root as) next.]
MUSIC. A kind of shawm introduced to the Balkans from the Middle East by Gypsies.

zurna /ˈzʊənə/ *noun*. **L19.**
[Turkish *zurnā*, Arab. *zurnā*, *zūrnā*, etc., ult. from Persian *sūr* feast+ *rāy* reed-pipe.]
MUSIC. A kind of shawm found in Turkey, Arabic-speaking countries, and various neighbouring regions.

zut /zyt/ *interjection*. **E20.**
[French.]
Expr. annoyance, contempt, impatience, etc.

zwanziger /ˈtsvantsɪɡər/ *noun*. **E19.**
[German, from *zwanzig* twenty.]
Hist. A former Austrian silver coin, equal to twenty kreutzers.

zwieback /ˈtsviːbak/ *noun*. **L19.**
[German = twice-bake (cf. BISCUIT).]
A (sweet) rusk or biscuit made by baking a small loaf, and then toasting slices until they are dry and crisp.

Zwinglian /ˈzwɪŋglɪən, ˈtsvɪ-/ *noun & adjective*. **M16.**
[from *Zwingli* (see below) + -IAN.]
▸**A** *noun*. A follower of the Swiss religious reformer Ulrich Zwingli (1484–1531). **M16.**
▸**B** *adjective*. Of or pertaining to Zwingli or his doctrine, esp. concerning metaphorical (and not real) presence of Christ in the Eucharist. **M16.**
■ **Zwinglianism** *noun* **L16.**

zwischenzug /ˈtsvaɪʃəntsuːk/ *noun*. **M20.**
[German, from *zwischen* between + *Zug* move.]
CHESS. A move interposed in a sequence of play in such a way as to alter the outcome.

zwitterion /ˈtsvɪtərʌɪən, ˈzwɪ-/ *noun*. **E20.**
[German, from *Zwitter* hybrid + *Ion* ION.]
CHEMISTRY. A molecule or ion having separate positively and negatively charged atoms or groups.
■ **zwitteriˈonic** *adjective* **M20.**

Zyban /ˈzʌɪban/ *noun*. **L20.**
[Invented name.]
(Proprietary name for) the antidepressant bupropion, used to relieve nicotine withdrawal symptoms in those giving up smoking.

Zydeco /ˈzʌɪdɪkəʊ/ *noun*. *US*. **M20.**
[Louisiana creole, perh. from a pronunc. of French *les haricots* in a dance-tune title.]
A kind of Afro-American dance music originally from southern Louisiana.

zyg- *combining form* see ZYGO-.

zygaena /zʌɪˈgiːnə, -ˈdʒiːnə/ *noun*. **L17.**
[mod. Latin (see below), from Greek *zugaina*. In sense 2 app. arbitrarily applied.]
1 *ZOOLOGY*. A hammerhead shark of the genus *Sphyrna* (formerly *Zygaena*); *esp.* the smooth hammerhead, *S. zygaena*. Now *rare* or *obsolete*. **L17.**
2 *ENTOMOLOGY*. A burnet-moth of the genus *Zygaena*. Now only as mod. Latin genus name. **M19.**
■ **zygaenid** *noun & adjective* (*ENTOMOLOGY*) (*a*) *noun* a moth of the family Zygaenidae, which comprises the burnets and foresters; (*b*) *adjective* of, pertaining to, or designating this family: **L19.**

zygal /ˈzʌɪg(ə)l/ *adjective*. *rare*. **L19.**
[from Greek *zugon* yoke + -AL¹.]
H-shaped.

zygantrum /zʌɪˈgantrəm, zɪ-/ *noun*. Pl. **-tra** /-trə/. **M19.**
[from ZYG(O- + ANTRUM.]
ZOOLOGY. A cavity on the posterior surface of the neural arch of a snake's vertebra, into which the zygosphene of the next vertebra fits.

zygapophysis /zʌɪgəˈpɒfɪsɪs, zɪg-/ *noun*. Pl. **-physes** /-fɪsiːz/. **M19.**
[from ZYG(O- + APOPHYSIS.]
ANATOMY & ZOOLOGY. Each of four lateral processes on the neural arch of a vertebra, articulating with the corresponding process of the next vertebra; an articular process.
■ **zygapophyseal**, **zygapophysial** /ˌzʌɪgəpəʊˈfɪzɪəl/ *adjectives* pertaining to a zygapophysis **L19.**

zygite /ˈzʌɪdʒʌɪt, -g-/ *noun*. **L19.**
[Greek *zugitēs*, from *zugon* thwart.]
GREEK ANTIQUITIES. A rower in one of the tiers of a bireme or trireme (believed to be the upper tier in a bireme, the middle tier in a trireme). Cf. THALAMITE, THRANITE.

zygo- /ˈzʌɪgəʊ, ˈzɪgəʊ/ *combining form*. Before a vowel also **zyg-**.
[from Greek *zugon* yoke: see -O-.]
Forming terms in *BIOLOGY* with senses (*a*) 'involving or pertaining to conjugation or zygosis'; (*b*) 'arranged symmetrically in pairs'.
■ **zygoˈdactyl** *adjective & noun* (*a*) *adjective* (of a bird) having the toes arranged in pairs, two before and two behind; (*b*) *noun* a zygodactyl bird: **E19.** **zygoˈdactylous** *adjective* = ZYGODACTYL *adjective* **E19.** **zygodont** *adjective* (of molar teeth) having an even number of cusps arranged in pairs; (of an animal, dentition, etc.) characterized by such teeth: **L19.** **zygoˈgenesis** *noun* reproduction involving the formation of a zygote **M20.** ˌ**zygogeˈnetic** *adjective* involving or reproducing by zygogenesis **M20.** **zygomere** *noun* (*CYTOLOGY*) a site on a chromosome thought to be responsible for the initiation of pairing between homologous chromosomes during zygotene in eukaryotes **M20.** **zygoˈnema** *noun* (*CYTOLOGY*) (now *rare*) (a chromosome at) zygotene **E20.** **zygophore** *noun* (*BOTANY*) in zygomycetes, a specialized hypha which bears a zygospore **E20.** **zygosome** *noun* (*CYTOLOGY*) = BIVALENT *noun* **E20.** **zygosphene** *noun* [Greek *sphēn* wedge] *ZOOLOGY* a wedge-shaped projection on the anterior surface of the neural arch of a snake's vertebra, which fits into the zygantrum of the next vertebra **M19.** **zygotene** *noun* (*CYTOLOGY*) the second stage of the prophase of the first meiotic division, in which homologous chromosomes begin to pair **E20.**

zygocactus /ˈzʌɪgəʊkaktəs/ *noun*. Pl. **-ti** /-tʌɪ/, **-tuses**. **M20.**
[from ZYGO- + CACTUS.]
Any of several ornamental Brazilian cacti constituting the genus *Schlumbergera* (formerly *Zygocactus*), with stems composed of flattened joints and pink or magenta flowers.

zygology /zʌɪˈgɒlədʒi/ *noun*. **L20.**
[from ZYGO- + -LOGY.]
The branch of technology that deals with joining and fastening.
■ **zygoˈlogical** *adjective* pertaining to or concerned with zygology **L20.** **zygologist** *noun* an expert in or student of zygology **L20.**

zygoma /zʌɪˈgəʊmə, zɪg-/ *noun*. Pl. **-mata** /-mətə/, **-mas**. **L17.**
[Greek *zugōma*, from *zugon* yoke: see -OMA.]
ANATOMY & ZOOLOGY. The zygomatic arch; a part of this.

zygomatic /zʌɪgə(ʊ)ˈmatɪk, zɪg-/ *adjective & noun*. **E18.**
[from Greek *zugōmat-*, *zugōma*: see prec., -IC.]
ANATOMY & ZOOLOGY. ▸**A** *adjective*. Pertaining to or forming part of the bone structure of the cheek. **E18.**
zygomatic arch a bony arch on each side of the skull in mammals, formed by the cheek-bone and its linkage with the temporal bone. **zygomatic bone** = ***cheek-bone*** (a) s.v. CHEEK *noun*. **zygomatic muscle** any of several muscles that arise from the zygomatic arch and assist in the movement of the lower jaw. **zygomatic process** a process of the temporal bone that forms part of the zygomatic arch.
▸**B** *noun*. A zygomatic bone or muscle. **E19.**

zygomorphic /zʌɪgə(ʊ)ˈmɔːfɪk/ *adjective*. **L19.**
[from ZYGO- + Greek *morphē* form + -IC.]
BOTANY. Of a flower, e.g. of a labiate plant: characterized by bilateral symmetry (and thus irregular). Opp. ***actinomorphic***.
■ **zygomorphism** *noun* zygomorphic character **L19.** **zygomorphous** *adjective* = ZYGOMORPHIC **L19.**

zygomycete /zʌɪgə(ʊ)ˈmʌɪsiːt/ *noun*. Orig. only in pl. **-mycetes** /-ˈmʌɪsiːts, -mʌɪˈsiːtiːz/. **L19.**
[Anglicized sing. of mod. Latin *Zygomycetes* (see below), formed as ZYGO- + Greek *mukētes* pl. of *mukēs* fungus.]
MYCOLOGY. A saprophytic or parasitic fungus of the subdivision Zygomycetina or class Zygomycetes, in which sexual reproduction is by fusion of usu. similar gametangia to produce a zygospore and asexual reproduction is by means of non-motile spores.
■ **zygomyˈcetous** *adjective* **E20.**

zygosis /zʌɪˈgəʊsɪs, zɪg-/ *noun*. **L19.**
[Greek *zugōsis*, from *zugoun* to yoke, from *zugon* yoke: see -OSIS.]
BIOLOGY. = CONJUGATION 4.

zygosity /zʌɪˈgɒsɪti/ *noun*. **M20.**
[from ZYGOS(IS + -ITY.]
GENETICS. **1** The genetic relationship of twins, triplets, etc., in respect of their being monozygotic, dizygotic, etc. **M20.**
2 The degree of genetic similarity between alleles which determines whether an individual is homozygotic or heterozygotic for the characteristic expressed. **M20.**

zygospore /ˈzʌɪgə(ʊ)spɔː/ *noun*. **M19.**
[from ZYGO- + SPORE.]
BOTANY. A thick-walled resting cell arising from the fusion of two similar gametes, as in zygomycetes and in certain algae.
■ **zygoˈsporic** *adjective* **E20.**

zygote /ˈzʌɪgəʊt/ *noun*. **L19.**
[from Greek *zugōtos* yoked, from *zugoun* to yoke, from *zugon* yoke.]
BIOLOGY. A diploid cell resulting from the fusion of two haploid gametes; a fertilized ovum.
Comb.: **zygote intrafallopian transfer** = *ZIFT*.
■ **zygotic** /-ˈgɒtɪk/ *adjective* pertaining to or of the nature of a zygote; produced or characterized by zygosis: **E20.** **zyˈgotically** *adverb* in the zygote; in terms of the zygote: **E20.**

Zyklon /ˈzʌɪklɒn/ *noun*. Also **Cyclon** /ˈsʌɪ-/. **M20.**
[German, of unkn. origin.]
Hydrogen cyanide adsorbed on, or released from, a carrier in the form of small tablets, used as an insecticidal fumigant and formerly as a lethal gas. Chiefly in ***Zyklon B***.

Zylonite *noun* var. of XYLONITE.

zym- *combining form* see ZYMO-.

zymase /ˈzʌɪmeɪz/ *noun*. **L19.**
[formed as next + -ASE.]
BIOCHEMISTRY. A mixture of enzymes which catalyse the breakdown of sugars in alcoholic fermentation, obtained from yeast.

zyme /zʌɪm/ *noun*. Now *rare*. **L19.**
[Greek *zumē* leaven.]
A fermenting enzyme, *esp.* (formerly) one believed to be the cause of a zymotic disease.

zymin /ˈzʌɪmɪn/ *noun*. Also †**-ine**. **M19.**
[formed as prec. + -IN¹.]
1 = ZYME. Now *rare* or *obsolete*. **M19.**
2 A pancreatic extract formerly used in medicine; a preparation of zymase. **E20.**

zymo- /ˈzʌɪməʊ/ *combining form*. Also †**zumo-**; before a vowel also **zym-**.
[from Greek *zumē* leaven: see -O-.]
Forming terms in *BIOLOGY* & *BIOCHEMISTRY* pertaining to enzymes or fermentation.
■ ˈ**zymodeme** *noun* a closely related subpopulation within one taxon, distinguished on the basis of the degree of similarity of certain enzymes **L20.** **zymogram** *noun* a strip of electrophoretic medium showing enzymes separated by a technique such as zone electrophoresis **M20.** **zymoˈlogical** *adjective* pertaining to or concerned with zymology **E19.** **zyˈmologist** *noun* an expert in or student of zymology **E19.** **zyˈmology** *noun* the branch of biochemistry that deals with the action of enzymes in fermentation; enzymology: **M18.** **zyˈmolysis** *noun* decomposition by means of enzymes; *esp.* fermentation: **L19.** **zymoˈlytic** *adjective* pertaining to or involving zymolysis **L19.** **zyˈmometer** *noun* an instrument for measuring the degree of fermentation in a fermenting liquor **M19.** **zymophore**, **zymoˈphoric** *adjectives* (now *rare*) designating a group of atoms in an enzyme, or in the receptors of a living cell, to which the enzymic activity is attributed **E20.** **zymoˈplastic** *adjective* producing an enzyme or enzymes **M20.** **zymosan** *noun* [after *glucosan*] an insoluble polysaccharide of the cell wall of yeast, used in the assay of properdins **M20.** **zymoˈsimeter** *noun* (now *rare*) = ZYMOMETER **E18.** **zymoˈtechnic**, **zymoˈtechnical** *adjectives* of or pertaining to zymotechnics **L19.** **zymoˈtechnics** *noun* the branch of science that deals with the production and control of fermentation; zymurgy: **L19.** **zymotechˈnologist** *noun* an expert in or student of zymotechnology **L19.** **zymotechˈnology** *noun* = ZYMOTECHNICS **E20.**

zymogen /ˈzʌɪmə(ʊ)dʒ(ə)n/ *noun*. **L19.**
[from ZYMO- + -GEN.]
An inactive enzyme precursor, which is converted into an enzyme when activated by another enzyme.
Comb.: **zymogen granule** a small dense vesicle containing zymogens, found in pancreatic cells that secrete digestive enzymes.
■ **zymoˈgenic** *adjective* producing an enzyme; now *spec.* causing fermentation: **L19.** **zyˈmogenous** *adjective* (*a*) (now *rare*) = ZYMOGENIC; (*b*) (of a soil micro-organism) dormant unless nutrients become available: **E20.**

zymosis /zʌɪˈməʊsɪs/ *noun*. Now *rare*. Pl. **-moses** /-ˈməʊsiːz/. **E18.**
[Greek *zumōsis* fermentation: see -OSIS.]
Fermentation; the development of a zymotic or infectious disease. Also, such a disease.

zymotic /zʌɪˈmɒtɪk/ *adjective & noun.* M19.
[Greek *zumōtikos* causing fermentation, formed as prec.: see -OTIC.]
▸ **A** *adjective.* Causing, caused by, or involving fermentation; *spec.* in MEDICINE, designating any infectious disease, formerly regarded as being caused by a process analogous to fermentation. M19.
▸ **B** *noun.* A zymotic or infectious disease. Now *rare.* M19.
▪ **zymotically** *adverb* (*rare*) M19.

zymurgy /ˈzʌɪməːdʒi/ *noun.* M19.
[from ZYM(O- + -*urgy*, after *metallurgy*, *thaumaturgy*.]
Orig., the art or practice of fermentation, in wine-making, brewing, and distilling. Now, the branch of biochemistry that deals with this.

Zyrian /ˈzɪrɪən/ *noun & adjective.* Also **Zyryan**. L19.
[from Russian *Zyryanin*: see -IAN.]
= KOMI.

zythum /ˈzɪθəm/ *noun. rare.* L19.
[Latin from Greek *zuthos*.]
Hist. A drink made in ancient times from fermented malt, esp. in Egypt.

Authors and publications quoted
References to the Bible and Shakespeare

Authors AND PUBLICATIONS QUOTED

Abbot, Robert, ?1588–?1662
Abbott, Claude Colleer, 1889–1971
Abbott, Edwin Abbott, 1838–1928
Abbott, John Stevens Cabot, 1805–77
Abercrombie, David, 1909–92
Abercrombie, John, 1726–1806
Abercrombie, Lascelles, 1881–1938
Abernethy, John, 1764–1831
Abingdon Herald
Abish, Walter, 1931–
Abney, William de Wiveleslie, 1844–1920
Abraham, Gerald Ernest Heal, 1904–88
Abrahams, Peter Hen;y, 1919–
Abrahams, Roger David, 1933–
Abrams, Meyer Howard, 1912–
Abse, Dannie, 1923–
Academy
Accountancy
Accountant
Achebe, Chinua, 1930–
Acheson, Dean Gooderham, 1893–1971
Achievement
Ackerley, Joe Randolph, 1896–1967
Ackland, Valen;ine, 1906–69
Ackroyd, Peter, 1949–
Acland, Thomas Dyke, 1809–98
Acorn User
Acton, Eliza, 1799–1859
Acton, Harold Mario Mitchell, 1904–94
Acton, John Emerin Dalberg, Lord 1834–1902
Adair, Gilbert, 1944–
Adair, James, *c* 1709–83
Adamic, Louis, 1899–1951
Adams, Andy, 1859–1935
Adams, Bronte Jane, 1963–
Adams, David Michael, 1933–
Adams, Douglas Noël, 1952–2001
Adams, Francis William Lauderdale, 1862–93
Adams, George, 1750–95
Adams, Henry, 1838–1918
Adams, Henry Cadwallader, 1817–99
Adams, James Truslow, 1878–1949
Adams, John, 1735–1826
Adams, John Quincy, 1767–1848
Adams, Pauline Ann, 1944–
Adams, Richard, 1920–
Adams, Samuel Hopkins, 1871–1958
Adams, Thomas, fl. 1612–53
Adamson, John William, 1851–1947
Adamson, Robert, 1852–1902
Addams, Jane, 1860–1935
Addis, John, d. 1876
Addison, Charles Greenstreet, d. 1866
Addison, Joseph, 1672–1719
Addison, Lancelot, 1632–1703
Ade, George, 1866–1944
Adler, George J., 1821–68
Adley, Charles Coles, *c* 1830–96
Advocate
Adweek (US)
Aeroplane
African Affairs
Agate, James Evershed, 1877–1947
Age (Melbourne)
Agee, James Rufus, 1909–55
Aiken, Conrad Potter, 1889–1973
Aiken, Joan, 1924–
Ainger, Alfred, 1837–1904
Ainsworth, William Harrison, 1805–82
Aircraft Illustrated
'Aird, Catherine' (Kinn Hamilton McIntosh), 1930–
Aird, Thomas, 1802–76
Air Enthusiast
Air Force Magazine
Air Gunner
Airgun World
Air International
Airy, George Biddell, 1801–92
Aitken, Jonathan William Patrick, 1942–
Akenside, Mark, 1721–70
Albee, Edward, 1928–
Albert, Arthur Lemuel, 1899–1990
Alcock, Vivien, 1926–
Alcott, Louisa May, 1832–88
Alday, John, fl. 1570
Aldington, Richard, 1892–1962
Aldis, Dorothy, 1896–1966
Aldiss, Brian Wilson, 1925–
Aldrich, Thomas Bailey, 1836–1907
Alexander, Alan, 1943–
Alexander, Cecil Frances, 1818–95
Alexander, Joseph Addison, 1809–60
'Alexander, Mrs' (Mrs Annie French Hector), 1825–1902
Algren, Nelson, 1909–81
Ali, Arif, 1935–
Ali, Rahmat, 1912–
Ali, Tariq, 1943–
Alice, princess of Great Britain and Ireland, 1843–78
Alison, Archibald, 1792–1867
Allan, Robert, 1774–1841
Allbeury, Theodore Edward le Bouthillier (known as 'Ted'), 1917–
Allen, Clifford Edward, 1902–
Allen, Ethan Nathan, 1904–93
Allen, Frederick Lewis, 1890–1954
Allen, Grant, 1848–99
Allen, Hervey, 1889–1949
Allen, Ira, 1751–1814
Allen, Marilyn, 1934–
Allen, William Sidney, 1918–
'Allen, Woody', (Allen, Stewart Konigsberg), 1935–
Alley, Norman William, 1895–1981
Allingham, Margery Louise, 1904–66
Allison, Dorothy E., 1949–
Allott, Kenneth, 1912–73
Allure
Allwood, Brian, 1920–44
Almon, John, 1737–1805
Alpers, Antony Francis, 1919–
Alter, Robert Bernard, 1935–
Alternative Service Book (1980)
Alther, Lisa, 1944–
Alvarez, Alfred, 1929–
Amadi, Elechi, 1934–
Amateur Gardening
Amateur Photographer
Amateur Stage
Ambit
Ambler, Eric, 1909–98
Ambrose, John, 1705–71
Ambrose, Katherine Charlotte (known as 'Kay'), 1914–71
American
American Accen;
American Banker
American Ethnologist
American Heritage
American Horticulturist
American Humorist
American Journal of Physiology
American Journal of Sociology
American Journal of Theology
American Mercury
American Naturalist
American Notes & Queries
American Poetry Review
American Quarterly
American Sociological Review
American Speech
Ames, Delano L., 1906–87
Amhurst, Nicholas, 1697–1742
Amiga Computing
Amiga User International
Amis, Kingsley William, 1922–95
Amis, Martin Louis, 1949–
Ammons, Archie Randolph, 1926–2001
Amor, Anne Clark, 1933–
Amory, Cleveland, 1917–98
Amory, Thomas, ?1691–1788
Ampleforth Journal
Amsterdam, Morey, 1914–
Amstrad PCW
Anderson, Barbara, 1926–
Anderson, Benedict Richard O'Gorman, 1936–
Anderson, Edward Lowell, 1842–1916
Anderson, George Kumler, 1901–80
Anderson (S. Carolina) *Independent*
Anderson, John Richard Lane, 1911–81
Anderson, Maxwell, 1888–1959
Anderson, Perry, 1938–
Anderson, Poul, 1926–2001
'Anderson, Rachel' (Rachel Bradby), 1943–
Anderson, Rasmus Björn, 1846–1936
Anderson, Robert Woodruff, 1917–
Anderson, Rufus, 1796–1880
Anderson, Scoular
Anderson, Sherwood, 1876–1941
Anderson, William, 1799–1873
Angadi, Patricia, 1914–2001
Angell, Roger, 1920–
Angelo, Henry, 1756–1835
Angelou, Maya, 1928–
Angier, Carole, 1943–
Angler
Angler's Mail
Animal World
Annabel
Annan, Noel Gilroy, 1916–2000
Annual Register
Ansoff, Harry Igor, 1918–
Anson, George, 1697–1762
Anstey, Christopher, 1774–1805
'Anstey, Frederick' (Thomas Anstey Guthrie), 1856–1934
Anstruther, Ian, 1922–
'Anthony, David' (William Dale Smith), 1929–
'Anthony, Evelyn' (Eve Stephens), 1928–
Anthony, Frank Sheldon, 1891–1925
'Anthony, J.' (John Anthony Paul Sabini), 1921–
Anthropology Today
Antiquarian Horology
Antiquaries Journal
Antique
Antique Collector
Antiques & Art Monitor
Antiquity
Apel, Willi, 1893–1988
Apollo
Appignanesi, Lisa, 1946–
Applied Linguistics
Aquaculture
Arab Times
Arber, Edward, 1836–1912
Arbuthnot, John, 1667–1735
Arch, Joseph, 1826–1919
Archaeological Journal
Archaeology
Archer, Jeffrey Howard, 1940–
Architects' Journal
Architectural Review
Archives of Neurology
Archives of Pediatrics
Ardagh, John Anthony, 1928–
Ardizzone, Edward Jeffrey, 1900–79
Ardrey, Robert, 1908–80
Arena
Arendt, Hannah, 1906–75
Argenti, John Ambrose, 1926–
Argosy
Argyle, John Michael, 1925–

Arizona Daily Star
Arkansas Historical Quarterly
Arkell, David, 1913–
'Arlen, Michael' (Dikran Kuyumjian), 1895–1956
Arlott, Leslie Thomas John, 1914–92
Armed Forces
Armstrong, Daniel Louis, 1900–71
Armstrong, Edward Allworthy, 1900–78
Armstrong, John, 1709–79
Armstrong, Margaret Neilson, 1867–1944
Armstrong, Neil, 1930–
Arnold, Edwin, 1832–1904
Arnold, Edwin Lester Linden, 1857–1935
Arnold, Frank Atkinson, 1867–1958
Arnold, Matthew, 1822–88
Arnold, Robert Arthur, 1833–1902
Arnold, Thomas, 1795–1842
Arnold-Forster, Mark, 1920–81
Arnott, Jake, 1961–
Arnott, Neil, 1788–1874
Arnould, Joseph, ?1814–86
Aronson, Alex, 1912–
Arrowsmith, Margaret Pat, 1930–
Art
Art & Artists
Art & Craft
Art & Design
Arthur, William, 1819–1901
Art in America
Artist
Art Line
Asbury, Herbert, 1891–1963
Ascham, Roger, 1515–68
Ash, Douglas, 1914–
Ash, William Franklin, 1917–
Ashbery, John, 1927–
Ashby-Sterry, Joseph, d. 1917
'Ashford, Jeffrey' (Roderic Graeme Jeffries), 1926–
Ashley, Bernard John, 1935–
Ashmolean
Ashworth, Andrea, 1969–
Asian Art
Asimov, Isaac, 1920–92
Askwith, Betty Ellen, 1909–
Asquith, Herbert, 1881–1947
Asquith, Herbert Henry, 1852–1928
'Astaire, Fred' (Frederick Austerlitz), 1899–1987
Astley, John Dugdale, 1828–94
ASTMS Industry News
Astrology
Athenaeum
Atherton, Gertrude Franklin, 1857–1948
Athill, Diana, 1917–
Athletic Journal
Athletics Today
Athletics Weekly
Atkins, Meg Elizabeth, 1932–
Atkins, Peter William, 1940–
Atkinson, John Christopher, 1814–1900
Atkinson, Kate, 1951–
Atlanta
Atlantic
Atlantic City
Atlantic Monthly
Attenborough, David Frederick, 1926–
Atterbury, Francis, 1662–1732
Attlee, Clement Richard, 1883–1967
Atwater, Mary Meigs, 1878–1956
Atwood, Margaret Eleanor, 1939–
Aubertin, John James, 1818–1900
Auchincloss, Louis Stanton, 1917–
Auckland, William Eden, Lord 1744–1814
Auckland Metro
Auckland Star
Audemars, Pierre, 1909–
Auden, Wystan Hugh, 1907–73
Audio Visual
Audubon
Audubon, John James, 1780–1851
Auel, Jean Marie, 1936–
Augarde, Anthony John, 1936–
Austen, Jane, 1775–1817
Auster, Paul, 1947–
Austin, Alfred, 1835–1913
Austin, John Longshaw, 1911–60
Austin, Sarah Taylor, 1793–1867
Austin, Vincent, 1929–
Australian Business
Australian Financial Review
Australian House & Garden
Australian Personal Computer
Authorized Version of the Bible (1611)
Autocar
Automobile Engineer
Autopart
Autosport
Avakian, George, 1919–
Avery, David, 1933–
Aviation News
Aviation Week
Ayckbourn, Alan, 1939–
Ayer, Alfred Jules, 1910–89
Ayerst, David George Ogilvy, 1904–
Ayliffe, John, 1676–1732
'Ayrton, Michael' (Michael Ayrton-Gould), 1921–75

B

Babington, Gervase, 1550–1610
Baby
Backhouse, Janet, 1938–
Backpacker
Back Street Heroes
Bacon, Francis, 1561–1626
Bacon, Nathaniel, 1593–1660
Bacon, Thomas, 1813–92
Badcock, John, fl. 1816–30 (*see also* 'Bee, Jon')
Baden-Powell, Robert Stephenson Smyth, 1857–1941
Bage, Robert, 1728–1801
Bagehot, Walter, 1826–77
Bagley, Desmond, 1923–83
Bagnall, Nicholas, 1924–
Bagnold, Enid, 1889–1981
Bagot, Richard, 1860–1921
Bailey, Henry Christopher, 1878–1961
Bailey, Hilary, 1936–
Bailey, Nathan, d. 1742
Bailey, Paul, 1937–
Bailey, Philip James, 1816–1902
Bailey, Trevor Edward, 1923–
Baillie, Donald Macpherson, 1887–1954
Baillie, Joanna, 1762–1851
Baillie, Matthew, 1761–1823
Baillie, Robert, 1599–1662
Bain, Alexander, 1810–77
Bain, Bruce, 1921–86
Bainbridge, Beryl, 1934–
'Bair, Patrick' (David Gurney), 1950–
Baird, Eric, fl. 1975
Baird, Irene, 1901–81
Baker, Dorothy, 1907–68
Baker, Elliott, 1922–
Baker, John Alec, 1926–
Baker, Nicholson, 1957–
Baker, Philip
Baker, Richard, 1568–1645
Baker, Samuel White, 1821–93
Bakewell, Robert, 1768–1843
Bakker, Elna Sundquist, 1921–
Balance
Balchin, Nigel, 1908–70
Baldwin, Faith, 1893–1978
Baldwin, James, 1924–87
Baldwin, Michael, 1930–
Baldwin, William, fl. 1547
Balfour, Arthur James, 1848–1930
Balfour, Edward, 1813–89
Ball, Robert Stawell, 1840–1913
Ballantine, Richard, 1959–
Ballantine, William, 1812–87
Ballantyne, David Watt, 1924–86
Ballantyne, Robert Michael, 1825–94
Ballard, James Graham, 1930–
Balogh, Thomas, 1905–85
Bancroft, Edward, 1744–1821
Bancroft, George, 1800–91
Bandinel, James, b. 1733
Banfield, Edmund James, 1852–1923
Bangladesh Times
Banker
Bankhead, Tallulah Brockman, 1902–68
Banks, Iain, 1954–
Banks, Lynne Reid, 1929–
Banks, Russell, 1940–
Bannerman, David Armitage, 1886–1979
Bannerman, Helen, *c* 1862–1946
Bannister, Roger Gilbert, 1929–
Banton, Michael Parker, 1926–
Banville, John, 1945–
Barber, Lynn, 1944–
Barber, Noël John Lysberg, 1909–88
Barber, Richard William, 1941–
Barckley, Richard, fl. 1598
Barclay, Alexander, ?1476–1552
Barclay, Florence Louisa, 1862–1921
Baret, John, d. ?1578
Bargrave, John, 1610–80
Barham, Richard Harris, 1788–1845
Baring, Maurice, 1874–1945
Baring-Gould, Sabine, 1834–1924
Barker, Arthur James, 1918–81
Barker, Christopher, b. 1815
Barker, George Granville, 1913–91
Barker, Paul, 1935–
Barker, Thomas, fl. 1651
Barling, Tom, 1936–
Barlow, David, 1943–
Barlow, Joel, 1754–1812
Barlow, William, d. 1613
Barnard, Robert, 1936–
Barnes, Djuna, 1892–1982
Barnes, Harold, 1908–78
Barnes, Julian Patrick, 1946–
Barnes, Peter, 1931–
Barnes, Robert Drane, 1933–
Barnes, William, 1801–86
Barnett, Anthony, 1942–
Barnett, Samuel Augustus, 1844–1913
Baron, Joseph Alexander, 1918–
Barr, Pat, 1934–
Barr, Robert, 1850–1912
Barr, Tony, 1921–
Barratt, Alfred, 1844–81
Barratt, Krome, 1924–
Barrett, Charles Leslie, 1879–1959
Barrett, Eaton Stannard, 1786–1820
Barrie, James Matthew, 1860–1937
Barrington, Jonah Paul, 1941–
'Barrington, Pamela' (Muriel Vere Mant Barling), 1904–
Barrough, Philip, fl. 1590
Barrow, Henry, ?1550–93
Barrow, Isaac, 1630–77
Barry, Alfred, 1826–1910
Barry, George, 1748–1805
Barry, Lording, 1580–1629
Barry, Philip, 1896–1949
Barstow, Stanley, 1928–
Barth, John Simmons, 1930–
Barthelme, Donald, 1931–1989
Bartholow, Roberts, 1831–1904
Bartlett, Ellis Ashmead, 1881–1931
Bartlett, William Henry, 1809–54
Barton, Alan, 1913–
Bartram, William, 1739–1823
Barzun, Jacques Martin, 1907–
Bascom, Harold, 1951–
Baseball Illustrated
Basse, William, d. 1653
Bate, Walter Jackson, 1918–99
Bateman, Colin, 1962–
Bates, Henry Walter, 1825–92
Bates, Herbert Ernest, 1905–74
Bath Herald
Batman, Stephen, d. 1584
Battiscombe, Esther Georgina, 1905–
Baum, Lyman Frank, 1856–1919
Bawden, Nina Mary, 1925–
Bax, Clifford, 1886–1962
Baxt, George Leonard, 1923–
Baxter, James Keir, 1926–72
Baxter, John, 1781–1858
Baxter, Richard, 1615–91
Bayer, William, 1939–
Bayley, John, 1925–
Bayliss, John Clifford, 1919–78
Baynard, Edward, b. 1641
Bayne, Peter, 1830–96
Bazaar Exchange & Mart
BBC Wildlife
Beadle, John Hanson, 1846–97
Beadle, Muriel, 1915–
Beano
Beardsley, Aubrey Vincent, 1872–98
Beaton, Cecil Walter Hardy, 1904–80
Beatson, Robert, 1742–1818
Beattie, Ann, 1947–
Beattie, James, 1735–1803

Beattie, Tasman, 1930–
Beaty, Arthur David, 1919–
Beaumont, William Blackledge (known as 'Bill'), 1952–
Beckett, Edmund, 1816–1905 (also quoted as E. Denison)
Beckett, Samuel, 1906–89
Beckford, Peter, 1740–1811
Beckford, William, 1760–1844
Becon, Thomas, 1512–67
Beddoes, Thomas, 1760–1808
Beddoes, Thomas Lovell, 1803–49
'Bede, Cuthbert' (Edward Bradley), 1827–89
Bedell, William, 1571–1642
Bedford, Arthur, 1668–1745
Bedford, Randolph, 1868–1941
Bedford, Sybille, 1911–
'Bee, Jon' (John Badcock), fl. 1816–30
Beebe, Lucius Morris, 1902–66
Beeching, Henry Charles, 1859–1919
Beekeeping
Beer, Patricia, 1924–99
Beer, Samuel Hutchison, 1911–
Beer, Stafford, 1926–
Beerbohm, Julius, 1854–1906
Beerbohm, Max, 1872–1956
Beeton, Isabella Mary, 1836–65
Behan, Brendan, 1923–64
Behn, Aphra, 1640–89
Behr, Edward, 1926–
Belben, Rosalind, 1941–
Belfast Telegraph
Belknap, Jeremy, 1744–98
Bell, Alan, 1942–
Bell, James, fl. 1551–96
Bell, Martin, 1918–78
Bell, Quentin Claudian, 1910–96
Bella
Bellamy, Edward, 1850–98
Bellamy, George Anne, ?1731–88
Belle (Australia)
Belloc, Joseph Hilaire Pierre René, 1870–1953
Bellow, Saul, 1915–
Belsham, William, 1752–1827
Belzoni, Giovanni Battista, 1778–1823
Bemis, Edward Webster, 1860–1930
Benford, Gregory, 1941–
Benham, William, 1831–1910
Benjamin, Park, 1849–1922
Benlowes, Edward, 1603–76
Benn, Tony, 1925–
Bennet, James Henry, 1816–91
Bennett, Agnes Maria, b. 1808
Bennett, Alan, 1934–
Bennett, Enoch Arnold, 1867–1931
Bennett, Geoffrey Martin, 1909–83
Bennett, John Godolphin, 1897–1974
Bennett, Ronan, 1956–
Benson, Arthur Christopher, 1862–1925
Benson, Edward Frederic, 1867–1940
Benson, Peter, 1956–
Benson, Richard Meux, 1824–1915
Bent, James Theodore, 1852–97
Bentham, Jeremy, 1748–1832
Bentley, Edmund Clerihew, 1875–1956
Bentley, Richard, 1662–1742
Bentley, Ursula, 1945–
Berckman, Evelyn Domenica, 1900–78
Beresford, James, 1764–1840
Beresford, Maurice Warwick, 1920–
Beresford-Howe, Constance, 1922–
Berger, John, 1926–
Berger, Thomas, 1924–
Bergman, Andrew, 1946–
Bergmann, Martin, 1913–
Berington, Simon, 1680–1755
Berkeley, George, 1685–1753
'Berlin, Irving' (Israel Baline), 1888–1989
Berlin, Isaiah, 1909–97
Berlins, Marcel, 1941–
Berman, Jeffrey, 1945–
Bermange, Barry, 1933–
Bermant, Chaim, 1929–
Bernal, John Desmond, 1901–71
Bernard, John, 1756–1828
Bernard, Richard, ?1567–1641
Berners, John Bourchier, Lord 1467–1533
Bernheimer, Charles, 1942–
Bernstein, Julius, 1839–1917
Berrill, Norman John, 1903–96
Berry, William, 1774–1851
Berryman, John, 1914–72
Berthoud, Roger, 1934–
Besant, Walter, 1836–1901
Best
Best, Thomas, fl. 1787
Beste, Raymond Vernon, 1908–
Best of Buster Monthly
Betjeman, John, 1906–84
Bettelheim, Bruno, 1903–90
Betterton, Thomas, ?1635–1710
Bevan, Aneurin, 1897–1963
Beveridge, Henry, 1799–1863
Beveridge, William, 1637–1708
Bewick, Thomas, 1753–1828
Bickers, Richard Leslie Townshend, 1917–
Bicycle
Bicycle Action
Biddlecombe, Terry, 1941–
Bierce, Ambrose, 1842–?1914
Bigg, Charles, 1840–1908
Big Issue
Bike Events
Biko, Stephen, 1946–77
Billingsley, John, 1657–1722
Billingsley, Nicholas, 1633–1709
Billings (Montana) *Gazette*
Binchy, Maeve, 1940–
Bingham, John Michael, 1908–
Bingley, William, 1774–1823
Binning, Hugh, 1627–53
Binyon, Robert Laurence, 1869–1943
BioFactors
Biological Bulletin
Biometrika
Birch, Samuel, 1813–85
Birch, Thomas, 1705–66
Bird, Golding, 1814–54
Bird, Isabella Lucy, 1831–1904
Birder's World
Birds Magazine
Bird Watching
Birdwood, George Christopher Molesworth, 1832–1917
'Birmingham, G. A.' (James Owen Hannay), 1865–1950
Birmingham Post
Birney, Earle, 1904–95
Birrell, Augustine, 1850–1933
Bischoff, James, 1776–1845
Bishop, Alan Gordon, 1937–
Bishop, Elizabeth, 1911–79
Bishop, James Alonzo, 1907–87
Bishop, Joseph Bucklin, 1847–1928
Bishop, Michael Lawson, 1945–
Bishop, Nathaniel Holmes, 1837–1902
Bissell, Richard Pike, 1913–77
'Black, Gavin' (Oswald Wynd), 1913–
Black, Ian Stuart, 1915–97
'Black, Lionel' (Dudley Raymond Barker), 1910–?80
Black, William, 1841–98
Black, William George, 1857–1932
Blackall, Offspring, 1654–1716
Black & White
Black Belt International
Blackburn, Thomas, 1916–77
Blackie, John Stuart, 1809–95
Blacklock, Thomas, 1721–91
Blackmore, Richard, d. 1729
Blackmore, Richard Doddridge, 1825–1900
Black Panther
Black Scholar
Blackstone, William, 1723–80
Blackwood, Caroline, 1931–1996
Blackwood, Helen Selina, 1807–67
Blackwood, John, 1818–79
Blackwood's Magazine
Black World
Blactress
Blades, James, 1901–99
Blagrave, Joseph, 1610–82
Blaine, James Gillespie, 1830–93
'Blair, Emma' (Iain Blair), 1942–
Blair, Hugh, 1718–1800
Blair, Peter Hunter, 1912–82
Blair, Robert, 1699–1747
'Blaisdell, Anne' (Barbara Elizabeth Linington), 1921–88 (*see also* 'Egan, Lesley', 'Shannon, Dell')
Blake, Forrester, 1912–
'Blake, Nicholas' (Cecil Day Lewis), 1904–72
Blake, William, 1757–1827
Blanchard, Paula, 1936–
Bleackley, Horace William, 1868–1931
Bleasdale, Alan, 1946–
Bligh, William, 1754–1817
Blincoe, Nicholas
Blishen, Edward, 1920–96
Blitz
Block, Lawrence, 1938–
Blomfield, Alfred, 1833–94
Blond, Anthony, 1928–
Blonsky, Marshall
Bloodworth, Dennis, 1919–
Bloomfield, Georgiana, 1822–1905
Bloomfield, Leonard, 1887–1949
Bloomfield, Robert, 1766–1823
Blount, Charles, 1654–93
Blount, Edward, fl. 1588–1632
Blount, Roy, 1941–
Blount, Thomas, 1618–79
Blower, Elizabeth, fl. 1788
Bloxam, Charles Loudon, 1831–87
Blue, Lionel, 1930–
Blue Jeans
Blueprint
Blues & Soul
Blume, Judy, 1938–
Blunden, Edmund Charles, 1896–1974
Blundeville, Thomas, fl. 1561
Blunt, John Henry, 1823–84
Blunt, Wilfred Scawen, 1840–1922
Bly, Robert, 1926–
Blyton, Enid, 1897–1968
BMX Action
Boardroom
Boards
Boate, Gerard, 1604–50
Bôcher, Maxime, 1867–1918
Boddam-Whetham, John, b. 1843
Boddy, Gillian, 1944–
Bodleian Library Record
Bodley, John Edward C., 1858–1925
'Bogarde, Dirk' (Derek Niven van den Bogaerde), 1921–99
Bogart, W. A.
Bogert, Lotta Jean, 1888–1970
'Boggis, David' (Gary Vaughan), 1946–
Bohr, Niels Henrik David, 1885–1962
Bohun, Ralph, *c* 1639–1716
Boland, Yasmin
'Boldrewood, Rolf' (Thomas Alexander Browne), 1826–1915
Bolger, Dermot, 1959–
Bolingbroke, Henry St John, 1678–1751
Boller, Paul Franklin, 1916–
Bolt, Robert, 1924–95
Bolton, Edmund Maria, ?1575–?1633
Bolton, Robert, 1572–1631
Bon Appetit
Bond, Edward Augustus, 1815–98
Bonfiglioli, Kyril, 1928–85
Bonington, Christian John, 1934–
Bonner, Geraldine, 1870–1930
Bonnycastle, John, ?1750–1821
Bookcase
Bookman
Book of Common Prayer (1662)
Books
Bookseller
Boorer, Wendy, 1931–
Booth, Martin, 1944–
Booth, Pat, 1942–
Booth, Stanley, 1942–
Boothby, Guy Newell, 1867–1905
Bordman, Gerald Martin, 1931–
Borlase, William, 1695–1772
Born, Max, 1882–1970
Borrow, George, 1803–81
Borwick, Malcolm, 1882–1957
Boscawen, William St Chad, 1854–1913
Bosse, Malcolm Joseph, 1926–
Boston
Boston, Thomas, 1677–1732
Boston Globe
Boston Herald
Boston Journal
Boston Sunday Globe
Boston Sunday Herald
Boston Transcript
Boswell, James, 1740–95

Botham, Ian Terence, 1955–
Bottomore, Thomas Burton, 1920–
Bottrell, William, 1816–81
Boult, Adrian Cecil, 1889–1983
Bourne, Geoffrey Howard, 1909–88
Boutell, Charles, 1822–77
Bouvier, John, 1787–1851
Bova, Benjamin William, 1932–
Bowden, Bertram Vivian, 1910–89
Bowen, Charles Synge C., 1835–94
Bowen, Elizabeth Dorothea Cole, 1899–1973
Bowen, Francis, 1811–90
Bowen, John Griffith, 1924–
Bowers, Fredson Thayer, 1905–91
Bowlby, Edward John Mostyn, 1907–90
Bowles, Paul Frederic, 1910–99
Bowles, Samuel, 1826–78
Bowles, Thomas Gibson, 1841–1922
Bowles, William Lisle, 1782–1850
Bowls International
Bowra, Cecil Maurice, 1898–1971
Bowyer, Jack Trory, 1927–
Boxing
Boxing News
Boxing Scene
Boycott, Geoffrey, 1940–
Boyd, Andrew Kirk Henry, 1920–
Boyd, William, 1952–
Boyer, Richard L., 1943–
Boyle, Andrew Philip, 1919–
Boyle, Charles, 1951–
Boyle, Jimmy, 1944–
Boyle, John, 1707–62
Boyle, Kay, 1902–92
Boyle, Robert, 1627–91
Boyle, T. Coraghesson, 1948–
Boy's Magazine
Boy's Own Paper
Bracken, Henry, 1697–1764
Brackenridge, Henry Marie, 1786–1871
Bradbury, John, fl. 1809
Bradbury, Malcolm, 1932–2000
Bradbury, Ray Douglas, 1920–
Bradby, Godfrey Fox, 1863–1947
Bradby, Mary Katharine, fl. 1920
Braddon, Mary Elizabeth, 1837–1915
Bradford, Barbara Taylor, 1933–
Bradford, Ernle Dusgate, 1922–86
Bradley, Omar Nelson, 1893–1981
Bradley, Richard, d. 1732
Bradshaw, Henry, d. 1513
Bragg, Melvyn, 1939–
Bragg, William Lawrence, 1890–1971
Bragge, Francis, 1664–1728
Brain
Brain, Walter Russell, Lord 1895–1966
Braine, John, 1922–86
Braithwaite, John Victor Maxwell, 1911–
Bramhall, John, 1594–1663
Bramson, Robert, 1925–
Bramwell, Vickie, fl. 1988
Brand, John, 1744–1806
Brande, William T., 1788–1866
Brandreth, Gyles Daubeney, 1948–
Branston, Frank, 1939–
Brasch, Charles, 1909–73
Brassey, Annie Allnutt, 1839–87
Brassey, Thomas, 1836–1918
Brathwait, Richard, ?1588–1673
Braun, Hugh Shornley, 1902–
Brautigan, Richard, 1935–84
Brawley, Ernest, 1937–
Bray, Denys de Saumarez, 1875–1951
Brayfield, Celia, 1945–
Brazil, Angela, 1868–1947
Brenan, Gerald, 1894–1987
Brent-Dyer, Elinor Mary, 1895–1969
Brereton, William, 1604–61
Brerewood, Edward, ?1565–1613
Brett, Michael John Lee, 1939–
Brett, Simon Anthony, 1945–
Brewer, John Mason, 1896–1975
Brewer, John Sherren, 1810–79
Brewerton, George Douglas, 1820–1901
Brewster, David, 1781–1868
Breytenbach, Breyten, 1939–
Brickhill, Paul Chester, 1916–91
Brides & Setting up Home
'Bridge, Ann' (Mary Dolling O'Malley), 1889–1974
Bridge Magazine
Bridges, Charles, 1794–1869
Bridges, Edward Ettingdene, 1892–1969
Bridges, Robert Seymour, 1844–1930
Bridges, Thomas, fl. 1759–75
Bridgman, Mary, 1853–1938
Brien, Alan, 1925–
Briggs, Asa, 1921–
Briggs, Charles Augustus, 1841–1913
Briggs, Julia, 1943–
Briggs, Susan Anne, 1932–
Brighouse News
Bright, James Franck, 1832–1920
Bright, John, 1811–89
Brill, Abraham Arden, 1874–1948
Brill, Steven, fl. 1978
Brimley, George, 1819–57
Brin, David
Brink, André, 1935–
Brinnin, John Malcolm, 1916–
Brinsley, John, fl. 1663
Bristed, Charles Astor, 1820–74
Bristowe, John Syer, 1827–95
British Birds
British Journal of Aesthetics
British Journal of Sociology
British Medical Bulletin
British Medical Journal
British Museum Magazine
Brittain, Vera Mary, 1893–1970
Brittan, Samuel, 1933–
Britten, Frederick James, 1843–1913
Broadcast
Broadcasting
Broadfoot, Barry, 1926–
Broadhurst, Henry, 1840–1911
Brock, Edwin, 1927–
Brockett, John Trotter, 1788–1842
Brockett, Linus Pierpont, 1820–93
Brodal, Alf, 1910–88
Brodie, Benjamin Collins, 1783–1862
Brodkey, Harold, 1930–1996
Brodrick, George Charles, 1831–1903
Brodsky, Joseph, 1940–96
Brome, Herbert Vincent, 1910–
Brome, Richard, ?1590–?1652
Bromfield, Louis, 1896–1956
Bronk, William, 1918–99
Bronowski, Jacob, 1908–74
Bronson, Po, 1964–
Brontë, Anne, 1820–49
Brontë, Charlotte, 1816–55
Brontë, Emily Jane, 1818–48
Brook, Peter, 1925–
Brooke, Frances, 1724–89
Brooke, Geoffrey Francis Heremon, 1884–1966
Brooke, Henry, ?1703–83
Brooke, Henry James, 1771–1857
Brooke, Jocelyn, 1908–66
Brooke, John, 1920–85
Brooke, Rupert Chawner, 1887–1915
Brooker, Bertram, 1888–1955
Brooke-Rose, Christine, 1923–
Brooklyn Eagle
Brookmyre, Christopher, 1968–
Brookner, Anita, 1938–
Brooks, Cleanth, 1906–94
Brooks, Frederick Tom, 1882–1952
Brooks, Thomas, 1608–80
Brooks, Van Wyck, 1886–1963
Broome, William, 1689–1745
Brougham, Henry Peter, 1778–1868
Broughton, Hugh, 1549–1612
Broughton, Rhoda, 1840–1920
Browder, Leon Wilfred, 1940–
Brown, Claude, 1937–
Brown, Frederic William, 1906–72
Brown, George Alfred, 1914–85
Brown, George Mackay, 1921–96
Brown, Hubert Rap, 1943–
Brown, Ivor John Carnegie, 1891–1974
Brown, James Alexander Campbell, 1911–64
Brown, James Baldwin, 1820–84
Brown, John, 1715–66
Brown, John Allen, 1831–1903
Brown, Michael Barratt, 1918–
Brown, Norman Oliver, 1913–
Brown, Peter Robert Lamont, 1935–
Brown, Robert Henry William, 1913–
Brown, Roger, 1941–
Brown, Thomas, 1633–1704
Browne, Sir Thomas, 1605–82
Browne, William, 1591–?1643
Brownie
Browning, Elizabeth Barrett, 1806–61
Browning, Robert, 1812–89
Brownjohn, Alan, 1931–
Brownjohn, John Nevil Maxwell, 1929–
Brubeck, Dave, 1920–
Bruccoli, Matthew Joseph, 1931–
Bruce, John, 1794–1880
Bruce, Lenny, 1925–66
Bruce, William, 1799–1882
Bruckberger, Raymond Leopold, 1907–98
Brugis, Thomas, fl. 1640
Bruton, Eric Moore, 1915–
Bryant, Jacob, 1715–1804
Bryant, William Cullen, 1794–1878
Bryce, James, 1838–1922
Bryson, William (known as 'Bill'), 1951–
Bubier, George Burden, 1823–69
Buchan, John, 1875–1940
Buchan, Peter, 1790–1854
Buchan, William, 1729–1805
Buchanan, Cynthia, 1937–
Buchanan, Jean Halket, 1947–
Buchanan, Robert, 1813–66
Buchanan-Gould, Vera, 1918–
Buchwald, Arthur, 1925–
Buck, George, d. 1623
Buck, Pearl Sydenstriker, 1892–1973
'Buckingham, David' (David Hugh Villers), 1921–
Buckland, Francis Trevelyan, 1826–80
Buckland, William, 1784–1856
Buckle, Henry Thomas, 1821–62
Buckley, Christopher Taylor, 1952–
Buckley, Theodore William Alois, 1825–56
Buckley, Wilfred, 1873–1933
Buckley, William Frank, 1925–
Buckman, Sydney Savory, 1860–1929
Bucks Examiner
Budd, George, 1808–82
Budgell, Eustace, 1685–1736
Budget (Ohio)
Building Today
Build It!
Bullein, William, d. 1576
Bullen, Frank Thomas, 1857–1915
Bulletin of Atomic Science
Bulletin of Hispanic Studies
Bulletin (Sydney)
Bullins, Ed, 1935–
Bullock, Alan Louis Charles, 1914–
Bulwer, John, fl. 1654
Bulwer-Lytton: *see* Lytton
Bunner, Henry Cuyler, 1855–96
Bunsen, Francis, 1791–1876
Bunting, Basil, 1900–85
Bunyan, John, 1628–88
Burchill, Julie, 1959–
Burge, Cyril Gordon, 1893–
Burger, Alfred, 1905–
'Burgess, Anthony' (John Anthony Burgess Wilson), 1917–93
Burgess, Melvin, 1954–
Burgon, John William, 1813–88
Burke, Carl F., 1917–
Burke, Colin, 1927–
Burke, Edmund, 1729–97
Burke, Thomas, 1887–1945
Burkitt, William, 1650–1703
Burl, Harold Aubrey Woodruff, 1926–
Burley, William John, 1914–
Burlington Magazine
Burn, Andrew, 1742–1814
Burn, Joshua Harold, 1892–1981
Burn, Richard, 1709–85
Burnand, Francis Cowley, 1836–1917
Burnet, Gilbert, 1643–1715
Burnet, Thomas, ?1635–1715
Burnett, Archibald, 1950–
Burnett, Frances Eliza Hodgson, 1849–1924

Burnett, William Riley, 1899–1982
Burney, Charles, 1726–1814
Burney, Fanny, 1752–1840
Burnford, Sheila, 1918–84
Burns, James Drummond, 1823–64
Burns, Olive Ann, 1924–90
Burns, Robert, 1759–96
Burritt, Elihu, 1810–79
Burroughs, Edgar Rice, 1875–1950
Burroughs, John, 1837–1921
Burroughs, William Seward, 1914–1997
Burrows, Edwin Grant, 1891–1958
Burt, Cyril Lodowic, 1883–1971
Burt, Mary Elizabeth, 1850–1918
Burthogge, Richard, ?1638–?1700
Burton, John Hill, 1809–81
Burton, Maurice, 1898–1992
Burton, Richard Francis, 1821–90
Burton, Robert, 1577–1640
Bury, Charlotte, 1775–1861
Busby, Roger, 1941–
Busby, Thomas, 1755–1838
Buses
Buses Extra
Bus Fayre
Bush, Ronald, 1946–
Bushnell, Horace, 1802–76
Business
Business Education Today
Business Franchise
Business Tokyo
Business Traveller
Business Week
Busk, Hans, 1772–1862
Butler, Alban, 1711–73
Butler, Arthur John, 1844–1910
Butler, Charles, d. 1647
Butler, Gerald Alfred, 1907–
Butler, Joseph, 1692–1752
Butler, Samuel, 1612–80
Butler, Thomas Belden, 1806–73
Butler, William Archer, ?1814–48
Butler, William Francis, 1838–1910
Butterworth, Michael, 1924–86
Buttes, Henry, fl. 16th cent.
Buying Cameras
Buzo, Alexander John, 1944–
Byars, Betsy, 1928–
Byatt, Antonia Susan, 1936–
Byfield, Richard, ?1598–1664
Byrne, John, 1940–
Byrom, John, 1692–1763
Byron, George Gordon, Lord, 1788–1824
Byron, Henry James, 1834–84
Bystander

C

Cabell, James Branch, 1879–1958
'Cable, Boyd' (Ernest Andrew Ewart), d. 1943
Cable, George Washington, 1844–1925
Cable, Mildred, 1878–1952
Cade, Anthony, ?1564–1641
Cage & Aviary Birds
Cain, James Mallahan, 1892–1977
Caine, Thomas Henry Hall, 1853–1931
Caird, Edward, 1835–1908
Caird, John, 1820–98
Cairncross, Alexander Kirkland, 1911–98
Calamy, Edmund, 1600–66
Caldcleugh, Alexander, d. 1858
Calder, Alan
Calder, Jennie, 1941–
Calder, Nigel David Ritchie, 1931–
Calderwood, David, 1575–1650
Caldwell, Erskine, 1903–87
Calhoun, John Caldwell, 1782–1850
California
California Bicyclist
Callaghan, Barry, 1937–
Callaghan, Leonard James, 1912–
Callaghan, Morley, 1903–90
Callender, Timothy, fl. 1975
Calverley, Charles Stuart, 1831–84
Calvert, Dennis
Calvert, Thomas, 1606–79
'Calvin, Henry' (Clifford Leonard Clark Hanley), 1922–
Cambrian News
Camden, William, 1551–1623
Camera Weekly
Cameron, Donald, 1939–
'Cameron, H. Lovett' (Caroline Emily Cameron), d. 1921
Cameron, Verney Lovett, 1844–94
Camp, William Newton Alexander, 1926–
Campaign
Campbell, Alistair, 1907–74
Campbell, Bruce, 1912–92
Campbell, George, 1824–92
Campbell, George Douglas, 1823–1900
Campbell, Ignatius Royston Dunnachie (known as 'Roy'), 1901–57
Campbell, Jane Montgomery, 1819–78
Campbell, John Gregorson, 1836–91
Campbell, Patrick Gordon, 1913–80
Campbell, Thomas, 1777–1844
Camplin, James Robert, 1947–
Canadian Journal of Linguistics
Canadian Magazine
Canal & Riverboat
Canaway, William Hamilton, 1925–
Canberra Times
Cancer Research
Canfield, Dorothy Frances, 1879–1958
Cannan, Joanna Maxwell, 1898–1961
Canning, Charlotte, 1827–67
Canning, George, 1770–1827
Canning, Victor, 1911–86
Canoeist
Capell, Richard, 1885–1954
Capern, Edward, 1819–94
Capes, Bernard, d. 1918
Cape Times
Capon, Paul, 1912–69
Capote, Truman, 1924–84
Captain
Car & Driver
Caravan Life
Caravan Magazine
Cardinall, Allan Wolsey, 1887–1956
Cardus, Neville, 1889–1975
Care, Henry, 1646–88
Carew, Jan Rynveld, 1925–
Carew, Richard, 1555–1620
Carew, Thomas, ?1598–?1639
Carey, Henry, ?1687–1743
Carey, John, 1934–
Carey, Peter, 1943–
Caribbean Quarterly
Caribbean Studies
Carkeet, David, 1946–
Carleton, George, 1559–1628
Carleton, William, 1794–1869
Carlson, Elof Axel, 1931–
Carlyle, Alexander, 1722–1805
Carlyle, Jane Baillie Welsh, 1801–66
Carlyle, Thomas, 1795–1881
Car Mechanics
'Carmichael, Harry' (Leopold Horace Ognall), 1908–79 (*see also* 'Howard, Hartley')
Carnegie, Andrew, 1835–1919
Carnegie, Dale, 1888–1955
Carpenter, Humphrey William, 1946–
Carpenter, Nathanael, 1589–?1628
Carpenter, Philip Pearsall, 1819–77
Carpenter, Richard, 1575–1627
Carpenter, William Benjamin, 1813–85
Carr, James Lloyd, 1912–94
Carr, John Dickson, 1906–77 (*see also* 'Dickson, Carter')
Carr, Lisle, fl. 1870
'Carrel, M.' (Lauran Bosworth Paine), 1916–
Carriage Driving
Carrier, Robert, 1923–
Carroll, James, 1943–
Carroll, John Bissel, 1916–
'Carroll, Lewis' (Charles Lutwidge Dodgson), 1832–98
Carroll, Martin, 1935–
Carson, Rachel, 1907–64
'Carstairs, John Paddy' (John Keys), 1914–70
Carswell, Catherine MacFarlane, 1879–1946
Carte, Thomas, 1686–1754
Carter, Angela Olive, 1940–92
Carter, Peter, 1929–
Carter, Philip Youngman, 1904–69
Cartwright, Christopher, 1602–58
Cartwright, George, 1739–1819
Cartwright, Justin James, 1944–
Cartwright, Thomas, 1535–1603
Cartwright, William, 1611–43
Carver, Raymond, 1939–
Cary, Alice, 1820–71
Cary, Henry Francis, 1772–1844
Cary, Joyce, 1888–1967
Caryl, Joseph, 1602–73
Casaubon, Méric, 1599–1671
Casement, Patrick John, 1935–
Casey, Gavin, 1907–64
Casey, John, 1939–
Cassell's Family Magazine
'Cassilis, Robert' (Michael Edwardes), 1923–
Castle, Barbara Anne, 1910–
Castlereagh, Robert Stewart, Viscount 1769–1822
Caswall, Edward, 1814–78
Catch
Cather, Willa Sibert, 1873–1947
Catholic Herald
Catlin, George, 1796–1872
Cattell, Raymond Bernard, 1905–98
'Caudwell, Christopher' (Christopher St John Sprigg), 1907–37
Caudwell, Sarah, 1939–
Causley, Charles, 1917–
Caute, John David, 1936–
Cavanaugh, Arthur, 1926–
Cave, Peter, 1940–
Cave, William, 1637–1713
Cavendish, George, 1500–?61
Caves & Caving
Caws, Mary Ann, 1933–
Caxton, William, ?1422–91
Cayley, Arthur, 1821–95
Cayley, George John, 1826–78
Cecil, Edward Christian David Gascoyne, 1902–86
'Cecil, Henry' (Cecil Henry Leon), 1902–76
Cell
Centlivre, Susannah, ?1667–1723
Century Magazine
Chabon, Michael, 1965–
Chadwick, William Owen, 1916–
Challoner, Richard, 1691–1781
Chalmers, George, 1742–1825
Chalmers, Mackenzie Dalzell, 1847–1927
Chalmers, Thomas, 1780–1847
Chaloner, Robert L., 1916–
Chamberlain, Lesley Veronica, fl. 1982
Chamberlayne, John, 1666–1723
Chambers, Aidan, 1934–
Chambers, Ephraim, ?1680–1740
Chambers, George Frederick, 1841–1915
Chambers, John David, 1805–93
Chambers, Robert William, 1802–71
Chambers, William, 1800–83
Chambers's Journal
Chamier, Frederick, 1796–1870
Chancellor, John, 1927–
Chandler, Raymond, 1888–1959
Chaney, Stephen G., 1944–
Chaplin, Charles, 1899–1977
Chaplin, Patrice, fl. 1984
Chaplin, Sid, 1916–86
Chapman, George, ?1559–1634
Chapman, Reginald Frederick, 1930–
Chapman, Robert William, 1881–1960
Chapman, Valentine Jackson, 1910–80
Chapone, Hester Mulso, 1727–1801
Chappell, Mollie, 1913–
Charles I, king of England, Scotland, and Ireland, 1600–49
'Charles, Gerda' (Edna Lipson), fl. 1971
Charles, Robert Henry, 1855–1931
Charlton, Mary, fl. 1794–1830
Charnock, Stephen, 1628–80
Chatelaine
Chatham, William Pitt, Earl of 1708–78
Chatwin, Charles Bruce, 1940–89
Chaucer, Geoffrey, ?1340–1400
Cheek, Mavis, 1948–
Cheetham, James Harold, 1921–
Cheever, John, 1912–82

Chemical Engineering
Chemistry in Britain
Chernin, Kim, 1940–
Cherry-Garrard, Apsley George Benet, 1886–1959
'Cherryh, C. J.' (Carolyn Janice Cherry), 1942–
Chesbro, George Clark, 1940–
Cheshire, David Frederick, 1935–
Chesney, George Tomkyns, 1830–95
Chess
Chesterfield, Philip Dormer Stanhope, Earl of 1694–1773
Chesterton, Gilbert Keith, 1874–1936
Cheyne, George, 1671–1743
Cheyne, Thomas Kelly, 1841–1915
Cheyney, Reginald Evelyn Peter, 1891–1951
Chicago
Chicago Daily News
Chicago Sun
Chicago Sun-Times
Chicago Tribune
Chichester, Francis, 1901–72
Child, Josiah, 1630–99
Childers, Robert Erskine, 1870–1922
Chile Pepper
Chillingworth, William, 1602–44
Chinese Economic Studies
Chitty, Susan Elspeth, 1929–
Choice
Cholmley, Hugh, 1600–57
Cholmondeley, Mary, 1859–1925
Chomsky, Avram Noam, 1928–
Choppin, Gregory Robert, 1927–
Christadelphian
Christian
Christian, Edward, 1788–1823
Christian Aid News
Christian Commonwealth
Christianity Today
Christian Science Monitor
Christiansen, Rupert Elliot Niels, 1954–
Christian Socialist
Christian World
Christie, Agatha Mary Clarissa, 1890–1976
Christie, Albany James, 1817–91
Chronicle
Church, Richard, 1893–1972
Church, Richard William, 1815–90
Churchill, Caryl, 1938–
Churchill, Charles, 1731–64
Churchill, Fleetwood, 1808–78
Churchill, Randolph Spencer, 1911–68
Churchill, Winston Leonard Spencer, 1874–1965
Church Times
Chute, Beatrice Joy, 1913–87
Cibber, Colley, 1671–1757
Ciccone, Madonna Louise, 1958–
Cincinnati Enquirer
Cisneros, Sandra, 1954–
Citizen (Ottawa)
City Limits
Civil Service Motoring
Clad, Noel Clovis, 1924–62
Claiborne, Craig, 1920–
Clancy, Lawrence Joseph, 1929–
Clancy, Thomas L., 1947–
Clapham, Alfred William, 1883–1950
Clapham, John, b. 1566
Clapperton, Richard, 1934–
Clare, Anthony Ward, 1942–
Clare, George Peter, 1920–
Clare, John, 1793–1864
Clarendon, Edward Hyde, Earl of 1609–74
Clark, Albert Curtis, c 1859–1937
Clark, Corbet
Clark, David, d. 1933
Clark, Douglas Malcolm, 1919–
Clark, Emily, 1795–1872
Clark, John Desmond, 1916–
Clark, John Grahame Douglas, 1907–
Clark, John Willis, 1833–1910
Clark, Kenneth McKenzie, 1903–83
Clark, Nigel George, fl. 1964
Clark, Ronald William, 1916–87
Clark, Thomas Alexander, 1937–
Clark, Walter van Tilburg, 1909–71
Clarke, Arthur Charles, 1917–
Clarke, Austin, 1896–1974
Clarke, Charles Cowden, 1787–1877
Clarke, James Freeman, 1810–88
Clarke, John, 1687–1734
Clarke, John Shipley, 1933–
Clarke, Laurence, fl. 1703–37
Clarke, Mary Cowden, 1809–98
Clarke, Peter Bernard, 1940–
Clarke, Samuel, 1599–1683
Clarke, William Malpas, 1922–
Classical Music
Classical Quarterly
Classical Review
Classic & Sportscar
Classic CD
Classic Racer
Clavell, James, 1953–94
Clay, Rosamund, 1944– (*see also* 'Oakley, Ann')
Cleary, Beverley, 1916–
Cleary, Brendan, 1958–
Cleary, Jon, 1917–
Cleeves, Ann, 1954–
Cleghorn, Sarah Norcliffe, 1876–1959
Cleland, John, 1709–89
Clements, Eileen Helen, 1905–
Clerke, Agnes Mary, 1842–1907
Cleveland, John, 1613–58
Climber
Clinton-Baddeley, Victor Clinton, 1900–70
Clissold, Frederick, fl. 1823
Clitheroe Advertiser & Times
Clodd, Edward, 1840–1930
Cloete, Edward Fairly Stuart, 1897–1976
Clothes Show Magazine
Clough, Arthur Hugh, 1819–61
Clouston, Joseph Storer, 1870–1944
Clubbe, William, 1745–1814
Club Cricketer
Club Tennis
Clune, Francis Patrick, 1894–1971
Clurman, Harold, 1901–80
Coarse Angler
Coarse Fishing
Cobb, John Boswell, 1926–
Cobb, Richard Charles, 1917–96
Cobb, Thomas, 1854–1932
Cobbett, William, 1763–1835
Cobbold, Thomas Spencer, 1828–86
Cobden, Richard, 1804–65
Cockayne, Thomas Oswald, 1807–73
Cockburn, Claud, 1904–81
Cockburn, Henry Thomas, 1779–1854
Cocker, Jarvis, 1963–
Cockshut, Anthony Oliver John, 1927–
Codrington, Robert, 1602–65
Cody, Liza, 1944–
Coe, Jonathan, 1961–
Coe, Malcolm James, 1930–
Coetzee, John M., 1940–
Cogan, Henry, fl. 1653
Cogan, Thomas, ?1545–1607
Cohen, Arthur Allen, 1928–86
Cohen, Leonard Norman, 1934–
Cohen, Philip, 1945–
Cohn, David Lewis, 1896–1960
Cohn, Nik, 1946–
Coin Monthly
Cokaine, Aston, 1608–84
Coke, Edward, 1552–1634
Coke, John, fl. 1549
Coke, Mary, 1726–1811
Coke, Roger, fl. 1696
Colborne, John, 1830–90
Colby, Averil, 1900–83
Colby, Frank Moore, 1865–1925
Cole, Henry Hardy, b. 1843
Cole, John Morrison, 1927–
Colebrooke, Henry Thomas, 1765–1837
Colegate, Isabel, 1931–
Coleridge, Ernest Hartley, 1846–1920
Coleridge, Hartley, 1796–1849
Coleridge, Henry Nelson, 1798–1843
Coleridge, Samuel Taylor, 1772–1834
Coles, William, 1626–62
Collier, Jeremy, 1650–1726
Collier, Richard Hugheson, 1924–
Collier's Quarterly
Collinges, John, 1623–90
Collingwood, Cuthbert, 1750–1810
Collingwood, Robin George, 1889–1943
Collingwood, William Gershom, 1854–1932
Collins, Anthony, 1676–1729
Collins, Edward James Mortimer, 1827–76
Collins, John, 1625–83
Collins, Mabel, 1851–1927
Collins, Merle, 1950–
'Collins, T.' (Joseph Furphy), 1843–1912
Collins, Wilkie, 1824–99
Collins, William, 1721–59
Collinson, William Edward, 1889–1969
Colman, George, 1762–1836
Coloradoan
Colquhoun, Patrick, 1745–1820
Columbus (Montana) *News*
Colvil, Samuel, fl. 1640–80
Colville, John Rupert, 1915–87
Colvin, Sidney, 1845–1927
Colwin, Laurie, 1944–92
Combat Handguns
Combe, Andrew, 1797–1847
Combe, William, 1741–1823
Commercials
Community Librarian
Company
Compton, Arthur Holly, 1892–1962
Compton-Burnett, Ivy, 1892–1969
Computer Bulletin
Computer Journal
Computers & the Humanities
Computer Weekly
Computerworld
Computing
Computing Equipment
Computing Review
Conacher, Brian, 1941–
Conan Doyle: *see* Doyle, Arthur Conan
Conder, Eustace Rogers, 1820–92
Coney, Michael Greatrex, 1932–
Confident Cooking
Congressional Globe
Congressional Record
Congreve, Richard, 1819–99
Congreve, William, 1670–1729
Conington, John, 1825–69
Conley, Robert Jackson, 1940–
Conn, Stewart, 1936–
Connecticut
Connell, Evan Shelby, 1924–
Connelly, Marcus Cook, 1890–1980
Conners, Bernard F., 1926–
'Connington, John Jervis' (Alfred Walter Stewart), 1880–1947
Connoisseur
Connolly, Cyril Vernon, 1903–47
Connor, John Anthony (known as 'Tony'), 1930–
'Connor, Ralph' (Charles William Gordon), 1860–1937
Conquest, Robert, 1917–
'Conrad, Joseph' (Teodor Josef Konrad Korzeniowski), 1857–1924
Conran, Caroline, 1939–
Conran, Shirley, 1932–
Conservation News
Constable, Henry, 1562–1613
Construction News
Consumer Reports
Contact
Contemporary Review
'Conway, Hugh' (Frederick John Fargus), 1847–85
Cook, Dutton, 1829–83
Cook, Eliza, 1818–89
Cook, James, Captain 1728–79
Cook, Theodore Andrea, 1867–1928
Cooke, Alfred Alistair, 1908–
Cooke, David Coxe, 1917–
Cooke, Deryck Victor, 1919–76
Cooke, Edward, fl. 1712
Cooke, John, fl. 1612
Cooke, Mordecai Cubitt, 1825–1914
Cooke, Rose Terry, 1825–1912
Cookery Year
Cook's Magazine
Cookson, Catherine, 1906–98
Cooley, Charles Horton, 1864–1929
'Coolidge, Susan' (Sarah Chauncey Woolsey), 1835–1905

Cooper, Colin Symons, 1926–
Cooper, Courtney Ryley, 1886–1940
Cooper, Duff, 1890–1954
Cooper, James Fenimore, 1789–1851
Cooper, Jeremy, 1946–
Cooper, Jilly, 1937–
Cooper, John Gilbert, 1723–69
Cooper, Kenneth Hardy, 1931–
Cooper, Susan Mary, 1935–
Cooper, Thomas, ?1517–94
Cooper, Thomas Mackay, 1892–1955
'Cooper, William' (Harry Summerfield Hoff), 1910–
Cooper, William Ricketts, 1843–78
Coover, Robert, 1932–
Copinger, Walter Arthur, 1847–1910
Copland, Aaron, 1900–90
Copland, Robert, fl. 1508–47
Coppard, Alfred Edgar, 1878–1957
Corbet, John, 1620–80
Corbet, Richard, 1582–1635
Corbett, Julian Stafford, 1854–1922
Corby, Herbert, 1911–
Corelli, Marie, 1854–1924
Coren, Michael, fl. 1989
Corlett, William, 1938–
Cornelisen, Ann, 1926–
Cornell, Katharine, 1898–1974
Cornhill Magazine
Cornish, Charles John, 1858–1906
Cornish Guardian
Cornishman
Cornish Times
'Cornwall, Barry' (Bryan Waller Proctor), 1787–1874
Cornwallis, Charles, 1738–1805
Cornwall Review
Cornwell, Bernard, 1944–
Cornwell, Patricia Daniels, 1956–
Correspondent
Coryat, Thomas, ?1577–1617
Cosgrave, Patrick John, 1941–
Cosmopolitan
Cotgrave, Randle, d. ?1634
Cotterell, Charles, ?1612–1702
Cottle, Basil, 1917–
Cotton, Charles, 1630–87
Cottrell, Alan Howard, 1919–
Coulter, John, fl. 1845
Coulton, George Gordon, 1858–1947
Country Companion
Country Homes
Country Life
Country Living
Countryman
Country Quest
Countryside Campaigner
Country Walking
County Cuisine
Coupland, Douglas, 1961–
Courier (N. Kent)
Courier & Advertiser (Dundee)
Courier-Mail (Brisbane)
Course, Edwin Alfred, 1922–
Courtier, Peter L., b. 1776
Courtney, William Prideaux, 1845–1915
Covarrubias, Miguel, 1904–57
Coverdale, Miles, 1488–1568
Coward, Noel Pierce, 1899–1973
Coward, Thomas Anthony, 1867–1933
Cowell, John, 1554–1611
Cowles, Frederick Ignatius, 1900–48
Cowley, Abraham, 1618–67
Cowley, Malcolm, 1898–1989
Cowper, Mary, 1685–1724
Cowper, Sarah, d. 1758
Cowper, William, 1731–1800
Cox, Charles Jeffrey (known as 'Jeff'), 1940–
Cox, David Roxbee, 1924–
Cox, Edward William, 1809–79
Cox, Greg, 1959–
Cox, Homersham, 1821–97
Cox, John Charles, 1843–1919
Cox, Michael Andrew, 1948–
Cox, Murray Newell, 1931–
Cox, Nicholas, *c* 1650–*c* 1731
Cox, Samuel, 1826–93
Coxeter, Harold Scott Macdonald, 1907–
Coxhead, Eileen Elizabeth, ?1909–79
Cozzens, James Gould, 1903–78
Crabbe, George, 1754–1832
Crace, Jim, 1946–
'Craddock, Charles Egbert' (Mary Noailles Murfree), 1850–1922
Crafts
Craig, Amanda, 1959–
Craig, Elizabeth Josephine, 1883–1980
Craig, Sandy, 1949–
Craig, William Marshall, fl. 1788–1828
Craik, George Lillie, 1798–1866
Cram, Ralph Adams, 1863–1942
Cramer, John Anthony, 1793–1848
Crane, Harold Hart, 1899–1932
Crane, Stephen, 1871–1900
Crankshaw, Edward, 1909–84
Cranmer, Thomas, 1489–1556
Crashaw, Richard, ?1613–49
Crawford, Francis Marion, 1854–1909
'Crawford, Robert' (Hugh Crauford Rae), 1935–
Crawley, Aidan Merivale, 1908–93
'Crawley, Rawdon' (George Frederick Pardon), 1824–84
Crawshay, Rose Mary, b. 1828
Creative Camera
Creative Review
Creech, Thomas, 1659–1700
Creighton, Mandell, 1843–1901
Crescendo
Crichton, Andrew, 1790–1855
Crichton, James Dunlop, 1907–2001
Crichton, Michael, 1942–
Crichton-Miller, Hugh, 1877–1959
Cricketer
Cricketer International
Cricket World
Crisis
Crisp, Norman James, 1923–
'Crisp, Quentin' (Denis Pratt), 1908–99
'Crispin, Edmund' (Robert Bruce Montgomery), 1921–78
Critchfield, Richard, 1931–94
Critchley, Julian, 1930–
Croall, Jonathan, 1941–
Crockett, David, 1786–1836
Crockett, Samuel Rutherford, 1860–1914
Crofts, Freeman Wills, 1879–1957
Croker, Bithia Mary, d. 1920
Croker, John Wilson, 1780–1857
Croll, James, 1821–90
'Crompton, Richmal' (Richmal Crompton Lamburn), 1890–1969
Cromwell, Oliver, 1599–1658
Cromwell, Thomas, ?1485–1540
Cronin, Archibald Joseph, 1896–1981
Cronin, Bernard, 1884–1968
Cronin, Vincent Archibald, 1924–
Crooke, Helkiah, 1576–1635
Crookes, William, 1832–1919
Croquet
Crosby, John Campbell, 1912–91
'Cross, Amanda' (Carolyn Heilbrun), 1926–
Cross, Brian
Cross, Ian Robert, 1925–
Crosse, Henry, fl. 1603
Crossley-Holland, Kevin, 1941–
Crossman, Richard Howard Stafford, 1907–74
Crowest, Frederick James, 1850–1927
Crowley, Robert, ?1518–88
Crowne, John, ?1640–1712
Cruise, William, d. 1834
Cruising
Crump, Arthur, fl. 1866
Crump, Barry John, 1935–
CU Amiga
Cudworth, Ralph, 1617–88
Cue World
Cullen, Countée, 1903–46
Cullen, William, 1710–90
Culpeper, Nicholas, 1616–54
Cumberland, Richard, 1732–1811
Cumberland News
Cumming, John, 1807–81
Cumming, Roualeyn Gordon, 1820–66
Cummings, Edward Estlin, 1894–1962
Cunningham, Daniel John, 1850–1909
'Cunningham, E. V.' (Howard Melvin Fast), 1914–
Cunningham, Henry Stewart, 1832–1920
Cunningham, Peter, 1816–69
Cunningham, William, 1849–1919
Cupitt, Don, 1934–
Cupples, Ann Jane, ?1839–98
Cupples, George, 1822–91
Curran, John Philpot, 1750–1817
Curran, Susan, 1952–
Currey, Ralph Nixon, 1907–2001
Currie, Elliot
Curtiss, Ursula Reilly, 1923–84
Curzon, Robert, 1810–73
Cusack, Ellen Dymphna, 1902–81
'Cushing, Paul' (Roland Arthur Wood-Seys), 1854–1919
Custom Car
Cutler, John Henry, 1910–2002
Cutler, Manasseh, 1742–1823
Cutting, Pauline Ann, 1952–
Cuyler, Theodore Ledyard, 1822–1909
Cycle World
Cycling
Cycling Weekly

D

Dacres, Edward, fl. 1640
Daedalus
Dahl, Roald, 1916–90
Daily Chronicle
Daily Colonist
Daily Express
Daily Graphic
Daily Graphic (Accra)
Daily Herald
Daily Mail
Daily Mirror
Daily Nation (Nairobi)
Daily News
Daily News (New York)
Daily Progress
Daily Sketch
Daily Star
Daily Telegraph
Daily Times (Lagos)
Dakyns, Henry Graham, 1838–1911
Dale, Alzina Stone, 1931–
Dale, Celia Marjorie, 1912–
'Dale, Frances' (Phyllis Nan Cradock), 1910–
Dale, Robert William, 1829–95
Dallas, William Sweetland, 1824–90
Dally, Peter John, 1923–
Dalrymple, James, fl. 1596
Dalrymple, William
Daly, Gay, fl. 1989
Dampier, William, 1652–1715
Dana, James Dwight, 1813–95
Dana, Richard Henry, 1815–82
Dance
Dance Theatre Journal
Dancing Times
Dandy
'Dane, Clemence' (Winifred Ashton), 1888–1965
Daniel, Glyn Edmund, 1914–86
Daniel, Samuel, 1562–1619
Darby, Henry Clifford, 1909–92
Dark, Eleanor, 1901–85
Darling, Malcolm Lyell, 1880–1969
Darts Player
Darwin, Charles Robert, 1809–82
Darwin, Erasmus, 1731–1802
Das, Manoj, fl. 1987
Dasent, George Webbe, 1817–96
Datamation
Dateline Magazine
Daubeny, Charles Giles Bridle, 1795–1867
Daughters of Sarah
Daus, John, fl. 1561
Davenant, William, 1606–68
Davenport, Robert, fl. 1623
David, Elizabeth, 1913–92
David, Hugh, 1954–
Davidson, Andrew Bruce, 1831–1902
Davidson, John, 1857–1909
Davidson, Lionel, 1922–
Davie, Donald Alfred, 1922–95
Davies, Andrew, 1936–
Davies, Charles, 1798–1876
Davies, Charles Maurice, 1828–1910

Davies, George Christopher, 1849–1922
Davies, Graeme John, 1937–
Davies, John, fl. 1662
Davies, Leslie Purnell, 1914–
Davies, Miles, 1662–1720
Davies, Paul Charles William, 1946–
Davies, Russell T.
Davies, William Henry, 1871–1940
Davies, William Robertson, 1913–95
Davin, Daniel Marcus, 1913–90
Davis, Andrew Jackson, 1826–1910
Davis, Angela Yvonne, 1944–
Davis, Charles Augustus, 1795–1867
Davis, George, 1939–
Davis, Jim, 1945–
Davis, Richard Harding, 1864–1916
Davison, Frank Dalby, 1893–1970
Davy, Humphry, 1778–1829
Dawkins, Richard, 1941–
Dawson, Alec John, 1872–1951
Dawson, Christopher Henry, 1889–1970
Dawson, George, 1821–76
Dawson, Jennifer, 1929–
Day, Angell, fl. 1586
Day, Clarence, 1874–1935
Day, George Edward, 1815–72
Day, Harvey, 1903–
Day, Thomas, 1748–89
Day Lewis: *see* Lewis, Cecil Day
Deacon, Richard, 1911–
'de Acton, Eugenia' (Alethea Brereton Lewis), 1749–1827
Deakin, James, 1929–
Dearmer, Geoffrey, 1893–1996
Debbie
Debonair (India)
Decanter
Decatur, Stephen, 1779–1820
Deccan Herald (Bangalore)
Decision
Dee, John, 1527–1608
Deedes, William Francis, 1913–
Deeping, Warwick, 1877–1950
Defence Update International
Defoe, Daniel, 1660–1731
Dehn, Paul Edward, 1912–76
Deighton, Leonard Cyril, 1929–
Dekker, Thomas, ?1570–?1641
'Delafield, E. M.' (Edmée Elizabeth Monica Dashwood), 1890–1943
de la Mare, Walter John, 1873–1956
Delaney, Shelagh, 1939–
Delany, Mary, 1700–88
de la Roche, Mazo, 1885–1961
Delaware Today
DeLillo, Don, 1936–
Delineator
De Lisser, Herbert George, 1878–1944
Delman, David, 1924–
De Lolme, Jean Louis, 1740–1806
de Man, Paul, ?1919–83
Demant, Vigo Auguste, 1893–1983
de Mauny, Erik, 1920–
Demille, Nelson Richard, 1943–
Deming, Philander, 1829–1915
De Morgan, Augustus, 1806–71
de Morgan, William Freud, 1839–1917
'Dempsey, Jack' (William Harrison Dempsey), 1895–1983
Denham, John, 1615–69
Denison, Edmund Beckett, 1816–1905 (also quoted as E. Beckett)
Denlinger, William Watson, 1924–
Denning, Alfred Thompson, Lord, 1899–1999
Dennis, John, 1657–1734
Dennis, John Gordon, 1920–
Dennis, Robert C., 1920–83
Denny, Ludwell, 1894–1970
Dent, Clinton Thomas, 1850–1912
'Dentry, Robert' (Osmar Egmont Dorkin White), 1909–91
De Quincey, Thomas, 1785–1859
Derby Diocesan News
Derham, William, 1657–1735
Desai, Anita, 1937–
de Sélincourt, Hugh, 1878–1951
de Seversky, Alexander Procofieff, 1894–1974
Deshpande, Shashi, 1938–
Design
Design Engineering
Design Week
de Silva, Colin, 1920–
Desoutter, Denis Marcel, 1919–
Detroit Free Press
Deutsch, Emanuel Oscar Menahem, 1829–73
Deutscher, Isaac, 1907–67
Deverell, William, 1937–
Devine, David McDonald, 1920–80
De Vinne, Theodore Low, 1828–1914
Devlin, Patrick Arthur, 1905–92
de Vries, Peter, 1910–93
Dewar, Michael, 1941–
Dewey, John, 1859–1952
de Windt, Harry, 1856–1933
Dexter, Colin, 1930–
Dhondy, Farrukh Jamshid, 1944–
Dialect Notes
Dibdin, Michael, 1947–
Dibdin, Thomas Frognall, 1776–1847
Dickens, Charles, 1812–70
Dickens, Monica Enid, 1915–92
Dickey, James Lafayette, 1923–97
Dickinson, Emily, 1830–86
Dickinson, Peter Malcolm, 1927–
Dickson, Adam, 1721–76
'Dickson, Carter' (John Dickson Carr), 1906–77
Dictionaries
Didcot Herald
Didion, Joan, 1934–
Diehl, Edith, 1876–1953
Digby, Kenelm, 1603–65
Digby, Kenelm Edward, 1836–1916
Digby, Kenelm Henry, 1800–80
Dilke, Charles Wentworth, 1843–1911
Dillard, Annie, 1945–
Dimensions
Diment, Adam, *c* 1945–
Dineley, David Lawrence, 1927–
Dinnage, Rosemary, fl. 1988
Direction
Dirt Bike
Dirt Rider
Dirty Linen
Discover
Discovery
Diski, Jenny, 1947–
Disraeli, Benjamin, 1804–81
D'Israeli, Isaac, 1766–1848
Dissent
Ditchburn, Robert William, 1903–87
Diver
Diver, Maud Katherine Helen, 1867–1945
Divine, Arthur Durham, 1904–87
Dixon, Norman Frank, 1922–
Dixon, Richard Watson, 1833–1900
Dixon, Robert Malcolm, 1939–
Dixon, William Hepworth, 1821–79
DIY Success!
DIY Today
Djoleto, Solomon Alexander Amu, 1929–
Dobell, Sydney Thompson, 1824–74
Dobie, James Frank, 1888–1964
Dobie, John Shedden, 1819–1903
Dobson, Henry Austin, 1840–1921
Doctorow, Edgar Laurence, 1931–
Dodd, Charles Harold, 1884–1973
Dodd, George, 1808–81
Dods, Marcus, 1834–1909
Dodsley, Robert, 1703–64
Dogworld
Doig, Ivan, 1939–
Do-It-Yourself
Dolan, Chris, 1958–
Doliner, Roy, 1932–
Dolman, John, fl. 1563
Donaldson, Frances Annesley, 1907–94
Donaldson, Greg
Donaldson, John William, 1811–61
Donaldson, Stephen, 1947–
Donleavy, James Patrick, 1926–
Donne, John, 1573–1631
Donnelly, Ross, ?1761–1840
Donoghue, Denis, 1928–
Donovan, Michael, d. 1876
Doolittle, Hilda, 1886–1961
Dopping, Olle, 1923–
Doran, John, 1807–78
Dorris, Michael Anthony, 1945–
Dos Passos, John Roderigo, 1896–1970
Doughty, Charles Montagu, 1843–1926
Douglas, Arthur, 1926–
Douglas, Gawin, ?1474–1522
Douglas, Howard, 1776–1861
Douglas, Keith Castellain, 1920–44
Douglas, Lloyd Cassel, 1877–1951
'Douglas, Norman' (George Norman Douglass), 1868–1952
Douglas, Robert Kennaway, 1838–1913
Douglas, William Sholto, 1893–1969
Douglas-Home, Alexander Frederick, 1903–95
Douglass, William, ?1619–1752
Dove, Patrick Edward, 1815–73
Dover, Kenneth James, 1920–
Dowden, Edward, 1843–1913
Dowden, John, 1840–1910
Dowell, Stephen, 1833–98
Down Beat
Down East
Downes, George, fl. 1822–32
Downey, Hal, 1877–1959
Downside Review
Dowson, Ernest Christopher, 1867–1900
Doyle, Arthur Conan, 1859–1930
Doyle, Richard, 1824–83
Doyle, Roddy, 1958–
Drabble, Margaret, 1939–
Drabble, Phil Percy Cooper, 1914–
Dragon Magazine
Drant, Thomas, d. ?1578
Drape, John William, 1811–82
Draper, Alfred Ernest, 1924–
Draw It! Paint It!
Draxe, Thomas, d. 1618
Drayton, Michael, 1563–1631
Dreiser, Theodore, 1871–1945
Dress
Dressage Review
Drew Magazine
Driscoll, Peter, 1942–
Drive
Driver, Samuel Rolles, 1846–1914
Drum
Drummond, Henry, 1851–97
Drummond, Ivor, 1929–
Drummond, June, 1923–
Drummond, Thomas, 1797–1840
Drummond, William, 1585–1649
Dryden, John, 1631–1700
DSNA Newsletter
D'Souza, Dinesh, 1961–
Dublin Review
Ducarel, Andrew Coltee, 1713–85
Duckett, Eleanor Shipley, ?1880–1976
Dudgeon, John Alastair, 1916–89
Dudgeon, Patrick Orpen, 1914–
Duff, Mountstuart Elphinstone Grant, 1829–1906
Duffy, Bruce, 1951–
Duffy, Maureen Patricia, 1933–
Dufton, William, d. 1859
Duggan, Alfred Leo, 1903–64
Duggan, Maurice Noel, 1922–74
Duke, Madelaine Elizabeth, 1925–
Dulles, John Foster, 1888–1959
du Maurier, Daphne, 1907–89
Dumfries & Galloway Standard
Dumfries Courier
Duncan, David, 1804–66
Duncan, James, 1804–61
Duncan, James Matthews, 1826–90
Duncan, Lois, 1934–
'Duncan, S. J.' (Sara Jeannette Cotes), 1861–1922
Duncan, Thomas William, 1905–87
Duncan-Jones, Austin Ernest, 1908–67
Duncombe, John, 1729–85
Duncumb, John, 1765–1839
Dunkin, Edwin, 1821–98
Dunmore, Helen, 1952–
Dunn, Douglas Eaglesham, 1942–
Dunn, Jane, fl. 1990
Dunnett, Dorothy, 1923–2001 (also quoted as D. Halliday)
Dunning, John, 1942–
Dunphy, Eamonn, 1945–
Dun's Review
Duppa, Richard, 1770–1831
Dupuy, Trevor Nevitt, 1916–95
D'Urfey, Thomas, 1653–1723

Durrant, Digby, 1926–
Durrell, Gerald Malcolm, 1925–95
Durrell, Lawrence George, 1912–90
du Toit, Alexander Logie, 1878–1948
Dwight, Timothy, 1752–1817
Dye, Dale A., fl. 1986
Dyer, John, 1699–1757
Dyke, Daniel, d. 1614
Dyke, Jeremiah, d. ?1620
Dykes, James Oswald, 1835–1912
'Dylan, Bob' (Robert Zimmerman), 1941–
Dyson, Edward George, 1865–1931

E

Élan
Eadie, John, 1810–76
Eager, Edward McMaken, 1911–64
Eagleton, Terence Francis, 1943–
Earbery, Matthias, fl. 1700
Earle, John, ?1601–65
Earle, Ralph, 1874–1939
Early Music
Early Music News
Earnshaw, Brian, 1929–
Earth Matters
Eastern Daily Press (Norwich)
Easton, Carol, 1933–
East (Tokyo)
Easyriders
Eaton, John, 1575–1641
Eaton, Mick, fl. 1981
Eaton, Theodore Hildreth, 1907–
EatSoup
Eberhart, Mignon Good, 1899–1996
Ebsworth, Joseph Woodfall, 1824–1908
Eby, Cecil De Grotte, 1927–
Ecclesiologist
Echard, Laurence A., ?1671–1730
Echewa, Thomas Obinkaram, 1940–
Echoes
Ecologist
Economist
Eddington, Arthur Stanley, 1882–1944
Eddison, Eric Rucker, 1882–1945
Edel, Joseph Léon, 1907–97
Edelman, Gerald Maurice, 1929–
Eden, Dorothy Enid, 1912–82
Eden, Richard, ?1521–76
Eden, Robert Anthony, 1897–1977
Edgar, Andrew, 1831–90
Edgar, David, 1948–
Edgar, John George, 1834–64
Edgar, Marriott, 1880–1951
Edgeworth, Maria, 1767–1849
Edib, Halidé, 1885–1964
Edinburgh Review
Edlin, Herbert Leeson, 1913–76
Educational Review
Edward VIII, king of Great Britain and Ireland, 1894–1972
Edwardes, Michael Owen, 1930–
Edwards, Ann Blanford, 1831–92
Edwards, David Lawrence, 1929–
Edwards, Edward, 1812–86
Edwards, John, 1637–1716
Edwards, Ruth Dudley, 1944–
Edwards-Jones, Imogen
'Egan, Lesley' (Barbara Elizabeth Linington), 1921–88 (*see also* 'Blaisdell, Anne', 'Shannon, Dell')
Egan, Pierce, 1772–1849
Egleton, Clive, 1927–
Einstein, Albert, 1879–1955
Eisenhower, Dwight David, 1890–1969
Ekwensi, Cyprian, 1921–
Eldred-Grigg, Stevan, 1952–
Electrical Review
Electrician
'Eliot, George' (Mary Ann Evans), 1819–80
Eliot, Thomas Stearns, 1888–1965
Elis, Islwyn Ffowc, 1924–
Elizabeth I, queen of England and Ireland, 1533–1603
Elkin, Stanley, 1930–
Elle
Ellicott, Charles John, 1819–1905
Elliot, John Herbert, 1918–97
Elliot, Robert Henry, 1837–1914
Elliott, Janice, 1931–95
Elliott, Sumner Locke, 1917–91
Ellis, Alexander John, 1814–90
Ellis, Alfred Burton, 1852–94
'Ellis, Alice Thomas' (Anna Margaret Haycraft), 1932–
Ellis, Henry, 1777–1869
Ellis, Robinson, 1834–1913
Ellis, William, d. 1758
Ellis-Fermor, Una, 1894–1958
Ellison, Ralph Waldo, 1914–94
Ellmann, Lucy, 1956–
Ellmann, Richard David, 1918–87
Ellroy, James, 1948–
Ellwood, Thomas, 1639–1713
Elmhirst, Edward Pennell, 1845–1916
Elphinston, James, 1721–1809
Elphinstone, Mountstuart, 1779–1859
Elstob, Elizabeth, 1683–1756
Elton, Ben, 1959–
Elyot, Thomas, ?1499–1546
Embleton, Clifford, 1931–
EMBO Journal
Embroidery
Emecheta, Buchi, 1944–
Emerson, Ralph Waldo, 1803–82
Empire
Empson, William, 1906–84
Emu
Encounter
Encyclopaedia Britannica (15th ed., 1974)
Endeavour
Engel, Carl, 1818–82
Engineer
Engineering
Engineering Today
England, Barry, 1934–
English Historical Review
English Language Teaching
English Review
English Studies
English World-Wide
Ennion, Eric Arnold Roberts, 1900–81
Enright, Anne, 1962–
Enright, Dennis Joseph, 1920–
Entertainment Weekly
Entick, John, ?1703–73
Entwistle, William James, 1895–1952
Environment Now
Epstein, Joseph, 1937–
Equals
Erdmann, Paul E., 1932–
Erdrich, Louise, 1954–
Erikson, Erik Homburger, 1902–94
Erondelle, Pierre, fl. 1586–1609
Erskine, Ebenezer, 1680–1754
Erskine, John, 1721–1803
'Erskine, Margaret' (Margaret Wetherby Williams), 1925–
Esposito, John Louis, 1940–
Esquire
Essays in Criticism
Essentials
Essex Review
Essex Weekly News
Esslin, Martin Julius, 1918–2002
Estates Gazette
Estcourt, Richard, 1668–1712
Estleman, Loren D., 1952–
Etherege, George, ?1653–91
Etonian
EuroBusiness
European
European Investor
European Sociological Review
Evangelical Times
Evans, Arthur John, 1851–1941
Evans, Emyr Estyn, 1905–89
Evans, George Ewart, 1909–88
Evans, Glyn, 1933–
Evans, Harold Matthew, 1928–
Evans, John Davies, 1925–
Evans, Lewis, d. 1756
Evans, Philip, 1944–
Evans, Sebastian, 1830–1909
Evans, Sian, 1912–
Evans-Pritchard, Edward Evan, 1902–73
Evelyn, John, 1620–1706
Evening Advertiser (Swindon)
Evening News
Evening News (Worcester)
Evening Post (Bristol)
Evening Post (Nottingham)
Evening Press (Eire)
Evening Standard
Evening Telegram (Newfoundland)
Evening Telegraph (Grimsby)
Evening Times (Glasgow)
Ewart, Gavin Buchanan, 1916–95
Ewing, Juliana Horatia, 1841–85
Examiner
Exley, Frederick Earl, 1929–
Expositor
Expression!
Express (Pennsylvania)
Eysenck, Hans Jurgen, 1916–97
Ezekiel, Nissam, 1924–

F

Faber, Frederick William, 1814–63
Faber, Geoffrey Cust, 1889–1961
Faber, George Stanley, 1773–1854
Fabyan, Robert, d. 1513
Face
Fairbairn, Andrew Martin, 1838–1912
Fairbairn, Patrick, 1805–74
Fairbairn, William, 1789–1874
Fairbairn, William Ronald Dodds, 1889–1964
Fairfax, Edward, d. 1635
Fairfax, Nathaniel, 1637–90
Fairfax, Thomas, 1612–71
Fairweather, Eileen, 1954–
Falconbridge, Alexander, d. 1792
'Falconer, Richard' (William Rufus Chetwood), d. 1766
Falconer, William, 1732–69
Family Circle
Family Practice
Fane, Julian Henry Charles, 1827–70
Fanshaw, Richard, 1608–66
Fantasy
Faraday, Michael, 1791–1867
Farah, Nuruddin, 1945–
Far Eastern Economic Review
Farjeon, Benjamin Leopold, 1833–1903
Farjeon, Eleanor, 1881–1965
Farmer, Penelope, 1939–
Farmer & Stockbreeder
Farmer's Magazine
Farmers Weekly
Farmers Weekly (Durban)
Farm Machinery
Farquhar, George, 1678–1707
Farrar, Frederick William, 1831–1903
Farrar-Hockley, Anthony Heritage, 1924–
Farrell, Brian Anthony, 1912–
Farrell, James Gordon, 1935–79
Farrell, James Thomas, 1904–79
Farrell, John Philip, 1939–
Farrell, Kathleen Amy, 1912–
Farrer, Austin Marsden, 1904–68
Farrer, Reginald John, 1880–1920
Farris, John, 1940–
Fast, Howard Melvin, 1914– (*see also* 'Cunningham, E. V.')
Fast Forward
Faulkner, John Meade, 1858–1932
Faulkner, William, 1897–1962
Faulks, Sebastian, 1953–
Fawcett, Henry, 1833–84
Fawkes, Francis, 1720–77
Fearon, Henry Bradshaw, b. *c* 1770
Feather, Leonard Geoffrey, 1914–94
Feather, William, 1889–1981
Featley, Daniel, 1582–1645
Federal Reporter
Feinstein, Elaine Barbara, 1930–
Felstead, Sidney Theodore, b. 1888
Feltham, Owen, ?1602–68
Felton, Cornelius Conway, 1807–62
Femina
Fenelon, Kevin Gerard, 1898–1983
Fenn, George Manville, 1831–1909
Fennell, John Greville, 1807–85
Fenton, Alexander, 1929–
Fenton, Elijah, 1683–1730
Fenton, Geoffrey, ?1539–1608
Fenton, James, 1949–
Fentick, Edwin Hurry, 1856–1905
Fenwick, Elizabeth, 1920–
Ferber, Edna, 1887–1968
Ferguson, Hugh, 1950–74
Ferguson, James, 1710–76
Ferguson, Patricia, fl. 1985
Ferguson, Robert, 1637–1714

Fergusson, Bernard Edward, 1911–80
Fergusson, Francis, 1904–86
Fergusson, Harvey, 1890–1971
Fergusson, James, 1808–86
Fergusson, Robert, 1750–74
Fermor, Patrick Michael Leigh, 1915–
Ferrari, Lilie
'Ferrars, Elizabeth' (Morna Doris Brown), 1907–95
Ferriar, John, 1764–1815
Ferrier, James Frederick, 1808–64
Ferrier, Susan Edmonstone, 1782–1854
Ferris, Timothy, 1944–
FHM
Fiction Magazine
Fiddes, Richard, 1671–1725
Fiddick, Peter, 1938–
Fiedler, Leslie Aaron, 1917–
Field
Field, Eugene, 1850–95
Field, Henry Martyn, 1822–1907
'Field, Joanna' (Marion Milner), 1900–
Field, Mary Katherine Keemle (known as 'Kate'), 1838–96
Field, William, 1768–1851
Field & Stream
Fielding, Helen, 1958–
Fielding, Henry, 1707–54
Fielding, Sarah, 1710–68
'Fielding, Xan' (Alexander Wallace Fielding), 1918–91
Fiennes, Celia, 1662–1741
Fiennes, Gerard Francis, 1906–85
Figes, Eva, 1932–
Film Monthly
Financial Review (Melbourne)
Financial Times
Financial Weekly
Finch, Henry, d. 1625
Fincham, John Robert Stanley, 1926–
Fine, Anne, 1947–
Fine, Reuben, 1914–93
Finescale Modeler
Fingleton, Jack, 1908–81
Finlayson, Hedley Herbert, 1895–
Finlayson, Roderick, 1904–
Finlayson, Thomas Campbell, 1836–93
Firbank, Arthur Annesley Ronald, 1886–1926
First Base
Firth, Raymond William, 1901–2002
Fisher, Graham George, 1926–
Fisher, Herbert Albert Laurens, 1865–1940
Fisher, John, 1459–1535
Fisher, Seymour, 1922–
Fisk, Robert, 1946–
Fiske, John, 1842–1901
Fiske, Minnie Maddern, 1865–1932
Fitch, Joshua Girling, 1824–1903
Fitter, Richard Sidney Richmond, 1913–
Fitzgeorge-Parker, Timothy, 1920–
FitzGerald, Edward, 1809–83
Fitzgerald, Frances, 1940–
Fitzgerald, Francis Scott Key, 1896–1940
Fitzgerald, Penelope, 1916–2000
Fitzgerald, Robert Allan, 1834–81
Fitzgibbon, Mary Agnes, 1851–1915
Fitzgibbon, Robert Louis Constantine, 1919–83
Fitzherbert, Margaret, 1942–86
Fitzpatrick, William John, 1830–95
Fixx, James Fuller, 1932–84
Flanagan, Mary, 1943–
Flandrau, Charles Macomb, 1871–1938
Flavel, John, ?1630–91
Flecker, James Elroy, 1884–1915
Fleming, Abraham, ?1552–1607
Fleming, Ian, 1908–64
Fleming, Joan Margaret, 1908–80
Fleming, John Ambrose, 1849–1945
Fleming, John Gunther, 1919–
Fleming, Nicholas, 1939–
Fleming, Robert Peter, 1907–71
Fletcher, David, 1940–
Fletcher, Giles, 1546–1611
Fletcher, John, 1579–1625
Fletcher, Phineas, 1582–1650
Flex
Flexner, James Thomas, 1908–
Flexner, Stuart Berg, 1928–
Flicks
Flight International
Flint, Austin, 1836–1915
Flintshire Leader
Florio, John, ?1553–1625
Florist's Journal
Flowers
Floyer, Ernest Ayscoghe, 1852–1903
Flying
'Flynt, Josiah' (Josiah Flynt Willard), 1869–1907
Flypast
Fly Rod & Reel
Focus
Foldes, Andor, 1913–
Folkingham, William, fl. 1610
Folk Roots
Fonblanque, Albany, 1793–1872
Fonda, Jane, 1937–
'Fonteyn, Margot' (Margaret Hookham), 1919–91
Food & Wine
Foot, Michael Mackintosh, 1913–
Foot, Michael Richard Daniell, 1919–
Football Monthly
Football News
Foote, Samuel, 1720–77
Footloose
Forbes
Forbes, Archibald, 1838–1900
Forbes, Bryan, 1926–
Forbes, Colin, 1923–
Forbes, Edward, 1815–54
Forbes, Frances Alice Monica, 1869–1936
Forbes, Gordon Sullivan, 1820–93
Forbes, Henry Ogg, 1851–1932
Forbes, James, 1749–1819
Ford, Charles, 1908–
Ford, Ford Madox, 1873–1939 (also quoted as F. M. Hueffer)
Ford, John, fl. 1639
Ford, Richard, 1796–1858
Ford, Sewell, 1868–1946
Fordyce, James, 1720–96
Forester, Cecil Scott, 1899–1966
Forestry
Forman, Harry Burton, 1842–1917
Forrest, John, 1847–1918
Forrest, Thomas, ?1729–?1802
Forrest, William, fl. 1530–81
Forsey, Eugene Alfred, 1904–91
Forster, Edward, 1769–1828
Forster, Edward Morgan, 1879–1970
Forster, Henry Rumsey, 1815–84
Forster, Margaret, 1938–
Forster, Thomas Ignatius Maria, 1789–1860
Forsyth, Frederick, 1938–
Forsyth, Joseph, 1763–1815
Forsyth, Peter Taylor, 1848–1921
Forsyth, Robert, 1776–1846
Forsyth, William, 1812–99
Fortescue, John, ?1394–?1476
Fortescue, Winifred, 1888–1951
Fortnightly Review
Fortnum, Charles Drury Edward, 1820–99
Fortune
Forum
Foster, Alan Dean, 1946–
Foster, Brian, 1920–
Foster, Harry La Tourette, 1895–1932
Foster, Jack Stroud, 1912–
Foster, John, 1770–1843
Foster, Michael, 1836–1907
Fotherby, Martin, 1559–1620
Fothergill, Jessie, 1851–91
Foulis, Henry, 1638–69
'Fowler, Gene' (Eugene Devlan), 1890–1960
Fowler, Henry Watson, 1858–1933
Fowler, Joseph Thomas, 1833–1924
Fowler, Thomas, 1832–1904
Fowler, William Warde, 1847–1921
Fowles, John, 1926–
Fownes, George, 1815–49
Fox, Robin James Lane, 1946–
Foxe, John, 1516–87
Frame, Donald Murdoch, 1911–
Frame, Janet, 1924–
Frame, Ronald, 1953–
'France, Ann' (Jennifer Ann Duncan), 1940–89
Francis, Arthur, 1944–
Francis, Clare, 1946–
Francis, Dick: *see* Francis, Richard Stanley
Francis, Francis, 1822–86
Francis, George William, 1800–65
Francis, John, 1810–86
Francis, Peter
Francis, Richard Stanley (known as 'Dick'), 1920–
Franck, Richard, ?1624–1708
Frank, André Gunder, 1929–
Frankau, Sydney Pamela, 1908–67
Franklin, Benjamin, 1706–90
Franklin, Kenneth James, 1897–1966
Franklin, Robert Michael, 1944–
Franklin, Stella Maria Sarah Miles Lampe, 1879–1954
Fraser, Antonia, 1932–
Fraser, David William, 1920–
Fraser, George Macdonald, 1925–
Fraser, George Sutherland, 1915–80
Fraser, Hugh, 1815–1922
'Fraser, James' (Alan White), 1922–
Fraser, James Baillie, 1783–1856
Fraser, Rebecca Rose, 1957–
Fraser's Magazine
Frater, Alexander, 1937–
Frayn, Michael, 1933–
Frazer, James George, 1854–1941
Freedman, Samuel G., fl. 1990
Freedomways
Freeland, Cynthia
Freeling, Nicolas, 1927–
'Freeman, Cynthia' (Bea Feinberg), ?1915–88
Freeman, Edward Augustus, 1823–92
Freeman, Gillian, 1929–
Freeman, John, 1880–1929
Freeman, Richard Austin, 1862–1943
Free Post (Detroit)
Freer, Martha Walker, 1822–88
Free-thinker
Freetime
Freight Distribution
Freight Guide
Freilich, Charles, 1905–55
Freke, William, 1662–1744
Fremantle, William Henry, 1831–1916
Fremdsprachen
Fremlin, Celia Margaret, 1914–
Fremont, John Charles, 1813–90
French, Herbert Stanley, 1875–1957
French, John, ?1616–57
French, Marilyn, 1929–
Frendz
Friedan, Betty Naomi, 1921–
Friedman, Michael Jan, 1955–
Friedman, Philip, 1944–
Friedrich, Carl Joachim, 1901–84
Friedrichsen, George Washington Salisbury, 1886–1979
Friend
Friends' Quarterly
Frisby, Terence Peter Michael, 1932–
Friswell, James Hain, 1825–78
Frith, John, 1503–33
Fromm, Erich, 1900–80
Frondel, Clifford, 1907–
Frost, Robert Lee, 1874–1963
Froude, James Anthony, 1818–94
Froude, Richard Hurrell, 1803–36
Frutkin, Mark
Fry, Alan, 1931–
Fry, Christopher, 1907–
Fry, Dennis Butler, 1907–83
Fry, Roger Eliot, 1866–1934
Fry, Stephen, 1957–
Frye, Herman Northrop, 1912–91
Frye, Richard Nelson, 1920–
Fryer, John, fl. 1698
Fugard, Athol Harold, 1932–
Fugard, Sheila, 1932–
Fulbecke, William, 1560–?1603
Fulbright, James William, 1905–95
Fulke, William, 1538–89
Fuller, Claude, 1872–1928
Fuller, Francis, 1670–1706
Fuller, John, 1937–
Fuller, Peter Michael, 1947–
Fuller, Roy Broadbent, 1912–91
Fuller, Thomas, 1608–61
Funny Fortnightly

G

H

Harmer, Thomas, 1714–88
Harper, John Lauder, 1925–
Harper, Thomas Norton, 1821–93
Harpers & Queen
Harper's Bazaar
Harper's Magazine
Harpsfield, Nicholas, ?1519–75
Harries, Richard Douglas, 1936–
Harris, Bartholomew, fl. 1659
Harris, Frank, 1856–1931
Harris, Geraldine, 1951–
Harris, James, 1709–80
Harris, James Howard, 1807–89
Harris, Joanne, 1964–
Harris, Joel Chandler, 1848–1908
Harris, Joseph, 1702–64
Harris, Miriam Coles, 1834–1925
Harris, Mollie, fl. 1969
Harris, Robert, 1581–1658
Harris, Theodore Wilson, 1921–
Harrison, Constance Cary, 1843–1920
Harrison, Frederick, 1831–1923
Harrison, Henry Sydnor, 1880–1930
Harrison, Jane Ellen, 1850–1928
Harrison, William, 1534–93
Harrogate Advertiser
Harsent, David, 1942–
Hart, Albert Bushnell, 1854–1943
Hart, Cyril, 1923–
Hart-Davis, Duff, 1936–
Harte, Francis Bret, 1836–1902
Harte, Walter, 1709–74
Hartley, David, 1705–57
Hartley, John, 1839–1915
Hartley, Leslie Poles, 1895–1972
Hartley Edwards, Elwyn, 1927–
Hartwig, Georg Ludwig, 1813–80
'Harvester, Simm' (Henry St John Clair Gibbs), 1909–75
Harvey, Gabriel, ?1545–1630
Harvey, John Robert, 1942–
Harvey, Thomas Edmund, 1875–1955
Harvey, William Fryer, 1885–1937
Haskell, Arnold Lionel, 1903–81
Hasluck, Peter Nooncree, 1854–1931
Hassel, Sven, 1917–
Hastings, MacDonald, 1909–82
Hastings, Selina, 1945–
Haston, Dougal, 1940–77
Hatcher, William Spottswood, 1935–
Hatton, Christopher, 1540–91
Hatton, Joseph, 1841–1907
Haughey, Charles James, 1925–
Haughton, Sidney Henry, 1888–1982
Havers, George, fl. 1665
Havighurst, Walter, 1901–94
Haweis, Hugh Reginald, 1839–1901
Hawes, James M., 1960–
Hawgood, John Arkas, 1905–71
Hawker, Peter, 1786–1853
Hawker, Robert Stephen, 1803–75
Hawkes, Jessie Jacquetta, 1910–96
Hawkesworth, John, 1715–73
Hawking, Stephen William, 1942–
Hawkins, Francis, 1628–81
Hawkins, Henry, 1817–1907
Hawkins, John, 1532–95
Hawkins, Laetitia Matilda, 1760–1835
Hawkins, Richard, *c* 1560–1622
Hawkins, Tristan
Hawthorne, Julian, 1846–1934
Hawthorne, Nathaniel, 1804–64
'Hay, Ian' (John Hay Beith), 1876–1952
Hay, John, 1838–1905
Hay, William, 1695–1755
Hayes, Colin Graham Frederick, 1919–
Hayford, Joseph Ephraim Casely, 1866–1965
Hayman, Higham Ronald, 1932–
Haymon, Sylvia T., 1918–
Hayward, John, ?1564–1627
Hayward, Samuel, 1718–57
Haywood, Eliza Fowler, ?1693–1756
Hazlitt, William, 1778–1830
Hazzard, Shirley, 1931–
Head, Bessie, ?1937–86
Head, Richard, ?1637–?86
Headlight
Heald, Timothy Villiers, 1944–
Healey, Denis Winston, 1917–
Healey, Edna May, 1918–
Healey, John, d. 1610
Health & Fitness
Health & Strength
Health Express
Health Guardian
Health Now
Health Promotion
Health Shopper
Healthy Living
Heaney, Seamus Justin, 1939–
Hearne, John, 1925–
Hearne, Thomas, 1678–1735
Heath, Edward Richard, 1916–
Heath, Francis George, 1843–1913
Heathcote, Ralph, 1721–95
Heath-Stubbs, John Francis Alexander, 1918–
Heaton, Mary Margaret, 1836–83
'Hebden, Mark' (John Harris), 1916–
Heber, Reginald, 1783–1826
Hecht, Anthony, 1923–
Hecht, Ben, 1893–1964
Hecht, Daniel
Hedgecoe, John, 1937–
Heffron, Dorris, 1944–
Heggen, Thomas, 1919–49
Hegland, Jean
Hegley, John, 1953–
Heilbroner, Robert Louis, 1919–
Heilbrun, Carolyn Gold, 1926– (*see also* 'Cross, Amanda')
Heinlein, Robert Anson, 1907–88
Heller, Joseph, 1923–99
Hellman, Lillian Florence, 1905–84
Helme, Elizabeth, d. 1816
Helmore, Thomas, 1811–90
Helps, Arthur, 1813–75
Hemans, Felicia Dorothea, 1793–1835
Hemingway, Ernest, 1899–1961
'Hemingway, Percy' (William Percy Addleshaw), 1866–1916
Henderson, Hamish, 1919–
Henderson, Lawrence, 1928–
Hendry, James Findlay, 1912–
Henfrey, Arthur, 1819–59
Henissart, Paul, 1923–
Hennessy, James Pope, 1916–74
Hennessy, John James, 1918–
Henry, Alexander, 1739–1824
Henry, John Joseph, 1758–1811
Henry, Matthew, 1662–1714
'Henry, O.' (William Sydney Porter), 1862–1910
Henry, Patrick, 1736–99
Henry, Robert, 1718–90
Henry, William, 1744–1836
Henry James Review
Hensley, Lewis, 1824–1905
Henty, George Alfred, 1832–1902
Herald (Melbourne)
Heraud, John Abraham, 1799–1887
Herbert, Alan Patrick, 1890–1971
Herbert, Edward, 1583–1648
Herbert, Frank Patrick, 1920–86
Herbert, George, 1593–1633
Herbert, Henry William, 1807–58
Herbert, James, 1943–
Herbert, Mary, 1561–1621
Herbert, Mary Elizabeth, 1822–1911
Herbert, Thomas, 1606–82
Herbert, Xavier, 1901–84
Here & Now
Heredity
Heren, Louis, 1919–95
Here's Health
Herford, Charles Harold, 1853–1931
Heritage Outlook
Herlihy, James Leo, 1927–
Herman, Henry, 1832–94
Herman, Nini Eleanor, 1925–
Herndon, William Henry, 1818–91
Herold, Jean Christopher, 1919–64
Herr, Michael, 1940–
Herrick, Robert, 1591–1674
'Herriot, James' (James Alfred Wight), 1916–95
Herschel, John Frederick William, 1792–1871
Herschel, William, 1738–1822
Hersey, John Richard, 1914–1993
Hervé, Peter, fl. 1816–29
Hervey, James, 1714–58
Hesketh, Phoebe, 1909–
Hewett, Dorothy Coads, 1923–
Hewitt, Foster, ?1903–85
Hewitt, James, 1928–
Hewlett, Esther, fl. 1829–41
Hewlett, Joseph Thomas James, 1800–47
Hewlett, Maurice Henry, 1861–1923
Heydon, Christopher, d. 1623
Heyer, Georgette, 1902–74
Heyes, Douglas, 1919–93
Heylin, Peter, 1600–62
Heywood, John, ?1497–?1580
Heywood, Oliver, 1630–1702
Heywood, Thomas, ?1574–1641
Hibbert, Henry, ?1600–78
Hickeringill, Edmund, 1631–1708
Hickes, George, 1642–1715
Hickin, Norman Ernest, 1910–
Hickman, Henry, d. 1692
Hickman, Katie, 1960–
Hieron, Samuel, ?1576–1617
Hi-Fi News
Hi-Fi Sound
Higgins, Aidan Charles, 1927–
Higgins, George Vincent, 1939–99
'Higgins, Jack' (Henry Patterson), 1929–
Higgins, Matthew James, 1810–68
Higginson, Thomas Wentworth, 1823–1911
Highland News
Highlife
High Magazine
Highsmith, Domini, 1942–
Highsmith, Patricia, 1921–1995
High Times
Highways & Transportation
Higonnet, Anne, 1959–
Higson, Charles, 1958–
Hildick, Edmund Wallace, 1925–
Hildrop, John, d. 1756
Hill, Aaron, 1685–1750
Hill, Geoffrey William, 1932–
Hill, Georgiana, fl. 1893–96
Hill, John Edward Christopher, 1912–
Hill, Peter, 1937–
Hill, Reginald Charles, 1936–
Hill, Susan Elizabeth, 1942–
Hillary, Edmund, 1919–
Hillary, Richard Hope, 1919–43
Hillerman, Anthony Grove (known as 'Tony'), 1925–
Hilton, Andrew John Boyd, 1944–
Hilton, Harold Horsfall, 1869–1942
Hilton, James, 1900–54
'Hilton, John Buxton' (John Greenwood), 1921–86
Hilton, Timothy, 1941–
Himmel, Richard, 1920–
Hinchliff, Peter Bingham, 1929–
Hinchliff, Thomas Woodbine, 1825–82
Hinde, George Jennings, 1839–1918
'Hinde, Thomas' (Thomas Willes Chitty), 1926–
Hindu
Hines, Barry Melvin, 1939–
Hinks, Arthur Robert, 1873–1945
Hinton, Nigel, 1941–
Hippocrates
Hislop, Ian David, 1960–
Hit Parader
Hoare, Richard Colt, 1758–1838
'Hobbes, John Oliver' (Pearl Mary Teresa Craigie), 1867–1906
Hobbes, Thomas, 1588–1679
Hobsbaum, Philip Dennis, 1932–
Hobsbawm, Eric John, 1917–
Hobson, Harold (known as 'Hank'), 1908–
Hobson, Laura Zametkin, 1900–86
'Hobson, Polly' (Julia Evans), 1913–
Hobson, Robert Frederick, 1920–
Hoccleve, Thomas, ?1370–?1450
Hockett, Charles Francis, 1916–2000
Hocking, Mary Eunice, 1921–
'Hodge, Merton' (Horace Emerton Hodge), 1903–58
Hodgkin, Thomas, 1831–1913
Hodgson, John, 1779–1845
Hodgson, Ralph, 1871–1962
Hodgson, William Hope, 1877–1918
Hodgson, William Noel, 1893–1916
Hodkinson, Mark, 1965–
Hodson, James Lonsdale, b. 1891

Hofstadter, Douglas Richard, 1945–
Hogan, Desmond, 1950–
Hogarth, William, 1697–1764
Hogg, Jabez, 1817–99
Hogg, James, 1770–1835
Hogg, Quintin McGaret, 1907–
Hogg, Thomas Jefferson, 1792–1862
Hoggart, Herbert Richard, 1918–
Holbrook, David Kenneth, 1923–
Holcroft, Henry, fl. 1640
Holcroft, Thomas, 1745–1800
Holden, Ursula, 1921–
Holder, William, 1616–98
Hole, Roger, 1932–
'Holiday, Billie' (Eleanora Fagan), 1915–59
Holiday Which?
Holinshed, Raphael, d. ?1580
Holland, John, 1794–1872
Holland, Josiah Gilbert, 1819–81
Holland, Philemon, 1552–1637
Holland, Richard, fl. 1450
Hollar, Wenceslas, 1607–77
Holliday, David, 1941–
Hollinghurst, Alan, 1954–
Hollingshead, John, 1827–1904
Hollingworth, Harry Levi, 1880–1956
Holloway, Christopher John, 1920–
'Hollyband, Claudius' (Claude de Sainliens), fl. 16th cent.
Hollybush, John, fl. 1561
Holme, Edith Constance, 1880–1955
Holme, Randle, 1627–99
Holmes, Arthur, 1890–1965
Holmes, Edward, 1797–1859
Holmes, James Clellon, 1926–
Holmes, Oliver Wendell, 1809–94
Holmes, Richard, 1945–
Holmes, Timothy, 1825–1907
Holroyd, Michael de Courcy Fraser, 1935–
Holt, Richard, 1948–
Holtby, Winifred, 1898–1935
Holyday, Barten, 1593–1661
Hom, Kenneth, 1949–
Home & Freezer Digest
Home Finder
HomeFlair
Home Office Computing
Home Plumbing
Homes & Garden
Hone, Joseph, 1937–
Hone, William, 1780–1842
Honey
Hongkong Standard
Honolulu Advertiser
Hood, Hugh John, 1928–
Hood, Stuart, 1915–
Hood, Thomas, 1799–1845
Hook, Theodore, 1788–1841
Hook, Walter Farquhar, 1798–1875
Hooke, Nathaniel, d. 1763
Hooke, Robert, 1635–1703
Hooker, Peter Jeremy, 1941–
Hooker, Richard, ?1554–1600
Hoole, John, 1727–1803
Hooper, John, ?1495–1555
Hooper, William Edmund James (known as 'Ted'), 1918–
Hope, Alec Derwent, 1907–2000
'Hope, Anthony' (Anthony Hope Hawkins), 1863–1933
'Hope, Ascott Robert' (Ascott Robert Hope Moncrieff), 1846–1927
Hope, Christopher, 1944–
Hopkins, Antony, 1921–
Hopkins, Ezekiel, 1634–90
Hopkins, Gerard Manley, 1844–89
Hopkins, Jane Ellice, 1836–1904
Hopkins, John, 1931–
Hopps, John Page, 1834–1911
Hornby, Nick, 1957–
Horne, George, 1730–92
Horne, Richard Henry, 1802–84
Horneck, Anthony, 1641–97
Horner, Tom, 1913–
Hornsby, Henry, 1934–
Hornung, Ernest William, 1866–1921
Horoscope
Horrobin, David Frederick, 1939–
Horrocks, Brian Gwynne, 1895–1985
Horse & Hound
Horse & Rider
Horse & Tack
Horse International
Horsley, Terence, 1904–49
Horticulture Week
Horton, Robert Forman, 1855–1934
Horwood, Harold Andrew, 1923–
Horwood, William, 1944–
Hosmer, James Kendall, 1834–1927
Hot Car
Hot Rod
Hot Shoe International
Hough, Emerson, 1857–1923
Hough, Graham Goulder, 1908–
Houghton, Richard Monckton Milnes, Lord 1809–85
Hounds
House & Garden
Household, Geoffrey Edward, 1900–88
Household Words
Housewife
Housman, Alfred Edward, 1859–1936
Houston, Margaret Bell, d. 1966
Howard, Edward, ?1793–1841
Howard, Elizabeth Jane, 1923–
'Howard, Hartley' (Leopold Horace Ognall), 1908–79 (*see also* 'Carmichael, Harry')
Howard, John, 1726–90
'Howard, Mary' (Mary Mussi), 1907–
Howard, Philip, 1933–
Howard Journal
Howarth, David Armine, 1912–
Howe, John, 1630–1705
Howell, George, 1833–1910
Howell, James, ?1594–1666
Howell, Laurence, ?1664–1720
Howells, William Dean, 1837–1920
'Howerd, Frankie' (Francis Alick Howard), 1917–92
Howes, James Philip, 1948–
Howitt, Mary, 1799–1888
Howitt, William, 1792–1879
Howker, Janni, 1957–
Howson, Albert Geoffrey, 1931–
Hoyle, Edmond, 1672–1769
Hoyle, Fred, 1915–
Hubbard, Philip Maitland, 1910–80
Hubbard, William, 1621–1704
Huddesford, George, 1749–1809
Hudson, Liam, 1933–
Hudson, Norman Webster, 1924–
Hueffer, Ford Madox, 1873–1939 (also quoted as F. M. Ford)
Hughes, Dorothy Belle Flanagan, 1904–93
Hughes, Edward James (known as 'Ted'), 1930–98
Hughes, Griffith, fl. 1750
Hughes, John, 1677–1720
Hughes, Langston, 1902–67
Hughes, Monica, 1925–
Hughes, Richard Arthur Warren, 1900–76
Hughes, Thomas, 1822–96
Hull, Edward, 1829–1917
Hull Advertiser
Hulme, Keri, 1947–
Hulme, Thomas Ernest, 1883–1917
Hume, David, 1711–76
Hume, Fergus, 1859–1932
Humphrey, George, 1889–1966
Humphreys, Henry Noel, 1810–79
Humphreys, Josephine, 1945–
Hungerford, Thomas Arthur G., 1915–
Hunt, Henry Cecil John, 1910–98
Hunt, James Henry Leigh, 1784–1859
Hunt, William Raymond, 1929–
Hunter, Alan James Herbert, 1922–
Hunter, Henry, 1741–1802
Hunter, John Kelso, 1802–73
Hunter, John Marvin, 1880–1957
Hunter, Mollie, 1922–
Hunter, Peter Hay, 1854–1940
Hunter, William Wilson, 1840–1900
Huntford, Roland, 1927–
Huntington, Gladys Parish, 1887–1959
Huntington, William, 1745–1813
Huntsberger, David Vernon, 1917–2002
Hurd, Douglas Richard, 1930–
Hurd, Richard, 1720–1806
Hurdis, James, 1763–1801
Hurlbut, Cornelius Searle, 1906–
Hurst, Fannie, 1889–1968
Hurston, Zora Neale, 1903–60
Hussein, Aamer, 1955–
Hussey, Robert, 1801–56
Hutchinson, George Evelyn, 1903–91
Hutchinson, Henry Neville, 1856–1927
Hutchinson, James R., 1933–
Hutchinson, Lucy, b. 1620
Hutchinson, Ray Coryton, 1907–75
Hutchinson, Thomas, 1711–80
Huth, Angela, 1938–
Hutschnecker, Arnold Aaron, 1898–
Hutten, Ernest Hirschlaff, 1908–
Hutton, Charles, 1737–1823
Hutton, James, 1726–97
Hutton, Richard Holt, 1826–97
Huxley, Aldous Leonard, 1894–1963
Huxley, Anthony Julian, 1920–92
Huxley, Elspeth Joscelin Grant, 1907–97
Huxley, Julian Sorell, 1887–1975
Huxley, Juliette, 1896–1994
Huxley, Leonard, 1860–1933
Huxley, Thomas Henry, 1825–95
Hyams, Edward Soloman, 1910–75
Hyams, Joe, 1923–
Hyde, John, 1833–75
'Hyde, Robin' (Iris Guiver Wilkinson), 1906–39
Hyland, Henry Stanley, 1914–
Hynes, James

I

Icarus
Ice Hockey News Review
Icon Thoughtstyle
Ideal Home
Idler Magazine
Idriess, Ian Llewellyn, 1890–1979
Iggulden, John Manners, 1917–
Ignatieff, Michael, 1947–
Ignatow, David, 1914–97
Ilkeston Advertiser
Illich, Ivan, 1926–
Illingworth, John Richardson, 1848–1915
Illingworth, Raymond, 1932–
Illustrated London News
Illustrated Weekly of India
Imison, John, d. 1788
Imms, Augustus Daniel, 1880–1949
Inchbald, Elizabeth, 1753–1821
Inchbald, Peter, fl. 1982
Independent
Independent on Sunday
Indexer
Indian Bookworm's Journal
Indian Express (Madurai)
India Today
Industry Week
Indy
Ingalls, Rachel, 1940–
Ingate, Mary, 1912–
Inge, William Ralph, 1860–1954
Ingelo, Nathaniel, ?1621–83
Ingelow, Jean, 1820–97
Ingersoll, Ernest, 1852–1946
Ingham, Sarah
Inglis, James, 1845–1908
Ingraham, Joseph Holt, 1809–60
Ink
'Innes, Michael' (John Innes Mackintosh Stewart), 1906–94
Innes, Ralph Hammond, 1913–98
Innes, Thomas, 1662–1744
Insight
Intercity Magazine
International Affairs
International Business Week
International Combat Arms
International Herald Tribune
International Musician
International Wildlife
Interview
Investors Chronicle
Ireland, David, 1927–
Ireland, Timothy, 1959–
Ireland, William Henry, 1777–1835
Irish Democrat
Irish Press
Irish Times
Irvine, Christopher, fl. 1638–85

'Kennedy, X. J.' (Joseph Charles Kennedy), 1929–
Kenny, Anthony John Patrick, 1931–
Kenyon, Michael Forbes, 1931–
Kerley, Peter, 1900–
Kermode, John Frank, 1919–
Kernahan, Coulson, 1858–1943
Kerouac, Jean-Louis Lebrid de (known as 'Jack Kerouac'), 1922–69
Kersh, Gerald, 1911–68
Kershaw, Kenneth Andrew, 1930–
Kesey, Ken Elton, 1935–2001
Kesson, Jessie, 1916–1994
Ketchum, William C., 1931–
Kethe, William, d. ?1608
'Keverne, Richard' (Clifford James Wheeler Hosken, 1882–1950
Keyboard Player
Keyes, Marian, 1963–
Keyes, Sidney Arthur Kilworth, 1922–43
Keynes, John Maynard, 1883–1946
Khan, Mohammed Masud Reza, 1921–
Khory, Rustomjee Naserwanjee, 1839–1904
Kiernan, Victor Gordon, 1913–
Kilian, Crawford, 1941–
Kilvert, Robert Francis, 1840–79
Kimenye, Barbara, ?1940–
Kindred Spirit
King, Adam, fl. 1580–90
King, Clarence, 1842–1901
King, Francis Henry, 1923–
King, Gordon John, 1922–
King, Henry, 1592–1669
King, Henry Churchill, 1858–1934
King, John, 1960–
King, Martin Luther, 1929–68
King, Norman, 1926–
King, Stephen, 1947–
King, William, 1663–1712
Kinglake, Alexander William, 1809–91
Kingsley, Charles, 1819–75
Kingsley, George Henry, 1827–92
Kingsley, Henry, 1830–76
Kingsley, Mary Henrietta, 1862–1900
Kingsley, Sidney, 1906–95
Kingsolver, Barbara, 1955–
Kingston, Maxine Hong, 1940–
Kingston, William Henry Giles, 1814–80
Kington, Miles, 1941–
Kinns, Samuel, 1826–1903
Kinsale, Laura
Kipling, Rudyard, 1865–1936
Kirby, William, 1759–1850
'Kirk, Eleanor' (Eleanor Hana Ames), 1831–1908
'Kirke, Edmund' (James Roberts Gilmore), 1822–1903
Kirkland, Caroline Matilda, 1801–64
Kirkman, Francis, 1632–?80
Kirkup, James, 1923–
Kirwan, Richard, 1733–1812
Kissinger, Henry Alfred, 1923–
Kitchen, Fred, 1891–1969
Kitchener, Horatio Herbert, 1850–1916
Kitchin, George William, 1827–1912
Kitto, John, 1804–54
Kittredge, George Lyman, 1860–1941
Kitzinger, Sheila, 1929–
Kizzia, Tom
Klauber, John David, 1917–87
Klawans, Harold Leo, 1937–
Klein, Josephine, 1926–
Kline, Morris, 1908–92
Kneale, Nigel, 1922–
Knight, Charles, 1791–1873
Knight, Edward Henry, 1824–83
Knight, George Wilson, 1897–1985
Knight, Stephen, 1951–
Knight, Thomas, d. 1820
Knights, Lionel Charles, 1906–97
Knolles, Richard, ?1550–1610
Knowles, James Sheridan, 1784–1862
Knowles, Robert Edmund, 1868–1946
Knox, Alexander, 1757–1831
Knox, Edmund George V., 1881–1971
Knox, John, 1505–72
Knox, Robert, 1791–1862
Knox, Ronald Arbuthnott, 1888–1957
Knox, Vicesimus, 1752–1821
Knox, William (known as 'Bill'), 1928–
Knox-Little, William John, 1839–1918
K.O.
Kocher, Paul Harold, 1907–98
Koestler, Arthur, 1905–83
Kohut, Heinz, 1913–81
Koontz, Dean Ray, 1945–
Koppett, Leonard, 1923–
Kops, Bernard, 1926–
Kormondy, Edward John, 1926–
Kosinski, Jerzy Nikodem, 1933–91
Kotzwinkle, William, 1938–
Kraft, Eric, 1944–
Kramer, Matt, 1951–
Krantz, Judith, 1928–
Krapp, George Philip, 1872–1934
Kroetsch, Robert Paul (known as 'Bob'), 1927–
Krutch, Joseph Wood, 1893–1970
Kunitz, Stanley Jasspon, 1905–
Kuper, Leo, 1908–94
Kurath, Hans, 1891–1992
Kureishi, Hanif, 1954–
Kurnitz, Harry, 1909–68
Kurth, Peter, 1953–
Kushner, Harold, 1935–
Kuwait Times
Kuzwayo, Ellen, 1914–
Kyd, Thomas, 1558–94
'Kyle, Duncan' (John Franklin Broxholme), 1930–
'Kyle, Robert' (Robert Terrall), 1914–

L

La Bern, Arthur Joseph, 1909–
Labour Monthly
'Lacy, Ed' (Len Zinberg), 1911–68
Ladies Homes Journal (US)
Lady
Lady's Pictorial
La Farge, Oliver, 1901–63
Laffan, Kevin Barry, 1922–
Lafitte, Paul, 1915–
Lagowski, Joseph John, 1930–
Laing, Kojo, 1946–
Laing, Ronald David, 1927–89
Lamb, Charles, 1775–1834
Lamb, David Alexander, 1954–
Lamb, Joseph Fairweather, 1928–
Lamb, Lynton Harold, 1907–77
Lambarde, William, 1536–1601
Lambert, Angela, fl. 1990
Lambert, Leonard Constant, 1905–51
Lamont, John, fl. 1649–71
Lampe, Geoffrey William Hugo, 1912–80
Lancashire Evening Telegraph
Lancashire Life
Lancaster, Osbert, 1908–80
Lancaster & Morecambe Guardian
Lancaster Guardian
Lancet
Lanciani, Rodolfo Amedeo, 1847–1929
Landau, Sidney I., 1933–
Lander, Richard Lemon, 1804–34
Landfall
Landon, Howard Chandler Robbins, 1926–
Landor, Walter Savage, 1775–1864
Landscape
Landsteiner, Ernest Karl, 1868–1943
Lane, Benjamin Ingersoll, 1797–1875
Lane, Edward William, 1801–76
Lane, Homer Tyrrell, 1876–1925
Lane, Maggie, 1947–
Lang, Andrew, 1844–1912
Lang, John, 1799–1878
Lang, William Cosmo Gordon, 1864–1945
Langbridge, Rosamund Grant, 1880–1964
Langhorne, John, 1735–79
Langley, Eve, 1908–74
Language
Lardner, Dionysius, 1793–1859
Lardner, Ringgold Wilmer, 1885–1933
Larkin, Philip Arthur, 1922–85
Larson, Charles, 1922–
Lasch, Christopher, 1932–
Laski, Audrey Louise, 1931–
Laski, Harold Joseph, 1893–1950
Laski, Marghanita, 1915–89
Lasky, Melvin Jonah, 1920–
Lassalle, Caroline, 1932–
Lassels, Richard, ?1603–68
L.A. Style
Latham, Henry, ?1828–71
Latham, Simon, d. 1618
Latimer, Hugh, ?1485–1555
Laud, William, 1573–1645
Laurence, Margaret, 1926–
Laurie, Peter Charles Somerville, 1937–
Lavin, Mary, 1912–96
Lavington, George, 1684–1762
Law, Denis, 1940–
Law, Edward, 1790–1871
Law, William, 1686–1761
Lawler, Ray, 1921–
Lawrence, David Herbert, 1885–1930
Lawrence, George Alfred, 1827–76
Lawrence, Henry, 1600–64
Lawrence, John, 1753–1839
Lawrence, Karen Ann, 1951–
Lawrence, Louise, 1943–
Lawrence, Starling
Lawrence, Thomas Edward, 1888–1935
Law Reports
Lawson, Henry Archibald Hertzberg, 1867–1922
Lawson, John, d. 1712
Lawson, Nigella Lucy, 1960–
Law Times
Lax, Eric, 1944–
Layard, George Somes, 1857–1925
Leach, Penelope Jane, 1937–
Leacock, Stephen Butler, 1869–1944
Leadam, Isaac Saunders, 1848–1913
Leadbeater, Mary, 1758–1826
Lean Living
Leapman, Michael, 1938–
Leary, Timothy Francis, 1920–96
Leasor, Thomas James, 1923–
Leavis, Frank Raymond, 1895–1978
Leavis, Queenie Dorothy, 1906–81
Leavitt, David, 1961–
Lebende Sprachen
'le Carré, John' (David John Cornwell), 1931–
Lecky, William Edward Hartpole, 1838–1903
Lecomber, Brian, 1945–
Lediard, Thomas, 1685–1743
Lee, Andrea, 1953–
Lee, Frederick George, 1832–1902
Lee, Harper, 1926–
'Lee, Holme' (Harriet Parr), 1828–1900
Lee, John Alexander, 1891–1982
Lee, Laurie, 1914–97
Lee, Maurice duPont, 1925–
Lee, Sophia, 1756–1824
'Lee, Vernon' (Violet Paget), 1856–1935
Leeds, Edward Thurlow, 1877–1955
Leeds Mercury
Lees, Gene, 1928–
Lees, James Cameron, 1834–1913
Lees-Milne, James, 1908–97
Le Fanu, Joseph Sheridan, 1814–73
Le Fevre, George William, 1798–1846
Le Gallienne, Richard, 1866–1947
Le Guin, Ursula, 1929–
Lehane, Jack, 1935–
Lehmann, Rosamond Nina, 1903–90
Lehmann, Rudolph Chambers, 1856–1929
Lehmann, Rudolph John Frederick, 1907–87
Lehrer, Thomas Andrew, 1928–
Leicester Chronicle
Leicester Mercury
Leigh, Benedicta, 1922–
Leigh Hunt: *see* Hunt, James Henry Leigh
Leighton, Frederic, 1830–96
Leighton, Robert, 1611–84
Leitch, Maurice, 1933–

M

'Macdonald, Ross' (Kenneth Millar), 1915–83
MacDonnell, George Alcock, 1830–99
McDougall, Joyce, 1926–
McDougall, William, 1871–1938
Macduff, John Ross, 1818–95
McEwan, Ian Russell, 1948–
Macfarlane, John, 1807–75
McGahern, John, 1935–
McGerr, Patricia, 1917–85
Macgill, Patrick, 1890–1963
Macgillivray, William, 1796–1852
McGinley, Patrick Anthony, 1937–
McGivern, William Peter, 1922–82
McGuane, Thomas Francis, 1939–
Machlin, Milton, 1924–
McIlvanney, William, 1936–
McIlwraith, Jean N., d. 1938
McInerney, Jay, 1955–
MacInnes, Colin, 1914–76
McInnes, Graham, 1912–70
MacInnes, Hamish, 1930–
McInnes, Neil, 1924–
'McIntosh, Louis' (Christopher Johnson), 1931–
Mackail, Denis George, 1892–1971
Mackail, John William, 1859–1945
Mackay, Aeneas James George, 1839–1911
McKay, Claude, 1890–1948
Mackay, George Eric, 1851–98
Mackay, Shena, 1944–
Mackay, William Paton, 1839–85
Mackenzie, Compton Edward Montague, 1883–1972
Mackenzie, Donald, 1918–
Mackenzie, George, 1636–91
Mackenzie, Henry, 1745–1831
Mackenzie, Morell, 1837–92
McKerrow, Ronald Brunlees, 1872–1940
Mackie, John Duncan, 1887–1978
Mackintosh, James, 1765–1832
Maclagan, Alexander, 1811–79
Maclaine, Archibald, 1722–1804
Maclaren, Alexander, 1826–1910
'Maclaren, Ian' (John Watson), 1850–1907
Maclaren-Ross, Julian, 1912–64
MacLean, Alistair Stuart, 1922–87
Maclean, Fitzroy Hew, 1911–96
Maclean's Magazine
McLean, Duncan, 1964–
Maclear, George Frederick, 1833–1902
McLeave, Hugh George, 1923–
MacLennan, John Hugh, 1907–90
Macleod, Charlotte Matilda, 1922–
'Macleod, Fiona' (William Sharp), 1855–1905
Macleod, Sheila
McLeod, John, ?1777–1820
McLuhan, Herbert Marshall, 1911–80
Macmillan, Daniel, 1813–57
Macmillan, Maurice Harold, 1894–1986
Macmillan's Magazine
McMurtrie, Henry, 1793–1865
McMurtry, Larry Jeff, 1936–
McNab, Andy, 1960–
McNabb, Vincent Joseph, 1868–1943
MacNeice, Frederick Louis, 1907–63
MacNeil, Robert, 1931–
McNeile, Alan Hugh, 1871–1933
McNeill, Anthony, 1941–
McPhee, John Angus, 1931–
McPherson, James Munro, 1936–
McQueen, John, 1929–
Macquoid, Katherine Sarah, 1824–1917
Macrae, Ann, 1948–
Macready, William Charles, 1793–1873
MacVicar, Angus, 1908–2001
McWilliam, Candia, 1955–
McWilliams, Carey, 1905–80
Madden, Deirdre, 1960–
Madden, Frederic, 1801–73
Maeterlinck, Maurice, 1862–1949
Magee, Bryan Edgar, 1930–
Magens, Nicholas, d. 1764
Maguire, Michael, 1945–
Mahaffy, John Pentland, 1839–1919
Mahon, Derek, 1941–
Mahony, Francis Sylvester, 1804–66
Mahy, Margaret May, 1936–
Maidenhead Advertiser
Maidment, James, ?1795–1879
Mailer, Norman, 1923–
Mailloux, Peter Alden, 1948–
Mail on Sunday
Maine, Henry James Sumner, 1822–88
Mair, Charles, 1838–1927
Maitland, Frederic William, 1850–1906
Maitland, Samuel Roffey, 1792–1866
Maitland, Sara, 1950–
Making Music
Malamud, Bernard, 1914–86
Malan, Rian, 1954–
Malcolm, John, 1936–
'Malcolm X': *see* 'X, Malcolm'
Maledicta
Maling, Arthur Gordon, 1923–
Malkin, Benjamin Heath, 1769–1842
Mallock, William Hurrell, 1849–1923
Mallon, Thomas, 1951–
Mallory, George Herbert Leigh, 1886–1924
Malory, Thomas, fl. 1470
Malouf, David, 1934–
Malthus, Thomas Robert, 1766–1834
Malvern Gazette
Mamet, David Alan, 1947–
Man
Management Today
Manby, George William, 1765–1854
Manchester, Henry Montagu, ?1563–1642
Manchester Evening News
Manchester Examiner
Manchester Weekly Times
Mandela, Nelson Rolihlahia, 1918–
Mandeville, John, d. 1372
Mandy
Mangan, James Clarence, 1803–49
Mangold, Thomas Cornelius, 1934–
Manley, Mary, 1663–1724
Manley, Thomas, 1628–90
Manlove, Colin Nicholas, 1942–
Mann, Anthony Philip, 1942–
Mann, Cecil, 1896–1967
Mann, Felix Bernard, 1931–
Mann, Horace, 1796–1859
Mann, Horace Kinder, 1859–1928
Mann, Jessica, 1937–
Mann, Leonard, 1895–1981
Mann, Robert James, 1817–86
Mannin, Ethel Edith, 1900–84
Manning, Aubrey William, 1930–
Manning, Frederic, 1882–1935
Manning, Henry Edward, 1808–92
Manning, Olivia, 1915–80
Manning, Robert, 1919–
Manning, Rosemary, 1911–88
Mansel, Henry Longueville, 1820–71
Mansfield, Charles Blachford, 1819–55
'Mansfield, Katherine' (Kathleen Mansfield Beauchamp), 1888–1923
Mansfield, Paul, 1922–
Manson, Patrick, 1844–1922
Mant, Richard, 1776–1848
Mantel, Hilary, 1952–
Mantell, Lorraine, ?1917–
Manton, Thomas, 1620–77
Manville Fenn: *see* Fenn, George Manville
Mapleson, James Henry, 1830–1901
Maplet, John, d. 1592
Marathon & Distance Runner
Marbeck, John, fl. 1541–85
March, Francis Andrew, 1825–1911
'March, William' (William Edward March Campbell), 1894–1954
Marcus, Stanley, 1905–2002
Marcy, Randolph Barnes, 1812–98
Marechera, Dambudzo, 1952–87
Marett, Robert Ranulph, 1866–1943
Mark, Janet Marjorie, 1943–
Marketing
Marketing Week
Markham, Albert Hastings, 1841–1918
Markham, Clements Robert, 1830–1916
Markham, Gervase, ?1568–1637
Markstein, George, 1929–87
Markus, Rixi, 1910–92
Marlowe, Christopher, 1564–93
Marmion, Shockerley, 1603–39
Marquand, John Phillips, 1893–1960
Marquis, Don, 1878–1937
Marrin, Minette, fl. 1988
Marriott, Wharton Booth, 1823–71
Marryat, Frederick, 1792–1848
Marryat, Horace, 1818–87
Marryat, Joseph, 1757–1824
Marsden, John Buxton, 1803–70
Marsh, Bryan, 1932–
Marsh, Edith Ngaio, 1899–1982
Marsh, George Perkins, 1801–82
Marsh, Jan, 1942–
Marsh, Richard, d. 1915
Marshall, Bruce, 1899–1987
Marshall, Charles, d. 1818
Marshall, John, 1755–1835
Marshall, John Sayre, 1846–1922
Marshall, Paule, 1929–
Marshall, Thomas Humphrey, 1893–1981
Marshall, William Leonard, 1944–
Marsh-Caldwell, Anne, 1791–1874
Mars-Jones, Adam Henry, 1954–
Marston, John, ?1575–1634
Martel, Yann, 1963–
Martin, Benjamin, 1704–82
Martin, Helen Reimensnyder, 1868–1939
Martin, Kingsley, 1897–1969
Martin, Theodore, 1816–1909
Martin, William Charles Linnaeus, 1798–1864
Martine, John, d. 1891
Martineau, Harriet, 1802–76
Martineau, James, 1805–1900
Marvell, Andrew, 1621–78
Marxism Today
Mascall, Eric Lionel, 1905–93
Masefield, John, 1878–1967
Maskell, William, ?1814–90
Maskelyne, Nevil, 1732–1811
Mason, Alfred Edward Woodley, 1865–1948
Mason, Anita, 1942–
Mason, Bobbie Anne, 1940–
Mason, Bruce Edward, 1921–82
Mason, Charles Peter, 1820–1900
Mason, Francis van Wyck, 1901–1978
Mason, John, 1706–63
Mason, Michael Henry, 1900–82
Mason, Richard Lakin, 1919–97
Mason, William, 1724–97
Masserman, Jules Homan, 1905–94
Massey, William Nathaniel, 1809–81
Massie, Allan Johnstone, 1938–
Massinger, Philip, 1583–1640
Masson, David, 1822–1907
Masson, Jeffrey Moussaieff, 1941–
Master Photographer
Masters, John, 1914–83
Match
Match Fishing
Mateer, Samuel, 1835–93
'Mather, Berkely' (John Evan Weston-Davis), 1909–96
Mather, Cotton, 1663–1728
Matheson, George, 1842–1906
Mathews, Anne, ?1782–1869
Mathews, Charles Edward, 1834–1905
Mathews, Richard, d. 1661
Mathewson, Christopher, 1880–1925
Mathias, Thomas James, ?1754–1835
Matthews, Henry, 1789–1828
Matthiessen, Peter, 1927–
Maudsley, Henry, 1835–1918
Maugham, Robert Cecil, 1916–81
Maugham, William Somerset, 1874–1965
Maundrell, Henry, 1665–1701
Maupin, Armistead, 1944–
Maurice, Frederick Denison, 1805–72
Maury, Matthew Fontaine, 1806–73
Max-Müller, Friedrich, 1823–1900
Maxwell, Gavin, 1914–69
Maxwell, James Clerk, 1831–79

N

Norton, Edward Felix, 1884–1954
Norton, John Bruce, 1815–83
Norton, Olive Marion, 1913–73
Norton, Thomas, 1532–84
'Norway, Kate' (Clive Manon Norton), 1913–73
Norwich Mercury
Notes & Queries
Novak, Michael, 1933–
'Novello, Ivor' (David Ifor Davies), 1893–1951
Noyes, Alfred, 1880–1958
Nuclear Energy
Number One
Numbers
Nursery World
Nursing
Nursing Times
Nye, Edgar Wilson, 1856–96
Nye, Nathaniel, b. 1624

O

'Oakley, Ann' (Rosamund Clay), 1944–
Oakley, Kenneth Page, 1911–81
Oastler, Richard, 1789–1861
Oates, Joyce Carol, 1938–
Oban Times
O'Brian, Patrick, 1914–2000
O'Brien, Edna, 1932–
'O'Brien, Flann' (Brian O'Nolan), 1911–66 (*see also* 'Na Gopaleen, Myles')
O'Brien, Timothy, 1948–
Observer
O'Casey, Sean, 1880–1964
Ockley, Simon, 1678–1720
O'Connell, Daniel, 1775–1847
O'Connor, Flannery, 1925–64
O'Connor, Thomas Power, 1848–1929
O'Conor, Charles, 1764–1828
Oddie, William Edgar (known as 'Bill'), 1941–
Odets, Clifford, 1906–63
O'Donnell, Peter, 1920–
O'Donovan, Edmund, 1844–83
O'Faoláin, Sean, 1900–91
O'Faolain, Julia, 1932–
Office
Off Road & 4 Wheel Drive
Offshore
Offshore Engineer
O'Flaherty, Liam, 1897–1984
Ogilvy, Charles Stanley, 1913–2000
Ogilvy, David Mackenzie, 1911–99
Ogle, George, 1704–46
O'Grady, Desmond, 1935–
O'Hara, John Henry, 1905–70
O'Hara, Kenneth, 1924–
Okakura, Kakuzo, 1862–1913
O'Keeffe, John, 1747–1833
O'Keeffe, Linda, 1951–
Okey, Thomas, 1852–1935
Okri, Ben, 1959–
Oldenburg, Henry, ?1615–77
Oldham, John, 1653–83
Oliphant, Laurence, 1829–88
Oliphant, Margaret Oliphant Wilson, 1828–97
Oliver, Daniel, 1830–1916
Oliver, Frederick Scott, 1864–1934
Oliver, Mary, 1935–
Oliver, Paul, 1927–
Olivier, Laurence Kerr, 1907–89
Ollier, Clifford David, 1931–
Olmsted, Frederick Law, 1822–1903
Olver, Robert
Oman, Carola Mary, 1897–1978
Oman, Charles William Chadwick, 1860–1946
Omni
Omnibus
On Board International
O'Neill, Eugene Gladstone, 1888–1953
Ong, Walter Jackson, 1912–
Onions, Charles Talbut, 1873–1965
Onions, George Oliver, 1873–1961
Opera Now
Optima
Options
Orbach, Susie, 1946–
Orcadian
Orczy, Baroness Emmuska, 1865–1947
Organic Gardening
Origo, Iris, 1902–76
Orlando (Florida) *Sen;inel*
Orme, Robert, 1728–1801
Ormerod, Paul
Ormsby, Frank, 1947–
Orr, James, 1844–1913
Ortiz, Elizabeth Lambert, 1928–
Orton, John Kingsley (known as 'Joe'), 1933–67
'Orwell, George' (Eric Hugh Blair), 1903–50
Osbaldistone, William Augustus, fl. 1795
Osborn, Henry Fairfield, 1857–1935
Osborne, Charles, 1927–
Osborne, John, 1929–1994
Osborne, Sidney Godolphin, 1808–89
O'Shaughnessy, Arthur William Edgar, 1844–81
Osmond, Humphrey Fortesque, 1917–
Ottawa Journal
Ottley, Roi, 1906–60
Otway, Thomas, 1652–85
Ouellette, Pierre, 1945–
'Ouida' (Marie Louise de la Ramée), 1839–1908
Ouseley, Frederick Arthur Gore, 1825–89
Outdoor Action
Outdoor Living (NZ)
Outing (US)
Outlook
Out of Town
Outrage
Overbury, Thomas, 1581–1613
Owen, George, 1552–1613
Owen, Jane, 1958–
Owen, John, 1616–83
Owen, Lewis, 1572–1633
Owen, Richard, 1804–92
Owen, Sidney James, 1827–1912
Owen, Wilfred Edward, 1893–1918
'Oxenham, John' (William Arthur Dunkerley), 1852–1941
Oxfam News
Oxfam Review
Oxford Art Journal
Oxford Diocesan Magazine
Oxford Economic Papers
Oxford English Dictionary (1st ed., 1933)
Oxford Journal
Oxford Journal of Legal Studies
Oxford Magazine
Oxford Mail
Oxford News
Oxford Star
Oxford Times
Oxford Today
Oxford University Gazette
Ozell, John, d. 1743

P

Pace, Eric, 1936–
Packard, Vance Oakley, 1914–96
Packer, Joy, 1905–77
'Packer, Vin' (Marijane Meaker), 1932–
Packet (Camborne)
Pae, David, 1828–84
Paffard, Mark, 1955–
Page, David, 1814–79
Page, Martin, 1938–
Paget, Francis Edward, 1806–82
Paget, James, 1814–99
Pagitt, Ephraim, 1575–1647
Paglia, Camille Anna, 1947–
Paine, Ralph Delahaye, 1871–1925
Paine, Thomas, 1737–1809
Painter, William, *c* 1525–95
Painting, Norman, 1924–
Pakenham, Simona Vere, 1916–
Paley, Frederick Apthorp, 1815–88
Paley, Grace, 1922–
Paley, William, 1743–1805
Palgrave, Francis Turner, 1824–97
Palgrave, Reginald Francis, 1788–1861
Palgrave, William Gifford, 1826–88
Pall Mall Gazette
Pall Mall Magazine
Palmer, Joel, 1810–81
Palmer, Samuel, d. 1724
Palmer, Vance, 1885–1959
Palsgrave, John, d. 1554
Paltock, Robert, 1697–1767
Pan Am Clipper
Pankhurst, Christabel, 1880–1958
Pantin, William Abel, 1902–73
Paragraph
Parent
Parenting
Parents
Paretsky, Sara, 1947–
Parish, Peter Anthony, 1930–
Park, Ruth, 1922–
Parker, Anthony (known as 'Tony'), 1923–
Parker, Charles Stuart, 1829–1910
Parker, Dorothy, 1893–1967
Parker, John Henry, 1806–84
Parker, Joseph, 1830–1902
Parker, Matthew, 1504–75
Parker, Robert Brown, 1932–
Parker, Samuel, 1640–88
Parker, William Hosken, 1910–
Parkes, Edmund Alexander, 1819–76
Parkinson, Cyril Northcote, 1909–93
Parkinson, Stephen, 1823–89
Parkman, Francis, 1823–93
Parks, Timothy, 1954–
Parliamentary Affairs
Parnell, Thomas, 1679–1718
Parr, Louisa, 1848–1903
Parrington, Vernon Lewis, 1871–1929
Parrish, Frank, 1929–
Parry, Charles Hubert Hastings, 1848–1918
Parsons, Abraham, d. 1785
Parsons, Eliza, d. 1811
Parsons, Talcott, 1902–79
Partisan Review
Partridge, Frances Catherine, 1900–
Pascoe, Charles Eyre, 1842–1919
Patches
Pater, Walter Horatio, 1839–94
Paterson, Andrew Barton, 1864–1941
Paterson, Samuel, 1728–1802
Patmore, Coventry Kersey, 1823–96
Paton, Alan Stewart, 1903–88
Paton, John Gibson, 1824–1907
Patrick, Simon, 1626–1707
Patten, Brian Arthur, 1946–
Patten, William, fl. 1548–80
Patten, William Gilbert, 1866–1945
Patterson, Arthur Henry, 1857–1935
Patterson, John Henry, 1867–1947
Patterson, Raymond M., 1929–
Patterson, Robert Hogarth, 1821–86
Pattinson, James, 1915–
Pattison, Ian
Pattison, Mark, 1813–84
Paul, Elliot Harold, 1891–1958
Paul, Herbert Woodfield, 1853–1935
Pawel, Ernst, 1920–94
Payn, James, 1830–98
Payne, Humfry, 1902–36
Payne, John, 1842–1916
Payne, Laurence, 1919–
Payne-Gallwey, Ralph William Frankland, 1848–1916
PC World
Peace News
Peacham, Henry, ?1576–?1643
Peacock, Edward, 1831–1915
Peacock, Thomas Love, 1785–1866
Peake, Mervyn, 1911–68
Peake, Richard Brinsley, 1792–1847
Pearce, Philippa, 1920–
Peard, Frances Mary, 1835–1923
Pearl, Raymond, 1879–1940
Pearson, Charles Henry, 1830–94
Pearson, Hesketh, 1887–1964
Pearson, John, ?1613–86
Pearson, Karl, 1857–1936
Pearson, William Harrison (known as 'Bill'), 1922–
Peattie, Donald Culross, 1898–1964
Pebody, Charles, 1839–90
Pecock, Reginald, ?1395–?1460
Pediatrics
Peel, John Hugh Brignal, 1913–83
Peel, Robert, 1788–1850
Peele, George, ?1558–?97
Pegge, Samuel, 1704–96
Pell, Daniel, fl. 1659

Pelton, Barry Clifton, 1935–
Pemberton, Max, 1863–1950
Pen International
Penman, Sharon Kay
Penn, Margaret, d. 1981
Penn, William, 1644–1718
Pennant, Thomas, 1726–98
Penning-Rowsell, Edmund Lionel, 1913–2002
Pennington, Arthur Robert, 1814–99
Penton, Brian, 1904–51
People
Pepys, Samuel, 1633–1703
Percival, Thomas, 1740–1804
Percy, Walker, 1916–
Percy, William Alexander, 1885–1942
Perelman, Sidney Joseph, 1904–79
Perkins, Emily, 1970–
Perle, Richard Norman, 1941–
Perriam, Wendy, 1940–
Perrin, Porter Gale, 1896–1962
Perronet, Edward, 1721–92
Perry, Frances Mary, 1907–
Perry, Ritchie John, 1942–
Person, Ethel Spector, fl. 1989
Personal Computer World
Personal Software
Perthshire Journal
'Peterley, David' (Richard Pennington), 1904–
Peters, Catherine, 1930–
'Peters, Elizabeth' (Barbara Mertz), 1927–
'Peters, Ellis' (Edith Mary Pargeter), 1913–95
'Peters, Ludovic' (Peter Ludwig Brent), 1931–84
Peterson, Roger Tory, 1908–1996
'Petrie, Rhona' (Marie Buchanan), 1922–
Petroleum Economist
Petroleum Today
Pettie, George, 1548–?89
Petty, William, 1623–76
Pevsner, Nikolaus Bernhard, 1902–83
Peyser, Joan, 1931–
Peyton, Edward, ?1588–1657
'Peyton, K. M.' (Kathleen Wendy Peyton), 1929–
Phaer, Thomas, 1510–60
Pharmaceutical Journal
Pharr, Robert Deane, 1916–89
Phelps, Austin, 1820–90
Phelps, Gilbert Henry, 1915–93
Philadelphia Inquirer
Philadelphia Record
Philidor, François André Danican, 1726–95
Philips, Ambrose, 1674–1749
Philips, Judson Pentecost, 1903–89
Philips, Susan Elizabeth
Phillip, William, fl. 1600
Phillips, Adam, 1954–
Phillips, Caryl, 1958–
Phillips, David Graham, 1867–1911
Phillips, Henry, 1838–95
Phillips, Jayne Anne, 1952–
Phillips, John, 1800–74
Phillips, Julia, 1944–
Phillips, Stephen, 1868–1915
Phillips, Wendell, 1811–84
Phillpotts, Eden, 1862–1960
Philosophical Quarterly
Philosophical Transactions
Photo Answers
Photographer
Photography
Physics Bulletin
Physiological Review
Physiology & Behaviour
Pi Magazine
Pickard, Nancy, 1945–
Pickering, John, 1772–1846
Piercy, Marge, 1936–
Pike, Edgar Royston, 1896–1980
Pike, Luke Owen, 1835–1915
Pike, Warburton Mayer, 1861–1915
Pike, Zebulon Montgomery, 1779–1813
Pilcher, Rosamunde, 1924–
Pilling, Ann, 1944–
Pilot
Pilots International
Pinckard, George, 1768–1835
Pinckney, Darryl, 1953–
Pinkerton, John, 1758–1826
Pinkney, Nathan, 1776–1825
Pink Paper
Pinter, Harold, 1930–
Pinto, Edward Henry, 1901–72
Piozzi, Hester Lynch, 1741–1821
Piper, David Towry, 1918–90
Pirsig, Robert M., 1928–
Pistone, Joseph D.
Pitman, Emma Raymond, b. 1841
Pitts, Denis, 1930–
Pitts, Joseph, 1663–?1731
Pizzey, Erin, 1939–
Plain, Belva, 1919–
Plain Dealer (Cleveland, Ohio)
Plamenatz, John Petrov, 1912–75
Planet
Plante, David, 1940–
Plants & Gardens
Plath, Sylvia, 1932–63
Platt, Kin, 1911–
'Player, Robert' (Robert Furneaux Jordan), 1937–
Playfair, John, 1748–1819
Playford, John, 1623–?86
Plays International
Plimpton, George
Plomer, William, 1903–73
Plot, Robert, 1640–96
Plowman, Max, 1883–1941
Plumb, Charles Theodore, 1905–
Plumptre, Edward Hayes, 1821–91
Podhoretz, Norman, 1930–
Poe, Edgar Allan, 1809–49
Poetry Nation Review
Poetry Review
Pohl, Frederik, 1919–
Police Chief
Police Review
Political Quarterly
Pollard, Ernest Charles, 1906–97
Pollock, Frederick, 1845–1937
Pollok, Robert, 1799–1827
Polunin, Nicholas Vladimir, 1909–97
Pony
Poole, Ernest, 1880–1950
Poole, George Ayliffe, 1808–83
Poole, Matthew, 1624–79
Pool Magazine
Poore, Benjamin Perley, 1820–87
Popcorn, Faith Beryl, 1948–
Pope, Alexander, 1688–1744
Pope, Mildred Katherine, 1872–1956
Pope Hennessy: *see* Hennessy, James Pope
Popple, William, d. 1708
Popular Hi-Fi
Popular Photography
Popular Science Monthly
Pordage, John, 1607–81
Porritt, Benjamin Dawson, 1884–1940
Porson, Richard, 1759–1808
Porter, Cole, 1891–1964
Porter, Eleanor Hodgman, 1868–1920
Porter, George Richardson, 1792–1852
Porter, Joyce, 1924–90
Porter, Katherine Anne, 1890–1980
Porter, Peter Neville Frederick, 1929–
Porter, Roy, 1946–
Portfolio Magazine
Pory, John, 1572–1636
Poste, Edward, fl. 1850–75
Postgate, Raymond William, 1896–1971
Postman, Neil
Pot Black
Potok, Chaim, 1929–
Potter, David, 1932–
Potter, Dennis, 1935–94
Potter, Helen Beatrix, 1866–1943
Potter, John, *c* 1674–1747
Potter, Stephen Meredith, 1900–69
Potts, Jean, 1910–99
Pough, Frederick Harvey, 1906–
Poultry World
Pound, Ezra Loomis, 1885–1972
Powell, Anthony Dymoke, 1905–2000
Powell, Dawn, 1897–1965
Powell, Edward Alexander, 1879–1957
Powell, Harry James, 1853–?1922
Powell, Thomas, ?1572–?1635
Power, Henry, 1623–68
Power, Maurice S., 1935–
Power Farming
Powers, James Farl, 1917–99
Powys, John Cowper, 1872–1963
Powys, Theodore Francis, 1875–1953
Poyer, Joe, 1939–
Practical Boat Owner
Practical Caravan
Practical Computing
Practical English Teaching
Practical Gardening
Practical Hairstyling & Beauty
Practical Health
Practical Householder
Practical Motorist
Practical Parenting
Practical Photography
Practical Wireless
Practical Woodworking
Practitioner
Praed, Rosa Caroline, 1851–1935
Praed, Winthrop Mackwath, 1802–39
Prater, Donald Arthur, 1918–2001
Pratt, Anne, 1806–93
Pratt, Josiah, 1768–1844
Pratt, Samuel Jackson, 1749–1814
Precision Marketing
Prediction
Premiere
Presbyterian Herald
Prescott, William Hickling, 1796–1859
Press, John Bryant, 1920–
Press & Journal (Aberdeen)
Preston, John, 1557–1628
Preston, Richard Graham, 1648–95
Preston, Thomas, 1537–98
Price, Anthony, 1928–
Price, Edward Reynolds, 1933–
Price, Langford Lovell, b. 1862
Price, Pamela Jean Vandyke, 1923–
Prichard, Katharine Susannah, 1883–1969
Prideaux, Humphrey, 1648–1724
Priest, Christopher McKenzie, 1943–
Priestland, Gerald, 1927–91
Priestley, John Boynton, 1894–1984
Priestley, Joseph, 1733–1804
Prima
Prime, William Cowper, 1825–1905
Primrose, Archibald Philip, 1847–1929
Princeton Alumni Weekly
Pringle, Henry Fowles, 1897–1958
Pringle, Thomas, 1789–1834
Prior, Matthew, 1664–1721
Pritchett, Victor Sawdon, 1900–97
Private Eye
Private Investor
Procter, Adelaide Anne, 1825–64
Procter, Bryan Waller, 1787–1874
Procter, Maurice, 1906–73
Proctor, Richard Anthony, 1837–88
Profession
Professional Photographer
Profumo, David, 1955–
Prokosch, Eduard, 1876–1938
Property Weekly (Oxon.)
Prout, Ebenezer, 1835–1909
Pryce-Jones, Alan Payan, 1908–2000
Prynne, William, 1600–69
Psychological Bulletin
Psychology Today
Publican Newspaper
Public Opinion
Publishers Weekly
Puck
Pudney, John Sleigh, 1909–77
Pugin, Augustus Welby Northmore, 1812–52
Pulling, Alexander, 1857–1942
Pulse
Punch
Punisher
Purcell, John, ?1674–1730
Purchas, Samuel, ?1577–1626
Purseglove, Jeremy John, 1949–
Purshall, Conyers, fl. 1705
Purves, Elizabeth Mary (known as 'Libby'), 1950–
Pusey, Edward Bouverie, 1800–82
Pusey, Philip, 1799–1855
Putnam, William Clement, 1908–63
Puttenham, George, *c* 1529–90
Puzo, Mario, 1920–99

Pycroft, James, 1813–95
Pyke, Magnus Alfred, 1908–92
Pyke, Vincent, b. 1827
Pyles, Thomas, 1905–80
Pym, Barbara Mary Crampton, 1913–80
Pynchon, Thomas, 1937–
Pyne, William Henry, 1769–1843

Q

Q
QL User
Quarles, Francis, 1592–1644
Quarry Magazine
QuarterBack
Quarterly
Quarterly Review
Quennell, Peter, 1905–93
Quest
Quick, Herbert, 1861–1925
Quiller-Couch, Arthur Thomas, 1863–1944
Quillin, Patrick, 1951–
Quilting Today
Quincy, Joseph, 1802–82
Quine, Willard Van Orman, 1908–2000
Quinn, Arthur Hobson, 1875–1960
Quinn, Susan, 1940–
Quirk, Randolph, 1920–
Quiver

R

Raban, Jonathan, 1942–
Racing Monthly
Racing Pigeon Pictorial
Racing Post
Radakovich, Anka, 1957–
Radcliffe, Ann, 1764–1823
Radio & Electronics World
Radio Times
'Radley, Sheila' (Sheila Mary Robinson), 1928–
Rae, Hugh Crauford, 1935– (*see also* 'Crawford, Robert')
Rae, John Malcolm, 1931–
Raeper, William, 1959–92
Raffald, Elizabeth, 1733–81
Raffles, Thomas Stamford, 1781–1826
Rage
Rail
Rail Enthusiast
Railnews
Railway Magazine
Railway World
Rainbowe, Edward, 1608–84
Raine, Craig, 1944–
'Raine, Richard' (Raymond Harold Sawkins), 1923–
Raine, William Macleod, 1871–1954
Raleigh, Thomas, 1850–1920
Raleigh, Walter, ?1552–1618
Rally Car
Rally Sport
Ramadge, Francis Hopkins, 1793–1867
Ramanujan, Attipat Krishnaswami, 1929–
Ramesey, William, fl. 1660
Ramparts
Ramsay, Allan, 1686–1758
Ramsay, Andrew Crombie, 1814–91
Ramsay, Balcarres Dalrymple Wardlaw, 1822–85
Ramsay, Edward Bannerman Burnett, 1793–1872
Rand, William, fl. 1655
Randall, Henry Stephen, 1811–76
Rand Daily Mail
Randolph, Bernard, 1643–?90
Randolph, Thomas, 1605–35
Ranken, Alexander, 1755–1827
Rankin, Ian James, 1960–
Rankin, Nicholas, 1950–
Rankine, William John Macquorn, 1820–72
Ransom, John Crowe, 1888–1974
Ransome, Arthur Mitchell, 1884–1967
'Ransome, Stephen' (Frederick Clyde Davis), 1902–77
Raphael, Chaim, 1908–94
Raphael, Frederick Michael, 1931–
Raritan
Rashdall, Hastings, 1858–1924
Rathbone, Julian, 1935–
Rattigan, Terence Mervyn, 1911–77
Raven, Ronald William, 1904–91
Raven, Simon Arthur Noel, 1927–
Ravenscroft, Edward, fl. 1671–97
Ravensworth, Henry Thomas Liddell, Lord 1797–1878
Rawlings, Marjorie Kinnan, 1896–1953
Rawlins, Gregory J. E.
Rawlinson, Alfred Edward John, 1884–1960
Rawlinson, George, 1812–1902
Ray, Cyril, 1908–91
Ray, John, 1627–1705
Ray, Rebecca
Raymond, Eric Steven
Raymond, Ernest, 1888–1974
Raymond, Rossiter Worthington, 1840–1918
Raymond, Walter, 1852–1931
Raynalde, Thomas, fl. 1540–51
Rayner, Claire Berenice, 1931–
Rayner, Richard, 1955–
Raz, Joseph, 1939–
Read, Allen Walker, 1906–
Read, Herbert Edward, 1893–1968
Read, Piers Paul, 1941–
Reade, Charles, 1814–84
Reade, Winwood, 1838–75
Reader
Reader's Digest
Reader's Report
Reading, Peter, 1946–
Real Estate
Rebound
Receiver
Recorde, Robert, ?1510–58
Redbook
Redemption
Redemption Tidings
Redgrove, Peter, 1932–
Redinger, Ruby Virginia, 1915–81
Redway, Jacques Wardlaw, 1849–1942
Reed, Edward James, 1830–1906
Reed, Henry, 1808–54
Reed, John Silas, 1887–1920
Reed, Thomas Baines, 1852–93
Rees-Mogg, William, 1928–
Reeve, Clara, 1729–1807
Reeves, William, 1815–92
Reichs, Kathleen J.
Reid, Andrew, d. 1767
Reid, Beryl, 1920–
Reid, Forrest, 1875–1947
Reid, Meta Mayne, 1818–83
Reid, Thomas, 1710–96
Reid, Victor Stafford, 1913–
Reisz, Karel, 1926–
Reith, John Charles Waltham, 1889–1971
Reitz, Deneys, 1882–1944
Relix
'Renault, Mary' (Mary Challans), 1915–83
Rendell, Ruth, 1930– (*see also* 'Vine, Barbara')
Renewal
Renouf, Peter le Page, 1822–97
Repton, Humphry, 1752–1818
Rescue News
Resurgence
Reveley, Edith, 1930–
Review of English Studies
Revised Version of the Bible (1885)
Reyner, John Hereward, 1900–
Reynolds, Dallas McCord (known as 'Mack'), 1917–83
Reynolds, Edward, 1599–1676
Reynolds, Frederick, 1764–1841
Reynolds, Henry Robert, 1825–96
Reynolds, Joshua, 1723–92
Reynolds, Simon, 1963–
Rhode, Eric, 1934–
Rhodes, Richard, 1937–
Rhone, Trevor D., 1940–
'Rhys, Jean' (Ella Gwendolen Rees Williams), 1894–1979
Rhythm
Rice, Alice Hegan, 1870–1942
Rice, Craig, 1908–57
Rice, Elmer Leopold, 1892–1967
Rice, Jennings, 1900–
Rich, Adrienne, 1929–
Rich, Jack C., 1914–
Richards, David Adam, 1950–
Richards, Ivor Armstrong, 1893–1979
Richardson, Albert Deane, 1833–69
Richardson, Alexander, 1864–1928
'Richardson, Henry Handel' (Ethel Florence Lindesay Robertson), 1870–1946
Richardson, Jonathan, 1665–1745
Richardson, Samuel, 1689–1761
Richey, Paul Henry Mills, 1916–
Richler, Mordecai, 1931–
Rickert, Edith, 1871–1938
Rickman, Thomas, 1776–1841
Riddell, Charlotte Eliza, 1832–1906
Rideout, Henry Milner, 1877–1927
Ridler, Anne Barbara, 1912–2001
Ridley, Jasper Godwin, 1920–
Riesenberg, Felix, 1913–62
Rinehart, Mary Roberts, 1876–1958
Ring
Risdon, Tristram, ?1580–1640
Ritchie, Leitch, ?1800–65
Ritz
Rivers, Anthony Woodville, Earl of, ?1442–83
Road, Alan, 1930–
Road Racer
Road Racing & Training
Road Racing Monthly
Roazen, Paul, 1936–
Robb, Frank, 1908–
'Robbins, Harold' (Harold Rubins), 1916–97
Robbins, Thomas Eugene, 1936–
Roberts, Andrew, 1963–
Roberts, Ann Victoria, 1953–
Roberts, Cecil, 1860–94
Roberts, Charles George Douglas, 1860–1943
Roberts, David, 1943–
Roberts, Francis, 1609–75
Roberts, Geoffrey Keith, 1936–
Roberts, John Morris, 1928–
Roberts, Keith, 1935–
Roberts, Michèle, 1949–
Roberts, William, 1830–99
Roberts, William Page, 1836–1928
Roberts-Austin, William Chandler, 1843–1902
Robertson, Alexander Cavaliere, 1846–1933
Robertson, Eben William, 1815–74
Robertson, Eileen Arbuthnot, 1903–61
Robertson, Frank, 1838–73
Robertson, Frederick William, 1816–53
Robertson, James, fl. 1794–1811
Robertson, John Mackinnon, 1856–1933
Robertson, Stuart, 1892–1940
Robertson, William, 1721–93
Robins, Elizabeth, 1865–1936
Robinson, Arthur Howard, 1915–
Robinson, Charles Napier, 1849–1936
Robinson, Derek, 1932–
Robinson, Donald Hannibal, 1906–
Robinson, Frederick William, 1830–1901
Robinson, John, 1774–1840
Robinson, Lennox, 1886–1958
Robinson, Mary, 1758–1800
Robinson, Nicholas, ?1697–1775
Robinson, Robert, 1927–
Robinson, Robert Spencer, 1809–89
Robinson, William Heath, 1872–1944
Roby, Mary Linn, 1930–
Rock, Daniel, 1799–1871
Rockstro, William Smyth, 1823–95
Rodger, Alexander, 1784–1846
Roe, Edward P., 1838–88
Roe, Sue, 1956–
Roebuck, John Arthur, 1801–79
Roethke, Theodore Huebner, 1908–63
Rogers, Daniel, 1573–1652
Rogers, Everett Mitchell, 1931–
Rogers, E. W., 1864–1913
Rogers, Henry, 1806–77
Rogers, James Edwin Thorold, 1823–90
Rogers, John, 1679–1729
Rogers, Leonard Robert, 1924–
Rogers, Samuel, 1763–1855
Rogers, William Penn Adair (known as 'Will'), 1879–1935
Rogers, Woodes, d. 1732
'Rohmer, Sax' (Arthur Henry Ward), 1883–1959

S

Sereny, Gitta, 1923–
Sergeant, John, 1622–1707
Serling, Robert Jerome, 1918–
Server
Seth, Vikram, 1952–
Seton, Anya, 1916–90
Seton, Ernest Evan Thompson, 1860–1946
Sewall, Samuel, 1652–1730
Sewall, William, 1797–1846
Seward, Anna, 1747–1809
Seward, William, 1747–99
Sewel, William, 1654–1720
Seymour, Gerald William, 1941–
Seymour, John, 1914–
Seymour, Miranda, 1948–
Seymour-Smith, Martin, 1928–
Shadbolt, Maurice Francis, 1932–
Shadwell, Thomas, ?1642–92
Shaffer, Anthony Joshua, 1926–
Shaffer, Peter Levin, 1926–
Shaftesbury, Anthony Ashley Cooper, Earl of 1671–1713
Shainberg, Lawrence, 1936–
Shairp, John Campbell, 1819–85
Shakespeare, William, 1564–1616
Shand, Alexander Innes, 1832–1907
Shanks, Edward Buxton, 1892–1953
'Shannon, Dell' (Barbara Elizabeth Linington), 1921–88 (*see also* 'Blaisdell, Anne', 'Egan, Lesley')
Sharp, John, 1645–1714
Sharp, Margery, 1905–91
Sharp, William, 1855–1905 (*see also* 'Macleod, Fiona')
Sharpe, Charles Kirkpatrick, ?1781–1851
Sharpe, Thomas Ridley (known as 'Tom'), 1928–
Sharrock, Robert, 1630–84
Shave, Neil, fl. 1985
Shaw, Albert, 1857–1947
Shaw, Flora Louisa, 1852–1929
Shaw, George Bernard, 1856–1950
Shaw, Irwin, 1913–84
Shaw, Robert Archibald, 1927–78
Shaw, Thomas Budd, 1813–62
She
Shearman, Montague, 1857–1930
Shebbeare, John, 1709–88
Sheed, Wilfrid, 1930–
Sheehan, George Augustus, 1918–
Sheffield, John, 1648–1721
Sheldon, Charles Monroe, 1857–1928
Sheldon, Sidney, 1917–
Shelley, Mary Wollstonecraft, 1797–1851
Shelley, Percy Bysshe, 1792–1822
Shell Technology
Shelton, Thomas, fl. 1612–20
Shelvocke, George, fl. 1690–1728
Shenstone, William, 1714–63
Shepard, Charles Upham, 1842–1915
Shepherd, Edwin Colston, 1891–1976
Sheppard, Elizabeth Sara, 1830–62
Sherard, Robert Harborough, 1861–1943
Sheridan, Elizabeth, 1758–1837
Sheridan, Frances, 1724–66
Sheridan, Richard Brinsley, 1751–1816
Sheridan, Thomas, 1719–88
Sherley, Thomas, 1564–?1630
Sherlock, Thomas, 1678–1761
Sherriff, Robert Cedric, 1896–1975
Sherring, Albert William, 1922–
Sherry, Norman, 1925–
Sherwood, Mary Martha, 1775–1851
Shetland Times
Shiel, Matthew Phipps, 1865–1947
Shields, Carol Ann, 1935–
Shields, David, 1956–
Shinwell, Emanuel, 1884–1986
Shipley, Orby, 1832–1916
Shipp, John, 1784–1834
Ships Monthly
Shirley, James, 1596–1666
Shirra, Robert, b. 1724
Shooting
Shooting Life
Shooting Magazine
Shooting Times
Shop Assistant
Short, Charles Christopher, d. 1978
Shorten, Lynda, 1955–
Shorthouse, Joseph Henry, 1834–1903
Showalter, Elaine, 1941–
Shub, David, 1887–1973
Shuckard, William Edward, 1802–68
Shulman, Max, 1919–88
Shute, Josiah, 1588–1643
'Shute, Nevil' (Nevil Shute Norway), 1899–1960
Sibbald, Robert, 1641–1722
Sibbes, Richard, 1577–1635
Siddons, Henry, 1774–1815
Sidgwick, Ethel, 1877–1970
Sidgwick, Henry, 1838–1900
Sidgwick, Nevil Vincent, 1873–1952
Sidhwa, Bapsi, 1938–
Sidney, Philip, 1554–86
Sight & Sound
Silk, Joseph Ivor, 1942–
Silliman, Benjamin, 1816–85
Sillitoe, Alan, 1928–
Silverberg, Robert, 1935–
Simak, Clifford Donald, 1904–88
Simeon, Charles, 1759–1836
Simmons, Charles, 1924–
Simmons, Jack, 1915–
Simmons, Thomas Frederick, 1815–84
Simms, Jacqueline, 1940–
Simms, William Gilmore, 1806–70
Simon, André Louis, 1877–1970
Simon, Edith, 1917–
Simon, Roger Lichtenberg, 1943–
Simond, Louis, 1761–1831
Simpson, Dorothy, 1933–
Simpson, Eileen, 1923–
Simpson, Louis Aston, 1923–
Simpson, Robert, 1795–1867
Sims, George Frederick, 1923–
Sims, George Robert, 1847–1922
Sinclair, Andrew Annandale, 1935–
Sinclair, Iain, 1943–
Sinclair, John, 1797–1875
Sinclair, May, 1863–1946
Sinclair, Upton Bell, 1878–1968
Singer, Charles Joseph, 1876–1960
Singer, Samuel Weller, 1783–1858
Singh, Vijay, 1952–
Singleton, Robert Corbey, 1810–81
Sipma, Pieter, 1872–1961
Sisson, Charles Hubert, 1914–
Sitwell, Edith Louisa, 1887–1964
Sitwell, Francis Osbert, 1892–1969
Skeat, Walter William, 1835–1912
Skelton, John, ?1460–1529
Skene, John, ?1543–1617
Sketch
Ski
Skiing
Skiing Today
Skin Diver
Skinner, Constance Livesay, 1879–1939
Skinner, Cornelia Otis, 1901–79
Skinner, Martyn, 1906–
Ski Survey
Skurray, Francis, 1774–1848
Skyline
Sky Magazine
Sky Warriors
Slater, Nigel, 1944–
Slaughter, Frank Gill, 1908–2001
Slimming
Slingsby, Henry, 1602–58
Slipstream
Sloan, John MacGavin, 1880–1926
Sloane, Hans, 1660–1753
SLR Camera
Smailes, Arthur Eltringham, 1911–84
Smart, Benjamin Humphrey, ?1786–1872
Smart, Hawley, 1833–93
Smart, John Jamieson Carswell, 1920–
Smart Set
Smash Hits
Smeaton, John, 1724–92
Smedley, Francis Edward, 1818–64
Smiles, Samuel, 1812–1904
Smiley, Jane, 1951–
Smith, Adam, 1723–90
Smith, Albert Richard, 1816–60
Smith, Alexander, 1830–67
Smith, Anthony, 1926–
Smith, Anthony Charles H., 1935–
Smith, Barnard, 1817–76
Smith, Betty, 1904–72
Smith, Bosworth, 1839–1908
Smith, Charlotte Turner, 1749–1806
Smith, David Marshall, 1936–
Smith, Delia, 1941–
Smith, Dodie, 1896–1990
Smith, Edmund, 1672–1710
Smith, Evelyn E., 1927–
Smith, Florence Margaret (known as 'Stevie'), 1902–71
Smith, Francis, fl. 1746–7
Smith, George Adam, 1856–1942
Smith, George Barnett, 1841–1909
Smith, Godfrey Sydney, 1926–
Smith, Goldwin, 1823–1910
Smith, Grover Cleveland, 1923–
Smith, Henry, ?1550–91
Smith, Herbert Maynard, 1869–1949
Smith, Horace, 1779–1849
Smith, Iain Crichton, 1928–
Smith, Ian Douglas, 1919–
Smith, James, 1759–1828
Smith, Joan, 1938–
Smith, John, Captain 1580–1631
Smith, Joshua Toulmin, 1816–69
Smith, Julie P., d. 1883
Smith, Kenneth, 1938–
Smith, Lloyd Logan Pearsall, 1865–1946
Smith, Martin Cruz, 1942–
Smith, Nancy, 1929–
Smith, Robert Kimmel, 1930–
Smith, Seba, 1792–1868
'Smith, Shelley' (Nancy Hermione Bodington), 1912–
Smith, Stevie: *see* Smith, Florence
Smith, Sydney, 1771–1845
Smith, Terrence Lore, 1942–88
Smith, Thomas, 1638–1710
Smith, Walter Chalmers, 1824–1908
Smith, Wilbur, 1933–
Smither, Elizabeth, 1941–
Smithsonian
Smollett, Tobias George, 1721–71
Smyth, Frank, 1941–
Smyth, Waring Wilkinson, 1817–90
Smyth, William Henry, 1788–1865
Smythe, Patricia Rosemary, 1928–96
Smythies, Harriet Maria, 1838–83
Snelgrave, William, fl. 1725
Snodgrass, William De Witt, 1926–
Snooker Scene
Snow, Charles Percy, 1905–80
Snow, Edgar, 1905–72
Snow, John Augustine, 1941–
Snowboard UK
Sobel, Dava, 1947–
Soccer
Soccer Special
Social History of Medicine
Socialist Leader
Socialist Review
Society
Society (Bombay)
Software Magazine
Soldier
Soldier of Fortune
Somerville, Alexander, 1811–85
Somerville, Mary, 1780–1872
Somerville, William, 1675–1742
Sommerstein, Alan Herbert, 1947–
Sontag, Susan, 1933–
Sorley, Charles Hamilton, 1895–1915
Sound Choice
Sounds
South, John Flint, 1797–1882
South, Robert, 1634–1716
South African Panorama
Southerly
Southern, Richard William, 1912–2001
Southerne, Thomas, 1660–1746
Southern Rag
Southern Star (Eire)
Southey, Robert, 1774–1843
South Oxfordshire Guardian
South Wales Echo
South Wales Guardian
Southworth, Louis, 1916–
Soviet Life
Soviet Weekly

Soyer, Alexis Benoit, 1809–58
Soyinka, Akinwande Oluwole (known as 'Wole'), 1934–
Spaceflight
Spackman, William Mode, 1905–1990
Spalding, Frances, 1950–
Spalding, John, 1609–70
Spalding, Linda, fl. 1988
Spalding, William, 1809–59
Spare Rib
Spark, Muriel, 1918–
Sparks, Bruce Wilfred, 1923–
Sparrow, William, 1801–74
Spectator
Speed, John, ?1532–1629
Speedway Star
Speight, Johnny, 1920–98
Spelman, Henry, ?1564–1641
Spence, Ferrand, fl. 1686
Spencer, Charles Bernard, 1909–63
Spencer, Herbert, 1820–1903
Spencer, John, 1630–93
Spencer, Thomas, fl. 1628–9
Spender, Stephen Harold, 1909–95
Spenser, Edmund, ?1552–99
Sphere
Spin
Spiritualist
Spock, Benjamin McLane, 1903–98
Sport
Sporting Dog
Sporting Gun
Sporting Life
Sporting Magazine
Sporting Mirror
Sporting News
Sports Illustrated
Spotlight Contacts
Spottiswood, John, 1565–1639
Spottiswoode, William, 1825–83
Sprigge, Joshua, 1618–84
Sprott, Walter John Herbert, 1897–1971
Spry, Constance, 1886–1960
Spufford, Honor Margaret, fl. 1989
Spurgeon, Charles Haddon, 1834–92
Spurling, Susan Hilary, 1940–
Spy
Squash World
Squire, John Collings, 1884–1958
St: *listed as if* Saint
Stacey, Nicolas David, 1927–
Stafford, Anthony, 1587–?1645
Stafford, Thomas, fl. 1633
Stafford, William Edgar, 1914–93
Stage
Stage & Television Today
Stained Glass
Stainer, John, 1840–1901
Stallworthy, Jon Howie, 1935–
Stamp, Laurence Dudley, 1898–1966
Stamps
Standard
Stanford, Charles, 1823–86
Stanford, Charles Villiers, 1852–1924
Stanhope, George, 1660–1728
Stanhope, Philip Henry, 1805–75
Stanley, Arthur Penrhyn, 1815–81
Stanley, Henry Morton, 1841–1904
Stanley, Thomas, 1625–78
Stanton, Martin, 1950–
Stanyhurst, Richard, 1547–1618
Stapledon, William Olaf, 1886–1950
Staples, Brett A., 1951–
Stapylton, Robert, d. 1669
Star & Style (Bombay)
Stardust (Bombay)
Stark, Freya, 1893–1993
'Starke, Barbara' (Dora Amy Turnbull), 1878–1961 (*see also* 'Wentworth, Patricia')
Starke, Linda Kathleen, 1948–
Starkey, Thomas, ?1499–1538
Star (Sheffield)
Star (Tarrytown, USA)
Stead, Christian Karlson, 1932–
Stead, Christina Ellen, 1902–83
Stead, William Thomas, 1849–1912
Steam Railway News
Stebbing, William, 1832–1926
Stedman, Edmund Clarence, 1833–1908
Steel, Allan Gibson, 1858–1914
Steel, Danielle, 1948–
Steel, Flora Annie Webster, 1847–1929
Steele, Richard, 1672–1729
Steen, Marguerite, 1894–1975
Steffens, Joseph Lincoln, 1866–1936
Stegner, Wallace Earle, 1909–93
Stein, Gertrude, 1874–1946
Stein, Mark Avrel, 1862–1943
Steinbeck, John Ernst, 1902–68
Steinem, Gloria, 1934–
Steiner, George, 1929–
Stephen, Henry John, 1787–1864
Stephen, James, 1789–1859
Stephen, Leslie, 1832–1904
Stephens, Henry, 1795–1874
Stephens, John Lloyd, 1805–52
Sterling, Bruce, 1954–
Sterling, Thomas L., 1921–
Stern, Gladys Bronwyn, 1890–1973
Stern, Joseph Peter, 1920–
Sterne, Laurence, 1713–68
Stevens, Anthony, fl. 1990
Stevens, John, d. 1726
Stevens, Wallace, 1879–1955
Stevenson, Adlai Ewing, 1900–68
Stevenson, Anne, 1933–
Stevenson, Robert Louis, 1850–94
Stevenson, Thomas, 1818–87
Stewart, Balfour, 1828–87
Stewart, Dugald, 1753–1828
Stewart, John Innes Mackintosh, 1906–94 (*see also* 'Innes, Michael')
Stewart, Linda, 1948–
Stewart, Mary Florence, 1916–
Stewart, Sophie, 1969–
Stewart, Walter, 1931–
Stewart, William, ?1481–?1550
Still, John, ?1543–1608
Stillingfleet, Benjamin, 1702–71
Stillingfleet, Edward, 1635–99
Stimpson, George William, 1896–1952
Stimson, Frederic Jesup, 1855–1943
Stivens, Dallas George, 1911–97
Stock & Land (Melbourne)
Stocker, Thomas, fl. 1569–92
Stoddard, Francis Hovey, 1847–1936
Stoddart, John, 1773–1856
Stoddart, Thomas Tod, 1810–80
Stoker, Bram, 1847–1912
Stoll, Cliff, fl. 1989
Stone, C. J., 1953–
Stonehouse, William Brocklehurst, 1792–1862
Stonor, Henry James, 1820–1908
Stopford, Edward Adderley, 1809–94
Stoppard, Tom, 1937–
Storey, David, 1933–
Stornoway Gazette
Storr, Anthony, 1920–
Storr, Catherine, 1913–2001
Story, Jack Trevor, 1917–91
Story, William Wetmore, 1819–95
Stott, Mary, 1907–
Stout, George Frederick, 1860–1944
Stout, Rex, 1886–1975
Stow, John, ?1525–1605
Stowe, Harriet Elizabeth Beecher, 1812–96
Strachey, Giles Lytton, 1880–1932
Strachey, Julia, 1901–79
Straker, John Foster, 1904–
Strand, Mark, 1934–
Strand Magazine
Strang, Barbara Mary Hope, 1925–82
Strange, Roderick, 1945–
'Strangford, Percy' (Percy Ellen Frederick William Smythe), 1826–69
Stratton-Porter, Gene, 1863–1924
Strauss, Victor, 1907–79
Strawson, Peter Frederick, 1919–
Strean, Herbert Samuel, 1931–
Streatfeild, Noel, 1895–1986
Street, George Slythe, 1867–1936
Strength & Health
Strength Athlete
Strong, Leonard Alfred George, 1896–1958
Struthers, John, 1776–1853
Strutt, Jacob George, 1790–1864
Strutt, Joseph, 1749–1802
Strype, John, 1643–1737
Stuart, Donald Robert, 1913–
Stuart, Douglas, 1918–
Stuart, Jesse, 1907–84
'Stuart, Robert' (Robert Meikleham), fl. 1824
Stubbes, Phillip, fl. 1583–91
Stubbings, George Wilfred, 1887–1951
Stubbs, William, 1825–1901
Studies in English Literature
Studio News
Studio Week
Sturgis, Howard Overing, 1855–1920
Sturmy, Samuel, 1633–69
Styron, William, 1925–
Successful Slimming
Sullivan, Edward Dean, 1888–1938
Sullivan, James, 1744–1808
Sullivan, John William Navin, 1886–1937
Sullivan, Martin Gloster, 1910–80
Sullivan, Richard Joseph, 1752–1806
Sully, James, 1842–1923
Summerskill, Edith Clara, 1901–80
Summerson, John Newenham, 1904–92
Sun
Sun (Baltimore)
Sun (Brisbane)
Sun (Melbourne)
Sun (Vancouver)
Sunday (Calcutta)
Sunday Australian
Sunday Correspondent
Sunday Dispatch
Sunday Express
Sunday Gleaner
Sunday Graphic
Sunday Mail (Brisbane)
Sunday Mail (Glasgow)
Sunday Mail (New Delhi)
Sunday Mirror
Sunday Pictorial
Sunday Post (Glasgow)
Sunday Star (Toronto)
Sunday Sun (Brisbane)
Sunday Telegraph
Sunday Times
Sundkler, Bengt Gustaf Malcolm, 1909–95
Superbike
Superman
Super Marketing
Surfing World
Surflet, Richard, fl. 1600–16
Surf Scene
Surr, Thomas Skinner, 1770–1844
Surrey, Henry Howard, ?1517–47
Surtees, Robert Smith, 1803–60
Survey
Surveyor
Survival Weaponry
Sutcliff, Rosemary, 1920–92
Sutcliffe, Halliwell, 1870–1932
Sutherland, John, 1938–
Sutherland, John Derg, 1905–
Swan, Annie Shepherd, 1859–1943
Swan, John, fl. 1635
Swannell, Julia Catherine, 1952–92
Swanton, Michael James, 1939–
Sweet, Henry, 1845–1912
Sweetman, David, 1943–
Swift, Graham, 1949–
Swift, Jonathan, 1667–1745
Swimming Times
Swinburne, Algernon Charles, 1837–1909
Swinburne, Henry, ?1560–1623
Swing
Swinhoe, Robert, *c* 1835–77
Swinnerton, Frank Arthur, 1884–1982
Switzer, Stephen, ?1682–1745
Syal, Meera, 1962–
Sydenham, Humphrey, 1591–?1650
Sydney Morning Herald
Sykes, Ernest, 1870–1958
Sylvester, Josuah, 1563–1618
Symington, Neville, 1937–
Symmons, Edwards, fl. 1648
Symonds, John Addington, 1840–93
Symons, Julian Gustav, 1912–94
Synge, Edmund John Millington, 1871–1909

Tucson (Arizona) *Citizen*
Tucson Magazine
Tufte, Edward Rolf, 1942–
Tuke, Diana Rosemary, 1932–
Tull, Anita Margaret Louise, 1955–
Tull, Jethro, 1674–1740
Tulloch, John, 1823–86
Tunis, Edwin, 1897–1973
Tuohy, John Francis (known as 'Frank'), 1925–
Turberville, George, ?1540–?1610
Turnbull, Andrew Winchester, 1921–70
Turnbull, Peter, 1950–
Turner, Charles Godfrey, d. 1922
Turner, Ernest Sackville, 1909–
Turner, George Reginald, 1916–97
Turner, George William, 1921–
Turner, Sharon, 1768–1847
Turner, Walter James Redfern, *c* 1889–1946
Turner, William, d. 1568
Turner, William Price (known as 'Bill'), 1927–
Turow, Scott, 1949–
Tusa, John, 1936–
Tuscaloosa News
Tusser, Thomas, ?1524–80
Tutuola, Amos, 1920–97
TV Guide (Canada)
TV Times
'Twain, Mark' (Samuel Langhorne Clemens), 1835–1910
Twentieth Century
Twenty Twenty
Twining, Louisa, 1820–1912
Twining, Thomas, 1776–1861
Tyler, Anne, 1941–
Tyler, Royall, 1757–1826
Tyler, William Seymour, 1810–97
Tylor, Edward Barnet, 1832–1917
Tynan, Kenneth Peacock, 1927–80
Tyndall, John, 1820–93
Tyrrell, George, 1861–1909
Tyrrell, James, 1642–1718
Tyrwhitt, Richard St John, 1827–95
Tytler, Patrick Fraser, 1791–1849
'Tytler, Sarah' (Henrietta Keddie), 1827–1914

U

Udall, Nicolas, 1505–56
Uglow, Jennifer, 1947–
Ukers, William Harrison, 1873–1954
Ulam, Adam Bruno, 1922–2000
Ulanov, Barry, 1918–2000
Ullmann, Stephen, 1914–76
Ulverston (Cumbria) *News*
Under 5
Undercurrents
Underdown, Thomas, fl. 1566–87
Underground Grammarian
Underhill, Evelyn, 1875–1941
Underwood, Benson J., 1915–
Underwood, Michael, 1736–1820
Unity
UnixWorld
Unsworth, Barry, 1930–
Unsworth, Walter, 1928–
Unwin, Stanley, 1884–1968
Updike, John Hoyer, 1932–
Upfield, Arthur William, 1888–1964
Urdang, Laurence, 1927–
Ure, Andrew, 1778–1857
Uris, Leon Marcus, 1924–
Urquhart, Thomas, 1611–60
US Air
USA Today
US News & World Reporter
Ussher, James, 1581–1656
Ustinov, Peter Alexander, 1921–
Uttley, Alison Jane, 1884–1976

V

Vachell, Horace Annesley, 1861–1955
Vanbrugh, John, 1664–1726
Vance, John Holbrook (known as 'Jack'), 1916–
Vancouver, Charles, fl. 1785–1813
Vancouver Province
van der Post, Laurens, 1906–97
van de Wetering, Janwillem, 1931–
Van Druten, John William, 1901–57
Vanity Fair
Van Loon, Henrrik Willem, 1882–1944
van Rjndt, Philippe, 1950–
Van Sommers, Peter, fl. 1988
Vardon, Harry, 1870–1937
Variety
Vaughan, Henry, 1622–95
Vaughan, Robert Alfred, 1823–57
Vaux, Edward, 1591–1661
Venables, Edmund, 1819–95
Veneer, John, fl. 1725
Venn, Henry, 1725–97
Venner, Tobias, 1577–1660
Venue
Verbatim
Vere, Francis, 1560–1609
Vernède, Robert Ernest, 1875–1917
Verney, Frances Parthenope, 1819–90
Verney, Margaret Maria, 1844–1930
Vernon, Christopher, fl. 1642–66
Vesey-Fitzgerald, Brian, 1900–81
Veterinary Record
Victoria, queen of Great Britain and Ireland, 1819–1901
Vidal, Gore, 1925–
Video for You
Videographic
Video Maker
Video Today
Video World
Village Voice
Villiers, George, 1628–87
Vilvain, Robert, ?1575–1663
Vince, Samuel, 1749–1821
'Vine, Barbara' (Ruth Rendell), 1930–
Vines, Sydney Howard, 1849–1934
Vinge, Vernor Steffen, 1944–
Viorst, Judith, 1931–
Virginia Quarterly Review
Viz
Vizetelly, Henry, 1820–94
Vogue
Voice of the Arab World
von Arnim, Mary Annette, 1866–1941
Vonnegut, Kurt, 1922–
von Troil, Uno, 1746–1803
Voynich, Ethel Lillian, 1864–1960

W

Wace, Henry, 1836–1924
Waddell, Helen Jane, 1889–1965
Waddington, Samuel, 1844–1923
Wade, Henry William Rawson, 1918–
Wade, Jonathan, 1941–73
Wagner, Geoffrey Atheling, 1927–
Wain, John Barrington, 1925–94
Wainwright, Geoffrey, 1939–
Wainwright, John William, 1925–
Wake, Charlotte, 1800–88
Wakefield, Gilbert, 1756–1801
Walcott, Derek, 1930–
Wales
Walford, Cornelius, 1827–85
Walford, Edward, 1823–97
Walker, Alice, 1944–
Walker, Clement, 1595–1651
Walker, David Maxwell, 1920–
Walker, Edward Joseph (known as 'Ted'), 1934–
Walker, Francis Amasa, 1840–97
Walker, Joe, 1910–
Walker, Martin, 1947–
Walker, Mary Richardson, 1811–97
Walker, Obadiah, 1616–99
Walker, Patrick, ?1666–?1745
Walker, Peter Norman, 1936–
Walker, Ted: *see* Walker, Edward
Walker, William, 1623–84
Wall, Thomas, fl. 1660–90
Wallace, Alfred Russell, 1823–1913
Wallace, Carlton, 1903–
Wallace, Dillon, 1863–1939
Wallace, Edgar, 1875–1932
Wallace, Edward Tatum, 1906–76
Wallace, Henry Agard, 1888–1965
Wallace, Irving, 1916–90
Wallace, Lewis, 1827–1905
'Wallace, Walter Adam' (Edward Adrian Woodruffe-Peacock), fl. 1890
Wallace, William, 1844–97
Wallant, Edward Lewis, 1926–62
Waller, Edmund, 1606–87
Wall Street Journal
Walpole, Horace, 1717–97
Walpole, Hugh Seymour, 1884–1941
Walpole, Spencer, 1839–1907
Walsh, John Evangelist, 1927–
Walshe, Robert Daniel, 1923–
Walters, Vanessa, 1977–
Walton, Izaak, 1593–1683
Wambaugh, Joseph, 1937–
Wandsborough Borough News
Wanley, Nathaniel, 1634–80
Wannan, William Fielding (known as 'Bill'), 1915–
Wanted
Warburton, William, 1698–1779
Ward, Adolphus William, 1837–1924
Ward, Artemas, 1848–1925
Ward, Barbara Mary, 1914–81
Ward, Edmund, 1928–
Ward, Edward, 1667–1731
Ward, Lester Frank, 1841–1913
Ward, Mary Augusta (Mrs Humphry Ward), 1851–1920
Ward, Nathaniel, ?1578–1652
Ward, Robert Plumer, 1765–1846
Ward, Samuel, 1577–1640
Ward, William, 1769–1823
'Warden, Florence' (Florence Alice James), 1857–1929
Ware, John Christie, b. 1880
Waring, William, d. 1793
Warmstry, Thomas, 1610–65
Warner, Alan, 1964–
Warner, Charles Dudley, 1829–1900
Warner, Francis, 1937–
Warner, Marina Sarah, 1946–
Warner, Philip, 1914–
Warner, Rex, 1905–86
Warner, Susan, 1819–85
Warner, Sylvia Townsend, 1893–1978
Warner, William, ?1558–1609
Warnock, Geoffrey James, 1923–
Warnock, Helen Mary, 1924–
Warren, Clarence Henry, 1895–1966
Warren, Kenneth, 1926–
Warren, Robert Penn, 1905–89
Warren, Samuel, 1807–77
Warren, Thomas, ?1617–94
Warsaw Voice
Warter, John Wood, 1806–76
Warton, Joseph, 1722–1800
Warton, Thomas, 1728–90
'Warung, Price' (William Astley), 1855–1911
Warwick, Christopher, 1949–
Washington, Booker Taliaferro, 1856–1915
Washington, George, 1732–99
Washington, Thomas, fl. 1585
Washington Flyer
Washington Journalism Review
Washington Post
Washington Times
Wastes Management
Watada, Terry, 1951–
Waten, Judah Leon, 1911–85
Waterhouse, Keith Spencer, 1929–
Waterland, Daniel, 1683–1740
Waterloo (Ontario) *Chronicle*
Waterski International
Waterson, David, d. 1942
Waterton, Charles, 1782–1865
Waterton, Edmund, 1830–87
Waterworth, James, 1806–76
Watkins, Henry William, 1844–1922
Watson, Alfred Edward Thomas, 1849–1922
Watson, Colin, 1920–83
Watson, Ian, 1943–
Watson, James Dewey, 1928–
Watson, John Broadus, 1878–1954
Watson, Richard, 1737–1816
Watson, Robert, ?1730–81
Watson, Thomas, d. 1686
Watson, William, 1858–1935
Watsonia
Watt, Ian Pierre, 1917–99
Watts, George Frederick, 1817–1904
Watts, Henry, 1815–84
Watts, Isaac, 1674–1748
Watts, Nigel, 1957–
Watts-Dunton, Walter Theodore, 1867–1940

Waugh, Alec Alexander Raban, 1898–1981
Waugh, Coulton, 1896–1973
Waugh, Evelyn Arthur St John, 1903–66
Waugh, Hillary Baldwin, 1920–
Way, Peter Howard, 1936–
Wayre, Philip, 1921–
Weatherhead, Leslie Dixon, 1893–1976
Weatherly, Keith, 1927–
Webb, Beatrice, 1858–1943
Webb, John, 1611–72
Webb, Mary Gladys, 1881–1927
Webb, Thomas Ebenezer, 1821–1903
Webster, John, ?1580–?1625
Webster, Noah, 1758–1843
Wedde, Ian Curtis, 1946–
Wedge, John, 1921–
Wedgwood, Cicely Veronica, 1910–
Wedgwood, Hensleigh, 1803–91
Wedgwood, Josiah, 1730–95
Weekend Australian
Weekend Magazine (Montreal)
Weekend Television
Weekend World (Johannesburg)
Weekly Dispatch
Weekly New Mexican
Weekly News (Cambridge)
Weekly Notes
Weekly Times (Melbourne)
Weekly World News (US)
'Weeton, Ellen' (Nelly Stock), b. 1776
Weever, John, 1576–1632
Weidman, Jerome, 1913–98
Weighell, Sidney, 1922–2002
Weight Watchers
Weigle, William Oliver, 1927–
Weinberg, Steven, 1933–
Weintraub, Stanley, 1929–
Weinzweig, Helen, 1915–
Weir, Archibald, 1859–1935
Weisskopf, Victor Frederick, 1908–2002
Welburn, Vivienne Carole, 1941–
Welby, Amelia Ball, 1819–52
Welch, John, 1942–
Welch, Maurice Denton, 1915–48
'Welcome, John' (John Needham Brennan), 1914–
Weldon, Fay, 1931–
Wellek, René, 1903–
Welles, George Orson, 1915–85
Wellington, Arthur Wellesley, Duke of, 1769–1852
Wells, Herbert George, 1866–1946
Wells, Kenneth McNeill, 1905–
'Wells, Tobias' (Deloris Stanton Forbes), 1923–
Wells, William Charles, 1757–1817
Welsh, Irvine, 1958–
Welton, Richard, ?1671–1726
Welty, Eudora, 1909–2001
'Wentworth, Patricia' (Dora Amy Turnbull), 1878–1961 (*see also* 'Starke, Barbara')
Wesker, Arnold, 1932–
Wesley, Charles, 1707–88
Wesley, John, 1703–91
'Wesley, Mary' (Mary Aline Siepmann), 1912–
Wesley, Samuel, 1662–1735
West, Anthony Panther, 1914–87
West, Donald James, 1924–
West, Jane, 1758–1852
West, Morris Langlo, 1916–99
'West, Nathanael' (Nathan Wallenstein Weinstein), 1903–40
'West, Rebecca' (Cicily Isabel Fairfield), 1892–1983
Westall, Robert Atkinson, 1929–93
Westall, William, 1781–1850
West Briton
Westcott, Brooke Foss, 1825–1901
Western Folklore
Western Mail (Cardiff)
Western Morning News
West Hawaii Today
Westheimer, David, 1917–
West Highland Free Press
Westlake, Donald Edwin, 1933–
Westmacott, Charles Molloy, 1787–1868
Westminster Gazette
Westminster Magazine
Westminster Review
Weston, Carolyn, 1921–
Weston, Frank, 1871–1924
Weston, Jessie Laidley, 1850–1928
Westrup, Jack Allan, 1904–75
Westworld (Vancouver)
Wevill, David Anthony, 1935–
Weyman, Stanley John, 1855–1928
Wharton, Edith, 1862–1937
Wharton, John Smith, 1816/7–67
Wharton, William, 1925–
What Car?
What Diet & Lifestyle
Whateley, William, 1583–1639
Whately, Richard, 1787–1863
What Food?
What Investment
What Mortgage
What Video?
Wheeler, Edward Lytton, ?1854–85
Wheeler, John Archibald, 1911–
Wheeler, Robert Eric Mortimer, 1890–1976
Whelan, Richard, fl. 1985
Wheler, George, 1650–1723
Whetstone, George, ?1544–?87
Whewell, William, 1794–1866
Which?
Which Computer?
Which Micro?
Which Motorcaravan
Which Video?
Whipple, Edwin Percy, 1819–86
Whipple, Fred Lawrence, 1906–
Whishaw, Frederick James, 1854–1934
Whistler, Alan Charles Laurence, 1912–
Whiston, William, 1667–1752
White, Antonia, 1899–1979
White, Edmund, 1940–
White, Edward, 1819–98
White, Ellen Gould, 1827–1915
White, Elwyn Brooks, 1899–1985
White, Gilbert, 1720–93
White, Henry Kirke, 1785–1806
White, James, 1803–62
White, Jim, 1958–
White, Patrick Victor Martindale, 1912–90
White, Percy, 1852–1938
White, Richard Grant, 1821–85
White, Robin Christopher Andrew, 1947–
White, Stewart Edward, 1873–1946
White, Terence Hanbury, 1906–64
White, Tryphena Ely, 1784–1816
White, William Lindsay, 1900–73
Whitehead, Alfred North, 1861–1947
Whitehead, Charles, 1804–62
Whitehead, William, 1715–85
Whitelock, Dorothy, 1901–82
Whitelocke, Bulstrode, 1605–75
Whitgift, John, ?1530–1604
Whiting, Nathaniel, ?1617–82
Whitinton, Robert, fl. 1520
Whitlock, Richard, b. ?1616
Whitman, Charles, 1916–
Whitman, Walter (known as 'Walt'), 1819–92
Whitney, Adeline Dufton Train, 1824–1906
Whitney, Josiah Dwight, 1819–96
Whitney, Phyllis Ayame, 1903–
Whitney, William Dwight, 1827–94
Whittaker, James, 1906–
Whittaker, Nicholas
Whittier, John Greenleaf, 1807–92
Whitworth, Charles, 1675–1725
Whole Earth Review
Whyte, John, ?1510–60
Whyte-Melville, George John, 1821–78
Wickham, Anna, 1884–1947
Wiebe, Ruby Henry, 1943–
Wiener, Norbert, 1894–1964
Wier, Albert Ernest, 1879–1945
Wiffen, Jeremiah Holmes, 1792–1836
Wiggin, Kate Douglas, 1856–1923
Wigginton, Brooks Eliot, 1942–
Wigglesworth, Vincent Brian, 1899–1994
Wigoder, David, 1942–
Wilberforce, Robert Isaac, 1802–57
Wilberforce, Samuel, 1805–73
Wilbur, Richard Purdy, 1921–
Wilcox, James, 1949–
Wilde, Oscar Fingall O'Flahertie Wills, 1856–1900
Wilder, Laura Ingalls, 1867–1957
Wilderness Odyssey
Wilenski, Reginald Howard, 1887–1975
Wilkes, Charles, 1798–1877
Wilkes, John, 1727–97
Wilkes, Roger, 1948–
Wilkie, William, 1721–72
Wilkins, Charles
Wilkins, John, 1614–72
Wilkins, Mary Eleanor, 1852–1930
Wilkinson, Denys Haigh, 1922–
Wilkinson, Frederick, 1922–
Wilkinson, John, fl. 1618
Wilkinson, Lancelot Patrick, 1907–85
Will, George, 1941–
Willet, Andrew, 1562–1621
Willey, Basil, 1897–1978
Williams, Bobby Joe, 1930–
Williams, Charles, 1886–1945
Williams, Charles Greville, 1829–1910
Williams, David, 1926–
Williams, George Huntington, 1856–94
Williams, Helen Marin, 1762–1827
Williams, Joshua, 1813–81
Williams, Kenneth, 1926–88
Williams, Laurence Frederic Rushbrook, 1890–1978
Williams, Martin T., 1924–
Williams, Nigel, 1948–
Williams, Raymond Henry, 1921–88
Williams, Samuel, 1743–1817
Williams, Thomas Lanier (known as 'Tennessee'), 1911–83
Williams, William, 1832–1900
Williams, William Carlos, 1883–1963
Williamson, Henry, 1895–1977
Williamson, Marianne, 1952–
Willis, Nathaniel Parker, 1806–67
Willmott, Peter, 1923–
Willock, John, fl. 1790
Wills, Charles James, 1892–1912
Wilmot, Catherine, ?1773–1824
Wilmot, Martha, 1775–1873
Wilson, Andrew Norman, 1950–
Wilson, Angus Frank Johnstone, 1913–91
Wilson, Augusta Jane, 1835–1909
Wilson, Colin Henry, 1931–
Wilson, Daniel, 1816–92
Wilson, Edmund, 1895–1972
Wilson, Frederick Richard, fl. 1870
Wilson, George Buckley Laird, 1908–84
Wilson, Harry Leon, 1867–1939
Wilson, Horace Hayman, 1786–1861
Wilson, James Harold, 1916–95
Wilson, John, 1785–1854
Wilson, John Fleming, 1877–1922
Wilson, Robert McLiam, 1964–
Wilson, Sloan, 1920–
Wilson, Snoo, 1948–
Wilson, Thomas, ?1525–81
Wilson, Thomas Woodrow, 1856–1924
Wilson, Walter, 1781–1847
Wilson Quarterly
Wilt, Frederick Loren, 1920–
Winchell, Alexander, 1824–91
Windham, William, 1750–1810
Windsurf
Wine
Wine & Spirits
Wine Spectator
Winnicott, Donald Woods, 1896–1971
Winning
Winokur, George, 1925–
Winsor, Diana, 1946–
'Winter, John Strange' (Henrietta Eliza Vaughan), 1856–1911
Winters, Arthur Yvor, 1900–68
Winterson, Jeanette, 1959–
Winthrop, John, 1588–1649
Wire
Wireless World
Wisden Cricket Monthly
Wise, Francis, 1695–1767
Wiseman, Richard, ?1622–76
Wister, Owen, 1860–1938
Wither, George, 1588–1667
Withering, William, 1741–99
Wittke, Carl Frederick, 1892–1971

Witts, Francis Edward, 1783–1854
Wodehouse, Pelham Grenville, 1881–1975
Wogan, Michael Terence (known as 'Terry'), 1938–
Wolcot, John, 1738–1819
Wolfe, Bernard, 1915–85
Wolfe, Charles, 1791–1823
Wolfe, Gary Kent, 1946–
Wolfe, Stephen Landis, 1932–
Wolfe, Thomas Clayton, 1900–38
Wolfe, Thomas Kennerly, 1931–
Wolff, Cynthia Griffin, 1936–
Wolff, Henry Drummond, 1830–1908
Wolff, Robert Lee, 1915–80
Wolff, Ruth, ?1909–72
Wollaston, William, 1660–1724
Wollff, Geoffrey, 1937–
Wollstonecraft, Mary, 1759–97
Wolseley, Garnet Joseph W., 1833–1913
Woman
Woman & Home
Woman's Day (US)
Woman's Home
Woman's Illustrated
Woman's Journal
Woman's Own
Woman's Realm
Women Speaking
Women's Review
Womock, Laurence, 1612–86
Wonder Woman
Wood, Annie
Wood, Anthony, 1632–95
Wood, Christopher, 1935–
Wood, Horatio Curtis, 1841–1920
Wood, James, 1760–1839
Wood, John George, 1827–89
Wood, Mrs Henry, 1814–87
Wood, Victoria, 1953–
Wood, William, 1679–1765
Woodall, John, ?1556–1643
Woodbridge, George, 1908–
Woodforde, James, 1740–1803
Woodhouse, Martin, 1932–
Woodhouse, Robert, 1773–1827
Woodruff, Hiram Washington, 1817–67
'Woods, Sara' (Sara Bowen-Judd), 1922–85
Woodward, George Moutard, ?1760–1809
Woodward, John, 1665–1728
Woodward, Samuel Peckworth, 1821–65
Woodworker
Woodworking
Woodworth, Robert Sessions, 1869–1962
Wooler, Neil, 1940–
Woolf, Adeline Virginia, 1882–1941
Woolf, Leonard Sidney, 1880–1969
Woolhouse, Roger Stuart, 1940–
Woolley, Charles Leonard, 1880–1960
Woolley, Hannah, fl. 1670
Woolner, Thomas, 1825–92
Worboise, Emma Jane, 1825–87
Worcester, Joseph Emerson, 1784–1865
Word
Word Study
Wordsworth, Christopher, 1807–85
Wordsworth, Dorothy, 1771–1855
Wordsworth, William, 1770–1850
Word Ways
Workbox
Working Woman
World Archaeology
World Magazine
World Monitor
World of Cricket Monthly
World Soccer
Worlidge, John, fl. 1669–98
Worsley, Philip Stanhope, 1835–66
Worsthorne, Peregrine Gerard, 1923–
Wotton, Henry, 1568–1639
Wotton, William, 1666–1727
Wouk, Herman, 1915–
Wraxall, Frederick Charles Lascelles, 1828–65
Wrenn, Charles Leslie, 1895–1969
Wright, Arthur, 1870–1932
Wright, Eric, 1929–
Wright, Frank Lloyd, 1867–1959
Wright, John, 1937–
Wright, Peter, 1923–
Wright, Ronald, 1948–
Wright, Thomas, 1810–77
Wrigley, Gordon, 1923–
Writer (US)
Wroth, Mary, fl. 1621
Wyatt, Thomas, ?1503–42
Wycherley, William, ?1640–1716
Wyclif, John, *c* 1325–84
Wyld, Henry Cecil Kennedy, 1870–1945
Wylie, Philip, 1902–71
Wymer, Norman, 1911–
Wyndham, Francis, 1924–
Wyndham, Henry Saxe, 1867–1940
'Wyndham, John' (John Wyndham Parks Lucas Harris), 1903–69
Wynter, Sylvia, fl. 1962

X

'X, Malcolm' (Malcolm Little), 1925–65

Y

Yachting World
Yalden, Thomas, 1670–1736
Yalom, Irvin David, 1931–
Yankee
Yarranton, Andrew, 1616–?84
Yates, Edmund Hodgson, 1831–94
Year's Work in English Studies
Yeates, Victor M., 1897–1934
Yeats, Jack Butler, 1871–1957
Yeats, John, fl. 1865
Yeats, William Butler, 1865–1939
Yeowell, James, ?1803–75
Yoga & Health
Yonge, Charles Duke, 1812–91
Yonge, Charlotte Mary, 1823–1901
York, Andrew, 1930–
Yorke, James, fl. 1640
Yorkshire Post
Youatt, William, 1776–1847
Young, Arthur, 1741–1820
Young, Bartholomew, fl. 1577–1600
Young, Edward, 1683–1765
Young, Emily Hilda, 1880–1949
Young, Filson, 1876–1938
Young, Francis Brett, 1884–1954
Young, John Zachary, 1907–97
Young, Nigel, 1938–
Young-Bruehl, Elisabeth, 1946–
Younge, Richard, fl. 1640–70
Your Business
Your Computer
Your Horse
Yours
Yudkin, John, 1910–95
'Yuill, P. B.' (Gordon Maclean Williams), 1934–

Z

Zaehner, Robert Charles, 1913–74
Zangwill, Israel, 1864–1926
Zephaniah, Benjamin Obadiah Iqbal, 1958–
Ziegler, Philip, 1929–
Zigzag
Ziman, John, 1925–
Zoologist
Zweig, Ferdynand, 1896–1988
Zweig, Paul, 1935–84
ZX Computing Monthly

References TO THE BIBLE AND SHAKESPEARE

Books of the Bible

Acts of the Apostles (*Acts*)
Amos
1 & 2 Chronicles (*Chron.*)
Colossians (*Col.*)
1 & 2 Corinthians (*Cor.*)
Daniel (*Dan.*)
Deuteronomy (*Deut.*)
Ecclesiastes (*Eccles.*)
Ecclesiasticus (*Ecclus*)
Ephesians (*Eph.*)
1 & 2 Esdras (*Esd.*)
Esther
Exodus (*Exod.*)
Ezekiel (*Ezek.*)
Galatians (*Gal.*)
Genesis (*Gen.*)
Habakkuk (*Hab.*)
Hebrews (*Heb.*)
Isaiah (*Isa.*)
James
Jeremiah (*Jer.*)
Job
Joel
John [gospel]
1 & 2 John [epistle]
Joshua (*Josh.*)
Judges (*Judg.*)
Judith
1 & 2 Kings
Lamentations (*Lam.*)
Leviticus (*Lev.*)
Luke
1 & 2 Maccabees (*Macc.*)
Mark
Matthew (*Matt.*)
Micah
Numbers (*Num.*)
Obadiah
1 & 2 Peter (*Pet.*)
Philippians (*Phil.*)
Proverbs (*Prov.*)
Psalms (*Ps.*)
Revelation (*Rev.*)
Romans (*Rom.*)
Ruth
1 & 2 Samuel (*Sam.*)
Song of Solomon (or Songs) (*S. of S.*)
Susanna (*Sus.*)
1 & 2 Thessalonians (*Thess.*)
1 & 2 Timothy (*Tim.*)
Titus
Tobit
Wisdom of Solomon (*Wisd.*)
Zechariah (*Zech.*)
Zephaniah (*Zeph.*)

Works by William Shakespeare

All's Well that Ends Well (*All's Well*)
Antony and Cleopatra (*Ant. & Cl.*)
As You Like It (*A.Y.L.*)
Comedy of Errors (*Com. Err.*)
Coriolanus (*Coriol.*)
Cymbeline (*Cymb.*)
Hamlet (*Haml.*)
Julius Caesar (*Jul. Caes.*)
The First Part of King Henry the Fourth (*1 Hen. IV*)
The Second Part of King Henry the Fourth (*2 Hen. IV*)
King Henry the Fifth (*Hen. V*)
The First Part of King Henry the Sixth (*1 Hen. VI*)
The Second Part of King Henry the Sixth (*2 Hen. VI*)
The Third Part of King Henry the Sixth (*3 Hen. VI*)
King John (*John*)
King Richard the Second (*Rich. II*)
King Richard the Third (*Rich. III*)
King Lear (*Lear*)
Love's Labour's Lost (*L.L.L.*)
Macbeth (*Macb.*)
Measure for Measure (*Meas. for M.*)
The Merchant of Venice (*Merch. V.*)
The Merry Wives of Windsor (*Merry W.*)
A Midsummer Night's Dream (*Mids. N. D.*)
Much Ado about Nothing (*Much Ado*)
Othello (*Oth.*)
Pericles (*Per.*)
The Phoenix and the Turtle (*Phoenix*)
The Rape of Lucrece (*Lucr.*)
Romeo and Juliet (*Rom. & Jul.*)
Sonnets (*Sonn.*)
The Taming of the Shrew (*Tam. Shr.*)
The Tempest (*Temp.*)
Timon of Athens (*Timon*)
Titus Andronicus (*Tit. A.*)
Troilus and Cressida (*Tr. & Cr.*)
Twelfth Night (*Twel. N.*)
The Two Gentlemen of Verona (*Two Gent.*)
Venus and Adonis (*Ven. & Ad.*)
The Winter's Tale (*Wint. T.*)